D1518946

CONGRESSIONAL QUARTERLY

Almanac®

105th CONGRESS
1st SESSION . . . 1997

VOLUME LIII

Congressional Quarterly Inc.

1414 22nd Street N.W.
Washington, D.C. 20037

Congressional Quarterly 1997 Almanac

Editor Jan Austin
Production Editor Melinda Nahmias

Congressional Quarterly Inc.

Congressional Quarterly Inc. is a publishing and information services company and a recognized leader in political journalism. For more than half a century, CQ has served clients in the fields of news, education, business and government with complete, timely and unbiased information on Congress, politics and national issues.

The flagship publication is the CQ Weekly, a weekly magazine offering news and analysis on Congress and legislation. The CQ Researcher (formerly Editorial Research Reports), with its focus on current issues, provides weekly, balanced summaries on topics of widespread interest.

CQ publishes the CQ Daily Monitor, a daily report on Congress and current and future activities of congressional committees, and produces several information sites on the World Wide Web, including CQ NewsAlert (www.cq.com)

CQ also provides news and analysis via the Internet: CQ.com On Congress is a legislative, regulatory and state tracking service with immediate access to both proprietary and public databases of legislative action, votes, schedules, profiles and analysis.

Another subscription online service, Politics for Pros, includes campaign news from House, Senate and gubernatorial races and extensive databases on political advertising, campaign finance and congressional districts.

Visit CQ on the World Wide Web at www.cq.com.

CQ also publishes a variety of books, including political science textbooks, under the CQ Press imprint to keep journalists, scholars and the public abreast of developing issues and events. CQ Books publishes information directories and reference books on the federal government, national elections and politics, including the Guide to the Presidency, the Guide to Congress, the Guide to the U.S. Supreme Court, the Guide to U.S. Elections, Politics in America, the Federal Regulatory Directory and Washington Information Directory.

The Congressional Quarterly Almanac®, published annually, provides a legislative history for each session of Congress. Congress and the Nation, published every four years, provides a record of government for a presidential term.

Printed in the United States of America
Library of Congress Catalog Number 47-41081
ISBN: 1-56802-268-9 ISSN: 0095-6007

What You Will Find in This Book

This is the 53rd edition of the Congressional Quarterly Almanac, an annual book that chronicles the course of major legislation and national political races.

Drawing on reporting and writing done throughout the year by the staffs of the CQ Weekly, the CQ Daily Monitor and House Action Reports, the Almanac organizes, distills and cross-indexes for permanent reference the full year in Congress and in national politics. The 1997 volume covers the first session of the 105th Congress.

The following are the major elements of the book:

● **Chapter 1 — Inside Congress.** The first chapter provides an overview of the year in Congress, including statistical data on the session, along with stories on the investigation into alleged campaign finance misdeeds and the failure to pass a bill to reform the campaign finance system. Also included is the story of House Speaker Newt Gingrich, R-Ga. — from his ethics woes, to his success in forging a bipartisan balanced-budget agreement, to an aborted attempt by Republicans to oust him.

● **Chapters 2-8 — Legislative Action.** The next seven chapters detail the year's action on bills covering economics and finance, government and commerce, energy and environment, social policy, defense and foreign policy. They include extensive detail on the pair of budget-reconciliation bills enacted to carry out the year's budget agreement.

● **Chapter 9 — Appropriations.** The ninth chapter contains legislative histories and summary charts for each of the 13 annual appropriations bills, as well as for the fiscal 1997 supplemental that provided funds for disaster aid in the Midwest and support for international peacekeeping operations.

● **Chapter 10 — Political Report.** Chapter 10 contains an original CQ study of the effects of changing demographics on the electorate, with separate stories on the suburbs, the cities and the nation's rural areas.

Details on governors' races and special elections are also provided.

● **Appendixes.** The volume includes appendixes on the following topics:

- **Glossary.** An 11-page glossary of terms used in Congress.
- **Congress and Its Members.** A description of the legislative process, a roster of members and a list of members' committee assignments.
- **Vote Studies.** Analyses of presidential support, party unity and conservative coalition patterns, as well as of the year's key House and Senate votes.
- **Texts.** Key presidential and other texts.
- **Public Laws.** A complete listing of public laws enacted during the session.
- **Roll Call Votes.** A complete set of roll call vote charts for the House and Senate during the session.

CQ

"By providing a link between the local newspaper and Capitol Hill we hope Congressional Quarterly can help to make public opinion the only effective pressure group in the country. Since many citizens other than editors are also interested in Congress, we hope that they too will find Congressional Quarterly an aid to a better understanding of their government.

"Congressional Quarterly presents the facts in as complete, concise and unbiased form as we know how. The editorial comment on the acts and votes of Congress, we leave to our subscribers."

Foreword, Congressional Quarterly, Vol. I, 1945
Henrietta Poynter, 1901-1968
Nelson Poynter, 1903-1978

SUMMARY TABLE OF CONTENTS

Table of Contents

Chapter 1 – Inside Congress

Chapter 2 – Economics & Finance

Chapter 3 – Government & Commerce

Chapter 4 – Environment & Energy

Chapter 5 – Law & Judiciary

Chapter 6 – Health & Human Services

Chapter 7 – Education, Housing, Labor & Veterans

Chapter 8 – Defense & Foreign Policy

Chapter 9 – Appropriations

Chapter 10 – Political Report

Appendixes

CQ

Chapter 1

INSIDE CONGRESS

CONGRESSIONAL OVERVIEW

Tone, Tenor of First Session Seemed Like Old Times

Voters, who turned the Capitol upside down in '94, opted for status quo two years later

The first session of the Republican-controlled 105th Congress marked a return to a more traditional style of legislating. Gone were the frenetic days of round-the-clock work that marked the GOP takeover of the 104th Congress in 1995. Gone, too, was the bravado of a new Republican majority trying to cow the Democratic White House, along with the unquestioned authority of a few newly empowered leaders.

In 1997, Republican leaders worked through the committee system to build majority coalitions — many of them bipartisan — to pass bills. Lawmakers looked more often for common ground with their adversaries rather than sticking to ideological purity. And the profile of controversial leaders such as House Speaker Newt Gingrich, R-Ga., receded into the background.

"For veteran Congress-watchers, the 105th is a lot more familiar," said Roger Davidson, a University of Maryland political scientist. "And one gets the impression it worked the way it should, or the way we've come to think it should."

Moderation and compromise won Republicans what confrontation and inflexibility had not. The most notable example was a landmark, bipartisan agreement to balance the budget by 2002 while providing the biggest tax cut since the Reagan administration — a goal that Republicans had found unattainable in the 104th Congress.

As part of the budget package, Congress made wide-ranging changes to Medicare, the federal health insurance program for the elderly, and Medicaid, the federal-state health program for the poor and disabled. It also created a new program to help states provide health insurance to about half the nation's estimated 10 million uninsured children.

GOP leaders also got all 13 regular appropriations bills enacted, abandoning the take-it-or-leave-it strategy that had triggered two government shutdowns and hurt Republicans during their first two years in power.

Beyond that, however, the 105th Congress was not notably productive in its first session. Highlights included enactment of a long-stalled overhaul of the Food and Drug Administration aimed at speeding up the approval of new drugs and medical devices; a bailout of Amtrak, the nation's troubled passenger railroad; and a bill to expedite the adoption of abused and neglected children by making it easier for local authorities to permanently remove children from abusive homes.

Unable to complete work on an ambitious, six-year highway bill, lawmakers cleared a short-term extension of existing law to keep federal transportation money flowing to the states in the interim.

On the foreign policy front, the Senate ratified an international chemical and biological weapons treaty, to the distress of conservative Republicans, and the House let stand the administration's decision to renew China's most-favored-nation trading status.

By contrast, items that had been high on the conservative agenda generally fell by the wayside — further proof that the GOP revolution was fading, dissipated by Republican infighting and the continuing ability of the Democratic minority to stand together to block crucial initiatives. Conservatives failed to win approval for constitutional amendments to impose term limits on members of Congress (11 versions failed to get the necessary two-thirds vote in the House) and to require a balanced budget (the Senate fell just short of a two-thirds majority March 4).

Social conservatives also met with defeat on a number of so-called wedge issues, including proposals to provide vouchers for private school education, create tax-free savings accounts for tuition, eliminate the National Endowment for the Arts, ban a controversial procedure that opponents dubbed "partial birth" abortion, and allow employers to offer compensatory time off instead of overtime pay. A House bill to end race and gender preferences by the government and its contractors was scuttled in committee.

Clinton lost a few items dear to his administration, as well. Congress refused to provide money he requested to underwrite a world currency stabilization program and to pay off U.S. debts to the United Nations, after the president infuriated conservatives by blocking legislation to ban U.S. aid for overseas organizations that performed or advocated abortions.

Clinton's most important defeat was on renewal of fast-track authority to negotiate trade deals. Republicans supported the measure, but it was pulled from consideration in the House after labor unions put heavy pressure on Democrats to vote no. Clinton also lost several confirmation battles with the Senate. His nominee for ambassador to Mexico, for-

First Session of the 105th at a Glance

The first session of the 105th Congress convened Jan. 7 and closed at 10:44 p.m. on Nov. 13, when the House adjourned sine die. The Senate had adjourned sine die hours earlier, at 7:56 p.m.

The chart below gives a statistical portrait of the session compared with the previous 10 years.

		1997	1996	1995	1994	1993	1992	1991	1990	1989	1988	1987
Days in Session	S	153	132	211	138	153	129	158	138	136	137	170
	H	132	122	168	123	142	123	154	134	147	129	169
Time in Session (hours)	S	1,093	1,037	1,839	1,244	1,270	1,091	1,201	1,250	1,003	1,127	1,215
	H	1,004	919	1,525	905	982	857	939	939	749	749	910
Avg. Length Daily Session (hours)	S	7.1	7.9	8.7	9.0	8.3	8.5	7.6	9.1	7.4	8.2	7.1
	H	7.6	7.5	9.1	7.4	6.9	7.0	6.1	7.0	5.1	5.8	5.4
Public Laws Enacted		153	245	88	255	210	347	243	410	240	471	242
Bills/ Resolutions Introduced	S	1,839	860	1,801	999	2,178	1,544	2,701	1,636	2,548	1,328	2,685
	H	3,662	1,899	3,430	2,104	4,543	2,714	5,057	2,769	4,842	2,412	4,857
	Total	5,501	2,759	5,231	3,103	6,721	4,258	7,758	4,405	7,390	3,740	7,542
Recorded Votes	S	298	306	613	329	395	270	280	326	312	379	420
	H*	640	455	885	507	615	488	444	536	379	465	511
	Total	938	761	1,498	836	1,010	758	724	862	691	844	931
Vetoes**		3	6	9	0	0	10	3	11	10	16	3

* includes quorum calls
**does not include line-item vetoes

mer Massachusetts Gov. William F. Weld, a Republican, was blocked, as were nominees Bill Lann Lee for assistant attorney general for civil rights and David Satcher for surgeon general. (Clinton subsequently appointed Lee as acting assistant attorney general.)

Clinton made the first use ever of the new line-item veto law, striking individual items in nine appropriations bills and the two reconciliation measures. While he used the power with relative caution, he provoked an angry bipartisan backlash when he struck 38 projects from the military construction spending bill. Congress ended the year poised to overrule him.

Learning To Live With Divided Government

Members of both parties agreed that the November 1996 elections sent a message that encouraged cautious legislating rather than the confrontational tone seen in the initial months of the 104th Congress.

Under sustained attack from Democrats who painted them as extremists, Republicans lost nine seats in the House and came close to seeing their majority slip away altogether. "With more and more polling data, they understand that if the election were held two weeks earlier, they would have lost the House," said Sen. John McCain, R-Ariz., himself a former House member. "A lot of them have recognized that there were excesses in 1995 that were very damaging to the party." *(1996 Almanac, pp. 11-23, 11-29)*

House Republicans' comfortable 37-seat majority of late 1996 fell to just 19 seats after the elections (227 Republicans, 207 Democrats, 1 Independent). As a result, GOP leaders had to focus much more on holding their ranks together on tough votes, since the defection of just 10 Republicans could give a solid Democratic bloc control on contentious issues.

While Senate Republicans increased their margin by two seats, from 53 to 55, they still fell well short of the 60 seats they needed to block a filibuster, a weapon Senate Democrats had used effectively in 1995 and 1996 to blunt GOP initiatives.

"The surviving freshmen of the 104th Congress learned the essential lesson that there are times it pays to be moderate instead of a hot spur," said Ross K. Baker, professor of political science at Rutgers University. "Incrementalism has gotten a new respectability."

And while voters kept Congress in GOP hands, they also re-elected the same Democratic president who had so frustrated Republicans in 1995-96. It was Clinton's deft use of the veto and the bully pulpit that helped slow and then all but stop the GOP revolution, and it was his relentless attacks on Republicans' plans to overhaul government that helped Democrats come close to snatching back control of the House in November 1996.

The decision by voters to continue divided government meant that both sides were now stuck with each other for at least the next two years and quite likely the next four, given the difficulty traditionally experienced by the president's party in off-year elections. That pushed both Congress and the White House to find ways to do business with one another, building on a series of last-minute compromises they had forged late in the last Congress.

In a single remarkable week just three months before the 1996 elections, Congress cleared legislation that overhauled welfare (PL 104-193), raised the federal minimum wage (PL 104-188), guaranteed the portability of health insurance (PL 104-191) and rewrote the nation's safe drinking water law (PL 104-182). Clinton quickly signed the bills, and both sides virtually overnight built a solid legislative record and showed they could work together — exactly what the voters seemed to want. *(1996 Almanac, p. 1-3)*

That grudging cooperation — both sides compromised key principles to get legislative accomplishments — set the tone for the 105th Congress.

Clinton, Too, Hears the Message

Clinton's first major public addresses in 1997 were clearly intended to set a bipartisan tone and extend an olive branch to congressional Republicans, many of whom resented what they felt had been Clinton's harsh and demagogic attacks on them during the 1996 campaign.

The president began his second term on a cold Jan. 20 with an Inauguration Day address that acknowledged the lesson of the 1996 election. "The American people returned to office a president of one party and a Congress of another," he said. "Surely they did not do this to advance the politics of petty bickering and extreme partisanship they plainly deplore. No, they call on all of us instead to be repairers of the breach and to move on with America's mission."

The speech was more somber than the one he had given four years earlier, when he stressed change and an energetic renewal. His words this time seemed tempered by the political battles of his first term and by a keener understanding of the limits of the presidency and the government.

The re-elected president strove to articulate a political philosophy he called a quest for the "vital center." Putting a new twist on a line often used by President Ronald Reagan, Clinton said: "Government is not the problem, and government is not the solution. We, the American people — we are the solution."

Still, he insisted, "where it can stand up for our values and interests around the world, and where it can give Americans the power to make a real difference in their everyday lives, government should do more, not less."

Clinton tried to strike a balance between fiscal realism and governmental protections, calling for "a nation that balances its budget but never loses the balance of its values; a nation where our grandparents have secure retirement and health care, and their grandchildren know we have made the reforms necessary to sustain those benefits for their time." *(Text, p. D-10)*

Little more than two weeks later, Clinton went to Capitol Hill on Feb. 4 to give his State of the Union address. Spelling out his second-term priorities, he again struck a chord of bipartisanship. "The people of this nation elected us all," the

Senate Invokes Cloture Seven Times

Senate Majority Leader Trent Lott, R-Miss., said the entire Senate agenda in 1997 would have been different if there had been five more Republicans. That would have given him 60 GOP votes — the number needed under Senate rules to invoke cloture. Not having them meant Republicans had to remain united and win over five Democrats in order to limit debate on a matter before the chamber. That was a telling obstacle: On every cloture vote that generated sharp partisan divisions, the Democrats prevailed.

The Senate held 24 cloture votes in 1997, slightly fewer than the 29 cloture votes in 1996 and more than the 21 votes in 1995. Attempts to limit debate succeeded on seven occasions, each time by a wide margin. The closest thing to a squeaker was the 69-31 vote to proceed to consideration of the fast-track trade bill (S 1269).

Some of the cloture votes disguised other disputes between the parties. For instance, the Senate failed four times to invoke cloture on a broadly popular six-year highway reauthorization bill (S 1173). Democrats stuck together at the request of Minority Leader Tom Daschle, D-S.D., not because they objected to the highway bill but to pressure Lott to agree to allow a clean vote the following year on unrelated campaign finance legislation. Daschle hailed his party's unity, calling it "the biggest test" Democrats faced all year.

Some cloture votes had only regional significance, such as the 93-2 vote to limit debate on the motion to take up the defense authorization bill (S 936), which contained a provision opposed by members from California and Texas.

Some cloture votes were needed to overcome resistance from a small but determined band of Democrats, such as the 89-5 vote to invoke cloture on proceeding to the Food and Drug Administration (FDA) overhaul bill (S 830) and the 94-4 vote to end debate on the bill.

Other cloture votes appeared constructed for purely political reasons. Members voted five times on ending debate on campaign finance legislation. But it was clear before the first votes were cast that proponents of the bill (S 25) could not surmount the 60-vote hurdle. The closest they came was 53 votes, as all 45 Democrats and eight Republicans sought to allow a vote on the bill.

In the list of cloture votes that follows, successful votes are shown in **bold**.

Date	Bill	Description	Vote
April 29	S 543	Volunteer Liability Limitation	53-46
April 30	S 543	Volunteer Liability Limitation	55-44
May 7	**S 672**	**Supplemental Appropriations**	**100-0**
May 15	S 4	Compensatory Time, Flexible Credit	53-47
June 4	S 4	Compensatory Time, Flexible Credit	51-47
July 8	S 936	Fiscal 1998 Defense Authorization	46-45
July 14		**Klein Nomination**	**78-11**
Sept. 5	**S 830**	**FDA Overhaul**	**89-5**
Sept. 16	**S 830**	**FDA Overhaul**	**94-4**
Sept. 30	S 1156	Fiscal 1998 D.C.Appropriations	58-41
Oct. 7	S 25	Campaign Finance Legislation	52-48
Oct. 7	S 25	Campaign Finance Legislation	53-47
Oct. 7	**S 1156**	**Fiscal 1998 D.C. Appropriations**	**99-1**
Oct. 8	S 25	Campaign Finance Legislation	52-47
Oct. 9	S 25	Campaign Finance Legislation	52-47
Oct. 9	S 25	Campaign Finance Legislation	51-48
Oct. 23	S 1173	Highway and Transit Reauthorization	48-52
Oct. 23	S 1173	Highway and Transit Reauthorization	48-50
Oct. 24	S 1173	Highway and Transit Reauthorization	43-49
Oct. 28	S 1173	Highway and Transit Reauthorization	52-48
Oct. 31	HR 2646	Education Savings Accounts	56-41
Oct. 31	**HR 1119**	**Fiscal 1998 Defense Authorization**	**93-2**
Nov. 4	HR 2646	Education Savings Accounts	56-44
Nov. 4	**S 1269**	**Fast Track Trade Procedures**	**69-31**

Clinton Limits Vetoes

President Clinton vetoed only three bills in 1997, compared with 11 blocked in 1996. However, he used his newly acquired line-item veto authority to strike individual provisions from 11 other bills during the year. *(Line-item veto, p. 2-63)*

Clinton's first veto was cast in the midst of a battle with the Republican-controlled Congress over a disaster-relief emergency spending bill (HR 1469). Republicans had attached two unrelated policy "riders" to the bill, and despite White House warnings of a veto, Senate Majority Leader Trent Lott, R-Miss., predicted Clinton would not block flood-relief aid over the GOP add-ons. Clinton vetoed the measure June 9, minutes after he received it, accusing Republicans of playing politics at the expense of flood victims

With polls showing the public siding with Clinton, neither chamber attempted to override the veto. Instead, three days later Congress hastily sent Clinton a new version of the spending bill without the policy provisions. The president signed the measure (HR 1871 — PL 105-18). *(Supplemental, p. 9-84)*

It was four months until Clinton vetoed another bill. On Oct. 10, he vetoed a measure (HR 1122) that would have banned a second- and third-trimester abortion procedure unless the woman's life was endangered. Clinton said so-called partial-birth abortions should be permitted if the woman's health was threatened. He had vetoed a similar bill in 1996. The question of whether to attempt an override was put off until 1998. *(Abortion procedure ban, p. 6-12)*

Clinton used his third veto to block legislation (HR 2631) that would have restored the 38 projects that he had struck from the fiscal 1998 military construction spending law (HR 2016 — PL 105-45), using his line-item veto. An attempt to override that veto was expected in early 1998. *(Appropriations, p. 9-61)*

president said. "They want us to be partners, not partisans. They put us all here in the same boat, they gave us all oars and they told us to row."

The address was short on new proposals (a July 4 deadline for campaign finance reform, designation of 10 rivers for environmental cleanup) and long on refashioned, poll-tested campaign initiatives such as expansion of the Family and Medical Leave Act and a $1,500 tax credit for college tuition.

Clinton touched on a range of issues. He called for a balanced budget but not a constitutional amendment requiring one. He urged the promotion of new technologies at home and of new democracies abroad, as well as the revitalization of the environment and the overhaul of campaign finance laws.

But the pillar of his address was education, which he described as a "national security issue for our future." Many Republicans welcomed the president's decision to make education his top priority and concurred with his goals but expressed serious reservations about his $51 billion proposal that called for national standards in curriculum and testing.

Those concerns aside, however, members of the GOP-controlled Congress sensed a bipartisan outreach in the signals Clinton sent in both his inaugural address and the State of the Union speech. "He encouraged bipartisan accord," Sen. Thad Cochran, R-Miss., said of Clinton. "I think he will get it from our side. . . . The Republicans are ready if he is." *(Clinton speech, p. D-17; GOP response, p. D-22)*

The Beleaguered Speaker

In one of the sharpest contrasts with the 104th Congress, Speaker Newt Gingrich, R-Ga., the undisputed leader of the GOP "revolution" that swept Capitol Hill in 1995, saw his hold on power severely weakened. Intraparty bickering over whether to retain him as Speaker was a subtheme through much of the year, repeatedly distracting House Republicans. *(Gingrich, p. 1-11)*

Dogged by ethics questions and viewed as too conciliatory by junior conservatives, Gingrich compounded his own problems by his widely perceived arrogance and his propensity for unilateral decisions that sometimes undercut his top lieutenants at key moments.

Following a two-year investigation, a special subcommittee of the House ethics committee had formally charged Gingrich the preceding December with violating House rules. Gingrich was charged with improperly using money raised by tax-exempt groups to pay for college courses that he taught from 1993 to 1995 — courses that Gingrich said had no partisan purpose, but which in fact appeared to have been designed to help the GOP take over the House in 1994. Gingrich was also charged with having misled the committee about the facts. *(1995 Almanac, p. 1-19; 1996 Almanac, p. 1-31)*

Negotiations with the committee produced a stunning public admission by Gingrich on Dec. 21, 1996, that he had broken House rules and given the committee inaccurate information, though he said that was unintentional. Gingrich had consistently claimed that the case against him was no more than a partisan vendetta by Democrats, and his admissions rocked House Republicans.

With disillusionment growing among the rank and file, Gingrich waged a no-holds-barred campaign to retain his post as Speaker. Even then, he barely squeaked by in the Jan. 7 balloting with 216 votes — just three more than what was needed for a majority of those present and voting. Six Republicans voted present, and four voted for various other Republicans. Minority Leader Richard A. Gephardt, D-Mo., received 205 votes. *(Vote 3, p. H-2)*

Ten days later, after receiving a report that concluded Gingrich had engaged in a pattern of "disregard and lack of respect for the standards of conduct," the ethics committee voted Jan. 17 to recommend that the Speaker be reprimanded for his transgressions and fined $300,000 to reimburse the committee for the costs of disproving his misleading statements. The House concurred Jan. 21 by a vote of 395-28; it was the first time the House had ever voted to reprimand a sitting Speaker. *(Vote 8, p. H-4)*

The episode left Gingrich with shaky control over his own troops, especially the hardline revolutionaries who had always been wary of his tendencies to compromise and now saw him as a tarnished leader to boot. Their discontent would grow into a serious attempt to topple Gingrich from power just four months later.

That disarray in the House left a power vacuum that was quickly filled by the more placid Senate, whose GOP leaders had taken a back seat to their brasher House colleagues in 1995-96. But while Senate Majority Leader Trent Lott, R-Miss., helped guide the post-revolutionary Republican Congress to deals on the budget and taxes, he displayed no appetite for the sort of larger role outside the institution that Gingrich sought.

A Balanced-Budget Deal

The central achievement of the year for both Republicans and Democrats was the deal to balance the budget, a goal that had eluded Washington for more than a quarter century. The negotiations succeeded in 1997, propelled by both a new spirit of compromise and a burgeoning economy that drove tax revenues higher than anyone had predicted.

Republicans had begun the year furious at partisan assertions during the fall election campaign that they were out to destroy Medicare, and wary of being hammered again for taking bold steps to balance the budget.

Speaking to the Republican National Committee on Jan. 17, Lott warned that when it came to balancing the budget, "we're saying to him, as we would say down home, 'Mr. President, you first, sir. Let's see the whites of your eyes, Mr. President.' . . . We're not going to be demagogued in the future like we have been occasionally in the past."

The first public sign that things were changing was Republicans' refusal to lambaste Clinton's Feb. 6 budget proposal. Instead, they bit their tongues and refused to criticize a budget they privately found disappointing, so as not to provoke a repeat of the acridly partisan atmosphere that had helped poison budget talks in 1995-96. "We will come up with a budget hopefully within six weeks or so that is supported by the administration and the Congress," Lott said confidently Feb. 6.

In fact, behind the scenes, Clinton budget operatives were already working with congressional budget drafters, first with the more receptive Senate, then with the House as well. Republicans and Democrats alike were eager for a deal that would put the divisive issue behind them.

Though Lott's prediction seemed almost naively optimistic at the time, it turned out to be right — if a bit off on how much time it would take. Little more than 12 weeks later, on May 2, Clinton and Republicans announced that a deal was at hand to balance the budget by 2002 while cutting taxes. In a last-minute twist that demonstrated the key role of the robust economy, the Congressional Budget Office (CBO) increased its five-year revenue estimates by $225 billion, enabling negotiators to eliminate or ease some of the most controversial proposals in their package.

Although some of the initial agreement was put into writing two weeks later, it was still only a sketch. Many of the details were left to be filled in by lawmakers writing the bills that would implement the deal later in the year.

GOP Troubles

Shortly afterward, Republican leaders staged an an ill-conceived showdown that seemed to signal that they had learned nothing from their disastrous confrontations with Clinton in 1995-96 — or from the win-win negotiations they had just completed with him on the balanced-budget deal. Despite repeated White House veto threats, GOP leaders in June tried to force the president to accept two controversial policy riders by attaching them to a must-pass disaster relief bill (HR 1469).

The first provision, aimed at increasing GOP leverage in future budget negotiations with the White House, would have guaranteed continued funding at existing levels to any agency whose regular appropriations bill had not become law by the Oct. 1 start of the fiscal year. The second would have blocked the use of GOP-opposed statistical sampling during the 2000 census. Democrats said the technique would ensure that the poor and minorities were not undercounted; Republicans feared it would lead to artificially inflated Democratic voter rolls.

Congressional Leadership
105th Congress, 1st Session

Senate

President Pro Tempore — Strom Thurmond, R-S.C.
Majority Leader — Trent Lott, R-Miss.
Majority Whip — Don Nickles, R-Okla.
Republican Conference Chairman — Connie Mack, R-Fla.
Republican Conference Secretary — Paul Coverdell, R-Ga.
Minority Leader — Tom Daschle, D-S.D.
Minority Whip — Wendell H. Ford, D-Ky.
Democratic Conference Secretary — Barbara A. Mikulski, D-Md.

House

Speaker — Newt Gingrich, R-Ga.
Majority Leader — Dick Armey, R-Texas
Majority Whip — Tom DeLay, R-Texas
Chairman of the Republican Conference — John A. Boehner, R-Ohio
Minority Leader — Richard A. Gephardt, D-Mo.
Minority Whip — David E. Bonior, D-Mich.
Chairman of the Democratic Caucus — Vic Fazio, D-Calif.

Republicans gambled that Clinton would not dare to follow through on his veto threat, or that if he did, he would pay a terrible political price for holding up badly needed flood aid for the Midwest.

That turned out to be a serious miscalculation. Clinton vetoed the bill minutes after he got it June 9, and the public directed its anger at congressional Republicans. There had been so many delays by Congress in getting the bill to Clinton in the first place that the GOP's message was overwhelmed by criticism from flood victims. Public pressure on Republicans quickly ratcheted up from uncomfortable to unbearable. "We're getting pounded," said Rep. Fred Upton of Michigan.

Lott — who had predicted that Clinton would never veto the measure and had promised to pass it again unchanged if the president did — faced a Democratic minority that tied up the Senate, insisting that no other bill would pass until a second flood aid measure came to the floor without the GOP riders.

In the House, Gingrich and Majority Leader Dick Armey, R-Texas, faced a rebellion from their own moderates, who demanded, in words from Clinton's veto message, a "clean, unencumbered" measure. *(Text, p. D-32)*

Gingrich and Lott finally decided to cut their losses. On June 12, they sent Clinton a second flood aid bill, which he immediately signed into law (HR 1871 — PL 105-18). To underscore his victory, Clinton held a hastily scheduled signing ceremony in the Oval Office, during which he underlined his signature twice and then raised his clenched fist in the air.

"It doesn't get any better than this," said Sen. Christopher J. Dodd, D-Conn.

Coup Plot Transfixes House

Republicans across the political spectrum were upset with the way their leadership had handled the episode. "It's another example, like the shutdown of the government, where peo-

Membership Changes

105th Congress, First Session

DEATHS

Name (District)	Date	Successor
Rep. Frank Tejeda, D-Texas (28)	Jan. 30, 1997	Ciro D. Rodriguez, D, sworn in April 17, 1997
Rep. Walter Capps, D-Calif. (22)	Oct. 28, 1997	Vacant at session's end

RESIGNATIONS

Name (District)	Date	Reason	Successor
Rep. Bill Richardson, D-N.M. (3)	Feb. 13, 1997	Ambassador to U.N.	Bill Redmond, R, sworn in May 20, 1997
Rep. Susan Molinari, R-N.Y. (13)	Aug. 1, 1997	CBS News anchor	Vito J. Fossella, R, sworn in Nov. 5, 1997
Rep.Thomas M. Foglietta, D-Pa. (1)	Nov. 11, 1997	Ambassador to Italy	Vacant at session's end
Rep. Floyd H. Flake, D-N.Y. (6)	Nov. 15, 1997	Pastor, Allen AME Church	Vacant at session's end

ple lose confidence in Republicans' ability to lead," said David M. McIntosh of Indiana, a leader of the firebrand GOP Class of 1994.

The debacle accelerated a revolt against Gingrich that had been brewing secretly for months. A core group of some 20 mostly junior conservative Republicans had been meeting in private to share their frustrations with the Speaker's leadership. Now, Gingrich's own top lieutenants —Armey, Majority Whip Tom DeLay of Texas, GOP Conference Chairman John A. Boehner of Ohio, and Bill Paxon of New York, who held an informal post as chairman of the leadership meetings — were drawn into the plotting.

The leaders later claimed that they were simply trying to learn what the rebels were up to and to intervene if necessary. But many of the junior lawmakers reported that the leaders had been more deeply involved. The plotting ended when Armey told the others he would no longer take part and informed Gingrich of the discussions.

Once word of the abortive coup leaked out, the House was transfixed by the destructive disarray at its highest levels. Gingrich demanded and received Paxon's resignation from his appointive post, but he did not move against the other three, who had all been elected to their positions by the Republican Conference.

Forced to re-evaluate his own performance, Gingrich tried thereafter to play a more traditional role as Speaker. He curtailed his travel, stuck close to the House and made frequent appearances on the floor to be available to rank-and-file members. By the end of the year, Gingrich seemed to have shored up his own standing, but his once formidable leadership team was unable to rebuild its close bonds.

Summer Focus: Reconciliation Bills

Despite the seemingly crippling disarray in the House, Republicans managed to pull together over the summer to finish negotiating and then pass twin reconciliation bills that wrote into law the balanced budget and tax cuts that the president and GOP leaders had agreed to in principle in May. The spending and tax bills (HR 2015 — PL 105-33, HR 2014 — PL 105-34) were signed Aug. 5.

The legislation was the last and most politically important item left over from the House Republicans' "Contract With America," the policy agenda with which the GOP had taken control of Congress nearly three years earlier.

As calculated by CBO in September, the five-year plan provided for a total of $116 billion in net deficit reduction, including $80 billion in net tax cuts. Clinton and the Democrats got more money for some domestic priorities, such as $20 billion for health care for poor children. And Republicans were able to deliver on their 1994 promises to cut taxes. The agreement included a $500-per-child tax credit for families and a reduction on individuals' taxes on profits from the sale of investments such as stocks.

The deal was also a boon for a president who, since his reelection in 1996, had been rediscovering his centrist Democrat roots and thinking about his legacy. Clinton called the legislation "the achievement of a generation."

As part of the package, projected Medicare spending was trimmed by $112 billion over five years and projected Medicaid spending was reduced by $7 billion. Medicare was expanded to include more managed care options, as well as a pilot program of tax-exempt medical savings accounts. In Medicaid, governors won wide latitude to place enrollees in managed care plans, no longer needing a waiver from the federal government to do so.

The children's health care initiative was financed in part by a 15-cent-per-pack increase in the federal tax on cigarettes.

Spending Bills Dominate As Session Winds Down

With the budget deal under its belt, Congress returned from its August recess to an agenda so anticlimactic that GOP leaders began talking about adjourning by Oct. 31, two weeks earlier than planned. In both chambers, the emphasis was on mopping up legislation that had been overshadowed by the budget deal. The top priorities: the 13 annual appropriations bills and a few other items important to constituents, such as a multibillion-dollar highway bill.

Also, in mid-September, the White House launched its campaign to win renewal of fast track authority — expedited treatment of trade agreements negotiated by the president.

The month of September was largely spent working on appropriations bills in advance of the Oct. 1 start of the new fiscal year. Just four of the bills cleared by Sept. 30, with a fifth completed the next day. Four of the remaining spending bills were snagged over controversial policy riders — abortion and family planning (foreign operations), vouchers for private schools (District of Columbia), national student testing (Labor, HHS and Education) and census sampling (Commerce, Justice, State).

By the end of October, the target adjournment date had slipped to Nov. 7. Five more spending bills had cleared, but the four that had been caught up in policy fights remained stuck. Work in October was also interrupted by a weeklong recess and by a series of procedural objections that House Democrats began raising to even non-controversial bills in an attempt to pressure the GOP to consider campaign finance legislation. Lawmakers also struggled to finish the FDA overhaul and the huge highway transportation bill.

With the exception of Clinton's voluntary national testing plan for schools, each of the disputed appropriations riders had been hashed out before — mostly to the dissatisfaction of conservatives. But conservatives refused to knuckle under, to the dismay of House Appropriations Committee Chairman Robert L. Livingston, R-La., who was determined to avoid having to bundle unfinished spending measures into a year-end omnibus appropriations bill. Twice before, Clinton had used such circumstances to maximize his leverage and force Republicans to cave to his priorities.

Clinton Loses on Fast Track

Meanwhile, Clinton was having troubles of his own as House Democrats refused to support the renewal of his fast-track trade negotiating authority. Despite an all-out blitz by the White House, Democratic vote-counters signaled that only about a quarter of the 205-member House Democratic Caucus would back the bill. Faced with all but certain defeat on the legislation, House GOP leaders delayed a scheduled vote from Nov. 7 to Nov. 9, and began using Clinton's weakness on fast track as leverage to try to seek concessions from him on the four stalled appropriations bills.

Gingrich warned the White House, which had threatened to veto all four spending bills, that conservative Republicans would oppose fast track in droves unless Clinton made concessions on those matters.

Compared with the tumultuous House, the Senate — traditionally more friendly toward trade initiatives — was an island of calm. In a pair of procedural votes taken Nov. 4 and Nov. 5, senators demonstrated their readiness to pass the trade bill by a surprisingly large margin. Then they waited for the House.

But the House never acted. Clinton was unable to rally Democrats, and the bill was shelved for the year on Nov. 10.

Campaign Finance: Scandal but No Reform

The final months of the session also saw bitter fights over campaign finance reform. The renewed emphasis on legislative compromise in the 105th Congress had not caused the parties to take a break from partisan warfare. Instead, they shifted most of the vitriol outside the legislative arena, where they took each other on over which side had more egregiously abused the campaign fundraising system in 1996.

A series of Senate hearings showcased both sides' embarrassing excesses, but the revelations generated no new momentum for tightening campaign finance laws. While Democrats and a handful of Republicans in the Senate backed an ambitious rewrite of those laws, there was not enough support to overcome a determined filibuster led by Lott and other GOP senators. The House declined to take up a similar measure. *(Campaign finance, pp. 1-20, 1-26)*

Republicans hoped they could seriously wound Clinton, the Democratic National Committee (DNC) and Democrats in general by exposing what the GOP felt were outrageous abuses of campaign laws.

Committees in the House and Senate promised explosive hearings. But the effort by Indiana Republican Dan Burton's House Government Reform and Oversight Committee barely got off the ground in 1997, leaving Chairman Burton to promise major revelations and a full set of hearings in 1998. By late October, Burton's committee had spent some $3 million while managing to hold just one hearing.

In the Senate, Tennessee Republican Fred Thompson's Governmental Affairs Committee produced more bang for the buck, spending $2.2 million to hold 32 hearings from July to October. But despite 12 weeks of hearings that Thompson formally ended Oct. 31, the chairman could never fully prove his opening contention that the government of China had hatched and carried out a plan to subvert U.S. elections with concealed donations to candidates.

Thompson's often contentious hearings painted an unflattering portrait of a White House and a DNC obsessed with raising campaign cash and often lax about where the money came from. Witnesses told of funneling foreign money through straw donors in the United States, but other testimony showed that much of the tainted money was returned. And while the committee showed again and again how donations bought access to Clinton, Vice President Al Gore and senior administration officials, there was no conclusive evidence that cash ever bought a change in White House policy.

Moreover, Democrats showed that then-Republican National Committee Chairman Haley Barbour pursued money he either knew or should have known was foreign, a revelation that helped offset the political damage to Democrats.

In the end, while the hearings exposed seamy behavior on both sides, they failed to outrage the public or embarrass Congress enough to overcome lawmakers' enormous resistance to changing the money-raising system that had gotten them elected.

Senate Democrats and a handful of Senate Republicans failed Oct. 7, 8 and 9 to garner the 60 votes necessary to stop a GOP-led filibuster against campaign finance legislation (S 25) sponsored by John McCain, R-Ariz., and Russell D. Feingold, D-Wis.

The Democrats embraced defeat as an opportunity to lay the blame on the GOP. But Republicans were unabashed about killing off what they said was a bad bill. "McCain-Feingold is dead," said Sen. Mitch McConnell, R-Ky., the lead opponent of attempts to tighten existing campaign fundraising restrictions. "This effort to put the government in charge of political discussion isn't going to pass now, isn't going to pass tomorrow, is not going to pass ever." For 1997, at least, McConnell was right.

Adjournment Welcomed

The session finally ground to a close Nov. 13, with weary lawmakers happy just to get out of town. The Senate departed first, adjourning at 7:55 p.m. The House followed suit at 10:44 p.m. It was the earliest end of a first session of Congress since 1965. *(First session at a glance, p. 1-4)*

Amid the partisan disputes over abortion and campaign finance, and the bitter family feud among Democrats over trade, the bonhomie and bipartisanship surrounding the budget deal had become a hazy summer memory. More immediate was the huge stack of bills that Congress had failed to

First Session Highlights

At the midpoint in the 105th Congress, lawmakers had cleared a few major pieces of legislation, but much remained on their agenda. The following are highlights:

What Congress Did

➤ Cleared legislation to balance the federal budget by 2002.

➤ Gave families a $500-per-child tax credit.

➤ Cut taxes on individual capital gains (profits from the sale of stocks and other investments) and sharply reduced the alternative minimum tax on corporations.

➤ Reduced spending for Medicare by $112 billion over five years, and for Medicaid by $7 billion.

➤ Created $20 billion in medical insurance for children of poor families.

➤ Cleared all 13 appropriations bills for fiscal 1998 separately, without a single government shutdown.

➤ Cut red tape at the Food and Drug Administration to allow new drugs and medical devices to come to the market sooner and to give terminal patients access to new treatments.

➤ Cleared stopgap legislation to keep federal transportation money flowing to the states in 1998 while work continued on a new six-year transportation bill.

➤ Bailed out Amtrak with $2.3 billion, saving the passenger rail service from bankruptcy.

➤ Made it easier to adopt abused and neglected children.

➤ Ratified the worldwide Chemical Weapons Convention, which outlawed chemical and biological weapons.

➤ Let stand President Clinton's decision to extend most-favored-nation status to China.

➤ Reprimanded and fined Speaker Newt Gingrich, R-Ga., for violations of House rules.

➤ Permitted a cost of living pay raise for lawmakers to take effect.

➤ Allowed the 1996 election of Democratic Sen. Mary L. Landrieu of Louisiana to stand despite a challenge from her Republican opponent.

What Congress Did Not Do

➤ Approve fast-track authority for the president to negotiate trade agreements.

➤ Revise the campaign finance laws to deal with fund-raising abuses identified in the 1996 elections.

➤ Produce a two-thirds majority to pass constitutional amendments to require a balanced budget and limit terms for members of Congress.

➤ Address the problem of juvenile crime.

➤ Overhaul the Internal Revenue Service.

➤ Enact GOP education policies, including vouchers and education savings accounts.

➤ Complete work on a major public housing overhaul.

➤ Cut off a Democratic filibuster blocking a bill aimed at allowing businesses to offer compensatory time off rather than pay overtime.

➤ End affirmative action hiring by the federal government and by federal contractors.

➤ Pass legislation deregulating the electric power industry.

➤ Pass legislation to limit businesses' exposure to lawsuits arising from faulty products.

➤ Ease regulations that industries found burdensome.

➤ Enact an omnibus banking bill.

➤ Act on a proposed settlement between 40 state attorneys general and the tobacco industry.

➤ Complete work on a House-initiated bill to make it easier for private property owners to appeal local zoning restrictions.

➤ Block new air quality regulations announced by the Environmental Protection Agency.

➤ Complete work on overhauling the superfund hazardous waste cleanup program and revising the Endangered Species Act.

➤ Override Clinton's veto of a bill banning an abortion procedure opponents called "partial birth" abortion.

➤ Reorganize the State Department and provide more than $800 million to pay off U.S. debts to the United Nations.

➤ Resolve the challenge to the election of Rep. Loretta Sanchez, D-Calif., launched by former GOP Rep. Robert K. Dornan.

send to the president. They included:

➤ The popular six-year reauthorization of the nation's highway and mass transit programs. Congress instead approved a short-term extension.

➤ Legislation to revamp the Internal Revenue Service. The House passed it, but the Senate postponed it to 1998.

➤ A major rewrite of the Endangered Species Act.

➤ An overhaul of campaign finance laws.

The session's final days were most painful for Clinton, who saw three of his major foreign policy initiatives go down in less than a week.

The president's desperate bid to win congressional approval of legislation renewing his fast-track trade negotiating authority had run into the brick wall of opposition erected by House Democrats.

A nettlesome dispute over abortion cost Clinton two other key priorities — a plan to pay off back debts to the United Nations and a proposed $3.5 billion commitment to help underwrite an International Monetary Fund (IMF) program to deal with global financial crises.

But it was not just Clinton's proposals that got buried. The cherished plans of Senate Foreign Relations Committee Chairman Jesse Helms, R-N.C., to restructure foreign policy agencies and revamp the United Nations (HR 1757) were stalled by the same imbroglio over abortion.

Lott badly wanted to move the six-year, $145 billion highway bill, which had wide bipartisan support. But that legislation was held hostage by Democrats to force a vote on a campaign finance bill. In the end, neither measure ever came to a vote in the Senate.

In one of its final actions, Congress cleared a bill aimed at rescuing Amtrak, the nation's passenger rail service, from bankruptcy (HR 2247 — PL 105-134).

But those bills were hardly the stuff of a rich legislative legacy. The limited output from the year was reflected in Republicans' post-adjournment wrap-ups, which repeatedly emphasized the importance of the budget deal.

Livingston reminded reporters that 1997 was the first year since Republicans took control of Congress in 1995 that all 13 annual appropriations bills had been enacted separately, rather than as pieces of year-end omnibus bills. Still, passing all of the nuts-and-bolts spending bills took six continuing resolutions.

The two sides essentially fought to a draw over the controversial appropriations riders. Clinton had to delay his national voluntary testing plan, while the conservatives' student voucher plan was scuttled by the Senate. On the census, the president could go forward with his plan to use statistical sampling, but Republicans won the right to an expedited court challenge of the procedure.

In their broader judgments of the first session, congressional leaders were predictably partisan. The Speaker pronounced the session "very productive," with the budget agreement ranking as the most important accomplishment. Senate Minority Leader Tom Daschle, D-S.D., chose to highlight the ability of Senate Democrats to use procedural maneuvers to block the GOP's agenda. Daschle said the unity of Democrats made it relatively easy to mount the 41 votes needed to sustain filibusters. "It keeps getting easier," he said. ■

Gingrich Weakened by Ethics Case

Once the undisputed leader of his party, House Speaker Newt Gingrich, R-Ga., began the year with bright hopes of recapturing the spirit of his early days in power. But he was unable to overcome the lingering backlash from an ethics case and the rank and file's misgivings about his erratic leadership. He was only narrowly re-elected as Speaker in January, and the forces of discontent within his own Republican conference dogged him for the rest of the year.

Gingrich was unable to reverse a slide in public opinion that made him one of the nation's most disliked politicians. His job performance ratings stood for most of the year at less than 35 percent. And he failed to shore up his standing with disgruntled House Republicans, many of whom had been swept into power with him in the 1994 elections but who gradually lost faith in his ability to carry the House GOP message and to lead them to victory against resurgent Democratic President Bill Clinton.

A mostly conservative group of junior members viewed Gingrich as too conciliatory toward moderates and the White House. But that, alone, was not enough to account for the disaster he confronted later in the year, when the rebels and some of his trusted lieutenants secretly plotted his ouster.

Among other things, Gingrich was hurt by his widely perceived arrogance. He traveled extensively to give speeches, taking him far away from the daily concerns of members. And while his missions often involved raising money for the party and for lawmakers' re-election campaigns, they were also designed to improve his standing in public opinion polls in advance of a possible campaign for president in 2000.

Gingrich was prone to unilateral decisions that took even some of his top lieutenants by surprise. In some cases, his on-the-spot proclamations undermined weeks or months of painstaking strategy. One such fateful error was his announcement in May that Republicans would be willing to separate the issue of tax cuts from the other elements of a major balanced-budget deal that the Republican-led Congress was negotiating with the White House. Conservatives howled, and Gingrich was forced to retreat.

Unhappiness with the Speaker culminated in July with an ill-conceived coup attempt plotted by a band of disgruntled House Republicans with behind-the-scenes encouragement from some of the leaders serving under Gingrich. The Speaker survived the ouster, which collapsed before it even got under way. But his hold on power was severely weakened, and Republicans for the first time began talking seriously about eventually finding a replacement for him.

Ironically, in spite of his problems and the almost nonstop attacks on his leadership by conservatives outside Congress, Gingrich managed to lead his party to victory on the budget legislation, forging an agreement that promised to yield the first balanced federal budget in 30 years. The legislation was the crown jewel of the policy agenda that House Republicans campaigned on when they took control of Congress. It would have been a career achievement for any Speaker, and especially for one who had aggressively led the effort to put the issue before the public in the first place.

Background

Republicans had managed to hold on to their majority in the House in the November 1996 elections, but by a much narrower margin than they had had in the 104th Congress.

Organizing for the new Congress, the House GOP caucused Nov. 20, 1996, and agreed to return Gingrich as Speaker, though the atmosphere was subdued. A small group of moderate Republicans had been outspoken in demanding that he step down until his ethics case was resolved, but the vote to return him was unanimous. Though the decision of the Republican Conference still had to be affirmed by the full House when the new Congress convened in January, Gingrich's re-election seemed assured.

Then on Dec. 31, in a kind of plea-bargaining arrangement with the House ethics committee, Gingrich acknowledged that he had failed to properly manage the financing of his political activities through charitable foundations. He also conceded a more serious offense — that he had given the committee misleading information in the course of its investigation. *(1996 Almanac, p. 1-31)*

In formal terms, Gingrich admitted that he had violated a House rule requiring that members act in a way that "shall reflect creditably on the House of Representatives."

The case grew out of a series of televised town hall meetings and college classes, called "Renewing American Civilization," that Gingrich created and taught between 1993 and 1995. They were financed through donations solicited by tax-exempt groups, an arrangement that allowed supporters to make undisclosed contributions and to claim tax write-offs as well — two benefits not available to them under election laws, which required full disclosure and provided no such tax write-offs.

While Gingrich maintained that the course was nonpartisan and thus eligible for tax-exempt support, an ethics investigatory subcommittee found that it was probably tied to party politics and to Gingrich's quest to lead a Republican takeover of Congress. Gingrich did not admit to improperly using tax-exempt groups for partisan politics, but instead acknowledged a lesser crime of failing to seek legal advice in his use of foundations to finance the course and town hall meetings.

He also acknowledged submitting misleading information to the panel about the course. However, he publicly blamed his attorney for the mistake and said he was unaware at the time that the attorney was conveying bad information to the ethics committee.

The sudden admissions of guilt jolted House Republicans, who had defended Gingrich through two years of repeated denials of wrongdoing. Gingrich had long claimed that the case was a partisan vendetta by Democrats. The new development also meant Republicans would be in the embarrassing position of having to vote on a punishment for their leader, not to mention having to cast highly visible votes to return him to the top House job.

Gingrich Re-Elected

The 105th Congress began with Gingrich in the midst of an all-out struggle to retain the speakership. The biennial election for House officers at the start of each new Congress — usually a prefabricated event that affirmed the majority party's choice for Speaker — had become an intrigue-filled drama.

A loosely aligned group of Republicans who had grown disillusioned with Gingrich's erratic style was engaged in a silent revolt, refusing to publicly proclaim their support of him.

Their votes were pivotal. The Speaker was chosen by a majority of lawmakers present and voting, and Republicans held a relatively slim 227-207 majority in the House, with one independent lawmaker. With all the Democrats and the one independent expected to vote for Minority Leader Richard A. Gephardt, D-Mo., it would take just 20 Republicans voting present rather than casting votes for Gingrich to tip the contest: Gephardt would win on a 208-207 vote, a disastrous scenario for Republicans.

The rebels hoped Gingrich would bow out before that happened, allowing some other prominent Republican leader to take over. However, it never was clear who that successor would be.

The Speaker's conservative allies outside the House deserted him, calling on him to step aside until all the questions about his ethics could be aired. They worried that Gingrich's weakness would make it impossible for the GOP to compete effectively with Clinton for control of the policy agenda, jeopardizing the strides Republicans felt they had made during the 104th Congress.

But the Speaker hunkered down for a fight, bringing to bear all the resources of the presiding officer of the House, and turning up the heat on wavering members with each passing day. Beginning in late December, Gingrich, Majority Leader Dick Armey of Texas, and other top GOP leaders and their aides waged a remarkable lobbying effort, undertaking a one-on-one, members-only campaign to put down the rebellion. Gingrich himself spoke to nearly every GOP member by phone during the holiday season.

The leaders faxed information on demand and held telephone conference calls connecting up to 200 members at a time. They established a 24-hour hotline, allowing members to check news developments daily and to ask questions. Gingrich and his advisers talked several times a day, and constantly updated whip checks.

One of their strongest arguments was the absence of a clear successor to Gingrich, which put Republicans in jeopardy of losing control of the election to the minority Democrats.

The no-holds-barred strategy worked. On Jan. 7, joyless House Republicans re-elected their Speaker, 216-205, over Gephardt — just three more votes than needed to attain a majority of those present and voting. Six Republicans voted present, and four voted for various other Republicans. *(Vote 3, p. H-2)*

In his acceptance speech, Gingrich apologized to his fellow lawmakers. "To whatever degree, in any way, that I have brought controversy or inappropriate attention to the House, I apologize," he said. "I feel humbled." *(Text, p. D-3)*

Speaker Reprimanded

While Gingrich's admission of guilt in December spared him the spectacle of a trial-like proceeding to defend himself, it posed another political problem for the GOP — the question of punishment.

Republicans on the Committee on Standards of Official Conduct, as the ethics committee was formally known, signaled that they would recommend a reprimand. A more serious penalty — censure — would automatically have disqualified Gingrich from serving as Speaker.

But ethics committee Democrats and the panel's special counsel, James M. Cole, were steadfast that no verdict on punishment would be made until after the evidence had been aired publicly at a sanctions hearing.

The two parties fought bitterly over the timing and duration of the hearing, as well as over the timing of the committee's report on the case. The committee itself, long a bipartisan island amid ethics storms, was torn asunder by the intensity of the feuding.

Chairman Nancy L. Johnson, R-Conn., and ranking member Jim McDermott, D-Wash., warred openly. The intense friction between the two thrust the chairmen of the subcommittee investigating Gingrich — Porter J. Goss, R-Fla., and Benjamin L. Cardin, D-Md. — into the role of leading the committee as the de facto chairmen.

In a bizarre side drama, McDermott was accused by Republicans of leaking to the press a clandestinely tape recorded conversation among Gingrich and his allies. The illegally recorded conversation, captured on tape by a Florida couple who happened to overhear the cellular phone transmissions on their police scanner, revealed Gingrich and his allies talking about ways to control damage and salvage his Speakership in advance of his admission of guilt in December. The release of the tape to the New York Times and other media outlets sparked a Justice Department investigation.

Panel Issues Report, Urges Reprimand

On Jan. 17, the ethics committee held a televised hearing, the first of its kind involving a House Speaker, where Cole outlined his findings. His report portrayed the Speaker's actions in a much harsher light than had GOP leaders.

Cole said he found that Gingrich had lied to the ethics subcommittee investigating the political connections of the tax-exempt networks that funded Gingrich's course. He said the financing arrangements violated federal tax law. The ethics panel declined to go as far as Cole in its findings, but said that Gingrich's actions were either intentional or reckless. "Neither choice reflects credibly on the House of Representatives," Cole said.

The report said Gingrich had engaged in a pattern of "disregard and lack of respect for the standards of conduct." It contradicted the Speaker's contention that he had decided to teach the course and some televised workshops to spread his ideas, and inadvertently brushed up against the tax code along the way.

"Mr. Gingrich ran a lot of very yellow lights. Orange lights. There were bells and whistles going off," Cole said at the hearing. "He was taking risks. Going right up to the edge."

Cole and the panel's investigatory subcommittee recommended that Gingrich be reprimanded and fined $300,000 to offset the cost of the investigation, particularly those portions devoted to discerning the truth from the Speaker's misleading submissions.

After hearing arguments from Cole and from Gingrich's attorneys, the committee voted 7-1 the same day to accept the subcommittee's recommendation. It also released Cole's 213-page report.

House Reprimands Gingrich

On Jan. 21, the House accepted the committee's recommendations, voting to reprimand the Speaker and impose a $300,000 penalty. The tally was 395-28, with five members voting present. Johnson called the sanctions "tough and unprecedented." *(Vote 8, p. H-4)*

Voting yes on the reprimand resolution were 196 Republicans, 198 Democrats and 1 Independent. Voting no were 26 Republicans and two Democrats, Gene Taylor of Mississippi and Earl F. Hilliard of Alabama. During the debate, Gingrich stayed out of public view, sequestered in his second-floor suite at the Capitol.

For all the partisan rancor the case had aroused, the actual vote was uneventful. Republicans were resigned to casting the first vote in history to reprimand a sitting Speaker. Democrats were uncharacteristically quiet, a strategy designed to focus public attention on Gingrich's punishment, not on their reaction.

While past Speakers had had brushes with House rules, Gingrich was the first to be hit with a formal sanction.

Jim Wright, D-Texas, was the first Speaker to be formally charged with rules violations, but he resigned in May 1989 before a trial-like disciplinary hearing could be held. Speakers Thomas P. "Tip" O'Neill, D-Mass., and Carl Albert, D-Okla., were tangentially tainted by allegations in a 1970s scandal involving bribes to lawmakers from Korean businessmen. But they were never accused of any crimes. Speaker John W. McCormack, D-Mass., attracted attention for his close ties to a lobbyist, but the speculation ended when he retired in 1970. *(Wright, 1989 Almanac, p. 36; McCormack, 1970 Almanac, p. 116)*

With the leadership under immense pressure to clean up its act, Armey took the immediate step of appointing James V. Hansen, R-Utah to replace Johnson as ethics chairman. Then, he and Gephardt agreed to temporarily disband the rest of the committee to foster a cessation of hostilities between the two parties. The two appointed a task force to come up with ways to make the panel more immune to partisan warfare. *(Ethics task force, p. 1-32)*

Although the vote put the ethics case to rest, the effects would be felt by the House's embattled leader and its dispirited rank-and-file for months to come. Gingrich, once considered one of the most influential figures of the modern Congress, was now a much weakened force.

Frustration Builds

Discontent with Gingrich's leadership grew as the year progressed and began to infect the upper reaches of the leadership. The Speaker's tendency to be only intermittently involved in problems that arose in the House and his penchant for unilateral decision-making began to grate.

His campaign to rehabilitate his image and his pursuit of a new vision for the Republican Party kept Gingrich on the road frequently. He traveled extensively to try out new themes for the GOP, such as tackling the problems of drug dependence, teenage pregnancy and substandard public schools. He delegated much of the responsibility for the day-to-day running of the House to Armey.

But at times, Gingrich would jump back into his Speaker's role, attempting to resolve differences between warring factions in the Republican Conference, doing political combat with the White House or setting the Republican message of the week. His on-again-off-again management style began to cause him increasing problems with Armey and the other leaders, especially at times of high stress for the party.

When he did play the role of full-time Speaker, Gingrich performed admirably. In the first part of the year, he, along with Senate Majority Leader Trent Lott, R-Miss., and the Republican chairmen of the House and Senate Budget committees began to make real progress is negotiating a balanced-budget deal with Clinton.

With his own re-election out of the way, Clinton conceded the need for deeper cuts in Medicare spending than he had the year before, when the two sides failed to reach a deal. He also signaled newfound flexibility on tax cuts, including cherished Republican priorities like a cut in the capital gains tax rate.

Extracting a big win from Clinton on tax cuts was perhaps Gingrich's best chance to reassure conservatives who were increasingly suspect of his leadership. And a show of force on tax cuts could insulate him from criticism from the right when it came time to make compromises on the spending side of the budget, which he invariably would have to do to get a deal with the Democratic White House.

But as was often the case over the course of the year, Gingrich squandered his political opportunities. In mid-March, he inflamed core GOP conservatives, including Armey, by announcing in the press that House Republicans would agree to temporarily postpone their tax cut proposals in order achieve a budget agreement with Clinton. Without tax cuts on the table, Gingrich reasoned, Clinton would have no excuse to back out of a budget deal. Later, Congress could present him with the tax cut package, perhaps in 1998 when the midterm elections would make it difficult for the president to say no.

But the logic did not fly with conservatives, who interpreted Gingrich's remarks as a retreat from a core GOP commitment. In a highly public split with Gingrich, Armey declared he would never support a budget deal without tax cuts. Another conservative member of the leadership, Whip Tom DeLay, also of Texas, said he supported Gingrich's strategy, but that did little to mollify angry lawmakers on the right.

Restless junior conservatives in the conference grew openly defiant. On March 20, 11 of them forced the defeat of a leadership-backed rule on the floor, humiliating Gingrich. The rule governed floor debate on a resolution to increase funding for standing committees, a betrayal, the rebels charged, of the institutional reforms they had ushered in two years earlier. The rule failed, 210-213. *(Vote 67, p. H-20)*

Even Gingrich's victories held a negative flip side for the beleaguered Speaker. On March 20, Gingrich led the House to pass, 295-136, a ban on the controversial procedure known as "partial-birth" abortion, a victory for conservatives. *(Vote 65, p. H-20)*

But the good news for conservatives was marred by the leadership's ham-handed treatment of popular Judiciary Committee Chairman Henry J. Hyde, R-Ill. Hyde had led his committee to pass one version of the abortion ban, but Gingrich summarily substituted the leadership's bill for the committee's handiwork, an insult to Hyde. Leadership aides conceded it was a mistake not to bring Hyde into the strategy much earlier.

Behind the scenes, a loosely aligned group of a dozen to 20 lawmakers began meeting in secret to discuss what to do about what they viewed as their increasingly ineffectual leadership. In late March, Gingrich's problems were summed up in one widely repeated phrase by GOP moderate Peter T. King of New York, who called the Speaker "road kill on the highway of American politics."

Discomfort Over Dole Loan

In the spring, Gingrich took steps to rebuild bridges with the party faithful.

He made what was deemed a highly successful trip to Asia during the Easter recess, leading a bipartisan group of House members to China, Taiwan, Hong Kong, Korea and Japan. Republicans applauded him for taking a tough stance with China, after Gingrich warned against repression in Hong Kong during the coming transition from British to Chinese rule.

Back home, the Speaker attempted to make amends with the right with a series of speeches in which he stumped for more far-reaching tax cuts than he had in the past. He called for eliminating all capital gains and estate taxes. And he reiterated his commitment to tax cuts in private meetings with House Republicans, including sessions with discontented junior members.

The only blot on his reformation campaign was continued speculation about how he would pay the $300,000 ethics committee fine, a festering issue among fellow Republicans who feared further embarrassment for the party.

A former history professor of modest financial means, Gingrich pondered for months over ways to pay the committee. On April 17, he announced an unusual arrangement in which he would borrow the money from former Senate Majority Leader and GOP presidential candidate Bob Dole of Kansas. Under the terms agreed to by the two men, Gingrich would not have to pay any of the principal or the 10 percent interest on the loan until 2005, after his term as Speaker had expired.

The arrangement kicked up a new round of criticism about the Speaker's judgment. Some Republicans thought Gingrich gave the appearance of accepting a special deal from Dole, who had gone to work for a major lobbying and law firm with dozens of clients interested in legislative outcomes on Capitol Hill.

Newly installed ethics committee Chairman Hansen and ranking member Howard L. Berman, D-Calif., refused to approve the deal. Gingrich finally settled for a modified arrangement in which he agreed to pay half the fine out of his own pocket and borrow the rest from Dole under more conventional terms. The loan was secured by a life insurance policy, Gingrich's house in Georgia and other of the Speaker's assets.

Although cloakroom talk of replacing Gingrich as Speaker grew steadily, Republicans were perpetually at a loss over who might replace him.

The next in succession, Armey, was considered too dogmatically conservative by many Republicans and not articulate enough for the television age. However, that did not discourage Armey from beginning to ready himself to take over at some point in the future. He began quietly holding weekly dinners with moderates to assuage their concerns about him. And he solicited critiques from members about his appearances on television news shows.

Other lawmakers considered promising but not ready for prime time were GOP Conference Chairman John A. Boehner of Ohio, former National Republican Congressional Committee Chairman Bill Paxon of New York, Budget Committee Chairman John R. Kasich of Ohio, and Appropriations Committee Chairman Robert L. Livingston of Louisiana.

Ironically, even as reservations about Gingrich spread among the rank-and-file, he was able to lead Republicans to their crowning achievement, a deal with Clinton to balance the budget in five years. The agreement, reached in early May, was the fruit of a long legislative quest undertaken by Republicans when they took control of Congress in 1995, and no one better symbolized that effort than Gingrich, the man who engineered the takeover.

Although the deal was a victory for the president as well, pride of ownership belonged to Gingrich. The plan included significant permanent tax cuts, so important to the GOP base and to Gingrich's precarious standing with core Republicans.

While conservatives still grumbled that the deal did not go far enough in trimming the size of the federal government, the plan attracted wide bipartisan support. After two weeks of discussions on the details, the House and Senate May 20-23 adopted nearly identical versions of a congressional budget resolution endorsing the pact.

The Last Straw

Gingrich was unable to savor the victory for long. The problem with his on-again, off-again stewardship of the House suddenly grew acute during work on an $8.6 billion supplemental spending bill to provide relief for flood ravaged states in the Midwest and Upper Plains.

Armey and other GOP leaders had adopted a strategy of attaching to the bill items they hoped Clinton could be forced to accept; they did not think he could veto such a popular piece of legislation. The most controversial riders were a provision that would effectively avert any further government shutdowns like the ones that had hurt Republicans in 1995-1996, and a second provision favored by the GOP to regulate how the 2000 census would be conducted.

The strategy failed miserably. Clinton vetoed the bill over the add-ons, and public attention was focused on television images of flood victims suffering while politicians in Washington squabbled. As in the earlier government shutdowns, the public blamed the GOP, not Clinton.

At that point, Gingrich stepped into the crisis and, without consulting Armey or the other leaders, swiftly replaced the earlier strategy. He and Lott ordered the bill stripped of extraneous provisions and sent to Clinton for his signature.

Although the House passed the bill June 12 by a vote of 348-74, all of Gingrich's top lieutenants — Armey, DeLay and Boehner — snubbed him by voting against it. Their strategy may have had serious weaknesses, but the leaders felt that they had once again been undermined by a Speaker arriving late on the scene. *(Vote 203, p. H-66)*

The humiliating events sparked a crisis in the leadership. Armey pointedly refused to defend the Speaker, and in an ominous turn of events, he, DeLay and Boehner began meeting secretly with the rebellious Republicans to hear their complaints about Gingrich.

Coup Plans Revealed

The breakdown of the leadership, which had mostly unfolded behind closed doors, exploded into public view with revelations in July that the leaders and some of the rebels had secretly discussed ways of ousting Gingrich. The coup never got off the ground, hampered by the continuing problem of deciding on a suitable successor. But plotting behind the Speaker's back by the men he had brought to power was nonetheless shocking.

As the press dug into the story, it became apparent that the chain of events began July 10, when Armey, DeLay, Boehner and Paxon, who held an informal post as chairman of the leadership meetings, engaged in a series of late-night meetings. At one of those sessions, Armey expressed frustration with Gingrich and said he was tired of taking the political heat for what he viewed as the Speaker's repeated blunders. The men decided that DeLay would meet with the rebels to find out whether they were serious about ousting Gingrich.

The leaders later claimed they were simply trying to find out what the rebels were up to and to intervene if necessary. But many of the junior lawmakers reported later that DeLay urged them to move ahead with a parliamentary maneuver called a motion to vacate the chair, which, on a simple majority vote, could be used to oust a Speaker.

It was also revealed that Armey, DeLay and Paxon discussed succession scenarios but could not agree on whose name would be put forward. If Republicans were unable to agree among themselves on a successor, the Democrats might be able to step forth and elect minority leader Gephardt as Speaker.

The plotting ended the next morning when Armey told the others he would no longer take part and informed Gingrich of the previous night's discussions.

The following days were tumultuous. Gingrich demanded and received Paxon's resignation from his appointive post, but he did not move against the other three, who were all elected to their positions by the Republican Conference. Despite their reservations about Gingrich, many Republicans felt their Speaker had been betrayed. Gingrich received a standing ovation when he arrived at a Republican caucus meeting held July 16 to fill low-rung leadership posts. Republicans chose Gingrich's candidate, Jennifer Dunn of Washington, to be vice chairman of the GOP Conference.

And in an extraordinary closed-door gathering on July 23, lawmakers compelled Armey, DeLay and Boehner to stand and describe their roles in the ouster talks. For the most part, the leaders blamed the bungled coup on fatigue, frustration and a series of miscues in which they inadvertently sent signals of readiness to the rebels.

Ironically, Gingrich's most valuable allies during that period were the institutionalists — the committee chairmen, the appropriations cardinals, the so-called go-along-get-along Republicans that he had once maligned for a defeatist acceptance of life in a permanent minority. Appropriations Chairman Livingston said the plotters demonstrated a "serious and appalling lack of judgment."

Coming Home

The near rebellion forced Gingrich to finally re-evaluate his own operation and the way he had redesigned the Speaker's role for himself.

He began to stick closer to the House and involve himself in the day-to-day concerns of fellow Republicans, giving up some of his self-assigned duties as party visionary. The experience taught him how dangerously isolated he had become, and he began to reach out to a circle of friends and advisers in the House to keep him closer in touch with the rank and file. He spent more time on the floor, so he could be seen by members and engage in informal, on-the-fly conversations.

He also began to keep tabs on the once trusted lieutenants who admitted varying degrees of complicity in the plotting. He broadened leadership meetings to include leaders other than the top three. In short, Gingrich strove to become what he likely had never thought he would be, a traditional Speaker.

As the year drew to a close, Gingrich's once formidable leadership team was unable to rebuild their close bonds. The members began to operate independently of one another, each concerned with his standing in the conference and his future in leadership.

Gingrich's own position was secure, but his future was very much in doubt. He began to toy with the idea of running for president in 2000, and many Republicans began to wonder whether he was looking for a graceful way to exit the House. ■

House Members Review Internal Operations

An innocuous sounding resolution to authorize funding for House standing committees sparked a brief mutiny by a group of junior Republicans. This and other internal House rules and personnel changes are summarized below.

Minor House Rules Changes

The House on Jan. 7 approved a package of new rules to govern the chamber for the 105th Congress. The vote was 226-202, along party lines. *(Vote 6, p. H-2)*

For the most part, lawmakers offered only limited debate on the package, concentrating on one element relating to a completion date for the ethics investigation of Speaker Newt Gingrich, R-Ga.

The ethics provision cleared the way for the members of the ethics committee (the Committee on Standards of Official Conduct) to continue serving on the panel until Jan. 21 to complete work on the Gingrich case. Many of those on the 10-member panel had wanted to rotate off the committee when their terms expired at the start of the 105th Congress on Jan. 7. *(Gingrich, p. 1-11)*

In large part, the rules changes were technical. Unlike 1995, when Republicans took control of the House and drew up a sweeping package of changes, the 1997 proposals were more narrowly crafted. Rules Committee Chairman Gerald B.H. Solomon, R-N.Y., called them "modest by comparison" to the changes adopted in 1995. *(1995 Almanac, p. 1-12)*

The most controversial change required non-governmental agencies that provided testimony before House committees to provide a list of the federal grants and contracts they had received in the previous three years. The change was a response to GOP concerns that nonprofit organizations that received federal funds had been improperly active in elections.

Another of the adopted rules directed the Speaker and minority leader to draw up a drug-testing policy for members and staff that was at least as strong as that which governed executive branch agencies. The final drug-testing plan was far weaker than an earlier proposal, which would have required that 10 percent of the House membership be randomly tested for drug use each month.

Other rules changes clarified earlier changes made by the Republican majority, and some reflected the GOP's experience in running the House. The Republicans moved to repeal a rule that prohibited committees from working in the afternoon while the House was conducting business. Republicans had discovered in 1996 that committees could not complete their markups in the morning hours, and had to go to the full House to get the rule waived.

The package also allowed committees to have a contingency fund for "unanticipated committee expenses." House Democratic Whip David E. Bonior of Michigan opposed the contingency fund, saying it would amount to "slush funds to conduct sham investigations."

Clarifying an existing rule, the package specified that any legislation to increase income tax rates would require a two-thirds majority vote of the House for approval. In 1996, Democrats had tried to apply the rule to all tax rate increases rather than just to income taxes.

Another rule banned members from distributing campaign contributions on the floor of the House, something Republican Conference Chairman John A. Boehner of Ohio was criticized for doing in the 104th Congress.

The rules also renamed the Committee on Economic and Educational Opportunities as the Committee on Education and the Workforce.

Committee Funding

The House on May 1 approved a resolution (H Res 129) funding 18 committees for the remainder of the 105th Congress, after an earlier version was blocked by a group of 11 angry GOP fiscal conservatives.

The resolution authorized $149.9 million, about 5 percent more than the panels received in the 104th Congress. The Appropriations Committee received its funds automatically, and the Government Reform and Oversight Committee had gotten its funds March 21, a day after the GOP rebels helped to derail the original version of the resolution.

The House approved the revised measure, 262-157. The only one of the 11 previous Republican dissidents who voted against the new funding was Mark W. Neumann of Wisconsin. The others were mollified by a $550,000 cut and by assurances from the leadership that the fiscal 1998 legislative appropriations bill would keep a lid on actual spending. *(Vote 98, p. H-32)*

The earlier dust-up occurred March 20, when 11 restless junior Republicans grew openly defiant of the leadership, preventing debate on the funding resolution and humiliating Speaker Newt Gingrich, R-Ga. The rebels joined with Democrats to defeat the rule for floor debate on the resolution (H Res 91 — H Rept 105-30), which would have increased committee funding by 14 percent over the previous year. They charged that the proposed increase was a betrayal of the institutional reforms they had ushered in two years earlier. The rule failed, 210-213. *(Vote 67, p. H-20)*

The bigger budgets had been pushed by the GOP leadership as a means of strengthening House committees' ability to oversee federal programs and agencies. Increased oversight was part of a leadership strategy to build a case for further cuts in what Republicans considered wasteful or unproductive programs.

After the vote, Gingrich further enraged conservatives by making the 11 defectors stand and explain their votes to their colleagues in a closed-door meeting of House Republicans. The action did nothing to improve the Speaker's standing in the ranks, which had hit a low point at that time. *(Gingrich, p. 1-11)*

After that confrontation, the leadership was able to win approval March 21 for funding for the Government Reform and Oversight Committee, which got $20 million, part of it for a high priority investigation of White House fundraising practices. The vote was 213-179. Also approved was a $7.9 million reserve fund for committees. *(Vote 71, p. H-22)*

After making minor cuts to appease the conservatives, the Oversight Committee approved the new resolution (H Res 129 — H Rept 105-79) by voice vote April 24. Adding together the reserve fund, the separate funding for the Government Reform and Oversight Committee and the $149.9 million the committee approved for the 18 committees, the sum total of committee funding was $177.8 million — only about $550,000 less than the funding level that had sparked the March mutiny.

New Chief Administrative Officer

James M. "Jay" Eagen III became the new chief administrative officer of the House, with the job of overseeing some 1,000 employees and the finances of the House's administrative offices. The House approved the appointment (H Res 207) by voice vote on July 31.

Eagen took over an office that had been plagued with accusations of mismanagement and abuse of authority by his predecessor, but the Republicans and Democrats who chose the 39-year-old staff director of the Education and the Workforce Committee for the job assured their colleagues that Eagen was the right person to restore the integrity of the office.

"Today I am losing my left arm, I am losing my right arm, but I can afford to lose both for the benefit of an institution I love," said Bill Goodling, R-Pa., chairman of the Education and the Workforce Committee. Eagen had worked for Goodling for 12 years, first as an administrative assistant and later as the top aide on the committee. "I can guarantee you he will serve this institution very, very well."

A four-member bipartisan task force recommended Eagen after a five-month search to replace Scot M. Faulkner, who was forced to resign in November 1996 after a rocky two-year tenure, which included an investigation launched by the House inspector general.

Democrats on the House Oversight Committee called on Chairman Bill Thomas, R-Calif., to release a report from the Inspector General on Faulkner and to hold hearings on his alleged mismanagement and abuse of authority. A draft report of the Inspector General's findings stated that Faulkner exhibited "poor judgment, mismanagement, abuse of authority and gross disregard for established policies and procedures." Faulkner said the report was false. *(1996 Almanac, p. 1-20)*

Vic Fazio, D-Calif., who served on the task force, said he

hoped Eagen would be "quite a contrast with the experience that we had during the first two years of the new majority's tenure here." Fazio said he backed the choice of Eagen because he found him to be "fair-minded and objective" and said he treated the minority "with the kind of respect that it is due."

When Republicans took over the House after the 1994 elections, they said they wanted a chief administrative officer from the private sector. But they had since come to favor hiring someone with a strong House background instead. Eagen's experience on the Hill dated to 1982, when he worked as a legislative assistant to Steve Gunderson, R-Wis., who eventually made Eagen his administrative assistant. In 1985, Goodling hired him as his administrative assistant, and he stayed there until 1991, when he became the minority staff director of the Education panel. ■

Senate Drops Landrieu Probe

A divisive and bitter investigation into charges that voter fraud tainted the outcome of the 1996 Louisiana Senate election ended with the Senate Rules and Administration Committee unanimously concluding that there was no evidence of widespread malfeasance to warrant unseating Democratic Sen. Mary L. Landrieu.

On Election Day, Nov. 5, 1996, Landrieu had narrowly defeated Republican state Rep. Louis "Woody" Jenkins by 5,788 votes out of 1.7 million cast. GOP Gov. Mike Foster certified Landrieu as the winner on Nov. 20, 1996.

But Jenkins, who had the strong backing of conservatives and the Republican right, alleged that skullduggery endemic to the Bayou state's Democratic Party cost him the election and propelled Landrieu to victory.

He leveled no specific charges at his opponent, but alleged that systematic illegality marred the contest. Jenkins' charges included vote buying, multiple voting, fraudulent voter registration, campaign finance violations, voting machine malfunctions, election commissioner wrongdoing and the illegal transporting of voters to the polls.

Jenkins initially pursued a challenge of the election results in the Louisiana courts, but abandoned that effort for lack of time and chose redress in the Senate, which is the final arbiter of its membership.

The Senate Rules and Administration Committee hired two outside counsels to investigate the charges and then, under pressure from conservatives who turned the case into a cause célèbre, rejected its independent lawyers' recommendations for a limited probe. On a party-line vote April 17, the panel chose to pursue an aggressive inquiry.

Over a six-month period, the investigation was marked by partisan fits and starts.

Democrats delayed the start of the investigation until ground rules were firmly established on the use of FBI agents and investigators from the General Accounting Office (GAO) and on the authority to issue subpoenas. John W. Warner, R-Va., chairman of the committee, directed that election-law attorneys from one of his home state's top law firms, McGuire Woods Battle and Boothe, spearhead the investigation.

In June, a few weeks after the second phase of the probe had begun, Democrats withdrew from the inquiry, saying investigators had found that a political operative for Jenkins, Thomas "Papa Bear" Miller, had paid witnesses to invent stories of voter fraud. The committee's minority referred incidents of alleged witness tampering to the Justice Department's criminal division.

In July, over the strong objections of the panel's Democrats, Republicans decided to pursue their own, open-ended investigation and granted Warner unprecedented subpoena power. The next month, the chairman was a one-man show in New Orleans, questioning Democratic officials and representatives from the gambling industry, which had had a gambling initiative on the ballot and had spent liberally during the 1996 campaign.

On Oct. 1, the committee concluded that there were isolated incidences of fraud, some election irregularities and lax record-keeping, but nothing on the scale of Jenkins' allegations of widespread, organized wrongdoing.

The committee voted 16-0 to end its investigation, saying "the evidence collected to date does not meet the applicable burden to justify further consideration" of Jenkins' petition that the Senate unseat Landrieu and order a new election.

Counsels Urge Limited Query

Hired by the Rules and Administration Committee in December 1996, Republican William B. Canfield III and Democrat Robert F. Bauer examined more than 8,000 pages of material submitted to the panel by Jenkins.

On April 8, the two lawyers reported to the committee that a limited investigation of three of Jenkins' claims was warranted. They recommended dismissal of four other charges relating to transporting voters, campaign finance violations, voting machine malfunctions and election commissioner malfeasance.

The counsels said they deemed Jenkins' charges of vote buying, multiple voting and fraudulent voter registration disturbing enough to examine whether "vote-by-vote, 5,788 or more illegal, fraudulent or stolen votes" were cast for Landrieu.

But they stressed that in all three claims, the evidence Jenkins provided to the committee added up to a limited probe, not a full-scale investigation. Specifically, they cited affidavits signed and sworn by Jenkins' campaign workers who said they interviewed individuals who might have participated in voter fraud or witnessed it.

"Affidavits based on hearsay [and in many cases double or triple hearsay] alone are not sufficiently reliable and credible to merit a full investigation," the counsels said.

The counsels sought the authority to conduct a four-week, limited investigation, and stressed the need for Jenkins to provide the names of those interviewed. The GOP candidate had withheld the names, contending that disclosing their identity would pose a threat to their safety.

Republicans Launch Full-Scale Probe

On April 17, Republicans on the committee, led by Chairman John W. Warner of Virginia, rejected the lawyers' recommendation and voted 9-7 along party lines for a broad-scale, everything-on-the-table investigation of the election. The committee also approved the appointment of a new investigative team, headed by prominent Republicans from Warner's home state of Virginia.

Members of the team included Richard Cullen, a former U.S. attorney who had been appointed by President George

Bush; George J. Terwilliger III, who served as deputy attorney general in the Bush administration; Frank B. Atkinson, who was deputy chief of staff to the attorney general in the Reagan administration; and James W. Dyke Jr., who worked as domestic policy adviser to Vice President Walter F. Mondale in the Jimmy Carter administration.

Working in conjunction — and keeping a close eye on the Republican-led team — was Democrat Bauer, one of the two independent counsels who had conducted the preliminary inquiry.

Angry committee Democrats said the efforts to overturn the election amounted to sour grapes on the part of Jenkins, who had failed three times in his attempts to win a Senate seat, beginning in 1978. "Hell hath no fury like a man beaten by a woman," said Dianne Feinstein, D-Calif., who had faced her own post-election challenge from former Republican Rep. Michael Huffington, whom she narrowly defeated in 1994.

Democrats saw the majority's push for an aggressive investigation as a move driven by the Republican leadership, particularly Senate Majority Leader Trent Lott of Mississippi. They reacted with surprise and vitriol to Warner's decision to carry out the leader's wishes.

Warner often had been at odds with the activist right in recent years, especially for his refusal to back Oliver L. North, the GOP Senate candidate in Virginia in 1994. North and Jenkins were political allies and personal friends.

But Warner was Jenkins' apparent mainstay, leading Democrats to speculate publicly that the chairman, elected to a fourth term in November 1996, had turned his focus to internal Senate politics — specifically the chance to succeed Senate Armed Services Committee Chairman Strom Thurmond, R-S.C. The 94-year-old Thurmond set the record for longevity in the Senate on May 25.

"John Warner wants to be the next chairman of the Armed Services Committee," said Senate Minority Leader Tom Daschle, D-S.D., on April 18, the day after the committee's partisan vote to pursue an aggressive investigation. "John Warner is willing to pay whatever dues necessary to see that that happens. He's being a good soldier."

Warner's office said the action by the Rules Committee was not related to Armed Services and that Warner knew of no reason to think Thurmond would be leaving. Thurmond did announce later in the year that he would step down as chairman of the panel at the end of the 105th Congress.

Democrats Pull Out

On May 1, committee Republicans and Democrats reached an uneasy truce on the protocol for the investigation. The probe would be a 45-day, $250,000 investigation employing outside counsels, FBI agents and detailees from the GAO. Subpoena and deposition power was limited to members of the committee, not staff or counsels — a key concession extracted by Democrats.

But within weeks of the agreement, a series of revelations dealt a blow to the investigation. Democrats withdrew their cooperation on June 25, saying the probe had exceeded its budget and 45-day deadline.

Investigators found that a convicted felon, Thomas "Papa Bear" Miller, working as a political operative for Jenkins, had paid individuals to fabricate stories of voter fraud.

FBI agents found that two witnesses said they had been paid to lie about selling their votes. Two other witnesses gave contradictory accounts in several interviews with agents. In addition, two GAO investigators detailed to the inquiry found that Jenkins' claims of illegal, phantom votes were completely without foundation.

Republicans had little or no comment on the revelations or Democratic calls for an end to the inquiry. Jenkins sharply criticized the Democrats for withdrawing and accused the minority of trying to block a full investigation.

In July, the investigation stalled as Republicans joined Democrats in asking the Justice Department to investigate tales of witness intimidation and witness tampering uncovered during the probe.

In addition, no money remained for the committee to pay outside counsels hired to investigate the charges, and the FBI agents who had participated in response to a bipartisan congressional request were withdrawn after Democrats pulled out.

Sparring Over When To Shut Down

With the probe in limbo, Daschle threatened a legislative slowdown to force resolution of the matter and hinted that Democratic senators might resort to describing the sordid details of the case on the Senate floor. Lott said it was the Democrats' refusal to cooperate that prevented the investigation from wrapping up.

Republicans and Democrats did agree that to date, the investigation had produced no evidence of fraud to warrant unseating Landrieu and ordering a new election. But the two sides were deeply divided over the scope and cost of the probe, and the timetable and means for concluding it.

Democrats wanted the investigation to end July 31, the day the contract expired on the office space committee investigators had leased in the Hale Boggs Federal Building in New Orleans. They argued that there was a dearth of evidence after seven months.

Republicans wanted to continue the investigation through Sept. 9, with as many as six FBI agents and the use of $450,000 in committee funds that had been designated for hearings on campaign finance legislation.

The GOP also wanted to issue subpoenas to New Orleans Democratic Mayor Marc Morial and his political organization, LIFE (Louisiana Independent Federation of Electors), and to the gambling industry.

Backing up the Democratic demands for an end to the inquiry was Bauer, who briefed reporters July 22 on why the minority withdrew from the investigation a month earlier.

Bauer said that at the outset of the all-out probe, investigators spoke to individuals associated with Jenkins' political organization, in particular those who had compiled the testimony of voter fraud from various witnesses. The investigators found that the claims came well after the election.

"At no time on Election Day or immediately thereafter was there known to anyone associated with Mr. Jenkins the name of any voter who claimed either to have seen illegal voting directly or to have participated in illegal voting," Bauer said. "It was their assumption that there must have been fraud."

Republicans Seek To Revive Probe

Rather than shutting down the dormant probe, Republicans on the committee voted July 31 to ratchet it up, creating an open-ended investigation and granting Warner the authority to subpoena "any individual, organization, corporation, or other entity who has or is believed to have, documents or other information related to the investigation." Warner could act without the consent of the minority.

Over the strong objections of the Democrats, Republicans voted 9-7 along party lines to revive the investigation with no deadlines, six FBI agents and outside counsels who would be paid from the GOP share of $450,000 that had been earmarked for campaign finance hearings. However, in the absence of a bipartisan request, the Justice Department was unwilling to provide FBI agents.

The action came after talks between Democrats and Republicans collapsed and a free-agent effort by Louisiana's senior senator, Democrat John B. Breaux, was rejected by his party.

In August, Warner issued 26 subpoenas, including ones to Morial's political organization, LIFE; to Carl Mullican Communications, an advertising company that worked for LIFE; and to Harrah's Entertainment, one of several casino operators interested in the gambling measure on the November 1996 ballot.

Warner also pleaded with Attorney General Janet Reno and FBI Director Louis J. Freeh to reverse the Justice Department policy of assigning FBI agents to committees only in response to bipartisan requests.

Warner traveled to New Orleans on Aug. 13-14 where he questioned city officials and reviewed documents. At the conclusion, he said he heard nothing to change his assessment of nearly a month before. "We have not, thus far, in my judgment seen a quantity of evidence that would overturn the election," he said.

When the Senate returned in September, from its August recess, Democrats held true to their threat and disrupted Senate business in an attempt to force Republicans to end the investigation. Daschle said the selective disruption, which included barring committees from meeting for more than two hours after the opening of the floor session, was a prudent step. An angry Lott recessed the Senate to allow the committees to convene.

Late in September, Republicans and Democrats indicated that the probe, which had found no evidence of widespread election malfeasance, was coming to an end. But Warner dispatched the committee's general counsel and a team of former FBI agents to New Orleans to continue the probe.

Investigation Closed

On Oct. 1, the committee met briefly behind closed doors and then opened the session as they voted unanimously to end the investigation.

The quick, unanimous vote was in sharp contrast to the months of partisan wrangling. A relieved Landrieu welcomed the decisions and said the committee was dead wrong to pursue the charges. "Never again should a legally certified senator be held hostage by wild, reckless and unproven allegations from a disgruntled loser," she said. Jenkins refused to concede the election and said Democratic obstruction had forced the Senate to end its probe.

In a final action, the committee decided against reimbursing either Landrieu or Jenkins for their legal fees, as lawmakers were leery of encouraging a losing candidate to challenge an election knowing the taxpayers would eventually foot the bill. ■

No Decision Reached On Sanchez Election

The House adjourned without resolving the contested election of California Democratic Rep. Loretta Sanchez, and angry Democrats vowed to resume parliamentary delaying tactics in January until the probe was ended. The investigation resulted in bitter partisan squabbling, which spilled onto the House floor in the days leading to adjournment.

A task force of the House Oversight Committee spent most of 1997 embroiled in investigating Sanchez's 1996 victory over former Republican Rep. Robert K. Dornan in California's 46th District. Dornan, a fiery conservative, had served 18 years in the House before his defeat. Dornan claimed Sanchez unseated him by 984 votes because of a rash of illegal voting by non-citizens. Sanchez, who was Hispanic, contended Dornan's charges were racially motivated.

Oversight Committee Chairman Bill Thomas, R-Calif., appointed a three-member task force — Republicans Vernon J. Ehlers of Michigan and Bob Ney of Ohio., and Democrat Steny H. Hoyer of Maryland — to conduct the investigation.

The panel subpoenaed and collected hundreds of documents, including files from Hispanic citizens groups, voter rolls from the Orange County, Calif., registrar, and databases from the Immigration and Naturalization Service to see if people who were not yet U.S. citizens cast votes in the election.

In particular, the task force looked at the activities of Hermandad Mexicana Nacional, a group that helped register Hispanic voters in California in 1996. By year's end, Ehlers claimed that at least 275 improperly cast ballots had been identified. But he also said that the task force was unable to conclude whether there was a sufficient number of bad ballots to justify throwing out the results and holding a new election.

On September, Dornan began using his privileges as a former member to visit the House floor. But after Dornan got into a nasty confrontation with Robert Menendez, D-N.J., about the probe, his floor access was denied. More than 100 Republicans joined a nearly unanimous bloc of Democrats to adopt a resolution (H Res 233) on Sept. 18 that barred Dornan from the House floor or surrounding areas until the contested election was resolved. *(Vote 415, p. H-126)*

On Oct. 24, the task force voted 2-1, with the lone Democrat Hoyer dissenting, to ask the California secretary of state for help. But many Republicans began to wonder if the investigation was out of steam.

Meanwhile, Democrats were raising a ruckus on the floor, introducing a slew of privileged resolutions to halt the probe, charging it targeted Hispanic voters. While none of the resolutions succeeded, Democrats did grind action on the floor to a halt several times.

Minority Leader Richard A. Gephardt, D-Mo., offered a privileged resolution (H Res 276) on Oct. 23 calling for an end to the probe by Oct. 29. The House rejected the proposal 204-222. *(Vote 525, p. H-160)*

Toward the end of the year, Republican and Democratic lawmakers began quiet, behind-the-scenes talks to try to find a face-saving way to end the probe. One much-discussed scenario would have allowed Republicans to issue a report condemning vote fraud in California while leaving Sanchez in her seat. But the talks collapsed when Thomas insisted that the investigation continue, according to a lawmaker involved in the negotiations.

(The House subsequently dropped the investigation on Feb. 12, 1998.) ■

Campaign Finance Probe Fizzles

Republicans began the year excited about the prospect of showcasing what they saw as egregious abuses of campaign finance laws by the Democrats during the 1996 elections.

Beyond the numerous stories of bent or broken campaign regulation, Republicans believed they had a particularly explosive mix that included conspiracy by the Chinese communist government to try to influence U.S. elections; the virtual sale of the White House and high-level access by President Clinton, Vice President Gore and the Democratic National Committee (DNC); and the spectacle of a variety of Asian and Asian-American fundraisers contravening U.S. laws by funneling foreign cash into Democratic campaigns.

This, House Speaker Newt Gingrich, R-Ga., promised in March, would be "bigger than Watergate."

By late fall, however, a year-long probe by the Senate Governmental Affairs Committee had turned up many incidents of fundraising excesses, but found no real smoking gun. A parallel investigation by the House Government Reform and Oversight Committee had barely gotten under way, with little indication that it would go much beyond territory already covered by the Senate probe.

While Senate investigators produced story after story of embarrassing behavior by Democratic fundraisers and painted a portrait of a White House and a Democratic Party desperate for re-election cash, there was no direct proof of a Chinese conspiracy, no proof that the White House ever knowingly accepted foreign money and no proof that the Clinton administration ever changed policy in exchange for campaign contributions.

Moreover, Senate Democrats managed to reveal that Republicans had in some cases been just as lax about letting foreign money infiltrate GOP political organizations.

The Senate probe wrapped up and shut down at the end of October. While the House investigation continued in the Government Reform and Oversight Committee and at least eight other committees and subcommittees, there was little sign by year's end that House members could do what their colleagues in the Senate had not by way of generating public outrage.

Oversold, costly and time-consuming, both chambers' investigations did little more than bolster the public's pre-existing belief that both parties were conducting business as usual. Republicans who had hoped for a clear political victory over Democrats were disappointed. And members of both parties who had thought the probes might finally ignite public demand for an overhaul of existing campaign finance laws were likewise frustrated. A campaign finance overhaul bill failed to overcome a filibuster in the Senate in October. The House did not take up campaign finance legislation in 1997. *(Campaign finance bill, p. 1-26)*

Senate Investigation

Though it produced few bombshells, the Senate Governmental Affairs Committee's high-profile probe into fundraising abuses demonstrated how the frantic scramble for money during the 1996 election campaigns caused both parties to bend fundraising laws.

The committee, chaired by Tennessee Republican Fred Thompson, a former Watergate prosecutor, held 32 hearings between July and October. Those sessions, which documented unabashed access-peddling by Clinton, Gore and the DNC as they sought cash to re-elect the president, were highlighted by the testimony of oil financier Roger Tamraz, who acknowledged donating $300,000 to Democrats in an effort to curry favor with the White House. And they showed how so many controls had broken down at the DNC that the party regularly accepted questionable contributions

The investigation also raised questions about possible obstruction of justice after the president and his allies only belatedly complied with longstanding requests for videotapes of White House "coffees," where Clinton schmoozed with big-money contributors.

But the committee also scrutinized questionable activities by Republicans, including the possible use of independent tax-exempt groups to evade federal spending limits.

Thompson announced Oct. 31 that the panel would hold no more hearings unless compelling new evidence warranted a resumption, and committee staff spent the rest of the year working on a report that was not issued until 1998.

Reinforcing Public Cynicism

With the public hardened by Watergate and subsequent scandals, nothing short of a president knee-deep in criminal conspiracy would have sufficed — and Republicans never proved that. "Watergate spoiled us a little bit. It kind of raised the bar for congressional hearings," Thompson acknowledged.

The Senate hearings did not tell people anything they did not expect from Washington, and they served to bolster the belief that both parties, not just the president's, were up to the same old shenanigans, according to pollsters tracking public response to the hearings.

"It's a Congress controlled by one party investigating the president of another party, and the public is highly suspicious of that," conceded committee member Sam Brownback, R-Kan.

Thompson claimed from the outset that he would expose a plot by the Chinese government to influence foreign policy with large and illegal political donations. While he was able to show that illegal foreign donations had indeed been accepted by the DNC — and returned in the glare of bad publicity from the scandal — he produced neither evidence of involvement by the Chinese nor proof that the Clinton administration altered policy to reward the Chinese or other contributors.

"That's the nexus most people are concerned about," Brownback said. "If contributors put money in, what did they get out of it? We were not able to close that loop."

Unable to meet its original objective, the Thompson committee kept moving the goal posts, depending on what the investigation turned up. More disappointments followed.

Thompson and the Republicans alleged that Clinton approved a scheme by the DNC to help the Teamsters raise money for the 1996 re-election campaign of union President Ron Carey in exchange for Teamster contributions to the DNC. They were unable to prove that the president knew of the arrangement, though the fundraising irregularities were highly embarrassing for the Democrats.

More eye-opening testimony came from a group of Buddhist nuns, who each gave $5,000 to the DNC after a speech by Gore at a Buddhist temple in California. The event was organized by John Huang, a former Commerce Department official suspected of raising money from foreign sources.

Although Thompson was attempting to show that the nuns and the temple were used as conduits for donations actually made by others, the committee was unable to say exactly where the money came from.

The committee also showed that the DNC accepted tainted donations from people acting as conduits for Asian-American businessmen and for the Lippo Group, an Indonesian conglomerate run by the Riady family, which had ties to the Clintons. What, if anything, Lippo or the Riadys received in exchange remained an unanswered question.

Key Moments

The origins of the Democrats' problems lay in their panicky response to the devastating loss of the House and Senate in 1994. Determined to stanch further erosion in Congress and re-elect the president in 1996, the party developed a voracious appetite for campaign cash. For television ads alone, former presidential adviser Dick Morris estimated that the Democrats spent roughly $85 million, double what the party spent to unseat President George Bush in 1992.

The Senate investigation focused on just a tiny portion of that: the $2.8 million that had been returned by the DNC because of questions about its origins. That money was raised in a way that Republicans said had intentionally skirted federal laws restricting political fundraising. Nearly 80 percent of the money came from the efforts of three people: former DNC fundraiser John Huang; California businessman Johnny Chung; and Yah Lin Trie, a former Arkansas restaurateur who became a top fundraiser for the party.

Following are some of the key developments from the Senate hearings:

• **Opening charges.** The Senate hearings opened July 8 as Republicans charged Democratic officials with accepting — and possibly encouraging — foreign cash donations they knew to be illegal.

Thompson charged that Democrats were in effect the willing accomplices of a conspiracy by the Chinese government to infiltrate the U.S. electoral system with infusions of cash aimed toward at least seven congressional candidates.

"I speak of allegations concerning a plan hatched during the last election cycle by the Chinese government and designed to pour illegal money into American political campaigns," Thompson said in his opening statement. Thompson said he based his charges on confidential information from U.S. intelligence sources and his committee's own investigations.

But ranking committee Democrat John Glenn of Ohio, who had gotten the same briefings and seen the same confidential documents, said he found "no evidence" to support Thompson's charges. Glenn said darkly that the allegations reminded him of the smears used by Sen. Joseph R. McCarthy, R-Wis. (1947-57), during his anti-communist hearings. "During the 1950s, we can all remember what happened," Glenn said.

The hearings quickly devolved into fruitless exchanges with former DNC Finance Director Richard Sullivan, whose earlier depositions had led Republican senators to believe he would clearly link Democrats to foreign fundraising schemes.

Instead, Sullivan repeatedly denied that there was any orchestrated attempt to raise foreign dollars. If foreign money came into the DNC, Sullivan insisted, it was an oversight and a mistake that followed an inexplicable lapse of vetting procedures designed to catch such illegal donations.

When they saw that Sullivan was failing to help make their case, Republicans leaned on documents to tell their story instead. They released records showing that two major Democratic contributors had accepted large wire transfers of money from banks in China and Japan at about the same time they gave big donations to the DNC — and at a time when their bank accounts held insufficient funds to make the contributions on their own. Republicans insisted that was strong proof that those big DNC donors were merely conduits for foreign cash.

But Democrats countered that the coincidence of wire transfers and big donations did not amount to proof the contributors were funneling foreign cash to Democrats, and by week's end, Republicans had produced little in the way of hard evidence that conclusively made their case.

What Republicans saw as a clear connection between foreign donors and a willfully ignorant or complicit DNC, Democrats viewed as questionable decision-making and sloppy background checks of donors.

• **John Huang.** Much of the probe focused on former Commerce Department official and DNC fundraiser John Huang. The question for Senate investigators was whether Huang was also an agent of the Chinese government, turning over U.S. secrets and helping to carry out a plot to infiltrate U.S. elections and influence American foreign policy with the lubricant of ready cash. Or was he simply passing industrial information to his former employer? Or was he just a zealous fundraiser gone awry?

Huang, who was secluded from the press and congressional investigators in his Glendale, Calif., home, was unwilling to tell his story without some form of immunity from prosecution on illegal fundraising charges. The committee never granted him that immunity, and he never appeared before the panel.

Republicans worked to portray Huang as a man who used his fundraising prowess to burrow his way into the federal government in a post at the Commerce Department, from which, they charged, he could have sent sensitive U.S. intelligence data back to his former employers at the Lippo Group, the Indonesian conglomerate with intimate ties to the Chinese government.

Democrats countered that Huang was nothing more than a careless fundraiser who cut corners and often disregarded even the most basic of fundraising rules in his quest to bring Asian-Americans to the forefront of U.S. politics. Half of the $3.4 million he raised in 1996 was returned as improper. Democrats scoffed at the espionage charges, insisting the evidence and the Republicans' own witnesses produced no proof that Huang was a spy.

Republicans also moved to link Huang and the Democrats to illegal foreign funds by laying out what appeared to be hard evidence that foreign money had infiltrated the DNC. Republicans produced a copy of a cancelled check for a $50,000 donation to the DNC in 1992 made by a California-based subsidiary of the Lippo Group that Huang ran. Documents showed that one week after pledging the money, Huang asked his superiors in Indonesia for reimbursement, an apparent violation of U.S. election law.

Federal law permitted political parties to accept contributions from U.S. subsidiaries of foreign corporations, but the money had to be earned on U.S. soil. The DNC said it would return the money.

Republicans called a series of witnesses to lay out what they said was at the very least a highly suspicious pattern of activity by Huang, who they said could have used his position at the Commerce Department to pass on highly classified information to the Lippo Group. Lippo was of particular concern because the multibillion-dollar real estate and banking conglomerate was partially owned by the Chinese government, and its relationship with Clinton dated back to Little Rock when it had a stake in the largest bank in town.

A CIA intelligence briefer testified that he met with Huang 37 times during his tenure at the Commerce Department, showing him hundreds of classified documents. Another witness testified that Huang routinely crossed the street from his Commerce office to use the phones and fax machine in the office of an investment bank with connections to the Lippo Group. Still another witness used subpoenaed phone records to show that Huang had made at least 29 calls or faxes to the parent company in Indonesia and 237 to its U.S. subsidiary while he was at Commerce.

Democrats said that proved nothing. "They are trying to make Huang into some sort of nefarious person who was placed at the Commerce and the DNC for nefarious purposes," Glenn said. "I have seen all of the intelligence stuff and I just don't see anything sinister."

• **Charlie Trie.** A onetime Chinese restaurant owner from Little Rock who had become friends with then-Gov. Clinton, Charlie Yah din Trie moved on to try his hand at other businesses after Clinton became president. While he was not a business success, he was able to give the appearance that he had access to the president. Lured by that apparent connection, foreign individuals and companies pumped some $1.4 million into his bank account, according to records introduced at the hearings.

Trie's chief benefactor was Ng Lap Seng, a business associate of Trie's from Macao, a Portuguese territory near Hong Hong. It was $905,000 from Ng that Trie used to make donations to the DNC and fuel one business venture after another, the hearings showed. Trie gave $220,000 of that to the DNC, according to an FBI agent who testified before the committee. The money was also used to reimburse individuals for donations they made at a February 1996 fundraiser at Washington's Hay-Adams Hotel where the Democrats raised $1.1 million.

Making a political contribution in the name of another person was against federal law, as were donations from foreign sources. Republicans said Trie was a prime example of how foreign money was funneled into the Democratic Party.

The DNC returned all of the money donated by Trie as well as an additional $425,000 he raised from others.

Investigators also produced evidence that Trie raised money in a suspicious way for the Presidential Legal Expense Trust, a private fund set up to help the Clintons pay their mounting legal bills. Trie tried on three occasions to give a total of $789,000 to the trust. Most of the money was contributed by hundreds of members of a Taiwan-based Buddhist sect called the Suma Ching Hai Meditation Association.

Even though the trust returned the money almost as soon as Trie turned it in, Republicans contended that there was a conspiracy at the White House to keep the donations secret until after the election.

• **Haley Barbour.** The Senate hearings offered Democrats few chances to showcase alleged GOP fundraising abuses. A key moment came when Democrats got a chance to grill former Republican National Committee (RNC) Chairman Haley Barbour over his alleged solicitation of foreign money for an RNC think tank called the National Policy Forum (NPF).

Barbour had created the NPF as a policy-generating arm of the RNC, but by the spring of 1994, the offshoot organization owed its parent $2.5 million — money the RNC badly needed to bankroll the fierce electoral battle for control of Congress just a few months away.

To get the money, the NPF turned to a wealthy Hong Kong businessman named Ambrous Tung Young. The patriarch of Young Brothers Development Co., a multibillion-dollar Asian building and aviation firm, Young agreed to guarantee a $2.1 million loan to the forum.

That foreign-backed loan to the NPF was at the core of the case Democrats brought against Republicans. Glenn charged that the Young Brothers' loan guarantee proved that the policy forum was nothing less than a "money-laundering machine" for the GOP, with the added benefit of offering donors a cloak of anonymity.

Coming after a parade of little-known officials, businessmen and obscure functionaries, Barbour offered the sluggish hearings their first star-quality witness, and Democrats attempted to put him on the hot seat in full public view. They charged him, in effect, with knowingly soliciting foreign money for GOP activities by funneling it through the NPF, which was seeking tax-exempt status and could legally accept such donations when a party committee could not.

Barbour's defense was to go on the offense and deny all allegations. When Democrats charged that he knew he was raising money in a questionable manner, he flatly denied it. When Democrats charged that the NPF was nothing more than a shell operation for the RNC, he insisted they were wrong. When two witnesses testified they had told Barbour beforehand that the money for the NPF came from a foreign source, he said he never heard them say that.

Some of the facts in the Democrats' case were undisputed: Young Brothers guaranteed the loan to the NPF by wiring money through its U.S.-based subsidiary, and the NPF quickly paid off $1.6 million of its debt to the RNC, infusing the cash-hungry party committee with funds just weeks before the crucial November 1994 election, according to Federal Election Commission records. Ultimately, the NPF defaulted on the loan, forcing Young to write off about $700,000. The remainder was paid by the RNC itself.

Beyond that, though, versions of what happened diverged. Democrats said the loan deal showed that Republicans were just as willing to overlook legalities in their zeal for campaign cash as Democrats were.

Republicans said Democrats, embarrassed by the scandals that had blemished the White House, were on a desperate prowl to hunt down a Republican example of wrongdoing. While some Republicans conceded the NPF had problems — it was ultimately denied tax-exempt status by the IRS for being too partisan and eventually closed down — Barbour insisted the policy forum did nothing the least bit illegal. As for the allegations that he knowingly solicited foreign money, he said he had "no idea that the money came from overseas."

Barbour's denials were contradicted by the testimony of a former NPF fundraiser. Houston businessman Frederick W. Volcansek testified that he told Barbour on several occasions that the money was coming from Hong Kong. When senators asked about Volcansek's testimony, Barbour said he "could not recall" Volcansek saying that.

• **Vice President Gore.** Following the August congressional recess, the focus of the Senate hearings shifted abruptly to Gore, who suddenly looked to be in very deep water.

The sharpest blow came Sept. 3, when Attorney General Janet Reno announced that she was opening a review of telephone calls Gore made from his office to solicit campaign donations. The review, the first step in requesting a court-appointed independent counsel, came the day The Washington Post published a story showing that $120,000 raised by Gore had gone into restricted "hard money" accounts, contradicting Gore's assertions that money from the calls had been deposited in soft-money accounts.

Tightly regulated hard money could go directly to candidates and campaigns; unrestricted soft money could go only to political party organizations for non-campaign use.

Reno had previously insisted that there did not appear to be enough "specific and credible" evidence involving the White House for her to recommend appointing an independent counsel, but that changed after the Post story.

"The Justice Department is reviewing allegations to determine whether [the charge that] the vice president illegally solicited campaign contributions on federal property should warrant a preliminary investigation under the Independent Counsel Act," the Justice Department wrote in a Sept. 3 statement.

No one disputed that Gore had made the ill-fated decision to dial for dollars from his White House office. What they disputed was exactly what the vice president knew when he made the calls. Was Gore aware that he was raising tightly regulated hard money in possible violation of a rarely enforced century-old law that seemed to ban soliciting funds on federal property, as Republicans asserted? Or did the vice president believe he was raising virtually unregulated — and possibly quite legal — soft money to pay for a media campaign, as the Democrats contended?

On its face, the law that Gore might have broken looked very simple. The statute prohibited anyone from asking for or receiving a political contribution "in any room or building occupied in the discharge of official duties."

But interpretations of exactly what that meant varied widely. One key question was whether "contribution" meant any donation or only hard money.

Some legal experts said that making phone calls on federal property was akin to jaywalking. The statute, first drafted over a century before, was originally intended to prevent the shakedown of federal employees, not phone calls to outside contributors for funds.

To appoint an independent counsel to investigate phone calls at the White House "is trivializing the whole use of the independent counsel," insisted Stanley Brand, a former House counsel who specialized in ethics law.

Compounding Gore's troubles, GOP members of the Senate committee began presenting evidence Sept. 4 that they said showed Gore knew or should have known that a controversial April 1996 luncheon at a Buddhist temple near Los Angeles was actually a fundraiser. Gore had consistently denied he knew it was a fundraiser.

Next came testimony from three Buddhist nuns whose revelations of illegal acts surrounding the temple event came as one of the few shocks in what so far had been lackluster hearings.

With their heads shorn, dressed in flowing, almond-brown robes and sandals, the nuns told the committee, in halting English, that the temple illegally reimbursed its members for $65,000 in political contributions after the luncheon. One nun said she destroyed documents when the controversy over the event first surfaced in the fall of 1996; another said she altered checks to protect Gore and the temple.

White House officials were quick to deride the evidence produced at the hearing as political posturing. They noted that Thompson, himself, was widely rumored to be considering running for president, which could put him in competition with Gore, the apparent front-runner for the 2000 Democratic presidential nomination. "This is all about 2000," said one White House official.

Gore's chief counsel Charles Burson said he was confident that Gore did not violate the law. Clinton likewise defended Gore, saying, "I believe what he did was legal."

There was no evidence that Gore knew anything about the donation scheme at the temple, but it was clearly no help to his political image to have his name so closely linked to the operation.

On Sept. 8, the Governmental Affairs Committee pursued the question of Gore's phone calls, with Republicans saying he knowingly skirted the law when he contacted some 46 donors from his White House office. Five of the contributions Gore raised — a total of $100,000 — were kept in the party's hard money account, according to officials of the DNC. The underlying agenda was clearly to build pressure on Reno to appoint an independent counsel.

In a subsequent decision that drew sharp criticism from Republicans, Reno announced Dec. 2 that she would not seek an independent counsel to look into fundraising phone calls by Gore or Clinton, though she said her department's internal investigations would continue.

• **Roger Tamraz.** Sheila Heslin, a former National Security Council official, appeared to give the committee its first clear example of quid pro quo, telling how a major contributor used large donations to override concerns about his controversial past and gain access to the White House on six different occasions, once even getting the chance to lobby Clinton directly.

In a detailed account that offered a rare glimpse of just how access was procured in Washington, Heslin told the panel that officials from the CIA, the Department of Energy and the DNC all pressured her to drop her objections to granting White House access to Roger Tamraz, an international oil financier she had determined was "shady and untrustworthy." Heslin said she was pointedly told that Tamraz had given the Democrats at least $200,000 and would give double that again if he could meet the president to discuss his proposal for building an oil pipeline across the Caspian Sea.

The fact that Tamraz did get access to Clinton and assistance from senior administration officials struck Republicans as evidence that the administration was auctioning off policy decisions. "This makes it clear that foreign policy was for sale," said Don Nickles, R-Okla.

Democrats countered that Tamraz never really got what he wanted. Richard J. Durbin, D-Ill., said that while it was clear that Tamraz received access in exchange for his donations, the financier never got the administration approval he was seeking for his pipeline project.

But committee chairman Thompson said Durbin was missing the point. Thompson argued that what Tamraz really wanted, and got, was access to the White House and the appearance of influence with the administration — commodities he could use to help sell his pipeline project to investors abroad. "The deal was not the pipeline; the deal was for him to go around the world and say what he got," Thompson said.

Tamraz himself freely admitted he was buying access by donating $300,000 to national and state Democratic Party committees during the 1996 elections. When asked by Joseph I. Lieberman, D-Conn., if he got his money's worth, Tamraz elicited much laughter in the hearing room by saying that next time he would give $600,000.

• **Interior Secretary Bruce Babbitt.** Babbitt's testimony concerned a 1995 decision by the Interior Department to deny an impoverished group of Indian tribes in Wisconsin permission to open a casino at an abandoned dog track in Hudson, Wis. Republicans suggested that the tribes lost out because of improper pressure from former White House Deputy Chief of Staff Harold M. Ickes in behalf of a rival group of wealthy tribes that eventually donated at least $300,000 to the Democratic Party to prevent competition.

Babbitt hotly denied the contention, saying the decision to deny the license was made by an 18-year veteran of the department because local officials opposed the casino. "The allegations that there was improper White House or DNC influence and that I was a conduit for that influence are demonstrably false," Babbitt told the committee.

The conflict was over a meeting Babbitt had had July 14, 1995, with Paul F. Eckstein, a lawyer who had been hired by several Chippewa tribes to lobby for their casino application. Eckstein, who had studied law at Harvard with Babbitt, campaigned with him and hiked the Grand Canyon with him, testified that his old friend told him the application was being nixed because Ickes had weighed in on the other side.

The Chippewa had asked the Interior Department for permission to run a casino in late 1993. On Nov. 15, 1994, the Bureau of Indian Affairs office in Minneapolis had given them the green light, forwarding the application to Washington.

The Chippewa faced stiff opposition from a group of seven other tribes who feared the dog track casino would siphon off profits from their own casino operations. The rival tribal group hired Patrick O'Connor, lobbyist and former DNC treasurer, to fight for them.

Republicans introduced evidence showing that O'Connor complained to Clinton at an event in Minneapolis on April 24, 1995, about White House inattention to his concerns. Evidence showed that presidential adviser Bruce Lindsey then took up the case with Ickes, as did DNC Chairman Donald L. Fowler after a meeting with O'Connor and the tribes.

Administration documents sent to Ickes showed awareness that the issue was "a hot potato."

The story went public in July 1996, when The Wall Street Journal wrote about the intertribal jockeying. Babbitt denied discussing the matter with Ickes but conceded in an Oct. 10 letter to Thompson that he had used Ickes' name in his conversation with Eckstein — but only in connection with the need for a final decision.

"Mr. Eckstein was extremely persistent in our meeting, and I used this phrase simply as a means of terminating the discussion and getting him out the door," Babbitt wrote.

Republican senators jumped on Babbitt when he testified. "I think you are getting in awfully deep water here," said Thompson, referring to the meeting. "Did you mislead him?"

Babbitt paused. "No sir, I don't think I did."

That was not good enough for Nickles. "Either Mr. Eckstein lied or you're not telling the truth," Nickles said.

Democrats led Eckstein to acknowledge that there were other opponents of the Chippewa casino, including Wisconsin's GOP Gov. Tommy G. Thompson.

The Chippewa remained convinced that they were outmuscled by political contributions. When asked why his group was turned down for the casino license, George Newago, the chairman of the Red Cliff Tribal Council, said succinctly: "Money talks."

Pulling the Plug

Continuing the hearings into campaign finance abuses held distinct disadvantages for the GOP. As the Thompson hearings wound down, the focus was threatening to drift from the Democratic White House to the activities of prominent members of Congress — including a number of Republican lawmakers. With Democrats pressing to open new areas of inquiry into Republican fundraising abuses, Senate Republicans decided to shut down the hearings.

Senate investigators found evidence that independent, GOP-leaning tax-exempt organizations might have been used to get around federal contribution and spending limits. Both senators and House members had been aided by these organizations, which offered anonymity to big-dollar contributors.

Committee documents showed that a consulting firm called Triad Management Services Inc. funneled millions of dollars from GOP contributors to nonprofit groups that then launched a $3 million advertising blitz for Republican congressional candidates in the closing weeks of the 1996 election.

One GOP aide warned that delving into congressional involvement could touch off a "holy war" that would pit members against one another.

Thompson reluctantly pulled the plug Oct. 31 after giving up efforts to win an extension beyond the original Dec. 31 deadline set by the Senate. Thompson tried to get an extension from Senate Majority Leader Trent Lott, R-Miss., but the impossibility of winning the few Democratic votes needed to block a filibuster doomed the effort.

Thompson insisted the hearings had been a success because they showed the need for legislation to overhaul the campaign finance system. "The cat is out of the bag when it comes to campaign finance legislation," he said. "We should not measure ourselves in terms of scalps on the wall."

"Hearings are not grand juries," he added. "They are not soap operas. What we are supposed to do is pull back the curtain on the activities of government."

Ranking Democrat Glenn was caustic about the suggestion of more hearings. "What for? More bloodletting of Democrats?" he asked. "I do not have a death wish."

House Committee

Meanwhile, the main House campaign finance investigation was just getting revved up. The House Government Reform and Oversight Committee, chaired by Dan Burton, R-Ind., had already been criticized for covering the same ground as the Thompson committee, and the general public apathy over the Senate hearings caused some House Republicans to wonder whether it was worthwhile to continue with a new round in the House.

"While I respect Dan Burton and there's probably more to look at, there comes a point when enough is enough, and I think we have passed that point," said Mark Foley, R-Fla. "More hearings are not going to produce anything further where the public says, 'Oh, there's the smoking gun.' It's expensive, time-consuming and redundant."

But John Shadegg, R-Ariz., a member of the Burton committee, said his constituents were just beginning to tune into the scandal now that they had seen the videotapes of the White House coffees on television. While he had once doubted whether the committee should hold hearings, Shadegg said, "Now I think we ought to push forward as aggressively as possible."

Partisan tensions had often impeded the working relationship between Thompson and ranking Democrat Glenn on the Senate committee, but the situation was even worse on Burton's panel.

The committee's credibility was whittled away by nonstop partisan sniping between Democratic and Republican members, and Burton was often forced onto the defensive by ranking member Henry A. Waxman, D-Calif., a savvy infighter. The strongest attack by the Waxman forces was on the issue of wasteful duplication after so much ground had been covered by the Thompson investigation.

Burton was also wounded politically by his own campaign activities. The Justice Department, which was conducting its own probe into illegal fundraising practices, slapped Burton's campaign committee in Indiana with a subpoena July 11 for financial records.

A Justice Department task force swept Burton into its probe after The Washington Post reported in March 1997 that a lobbyist for Pakistan had been "shaken down" by Burton for a $5,000 campaign contribution.

"Dan Burton's campaign is a clean and honest campaign," said Kevin Binger, chief of staff of the Government Reform and Oversight Committee. "The Justice Department will only find evidence of honest, ethical and legal behavior."

The panel's low productivity also raised doubts about the wisdom of continuing. Democrats charged that by the end of October, Burton's committee had spent nearly $3 million and held just one hearing, on Oct. 9. Committee Republicans did not contest that dollar figure but declined to provide one of their own. By contrast, Thompson's committee had spent $2.2 million and held 32 hearings.

Burton contended that he would cover new ground and that he would focus on the Chinese money connection. He and other Republicans said it was unfair to judge the panel's hearing-to-dollars-spent ratio yet because the committee was still in the early stages of its investigation. Burton's investigation had an open-ended timetable and the option of supplementing its $3.8 million budget by tapping into a special $7.9 million reserve fund controlled by the House GOP leadership.

But there were signs the House probe was running into the same problem that Thompson did in trying to prove that the Chinese government attempted to buy influence over Clinton's foreign policy. "There is a strong indication of money coming from that area of the world," Burton said. "Now, pinning it down to specific sources is going to take a little more work."

Despite the low productivity, Burton continued to enjoy the backing of Gingrich and other House leaders.

Republican Conference Chairman John A. Boehner of Ohio said the Burton hearings, most of which were expected to occur in 1998, would put continued pressure on Attorney General Reno to appoint an independent counsel to look into alleged wrongdoing by the president and vice president. Most Republicans believed that a full-fledged investigation by an independent counsel was the best way to pick up where the hearings left off.

"The picture is clear," Boehner said. "[Democrats] orchestrated a conspiracy to evade campaign limits to further their political objectives. And from what little evidence we have, we know the president and vice president were deeply involved in it."

Political professionals said the hearings had limited voter appeal aside from their value in exciting party activists. "I don't see it playing among the general public, but I don't minimize the importance of reaching core Republican voters who might have no reason to care about the '98 election," said political analyst Stuart Rothenberg, who published a political newsletter. "That alone might be a significant benefit to Republicans."

Postscript

Using the hearings to influence potential voters beyond the GOP base may have been a doomed strategy from the start. Congressional Republicans began with objectives that, by the end of the year, looked fatally contradictory: They wanted to raise the issue of campaign finance abuses but keep the spotlight focused on the Democratic White House, despite evidence of similar abuses by the GOP.

Larry J. Sabato, a University of Virginia political scientist who had written extensively about fundraising abuses, said, "No one was going to believe that only the Democrats did smarmy things. Just like no one is going to believe that only Democrats want real campaign finance reform. Everyone knows it takes both parties working together."

And even as they were highlighting the flaws of the existing campaign finance system, Republicans were fending off suggestions that it was time to change that system — which served their bottom-line needs as well as it served the Democrats' come election time.

The hearings also did little to penetrate the political Teflon that seemed to protect Clinton from Republican accusations of wrongdoing. In fact, the hearings reinforced a trend in public opinion that was maddening for the Republicans. People said they liked the job Clinton was doing despite their perception of him as untrustworthy. The president's job approval percentage ratings continued to range in the mid-50s, while his disapproval ratings remained in the mid-30s.

The hearings did more political damage to Gore. Opinions of the likely contestant for the Democratic presidential nomination in 2000 began a long, slow slide when the scandal started to unfold late in 1996, according to Gallup pollsters. Gore's positive ratings dropped from 57 percent in March 1997 to 47 percent in October 1997, a reflection of the higher expectations the public had of him versus Clinton, Gallup concluded.

No Momentum for Changing the Law

Campaign finance experts said the hearings showed both parties playing fast and loose with election law.

"There's no doubt that the Clinton people went as far as they could to open the envelope on the parameters of the law," said Herbert E. Alexander, director the Citizens' Research Foundation and a former consultant to the Senate Watergate committee.

Bill Hogan, of the Center for Public Integrity, said the hearings "gave the public an unprecedented view inside the world of high campaign finance. It's a system that is just totally polluted."

But public indifference to the hearings meant that there was no clamor for more of them, and little political pressure on members of Congress to pass legislation closing the legal loopholes exposed by the hearings.

Attention paid the Thompson hearings was weak even by the low standards of congressional hearings. Just one in 10 Americans followed them closely, according to a Pew Research Center survey, and more than a third paid almost no attention at all. In recent years, only the hearings into the Whitewater land deal involving the Clintons and into the Ruby Ridge shootout had attracted so little interest.

Much of the reason for that was the public's cynicism that anything would change, said Karlyn Bowman, a public opinion specialist at the American Enterprise Institute. "They think that whatever is done, the politicians and the parties will find new loopholes," she said.

"If the parallel to Watergate is apt, the situation today seems quite different," she said. "It may be that the public is just 'scandaled' out. Unless there's an awful lot new that comes . . . I'm not sure something like this has legs." ■

Filibuster Halts Campaign Finance Bill

Another year of partisan debate — this time following on the heels of unprecedented campaign spending during the 1996 election cycle — left Congress little closer to agreement on new ground rules for financing campaigns for federal office.

Months of Senate hearings and intermittent proceedings in two House committees provided new evidence of what critics pointed to as campaign finance violations and huge loopholes in existing law. But Democratic-led efforts to overhaul the post-Watergate regulations did not generate enough momentum to break through the procedural roadblocks erected by GOP leaders.

Republicans offered their own version of campaign finance reform, focusing on curtailing the political activities of labor unions.

Democratic backers of the leading campaign finance bill (S 25) stalled other legislation near the end of the session in an effort to persuade Majority Leader Trent Lott, R-Miss., to bring the measure to the floor. But both the campaign finance bill and an attempt by Lott to add language curbing union political activity were blocked by filibusters.

Companion House legislation never made it to the floor of that chamber.

Democrats were quick to blame the GOP for leaving a discredited campaign finance system in place for the 1998 election cycle. But Republicans made no apology for blocking what they said was a bad bill. "This effort to put the government in charge of political discussion isn't going to pass now, isn't going to pass tomorrow, is not going to pass ever," said leading Senate opponent Mitch McConnell, R-Ky.

Leaders in both chambers agreed that they would permit floor action on campaign finance legislation early in 1998.

Earlier in the year, the Senate rejected, 38-61, a proposed constitutional amendment (S J Res 18) that would have allowed Congress to impose mandatory limits on campaign spending. The March 18 vote on the resolution sponsored by Ernest F. Hollings, D-S.C., and Robert C. Byrd, D-W.Va., was far short of the two-thirds majority necessary for passing a constitutional amendment. *(Vote 31, p. S-8)*

Background

The House and Senate had struggled since 1980 to overhaul the campaign finance system put in place after the Watergate scandal in 1974 (PL 93-433).

Both chambers passed versions of a campaign finance bill in 1993. But though President Clinton had made much of the issue in his 1992 campaign, the Democratic majority in Congress allowed the legislation to languish until the final days of the 103rd Congress, when Senate Republicans used a filibuster to block a conference with the House. *(1994 Almanac, p. 32)*

GOP and Democratic leaders — including Clinton and House Speaker Newt Gingrich, R-Ga. — repeatedly promised action on campaign finance reform in 1995, but made little effort to deliver, leaving it to rank-and-file members to push the issue. House and Senate committees took no action, but House Republicans appointed a task force to study the matter. *(1995 Almanac, p. 1-44)*

In 1996, a bipartisan bill including voluntary spending limits and a ban on contributions by political action committees (PACs) was stopped by a filibuster in the Senate, while the House defeated both a GOP bill to impose new contribution limits and a Democratic alternative. *(1996 Almanac, p. 1-21)*

But with revelations of questionable 1996 fundraising shining a public spotlight on the ineffectiveness of the existing restrictions, 1997 appeared to offer a favorable climate for rewriting the laws governing campaign finance.

The parties' unprecedented use in 1996 of more than $263 million in largely unregulated donations from corporations, unions and wealthy individuals made "soft money" the leading issue in the debate.

Soft money was supposed to be used for party-building efforts such as get-out-the-vote and voter registration drives, but it was often spent on thinly veiled campaign activities. The U.S. Supreme Court opened the door for the broader use of soft money with a June 1996 ruling that parties could spend an unlimited amount to promote their positions on issues as long as they did not coordinate that activity directly with candidates. *(1996 Almanac, p. 5-47)*

The focal point for the 1997 debate was a bill (S 25) sponsored by John McCain, R-Ariz., and Russell D. Feingold, D-Wis. The legislation had the backing of all 45 Senate Democrats and three Republicans — McCain, Susan Collins of Maine and Fred Thompson of Tennessee.

The bill proposed to ban soft money, provide free or discounted television advertising and postage for candidates who adhered to voluntary spending limits, reduce ceilings on PAC contributions, tighten disclosure requirements, impose tougher penalties for violations, and impose new restrictions intended to draw a clearer line between spending to promote candidates and expenditures to promote issues.

Companion legislation (HR 1776 and HR 1777) was introduced in the House by Christopher Shays, R-Conn., and Martin T. Meehan, D-Mass.

Senate Committee Action

The Senate Governmental Affairs Committee, chaired by Thompson, held a series of 32 hearings between July and October that established the parties' pursuit and use of soft money as the leading campaign finance issue.

However, there was no committee action in the Senate on campaign finance legislation, which fell under the jurisdiction of the Rules and Administration Committee.

Thompson's high-profile probe into fundraising abuses suggested that during the frantic scramble for 1996 campaign money, both parties had bent the fundraising laws. The hearings documented access-peddling by the Clinton-Gore reelection campaign, but also scrutinized questionable activities by Republicans, including the possible use of independent tax-exempt groups to evade federal spending limits. *(Campaign finance probe, p. 1-20)*

In an effort to build pressure on his colleagues to take up campaign reform legislation, Thompson abruptly shifted the course of the hearings in late September away from specific abuses to what was wrong with the existing system and how to fix it.

The panel heard repeated calls for banning soft money. Thomas E. Mann, director of governmental studies at the Brookings Institution, told senators that a soft money ban would "remove the primary incentive behind most of the offensive behavior."

Former Vice President Walter F. Mondale and former Kansas Republican Sen. Nancy Kassebaum Baker gave the panel a statement signed by 81 former members of Congress calling for legislation banning soft money, increasing disclosure of contributions and stepping up enforcement of campaign finance laws.

"Practically every horror story that you heard either directly or indirectly is as a result of soft money," said Mondale. Kassebaum said the growth of unregulated donations of soft money had reached a "crisis point."

Senate Floor Action

Lott — who strongly opposed the McCain-Feingold bill on the grounds that it would favor Democrats and restrict political free speech — kept the measure off the floor for most of the year. But during the fall, supporters used threats and delaying tactics to force Lott to bring the bill up and let supporters take a shot at rounding up the 60 votes needed to overcome a filibuster.

McCain-Feingold Scaled Back

To maximize GOP support for the bill, McCain and Feingold decided to scale it back. The goal, McCain said, was simple: "We wanted to present a package that is hardest to vote against."

Three key elements were central to the revised bill. Most important, it proposed to ban contributions of soft money. In addition, the legislation would require labor unions to notify non-union members that they could seek refunds of dues used to make political contributions.

Finally, the bill attempted to place some conditions on the use of so-called issue advocacy television commercials. Because the ads ostensibly focused on issues, they were not covered by federal election laws, even though they often implicitly supported individual candidates. The bill addressed this complex issue by proposing to modify the statutory definition of what was termed "express advocacy," drawing what McCain said would be a "bright line" between expenditures on ads promoting issues and those promoting candidates.

The bill also included provisions to require more public disclosure of contributions and expenditures and impose tougher penalties on violators. And it proposed to bar political parties from making "coordinated expenditures" in behalf of Senate candidates who did not agree to limit their personal spending on their campaigns to $50,000 per election.

Dropped from the original bill were provisions that would have imposed lower limits on PAC contributions, provided bargain-rate television time for candidates who accepted voluntary spending limits, and set voluntary campaign spending limits to restrict both total spending by a campaign and personal spending by a candidate.

Lott Sets Up Roadblocks

After repeatedly declaring that he would not be pressured into bringing the McCain-Feingold bill to the floor, Lott reversed himself in mid-September.

An initial deal to bring up the bill collapsed amid angry charges by Minority Leader Tom Daschle, D-S.D., that Republicans — who would retain control of the timing and process — were trying to blindside Democrats. But after Clinton upped the ante Sept. 23, threatening to call Congress into special session if leaders adjourned without allowing a vote, Lott agreed to bring up the bill.

But Lott was able to use his power as majority leader to erect a formidable series of procedural roadblocks. He opened debate on the bill Sept. 26, after springing the news on McCain just the day before. McCain's staff had to work into the night to get ready, fine-tuning the legislation, which was at least 10 votes short of the number needed to break a filibuster.

Then, on Sept. 29, Lott changed the dynamics by offering an amendment that would force unions to seek prior consent from workers before using their dues to make political donations or conduct political education campaigns. The effect would be to force unions to scale back their political activities dramatically.

The amendment, dubbed the "Paycheck Protection Act" by Republicans, offered Lott an opportunity to pursue two key political objectives: targeting political activity by labor unions, which had dumped millions of dollars into Democratic congressional campaigns in 1996, and, presuming the amendment was adopted, forcing Democrats to scuttle McCain-Feingold rather than see the restriction enacted.

Lott used his power as majority leader to block any changes to his amendment by "filling up the amendment tree," a time-honored procedure under which Senate leaders foreclosed all the procedural possibilities for amendments with slightly different versions of their own proposal.

Precluded from amending Lott's amendment, McCain and Feingold had to come up with 50 votes to table (kill) it, assuming the 51st and deciding vote was cast by Vice President Al Gore. But Democrats had just 49 presumably solid votes, which left them with few options other than to filibuster.

Lott had been hinting at such a strategy for weeks, making it clear that his preferred scenario was one in which Democrats were blamed for bringing down the bill. "They're going to be filibustering, not us," he had told reporters a few weeks earlier.

Lott had invested considerable prestige in the fight over his amendment, but even if he lost that round, Republicans still had the option of blocking the underlying bill with a filibuster of their own.

Republicans Olympia J. Snowe of Maine and James M. Jeffords of Vermont tried unsuccessfully to broker a compromise that would expand Lott's union proposal to cover advocacy groups such as the National Rifle Association and the Sierra Club. But Daschle told Snowe that Democrats would not agree to support the deal.

Dueling Filibusters

The Senate struggle came down to a pair of procedural votes on Oct. 7. The first was a motion to invoke cloture on Lott's union-dues amendment, thereby limiting debate and allowing an up-or-down roll call. Republicans fell eight votes short of the 60 they needed to stop a Democratic filibuster. The tally was 52-48. *(Vote 266, p. S-45)*

The second vote was on limiting debate on the underlying McCain-Feingold bill. This time, the Democrats fell seven votes short of the 60 needed for cloture. The vote was 53-47, with all 45 Democrats and eight Republicans — Collins, McCain, Thompson, Snowe, Jeffords, Arlen Specter of Pennsylvania, John H. Chafee of Rhode Island, and Tim Hutchinson of Arkansas — supporting cloture. *(Vote 267 p. S-45)*

"These two votes put an end to campaign finance reform," Lott declared. "It puts an end to phony reform." Said McConnell: "McCain-Feingold is dead."

Daschle forced more votes on Oct. 8 and 9, but without significantly different results. Hutchinson changed his stance and opposed cloture on McCain-Feingold in the later votes. *(Votes 270, 273, 274 — pp. S-45, S-46)*

The early October showdown, however, did not end the Senate's campaign finance debate. Democrats renewed their pressure on Lott to set a date for considering the McCain-

Feingold bill early in 1998 under procedures that would assure an up-or-down vote.

The Democrats filibustered a massive six-year transportation bill (S 1173), defeating four attempts to invoke cloture and prompting Lott to abandon the bill until the new year. Democrats also threatened to block all other legislation except appropriations bills. *(Votes 275, 277, 278, 282; pp. S-47, S-48)*

On Oct. 30, under a carefully crafted agreement, Lott promised to bring campaign finance legislation back to the Senate floor no later than March 6, 1998.

House Action

While the House Government Reform and Oversight Committee faltered in its efforts to mount hearings parallel to the Senate committee's probe, the House Oversight Committee heard testimony from lawmakers on campaign finance overhaul proposals. Chairman Bill Thomas, R-Calif., said he wanted to wait until 1998 for legislative action and suggested that Congress move in small, unified steps. During hearings that grew testy, Democrats accused Republican leaders of blocking campaign finance legislation to protect a GOP fundraising advantage.

House Democrats began an effort to gather the 218 signatures needed for a discharge petition to force floor action on campaign finance legislation. But the House took no action on overhaul proposals.

GOP leaders agreed to permit votes in February or March on unspecified proposals aimed at addressing various concerns, including foreign contributions and the violation of presidential campaign spending limits. ■

Term Limits Plan Fails in the House

Despite a strong push early in the session, term limits advocates failed to muster the necessary votes in the House to pass a constitutional amendment limiting the number of terms a member of Congress could serve. The Senate did not consider the amendment.

Bill McCollum, R-Fla., a key proponent of the main term limits proposal in the House, could not put together more than a simple majority for his plan, which left him 69 votes shy of the two-thirds majority necessary to pass a constitutional amendment. That was the high-water mark for term limit advocates: 10 alternative term limits proposals failed to get even a simple majority.

McCollum's bill would have limited House and Senate service to 12 years, not counting time already served in Congress. Had it passed in both chambers, three-quarters of the states, or 38, would have had to ratify the measure within seven years for it to take effect.

Term limits at the state level were also dealt a blow when a federal court overturned the state's term limits for California legislators. And a faction of the term limits movement, U.S. Term Limits, lost at least one of its attempts to highlight those members of Congress who voted against term limits proposals. *(California ruling, p. 1-29)*

BOXSCORE

Congressional Term Limits Amendment — H J Res 2. The proposed constitutional amendment would have limited members to 12 years in Congress; it was not retroactive.

Report: H Rept 105-2.

KEY ACTION

Feb. 12 — House rejected H J Res 2, 217-211; a two-thirds majority was needed for passage.

Background

Support for term limits — a key plank in the House Republicans' agenda-setting 1995 "Contract With America" — had been waning for several years.

In the 1995 case *U.S. Term Limits v. Thornton*, the Supreme Court struck down state-initiated term limits for members of Congress as unconstitutional. That year the House voted on several term limits proposals sparked by the contract, but none won the necessary two-thirds majority. *(1995 Almanac, p. 1-35)*

In 1996, the Senate failed to cut off debate on a term limits constitutional amendment, killing the measure for the year. *(1996 Almanac, p. 1-25)*

Given those votes, U.S. Term Limits decided to try a new strategy. The group won spots on the ballot in nine states in 1996 for an initiative that threatened members who failed to vote for a specific term limits proposal with a so-called "scarlet letter." Members who did not support the "exact language" of the term limits measure approved by their own state would have a statement next to their name on the next ballot that read: "Disregarded voter instructions on term limits."

The initiative won in all nine states, but the restrictive wording backfired in the House, where it helped to splinter the vote. For while each state's basic term limits proposal was the same — six years for House members and 12 years for the Senate — some of them differed in very minor ways, and members of the House were unwilling to vote for anything other than the exact language of their state's ballot.

Also, on Feb. 24, the Supreme Court let stand an Arkansas ruling overturning the U.S. Term Limits scarlet letter in that state. The Arkansas court had ruled in *Arkansas Term Limits v. Donovan* that the initiative was a coercive attempt to get around Article 5 of the U.S. Constitution, stating that amendments must originate in Congress or in constitutional conventions, not in ballot initiatives. The Supreme Court refused to hear an appeal.

House Committee

The House Judiciary Committee on Feb. 4 voted 19-12, largely along party lines, to send the term limits constitutional amendment to the House floor without recommendation (H J Res 2 — H Rept 105-2). The action came after the panel defeated a variety of alternatives to the proposal authored by McCollum to limit House and Senate members to 12 years in office.

The markup began with Chairman Henry J. Hyde, R-Ill., announcing he was unalterably opposed to term limits but would vote to send the measure to the floor. He later spoke in favor of an amendment to make the proposal retroactive — then voted against it.

Barney Frank, D-Mass., also expressed deep philosophical problems with limiting terms, then offered the most restrictive amendments of all. One would have limited House and Senate members to six years. The other would have made the limits retroactive. Both were rejected, 12-16. Frank called his actions "honest mischief."

Then two African-American Democrats from the South took up the cause of states' rights. Robert C. Scott, D-Va., and Sheila Jackson-Lee, D-Texas, offered amendments to give states the authority to set congressional term limits. Scott's proposal would have allowed states to set limits more restrictive than the 12-year national standard. It was rejected, 13-15. Jackson-Lee's would have left the matter to the states. It was rejected, 7-22.

Jackson-Lee said her amendment was difficult for her "inasmuch as I suffered under states' rights as an African-American." But she said she was doing it in the spirit of comity, to help capture the essence of what Republicans wanted.

McCollum said "good government" would not be served by allowing states discretion to set terms. He argued that a national guidepost was necessary for term limits to be effective — otherwise Congress would be governed by a "crazy quilt" of varying standards. Several Democrats took up the quilt analogy before Frank put it to rest.

"Not to be a wet blanket on the crazy quilt, but there is an inconsistency here," Frank said. "The great majority of Republicans are going to say — on the matter of term limits — 'States, shut up. We don't want to hear from you.' "

The gamesmanship illustrated the problems McCollum had in building a consensus for his proposal, which was criticized both by those who opposed term limits and by those who felt 12 years was too long, particularly for House members.

Republicans who opposed term limits generally felt that bringing the amendment to the floor for almost certain rejection would do no harm and could boost the party's image as being responsive to popular sentiment. In most public opinion polls, strong majorities supported term limits.

The Judiciary panel considered — and defeated — two versions designed to satisfy U.S. Term Limits' call for limits of six years and 12 years. One, offered by Bob Inglis, R-S.C., would have set terms at six years and 12 years, but not retroactively; it was rejected 4-24. The second, by Asa Hutchinson, R-Ark., would have made the limits retroactive; it was rejected 3-25.

H J Res 2 was slightly different from the version approved by the committee in 1995 but virtually identical to the resolution that went to the floor that year. The committee version would have banned more than 12 consecutive years in office, rather than 12 years total. The Rules Committee changed the proposal to 12 years total before sending it to the floor.

This time, the committee rejected, 11-19, a proposal by Jerrold Nadler, D-N.Y., to adopt the 12-consecutive-years approach.

Appeals Panel Strikes California Limits

A federal appeals court Oct. 7 struck down a California law limiting state legislators' terms.

The statute, which had resulted from a successful ballot initiative in 1990, held members of the state Assembly to three two-year terms and state senators to two four-year terms. The California Supreme Court, which reviewed the law in 1991, interpreted those limits as referring not just to consecutive terms but as being effective for the span of a person's life.

That led to a challenge filed by several legislators and a federal court ruling on April 24 that found the lifetime ban violated legislators' First Amendment and 14th Amendment rights of voting, expression and association.

However, the Oct. 7 ruling by a panel of three judges from the 9th U.S. Circuit Court of Appeals did not strike down the lifetime limits themselves, as the district judge had. The panel, on a 2-1 vote, ruled only that the law was invalid because voters in 1990 had not been adequately informed that the limits amounted to a lifetime ban.

California was one of the first states to pass ballot initiatives limiting terms, both for state legislators and members of Congress. Willie Brown, a Democrat who had held the Assembly Speakership for 14 years, was widely acknowledged as the primary target of the 1990 state term limits initiative. Brown bowed to the new limits and was elected mayor of San Francisco in 1995.

"The people of California want these term limits, want them more now than when they voted for them," said Adam Bromberg, communications director for U.S. Term Limits. "Once again, judges made a decision without regard to the law — they were clever to sidestep the issue and say that people didn't know," Bromberg said.

House Floor Action

The House on Feb. 12 rejected 11 versions of the term limits amendment. Only the underlying plan (H J Res 2) attained a simple majority of 217-211. The tally was 69 votes short of the necessary two-thirds majority needed for passage and 10 votes short of the support garnered by a similar measure in 1995. *(Vote 21, p. H-8)*

"In a very sad way, this amendment demeans public service as a corrupting influence," said Hyde. "It reeks of cynicism and pessimism."

Members considered 10 proposals beyond McCollum's plan. These would have made the limits retroactive, given states the authority to adopt stricter limits, or restricted House members to six years or eight years. They were all soundly defeated.

The debate was heavily influenced by the U.S. Term Limits scarlet letter strategy, which others blamed for splintering the votes and preventing members from supporting any single proposal.

Seven of the 11 versions voted on by the House reflected efforts to comply with individual state initiatives. All of them would have restricted House members to six years and senators to 12. All but one were identical except for technicalities as minor as punctuation. The seventh, the Missouri version, added a clause allowing states to shorten or lengthen the terms.

But with the threat of a scarlet letter on the next ballot, members from these states, particularly Republicans, were generally eager to comply with the exact letter of their state's law.

Some delegations appeared to have more leeway than others. Nebraska members, for instance, were told by their secretary of state that they could vote for the other six-year-12-

year plans. But members from Colorado and Arkansas received stern warnings not to vote for any other proposals. "The terms 'exact language' are seldom used in constitutional or statutory drafting," said Colorado Attorney General Gale Norton in a letter to the state delegation. "They unambiguously require strict compliance."

Scott McInnis, R-Colo., compared members from states with the strictest initiatives to Siamese fighting fish. "We've been bred to eat each other," he said. "This is the first time that I've been forced to vote against some reasonable term limits proposals."

The Colorado version was the most successful of the seven because it had the largest delegation behind it and because that delegation could not reciprocate the support its version got from other states. It was rejected, 87-339. *(Vote 12, p. H-6)*

The other measures failed as follows: Arkansas, 85-341; Idaho, 85-339; Missouri, 72-353; Nebraska, 83-342; Nevada, 85-339; and South Dakota, 83-342. *(Votes 11, 13-17, p. H-6)*

Members also debated several other alternatives. One, offered by Tillie Fowler, R-Fla., would have set House limits at eight consecutive years and Senate limits at 12. Billed as a compromise between those who insisted on six years in the House and those who favored 12, the amendment was soundly rejected, 91-335. *(Vote 18, p. H-6)*

Scott offered a version that would have set the limits at 12 years for both chambers, but given states the option to draft limits. It was rejected, 97-329. *(Vote 19, p. H-8)*

The only alternative to McCollum that received more than 100 votes was offered by Joe L. Barton, R-Texas, and John D. Dingell, D-Mich. It would have made the McCollum proposal retroactive to time served at the time of state ratification of the amendment.

Democrats used the Barton-Dingell debate to ridicule those who would vote for a term limits amendment as long as it was unlikely to affect their own careers. But proponents of the McCollum version saw Barton-Dingell as a mischievous attempt to derail the fragile consensus behind their effort.

Barton-Dingell was rejected, 152-274. Its support came both from hard-core term limits advocates, who saw it as an improvement to H J Res 2, and from some Democrats who opposed H J Res 2. *(Vote 20, p. H-8)* ■

Lawmakers Grant Themselves a Raise

Shrugging off a spate of critical news stories, lawmakers in September allowed the first pay raise for members of Congress in five years. The raise boosted lawmakers' yearly $133,600 salary by 2.3 percent, to $136,700 (the salary was customarily rounded to the next hundred dollars). It took effect Jan. 1, 1998.

By law, members of Congress were entitled to an automatic yearly cost of living adjustment (COLA). But the raise had been blocked every year since fiscal 1993, typically after a lawmaker — often one in a tight re-election contest — introduced an amendment to the Treasury-Postal Service appropriations bill blocking the COLA for that year. Though most members wanted a raise, they were not inclined to go on record in support of one, so year after year they voted to deny themselves the extra pay. *(1996 Almanac, p. 1-27)*

The underlying Treasury-Postal bill did not contain the automatic pay raise provision, but as one of the 13 must-pass appropriations bills, it was an attractive vehicle for carrying the amendment.

In 1997, a number of younger lawmakers, many of whom came into office promising to eliminate congressional perks and privileges, staunchly opposed the pay raise. But congressional leaders from both parties worked quietly behind the scenes to squelch opposition before it could gain momentum. The leadership was bolstered by polls showing a reversal in the downward slide in public opinion about Congress and by the overwhelming majority of members who wanted the raise.

House GOP leaders used their control of the rules governing floor debate on legislation to make it extremely difficult for opponents to add the pay-raise language. They also used the element of surprise on Sept. 17, calling for a vote before opponents expected one and catching them off guard.

The Senate attached a COLA-blocking provision to its version of the Treasury-Postal appropriations bill, but it was dropped in conference. Although lawmakers took some heat from newspaper columnists and radio talk show hosts back home, they cleared the Treasury-Postal Service appropriations bill Oct. 1, with no COLA blocking provision. The president signed the bill (HR 2378 — PL 105-61) on Oct. 10.

Background

In 1989, Congress tried to take the politics out of the pay raise issue with bipartisan legislation that gave members a big boost in pay in return for giving up lucrative speaking fees. The legislation also provided for an annual COLA thereafter. At the time, House Speaker Thomas S. Foley, D-Wash., and Minority Leader Robert H. Michel, R-Ill., worked together to put the weight of their offices and their personal prestige behind the pay raise. *(1989 Almanac, p. 51)*

But the arrangement fell apart beginning in 1993 when members began offering amendments to block the COLA that invariably passed by large margins. Since then, salaries had remained at $133,600 for most members, with leaders paid more.

The hope of reviving the annual COLA for members in 1997 began with a group of rank-and-file lawmakers in both parties who were active in the campaign to return institutional civility to Congress. It was among the issues that the group believed could improve the quality of life for members, many of whom were juggling two residences — one in their district and one in Washington.

Reps. Ray LaHood, R-Ill., and David E. Skaggs, D-Colo., led a group that organized a bipartisan retreat for members in Hershey, Pa. The two pressed for party leaders in the House to meet to discuss the raise and other institutional issues.

LaHood and Skaggs asked Speaker Newt Gingrich, R-Ga., to set up a meeting with Minority Leader Richard A. Gephardt, D-Mo., but members of the leadership and top aides said Gingrich and Gephardt, who rarely spoke and almost never met, were not in a position to tackle such a sensitive issue. "You need to have an element of trust between the leaderships and you don't have that," said a senior Republican aide.

Another necessary ingredient was for the leaders to be on a solid footing with their followers and to have political capital to spend. Gingrich's leadership was subject to constant scrutiny and second-guessing by GOP members, especially after the Republicans lost a public relations battle with the

Democratic White House over a major disaster relief bill. *(Gingrich, p. 1-11)*

Gephardt's widely publicized break with Clinton on budget and trade issues had raised concerns among some Democrats about his leadership as well.

Finally, on July 9, the two leaders met to discuss the possibility of a members' pay raise. Also at the meeting were Majority Leader Dick Armey of Texas, and the party whips, Tom DeLay, R-Texas, and David E. Bonior, D-Mich.

The leaders agreed to poll members of their respective caucuses to test whether a détente on the politically explosive issue was possible. If lawmakers on both sides could be persuaded to refrain from offering amendments to kill the COLA, the increase could go through automatically. "We talked about it," Gephardt said after the meeting. "We'll have to see where [members] are. I have no idea what the sentiment will be."

Some members in both chambers said Congress should continue the salary freeze until it erased the federal deficit, which was unlikely to happen before 2002. "This is not the time to be giving Congress a pay increase, when the budget is still unbalanced," said Rep. Jon Christensen, R-Neb.

Legislative Action

Unable for political reasons to launch a frontal assault against a COLA amendment, House and Senate leaders took different tacks.

The House approach was to sit on the bill. Leaders refused to field questions about the pay raise issue, despite the Sept. 30 deadline to clear the Treasury-Postal bill before the start of the 1998 fiscal year. They blamed their lack of action on a scheduling conflict. "I don't talk congressional pay raise," House Appropriations Chairman Robert L. Livingston, R-La., said on July 16.

Meanwhile, both parties were informally whipping the issue in the House to test support for a rule that would bar a pay raise amendment.

Unlike his House counterparts, Senate Appropriations Committee Chairman Ted Stevens, R-Alaska, moved the Treasury-Postal bill quickly. On July 17, the Senate agreed by voice vote to add language offered by Sam Brownback, R-Kan., to eliminate the COLA. The Senate also adopted, by voice vote, a subsequent amendment by Orrin G. Hatch, R-Utah, to ensure that federal judges, whose salaries were tied to those of lawmakers, did receive a cost of living adjustment.

The Senate then passed its version of the Treasury-Postal bill (S 1023) on July 22 by a vote of 99-0. *(Vote 191, p. S-34)*

Stevens waited until the COLA-blocking amendment was approved to warn that the pay freeze could discourage talented politicians from running for Congress. "What will be the decision made by young people who are thinking of coming here?" he asked.

The House Responds

House leaders finally acted on the bill in September, when they managed to outwit the pay raise opponents.

They brought the bill to the floor Sept. 17 without warning and without sending it through the Rules Committee, where opponents typically introduced their COLA-blocking amendment. Caught off guard, opponents led by Linda Smith, R-Wash., had too little time to organize an effort on the floor. One top Republican close to the leadership said that while opponents were not expressly denied the chance to bring up the pay raise issue, "no one sent them a telegram inviting them to do so, either."

Congressional Pay History

Year	Salary
1789-1795	$6 per diem
1795-1796	$6 per diem (House) $7 per diem (Senate)
1796-1815	$6 per diem
1815-1817	$1,500 per year
1817-1855	$8 per diem
1855-1865	$3,000 per year
1865-1871	$5,000 per year
1871-1874	$7,500 per year
1874-1907	$5,000 per year
1907-1925	$7,500 per year
1925-1932	$10,000 per year
1932-1933	$9,000 per year
1933-1934	$8,500 per year
Feb.-July 1934	$9,000 per year
July 1934-1935	$9,500 per year
1935-1947	$10,000 per year
1947-1955	$12,500 per year
1955-1965	$22,500 per year
1965-1969	$30,000 per year
1969-1975	$42,500 per year
1975-1977	$44,600 per year
1977-1979	$57,500 per year
1979-1982	$60,662.50 per year*
1982-1983	$69,800 per year (House)
1983-1984	$69,800 per year (Senate)
1984	$72,600 per year
1985-1986	$75,100 per year
January-February 1987	$77,400 per year
March 1987-1990	$89,500 per year
1990	$96,600 per year (House) $98,400 per year (Senate)
January-August 1991	$125,100 per year (House) $101,900 per year (Senate)
Balance of 1991	$125,100 per year (Both)
1992-1993	$129,500 per year
1993-1997	$133,600 per year

**Salary increases were generally rounded to the nearest $100. The 1979 increase was not rounded because of specific language in the enacting legislation.*

Note: The top six leaders of Congress — the Speaker of the House, the Senate president pro tempore and the majority and minority leaders of both chambers — received additional pay. Highest paid was the Speaker, who received $171,500 in 1997.

Sources: Congressional Research Service; House Sergeant at Arms; Senate Disbursing Office.

The bill passed, 231-192, without the pay freeze language. *(Vote 403, p. H-122)*

By the following week, however, Smith was joined by other Republicans, a few Democrats and several national organizations, ranging from consumer activist Ralph Nader's Congressional Accountability Project to conservative commentator Paul M. Weyrich's Coalitions for America. They argued once again that Congress did not deserve a pay raise until the federal budget was actually balanced. Some objected less to the COLA than to the leadership's deft maneuvering to avoid a vote, which they likened to the old days of Democratic rule in the House. "They are acting like the old Congress that used to slip things through," Smith said. "This was supposed to be a new Congress."

The Smith forces threatened to raise the COLA issue on other spending bills, including the Commerce, Justice, State bill (HR 2267), which was already bogged down by several contentious issues. On Sept. 24, as that bill was heading to the floor, DeLay brokered a compromise with Smith, J.D. Hayworth, R-Ariz., and David M. McIntosh, R-Ind.

The leadership agreed to hold a roll call vote on a procedural motion on the Treasury-Postal bill as the House prepared to send it to conference. If the motion, called "ordering the previous question," passed, Smith would be barred under House rules from amending the bill with a COLA block. But if it failed, she could offer her amendment.

The motion prevailed, 229-199, and Smith was unable to offer her amendment. Republicans backed the motion, 114-110; Democrats supported it, 115-88. Gingrich who worked behind the scenes to negotiate bipartisan agreement in favor of the pay raise, cast one of the early votes in favor of the motion. The House Speaker rarely voted. *(Vote 435, p. H-132)*

In the personal and sometimes angry debate that preceded the vote, members defended their job performance. Livingston, who noted that he was not a wealthy man and had just put his last child through college, said, "It is not politically wise for me to stand here and make this speech. . . . But I believe strongly that for members to demagogue and say we are not worth what every other American citizen is worth . . . is to say the U.S. Congress is not worth the people's attention and their investment, and I do not believe that."

Peter T. King, R-N.Y., accused pay raise foes of pandering to the public and called their claims that Congress was undeserving of a pay raise "intellectually vapid." If lawmakers were continually denied pay raises, he said, the country would end up with "a Congress of wackos and millionaires."

The Senate Agrees

House and Senate conferees agreed Sept. 29 to a final version of the bill (H Rept 105-284) that dropped the Senate pay freeze provision. After deliberating only four minutes, the Senate negotiators had deadlocked, 3-3, on retaining it. With House conferees united behind the raise, the House position prevailed.

That left the bill silent on the issue, permitting the scheduled pay increase to take effect in fiscal 1998. The change translated into an extra $3,073 per year for lawmakers, which was rounded up to $3,100.

The House approved the conference report Sept. 30 by a vote of 220-207. The Senate cleared the bill Oct. 1, 55-45. Underscoring the skittishness with which senators approached the issue, 19 of the 30 senators facing re-election in 1998 voted against the underlying bill. *(House vote 474, p. H-144; Senate vote 264, p. S-44)* ■

Gingrich Case Prompts Ethics Overhaul

The highly partisan atmosphere surrounding the ethics investigation of House Speaker Newt Gingrich, R-Ga., and the near-breakdown of the ethics committee that resulted, prompted the House to revamp its self-policing process.

Leaders of both parties put together a task force to study the situation and recommend changes to the full House. While the task force was deliberating, the Committee on Standards of Official Conduct, as the ethics committee was officially named, was not constituted, and there was a moratorium on filing ethics complaints against members.

The task force completed its work and issued a report in June. In September, the House adopted new rules (H Res 168) based largely on the group's recommendations, aimed at making the ethics process more timely and bipartisan. However, the vote was more partisan than the members of the task force had hoped. After the House made two important changes to the task force recommendations, many Democrats voted against it.

In the most controversial vote, the House barred outside groups and individuals from filing ethics complaints against members of Congress. That was a change from the panel's recommendations, which would have allowed such filings if the filer had "personal knowledge" of an infraction.

The rules changes adopted by the House also included:

➤ A time limit of 45 days during which the committee was required to either dismiss a complaint, resolve it with a letter to the lawmaker or establish a subcommittee to open an investigation. If the committee failed to act within 45 calendar days — or five legislative days, whichever was longer — a complaint would automatically go to the investigation stage. But the panel also could extend the review period for an additional 45 calendar days.

➤ Enhanced powers for the chairman and ranking member, who were empowered to refer a complaint to an investigative subcommittee on their own. Under previous rules, only a vote of the full committee could kick off an investigation. The ranking member also was given greater power to place items on the committee's agenda.

➤ Creation of a nonpartisan professional staff and a 20-member pool of lawmakers who could be called on to serve on the subcommittees.

Overall, however, the task force opted to maintain the existing bifurcated system, in which an investigatory subcommittee reviewed a complaint and then made recommendations to an adjudicatory subcommittee that took over the trial-like phase of the process. The system, established under ethics legislation passed in 1989, had been in place since 1991. *(1989 Almanac, p. 16; 1991 Almanac, p. 44)*

Ethics Task Force

On Feb. 12, House leaders announced the creation of a 10-member ethics task force, evenly divided between the two parties, to begin a review of the ethics process. The announcement was accompanied by a two-month moratorium on the filing of new ethics cases. Majority Leader Dick Armey, R-Texas, and Minority Leader Richard A. Gephardt, D-Mo., made the announcement jointly on the House floor.

"After the past few tumultuous months, I think we must have a brief cooling-off period where members can sit back and examine where the ethics process works, where it does not and how it might be improved," Armey said.

"We agree on the Democratic side there needs to be a complete review of the ethics process, with a view toward recommending changes to the whole body," said Gephardt.

The two co-chairman of the task force were Robert L. Livingston, R-La., chairman of the House Appropriations Committee, and Benjamin L. Cardin, D-Md.

The other Republicans were: Porter J. Goss of Florida; Michael N. Castle of Delaware; Bill Thomas of California;

and Rules Committee Chairman Gerald B.H. Solomon of New York.

The other Democrats were: Nancy Pelosi of California, who had served on the ethics panel during the Gingrich case; Louis Stokes of Ohio, a former ethics committee chairman; Martin Frost of Texas; and Joe Moakley of Massachusetts.

The most controversial issue facing the panel was whether to allow former lawmakers or other public luminaries to handle at least a part of the procedures, such as the reviewing of initial complaints or the investigatory stages. The idea was to give the process more independence and to ease the workload for the committee.

Both the co-chairmen were lukewarm to the idea. Livingston said he was willing to listen to proposals for outsider involvement, but added, "I do believe that the House is the primary arbiter on ethics." He said the Constitution "did not envision setting up a commission every time there's a problem." Livingston said he preferred to try to improve the existing internal system. He said the aim of the task force was "to do whatever possible to avert political wars inside the ethics committee."

Cardin had previously suggested using panels of former lawmakers for the investigatory stages because they would not have the time constraints of House members. But he said he did not think lawmakers policing themselves was a "central problem."

"I've drawn no conclusions," he said, suggesting there were other ways of dealing with the workload problem. One was to have leaders from both parties actively discourage frivolous or tit-for-tat complaints, he said.

In addition to resolving the issue of outside assistance, the task force was charged with reviewing: changes in the standards for initiating an investigation, possible limits on who could file complaints, evidentiary standards during a probe, whether to impose time limits on investigations, and whether the existing system worked well.

Under the two-stage system that had been in place since 1991, the ethics committee initially reviewed complaints and decided whether to open an investigation. If so, an investigatory subcommittee gathered evidence. If it issued formal charges, the members who did not serve on the subcommittee conducted the second phase, a trial-like process called a disciplinary hearing. The findings of the adjudicatory subcommittee went to the full committee for action.

In the Gingrich case, the investigatory subcommittee, run by Goss and Cardin, was able to reach bipartisan consensus. That resulted in the Speaker admitting to a two-part formal charge: that he failed to get useful legal advice in setting up charitable foundations to pay for his political activities and that he gave the committee false information. *(Gingrich, p. 1-11)*

But problems arose on the full committee, where Chairwoman Nancy L. Johnson, R-Conn., and ranking member Jim McDermott, D-Wash., were under heavy pressure from their respective political parties. Johnson was roundly criticized for delays in the case and for failing to follow procedure; McDermott was criticized for appearing to be biased against Gingrich and for allegedly leaking a tape-recorded conversation of the Speaker discussing strategy with his allies. *(1996 Almanac, p. 1-31)*

The matter was resolved Jan. 21, when the House voted to accept the committee's recommendation to reprimand the Speaker.

Task Force Issues Report

The task force issued its report June 18, but not before being snagged in the ongoing battles within the House Republican leadership.

Just hours before the long-awaited report was to be released, Livingston suddenly announced he had "pulled the plug" on both the panel and its report. Hours later, as task force Democrats proceeded with the planned release, Livingston just as abruptly reversed himself and revived the report and its 30 recommendations. "I was off the reservation for a while, but I'm back on the reservation," he said.

The 30 recommendations faced serious political obstacles to their adoption by the full House, not the least of which was the disarray within the Republican leadership that was responsible for Livingston's June 18 flip-flop.

One senior member of the leadership said later that the initial decision to kill the task force was simply "an immediate overreaction" to the unreleased report. The task force had labored for months in relative secrecy, keeping even top leadership in the dark. Now, from the leadership's perspective, Livingston and Cardin were dropping a 50-page report on the House and pushing for a vote the following week.

There was a personal element to the fracas as well: the increasing friction between some of the leadership and Livingston. "There was a feeling that Livingston was just trying to shove this thing out, so he could get on with his own thing," the senior leader said, referring to an appropriations process that was well behind schedule.

Rather than endure another political black eye over the ethics process, Republican leaders decided to allow planned hearings on the recommendations to proceed before the House Rules Committee on June 20. But Livingston's bid for a floor vote as early as June 24 was deferred until after the July 4th recess.

Largely lost amid the rancor was the substance of the report itself. Reformers had hoped the task force would respond to complaints that the House could not police itself by recommending that ethics complaints be referred to outside investigators and adjudicators.

But the task force shied away from anything that far-reaching. Under the proposed new rules, outside watchdog groups would gain the right to file ethics complaints without the sponsorship of a House member. But those groups would have to meet a higher standard of evidence than members themselves. They would need "personal knowledge" of the ethical transgression alleged.

Under the proposal, watchdog groups would also lose a key means of bringing complaints. Under the existing rules, outsiders' ethics complaints had to be introduced by a member of the House, but three formal letters from members refusing sponsorship also sufficed if a sponsor could not be obtained. Critics of the so-called three-refusal rule said it allowed members who did not want to bring complaints in public to do so, in effect, by refusing to do so. Defenders said the rule allowed outsiders to file complaints against powerful members who might retaliate against their colleagues.

In voting to repeal the three-refusal rule, task force members of both parties said it had been abused. But Gary Ruskin, director of the Congressional Accountability Project, a Ralph Nader-affiliated organization, said repeal would leave watchdog groups more shut out of the process than they already were. "We're calling this the Corrupt Politicians Protection Act," Ruskin said.

Other task force recommendations included:

➤ Formation of a 20-member pool, 10 members from each party who were not on the ethics committee, to serve on the panel's investigatory subcommittees. This was designed to relieve the time demands of serving on ethics, a common complaint of past members, and to increase understanding of the difficulty of handling ethics complaints. Much of the pressure on the committee during the Gingrich case stemmed from the partisan war waged just outside its doors as it struggled to maintain fairness.

➤ Creation of a permanent, nonpartisan ethics committee staff.

➤ Reduction of the term on ethics from six years to four, with the chairman and ranking member permitted to stay longer.

➤ Explicit rights for the ranking minority member to place items on the committee's agenda.

➤ Strict new standards of confidentiality that would require committee members to take non-disclosure oaths, close almost all investigative deliberations to the public, restrict the release of evidence and hide roll call votes unless the committee voted to divulge them.

The task force was largely united behind the report, voting 8-1 on June 17 to support it (three members were absent). The "no" vote was cast by Thomas.

Castle said the panel had endured late nights, heated arguments and walk-outs in its effort to open up the ethics process to a wider array of participants while insulating it from partisan witch hunts. "Nobody thinks it's going to satisfy everyone, but I think it is a very carefully thought-out product," Castle said.

House Floor Action

After a day of frequently personal and emotional debate, the House on Sept. 18 approved a new set of rules for its ethics process. The vote on the resolution (H Res 168) was 258-154. But the action came after the House made two major changes to the package put forward by the task force and defeated a third. Republicans voted 210-6 for the resolution. Democrats, many of them angered by the changes made on the floor, opposed it, 48-147. *(Vote 413, p. H-126)*

● **Outside complaints barred.** In what was the most controversial change adopted by the House, the new rules barred non-members from filing complaints with the ethics committee.

In place of the task force recommendation that outside groups be allowed to file complaints if they had "personal knowledge" of a transgression," the House approved, 228-193, the outside filing ban sponsored by John P. Murtha, D-Pa. He and other advocates argued that members needed to be protected from frivolous ethics complaints, especially from their political foes during re-election campaigns. *(Vote 409, p. H-124)*

Under the approved change, outsiders were required to find a lawmaker to sponsor the complaint, which meant they had to go a long extra mile to find a member willing to risk political oblivion by bringing a formal complaint against a House leader or an influential committee chairman.

The case that started the House on the road to reflection and self-improvement — the highly contentious ethics investigation of Speaker Gingrich — might not have seen the light of day under the new rule. The case had been instigated in 1994 by Gingrich's political opponent at the time, Georgia Democrat Ben Jones. *(1994 Almanac, p. 54)*

Cardin argued vehemently against the change, calling it "the first time in the history of this chamber since we adopted ethics procedures that we will close the doors on outsiders" and warning: "We will lose the confidence of the outside world, and rightly so."

Cardin said he could envision circumstances in which, for example, a staff member received unwanted sexual advances from a House member and then was compelled to try to find another lawmaker willing to press the case against the out-of-bounds colleague.

Livingston, who opposed the Murtha amendment, said he hoped it would not impede the filing of legitimate complaints. He noted that the ethics committee retained the power to act on its own on information provided by outsiders.

"We were better off under the old rules," said task force member Pelosi, who voted against the rules package because of the Murtha amendment. "We've succeeded in building a cocoon around Congress. I believe in giving members some level of protection, but we should not create a shield against outside complaints."

● **Full committee approval required.** A second modification approved by the House required a majority vote of the full committee to expand the scope of a subcommittee investigation when additional information was uncovered. The vote was 221-194. The task force had recommended that the investigative subcommittee that handled the initial steps of a case have the power to expand the scope. The intent was to safeguard the subcommittee's autonomy. *(Vote 411, p. H-126)*

● **Expiration of complaints rejected.** The House rejected, 181-236, a third amendment, which critics said had the greatest potential to do long-term damage to the ethics process. Sponsored by W.J. "Billy" Tauzin, R-La., it would have required that complaints against members be dismissed if the committee deadlocked for six months over the issue of whether to open an investigation. *(Vote 410, p. H-124)*

Supporters of the amendment argued that lawmakers needed protection from election-year opponents who filed baseless ethics complaints with the intent of having them linger long enough to do political damage. "These accusations are going to be there, and the truth will have a difficult time catching up with them," said Judiciary Chairman Henry J. Hyde, R-Ill.

But critics said the amendment would encourage stalemate by giving committee members favoring dismissal an incentive to dig in and wait for the clock to run out. "This amendment kills the ethics process because it promotes partisanship and deadlock throughout the whole process," said Howard L. Berman, D-Calif.

The task force position prevailed. If the committee were to deadlock, it would notify the target of the investigation of the delay but would not automatically dismiss the case.

Ethics Committee Revived

Following the approval of new ethics rules, the House leadership revived the ethics committee. Ending a hiatus of nearly seven months, the panel held its first meeting the week of Sept. 29 with a roster of new members.

James V. Hansen of Utah, the new chairman, and Berman, the ranking Democrat, quickly got down to work with their new committee members, acting on complaints against Gingrich, Majority Whip Tom DeLay, R-Texas, and Transportation and Infrastructure Chairman Bud Shuster, R-Pa. *(Ethics cases, p. 1-35)*

Lawmakers chosen for the 10-member committee, arguably the least popular assignment among the 20 standing committees, were typically relatively junior members from safe districts who had reputations as leadership loyalists. One exception on the seniority issue in the new group was Martin Olav Sabo, D-Minn., a 19-year veteran and former chairman of the Budget Committee.

Other Democratic members were: Chaka Fattah of Pennsylvania, Ed Pastor of Arizona and Zoe Lofgren of California.

The Republicans were Lamar Smith of Texas, an 11-year lawmaker who chaired the Judiciary Committee's immigration subcommittee; Joel Hefley of Colorado; Robert W. Goodlatte of Virginia; and Joe Knollenberg of Michigan.

The New Ethics 'Pool'

As required by the new House ethics rules, members who did not sit on the committee itself were named to a "pool" that would investigate charges of impropriety by their colleagues. Although the rules allowed for a 20-member pool, only 19 members were named: 10 Republicans and nine Democrats.

The 10 Republicans selected for the investigative pool were: Herbert H. Bateman of Virginia, Ed Bryant of Tennessee, Nathan Deal of Georgia, Richard "Doc" Hastings of Washington, Jim McCrery of Louisiana, Howard P. "Buck" McKeon of California, Dan Miller of Florida, Rob Portman of Ohio, James M. Talent of Missouri, and William M. "Mac" Thornberry of Texas.

Democrats named were: James E. Clyburn of South Carolina, Mike Doyle of Pennsylvania, Chet Edwards of Texas, Ron Klink of Pennsylvania, John Lewis of Georgia, Carrie P. Meek of Florida, Robert C. Scott of Virginia, Bart Stupak of Michigan, and John Tanner of Tennessee. ■

Congressional Ethics Cases Get Attention in 1997

Once again, the troubles of Speaker Newt Gingrich, R-Ga., dominated the headlines on congressional ethics. But a number of other House members and former members made news on the ethics front in 1997. The following is a summary:

DeLay Complaint Dismissed

On Nov. 7, the House ethics committee dismissed a complaint against Majority Whip Tom DeLay, R-Texas, brought by a government watchdog group that raised questions about his prodigious fundraising and about whether he helped clients of his lobbyist brother.

In a letter to DeLay, the Committee on Standards of Official Conduct said it "found no basis for launching an investigation" of influence-peddling by DeLay, and that his contacts with brother Randy DeLay's clients either predated his brother's hiring or could be considered normal constituent services.

The committee also dismissed an allegation that DeLay might have linked favors to campaign contributions. As part of its complaint, the Congressional Accountability Project cited a 1995 Washington Post story that described how DeLay checked the frequency and amount of campaign contributions from lobbyists when they visited his office, leaving the impression that they had better give to GOP candidates.

The group, which was affiliated with Ralph Nader, had filed the complaint in September 1996.

The committee noted that DeLay's written response to the committee "did not contain a denial that the event mentioned in the newspaper story occurred."

The committee appeared to caution DeLay about his fundraising. The statement noted that fundraising was illegal in the Capitol or congressional office buildings and added: "Rep. DeLay was advised that it is particularly important that a member not make statements that create the impression that the member would consider an individual's requests for access or for official action based on such campaign contributions."

DeLay issued a statement saying, "As I have maintained from the start, these complaints were politically motivated and not true. I have always honestly and forthrightly fought for the people of the Houston area. The committee's decision confirms that fact."

"Do they just ask Congressman DeLay and take his word for it?" asked Gary Ruskin, director of the Congressional Accountability Project. "What evidence do we have that they did any investigation whatsoever?"

Among other things, the complaint alleged that DeLay worked to round up congressional support for a letter to then-Commerce Secretary Ronald H. Brown and then-U.S. Trade Representative Mickey Kantor urging them to support Cemex, a Mexican cement-making company that was embroiled in a trade dispute with the United States and a foreign company represented by Randy DeLay.

Kim Pleads Guilty

After four years of protesting his innocence, Rep. Jay C. Kim admitted in federal court Aug. 11 that he had accepted illegal campaign contributions. The California Republican and his wife, June, pleaded guilty in Los Angeles federal court to a total of 10 counts stemming from the receipt of more than $230,000 in illegal contributions.

The Kims were initially to be sentenced Oct. 23 but won delays of the sentencing until well into 1998. According to the terms of their plea agreement with federal prosecutors, they faced up to six months in jail and fines totaling $635,000. Judge Richard A. Paez warned the Kims that he would not be bound by the agreement and could impose stiffer penalties.

Because the charges against Kim were misdemeanors, he was not covered by a House Republican Conference rule that would have stripped him of his subcommittee chairmanship for a felony conviction. Kim chaired the Transportation and Infrastructure Subcommittee on Public Buildings and Economic Development.

On behalf of his campaign committee, Kim pleaded guilty to five felony counts. The committee faced potential fines of as much as $2.5 million; Kim himself would not be personally liable.

Kim did plead guilty to three misdemeanor charges for which he was personally culpable: that he knowingly accepted a $50,000 campaign contribution from a Taiwanese national and laundered it through his personal bank account; that he accepted an illegal $12,000 corporate contribution from Nikko Enterprises Inc.; and that he directed his firm, JayKim Engineers Inc., to give more than $83,000 in illegal corporate contributions to his campaign.

June Kim pleaded guilty to two charges that stemmed from her acceptance of more than $19,000 in illegal corporate campaign contributions. The bulk of that amount, $14,000, had been laundered through an electronics firm owned by Kim campaign treasurer Seokuk Ma. Ma was convicted in April 1997 of having accepted and concealed at least $23,000 in illegal contributions and was sentenced to five year's probation and fined $12,000. *(1996 Almanac, p. 1-38)*

The Los Angeles Times broke the story in 1993 that Kim had directed his firm to illegally contribute $485,000 in funds and services to his 1992 campaign. The paper, which had supported Kim in his first campaign, called for his resignation in an Aug. 13 editorial.

McDermott Faces Suit

Frustrated by the amount of time the Justice Department had taken to investigate the illegal tape recording of a conference call among House GOP leaders in December

1996, Rep. John A. Boehner, R-Ohio, turned to the courts.

Boehner was preparing to sue Rep. Jim McDermott, D-Wash., alleging that he made public the contents of the tape. A spokesperson for McDermott said the congressman would not comment on the case until the investigation was complete.

On Dec. 21, 1996, Boehner, head of the House GOP Conference, was driving in Florida talking to other Republican leaders on a cell phone about the predicament facing House Speaker Newt Gingrich, R-Ga. *(1996 Almanac, p. 1-31)*

That same day, Gingrich admitted that he had violated House rules by failing to properly manage the financing of his political activities through tax-exempt foundations and by giving the ethics committee inaccurate information about the matter.

The call was intercepted by a Florida couple listening to their police scanner. They said they taped the call because they thought it had historic value. The contents of the tape eventually showed up in The New York Times and The Atlanta Journal-Constitution.

Democrats immediately charged that the tape showed that Gingrich had violated an agreement not to rally opposition to an ethics committee decision to reprimand him.

A Boehner aide said the lawsuit would be filed under the Electronic Communications Privacy Act. If successful, Boehner could receive $10,000. In early 1997, Boehner won permission from the House ethics committee and the Federal Election Commission to use campaign funds to pay for the lawsuit.

Shuster Probe Launched

The House ethics committee announced Nov. 14 that it had launched an investigation into charges that House Transportation and Infrastructure Committee Chairman Bud Shuster, R-Pa., accepted improper favors from a lobbyist who also acted as his campaign fundraiser.

The committee issued a brief statement, saying it had created an investigative subcommittee to look into a complaint against Shuster by the Congressional Accountability Project, a Ralph Nadar-affiliated group.

The subcommittee was chaired by Joel Hefley, R-Colo., and the ranking member was Zoe Lofgren, D-Calif. The other two members were Jim McCrery, R-La., and Chet Edwards, D-Texas.

"I'm pleased that the committee is moving expeditiously," Shuster said in a statement Nov. 14. "This is the proper procedure."

Citing a slew of newspaper accounts, the watchdog group asked the committee to investigate Shuster's relationship with Ann Eppard, a former top aide who had become a lobbyist.

Many of Eppard's clients were transportation businesses with an interest in legislation before Shuster's committee. Eppard also served as Shuster's fundraiser, soliciting contributions from many of those same transportation clients, according to the news stories. Shuster also often stayed with Eppard at her $823,000 waterfront home.

The opening of a congressional investigation followed months of reports that Shuster also was the subject of a federal grand jury investigation.

On Feb. 3, the Boston Globe reported that a grand jury in Boston was examining whether Shuster used his influence to help two Boston businessmen whose properties were threatened by a federally funded highway project in that city. Both businessmen had contributed thousands of dollars to Shuster's congressional campaign committee.

The paper said the investigation was part of a broader probe of the relationship between Shuster and Eppard. Shuster told reporters after the story was published that he had not been notified by prosecutors of the grand jury investigation.

Under House Republican rules, Shuster would have to relinquish his committee chairmanship if he were indicted.

Former Members

Cooley Sentenced

Former Rep. Wes Cooley, R-Ore., was found guilty March 18 of lying about his military record in official state voters' pamphlets. He was sentenced to two years' probation and ordered to perform community service and pay fines and expenses.

Cooley, 64, did not challenge facts presented by state prosecutors. He served in the House from 1995 to 1997, withdrawing his re-election bid under pressure from Republicans after questions were raised about a number of his past statements. He was indicted in December 1996 for claiming in 1994 primary and general election pamphlets that he had been a member of the Army Special Forces in Korea. Prosecutors told the court they could prove that Cooley was in the United States during the Korean War. *(1996 Almanac, p. 1-36)*

Federal officials were still investigating allegations that Cooley and his wife lied about their marital status so she could continue to collect widow's benefits from her first husband through the Veterans' Administration.

Oakar Pleads Guilty

Former Rep. Mary Rose Oakar, D-Ohio, pleaded guilty Sept. 30 to a misdemeanor conspiracy charge and a misdemeanor campaign finance violation.

Oakar served in the House from 1977 until she was unseated in 1992 amid accusations that she had abused the House bank by writing 213 checks she could not cover. The House bank closed in 1991.

Subsequent scrutiny of her 1992 campaign accounts by federal investigators revealed that she had shifted $16,000 in campaign contributions from her House bank account to her campaign using false names to evade individual contribution limits.

Oakar admitted the shift and admitted giving false information to the Federal Election Commission. Oakar was the 11th person (and fourth former House member) to plead guilty to charges stemming from the House bank scandal. *(1996 Almanac, p. 1-40)*

On Jan. 21, 1998, Oakar was sentenced to two years of probation and fined $32,000 on two misdemeanor counts. As a part of her agreement, Oakar was required to perform 200 hours of community service.

Collins Findings Issued

The House ethics committee announced Jan. 2 that it had found reason to believe that former Rep. Barbara-Rose Collins, D-Mich., violated laws and House rules.

The panel said Collins improperly used congressional staff members to do personal chores or campaign work and misused official, campaign and scholarship funds. She improperly directed congressional staff members to clean her house and arrange campaign fundraising events on office time, the panel said.

The subcommittee also found evidence that Collins used House office funds for her 1995 campaign. For example, a plane ticket was purchased with office funds for a friend to go to a campaign event. In another instance, a campaign hotel bill was paid with office funds. The subcommittee said it believed Collins was aware that in both cases congressional funds were used.

Collins, whose term expired Jan. 3, 1997, was defeated for re-election in an August 1996 primary by Democrat Carolyn Cheeks Kilpatrick, who was sworn in Jan. 7. The full House did not act on a punishment for Collins. But a Justice Department probe was expected to continue. *(1996 Almanac, p. 1-37)*

Rostenkowski Released From Jail

After spending 13 months in jail and two more at a halfway house, one of the most formidable former members of the House, Dan Rostenkowski, D-Ill., was allowed to go home.

In the early morning hours of Oct. 15, the 69-year-old Rostenkowski left a Chicago halfway house and silently brushed past a throng of reporters to enter a waiting car. Friends and colleagues said he was trim, rested and ready — though ready for what was not certain.

Since his transfer to the halfway house in August, after serving 13 months at a minimum security prison in Wisconsin, Rostenkowski had been quietly plying his trade as a political consultant, working in a storefront office next to the home his grandfather built on Chicago's Near West Side.

But his friends expected that, sooner or later, Rostenkowski would return to Washington, the scene of his greatest triumphs and most humiliating defeats. He no longer shaped federal policy on taxes or health care, as he once did, but his expertise on those subjects could make him a valuable commodity.

"There aren't many people who have the background that Rosty's got," said former Oklahoma Republican Rep. Mickey Edwards, who had become a lecturer on government at Harvard University's John F. Kennedy School of Government.

But Rostenkowski also carried the heavy burden of being a convicted felon. In 1994, federal prosecutors issued a 17-count indictment that accused him of padding his payroll with no-show employees, stealing cash from the House Post Office, using campaign funds to buy cars for his family and obstructing the investigation against him. In all, he was charged with misusing or embezzling more than $700,000. *(1994 Almanac, p. 45)*

Most of those charges were dropped as part of a 1996 plea agreement, under which he admitted he had put employees on his payroll to "perform personal and political service" and misused federal money to buy gifts for friends. *(1996 Almanac, p. 1-40)*

For many Americans, the case against Rostenkowski symbolized all that was wrong with four decades of Democratic rule in the House — the arrogance of power, the lavish lifestyles financed with taxpayer funds.

Just months after the May 1994 indictment, Republicans took control of Congress. And Rostenkowski, for all his success at bringing home the bacon to his Chicago district, was turned out in favor of Michael Patrick Flanagan, a lightly regarded Republican who lost his own re-election try in 1996.

Edwards conceded that, while older members could still be a bit in awe of Rostenkowski, "the downside for Rosty is that for a lot of younger members, all they know is that he went to jail."

Back in Chicago, it seemed that all was forgiven. At Sophie's Busy Bee, a famous Polish diner in Rostenkowski's old district, "The people are saying they love him, they respect him," said owner Sophie Madej in a telephone interview. "They are just glad to have him home."

Had the newly svelte Rostenkowski, who lost 60 pounds in prison, come for his customary cup of chicken soup and grilled pork chop sandwich? "No, we're still waiting," Madej said, laughing. "He might want something different now."

Rota Sentenced

Robert V. Rota, the former House postmaster, was sentenced Feb. 20 to four months in prison for his role in the House Post Office scandal. Rota had pleaded guilty to misdemeanor charges for supplying former Democratic Reps. Dan Rostenkowski of Illinois and Joe Kolter of Pennsylvania with cash in exchange for government-purchased stamps.

U.S. District Court Judge Norma Holloway Johnson of Washington also ordered Rota to pay a $2,000 fine and to pay Congress $5,000 in restitution for his role in the scam.

Despite his cooperation with federal investigators, Johnson rejected probation and accepted U.S. prosecutor Thomas J. Motley's argument that Rota should be punished more harshly for lying to investigators in 1980, coercing others to lie and covering up the crimes.

Johnson said that she understood Rota came under intense pressure from Rostenkowski, then a powerful member of the Ways and Means Committee, to cover up the transactions. But, she said, she could not give him probation.

"I know that those powerful men perhaps had such an influence on you that it was difficult to overcome," Johnson told Rota, who wept and grabbed a podium for support as she imposed the sentence. "I do concern myself with the fact that there was a time when you could have come clean," she said.

Rota denied the existence of a cash-for-stamps scheme in 1980 and persuaded another post office employee to lie to investigators. The allegations resurfaced in 1991, and Rota again lied. But this time, another employee cooperated. In 1993, Rota was indicted and made a deal to cooperate. He confessed that he gave Rostenkowski and Kolter several thousand dollars in cash for stamps over 15 years. *(1993 Almanac, p. 64)* ■

CQ

Chapter 2

ECONOMICS & FINANCE

BUDGET

Five-Year Balanced-Budget Deal Shapes Year's Fiscal Debate

Putting the budget wars of the 104th Congress behind them, White House, GOP agree to erase the deficit by 2002

Riding the tailwind of a boisterous economy and building on the remnants of their scuttled 1995-96 budget talks, President Clinton and the Republican-controlled 105th Congress concluded a budget deal that promised to eliminate the federal deficit by 2002, producing the first balanced budget since the late 1960s.

The agreement was reached in May, though it took lawmakers much of the remainder of the session to fill in the details. The bipartisan effort would have seemed unimaginable two years earlier, when congressional Republicans challenged Clinton to a budget duel that forced the temporary shutdown of a large portion of the government. But striking a deal became easier after the split decision in the 1996 elections, which retained Republican control of Congress and Democratic control of the White House. Both sides read the election as a mandate to work together.

The unseen hand in it all was the strong economy. Its salutary effect on the budget made it possible for negotiators to eliminate the deficit in five years, while providing both a net tax cut calculated at the time as $95 billion over five years ($275 billion over 10) and increased spending for administration priorities.

Budget-Related Stories

Budget Deal Sets Stage

The first public sign that things were changing was Republicans' refusal to lambaste Clinton's Feb. 6 budget proposal for fiscal 1998. Although they found it disappointing, they held their criticism so as to avoid a repeat of the acridly partisan atmosphere that had helped poison budget talks in 1995-96. Behind the scenes, key White House budget aides were already working with congressional budget drafters to lay the groundwork for an agreement.

It took weeks of back-channel talks, but on May 2 the White House and congressional leaders announced they had reached a deal. Two more weeks of bargaining enabled them to fill in enough of the details to allow Congress to translate the agreement into a congressional budget resolution (H Con Res 84). Though the resolution was late — it was not completed until June 5, well past the April 15 statutory deadline — the result was a bipartisan blueprint, the first in recent memory, setting the ceiling for the annual appropriations bills and providing guidelines for tax and spending decisions.

The budget resolution called for two reconciliation bills aimed at reconciling existing law with the budget agreement. Republicans were determined to have the two huge bills completed before Congress left for its August recess, and they succeeded. The bills were cleared July 31 and signed into law Aug. 5.

The first (HR 2015 — PL 105-33) was projected to achieve $127 billion in net deficit reduction over five years through a combination of cuts in mandatory and discretionary programs, and new revenue from an increase in the cigarette tax, auctions of electromagnetic spectrum and other sources. Lawmakers also made room for $33 billion in new spending sought by Clinton, including $20 billion for children's health insurance and $13 billion to restore some cuts made in the 1996 welfare law. The bill continued "pay-as-you-go" rules for entitlement and tax changes, extended existing limits on discretionary appropriations and increased the statutory federal debt ceiling.

The second bill (HR 2014 — PL 105-34) contained a projected $95 billion in net tax cuts over five years.

In September, the Congressional Budget Office (CBO) recalculated the numbers, estimating that together the bills would achieve $116 billion in net deficit reduction over five years — $195.7 billion in savings offset by what Congress' Joint Committee on Taxation calculated would be $80 billion in net revenue reduction.

Advocates of a balanced-budget amendment to the Constitution had met with disappointment in March, when the Senate fell one vote short of the two-thirds majority needed to approve a constitutional amendment. With a balanced-budget deal in place and economic growth working to shrink the deficit, the amendment's future prospects looked dim.

Appropriations Bills Clear, Line-Item Veto Used

With the budget-reconciliation bills enacted, lawmakers spent much of September working on the 13 regular appropriations bills. Each of the spending bills was ultimately enacted — the first time that had happened since Republicans took control of Congress in 1995. But four of them became stalled by fights over issues such as abortion and private school vouchers did not clear until the end of the session.

Clinton used his new line-item veto authority, which took effect Jan. 1, to cancel individual items in nine of the 13 appropriations bills. After provoking a furor by striking 38 projects totaling $287 million from the military construction bill, Clinton wielded the line-item-veto pen with a relatively light hand. (His first use of the veto came earlier, when he cancelled three items from the twin tax and spending bills.)

The Supreme Court dismissed an early challenge to the law's constitutionality, but further lawsuits were working their way through the courts. ■

Clinton Budget: 'Alive on Arrival'

The President's Budget

(By fiscal year; in billions of dollars)

	1997	1998	1999	2000	2001	2002
Budget authority	$1,652.9	$1,709.5	$1,777.4	$1,831.7	$1,880.0	$1,922.3
Outlays	1,631.0	1,687.5	1,760.7	1,814.4	1,844.5	1,879.7
Revenues	1,505.4	1,566.8	1,643.3	1,727.3	1,808.3	1,896.7
Deficit	−125.6	−120.6	−117.4	− 87.1	− 36.1	17.0

SOURCE: Office of Management and Budget

President Clinton sent a $1.69 trillion fiscal 1998 budget to Capitol Hill on Feb. 6 amid widespread speculation that this might be the year when Republicans and Democrats would at last reach agreement on a budget-balancing plan.

By GOP lights, Clinton's budget still proposed to spend too much, cut taxes too little and achieve only about half the deficit reduction needed to balance the budget by 2002. Indeed, Republicans probably would have dismissed the same package out of hand during budget talks in 1995-96. This time, however, most of them bit their tongues, declared the budget "alive on arrival" and predicted that they could tweak it into something both sides could embrace.

The change reflected both Republicans' success in forcing Clinton to accept their goal of balancing the budget by 2002 and the scars they carried as a result of the politically disastrous government shutdowns they had provoked in 1995. They spent the next year fighting Democratic accusations that they were "Medicare killers," and struggled to survive an election that looked for a time as if it might cost them control of the House. Now, battered Republicans were looking for a deal.

Clinton's budget laid down a White House marker for such negotiations — and it showed how much distance still had to be crossed before the two sides had an agreement. *(Provisions, p. 2-7)*

The following are major elements of Clinton's budget:

• **Deficit reduction.** Clinton proposed to balance the budget by fiscal 2002 with net deficit reduction of $252 billion. For 2002, he promised a $17 billion surplus. The administration was able to avoid deeper cuts because it insisted that the future was not nearly as gloomy as the Congressional Budget Office (CBO) projected. Instead, the White House used the more optimistic deficit estimates of its own Office of Management and Budget (OMB).

By contrast, GOP budget-drafters said it would take at least $435 billion to do the job, based on CBO's higher deficit estimates. In its own "illustrative path" to a balanced budget, CBO projected that it would take some $500 billion in net deficit reduction over five years to balance the budget by 2002.

Republicans had made the use of CBO numbers, which were required for calculating any budget Congress produced, an object of near-religious faith in 1995-96.

The administration defended its estimates, noting that recent OMB deficit projects had been more accurate than those of CBO, which had had to sharply downgrade its forecast deficits from 1996 to 1997. Clinton even boasted that his proposal would eliminate the deficit not just in 2002, but for two decades beyond — a claim widely doubted since the package contained virtually none of the fundamental reforms to Medicare and Social Security that analysts said would be needed to avoid huge deficits when Baby Boomers began to retire in the 21st century.

To protect itself, the administration included a "trigger" mechanism designed to suspend most of the tax cuts and impose a 2.25 percent across-the-board cut in all spending except Social Security in 2001-2002 if deficits turned out to be worse than OMB's forecast. The plan, derided by Republicans, was estimated to add $95 billion in net deficit reduction.

"The budget offers what may be temporary tax relief combined with permanent tax hikes, adding up to an excessive tax burden," said House Ways and Means Committee Chairman Bill Archer, R-Texas. "This aspect of the budget has to be improved."

• **Tax cuts.** Clinton proposed $98.4 billion in gross tax cuts over five years, including a $500-per-child tax credit and a capital gains break on the sale of a principal residence. More than a third of the proposed tax cuts — $38.4 billion over five years — was aimed at helping families send their children to college.

Clinton called for offsetting all but about $22.4 billion of the lost revenue by extending expiring taxes and ending a variety of corporate tax breaks.

Republicans wanted gross tax cuts almost twice as big as Clinton's — about $200 billion over five years, according to Senate Majority Leader Trent Lott, R-Miss. — and net tax cuts as much as six or seven times as large — between $120 billion and $150 billion.

Administration officials sent a clear message that they were prepared to bargain. "I think there is the prospect of finding common ground," said Deputy Treasury Secretary Lawrence H. Summers. But Summers also suggested that it was up to Republicans to find acceptable offsets to pay for any bigger tax cuts.

"Obviously, to reach a balanced budget the president and the Congress have to reach an agreement on taxes. But we do not believe that it is appropriate . . . or supported by the American people to make large cuts in programs like Medicare in order to make tax cuts that are targeted at a small minority of Americans," Summers said. "We will be very concerned to see how any further tax reductions are paid for."

• **Domestic spending.** The White House called for a series of ambitious increases in education (a 31 percent increase in selected areas from 1997 to 1998), welfare (about $22 billion) and health care (expansion of health coverage for children and other initiatives). Clinton said his spending proposals were part of a plan that would "balance the budget while maintaining the balance of our values."

• **Welfare.** Clinton called for restoring about $18 billion of the $54.6 billion in savings expected from the 1996 welfare overhaul (PL 104-193) through 2002, much of it to overturn the ban on an array of federal social services to legal immigrants. Clinton also called for $3.6 billion in new spending, chiefly to get welfare recipients into jobs. The budget included proposals to:

• Make legal immigrants who became disabled after entering the country eligible for Supplemental Security Income (SSI) and Medicaid, the federal-state health insurance program for the poor; provide Medicaid to legal immigrant children of poor families; and make refugees and those granted

A Budget Glossary

Appropriations: The process by which Congress provides budget authority, usually through the enactment of 13 separate appropriations bills.

Budget authority: The authority for federal agencies to spend or otherwise obligate money, accomplished through enactment into law of appropriations bills.

Budget outlays: Money that is actually spent in a given fiscal year, as opposed to money that is appropriated for that year. One year's budget authority can result in outlays over several years, and the outlays in any given year result from a mix of budget authority from that and prior years.

Budget authority is similar to putting money in a checking account; outlays occur when checks are written and cashed.

Discretionary spending: Programs that Congress can finance as it chooses through appropriations. With the exception of paying entitlement benefits to individuals (see below), almost everything the government does is financed by discretionary spending. Examples include all federal agencies, Congress, the White House, the courts, the military and activities from space exploration to child nutrition. About a third of all federal spending falls into this category.

Fiscal 1998: The budget year, which runs from Oct. 1, 1997, through Sept. 30, 1998.

Mandatory spending: Made up mostly of entitlements, which are programs whose eligibility requirements are written into law. Anyone who meets those requirements is *entitled* to the money until Congress changes the law.

Examples include Social Security, Medicare, Medicaid, unemployment benefits, food stamps and federal pensions. Another major category of mandatory spending is the interest paid to holders of federal government bonds. Social Security and interest payments are permanently appropriated. And although budget authority for some entitlements is provided through the appropriations process, appropriators have little or no control over the money. Mandatory spending accounts for about two-thirds of all federal spending.

Pay-as-you-go rule (PAYGO): This rule requires that all tax cuts, new entitlement programs or expansions of existing entitlement programs be budget-neutral — offset either by additional taxes or cuts in existing entitlement programs.

Reconciliation: The process by which tax laws and spending programs are changed, or reconciled, to reach outlay and revenue targets set in the congressional budget resolution. Established by the 1974 Congressional Budget Act, it was first used in 1980. Two reconciliation bills were enacted in 1997 — the first (PL 105-33) to adjust tax laws and the second (PL 105-34) to cut entitlement programs and place caps on discretionary spending.

Rescission: The cancellation of previously appropriated budget authority. This is a common way to save money that already has been appropriated. A rescissions bill must be passed by Congress and signed by the president (or enacted over his veto), just as an appropriations bill is.

The president gained "enhanced rescissions" authority, which allows him to strike items within a larger spending bill, on Jan. 1 (PL 104-130). *(Line-item veto, p. 2-63)*

Revenues: Taxes, customs duties, some user fees and most other receipts paid to the federal government. Some receipts and user fees show up as "negative outlays," however, and do not count as revenue.

Sequester: The cancellation of spending authority as a disciplinary measure to corral spending above pre-set limits. Appropriations that exceed annual spending caps can trigger a sequester that would cut all appropriations by the amount of the excess. Similarly, tax cuts or new or expanded entitlement spending programs that are not offset under pay-as-you-go rules would trigger a sequester of non-exempt entitlement programs.

asylum eligible for federal benefits for seven years instead of five. The estimated cost was $14.6 billion.

- Allow disabled children to continue receiving Medicaid if they lost their SSI because of changes in the definition of childhood disability.
- Help states and cities provide subsidies and other incentives to businesses to hire welfare recipients. Clinton also proposed to allow employers to claim a 50 percent tax credit on the first $10,000 a year of wages, for up to two years, for newly hired long-term welfare recipients.

- **Education.** In addition to his proposed tax benefits for education, Clinton requested significant spending increases for selected education programs, including school modernization, student loans, remedial education for low-income students and a new program to promote reading.
- **Health.** Clinton signaled a desire for a truce with Republicans on Medicare, the health insurance program for the elderly and disabled. He proposed to cut projected spending for the program by $100 billion over five years, mostly by reducing payments to health care providers such as hospitals, doctors, and health maintenance organizations (HMOs).

While the budget included no fiscal 1998 savings in Medicaid, it proposed to cut projected Medicaid spending by $9.3 billion over five years, chiefly through a "per capita cap" that would limit federal contributions to states to a set amount per beneficiary.

Together, the proposed cuts in projected spending for Medicare and Medicaid accounted for $109 billion, or 43 percent of the net deficit reduction in Clinton's budget.

On the other hand, Clinton called for increasing health insurance coverage for children and for temporarily unemployed workers.

- **Defense.** The budget called for spending $247.5 billion in outlays on defense in fiscal 1998, a decline from the $254.3 billion provided for fiscal 1997.

Supplemental Requests

Along with his budget for fiscal 1998, Clinton also submitted several requests for additional fiscal 1997 appropriations. The largest of these supplemental requests was $2 billion to finance added costs for operations in Bosnia and other military contingencies.

He also asked for $921 million to clear U.S. debts to the United Nations. The money, intended to provide incentives for the United Nations to implement sweeping reforms, was not to be spent until the start of fiscal 1999.

Clinton also sought $753 million more in fiscal 1997 to fund cost-of-living increases in veterans' programs and $100 million for the special nutrition program for low-income women and children. *(Supplemental, p. 9-84)* ■

The President's Tax Proposals

The five-year tax package submitted as part of President Clinton's fiscal 1998 budget contained $98.4 billion in tax cuts, as scored by the White House's Office of Management and Budget. To offset some of the revenue that would be lost to the Treasury, Clinton called for eliminating about $34 billion in corporate tax preferences and continuing or reinstating about $42 billion in excise taxes. That brought the net proposed tax cut to $22.4 billion over five years.

If by fiscal 2000 it appeared that the budget would not be in balance by 2002, then most of the tax cuts would be suspended starting in 2001, reducing the size of the tax package by about $30 billion over the five-year period, according to administration officials. (There would be additional cuts in spending as well.) At least two of the tax cuts would remain in place, however: a capital gains tax break for home sellers and expanded individual retirement accounts (IRAs).

● **Child tax credit.** The most costly item in the package was a proposed tax credit for children under age 13 whose families earned $75,000 a year or less in gross adjusted income. An eligible family's tax liability would be reduced by $300 a year in 1997, 1998 and 1999 and by $500 in 2000 and thereafter. The credit was to be phased down for families earning between $60,000 and $75,000 annually. The credit would be non-refundable, meaning that families that earned too little to pay income taxes would not benefit. The proposal was expected to cost $46 billion over five years.

● **Education tax cuts.** Tax cuts for education were the second costliest piece of the package totaling $38.4 billion over five years. Virtually all of that was to be used for a two-year tax credit and a deduction of up to $10,000 per year — both for postsecondary education; eligible taxpayers could take one, but not both.

• **Hope Scholarship credit.** Students from families with adjusted gross incomes of less than $80,000 a year would be eligible for a $1,500 tax credit for two years of postsecondary education. The credit was to be phased out for couples earning more than $100,000 a year. It only would be available for the second year if the student maintained a "B" average or better. The credit was expected to result in a revenue loss of $18.6 billion over five years.

• **$10,000 deduction.** Couples with adjusted gross incomes of less than $80,000 a year could take a sizable tax deduction to offset the cost of any postsecondary education, including job training, for themselves or their children. The credit — worth $5,000 a year for tax years 1997 and 1998 and $10,000 in 1999 and thereafter — would be phased out for couples earning more than $100,000 annually. It was expected to result in a revenue loss of $17.5 billion over five years.

Administration economists said higher-income people would be more likely to take the deduction, while lower-income families would choose the credit.

• **Employer-provided assistance.** The package included several smaller education tax cuts, among them an extension of the tax exclusion for employer-provided educational assistance. The extension would allow workers to exclude from their income the cost of any graduate or undergraduate course work paid for by their employers through Dec. 1, 2000. A separate provision proposed giving small businesses a tax credit worth 10 percent of the cost of funding education for their employees. The exclusion and credit were expected to cost $2.3 billion over five years.

● **Capital gains cut.** Clinton proposed a limited capital gains tax cut targeted at homeowners. Under his proposal, profits of up to $500,000 on the sale of a principal residence would be tax-free. The Treasury Department said the provision would cover 99 percent of all home sales. The proposal was projected to cost $1.4 billion over five years.

Under existing law, capital gains — profits on the sale of appreciated assets such as stock, real estate and artwork — were taxed at a maximum rate of 28 percent. Homeowners could defer the tax on profits from selling their home, but only if they purchased a new home of equal or greater value within a specified time. Taxpayers over age 55 were eligible for a one-time exclusion of up to $125,000 in profits on the sale of a home.

● **IRAs.** Also in the tax package was a reprise of Clinton's proposal to expand eligibility for traditional tax-deferred IRAs and create a special IRA that would allow investors to avoid taxes on the accumulated interest when they withdrew their savings. The existing limit of $2,000 per year for contributions would continue but be adjusted for inflation.

Under Clinton's plan, traditional IRAs would be available to taxpayers with annual adjusted gross incomes of up to $70,000 for individuals and $100,000 for couples. The plan would be phased in fully by 2000. Existing law limited the eligibility for tax-deferred IRAs to individuals with annual adjusted gross incomes up to $35,000 and couples with incomes of less than $50,000.

Investors could withdraw money without penalty to purchase a first-time home, pay for postsecondary education or cover living expenses of a taxpayer who had been unemployed for at least 12 consecutive weeks. The provision was projected to cost $5.5 billion over five years.

As an alternative, individuals eligible for tax-deferred IRAs could instead put their contribution into a new, backloaded IRA. Contributions to this special IRA would not be tax deductible, but they could be withdrawn tax free. If the contribution remained in the account for at least five years, the earnings could also be withdrawn tax free.

● **Tax incentives.** Clinton also proposed a series of incentives for distressed areas — polluted sites, inner cities, poor rural areas and the District of Columbia. There was also a small welfare-to-work tax credit of up to 50 percent of the first $10,000 in wages for employers who hired long-term welfare recipients. The revenue loss from these provisions was estimated at $3.2 billion.

● **Corporate taxes.** To offset part of the anticipated revenue losses, Clinton proposed $34 billion in tax increases over five years, aimed primarily at large corporations and Wall Street investors. One of the largest items — worth $3 billion over five years — was a plan to require investors to calculate their profits or losses from sales of stock or mutual funds by using the "average cost" accounting technique.

That meant that investors could end up paying higher capital gains taxes because they would have to figure out the average cost of stock bought over a period of time, instead of selling the shares that would give them the smallest gain.

In describing the package of revenue-raisers, Treasury Secretary Robert E. Rubin — former co-chairman of the investment firm Goldman, Sachs & Co. — defended the decision to eliminate what he called "unwarranted tax subsidies" to Wall Street firms. He quipped that these provisions were "things I always used to take advantage of. . . . That's what happens when you put the hen in the chicken coop."

Business lobbyists conceded privately that they had anticipated most of the proposals; if anything, they assumed that Congress would end even more corporate preferences in the search for revenue to offset additional tax cuts.

● **Excise taxes.** Among the excise taxes that Clinton sought to renew were the ticket tax on air travel; taxes under the superfund hazardous waste program that corporations paid to finance environmental cleanup; and the tax on oil that helped pay for oil spill cleanups. The renewal or continuation of the excise taxes was projected to raise $42 billion over five years.

Highlights of Clinton's Budget

The following are highlights of the spending proposals in President Clinton's fiscal 1998 budget, submitted to Congress on Feb. 6.

As required by law, the budget was organized by broad functional categories, such as agriculture, international affairs and transportation. In some cases, these categories lumped together programs from various agencies; in others, individual agencies had their budgets divided among several functions. (The functional categories were different from those used in the 13 annual appropriations bills.)

The budget was presented in two forms: budget authority (BA) — the amount of new federal commitments that agencies could make during the fiscal year — and outlays — the amount of money that actually would be spent in a given fiscal year. One year's budget authority could result in outlays over several years.

The following summary refers to projected outlays, unless otherwise designated:

SPENDING CATEGORIES

Agriculture

Clinton proposed $12.3 billion in fiscal 1998 outlays for programs under the agriculture function, more than $2 billion more than the $10.3 billion provided in fiscal 1997.

That total only covered programs that directly affected farming and food, such as subsidies to farmers, farmland conservation, agricultural research, food inspection and foreign food assistance. Those programs constituted only a little over a fifth of the $58.8 billion in outlays that Clinton was requesting for the Agriculture Department as a whole. The department's remaining activities, including the food stamp program and the Forest Service, were covered under other budget functions.

The agriculture function was made up mostly of mandatory programs that were authorized under the sweeping 1996 farm law overhaul (PL 104-127). Those programs were not expected to produce budget savings for the government, at least in the short term. *(1996 Almanac, p. 3-15)*

Mandatory programs administered by the Commodity Credit Corporation, which made most of the payments to farmers, were projected to rise to $7.7 billion in fiscal 1998, up from $5.8 billion in fiscal 1997. The figure was projected to decline to $5.3 billion in fiscal 2002.

In the past, the Agriculture Department had increased subsidies to farmers whenever prices fell. The 1996 farm law replaced that policy with a system of fixed, declining payments to farmers regardless of market conditions.

In an effort to address widespread concerns among farmers about how they would ride out lean years under the new system, Clinton proposed to increase spending on federally backed crop insurance. Specifically, he proposed to expand "revenue insurance" — already available in limited areas under a pilot program — to farmers nationwide. Revenue insurance was designed to protect farmers from price and yield fluctuations by guaranteeing an estimated harvest price at an average yield.

Funding for the Risk Management Agency, which ran the crop insurance program, was slated to increase $37 million from fiscal 1997 to a proposed $1.8 billion in fiscal 1998 outlays, according to the Agriculture Department.

Perhaps the most controversial element in the function was an Agriculture Department proposal to collect $390 million in new user fees from meat and egg processing companies to help pay the cost for modernized inspection of meat, poultry and egg products. Prior attempts to institute such fees had failed.

The department's budget called for a $31 million increase in outlays for research and education programs, and a $7 million increase, to $646 million, for marketing and regulatory programs.

Also included was a $272 million increase for agriculture export programs. The Export Enhancement Program stood to be a big winner under the president's budget, rising from $100 million in 1997 to $500 million in 1998. The program provided bonus payments to U.S. exporters of agriculture commodities to help them compete better with overseas suppliers that were subsidized by their own governments.

Agriculture Department officials said that as part of a reorganization effort begun in 1994, they planned to produce savings by continuing to streamline the department and reduce the number of employees.

Commerce/Community Development

The budget called for a total of $14.8 billion in fiscal 1998 outlays for the two broad categories of commerce and housing credit, and community and regional development. That figure was somewhat misleading, however, since it included deposit insurance and mortgage credit activities that were expected to result in substantial surpluses — $4 billion in the deposit insurance funds and another $2.5 billion from mortgage credit activities, partly from proposals to restructure certain multifamily family mortgages. Without those accounts, the bottom line for commerce and housing credit would have grown by more than $6.5 billion.

● **Deposit insurance.** The budget projected that revenues would continue to exceed losses from bank and thrift failures and that the government would run a $4 billion deposit insurance surplus in fiscal 1998. That was down from $12.1 billion in fiscal 1997. Although deposit insurance was off-budget, the surpluses or deficits on the ledgers of the federal deposit insurance funds counted toward deficit calculations.

● **Financial institutions.** The budget called for $125 million in new budget authority to help build up a special fund established in 1994 to nurture "community development financial institutions" — a small but growing network of alternative lenders that provided community development loans to borrowers that would otherwise have difficulty raising capital. The fund received $45 million in fiscal 1997.

The administration also dusted off a hardy perennial: a proposal to impose fees on state-chartered banks to defray the costs of examinations by the Federal Deposit Insurance Corporation and the Federal Reserve. Bank opposition had guaranteed dead-on-arrival status since the administration first proposed the examination fee in 1993.

● **Commerce research and development.** Clinton sought additional funding for two programs at the National Institute of Standards and Technology (NIST).

He proposed $275 million in budget authority, a $50 million increase over fiscal 1997, for the Advanced Technology Program, which provided grants to help industry develop cutting-edge technologies. The program was a favorite target of GOP critics, who denounced it as "corporate welfare."

Clinton also requested $129 million in budget authority — a 36 percent increase — for the Manufacturing Extension Partnerships program, which helped industries adopt modern and efficient manufacturing techniques.

Research facilities operated by NIST were slated to get $276 million under the president's plan.

Clinton also proposed $36 million for the National Information Infrastructure grants program, which helped nonprofit institutions hook up to the Internet.

● **Small Business Administration.** The budget assumed that the Small Business Administration (SBA) would guarantee a record $14.4 billion in loans in fiscal 1998, up from $13.8 billion in fiscal 1997.

Overall, however, SBA outlays were expected to plummet from $648 million in fiscal 1997 to $186 million in fiscal 1998 because of an anticipated increase in the liquidation of assets from defaulted loans and sales of performing loans on the secondary market. The request for new budget authority dropped from $852 million in 1997 to $702 million for fiscal 1998, mostly because the agency had leftover money for disaster loans and did not request an appropriation for the program. The fiscal 1997 appropriation was $218 million.

● **Postal Service.** Although the Postal Service's annual budget had been kept separate from the overall federal budget since 1971, its revenues and expenses counted toward the deficit. Outlays were expected to rise from $2 billion in fiscal 1997 to $4.1 billion in 1998, due mostly to capital expenditures. The Postal Service projected surpluses starting in 2000.

The Postal Service also received an annual appropriation to subsidize mail for the blind and for oversees voting. The fiscal 1998 estimate was $86 million.

The administration again requested that $35 million for pre-1973 workers' compensation payments be financed by postal revenues rather than through an annual appropriation. Congress had rejected the idea in 1996.

● **Housing credit.** As in each of the previous two years, the budget proposed overhauling the Federal Housing Administration's multifamily housing mortgage operations, in part by selling off mortgages and moving rent-subsidized units toward a more market-driven basis.

The budget called for $110 billion in authority for fiscal 1998 mortgage insurance commitments aimed at first-time home buyers, minorities, low-income families and residents of rural areas and inner cities. The same commitment level was sought in both fiscal 1996 and 1997.

● **Community development.** For the fourth year in a row, the administration requested $4.6 billion in budget authority for Community Development Block Grants. Intended to promote economic development, spark urban renewal and pay for affordable housing, the program provided grants to states and localities, which got virtually total control of the money.

The budget also included requests of: $50 million in budget authority for economic development grants; another $50 million to promote homeownership in targeted geographic areas; $100 million to create empowerment zones and enterprise communities; and $60 million for a program aimed at reducing the hazard of lead-based paint. Another $1.3 billion in budget authority was requested for the HOME Investment Partnership, a program that provided grants to states to expand the supply of affordable housing.

● **Area and regional development.** Direct outlays for development programs run by the Agriculture Department were projected to decrease by $38 million from fiscal 1997 levels, to $2.2 billion.

The budget proposed to fully carry out the Rural Community Advancement Program, created in the 1996 farm bill (PL 104-127) to coordinate funding for housing, utilities and business assistance and to allow greater state and local control over initiatives. Loans and grants under this program were expected to generate an estimated $9.7 billion in projects, a $1 billion increase over fiscal 1997, partly because of a projected decline in interest rates.

Defense

Clinton requested $265.3 billion in budget authority for the national defense function, nearly $11 billion more than he sought for fiscal 1997, but only about $200 million more than Congress appropriated for that budget year. In terms of outlays, or actual spending, Clinton's fiscal 1998 request translated into $259.4 billion, nearly $9 billion less than the anticipated level for fiscal 1997.

Measured in inflation-adjusted terms, the Clinton budget continued a 13-year decline in purchasing power for the defense budget. Compared with the fiscal 1985 defense budget, which was the largest since the Korean War, Clinton's request translated into about 40 percent less purchasing power.

● **Pentagon.** Most of the funding requested under the defense function — $250.7 billion in budget authority — was for military operations of the Department of Defense. (That did not include the civil works program of the Army Corps of Engineers, which was budgeted separately.)

The Pentagon request was $2.6 billion more than Clinton had projected the previous year, but $2.1 billion less than Congress appropriated for fiscal 1997. Taking inflation into account, the fiscal 1998 request amounted to a 3.4 percent reduction in purchasing power from the fiscal 1997 appropriation.

The fiscal 1998 request was part of a six-year plan that budgeted a total of nearly $1.6 trillion for the Pentagon through fiscal 2003. Compared with the long-term plan Clinton had outlined the year before, the new plan called for nearly $14 billion in additional purchasing power. In addition to the $2.6 billion Clinton added to his fiscal 1998 request, he added a total of $7 billion to the budgets projected for future years.

Clinton proposed to further increase long-term Pentagon spending by not deducting from his budget the $4 billion in savings expected to result from lower inflation and better prices in future years. This was the fifth time in four years that he had increased his long-range defense budget plan.

Administration officials acknowledged that the fiscal 1998 budget was a place-holder that would continue for one more year the defense program Clinton had adopted in 1993 while two long-range reviews of U.S. defense requirements were conducted. The two studies — the Pentagon's internal Quadrennial Defense Review, and a legislatively-chartered review by a National Defense Panel of outside experts — were slated for completion later in 1997.

In the meantime, the fiscal 1998 budget was based on the goal adopted by Clinton in 1993 of a force that could win two major regional wars breaking out several weeks apart, even if they were in areas far from each other and from the United States.

The Defense Department budget included the following major categories of budget authority:

● **Military personnel.** The $69.5 billion requested for pay and benefits of active-duty, reserve and National Guard forces assumed only modest reductions below fiscal 1997 manpower levels. It would support an active-duty force of 1,431,000 — down only 21,000 — and a Guard and reserve force of 892,000, down 10,000 compared with the previous year.

The budget included funds for a 2.8 percent military pay raise, the amount called for by the formula enshrined in law for calculating annual cost of living hikes in military pay.

● **Operations and maintenance.** To cover the cost of operations, training and maintenance — the part of the budget most closely linked to the day-to-day combat-readiness of the force — Clinton requested $93.7 billion. As had been the case in previous years, this part of the budget was larger than Clinton had projected the year before.

The request included $1.47 billion to cover the cost of military operations in Bosnia through June 1998, when U.S. forces were scheduled to be withdrawn. It also included about $700 million for military operations in the vicinity of Iraq. To continue the Nunn-Lugar program, designed to help former Soviet states dispose of their nuclear weapons, the budget included $382 million.

● **Procurement.** The boost in operations funding forced the administration to defer a planned increase in procurement funding for the third consecutive year. The $42.6 billion procurement request was $1.5 billion less than Congress appropriated for fiscal 1997 and $2.9 billion less than the fiscal 1998 procurement budget Clinton had projected the previous year. However, the administration's long-range budget plan still projected that procurement funding would reach $60 billion by 2001.

● **Research.** The $35.9 billion request for research and development included $2.6 billion for anti-missile defense programs. Additional amounts requested for procurement brought the total anti-missile related funding in the budget to $3.5 billion, about $500 million less than Congress appropriated for fiscal 1997.

● **Energy Department.** Much of the rest of the national defense budget — $13.6 billion — was for defense-related programs conducted by the Energy Department. Most of these involved nuclear energy, including storage and maintenance of nuclear weapons and the development of nuclear power plants for warships. Nearly 40 percent of the Energy Department's defense program — $5.2 billion — was for environmental cleanup of the agency's far-flung U.S. nuclear weapons production complex.

Another large element of the Energy Department account was the $4 billion requested for programs intended to ensure that stockpiled nuclear weapons remained operable without actual nuclear testing.

● **Other.** The remainder of the national defense budget, nearly $1 billion, was for assorted other programs such as Maritime Administration subsidies for commercial cargo ships that the Pentagon could use in case of war, and the Selective Service System.

● **Supplemental request.** The administration also asked Congress for a $2 billion supplemental appropriation for fiscal 1997 to cover the previously unbudgeted cost of keeping U.S. forces in Bosnia through fiscal 1997. *(Supplemental, p. 9-84)*

To prevent an increase in defense outlays, which would increase the deficit, the administration also requested authority to rescind (or cancel) $4.8 billion in fiscal 1997 defense budget authority. The outlay reductions resulting from these unspecified cuts were intended to cancel out the anticipated $1.5 billion increase in Bosnia-related outlays in fiscal 1997 as well as other unplanned outlay increases in fiscal 1997 and future years.

Since the unanticipated expenses of the Bosnia operation already were being incurred, Pentagon officials warned that if Congress did not approve supplemental funding by early April, the services would have to begin cancelling planned training and maintenance to free up funds to cover those costs.

Education

Clinton proposed major investments in education and related programs following his call in his State of the Union address for a "national crusade" to improve educational achievement. *(Text, p. D-17)*

The budget included $56.2 billion in overall outlays for education and related programs in fiscal 1998, an increase of $4.9 billion, or nearly 10 percent, from fiscal 1997.

Much of the proposed increase was for the Education Department. Clinton requested $29.1 billion in discretionary budget authority, an 11 percent increase over the 1997 level. Budget authority for the department's mandatory programs was expected to nearly triple to $10.4 billion, much of it for a school building program.

● **Elementary and secondary education.** The administration proposed a one-time appropriation of $5 billion to stimulate state and local efforts to modernize schools, especially in urban areas. Clinton wanted the program to pay for up to half the interest on construction bonds or similar financing, with the goal of encouraging $20 billion in new construction or renovation.

The administration also requested $200 million in budget authority — as part of $1.4 billion over five years — for a new program to enlist and train 1 million tutors to help children read independently by the end of third grade.

Clinton continued to emphasize the Goals 2000 program, which provided grants aimed at upgrading teaching and learning standards. The program, which was opposed by many GOP conservatives, was slated to receive $620 million in budget authority under Clinton's budget, a $129 million increase.

The budget also included:

- $425 million in budget authority, a $225 million increase, for the Technology Literacy Challenge Fund to help meet Clinton's goal of linking every school to the Internet by 2000.
- $7.6 billion in budget authority, an increase of $347 million, for Title I remedial education program grants for low-income students. Title I was the largest source of federal funds for elementary and secondary education.
- $4.2 billion in budget authority, an increase of $174 million, for special education programs, most of it for state grants.

● **Higher education.** Student loan volume for higher education was expected to total $36.5 billion in budget authority, up from an estimated $33.7 billion in fiscal 1997. Loans made through commercial lending institutions would still account for a larger share of the volume than those made directly by the federal government, but the gap between the two would continue to narrow.

The maximum award for the Pell grant program, which distributed tuition funds based on students' need and merit, would be increased to $3,000 from $2,700 in fiscal 1997.

● **Labor Department.** The administration requested $37.5 billion in budget authority for the Labor Department, an increase from $34.4 billion in fiscal 1997.

Consistent with Clinton's emphasis on education and training, the budget again focused on initiatives aimed at youths. It included $1.2 billion in budget authority for the Job Corps program for young adults, an increase of about $93 million from fiscal 1997.

It also included $871 million in budget authority for the Summer Youth Program, the same level as in fiscal 1997. School-to-work, a state grants program aimed primarily at helping non-college bound high school students make the transition to the work force, was to receive $400 million in budget authority, the same as in fiscal 1997.

● **Social services.** The administration requested $4.3 billion in budget authority for Head Start, an increase of $324 million. The program provided low-income preschoolers and their families with early education, health care, nutrition and social services.

Clinton requested $809 million, an increase of $93 million, for his national service initiative, a program that provided education grants in exchange for community service.

Energy

Using enhanced revenue sources and some program reductions, the administration hoped to provide funding for priority research programs that had been cut by the Republican-controlled 104th Congress. The administration projected that by 2002, receipts from huge, federally owned utilities, the sale of energy-related assets and nuclear waste fees paid by electricity consumers would greatly exceed the costs of energy research, development and regulatory efforts.

Clinton's budget called for $2.3 billion in outlays under the energy function in fiscal 1998, compared with an estimated $2.1 billion in fiscal 1997 and $2.8 billion in fiscal 1996. But the actual spending requested for energy programs in fiscal 1998 was $5 billion ($79 million more than in 1997).

The smaller outlay figure was arrived at after taking account of what the administration said would be $2.8 billion in federal receipts in fiscal 1998. These included $175 million from the proposed sale of the Naval Petroleum Reserve in Elk Hills, Calif., and $1.1 billion in profits generated by federally owned utilities.

In a potentially controversial proposal, the White House called for changes in the Tennessee Valley Authority (TVA), a network of economic development, flood control and hydroelectric projects in the South established during the New Deal era.

Clinton called for the TVA to drop all of its activities not related to power generation — in other words, the ones that did not make money. Under the plan, receipts were projected to jump from an estimated $111 million in fiscal 1997 to $285 million in 1998 and to $443 million in 2002.

The administration proposed to increase energy research and development by $8 million, to $3.5 billion in fiscal 1998. Within that program area were perennial budget targets, such as solar and renewable energy research, slated to rise from $266 million in fiscal 1997 to $343 million, and fusion energy research, slated to fall from $231 million to $225 million. Conservatives in Congress contended that energy research should be wholly conducted and funded by the private sector.

Clinton requested $186 million for the controversial nuclear waste storage project at Yucca Mountain, Nev., up from $166 million appropriated in 1997. The cost of ongoing scientific studies of Yucca

Mountain, and the planned construction of a waste repository at the site, were to be borne in large part by receipts from the electric utilities that were planning to use it.

The administration was counting on those receipts reaching $655 million in fiscal 1998, up from $649 million expected in 1997. The budget anticipated that nuclear waste fund receipts would total $3.3 billion through 2002. However, 33 utilities had sued to halt their payments into the trust fund over contractual disputes with the Energy Department, which said it could not meet a January 1998 deadline to take possession of the utilities' nuclear waste.

Clinton sought to restore funding levels for another GOP target, the federal effort to enhance energy conservation in buildings, industry and transportation. Funding for the program dropped from $624 million in fiscal 1996 to an estimated $565 million in 1997. Clinton requested $589 million for fiscal 1998.

Funding for the energy function was not the same as the budget for the Department of Energy. Fully two-thirds of the department's spending went to nuclear weapons research, production and cleanup programs funded under the defense portion of the budget.

Other parts of the agency's funding came under the administration's general science, space and technology request.

Environment

The budget provided for a slight decrease in funding for the natural resources and environment function, calling for $22.3 billion in outlays for fiscal 1998, $459 million less than estimated fiscal 1997 spending.

The natural resources category spanned almost all of the hotly contested environmental and public lands programs. It covered Interior Department agencies, including the Bureau of Land Management; the Forest Service, administered by the Agriculture Department; and the Army Corps of Engineers. It also included the Environmental Protection Agency (EPA).

The administration contended its fiscal 1998 budget would continue efforts to balance environmental protection and economic costs. The budget statement pointed to efforts to cut "excessive regulation and [target] investments in programs that will have the biggest impact on improving the environment."

● **EPA.** Clinton requested $7.7 billion in budget authority for the EPA, a 17 percent increase over the $6.6 billion provided in fiscal 1997 and 22 percent more than the $6.3 billion provided in fiscal 1996.

A major portion of the EPA's budget — $2.1 billion in budget authority — was for the superfund hazardous waste program. That was an increase of $700 million, or 33 percent, over fiscal 1997 levels. The budget also called for reauthorizing the taxes that had financed the program before they expired in 1995.

The administration argued that it needed the funds to help meet its goal of nearly doubling the pace of superfund cleanups. The EPA wanted to clean up an additional 250 sites over the coming four years.

Congress had been engaged in a four-year fight over whether to overhaul the superfund program, which had been slowed by seemingly endless litigation. Republicans wanted a major overhaul and were wary of increasing funding for superfund until the program had been restructured.

Clinton requested a $50 million increase, to about $88 million, for the "brownfields" program, which was aimed at cleaning up polluted industrial sites to make them suitable for redevelopment.

● **Flood control, dams.** Clinton proposed a slight decrease from fiscal 1997 for the two agencies responsible for overseeing flood control and dam projects. The budget included about $800 million for the Bureau of Reclamation and $3.4 billion for the Army Corps of Engineers.

● **Land management.** Major land management agencies were on a similar downward path. The budget included $2.4 billion for the Forest Service, $221 million less than in fiscal 1997, and $1 billion for Interior's Bureau of Land Management, down from $1.1 billion in fiscal 1997.

● **Other programs.** Repeating a proposal that fell flat in the 104th Congress, Clinton called for a 1-cent-a-pound fee on Florida sugar to help finance restoration of the Everglades.

The budget also included start-up money for management of the Escalante National Monument in Utah. The project was bitterly opposed by Utah's two Republican senators and many of their Western colleagues.

Health/Medicare

Clinton proposed outlays of $345.3 billion for health care programs in fiscal 1998. Medicare and Medicaid made up the bulk of that; other programs included expanded health coverage for children and the temporarily unemployed, medical research, food safety, and substance abuse treatment and prevention. The total did not include spending on military and veterans' medical programs.

Proposals to slow the growth in spending for Medicare and Medicaid were a major element of Clinton's overall plan to balance the budget by 2002. Of the $252 billion in planned deficit reduction over five years, changes in Medicare and Medicaid — the bulk of them in Medicare — accounted for $109 billion, or 43 percent.

● **Medicare.** Clinton proposed to shrink projected spending on Medicare, the health insurance program for the elderly and disabled, by $100 billion over five years, largely by reducing payments to Medicare health care providers such as hospitals, doctors, and health maintenance organizations (HMOs).

For fiscal 1998, the budget called for spending $207.1 billion on the program. That was 6.6 percent more than the $194.3 billion expected to be spent in fiscal 1997 — but $4.3 billion below the amount that had been projected for fiscal 1998. The Medicare budget included the following:

● **Hospitals.** A $33 billion reduction over five years in reimbursements to hospitals, to be achieved mainly by reducing their regular inflation increase and by cutting payments for capital expenses.

At the same time, Clinton proposed to help hospitals by allowing them to form provider-sponsored organizations that could compete for the Medicare managed care business. These organizations would contract directly with the federal government to offer a benefits package to Medicare enrollees at a fixed cost — an arrangement already used by HMOs that participated in Medicare. Clinton also proposed to increase funding for hospitals that trained doctors and that treated a disproportionate share of poor or uninsured patients.

● **HMOs.** A $34 billion reduction over five years in payments to HMOs. Under existing law, HMOs were paid a fixed cost per beneficiary based on 95 percent of the average cost for a Medicare beneficiary. Clinton proposed to reduce that to 90 percent by 2000.

HMOs participating in Medicare also stood to lose from Clinton's proposal to allow hospitals to compete with them for Medicare managed care patients. Moreover, when payments to hospitals dropped, payments to HMOs dropped. And the additional money to hospitals to train doctors or treat poor people was to be carved out of the HMO reimbursement calculation.

● **Other providers.** A reduction of $7 billion over five years in payments to doctors. Reimbursements to skilled nursing facilities would be cut $7 billion over five years, and payments to home health care providers would be cut $14 billion.

Clinton also proposed to shift most home health care expenses from Medicare Part A to Part B as part of an effort to extend the life of the Part A trust fund to 2007. Without Medicare changes, the government estimated the trust fund would be broke in 2001. Medicare Part A generally paid for hospital expenses; Part B generally covered doctors' bills.

● **Medicaid**. The budget included no fiscal 1998 savings from Medicaid, the federal-state health insurance program for the poor. Over five years, however, it proposed to slow spending on the program by a total of $9.3 billion. Proposed program changes were expected to save $22 billion, but Clinton also included $13 billion in spending increases.

The core of the administration's plan was a "per capita cap" that would limit federal contributions to states to a set amount per beneficiary. In exchange, the administration proposed giving states, which were required to offer certain benefits to certain populations, more flexibility in administering the program.

For fiscal 1998, the budget assumed that spending on Medicaid grants to states would grow to $105.9 billion from $98.5 billion in fiscal 1997 — an increase of $1.4 billion compared to existing law.

● **Expanded health insurance.** The administration proposed to increase health insurance coverage for children and for temporarily unemployed workers.

Clinton wanted to give health coverage to up to 5 million more children by finding those who were eligible for Medicaid but not enrolled, by extending Medicaid coverage for one year to children who would have been dropped, and by giving states $750 million a year to work with private insurers to cover more children.

He also proposed spending $9.8 billion over five years to help finance six months of coverage for workers who lost insurance when they lost their job.

The president budget also included $25 million to make it easier for small businesses to pool their resources to buy health coverage for their employees.

● **Other health programs.** The budget proposed $12.8 billion in outlays for the National Institutes of Health, an increase of $643 million over fiscal 1997, for research in areas including AIDS, breast cancer, prevention and genetic medicine. The administration also proposed:

● $201 million in outlays on food safety and inspection, down from $572 million in fiscal 1997. Spending on consumer and occupational health and safety was to decrease to $1.9 billion in outlays from $2.1 billion in 1997.

● Increases in substance abuse programs and mental health service funding, which would receive $2.1 billion, up from $1.9 billion.

● $1.8 billion in outlays for the Indian Health Service, the same as in fiscal 1997.

● Increased funding for the Centers for Disease Control and Prevention. Clinton proposed $2.3 billion in outlays, up from $2.2 billion, including more money for childhood immunizations and control of infectious diseases.

Income Security

For income security programs, Clinton requested $247.5 billion in fiscal 1998, an $8.6 billion increase over estimated fiscal 1997 levels.

Most of the increases were in mandatory programs, for which Congress did not set annual spending levels, including disability, federal retirement and unemployment programs. The biggest increase among discretionary programs was for housing assistance.

● **Social Security.** Outlays for Social Security were expected to rise to $384.3 billion, a $16.6 million increase over fiscal 1997. The figure included a projected 2.7 percent cost of living increase.

● **Housing.** For the Department of Housing and Urban Development, which had been cut significantly in recent years, the administration requested $23 billion in budget authority, up from $19.4 billion in fiscal 1997. The increase reflected the need to renew expiring contracts in the Section 8 program, which provided subsidized housing for low-income families, the elderly and the disabled.

To expand access to affordable housing, the budget called for $305 million in budget authority to issue 50,000 new Section 8 program vouchers.

The administration also requested $524 million in budget authority to demolish the 100,000 worst units of public housing by 2000, replacing them with low-rise public housing and expanded Section 8 assistance. In addition, the administration requested $50 million in budget authority to strengthen enforcement against landlords who received federal housing dollars.

The administration asked for $50 million in additional budget authority in fiscal 1998 for Economic Development Initiative grants that financed large-scale urban renewal projects.

The budget also included additional assistance for several housing-related programs to help former welfare recipients enter the work force.

● **Nutrition.** Budget authority for the special supplemental nutrition program for Women, Infants and Children (WIC) was estimated at $4.1 billion, an increase of $278 million from fiscal 1997. WIC helped low-income women buy nutritious food for themselves during and after pregnancy, and for their children under age 5. The funding would allow the program to reach all eligible applicants by the end of fiscal 1998.

The budget assumed $25 billion in outlays for the food stamp program in fiscal 1998, up $534 million from fiscal 1997, to serve an average of 23.4 million people each month. The administration proposed an additional $836 million in budget authority in fiscal 1998 to mitigate some of the effects of the welfare overhaul law (PL 104-193) enacted in 1996.

Spending on child nutrition programs, which provided free or reduced-price meals for students and some elderly adults, was projected to rise to $8.5 billion in fiscal 1998, a $227 million increase from the year before.

● **Welfare.** The budget projected spending $16.7 billion in fiscal 1998 for the new welfare program known as Temporary Assistance for Needy Families and for related programs. It also included $1.9 billion in outlays to help states find child care for welfare recipients and low-income working families plus $998 million in outlays for the Child Care and Development Block Grant, which served low-income families.

● **LIHEAP.** Clinton requested $1 billion in budget authority for the Low Income Home Energy Assistance Program (LIHEAP), which gave states grants to help low-income households with heating and cooling costs, weatherization and emergency energy assistance. That was $5 million less than in fiscal 1997.

● **Unemployment compensation.** The budget anticipated $29.3 billion in spending for unemployment compensation in fiscal 1998, an increase over the fiscal 1997 estimate of $27.2 billion.

● **Other income security.** Spending on Supplemental Security Income, which provided cash to the low-income aged, blind and disabled, was projected to be $25.5 billion in fiscal 1998, $1.1 billion less than in the previous year. The figures included a projected 2.7 percent cost of living adjustment. In addition, the administration proposed a series of changes in the new welfare overhaul law, worth $1.7 billion in fiscal 1998 outlays, to make it easier for certain legal immigrants to receive money under the program.

International Affairs

The central elements of the Clinton administration's international affairs budget were proposals to pay off sizable U.S. debts to the United Nations and to significantly increase economic aid for Russia and other former Soviet republics.

Overall, Clinton requested $19.5 billion in budget authority for international affairs, an increase over the $18.2 billion approved by Congress for fiscal 1997. That translated into $14.9 billion in outlays, a modest increase of nearly $100 million from fiscal 1997.

Not included in these figures was $3.5 billion in budget authority requested by the Treasury Department to cover the U.S. share of a new International Monetary Fund account being established to deal with global financial emergencies. The administration did not include this request in the foreign affairs budget because it entailed no outlays and would not increase the deficit.

Clinton and Secretary of State Madeleine K. Albright had already launched an aggressive campaign to persuade Congress to increase funding for foreign affairs. During his State of the Union speech Feb. 4, Clinton told lawmakers: "If America is to continue to lead the world, we here who lead America simply must find the will to pay our way." *(Text, p. D-17)*

The State Department planned to clear about $1 billion in debts to the United Nations and other international organizations in return for management reforms by those institutions.

The administration included only $100 million of that money in the fiscal 1998 budget. The remaining $921 million was being requested as a supplemental appropriation for fiscal 1997, though it was not to be made available until Oct. 1, 1998. The highly unusual funding formula was intended to give U.N. officials an inducement to enact painful budget cuts. *(Supplemental, p. 9-84)*

The Treasury Department was seeking more than $1 billion to finance new commitments and debts to the International Development Association, the World Bank affiliate that provided interest-free loans to poor nations, especially in Africa. Overall, the budget included $1.5 billion for multilateral development banks, an increase of more than $500 million from fiscal 1997.

In unveiling the budget, Albright focused particular attention on the administration's $900 million aid request for countries of the former Soviet Union, an increase of nearly $300 million from fiscal 1997. Included in the request was $528 million for a new "Partnership for Freedom" aimed at stimulating the growth of the private sector in those nations. Albright said the request was a top administration priority because "the ultimate victory over despotism" in the former Soviet Union "is not yet assured."

The rest of the foreign affairs budget contained few surprises. It included $3 billion in economic and military aid for Israel and $2.1 billion for Egypt — the same levels as in recent years and far more than requested for any other country.

The budget continued the long-term reduction in military aid for Greece and Turkey, key NATO allies that had received billions of dollars in security assistance during the Cold War. The administration requested $33 million to subsidize $175 million in military loans for Turkey and nearly $13 million to back $123 million in loans for Greece.

The budget proposed modest reductions in subsidies for loans by the Overseas Private Investment Corporation (OPIC) and the Export-Import Bank, which promoted U.S. exports abroad. The programs were targets for a bipartisan congressional group seeking to end "corporate welfare." Clinton requested $60 million for OPIC's loan program, $12 million below the fiscal 1997 level. The budget included $632 million for the Export-Import Bank's loan program, a reduction of $94 million from fiscal 1997.

Justice

Outlays for justice-related agencies were slated to rise by 16.6 percent to $24.2 billion under Clinton's budget because of previously established grants to states for police officers, new prisons and other anti-crime programs. The cost of these grant programs, most of them called for under the 1994 anti-crime law (PL 103-322), was expected to more than double to $4.3 billion in fiscal 1998.

Under Clinton's proposal, the Justice Department was to receive $18.9 billion in outlays, a 19 percent increase over fiscal 1997. About $5.2 billion of that was to come from the special anti-crime trust fund established under the 1994 law. Another $2 billion was expected to come from border crossing and other fees.

- **Crime.** Funding for federal law enforcement besides the grant programs also was slated to grow. The administration requested $3.9 billion for criminal investigations under the FBI, Drug Enforcement Administration (DEA) and several smaller agencies, up from $3.5 billion in fiscal 1997. It proposed $504 million for the Bureau of Alcohol, Tobacco and Firearms, an 11 percent increase.

Overall, the budget called for an increase in outlays for federal law enforcement from $9.1 billion in fiscal 1997 to $9.9 billion.

The request included funding for significant increases in personnel: 363 new positions at the DEA; 144 at the FBI, and 56 at the U.S. Attorneys' offices.

The budget also took aim at juvenile crime. The Justice Department targeted $227.5 million to deal with juvenile issues — more than twice the $103 million in outlays in fiscal 1997 and almost four times as much as the $60 million spent in fiscal 1996. The funds were to go to establish special courts dealing with juvenile crime and to finance several grants to communities to improve law enforcement and crime-prevention programs.

Clinton's plan to put 100,000 police officers on the street remained one of his most controversial crime initiatives. The state grants included in the fiscal 1998 budget were aimed at bringing the number up to 80,000, according to the Justice Department. Republicans preferred to let states spend the money as they saw fit, and they argued that the number of officers was illusory because the grant money would begin to dry up early in the next century.

- **Immigration.** Clinton called for putting the Immigration and Naturalization Service and the Border Patrol — which already had received major budget increases to enhance border controls and stem the flow of illegal immigrants — on a steady course. The budget included discretionary outlays of $3.9 billion for border enforcement, a nominal increase over fiscal 1997, when the INS's budget went up 30 percent. The request included funding for 500 new border agents.
- **Other law enforcement.** Clinton proposed an 8 percent increase to $6.2 billion for federal litigation and judicial activities. The FBI's new crime lab, in its third year, was slated to get significant new outlays — $36 million, compared with $8 million in fiscal 1997. A special counterterrorism fund created in the wake of the 1995 bombing of a federal building in Oklahoma City was to get its first allocation of $29.5 million.

Once again, Clinton requested $340 million for the Legal Services Corporation, a perennial target for GOP budget-cutters. In fiscal 1997, he asked for that amount but got only $283 million.

Science, Space and Technology

Clinton offered a five-year science and technology budget aimed at gradually reducing funding for space programs while holding spending relatively steady in most research fields.

The general science, space and technology category in the president's budget included the National Science Foundation (NSF), the Department of Energy's general science programs and programs of the National Aeronautics and Space Administration (NASA).

Clinton requested $16.5 billion in total outlays for these areas in fiscal 1998, a modest $63 million drop from estimates for fiscal 1997. Under the administration plan, total spending for general science, space and technology would continue to slide gradually to $16.1 billion by 2002.

The long-term decrease was to come largely at the expense of NASA, whose space flight, research and supporting activities were slated to decline $611 million from estimated 1997 levels, to $11.7 billion in 2002.

Science and technology spending represented a priority for Clinton, though many of his favored programs had been criticized by Republicans as "corporate welfare."

"It is time to put that debate [over federal support for science and technology funding] behind us and rebuild the historical bipartisan support for a strategy to maintain America's world leadership in science and technology," John H. Gibbons, the president's science adviser, said Feb. 6.

- **NASA.** Overall, funding for NASA's science, aeronautics and technology programs — which included Mission to Planet Earth and research, development, construction and operations of other NASA unmanned spacecraft — was slated to increase in fiscal 1998 from $4.5 billion to $4.6 billion, reaching $5 billion by 2002.

Within NASA, the president wanted more money for Mission to Planet Earth, an environmentally oriented program that had drawn fire from some Republicans. Funding for the program, a constellation of observation satellites trained on the planet's atmosphere, was to rise by $55 million under the president's plan, to $1.4 billion. Some conservatives saw the program as unnecessary; others said it could be completed for less money.

For human space flight programs, including the space shuttle, Clinton requested an increase from $5.4 billion in fiscal 1997 to $5.6 billion in 1998. But within that category, funding for the international space station was to fall by $27 million, to $2.1 billion.

Spending on the X-33 reusable launch vehicle, intended as the successor to the space shuttle, was to rise 35 percent in 1998 to $330 million from 1997's $245 million.

By 2002, total funding for human space flight programs was projected to decline to $4.7 billion.

- **NSF.** Funding for the National Science Foundation, which supported research and education through competitively selected grants, was slated to fall slightly in fiscal 1998 to $3.2 billion, down $23 million from estimated 1997 levels. But outlays were projected to rise slowly to $3.3 billion by 2002.

● **Energy.** The Energy Department's general science programs in high energy and nuclear physics — a small part of the $16.8 billion budget request for the department — were slated to hold their own, slipping slightly from $989 million to $988 million. Spending was to rise in the ensuing four years.

The administration sought an increase from $15 million to $35 million for the Large Hadron Collider, a giant atom smasher under construction in Switzerland. The project — which when completed in 2005 would be the largest particle accelerator in the world — was to serve many of the same scientific functions as the Superconducting Super Collider, an expensive project in Texas that Congress killed in 1995.

Transportation

Clinton requested $39.3 billion for programs under the transportation function, almost exactly the same as the estimated outlays in fiscal 1997.

The largest single transportation item — and perhaps the most contentious — was $18.5 billion for the Federal Highway Administration, a $300 million cut from fiscal 1997. While Clinton was essentially proposing to freeze discretionary highway funding at about $18 billion annually over five years, a majority of senators were backing a proposal to boost authorized spending on highways to $26 billion yearly. (*Highways, p. 3-18*)

In a further worry for highway advocates, the administration proposed, for the first time, to dip into the federal Highway Trust Fund to subsidize Amtrak, the troubled national passenger railroad. Even with this stable funding source, Amtrak's capital and operating funding was projected to decline from $842 million in fiscal 1997 to $767 million in fiscal 1998 — well below the $1 billion requested by Amtrak officials.

Another potentially controversial initiative was a proposed 30 percent increase in funding for the Congestion Mitigation and Air Quality Improvement Program. The program, which was authorized at $1 billion a year, promoted transportation alternatives such as ride sharing but was opposed by powerful highway lobbies that wanted the money spent for more roads.

Clinton sought to hold authorization levels for public transit programs stable at $4.4 billion. The budget proposed to give transit systems more flexibility over spending their capital funds, and eliminate the separate operating fund category for areas with populations of more than 200,000.

Airport grants were to decline by about 30 percent to $1 billion under Clinton's budget. Transportation Department officials said small airports would continue to get government funding for runway expansion and other construction projects, while larger airports could raise money from other sources, such as aircraft and passenger charges.

Focusing on safety, Clinton requested an 8.7 percent increase in the operating budget of the Federal Aviation Administration (FAA), bringing it to $5.4 billion. The administration said that would enable the agency to hire 500 additional air traffic controllers, as well as hundreds of security staffers and safety inspectors.

Clinton proposed to increase funding for railroad safety programs by 12 percent, to $57 million, enabling the government to buy an automated track inspection vehicle. He sought a $9 million increase in funding for programs designed to combat drunken driving.

Proposed funding for other safety efforts included $8 million for a research and education program on the danger air bags posed to children and young adults; $9 million for a program to promote safety belts and $2 million for a pilot program to test driver's license applicants for drug use.

Other initiatives included a $100 million program to help transport welfare recipients to jobs and training, and a $34 million increase for the Coast Guard to prevent illegal drugs from entering the country.

Hinting at a change in tax policy, the budget called for the eventual financing of the FAA through unspecified user fees, an approach favored by major carriers such as Northwest but opposed by discount airlines.

Veterans' Benefits

Clinton requested a slight increase in spending for veterans' health care and benefits programs — $41 billion in outlays, up $1.3 billion from fiscal 1997. But he proposed to continue cutting spending for construction projects at veterans facilities and requested no money for new veterans hospitals.

● **Health care.** The bulk of the discretionary funds spent by the Department of Veterans Affairs (VA) went for veterans' medical care. The VA estimated it would treat 3.1 million veterans during fiscal 1998 through its network of 173 veterans hospitals, 133 nursing homes and 398 outpatient clinics.

The budget included $17.6 billion in outlays for veterans' medical treatment, a $200 million increase from fiscal 1997.

The five-year plan provided for moderate increases in health care spending through fiscal 2002, when outlays were expected to reach $18.2 billion. The small but steady increases differed from the plan Clinton had presented the previous year. That six-year plan proposed that spending on veterans' health care drop to $13.3 billion in fiscal 2000 before returning close to existing levels in 2002.

Veterans' advocates wanted the White House to restore the cuts, and the president proposed to do so.

● **Compensation benefits.** The VA's other primary responsibility was to provide benefits to disabled veterans and their surviving dependents.

The budget called for $16.7 billion in mandatory outlays for compensation benefits in fiscal 1998, a $557 million increase from fiscal 1997. Most of the increase was to cover a 2.7 percent cost of living adjustment in monthly payments to beneficiaries — 2.3 million veterans with injuries connected to their military service and 307,000 survivors of veterans who died from service-connected injuries.

● **Construction.** Outlays on VA medical construction were slated to drop for the second consecutive year, from an estimated $547 million in fiscal 1997 to $470 million in fiscal 1998.

Under the Clinton plan, construction spending was to decline each year through fiscal 2002, down to $292 million. The government spent $696 million on medical construction in fiscal 1996.

Clinton did not request money to build any new VA hospitals, reflecting the administration's goal of treating more veterans in less expensive outpatient clinics and contracting out services to the private sector.

Most spending on medical construction was to go toward renovating aging hospitals and improving outpatient clinics and nursing homes.

The budget did, however, include increased funds for the VA's cemetery system, including money for a new veterans cemetery in Cleveland. Spending on the cemetery system was slated to increase by $8 million, from $76 million in fiscal 1997 to $84 million in fiscal 1998.

The budget projected increased spending on veterans cemeteries each year through 2002, when outlays were expected to reach $88 million. The VA expected to bury more than 92,000 veterans in 2002, compared with just under 72,000 in 1996.

● **Staff reduction.** Clinton proposed to reduce the size of the VA's staff by almost 5,000, to 210,625. The number of VA employees had decreased each year since 1993, when the department had more than 234,000 employees.

● **Legislative proposals.** The budget called for legislation to allow the VA to keep user fees and payments it received from private insurance companies, which reverted to the general Treasury under existing law. The VA estimated that the proposal would allow it to retain $468 million in fiscal 1998, increasing to $768 million by 2002.

The budget also proposed a pilot project to allow the VA to keep payments it received from veterans covered by Medicare. Those payments also went to the Treasury under existing law. ■

Budget Authority, Outlays by Agency

(Fiscal years; in millions of dollars †)

AGENCY	BUDGET AUTHORITY 1996 actual	1997 estimate	1998 proposed	OUTLAYS 1996 actual	1997 estimate	1998 proposed
Legislative Branch	$ 2,465	$ 2,526	$ 2,754	$ 2,273	$ 2,531	$ 2,772
Judiciary	3,174	3,364	3,751	3,059	3,617	3,693
Executive Office of the President	203	212	230	202	222	233
Funds Appropriated to the President	10,243	10,579	14,876	9,713	9,738	10,156
Agriculture	58,734	60,615	60,275	54,344	56,954	58,779
Commerce	3,612	3,697	4,168	3,702	3,808	4,080
Defense — Military	254,406	249,990	250,697	253,253	254,284	247,492
Defense — Civil	32,390	33,774	35,190	32,536	33,873	34,798
Education	29,097	29,358	39,470	29,727	28,340	32,134
Energy	14,136	14,225	17,018	16,203	15,423	14,562
Health and Human Services	318,454	357,276	370,026	319,803	351,086	376,147
Housing and Urban Development	21,093	19,386	23,003	25,508	29,928	32,302
Interior	7,211	7,065	7,299	6,725	7,404	7,101
Justice	15,185	17,421	17,784	11,954	14,520	17,350
Labor	33,434	34,421	37,475	32,492	32,874	35,624
State	5,080	5,209	5,542	4,951	5,487	5,523
Transportation	35,716	42,953	43,254	38,780	38,388	38,456
Treasury	365,768	382,575	392,936	364,629	380,559	390,381
Veterans Affairs	38,714	39,391	41,086	36,920	39,619	40,890
Environmental Protection Agency	6,268	6,590	7,659	6,046	6,272	6,701
General Services Administration	217	709	219	732	1,243	521
National Aeronautics and Space Administration	13,886	13,710	13,501	13,881	13,697	13,595
Office of Personnel Management	43,814	44,834	47,810	42,870	44,838	46,527
Small Business Administration	1,089	865	652	873	460	137
Social Security Administration	377,329	395,662	412,710	375,234	395,943	413,000
Other Independent Agencies	24,342	27,011	25,839	8,917	10,445	20,198
Undistributed Offsetting Receipts	-134,997	-150,537	-165,677	-134,997	-150,537	-165,677
TOTAL	**$1,581,063**	**$1,652,881**	**$1,709,547**	**$1,560,330**	**$1,631,016**	**$1,687,475**
On Budget	1,274,092	1,332,287	1,378,612	1,259,872	1,316,014	1,358,896
Off Budget	306,971	320,594	330,935	300,458	315,002	328,579

† Figures may not add to totals due to rounding.

SOURCE: President's fiscal 1998 budget

Administration Economic Assumptions[1]

(Calendar years; dollar amounts in billions)

	Actual	Projections						
	1995	1996	1997	1998	1999	2000	2001	2002
Gross domestic product								
Dollar levels:								
Current dollars	$ 7,254	$ 7,577	$ 7,943	$ 8,313	$ 8,717	$ 9,153	$ 9,610	$ 10,087
Real, chained (1992) dollars[2]	6,743	6,901	7,056	7,197	7,355	7,525	7,699	7,877
Chained price index (1992 = 100), annual average[2]	107.6	109.9	112.7	115.7	118.7	121.8	125.0	128.2
Percentage change, fourth quarter over fourth quarter:								
Current dollars	3.8	5.0	4.6	4.7	5.0	5.0	5.0	5.0
Real, chained (1992) dollars[2]	1.3	2.8	2.0	2.0	2.3	2.3	2.3	2.3
Chained price index (1992 = 100)[2]	2.5	2.3	2.5	2.6	2.6	2.6	2.6	2.6
Percentage change, year over year:								
Current dollars	4.6	4.5	4.8	4.7	4.9	5.0	5.0	5.0
Real, chained (1992) dollars[2]	2.0	2.3	2.2	2.0	2.2	2.3	2.3	2.3
Chained price index (1992 = 100)[2]	2.5	2.2	2.5	2.6	2.6	2.6	2.6	2.6
Incomes (current dollars)								
Corporate profits before tax	$ 599	$ 652	$ 676	$ 714	$ 757	$ 796	$ 816	$ 849
Wages and salaries	3,431	3,628	3,808	3,982	4,168	4,374	4,590	4,810
Other taxable income	1,532	1,612	1,684	1,748	1,809	1,882	1,967	2,068
Consumer price index (all urban)[3]								
Level (1982-84 = 100), annual average	152.5	156.9	161.2	165.5	170.0	174.6	179.3	184.1
Percentage change, fourth quarter over fourth quarter	2.7	3.1	2.6	2.7	2.7	2.7	2.7	2.7
Percent change, year over year	2.8	2.9	2.7	2.7	2.7	2.7	2.7	2.7
Unemployment rate, civilian (percent)[4]								
Fourth quarter level	5.5	5.3	5.4	5.6	5.5	5.5	5.5	5.5
Annual average	5.6	5.4	5.3	5.5	5.5	5.5	5.5	5.5
Federal pay raises, January (percent)								
Military	2.6	2.6	3.0	2.8	3.0	3.0	3.0	3.0
Civilian[5]	2.6	2.4	3.0	2.8				
Interest rates (percent)								
91-day Treasury bills[6]	5.5	5.0	5.0	4.7	4.4	4.2	4.0	4.0
10-year Treasury notes	6.6	6.5	6.1	5.9	5.5	5.3	5.1	5.1

[1] *Based on data available as of mid-November 1996.*

[2] *In January 1996, the Commerce Department's Bureau of Economic Analysis replaced the traditional method of adjusting Gross Domestic Product calculations for inflation. Instead of using a price index based on the relative weights of certain goods from a single year, the calculation now uses a moving two-year average of relative prices, where the index is set at 100 for 1992. GDP has been recomputed using this method back to 1959.*

[3] *CPI for all urban consumers. Two versions of the CPI are now published; the index shown here is used, as required by law, in calculating automatic adjustments to individual income tax brackets. Projections reflect scheduled changes in methodology.*

[4] *Percent of civilian labor force, excluding military personnel residing in the United States.*

[5] *Percentages for 1995-1998 include locality pay adjustments. Percentages to be proposed after 1998 have not yet been determined.*

[6] *Average rate on new issues within period.*

SOURCE: President's fiscal 1998 budget

Fiscal 1998 Budget by Function

(Figures for 1997 and 1998 are estimates; in millions of dollars †)

	BUDGET AUTHORITY			OUTLAYS		
	1996	1997	1998	1996	1997	1998
NATIONAL DEFENSE						
Military Defense	$ 254,406	$ 249,990	$ 250,697	$ 253,187	$ 254,272	$247,492
Atomic energy defense activities	10,690	11,327	13,600	11,639	11,939	10,902
Defense-related activities	911	989	979	922	965	994
TOTAL	266,007	262,306	265,276	265,748	267,176	259,388
INTERNATIONAL AFFAIRS						
International development/humanitarian assistance	6,084	6,110	7,242	6,160	6,498	6,086
International security assistance	5,038	5,088	5,233	4,565	5,080	5,407
Conduct of foreign affairs	3,833	3,893	4,167	3,761	4,060	4,153
Foreign information and exchange activities	1,131	1,100	1,135	1,187	1,165	1,138
International financial programs	310	1,201	4,032	-2,177	-1,981	-1,879
TOTAL	16,396	17,392	21,809	13,496	14,822	14,905
GENERAL SCIENCE, SPACE AND TECHNOLOGY						
General science and basic research	4,146	4,241	4,346	4,016	4,203	4,179
Space flight, research and supporting activities	12,570	12,426	12,131	12,693	12,348	12,309
TOTAL	16,716	16,667	16,477	16,709	16,551	16,488
ENERGY						
Energy supply	1,784	244	800	1,646	1,220	1,277
Energy conservation	533	550	688	624	565	589
Emergency energy preparedness			209	141	31	226
Energy information, policy and regulation	330	167	193	425	237	187
TOTAL	2,647	961	1,890	2,836	2,053	2,279
NATURAL RESOURCES AND ENVIRONMENT						
Water resources	4,254	4,478	4,688	4,617	5,008	4,196
Conservation and land management	5,577	5,451	5,507	5,396	5,920	5,592
Recreational resources	2,651	2,763	2,863	2,673	2,746	2,885
Pollution control and abatement	6,430	6,753	7,828	6,180	6,448	6,865
Other natural resources	2,698	2,661	2,797	2,748	2,651	2,776
TOTAL	21,610	22,106	23,683	21,614	22,773	22,314
AGRICULTURE						
Farm income stabilization	6,894	8,561	9,281	6,477	7,474	9,447
Agricultural research and services	2,733	2,882	2,838	2,682	2,778	2,894
TOTAL	9,627	11,443	12,119	9,159	10,252	12,341
COMMERCE AND HOUSING CREDIT						
Mortgage credit	1,289	261	-1,839	-4,753	-3,220	-1,617
Postal Service subsidy (on budget)	122	121	86	122	121	86
Postal Service (off budget)	3,441	8,000	4,967	-626	1,976	4,094
Deposit insurance	11	-25	-113	-8,394	-12,056	-4,000
Other advancement of commerce	3,477	4,483	5,182	3,005	4,371	4,796
TOTAL	8,340	12,840	8,283	-10,646	-8,808	3,359
(On budget)	(4,899)	(4,840)	(3,316)	(-10,020)	(-10,784)	(-735)
(Off budget)	(3,441)	(8,000)	(4,967)	(-626)	(1,976)	(4,094)
TRANSPORTATION						
Ground transportation	23,346	29,440	29,128	25,650	25,591	25,457
Air transportation	9,576	10,565	11,227	10,135	9,929	10,139
Water transportation	3,379	3,495	3,640	3,460	3,418	3,460
Other transportation	312	330	203	320	324	203
TOTAL	36,613	43,830	44,198	39,565	39,262	39,259
COMMUNITY AND REGIONAL DEVELOPMENT						
Community development	5,083	5,090	5,138	4,860	5,611	5,115
Area and regional development	2,767	3,230	2,963	2,667	2,968	2,800
Disaster relief and insurance	4,693	2,128	3,226	3,158	4,173	3,520
TOTAL	12,543	10,448	11,327	10,685	12,752	11,435
EDUCATION, TRAINING, EMPLOYMENT, SOCIAL SERVICES						
Elementary, secondary and vocational education	13,697	16,946	23,301	14,871	16,215	17,718
Higher education	12,725	9,462	13,221	12,191	9,154	11,361
Research and general education aids	2,102	2,331	2,391	2,215	2,283	2,378
Training and employment	6,911	7,623	7,533	7,030	6,835	7,226
Other labor services	957	1,003	1,063	925	1,004	1,053
Social services	15,593	16,522	17,160	14,769	15,800	16,468
TOTAL	51,985	53,887	64,669	52,001	51,291	56,204

Fiscal 1998 Budget by Function

(Figures for 1997 and 1998 are estimates; in millions of dollars †)

	BUDGET AUTHORITY			OUTLAYS		
	1996	**1997**	**1998**	**1996**	**1997**	**1998**
HEALTH						
Health care services	$95,459	$114,695	$118,369	$106,622	$112,822	$123,012
Health research and training	12,434	13,381	13,529	10,827	12,741	13,330
Consumer and occupational health and safety	1,976	2,041	1,871	1,929	2,067	1,899
TOTAL	109,869	130,117	133,769	119,378	127,630	138,241
MEDICARE	179,652	194,070	206,875	174,225	194,256	207,084
INCOME SECURITY						
General retirement and disability insurance	6,185	5,945	5,905	5,234	4,631	4,620
Federal employee retirement and disability	69,754	72,660	75,579	68,093	71,214	73,984
Unemployment compensation	24,964	25,139	27,207	24,898	25,117	27,127
Housing assistance	16,430	15,235	20,159	26,754	29,046	29,401
Food and nutrition assistance	40,434	41,414	41,234	37,933	37,995	39,267
Other income security	64,277	72,187	69,334	63,077	70,852	73,100
TOTAL	222,044	232,580	239,418	225,989	238,855	247,499
SOCIAL SECURITY	352,136	367,280	385,821	349,676	367,713	384,338
(On budget)	(5,821)	(6,943)	(7,626)	(5,807)	(6,944)	(7,626)
(Off budget)	(346,315)	(360,337)	(378,195)	(343,869)	(360,769)	(376,712)
VETERANS BENEFITS AND SERVICES						
Income security	19,703	20,442	21,070	18,201	20,540	21,164
Education, training and rehabilitation	1,013	1,047	1,143	1,114	1,079	1,220
Hospital and medical care	16,812	17,374	17,572	16,586	17,487	17,472
Housing	212	-442	323	66	-517	70
Other benefits and services	1,023	1,015	1,058	1,018	1,061	1,045
TOTAL	38,763	39,436	41,166	36,985	39,650	40,971
ADMINISTRATION OF JUSTICE						
Federal law enforcement activities	7,976	9,413	10,087	7,022	8,520	9,315
Federal litigative and judicial activities	6,060	6,476	7,120	6,067	6,674	7,007
Federal correctional activities	2,881	3,189	3,245	3,013	3,104	3,287
Criminal justice assistance	4,134	4,693	4,416	1,446	2,486	4,619
TOTAL	21,051	23,771	24,868	17,548	20,784	24,228
GENERAL GOVERNMENT						
Legislative functions	1,925	1,973	2,170	1,965	2,032	2,157
Executive direction and management	270	402	548	252	299	465
Central fiscal operations	7,678	7,472	8,392	7,459	7,543	7,772
General property and records management	415	756	428	820	1,094	645
Central personnel management	154	150	148	103	153	148
General-purpose fiscal assistance	1,994	2,088	2,162	1,981	2,090	1,925
Other general government	851	1,195	966	1,006	1,082	945
Deductions for offsetting receipts	-1,694	-1,184	-1,184	-1,694	-1,184	-1,184
TOTAL	11,593	12,852	13,630	11,892	13,109	12,873
NET INTEREST						
Interest on the public debt	343,955	356,740	366,107	343,955	356,740	366,107
Interest received by on-budget trust funds	-60,869	-62,812	-63,746	-60,869	-62,812	-63,746
Interest received by off-budget trust funds	-36,507	-41,238	-45,199	-36,507	-41,238	-45,199
Other interest	-5,488	-5,308	-7,303	-5,489	-5,308	-7,303
TOTAL	241,091	247,382	249,859	241,090	247,382	249,859
(On budget)	(277,598)	(288,620)	(295,058)	(277,597)	(288,620)	(295,058)
(Off budget)	(-36,507)	(-41,238)	(-45,199)	(-36,507)	(-41,238)	(-45,199)
UNDISTRIBUTED OFFSETTING RECEIPTS	-37,620	-46,487	-55,590	-37,620	-46,487	-55,590
(On budget)	(-31,342)	(-39,982)	(-48,562)	(-31,342)	(-39,982)	(48,562)
(Off budget)	(-6,278)	(-6,505)	(-7,028)	(-6,278)	(-6,505)	(-7,028)
TOTAL	**$1,581,063**	**$1,652,881**	**$1,709,547**	**$1,560,330**	**$1,631,016**	**$1,687,475**
(On budget)	(1,274,092)	(1,332,287)	(1,378,612)	(1,259,872)	(1,316,014)	(1,358,896)
(Off budget)	(306,971)	(320,594)	(330,935)	(300,458)	(315,002)	(328,579)

† Figures may not add due to rounding.

SOURCE: President's fiscal 1998 budget

Pact Aims To Erase Deficit by 2002

Building on a strong economy and two earlier rounds of deficit reduction, President Clinton and the Republican majority in Congress struck a historic agreement to balance the budget in five years, while cutting taxes and increasing spending for selected administration priorities in areas such as children's health care.

The sprawling pact promised to eliminate the deficit for the first time since 1969 and produce a small surplus in 2002. It included tax cuts that Republicans had sought for more than a decade, along with cutbacks in government-subsidized health insurance that both sides had gingerly embraced only in the previous two years.

The move by both sides toward the middle was an extraordinary departure from the revenge-seeking warfare over the budget that had come to be Congress' chief preoccupation over most of the previous two decades.

The agreement was announced with much fanfare May 2, following two months of on-again, off-again talks between the administration and congressional leaders. "I wanted a balanced budget with balanced values," Clinton said. "I believe we have got it today."

"Clap your hands together!" shouted an unusually effusive Senate Budget Chairman Pete V. Domenici, R-N.M. Senate Majority Leader Trent Lott, R-Miss., said the effects of the deal on Americans would be "nothing less than revolutionary."

The enthusiasm proved somewhat premature. Critical details of the deal had been left vague, and it had not been put into writing. Almost immediately, each side began disputing exactly what had been agreed to. With complaints escalating on both sides of the aisle, the White House and congressional leaders quickly resumed their talks with the goal of producing written documents giving greater specificity to the deal.

It took two more weeks of horse-trading, but on May 15, bipartisan negotiators announced a more detailed, written version. It was almost immediately translated into a congressional budget resolution that formally set Congress' budget guidelines and paved the way for later enactment of two reconciliation bills and 13 fiscal 1998 appropriations bills. *(Budget resolution, p. 2-23; reconciliation bills, p. 2-27; appropriations, p. 9-3)*

Both Sides Swallow Bitter Pills

The budget deal gave Republicans tax cuts and spending cuts, but much smaller ones than they initially had demanded. There was virtually none of the radical overhaul of entitlement programs, the death of entire Cabinet departments or the stringent lowering of spending levels for domestic programs that the GOP had refused to bargain away when they had a chance to strike a deal with Clinton in January 1996.

In some ways, however, Clinton had moved just as far as the Republicans. This was not the same elusive chief executive who lured Republicans into prolonged and politically devastating budget fisticuffs in late 1995 and early 1996. This time, to Republicans' surprise and delight, the president clearly wanted a deal.

And the deal put Clinton's name on upper-income tax cuts that would have been unthinkable to most Democrats when Clinton was raising taxes on wealthy taxpayers amid class-warfare rhetoric in 1993. The agreement gave the president limited money for selected priorities, but it also accelerated a trend toward squeezing domestic spending that seemed likely to force the further elimination of programs as inflation steadily eroded real purchasing power over the five years leading to 2002.

Clinton's embrace of a balanced budget itself was a huge shift from the stand-pat stance he and Democrats took after they enacted an ambitious deficit-reduction package in 1993.

While both Democrats and Republicans had political incentives to strike a deal in 1997, what made it all possible in the end was a plummeting deficit, driven down by past budget deals and a surging economy to lows that would have been fantasy two years before.

In 1995, when Republicans took control of Congress and began their balanced-budget drive, they were looking at a 2002 deficit of $299 billion, even after subtracting the "fiscal dividend" that the Congressional Budget Office (CBO) said would come from getting the budget to balance.

This time, CBO was projecting a deficit in 2002 — the year when the budget was to be in balance — of just $105 billion. The job, in effect, was about two-thirds easier than it had been only two years earlier. The joke among budget watchers was that Clinton and the Republican Congress were in a hurry to seal their deal before the budget balanced itself.

The agreement seemed reasonably likely to produce the longed-for balanced budget in 2002, so long as the economy did not falter precipitously. The plan was based on CBO's relatively conservative growth projections, which saw the economy expanding at just 2.1 percent a year.

But veteran budget watchers also noted that most of the spending cuts would come after Clinton left office and the 105th Congress was a memory. "President Clinton and the 105th Congress agreed that President Gore and the 107th Congress should sacrifice," quipped former CBO director Robert D. Reischauer.

Highlights

In its final form, the agreement included the following major elements:

- **Deficit reduction.** The deficit was slated to disappear in 2002, but in the short term, it was projected to head up, not down. That was largely because of the bipartisan thirst for tax cuts, which traditionally kicked in much more quickly than spending cuts. About half the net tax cuts would come in the last two years of the five-year deal, while more than 70 percent of the net spending cuts were deferred to those last two years.

That produced an odd-looking deficit path: From $67 billion in fiscal 1997, the deficit was expected to rise to $90.4 billion in 1998 before inching down to $89.7 billion in 1999 and then to $83 billion in 2000. Only in 2001 would the deficit finally fall below the 1997 level, to $53.3 billion, before turning into a $1.3 billion surplus in 2002.

- **Taxes.** The only two absolute numbers in the initial tax package were net cuts of $85 billion over five years and $250 billion over 10 years. (The gross cuts in the first five years were expected to be $135 billion, $50 billion of that offset by revenue-raisers, including extension of the airline ticket tax.)

Two letters from the GOP leadership set out several other points of understanding.

The first, a letter to Clinton, stated that the cuts would include a permanent, broad-based capital gains tax cut, a $500-per-child tax credit, expanded individual retirement accounts (IRAs), a reduction in the estate tax and "roughly" $35 billion over five years to help middle-income families pay postsecondary education costs, a key Clinton initiative. Also mentioned, although less securely guaranteed, were a welfare-to-work tax credit, capital gains tax relief for home sales, tax incentives for businesses to clean up environmentally damaged areas and tax incentives for the District of Columbia.

The second letter, to White House Chief of Staff Erskine Bowles, said that Congress' Joint Committee on Taxation would consult with the Treasury Department on how to estimate the cost of the tax provisions. In the past, Joint Tax and Treasury had disagreed, especially on how to score capital gains tax cuts.

• **Medicare.** The agreement assumed $115 billion in net savings over five years from Medicare, the health insurance program for the elderly and disabled. Initially, negotiators expected to achieve all of that by reducing reimbursement rates for providers such as hospitals, doctors and health maintenance organizations.

In the written pact, negotiators reduced the amount coming from providers to about $100 billion, with Medicare beneficiaries making up the $15 billion difference through an increase in the monthly premiums for the Part B portion of Medicare, which covered outpatient doctor visits. Low-income beneficiaries were protected from higher premiums by the addition of $1.5 billion in spending to subsidize their costs.

Four new benefits were included: colo-rectal screenings, mammograms, diabetes self-management and preventive vaccinations.

• **Medicaid.** Spending on health care for the poor and disabled was to be reduced by a net of $13.6 billion over five years. Gross spending reductions would be about $16 billion. The difference was a result of new spending planned for the District of Columbia and for Puerto Rico and other territories and for the low-income elderly under Medicare. The savings were to come largely from reducing reimbursements to hospitals.

• **Welfare.** The agreement included a key Clinton initiative — restoring Supplemental Security Income (SSI) and Medicaid benefits for disabled legal immigrants who had entered the country before Aug. 23, 1996. The benefits had been terminated as part of the 1996 welfare overhaul law (PL 104-193). Under the deal, those disabled legal immigrants who entered the country after Aug. 22, 1996, and were on the rolls before June 1, 1997, would also be eligible. The cost of restoring the benefits was $9.7 billion over five years.

Negotiators also agreed to restore $1.5 billion over five years in food stamp spending. The welfare law had cut the amount for food stamps by $23 billion over five years.

• **Children's health and other presidential priorities.** Clinton also got guarantees that Congress would spend $16 billion over the first five years to insure up to 5 million children whose parents were too poor to afford health insurance.

Within the domestic discretionary accounts, Clinton also got guarantees that Congress would fund at his requested levels top-priority programs including the National Institute of Standards and Technology; bilingual and immigrant education; an increase in Pell grants, which aided low-income college students; child literacy initiatives; Head Start; national parks, including the Everglades Restoration Fund; the Bureau of Indian Affairs' tribal priority allocations; training and employment services, including Job Corps; and the Violent Crime Reduction Trust fund.

Background

The bipartisan agreement was a major breakthrough after more than two years of bitter partisan fighting over the budget. The Republican congressional majority had taken over in early 1995 determined to make a balanced budget and tax cuts their vehicle for radically reshaping the federal government. But they had underestimated Clinton's will and his ability to stymie them.

By the time they conceded defeat in budget talks that dragged into 1996, Republicans had triggered two federal shutdowns that closed much of the government and brought them a drubbing in public opinion polls. *(1996 Almanac, p. 2-5; 1995 Almanac, p. 11-3)*

The residue of those battles — and of the ensuing fall 1996 elections, in which Democrats tarred Republicans as "Medicare killers" — was a deep bitterness that seemed likely to poison the relationship indefinitely.

Dramatic Turnaround in 1997

There were many reasons for the dramatic turnaround in 1997. One was sheer exhaustion. Each side had been brutalized by the other over the previous four years: Clinton and the Democrats in 1993-94 when Republicans attacked their tax-heavy budget package, and Republicans in 1995-96 when Democrats savaged their proposed cuts in projected spending for Medicare.

"Some Republicans came back [from the 1996 elections] frankly shellshocked," said Rep. Christopher Shays, R-Conn. They also came back to a smaller majority in the House and the reality that the White House would be occupied by a Democrat for the next four years. Republicans and Democrats alike also wanted a big legislative achievement to divert attention from scandals, investigations and ethics difficulties.

And congressional Republicans were in a bind on the budget in 1997. Clinton released his fiscal 1998 budget in early February, promising to eliminate the deficit by 2002 based on the more optimistic deficit forecasts of the Office of Management and Budget (OMB), which said about $252 billion in net cuts would do the job. *(Clinton budget, p. 2-4)*

Congressional Republicans wanted far bigger tax cuts than the president proposed, but they also needed to balance the budget based on CBO forecasts. At the time, CBO was projecting that it would take about $500 billion in net deficit reduction over five years to wipe out the deficit by 2002. That meant coming up with as much as $300 billion in additional spending cuts over five years, making Republicans vulnerable to charges that they were out to gut critical federal programs — the same attacks that had hurt them badly in 1995-96.

GOP leaders also worried that internal splits over spending and taxes could lead them into chaos if they had to pass a budget on their own. Fights already were brewing between House and Senate Republicans over appropriated spending, and among Republicans in both chambers over whether to delay the promised tax cuts to ensure a balanced budget.

Even if they resolved all those battles, they still faced the prospect of drawn out negotiations with the White House. "You want to talk about a journey that never gets to a destination?" asked a senior Republican.

Clinton, meanwhile, was searching for a landmark achievement to help define his second term and divert attention from ongoing investigations into his and other Democrats' alleged campaign fundraising irregularities. Also, administration officials said Clinton had come to believe that concluding a budget deal with Republicans offered a compelling long-term strategy for Democrats — even though many congressional Democrats strongly disputed that.

"There's an honest disagreement between the leaders of the Democratic Party in the House and the president about the future of the Democratic Party," said a White House offi-

1997 Budget Agreement

(in billions of dollars)

Category	Five-year total
Gross tax relief (maximum)	$135.0
Net tax relief	85.0
Defense (change from current services)	-76.8
Non-defense discretionary changes (from current services)	-64.1
Presidential initiatives	31.7
Medicare	-115.0
Medicaid	-16.0
Earned-Income Credit	-0.1
Student loans	-1.8
Federal retirement provisions	-4.9
Veterans provisions	-2.7
Spectrum auctions	-26.3
Housing	-1.6
Transportation	-0.2
Other mandatory provisions	-2.0

cial. "The president really believes that if the Democrats are going to move into the 21st century in a way that they are able to protect their priorities, they need to get this monkey of 'tax and spend' off their backs. They have to get credibility for being fiscally responsible."

The movement toward compromise was also eased by a change of players at the White House. Former lead budget negotiator and Chief of Staff Leon E. Panetta's steely reluctance to make concessions infuriated even those Republicans who had long considered him a friend. After Panetta resigned to return home to California in early 1997, he was replaced by a troika of negotiators — OMB Director Franklin D. Raines, new Chief of Staff Bowles and White House legislative liaison John Hilley — whom Republicans found much more to their liking.

Economic Growth Underpins Deal

As the negotiators worked, they got an unexpected boost from the economy, whose surprisingly strong growth was driving the deficit to remarkable lows. The plummeting deficits enabled CBO to hand negotiators a huge, last-minute windfall of extra projected revenues over the following five years, money they "spent" largely to remove elements of the deal that were unpopular with one or both sides.

Among the items dropped before the deal was announced May 2 was a proposed per capita cap on Medicaid spending that had infuriated liberal Democrats and governors of both parties. Gone, too, was a controversial plan to legislate a reduction in the Consumer Price Index (CPI), which was used to calculate the annual cost of living increase in Social Security checks and to index tax brackets.

Ironically, the good news on the deficit was at least partly the result of two much-derided earlier rounds of deficit reduction. "We wouldn't be talking about a balanced budget in 1997 if we didn't have the budget deals of 1990 and 1993," said Allen Schick, a University of Maryland professor of public policy. Schick and others said that the tax increases and spending cuts in those two earlier budget packages helped chip away at a deficit that had soared to more than $220 billion when negotiators were working out the 1990 budget agreement. *(1990 Almanac, p. 111; 1993 Almanac, p. 107)*

Updated to 1997 dollars, the 1990 package was worth about $593 billion; the 1993 deal was worth about $487 billion. By contrast, the 1997 agreement was expected to save only about $204 billion over five years.

The Search for a Deal

Low-keyed budget negotiations began shortly after Clinton submitted his $1.69 trillion fiscal 1998 request Feb. 6. Senior White House officials held a series of private meetings with members of Congress that included intense talks with Budget Chairman Domenici and other Senate Republicans.

While quietly pursuing a compromise, Democrats were also pushing Republicans to put up their own budget. The implicit message: Republicans had better make a deal with Clinton soon or risk writing their own budget resolution with much deeper spending cuts.

Unwilling to try drafting their own budget, Republicans concentrated on attacking Clinton's — particularly after CBO released an analysis March 3 showing the president's proposal generating not the $17 billion surplus he claimed it would in 2002, but a $69 billion deficit. CBO said the difference stemmed largely from the White House's more optimistic view of the economy.

CBO also said that more than 80 percent of the president's overall deficit reduction would not come until the final two years of the plan in 2001 and 2002 — after Clinton left office.

On March 12, House Republicans passed a non-binding resolution (H Res 89) calling on the president to scrap his budget and send them a new one that would eliminate the deficit using CBO numbers. The resolution passed 231-197. *(Vote 44, p. H-16)*

Democrats, eager to see Republicans walk the plank, shot back that the GOP ought to put its own budget proposals on the table before taking shots at Clinton's.

Tax Cut Free-for-All

With no clear path to a budget compromise, lawmakers outdid one another with proposals for cutting taxes. The free-for-all fueled concerns among deficit hawks, both Republican and Democratic, that the demand for tax cuts could make it more difficult to reconcile lawmakers to the limited cuts that were likely to fit into a balanced-budget package. Alternatively, many Democrats feared, the drive for larger tax cuts could necessitate deeper spending cuts, ultimately making it more difficult to sell a balanced-budget plan on their side of the aisle.

Both parties had lists of cuts that they considered essential to a final deal. For Republicans, the three must-haves were a broad-based reduction in capital gains taxes, a $500-per-child tax credit and a reduction in estate taxes. Under proposals introduced by Senate Republicans in January (S 1, S 2), those alone were projected to cost $161 billion over five years and $395 billion over 10 years.

The Senate GOP leadership added an expansion of IRAs, a proposal strongly advocated by Senate Finance Committee Chairman William V. Roth Jr., R-Del., that was expected to cost $33 billion over five years and $113 billion over 10 years. Altogether, Republicans were talking about net tax cuts of as much as $170 billion over five years.

Clinton's budget proposed gross tax cuts of $98.4 billion, with all but about $22.4 billion of that offset by tax increases. His plan included a more modest version of the child tax credit and a much smaller capital gains tax cut targeted to homeowners. Clinton also called for several new tax reductions. The most costly of these were incentives for higher education, including a $1,500-per-student tax credit and a $10,000 deduction, that together were projected to cost nearly $41 billion over five years and about $84 billion over 10 years in lost revenue.

The Joint Tax Committee said Clinton's gross tax cuts would actually cost $117 billion over five years and $281 billion over 10 years.

Budget hawks warned that the high long-term cost of some of the proposed tax cuts would all but guarantee that even if the budget could be balanced in fiscal 2002, it would remain at zero only fleetingly. Some of the cuts were designed so that the biggest revenue losses would come after five years.

But for Republicans intent on remaking government, the rising cost of any cuts was not necessarily a bad thing. "This debate is not about a balanced budget," said Bill Archer, R-Texas, chairman of the tax-writing House Ways and Means Committee. "It is about whether we will downsize the size of government."

Compromise Resisted by Hard-Liners

Attempts to find a middle ground were continually complicated by pressure from hard-liners in both parties.

On the Democratic side, for example, liberals sharply opposed a plan by budget negotiators to mine huge savings from a proposed change in the way the CPI, the chief measure of inflation, was calculated. Budget drafters saw the change as a "magic bullet" that would enable them to balance the budget while also meeting lawmakers' demands for tax cuts.

There was widespread belief among economists that the CPI overstated actual changes in the cost of living. A special commission assembled by the Senate Finance Committee, and led by Michael Boskin, onetime chief economist for President George Bush, had concluded in December 1996 that the CPI overstated cost of living increases by about 1.1 percentage points.

The effect of revising the index downward would be to lower future cost of living adjustments for Social Security recipients, reduce benefits increases in several other federal programs, and accelerate the "bracket creep" that kicked taxpayers into higher tax brackets, effectively raising their taxes.

The deficit-reduction potential was enormous. CBO estimated that a 1 percentage point reduction in the CPI could slice $141 billion off the deficit over five years — more than half the net deficit reduction in Clinton's budget and plenty to pay for much bigger tax cuts.

But to take advantage of the politically risky fix, lawmakers from both parties clearly had to join hands and take the heat together. Bipartisan cover was essential.

In the House, Budget Committee Chairman John R. Kasich, R-Ohio, and Appropriations Committee Chairman Robert L. Livingston, R-La., were both vocal supporters of the CPI change. On Feb. 24, Lott called for a commission of four experts to determine the amount by which the existing CPI should be recalculated.

Clinton welcomed Lott's proposal, and senior White House officials hinted he might follow it. But a CPI change was vehemently opposed by House Minority Leader Richard A. Gephardt, D-Mo., and other liberal Democrats. Along with organized labor and advocates for the elderly, they said the idea was simply a cover for cutting Social Security benefits and raising taxes.

Clinton bowed to the liberals in early March, dropping the commission idea. The move infuriated Lott and contributed to a mood of pessimism about the chances of a budget deal. Though plans to legislate a CPI change were later included in the bipartisan plan, the provision was dropped before the May 2 announcement.

On the Republican side, efforts to get around the cost of the huge GOP-proposed tax cuts brought a backlash from the party's right wing, for whom tax cuts were at least as important as balancing the budget.

Centrist budget balancers from both parties had long advocated postponing tax cuts until the deficit was clearly being eradicated. House Speaker Newt Gingrich, R-Ga., told reporters March 17 that he favored a postponement in order to focus on balancing the budget.

House Majority Leader Dick Armey, R-Texas, quickly rebuked the Speaker, and in the Senate, 17 conservative Republicans sent Lott a letter implying they would not support any deal that split tax cuts from a balanced budget. Lott pointedly disagreed with the Speaker, as did the chairmen of the two tax-writing committees, and the idea was quickly dropped.

Pressure Builds for a Deal

Despite often gloomy assessments of their progress, Republican leaders were loath to draft a fiscal 1998 budget resolution before they had a bipartisan deal in hand. As the statutory target date of April 15 for Congress' budget grew nearer, Clinton's leverage grew.

Intense negotiations finally began the week of April 7 among the chairmen and ranking members of the House and Senate Budget committees and a White House team made up of OMB's Raines, legislative liaison Hilley and Gene Sperling, director of Clinton's National Economic Council.

Kasich said each side was trying to determine how much the other was willing to give up without violating core principles. "It may be a bridge too far. We just don't know yet," he said.

Each day was devoted to a particular topic. First came Medicare. The administration agreed to bring its savings level up to $100 billion over five years as scored by CBO. Previously, CBO had estimated that Clinton's program changes would achieve $82 billion in savings. The administration proposed a new $8 billion cut in payments to hospitals and reductions in physician and nursing home payments. Domenici declared the discussions "a healthy start."

Next came non-defense discretionary spending, where the two sides were at loggerheads. The administration vigorously pushed Clinton's priorities, including additional spending in areas such as education. Appropriators complained that the White House was not offering any savings beyond the $79 billion over five years already in its plan.

On taxes, both sides laid out their priorities, but no compromises were discussed. The chairmen of the tax-writing committees expressed their commitment to a tax cut of as much as $180 billion over five years, but Domenici reportedly argued that taxes should not drive the rest of the budget numbers.

On April 11, Clinton aides presented the president's rationale for new spending on children's health care, education and new Medicare benefits for the elderly. GOP lawmakers greeted the presentation with what Sen. Frank R. Lautenberg, D-N.J., described as "a thunder of silence."

Despite saber-rattling talk from Republican leaders that the week of April 14 would be "make or break" time, April 15 came and went with the negotiations still stuck.

Lead appropriators warned that they would have to begin marking up fiscal 1998 spending bills in May, budget or no budget, in order to finish by Oct. 1, the start of the new fiscal year. Lott and Assistant Senate Majority Leader Don Nickles, R-Okla., warned that prolonging the talks would only reduce bargaining room and make a deal less likely.

Ten conservative senators, led by Phil Gramm of Texas and Sam Brownback of Kansas, wrote Lott insisting that he stick with core GOP principles on tax cuts, spending and other issues. Meanwhile, other Senate Republicans were signaling that if talks with the White House broke down, they would look for common ground with a group of moderates led by John H. Chafee, R-R.I., and John B. Breaux, D-La.

In the House, GOP leaders were pressing Kasich to get on with the long-delayed budget resolution markup April 30, with or without a deal. House Republicans had no safe harbor comparable to that offered by Chafee-Breaux in the Senate. The budget proposed by conservative "Blue Dog" Democrats relied on a CPI change and offered no tax cuts until the budget was balanced — both anathema to Republican strategists.

That left Kasich with the prospect of going ahead with a budget that appealed to the vast majority of House Republicans, rather than with a more bipartisan, Senate-style plan. The likely upshot: House and Senate budgets that would be almost as tough to compromise as the split between Clinton and the GOP.

Clinton had difficulties on his side, too. He was gradually alienating liberal Democrats as he inched up his cuts in projected spending for Medicare and tightened up on domestic spending. Fully 109 Democrats, more than half of those in the House, wrote to warn the president that he should not hold defense spending harmless while cutting domestic programs. "The president is making a fundamental mistake," said Barney Frank, D-Mass."You can't leave the military off the table."

Clinton worked to soothe the potential rebellion, hosting House Democratic leaders and Budget Committee members for a lengthy clear-the-air session April 23; Senate leaders and Budget Committee members followed April 24. Clinton reportedly stressed that he would not walk away from Democratic priorities. But he also said it made no sense to force Republicans to write their own budget, arguing that that would only harden their position and make it tougher to get a deal.

On Capitol Hill, Democrats sounded less anxious for a deal than Republicans. "Deadlines here come and go," said Lautenberg, ranking Democrat on the Budget Committee, after an April 24 meeting with Clinton. "The discussion can go on for a while."

Reaching Accord

By April 30, the White House and congressional Republicans seemed to be closing in on a deal.

Angry Democrats denounced the closed-door negotiations and objected to their second-class status as Clinton and the Republicans made their final compromises. "It is unfortunate that this has not been a budget summit arrangement that has included House Democrats," said Gephardt, adding that he was "not optimistic" about getting a majority of House Democrats to support the plan.

Gephardt was widely viewed as a contender for the Democratic presidential nomination in 2000, and many had assumed for months that if Clinton struck a deal with Republicans, Gephardt would oppose it both on principle and as a way of distinguishing himself from his chief rival, Vice President Al Gore.

But the White House was taken aback when Senate Minority Leader Tom Daschle, D-S.D., denounced the final bargaining early May 1 and suggested he might oppose the deal. "It's atrocious that deals would be cut and that decisions would be made behind closed doors with very, very few, if anybody, knowing what this whole package looks like," Daschle told reporters. "It's going to take several weeks before I can persuade my colleagues that this is a budget that they ought to support," he said, adding, "I'm not going to sell it if I don't believe in it."

After an afternoon briefing from White House budget director Raines, however, Daschle became more conciliatory. "A majority of our caucus would support the budget agreement," he said.

Eleventh-Hour Windfall

The job of rounding up the Democratic votes got much easier the night of May 1. As weary negotiators were fine-tuning the complex deal, they received late word from CBO that the fiscal 1997 deficit would be nearly $50 billion lower than previous estimates. Speculation of an impending windfall had been rampant — in fact there was some fear that the extra money would shatter the deal — but the official word did not come until the eleventh hour.

CBO projected that, because of higher-than-expected income tax receipts in April, the fiscal 1997 deficit would be $75 billion, not the $124 billion forecast in January. Over the five-year time frame of the agreement, CBO projected extra revenues of $225 billion, about $114 billion of which was available to the negotiators. (The other $108 billion was soaked up by an agreement to use some of OMB's economic assumptions.)

The negotiators agreed to count $64 billion of the extra revenue toward making the projected deficit smaller in coming years, which won over the fiscal conservatives. Another $24 billion was used to eliminate the need for legislation mandating a reduction in the CPI. The rest was used to jettison some controversial provisions still in the accord, such as the per capita cap on Medicaid, and to reduce the fiscal hit to Medicare. Some of the extra revenue was earmarked for extra spending on Clinton priorities, such as health care for children, the administration's welfare-to-work program and transportation.

The windfall raised questions about CBO's integrity, with some Republicans and Democrats wondering about the recalculation three months before new estimates typically came out. But even the critics conceded that the numbers were a reflection of fiscal reality.

Bargain Tests Unity in Both Parties

When Clinton announced May 2 that a deal had finally been reached, it was before a subdued group of Democrats at a congressional retreat in Baltimore. The White House already knew it faced a tough selling job.

While pro-business, conservative and moderate Democrats were pleased, their more liberal, blue-collar counterparts viewed the package as tilted against the poor and the tax cuts as stacked in favor of the rich. They also feared the agreement would hand the GOP the sort of positive accomplishment it could use to gain ground in the 1998 congressional elections.

Senate Democrats had been frustrated for weeks by a negotiating process that largely ignored them, but many were resigned to accepting the budget as better than nothing. The real test was expected to come in the House, where opposition was stronger and the vitriol higher.

"It's the poor people who are being singled out to suffer . . . and it's unworthy of a Democratic president," said Rep. Henry A. Waxman, D-Calif.

Clinton got started even before the deal was final, working overtime to placate Democrats and secure some last-minute concessions, including scuttling the per capita cap on Medicaid and adding $20 billion in domestic spending.

The mood May 2 was markedly different in the Rotunda of the Capitol, where Republican leaders were giddy as they held their own simultaneous announcement of the deal.

Despite its flaws, the budget deal offered Republicans a political trifecta: a balanced budget in five years; significant, permanent tax cuts; and a plan to keep Medicare solvent for another decade. "To our base, to our folks, those three issues are paramount," said House GOP Conference chairman John A. Boehner, R-Ohio.

Not all Republicans agreed, however. Gramm blasted the agreement as "a good political deal and a bad budget," complaining that it failed to adequately cut taxes and spending.

Refining the Deal

Difficult as it was to reach an agreement, the bargaining was hardly finished. Within a week, congressional and White House negotiators were wrangling anew over exactly what it was they had agreed to. Disputes arose over issues such as the size and composition of tax cuts, who would get how much new spending and how to make the deficit drop steadily until the budget was balanced in 2002.

One bone of contention was how much of the $115 billion in Medicare savings should come from different sectors of the health care industry. The administration wanted HMOs to accept lower reimbursement rates, but some lawmakers objected. HMOs generally reined in costs by strictly limiting access to sophisticated tests and specialists.

Another battle loomed over how large an education tax cut the GOP leadership had promised. The White House insisted it had won agreement to $35 billion over five years in tax credits and deductions for higher education. But Republicans on the tax-writing committees worried that giving Clinton that much would leave precious little room for cuts in capital gains and other areas that they held dear.

A fight was also brewing over how far to go in restoring welfare benefits to elderly, disabled and blind legal immigrants. And members of the House Transportation Committee were holding out for additional spending for the six-year, $180 billion transportation bill they were working on.

Back to the Negotiating Table

With so many issues at play — and with GOP leaders pressing an ambitious schedule for implementing the agreement — the two sides quickly resumed negotiations.

The haggling centered on a number of mostly small items — spending programs for which the White House wanted more money and tax cuts Republicans wanted to keep on the table. Negotiations stalled repeatedly when one side put down on paper its version of what they had verbally agreed to — and opponents discovered items they insisted had never been approved.

Part of the holdup, too, was caused by a delicate dance between the White House, which wanted as specific an agreement as it could rope congressional Republicans into, and GOP leaders, who were worried about dictating too much to the stubborn committee chairmen who would draft the tax and spending bills.

In the end, the negotiators settled for substantial specificity. On May 15, they presented a written version of the accord. In 24 pages they spelled out details of the more than $33 billion Clinton won in restored or new spending for legal immigrants, food stamp recipients, children without health insurance and other administration priorities, plus protection for other domestic programs.

The talks also produced the two letters to the White House from Lott and Gingrich committing Republicans to "roughly $35 billion" for Clinton's education tax cuts and credits, while urging cooperation among congressional and administration tax estimators, with a pledge that the tax cut package "shall not cause costs to explode in the outyears."

Although both sides claimed victory, the White House sounded a little happier than Republicans did — just the reverse of the satisfaction index when both sides made separate announcements of the initial deal May 2. "We got 98 percent of what we needed or wanted," said Hilley, who described Clinton as "ecstatic."

Republicans released a four-page document titled, "What the President Did Not Get From This Agreement." Among other things, it noted the deal included much bigger net tax cuts than Clinton originally proposed and "substantially scales back the President's insatiable appetite for more government spending programs." ■

Budget Resolution Mirrors Pact

For the first time in recent memory, Congress adopted a broadly supported, bipartisan budget resolution to guide its tax and spending decisions. The measure was the first formal step on the five-year path to a balanced budget agreed to in May by President Clinton and congressional leaders.

The fiscal 1998 budget resolution (H Con Res 84) aimed to reduce the deficit by $204.3 billion over five years, including $115 billion in savings from Medicare. It provided for $85 billion in net tax cuts, a $16 billion children's health care initiative, restoration of Supplemental Security Income (SSI) and other benefits for disabled legal immigrants and increases in domestic appropriations, at least in the short term.

The budget assumed the deficit would rise slightly to $90.4 billion in fiscal 1998, gradually decline in subsequent years and give way to a small surplus of $1.6 billion in fiscal 2002.

Though the measure was a critical step in the budget process, it provided only a semi-binding roadmap. It was not signed by the president, and its recommendations did not have the force of law — though Congress' own rules required it to abide by the resolution's broad outlines.

The resolution set the overall limit for the 13 regular fiscal 1998 appropriations bills — a total of $526.9 billion in budget authority for discretionary spending, up about 3 percent from fiscal 1997. Although it built in specific protections for some White House priorities, it did not set individual spending levels for the 13 bills, a fact that virtually guaranteed fights between the president and Congress over several of the measures.

H Con Res 84 also contained instructions for writing two separate reconciliation bills, so named because their purpose was to reconcile tax and spending policy with deficit-reduction goals. The first was to be written by Congress' authorizing committees to cut spending in various entitlement programs such as Medicare. The second, the responsibility of the tax-writing committees, was supposed to produce tax cuts that matched those in the budget deal.

The White House had insisted on splitting the reconciliation process in two so that Democrats could vote for balancing the budget but against tax cuts if they felt the tax bill was excessively tilted toward the wealthy. That strategy also preserved White House leverage over the shape of the tax cuts by allowing Clinton to veto a tax-cut bill without also killing the balanced-budget package.

House authorizers were required to report their entitlement cuts to the Budget Committee for consolidation by June 12. The revenue portion of the agreement was due June 13. The deadlines for Senate committees were June 13 and June 20.

BOXSCORE

Fiscal 1998 Budget Resolution — H Con Res 84. The resolution reflected the five-year bipartisan balanced-budget agreement reached by the White House and congressional leaders in May.

Reports: H Rept 105-100; conference report, H Rept 105-116.

KEY ACTION

May 21 — House passed H Con Res 84, 333-99.

May 23 — Senate passed H Con Res 84, amended, 78-22.

June 5 — House agreed to the conference report, 327-97; **Senate** agreed, 76-22.

Background

The Budget committees did not begin drafting the measure until mid-May, a month past the April 15 statutory deadline for completing work on the budget. The task had been postponed while Republican leaders negotiated with the White House over a five-year bipartisan budget-balancing agreement. *(Budget deal, p. 2-18)*

The alternative — pushing through a GOP-only budget resolution with spending cuts deep enough to meet the relatively pessimistic deficit projections of the Congressional Budget Office (CBO) — would have left Republicans vulnerable to the kind of savaging from Democrats that had weakened them in the 1996 congressional elections.

The White House had worked from the more cheerful economic forecasts of its own Office of Management and Budget (OMB), which required $252 billion in deficit reduction over five years to balance the budget. By contrast, CBO said it would take some $500 billion in net deficit reduction to do the job. Add to that the much deeper tax cuts being proposed by the GOP and Republicans would have had to come up with as much as $300 billion more in spending cuts over five years than the White House.

A bipartisan budget deal was finally announced with much fanfare May 2, and Republican leaders laid out an ambitious legislative schedule that called for passing identical budget resolutions in both chambers, eliminating the need for a conference, and wrapping up the first part of the job before Congress left for its Memorial Day recess May 23. House Speaker Newt Gingrich, R-Ga., said he wanted to have both reconciliation bills cleared and headed to Clinton by July 4, "to give the American people a birthday gift."

But the May 2 announcement turned out to be premature. Disputes broke out almost immediately over just what was contained in the budget agreement, which had not been put into writing. So the Budget committees waited while the two sides returned to the bargaining table to haggle over an array of issues large and small. This time the negotiators got more specific, and they put key parts of the deal into writing. On May 15, the refined agreement was ready.

House, Senate Committees

Just hours after the bargaining ended late on May 15, the House Budget Committee approved a draft budget resolution that reflected the bipartisan deal. The vote on the measure — later introduced as H Con Res 84 (H Rept 105-100) — was 31-7.

Voting along party lines each time, the committee rejected 11 Democratic amendments aimed at assuring that the tax cuts would benefit people of all income levels, that the revenue losses would not explode after the budget's five-year time frame and that several domestic programs would be added to the written list of priorities that both sides agreed to protect.

"We're not going to start adding additions to the list that took us four months to put together," said committee Chairman John R. Kasich, R-Ohio. The resolution moved through the committee effectively unaltered.

A virtually identical budget sailed through the Senate Budget Committee in less than three hours May 19, winning approval on a 17-4 vote.

Ten Republicans and seven Democrats backed the centrist package. Three of the "no" votes were cast from the ideological wings by GOP conservatives Phil Gramm of Texas and Rod Grams of Minnesota, and by liberal Democrat Paul S. Sarbanes of Maryland.

Ernest F. Hollings, D-S.C., voted "no" after reiterating his view that this budget, like most, deceptively used excess payments to the Social Security trust fund to mask the true deficit. On a voice vote, the panel rejected a Hollings amendment to bring the budget closer to actual balance by striking both Clinton's extra spending and the GOP-inspired tax cuts.

The committee defeated, 10-11, two amendments by Patty Murray, D-Wash. One would have put the sense of the Senate behind extra funding for technology training for teachers; the other would have urged extra spending on childhood and parental programs.

By 6-15, the committee defeated an amendment by Ron Wyden, D-Ore., that would have cut defense spending by about $17 billion and allowed that money to go to non-defense programs by doing away with the "firewall" negotiators had agreed to erect in order to prevent raids of defense funds in 1998 and 1999.

House Floor Action

After 11 hours of floor debate that ran past 3 a.m. on May 21, the House gave overwhelming approval to the budget resolution; the vote was 333-99. Democrats delivered enough votes to satisfy Clinton's promise that he would only back a deal that had the support of more than half his party's caucus —132 of the 206 House Democrats (64 percent) voted for the deal. *(Vote 148, p. H-48)*

No one in the House was totally pleased with the bipartisan budget deal, but a majority of members in both parties found something in it to endorse. For most Republicans, it was the hefty package of tax cuts, the first net tax cut since 1981. For many Democrats, it was a significant increase in spending on education. Above all, the agreement allowed both parties to claim ownership of the balanced-budget issue.

"Every liberal could write a budget that is better than this by their values: fewer tax cuts, more domestic spending, less defense. Every conservative can write a budget that is better than this: more tax cuts, more defense, less domestic spending," said Gingrich.

"We were faced with a choice — four years of deadlock, four years of the American people growing even more cynical . . . or something which frankly we did not do enough of last time: Get in a room, lay out what we really want, listen to the other side and try to find a common ground," Gingrich said.

Democratic budget supporters expressed similar sentiments. "This is a divided government and to do a deal, none of us gets to do it alone," said John M. Spratt Jr. of South Carolina, the ranking Democrat on the House Budget Committee. "We have . . . a choice between gridlock and compromise, and what we have before us is just that — it is compromise. It is not a perfect solution."

While the wings of both parties — conservative Republicans and liberal Democrats — offered alternative budget resolutions during the debate, they amounted to little more than gestures.

The deal even drew support from Democrats often considered solidly in the liberal camp, such as Minority Whip David E. Bonior of Michigan, Rosa DeLauro of Connecticut, and Congressional Black Caucus members Sanford D. Bishop Jr. and Cynthia A. McKinney, both Georgians. Support also came from passionate GOP conservatives, such as Mark W. Neumann of Wisconsin and Mark Souder and Dan Burton, both of Indiana.

However, the bipartisan tone of compromise and hard-won respect barely masked the many trouble spots that lay ahead. In speech after speech, members cited specific concerns, including programs they said they would fight to protect or to eliminate. Many warned that while they were voting for the budget resolution, they were making no guarantee that they would support the reconciliation measures needed to make the savings and tax cuts a reality.

Shuster's Proposal

The potential shallowness of support for the deal was underscored by a challenge mounted by Transportation and Infrastructure Committee Chairman Bud Shuster, R-Pa., whose alternative budget was barely defeated, 214-216. It would have reduced both spending and tax cuts to get another $12 billion beyond the $125 billion contained in the budget deal for roads, bridges and other transportation projects. *(Vote 147, p. H-48)*

Shuster's amendment won the support of three-fourths of the House Democrats, despite pleas from the White House to vote against it. The proposal was defeated only after a late night, closed-door Republican conference where Gingrich and Kasich pleaded with their members to put the balanced-budget agreement ahead of their concerns for specific road and bridge projects.

Their entreaties continued on the floor. "Yes, I am here to represent my district. But the country, the country wants us tonight to look beyond our district, to look to a degree beyond our own priorities and be part of America's team," said Kasich, speaking passionately to both sides of the aisle.

Opponents Come From all Corners

The most significant opposition among Democrats came from House Minority Leader Richard A. Gephardt, D-Mo., who voted with Shuster and against the resolution. Gephardt, considered a likely presidential candidate in 2000, did not rally opposition, however. He took care to avoid even the appearance of attempting to marshal votes against the budget, holding off on announcing his own position until the day the resolution came to the floor.

The other 98 votes against the resolution came from every corner of the political spectrum. Among the 26 Republicans who voted "no" were some of the younger and most conservative members of the conference, such as David M. McIntosh of Indiana, but also several senior members, such as Judiciary Committee Chairman Henry J. Hyde of Illinois.

Crane and other Republicans objected to the deal because it would increase the deficit in fiscal 1998 and would not significantly reduce it until fiscal 2001. Conservatives also criticized the tax cut package as too small to accommodate the many provisions that members had said they would deliver to taxpayers.

Of 72 Democrats who opposed the resolution, the majority were members of the Congressional Black Caucus or the Progressive Caucus. They complained that the deal failed to restore enough spending for food stamps, cut as part of the 1996 welfare system overhaul (PL 104-193), and they protested that the spending cuts would disproportionately hit the poor and elderly while the tax cuts would favor higher income Americans.

Missing from the list of dissenters were all but one of the "Blue Dogs," conservative Democrats who in the past had promoted rigorously spartan budgets that resisted tax cuts before the deficit reached zero. Despite the failure of the budget agreement to provide enforcement mechanisms to ensure that the deficit would be zeroed out, only one of the Blue Dogs — William O. Lipinski of Illinois — was willing to go against the tide.

"I am disappointed that we missed the opportunity to make real reforms in the long-term costs of entitlements," said Charles W. Stenholm, D-Texas. But, he added, "this is the best we could do in a bipartisan way, and I will support this resolution to keep the process moving forward."

Alternative Offerings

Four alternative budgets were offered during the debate, which started on May 20 and ran until nearly dawn on May 21.

- **Congressional Black Caucus.** Sponsors said their proposal would balance the budget by 2001 while preserving health care spending and sharply increasing aid for education. To pay for the increases, they proposed to end $195 billion worth of corporate tax "loopholes," delay tax cuts until the budget was balanced, and reduce defense spending by $190 billion in lieu of reducing Medicaid and most domestic discretionary accounts. The caucus's budget was rejected, 72-358. *(Vote 143, p. H-48)*
- **Conservative Action Team.** The proposal would have more than doubled the net tax cuts in the budget agreement, from $85 billion to $192.5 billion over five years. The additional tax cuts would have been paid for by deeper cuts in non-defense discretionary spending. The proposal failed, 119-313. *(Vote 144, p. H-48)*
- **Brown.** George E. Brown Jr., D-Calif., offered an amendment to rearrange spending priorities in the budget. He proposed to increase spending for transportation, education, energy, environmental cleanup and most notably scientific research. Brown was the ranking Democrat on the House Science Committee. The additional spending was to be paid for by eliminating the tax cuts and reducing defense spending. Brown's plan failed, 91-339 *(Vote 145, p. H-48)*
- **Kennedy.** Joseph P. Kennedy II, D-Mass., offered a plan that called for no net tax cut and for deeper cuts in defense spending in order to pay for $103 billion in additional spending on health, education, transportation and economic development. Kennedy would have allowed up to $60 billion in tax cuts, but only if they were paid for within the tax code by increasing existing taxes and eliminating

1997 Budget Resolution

(in billions of dollars)

Fiscal Year	1998	1999	2000	2001	2002	5-year total
Discretionary Spending						
Defense						
BA	$ 269	$ 272	$ 275	$ 282	$ 290	$ 1,387
Outlays	267	267	269	271	273	1,346
Non-Defense						
BA	258	261	262	260	261	1,303
Outlays	286	293	295	294	288	1,456
Total						
BA	**527**	**533**	**537**	**542**	**551**	**2,690**
Outlays	**553**	**559**	**564**	**564**	**561**	**2,802**
Entitlement Spending						
Medicare	221	233	253	261	280	1,248
Medicaid	105	112	120	129	138	605
Other	564	597	625	662	673	3,121
Total	**890**	**942**	**999**	**1,052**	**1,091**	**4,974**
Grand Total						
Total spending (outlays)	**$ 1,692**	**$ 1,754**	**$ 1,811**	**$ 1,858**	**$ 1,889**	**$ 9,005**
Total revenues	**1,602**	**1,664**	**1,728**	**1,805**	**1,890**	**8,690**
Deficit/Surplus	**-90.4**	**-89.7**	**-83.0**	**-53.3**	**1.3**	**—**

Note: Figures may not add due to rounding

SOURCE: House Budget Committee

tax preferences. His proposal was rejected, 123-306. *(Vote 146, p. H-48)*

Senate Floor Action

More than 50 amendments spread through four days of Senate debate May 20-23 highlighted nearly all the ways members of both parties disliked the bipartisan budget deal. But in the end, the Senate left the budget virtually unchanged, approving it May 23 by a vote of 78-22; just 14 Republicans and eight Democrats voted no. *(Vote 92, p. S-17)*

A final, hours-long "vote-a-rama" on May 23 let senators vent their frustrations before the final vote. "This agreement responds to the American people, who clearly sent a message in the last election," said Senate Budget Committee Chairman Pete V. Domenici, R-N.M. "The people said, 'Work together. . . . Do not fight all the time.' So we have done just that."

"I am hopeful that this agreement represents a turning point in contemporary American politics," echoed Budget Committee ranking Democrat Frank R. Lautenberg of New Jersey. "This agreement shows Democrats and Republicans are ready to put aside partisan differences, rise above petty bickering and make the hard decisions that our people across the country want us to do."

Although the Senate version was nearly identical to the House-approved resolution, a plan to quickly combine the two into a single measure collapsed late May 22. Senate Minority Leader Tom Daschle, D-S.D., was furious that Congress was adjourning for the Memorial Day recess without finishing work on a separate supplemental appropriations bill (HR 1469) to provide relief to victims of Midwest flooding, which was bogged down by controversial Republican riders. In protest, Daschle, whose own state was inundated by spring floods, declined to help work through the complex process that would have allowed Congress to finalize the budget resolution before heading home. *(Supplemental, p. 9-84)*

A Barrage of Amendments

Ironically, a chief theme during the four days of Senate floor debate on the resolution was that the deal — whose goal was to balance the budget — offered too little new spending for both parties. Republicans and Democrats alike tried to wring out more money for children without health insurance, highway projects without sufficient funding and other bipartisan priorities.

Leaders were on the defensive from the start, warning that any substantive change risked killing the fragile agreement. But they were peppered with amendments from disgruntled members from the wings of both parties trying to embarrass the majority and build a record to campaign on.

Although Republicans accused Democrats of reneging on the spirit of the deal by refusing to vote against killer amendments, Democrats insisted they had promised only to provide the votes for final passage.

The severest test came on an amendment by Orrin G. Hatch, R-Utah, and Edward M. Kennedy, D-Mass., to raise the tax on cigarettes by 43 cents a pack and divide the proceeds between deficit reduction ($10 billion) and additional health insurance coverage for uninsured children ($20 billion).

The proposal was almost irresistible to many members of both parties, especially after Hatch and Kennedy boiled their appeal down to a choice between tobacco companies and a towheaded child named Joey, whose photo appeared on the posters and newspaper ads they used to buttress their pitch.

GOP leaders were first worried and then angry, especially after word spread that Vice President Al Gore might come to the Senate, ready to vote for the amendment in case of a tie. Senate Majority Leader Trent Lott, R-Miss., warned he would pull the budget off the floor if it even looked as if the amendment would be adopted.

Republicans had visions of 30-second TV spots attacking them for being against children, and they demanded Democratic cover — starting with the president. Clinton himself did not speak publicly, but White House spokesman Mike McCurry did.

"As a free-standing matter, I think this president's sympathies are pretty clear around the thrust of the legislation," McCurry said May 21. "The problem is, the amendment doesn't stand freely. It stands encumbering the balanced-budget agreement that we also fought very hard for. The president is not about to see all that hard work go down the drain."

In the end, the Senate voted 55-45 to table, or kill, the Hatch-Kennedy amendment, with eight Democrats voting to table, offsetting eight Republicans who voted to preserve the amendment. *(Vote 76, p. S-15)*

Other amendments with the potential to complicate subsequent legislation on the budget deal included proposals by:

➤ Christopher J. Dodd, D-Conn., to increase appropriations caps by $15.8 billion over five years, offset that by ending corporate tax breaks, and spend the money on programs for infants, toddlers and young children. The amendment was tabled, 61-39, with nine Democrats joining the vote to kill it. *(Vote 72, p. S-15)*

➤ John W. Warner, R-Va., and Max Baucus, D-Mont., to increase transportation funding by $12 billion over five years, with offsets to be determined. Like Shuster's amendment in the House, this came within two votes of passing. The vote was 51-49 to table it. *(Vote 80, p. S-16)*

Final Action

After returning from the Memorial Day recess, House and Senate conferees met briefly June 4 to resolve the relatively minor differences between the two chambers' resolutions to produce a conference report (H Rept 105-116).

The House approved the conference report the following day, June 5, 327-97. The Senate acted just hours later, approving the measure, 76-22. That completed work on the budget resolution since the president's signature was not required. *(House vote 166, p. H-56; Senate vote 96, p. S-18)* ■

Reconciliation Package: An Overview

With flags flying and a military band playing, President Clinton on Aug. 5 signed a pair of budget-reconciliation bills that promised to eliminate the federal deficit by 2002, while providing substantial tax cuts over five years and expanding access to health care for children. Together with Republican lawmakers, veterans of some of the bitterest budget battles in recent memory, Clinton heralded the bills as a victory for bipartisanship.

RELATED STORIES

Tax Bill	2-30
Provisions	2-39
Spending Cuts	2-47
Provisions	2-52
Vetoed Provisions	2-61
Airline Taxes	3-28
Education	7-5
Medicare	6-3
Spectrum Auction	3-34
Welfare	6-31

Congress had cleared the separate spending and tax bills with relative ease on July 31, following intense negotiations that dominated the month of July.

The spending bill — officially the Balanced Budget Act of 1997 (HR 2015 — PL 105-33) — was expected at the time to result in gross spending cuts of $263 billion over five years. Nearly half that total — $140 billion over five years — came from extending caps on discretionary spending, the money over which the appropriators had annual authority. The remainder resulted mainly from cuts in Medicare and Medicaid, and from revenues from auctioning portions of the electromagnetic spectrum and increasing the tax on cigarettes.

The spending cuts were partly offset by $33 billion in new spending sought by Clinton and the Democrats for a children's health insurance initiative and to restore some cuts made in the 1996 welfare law (PL 104-193). The bill also continued "pay-as-you-go" rules for entitlement and tax changes, and increased the statutory ceiling on the federal debt.

The tax bill — dubbed the Taxpayer Relief Act of 1997 (HR 2014 — PL 105-34) — promised net tax cuts of $95 billion over five years, $275 billion over 10 years. The most costly item was a $500-per-child tax credit targeted at the middle class. The tax cuts were partially offset by a set of revenue raisers, including the renewal and restructuring of taxes on air travel, projected to bring in $33.2 billion over five years

Satisfaction on Both Sides

For Republicans, the legislation capped a balanced-budget and tax-cutting drive that had consumed them since they took over Congress in 1995, though it came through incremental change, not revolution.

"We are reversing the decades-old trend of bigger government, bigger taxes and bigger spending," said Senate Finance Committee Chairman William V. Roth Jr., R-Del. "Balancing the budget and cutting taxes are Republican ideas — make no mistake about that."

The bills also marked perhaps Clinton's greatest legislative triumph. His team left the bargaining table with more of what he wanted on the details — including the scope of the child tax credit, a new children's health initiative, restoration of welfare benefits for disabled legal immigrants and a score of other issues — than most in Congress had expected.

"When this administration took office, America's budget deficit was $290 billion and rising. We put in place a comprehensive economic strategy to cut the deficit and invest in our people," Clinton told a cheering gathering of Democrats on the White House lawn July 29, the day the final negotiations on the package were completed.

CBO Recalculates the Numbers

When the dust had settled, the Congressional Budget Office (CBO) provided a more sober projection of the combined impact of the two bills. In its end-of-fiscal-year report issued in September, CBO estimated that the bills would provide a total of $115.7 billion in net deficit reduction over five years. That broke down into $195.7 billion in spending cuts ($88.8 billion from discretionary spending accounts and $106.9 billion from mandatory programs), partially offset by $80 billion in net tax cuts.

CBO also concluded that the two bills would not only result in a slight surplus in fiscal 2002, but that they would put the federal deficit on a path that "hovers near zero for the next 10 years."

Conflicting estimates of the effects of major deficit-reduction bills were not unusual. For one thing, the legislation was enormously complex. Also, those backing the bill often had a tendency to emphasize the best-case numbers. In an effort to standardize their assessments, budget experts tended after the fact to use CBO's estimates. However, the numbers used at the time the bills were being crafted and debated in Congress were the basis for decision-making and are the numbers used in the legislative history that follows.

The Foundations of Success

The negotiators were only able to draft a plan that satisfied staunch conservatives such as House Ways and Means Chairman Bill Archer, R-Texas, and liberals such as Sen. Edward M. Kennedy, D-Mass., because of the groundwork laid by the politically wrenching anti-deficit battles of 1990 and 1993.

And without a roaring economy churning out revenue greater than anyone expected, the agreement would not have been possible. "The true hero is this stupendous economy. . . . The economy has done more to reduce the deficit than the politicians have," said Martha Phillips, executive director of the Concord Coalition, a balanced-budget advocacy group. Referring to deficit-reduction packages enacted in 1990 and 1993, she added, "This is probably No. 3 in terms of size and momentousness, but it's the last little piece."

For budget purists, the final product put off until later the tough choices needed to address the crisis that would occur when the Baby Boomers began to retire and claim Social Security and health care benefits. While the Senate had voted to increase the eligibility age for Medicare coverage and take other dramatic cost-saving steps, the final bill did none of that, deferring to a bipartisan study commission.

The pact was also criticized for relying on predictions that there would be no recession in the next five years, as well as on discretionary spending caps that would not really bite until after the 2000 elections, and on one-time (and perhaps illusory) savings from auctions of the electromagnetic spectrum.

But for the overwhelming majority in Congress, which had been obsessed with the deficit since the 1980s, such long-term concerns were secondary to getting the deficit monkey off its back.

Background

The two bills grew out of bipartisan budget talks in the spring, primarily between congressional Republicans and the White House, that culminated in an agreement to balance the federal budget by 2002. *(Budget deal, p. 2-18)*

Though much remained to be nailed down, that agreement marked a dramatic shift from the rancorous, partisan budget warfare that had dominated the 104th Congress. When the Republican majority first stormed the Capitol in 1995, they vowed to eliminate the deficit, then about $200 billion, by 2002. To that end, they planned to cut projected spending by $894 billion over seven years, while also cutting taxes by $245 billion.

Republicans ended the 104th Congress far short of their goal. They could point to two principal areas of savings: $49 billion from reduced domestic appropriations and another $55 billion estimated to flow from the 1996 welfare overhaul law. And while they had successfully reframed the debate — Clinton and even liberal Democrats agreed on the goal of a balanced budget — Republicans lost the political battle by refusing to accept incremental gains, instead forcing two disruptive shutdowns of much of the federal government. *(1995 Almanac, 11-3; 1996 Almanac, 2-5)*

In the 1996 elections, Clinton savaged them as a threat to the future of Medicare. Although Republicans held onto the House, their margin was trimmed.

Budget Deal Paves the Way

As the 105th Congress began, both sides read the split electoral decision — a Clinton victory and GOP retention of control in Congress — as a mandate for bipartisanship. The vigorous growth of the economy provided a strong tailwind, giving both sides an opportunity to balance the budget with relatively little pain.

Full-fledged negotiations began in the spring, and Clinton and Republicans announced separately May 2 that a deal was at hand. The initial agreement, some of which was put into writing two weeks later, was still only a sketch, however. Many of the details were left to be filled in later by lawmakers writing the bills that would implement the deal. The next step came in June, when lawmakers adopted a bipartisan fiscal 1998 budget resolution (H Con Res 84) that reflected the budget agreement. *(Budget resolution, p. 2-23)*

The resolution, which received final approval June 5, called for two reconciliation bills — so named because they were intended to reconcile tax and spending policies with balanced-budget goals. One was designed to cut taxes, the other to reduce spending so as to balance the budget and finance the tax cuts. Authorizing committees in the House and Senate were assigned to contribute pieces of the two bills, with the most significant responsibility assigned to the House Ways and Means and Senate Finance committees, which had jurisdiction over both taxes and Medicare.

The committees got started even before the budget resolution became final. Their reconciliation proposals were sent to the House and Senate Budget committees, which in turn compiled them for floor action.

House/Senate Floor Action

The momentum quickened the week of June 23, as both chambers easily passed versions of the spending and tax bills that made up the reconciliation package.

In the House, the two measures moved on separate tracks, accompanied by highly partisan negotiations over possible changes. The spending bill passed 270-162, with only seven Republican "no" votes; Democrats opposed the bill by about 3:1. The vote on the tax bill was even more partisan: It passed, 253-179, with just one Republican opposed and only 27 Democrats voting "yes." *(Votes 241, 245, pp. H-76, H-78)*

By contrast, a bipartisan tone prevailed in the Senate as it worked through the two bills. The spending bill passed 73-27, with just three GOP defections. Democrats, deeply divided over proposals for Medicare means testing among others, split almost evenly, with 21 in favor and 24 voting "no." *(Vote 130, p. S-24)*

On the tax bill, Senate Republicans held all but four of their own. Democrats were still divided, but less so: 29 voted "yes," while 14 opposed the bill. The final tally was 80-18. *(Vote 160, p. S-28)*

Lawmakers left for the July Fourth recess, knowing they would return to an arduous and potentially explosive set of conference negotiations. They would have less than a month left if they were to meet the Republicans' goal of completing before Congress departed for the August recess.

Conference/Final Action

The final stage began July 10 and 11, as negotiators on the two bills convened ceremonial opening sessions.

Despite all the talks that had gone on before, a number of highly emotional issues remained to be resolved. Among them: whether to require higher-income senior citizens to pay bigger Medicare premiums on doctor bills, and whether to increase the eligibility age for the federal health insurance program. Also on the table: whether to retain a Senate-passed increase of 20 cents per pack in the cigarette tax to expand a new children's health care initiative, and which legal immigrants should be eligible for cash benefits for the elderly and disabled under the Supplemental Security Income program.

But the possibility of bringing the federal budget into balance for the first time since 1969, and producing the first sweeping tax cuts since Ronald Reagan came into office, propelled Republicans into the conference with a degree of flexibility that would have seemed unthinkable during the budget wars of 1995. "We're going to do everything we can to get the two bills signed by the president," said House Speaker Newt Gingrich, R-Ga.

Clinton, too, had an enormous stake in a successful outcome. His initiatives to expand child health care, provide education tax credits and increase spending on domestic priorities hung in the balance.

The first week yielded little visible progress. Negotiators met behind closed doors in 13 separate "subconferences" that seemed devoted largely to speechifying. In Republican-only strategy sessions there were divisions over whether to push for a quick deal with Clinton or try to keep the final package tilted toward the GOP agenda.

By July 18, Gingrich and Senate Majority Leader Trent Lott, R-Miss., had decided to exclude Democrats and White House officials and convene a smaller group of top Republicans to adopt a unified House-Senate GOP position. They staked out hard line positions on a number of hot-button issues that seemed certain to antagonize the White House, such as making the portion of capital gains attributable to inflation exempt from tax and refusing disability benefits to legal immigrants who became disabled after the 1996 welfare overhaul was signed into law.

Democrats had expressed some concern that Clinton might be too eager to close a deal and yield to Republican pressures. "Sometimes, you know," said George Miller, D-Calif., "he lays his cards down a little early."

But once serious talks began July 24, the Clinton administration showed no signs of backing down. Even Democrats who had been nervous that Clinton might cut a deal prematurely said they were more assured than they had been that he would play his cards well. "The president has a tremendous amount of leverage right now," said Sen. John D. Rockefeller IV, D-W.Va., one of a group of Democrats who huddled with Clinton at the White House on July 23.

Even the timing seemed to work in Clinton's favor. As their self-imposed deadline to get the bills finished before the August recess approached, Republicans were feeling more pressure than the Democrats. "We've said all along what we want is a good deal," said White House Chief of Staff Erskine Bowles. "That good deal could take one day or 30 days."

In addition, Clinton was enjoying a wave of popularity, with a record 64 percent approval rating in the Washington Post/ABC News poll. Public opinion surveys indicated he was winning the public-relations war over whether the GOP-drafted tax plans would give wealthier tax payers too high a percentage of the tax relief.

Meanwhile, House GOP leaders were reeling from the stunning and highly publicized revelation of a plot within their ranks to topple Gingrich. Republicans across the spectrum were anxious to get beyond the embarrassment of the aborted coup and deliver tax cuts and a balanced budget to their constituents. "You will see members support the compromise enthusiastically, given the fact that the overall agreement is 4-to-1 favorable . . . to the American people at a time where our conference needs to show that we can move the ball down the field," said Rep. Zach Wamp, R-Tenn. "If some people have to hold their nose and vote "yes" with a smile on their face, that's what they'll do." *(Gingrich, p. 1-11)*

Last-Minute Dealing

The final negotiations took place in the Capitol, including discussion over the July 26-27 weekend. Gingrich and Lott faced a White House team headed by Bowles, Treasury Secretary Robert E. Rubin and budget director Franklin D. Raines.

Negotiators made early progress on the spending bill, though snags emerged on such issues as how much money to dedicate to the new children's health initiative and a Clinton demand to give so-called workfare recipients the same rights under the Fair Labor Standards Act as regular workers. Clinton carried the day on both subjects, winning $24 billion over five years for children's health care and forcing Republicans to back down on welfare — although Armey and others pledged to revisit the issue in coming months.

After closing gaps in the tax bill, Lott emerged from his office on Monday, July 28, to declare a tentative agreement. "We gave ground, and the administration gave ground, and we found common ground," Lott said.

The news reached Clinton at a golf course in Las Vegas, where he was attending a meeting of the National Governors' Association. Although the president withheld public comment before returning to Washington, Bowles said, "We couldn't be more pleased with the outcome."

Still, smaller issues proved nettlesome. For example, Clinton issued an 11th-hour threat to veto the tax bill over a provision by Sen. Paul Coverdell, R-Ga., that would have permitted withdrawals from Individual Retirement Accounts to pay for private school tuition. The provision was quickly stripped.

The White House failed in a last-minute attempt to include a free-trade provision giving parity to island nations that were competing with Mexican exports favored under the North American Free Trade Agreement. And Finance Chairman Roth failed to get the White House to sign off on language that would have revamped Amtrak operations.

The next day, Republicans leaders gathered on the East Steps of the Capitol with a group of Boy Scouts from Georgia for a balloon festooned announcement of the deal. An exuberant House Budget Committee Chairman John R. Kasich, R-Ohio, dismissed questions about potential opposition on the House floor, declaring: "I'm beyond the vote count."

And buses took many congressional Democrats to a victory party at the South Lawn of the White House, where Clinton declared that the agreement would make the nation "stronger, more vibrant, more united than ever."

Exuberance on the Floor

Final passage in the House and Senate took place with remarkable ease.

On July 30, GOP leaders brought the spending bill to the House floor. Members rose in a standing ovation as Kasich declared this "the dawning of a new era, an era where we recognize the limits of government." The House adopted the conference report, 346-85, after a 90-minute debate, with much of the opposition coming from liberal Democrats, as well as tobacco-state lawmakers opposed to a higher cigarette tax. *(Vote 345, p. H-104)*

Moving with rare dispatch, the Senate cleared the spending bill July 31, 85-15, with liberals such as Kennedy and conservatives such as Majority Whip Don Nickles, R-Okla., joining in support. Lott was so caught up in the goodwill of the moment that he told his colleagues he was ready to hum "Hail to the Chief." *(Vote 209, p. S-36)*

Lawmakers in both parties and both chambers voted for the conference report on the tax bill July 31 by overwhelming margins.

In the House, the tally was 389-43, with just one Republican, Tom Campbell of California, opposed. In the Senate, the vote was 92-8, with all the "nay" votes cast by liberal Democrats. *(House vote 350, p. H-106; Senate vote 211, p. S-36)*

Even as lawmakers raced to go home and tout their accomplishments, however, there were a few skunks at the picnic. Some liberals worried that the benefits would accrue mostly to the better-off, and a handful of deficit hawks attacked the end result as a missed opportunity to address demographic and generational problems that loomed when Baby Boomers began to retire.

House Minority Leader Richard A. Gephardt, D-Mo., the most prominent dissenter, attacked the final bills as unfairly tilted toward the wealthy and insufficiently aggressive on the deficit. "Unfortunately, this agreement sacrifices tomorrow's hopes for today's headlines," Gephardt said. And in the Senate, Republican Phil Gramm of Texas worried that the agreement would do little to contain the burgeoning costs of entitlement programs such as Medicare. ■

Reconciliation Package: Tax Cuts

BOXSCORE

Tax Reconciliation — HR 2014 (S 949). The tax portion of the budget-reconciliation package provided for $95 billion in net tax cuts over five years and $275 billion over 10 years.

Reports: H Rept 105-148, S Rept 105-33; conference report, H Rept 105-220.

KEY ACTION

June 26 — House passed HR 2014, 253-179.

June 27 — Senate passed HR 2014, 80-18, after substituting the text of S 949.

July 31 — House adopted the conference report, 389-43; **Senate** cleared the bill, 92-8.

Aug. 5 — President signed HR 2014 — PL 105-34.

With Republicans committed to cutting individual and corporate tax rates and Democrats promising to aid low- and middle-income workers, Congress succeeded in clearing the deepest tax cut since 1981. The biggest benefits went to those who had children, sought higher education, had capital gains on investments or wanted to save for retirement

The compromise tax package — which grew out of the bipartisan balanced-budget agreement reached in May — won overwhelming approval in both chambers July 31. President Clinton signed it into law Aug. 5 (HR 2014 — PL 105-34).

The price of such comity, however, was a highly complicated bill that contained more tax cuts than could fit within the parameters agreed to in May. The price tag on the final bill was $95 billion in net tax cuts over five years, growing to $275 billion over 10 years. The original agreement was for $85 billion in net cuts over five years and $250 billion over 10 years.

To keep from busting the limits even more, negotiators used a host of convoluted provisions to constrain short-term costs and push the revenue losses into future years.

The tax-reduction measure was one of a pair of budget-reconciliation bills that aimed to eliminate the federal deficit by 2002 while providing significant tax cuts. That overarching goal, and some of the details for getting there, had been agreed to during lengthy bipartisan negotiations that culminated in a balanced-budget accord announced May 2. *(Budget deal, p. 2-18; reconciliation, p. 2-27)*

While the tax and spending bills moved through Congress in tandem, the tax package was, by all accounts, the more difficult of the two to complete. It ultimately succeeded because it gave major victories to both sides.

Republican gains included the largest reduction in capital gains tax rates since 1981, a $500-per-child tax credit, a significant increase in the tax exemption for estates, and an expansion of tax-preferred Individual Retirement Account (IRA) savings plans.

Clinton and his Democratic allies won hefty new tax incentives for education, and they managed to shape the $500-per-child tax credit to make it available to most working poor families, including some too poor to owe any income taxes.

Clinton joined with congressional Democrats on the South Lawn of the White House on July 29 to announce agreement on the bill. He thanked the GOP leadership for "work[ing] with us across the lines of substantial philosophical and practical differences to reach a good faith agreement that is an honorable and principled compromise."

Charles B. Rangel of New York, top Democrat on the House Ways and Means Committee, expressed relief: "We have now shattered the myth that we are spending Democrats and taxing Democrats," he said.

Republicans made their own announcement on the steps of the Capitol, surrounded by Boy Scouts from Georgia and other visitors. Senate Budget Chairman Pete V. Domenici of New Mexico, veteran of many budget wars, was euphoric. "I've been working at a balanced budget for two decades now, and so I'm kind of overwhelmed," he said. "But I think it's time that we in the Congress who claim we're the adult leaders of America pay our own bills and not pass the bills on to our children."

Gross tax cuts in the final package were about $152 billion over five years, with an offset of $56 billion in tax increases, according to estimates by the Joint Committee on Taxation. Over 10 years, the gross tax cut was projected to be $401 billion, with $126 billion in offsetting tax increases.

Still, it was a modest plan when compared with the tax cuts that Republicans had crusaded for when they took control of Congress in 1995. Their target then: $600 billion in tax cuts over 10 years. In reality, the final number was not a great deal more generous than the net five-year, $75 billion figure that Clinton had offered before budget negotiations blew up at the end of 1995.

Tax experts noted that the tax cut was about one-tenth the size of President Ronald Reagan's legendary 1981 income tax reduction — and that it was much more complicated.

"The middle class is going to enjoy the same complexity that previously we restricted to the wealthy," said former Congressional Budget Office Director Robert D. Reischauer, a senior fellow at the Brookings Institution. "You're going to have to be a masochist to do your tax return yourself," agreed economist Rudolph G. Penner, another former CBO director.

Tax Bill Highlights

Major elements of the tax bill included:

- **Child tax credit.** A $500-per-child tax credit ($400-per-child in 1998) for families with children under age 17. The full credit would be available to single filers with up to $75,000 in adjusted gross income and married couples with up to $110,000. The credit was partially refundable to low-income families with three or more children, which meant that the parents could receive it as a payment even if they owed no income tax.

The child tax credit accounted for more than half the bill's gross five-year tax cuts; making it more available to low-income families was the main factor in increasing the overall size of the tax bill.

- **Education.** Eleven education tax incentives, including:
  - A non-refundable HOPE tax credit of as much as $1,500 per student for each of the first two years of college. Joint filers with up to $80,000 in adjusted gross income ($40,000 for single filers) would be eligible for the full credit.
  - A non-refundable lifetime learning credit worth up to $1,000 per year through 2002, rising to a maximum of $2,000 per year after that.
  - A new education savings account. Individuals could make non-deductible contributions of up to $500 per child per year and withdraw the principal and earnings tax free to help pay for a child's college or graduate education.
  - Penalty-free withdrawals from all IRAs for education expenses.
- **Capital gains.** A cut in the maximum individual tax rate on capital gains from 28 percent to 20 percent for investments held for more than 18 months, dropping to 18 percent after 2000 for assets held for at least five years.

In addition, the bill provided a capital gains tax exemption for profits from the sale of a primary residence. Single filers could exempt up to $250,000; couples filing jointly could exempt up to $500,000.

- **IRAs.** A new, "back-loaded" savings acount, known as the "Roth IRA" after its chief sponsor, Senate Finance Committee Chairman William V. Roth Jr., R-Del. While contributions were not tax deductible, the principal and earnings could be withdrawn tax free after five years if the holder was age 59 1/2, disabled or deceased, or the money was used for a first-time home purchase. Taxpayers with adjusted gross incomes up to $100,000 could convert their existing IRAs to Roth IRAs after paying taxes on the funds.

The bill also increased the existing income limit for individuals making tax-free contributions to traditional IRAs, and it allowed penalty-free withdrawals to finance a first-time home or for educational purposes.

- **Estate tax.** A gradual increase in the amount exempt from gift and estate taxes from $600,000 to $1 million by 2007, and an immediate increase to $1.3 million in the exemption for family farms and businesses.
- **Corporate AMT.** Repeal of the alternative minimum tax (AMT) for small businesses and a faster depreciation schedule for large businesses.
- **Gasoline tax.** Repeal of a requirement that 4.3 cents per gallon in federal gasoline taxes go to deficit reduction. Instead, the money, like the rest of the gasoline tax, was dedicated to the Highway Trust Fund, a shift sought by proponents of increased highway spending.
- **Airline ticket tax.** The bill reduced the tax on domestic airline tickets from 10 percent to 7.5 percent, but it added a new per-passenger fee for each flight segment — $1 per segment in 1998, rising to $3 in 2002. Also, the existing $6 departure tax on international fights was replaced with a tax of $12 each for arrivals and departures.

The estimated revenue from the airline tax provisions was $33.2 billion over five years and $79.7 over 10 years. Because the existing tax had expired, the full amount was counted as deficit reduction.

Background

House Budget Chairman John R. Kasich, R-Ohio, and other Republican negotiators had tried to settle many of the details of the tax bill during balanced-budget talks in the spring. But they were blocked by protests from House Ways and Means Committee Chairman Bill Archer, R-Texas, who insisted on retaining jurisdiction over the tax provisions.

As a result, the bipartisan budget agreement reached in May specified little more than that net tax cuts would equal $85 billion over five years and $250 billion over 10 years. Republican lawmakers hoped that the gross tax cuts in the final bill would reach $135 billion over five years and as much as $350 billion over 10 years.

Two side letters from the GOP leadership provided some additional detail. The first stated that the cuts would include a permanent, broad-based capital gains tax cut, a $500-per-child tax credit, expanded IRAs, a reduction in the estate tax and "roughly" $35 billion over five years to help middle-income families pay postsecondary education costs.

The second letter said that Congress' Joint Committee on Taxation would consult with the Treasury Department on how to estimate the cost of the tax provisions. In the past, Joint Tax and Treasury had disagreed, especially on how to score capital gains tax cuts.

That still left a great deal of bargaining for the summer when it came time to write the myriad tax provisions into law.

There was significant disagreement between House and Senate Republicans over which tax cuts and credits should be included in the bill. Those negotiations proved far more difficult than the debate over the companion spending bill (HR 2015). Among the most contentious issues were the size and scope of corporate tax breaks (the House wanted to lower the corporate capital gains tax rate and the corporate AMT, while the Senate sought neither) and eligibility for the $500-per-child tax credit (the Senate wanted to make it partially refundable, meaning that workers too poor to owe income taxes could still take advantage of it; the House rejected that as "welfare").

Clinton raised the stakes in late June, insisting that the tax package be aimed at middle-income and working-poor families. Republicans reacted at first by producing a bill in closed-door, GOP-only negotiations that moved away from Clinton and toward the House version of the package on such key issues as making the $500-per-child tax credit non-refundable.

But within days, after another round of tense negotiations, the GOP challenge dissipated and a final deal was struck. Some of the partisan bitterness lingered, however, evidenced in the separate announcements held by the two sides July 29.

Line-Item Veto

On Aug. 11, Clinton used his new line-item veto authority for the first time to strike two relatively obscure provisions from the bill. As required under the 1996 line-item veto law (PL 104-130), the Joint Committee on Taxation had identified 79 "limited tax benefits" that were expected to benefit 100 or fewer taxpayers, or "transition rules" that would help 10 or fewer taxpayers. *(Line-item veto, p. 2-63; 1996 Almanac, p. 2-28)*

The items selected by Clinton were a provision to permit deferral of taxes on the sale of food-processing facilities sold to farmer co-operatives, and language sought by the financial services industry to allow banks and other institutions to defer taxes on interest income that was produced by overseas subsidiaries and subject to taxes by the host country.

Lawmakers and the White House ultimately agreed on

compromise language, but efforts to pass it as separate legislation before Congress adjourned for the year were not successful. *(Reconcilation vetoes, p. 2-61)*

House Ways and Means Committee

The tax bill began in the House Ways and Means Committee, which approved its version, 22-16, after an acrimonious two-day markup that began June 12 and ran into the predawn hours of the following day. The draft received no Democratic votes.

Because the measure was a budget-reconciliation bill, the job of reporting it to the floor fell to the Budget Committee. The budget panel agreed, 20-12, on June 20 to send the bill to the full House (H Rept 105-148).

The Ways and Means package proposed to cut taxes by $133 billion over five years, offset by $48 billion in tax increases, for a net tax cut of $85 billion — the target set in the May accord and the budget resolution. The offsetting revenues came mostly from a proposal to expand excise taxes on airline tickets.

Archer had scaled back his initial proposals for corporate tax breaks under pressure from GOP leaders. But the measure still faced criticism from rank-and-file Republicans who were being pressed by lobbyists to tilt the bill's benefits more toward farmers and small-business owners and less toward big corporations.

The conservative Archer held his ground during the markup, but he conceded that his version of the bill was not what Clinton wanted and that changes were inevitable. "We want to continue to work with the president [to produce] a bill he can sign," Archer said. "We would not be here today without his cooperation."

Committee Provisions

As approved by the committee, the bill included the following major proposals:

- **Child tax credit.** A $400 credit in 1998, rising to $500 in 1999, for each child under age 17. The full credit would be available to couples with up to $110,000 annually in adjusted gross income, and single filers with up to $75,000. Poor working families eligible for the refundable earned-income tax credit (EITC) could only get the child credit if they still owed taxes after counting the EITC.

After 1999, the child credit would be reduced by one-half the amount taken under the existing dependent care credit. This provision would apply to couples with more than $60,000 in adjusted gross income ($33,000 for single filers).

- **Education.** $31 billion in education tax incentives, including a non-refundable HOPE credit of up to $1,500 per student for each of the first two years of college. The full credit would be available to single filers with up to $40,000 a year in gross adjusted income and couples making up to $80,000 per year.

Alternatively, parents could take a deduction of up to $10,000 per student in a given year (up to a cumulative total of $40,000 per student) for money withdrawn from a special education investment account or a qualified pre-paid tuition program and used to pay for higher education. The special education account would be similar to an IRA; a taxpayer could invest up to $5,000 a year per student in after-tax contributions.

- **Capital gains.** A cut in the maximum tax rate on individual capital gains — profits from the sale of investments — from 28 percent to 20 percent. For taxpayers in the 15 percent bracket, the rate would drop from 15 percent to 10 percent. After 2000, gains on assets held more than three years would be indexed to inflation, making the portion of the gain that was due to inflation tax exempt.

The top corporate capital gains would be reduced to 30 percent by 2000 for assets held more than eight years. Under existing law, corporate capital gains were taxed as ordinary income, with a top rate of 35 percent.

- **AMT.** Repeal of the alternative minimum tax for small businesses — those with $5 million or less in gross annual receipts. Larger businesses would be allowed to use faster depreciation schedules than under existing law.

The bill also proposed a gradual increase in the amount of individual income exempt from the AMT. From 1999 to 2007, the exemption would increase by $1,000 per year for married couples and $750 per year for single filers; after that, it would be indexed for inflation.

- **Estate tax.** A gradual increase in the amount exempt from gift and estate taxes — from $600,000 under existing law to $1 million by 2007; the exemption would be indexed for inflation after 2007.
- **IRAs.** A new IRA to which individuals at any income level could make nondeductible contributions of up to $2,000 a year. Principal and interest could be withdrawn tax free after five years if the holder was 59-1/2, disabled or deceased, or the money was used to finance the purchase of a first home. The $2,000 would be in addition to contributions made to a traditional, tax-deductible IRA.

Democrats Shut Out

A Democratic alternative that had Clinton's endorsement and the backing of the full Democratic caucus — from the most liberal members to the most conservative — was rejected on a party-line vote.

The Democratic proposal had many of the same elements as the GOP bill — a per-child tax credit, a capital gains tax cut, education tax breaks, estate tax relief and expanded IRAs — but every provision was designed to give the maximum benefit to low- and middle-income workers and their families.

For example, the Democrats' version of the $500-per-child tax credit was limited to couples with adjusted gross annual incomes of less than $75,000 instead of $110,000 as in the GOP bill. The capital gains cut — with a top rate of 18 percent — was restricted to the first $600,000 in gains over a lifetime. The education tax credits were similar to those offered by Clinton but were more beneficial to low-income students, allowing them to use both the Clinton tax credit and a Pell grant scholarship to offset the costs of tuition.

Protest Precedes Markup

Archer's bill provoked an outcry even before the markup. When Archer announced the details June 9, Clinton and House Democrats quickly charged that he had violated the spirit, if not the letter, of the May budget agreement. "Every part is skewed against low-income people," said Rangel. "I don't find any violation of what was put down in the agreement, it's just that he pushed this envelope as far to the right as he could." Clinton weighed in June 10, saying Archer's plan was not "consistent with the budget agreement."

According to the Treasury Department's distributional tables, families with adjusted gross incomes in the top 20 percent — or above $93,222 a year — stood to get 67.9 percent of the bill's tax cuts when they were fully phased in. Congress' Joint Tax Committee disputed those numbers, saying more than half the benefits would go to taxpayers with incomes below the top fifth, although the committee's distributional tables did not show the effect of the tax bill when it was fully phased in.

Archer also faced serious rebukes from within his own party. GOP lawmakers said they were uncomfortable with the size of the proposed corporate tax breaks and with provisions that would impose a new tax on Indian tribal income from gambling casinos, and eliminate an existing tax break for ethanol.

Hot-Button Issues

• **AMT vs. estate tax relief.** Before the markup, Republican leaders nixed a plan by Archer to give a smaller break than advocates wanted for estate taxes in order to make room for a very expensive proposal to repeal the corporate AMT. Archer was perhaps the most ardent supporter in Congress of such a repeal, which was projected to cost almost $34 billion over 10 years.

Inserted in the tax code as part of the 1986 overhaul, the corporate AMT was intended to ensure that all corporations paid at least some income tax. Archer had repeatedly tried to repeal it, arguing that it was too complicated.

However, lowering the estate tax was the No. 1 priority for the small-business lobby, a staunch friend of the GOP. Estate tax relief was also a favorite cause of Senate Majority Leader Trent Lott, R-Miss.

Under Archer's original draft, the increase in the estate tax exemption from $600,000 to $1 million would have taken 17 years to complete. According to advocates, that would not have kept up with inflation.

When the provision became public, a cry of indignation went up from lobbyists for the National Federation of Independent Business (NFIB), the Association of Wholesaler-Distributors, the National Retail Federation and the Farm Bureau. Within hours, they had launched a campaign among the congressional rank and file and the leadership aimed at forcing Archer to rewrite the bill.

Their protests fell on sympathetic ears. "We voiced our concerns to the chairman," said John A. Boehner, R-Ohio, chairman of the Republican Conference. "The AMT [repeal] may be good policy, but we open ourselves up to political attacks," he said, referring to Democratic reminders that in the pre-AMT days of the early 1980s, a number of very profitable corporations paid no taxes at all.

The leadership forced Archer to confine the AMT repeal to small corporations — those with gross receipts of less than $5 million a year — and accelerate the estate tax cut. The change was made in advance of the committee markup.

• **Ethanol.** Rural Republicans, who lent their support to the increase in the estate tax, also balked at a proposal by Archer to terminate the tax credit for ethanol, a fuel made from corn. A bipartisan effort to amend the bill to restore the ethanol tax credit failed, 17-21.

Jim Nussle, R-Iowa, underscored the depth of Farm Belt feeling about the ethanol provision by becoming the only Republican to vote against the committee bill.

Archer had waged an identical fight — and lost — in 1995. During the drafting of the tax bill that was part of the House GOP's "Contract With America," Speaker Newt Gingrich, R-Ga., forced Archer to remove the proposed termination of the ethanol credit before the bill went to the floor because of threats of revolt from Farm Belt Republicans. *(1995 Almanac, p. 2-71)*

• **Indian gaming.** Like ethanol, Indian gaming was a regional issue; it pitted lawmakers whose states had private casinos or riverboat gambling against those with Indian tribes that ran casinos.

Archer's original draft would have levied income taxes on all commercial businesses run by Indian tribes. According to Joint Tax Committee analysts, 80 percent of the revenues would have come from a tax on gambling income.

Attorney General Janet Reno sent a letter to committee members saying the administration opposed the provision because it had potential constitutional problems and violated a history of avoiding taxation of Indian tribes, which were considered sovereign nations.

J.D. Hayworth, R-Ariz., whose state had one of the largest Indian populations in the country, led the fight to eliminate the proposal and rallied enough of his colleagues to defeat Archer, who spoke passionately against Hayworth's effort. "You may win this amendment tonight, and it is not a personal affront to this chairman, but it is an affront to business people across this country who pay taxes," he said, waving a General Accounting Office report that charted how much tribes' revenues had risen since they began to operate casinos.

Hayworth's amendment won, 22-16, with seven Republicans banding with united Democrats.

• **Airline tax.** Despite considerable resistance from the aviation industry, the Ways and Means Committee agreed to a complicated plan to increase aviation taxes by about $34 billion over five years and $82.3 billion over 10 years.

Under the committee-approved bill, the existing 10 percent tax was to be divided into two separate levies on domestic flights: a 7.5 percent ticket tax and a per-passenger charge on each segment of a flight. The per-passenger charge would start at $2 in fiscal 1998 and gradually increase to $3 in fiscal 2002.

The plan essentially split the difference between discount airlines that preferred the existing 10 percent ticket tax, and hub-and-spoke airlines that were lobbying for various per-passenger and per-mile charges. *(Airline tax, p. 3-28)*

In addition, the committee proposed increasing the per-passenger charge on international departures from $6 to $10, and levying a new $10 charge on international arrivals.

Those charges were further increased to $15.50 each way under a portion of Hayworth's amendment intended to make up for the revenue that would have come from taxing gambling and other commercial activities of American Indian tribes.

Finally, the bill included a 7.5 percent tax on frequent flier miles that credit card and other companies purchased from airlines (usually for about 2 cents per mile) to reward to their customers.

The airline industry bitterly fought the package, with corporate chief executives flying to Washington to lobby against it personally. They said that every 1 percent increase in fare prices would reduce passenger traffic by a corresponding 1 percent.

"None of us likes it," committee member Rob Portman, R-Ohio, said of the proposed tax increases. "But there's an acknowledgment on the part of members that we need that revenue in order to give needed tax relief."

House Floor Action

The House passed the bill June 26 on a 253-179 tally, with a nearly unified Democratic caucus voting against the package. Only 27 Democrats voted "yes" — the same number that voted for the GOP's Contract With America tax-cut bill in 1995. Republicans lost only one of their own. House consideration of the tax bill followed earlier passage of the companion spending bill. *(Vote 245, p. H-78)*

Archer overcame many of the earlier GOP criticisms by agreeing to several modifications that were incorporated into the bill as part of the rule for floor debate (H Res 174).

Foremost among the changes, Archer agreed to retain the tax credit for ethanol. He also agreed to modify the per-child and dependent care tax credits so that joint taxpayers with adjusted gross incomes of under $60,000 could claim both credits in full. Under the committee bill, in 2002, the $500-per-child-tax credit would have been reduced by half for taxpayers who also claimed the dependent and child care credit.

Archer also offered a break to airline companies by delaying for two weeks the deadline for depositing the proposed ticket tax in 1998, thereby allowing the airlines an additional two weeks to invest the tax revenues.

Sharply Partisan Debate

During the rancorous 4-1/2 hour floor debate, Republicans and Democrats sparred over the fairness of the proposed tax cuts, with both sides claiming their proposals were best for middle-income Americans.

It was clear that the per-child tax credit would be one of the stickiest points as the bill moved through Congress. The core dispute involved whether the working poor who paid little or no income taxes should be eligible for the credit in the form of a check that in theory would offset their payroll taxes.

"This is a bill for people who pay income taxes. It will be very hard for the American people to accept the president's proposal to increase welfare spending by providing tax relief to people who pay no taxes," said Archer.

But Clinton and the Democrats wanted the $500 tax credit to be fully refundable. "It is, to me, a breathtaking conclusion," said Minority Leader Richard A. Gephardt of Missouri, "to say that people that work hard every day and are out there trying to support their family are somehow welfare recipients because they get the earned-income credit."

On another issue, conservative and moderate Democrats expressed fears that the bill would cause the deficit to explode in the years not covered by the budget accord. Charles W. Stenholm, D-Texas, a deficit hawk who often sided with Republicans on budget issues, argued that the potential deficit due to the tax cuts in the years beyond the scope of the budget agreement would "overwhelm any benefit that this tax cut will have in the short run."

Chafing against Democratic arguments that the tax cuts would benefit the rich, Republicans said Democrats were relying on "class warfare" and distorting the definition of "rich" to refute Republican goals. "You're making everybody in America rich trying to get the numbers up," said Lindsey Graham, R-S.C.

"For too long, liberals have treated the middle class as their personal ATM machine — a cash cow," said Bill Paxon, R-N.Y.

But Democrats said the bill would do little for the poorest Americans. Rangel repeatedly cited statistics showing that about half the children in many states would not be eligible for the child credit. Said Gephardt: "We want everybody to have a tax cut, but we want the lion's share to go to hard-working, middle-class families and families struggling to get into the middle class."

Democratic Substitute Rejected

The only amendment allowed under the rule — a Democratic substitute offered by Rangel — was defeated on a nearly party-line vote, 197-235. *(Vote 243, p. H-78)*

As they had in committee, Democrats sought to limit the tax cuts that would go to higher-income investors in areas such as capital gains. They called for restricting the per-child tax credit to couples with adjusted gross incomes of less than $75,000 annually, as opposed to the $110,000 in the GOP bill, and for making the child credit refundable.

Barred by the rule from offering a separate amendment, conservative "Blue Dog" Democrats led by Collin C. Peterson of Minnesota offered a motion to recommit the bill to the committee with instructions to target the capital gains tax reduction to investors who held the assets for longer periods, as well as to increase the amount exempt from estate taxes. The proposal was defeated 164-268, with both liberal Democrats and the majority of Republicans opposing it. *(Vote 244, p. H-78)*

Though Treasury Secretary Robert E. Rubin wrote Gingrich saying the administration "strongly opposes" the House bill, Gingrich and fellow Republicans were exultant over the passage of their tax-cut measure. "We're going home for the Fourth of July break with a very good sense that we did what the American people sent us here to do," Gingrich said.

Senate Finance Committee

In contrast to the sharp wrangling over the House bill, the Senate Finance Committee approved a bipartisan draft bill June 19 by a vote of 18-2. Every Democrat voted for the measure; the "no" votes came from two conservative Republicans, Don Nickles of Oklahoma and Phil Gramm of Texas, who blasted decisions to raise the tobacco tax and increase spending for children's health.

The bill, which Roth subsequently introduced as S 949 (S Rept 105-33), provided for $77 billion in net tax cuts over five years. That was $8 billion less than the amount allowed in the budget resolution and approved by the House Ways and Means Committee, though S 949 did meet the $135 billion in gross cuts allowed by the budget deal. The net 10-year tax cut, like that in the House bill, was roughly $250 billion.

The bill won ringing endorsement from committee Democrats who spanned the ideological spectrum from centrists like John B. Breaux of Louisiana to liberals like Carol Moseley-Braun of Illinois and John D. Rockefeller IV of West Virginia.

Freewheeling Markup Transforms Bill

The bipartisan bill came out of a freewheeling markup that surprised just about everyone.

When committee members went behind closed doors to winnow the 110 amendments that senators wanted to add to the measure, they were expected to return in a couple of hours with a few modifications.

But as the hours dragged on and the ranks of lobbyists outside the committee room swelled to more than 200, it was clear that more was at stake than minor changes. At one point, most of the staff was even asked to leave the room.

When the senators emerged eight hours later, they unveiled a startling bipartisan deal that called for nearly doubling the federal cigarette tax from 24 cents per pack to 44 cents. The resulting revenue — as much as $15 billion over five years, according to initial estimates — allowed for horse-trading in a number of other areas.

About half the money was targeted for new block grants to states for children's health care. Nearly $3.5 billion was used to reduce the ticket tax on international flights that Roth had included in the draft bill. About $800 million went to boost the capital gains tax break for real estate, and $3 billion was used to increase the number of working poor families that would be eligible for the $500-per-child tax credit.

Another significant amendment added in committee proposed taking the 4.3 cents-per-gallon gas tax that had been dedicated to deficit reduction since 1993 and deposit it into the highway trust fund. A laundry list of 28 special-interest amendments requested by Finance Committee members also was added to the bill.

In 90 minutes of public discussion that preceded the final vote, the mood among Finance Committee members was victorious. "We're going to work as a bipartisan team," Roth said. "We combined the best ideas from both sides of the aisle and both ends of Pennsylvania Avenue." Roth drew extravagant praise from panel Democrats, led by ranking member Daniel Patrick Moynihan of New York, for including them fully in drafting the bill.

The Finance Committee deal came together as a result of a combination of forces that virtually no one had foreseen. Chief among them was intense lobbying by the seven major airline companies for a reduction in the proposed ticket tax and by the real estate industry for a bigger capital gains tax break.

Because nine proposed amendments called for increased tobacco taxes to offset reduced levies on real estate, estates and other items, it was clear that if the Finance Committee did not act, there were enough votes for a higher tobacco tax on the floor. Panel members made the calculation that they would rather control how the revenue was spent, Breaux said.

Hatch led the charge to put some of the revenue into children's health care, warning colleagues not to underestimate how the Democrats would pillory them if they raised the tobacco tax but did nothing for children. Backing him up were fellow Republicans John H. Chafee of Rhode Island, Alfonse M. D'Amato of New York and Frank H. Murkowski of Alaska.

Democrats were more than happy to add money for children's health, and if the price was helping airlines and real estate, they had no complaints. Many of them had drafted amendments of their own to help those industries.

Clinton Hints at Compromise

Overall, Clinton indicated he preferred the Finance Committee approach to that of the Ways and Means bill, though Treasury Secretary Rubin still complained to Roth that the Finance bill skewed the proposed tax cuts too much toward upper-income taxpayers.

In fact, Clinton appeared to be preparing Democrats — especially liberals — for the possibility that he would pick his tax battles carefully and was resigned to a tax cut that tilted toward the rich. In an interview published June 19 in The Wall Street Journal, Clinton said, "The distribution pattern of any tax plan will look somewhat skewed to upper-income people if there is any kind of capital gains tax and estate tax relief in it. But that was the price of a [budget] agreement."

Barbs were quick in coming from liberal Democrats who disagreed with the Finance Committee's approach and were disappointed that Clinton had held his fire. "The president could and should and must be a lot stronger," said Paul Wellstone, D-Minn. "If Democrats don't stand for tax breaks for working families more than for the wealthy, then what do Democrats stand for?"

Senate Bill Highlights

As approved by the Finance Committee, the bill included the following major proposals:

- **Child tax credit.** A $500-per-child tax credit for children under age 17 (age 18 after 2002). For children ages 13-16 (13-17 after 2002) the credit would have to be deposited into an education savings account or a prepaid tuition program. The adjusted gross income thresholds for the full credit were the same as in the House bill: $75,000 for single filers, $110,000 for couples.

The Senate bill moved in Clinton's direction by allowing for eligible low-income families to take half the EITC after taking the per-child credit. The Senate bill did not link the credit to the separate dependent care credit.

- **Education.** Incentives similar to those in the House bill, including an almost identical tax credit. The bill also included an education investment account, but instead of allowing a $10,000 deduction for withdrawals as in the House bill, any amount could be withdrawn tax free if the money was used for tuition, room, board or graduate education. Taxpayers could put $2,000 of after-tax dollars into the account, in addition to money from the child tax credit.
- **Capital gains.** A reduction of the top individual rate, like that in the House bill, from 28 percent to 20 percent. However, the Senate bill did not call for indexing gains for inflation, nor did it call for a reduction in the corporate capital gains rate.
- **AMT.** No reduction in the corporate AMT. For individuals, exemptions allowed in calculating the AMT would be increased, though at different rates than provided in the House bill.
- **Estate tax.** A gradual increase from $600,000 to $1 million over 10 years.
- **IRAs.** A new backloaded IRA, similar to that in the House bill. The Senate also proposed raising the income limits on taxpayers eligible to use traditional tax-deferred IRAs and removing the existing rule that barred an individual from using a tax-deferred IRA merely because his or her spouse had an employer-sponsored retirement plan.
- **Airline ticket tax.** Continuation of the 10 percent tax for domestic fights. The Senate proposed to replace the $6 departure tax for international flights with an $8 tax each on arrivals and departures, plus a 10 percent tax on the domestic segments of international flights.
- **Tobacco tax.** A 20-cents-per-pack increase in the federal tobacco tax.

Senate Floor Action

The Senate took up the tax bill June 27, one day after the House had acted, and passed it 80-18, with 29 Democratic votes including that of Minority Leader Tom Daschle of South Dakota. "There's a lot of good things in it," Daschle said, though he continued to criticize some of the provisions as unnecessarily favoring the wealthiest. (The Senate voted on HR 2014, after substituting the amended text of its own bill.) *(Vote 160, p. S-28)*

Lott all but disowned some provisions of the bill and predicted they might disappear "as we pass through the Rotunda" to conference. In particular, he said he opposed the increased tobacco taxes and would demand that the net tax cut of $77 billion over five years be increased to the full $85 billion allowed by the budget resolution and included in the House bill.

Senate GOP leaders worked to bury amendments from their own ranks that threatened to undermine the Finance Committee version of the bill. Though conservatives were frustrated by the final product, most backed the leadership in the final vote. "Most of us recognize that while we haven't done as much as we'd like to do . . . it's a step in the right direction," said Wayne Allard, R-Colo.

Major Amendments

- **Democratic substitute.** Daschle offered a substitute amendment that would have made the child credit refundable, targeted a sizeable portion of the capital gains tax cuts to investments in small and start-up companies, and created a special estate tax exemption for family-owned businesses and farms.

The amendment failed, 38-61, with seven Democrats voting against it; six were Finance Committee members who felt bound to resist all efforts to change the committee package. *(Vote 134, p. S-25)*

- **Capital gains.** The Senate defeated two attempts by Byron L. Dorgan, D-N.D., to restrict the capital gains break. The first, rejected 24-75, would have imposed a $1 million lifetime cap on an individual's capital gains deductions. *(Vote 132, p. S-25)*

A second Dorgan amendment — to temporarily halt the capital gains tax cut after 2002 if the budget was not in balance — failed, 34-64, on a procedural vote. *(Vote 133, p. S-25)*

The Senate also rejected, 41-57, an amendment by Allard to index capital gains for inflation. *(Vote 159, p. S-28)*

- **Tobacco tax.** The sharpest exchanges on the Senate floor came over proposals to increase federal tobacco taxes.

Tobacco-state members were critical of the Finance Committee's proposal for a 20-cents-per-pack increase, and the debate became a shouting match when several senators tried to increase the tax even further.

Freshman Richard J. Durbin, D-Ill., proposed an additional 10 to 11 cents in order to expand the tax deduction for health insurance for the self-employed. Later, Edward M. Kennedy, D-Mass., tried to add 23 cents, in part to provide full health insurance for children who had none.

"I have 65,000 farm families that this legislation will put out of business," said Wendell H. Ford, D-Ky. "You take care of my farmers, and I'll talk about taxes after that." Durbin, an anti-tobacco crusader, said coldly: "The product you defend kills people."

Durbin's amendment was defeated, 41-58, on a procedural motion; Kennedy's fell, 30-70, also on a motion of procedure. *(Votes 137, 149, pp. S-25, S-27)*

Clinton Weighs In

In anticipation of a House-Senate conference on the bill, Clinton released a revised tax cut plan of his own June 30, staking out a position for Democrats and making clear his price for approving the final product.

Clinton proposed gross tax cuts of $135 billion over five years and $341 billion over 10 years. The net cut, as agreed to in the May budget pact, was $85 billion over five years and $241 billion over 10 years.

Although Clinton had previously criticized both the House and Senate tax bills in detail, this was the administration's first comprehensive proposal since the president's fiscal 1998 budget was submitted to Congress on Feb. 6.

The White House proposal tracked closely most of the elements in the House and Senate Democratic proposals. It also included versions of several key GOP proposals, including a capital gains tax cut and a significant reduction in estate taxes for small businesses and farms. *(Clinton plan, p. 2-37)*

Most notably, Clinton's plan included $122 billion in education-related tax cuts over 10 years, more than in either the House or Senate version. Clinton aimed his education tax cuts almost entirely at middle- and lower-income taxpayers by proposing credits to offset tuition costs. In contrast, the GOP bills devoted nearly one-third of the education tax cuts to IRAs that targeted education. Lower-income taxpayers typically lacked the money to contribute to an IRA, so the benefit would be enjoyed primarily by higher-income people.

"Just as a tax cut bill is the Republicans' crown jewel, our crown jewel is the education piece," said a White House aide. "If they are going to get a tax bill, we've got to get our education piece and it has to have signature-type Clinton stuff."

Clinton's new capital gains proposal — to allow taxpayers to exclude up to 30 percent of a gain from taxation — was designed to minimize benefits to high-income taxpayers; their effective capital gains tax rate would drop by less than 1 percent under the plan.

Conference

The surface similarities between the House and Senate bills, both of which sought to implement the balanced-budget agreement, obscured the political and the policy differences that separated the two chambers.

Beyond the bare-bones requirements of the budget agreement, House Republicans had made virtually no concessions to Democrats, who denounced the GOP bill as favoring the rich and threatening to send the deficit soaring in future years.

In contrast, Senate GOP leaders risked losing support from their conservative wing, tilting their bill toward lower-income workers and away from big business in order to court Democratic votes.

"You have differences in the size of the packages in the Senate and the House, and you certainly have differences in the tax policies," said Gramm. "People think that because the bills flowed from the same budget agreement they are much the same, but it's going to be a difficult conference, a very important conference."

In addition to reconciling conflicting approaches in the House and Senate bills, negotiators had to deal with the White House. Leaders in both chambers said their goal was to produce a signable bill, which meant that the president's surrogates would have to be intimately involved in shaping its provisions.

"I see the president as being a significant player in the conference because we don't want to send him a bill that he will veto," said Archer, adding: "And he doesn't want to veto a bill that we send him."

Both Sides Harden Stance

Republicans spent much of the four-week period following passage of the House and Senate bills trying to get their own house in order. In sessions that began July 18 and finished July 23, they met among themselves to develop a unified GOP plan that they could take to the White House.

Clinton kept up the pressure, at one point inviting top congressional negotiators to the White House, where among other things, he made it clear that he intended to be a player in the tax negotiations. Republicans had long claimed that Clinton got increased spending for his priorities as part of the May budget pact, in exchange for giving Republicans a free hand over the tax bill.

"It is unrealistic for anyone to think that the president of the United States will not be an active participant in the negotiations on the tax bill," Office of Management and Budget (OMB) Director Franklin D. Raines declared July 16.

On July 19, Clinton sent a letter to Lott laying out his tax priorities:

➤ He would not sign a bill that indexed capital gains. He had argued repeatedly that indexing would have high costs in the second five years of the budget agreement and beyond, and would essentially provide a double tax cut for capital gains.

➤ He insisted that the $500-per-child credit be refundable to low-income families.

➤ He wanted most of the GOP education proposals replaced with his own, which he said were aimed at middle income families.

Those concessions were hard for some Republicans to

Clinton Plan vs. GOP Bills

President Clinton released a revised set of tax cut proposals June 30. Following are the key differences between his package and the competing House and Senate versions of the tax-reconciliation bill (HR 2014):

● **Capital gains.** Clinton proposed a top effective capital gains tax rate for individuals of 27.7 percent. That was a change from his Feb. 6 budget, which called for a capital gains tax break limited to those selling a home.

For better-off taxpayers, Clinton's new plan offered only a slight drop from the existing top rate of 28 percent. It was more generous to taxpayers in lower brackets offering those in the 28 percent bracket an effective capital gains tax of about 20 percent. The lowest rate — for taxpayers in the 15 percent bracket — would be roughly 11 percent.

Both House and Senate bills aimed to reduce the top rate to 20 percent (10 percent for those in the 15 percent bracket). The House also wanted to index capital gains to inflation, a provision Clinton said would prompt a veto.

Clinton's plan, like the Senate bill, proposed no capital gains tax relief for corporations. The House bill called for a cut in corporate capital gains taxes.

● **Child tax credit.** This provision was largely unchanged from Clinton's earlier proposals. He called for a $400-per-child tax credit in 1998, rising to $500 in 1999 and indexed for inflation thereafter. It was to be available for children under 17, with the age limit rising to 19 after 2002.

Until 2000, Clinton wanted the full credit to be available to families with adjusted gross incomes of up to $60,000, phasing out completely for those making more than $75,000. After 2000, the respective income thresholds would rise to $80,000 and $100,000.

Republicans were proposing to make the credit available to single taxpayers with up to $75,000 per year in gross adjusted income and couples with up to $110,000 per year.

Unlike the GOP plans, Clinton wanted to make the credit partially refundable. Taxpayers too poor to owe any income tax would still qualify for the credit, depending on whether they also receive the earned income tax credit (EITC). If they received the EITC and it did not cancel their payroll tax liability, the per-child tax credit could be used to eliminate the remaining portion of their payroll tax liability.

● **Education.** Like the House and Senate bills, Clinton included numerous education-related tax incentives, but two of them accounted for most of the revenue loss: a $1,500 HOPE tax credit and a $1,000 tuition-tax credit. The latter was a slight change from the education deduction that Clinton previously proposed.

The HOPE credit would be available for two years of a student's educational costs and would be worth up to $1,500 per year. After 2002, the maximum credit would increase to $2,000. The full credit would be available for couples with adjusted gross incomes of up to $80,000 and phase out completely for taxpayers with incomes of more than $100,000. Eligible students could receive both a HOPE tax credit and a Pell grant. Both the House and Senate proposals included a similar credit.

The second proposal was a 20 percent tuition tax credit for third- and fourth-year college students, graduate students and workers returning to school. The credit was to be worth up to $1,000 through 2002; it would increase to $2,000 thereafter. The tuition tax credit would be available for taxpayers of the same income levels as the HOPE credit.

Neither the House nor the Senate plans included such a credit.

Like the GOP bills, Clinton called for penalty-free withdrawals from Individual Retirement Accounts (IRAs) for undergraduate, vocational and graduate education expenses.

Also, under Clinton's new proposal, families receiving the child tax credit could put the money into a special IRA along with a $500 after-tax contribution of their own. Interest and principal could be withdrawn tax-free if the money was used for education, purchase of the child's first home or the taxpayer's retirement.

● **Tobacco tax.** Clinton endorsed the 20-cent per-pack increase in tobacco taxes that was part of the Senate bill, but he wanted to put all money in a trust fund for children's health care. The Senate wanted to devote part of the cigarette tax revenue to children's health insurance and use the rest to offset other tax breaks.

● **Estate taxes.** While Clinton had previously proposed only minor changes in estate tax payment schedules, his new plan called for allowing family-owned businesses and farms to exempt an additional $900,000 in value. Under existing law, heirs, other than spouses, could avoid taxes on the first $600,000.

Clinton did not propose increasing the exclusion from estate and gift taxes for individuals, a plan strongly supported by many congressional Republicans. The GOP bills sought to increase the existing $600,000 exemption gradually to $1 million over about nine years.

● **Alternative minimum tax.** Unlike the GOP bills, Clinton did not propose any reduction in the alternative minimum tax (AMT).

swallow, and the GOP-only negotiations seemed to move at a snail's pace.

Initially, Republicans took a hard line, embracing the very elements of the House bill — such as indexing capital gains and making the $500-per-child tax credit non-refundable — that Clinton had labeled unacceptable. GOP conferees also agreed to sharply reduce the AMT for big businesses and allow businesses to reclassify some workers as independent contractors, making it easier to deny them benefits.

The strong GOP reluctance to make big concessions left some White House officials astonished. Why, they asked, would the Republicans not be willing to give up indexing — dear as it was to Archer — when they could still get a lower rate on capital gains, the child tax credit and a cut in estate taxes, all proposals from their Contract With America?

"The crown jewel is within their reach and they don't know how to grab it," said a senior White House official.

But House GOP leaders faced a complicated task. They were just recovering from an aborted mid-July coup attempt against Gingrich, fueled by conservative angst over what the Speaker might give away to Clinton. GOP leaders were thus anxious to prove that they had fought hard for the House version of the tax bill. *(Gingrich, p. 1-11)*

Also, the leadership had to figure out how to hold or replace a bloc of 15 to 20 Republicans from tobacco growing states whose support was tied to the fate of the tobacco tax. And the turmoil at the top of the GOP ranks was interfering with the leadership's ability to get firm vote counts on the different options.

Finally, a Deal

The final round of give and take on the tax bill began July 25 with intensive meetings in the offices of Gingrich and Lott attended by top administration officials. It had been suggested that two of the most contentious players — Archer and Rubin — might be left out of the closing negotiations. But they were not, and the final tax bill bore the imprint of both men, particularly in the compromise on capital gains taxes.

● **Capital gains.** In one of the most obvious trade-offs, the administration accepted the Republican demand to lower the top capital gains tax rate to 20 percent (10 percent for those in the 15 percent bracket) for assets held for more than 18 months.

Republicans, in turn, gave up their indexing proposal, though they made up a little of what they lost by dropping the top rate to 18 percent for assets bought after 2001 and held at least five years. The House proposal to reduce corporate capital gains was dropped.

- **Child tax credit.** Republicans acceded to Clinton's demand that the new $500-per-child tax credit be available to low-income working families that paid only payroll taxes, not income taxes. In return, Clinton accepted GOP demands that the full credit be available to single filers with as much as $75,000 a year in gross adjusted income and couples with up to $110,000 a year.

To help pay for this expansion of the GOP proposal, eligibility requirements for the EITC were tightened to raise $5 billion annually. The Senate provision requiring that the credit be deposited toward education expenses was dropped.

- **Education.** The president got the $35 billion in education tax breaks that were a key goal for him in the budget deal, but the GOP shaped some of the fine points. Clinton got his treasured Hope scholarship of $1,500 tax credits for the first two years of college.
- **Estate taxes.** The GOP won essentially what it wanted: an increase in the amount of inheritance exempt from taxes from $600,000 to $1 million over 10 years, as well as an additional exemption that brought the total allowable for small businesses and family farms to $1.3 million.
- **AMT.** The House won repeal of the corporate AMT for small businesses and faster depreciation for large businesses. The final bill did not include either the House or the Senate plan to increase the amount exempt from the individual AMT.
- **Airline ticket tax.** The conferees went with the House proposal to restructure domestic passenger taxes, moving to a 7.5 percent ticket tax combined with a per-passenger tax on each segment of a flight. As proposed by both chambers, the international departure tax was increased and augmented with a tax on international arrivals. The White House did not object to the compromise GOP plan, which was expected to raise $33.2 billion over five years and $79.7 billion over 10 years.
- **Tobacco tax.** The addition to the federal tobacco tax — 10 cents per pack in 2000, rising to 15 cents in 2002 — was moved to the conference report on the separate spending-reconciliation bill, where it was used in part to pay for children's health programs.

Lott had tried to put off the issue, arguing that Congress should not increase cigarette taxes while it was considering a settlement between the tobacco industry and 40 state attorneys general that had been announced June 20.

Although Lott lost that fight, tobacco firms succeeded in persuading GOP leaders — with the apparent acquiescence of the White House — to reduce the amount of the proposed tobacco settlement ($368.5 billion over 25 years) by the amount raised by the higher cigarette tax. The provision, which was quietly inserted just hours before the bill was printed, was subsequently repealed as part of the spending bill for the departments of Labor, Health and Human Services and Education (PL 105-78). *(Tobacco settlement, p. 3-3; appropriations, p. 9-50)*

Last-Minute Tangles

In the end, it was not big-picture disagreements over tax policy that prolonged work on the bill, but disputes about finer points.

- **Private and parochial schools.** At the last minute, the administration threatened to veto the entire bill over a provision inserted at the behest of Sen. Paul Coverdell, R-Ga., which would have allowed IRA savings to be used by families to pay tuition at parochial and private elementary and secondary schools. *(Private school proposals, p. 7-6)*

The Senate had voted for the provision, and GOP leaders said they were not willing to abandon it unless Clinton put the veto threat in writing — which he did in a brief letter to Gingrich saying the provision "would undermine public education." The provision was dropped.

- **Amtrak and Caribbean trade.** The budget agreement included $2.3 billion for financially troubled Amtrak — but only if accompanied by GOP legislation to change labor laws governing the railroad's unionized workers. That legislation was later enacted. *(Amtrak, p. 3-22)*

Roth said that he would include an unrelated administration request to expand the special trade treatment given to 24 Caribbean and Central American countries — if the president would sign off on Amtrak labor restrictions. Clinton did not go along, so both provisions were dropped.

- **IRAs.** Another last-minute fight focused on eligibility for IRAs. Roth fought for higher income limits, while the White House tried to tailor them to middle-income Americans. Roth won that round; all but the wealthiest 3 to 4 percent of Americans were allowed a tax break for using the savings accounts. However, the administration insisted that annual caps be placed on the amounts that could be deposited.

Final Passage

Lawmakers in both parties and both chambers voted for the conference report July 31 by overwhelming margins. In the House, the vote was 389-43, with just one Republican, Tom Campbell of California, opposing it. In the Senate, the vote was 92-8; all the "nay" votes came from Democrats. *(House vote 350, p. H-106; Senate vote 211, p. S-36)*

Although dissenters on the final votes were few, the main argument against the bill — and the most oft-repeated theme of Democrats throughout the negotiations — was that it was tilted too far toward higher-income Americans.

While the tax package had many benefits for middle-income taxpayers, especially in the first five years, the final package also rewarded the wealthy, according to economists. "Certainly this tax bill heaps benefits on the upper middle class and the upper class when private markets have rewarded them spectacularly," said Reischauer, who noted that even the largest of the so-called middle class tax benefits — the $500-per-child tax credit — would go to all but the wealthiest 10 percent of taxpayers.

Leading the charge on fairness, Gephardt lambasted Republicans for such provisions as the reduction in capital gains tax rates and deep cuts in the corporate AMT. "I believe in building this economy from the bottom up, not the top down," Gephardt said. "Unfortunately, this tax bill will make the tax code less progressive."

In contrast, Rangel, whose district was centered in Harlem, drew laughter when he ribbed his GOP colleagues during the floor debate on their allegiance to indexing capital gains for inflation. "I do not know your districts as well as I know my own, but really, people do not run inside my [political] clubhouse asking, 'How did you do on indexing? And for God's sake, did you reduce capital gains?' "

The fairness debate seemed likely to come back over and over in the coming years, especially since Republicans promised that this was just the first in a series of tax-cut bills. "We're just warming up," said Archer. ■

Provisions of Tax-Cutting Plan

Following are major provisions of the revenue-reconciliation bill signed into law Aug. 5 (HR 2014 — PL 105-34). According to estimates by the Joint Committee on Taxation, the bill contained gross tax cuts of $152 billion over five years, with an offset of $56 billion in tax increases. Over 10 years, the projected gross tax cut was $401 billion, with $126 billion in offsetting tax increases.

The provisions detailed below are those that were expected to raise more than $100 million in revenue over 10 years, or cost the Treasury that much in lost revenues, according to Joint Tax. The list also includes a handful of significant provisions that involved a smaller tax gain or loss. It does not include the minor provisions cancelled under the line-item veto. (Vetoes, p. 2-61)

MAJOR PROVISIONS

Family, Education Tax Cuts

● **Child credit.** Families with children under age 17 could take a $400-per-child tax credit starting in 1998, rising to $500 per child in 1999. Grandparents could claim the credit if they claimed the child as a dependent on their tax form.

The tax credit began to phase out for single taxpayers with adjusted gross annual incomes of more than $75,000 and for couples with incomes of more than $110,000. The maximum child credit available to the taxpayer ($500 times the number of qualifying children) was reduced by $50 for each $1,000 that the taxpayer's adjusted gross income exceeded the threshold amounts. The more children a family had, the higher the income level at which the tax credit phased out entirely. For instance, a couple with an income of $150,000 and five qualifying children would still be eligible for a $500 credit.

Low-income families that were eligible for the earned-income tax credit (generally those with incomes of $30,000 a year or less) could take the child credit before they figured their earned-income credit. If the child credit exceeded a taxpayer's regular tax liability, the taxpayer was required to calculate whether the tax liability plus the employee share of federal payroll taxes exceeded the earned-income credit. If so, the new law provided that the amount by which the child credit exceeded the amount calculated above was refundable to the taxpayer. This applied only to taxpayers with three or more children.

Effective date: Jan. 1, 1998. Estimated cost: $85 billion over five years; $183.4 billion over 10 years.

Education Incentives

● **HOPE college tax credit.** Taxpayers could receive a non-refundable credit of up to $1,500 per student for each of the first two years of college. The credit could be applied to to 100 percent of the first $1,000 of tuition and fees, and 50 percent of the next $1,000 in costs. The credit could not be claimed against the purchase of books or the cost of student activities. The credit would be indexed for inflation starting in 2002.

A single taxpayer would be eligible for the full credit if his or her adjusted gross annual income was less than $40,000; the ceiling for joint filers was $80,000. The first taxable year in which the income limits would be adjusted for inflation was 2001.

● **Lifetime learning credit.** For the second two years of college, or for graduate and post-graduate education and thereafter, a lifetime tax credit was available equal to 20 percent of up to $5,000 in tuition and related school expenses; after 2002, the credit would be equal to 20 percent of up to $10,000. Taxpayers would be eligible for the full credit if their adjusted gross annual incomes were less than $40,000 for single filers and $80,000 for joint filers. The first taxable year in which the income limits could be increased to reflect inflation was 2001.

Effective date for both the HOPE credit and the lifetime learning credit: Dec. 31, 1997. Estimated cost of both: $31.6 billion over five years and $76 billion over 10 years.

● **Education savings accounts.** Modeled on individual retirement accounts (IRAs), these accounts allowed taxpayers to make nondeductible contributions of up to $500 per year for each child under age 18. The principal and interest could be withdrawn tax-free at any time to help pay for a child's college or graduate education. Virtually all taxpayers — except those with incomes in the top 3 percent or so — were eligible to make use of the accounts. The adjusted gross annual income limit for single filers was $95,000; for joint filers, $150,000.

Any balance remaining in an education account at the time a beneficiary reached 30 years old had to be distributed, and the earnings portion of such a distribution would be subject to tax and to an additional 10 percent penalty.

Effective date: Dec. 31, 1997. Estimated cost: $3.9 billion over five years and $14.2 billion over 10 years.

Each year, for each student, the taxpayer could choose either the HOPE credit, the lifetime learning credit, or a tax-free distribution from an education savings account.

● **Penalty-free IRA withdrawals.** Penalty-free withdrawals could be made from all IRAs for undergraduate, postsecondary vocational and graduate education expenses.

Effective date: Dec. 31, 1997. Estimated cost: $812 million over five years and $1.7 billion over 10 years.

● **Student loan interest deduction.** A deduction of up to $1,000 was permitted for interest payments on student loans starting in 1998, rising to $2,500 in 2001. The deduction was available to individual taxpayers with adjusted gross annual incomes of up to $40,000 and couples with incomes of up to $60,000. Income ranges would increase for inflation after 2002. (This provision largely reversed a provision of the 1986 tax act, which disallowed the deduction of personal interest, including student loan interest.)

Effective date: Dec. 31, 1997. Estimated cost: $690 million over five years and $2.4 billion over 10 years.

● **Deduction for state-sponsored tuition programs.** Deductions for state-sponsored prepaid tuition programs and other state savings programs were expanded to include the costs of room and board in addition to tuition.

Effective date: Dec. 31, 1997. Estimated cost: $533 million over five years and $1.5 billion over 10 years.

● **Exemption for employer-provided educational assistance.** The law extended through May 31, 2000, the exemption from taxation of employer-provided educational assistance for undergraduates. The exclusion had previously applied to graduate as well as undergraduate education, but the 1996 small-business tax bill (PL 104-188) limited the exemption to undergraduate courses beginning after June 30, 1996.

Estimated cost: $1.2 billion over five years.

● **Tax credit for qualified zone academy bonds.** The bill made it easier for public schools in impoverished neighborhoods to form partnerships with corporations to provide job training. The school districts could borrow money and pay only 50 percent of the present value of the loan — half the total interest payments due over the term of the loan, plus the principal. The government would pay the lender, such as a bank or insurance company, the other 50 percent.

Corporations would have to make an investment in the school worth at least 10 percent of the value of the bond. All investments had to be in schools in designated "enterprise zones," or in areas where at least 35 percent of the students qualified for the school lunch program. Up to $400 million of "qualified zone academy bonds" could be issued in 1998 and $400 million in 1999. The bonds could be issued by a state or a local unit of government.

Effective date: Dec. 31, 1997. Estimated cost: $172 million over five years and $408 million over 10 years.

• **Deduction for corporate contributions of computer technology.** Companies became eligible for an income tax deduction when they contributed new or unused computers, computer printers and computer technology such as software to educational organizations with students in kindergarten through 12th grade. The provision was effective from Jan. 1, 1998, until Jan. 1, 2001.

Estimated cost. $225 million over five years.

• **Repeal of limit on bonds issued by non-profits.** Nonprofit entities — those organized under section 501(c)(3) of the tax code — were allowed to issue an unlimited amount of tax-exempt bonds. Interest paid on the bonds was not subject to federal tax.

The provision reversed a policy in place since the 1986 tax act, which placed a $150 million cap on the amount of tax-exempt debt that each nonprofit entity could issue. However, any bonds above the prior cap could only be issued for new projects, not to help finance existing projects. The provision was expected to be used primarily by universities and nursing homes.

Effective date: Aug. 5, 1997. Estimated cost: $315 million over five years and $962 million over 10 years.

• **Cancellation of certain student loans.** Under existing law, the forgiveness of indebtedness with respect to student loans did not count as gross income when the student agreed to work in certain professions. The new law expanded the exemption to include student loans that were forgiven by tax-exempt charitable organizations and foundations.

Estimated cost: Negligible.

• **Bonds for public school construction.** Government units (such as a school district) that were classified as "small issuers" of tax-exempt bonds because their issues were worth $5 million or less could issue an additional $5 million in bonds to finance public school capital expenditures. These bonds were not subject to the rebate-on-earnings requirement that governed larger issues. That meant the issuer could sell the bonds months before the building project got under way and invest the bond proceeds until needed without having to rebate the earnings to the federal government. Larger issuers had to rebate the earnings.

Effective date: Dec. 31, 1997. Estimated cost: $36 million over five years and $199 million over 10 years.

Capital Gains, IRAs

• **Capital gains.** The bill created a new rate structure for taxes on individual capital gains — profits from the sale of stocks or other investments — giving progressively lower rates for assets held for longer periods of time. The new law:

• Reduced the top individual tax rate on capital gains from 28 percent to 20 percent. To qualify, assets had to be held for more than 18 months. For individuals in the 15 percent tax bracket, the new top rate was 10 percent.

• Reduced the top rate to 18 percent for assets purchased after 2000 and held for at least five years. Taxpayers with assets bought before 2000 could pay a "tollgate tax" at the 20 percent rate on the gain on their assets up until 2000 and then take advantage of the 18 percent rate.

• Retained the existing top rate — 28 percent, 15 percent for individuals in the 15 percent bracket — for assets held for at least 12 months but not more than 18 months. Collectibles such as art and antiques would continue to be taxed at this rate regardless of how long they were held.

• Taxed short-term gains — those on assets held for less than 12 months — at ordinary income rates, which could go as high as 39.6 percent.

• Taxed profits from investments in real estate (so called real estate recapture) subject to the capital gains tax at a 25 percent rate. Effective date: retroactive to May 7, 1997. Estimated cost: $123 million increase in revenues over five years but a loss of $21.2 billion over 10 years.

• **Primary residence exclusion.** The new law eliminated capital gains taxes on profits from the sale of a primary residence that netted the seller up to $250,000 for individual taxpayers and $500,000 for couples.

The law erased a taxpayer's prior ability to take the profit from the sale of one house and put it immediately into the purchase of another house that was equal or greater in cost without paying tax on the gain. Also eliminated was the $125,000 exclusion for the sale of principal residence for those 55 or older.

Effective date: May 6, 1997. Estimated cost: Negligible.

• **Rollover of gain from the purchase of small-business stock.** In a step designed to spur venture capital investment, the bill expanded a 1993 provision that provided individuals a 50 percent exclusion for gains from the sale of certain small-business stock. The stock had to have been acquired when the company first issued it. The amount of gain eligible for the 50 percent exclusion was the greater of 10 times the taxpayers' tax basis in the stock, or $10 million.

Previously, a corporation could not qualify as a small business if its gross assets exceeded $50 million. The new law doubled that threshold to $100 million. An individual could roll over the gain from the sale of such stock tax-free, so long as the proceeds were used to purchase qualified small business stock.

Effective date: The increase in the size of eligible corporations was effective Aug 5, 1997. The remaining provisions applied to stock issued after Aug. 10, 1993, the original effective date of the small business provision.

Individual Retirement Accounts

The law provided for two new types of individual retirement accounts. One was the education savings account (see above). The other was the "backloaded" Roth IRA, named for its chief sponsor, Sen. William V. Roth Jr., R-Del. The law also changed the rules for traditional, tax-deferred IRAs, which allowed taxpayers to save pre-tax dollars and withdraw them at retirement.

• **Roth IRA.** Single filers with adjusted gross annual incomes up to $95,000 and joint filers with incomes up to $150,000 could make after-tax contributions to a Roth IRA ($2,000 for individuals, $4,000 for couples). Individuals making up to $110,000 and couples making up to $160,000 could make partial contributions.

While contributions to the Roth IRA were not tax deductible, both the interest and principal could be withdrawn tax-free if the account had been open for five years and the account holder was age 59 1/2, disabled or deceased, or was withdrawing the money for a first-time home purchase.

The contributions to a Roth IRA could be withdrawn early without penalty.

Taxpayers with adjusted gross annual incomes under $100,000 could convert all or part of the funds they had accumulated in a traditional, tax-deferred IRA to a Roth IRA. The withdrawals (pre-tax contributions and earnings) were subject to income tax at the time of the rollover, but there was no penalty. If the rollover was done before Jan. 1, 1999, the tax could be spread over four years.

Future earnings could be withdrawn tax free after five years as long as the distribution was used for a first-time home purchase or the individual was 59 1/2, disabled or deceased.

• **Tax-deferred IRA.** Previously, taxpayers who participated in employer-sponsored retirement plans had to have relatively low adjusted gross incomes — less than $25,000 for single filers and less than $40,000 for couples — to make a fully deductible $2,000 annual contribution to an IRA.

The new law increased the income limits by $5,000 for single filers and by $10,000 for joint filers in 1998, and by $1,000 each year thereafter through 2002. After that, the limits would gradually rise to $50,000 for single filers and $80,000 for joint filers.

The new law also allowed penalty-free withdrawals to finance a first-time home purchase or for educational purposes.

Beginning in 1998, a spouse who was not an active participant in an employer-sponsored plan could make a fully deductible IRA contribution up to $2,000 if the couple's adjust gross income was less than $150,000 — even if the other spouse was covered by a retirement plan at work.

● **Coins and bullion.** Starting in 1998, IRAs could be invested in platinum coins and bullion.

● **Effective date, cost.** Effective date for all IRA provisions: Dec. 31, 1997. Estimated cost of all IRA provisions: $1.8 billion over five years and $20.2 billion over 10 years.

Other Deductions

● **Home office deduction.** The new law expanded the deduction for home offices to cover taxpayers who worked outside the home but did their billing, administrative work and management from their home offices. The deduction was available as long as the office was the taxpayer's principal place of business, defined as the place where the taxpayer "conducts substantial administration or management of the trade or business."

The provision overturned a 1993 U.S. Supreme Court decision *(Commissioner v. Solliman)* that disallowed a deduction for an anesthesiologist who went from hospital to hospital but had no office in those places and did his billing from a home office.

The new law allowed the deduction even for people who had an office outside the home but chose not to do their administrative and management work there. This could apply, for instance, to independent contractors who were consultants, free-lance writers or the shopkeeper who sold merchandise in a store but kept his accounts in an office at home.

Estimated cost: $880 million over five years and $2.4 billion over 10 years.

● **Health insurance for self-employed persons.** The deductibility of premiums paid by the self-employed was increased to 100 percent by 2007. Previously, it was to have been increased to 80 percent by 2006. Estimated cost: $383 million over five years and $3.5 billion over 10 years.

● **Standard mileage rate for charitable deduction.** Taxpayers who used personal vehicles for charitable purposes (such as delivering meals to homebound people) could deduct 14 cents per mile, an increase from the previous 12 cents per mile deduction.

Effective date: Jan. 1, 1998. Estimated cost: $247 million over five years and $621 million over 10 years.

Corporate AMT

● **Depreciation conformity.** For all businesses, the depreciation adjustment under the alternative minimum tax (AMT) was altered to make it the same as depreciation under the regular tax system. That meant a shorter life for all property taxed under the AMT and sharply reduced the AMT liability of those firms that were subject to it.

The AMT was designed to ensure that even corporations that did not owe regular income taxes still paid some tax. The AMT was used only when a taxpayer's alternative minimum tax liability exceeded its regular tax liability. The corporate AMT was 20 percent on alternative minimum taxable income in excess of a phased-out $40,000 exemption.

Effective date: Jan 1, 1998. Estimated cost: $6.8 billion over five years; $18.3 billion over 10 years.

● **Small business exemption.** Businesses with average gross annual receipts of less than $5 million were no longer subject to the AMT.

Effective date: Jan 1, 1998. Estimated cost: $577 million over five years and $762 million over 10 years.

● **Repeal of installment accounting method for farmers.** The new law allowed farmers to defer counting the income on sales of crops and other products from the year in which the product was sold into the following year without incurring any additional alternative minimum tax liability. Previously, deferred sales were counted as preference items for minimum tax purposes, which increased farmers' minimum tax liability. It had been unclear since 1986 how the deferral law applied to farmers, and after wrangling with the IRS, farmers asked Congress to clarify that deferral of income from crop sales was permissible.

Effective date: Retroactive to tax year 1987. Estimated cost: $811 million over five years and $872 million over 10 years.

Estate and Gift Taxes

● **Increase in unified estate and gift tax credit.** Since 1976, the tax on gifts (given during the donor's lifetime) and estates (transferred at death) had been unified, with a single, graduated rate for the cumulative transfers made by a taxpayer during his lifetime and at death. Under existing law, $600,000 was effectively exempt from the estate and gift tax rate, which began at 37 percent and reached a maximum of 55 percent.

The new law increased the amount of an estate that was exempt from the federal estate tax from $600,000 to $1 million. The schedule for the exemption rose gradually and erratically, with just $100,000 of the increase occurring before 2003. The exemption would increase to $625,000 in 1998, to $650,000 in 1999 and to $675,000 in 2000 and remain at that level in 2001. Then it would jump to $700,000 in 2002 and remain at that level in 2003, to $850,000 in 2004, to $950,000 in 2005 and finally to $1 million in 2006.

● **Gift tax exclusion.** Previously, a benefactor could give $10,000 per year to any number of recipients without paying tax on the gift or affecting his total estate tax exemption. The new law indexed the $10,000 exclusion for inflation after 1998.

● **Generation-skipping tax exemption**. Existing law allowed a grandparent to transfer up to $1 million to a grandchild whose parent was dead without paying a generation-skipping tax on the gift. The bill indexed this exemption for inflation after 1998.

● **Special use valuation.** So-called special use valuation allowed farmers to value their property at its current value rather than its highest and best-use value and reduce the total value of their property for estate tax purposes by up to $750,000. The bill indexed this exemption for inflation after 1998.

Effective date: Jan. 1, 1998. Total estimated cost: $5.9 billion over five years; $33.1 billion over 10 years.

● **Exemption for family farms and family-owned small business.** A new estate tax exemption of $700,000 was created for family farms and family-owned businesses starting in 1998. However, in future years as the unified credit rose to $1 million (see above) the family business exemption would fall to $300,000. In any given year, the combination of the unified credit and the exemption for family owned farms and businesses was to equal $1.3 million.

To be eligible for the exemption, 50 percent of the business had to be under the ownership of one family; alternatively, 70 percent could be under the ownership of two families or 90 percent under the ownership of three families. In addition, an heir had to participate in the management of the business for five years out of any eight-year period in the 10 years after the death of the previous owner. (An heir also had to be a relative of the previous owner, such as a child, spouse or lineal descendent.) In addition, the business had to constitute at least half of the previous owner's estate in order to qualify for the exemption.

If the heir decided to withdraw from material participation in the business within 10 years of the previous owner's death, the estate tax benefit would be subject to recapture, meaning that the IRS could assess the taxpayer for the difference between the estate taxes paid and the estate tax that would have been paid if there had been no exemption.

Estimated cost: $5.9 billion over five years and $33.1 billion over 10 years.

● **Installment payments.** Closely held businesses and family farms had been able to pay estate taxes on an installment plan over 14 years with an especially low interest rate. Under the bill, the interest rate was reduced from 4 percent to to 2 percent. However, the interest was no longer deductible for estate or income tax purposes.

Effective date: Jan. 1, 1998. Estimated cost: $84 million over five years and $349 million over 10 years.

● **Exclusion for permanent conservation easement.** If a permanent easement was put on a piece of land, meaning that it could not be subdivided for development purposes, then the executor of an estate could exclude from tax 40 percent of the value of the land so long as the exclusion was not in excess of $1 million. To qualify for the exclusion, the land had to be within 25 miles of a metropolitan area or within 10 miles of an Urban National Forest; it also had to have been owned by the person who died or a member of his family during the preceding three years.

Effective date: Jan. 1, 1998. Estimated cost: $82 million over five years and $349 million over 10 years.

● **Limit on gift re-evaluation.** When a taxpayer made a gift, its value was counted against his unified credit. At death, the value of the gift was subtracted from his unified credit, and the remainder of the credit was available to reduce the taxes on his estate. This provision halted the occasional practice by the IRS of revaluing (and, in some cases, increasing the imputed value of) a taxpayer's gifts when he died.

Effective date: Aug. 5, 1997. Estimated cost: $81 million over five years and $310 million over 10 years.

● **Modification of generation-skipping tax for transfers to persons with deceased parents.** The new law expanded to collateral heirs, such as grandnieces and grandnephews, the provision allowing a grandparent to transfer money to a grandchild whose parent was dead without paying a generation-skipping tax on the gift.

Effective date: Jan. 1, 1998. Estimated cost: $16 million over five years and $41 million over 10 years.

Expiring Tax Provisions

● **Research tax credit.** The research and development tax credit was extended for 13 months — from June 1, 1997, to June 30, 1998. The credit was equal to 20 percent of a company's research expenditures; if the company gave a grant to a university to do basic research, a portion of that expenditure was eligible for the tax credit.

Estimated cost: $2.24 billion over five years and $2.27 billion over 10 years.

● **Stock donated to private foundations.** The bill extended for 13 months — from June 1, 1997, to June 30, 1998 — a provision that allowed taxpayers who gave stock to charitable organizations to deduct not only their basis in the stock but also any capital gain.

Estimated cost: $112 million over five years and $112 million over 10 years.

● **Work opportunity tax credit.** The law extended for nine months the credit for employers who hired workers from one of seven needy groups and added one new group: Supplemental Social Security recipients. The other groups included people trying to get off welfare, high-risk youths, qualified veterans and qualified ex-felons.

The maximum credit was generally $2,400 per individual. An employee had to work for at least 120 hours before his or her wages were eligible for the credit. The credit was available for wages paid for qualified individuals who began work after September 30, 1997, and before July 1, 1998.

Estimated cost: $383 million over five years and $385 million over 10 years.

● **Orphan drug tax credit.** The bill made permanent a 50 percent tax credit for qualified clinical testing expenses incurred in testing of certain drugs for rare diseases or conditions. Rare diseases and conditions were defined as those that affected fewer than 200,000 people nationwide, or more than 200,000 but for which there was no reasonable expectation that businesses could recoup the costs of developing a drug for such disease from U.S. sales.

Effective date for clinical testing expenses incurred: May 31, 1997. Estimated cost: $152 million over five years and $346 million over 10 years.

District of Columbia

● **Enterprise zone**. Most of the nation's capital was included in an enterprise zone created under the bill. The zone included those census tracts that had been in Washington's enterprise community (portions of Anacostia, Mt. Pleasant, Chinatown and the easternmost part of the District) and all other census tracts where the poverty rate was more than 20 percent. Employers who moved there were eligible for a 20 percent wage credit, increased expensing and expanded tax-exempt financing.

Effective date: Jan. 1, 1998, through Dec. 31, 2002. Estimated cost: $539 million over five years and $582 million over 10 years.

● **Zero-percent capital gains rate.** Capital gains on sales of business property in such neighborhoods was reduced to zero if the property was held for at least five years.

Effective date: Jan. 1, 1998, though Dec. 31, 2002. Estimated cost: $73 million over five years and $502 million over 10 years.

● **Credit for homebuyers.** Purchasers of homes in the District were eligible for a new, $5,000 credit if their adjusted gross annual incomes were less than $70,000 for single filers and less than $110,000 for joint filers.

Effective date: ended Dec. 31, 2000. Estimated cost: $74 million over five years.

Miscellaneous

Welfare to Work

● **Wage credit.** The bill offered a wage credit to employers who hired former welfare recipients. The credit was worth 35 percent of the first $10,000 in wages in the first year of employment and 50 percent on $10,000 of wages in the second year of employment. The maximum credit was $8,500 per qualified employee.

Eligible wages included cash wages plus educational assistance covered by the tax exclusion for employer-provided tuition assistance, health plan coverage and dependent care assistance.

Effective for wages paid or incurred from Dec. 31, 1997, through April 30, 1999. Estimated cost: $99 million over five years and $106 million over 10 years.

Excise Taxes

● **Gas tax and Highway Trust Fund.** Revenue from a 4.3-cents-per-gallon federal tax on gasoline, motor fuels and diesel was channeled into the Highway Trust Fund instead of the general fund. The 4.3-cents-per-gallon tax was only a portion of the total 18.3-cents-per-gallon federal tax; it was added in 1993 as part of President Clinton's deficit-reduction plan. Although the change had no overall effect on government revenues, it limited the money available in domestic accounts for non-highway trust fund spending.

Effective date: Oct. 1, 1997. Estimated cost: None.

● **Alternative fuels excise tax.** The bill equalized the taxation of alternative fuels so that it was based on their energy content. The result was a tax cut for propane, liquefied natural gas and methanol.

Effective date: Oct. 1, 1997. Estimated cost: $82 million over five years and $186 million over 10 years.

● **Vaccine excise rates.** The tax paid by manufacturers of vaccines was leveled so that all vaccines would be taxed at the same rate of 75 cents per dose. Combination vaccines, such as measles, mumps and rubella (MMR) vaccines, would be taxed at 75 cents times the number of components in the combined vaccines; the tax on MMR would be $2.25 per dose.

In addition, three new vaccines were made subject to the tax: haemophilus influenza, hepatitis B and chicken pox.

Amounts equal to the revenues from the tax were deposited in the Vaccine Injury Compensation Trust Fund to finance awards to individuals who suffered certain injuries following administration of the taxable vaccines.

Effective for vaccines purchased after Sept. 30, 1997. Estimated cost: $74 million over five years and $146 million over 10 years.

'Brownfields'

● **Deduction.** Under the bill, a business could deduct the cost of cleaning up environmental contamination in so-called brownfields sites in targeted areas. Such sites were not hazardous enough to come under superfund but had been certified by a state environmental agency to contain or potentially contain a hazardous substance. A targeted area was an empowerment zone or enterprise community or any census tract with a 20 percent or greater poverty rate.

The deduction could be taken starting in the year after the date of enactment, and it expired on Jan. 1, 2001. However, if the property was sold or disposed of before the environmental cleanup was complete, the taxpayer would have to include the prior deductions as income.

Effective date: For expenses in taxable years ending after Aug. 5, 1997. Estimated cost: $417 million over five years and $352 million over 10 years.

Empowerment Zones

● **Two new urban zones.** The bill provided for the creation of two new urban empowerment zones, in addition to the six created under the 1993 budget-reconciliation act (PL 103-66). The new zones had to be designated within 180 days.

The existing urban zones were in New York City, Baltimore, Atlanta, Philadelphia-Camden, Detroit and Chicago. Qualified businesses located in the zones were eligible for special tax incentives, such as a credit for wages paid to zone residents, additional expensing and special tax-exempt financing. *(1993 Almanac, p. 107)*

● **Additional zones.** The new law also authorized the creation of 20 additional empowerment zones — 15 in urban areas and five in rural areas. The zones would have a range of incentives similar to those enjoyed by existing empowerment zones, though businesses would not be eligible for the work opportunity tax credit, which offset the cost of hiring employees. The new brownfields deduction would be available in all the new empowerment zones.

The zones had to be designated before 1999; the designations generally would remain in effect for 10 years.

Effective date: Aug. 5, 1997. Estimated cost: $717 million over five years and $1.2 billion over 10 years.

Other Domestic Provisions

● **Inventory accounting estimates.** Targeted at large retailers, manufacturers and other businesses with significant tangible inventories, this provision clarified that estimates of inventory shrinkage — due to breakage, undetected theft and bookkeeping errors — would be considered valid even if they were not taken at the end of the year, but were based on physical estimates earlier in the year and adjusted at year's end. A complex formula was set up specifically for retailers who had recently tangled with the IRS in a number of cases involving inventory shrinkage estimates.

Effective date: Aug. 5, 1997. Estimated cost: $103 million over five years and $268 million over 10 years.

● **Treatment of workers' compensation.** The tax treatment of workers' compensation payments was brought into conformity with the treatment of structured settlements in personal injury cases. Such payments were tax-exempt because the injured party was being compensated for loss, not realizing a gain.

Effective date: Aug. 5, 1997. Estimated cost: $27 million over five years and $164 million over 10 years.

● **Income averaging for farmers.** The new law set up a formula for farmers so that they were taxed annually based on their average income over a three-year period. Income averaging, which generally reduced a taxpayer's liability, had been repealed for all taxpayers by the 1986 act.

Effective date: Dec. 31, 1997, through tax year 2000. Estimated cost: $161 million over five years.

● **Increased deduction for business meals.** The bill increased from 50 percent to 80 percent the deduction for meals taken while a person subject to the Department of Transportation hours-of-service limitations was away from home during a period of duty or incident to a period of duty. The increased deduction was to be phased in over 11 years with the first increase taking effect in 1998.

Workers covered included truck drivers, who because of hours-of-service limitations had to stop driving after 10 hours; certain air transportation employees such as airplane pilots, crew dispatchers, mechanics and control tower operators; railroad employees including engineers, conductors, train crews, dispatchers and control operations personnel; and certain merchant mariners subject to Coast Guard regulations.

Effective date: Jan. 1, 1998. Estimated cost: $138 million over five years and $600 million over 10 years.

Foreign Business Provisions

● **Foreign sales of computer software.** Profits on computer software sold for reproduction through a foreign sales corporation to overseas buyers were tax exempt under the bill. This was the same tax benefit received by other products sold through a foreign sales corporation.

Software giants Microsoft and Oracle were the two companies that pushed hardest for the provision, but numerous other computer software companies were expected to take advantage of it.

Effective for software licenses after Dec. 31, 1997. Estimated cost: $568 million over five years and $1.7 billion over 10 years.

● **Passive foreign investment asset valuation and other tax reduction provisions.** The new law drew a brighter line between passive foreign investment companies (PFICs) and controlled foreign corporations (CFCs), making it easier for some overseas subsidiaries of U.S. firms to qualify as CFCs.

Under the law, a PFIC (such as a foreign mutual fund) taxed a U.S. investor on earnings, whereas a shareholder of a CFC was not taxed until the income was repatriated. A PFIC was any company in which either 75 percent or more of its gross income was passive (from investments), or 50 percent or more of the fair market value of its assets consisted of assets that produced passive income.

Another section of the provision, sought by Amway, allowed foreign subsidiaries of publicly traded U.S. companies to be defined as PFICs only if their assets met the fair-market value test. This assured that they would continue to be classified as CFCs, which was preferable from a tax standpoint.

Effective date: Jan. 1, 1998. Estimated cost: $124 million over five years and $280 million over 10 years.

● **Foreign tax credit on interests in foreign joint ventures.** The foreign tax credit system was streamlined for U.S. firms that owned between 10 percent and 50 percent of the stock of a joint venture with an overseas firm. Previously, a U.S. company had to apply a separate foreign tax credit against dividends received from each venture; some firms had hundreds of such ventures. This provision allowed U.S. firms to combine their dividends and their offsetting credits instead of calculating each one individually.

Effective date: Jan. 1, 2003. Estimated cost: $982 million over 10 years.

● **Tax exempt income of U.S. citizens overseas.** The bill increased from $70,000 to $80,000 the amount of annual income that a U.S. citizen working overseas could earn without paying U.S. income tax. The increased exemption was to be phased in at a rate of $2,000 per year starting in 1998. The exemption was designed to offset the tax that U.S. citizens paid to the country where they were residing. The provision was strongly supported by multinational companies that had foreign subsidiaries or subcontracted with overseas companies that employed U.S. citizens.

Estimated cost: $244 million over five years and $801 million over 10 years.

Amtrak

The imperiled passenger railroad system was granted a refund — known as a net operating loss carry-back — on taxes paid by the predecessor railroad lines that merged their passenger operation in 1971 to form Amtrak. However, the tax break was contingent on the company embracing management changes that had to be ratified by Congress in a separate bill. (An Amtrak restructuring bill was signed into law Dec. 2, freeing the $2.3 billion that had been set aside.)

Estimated cost: $2.3 billion over five years.

Revenue Raisers

Excise and Employment Taxes

● **Airline ticket tax.** Under the new law, the existing 10 percent tax on domestic airline tickets was reduced to 9 percent in fiscal

1998, 8 percent in fiscal 1999 and 7.5 percent in 2000. A new per-passenger tax was imposed on each segment of a domestic flight, beginning at $1 in fiscal 1998, gradually increasing to $3 in fiscal 2002 and then changing to reflect inflation, based on the Consumer Price Index (CPI). Flights to small airports in isolated rural areas were exempt from the segment tax.

The tax on international departures was increased from $6 to $12, and a new $12 tax was imposed on international arrivals, with those taxes indexed to the CPI beginning in January 1999. The bill kept the existing $6 tax on flights to Alaska and Hawaii, but indexed it to the CPI beginning in 1999. It also imposed a 7.5 percent tax on purchases of frequent-flier miles by credit card companies and others. Taxes on air cargo and aviation fuel were extended.

Estimated revenue: $33.2 billion over five years and $79.7 billion over 10 years.

● **Tax on kerosene.** The bill required that kerosene be taxed when it was removed from the terminal where it was stored unless it was indelibly dyed and destined for a non-taxable use such as home heating fuel or aviation fuel. Like diesel fuel, kerosene was supposed to be taxed at the wholesale level when it was destined for use as a transportation fuel. However, the IRS had had problems enforcing the taxation in the case of kerosene because previously there had been no dying requirement.

Effective date: July 1, 1998. Estimated revenue: $226 million over five years and $461 million over 10 years.

● **Leaking underground storage tanks.** The bill reinstated the 0.1 cent per gallon excise tax on gasoline, diesel fuel, special motor fuels, aviation fuels and inland waterway fuels through March 31, 2005. The tax revenue was used to help gas stations convert to new, non-leaking tanks.

Effective date: Oct. 1, 1997. Estimated revenue: $645 million over five years and $983 million over 10 years.

● **Excise tax on prepaid phone cards.** The bill specified that phone cards were subject to the 3 percent telephone excise tax. In theory, the cards were already subject to the tax, but there had been confusion as to whether the tax was supposed to be levied by the retailer selling the card or by the communications company that sold the service. The bill required that the tax be built into the face value of the card and be charged by the communications service provider (the company that bought time from the owners of the telephone lines).

Effective date: Aug. 5, 1997. Estimated revenue: $193 million over five years and $684 million over 10 years.

● **Excise tax on trucks and truck tires.** The bill consolidated the taxes on trucks and truck tires. Previously, the truck tax was based on the selling price, but the buyer was allowed to subtract the value of the tires in determining the price of the truck and then pay a tax on the tires that was based on weight.

Effective on sales after Dec. 31, 1997. Estimated revenue: $452 million over five years and $979 million over 10 years.

● **FUTA surtax extended.** The bill extended through Dec. 31, 2007, the existing federal unemployment surtax of 0.2 percent on the first $7,000 paid annually by covered employers to each employee. In addition to the temporary 0.2 percent surtax, which was first enacted in 1976, there was a 0.6 percent permanent federal unemployment tax (FUTA). The revenue went to finance administration of the system, half of the federal-state extended-benefits program and a federal account for state loans. The provision also allowed more money to accumulate in the federal unemployment trust fund.

Effective date: Jan. 1, 1999. Estimated savings: $6.4 billion over five years; $6.7 billion over 10 years.

Individual Tax Simplification

● **Standard deduction for dependents.** The bill increased slightly the allowable standard deduction for dependents both under the regular tax system and the alternative minimum tax system.

Effective date: Tax years after Dec. 31, 1997. Estimated revenue: $146 million over five years and $327 million over 10 years.

● **Estimated tax.** Existing law required individual taxpayers to make up any income taxes that they owed beyond what was withheld from their paychecks by making quarterly estimated payments. If the remaining tax liability was $500 or more, the taxpayer was fined.

The new law increased the *de minimus* threshold for estimated tax payments to $1,000.

Effective for tax years after Dec. 31, 1997. Estimated revenue: $208 million over five years and $326 million over 10 years.

Corporate Operations, Financial Products

● **Recognition of gain on certain stock positions.** The bill specified that profits from certain transactions that were economically equivalent to an outright sale — such as the practice known on Wall Street as "selling short against the box" — be treated as sales that could be taxed as a capital gain.

Effective date: June 8, 1997. Estimated revenue: $708 million over five years; $1.2 billion over 10 years.

● **Gains or losses from certain terminations with respect to property.** The bill required that any loss resulting from the termination of a capital asset — for example, when a bond was paid off — be treated as a capital loss for tax purposes. Previously, such losses could be treated as ordinary losses, deductible against ordinary income; that was more advantageous than a capital gains loss since ordinary income was taxed at a higher rate than capital gains. In addition, a capital loss was limited to $3,000 a year and was netted against capital gains.

Effective date: June 8, 1997. Estimated revenue: $117 million over five years and $242 million over 10 years.

● **Interest of pooled credit card receivables or debt obligations.** This provision was primarily designed to force credit card companies to include in their taxable income the interest they expected to receive from credit card debt. Companies rarely received all the interest they were owed, since a portion of credit bills went unpaid and had to be written off.

Previously, credit card companies could defer taxes on the interest until it was paid by borrowers. The new law required them to estimate how much they would ultimately receive and include it as taxable income.

Effective date: Jan. 1, 1998. Estimated revenue: $1.3 billion over five years; $1.9 billion over 10 years.

● **Denial of interest deduction on certain debt instruments.** The bill required that when a corporation issued a financial instrument that was payable in stock when it was redeemed, the issuer could not deduct interest earned on the instrument. This was designed to limit the tax advantage for certain types of exotic financial instruments that were being called "debt" but had the characteristics of equity.

Effective for transactions after June 8, 1997. Estimated revenue: $148 million over five years and $469 million over 10 years.

● **Tax treatment of certain extraordinary dividends.** Large one-time dividends resulting from corporation-to-corporation transactions had to be recognized as capital gains for tax purposes. Previously, corporations could take so-called dividend-received deductions, which were worth 70 percent of the total dividend, and pay tax on the balance.

Effective date: Sept. 13, 1995. Estimated revenue: $68 million over five years; $375 million over 10 years.

● **Gain recognition on certain distributions of controlled corporation stock (Morris Trust provision).** Triggered by several highly publicized transactions in which corporations effectively sold a trade, business or subdivision without paying tax, this provision required that when a company spun off a subsidiary, gain was recognized and the company paid tax on the transaction.

Effective for acquisitions of stock that occurred after April 16, 1997. Estimated revenue: $1.1 billion over five years and $1.5 billion over 10 years.

● **Holding period for dividends-received deduction.** The dividends-received deduction was limited to those corporate taxpayers who held stocks that carried a genuine risk of loss on the investment. Corporate investors in stock could deduct 70 percent of the value of dividends received.

Previously, there were some financial products that allowed corporate investors to buy stock, but for much of the holding period hedge the risk that usually accompanied equity investment and still take the dividend deduction.

Effective for dividends received or accrued 30 days after the date of enactment with exceptions for stock held on June 8, 1997. Estimated revenue: $71 million over five years and $156 million over 10 years.

● **Registration relating to confidential corporate tax shelters.** The bill tightened rules for registering tax shelters, including a requirement that shelters be registered one day after they were first offered to potential investors.

Effective as soon as Treasury issued regulations. Estimated revenue: $170 million over five years and $392 million over 10 years.

● **Certain preferred stock treated as "boot."** The bill required that in certain corporate transactions, such as reorganizations, in which stockholders exchanged equity for preferred stock, any gain be recognized and taxed at the preferred stocks' fair market value. There were numerous exceptions, such as for a taxpayer who exchanged one type of preferred stock for a comparable type of preferred stock and for recapitalization of a family-owned business.

Effective for transactions after June 8, 1997. Estimated revenue: $194 million over five years and $248 million over 10 years.

IRS Authority

● **Disclosure of tax return information for certain veterans' programs.** The bill permanently extended the right of the IRS to disclose certain information about self-employment and other areas to the Department of Veterans Affairs so that it could accurately determine benefit amounts for needs-based pensions, health care and other programs.

Effective date: Oct. 1, 1998, through Sept. 30, 2003. Estimated revenue: $116 million over five years and $152 million over 10 years.

● **IRS levy on benefits.** The IRS was allowed to place a continuous levy on non-means-tested federal benefits, such as Social Security, if a taxpayer failed to pay his tax bill. A levy allowed the IRS to seize or sell non-exempt taxpayer property to satisfy tax obligations. The levy would go into effect 10 days after notice and demand for payment by the IRS. In addition, the Treasury secretary was authorized to place a continuous levy on workers' compensation payments, annuity or pension payments under the railroad retirement act and the railroad unemployment insurance act, unemployment benefits and public assistance benefits.

Effective date: Aug. 6, 1997. Estimated revenue: $1.3 billion over five years and $1.8 billion over 10 years.

Earned-Income Tax Credit

● **EITC compliance.** Complaints about fraud and inaccuracy in the EITC system prompted Congress to enact a series of measures designed to clamp down on the problem.

A taxpayer who fraudulently claimed the credit would become ineligible for the subsequent 10 years. If the claim was a result of intentional or reckless disregard of the rules, then the taxpayer would be ineligible for the subsequent two years.

Taxpayers who were disqualified from claiming the EITC because they failed to provide the correct taxpayer identification number would have to go through a recertification process put in place by the secretary of the Treasury.

Tax return preparers who failed to meet due diligence requirements in preparing EITC claims would be subject to an additional $100 penalty per return beyond the existing penalties, which varied depending on the error and the preparer's intent but could cost as much as $1,000 per return.

Effective date: Dec. 31, 1996. Estimated savings: $88 million over five years and $193 million over 10 years.

● **Change in gross income eligibility.** Taxpayers were required to include tax-exempt interest and non-taxable distributions from pensions, annuities and IRAs when calculating their adjusted gross income for EITC eligibility purposes. In addition, 75 percent of losses from a business, such as a small family-owned firm, had to be disregarded when calculating adjusted gross income.

Effective date: Dec. 31, 1997. Estimated savings: $312 million over five years and $788 million over 10 years.

● **Federal case register data.** By Oct. 1, 1999, the secretary of the Treasury Department was required to have access to the registry at the Department of Health and Human Services of all child support orders and the Social Security numbers of all children covered by the orders. It was anticipated that the IRS could use the Social Security numbers to identify questionable claims for the EITC, the dependent exemption and other tax benefits before the refunds were paid out.

Effective date: Aug. 5, 1997. Estimated savings: $30 million over five years and $350 million over 10 years.

● **Workfare wages not qualified as income.** Wages received by former welfare recipients as part of "workfare" programs would not be counted as wages for the purpose of qualifying for the EITC.

Effective date: Aug. 5, 1997. Estimated savings: Negligible.

Other Provisions

● **Repeal of 1986 grandfather rules for certain pension operations.** Under existing law, a non-profit organization could not be exempt from tax if a substantial aspect of its work included providing commercial insurance. There was a partial exception for Blue Cross/Blue Shield organizations. The bill overturned the exception for two other companies: Mutual of America, which was established to handle pension plans for social workers, and Teachers Insurance Annuity Association — College Retirement Equity Fund, which handled the pension business of college teachers.

Effective date: Dec. 31, 1997. Estimated revenue: $450 million over five years and $1.2 billion over 10 years.

● **Foreign tax credits holding period.** The bill required shareholders that received dividends from foreign corporations to hold the stock for at least 16 days for common stock and 46 days in the case of preferred stock before receiving foreign tax credits for foreign income taxes paid on the dividend.

Previously, there was no holding period, which led taxpayers who could not use the foreign tax credits (for instance, because they were tax-exempt entities) to engage in tax-motivated transactions that involved trading the dividends to taxpayers who could use the foreign tax credits. The provision aimed to limit those practices.

Effective for dividends paid or accrued 30 days or more after the date of enactment, Aug. 5, 1997. Estimated revenue: $230 million over five years and $552 million over 10 years.

● **Parking or cash compensation.** Employers gained the option of offering employees either tax-free parking worth up to $165 a month or taxable cash compensation equivalent to that amount. The aim was to give employers and employees more choice, reward people for taking public transportation and give the government the potential to raise some revenue: If the employee took the cash, it would be taxed.

Effective date: Dec. 31, 1997. Estimated revenue: $46 million over five years and $118 million over 10 years.

● **Basis recovery method.** The bill created a new formula that reduced the amount of a pension annuity excludable from income when the annuity was a joint and survivor annuity, as opposed to a single life annuity.

Effective date: Dec. 31, 1997. Estimated revenue: $30 million over five years and $130 million over 10 years.

● **Terminate suspense accounts for family farm corporations.** The bill tightened accounting rules that had allowed primarily large farms to effectively defer paying taxes for years. The new rules prohibited so-called suspense accounts; those farms that had them were required to phase them out, paying tax on the money in them over 20 years.

Effective date: June 8, 1997. Estimated revenue: $170 million over five years and $377 million over 10 years.

● **Two-year carry-back and 20-year carry-forward.** The bill reduced from three years to two years the amount of time that a taxpayer could carry back a net operating loss, but extended the amount of time it could be carried forward to 20 years from 15 years.

Estimated revenue: $1.1 billion over five years and $1.7 billion over 10 years.

● **Company-owned life insurance.** Further restrictions were placed on deductions for life insurance contracts. The provision arose after it became public that some large mortgage companies planned to sell their contracts to borrowers. The tax treatment of life insurance contracts had been sharply curtailed in 1996, following widespread reports that corporate investors were avoiding tax on the contract's inside buildup.

Effective date: June 8, 1997. Estimated revenue: $500 million over five years and $2.2 billion over 10 years.

● **Basis allocation rules for distributee partners.** The bill tightened rules governing the allocation of the assets of a partnership when the partnership was sold in order to eliminate disguised sales made through partnerships.

Effective date: Aug. 5, 1997. Estimated revenue: $249 million over five years and $581 million over 10 years.

● **Eliminate the substantial appreciation requirement for inventory of a partnership.** Partnerships could no longer exempt the first 20 percent of inventory appreciation; all inventory appreciation had to be taxed as ordinary income. This provision applied only to individuals with partnership interests and affected the tax consequences only of the inventory. Any appreciation in the partnership shares would be taxed as a capital gain.

Effective date: Aug. 5, 1997. Estimated revenue: $316 million over five years and $760 million over 10 years.

● **Income forecast method for depreciation restricted.** The provision limited use of the income forecasting method of calculating depreciation to the types of products for which it was designed — such as movies, books and other intellectual property whose value was not affected by the passage of time in the same way as other durable goods. This depreciation methods was not to be used for other leased property.

Effective date: Dec. 31, 1997. Estimated savings: $248 million over five years and $352 million over 10 years.

● **Property losses to be replaced with property acquired from an unrelated person.** The bill specified that a taxpayer who involuntarily lost property (such as a small-business owner whose store burned down) had to acquire replacement property from an unrelated party, meaning not a relative. Property replaced as a result of such an involuntary conversion was not subject to tax if the replacement property was more valuable than the original property. However, if the replacement property was acquired from a relative — a spouse, sibling or parent — it could be a way of avoiding tax.

Effective for involuntary conversions occurring after June 12, 1997. Estimated savings: $30 million over five years and $115 million over 10 years.

● **One-year carry-back and 20-year carry-forward on general business credit.** The bill limited to one year the length of time that all general business credits could be carried back and extended from 15 years to 20 years the length of time the credits could be carried forward. The credits covered by the bill included, but were not limited to, the empowerment zone credit, energy credit, reforestation credit, alcohol fuels credit and the low-income housing credit.

Effective date: Dec. 31, 1997. Estimated savings: $471 million over five years and $527 million over 10 years.

● **Installment sales grandfather rules repealed.** An exception in the 1986 tax overhaul that allowed farm machinery manufacturer John Deere and major automakers to use the installment sales method of accounting was ended. The installment sales method allowed those companies to avoid recognizing the sale of a vehicle until the dealer sold it and paid them for it, similar to a consignment sale. The exception was put in place when John Deere was in dire straits.

Effective date: Dec. 31, 1998. Estimated savings: $353 million over five years and $507 million over 10 years.

Miscellaneous Revenue Reductions

● **Repeal unrelated business income tax on an employee stock ownership plan (ESOP) that was a shareholder in a subchapter S corporations.** The bill exempted ESOPs from paying income tax on the distributions from a subchapter S corporation until the ESOP distributed the income to the ESOP participants.

Effective date: Dec. 31, 1997. Estimated cost. $149 million over five years and $400 million over 10 years.

● **Limit on employer stock in 401(k) retirement plans.** The bill restricted the amount of its own stock that an employer could hold in a 401 (k) plan to 10 percent of the assets derived from employees' elective deferrals.

Effective date: Aug. 5, 1997. Estimated cost: Negligible.

● **Full-funding limit for defined-benefit plans.** Businesses were allowed to increase the funding of their defined-benefit pension plans beyond the existing full-funding limit, which was defined as the lesser of a plan's accrued liability or 150 percent of the current liability. Under the act, plans could be funded up to 155 percent of liability beginning in 1999, up to 160 percent beginning in 2001, up to 165 percent beginning in 2003 and up to 170 percent in 2004 and thereafter. When corporations contributed to employee pension plans, they did not have to count the money as part of their taxable income.

Effective date: Dec. 31, 1997. Estimated cost: $48 million over five years and $164 million over 10 years.

● **Modify limits for state and local plans.** Under the bill, state and local employees could credit previous pension participation in other states or in the private sector toward their current state or local government retirement plan. Employees were given the chance to buy into their new employer's plan by making a contribution equal to the amount that they would have paid if they had worked the requisite number of years.

Previously, people were prohibited from contributing the lesser of $30,000 or 25 percent of their annual salary at any one time to a state or local plan.

That created a problem for some workers, such as public school teachers who had taught for five years in a private school and then went to teach in the public school system. Many teachers were reaching retirement age only to discover that they could not retire with a pension. While they could theoretically buy into the state or local plan, they could not do so all at once because of the cap on contributions. This provision raised the cap to $30,000 or a maximum annual pension benefit of $125,000.

Effective date: Dec. 31, 1997. Estimated cost: $111 million over five years and $246 million over 10 years.

● **Repeal 30 percent gross income limitation for regulated investment companies.** Aimed at giving mutual funds more flexibility, this provision allowed mutual funds to get more than 30 percent of their income from stocks and bonds held for less than three months without losing preferential tax status. Under preferential status, tax liability passed through to the shareholders, and the mutual fund effectively paid no corporate tax.

Existing law allowed mutual funds to deduct their dividends to their shareholders; since virtually all their dividends went to shareholders, mutual funds had almost no tax liability. However, to retain that favorable tax treatment, a fund had to get less than 30 percent of its income from stocks or bonds held for less than three months. If it exceeded the 30 percent rule, the fund lost its status as a pass-through entity and was liable for the tax.

Effective date: Dec. 31, 1997. Estimated cost: $138 million over five years and $408 million over 10 years.

Trade

● **Generalized System of Preferences.** To spur economic development around the world, Congress in 1974 began granting the president authority to extend duty-free treatment to imports from countries designated as developing nations. That authority had last expired on May 31, 1997. The law reauthorized the program from June 1, 1997, through June 30, 1998.

Estimated cost: $378 million over five years. ■

Reconciliation Package: Spending Cuts

After months of balanced-budget negotiations, Congress and the White House agreed on a huge package of spending cuts that promised to reduce net federal deficit by $127 billion over five years. Dubbed the Balanced Budget Act of 1997, the measure was cleared by Congress on July 31. President Clinton signed it into law, along with a companion tax-reconciliation bill, at a White House ceremony Aug. 5 (HR 2015 — PL 105-33).

Together, the two bills were expected to result in a balanced federal budget by 2002, while allowing for significant tax cuts.

The spending reductions were almost evenly divided between entitlement programs ($122 billion) and discretionary appropriations (about $140 billion). The biggest savings — $115 billion over five years — came from Medicare, the government-subsidized health insurance program for the elderly

The bill also cut projected Medicaid spending, authorized new auctioning of portions of the broadcast spectrum, and affected programs ranging from student loans to housing and veterans' benefits.

The hard bargaining required to produce the bill yielded rewards for both sides. Clinton carried the day on restoring benefits to legal immigrants who were in the country when the 1996 welfare overhaul law (PL 104-193) was signed. He also won the inclusion of a new children's health care initiative, funded in part by an increase in the federal tax on cigarettes.

Republicans won spending cuts large enough to deliver on their promise to both balance the budget and provide hefty tax reductions. They also won inclusion of a pilot program for 390,000 seniors to purchase "medical savings accounts."

BOXSCORE

Spending Reconciliation — HR 2015 (S 947). The bill provided for $263 billion in deficit reduction over five years, mainly through cuts in entitlement programs and caps on discretionary spending.

Reports: H Rept 105-149; conference report, H Rept 105-217.

KEY ACTION

June 25 — House passed HR 2015, 270-162. **Senate** passed S 947, 73-27, then passed HR 2015, amended, by voice vote.

July 30 — House adopted the conference report, 346-85.

July 31 — Senate cleared the bill, 85-15.

Aug. 5 — President signed HR 2015 — PL 105-33.

Bill Highlights

The following are highlights of the spending-cut package:

• **Medicare.** The bill cut the projected growth of the Medicare program by 12 percent, or $115 billion, over five years, primarily by reducing payments to doctors, hospitals and other health care providers. It also increased Medicare Part B premiums, which paid for doctor visits and other outpatient services. *(Medicare, Medicaid and children's health p. 6-3)*

At the same time, the bill provided for Medicare to cover more preventive tests, including prostrate screenings, bone-density tests and blood testing and diet counseling, for beneficiaries needing them.

Although the changes were the most extensive made in the Medicare program since it began in 1965, the final bill did not include key structural changes endorsed by the Senate. The Senate wanted to gradually increase the Medicare eligibility age from 65 to 67, require wealthier seniors to pay a higher Medicare premium, and require beneficiaries to pay a $5 co-payment for each home health care visit.

These proposals, which addressed the program's long-term financial problems, were deemed too controversial by both the House and the administration.

• **Medical savings accounts.** The bill created a pilot program to allow about 390,000 people to use new, medical savings accounts instead of traditional Medicare to pay for health expenses.

• **Medicaid.** The bill reduced projected spending on Medicaid, the government-backed health insurance program for the poor, by about $10.4 billion over five years. Most of the savings came from reducing payments to states for hospitals that served a disproportionate share of low-income patients.

Additional savings were achieved by giving states more flexibility in setting provider payment levels. The bill repealed the so-called Boren Amendment, which required state Medicaid programs to pay hospitals and nursing homes a "reasonable and adequate" rate.

The bill also established a $1.5 billion block grant to states to help low-income Medicaid enrollees pay their Part B Medicare premiums.

• **Children's health initiative.** The bill provided $23.4 billion to expand health coverage to uninsured children. The costs were partially offset by a 15-cent-per-pack increase in the federal cigarette tax.

States were given flexibility to determine eligibility for the program, though it was generally limited to children from families with incomes up to 200 percent of the poverty level.

States could decide to expand their Medicaid programs, provide health insurance programs for these children, use up to 10 percent of their funds for direct services to children, or some combination of these options. Some of the money could go to hospitals and other health care providers, but most had to be used to pay for insurance.

• **Welfare.** Legal immigrants who were in the United States on Aug. 22, 1996, the date the 1996 welfare overhaul bill was signed, were made eligible for Supplemental Security Income (SSI) cash benefits for the low-income aged and disabled, whether they were disabled then or became disabled later. Without the change, all non-citizens would have been removed from the SSI rolls Oct. 1, 1997. *(Welfare, p. 6-31; 1996 Almanac, p. 6-3)*

In addition, the bill:

• Continued Medicaid coverage for disabled children who lost their SSI benefits because of eligibility changes contained in the welfare law.

• Created a fund worth $3 billion to help states place long-term welfare recipients into the work force in fiscal 1998 and 1999. The final bill did not include controversial House provisions that would have exempted recipients in certain "workfare" positions from the federal minimum wage law.

• Increased spending by a total of $1.5 billion over five years for food stamps and employment and training benefits for people who might otherwise have lost their eligibility under the welfare overhaul law.

• **Spectrum auction.** The bill raised a total of $21.4 billion over five years by extending and expanding the authority of

Spending Caps, 'PAYGO' Rules . . .

As part of the Balanced Budget Act of 1997, Congress extended key budget enforcement rules through 2002. Those rules imposed spending cuts if Congress failed to abide by specific limits on discretionary spending or if it changed the tax code or mandatory programs in ways that resulted in a net increase in the deficit.

House deficit hawks attempted to go much further, calling for tough new rules that would automatically force Congress to achieve its stated goal of eliminating the deficit by 2002. But they ran into entrenched opposition, offended committee chairmen and won little support. In the end, their attempts both to include their more stringent enforcement provisions in the reconciliation package and to pass them as a separate bill were unsuccessful.

Budget Rules Extended

The spending portion of the budget-reconciliation package (HR 2015 — PL 105-33) included a budget-enforcement section that mainly extended a set of rules first enacted in 1990 (PL 101-508) in an effort to curb the deficit. Those rules — limits on discretionary spending and so-called pay-as-you-go procedures for entitlements and taxes — had been extended once in 1993, but they were due to expire Sept. 30, 1998. *(1990 Almanac, p. 161; 1993 Almanac, p. 138)*

The following were the key budget-enforcement provisions of HR 2015:

• **Discretionary spending caps.** The bill extended the limits on discretionary spending — the money appropriated through annual spending bills. The caps placed limits on both budget authority and outlays.

The White House could adjust the annual caps to account for emergency appropriations and differences between the Congressional Budget Office (CBO) and the White House Office of Management and Budget (OMB) in estimating outlays, as under existing law. But the caps could no longer be adjusted for inflation or for differences in estimating budget authority.

• **Firewalls.** The bill revived and modified so-called firewalls erected in the 1990 law to separate defense and nondefense discretionary spending. The purpose of the walls was to keep Congress from cutting defense to pay for domestic programs, or vice versa. The firewalls had expired at the end of fiscal 1993. HR 2015 renewed them for fiscal 1998-99, then combined categories under a single discretionary cap for fiscal 2000-2002.

The bill also created a separate category under the budget law for fiscal 1998-2000 for the Violent Crime Reduction Trust Fund. This extended and replaced provisions of the 1994 crime law (PL 103-322) that created separate limits for the crime trust fund.

• **PAYGO.** The law extended pay-as-you-go procedures, known as PAYGO, for revenues and mandatory spending. Under PAYGO, the cost of any new or expanded entitlement program, or any tax cut, had to be offset by cuts in other entitlement spending or by tax increases.

PAYGO applied only to legislative changes made by Congress — for example, the creation of a new entitlement program or a change in eligibility rules for an existing one. It did not come into play if other factors caused an increase in the deficit — for example, an economic downturn that caused more people to qualify for existing benefits or reduced income tax revenues.

• **Sequestration.** The discretionary caps and PAYGO rules were enforced through what was known as sequestration — automatic, across-the-board spending cuts in non-exempt programs. A sequester was triggered for discretionary programs if the annual spending cap was exceeded. Under PAYGO, a sequester was triggered if the net effect of tax and entitlement legislation was to increase the deficit.

Legislative Path

The budget-enforcement provisions were written by the House and Senate Budget committees, in consultation with CBO and OMB.

The House passed them as part of HR 2015, the spending-cut portion of the budget-reconciliation package. They were incorporated as part of the rule for floor consideration of the bill, approved June 25. In the Senate, similar budget rules were added to HR 2014, the tax portion of the reconciliation package. They were added in a floor amendment by Budget Committee Chairman Pete V. Domenici, R-N.M., that was adopted, 98-2, on June 27. *(Vote 141, p. S-26)*

---

the Federal Communications Commission to auction electromagnetic spectrum, including spectrum returned by television broadcasters after they converted to digital broadcasts. *(Spectrum auction, p. 3-34)*

• **Discretionary spending caps.** Budget enforcement provisions in the bill extended existing caps on appropriated spending through 2002, for an estimated five-year savings of $140 billion.

• **Other deficit reduction.** The bill included the following additional savings and revenue over five years:

• $2.7 billion in savings by reducing spending on veterans' programs.

• $4.8 billion in savings by increasing federal agency and federal employee contributions to federal employee retirement plans.

• $1.8 billion in savings from changes in federal student loan programs. *(Student loans, p. 7-8)*

• $Another 1.8 billion in savings from replacing the Federal Housing Administration's foreclosure relief program and reducing subsidies in the Section 8 rental housing program.

• $736 million in increased revenues from extending vessel tonnage fees, selling Governors Island in New York harbor and selling air rights over Union Station.

• **Debt limit.** In a little-noticed provision, the bill also increased the statutory limit on the public debt from $5.5 trillion to $5.950 trillion. Under existing estimates, that was considered sufficient to last until Dec. 15, 1999.

Background

The broad parameters for the tax and spending bills had been set in the bipartisan budget deal reached in May, and

. . . Extended Through 2002

Conference negotiators agreed to put the rules in the spending bill.

Deficit Hawks Rebuffed

A small but persistent band of deficit hawks in the House — led by Republicans Joe L. Barton of Texas, Michael N. Castle of Delaware and Zach Wamp of Tennessee, joined by "Blue Dog" Democrats such as David Minge of Minnesota and Charles W. Stenholm of Texas — wanted more.

Their plan was to use the levels set in the fiscal 1998 budget resolution (H Con Res 84) to create annual statutory caps on spending for entitlement programs, such as Medicare and Medicaid, as well as a floor for revenues and a limit on the total deficit. If those limits were breached, Congress and the White House would have until Dec. 15 of a given year to find a way to make up the difference.

If they failed, the president would be required to curb any entitlement program that had grown too quickly; the sequestered funding would be permanently cancelled. If revenues were lower than required, the tax cuts enacted in the tax-reconciliation bill would be temporarily suspended.

Congress and the president could also punt and change the caps, but they would have to pass a law to do so.

Without such caps, supporters argued, the deficit effects of entitlement and tax provisions could end up being much different than anticipated without triggering any action.

Amendment Bid Rejected

In a high-stakes standoff with GOP leaders, Barton, Castle and Minge appeared before the House Rules Committee June 24 and threatened to defeat the rule for floor debate on the budget-reconciliation bills if they were not given a chance to add their enforcement language. The committee rejected their demand.

The next morning, the rule was in trouble, and Barton pressed his case with GOP leaders. Finally, just an hour before the rule went to the floor, he backed off in exchange for the promise of a stand-alone vote by July 24.

In an unusual move, Rules Committee Chairman Gerald B.H. Solomon, R-N.Y., announced the promise on the floor. Barton then urged the rebels to vote for the rule, which passed 228-200. *(Vote 239, p. H-76)*

"I took the July 24 vote, which gets us some support and time to build more support, over having to go through a dogfight to beat a rule," Barton said. "I think we would have defeated it, but it would have left a lot of bad feelings."

Stand-Alone Bill Falls

Although the rebels got their vote, they failed to pass their bill. The separate measure (HR 2003) went down in flames July 23 under attack from all sides. The House vote was 81-347. *(Vote 301, p. H-92)*

The idea of putting teeth into the budget agreement had an intrinsic appeal, especially given the failure of every recent balanced-budget pronouncement to come true. But even many of the bill's supporters argued that the procedures outlined in HR 2003 were too convoluted and needed further refinement.

The rebels' use of threats to bring the measure to the floor won them little sympathy from the leadership. On July 22, the Rules Committee issued a closed rule (H Res 192) that denied Barton and his allies any chance to offer amendments that might improve their bill.

Minge and others charged that the leadership wanted to see the "weakest possible bill before the body for a vote, hoping that this bill could be defeated." Solomon countered that the leadership agreement with the rebels was to bring up HR 2003 as introduced.

The short-circuiting of the committee process did not go over well and was another major element of the defeat. In addition, many Republicans disliked the plan because of its potential to slow down implementation of their tax cuts. And Democrats and Republicans alike complained that they and other members did not fully understand what the effect might be on key programs, such as Social Security and veterans' benefits.

Others argued that the existing budget enforcement rules had worked. "This bill deals with a problem that has not presented itself for the last five years," said Spratt.

The rebels made one last try after the vote, offering a motion that would have brought up a revised version. They lost, 148-279. *(Vote 300, p. H-92)*

refined in the fiscal 1998 budget resolution (H Con Res 84). The budget resolution instructed eight committees each in the House and Senate to contribute pieces to the spending-cut bill, with the most significant responsibility assigned to the House Ways and Means Committee and the Senate Finance Committee. The budget resolution included specific recommendations for meeting the targets, but most of the details were advisory. *(Budget resolution, p. 2-23)*

In many cases, work on the spending cuts proceeded smoothly. In the House, Ways and Means easily approved Medicare provisions by a 36-3 vote.

But in areas such as welfare and children's health, House Republicans adopted positions that drew objections from the administration. In the Senate, action proceeded on a more bipartisan basis, typified by freewheeling Finance Committee proposals to raise the cigarette tax by 20 cents per pack to pay for a larger children's health care initiative.

The spending-cut bills that reached the House and Senate floors were stitched together by the respective Budget committees from the pieces produced by the individual panels.

House Committee Action

The House Budget Committee worked into the evening June 20 before approving its version of the spending-cut bill, 25-5 (HR 2015 — H Rept 105-149). The markup had convened after a day's worth of negotiations involving Budget Chairman John R. Kasich, R-Ohio, ranking member John M. Spratt Jr., D-S.C., and the White House over what changes would be made to the bill on the floor.

The administration and Spratt complained that many of

the GOP-written provisions did not live up to the letter and spirit of the May budget deal. However many lawmakers, including some Democrats, felt free to go against the wishes of the White House. The budget negotiators, said Majority Leader Dick Armey, R-Texas, "must understand that the agreements requiring execution by other people have certain limitations on them."

Among the most significant in a lengthy list of administration objections:

• **Welfare.** The bipartisan budget agreement, reflected in the budget resolution, called for making legal immigrants who were in the country as of Aug. 22, 1996, eligible for SSI no matter when they became disabled.

By contrast, the House provisions, written by the Ways and Means Subcommittee on Human Resources, proposed covering only legal immigrants who were already receiving SSI as of Aug. 22, 1996. Legal immigrants who were in the country at that time but were not receiving SSI benefits would not be eligible for SSI if they subsequently became disabled.

• **Children's health care.** The House bill included a new $16 billion block grant program to expand health coverage for uninsured children. States could purchase private health insurance for low-income families or expand Medicaid to cover more children. Democrats said the plan would cover only half the nation's 10 million uninsured children and would give states officials too much spending latitude. They said there were not enough protections to ensure that the money would be used to cover more children, rather than serving as a slush fund for the states.

• **Minimum wage.** The House bill sought to reverse a Labor Department directive issued in May that required states to pay the minimum wage to "workfare" beneficiaries — welfare recipients who were required to work in public or nonprofit jobs as a condition of receiving welfare benefits. Under the House bill, states could count federal benefits as part of the compensation for minimum wage purposes.

• **Medicaid.** Democrats argued that Republicans were reneging on a promise to help low-income elderly people pay higher Medicare premiums for doctor visits. Republicans argued that the budget agreement was not that broad.

Negotiations continued even after the committee had approved the bill. Although Kasich was walking a tightrope between Democratic demands and strong-willed GOP chairmen, he managed to give Spratt and the administration some, though not nearly all, of what they were seeking.

House Floor Action

The House passed the bill June 25 by a vote of 270-162. No Democratic amendments were allowed. While the compromises negotiated prior to the vote did not address all of the Democratic concerns, they represented enough of a good faith effort to win the votes of 51 Democrats. *(Vote 241, p. H-76)*

"We're not totally, completely satisfied on the spending side. We've got a long way to go," said Gary A. Condit of California, a leader of the conservative "Blue Dog" Democrats. "We understand the obstacle course [Kasich] has [to run] to get it through the House."

Other Democrats responded with outrage at what they said were GOP breaches of the May agreement. "What we have here is a replay, really, of the last Congress," said Minority Whip David E. Bonior, D-Mich. "They are taking dollars out of children's hospitals; they are taking dollars that were intended for children's health insurance benefits."

The changes had been automatically incorporated into the spending bill when the House adopted a "self-executing" rule (H Res 174) that allowed the tax and spending bills to come to the floor.

Among the changes, the rule:

➤ Added $1 billion to the $500 million already in the bill to help pay Medicare Part B premiums for low-income beneficiaries, bringing the total to $1.5 billion.

➤ Modified the "workfare" provisions so that only cash welfare benefits and food stamps could be counted toward compensation.

➤ Increased access to the new health care coverage for children.

➤ Revised spectrum auction provisions to raise an additional $10.6 billion over five years, bringing the total amount expected from the auctions to $20.3 billion. That was still short of the $26.3 billion called for under the budget resolution.

➤ Added a set of budget enforcement procedures that extended caps on discretionary spending and so-called PAYGO rules through fiscal 2002. Under PAYGO, congressional action to cut taxes or expand entitlement spending had to be offset by tax increases or entitlement cuts.

A small, bipartisan group of deficit hawks threatened to defeat the rule for floor consideration of the reconciliation bills if they were not allowed to offer an amendment containing stricter enforcement rules. Republican leaders persuaded them to back off in exchange for a separate vote on their bill, and the rule was adopted, 228-200. The separate bill was subsequently defeated. *(Vote 239, p. H-76; budget enforcement, p. 2-48)*

Senate Committee Action

The Senate Budget Committee approved its own version of the spending-cuts bill (S 947) on June 20 by a vote of 18-3. The panel made no changes to the provisions it received from the eight committees, and it issued no written report.

The Medicare, Medicaid and welfare provisions that were the heart of the bill came with bipartisan support from the Finance Committee, which approved them, 20-0, on June 18.

The following were among the major differences between the Senate and House bills:

• **Minimum wage.** At the behest of Chairman William V. Roth Jr., R-Del., the Senate Finance Committee took no position on whether workfare beneficiaries should be exempt from minimum wage laws, effectively leaving in place Clinton's decision.

• **Welfare.** The committee endorsed a Roth compromise on legal immigrants' access to SSI benefits: Legal immigrants who were collecting SSI by Aug. 22, 1996, would remain eligible for the aid. Legal immigrants who were in the country at that time and later became disabled could apply for SSI until Sept. 30, 1997.

• **Medicare changes.** The Finance bill proposed a radical change in Medicare, linking the annual deductible for Medicare's Part B program to seniors' incomes.

Phil Gramm, R-Texas said the proposal, added in committee, would represent "the most dramatic reform of Medicare in this country. . . . If it is sustained, we will have done more in one markup than all the talk" on changing Medicare. The bill also included provisions to gradually raise the eligibility age for Medicare benefits from 65 to 67 by 2027, and to require a $5 co-payment for some home health care services.

The White House vigorously opposed the means testing and eligibility age increase, as did the American Association of Retired Persons.

• **Medical savings accounts.** The committee scaled back a House proposal to allow 500,000 Medicare beneficiaries to shift from the traditional fee-for-service program to tax-exempt medical savings accounts. The federal government would deposit a lump sum annually into these accounts, which beneficiaries could use to pay for qualified medical services.

Those who chose them would also have to purchase high-deductible insurance policies to cover catastrophic illnesses. The House proposal allowed catastrophic policies with deductibles as high as $6,000 and placed no limit on beneficiaries' out-of-pocket expenses.

The Finance version called for a demonstration program of 100,000 people, deductibles between $1,500 and $2,250, and a cap on out-of-pocket expenses.

• **Children's health.** The Finance Committee rejected attempts to change the children's health provisions in the spending bill. However, Sen. Orrin G. Hatch, R-Utah, won committee approval for an amendment to the companion tax bill to increase cigarette taxes by 20 cents a pack, netting an additional $8 billion to pay for new health coverage for uninsured children.

That brought the Senate total for the initiative to $24 billion, compared to $16 billion in the House.

Senate Floor Action

Acting on the same day as the House, the Senate passed its spending-cut bill June 25 by a vote of 73-27. It later agreed by voice vote to pass HR 2015, after substituting the Senate text. *(Vote 130, p. S-24)*

The vote reflected the bill's bipartisan support in the Senate, as well as the uncomfortable splits it had created in the Democratic caucus: 21 Democrats voted for the bill; 24 voted "no."

Efforts by Democratic liberals such as Edward M. Kennedy of Massachusetts to eliminate the proposals to restructure Medicare were crushed by surprisingly large margins. When the bill came to the floor June 23, Kennedy attacked it as a continuation of the "Republican assault on Medicare that began in the last Congress." But the next day, the three most controversial elements were affirmed by sweeping votes.

First, the Senate tabled (killed), 59-41, an amendment by Kennedy and Paul Wellstone, D-Minn., that would have removed the requirement for a $5 co-payment for some home health care services. The Senate then voted 62-38 to waive the so-called Byrd rule — which barred extraneous material in reconciliation bills — to retain the proposed increase in the Medicare eligibility age. Finally, senators voted overwhelmingly, 70-30, to kill an an attempt by Kennedy to eliminate the provision requiring that higher-income seniors pay higher Medicare Part B premiums for outpatient services. *(Votes 111, 112, 113, p. S-22)*

With virtually no discussion, the Senate on June 25 gave voice vote approval to an amendment by Frank R. Lautenberg, D-N.J., to make legal immigrants who were in the country as of Aug. 22, 1966, eligible for SSI no matter when they became disabled.

The Senate also adopted by voice vote a package of changes from John H. Chafee, R-R.I., and John D. Rockefeller IV, D-W.Va., to ensure that expanded children's health coverage was equivalent to that provided to federal workers, and to limit premiums, deductibles and co-payments for low-income families.

Conference/Final Action

The House-Senate conference on the bill proceeded slowly at first, with one ceremonial opening session July 10 and 13 separate "subconferences," where negotiators met behind closed doors. Republicans soon tossed Democrats and White House officials out of the rooms and set about adopting a unified House-Senate GOP position to take to Clinton.

Serious negotiations with the White House began July 24 and intensified over the weekend of July 26-27. Republicans at first took a hard line, for example, rejecting proposals to allow SSI benefits to legal immigrants who became disabled after the welfare law was enacted. The provision was the only one in the spending bill to draw an explicit veto threat.

But Republicans knew they would have to make concessions if they were to reach their goal of getting a bill enacted before the August recess — particularly given Clinton's rising ratings in the polls and the discord in their own ranks evidenced in a recent coup attempt against Speaker Newt Gingrich, R-Ga. *(Gingrich, p. 1-11)*

Finally, the number of negotiators shrank sharply, with Gingrich and Senate Majority Leader Trent Lott, R-Miss., White House Chief of Staff Erskine Bowles and Office of Management and Budget Director Franklin D. Raines in the most critical roles. Racing to meet the August recess deadline, Republican negotiators started making concessions in weekend talks July 26-27 that finally produced agreement on Monday, July 28.

The House adopted the resulting conference report (H Rept 105-217) on July 30 by a vote of 346-85. The Senate cleared the bill, 85-15, the following day. *(House vote 345, p. H-104; Senate vote 209, p. S-36)*

The Final Deals

Amid the scores of compromises made to reach that point, the following stood out:

• **Children's health.** In the end, the cigarette tax, which had begun as part of the companion tax bill, was assigned to the spending bill. The 15-cents-a-pack increase provided financing for the children's health insurance initiative, which was funded at the $23.4 billion level favored by the Senate.

Though the children's health plan was not in Clinton's initial budget, once the president was on board, he promoted it heavily and its inclusion was a major victory for the administration. On Capitol Hill, the proposal had been pushed hard by Kennedy, Minority Leader Tom Daschle, D-S.D., and prominent Republicans such as Hatch.

• **Medicare.** At the insistence of both the House and the administration, the final bill did not include Senate proposals for means testing, increasing the eligibility age and requiring a $5 co-payment for each home health care visit for Medicare beneficiaries..

Instead, it provided for the establishment of a National Bipartisan Commission on the Future of Medicare to report in 1999 on the financial impact of the pending retirement of the Baby Boomers and recommend structural changes.

• **Medical savings accounts.** The final bill included the House plan for a pilot medical savings account program, though the number of participants was reduced to 390,000. As in the House bill, annual deductibles as high as $6,000 were allowed.

• **Medicaid.** The bill established a $1.5 billion block grant to states to assist low-income Medicaid enrollees to pay their Part B Medicare premiums.

• **Welfare.** Clinton insisted on the Senate provisions, which made legal immigrants who were in the country Aug. 22, 1996, eligible for SSI benefits regardless of when they became disabled.

The bill also continued Medicaid coverage for disabled children who lost their SSI benefits because of changes in eligibility contained in the welfare law.

● **Workfare.** Clinton and congressional Democrats dug in their heels and eliminated the House language aimed at relaxing minimum wage and other federal labor requirements for welfare recipients who were required to work in state and nonprofit jobs.

● **Budget enforcement.** The final bill included a set of budget enforcement provisions extending discretionary caps and PAYGO requirements through 2002.

The House had added the enforcement language when HR 2015 first came to the floor. The Senate spending-cut bill did not address budget enforcement, but the Senate had adopted similar provisions during floor consideration of the companion tax-reconciliation bill. That amendment, by Senate Budget Committee Chairman Pete V. Domenici, R-N.M., had been adopted, 98-2. *(Vote 141, p. S-26)* ■

Spending Bill Provisions

Following are major provisions of the Balanced Budget Act of 1997 (HR 2015 — PL 105-33), the portion of the budget-reconciliation package that dealt with mandatory and discretionary spending. Enacted Aug. 5, the bill contained savings sufficient to balance the budget by 2002 and help finance a companion bill (HR 2014 — PL 105-34) that made the first major tax cuts since 1981.

The spending-cut bill was expected to achieve $127 billion in net deficit reduction over five years (fiscal 1998 through fiscal 2002).

Gross deficit reduction was expected to be $160 billion, achieved chiefly through $112 billion in savings from Medicare, $21 billion from electromagnetic spectrum auctions, $7 billion in Medicaid savings, $5 billion in cigarette tax increases, and $15 billion in other savings and taxes.

The bill also included $33 billion in new spending sought by President Clinton and congressional Democrats: $20 billion for a children's health insurance initiative and $13 billion to restore certain welfare cuts made in the 1996 welfare law (PL 104-193).

The Medicare and Medicaid changes in the bill included some of the most significant alterations to the two federal health insurance programs since they were created in 1965. The bill also included an expanded children's health care program.

MAJOR PROVISIONS

Budget Provisions

HR 2015 extended two key mechanisms for enforcing budget limits established by the 1990 budget law (PL 101-508). The rules, which had been renewed in 1993, had been set to expire at the end of fiscal 1998. *(1990 Almanac, p. 161; 1993 Almanac, p. 138)*

The bill also updated and revised the Congressional Budget and Impoundment Control Act (PL 93-344), which had been amended numerous times since it became law in 1974. Most provisions involved technical changes and corrections, elimination of redundancies and revisions to reflect evolution in budget practices.

Major budget provisions:

Budget Enforcement

● **Discretionary spending caps.** Extended limits on discretionary spending — the money provided annually through the appropriations bills — through 2002. The limits applied to both budget authority and outlays. As before, they were enforceable through sequestration — automatic across-the-board cuts in non-exempt discretionary programs.

The White House could adjust the annual caps to account for emergency appropriations and differences between the Congressional Budget Office (CBO) and the White House Office of Management and Budget (OMB) in estimating outlays, as under existing law. The caps could also be raised if legislation was enacted to provide funding for the International Monetary Fund, international arrearages in United Nations dues and other accounts, and efforts to curb fraud in the earned-income tax credit program, which provided tax relief for low-income workers.

But the caps could no longer be adjusted for inflation or for differences between CBO and OMB in estimating budget authority.

Separately, the chairmen of the House and Senate Budget committees could adjust budget levels set forth in the annual budget resolution to reflect certain action on legislation, generally mirroring adjustments made by the president in discretionary caps.

● **'Firewalls.'** Revived and modified "firewalls" separating specific discretionary spending accounts. Those barriers, first set up under the 1990 law and since expired, had separated domestic, defense and international accounts; only those accounts within the subcategory that was breached were subject to a sequester. The effect was to prevent Congress from cutting defense to pay for extra domestic spending, or vice versa.

The new firewalls separated defense and non-defense discretionary spending in fiscal 1998 and 1999. In fiscal years 2000, 2001 and 2002, all discretionary spending would be in a single category.

In addition, the bill incorporated into the budget rules caps on discretionary spending for crime prevention enacted under the 1994 crime law (PL 103-322). Those limits were effective from fiscal 1998 through 2000.

The bill extended the caps as follows (in billions of dollars):

Fiscal Year	Category	Budget Authority	Outlays
1998	Defense	$ 269.0	$ 269.8
	Non-defense	252.4	282.9
	Violent Crime reduction	5.5	3.6
1999	Defense	271.5	266.5
	Non-defense	255.7	287.9
	Violent Crime reduction	5.8	5.0
2000	Discretionary	532.7	558.7
	Violent Crime reduction	4.5	5.6
2001	Discretionary	542.0	564.4
2002	Discretionary	551.1	560.8

● **PAYGO rules.** Extended through 2002 pay-as-you-go rules, known as PAYGO, for legislation affecting direct or mandatory spending or revenues. Under PAYGO, the cost of any new or expanded entitlement program or any tax cut had to be offset by cuts in other entitlement spending or by tax increases. A sequester was triggered if the net effect of tax and entitlement legislation was to increase the deficit.

Any sequestration was to be evenly divided between non-exempt defense accounts and non-exempt non-defense accounts. Exempt accounts included Social Security, veterans' programs, net interest payments on the debt and programs for low-income people. Sequestration of many other programs was governed by limitations, special rules and exceptions; for example, any sequestration of Medicare was limited to a 4 percent cut.

The bill extended PAYGO enforcement procedures through fiscal 2006. Any legislation enacted through 2002 was subject to pay-as-you-go rules and enforcement by sequester for five years. (The goal was to prevent Congress from passing legislation that met pay-as-you-go requirements prior to 2002, but resulted in a deficit afterward.)

PAYGO applied only to legislative changes — for example the creation of a new entitlement program or the expansion of an existing one. It did not cover factors considered outside Congress' control such as a recession.

● **PAYGO balances.** Eliminated existing balances on the so-called PAYGO scorecard, a running tally that combined the deficit effects of enacted legislation. If the PAYGO scorecard reflected deficit reduction, this balance could, in effect, be used to prevent a sequester if other legislation increased the deficit by an amount less than the PAYGO balance.

The 1997 PAYGO scorecard reflected a negative PAYGO balance caused by deficit reduction resulting chiefly from savings from the 1996 welfare overhaul (PL 104-193) and the 1996 farm bill (PL 104-127).

The bill exempted from PAYGO balances the savings and revenue losses from the companion 1997 tax law. The aim was to prevent such savings from being used to finance legislation to reduce revenues or increase direct spending.

Budget Act Amendments

● **Budget resolution.** Required Congress' annual budget resolution to cover a minimum of five years, making permanent a temporary five-year requirement — set to expire at the end of fiscal 1998 — enacted as part of the 1990 budget law. The House and Senate Budget committees could recommend that the budget resolution cover a longer period.

The budget provisions made optional (instead of mandatory) inclusion in the budget resolution of total direct loan obligation and total primary loan guarantee commitment levels. The Federal Credit Reform Act of 1990 had rendered the requirement obsolete.

● **Appropriations allocations.** Changed the procedure for providing contingent budget allocations to the House Appropriations Committee in the event that a budget resolution was not adopted by the April 15 deadline. Such contingent allocations were to be be based on the discretionary spending limits in the prior year's budget resolution, instead of those in the president's budget.

● **Senate task force.** Provided for the appointment of a six-member bipartisan task force to study Senate floor procedures for considering the budget resolution and budget-reconciliation bills. This responded to criticism that senators sometimes voted on numerous amendments — with very little debate — during so-called vote-a-thons after the time for debate had expired.

Debt Limit

The bill increased the statutory limit on the national debt from $5.5 trillion to $5.95 trillion. The increase was expected to provide sufficient borrowing authority for the federal government until approximately Dec. 15, 1999.

Medicare

The bill included some of the most significant alterations to Medicare, the federal health insurance program for the elderly and disabled, since the program was created in 1965. Among other things, the bill broadened the options available to seniors to include several managed care alternatives, such as preferred provider organizations and provider sponsored organizations. It also allowed up to 390,000 seniors to open medical savings accounts, which could be used for qualified medical expenses but had to be coupled with high-deductible health insurance plans to pay for catastrophic illnesses.

Legislators decided to leave to a commission some of the toughest decisions about Medicare: its long-term solvency, and whether to raise the eligibility age, require higher-income beneficiaries to pay more for their care and require a copayment on some home health care services.

Major Medicare provisions:

● **Expanded choices.** Permitted seniors to receive their health care from an expanded set of managed care options that went beyond the standard health maintenance organization (HMO) option that had been available to Medicare beneficiaries. An HMO provided health care in a geographic area with set benefits at a set fee. A primary care doctor often served as a "gatekeeper," controlling access to specialists and medical procedures.

The new "Medicare+Choice" options, as well as changes in payments to managed care providers, were expected to save $22.5 billion over five years. All Medicare+Choice enrollees would continue to pay monthly premiums ($43.50 in 1997) for Medicare Part B, which paid for doctor's visits and outpatient services, with additional out-of-pocket costs varying with the plan selected. Options included:

● **PPOs and PSOs.** Preferred provider organizations and provider sponsored organizations could collect monthly premiums and small copayments from beneficiaries, and would generally restrict enrollees to visiting doctors on a specific list.

A PSO, however, would not have a separate administrative entity. Doctors and hospitals would run the plans themselves. PSOs had to apply first to state authorities for licensing. If state officials failed to complete action on the license within 90 days, or if the application was improperly denied, the PSO could apply to the federal government for a waiver. A federal waiver would be good for 36 months and could not be renewed.

● **Medical savings accounts.** These plans, open to 390,000 people as a pilot program, allowed seniors to use special tax-exempt accounts for qualified medical expenses. Seniors who selected this option had to also purchase a high-deductible insurance policy (up to $6,000 deductible) to cover catastrophic illnesses.

They could spend some of the money in their accounts — up to 40 percent of the policy deductible — for purposes other than medical expenses, although such money would be included in taxable income. Seniors who withdrew more than 40 percent would face a 50 percent penalty tax. When an account holder died, the beneficiary could continue the account, but no new contributions could be made.

The demonstration program was scheduled to sunset Dec. 31, 2002. Those with the accounts could keep them.

● **Private fee-for-service.** These private indemnity plans covered at least the same services as Medicare's fee-for-service program but did not have to abide by the same fee schedule. Premiums were not capped and doctors and other providers could charge patients up to 115 percent of what the indemnity plan paid providers. Backers of the provision said it would give Medicare beneficiaries more choice in providers and a greater say in the quality of their medical care.

● **Private contracting.** This option allowed physicians not in the Medicare program to enter into private contracts with beneficiaries for a particular service covered by Medicare. The doctors could charge the beneficiary more than what was allowed under Medicare's fee-for-service schedule. Physicians who participated in private contracting could not participate in the Medicare program for two years. To help protect beneficiaries, they were not allowed to enter into a contract when facing an emergency or urgent health problem. The contract the beneficiary signed had to state clearly that no Medicare claims would be submitted, nor would any supplementary insurance pick up part of the cost. The provision was effective Jan. 1, 1998.

● **Payment rates.** Changed payment rates for providers in the Medicare+Choice program. Providers were previously paid under a system of county rates, a fixed monthly amount per beneficiary per county. Under the bill, providers were to be paid according to a system that more evenly blended local county rates with national rates over the five-year period.

Every health plan would be paid a minimum, or "floor," of $367 per month per beneficiary, starting in 1998. That amount was to be updated annually to reflect the growth in Medicare fee-for-service payments minus 0.8 percentage point in fiscal 1998 and minus 0.5 percentage point each year through fiscal 2002. Each plan would receive at least a 2 percent increase every year. Starting Jan. 1, 2000, Medicare payments to managed care providers would reflect updated factors that affected health costs, such as demographics and patients' health history.

In a change from prior practice, payments for graduate medical education were to be "carved out" of payments to Medicare+Choice plans over the following five years. Instead, those payments would be distributed directly to teaching hospitals when they provided inpatient care to Medicare+Choice enrollees. The change was made, in part, to help teaching institutions compete for managed care patients.

● **Services covered.** Allowed managed care plans participating in Medicare to offer coverage beyond what Medicare's traditional fee-for-service plan covered. For example, they could cover prescription drugs. The plans also had to cover emergency medical treatment — including treatment for severe pain — that would be sought by a "prudent layperson," someone with an average knowledge of health or medicine. Seniors could not be rejected from managed care plans because of their health status.

● **Enrollment.** Generally required new or expanded options to be in place by Jan 1, 1999. The secretary of Health and Human Services (HHS) was directed to conduct an education and publicity campaign in November 1998 to tell seniors about their new options in Medicare coverage and how to select them. A coordinated, open enrollment campaign was set to begin in November 1999, with health information fairs throughout the country scheduled for November of each year.

Health plans were required to disclose, in a clear, accurate and standardized form, information such as the plan's service area, benefits offered, the number of providers participating in the plan, and out-of-network coverage provided.

● **Disenrollment.** Allowed seniors to change their Medicare options on a monthly basis through 2001. In 2002, seniors would be allowed to leave a managed care plan only during their first six months of enrollment. By 2003, that would drop to three months. Exceptions included first-time enrollees, who could leave any month during the first year, or seniors who moved out of a plan's service area.

● **50:50 rule.** Repealed as of Jan. 1, 1999, a regulation requiring that at least half of enrollees in Medicare HMOs be people who were not enrolled in Medicare or Medicaid. Until then, the HHS secretary had broad authority to waive the 50:50 rule.

● **Guaranteed Medigap renewal.** Assured that in the first year in which seniors left traditional fee-for-service plans, leaving behind their supplemental insurance known as Medigap, they could in most cases return to their same Medigap policy should they decide to drop out of a Medicare+Choice plan.

In other Medigap changes, the bill limited insurers' ability to exclude beneficiaries from coverage because of pre-existing medical conditions if they enrolled during specific periods. It also permitted a new high-deductible option for Medigap insurance, with two new standard benefit plans that charged a $1,500 deductible before the policy began paying benefits.

● **Information on quality factors.** Required Medicare+Choice plans to give beneficiaries information about quality of care and specific procedures for grievances and appeals. The health plans also had to comply with specific quality assurance requirements, such as monitoring how the plans dealt with seniors suffering from acute and chronic conditions. The plans also had to disclose on request how they compensated participating physicians.

● **Anti-gag clause.** Prohibited Medicare+Choice plans from restricting communications between physicians (and other medical providers) and Medicare patients. Such restrictions, known as gag-clauses, limited what doctors could discuss with their patients, stipulating that they could not discuss treatments or specialists not covered by the health plan. Conscience clauses exempted religious institutions and others with similar concerns from being forced to discuss treatments or services — such as abortion or family planning — that they found objectionable. Such concerns had to be made clear to beneficiaries at the time of enrollment.

Hospitals

The bill took steps to trim hospital costs that were expected to save $39.8 billion through fiscal 2002. They included changes in payment rates in Part A of Medicare, which covered hospital costs, and a widening of the prospective payment system, which governed Medicare reimbursements to most hospitals. Prospective payments were a fixed, predetermined amount paid according to the patient's diagnosis. The bill called for the prospective payment system to be broadened to outpatient, skilled nursing facilities, home health services, and rehabilitation hospitals. Hospital provisions in the bill:

● **Payments update.** Kept prospective payments to hospitals flat for fiscal 1998. Payments over the following four years would be tied to the market basket index, which measured the costs of goods and services purchased by hospitals. The market basket was projected to rise by 3 percent in fiscal 1998, 3.5 percent in fiscal 1999-2001, and 3.4 percent in fiscal 2002.

Prospective payments would increase by the rise in the market basket index minus 1.9 percentage points in fiscal 1999; minus 1.8 percentage points in 2000; and minus 1.1 percentage points in fiscal 2001 and 2002.

Slightly higher payments would be given to certain hospitals, such as those that were dependent on Medicare for large amounts of revenue but did not receive "disproportionate share" payments. Such payments went to hospitals that served many of the poor and uninsured. In fiscal 1998, those hospitals would receive a payment equal to the update provided for all other hospitals plus 0.5 percentage point; it would be plus 0.3 percentage point in fiscal 1999.

● **Disproportionate share payments.** Reduced payment formula amounts for hospitals that served a disproportionate share of low-income patients by 1 percent in fiscal 1998; 2 percent in fiscal 1999; 3 percent in fiscal 2000; 4 percent in fiscal 2001; and 5 percent in fiscal 2002, with no reductions in fiscal 2003 and beyond.

Within a year of the bill's enactment, the HHS secretary was to submit a report to the House Ways and Means Committee and the Senate Finance Committee that included a formula for determining any additional disproportionate share payments to hospitals.

● **Graduate medical education payments.** Cut the indirect medical education (IME) adjustment that compensated teaching hospitals for higher costs involved in having residents treat patients and in treating patients who required special services available only in teaching hospitals.

Under prior law, the IME adjustment increased Medicare's hospital payments by about 7.7 percent for each 10 percent increase in a hospital's ratio of interns and residents to beds. The new adjustment reduced those reimbursement rates from 7.7 percent to 7 percent in fiscal 1998, 6.5 percent in fiscal 1999, 6.0 percent in fiscal 2000 and 5.5 percent in fiscal 2001 and subsequent years.

The bill also provided incentive payments to teaching hospitals to voluntarily reduce the number of medical residents in training.

● **Payment reductions to specialty hospitals.** Cut Medicare payments to five types of specialty hospitals and psychiatric and rehabilitation units in general hospitals that were exempt from the program's prospective payment system. Those facilities were to receive no update in fiscal 1998. For fiscal 1999-2002, updates would vary depending on several factors, including how much a hospital spent on each patient.

● **Capital payments.** Cut 17.8 percent from payments to hospitals covered by the prospective payment system for so-called inpatient capital, such as land and buildings, for fiscal 1998-2002. For hospitals not participating in the prospective payment system, the reduction would be 15 percent over five years.

● **New prospective payment systems.** Required the HHS secretary to establish prospective payment systems for psychiatric, rehabilitation and long-term care hospitals and skilled nursing facilities, as well as psychiatric and rehabilitation units in general hospitals.

Physicians and Other Providers

The bill included savings of $33.6 billion over five years from reducing payments to providers. The bill:

- **Physician services.** Saved $5.3 billion over five years by reducing payments for physician services.
- **Physician practice expense.** Postponed until Jan. 1, 1999, implementation of regulations governing reimbursements for physician practice expenses, which included overhead costs. With a three-year phase-in, the new regulations would become fully effective Jan. 1, 2002. The HHS secretary was required to report to Congress by March 1, 1998, on the data and methodology used in crafting the regulations
- **Single conversion factor.** Established a single so-called conversion factor beginning in 1998 for Medicare reimbursements for physician services, replacing the existing three. Medicare's fee schedule assigned relative values to services reflecting three factors: a physician's time, skill and intensity involved in performing the service; practice expenses; and malpractice costs. The schedule was also adjusted for geographic cost variations.
- **Durable medical equipment.** Eliminated scheduled payment increases for fiscal 1998 through fiscal 2002 for durable medical equipment such as wheelchairs. In addition, oxygen and oxygen equipment payments were to be cut 25 percent in fiscal 1998 and an additional 5 percent in 1999. The HHS secretary was required to overhaul reimbursement regulations governing durable medical equipment and oxygen. Payment increases for prosthetics and orthotics were limited to 1 percent a year for fiscal 1998-2002.
- **Chiropractic services.** Eliminated by Jan. 1, 2000, a requirement that Medicare recipients first receive an X-ray before seeking coverage for certain chiropractic services. In the past, Medicare did not pay for X-rays if they were performed or ordered by a chiropractor, forcing Medicare recipients to visit a doctor first. With that requirement removed, use of chiropractic services was expected to increase.
- **Ambulance services.** Maintained "reasonable cost and charge limits" for ambulance services through fiscal 1999, with annual increases equal to the Consumer Price Index minus 1 percentage point. A new payment schedule for ambulance services was to be negotiated by 2002.
- **Clinical laboratory services.** Froze fee schedule payments for clinical laboratory services from 1998 to 2002. Beginning in 1998, the cap on payment amounts was to fall to 74 percent of the median of all laboratory fee schedules nationwide.
- **Outpatient services.** Froze, then gradually reduced, the Medicare beneficiary's share of payments for outpatient services to lower the beneficiary's out-of-pocket expenses. Previously, beneficiaries paid 20 percent of what a hospital charged. Medicare paid 80 percent of the so-called reasonable and customary amount established by the government — often considerably less than what the hospital charged. In some cases, beneficiaries ended up paying much more than 20 percent of "reasonable and customary" amounts. The HHS secretary was directed to develop a prospective payment system for covered outpatient services.

Other Medicare Provisions

Other provisions in the bill:

- **Commission on the future.** Established a 17-member national bipartisan commission to report to Congress by March 1, 1999, on the long-term financial condition of Medicare. The panel was to identify problems that threatened the financial integrity of the Medicare Part A trust fund, which paid hospital costs, and to analyze potential solutions. The commission was required to report any findings that were approved by at least 11 commission members.
- **Commission on payments.** Created the Medicare Payment Advisory Commission to replace the Physician Payment Review Commission and the Prospective Payment Assessment Commission. The new commission was to advise Congress on Medicare payments.
- **Competitive bidding.** Required the HHS secretary to set up several competitive bidding demonstration projects that covered Part B items other than physician services. Under existing law, Medicare did not use competitive bidding to select providers. The HHS secretary was also directed to study coordinated care and case management for chronically ill seniors.
- **Fraud and abuse.** Strengthened civil and criminal penalties for Medicare fraud and abuse. Individuals convicted of three health-related crimes would be permanently excluded from the Medicare program. Those convicted of two health-related offenses would be excluded from federal health programs for 10 years.

The HHS secretary could impose new civil penalties on people who contracted with an excluded provider.

Providers were required to provide surety bonds and certain identification numbers to HHS. Beneficiaries were allowed to request an itemized bill for Medicare services. Providers could seek written advisory opinions concerning whether certain physician self-referrals were prohibited under federal law.

- **Part B premiums.** Kept the monthly premiums that Medicare beneficiaries paid for Part B, which covered doctor's visits and other outpatient costs, at 25 percent of the cost of Part B. Premiums, $45.80 at the time, were slated to rise to $67 a month in fiscal 2002. Part of the increase was due to the transfer from Part A to Part B of home health benefits, whose costs were growing rapidly.
- **Home health transfer.** Gradually transferred from Part A to Part B the cost of home health visits that were not part of the first 100 visits following a beneficiary's stay in a hospital or skilled nursing facility. The transfer was to be phased in over six years, from 1998 through 2003. The increase in the Part B premium attributable to the transfer was to be phased in over seven years, beginning in 1998. The bill directed the HHS secretary to create a prospective payment system for home health agencies by Oct. 1, 1999.
- **Low-income beneficiaries.** Required the federal government, instead of states, to pay the costs associated with expanding Medicare Part B premium assistance from people with incomes at 120 percent of the federal poverty level to those at 135 percent, as well as the extra premium costs attributable to the home health transfer for people at between 135 percent and 175 percent of the poverty level. The $1.5 billion allocated applied to payments between January 1998 and December 2002.
- **Prevention initiatives.** Broadened standard Medicare coverage on Jan. 1, 1998, to include preventive services such as annual mammograms for women 40 and over, waiving the deductible, and pelvic exams and clinical breast examination every three years, with coverage authorized yearly for Pap smears and pelvic exams for women at high risk of developing cervical or vaginal cancer. Yearly coverage was also authorized for women of childbearing age who had had a positive test in any of the three preceding years.

The bill covered colorectal screening tests, diabetes screening tests and diabetes outpatient self-management training services. As of Jan. 1, 2000, prostate cancer screening tests were to be covered for men 50 or older. Bone mass measurement would be covered for high-risk patients, such as an estrogen-deficient woman at clinical risk for osteoporosis, as of July 1, 1998.

- **Rural initiatives.** Established a telemedicine program for patients in rural areas, with programs to be in operation by Jan. 1, 1999. Telemedicine programs allowed patients in rural areas to contact medical providers through telecommunications systems, such as televisions and computers, for diagnosis and treatment of some illnesses.

Medicaid

The changes in Medicaid, the federal-state health insurance program for the poor, gave states more flexibility to put enrollees in managed care. The bill also reduced so-called disproportionate share payments from the federal government that helped states care for the poor or uninsured.

Medicaid provisions in the bill:

- **Boren Amendment.** Repealed the Boren Amendment, which required state Medicaid programs to pay hospitals and nursing homes "reasonable and adequate" rates to help the facilities cover operating costs. The amendment was named for its creator, former Sen. David

Boren, D-Okla. (1979-94), who said it was needed to guard against state governments squeezing nursing home budgets, which could reduce the quality of care.

The amendment's repeal gave states more flexibility in setting provider payment levels, but it required them to do so through a public process. The bill required a study to determine how repeal of the Boren Amendment affected patient access to hospitals, quality and safety. The repeal applied to payment for items and services beginning Oct. 1, 1997.

● **Disproportionate share payments.** Reduced federal disproportionate share allotments to states by imposing freezes and making graduated proportional reductions. The legislation also placed additional caps on state disproportionate share allotments starting in fiscal 1998, with specified caps through fiscal 2002. For 2003 and beyond, allotments would be equal to the previous year's allotment plus the percentage change in the Consumer Price Index for medical services. They could not exceed 12 percent of a state's medical assistance expenditures.

● **Managed care.** Permitted governors to place Medicaid enrollees in managed care without first seeking a waiver from the federal government.

States were required to provide beneficiaries with at least two plans to choose from and to meet quality assurance standards established by the HHS secretary. States could establish a minimum enrollment period of up to one year. Plans had to cover emergency medical treatment, including severe pain. Covered services had to be specified to beneficiaries, with grievance procedures in place and penalties applied if a managed care firm did not provide required services.

Medicaid beneficiaries who where exempt from state requirements that they enroll in managed care included children with special needs and certain Medicare patients.

● **Cost-sharing.** Permitted deductibles, copayments and other cost-sharing to be applied to Medicaid beneficiaries in managed care, but only to the same extent that states imposed cost-sharing on fee-for-service beneficiaries. Managed care providers could not withhold services even if a patient was unable to pay a cost-sharing amount. Eligible pregnant women and children under 19 were exempt from deductibles and cost-sharing.

A related provision gave states the option of not paying Medicare cost-sharing amounts to providers if they exceeded Medicaid reimbursement rates. Previously, states had been required to pay Medicare cost-sharing charges, which were higher than Medicaid's, for people who were beneficiaries under both Medicare and Medicaid, and for other low-income Medicare beneficiaries. The beneficiary would not be liable for payment to a managed care entity or other provider.

● **Anti-gag clause.** Prohibited managed care plans from restricting communications between Medicaid patients and their physicians or other medical providers. Such clauses limited what doctors could discuss with their patients, stipulating they could not discuss treatments or specialists not covered by the health plan. Conscience clauses exempted religious institutions and others with similar concerns from being forced to discuss treatments or services — such as abortion or family planning — that they found objectionable.

● **Immigrants' eligibility.** Restored Medicaid eligibility for legal immigrants who entered the country by Aug. 22, 1996, and who were elderly or disabled and qualified for Supplemental Security Income (SSI) benefits, or who subsequently became disabled and then eligible for SSI.

The bill also gave states the option of guaranteeing that legal immigrant children under age 19 who were determined to be eligible for Medicaid would continue to receive it for up to 12 months without a redetermination of eligibility. Also, states could extend Medicaid coverage to children on the basis of "presumptive" eligibility until a formal determination could be made.

● **Disabled children.** Required that states extend Medicaid coverage to disabled children who were no longer eligible for SSI disability payments under the 1996 welfare law (PL 104-193).

● **75/25 rule.** Repealed as of June 20, 1997, a rule that required at least 25 percent of enrollees in Medicaid managed care organizations to be beneficiaries who were not in Medicaid or Medicare.

● **Matching payments.** Permanently raised the matching rate — the federal share of a state's expenditures for Medicaid items and services — in several places. For example, the rate for the District of Columbia was raised from 50 percent to 70 percent. For Alaska, the federal matching rate was to increase from 50 percent to 59.8 percent over three years.

The bill also authorized $25 million a year for the following four years to reimburse the 12 states with the most illegal immigrants to offset costs for emergency health services for them.

● **Disabled workers.** Permitted disabled SSI beneficiaries with incomes up to 250 percent of the federal poverty level to buy into the Medicaid program, with premiums based on a sliding scale.

● **PACE.** Permitted states to offer Programs of All-Inclusive Care for the Elderly (PACE) as an optional benefit, with states allowed to limit enrollment. PACE programs provided health and long-term care services to frail elderly people who might otherwise be institutionalized. Previously, PACE programs were limited and experimental.

● **Waste and fraud.** Created protections against Medicaid waste, fraud and abuse, including requiring a surety bond of at least $50,000 for home health agencies and durable medical equipment suppliers. States could refuse to allow any person or entity convicted of a felony from serving as a Medicaid provider.

Children's Health

The bill provided $20 billion to expand children's health insurance coverage over five years, with the costs offset by an increase of 15 cents per pack in cigarette taxes. States were given broad flexibility in determining benefits packages. The children's health provisions:

● **Funding.** Guaranteed each state a fixed allotment based on a blend, over time, of its percentage of all children who were uninsured and its percentage of children who lived in families with incomes less than 200 percent of the poverty level. States were required to provide matching funds.

A state could participate in the program by selecting a capped block grant, expanding its Medicaid program above its existing state eligibility requirements for children's coverage or combining both approaches. Existing children's health programs in New York, Pennsylvania and Florida could continue. States were eligible to receive federal grants as of Oct. 1.

● **Capped grants.** Required states to provide coverage equivalent to one of several benchmark packages: the federal employees Blue Cross/Blue Shield standard option coverage; any health benefits plan available to state employees; or the health maintenance organization in the state with the largest commercial enrollment.

The plans had to include, at a minimum, coverage of inpatient and outpatient hospital services, physician medical and surgical services, laboratory and X-ray services and well-baby and well-child care, including immunizations and other services.

Additional benefits could include coverage of prescription drugs, mental health, and vision and hearing services, but coverage of these additional services had to have an actuarial value that was at least 75 percent of the value of coverage in a benchmark package. Only 10 percent of an allotment could be spent on items such as administrative costs and outreach activities. States also could seek a waiver from the HHS secretary to craft a package that departed from these requirements.

● **Medicaid expansion.** Permitted states to receive additional federal funds to expand Medicaid coverage of children beyond the Medicaid eligibility in their state as of March 31, 1997. The enhanced match would apply to costs for covering children in the expanded eligibility category until the allotment for the year was spent. After that, regular federal Medicaid matching rates would apply.

● **Expanded eligibility.** Broadened eligibility for Medicaid to permit states to serve children in families with incomes up to 200 percent of the federal poverty level, or up to 50 percentage points higher than its Medicaid eligibility level.

● **Cost-sharing.** Limited the amount of deductibles, coinsurance or copayments that could be charged on children enrolled in programs financed with capped block grant funds. No cost-sharing could be imposed for well-baby and well-child care, including immunizations. Only "nominal" cost-sharing requirements could be levied against families whose income was at or below 150 percent of the poverty level. For families above that level, cost-sharing would be imposed on a sliding-scale basis. States could not count money raised through premiums or cost-sharing toward a matching funds requirement.

● **Abortion.** Mandated that the children's health initiative be governed by the so-called Hyde Amendment, named for its author, Rep. Henry J. Hyde, R-Ill. The amendment, a perennial appropriations rider, prohibited federal funding of abortions except in cases of rape or incest or to save the woman's life. But states could spend their own money to pay for abortions as long as the funds were not mingled with federal funds.

● **Diabetes grant program.** Created a $30 million a year grant program from fiscal 1998 through 2002 to support prevention and treatment services and research for type I diabetes in children. The legislation also established a separate grant program to support prevention, treatment and research on diabetes in American Indians, with $30 million a year for fiscal 1998 through 2002.

Welfare

Food Stamps

Food stamp provisions in the bill:

● **Exemptions from work requirement.** Allowed states to exempt from work requirements up to 15 percent of food stamp recipients who would otherwise be required to work. States that exempted more or less than 15 percent would have their allowable exemptions adjusted by the same amount the following year.

The 1996 welfare overhaul law (PL 104-193) required able-bodied food stamp recipients between the ages of 18 and 50 who did not have dependents to work an average of at least 20 hours per week or to participate in a state-approved work, training or workfare program. Otherwise, they could receive no more than three months of food stamps out of every three years, plus an additional three months if they re-established their food stamps eligibility through work or a work-related activity and then became unemployed.

● **Federal funding.** Increased federal funding for food stamp employment and training programs from the amounts established in the welfare law. The new amounts were $212 million in fiscal 1998, $215 million in fiscal 1999, $217 million in fiscal 2000, $219 million in fiscal 2001 and $165 million in fiscal 2002.

States had to use at least 80 percent of these funds to help food stamp recipients who were required to participate in the work-related activities.

To receive the new federal funds — beyond the amounts set in the welfare law — states had to spend at least as much on employment and training programs for food stamp recipients as they did in fiscal 1996.

● **Prisoners.** Required states to ensure that prisoners incarcerated for more than 30 days did not receive food stamps. However, the secretary of Agriculture could decide that "extraordinary circumstances" prevented a state from complying. States were required to abide by this provision by Aug. 5, 1998, a year after the law's enactment. The Agriculture secretary could grant states an extra year to comply.

Welfare-to-Work Grants

The legislation provided $3 billion to states and localities to support welfare-to-work efforts. The Department of Labor was responsible for administering the program. The welfare-to-work provisions:

● **Distribution of funds.** Made available $1.5 billion in fiscal 1998 and in fiscal 1999. Of that amount, 75 percent was to be distributed as formula grants to states, and 25 percent as competitive grants.

● **Set-asides.** Set aside some of the money as follows:

• 0.8 percent for evaluations of the welfare-to-work grant by the HHS secretary. Of that amount, up to $6 million could be used to evaluate abstinence programs.

• 1 percent for Indian tribes that chose to run their own programs.

• $100 million for performance bonuses (to be set aside from fiscal 1999 funding and paid to states in fiscal 2000).

● **Matching requirements.** Required states to spend 50 cents for every $1 in federal welfare-to-work funds they received. Indian tribes were not required to match their funds.

● **State spending.** Required states receiving the aid to meet the maintenance of effort requirements in the temporary assistance for needy families (TANF) block grant created by the 1996 welfare overhaul. That meant states had to spend at least 75 percent of the state funds they spent for welfare-related programs in fiscal 1994. States that did not place the required percentage of welfare recipients into the work force had to spend 80 percent of their funds. (States were required to have a certain percentage of their welfare caseload participating in work activities, starting at 25 percent in fiscal 1997 and rising to 50 percent in fiscal 2002.)

● **State shares.** Apportioned the funds made available under the formula based on a state's pro rata share of the national poverty population and pro rata share of the national population receiving temporary assistance for needy families.

● **Distribution of funds within states.** Required that at least 85 percent of a state's formula grant be used in areas with high unemployment rates and high rates of people who had been on temporary assistance for at least 30 months.

● **Competitive grants.** Required the secretary of Labor to award competitive grants to projects that would expand knowledge about moving people into the work force. Eligible grant recipients included private industry councils, cities or counties, or private entities that applied in conjunction with private industry councils, cities or counties.

● **Use of funds.** Allowed funds to be used for such activities as community service and work experience programs; job creation through wage subsidies; on-the-job training, and contracts or vouchers for employment-related services. At least 70 percent of the funds had to be used to help people who met at least two of the following three criteria: They had not graduated from high school, they required treatment for substance abuse, and they had a poor work history.

In addition, recipients had to have received welfare payments for at least 30 months (not necessarily consecutively) or be within 12 months of reaching the state's time limit for benefits. States were permitted to assist recipients after they had reached the five-year time limit on welfare benefits.

● **Penalties.** Allowed states, notwithstanding minimum wage requirements, to penalize a family on welfare for not complying with the program's rules.

● **Worker protection.** Applied the following provisions to welfare-to-work participants, but not necessarily to other recipients of temporary assistance:

• **Non-displacement.** They could not fill a position created by a layoff or fill a vacancy created when an employer fired a worker specifically to create an opening for a welfare-to-work participant. Nor could an employer reduce an employee's hours of work to accommodate a welfare-to-work participant. A work activity could not violate an existing contract for services or collective bargaining agreement.

• **Non-discrimination.** A welfare-to-work participant could not be discriminated against because of gender, in addition to other anti-discrimination provisions included in TANF.

• **Health and safety.** Federal and state health and safety standards, including worker's compensation, applied to welfare-to-work participants.

• **Grievances.** States had to establish grievance procedures for complaints that a program violated worker protection requirements.

Temporary Assistance for Needy Families

The 1996 welfare overhaul created Temporary Assistance for Needy Families (TANF) to replace Title IV-A of the Social Security Act, which provided Aid to Families with Dependent Children (AFDC).

In doing so, the law ended the 61-year-old federal guarantee of providing welfare checks to all eligible low-income mothers and children. In its place, federal funding was provided to states in predetermined lump sums, known as block grants, giving states almost complete control over eligibility and benefits. However, the law also imposed certain requirements on the states and on welfare recipients.

The TANF provisions in the budget bill:

● **Limit on funds transfer.** Clarified that states could transfer only up to 10 percent of their TANF funds to the social services block grant, which provided money to states for services such as child care.

● **Limit on education activities.** Allowed no more than 30 percent of a state's TANF participants who were counted toward the state's work requirement to fulfill that requirement by taking part in educational activities. However, in fiscal 1998 and 1999, an unlimited number of teen parents participating in educational activities could be counted as working. Beginning in fiscal 2000, teen parents would be included in the 30 percent cap.

● **Penalties for not working.** Made states that did not reduce TANF participants' benefits for every hour that they refused to work subject to reductions of 1 percent to 5 percent in the state's TANF grant.

States that failed to meet their work participation rates would lose 5 percent of their TANF grant for the first year of non-compliance, rising in subsequent years by 2 percentage points, for a maximum penalty of 21 percent. Previously, the HHS secretary had the option to penalize states up to 5 percent the first year, with up to 2 percent added in additional years. The secretary could reduce the penalty because of extraordinary circumstances, which had to be specified in writing and provided to Congress.

Supplemental Security Income (SSI)

The legislation included provisions that:

● **Redetermination.** Gave the Social Security Administration until February 1998 to determine whether children who were receiving SSI — which provided cash to the low-income aged and disabled — still qualified for the aid. The redeterminations were needed because the welfare law put in place a stricter definition of disability for children. The welfare law would have required the redeterminations to be finished by August 1997.

● **State supplements.** Increased the fees to states for having the federal government administer state supplementary SSI payments.

Aid to Legal Immigrants

● **Refugees and others.** Made refugees, those granted asylum and aliens whose deportation had been withheld eligible for SSI and Medicaid for seven years after entering the United States. Cuban and Haitian entrants, as well as certain Amerasian immigrants, were also allowed to qualify for aid under these terms. The law previously granted them the aid for five years after arrival.

● **Eligibility for legal immigrants.** Allowed legal immigrants who were receiving SSI on Aug. 22, 1996 — the day Clinton signed the welfare law — to continue to be eligible for SSI. This provision applied regardless of whether the immigrants were receiving the aid because they were aged or disabled. In addition, legal immigrants who were in the United States by Aug. 22, 1996, and subsequently became disabled, would be eligible for SSI. The welfare overhaul law would have ended SSI eligibility for legal immigrants.

● **Elderly immigrants.** Allowed legal immigrants who had been receiving SSI on the basis of applications filed before Jan. 1, 1979 (before the Social Security Administration tracked citizenship), to remain eligible for SSI.

District of Columbia

The bill made the most far-reaching changes to the federal government's relationship with its capital city since Congress granted home rule to the District of Columbia in 1993. The initiatives were expected to cost the federal government $928 million over five years, lifting a sizable financial burden from a city chronically in the red. The bill:

● **Pension liability.** Resumed federal responsibility for a costly pension plan for city teachers, police and firefighters who retired by June 30, 1997. The federal government had transferred responsibility for the fund to the District in a 1979 law (PL 96-122). At that time the fund had unfunded liabilities of $1.9 billion. That liability had grown to $4.8 billion by fiscal 1997, about the same amount as the District's total annual budget.

Under the bill, pension payments for city workers were to come from a federal trust fund run by the Treasury Department. The bill left the District with $1.275 billion from its old pension fund to start another plan for teachers, police and firefighters who retired or became disabled after June 30.

● **Management changes.** Required a federally created control board overseeing the city's finances to hire, no later than 30 days after enactment of the bill, consultants to develop management overhaul plans for nine city departments: Administrative Services, Consumer and Regulatory Affairs, Corrections, Employment Services, Fire and Emergency Medical Services, Housing and Community Development, Human Services, Public Works and Public Health.

The bill declared vacant the director positions for those departments, which meant that incumbent department heads had to be reappointed or replaced. It made mayoral appointments to head those departments subject to an affirmative vote of a financial control board created by the federal government in 1995. The control board could appoint a department head if the mayor did not act within 30 days of a vacancy. It also gave the board the power to remove any department head.

The fiscal 1998 spending bill for the District of Columbia (HR 2607 — PL 105-100) clarified that the city council could veto mayoral appointments to head the nine departments. *(Appropriations, p. 9-27)*

● **Penal system transfer.** Required that the District's Lorton Prison complex in Northern Virginia be closed no later than Dec. 31, 2001. All prisoners were to be transferred by Oct. 1, 2001, to a facility operated by or under contract to the Federal Bureau of Prisons. The District was required to provide for the prisoners at Lorton until it closed, or until the last prisoner had been moved.

The Bureau of Prisons was required to house at least 2,000 D.C. inmates in private prisons by Dec. 31, 1999, and at least 50 percent of D.C. inmates in such facilities by Sept. 30, 2003. The Bureau of Prisons was authorized to buy land and contract to build a new facility for felony inmates, but the bill specified that no facility could be built on the Lorton site or surrounding Lorton lands.

The bill transferred the highly desirable land occupied by the Lorton Prison complex to the Interior Department, with the exception of two small pieces that were to go to the Fairfax County Water Authority and the Fairfax County Parks Authority. It was unclear what would eventually happen to the rest of the land. Some Virginians wanted it to become a park, but others hoped to use it for housing or retail developments.

● **Truth in sentencing.** Established a seven-member commission led by a Justice Department nominee to recommend changes to make the District's criminal code comparable to federal truth-in-sentencing laws for felonies. Such laws required inmates to serve out the majority of their prison terms. The recommendations, due within 180 days of the bill's enactment, would be transmitted to the city council and to the D.C. Superior Court. If the commission failed to make a recommendation or the council failed to act on it within 270 days of the bill's enactment, the attorney general could promulgate regulations to change the District code.

● **Parole.** Required the U.S. Parole Commission to assume authority to grant and deny parole to D.C. offenders within one year after the bill's enactment.

● **Reorganizing criminal justice.** Required the attorney general, in consultation with the chairman of the control board and the mayor, to appoint a trustee to reorganize pretrial and defense services, parole and probation. The bill created an Offender Supervision, Defender and Courts Services Agency to supervise those on parole, probation or early release. Pretrial and public defender services would also be provided by the agency. The director would be appointed by the president.

● **Courts transfer.** Established separate federal appropriations for the D.C. Superior Court, the D.C. Court of Appeals and the D.C. Court

System to be made through the State Justice Institute. Lawmakers later determined that the institute was too small to handle the duty. The fiscal 1998 spending bill (HR 2607 — PL 105-100) for the District of Columbia transferred responsibility for the appropriations to the Office of Management and Budget.

The bill also set up a new retirement plan for judges and their survivors, encompassing money the judges and the District government had put into the D.C. Judges' Retirement Fund. Under the bill, non-judicial employees of the courts were to be treated as federal employees for purposes of retirement.

- **Crime studies.** Authorized funds to set up a District institute or corporation to study and implement demonstration projects on preventing and solving crimes and punishing offenders.
- **Penalty for blocking bridges.** Instituted fines of $1,000 to $5,000 and prison terms of up to 30 days for anyone "knowingly and willfully" obstructing a bridge between D.C. and Virginia. "Janitors for Justice," a group made up mostly of Service Employees International Union members, had blocked the 14th Street Bridge several times in the mid-1990s to picket for better working conditions. Their protest angered many commuters who were tied up for hours in traffic jams.
- **Garnisheeing wages.** Allowed private entities, such as businesses, and public entities, such as child support enforcers, to garnishee the wages, retirement benefits or disability pay of city workers.

For decades the federal government had shielded its workers from collections for debts, alimony, or the like, and before Home Rule, District employees were part of the federal work force. After the city gained autonomy, it continued to shield employees from collectors, even when the federal government dropped that policy in the mid-1990s.

- **Collecting taxes.** Allowed the District's chief financial officer to contract with a private entity to collect the District's taxes.
- **Financing debt.** Authorized the District government to borrow from the federal Treasury up to $300 million for a 10-year term to pay down the city's $500 million accumulated operating deficit. The loans would incur the standard Treasury interest rate at the time.
- **Other financing.** Authorized the city council to issue general obligation bonds and taxable or tax-exempt revenue bonds to finance capital projects. The Home Rule Act of 1973 had restricted the District's ability to sell bonds for many purposes, including economic development.
- **Federal payment.** Repealed requirements that the federal government provide an annual payment to the city, but authorized a $190 million payment in fiscal 1998, an amount enacted in the subsequent appropriations measure. Because of federal requirements that limited the District's earning potential — for example, by limiting the height of buildings and exempting some groups from local property taxes — the bill authorized unspecified sums to be appropriated in subsequent years.
- **Balancing the budget.** Required that the District balance its city budget in 1998, one year earlier than required by the 1995 law (PL 104-8) that created the control board. *(1995 Almanac, p. 3-23)*
- **Writing the budget.** Removed several cumbersome federal requirements on how the mayor, city council and financial control board had to interact when writing the District's annual budget. If the three entities agreed on a budget, the bill allowed them to submit it to Congress and the president.
- **Regulatory overhaul.** Required the control board to complete within six months of bill enactment a review of the District's regulations, particularly permit and application processes. The board's recommendations, which the bill said should focus on regulations that "unnecessarily and inappropriately impair economic development," were to be submitted to the mayor, city council and Congress. The control board could implement the recommendations, but it was required to consider the views of the city council and mayor.
- **Clean Air fee.** Wiped from the District code a 1994 ordinance assessing a "Clean Air" fee on federal employees who parked in federal lots in the District.
- **Utility mergers.** Eliminated a requirement that Congress approve mergers involving District utility companies.

Civil Service Pensions

Federal departments and federal employees were required to contribute more to their pension and disability plans, saving the Treasury $5.94 billion over five years. The bill:

- **Pension contributions.** Required federal agencies to increase their contributions to the Civil Service Retirement System (CSRS) by $2.9 billion, or about 1.5 percent, beginning Oct. 1, 1997, and continuing through Sept. 30, 2002. Only the Postal Service and the Metropolitan Washington Airports Authority were exempt from the increase.

Workers participating in CSRS or the Federal Employees Retirement System (FERS) — the other retirement plan — were required to pay $1.8 billion more, increasing their existing contributions by about 0.5 percent by 2001.

The bill prohibited agencies from decreasing their contribution to FERS in light of employees' increased contributions.

- **Health benefits.** Established a permanent formula for calculating the amount the government would contribute for employees and their families under the Federal Employees Health Benefits Program. The existing formula was set to expire in 1999.

The bill required the Office of Personnel Management to calculate the rate by Oct. 1 of each year. Under the formula, the government would pay a "weighted average" based on the number of subscribers in specific health insurance plans. The government would contribute 72 percent of that average. However, the provision stipulated that the government could not pay more than 75 percent of a plan's premium.

Without the changes, federal employees and retirees would have faced an average premium increase of $276 a year, according to the Senate Governmental Affairs Committee.

- **Injured postal workers.** Ended an annual payment to the Postal Service of about $35 million to compensate workers injured before the Post Office Department became the quasi-independent Postal Service in 1970. Instead, the Postal Service had to use its own revenue to pay these claims.

Housing Programs

Congress made permanent three changes that had been reducing costs at the Department of Housing and Urban Development (HUD) since they were enacted in fiscal 1996 as part of the omnibus spending measure (PL 104-134) funding the department. The housing provisions were projected to save $1.77 billion over five years. The bill:

- **Foreclosure relief limits.** Eliminated a HUD program that provided up to three years of foreclosure relief for borrowers who had defaulted on their federal home mortgages but who showed some potential for resuming payments. Lawmakers said the federal losses from this program were too great.

To minimize those losses but still provide some foreclosure relief, the bill allowed the Federal Housing Administration (FHA) and HUD to grant up to 12 months of relief from mortgage payments. In exchange for the government assuming the cost of those payments, lenders would be required to alter the terms of the loan, at least on a short-term basis, to make it easier for the borrower to pay.

- **Section 8 rent increases.** Curbed rent increases for federally subsidized (Section 8) units priced at or above market rates. Rent increases would have to reflect actual increases in operating costs rather than inflation in the housing market. Landlords could increase rents only if they demonstrated that the increases would not make the unit's rent higher than the rent for a similar unsubsidized unit.

Owners of new or recently renovated units could adjust rents for inflation only if their units did not exceed the fair market rents for that area.

These changes were to take effect in fiscal 1999.

- **Section 8 subsidy reductions.** Reduced annual rent increases by 1 percentage point for owners of Section 8 properties in which there had been no tenant turnover since the last rent increase. However, the Annual Adjustment Factor, the formula on which the federal government based rent increases, could not be reduced to less than 1 percent, so landlords could increase rents at least that much. The changes were to take effect in fiscal 1999.

Veterans Programs

Most provisions on veterans extended cost-saving programs already in place, to further reduce spending by $2.7 billion over five years. The bill:

- **Loan guarantees.** Extended Department of Veterans Affairs (VA) authority to guarantee, on the secondary market, loans that the VA had made to purchasers of its property. This authority was extended through Dec. 31, 2002.
- **Mortgage fees.** Extended through Oct. 1, 2002, fees on VA-guaranteed, insured or direct home loans. For first-time loans, the fee ranged from 0.5 percent to 2 percent, depending on the amount of the down payment and whether the veteran was on active duty or in the reserves. Veterans paid 3 percent in fees for all subsequent loans except those in which they had made down payments of more than 5 percent.
- **Decisions on foreclosed properties.** Extended through Oct. 1, 2002, the VA's authority to use a "no-bid" procedure to determine whether it should purchase foreclosed properties it had guaranteed and resell them, or pay the guaranteed amount to the holder of the loan.
- **Income verification.** Extended through Sept. 30, 2002, the VA's access to financial records at the Department of Health and Human Services, Social Security Administration and Internal Revenue Service to determine eligibility for needs-based pensions and health care services.
- **Pension limits.** Extended through Sept. 30, 2002, limits on the amount of VA pensions that could be paid to veterans or spouses who were eligible for Medicaid, lived in nursing homes that received Medicaid payments, and had no dependents. As under existing law, which was set to expire Sept. 30, 1998, such veterans and spouses were limited to $90 in pensions per month.
- **Veterans' copayments.** Extended through Sept. 30, 2002, existing laws that required veterans with higher incomes to pay for a portion of their medical and nursing home care. Also, veterans without service-connected disabilities or low incomes were required to pay $2 for each 30-day prescription provided on an outpatient basis.
- **Cost recovery.** Extended through Oct. 1, 2002, the VA's ability to collect reimbursement from health insurance companies and other third-party payers for VA treatment of veterans with conditions not related to their service.
- **New fund.** Established a Medical Care Collections Fund, which began receiving payments Sept. 30, to replace the Medical-Care Cost Recovery Fund.

The new fund provided a more reliable stream of funding to the VA, because the Treasury Department was required to subsidize it if receipts did not meet CBO projections in fiscal 1998, 1999 and 2000. If income was at least $25 million less than projected in those years, the Treasury Department would be required to deposit the estimated shortfall in the account. If additional receipts came in, the VA would be required to use them to repay the Treasury.

- **Inflation adjustments.** Stipulated that increases in disability and survivors benefits could not exceed the rate of growth in Social Security payments from 1998 through 2002. Any increase in benefits was to be rounded to the next lowest dollar figure.
- **Fees on foreclosed properties.** Increased from 1 percent to 2.25 percent the loan fee that borrowers had to pay if they purchased, through a VA loan, a property that the VA had repossessed.
- **Recovery of loan losses.** Eliminated requirements that the VA obtain consent from veterans or surviving spouses who were defaulting on a VA loan before it attempted to mitigate its losses by reducing other federal payments or benefits to them, such as federal salaries or tax refunds. The bill eliminated provisions that required courts to determine whether a veteran or surviving spouse was liable for the loan. Instead, the VA had to notify the veteran or surviving spouse by certified mail and give him or her a chance to request that the VA secretary waive the debt.

Education Provisions

The education portion of the bill reduced spending by $1.76 billion over five years, largely by reducing funding for administrative functions and by requiring student loan agencies to transfer much of their reserve funds to the federal treasury. The bill:

- **Return of reserve funds.** Required agencies that guaranteed student loans to return $1 billion in reserve funds to the federal Treasury by Sept. 1, 2002. GOP aides said this represented about half the agencies' reserves. Most agencies were required to return the money in five equal annual installments. The measure also reduced mandatory administrative accounts for both the direct student loan and guaranteed student loan programs.
- **Repealing institution payments.** Eliminated the $10 payment per loan that the federal government gave to institutions that made direct student loans.
- **Student aid programs.** Extended student loan programs through 2006, including guaranteed student loans and loan consolidation programs.
- **Vocational education.** Repealed a 1917 law known as the Smith-Hughes Vocational Education Act, which authorized grants to states to provide vocational education. That mandate had been usurped in 1963 by the Perkins Vocational Act. Funding for the Smith-Hughes Act was redirected to the Perkins program, long the main grant provider to states.

Broadcast Spectrum Sales

Lawmakers looked to an invisible but lucrative government commodity to help reduce the deficit. CBO estimated that the government would take in $21.4 billion through 2002 from the auction of electromagnetic spectrum, the airwaves used to carry the signals for communications such as cellular telephones, radio and television. The legislation broadened and extended the authority of the Federal Communications Commission (FCC) to auction spectrum.

The bill included provisions that:

- **FCC auction authority.** Extended the FCC's authority to use competitive bidding to assign licenses for the use of spectrum until Sept. 30, 2007. The agency's previous authority was set to expire Sept. 30, 1998.

The bill also expanded the FCC's auction authority, generally allowing it to use competitive bidding for all radio-based licenses for mutually exclusive rights to use a portion of the spectrum. Auctions could not be used for assigning public broadcasting licenses, providing additional spectrum to television stations to broadcast advanced digital signals or for public safety radio services.

Previously, the FCC could only use auctions to award spectrum to companies that resold communications services, such as paging or cellular telephone services, to subscribers.

Radio or television licenses that were in dispute prior to July 1, 1997, also were to be auctioned under the new bill.

- **Auction of new spectrum.** Required the auction of a total of 120 megahertz of spectrum for commercial uses by the end of fiscal 2002: 45 megahertz that had been set aside for government use, an additional 55 megahertz to be located by the FCC, and 20 megahertz to be located by the secretary of Commerce from spectrum that had been reserved for government use. Federal agencies could be reimbursed for the cost of relocating federal broadcast operations to another frequency to accommodate a private party's use of the spectrum.
- **Reclaiming analog spectrum.** Required the FCC to reclaim by Dec. 31, 2006, spectrum that was being used by broadcasters to transmit analog television signals. The FCC had allocated broadcasters an additional channel of spectrum to allow them to transmit both analog and digital signals while they made the transition to digital.

Because of concern that some consumers might be left without free over-the-air television on Jan. 1, 2007, however, the bill required the FCC to grant broadcasters an extension under certain conditions, including:

- If one or more of the affiliates of the four largest networks in a market was not broadcasting in digital.

- If technology allowing analog television sets to receive digital signals was not generally available in a market.
- If at least 15 percent or more of television households in a market did not subscribe to a multichannel video programming distributor, such as cable television, that carried the digital signals of local broadcasters, or did not have at least one digital television set or at least one analog television set with a converter box allowing it to receive digital TV signals.

- **Auctioning reclaimed spectrum.** Required the FCC to auction the reclaimed analog spectrum by the end of 2002. Critics cited the disparity between the deadlines for reclaiming and auctioning the spectrum as evidence that the spectrum provisions would not raise as much as estimated.
- **Duopoly and cross-ownership waivers.** Required the FCC to grant a waiver from its "duopoly" and "cross-ownership" rules in cities of more than 400,000 to allow newspapers and broadcasters to bid on the reclaimed analog spectrum.

The duopoly rule barred a broadcaster from owning more than one television station in the same market. The cross-ownership rules barred a newspaper from owning a television station in the same market in which it circulated or a television station from owning a newspaper in the same market in which it broadcast.

- **Spectrum for public safety use.** Reallocated 60 megahertz of spectrum being used for channels 60-69, which were adjacent to spectrum already being used for public safety purposes. The FCC, after consulting with the secretary of Commerce and the attorney general, was required to reallocate 24 megahertz of this amount for public safety services use. The rest, 36 megahertz, had to be auctioned for commercial use after Jan. 1, 2001.

The FCC was required to begin assigning public safety licenses by Sept. 30, 1998. Before granting the licenses, the FCC had to make five findings, including ensuring that spectrum was not immediately available on a frequency already allocated to public service and determining that granting the application was consistent with the public interest.

- **Universal Service Fund.** Required an appropriation of $3 billion in 2001 to the universal service fund, which was established to ensure that affordable telecommunications services were available to all regions of the country.

The $3 billion was to then be repaid to the federal government from the universal service fund in 2002. To accommodate this, telecommunications carriers and providers would be directed in 2001 to defer $3 billion in payments to the universal service fund until 2002. The CBO estimated that this provision would have a neutral impact on the budget but would be counted as a net increase in revenues in 2002, the year the budget was supposed to be balanced.

Other Provisions

The bill also:

- **Petroleum reserve.** Anticipated raising $13 million through 2002 by allowing foreign governments to lease unused space in Louisiana salt caves that stored the nation's Strategic Petroleum Reserve. Key members of the Senate Energy and Natural Resources Committee approved the change in May after securing a commitment from budget writers that those foreign leases would be used after 2002 to restock the depleted, 564-million barrel reserve.
- **Transportation.** Ordered the sale of Governor's Island, the site of a Coast Guard base, by 2002 to raise an estimated $500 million. The bill also ordered the sale of 16 acres of air rights over tracks behind Washington's Union Station for $40 million. And it extended vessel tonnage fees, which expired in 1998, through 2002, to raise an estimated $245 million. ■

Clinton Tests New Power On Budget Package

President Clinton made the first-ever use of his new line-item veto authority to cancel three provisions in the budget-reconciliation package — two special-interest tax breaks and a New York Medicaid provision. Clinton announced his decision to strike the items from the twin spending and tax bills (PL 105-33, PL 105-34) on Aug. 11. The White House said the cancellations would save taxpayers $615 million over five years. *(Text, p. D-35)*

Clinton said he saw merit in the two tax provisions and would work with Congress to narrow their reach. The first was a one-year tax deferral for U.S. financial services firms on interest and other income earned abroad. The second was a deferral on capital gains realized from the sale of agricultural processing plants to farm cooperatives.

The third vetoed provision, enacted as part of the spending bill, granted a special exception for New York to permit the state to use taxes and other assessments collected from health care providers to match federal contributions for the Medicaid program. No other state stood to benefit from the provision.

Though some top officials and members of Congress urged Clinton to hold off using the veto until he received the annual appropriations bills, the White House decided to make a show of presidential strength in advance of the appropriations season. *(Line-item veto, p. 2-63)*

The House passed a scaled-back version of the two tax breaks Nov. 8, but the effort collapsed at the end of the session under pressure from senators unhappy with revisions agreed to by the House and the administration. The City of New York took the Medicaid veto to court, where the suit was pending at year's end.

Background

Clinton vetoed the three provisions using authority provided him under the 1996 line-item veto law (PL 104-130). The main purpose of the 1996 law was to enable the president to cancel individual items buried in already enacted appropriations bills, but it also applied to narrowly focused tax breaks — provisions that benefitted 100 or fewer taxpayers and "transition rules" that would help 10 or fewer taxpayers. Under the law, the Joint Committee on Taxation was required to identify any eligible tax provisions. In the case of the twin reconciliation bills, Joint Tax compiled a list of 79 items of which the administration chose three:

- **Financial services.** Backed by a potent coalition of financial services providers, the one-year tax deferral on foreign income was intended to help U.S. financial services firms compete with foreign companies that were not subject to home-country taxes.

U.S. manufacturers and service companies generally were allowed to defer paying taxes on overseas income until the profits were paid back to the U.S. parent. Financial services companies had once been able to do the same thing, but Congress cut off the opportunity in 1986 after a few corporations used it to shift income to tax havens.

The provision was to have taken effect Jan. 1 and expire after one year, though supporters had hoped it would be renewed annually. It had the backing of Senate Majority Leader Trent Lott, R-Miss., along with Democratic Sens. John B.

Breaux of Louisiana and Richard H. Bryan of Nevada, and a majority of the House Ways and Means Committee — including Clinton loyalists such as Democrats Robert T. Matsui of California and Barbara B. Kennelly of Connecticut.

But the proposal fell prey to protests from the Treasury Department, which said it was drawn too permissively and could be used by corporations to shift foreign income to tax havens such as the Cayman Islands and avoid all tax. "While the primary purpose of the provision was proper, it was drafted in a manner that would have permitted substantial abuse and created major tax loopholes," said a White House statement.

The administration indicated it was willing to consider a revised version of the provision. "We're still willing to work with the Congress to figure out how to do this right," said a Treasury official.

The Treasury Department estimated that cancelling the provision saved $317 billion in revenue over five years, while the Joint Tax Committee, which provided the official estimates for Congress, put the figure at $94 million.

• **Sales to farm co-ops.** The more controversial vetoed tax item would have permitted a tax-free rollover of a gain on the sale of an agriculture processing plant to a farmers' cooperative.

It had attracted attention even before the veto because it had been sought by Harold C. Simmons, a wealthy Republican donor from Texas who made $250 million on the sale of sugar beet refineries to the Snake River Sugar Co., a farmers' cooperative.

Proponents of the provision, including Charles W. Stenholm, D-Texas, said inaccurate press reports casting the provision as a Simmons windfall poisoned the atmosphere and led to the veto. Even the value of the veto was somewhat in dispute. Rubin estimated the savings would be about $98 million over five years. Joint Tax put the figure at around $84 million. A Stenholm aide said all those figures were illusory because they were based on taxes a corporation would pay in a straight sale of assets to a co-operative. Absent the tax provision, the aide said, no such sales would be consummated, meaning no gain at all for the Treasury.

In his veto message, Clinton lauded the ostensible goal of the provision — making it easier for farmers to move away from producing only raw materials, such as sugar beets, toward manufacturing finished products such as processed sugar — and promised to work on a separate bill with that aim.

• **New York aid.** The only item vetoed from the spending bill was a provision designed to settle a long-running dispute between the federal government and the state of New York over Medicaid funding. In 1991, Congress had passed a law (PL 102-234) that limited the way states could raise funds to pay their share of the joint federal-state health program for the poor. The purpose was to stop states from artificially boosting their matching funds to get extra federal money.

New York had sought a waiver after federal officials ruled that the state's system of provider taxes was not allowable under the law, but the waiver had not been granted.

The vetoed provision, inserted into HR 2015 by New York's senators — Republican Alfonse M. D'Amato and Democrat Daniel Patrick Moynihan — sought to solve the problem by allowing any provider taxes that New York collected before June 1 and for which a waiver had been sought to be considered permissible.

Clinton said he vetoed the provision because it would have allowed New York to "tap into the federal Treasury to reduce its state expenditures through the use of the health-provider tax to match federal Medicaid dollars that are impermissible in every other state in the country." The White House said the veto would save $200 million in fiscal 1998.

Charles B. Rangel, D-N.Y., the ranking Democrat on the House Ways and Means Committee, said he was unaware of any White House objections to the provision until the president vetoed it. "I received no notice to watch out for this," Rangel said. "He was at the table with us; he could have taken this out." Moynihan, D'Amato and Rep. Gerald B. H. Solomon, R-N.Y., expressed outrage as well.

New York Governor George E. Pataki called the veto "a body blow to our health care network that could endanger $2.6 billion for the health care of our children and our neediest citizens. . . . We will fight in Congress and in the courts to protect our children and needy families."

Legislative, Court Challenges

Supporters sought to salvage all three of the vetoed items. The two tax provisions were rewritten in an unsuccessful effort to enact them separately. Any attempt in Congress to revive the Medicaid provision would have benefitted only New York and was regarded as having no chance of passing. Instead, on Oct. 16, New York City Mayor Rudolph W. Giuliani filed suit in U.S. District Court in Washington challenging the constitutionality of the line-item veto.

That suit, *City of New York v. Clinton*, was subsequently expanded to include a second suit, *Snake River Potato Growers Inc. v. Rubin*, with oral arguments scheduled for Jan. 14, 1998, before Judge Thomas F. Hogan of the U.S. District Court for the District of Columbia.

Attempt To Rewrite Tax Breaks Stalls

After Clinton said he saw merit in both tax provisions and would work with Congress to narrow their reach, the House Ways and Means Committee on Sept. 23 gave voice vote approval to a new bill (HR 2513 — H Rept 105-318, Part 1) containing scaled back versions of the two items. Though the compromise language had the backing of the White House, enactment proved too difficult. The bill was subject to Senate "holds," and lawmakers feared it could become an end-of-session magnet for other pet tax breaks.

The Ways and Means bill narrowed the financial services provision and limited the deferral to 1998 taxes. The revised provision was estimated to cost the Treasury $57 million.

The tax break on sales of agriculture processing facilities to a farmers' cooperative was rewritten to target small farmers: The amount of tax that could be deferred was limited to $75 million, and the processing plant would be required to purchase at least 50 percent of its raw materials from the cooperative or its members. The projected cost of the provision was reduced to $15 million over five years.

The bill sailed through the House on Nov. 8 by voice vote. But in the Senate, Larry E. Craig, R-Idaho, denounced the compromise, which could not be used to help restructure the Snake River deal. Craig represented farmers in the deal with Simmons as well as those in another large potato growers' co-op.

"I will attempt to block the effort on the floor of the United States Senate," Craig said. "This single senator plans to be a real problem for them." Craig got help from Senate Finance Chairman William V. Roth Jr., R-Del., who insisted the bill be referred to his committee.

Despite a push by Lott and lobbyists for banking, securities, credit card and insurance companies, the bill remained stalled. ■

Line-Item Veto Makes Rocky Debut

President Clinton won, lost, regained and then used the long-sought line-item veto — all in 1997. But before the year was out, his use of the veto to excise individual items in spending and tax bills was challenged yet again — on two fronts.

The line-item veto — actually, an enhanced rescissions power over tax and spending bills — took effect Jan. 1. In theory, it represented a huge transfer of power from Congress to the president, but Clinton found it to be a double-edged sword. After causing a furor in October when he vetoed 38 projects totaling $287 million from the military construction appropriations bill, he wielded it thereafter with a light hand.

In all, Clinton used the veto on 11 bills — two budget-reconciliation measures and nine of the 13 regular appropriations bills. The four untouched spending bills were for the District of Columbia, foreign operations, the legislative branch and the departments of Labor, Health and Human Services, and Education. He cut 82 items from the appropriations bills totaling $1.9 billion over five years — a fraction of the $9 trillion federal budget over that period.

While the Supreme Court dismissed an early challenge to the law's constitutionality, further lawsuits were working their way through the courts at year's end. In one case, the administration agreed out of court to restore a vetoed provision. And Congress was poised to override Clinton's attempt to eliminate the military construction projects.

Background

The power to strike items buried in bills sent to the White House had been sought by presidents since Ulysses S. Grant. The House had passed versions of the veto in 1992, 1993 and 1994, but each time the legislation was blocked in the Senate.

In the fall of 1994, House Republicans made enactment of a line-item veto a top priority in their "Contract With America," which set the agenda for the House in the GOP-controlled 104th Congress. The bill (PL 104-130) was cleared by Congress and signed into law in 1996. *(1993 Almanac, p. 22; 1995 Almanac, p. 2-40; 1996 Almanac, p. 2-28)*

Though Republicans had pushed hard for the line-item veto law, they were not eager to see it used by Clinton on their bills. They delayed the law's effective date until 1998 in the vain hope that by then a Republican would be sitting in the White House.

Actually, the law was not a true line-item veto, which would have allowed the executive to strike individual items or lines or words from bills that he wanted to sign. That would have required a constitutional amendment, which proved a politically impossible task.

Instead, Republicans devised a way to strengthen the president's existing ability to propose rescissions of spending from already enacted appropriations bills. The new power also permitted the president to "cancel" limited tax provisions and new entitlement spending.

The law specified that any savings from a vetoed item had to be used to reduce the deficit and could not be used by appropriators for other spending. This deficit-reduction "lockbox" created incentives for Congress and the White House to work together to avoid many vetoes in order to make full use of the pool of money available for discretionary spending.

The law gave Congress 30 days in which to clear a bill disapproving the president's cancellations. If the president vetoed that bill, Congress would need a two-thirds majority to override him. Other alternatives for lawmakers were to pass a modified version of the provisions in hopes of getting the president's support, or going to court.

The veto was set to expire Jan. 1, 2005.

Early Court Case Dismissed

On Jan. 2, the day after it took effect, the new law was challenged by a group of lawmakers led by Sen. Robert C. Byrd, D-W. Va., who argued that it violated the procedures laid out in the Constitution for enacting bills into law. Article I of the Constitution vested all legislative power to write and amend law with Congress; the president could only accept or reject bills. The plaintiffs argued that the new line-item veto gave the president the power to change or amend a law after he signed it.

Byrd was joined in the suit, *Byrd v. Raines,* by former Senate Appropriations Committee Chairman Mark O. Hatfield, R-Ore. (1967-97); Sens. Carl Levin, D-Mich., and Daniel Patrick Moynihan, D-N.Y.; and Reps. Henry A. Waxman, D-Calif., and David E. Skaggs, D-Colo.

U.S. District Judge Thomas P. Jackson agreed with the lawmakers and struck down the law April 10. "Rather than making expenditures of federal funds appropriated by Congress matters of presidential discretion, the Act effectively permits the President to repeal duly enacted provisions of federal law," Jackson wrote. "This he cannot do."

Byrd and other veto opponents were predictably jubilant. "It was a great day for the Constitution and the American people because it was their power — not mine — their power of the purse that was preserved," said Byrd. "As long as Congress has the power of the purse, the people's liberties are preserved."

Urged on by conservative lawmakers, Clinton vowed to appeal Jackson's decision directly to the Supreme Court, a step that was allowed under the law.

High Court Says Plaintiffs Not Injured

When the Supreme Court heard arguments May 27, it became clear that the constitutional merits of the law would be secondary in this case to whether Byrd and his colleagues had legal standing to file their lawsuit — especially since Clinton had not yet used the veto power.

Indeed, that was the basis of the court's 7-2 decision, announced June 26, which overturned the district court and reinstated the veto. The majority decision, written by Chief Justice William H. Rehnquist, held that Byrd and the others did not have standing because they had not yet been injured by the veto.

Referring to the lawmakers' argument that the threat of a veto could affect their votes and actions, Rehnquist wrote: "Appellees' claim of standing is based on a loss of political power . . . [but] the institutional injury they they allege is wholly abstract and widely dispersed, and their attempt to litigate this dispute at this time and in this form is contrary to historical experience." *(Supreme Court, p. 5-21; excerpts, p. 5-26)*

"I intend to use it whenever appropriate, and I look forward to using it wisely," Clinton said in a statement issued by the White House. "With it, the president will be able to prevent Congress from enacting special-interest provisions under the cloak of a 500- or 1,000-page bill."

The lawmakers who brought the lawsuit insisted it was only a matter of time before the veto would be declared unconstitutional. "Losing on a technicality just delays the time when the court must decide the fundamental issue," said Levin. In fact, one of the dissenting justices, John Paul Stevens, said he would have granted the lawmakers standing and would have voted to strike down the veto act as unconstitutional.

Reconciliation Bills

Clinton got his first chance to use the line-item veto in August, after he signed the huge spending and tax bills (PL 105-33, PL 105-34) that made up the budget-balancing reconciliation package. *(Reconciliation vetoes, p. 2-61)*

Though the procedure was intended primarily for use on appropriations bills, the law also required the Joint Committee on Taxation to identify for possible veto tax provisions that benefited 100 or fewer taxpayers, as well as "transition rules" that would help 10 or fewer taxpayers.

Joint Tax identified 79 narrowly focused tax provisions that were eligible for the veto. On Aug. 11, Clinton cancelled two provisions from the tax bill and one from the spending measure — a Medicaid provision aimed at helping New York. White House aides claimed the trio of vetoes would save $615 million over five years.

Some experts questioned whether Clinton was too quick to use his new power on three obscure provisions in the budget bills. Clinton ignored advice to wait and use the veto against appropriations measures, where legal analysts said he would be on more solid constitutional ground.

That was because the president had been permitted for much of the nation's history to "impound" appropriated funds and not spend them — though the authority had been sharply rolled back in the 1974 Budget Act after President Richard M. Nixon made sweeping use of the power. *(1974 Almanac, p. 145)*

The veto was more suspect when it came to tax provisions, because it could be argued that Clinton, in effect, was amending the reconciliation bills after signing them into law.

"What Congress has taken away in the 1974 Budget Act, it can certainly restore by statute," said Dave Mason, a senior fellow in congressional studies with the Heritage Foundation. On taxes, Mason said, the constitutionality of the veto was a "much more open question."

Sen. John McCain, R-Ariz., perhaps the single most ardent booster of the line-item veto, advised Clinton to wait for an appropriations bill. "I fear the president has risked the future of this important budget cutting tool," McCain said.

Looking Toward the Fall

But the president's Aug. 11 action was seen as setting the stage for the fall, when the White House would get the 13 appropriations bills for fiscal 1998. Clinton himself argued that the threat of the veto could prevent appropriators from larding spending bills with pet earmarks. "It may be that the use of the line-item veto here will mean that it won't have to be used as much in the appropriations process, and that would please me greatly," Clinton said.

The president called the veto "a powerful new tool to protect taxpayers . . . a tool designed to fight against waste and unjustifiable expenditures." He added: "In the past, good legislation could be cluttered up with unjustifiable or wasteful spending or tax provisions, leaving the president no choice but to sign or veto the overall legislation." *(Text, p. D-35)*

The decision to strike the items came after an in-house debate in which top advisers such as Treasury Secretary Robert E. Rubin and Chief of Staff Erskine Bowles reportedly recommended caution, not desiring to spoil any bipartisan spillover from the successful completion of the balanced-budget legislation. But other presidential advisers, such as National Economic Council Chairman Gene Sperling and senior aide Rahm Emanuel, urged Clinton to demonstrate presidential mettle in advance of the appropriations season.

"This was a political decision done by the political folks at the White House," said Stanley Collender, managing director of Burson-Marsteller's budget consulting group. "I think the substance was far less important than the act of doing it."

Thomas E. Mann, director of governmental studies at the Brookings Institution, said Clinton "acted at the first opportunity, which sends a signal that he is perfectly willing to make use of this weapon." Mann said it "would have been a sign of weakness for him to take a bye on it."

The three items that Clinton vetoed were:

- A provision in the tax bill to permit deferral of taxes on the sale of food-processing facilities sold to farmer cooperatives.
- Language sought by the financial services industry, also in the tax bill, allowing banks and other institutions to defer taxes on interest income produced by overseas subsidiaries and subject to taxes by the host country.
- A special exception in the spending bill that would have permitted the state of New York to use taxes and other assessments collected from health care providers to match federal contributions for the Medicaid program. No other state would have benefited from the provision.

Members of Congress who had fought for the provisions were furious. Charles B. Rangel of New York, the ranking Democrat on the House Ways and Means Committee, said he was unaware of any White House objections to the Medicaid provision until the president vetoed it. "I received no notice to watch out for this," Rangel said.

A spokesman for House Speaker Newt Gingrich, R-Ga., complained that Congress had been "blindsided," because potential vetoes were not mentioned during the budget talks. But other Republicans, such as Senate Majority Leader Trent Lott, R-Miss., and House Ways and Means Committee Chairman Bill Archer, R-Texas, were more restrained. "The president has asserted his prerogative," Archer said. Archer had long advocated the line-item veto, though he resisted having it apply to narrowly targeted tax benefits.

Military Construction

The howls of protest grew louder Oct. 6, when Clinton struck more than three dozen projects worth $287 million from the $9.2 billion fiscal 1998 military construction spending bill (HR 2016 — PL 105-45). Setting a pattern for the rest of the appropriations season, he took the full 10 days he was allowed under the veto law to give his budget aides time to scour the bill. *(Appropriations, p. 9-61)*

"The old rules have, in fact, changed," Clinton declared. He said he had made "tough calls involving real money and hard choices," but he pointedly did not describe the projects as wasteful or unnecessary. For one thing, 32 of the 38 projects he cancelled were included in long-range Pentagon plans. *(Text, p. D-43)*

Lawmakers had simply accelerated the projects — a longstanding congressional tradition — and most members whose projects got tagged were at first dumbstruck, and then outraged. Among the most common complaints was the lack of advance notification to members, who were unable to fight for their projects. "I was stunned," said Sen. Bob Graham, D-Fla., who watched his state lose two projects. "They didn't handle it right."

"Porkbusters" such as McCain, meanwhile, said Clinton had not gone far enough. McCain had identified 129 projects in the bill that had not been requested by the administration for funding in fiscal 1998.

Clinton said he struck projects that met three criteria: They were not requested in his fiscal 1998 budget; there had not been enough design work done on them to ensure that construction could begin in 1998; and they would not "substantially improve the quality of life of military service members and their families."

But in several cases, White House budget aides acknowledged that they were working from outdated or erroneous material — a fact drilled home Oct. 9 at a hastily arranged Senate Appropriations Committee hearing. Several senators got Pentagon officials to acknowledge that construction of their projects could get under way in 1998.

Highlighting the session was an I-told-you-so performance by Byrd, the most vociferous opponent of the line-item veto. "I did not vote for this horror, and I wonder how some members who did make the very unwise choice to support it are feeling now that their legislative initiatives have felt the line-item meat cleaver," Byrd said.

Several Republicans were quick to admit a change of heart on the veto. Larry E. Craig of Idaho, told Byrd: "The president's actions . . . increasingly impress upon me the wisdom of our Founding Fathers. I think you know what I'm saying." Byrd responded: "I thought that when I voted against it."

"I feel like I need to eat a little crow," said Robert F. Bennett, R-Utah. "I'm prepared . . . to reconsider my previous position, based on the experience here."

Panel Democrats could not resist piling on. "There is certainly a part of me that is gloating right now," said Harry Reid of Nevada. "As my mother told me many times, 'I hope everybody's happy now.' "

As soon as the final gavel dropped, Appropriations Committee Chairman Ted Stevens, R-Alaska, marched to the Senate floor and introduced a "disapproval bill" (S 1292) to restore all but two of the vetoed projects.

Other Spending Bills

After infuriating so many members with his aggressive use of the veto on the military construction bill, Clinton eased up, wielding his veto pen with more caution on eight other fiscal 1998 appropriations bills:

- **Defense.** Clinton took a gentle swipe at the huge $247.7 billion defense appropriations bill (HR 2266 — PL 105-56) on Oct. 14, striking just 13 projects totaling $144 million.

"I know that a lot of members who voted for the line-item veto in Congress now wonder whether they did the right thing, now that I'm exercising it. But I'd like to remind you that again I have deferred in great measure to Congress," Clinton said. "I'm hoping that in the years ahead, I won't be using it as much . . . because it will lead to a different kind of negotiation in the budgeting process." *(Appropriations, p. 9-17; text, p. D-42)*

The White House decision-making process was strikingly different from the approach used on the military construction bill. Most important, Pentagon officials were involved in making the decisions, and members of Congress were permitted to justify their projects.

Still, Clinton's inconsistent application of the veto earned him a scorching letter from McCain. After first complaining that the "administration's process for determining items to veto has been unduly influenced by political considerations," McCain scolded Clinton for not killing projects that "clearly have no relevance to national security." An example: a much-publicized $250,000 earmark inserted by Sen. Daniel K. Inouye, D-Hawaii, to help develop two cruise ships for a company servicing the Hawaiian islands.

- **Treasury-Postal Service.** On Oct. 16, Clinton vetoed a single provision in the Treasury Department and Postal Service bill (HR 2378 — PL 105-61), saying it would keep "a hastily conceived, undebated provision from becoming law." The administration said the veto would save $854 million over five years. *(Appropriations, p. 9-71; text, p. D-42)*

Under the provision — added in conference by Senate Appropriations Chairman Stevens — about 1.1 million federal workers hired before 1983 would be allowed to switch from the old Civil Service Retirement System to the Federal Employees Retirement System. They could then take greater advantage of a tax-deferred savings plan, and widowed federal employees could to receive higher Social Security survivor's payments.

- **Energy and water.** On Oct. 17, Clinton vetoed eight projects totaling $19 million from the $21.2 billion energy and water development bill (HR 2203 — PL 105-62). The measure was one of the most popular in Congress because it financed about $5 billion in water projects.

Among those hit by the cuts were Senate Majority Leader Lott, whose state lost $1.9 million that was intended to dredge Sardis Lake in Mississippi for a private marina and convention center in northern Mississippi. *(Appropriations, p. 9-31)*

- **Transportation.** Another Senate leader's home state got hit Nov. 1, when Clinton excised three projects worth just over $6 million from the $42.2 billion transportation appropriations bill (HR 2169 — PL 105-66). Of that, $5 million was for a railroad dock improvement project in Seward, Alaska, that had been pushed by Stevens. *(Appropriations, p. 9-66)*

Administration officials argued that the money was to have come from the Federal Railroad Administration, whose job was to oversee rail safety; the Seward project was for economic development. McCain again was critical, saying earmarks in the bill should have been left to the discretion of the secretary of the Department of Transportation and agency directors.

- **VA-HUD.** Also on Nov. 1, Clinton dropped seven projects from the appropriations bill for the departments of Veterans Affairs (VA) and Housing and Urban Development (HUD) and 17 independent agencies (HR 2158 — PL 105-65). The cancellations saved $14 million out of a $90.7 billion package. *(Appropriations, p. 9-77)*

As on previous bills, Clinton targeted projects not included in his budget request and those whose removal, he said, would not "impair any essential government functions" or "harm the national interest." The most expensive, for NASA telescopes in Arizona and Chile, was worth $10 million.

"It wasn't pork," said Senate Majority Whip Don Nickles, R-Okla., who lost $900,000 to finish planning a new national cemetery in Oklahoma. "It was a project we worked on for 10 to 12 years."

- **Agriculture.** On Nov. 20, Clinton used a particularly light touch with the agriculture spending bill (HR 2160 — PL 105-86), slicing five projects worth $1.9 million from a $49.7 billion measure that critics said was loaded with "pork barrel" projects. *(Appropriations, p. 9-5)*

• **Interior.** Also on Nov. 20, Clinton struck two projects worth $6.2 million from the $13.8 billion spending bill for the Interior Department (HR 2107 — PL 105-83). *(Appropriations, p. 9-44)*

• **Commerce-Justice-State.** Clinton closed out the first year of the line-item veto on Dec. 2, striking just one project worth $5 million from the $31.8 billion appropriations bill for the departments of Commerce, Justice and State (HR 2267 — PL 105-119). *(Appropriations, p. 9-11)*

Veto Challenged

Despite the grumbling from lawmakers when they lost projects, most of Clinton's line-item vetoes went unchallenged. In two cases, however, Congress tried to revise or restore vetoed provisions. Although neither effort was successful in 1997, lawmakers appeared likely to prevail on the military construction bill when Congress began its second session in 1998. Also, in several instances, the affected parties went to court to challenge the constitutionality of the line-item veto law.

• **Tax provisions.** Rather than trying to overturn Clinton's vetoes, the House easily passed a slimmed-down version of the two narrow tax breaks (HR 2513 — H Rept 105, 318, Part 1) by voice vote Nov. 8. But the effort fizzled at the end of the session under pressure from senators who were unhappy with the compromise that had been struck by the House and the Clinton administration.

Craig, in particular, balked at the changes that had been made to focus the farmers' co-op provision on small farmers. With help from Finance Chairman William V. Roth Jr., R-Del., he blocked floor consideration of the bill.

• **Military construction.** Prospects were much brighter for the 38 vetoed military construction projects.

From the outset, angry appropriators ignored offers from the White House to cooperate in redrafting some of the vetoed provisions. Instead, the Senate on Oct. 30 passed Steven's bill (S 1292) rejecting 36 of the 38 vetoes. The vote was 69-30, giving sponsors a three-vote cushion over the two-thirds majority needed to override a veto. *(Vote 287, p. S-49)*

On Nov. 8, the House overwhelmingly passed a bill (HR 2631) disapproving of all 38 vetoes; the vote was 352-64. "I think the manner in which the White House has handled these line-item vetoes in recent weeks is an affront to responsible government and deserves the type of public repudiation that this resolution provides," said David R. Obey of Wisconsin, ranking Democrat on the House Appropriations Committee. The Senate agreed to the House bill the next day, clearing it by voice vote. *(Vote 617, p. H-184)*

As expected, Clinton vetoed the new bill Nov. 13. While acknowledging that the Defense Department had given his budget aides outdated information on some of the projects when he decided to strike them, Clinton defended his second veto, insisting the projects "would not substantially improve the quality of life of military service members and their families."

But with veto-proof margins in both chambers, Congress appeared poised to override the president in 1998.

• **Treasury-Postal Service.** Clinton's veto of the retirement system provision in the Treasury-Postal bill brought an immediate reaction from the National Treasury Employees Union, which filed suit Oct. 16 in the U.S. District Court in Washington. In this case, the vetoed provision was a policy "rider" that changed the underlying authorization law. It did not carry an appropriation, and Clinton's veto message erroneously characterized it as a "dollar amount of discretionary budget authority."

The case was combined with two others, with oral arguments scheduled for Jan. 14, 1998, before Judge Thomas F. Hogan of the U.S. District Court for the District of Columbia.

Before oral arguments could begin, however, the Justice Department reached an agreement with the union in which it admitted that the president had exceeded his authority in striking the item. On Jan. 6, Judge Hogan signed a consent order invalidating Clinton's use of the line-item veto in this instance. The result of the consent decree was that the provision remained in the bill.

• **New York Medicare provision.** On Oct. 16, lawyers for New York City Mayor Rudolph W. Giuliani, local hospitals and two labor unions filed suit in the U.S. District Court in Washington challenging Clinton's Aug. 11 veto of the Medicaid provision. The suit, *City of New York v. Clinton*, was subsequently expanded to include *Snake River Potato Growers Inc. v. Rubin* and, briefly, the *Treasury Employees Union's* suit. Oral arguments were scheduled for Jan. 14, 1998, before Judge Hogan. ■

Balanced-Budget Amendment Falls

Advocates of a constitutional amendment to require a balanced federal budget had their hopes dashed once again, as a handful of Senate Democrats switched their positions to defeat the proposal.

The potential impact of the amendment on Social Security — the political wedge issue that had sunk the amendment two years before — once again cost votes. Also undercutting the Republican-led drive for the amendment was the expectation that Congress and President Clinton would finally reach a deal to balance the budget on their own later in the year. *(Budget deal, p. 2-18)*

The amendment (S J Res 1, H J Res 1) would have required a balanced budget by fiscal 2002 or two years after ratification by three-fourths of the states, whichever came later. A three-fifths supermajority vote in both the House and Senate would have been required to waive the balanced-budget requirement, as well as to raise the national debt limit.

Although the makeup of the Senate after the 1996 elections suggested the measure would pass that chamber with 68 votes, the count again stalled at 66, just one short of the two-thirds required for a constitutional amendment. Democrats Robert G. Torricelli of New Jersey and Tim Johnson of South Dakota — both of whom had voted for an identical amendment when it passed the House in 1995 — switched to "nay," and the amendment died.

Even had the amendment passed in the Senate, however, supporters would have had difficulty getting it through the House. Democratic gains in the 1996 elections had buoyed opponents' prospects for killing the measure, which had passed the House in 1995 with a dozen votes to spare. Labor unions lobbied hard, and whip counts showed amendment supporters perhaps a dozen votes shy in the House.

Republican leaders in the House indicated privately that they were in no hurry to force members to cast a potentially uncomfortable Social Security-related vote unless the Senate acted first. When the Senate killed the amendment, it was shelved in the House.

Clinton's Opposition

After initially hinting that he could live with the amendment if it were modified to provide flexibility in times of recession, Clinton dug in and waged a hard fight to defeat it.

At a Jan. 17 hearing, Treasury Secretary Robert E. Rubin told the Senate Judiciary Committee that while the administration was fully committed to reaching a balanced-budget agreement, writing such a mandate into the Constitution was a very bad idea.

"First, a balanced-budget amendment could turn slowdowns into recessions and recessions into more severe recessions or even depressions. . . . It could prevent us from dealing expeditiously with emergencies such as natural disasters or military threats," Rubin said.

In addition, he said, "the amendment poses immense enforcement problems that might well lead to the involvement of the courts in budget decisions, unprecedented impoundment powers to the president or the temporary cessation of all federal payments."

Clinton made his own position clear at a Jan. 28 news conference."Congress has an obligation to think of what could happen here in the future and ask themselves whether they really want to straitjacket the United States," he said. "What we ought to do is follow prudent policies, balance the budget and go forward. But we shouldn't compromise what might happen 10, 15 years from now with an amendment to the Constitution. I think it's bad economic policy and bad policy."

The administration faced an uphill climb to defeat the proposal, however. (If Congress had approved the amendment, it would have gone directly to the states for ratification.)

Judiciary Committee Chairman Orrin G. Hatch, R-Utah, announced Jan. 17 that Senate supporters had already locked up 62 cosponsors for the measure. If all returning senators voted as they previously had and no freshman Democrat broke a campaign promise, Hatch said, the amendment would win approval with 68 votes, one more than the 67 votes that were required.

In the House, Republican leaders were more uncertain. "This is going to be tough. . . . It's going to be unlike the last Congress," said House Majority Whip Tom DeLay, R-Texas. "We are calling on the American people to call, write, telegraph, fax their congressmen and tell them that they want a balanced-budget amendment to the Constitution."

"In the House, the supporters have to win over the swing votes to win," said a Senate GOP staff aide. "In the Senate, the opponents have to pick up the swing votes to win."

Lobbying Blitz

Interest groups on both sides of the issue mounted grass-roots campaigns in the districts and states of key swing members.

Pro-amendment groups — led by the National Taxpayers Union, the Business Roundtable, the U.S. Chamber of Commerce, the Concord Coalition and a bevy of other business and conservative organizations — financed media buys and news conferences in states such as New Jersey, Louisiana and Ohio aimed at building public pressure on wavering lawmakers.

A coalition on the other side of the issue, led by labor unions, advocates for senior citizens and left-leaning interest groups, launched its own grass-roots campaign aimed especially at House Democratic freshmen. Unions in particular, led by the American Federation of State, County and Municipal Employees, worked closely with Democratic leaders to try to kill the amendment in the House.

BOXSCORE

Balanced-Budget Constitutional Amendment — S J Res 1, H J Res 1. The resolution proposed to amend the Constitution to require a balanced budget by fiscal 2002 or two years after ratification by three-fourths of the states, whichever came later.

Report: S Rept 105-3.

KEY ACTION

March 4 — Senate fell one vote shy of the two-thirds majority needed to pass S J Res 1; the vote was 66-34.

Background

The idea of amending the Constitution to require a balanced budget had been raised frequently since the early 1980s. Support had built gradually as frustration mounted over the seemingly permanent budget deficit and the resulting $5.3 trillion gross national debt. The text of the amendment had been crafted and massaged by members of both chambers and both parties. But supporters had never been able to muster the two-thirds vote required in both chambers for a constitutional amendment.

"This may be one of those things that enough people are for, but it never seems to happen," said amendment opponent Sen. Joseph I. Lieberman, D-Conn. "And that's OK with me."

Backers Fall Short in 104th Congress

When Republicans took control of the House in 1995, the centerpiece of their ambitious agenda was passage of a balanced-budget amendment. Shellshocked at their loss of control for the first time in 40 years, Democratic leaders did not mount a fight, and on Jan. 26, 1995, the House endorsed the amendment by an overwhelming vote of 300-132.

By contrast, both sides knew the Senate vote would be a cliffhanger. Majority Leader Bob Dole, R-Kan. — presidential hopeful and lead sponsor of the Senate resolution — had a huge stake in securing a two-thirds majority. Dole held off final balloting for two days while he scrambled to find a 67th vote, but he could not pry one loose. After Dole switched to "no" to preserve his ability to call for a revote later in the session, the final tally on March 2 was 65-35. *(1995 Almanac: balanced-budget amendment, p. 2-34; history, p. 2-35)*

Dole tried again in 1996 — primarily to emphasize his credentials as a deficit hawk before he departed the Senate in June to run full-time for president. The amendment failed June 6 on a 64-35 vote. *(1996 Almanac, p. 2-32)*

Arguments Pro and Con

The central argument behind the amendment remained compellingly simple: Nothing short of a constitutional mandate would reverse the chronic inability of Congress and the president to stop deficit spending.

"I do not lightly suggest amending our founding document," said Hatch. "Yet, all other avenues having failed us, I believe it is appropriate to take recourse to our basic charter to rein in an abused power of the purse . . . in order that we might save future generations from the heavy burden of irresponsible government borrowing."

Opponents attacked the amendment on many familiar fronts: its treatment of surplus Social Security revenues, questions over whether it would give federal judges power to make budget decisions and resistance to writing fiscal policy into the Constitution.

"This proposed constitutional amendment risks seriously undercutting the protection of our constitutional separation of powers," said Patrick J. Leahy of Vermont, top Democrat on the Senate Judiciary Committee. "No one has yet convincingly explained how the proposed amendment would work and what role would the president play and what role the courts play in its implementation and enforcement."

There also was a new element in the debate in 1997: the expectation that the Republican Congress and Clinton would reach a balanced-budget deal. "This whole debate started in earnest in the early 1980s, when the deficit was skyrocketing. . . . There was a sense that there was nothing we could do but pass a constitutional amendment to give Congress the muscle to do the job," said Senate Democratic Leader Tom Daschle of South Dakota. "That has changed quite dramatically. We have brought the deficit down by 60 percent."

Senate Budget Committee Chairman Pete V. Domenici, R-N.M., did not see it that way. "History would reveal you get one big effort, but where's the staying power?" he asked. "It's probably going to be very, very tough to stay in balance without a constitutional amendment."

The Social Security Hot Button

In the Senate, at least eight Democrats said they would not vote for a balanced-budget amendment unless it exempted Social Security. They were Daschle, Kent Conrad and Byron L. Dorgan of North Dakota, Harry Reid of Nevada, Dianne Feinstein of California, Wendell H. Ford of Kentucky, Ernest F. Hollings of South Carolina and Ron Wyden of Oregon.

In the House, GOP leaders were blocked in part by a simmering revolt among some conservatives who agreed with liberal Democrats that Social Security should be exempted from the amendment.

Under existing law, the Social Security trust funds were officially "off budget," but the surpluses they were piling up to cover benefits once Baby Boomers started to retire were being counted toward bringing the overall deficit into balance. Opponents argued that the amendment would recklessly enshrine this practice in the Constitution. And they warned that when the surpluses began to dry up, as they were expected to do around 2019, the balanced-budget amendment would give Congress powerful incentives to reduce Social Security benefits or raise payroll taxes to finance other government programs.

Amendment supporters countered that the Social Security issue was purely a political fig leaf to justify a "no" vote on the amendment. Most budget analysts agreed with the GOP majority on the substance, but Democrats had a potent weapon in the political battle.

They pointed out that Clinton's fiscal 1998 budget relied on Social Security surpluses. And they said that exempting Social Security from the so-called unified budget would require extraordinary cuts in other programs, including Medicare, education and most discretionary spending, to bring the budget into balance.

On the flip side, when Social Security trust funds started to deplete in 2019, an exemption would allow huge deficits to finance benefits, because the trust funds would be excluded from balanced-budget calculations.

"If it is true that excluding Social Security from the balanced-budget amendment would force us to 'save' the short-term surplus, it is equally true that excluding Social Security would allow us to run massive budget deficits . . . beginning in 2019," said Domenici. "Ironically, these massive and unprecedented deficits would be specifically sanctioned by an amendment to the Constitution."

Splits Among Conservatives

Although there was a down-the-line allegiance to the amendment among congressional Republicans, there were cracks elsewhere in conservative quarters. For example, Federal Reserve Board Chairman Alan Greenspan, whose views ordinarily carried great weight among Republicans, opposed the amendment.

"I've always believed that the Constitution should be sets of principles . . . from which enabling legislation is enacted by Congress to implement certain general purposes," Greenspan said at a Senate Budget Committee hearing in January. "It is very difficult to implement technical economic policy through the Constitution."

And The Wall Street Journal, whose conservative editorials were closely watched in GOP circles, weighed in Feb. 4 with an editorial titled "Constitutional Boondoggle." It said: "The president is right and Republicans are wrong on item one of the GOP congressional agenda. . . . Politically it's empty symbolism. Legally it clutters the Constitution with dubious prose."

Senate Committee

The Senate Judiciary Committee got started quickly in the 105th Congress, approving the GOP's version of the balanced-budget amendment Jan. 30 by a vote of 13-5 (S J Res 1 — S Rept 105-3).

Republicans generally acted as a bloc during the markup to defeat several Democratic amendments, including a wide-ranging proposal by Feinstein that hit on virtually all of the key issues raised by the opponents. The amendment, defeated on a party-line vote of 8-9, sought to:

➤ Cut off the use of Social Security trust fund surpluses to offset the deficit by 2003.

➤ Allow the government to run deficits within a separate capital budget dedicated to infrastructure improvements. Feinstein and others pointed out that virtually every state issued bonds to finance long-term capital projects such as highway spending that were not subject to state balanced-budget requirements. Balanced-budget amendment advocates responded that the idea would create a huge loophole allowing permanent deficits.

➤ Drop the proposed requirement for a three-fifths vote in Congress to raise the debt ceiling. The idea had drawn criticism on the grounds that it would increase the potential for a default on the federal debt, which would send shock waves through financial markets and raise interest rates. Critics also said the requirement for a supermajority would give extraordinary power to the minority in Congress, enabling it to hold must-pass debt limit legislation hostage.

Defenders responded that the requirement would act as a backstop to ensure the amendment worked as designed. In theory, if the budget was balanced, there would be no need to raise the debt limit.

➤ Waive the balanced-budget amendment if Congress declared a "national economic" emergency.

Concern that the balanced-budget amendment would aggravate recessions was one of the most powerful arguments against it. The fear was that the amendment would require budget cuts that would undermine so-called built-in stabilizers, such as reduced tax revenues and increased unemployment benefits, that would otherwise help cushion an economic downturn. Clinton and Rubin emphasized this point, as did a group of more than 1,000 economists who signed a petition against the balanced-budget amendment.

Amendment supporters countered that the amendment had a built-in "escape hatch": Congress could permit a deficit during a recession, provided three-fifths of each chamber voted to do so.

The Judiciary Committee also rejected amendments by:

➤ Torricelli, who offered a proposal that resembled Feinstein's but would have immediately blocked using Social Security trust fund surpluses in balanced-budget calculations. It failed 8-9.

➤ Edward M. Kennedy, D-Mass., to exempt Social Security from the strictures of the amendment. It failed, 9-9, with Republican Arlen Specter of Pennsylvania breaking ranks.

Senate Floor Action

The measure went to the Senate floor Feb. 5 with every Republican pledged to vote for it. But GOP leaders were unable to win over all of the 12 Democrats they needed to prevail. When the Senate finally acted March 4, the vote was 66-34, one vote shy of the required two-thirds margin. *(Vote 24, p. S-6)*

Majority Leader Trent Lott, R-Miss., declined to switch his vote to "no," which would have permitted him to call up the amendment at any time for a revote. To have done so would have interfered with the GOP message of the day: All 55 Republicans supported the measure, and its defeat came at the hands of Democrats who broke campaign promises that they would back the amendment.

The Four Undeclared Freshmen

The substance of the monthlong debate on S J Res 1 had been overshadowed by almost daily news conferences, competing grass-roots campaigns and a spotlight on four initially undeclared Democratic freshmen, each of whom had supported the amendment during his or her 1996 campaign or voted for it as a House member. The four were: Max Cleland of Georgia, Mary L. Landrieu of Louisiana, Johnson and Torricelli.

One by one, the four made their decisions known. Cleland went first, confirming Feb. 14 that he would vote for the GOP-drafted amendment. On Feb. 20, Johnson announced that he would vote no because of concern over the potential effect on Social Security. That meant that if either Torricelli or Landrieu switched, the amendment would die. After sounding very much like she was paving the way for a switch, Landrieu announced Feb. 25 that she would keep her campaign promise to vote for the amendment.

That left it to Torricelli, a Democratic loyalist who had voted three times for a virtually identical amendment in the House and who had also supported it during a nasty Senate campaign. In a dramatic announcement Feb. 26, the freshman senator said he would vote no, dooming the amendment.

"In considering what I think are the failings of the balanced-budget amendment . . . I am left with doubts," Torricelli said. "But I have adopted at least this philosophy for myself — that all doubts concerning amendments to the Constitution must be settled in leaving the genius of the Founding Fathers undisturbed. Those doubts compel me to deny the 67th and deciding vote for a constitutional amendment requiring a balanced budget."

Torricelli and Johnson had been led patiently back into the fold by Daschle, aided by Clinton, Treasury Secretary Rubin and Senate opponents such as Robert C. Byrd, D-W.Va., and Daniel Patrick Moynihan, D-N.Y. By all accounts, Daschle was masterful, pressing the issue with a light but determined hand.

"He wasn't pushy at all," Torricelli said. "He asked me only to consider the consequences of being the deciding vote to amend the Constitution."

"He was gently persuading them," said Leahy. "And when that didn't work, you send them downstairs to see Bob Byrd."

In the days preceding the final vote, Lott indicated that he might agree to modify the amendment to garner the critical 67th vote. He told CBS' "Face The Nation" on March 2 that he was willing to permit greater flexibility in times of recession or national security emergency. He also had indicated earlier that he might permit a limited "capital budget" to pay for infrastructure improvements through deficit financing.

But there were no real attempts at negotiation. Once Torricelli's announcement made the outcome clear, the level of partisanship began to rise. Lott on Feb. 28 attacked Torricelli and fellow freshman opponent Johnson from the Senate floor, though not by name.

"This is a question of honesty. It is a question of truth in government. We wonder why people are cynical, why people wonder about us, why they question us," Lott said. "This is exhibit A. When you give your word to your constituency in your state during the election campaign . . . and then six months later you say, 'Gee whiz, I have learned something new,' it is hard to take."

Ironically, the changes that Lott suggested he was willing to make closely mirrored those sought by Torricelli. But Lott never called, and Torricelli lashed back.

"Sen. Lott's comments are at best disingenuous. He indicates on the floor of the Senate and then before the national news media that he's engaged in negotiations and compromises to pass the balanced-budget amendment, but we can find no member of the Senate who's ever heard from him," Torricelli said. "I'm left to conclude that he doesn't want to pass the amendment. He may find it a better [political] issue."

Floor Amendments

During the floor action, senators took a number of votes on amendments.

The week of Feb. 10, Republicans easily voted down Democratic amendments by:

➤ Richard J. Durbin of Illinois, to permit Congress to pass a joint resolution to waive balanced-budget requirements during a recession or serious economic emergency. Tabled (killed) Feb. 10 on a 64-35 vote. *(Vote 7, p. S-3)*

➤ Paul Wellstone of Minnesota, to declare that it was U.S. government policy that spending on education, nutrition and children's health should not be disproportionately cut to achieve a balanced budget. Tabled on Feb. 11 by a 64-36 vote. *(Vote 8, p. S-3)*

➤ Christopher J. Dodd of Connecticut, to make it easier to waive the strictures of the amendment when the United States faced a "serious military threat." A waiver in the Republican version would have kicked in when the country was "engaged in military conflict." Tabled Feb. 12 on a 64-36 vote. *(Vote 10, p. S-3)*

The pace of the Senate floor debate quickened the week of Feb. 24, with a vote on the hot-button Social Security issue, as well as votes on a host of other issues, such as proposals to permit a capital budget for infrastructure projects, and to waive the constitutional amendment in times of recession and military threat.

Prominently displayed on the floor was a stack of 28 unbalanced presidential budgets, which Hatch frequently stood behind to illustrate the need for the amendment. Ernest F. Hollings, D-S.C, derisively referred to it as the "Reagan-Bush memorial deficit pile."

The most passionate debate came on an amendment by Harry Reid, D-Nev., to exclude the Social Security trust funds.

Republicans, bolstered by an analysis by the bipartisan budget watchdog Concord Coalition that termed the Democratic arguments on Social Security "nonsense," accused Reid and other Democrats of hiding behind the politically charged issue to justify "no" votes. But Republicans admitted privately that the issue was working for Democrats.

Democrats fought back with the results of a petition drive by the National Committee to Preserve Social Security and Medicare, a senior-citizens advocacy group. Nearly 1 million signers urged Congress to reject any measure that failed to explicitly protect Social Security. In the end, Republicans on Feb. 25 tabled (killed) Reid's amendment, 55-44. *(Vote 14, p. S-4)*

Republicans also voted in unison to kill amendments by:

➤ Feinstein, to permit the use of Social Security trust fund surpluses to offset the deficit for one year after the amendment took effect; permit Congress to raise the debt ceiling by majority vote; allow a capital budget, and permit Congress to waive balanced-budget mandates in times of military conflict, national economic emergency or natural disasters. Tabled Feb. 26, 67-33. *(Vote 15, p. S-4)*

➤ Torricelli, to permit deficits for a capital budget and to make it easier to waive balanced-budget requirements in times of recession or when Congress declared a national security emergency. Rejected Feb. 26, 37-63. *(Vote 16, p. S-4)*

➤ Kennedy, to vest sole enforcement authority under the amendment with Congress, unless Congress passed a law to grant such authority to the president or the courts. Tabled Feb. 27, 61-39. *(Vote 20, p. S-5)*

The role of the courts was a touchy issue. In 1995, Dole had agreed on the Senate floor to add language that would block the courts from enforcing the amendment. He did so as the price for obtaining the vote of then-Sen. Sam Nunn, D-Ga. But the so-called judicial review language was strongly opposed in the House and was not especially popular in the Senate. It was not included in S J Res 1.

House Committee

The House Judiciary Committee took up an identical resolution (H J Res 1) on Feb. 5, the same day the Senate began its floor debate. But Chairman Henry J. Hyde, R-Ill., abruptly adjourned the markup after only two hours of debate and no votes, saying further committee action was on hold until after the Senate voted.

Hyde acted after it appeared he lacked the votes in committee to block an amendment on Social Security offered by top committee Democrat John Conyers Jr. of Michigan "The plan right now is to wait for the Senate to vote on it," Hyde said. "There is a high antsy quotient around here."

Conyers' amendment would have stopped the practice of using surplus Social Security revenues to help bring the budget closer to balance. The effect would have been to require draconian budget cuts in the short term, and its adoption would likely have killed the underlying measure.

House Leaders Decline To Push Floor Vote

House GOP leaders saw no point in pushing for a vote if the Senate was going to defeat the measure anyway. Beyond the problems in Judiciary, whip counts for the measure were stalled about 10 votes short of the necessary two-thirds, and Democratic undecideds appear to be breaking toward the opponents' camp.

A small but potentially decisive rump group of conservatives, mostly sophomores from political swing districts, were agitating to exempt Social Security from the balanced-budget amendment. They wanted some chance for a floor vote, perhaps on legislation to permit Social Security surpluses to be invested in securities other than government bonds

If not satisfied, the group held out the option of voting against the amendment or even voting with Democrats on a procedural motion to send the measure back to the Judiciary Committee.

A less troubling but still nettlesome issue for House GOP leaders involved how to deal with conservatives who believed the balanced-budget amendment should require a two-thirds vote in both chambers to raise taxes. This so-called tax limitation concept was included in the House Republicans' 1994 "Contract With America." The reasoning behind it was that it would force budget cuts instead of tax increases to balance the budget.

The issue had threatened House passage of the balanced-budget amendment in 1995, as GOP leaders were forced to whip disappointed freshmen into line. The top sponsor of the tax supermajority requirement, Joe L. Barton, R-Texas, was again trying to attach it to the amendment.

Torricelli's declaration on Feb. 26 seemed to signal the end for the amendment in the House. "There's no reason to go ahead in the House right now," said Rep. Charles W. Stenholm, D-Texas, by far the most active Democrat supporting the idea. "I think we ought to get on with the budget, get serious."

In the wake of the Senate vote, top House Republicans briefly considered bringing H J Res 1 to the floor after all in what Majority Leader Dick Armey, R-Texas, described as an attempt to "reincarnate" the amendment.

But faced with pessimistic vote counts, the leadership put the plan on the back burner and turned instead to the bipartisan budget talks with Clinton. ■

IRS Overhaul Sails Through House

Barely on the radar screen early in the year, proposals to overhaul the perpetually unpopular Internal Revenue Service took off late in 1997.

After a series of emotionally charged hearings before the Senate Finance Committee in late September, the House moved quickly to pass a bill (HR 2676) calling for a series of management changes at the IRS, including the creation of an oversight board dominated by private-sector management experts.

The Senate did not take up the bill before it quit for the year, however. Finance Committee Chairman William V. Roth Jr., R-Del., insisted that he needed more time to hold hearings and review specific provisions. Democrats complained that Senate Republicans were stalling to give themselves a political issue as the 1998 midterm elections approached, but Roth and other GOP leaders remained resolute. "This is a very important reform," Roth said. "We have to do it right."

Congress did clear a smaller bill (HR 1226) aimed at punishing IRS employees for unauthorized "browsing" through tax returns and other documents.

Background

The drive to overhaul the IRS kicked off June 25, when a congressionally created, bipartisan commission recommended that oversight of the agency be shifted from the Treasury Department to an independent board of governors. The commission recommended a seven-member board, including five presidentially appointed executives from the private sector, plus the Treasury secretary and a representative of the IRS employees' labor union. The board would name the IRS commissioner, who would serve a five-year term.

The National Commission on Restructuring the Internal Revenue Service was co-chaired by Republican Rep. Rob Portman of Ohio and Democratic Sen. Bob Kerrey of Nebraska. House Speaker Newt Gingrich, R-Ga., and other GOP leaders immediately endorsed the plan, but the Clinton administration opposed it.

Kerrey said the commission's 52 recommendations, which resulted from a year of hearings and debate, were aimed at making the IRS more service oriented. "These recommendations," he said, " are based on a simple idea: The IRS works for the taxpayers, not the other way around."

Among the recommendations: Take steps to achieve 80 percent electronic filing within 10 years, eliminate the alternative minimum tax, and move the deadline for filing personal income tax returns from April 15 to May 15 for people who continued to file returns on paper and to June 15 for those filing electronically. The commission also proposed more safeguards for taxpayers, including compensation for misdeeds by IRS agents.

Portman and Kerrey introduced bills (HR 2292, S 1096) embodying the commission's recommendations over the summer, but there was little initial action in the face of strong objections from the Clinton administration.

Treasury Secretary Robert E. Rubin called the recommendation for an independent board of governors "substantially and seriously flawed." He said business leaders appointed to the board would have the appearance, if not the reality, of a conflict of interest with IRS tax policies. "I think that you run a real risk of undermining that sense of fairness if the American people feel that the law enforcement, auditing and compliance functions of the IRS are being controlled by a group of private-sector chief executive officers," Rubin said.

The administration maintained its position into the fall. Appearing before the House Ways and Means Committee on Sept. 17, Rubin said the board of overseers "just isn't very likely to work altogether."

Rubin and other administration officials insisted they had already initiated management changes at the IRS, including the establishment in 1996 of an oversight board with members drawn from the government — senior officials from Treasury, the Office of Management and Budget, and the IRS. The Clinton administration wanted to make that board permanent, and legislation to that effect (S 1174, HR 2428) was introduced in September by Sen. Daniel Patrick Moynihan and Rep. Charles B. Rangel, both New Yorkers and the top Democrats, respectively, on the Senate Finance Committee and the House Ways and Means Committee.

But supporters of the Kerrey-Portman recommendations argued that private-sector expertise was needed to address the strategic modernization and customer service issues dogging the IRS, and that government officials with short tenures would not offer the continuity or independence needed to overhaul the agency.

Senate Hearings

Three days of emotional testimony on IRS abuses before the Senate Finance Committee brought a sea change in the administration's position. In hearings held Sept. 23-25, four taxpayers told of being harassed by IRS agents, and seven active and former IRS employees said the agency's culture endorsed improper tactics.

Nancy Jacobs of Bakersfield, Calif., cried as she described a 17-year battle to correct confusion over a debt owed by someone with a name similar to that of her optometrist husband. Both had been assigned the same employer-identification number. Jacobs said she and her husband were still owed more than $10,000.

Monsignor Lawrence Ballweg of New York said he lost sleep for eight months after the IRS insisted he owed $18,000 on his late mother's charitable trust, but the agency refused to give him a copy of the tax return. It turned out he had simply filed the wrong form.

IRS revenue agent Jennifer Long testified that "egregious tactics" were used with the support of supervisors "to extract unfairly assessed taxes from taxpayers, literally ruining families, lives and businesses — all unnecessarily and sometimes illegally."

The hearings culminated in an extraordinary, public apology from acting IRS Commissioner Michael P. Dolan. "No one should have endured what these citizens describe as their experience at the hand of the tax system," Dolan said. He and other IRS officials vowed rapid reforms, including a ban on ranking district offices based on tax collections, a practice that amounted to unofficial quotas and put pressure on managers and agents.

Still, Dolan and other officials defended the IRS' overall record. In 1996, the agency collected nearly $1.5 trillion from 209 million tax returns. Of those returns, just 1.4 percent were audited, and of the audited returns, only 3.8 percent resulted in penalties. Dolan said that in 435 cases over the previous three years, IRS employees had been disciplined for some form of taxpayer mistreatment.

There were other voices of caution, as well. Pamela F. Olson, vice chairman of committee operations for the American Bar Association's section on taxation, said the hearings focused on a handful of egregious violations, not "what's actually going on out there." She said they "got out of hand." And Robert Tobias, president of the National Treasury Employees Union, warned that "the IRS cannot survive two more years of this kind of bashing."

House Committee Action

In the House, Ways and Means Committee Chairman Bill Archer, R-Texas, scheduled a markup for Oct. 22 on the first comprehensive overhaul of IRS operations since 1952. That forced the Clinton administration and congressional Democrats to decide how to confront the issue.

On Oct. 10, Clinton offered a set of initiatives designed to make the IRS more consumer-oriented. His proposals included creating an eight-member "board of trustees" with a strictly advisory role, along with 33 regional "citizen advocacy panels" to review taxpayer grievances.

GOP critics said such changes would be too little, too late. Archer labeled Clinton "part of the problem" for resisting a sweeping overhaul that would include an independent governing board. Sen. Charles E. Grassley, R-Iowa, a member of the Kerrey-Portman commission, called Clinton's plan "paper thin," while Sen. Phil Gramm, R-Texas, decried it as "reaction, not a reform."

Democrats Climb Aboard

On Oct. 22, the Ways and Means Committee approved the restructuring bill (HR 2676 — H Rept 105-364, Part 1) by a lopsided vote of 33-4. Only Democrats John Lewis of Georgia, Robert T. Matsui of California, Jim McDermott of Washington and Pete Stark of California voted no.

By the time of the markup, Democratic opposition had crumbled under an onslaught of popular anger triggered by the Senate Finance Committee hearings. Following a week of intense negotiations, Minority Leader Richard A. Gephardt, D-Mo., Rangel, Clinton and Rubin had all jumped on board. "Now, David, the taxpayer, will get the stronger slingshot he needs in his dealings with Goliath, the IRS," Archer crowed.

Kerrey had gone through the bill's provisions line by line with Clinton during the week of Oct. 13, and said he sensed the president was softening.

On the morning of Oct. 21, Rubin conferred with a handful of Ways and Means Democrats to confirm reports that Gephardt was going to endorse the bill. When he was assured that it was true, the Treasury secretary met with top White House aides, who urged Rubin to follow suit. That afternoon, Gephardt announced his support for what he called "a plan to dramatically reform the IRS." An hour later, Rubin followed with a more tepid endorsement, calling the proposed legislation "workable."

"When Gephardt went over, things pretty much collapsed," said bill critic Matsui.

The switch left the White House open to a few snide quips from Republicans. Archer congratulated Clinton for his "healthy amount of, shall we say, philosophical flexibility." But it also deprived GOP leaders of the political bludgeon they had been wielding for weeks.

"The president is smart enough to understand a piece of legislation and like it," Kerrey said. "He knew he would be criticized for switching positions, but he had the courage to do it anyway."

Archer Makes Changes

Also, Archer had agreed to some important concessions to the administration. Under the revised bill, the president would retain the power to nominate and remove the IRS commissioner, a power that the earlier version would have granted to the oversight board. The new board would review the IRS budget, consult on strategic plans and oversee operational functions, although it would have no powers over tax law enforcement.

But some changes in the chairman's version of the bill seemed like a poke in Clinton's eye. Despite administration concerns over private-sector board members, Archer increased the number of non-government professionals to eight, up from the five proposed by the Kerrey-Portman commission.

Archer also added a provision to make it a felony for executive branch officials to use IRS audits for political purposes. Clinton critics had questioned a 1997 audit of Paula Jones, the former Arkansas government employee who was suing the president for alleged sexual harassment. "We have no substantive evidence that has occurred," Archer said, referring to the use of audits as a political tool. "But there is a perception in the minds of people that undermines the system."

Finally, Archer added a provision that would shift the burden of proof from the taxpayer to the IRS in disputes that reached tax court. The Kerrey-Portman commission had considered such a change but declined to include it in its recommendations.

Other provisions of the bill were never under dispute, including proposals to allow taxpayers to sue the IRS for up to $100,000 in damages arising from negligence; to make it easier for taxpayers to recover legal fees incurred in disputes with the IRS; to help those who inadvertently signed unlawful tax documents prepared by their spouses; to encourage electronic filing of tax returns; to ease personnel restrictions at the agency; and to place congressional oversight under a new joint committee.

Critics Warn of More Tax Cheating

Behind the House momentum, however, doubts still lingered, particularly over the proposal to shift the burden of proof from the taxpayer to the IRS, and the plan to create an independent board dominated by private-sector representatives. "It will do some harm," Matsui said of the bill. "But nobody's willing to stand on the railroad tracks to stop it."

It was the burden-of-proof provision that raised the most eyebrows among tax professionals. To advocates, it was a simple question of fairness: Why should an accused murderer be considered innocent until proven guilty, while a taxpayer had to prove his innocence against the IRS' presumption of guilt?

But even conservative tax groups such as the National Taxpayers Union raised questions about a broad change in the burden of proof. They suggested that tax cheats could conceal documentation of claimed deductions, then dare the IRS to prove them wrong. That could have the consequence of making the IRS more aggressive and intrusive in its subpoenaing of documents. And with more tax cheating, law-abiding taxpayers would have to make up the shortfall, the critics said.

In a strongly worded letter to Archer, Paul Cherecwich Jr., president of the Tax Executives Institute and an executive of Thiokol Corp., called the proposal "misguided" and "facile," saying a 1 percent drop in voluntary tax compliance would necessitate a $10 billion increase in revenues. "The issue is not whether a taxpayer is assumed 'guilty' until proven innocent; it is whether the taxpayer is accountable for what is claimed on the tax return," Cherecwich wrote.

Supporters countered that the legislative language was crafted to avoid those pitfalls. Taxpayers would still have the burden of proof throughout the administrative process with the IRS and would be legally bound to release all relevant tax documentation. Only in tax court would the burden of proof shift.

Kenneth J. Kies, director of the Joint Tax Committee, said that would make the shift applicable in only a tiny fraction of IRS disputes. Of the 25,000 to 30,000 cases filed in tax court each year, only 1,000 to 1,500 would go to trial, he said.

But even the Joint Tax Committee conceded that the provision would increase tax cheating, albeit by a minuscule amount. In its calculations of cost, Joint Tax said the burden-of-proof provision was expected to cost $795 million through 2002, the largest piece of the bill's total cost of $2.6 billion. Of that $795 million, 15 percent — or $119 million — would come from tax fraud. The rest would come from legitimate tax disputes that would have been resolved in the IRS' favor under existing rules but would be won by taxpayers under the new rules.

Cherecwich was unimpressed by the limitations on the burden-of-proof shift. He said they would only encourage tax cheats to take their cases to court — "thereby consuming time and resources of not only the IRS but also the tax courts. Stated differently, delaying a bad idea does not make it a good one."

But the measure's advocates argued that a small increase in tax cheating was the price to be paid for fairness. "It is clearly the right thing to do," said House Majority Leader Dick Armey, R-Texas.

Stark attempted to amend the bill by restricting board members from representing any clients with business or disputes before the IRS. But Portman said the legislation already applied existing federal conflict-of-interest restrictions. Stark's amendment failed, 14-23, generally along party lines.

The committee did adopt by voice vote an amendment by Gerald D. Kleczka, D-Wis., tightening reimbursement of board members' travel expenses.

House Floor Action

The House passed the bill Nov. 5 by an overwhelming vote of 426-4, with no amendments. The only dissenters were Democrats Steny H. Hoyer of Maryland and Ways and Means members McDermott, Matsui and Stark. *(Vote 577, p. H-174)*

Most of the floor debate was given over to GOP claims that the bill was simply the first salvo in a war against the graduated income tax system — though their party was divided into two camps on that issue. One, led by Armey, favored a a flat 17 percent income tax rate. The other, led by W.J. "Billy" Tauzin, R-La., supported a national sales tax. Tauzin and Armey had launched a "Scrap the Code" tour in October, during which they visited several cities to debate which option was best.

Some critics suggested, however, that what was good for the GOP could prove bad for the Treasury. They predicted that IRS bashing could raise a serious new question: How far could Congress go before a climate of contempt for the IRS began to undermine a collection system that was historically based on voluntary compliance?

IRS 'Browsing' Barred

In separate action, Congress cleared a bill making it a crime for IRS employees to snoop through tax returns and other records. Under the legislation, signed into law Aug. 5 (HR 1226 — PL 105-35), IRS workers risked a Class A misdemeanor charge for "browsing" through tax records of cases they were not authorized to review. Anyone convicted could face up to one year in prison and a $1,000 fine.

Sponsors said more than 3,300 cases of unauthorized snooping had been recorded by the IRS since 1991. Among those whose privacy had been invaded were celebrities such as actors Tom Cruise and Elizabeth Taylor and basketball star Michael Jordan. Under the bill, a taxpayer whose records had been improperly accessed would be notified by the IRS once an employee was convicted. The victim could then seek civil damages from the employee.

The measure, sponsored by Archer, began in the House Ways and Means Committee, which approved it by voice vote April 9 (H Rept 105-51). The House passed the bill on tax-filing day, April 15, by a vote of 412-0. Speaker Newt Gingrich, R-Ga., called it "only the first step in what I think will be a real landmark Congress in bringing the IRS under control." *(House vote 76, p. H-26)*

The Senate passed a similar bill (S 522) the same day by a vote of 97-0, but the Senate version had additional provisions not in the House bill. Senate sponsors later agreed to drop the extra provisions in favor of the House bill, clearing the measure by voice vote July 23. *(Vote 43, p. S-10)* ■

Financial Services Overhaul Stalls

Once again, congressional leaders fell short in their efforts to advance a plan that would partially deregulate the financial services industry. Although House leaders steered a sweeping proposal through two committees, they failed to bring it to the floor due to a longstanding feud between the banking and insurance industries, in addition to disagreements over regulating securities and ending the national charter for thrift institutions.

The Senate took no action on the bill.

Top House leaders vowed to pursue the issue early in 1998. However, with powerful financial industries sharply at odds over the measure, it appeared the 105th Congress would go down as the fourth since 1988 to fail to overhaul decades-old banking laws.

As a result, regulators and the courts, rather than lawmakers, were expected to continue setting the rules for changes in the financial industry as they had for a decade.

Much of the House action took place in the Banking and Financial Services Committee and the Commerce Committee. The two panels approved sharply different versions of a sweeping bill (HR 10) that aimed to repeal Depression-era restrictions on affiliations between banks, insurance companies and securities firms, allowing major mergers and reshaping the entire industry.

Proponents, including senior lawmakers and top administration officials, said updating the laws would save consumers money and create a "one-stop shopping" approach for financial transactions. But opponents, such as small banks and some consumer advocates, warned that it could lead to a dangerous consolidation of financial power.

After the Commerce Committee finished its work Oct. 30, Republican Conference Chairman John A. Boehner, R-Ohio, brought together senior Democrats and Republicans on the Banking, Commerce and Rules committees to try to move a consensus version of the bill through the Rules Committee. He and other top leaders had planned all year to bring the legislation to the floor by the fall.

But the two committee versions clashed over such basic issues as whether to allow partial mergers between financial firms and commercial companies, and the extent to which bank sales of insurance and securities would be regulated. Lawmakers were also at odds over provisions in both versions that would end the national thrift charter.

Rules Committee Chairman Gerald B.H. Solomon, R-N.Y., and senior Commerce Committee Democrat John D. Dingell of Michigan, both of whom were close to the insurers, pressed to sharply limit bank sales of insurance — a position opposed by bank allies on the Banking Committee, such as Chairman Jim Leach, R-Iowa. Commerce members also supported provisions to step up regulations on bank sales of securities, despite objections from Banking members.

Talks collapsed shortly before the end of the session, when Commerce Committee members failed to attend a Nov. 8 meeting. In a terse written statement, House Majority Leader Dick Armey, R-Texas, and others vowed to continue pressing for consensus early in 1998.

In the Senate, Banking, Housing and Urban Affairs Committee Chairman Alfonse M. D'Amato, R-N.Y., introduced a bill (S 298) that would allow a broad mixing of banking and commerce. But his deeply divided committee failed to hold any hearings on it, and D'Amato said he would wait for House floor action before moving ahead.

BOXSCORE

Financial Services Modernization — HR 10. The bill sought to partially deregulate the financial services industry, allowing affiliations among banks, securities firms and insurance companies.

Report: H Rept 105-164, Parts 1, 2, 3.

KEY ACTION

June 20 — House Banking Committee approved HR 10, 28-26.

Oct. 30 — House Commerce Committee approved HR 10, amended, 33-11.

Background

All sides generally agreed that the 1933 Glass-Steagall Act, enacted in the wake of widespread bank failures, was out of date and that its restrictions preventing affiliations between different types of financial institutions should be repealed. But any effort to overhaul banking laws inevitably started fights among competing financial services interest groups.

The financial world had changed dramatically since the 1930s, in part because of new technology. Thanks to innovations such as automated teller machines, telephone banking and computer transactions, consumers could conduct their financial business at electronic speed, breaking down international investment borders as well as the boundaries between different types of financial institutions.

In addition, companies offered hybrid products — such as mutual funds with check-writing options or savings accounts that resembled insurance annuities — that did not easily fit into the old definitions of banking,

"Revolutionary improvements in technology and escalating competition are redefining the financial services business," William T. McConnell, president-elect of the American Bankers Association, said at a May House Banking Committee hearing. "The lines between different types of financial service firms have been blurred beyond recognition."

The movement of money also changed the competitive dynamics among various types of financial institutions. As more money flowed out of banks and into mutual funds and other investments, bank holding companies began offering such services as limited insurance policies in order to hold on to their share of the financial marketplace.

Securities firms started to expand by offering certain banking services, such as checking accounts. Insurance companies laid the groundwork to set up thrifts, thereby competing for savings accounts. And commercial giants such as General Electric offered credit cards and brokerage services.

Further blurring the lines, moves such as the $9 billion consolidation of Travelers Group and Salomon Inc., announced in the fall of 1997, created giant brokerage and financial services companies.

Regulators, including the Federal Reserve Board and the Office of the Comptroller of the Currency (OCC), found themselves scrambling to keep up. In 1986, the OCC issued a letter allowing nationwide sales of insurance by banks. One year later, the Fed issued the first of a series of opinions that allowed bank holding companies to set up subsidiaries to sell securities. *(Key rulings, p. 2-77)*

These and other rulings, coupled with a 1994 law enabling banks to set up branch offices nationwide (PL 103-328), helped banks post double-digit profits for many areas of their business. *(1994 Almanac, p. 93)*

Buoyed by regulatory rulings that were expanding their reach, bank officials became ambivalent about congressional action to update financial services laws. But the expansion of bank powers raised alarms in other quarters.

Securities and insurance executives charged that banks were enjoying an unfair competitive advantage. Securities firms in particular contended that government rules had become dangerously unbalanced, allowing overseas banks to acquire U.S. securities firms and potentially undermine the premier position of the American investment banking industry. "You're a sitting duck right now — they can come in and buy you," said Bruce Thompson, director of government relations for Merrill Lynch & Co.

Other concerns were voiced by consumer groups, which contended that bank holding companies could pressure consumers into buying risky financial products offered by a subsidiary in order to get a loan. They also said consumers could be misled into thinking products offered by a bank holding company subsidiary were covered by the Federal Deposit Insurance Corporation, the independent agency that insured bank deposits up to $100,000.

"Consumers have already experienced problems with bank sales activities and, as bank powers expand, can expect more deceptive and misleading practices," said Mary Griffin, the insurance counsel with Consumers Union, the publisher of Consumer Reports.

With the financial marketplace in flux and a series of regulatory and court rulings creating confusion, a growing number of experts urged Congress to weigh in.

"Every new ruling has a way of exposing fresh inequities and creating new uncertainties," former Federal Reserve

Board Chairman Paul A. Volcker told a congressional panel in May. "In the absence of clear and up-to-date congressional mandates, there is seemingly endless squabbling in the courts. . . . Unfortunately, in some instances, important safeguards are being weakened and the playing field is uneven. Legislation is overdue."

Throughout the year, House Republican leaders, too, maintained that overhauling financial laws was a top priority. "Congress wants to preserve our right to write laws, which frankly has been overshadowed by the OCC and other regulators," said Boehner, the GOP leadership's point man on financial issues. "If we don't modernize our financial services industry, America's ability to compete in the world is going to be severely undermined."

But the record of previous congressional attempts was not encouraging.

Past Efforts Frustrated

Three efforts in the previous decade had foundered in the face of seemingly intractable industry divisions.

Democrats tried but failed to muster a consensus for change in 1988 and 1991. *(1991 Almanac, p. 75; 1988 Almanac, p. 230)*

The Republican-led 104th Congress did no better despite determined efforts by Leach in his first term as banking chairman. Leach struggled for more than a year to bring an ambitious rewrite of banking law to the floor, repeatedly redrafting a bill in his search for a legislative mix that would suit various financial services industry groups. *(1996 Almanac, p. 2-43)*

But the redrafts did not sufficiently ease the opposition from banks, which objected to a provision that would have curbed the OCC's ability to expand their powers to sell certain insurance products. In March 1996, the Supreme Court confirmed the ability of national banks to sell insurance from small towns without interference from state regulators — meaning the banks no longer needed much help from Congress.

Also bedeviling Leach's effort was the indifference of Senate Banking Chairman D'Amato. Publicly, D'Amato said he would mark up a bill once the House acted. But he was confident that Leach would fail and made no preparations to act. D'Amato's inaction reinforced the belief on the part of House leaders that the bill had no chance to become law and therefore was not worth requiring members to cast politically uncomfortable votes.

Nor did the Clinton administration display any interest in advancing the bill. And, roiling the waters, Comptroller of the Currency Eugene Ludwig waged a behind-the-scenes war against the measure, which would have shifted some regulatory authority from his agency to the Federal Reserve.

After the legislation stalled, regulators issued new rulings that further strengthened the market position of banks. Particularly important was a Federal Reserve Board rule to ease restrictions on the securities activities of banking companies.

This set the stage for a major merger announced in early 1997 between Bankers Trust New York Corp., the seventh-largest U.S. banking company, and Alex. Brown Inc., a major regional brokerage based in Baltimore. The merger was the biggest breach of the Glass-Steagall walls to date.

Trying Again in the 105th Congress

Thanks to the regulatory rulings, banks already appeared close to offering most of the services they wanted without rewriting the law. Other elements of the financial services industry also seemed unenthusiastic about congressional action. The banks' reluctance contributed to a sense of futility, and many of the affected parties did not feel like going through a reprise of the lobbying wars of recent years. And there were enough avenues in existing law to allow almost everyone to offer new products and services.

"We've got to go back to the drawing board a bit here," said Sen. Christopher J. Dodd, D-Conn., a senior Banking Committee member and an essential player if the effort was to succeed. "The financial services sector, basically, isn't showing a lot of interest in legislation."

Against this backdrop, the Treasury Department issued a long-awaited proposal in June that punted some of the most contentious issues to Congress.

Under the Treasury plan, banking companies would be allowed to engage in a full range of insurance and securities underwriting and sales activities, either as subsidiaries of a bank or as affiliates within a holding company. Insurance companies and agents vehemently opposed the plan, saying it would give the OCC too much leeway to define which financial products were insurance and thus potentially exempt banks from scrutiny by state insurance regulators.

On the controversial issue of banking and commerce, Treasury offered two options.

Under the first, a limited portion (or "basket") of a holding company's revenues could come from non-financial activities. The federal thrift charter would be eliminated, and banks would still be barred from affiliating with any of the 1,000 largest non-financial companies.

But that notion sparked opposition from consumer groups, labor unions and small banks, which said it would lead to a dangerous concentration of financial power and make it more difficult for average citizens to get loans. Treasury backed off promoting full-blown banking and commerce affiliations after the interest groups and Paul S. Sarbanes of Maryland, the top Democrat on the Senate Banking Committee, expressed opposition.

The other Treasury option would block any commercial activities by banking companies, though such activities could still be carried out through thrift affiliates with unique powers.

A class of wholesale banks would be created that could only accept deposits of more than $100,000 and would not carry deposit insurance. These entities could have unlimited commercial activities. But in a politically nettlesome requirement, such "wholesale financial institutions" would be subject to the Community Reinvestment Act, which pressured banks to lend in underserved communities.

House Banking Committee

The congressional debate got off to a dramatic start, with the House Banking and Financial Services Committee barely approving the bill on June 20 (H Rept 105-164, Parts 1 and 2). After a four-day markup, the committee was so divided that it voted by just 28-26 to approve the measure. Leach, who introduced HR 10, said the close vote showed "how extraordinarily balanced the bill is," adding, "It will be a close call on the House floor."

However, one of the "yes" votes was cast by Leach, who said he might not support the bill on the floor due to two amendments, added in committee over his objections, to allow the mixing of banking and commerce.

The committee also voted to end the federal thrift charter within two years, narrowly defeating a rival amendment that would have retained it. That spurred the thrift industry to join with small banks and consumer groups in opposing the bill and nearly sinking it in committee.

Leach's Proposals

There was ample reason for controversy: HR 10 contained the potential for the most sweeping change to the financial services industry in 60 years.

Building on the administration plan, the bill, as introduced by Leach, proposed to repeal the Glass-Steagall restrictions on banks affiliating with securities firms, thereby allowing the combination of commercial and investment banking. It also proposed to repeal restrictions on banks affiliating with insurance companies and to override state laws prohibiting such affiliations.

Leach's bill called for the creation of a new type of bank, known as a Wholesale Financial Institution, which would accept only wholesale, non-federally insured deposits of $100,000 or more.

The bill also proposed to lift cross-marketing and activity restrictions on non-bank banks (banks which, before 1987, did not both take demand deposits and make commercial loans). National banks would be allowed to underwrite municipal revenue bonds within the bank. Small banks could get Federal Home Loan advances for small business and other community development loans.

Finally, the measure provided for creating a Council on Financial Services composed of banking, insurance and securities regulators. The council would have wide authority in defining financial products and determining new permissible financial activities.

Supporters hoped the bill would spur competition and help financial companies adapt to changing technologies. Treasury Secretary Robert E. Rubin, who presented the administration's plan to the committee on June 3, estimated that increased competitiveness could reduce customer costs by as much as $15 billion a year.

Leach said his plan, "looks to the future financial marketplace by dramatically expanding opportunities for all."

Mixing Banking and Commerce

But Leach's support of his own bill was shaken during the marathon markup by the adoption of two amendments that aimed to partially dismantle the walls between financial and non-financial companies.

First, the committee approved, 35-19, a bipartisan amendment by Marge Roukema, R-N.J., and others to allow a bank holding company to invest up to 15 percent of its domestic gross revenues in a non-financial company. The commercial firm could not have more than $750 million in assets.

Supporters said such a 15 percent basket would allow insurance and securities companies with non-financial holdings to affiliate with banks. Otherwise, such companies would have to divest their commercial holdings if they were to engage in new activities. "Without this amendment . . . we may well be condemning many of our firms to secondary status," warned Charles E. Schumer, D-N.Y.

Some members said they would prefer a largely unrestricted mixing of banking and commerce, rather than stopping at 15 percent.

But Leach and the committee's senior Democrat, Henry B. Gonzalez of Texas, argued that the amendment could allow a small number of companies to dominate the financial services industry. They also warned that it could create conflicts of interest, with banks providing credit to commercial affiliates regardless of their soundness.

"The amendment goes much farther than it needs to, inviting rapid growth of combinations that we do not understand, and creates risks which regulators are ill-prepared to deal with and may not be able to control," Gonzalez said.

The committee then narrowly approved, 25-23, a second amendment to create a "reverse basket," allowing non-financial firms to invest up to 15 percent of their gross revenues in a financial institution. A commercial company could buy a bank with assets of up to $500 million.

Supporters said such an amendment was necessary to retain a balance between financial and non-financial firms, but opponents said it went too far.

After the markup, Leach warned that he could oppose the bill if the baskets were retained. "I supported committee approval of the bill as a steward of the committee," he said, "but like all members I will reserve final judgment on the bill, particularly in light of how the banking and commerce issue is resolved."

A Battle Over Thrifts

Another impassioned debate erupted over the issue of whether to continue or eliminate the federal thrift charter, a politically difficult issue that pitted banks against savings and loan institutions.

Leach's original language would have abolished the thrift charter and treated state-chartered thrifts as banks. Conversion of all thrifts, both federal and state, to banks was effectively assumed by the 1996 legislation (PL 104-208) that recapitalized the Savings Association Insurance Fund (SAIF). That law called for the SAIF to be merged with the Bank Insurance Fund when Congress acted to eliminate the thrift charter.

But Leach conceded that his approach had little support, and the thrift debate turned instead on a pair of competing amendments.

The first, offered by Bill McCollum, R-Fla., proposed ending the federal thrift charter after two years, with federal savings associations becoming national banks at that time. The savings associations could retain their branches and agencies after the conversion.

John J. LaFalce, D-N.Y., and Jack Metcalf, R-Wash., then tried to modify McCollum's proposal with language that retained the thrift charter. That set off a wide-ranging debate over the value of savings and loans.

Advocates of the thrifts contended that Congress could throw financial competition out of balance by forcing thrifts to become banks. They also painted the issue as a David vs. Goliath struggle, with small neighborhood thrifts providing vital home loans to low-income families that could not obtain financing from large banks.

"Some of us have very, very strong memories of who provided the housing opportunities in some communities," said Maxine Waters, D-Calif. "Leave these thrifts alone."

On the other side, members contended that existing law unfairly favored thrifts by allowing them to affiliate with commercial businesses and operate under fewer government regulations than banks. They also warned that the government could face another savings and loan bailout without some sort of action.

"The merger [of thrifts and banks] is a public policy necessity in order to protect the taxpayers from future deficits," McCollum said.

Members narrowly rejected the LaFalce-Metcalf amendment, 23-26. Then they adopted the McCollum amendment, 42-4.

Consumer Protection

The committee also adopted, by voice vote, an amendment by Waters to require bank holding company affiliates to provide low-cost "lifeline" banking services, such as basic

Key Rulings Expand Bank Powers

With Congress deadlocked for years over banking legislation, regulators and judges stepped into the breach with a series of decisions expanding the reach of banks — sometimes over the objections of insurers and securities firms. The following is a summary of major recent regulatory and court decisions that affected the banking industry:

1986: The Office of the Comptroller of the Currency issued a letter permitting banks to sell insurance nationwide. The comptroller based the decision on a provision of the National Bank Act of 1916 that authorized national banks located in towns of 5,000 or fewer residents to sell insurance.

However, the 1916 provision did not explicitly state whether banks could sell insurance outside those small towns, and it had been the subject of considerable debate. For years before the comptroller's letter, national banks had been restricted to selling insurance in small towns and surrounding rural areas where insurance might not be readily available.

1987: The Federal Reserve Board authorized bank holding companies to engage in limited securities activities. It allowed bank holding companies' subsidiaries to derive up to 5 percent of their gross revenue from underwriting and dealing in securities such as commercial paper and municipal revenue bonds.

The ruling was based on section 20 of the Glass-Steagall Act of 1933, which stated that no bank could be affiliated with an organization that "engaged principally" in activities that were generally off-limits to banks, such as securities underwriting.

1989: The Fed expanded the activities of so-called section 20 subsidiaries, allowing them to derive up to 10 percent of their revenues from securities underwriting. Large bank holding companies were permitted to engage in longer-term corporate debt securities.

1991: The Fed authorized foreign banks to underwrite securities in the United States directly through subsidiaries, instead of through the subsidiary of a holding company as required of domestic banks.

1993: Upholding the interpretation of the Comptroller of the Currency, a Circuit Court judge in Washington, D.C., ruled in a case brought by the Independent Insurance Agents of America that banks could indeed sell insurance from towns of 5,000 or fewer residents. The insurance agents decided against appealing the case to the Supreme Court, but the issue continued to spawn various legal and regulatory disputes.

1995: Amid debate over whether certain products should be defined as insurance or banking, the Supreme Court ruled that annuities were a banking product and could be sold by banks. "Annuities . . . are functionally similar to other investments that banks typically sell," the court stated.

Insurers had contended that annuities involved the pooling of risk, and therefore should be regulated as insurance products.

1996: In a landmark decision, *Barnett Bank v. Nelson*, the Supreme Court ruled in March that banks could sell insurance from offices in small towns, even in states that had laws prohibiting such sales. The ruling overrode a Florida law barring affiliations between banks and insurance agents. *(1996 Almanac, p. 2-51)*

1996: On Dec. 15, the Fed issued a series of rulings greatly expanding the ability of bank holding companies to underwrite securities. It increased the amount of gross revenue that a bank subsidiary could derive from securities activities from 10 to 25 percent. It also eased "prudential limitations," or firewalls, between bank holding companies and their bank and securities subsidiaries, allowing bank directors, officers or employees to serve on the board of the securities subsidiary, so long as they did not constitute the majority.

The rulings cleared the way for bank holding companies to acquire major securities firms in a series of takeovers in 1997.

checking accounts. Hours later, when bank lobbyists began objecting to the language, McCollum said the amendment should be reconsidered because it would place a regulatory burden on banks. He backed down after Waters accused him of submitting to special interests.

The panel rejected, 25-25, another Waters amendment that would have prevented federal pre-emption of state consumer protection laws.

But it agreed, 33-7, to an amendment by LaFalce to require that banks clearly label which of their financial products were federally insured, and prohibit them from pressuring consumers to buy products in order to get credit.

Other Amendments

In action on other amendments, the Banking Committee:

➤ Approved, by voice vote, an amendment by Richard H. Baker, R-La., and others to provide for voluntary membership in federal home loan banks and broaden the ability of smaller depository institutions to use advances.

➤ Gave voice vote approval to an amendment by Michael N. Castle, R-Del., providing for an expedited review of new financial products. The Federal Reserve Board would consider appeals involving disputes over the definition of insurance and financial products.

➤ Rejected, along party lines, amendments that would have expanded information about sales and underwriting by race and gender, and required federal regulators to examine the minority lending practices of bank holding company affiliates.

➤ Approved, by voice vote, a pair of amendments to add a state securities regulator and an individual with state bank supervisory experience to the National Council on Financial Services. However, the Commerce secretary would not serve on the board, as had been required in Leach's original bill.

House Commerce Committee

Undaunted by the divisions during the Banking markup, House Commerce Committee members prepared to take up the bill in early September. GOP leaders spoke of combining elements of the Banking and Commerce committee products in time for a showdown vote on the House floor in the fall. Then reality hit.

To put together a financial bill, the committee faced the

Interstate Banking

A bill clarifying who should regulate branches opened by out-of-state banks under a 1994 law was signed by President Clinton on July 3 (HR 1306 — PL 105-24).

The 1994 interstate banking law (PL 103-328) allowed both state-chartered banks and federally chartered national banks to open branches in states other than their own. But the law was unclear on whether the new branches were to be regulated by officials in the bank's home state or the state in which the branches were located. *(1994 Almanac, p. 93)*

Under the bill, sponsored by Marge Roukema, R-N.J., the state hosting the branch was charged with regulating the branch in most instances. In cases in which the law of the host state did not apply to a branch of an out-of-state bank, the branch was to be governed by the law of its home state.

Under the 1994 law, the branches of state-chartered banks opened in other states were supposed to be regulated and have the same powers as the state-chartered banks of the host state. However, in some states, existing regulations gave greater powers to national banks. As a result, some state-chartered banks wishing to branch into other states had changed to national bank charters to take advantage of those powers. Such conversions caused concern that other state-chartered banks would do the same thing, thereby weakening the nation's dual banking system, which gave banks the option of operating and being regulated under either federal banking rules or separate state rules.

At the time, 43 states had so-called "wild card" or "parity" laws that granted state-chartered banks the same powers enjoyed by national banks operating in their state. The bill was intended to address the disparity in regulation that occurred in the remaining seven.

The bill began in the House Banking and Financial Services Committee's Financial Institutions and Consumer Credit Subcommittee, which approved it May 7 by voice vote.

At the time, five pro-consumer organizations protested that the measure would "grossly undermine the traditional authority of states to regulate businesses that operate within their borders ... [and] force consumers to rely on the legislatures of other states for protection when the banks in their states engage in unfair or deceptive practices."

Banking Committee Chairman Jim Leach, R-Iowa, argued that the bill would "enhance competition between state and national banks, which in turn creates benefits for consumers."

The full Banking Committee did not act on the bill. Instead, it went directly to the floor, where it was passed May 21 by voice vote. The bill was taken up under suspension of the rules, a procedure that allowed no amendments.

The Senate passed the measure by voice vote June 12, along with several technical amendments, including one by Paul S. Sarbanes of Maryland, ranking Democrat on the Banking Committee, that increased reporting requirements on the Comptroller of the Currency.

The House accepted the changes June 24 by voice vote, clearing the bill.

task of assembling a nearly impossible jigsaw puzzle of competing interests. The main issues to be resolved included how to regulate the insurance products of national banks, whether to allow the mixing of banking and commerce, and whether to step up regulations of new banking products. Making the politics more combustible, lobbyists for several of the industries threatened to use their considerable clout to wage all-out war against the measure unless they got their way.

"We're thrust in the middle of this holy war," said Michael G. Oxley, R-Ohio, chairman of the Commerce Committee's Finance and Hazardous Materials Subcommittee.

The committee repeatedly postponed action as Oxley and full committee Chairman Thomas J. Bliley Jr., R-Va., struggled to cobble together enough support to move the bill forward. Indicative of the difficulties, one draft bill drew withering fire from the insurance lobby even before it was circulated the week of Sept. 15. "If the bill is offered as described, we will invoke all our resources to oppose the bill," the Independent Insurance Agents of America and the National Association of Life Underwriters warned Sept. 12 in a letter to panel members.

Taking up the insurers' cause, the committee's senior Democrat, Dingell of Michigan, prepared an amendment to empower state insurance commissioners to define and regulate bank insurance products. He appeared to have the support of roughly half the committee.

In late September, Bliley indefinitely postponed the markup. But the bill's advocates continued to press for action.

"The goal of the Congress . . . should be to enact legislation which is in the public interest and which provides balance among all affected parties — criteria which may also cause angst for everybody," Leach wrote in a seven-page letter to House Speaker Newt Gingrich, R-Ga. "Congress should not allow yet another opportunity to act in the national interest slip away."

Commerce Subcommittee Approves Bill

Oxley's subcommittee finally took action Oct. 24, approving HR 10, 23-2 in a disarmingly quick markup. Apparently putting away their knives for the moment, members discussed, but then withdrew, a variety of amendments.

Oxley's compromise met a key banking demand by defining certain products as insurance, thereby taking a step toward preventing insurance commissioners from expanding beyond those definitions and regulating traditional banking products.

But to satisfy Dingell, Oxley bowed to an insurance industry demand that the bill reduce the regulatory clout of the OCC. In addition, bankers said Oxley's bill could give states considerable power to restrict, or even bar, insurance sales by banks.

Insurance and securities lobbyists generally praised the new version. But bank officials blasted it, underscoring the battles to come. "We are adamantly opposed to the course and direction of this print, which runs counter to financial modernization," said Alfred M. Pollard, senior director for legislative affairs for The Bankers Roundtable, a consortium of major banks. "Instead of moving all parties forward, it seeks to give advantage to certain sectors in the marketplace," he said.

But the contentious divide between insurers and banks was barely alluded to during the two-and-a-half hour subcommittee markup. Instead, members offered, and then withdrew, amendments to reduce Federal Reserve oversight of financial holding companies, allow limited affiliations between financial and commercial companies, and protect consumers from coercive sales techniques. Lawmakers agreed to discuss such issues before the full committee markup.

The committee approved, by voice vote, an amendment by Paul E. Gillmor, R-Ohio, that would define certain financial activities in the statute, reducing the authority of the Federal Reserve to make such definitions.

It rejected, 9-15, a proposal by Rick A. Lazio, R-N.Y., that would have given thrifts more powers after the thrift charter was repealed.

Full Committee Gives Its Assent

Moving the debate forward, the Commerce Committee on Oct. 30 easily approved its version of HR 10 by a vote of 33-11 (H Rept 105-164, Part 3). However, most banks continued to strongly oppose the bill, and House leaders faced an uphill task getting it ready for floor action before Congress recessed for the year.

The committee version mainly hewed to Oxley's mark. But a manager's amendment, offered by Bliley and approved by voice vote, added language that would generally allow a bank holding company to invest up to 5 percent of its gross revenues in a commercial company.

Meeting a priority of the securities industry, the committee gave voice vote approval to a proposal by Gillmor to limit the authority of the Federal Reserve to regulate non-bank affiliates of financial holding companies.

The committee also gave voice vote approval to an amendment by Diana DeGette, D-Colo., that would bar financial companies from discriminating against victims of domestic violence when selling insurance products.

Bank lobbyists expressed confidence that they would rebound from their setbacks in the Commerce Committee when the bill went to the floor, where they said they had more clout. "There are bankers in everybody's district," said Edward L. Yingling, chief lobbyist for the American Bankers Association. "We have strong grass roots."

GOP Leadership Steps In

With Commerce Committee action out of the way, Boehner launched a full-scale press to produce a consensus bill. But with only a short time remaining in the session, veteran lawmakers expressed doubt that there was still time for floor action. "It's still got too many problems," said John Linder, R-Ga., a close ally of Gingrich. "We don't want to have a mess on the floor where Republicans are fighting Republicans."

Further clouding the picture, an influential senator took the unusual step of assailing the Commerce version in a printed statement as soon as it won committee approval. "The banking legislation reported by the House Commerce Committee today will be . . . dead on arrival in the Senate," said Lauch Faircloth, R-N.C., chairman of the Senate Banking Subcommittee on Financial Institutions. "Rather than hastily passing a bill before recess, the House would be well advised to craft a bill that enjoys the support of the majority of banks and savings and loans."

Nevertheless, Boehner held a series of bipartisan meetings with members of the Banking, Commerce and Rules committees. By making some concessions to the banking industry, he hoped to bring some major banks on board without losing the support of other financial industries. "There's progress being made," he said Nov. 6. "We're going ahead . . . as soon as is practicable."

Just two days later, however, Boehner finally threw in the towel. The final blow came Nov. 8, when Commerce leaders failed to show up for a meeting with Leach and other Banking Committee members in Boehner's office. "Our people were just absolutely flabbergasted that they had been stood up," said a Banking aide.

Commerce members missed the meeting because of an unavoidable scheduling conflict, said a spokeswoman for Oxley. "You can't be in two places at once," said Peggy Peterson.

Boehner pledged to continue pressing the measure. "We remain committed to completing our work and putting this legislation on the House floor early next year," he said in a written statement.

In the Senate, D'Amato continued to rule out action unless the House could figure out a compromise. "Let the House deal with it," he said tersely. "It has a long way to go." ■

Mortgage Insurance Bill Advances

Responding to consumer complaints, the House and Senate passed similar bills (HR 607, S 318) to make it easier for homeowners to cancel private mortgage insurance. Despite broad support for the legislation, however, industry objections made for slow-going at virtually every stage in the process, and Congress was not able to clear the bill before adjourning for the year.

Both versions of the legislation specified that homeowners would no longer have to carry private mortgage insurance once they paid off at least 20 percent of their loans. Although the thresholds differed slightly, both bills also required mortgage holders to automatically cancel a private insurance policy once a certain portion of the loan's principal was paid off.

Lenders typically required private mortgage insurance when a buyer put down less than 20 percent of the cost of the house at the time of purchase. Premiums ranged from $20 to $100 a month. Once a consumer had built up equity in the home, generally a 20 percent stake, the insurance could be dropped.

But supporters of the bill said many homeowners continued to pay monthly premiums for mortgage insurance even after they had significant equity and could no longer be reasonably considered a risk to lenders. The industry said about 5 percent of the 5 million homeowners with policies no longer needed the coverage; consumer advocates argued that the figure was as high as 20 percent.

Senate bill sponsor Alfonse M. D'Amato, R-N.Y., chairman of the Banking Committee, said many homeowners were unaware when they could cancel policies, had entered into mortgage agreements that required them to carry insurance throughout the life of the loan, or ran into "technical hurdles" when they tried to terminate their coverage.

"For many creditworthy, cash-poor potential home buyers, private mortgage insurance has been a blessing. Unfortunately, it can also become a curse," he said.

House Committee Action

The House version of the bill sailed through the Banking Committee on March 20 on a nearly unanimous vote of 36-1 (HR 607 — H Rept 105-55). Its sponsor, James V. Hansen, R-

Utah, had wrangled with his mortgage servicer for four years before being able to terminate the mortgage insurance on his Alexandria, Va., condominium.

As introduced, the bill would have required mortgage servicers to provide periodic notices to consumers of their right to cancel their mortgage insurance policies. But committee Democrats complained that neither the original bill nor a GOP substitute would make lenders clearly liable for failing to cancel the policy or informing the homeowner of his right to cancel.

Instead, the panel gave voice vote approval to an amendment requiring that a mortgage holder automatically cancel a private insurance policy once 25 percent of the loan's principal was paid off.

The panel also approve an amendment by Maxine Waters, D-Calif., to prevent the bill's provisions from pre-empting state disclosure laws dealing with mortgage insurance. The vote was 22-12.

The committee rejected an amendment that would have applied the bill to existing mortgages. The House bill applied only to mortgage loans issued one year after enactment of the measure.

BOXSCORE

Mortgage Insurance Cancellation — HR 607, S 318. The bill provided for automatic cancellation of private mortgage insurance once a homeowner had paid off a certain portion of the mortgage.

Reports: H Rept 105-55, S Rept 105-129.

KEY ACTION

April 16 — House passed HR 607, 421-7.

Nov. 9 — Senate passed S 318 by voice vote.

Nov. 13 — Senate passed HR 607 by voice vote, after substituting provisions of S 318.

The bill required that mortgage insurance be automatically cut off when a homeowner built up a 25 percent equity stake in the home. The automatic cutoff would apply to loans made after the bill became law, not existing mortgages.

The bill also included provisions to create a legal right for consumers to cancel their private mortgage insurance before the 25 percent equity threshold was reached, provided certain termination criteria set by the lender were met.

Mortgage servicing firms would be required to disclose to homeowners — as part of existing annual disclosures of mortgage status — their right to cancel mortgage insurance and the terms and conditions for doing so. The insurance would have to be canceled if they met those criteria.

One provision that contributed to the measure's being pulled from the floor April 8 was a requirement that insurance companies and mortgage holders provide information to mortgage servicers, so that the servicers could make the required disclosures to the homeowner. Elements of the mortgage industry worried about assuming legal liability for transmitting erroneous information.

House Floor Action

The bill was scheduled for House floor action April 8 but was abruptly pulled from the schedule by Majority Leader Dick Armey, R-Texas, after objections from the insurance industry were relayed by several GOP members. While the mortgage insurance industry said it supported the idea, it claimed that the version approved by the House Banking Committee would create a compliance burden on the industry and require unnecessary oversight by the Department of Housing and Urban Development.

House Democrats seized on the delay as evidence that lobbyists were exerting too much control over the congressional agenda. "That bill came out of the Banking Committee 36-1 and was ready for floor action, and now, because the insurance lobby has talked to the Republican leadership, apparently the bill's not going to come up," Minority Leader Richard A. Gephardt of Missouri charged at an April 10 news conference.

Bill Wins Overwhelming Support

Moving quickly to revive the popular bill, House leaders returned it to the schedule April 16. The House passed the measure that day, 421-7, although several members remained concerned that it might lead to unnecessary and frivolous lawsuits and add costs on mortgage servicers and lenders. *(Vote 80, p. H-26)*

"I am so proud. We beat the special interests on this bill," Waters said.

The House-passed version was identical to that approved by the Banking Committee. Armey had insisted that the delay was needed to allow time to "fix some of the concerns with the bill." But Leach was unwilling to alter his committee's bipartisan measure or to risk accusations of yielding to special interests.

GOP and Democratic staff aides said there was a general sense that changes would be made in conference.

Senate Action

Delays were not confined to the House. D'Amato was forced to call off a markup of his companion bill (S 318) scheduled for March 18, after Republicans protested that the measure would impose too much additional regulation on the mortgage industry.

"The private mortgage insurers should be ashamed for ripping off so many people and for attempting to block legislation to stop their abusive practices," D'Amato said after the House vote.

The Senate Banking Committee finally took up the measure Oct. 23, approving it, 16-1 (S Rept 105-129). D'Amato predicted it would save working families $20 to $100 a month.

Under S 318, homeowners would be allowed to end their mortgage insurance without penalty if they had paid off 20 percent of their mortgage and were current on payments. Such policies would be canceled automatically after 22 percent of the mortgage was paid, not 25 percent as in the House bill. (D'Amato had initially proposed 20 percent.) There was an exception for high-risk borrowers.

Wayne Allard, R-Colo., the lone dissenter, warned that the bill could expose lenders to more risk.

The Senate bill also included the abolition of the Thrift Depositor Protection Oversight Board, which had monitored the defunct Resolution Trust Corporation. The House passed its version of that bill (HR 2343) on Sept. 23. *(Oversight board, p. 2-84)*

Senate Floor Vote

The Senate passed S 318 by voice vote Nov. 9. On Nov. 13, the Senate passed HR 607 by voice vote, after substituting the provisions of S 318. That gave the House and Senate a common bill to work on, but the House did not have time to react before adjournment. ■

Crackdown on Mortgage Scams Held Over to 1998

The House and Senate passed nearly identical versions of a bill (S 562) designed to protect elderly homeowners from scam artists selling referrals to a free federal mortgage program. But the legislation failed to clear because of technical differences.

The bill required the Department of Housing and Urban Development (HUD) to issue rules that would prevent organizations from charging excess fees for advising senior citizens on the availability of so-called reverse mortgages. It also required mortgage lenders to fully disclose to borrowers all the costs of going through the lenders to obtain such mortgages, including any costs of estate planning or financial advice.

At issue was a HUD program that allowed senior citizens — defined as people ages 62 and older — to borrow against the equity in their homes for everyday expenses without having to make monthly interest or principal payments. The loan was repaid when the house was sold, usually after the owner's death.

About 20,000 such Home Equity Conversion Mortgages had been taken out since the program was established in 1987, most of them by low- and moderate-income senior citizens.

In New York and several other states, however, authorities reported that unscrupulous mortgage brokers, often going door-to-door in older middle-income neighborhoods, were pitching these loans to unwitting homeowners. Typically, the broker skimmed as much as 10 percent off the top of the loan for supplying forms and other information that HUD provided for free.

HUD Secretary Andrew M. Cuomo had attempted earlier in the year to prohibit the high fees, but organizations charging the fees obtained a court order blocking HUD from acting. Cuomo appealed to Congress, where Rep. Rick A. Lazio and Sen. Alfonse M. D'Amato, both Republicans from New York, sponsored a bill authorizing HUD to issue the rules.

D'Amato took S 562 directly to the Senate floor, where it passed by voice vote April 25 with support from conservatives and liberals alike.

The House took up S 562 on Sept. 16, passing it by an overwhelming vote of 422-1. Ron Paul, R-Texas, was the lone dissenter. *(Vote 397, p. H-120)*

The House had passed similar provisions in May as part of HR 2, a sweeping public housing overhaul that subsequently got bogged down in the Senate. *(Housing overhaul, p. 7-12)*

So, before passing the reverse-mortgage bill, the House added numerous other provisions, including extensions of several expiring federal housing programs whose permanent extensions were stalled in HR 2. The amended bill also included a two-year reauthorization for the National Flood Insurance program.

The changes, which were made as part of the motion to suspend the rules and pass the bill, meant that the measure had to go back to the Senate for approval.

As the session drew to a close, the two chambers batted the bill back and forth, each making minor changes. The Senate approved the House version, with a modification, by voice vote Nov. 9. The House returned the favor Nov. 13, approving a small revision by voice vote and requiring yet another trip for the bill to the Senate. By that point, the session was over, leaving the measure for final action in 1998. ■

Creditors Call for Bankruptcy Reform

Banks and other creditors began a formidable lobbying campaign in 1997 aimed at revamping federal bankruptcy laws and making it harder for consumers to walk away from their debts. Bankruptcy overhaul bills (HR 2500, S 1301) were introduced in both chambers, setting the stage for what was expected to be a significant battle in the second session.

In the meantime, both chambers started work on narrower bankruptcy bills, though none of them became law in the first session.

The increased attention was the result of the skyrocketing rate of bankruptcies across the country. A record 1.4 million Americans were expected to declare bankruptcy in 1997 — more than double the number of a decade earlier — leaving unpaid bills worth more than $40 billion. Lenders said the write-offs were costing the average household more than $400 a year in the form of higher interest rates and merchandise prices.

A coalition of banks, credit card companies, retailers and other lenders blamed the problem on laws that made it easy to file for bankruptcy, coupled with a relaxed societal attitude toward financial delinquency. They pressed Congress to tighten the bankruptcy code so that people who had money could not escape their debts, steps the lenders said might enable them to recover several billion dollars each year.

Topping the list of lobbyists working on their behalf were former Democratic Sen. Lloyd Bentsen of Texas, who had served as chairman of the Senate Finance Committee and President Clinton's first Treasury secretary, and Haley Barbour of Mississippi, former head of the Republican National Committee. "Congress and the administration should act to stem the expensive and corrosive spread of bankruptcy abuse," Bentsen argued in a Sept. 19 Washington Times column.

On the other side, bankruptcy lawyers and many consumer groups generally defended existing bankruptcy law, saying the chief problem was the reckless marketing of credit. They denounced credit card companies for mailing as many as 2.8 billion solicitations a year to potential cardholders, and they warned that the proposed bankruptcy changes amounted to "the next step before debtor's prison."

Background

By any measure, Americans were filing a staggering number of bankruptcy suits. Despite the ongoing economic boom, the bankruptcy rate per household so far in the 1990s was nearly eight times higher than the rate in the economically depressed 1930s — and it was continuing to climb every year.

"The rate of filing and the number of cases is unprecedented," said Samuel Gerdano, executive director of the American Bankruptcy Institute, a non-partisan research organization.

Neither Gerdano nor anyone else could pinpoint the precise reason for the increase, although analysts pointed to increased consumer lending, the reduced stigma of bankruptcy, job insecurity, the growth of legalized gambling and aggressive advertising by bankruptcy attorneys. In addition, a number of consumer bankruptcies — one in five, by some estimates — were declared by small-business owners who lost their own savings when their companies foundered.

Whatever the causes, the delinquency rate had reached more than one bankruptcy filing for every 100 households, and both creditors and taxpayers were beginning to feel the pinch.

Creditors warned that the billions of dollars in losses were forcing them to tighten their lending policies and raise their interest rates. They said marginal loan applicants, especially lower-income Americans, were finding it increasingly difficult to get reasonably priced loans. "It is getting more difficult to determine those who will pay and those who will declare bankruptcy," said Reid Pollard, president and chief executive officer of Randolph Bank & Trust in Asheboro, N.C.

Bank credit card companies were bracing for about $10 billion in bankruptcy-related losses in 1997, according to a Visa U.S.A. spokesman. Credit unions, diversified financial companies such as American Express, and retailers that sold on credit were losing billions more.

Although some analysts believed the surging rate might eventually exact a toll on the nation, the credit-driven economy so far seemed to be shrugging off any ill effects.

Annual consumer debt topped $1 trillion (although a portion of that included credit card balances that were paid off in full every month), and the economy had become so oriented toward credit that it was difficult to conduct certain transactions, such as renting a car or reserving a hotel room, without a credit card. There were more than 383 million Visa and MasterCard cards in circulation in the United States in 1997.

Due to the growth of consumer lending and other factors, banks were generally enjoying flush times. Although credit card profits had dipped from a high in 1993, "credit card earnings still compare favorably to returns on all commercial bank activities," concluded a report by the Federal Reserve Board.

Given such profits, bankruptcy attorneys questioned whether the delinquency rate was really causing so much financial havoc for creditors that an overhaul of the law was required. "It seems to me pretty disingenuous for them to be complaining about their losses when this is the most profitable part of their portfolio," said Norma Hammes, president of the National Association of Consumer Bankruptcy Attorneys.

National Commission

The debate officially kicked off Oct. 20, when the National Bankruptcy Review Commission issued its findings. The nine-member panel — created by Congress in 1994 to recommend changes to the bankruptcy code — presented a list of 172 relatively modest recommendations. It did not take up the issue of requiring consumers with money to repay their debts. *(1994 Almanac, p. 175)*

The commission, which split 5-4 on some issues, recommended that the federal government adopt uniform exemptions for assets in bankruptcy cases to prevent debtors from targeting a state and sinking thousands of dollars into a protected asset, such as a house or a racehorse.

In addition, the commission sought to bar "reaffirmations" of certain types of debt, meaning lenders could not work with a borrower to recover assets outside the bankruptcy process. It said debtors should be limited to no more than two Chapter 7 filings every six years to prevent ineligible debtors from repeatedly filing to temporarily evade debts. And it proposed that student loans be treated as dischargeable debts, like any other loan.

Commissioner Edith Jones, a U.S. Court of Appeals judge in Houston, drafted a blistering dissent contending that the majority report was so tilted against creditors that it "should not be taken seriously."

"The system itself is always going to be unpopular, and the system itself is always going to be controversial," said Brady C. Williamson, a Madison, Wis., lawyer who chaired the bankruptcy review commission. "The very nature of bankruptcy is that people don't get paid . . . What the commission has really tried to find over the last 18 months is balance, and balance doesn't really have a lot of advocates."

Lenders had started mobilizing three months earlier and were poised for war. The National Consumer Bankruptcy Coalition — an alliance of banking, credit union and retail trade groups — sent letters to top lawmakers and administration officials warning that the recommendations would only spur more bankruptcy filings and make it harder for creditors to repossess goods.

They claimed the exemption levels proposed by the commission were so high that a bankrupt family could have a higher net worth than three-quarters of American families. "Unfortunately and inexplicably, in the face of record consumer bankruptcy filing during strong economic conditions, the commission has adopted recommendations which would make filing for bankruptcy far more attractive and lead to a substantial further increase in total bankruptcy filings," the coalition's letter stated.

Top creditors flew to Washington in September for a day of meetings with congressional leaders, including Senate Majority Leader Trent Lott, R-Miss. They orchestrated a media campaign to stress that bankruptcy laws were hurting responsible consumers, and they helped draft a House overhaul bill (HR 2500).

Overhaul Bills

The well-moneyed creditors surged ahead in the early rounds of the debate on Capitol Hill. "Congress is already convinced we need a needs-based bankruptcy system," said Philip S. Corwin, a lobbyist for the American Bankers Association. "Now they're debating how that is going to be implemented."

The lead House bill was HR 2500, introduced by Bill McCollum, R-Fla., and Rick Boucher, D-Va. Under its provisions, debtors who met certain income tests would be required to partially repay their debts. They would have to file for Chapter 13 bankruptcy, under which they could enter into a discounted repayment plan, rather than Chapter 7, which did not require debt repayment. "Bankruptcy was never meant to be used as a financial-planning tool or for mere convenience," McCollum said.

"It does not stop anyone from getting bankruptcy relief," said Peter Kravitz, legislative counsel for the Independent Bankers Association of America. "All we are saying is, if you have the ability to repay, you ought to repay."

In the Senate, Charles E. Grassley, R-Iowa, and Richard J. Durbin, D-Ill., introduced a bill (S 1301) generally requiring that consumers enter into repayment plans if they had the means to pay off 20 percent or more of their debts. Creditors would be able to file legal motions to have bankruptcy cases dismissed. To protect consumers, the bill called for stiffer penalties against lenders who used certain heavy-handed techniques to recoup their debts.

"It will crack down on bankruptcy abuses on both sides of the equation," said Grassley, who chaired the Judiciary Subcommittee on Administrative Oversight and the Courts. "And it will tell those who don't want to take personal responsibility for their debts that the free ride is over."

Bankruptcy attorneys and some consumer advocates blasted both bills. They said requirements in S 1301 that debtors file numerous financial reports, including several years of tax returns, would make the process too expensive for destitute consumers. "It's all going to drive up the cost of bankruptcy, which I think is one of the creditors' goals," said Henry Sommer, a Philadelphia bankruptcy attorney who was monitoring the legislation.

In addition to striking early to attack the commission report and helping to draft the McCollum bill, the financial community also started to contribute campaign dollars, including $9,000 as of October to Grassley, who was up for re-election in 1998. In contrast, the bankruptcy lawyers had no full-time lobbyists and no political action committee, and they had yet to draft a bill.

But final congressional action was a long way off. The last time a bankruptcy commission had issued a report was in 1973, and it took five years for Congress to act on it. With the opposing camps staking out sharply conflicting positions in the fall, lawmakers clearly faced another multi-year battle.

Narrow Bankruptcy Bills

The House and Senate each took up less sweeping bankruptcy bills:

- **Bankruptcy judges.** The House voted in July to authorize 18 additional bankruptcy judgeships in an attempt to catch up with a burgeoning caseload of personal bankruptcy filings. The measure (HR 1596) went no further.

Under the bill, seven of the 18 new judgeships would be permanent. Central California would get four, raising its total to 25, while Maryland, New Jersey and western Tennessee would each get one.

The remaining 11 judgeships would be temporary, with appointments lasting at least five years. They would go to districts in California, Florida, Maryland, Michigan, Mississippi, New York, Pennsylvania and Virginia. An existing temporary judgeship in Delaware would be extended at least through 2003.

The bill began in the House Judiciary Committee, which approved it by voice vote July 16 (H Rept 105-208). The House followed suit July 28, passing the bill by voice vote.

- **Boaters, real estate.** The House passed a package of technical amendments to the bankruptcy code by voice vote Nov. 12, but the Senate did not take it up.

The bill (HR 764 — H Rept 105-324), which had been approved July 16 by the House Judiciary Committee, included a proposal to make those convicted of drunken operation of a boat or aircraft liable for damages even if they entered bankruptcy. Such liability already applied to drunk automobile drivers.

The bill also proposed to increase from $4 million to $15 million the debt ceiling on bankruptcy cases involving "single asset real estate" debtors eligible for expedited proceedings. Single asset real estate was a property that generated the majority of a debtor's gross income. Family farms would be exempt from the change. Supporters hoped that raising the ceiling would allow creditors quicker recovery of their assets.

- **Farmers, schools.** The Senate passed two measures by voice vote Oct. 30 containing minor adjustments to bankruptcy law aimed at helping farmers and schools. The two bills attracted little controversy, but went no further.

The first bill (S 1024) sought to make Chapter 12 of the U.S. bankruptcy code permanent. Created in 1986, Chapter 12 allowed farmers to reorganize their debts with little interference from banks. The bill, sponsored by Grassley, would prohibit banks from foreclosing on a family-owned farm as long as the farmer could continue to make payments on rental equipment.

The second measure (S 1149), also sponsored by Grassley, sought to prevent local school districts from having to repay money already received in the event that local bankruptcies lowered assessed valuations and the amount of money received from property taxes. The bill also proposed to put local government liens on an equal level with those filed by other creditors in bankruptcy cases. ■

Other Financial Legislation Considered in 1997

Lawmakers took up a number of relatively narrow or slow-moving bills dealing with taxes, banking, the budget and other economic and financial issues.

Supermajority for Tax Increases

The House considered — and rejected — a proposed constitutional amendment (H J Res 62 — H Rept 105-50) to make it more difficult for Congress to increase taxes. The amendment would have required a two-thirds "supermajority" in both chambers to pass any bill increasing revenues, except in time of war or military conflict.

Proponents fell 49 votes short of the two-thirds majority needed to approve an amendment to the Constitution. The vote was 233-190, with 25 Democrats voting "yes" and 15 Republicans voting "no." *(Vote 78, p. H-26)*

The House had failed to pass a similar measure in 1996, falling 37 votes short of the required two-thirds majority. The Senate did not take up that resolution and was not scheduled to consider H J Res 62. *(1996 Almanac, p. 2-41)*

Double Taxation

The House passed a bill (HR 1953) by voice vote July 28 to end the double income tax liability of employees at federal institutions that straddled state lines. The Senate took no action on the measure.

The bill was designed to address a controversy that arose at Fort Campbell, a military installation straddling the Kentucky-Tennessee border. Both states had tried to collect income taxes from base workers regardless of which state they lived in.

The bill stipulated that, effective upon its enactment, such workers could be taxed only by the state in which they lived.

The bill also sought to clarify the tax liabilities of employees at two other federal facilities — a hydroelectric plant on the Columbia River that was in both Oregon and Washington, and a second hydroelectric plant on the Missouri River that sat in both Nebraska and South Dakota.

The bill had won voice vote approval from the Judiciary Committee on July 16 (H Rept 105-203).

Penny Stocks

In the face of congressional action, the New York Stock Exchange June 5 voted to begin pricing stocks by the penny rather than in eighths of a dollar as they had for more than a century. The change was set to occur "as soon as the essential systems are in place in the securities industry," which could take up to a year, according to a statement issued by the exchange.

Legislation to force the change had been moving through the House, but sponsors pulled the bill (HR 1053) after the stock exchange acted. House Commerce Committee Chairman Thomas J. Bliley Jr., R-Va., said the bill's sponsors had "accomplished in three months what it took the markets more than 200 years to do."

The panel's Subcommittee on Finance had approved HR 1053 by voice vote May 21. The bill had been opposed by the brokerage industry, which made its profits from the eighth-of-a-dollar (12.5 cent) spread between each price point. Subcommittee Chairman Michael G. Oxley, R-Ohio, said every penny by which the 12.5 cent spread was narrowed would collectively benefit investors by $1 billion or more a year.

Coin Designs

The House on Nov. 13 cleared a bill requiring the U.S. Mint to strike new quarters commemorating each of the 50 states. President Clinton signed the measure into law Dec. 1 (S 1228 — PL 105-124).

The measure did not alter the front side of the quarter, which featured George Washington's profile, but the spread-winged eagle on the reverse side was to be replaced with alternating designs honoring each state.

The bill required the Mint to issue five versions of the new quarter each year for 10 years, beginning in 1999, with the states honored in the order they entered the union. Mottoes, symbols and other designs were allowed, but no faces or "frivolous" elements were permitted. The bill also prohibited portraits and "head and shoulders busts" of either the living or the dead.

The designs were to be selected by a group including state and federal officials, the Citizens Commemorative Coin Advisory and the Commission on Fine Arts.

The bill also called for the Treasury Department to create and design a gold-colored dollar coin to replace the Susan B.Anthony dollar, which was minted from 1979 to 1981. Treasury was to determine the design of the new coin, which was intended to supplement the nation's supply of paper dollars.

The bill, sponsored by John H. Chafee, R-R.I., began in the Senate Banking, Housing and Urban Affairs Committee, which approved it by voice vote Oct. 23 (S Rept 105-130). The Senate passed it by voice vote Nov. 9. The House passed the measure by voice vote Nov. 13, after approving a companion bill (HR 2414) on Sept. 23, by a vote of 413-6 *(Vote 417, p. H-128)*

SEC Reauthorization

The House Nov. 13 passed a bill (HR 1262) to reauthorize the Securities and Exchange Commission (SEC) for two years and approve a $320 million budget for the agency in fiscal 1998, slightly more than the $317 million requested by President Clinton. The SEC, which regulated the nation's stock markets, would get a budget boost to $343 million in fiscal 1999 under the bill. The Senate took no action on the measure.

Proponents said the additional funding would allow the SEC to conduct cost-benefit analyses of proposed new rules, as required under a 1996 law (PL 104-290) aimed at streamlining the regulation of the securities and mutual funds industries. *(1996 Almanac, p. 2-55)*

The House Commerce Committee approved the bill by voice vote July 23 (H Rept 105-274). The full House took it up Oct. 1 on the suspension calendar, which was used for non-controversial measures, but the bill fell victim to an unrelated partisan battle over the House agenda. The vote on the SEC measure was 230-170, well short of the two-thirds majority needed for a suspension bill. *(Vote 489, p. H-148)*

The bill was subsequently passed Nov. 13 by voice vote.

Thrift Oversight Board

The House passed a bill (HR 2343) to abolish the Thrift Depositor Protection Oversight Board and transfer its remaining responsibilities to the Treasury Department. The vote on Sept. 23 was 420-0. *(Vote 416, p. H-128)*

The Senate passed a similar proposal as part of its version of a bill on private mortgage insurance (S 318 — S Rept 105-129). *(Mortgage insurance, p. 2-79)*

The thrift oversight board monitored the activities of the Resolution Trust Corporation, which managed the savings and loan bailout. The RTC was created in 1989 to sell failing thrifts, manage and dispose of their assets, and protect their insured depositors. That work had been completed, and the Treasury Department requested in June that the board be dissolved.

Two of the board's remaining responsibilities were to oversee the payoff of $30 billion worth of bonds issued from 1989 to 1991, and to be a non-voting member of the Affordable Housing Advisory Board. Those tasks would be assumed by Treasury under the bill.

An amendment to HR 2343 offered by Spencer Bachus, R-Ala., and approved by voice vote in the House Banking and Financial Services Committee proposed to simplify the meeting requirements for the Affordable Housing Advisory Board. The Banking Committee approved the bill by voice vote Sept. 9 (H Rept 105-249).

Two-Year Budget Cycle

The Senate Governmental Affairs Committee voted 12-1 on May 22 in favor of creating a two-year federal budgeting cycle (S 261 — S Rept 105-72). Under the bill — sponsored by Budget Committee Chairman Pete V. Domenici, R-N.M. — Congress would complete all budget and appropriations measures during the first year of the two-year cycle, leaving the second year for oversight of agencies.

The committee defeated, 4-10, an amendment by Richard J. Durbin, D-Ill., that would have allowed budget resolutions to cover two years but would have kept the existing one-year appropriations cycle. Durbin argued it was unrealistic to expect Congress to accurately predict what spending needs would be over two years. Durbin provided the sole vote against the measure. ■

Clinton Loses 'Fast Track' Trade Bid

President Clinton suffered a major setback late in the year when House Democrats and their allies in organized labor denied him a renewal of "fast track" authority for newly negotiated trade agreements.

Fast-track authority guaranteed that, once the president submitted a trade agreement to Congress, lawmakers would take an up-or-down vote within 90 days, with no amendments allowed. Without such restrictions, trade experts said, foreign countries were reluctant to begin serious trade negotiations with the United States for fear that members of Congress would force a second round of bargaining to try to get concessions beneficial to their states or districts.

Congress had granted fast-track authority to every president from Gerald R. Ford on. The most recent extension had lapsed at the end of 1994.

While the demise of the legislation (HR 2621) appeared to have little short-term trade impact, it left long-term U.S. trade policy adrift. Clinton's ability to negotiate trade agreements with South American countries such as Chile was in severe doubt, as were plans to enter into industry-specific World Trade Organization talks aimed at boosting exports of agricultural goods, services and intellectual property.

Clinton had delayed submitting his fast-track bill to Congress until mid-September, when it was quickly attacked by members of both parties. Democrats demanded that labor and environmental issues play a central role in trade negotiations, while Republicans successfully insisted on limiting any reference to labor and environmental issues to their direct impact on trade.

To make matters more difficult for Clinton, the number of free-traders in Congress, both Republican and Democratic, had diminished. And with no major trade agreement in the offing to create a lobbying push, the business community mounted a weak effort for the legislation.

Lawmakers and lobbyists focused almost all their attention on the House. The Senate, traditionally more friendly toward trade initiatives, demonstrated on two procedural votes that it could pass the legislation by a filibuster-proof margin.

House GOP leaders made a major push at the end of the session to pass the fast-track bill. Most House Republicans supported the renewal, despite their reservations about Clinton. But about 60 Republicans — generally labor-friendly members and those from the party's protectionist wing — were poised to vote "no."

On the other side of the aisle, labor unions and environmentalists had worked against the bill for months and had lined up opposition from 80 percent of House Democrats.

Fast-track opponents turned the debate into a referendum on the North American Free Trade Agreement (NAFTA), which had failed to live up to some of the promises that had been made for it in 1993 when it won congressional approval. The opponents pointed to U.S. job losses in manufacturing sectors and laid the blame on NAFTA "side agreements" that failed to tighten labor and environmental standards in Mexico. *(1993 Almanac, p. 171)*

House GOP leaders did not want to bring the bill to the floor until 70 Democrats had been lined up to vote for it, but Democratic supporters prevailed on House Speaker Newt Gingrich, R-Ga., to schedule a vote as a way to push the undecideds off the fence.

The vote was announced for Nov. 7, then rescheduled for Nov. 9 after initial tallies lagged well short of the votes needed for passage. Steady pressure built the GOP tally, but Clinton could not rally Democrats, and the bill was shelved.

The episode highlighted a schism between Clinton and House Democrats, and it was regarded as both a potential sign of Clinton's lame-duck status and a possible opening salvo in the 2000 Democratic primary, where the leader of the anti-fast-track forces in the House, Minority Leader Richard A. Gephardt, D-Mo., was considering a race against Vice President Al Gore.

Background

Negotiations over Clinton's bid for fast-track authority had been stalled for nearly three years. The hangup was over how to reconcile GOP insistence that trade talks focus strictly on trade issues, with the demand by many Democrats that labor and environmental standards be addressed in the "core" of any trade agreement, thus making them enforceable by trade sanctions. *(1995 Almanac, p. 2-94)*

In April, Gingrich indicated that the GOP was open to some compromise. "We're willing to consider those legitimate areas that relate to trade on labor and the environment. What we're not willing to do is impose on our neighbors a European socialist-style social contract, which we think is profoundly wrong," the Speaker told reporters April 29.

"We're describing a middle ground," Gingrich said. "If we had a purely free-trade position, it would be nothing on labor, nothing on the environment, only trade."

California Rep. Robert T. Matsui, ranking Democrat on the Ways and Means Trade Subcommittee, said Gingrich's proposal would not attract significant Democratic support.

And administration officials made it clear that, while fast track remained a priority, the president planned to wait until autumn before moving ahead, given the need to concentrate on balanced-budget talks that were certain to run through the spring and summer. "The president has come to the conclusion that we should push hard for fast-track authority, beginning in the fall, in September," said White House Press Secretary Mike McCurry. *(Budget deal, p. 2-18)*

That frustrated free-traders on Capitol Hill. On May 21, Sen. Bob Graham, D-Fla., a Clinton ally, announced his intention to introduce a fast-track bill in consultation with Senate Republicans, unless the president moved forward by mid-June. "I think that the window is closing. The next couple of months are critical," said Graham, a member of the Senate Finance Committee. Joining him were Senate Commerce Committee Chairman John McCain, R-Ariz., Charles E. Grassley, R-Iowa, and Kay Bailey Hutchison, R-Texas.

In the House, some Republicans said they were all but ready to give up on fast track because the administration had delayed for so many months. "I have been urging an early focus on fast track in order to avoid direct conflict with congressional action on the budget and extension of [most-favored-nation] status for China that will occur in June or July," Ways and Means Committee Chairman Bill Archer, R-Texas, said in a May 15 letter to Clinton.

But even as the budget negotiations took precedence, the administration continued discussions with Congress on trade policy. On July 24, Clinton invited two dozen Democratic lawmakers to the White House to discuss the upcoming trade debate.

Clinton announced he had assembled a team of private-sector, Cabinet and sub-Cabinet officials to draft a fast-track bill and shepherd it through Congress in September and October.

"I am calling on the Congress to enact fast-track legislation so we can continue our aggressive drive to open markets to our goods and services and create more high-skilled jobs for the American people," Clinton said, as he announced his appointment of Jason S. Berman, chairman and CEO of the Recording Industry Association of America, to coordinate the administration's efforts.

Leading the effort within the administration was U.S. Trade Representative Charlene Barshefsky, along with White House Chief of Staff Erskine Bowles, Treasury Secretary Robert E. Rubin, Secretary of State Madeleine K. Albright and Commerce Secretary William M. Daley. The four Cabinet-level officials joined Clinton in the White House session with congressional Democrats, which lasted for more than two hours.

"He asked members who are on the fence or uncommitted to keep their powder dry until he unveils his proposal and he has a chance to talk with them again," Matsui said. "You could really feel his commitment to the issue."

Clinton's Request

Clinton officially kicked off his campaign for renewed fast-track authority Sept. 10. But instead of offering a detailed request, the White House event amounted to little more than a pep rally. In deference to objections from Senate Minority Leader Tom Daschle, D-S.D., and others who complained that they had not been adequately consulted as the administration prepared to unveil its bill, Clinton delayed by at least a week revealing any specifics.

In his speech, Clinton vowed to "continue to seek even further adherence around the globe to fundamental worker rights and environmental protection, as we have for decades."

Clinton said he firmly believed that trade was essential to sustaining the economic expansion that helped him win reelection in 1996. "Every president of either party has had this authority since 1974 for a very good reason: It strengthens our ability to break down trade barriers and unfair trade restrictions," he said. "Every single trade agreement we will reach will tear down barriers to our goods and services, and that is good for America."

While the assembled audience of export-oriented business people applauded, congressional Republicans boycotted the East Room event over the lack of specifics. "Fast track will be a very difficult debate, but it doesn't get any easier by delaying it," said Grassley. "The president must face up to divisions in his political party and make some tough decisions."

To avoid distancing his Democratic opponents, Clinton pointedly did not mention NAFTA during his address. An administration assessment of NAFTA said the agreement had only modestly improved net exports, income, investment and job creation. Mexican wages along the border had dropped, and illegal immigration, pollution and drug trafficking remained serious problems.

Administration officials sought to downplay the importance of not having legislative language ready on the day of the big show.

Said Gene Sperling, director of the National Economic Council: "There's nothing complicated here. . . . It was very clear to us that it would be more helpful in getting bipartisan support, more helpful in creating a tone and an atmosphere of inclusiveness, if we took a few more days to consult and to hear more people out."

Gephardt said, "The delay in sending up a detailed bill is hopefully a sign that a majority of Democrats and their concerns are being heard."

Cool Reception From Democrats

But when Clinton went to the Capitol to unveil his long-awaited plan Sept. 16, he immediately ran into a skeptical — and sometimes hostile — caucus of House Democrats who said the bill did not place enough emphasis on labor and environmental issues in trade negotiations.

They were emboldened by labor unions, which had launched a major campaign against the measure. The union lobbying was intense and also personal; many Democrats, especially freshmen who had yet to face a key trade vote, owed their seats in large part to labor-financed campaigns against their opponents. The AFL-CIO vowed a $1 million advertising campaign to whip up voter sentiment in the districts of undecided members.

The opponents also found support in public opinion polls. A Business Week poll conducted Sept. 3-7 by Louis Harris and Associates Inc. found 54 percent of the public against renewing fast-track authority, with only 36 percent in favor. That and other polls showed the public was skeptical of free trade and, by a wide margin, supported the idea of using trade agreements to protect the environment and raise labor standards.

Gephardt said Clinton's proposal "sends the wrong signal to the world community about what our priorities and standards in trade should be. With the president's bill, we are compromising the basic goals of growth, opportunity, the dignity of work, environmental quality and democracy."

Clinton's plan came under attack from the opposite direction the next day, when Rubin and Barshefsky appeared before the Senate Finance Committee, normally a sympathetic forum on trade issues.

Republicans lambasted the plan for its language encouraging the president to negotiate trade pacts that would require "trade-related" labor and environmental improvements. They said such requirements could impede trade, and complained that, at least in theory, the bill could give the president license to negotiate trade deals that would change U.S. environmental and labor laws.

Phil Gramm, R-Texas, a staunch advocate of free trade, lit into the administration's plan as "totally and absolutely unacceptable. It will never be approved by the United States Senate as it is written," he said, adding: "I would rather that the U.S. sit on the sidelines than to see us destroy the world trading process by injecting into it labor and environmental conditions that will disrupt trade and reduce the volume of trade in the world."

Majority Leader Trent Lott, R-Miss., agreed. "Fast track is not, emphatically not, a vehicle for special-interest agendas," he said.

Senate Action

By the time the Finance Committee marked up its version of the bill Oct. 1, most senators' concerns had been mollified. Members met first behind closed doors with Barshefsky and then approved the measure (S 1269 — S Rept 105-102) by voice vote in a markup that itself lasted less than a minute. Only Kent Conrad, D-N.D., voted "no."

The committee bill said labor and environmental issues should be considerations when negotiating trade agreements, but only to the extent needed to prevent trading partners from lowering their standards to boost exports. Also, any such agreements could not restrict U.S. autonomy.

The GOP-drafted bill also proposed to narrow the scope of issues that could be added to bills eligible for fast-track treatment. Under previous fast-track rules, anything deemed "necessary or appropriate" to implement an agreement was allowed. The Finance bill proposed tightening that to include only provisions that would be "necessary to implement such agreement" or "otherwise related to the implementation, enforcement . . . and are directly related to trade."

For their part, committee Democrats won a two-year extension of trade assistance programs that would help workers and companies who lost jobs and business to foreign competitors. Funding was to come from a $5 surcharge on airline and ship passengers arriving from Canada, Mexico and the Caribbean.

Also added was language requiring that the administration consult with Congress before initialing any trade agreements — typically the time when the most controversial items in the negotiations were added or dropped.

Supporters said the panel's markup was timed, in part, to give a political boost to fast-track renewal. "We just concluded that to not do anything this week was to have no bill," said Gramm. "New life has been breathed into fast track by the Finance Committee," said John B. Breaux, D-La.

Senate Floor Votes Show Support

Shortly after meeting with Clinton at the White House, Lott announced that he would bring the bill to the Senate floor in late October or early November. Top administration officials wanted the Senate to take the bill up quickly, on the theory that a big vote there would provide momentum in the House.

On Nov. 4, the Senate easily invoked cloture on the motion to proceed to the fast-track bill. The margin was surprisingly large, 69-31, and despite its procedural nature was taken as a definitive sign that the Senate would be able to pass the legislation. *(Vote 292, p. S-50)*

On Nov. 5, the Senate agreed by a similar margin to proceed to floor consideration of the bill. The vote was 68-31. *(Vote 294, p. S-50)*

Then the Senate stopped and waited for the House to act.

House Committee

Clinton's problems in the House were evident at a Ways and Means Trade Subcommittee hearing Sept. 30. Top Democratic supporter Matsui warned that fast track "is in deep trouble at this particular time." Gingrich echoed the sentiment, saying, "I do not today see the votes to pass fast track."

According to vote counters on both sides of the aisle, House passage required 60 to 80 Democratic votes in addition to those of 150 or so Republicans. Both sides were well short of their respective goals.

Republicans faulted Clinton for not being active enough on the issue and insisted that only the president could lift fast track over the finish line. "There's just no leadership from the White House," complained Jim Kolbe, R-Ariz., a leading GOP voice on trade issues. "President Clinton needs this, but he's made it clear he doesn't want to antagonize the labor vote."

Matsui countered that the business lobby was not doing enough to line up support. "They will tell you they are working hard, but they have to show a little more intensity," Matsui said. "This is labor's No. 1 issue. Business really has to decide if they want to make this their No. 1 issue."

In part, the lack of intensity was due to the fact that fast track was a procedural measure that did not promise any immediate benefit to business like NAFTA or approval of the Uruguay Round of the General Agreement on Tariffs and Trade (GATT). *(NAFTA, 1993 Almanac, p. 171; GATT, 1994 Almanac, p. 123)*

Ways and Means Approves Bill

The Ways and Means Committee approved its version of the bill on Oct. 8 by a vote of 24-14 (HR 2621 — H Rept 105-341, Part 1). But the most closely scrutinized factor — how many Democrats supported the measure — provided an ominous signal to the White House.

Only four of the panel's 16 Democrats voted for the bill, despite a personal push by Clinton, who met with about half of them on the eve of the markup. Before the session, Clinton had the support of Democrats Matsui and John Tanner of Tennessee. The president's pleas brought over only two more: Jim McDermott of Washington and William J. Jefferson of Louisiana.

The tepid show of Democratic support rankled panel Republicans, some of whom were clearly not happy doing the heavy lifting for a Clinton priority. "Obviously, the president didn't do his job," said Jim Nussle, R-Iowa. "If this is such an important issue for the president, why is it he could only get four votes?"

Archer had hoped to approve the bill by voice vote, allowing members to go officially unrecorded. But panel Democrats scotched that plan, and in a GOP caucus before the vote several Republicans expressed displeasure at being put in a position of voting for a controversial bill that might never reach a floor vote.

In an indication of how unhappy they were, eight GOP members initially voted "pass," apparently to watch the Democrats vote first. While the display added some drama, in the end, party discipline prevailed.

Archer Makes Last-Minute Changes

As in the Senate Finance Committee markup, the stage was set by a round of last-minute negotiations with the Office of the U.S. Trade Representative. Early the morning of Oct. 7, those talks produced a deal between Archer and the administration.

Only 48 hours before, Archer and the White House had been on a collision course. Archer had produced an initial draft that the administration objected to on three counts: The negotiating authority was too narrow in scope; the White House disagreed with the way labor and environmental issues were addressed; and language governing the issues that could be included in implementing legislation was too strict.

When Archer was notified that his first draft was not going to receive administration support — or any Democratic votes in committee — he gave ground. The administration said the resulting bill, though it used different language, closely tracked the Senate Finance measure.

Like the Senate version, it allowed for labor and environmental issues to be part of fast-track trade deals when they were directly related to trade. Both bills said the president would be free to pursue those issues in the International Labor Organization and World Trade Organization, but that any "side agreements" would be subject to the normal legislative process — open to amendments and vulnerable to Senate filibusters.

Clinton, who left Oct. 12 for a seven-day visit to three South American countries to talk trade, hailed the panel's action.

But Archer echoed the sentiments of other House GOP leaders, who said they wanted 80 to 90 Democratic votes when and if fast track came to the floor. Such a tally was all but impossible: Democratic vote counters said the maximum number of Democratic votes was 70, and that could be reached only if nothing changed.

House Floor

Although House GOP leaders had said they would not bring the bill to the floor until Clinton obtained commitments from at least 70 Democrats, they agreed Oct. 29 to schedule a floor vote before Congress adjourned for the year.

With the vote count on their side stalled and undecideds dribbling into the opponents' camp, Democratic supporters had pleaded for a do-or-die vote in hopes of pushing some undecided Democrats into their column. "Those guys came over and said, 'If we don't get a vote this year, it's dead for sure,'" said David L. Hobson, R-Ohio, a Gingrich intimate. "I think it put our guys on the spot. . . . We're not going to get hung for killing it."

Once a Nov. 7 date was announced, the White House made a furious push, extending to undecided House Democrats the best it had to offer — even promises of presidential visits to their districts to help raise funds before the 1998 election.

On Nov. 5, Clinton unveiled a $4 billion package for job retraining and other aid for communities that lost jobs to trade. Less than half the money represented increases in future funding; the rest was already anticipated.

The following day, Clinton flew to Texas for the dedication of the presidential library of his predecessor, George Bush. Ex-presidents of both parties joined Clinton in pushing for fast-track renewal. "We hope and pray you get the votes tomorrow," Ford said.

Clinton hurried back to Washington to work the phones and visit with lawmakers. But by late that evening, the count of Democratic supporters was stuck in the low 40s — a figure that would require Republicans to deliver more than 170 votes to pass the bill.

By Nov. 7, the White House was still not sure it had the votes. So at Clinton's request, House leaders pushed the vote into the weekend of Nov. 8-9, when lawmakers planned to stay in town for a vote-a-thon leading up to adjournment. Clinton's frustration was evident Nov. 7, at his third news conference on fast track in as many days. "This is a no-brainer on the merits," he told reporters.

The all-out lobbying blitz continued into Monday, Nov. 10. House Republican leaders produced more GOP votes than had been promised, but Clinton was still unable to move enough Democrats to clinch the victory.

Clinton's aides said he drew the line when several swing members demanded concessions on non-related bills that were also in danger in the session's final hours. Rather than seeing fast track defeated, Gingrich and Clinton shelved the bill Nov. 10.

Gephardt, who had led the opposition, said he was willing to work with Clinton to craft a new bill for consideration in 1998. "The real question before us now is whether we can connect our values of environmental quality, worker and human rights to our economic policy," Gephardt said. "Americans want a trade policy that ensures that future trade agreements address all these issues."

But opinions were mixed about the chances of reviving fast track as the 1998 election neared. "After this massive effort, after the Senate doing its part, and after all the work that went into trying to get the votes in the House, I don't see it happening at this point," Lott said. "So it would appear to me that it's dead." ■

Caribbean Nations Fail in Bid For New Trade Preferences

With opponents arguing that U.S. imports from the region had grown, not shrunk, the House on Nov. 4 defeated a bill (HR 2644) aimed at expanding trade preferences for goods from 26 Caribbean and Central American countries. The measure fell, 182-234, with 83 Republicans, 150 Democrats and Bernard Sanders, I-Vt., voting "no." *(Vote 570, p. H-172)*

The bill would have granted preferential tariff and quota treatment, equivalent to that accorded to Mexico under the North American Free Trade Agreement (NAFTA), to specific products from nations in the Caribbean Basin Initiative (CBI).

The CBI, launched by President Ronald Reagan in 1983, provided preferential access to the U.S. market as a way of encouraging industrial development and promoting political stability in the Caribbean. CBI trade benefits were made permanent in 1990. *(1983 Almanac, p. 252; 1990 Almanac, p. 211)*

But Jamaica and other CBI countries had complained that they were suffering as an unintended result of NAFTA, which went into effect in 1994. Under NAFTA, all tariffs between the United States and Mexico were being eliminated over a 15-year period. *(NAFTA, 1993 Almanac, p. 171)*

HR 2644 was intended as temporary relief, lasting for 14 months or until the Caribbean countries joined NAFTA or another reciprocal free-trade agreement, whichever came sooner. The bill included a statement that it was U.S. policy to include these Caribbean countries in NAFTA or a comparable free-trade agreement at the earliest possible date.

The relief would have applied to such products as textiles, apparel, canned tuna, petroleum and petroleum products, footwear, handbags and luggage, which did not receive duty-free treatment under the CBI. The projected cost was $243 million in lost revenue in fiscal 1998-99, to be offset by tightening deductions for employment severance pay.

The bill originated in the House Ways and Means Committee, which approved it by voice vote Oct. 9 (H Rept 105-365).

But when the bill reached the floor, opponents argued that Caribbean exports had increased since NAFTA took effect and that they continued to outstrip Mexican exports in some key sectors. U.S. imports of textile and apparel goods — including finished products made from U.S.-supplied materials — totaled $6.1 billion from Caribbean countries in 1996, compared with $3.6 billion worth of such goods from Mexico.

Some lawmakers also complained that the expanded Caribbean bill included fewer safeguards than NAFTA required of Mexico. "There are no requirements for sanctions against sweatshops or child labor; for requirements for cooperation on drug interdiction or money laundering or illegal immigration; no requirements to remove trade barriers from U.S. exporters," said Benjamin L. Cardin, D-Md.

Other opponents argued that NAFTA had cost U.S. jobs, and that expanding Caribbean preferences would only aggravate those losses.

The House had approved identical CBI provisions earlier in the year as part of the tax-reconciliation bill (HR 2014), but they were dropped in conference at the insistence of the Senate, which had not yet considered them. As negotiations on the final tax bill were reaching a conclusion, the White House made a last-minute attempt to win inclusion of the CBI proposal but was unsuccessful. *(Tax reconciliation, p. 2-30)* ■

Lawmakers Reauthorize Ex-Im Bank

Congress agreed to a four-year reauthorization for the Export-Import Bank, an independent agency established in 1945 to help finance foreign purchases of U.S. goods through low-interest direct loans, loan guarantees and export credit insurance.

Previous authorization for the bank had expired on Sept. 30; the bill extended it to Sept. 30, 2001. The legislation did not include a specific funding level, leaving that up to appropriators. President Clinton signed the bill into law Nov. 26 (S 1026 — PL 105-121).

Some lawmakers were critical of the Ex-Im Bank, calling its activities "corporate welfare." On the other side, proponents argued that the bank was essential in helping U.S. firms compete with foreign companies that received significant assistance from their governments. House sponsor Michael N. Castle, R-Del., said the reauthorization would help ensure that U.S. businesses and workers "are able to compete and win against subsidized foreign competition in today's global market."

In addition to the overall reauthorization, the bill included provisions to:

➤ Reauthorize the Tied-Aid Credit Fund for four years. Tied-aid grants were paired with traditional export financing by the bank to encourage foreign purchasers to buy U.S. goods and services. The program was designed to counter similar tied-aid programs of other nations such as Japan, Germany and France.

➤ Extend the Ex-Im Bank's authority to help finance the export of nonlethal defense articles.

➤ Establish an assistant general counsel for administration at the bank to deal with ethics issues, and a new advisory committee to facilitate U.S. exports to sub-Saharan Africa.

➤ Require that two labor representatives be included on the Bank's Advisory Committee, and require the bank to design an outreach program for companies that had never used its services.

➤ Deny export financing for sales to the Russian government or military if that country transferred SS-N-22 missile systems to China.

➤ Create an advisory committee to recommend ways to increase exports to sub-Saharan Africa.

BOXSCORE

Export-Import Bank — S 1026 (HR 1370). The bill reauthorized the Ex-Im Bank through Sept. 30, 2001.

Reports: S Rept 105-76, H Rept 105-224; conference report, H Rept 105-392.

KEY ACTION

Sept. 16 — Senate passed S 1026 by voice vote.

Oct. 6 — House passed HR 1370, 378-38, then passed S 1026 by voice vote after substituting the text of its own bill.

Nov. 8 — Senate adopted conference report on S 1026 by voice vote.

Nov. 9 — House cleared the bill by voice vote.

Nov. 26 — President signed S 1026 — PL 105-121.

Senate Action

The Senate version of the bill, sponsored by Rod Grams, R-Minn., began in the Banking Committee, which approved it, 16-0, on July 31 (S 1026 — S Rept 105-76). The Senate passed the bill by voice vote Sept. 16.

The committee approved, 17-0, an amendment by Michael B. Enzi, R-Wyo., directing the bank to do more to inform small and rural companies about its programs. Enzi withdrew a second amendment that would have required the bank to give preference to companies that did not regularly use the bank's services.

House Action

The House Banking Committee actually started first on the legislation, with the Subcommittee on Domestic and International Monetary Policy giving voice vote approval to a companion bill (HR 1370) on May 8.

The panel rejected a series of amendments offered by Bernard Sanders, I-Vt., to bar Ex-Im Bank assistance in exporting goods that had any foreign content or that were going to countries that did not protect internationally recognized worker rights.

Also rejected, 8-11, was a proposal by Barney Frank, D-Mass., that would have required members of the boards of directors of companies receiving Ex-Im Bank assistance to perform eight hours of community service a month.

The full Banking Committee approved the bill by voice vote July 9 (H Rept 105-224).

Sanders had better luck there, winning approval of two amendments. The first, adopted by voice vote, required that the bank have at least two labor representatives on its advisory committee. The second, approved 24-19, directed the bank to ensure that preference be given to assisting firms with a commitment to investing and creating jobs in the United States.

Frank failed, 9-29, to win support for his proposal to require community service from the boards of companies receiving Ex-Im bank financing. The panel also defeated, 8-35, a proposal by Walter B. Jones Jr., R-N.C., to restrict the bank to guaranteeing no more than 90 percent of the interest and principle on a loan.

House Floor Action

The House passed the bill Oct. 6 by a vote of 378-38, then inserted the text into S 1026 and passed that bill by voice vote. *(Vote 492, p. H-150)*

The House first agreed to amendments to:

➤ Prohibit bank subsidies of exports to Russia if the former superpower transferred certain missile systems to China. The amendment, by Gerald B.H. Solomon, R-N.Y., was approved by voice vote.

➤ Bar Ex-Im Bank financial assistance to companies that employed child labor. Offered by Bruce F. Vento, D-Minn., the amendment was approved by voice vote.

➤ Give preference to U.S. companies seeking help for operations in China that: avoided the use of child or prison labor; avoided discrimination based on religion, race or gender; and, in general, respected human and worker rights. The amendment, by Lane Evans, D-Ill., was adopted, 241-182. *(Vote 472, p. H-142)*

➤ Change the name of the bank to the United States Export Bank. Offered by John J. LaFalce, D-N.Y., it was adopted, 362-56. *(Vote 473, p. H-144)*

Frank's community service amendment was rejected by voice vote, as was a proposal by Dana Rohrabacher, R-

Calif., to bar assistance to companies that were at least 50 percent owned by a foreign government. Rohrabacher tried again with an amendment to prohibit aid to companies owned by non-democratic foreign governments, but that too failed on a voice vote.

Conference/Final Action

House and Senate negotiators reached agreement on the bill Nov. 7. The Senate adopted the conference report (H Rept 105-392) by voice vote Nov. 8, and the House cleared the bill Nov. 9, also by voice vote.

Senate conferees balked at the House-passed proposal to change the bank's name, and it was dropped.

Conferees also decided, on a vote of 8-2, to modify the House-passed provision to prohibit the bank from subsidizing exports to Russia if the former superpower transferred certain missile systems to China. The new language applied only to the sale of SSN-22 missiles. It required the president certify that the transfer occurred and that it posed "a significant and imminent threat to the United States" before the subsidies could be banned.

The final bill included a provision stating that it was U.S. policy to foster the expansion of exports, thereby contributing to a commitment to reinvestment and job creation in the United States. The bill also added child labor to the list of human rights abuses that could serve as a basis for the president to deny Ex-Im Bank credits. ■

Other Trade-Related Bills Considered in 1997

Congress considered a number of bills aimed at facilitating or liberalizing trade relations with various countries. Legislation reauthorizing the Overseas Private Investment Corporation and extending the Generalized System of Preferences cleared; work on other bills was unfinished at the end of the session.

GSP

Congress extended the Generalized System of Preferences (GSP) from June 1, 1997, through June 30, 1998, as part of the tax bill (HR 2014 — PL 105-34) enacted Aug. 5 as part of the year's budget-reconciliation package.

GSP provided duty-free status to products imported from developing nations with the aim of spurring economic growth in those countries. The most recent extension, enacted in 1996, had expired May 31, 1997. *(1996 Almanac, p. 2-62)*

MFN Bills

The Senate Finance Committee on Sept. 11 voted to permanently extend most-favored-nation (MFN) trading status to products from Mongolia and Laos. The panel also approved a bill to change the MFN designation to "normal trade relations." Each of the measures was approved by voice vote. None of the bills saw further action in the first session.

Committee Chairman William V. Roth Jr., R-Del., said the MFN bill for Mongolia (S 343 — S Rept 105-81) reflected the fact that that country had been making economic and political reforms and had joined the World Trade Organization. He said the bill for Laos (S 1093 — S Rept 105-83) was needed to implement a recent bilateral trade agreement between that Southeast Asian country and the United States.

The third bill (S 747 — S Rept 105-82) was aimed at avoiding the confusion often created by the term "most favored nation." Despite the name, MFN status referred to the non-discriminatory, low-tariff treatment that the United States made available to all but a very few nations. A similar Senate bill died in 1996. *(1996 Almanac, p. 2-61)*

In the House, the Ways and Means Trade Subcommittee approved bills to grant MFN status to Mongolia (HR 2133) and Laos (HR 2132) by voice vote July 15. The full committee did not take up the measures.

OPIC

Congress agreed to reauthorize the Overseas Private Investment Corporation (OPIC) for two years as part of the fiscal 1998 foreign operations appropriations bill. OPIC provided loan guarantees and political risk insurance for U.S. companies operating abroad.

The spending bill, signed into law Nov. 26 (HR 2159 — PL 105-118), raised OPIC's combined statutory ceiling for financing and risk insurance from $23 billion to $29 billion.

Earlier in the year, two committees and the full Senate had speedily approved reauthorization legislation. However, OPIC had legions of critics in Congress — both conservatives and liberals — many of whom criticized its activities as "corporate welfare."

The House International Relations Trade Subcommittee gave voice vote approval July 16 to a two-year authorization bill (HR 2064) that proposed raising OPIC's combined statutory ceiling to $29 billion. The bill, sponsored by Donald Manzullo, R-Ill., also called for several changes aimed at improving congressional oversight of the agency, including creation of an OPIC inspector general.

Manzullo said the changes would mollify many OPIC critics, who had banded together in 1996 to overwhelmingly defeat a five-year OPIC authorization on the House floor. The agency was authorized through fiscal 1997 in the fiscal 1997 foreign operations appropriations bill (PL 104-208). *(1996 Almanac, p. 2-60)*

But Manzullo opposed an amendment, offered by California Republicans Dana Rohrabacher and Tom Campbell, to bar OPIC from aiding projects in countries that did not hold free and fair elections, that engaged in armed aggression, lacked independent judiciaries, or did not respect freedom of speech. The amendment was adopted by voice vote.

Campbell said that by promoting trade in countries that did not meet these criteria, OPIC forestalled democratic reforms. Manzullo countered that the amendment language was too restrictive and vague.

Later on July 16, the Senate adopted roughly the same OPIC language, without the oversight items, as an amendment to its version of the foreign operations spending bill (S 955). The next day, before the Senate took final action on the spending measure, the Senate Foreign Relations Committee hastily approved a bill (S 1032) authorizing the OPIC appropriation.

Conferees agreed to include the authorization in the final foreign operations bill, along with $60 million for OPIC program expenses.

Sub-Saharan Africa

A bill (HR 1432) designed to promote economic development and investment in sub-Saharan Africa was approved by two House panels but got no further in the first session.

The long-range goal of the bill, introduced by Ways and Means Trade Subcommittee Chairman Philip M. Crane, R-Ill., was to reduce the region's dependence on U.S. financial assistance. To that end, it proposed to authorize some short-term aid, such as technical assistance, to help countries move toward compliance with World Trade Organization standards and liberalize their agricultural markets.

The legislation included the permanent extension to sub-Saharan Africa of the Generalized System of Preferences (GSP), which gave duty-free treatment to certain goods from eligible developing countries. It also proposed allowing the president to admit additional goods and products not covered under GSP, provided they did not threaten U.S. jobs.

Action on the bill began in the Africa Subcommittee of the House International Relations Committee, which approved it by voice vote May 22. The full International Relations Committee approved the measure by voice vote June 25, after adopting several amendments.

The panel approved two amendments by voice vote, one by Chairman Benjamin A. Gilman, R-N.Y., and the other by Christopher H. Smith, R-N.J., to bar economic and investment benefits under the bill to nations that violated basic human rights.

Panel member Alcee L. Hastings, D-Fla., argued that the amendments appeared hypocritical in view of the June 24 House vote upholding most-favored-nation trade status for China, which many lawmakers sought to deny because of that nation's human rights violations. *(China MFN, p. 8-37)*

Donald M. Payne, D-N.J., offered an amendment, approved by voice vote, that would require the president to notify Congress before waiving any provisions under the bill.

The bill went next to the Ways and Means Committee, where the Trade Subcommittee approved it by voice vote Oct. 23. The full committee did not take it up. ■

Barshefsky Wins Waiver To Take USTR Post

Charlene Barshefsky was sworn in as U.S. trade representative March 18, a day after President Clinton signed a waiver allowing her to assume the post (S J Res 5 — PL 105-5). Barshefsky had been named deputy trade representative in 1993 and was promoted to acting trade representative in April 1996 when Mickey Kantor left to become secretary of Commerce.

The Senate easily confirmed her nomination, 99-1, on March 5. *(Vote 27, p. S-6)*

But to assume the job, she also needed a waiver from both chambers of provisions in a 1995 lobbying law (PL 104-65) that barred anyone who had advised a foreign government from becoming the U.S. trade representative. As a lawyer in private practice, Barshefsky had briefly advised the government of Canada and the province of Quebec in a trade dispute. *(1995 Almanac, p. 1-38)*

The Senate passed the waiver, 98-2, on March 5 when it confirmed Barshefsky. The House cleared it by voice vote March 11. *(Vote 26, p. S-6)*

Senate Committee

The Senate Finance Committee approved Barshefsky's nomination by voice vote on Jan. 30, approving the conflict-of-interest waiver at the same time.

Barshefsky used her confirmation hearing to make a strong pitch for renewing fast-track authority, which provided expedited procedures for congressional consideration of trade agreements. "Absent fast track, other countries will not deal with us," she said, adding that if the United States was not at the bargaining table, it would lose leverage in setting trade rules worldwide.

The fast-track renewal bill was blocked in the Senate at the end of the session. *(Fast track, p. 2-85)*

Barshefsky drew so much praise from members of the Finance Committee that the waiver was barely an issue. Rather, most committee members ridiculed the provision. "This takes the naive approach that if anybody has ever worked for a foreign interest they are tainted," said Phil Gramm, R-Texas. "I hope we have people who are qualified enough that everyone in the world would want their services."

"I think we ought to change this thing," agreed John H. Chafee, R-R.I. "I believe that not a single one of the past U.S. trade representatives could have been confirmed under this legislation."

The willingness to criticize the prohibition was a slap at former Senate Majority Leader Bob Dole, R-Kan., who had added the prohibition to the lobbying law without consulting the Finance Committee. "That's the problem with adding proposals at midnight," said committee Chairman William V. Roth Jr., R-Del.

Senate Floor Action

The 99-1 floor vote confirming Barshefsky March 5 reflected lawmakers' strong approval of her hard-nosed negotiating style. As acting trade representative, she had pushed hard for trade concessions from China and Japan. She had walked away from a telecommunications agreement in 1996 because its terms were not favorable enough to the United States.

"Charlene Barshefsky won me and a lot of other people over because she is a tough negotiator. So it was more of a vote of confidence in her, rather than a prediction of how senators feel about fast track or other trade policies," said freshman Sen. Susan Collins, R-Maine.

Repeatedly, senators underscored how much confidence it had given them that Barshefsky had the courage to drop the global telecommunications deal. She only signed off on it in April 1997, when all the parties came back to the table and offered better terms. That approach was clearly the one senators wanted her to take in future trade negotiations.

Trouble Over the Waiver

The only significant obstacle to Barshefsky's confirmation was the accompanying conflict-of-interest waiver. Majority Leader Trent Lott, R-Miss., said repeatedly that it made him uncomfortable. "I don't think you can lightly dismiss a law that's on the books," he said.

Lott was one of two senators to vote against the waiver, though he voted for confirmation. The other was Wayne Allard, R-Colo., who was the lone vote against confirming Barshefsky.

The other threat to the waiver was eliminated when the Senate handily defeated an amendment by Ernest F. Hollings, D-S.C., that would have required Congress to vote on all international trade agreements that would "in effect" amend or repeal U.S. laws.

Senate action on the nomination had been stalled for weeks while the White House and leading Democrats tried to talk Hollings out of offering the amendment. The Clinton administration was adamantly opposed to the proposal, saying it would completely hamstring U.S. trade policy.

Even under existing law, there was a battle every time Congress was asked to vote on the implementing legislation necessary for major trade agreements to go into effect. As recently as September 1996, the House had effectively killed a relatively limited shipping agreement with the 29 member nations of the Organization for Economic Cooperation and Development.

But Hollings, a strong protectionist, would not relent, and Minority Leader Tom Daschle, D-S.D., finally made an agreement with Lott to allow Hollings a chance to offer his amendment on the floor.

Roth, a strong Barshefsky supporter, argued that the Hollings amendment could "immobilize our ability to negotiate trade agreements, even on relatively minor issues, as Congress would be required to approve tens if not hundreds of such agreements. . . . All of these agreements would also be fully amendable," Roth said.

Hollings argued that in the recently concluded telecommunications agreement, Barshefsky had bypassed Congress and agreed to relax regulations restricting foreign ownership of telecommunications services, a policy change that should have required congressional action.

In the end, Hollings' proposal won some warm words but few votes. Democrats who might have supported his approach in the abstract wanted to avoid hurting a Clinton nominee, and on the Republican side, free-trade lawmakers objected to Hollings' amendment on principle.

"The Hollings amendment represents a different view of trade," said John McCain, R-Ariz., "I believe that the American worker can compete with anyone in the world, and with that fundamental belief I'm in favor of reducing barriers to trade," he said.

The amendment was tabled (killed) by a vote of 84-16. Sixteen senators supported Hollings — nine Democrats and seven Republicans, including Republican conference Chairman Larry E. Craig of Idaho and Democratic Whip Byron L. Dorgan of North Dakota. *(Vote 25, p. S-6)*

The debate in the House, by contrast, was brief and relatively calm. Ways and Means Chairman Bill Archer, R-Texas, said he supported the waiver because Barshefsky had only "a minimal advisory role to the Canadian government a number of years ago." ■

Ferguson, Gramlich Confirmed at Fed

The Senate confirmed two nominees — Roger Ferguson and Edward Gramlich — for the Federal Reserve's board of governors by voice vote Oct. 30. President Clinton had nominated the two men to the posts July 10.

Ferguson had been a New York-based partner at the international consulting firm McKinsey and Co., where he specialized in bank restructuring and payments systems. He had a law degree and a doctorate in economics from Harvard University.

Gramlich was dean of the School of Public Policy at the University of Michigan, where he had been an economics professor for more than 20 years. He had once served as acting director of the Congressional Budget Office. Earlier in the year, Gramlich had served as chairman of a government advisory council on ways to shore up the Social Security system.

Ferguson filled a vacancy on the seven-member board created when Lawrence Lindsey left to join the American Enterprise Institute. Ferguson's term ran to Jan. 31, 2000.

Gramlich took the seat vacated by Janet Yellen, who became chairman of the president's Council of Economic Advisers earlier in the year. His term was up Jan. 31, 2008.

The Senate Banking Committee recommended the two for confirmation without objection Oct. 8, following hearings Sept. 30. Chairman Alfonse M. D'Amato, R-N.Y., praised both men's "extraordinary backgrounds" and predicted they would be easily confirmed. Paul S. Sarbanes of Maryland, the committee's ranking Democrat, also endorsed the nominations.

The two Fed nominees were circumspect in discussing their views on monetary policy during the hearing. Ferguson expressed cautious optimism about the continued expansion of a robust economy, but he would not commit to altering assumptions about maintaining low unemployment without inflation.

"With current uncertainties, Federal Reserve governors should be open to the possibility that underlying dynamics of the economy might be changing, but they should seek evidence for such developments and not act on the presumption of change," he said.

The Senate vote came after Democratic critics of the Fed's monetary policy, led by Iowa Sen. Tom Harkin, dropped holds on the nominations in exchange for an agreement from Majority Leader Trent Lott, R-Miss., to give Harkin 90 minutes of floor time.

Harkin said that under Chairman Alan Greenspan, the Federal Reserve Board had allowed interest rates to remain too high for working Americans, on the belief that higher rates were keeping inflation in check. Harkin said the nominees' positions were "too much in line with the present thinking at the Fed. . . . And I think that is going to cost us dearly in the years ahead."

Byron L. Dorgan, D-N.D., joined Harkin, saying the Fed's board would not gain new perspective with these nominees. The governors "all come from the same area. They all look the same. They all wear the same suits. They all have the same educational background," Dorgan said. "If you put them in a barrel and shake it up, the same person winds up on top — gray suit, Ivy League background." ■

Carey, Unger Take Slots at SEC

With no debate, the Senate on Oct. 21 confirmed by voice vote two nominees for the Securities and Exchange Commission (SEC). They were Paul R. Carey, a White House legislative aide and the son of former New York Gov. Hugh Carey, and Laura S. Unger, securities counsel for the Banking Committee. Unger had also served as an aide to Banking Chairman Alfonse M. D'Amato, R-N.Y.

Carey's term ran until June 5, 2002. Unger's expired June 5, 2001.

The Senate Banking Committee had approved the nominations without objection on Oct. 8 following a confirmation hearing Sept. 30. "In my opinion, the president could not have chosen two more qualified people to serve on the SEC," D'Amato said.

In testimony, Unger warned that the SEC should not regulate the stock markets too tightly in its effort to protect investors. "Too much regulation will make the markets an unattractive source of financing to companies. If confirmed, I will work to ensure that the commission's programs strike the appropriate balance," she said.

Unger told senators she also wanted to focus on challenges that would face regulators in the next century, including technological advances, internationalization, continued growth in mutual funds and financial modernization.

Carey said one of the SEC's greatest challenges would come in defining the relationship between U.S. markets and those of other nations. "Ongoing efforts to arrive at international accounting standards as well as cooperation on enforcement matters should permit us to accommodate the growth of cross-border transactions without diminishing investor protection," he said. ■

Rossotti Confirmed To Head Internal Revenue Service

The Senate on Nov. 3 voted, 92-0, to confirm Charles O. Rossotti, a Virginia business executive, as the new commissioner of the Internal Revenue Service. He replaced acting commissioner Michael P. Dolan. *(Vote 290, p. S-50)*

Giving up his job as chairman of American Management Systems Inc., Rossotti became the first IRS commissioner since World War II not drawn from the nation's legions of tax lawyers. Since founding the company in 1970, Rossotti had piled up an impressive record dealing with complicated technology projects at clients such as IBM, the National Football League and the California Franchise Tax Board. His company had grown to about 7,500 employees worldwide.

The White House purposely picked a business executive for the job, saying a skilled manager with technology experience would be better suited to modernize the IRS than another tax lawyer. In particular, it was hoped that his experience would help in dealing with the ongoing problems in updating the IRS's computer system.

The Senate Finance Committee had approved the nomination by voice vote Oct. 29. Despite the bipartisan assault that was under way against the IRS, Rossotti gained far more sympathy than spite when he appeared before the panel Oct. 23. "You're going to get an idea in this hearing what a bad job this really is," said Phil Gramm, R-Texas. "And if you don't change your mind, we will probably confirm you."

Finance Committee Chairman William V. Roth Jr., R-Del., said Rossotti would bring to the job a background that "breaks the mold." Said Roth: "The IRS needs a leader who will buck tradition."

Rossotti told the Finance Committee he was up to the challenge. He pledged to recruit another outsider for the post of taxpayer advocate and to better publicize the advocate's services.

He also said he would move quickly to institute 33 citizen advocacy councils that Clinton had recently proposed. In the long term, he said, he would "get the entire organization to think of themselves effectively as taxpayer advocates" with "managers who actually understand what's going on."

When the nomination reached the floor, the debate was perfunctory but filled with high praise for the nominee. It did nothing, however, to prod the Senate on a bill to overhaul the IRS, despite pleas from Charles E. Grassley, R-Iowa, that "Mr. Rossotti needs the tools that are in our bill in order for him to fully succeed in his job." *(IRS overhaul, p. 2-71)* ■

President Chooses Yellen For Economic Council

Janet Yellen won confirmation Feb. 13 to serve as chairman of President Clinton's Council of Economic Advisers, one day after receiving a 17-0 endorsement from the Senate Banking Committee. Senate approval was by voice vote.

A former economics professor at the University of California at Berkeley, Yellen replaced Joseph E. Stiglitz. She gave up a seat on the Board of Governors of the Federal Reserve that she had held since 1994.

"I am tremendously pleased you will be taking on this assignment," Banking Committee Chairman Alfonse M. D'Amato, R-N.Y., told Yellen at her Feb. 5 confirmation hearing.

GOP committee members pressed for her views on the balanced-budget amendment, taxes and economic growth. In response to a question from Lauch Faircloth, R-N.C., Yellen said she strongly opposed amending the Constitution to require balanced budgets. Echoing the president and other administration officials, she said the amendment could precipitate a recession or depression by eliminating the government's ability to lower taxes or increase spending during economic downturns.

Yellen said she would not give "high priority" to a broad-based capital gains tax cut advocated by many Republicans.

She also told the committee that she considered it a "very important priority" to promote policies aimed at improving the economy's 2.5 percent annual growth rate. Republicans encouraged her to press that view in the White House. "Many people, including President Clinton, now consider a growth rate of 2.5 percent to be acceptable, even laudable," said Connie Mack, R-Fla. "We should not accept such mediocrity." ■

CQ

Chapter 3

GOVERNMENT & COMMERCE

COMMERCE

Passions Run High as Congress Wades Into Tobacco Issue

Wary lawmakers examine fine print of deal worked out between states and tobacco companies

The nation's biggest tobacco companies and 40 state attorneys general reached a landmark $368.5 billion agreement June 20 to help the states pay for illnesses caused by cigarettes and finance an unprecedented public education campaign against smoking. In exchange, the companies would get reduced vulnerability to lawsuits by individuals, groups and government officials.

Much of the deal had to be written into law if it was to take effect, and the participants, particularly the tobacco companies, begged Congress to act quickly before the agreement could unravel.

But lawmakers were extremely reluctant to wade into the controversy. Instead, the focus in 1997 was on holding hearings and setting up task forces. Still, by year's end, members of both parties agreed that action was necessary, and they said they were committed to taking up broad tobacco legislation in early 1998.

Tobacco-state lawmakers were coming to see the deal as a vehicle to ensure infusions of economic development funds for their tobacco farmers. At first, anti-tobacco lawmakers had pounced on the settlement as too weak and too easy on the industry, but the tobacco control provisions were beginning to woo them.

Meanwhile, President Clinton announced Sept. 17 that he would demand five key changes in the agreement, including stiffening the penalties on companies if they failed to reach goals to reduce teen smoking.

Several pending court cases were moving forward in the states that could affect the settlement. And a high-priced, high-profile cortege of lobbyists kept up the pressure for action in 1998.

Congress was expected to take its time in 1998 reviewing the deal before deciding whether to approve key provisions, including restrictions on future lawsuits against tobacco manufacturers, limitations on tobacco advertising and authority for the Food and Drug Administration (FDA) to regulate tobacco.

Background

The tobacco industry's interest in reaching a settlement reflected the industry's rapid change of fortunes in the 1990s. The companies faced lawsuits brought by 40 state attorneys general demanding payment of costs incurred by state Medicaid programs as a result of tobacco-related illnesses.

The industry had won one victory in Florida on May 5, when a jury cleared R.J. Reynolds Tobacco Co. of responsibility for the cancer death of smoker Jean Connor. But the attorneys general were taking a different tack, arguing that the ordinary taxpayer should not be liable for tobacco-related costs. The argument circumvented tobacco-industry arguments that smokers knew the risks when they took up the habit.

Meanwhile, pressure was growing on a number of other fronts. A separate settlement by The Liggett Group Inc. with 22 state attorneys general in March was spurring the release of documents purporting to show that, despite fierce denials, industry officials had known years before about the dangers of cigarette smoking.

On April 25, U.S. District Court Judge William L. Osteen Sr. ruled in Greensboro, N.C., that the FDA could regulate nicotine-laden tobacco products as drugs — a policy change that anti-smoking lawmakers had tried but failed to enact in years past.

If upheld, Osteen's ruling, issued in the heart of tobacco's home turf, would deprive the companies of an important bargaining chip in the settlement talks: the offer to submit voluntarily to FDA regulation. Osteen did say the FDA lacked the statutory authority to dictate the terms of tobacco advertising. But the Justice Department planned to appeal that part of the decision, and a Supreme Court ruling in another case just a week later suggested that the appeal could succeed.

In that instance, the Supreme Court let stand a lower-court ruling permitting the city of Baltimore to bar cigarette and alcoholic beverage advertisements from most city billboards.

In short, without a settlement, the tobacco companies faced the possibility of future legal judgments requiring them to pay potentially ruinous financial damages to individuals claiming they were harmed by the industry's products.

The Settlement

Under the proposed 68-page settlement, tobacco companies agreed to accept restrictions on their marketing and sales practices, and conditional federal regulation of the nicotine in their products. In exchange, all pending class action and state lawsuits were to be dismissed. Future litigants would be prohibited from banding together in class action suits, and individuals could not sue for punitive damages.

The deal included a number of initiatives aimed at protecting children that had long been sought by tobacco's opponents. For example, billboard advertising was to be banned, as well as outdoor signs at sports stadiums. Images such as Joe Camel and the Marlboro Man would be eliminated from all advertising. Industry critics contended that tobacco companies used those images to romanticize their products.

Tobacco companies would be required to compensate private litigants, state governments and public anti-smoking and health education campaigns, with the bulk of the money going to reimburse state Medicaid programs for the cost of treating smoking-related illnesses.

The tobacco industry portrayed the deal as a framework to reduce the nation's smoking habit and pay its share of the devastating consequences. Anti-smoking advocates said it did not contain sufficient penalties for the industry and fell short of protecting public health. They said the industry was up to its old tricks, looking to Congress for the best deal possible after winning a settlement that for the first time gave it the promise of legal immunity.

Initial Reactions

The tobacco industry wanted the deal approved as written in June. The attorneys general of the states suing the tobacco companies concurred, saying it was the best deal they could hope for and warning Congress against tampering with it.

But almost immediately, members of Congress, both allies and opponents of the tobacco industry, pounced on the settlement, declaring they would not rubber stamp any legislation.

"Congress cannot and will not be bound to ratify a privately negotiated resolution of this," said House Speaker Newt Gingrich, R-Ga. "I can tell you one of my concerns," said Ron Wyden, D-Ore., "is that the United States Senate is not here to staple this deal together and salute it."

Clinton said some of the provisions were not tough enough, singling out strict limits to be placed on the FDA's ability to issue new tobacco regulations. Public interest groups protested that limiting tobacco's liability in lawsuits would hurt consumers.

On July 9, Philip Morris Inc., R.J. Reynolds Tobacco Co., Brown & Williamson Tobacco Corp., Lorillard Tobacco Co. and the United States Tobacco Co. issued a joint statement warning against tampering with the settlement.

In particular, they wanted to preserve a requirement that the FDA prove that nicotine restrictions would not foster a black market for tobacco products — precisely the provision Clinton said that he opposed. "The risk of creating a substantial black market in tobacco products should be a legitimate concern to all Americans for a variety of reasons," the statement said. "The industry believes that the proposed resolution appropriately balances the various factors that should be considered in any determination to ban nicotine."

The federal government added a new twist in November, laying claim to half the money that the states recovered from the tobacco companies to pay for the costs of treating Medicaid beneficiaries with smoking-related illnesses. The Health Care Financing Administration, responsible for overseeing Medicare and Medicaid, notified the states Nov. 3 that they were required under the Social Security Act to reimburse the federal government for its share of Medicaid expenses when damages were recovered.

The states insisted they should control the settlement money because they had fought the tobacco industry without help from Washington. "Now the federal government, without having lifted a finger to assist the states, is claiming a right to a portion of any settlement funds," said Sen. Bob Graham, D-Fla., a former governor.

Congressional Action

There were few major votes on the tobacco deal in 1997, although both chambers held hearings and leaders on both sides of the aisle created task forces to study the settlement. But several votes that went against the industry, particularly in the Senate, led even the most ardent defenders of the settlement to conclude that the companies would have to accept much tougher terms.

- **Tax break repeal.** The most telling sign of growing momentum in Congress for a tougher settlement came after industry allies slipped a last-minute provision into the budget-reconciliation tax bill (HR 2014 — PL 105-34) stipulating that any money raised by a cigarette tax increase in the accompanying spending-cut bill (HR 2015 — PL 105-33) be applied toward the total amount the industry had agreed to pay in the settlement. The provision effectively would have shaved about $50 billion from the tobacco industry's liabilities over the expected 25-year life span of the settlement

The ploy backfired on the industry, with adversaries saying it was a backroom deal that symbolized Congress' continuing coddling of the cigarette-makers.

On Sept. 10, after some parliamentary maneuvering, Richard J. Durbin, D-Ill., won Senate support for repealing the tax break. His amendment — to the Senate version of the appropriations bill for the departments of Labor, Health and Human Services and Education (S 1061) — was adopted, 95-3. *(Vote 227, p. S-38)*

On Sept. 17, the House followed suit, approving repeal language by voice vote. The amendment was included in the final version of the bill, enacted Nov. 13 (HR 2264 — PL 105-78). *(Appropriations, p. 9-50)*

- **Anti-smoking programs.** A week earlier, the Senate had overwhelmingly voted to appropriate more money for anti-smoking programs. The vote came on an amendment by Tom Harkin, D-Iowa, to the fiscal 1998 agriculture spending bill.

Harkin proposed to increase funding for FDA anti-smoking programs from the $4.9 million originally approved by the Senate, to $34 million, the level requested by the Clinton administration. The administration wanted the money to expand an FDA program aimed at reducing children's access to tobacco products through such measures as requiring retailers to check the identification of purchasers to ensure that they were 18 or older.

A month and a half earlier, on July 23, the Senate had rejected a similar Harkin amendment, voting 52-48 to table (kill) it. More than 20 senators reversed themselves Sept. 3, when Harkin offered a revised amendment. An attempt to table the proposal failed, 28-70, and the Senate then adopted the amendment by voice vote. *(Votes 198, p. S-35; 212, p. S-37)*

Harkin and others attributed the turnaround in part to a change in the financing mechanism; the earlier amendment would have required approval from the House Ways and Means Committee, complicating the bill's chances for clearing. But Harkin also said he believed publicity during the August recess about the $50 billion tobacco industry tax break had prompted some senators to change their votes.

The House did its own, if less dramatic, turnaround. The House version of the agriculture spending bill, passed July 24, included $24 million for the tobacco initiative. An attempt by Martin T. Meehan, D-Mass., to add another $10 million on the floor was rejected, 177-248. But the House subsequently voted 299-125 on Sept. 3 for a non-binding motion instructing its conferees to agree to the Senate funding level. *(Vote 309, p. H-94; vote 353, p. H-106)*

Conferees included the full $34 million in the final bill, which was signed into law Nov. 18 (HR 2160 — PL 105-86). *(Appropriations, p. 9-5)*

Other Congressional Action

After an initial period of silence on the settlement, House GOP leaders ended the session calling for Congress to weigh in. Gingrich said he wanted action on the settlement in early 1998, but would insist on broadening its reach to include controls on teen alcohol and drug use. GOP leaders also said any settlement would have to include strict limits on fees paid to the trial lawyers who helped negotiate it.

House Commerce Committee Chairman Thomas J. Bliley Jr., R-Va., a traditional ally of the tobacco industry, shocked observers Nov. 13 at his first hearing on the settlement when he demanded that cigarette manufacturers release hundreds of internal documents that he said the panel needed to evaluate the deal. The companies gave up the material Dec. 5, but only after Bliley had issued subpoenas.

Philip Morris, Lorillard, R.J. Reynolds Tobacco, and Brown and Williamson Tobacco had been withholding the documents as part of a suit filed against the industry by Minnesota Attorney General Hubert H. Humphrey III. The companies said the papers should be secret because of attorney-client privilege. But a court-appointed official who reviewed the papers recommended to the judge in the case that the argument be rejected.

In the Senate, leaders on both sides of the aisle created task forces to study the settlement. Hearings began in the Judiciary; Commerce, Science and Transportation; Labor and Human Resources; Agriculture, Nutrition and Forestry; and Indian Affairs committees.

Judiciary Committee Chairman Orrin G. Hatch, R-Utah, a tobacco industry opponent, volunteered to shepherd the settlement through the legislative maze, and he introduced legislation (S 1530) that would require the industry to pay $30 billion more than the settlement envisioned, while boosting the penalties the industry would have to pay for failing to meet targets for reducing underage smoking.

Edward M. Kennedy of Massachusetts, ranking Democrat on the Labor and Human Resources Committee, introduced his own tough, anti-tobacco legislation (S 1492) based on the settlement. Commerce Committee Chairman John McCain, R-Ariz., introduced two nearly identical bills (S 1414; S 1415) that aimed to codify most of the original settlement.

Court Action

Even as the national tobacco settlement awaited congressional action, individual states continued to negotiate their own deals with the tobacco companies.

• **Mississippi.** Under a settlement announced July 3, the tobacco companies agreed to pay Mississippi nearly $3.4 billion over 25 years to compensate the state for tobacco-related health care costs. The suit, filed in May 1994, made Mississippi the first state to attempt to recover its health care costs from the tobacco industry.

• **Florida.** A landmark legal settlement Aug. 25 between Florida and the tobacco industry sowed further confusion about Congress' already uncertain efforts to enact a far broader national settlement of tobacco litigation.

Tobacco industry officials agreed that their companies would pay $11.3 billion over 25 years to reimburse the state for tobacco-related Medicaid expenses and pay for substance abuse mitigation programs, children's health care programs and anti-tobacco educational campaigns aimed at minors.

Tobacco industry officials said the Florida deal showed they could bypass the national settlement and settle each case individually if Congress or the White House tried to toughen the terms of the June deal. Tobacco industry opponents in Congress said Florida proved that states could win money and concessions from the industry and give almost nothing in return.

But Mississippi attorney Richard F. Scruggs, one of the lead negotiators in the national deal, warned that the industry was clearing the way for a state-by-state approach that could take years and yield at least a third less money and fewer restrictions on the industry than the national settlement envisioned.

Buried in the documents relating to the case were numerous references, dating to the 1960s, to the tobacco industry's efforts to influence Congress and how well it had succeeded. For example:

➤ In May 1964, while preparing for congressional hearings on proposed cigarette warning labels, industry attorneys at the Washington law firm of Arnold, Fortas & Porter met to discuss a survey on the public's knowledge of the health effects of smoking. If it could be shown that the public was already aware of such effects, the lawyers reasoned, Congress could be convinced that mandating health warnings on labels and in cigarette ads was superfluous.

➤ On Sept. 10, 1981, industry lawyers brainstormed on how to cultivate defense witnesses, including how to "stimulate the interest of doctors." But they fretted about the unpredictability of such witnesses when called to testify to Congress.

➤ An undated confidential paper, drafted by R.J. Reynolds Tobacco to deal with a clamor to disclose the ingredients added to cigarettes, hailed Congress' confirmation of companies' rights to keep such additives secret.

"Even Congress recognized the legitimacy of the industry's claims of secrecy when it required that disclosure of ingredients be made on an industry-wide, rather than company or brand, basis," the document said.

• **Airline attendants.** A surprise announcement Oct. 10 that four tobacco companies had reached a $300 million settlement in a flight attendants' class action lawsuit emboldened anti-tobacco groups to demand that Congress strengthen the terms of the June settlement.

In particular, they called for eliminating what was perhaps the most important provision to the industry: protection from future class action lawsuits.

"Any legislation that exempts them for all practical matters from liability will be seen as letting them off the hook just as they are getting their comeuppance," said Richard Daynard, president of Northeastern University Law School's Tobacco Control Resource Center.

The 60,000 suing attendants, none of them smokers, argued that they had gotten sick breathing secondhand smoke on airliners. Among the ailments were lung cancer, emphysema and chronic bronchitis.

Under the terms of the settlement, Philip Morris, R.J. Reynolds Tobacco, Brown & Williamson Tobacco and Lorillard Tobacco agreed to pay $300 million to establish a foundation for scientific research on diseases associated with cigarette smoking. No money was to go directly to the flight attendants, although the companies agreed to pay $49 million in fees and other costs for the attendants' attorneys.

The companies also agreed to support federal legislation prohibiting smoking on segments of international flights beginning or ending in the United States. Such legislation would extend the reach of a 1989 measure, fought strongly by the tobacco industry, that permanently banned smoking on virtually all domestic air flights. *(1989 Almanac, p. 749)*

In exchange, the class action suit was scuttled, leaving each flight attendant to pursue his or her claims separately. Those individual lawsuits could not seek punitive damages.

Clinton

In a long-anticipated announcement Sept. 17, Clinton chose to neither explicitly endorse nor reject the proposed

Tobacco Deal Highlights

The following are the major provisions from the June 20 settlement reached by the nation's biggest tobacco companies and 40 state attorneys general. Many of the provisions required legislative action to take effect.

● **Industry payment.** The participating manufacturers agreed to provide $368.5 billion to the states, lawsuit plaintiffs and public health campaigns over 25 years. An initial commitment of $10 billion was payable at the time legislation was enacted. Ensuing payments were to be made annually for 25 years following a schedule in the agreement. After the first 25 years, $15 billion a year would be paid indefinitely.

● **Civil liability.** Pending lawsuits against the tobacco industry — including addiction/dependency claims, the cases brought by the 40 state attorneys general and class action cases — were to be legislatively settled for a yet-to-be-confirmed sum that would be included in the $368.5 billion to be paid by the tobacco companies. All future prosecutions of such claims would be barred.

Individual plaintiffs in cases involving past actions of the tobacco companies would be entitled to claim damages for medical services and lost wages, but not for punitive damages.

Provisions for civil liability for "future conduct" cases — those based on actions of the tobacco industry after the proposed settlement was ironed out — would follow the same guidelines as past conduct cases, except that parties could claim actual and punitive damages.

The settlement included an annual aggregate cap for judgments/settlements of 33 percent of the annual industry base payment. If the total payout exceeded the cap, the excess amount would be rolled over. If an individual settlement exceeded $1 million, the excess amount would not be paid that year unless every other judgment/settlement could be satisfied within the annual aggregate cap.

If the annual aggregate cap was not spent in any given year, a commission appointed by the president was to determine the manner in which the excess money would be used.

● **Product development and manufacturing.** For the first time, the development and manufacturing of tobacco products was to be subject to federal regulation. Manufacturers would be required to notify the Food and Drug Administration (FDA) of any technology that would reduce health risks from use of tobacco products. In the event that a "less hazardous tobacco product" was developed, the FDA would have the authority to mandate the introduction of the product into the market.

The negotiators deferred the elimination of nicotine until at least 12 years after the deal's implementation because they feared that a more rapid move would create a black market for nicotine-laden tobacco products.

● **Non-tobacco ingredients.** The FDA would gain the authority to evaluate all additives in tobacco products.

● **Reducing tobacco use by children.** The agreement included provisions aimed at drastically reducing the number of underage consumers of tobacco products. The minimum age required for the purchase of tobacco products would be set at 18. Photo identification would be required for purchase, and the sale would have to be face to face. Vending machine sales would be banned. Tobacco products would have to be placed out of reach of customers, except in adult-only facilities, and be sold only by licensed vendors.

● **Reduction goals.** The settlement set goals for reducing tobacco use among youths. It called for cutting underage use of cigarette products by at least 30 percent from existing levels by the fifth year after implementing legislation took effect, by at least 50 percent by the seventh year, and by at least 60 percent by the 10th year. If those goals were not attained, both manufacturers and states would suffer financial penalties.

Underage use of smokeless tobacco was to decline by at least 25 percent from the baseline levels by the fifth year after implementing legislation took effect, by 35 percent by the seventh year, and by at least 45 percent by the 10th year.

● **Industry penalties.** Should future FDA calculations show that requirements to reduce underage tobacco use were not met, the agency would impose a surcharge on the manufacturer. The surcharge for cigarette manufacturers would be $80 million for each percentage point by which the goal was missed. This amount was determined as an approximation of the present value of the profit the cigarette industry would earn over the life of underage smokers. The industrywide surcharge could not exceed $2 billion a year. The surcharge for smokeless tobacco products would follow the same guidelines.

● **State enforcement.** States would be subject to a similar enforcement plan regarding underage tobacco consumption. Under the agreement, each state would set standards for determining whether it had "pursued all reasonably available measures to enforce" the prohibition on sales of tobacco products to children and adolescents.

If a state did not meet the "no sales to minors" requirement, the FDA could withhold money the states would otherwise receive for enforcing the requirement. The amount withheld could be as much as 1 percent of the expected federal payment for each percentage point by which the state's performance failed to meet the performance targets for that year. In no case would more than 20 percent of the allocable money be withheld from the state.

● **Marketing and advertising restrictions.** The FDA would be given statutory authority to drastically curtail tobacco advertisements. The agreement banned non-tobacco merchandise, such as clothing decorated with brand names of tobacco products. It also banned outdoor and Internet advertising of tobacco products.

Product descriptions such as "light" or "low tar," which might lead a customer to believe the product was less hazardous than other cigarettes, would have to be accompanied by a disclaimer, such as "Brand X not shown to be less hazardous than other cigarettes."

● **Warnings, labeling and packaging.** The settlement proposed amendments to the Federal Cigarette Labeling and Advertising Act and Comprehensive Smokeless Tobacco Health Education Act to mandate a new set of warnings on product packages. New wording would include, "WARNING: Smoking can kill you." The warnings were to be alternated quarterly and occupy the upper 25 percent of the front panel on cigarette packaging. On smokeless tobacco products, the warnings would occupy 25 percent of the display panel.

● **Involuntary exposure to tobacco smoke.** The agreement included rules to restrict indoor smoking in "public facilities" — defined as any building regularly entered by 10 or more individuals at least one day per week — to ventilated areas that followed specific guidelines. Employees would not be required to enter a designated smoking area while smoking was occurring.

Such public accommodations as restaurants, bars and casinos would be excluded from the "public facility" guidelines; however, fast-food restaurants would be required to meet the requirements because they typically drew large numbers of underage customers.

● **Allocation of grant monies.** Of the $368.5 billion that the tobacco industry agreed to pay, a set amount would be reserved to finance programs including: promotions to discourage underage tobacco consumption, assistance to individuals who wanted to quit using tobacco products, and establishment of a Public Health Trust Fund to finance specific tobacco-related medical research.

● **Industry associations.** Within 90 days of the effective date of implementing legislation, the tobacco product manufacturers were to disband and dissolve any trade associations, such as the Tobacco Institute, the industry's lobbying arm in Washington, D.C. ■

$368.5 billion settlement. Instead he demanded five key changes. And, rather than laying out a specific legislative proposal, he said he would meet with congressional leaders to craft a plan. Informal, bipartisan meetings began Oct. 1. *(Text, p. D-37)*

That put Congress in the hot seat and further ensured that the issue would be kicked into 1998, giving Democrats a potentially fertile campaign topic for the midyear elections.

The major provisions Clinton said he wanted included in tobacco legislation were:

➤ An increase in the penalties that tobacco companies would have to pay if they failed to meet targets for reducing teen smoking. He called for a combination of payments and penalties to boost the price of a pack of cigarettes by $1.50, adding that such penalties should not be tax-deductible as requested by the tobacco companies.

The original settlement was estimated to raise the price of cigarettes by about 62 cents a pack, but industry officials said that when inflation and other factors were taken into account, the figures were close to each other.

➤ Full authority for the FDA to regulate tobacco.

➤ Greater disclosure of tobacco industry documents.

➤ Meeting other health care goals, including reducing secondhand smoke, strengthening international efforts to control tobacco and providing funding for medical research.

➤ Protection for tobacco farmers and communities that might be hurt if tobacco sales declined.

Lobbying

The tobacco industry geared up for a major lobbying push, hiring some of the biggest names in the nation's capital to campaign for its version of the tobacco settlement.

The industry spent $42 million of its own money on lobbying in 1996 and the first half of 1997, and nearly $8 million in the first half of 1997 hiring outside lobbyists.

Among the biggest names on its payroll were former Senate Majority Leaders George J. Mitchell, D-Maine, and Howard H. Baker Jr., R-Tenn., who resigned from the board of the Mayo Clinic because of his tobacco ties.

Several former members of the House also worked for the industry, including Republican Stan E. Parris of Virginia and Democrats James V. Stanton of Ohio, Ed Jenkins of Georgia and Alan Wheat of Missouri. ■

Slow Start on Electricity Deregulation

Efforts to deregulate the nation's $208 billion electric power industry, once touted as a priority for the 105th Congress, turned out to be much more difficult than many lawmakers had anticipated.

By year's end, the Senate Banking Committee had agreed on a narrow proposal, backed by the utilities, to repeal the 1935 Public Utilities Holding Companies Act (PUHCA), the main federal law regulating the growth and business activities of multistate electric utilities. Banking Committee Chairman Alfonse M. D'Amato, R-N.Y., was eager to get the measure to the Senate floor, but its path was blocked by a threatened filibuster.

In the House, Dan Schaefer, R-Colo., chairman of the Commerce Subcommittee on Energy and Power, put together a much broader bill but was unable to hold a markup before adjournment. The lack of consensus among committee Republicans forced him to wait while he looked for a compromise acceptable to Democrats.

"Everybody came out of the gate too quickly," said Roger Gale, president of the Washington International Energy Group, an energy consulting firm. "It's the kind of thing that takes two years, and maybe four or five, to happen."

Under existing law, state-regulated utilities held a monopoly over retail service to customers in specific areas, with the prices set by state regulators. The price of transmitting electricity between different states was regulated by the Federal Energy Regulatory Commission (FERC).

As envisioned by proponents, deregulation would allow utilities to sell to any customer, and consumers would be able to choose their electricity providers much the way they chose their long-distance phone carrier. States would allow the price of electricity to be set in a competitive market, while federal regulators would retain their existing control over power lines.

But there were many unresolved questions about how to approach deregulation and how big a role the federal government should have. The debate pitted House Republicans who wanted broad, federally mandated deregulation, against powerful Senate Republicans who favored incremental change.

House Republicans were allied with large consumers of electricity, who stood to save millions of dollars in a competitive market, and independent power producers eager to enter a market that had been dominated by large utility companies in what amounted to the nation's last big regulated monopoly.

Senate Republicans were more attuned to the utility companies, which argued that deregulating the industry should be left to the states.

Democrats, too, were divided between allies and foes of deregulation, with each side accusing the other of intransigence.

At the end of the session, House and Senate Republicans remained at loggerheads. House Commerce Committee Chairman Thomas J. Bliley Jr., R-Va., said he would not consider a stand-alone repeal bill. John D. Dingell of Michigan, the panel's ranking Democrat, also opposed such an approach. On the other side, Frank H. Murkowski, R-Alaska, chairman of the Senate Energy and Natural Resources Committee, wanted to simply repeal PUHCA and leave regulation to the states; he opposed any federal mandate.

At stake in the debate were hundreds of billions of dollars in annual savings to consumers and big financial gains or losses to energy companies that would be forced to compete in the marketplace. The Clinton administration projected that deregulation could save consumers as much as $20 billion a year — roughly a tenth of the nation's electricity bill. It estimated savings of about $19 a month in the electricity bill of an average family of four.

With such big stakes, well-funded electric utilities mounted a strong effort to slow the pace of deregulation, hiring lobbyists and flooding congress with campaign money.

Meanwhile, with Congress moving slowly, some states were racing ahead with deregulation, selling cheaper electricity that was lighting up such landmarks as the Golden Gate Bridge and offices and homes. In all, 15 states had programs to introduce competition to local utilities over the next seven years.

Background

At the root of the movement to deregulate was a gap in comparative electricity rates between such states as Washington and Kentucky, where electricity cost about 4 cents per kilowatt-hour, and states such as New York and California, where prices were more than twice as much.

Advocates said deregulation would allow cheaper electricity — produced, for example, by hydropower dams in the Northwest and power plants in coal-belt states with low transportation costs — to flow from utilities in one region to customers in another. Under existing law, utilities could only sell wholesale electricity to energy companies in other states.

Proponents found support in a study by the Center for Market Processes, a research center based at George Mason University in Fairfax, Va. The study predicted that electric utilities would give consumers benefits similar to those given by four other industries that had undergone deregulation in the previous two decades: long-distance telephone service, airlines, trucking and railroads. The study said deregulation produced cuts in real prices from 25 percent to over 50 percent within 10 years.

"Consumers gained substantially — not just because of rate reductions, but also because of improvements in the quality of service. All broad consumer groups shared in the price reductions, though some benefited more than others," concluded Robert Crandall and Jerry Ellig, authors of the report.

But critics said the primary beneficiary would be industry. They predicted a "Big Dog eats first" scenario in which big businesses cut deals for the cheapest power, while leaving residential customers with electricity from higher-cost sources including nuclear plants.

"The big question is whether residential and small-business consumers will be left holding the bag with higher rates than big companies that are able to negotiate big power contracts at lower rates," said Eleanor Miller, a manager of media and public affairs for the National Rural Electric Cooperative Association, which represented energy cooperatives that served rural customers. The group's members feared that deregulation could open their territories to competition from big rivals and encourage legislative attacks on cheap financing enjoyed by cooperatives and municipal utilities.

Carl K. Oshiro, a former adviser to the president of the California Public Utilities Commission, said in a study for the Consumer Research Foundation, a California-based nonprofit group, that utilities would probably give their best deals to large industrial customers who were leading the push for deregulation. "For residential consumers with little economic power such as low-income customers and those in rural areas, restructuring could mean few, if any, choices, higher rates and poorer service," he said.

Senate Committee

The Senate Banking, Housing and Urban Affairs Committee on June 5 easily approved D'Amato's plan (S 621 — S Rept 105-41) to repeal PUHCA, the Depression-era law that was enacted to restrain utility monopolization. But the voice vote approval of the legislation belied the difficult road ahead. A similar bill (S 1317) had sailed through the Banking Committee the previous June, but was never considered by the full Senate. *(1996 Almanac, p. 3-6)*

Consumer groups, galvanized by a move toward consolidation in the electric power industry in anticipation of deregulation, argued that the 1935 holding company law was holding back the re-monopolization of electric power. Utilities covered by the holding company act could only expand into contiguous states. Exempt utilities had an incentive to stay small, since a rapid expansion would also force them to register with the Securities and Exchange Commission (SEC).

But Banking Committee senators said they saw no reason to wait to repeal a law they said was hampering the industry's ability to prepare for competition. "I'm not a person who believes we have to make the world perfect before we make it better," said Phil Gramm, R-Texas.

D'Amato and the committee's ranking Democrat, Paul S. Sarbanes of Maryland, said provisions had been added to the bill specifically to address the concerns of consumer groups. They included expanding the powers of federal and state regulators to examine the financial records of utility holding companies and their subsidiaries.

In fact, proponents argued, repealing the holding company act would actually strengthen controls over market abuses. Under existing law, the 12 electric utilities and three natural gas companies that fell under PUHCA were regulated by both the SEC and the FERC. If the companies did not like a FERC order, they could turn to the SEC for protection.

D'Amato said repealing the holding company act would end that practice, increase consumer protections and lower electricity rates. "Certainly that's the goal. I hope it would be the case," he said before the markup.

Key lawmakers hedged, saying they could support the repeal — but only in the context of broad legislation to bring retail competition to the electric power industry. One such member was Dale Bumpers of Arkansas, the ranking Democrat on the Senate Energy and Natural Resources Committee, who put a hold on the repeal bill, threatening to block it with a filibuster if it came to the Senate floor.

Bumpers collected 17 signatures from Senate Democrats on a letter saying that D'Amato's proposal should be part of a broader review of bills to restructure the electric utility industry.

Later, on Nov. 7, Bumpers and Sen. Slade Gorton, R-Wash., unveiled a bipartisan bill (S 1401) that proposed setting a deadline of Jan. 1, 2002, for states to deregulate the industry. The bill took aim at one of the potential obstacles to comprehensive legislation: fear that deregulation might draw power away from states with low-cost electricity, pushing up their prices for consumers.

The bill proposed to require utilities in low-cost power regions, whose profits would increase because of competition, to reimburse consumers for increases in the cost of their power. Utilities would be required to draw a certain percentage of their power from renewable sources, including hydropower.

House Bills

In the House, Schaefer held hearings in his Commerce Energy and Power Subcommittee the week of Oct. 20 on three comprehensive deregulation bills. The lead bill (HR 655), sponsored by Schaefer, sought to require nationwide retail competition by 2000. States would be free to develop their own programs before that deadline, but if a state did not have a program by then, the FERC would establish retail competition in that state.

The idea of requiring retail competition for all consumers by "a date certain" had strong backing from Bliley.

A second bill (HR 1230), sponsored by Majority Whip Tom DeLay, R-Texas, proposed requiring retail competition by 1999. A third bill (HR 1960), sponsored by Edward J. Markey, D-Mass., sought to leave most decisions on retail competition to the states. Utilities whose territories were not open to retail competition would be barred from serving states with retail competition.

The subcommittee also considered two narrow bills. One (HR 338), sponsored by Cliff Stearns, R-Fla., called for the repeal of a section of the Public Utility Regulatory Policies Act of 1978 (PURPA) that required utilities to buy electricity from independent producers including power generated from wind or solar energy or from co-generation plants that produced steam for industrial use.

The second bill (HR 1359), sponsored by Peter A. DeFazio, D-Ore., sought to amend PURPA to establish a fund to support programs for electric energy conservation, energy efficiency, renewable energy and affordable service for consumers.

The Administration's Position

Elizabeth Anne Moler, deputy secretary of the Department of Energy, told the subcommittee that the administration was still developing its policy on how to promote more retail competition between utilities. FERC Chairman James J. Hoecker said that if there was going to be a federal mandate, Congress should "order such access by a date certain but leave the details of such programs to the states." ■

Senators Offer Plan To Revamp Federal Rule-Making Process

Senate Governmental Affairs Committee Chairman Fred Thompson, R-Tenn., and Carl Levin, D-Mich., a senior committee member, teamed up in 1997 to produce a modest regulatory overhaul bill they hoped would avoid the pitfalls that killed more sweeping proposals in the 104th Congress.

The new bill (S 981) was aimed at refining the process used by federal agencies to write regulations. Lawmakers did not act on it in the first session.

The bill proposed that agencies be required to conduct a peer-reviewed, cost-benefit analysis before issuing any rule that would have an impact on the economy of $100 million or more a year. The agency would have to assess whether the benefits of the rule justified its costs and whether the choice of regulatory action was more cost effective and would provide greater benefits than other options. In addition, risk assessments would be required for proposed federal standards affecting health, safety and the environment.

Senate Democrats who signed on along with Levin included John Glenn of Ohio, ranking Democrat on Governmental Affairs; Charles S. Robb of Virginia; and John D. Rockefeller IV of West Virginia.

Supporters said the bill would not change existing rules or establish a standard for agencies to meet, unlike a bill that senators filibustered in the 104th Congress. While agencies would be required to analyze prospective rules, they could go ahead with a rule that was not found to be cost effective as long as they explained their reasons for doing so.

In the previous Congress, Republicans were forced to abandon sweeping proposals to "tame the regulatory beast," and Democrats were able to capitalize on the GOP's miscues to portray the party as out to gut popular health and environment laws. *(1996 Almanac, p. 3-3)* ■

Property Rights Bill Advances in House

After months of intensive lobbying, home builders and developers won House passage of a bill (HR 1534) designed to give property owners greater access to federal courts and greater clout with local zoning boards.

While the effort had strong backing from Republican leaders in the Senate, there was no action on the bill in that chamber. Senate Judiciary Committee Chairman Orrin G. Hatch, R-Utah, said he hoped to pass a bill in the second session. But the measure also faced a potential Senate filibuster and a veto from the president.

The House bill, passed in October, sought to give landowners and business developers a new legal tool to challenge local zoning laws that prevented them from developing their property. Such laws qualified as "takings" under the Fifth Amendment to the Constitution, which prohibits the federal government from taking property without compensating the property owner.

Under existing law, takings claims were handled primarily by local administrative review panels and state courts. If they did reach the federal courts, bill supporters said, it was only after many years. Under the bill, landowners would be able to go straight to federal court after an appeal to a local administrative board had been denied.

"The sole purpose of this," said House bill sponsor Elton Gallegly, R-Calif., is to give the landowners their day in federal court, as the Constitution requires."

Democratic opponents, however, maintained that the legislation contradicted much of what the GOP had been saying about handing federal powers back to state and local government. They also noted that Republicans were generally critical of what they saw as federal courts usurping powers from elected officials. Yet, in this case, the GOP wanted to hand the same courts broad new powers at the expense of local government in the name of helping landowners.

"It is so obviously contrary to everything my Republican colleagues have been preaching about in the last four years," said Melvin Watt, D-N.C.

One of the developers' biggest complaints about existing law was that it required them to exhaust appeals to planning agency decisions in state courts and be denied compensation before a federal court would hear a Fifth Amendment takings claim. Bill proponents said the process could stretch on for years, forcing average homeowners and developers into legal limbo. It also offered little incentive for planning boards to act expeditiously on building requests. Boards could keep developers at bay by turning down proposals and asking for endless revisions to building plans, proponents argued.

"It turns into a process of gamesmanship," said Nancie G. Marzulla, president and chief legal counsel of Defenders of Property Rights. "The process, particularly at the local zoning level, can go on for years and years and cost thousands of dollars."

Under HR 1534, property owners would have the option of taking their case directly to a federal court after filing at least two appeals to a planning board decision. At least one of the appeals would have to be to an elected body, such as a city council, if available in the locality. Other appeals could be filed to the planning board or other agency with jurisdiction over planning decisions.

Lobbyists for the 190,000-member National Association of Home Builders put on a full court press as the bill reached the House floor, buttonholing members in the corridors and in the dimly lit tunnels under the Capitol as they raced from their offices to vote. The day was the culmination of a months-long campaign by the home builders, which involved everything from helping to write the bill, to organizing grass-roots pressure in members' districts.

Opposing the measure was a hastily assembled coalition of historic preservationists, governors, state and local government federations and environmental groups. The U.S. Judicial Conference also opposed it, saying it would add to the demands on an already overburdened federal bench.

Background

The narrow focus of HR 1534 reflected lessons learned by Western lawmakers and other property rights activists in the 104th Congress, when attempts to enact more sweeping legislation met with defeat. Those bills, including one sponsored by then-Senate Majority Leader Bob Dole, R-Kan., were aimed at compensating owners for government actions that diminished property values. *(1996 Almanac, p. 3-3)*

Property rights advocates argued in 1995 and 1996 that federal regulators were flouting the Fifth Amendment when they imposed money-losing restrictions on property owners but offered no compensation to make up for the losses. But environmentalists prevailed in the 104th Congress using the counter argument that requiring greater compensation would tie agencies in knots. Also, many fiscal conservatives worried the approach would bankrupt agencies with costly compensation claims.

In 1997, the home builders abandoned the compensation tack, focusing instead on a narrower procedural question. Early work on the new bill took place at the office of Linowes and Blocher, a Silver Spring, Md., law firm retained by the association. Any provisions dealing directly with compensation were dropped. Instead, HR 1534 zeroed in on providing property owners more power to get their proposals addressed by local zoning boards.

"We've learned from past experiences," said bill supporter W.J. "Billy" Tauzin, R-La. "You take the victories you can win. It's called incrementalism."

House Action

The House Judiciary Subcommittee on Courts and Intellectual Property approved HR 1534 on Sept. 30 by a 7-4 vote. The full Judiciary Committee followed suit Oct. 7, approving the bill (H Rept 105-323) by a vote of 18-10, with only Steven R. Rothman, D-N.J., crossing party lines to support it.

The House passed the bill Oct. 22 by a vote of 248-178, in the midst of an intense grass-roots lobbying campaign by the home builders. The opposition came from 147 Democrats and 30 Republicans, 16 from the Northeast and 10 from the Midwest. *(Vote 519, p. H-158)*

The floor debate brought out long-festering tensions between Western and Eastern House Republicans. The Westerners had long been frustrated with their Eastern colleagues, who often allied themselves with environmental groups to defeat legislation important to Western constituents.

On the property rights bill, Westerners were not about to brook opposition. They issued a blunt warning to their colleagues: Pass HR 1534, or the Westerners would work to defeat a bill (HR 2247) to reauthorize Amtrak, the national passenger railroad network. The Amtrak bill, which was next on the floor schedule that week, was a priority for many Easterners, whose constituents rode the rails every day. *(Amtrak, p. 3-22)*

Some moderate Republicans, including Sherwood Boehlert of New York, argued that HR 1534 would intrude into local land use planning and would benefit developers at the expense of average citizens. Boehlert tried to delete the provisions that would allow landowners to appeal local land-use decisions in the federal courts, while retaining expedited federal court consideration in land-use disputes that involved the federal government. The amendment was rejected, 178-242. "The home builders flexed their muscles," Boehlert said afterward. *(Vote 518, p. H-158)*

Senate Bill

Paul Coverdell, R-Ga., introduced similar legislation (S 1204) in the Senate. Coverdell's bill also included a provision from a separate bill (HR 992) passed by the House in March and aimed at giving landowners greater leeway in suing the federal government for takings. Under the bill, such suits could be heard either in the U.S. District Court or in the U.S. Court of Federal Claims.

But key Democrats, such as the Judiciary Committee's ranking member, Patrick J. Leahy of Vermont, said the bill would upset a delicate balance between developers and average citizens. "We know this would just trample on the people of the state of Vermont," he said. "It's going to have to be changed considerably before it is considered on the floor." ■

Congress Overhauls Federal-D.C. Ties

After years of being either ignored or lambasted by federal leaders, the District of Columbia saw the promises of GOP leaders and President Clinton come to fruition in 1997, as the two forged a new federal relationship with the nation's capital. After including a plan to take over a host of costly District services in the budget-reconciliation package enacted Aug. 5, Republican leaders agreed to include funding to implement the measure in the fiscal 1998 spending bill for the District.

Under the plan, the federal government assumed responsibility for a highly underfunded pension system for some District workers that had been shifted to the city years before. It picked up 70 percent of the tab for the city's Medicaid program, compared with 50 percent before, and agreed to lend up to $300 million to the city for 10 years.

It also assumed control of the city's prison and court systems and provided three tax incentives for District residents, including a $5,000 tax credit for many first-time home buyers. The Office of Management and Budget (OMB) estimated the plan would cost the federal government — and save the District — $928 million over five years.

In exchange, the city gave up its annual federal payment, although the plan authorized a $190 million stipend to the city for fiscal 1998. Congress eventually provided that amount. Locals had long asserted that the federal payment — $660 million in fiscal 1997 — was not a "gift" but reimbursement for the costs of being the nation's capital, mainly the taxes the city could not collect from the many federal, non-taxable entities located within its borders. But the loss of the federal payment did not draw much response from city officials.

Instead, they concentrated on a provision that they charged nullified any good done by the rest of the plan. It removed the mayor and City Council's control over nine of the city's largest departments, transferring the right to confirm and fire heads of departments to a federally appointed control board created by Congress and Clinton in 1995 to oversee the city's finances. *(1995 Almanac, p. 3-23)*

Democratic Mayor Marion S. Barry Jr., decried the move as a "rape" of democracy, and some city residents futilely demanded that Clinton veto the bill. Eleanor Holmes Norton, the District's Democratic House delegate, said she would introduce legislation to return city officials' powers.

Norton created a stir shortly after the overhaul measure was passed by first calling the plan "a big win for the District" and then speaking out strongly against plans to reduce the city's powers over major departments.

In an effort to ease city concerns, the D.C. appropriations bill contained a provision stating that the City Council retained the power to reject Barry's appointments.

Legislative Action

A District aid bill initially was thought to face a long, hard road. It was generally assumed that a stand-alone bill to assist the nation's capital would be caricatured as a giveaway to a city that had become a symbol of wasteful government, as well as a sign of an "inside the Beltway" mentality on Capitol Hill. So the city's advocates looked for a legislative train to carry their plan. Late July 29, they succeeded in grabbing hold of the budget-reconciliation caboose. Sen. John W. Warner, R-Va., who was most interested in a provision to close the District's much maligned Lorton prison in Northern Virginia, declared, "It's on a train which is going to move, which is going to become law."

It would not have gotten there without a lot of help.

Putting the Plan Together

The blueprint for the "D.C. rescue plan" came in Clinton's fiscal 1998 budget request in February. White House budget director Franklin D. Raines, a one-time D.C. financial adviser, determined that the District needed an entity to act as its "state government" by taking greater responsibility for Medicaid health insurance, criminal justice and other programs. In exchange, the federal government would discontinue its annual payment to the city and demand changes in city ordinances.

The House Government Reform and Oversight Committee's District of Columbia Subcommittee pared back the plan June 19 and added a provision to provide a $140 million federal payment to the city in fiscal 1998.

Congressional leaders agreed to form several discussion groups on different provisions relating to the District, such as management initiatives and the debt provisions. Sen. Connie Mack, R-Fla., was appointed to oversee the efforts. But lawmakers made little headway in three weeks of discussions, and a proposal by Senate D.C. Appropriations Subcommittee Chairman Lauch Faircloth, R-N.C., to install a city manager to run the District government threatened to derail the whole plan. Norton, who had earned bipartisan respect on city issues, fought that proposal. "I convinced members who wanted a city manager that it was unworkable," she said later.

Other issues also needed to be resolved. Virginia lawmakers demanded that Lorton be closed, while Sam Brownback, R-Kan., chairman of the D.C. subcommittee of the Senate Governmental Affairs Committee, insisted that the District contract out its prison operations to the private sector. Brownback and Norton joined to push her plan to cut federal taxes in the city.

At that point, House Speaker Newt Gingrich, R-Ga., Senate Majority Leader Trent Lott, R-Miss., and Clinton administration officials stepped in to work out the details. The package, which came together in the last hours of the budget negotiations, provided unprecedented federal aid for the city. But it also stripped power from the District's elected government, including the controversial Barry, and gave the financial control board wide latitude to reorganize the city's troubled bureaucracy.

Barry and the City Council would have to give up power over nine major city departments. The control board would approve nominees to run the departments, and only the board could fire them. Consultants would be hired to recommend and implement changes to departments.

Barry charged that Republicans were trying to "re-colonize" the District by undoing the home rule system in effect since 1973. He singled out Faircloth for the harshest criticism, saying he "has raped democracy and freedom."

But others said Barry prompted the takeover by failing to cooperate with the control board until it was painfully clear he had no other option. "He brought it on himself," said Thomas M. Davis III, R-Va., chairman of the House Governmental Reform and Oversight D.C. subcommittee.

"I think all of us have to regard this as a statement on how the District was run," Norton said, though she insisted that Republicans had never mentioned Barry by name during the negotiations.

Details of the Overhaul

The plan for overhauling the District was split, with some provisions appearing in the reconciliation spending bill (HR 2015 — PL 105-33), and others enacted as part of the companion tax bill (HR 2014 — PL 105-34). *(Spending, p. 2-30; taxes, p. 2-47)*

Under the legislation, the federal government agreed to:

- Resume responsibility after 18 years for a fund that provided pensions to city police officers, firefighters and teachers. The fund's liabilities exceeded available resources by nearly $5 billion.
- Pay 70 percent of the cost of the District's Medicaid program, up from 50 percent.
- Provide a $190 million federal payment in fiscal 1998. Such payments were not guaranteed in future years.
- Lend the city up to $300 million for a 10-year period.
- Transfer prison administration to the Federal Bureau of Prisons, with the Lorton facility to close by 2002. Half the prison population would have to be sent to privately run facilities. A seven-member board headed by a Justice Department designee would recommend changes to the District's sentencing guidelines.
- Provide a $5,000 tax credit for single first-time home buyers with adjusted gross incomes of less than $70,000 and joint filers with adjusted gross incomes of less than $110,000.
- Include much of the city in a new enterprise zone. Employers who moved into the zone would be eligible for a 20 percent wage credit. Capital gains on sales of business property in such neighborhoods was reduced to zero.

Appropriators Lend Support

At the request of the leadership, House and Senate appropriators waited until plans to revamp the federal-District relationship were completed before marking up the fiscal 1998 District of Columbia appropriations bill. As a result, the spending bill implemented many of the planned changes. It provided a total of $855 million in federal funds for the District, $136 million more than the fiscal 1997 level and $78 million more than Clinton had requested.

Of the total, only $190 million went directly to the city. The remaining $665 million went to the agencies and trustees charged with assuming responsibility for courts, prisons and other city services. The bill was signed into law Oct. 10 (HR 2607 — PL 105-100). *(Appropriations, p. 9-27)* ■

House Committee OKs Bill for Puerto Rico Referendum

The House Resources Committee approved a bill May 21 that would allow residents of the U.S. commonwealth of Puerto Rico to vote in 1998 on their political destiny.

The bill (HR 856 — H Rept 105-131, Part 1), approved 43-1, would require a referendum by Dec. 31, 1998, in which Puerto Ricans could vote to continue their commonwealth relationship with the United States, support independence or seek statehood.

A vote for statehood would require the president to submit legislation to Congress that would allow for a transition plan spanning no more than 10 years. If voters chose independence, a constitutional convention would be held on the island. If the commonwealth status prevailed, a new referendum would be held every 10 years.

Puerto Rico's House delegate, Democrat Carlos Romero-Barceló, spoke in support of the bill during the markup. He said the referendum would put to rest a "misrepresentation" perpetuated by the United States since 1950 that Puerto Rico had fiscal autonomy and its people had full U.S. citizenship. "The fact is that ours is a colonial relationship that clearly contradicts the basic tenets of democracy and full self-government," Romero-Barceló said.

He was backed by Resources Committee Chairman Don Young, R-Alaska, the bill's sponsor. "It is time for Congress to permit democracy to fully develop in Puerto Rico," Young said.

Before the committee approved the bill, it rejected, 10-32, an amendment by George Miller, D-Calif., that would have broadened the definition of commonwealth status to allow greater Puerto Rican autonomy. Miller said HR 856 did not fairly represent the views of the island's Commonwealth Party leaders.

"None of us would tolerate allowing our political opponents to define our views on the ballot," Miller said. But Romero-Barceló said Miller's amendment was misleading, proposing benefits from commonwealth status that Congress would never enact as law.

W.J. "Billy" Tauzin, R-La., underscored the point, calling Miller's definition of commonwealth too generous. Tauzin interpreted Miller's amendment as specifying that federal benefits to residents of Puerto Rico would have to be comparable to those received by other Americans, though Puerto Ricans did not face tax obligations equal to those of other Americans. "This would be an extraordinary option for the people of Puerto Rico," Tauzin said. "Who wouldn't accept it?"

The committee had approved a similar bill in 1996, but Young pulled it from the House floor after a dispute over a proposal by Rules Committee Chairman Gerald B.H. Solomon, R-N.Y., to require that English be the official language in Puerto Rico. *(1996 Almanac, p. 3-8)*

Puerto Rico was ceded to the United States in 1898 under the treaty ending the Spanish-American War. Puerto Ricans were granted U.S. citizenship in 1917, and the island became a U.S. commonwealth in 1952.

In a nonbinding election held in 1993, 49 percent of Puerto Ricans who voted chose to keep the island as a territory. Those voters chose an "enhanced commonwealth" status, which would allow Puerto Ricans to collect federal benefits such as food stamps and Social Security but would exempt them from federal taxes. Another 46 percent chose statehood, and 4 percent voted for independence. ■

Product Liability Bill Loses Momentum

Advocates of overhauling federal product liability law came close to reaching a compromise with the White House in the fall, but as time ran out on the session so did the steam that had been driving a potential deal.

The legislation sought to limit manufacturers' legal liability for injuries or deaths caused by their products. The Senate Commerce, Science and Transportation Committee had approved an early version (S 648) in May, but that bill was simply viewed as a starting point for negotiations. A compromise appeared possible after John D. Rockefeller IV, D-W.Va., the Senate's chief proponent of product liability overhaul, negotiated a draft bill with the White House.

The draft, details of which emerged in the fall, was narrower in scope than a 1996 bill that had drawn a veto from President Clinton. Business leaders and others expressed disappointment with the revisions, but Rockefeller insisted the White House would not move much beyond the measure he had negotiated.

Slade Gorton, R-Wash., the Senate GOP's point man on the issue, developed a counteroffer, but negotiations over that version were stalled at the end of the session.

When it became clear that a product liability bill would not be completed before Congress adjourned for the year, some representatives of the health manufacturing industry tried to move provisions on biomaterials as a separate bill. The legislation sought to make it more difficult to sue suppliers who provided raw materials for medical devices. A House subcommittee marked up the bill (HR 872), but Rockefeller opposed moving it and it went no further. Rockefeller was concerned that it could derail prospects for passing a broader product liability bill in the second session.

Background

The policy battle over product liability had raged for nearly two decades.

Most Republican lawmakers and some business-oriented Democrats said multimillion-dollar judgments in product liability cases, and the high insurance costs businesses had to carry to defend against them, were a job-killing drag on the economy. They also maintained that concern over potential litigation had helped drive manufacturers and suppliers of raw materials out of the market for some products, a problem they said was particularly acute in the medical devices industry.

Opponents, led by trial lawyers and some consumer groups, argued that limiting awards in such cases would damage protections for consumers against injury or death caused by the negligence of product manufacturers or marketers. Critics also objected to the federal government interfering in an area they said was being adequately handled by states, many of which allowed larger awards than would be permitted under the federal proposal.

GOP Bill Vetoed in 104th Congress

Having made "tort reform" part of their 1994 "Contract With America" manifesto, House Republicans moved quickly in 1995, passing a broad bill that included limits on medical malpractice awards and would have applied to all civil cases, not just product liability. As with other planks in their contract, the legislation ran into trouble in the Senate, which passed a less far-reaching measure that was limited to product liability cases.

House negotiators initially held out for their version, but they ultimately were forced to accept the narrower Senate bill to avoid a repeat of the Democratic-led filibusters that had prevented any product liability bill from even getting past the Senate floor prior to the 104th Congress.

The final bill, cleared in March 1996, was still unacceptable to Clinton, who said it would go too far in denying injured parties their day in court. The bill would have pre-empted the existing patchwork of state and local laws governing product liability and placed limits on punitive damage awards, which were intended to punish negligent behavior.

Punitive damages against big businesses would have been limited to the greater of $250,000 or two times the total of economic damages, such as lost wages, and non-economic damages, such as pain and suffering. The cap for small businesses would have been the lesser of the two limits.

Clinton vetoed the bill May 2, 1996, saying that it "inappropriately intrudes on state authority and does so in a way that tilts the legal playing field against consumers." His specific objections included the imposition of "arbitrary ceilings on punitive damages" and a proposal to eliminate joint liability for noneconomic damages such as pain and suffering. Under joint liability, each company in a multi-company suit could be held liable for all the damages, regardless of how much they contributed to the plaintiff's injuries.

However, Clinton left the door open by saying he could support "real common sense product liability reform." *(1996 Almanac, p. 3-9)*

Legislative Action

In 1997, Senate Republican leaders included product liability legislation among their top 10 agenda items for the 105th Congress. "We owe it to the American people to try again," Senate Majority Leader Trent Lott, R-Miss., said in January. In contrast to their aggressive approach in the 104th Congress, House leaders waited for the Senate to make the first move and provide an indication of the type of bill it would accept.

On May 1, the Senate Commerce, Science and Transportation Committee approved a modified version of the vetoed 1996 bill. The new measure (S 648 — S Rept 105-32), introduced by Gorton, was approved on a 11-9 party-line vote, without amendments. However, it did not have the support of Rockefeller.

Rockefeller said S 648 did not address the major issues that Clinton had outlined in his veto. He insisted that supporters craft a bill that would not only pass Congress, but also gain Clinton's signature. "I look at this as kind of a work in progress," he said. "I look at my vote today as trying to say this bill won't get us there."

Like the vetoed bill, S 648 proposed to cap punitive damage awards against big businesses at the greater of $250,000 or two times the total of economic damages such as lost wages and non-economic damages such as pain and suffering. The cap for small businesses would be the lesser of the two limits.

Gorton attempted to fix some of the lesser problems cited by Clinton. For example, the authors made it clear the bill would not set limits on damages in "negligent entrustment" cases, those involving businesses that sold items such as guns or liquor to people who later caused harm with those products.

S 648 also attempted to assuage the White House by exempting cases involving silicone breast implants from a title in the bill limiting lawsuits against suppliers of raw materials. That title would allow dismissal of faulty-product claims against a raw material supplier when the supplier provided materials as specified and could not also be classified as the seller or manufacturer of the product.

But Rockefeller and Byron L. Dorgan, D-N.D., both of whom had supported the 1995 bill, said S 648 raised new points of conflict. For example, while S 648 extended the proposed deadline for filing a product liability suit from 15 years in the 1996 bill, to 18 years after the product had been delivered, Rockefeller and Dorgan said it would apply time limits to all products, not just durable goods as in the earlier bill.

Rockefeller warned repeatedly that supporters would not get the number of Democratic votes needed to end a likely filibuster of the bill unless further changes were made to S 648. The point was not lost on Gorton and others. "I know this is not the final version of this proposal," Gorton said.

Rockefeller Seeks a Middle Ground

In early October, key Republicans met with administration officials to discuss a compromise that Rockefeller and the White House had been working on for several months. The draft was much narrower than S 648. For example, it called for caps on punitive damage awards only against small businesses. Republicans pushed for changes, but Rockefeller urged them to take what they could get from Clinton, given that the administration would be happy with no bill. "President Clinton will not lose a millisecond of a night's sleep if they walk away from the whole thing," he said.

Republicans came back with a counteroffer, reflecting the concerns that Republicans and business leaders had with Rockefeller's bill, but the negotiations stalled over a handful of issues, including language concerning liability in accidents involving drunken drivers who were injured. Business leaders wanted to make sure that a drunken driver could not seek damages from an automaker if he or she caused the accident.

Stand-Alone Bill

On Sept. 11, a House Judiciary subcommittee approved a narrow measure (HR 872) aimed at making it more difficult to sue suppliers of raw materials for liability in cases involving medical devices. The Commercial and Administrative Law Subcommittee approved the bill, sponsored by subcommittee Chairman George W. Gekas, R-Pa., by voice vote.

Supporters said the legislation was necessary to ensure that materials were available for medical devices. Gekas and others said many suppliers of medical devices had stopped providing raw materials for such products because of the high costs of liability insurance.

Under the bill, suppliers could be dismissed from a liability case if the material used in a medical device met the manufacturer's requirement and the supplier did not make or sell the whole product. Clinton had cited similar provisions in his list of objections to the vetoed 1996 bill. He expressed concern that the legislation would shield from liability even suppliers who were found to bear some responsibility for an injury from a medical device.

The bill excluded cases involving breast implants, an exemption not in the earlier bill.

Before approving HR 872, the subcommittee adopted by voice vote a substitute amendment that would create a post-trial process allowing a plaintiff or manufacturer to file a motion to bring a supplier back into a case if evidence surfaced showing that the supplier had been negligent.

Jerrold Nadler of New York, the panel's ranking Democrat, said that while the amendment improved the legislation, he was concerned that evidence showing that a supplier was negligent could be ruled as irrelevant before the supplier was brought back into the case. As a result, the manufacturer or plaintiff would have a more difficult time proving the supplier's negligence in court, said Nadler, who opposed the bill in subcommittee.

Some panel Democrats who support HR 872 said they would oppose attempts to attach it to a broader product liability bill. "The last thing in the world we ought to do to this bill is fold it into a product liability bill, because if we do that, this bill . . . will remain just that, a bill, rather than having it become law," said Martin T. Meehan of Massachusetts.

Further action on the smaller bill was thwarted the week of Nov. 3, when Rockefeller said he would block it from coming to the Senate floor. "Any effort to move biomaterials will make passage of product liability much less possible because we need in the product liability bill all those factors that can appeal to people," Rockefeller said. ■

Patent Overhaul Sparks Lively Debate

The House voted in April to alter the way patents were granted and reviewed — but only after critics significantly scaled back a controversial provision that would have required the publication of all patent applications 18 months after they were filed. Under existing law, patents remained confidential until they were granted. The Senate Judiciary Committee approved a companion bill (S 507), but it went no further in the first session.

The House-passed bill (HR 400) exempted small businesses, independent inventors and universities from the advance publication requirement. Critics argued that allowing publication after 18 months would give foreign companies and others the opportunity to "steal" the ideas of U.S. inventors, and also allow big businesses to prey on small companies and independent inventors.

Supporters of the original provision said it was needed to bring intellectual property protections in the United States into line with those in the rest of the industrialized world.

Other provisions of HR 400 included converting the U.S. Patent and Trademark Office from a division of the Commerce Department into a wholly owned government corporation. The office's managers would run its daily activities without the supervision of a government agency but would still be subject to policy direction by the Commerce secretary and the White House.

The patent office, which did not receive tax dollars, would be allowed to keep all the money it collected through applications and user fees. Under existing law, some of the money was diverted to other government agencies.

BOXSCORE

Patent Overhaul — HR 400, S 507. The bills proposed converting the patent office into a wholly owned government corporation and limiting the confidentiality of some patent applications.

Reports: H Rept 105-39, S Rept 105-42.

KEY ACTION

April 23 — House passed HR 400 by voice vote.

May 22 — Senate Judiciary Committee approved HR 400 by voice vote, after substituting the text of S 507.

House Committee

The House Judiciary Subcommittee on Courts and Intellectual Property approved HR 400 by voice vote March 5. The full Judiciary Committee followed suit March 12, also by voice vote (H Rept 105-39).

The legislation sponsored by subcommittee Chairman Howard Coble, R-N.C., contained provisions requiring that patent requests be published 18 months after they were filed, and that the patent office become a wholly owned government corporation.

The subcommittee added the proposal to allow the patent office to retain all money it received from application and user fees, blocking a Clinton administration proposal to divert $92 million in fees from the patent office to other parts of the budget in fiscal 1998. Coble called President Clinton's plan an "unwarranted tax on innovation."

The attempt to allow publication of patent proposals 18 months after they were filed drew the criticism of a group of lawmakers led by Dana Rohrabacher, R-Calif., who argued that it would weaken the ability of American inventors to protect their innovations. Rohrabacher referred to the bill as the "Steal American Technology Act."

Supporters of the legislation countered that, in addition to making U.S. patent law more compatible with that of many other industrialized countries, the provision would allow U.S. companies to more quickly utilize technological advances — including those for which patents were never granted.

House Floor Action

The House passed HR 400 by voice vote April 23 with all but the advance publication provision intact.

Members had begun work on the bill April 17. At that time, supporters successfully fended off an attempt by Rohrabacher to scrap the committee-approved 18-month advance publication requirement. But before completing action on the legislation April 23, the House reversed itself, agreeing to much of what Rohrabacher and other critics wanted.

Early Publication Survives First Test

In a victory for bill supporters, the House on April 17 defeated, 178-227, a substitute amendment offered by Rohrabacher that would have dropped the 18-month limit on confidentiality. *(Vote 85, p. H-28)*

The amendment, introduced earlier as a separate bill (HR 811), also would have changed the term of a patent. Under existing law, a patent was good for 20 years from the date the application was filed. Rohrabacher proposed giving inventors patent protection for 17 years from the date a patent was granted or 20 years from the date of filing, whichever was later.

Rohrabacher argued unsuccessfully that the bill would give individuals and foreign businesses too easy access to the ideas of American inventors.

Bill supporters argued that the 18-month limit was aimed at ending "submarine patenting," a practice involving the deliberate delay by the applicant of the issuance of a patent for several years and constant changing of the claims to cover a developing technology, in order to extract money from those who came to depend on the technology. "The only way to effectively dispel . . . gaming of the system is to expose the applicant to publication after a reasonable length of time," said Judiciary Committee Chairman Henry J. Hyde, R-Ill.

Backers of HR 400 also said the publication provision would help U.S. companies. Because most foreign countries published patent applications after 18 months, they said, foreign competitors had access to U.S. technology in their native tongue. But under existing U.S. law, foreign companies did not have to reveal their technology innovations in the United States until their patents were granted.

"Foreign companies are . . . able to study our latest technological developments abroad, but are not required to reveal their work to our inventors on these same terms here," said Coble. "Eighteen-month publication therefore levels the international playing field."

"Don't be fooled by this idea that you have to cut your limb off to cure the hangnail," Rohrabacher responded. He said his substitute addressed the submarine patenting problem, but without jeopardizing the rights of the inventor. HR 400's supporters said Rohrabacher's plan had too many loopholes.

Opponents of HR 400 also objected on a number of other grounds. They said the bill's supporters were trying to change a system that worked, in order to please big corporations at the expense of the little guy. They said the bill would "corporatize" the patent office by turning it into a government-owned corporation.

"Don't fix a system that isn't broken," said Democrat Marcy Kaptur of Ohio.

The House gave voice vote approval April 17 to an amendment aimed at accommodating the concerns of small businesses and inventors. The amendment provided for a three-month delay in publishing patent requests made by small businesses and inventors in cases when the inventor had received at least two determinations indicating whether the patent would be granted. Backers said this would allow inventors who knew their requests would not be approved to withdraw their patent applications and avoid publication.

Supporters also noted that the bill would allow patent holders to sue for patent infringement after their patent was granted if someone tried to commercialize their idea between the time their patent was published and the date it was granted. Under existing law, inventors were eligible for royalties from the use of their inventions only after patents were granted.

Fighting Internet Theft

A bill signed into law Dec. 16 criminalized the piracy of copyrighted works on the Internet. The legislation (HR 2265 — PL 105-147) prohibited unlawful electronic transmission of copyrighted works for "commercial advantage or financial gain." The definition of "financial gain" included the value of the copyrighted work itself, making it illegal to give away software, for example.

Howard Coble, R-N.C., chairman of the House Judiciary Subcommittee on Courts and Intellectual Property, said the bill would help reduce the nearly $20 billion in royalty fees lost to unlawful software, music and movie distribution in 1997. Coble said previous copyright law was insufficient to address these problems because it did not specifically criminalize transferring copyrighted material via computer. In addition, much Internet piracy involved material that was given away, not sold for profit. Those offenses also were not covered by previous law, he said.

The new law made it a crime to steal one or more copies of one or more copyrighted works having a total retail value of $1,000, or to reproduce or distribute 10 or more copies of one or more copyrighted works, having a total retail value of $2,500 or more. Violators would be subject to up to $250,000 in fines and prison terms of up to six years.

The bill did not address the issue of who was liable when the Internet was used for criminal purposes. Coble introduced a separate bill that covered that subject, but it did not get beyond the hearing stage in 1997.

HR 2265, introduced by Robert W. Goodlatte, R-Va., began in the House Judiciary Subcommittee on Courts and Intellectual Property, which approved it by voice vote Sept. 30. The panel adopted an amendment, also by voice vote, specifying that the bill was intended only to address "willful misconduct" and reducing the retail value threshold to $2,500 from $5,000 under the original bill, among other changes.

The full Judiciary Committee approved the bill by voice vote Oct. 7 (H Rept 105-339) after loosening the definition of crime to cover theft and distribution of information even if it was given away.

The House passed the bill by voice vote Nov. 4 under suspension of the rules, and the Senate cleared it Nov. 13, also by voice vote.

Key Provision Watered Down

However, in a surprising turnaround April 23, the House adopted an amendment by Kaptur to bar publication of patent applications by small businesses, independent inventors and universities until the patents were granted. The vote was 220-193. Lawmakers on both sides of the issue said the fact that Kaptur was a Democrat aided the amendment. It received 36 more Democratic votes than did Rohrabacher's. *(Vote 88, p. H-30)*

Kaptur and others argued that allowing publication after 18 months would give foreign companies and others the opportunity to "steal" the ideas of U.S. inventors, and also allow big businesses to prey on small companies and independent inventors. The amendment also removed a provision that opponents said would expand opportunities for third parties to challenge the validity of U.S. patents.

Adoption of the amendment was a coup for bill opponents, who had appeared defeated the week before when they tried to kill the entire provision. This is the victory of the "little guy over the big guy," Rohrabacher said after Kaptur's amendment passed.

Kaptur and her supporters said her amendment would address submarine patenting by establishing circumstances under which a patent could be published early. Kaptur and others argued that while submarine patenting did occur, the problem was not as great as HR 400's supporters maintained. "They tried to make it the whole issue," Kaptur said.

Opponents of submarine patenting said that Kaptur's language, which was similar to Rohrabacher's, still provided too many loopholes.

Other Amendments Defeated

The House rejected three other attempts to amend HR 400.

➤ The first, by Tom Campbell, R-Calif., addressed the "prior use" provision, which would allow anyone who had been using an invention commercially before a patent was filed to continue using it, even after a patent was granted. Campbell's amendment, defeated 185-224, sought to limit, in scope and volume, the prior user's right to use the patented technology. *(Vote 86, p. H-30)*

➤ The second, also by Campbell, would have restricted publication of a patent application until there had been two substantive actions by the patent office that indicated whether it intended to grant the patent. The amendment was rejected 167-242. *(Vote 87, p. H-30)*

➤ The third, by Duncan Hunter, R-Calif., proposed to remove the patent office from deficit calculations, exempt it from federal full-time-equivalent employee requirements and require patent office employees to spend at least 5 percent of their annual work time in training. It was rejected, 133-280. *(Vote 89, p. H-30)*

Senate Committee

Following the lead of the House, the Senate Judiciary Committee on May 22 approved a bill to revamp the nation's patent system, after making changes to address concerns about its potential effect on independent inventors and small businesses. The committee approved the bill (S 507 — S Rept 105-42) by voice vote. The panel then called up HR 400 and agreed by voice vote to replace its text with that of S 507 as amended.

Before approving the bill, the committee adopted a substitute amendment by Chairman Orrin G. Hatch, R-Utah, and ranking Democrat Patrick J. Leahy of Vermont aimed at bringing the measure more in line with the House-passed bill. Originally, S 507 had included the requirement that patent applications be published 18 months after they were filed, regardless of whether a patent had been granted.

The substitute allowed for patent seekers who certified that they were filing for patents only in the United States and not overseas to keep their applications secret until they were granted. All others would be subject to the 18-month requirement.

The bill would allow patent holders to sue for royalties if someone attempted to market their ideas between the time their patents were published and granted. Opponents argued that small businesses and independent inventors did not have the resources to fight for their rights in court.

Some opponents remained unhappy with other portions of the bill, including the proposal to convert the Patent and Trademark Office into a wholly owned government corporation. "It's a bad bill, and we're not going to retreat on it," said Kevin DeLaney, president of the National Patent Association, a group of inventors formed to oppose the legislation.

The committee also gave voice vote approval to an amendment by Charles E. Grassley, R-Iowa, that deleted language from the bill aimed at excluding hospitals and health maintenance organizations (HMOs) from a statute that allowed HMOs, hospitals and doctors to avoid paying royalties for using patented medical procedures. ■

Lawmakers Reauthorize Several SBA Programs

Congress cleared legislation reauthorizing a number of Small Business Administration (SBA) programs through fiscal 2000, including $12 billion in fiscal 1998 for the SBA's popular "7(a)" general business loan program. Other provisions established a microloan program for former welfare recipients, provided incentives for small businesses to locate in low-income areas and permitted the SBA to conduct criminal background checks on applicants for certain loan programs.

President Clinton signed the measure into law Dec. 2 (S 1139 — PL 105-135).

The bill, sponsored by Christopher S. Bond, R-Mo., began in the Senate, where it won approval from the Small Business Committee on an 18-0 vote June 26 (S Rept 105-62). The full Senate passed the measure Sept. 9 by voice vote.

In the House, the Small Business Committee marked up its own version of the bill (HR 2261 — H Rept 105-246), approving it June 30 by voice vote.

Two significant provisions were added to the bill in committee. The first proposed that the SBA be allowed to accept money from other federal agencies to provide additional grants to microloan borrowers who were on welfare. The second would direct existing SBA aid programs to provide counseling to small businesses that had been hurt by the North American Free Trade Agreement (NAFTA) or by the relocation of jobs overseas for any reason.

The House passed the bill Sept. 29 by a vote of 397-17. It then substituted the text for that of S 1139 and passed the amended Senate bill by voice vote. *(Vote 463, p. H-140)*

Rather than hold a conference to resolve their differences, members held informal negotiations, opting to use the original text of S 1139, with only a few provisions added from the House version of the bill. The Senate approved the compromise by voice vote Oct. 31. The House agreed to the changes Nov. 9, clearing the bill by voice vote.

Major Provisions

The SBA bill included provisions to:

- **7(a) business loan program.** Authorize $39.5 billion over three years for the 7(a) program, which helped small businesses get access to loans that would otherwise be unavailable to them. The program guaranteed to pay part of any loss sustained by the lender.
- **Long-term development loans.** Authorize $11 billion over three years for the "504" program, which guaranteed long-term loans for capital improvements and equipment.
- **Microloans.** Make permanent the SBA's existing microloan program, which worked through community nonprofit organizations to provide small-business entrepreneurs with short-term loans of up to $25,000. The program also provided technical assistance, such as information on account-

ing, marketing and advertising.

In addition, the bill established a three-year program to extend similar loans and technical assistance to former welfare recipients in an effort to help them start businesses and stay off government assistance. The program included some business training and encouraged supplemental grants from other sources to help cover the recipients' child care and transportation expenses.

- **'HUBZones.'** Create a program to encourage small businesses to locate in economically disadvantaged inner-city and rural areas defined as historically underutilized business zones, or "HUBZones." Inner-city HUBZones were areas where 50 percent or more of the households had incomes of less than 60 percent of the median income for the larger metropolitan area. Rural HUBZones comprised areas where household income was less than 80 percent of the median rural income.

The bill permitted federal agencies to give preference to "qualified HUBZone small business concerns" in procurement contracts. For example, if at least two HUBZone small businesses bid on a contract worth more than $100,000, then an agency could limit the competition to HUBZone small businesses.

When there was only one such bid, the bill encouraged federal agencies to award sole-source contracts to HUBZone small businesses, if the award could be made at a fair and reasonable price.

The HUBZone provisions had been approved, 18-0, by the Committee on Small Business and subsequently added to the bill. The administration objected to the proposals, which were not in the House version, saying they would draw funding away from other SBA programs.

- **Women-owned businesses.** Authorize $8 million a year for Women's Business Centers, which provided information and assistance to female business owners. The bill also expanded the number of federal agencies that participated in a contracting preference program, and added five members to the National Women's Business Council Board in an effort to increase private-sector participation.
- **Criminal background checks.** Permit the SBA to conduct criminal background checks on loan applicants for the 7(a) and 504 programs, using the best available means. The House version would have required the checks.
- **Contract 'bundling.'** Define "bundling" of federal contracts, a practice of consolidating several smaller contracts into one large contract, and grant the SBA greater authority to challenge such contract consolidations. Critics said the practice of bundling often precluded small businesses from competing for government work because it made jobs too large for them to bid on.
- **NAFTA aid.** Direct the SBA to offer specific assistance to small businesses hurt by NAFTA. ■

Baseball Antitrust Exemption

On an 11-6 vote and after months of delay, the Senate Judiciary Committee on July 31 approved a bill (S 53 — S Rept 105-118) to partially lift the antitrust exemption that had governed major-league baseball for more than 70 years. Although the legislation was based on an agreement between team owners and players, the owners opposed it, and it went no further in 1997.

The bill sought to end the antitrust exemption as it applied to labor talks, without affecting other key aspects of professional baseball, such as team franchise relocations, the ties between the major and minor leagues, and broadcasting rights.

The exemption dated to a 1922 Supreme Court decision, *Federal Baseball Club v. National League*. In that case, a unanimous court held that professional baseball was a sport involving state exhibitions, not a business spawning interstate commerce within the meaning of the antitrust laws. The exemption prevented players from going to court on antitrust grounds if the owners imposed unilateral conditions, such as a salary cap.

Major-league players and owners — whose adversarial relationship resulted in a strike that forced cancellation of the 1994 World Series and delayed the 1995 season — had concurred as part of a 1996 collective bargaining agreement to seek legislation providing a limited rollback of the antitrust exemption. A markup of S 53 was scheduled and postponed several times to give major-league team owners and players a chance to agree on bill provisions.

Although the two parties reached a compromise in June, the owners drew back, saying the legislation did not specify clearly enough that the minor leagues' antitrust exemption would remain intact.

During the markup, bill sponsor and committee Chairman Orrin G. Hatch, R-Utah, offered an amendment clarifying that the bill was not intended to address the antitrust status of the minor leagues. Though it was adopted, the owners still did not support the bill.

Hatch said his amendment addressed the concerns about the minor leagues, "and then some." But ranking Democrat Joseph R. Biden Jr. of Delaware — whose home city of Wilmington hosted a minor-league affiliate of the Kansas City Royals — warned that the bill was "paving the road to hell" because it could weaken the binding relationship between minor-league teams and their major-league sponsors.

Hatch had won his committee's approval for a similar bill in 1995, but it went no further in the 104th Congress. *(1995 Almanac, p. 3-45)* ■

Armored Car Guards

The House passed a bill Feb. 26 aimed at making it easier for armored car guards to carry their guns across state lines. The legislation (HR 624), which passed 416-0, was the second attempt in as many years to amend the 1993 Armored Car Industry Reciprocity Act (PL 103-55). *(Vote 25, p. H-10)*

The 1993 law was intended to relieve guards of having to obtain a separate permit from each state they entered. It required states to recognize weapons permits issued by another state to armored car guards if the issuing state required annual criminal background checks and firearms training. However, only five states met the law's eligibility requirements for reciprocity. Most, for example, renewed their permits every two years to cut costs.

Under HR 624, the permits could be renewed every two years. In addition, states would only have to conduct a criminal background check when an individual first applied for a license. The 1993 law ordered such checks for renewals as well. The bill clarified that states, not third-party entities, should conduct the background checks.

The bill had won voice-vote approval from the Commerce Committee's Telecommunications, Trade and Consumer Protection Subcommittee on Feb. 11, and from the full panel Feb. 13 (H Rept 105-6).

Bill sponsor Edward Whitfield, R-Ky., had won House passage for a similar bill in 1996, but the Senate did not act on it in the press of business at the end of the session. *(1996 Almanac, p. 3-13)* ■

Highway Bill Showdown Postponed

Congress' struggle to reauthorize the nation's pre-eminent transportation law ended for the year Nov. 12 with a $9.8 billion rain check and a "wait until next year."

Lawmakers' inability to pass a long-term extension of the 1991 Intermodal Surface Transportation Efficiency Act was seen by state and local governments — and by many members of Congress themselves — as the most glaring failure of the legislative year.

Reauthorizing the landmark six-year law known as ISTEA (pronounced "ice tea") was considered a must when the 105th Congress convened in January. The law, which was due to expire Sept. 30, authorized the federal funding of virtually all highway, bridge and mass transit construction and maintenance programs, as well as traffic safety efforts and other surface transportation projects.

Unlike other federal programs that could get new federal funding through appropriations bills even if the authorization for them had expired, federal highway programs were directly funded through so-called contract authority that was part of the highway bill itself.

Without a successor, the Federal Highway Administration was expected to shut down by January 1998. Although most states would have unspent federal money and state reserves to get their highway construction projects through the first of the year, no new long-range road contracts could be signed. Smaller states that were more reliant on federal highways than local roads and lacked flexibility to use local money would be especially hard hit.

Even with so much advance notice, however, Congress could not overcome all the obstacles — some anticipated, some not.

Instead, in the final days of the session, lawmakers agreed to a $9.8 billion short-term extension of existing law that included about $5.5 billion in new highway money. The stop-gap measure was expected to help the states financially until the spring of 1998, when Congress hoped to finish a new long-term bill.

BOXSCORE

Highway and Transit Reauthorization — HR 2400, S 1173. The bills provided for a six-year reauthorization of the 1991 Intermodal Surface Transportation Efficiency Act (ISTEA). Pending enactment, Congress cleared S 1519 (PL 105-130), which provided a $9.8 billion short-term extension of existing law.

Report: S Rept 105-95 (S 1173).

KEY ACTION

Sept. 24 — House committee marked up, but did not report, HR 2400.

Oct. 28 — Senate rejected fourth cloture motion; S 1173 pulled from the floor for the year.

A Year-Long Struggle

The job of drafting bipartisan ISTEA bills that could get out of the House and Senate committees of primary jurisdiction took most of the legislative year.

The effort came close to exploding in the House, where Transportation and Infrastructure Committee Chairman Bud Shuster, R-Pa., pushed a six-year $218.3 billion bill (HR 2400) that threatened to shatter spending limits established by the bipartisan balanced-budget agreement reached in May. As part of that plan, Clinton and congressional leaders agreed to cap highway spending at $22 billion a year and limit overall spending on transportation to roughly $29.5 billion a year.

House Speaker Newt Gingrich, R-Ga., refused to bring Shuster's bill to the floor, and Shuster refused to scale it back, hoping instead that a roaring economy would hold down social spending and bring in greater tax receipts than were anticipated when the budget deal was concluded. Those extra dollars would not be secured until 1998.

In the Senate, committee leaders were committed to staying within the limits set in the budget deal. As a result, they produced a much smaller six-year bill (S 1173) with $145 billion for highways and $35.7 billion for transit.

While House committee leaders tried to give virtually everything to everybody, their Senate counterparts had to make tough choices that displeased some members. The Senate bill proposed to shift billions of dollars from Northeastern states to Southern and Midwestern states that had traditionally paid more in federal gas taxes than they had received in transportation funding.

Making those decisions and cobbling together a large enough coalition to ensure passage took months. By the time the bill reached the Senate floor in October, the House had given up for the year. A plethora of controversial floor amendments awaited. And to seal the bill's fate, Democrats decided to use it as a vehicle for unrelated efforts to revamp the campaign finance system. The bill died of its own weight.

Background

When the law widely known as ISTEA was enacted in 1991, the debate was framed in revolutionary terms. The law was to take the nation into the "post-interstate era," when the massive, interconnected national grid of highways created under the Eisenhower administration would finally be complete.

Advocates, such as Sen. Daniel Patrick Moynihan, D-N.Y. — then chairman of the Senate Environment and Public Works Committee with jurisdiction over the legislation — called for sweeping change. They wanted more flexibility for municipal and state governments to decide their transportation priorities; a greater emphasis on mass transit, bike paths and other alternatives to the automobile; an air bag in every car; and funds to help states improve their air quality.

Moynihan ended up getting much, though not all, that he wanted. The $157 billion law (PL 102-240) was a landmark. Although most of the money was still earmarked for highways, roads and bridges, billions of dollars were also set aside under the Congestion Mitigation and Air Quality improvement program and other new programs for transportation alternatives.

In addition, new controls were placed on outdoor advertising. A special $30 million fund was established for national scenic and historic roads. And the federal government threw its weight behind bicycle and pedestrian walkways. *(1991 Almanac, p. 137)*

1997 Sees Shift in Priorities

By the time the battle lines were drawn for the law's reauthorization in 1997, however, the political terrain had shifted dramatically. Republicans from highway-centered Southern states controlled both sides of the Capitol. The environmentalists who held such sway in 1991 seemed to be on the outs, while the road builders and contractors appeared ready to dictate the terms of the new law.

Initial proposals demanded an end to many of the 1991 law's categories, especially its environmental and alternative transportation accounts. Some conservatives even pushed to repeal all federal gas taxes, get Washington out of the transportation business and leave it to the states to decide their traveling futures.

For their part, environmentalists and transit advocates sought to protect their gains from 1991 while tapping the highway trust fund — which was filled by dedicated gas and transportation taxes — to rescue Amtrak, the nation's passenger rail system, from a looming bankruptcy. *(Amtrak, p. 3-22)*

Environmentalists had a powerful ally in John H. Chafee, R-R.I., chairman of the Senate Environment and Public Works Committee, who resolutely demanded that alternative transportation and air quality accounts remain intact. In the House, Shuster needed the environmentalists and their Democratic allies on his side in his virulent battles with the GOP leadership.

President Clinton weighed in March 12 with a six-year $175 billion transportation funding proposal that focused on increased environmental protection and assistance for welfare recipients getting to work, rather than on boosting highway spending. The proposal stressed alternatives to highway construction, such as buses, trains, bicycle paths and intermodal links between different transportation systems. And it called for additional emphasis on transportation safety.

Within months, however, those issues proved to be sideshows to the main event. Instead of a transportation policy debate, the reauthorization bill became entangled in disputes over money — how much money highway advocates could extract from the budget writers and how that money would be apportioned among the states.

Regional Conflicts Over Funding

There were two competing philosophies on how to distribute highway funds.

Should Congress direct dollars to the areas with greatest need? If so, then money would continue to flow to the Northeast with its crumbling highways and massive congestion, and to some sparsely populated Western states that did not have the tax base to maintain highways used largely by out-of-state travellers.

Or should Congress direct dollars to the areas that contributed the most gas revenue to the federal Treasury? If so, then more money should go to California and to many Southern and Midwestern states, some of which received considerably less than they remitted to the Highway Trust Fund.

Under existing law, a large portion of federal gasoline tax dollars flowed to states in the Northeast and the West. For decades, Southerners and Midwesterners had complained that the formula ensured that states such as Massachusetts and Rhode Island received up to $2.35 to the dollar of tax expenditures while a state such as South Carolina reaped as little as 56 cents.

Congress had last revised the formula in 1991, supposedly to iron out many of the historic funding differences. However, lawmakers also agreed to lock in certain age-old calculations such as miles of postal routes, thereby allowing Northeastern and Western states to maintain their traditional advantages.

States on the short end of the deal generally rallied in 1997 behind a funding formula known as STEP 21 (for "Streamlined Transportation Efficiency Program for the 21st Century"), which proposed to guarantee each state a return of at least 95 percent of the funds it remitted to Washington. Northeasterners, on the other hand, backed the "ISTEA Works" coalition, which advocated the status quo.

Shuster's Answer: Spend More Money

Shuster aimed to spread federal money more evenly among the states, but that required a large pot of money to ensure that states that did well under the existing funding formulas (including his home state of Pennsylvania) did not lose hundreds of millions of dollars.

To that end, he launched a crusade to boost annual highway funding from the existing level of $20 billion to as much as $32 billion, $10 billion a year above the cap set in the budget deal. That brought Shuster into a head-on confrontation with the Republican leadership, whose No. 1 priority was balancing the budget.

In a chaotic floor vote May 21, Shuster demonstrated the widespread support that existed in the House for more highway spending. He nearly succeeded in adding $12 billion over five years for highways by cutting other discretionary programs by 0.39 percent and scaling back proposed tax cuts by 0.39 percent. The effect would have been to reduce defense spending over five years by $6 billion, domestic programs by $5 billion and proposed tax relief by about $1 billion. His amendment, offered to the fiscal 1998 budget resolution (H Con Res 84), failed 214-216. *(Vote 147, p. H-48)*

Shuster's near-miss inspired a similar movement in the Senate the following day, with similar results. An amendment by John W. Warner, R-Va., and Max Baucus, D-Mont., to increase transportation funding was tabled (killed) on May 22 by a vote of 51-49. *(Vote 80, p. S-16)*

Far from giving up, highway enthusiasts pinned their hopes on a provision in the Senate version of the tax-reconciliation bill (S 949) that called for shifting 4.3 cents per gallon in federal gasoline taxes from deficit reduction to the Highway Trust Fund. The remainder of the 18.3-cents-per-gallon federal gas tax already went to the trust funds.

The 4.3 cents portion had been used for deficit reduction since it was enacted in 1993 as part of Clinton's first budget package. The change was projected to yield about $6.5 billion a year in additional funds for general transportation use.

Despite strong opposition from Senate Budget Committee Chairman Pete V. Domenici, R-N.M., and administration officials — who wanted to continue using the 4.3 cents for deficit reduction — the provision prevailed in conference. The final tax bill enacted Aug. 5 (HR 2014 — PL 105-34) made the shift effective Oct. 1, 1997. *(Tax reconciliation, p. 2-30)*

House Action

The possibility of more money spurred Shuster and his committee's ranking Democrat, James L. Oberstar of Minnesota, to defer negotiations on ISTEA reauthorization until the budget bill was completed.

Shuster finally unveiled his $103.2 billion three-year bill (HR 2400) on Sept. 4. At a news conference with the bipartisan leaders of his committee, Shuster declared that he had made "Solomonlike" choices in crafting the bill, dubbed the Building Efficient Surface Transportation Equity Act, or BESTEA.

In reality, however, he had been able to finesse the hard choices by increasing funding for every region and virtually every mode of travel. Southerners would get the 95 percent minimum return on federal gas taxes they demanded, environmental spending would increase and funds would continue to flow generously to the Northeast.

Total transportation spending for highways and other programs would rise from $23 billion a year to $30.3 billion in fiscal 1998, $34.4 billion in fiscal 1999 and $38.4 billion in fiscal 2000. Over that time, highway funds would jump from $20 billion to $24.9 billion to $28.5 billion to $32 billion.

Projecting Shuster's spending levels to the end of the budget deal's life in 2002, budget hawks estimated HR 2400 would exceed allocations under the budget deal by $34 billion.

Although he had his sprawling 74-member committee behind him, Shuster was immediately in trouble with the GOP leadership. "It's not against the law to dream," House Republican Conference Chairman John A. Boehner, R-Ohio, said of Shuster's bill.

"This is now between Newt Gingrich and Bud Shuster," said Oberstar. "If this bill reaches the [House] floor, it will pass. And if the Republican leadership stops it, it means they aren't listening to their own members."

Bill Sails Through Subcommittee

Transportation and Infrastructure Committee leaders thumbed their noses at the Republican leadership Sept. 10, ramming HR 2400 through the Surface Transportation Subcommittee by voice vote in a unanimous show of force. The markup lasted a matter of minutes. Amendments were put off until the full committee markup, scheduled for Sept. 17, so Shuster could show the GOP leadership a united front.

Little attention was paid to the spending limits in the balanced-budget agreement. Instead subcommittee members focused on gas tax dollars that were collected each year but held in surplus to offset the size of the deficit. The surplus was estimated at $23.9 billion.

"For far too long, gas taxes paid by the American people have been held hostage to the whims and caprices of the budgeteers as the nation's transportation infrastructure crumbles," declared Nick J. Rahall II of West Virginia, the subcommittee's ranking Democrat. "Let it be known across this great land, this is a day of liberation."

But the GOP leadership prevailed upon budget hawks to hold the line, and Shuster watched his support in the full House slip.

Republican Rep. Joe Scarborough's home state of Florida would have received a bonanza under the Shuster bill. The state's allocation of federal transportation dollars would have risen annually from $763 million a year to an average of $1.1 billion. Yet Scarborough insisted he would vote against the bill on the House floor "even if they had the Joe Scarborough Memorial Highway from Pensacola to Miami."

Faced with such rank-and-file opposition, Shuster postponed the full committee markup, trying to reach a compromise with Gingrich in a series of one-on-one meetings. Just what Gingrich promised Shuster in those meetings was unclear. Gingrich said he simply told the chairman he would reexamine transportation allocations during the budget process in the spring of 1998. Shuster said he was told highways would be the first in line if a burgeoning economy produced an unexpected surplus.

Full Committee Pulls Back

In either case, Shuster blinked under the pressure of a united Republican leadership. The Transportation Committee on Sept. 24 tabled HR 2400 until 1998, then approved by voice vote an $11.9 billion six-month extension of existing law (HR 2516 — H Rept 105-270).

The action enabled Gingrich to head off an intraparty battle, but the truce also bought Shuster and his allies time to make their claim for more infrastructure spending.

To formalize that claim, the committee went ahead and marked up HR 2400 on Sept. 24, adopting by voice vote an amendment by Tom Petri, R-Wis., chairman of the Surface Transportation Subcommittee, to extend the bill from three years to six and raise its total funding level to $218.3 billion.

Committee members also approved by voice vote an amendment by Shuster stipulating that annual funding levels would fall automatically if anticipated tax revenues failed to materialize. Finally, the panel gave voice vote approval to a resolution backing the principles and funding levels of HR 2400 before setting the bill aside. No vote was taken to report the measure out of committee.

By deferring the highway bill to an election year, Shuster added pressure on House leaders who might wish to use transportation projects to shore up voter support. If Gingrich denied the committee the funding it demanded, Rahall said, the Speaker would create "the type of road rage that may show up in the polls."

The House then approved the stopgap bill (HR 2516) Oct. 1, by voice vote and with no debate.

Senate Committees

With Senate leaders committed to holding the line on spending, the Environment and Public Works and the Banking, Housing and Urban Affairs committees produced a bill authorizing $180.7 billion over six years — $145 billion of it for highways and another $35.7 billion for mass transit. Additional pieces were provided by the tax-writing Finance Committee and the Commerce Committee.

Environment and Public Works Takes Lead

The staff of the Environment and Public Works Committee — whose chairman, Chafee, was a devotee of fiscal restraint — spent the better part of a year working on a compromise that could garner enough votes to get through the Senate. Committee leaders finally unveiled the fruits of that labor Sept. 11 — a six-year $145 billion highway bill (S 1173) that proposed shifting billions of dollars from large states in the Northeast to the South and Midwest.

The bill called for a 20 percent increase in highway funding, compared with 30 percent in the House version. The Northeast stood to lose somewhat, with a smaller percentage of the pie. But with that pie expanding considerably, Massachusetts was the only state that would see its actual dollars decline.

To ensure passage, committee negotiators assembled a delicate compromise, allying Southerners and Midwesterners with the Westerners who fared well under the existing funding formulas. They then added some key small states in the Northeast, such as Chafee's home state of Rhode Island, and New Hampshire, home to Republican committee member Robert C. Smith. Under the proposed funding formulas, no state would receive less than 90 cents for every dollar it paid in federal transportation taxes.

In an impressive show of legislative finesse, Chafee pushed the 383-page highway bill through the full committee Sept. 17 by an 18-0 vote (S Rept 105-95).

His whip hand, coupled with a few choice carrots, turned an expected rebellion into a love-fest. Chafee mollified New Jersey Democrat Frank R. Lautenberg with $120 million for his state over six years. He promised Tim Hutchinson, R-Ark., and Jeff Sessions, R-Ala., that he would try to find more funds for their states, and in a gesture to Sessions, he named Alabama's higher education system as a new transportation research center. The markup was over in less than three hours.

The Massachusetts delegation remained overtly bitter

over the state's potential decline in annual transportation funding from $831 million a year to $392 million. However, the Bay State's average under the 1991 law had been bolstered by the ongoing Central Artery project burrowing under Boston Harbor. Its completion early in the 21st century accounted for most of the fall-off. Without a seat on the committee, the state's delegation could not even raise its concern.

The only real controversy came over a proposal, tucked into Chafee's multifaceted "manager's amendment," that had the potential to change the way air bags were designed for cars.

The provision, authored by Dirk Kempthorne, R-Idaho, proposed to abolish a requirement that air bags be strong enough to save the life of a 170-pound man not using a seatbelt. Kempthorne said the requirement forced safety engineers to design heavy, rapidly deploying air bags that had killed dozens of children and small adults.

Under the Kempthorne proposal, safety engineers would design air bags as supplemental safety systems useful mainly for passengers wearing seatbelts. Consumer and transportation safety groups strongly opposed him.

Ricardo Martinez, the administrator of the National Highway Traffic Safety Administration, implored senators to allow federal engineers to design safer air bags before altering existing standards by legislative fiat. He said Kempthorne's provision might be aimed at saving children, but that it would be "a death knell for teenagers and young adults" — the passengers least likely to be wearing seatbelts and most likely to crash.

Kempthorne was unyielding, pounding the table when he said, "I am not content to sit here and talk about the body count of America's children because of a flawed federal standard." Ultimately, Barbara Boxer, D-Calif., withdrew a motion to strike the provision.

The committee adopted several non-controversial amendments by voice vote. Republican Smith of New Hampshire and Democrats Ron Wyden of Oregon and Bob Graham of Florida won acceptance of a proposal to speed up the environmental review process for transportation construction. Smith added another provision allowing motorcycles to be included in research projects for so-called Intelligent Transportation Systems aimed at finding high-tech advances.

Banking Panel Adds Transit Funding

Keeping the bill on track, the Senate Banking, Housing and Urban Affairs Committee on Sept. 25 approved $35.7 billion over six years for mass transit programs. The proposal, endorsed by a vote of 17-1, was to be married to S 1173 on the Senate floor. The total represented a 13 percent increase over the $31.5 billion allocated under the 1991 law.

Only Connie Mack, R-Fla., voted "no," in protest of what he called an unfair allocation for his state. Another Southerner, Lauch Faircloth, R-N.C., called the legislation "absolutely the most unfair allocation of federal dollars I've ever seen" but voted for it.

There was little the Southerners could do. The much larger highway portion of the bill was already slanted in their favor. The mass transit authorization — steered through the Banking Committee by Chairman Alfonse M. D'Amato, R-N.Y., ranking Democrat Paul S. Sarbanes of Maryland, John Kerry, D-Mass., and Christopher J. Dodd, D-Conn. — was something of a consolation prize to the Northeast.

The committee also adopted, 11-7, a proposal to authorize a $100 million-a-year, welfare-to-work program sought by the Clinton administration. Under the amendment, offered by Carol Moseley-Braun, D-Ill., states and local governments would have to put up half the money to attain federal matching grants designed to help welfare recipients, most of whom lived in cities or rural areas, reach jobs in the suburbs.

Funds for the program were to be appropriated out of the general Treasury, not the Highway Trust Fund. That put the program's future at the mercy of Richard C. Shelby, R-Ala., chairman of the Senate Transportation Appropriations Subcommittee, who voted against the Moseley-Braun amendment.

Finance Committee OKs Taxes

The Senate Finance Committee added its piece to the puzzle Oct. 1, giving voice vote approval to the extension of existing transportation taxes and tax credits.

In a partial victory for farm state lawmakers and a defeat for budget cutters, the committee approved a 10-year extension of a tax exemption for the purchase of ethanol, a fuel made primarily from fermented corn. The exemption was scheduled to expire in 2000. Under the Finance Committee plan, the 5.4-cents-per-gallon exemption was to fall to 5.3 cents in 2001, 5.2 cents in 2003, and 5.1 cents in 2005.

The 18.3-cent tax on gasoline would remain the same through the life of S 1173, as would the 24.3-cent tax on diesel fuel, the 4.3-cent tax on compressed natural gas and the 18.3-cent tax on other motor fuels. The committee proposed to repeal a tax of 1.25 cents per gallon on diesel fuel used by trains and raise the tax exemption for employer-provided transit passes from $65 a month to $100 a month, beginning in 2003.

The package of fuel taxes, expected to raise an extra $91 million through 2007, was scheduled to be added to S 1173 on the Senate floor.

The final element of the bill was approved Oct. 23 by the Commerce Committee — a $1.1 billion safety component to provide state grants to combat drunken driving, stiffen regulations on transport of hazardous materials, encourage stronger laws protecting underground pipelines and telecommunications cables and toughen penalties for attacks against railroad passengers and personnel.

By voice vote, the panel adopted an amendment drafted by Byron L. Dorgan, D-N.D., to provide $1 million in grants to states for training law enforcement officials in high-speed pursuits. Also by voice vote, the committee adopted a proposal by Slade Gorton, R-Wash., to authorize $10 million for capital improvements on light-density rail lines.

Senate Floor Action

The committee work proved to be the easy part. When the bill reached the Senate floor in early October, it was engulfed in a war over a separate campaign finance bill (S 25). To punish the Republicans for filibustering S 25, a united Democratic front set out to block the highway measure.

Chafee brought the highway bill to the floor Oct. 8, and, with the support of GOP leaders, attempted a procedural maneuver to load up the bill's "amendment tree" with minor amendments, thus precluding the Democrats from attaching the campaign finance legislation. *(Campaign finance bill, p. 1-26)*

Catching wind of Chafee's efforts, Robert C. Byrd, D-W.Va., used his legendary parliamentary prowess to seize the floor and force a quorum call. When Democrats refused to waive the quorum call without a vote, Majority Leader Trent Lott, R-Miss., was forced to call members to the floor to answer the roll call. By then, at least an hour had passed, and it was clear the Democrats would wreak havoc on GOP desires to finish work on the transportation bill.

If Republicans were flummoxed by the parliamentary maneuvering, Democrats were left furious. Lott announced he would make room only for amendments he deemed relevant to the transportation law, a stance Democratic leaders declared intolerable.

The Democrats took their revenge. Although they were under pressure from the transportation lobby, they held firm through four GOP attempts to break their filibuster. The fourth vote to cut off debate and move toward consideration of the bill came Oct. 28. It fell well short of the 60 votes needed, 52-48. Lott then pulled the bill off the floor and declared the debate over for the year. *(Vote 282, p. S-48)*

Earlier motions to invoke cloture were defeated Oct. 23 by votes of 48-52 and 48-50, and Oct. 24, by a vote of 43-49. *(Votes 275, 277, 278, pp. S-47, S-48)*

Both Lott and Chafee vowed not to pass a short-term extension in the hope that they could force quick action on a long-term bill in February 1998.

Road contractors, state officials, and highway safety workers were incensed. "It's idiotic. Every year, every time we come up with a highway reauthorization, whether its Democrats or Republicans, somebody is always holding it hostage to something else," fumed Duane Kraft, the executive director of the Associated General Contractors chapter in Jefferson City, Missouri.

The House Transportation and Infrastructure Committee could not resist a round of "I told you so's." For weeks, House members had been saying the Senate was running out of time. "Let it be known, when the chips were down and the need to act was there, this committee came together and passed a [six-month extension] bill on the House floor in 55 seconds," Oberstar gloated.

Such displays only angered senators, whose frustration was aimed not only at the other party but at the House as well. Even the lobbyists who were pushing a short-term extension instead of a full, six-year bill came under fire in the end.

"For those governors and those highway people that now would like some additional action, where were they a week ago?" asked Lott. "Why weren't they talking to the senators that were opposing cloture that would allow us to get onto this highway bill?"

Short-Term Bill

Senators resisted until the final days of the session before agreeing to a compromise bill that would enable states to continue funding highway programs through March.

The simplest approach would have been to endorse the House-passed bill extending existing law for six months. But Senate pride, along with regional sensitivities over funding, made that idea a non-starter. Senators from the Midwest and South said they could not stomach approving even a six-month continuation of existing funding formulas skewed against their states in favor of the Northeast and Upper Plains.

The Senate's resolve to leave the states dry began to erode in early November, however, under a barrage of lobbying by governors, state highway officials, contractors and labor unions. The Senate Environment and Public Works Committee held a hastily convened hearing Nov. 4, at which Democratic Gov. Paul E. Patton of Kentucky and state highway officials detailed numbing lists of programs and people threatened by congressional inaction.

Still unwilling to approve a straight extension, senators coalesced around a proposal by Christopher S. Bond, R-Mo. The bill (S 1454), which the Senate passed by voice vote Nov. 7, provided for states to shift leftover money from well-stocked accounts to depleted highway and transit projects with the proviso that the funds be reimbursed when Congress enacted a long-term reauthorization.

It also proposed to "advance" $1.3 billion in new money to states that lacked sufficient reserves, an amount Shuster quickly rejected as wholly inadequate.

With the session drawing to a close, House and Senate transportation leaders finally agreed on a complicated compromise (S 1519) that extended authority for highway and transit spending for approximately six months while Congress worked to enact a long-term reauthorization.

The short-term bill provided an advance of $5.5 billion in new highway contract authority; it also included Bond's provision allowing states to shift existing contract authority from one highway program to another, as long as the funds were later repaid.

Overall, it capped states' combined spending of reserves and new money at $9.8 billion, roughly enough to get them comfortably through March of 1998.

And to satisfy Lott's demand to keep the pressure on Congress, the bill set a firm deadline of May 1, 1998, after which the states could obligate federal funds only if Congress had passed a new reauthorization bill.

The Senate passed S 1519 by voice vote Nov. 10, and the House cleared it by voice vote on Nov. 12, the penultimate day of the session. Clinton signed it into law Dec. 1 (PL 105-130). ■

Amtrak Bill Clears in Final Hours

Legislation to rescue Amtrak from the brink of bankruptcy overcame a last-minute obstacle Nov. 13, and cleared just minutes before Congress adjourned for the year. President Clinton signed the bill into law Dec. 2 (S 738 — PL 105-134).

The legislation — more than two years in the making — restructured the management of the nation's ailing passenger railroad and authorized $5.2 billion in operating subsidies, capital improvement and retirement funds through fiscal 2002. It gave Amtrak managers new flexibility to cut expenses and operate in a more businesslike manner, with the aim of enabling the railroad to operate without federal subsidies by 2002. And it freed up $2.3 billion for rail capital improvement set aside under the 1997 tax reconciliation bill (HR 2014), with all but $100 million of that money reserved for Amtrak.

The bill barred the use of federal funds for Amtrak operating expenses beginning five years after enactment, and it specified that none of the $2.3 billion provided under the budget bill could be used for anything but capital expenses. *(Provisions, p. 3-27)*

Enactment was vital to the railroad, which was scheduled to go to creditors in December for an extension of its $150 million line of credit. Amtrak had already borrowed $83 million just to meet payroll in fiscal 1997, and expected to borrow $100 million in fiscal 1998. Failure to clear the bill could have prompted the banks to shun the risk, potentially hastening a bankruptcy of the railroad that had been expected as early as the spring of 1998.

With new management tools and an infusion of capital, Congress hoped Amtrak managers would be able to wean the railroad off of federal subsidies by fiscal 2002, the last year of federal support envisioned by the legislation.

Final passage seemed to surprise even House and Senate negotiators who had labored to make it happen.

The Senate had passed the bill Nov. 7 by voice vote after a grueling round of negotiations between Democrats and Republicans. But an objection lodged Nov. 12 by House Transportation and Infrastructure Committee Chairman Bud Shuster, R-Pa., over an obscure provision appeared to doom the bill for the year.

Frantic midnight negotiations resolved the impasse just in time, giving the 105th Congress what Rep. Benjamin L. Cardin, D-Md., called "a major accomplishment that just 24 hours ago we thought was impossible."

"It looked very dubious," agreed Michael N. Castle, R-Del., an Amtrak supporter who pleaded with his House colleagues to pass the measure.

Shuster wanted to revamp Amtrak's board of directors, and he was willing to bring down the bill over the issue. His own version of an Amtrak reform bill (HR 2247) had been defeated on the House floor Oct. 24, when an unusual coalition of Democrats, pro-union Republicans and deficit hawks teamed up to defeat key labor provisions that Republican leaders insisted remain in the bill.

While enactment of S 738 gave the railroad a new lease on life, it did not ensure its long-term survival. In the short run, labor strife could rock the railway. And House GOP staff expressed grave doubts whether the bill itself would really give Amtrak management sufficient flexibility to cut costs enough to make Amtrak competitive with airline and automobile travel.

Even Amtrak supporters were less than certain that the bill would realize its goal of ending federal subsidies by fiscal 2002. Both Castle and Rep. Jerrold Nadler, D-N.Y., said the goal was unrealistic, and Nadler vowed to revisit the issue before Amtrak was cut from the government's purse strings.

Let them try, warned John McCain, R-Ariz., chairman of the Senate Commerce, Science and Transportation Committee, and a reluctant supporter of the bill. Amtrak had already received more than $20 billion in federal subsidies since its inception, he said. "I say enough is enough," he vowed. "And I commit now that if this reform and reauthorization plan does not make Amtrak financially viable, I will do everything in my power . . . to see that it comes to an end."

BOXSCORE

Amtrak Reauthorization — S 738 (HR 2247). The bill restructured Amtrak management and labor, authorized funds through fiscal 2002 and released $2.3 billion in capital funds set aside by the balanced-budget agreement.

Reports: S Rept 105-85, H Rept 105-251.

KEY ACTION

Nov. 7 — Senate passed S 738 by voice vote.

Nov. 13 — House passed S 738, revised, by voice vote; **Senate** cleared the bill by voice vote.

Dec. 2 — President signed S 738 — PL 105-134.

Background

Amtrak, officially known as the National Railroad Passenger Corporation, was created when Congress passed the Rail Passenger Service Act of 1970 to relieve privately owned railroads of their money-losing passenger lines.

A private corporation whose stock was held mostly by the Transportation Department, Amtrak began operations with a $50 million grant, $100 million in loan guarantees for new equipment, and the expectation that it would eventually turn a profit. But the venture quickly proved to be no more profitable under federal control than it had been in private hands, and Amtrak went through 80 percent of its first grant within two months.

Congress added to Amtrak's problems by requiring service on unprofitable routes and imposing labor rules that deterred layoffs and private contracting. In the 1980s, Congress also made deep cuts in capital grants, saddling the railroad with aging, costly equipment and leaving it ill-prepared to compete in the 1990s with airlines and intercity bus services that were cutting their fares.

The rail system hit the wall in 1994 as its operating deficit climbed near $200 million. In response, Amtrak management announced plans to slash service, and officials told Congress that their goal was to survive without operating subsidies by fiscal 2002. They made it clear, however, that they would have to continue relying heavily on federal support for capital, and they sought a large, steady stream of money for new equipment and facilities. House and Senate committees approved bills in 1994 to reauthorize Amtrak and boost its funding, but neither measure made it to the floor. *(1994 Almanac, p. 171)*

When Republicans took control of Congress in 1995, many Amtrak supporters feared for the railroad's continued existence, given conservative Republicans' historic opposition to Amtrak subsidies. Fortunately for Amtrak, the railroad had influential GOP allies who moved into key positions in the new Congress. Still, their support was tempered by a desire to trim federal spending. Some Amtrak supporters considered it a victory when the budget resolution for fiscal 1996 stopped short of calling for an immediate cutoff of Amtrak aid. Instead, it proposed that Amtrak's operating assistance be phased out over seven years.

In 1995, the House overwhelmingly passed legislation (HR 1788) to reform and modify Amtrak to enable the railroad to wean itself from operating subsidies. But the bill stalled in the Senate because of bipartisan concerns over proposed limits on Amtrak's liability in case of rail accidents. *(1995 Almanac, p. 3-65)*

In early 1997, the General Accounting Office reported that Amtrak — despite streamlining its operations, cutting its route system by 15 percent and taking other measures to stem losses — was sliding deeper into debt, losing $1.6 billion in 1995 and 1996. Amtrak officials did not dispute these findings. On the contrary, Amtrak President Thomas M. Downs warned Congress that the railroad faced bankruptcy as early as the spring of 1998, when it would exhaust its line of credit.

1997 Rescue Proposals

In response to Amtrak's plight, efforts to save the railroad moved along several different paths. In late March, Shuster and other senior members of the House Transportation and Infrastructure Committee formed a bipartisan "blue ribbon panel" of transportation experts to develop an emergency plan to save Amtrak from bankruptcy and preserve inter-city rail services for the long term.

The panel released its recommendations June 23. In what critics considered a somewhat radical proposal, it called for dividing Amtrak into a federal rail infrastructure agency, which would own and maintain the Washington-Boston Northeast rail corridor, and a separate passenger rail service that would be privatized and would have to compete against other passenger rail operators that would offer services on the Northeast corridor and elsewhere.

Passenger train boosters at the National Association of Railroad Passengers opposed the restructuring proposal, saying it would "lead to a dramatic reduction in route miles and states served. This, in turn, would quickly lead to the end of federal funding for intercity passenger rail."

Frank R. Wolf, R-Va., chairman of the House Appropriations Subcommittee on Transportation, offered an alternative plan. In the draft fiscal 1998 transportation appropriations bill approved by his subcommittee June 24, Wolf included a provision calling for an independent commission, patterned after the military base realignment and closure commission, to examine Amtrak's problems and recommend train routes to close or restructure.

Congress would have to approve or reject the commission's recommendations in their totality. The object was to eliminate many unprofitable, long-distance routes that had been forced on Amtrak by members of Congress eager to maintain rail service to their districts and states.

However, Wolf's proposal was later deleted from the spending bill when the measure was being considered on the House floor. *(Appropriations, p. 9-66)*

Congress OKs Capital Funds, Requires Reform

Most lawmakers believed that solving Amtrak's problems involved providing it with adequate funding for operations and capital improvements, while also reforming Amtrak operations to allow the railroad to run more efficiently.

In the Senate, William V. Roth Jr., R-Del., and Daniel Patrick Moynihan, D-N.Y. — the chairman and ranking member, respectively, of the Finance Committee — were both major supporters of Amtrak. They wrote into the Senate version of the tax reconciliation bill (S 949 — S Rept 105-33) provisions that would create a dedicated source of annual funding for Amtrak. Under their proposal, a half cent of the existing federal gas tax would be used to finance an Amtrak trust fund, which could yield up to $650 million a year in dedicated funding for the railroad.

During the House-Senate conference on the tax bill, the provision was modified to instead provide a total of up to $2.3 billion in subsidies for rail capital improvements only. Under the final version signed into law Aug. 5 (PL 105-34), the assistance was to be provided over two years in the form of a refund of taxes previously paid by the private railroads that merged in 1971 to form Amtrak. Up to $2.2 billion would be reserved for Amtrak and the remainder used for other intercity rail or bus services. But the tax bill included an important condition: The funding could only be released after the enactment of Amtrak reform legislation. *(Tax reconciliation bill, p. 2-30)*

Roth tried to attach a set of Amtrak reforms to the final tax bill as a means of fulfilling this requirement, but the administration opposed the liability limits and labor provisions in the proposal. Roth subsequently offered to support an unrelated administration request to lower tariffs for certain Caribbean and Central American imports, in exchange for including the Amtrak reforms. But the White House continued to oppose the Amtrak language, and neither the Caribbean trade nor Amtrak reform provisions were added to the final bill.

The White House's actions were applauded by rail unions. "My basic position is a real simple one: They're not going to save Amtrak on the backs of its employees," said Edward Wytkind, executive director of the AFL-CIO's transportation trades department.

Republicans retorted that the unions and their Democratic allies were threatening to bring down the railroad in the name of labor protection. "I believe a very sad miscalculation is being made here," said Shuster.

On the other side, Amtrak critic McCain called the $2.3 billion for capital subsidies "the greatest train robbery since the [Jesse] James boys went out of business." He said he was skeptical that Congress would have the fortitude to hold out for fundamental changes in Amtrak, with $2.3 billion riding on the outcome. "It's all in the definition of 'reform.' Anything can be reform," McCain said. "It's a scam."

Trapped in the middle was Amtrak, whose officials recognized that the railroad would go bankrupt without the money, putting at risk all of its 24,000 employees. "This is not a game of our own making," said Thomas J. Gillespie Jr., Amtrak's vice president for government affairs. "We feel like we're tied to the railroad tracks."

Senate Committee

The Senate Commerce, Science and Transportation Committee approved an Amtrak reform bill (S 738 — S Rept 105-85) by voice vote June 26.

Similar to a version that had stalled in the Senate in 1995, the measure included operating and labor reforms aimed at reducing the railroad's business costs and enabling it to run without operating subsidies after fiscal 2002. Bill sponsor Kay Bailey Hutchison, R-Texas, said the legislation would "give Amtrak a fighting chance to succeed."

S 738 proposed a $5.2 billion authorization for Amtrak through fiscal 2002, well above the existing annual rate of federal support. The measure assumed, however, that the funding would come largely from dedicating a half cent of the federal gas tax to Amtrak — a provision that at the time was included in the pending Senate tax reconciliation bill.

The committee-approved bill proposed to repeal statutory labor protections that required Amtrak to give severance payments of up to six years worth of pay to employees who were laid off because of route changes and that prevented Amtrak from contracting out any support work other than food and beverage services.

The bill also included provisions to limit punitive damages sought by those injured in Amtrak accidents to $250,000 or twice compensatory damages, whichever was greater. Amtrak would be required to absolve freight rail carriers on whose tracks it traveled from any liability in the event of a passenger rail accident.

Committee Democrats were narrowly defeated on two amendments that would have stripped the bill of both controversial liability provisions. The first, by Wendell H. Ford of Kentucky, would have eliminated the proposed cap on punitive damages; it was rejected, 9-10. The second, also offered by Ford, would have eliminated the provisions requiring Amtrak to indemnify freight railroads for accidents; it was rejected on a tie vote of 9-9.

Ford and Ernest F. Hollings, D-S.C., argued that the provisions would reduce incentives for both Amtrak and freight railroads to operate safely. In the event of a catastrophic accident, they said, the indemnification clause could bankrupt Amtrak. But Hutchison contended that without indemnity, the access fees charged by freight railroads for Amtrak to use their track could triple from $90 million to $270 million a year.

The committee also rejected, by voice vote, an amendment by John Ashcroft, R-Mo., that would have prohibited Amtrak from submitting below-cost bids to perform services that could otherwise be contracted out to private vendors.

Amtrak Strike Temporarily Averted

If the raging controversies over Amtrak labor and liability provisions were not enough to tie Congress in knots while it considered Amtrak reform legislation (S 738, HR 2247), a threat by Amtrak workers to strike complicated matters further. *(Amtrak, p. 3-22)*

In August, the Brotherhood of Maintenance of Way Employees, which represented more than 2,300 Amtrak workers who built and maintained Amtrak's rail lines, announced its intention to strike. The union said that union employees with identical jobs at the freight rail companies earned as much as $6 an hour more than Amtrak workers. Amtrak, which was borrowing million of dollars in short-term loans just to stay in operation, contended it simply could not afford the union wage demands.

On Aug. 21, President Clinton postponed the initial strike deadline by establishing a Presidential Emergency Board to help resolve the impasse. Clinton was acting under authority of the Railway Labor Act, which governed collective bargaining in the rail industry. The emergency board came back in September to declare that the union was correct in its wage demands, but it acknowledged "the difficult political, financial and fiscal quandary in which Amtrak finds itself." "The issue of Amtrak's survival lies properly in Congress," the board concluded.

Release of the emergency board's report also triggered a 30-day "cooling off" period, after which the union would be free to strike. (The union later extended the initial strike deadline of midnight Oct. 21, to midnight Oct. 28, and then agreed not to strike during the year-end congressional recess if Congress was unable to complete action on Amtrak reform legislation.)

The threat of a strike increased the urgency of completing Amtrak reforms, which would release $2.3 billion set aside for rail capital improvements under the tax-reconciliation bill (PL 105-34). Without this support, Amtrak was expected to go bankrupt in the spring of 1998; a protracted labor strike would likely force Amtrak into bankruptcy even sooner.

Secretary of Transportation Rodney Slater also raised the specter of traffic gridlock in the event of a strike, with more than 500,000 commuters crowding airports and highways from Washington to Boston. "Amtrak handles about 40 percent of the traffic between Washington and New York," Slater said at a news conference in Washington's Union Station. "The highways and airports could not handle that."

Temporary Settlement Reached

Slater worked to broker a deal between Amtrak and the union, encouraging Amtrak's board of directors to become more directly involved in the negotiations. On Nov. 2, he announced that Amtrak and the union had reached a tentative agreement to avert a walkout.

Under the agreement, the Brotherhood of Maintenance of Way Employees would receive the 3.5 percent wage increases that its leaders were demanding for fiscal 1998 and 1999, plus a retroactive pay raise for salaries dating to 1995. In exchange, the union agreed to productivity improvements aimed at reducing costs.

The union said it could save Amtrak $7 million a year through improvements such as reduced costs of injury compensation, better use of materials on the job, and more productive performance on track construction, railroad tie installation and bridge reconstruction. In addition, labor and management agreed to form a productivity council to find $6 million more in labor savings.

All of this was contingent on congressional action. The first step was enactment of a bill overhauling Amtrak management and labor, which would free up the $2.3 billion set aside under the tax-reconciliation bill. That occurred Dec. 2 (PL 105-134).

Conditions Unlikely To Be Met

But the settlement included several other suppositions that seemed less likely to be realized. It assumed that Congress would:

- Appropriate $41.5 million more in operating subsidies for fiscal 1998 than was authorized under the balanced-budget agreement.
- Come up with $134 million to make up for operating subsidies that Amtrak requested in fiscal 1996 and 1997, but did not receive.
- Reverse a technical provision in the fiscal 1998 transportation appropriations law (PL 105-66) that in effect reduced the $2.3 billion set aside in the tax bill by $199 million — the amount of capital funding provided to Amtrak for fiscal 1998 in the appropriations measure. Democrats said the provision — which had been inserted into the appropriations bill by Senate Transportation Appropriations Subcommittee Chairman Richard C. Shelby, R-Ala. — was the key assumption, since the balanced-budget deal had already made room for the expenditure of both the $2.3 billion and the $199 million. An aide to Sen. John Kerry, D-Mass., said that would be more than enough in the short run to meet labor's demands.

Members, however, said these steps simply would not occur. As a consequence, the proposed settlement landed on Capitol Hill with a thud Nov. 3. Republicans denounced what Senate Majority Leader Trent Lott, R-Miss., called a politically untenable "non-starter." The unions, in turn, were furious that Republicans were trampling on a collective bargaining agreement before it had even been codified.

In fact, the unions and Amtrak supporters were hoping that Amtrak would be able to creatively use the newly released $2.3 billion to resolve the crisis, including using the funds to pay wages. In the final Amtrak reform bill, however, Republicans insisted on language specifying that none of the funds from the tax bill could be used for anything other than capital expenses.

In the end, the union-management deal was more of a stalling tactic than a permanent solution. If proposed funding failed to materialize, Amtrak and the union would have 30 days to negotiate a new deal, and another 30 days to cool off before the union could strike. That clock would start ticking when the Amtrak board determined Congress would not appropriate the money for fiscal 1999.

Consequently, the settlement was expected to fall apart sometime in 1998, when Amtrak management would have to officially tell the union that Congress would not appropriate the hundreds of millions of extra dollars upon which the deal depended.

House Bill

The impetus for Congress to enact Amtrak reform legislation intensified following the July 28 decision by House-Senate budget negotiators to include the $2.3 billion for passenger rail capital improvements in the reconciliation tax bill.

Just two days later, on July 30, the House Transportation and Infrastructure Committee voted 36-30 to approve a bill (HR 2247 — H Rept 105-251) nearly identical to the measure that had passed the House with overwhelming bipartisan support in 1995. Like the earlier bill, HR 2247 sought to end Amtrak's annual federal subsidy by fiscal 2002 and help make the railroad self-sufficient by giving its management added flexibility to reduce operating costs.

This time, however, Democrats objected to the labor provisions, particularly those that would do away with the statutory work force protections — the guarantee of up to six years' pay for certain workers laid off due to route restructuring, and the prohibition on contracting out most Amtrak operations. The bill proposed to make both of those matters subject to collective bargaining through a special, expedited bargaining process.

While Democrats had signed off on identical labor provisions in 1995, they pointed out that since that time Amtrak had laid off more than 2,000 employees with only minimal expense — which showed, they argued, that those labor protections were not as onerous as Republicans contended.

Democrats also objected to the bill's liability provisions — the cap on punitive damages for persons injured in Amtrak accidents, and the proposal to allow Amtrak to indemnify freight rail companies against lawsuits brought by Amtrak passengers injured while traveling on tracks owned by the freight companies.

James L. Oberstar of Minnesota, the ranking Democrat on the committee, attempted to drop the controversial labor and liability provisions, but his amendment was rejected, 31-37, along party lines.

Shuster said he would move ahead with the bill in September, after the August congressional recess, and he expressed hope that Clinton would not veto it, given Amtrak's dire straits. But he also took a poke at Clinton's opposition to the bill's labor provisions, saying, "The president is dancing like a marionette, with rail labor pulling the strings."

Bill Pulled From House Floor

The House took up the bill Oct. 22, but Republican leaders abruptly yanked it two days later after Democrats — bolstered by an unlikely assortment of GOP budget hawks, pro-labor Republicans and angry Western conservatives — defeated a leadership-backed labor amendment. Without the amendment, the leadership feared the $2.3 billion would be spent without enactment of labor law changes. "I believe we have jeopardized the future of Amtrak's existence," fumed Shuster.

The bill's collapse took a tortuous parliamentary path. Steven C. LaTourette, R-Ohio, and James A. Traficant Jr., D-Ohio, offered an amendment to reinstate the Amtrak labor protections but make them subject to bargaining in union-management contract negotiations. The amendment also clarified that changes in labor protections in the Amtrak bill would not affect freight rail and transit workers. This was a major concern of the freight and transit unions.

The Republican leadership backed a substitute offered by Jack Quinn, R-N.Y., a traditional union ally who had helped negotiate the original labor provisions. Quinn proposed to strip out all the language in the LaTourette-Traficant amendment except for the provision maintaining protections for freight and transit employees.

But Quinn's amendment failed by a vote of 195-223, with 26 Republicans joining a nearly united Democratic front. *(Vote 529, p. H-162)*

Most of the Republicans who voted against Quinn sided with the unions, but a handful cast their votes to prevent the expenditure of the $2.3 billion. Still others from the West were trying to punish their colleagues from the Northeast who had opposed property-rights legislation and whose region depended on Amtrak service. "Sometimes it is hard to get people's attention," said George P. Radanovich, R-Calif., who voted for the Quinn amendment but promised to lead Western conservatives against the bill's final passage. "We got their attention."

With Quinn's substitute defeated and adoption of the LaTourette-Traficant amendment virtually assured, Shuster and GOP leaders immediately pulled the bill from the House floor.

The collapse only raised the stakes for Amtrak. The lack of a bill deemed by GOP leaders as providing "reform" threatened to leave the railroad without the subsidy it was counting on to put it on a path toward solvency. Amtrak supporters also had been hoping that some of the money could be used to placate labor demands that had brought Amtrak's maintenance union to the brink of a strike.

"There are maybe a half dozen people in there who understand how all these things are interlocked and how precarious the situation is," said a frustrated Castle, whose home state of Delaware was uniquely dependent on passenger rail.

Senate Floor Action

After the bill was derailed in the House, the White House and a bipartisan group of senators set out to find a compromise on the labor and liability issues. They finally reached agreement Nov. 6. The following day, the Senate amended its committee-reported bill and passed the compromise (S 738) by voice vote.

While neither Amtrak management nor labor were completely thrilled with the accord, both said they could live with it. "It's reasonable. It's not a bad deal," said Amtrak vice president Gillespie. "It's like they've made us a deal we couldn't refuse," said James M. Brunkenhoefer, national legislative director for the United Transportation Union.

Under the compromise, statutory protection of both disputed labor provisions would end. The six-year severance clause would be immediately subject to collective bargaining between Amtrak's unions and management, and if no agreement was reached in six months, the unions would lose the severance protection so anathema to most Republicans. In reality, said Hutchinson, who brokered the compromise, since Amtrak managers could simply stall for six months, the provision was as good as gone.

The prohibition on contracting-out would remain in existing collective bargaining agreements until late 1999, but it could be modified through negotiations before that time. "This works for us," said Amtrak's Gillespie. "We can now, at some point, say with the employees at the bargaining table, these are the things we need to negotiate. That's the key."

On the issue of civil liability, the deal set a global cap of $200 million for all passengers in a given train accident, rather than limiting liability for each person based on the individual's economic losses. The deal also stipulated that Amtrak could enter into agreements with freight rail companies to assume all legal liability in the event of accidents on freight

Final Bill Provisions

The following are the major features of the Amtrak overhaul signed into law Dec. 2 (S 738 — PL 105-134). The new law:

- **Contracting restrictions.** Eliminated statutory restrictions that generally prohibited Amtrak from contracting out for work or services. Those contracting restrictions, however, were "deemed" to be a part of all existing Amtrak labor contracts, thereby continuing the prohibition until contracts were renegotiated — at which time the restrictions would be subject to negotiation. Contract negotiations on this issue had to begin no later than Nov. 1, 1999.
- **Labor protections.** Eliminated statutory labor protections for Amtrak employees 180 days after enactment. These included the guarantee of severance benefits equal to a year of wages for every year worked, up to a maximum six years' pay, for employees who lost their jobs because of rail service reductions. The bill established a special, expedited process for Amtrak and its unions to negotiate new labor protections, and it specified that nothing in the measure would affect similar labor protections provided to workers of freight railroads and transit systems.
- **Liability limits.** Capped Amtrak's liability for rail accidents to a total of $200 million per accident for all claims made by passengers for economic, non-economic and punitive damages. This cap, however, applied only to claims made by Amtrak passengers, and not to claims made by other parties harmed by an Amtrak accident. The measure also gave Amtrak authority to indemnify freight railroads — i.e., to assume their legal liability — for Amtrak accidents that occurred on track owned by freight railroads.
- **Board of directors.** Eliminated Amtrak's existing nine-member board of directors, and established a seven-member temporary Reform Board, with six of the seven members to be appointed by the president, subject to Senate confirmation, after consultation with congressional leadership.
- **Route flexibility.** Eliminated statutory requirements that Amtrak operate a specified "basic system" of routes in the country, composed primarily of the routes Amtrak inherited from predecessor private railroads in 1971. The bill also eliminated restrictions on Amtrak's ability to discontinue service on a route, thereby allowing Amtrak to evaluate and modify its route system according to commercial potential, rather than statutory requirements. The bill doubled from 90 days to 180 days the advance notification that Amtrak was required to give state and local governments before discontinuing service on any route.
- **Privatization.** Provided for the eventual privatization of Amtrak by, among other things, removing the Transportation Department as a preferred creditor, and requiring Amtrak to redeem all of its common stock by the end of fiscal 2002. The stock had been issued to freight railroads in exchange for donations of equipment when Amtrak was formed.
- **Performance requirements.** Established a special independent commission — the Amtrak Reform Council — to continually evaluate Amtrak's financial performance. If after two years the reform council found that Amtrak was either failing to meet its financial performance goals, or would need continued federal operating subsidies after fiscal 2002, Congress would be required to consider legislation to restructure or liquidate Amtrak. ■

tracks. However, this authority to indemnify freight railroads would not have the force of law.

Sen. John B. Breaux, D-La., who headed negotiations on the liability issues, said that by not explicitly writing indemnification into law or backing it with federal enforcement powers, as previously had been proposed, the legality and enforceability of each indemnification agreement would instead be left for the courts to decide. Courts, for instance, would decide whether Amtrak could shield freight companies from liability in cases where freight workers were clearly negligent.

Final Action

While most members hailed the Senate compromise, Shuster opposed it on the grounds that the Senate deal did not include a sweeping overhaul of Amtrak's board of directors. Shuster wanted the existing board replaced by a new professional board with a majority of Republican nominees.

Under Shuster's plan, the president would select a seven-member board, subject to Senate confirmation, with six of the seven appointments made after consultations with congressional leaders. Neither the secretary of Transportation nor Amtrak's president would be permitted to serve on the board, as they did under existing law.

Shuster brandished a letter from the Department of Justice questioning the constitutionality of the board in the Senate bill. "As chairman of the committee, I would be derelict in my duties if I were to bring this bill to the floor recognizing that it's been said by the Justice Department that what I bring to the floor is unconstitutional," he said.

Under the Senate-passed bill, the number of Amtrak board members appointed by the president would increase; the president would be required to choose a governor and a mayor with interests in rail transportation, a labor representative and a commuter rail representative. The Justice Department letter said that such constrained choices would not leave sufficient "scope for the judgment and will" of the president, as demanded by the Constitution, and it suggested a change to the bill.

However, the Justice Department's letter was not actually as definitive as Shuster implied. Secretary of Transportation Rodney Slater insisted that the Senate bill could be implemented in a constitutional manner.

Moreover, it turned out that the letter was not new information, as Shuster said, but a correspondence sent to the Senate Commerce Committee on July 24. Shuster also conceded that under the letter's interpretation, the existing Amtrak board had been unconstitutional since its inception in 1971, yet it had never been challenged.

House and Senate negotiators were furious. Labor leaders charged that Shuster was simply trying to get back at them for unhinging his original Amtrak bill. "You shouldn't allow the chairman of a committee to not only bring a bill down but bring a corporation down," said the AFL-CIO's Wytkind.

The labor unions mobilized to thwart Shuster. Wytkind and Peggy Taylor, the AFL-CIO's chief lobbyist, blanketed the House with letters opposing Shuster's board provision. "Very tough concessions were made by labor on this bill because we know Amtrak needs this money," Wytkind said. "Enough is enough."

They had reason to protest. Since existing labor protections and restrictions on contracting would become subject to collective bargaining under the compromise, a board dominated by Democrats would help the union cause.

Republicans, meanwhile, were already angered over a settlement reached Nov. 2 between Amtrak's existing board and the railroad's maintenance union to avert a threatened strike. Republicans believed that the board, under pressure from the administration, had cut too generous a deal. *(Amtrak strike, p. 3-25)*

Shuster persuaded the House Rules Committee to bring the Senate Amtrak bill to the House floor with an amendment already attached that would insert his board of directors language. But Oberstar, the ranking Democrat on the Transportation Committee, devised a parliamentary maneuver of his own that would have, in effect, dropped Shuster's provision and sent the original Senate bill to the White House.

When it appeared that Oberstar might prevail, the Republican Conference ducked into a closed-door meeting the night of Nov. 12. Shuster implored the GOP to stay with him, but Castle said too much was at stake to derail the Senate bill. He noted that S 738 already included creation of an Amtrak reform council to oversee the board of directors, and that it stiffened congressional oversight of Amtrak.

"Before we leave, I hope each and every one of us will understand the future of passenger rail travel in this country is at hand," Castle said.

Shuster pulled the bill from the floor for the day. Around 11 p.m., Castle received word that staff members were beginning to negotiate a compromise. By midnight, a deal was at hand.

The final compromise allowed Shuster to say he had prevented Congress from clearing a possibly unconstitutional bill, and allowed Democrats to claim that the board would not be dominated by Republicans.

The existing board was to be replaced no later than March 1998 by a seven-member "reform board" — six of whose members would be chosen by the president in general consultation with all the House and Senate's top leadership. Unlike Shuster's proposal, it did not allow each congressional leader to effectively chose a specific number of board members. The final deal also allowed the secretary of Transportation to be appointed to the board as the seventh member, but without Senate confirmation.

Even Castle, who had earlier questioned Shuster's "brinkmanship," conceded that the final deal was an improvement over the Senate-passed version. "He's a better negotiator than I," Castle said. "It's a very good compromise, an excellent compromise."

The House passed the amended Amtrak bill by voice vote Nov. 13, and the Senate cleared it shortly afterward, also by voice vote. ■

Airline Ticket Taxes Restructured

A major battle between the big airlines and their discount competitors over airline ticket taxes ended in somewhat of a draw, with Congress clearing a tax bill that included concessions to both sides.

The bill, signed into law Aug. 5 (HR 2014 — PL 105-34) was part of a five-year balanced-budget deal reached by the Republican-controlled Congress and the White House. It included provisions that boosted airline ticket taxes from about $30 billion to $33.2 billion over five years, rising to $79.7 billion over 10 years. It also restructured the taxes in a way that split the difference between big carriers such as American and Delta that had lobbied vigorously for a new system of fees tied to the distance a passenger traveled, and discount airlines such as Southwest that wanted to continue the existing 10 percent tax on the price of an airline ticket.

The bill reauthorized the ticket excise tax for 10 years, but at a gradually declining rate. Beginning in 1998, the excise tax would be supplemented by a per-passenger tax on each segment of a domestic flight that would increase gradually in subsequent years. In addition, the bill imposed a $12 tax on international arrivals and a separate $12 tax on departures. Previously, the only international tax was $6 for departures.

Republicans needed the revenue from the airline taxes to help offset the huge tax cuts contained in the tax-reconciliation bill. So, although the airline ticket tax had expired at the end of 1996, the long-term reauthorizing did not come until August, when the tax bill was signed. In the meantime, a stopgap bill enacted in February kept the existing taxes in place.

Background

The 10 percent tax on domestic airline tickets fed the Airport and Airway Trust Fund, which provided the Federal Aviation Administration (FAA) with a majority of its funding. The trust fund got additional money from the $6-per-passenger departure tax and from taxes on cargo and non-commercial aviation fuel. Together, the taxes brought in about $500 million a month.

Since the 10 percent tax was directly related to the price of a ticket, it tended to favor discount airlines such as Southwest and ValuJet (later renamed AirTrans). Geographically, this helped passengers with access to airports serviced by those airlines, such as Baltimore-Washington International and Midway in Chicago.

When the longstanding levies expired in December 1995, the big airlines demanded that Congress dump the 10 percent ticket tax and replace it with a tax structure more favorable to them. Seven of the biggest U.S. carriers — American, Continental, Delta, Northwest, TransWorld, United and USAir — pressed Congress to adopt a three-part tax formula consisting of $4.50 per passenger, $2 per seat on jets with more than 70 seats ($1 on smaller airplanes) and half a cent per nonstop passenger mile.

"The 10 percent ticket sales tax is inherently inefficient, outmoded and unfair, and should be replaced with a usage-based system which charges passengers only for the services they use — no more and no less," said Northwest Airlines Executive Vice President Michael E. Levine.

The big carriers had a great deal working for them. They had contributed about $2.5 million to federal campaigns in the 1995-96 election cycle. According to the nonpartisan Center for Responsive Politics, the discount carriers contributed only about $70,000. Most of them did not even have political action committees.

The major carriers retained a massive team of lobbyists to make their case, including former Republican National Committee Chairman Haley Barbour and former Transportation Secretary James Burnley. At first, they found a sympathetic audience with many lawmakers, as well as with the Clinton administration. They contended that a tax system based on passenger use of the air traffic control system (such as a set fee for each takeoff and landing) rather than on widely varying fares, would lead eventually to better funding for the FAA.

Big Carriers Overreach

But in their eagerness to change the taxes, the big carriers overreached. They ended up drawing attention to themselves not so much as an aggrieved party, but as a potential source of new federal revenue at a time when Republicans were looking for ways to pay for tax cuts.

For example, the major carriers told members of the House Ways and Means and Senate Finance committees that they were paying for more than their fair share of the air traffic control system. But once congressional analysts began digging into the issue, they found that the big airlines actually enjoyed some tax breaks. Passengers on international flights, for example, were paying a round-trip tax of just $6, far lower than the tax on domestic flights.

Moreover, Transportation Department estimates showed that, while passengers on the seven major airlines would save $400 million or more under the plan, Southwest passengers could pay $195 million more yearly into the airport trust fund. ValuJet passengers would pay $40 million more and America West passengers about $28 million more.

"The proposal would dramatically redistribute the taxes among airlines and could have substantial implications for domestic competition," warned John H. Anderson Jr., director of transportation issues at the General Accounting Office (GAO).

As the debate continued, the major airlines vowed to fight congressional efforts to reinstate the expired 10 percent ticket tax, even though the FAA was running out of money. "They wanted to play a game of chicken with Congress," said a former aviation staff member. At that point, the tax-writing Ways and Means and Finance committees were looking for narrowly focused tax increases to offset planned tax cuts. "The large airlines placed a big bull's-eye on their backs," said Tim Hannegan, assistant director of aviation issues for the GAO.

Lawmakers renewed the tax in August 1996, but it was a temporary extension that lasted only through the end of the year. They saved a longer term solution for inclusion in a reconciliation bill in 1997. *(1996 Almanac, pp. 2-34, 3-34)*

The discount carriers launched a campaign of their own, hiring former House Ways and Means members Thomas Downey (1975-93) and Rod Chandler (1983-93) to lobby Congress. Southwest and its allies had the advantage of playing defense. They also enjoyed some good will for having introduced low-cost service to numerous small cities. "I believe the lower-cost airlines have been a tremendous boon to certain parts of the country," said Senate Environment and Public Works Committee Chairman John H. Chafee, R-R.I.

Southwest even announced in February that it would inaugurate service to Jackson, Miss. Although airline officials insisted the expansion was purely for business reasons, the decision followed years of complaints by Senate Majority Leader Trent Lott, R-Miss., that airlines underserved his state. The discount carriers also got help from influential aviation industry groups, including some manufacturers and private pilots. "The current tax structure works," said Edward M. Bolen, president of the General Aviation Manufacturers Association. "We know it, we know how to pay it. We've had our business plans based on it."

Temporary Extension

With the FAA nearly out of money for airport construction projects and a reconciliation bill still months away, Congress on Feb. 27, 1997, cleared another short-term bill renewing the airline taxes through Sept. 30. Clinton signed the bill into law Feb. 28 (HR 668 — PL 105-2).

The action came none too soon for the FAA, which was so strapped for funds that it had begun to defer some airport grants for projects such as runway expansion and radar upgrades. The temporary bill raised an estimated $2.7 billion for the trust fund. It also corrected a problem that resulted when the administration allowed the airlines to defer paying $1.2 billion in taxes, only to discover belatedly that it lacked the authority to move the delayed funds from the general Treasury into the Airport and Airway Trust Fund. The bill gave the FAA access to the waylaid $1.2 billion and barred the airlines from deferring tax payments.

Despite the temporary infusion of revenue, however, airport managers remained uncertain in the absence of a longer term decision on taxes. "It continues to throw airport planning into chaos because, from one month to the next, airports are continually faced with uncertainty over whether the revenue stream is on or off, and how long it will take to get it back on," said Todd J. Hauptli, a lobbyist with the American Association of Airport Executives.

Legislative Action

The short-term extension began in the Senate Finance Committee, which approved it by voice vote Feb. 5 (S 279 — S Rept 105-4). But it was put on hold pending action by the House, which was charged by the Constitution with originating any tax measure. The House Ways and Means Committee approved its bill (HR 668 — H Rept 105-5) by voice vote Feb. 12. The temporary extension cleared easily the week of Sept. 30, though members in both chambers kicked up something of a fuss. The House passed it Feb. 26 by a vote of 347-73, squelching a revolt by some anti-tax members. The Senate cleared the bill by voice vote Feb. 27. *(House vote 27, p. H-10)*

Van Hilleary, R-Tenn., and other conservatives delayed the House vote for a day, arguing that the taxes should not be reinstated without an offsetting cut in other taxes, such as the 4.3-cent-per-gallon portion of the federal gasoline tax instituted in 1993. "There is no reason why we need to be steamrolling taxpayers just to continue paving runways," Hilleary said. The National Taxpayers Union supported the conservatives' cause, saying it would score the vote as a tax increase.

But Ways and Means Chairman Bill Archer, R-Texas, said that essential airport operations, including safety enhancements, would be in jeopardy without the legislation.

In the Senate, Democrat Bob Graham of Florida briefly held up final action to contend that the taxes should be extended through Dec. 31. Otherwise, he said, they were likely to expire again before lawmakers could come up with a long-range funding plan that satisfied competing interests in the industry. Other senators had considered offering unrelated amendments to redirect more gas tax money into the Highway Trust Fund or provide aid to farmers, but airport managers lobbied them to hold off and let the bill through.

Tax-Reconciliation Bill

When it came time to write the tax-reconciliation bill, lawmakers already had their sights set on the aviation industry.

On June 13, the House Ways and Means Committee approved a draft tax bill that called for $34 billion in airline taxes over five years, an increase of nearly $5 billion, with most of the proposed hikes falling on international flights. The draft, approved on a partisan, 22-16 vote, was subsequently introduced as HR 2014 (H Rept 105-148).

Ways and Means proposed splitting the existing 10 percent ticket tax into two separate levies on domestic flights: a 7.5 percent ticket tax and a per-passenger charge on each segment of a flight. The per-segment charge would start at $2 in fiscal 1998, increase gradually to $3 by fiscal 2002 and be indexed to the Consumer Price Index (CPI) after that.

For international flights, the draft proposed increasing the existing per-passenger departure tax from $6 to $15.50. In addition, it called for a new $15.50 charge on international arrivals. Archer had originally proposed taxes of $10 each on international arrivals and departures, but J.D. Hayworth, R-Ariz., succeeded in increasing them by $5.50 each way. He wanted to substitute the additional revenue for money Archer had planned to get from a tax on gaming and other commercial activities carried out by American Indian tribes. Hayworth's amendment was adopted, 22-16.

The Ways and Means plan also called for a 7.5 percent tax on frequent-flier miles purchased by credit card companies and others to use as an incentive to their customers.

Before taking the bill to the House floor, Archer made a number of changes, including giving airlines a two-week delay in the deadline for depositing the proposed ticket tax in 1998, thereby allowing them to invest the tax revenues for an additional two weeks.

The big carriers saw the Ways and Means bill as a major setback, but they disliked the bipartisan version produced by the Senate even more. Approved 18-2 by the Finance Committee on June 19, it called for simply reinstating the 10 percent ticket tax on domestic flights. In addition, it proposed replacing the $6 departure tax for international flights with an $8 tax each on arrivals and departures. And, in a move that particularly rankled the big carriers, it proposed adding a 10 percent tax on the domestic segment of international flights.

Conferees Agree To Spread the Pain

As the tax bill moved to conference, the major airlines found themselves holding a rally on the Capitol steps July 9 to urge Archer to hold fast to the same House position they had assailed just a few weeks before.

Since neither congressional Democrats nor the Clinton administration made the airline tax increase a priority, the matter was largely left to the Republicans to decide among themselves, and it provoked a split among top GOP leaders. House Speaker Newt Gingrich, R-Ga., took the side of the major carriers, in part because many employees of Atlanta-based Delta lived in his district. Lott leaned toward Southwest. "Both positions, strongly held and fairly come to, are reflective of their experiences with airlines in their districts and states," said aviation lobbyist Hauptli.

The compromise that ultimately came out of conference was not entirely satisfactory to any of the parties. The bill provided for $33.2 billion in aviation taxes over five years, $79.7 billion over 10 years. Conferees agreed to:

➤ Authorize the Airport and Airway Trust fund taxes for 10 years, through Sept. 30, 2007. The levies included the airline ticket tax, as well as taxes on air cargo and aviation fuel.

➤ Reduce the 10 percent tax on domestic airline tickets to 9 percent in fiscal 1998, 8 percent in fiscal 1999 and 7.5 percent in 2000.

➤ Impose a new per-passenger tax on each segment of a domestic flight, beginning at $1 in fiscal 1998, gradually increasing to $3 in fiscal 2002 and then changing to reflect inflation. Flights to small airports in isolated rural areas would be exempt from the per-segment tax.

➤ Impose a tax of $12 each way on international arrivals and departures. The taxes would be indexed to the CPI beginning in January 1999. The bill kept the existing $6 tax on flights to Alaska and Hawaii, but indexed it to the CPI beginning in 1999.

➤ Impose a new, 7.5 percent tax on purchases of frequent-flier miles by credit card and other companies to reward to their customers.

In the end, the big airlines had to accept the continuation of the ticket excise tax, though they were pleased that it would be reduced over several years and be partially replaced by a new levy based on each segment of a domestic flight. The airlines also won a brief delay in depositing the taxes. While the big carriers were unhappy over the international arrival and departure taxes, they succeeded in killing the Senate proposal for a new tax on the domestic segments of international flights.

"I think it's ironic that the debate was started by the large carriers last year in the expectation that they would reduce their tax burden by several hundred million dollars . . . and they now are facing a [big] tax increase . . . over the next five years," said the GAO's Hannegan. "It's hard to call these efforts successful." ■

Other Transportation Issues Considered in 1997

Lawmakers worked on several other transportation measures, including a reauthorization of Federal Aviation Administration research, engineering and development programs.

FAA Reauthorization

A bill reauthorizing Federal Aviation Administration (FAA) research, engineering and development programs came close to enactment at the end of the session and was subsequently signed into law Feb. 11, 1998 (HR 1271 — PL 105-155).

The bill authorized a total of $457 million for the programs through fiscal 1999 — $226.8 million in fiscal 1998 and $229.7 million in fiscal 1999. It also established a new undergraduate research grants program. The measure urged the FAA to address the year 2000 computer problem, and it barred contractors from receiving FAA research grants if they received any other federal grants through a non-competitive process.

Congress had reauthorized most FAA activities, including FAA operations and the airport improvement grant program, through fiscal 1998 as part of the last authorization bill enacted in 1996. But the research, engineering and development programs had only been authorized for one year. *(1996 Almanac, p. 3-34)*

The programs — aimed at improving the safety, security, capacity and productivity of the airways and the air traffic control system — were generally conducted by FAA technical personnel and by colleges and universities.

Legislative Action

The bill began in the House Science Committee, which approved it by voice vote April 16 (H Rept 105-61). The House passed the bill April 29 by a vote of 414-7. *(Vote 95, p. H-32)*

The House-passed bill was a three-year authorization that called for a total of $672 million for the programs through fiscal 2000 — $217 million in fiscal 1998, $224 million in fiscal 1999 and $231 million in fiscal 2000. The bill included the establishment of a new undergraduate research program.

Also under the bill, FAA research grants could not go to contractors who received any other federal grants through a non-competitive process, and recipients of FAA research, engineering or development funds would be barred from using that money to lobby Congress.

The House gave voice vote approval to an amendment by bill sponsor Constance A. Morella, R-Md., aimed at alleviating jurisdictional concerns raised by House Transportation and Infrastructure Committee Chairman Bud Shuster, R-Pa.

Members also approved by voice vote an amendment by Sheila Jackson-Lee, D-Texas, to clarify that historically black colleges and universities and those that served Hispanics could participate in the undergraduate research program that HR 1271 would establish. Jackson-Lee said the amendment would send a message "to our population that we want all people involved in this very important research."

On Nov. 4, the Senate Commerce, Science and Transportation Committee gave voice vote approval to a revised version of HR 1271 (S Rept 105-152). The Senate passed the bill by voice vote Nov. 13, the last day of the session.

The Senate version included two significant changes to the bill. It struck the fiscal 2000 authorization, and it increased the amount for research, engineering and development by $5.6 million in fiscal 1999. The changes required House approval, which occurred on Feb. 3, 1998, when the House accepted the Senate amendments by voice vote, clearing the bill.

Ocean Shipping

The Senate Commerce, Science and Transportation Committee approved a bill (S 414) aimed at revising shipping laws to allow companies greater flexibility in contracting for ocean shipping. The bill was approved May 1 by a vote of 20-0.

Ocean shipping of goods between the United States and foreign countries was generally governed by the Shipping Act of 1984, which was administered by the Federal Maritime Commission (FMC), an independent agency that regulated domestic and international shipping in U.S. waters.

The 1984 act prohibited confidential service contracts and required that all rates be publicly available. Supporters said public disclosure sometimes put companies at a competitive disadvantage because many foreign countries, such as Japan, let companies keep their rates and contracts confidential.

The bill proposed to eliminate existing requirements that carriers file rate increases or decreases with the FMC. The only demand for posting would be that it be easily accessible. For example, carriers would be responsible for publicly posting their shipping rates on an Internet home page. The bill also would allow limited, confidential service contracting by shippers and common carriers, but shippers would have to stay within the bounds of antitrust law.

Also under the bill, the FMC would merge with the Surface Transportation Board, which regulated ground transportation, to form a new agency to be called the Intermodal Transportation Board.

The bill included a requirement that the Transportation secretary verify that a vessel operator had not violated U.S. shipping laws before granting a shipbuilding loan guarantee. The provision was added because of concerns among some members that the China Ocean Shipping Company (COSCO) was granted a loan guarantee while being investigated for unfair pricing practices. COSCO, owned by the Chinese government, also was in line to receive property for a facility on U.S. land.

The bill also included burial benefits for certain World War II merchant marine veterans.

FMC Chairman Harold J. Creel told the Surface Transportation and Merchant Marine Subcommittee during a hearing March 20 that the proposal to allow limited confidential contracts would "go too far and risk discrimination and abuse adverse to U.S. trade interests." Creel, however, said he generally supported the measure.

The House passed a similar measure in the 104th Congress, but it stalled in the Senate because of fears that relaxed regulations on shipping-rate structures would allow bigger shipping companies to underbid their smaller competition. Bill sponsor Kay Bailey Hutchison, R-Texas, said S 414 would address those fears. *(1996 Almanac, p. 3-38)*

Trust Funds

The House Transportation and Infrastructure Committee gave voice vote approval Feb. 5 to a bill (HR 4) sponsored by panel Chairman Bud Shuster, R-Pa., to move four transportation trust funds "off-budget." Although the bill went no further, the proposal was incorporated into the House version of the surface transportation reauthorization bill (HR 2400). It was strongly opposed by the Clinton administration.

The intent of HR 4, which was backed by powerful road-building lobbies, was to force the government to stop using the trust fund balances to offset the deficit. Supporters said it could lead Congress to spend an additional $3 billion or more a year on transportation projects, instead of letting the money pile up in the trust funds. "That means highways. That means improvements. That means benefits to every congressional district in the country," said the committee's ranking Democrat, James L. Oberstar of Minnesota.

The bill was virtually identical to legislation that easily passed the House in 1996 but was never taken up in the Senate. *(1996 Almanac, p. 3-40)*

The four trust funds — covering programs for highways and mass transit, aviation, harbors and inland waterways — were fed by taxes on items such as fuel, tires and cargo. Although the trust funds generally had sizable cash balances, appropriators routinely spent less on transportation projects than Congress had authorized, largely because of overall caps on discretionary spending.

Supporters of HR 4 contended that it was dishonest for the government to hold back money in the trust funds to reduce the size of the deficit. But even some supporters conceded privately that the proposal faced long odds. Deficit hawks in both Congress and the Clinton administration said it could fragment the budget, making it more difficult for the government to control spending. "The majority of senators want to keep it on-budget," said Sen. John W. Warner, R-Va., chairman of the Environment and Public Works Transportation and Infrastructure Subcommittee. ■

House Backs Grazing Fees Increase

The House passed a bill late in the session to increase grazing fees on federal lands, but the Senate took no action on the legislation.

The bill (HR 2493) proposed raising the fees for grazing cattle on most public lands by an average of 15 percent over the following five years, while reducing the grazing fee for sheep by about one-third. The measure was supported by livestock groups but opposed by the Clinton administration and by environmental organizations.

House endorsement of HR 2493 was an important turning point for bill supporters. In the 104th Congress, the House served as a burial ground for grazing bills as Westerners failed to bridge differences with Eastern colleagues, who raised objections on environmental grounds. *(1996 Almanac, 10-58)*

Since their inception, grazing fees had caused conflict between ranchers, who wanted to keep the fees down, and environmentalists, who asserted that lower fees resulted in overgrazing and deterioration of public lands through runoff pollution and excessive foraging. The environmentalists were joined by deficit hawks who contended that ranchers were subsidized by low grazing fees.

Under existing law, grazing fees were established by executive order and varied based on market conditions. They were determined by several factors, including the price of cattle, the private lease rate for grazing land and the costs associated with beef production. The fee was measured in "animal unit months" (AUM), the amount of forage needed to feed one cow, five sheep or one horse for a month. The minimal fee for the 1996 and 1997 grazing seasons was $1.35 per AUM.

The bill proposed a new, statutory grazing fee formula based primarily on two factors that would fluctuate over time — the value of beef cattle, as determined by the Department of Agriculture, and the interest rate over the previous 12 months. The new formula did not include a minimum amount, or floor, below which the fees could not fall. The effect would be to increase the fee for grazing cattle to $1.84 per AUM.

The bill also proposed modifications to the existing grazing policy advisory panels, established by Interior Secretary Bruce Babbitt to increase state and local participation.

The Clinton administration and environmental groups said the bill would tip the balance in grazing decisions toward ranchers and away from environmental interests. Environmental groups said the proposed grazing fee increase was little more than window dressing, and would not represent a fair return to taxpayers.

The administration had made a push in 1993 to almost triple grazing fees to $4.28 per AUM over three years — still far lower than many private fees — but it was stymied by fierce opposition from ranchers. *(1993 Almanac, p. 273)*

House Action

The House Agriculture Committee approved HR 2493 (H Rept 105-346, Part 1) on Sept. 24 by voice vote and with relatively little debate.

Bill supporters, including committee Chairman Bob Smith, R-Ore., and many ranchers, said the measure would streamline management of federal land used for grazing livestock and provide stability to ranching communities. Smith said such communities often bore the brunt of abrupt changes in grazing policy.

But on the day of the markup, Babbitt sent a letter to Smith saying he would recommend a veto of the bill. "Rather than helping to forge consensus about improving the public rangelands, the bill instead would lead to yet another contentious, lengthy and unnecessary debate in Congress over livestock grazing on Western public land," Babbitt said.

Babbitt said the legislation would undermine the advisory councils by requiring that decisions be approved by a majority vote, rather than by consensus.

The House Resources Committee approved the bill Oct. 8 by a vote of 23-3 (H Rept 105-346, Part 2).

Modified Bill Wins House Support

In a big win for Western Republicans, the House passed the measure Oct. 30 by a vote of 242-182. But the comfortable margin was assured only after the Westerners brokered a decisive compromise with their Eastern colleagues. *(Vote 549, p. H-166)*

Smith said the new grazing fee formula would end the fluctuations and instability associated with the existing formula, which moved up or down depending on market conditions. The added certainty, he said, would make it far easier for small ranchers to get bank financing.

Smith had worked beforehand to resolve differences with Sherwood Boehlert of New York, House Republicans' leading voice on environmental issues. To satisfy Boehlert, Smith dropped a handful of provisions, including one to give ranchers greater influence over grazing policy developed by panels advising federal land managers.

"I'm not standing up and cheering," said Boehlert. "But I basically think it's a good bill." Boehlert's support was pivotal in enabling Smith to defeat attempts to sharply increase the proposed grazing fee. If those amendments had been adopted, the Westerners and their allies in the ranching community would likely have withdrawn their support for the bill.

Boehlert credited Smith with soothing the bitter feelings over federal land management issues. House Speaker Newt Gingrich, R-Ga., also got personally involved in spurring both sides to reach a compromise. "Bob Smith and I both got elected in 1982," observed Boehlert. "We've been able to reason together. The junior ideologues have not yet achieved that experience. It takes time, so they are less likely to work out sensible compromises."

Higher Fee Rejected

The unsuccessful attempts to increase the fee were backed by a coalition of fiscal conservatives and environmentalists, who argued that the increase in HR 2493 was little more than a fig leaf and that ranchers supported it to stave off much larger hikes. Their efforts included:

➤ A proposal by Scott L. Klug, R-Wis., rejected 205-219, that would have tied the federal grazing fee to the fee charged by the state where the rancher was located. Because state fees were much higher, that would have amounted to a significant increase. *(Vote 546, p. H-166)*

Klug said the amendment failed, albeit narrowly, for a handful of reasons. He said Boehlert had worked hard to fashion a compromise, and key Republicans wanted to support Boehlert by opposing the bigger fee increase. In addition, he said, the House seemed to be lacking hard-core deficit hawks, particularly in the freshman class.

➤ An amendment by Bruce F. Vento, D-Minn., rejected 208-212, to require large ranchers to pay either the average grazing fee for the state in question, or the bill"s grazing formula plus a 25 percent federal fee, whichever was higher. *(Vote 547, p. H-166)*

➤ Another Vento amendment, rejected 176-244, to remove language in the bill that would have the effect of reducing grazing fees for sheep and goats. *(Vote 548, p. H-166)*

Smith argued that the fee increase in HR 2493 struck the right balance, and that the ranching industry should be praised for supporting it. "How many industries in America would come to Congress and ask for a 36 percent increase in the cost of doing business?" he asked. ■

Other Legislation Related To Agriculture

Lawmakers worked on several agriculture reauthorization bills, none of which made it into law in the first session.

Agricultural Research

The House and Senate passed conflicting versions of a five-year authorization for agricultural research and education programs. Objections to the Senate bill by members in the House prevented the legislation from going to conference in the first session. House complaints focused on provisions in the Senate bill that they said would create more than $1 billion in new mandatory spending for agricultural research, with the funds taken out of the food stamp program.

The House version of the bill (HR 2534), sponsored by Larry Combest, R-Texas, proposed authorizing $14.7 billion for the programs through fiscal 2002. It also included provisions requiring the Agriculture Department to consider public input when setting funding priorities and directing that all the department's research programs be subject to scientific peer review.

Authorization for most of the programs expired at the end of fiscal 1997. Congress had not conducted a comprehensive review of the department's research, education and extension programs since 1977.

The bill included a requirement that land-grant universities receiving federal research grants match those funds one to one with non-federal dollars. Originally established with federal funding in the 1890s to promote agricultural education, the nation's 17 land-grant universities played a large part in conducting federally funded agricultural research programs. Under existing law, they were able to receive up to $100,000 match-free from the federal government.

A provision in the original bill would have expanded a number of federal research grant programs open only to land-grant institutions to allow all universities to compete for the funding. However, the language was removed during subcommittee markup, after several panel members strongly objected to the proposed expansion.

The House Agriculture Subcommittee on Forestry, Resource Conservation and Research approved the amended bill by voice vote Sept. 25. The full committee approved it by voice vote Oct. 29 (H Rept 105-376). The House passed the bill Nov. 8 by a vote of 291-125. *(Vote 618, p. H-184)*

The Senate passed its version of the bill (S 1150) by voice vote Oct. 29. Supporters said it would authorize $780 million in mandatory spending for federal agricultural research programs through fiscal 2002.

Bill sponsor Richard G. Lugar, R-Ind., said the amount represented about a 10 percent increase in the overall authorization, but that the increase would be offset by cuts in the food stamp program and administrative spending at the Agriculture Department. He said making the spending mandatory would free the programs from the annual appropriations struggle and allow more continuity in research efforts.

The Senate bill also proposed establishing stricter criteria for awarding research grants with a greater emphasis on multistate and multidisciplinary efforts. Projects that focused on increasing food production while protecting the environment also would receive priority.

The Senate Agriculture Committee approved the bill July 30 by a vote of 18-0 (S Rept 105-73).

Dairy Recalls

The House voted to reauthorize a program that helped dairy farmers recoup losses on recalled products, but the Senate did not take up the bill (HR 1789).

The measure, sponsored by Charles W. Stenholm, D-Texas, proposed reauthorizing the Dairy Indemnity Program through fiscal 2002. The program compensated farmers whose dairy products were pulled from the consumer market because of contamination from toxins, pesticides, chemicals or other substances through no fault of the producer.

The program's fiscal 1997 budget had been depleted in February by a large-scale milk recall affecting 30 milk producers, and the Farm Service Agency had stopped accepting claim requests. Under the bill, funds appropriated in fiscal 1998 could be used to pay claims arising from the 1997 shortfall.

The House Agriculture Subcommittee on Livestock, Dairy and Poultry approved the measure by voice vote June 26, and the full committee approved it by voice vote Sept. 24 (H Rept 105-294). The House passed it by voice vote under suspension of the rules Oct. 21.

Environmental Conservation

The Agriculture Department announced May 22, that it was enrolling 16.1 million acres into the Conservation Reserve Program, which paid farmers to idle environmentally sensitive land.

The move removed the impetus for a bill (HR 1342 — H Rept 105-80) passed by the House in April that would have provided a one-year extension to certain farmers of winter crops whose contracts with the Conservation Reserve Program were set to expire in 1997. A provision in HR 1342 said the bill would be void if the Agriculture Department took action on the program's contract renewals.

A Senate Agriculture Committee aide said Chairman Richard G. Lugar, R-Ind., helped broker the deal to pay farmers an average of nearly $40 an acre to idle the land. Lugar praised the department's move, saying it meant the program would be "more environmentally targeted and economical." But Lugar's counterpart on the House Agriculture Committee, Chairman Bob Smith, R-Ore., said the administration's plan did not enroll enough land and was "completely inadequate."

The House had passed HR 1342, sponsored by Smith, on April 29 by a vote of 325-92. The bill passed over the objections of some lawmakers who believed it would prevent the Agriculture Department from enrolling other, more environmentally pivotal land in the program. *(Vote 92, p. H-32)* ■

FCC To Auction Additional Spectrum

The federal government was authorized to step up its auctions of electromagnetic spectrum as part of an effort to raise revenues to balance the budget. The Congressional Budget Office (CBO) estimated that the Treasury would net $21.4 billion over five years from the spectrum auction provisions, which were included in budget-reconciliation legislation (HR 2015 — PL 105-33) signed into law Aug. 5.

Budget negotiators originally had hoped the auctions would raise $26.3 billion. But members of the committees with jurisdiction — House Commerce and Senate Commerce, Science and Transportation — refused to include some controversial provisions that might have boosted the CBO score to that level. The rejected proposals included a White House plan to impose fees on spectrum users, which was staunchly opposed by broadcasters, and another provision to auction toll-free "vanity" telephone numbers.

Lawmakers in both chambers, particularly Democrats, expressed doubt throughout the process that the spectrum provisions would yield the expected revenues.

Many members also said that forcing the auction of spectrum to meet budget goals instead of auctioning it when there was market demand would reduce its value.

The reconciliation bill extended the auction authority of the Federal Communications Commission (FCC) and outlined which pieces of spectrum were to be auctioned by 2002 in order to help balance the budget.

The bill included the following provisions:

- **FCC auction authority.** The FCC's authority to use competitive bidding to assign licenses for the use of the electromagnetic spectrum was extended until Sept. 30, 2007. Its existing authority was due to expire Sept. 30, 1998.

The FCC's auction authority was also expanded. Previously, the agency could use auctions only to award spectrum to companies that resold communications services — such as for paging, cellular telephone or personal communications services — to subscribers. Under the new law, auctions could generally be used for all radio-based licenses for mutually exclusive rights to use a portion of the spectrum.

Auctions could not be used for assigning public broadcasting licenses, providing additional spectrum to televisions stations to broadcast advanced digital signals, or licensing noncommercial public radio services.

- **Spectrum reallocation and sales.** The bill required the FCC to find 100 megahertz of spectrum to auction by the end of 2002, including 45 megahertz being used by the federal government and scheduled for auction in 2006. The National Telecommunications and Information Administration was directed to locate an additional 20 megahertz being used by federal agencies. The bill also set aside 24 megahertz of spectrum from channels 60-69 for public safety use, while the remaining 36 megahertz was to be auctioned.

- **Recaptured television spectrum.** One of the most controversial provisions set a deadline for the FCC to auction spectrum that television broadcasters were expected to return to the government after making the transition from analog television signals to digital technology.

The bill required that television stations return the analog spectrum by the end of 2006.

But it required the FCC to auction the returned spectrum by Sept. 30, 2002 — more than four years before the giveback deadline — so that the revenues could be counted within the five-year time-frame of the bill.

It also directed the FCC to grant any broadcaster an extension to retain its analog spectrum space if one of the following circumstances existed at the end of 2006: at least one major network in a TV market was not broadcasting in digital; converter boxes enabling analog TV sets to receive digital signals were not generally available in a market; or 15 percent or more of local households did not have digital sets, subscribe to cable or digital satellite, or have at least one analog TV set with a digital converter.

The administration wanted a more certain spectrum giveback date, but lawmakers such as W.J. "Billy" Tauzin, R-La., chairman of the House Commerce Telecommunications Subcommittee, argued that Congress had to provide some leeway to ensure that consumers did not lose access to free over-the-air television.

- **Waivers.** Another controversial provision, pushed hardest by Tauzin, required the FCC to grant a waiver of its "duopoly" and "cross-ownership" rules in cities of more than 400,000 people. Those rules barred any broadcaster from owning more than one TV station in the same market and any newspaper from owning a TV station in the same area in which it circulated.

Under the bill, newspapers and TV stations in such cities could bid for recaptured spectrum in their own market if it was to be used to broadcast digital television signals. Proponents argued that this would encourage more active bidding for the returned spectrum.

Background

The FCC had adopted rules April 3 giving each broadcaster an additional channel of spectrum to make the conversion from analog to more technologically advanced digital television. The agency had set a target date of 2006 for broadcasters to return their analog spectrum and begin broadcasting exclusively in digital form.

The commission also required affiliates of the four major networks in the top 10 television markets to operate in both digital and analog by May 1, 1999. Digital television sets, which initially could cost as much as $5,000, were expected to be available by late 1998.

Critics had tried without success to forestall what they said was a giveaway of a valuable asset: remaining space on the broadcast spectrum. Before leaving the Senate in 1996, Majority Leader Bob Dole, R-Kan., attempted to require broadcasters to pay for additional spectrum space to provide digital television. His efforts were stymied by opposition from the National Association of Broadcasters and its allies in Congress. *(1996 Almanac, p. 3-47)*

Senate Commerce, Science and Transportation Committee Chairman John McCain, R-Ariz., who had supported Dole's efforts to auction the additional television spectrum space, urged the FCC and the broadcast industry to move quickly to make the transition to digital. "It is only by enjoying the benefits of digital television service and by auctioning the returned analog channels at the earliest possible date that the public can be compensated," he said.

House Committee Action

Despite catcalls from Democrats and concern by some Republicans, the House Commerce Committee narrowly approved its version of the spectrum auction provisions June 11. The 27-23 vote came one day after the panel's Telecommunications, Trade and Consumer Protection Subcommittee squeezed the legislation through on a 13-12 vote.

Under the fiscal 1998 budget resolution (H Con Res 84), the committee was supposed to figure out a way to raise $26.3 billion over five years from such auctions.

Members of both parties expressed doubts that the auctions would raise anything near that. "I think everyone recognizes that the number is pure fantasy," said John D. Dingell of Michigan, the Commerce Committee's ranking Democrat.

Michael G. Oxley, R-Ohio, noted, as did others, that recent spectrum auctions by the FCC had not generated the amounts they were estimated to bring in to the federal Treasury. He pointed to an April auction mandated by a fiscal 1997 catchall spending bill (PL 104-208) that brought in only a fraction of the estimated amount. "This, in a word, is a farce," said Oxley.

Still, most Republicans played down their concerns and voted for the plan in the interest of advancing a big chunk of money for the spending-reconciliation bill then working its way through Congress.

Auction Provisions

The committee proposed to extend the FCC's auction authority through fiscal 2002.

The panel called on the FCC to find 100 megahertz of spectrum, including 45 megahertz that was being used exclusively by the federal government, to auction by Sept. 30, 2002. The National Telecommunications and Information Administration was directed to locate an additional 20 megahertz.

Under the bill, broadcasters would be required to return the 78 megahertz of spectrum being used for analog broadcasting by the end of 2006. The FCC would be required to begin auctioning the returned spectrum by July 1, 2001. The agency would also be required to extend the deadline for returning analog spectrum for stations in areas where more than 5 percent of households continued to rely exclusively on over-the-air analog television signals.

Democrats argued that this loophole would reduce the dollar value of analog spectrum, as businesses would not want to bid in 2001 for slots that they might not receive for several years. "Who in the world is going to bid for these frequencies?" asked Edward J. Markey of Massachusetts, the ranking Democrat on the subcommittee.

The bill also required that the FCC allocate the 60 megahertz of spectrum being used for UHF TV channels 60-69, with 36 megahertz to be auctioned off for commercial uses and the remaining 24 megahertz to be set aside for public safety use.

Subcommittee Markup

During subcommittee consideration June 10, members voted 15-10 to adopt an amendment by Tauzin that was later refined in the full committee. Under Tauzin's proposal, the FCC would be required to void auctions if it determined that the aggregate proceeds from such sales would total less than two-thirds of the amount CBO had earlier estimated such auctions would generate.

The amendment was offered as a substitute to a proposal by Dingell that the FCC be required to set minimum bids but also be allowed to hold an auction only when it believed it was needed, not necessarily within the time frame outlined in the budget resolution. Tauzin said Dingell's amendment could allow the FCC to postpone the auctions beyond 2002, the last year of the budget agreement.

Dingell offered the same amendment in full committee, but the language was again overridden by a Tauzin amendment that was approved on a 26-20 vote.

The subcommittee rejected by voice vote a Markey amendment that would have required the Treasury secretary to reduce the capital gains tax cut that Republicans planned to include in the reconciliation package if spectrum auctions failed to bring in the amount estimated by CBO.

The panel adopted by voice vote an amendment by Joe L. Barton, R-Texas, to ensure that the FCC would not auction any spectrum being used by the National Aeronautics and Space Administration and the National Oceanic and Atmospheric Administration.

Full Committee Approval

During the full committee markup, Markey offered an amendment that he contended would help increase the value of the analog spectrum by accelerating broadcasters' conversion to digital. His proposal, rejected 11-31, would have required that all television sets sold after the 2001 analog auction be able to receive digital signals.

Elizabeth Furse, D-Ore., made a similar attempt. Her amendment, rejected 16-30, would have required TV set manufacturers to include a label on any analog television set sold beginning three years before the issuance of licenses for the use of auctioned analog spectrum. The label would have informed consumers that the set might be incapable of receiving over-the-air signals after 2006.

The committee voted 26-23 to approve an amendment by Oxley to relax the rules against allowing a broadcaster to own more than one TV station in a broadcast market and a newspaper from owning a TV station in its circulation market. The close vote reflected protests by several Democrats that such a key change in broadcasting law should not be tucked into a budget bill.

House Floor Action

Before passing the reconciliation-spending bill, 270-162, on June 25, the House agreed to several changes, including alterations aimed at increasing the revenue generated by the spectrum auction provisions. The changes were adopted automatically as part of the rule for floor debate on the bill. *(Vote 241, p. H-76)*

CBO had dealt a blow to the Commerce Committee's spectrum plan June 16 by estimating that it would raise only $9.7 billion over five years. That was $16.6 billion short of the amount required under the budget resolution.

Among the reasons cited by CBO was the loophole for stations to retain their analog spectrum after 2006 if 5 percent of their viewers continued to rely exclusively on over-the-air analog television signals. CBO also cited the proposed requirement that the FCC void the results of an auction if the bids did not meet a certain minimum. CBO said the provision would void many auctions, resulting in decreased collections.

The changes — which increased the projected revenue to $20.3 billion over five years — included allowing, rather than requiring, the FCC to extend the spectrum giveback deadline; requiring the FCC to complete the auction of returned analog television spectrum by Sept. 30, 2002; and striking the language requiring the agency to void auctions that failed to meet bid standards.

Senate Action

The Senate Commerce, Science and Transportation Committee approved its version of the spectrum provisions, 15-5, on June 17.

The committee proposals were based on recommendations by the White House Office of Management and Budget (OMB). A preliminary CBO estimate put the proceeds from the OMB proposal at $21.4 billion, but the total was subsequently reduced to $15.9 billion.

As in the House, members voiced skepticism about the amount that budget negotiators hoped to raise through spectrum auctions. "We've got one grand fraud on course," said Ernest F. Hollings of South Carolina, the ranking Democrat on the Commerce Committee.

Like the House version, the Senate proposal called on the FCC to find 100 megahertz of spectrum to auction. It also required the auction of 36 megahertz of spectrum being used for TV channels 60-69, while setting aside 24 megahertz from these channels for public safety use.

The legislation also contained provisions — the source of much of the bill's controversy — requiring that the FCC recapture by 2006, but auction by Sept. 30, 2002, the spectrum that broadcasters were using for analog television.

The committee approved by voice vote an amendment by McCain codifying the 2006 giveback date, but also ordering the FCC to provide any broadcaster an extension if 5 percent of households in its TV market did not have access to local digital television signals, either by direct over-the-air reception or other means, which could include cable television or other services.

The Senate panel did not adopt all of OMB's recommendations. The committee agreed by voice vote to strike a provision, opposed by broadcasters and others, that would have authorized the FCC to impose fees on spectrum users. James C. May, executive vice president for government relations for the National Association of Broadcasters, had said that if this provision was included, broadcasters would not rest "until it is knocked out."

Also by voice vote, the panel struck language calling for the auction of toll-free vanity telephone numbers.

Committee members rejected an effort by Byron L. Dorgan, D-N.D., to give the FCC more leeway in deciding when to conduct spectrum auctions. His amendment would have allowed the FCC to hold an auction when it determined it would yield maximum returns to the government, not necessarily within the five-year budget time frame.

McCain expressed concern that Dorgan's amendment would prompt CBO to "dramatically downgrade" its scoring of potential revenue.

The panel instead approved, 11-7, an amendment by Republican Sam Brownback of Kansas to Dorgan's amendment specifying that the auctions had to be held within the five-year budget time frame.

Senate Floor Action

The Senate passed the overall spending-reconciliation bill June 25 by a vote of 73-27. *(Vote 130, p. S-24)*

During floor debate, senators gave voice vote approval to an amendment by Budget Committee Chairman Pete V. Domenici, R-N.M., adding about $4 billion to the $15.9 billion in revenue expected under the committee spectrum auction provisions. Most of the revenue came from deleting a committee-approved provision that would have allowed the FCC to delay or cancel auctions that might have pushed revenue collections beyond the 2002 closure of the scorekeeping window.

Conference, Final Action

House and Senate conferees working on the spectrum provisions managed to get their total revenue estimate up to $21.4 billion over five years.

That was accomplished in part by adding an accounting mechanism under which $3 billion was to be appropriated in fiscal 2001 for the Universal Service Fund, which subsidized local phone service. The fund was required to return an equal amount to the Treasury in 2002 so that the money could be counted as a revenue increase within the five-year period covered by the reconciliation bill.

The provision brought criticism from Hollings, among others, who called it an effort "to float an interest-free loan to the government" at the expense of small telephone companies.

The House adopted the conference report on the reconciliation bill (H Rept 105-217) on July 30, 346-85. The Senate cleared the bill the next day, 85-15. *(House vote 345, p. H-104; Senate vote 209, p. S-36)* ■

No Clarity on Encryption Exports

House committees produced five conflicting versions of a bill (HR 695) to ease restrictions on the commercial export of encryption equipment and technology. The committees' actions reflected sharp disagreements in Congress over how far to go in allowing dissemination of technology to protect electronic communications from unauthorized access. Encryption worked by using mathematical formulas to scramble data; the data could then be decoded only through a string of digits that composed an electronic "key."

A Senate version of the bill (S 909) was approved by the Commerce, Science and Transportation Committee but got no further in the first session.

Computer software companies and others argued that existing export restrictions put them at a disadvantage with foreign competitors who could export much stronger forms of commercial encryption. They backed HR 695, introduced by Rep. Robert W. Goodlatte, R-Va., because it would allow them to export encryption software, as well as hardware with encryption capabilities, that was equal in strength to products that were generally available overseas.

National security and law enforcement officials, however, said widespread use of robust encryption would hamper intelligence gathering and crime fighting.

Given these concerns, the Clinton administration was reluctant to ease export controls unless encryption products included a recovery feature. Such a feature would allow law enforcement officials, when authorized, to gain access to the keys needed to decode encrypted communications. Computer industry officials were opposed to mandatory key recovery.

FBI Director Louis J. Freeh, who opposed HR 695, went a step further, calling for controls on the domestic use of encryption, a move that other administration officials said they did not support.

Attempts To Thwart Criminals, Spies

Freeh and other law enforcement officials had a sympathetic ear in the House Intelligence and National Security committees. Before approving HR 695, the National Security

Committee on Sept. 9 added language to allow the president to ban exports of encryption products that he determined might harm national security.

On Sept. 11, the House Intelligence Committee voted to require manufacturers to include a recovery feature in encryption products that were distributed domestically or imported into the United States. (The House Commerce Committee rejected a similar amendment Sept. 24.) The Intelligence panel also approved a provision requiring that encryption products exported for sale overseas include a recovery feature.

The job of sorting out which version to send to the House floor fell to Rules Committee Chairman Gerald B.H. Solomon, R-N.Y., who said he would not move any encryption bill unless it addressed the concerns of law enforcement officials.

On the Senate side, the Commerce, Science and Transportation Committee approved a bill (S 909) on June 19 that was close to the administration's position and included provisions aimed at fostering the White House's goal of an international key recovery infrastructure. Opponents in the computer software industry said it would provide only token relief from existing export restrictions. Commerce Committee Chairman John McCain, R-Ariz., one of S 909's chief sponsors, and others tried to find a compromise acceptable to both the software industry and law enforcement, but they had little luck.

BOXSCORE

Encryption Exports — HR 695, S 909. Committee-approved versions of the bills sought, in varying degrees, to relax export restrictions on commercial encryption technology.

House committee reports:

Judiciary — HR 105-108, Part 1.

International Relations — HR 105-108, Part 2.

National Security — HR 105-108, Part 3.

Intelligence — HR 105-108, Part 4.

Commerce — HR 105-108, Part 5.

Background

As the private sector's reliance on computers and online communications continued to soar, so too did the demand for products to ensure that criminals could not get access to sensitive information.

There were no restrictions on the domestic use of encryption. But up until Jan. 1, 1997, the Clinton administration had limited encryption exports to products with a strength of 40 bits or less, a level that computer industry representatives said provided only minimal security. Their claim was bolstered in early 1997 when a graduate student at the University of California at Berkeley, who was answering a challenge from a California software company, broke a 40-bit code in a matter of hours.

Industry representatives said export restrictions not only threatened the technological edge that U.S. companies held over foreign competitors, but might also enable foreign companies that did not face the same restrictions to gain a toehold in the U.S. market. "We're one of world leaders in cryptography, yet we're handicapped by these export controls," said Kelly Blough, director of governmental relations for Pretty Good Privacy, a company that marketed encryption products.

Clinton Opens Door a Crack

Such arguments struck a nerve with the Clinton administration, which touted increased high-tech exports as crucial to future U.S. prosperity. Under pressure from business interests and their allies in Congress, the administration announced in December 1996 that it would allow the export of more sophisticated encryption products — provided they were equipped with a key recovery system and cleared a review by the departments of Commerce, Justice and Defense.

The recovery system would allow law enforcement officials acting under court order to gain access to the electronic keys that would enable them to decode encrypted communications. The administration's goal was the development of a key recovery infrastructure to be used worldwide.

Under the new policy, companies could export 56-bit or equivalent products for two years if they submitted plans showing they were working to develop a key recovery system. Companies would be required to tell the government who possessed the keys to the encrypted products.

But business interests and some lawmakers wanted more freedom and fewer caveats. They argued that continued limitations were ineffectual, as producers in other nations were marketing stronger encryption programs, without a key recovery feature, than U.S. companies were allowed to sell overseas.

At a hearing held March 19 by the Senate Commerce, Science and Transportation Committee, the administration's chief spokesman on the issue, William A. Reinsch, head of the Commerce Department's Bureau of Export Administration, said the administration understood there was a business need for strong encryption, but that it had to be balanced with the national interest.

"Businesses and individuals need encrypted products to protect sensitive commercial information and to preserve privacy," Reinsch told the hearing. "But the increased use of encryption carries with it serious risks for law enforcement and our national security."

FBI Director Freeh, who also appeared at the March 19 Commerce hearing, said law enforcement officials were concerned about the "wide dissemination and use of robust and unbreakable encryption," which he warned would increase the likelihood of its use by criminals.

Freeh noted that criminals were already using encryption. For example, a laptop computer seized by the FBI from Ramzi Yousef, who was convicted on terrorism charges in 1996, contained encrypted files with plans to blow up several U.S.-owned commercial airliners. Freeh argued that a key recovery system would enable law enforcement agencies to obtain encrypted information from criminals without their knowledge.

Freeh and other administration officials said that, while strong encryption was available worldwide, its use was not yet widespread. They argued that it was important for the United States to encourage key recovery before the use of strong, non-recoverable encryption products became pervasive.

Industry representatives disputed Freeh's claim that strong encryption was not widely used around the world. Opponents of Clinton's proposals also said there was no guarantee that criminals would use software that included a key recovery system.

While some businesses might want products with a key recovery feature, industry representatives said, other customers feared that the keys could end up in the wrong hands. "We believe customers, individuals and corporate customers will not want to buy products that have a back door," said Todd Coffin, a spokesman for Pretty Good Privacy.

House Judiciary Committee

The first markup took place in the House Judiciary Committee. With bipartisan support, the committee approved HR 695 by voice vote May 14. The panel's Subcommittee on Courts and Intellectual Property had endorsed the measure by voice vote and without amendment April 30. The Judiciary Committee had primary jurisdiction over the bill, though not over the export provisions.

Under the committee-approved bill, U.S. companies would be allowed to export encryption software equal in strength to products that were generally available overseas. The standard would also apply to hardware with encryption capabilities. In direct contradiction of Clinton administration policy, the bill would prohibit the government from requiring participation in a key recovery system. For those who used encryption to further crime, the bill proposed to establish criminal penalties.

Proponents, including California Rep. Zoe Lofgren, the bill's leading Democratic supporter, said that if the administration failed to gain international acceptance of a key recovery infrastructure — which so far had been the case — such a system would never work domestically and would damage the ability of U.S. businesses to compete with foreign companies.

HR 695 had the support of an unusually broad coalition, including not only the computer software and hardware industries, but also organizations such as the liberal American Civil Liberties Union and the conservative Eagle Forum that were usually at cross-purposes.

Before approving the bill, the full committee gave voice vote approval to an amendment specifying that the proposed criminal penalties would apply only to instances in which a person, in the commission of a felony, knowingly and willfully encrypted incriminating information to avoid detection by law enforcement officials. The amendment, by Bill Delahunt, D-Mass., was intended to alleviate concerns that the penalty provision might be extended to cover everyday, innocent use of encryption.

House International Relations Committee

The International Relations Committee approved HR 695 by voice vote July 22, after rebuffing a key amendment aimed at weakening the legislation. The panel's Subcommittee on International Economic Policy and Trade had approved it, 14-1, on June 24. The International Relations Committee had jurisdiction over the bill's export provisions.

The full committee rejected, 12-22, an amendment by Chairman Benjamin A. Gilman, R-N.Y., that would have allowed the president to block the export of encryption software or hardware with encryption capabilities if he determined the products would adversely affect national security.

Sam Gejdenson, D-Conn., said that while national security and law enforcement officials predicted "the end of Western civilization as we know it" if HR 695 was enacted, powerful encryption products already were widely available around the world and in the United States. "You're fooling yourselves if you think you are giving the president the ability" to stop the use of powerful encryption, he said of the Gilman amendment.

House National Security, Intelligence Committees

The bill went next to the National Security and Intelligence committees, whose members were far more sympathetic to the argument that the increased availability and use of unbreakable encryption in the United States and overseas would hinder efforts to catch terrorists and other criminals.

The National Security Committee delivered the first blow Sept. 9, voting 45-1 to give the president the power to limit encryption exports to a strength level that would not compromise national security. The level would be reviewed each year. The amendment also proposed giving the Defense secretary virtual veto power over whether an encryption product could be exported to a particular country or user. Adam Smith, D-Wash., cast the lone vote against the amendment. The committee then approved the amended bill by voice vote.

The Intelligence Committee went even further on Sept. 11, voting to place controls on domestic encryption to give authorities a tool to use against terrorists and other criminals who wanted to hide information.

The amendment, adopted by voice vote, required that encryption products manufactured and distributed domestically or imported into the United States after Jan. 31, 2000, include a feature that would allow authorities, upon presentation of a court order, to gain immediate access to plaintext data or decryption information. The panel also approved a provision requiring that encryption products exported overseas include a recovery feature. The decision of whether to activate the feature would rest with the foreign users, however.

The committee approved its version of the bill by a voice vote. The Commerce Department's Reinsch indicated the panel might have gone too far. "We believe the solution lies in a voluntary key recovery system, and we are prepared to work with Congress and the industry to develop a balanced approach. Neither the committee action nor HR 695 as introduced meets this test," he said.

Action in the two committees came as the FBI and national security officials stepped up their efforts, through closed briefings with lawmakers, to warn about the bill. They said unrestricted use of strong encryption would hamper their ability to use wiretaps and other measures to catch criminals and terrorists.

Freeh publicly highlighted his concerns during testimony Sept. 3 before a Senate Judiciary subcommittee, giving the strongest indication yet of his desire to see controls placed on encryption products used in the United States.

Freeh said he favored legislation requiring manufacturers to include some form of recovery feature in encryption products sold in the United States, so that law enforcement agents would have a means of decoding information when necessary.

Computer software industry representatives blasted the comments as a dramatic shift in administration policy. Administration officials, however, distanced themselves from Freeh's remarks, saying there had been no change in their policy of support for Americans' right to use any form of encryption.

Goodlatte and others complained that Freeh's warnings were out of touch with reality. They said strong encryption was already widely available throughout the world, and that U.S. efforts to control its use would fail.

But both committees appeared to heed Freeh.

House Commerce Committee

The Commerce Committee, the fifth and last House panel to weigh in on the bill, approved yet another version of HR 695 on Sept. 24; the vote was 44-6. The panel had been given a two-week extension in hopes that it could find a middle ground that would take into account the needs of the software industry and other business interests, while ensuring that the bill did not threaten national security. But the bill that came out of the committee did not appear strong enough to satisfy law enforcement interests.

The committee rejected, 16-35, an attempt to place new restrictions on domestic use of encryption. The amendment, backed by Solomon and law enforcement groups, was offered by Michael G. Oxley, R-Ohio, and Thomas J. Manton, D-N.Y. It would have required that encryption products manufactured for sale in the United States include a feature that would enable law enforcement officials, with the proper legal authority, to decode encrypted information into plain text without the knowledge of the user. "I support American business and American exports, but not at any cost," said Manton, a former New York City police officer.

The amendment's opponents said it would require manufacturers to build a "back door" into their products that would give government officials unprecedented access to Americans' private communications. They said criminals would evade the obstacle by buying encryption products overseas that did not have such a recovery feature. "We could legislate until the cows come home, and bad guys will have encryption," said Rick White, R-Wash.

Oxley, a former FBI agent, said his amendment would not give law enforcement new authority but instead give it the tools to adapt to changing technologies.

After rejecting the Oxley-Manton amendment, the panel voted 40-11 to adopt a weaker proposal by White and Edward J. Markey, D-Mass. Their amendment called for establishing a National Electronic Technologies Center that would tap the expertise of industry and government in order to help law enforcement figure out how to break encryption codes. The amendment also called for doubling the penalties in HR 695 for the use of encryption in committing a felony.

On the eve of the Commerce Committee markup, Solomon sent a letter saying he would not send the bill to the floor unless it addressed law enforcement concerns.

Senate Commerce Committee

In the midst of the House markups, the Senate Commerce, Science and Transportation Committee gave voice vote approval June 19 to S 909. The measure, sponsored by McCain and Bob Kerrey, D-Neb., the measure was aimed at breaking the long deadlock over encryption policy, but it did little to resolve the dispute.

Critics, including computer software makers and free-speech advocates, said the bill offered only token relief from the existing rules and would actually take a step backward on domestic use of such technology.

Under the bill, companies would be allowed to export encryption technology with 56-bit strength without key recovery. But they would have to include key recovery in their products in order to export anything above that level.

The bill also sought to promote the establishment of a "secure public network" for businesses, government and individuals to communicate electronically by encouraging the use of products with key recovery. Encryption products purchased by federal agencies would have to have key recovery, as would any products purchased with U.S. funds for the development of encrypted public networks.

The bill outlined conditions under which keys could be released to others, limits on using encryption and circumstances for recovering damages when a key was illegally released. It also proposed setting up a voluntary registration system for public authorities and other agents that would administer key recovery programs.

Although S 909 stated that it was not mandating domestic use of encryption with key recovery, opponents of the legislation said it would have that effect. "It would impose significant incentives and therefore try to get key recovery implemented domestically," said John Scheibel, vice president and general counsel for the Computer and Communications Industry Association.

Scheibel's group and others instead favored an approach taken by Conrad Burns, R-Mont., who opposed S 909 in committee and introduced a bill (S 377) that proposed to go much further in liberalizing encryption export restrictions. Burns' bill did not try to encourage key recovery.

Burns offered a stripped-down version of the bill as an amendment to S 909, but it was rejected, 8-12. The amendment would have allowed the export of non-recoverable encryption products with a strength that was generally available overseas and export of products with unlimited strength as long as they included key recovery.

The committee, however, did approve by voice vote an amendment by John Kerry, D-Mass., aimed at providing the software industry with more relief from export restrictions. The amendment sought to establish a board with representatives from the CIA, FBI, National Security Agency and the White House to evaluate whether a market existed overseas for encryption products without key recovery that were stronger than the bill would allow and make recommendations to the president about whether to allow an export exemption.

Burns was not satisfied. He argued that such a board could not work fast enough for businesses to compete. "Let's deal with reality here in the business world," he said. "You're going to be a day late and a dollar short."

McCain acknowledged that S 909 was "not perfect" and invited critics to work with him on a consensus bill, but he was unable to bridge the gap before the session ended. ■

Broadcasters Agree To Rate Television Programs

After months of mounting pressure by members of Congress and family advocacy groups, the broadcast industry agreed in July to alter the voluntary television ratings system they had put in place at the beginning of the year to include more information about the content of programs.

The broadcasters' move came in response to complaints by lawmakers and advocacy groups that the industry's age-based system did not give viewers enough information about the content of television programs. The industry's original system was based on the guidelines used for movies, with ratings based on their suitability for certain ages. It included the following ratings:

- **Children's programs:**

TV-Y — Designed for all children, particularly for a very young audience, including children ages 2-6.

TV-Y7 — May contain mild physical or comedic violence; aimed at children ages 7 and above.

- **Programs aimed at all audiences:**

TV-G — Contains little or no violence, no strong language and little or no sexual dialogue or situations.

TV-PG — May contain infrequent coarse language, limited violence and some suggestive sexual dialogue and situations.

TV-14 — Unsuitable for children under age 14. Programs may contain sophisticated themes, sexual content, strong language and more intense violence.

TV-M — Unsuitable for children under age 17. Programs

may contain adult themes, profane language, graphic violence and explicit sexual content.

Background to the Ratings Dispute

The call for a television ratings system grew out of a provision included in the 1996 telecommunications law (PL 104-104) requiring that new television sets include a "v-chip," technology that would allow viewers to block out objectionable programs. The v-chip blocked programs based on their ratings. Broadcast and cable companies were given until Feb. 8, 1997, to develop their own ratings system. If they did not comply, the law required the Federal Communications Commission (FCC) to develop ratings guidelines with the help of a panel of parents and industry representatives. *(1996 Almanac, p. 3-43)*

After a meeting at the White House and considerable prodding by the president and members of Congress, broadcast industry executives announced Feb. 29, 1996, that they would develop a voluntary ratings system.

They formally unveiled the guidelines Dec. 19, 1996. The system, however, was met with a chorus of criticism by parents, education officials and some lawmakers such as Rep. Edward J. Markey, D-Mass., one of the chief authors of the v-chip provision.

During a hearing Feb. 27, 1997, before the Senate Commerce Committee, Motion Picture Association of America President Jack Valenti, who helped develop the ratings system, said the industry was not opposed to making changes if they were needed. But he defended the industry's system as easy to understand and urged Congress to give it a chance.

Critics Force Revisions

Hoping to prod the industry to take action, the Senate Commerce, Science and Transportation Committee on May 1 approved a bill (S 363 — S Rept 105-89) that would give broadcasters a choice: adopt a content-based system or restrict violent programming to late-night hours. The committee approved the bill on a 19-1 vote.

Under the bill, sponsored by Ernest F. Hollings, D-S.C., the FCC would be required to define television violence and establish "safe harbor" viewing times for children. Broadcasters would be prohibited from showing violent programming during the safe-harbor hours unless they adopted a content-based ratings system. In addition, they could lose their licenses if they repeatedly violated the safe-harbor provision.

Among those voting for Hollings' bill was Commerce Committee Chairman John McCain, R-Ariz., who had opposed similar legislation in 1996. He said he changed his position, in part, because of his frustration with broadcasters. "The lack of any measurable progress on the part of broadcasters and, most importantly, the program producers in developing an effective content-based ratings system [leads] me to support S 363," he said.

At the same time, McCain, Markey and others continued to urge the industry to act voluntarily.

Finally in July, the industry agreed to make many of the changes called for by the critics. The revised system added the icons "S," "V," "L" and "D" for sex, violence, course language and suggestive dialogue to the original age-based rating system to indicate whether a program contained those elements. The revised system went into place Oct. 1, 1997.

The industry, in turn, secured a promise from lawmakers — including McCain, Senate Majority Leader Trent Lott, R-Miss., and Minority Leader Tom Daschle, D-S.D. — that they would refrain for "several years" from pushing legislation that would change the ratings. Broadcasters were given similar assurances by House Commerce Telecommunications Subcommittee Chairman W.J. "Billy" Tauzin, R-La., and Markey, the panel's ranking Democrat, who had sponsored a House version (HR 910) of Hollings' bill.

But McCain said his promise not to push any legislation did not apply to those networks that refused to sign on to the new ratings system, which included NBC and the cable network BET. ■

Subcommittees Advance Bills To Restrict Internet Taxes

Committees in both the House and Senate took initial steps in 1997 to halt state and local authorities from instituting new taxes specifically targeted at the Internet. The legislation (HR 1054, S 442) came in response to complaints from businesses and on-line service providers that the imposition of myriad taxes by the thousands of U.S. taxing jurisdictions would hinder the growth of the Internet.

The sponsor of S 442, Democratic Sen. Ron Wyden of Oregon, said 20 states and the District of Columbia had imposed taxes on electronic commerce with differing results. New York, for example, taxed gross receipts on "furnishing information," but not on personal information.

Alabama's Revenue Department, on the other hand, Wyden said, had declared that Internet service providers such as America Online were utilities and had to pay a 4 percent public utilities tax like providers of electricity and water.

Bill supporters said a moratorium was needed while the federal government determined what kind of taxes were reasonable and would not hinder business opportunities.

HR 1054, sponsored by Rep. Christopher Cox, R-Calif., won approval in two House subcommittees — the Judiciary Subcommittee on Commercial and Administrative Law, and the Commerce Subcommittee on Telecommunications, Trade and Consumer Protection.

Wyden's bill was approved by the Senate Commerce, Science and Transportation Committee.

Background

Supporters of a moratorium warned that overzealous state and local officials in the nation's 30,000 taxing jurisdictions could obstruct the growth of the Internet by imposing new taxes. While acknowledging that there was no widespread effort to do this, they argued that the Internet would become an irresistible target. "Tax collectors around the country and globe are eyeing the Net," Cox said.

Opponents, including the National Governors' Association (NGA) and the National League of Cities, claimed the bills would pre-empt state taxing authority. They expressed particular concern about the impact on sales taxes, which the NGA said made up almost half of state revenues. They were worried that a loophole used by mail-order companies would have a devastating effect on their sales tax revenues as shopping on the Internet became more popular. The Supreme Court had ruled that companies were not required to collect sales taxes from customers in states where the companies did not have a physical presence.

While both bills proposed exempting sales, income and other traditional taxes, they did not call for closing the out-of-state sales tax loophole.

House Subcommittee

The House was first out of the box Oct. 9, when the two subcommittees approved nearly identical versions of HR 1054, both by voice vote. The bill sought to bar federal and state governments from implementing or enforcing taxes on Internet commerce for six years.

During that time, the Treasury, Commerce and State departments would work with state and local governments and consumer and business groups to build a consensus on how business transactions conducted over the Internet or other interactive computer services should be taxed. The president would be required to submit policy recommendations to Congress two years after the bill was enacted.

The moratorium would not apply to taxes on net income earned from Internet services, business license taxes or sales and use taxes on interstate electronic transactions that were consistent with mail-order or telephone transactions.

The president would be required to seek agreements through various international trade organizations to make international activity on the Internet and interactive computer services tariff- and taxation-free.

Both panels adopted changes made by Cox in response to criticism from state and local leaders about the potential impact on their taxing authority. The substitute expanded the list of specific taxes that would be exempt from the moratorium, such as property taxes and levies paid by common carriers when they were providing telecommunications services such as phone service. In addition, it limited the proposed moratorium to six years rather than making it indefinite, as in the original version.

While there was little debate in the Judiciary subcommittee, Edward J. Markey of Massachusetts, the ranking Democrat on the Commerce subcommittee, expressed concern that the Internet was being singled out for special treatment, saying Congress must "tread very carefully in this area before we unwittingly create a cyberspace Cayman Island-like tax haven."

Senate Committee

The Senate Commerce, Science and Transportation Committee approved S 442 by a vote of 14-5 on Nov. 4.

Before voting to report the bill, the panel adopted a substitute amendment offered by Wyden, Committee Chairman John McCain, R-Ariz., and others. Wyden's substitute added an end date for the moratorium, Jan. 1, 2004, and made many of the same changes that Cox had made regarding which taxes would be exempted from the moratorium.

Despite the changes, several senators voiced concerns about the legislation's impact on local and state governments. "The easiest tax cuts for us to vote for, of course, are tax cuts we don't have to pay for," said Slade Gorton, R-Wash.

Wyden had delayed the markup, first scheduled for June, while he tried to resolve concerns raised by Ted Stevens, R-Alaska. Stevens' concerns related mainly to questions about the impact of the Internet on universal service, which sought to ensure that all Americans had access to affordable telephone service. Stevens was critical of an FCC decision to exclude Internet service providers from having to pay into the fund established in the 1996 telecommunications overhaul (PL 104-104) to support universal service. He feared telecommunications providers might try to use the exemption to avoid paying to support universal service.

After working out some changes with Wyden on the bill, he agreed to address his concerns in fiscal 1998 Commerce, Justice, State spending bill, which funded the FCC. He included language in that measure (HR 2267 — PL 105-119) requiring the FCC to conduct a study on its rules implementing the universal service provisions. *(Appropriations, p. 9-11)* ■

Despite Concerns, Panel OKs Four Nominees for FCC

The Senate in late October confirmed William E. Kennard as the new chairman of the Federal Communications Commission (FCC), and endorsed three other new members of the five-member commission.

The need to fill four vacancies presented lawmakers with an opportunity to express their dissatisfaction over how the FCC was implementing the 1996 telecommunications overhaul, and to try to influence the agency's direction. As a result, Congress gave an unusual amount of attention to the confirmation process. "We vested a great deal of authority in the FCC," said Rep. Michael G. Oxley, R-Ohio. "It's natural to follow the power."

The Senate Commerce Committee approved the nominations after confirmation hearings Sept. 30 and Oct. 1. The commissioners occupied full-time jobs that paid at least $115,000 a year. The only holdover was Susan Ness, who held one of the FCC's three Democratic seats.

The New Commissioners

Kennard, who succeeded Reed E. Hundt as FCC chairman, was confirmed Oct. 29 by a vote of 99-1. Conrad Burns, R-Mont., cast the lone "no" vote. *(Vote 284, p. S-49)*

Kennard, 40, had served as FCC general counsel since 1993. Before that, he had been a partner in the law firm of Verner, Liipfert, Bernhard, McPherson and Hand. During his 10-year tenure there, he specialized in communications law. Prior to joining the law firm, he spent a year at the National Association of Broadcasters as a legal adviser on regulatory and First Amendment issues. Kennard was the first African-American to head the commission.

Sen. Ernest F. Hollings of South Carolina, ranking Democrat on the Commerce Committee, had pushed Ralph B. Everett, his former staff member on the committee, for the chairman's slot. Everett also was backed by the Congressional Black Caucus. But the White House chose Kennard, who had already been nominated for a Democratic seat on the commission.

The other three nominees, all of whom were confirmed by voice vote Oct. 28, were:

➤ Michael Powell, chief of staff in the Justice Department's antitrust division, who took one of the Republican seats on the commission. Powell, 34, was the son of former Joint Chiefs of Staff Chairman Colin L. Powell. He joined the Justice Department in late 1996 after a two-year stint at the Washington law firm of O'Melveny & Myers. He also had served as a law clerk at the U.S. Court of Appeals for the District of Columbia and spent three years in the Army. Powell had the strong support of Commerce Committee Chairman John McCain, R-Ariz.

➤ Harold W. Furchtgott-Roth, who took the other GOP seat and was the only non-lawyer on the commission. Furchtgott-Roth, 40, had served as chief economist to the House Commerce Committee since 1995 and was one of the key staffers involved in helping to craft the 1996 Telecommunications Act. Before joining the committee, he had worked as a senior economist at Economists Incorporated, providing clients with economic support for litigation and regulatory proceedings.

➤ Gloria Tristani, 43, who took over a Democratic slot. Tristani had served since 1995 on the New Mexico commission that regulated state utilities and had practiced law with an Albuquerque firm before that. A native of Puerto Rico, she was the granddaughter of former Sen. Dennis Chavez (House 1931-35; Senate 1935-62). Her appointment enabled the White House to accommodate the demands of rural-state lawmakers who wanted someone sympathetic to the concerns of rural residents for the second Democratic seat.

Pressure on the FCC

For many lawmakers, the most pressing issue facing the FCC was the implementation of the 1996 Telecommunications Act (PL 104-104), which swept away 62 years of telecommunications policy in an effort to open the telecommunications market to competition. *(1996 Almanac, p. 3-43)*

The act's supporters had promised consumers that they would have more choices at lower prices as telecommunications companies moved into one another's markets. Supporters envisioned cable companies offering telephone services, local phone companies moving into the long-distance market and long-distance companies expanding to offer local phone service. But, thus far, many of the promises had not come to fruition.

"The law has not lived up to the rhetoric that accompanied its passage," said McCain, who had voted against the bill, saying it would not go far enough in deregulating the telecommunications industry. McCain said that while many of the problems that had emerged since then were inherent to the act itself, the FCC had exacerbated the problem by interpreting the law "in the most bureaucratic fashion."

"My first wish is that they would simply read the bill we passed," said W.J. "Billy" Tauzin, R-La., chairman of the House Commerce telecommunications subcommittee. "If they follow it . . . we can begin the process that the bill promises in terms of competition."

Others blamed the local telephone companies, saying they were blocking competition while at the same time complaining about the FCC's refusal so far to allow any of the Bell companies to enter the long-distance telephone market. Under the act, a Bell could offer long-distance service in its region only after it opened its local service network to competition. "It is important for the new FCC to continue to remain tough on companies that want the best of both worlds, that is to retain monopolies in their own marketplaces while competing in other areas of telecommunications," said Rep. Edward J. Markey, D-Mass.

Many lawmakers and even outgoing FCC Chairman Hundt expressed frustration about the slow pace of competition in the local telephone market. All four nominees indicated that ensuring competition would be one of their chief goals. "If confirmed, I intend to ask the hard-working FCC staff to roll up their sleeves once again and mount a new offensive for competition," Kennard said.

Raising the Bell's complaint that the FCC had erected hurdles to their entry into the long-distance market that went beyond requirements of the 1996 law, Sen. Wendell H. Ford, D-Ky., said it appeared that the commission was "moving the goal posts." Kennard agreed that for competition to grow, it was "vitally important" for the FCC to be clear about what the standards were for entry into the long-distance market.

FCC Rules Challenged in Court

In the meantime, elements of the 1996 act were being challenged in court. In the broadest threat to the law, a federal judge in Texas ruled Dec. 31 that key provisions — those barring the regional Bells from providing in-region long distance service until they had opened up their local telephone market to competitors — unfairly singled out the Bells.

U.S. District Court Judge Joe Kendall ruled in favor of regional Bells SBC Communications Inc. and U.S. West Communications Inc., which challenged the law after the FCC denied a request by SBC to offer long distance service in Oklahoma. In light of Kendall's decision, SBC said it would move again to provide long distance.

Kendall said the provisions challenged by SBC and U.S. West were unconstitutional because they represented "a bill of attainder," a legislative act that inflicted punishment without a trial. He said the provisions stripped the Bells "of their ability to enter new markets and tied their hands while their competitors such as GTE, AT&T and MCI take their punches."

Kennard, who by then had been sworn in as FCC chairman, said the government would appeal the decision, which he said "guts the incentive" for the regional Bell companies to open their markets to competition. Regional telephone companies, such as the Bells, still controlled 99 percent of the local market, Kennard said. "This may be a wakeup call to everyone, including the FCC, that they need to carry out the intent of Congress," said Oxley.

Earlier, in July, the 8th U.S. Circuit Court of Appeals, based in St. Louis, struck down major parts of the commission's interconnection order, which set out the conditions and rates under which new competitors could enter the local telephone market. Local telephone companies argued that the FCC rules required them to offer their networks at "bargain basement prices," handing their competitors an advantage. The court said the FCC did not have the authority to set the rates that competitors would have to pay to incumbent local phone companies to use their networks.

In September, local telephone companies and state regulators went to court separately to argue that the FCC was trying to get around the appellate court's decision by requiring the Bells to accept the FCC pricing mechanism as one of the conditions for gaining entry into the long-distance market. ■

Other Legislation Related To Communications

The Senate worked on bills aimed at curbing illegal use of cellular telephone services and punishing gambling on the Internet. Neither measure was enacted in the first session.

Cellular Phone 'Cloning'

The Senate passed legislation by voice vote Nov. 10 designed to crack down on illegal "cloning" of cellular telephones. Bill sponsor Jon Kyl, R-Ariz., said the measure (S 493) was aimed at thieves who used high-tech software to "clone" the electronic serial numbers of legal cellular phones. The numbers were then used to obtain free phone service, with the calls charged to the unsuspecting user of the legal phone. In addition to costing consumers more than $650 million a year, Kyl said the fraudulent calls often were used to conduct illegal activity such as drug trafficking.

The bill, which the Senate Judiciary Committee had approved Sept. 18 by voice vote, proposed to criminalize the manufacture, sale or possession of computer software and hardware used for cloning, except for legitimate uses by law enforcement or the telecommunications industry. Under existing law, prosecutors had to prove that a defendant intended to use such equipment illegally.

The legislation also included penalties for violators. First-time offenders could face up to 15 years in prison and a fine reflecting the cost of the crime. Repeat offenders could face a fine and a prison sentence of up to 20 years.

"Cloned phones are popular among the most vicious criminal element," said Kyl. "Except for law enforcement and telecommunications carriers, there is no legitimate purpose for which to possess equipment used to modify cellular phones," he said.

The House Judiciary Committee approved a similar bill (HR 2460) by voice vote Oct. 29. Sam Johnson, R-Texas, introduced the legislation after discovering that his cellular telephone had been cloned when $6,000 worth of calls he did not make appeared on his bill.

Like the Senate bill, HR 2460 proposed to expand the definition of "scanning receiver" to include reception of cellular phone codes. Scanning receivers were legal devices used to receive voice radio transmissions but they could also be used to steal electronic serial numbers.

Internet Gambling

The Senate Judiciary Committee took the first step in trying to crack down on unregulated and rapidly growing cyberspace gambling parlors Oct. 23, giving voice vote approval to a bill (S 474 — no written report) that would specifically prohibit gambling on the Internet.

Existing law banned interstate gambling over telephone or other wire communications but did not specifically outlaw wagering on the Internet. Jon Kyl, R-Ariz., the bill's chief sponsor, said the legislation was needed to ensure that "activity which is illegal in one forum is not allowed in another."

Under a substitute amendment offered by Kyl and approved by the committee, those convicted of running an Internet gambling business in the United States could face up to four years in jail and fines up to $20,000 or equal to the amount of bets received, whichever was greater. Internet gamblers also could face up to six months in jail and a fine of $2,500 or the amount of the bets placed, whichever was greater.

Most Internet gambling operations were located outside the United States and out of reach of U.S. law, according to industry representatives. S 474 took aim at those businesses with a provision that would allow state and federal law enforcement officials with a court order to require an Internet service provider to block service to gambling sites.

The legislation also required that the secretary of State begin negotiating agreements with foreign countries to allow U.S. officials to enforce the measure outside the United States.

Internet gambling was a mushrooming industry. The number of sites had grown from about 15 at the beginning of the year to 60, according to Sue Schneider, managing editor of Rolling Good Times Online, a magazine that followed the gambling industry.

S 474's supporters said Internet gambling was particularly open to addiction, fraud and access by minors because it was unregulated and available in the privacy of the user's home. Kyl painted the nightmarish scenario of a child gaining access to his parents' credit card and losing thousands of dollars to an on-line casino.

The bill had the backing of traditional regulated-gambling allies such as Sen. Richard H. Bryan, D-Nev. And it was not opposed by traditional gambling interests. Frank J. Fahrenkopf Jr., president of the American Gaming Association, said his group opposed Internet gambling because "we don't see any mechanism at present" for regulating it.

But Internet gambling site operators argued that the legislation was unworkable and would open the door to other forms of regulation on the Internet. Kevin A. Mercuri of the Interactive Services Association, which represented about 35 gambling sites and some Internet service providers, said the bill would place "undue if not impossible burdens on Internet service providers." Mercuri and other opponents of S 474 said Internet gambling was impossible to stop, and that the federal government should focus instead on regulating and taxing it.

Before approving S 474, the committee agreed to delete language in the bill that would have allowed states to pass laws legalizing Internet gambling within their own borders. The amendment, by Orrin G. Hatch, R-Utah, was adopted by voice vote.

Jeff Sessions, R-Ala., and Joseph R. Biden Jr., D-Del., said that the original language would have created new opportunities, not specifically allowed under federal law, for states to allow Internet gambling. "I'm not going to vote for something that even allows that possibility," Biden said.

Kyl and others indicated that the provision was added at the urging of the horse racing industry, which viewed Internet betting as a potential source of new revenues. ■

House Panels Advance Several Science-Related Bills

The House Science Committee took a bipartisan path in 1997, approving a series of bills authorizing spending for federal agencies' scientific research and development activities. The approach stood in sharp contrast to the partisan battles that divided the panel in the 104th Congress. However, the committee did have jurisdictional run-ins with other House panels over three of the bills — for the National Oceanic and Atmospheric Administration (NOAA), the Environmental Protection Agency (EPA) and research programs at the Department of Energy. None of those bills passed the House.

The House did pass reauthorization bills for the National Aeronautics and Space Agency (NASA), the Commerce Department's National Institute of Standards and Technology (NIST) and the National Science Foundation (NSF), as well as a measure to encourage private-sector involvement in space.

Prospects for Senate action, however, were uncertain. In recent years, the Senate had eschewed science authorizations and preferred to act on the programs through the appropriations process.

The bipartisan tenor of the Science Committee coincided with the departure of its combative former Chairman Robert S. Walker, R-Pa., who had retired at the end of the 104th Congress. The new chairman, F. James Sensenbrenner Jr., R-Wis., took a more low-key approach. Most controversies over provisions were settled through amendments. The committee's ranking Democrat, George E. Brown Jr. of California, who had had a rocky relationship with Walker, praised Sensenbrenner for working cooperatively with Democrats. In the 104th Congress, Democrats had complained they were frozen out of the decision-making process.

Sensenbrenner said the committee provided a good lesson

to Congress. With "bipartisan cooperation and civility, this Congress can get a lot of work done," he said.

NASA

The House passed a $13.8 billion authorization bill for NASA (HR 1275 — H Rept 105-65) by voice vote April 24. The measure had been approved by the Science Committee April 16, also by voice vote.

During the committee markup, members vented their frustration with the agency's handling of the international space station project — though they rebuffed efforts to cut the $2.1 billion included for the program in fiscal 1998. NASA officials had announced April 9 that they were delaying the start of construction of the space station because of Russia's inability to deliver the service module, a key component, on time. Construction had been scheduled for November but was pushed back to no later than October 1998.

Sensenbrenner, a space station supporter, criticized the administration for not heeding his warnings about making the Russians such a key player in the project. He and Brown offered an amendment, adopted 25-0, to force the administration to develop guidelines to govern future relations with Russia on the space station. Under the amendment, NASA would be barred from giving Russia any funds to help it pay its portion of the program, and the NASA administrator would have to report to Congress every month on Russia's progress on the project.

"Some will ask why we have not demanded immediate removal of Russia from the program," Sensenbrenner said. "The fact is that we are now well down the road of relying on the Russians."

Later, the committee rejected, 2-16, an amendment by leading space station opponent Tim Roemer, D-Ind., to remove the Russians from participation in the project. The committee also soundly rejected amendments by Roemer to kill the space station and to reduce funding for the project by $75 million.

Unlike in recent years, the committee spent little time debating another controversial NASA program, Mission to Planet Earth, which consisted of a series of satellites monitoring the Earth's environment. The program had been a favorite target of former Chairman Walker and other Republicans.

This time, Republicans gave in, agreeing to the $1.4 billion requested for the program in each of fiscal years 1998 and 1999. Through an amendment adopted by the committee, Dana Rohrabacher, R-Calif., chairman of the Space and Aeronautics Subcommittee, also agreed to remove a provision in the bill that would have required NASA to use $200 million from an existing reserve fund to help pay part of the program's budget.

House Floor Action

Before passing the bill April 24, members rejected, 112-305, an attempt by Roemer to terminate the space station project. The floor amendment had become an annual ritual for Roemer, but he had been losing ground. His high-water mark was in 1993, when his amendment to kill the project lost by one vote. Roemer garnered 127 votes for a similar amendment to an omnibus science bill in 1996. *(Vote 90, p. H-30)*

Roemer argued that the project would not provide the scientific benefits its supporters claimed and that it was siphoning funding from more beneficial NASA programs. He and others also noted the delay caused by Russia's failure to deliver the service module and warned that further problems with the Russians would likely drive up the project's cost. "We are not getting good science out of this project; we are not getting a return on the dollar," Roemer said.

His opponents, however, argued that the space station was too far along to kill and that, once functioning, it would be an important platform for research into cures for many diseases. "It's just too late to turn our back on this program," said Robert E. "Bud" Cramer of Alabama, ranking Democrat on the Science Subcommittee on Space and Aeronautics.

The House also defeated, 186-226, an amendment by Sheila Jackson-Lee, D-Texas, to increase funding under NASA's minority research and education program for universities other than historically black universities and colleges that had large minority enrollments. *(Vote 91, p. H-30)*

NIST

Also on April 24, the House passed a reauthorization bill (HR 1274 — H Rept 105-64) for NIST by voice vote. The Science Committee had approved it by voice vote April 16.

The bill called for authorizing $609 million in fiscal 1998 for the NIST, but it proposed reducing the funding for the agency's Advanced Technology Program, which provided grants to assist industries in developing cutting-edge technologies. The program was a high priority for the Clinton administration, but conservative Republicans attacked it as a form of corporate welfare.

The bill proposed $185 million for the program in fiscal 1998, $90 million less than the administration requested for fiscal 1998 and $40 million less than was appropriated for fiscal 1997. Walker's 1996 omnibus authorization bill had included no funding for the program.

Debbie Stabenow, D-Mich., offered an amendment in the committee to bring the funding up to the fiscal 1997 level, calling the program "extremely beneficial" in bringing public and private sectors together to fund projects that might not otherwise be pursued. The amendment was rejected on a close vote of 19-20.

Sensenbrenner noted that unlike his predecessor, he was not "philosophically opposed" to the program. But he said he was concerned that some companies had abused it by not first seeking funding from the private sector before turning to the federal program.

NOAA

The Science and Commerce committees knocked heads on a two-year reauthorization bill (HR 1278) for several NOAA activities, including atmospheric, weather and satellite programs; oceanographic and marine research; and hydrographic and coastal assessment and monitoring.

The Science Committee gave voice vote approval April 16 to a version of the bill (H Rept 105-66, Part 1) that recommended $1.45 billion for the programs in fiscal 1998. It included an increase of $26.8 million over fiscal 1997 levels for the National Weather Service.

The House Resources Committee weighed in June 11, giving its voice vote approval to a version (H Rept 105-6, Part 2) that would authorize $1.2 billion for the programs in fiscal 1998.

The panel stripped out about 10 percent of the funds approved by the Science Committee, money directed toward programs that Resources Committee Chairman Don Young, R-Alaska, argued fell solely within his panel's jurisdiction. Among the programs chopped from the bill were navigation services provided by the National Ocean Service and coastal and ocean assessments. The Resources Committee also removed a Science panel provision to eliminate NOAA's corps of commissioned officers.

The Resources Committee adopted by voice vote an amendment by Ken Calvert, R-Calif., to cut NOAA administration funding by 5 percent, to $18.2 million in fiscal 1998, and 5 percent more to $17.3 million in fiscal 1999.

Energy R&D

A turf fight between the Science and Commerce committees produced conflicting versions of a bill (HR 1277) to reauthorize civilian research and development activities at the Department of Energy. The committees were playing for pride on the bill, which had little chance for enactment. The Senate had not acted on an Energy Department authorization since the early 1980s, preferring to handle agency issues through the appropriations process.

Science Committee Approves Bill

The Science Committee gave voice vote approval April 16 to a version of the bill (H Rept 105-67, Part 1) that recommended $4.6 billion for the programs in fiscal 1998, about $200 million less than the amount requested by the president. Democrats and some Republicans expressed concern about funding limitations on numerous Energy Department programs such as the Solar Building Technology Research Space Conditioning and Water Heating Quality Assurance program.

The American Wind Energy Association and other groups objected to a provision they said would "arbitrarily slash funding" for renewable energy and energy efficiency programs. Some committee Republicans, including Matt Salmon of Arizona, expressed similar concerns. In response, Energy and Environment Subcommittee Chairman Calvert offered an amendment, approved without objection, deleting the provision.

The bill included a provision to prohibit the department from using $50 million for a "clean coal" plant in China. "Corporate welfare is bad enough, but it is even worse when government sends the money to another country," Calvert said following the markup.

The committee also revived its debate over the controversial superconducting super collider project, an $11 billion giant atom smasher that was being built in Texas when its funding was killed by Congress in 1993. The debate came over the U.S. share of funding for the Large Hadron Collider in Switzerland, a high-energy physics project similar to, though on a much smaller scale than, the superconducting super collider.

Joe L. Barton, R-Texas, tried to eliminate funding for the Large Hadron Collider, which amounted to $35 million for fiscal 1998. He said he was concerned about providing funding for a non-U.S. project without having adequate knowledge of how it would be managed and without sufficient guarantees that U.S. scientists would have equal access and partnership in the project. Barton said that while he was not opposed to the collider, he was "opposed to the U.S. paying ransom for our scientists to participate" in the project. His amendment was supported by some other Texans on the panel.

Sherwood Boehlert, R-N.Y., who supported the project, countered that it was important for those who had argued in favor of saving the super collider on the merits of the scientific benefits to support the collider in Switzerland. "Some may argue that the Europeans didn't help the [superconducting super collider], so we shouldn't help them," Boehlert said. "This is petty and counterproductive."

The committee rejected the Barton amendment by a 12-20 show of hands. The panel, however, retained language in the bill to prohibit funding for the project unless Energy Secretary Federico F. Peña reported on the impact that funding the project would have on U.S. high-energy and nuclear physics facilities.

Sensenbrenner said the committee "should put the brakes" on funding until questions had been answered by the Europeans.

Commerce Committee Cuts Funding

On June 4, the House Commerce Committee gave voice vote approval to a pared-back $3.7 billion version of HR 1277 (H Rept 105-67, Part 2). The committee excluded about $924 million in projects that were approved by the Science Committee. The panel's Energy and Power Subcommittee had stripped those projects at a May 22 markup, saying they were under the jurisdiction of Commerce, not Science, and therefore should not have been included in the bill.

Led by Chairman Thomas J. Bliley Jr., R-Va., the Commerce Committee objected that many projects in the Science panel's version — including isotope manufacturing, safety oversight, environmental cleanup and uranium production — had little to do with scientific research and fell within Commerce's vast jurisdiction. In one area of agreement, though, both committees rejected funding for the White House's high-profile $300 million Next Generation Internet program.

Democrats, too, were also at odds over the bill. Brown, ranking Democrat on Science, said the June 4 action marked "a continuation of the egregious grab for power" he said was begun by John D. Dingell, the Michigan Democrat who headed the Energy and Commerce Committee from 1981 to 1995 and had become the ranking member on Commerce.

NSF

The House on April 24 passed a $3.5 billion authorization bill (HR 1273 — H Rept 105-63) for the National Science Foundation (NSF), up from the president's request of $3.4 billion. This measure, too, won voice vote approval from the Science Committee April 16.

Before passing the measure, the House adopted by voice vote an amendment by Republican Tom Coburn of Oklahoma, to prohibit the agency from providing money for the Man and Biosphere Program, a U.N.-sponsored environmental preservation program.

Helen Chenoweth, R-Idaho, contended that the program would give "the international community an open invitation to interfere in domestic land use decisions." Brown, ranking Democrat on the Science Committee, disputed this notion, saying, "There is nothing here which provides the U.N. any authority whatsoever over any territory of the United States."

Private Sector Role in Space

The House passed a bill (HR 1702) by voice vote Nov. 4 aimed at encouraging private-sector competition in the development of industrial space products. The Science Committee had approved the measure (H Rept 105-347) by voice vote June 18, following a markup in the panel's Space and Aeronautics Subcommittee on June 12.

The bill, introduced by committee Chairman Sensenbrenner, called on NASA to buy space transportation services from private companies to the maximum extent practical and included a variety of other provisions to encourage commercial activities in space.

EPA

The House Science and Commerce committees also locked horns over a bill (HR 1276) to authorize research, development and demonstration activities at the EPA. The Science Committee went first, approving a $640 million authorization bill (H Rept 105-99, Part 1) by voice vote April 16.

The House Commerce Committee then approved a revised version (H Rept 105-99, Part 2) by voice vote June 25, after deleting $208 million. Commerce members said the Science Committee had no jurisdiction over several items in the original bill, including projects associated with the Safe Drinking Water and Clean Air acts.

The amendment, offered by Michael G. Oxley, R-Ohio, was adopted by voice vote. Oxley said it limited the bill to matters within the Science panel's purview and removed projects that already had authorizations in place. The amendment deleted $115 million for drinking water and air pollution research by EPA's Office of Research and Development and $82 million for the Office of Air and Radiation.

"Had the Science Committee chosen to stay within the bounds of the environmental research and development programs, we would not be here today," fumed Commerce Committee member Sherrod Brown, D-Ohio. ■

Daley Vows To Avoid Politics At Commerce Department

William M. Daley won easy confirmation to head the Commerce Department, though he did garner the first "no" votes of any Clinton nominee in 1977. The Senate confirmed him, 95-2, on Jan. 30. The Commerce, Science and Transportation Committee had approved the nomination, 19-1, the previous day. *(Vote 3, p. S-2)*

Daley, 48, succeeded retiring Secretary Mickey Kantor, who took over Commerce after his predecessor, Ronald H. Brown, was killed in an April 1996 plane crash while on a trade mission to Bosnia-Herzegovina and Croatia. *(1996 Almanac, p. 3-14)*

Daley had run the fundraising effort for the 1996 Democratic National Convention in Chicago. A lawyer, Daley was a member of that city's royal political family. His brother, Richard M. Daley, was elected mayor of Chicago in 1989; his father, Richard J. Daley, dominated as mayor from 1955 to 1976.

Daley had been associated with Clinton since the 1992 presidential campaign. As Illinois chairman of Clinton's campaign that year, Daley — along with his brother — helped Clinton win big victories in the state's Democratic presidential primary and in the general election.

He had been seen as the front-runner to head the Transportation Department in Clinton's first term, but he was passed over for former Denver Mayor Federico F. Peña — leaving the Daley family feeling slighted for a time. But Clinton appointed Daley in 1993 to the board of the Federal National Mortgage Association (Fannie Mae), a government-sponsored enterprise. He also gave him a more public role as his special counsel on the North American Free Trade Agreement, the only official position Daley had held until his confirmation to head Commerce.

The Daleys were fully on board for the 1996 campaign, helping Clinton win a near landslide in Illinois in the general election.

William Daley was a partner at the Chicago law firm Mayer, Brown & Platt, working primarily in corporate and government relations. He earned nearly $1 million in 1996 from his work as a lobbyist and corporate adviser. He also served on boards of directors of a handful of companies, in addition to Fannie Mae.

Daley Pledges No Politics at Commerce

Daley launched a pre-emptive strike during his confirmation hearing Jan. 22 aimed at quelling Republican allegations that the Clinton administration had turned the Commerce Department into a Democratic political operation. He declared that he would eschew partisanship and keep the department free of political activity during his tenure.

Wendell H. Ford, D-Ky., asked Daley to respond to questions that were raised about his service as a Fannie Mae board member that coincided with work that his law firm had done for the federally chartered corporation. Daley denied that there were any connections between the two, saying that if the law firm was not qualified to work for Fannie Mae, "we wouldn't be representing them."

Responding to concerns that Chicago might benefit disproportionately from his position at the helm of Commerce, Daley promised to recuse himself from specific matters in which Chicago was a party. He also promised to sever his professional ties with his law firm while at Commerce.

Overall, the hearing was relatively easy for Daley. Even Spencer Abraham of Michigan and Sam Brownback of Kansas — committee Republicans who said Commerce was a wasteful bureaucracy that should be eliminated — took a gentle approach in questioning the nominee.

Daley pledged several times during the hearing to keep politics out of the department. "There is a place for politics in our public life, but there is no place for politics in the Department of Commerce," he said. He then offered two concrete actions as proof of his intentions.

First, he promised to reduce the number of political appointees in the department from 256 slots to 156. Second, he promised to defer all overseas trade missions by Commerce Department officials while he conducted a 30-day review of the "procedures, rules and criteria" that governed such missions. Some Republicans had accused the administration of turning Commerce trade missions into junkets to reward businesses that contributed to the Democratic Party.

Republican concerns were further heightened by reports that first emerged late in the 1996 campaign cycle that detailed questionable fundraising practices on behalf of the Democratic National Committee by John Huang, a former Commerce Department employee. *(Campaign finance investigation, p. 1-20)*

To some conservative Republicans, however, the issue of partisan politics at Commerce was secondary to a larger theme: whether the department should exist at all. In the 104th Congress, the Commerce Department had emerged as one of the top targets of Republicans interested in eliminating departments they saw as wasteful. *(1995 Almanac, p. 3-34)*

While acknowledging that changes needed to be made, Daley defended the department, describing it as a vital advocate for U.S. businesses. "We cannot step back in a world in which our global competitors are aggressively pursuing market opportunities for their companies," he said. "But we can ensure that all of the department's programs meet the standards of excellence and integrity that the American people expect." ■

Rodney Slater Confirmed For Transportation Post

Rodney Slater won Senate confirmation Feb. 6 as the new Transportation secretary, after breezing through the confirmation process. The vote was 98-0. Slater succeeded Federico F. Peña, who became Energy secretary in the second Clinton administration. *(Vote 6, p. S-3)*

Slater had headed the Federal Highway Administration since 1993 and had received high marks from lawmakers of both parties. A longtime Clinton ally, he had served as head of the Arkansas highway program under then-Gov. Bill Clinton.

The Senate Commerce, Science and Transportation Committee had unanimously recommended Slater's confirmation. The panel approved his nomination by voice vote Feb. 5, after Slater won strong bipartisan praise at a Jan. 29 confirmation hearing.

At the hearing, Slater pledged to make transportation safety his top priority. With recent passenger airline disasters causing widespread public concern, Slater said that ensuring safety would be "the true North Star that guides our moral compass."

No senator spoke against Slater. However, committee Chairman John McCain, R-Ariz., chided him about his role in a 1996 Clinton campaign strategy group. A planning memo by the African American Working Group — headed by Alexis Herman, the White House director of public liaison and Clinton's nominee for Labor secretary — suggested highlighting key black officials in the administration as a means of promoting voter turnout. But it also took an apparent slap at Republicans by labeling opponents of Democrats as "enemies of civil rights."

Slater, who was a member of the working group, described the civil rights language as "unfortunate." Apparently mollified, McCain called the response "important." ■

Senate Confirms Alvarez To Head SBA

Investment banker Aida Alvarez won voice vote confirmation from the Senate on Feb. 13 to head the Small Business Administration. She had won approval by the Senate Small Business Committee on a vote of 18-0 the previous day.

"She will be an extremely effective advocate for small business," Spencer Abraham, R-Mich., said in introducing Alvarez at the panel's confirmation hearing.

Senators applauded Alvarez's previous performance as the first director of the Office of Federal Housing Enterprise Oversight. The independent regulatory office oversaw the financial safety and soundness of the nation's largest housing finance institutions, the Federal National Mortgage Association (Fannie Mae) and the Federal Home Loan Mortgage Corporation (Freddie Mac).

In her testimony, Alvarez stressed her humble origins as a child from rural Puerto Rico who emigrated with her family to New York City and took her first job in a small business — waiting tables in her family's restaurant. Alvarez graduated cum laude from Harvard College and became a television journalist before embarking on a career as an investment banker.

"What worked for the Alvarez family has worked for millions of Americans," Alvarez said. "Small business is the incubator of America's entrepreneurial spirit." ■

CQ

Chapter 4

ENVIRONMENT & ENERGY

ENVIRONMENT

Westerners Adjust Their Sights And Take Home Some Wins

Reaching out to Easterners and moderating their goals, lawmakers win House passage for bills on federal grazing and landowner power

After being roughed up in the 104th Congress as extremists out to gut environmental protections, Western lawmakers regrouped in 1997. They abandoned efforts to enact sweeping legislation to transform the nation's environmental policies. Instead, they focused on narrower bills and incremental change. They also became more astute in packaging their bills, doing the spadework to educate members and running their own whip operation.

"Two years ago we assumed as a new majority that it would be easy to solve some of these problems," said Richard W. Pombo, R-Calif. This time, "legislation is definitely more targeted, a lot simpler, and we're doing a lot more groundwork than we were doing."

Republicans who lived west of the Mississippi River did not win every fight in 1997, but their new-found moderation was beginning to pay off, at least in the House. They built coalitions with some Eastern colleagues, got the support of the leadership and, when necessary, played hardball. Late in the session, they succeeded in pushing through a handful of bills in the House aimed at revising federal grazing policy, giving landowners new legal clout and curbing presidential power to protect environmentally sensitive federal lands.

The legislation still faced an uphill climb in the Senate, as well as veto threats from the Clinton administration. Nevertheless, Western Republicans had gained significant ground compared with the start of the 104th Congress. Then, they were regarded as such pariahs that they were unable to build coalitions or get major bills passed by the House, let alone signed into law. *(1995 Almanac, p. 5-3)*

Bob Smith, R-Ore., chairman of the House Agriculture Committee, said many Western Republicans realized that they had overreached, assuming that members would automatically embrace their agenda.

Some of their successes in 1997:

➤ Giving property owners greater access to federal courts and new clout with local zoning boards.

➤ Revising grazing policy on federal lands, while agreeing to a modest increase in grazing fees.

➤ Curbing presidential authority, granted under the 1906 Antiquities Law, to set aside federal tracts vulnerable to environmental threats.

Intraparty Tensions Not Gone

Tensions still ran high between Eastern Republicans, who often voted against the Westerners on environmental grounds, and the Westerners, who resented them for it. But in some cases, the differences were overcome. "There's a kind of recognition that this party has to reach out East and West," said Smith.

The Westerners also benefited from stronger leadership support, as House GOP leaders looked to shore up their backing in the party in the wake of an aborted summer coup attempt against House Speaker Newt Gingrich, R-Ga. The Western caucus made up about a third of the GOP Conference and contained some of its most outspoken members. *(Gingrich, p. 1-11)*

In May, Westerners tried in vain to pass a bill easing requirements of the 1973 Endangered Species Act for flood control projects. The leadership offered them little support, even declining to engage its vote counting operation. In contrast, the leadership worked actively to pass Smith's grazing bill the week of Oct. 27. "People are starting to see that the Westerners have some rights, that we're not asking for ridiculous things, but things of moderation," said James V. Hansen, R-Utah, a senior member of the House Resources Committee.

A New Direction

It was not that the Westerners had changed their stripes. They still were fighting against efforts by land managers and environmental groups to restrict activities on federal land. They continued to favor the rights of property owners and back commercial uses of public land, and they championed such causes as federal funding for building logging roads in national forests. But they sought to portray their efforts as moderate and friendly to the environment, sloughing off the "extremist" label they had acquired in the 104th Congress.

"We've come to the conclusion that our policies provided for greater environmental protection," said George P. Radanovich, R-Calif., a leader on Western issues. "So our strategy has changed. The challenge has been how do we 'outgreen' the greens."

At the same time, Radanovich said, the Westerners were pushing more incremental legislation. On the grazing bill, for example, Smith worked closely with an Easterner, Sherwood Boehlert, R-N.Y., a leading voice on environmental issues, to craft a compromise that proved decisive in getting the bill through the House. In the end, the bill was far narrower than a grazing bill considered in the 104th that would have overturned Clinton administration rules for grazing on public land. Boehlert gave Smith high marks, saying he was a big factor in Westerners' success in 1997. "People ask, 'How come you guys worked this out?' " said Boehlert. "I say, 'That's easy, we're both adults.' "

While his willingness to work with the Westerners helped bridge differences in the party, Boehlert also laid himself and other moderates from the Northeast open to attack from environmental groups, which strongly opposed the grazing bill and other Western-favored initiatives.

For their part, the Westerners only saw their clout increasing. With the population continuing to shift from the Northeast and flow West, they looked forward to gaining seats through redistricting after the 2000 census. ■

Dolphin Deal Sails Through Congress

After nearly two years of trying, Congress cleared legislation July 31 implementing a 1995 international pact aimed at protecting dolphins from potentially deadly tuna nets. President Clinton signed the bill into law Aug. 15 (HR 408 — PL 105-42).

The bill lifted an ongoing U.S. embargo on tuna from Mexico, Venezuela and other Latin American nations that were eager for access to the $1.4 billion a year U.S. canned tuna market. The embargo was originally imposed because those nations' fishermen caught tuna in the eastern tropical Pacific Ocean using encircling nets that also snagged and killed dolphins.

The Latin American countries insisted they had revised the fishing method so that it protected dolphins, and they argued that the embargo was unfair under the General Agreement on Tariffs and Trade (GATT).

The bill also provided a process for relaxing the dolphin-safe standard used in the United States to label tuna cans. Existing law barred the use of the label on tuna caught in the eastern tropical Pacific Ocean by a vessel that was using encircling nets.

Under the bill, the Commerce Department was required to conduct a three-year scientific study on the effects of encircling nets on dolphins. As early as March 1999, the Commerce secretary could ease the standard to allow the use of encircling nets, as long as no dolphins were killed or seriously injured. The decision was to be based in part on the preliminary results of the study.

The bill also directed the Commerce Department to design an official dolphin-safe label, though tuna canners were not required to use it. They could use the label of their choice, as long as the tuna met protection standards as strong as those in the bill, as well as other requirements, such as not making misleading claims as defined by the Federal Trade Commission Act. Only one label design could be attached to an individual can. *(Bill highlights, p. 4-6)*

The measure drew strong support from the White House, but it provoked the ire of many congressional Democrats and created an unusually deep division among environmental groups.

Some activists hailed it for implementing the 1995 agreement, known as the Declaration of Panama, which for the first time brought many countries into a compact to protect dolphins and the ecosystem as a whole. Others, however, viewed the legislation as a weakening of the dolphin-safe standard in the United States and said it was a sellout to U.S. trading partners.

BOXSCORE

Dolphin-Safe Tuna — HR 408, (S 39). The bill ended a ban on tuna imports from certain Latin American countries and created a process for redefining the dolphin-safe label on canned tuna.

Report: H Rept 105-74, Parts 1 and 2.

KEY ACTION

May 21 — House passed HR 408, 262-166.

July 30 — Senate passed compromise version of S 39, 99-0. It then passed HR 408 by voice vote after substituting the text of S 39.

July 31 — House agreed to Senate amendment, clearing HR 408.

Aug. 15 — President signed HR 408 — PL 105-42.

Critics Force Compromise

After sailing easily through the House, the bill temporarily stalled in the Senate, where Barbara Boxer, D-Calif., threatened a filibuster. A similar threat had torpedoed the legislation in the final weeks of the 104th Congress.

Hoping to avoid the same fate for this bill, members on both sides reached a compromise that delayed a label change for 18 months and required a scientific study that Boxer said could potentially be used by critics to bolster their case. Boxer had objected to the argument that the United States was required by the Panama agreement to change the legal definition of dolphin-safe tuna. "I think Americans should make American law," she said.

John Kerry, D-Mass., said the compromise included "the critical element missing from the original bill: enhanced protection for depleted dolphin stocks on the basis of sound science before any changes are made to U.S. law."

Supporters of the bill voiced confidence that evidence produced by the study would vindicate them and convince Commerce to change the label to a definition that they favored.

Mark J. Robertson, a consultant to the Mexican fishing industry, said he and his clients were not happy with the delay in changing the label, but supported the bill nonetheless. "Due to politics, an 18-month delay will be necessary to bring this into place," he said.

"I think the compromise seems reasonable on its face," said William Snape, legal director for Defenders of Wildlife, who had criticized the Clinton administration for signing the Panama agreement, saying it went too far to satisfy trading partners and was selling out environmental protections.

Nina Young, a marine mammal scientist with the Center for Marine Conservation who had supported the House bill, said the final bill illustrated that "we can make this whole trade-and-the-environment issue work."

The House agreed to accept the Senate compromise. After more than a year of fighting over the issue, proponents said they had struck the best deal possible. "There's an end to this," said Wayne T. Gilchrest, R-Md., lead sponsor of the House-passed version, in explaining his support for the compromise. "That's what we want."

Background

The dolphin-safe tuna bill was closely watched as it moved through Congress. With Latin American nations pushing to open international markets, it was seen as a test of how the United States would balance its pursuit of free trade with environmental protections.

Before the enactment of HR 408, only tuna determined to be "dolphin safe" could be imported into the United States, and tuna could be labeled dolphin-safe only if it was caught using fishing methods that did not harm dolphins.

The prohibition grew out of an effort to protect dolphins in the eastern tropical Pacific Ocean (5 million square miles stretching from Southern California to Chile), where dolphins regularly swam above schools of large yellowfin tuna.

Since the late 1950s, commercial fishermen had deployed large purse seine nets around schools of dolphin to harvest the tuna swimming below. These nets encircled the fish and were then drawn shut, like a purse. During this process, dolphins often became trapped in the nets and drowned.

Concern over this killing led to enactment in 1972 of the Marine Mammal Protection Act (PL 92-522), which called for U.S. efforts to virtually eliminate the incidental killing of marine mammals during commercial fishing. In 1984, the law was amended to prohibit foreign nations from selling yellowfin tuna in U.S. markets if they did not have dolphin-protection programs similar to those in the United States. The restriction was further strengthened in 1988. *(1972 Almanac, p. 961; 1984 Almanac, p. 336; 1988 Almanac, p. 168)*

The United States followed through in 1990 by banning the import of tuna products from Mexico. Mexico challenged the ban as an unfair trade practice under GATT, and a GATT dispute panel supported Mexico's challenge. The United States, however, was able to block consideration of the panel's report by the full GATT council.

In the meantime, confronted by a consumer boycott boosted by footage of dolphins being savagely killed on tuna boats, major U.S. tuna companies announced in 1990 that they would stop buying any tuna caught in association with dolphins, and they began applying dolphin-safe labels to their products.

Congress gave the definition the force of law the same year, specifying that dolphin-safe labels could not be used on eastern tropical Pacific tuna that were caught during fishing trips in which purse seine nets were used to encircle dolphins. Congress also specifically prohibited the import into the United States of tuna not considered dolphin-safe. *(1990 Almanac, p. 399)*

To help resolve the Mexican challenge and further promote international dolphin protection, Congress in 1992 called for a five-year global moratorium on the practice of intentionally encircling dolphins with purse seines in the harvesting of tuna. To give nations time to respond, the law lifted the existing tuna import embargoes until 1994.

With no nation formally observing the moratorium, the United States in 1994 banned the import of tuna products from Mexico, Colombia, Panama, Vanuatu and Venezuela. But changes were already under way.

In 1992, nations that fished the eastern tropical Pacific had gathered in La Jolla, Calif., to try to determine how to reduce dolphin mortality and thereby persuade the United States to end its embargo.

They agreed to use nets that would not ensnarl dolphins, to use a procedure that allowed the back edge of the net to sink below the surface so that dolphins could swim out, to use rafts and divers to help herd dolphins out of nets, to have in place international observers who would monitor fishing practices and dolphin mortalities, and to place restrictions on fishing vessels that exceeded annual dolphin mortality limits.

In the wake of this voluntary agreement, estimates of dolphin mortality in the eastern tropical Pacific declined from more than 100,000 in 1991 to 2,547 in 1996.

In October 1995, the United States, several international environmental groups and 11 other nations met in Panama to develop a binding international agreement to lock in these gains, as well as to protect other marine species (such as sea turtles, sharks and billfish) in the eastern tropical Pacific that were being harmed by alternative (i.e., non-purse seine) tuna fishing practices.

Under the resulting Declaration of Panama, the 12 signatory nations agreed to continue using the dolphin-protection fishing practices agreed to in La Jolla; they also established an annual limit of 5,000 dolphins that could be killed during such fishing.

In return for other nations' agreeing to adhere to safer tuna fishing practices, the United States agreed to lift its embargo on tuna imports, allowing the import of all tuna caught in compliance with the La Jolla agreement. It also agreed to modify the definition of dolphin-safe tuna to include tuna caught with purse seines in which no dolphin mortalities were observed.

In July 1996, the House voted 316 to 108 to pass a bill that would have changed U.S. laws to comply with the Panama accord. However, the measure died in the Senate at the end of the 104th Congress under filibuster threats from Boxer and Joseph R. Biden Jr., D-Del., authors of the 1990 dolphin-safe label law. *(1996 Almanac, p. 4-25)*

Arguments Pro and Con

Supporters of the legislation, including Clinton, many Republicans in Congress and some environmental groups, argued that the Panama Declaration was a model for reconciling the often competing pressures of global economics and environmental protection.

They said the bill would not only settle a closely watched trade dispute, but would also bind Latin American nations to an international agreement to safeguard the marine ecosystem in the eastern tropical Pacific Ocean.

Opponents, including other environmental groups and many Democrats, said the Panama agreement was the kind of sellout of U.S. environmental laws that they argued was becoming increasingly frequent as the Clinton administration bent over backward to accommodate trading partners.

Some of the most vocal critics of the 1993 North American Free Trade Agreement (NAFTA) pointed to the tuna accord as evidence that free-trade pressures were forcing the White House to do whatever it took to bolster Mexico's fragile economy and ensure NAFTA's success.

For Clinton, Vice President Al Gore (a presidential aspirant for 2000) and their fellow Democrats, the legislation also exposed fierce intraparty divisions over trade policy, as well as the split among traditional allies in the environmental community.

"Mexico gets virtually everything it wants, and no one holds its feet to the fire on environmental issues," said House Minority Whip David E. Bonior of Michigan, the Democratic Party's leading opponent of NAFTA. "It's greed being masqueraded as progressivism."

Other opponents included Defenders of Wildlife and the Humane Society of the United States, which argued that the measure would allow dolphins to be killed unnecessarily.

Critics also argued that U.S. law regarding dolphin-safe tuna labeling should never have been part of the Panama negotiations.

Proponents of the bill said such arguments were misplaced and showed a poor appreciation of the world of international trade. "In order to effectively manage the international fishery, you need international cooperation," said Mexico consultant Robertson. "That is not established through unilateral action."

Among environmental groups, Greenpeace supported HR 408, even though it was a critic of NAFTA. Gerry Leape, legislative director for ocean issues at Greenpeace, said the Panama agreement was "not a degradation of our environmental laws but a strengthening." He said the change in the dolphin-safe label would better protect marine life as a whole and safeguard dolphins while aiding Latin American fishermen.

The Center for Marine Conservation also supported HR 408. "What we want to do is end dolphin mortality," said

Dolphin-Safe Tuna Bill Highlights

Following are the key provisions of the bill (HR 408 — PL 105-42), which lifted a U.S. embargo on tuna imports from certain Latin American countries and changed the definition of "dolphin safe" tuna.

● **Study.** The Commerce secretary was required to conduct a three-year study of the effects in the eastern tropical Pacific Ocean of the use of encircling fishing nets, which captured tuna but could also trap and kill dolphins swimming above tuna schools. The provision was inserted to satisfy bill opponents, who argued that, despite the use of revised techniques to minimize dolphin deaths, the nets could still injure dolphins.

The study, scheduled to begin Oct. 1, was to include an examination of stress that dolphins experienced when encircled. The bill also called for an "experiment involving the repeated chasing and capturing of dolphins by means of intentional encirclement."

● **Defining 'dolphin safe.'** The bill redefined the "dolphin safe" label affixed to tuna cans. Previously, tuna was defined as dolphin-safe if it was caught without using encircling nets. The bill initially tightened the definition: Encircling nets could not be used during the entire fishing trip. However, the definition could be loosened as early as March 1999, if the Commerce secretary made a preliminary finding, based on the study and "any other relevant information," that encircling nets did not have a "significant adverse impact on any depleted dolphin stock." Encircling nets then would be allowed so long as the tuna were caught without killing or seriously injuring dolphins. The definition could be revised again after July 1, 2001, based on the final outcome of the study.

● **Label.** Only one dolphin-safe label could be attached to each tuna can. The Commerce secretary was directed to develop an official dolphin-safe label, but tuna canners were free to use the label of their choice, including, for example, a label developed by an environmental group. The definition for any label had to be at least as strong as that embodied in the bill. Tuna canners had been worried that allowing more than one label would open them to pressure exerted by environmental groups to choose a more restrictive label. To help allay these concerns, a provision was inserted making it a violation of the Federal Trade Commission Act to "willingly or knowingly" use a label "to mislead or deceive consumers" about the protections for dolphins under the bill.

● **Limits.** As many as 5,000 dolphins could be killed each year in the eastern tropical Pacific Ocean, with the objective of entirely eliminating dolphin deaths through the setting of annual limits. An overall annual mortality limit was to be set through 2000 at between 0.1 percent and 0.2 percent of the estimated minimum dolphin populations. The level in 2001 was to drop to 0.1 percent. Rights to fish for tuna with dolphins swimming in close proximity would be suspended if the limits were breached.

● **Bycatch.** The secretary of State was directed to seek an international agreement for a program in the eastern tropical Pacific Ocean to reduce the incidental killing of sea turtles, sharks and other species during tuna fishing. The bycatch reduction program was to include measures to release threatened and endangered species alive and minimize overall mortality. ■

Young, the group's marine mammal scientist. "If you're going to end dolphin mortality, you've got to go to the people who are responsible for maintenance of the fishery. This is a model for what we want to do with all fishery trade agreements."

House Committee

HR 408 began in the House Resources Subcommittee on Fisheries Conservation, Wildlife and Oceans, which approved it by voice vote April 10. The full committee gave its voice vote approval April 16. The House Ways and Means Committee, which had jurisdiction over the bill's trade-related provisions, approved the bill without amendment April 30 by a vote of 28-9 (H Rept 105-74, Parts 1 and 2).

The bill contained provisions endorsing the dolphin conservation program put in place under the Panama agreement.

It proposed to end the embargo on tuna caught using nets that encircled dolphins and to cap at 5,000 the number of dolphins that could be killed annually in Latin American fisheries. It also proposed to revise the U.S. standard for dolphin-safe tuna to include fish caught by encircling nets so long as an observer on the tuna boat certified that no dolphins had been killed in that catch.

The bill also called for the Commerce Department to study the impact of encirclement techniques on dolphins in the eastern tropical Pacific, and it proposed to authorize $1 million for the study.

Leading the opposition to the bill in the House was George Miller of California, the senior Democrat on the Resources Committee. He said the Panama agreement was poorly conceived and that Congress should not bow to international pressure to accept it.

He said the new dolphin-safe standard proposed in the bill was unenforceable, that it would allow needless dolphin deaths and that it would be a sweetheart deal for Latin American fishermen, who could market their product to U.S. consumers with a dolphin-safe label that Miller said would be misleading.

Gilchrest warned that if his legislation was not enacted, the 1995 agreement would collapse and other nations would feel free to return to dolphin-killing practices.

Gilchrest and his supporters argued that HR 408 offered the best protection for the marine ecosystem as a whole. He said the ban on tuna caught with encircling nets simply encouraged alternative tuna fishing practices that ensnared and led to the deaths of species other than dolphins, such as sea turtles.

The dolphin-safe label needed updating, he said, to more accurately reflect the fact that Mexican and other Latin American fishing fleets had revised encircling fishing practices to reduce dolphin deaths.

Supporters argued that the new definition was an improvement because it would give the dolphin-safe standard the added weight of an independent observer. But opponents in the environmental community said the standard could not be enforced because fishermen could easily conceal dolphin deaths from independent observers.

"It's difficult to monitor every square foot of sea in the blinding glare of sunlight, downpour of rain or a 20-knot or greater wind creating a choppy sea," said Christopher Croft, a biologist and president of an organization known as Environmental Solutions. "Indeed, whales have breached near vessels unnoticed by observers."

Miller's Amendment Fails

At the Resources subcommittee markup, Miller pushed a substitute amendment, rejected 4-7, that would have lifted the embargo only for dolphin-safe tuna and revised the existing standard to include a more stringent prohibition on activities such as chasing or seriously injuring dolphins.

The failed amendment also would have required that

threatened species such as sea turtles be released alive, which was a response to the assertion by supporters of HR 408 that it would better protect the ecosystem as a whole.

Gilchrest contended that the amendment would undercut the 1995 Panama agreement. But Miller countered, "HR 408 would weaken the meaning of the famous dolphin-safe label by allowing dolphins to be seriously injured and harassed without limits . . . and still have the tuna called safe for dolphins."

House Floor Action

The House easily passed the bill May 21 on a 262-166 vote that fell roughly along party lines. The measure won the support of 204 Republicans and 58 Democrats; 146 Democrats and 19 Republicans opposed it. The opposition was stronger than it had been the previous year. *(Vote 151, p. H-50)*

The debate revolved largely around the issues of environmental protection, international trade and an alleged connection between Latin American tuna boats and the drug trade.

"If we really, truly believe in conservation and believe in saving the dolphins, this is a piece of legislation that must pass," said House Resources Committee Chairman Don Young, R-Alaska.

But foes said the bill would lead to the killing of more dolphins while doing little to protect other marine life. "Tuna would be labeled as dolphin-safe and permitted to enter the United States even if dolphins were chased, netted or harmed, seriously injured or even killed, as long as the dead dolphins were not observed," said Frank Pallone Jr., D-N.J.

Opponents also argued that Latin American tuna boats would increasingly be used for drug trafficking, a charge that the White House and the Mexican fishing industry denied. "Increasing the number of tuna boats will simply increase the ability of drug lords to use them for smuggling," said Charles E. Schumer, D-N.Y.

Senate Committee

The Senate Commerce, Science and Transportation Committee joined the fray June 26, giving voice vote approval to a bill (S 39) similar to the House-passed measure.

Under an amendment offered by Maine Republican Olympia J. Snowe and adopted by voice vote, the dolphin-safe label could also be applied to tuna from a catch that did not immediately kill dolphins but seriously or mortally wounded them.

Snowe's amendment required that the State Department issue emergency regulations if the new safety standards proved to have an adverse effect on the dolphin population. If signatories to the Panama agreement failed to comply with the emergency rules, the U.S. embargo would be reimposed. The House version allowed but did not require such regulations.

Snowe's amendment also brought the Senate bill into line with House language sponsored by Neil Abercrombie, D-Hawaii, in directing the State Department to work with the signatories to reach additional agreements on other species such as sea turtles that were sometimes injured in tuna fishing.

The Senate bill proposed to authorize $8 million for research on the effect of encirclement fishing methods on dolphin safety, $7 million more than in the House bill.

Senate Floor Action

After weeks of behind-the-scenes maneuvering aimed at avoiding a filibuster by Boxer and others, the Senate passed a revised version of S 39 on July 30 by a vote of 99-0. Senators then took up the House version (HR 408), substituted the text of S 39 and passed it by voice vote. *(Vote 207, p. S-36)*

The House accepted the Senate changes and cleared HR 408 by voice vote July 31.

The breakthrough on the bill came July 25 when Snowe and others announced a compromise: The embargo would be lifted, but the easing of the definition of dolphin-safe tuna would be postponed for at least 18 months. The deal also required a three-year study on the effects of "intentional encirclement on dolphins and dolphin populations." If the Commerce secretary found that encircling nets were depleting dolphin populations, then the definition for the dolphin-safe label would not change. However, the Commerce secretary could make an interim decision about changing the label in March 1999.

Boxer supported the compromise, calling it "a victory for American consumers." She later warned that she planned to keep a close eye on the results of the study and that bill proponents should not take anything for granted. "We have won 18 months of the status quo," she said. "Eighteen months when consumers know that the dolphin-safe label means just that. And after that, we will live to see the preliminary results of the study." ■

Senate Starts on Species Act Rewrite

On Sept. 30, the Senate Environment and Public Works Committee gave a thumbs up to a major rewrite of the federal Endangered Species Act. On the same day, The Washington Post endorsed the bill (S 1180) and the Clinton administration announced its support.

The events were the culmination of more than a year of painstaking work by Dirk Kempthorne, R-Idaho. With little fanfare, Kempthorne assembled a bill that had the support of committee Chairman John H. Chafee, R-R.I., who frequently sided with environmentalists in Congress, and of senior panel Democrats Max Baucus of Montana and Harry Reid of Nevada.

Many hurdles still lay ahead, however. Even if the bill got through the Senate in the second session, it faced a big challenge in the House, where Republicans had backed off earlier efforts to overhaul the law after taking a pasting on environmental issues in the 104th Congress. Resources Committee Chairman Don Young, R-Alaska, indicated that he would demand stronger property rights protections. "I'm not going to promote something if it doesn't deal with the basic problem," he said.

The key to Kempthorne's bill was its moderation. It proposed a new process for recovering species and offered greater involvement to ranchers, property owners and communities in federal decision-making. The bill had the support of industry groups, including timber companies, home builders and ranchers, who saw it as a moderate but important step toward revamping what they considered an onerous law.

Endangered Species Act Waived . . .

Costly winter flooding across the country unleashed a debate in Congress over what role, if any, environmental laws might have played in limiting efforts to protect against loss of life and property. The fight exposed divisions within the Republican Party on environmental issues and highlighted the extreme difficulty of making even narrowly crafted changes to the Endangered Species Act.

House conservatives tried but failed to pass a flood-control bill (HR 478) that would have waived certain provisions of the Endangered Species Act as they pertained to flood-control projects. In the end, a less sweeping waiver was enacted June 12 as part of a fiscal 1997 supplemental spending bill (HR 1871 — PL 105-18) that sent millions of dollars in disaster relief to flood-ravaged areas in the Midwest, the South, California and other areas.

Republican conservatives — including Reps. Richard W. Pombo and Wally Herger, whose California districts were hurt by the floods — put part of the blame for the damage on the species act. The act required a review of flood-control projects to ensure that they would not harm threatened plants or animals. Pombo said such reviews were often so protracted that they delayed and discouraged upkeep of earthen levees, which collapsed in part because of their weakened condition.

Federal officials and opponents of the bill dismissed the argument that the species protection law played any role in weakening the levees. They said the law already allowed emergency levee repairs.

HR 478

Pombo and Herger introduced a bill (HR 478) aimed at allowing local reclamation districts and others responsible for maintaining the nation's levee system to conduct basic maintenance without first submitting to review under the species act.

House Committee Gives OK

The House Resources Committee approved the bill April 16 by a vote of 23-9 (H Rept 105-75). "This bill will protect both people and wildlife," said Pombo. "It will also make future disasters much less expensive by allowing for regular ongoing maintenance of levees, instead of waiting for a disaster and then scrambling to clean up afterwards."

Pombo said the bill was meant to address problems with ongoing levee repairs, not to permit new development. But critics said it was written so broadly that it would provide a huge opening for legal challenges to virtually any project related to flood control — even massive Western dam projects.

Pombo responded by offering an amendment, approved by voice vote, to narrow the scope of the bill to existing flood-control projects. "The amendment makes it clear that the legislation does not open the door for new construction of dams and other development," he said. But George Miller of California, the panel's ranking Democrat, said the bill would go too far even with the amendment. "We are still well beyond the issue of levee repairs," he said.

Proponents Outflanked on House Floor

Pombo and Herger wagered they would prevail on the House floor by portraying their bill as a choice between protecting people or safeguarding bugs and rodents. Instead, they were outflanked by Republican moderate Sherwood Boehlert of New York, who won House approval May 7 for an amendment that all but gutted the measure. Conceding defeat, bill supporters then pulled HR 478 from the floor, saying it had become a shell of its former self.

Boehlert's amendment would have allowed emergency repairs without the usual review — but only in federally declared disaster areas and for other flood-control projects that addressed a "substantial threat to human lives and property." Even those limited waivers would have expired at the end of 1998. The proposal was approved, 227-196. *(Vote 108, p. H-36)*

It was the first big environmental vote in the 105th Congress, and it drew together a coalition of moderate Republicans and liberal Democrats — much like the one in the 104th Congress that beat back a number of initiatives pushed by Republicans and Democrats from the West and South to restrict environmental regulations. As on those previous issues, party crossover favored the environmentalist position. While 27 Democrats opposed the Boehlert amendment, 54 Republicans supported it.

The vote, which underscored the continuing rift among Republicans over environmental issues, came about a year

---

Many environmental groups hated it, arguing that it would undermine a popular environmental law, and conservative senators wanted more protections for property owners. But the bill appeared to have enough attractions to win the support of moderate Democrats and dissuade Western Republicans from bolting. All the Republicans on the committee voted for the bill; the three dissenters were Democrats.

"It's not strong enough in terms of property rights," said James M. Inhofe, R-Okla., a panel member. "But it's slightly better than no bill at all. I support it. I think it will pass."

With prospects for a rewrite brightening in the Senate, environmentalists put most of their energy into stopping the bill in the House, where they hoped a bipartisan coalition would get behind an alternative (HR 2351) by George Miller of California, the ranking Democrat on the Resources Committee. They contended that Miller's bill would correct the deficiencies in the act by providing tax incentives and other sweeteners to landowners, but without compromising species protection.

House conservatives wanted their issues addressed as well. Richard W. Pombo, R-Calif., a senior member of the Resources panel and longtime critic of the species protection law, said any House bill would have to include strong protections for landowners. "There has to be an effort to protect private property owners in the legislation to make it worth passing," he said.

Congress took a modest step earlier in the year, agreeing to waive certain provisions of the species law as they pertained to flood control projects. The provisions were enacted as part of a fiscal 1997 supplemental spending bill (HR 1871 — PL 105-18) signed into law June 12. *(Flood waivers, this page)*

. . . For Emergency Flood Control

after Republican conservatives and moderates had pledged to find common ground through a leadership-appointed task force on the environment — headed by Pombo and Boehlert. "Nothing really came from all of that," said W. J. "Billy" Tauzin, R-La. "In the end, it was a lot of nice hand-holding."

Resources Committee Chairman Don Young, R-Alaska, said he was aghast that Boehlert undercut his fellow Republicans on the floor. He said Boehlert never talked to him directly about a compromise, instead allying with Democrats to undercut the bill. "He could have simply talked against [HR 478]," said Young. "But to offer a substitute to a Republican bill, to embarrass Richard Pombo and Wally Herger and endanger their seats, is very unprofessional and uncalled for."

Portraying the conservatives as uncompromising, Boehlert said his position was well-known and that he had kept open the lines of communication. "I talked to my colleagues every single day," he said. "I would tell the other side that they need to look in the mirror if they want to see the source of the problem."

Supplemental

Ultimately, provisions similar to the Boehlert amendment were attached to the Senate version of the fiscal 1997 supplemental spending bill and survived in conference.

The House Energy and Water Appropriations Subcommittee initially included language in its version of the spending bill (HR 1469) to allow suspension of the usual review required by the species act in the case of projects to repair, construct and maintain levees damaged in the 1997 floods. Vic Fazio of California, the ranking Democrat on the subcommittee, insisted the provisions would simply codify existing Interior Department policy.

However, at the insistence of subcommittee Chairman Joseph M. McDade, R-Pa., the amendment was extended to protect against future levee failures as well. Reviews could be bypassed through the end of 2000 in cases of an "imminent threat" to nearby citizens and property. The subcommittee approved the draft spending bill, including the endangered species provisions, on April 16.

Environmentalists immediately decried the proposal as an overly broad, dangerous exemption from environmental review. Miller said it could be as politically disruptive as the "timber salvage rider," a sleeper provision to a fiscal 1995 spending rescissions bill that enraged environmentalists, divided Republicans and embarrassed the White House. "This is salvage rider II," said Miller. "I believe we are about to repeat history."

In response, McDade agreed to narrow the scope of the provision. The new version, adopted by voice vote in the full Appropriations Committee April 25, sought to put into law a U.S. Fish and Wildlife Service policy issued in February that allowed for emergency repairs to levees without the usual review. The emergency repair policy was to apply to all federally declared disaster areas in 1997 and to repairs on flood-control projects that responded to "an imminent threat to human lives and property." It was to expire by the end of 1998 and did not apply to basic maintenance.

At that point, however, Pombo and Young were still hoping to win House support for the more sweeping standalone bill. In an effort to rally votes for HR 478, Young persuaded the GOP leadership to drop the McDade amendment from the supplemental.

Meanwhile, the Senate Appropriations Committee on April 30 approved a version of the supplemental spending bill (S 672) that contained language by Larry E. Craig, R-Idaho, to exempt the operation and repair of flood-control projects from review procedures. The administration said the provision was so broadly drafted as to waive the act in non-emergency situations.

Craig also faced opposition from moderates within his own party and from Senate Democrats, who pushed a narrower provision. In the end, Senate conservatives struck a compromise with the moderates that closely resembled the Boehlert provision. "I think the vote in the House [on the Boehlert amendment] was very important," said Harry Reid, D-Nev., who credited it with showing the extent of opposition to broader exemptions.

The version accepted by conferees and included in the final bill waived the reviews required under the Endangered Species Act for those repairs that were determined to be necessary to respond to an imminent threat to human lives and property in 1996 or 1997.

Background

Efforts by Congress to revise the 1973 Endangered Species Act (PL 93-205) had been bogged down for years by fierce disagreements over how to protect species without trampling on the rights of property owners.

The 1973 act made it illegal to kill, injure, trap, harass or otherwise "take" any animal or plant that was deemed endangered or threatened. It also established a process for designating an endangered or threatened species, and required development of a plan for its recovery.

Revamping the law was a top priority for many Westerners and some Southerners, who argued that it imposed unjustified restrictions on land use while doing too little toward recovery of endangered plants and animals. Critics said the burdens of the law were so onerous that landowners sometimes preferred to destroy the habitat to get rid of any sign of threatened species on their land rather than allow federal regulators to put strict restrictions on the use of their property.

The law had expired in 1992, but the enforcement mechanisms were kept alive through annual appropriations bills.

The House Resources Committee approved a major overhaul of the act in 1995, but the bill stalled when moderate and conservative Republicans were unable to resolve differences over property rights and other issues. *(1995 Almanac, p. 5-13)*

Senate Bill Highlights

Kempthorne said his goal was to do a better job of recovering species while cutting through the red tape that frustrated average citizens. The bill sought to create greater flexibility and incentives for landowners to protect plants and animals on their own. It included provisions to:

- **Habitat agreements.** Allow private landowners to develop "habitat conservation plans" to protect a number of species in a single habitat. If the plan was approved by the Interior Department, the landowner would be guaranteed that he would not have to spend additional money or set aside more land to protect a species covered.
- **'Safe harbor.'** Allow landowners to enter into voluntary "safe harbor" agreements with the Interior Department. The landowner would agree to maintain, create, restore or improve habitat in return for being exempted from additional liability under the act.
- **Recovery.** Require the federal government to issue final recovery plans within 30 months of placing a species on the endangered list. There was no such deadline under existing law. The overall economic effects on the public and private sectors would have to be outlined if the plan imposed significant costs on a municipality, county, region or industry.
- **Consultation.** Streamline the consultation process under which federal agencies were required to consult with the U.S. Fish and Wildlife Service, which ran the program, to ensure that their actions did not harm threatened or endangered species or destroy critical habitat. Under the bill, if an agency determined that its actions were not likely to affect a species, it would not be required to consult with Fish and Wildlife. Fish and Wildlife would have 60 days to object in writing.
- **Listing.** Require certain minimum scientific evidence for listing a species as endangered, including specific threats to the species. All listing and delisting decisions would have to be reviewed by three scientists nominated by the National Academy of Sciences and appointed by the Interior secretary. The bill included a procedure for delisting a species once its recovery goal had been reached.

Senate Committee

The Environment and Public Works Committee approved the bill, 15-3, on Sept. 30, with few amendments (S Rept 105-128). Kempthorne, chairman of the panel's Drinking Water, Fisheries and Wildlife subcommittee, and his core supporters lobbied hard to fend off changes that could fragment their coalition. They prodded and cajoled colleagues, particularly from the West, to hold off on amendments on property and water rights, which would have undercut administration and Democratic support for the bill.

Committee member Craig Thomas, R-Wyo., said that while many Westerners might not like the bill, they had to recognize that the political climate was unlikely to yield anything better. "You either take what you can get or get nothing at all," he said.

Kempthorne acknowledged the constraints at the markup. In what he said was a symbolic move, he proposed and then withdrew an amendment to provide compensation to landowners for federal decisions that affected property values. "It was just to demonstrate how strongly I feel," he said. "We need to keep showcasing the issue."

While the amendment was popular among Westerners, it would have been a deal breaker for many Democrats and some Republicans, including Chafee. Kempthorne contended that property owners should be afforded greater protection against federal decisions, while the opponents said the provision would break the bank and cripple enforcement of the species law.

The other Westerners on the panel showed similar restraint, in part out of deference to Kempthorne and the work he had put into the bill. Thomas, for example, withdrew an amendment popular in the West that would have given states greater control over water rights.

Westerners said that the federal government held too much control over the flow to water-dependent ranchers and others, but environmental groups and many Democrats said turning over more power to the states would put ecosystems at risk. "The whole subject of water rights is a morass," said Chafee. "If you start down the road of putting any language in, it would lead to all kinds of problems you don't want to get into."

Kempthorne opposed the water-rights amendment, but played the part of a sympathetic Westerner. "I don't know of any issue more important than water," he told Thomas. "I will pledge that we will work diligently to find language that will accomplish our needs and desires in the West. It is a tough one. But I am not ready to let go of it."

The committee approved a handful of amendments, including a proposal by Ron Wyden, D-Ore., adopted by voice vote, to allow states to establish conservation agreements to protect species and avoid their inclusion on the federal endangered list. It also gave voice vote approval to an amendment by Inhofe to temporarily suspend some federal oversight of species during an emergency repair of a pipeline or utility line.

Administration Support

Before the markup, the Clinton administration flirted with an outright endorsement but held back. Officials said they feared that the Kempthorne bill would saddle them with a dizzying array of mandates and deadlines and that Congress would not provide enough money to carry them out.

Of particular concern was a requirement in the original bill that recovery plans for all listed species be put in place within five years, with half the plans to be completed within 36 months. To bring the administration on board, the committee gave voice vote approval to an amendment that would give the administration more flexibility.

For example, it included a provision to allow the Fish and Wildlife Service to prioritize completion of recovery plans so that it could focus on the most pressing threats, even during funding shortfalls. "Our main concern was the amount of process and deadlines in the bill," said Daniel M. Ashe, assistant director for external affairs at the Fish and Wildlife Service.

The changes, however, were not enough to satisfy environmental groups and their allies in Congress, who continued to charge that the bill would cripple species protection. Frank R. Lautenberg, D-N.J., who voted against the bill, said that the funding question loomed largest. Without enough money, Fish and Wildlife will not be able to carry out its mission. "It's principally the financial question," he said. "It obviates the rest of it."

Kempthorne said that as an authorizer he had only limited sway over the appropriators. But he said that pushing through an authorizing bill was the necessary first step for securing more money. "This new bill is the catalyst for further funding," he said.

Ralph Regula, R-Ohio, chairman of the House Interior Appropriations subcommittee concurred. "If we can get an agreement on an Endangered Species Act bill, then we will do what is necessary," he said.

Among the issues of particular concern to environmentalists was the chance for agencies, such as the Forest Service, to bypass the Fish and Wildlife Service. "Kempthorne's bill is a thinly veiled effort to gut the Endangered Species Act," said Peter Galvin of the Southwest Center for Biological Diversity, a conservation group based in Tucson, Ariz. "The self-consultation is like asking Jack Kevorkian to serve on a commission to discuss doctor-assisted suicide. It is setting up a conflict of interest. You are asking an agency to police itself. It just doesn't work in this context." ■

Partisan Disputes Stop Superfund Bill

Partisan bickering over how far to go in rewriting the superfund hazardous waste law once again stymied efforts to overhaul the beleaguered program. Although Senate Republican leaders placed a rewrite on their top 10 list of legislative priorities for the year, the session ended without a committee markup in either chamber. Bipartisan negotiations broke down in the early summer, and a GOP attempt late in the year to go it alone fizzled in the face of stiff Democratic opposition.

Among the perennial disagreements that kept lawmakers apart were differences over how to clean up sites, who should pay the tab and how to remedy damage done by superfund sites to rivers, streams and other natural resources. Perhaps the biggest bone of contention between Republicans and the administration was how far to go in scaling back existing retroactive liability provisions, which allowed the government to hold a company responsible for the costs of cleaning up toxic waste dumped before the superfund law was enacted in 1980.

Republicans argued that exempting some businesses from such costs would actually speed cleanups by clearing away much of the litigation that had bogged down the program. They also argued that it was unfair to punish a company later for something that was legal at the time. But the administration and its Democratic allies in Congress opposed broad liability repeal, saying it would "let polluters off the hook" and shift more of the cost to taxpayers.

GOP Sens. Robert C. Smith of New Hampshire and John H. Chafee of Rhode Island introduced a bill (S 8) at the start of the session that stopped short of seeking an outright repeal of retroactive liability, but proposed to loosen it considerably. Senate staffers said it would exempt from liability as much as 75 percent of the businesses and other parties that could be required to pay under existing law.

As introduced, the bill included provisions to:

➤ Exempt from liability small businesses and others who dumped small amounts of wastes at a superfund site. Those who sent waste legally to a municipal landfill would also be exempt.

➤ Assign liability in proportion to the amount of waste a polluter actually dumped at a site, replacing the "joint and several liability" in the law.

➤ Give states primary responsibility for conducting superfund cleanups.

➤ Link cleanup standards to a site's future use.

Republicans modified the bill during the course of the year but were unable to win over the administration. The measure did not get beyond the hearing stage.

Under active discussion at the end of the session was a more limited repeal of financial liability for small businesses that generated office and household trash. Environmentalists and business groups agreed that many of these businesses were unfairly caught in the superfund liability net.

Bickering Over 'Brownfields' Bill

Typical of the jockeying for position by both parties that helped stall efforts to rewrite superfund legislation was a dispute over where so-called brownfields fit into the mix.

Democrats unveiled a stand-alone bill (HR 1120) on March 19 aimed at cleaning up and redeveloping brownfields — sites that were not hazardous enough to come under superfund but that had been certified by a state environmental agency as containing or potentially containing a hazardous substance.

"This isn't a serious legislative effort. It's a photo op," responded House Commerce Committee Chairman Thomas J. Bliley Jr., R-Va. "They care more about politics than toxic waste cleanups."

The problem was not that Republicans opposed brownfields relief. Members of both parties embraced the concept of reducing potential financial liability for businesses willing to purchase the sites. Both parties also supported providing millions of dollars in grants to help states and localities encourage development.

But formal bipartisan House staff negotiations on a broad superfund overhaul had begun March 18, and Republicans were piqued that Democrats unveiled a separate brownfields bill the very next day, without consulting them. Among other things, GOP members believed that breaking out the popular brownfields proposals would reduce pressure for an overall deal.

Also, there were some key differences in the legislation. For example, while both S 8 and HR 1120 proposed absolving brownfields sellers and purchasers of superfund liability, HR 1120 outlined clear exceptions under which the Environmental Protection Agency (EPA) would be able to recover cleanup costs if additional contamination was found after the property had been certified as clean by the state in which it was located. These would include cases in which a site posed an imminent danger.

Making it clear they were staking out a political position, Democrats presented their bill at a news conference headlined by House Minority Leader Richard A. Gephardt, D-Mo., and Carol M. Browner, head of the EPA. Gephardt urged Republicans to work together to pass the bill, but he also lambasted the GOP approach to revamping the superfund law. He reaffirmed Democratic opposition to easing the liability provisions, saying it would violate a key principle of the superfund statute — that the "polluter should pay."

"We won't allow them to shift the multibillion-dollar cleanup tab from polluters to taxpayers and the states," Gephardt said.

Background

Long countenanced as the inevitable byproduct of industrial progress, toxic waste sites came to be seen as intolerable threats to public health in the 1970s. Among the high-profile environmental disasters that grabbed public attention was the 1977 discovery in Niagara Falls, N.Y., that the Love Canal residential subdivision had been built atop a former chemical dump. The public clamored for action.

In 1980, Congress responded by enacting the superfund law (PL 96-510), founded on the basic principle that those responsible for toxic-waste pollution, not the government, should pay for cleanup, even if they broke no environmental laws at the time of disposal.

The law created a trust fund, better known as the "superfund," fed by taxes on petroleum and hazardous chemicals, a broad-based environmental tax on large companies and annual appropriations. The EPA was charged with creating a priority list of contaminated sites around the country that were most in need of attention. The government was authorized to make a single individual or business pay to clean up a site, even if others contributed to the pollution. *(1980 Almanac, p. 584)*

However, the program quickly became tangled in a web of endless litigation. Polluters went to court to find other polluters, such as municipalities that hauled household garbage to toxic waste sites, to share the cleanup costs. Polluters also often sued their insurance companies when they balked at paying claims filed to recover cleanup costs. By 1997, the federal government had spent $17.9 billion on the program. In all, 504 of the nation's most dangerous toxic waste sites had been cleaned, but nearly 1,300 remained on the priority list.

The program had last been reauthorized in 1986 and extended through fiscal 1994 as part of the 1990 budget-reconciliation bill. The taxes that helped finance the cleanups were authorized through fiscal 1995. Both authorizations had expired. *(1986 Almanac, p. 111; 1991 Almanac, p. 527)*

According to the Congressional Budget Office, there was still enough money in the trust fund to pay for the program through 2000. The EPA estimated that by the end of fiscal 1997, the fund would have an unobligated balance of $2.5 billion. House Ways and Means Committee Chairman Bill Archer, R-Texas, said he would not agree to renew the taxes until the program had been revamped.

For nearly five years, Congress had been struggling over how to rewrite the superfund law. Despite bipartisan approval from five committees and the Clinton administration, overhaul legislation died in the final weeks of the 103rd Congress, the victim of divisions over proposed taxes, new cleanup standards and wages paid by federal contractors. In the 104th Congress, the Republican majority pushed to repeal retroactive liability, but gave up in the face of strong opposition from most congressional Democrats and the Clinton administration. Republicans conceded that they could not find the money to pay for a full repeal. *(1994 Almanac, p. 231; 1996 Almanac, p. 4-13)*

Clinton Resists Major Rewrite

The Clinton administration wanted to reauthorize the superfund taxes, which raised about $1.7 billion a year. It also wanted to increase federal funding for the program from $1.4 billion in fiscal 1997 to $2.1 billion annually beginning in fiscal 1998 in order to clean up an additional 250 toxic waste sites over the following four years.

Some officials seemed to indicate support for a major overhaul of the superfund program, as well. But in a statement of principles for superfund reform released May 7, the administration emphasized that any legislative fix must be "narrowly targeted," and it strongly opposed GOP proposals to revise existing superfund liability standards. Administration officials touted what they said was improved management of the program, leaving the impression that they did not want a significant bill.

Senate Bill

Senate Republicans scheduled a markup of S 8 in September, but backed off in the face of stiff Democratic opposition.

Among other things, the bill proposed to eliminate an existing requirement that the EPA pursue cleanups that offered permanent remedies. Bill supporters said the requirement could add millions of dollars to the cost of a cleanup and that the EPA needed greater flexibility to balance costs against other factors such as human health protection and the long-term effectiveness of the treatment. But some Democrats and many environmentalists said the law already provided significant flexibility and worried that easing standards would lead to less thorough cleanups, putting communities at risk.

Another issue, which became prominent in 1997, was liability for damage to natural resources. S 8 proposed to limit the damages that could be recovered from a polluter, including some of the costs unrelated to site restoration. Businesses, municipalities and others worried that they could be required to pay for waste site cleanups, only to face more costs for damage to nearby rivers, streams and other natural resources. But senators from states where the damage to natural resources was an issue — such as Max Baucus of Montana, the ranking Democrat on the Environment and Public Works Committee — warned against pushing the limits too far. The Clinton administration opposed the provisions in S 8, saying they could stand in the way of cleanups.

Back to the Negotiating Table

The decision to delay the markup and resume negotiations, announced at a Sept. 4 hearing before the Environment and Public Works Committee, was the culmination of weeks of behind-the-scenes maneuvering.

Senate Republicans had broken off bipartisan negotiations earlier in the summer. Then, much to the chagrin of Democrats and the Clinton administration, they decided to move ahead with a revised version of S 8. By setting a firm markup date, Republicans hoped to force action, and even a possible compromise. "We decided months ago if we don't impose a deadline on ourselves we're not going to get anywhere," said bill sponsor Smith, a senior member of the committee.

But despite some concessions, the draft provoked strong opposition and a stern warning that a superfund bill without bipartisan support would be doomed. "I don't think there will be much of a super response to the Republican superfund bill," Senate Minority Leader Tom Daschle, D-S.D., said the day before the hearing. "It is a mistake to move ahead without Democratic support. And it will not pass into law, I can assure you that."

"We are deeply concerned that the markup of S 8, scheduled for next week, will not produce a bill that enjoys the support of the administration, Senate Democrats or a broad range of superfund stakeholders," the EPA's Browner warned at the Sept. 4 hearing. "Without this consensus, a superfund bill will simply not be enacted this year."

In her testimony, Browner said the latest draft of S 8 was a step forward. She singled out for praise provisions that would allow for more public participation, require that groundwater be cleaned up under the same standards as drinking water and create a legal settlement process for businesses that contributed small amounts of waste.

But Browner objected to provisions that she said would not go far enough to clean up groundwater, allow states to assume more responsibility over the program but shut the public out of decision-making and put too many limits on legal claims for damage to natural resources. In addition, she said S 8 would not provide sufficient cleanups for the most toxic waste sites.

Narrow House Bill

Late in the session, Michael G. Oxley, R-Ohio, chairman of the House Commerce Subcommittee on Finance and Hazardous Materials, introduced a narrower superfund bill (HR 3000) cosponsored by a nearly equal number of Democrats and Republicans. The bill proposed to exempt from cleanup responsibility those whose waste "did not contribute significantly to the cleanup costs" at a priority site. It also proposed exemptions for those who generated or transported only municipal solid waste to the site.

Bliley endorsed the bill in November, but the measure failed to pick up the support of key Democrats, including John D. Dingell of Michigan, the senior Democrat on the Commerce Committee. In the absence of such backing, the measure never moved. ■

Environmental Agency Tightens Clean Air Rules

Stringent new clean air regulations finalized by the Environmental Protection Agency (EPA) in July divided Congress along regional and ideological lines. Although opponents threatened to try to block the rules, they were unable to muster enough support in either chamber to pass a bill that could withstand a presidential veto. As a result, no bill moved forward.

The regulations, which first were brought forward in November 1996, tightened existing environmental regulations for ozone, a main component of smog, and created a standard for tiny airborne particles of soot produced by sources such as coal-fired power plants and diesel engines.

Democrats from Midwest and oil states joined the mainly Republican opposition because power plants and refineries in their states could suffer under the rules. Many Republicans from states that were downwind from such facilities joined Democrats in support of the rules.

Critics argued that the Clean Air Act was working well as it was, that the new standards were based on flimsy science, and that they would impose millions of dollars in compliance costs with no appreciable benefit. They were backed by a coalition of businesses, such as power plant operators, automobile makers, and oil and gas refiners, which would be forced to reduce emissions under the regulations.

Proponents, including environmental and health groups, said the new rules were based on strong scientific evidence and would protect the health of the public in general, and children and the elderly in particular. EPA Administrator Carol M. Browner, who appeared several times before congressional panels during the year, said the rules were needed to protect asthmatics, children and the elderly and were primarily aimed at utilities and smokestack industries.

President Clinton came out in favor of the new rules June 25, drawing cheers from environmentalists and their allies in both parties. But he also elicited jeers from members such as John D. Dingell, D-Mich., whose constituents feared they would have to pay millions of dollars in compliance costs. Dingell called a press conference to denounce the rules as "asinine" and pledged to fight them in Congress. "The Clean Air Act is working and would have worked better if not for the actions today," he said of Clinton's announcement.

Opponents Fall Short

Opponents in the House introduced a bill (HR 1984) in June calling for a four-year moratorium on implementing the new rules and requiring more scientific studies. Sponsor Ron Klink, D-Pa., called it "an issue we will go to war on." Shortly before the August recess, House Commerce Committee Chairman Thomas J. Bliley Jr., R-Va., pledged to move ahead on a bill — if it could win the two-thirds majority necessary to overturn a presidential veto. But it became evident that goal was out of reach, and the bill never moved in the House.

Ray LaHood, R-Ill., threatened to attach it as an amendment to the appropriations bill for housing and veterans' affairs (HR 2158). But partly at the urging of Bliley, he agreed to withdraw it.

In the Senate, a moratorium bill had little chance. Environment and Public Works Committee Chairman John H. Chafee, R-R.I., did not support overturning the rules through legislation. Northeastern Republicans, whose states were downwind from polluting Midwestern power plants, had been strongly supportive of the rules. Their ranks included Olympia J. Snowe and Susan Collins of Maine and Alfonse M. D'Amato of New York, who was looking to shore up his environmental credentials in time for his 1998 re-election campaign.

James M. Inhofe, R-Okla., said he would lead a bipartisan effort to block the EPA rules with legislation that mirrored the House bill. But Inhofe said he wanted the House to act first, which never happened.

Hearings Used To Vent Anger

House Republicans George W. Gekas of Pennsylvania and David M. McIntosh of Indiana, among others, used hearings to lambaste the new rules and challenge their legality.

Gekas accused the EPA of failing to analyze the effect of the rules on small business as required by the Regulatory Flexibility Act (PL 96-354); ignoring the requirement that federal agencies consult with small businesses under the Small Business Regulatory Enforcement Fairness Act (PL 104-121); and neglecting consideration of how the rules would affect state and local governments as required by the Unfunded Mandates Act (PL 104-4).

Browner countered that the Clean Air Act, amended in 1990 (PL 101-549), required the EPA to consider first and foremost the adequacy of existing standards to protect public health in proposing new rules. Based on 250 studies, Browner said, the EPA concluded that the previous standards were not sufficient to protect public health. *(1990 Almanac, p. 229)*

Browner added that the Clean Air Act prohibited the agency from considering the cost of proposed rules as it developed new standards and that such concerns could be addressed only as ways were developed to implement the new standards. ■

Hill Cool to Global Warming Pact

An international treaty on global warming, which was concluded at a conference Dec. 1-11 in Kyoto, Japan, was in trouble on Capitol Hill before the meeting even occurred.

"The Kyoto deal is dead on arrival," said Frank H. Murkowski, R-Alaska, chairman of the Senate Energy and Natural Resources Committee. Murkowski, who delivered his warning at a news conference Dec. 10, was not alone. Even some of the treaty's staunchest supporters feared that without additional revisions to the pact Murkowski would not be far from the mark.

The reason: Under the treaty, the United States would have to reduce its greenhouse gas emissions to 7 percent below 1990 levels by 2012. However, developing nations would not be required to adhere to any firm limits.

In the months leading up to the Kyoto conference, it was clear that the linchpin for members of Congress was the participation of India, China and other developing nations in cutting emission levels. But those countries argued that because the United States and the other industrialized nations had produced the bulk of the pollution, they should take the first step toward cleaning it up.

In its only legislative action of the year on the issue, the Senate fired a warning shot July 25, voting 95-0 in favor of a non-binding resolution (S Res 98) stating that the administration should sign such a deal only if it included commitments from developing countries. *(Vote 205, p. S-36)*

Senators on both sides of the aisle, including Majority Leader Trent Lott, R-Miss., and Minority Leader Tom Daschle, D-S.D., worried that a double standard could put U.S. businesses at a competitive disadvantage, raising the price of energy at home and causing jobs to move overseas where costs were lower.

"I would urge President Clinton not to submit the treaty to the Senate for ratification until developing countries have agreed to participate in a meaningful way," Daschle said.

The Clinton administration seemed to get the message. Vice President Al Gore said the treaty would not be submitted for ratification until after the administration hammered out additional agreements with developing nations on reducing emissions. "Let's be clear," he said. "We will not submit this agreement for ratification until key developing nations participate."

John Kerry, D-Mass., a backer of the treaty, supported the administration's decision to hold off submitting it for ratification. "No one in their right mind is going to say it's OK for the U.S. to make these significant changes and allow our competitors to remain free of them," he said in Kyoto.

Despite the cool reaction, however, the Clinton administration, some moderate Senate Republicans and many Democrats as well as environmental groups hailed the treaty as a big step forward. Getting diverse nations to agree on anything was difficult enough, they said, but getting them to sign off on a goal to reduce greenhouse gas emissions was especially daunting.

Background

Global warming was caused by the increasing buildup of carbon dioxide, methane and other gases from the burning of fossil fuels, such as oil, coal and natural gas. Those gases were collecting in the atmosphere, wrapping the earth in a layer of insulation and heating the climate. Many scientists predicted that warmer weather could melt ice caps, leading to disappearing shorelines, and cause severe drought and more intense storms. According to the federal Energy Information Administration, the United States was producing 24 percent of worldwide carbon dioxide emissions, regarded as the chief culprit in global warming.

In advance of the Kyoto talks, the president on Oct. 22 proposed reducing so-called greenhouse gas emissions to 1990 levels sometime between 2008 and 2012. That drew opposition from environmental groups who favored stricter limits and business groups that were resisting tough restrictions. Clinton also was criticized by European allies for not going far enough. U.S. emissions of the main greenhouse gas, carbon dioxide, were 8 percent above 1990 levels and were expected to grow by 34 percent above 1990 levels by 2010.

Pushing for strict controls were environmental groups and their allies in Congress, including legislators from areas that stood to benefit from them, such as coastal communities and states that were downwind from aging coal-fired power plants in the Midwest.

But a well-financed coalition of automobile makers, coal-fired power plants, refineries and other energy-dependent industries and their unions strongly opposed stringent new controls. They also could count on some powerful allies in Congress, including House and Senate GOP leaders, Democrats from coal-dependent states, and allies of unions, particularly the coal miners and automobile workers, who warned that the treaty might bring layoffs.

No technology existed to control carbon emissions. That meant the only way to reduce greenhouse gases was to burn less fuel or find alternative sources of energy. Industries said the federal government would be forced to place costly requirements on them to reduce emissions.

Under the "Berlin Mandate," signed by the United States and European nations in 1995, developing countries such as Mexico, China and India did not have to commit in Kyoto to legally binding limits on greenhouse gas emissions. The agreement was aimed at providing the poorer developing nations greater flexibility in reducing such gases.

Senate Action

The Senate resolution adopted in July was sponsored by Robert C. Byrd, D-W.Va. In pushing his measure, Byrd said developing countries should have to live by the same rules as everyone else. He noted that Third World nations produced an abundance of greenhouse gases and might gain a competitive advantage if they did not have to impose costly pollution controls.

"I am not out to kill the treaty," Byrd said, adding that if it left out developing countries, "count me in, in the assassination of the treaty."

The resolution initially drew fire from environmental groups. They feared it was a thinly veiled attempt by Byrd, who was worried that emissions restrictions would hurt coal-producing states such as West Virginia, to undermine treaty negotiations by pushing the administration to abandon the earlier Berlin accord.

Prior to the debate, Kerry expressed concern that it might undercut the administration's negotiating position in Kyoto. But Kerry said on the floor that a closer reading of the resolution had convinced him that it would not tie the negotiators' hands.

"It's so flexible as to mean very little," Daniel Lashof, a senior scientist at the Natural Resources Defense Council, said of the resolution later. "That's why 95 people voted for it, and nobody voted against it." ■

House Passes Oil Leaks Bill

The House on April 23 easily passed a bill aimed at speeding the cleanup of leaking underground storage tanks by assuring states that they would receive a set share of federal funding to do the job. The bill passed by voice vote with bipartisan support and relatively little debate.

The measure (HR 688), sponsored by Dan Schaefer, R-Colo., required that the Environmental Protection Agency (EPA) transfer to the states at least 85 percent of federal money appropriated to the agency each year from the Leaking Underground Storage Tank Trust Fund (LUST).

The EPA traditionally turned over roughly that percentage to the states for use in cleaning up petroleum and other hazardous liquids leaking from underground tanks at gasoline stations and other sites. But bill proponents said states needed additional assurances that the funds would be there. "The 85 percent provision helps satisfy us that the EPA will keep following good practices regardless of budget fluctuations," said Commerce Committee Chairman Thomas J. Bliley Jr., R-Va.

The bill also sought to give states more flexibility in determining how to spend the money, which totaled $60 million in fiscal 1997. "The states know better how to use this money than the federal government," Schaefer said. "It is only right and sensible that they should have the discretion to clean up and repair existing gasoline storage tanks."

HR 688 began in the Commerce panel's Finance and Hazardous Materials Subcommittee, which approved it by voice vote March 20. The full Commerce Committee approved the measure without change by voice vote April 16 (H Rept 105-58, Part 1).

In a hearing before the markup, the Clinton administration expressed qualms that the bill would let tank owners off the hook for pollution that they should be paying to clean up.

LUST was created in 1986 to ensure a reliable stream of federal funding to clean up and contain toxic substances leaking from underground tanks. It was financed by a 0.1-cent-per-gallon gasoline tax that expired in December 1995; it had a balance of about $1 billion. Of the 1 million active and regulated petroleum tanks, Schaefer said 33,345 leaking tanks were reported to the EPA for cleanup in 1996 alone.

An identical measure sponsored by Schaefer passed the House in the 104th Congress but was not taken up in the Senate. *(1996 Almanac, p. 4-27)* ■

Balancing Conservation, Recreation

Overcoming past disputes between conservationists and recreational users, Congress cleared legislation revamping management of the National Wildlife Refuge System.

The measure (HR 1420) officially established conservation, including restoration of fish, wildlife and plant populations, as the basic mission of the system. It was the first time the refuges had been given a clearly defined legal purpose. To the satisfaction of hunters and fisherman, the bill also recognized hunting and other recreation as a priority in the refuges whenever it was compatible with conservation.

An earlier version of the legislation would have put recreational activities on an equal footing with conservation efforts in the system's mission statement. That measure was opposed by Interior Secretary Bruce Babbitt, who said he would urge Clinton to veto it.

HR 1420, by contrast, represented a bipartisan compromise that had the endorsement of the Interior Department. President Clinton signed the bill into law Oct. 9 (PL 105-57).

"Together we have been successful in crafting a bill that will effectively conserve and manage our fish and wildlife for the future, while allowing millions of Americans to enjoy wildlife-dependent recreation within our refuge system," said House Resources Committee Chairman Don Young, R-Alaska.

Democrats had equal praise. "This is in fact a bona fide compromise, which resulted from concessions on both sides," said George Miller of California, the committee's senior Democrat and an energetic critic of most Republican environmental efforts.

BOXSCORE

National Wildlife Refuges — HR 1420. The bill established conservation and preservation of fish, wildlife and plant resources as the primary mission of the refuge system, while making hunting and other recreation a priority when such activities were compatible with the main mission.

Report: H Rept 105-106.

KEY ACTION

June 3 — House passed HR 1420, 407-1.

Sept. 10 — Senate passed HR 1420, amended, by voice vote.

Sept. 23 — House cleared the amended bill, 419-1.

Oct. 9 — President signed HR 1420 — PL 105-57.

Bill Highlights

The bill contained provisions to:

- **Mission.** Establish as the refuge system's overall mission the management and conservation of fish, wildlife, plants and their habitats for "present and future generations of Americans."
- **'Compatible' uses.** Define a "compatible" use as one that would not materially interfere with or detract from the fulfillment of the mission of the system or the additional purposes of a particular refuge. This was a regulatory definition that the Fish And Wildlife Service had used for many years.

New activities would only be permitted if they were specifically found to be compatible. Existing uses that had been determined to be compatible could continue unless the determination was modified. Incompatible activities were to be eliminated as quickly as possible.

- **Hunting, fishing.** Recognize that "wildlife-dependent" recreational uses, including fishing and hunting, were appropriate if they were found to be compatible with a refuge's purposes, and require that they be facilitated. The bill also made clear that uses other than those directly related to wildlife could be judged compatible with a refuge's purposes.
- **Conservation plans.** Require comprehensive conservation plans for each of the nation's 509 refuges.
- **Water rights.** Clarify that the bill did not affect existing water rights.

Background

The 92 million acre National Wildlife Refuge System, first established in 1903, was a sprawling and diverse system designed to protect plants and wildlife and provide recreation for millions of Americans. Run by the Interior Department's Fish and Wildlife Service, the system's 509 refuges were scattered across all 50 states and served a variety of users.

Some refuges offered isolation and sanctuary for threatened plants and animals, as well as a solitary experience for campers and backpackers. Others had become tourist meccas; the Chincoteague National Wildlife Refuge off the Virginia coast, for example, got more than 1 million visitors each year.

According to Interior Department figures, 283 refuges allowed hunting and 276 allowed fishing.

The majority of acreage was in Alaska, but refuges were found amid the sprawl of West Coast subdivisions as well as in the isolation of Alaska's Arctic National Wildlife Refuge.

Refuge property was purchased with money from a handful of sources, including annual appropriations from the Land and Water Conservation fund and funds from the Migratory Bird Conservation account.

The system — which was managed under the Refuge Recreation Act of 1962 and the 1966 National Wildlife Refuge System Administration Act — labored under funding constraints and a lack of management oversight. In particular, there was broad agreement that the system suffered from the lack of an explicit, singular mission. While existing federal law allowed uses "compatible" with the major purposes of the system, it did not state what those purposes were, nor did it define "compatible."

Attempts to clarify the law had bogged down in previous Congresses, stymied by disputes between conservationists, who wanted to ensure that the refuges focused on protecting plants and wildlife, and hunters and other recreational users, who wanted to protect their access to the refuges.

A House-passed bill that would have elevated the priority given to recreational activities was halted in 1996 by Senate opposition and a presidential veto threat. *(1996 Almanac, p. 4-22)*

As the 105th Congress began, a rematch seemed in the offing. Young introduced a bill (HR 511) that would have established a list of six purposes for the refuge system, including conservation and compatible recreational uses, and permitted fishing and hunting on a refuge unless a specific finding was made to bar it.

At a March 6 hearing, hunting groups supported Young's bill. "The sporting community needs a statutory shield from the animal rights fanatics who have made it their mission to terminate all fishing and hunting on the public's refuge lands," said William Horn of the Wildlife Legislative Fund of America, a pro-hunting group.

But Babbitt said HR 511 would wrongly elevate hunting and recreation to equal footing with the "traditional conservation purposes of the refuge system."

The legislation seemed once again headed for the ash heap. But within two months of the contentious hearing, and after weeks of intense talks between the Clinton administration and key House Republicans and Democrats, negotiators produced a compromise bill that both sides seemed ready to support.

"HR 1420 addresses all of the concerns raised in my March 6, 1997, testimony," Babbitt wrote in a letter April 29, "while securing an appropriate role for America's sportsmen and women and fish and wildlife-dependent recreation generally in the refuge system."

Babbitt gave himself an escape clause, however: "Any substantive change would obligate the parties now supporting it to re-evaluate their positions," he wrote. "In particular, enactment of any amendment weakening existing protections for the refuge system or any individual refuge would force us to withdraw our support."

Legislative Action

On April 30, the House Resources Committee approved the compromise bill by voice vote (H Rept 105-106). The measure had bipartisan support and provoked relatively little debate, a contrast to the panel's tradition of partisan fighting over management of federal lands.

Young gave it his support, as did Miller. Young said he believed the bill would achieve his goal of creating "a statutory shield to ensure that hunting and fishing . . . could continue within the system and to facilitate these traditional activities where compatible with conservation."

The bill also had the support of John D. Dingell of Michigan, the ranking Democrat on the Commerce Committee, author of the 1966 legislation, and a senior member of the influential Congressional Sportsmen's Caucus.

Environmental groups, however, had a mixed reaction, cheering some provisions that they had sought for years but taking issue with others. Groups were pleased that the bill would, for the first time, require conservation plans for each refuge, and that it called for the refuges to "ensure that the biological integrity, diversity, and environmental health of the system are maintained for the benefit of present and future generations of Americans."

"Frankly, we're still concerned the bill is skewed [away from conservation]," said Jim Waltman, director of refuges and wildlife for the Wilderness Society. "But it's moving substantially back in the right direction," compared with earlier Republican proposals.

At the markup, Miller, traditionally an ally of the environmentalists, played down such concerns.

House, Senate Floor Action

The House gave the bill a ringing endorsement June 3, passing it, 407-1. Ron Paul, R-Texas, an advocate of limiting federal government activities, cast the lone "no" vote. *(Vote 156, p. H-52)*

The Senate made only minor adjustments to HR 1420 before passing it by voice vote Sept. 10. Among the Senate changes were provisions to clarify that activities did not have to be wildlife-dependent to be considered compatible with the primary purpose of a refuge.

Also included by the Senate was a provision requiring the Interior Department to monitor the condition of fish, wildlife and plants in the refuges.

The House accepted the Senate amendments and cleared the bill Sept. 23 by a vote of 419-1. *(Vote 424, p. H-130)* ■

House Seeks To Limit Designation Of National Monuments

The House passed legislation (HR 1127) aimed at curbing presidential authority, first created under President Theodore Roosevelt, to protect environmentally sensitive land. Western Republicans pushed the bill as a countermove to a 1996 decision by President Clinton to set aside 1.7 million acres in Utah as the Grand Staircase-Escalante National Monument.

Although the House-passed bill was not as restrictive as Westerners had hoped, it still drew vigorous protests from environmental groups and a veto threat from the Clinton administration.

The original bill would have amended the 1906 Antiquities Act to bar the president from designating more than 50,000 acres as a national monument without first getting authorization from Congress. As amended by the House, HR 1127 allowed the president to designate any size area as a national monument without prior authorization. However, for monuments larger than 50,000 acres, the designation would expire after two years unless Congress passed a joint resolution supporting it.

Clinton's Sept. 18, 1996, designation of the national monument in Utah won plaudits from environmental groups, which had made it one of their priorities during the 1996 presidential campaign. But it provoked Utah's congressional delegation, many Western Republicans and some Democrats, who claimed it was a shameless land grab on the part of the administration, exercised with little regard for local concerns.

The designation was issued after Congress had reached an impasse on legislation in the 104th Congress to create a new

Utah wilderness area. Much of the land that was included in that effort was folded into the Escalante monument. *(1995 Almanac, p. 5-19; 1996 Almanac, p. 4-18)*

Background

The 1906 Antiquities Act had been invoked by 13 presidents to designate more than 100 national monuments, including the Muir Woods in California, Death Valley in Nevada and California, the Edison Lab in New Jersey and Bryce Canyon in Utah. Many were later designated as national parks, historic sites or historical parks.

The administration said the 1906 act was one of the most successful environmental laws of the century, and Interior Secretary Bruce Babbitt had told lawmakers earlier in the year that Clinton would veto an attempt to weaken it.

Bill sponsor James V. Hansen, R-Utah, agreed that the law had been a valuable asset in protecting environmentally sensitive properties. But in issuing the Utah designation, he and other Westerners said, Clinton overstepped the bounds.

They dismissed it as having less to do with preservation than with unvarnished election-year politics aimed at satisfying environmental groups. Hansen, for instance, asserted that much of the monument was an unsightly landscape that included "one of the ugliest places in the state of Utah." At the same time, Hansen said, the designation locked up access to 200,000 acres of income-producing land set aside in trust for public education in the state and an energy reserve valued at more than $1 trillion. For the critics, the Clinton decision amounted to trampling on the rights of average citizens.

"When I stand out there as a federal official and they say, 'Where is the monument?' I say, 'Friend, you are standing on it,' " said Hansen. "They say, 'Well what am I supposed to see?' I say, 'I don't know, look around and enjoy it.' "

"If the Utah delegation is unhappy with the designation, they should address the issue rather than gutting the act that created so many of our treasured national parks," said Carol F. Aten, executive vice president of the National Parks and Conservation Association.

House Action

The House Resources Subcommittee on National Parks and Public Lands approved the original version of the bill by voice vote May 8. The full Resources Committee approved it June 25, also by voice vote (H Rept 105-191).

Hansen, who chaired the subcommittee, accused Clinton of trampling Utah's state and local interests in a move that he called "purely political, designed to appease the environmental community and timed according to the November [1996] election." Bruce F. Vento, D-Minn., agreed that Clinton should have consulted with Utah officials, but he warned that the bill was too restrictive. "It will be fiercely fought," he said. "It will not become law."

The measure included the 50,000-acre limit on the areas that could be designated as a national monument without the prior approval of Congress and the governor and legislature of the state in which the monument was to be established.

The full committee added language to limit the president to designating no more than one monument per state each year. The amendment, by Helen Chenoweth, R-Idaho, was adopted by voice vote. "This administration has demonstrated a very voracious attitude for the acquisition of land," said Chenoweth, who was a leading property rights advocate.

Critics Weaken Bill on House Floor

The House passed the bill Oct. 7 by a vote of 229-197, but conservatives had to make concessions to party moderates to get the bill through. *(Vote 495, p. H-150)*

Sherwood Boehlert, R-N.Y., a leading moderate on environmental issues, objected to the requirement that the president get congressional approval for any designation greater than 50,000 acres. He said the proviso would allow designations to be blocked through congressional inaction.

Boehlert supported a substitute amendment, adopted 222-202, that contained language allowing the president to make a designation of any size, without first securing congressional approval. For monuments larger than 50,000 acres, the designation would expire within two years unless Congress passed a joint resolution endorsing it. "The compromise improves on the bill by allowing a monument declaration to take effect immediately, rather than requiring a wait for congressional approval," said Boehlert. *(Vote 494, p. H-150)*

Boehlert said, however, that he would drop his support for the bill unless he got additional concessions ensuring that Congress would act expeditiously on designations.

Earlier, the House rejected, 201-224, a proposal by Vento to drop the 50,000-acre restriction in the bill and instead establish a one-year delay from the time the president announced a monument designation to the date it would take effect. *(Vote 493, p. H-150)* ■

Other Environmental Issues Considered in 1997

Lawmakers considered a number of smaller bills related to public land and national recreation areas, several of them aimed at revising particular federal rules or blocking the designation of sites for environmental attention. None of the measures were enacted in the first session.

Alaska Land Swaps

A bill (S 967 — S Rept 105-119) to allow development and land swaps in Alaska was approved Sept. 24 by the Senate Energy and Natural Resources Committee. The measure, sponsored by Frank H. Murkowski, R-Alaska, was endorsed on a 12-8 vote. Most Democrats voted "no" to support the administration, which threatened to veto the bill because of environmental concerns.

The bill sought to amend land claims laws for Alaska to allow a land exchange with the Calista Native Regional Corporation in which the government would get about 225,000 acres of land within the Yukon Delta National Wildlife Refuge. It would also affect traditional fishing rights in Glacier Bay National Park. Other provisions sought to allow property owners to retain ownership of cabins on certain lands and permit continued helicopter use on designated land under regulation by the Interior secretary.

American Heritage Rivers

A plan by President Clinton to designate 10 of the nation's rivers for special attention in 1998 came under assault in the House Resources Committee, which approved a bill Oct. 22 to bar the use of federal funds to develop or carry out the initiative. The bill (HR 1842) was approved 15-8, but went no further in the first session.

Clinton announced the initiative in his Feb. 4 State of the

Union address, saying he would designate 10 American Heritage Rivers "to help communities alongside them revitalize their waterfronts and clean up pollution." The plan found support from communities and some governors of both parties across the country. It was also backed by lawmakers in both parties who hoped rivers in their states might be selected.

But Helen Chenoweth, R-Idaho, the bill's sponsor, said the initiative violated the property and water rights of residents living near the rivers. Supporters of the bill said the program could lead to federal officials testifying on zoning matters against local residents.

Clinton signed an executive order Sept. 11 directing federal agencies to use already authorized programs to help communities refurbish waterfronts and improve water quality in rivers that were selected.

An effort to quash the initiative in the Senate failed Sept. 18 when an amendment offered by Tim Hutchinson, R-Ark., to the fiscal 1998 Interior appropriations bill (HR 2107) was tabled (killed), 57-42. The amendment would have required congressional approval of the program. *(Vote 247, p. S-42)*

Two Republicans, John H. Chafee of Rhode Island and Alfonse M. D'Amato of New York, spoke in favor of Clinton's initiative. D'Amato said it would be driven by local efforts and not dictated by Clinton. He noted that the Hudson River in New York was a possible candidate. "This is not a question [of] where the president or Washington or Big Brother designates a river," he said.

Boundary Wilderness

House and Senate panels approved versions of a bill to ease motorboat and truck restrictions in the Boundary Waters Canoe Area Wilderness in northern Minnesota, bringing cheers from recreational boaters and boos from environmental groups.

The Senate Energy and Natural Resources Committee was the first to act, approving its version of the bill (S 783 — S Rept 105-80) on an 11-9 party-line vote July 30. Sponsored by Rod Grams, R-Minn., the legislation proposed allowing trucks to transport boats over three portage routes connecting five lakes in the area. It also proposed to delete a provision in the 1978 Boundary Waters Act (PL 95-495) that phased out motorboats on part of Sea Gull Lake, located within the wilderness.

Stretching nearly 150 miles along the U.S.-Canadian border from Voyageurs National Park to Lake Superior, the wilderness was a popular tourist destination, attracting about 200,000 visitors a year. Heavy use had led to a dispute in Minnesota over whether trucks and motorboats should be barred permanently.

Echoing the concerns of environmental groups, Dale Bumpers of Arkansas, the ranking Democrat on the panel, said the bill could damage the land and disrupt the placid wilderness. Paul Wellstone, D-Minn., also opposed the bill.

Grams disputed their claims, arguing that expanded access would benefit senior citizens and northern Minnesota families. Boaters had been frustrated that they could use motorboats on the five lakes but had to haul the boats by hand between lakes.

A House subcommittee on Oct. 7 approved a companion bill (HR 1739) sponsored by James L. Oberstar, D-Minn. The Resources Subcommittee on Forests and Forest Health approved the measure, 5-2, after rejecting six amendments by bill foe Bruce F. Vento, D-Minn. Vento sought to bar motorboats on Sea Gull Lake and several other lakes, prohibit trucks from hauling boats on a 4-mile portage and bar federal subsidies for private portage services.

Vento resurrected his amendments when the bill came before the full House Resources Committee on Oct. 22. The panel approved the bill, 22-7. Most of Vento's attempts failed, but two were approved as part of a proposal offered by Helen Chenoweth, R-Idaho. Her amendment, adopted by voice vote, clarified that the bill would apply only to portages opened in 1992. It also sought to bar federal subsidies for private portage services, and prohibit the use of commercial equipment on portages.

Hells Canyon

Committees in both chambers approved legislation to lift a restriction on jetboats using the Snake River inside the Hells Canyon National Recreation Area in Oregon and Idaho. Rafters and jetboat users were facing off over use of the river.

Under a Forest Service management plan, jetboats were not allowed on the river on certain summer days. The legislation proposed removing the restriction and allowing jetboats to use the river at any time.

The Senate Energy and Natural Resources Committee approved the bill (S 360 — S Rept 105-78) on July 30 by a vote of 11-9. Bill sponsor Larry E. Craig, R-Idaho, said the Forest Service restrictions threatened to "wipe out an entire industry. . . . I'm willing to limit jetboating, but I'm not willing to take them off the river," he said.

Ron Wyden, D-Ore., disagreed, saying the restrictions were not putting jetboaters out of business and that limits were necessary to protect the river ecosystem as well as commercial operators who ran rafting trips on the river. "You have two industries here who are at odds over the use of a natural resource," said Gordon H. Smith, R-Ore.

The House Resources Committee approved a companion bill (HR 838 — H Rept 105-378) on July 16.

U.N. Lands Designation

The House passed legislation to sharply curtail U.S. participation in a United Nations-sponsored international program to recognize and preserve environmentally sensitive areas, but the bill faced an uncertain fate in the Senate and a presidential veto threat.

Supporters portrayed the bill (HR 901) as an attempt to protect federally controlled property from designations — known as World Heritage sites and biosphere reserves — issued by the United Nations Educational, Scientific and Cultural Organization (UNESCO).

Under a 1972 treaty approved by the United States and more than 100 other countries, 22 sites in the United States, including Yellowstone National Park in Wyoming, had been designated as World Heritage sites; 47 sites had been selected for the biosphere program. The designations were aimed at enhancing international cooperation in scientific research and establishing international alliances to protect the world's most valued cultural and natural sites.

The bill proposed that congressional approval be required for any new biosphere reserve or heritage sites and that existing biosphere reserve designations be terminated by 2000 unless they were authorized by Congress.

House Committee Gives OK

The House Resources Committee approved the bill June 25 by a vote of 26-9 (H Rept 105-245). "This bill will protect our domestic land use decision-making process from unnecessary international interference," said Committee Chairman Don Young, R-Alaska.

But opponents, including the Clinton administration, said the bill was unnecessary and would undercut international research and recognition that had benefited many of the designated areas. Edward J. Markey, D-Mass., ridiculed the legislation, saying its proponents had created a conspiracy theory of international control of U.S. lands. "This legislation is dealing with a problem that doesn't exist," Markey said.

"No one has brought forward any evidence of adverse effects in the United States because of these designations," said committee Democrat Bruce F. Vento of Minnesota. According to a June 6 Congressional Research Service report, the biosphere reserve designation did not "convey any control or jurisdiction over such sites to the United Nations or any other entity."

Floor Vote Revises Bill

The House passed the bill Oct. 8 by a vote of 236-191, but only after agreeing to add language intended by opponents to gut the measure. *(Vote 504, p. H-152)*

Young and other proponents argued that HR 901 would protect the nation's ability to manage its own land without foreign influence. He said the issue was one of sovereignty and of Congress' right to exercise authority over land management. "This is the right thing to do for America," said Young.

Opponents again dismissed it as concocted by conspiracy theorists. "I have been here 23 years," said George Miller of California, ranking Democrat on the Resources Committee. "This is the craziest damn bill I have ever seen."

As a legislative countermove, Miller joined with Vento to propose an amendment, adopted 242-182, to require congressional approval when a foreign company wanted to mine or otherwise commercially develop federally controlled lands. *(Vote 502, p. H-152)*

In handouts distributed to members on the floor, Vento portrayed the amendment as a move to stop foreign companies from picking up cheap leases to mineral rights and otherwise using public lands at taxpayer expense. "Stop foreign exploitation of U.S. lands," read the flier. Vento said Young's true agenda in pushing the legislation was to ease the way for greater commercial development. Young denied this, saying Vento's amendment was a toothless tiger that did not change the intent of his bill.

"I think we turned the whole bill inside out," countered Vento.

Wildfires

The House on July 9 gave overwhelming support to a bill (HR 858) aimed at creating pilot projects in three Northern California forests to reduce the risk of catastrophic wildfires. The bill passed by a vote of 429-1. The Senate Energy and Natural Resources Committee approved an amended version of the plan in late October. *(Vote 251, p. H-80)*

The bill directed forest managers to take certain steps, including thinning timber stands and building firebreaks. It was intended to implement a proposal by what was known as the Quincy Library Group — a group of environmentalists, timber industry officials and Northern California community representatives who met in Quincy, Calif., in 1993 to seek out more effective ways to prevent forest wildfires.

However, the one-sided House vote obscured the largely partisan disputes that had threatened to slow or possibly kill the bill.

When the measure was before the House Resources Committee in May, environmental groups and liberal House Democrats urged that it be withdrawn or rejected. They said it did not effectively reflect the ideas and goals of the Quincy group and that the committee had not had time to assess all of the environmental implications.

George Miller of California, ranking Democrat on the Resources Committee, led the opposition during the markup. He said there was even disagreement over the bill among members of the Quincy Library Group. Seven environmental groups also had urged the committee to postpone the markup.

The Resources Committee nevertheless approved the bill by voice vote May 21 (H Rept 105-136, Part 1).

Before taking the measure to the floor, Resources Committee Chairman Don Young, R-Alaska, picked up the support of moderate Republicans — including Sherwood Boehlert of New York, a leading voice on environmental issues — by accepting a compromise amendment to strengthen environmental provisions.

But in the opening hour of the floor debate, Miller continued to lambaste the bill, saying the amendment would not go far enough to bolster environmental provisions. Though Miller and other opponents, mostly Democrats, said they supported the Quincy Library agreement, they argued that the bill was not true to it. They said it would skirt environmental laws, a point contested by supporters of the revision backed by Young.

Opponents flagged provisions on maintaining areas around streams and other waterways, known as riparian management, and on the degree of scientific justification needed for forest management decisions. They initially backed a Miller amendment to correct the problems.

But just as the House was poised to begin the major part of the debate on HR 858, Young announced a new compromise, supported by Miller and approved by voice vote as an amendment. Miller said the compromise addressed the main contested points. The key provision, he said, was a more explicit statement that agencies carrying out the bill's provisions should comply with environmental laws.

The compromise also increased the time for assessing the environmental impact of the project and provided for an environmental impact study of the project as a whole. ■

Nevada Waste Site Plan Again Stalls

Nuclear utilities won passage in both chambers of legislation to establish a temporary site in the Nevada desert to store the high-level nuclear waste that was piling up at power plants across the country. But the Senate vote fell short of the two-thirds majority needed to counter a threatened veto, and conference action was postponed indefinitely.

The legislation directed the Energy Department to open a temporary site for nuclear waste near Yucca Mountain, about 100 miles northwest of Las Vegas. The House bill proposed a deadline of January 2002; the Senate opted for Nov. 30, 1999.

The plan was intended to sidestep the lengthy process of building a permanent dump at the mountain site — a battle that had entangled Congress for more than a decade. Utilities pressured Congress and the White House for quick action, saying they were running out of room in storage pools for spent nuclear fuel.

But Clinton administration officials remained resolute in their opposition to the supposedly temporary solution, which they feared could kill efforts to implement long-term underground waste disposal. They argued that a temporary location would bias scientific studies of the waste site and drain resources aimed at a permanent solution.

Nevada's congressional delegation was vehemently opposed to storing the waste in their state. The state's two Democratic senators, Harry Reid and Richard H. Bryan, warned they would use every tactic they could to slow or thwart final passage of a bill that their constituents detested. "It's Armageddon," Bryan warned, vowing to repeat his lengthy 1996 filibuster on similar legislation. Although the 1996 bill ultimately passed the Senate with 63 votes, the total was short of a veto-proof majority and the House declined to take up the measure. *(1996 Almanac, p. 4-30)*

But proponents of a temporary site were optimistic that they would succeed in the 105th Congress. Two opponents of the legislation, Democratic Sens. Jim Exon of Nebraska and David Pryor of Arkansas, had retired. Republicans Chuck Hagel and Tim Hutchinson, who took their seats, were expected to vote for the measure, potentially bringing the total number of Senate supporters to 65. Proponents also hoped that changes made to the Senate bill could help pick up votes. But when the Senate voted April 15, they were still two votes short of the two-thirds majority needed for a veto override.

Initially, House Commerce Committee Chairman Thomas J. Bliley Jr., R-Va., seemed reluctant to deal with the nuclear waste issue. Among other things, the same utilities that were demanding action on the waste bill were vigorously opposing one of Bliley's legislative priorities — electricity deregulation. Bliley also said there were better things for his panel to do than take up a bill that was almost sure to be vetoed.

But the committee eventually approved the bill in mid-September. Supporters — led by Dan Schaefer, R-Colo., Fred Upton, R-Mich., and Dennis Hastert, R-Ill. — also won strong bipartisan support on the House floor Oct. 30.

Nevada's two House members — junior Republicans John Ensign and Jim Gibbons — tried to build a coalition among members who opposed nuclear power and those who had no nuclear waste in their districts but would have it transported through their home turf. But the effort was not sufficient to thwart the bill.

By then, however, the session was winding to a close. Advocates of the temporary site hoped the federal courts would give lawmakers an extra push by enforcing a Jan. 31, 1998, statutory deadline for the Energy Department to accept spent nuclear fuel stored at commercial nuclear plants. But on Nov. 14, the U.S. Court of Appeals for the District of Columbia gave nuclear utilities only a partial victory. The court said the Energy Department had to begin taking possession of spent fuel on Jan. 31, 1998, but it did not require that the spent fuel be moved.

President Clinton said repeatedly that he would veto legislation mandating a specific location for temporary nuclear waste storage before the viability of Yucca Mountain, the only site being studied for permanent high-level nuclear waste storage, was determined. The Energy Department was not expected to complete its viability study until September 1998 at the earliest. A more rigorous "suitability study" was due out in 2000.

BOXSCORE

Nuclear Waste Storage — HR 1270, S 104. The bill required construction of an interim nuclear waste storage site at Yucca Mountain, Nev.

Reports: H Rept 105-290, Parts 1, 2; S Rept 105-10.

KEY ACTION

April 15 — Senate passed S 104, 65-34.

Oct. 30 — House passed HR 1270, 307-120.

Background

The 1982 Nuclear Waste Policy Act (PL 97-425) established a national nuclear waste disposal system and gave the Energy Department until 1998 to open a permanent underground repository for high-level nuclear waste. The department was required to take possession of the waste by Jan. 31, 1998. To finance development of the facility, the law also established the Nuclear Waste Fund to collect fees from nuclear utilities. About $12 billion had been raised by the fund, about $5 billion of which had been spent on the program. *(1982 Almanac, p. 304)*

In 1987, Congress directed the department to limit its evaluation of potential nuclear waste repository sites to one location, an arid ridge called Yucca Mountain on Nevada's former nuclear weapons testing grounds, and to subject only that site to a series of intensive geological and hydrological studies. If the studies determined that the site was suitable, it would then be formally selected. The department expected to complete the initial viability assessment in 1998, but its target date for opening a permanent repository had been put off until 2010.

The 1987 law also directed the Energy Department to develop a temporary facility to store nuclear waste until a permanent site was ready. But attempts to place that site at Yucca Mountain had been unsuccessful. In the meantime, storage space for spent nuclear fuel was being exhausted at dozens of nuclear utilities. *(1987 Almanac, p. 307)*

Senate Committee

After weeks of delay, the Senate Energy and Natural Resources Committee approved its version of the bill March 13 by a vote of 15-5 (S 104 — S Rept 105-10). The committee-approved bill gave the president until the Dec. 31, 1998, to halt construction of a temporary waste site at Yucca Mountain if he determined that the site was not viable for permanent storage. He then would have 18 months to find an alternative location that Congress would have to approve within 24 months.

Amendments Adopted

During committee action on the bill, members adopted amendments by:

- **Hanford site.** Ron Wyden, D-Ore., to bar the president from considering Washington state's Hanford nuclear reservation, a sprawling Energy Department nuclear weapons plant, as an alternative to Yucca Mountain. The use of Hanford was opposed by the committee's large contingent from the Pacific Northwest.

Jeff Bingaman, D-N.M., complained that the restriction would open the bill to any number of amendments from members seeking to disqualify their own states. Also, by removing Hanford from consideration, the amendment could make it more difficult for Clinton to meet the 18-month deadline. Under the draft bill, if the president failed to meet that deadline, construction of the interim site at Yucca Mountain would begin automatically.

But the committee included five senators from Washington, Oregon, Idaho and Montana, and over the objections of four other members, Chairman Frank H. Murkowski, R-Alaska, declared the Wyden amendment approved by voice vote.

- **Transportation standards.** Wyden, adopted by voice vote, to tighten nuclear waste transportation standards. Wyden, who had opposed the bill in 1996, subsequently voted to report S 104 out of committee.
- **Oversight.** Bingaman, adopted by voice vote, to restore the oversight authority of the independent Nuclear Waste Technical Review Board, which the draft bill would have undercut.
- **Military waste.** Larry E. Craig, R-Idaho, to reserve at least 5 percent of the interim storage site for military and Energy Department nuclear waste. A growing pile of spent naval reactor fuel and radioactive Energy Department refuse in eastern Idaho had been a political liability for Craig during his 1996 re-election campaign. The amendment was adopted by voice vote.

Amendments Rejected

The biggest committee battle came when Bingaman tried to address White House objections by introducing four broad amendments, all of which were defeated. Bingaman's proposals would have:

➤ Ratcheted up radiation safety standards, barred construction of a temporary Yucca site if the Energy Department determined the location was unsuitable for permanent storage and pushed back the first waste shipments from 1999 to 2002. That time frame would have allowed the Energy Department to complete the final suitability study, due in 2000.

The amendment also would have reduced the dump's capacity from 60,000 metric tons of waste to 18,000 metric tons and shortened its license from 100 years to 40 years to ensure that the temporary site did not become a de facto permanent repository.

➤ Removed a provision to pre-empt all federal, state and local laws that conflicted with the waste legislation.

➤ Made it more difficult for Congress to use fees collected from utilities for nuclear waste disposal for other purposes.

The first three amendments failed largely along party lines, 8-12, with Bob Graham of Florida the only Democrat to side with the committee's united Republicans.

➤ Mitigated financial claims against the federal government that could arise if it missed the 1998 deadline for assuming control over utilities' nuclear waste. The amendment failed, 7-13, with Byron L. Dorgan, D-N.D., joining Graham to vote "no."

Democrats complained that Murkowski gave little serious thought to Bingaman's proposals, which Republican Pete V. Domenici of New Mexico said would give "pretty fair treatment to a major national issue that the president has avoided year after year." "You want to drive this bill out of here, and we want to work it out before driving it out," said Democrat Wendell H. Ford of Kentucky.

Senate Floor Action

After several days of debate, the Senate passed the bill April 15, but the 65-34 tally was still two votes shy of the margin needed to override Clinton's threatened veto. *(Vote 42, p. S-10)*

Bill sponsors fell short of a veto-proof majority because of "no" votes by two first-year Democrats who succeeded retired members of their own party who had supported the Yucca site. Sens. Paul Simon of Illinois and J. Bennett Johnston of Louisiana had backed the bill in 1996. But their successors, Richard J. Durbin of Illinois and Mary L. Landrieu of Louisiana, voted against the measure in 1997.

When the Senate first began work on the bill April 9, Murkowski, known for his uncompromising stands, made several concessions aimed at swaying key Democratic votes. The changes, which surprised even the Democrats, included tightening environmental rules on the waste site, bolstering training provisions for transportation workers and moving the opening date for the repository from 1999, as originally proposed, until at least June 30, 2003.

But the modifications were not enough to change minds in the White House. "The president has made it clear that he would veto the Senate version of this bill, and nothing that happened on the Senate floor has changed his position," said Office of Management and Budget spokesman Lawrence J. Haas.

Bill proponents lost their chance to cross the veto-proof threshold when they came out against a key amendment by Bingaman, who was highly regarded by Democrats for his acumen on nuclear issues. Bingaman's amendment would have barred interim storage at the Nevada site if Energy Department scientists found Yucca Mountain to be unsuitable for permanent storage.

Murkowski said he was 90 percent sure Yucca would be suitable but he refused to give in, saying the Bingaman amendment would invite the president to find the site wanting and do nothing. In the end, Murkowski's motion to table (kill) Bingaman's amendment passed, 59-39. Landrieu said she would follow Bingaman and vote against the bill. *(Vote 40, p. S-10)*

Other Floor Amendments

Wyden's provision added in committee to make the Hanford site off-limits as an alternative to Yucca Mountain sent other senators scrambling to protect their own states in the event an alternative was sought.

On April 10, the Senate agreed by voice vote to an amendment by Republican Strom Thurmond and Democrat Ernest F. Hollings of South Carolina to exempt their state's Savannah River nuclear weapons plant from consideration. Republicans Bill Frist and Fred Thompson of Tennessee followed with an amendment to exempt the federal nuclear complex at Oak Ridge, Tenn., which was adopted, 60-33. *(Vote 37, p. S-9)*

With each exemption, Clinton gained ammunition to argue that the bill would give him no choice but to build the dump at Yucca Mountain, regardless of pending scientific findings. Late on April 10, the Senate rejected, 36-56, an amendment by Bingaman to strike all the exemptions the Senate had passed. *(Vote 39, p. S-9)*

In other action, the Senate:

➤ On April 10, rejected, 24-69, a non-binding resolution by Dale Bumpers, D-Ark., that would have absolved the Energy Department of blame if the department was unable to fulfill utility contracts that required it to take control of nuclear waste by January 1998. The amendment would have attributed a missed deadline to issues beyond the Energy Department's control. Such a resolution would have helped the department fight the utilities' lawsuit, which demanded financial damages for the department's impending breach of those utility contracts. *(Vote 38, p. S-9)*

➤ Also on April 10, rejected an attempt by Reid and Bryan to forbid the shipment of nuclear waste through a state without the approval of the state's governor. Their amendment was tabled (killed), 72-24. *(Vote 36, p. S-9)*

The final vote on the bill provided a tense moment. Nearly 15 minutes after voting was supposed to have ended, Daniel R. Coats, R-Ind., Durbin and Tom Harkin, D-Iowa, stood staring at each other at the front of the chamber. None wanted to be the decisive vote. Finally, Durbin approached Coats and conferred. All three then voted: Coats and Durbin against the bill, Harkin in favor.

House Subcommittee

House action on the issue began in the Commerce Subcommittee on Energy and Power, which approved its version of the bill (HR 1270) July 31 by an overwhelming vote of 21-3, despite dogged efforts by Edward J. Markey, D-Mass., to derail the measure.

The draft bill mandated opening the temporary waste site by 2002. In a compromise with the nuclear power industry, the bill proposed setting up new formulas to allow the amount of money taken from ratepayers for the project to increase by as much as 50 percent in some years. In exchange, the utilities' payments would be lower in other years.

The draft bill also proposed limiting the capacity of the temporary site to 40,000 metric tons of waste, considerably less than the total amount of nuclear waste that was expected to be generated by the end of the next century. The limit was meant to ensure that the temporary site did not become the de facto permanent site. The bill also proposed to require the Energy Department to develop a nationwide rail and truck transportation system, including help for towns along the way to plan for potential emergencies; pre-empt environmental laws; and set a deadline of January 2010 to open a permanent repository at Yucca Mountain.

Five Markey Amendments Rejected

Markey, a longtime foe of the nuclear industry, began his battle against the bill with a series of amendments, all of which were defeated. He proposed to:

➤ Strike a clause forbidding the Environmental Protection Agency (EPA) from setting radiation protection standards for the project. The House bill included allowable radiation exposure levels for humans that the White House said were higher than those of comparable facilities. For instance, Markey said, the Energy Department's Waste Isolation Pilot Project in New Mexico had a standard that was six times lower. The amendment failed, 6-18.

➤ Strike mandated restrictions on an environmental impact statement that the Energy Department would have to conduct before construction began. Under the bill, the impact statement would not consider the need for the repository, or alternative sites, designs and construction timetables. The amendment was rejected, 6-21.

➤ Cut the size of the temporary site by 75 percent, to a capacity of 10,000 metric tons, and prevent initial construction until a license for the site was issued. The proposal failed, 3-21.

➤ Remove all caps on the amount that utilities would have to pay in a given year for site construction. Studies suggested that increasing competition in the electric power industry could force up to 40 percent of the nation's nuclear power plants to shut down prematurely. Markey said that could leave the nuclear waste fund with a large shortfall. The amendment was defeated by voice vote.

➤ Ensure that the permanent waste site would be large enough to handle all the civilian and defense nuclear waste the nation would generate. That amendment also failed on a voice vote.

House Full Committee

The full Commerce Committee shucked off more than a half dozen Democratic amendments Sept. 18, then approved the measure by a lopsided 43-3 vote (H Rept 105-290, Part 1).

Energy and Power Subcommittee Chairman Schaefer tried to placate some Democratic concerns with a new version of the bill that allowed for a more diligent environmental review and gave a larger oversight role to the EPA. His substitute also included a provision specifically aimed at committee member Elizabeth Furse, D-Ore., to make it easier for shutdown reactors to get their waste included in the interim storage site. Oregon was home to such a reactor.

Markey Again Fails To Alter Bill

The imperative of the committee session was clearly to remove nuclear waste from power plants scattered throughout the country and place it in one location and one congressional district, and Markey's continued opposition could not derail that sentiment. As he had done in the subcommittee, Markey peppered the proceedings with amendments, none of which came close to passage. He proposed to:

➤ Deny nuclear waste transport contractors immunity from civil liability in the event of an accident. Under existing law, all Energy Department nuclear contractors had such immunity, but Markey held that in the case of waste transport, civil indemnification would mean shipping companies would have no incentive to perform their jobs safely. The amendment failed, 13-22.

➤ Strip the bill of a radiation-exposure standard that he contended was dangerously loose. Markey said the allowable exposure in the bill was four times higher than France's standard and 10 times higher than the standards of Sweden, Finland and Switzerland. The amendment was rejected, 11-25.

➤ Force the Energy Department to consider the possibility that in the future, people could stumble onto the nuclear waste site, possibly releasing radiation. The amendment failed, 8-27.

➤ Bar selection of an interim storage site until the suitability of Yucca Mountain had been determined. This amendment went to the heart of the president's position. It also would have limited the size of the temporary waste site to 10,000 metric tons, ensuring that it could not become the de facto permanent site. It was rejected, 4-34.

➤ Eliminate the annual cap on fees the Energy Department could charge nuclear utilities to pay for nuclear waste activities. The amendment was defeated by voice vote.

Bill supporters were in no mood to entertain any changes to the bill, no matter the source. By voice vote, they rejected amendments by:

➤ Tom Sawyer, D-Ohio, requesting that waste transport routes avoid the most populous areas.

➤ Diana DeGette, D-Colo., to strip the bill of restrictions on environmental assessments.

➤ Karen McCarthy, D-Mo., stipulating that no waste shipments could go through communities until emergency training had been completed.

Resources Committee Opposes Bill

The House Resources Committee, which shared jurisdiction over the bill, voted Oct. 8 to report the measure unfavorably (H Rept 105-290, Part 2). The decision, approved by voice vote, meant the committee recommended that the House not pass the bill. That left it to the Rules Committee to choose between two competing versions of the legislation.

The unfavorable report by the Resources Committee, chaired by Don Young, R-Alaska, served notice that Nevada was not without allies. Nevada's Ensign called the bill a "war on the West," echoing a battle cry started in the 1980s, when Congress decided to build a repository in the remote West rather than on the East or West coasts or in the Midwest, South or Northeast, where much of the nation's nuclear power was generated

The panel's bill did not include amendments by the Commerce Committee, such as specifying an oversight role for the EPA. It had a narrower pre-emption of federal laws and would have opened the interim dump in 2000, two years earlier than the Commerce version.

House Floor Action

As expected, the House Rules Committee made the Commerce Committee's version of the bill in order. After considering numerous amendments, the House passed the measure Oct. 30 by a vote of 307-120. *(Vote 557, p. H-168)*

Nevadans Ensign and Gibbons led the floor fight against the bill. They complained the Republican leadership did not allow consideration of enough key amendments. In preparing the measure for floor action, the Rules Committee on Oct. 23 had rejected several amendments, including one offered by Dennis J. Kucinich, D-Ohio, to prohibit companies from transporting high-level radioactive waste through cities with more than 50,000 residents.

Markey tried to recommit the bill before final passage, with instructions to insert language to remove indemnification for nuclear waste transporters that were involved in accidents. The motion to recommit failed by a 142-283 vote. *(Vote 556, p. H-168)*

Floor Amendments

House debate included consideration of the following amendments.

● **Rail routes.** The House approved by voice vote an amendment offered by Schaefer, who managed the bill on the floor, to require the Transportation Department to set procedures within a year for picking preferred rail routes to the interim facility and to set standards for training waste transporters. Among the members who had expressed concern was Karen McCarthy, D-Mo. She supported the amendment but said she worried that many of the nuclear shipments would travel through her state.

● **Tribal consultation.** The House approved, 408-10, an amendment by Dale E. Kildee, D-Mich., to require the Energy Department to consult about the project with Indian tribes whose reservations were near Yucca Mountain. *(Vote 543, p. H-166)*

● **Foreign waste.** By a 407-11 vote, the House approved an amendment by James A. Traficant Jr., D-Ohio, providing that only nuclear waste produced in the United States could be stored in the repository. Traficant said the United States should not become the world's nuclear "dumping ground." *(Vote 544, p. H-166)*

The House considered, but defeated, amendments that would have:

➤ Required a risk assessment study. The proposal, by Ensign, failed by a 135-290 vote. *(Vote 550, p. H-168)*

➤ Barred nuclear waste transportation planning if the Federal Emergency Management Agency found insufficient funds for emergency response teams on the transportation routes. The amendment, by Ensign, failed by a 118-305 vote. *(Vote 552, H-168)*

➤ Required governors of states on transportation routes to certify that there were adequate "emergency response teams" for accidents. The amendment, by Gibbons, failed, 112-312. *(Vote 551, p. H-168)*

➤ Deleted the cap — one-tenth of 1 cent per kilowatt hour — placed on the utility nuclear waste disposal fees after the interim facility opened. The proposal, also by Gibbons, failed by a 67-357 vote. *(Vote 554, p. H-168)*

➤ Deleted the provision removing the EPA's authority to set radiation protection standards for the permanent repository. The amendment, by Markey, failed, 151-273. *(Vote 553, p. H-168)* ■

Tri-State Radioactive Waste Pact Gets House Endorsement

A bill (HR 629) approving a three-state compact for disposing of low-level radioactive waste in western Texas won House approval in October. The Senate Judiciary Committee approved a companion bill (S 270) by voice vote March 20.

The legislation provided for creating a new disposal site in Texas to accept low-level radioactive waste from Maine and Vermont. Maine and Vermont would be required to ensure the safe transport of the waste and pay $25 million each to build and operate the facility. The compact had been endorsed by the governors and state legislatures of the three states.

While the measure was approved with large majorities at each stage, it was vigorously opposed by two congressmen from western Texas, reflecting strong local opposition to the compact.

Background

The Low Level Radioactive Waste Policy Act, enacted in 1980 (PL 96-573) and amended in 1985 (PL 99-240), made states responsible for disposing of low-level radioactive waste generated within their borders. Examples of such waste included protective clothing worn by nuclear power workers, and radiological and other waste generated by hospitals.

The act encouraged states to form regional waste disposal compacts in order to limit the number of disposal sites. Congress had consented to nine such interstate compacts involving 41 states. States participating in a congressionally approved disposal compact could exclude from their disposal facilities any waste generated in states that were not members of that compact.

Despite bipartisan support, the proposed Texas compact had had a difficult time in Congress. A nearly identical measure had breezed through the Commerce Committee in 1995 but was defeated on the House floor. *(1995 Almanac, p. 5-18)*

The plan received mixed reviews, including an even split among the Texas delegation. Supporters of the bill asserted that Congress was simply fulfilling its role in approving a compact already agreed to among the states. Opponents contended that the proposed waste site — a ranch about 15 miles from the Rio Grande, near the border town of Sierra Blanca — would violate accords with Mexico that prohibited environmental degradation within 60 miles of the U.S.-Mexico border.

Two west Texas House members, Democrat Silvestre Reyes and Republican Henry Bonilla, argued that the area's population, predominantly poor and Latino, felt betrayed.

House Action

Those ill feelings were evident when the House Commerce Energy and Power Subcommittee held a hearing prior to approving the bill May 13. Texans squared off against Texans, with Bonilla and Reyes dueling with Republican Joe L. Barton and Democrat Gene Green, who supported the bill.

Also, Texas and Maine state officials clashed with a Sierra Blanca rancher and a west Texas county attorney, giving the hearing some of the passion of a local zoning board meeting. "It grieves me deeply that, because of the love of money, my home and state could become the radioactive pay toilet for the unwanted wastes of the whole United States," said rancher Bill Addington.

But the subcommittee shrugged off the opposition as a matter for Texans to resolve among themselves. Both Dan Schaefer, R-Colo., the subcommittee's chairman, and Ralph M. Hall of Texas, its ranking Democrat, noted that nowhere in the bill was Sierra Blanca designated as the site for the waste dump. That had been determined by Texas officials and endorsed by Republican Gov. George W. Bush and his predecessor, Democrat Ann W. Richards.

The full Commerce Committee gave voice vote approval to the bill on June 25 with little debate (H Rept 105-181).

House Floor Action

The House passed the bill Oct. 7 by a vote of 309-107. During the floor debate, supporters of the bill, including many members of the Texas delegation, argued that Congress should give its consent to an agreement that had been reached by local officials. *(Vote 497, p. H-150)*

Others said that choosing one site was a much preferable alternative to storing waste at individual hospitals and other sites. "It is much more heinous to have it scattered everywhere," said Texas Democrat Eddie Bernice Johnson.

But Bonilla and Reyes again argued against the bill. "Who would want radioactive waste shipped to their district?" Reyes asked. Reyes argued that the Sierra Blanca site was prone to earthquakes and said the compact would disproportionately affect Hispanics, who made up 75 percent of the population surrounding the site. ■

Other Energy-Related Issues Considered in First Session

Lawmakers considered several energy-related initiatives in 1997, including an agreement to stop funding non-power operations at the Tennessee Valley Authority, and a decision to continue a study of the potential health effects of electric and magnetic fields created by power lines and other carriers of electricity.

TVA

The federal subsidy for the once-sacrosanct Tennessee Valley Authority (TVA) survived for another year — but only barely. The fiscal 1998 Energy and Water appropriations bill (HR 2203 — PL 105-62) provided $70 million for the giant federally owned utility, well short of the president's $106 million request and considerably less than the $86 million initially approved by the Senate.

Moreover, an unyielding House contingent won explicit legislative language ensuring that the federal subsidy — which financed programs not related to the company's lucrative power production arm, such as environmental and economic projects — would be the last. The House had initially voted to zero out the agency in fiscal 1998.

With the electricity industry inching into an era of competition and deregulation, TVA foes argued that federal subsidies were distorting prices, giving an unfair advantage to federal power agencies. Also, lawmakers in the Northeast and Midwest complained that their regions were the only ones not benefiting from federally generated, low-cost electricity. TVA served large portions of the Southeast.

"Some things do have to come to an end sometime," said Joe Knollenberg, R-Mich., a member of the House Energy and Water Development Appropriations Subcommittee.

TVA supporters responded that the Depression-era agency had special responsibilities — such as maintaining waterways, protecting stretches of wilderness and protecting their customers from floods — that other utilities did not have to shoulder. If the TVA stopped performing those functions, they said, the Army Corps of Engineers or some other federal agency would have to step in.

House conferees entered the House-Senate negotiations on the appropriations bill gunning for the TVA, in large part because TVA Chairman Craven Crowell had stepped on toes earlier in the year when he asserted that his federal utility should be able to compete with private electric utilities in surrounding states. "TVA may be one of the most arrogant agencies I have ever seen in government," said Mike Parker, R-Miss.

But the House was taking on a region represented by mostly Republican senators, who applied a full press to hold the line. Sens. Jeff Sessions and Richard C. Shelby of Alabama, and Bill Frist and Fred Thompson of Tennessee, wrote the White House to "respectfully request" a veto if the TVA lost its funding.

After deadlocking for weeks, the Senate prevailed, but at a price. As recently as fiscal 1995, TVA's non-power subsidy had been nearly twice as large as the $70 million in the final bill.

The TVA's Changing Fortunes

Created in 1933 under emergency legislation enacted during the landmark first 100 days of President Franklin Delano Roosevelt's administration, the TVA's origins were humble compared with its scope in 1997. The TVA had come to serve

7.3 million customers in seven Southern states using 44 power sources. Even at the start, however, the agency's size and influence were questioned by private utilities that saw a threat of competition. In 1936 and 1939, private power companies took their case to the Supreme Court, challenging the TVA's right to sell power in the region.

In both cases, the Supreme Court upheld the TVA, and its major expansion across the Tennessee Valley pressed on. Between 1933 and 1942, the TVA began construction of 18 hydroelectric dams. The TVA got another boost in 1959, when Congress allowed it to finance construction projects through revenue bonds, giving it the freedom to construct or improve electric power facilities without relying on prior congressional approval. To appease private competitors, the same bill also restricted the areas into which the TVA could expand.

For decades, the TVA enjoyed favorable treatment from members of both parties whose districts were served by it. But after Republicans took control of the House in 1995 calling for budget cuts and a smaller federal role, the idea of privatizing the TVA began to catch on.

Scott L. Klug, R-Wis., a moderate with a reputation as a deficit hawk, offered amendments to cut the TVA's ties to the federal government in the fiscal 1996 and 1997 energy-water spending bills. The first attempt failed, 144-284, with Republicans split almost evenly and Democrats overwhelmingly opposed. In 1996, Klug tried to remove $16 million intended for the TVA's economic development program from the $120 million requested. That move was rejected, 184-236. *(1995 Almanac, p. 11-34; 1996 Almanac, p. 10-42)*

The situation changed in January 1997, when TVA Chairman Crowell announced that he favored doing away with the agency's federal subsidy. Crowell wanted to wait a year, but his stance — controversial within the agency and opposed by many of its supporters — was virtually an invitation to Congress to cut the TVA's historic ties to the government.

Strategic Petroleum Reserve

Lawmakers in both chambers favored reauthorizing the Strategic Petroleum Reserve and allowing the United States to continue its participation in the International Energy Agency (IEP). The two programs were set to expire Sept. 30, 1997. But the House and Senate could not agree on what vehicle to use.

The House bill (HR 2472 — H Rept 105-275) proposed to reauthorize the programs for one year. The Commerce Committee approved the measure Sept. 18 by voice vote, and the full House passed it Sept. 29 by a vote of 405-8. *(Vote 464, p. H-140)*

The Senate bill (S 417 — S Rept 105-25) proposed extending the programs through Sept. 30, 2002. In addition, it included antitrust provisions aimed at allowing U.S. oil companies to participate in international energy programs.

The Strategic Petroleum Reserve was created in 1975 to reduce the impact of future oil import disruptions. The same act authorized U.S. participation in the IEP, an international agreement to coordinate the responses of oil-consuming nations to interruptions in the global supply of oil.

Power Line Health Study

A bill enacted July 3 (HR 363 — PL 105-23) provided a one-year extension for a Department of Energy study on the health effects of electromagnetic fields created by electricity running through power lines and cords.

The bill extended the Electric and Magnetic Fields Research and Public Information Dissemination Program, established by the Energy Policy Act of 1992 (PL 102-486). Supporters said the extension was necessary to complete the program's objectives. They also noted that half the funding was being provided by non-governmental sources. Although the program had been created in 1992, money was not appropriated until 1994.

Research into the effects of electric and magnetic fields began in the 1960s in what was then the Soviet Union, after power workers complained of various maladies. In the 1970s, the Energy Department began researching the potential health effects of magnetic fields created by power lines because of indications that people in the vicinity of such lines developed brain cancers and leukemia more often than others. To date, the research had been inconclusive.

The House passed the bill April 29 by a vote of 387-35, after separate versions were approved by the Commerce and Science committees (H Rept 105-60, Parts 1, 2). *(Vote 94, p. H-32)*

The Senate Energy and Natural Resources Committee approved the measure June 12 (S Rept 105-27), and the Senate cleared it by voice vote June 20. ■

Waste Disposal Controversy Delays Peña Confirmation

The Senate on March 12 voted 99-1 to confirm Federico F. Peña as Energy secretary, nearly three months after President Clinton nominated him for the post. Peña replaced Hazel R. O'Leary, who retired. *(Vote 30, p. S-7)*

The lopsided tally belied a contentious process in which Senate action on Peña became enmeshed in a separate dispute over a bill to establish a temporary nuclear waste repository at Yucca Mountain in Nevada.

Senators did not object to Peña's qualifications for the Department of Energy post, despite his lack of background on energy issues. His abilities were proven, they said, during Clinton's first term, when Peña served as Transportation secretary.

But Frank H. Murkowski, R-Alaska, chairman of the Senate Energy and Natural Resources Committee, and a handful of other committee Republicans tried to use Peña's confirmation to pressure the White House to drop a veto threat against the waste bill (S 104). *(Yucca Mountain, p. 4-20)*

Murkowski twice canceled committee action on the Peña nomination in February. "It's patently unfair to hold a perfectly good man hostage to a particular issue," said Dale Bumpers of Arkansas, ranking Democrat on the Energy Committee. Murkowski conceded that he saw no reason Peña would not be confirmed. "I've been accused of holding Secretary Peña hostage. That isn't the issue. The issue here is the administration holding this nuclear waste issue hostage," Murkowski said.

The committee finally voted, 19-0, on March 6 to send the nomination to the Senate floor. Committee member Rod Grams, R-Minn., voted present that day to protest the White House's nuclear waste policies, then blocked the full Senate from moving quickly under unanimous consent rules to approve Peña's nomination.

Eager to clear away unfinished business, Senate Majority Leader Trent Lott, R-Miss., agreed to allow Grams to voice his position on the waste bill from the Senate floor. Grams then voted against Peña, the only senator to do so.

Lott had hoped a final confirmation vote would be followed by Senate consideration of the nuclear waste bill the week of March 17. But a parliamentary maneuver by Richard H. Bryan, D-Nev., just before the Peña vote delayed progress on the waste bill and made it clear that bill opponents would not accept the deal Lott had hoped for.

Critics Focus on Policies, Not Nominee

Throughout the process, Peña encountered little personal opposition.

Sen. Charles E. Grassley, R-Iowa, had raised concerns over charges that Peña, as Transportation secretary, reinstated a contract with a minority-owned firm in Florida even after the Coast Guard terminated it for poor performance. A former Coast Guard auditor, Robert Baggan, filed a $30 million "whistleblower" lawsuit against Peña and the department over the issue. But Transportation Department investigators cleared Peña of any wrongdoing, and Grassley said he did not wish to hold up Peña's confirmation.

Peña's nomination was initially clouded by widespread speculation that Clinton had picked him mainly to preserve the Cabinet's ethnic diversity. Clinton had been leaning toward Elizabeth Moler, chairman of the Federal Energy Regulatory Commission, for the Energy post, and Peña had planned to leave the government. But with Housing and Urban Development Secretary Henry G. Cisneros retiring, Peña's departure would have left the Cabinet with no Hispanic members. Clinton asked Peña to stay as Energy secretary.

Apart from the ethnicity issue, some senators questioned whether Peña's last-minute nomination meant the administration viewed the job, in Murkowski's words, as a "throwaway" position.

But most of the questions during Peña's confirmation hearing before the Energy Committee Jan. 30, focused not so much on the nominee, as on the department he was seeking to lead.

Committee members raised issues — such as nuclear waste disposal, a nuclear weapons test ban, oil drilling in the Arctic and the future of federally owned power plants — that had vexed the department in recent years and led critics to argue it should be eliminated. "Some are going as far as to say you are here today to interview for the position of captain of the Titanic," Murkowski told Peña.

Many in Congress were critical of O'Leary's stewardship of the department, and Peña was warned that inertia at Energy would not be tolerated. "We can accept that you are not an energy expert. . . . What we won't accept is a department that believes that if it ignores these problems, they will go away," Murkowski said.

Hot Issues on Senators' Minds

The long-stymied effort to establish a central repository for the nation's nuclear waste spurred heated discussion at the hearing. GOP Sens. Murkowski, Grams and Larry E. Craig of Idaho blasted the administration's opposition to building a temporary storage site at Yucca Mountain for the waste products piling up at civilian nuclear reactors and government facilities.

"This administration struts around the country saying they're the No. 1 environmental administration ever," Craig said. "Yet they have flatly stuck their heads in the sand" on nuclear waste, which he declared the most critical environmental issue facing the nation.

Peña also found himself challenged, this time by Democrat Bumpers, on the administration's approach to deregulating the electric power industry. Bumpers wanted to mandate electric power deregulation nationwide by 2003, but top Energy Department officials favored letting the states decide when or whether to allow competition in their markets.

"To allow states to do this on a harum-scarum basis according to their own rules is going to be chaotic not just for the nation, but for the utilities themselves," Bumpers said. *(Electricity deregulation, p. 3-7)*

Three committee members from the Pacific Northwest — Ron Wyden, D-Ore., Gordon H. Smith, R-Ore., and Conrad Burns, R-Mont. — told Peña they would never consent to selling the region's federal power operations, especially the Bonneville Power Administration.

Though Grams continued to press for dismantling the Energy Department, as he had during the 104th Congress, he appeared to have little support. Murkowski said energy issues needed an advocate in the Cabinet, though he complained that the department's voice often went unheeded by the White House. ■

CQ

Chapter 5

LAW & JUDICIARY

CURBING JUVENILE CRIME

Myriad Disputes Slow Progress Of GOP Juvenile Crime Bills

Democrats resist efforts to try more violent youths as adults, call for greater emphasis on preventive programs

Efforts to find common ground on legislation aimed at reducing juvenile crime remained stalled at the end of the first session. The House passed a juvenile crime bill (HR 3) in May aimed at getting more of the nation's violent juvenile offenders prosecuted in adult courts and ensuring that all crimes by juveniles met with some punishment. The Senate Judiciary Committee approved a broader companion bill (S 10) in July but put off floor action.

The centerpiece of each was a $500 million-a-year program of grants to states that agreed to cooperate in the effort.

The principal area of partisan dispute centered on whether juveniles should be tried as adults and, if so, which ones and who should decide.

Republicans argued that juvenile justice systems across the country were failing to hold violent offenders accountable for their wrongdoing. When juveniles committed serious crimes usually committed by adults, they said, they should expect to be tried and punished as adults. Bill supporters also argued that the surge in the youth population expected shortly after the turn of the century, could produce gang violence on an unprecedented scale if steps were not taken quickly.

Democrats were split on the issue of trying youths as adults. Some moderates were willing to do so in the case of unusually dangerous criminals. But liberals argued that the best way to reduce juvenile crime was through prevention programs. They said trying juveniles as adults would foreclose any chance of reforming young people before they became lifelong criminals.

President Clinton produced a plan of his own that combined get-tough policies with money for prevention programs. To the dismay of many liberal Democrats, the administration used the plan as the basis for negotiations with House Republicans aimed at producing a compromise that could win the support of moderate Democrats. Clinton pressed Republicans to add several of his provisions to their legislation, including stepped up prosecution of gun-related crimes, a requirement that hand guns be sold with childproof gun locks, and more money for prevention programs.

For a time, a bipartisan compromise bill seemed imminent, but the negotiations fell apart at the last minute. GOP leaders feared that adding administration proposals on the House floor would create a procedural opening for Democrats to force a vote on the gun lock proposal.

Both sides still held out hope for a compromise, however, especially because the talks collapsed over procedural, rather than philosophical, differences. Additionally, an October announcement by eight of the largest U.S. firearms manufacturers that they would voluntarily provide child safety locks with new handguns held the potential for reducing tensions over the issue.

BOXSCORE

Curbing Juvenile Crime — HR 3, S 10. The bills contained provisions to require the federal government and encourage the states to try violent juveniles as adults and to punish all juvenile crimes.

Reports: H Rept 105-86, S Rept 105-108.

KEY ACTION

May 8 — House passed HR 3, 286-132.

July 24 — Senate Judiciary Committee approved S 10, 12-6.

House and Senate Bills

The House bill (HR 3), sponsored by Bill McCollum, R-Fla., essentially tracked a bill that Republicans had pushed in the 104th Congress. That bill had come under vociferous attack from Democrats and never made it out of the Judiciary Committee despite a markup that spanned four days. This time, however, GOP leaders put the issue near the top of their agenda. *(1996 Almanac, p. 5-29)*

HR 3 was designed to work in tandem with a smaller funding bill (HR 1818) that proposed to combine several juvenile crime prevention programs into block grants to the states. That bill passed the House in July. *(Juvenile crime prevention, p. 5-4)*

HR 3 called for providing $1.5 billion over three years in grants to states that agreed to try violent juvenile offenders age 15 and over as adults. The states would have to develop a graduated system of penalties that ensured a sanction for every delinquent or criminal act and escalated the sanction with each more serious crime.

State and local authorities would also be required to collect fingerprints and criminal records of juvenile offenders, and make them available to law enforcement agencies and school officials. Under existing law, these records, if collected at all, remained sealed until the offender's 18th birthday, when they were expunged.

The bill also proposed what backers said would be a model federal system of juvenile justice. For the few federal crimes involving juveniles — perhaps including crimes against federal property, Indian reservations or those involving interstate travel — the bill would make it easier for federal authorities to prosecute and try as adults juveniles ages 14 years and older who committed violent federal crimes or federal drug-trafficking offenses. With the approval of the attorney general, teenagers 13 years old who broke such laws could be prosecuted as adults. Existing law allowed youths ages 15 and older to be tried as adults.

The attorney general could make exceptions if it was in the interest of public safety.

The federal government would also be required to keep

House Passes Juvenile Crime Prevention Bill

The House passed a bill (HR 1818) aimed at combining several juvenile crime prevention programs into a block grant to the states.

Republican supporters presented the bill as the prevention arm of an effort to reduce juvenile crime that included a separate House bill (HR 3) focusing on punishment. That measure passed the House May 8. "Combined with HR 3, it provides the missing link in our efforts to combat juvenile crime," said bill sponsor Frank Riggs, R-Calif.

The Senate included prevention provisions in its companion bill to HR 3 (S 10), which was reported by the Senate Judiciary Committee but stalled thereafter. *(Juvenile crime, p. 5-3)*

HR 1818 proposed to consolidate several prevention programs — such as boot camps, treatment for abused and neglected children, and gang-prevention programs at school — into a single Juvenile Delinquency Prevention Block Grant Program, giving states and localities wide leeway to decide how to spend the money.

The grants would be authorized through 2001 at unspecified levels. Funding was to be allocated to the states according to a formula: 50 percent would be based on population and 50 percent on each state's three-year annual average number of arrests of juveniles for serious crimes.

In addition to creating block grants, the bill called for relaxing existing requirements on states that received federal money. Most notably, it proposed giving the states more flexibility to temporarily detain juveniles in adult prisons. With few exceptions, existing law allowed juveniles to be housed in adult facilities for only 24 hours before their initial court appearance. The bill proposed extending that limit to 48 hours.

The House Education Subcommittee on Early Childhood, Youth and Families approved HR 1818 by voice vote June 12.

The subcommittee adopted an amendment, by James C. Greenwood, R-Pa., to ensure that courts had access to the child welfare records of troubled juveniles. It also agreed to add language by Michael N. Castle, R-Del., authorizing $5 million a year for five years for the National Center for Missing and Exploited Children. Both amendments were adopted by voice vote.

The full Committee on Education and the Workforce approved the bill by voice vote June 18 (H Rept 105-155).

While Democrats backed the bill, some on the panel supported an amendment by Donald M. Payne, D-N.J., to require states to set aside half of the block grant money for programs targeting juveniles before they committed a crime. Payne said that without such a requirement, state and local governments would use most of the money on juveniles already in the juvenile justice system, shortchanging efforts to keep them out. Republicans said they did not want to tell local agencies how to spend the money. The amendment was defeated by voice vote.

The House easily passed the bill July 15 by a vote of 413-14. *(Vote 267, p. H-84)*

records and devise graduated sanctions.

The Senate bill (S 10), sponsored by Judiciary Committee Chairman Orrin G. Hatch, R-Utah, was more sweeping than the two House bills combined. Like HR 3, it included provisions to require the federal government and urge the states to try the most violent juveniles in adult court. It called for $500 million a year in incentive grants to the states over five years, for a total of $2.5 billion.

Like HR 1818, the Senate bill authorized funding for juvenile crime prevention programs. It proposed combining several programs — such as boot camps, treatment for abused and neglected children and gang-prevention programs in schools — into a single Juvenile Delinquency Prevention Block Grant Program, giving states and localities wide leeway to decide how to spend the money. The programs would be reauthorized at $750 million over five years.

The Senate bill also called for allocating $100 million to the Boys and Girls Clubs of America and ordering the Justice Department to use the money to help create another 1,000 local clubs, bringing the total to 2,500. This was a high priority for Judiciary Committee Chairman Hatch, who said he would rather have prevention money go to these groups than "to the bureaucrats in Washington."

Background

Juvenile crime, especially when it included violence, had become a hot issue for lawmakers in both parties, partly as a function of the numbers.

Although violent crime arrest rates for juveniles ages 10 to 17 had dropped 2.9 percent in 1995, they remained nearly 70 percent higher than in 1985. For murders by juveniles, arrests rose 96 percent over the same time period. In contrast, violent crime arrest rates for adults had risen only slightly in the previous decade and murder arrest rates had fallen.

Teenagers accounted for the largest portion of all violent crime in the country, and those ages 17 to 19 were the most violent of all age groups. More murder and robbery was committed by 18-year-old males than by any other group, and more than one-third of all murders were committed by offenders under age 21.

The vast majority of juvenile offenses were handled by state authorities. Only 10 percent of violent juvenile offenders — those convicted of murder, rape, robbery and assault — received any secure confinement in the states. According to the Justice Department, 43 percent of juveniles in state institutions had more than five prior arrests, and 20 percent had been arrested more than 10 times.

Hurdles for Bill Sponsors

The question of what the federal government could do to deal with the stubbornly high rates of juvenile crime posed several key challenges for bill sponsors. First, they needed to overcome deep partisan differences. Second, they had to prevent the debate from turning into one on gun control, the death penalty or other hot-button issues.

More broadly, lawmakers faced the question of whether the federal government should or could play an effective role in fighting juvenile crime, which in most cases involved local statutes and prosecution.

Fewer than 200 juveniles were prosecuted in federal courts annually; the vast majority were tried in state courts.

Congress was limited primarily to improving federal enforcement, authorizing funds to localities and placing conditions on those funds. Moreover, some critics contended that the problem of juvenile crime went well beyond the limits of federal authority to an inability or unwillingness at all levels of government to face a systemic problem that could get worse as the teenage population grew.

Clinton Weighs In With His Proposal

The Clinton administration, which made reducing crime by minors a high priority, spent the three-month interregnum between the 104th and 105th Congresses devising legislation from scratch.

The Justice Department held brainstorming sessions with participants ranging from the Office of Juvenile Justice and Delinquency Prevention, to the Immigration and Naturalization Service and the U.S. Marshals office, among others. The brainstormers threw out some ideas as unworkable in order to limit the bill's scope to juvenile issues. The final product (HR 810) was introduced in late February by Charles E. Schumer, D-N.Y.

The administration's bill was much less stern than HR 3 on the issue of trying juveniles as adults. It proposed allowing, but not requiring, federal prosecutors to do so. It also called for giving federal judges considerable discretion to throw a case back into the juvenile system — an important selling point in getting Democrats to support the measure. The bill would not have much potential effect on how states tried juveniles.

In another key difference with the GOP bill, Clinton sought to combine punishment with prevention. The bill proposed giving money to schools and communities to develop anti-truancy programs and after-school programs to keep juveniles occupied when they might otherwise commit crimes. Fifty-one percent of weekday juvenile crimes occurred between 2 p.m. and 7 p.m.

Otherwise, much of HR 810 sounded like a Republican bill. It had a long section on new penalties for gang, gun and drug crimes. It proposed expanding the use of the Racketeering Influenced and Corrupt Organizations (RICO) statute in prosecuting gangs, which would allow prosecutors to go after more perpetrators by charging them with conspiracy to commit crimes. It also proposed eliminating statutes of limitations on murders, and increasing protection for people who were willing to testify against gangs.

Other provisions included increased penalties for firearms-related conspiracies and for discharging a firearm during a crime, a requirement that safety locks be sold on all firearms in an effort to prevent accidental shootings by children and requirements for how gun merchants stored their merchandise.

House Committee

The House Judiciary Committee approved its juvenile crime bill (HR 3 — H Rept 105-86) on April 29, after two long and contentious markup sessions in which Republicans turned back numerous Democratic amendments. The final 15-9 vote fell along party lines with the exception of Schumer, the ranking Democrat on the panel's crime subcommittee, who supported the bill.

Much of the real negotiation was taking place behind the scenes, however. Talks among Republicans, the Clinton administration and moderate committee Democrats such as Schumer were expected to lead to the addition of several "get-tough" proposals from Clinton's bill to HR 3. The bargaining left many of the committee's traditional liberals feeling left out and frustrated. "The administration is wrong. Please don't listen to what they say," entreated Maxine Waters, D-Calif.

During the initial committee markup session April 24, several Democrats sought to defeat, or at least delay, the bill, saying it was unnecessarily harsh and counterproductive. Melvin Watt, D-N.C., ordered that the entire 36-page bill be read aloud. Other Democrats offered a string of amendments aimed at substantially altering the legislation's direction.

Democrats argued vehemently that trying juveniles as adults would not necessarily reduce crime and that requiring states to do so was inconsistent with the GOP philosophy that Washington should not tell states how to run their affairs.

But McCollum, who did virtually all the talking for Republicans, said the approach was necessary to fix a juvenile justice system that simply did not work in many states.

Key Democratic amendments rejected during the markup included a package of proposals by Schumer to provide block grants to pay for juvenile correctional facilities and additional prosecutors, after-school programs for at-risk young people, and grants for youth violence courts for young offenders. The proposal was defeated, 10-11.

An attempt by Schumer to add language requiring gun dealers to sell safety locks with every gun was ruled nongermane.

John Conyers Jr. of Michigan, the ranking Democrat on the full committee, offered a substitute that would have prohibited people who committed violent crimes as juveniles from owning a gun, established special sentences for drug dealers, set up drug treatment programs for incarcerated juveniles and included a host of crime prevention programs. It was rejected, 7-17.

In the second markup session, April 29, Republicans again held together, turning away a dozen Democratic amendments.

The committee defeated two amendments by Watt, both on votes of 9-16. The first would have deleted the provision allowing 13-year-olds to be tried as adults; the other would have allowed judges, rather than prosecutors, to decide on a case-by-case basis whether to try juveniles as adults.

After a lengthy debate, the panel also rejected, 11-14, an amendment by Waters that would have prohibited adult prosecution of juveniles for conspiracy under certain federal drug laws. Waters argued that the provision could lead to adult prosecution for juveniles who were tricked into transporting drugs by older, more sophisticated criminals. But McCollum said that only juveniles who showed intent to commit a crime could be tried as adults under the conspiracy provision.

Democrats were successful with three relatively minor amendments. The committee approved by voice vote:

- A proposal by Zoe Lofgren, D-Calif., to allow states to use the block grants to hire additional juvenile judges, probation officers and court-appointed defenders, as well as to provide pre-trial services for juveniles.
- An amendment by Robert C. Scott, D-Va., to add "reducing recidivism" as a goal for juvenile courts and probation officers who received block grant money.
- A Scott amendment clarifying that juveniles should not be housed with adult criminals either before or after their trials.

Before the final vote, McCollum made some changes to accommodate administration requests, including language clarifying that juveniles, even if tried as adults, would have to be housed with other juveniles, and restricting the application of mandatory minimum sentences only to older and more violent juveniles.

The committee did not, however, include the administration's proposal that safety locks be sold with each gun. The administration also objected to a lack of funding in the bill for crime prevention, such as after-school programs and anti-truancy efforts.

House Floor Action

Despite talk of a grand compromise that would win the support of moderate Democrats, the House passed HR 3 on May 8 by a mostly party-line vote of 286-132. The bill looked much the same as it had when it left the committee. *(Vote 118, p. H-38)*

McCollum had anticipated adding much of Clinton's juvenile crime bill to HR 3 in a manager's amendment that was to include new penalties for gun, gang and drug crimes; expanded use of RICO in prosecuting gangs; and expanded witness protection programs. But those plans unravelled shortly before the bill reached the floor.

McCollum backed off not because of objections to the substance of the administration proposals — indeed, much of Clinton's bill read like a GOP remedy for juvenile crime. Rather, he was worried that the amendment would give liberal Democrats a chance to try to recommit the bill, sending it back to committee with instructions to add the safety lock language. Democrats could not do that as long as the underlying bill had no gun provisions. "We don't have to provide them an opportunity to play games," McCollum said of the Democrats.

McCollum also said the administration had been unwilling to close a deal, perhaps in hopes of gaining more leverage later. "They felt more comfortable waiting to see what happens in the Senate," he said.

With the collapse of the negotiations, partisan fault lines resurfaced. Democrats put aside most of their internal differences and united behind an alternative measure, which was defeated along party lines. Clinton formally opposed HR 3, though both sides held out the hope of future accommodation. Schumer, who had supported the bill in committee, voted against it on the floor.

Democratic Amendments Rejected

There was one Democratic rift that was not completely closed, however, and that concerned the content of the party's alternative.

During the committee markup, Schumer and Conyers had offered a substitute that included stepped up penalties for juvenile offenders, as well as more traditional Democratic crime prevention measures.

The package did not go over well with some of the more junior and more liberal members of the caucus, who saw it as aimed at helping Schumer's upcoming campaign for a Senate seat rather than as representing party views. Through the caucus, they outvoted and circumvented Schumer and Conyers and produced an alternative to the alternative, which was what Democrats brought to the floor.

Pushed aside, neither Schumer nor Conyers, the two senior House Democrats on crime issues, played a significant role during the floor debate. Sheila Jackson-Lee, D-Texas, managed general debate on HR 3 for the Democrats.

The Democratic alternative was spearheaded by Bart Stupak, D-Mich., who was not a member of the Judiciary Committee. Liberals liked the Stupak alternative because it focused heavily on crime prevention, with 60 percent of its $1.5 billion in grants targeted to programs such as education, drug treatment and after-school activities. The alternative was rejected, 200-224, along party lines. *(Vote 111, p. H-38)*

Several other Democratic amendments went down as well, including:

➤ An attempt by Waters to delete language requiring that juveniles convicted of conspiracy to commit drug crimes be tried as adults. She was rebuffed, 100-320. *(Vote 112, p. H-38)*

➤ A Conyers amendment to delete the provision allowing 13-year-olds in some instances to be tried as adults, defeated, 129-288. *(Vote 113, p. H-38)*

➤ An amendment by Scott to prevent grants from being used for prison construction, rejected, 101-321. *(Vote 114, p. H-38)*

➤ An amendment by Lofgren to allow half the bill's funding to be spent on prevention programs, rejected, 191-227. *(Vote 115, p. H-38)*

Much of the House debate focused on whether the measure amounted to undue meddling by Washington in an area some felt was best left to states and localities

Democrats pointed out that most states would have to change their laws to qualify for grants under the bill. McCollum responded that that was the purpose of the legislation. "The fact that we don't have a lot of states that already qualify is no reason to vote against this bill," he said. "In fact it is the essence of why to vote for it."

Senate Committee

After eight sessions spanning almost two months, the Senate Judiciary Committee concluded work on its own juvenile crime bill July 24, approving the broad measure by a 12-6 vote (S 10 — S Rept 105-108).

Senate Democrats argued that in getting tough on violent youths, the bill was overly harsh on kids who were not beyond rehabilitation. Patrick J. Leahy of Vermont, the panel's ranking Democrat, called it, "a sledgehammer for a gnat." But Hatch succeeded in holding off Democratic amendments aimed at softening the core proposals.

Work on the bill was delayed repeatedly for lack of a quorum. Hatch spent several hours over the eight sessions waiting — sometimes alone — for enough colleagues to show up. His pleas for staff members to round up their bosses were a constant refrain.

To end the seemingly interminable markup, several senators from both parties finally agreed to withhold further amendments until the bill reached the floor.

At the committee's opening session June 12, the bill came under attack from several fronts. Joseph R. Biden Jr., D-Del., said it lacked sufficient funding for prevention programs and was overly harsh on those teens who were not beyond rehabilitation.

Arlen Specter, R-Pa., questioned the wisdom of telling states they should try violent youths as adults and Fred Thompson, R-Tenn., said the bill might constitute federal intrusion into criminal justice areas best left to states.

Changes to the Bill in Committee

The markup did not resume until a month later, after Hatch had modified his bill to address some Democratic concerns. For example, he removed a provision that would have allowed juveniles convicted as adults of capital offenses to be subject to the death penalty.

The committee agreed by voice vote July 11 to add language by John Ashcroft, R-Mo., to increase penalties for drug traffickers who distributed drugs to minors or used minors to commit drug-related crimes.

In the final days of the markup, July 23 and 24, the committee further modified the bill, giving voice vote approval to amendments:

➤ By Biden, specifying that the grant money could not be used to build prisons for adults, although it could be used to modify or add to an adult facility to create juvenile wings.

➤ By Biden, to retain some existing restrictions on the housing of juveniles together with adults in federal detention centers. Existing law required that adults and juveniles not be close enough to see or hear each other. The bill's proposal to allow some incidental physical contact during the first 72 hours of incarceration, and visual contact thereafter, would still apply to state facilities.

➤ By Biden, incorporating some of Clinton's proposals for enhanced federal penalties for gun crimes — for example, increased penalties for crimes such as selling or purchasing a gun with an obliterated serial number, and selling a weapon with the knowledge that it would be used in a violent drug-trafficking crime. Members approved the amendment after deleting a section that would have allowed for forfeiture of weapons used in such crimes.

➤ By Charles E. Grassley, R-Iowa, to require that juveniles convicted of sex crimes be tested for sexually transmitted diseases.

Gun Lock Requirement Rejected

After one of the more contentious debates, Republicans on July 15 defeated, 8-9, an attempt to add the gun lock provision to the bill. The amendment, by Herb Kohl, D-Wis., would have required firearm dealers to sell safety locks with each handgun. Democrats argued that it was sensible consumer product safety legislation directed at children, likening it to childproof caps on dangerous medicines.

But Hatch said that forcing dealers to sell one lock with each pistol made no sense. He offered an alternative, adopted 10-7, to require all dealers to have gun locks or other safety devices available for sale, and to allow federal crimefighting funds to be used to train private citizens in gun safety.

Other Amendments Defeated

The committee defeated a number of other Democratic amendments, many of them intended to soften the proposed treatment of juvenile offenders, including proposals to:

➤ Give state courts the right of first refusal in cases involving juveniles charged with less serious violent crimes or less serious drug crimes before a federal court could take the case, if there was a jurisdictional conflict. The amendment, by Leahy, was rejected, 7-9, on July 10.

Jon Kyl, R-Ariz., argued that the amendment was unnecessary because U.S. attorneys generally did not want to take less serious cases involving juveniles, and those cases usually ended up in state court anyway. But Leahy said he wanted to clarify that the bill would not change existing practice. "I want to make it clear that this committee is not expanding [federal prosecutors'] ability to step in and trample the law," Leahy said.

➤ A Leahy proposal, defeated 6-10 on July 10, that would have allowed a juvenile charged as an adult in certain felony cases to petition to be transferred to a juvenile court. Leahy cited a high-profile Wisconsin case in which a 17-year-old was charged as an adult for statutory rape after his 15-year-old girlfriend became pregnant. Hatch argued that the amendment would open the door to more appeals.

➤ A proposal by Biden, defeated 7-8 on July 15, that would have made it more difficult for the federal government to assert jurisdiction in minor crimes committed by juveniles.

➤ An amendment by Richard J. Durbin, D-Ill., to make it more difficult for juveniles to waive their right to counsel in judicial proceedings, stipulating that it could occur only after the juvenile talked with a lawyer and the court made a reasonable effort to contact the juvenile's parents. It was defeated, 6-10, on July 15.

Other amendments rejected during the course of the debate included proposals:

➤ By Specter, defeated 8-9 on July 15, to require that at least 50 percent of the incentive grants be spent on crime prevention programs, particularly those aimed at helping people released from prison. Other Republicans argued that the federal government already had plenty of prevention programs, many of which did not work.

➤ By Biden, rejected 6-12 on July 24, to place new safety requirements on how gun dealers stored their firearms, with a civil penalty of up to $10,000 for failure to comply. Biden argued that the penalties would give authorities greater flexibility in punishing gun dealers.

Floor Action Delayed

By the time the committee approved S 10, Congress was preparing to leave for its August recess. When lawmakers returned in September, the focus was largely on finishing the must-pass appropriations bills. With Senate Democrats threatening to elicit support from moderate Republicans on amendments to increase funding for crime prevention, the juvenile crime bill was put on the back burner. ■

GOP Rethinks Affirmative Action Plan

Republican opponents of affirmative action planned a major offensive during the first session, but they found the issue too controversial to handle, even within their own ranks.

A bill (HR 1909) aimed at banning consideration of race and gender in federal hiring and contracting made it through the House Judiciary Subcommittee on the Constitution in July. But it was tabled in November by the full Judiciary Committee, after four Republicans joined Democrats to oppose it.

The four said the bill could hurt the party's standing with women and minorities. Some cited philosophical objections, while others said the legislation merely needed to be fine-tuned or more effectively promoted to the public.

The only other affirmative action flashpoint during the first session — a controversy over President Clinton's nomination of NAACP lawyer Bill Lann Lee to be assistant attorney general for civil rights — was doused at least temporarily in December. Clinton appointed Lee as acting assistant attorney general, rather than using his powers to make a recess appointment, a step that would have escalated tensions with Republicans. *(Lee appointment, p. 5-9)*

The decision by congressional Republicans to back off on HR 1909, and the rejection in November of a Houston initiative to limit affirmative action, appeared to mark a slowing in the movement's momentum in 1997.

In 1996, California voters had approved a sweeping ballot initiative ending affirmative action in state hiring, contracting and university admissions. That measure, known as Proposition 209, passed a crucial test Nov. 3 when the Supreme Court let stand lower court rulings finding it constitutional. Meanwhile, parties to a major court challenge to affirmative action, *Piscataway Township Board of Education v. Taxman*, settled their case in November, effectively removing it from the Supreme Court's calendar.

Background

Republicans had taken over Congress in 1995 pledging to curtail or eliminate affirmative action programs designed to help minorities and women overcome the disadvantages of past or current discrimination.

They were encouraged by a Supreme Court ruling in June of that year — in the case of *Adarand Constructors v. Peña* — that made federal affirmative action programs subject to the most rigorous level of court review, known as strict scrutiny. Though the court did not strike down any specific programs, it criticized the moral justification for affirmative action, saying that race-conscious programs could amount to unconstitutional reverse discrimination. *(1995 Almanac, pp. 6-24, 6-38)*

Clinton weighed in July 19, 1995, following a months-long review of the issue, by giving a strong endorsement to affirmative action. While some programs might need to be changed or eliminated, he said, his review showed that affirmative action was still needed. "Mend it, but don't end it," he said. That sentiment was echoed by many, though not all, Democrats, while Republicans remained divided over how to proceed.

In the end, opponents of affirmative action were unable to translate the momentum from the court decision into legislation in the 104th Congress. A bill sponsored by Charles T. Canady, R-Fla., got only as far as a House subcommittee, which approved it in March 1996. Nervous about the November elections, Republicans scuttled efforts to move the legislation further. *(1996 Almanac, p. 5-37)*

House Subcommittee

The House bill passed its first milestone in the 105th Congress on July 9 when it gained voice vote approval from the Judiciary Subcommittee on the Constitution.

Sponsored by Canady, who chaired the subcommittee, the legislation sought to bar the federal government from using a series of laws, rulings and executive orders enacted over the previous three decades to redress discrimination against minorities and women.

The vote on HR 1909 came after several hours of tense partisan debate. All of the amendments offered by Democrats were defeated along party lines, as both sides argued at cross-purposes.

Republicans, led by Canady, argued that programs setting preferences for minority hiring and contracting were misguided because they discriminated against non-minorities. They maintained that such programs put individuals at a disadvantage by using them to correct discrimination problems for which they were not responsible.

Democrats argued that preference programs under affirmative action were only a modest attempt to reverse widespread and longstanding discrimination. They spoke in terms of broad categories and percentages, pointing out that white men still got most of the economic opportunities in America.

Typical of the debate was an amendment offered by Virginia Democrat Robert C. Scott, who proposed changing the official name of HR 1909 from the Civil Rights Act of 1997 to the Equal Opportunity Repeal Act of 1997. It was defeated by voice vote.

Canady called his bill an "incremental approach" to ending preferences. He noted that it would apply only to the federal government, so it would not affect one of the biggest battlegrounds over affirmative action: admissions to state-run universities and graduate schools.

Furthermore, Canady said, it would not apply to remedial action ordered by a court or administrative body to address instances of discrimination. Democrats argued that this provision was not clear enough; Scott offered an amendment to shore it up, but it was defeated, 5-7.

Meanwhile, however, a second debate was taking place — among House Republicans. Most of the GOP caucus supported the aims of Canady's bill, at least in principle. But several House leaders expressed concern about the political consequences of opposing affirmative action when the party was trying to attract support among minorities.

Speaker Newt Gingrich, R-Ga., tried to find a way to link new limits on affirmative action with alternatives for promoting minority opportunities. In a June 18 speech, Gingrich outlined a program for aiding the economically disadvantaged, while also endorsing Canady's bill.

House Full Committee

Despite strong backing from conservatives, the bill fell in the face of opposition from GOP moderates when the full Judiciary Committee took it up Nov. 6. The committee tabled (killed) the bill by a vote of 17-9.

The week had started well for affirmative action opponents. On Nov. 3, the Supreme Court let stand a ruling by the 9th U.S. Circuit Court of Appeals upholding California's Proposition 209. The outlook started to change Nov. 4, when voters in Houston rejected an effort to end affirmative action programs. Polls had predicted the opposite outcome.

A Nov. 5 Republican strategy session turned into a virtual shouting match as members debated whether to move forward. Republicans were deeply divided. Some still felt that opposing what they considered to be discriminatory programs constituted the moral high ground. Others were having doubts. "We want to be thoughtful about this process," Henry Bonilla, R-Texas, said later. "We want to make sure our message is right."

At the markup, four Republicans — Elton Gallegly of California, Steve Buyer of Indiana, George W. Gekas of Pennsylvania and Ed Pease of Indiana — crossed over to vote with 13 committee Democrats to kill HR 1909. The upset reflected both a short-term political calculus and a major rethinking of how the party should handle the racially charged issue.

Some Republicans doubted the wisdom of approving such a bill in committee just days before adjournment, allowing opponents to attack them with impunity in the months Congress was not in session. This won over Gallegly, who voted to table a bill he cosponsored. "People are going to demagogue this thing and twist it in ways that are very hard to respond to," Gallegly said.

Others cited deeper reservations. They argued that the GOP was in danger of alienating non-white citizens, which was unwise politically and philosophically. "As the party of Lincoln, we need to stand up against discrimination," said Buyer.

The success of the tabling motion appeared to be part of a wider effort to package conservative social policy issues in a more saleable form. Several Republicans, supporters and opponents of Canady's bill, said the measure needed to be sharpened, narrowed or otherwise modified to keep it from attracting such virulent opposition. Others said it should be paired with an alternative to affirmative action — aid to inner cities, for example — to demonstrate that the party was not anti-minority.

Republican opponents of the Canady bill handed out the affirmative action section of a recent survey by Frank Luntz, one of many GOP pollsters who had been probing the populace on social policy matters.

Luntz concluded that Republicans had to be careful about how they presented their plans to end affirmative action. The issue had to be posed in terms of ending preferences and set-asides and had to be balanced with an understanding that discrimination still existed, Luntz said. "Any discussion . . . must begin with an acknowledgment of the problem *and* include alternatives to affirmative action," he said.

If Republicans were divided on the matter, Democrats and their supporters were not. So many representatives of civil rights organizations showed up at the markup that they blocked most entrances to the room.

Former presidential candidate Jesse Jackson arrived and led the group in a prayer. At other times the gathering looked more like a pep rally. When Judiciary Committee Chairman Henry J. Hyde, R-Ill., announced the outcome and gaveled the meeting to an end, the room filled with cheers.

The crowd may have prevented some members from getting into the room to vote. Several Democrats initially voted "pass" to give colleagues more time to get in. When they were in the room, they voted "aye."

Most Democrats made it through the throngs. Seven Republicans did not show up. A party caucus occurred at the same time, and Canady said some members had not rushed quickly enough. Others may have avoided weighing in on the controversial matter. ■

Clinton Names 'Acting' Civil Rights Chief

President Clinton announced Dec. 15 that he was appointing Bill Lann Lee, a lawyer for the NAACP Legal Defense and Education Fund, as acting assistant attorney general for civil rights. The move came a month after Lee's nomination was effectively blocked by Senate Judiciary Committee Republicans who opposed his views on affirmative action.

The decision to put the word "acting" before Lee's title as the Justice Department's civil rights chief allowed Clinton and Senate Republicans to avoid a confrontation, at least temporarily. The alternative — giving Lee a recess appointment, thereby allowing him to serve through the end of the 105th Congress without Senate confirmation — would have sparked a new battle between Clinton and Congress.

For Lee, the appointment as an "acting" official meant he would have less prestige but more time in office. A recess appointment made during the winter break would have allowed him to serve only until the following fall. There were no tenure limits on an acting appointment.

Lee replaced Deval L. Patrick, who had resigned earlier in the year.

A Difficult Choice for Republicans

In nominating Lee, Clinton found someone who supported his views and presented Republicans with a dilemma. Allowing him to be confirmed threatened to upset party regulars who opposed affirmative action. But challenging Lee — a Chinese-American with a compelling background of overcoming humble origins — worried GOP moderates who feared the party would alienate Asian-Americans, an increasingly important swing vote.

The son of a Chinese immigrant who owned a laundry shop in Harlem, Lee had attended Yale University and Columbia Law School before becoming a civil rights lawyer. His decision to go into civil rights was heavily influenced by the experiences of his father, who was denied housing and employment opportunities even after serving in the U.S. Army in World War II.

Lee opposed California's Proposition 209, which forbade consideration of race in state hiring, contracting and school admissions. That made him a target of conservative groups that hoped to use the nomination as a Senate referendum on the 1996 initiative.

Confirmation Hearing

At Lee's confirmation hearing before the Senate Judiciary Committee on Oct. 22, Republicans alternated between questioning him and apologizing for having to do so. "I like you very much personally, there is no doubt of that," said Chairman Orrin G. Hatch, R-Utah. "But you're going to have to answer some of these questions."

Conservatives portrayed Lee as a liberal ideologue wedded to views of affirmative action that were increasingly being struck down by the courts. Democrats described him as a pragmatist who favored settling cases out of court and making reasonable accommodations to his adversaries.

Lee's testimony was of little help to either side. He declined to give substantive answers to questions about his views on busing and on what he believed his role in the administration would be on Proposition 209. He cited several reasons for deflecting questions: Some issues, he said, might come before him as assistant attorney general; others would be better addressed to people higher in the administration.

Republicans said later they were not comfortable with some of Lee's answers. His testimony, under hostile questioning, was cautious and technical. When Mike DeWine, R-Ohio, asked what he would say to parents concerned about busing, Lee gave a legalistic answer. When asked if his question was answered, DeWine said, "With all due respect, it is not."

Following Lee's testimony, Republicans brought in two minority witnesses — Gerald A. Reynolds, president of the Center for New Black Leadership, a conservative African-American organization, and Susan Au Allen, president of the U.S. Pan Asian Chamber of Commerce. Reynolds said Lee's opposition to Proposition 209 was undemocratic. Allen said Lee was ideologically predisposed to quotas.

Democrats cited support from Republican Mayor Richard Riordan of Los Angeles and brought in two white witnesses to back the nominee — Andrew C. Patterson, an attorney for several companies that Lee had sued for sex or race discrimination, and Barbara Towers, a self-described conservative Republican and California homeowner whom Lee represented in a class-action suit.

Both Patterson and Towers said they had firsthand knowledge that Lee was pragmatic and easy to work with. Patterson said Lee never insisted on quotas, was always willing to negotiate, and, in one case, dropped a suit when the preliminary "discovery" process led to a new understanding of the company's promotion policy.

Nomination Stalls

The Senate Judiciary Committee met twice to consider acting on the nomination, but Democrats — aware that they did not have the support they needed — delayed and ultimately blocked a vote.

In the first meeting Nov. 6, committee Democrats forced Chairman Hatch to delay the vote for at least a week to give them more time to turn up the heat on Republican moderates. Democrats were courting Arlen Specter of Pennsylvania, Spencer Abraham of Michigan and Fred Thompson of Tennessee. Strom Thurmond of South Carolina had written a letter supporting Lee but was firmly in the opposition camp by Nov. 6.

Two days before the committee met, Hatch had announced his own opposition to Lee on the basis of the nominee's support for Proposition 209 and his interpretation of court rulings on affirmative action. "Mr. Lee is prepared to support racial preference programs until every possible exception under the law is unequivocally foreclosed by the Supreme Court," Hatch said in a floor statement.

The administration argued that rejecting Lee would set an unfortunate precedent. "The Constitution's framers simply did not envision a process where the Senate would only confirm nominees who denounced the views of the president who nominates them," said Attorney General Janet Reno.

Democrats Fall Short

By the time the committee met for a second time, Nov. 13, Republicans clearly had the votes to keep the nomination from reaching the floor. Recognizing that they would lose, Democrats kept the panel from taking a formal vote. Such a vote would have been 9-9 to recommend Lee and 9-9 to report him, or send his name to the full Senate. Specter was the only Republican to cross party lines and support Lee.

A nominee needed a majority to be reported, and could be reported even if the recommendation was unfavorable. In the Judiciary Committee, at least one Democrat had to agree to allow a vote to be taken. Unable to formally block a confirmation vote on the floor, the nine Republicans who opposed Lee entered into the record a letter from Majority Leader Trent Lott, R-Miss., saying how they would have voted.

Said Hatch, "Mr. Lee fails to comprehend the now established constitutional principle that racial preference programs are impermissible in all but the most extraordinary circumstances."

The panel's ranking Democrat, Patrick J. Leahy of Vermont, said Republicans should repeal the laws they disliked, rather than expressing their views by blocking Lee. "You have the majority in the House and Senate," Leahy said. "If you really think the laws are wrong, change them. Don't sacrifice this good nominee to the politics of the far right."

Had Lee's nomination gone to the floor, he probably could have attracted enough GOP votes to win confirmation. Democrats said the vote, at worst, would have been a tie — which Vice President Al Gore could have broken. Specter said Lee would have easily prevailed.

Lee had garnered widespread support among Asian-Americans, and local chapters of various Asian-American groups had been turning up the heat on Republican senators. Though much of it was directed at those thought to be least comfortable with the GOP position, even Hatch had been under fire in his home state. The Deseret News, a Salt Lake City newspaper owned by the Mormon church, ran a cartoon of Hatch being carried on the shoulders of hooded Ku Klux Klan members congratulating him for his stance on Lee.

Clinton Acts

With Lee's nomination stuck in the Judiciary Committee, the focus turned to the White House. The decision involved a difficult calculus for Clinton, who was under pressure from liberal groups to go forward with a recess appointment but was also loath to pick a fight with a Senate that could retaliate.

Recess appointments were provided for in Article II Section 2 of the Constitution, a remnant of the days when members of Congress could be out of touch from Washington for months, traveling to and from their states and districts by horseback. While there was no longer much practical need for such appointments, opponents were resigned to them since they were specifically created in the Constitution.

Presidents were generally reluctant to use this appointment power for all but routine nominations, however. Of the 37 people Clinton had appointed so far using this method, none had created an uproar. The highest ranking was Mickey Kantor, who was appointed Commerce secretary after Ronald H. Brown died in a plane crash in 1996.

After Clinton's Dec. 15 announcement that he would make Lee acting assistant attorney general for civil rights, rather than using his recess powers, Republicans grumbled but overall their response was remarkably muted. Hatch said he was pleased that the president had "not directly ignored the advice and consent of the Senate by giving Mr. Lee a recess appointment."

For Clinton, the acting appointment meant not having to wage a fight with the Senate, many of whose members took their confirmation powers very seriously. A recess appointment would have upset Democrats as well as Republicans. Sen. Robert C. Byrd, D-W. Va., publicly warned Clinton not to take that route, and several others did so privately.

Clinton left open the possibility of a future confirmation vote, however. "While he will have the full authority and support to carry out the duties of the assistant attorney for civil rights," Clinton said, "I still look forward to striking the word 'acting' from his title." ■

House Supports Amendment Barring Flag Desecration

By an overwhelming, bipartisan vote, the House on June 12 approved a proposed constitutional amendment (H J Res 54) that would allow Congress to ban physical desecration of the U.S. flag. The strong vote buoyed backers' hopes of winning passage in the Senate, where the real fight was expected to take place, but the Senate did not take up the amendment in the first session.

Supporters argued that the flag amendment was necessary to prevent people from defiling a sacred symbol of American democracy and patriotism. "There still are some standards that ought to be maintained," said House Judiciary Committee Chairman Henry J. Hyde, R-Ill.

Opponents maintained that it was impossible to force people to be patriotic, and that prohibiting desecration of the flag would violate the constitutionally protected right to free speech. "What's more important to me than even the flag is the Constitution of the United States," said Rep. Melvin Watt, D-N.C.

As required by the Constitution, the amendment had to garner a two-thirds majority in each chamber to be sent to the states for ratification. Ratification by three-fourths (38) of the state legislatures was required for the amendment to take effect. H J Res 54 provided seven years for the states to act. The president played no constitutional role in the consideration of a constitutional amendment, but the White House opposed this one.

Background

The 1997 effort marked the third time lawmakers had pushed a resolution to protect the flag since the U.S. Supreme Court struck down state and federal flag desecration statutes in 1989 and 1990. In both cases, the court held that flag desecration was a form of political expression protected under the First Amendment.

The first attempt came in 1990, when the House fell 34 votes short of the required two-thirds majority. In 1995, the House easily passed the resolution, but a companion measure failed in the Senate, 63-36 — three votes shy of the two-thirds mark. *(1989 Almanac, p. 307; 1990 Almanac, p. 524; 1995 Almanac, p. 622)*

The proposal that passed the House in 1995 would have given both Congress and the states the constitutional authority to pass laws banning flag desecration. Some opponents argued that that would create a hodgepodge of different laws in the states. H J Res 54 proposed giving that authority only to Congress, a change that sponsor Gerald B.H. Solomon, R-N.Y., accepted in hopes of picking up additional support.

BOXSCORE

Constitutional Amendment Banning Flag Desecration — H J Res 54. The resolution proposed submitting to the states for ratification a constitutional amendment stating: "The Congress shall have the power to prohibit the physical desecration of the flag of the United States."

Report: H Rept 105-121.

KEY ACTION

June 12 — House agreed to H J Res 54, 310-114.

House Action

The House Judiciary Subcommittee on the Constitution approved H J Res 54 by voice vote May 8, though most, if not all, panel Democrats could be heard voting "no."

At the markup, Hyde argued that those who would burn a U.S. flag deserved no more protection than those who would vandalize a synagogue or tip over tombstones. "I would say it's a hate crime," he said.

The full Judiciary Committee approved the resolution May 14 by a vote of 20-9 (H Rept 105-121). Critics argued that flag desecration was a form of free speech, but Hyde said that banning flag desecration would be an acceptable limit on that freedom.

Some Democrats also argued that the resolution was not specific enough in defining a flag or desecration. "Any criminal statute enacted under this amendment will be inherently . . . unworkable," said Robert C. Scott, D-Va. "Wearing a flag tie will be an offense punishable by jail time."

Zoe Lofgren, D-Calif., offered an amendment to replace the resolution with a requirement that all U.S. flags be made of flameproof material. She then withdrew it, saying she only wanted to point out alternative measures that would be "less intrusive to the constitutional scheme and constitutional rights."

Two Democrats, Steven R. Rothman of New Jersey and Robert Wexler of Florida, supported the resolution, saying it was worth limiting a form of expression to protect the symbol of the nation.

House Gives Strong Support

The House adopted the resolution June 12 by a vote of 310-114 — 27 more than the necessary two-thirds. Republicans backed the measure by an overwhelming majority, 210-13, while Democrats were evenly split — 100 yeas and 100 nays. *(Vote 202, p. H-66)*

Solomon said he and his Senate counterpart, Orrin G. Hatch, R-Utah, would step up efforts to gain support from a handful of senators who could change the outcome in that chamber.

Most Republicans and many Democrats spoke for the measure, saying it would fulfill the public's wish to protect the flag. Some liberal Democrats and a handful of Republicans opposed it on the grounds that it would violate the First Amendment right of free speech.

"Too many brave Americans have marched behind it," Hyde said of the flag. "Too many have come home in a box covered by a flag. Too many parents and widows have clutched that flag to their hearts as the last remembrance of their beloved one, to treat that flag with anything less than reverence and respect."

But David E. Skaggs, D-Colo., said "Respect cannot be mandated," adding that supporters, "in their understandable passion to protect the flag . . . ask us to undermine the Bill of Rights."

The wishes of the nation's veterans factored heavily in the debate. As about 30 members of the American Legion watched from the gallery, Solomon's staff carted out two stacks of signatures on a petition asking Congress to protect the flag. Most of the 3 million signatures came from veterans and religious groups. ■

GOP Relaxes Stance on Immigration

Republicans in 1997 backed away from several of the tough immigration policies they had enacted the previous year.

In August, they agreed to restore certain welfare benefits to legal immigrants who were already in the United States when the 1996 welfare overhaul law (PL 104-193) was enacted — a move made to avert a political backlash in states with large immigrant populations such as California and Florida. The change was included in the spending portion of the budget-reconciliation package (PL 105-33), signed Aug. 5. *(Welfare, p. 6-31; spending-reconciliation, p. 2-47)*

Then, facing a late September deadline, lawmakers were confronted with two problems stemming from the 1996 immigration law (PL 104-208) aimed at clamping down on illegal immigrants. *(1996 Almanac, p. 5-3)*

The first problem was the imminent deportation of some 280,000 refugees from El Salvador, Guatemala and Nicaragua, who had come to the United States in the 1980s when their homelands were caught up in civil wars. Congress included provisions to ease their situation as part of the fiscal 1998 appropriations bill for the District of Columbia (PL 105-100).

The second issue involved a "Catch-22" situation created by the 1996 law for hundreds of thousands of illegal immigrants who were working toward permanent resident visas. Provisions to help them were included in the fiscal 1998 spending bill for the departments of Commerce, Justice and State (PL 105-119).

Central American Refugees

The 1996 immigration law made most of the 280,000 Salvadoran, Guatemalan and Nicaraguan refugees who had come to the United States in the 1980s subject to deportation.

Under prior law, they would have been exempt from deportation if they stayed in the United States for seven years and showed that deportation would cause hardship to a family member legally in the United States, such as a child born here. The 1996 law stopped the clock for most refugees, and required them to have been in the country for 10 years to be exempt from deportation.

Rep. Lamar Smith, R-Texas, an author of the language making the Central Americans deportable, argued that, with the civil wars over and elected governments in power, refugees from these three countries should be required to return home. Refugee status was not meant as an alternative form of legal immigration, Smith and others said.

But the governments of Nicaragua, El Salvador and Guatemala argued strenuously that their fragile economies could not handle a massive repatriation. President Clinton was deluged by their appeals when he toured Mexico and Costa Rica during the spring. In July, he announced he would do as much as he could through executive action.

"We want to make sure the people who sought refuge in our country and who have contributed greatly to their local communities here in the United States are treated with fairness and dignity," Clinton said.

Some elements of the 1996 law could only be altered through legislation, however. For example, the law said that under no circumstances were more than 4,000 people per year to be exempt from deportation proceedings. That made it virtually impossible for a person with a pending application for refugee status to avoid being deported.

Rep. Lincoln Diaz-Balart, R-Fla., and Sen. Connie Mack, R-Fla., introduced legislation (HR 2302, S 1076) to remove that cap and exempt about half the Central American refugees from the new law. Their strategy was to add the provisions to must-pass legislation in the Senate, where they faced less opposition than in the House.

Joined by Sens. Edward M. Kennedy, D-Mass., and Bob Graham, D-Fla., Mack set out to attach an amendment protecting the refugees to the D.C. appropriations bill (S 1156). The three succeeded Oct. 8 by a vote of 99-1. Sen. Robert C. Byrd, D-W.Va., cast the lone "no" vote, to protest the fact that the amendment was unrelated to the underlying spending bill. *(Vote 269, p. S-45)*

However, Sen. Carol Moseley-Braun, D-Ill., held up further action on the bill while she demanded similar protection for more than 10,000 Haitians who had entered the country by the early 1990s.

With the Senate version of the D.C. bill stalled, Republican leaders put together a revised bill that finally cleared Nov. 13, the last day of the session, and was signed into law Nov. 19 (PL 105-100). *(Appropriations, p. 9-27)*

The final bill included the immigration provisions, expanded to affect some other immigrants but without any protection for the Haitians. Members of the Black Caucus continued to object, but the administration assuaged them with an assurance that it would not deport the Haitians until Congress had had a chance to act separately on their fate.

Under the bill, refugees from Nicaragua and Cuba who entered the United States before Dec. 1, 1995, were eligible to apply for permanent residence if they did so prior to April 1, 2000. Additionally, certain refugees from Guatemala, El Salvador, the former Soviet republics and former eastern bloc countries who sought asylum before 1990, could have their cases reviewed under the rules in place before the 1996 immigration law was enacted.

245(i)

The second issue involved the pending expiration of a 1994 provision affecting illegal immigrants who were working toward obtaining legal status. The provision — known as 245(i) after a section of the 1994 State Department spending law (PL 103-317) — allowed them to get permanent resident visas in the United States after paying a $1,000 fine, rather than first returning to their country.

The provision was due to expire Sept. 30, after which time permanent visas would only be issued by U.S. embassies and consulates overseas. That created a dilemma for hundreds of thousands of immigrants. Under the 1996 immigration law, illegal aliens who left the United States after Sept. 27 could not come back for three years. After April 1, they would be barred for 10 years.

The 245(i) issue was fought out on the fiscal 1998 appropriations bill for the departments of Commerce, Justice and State.

Lawmakers who wanted to stay tough on illegal aliens, such as Reps. Smith and Elton Gallegly, R-Calif., led the opposition. In a letter to the House Rules Committee, Smith argued that the statute "rewards those who have jumped the line by entering the U.S. illegally or overstaying a visa . . . Section 245(i) thus rewards illegal behavior, provides an incentive for continued illegal immigration, and compromises the integrity of the immigrant admissions process."

Supporters of the extension argued that forcing so many people to leave the United States — or go underground — would have an adverse effect on immigrant communities and on businesses that relied on immigrants.

Employers were interested because 245(i) had become the most practical way for them to deal with immigration problems. For example, transferring an immigrant employee to a new city could violate the terms of a temporary visa, making the immigrant an illegal alien. In the past, businesses had not worried about their employees going temporarily "out of status" because when they needed a green card they could go through the 245(i) process.

Laura F. Reiff, a partner at the law firm of Baker & McKenzie, said self-interest prompted the corporate world to get behind an extension. "The National Association of Manufacturers and the U.S. Chamber don't do something because immigration lawyers tell them to," she said.

Others noted that the State Department was not prepared to go back to screening permanent visa applications at its overseas missions. "Once 245(i) happened, consulates were shrunk," said Ana Navarra, a Miami immigration lawyer. "They just don't have the people."

Money also played a role. The $1,000 charged to process a visa application from an illegal immigrant in the United States under 245(i), was expected to bring in more than $200 million in 1997.

The Senate version of the Commerce, Justice, State spending bill (S 1022), passed July 29, included a provision to extend the 245(i) program permanently. By contrast, the slow-moving House version (HR 2267) was silent on the issue, a stance that would have allowed 245(i) to expire at the end of fiscal 1997.

The House did not pass the bill until Sept. 30 — the end of the fiscal year and the expiration date for section 245(i). To keep agencies operating until this and other unfinished appropriations bills were completed, lawmakers passed a series of stopgap appropriations bill, which also kept the 245(i) program alive — first until Nov. 7 and then until Nov. 14.

Meanwhile, pro-immigration forces were working with religious groups and major corporations to get the program extended. They won a significant victory Oct. 29, when the House took a non-binding, though highly revealing, vote on the issue. Dana Rohrabacher, R-Calif., moved to instruct conferees on the Commerce, Justice State bill to terminate the 245(i) program. The motion was rejected, 153-268, virtually ensuring that the conference report would include an extension. *(Vote 541, p. H-164)*

Under the compromise ultimately contained in the conference report (H Rept 105-390), most future permanent visas would be issued only in an immigrant's home country. But anyone in the United States who submitted an application by Jan. 14, 1998, would be allowed to get one here.

The language included two exceptions for immigrants seeking permanent status through an employer. They did not need a pending green card application by Jan. 14, just a pending application for Labor Department certification that they possessed a job skill in high demand. Such a certificate was a prerequisite for applying for an employment-based permanent visa.

Also, any skilled immigrant who fell into the status of an illegal alien for less than six months while waiting for paperwork could get a permanent visa in the United States.

The Senate adopted the conference report Nov. 13, and the House cleared it late the same day. The bill was signed into law Nov. 26 (PL 105-119). *(Appropriations, p. 9-11)* ■

House Panel Approves Anti-Cloning Bill

When scientists in Scotland announced in February 1997 that they had successfully used cloning to produce a sheep named Dolly, lawmakers on Capitol Hill vowed to prevent that from ever happening with human beings. But as the House Science Committee approved the first anti-cloning bill July 29, they discovered how difficult their task was.

The bill (HR 922 — H Rept 105-239, Part 1), sponsored by Vernon J. Ehlers, R-Mich., and approved by voice vote, proposed banning federal funding of research on human cloning. Committee Chairman F. James Sensenbrenner Jr., R-Wis., hailed his panel for being the first to stake out a "morally and ethically" responsible position on cloning.

But biotechnology companies vowed to fight the legislation, arguing that it would interfere with legitimate medical research. They said the bill as written would not just affect the creation of human life through cloning; they said it could halt a wide array of scientific research conducted by private companies.

Ehlers' specifically called for a ban on federal funding for "the use of human somatic cell nuclear transfer technology to produce an embryo." The use of the word "embryo" rather than "human being" was what alarmed the biotechnology companies. The word "embryo" reflected lobbying by conservative religious groups, which argued that an embryo, however created, constituted human life.

The biotechnology companies said Ehlers had seized on the publicity surrounding Dolly to impose new restrictions on genetic research. "He is going off in a wholly new direction on this issue," said Charles E. Ludlam, vice president for governmental relations for the Biotechnology Industry Organization, a lobbying group for private companies.

Federal funding of human embryo research already was banned under language in the annual appropriations bill for the departments of Labor and Health and Human Services (HR 2264). Ehlers was trying to make that ban permanent.

During the Science Committee markup, Lynn Rivers, D-Mich., offered an alternative that would have banned funding for the use of cloning technology in the "creation of a human being." It also would have more specifically defined the procedure that could not be federally funded. It was defeated by voice vote.

Ehlers Sees 'Major Battle' Ahead

Ehlers said the proposed funding ban was just a dry run for his second bill, HR 923, which sought to ban human cloning — including certain types of embryonic research — outright. It was that prospect that had biotechnology companies and their congressional allies preparing to take on Ehlers and the conservative religious groups behind him. "Obviously," said Ehlers, "this is going to be a major battle."

Biotechnology companies said Ehlers' bills could impede research into such areas as regeneration of diseased organ tissue and new forms of fertility treatment.

Cloning was generally defined as the reproduction of a cell or entire organism that was genetically identical to an existing organism. The bill approved by the Science Committee would affect the form of cloning in which scientists transferred the nuclei of certain cells into others to create an embryo. It would not affect other forms of cloning, such as the splitting of embryos, which occurred spontaneously in nature in the case of identical twins.

The nuclear transfer technique used to create Dolly, and which could theoretically be used to create a human clone, could also be used for medical purposes — regenerating the skin cells of burn victims, for example. Another possibility was to implant human genes into certain animals to prompt them to produce human proteins and antibodies that could be used to attack diseases.

Proposal Called 'Overly Broad'

At the markup, Republicans Constance A. Morella and Roscoe G. Bartlett, both of Maryland, expressed deep reservations about interfering with research, as did several of their Democratic colleagues. "It is overly broad, overly prescriptive," Morella said of the legislation. "It would inhibit biomedical research that could really improve the quality of life for so many people."

Morella, whose district in the Washington suburbs included the nation's third-largest concentration of biotechnology firms, pointed to the lack of endorsements that HR 922 had garnered. She said there was a national and international consensus that cloning a human being was ethically wrong. Scientists — including Dr. Ian Wilmut, Dolly's creator — said they could foresee no justification for cloning a human. Yet no scientific organization endorsed Ehlers' bill, Morella pointed out.

Ehlers, a physicist, countered that it was the biotechnology companies that wanted to take the government in a new direction. He said the Rivers amendment, which the companies had helped write, would specifically allow research on embryos despite widespread opposition to it. He also said that biotechnology companies could not answer the question of how the bill's language would affect future research.

The version of HR 922 approved by the Science Committee was produced just hours before the panel met. The issue engendered lively discussion, but the markup served little more than to introduce the issue. No roll call vote was requested, and Sensenbrenner made clear that he wanted the panel to approve the bill and to leave much of the debate for the Commerce Committee or the House floor.

Morella said the issue was so new and complex that many Science panel members had not given it much thought.

Ehlers' approach in both HR 922 and HR 923 differed substantially from that advocated by the National Bioethics Advisory Commission. President Clinton ordered that panel to study the ramifications of cloning after Dolly's arrival.

The commission studiously avoided addressing questions of embryonic research, saying that that issue had been dealt with in the Labor-HHS spending bill. In a June report, it endorsed a legislative ban on cloning to create a human being. It also suggested that such legislation should automatically sunset after several years, so it could be revisited in the wake of scientific developments.

The commission concluded: "It is notoriously difficult to draft legislation at any particular moment that can serve to both exploit and govern the rapid and unpredictable advances of science." ■

House Panel Again Considers Prayer Amendment

After nearly two years of negotiations, a House panel took the first step Oct. 28 toward amending the Constitution to expand the right to religious expression in public settings.

The measure (H J Res 78), sponsored by Ernest Istook, R-Okla., was approved in an 8-4 party-line vote by the Judiciary Committee's Subcommittee on the Constitution. Similar legislation had remained bottled up in subcommittee throughout the 104th Congress because supporters could not agree on the wording. *(1995 Almanac, p. 6-28)*

However, full committee action was put off until 1998, and a House floor vote was judged almost certain to fall short of the two-thirds majority needed to send a constitutional amendment to the states. The Senate had no plans to consider the measure.

The proposal, called the "religious liberties" amendment by its sponsors, was an expansion of the school prayer amendments that Congress began considering in 1966. Those measures focused on allowing prayer in the public schools. The 1997 version covered school prayer and other forms of religious expression on public property, such as placing a Nativity scene in front of a town hall. *(School prayer, 1984 Almanac, p. 245)*

The most controversial element was a provision stating that the government could not deny "equal access to a benefit on account of religion." The benefits clause could allow for school voucher programs that provided tuition money for parents to use for private or parochial schooling. The constitutionality of such programs had not yet been resolved by the Supreme Court. Depending on interpretation, the clause might even require government financing of religious schools. Supporters, however, said it would only require government support of religious schools if the government supported private non-religious schools.

The resolution effectively sought to amend the First Amendment, which bans laws that prohibit "the free exercise of religion" while also banning laws that provide for the "establishment of religion." Supporters said it was needed not because the First Amendment's wording on religion was flawed, but because courts had misinterpreted it. They cited a string of rulings as evidence that the Supreme Court had taken the separation of church and state doctrine implicit in the First Amendment to absurd lengths.

Judiciary Committee Chairman Henry J. Hyde, R-Ill., said H J Res 78 was needed because of "judicial amendments to the Constitution" — court rulings that went beyond the intended meaning of the Constitution.

Opponents of the resolution, which would amend the Bill of Rights for the first time, said the Founding Fathers' language was clearer than anything the Judiciary Committee might come up with. If the problem was court interpretation, they added, why assume the courts would do any better with the new language?

At the Oct. 28 markup, lawmakers adopted by voice vote a substitute amendment by Asa Hutchinson, R-Ark., adding language specifying that the government could not establish an "official religion" or "prescribe" any school prayer. The previous version said the government could not "initiate or designate" prayer. Hutchinson's substitute also clarified that states, as well as the federal government, were subject to the amendment.

Melvin Watt, D-N.C., offered an amendment, defeated by voice vote, that would have added a clause deleting all portions of the First Amendment dealing with religion. He said the new language would clash with the old.

An amendment by Robert C. Scott, D-Va., defeated by voice vote, would have required any religious institution that received a government "benefit" to follow civil rights laws. Religious institutions were exempt. ■

Other Legislation Aimed At Crime Prevention

The House Judiciary Committee approved a number of bills in 1997, including measures to limit federal asset seizures, increase minimum sentences for federal crimes involving guns, expand registration requirements for sexual offenders, increase protection for witnesses and give victims more rights in the court room.

Several of the bills passed the House, but only two became law — the victims' rights measure and a bill aimed at protecting volunteers from civil suits.

Efforts to win support for a constitutional amendment protecting religious expression in public places got no further than a House subcommittee.

Asset Seizures

After six years of negotiations with the Justice Department and interest groups, the House Judiciary Committee on June 20 agreed on legislation to make it more difficult for the government to seize assets as part of federal prosecutions. The bill (HR 1965 — H Rept 105-358, Part 1) was approved, 26-1, with dissent from Bob Barr, R-Ga.

The measure, sponsored by Judiciary Committee Chairman Henry J. Hyde, R-Ill., was also referred to the House Ways and Means Committee, which did not act on it in 1997.

The bill went no further in the first session.

Changing the nation's forfeiture laws had been a longtime goal for Hyde, who argued that existing law was contrary to most jurisprudence in that it required people to prove their assets were not used in a crime, rather than requiring the government to prove they were. The Justice Department was equally adamant that revising the law could reduce its prosecutorial abilities.

Hyde's bill proposed to shift the burden of proof from the individual to the government, which would have to produce a preponderance of evidence that the asset was used in connection with a crime. The change would primarily affect civil forfeiture proceedings that were sometimes employed in connection with criminal prosecutions. The main effect would be to make it tougher for the government to seize boats, planes, real estate, currency and other assets used in crimes such as drug smuggling and money laundering.

The bill included several protections for people at risk of having their assets seized, including an automatic "innocent owner" defense for people who took reasonable measures to make sure their property was not used illegally. It provided for counsel for the indigent and would allow the return of assets in cases of economic hardship.

At the same time, the bill contained provisions to enhance the government's ability to seize assets as part of criminal proceedings.

The Justice Department signed off on Hyde's proposal after winning some concessions, such as lowering the required standard of evidence from "clear and convincing" to a "preponderance." It also won some exceptions to what should be returned in hardship cases. Contraband, currency (in many cases), and items well-suited for use in a crime would be exempt from the return provision.

Despite the lopsided committee vote, the bill still faced a number of hurdles. "It is a balance of a lot of delicate positions," Hyde said, cautioning that "any gust of wind could knock it over."

Potential problems included concerns over language mandating payment of legal representation costs for the indigent, placing the burden of proof on the government, and allowing owners to sue the government for non-negligent damage done to their property while it was in the government's possession.

The National Association of Criminal Defense Lawyers objected to several provisions, including the proposed expansion of the government's forfeiture powers in criminal cases.

Drug Czar's Office

The House on Oct. 21 passed a two-year reauthorization of the Office of National Drug Control Policy, the agency responsible for coordinating the federal fight against illegal drugs. The bill (HR 2610), which passed by voice vote, also contained specific goals for reducing drug consumption, standards that Democrats decried as "unrealistic."

Sponsored by Dennis Hastert, R-Ill., the bill included requirements that by the end of 2001: drug usage drop from 6.1 percent of the population to 3 percent; the availability of cocaine, heroin, marijuana and methamphetamines be cut by 80 percent; the street purity levels of these drugs be cut by 60 percent, and drug-related crime be reduced 50 percent.

Republicans maintained that the provisions would hold the office's director, the so-called drug czar, responsible for reducing drug use. "We want to win the fight against drugs, and we have to take extraordinary efforts to get it done," Hastert said.

Democrats and the White House argued that the bill would put unrealistic expectations on the office, apparently to set up the administration for political failure. "Judging by its major provisions, the bill appears designed to achieve political advantage in the 1998 and 2000 election," said Thomas M. Barrett, D-Wis.

The White House issued a statement saying that the targets could not be met in the allotted time, because they did not take into account budget constraints, time needed to train personnel, and the lag time between changes in attitudes about drugs and changes in behavior. The administration also faulted the bill for proposing only a two-year reauthorization rather than the 12-year renewal it was seeking, and it called the measure's reporting requirements overly burdensome.

The bill had begun in the House Government Reform and Oversight Committee, which approved it by voice vote Oct. 7. The panel rejected a number of Democratic amendments, including proposals by Barrett to add tobacco and alcohol to the agency's mandate, rejected 5-22, and to reauthorize the drug agency through 2001, rejected by voice vote.

The Senate Judiciary Committee approved a revised version of the bill Nov. 6, by voice vote and without debate. The two-year reauthorization included requirements that the agency submit to Congress a 10-year strategy for reducing illegal drug use and develop short-term, measurable objectives that could realistically be achieved in two years.

The office of the so-called drug czar had been created in 1988 to coordinate government efforts to stem growing use of illegal drugs. *(1988 Almanac, p. 85)*

Mandatory Minimum Sentences

Renewing a long-simmering debate over mandatory minimum sentences, the House Judiciary Committee approved a bill (HR 424) Sept. 9 calling for tougher sentences for crimes committed with firearms. The measure went no further in the first session.

The main purpose of the legislation was to clarify and expand on a 1988 law (PL 100-649) that created mandatory penalties for using a gun while committing a crime. The bill was a response to a 1995 Supreme Court decision in *Bailey v. United States*, in which the court ruled that overt use, not mere possession, of a weapon was necessary for the mandatory sentencing requirement to take effect. *(1988 Almanac, p. 82)*

HR 424, sponsored by Sue Myrick, R-N.C., specified that the criminal merely had to possess the weapon. It also proposed a graduated series of penalties for possessing, brandishing or discharging a firearm in a federal crime involving violence or drug trafficking.

Under existing law, the sentence for a first offense was five years in addition to whatever sentence was imposed for the crime itself.

HR 424 proposed replacing that with mandatory minimum sentences of: 10 years for a first offense involving possession of a gun while committing the crime; 15 years for brandishing the firearm; 20 years for discharging the weapon; and 30 years if the gun was equipped with a silencer. The penalties would increase for a second offense. In all cases, they would be added to the sentence for the underlying crime.

The bill also barred probationary sentences or concurrent sentences for people convicted under its provisions.

Myrick's measure began in the House Judiciary Committee's Crime Subcommittee, which approved it by voice vote July 16. The full Judiciary Committee approved the bill, 17-8, on Sept. 9, after Democrats made several attempts to gut the legislation (H Rept 105-344). Crime Subcommittee Chairman Bill McCollum, R-Fla., said the bill aimed to send the message that Congress was serious about gun crimes. "If you use a gun in the commission of a crime, you will get the book thrown at you," he said.

Democrats charged that Congress should not be in the business of micromanaging criminal justice procedures. Bill Delahunt, D-Mass., said the types of mandated sentences in HR 424 would encroach on the mission of the U.S. Sentencing Commission, which was created to take politics out of sentencing. "We are legislatively beating ourselves on the chest," Delahunt said. "It just doesn't make sense."

Democrats Melvin Watt of North Carolina, Sheila Jackson-Lee of Texas, Robert C. Scott of West Virginia and ranking member John Conyers Jr. of Michigan offered amendments to reduce the number of years in each sentence or completely remove all of the sentencing language. Conyers argued that no hearings had been held on the issue, and the Democrats said there was no evidence that the increased sentences would be useful.

All of the amendments were rejected.

Sex Offenders

The House passed a bill (HR 1683) Sept. 23 aimed at strengthening state registration programs for convicted sex offenders and closing several loopholes in existing law. The Senate did not act on the measure in the first session.

Under the bill, sex offenders convicted in military and federal courts would be required to register under existing state programs. In an effort to track offenders who crossed state borders, the bill would require them to register in the state where they lived and any state where they were employed or enrolled as a student.

"Some child sex offenders are slipping through the cracks," said the bill's sponsor, Bill McCollum, R-Fla. "It is well-recognized that sexual predators are remarkably clever and persistently transient. These offenders are not confined within state lines, and neither should be our efforts to keep track of them."

Legislation requiring states to set up registries of sex offenders was first enacted as part of the 1994 omnibus crime law (PL 103-322). *(1994 Almanac, p. 273)*

The 1994 law required states to register the names, addresses and other pertinent information on anyone being released from prison who had kidnapped or sexually molested a child, or who had committed sexually violent crimes. Local law enforcement officials were authorized to release information to the public if it was considered necessary for public safety.

The states were given until September 1997 to establish a registration system using guidelines drawn up by the Justice Department. Those that did not would lose 10 percent of their federal crime-fighting funds available under the so-called Byrne grant program.

Two laws enacted in 1996 expanded the sexual offender registration provisions. *(1996 Almanac, p. 5-45)*

The first, known as Megan's Law, required state and local law enforcement agencies to make public "relevant information" about the release and whereabouts of sexual offenders who were required to register under the 1994 law. It mandated that local communities be notified when sex offenders moved into their neighborhoods. The law (PL 104-145) was named after 7-year-old Megan Kanka of Hamilton, N.J., who was raped and murdered in 1994 by a twice-convicted sex offender who lived across the street from her home.

The second 1996 law (PL 104-236) required the FBI to keep a national database of sexual offenders registered on state lists to enable law enforcement officers to track them across state lines. Sex offenders were required to verify their addresses regularly by returning cards with fingerprints to the FBI.

By May 1996, all 50 states and the District of Columbia had some sort of registration system in place, and at least 40 had some form of notification program to inform residents when sex offenders moved into their neighborhoods. By 1997, however, most states still had not complied with all the technicalities of the law.

McCollum's bill proposed to give states two additional years to comply, and to allow states more flexibility to implement what the report accompanying the bill described as "ideas that may not have come from Congress but may be equally effective or even more effective in keeping track of sex offenders."

Legislative Action

The bill began in the Judiciary Subcommittee on Crime, chaired by McCollum, which approved the measure by voice vote June 12. The full Judiciary Committee followed suit Sept. 9, also by voice vote (H Rept 105-256).

While the bill was relatively non-controversial, Charles E. Schumer of New York and other Democrats raised a potential problem with the registries. Schumer said five states that had anti-sodomy laws — Arizona, Mississippi, Kansas, Louisiana and South Carolina — had indicated that they would put consenting adults convicted of sodomy on state sex offender registries.

Schumer proposed cutting federal Byrne grants by 10 percent to any state that put such consenting adults in the registries, but the committee defeated the amendment, 12-19, in a party-line vote.

Schumer argued that any state that published names of people who engaged in consensual sex acts was perverting the purpose of the legislation. McCollum countered that nothing in the original legislation authorized the names of non-violent sex offenders to be placed in the registries. He also said the federal government should not pass judgment on state laws.

The House passed the bill under suspension of the rules Sept. 23 by a vote of 415-2. *(Vote 420, p. H-128)*

Victims' Rights

Expanding the rights of crime victims and their families, President Clinton signed legislation March 19 (HR 924 — PL 105-6) that allowed certain relatives of the victims of the 1995 Oklahoma City bombing to attend the trial of the accused bombers in Denver.

The bill, sponsored by Bill McCollum, R-Fla., prevented federal judges from barring people from their courtrooms who planned to testify during the penalty phase of the trial. Under previous law, witnesses could be barred from hearing courtroom testimony if the judge believed their testimony could be tainted by observing the proceedings.

Under the new law, judges could still bar anyone subpoenaed to testify in the guilt-or-innocence phase of the trial.

Although the bill did not specifically cite any case, it was passed in response to a 1996 ruling by U.S. District Judge Richard Matsch, the presiding judge in the bombing case. Matsch ruled that victims who planned to make statements at sentencing could not attend other trial proceedings because seeing the defendants in court could influence their testimony.

Critics of the bill said it represented an interference by Congress in the judicial process and could even have an impact on the trial. Supporters maintained it was only a minor clarification of laws affecting victims' rights.

The bill was considered with unusual alacrity in anticipation of the trial beginning March 31. It began in the House Judiciary Subcommittee on Crime, which approved it by voice vote March 6.

The full Judiciary Committee approved the measure March 12 (H Rept 105-28), after amending it to clarify that victims could testify at a sentencing hearing even if they attended the trial. The committee rejected amendments by Democratic opponents that would have exempted cases then pending in court and cases in which the death penalty might be invoked.

The House passed the bill March 18, by a vote of 418-9, and the Senate cleared it by voice vote the following day. *(Vote 52, p. H-18)*

War Crimes

The House on July 29 passed a bill (HR 1348) aimed at expanding the government's authority to try and prosecute war criminals. The Senate did not act on the measure in the first session.

HR 1348, sponsored by Walter B. Jones Jr., R-N.C., sought to broaden the definition of the crimes covered by a 1996 law (PL 104-192). That statute allowed federal prosecution of war crimes committed by or against U.S. military personnel or nationals. Punishments included the death penalty if the victim was killed. War crimes were defined as grave breaches of the 1949 Geneva Conventions for the Protection of Victims of War. Enactment of the 1996 law fulfilled obligations assumed by the United States when the Senate ratified the Geneva Conventions in 1955. *(1996 Almanac, p. 5-46)*

The new bill proposed extending the law to cover violations of other conventions signed by the United States, including the 1907 Hague Convention. The crimes included torture and murder of civilians and prisoners of war, use of weapons that caused unnecessary suffering, bombing of undefended towns, unnecessary bombardment of hospitals or religious buildings, and the pillaging of towns.

The bill also proposed to cover some crimes involving booby traps or land mines that could be prosecuted should the Senate ratify pending international treaties to ban them. *(Land mines, p. 8-26)*

Jones, who also sponsored the 1996 law, said the legislation would "rectify the existing discrepancies between our nation's intolerance of war crimes and our inability to prosecute war criminals."

The bill was approved July 15 by the House Judiciary Subcommittee on Immigration and Claims, by voice vote and without amendment. The full House Judiciary Committee approved it without amendment on a 17-4 vote July 23 (H Rept 105-204). The House passed the bill, 391-32, under suspension of the rules July 29. The only objections came from members opposed to the death penalty. *(Vote 340, p. H-104)*

Witness Protection

The House Judiciary Committee voted 20-4 on July 23 to report a bill (HR 2181 — H Rept 105-258) aimed at curtailing the intimidation of witnesses, particularly in gang-related cases. The measure got no further in the first session.

Under the bill, it would be a federal offense to cross state lines or international borders with the intent to influence the testimony of a witness in a state criminal proceeding by bribery, force or a threat. The offense would also include using such means to get someone to destroy, alter or conceal evidence of a crime.

Violators could be subject to fines and up to 10 years in prison — 20 years in prison for harming a witness. The death penalty could be invoked if the witness was killed.

The bill also called for stiffer penalties for obstruction of justice involving victims, witnesses or informants, and it contained provisions aimed at increasing cooperation among state and local witness protection programs.

Supporters said prosecutors needed new weapons to secure witnesses in gang- and drug-related cases. Bill McCollum, R-Fla., chairman of the panel's Subcommittee on Crime, said that prosecutors in many areas of the country were hamstrung when key witnesses refused to testify in such cases for fear of retaliation from defendants.

While the bill's intent had universal support in the committee, a group of Democrats argued that the provisions went too far. Democrat Jerrold Nadler of New York tried to eliminate the death penalty provision, but his amendment was rejected 7-17. Some Democrats said they would not support the bill if the death penalty provision remained.

Volunteer Protection

Volunteers gained new legal protections under a bill signed into law June 18 (S 543 — PL 105-19). The bill shielded volunteers from personal civil liability for harm caused while they were acting on behalf of a nonprofit organization, as long as they were not guilty of negligence, or willful, malicious or criminal conduct. Even in cases where they could be held liable, they would be partially protected.

Volunteers could only be forced to pay non-economic penalties — for such things as causing mental anguish or pain and suffering — in proportion to their level of responsibility. This was aimed at preventing litigants from seeking out the wealthiest person with some level of liability — a nonprofit organization board member, for instance — and forcing that person to pay the entire penalty. The practice could still be used to impose economic penalties such as for hospital costs or lost work.

Supporters said the measure would protect volunteers from "frivolous lawsuits" that could discourage them from volunteering.

Legislative Action

The first action on the bill came on the Senate floor, where the measure passed May 1, 99-1. Fred Thompson, R-Tenn., cast the lone dissenting vote, saying the issue was better addressed at the state level. *(Vote 55, p. S-12)*

Democrats had temporarily delayed the floor action to protest the fact that the bill had not gone through the usual committee process — as well as to show their unhappiness over a separate GOP delay in taking up the nomination of Alexis Herman to be Labor secretary. *(Herman, p. 7-10)*

Republicans tried twice and failed to cut off debate and proceed to the bill. The first attempt — which was also the year's first cloture showdown — failed April 29 by a vote of 53-46, seven votes short of the 60 votes required to cut off debate. The second attempt failed April 30, 55-44. *(Votes 52, 53, p. S-12)*

After the second cloture vote, Herman was confirmed and Democrats allowed the volunteer liability bill to come to the floor. Before the final vote, however, Democrats objected that the bill, as written, could provide unintended protections to hate groups such as the Ku Klux Klan and to volunteers who abused children.

Senators approved by voice vote an amendment to ensure that the bill's protections would not be extended to members of hate groups.

Another amendment approved by voice vote allowed states to opt out of the federal law if they determined that their own laws protecting volunteers from frivolous lawsuits were adequate. The original bill would have pre-empted state law.

Less than two weeks after the Senate vote, a similar bill began moving in the House.

The House Judiciary Committee approved the measure (HR 911 — H Rept 105-101, Part 1) on May 13 by a vote of 20-7. The panel first adopted by voice vote a substitute amendment by Bob Inglis, R-S.C., aimed at bringing the House bill more in line with the Senate-passed version. Under Inglis' amendment, the federal statute generally would supplant state laws, though it would not supersede those state laws that provided more protection for volunteers than the federal legislation. Also under Inglis' substitute, states could pass legislation to opt out of the bill's requirements.

The original House bill would have increased block grants for social services if states without laws shielding volunteers from liability adopted such statutes. Inglis' substitute did not. An amendment by John Conyers Jr., D-Mich., to restore the incentives was rejected, 5-21.

The House passed HR 911 on May 21 by a vote of 390-35, then passed S 543 by voice vote, amended to reflect the House version. Later that day, the Senate accepted the House version by voice vote, clearing it for the president. *(Vote 150, p. H-50)* ■

Federal Judicial Circuits To Be Examined

Congress cleared legislation creating a five-member commission to study the nation's 12 federal judicial circuits, with special attention to the massive 9th Circuit. The panel members were to be appointed by the chief justice of the United States. The plan was enacted as part of the fiscal 1998 spending bill for the departments of Commerce, Justice, State and the federal judicary (HR 2267 — PL 105-119), signed into law Nov. 26.

The House had initially passed a separate bill (HR 908) providing for a 10-member commission, while the Senate attached language to its version of the Commerce, Justice, State bill (S 1022) that called for splitting the 9th Circuit.

The commission was a fallback position for Mountain State lawmakers eager to break up the 9th Circuit, which sprawled over California, eight other states and two Pacific territories. "It's an empire," said Rep. Don Young, R-Alaska. "It covers a land mass the size of Western Europe."

The issue went beyond practical considerations, however. At bottom, it was a fight over the direction of the federal judiciary in Western states. The loudest calls for splitting the 9th came from mountain state Republicans. They argued that the circuit was dominated by liberal judges based in San Francisco, who did not understand the needs of their more rural, resource-rich economies.

But Democrats, particularly those allied with environmental interests, were leery of creating a new circuit dominated by Republican-leaning states. Splitting up the circuit also ran into fierce opposition from California and nearby states such as Nevada and Arizona, which worried about dividing regions that were economically linked. Maritime interests argued that having all Western ports in one circuit made sense. And legal scholars pointed out that another circuit would mean more cases in which the Supreme Court would have to resolve differing opinions.

Background

The 9th Circuit, based in San Francisco and roughly twice the size of other circuits, was made up of California, Oregon, Washington, Montana, Idaho, Nevada, Arizona, Alaska, Hawaii, Guam and the Northern Mariana Islands. It had 28 appellate judgeships, about twice the number of the other regional circuits.

Separating California from the more conservative states in the 9th was a longtime goal of many Republicans, who wanted to create a new circuit among the Western mountain states.

The Senate had taken up a bill in 1996 that would have left California, Hawaii and the territories in the 9th, while creating a new 12th Circuit for the remaining states. But before passing the legislation, the chamber agreed instead to set up a commission to study the circuits. The House never acted on the measure. *(1996 Almanac, p. 5-46)*

Democrats said that, though the idea of splitting the circuit had been on the table for more than two decades, its practical consequences had not been thought through. "Do we need new judges?" asked Sen. Harry Reid, D-Nev. "Do we need new courthouses? It seems very clear to me that with what we are doing now, we will need both."

Other Democrats argued that if Congress was going to go to the trouble of reconfiguring the 9th Circuit, it ought to examine all 12 circuits to see whether and how they should be altered. The federal judiciary was full of imbalances, they said, in terms both of the population of the circuits and the number of judges assigned to each.

Legislative Action

The House bill (HR 908) began in the Judiciary Subcommittee on Courts and Intellectual Property, which approved it March 5. The full Judiciary Committee followed suit March 12 (H Rept 105-26). Both were voice votes. The House passed the measure June 3, also by voice vote, under suspension of the rules.

The bill called for the creation of a 10-member commission, to be appointed by the president, congressional leaders and the Supreme Court. The commission was to have 18 months to propose changes to any of the 11 regional circuits or the District of Columbia circuit. The House and Senate Judiciary committees would be required to take action 60 days after receiving the panel's report.

Commerce, Justice, State Bill

The Senate Appropriations Committee waded into the controversial issue of what to do about the 9th judicial circuit July 15, voting to split the mammoth circuit as part of the Commerce, Justice, State spending bill (S 1022). The amendment, offered by Judd Gregg, R-N.H., was approved by voice vote.

Putting the language on a must-pass appropriations bill was an attempt to get around the Senate Judiciary Committee, which had not taken any action on the proposal.

Shortly before the vote on the Gregg amendment, the committee rejected, 13-15, an alternative proposed by Reid that would have commissioned a study of the issue without any immediate action to divide circuits.

Gregg's amendment called for separating California and the Pacific territories from six other states: Oregon, Washington, Montana, Idaho, Arizona and Alaska. Nevada and Hawaii would have their choice of circuits.

An earlier version of the amendment, abandoned shortly before the vote, called for a three-way split, with California being cut in half. Southern California would have been linked with Arizona; Northern California with Nevada, Hawaii and the territories. The other states would have been lumped together in a third circuit.

The proposal to split California was based on the belief that Arizona had more economic ties to Southern California, and Nevada more to Northern California, than the two California regions had with each other. That plan was scratched because of vociferous objections from the California delegation.

Final Action

Backed by pressure from the 52-member California delegation, House conferees prevailed during negotiations over what to do with the 9th Circuit. The result was a modified version of the House plan to create a commission to study the matter. *(Appropriations p. 9-11)* ■

House Panel Votes To Limit Federal Judges' Powers

Legislation to limit the power of federal judges won a narrow vote of approval in a House Judiciary subcommittee, but did not advance further before Congress adjourned for the year. The Judiciary Committee's Courts and Intellectual Property Subcommittee approved the bill (HR 1252) on June 10 by a vote of 8-7.

The measure, introduced by committee Chairman Henry J. Hyde, R-Ill, was aimed at reining in federal judges who issued what Republicans said were unpopular and expansive rulings, in what they called "judicial activism." Republicans were particularly angry over recent rulings striking down two ballot initiatives in California — one disbanding affirmative action programs and the other cutting public services to immigrants — and one in Colorado limiting the application of civil rights laws to homosexuals.

As approved by the subcommittee, HR 1252 also included provisions to limit court-ordered tax increases, stipulate that only a three-judge panel (not a single judge) could overturn a law resulting from a public referendum, and give attorneys the right to reject the first judge assigned to their case.

Democrats saw GOP complaints about activism as an assault on the independence of the judicial branch and a pretext for opposing President Clinton's judicial nominees. Much of that debate took place in the Senate, which had the power to confirm or reject judicial nominees. There, Republicans and Democrats were locked in a bitter dispute over how quickly the Senate Judiciary Committee should consider Clinton's nominees. *(Judicial nominees, this page)*

Hyde's bill allowed House Republicans to get into the debate. It also provided an alternative to the approach espoused by Majority Whip Tom DeLay, R-Texas, who called for widespread impeachment of unpopular judges.

The subcommittee markup began on an acrimonious note when Howard Coble, R-N.C., showed up with a Hyde substitute that added language separating judicial pay from that of members of Congress. U.S. District Court judges earned the same annual salary as members of Congress: $133,600. The highest paid member of the judiciary, Chief Justice William H. Rehnquist, made $171,500, which was also the salary of Vice President Al Gore and House Speaker Newt Gingrich, R-Ga.

Hyde proposed giving federal judges automatic cost of living increases. Under existing law, judges, like senior members of the executive branch, received raises only when Congress approved a pay increase for itself, and lawmakers had refused to accept an increase since 1993. Congress subsequently cleared a raise for itself in fiscal 1998. *(Pay raise, p. 1-30)*

Hyde said that if judicial pay were held hostage by Congress, good lawyers would turn down the chance to sit on the federal bench. F. James Sensenbrenner Jr., R-Wis., countered that the provision would violate the equality of the three branches of government. He tried to strike the judicial pay provision, but was defeated, 1-8. Several Republicans, including Coble, were sympathetic but apparently unwilling to take on Hyde.

In other action, Bill Delahunt, D-Mass., won voice vote approval for an amendment addressing what was arguably the most far-reaching element in the bill — the proposed limit on tax increases. As originally written, the bill would have banned any court ruling that "required" a tax increase. Delahunt's amendment changed "requires" to "expressly directs."

Under the original bill, a judge would have been barred from making any ruling that would force a government to raise taxes. Under the new language, the judge could impose a stiff penalty on a government, but could not order it to raise taxes to meet the costs.

The subcommittee rejected this change of wording, 5-7, when it was part of an amendment that also sought to strike several pages of text aimed at limiting tax increases. A slightly different version of the amendment then was approved by voice vote.

Several other Democratic amendments did not fare as well. One by Howard L. Berman, D-Calif., to strike the language requiring challenges of referendums to go to a three-judge panel, was defeated 6-9. A Delahunt amendment to limit who could bring suit challenging a tax increase was defeated, 6-8. ■

Senate Under Fire for Slow Pace On Judicial Nominations

Under pressure from conservatives inside Congress and out, the number of judicial nominees confirmed by the Senate slowed to a trickle in 1997.

The Senate confirmed 36 federal district and appellate judges in the first session. Though that was an increase from the 20 confirmed in 1996, it was not enough to keep up with attrition. Thanks to a flurry of confirmations at the end of the session, the number of vacancies fell from over 100 in the late summer to 82 at year's end. But the final count, which constituted about one-tenth of the federal bench, was still high enough to prompt stern words from an unusual source: the nation's top judge.

Conservative Chief Justice William H. Rehnquist used his annual report on the state of the judiciary, released Jan. 1, 1998, to deliver some tough criticism of Congress. He warned that the high level of vacancies could not continue without "eroding the quality of justice" on the federal bench.

In his report, Rehnquist noted that the number of cases in federal courts continued to climb in 1997, due partly to

Waxman Confirmed

The Senate easily confirmed Seth P. Waxman, President Clinton's nominee for solicitor general, by voice vote Nov. 7.

Waxman, who received generous praise from Republicans and Democrats alike, became the nation's top litigator, in charge of arguing the government's position before the Supreme Court and deciding which lower court rulings to appeal.

Waxman had been acting solicitor general since Sept. 1 and previously was deputy solicitor general. Before coming to the government he had worked for the Washington law firm of Miller, Cassidy, Larroca & Lewin.

Waxman's confirmation hearing before the Senate Judiciary Committee Nov. 5 came as NAACP lawyer Bill Lann Lee, Clinton's nominee for assistant attorney general for civil rights, was facing increasing Republican opposition for his support for affirmative action programs. *(Lee appointment, p. 5-9)*

Waxman secured the support of Republicans by promising to defend any future laws that banned affirmative action programs as long as he could make a "reasonable" argument in support of the law. "I don't think anybody can deny that there are reasonable arguments on both sides," he said, adding that a decision not to defend a law "should be very, very rare."

laws passed by Congress expanding their jurisdiction, while at the same time nearly one in 10 federal judgeships remained vacant.

While suggesting that the White House could have acted more quickly to nominate judges, Rehnquist emphasized the Senate's sluggish pace. "The Senate is surely under no obligation to confirm any particular nominee, but after the necessary time for inquiry it should vote him up or down. In the latter case, the president can then send up another nominee," he said.

With numerous vacancies, some circuits were relying on semi-retired senior judges and judges brought in from other parts of the country. Hardest hit was the 9th U.S. Circuit Court of Appeals, which consisted of California, eight other states and two Pacific territories. It was missing 10 of its 28 judges, which had made its chief judge, Proctor Hug Jr., an outspoken critic of the Senate.

Much of the slowdown in confirming judges was the result of pressure from a handful of conservative groups — most notably the Free Congress Research and Educational Foundation, a think tank and fundraising organization that made a crusade out of keeping Clinton from staffing the federal bench. The group contended that those who had already been confirmed were "judicial activists," meaning they were deemed to "legislate from the bench," taking a broad rather than a restrictive view of the Constitution and federal law.

The issue resonated among conservative voters incensed by rulings striking down ballot initiatives or imposing church-state separation. A decision by an Alabama federal judge prohibiting the display of the Ten Commandments in public places, for example, created a stir among religious conservatives. By shedding light on existing rulings, the critics were able to drum up opposition to Clinton nominees and exert pressure on Senate Judiciary Committee Chairman Orrin G. Hatch, R-Utah.

Pressure came from within Congress as well. Republicans in both chambers complained that Clinton's nominees wrote opinions that were only loosely based on constitutional principles.

Worried that Hatch would go easy on Clinton's nominees, conservatives in April nearly stripped the chairman of much of his power over the confirmation process. On April 29, the 55-member Senate Republican Caucus came within a few votes of accepting two proposals that would have given individual senators greater power to block the nominations.

The first, by Phil Gramm of Texas, would have made nominees to the 11 regional Circuit Courts of Appeals subject to a veto by a majority of the senators from the affected circuit. The second proposal, offered by Slade Gorton of Washington, would have given Republicans greater power to quietly block a nomination before the president made it formal. In lieu of the two proposals, the caucus approved language saying the Senate should reject judicial nominees with "activist" philosophies.

Democrats maintained that there was nothing particularly activist about Clinton's nominees and charged that Republicans hoped to slow the process until they could retake the White House and the power to nominate judges. "It's something I've never seen in 22 years," Patrick J. Leahy of Vermont, the ranking Democrat on the Judiciary Committee, said during the Spring. "It seems to me the Republican majority can't get over the fact that not only was Bill Clinton elected for a first term, he was re-elected by a comfortable margin."

Clinton, however, was not particularly helpful to Democrats on the Hill. Through most of the year, he was slow to nominate judges and rarely expended political capital on their behalf. Of the 82 openings at the end of the year, only 42 had pending nominees, and many of those came in the summer and fall.

The conflicting pressures left Hatch with a delicate balancing act. In response to Rehnquist's criticisms, he defended the Senate and asserted that the White House bore much of the blame. "The Senate cannot confirm judges that the president does not nominate," he said in a statement Jan. 2, 1998.

But in an interview, Hatch made it clear he was taking Rehnquist's criticisms to heart, saying the Senate could "do a better job." Still, he acknowledged the limits he felt in the face of conservative pressures. "I can't be much more assertive than I've been," he said. ■

1997 Supreme Court Decisions

Key Supreme Court rulings in 1997 showed a growing willingness by the high court to rein in the powers of Congress, particularly when those powers came at the expense of the states. Indeed, when combined with several decisions in recent years, they represented the most significant effort by the court to limit congressional powers since the New Deal era.

Two major cases allowed the court to pursue its re-examination of the proper federal role in 1997. The first concerned the constitutionality of the 1993 Brady Act (PL 103-159) — particularly its requirement that local police conduct background checks on prospective gun owners.

The second was a challenge to the 1993 Religious Freedom Restoration Act (PL 103-141), which limited state and local governments' ability to restrict religious liberties by saying they could do so only if they had a "compelling interest" — a high legal standard to meet.

In both cases, the court ruled that Congress had ventured into areas where it had no right to be. The effect of these and earlier rulings was to reinterpret and narrow the scope of certain parts of the Constitution — specifically the 10th and 14th Amendments — that had long been viewed as giving Congress broad powers.

The reasons for the courts' interest in re-evaluating Congress' legislative authority were a subject of conflicting interpretations.

Conservatives hoped it was the sign of a restrained court ready to undo years of activist rulings that had expanded federal power. Some liberals, on the other hand, saw it as a new form of conservative activism: a court dominated by Republican appointees, reinterpreting the Constitution to undo the work of Congress.

In either case, the rulings meant future Congresses would have to be much more careful in drafting legislation. In many cases, bills would have to be more closely tied to interstate commerce. Mandates on states would have to be cast as voluntary and perhaps linked to federal funding. Legislation creating new rights would need to be limited to redressing specific wrongs.

"There are enough cases now where I think Congress ought to think of it as a wake-up call," A.E. Dick Howard, a law professor at the University of Virginia, said even before the Brady and religious freedom rulings came down. "Surely all this adds up to changing the way Congress does its business. Routine congressional drafting becomes freighted with constitutional consideration."

Orrin G. Hatch, R-Utah, chairman of the Senate Judiciary Committee, said he was "very happy with these decisions" because they indicate that "we have a Congress that operates under limited and enumerated powers."

Civil rights organizations, on the other hand, expressed concern, especially at the attention being paid by the court to the 14th Amendment. The 1965 Voting Rights Act and the fair employment title of the 1964 Civil Rights Act, among other statutes, relied on a fairly broad interpretation of Congress' discretionary powers under the 14th Amendment.

The following is a summary of the Brady and religious freedom cases, along with a number of other cases of special interest to members of Congress:

Brady Gun Control Law

A deeply divided U.S. Supreme Court struck down a major portion of the 1993 Brady gun control law on June 27.

The 5-4 ruling in the combined cases of *Mack v. United States* and *Printz v. United States* struck down a portion of the law that required local law enforcement officials to conduct background checks on prospective handgun purchasers. The court concluded that Congress had no authority to require such checks.

"The federal government may neither issue directives requiring the states to address particular problems, nor command the states' officers, or those of their political subdivision, to administer or enforce a federal regulatory program," Justice Antonin Scalia said in the majority opinion. *(Excerpts, p. 5-23)*

The ruling left intact the law's five-day waiting period for gun purchases, which was supposed to sunset in November 1998, when a national database for instant background checks was to become available for use by gun dealers.

Brady Act supporters minimized the ruling's practical effects. "I'm heartened that the rest of the law, especially the waiting period, survived intact," said Sen. Edward M. Kennedy, D-Mass.

The National Rifle Association, a longtime opponent of the Brady Act, hailed the decision.

Building on Earlier Cases

The decision came on the heels of two earlier rulings — in *Lopez v. United States* and *New York v. United States* — that had prompted lawmakers and constitutional scholars to pay close attention to the court's direction.

In the 1995 *Lopez* case, the court struck down a federal ban on the possession of firearms near schools that had been enacted as part of the 1990 crime bill (PL 101-647). The statute was thrown out on the grounds that the Constitution did not give Congress the power to enact such legislation. The court rejected the government's argument that the statute was enacted as part of Congress' authority to regulate interstate commerce.

The *Lopez* decisions followed and drew on the court's 1992 ruling in *New York v. United States*. In that case, the court threw out part of a 1985 federal statute dealing with low-level nuclear waste generated by nuclear power facilities. Under certain circumstances, the statute had required states to take possession of, and be held liable for, nuclear waste. The court said the federal government was unconstitutionally commandeering the states to carry out federal policy.

The majority opinion on the Brady Act was based heavily on the *New York* case, as well as a reading of the Constitution, the Federalist Papers, and historical precedent. "Now we have a set of rulings showing the court wants to limit Congress to its enumerated powers," said Cass Sunstein, law professor at the University of Chicago. "The court hasn't been in that business since the early New Deal."

Challenging Brady

The Brady law (PL 103-159) was named after President Reagan's press secretary James S. Brady, who was injured by a handgun in the 1981 assassination attempt on the president. It imposed a five-day waiting period for gun purchases and required that, during that time, local police make "reasonable efforts" to verify that the prospective purchaser did not have a criminal background and was not an illegal immigrant, mentally incompetent, or otherwise disqualified from owning a gun. *(1993 Almanac, p. 300)*

Two sheriffs, Richard Mack of Graham County, Ariz., and Jay Printz of Ravalli County, Mont., brought suit against the background check, calling it burdensome. District courts in both states agreed, finding that Congress had exceeded its authority under the 10th Amendment, which limited Congress to those powers specifically enumerated in the Constitution.

These decisions, however, were reversed on appeal by the 9th Circuit.

Lawyers for Mack and Printz argued that the federal government was essentially forcing them to use limited resources to carry out a federal mandate.

The Justice Department argued that the background check was not comparable to the *New York* mandate because it did not require states to make laws. It said the background check was a routine, ministerial requirement of the type that had been upheld previously. The government argued that throwing out background checks could also call into question routine state-federal cooperation on such matters as sharing crime statistics.

The Supreme Court, however, rejected the Brady background check, saying Congress had exceeded its authority and was essentially commandeering or "dragooning" local law enforcement officers.

"We held in *New York* that Congress cannot compel the States to enact or enforce a federal regulatory program," Scalia wrote in the majority opinion, which was joined by Chief Justice William H. Rehnquist and Justices Sandra Day O'Connor, Anthony M. Kennedy and Clarence Thomas. "Today we hold that Congress cannot circumvent that prohibition by conscripting the State's officers directly."

In his dissent, Justice John Paul Stevens argued that the ruling amounted to a sweeping denial of the sovereignty of the national legislature. In the future, he said, Congress might have trouble drawing on local support during emergencies such as wars, natural disasters or epidemics.

Stevens questioned the wisdom of basing the ruling on the *New York* case, which was handed down by many of the same justices ruling in Brady. He also said the analysis of the Constitution and historical precedent was deeply flawed.

"Historical materials strongly suggest the founders intended to enhance the capacity of the federal government by empowering it — as a part of the new authority to make demands directly on individual citizens — to act through local officials," Stevens wrote, adding that the reasoning in the case would "undermine most of our post-New Deal Commerce Clause jurisprudence."

Reacting to the court decision, President Clinton ordered top law enforcement officials to remind local police agencies that they could still make background checks voluntarily.

One irony was that the ruling could slow the purchase of handguns. Under the law, prospective buyers did not have to wait the entire five days once they had been cleared in a background check. If no one conducted the check, they would have to wait the five days.

Court's Inclination Not Anticipated

When Congress first debated the Brady Act, most of the discussion centered on the Second Amendment, not the 10th. Gun law opponents, following up on the 1992 *New York* ruling in the nuclear waste case, raised some questions about federal power. But these were secondary to their arguments that the proposed Brady law violated the constitutional right to bear arms.

In hindsight, Brady law proponents might have skirted the question of federal power by making the background check voluntary — while tying a significant amount of federal funding to local cooperation.

But they did not believe the mandate would run into problems. They saw the background check as similar to other minor administrative duties imposed on the states, such as providing statistics on crime and traffic fatalities.

"I guess it is hard to believe the court would strike down the Brady mandate without adopting a rule against any requirements from federal officials," said Dennis Henigan, legal counsel at Handgun Control Inc., the organization that Brady founded.

"This court is clearly more protective of state interests," Henigan added. "They seem to be out to strike a different balance between state power and federal power. A decision striking down the mandatory background check would have been inconceivable, even in the Burger court," he said, referring to Chief Justice Warren E. Burger.

The 10th Amendment

Despite the seemingly apparent meaning of the 10th Amendment, the court and Congress had struggled with it for much of U.S. history. The Amendment stated simply that: "The powers not delegated to the United States by the Constitution, nor prohibited by it to the States, are reserved to the States respectively, and to the people."

In the early days of the republic, the government's powers seemed fairly straightforward: It could coin money, declare war, administer patents, borrow money, establish a postal service, and do other things specifically mentioned in the Constitution, including regulating commerce "among the several states."

But since then, the amendment's meaning had been significantly eroded, particularly after the Civil War. The 13th, 14th and 15th amendments adopted in the war's wake aimed to shift power to Washington in a way seemingly at odds with the 10th Amendment.

Also helping erode the 10th Amendment was the ever-growing interpretation of what constituted interstate commerce. Until well into the 20th century, the court took a fairly limited approach to interstate commerce. President Franklin D. Roosevelt became so frustrated with the Supreme Court for failing to see the interstate commerce dimensions of his New Deal laws that he launched an unsuccessful and highly controversial "court-packing" campaign to allow him six new appointments.

In the late 1930s, however, the court reversed course. Perhaps the most notable example was the 1942 ruling in *Wickard v. Filburn*. The court upheld a federal law regulating the seemingly non-commercial act of raising crops for home consumption. The reasoning was that such crops affected overall supply and demand, which in turn affected interstate commerce.

With rulings like that, the 10th Amendment soon came to be seen as little more than a minor obstacle for federal lawmakers. For Supreme Court justices, it became increasingly difficult to reconcile with a growing body of case law.

In a 1985 case, *Garcia v. San Antonio Metropolitan Transit Authority*, Justice Harry Blackmun indicated he could no longer find a meaningful 10th Amendment doctrine. He went on to reason that lawmakers — particularly senators — rather than judges, were in the best position to protect states from an overreaching federal government.

Except for a brief resurgence of interest in the 10th Amendment in the mid-1970s, the court's major rulings since the New Deal had effectively expanded federal powers. That remained true up until *Lopez* and *New York*.

Handgun Decision Excerpts

Excerpts from the Supreme Court's decision on the Brady Handgun Violence Prevention Act (PL 103-159) in the cases of Printz v. United States *and* Mack v. United States.

From the majority opinion, written by Justice Antonin Scalia:

"The Constitution ... contemplates that a State's government will represent and remain accountable to its own citizens. ... This separation of the two spheres is one of the Constitution's structural protections of liberty.

"We held in [a previous case] that Congress cannot compel the States to enact or enforce a federal regulatory program. Today we hold that Congress cannot circumvent that prohibition by conscripting the State's officers directly.

"The Federal Government may neither issue directives requiring the States to address particular problems, nor command the States' officers, or those of their political subdivisions, to administer or enforce a federal regulatory program. It matters not whether policymaking is involved, and no case-by-case weighing of the burdens or benefits is necessary; such commands are fundamentally incompatible with our constitutional system of dual sovereignty."

From the concurring opinion written by Justice Sandra Day O'Connor:

"The Court appropriately refrains from deciding whether other purely ministerial reporting requirements imposed by Congress on state and local authorities pursuant to its Commerce Clause powers are similarly invalid. . . . The provisions invalidated here, however, which directly compel state officials to administer a federal regulatory program, utterly fail to adhere to the design and structure of our constitutional scheme."

From the dissenting opinion, written by Justice John Paul Stevens: "

When Congress exercises the powers delegated to it by the Constitution, it may impose affirmative obligations on executive and judicial officers of state and local governments as well as ordinary citizens.

"The provision of the Brady Act that crosses the Court's newly defined constitutional threshold is more comparable to a statute requiring local police officers to report the identity of missing children to the Crime Control Center of the Department of Justice than to an offensive federal command to a sovereign state.

"If Congress believes that such a statute will benefit the people of the Nation, and serve the interests of cooperative federalism better than an enlarged federal bureaucracy, we should respect both its policy judgment and its appraisal of its constitutional power."

Religious Freedom

In a sweeping decision June 25, the Supreme Court overturned a 1993 religious freedom law and significantly narrowed Congress' discretion under its 14th Amendment duty to implement equal protection laws.

In a 6-3 decision in *City of Boerne v. Flores*, the court ruled that the Religious Freedom Restoration Act (PL 103-141) exceeded Congress' authority because it did not aim to remedy a specific act of religious discrimination. The religious freedom law prohibited a government from infringing on religious practices unless it had a "compelling interest" in the matter, such as protecting public health or safety.

"The court, led by Justice Anthony M. Kennedy, said Congress had interfered with states' rights and had infringed on the court's power to interpret the Constitution's religious protections.

"The power to interpret the Constitution in a case or controversy remains in the judiciary," Kennedy wrote in the majority opinion, which was joined by Chief Justice William H. Rehnquist and Justices Antonin Scalia, Clarence Thomas, John Paul Stevens and Ruth Bader Ginsburg.

The case had been brought before the court by a small town in Texas named Boerne. The town had blocked the tiny St. Peter's Catholic Church from expanding, saying the church resided in a historic district and could not change the building. The church filed suit, arguing that the local statute creating the district violated its First Amendment right to free exercise of religion, and also violated the Religious Freedom Restoration Act because the city had no "compelling interest" in restricting church activities. The court's ruling left the church unable to expand.

The decision was a blow to those who had supported the religious freedom law in response to a court they believed was too willing to undermine religious freedom. "The decision shows the court's blindness to a pervasive trend in society, which does not just discriminate against, but is expunging, religion," said Orrin G. Hatch, R-Utah, chairman of the Senate Judiciary Committee.

The 1993 religious freedom law had, itself, been enacted in response to a 1990 Supreme Court ruling in Employment Division v. Smith, which held that there was no religious exemption from laws that applied equally to everyone, as long as the law did not single out a particular religion for discrimination.

Prior to *Smith*, the government could infringe on religious liberties only if it had a "compelling interest" to do so. The *Smith* case determined that a government did not have to meet such a standard. Before *Smith*, for example, a county government could not ban wine at communion as part of a ban on alcohol unless it could show a specific problem associated with communion. After *Smith*, the county only had to say the ban on wine at communion was incidental to its larger interest in preventing drunkenness.

The Smith ruling did not sit well with a broad coalition of conservatives, moderates and liberals, including the Christian Coalition and the ACLU, which banded together to push a new statute. The Religious Freedom Restoration Act essentially aimed to reinstate the "compelling interest" standard.

Authors of the new law used as justification the 14th Amendment, citing Congress' power to enforce provisions that protected equal rights and prohibited discrimination. *(1993 Almanac, p. 315)*

But in *Boerne*, the court said that any law based on the 14th Amendment had to aim to remedy a specific instance of discrimination. "Any suggestion that Congress has substantive, non-remedial power under the 14th Amendment is not supported by our case law," Kennedy wrote.

The court then found that the religious protections under the statute were not remedial, but amounted to an expanded interpretation of the First Amendment's guarantee of "free exercise of religion." Kennedy noted: "Congress does not enforce a constitutional right by changing what it is."

New Focus on the 14th Amendment

The re-examination of Congress' powers under the 14th Amendment in *Boerne* marked a departure for the court. Previous court rulings on matters of state and federal power had been based largely on the 10th Amendment, which assigned to the states those powers not specifically given to the federal government by the Constitution.

Arguably the most significant amendment since the Bill of Rights, the 14th Amendment conferred citizenship on all people born or naturalized in the United States, regardless of race; required states to provide equal protection under the law to all people; and barred states from denying life, liberty, or property without due process.

Adopted after the Civil War, the 14th Amendment restructured the relationship between the federal government and the states. Previously, few powers resided in Washington. The 14th Amendment imposed direct restrictions on states, empowered Congress to adopt further restrictions, and — through a series of court rulings known as the incorporation doctrine — applied much of the rest of the Bill of Rights to the states.

The amendment's fifth and final section said: "Congress shall have the power to enforce, by appropriate legislation, the provisions of this article."

Through the incorporation doctrine, the court determined that Congress' Section 5 enforcement powers allowed it to pass laws protecting other constitutional rights as well.

For years the court had struggled to determine how broad the Section 5 power was. The ruling in *Boerne* appeared to be a substantial limitation, though it left much to interpretation. "While the line between measures that remedy or prevent unconstitutional actions and measures that make a substantive change in the governing law is not easy to discern. . . . the distinction exists and must be observed," Kennedy wrote.

Not everyone opposed the ruling's limits on Congress. A coalition of states filed a friend-of-the-court brief against the religion statute. And many conservative legal scholars believed Congress had gotten away with too much under Section 5. "I think the decision is a much-needed corrective," said University of Virginia law professor A.E. Dick Howard. "It's very important to remind Congress that its powers under Section 5 are not infinitely elastic."

On a practical level, the ruling put some social conservatives in Congress in the uncomfortable position of having to choose between their interest in limiting federal power and their interest in supporting religious values. Most previous rulings limiting congressional power had affected laws pushed by liberals, such as those to restrict guns or prevent violence against women.

Alaska's Open Primary

Open primary laws won a quiet but potentially important round May 12 when the U.S. Supreme Court declined to review a decision by the Alaska Supreme Court upholding the state's open primary system.

The court's refusal to review the decision was issued without comment, giving no clue as to why the justices did not feel it necessary to hear the case — or how they might deal with another case pending on the subject.

Open primaries allowed voters who were not registered in a party to vote in that party's primary to select nominees for state or federal office. Open primaries were traditional in states that did not register voters by party, and they were catching on elsewhere.

Alaska's open primary was a state tradition until 1990, when the Alaska GOP changed its rules to bar Democrats from voting in Republican primaries (independents were still allowed). That change was disallowed in March 1996 by a ruling of the Alaska Supreme Court, which said the GOP could not be in conflict with state law.

Alaska Republicans appealed that ruling to the U.S. Supreme Court, citing their freedom of association and characterizing the selection of nominees as an act of political expression. The state responded that the issue had been resolved at the highest level of the state's judiciary system and that the Constitution allowed individual states jurisdiction over their own elections.

The Supreme Court apparently saw nothing to object to in the Alaska court's decision.

Cable TV

In a victory for broadcasters over the cable television industry, the Supreme Court on March 31 upheld a law requiring cable operators to carry local broadcast stations on their systems. In a 5-4 decision, the Supreme Court affirmed the "must-carry" provision of a 1992 law (PL 102-385) designed to control cable TV rate increases until competition increased in the industry. *(1992 Almanac, p. 171)*

The law was challenged by the Turner Broadcasting System, other cable companies and the National Cable Television Association. Plaintiffs argued that the must-carry provision violated their constitutional right to free speech by forcing them to give preference to broadcast stations over some cable programmers.

But in writing for the court, Justice Anthony M. Kennedy said, "Congress has an independent interest in preserving a multiplicity of broadcasters to ensure that all households have access to information and entertainment on an equal footing with those who subscribe to cable."

Edward O. Fritts, president of the National Association of Broadcasters, praised the decision as important to helping preserve free over-the-airwaves television, a notion echoed by Rep. Edward J. Markey, D-Mass., a chief sponsor of the 1992 law. "With this decision, local television stations have been given the cable carriage assurance they need to ensure that the U.S. system of universal broadcasting will remain the envy of the world," Fritts said in a statement.

Cable operators expressed disappointment but said the decision would not have much effect on programming because cable systems already carried most broadcast stations.

The law, which went into effect after Congress overrode a veto by President George Bush, required cable operators to set aside up to one-third of their channel capacity to carry local broadcast stations. The provision was aimed at helping smaller UHF broadcast stations and other TV programmers who were in danger of being dropped by cable companies.

The court ruled that, in writing the law, Congress "could reasonably conclude from the substantial body of evidence before it that attaining cable carriage would be of increasing importance to ensuring broadcasters' economic viability, and that, absent legislative action, the free local off-air broadcast system was endangered."

The court went on to say that despite arguments by cable operators to the contrary, the must-carry provision had not had a significant effect on cable operators, noting that only 5.5 percent of cable systems nationwide had had to drop programming because of it.

Endangered Species Act

The Supreme Court ruled unanimously March 19 that property owners and other citizens could sue the federal government for actions taken under the Endangered Species Act, even if they were seeking less, not more, protection for species.

The decision, in *Bennett v. Spears*, overturned a ruling by the 9th U.S. Circuit Court of Appeals, which had jurisdiction over nine Western states.

The appeals court had determined that individuals could sue for actions taken under the Endangered Species Act only in behalf of species protection. The Supreme Court decided that landowners could also sue on grounds that they had suffered economic harm because of government actions to protect certain plants and animals.

The plaintiffs — ranchers and irrigation districts in Oregon — contended that the government had gone too far by reducing water flows in an attempt to protect an endangered fish species.

The Supreme Court's ruling was a defeat for the Clinton administration, which had sought a "one-way" interpretation that would have allowed only species protection as grounds to sue under the law.

Internet 'Indecency'

In a far-reaching defense of First Amendment rights, the Supreme Court on June 26 struck down provisions of the 1996 telecommunications law (PL 104-104) aimed at barring "indecent" communications on the Internet and other online communications.

The provisions, labeled the Communications Decency Act and under legal injunction since shortly after they were enacted, would have banned the dissemination to minors of material that was "indecent" or "patently offensive."

The court ruled 7-2 in *Reno v. ACLU* that the statute committed a fundamental violation of free speech rights. The court ruled that the law, aimed at protecting children, was so broad that it would also impose limits on adult conversation. The court said the law was so vague that it would chill speech of people uncertain of whether they could be prosecuted.

Contrary to the government's assertion, the court said parents had narrower alternatives, such as special software programs, to screen out objectionable material.

"It is true that we have repeatedly recognized the government interest in protecting children from harmful materials," said Justice John Paul Stevens in his majority ruling. "But that interest does not justify an unnecessarily broad suppression of speech addressed to adults."

Stevens' opinion was hailed by a coalition of groups that had tried to stop the provisions from becoming law and had subsequently fought them in the courts. "The Supreme Court has written the Bill of Rights for the 21st Century," said Jerry Berman, executive director of the Center for Democracy and Technology, a First Amendment rights group.

While President Clinton strongly favored the decency provisions and his Justice Department argued in favor of them, it was the bill's authors who took most umbrage at the ruling and vowed to introduce new legislation. "It is telling families to fend for themselves in an Internet of raw indecency," said Sen. Daniel R. Coats, R-Ind.

The ruling was a complete repudiation of the law, striking down its bans on both indecent and patently offensive materials as applied to all forms of "cybercommunications."

Some legal experts had predicted that the court might uphold the bans when applied to person-to-person communications, such as electronic mail, where it could be easier to know if a minor was involved. Much harder to monitor were public forums such as "chat rooms," "bulletin boards," and pages on the portion of the Internet known as the World Wide Web that transmitted graphic materials.

But only the dissenters, Justice Sandra Day O'Connor and Chief Justice William H. Rehnquist, raised this issue. They would have upheld the statute as it applied to direct communication between an adult and one or more minors.

The ruling effectively established that online communications had the same free speech protections as print media such as newspapers and magazines — as opposed to the more restricted rights of broadcasters. The courts had upheld greater content restrictions on radio and television, on the grounds that they were more pervasive and that they reached their audiences through the publicly owned airwaves.

Had it prevailed in its entirety, the decency law could have posed a dilemma for some print publications. Though their right to publish indecent material on paper was constitutionally protected, online distribution of the same material would have exposed them to criminal sanctions of as much as $250,000 and two years in prison.

The Communications Decency Act originated in the Senate, where it was added to that chamber's version of the telecommunications law overhaul in 1995. The House took the approach of fostering screening technologies when it passed its version of the bill later that year. *(1995 Almanac, p. 4-3)*

House conferees initially offered a compromise plan that took the Senate approach but used the standard of "obscenity" rather than "indecency." Obscenity was a much higher threshold: The material had to appeal to people's prurient interest in sex and be completely without redeeming values.

Then, as congressional negotiators closed in on a deal, the House conferees agreed, though barely, to go one step further and change the prohibition from obscenity to indecency.

The Supreme Court ruling was not unexpected. A three-judge federal panel in Philadelphia that heard the case in 1996 had ruled that the statute was unconstitutional. *(1996 Almanac, p. 3-46)*

Line-Item Veto

In its first decision on the controversial 1996 Line-Item Veto Act (PL 104-130), the Supreme Court left the law in place but made no decision on the underlying separation of powers issue.

The court on June 26 announced a 7-2 decision that reversed a lower court and dismissed a lawsuit brought by six members of Congress who argued that the Line-Item Veto Act unconstitutionally transferred too much lawmaking power to the president. *(Line-item veto, p. 2-63)*

The court's majority decision, written by Chief Justice William H. Rehnquist, did not address the constitutional merits of the law, leaving the door open to further suits. The case, *Byrd v. Raines*, was dismissed because the court found that the members of Congress who brought it lacked legal standing to sue. They had not suffered any injury under the law, since at that point the veto had yet to be used.

Line-Item Veto Excerpts

Excerpts from the Supreme Court's decision on the Line-Item Veto Act (PL 104-130) in the case of Byrd v. Raines.

From the majority opinion, written by Chief Justice William H. Rehnquist:

"The District Court for the District of Columbia declared the Line Item Veto Act unconstitutional. On this direct appeal, we hold that appellees lack standing to bring this suit, and therefore direct that the judgment of the District Court be vacated and the complaint dismissed. . . .

"We have consistently stressed that a plaintiff's complaint must establish that he has a 'personal stake' in the alleged dispute, and that the alleged injury suffered is particularized as to him. . . . We have also stressed that the alleged injury must be legally and judicially cognizable. This requires, among other things, that the plaintiff have suffered 'an invasion of a legally protected interest which is . . . concrete and particularized,' and that the dispute is 'traditionally thought to be capable of resolution through the judicial process.' . . .

"In the light of this overriding and time honored concern about keeping the Judiciary's power within its proper constitutional sphere, we must put aside the natural urge to proceed directly to the merits of this important dispute and to 'settle' it for the sake of convenience and efficiency. Instead, we must carefully inquire as to whether appellees have met their burden of establishing that their claimed injury is personal, particularized, concrete, and otherwise judicially cognizable. . . .

"They have not alleged that they voted for a specific bill, that there were sufficient votes to pass the bill, and that the bill was nonetheless deemed defeated. In the vote on the Line Item Veto Act, their votes were given full effect. They simply lost that vote. Nor can they allege that the Act will nullify their votes in the future. . . . In the future, a majority of Senators and Congressmen can pass or reject appropriations bills; the Act has no effect on this process.

"In addition, a majority of Senators and Congressmen can vote to repeal the Act, or to exempt a given appropriations bill (or a given provision in an appropriations bill) from the Act; again, the Act has no effect on this process. . . .

"In sum, appellees have alleged no injury to themselves as individuals, the institutional injury they allege is wholly abstract and widely dispersed, and their attempt to litigate this dispute at this time and in this form is contrary to historical experience.

"We attach some importance to the fact that appellees have not been authorized to represent their respective Houses of Congress in this action, and indeed both Houses actively oppose their suit. . . . We also note that our conclusion neither deprives Members of Congress of an adequate remedy (since they may repeal the Act or exempt appropriations bills from its reach), nor forecloses the Act from constitutional challenge (by someone who suffers judicially cognizable injury as a result of the Act). Whether the case would be different if any of these circumstances were different we need not now decide.

From the dissenting opinion of Justice John Paul Stevens:

"The Line Item Veto Act purports to establish a procedure for the creation of laws that are truncated versions of bills that have been passed by the Congress and presented to the President for signature. If the procedure were valid, it would deny every Senator and every Representative any opportunity to vote for or against the truncated measure that survives the exercise of the President's cancellation authority.

"Because the opportunity to cast such votes is a right guaranteed by the text of the Constitution, I think it clear that the persons who are deprived of that right by the Act have standing to challenge its constitutionality.

"Moreover, because the impairment of that constitutional right has an immediate impact on their official powers, in my judgment they need not wait until after the President has exercised his cancellation authority to bring suit.

"Finally, the same reason that the respondents have standing provides a sufficient basis for concluding that the statute is unconstitutional."

The court had always held that a plaintiff had standing if his case involved a "case or controversy" in which there was a concrete personal injury. The plaintiffs, led by Sen. Robert C. Byrd, D-W.Va., argued that the mere existence of the law eroded their power as legislators, in part because the threat of a veto might be used to affect their votes and actions.

The court was not convinced. "Appellees' claim of standing is based on a loss of political power," Rehnquist wrote, adding that the plaintiffs in the case "have alleged no injury to themselves as individuals, the institutional injury they allege is wholly abstract and widely dispersed, and their attempt to litigate this dispute at this time and in this form is contrary to historical experience."

Justices John Paul Stevens and Stephen G. Breyer dissented from Rehnquist's opinion. Stevens said he would have found the law unconstitutional; Breyer said the plaintiffs had standing, but he did not express any views on the constitutional merits. *(Excerpts, this page)*

President Clinton supported the line-item veto, as had presidents dating back to Ulysses S. Grant. "I intend to use it whenever appropriate, and I look forward to using it wisely," he said in a statement. "With it, the president will be able to prevent Congress from enacting special-interest provisions under the cloak of a 500- or 1,000-page bill."

The 1996 act was not a true line-item veto. A true line-item veto would have permitted the president, unless overridden by a two-thirds vote in both House and Senate, to strike individual provisions of a bill while letting the rest of the measure become law. But such an explicit veto required amending the Constitution, a virtually impossible job.

Instead, congressional budget hawks had devised an "enhanced rescissions" procedure that permitted the president to "cancel" specific dollar items in appropriations bills, new entitlement spending or certain narrowly targeted tax breaks. Such cancellations were to take effect unless Congress passed a bill to reverse them; the president could then veto the disapproval measure. *(1996 Almanac, p. 2-28)*

The Supreme Court's decision came as a bitter pill to Byrd

and his colleagues, who had won a resounding victory in April from U.S. District Court Judge Thomas P. Jackson. Jackson accepted the lawmakers' argument that the law was unconstitutional because it changed the procedure laid out in the Constitution for making law.

When Congress sent the president a bill for his signature, the president was required to sign it, veto it or let it become law without his signature. The new "enhanced rescissions" power would, according to Judge Jackson, permit "the president to repeal duly enacted provisions of federal law."

"Losing on a technicality just delays the time when the court must decide this fundamental issue," said Sen. Carl Levin, D-Mich., one of the plaintiffs.

In addition to Byrd and Levin, the plaintiffs included Sen. Daniel Patrick Moynihan, D-N.Y.; former Sen. Mark O. Hatfield, R-Ore. (1967-97); and Reps. Henry A. Waxman, D-Calif. and David E. Skaggs, D-Colo.

Minority Districts

• **Virginia.** Confirming its position on race-based redistricting, the Supreme Court on June 27 upheld a lower court decision that had nullified Virginia's 3rd District.

The Richmond-based 3rd threaded its way for 225 miles through the Tidewater area and bordered on four other districts. Its population was 62 percent black. In 1992, Democratic Rep. Robert C. Scott was elected from the 3rd as the first African-American to represent Virginia in Congress since Reconstruction.

Two Republican activists filed a lawsuit in November 1995, claiming that the district was unconstitutional under the equal protection clause of the 14th Amendment. On Feb. 7, 1997 a federal three-judge panel in Richmond agreed, and that was the ruling that the Supreme Court let stand.

The state's attorney general appealed, in part to seek further guidance for the legislature in its task of redrawing the map. "We were told it was bad but we weren't really told how to make it better," said deputy state attorney general Claude Allen.

Defenders of the existing map, in use since 1992, had argued that the Voting Rights Act of 1965 not only permitted but encouraged the consideration of race in redistricting. Nearly one Virginian in five was black, but aside from Scott the state's 11-member House delegation was entirely white.

But since 1993, the Supreme Court had ruled against districts in several states that were deliberately drawn so that one racial minority group would constitute a majority. The court said the use of race as the "predominant factor" in drawing district lines was unconstitutional. *(*Shaw v. Reno, *1993 Almanac, p. 325;* Miller v. Johnson, *1995 Almanac, p. 6-39)*

• **Georgia**. In another 5-4 decision affirming its views on race-based redistricting, the Supreme Court on June 19 upheld the map of districts drawn for Georgia's 1996 congressional elections by a three-judge panel in that state.

The decision left Georgia's 11 districts unchanged until after the 2000 census, barring a highly unlikely intervention by the Legislature. The three judges had drawn the map in 1995 after the Legislature failed to do so.

The map used in 1994 and 1992 had been declared an unconstitutional racial gerrymander by the Supreme Court. The earlier map had three black-majority districts; the current map had just one. *(1995 Almanac, p. 12-3; 1996 Almanac, p. 11-37)*

In writing for the majority, Justice Anthony M. Kennedy said it would not have been possible to draw a map creating more black seats without using race as the predominant factor. He also noted that black incumbents in the two formerly black-majority districts still won re-election in 1996.

Term Limits

The Supreme Court struck another blow to the term limits movement Feb. 24 when it let stand an Arkansas court ruling against a law designed to pressure members of Congress to support such limits. *(Term limits, p. 1-28)*

The decision, in *Arkansas Term Limits v. Donovan*, was a one-sentence statement that the court would not take up the case. That left term limits supporters with few clear options other than to hope the court would agree to hear one of the other pending state cases.

Voters passed the Arkansas law in November 1996 as part of a ballot initiative. It would have required members of the state's congressional delegation to support only one term limits measure: a six-year limit on service in the House and 12 years in the Senate.

The penalty for not doing so would have been a note — a so-called scarlet letter — alongside the lawmaker's name the next time it appeared on the ballot. The note would have read: "Disregarded voter instructions on term limits."

Term limits supporters fell back on the scarlet letter law when the court, in its 1995 ruling in *U.S. Term Limits v. Thornton*, rejected a more direct approach — one that would have denied candidates a place on the ballot once they had served more than six years in the House or 12 in the Senate. *(1995 Almanac, p. 6-37)*

The Arkansas court ruled that the latest initiative was a coercive attempt to get around Article 5 of the Constitution stating that amendments were to originate in Congress or constitutional conventions, not in ballot initiatives.

Besides Arkansas, eight other states had passed scarlet letter laws. Lawsuits were pending in five of them: Maine, Idaho, Colorado, Nebraska and Missouri.

The Supreme Court did not say why it let the Arkansas ruling stand. Opponents of term limits interpreted the action as a rejection of the scarlet letter law. Supporters hoped it merely meant the court was not ready to examine the issue.

Other Closely Watched Cases

In its closing days the week of June 23, the Supreme Court handed down rulings in several other cases closely watched by some members of Congress.

• **Assisted suicide.** In the cases *Vacco v. Quill* and *Washington v. Glucksberg*, the court ruled that states could bar assisted suicide and that individuals did not have a constitutional right to end their lives.

Congress raised its objections to assisted suicide when, on April 16, the Senate cleared legislation (HR 1003 – PL 105-12) banning federal funding of such procedures. Had the court ruled otherwise, lawmakers might have initiated measures to limit assisted suicides. *(Assisted suicide, p. 6-29)*

• **Donor disclosure rules.** The Supreme Court on Jan. 6 refused to hear an appeal from the Republican Party regarding disclosure requirements for individuals who donated more than $200 to a political campaign. The GOP had objected to a Federal Election Commission rule requiring that political committees exert their "best efforts" to identify campaign contributors by occupation, employer and address.

The rule required committees to seek the donor information at least once after the gift in a communication dedicated solely to that purpose. The party argued that this constituted a restraint on its free speech — as well as a costly and onerous burden.

● **Parochial education**. In *Agostini v. Felton* the court allowed public funding of remedial education inside parochial schools. Under existing law, parochial school students were entitled to federally funded remedial education if they qualified. But a 1985 court ruling said that such education could not take place inside parochial schools. As a result, much of it took place in vans parked outside the schools.

Some conservative lawmakers viewed the opinion as a prelude to a ruling in favor of school voucher programs, which allowed parents to directly use taxpayer funding for religious schools. ■

CQ

Chapter 6

HEALTH & HUMAN SERVICES

HEALTH

Big Medicare, Medicaid Changes Enacted in Budget Bills

Package also includes new $20 billion program to expand health care coverage for low-income children

Congress made sweeping changes to two federal health entitlement programs in 1997 and created a new initiative to broaden health care coverage for uninsured children. The legislation was the centerpiece of a massive budget-reconciliation package that President Clinton signed into law Aug. 5 (HR 2015 — PL 105-33).

The bill trimmed Medicare spending by $112 billion over five years, reduced Medicaid spending by $7 billion and created a $20 billion state grant program to provide health insurance to approximately 3.4 million children, about 2 million of them previously uninsured.

- **Medicare.** The Medicare changes were the most sweeping ever made to the 32-year-old program, which provided health care to more than 38 million elderly or disabled Americans. In hopes of reducing federal spending, lawmakers included more managed care alternatives, such as provider sponsored organizations and preferred provider organizations. The alternatives were offered in addition to the health maintenance organizations (HMOs) already available to Medicare beneficiaries.

The legislation also established a pilot program for medical savings accounts, which allowed seniors to use tax-exempt accounts for qualified medical expenses. Those who selected this option, available to up to 390,000 seniors, were also required to purchase a high-deductible insurance policy (up to $6,000 deductible) to cover catastrophic illnesses.

- **Medicaid.** The cuts in Medicaid, the federal-state health insurance program for the poor, were achieved primarily by reducing so-called disproportionate share payments, which went to states with hospitals that served large numbers of poor and uninsured patients.

State governors won wide latitude to place Medicaid enrollees in managed care plans, no longer needing a waiver from the federal government to do so. They argued successfully that this would help them reduce costs.

- **Children's health.** Congress also agreed to provide $20 billion in grants to help the states tackle the growing problem of uninsured children. States could choose from several options, including expanding Medicaid or enrolling children in one of several "benchmark" plans. The initiative was financed partly by a 15-cent-per-pack increase in the federal cigarette tax.

The new program was governed by the so-called Hyde amendment, named for its author, Rep. Henry J. Hyde, R-Ill. The amendment, a perennial appropriations rider, prohibited federal funding for abortions except in cases of rape or incest or to save the woman's life. States could spend their own money to pay for abortions as long as the funds were not mingled with federal funds.

The changes in Medicare and Medicaid and the creation of the children's health initiative were made in an unusual atmosphere of bipartisanship. The administration worked closely with congressional Republicans to broker the changes, particularly those made to Medicare. Both sides generally stuck to parameters established in the balanced-budget deal that Republicans and the White House had agreed to in May. *(Budget deal, p. 2-18; budget resolution, p. 2-23)*

Still smarting from accusations in the fall 1996 election campaigns that they had tried to dismantle Medicare, Republicans needed Democrats and Clinton on board before they threw their support behind the changes.

Even then, House Republicans, who received the worst blistering over the Medicare issue in 1996, were only willing to go so far. They refused to support proposals put forward by their Senate counterparts that would have gradually raised the eligibility age for Medicare to 67 from 65, required a $5 copayment for some home health care visits and forced some better-off beneficiaries to pay more of their Medicare Part B premiums. Part B was the voluntary portion of Medicare that paid for doctor bills and related services. All three initiatives were dropped in conference.

As a result, while the final bill provided several short-term fixes to buck up the ailing Medicare program, lawmakers fell short of making the comprehensive adjustments needed to sustain Medicare's long-term financial health. "The leadership on our side of the aisle did not have the courage to stand up and fix this program," said Republican Rep. Tom Coburn of Oklahoma, a physician.

The legislation did, however, create a bipartisan commission to make recommendations on how the Medicare program might handle the financial impact of the pending retirement of millions of Baby Boomers beginning about 2010. *(Highlights, p. 6-5; spending-reconciliation bill, p. 2-47; provisions, p. 2-52)*

Background

Despite partisan disagreements, the Medicare debate went far more smoothly than it had in 1995, when partisan bickering prevailed and Clinton eventually vetoed the GOP package. *(1995 Almanac, p. 7-3)*

There were several differences in 1997. One was the size of the cuts. In 1995, Republicans sought to reduce the growth of federal spending on Medicare by $270 billion, compared with $115 billion in 1997.

Attitudes had also changed. "The partisan, in-your-face fervor and self-righteousness has abated," said Rep. Sherrod Brown, D-Ohio. He and other Democrats were pleased that the Republican Medicare proposals included several items they favored such as broader consumer protections and coverage for some preventive medicine. "It's clearly better" than the 1995 proposal, Brown said.

"I just think the entire environment is different this time," said House Ways and Means Committee Chairman Bill Archer, R-Texas. "That's what the people of this country want to see. They would rather see us work together than fight each other."

Both Clinton and GOP lawmakers recognized the need to turn to Medicare for savings as part of an overall drive to get government spending in check and balance the federal budget. By the time the health provisions were being drafted, the Medicare blueprint had been written into the budget resolution (H Con Res 84). For the most part, both parties stuck to the deal. Their disagreements focused more on policy — what changes to make to the Medicare program — than on how much to cut spending.

Republicans sought long-term changes — in particular the integration of more managed care into Medicare, while the president's plan focused on reducing payments to providers, such as doctors, hospitals and health maintenance organizations.

Of immediate concern was improving the prospects of the Part A trust fund, which covered inpatient hospital care and was financed by a dedicated payroll tax. In 1995, the trust fund began to take in less money than it spent, and the fund's reserves were expected to run out by fiscal 2001. The number of people contributing to the fund continued to decline. In 1995, 144 million workers supported 37 million beneficiaries, which translated into 3.9 workers per beneficiary. In 2030, there were expected to be 2.2 workers per beneficiary.

Clinton proposed extending the trust fund to 2007 by cutting provider payments and shifting about $50 billion in home health costs from the Part A program to Part B, which was financed by patient premiums and general revenues. "It's clearly a short-term proposal," Health and Human Services Secretary Donna E. Shalala acknowledged in a Feb. 12 appearance before the House Ways and Means Committee.

Republican Proposals

The real wrangling over Medicare began, however, once Republicans made their proposal public in June.

Directed by House leaders to assemble the Republicans' Medicare initiative, House Ways and Means Health Subcommittee Chairman Bill Thomas, R-Calif., worked with Democrats to structure a package that would trim the growth of federal spending by $115 billion over five years. Like Clinton, Thomas proposed to reduce payments to doctors and hospitals, but he also added a package of preventative health services and managed care plans.

In the Senate, Finance Committee Chairman William V. Roth Jr., R-Del., also aimed to cut $115 billion from the growth in Medicare spending, but he incorporated several key provisions not in the House bill. Roth proposed to gradually increase the eligibility age for Medicare beneficiaries from 65 to 67 in the period 2003-2027. He also called for a $5 copayment per visit for some Medicare home health care services.

Both plans called for a demonstration project, open to 500,000 seniors, to test how medical savings account would work in the federal Medicare program. Both proposed to expand the managed care options open to seniors. And both called for slightly higher Medicare Part B premiums.

The House and Senate Medicaid proposals mirrored one another, with the House calling for a reduction of about $15.3 billion over five years and the Senate providing for a $13.6 billion reduction. Both plans proposed to get much of the savings by reducing the level of disproportionate share payments to states with hospitals serving large numbers of poor and uninsured patients, and both proposed allowing states to move more Medicaid beneficiaries into managed care. The plans also called for repealing a federal law that required state Medicaid programs to pay "reasonable and adequate" rates to nursing homes.

On the issue of health insurance for children, the House and Senate were also in sync. The GOP plans proposed a new, $16 billion grant program to expand coverage, giving states the choice of expanding Medicaid to cover more children or purchasing private health insurance for low-income families.

House Action

Two House committees — Ways and Means, and Commerce — moved quickly to approve portions of the legislation. The two panels shared jurisdiction over Medicare; the Commerce Committee also oversaw Medicaid and the creation of the children's health insurance program. Democrats on both panels worked, often without success, to amend the Republican proposals.

Ways and Means Committee

The Ways and Means Health Subcommittee voted 13-0 on June 4 to approve Thomas' proposals, which the subcommittee chairman described as a down payment on fixing Medicare's long-term problems. The full Ways and Means Committee approved the same legislation June 9 by a 36-3 vote.

A bipartisan spirit clearly dominated the June 4 subcommittee markup, with Thomas describing the cooperation between panel Democrats and Republicans as "extraordinary." Ranking subcommittee Democrat Pete Stark of California, who rarely hesitated to criticize Republicans, praised the package and the behind-the-scenes work that had produced the legislation. "This bill and its drafting are a striking and welcome contrast to the contentious days of the 104th Congress," Stark said.

The proposal sought to expand the role of managed care in the Medicare program, allowing seniors to get their medical care from HMOs, provider sponsored organizations or preferred provider organizations. Managed care plans aimed to control costs by monitoring access to treatment and specialists. Seniors would also retain the option of staying in a traditional fee-for-service plan.

To address criticism that Medicare had not focused enough on preventive care, the proposal included coverage for services such as mammograms, Pap smears and screenings to detect prostate and colorectal cancer.

- **Medical savings accounts.** The medical savings account portion of the Thomas plan called for a pilot program in which up to 500,000 seniors would be allowed to put Medicare money into tax-exempt accounts that could be used to pay for qualified medical expenses. Beneficiaries who chose the accounts would also be required to select a government-provided high-deductible health insurance policy to cover catastrophic injuries or illnesses. The maximum deductible would be $6,000 in 1999, a figure that would be indexed to inflation in subsequent years.

Enrollment would begin Jan. 1, 1999, and end Dec. 31, 2002, at which point any Medicare beneficiary with a savings account could keep it. The Department of Health and Human Services (HHS) would make an annual, lump sum payment into each savings account. The amount would be no less than the usual sum that the department paid for Medicare benefi-

Health Provisions in the Budget Package

The following are key elements of the spending-cut bill (HR 2015 — PL 105-33) that affected Medicare, Medicaid and children's health insurance programs. Senate-passed provisions to raise the Medicare eligibility age, link Medicare Part B premiums to income for better-off seniors, and add a $5 copayment for certain home health care visits were dropped.

The final bill included provisions to:

Medicare

● **Spending reductions.** Cut spending growth by $115 billion over five years, mostly through reductions in Medicare payments to hospitals, doctors and other health care providers. Under previous law, the basic payment to hospitals for inpatient care increased each year by the rate of growth in the "hospital market basket," a measure of the goods and services that hospitals purchased. The market basket was projected to increase by 3 percent in fiscal 1998 and by 3.5 percent in subsequent years. However, the legislation froze 1998 payments at 1997 levels, and set the increase at 1.9 percent in fiscal 1999 and 1.8 percent in fiscal 2000 and thereafter.

The bill also changed the formula for determining payments to physicians and introduced prospective payment systems, or fee schedules, to pay skilled nursing facilities, rehabilitation hospitals, outpatient hospital services and home health services.

● **Trust fund.** Delay the projected depletion of the Medicare Part A trust fund, which paid for inpatient hospital care, until fiscal 2007. It was otherwise projected to run dry in fiscal 2001. Insolvency was postponed primarily by transferring the payment of certain home health services from Part A, which was financed by a payroll tax, to Medicare Part B. Part B, which paid doctors bills, was financed by patient premiums and general revenues.

● **Expanded options.** Give beneficiaries the option of remaining in the traditional fee-for-service program, or enrolling in a managed care plan such as a health maintenance organization or provider sponsored organization. Some seniors also could choose to combine a tax-free medical savings account with a high-deductible insurance plan.

● **Medical savings accounts.** Allow 390,000 Medicare beneficiaries to set up medical savings accounts to pay for qualified medical expenses. Participating seniors also had to buy a high-deductible health insurance plan to pay for catastrophic illnesses. The government would deposit a part of the individual's Medicare benefit into the medical savings account. Interest accrued and withdrawals to pay medical expenses would not be taxable. The insurance plan would pay benefits after the beneficiary paid the deductible, which could not exceed $6,000.

● **Premium increases.** Increase Part B premiums, $43.80 a month at the time of enactment, enough to continue to cover 25 percent of Part B program costs (the other 75 percent came from general revenues).

Prior to enactment of the new law, the Part B premium was going to be indexed to the cost of living increase for Social Security benefits beginning in 1999. This increase generally was lower than the increase in Part B costs, so the Part B premium would have covered a declining share of costs after 1999. Part B also had to absorb the cost of transferring home health care costs to Part B from Part A. By 2002, premiums would be $67 a month, as opposed to $51.50 in 2002 under prior law.

● **Preventive care.** Increase Medicare spending by $4 billion over five years to provide expanded benefits aimed at preventing seniors from getting sick. The benefits included mammography, Pap smears, screening for prostate and colorectal cancer, and diagnosis of osteoporosis.

● **Medicare commission.** Establish a 17-member National Bipartisan Commission on the Future of Medicare. It was charged with reporting in 1999 on the financial impact on Medicare of the pending retirement of the Baby Boomers and making recommendations on structural changes to Medicare.

Medicaid

● **Spending reductions.** Reduce Medicaid spending by about $10.4 billion over five years, mostly by reducing payments to states for hospitals that served a disproportionate share of low-income patients.

● **Boren Amendment.** Repeal the so-called Boren Amendment, which required state Medicaid programs to pay hospitals and nursing homes a "reasonable and adequate" rate. States would have more flexibility in setting provider payment levels.

● **Low-income beneficiaries.** Establish a $1.5 billion block grant to states to assist Medicaid enrollees with incomes between 120 percent and 150 percent of the federal poverty level to pay their Part B premiums. Previously, states were required to pay premiums for beneficiaries with incomes between 100 percent and 120 percent of the poverty level.

Children's Health Insurance

● **New program.** Provide $23.4 billion to expand health coverage to uninsured children, with costs partially offset by a 15-cent-per-pack increase in federal cigarette taxes.

● **State options.** Give states flexibility to determine eligibility for the program, while generally limiting eligibility to children from families with incomes up to 200 percent of the poverty level. States could decide to increase their Medicaid spending, provide health insurance programs for these children, use up to 10 percent of their funds for direct services to children, or some combination of these options. ■

---

ciaries in health maintenance organizations. Medicare HMOs were paid 95 percent of the average cost per beneficiary in the traditional fee-for-service program.

Participants would use their accounts to pay their deductibles, after which the catastrophic policies would kick in, reimbursing providers for the same amount that would have been paid by Medicare under the traditional fee-for-service plan. Beneficiaries, however, would incur so-called balanced billing, which meant they would pay the full amount charged by a provider, even if it exceeded Medicare's set reimbursement.

Money left in seniors' accounts would accrue, a feature sponsors believed would make the elderly more judicious about their medical care spending. The Congressional Budget Office (CBO) estimated that the savings accounts would cost taxpayers about $2 billion over five years in lost tax revenue, but Republicans said they would reduce Medicare spending over the long haul.

Democrats criticized the program, saying only the healthiest and wealthiest seniors would choose medical savings accounts, while the ill and less affluent would remain in fee-for-service plans. "This is the fastest and surest way to undermine the Medicare system and create new problems down the road for its financial solvency," said House Minority Leader Richard A. Gephardt, D-Mo.

● **Provider payments.** To trim Medicare spending and offset the cost of the medical savings accounts, Thomas included about $102 billion in payment reductions to Medicare providers. Payment rates to hospitals would be frozen for one year. Other providers, including doctors, HMOs and skilled nursing facilities, would face lower rates of growth in their Medicare reimbursement schedules.

Doctors, however, won some concessions, including a one-year delay in a government plan to change the way Medicare reimbursed physicians for office expenses such as supplies and rent. The American Medical Association (AMA) had charged that a government study on the issue was flawed and that the scheduled changes would result in dramatic reductions, with some physicians' payments being cut by as much as 40 percent.

The AMA also pressed for — and won — a $250,000 cap on non-economic damages in medical malpractice cases.

• **Part B premium increase.** Medicare beneficiaries were asked to share in the cost of trimming the program.

Under existing law, Part B premiums would be indexed to the cost of living increase for Social Security benefits beginning in 1999. The result would be an increase from $45.80 per month in 1998 to $51.50 per month in 2002. But that was lower than the projected increase in Part B costs, meaning it would cover a declining share of costs after 1999.

Under Thomas' plan, Part B premiums would rise to $67 per month by 2002. The aim was to cover more of the program's costs and to pay for certain home health care services that would be transferred from Part A to Part B under the bill in an effort to delay insolvency in the Medicare Part A trust fund. "That's a pretty significant premium increase over five years," said Martin Corry, director of legislative affairs for the American Association of Retired Persons (AARP).

• **Consumer protection**. The plan sought to expand consumer protections for people who chose managed care. It proposed to curb so-called gag clauses, which limited the information doctors could share with their patients. Such clauses stipulated that doctors could not discuss treatments or specialists that the HMO would not cover.

The plan also included a requirement that health plans pay for emergency care if a "prudent layperson" would determine that a trip to the emergency room was necessary.

Subcommittee Amendments

Several Democrats and one Republican offered unsuccessful amendments to the plan during the subcommittee markup:

➤ Stark proposed trimming the medical savings account project to 100,000 people, with $1.6 billion in savings redirected to pay for 16 hours a week of respite care for families of beneficiaries suffering from Alzheimer's disease. His amendment failed, 5-7.

➤ Benjamin L. Cardin, D-Md., offered, then withdrew, a proposal to levy a 1 percent user fee on health care plans to help fund graduate medical education. Thomas said he would work with Cardin on the issue before the full committee markup. Another attempt by Cardin to boost money for graduate medical education and hospitals that served a large number of poor people failed on a voice vote.

➤ An amendment by Gerald D. Kleczka, D-Wis., to strike the $250,000 cap on non-economic damages in malpractice suits failed, 5-8.

➤ Nancy L. Johnson, R-Conn., tried to strike a provision in the bill that would revert to a pre-1992 policy under which hospitals were reimbursed by Medicare for certain capital expenses based on their actual costs, not a set amount based on a formula. She said the policy would favor for-profit hospitals and take money away from nonprofits. Her amendment failed, 6-7.

Full Committee Amendments

There was slightly more dissent when the plan reached the full Ways and Means Committee, but it still received surprising bipartisan backing. Democrats stepped up their attacks in an effort to reshape major portions of the package, particularly the medical savings account demonstration project, but for the most part, those attempts failed. Amendments considered during the markup included proposals by:

➤ Xavier Becerra, D-Calif., to scrap the medical savings accounts and use the money to pay Medicare Part B premiums for individuals earning from 120 percent to 150 percent of the federal poverty level. Becerra said the payment was supposed to be part of the bipartisan budget deal, but Thomas disagreed. Becerra's amendment failed, 15-22.

➤ Jim Nussle, R-Iowa, and other rural state lawmakers to boost Medicare payments to rural providers. The amendment, adopted by voice vote, proposed to gradually change the formula for reimbursing doctors and hospitals in rural areas to a 50-50 blend of newly created local and national payment rates. National payment rates would generally be higher than local rural rates. Under existing law, the reimbursements were fixed. The bill had proposed a 70-30 blend of local and national rates. Nussle said his change was needed to encourage managed care providers to do business in rural areas.

➤ John Lewis, D-Ga., to strike the provision in the bill calling for a reversion to the pre-1992 policy of reimbursing hospitals for certain capital expenses based on their actual costs, not a set amount based on a formula. Lewis and others argued that returning to the earlier policy would take money from nonprofit hospitals and redirect it to for-profits. Representatives of for-profit hospitals said that because they paid property taxes and nonprofits often did not, they were entitled to larger reimbursements.

Lewis' amendment was approved, 20-19, with support from four Republicans, including Committee Chairman Archer, who said he was reluctant to take money away from nonprofit hospitals that depended on it.

Commerce Committee: Medicare

Sounding a far less bipartisan tone, the Commerce Committee's Health and Environment Subcommittee approved its package of Medicare changes June 10 by a vote of 15-11. The full Commerce Committee approved the proposals June 12 on a 29-17 vote, with only two Democrats — John D. Dingell of Michigan and Ralph M. Hall of Texas — voting "yes."

Democrats were just as unsuccessful as they had been in the Ways and Means Committee at stripping medical savings accounts and malpractice caps from the bill.

Like the Ways and Means package, the Commerce plan proposed to cut $115 billion from spending growth in Medicare, mostly through lower payments to doctors and hospitals participating in Medicare's traditional fee-for-service as well as managed care plans. It asked beneficiaries to pay a bit more in premiums, but promised them an expanded package of preventive health services and the ability to choose from more managed care options. And it included consumer protections for those who chose managed care.

One important difference, however, was the way the Commerce plan would pay managed care companies. It proposed to take away, or "carve out," the portion of HMO reimbursements that was targeted to fund graduate medical education and help finance hospitals serving a disproportionate share of low-income and uninsured patients. The money — about $11 billion over five years — would instead be paid directly to the institutions that trained medical residents and provided charity care.

The Commerce change responded to criticism that managed care providers often did not contract with such institutions, which typically had higher overhead costs than other providers, cutting into profits. Managed care groups rejected such accusations and argued that they did contract with academic health centers and provided some charity care. The Ways and Means plan called for an extensive study into the payment rate system. Both plans called for a 0.5 percent reduction in Medicare payments to health maintenance organizations.

During the subcommittee markup, Democrats and some Republicans joined forces to broaden the consumer protections in the legislation. Republicans Coburn and Greg Ganske of Iowa, both doctors, and Charlie Norwood of Georgia, a dentist, fought to let physicians and patients, rather than managed care companies, have the final say on when patients should check out of the hospital. Coburn said he wanted such decisions to be taken away from "an insurance clerk 600 miles away."

Democrats backed their efforts, and the subcommittee approved the amendment, 17-10. The provision was not challenged at the full committee markup. But some managed care proponents such as Peter Deutsch, D-Fla., said the change would damage managed care's ability to control costs. "The system, with all its faults . . . has worked," Deutsch said.

Commerce Committee: Medicaid, Children's Health Insurance

The Commerce Committee also approved a package of Medicaid overhaul proposals projected to reduce federal spending by $15.3 billion over five years, primarily by lowering payments to states with hospitals that treated large numbers of low-income and uninsured people. Also, states would be allowed to move more Medicaid patients into managed care.

The Health and Environment Subcommittee approved the Medicaid package June 10 on a 16-12 vote. The full Commerce panel approved it by a 28-18 vote June 12.

Democrats charged that several elements of the plan were inconsistent with the budget deal brokered by Republicans and the White House. Henry A. Waxman of California said Republicans were reneging on a promise to help low-income elderly people pay their Medicare Part B premiums.

The budget agreement called for spending $1.5 billion over five years to ease the impact of increasing Medicare premiums on low-income beneficiaries. The Commerce Committee bill included $500 million targeted specifically to offsetting the portion of the Part B premium increase attributable to the proposed transfer of home health services from Part A to Part B.

Waxman offered an amendment in the full committee to pay Part B premiums for seniors with incomes below 150 percent of the poverty level, as opposed to 120 percent under existing law, but he failed in a 19-25 party-line vote.

The White House also expressed concern. In a letter to Health Subcommittee Chairman Michael Bilirakis, R-Fla., Office of Management and Budget Director Franklin D. Raines said the proposal might not protect some low-income Medicare beneficiaries "as was intended in the [budget] agreement."

Raines also opposed the GOP's plan to significantly reduce the level of disproportionate share payments to states with hospital that served large numbers of low-income and uninsured patients. Some states would see reductions as large as 40 percent over five years. "Although we agree that there have been abuses," Raines wrote, "taking such large reductions in certain states . . . will likely affect their ability to cover services."

Another point of dispute between the White House and Democrats concerned the so-called Boren Amendment. Named for its creator, former Sen. David L. Boren, D-Okla. (1979-94), the amendment required state Medicaid programs to pay "reasonable and adequate" rates to nursing homes and hospitals. Boren said it was needed to guard against state governments squeezing nursing home budgets, which could reduce the quality of care.

But Clinton and many governors called for repealing the requirement because of the burden it placed on state budgets. The Commerce Committee included the repeal in its Medicaid proposal.

Some Democrats and moderate Republicans on both the subcommittee and the full committee wanted the Boren Amendment to remain in place. On June 10, the Health Subcommittee voted 15-13 to drop the repeal; on June 12 the full committee voted 28-19 to reinstate it.

Children's Health Initiative

The committee voted 39-7 to approve the new $16 billion grant program to expand health coverage for uninsured children.

Democrats voiced concern that the GOP proposal would give state officials too much spending latitude, and they objected to inclusion of the Hyde language on abortion. But an attempt by Diana DeGette, D-Colo., to strip the Hyde Amendment failed in the full committee on a 17-30 vote.

Republicans sought other changes in the children's health provisions. Nathan Deal, R-Ga., succeeded in removing language that would have guaranteed that disabled children who lost Social Security disability payments under the 1996 welfare law (PL 104-193) could continue to receive medical coverage through Medicaid. Deal and others charged that the program had been widely abused. His amendment, which directed the savings to emergency rooms providing care for illegal aliens, was approved, 27-18. *(1996 Almanac, p. 6-3)*

House Floor Action

The House acted quickly on the spending-cut bill (HR 2015 — H Rept 105-149), which had been assembled from the provisions produced by Ways and Means, Commerce and a number of other authorizing committees. The rule governing floor debate allowed no Democratic substitutes. The House passed the bill June 25 on a 270-162 vote. *(Vote 241, p. H-76)*

The rule also automatically made several changes to the bill. Among other things, it:

➤ Added $1 billion to the $500 million already in the bill for Medicaid to help pay Part B premiums for low-income beneficiaries, bringing the total to $1.5 billion.

➤ Stripped out the provision that would have allowed only doctors and patients, rather than insurers, to decide when a patient would be discharged from the hospital. The provision was deleted in response to a CBO estimate that it would increase federal Medicaid spending by $800 million over five years.

The House turned back a Democratic attempt to drop the children's health insurance block grant and instead expand the existing Medicaid program to supply additional coverage and permit states to establish their own programs to provide health coverage to uninsured children. The amendment, offered by Brown of Ohio, was defeated on a 207-223 vote. *(Vote 240, p. H-76)*

Brown and other Democrats said they feared Republicans had not put enough protections in the bill to guarantee that the money would be used to cover more children. "We want to make sure this money goes to insure millions of children . . . not frittered away so the governors have some kind of slush fund to plug holes in their budgets," Brown said.

Senate Action

In the Senate, the Medicare, Medicaid and children's health insurance provisions of the budget-reconciliation bill all came under the purview of the Finance Committee.

In many ways, the Finance Medicare package resembled the plans approved by the House Ways and Means and Commerce committees. All three plans aimed to trim about $115 billion from Medicare's projected growth in spending over five years, with most of the savings coming from reduced payments to doctors, hospitals and other medical providers participating in Medicare's traditional fee-for-service and managed care plans.

Finance Committee: Medicare

The Senate Finance Committee approved its package of Medicare changes June 18 on a bipartisan vote of 20-0, after revising key elements of Roth's medical savings account proposal and adding a plan to link Medicare Part B deductibles to patients' income.

The package already included the proposed increase in the eligibility age for Medicare benefits — from 65 to 67 from 2003 to 2027 — as well as the $5 copayment per visit for some Medicare home health care services.

The committee's two-day, 19-hour markup opened June 17 with a list of 263 amendments that was eventually whittled to about 65.

As the markup began, Roth described the package as a compromise "between differing political philosophies; between deeply held views. . . . I doubt that anyone is entirely satisfied with it." Daniel Patrick Moynihan of New York, the panel's ranking Democrat, praised Roth's plan for moving "this 1960s program into the present age" of managed care.

Savings Account Plan Modified

With some bipartisan support, the committee approved two amendments that effectively gutted key elements of Roth's medical savings account experiment.

The committee adopted, 12-8, an amendment by John H. Chafee, R-R.I., and Bob Graham, D-Fla., that reduced the size of the proposed demonstration program to 100,000 people from 500,000 in Roth's plan. Savings from that change were directed to other areas, including $300 million to cover copayments for mammograms and $400 million to fund a "telemedicine" project for rural areas.

The committee also accepted, 11-9, an amendment by John D. Rockefeller IV, D-W.Va., to lower the maximum deductibles allowed for Medicare recipients who chose to open a medical savings account and to cap the beneficiary's out-of-pocket expenses — both significant departures from the proposals approved by the House Ways and Means and Commerce committees.

Under the amendment, the maximum deductibles for the catastrophic insurance policy would fall to between $1,500 and $2,250 from the $6,000 in the Roth plan. Beneficiaries' out-of-pocket payments would be capped at $3,000, thereby reinstating protection against balanced billing and shielding beneficiaries from having to pay the full amount charged by a provider if it exceeded Medicare's set reimbursement.

Rockefeller said his amendment would give seniors the same consumer protections available under the 1996 health insurance portability law (PL 104-191). That bill also included a pilot program for medical savings accounts. *(1996 Almanac, p. 6-28)*

Majority Leader Trent Lott, R-Miss., who was unhappy with the changes, pledged to increase the number of seniors eligible to participate. "When it comes out of conference it will not be at 100,000," he said.

Means-Testing Provision Added

In what had the potential to become the most significant change in the Medicare program since its inception, the Finance Committee added language linking some beneficiaries' insurance deductibles under Medicare Part B to their income. If enacted, it would be the first time that any so-called means-testing was applied to the program. The amendment, sponsored by Chafee and Bob Kerrey, D-Neb., was approved 18-2 in a late-night vote June 17, with Roth and Carol Moseley-Braun, D-Ill., casting the dissenting votes.

Under the amendment, the annual deductible of $100 for all enrollees would increase to about $540 for people with adjusted gross incomes above $50,000 and couples with incomes above $75,000. The deductible would climb to a maximum of $2,160 for people with adjusted gross incomes above $100,000 and couples above $125,000.

Under existing law, Medicare beneficiaries paid the $100 deductible for doctors' expenses each year, and Medicare paid 80 percent of the rest. Many beneficiaries also had supplemental insurance, or Medigap, to pay expenses not covered by Medicare.

Amendment supporters said pegging the deductible increase to income would influence beneficiaries' behavior, making them think twice about spending their own money when using health services. Phil Gramm, R-Texas, said the change represented "the most dramatic reform of Medicare in this country. . . . If it is sustained, we will have done more in one markup than all the talk" on changing Medicare. Lott called the amendment "courageous."

But the proposal faced heavy opposition from liberal lawmakers such as Edward M. Kennedy, D-Mass. "Means testing the deductible affects only those who actually use health services," Kennedy said. "It therefore imposes a 'sickness tax' that undermines Medicare's fundamental policy of spreading risks and costs across all beneficiaries."

The White House also expressed concerns about the proposal, which spokesman Mike McCurry said was a possible violation of the budget deal. "This kind of flies in the face of that agreement," he said.

Lott urged the White House to stay away from such snap judgments, stressing that the debate over restructuring Medicare would be a long one. "This is not a sprint," Lott said. "This is a seven-hurdle distance race."

Corry of the AARP called the means-testing proposal "unworkable" and said it would open the door to the further deterioration of benefits. The powerful seniors lobbying group also vowed to fight Roth's proposals to gradually raise the Medicare eligibility age and to impose a $5 copayment for some Medicare home health services.

Other Medicare Amendments

Managed care providers complained loudly that they would be adversely affected by several provisions in the bill, including the proposed payment reductions. The changes were included to respond to criticism of HMOs, including charges that historically they had made handsome profits off healthy seniors, who tended to gravitate to HMO plans, while less healthy, less affluent seniors remained in traditional fee-for-service plans.

Like the Commerce Committee plan, the Finance package proposed to "carve out" funds intended for graduate medical education and disproportionate share hospitals, and send the money directly to those institutions. In addition, the Finance plan included a "risk adjuster" that would be applied to Medicare managed care provider payments for new enrollees. In the first year, the base payment would be trimmed 5 percent, declining to 1 percent the fifth year.

An attempt by Orrin G. Hatch, R-Utah, to strip the risk adjustment provision failed, 2-18. But Max Baucus, D-Mont., won voice vote approval for an amendment to give new managed care plans under Medicare a one-year reprieve from the risk adjustment. The amendment was an incentive to managed care providers to enroll seniors who lived in rural areas. Managed care companies sometimes avoided rural areas because their reimbursement rates were often lower than rates in urban areas.

To further boost the appeal of rural areas, Charles E. Grassley, R-Iowa, won support for a plan to raise the $350 minimum payment per month per beneficiary for Medicare managed care providers to about $400. His amendment was adopted, 11-9.

In other action, Chafee and Graham succeeded in broadening the bill's definition of conditions requiring emergency care to include "severe pain," such as chest pains. They also added language requiring the HHS secretary to develop rules detailing under what conditions so-called post-stabilization care was covered and how promptly an HMO had to respond to requests to authorize treatment. The amendment, approved 17-3, aimed to assuage concerns that some HMOs intentionally ignored emergency room requests for authorization of care after a patient had been stabilized.

Karen Ignagni, president and chief executive officer of the American Association of Health Plans, a trade group representing more than 1,000 managed care providers, said the Finance provisions affecting HMOs would "hurt real people by increasing out-of-pocket expenses and significantly cutting the benefits of Medicare beneficiaries in HMOs." Such benefit reductions could include eliminating prescription drug and dental coverage, Ignagni said.

The Senate plan did not include the proposal to allow physicians and patients, rather than a managed care plan, to decide when patients should be discharged from the hospital. Managed care advocates said such curbs would hurt their ability to control costs.

The Finance package also steered clear of the caps proposed in the House bill for non-economic damages in malpractice lawsuits. Lott said he favored such caps but doubted they would survive in the Senate. "I'd like to do it, but there's a lot of resistance," he said.

Finance Committee: Medicaid, Children's Health Insurance

The Senate Finance Committee's proposals to trim Medicaid by $13.6 billion and boost spending on children's health by $16 billion received the same 20-0 bipartisan backing on June 18 as the panel's package on Medicare.

As in the House plan, most of the proposed Medicaid savings came from reducing disproportionate share payments to hospitals. States would be allowed to move more Medicaid beneficiaries into managed care, and the federal requirement that state Medicaid programs pay "reasonable and adequate" rates to nursing homes would be repealed.

Like the initial House bill, the Senate plan did not include the full $1.5 billion to pay the Medicare Part B premiums for some low-income seniors. As he had done with House leaders, OMB's Raines complained that this was a violation of the bipartisan budget agreement.

Some Finance Republicans agreed with the administration. Arlen Specter, R-Pa., told Lott he faced a "major revolt from elements in both parties" if the money was not restored. Specter, along with Republicans Rick Santorum of Pennsylvania, and Susan Collins and Olympia J. Snowe of Maine, sent a letter to Lott on June 19 urging him to reinstate the funds.

Nor did the Senate plan include funding to restore Medicaid benefits for disabled children who lost Social Security disability payments as a result of the 1996 welfare overhaul. However, the committee agreed to provide $200 million to cover some children of lower-income legal immigrants who lost their Medicaid coverage under the new law. The amendment, offered by Graham and Chafee, reduced the scope of the medical savings accounts in the Medicare portion of the package and redirected the savings. It was approved, 12-8.

Children's Health Initiative

Chafee's luck, however, did not continue when he tried to revise the children's health provisions. Despite White House backing, Chafee and Rockefeller failed in a bid to substitute their own proposal for Roth's.

The Chafee-Rockefeller amendment, which failed 9-11, would have spent $12 billion to expand the existing Medicaid program and $4 billion on federal block grants to states. Roth's approach, which also would cost $16 billion, allowed states to choose a block grant or an enhanced federal funding match to expand Medicaid.

The day before the vote on the amendment, Clinton urged Roth to embrace the Chafee-Rockefeller approach. Rockefeller said he was pleased with the White House support, but said it might have helped more had it come earlier. "They weren't there until quite recently," Rockefeller said after the final Finance vote.

Don Nickles, R-Okla., succeeded on a 12-8 vote in adding the Hyde language on abortion to the children's health initiative.

Hatch tried to add language increasing the federal excise tax on cigarettes and tobacco products to provide an additional $20 billion for expanding children's health coverage, but Roth ruled Hatch's amendment out of order.

On June 19, however, the Finance Committee approved a variation of Hatch's tobacco tax plan as part of a second reconciliation bill (HR 2014), this one aimed at cutting taxes by $85 billion over five years. That victory netted about $8 billion to pay for new health coverage for uninsured children. *(Tax reconciliation, p. 2-30)*

Senate Floor Action

In contrast to the tight framework that governed debate on the House floor, the Senate undertook an eight-hour voting marathon before passing its version of the spending-cut bill (S 947) June 25 by a vote of 73-27. *(Vote 130, p. S-24)*

Some senators expressed dismay that they were voting on critical provisions that were not adequately explained. "That's no way to operate," said Robert C. Byrd, D-W.Va.

Many of the votes involved waiving the 1974 Budget Act, which restricted the types of amendments that could be offered to reconciliation bills on the Senate floor; 60 votes were required to waive the budget act.

By voice vote on June 24, the Senate adopted an amendment by Roth and Moynihan to require some higher-income Medicare beneficiaries to pay a larger share of their premiums for Part B. (The focus on premiums replaced the earlier committee plan to means test Part B deductibles.)

Under existing law, all beneficiaries paid 25 percent of their Part B costs. Under the amended Senate bill, that share would begin to increase for individuals whose adjusted gross incomes were $50,000 or greater and for couples with incomes of $75,000 or more. Individuals with adjusted gross incomes of $100,000 or more and couples with incomes of $125,000 or more would pay the whole Part B premium.

The savings from the premium increase would go in part to help low-income seniors pay their Part B premiums, bringing the total in the bill to $1.5 billion.

Senate Budget Committee Chairman Pete V. Domenici, R-N.M., said the plan would raise about $4 billion and affect about 5 percent of Medicare's 38 million beneficiaries.

Senate Backs Committee on Medicare

On June 24, the Senate reaffirmed the most controversial elements of the committee proposal.

First, the Senate tabled (killed) an amendment by Kennedy and Paul Wellstone, D-Minn., to remove the requirement for a $5 copayment for some home health care services. Then the Senate voted 62-38 to bar an attempt by Kennedy to challenge the proposed increase in the eligibility age for Medicare. *(Votes 111, 112, p. S-22)*

Lastly, the Senate voted 70-30 to table (kill) a Kennedy amendment to strike the provisions linking Part B premiums to incomes for better-off beneficiaries. Kennedy then tried to delay the onset of means testing by two years, having it begin in 2000 rather than 1998. His motion to waive the budget act and permit the change failed, 37-63. *(Votes 113, 114, p. S-22)*

Kennedy did succeed with a proposal, approved by voice vote, to apply means testing to senators. Senators who earned more than $100,000 per year — and all of them did — would be required to pay the full amount of their Part B premiums if the means testing provision became law.

The Senate subsequently rejected, 25-75, a substitute offered by Jack Reed, D-R.I., that would have deleted the increase in the eligibility age, the copayment for home services and the means testing for Part B premiums. The amendment was rejected on a procedural motion. *(Vote 115, p. S-22)*

In other action, the Senate:

➤ Adopted by voice vote an amendment by Jon Kyl, R-Ariz., to permit Medicare beneficiaries to use their own money to pay for services from physicians who did not participate in the Medicare program.

➤ Rejected, 66-34, on a procedural motion an attempt by Barbara A. Mikulski, D-Md., to strike the section of the bill calling for repeal of the Boren Amendment. *(Vote 124, p. S-23)*

➤ Defeated, 39-61, a motion by Kerrey to strike the Hyde Amendment language from the children's health initiative. *(Vote 129, p. S-24)*

➤ Adopted by voice vote a package of changes from Chafee and Rockefeller requiring states that expanded children's health coverage to make sure children's benefits packages were equivalent to the services provided to children under the Federal Employees Health Benefits Program's standard Blue Cross/Blue Shield plan. The amendment also proposed to limit premiums, deductibles and copayments for low-income families.

➤ Adopted by voice vote a proposal by Domenici and Wellstone to require that states using the federal block grant money to expand children's health care purchase only health plans that offered equal levels of coverage for severe mental illness and physical ailments.

Conference/Final Action

The House-Senate conference on the spending-cut bill began with a ceremonial opening session July 10 but quickly broke into smaller subconferences that met behind closed doors. The subconference on Medicare convened immediately, though the negotiations were mostly a GOP-only affair.

On July 24, Republican leaders took their preliminary agreements to the White House and began a final round of bargaining with top administration officials. At that point, House and Senate Republicans still had not decided what to do with the Senate's eligibility, copayment and means-testing provisions.

The GOP initially staked out a hard line in a number of areas, including some of the health provisions. On the children's health care initiative, for example, Republican negotiators opted for the $16 billion House proposal that relied heavily on block grants to states, rather than for the Senate's bipartisan $24 billion proposal that required states to offer a uniform package of children's health benefits. The cost had to be trimmed because the House GOP insisted that the Senate-approved increase in tobacco taxes be dropped.

On medical savings accounts, Republicans went with the House proposal to allow 500,000 seniors to sign up, rather than 100,000 as in the Senate version. The House proposal also permitted a maximum deductible of $6,000 and included no caps on beneficiaries' out-of-pocket expenses. The Senate had proposed capping out-of-pocket costs at $3,000 and deductibles at between $1,500 and $2,250.

But Clinton's influence over the bill was growing. Rank-and-file Republicans were eager to finish before the August recess so they could take the results home to their constituents. And the House GOP was still reeling from an aborted effort by conservative dissidents to oust Speaker Newt Gingrich, R-Ga. "The president has a tremendous amount of leverage right now," observed Rockefeller. *(Gingrich, p. 1-11)*

The White House pushed for a number of changes, including reducing the medical savings account test program to as few as 100,000 participants, and dropping unrestricted fee-for-service health plans as an option in Medicare. In addition, Clinton began to press for changes to the children's health initiative. He wanted the legislative package to mandate coverage for prescription drugs, vision and hearing services. He also wanted plans to provide the same level of coverage for mental health illnesses as for physical ailments. And he urged House Republicans to agree to use the cigarette tax increase, which the Senate had passed as part of the companion tax bill, to boost the children's health package to $24 billion, up from the $16 billion agreed to in the budget deal.

Debates Over Means Testing, Eligibility

The toughest disagreements to resolve were over the Senate proposals to raise the eligibility age for Medicare, apply means testing to Part B premiums, and require a $5 copayment for some home health care.

Archer had said early on that it was "unlikely" the proposals would be included in the final legislation. He described them as "premature," particularly since no public hearings had been conducted. "This is a massive difference between our bills," Archer said. "It will not be easily resolved."

AARP, the powerful lobbying group for the elderly, weighed in, with Executive Director Horace B. Deets calling the Senate proposals "harmful provisions that would jeopardize Medicare's future."

White House spokesman Toiv said the provisions would be difficult to retain because they did not have widespread bipartisan support in the House and were not part of the budget deal.

The increase in the eligibility age for Medicare benefits had long seemed like a non-starter, though it remained part of the talks.

The House opposed it, as did the Clinton administration. On July 10, the House voted 414-14, to approve a motion by John M. Spratt Jr., D-S.C., urging conferees to reject the Senate provision. Though the motion was non-binding, the overwhelming vote signaled that the provision had little chance. *(Vote 257, p. H-82)*

Negotiations over Medicare means testing stalled over both philosophical and practical disagreements. Medicare had traditionally been a "middle-class" entitlement that did not distinguish between rich and poor. While the means-testing plan would affect a select few — seniors in about the top 6 percent in the income bracket — it could be seen as the first step in turning Medicare into a welfare program.

On the practical side, there was the question of how such a proposal would be implemented. The White House proposed using the tax system, requiring the IRS to add a line to the 1040 tax form. Republicans feared that could be viewed as a tax increase and wanted means testing to be handled by HHS. Administration officials said that was too cumbersome.

Negotiators also tried to assess which method would bring in the most money. A CBO analysis found that having the IRS collect premiums would raise $8.9 billion over five years, while relying on HHS would raise only $3.9 billion. That was because the IRS already had access to seniors' income records; HHS did not.

Clinton seemed to gradually warm to the idea of means testing. At a July 9 news conference at the NATO summit in Madrid, he said he had "never been opposed to means-testing Medicare" but wanted to make sure that any such change was "fair and workable."

Bruce Vladeck, administrator of the Health Care Financing Administration expressed similar concerns July 10 in an appearance before the subconference on Medicare. While Vladeck said the administration was "not uncomfortable with" the idea of linking Part B premiums to income, the Senate plan was "cumbersome" and would be "hard to administer."

Vladeck also said that phasing out the federal subsidy entirely would "cause a significant deterioration in the risk pool for the Part B program," with wealthier, and often healthier, beneficiaries abandoning the program altogether.

On July 22, Clinton came out with a fairly strong endorsement of means testing for Part B premiums. This time he proposed having them send a check made out to the "Medicare Trust Fund" with their tax returns every April 15, but Republicans rejected the tax connection.

Final Action

After lengthy negotiations that dominated much of June and July, House and Senate conferees finally reached agreement July 30 on the conference report to the budget-reconciliation bill (HR 2015 — H Rept 105-217). The House acted first, voting 346-85 on July 30 to adopt the report. The Senate followed the next day, clearing the bill by a vote of 85-15. *(House vote 345, p. H-104; Senate vote 209, p. S-36)*

In the end, conferees agreed to stave off Medicare's immediate problem — the expected depletion of the Part A trust fund by 2001 — putting insolvency off until fiscal 2007. But they left the question of how to ensure Medicare's long-term financial health unanswered.

The three controversial Senate proposals — raising the eligibility age, adding means testing for Part B premiums, and requiring a copayment on some home health services — were dropped in the face of strong House opposition. "It was a clear failure of American government to act in a crisis," said Gramm. "The disappointment is we had a golden opportunity here."

But Thomas, the Ways and Means Health Subcommittee chairman, was more upbeat, saying that bipartisan backing in both chambers signaled that legislators could make further changes without fear of political damage. "We have broken the logjam," Thomas said. "We can adjust Medicare."

One gesture Congress did make toward the future was the creation of a 17-member bipartisan commission to address Medicare's long-term structural and financial problems. The panel was to begin its deliberations in 1998.

The bill postponed the Medicare Part A trust fund problems mainly by shifting home health care costs, the fastest growing element of Medicare spending, from Part A to Part B, which came from general Treasury revenues and patient premiums. The shift increased Part B premiums from $43.80 at the time of enactment, to $67 in fiscal 2002.

"We have to have a further wave of reform in the future," said Gingrich. "We knew the most we could do in one jump was save Medicare for a decade." Gingrich said the Senate had demonstrated "courage" in trying to raise the Medicare eligibility age and increase premiums for better-off seniors, even though the House did not follow the Senate's lead.

"In the end, we reached the conclusion it was better to do none of them in isolation," Gingrich told a gathering of senior citizens July 29. "There's a point here where every reasonable person knows this is something that has to be rethought."

Medicare Changes

The conference report retained the original principles included in the House and Senate Medicare proposals. It gave seniors an expanded set of managed care choices that went beyond the standard HMO option already available to them. It broadened Medicare coverage to include preventive services, and it added medical savings accounts to the program. Some legislators hoped the additional benefits would lure the elderly to such plans.

The bill also included two changes in Medicare that seniors' advocates feared would end up costing beneficiaries more. One change allowed seniors to choose an unrestricted fee-for-service plan that allowed them to select their own doctors. Such plans did not have to follow the Medicare fee schedule. Doctors and other providers could charge patients up to 115 percent of what their insurance plan paid.

The other change permitted private contracting — the ability of physicians not in the Medicare program to enter into private contracts with beneficiaries for services otherwise covered by Medicare. However, doctors who wanted to privately contract with patients had to agree to not participate in the Medicare program or accept any Medicare reimbursement for two years.

Kyl led a fight to delete the two-year ban, but seniors groups such as the AARP charged that lifting the restriction could lead to two-tiered system of medical care for the elderly.

- **Medical savings accounts.** The final bill included the House version of the medical savings account plan, though the number of participants was reduced to 390,000. As in the House bill, annual deductibles as high as $6,000 were allowed and there was no cap on out-of-pocket expenses.
- **Preventive care.** The bill increased Medicare spending

by $4 billion over five years to provide a package of preventive care initiatives, including mammograms, Pap smears, screening for prostrate and colorectal cancer, diabetes self-management and the diagnosis of osteoporosis.

• **Consumer protection.** Protections for beneficiaries in managed care programs included a requirement that the plans provide coverage for care that a "prudent layperson" would consider to be an emergency, and a ban on so-called gag clauses restricting the advice that doctors could give their patients.

Negotiators also agreed to permit Medicare beneficiaries who enrolled in managed care plans to drop out on a monthly basis, as they could under existing law, over the following four years. After that, seniors would have to enroll for longer — eventually for at least a year.

• **Rural areas.** The final package included several incentives to encourage managed care providers to set up business in rural areas, including a guaranteed minimum payment of $367 per month per beneficiary; existing payments were as low as $223 per month. Another change called for a gradual blending of local and national reimbursement rates, a departure from the fixed-payment, county-based system in which urban rates often were much higher than rural rates.

• **Provider payments.** Other provisions in the bill, however, reduced payments to managed care providers. Conferees agreed to "carve out" money previously included in Medicare payments to managed care companies but designated for graduate medical education. Instead, the money would be sent directly to teaching hospitals when they cared for Medicare patients. The change was made in part to help teaching institutions compete for managed care patients.

However, the agreement also provided for Medicare managed care providers to receive at least a 2 percent payment increase annually, guaranteeing that HMOs doing business in higher-cost areas would get some increase in reimbursements.

The bill expanded Medicare's prospective payment, or fee schedule, system to the rapidly growing home health care and skilled nursing sectors in order to curb costs.

• **Fraud.** The agreement also included tough measures to punish fraud, such as Medicare overpayments to hospitals, doctors and other providers. In a widely expected move, negotiators dropped the controversial House proposal to cap non-economic damages in medical malpractice cases at $250,000.

Medicaid Changes

While the final package reduced Medicaid spending by reducing so-called disproportionate share payments, at the last minute $600 million was added back to aid states such as Texas and New York that had many low-income and uninsured residents. In an effort to appease lawmakers angry at the cuts, conferees decided that no state's reimbursement would be reduced more than 3.5 percent below its fiscal 1995 Medicaid funding.

The Medicaid package also included medical coverage for disabled children who were no longer eligible for Supplemental Security Income disability payments under the 1996 welfare law, and a $1.5 billion block grant to the states to pay Medicare Part B premiums for Medicaid beneficiaries whose family income was between 120 percent and 150 percent of the poverty level. (Those below 120 percent were already covered under existing law.)

Conferees agreed to repeal the Boren Amendment that had required Medicaid programs to pay hospitals and nursing homes a "reasonable and adequate" rate.

Children's Health Initiative

The agreement provided $20 billion over five years for the children's health initiative. This was expected to provide health care coverage for up to 5 million of the estimated 10 million uninsured children.

The increase was made possible by a decision to incorporate the 15-cents-a-pack increase in the federal cigarette tax that had begun as part of the companion tax bill.

States could choose from several options, such as broadening their existing Medicaid coverage or enrolling uninsured children in private health plans. Benefits packages had to be equivalent to one of several benchmark plans, such as the standard Blue Cross/Blue Shield preferred provider option offered under the Federal Employees Health Benefits plan.

States also could develop their own plans as long as they were similar financially to a benchmark package and included a specific list of services. Existing children's health programs in New York, Pennsylvania and Florida could continue as they were.

Only 10 percent of the federal grant money could be spent on so-called direct services, such as community outreach programs, or administration. ■

Clinton Again Vetoes Abortion Ban

For the second year in a row, lawmakers cleared legislation outlawing a controversial abortion procedure, and for the second time, President Clinton vetoed the bill. Supporters chose to defer an override attempt until 1998. Though their vote margin in the House was wide enough to easily override a veto, they remained three votes short in the Senate.

The bill (HR 1122) sought to ban what opponents called "partial birth" abortion, except in cases where no other medical procedure would save the woman's life. Under the measure, a doctor who performed the procedure could be subject to fines and up to two years in prison. The woman would be exempt from criminal penalties.

A partial-birth abortion was defined in the bill as one in which "the person performing the abortion partially vaginally delivers a living fetus before killing the fetus and completing delivery."

As initially passed by the House in March, the bill was identical to the version that had been vetoed in 1996. The Senate modified the bill slightly in an effort to win broader support before passing it in May.

Crafted by Sen. Rick Santorum, R-Pa., the alterations included clarifying what constituted the procedure, one of several abortion methods used in the second and third trimesters of pregnancy.

The bill further defined the offense as to "deliberately and intentionally deliver into the vagina a living fetus, or a substantial portion thereof, for the purpose of performing a procedure the physician knows will kill the fetus, and kills the fetus."

Santorum also streamlined bill language aimed at shielding doctors from criminal penalties if a physical life-threatening medical emergency forced them to use the procedure. Under the revised bill, a physician accused of violating the law could first seek a hearing before a state medical board to determine whether his or her actions were "necessary to save the life of the mother whose life was endangered by a physical disorder, illness or injury." Santorum said the proceedings would provide "a legitimate peer review mechanism," evidence that could be used in later court proceedings.

The House agreed in October to send the revised bill to the president, who vetoed it, as promised, Oct. 10. Clinton said he would continue to oppose the bill unless it was modified to allow such abortions to take place to protect the health of the woman.

Supporters of the bill expressed optimism that they could override the veto. But even if they were unable to enact the legislation under a Democratic president, the issue had allowed them to go on the offensive in a debate where they had largely been in retreat. The move forced Clinton to defend such abortions. Abortion foes also hoped it would cause some re-examination of the issue by a public that was at once reluctant to restrict abortion rights yet uncomfortable with the number of abortions performed.

BOXSCORE

Abortion Procedure Ban — HR 1122 (HR 929, S 6). The bill proposed to ban so-called partial birth abortions, except to save the life of the woman.

Report: H Rept 105-24 (HR 929).

KEY ACTION

March 20 — House passed HR 1122, 295-136.

May 20 — Senate passed HR 1122, amended, 64-36.

Oct. 8 — House accepted Senate changes, clearing HR 1122, 296-132.

Oct. 10 — President vetoed HR 1122.

Background

If enacted, the bill would have marked the first time Congress had made a specific abortion procedure illegal.

In its 1973 decision in *Roe v. Wade*, the U.S. Supreme Court ruled that women had a legal right to have an abortion. Under *Roe* and a key successor case, *Planned Parenthood of Southeastern Pennsylvania v. Casey* (1992), federal and state governments were prohibited from setting restrictions on abortion that would place an "undue burden" on the woman until the fetus was "viable," or could live outside the womb. After viability, Congress and state legislatures could restrict abortions as long as exceptions were made to protect a woman's life and health. Courts had defined health broadly to include a variety of physical and psychological factors.

Most states had passed laws leaving to doctors the questions of viability and what constituted a health concern for the woman. New York and Pennsylvania were the principal exceptions; they defined viability as 24 weeks.

Constitutional Arguments

The anti-abortion bill was supported by the American Medical Association (AMA) and by anti-abortion groups including the National Right to Life Committee, the U.S. Catholic Conference and the Christian Coalition.

Opponents included Planned Parenthood, the American Civil Liberties Union, the National Abortion and Reproductive Rights Action League and the National Organization for Women.

Proponents argued that the bill was consistent with the Constitution. They said the procedure in question was not protected under *Roe v. Wade* because the fetus was mostly outside the woman's body during the procedure. "Location is critical," said Helen Alvare of the National Conference of Catholic Bishops.

But the American Civil Liberties Union disagreed. "By making no exceptions for maternal health and inadequate exceptions to save a woman's life, this bill flies in the face of well-established Supreme Court precedents," said Catherine Weiss, director of the group's Reproductive Freedom Project.

Kathryn Kolbert, vice president of the Center For Reproductive Law and Policy, a nonprofit group that supported abortion rights, said "nothing" in previous cases supported the view that the partial-birth procedure was outside the scope of *Roe.*

Kolbert argued that the bill, if enacted, would ultimately be declared unconstitutional because it "outlaws abortion without regard for a woman's health and prevents doctors from exercising their best medical judgment for a particular patient."

Action in the 104th Congress

Passage of a bill to ban the abortion procedure was the biggest victory scored by anti-abortion forces in the 104th Congress. In debate that was emotional and graphic, bill proponents were able to focus on the details of a specific procedure that much of the public found unacceptable. That put them in a stronger position than when the focus was on the traditional, more philosophical question of a woman's right to have an abortion.

Most of the legislative action on the bill occurred in 1995. The House passed the measure 288-139 on Nov. 1, and the Senate passing a revised version Dec. 7 by a vote of 54-44. The bill would have made it a crime to perform a partial-birth abortion throughout the term of the pregnancy, unless it was necessary to save the life of the woman.

Senate changes included an amendment shifting the burden of proof to the prosecutor for establishing beyond a reasonable doubt that the procedure was not necessary to save the woman's life, or that another procedure would have saved her life. The House cleared the bill March 27, 1996, by a vote of 286-129.

Clinton vetoed the bill April 10 of that year, saying that he would sign it only if the exception were broadened to include not only the life but also the health of the woman.

Republicans waited until September, close to the fall elections, to attempt an override. The effort was seen as largely symbolic, however, because bill supporters were well short of the necessary two-thirds majority in the Senate. The House voted 285-137 to override the veto, but the Senate vote was 57-41, nine votes short. *(1995 Almanac, p. 7-30; 1996 Almanac, pp. 6-43, D-13)*

New Momentum in 1997

As abortion foes renewed their efforts in 1997, they gained momentum from two unlikely sources: abortion rights advocate Ron Fitzsimmons, executive director of the National Coalition of Abortion Providers, and the AMA.

In an emotional hearing held March 11 by the House and Senate Judiciary committees, Republicans spotlighted statements made by Fitzsimmons in several recent interviews acknowledging that he had lied the previous year when he said the procedure was rarely performed. Abortion rights advocates had argued that only a few hundred such procedures were performed each year and that they were mostly cases involving health concerns of the woman.

Also since the 1996 debate, The Washington Post and the

Abortion Battle Fought . . .

Efforts to add abortion restrictions — or to remove them from existing law — figured in several bills in the first session of the 105th Congress.

• **State Department authorization.** A dispute between Congress and the White House over abortion restrictions on international family planning aid stymied efforts to enact a State Department authorization bill for fiscal 1998-99 (HR 1757).

The provision, added to the bill on the House floor by Christopher H. Smith, R-N.J., sought to bar aid to international family planning groups that promoted, performed or supported abortion except in cases of rape, incest or danger to the life of the woman. The House adopted the proposal June 5 by a vote of 232-189. *(Vote 168, p. H-56)*

Smith had been trying for some time to reinstitute the Reagan-era "Mexico City policy," which barred U.S. aid to groups that practiced or advocated abortion, even if they used their own money to do so. (Since 1973, U.S. law had outlawed direct funding of overseas abortions.)

President Clinton had overturned the policy by executive action in 1993, and Republicans had been seeking ever since to restore it. Smith, who led the anti-abortion forces in the House, argued that providing U.S. funding to such groups simply allowed them to use their own money to perform or promote the use of abortion. *(1993 Almanac, p. 348)*

The Senate-passed version of the bill contained no such restriction. Though Senate Foreign Relations Committee Chairman Jesse Helms, R-N.C., was a strong foe of abortion, he struggled to get the matter dealt with in another bill to protect the State Department authorization from a certain veto. But an end-of-session decision by Republican leaders to drop similar Smith language from the foreign aid operations bill (HR 2159) removed that option and left the conference on the State Department bill in disarray. *(State Department, p. 8-32)*

• **Foreign operations appropriations.** Smith succeeded in adding essentially the same language to the House version of the fiscal 1998 foreign operations spending bill (HR 2159).

The amendment, which the House approved Sept. 4 on a 234-191 vote, sought to prohibit aid to international family planning groups that promoted, performed or supported abortion except in cases of rape, incest or danger to the life of the woman. In addition, it called for barring funding for any foreign organization that lobbied for or against abortion, and for the U.N. Population Fund unless it ceased all activities in China. *(Vote 363, p. H-110)*

As was the case on the State Department bill, the abortion language was not part of the Senate version of the foreign aid spending bill. Though conferees quickly resolved most of their other differences on HR 2159, the conflict over abortion proved too difficult and was punted to the leadership. Republican leaders attempted to win support for a modified version of the abortion ban but were rebuffed by moderate House Republicans.

Finally, with the session drawing to a close, they bowed to Clinton and dropped the abortion provision. The concession allowed the bill to become law, but at a price. GOP conservatives insisted that the final bill drop a package of carefully negotiated provisions that included funding for the International Monetary Fund, partial repayment of U.S. debts to the United Nations, and a plan to reorganize the country's foreign affairs bureaucracy.

Clinton signed the bill into law Nov. 26 (PL 105-118). *(Appropriations, p. 9-37)*

• **International family planning aid.** In one of their first actions of the year, the House and Senate agreed to release $385 million in previously appropriated international family planning aid without abortion restrictions. A compromise the previous year had removed the restrictions but prevented the president from using the money until July 1, 1997, unless he determined that the delay was harming U.S. family planning programs.

Clinton made that finding Jan. 31, triggering a congressional vote on legislation (HJ Res 36) to begin releasing the

Bergen County (New Jersey) Record had published articles that included evidence that the procedure was more common than was previously believed.

"Recent statements by [Fitzsimmons] are revealing what many already knew — that there has long existed voluminous and convincing evidence that there are thousands of elective partial-birth abortions performed every year," said Senate Judiciary Committee Chairman Orrin G. Hatch, R-Utah.

Supporters of abortion rights countered that the precise number of these abortions — which was hard to estimate because nationwide records were not kept — was not the issue. Rather, they argued that banning the procedure was an attempt to slowly eat away at rights conferred on women in the *Roe* decision.

"If you ban this, doctors could use a different procedure," said Renee Chelian, president of the National Coalition of Abortion Providers. "My concern is that you will then try to ban that one, and the next and the next. And suddenly abortion is no longer available."

Abortion rights advocates argued that even if the numbers were revised upward, partial-birth abortions still represented a tiny fraction of all abortions performed. Kate Michelman, president of the National Abortion and Reproductive Rights Action League, said 99 percent of all abortions were performed in the first 20 weeks of pregnancy, when the partial-birth procedure was not used.

Revisions Win AMA Backing

Santorum's revised bill won the unexpected endorsement of the AMA, whose board of trustees came out in support of the legislation May 19, just as the Senate was about to vote on it. The AMA previously had never endorsed an abortion ban. Unlike the AMA, the American College of Obstetricians and Gynecologists opposed Santorum's bill.

Dr. Nancy Dickey, chairman of the AMA board of trustees, said the group decided to support the legislation because Santorum's changes made it clear that the "accepted abortion procedure known as dilation and evacuation is not covered by the bill." Doctors referred to the so-called partial-birth procedure as intact dilation and extraction

. . . On Multiple Fronts

funds March 1. During the debate, administration and abortion rights supporters in Congress succeeded in shifting the focus to the urgent need for family planning in developing countries and away from the emotionally charged issue of abortion.

The House passed the legislation Feb. 13, on a 220-209 vote, and the Senate cleared it Feb. 25, by a vote of 53-46. Clinton signed the measure into law Feb. 28 (PL 105-3) *(House vote 22, p. H-8; Senate vote 13, p. S-4; appropriations, p. 9-40)*

• **Treasury, Postal Service appropriations.** The fiscal 1998 Treasury, Postal Service spending bill, signed into law Oct. 10 (HR 2378 — PL 105-61), continued for a third year a ban on the use of federal employee health plans to pay for abortions, except in cases of rape or incest, or to protect the life of the woman. The abortion ban had been included in the bill from 1984 to 1993, when Clinton took office and lifted it. The restriction was reinstituted in the fiscal 1996 bill.

The Senate added the language during floor action on its version of the fiscal 1998 bill, approving an amendment by Mike DeWine, R-Ohio, by a vote of 54-45 on June 22. The same day, House appropriators adopted a similar amendment by Appropriations Committee Chairman Robert L. Livingston, R-La., during their subcommittee markup of the bill. *(Vote 190, p. S-34; appropriations, p. 9-71)*

• **Labor, HHS appropriations.** The fiscal 1998 spending bill for the departments of Labor and Health and Human Services (HHS), signed into law Nov. 13 (HR 2264 — PL 105-78), expanded the traditional ban on federally funded abortions to cover managed care plans offered under Medicaid.

The ban — known as the Hyde amendment after its author, Rep. Henry J. Hyde, R-Ill. — barred federal funding of abortion except in cases of rape or incest or to save the woman's life. The expanded version specified that Medicaid funds could not be used either to pay for abortions or to pay for health plans that covered abortions. The exceptions for rape, incest or danger to the life of the woman remained.

The House added the expanded language during floor action on the bill Sept. 11. The amendment, offered by Hyde, was adopted by a vote of 270-150. The Senate gave voice vote approval the same day to a similar amendment by John Ashcroft, R-Mo. *(House vote 388, p. H-116; appropriations, p. 9-50)*

• **Defense authorization.** The fiscal 1998 defense authorization bill, signed into law Nov. 18 (HR 1119 — PL 105-85) continued a ban on abortions in overseas military hospitals, even if the woman offered to pay for the procedure herself. Both chambers had included the language in their versions of the bill. The House on June 19 defeated an amendment by Jane Harman, D-Calif., that would have repealed the prohibition. The vote was 196-224. On July 10, the Senate rejected a similar amendment by Patty Murray, D-Wash., by a vote of 48-51. *(House vote 217, p. H-70; Senate vote 167, p. S-30; defense authorization, p. 8-3)*

• **Budget reconciliation.** As part of the budget-reconciliation bill signed into law Aug 5 (HR 2015 — PL 105-33), Congress created a $20 billion program to help states expand health insurance to approximately half the nation's 10 million uninsured children. The bill made the Hyde amendment a permanent feature of the program. The language prohibiting federal funding for abortions except in cases of rape or incest or to save the woman's life was included in both the House- and Senate-passed versions of the bill. *(Children's health initiative, p. 6-3)*

• **'Partial birth' abortion.** For the second time in two years, Congress cleared a bill to outlaw a controversial procedure known as "partial birth" abortion that was used to terminate pregnancies in the second and third trimesters. As he had in 1996, Clinton vetoed the bill. *(Abortion procedure ban, p. 6-12)*

The Senate passed the bill (HR 1122) May 20 by a vote of 64-36 , three short of the 67 needed to override the anticipated presidential veto. The House cleared it Oct. 8, 296-132. Clinton vetoed the measure Oct. 10. *(Senate vote 71, p. S-15; House vote 500, p. H-152; text, p. D-43)*

The board's decision was confirmed in June by the group's governing House of Delegates. The decision ran counter to action in December 1996, when the delegates had declined to vote on the partial-birth issue, calling instead for a study of late-term pregnancy "terminations and circumstances." That study, released just as the Senate focused on Santorum's bill, made it clear that the AMA was not endorsing any specific legislation.

AMA spokesman James H. Stacey rejected allegations made by bill opponents that the association supported the bill in exchange for favorable treatment, such as relief for physicians, in separate budget-reconciliation legislation (HR 2015). Congress was determining which Medicare providers would get lower reimbursements as part of the plan to carve $115 billion in net savings from Medicare by 2002. *(Medicare, p. 6-3)*

"Nothing like that was ever discussed," Stacey said. Santorum, who consulted with AMA officials in crafting his changes, concurred: "The word Medicare never came up in any discussion we ever had," he said.

House Committee

The House Judiciary Committee approved the bill (HR 929 — H Rept 105-24) March 12 on a party-line vote of 20-11, after defeating a series of Democratic amendments aimed at softening the proposed ban.

The committee-approved bill was similar to the vetoed 1996 measure, but it specifically stated that the procedure could be performed to save a woman whose life was endangered by the pregnancy itself. It also contained provisions to prevent a prospective father who had abused or abandoned the woman from suing the person performing the abortion.

The Judiciary Committee markup was largely a display of partisan differences that portended another bitter fight over the issue.

The panel gave voice vote approval to two amendments by Jerrold Nadler, D-N.Y., that added the language barring a man who abused or abandoned a woman from suing the doctor who performed her partial-birth abortion.

But other amendments were beaten back on party-line

votes. The principal Democratic alternative, offered by Robert C. Scott of Virginia, would have banned the procedure in question only after the fetus was viable and only if the health of the woman was not an issue.

The Scott amendment reflected Clinton's position and, according to Democrats, was necessary to make the bill acceptable to the courts. "Time after time," Barney Frank, D-Mass., told his GOP colleagues, "you reject attempts to make the bill constitutional or passable."

But abortion opponents called the amendment a sham that would do nothing new to limit abortions. "[This] phony ban would allow the 4,000 or more partial-birth abortions that are performed annually on perfectly healthy babies of perfectly healthy mothers," said Douglas Johnson, legislative director of the National Right to Life Committee.

The amendment was rejected, 13-18.

An amendment offered by Sheila Jackson-Lee, D-Texas that would have granted an exception for the woman's health but would not have limited the ban to viable fetuses was rejected, 13-18, largely along party lines.

Amendments by Frank and Nadler to limit the liability of doctors performing partial-birth abortions were defeated, as was a Jackson-Lee proposal to replace the word "infant" in the bill text with "fetus."

House Floor Action

The House passed the partial-birth abortion ban March 20 by a vote of 295-136, a margin wide enough to easily override the expected veto. Rather than taking up the committee-approved bill, the GOP leadership chose to substitute a version (HR 1122) that was the same as the vetoed 1996 bill. *(Vote 65, p. H-20)*

Three members, apparently persuaded by the Fitzsimmons revelation, switched their votes from 1996 to support the bill: Christopher Shays, R-Conn., Rodney Frelinghuysen, R-N.J., and Sue W. Kelly, R-N.Y.

Peter J. Visclosky, D-Ind., also changed his vote, but he was not a new switcher — he had changed his mind earlier and voted in September 1996 to override Clinton's veto. Martin Frost, D-Texas, switched his vote the other way to oppose the bill.

Under the bill, doctors who performed partial-birth abortions could face fines and up to two years in prison. The woman would be exempt from criminal penalties, but the prospective father could sue the doctor for damages if he was married to the woman at the time of the abortion.

"This bill tramples on *Roe v. Wade*," said abortion-rights supporter Nita M. Lowey, D-N.Y.

Anti-abortion lawmakers chose to resurrect the 1996 bill partly because they felt it had gained momentum following Fitzsimmons' public admission that he had lied when he said the procedure was performed rarely and usually only on deformed fetuses.

Some bill supporters challenged the need for the exception to save the woman's life — which was part of the committee-approved bill — maintaining that the procedure was not performed to do so. "It's done for the convenience of an abortionist. It is never done for any other reason," said Tom Coburn, R-Okla., a physician.

Also, since HR 1122 was identical to the version that had been introduced in the Senate (S 6), substituting it for the committee bill was expected to speed things up by eliminating the need for a House-Senate conference.

Abortion opponents tried to keep the floor debate focused on the procedure. "This is about the killing of an infant. It's time to put an end to this barbaric procedure," said Jim Bunning, R-Ky. "Don't lose sight of the focus of this debate: The horrible procedure known as partial-birth abortion," said Sue Myrick, R-N.C. "We are not talking about the general issue of abortion in this debate."

Ban opponents used the key concept of viability to push an alternative measure that had been defeated in committee. Backed by Steny H. Hoyer, D-Md., and James C. Greenwood, R-Pa., the proposal would have allowed any procedure before viability, but banned all post-viability abortions except those needed to save the woman's life or protect her from serious adverse health conditions. "The issue isn't how it is performed, but when it is performed," Greenwood said.

Hoyer tried to send the bill back to committee with instructions to substitute his proposal, but the motion was ruled out of order as not germane. He made another motion to appeal the ruling, but it was tabled (killed), 265-165. *(Vote 63, p. H-20)*

Frank also tried to send the measure back to committee, with narrower instructions. His proposal would have inserted a health exception into the bill covering "life-endangering physical conditions caused by or arising from the pregnancy itself, or to avert serious adverse long-term physical health consequences to the mother." The House rejected his motion, 149-282. *(Vote 64, p. H-20)*

Senate Floor Action

The Senate passed a revised version of the House bill May 20, 64-36. Supporters scored a net gain of 10 votes compared with the December 1995 Senate tally of 54-44, but they were still three votes shy of the 67-vote majority needed to override the promised veto. *(Vote 71, p. S-15)*

Senators who reversed their stance from 1995 and supported rather than opposed the bill included Minority Leader Tom Daschle, D-S.D., Robert C. Byrd, D-W.Va., and Ernest F. Hollings, D-S.C. Daschle and Hollings were up for re-election in 1998, and Byrd faced re-election in 2000. Additional support came from some newly elected Republicans.

Patrick J. Leahy, D-Vt., and Arlen Specter, R-Pa., also flipped their votes to "yes" from the "no" votes they cast in 1995, but both had signaled the switch in September 1996 when they voted to override Clinton's veto of the ban.

Santorum's Changes

Before the bill reached the floor May 14, Santorum, who had sponsored the original Senate bill (S 6) made what he termed "technical" changes to broaden the bill's appeal. They included a clarification of the procedure covered in the bill and provisions aimed at shielding doctors from criminal penalties if they used the procedure in a medical emergency to save a woman's life.

Santorum's efforts won the endorsement of the AMA on the eve of the floor vote. The AMA's backing was not enough to win a veto-proof majority for the bill, but it was a factor in some senators' decisions. Byrd cited the AMA in his floor statement explaining his vote for the bill. Dale Bumpers, D-Ark., said the endorsement influenced him, although he ultimately voted against the measure.

But others, including John H. Chafee, R-R.I., said the AMA had no impact on their opposition to the bill. "I'm just opposed to Congress getting into these things," he said. Chafee termed the AMA's announcement "odd," in part because of its timing. "Where have they been? . . . They didn't do it before the House [vote]," he said.

Barbara A. Mikulski, D-Md., viewed the endorsement with

suspicion. "Is the AMA worried about saving lives or saving doctors?" she asked. She also joined some other senators who expressed frustration over the lack of any middle ground. "What bothers me is the rigidity of both the right and the left on the issue," Mikulski said.

In a floor statement after the vote, Daschle said the debate had become muddied. "In spite of the personal nature of this debate, its complexity . . . and its seriousness, this issue has become politicized to the extent that much of the rhetoric has substantially diminished the potential for real discourse," he said.

Daschle warned that failure to find a middle ground in Congress would leave key decisions to the Supreme Court. He predicted that the court would find the bill's constitutionality questionable, which will "certainly force those unwilling to compromise now to a more conciliatory position later."

Emotionally Charged Debate

As HR 1122 made its way to the Senate floor, abortion opponents turned up the pressure with a media campaign targeting senators who opposed the Santorum bill but were considered most likely to change their minds. Abortion rights supporters battled back with their own ad push and an intensive lobbying effort on Capitol Hill.

As the debate began May 14, three camps formed: Santorum led the campaign to back his basic bill, while Daschle, on the one hand, and California Democrats Barbara Boxer and Dianne Feinstein, on the other, offered separate proposals to soften the ban.

Santorum and other abortion opponents maintained that the partial-birth procedure was violent and unnecessary. In graphic detail, Santorum outlined the procedure, illustrating his remarks with pictures of a fetus undergoing the partial-birth process. "We can't hide anymore from the truth of what's happening out there," Santorum said. "It's killing a little baby that hasn't hurt anyone, that just wants a chance."

The debate veered from such impassioned moments to adamant assertions that women and their doctors should always be the ultimate arbiters when deciding what procedures were used and when. "It is the height of ego, to me, to decide we're going to be not only lawmakers but doctors," Boxer said.

Both sides used recent reports from various medical groups to back up their views. Both relayed the personal stories of infants and their mothers, and how the decision to have a partial-birth abortion or decline the procedure had changed their lives forever.

Daschle's Amendment

Daschle offered an alternative that proposed to outlaw all abortions for a viable fetus, except in cases where the woman's life was in danger or to prevent any "grievous injury" to her physical health. Daschle described it as a compromise that would narrow the health exception for a late-term abortion.

Abortion opponents said Daschle's measure would do nothing to curb the procedure, because the health exception would be interpreted broadly anyway. "It is a sham," Douglas Johnson, legislative director of the National Right to Life Committee, wrote in a letter to senators. "A vote for this political gimmick will not stand the test of time."

Marty Dannenfelser, director of government relations for the Family Research Council, said Daschle's amendment "would not deal with 90 percent of the partial-birth abortions done in America."

Daschle disagreed. "Anybody that would read my amendment would know that calling my amendment a loophole is as far off the mark as you can get," he said. "We tie it down as tightly as we can to lifesaving circumstances or to circumstances where the health of the mother is at stake in a very, very grievous sense." He said that under his proposal, mental anguish would have to manifest itself in a physical manner in order to qualify as seriously threatening to a woman's health or life.

Tom Harkin, D-Iowa, who voted for Daschle's amendment, termed it "the moderate center that so many of us are looking for."

Daschle argued that senators should back his amendment because it would outlaw all abortion procedures on a viable fetus, while Santorum's bill focused on one procedure. "It is the best, tightest, toughest language that we can come up with," Daschle said.

Santorum countered that Daschle's bill was "no ban, either" because it would allow physicians wide latitude in deciding when the procedure was needed.

Johnson of the Right to Life Committee said Daschle's proposal would have little real impact on curbing late-term abortions and called the amendment a trick "that would have allowed partial-birth abortion on demand."

Critics Say Abortion Ban Incompatible With *Roe*

The Supreme Court's 1973 ruling in *Roe v. Wade* struck down all state laws banning abortion. The 7-2 ruling vastly extended the constitutional right of personal privacy — a right never explicitly mentioned in the Constitution — to include a woman's right to end a pregnancy.

Some critics of the bill to ban so-called partial-birth abortions (HR 1122) argued that the measure could be interpreted as unconstitutional under the *Roe* decision for two reasons.

First, the bill sought to ban an abortion procedure that was performed in the second trimester of pregnancy, before the fetus was viable, or could live outside the womb. *Roe* prohibited government intervention in abortions before the fetus was viable — although the ruling did not define when viability occurred. Second, in banning the procedure in the third trimester as well, the bill failed to include an exception for the woman's health.

The following is a summary of the court's decision in *Roe v. Wade*:

The ruling prohibited government intervention in abortions in the first trimester of pregnancy, holding that the state had no compelling interest in interfering with the decision. In the second trimester, the ruling recognized a state interest in protecting the health of the woman. States could, for example, pass laws requiring that abortions be performed by a doctor or other licensed professional. In the third trimester, when the fetus was viable, the *Roe* ruling recognized a state interest in protecting the fetus. It said states could ban third-trimester abortions, except when they were necessary to protect the life or health of the woman. A related ruling defined "health" broadly, to include a variety of physical and psychological factors.

Before the vote, Daschle's campaign got a boost from Clinton. White House spokesman Mike McCurry said Daschle's bill was consistent with Clinton's own record as governor of Arkansas, when he signed legislation barring third-trimester abortions with "the appropriate exception for life or health of the mother."

Daschle's amendment failed May 15 by a vote of 36-64. *(Vote 70, p. S-14)*

After the vote, which Daschle had predicted would be close, he said May 16: "At one point, I think we had more than 40 votes, but there was intense lobbying throughout the day, and as a result of that effort, we came up short. . . . We had the impression that we were going to get a lot more Republican support than we did. And my sense is that they were feeling a lot of pressure not to leave the party, and they were successful."

Boxer-Feinstein Amendment

Daschle maintained that his amendment fell within the parameters of *Roe*, but Boxer and Feinstein disagreed. They proposed banning post-viability abortions except to save the woman's life or protect her health, saying this was a broader health exception than Daschle's. Their proposal, which in essence would have provided the same scope for abortion as *Roe*, failed May 15, 28-72. *(Vote 69, p. S-14)*

Feinstein said Santorum's bill intentionally included a "vague definition" of partial-birth abortion because its intent was to "essentially stop second- and third- trimester abortions with no consideration for the woman's health."

Santorum, however, had consistently said he believed that the procedure was never necessary to save a woman's life. "There is never a case where this procedure has to be performed to protect the life of the mother. Period," Santorum said in floor debate.

Senate Majority Leader Trent Lott, R-Miss., said some middle ground was possible. "There are some aspects of [Daschle's amendment] that are worth considering, maybe in some other form, maybe free-standing later on, maybe as part of another bill," Lott said.

But Lott said that Daschle's proposal, itself, was not the ticket. "It's too broad, that's the problem." Lott said. "Still, it's movement for a Democrat, and I don't want to dismiss that."

For his part, Daschle also signaled a willingness to discuss alternatives but stressed, "I will not compromise on the issue of health. . . . I think it's important to emphasize that we can't compromise on some fundamental constitutional principles, including health and the rights of women prior to viability."

Final Action/Veto

The House easily accepted the Senate changes, clearing the revised bill, 296-132, on Oct. 8. *(Vote 500, p. H-152)*

Clinton vetoed the bill Oct. 10, saying he was objecting for the same reason he had in 1996, namely that the bill did not allow an exception for the health of the woman. *(Text, D-43)*

Charles T. Canady, R-Fla., who led the House floor fight to endorse the Senate changes, said he did not expect the House to vote on the override until 1998. He said the House had voted on the Senate revisions because leaders wanted to "move forward with this phase" of the debate.

Lott sounded more optimistic about a vote before the year was out, saying he saw "a real opportunity" to override the veto. However, bill supporters were unable to secure the last few votes, and the issue was put off until 1998. ■

Bipartisan FDA Overhaul Enacted

Republicans saw their longtime goal of streamlining the Food and Drug Administration's (FDA) regulatory process come to fruition as they worked with Democrats and the Clinton administration to write a bill that easily cleared Congress at the end of the session. President Clinton signed the bill into law Nov. 21 (S 830 — PL 105-115) with a host of members from both parties looking on.

With regulatory oversight of nearly one-third of the products in the U.S. marketplace, the FDA often spent years testing and retesting prescription drugs, medical devices and foods. Republicans and some Democrats argued that the painstaking product studies had kept life-improving remedies and foods from reaching the U.S. market as quickly as similar products in other countries, causing hardship for consumers and manufacturers.

The bill's prescription for a speedier FDA combined the use of other federal agencies and private consultants to review some products, with a renewed focus on testing medical devices for their specific intended use.

A similar but more strident bill (S 1477) introduced in the 104th Congress never made it further than committee in either chamber because of GOP fights with Democrats and affected industries over how far to go in remaking the FDA.

Republicans avoided a similar fate for the 1997 bill by attaching FDA overhaul plans to the reauthorization of the popular Prescription Drug User Fee Act (PL 102-571), which was due to expire Oct. 1. The user fees, which drug companies paid annually and upon the submission of drugs, had enabled the FDA to increase its work force, significantly reducing the time it took to review new drugs.

By tying their FDA overhaul plans to a five-year reauthorization of the drug user fee law, Republicans managed to get more support from Democrats and the industry from the outset. In addition, they agreed to tone down some of their proposals to speed up the review of prescription drugs, medical devices and food packaging, and they compromised on a number of controversial issues early in the process.

Their flexibility paid off. Both chambers passed the final bill by voice vote Nov. 9.

Bill Highlights

The bill made a host of changes to the FDA, many of which broadened the scope of pilot projects already in place. The legislation:

• **Prescription drugs.** Reauthorized the drug user fee act, increasing the fees and requiring the FDA to try to speed the pre-review, or development, stage for drugs, which typically was about seven years.

The bill also made treatments not yet approved by the FDA widely available to patients with serious conditions. Previously, only cancer patients or people with HIV and AIDS were eligible for such expedited help. And it established procedures to speed up the review of drugs with the potential to help patients who had conditions or diseases for which there were few existing treatments.

• **Medical devices.** Expanded a pilot program that allowed outside groups, such as university laboratories, to evaluate medical devices submitted to the FDA for approval. Manufacturers could contract with FDA-accredited consultants to review some products that manufacturers said were "substantially equivalent" to ones already on the market, though the FDA would still make the final decision. Risky medical products were exempt from such outside reviews.

The bill required the FDA to focus on the intended use listed on manufacturers' labels when reviewing medical devices for which the manufacturer said a "substantial equivalent" already existed.

- **Food labeling.** Allowed food manufacturers to use health and nutrient claims made by federal scientific agencies, such as the Centers for Disease Control and Prevention, on their packaging, unless the FDA objected.

BOXSCORE

FDA Overhaul — S 830 (HR 1411). The bill streamlined Food and Drug Administration (FDA) procedures for regulating food, medical devices and pharmaceuticals, and reauthorized the 1992 Prescription Drug User Fee Act.

Reports: S Rept 105-43, H Repts 105-310, 105-306, 105-307; conference report, H Rept 105-399.

KEY ACTION

Sept. 24 — Senate passed S 830, 98-2.

Oct. 7 — House passed S 830 by voice vote, after substituting the text of HR 1411.

Nov. 9 — Senate adopted the conference report by voice vote. **House** cleared S 830 by voice vote.

Nov. 21 — President signed S 830 — PL 105-115.

Background

Founded in 1909 as a bureau of the Agriculture Department, the FDA's original mandate was to examine foods and drugs after they went to market. In 1938, Congress passed the Federal Food, Drug and Cosmetic Act, which made the FDA responsible for assessing a product's safety before it reached consumers. Increasingly strict federal regulations in subsequent years gave the agency more and more authority to control access to the marketplace.

Funded at $887.6 million in fiscal 1997, the FDA set food standards, inspected plants and laboratories, and regulated product labels for clarity and accuracy. It also tested all new drugs and medical devices before they were marketed and monitored them after they were approved. The agency estimated that 25 cents of every U.S. dollar was spent on products it regulated.

Demands for Change

It was the agency's process for approving new drugs and medical devices that drove critics to demand an overhaul.

Aggressive Republican deregulators in both chambers said Congress and the FDA had gone too far, that the process was interminable. They said the FDA had moved beyond its role as consumer protector and instead acted as an abusive regulator that denied the public valuable, sometimes lifesaving, products.

Although most Republicans toned down their rhetoric in the 105th Congress, cognizant that it might alienate Democrats they wanted on their side, they still had plenty about which to complain.

The FDA was required by statute to act within 180 days on applications to market most new drugs and devices. But that deadline was so rarely met that it had become almost irrelevant. In 1992, for instance, the average approval time for a new drug was 19 months. That dropped to 15 months in 1996, largely because of extra reviewers hired as a result of the user fee act.

Even before drug manufacturers could apply for approval of a new product — starting the 180-day clock — they had to go through a much lengthier approval process that could last many years. It involved "pre-clinical testing" of the drug on animals, followed by three phases of clinical tests on humans.

Manufacturers complained that after the FDA agreed to an approval process, the agency raised the bar, requiring more data or tests. As a result, Republicans said, it took an average of 12 years and $359 million to bring a new drug from the test tube to the patient.

The FDA's Response

The FDA had tried to neutralize its critics by healing itself, rather than submitting to a broad congressional overhaul.

Enactment of the prescription drug user fee helped by giving the agency more money and staff. The General Accounting Office said the equivalent of 700 full-time employees had been added since 1992; the House Commerce Committee and the FDA put the estimate at 600. The agency had a total of 9,500 employees. The user fee law also required the FDA to review increasingly higher percentages of new drug applications within one year, which was still more than twice the statutory time limit. *(1992 Almanac, p. 418)*

In 1995, then-FDA Commissioner David A. Kessler boasted that the agency was far exceeding the standards set in 1992. The FDA also simplified the approval process for most biological drugs — such as vaccines and blood products — by eliminating the need to license the manufacturing facilities. And the agency cut the backlog of pending applications for medical devices, which included products ranging from tongue depressors to pacemakers.

The FDA also made efforts to get treatment to the sickest patients more quickly — for example, allowing patients with cancer and AIDS to use possibly life-sustaining drugs that had not yet been approved. And, in a small pilot project, it allowed some private contractors to test medical devices to see if they were "substantially equivalent" to another product already on the market.

Developing Legislation

Though Republicans wanted broader changes, they could do little as long as the GOP was the minority party in Congress. But when Republicans took control of both chambers in 1995, they put an FDA overhaul high on their list.

After hundreds of hours of hearings, however, action on the Republican FDA bills stalled at the end of the 104th Congress. Members disagreed on the scope of the proposed changes, and the support of some industry groups waned. *(1996 Almanac, p. 6-45)*

When the 105th Congress began, FDA reformers took a new tack, harnessing an FDA overhaul to reauthorization of the expiring prescription drug user fee law.

Senate Labor and Human Resources Committee Chairman James M. Jeffords, R-Vt., started the ball rolling by announcing in June that he would attach an FDA streamlining bill to a user fee reauthorization.

House Commerce Committee Chairman Thomas J. Bliley Jr., R-Va., agreed that the two issues should be linked, though he was slower to make such commitments public, in part because he had delegated responsibility for developing an FDA measure to a cadre of junior Republicans, including Richard M. Burr of North Carolina, James C. Greenwood of Pennsylvania, Scott L. Klug of Wisconsin, Edward Whitfield of Kentucky and Joe L. Barton of Texas.

Barton and Anna G. Eshoo, D-Calif., got a head start on the others by introducing a bipartisan measure (HR 1710) early on that proposed restructuring the FDA's reviews of medical devices. Burr, Greenwood, Klug and others subsequently developed the prescription drugs section (HR 1411), and Whitfield assembled a measure on food regulation (HR 2469).

Senate Committee

The Senate Labor and Human Resources Committee took up Jeffords' bill (S 830) the weeks of June 9 and 16, approving it June 18 by a vote of 14-4 (S Rept 105-43). Half the panel's Democrats and all 10 Republicans voted for it.

The four Democrats who supported the bill — Christopher J. Dodd of Connecticut, Barbara A. Mikulski of Maryland, Paul Wellstone of Minnesota and Patty Murray of Washington — also helped in the adoption of a handful of Republican amendments during the markup.

"The strong bipartisan vote shows that this is a moderate proposal which will ensure we have a strong FDA into the future," Jeffords said. "The FDA needs us to get on with it," said Mikulski. "The American people need us to get on with it."

Edward M. Kennedy of Massachusetts, the committee's ranking minority member, led the opposition, offering a glimpse of the problems that lay ahead for the bill. While he said it was imperative to reauthorize the drug user fee law, which he had cosponsored, he said he would let the law die before accepting some of the bill's contentious proposals. "Timely reauthorization is tremendously important, but it is not so important that Americans should accept the threats to public health included in this bill," he said.

Joining him in voting against the legislation were Democrats Tom Harkin of Iowa, Jeff Bingaman of New Mexico and Jack Reed of Rhode Island.

Committee approval was eased by a series of bipartisan compromises, which helped reduce the number of potential amendments from 68 on June 11 to 49 the week of June 16 and to just 11, including technical changes, during about three hours of debate June 18.

Donna E. Shalala, the secretary of Health and Human Services (HHS), indicated a willingness to work with the committee on the FDA bill to ensure renewal of the user fee law. Shalala spelled out the Clinton administration's problems with the bill in a June 11 letter to Jeffords, but stopped short of threatening a veto. Among the provisions the administration opposed were planned changes in food labeling and the expanded use of third-party reviews of medical devices.

Food Labeling Claims

The most contentious issue for the committee involved prospective changes in food labeling, which pitted Kennedy against Judd Gregg, R-N.H., in several high-volume exchanges.

The bill included a proposal to amend the 1990 Nutrition Labeling and Education Act (PL 101-535) to allow the use on food labels of health claims approved by "an authoritative scientific body of the United States government" other than the FDA — such as the Centers for Disease Control and Prevention, the National Institutes of Health and the National Academy of Sciences or its subdivisions.

Under the original bill, a food manufacturer would have had 90 days to notify the FDA of plans to use such a health claim on a label, time for the agency to either accept or dispute the statement. The committee agreed by voice vote to a modification offered by Gregg increasing the time frame from 90 days to 120 days.

Several committee Republicans complained that the FDA had dragged its feet in approving health claims. They cited a four-year lag from the time the Public Health Service in 1992 announced the benefits of folic acid in preventing birth defects, such as spina bifida, until the FDA approved the use of the information on food labels in March 1996. "We want to get this kind of information out, and the best way is through food labeling," said Susan Collins, R-Maine.

Kennedy attacked the provision and Gregg's modification, charging that it would undermine the food labeling act and confuse consumers. Gregg responded that the agencies that would approve the claims were premier, credible agencies that made significant decisions on health issues, and that the FDA would be authorized to dispute the claims.

A Kennedy amendment to strike the provision failed, 5-13, with Dodd, Harkin and Mikulski joining the Republicans in opposition.

Non-Prescription Warning Labels

Another Gregg amendment, to establish national uniformity for warning labels on non-prescription drugs and cosmetics, also touched off a lengthy and sometimes angry debate.

Kennedy argued that the amendment would pre-empt a state's ability to attach such labels to over-the-counter drugs or cosmetics. Gregg said it was not a pre-emption and that a state could change the status of a drug to require a prescription if it wanted to ensure that a warning accompanied the medication.

Murray questioned whether states could continue requiring "Mr. Yuk" poison stickers on items such as Tylenol to warn children against consuming the drug without adult supervision. Gregg promised to work with Murray to ensure that states continued to have that right. The Gregg amendment prevailed, 15-3, with opposition from Kennedy, Murray and Mike DeWine, R-Ohio.

Third-Party Review of Medical Devices

Democrats also objected to a proposal in the bill to expand an FDA pilot program that farmed out reviews of low-risk medical devices such as surgical gloves or electronic thermometers. They warned about potential conflicts of interest, including the possibility that outside experts would approve products in hopes of continuing a potentially lucrative business arrangement.

Under the bill, a manufacturer would notify the FDA that it wanted its product reviewed by an accredited outside expert. The FDA would select two organizations, and the manufacturer would contract with one for review of the device. The FDA would have the final say on the recommendations of the outside expert.

Harkin wanted to require the FDA to review the compensation agreement between the manufacturer and the third party. But Daniel R. Coats, R-Ind., argued that the FDA already had that authority and warned against creating another layer of bureaucracy to handle a pre-approval process for contracts. Harkin modified his amendment to say the FDA "may" review agreements, but Coats remained firmly opposed, and the amendment failed on an 8-10 party-line vote.

An amendment by Harkin to exempt some more sophisticated devices, such as heart valves and pacemakers, from the possibility of third-party review failed on a vote of 7-11, with Dodd joining Republicans in opposition.

The committee also rejected, 6-12, an amendment by Kennedy that would have imposed civil penalties on companies that failed to complete the required final stage of research trials on an approved drug.

Senate Floor Action

Despite the overwhelming support for the bill in committee, Kennedy's concerns came back to haunt Republicans. Jeffords delayed floor action until the week of Sept. 1 in hopes of assuaging Kennedy and the Clinton administration, but when that seemed impossible they finally decided to move forward without them. Even then, it took two weeks of debate before the Senate passed the measure Sept. 24 by a vote of 98-2. The "no" votes were cast by Kennedy and Reed. *(Vote 256, p. S-43)*

The decision to go ahead on the bill seemed validated on Sept. 5, the first day of debate, when the vast majority of Democrats joined all of the Republicans in voting 89-5 to invoke cloture, or stem debate, on a motion to proceed to the bill. The four Democrats who joined Kennedy in voting against cloture were Daniel K. Akaka of Hawaii, Max Cleland of Georgia, Richard J. Durbin of Illinois, and Reed. "Today is just the first step, but it could hardly be a better one," Jeffords said afterward. *(Vote 220, p. S-38)*

The chamber then began an eight-hour debate on proceeding to the bill, kicking off two weeks of floor discussion. Jeffords and other committee Republicans had not expected such a drawn-out attack. They had spent months during the summer trying to negotiate with Kennedy and HHS, managing to reach agreement on about three dozen changes to the bill, including alterations to several key provisions.

Among the sections amended was the proposal to expand an existing pilot program that allowed third-party review of low-risk medical devices. The negotiators left the expansion in place, but agreed to reserve review of so-called Class III devices — those with the most potential for serious health effects — for the FDA alone. However, Kennedy and Shalala said the changes to the bill did not go far enough. They continued to oppose several provisions, and Shalala said she would recommend a veto unless those items were removed.

Compromise on Cosmetic Labeling

The main sticking point was the plan to establish national uniformity in warning labels on non-prescription drugs and cosmetics. In charged floor debate replete with graphic photos of peeling feet and deformed faces, Kennedy argued that having the FDA regulate such products — a job that had been left largely to the states — would endanger the products' consumers, most of whom were women. He said the FDA had neither the legal authority nor adequate staffing to accurately regulate cosmetics.

But Jeffords said many states did not efficiently regulate cosmetics, and that many consumers were going unprotected. He also agreed to "grandfather in" existing state laws regarding the products.

Kennedy, Gregg and the Clinton administration finally forged an agreement the week of Sept. 11 under which states could continue to regulate cosmetics as they had been doing. But the FDA also could issue warning labels, and states could not issue their own labels in cases in which the FDA already had ruled on the need for labels.

Kennedy said he was pleased with the compromise, in part because the FDA had rarely issued cosmetics regulations that conflicted with those of the states. Republicans were happy that it included their plans for national standards on cosmetics and non-prescription drugs.

Kennedy Fights Focus on Intended Use

But there were other things on Kennedy's mind. He had not succeeded in changing a provision that would require the FDA, when evaluating a lower-risk medical device "substantially equivalent" to a device already approved, to judge the device only by the intended use described on the manufacturer's label. The FDA already focused its evaluations on the intended use, but sometimes considered other factors, bill supporters said. The provision prompted Kennedy to again stall the Senate, this time the week of Sept. 15.

Kennedy said he thought it was "really the last remaining issue," but Republicans were skeptical. "Many of us are concerned that even if this issue is resolved, we will suddenly have a new issue appear" said Coats. On Sept. 16, the Senate voted 94-4 to invoke cloture, thereby preventing a filibuster. *(Vote 239, p. S-41)*

Bill supporters said the provision that Kennedy objected to would not interfere with the FDA's ability to judge a product for safety and efficacy, nor would it stop the FDA from rejecting a device that was not "substantially equivalent" to the original device.

Kennedy argued that the provision should be amended to specifically give the FDA the ability to investigate whether the label was "false or misleading." Without such words, Kennedy maintained, the bill "will create a loophole through which unscrupulous manufacturers of medical devices can drive a truck." Kennedy cited the example of a company that he said misrepresented its product to the FDA by submitting a needle intended to remove breast tumors as "substantially equivalent" to a needle the FDA had approved to take small samples of tissue to test for cancer.

Dodd argued that if Kennedy's language were added to the bill, "then there's no end to the studies that could be required of manufacturers" because the FDA could "look into the crystal ball" to come up with any number of additional uses and force manufacturers to produce data on how the device would stand up.

An attempt by Kennedy and Reed to alter the medical device language was tabled (killed) Sept. 23 by a vote of 65-35. *(Vote 254, p. S-43)*

The Senate also defeated 40-59, an amendment by Durbin that would have imposed conflict of interest standards on private parties chosen to evaluate medical devices under the bill's third-party review provisions. A second Durbin amendment, defeated 39-61, would have retained existing law requiring the FDA and medical device manufacturers to keep lists of patients who had had devices implanted. *(Votes 252, 253, p. S-43)*

Faced with a strong Senate vote to retain the provision he found most objectionable, Kennedy finally relented, dropping a last chance to delay the bill. Although outnumbered throughout the negotiations, he had nevertheless succeeded in modifying dozens of provisions, including such high GOP priorities as national standards for cosmetic regulations. "If you get 19 of 20 . . . you ought to be very pleased," Jeffords reminded him.

In fact, the concessions made by Jeffords and other moderates to get a bipartisan bill risked the loss of some conservative GOP support. Coats termed the resulting measure "watered down," saying, "It's no secret I would have preferred a stronger bill." But he and other conservatives said the attempts to streamline the FDA, reduce product review times and make new treatments more readily available to the seriously ill, were still worthwhile.

Coats signaled, however, that he would not be receptive to continued negotiations with Kennedy on the bill. "I would hope it would survive in its current form," he said. But Kennedy said he would not back down from trying to change the medical device language in conference. "I'm convinced we're absolutely correct," he said. The Clinton administration also weighed in against the provision, but dropped earlier threats of a veto.

Other Amendments

The Senate accepted by voice vote several other amendments, including two by Jeffords that addressed Democratic concerns. One added a disclaimer that nothing in the bill would limit the FDA's ability to regulate tobacco. The other removed provisions that would have exempted most manufacturers with reviews pending at the FDA from filing environmental review reports.

Tim Hutchinson, R-Ark., won voice vote approval for an amendment to allow the FDA to regulate "compounding," or drug-making, when it involved more than just a pharmacist custom-making a prescription for a patient. The amendment included standards for FDA intervention.

Pharmacy regulation generally had been left to the states, but the FDA said that some unscrupulous, makeshift drug manufacturers had been hiding behind compounding laws to shield themselves from federal requirements on ingredients and practices.

House Subcommittee

While the Senate was locked in debate over S 830, the House Commerce Committee's Health and Environment Subcommittee marked up three separate bills to revamp the FDA's prescription drug, medical device and food safety oversight programs. All three were approved in voice votes Sept. 17.

Ranking subcommittee Democrat Sherrod Brown of Ohio hailed the markup as a "James Monroe era of good feeling," while Chairman Michael Bilirakis, R-Fla., called it "a perfect illustration of what the public wants us to do."

Democrats withdrew several amendments when Republicans said they would discuss the issues further. But, following Kennedy's lead, House Democrats signalled they would be less cooperative as the bills moved forward unless Republicans compromised on such issues as the scope of medical device reviews.

"Quite honestly, I've already accommodated a lot. . . . At some point in time, there's just a philosophical difference of opinion," responded bill sponsor Barton.

- **Prescription drugs.** The first of the three bills (HR 1411) proposed to reauthorize the drug user fee law for five years and modify the FDA's oversight of prescription drugs, expediting the approval process for drugs aimed at life-threatening or serious illnesses, and allowing more seriously ill patients to gain access to medical treatments before the FDA had approved them.

Under the bill, drug companies would be allowed to share information with medical providers, pharmacies, insurance agencies, group plan managers and government agencies on some off-label uses of their drugs — uses for which the FDA had not tested the drug — if the companies met several conditions. Under existing law, manufacturers shared such information without FDA review.

The panel accepted a proposal by Peter Deutsch, D-Fla., to give makers of generic drugs the same right as would be given to other manufacturers to work out differences with FDA officials one-on-one. Frank Pallone Jr., D-N.J., won approval for a proposal to require the FDA to study the health effects of mercury in nasal sprays. Both changes were approved by voice vote.

- **Medical devices.** The second bill (HR 1710) proposed to limit FDA evaluations of medical devices to the intent submitted on the manufacturers' label. It proposed to allow FDA-accredited third-party reviewers to evaluate all medical devices, except those that would be permanently implanted or were otherwise life-sustaining, and those classified as potentially dangerous Class III devices, such as pacemakers.
- **Food labeling.** The third bill (HR 2469) proposed changing the way the FDA evaluated health and nutrient claims on foods, allowing manufacturers to use health rulings by qualified agencies other than the FDA on their labels. Qualified outside agencies would be limited to those, such as the National Institutes of Health, that dealt with scientific issues. The bill included an 18-month deadline for FDA action on proposed new labels.

The panel agreed to require the FDA to rule within 60 days of enactment on long-pending applications to use irradiation to kill food-borne pathogens in red meat. The amendment, by Greg Ganske, R-Iowa, was approved by voice vote.

House Full Committee

The House Commerce Committee took up the three separate bills Sept. 25 and 26, approving the drug and food labeling measures with little opposition the first day. But the vote on the medical device bill was put off until Sept. 26 to allow more time for a compromise.

- **Prescription drugs.** Most discussion Sept. 25 centered on the prescription drug reauthorization, which was approved, 43-0 (H Rept 105-310).

The committee adopted, 21-20, an amendment by Pallone to require that the sole manufacturer of a life-sustaining, life-supporting or preventive drug or vaccine notify the HHS secretary at least six months before it stopped making the product.

The panel rejected, 7-36, an attempt by Brown to slow implementation of the provision allowing drug companies to share more information with doctors and other health care officials on alternate uses of their drugs. Under the bill, the FDA would be charged with monitoring the information — much of it in the form of articles and peer reviews — that the companies circulated. Brown argued that the FDA was not equipped to do such research, and he proposed delaying the program until appropriators funded it properly.

Brown warned of problems like the ones that prompted drugmakers to pull two diet drugs from the market the week of Sept. 15. One of them, fenfluramine, was often prescribed in combination with another drug, phentermine, not pulled from the shelves. The FDA had approved both drugs separately, but had not tested "fen/phen" together. Subsequent studies indicated that the combination could cause heart damage. Had the bill's "off-label" provision been in effect, Brown argued, many more people could have had fen/phen prescriptions because drug company sales people would have been allowed to aggressively market off-label uses to doctors.

The committee also rejected, by voice vote, a proposal by Pallone to allow states to adopt California's Proposition 65, which required health warnings on all products that contained certain toxins.

- **Food labeling.** The food labeling bill won 43-0 approval Sept. 25 (H Rept 105-306), after the committee agreed to several amendments. The most significant was one by Bart Stupak, D-Mich., to attach a Senate provision that would require food producers to notify the FDA of the type of packaging and other surfaces that had come into contact with the food. If the FDA did not object within 120 days of receiving notification, the manufacturer could market the product. Under existing law, the FDA was required to put "food contact surfaces" through the same lengthy tests as food additives, such as dyes.

- **Medical devices.** The panel had planned to take up the medical device bill with the others Sept. 25, but Bliley put off consideration to give Barton and Eshoo more time to try to work out a compromise. Despite long odds against them, the pair managed to develop language that appeased committee Democrats. The committee approved it Sept. 26 by voice vote (H Rept 105-307).

Several Democrats, led by Henry A. Waxman of California, had objected to tying FDA evaluations of lower-risk devices to the manufacturers' intended use. They said, as Kennedy had, that consumers could be at risk if companies submitted inadequate labels.

Under the compromise, the FDA could authorize reviewers to test for other purposes if they believed there was a reasonable chance the device would be used for a purpose other than that listed on the label, and that that purpose could cause harm. The manufacturer would have to be notified of the decision and given a chance to respond. The manufacturer could continue to market the device, but the FDA could require that it include a warning that the product had not been found safe for certain uses.

If the product was judged to be safe and equivalent to other products already on the market, the FDA could allow it to go to market while it was evaluating its safety for other uses.

The Barton-Eshoo compromise won the approval of Kennedy and Reed, as well as of the FDA.

With the labeling issue resolved, panel Democrats expressed concerns about other parts of the bill, such as the proposal to allow third-party reviews of low-risk devices. Several amendments were offered, then withdrawn, with sponsors hoping their concerns would be resolved before the legislation headed to the House floor.

House Floor Action

With strong bipartisan support, the House took up a merged version of its FDA bills (HR 1411) on Oct. 7 under "suspension of the rules," an expedited floor procedure generally reserved for non-controversial legislation. After passing the measure by voice vote, the House took the procedural step of inserting the text into S 830 and passing that bill by voice vote.

The bill's appearance on the floor had been delayed while members tried to work out differences with the White House. The Clinton administration had indicated that it might consider the drug user fee act reauthorized for one year under the agriculture appropriations bill (HR 2160), which provided annual funding for the FDA. Fearful of losing the engine behind their FDA bill, Republicans scrambled to slow down the agriculture appropriations — then just two steps away from the president's desk. *(Appropriations, p. 9-5)*

Democratic backers played a major role in moving the FDA bill forward. John D. Dingell of Michigan, the ranking Democrat on the Commerce Committee, persuaded party leaders to allow the measure to pass through a legislative logjam set up to protest a lack of minority party initiatives on the House calendar.

After the House vote, Dingell credited bipartisanship for turning the bill from one "which started out . . . seriously flawed" to one which "is a good consensus arrangement." Bliley hailed it as a product of three years of work in which Republicans conferred with Democrats, the FDA, the Clinton administration, industry groups, consumer groups and others. "Congress had to act . . . with prudence and balance," Bliley said.

The measure drew only faint criticism on the floor. Waxman reiterated his concern about focusing FDA evaluations of medical devices on the manufacturer's intended use, predicting that "over the long run, we will regret that we have changed FDA law in this way." He nevertheless supported the compromise.

Dingell declared the differences between the House and Senate bills "easily resolvable." Prospects for an easy conference were further buoyed when the Clinton administration, despite some concerns, announced support for the bill Oct. 7, and Kennedy said he would accept the House compromise on the medical device testing provision.

Conference

Despite bipartisan predictions that resolving differences would take little time, the conference report was not completed until Nov. 9 (H Rept 105-399).

Though nearly two-thirds of the House and Senate bills were identical, when it came to the details, they often took different routes to the same goal, and some controversies remained. House and Senate conferees gave staff several weeks to resolve as many of the differences as possible before finally meeting Nov. 5.

With the session rapidly coming to a close, the conference committee did not have time to meet again. Instead, staff and members worked behind the scenes to iron out differences on a dozen issues, with the final details agreed to the weekend of Nov. 8-9.

Conservative Republicans, led by Coats, signaled that they preferred the Senate bill's controversial language on medical device reviews, the language Kennedy had fought against so vociferously.

In a letter to conferees Nov. 4, Shalala reiterated that she would advise Clinton to veto the bill if it included the Senate medical devices language instead of the compromise House provision. Jeffords and Bliley appealed to conservatives to accept the compromise device language in an effort to move the bill.

Most provisions in both bills made it into the final version, some with modifications. The following were among the main compromises:

- **Scope of FDA review.** The final bill required the FDA to base its evaluations on the intended use specified in the manufacturer's labeling when determining whether a medical device was substantially equivalent to one already on the market. However, it allowed the FDA to require manufacturers to include warning labels on their product if the agency believed the device would be used in another way that could cause harm.
- **Third-party reviews.** Conferees agreed to limit the types of medical devices that could be reviewed by FDA-accredited outside consultants. Besides excluding Class III medical devices — risky products such as heart-lung machines and pacemakers — and other permanent implants, the bill also exempted any less risky Class II medical devices — such as digital mammography machines — from outside review if the FDA needed clinical data to review them.

However, the FDA could only exclude a certain percentage of devices — up to 6 percent of those submitted to the FDA's main review program — from third-party evaluation because of the need for clinical information.

• **Information sharing.** The final bill allowed drug and medical device manufacturers to distribute information on uses for their products that the FDA had not yet approved, if the information came from medical journals or textbooks. The manufacturer had to agree to conduct the research necessary to submit a supplemental application to the FDA on the proposed use, and the FDA could require the manufacturer to share contrary information on the product.

• **Drug compounding.** The bill clarified the parameters under which compounding was legal and to be regulated by the states. However, it specified that pharmacists who used drugs removed from the market for safety reasons, or who regularly copied commercially available drugs, would be subject to federal regulation. Lawmakers, staff aides, the pharmacy industry and the FDA spent months negotiating the language, an early version of which appeared in the Senate bill.

• **Prescription drug user fees.** The bill increased the annual user fees that most drug manufacturers paid and fees charged upon submission of drug applications to the FDA. In exchange, the FDA would try to reduce the time it took to get drugs through the pre-review, or development, stage.

Conferees agreed to retain the existing mechanism for increasing the amount to be appropriated annually for the FDA. As in the original law, recommendations for FDA spending would be based on the lower of two inflation indicators — the Consumer Price Index or the growth in discretionary budget authority for domestic spending. The House had proposed retaining the original trigger, while the Senate bill had included a trigger that would have increased Congress' spending obligations more quickly. The administration had backed a trigger that would have increased appropriations more slowly than either version.

• **Food labeling.** Conferees agreed to allow manufacturers to use health claims from scientific federal agencies unless the FDA objected within 120 days of receiving notice of the manufacturer's intent to use the claim.

• **Cosmetic standards.** The bill allowed the FDA to create national standards, including those for labeling, for cosmetics and over-the-counter drugs. However, states could continue regulating cosmetics — and issuing warning labels — in cases in which the FDA did not act.

Final Action

The Senate took up the conference report during a rare Sunday session Nov. 9 and adopted it by voice vote. The House cleared the bill later the same day, also by voice vote.

Final debate on the measure generated no controversy as both Republicans and Democrats celebrated the bill's passage.

Bliley declared the bill would "do more to help patients than any legislation passed in decades." Even Kennedy, who had stymied action on the bill for so long, spoke in favor of the final product. "I am convinced that as a result of this legislation the health of the American people will be enhanced through faster availability of pharmaceutical drugs and medical devices," he said.

Kennedy had been won over by Jeffords' and Bliley's willingness to compromise. While conservative Republicans had wanted more stark changes, they still backed the consensus bill as a first step in their plans to revamp the FDA.

In the House, Burr said he expected Congress to revisit FDA streamlining in a few years, while Whitfield called the food section of the bill he had compiled "a responsible down payment." ■

Provisions of the FDA Overhaul

The Food and Drug Administration (FDA) overhaul, signed into law Nov. 21 (S 830 — PL 105-115), streamlined FDA procedures for regulating food, medical devices and pharmaceuticals, and reauthorized the 1992 Prescription Drug User Fee Act.

Drug User Fees

Prescription drugs went through a mazelike approval process before they reached consumers. A handful of new over-the-counter drugs were also tested in this way.

When a company developed a new drug, it first conducted "preclinical testing" during which the compound was tested on animals to determine if it was safe to test on humans. If the animal tests were successful, the company developed a blueprint for clinical trials on humans, called a protocol.

The second stage was a pre-approval process. With animal test results and its protocol in hand, the company contacted the FDA and filed an Investigational New Drug application. If the FDA accepted both the animal test results and the protocol, the company could begin a three-phase clinical-trial period.

During the first phase, the drug was tested on about 20 to 80 healthy volunteers to determine its safety, dosage range and how it was absorbed, metabolized, distributed and excreted by the body.

The second phase of the clinical trials was controlled, using about 100 to 300 volunteers afflicted with the disease targeted by the new drug, to test effectiveness and monitor side effects.

The third phase was similar, but involved about 1,000 to 3,000 patients in clinics and hospitals. Doctors tried to verify effectiveness and track reactions to long-term use.

After the clinical trials were complete, the company compiled its data and presented its case to the FDA in a New Drug Application, asserting that the new product was safe and effective.

The final stage was the approval process. While the FDA was required by law to review the application within six months, it typically took much longer. Under the 1992 law, the approval stage had decreased from an average of 19 months to 15 months. If the application was approved, the drug went to market and the FDA continued to monitor it.

The new law included provisions to:

• **Reauthorization.** Reauthorize the Prescription Drug User Fee Act of 1992 (PL 102-571), which expired Oct. 1, through Oct. 1, 2002. Under the act, drug companies paid both annual fees and fees upon submission of drugs for review. The revenue was used to hire additional FDA staff.

• **New fees.** Increase user fees by about 21 percent. The 1992 law created three types of fees. Application fees were paid by most manufacturers submitting a drug or biological product, such as a vaccine, to the FDA for review. Establishment fees were paid annually by drug companies that manufactured at least one approved prescription drug but had an application pending for another drug or a supplemental use of the marketed drug. Product fees were paid annually by those with pending applications for drug approvals.

The bill increased the fee for new drug applications from $233,000 in fiscal 1997 to $250,704 in fiscal 1998 and ultimately to $258,451 in fiscal 2002. Annual establishment fees were about half that amount, while product fees were significantly less — $14,000 in fiscal 1997. The Congressional Budget Office estimated the fees would bring in $601 million over five years.

● **Trigger.** Leave intact a "trigger" mechanism that suggested annual FDA appropriations levels. Recommended funding increases for the FDA would continue to be based on the lower of two inflation indicators: the Consumer Price Index or the growth in discretionary budget authority for domestic spending. The bill authorized $549 million in funding over five years.

● **Pre-approval process.** Pledge, in exchange for the higher fees, a reduction in the time it took the FDA to get drugs through the pre-approval process, or clinical trial phase. That process, the second of the three stages that drug companies went through when trying to move their products to market, had been taking about seven years.

Prescription Drugs

● **Pediatric studies.** Allow the secretary of Health and Human Services (HHS) to ask drug companies to study how a specific product could be used to treat children. As a reward for completing the study within the secretary's time frame, the companies would be granted six additional months of patent protection. Extending patent terms benefited the company by delaying the marketing of generic replicas.

The provision addressed a question that had long plagued parents and doctors: How much of an adult medicine should be given to a child? Few companies studied the effects of their products on children, prompting many parents to mash pills or break them in half to give children an amount commensurate with their size.

Within 180 days of the law's enactment, the HHS secretary was required to develop a list of approved drugs on which additional pediatric information might be of benefit. To receive the patent extension, drug companies had to submit the product to the FDA for review by Jan. 1, 2002. The secretary could waive that deadline if the drug was on the market before enactment, if it was included in the priority list the secretary had developed and if he or she felt it would be beneficial to have pediatric information about the drug. The secretary was required to report to Congress by Jan. 1, 2002, on the effect and adequacy of the provision.

The provision differed from a pending Clinton administration proposal to require drug manufacturers to test their products to determine proper doses for children; Clinton's plan did not include patent incentives.

● **'Fast-track' process.** Expand the FDA's "fast-track" process to expedite reviews for all new drugs and biological products, including vaccines, intended to treat life-threatening or serious conditions. The FDA already had such policies, but they chiefly benefited AIDS and cancer patients.

Manufacturers could apply to the HHS secretary to have their products considered for fast track.

The process aimed to allow certain drugs onto the market more quickly by allowing the HHS secretary to approve them if preliminary FDA assessments showed that they met certain goals (known as surrogate end points), such as reducing the amount of HIV virus in an AIDS patient's blood, but that further study was needed to determine the drug's ultimate effectiveness.

The FDA could require the manufacturer to conduct further studies and to submit proposed promotional material to the FDA at least 30 days before the material was disseminated. The agency could withdraw its approval of the product if follow-up tests indicated such action was warranted.

The HHS secretary was required to issue guidelines for the process within one year of the law's enactment and to disseminate information on the program to health care professionals and biomedical companies.

● **Clinical trials database.** Require the HHS secretary to work with the National Institutes of Health (NIH) to establish a data bank of information on clinical trials for drugs intended to treat serious or life-threatening diseases and conditions. The information was to be distributed to the public through a toll-free number and other venues.

The information provided would include a description of eligibility criteria for the trials, the trial sites and contact information for those who wanted to enroll in the trials. If manufacturers consented, the database could also include information on the results of clinical trials.

The bill required the HHS secretary to submit within two years to the Senate Labor and Human Resources Committee and the House Commerce Committee a study on whether information about medical device trials should be included in the data bank. The FDA already ran a data bank on clinical trials relating to AIDS; the National Cancer Institute ran one relating to cancer.

● **Economic benefits.** Define the detailed economic information that drugmakers and biological product manufacturers were allowed to share with managed care providers and others who selected drugs.

The bill required that the information made available be directly linked to the drug's main purpose. For instance, the maker of a drug used only to treat the symptoms of rheumatoid arthritis could not claim the prevention of deformities as part of the drug's economic benefits. Also, the information had to be based on "competent and reliable scientific evidence," but it no longer had to be substantiated by two adequate and well-controlled clinical trials.

The HHS secretary could request information on how the company devised the economic information.

The comptroller general was required to study the effects of this provision on health care delivery and consumers and to report to Congress no later than four years and six months after enactment.

● **Clinical investigations.** Allow the HHS secretary to determine that a single "adequate and well-controlled" clinical trial could provide enough information for a specific new drug approval. Previous law required the FDA to base approval on "substantial evidence of effectiveness." Officials within the FDA had differed over whether that meant one trial or at least two. The new law specified that one investigation could be "substantial evidence."

The secretary was required to consult with the NIH and the drug industry to develop guidelines for including women and minorities in clinical trials.

● **Manufacturing changes.** Allow the FDA to devise a list of minor manufacturing changes to already approved drugs, animal drugs or biological products that did not require FDA approval. Manufacturers would have to prove that the changes did not alter the product's identity, strength, quality, purity or potency.

For major changes, drug companies would only be able to market the newly made product after the FDA approved a supplemental drug application submitted by the company.

The FDA had allowed manufacturers to make some changes without approval, but the industry charged that the agency was not flexible enough. The law allowed more changes without FDA approval, but manufacturers were required to keep a record of changes and make it available to the FDA.

Previous regulations would stay in effect for two years or until the secretary promulgated new regulations.

● **Streamlining clinical research.** Reduce the amount of information the manufacturer was required to submit to the FDA before clinical trials could begin, allowing a trial to begin 30 days after the manufacturer submitted detailed plans and tabulations from past tests.

● **Streamlining data.** Require the HHS secretary, acting through the FDA commissioner, to compile within one year of bill enactment guidelines for when manufacturers could submit abbreviated information on clinical trials as they entered the FDA's final drug approval phase.

● **Regulatory changes.** Require the HHS secretary to issue guidelines advising FDA reviewers on the importance of "promptness, technical excellence, lack of bias and conflict of interest, and knowledge of regulatory and scientific standards" in their work.

Also, the secretary was required to meet with the maker of a drug or biological product with a pending application if the manufacturer made a "reasonable" request to discuss review of the product. Any agreement reached between the secretary and the company would have to be followed unless the manufacturer requested a change or the director of the reviewing division at the FDA certified that an essential element in determining the product's safety or efficacy was identified after testing began.

An identical procedure was established for the makers of generic drugs, which had to be found "bioequivalent" to a drug already on the market.

This section responded to industry complaints that different FDA reviewers requested varying amounts of information about products and that the review process was not uniform.

● **Scientific advisory panels.** Require the HHS secretary to create panels of experts or utilize existing ones to provide expertise regarding clinical trials and drug approvals. The bill changed the makeup of the panels, adding several new types of experts, including at least two people expert in the disease or condition for which the drug would be used. It set stricter statutory deadlines, including reviewing products within 60 days of when they were ready for consideration and giving the FDA 90 days after the panel's recommendation to announce the agency's decision.

● **Positron emission tomography.** Remove existing FDA requirements that makers of Positron Emission Tomography (PET), a class of short-lived drugs used to diagnose ailments such as cancer, submit applications to the FDA. Such drugs were usually mixed by pharmacists, who traditionally were regulated by states. The FDA had moved recently to regulate them.

Within two years of bill enactment, the HHS secretary had to establish procedures for approving PET products and outline good manufacturing processes for them. Drug manufacturers could not be required to file approval applications until at least two years after those guidelines were established.

● **Radiopharmaceuticals.** Require the HHS secretary to issue within 180 days of enactment regulations for the radiopharmaceutical industry. Final regulations had to be promulgated within 18 months. Radiopharmaceuticals are drugs intended to diagnose or monitor a disease. They emit nuclear particles or photons when they disintegrate.

● **Modernizing regulations.** Incorporate a Clinton administration initiative to require only one license for biological products and their manufacturing plants. Previously, each needed to be licensed separately. Biologicals are "live" products, such as vaccines, blood products and viruses.

● **Small-scale manufacturing.** Allow the FDA to approve new human or animal drugs made on a small-scale or pilot basis before the manufacturer upgraded to a larger facility. The policy had been in place for biological products for two years.

● **Insulin and antibiotics.** Allow the makers of new insulin and antibiotics to claim the same extended patent protection that manufacturers of some other new drugs received. The manufacturer had to submit the new product for approval after bill enactment to qualify for the market exclusivity.

● **Labeling requirements.** Eliminate mandates that prescription drugs contain the following two statements: "Caution: Federal law prohibits dispensing without a prescription" and "Warning: May be habit forming." Henceforth, labels had to include "Rx only," unless manufacturers chose to add other warnings.

● **Pharmacy regulation.** Clarify the parameters under which "compounding" was legal and to be regulated by the states. Compounding is the practice of a licensed pharmacist or physician making a custom medicine for a patient based on a valid prescription.

However, pharmacies that compounded too many drugs that were essentially copies of a commercially available product or pharmacies that used ingredients that the FDA had pulled from the market because of safety concerns would be be subject to federal regulation.

Advertising a compounded drug was prohibited under the bill, although pharmacists could advertise their ability to compound prescriptions. The measure required the FDA to consult with the U.S. Pharmacopoeia Convention and other groups to develop a list of bulk drug substances that could be used in compounding. The provision was effective one year after bill enactment.

● **Clinical pharmacology.** Authorize $3 million for each fiscal year through 2002 for the Clinical Pharmacology Training Program (PL 102-222). The program, which began in 1991, provided funding for colleges and universities that established pilot programs to train students in clinical pharmacology.

● **Sunscreens.** Require the secretary to issue regulations no later than 18 months after bill enactment for over-the-counter products that prevented or treated sunburns. The FDA had been working on such regulations for years.

● **Post-marketing studies.** Mandate that drug manufacturers required by the FDA to conduct post-marketing studies of their product report annually to the agency on the status of those studies. The status would be printed each year in the Federal Register. The secretary was required to submit no later than Oct. 1, 2001, a report to the Senate Labor and Human Resources Committee and the House Commerce Committee about manufacturers' compliance with the requirements and the FDA's response to any completed studies.

● **Notice of discontinuing a drug.** Require manufacturers who were the sole makers of drugs that were life-sustaining, life-supporting or intended to prevent debilitating conditions to notify the HHS secretary at least six months before discontinuing production of the drug. The secretary could grant exceptions to the six-month period if manufacturers certified that they faced hardships in continuing production that long. Upon receiving notice, the secretary was required to distribute the information to appropriate physician and patient groups.

Medical Devices

Medical devices — ranging from simple items such as toothbrushes to more complex ones such as pacemakers and artificial heart valves — took one of two routes through the FDA approval process.

Devices employing breakthrough technologies went through the pre-market approval process, which put them through a series of clinical trials to ensure that they were safe and effective for market use. The FDA approved about 30 products through this process in 1996.

Far more products — about 6,000 — were approved by the generally less rigorous process known as the 510(k) process. Products eligible for this option were similar to products already on the market. To achieve FDA approval, the products had to be found to be "substantially equivalent" to a previous product.

The FDA classified medical devices into three categories based on their ability to cause harm. Class I devices, such as bandages, toothbrushes and tongue depressors, faced less scrutiny than Class II devices — products such as hearing aids, catheters and contact lenses. The most extensive FDA scrutiny was reserved for Class III devices — high risk products such as artificial heart valves, heart-lung machines and pacemakers.

The FDA overhaul included provisions to:

● **Manufacturing changes.** Require the secretary to establish no later than a year after bill enactment guidelines on changes manufacturers could make to devices in the clinical trial review phase without having to submit an additional application for approval. An additional application would not be required for insignificant alterations in the way the device was made or for modifications to clinical testing protocols that would not affect the validity of data or scientific outcome, or harm people taking part in the trials. Manufacturers would have to notify the FDA no later than five days after making the changes.

The provision required the HHS secretary to meet with the makers of Class III or implantable medical devices no later than 30 days after they requested a meeting to discuss clinical protocols for their product. Any agreement reached could not be changed unless the manufacturer agreed to the change or the director of the office reviewing the device identified an additional "substantial scientific issue essential to determining the safety or effectiveness of the device involved."

● **Breakthrough devices.** Require the secretary to give priority to reviewing devices that were breakthrough technologies for which no approved alternative existed, which offered a significant advantage over existing alternatives or which would benefit patients.

● **Rare conditions.** Allow the HHS secretary to permit doctors to use devices that had not yet been determined to be effective to treat small groups of patients for whom treatment was not generally available. The secretary had to rule within 75 days on an application to use the device.

Underlying law required that such devices only be used at facilities that had established committees to oversee clinical testing. The bill allowed physicians to use the device before gaining approval from an institutional review committee if the doctor believed waiting would cause the patient harm or death. The physician had to notify the committee afterward that the device was used.

● **Device standards.** Authorize the FDA to recognize all or part of the medical device performance standards developed by national or international standards-setting organizations, such as the American Association of Mechanical Instrumentation. This would allow manufacturers to declare conformity with outside groups' standards accepted by the FDA to fulfill all or part of pre-market requirements. Bill sponsors believed this would speed review of new medical devices and allow manufacturers to comply with standards recognized in other countries.

● **Scope of review.** Require the HHS secretary to meet with device manufacturers to determine what type of scientific evidence would be necessary for the FDA to determine the effectiveness of a device that the manufacturer planned to submit later for pre-market approval. No later than 30 days after the meeting, the secretary was required to send the manufacturer a document outlining the scientific evidence that would be required. The secretary was required to consider the "least burdensome" means of effectively evaluating the device.

The bill also required the secretary, when considering 510(k) devices, to only request information necessary to determine whether the product was substantially equivalent. That determination had to be based on the intended use as indicated on the proposed labeling submitted by the manufacturer. The secretary was required to take the "least burdensome" approach to determining whether it was equivalent.

However, if the director of the FDA unit which regulated devices determined that there was a "reasonable likelihood" that the 510(k) device had other intended uses and that those uses could cause harm, the director could require the manufacturer to disclose such information to purchasers, through labels or other means. Those FDA powers would expire five years after bill enactment.

The secretary would permanently retain the power to take into account whether the originally proposed label was "false or misleading" and to keep the product off the market if he or she determined that the labeling was incorrect.

● **Changes to devices.** Maintain existing requirements that manufacturers of devices considered under the pre-market approval process submit a supplemental application for the product to the FDA if they made changes that might affect its safety or efficacy.

If the changes only altered manufacturing practices, the company could submit a notice to the FDA detailing the changes. The product could be marketed 30 days after the secretary received the notice, unless the secretary requested additional information. If the secretary required the manufacturer to submit a supplemental application for product approval, the secretary had to complete the review within 135 days.

● **Repealing some reviews.** Exempt Class I medical devices from 510(k) reviews unless they were of "substantial importance" in preventing impairments or if the device posed a "potential unreasonable risk of illness or injury."

The secretary was required to publish, within 60 days of the law's enactment, a list of Class II devices that could be exempted from such review. After the list came out, the secretary could exempt additional Class II devices from review if manufacturers petitioned for it or the secretary otherwise determined a review was not needed. Products exempt from such reviews would still be subject to other FDA regulations, such as good manufacturing practice guidelines.

Since most medical devices were not entirely new products, they were categorized with similar products already on the market. For instance, a new bandage would be classified as a Class I device, like other bandages.

The provision also required that the secretary base a decision on classifying the 510(k) device only on information about whether it was "substantially equivalent" to a device already on the market. The secretary was prohibited from withholding a classification because of a manufacturer's previous failure to comply with unrelated provisions, including good manufacturing requirements.

● **Class III designation.** Allow manufacturers of devices the FDA had classified as Class III, or the most risky, to appeal the decision. The FDA was required to rule on the appeal within 60 days. Under existing law, devices for which there was no substantially equivalent precedent were automatically classified as Class III.

● **Classification panels.** Allow manufacturers to participate fully in panels convened to review classification of devices. They were to receive the same access to information, opportunity to submit data and chance to participate in debate as the FDA.

● **Review details.** Clarify that the FDA had to review a 510(k) submission within 90 days — a time frame that was already part of the agency's guidelines. The provision also required the secretary to meet with manufacturers with device applications pending within 100 days of their request to discuss the status of the review. Before the meeting, the secretary had to provide in writing a list of any deficiencies in the application that the FDA had noticed.

● **Third-party review.** Expand an FDA pilot program to require the secretary, no later than one year after enactment, to accredit consultants, such as university or private laboratories, to review 510(k) devices. After the reviewer submitted a written recommendation, the secretary would have 30 days to make a determination.

Certain devices were exempt from outside review: All Class III devices; Class II devices that were intended to be permanently implanted or life-sustaining or -supporting; or Class II devices which required clinical data. Exemptions based on clinical data had to be limited to 6 percent of the total number of 510(k) reports submitted to the FDA in that year.

Within 180 days of the law's enactment, the secretary was required to publish guidelines for reviewers. In addition to the technical requirements the secretary would propose, the bill specified that reviewers had to be independent of the government and of manufacturers, suppliers and vendors of devices.

They were to be paid by the manufacturer submitting the application. The manufacturer could only choose consultants from the accredited list, though the FDA had to give the company at least two accredited choices. The secretary was required to oversee the private consultants and could withdraw their accreditation if they did not comply with health and safety laws or if they had a conflict of interest in considering the device.

This section expired five years after the secretary notified Congress that at least two consultants were accredited to review at least 60 percent of the 510(k) submissions or four years after the secretary notified Congress that he or she used third-party consultants in at least 35 percent of the reviews completed by the FDA.

The secretary was required to submit a report to the House Commerce Committee and the Senate Labor and Human Resources Committee no later than three years after enactment on whether outside consultants should be permitted to review Class II devices requiring clinical data.

The comptroller general was required to report to both committees, no later than five years after bill enactment, on the extent to which the FDA had implemented this section. At least six months before the section was to expire, the comptroller was to submit a report to the committees evaluating the program's role in helping HHS carry out its duties.

● **Post-market surveillance.** Allow the HHS secretary to reduce the number of Class II and III devices which manufacturers needed to track after they had been used or implanted in patients. The Safe Medical Devices Act of 1990 (PL 101-629) had required tracking every permanently implanted or life-sustaining device that could have serious adverse health effects had it failed. Tracking involved keeping a list of every patient in whom the device was implanted or on whom it had been used.

Post-market surveillance involved follow-up studies of people involved in clinical trials of the product to ensure that the device was safe and effective for the long run. The secretary could require manufacturers to carry out such surveillance for as long as 36 months, unless the manufacturer agreed to do so for a longer period.

● **Distributors.** Reduce reporting requirements on distributors and some paperwork requirements for manufacturers.

● **Device data.** Allow the secretary to use information from premarket approval reviews of a device to assist the FDA's review of subsequent devices for up to six years after the first device was approved.

● **Clinical investigations.** Clarify that one clinical trial could be sufficient to determine a device's efficacy. The FDA had debated how many were needed.

Food Labels and Claims

● **Nutrient and health claims.** Create an expedited rule-making procedure for nutrient and health claims that food manufacturers planned to include on their product's labeling. If manufacturers petitioned to use a claim and the FDA did not approve the use within 100 days, the application would be deemed denied unless the secretary and the manufacturer mutually agreed to give the FDA more time to consider it. If the FDA did not propose a regulation to authorize or deny a claim within 90 days of receiving it, it was deemed denied, unless there was mutual agreement to extend the time. The bill also required the secretary to complete final rule-making on a claim within 18 months of proposing a regulation.

● **Expanding use of claims.** Allow manufacturers to use on their food packaging authoritative statements published by scientific federal agencies, such as the Centers for Disease Control and Prevention (CDC) and the National Academy of Sciences.

The statements had to refer to "the relationship between a nutrient and a disease or health-related condition to which the claim refers." An example of such a statement was one the CDC issued in 1992 recommending that women of child-bearing age consume 0.4 milligrams of folic acid per day to reduce the risk of birth defects. The FDA did not approve the use of such a claim on products containing folic acid until 1996.

Manufacturers intending to include health claims on their labels had to submit notice to the FDA at least 120 days before the product was marketed across state lines. Those intending to use nutrient claims, such as "contains only 5 grams of fat," were required to notify the FDA at least 120 days before the product was marketed. The FDA could block a proposed label.

● **Labeling requirements.** Allow the secretary, when considering a nutrient claim on a product, to require that the manufacturer include labeling referring to the mandatory nutrition information elsewhere on the package. This would be done if the food contained levels of a nutrient that would increase the risk of diet-related disease or conditions in the general public.

● **Irradiation.** Repeal requirements that packages of foods treated with irradiation — low doses of radiation that killed most pathogens — state so in type more prominent than the ingredients section. The bill also required that within 60 days of enactment the FDA rule on a New Jersey company's 3-year-old petition to use irradiation to treat red meat. On Dec. 2, the FDA approved the petition.

● **Glass and ceramic ware.** Prevent the secretary from banning the use of lead- and cadmium-based enamel in the lip and rim area of glass and ceramic ware less than one year after it published its intention to do so. The secretary was also prohibited from banning it before Jan. 1, 2003, unless the use of such enamel as decoration in glass or ceramic ware not intended for children was determined to be unsafe. The FDA had authority over such products because they could be considered food additives.

● **Food contact surfaces.** Simplify the process for FDA approval of substances used in food preparation, packaging, transporting and holding if appropriators provided $3 million for fiscal 2000 and following years, or the amount in the president's budget request, to meet the FDA's costs. Under existing law, the FDA had to subject "food contact surfaces," such as plastic packaging, to the same rigorous tests it used for food additives, such as dyes. Under the bill, the FDA would have 120 days to disapprove after a manufacturer notified the agency of its intent to use a "contact surface."

Other Provisions

● **Off-label uses.** Allow drug and medical device manufacturers to distribute information to doctors, pharmacists, insurance officials and state and federal officials on unapproved or unofficial uses for their FDA-approved products, if the information came from medical journals and textbooks. The FDA based its testing and approval primarily on the use for which the manufacturer intended to market the item, but many products were also used in other ways supported by new research. For example, most drugs used to treat cancer were approved for other uses.

Manufacturers planning to distribute information on such "off-label" uses had to agree to submit to the FDA a supplemental application on the additional proposed use. The FDA could require manufacturers to share contrary information or could prevent them from disseminating information on "off-label" uses if the secretary determined that the information did not comply with the law.

The changes were to take effect one year after enactment, or when the secretary issued final regulations on it. It would expire seven years after those regulations were promulgated or Sept. 30, 2006, whichever was later.

Prior to 1996, manufacturers were not supposed to circulate such information. The FDA had allowed limited circulation of some journal and textbook articles beginning in October 1996.

The bill also required several studies on off-label uses. The comptroller general was required to determine the section's effects on HHS resources, reporting results to the House Commerce Committee and the Senate Labor and Human Resources Committee no later than Jan. 1, 2002. The National Academy of Science's Institute of Medicine was required to study the effectiveness of the provision and the quality of information being disseminated, reporting to the two committees no later than Sept. 30, 2005.

● **Unapproved treatments.** Allow a physician to use a drug or medical device not yet approved by the FDA to diagnose, monitor or treat a serious disease or condition if there was no satisfactory alternative, if the FDA certified that there was sufficient evidence that the drug or device was safe and effective, if the FDA determined that use of the product would not interrupt ongoing testing and if the manufacturer or clinical investigator told the FDA how the physician intended to use it.

The drug or medical device could be used to treat one patient or a group of patients. The FDA could immediately terminate the expanded access if the secretary determined that it no longer met the requirements. The FDA's previous policies to allow for expedited use of some drugs and devices benefited mostly cancer and AIDS patients.

● **Cosmetics and non-prescription drugs.** Allow the FDA to create national standards, including warning label standards, for cosmetics and over-the-counter drugs, pre-empting state laws. But states could petition the FDA to continue using their own regulations, including warning labels, when their rules conflicted with the FDA's. In addition, states could continue requiring labels in cases in which the FDA had not acted. State regulations in place before Sept. 1, 1997, would stand, including California's Proposition 65, which required warning labels on products containing certain toxins. Previously, states had had almost exclusive regulation of cosmetics and over-the-counter drugs.

● **Expert review.** Allow the secretary to contract with outside experts to review part or all of an application or petition. The FDA would retain the right to make final decisions.

● **Supplemental reviews.** Require the secretary no later than 180 days after bill enactment to publish standards to promptly review additional uses for drugs and biological products that the FDA had already approved.

● **Dispute resolution.** Require the secretary to establish a procedure to allow manufacturers of drugs and medical devices to dispute scientific decisions in a product review.

● **Mission statement and reports.** Establish a formal mission for the FDA stipulating that the agency aimed to "promote the public health by promptly and efficiently reviewing clinical research and taking appropriate action on the marketing of regulated products within a timely matter."

The bill also required the HHS secretary to develop a plan within one year to bring the FDA into compliance with bill provisions. The secretary had to report annually on the FDA's progress.

- **Tracking applications.** Require the secretary to maintain information to monitor the progress of all applications and requests submitted to the FDA. Within one year of enactment, the secretary had to report to the House Commerce Committee and the Senate Labor and Human Resources Committee on the status of the system, its projected costs and how it would deal with confidentiality concerns.
- **Training.** Require the FDA to provide scientific and specialized training for its employees and to provide fellowships and training to students. The latter provision also applied to other public health agencies.
- **Information on therapy.** Authorize $11 million through fiscal 2002 for a demonstration grant project to be run by the Agency for Health Care Policy and Research to study and increase awareness of new drugs, biological products and medical devices and the risks of using them or using them in combination with another product.
- **Global agreements.** Require the secretary, within 180 days of bill enactment, to release a strategy for implementing worldwide standards on good manufacturing practices for drugs, devices and foods. The bill required the secretary to work with the Office of the U.S. Trade Representative on international biomedical and food issues. The secretary was not required to work on global agreements about dietary supplements.
- **Environmental impact.** Codify existing policy exempting manufacturers of certain categories of drugs and biological products from having to file environmental impact reports.
- **Mercury.** Require the secretary within two years of enactment to compile a list and undertake a study of drugs and foods that contained intentionally introduced mercury compounds, and to issue regulations restricting the sale of products containing mercury, if the secretary found that they posed a human health risk. The secretary was required to study the health effects of using nasal sprays containing mercury.
- **Interagency cooperation.** Require the secretary to foster collaboration among the FDA, the NIH and other science-based federal agencies regarding emerging medical therapies and advances in nutrition and food science.
- **Classification of products.** Allow manufacturers to petition the secretary to determine within 60 days whether their product should be classified as a drug, a biologic or a medical device. If the secretary failed to issue a decision in 60 days, the recommendation of the applicant would be accepted.
- **Foreign manufacturers.** Require foreign companies that made drugs or medical devices to register their U.S. agents with the secretary. The secretary could contact foreign governments to determine whether the product met U.S. standards.
- **Interstate commerce.** Extend the FDA's jurisdiction over matters involving interstate commerce to include food, drugs and cosmetics. Previously, it applied only to medical devices.
- **Disclaimers.** Specify that entities required to file reports about adverse reactions to a product were not necessarily admitting that the product malfunctioned. Such a disclaimer had already been in place for drug and medical device manufactures. The bill extended it to the makers of foods, dietary supplements and cosmetics.
- **Labeling.** Repeal a prohibition against using "FDA approved" on product labeling.
- **Tobacco.** Specify that nothing in the bill affected the secretary's authority to regulate tobacco products ■

Congress Bans Funding For Assisted Suicide

President Clinton signed a bill April 30 prohibiting the use of federal funds for physician-assisted suicide (HR 1003 — PL 105-12). The Senate cleared the bill April 16 a week after the House passed it, making it one of the first bills of the 105th Congress to reach Clinton's desk. Clinton said he had no objection to the measure, but considered it a reiteration of existing policy.

The measure had the support of a wide range of religious and medical organizations. The chief criticisms came from Democrats who argued that it was "a solution in search of a problem" and that it was more important to focus on suicide prevention.

At the time, no federal agency funded such suicides. But bill supporters said it was necessary to clarify the government's position, particularly if states started to legalize assisted suicide and judges ruled that it qualified for federal funding. "All it would take is for one district court judge to rule that it falls under the guidelines for federal support," said bill sponsor Ralph M. Hall, D-Texas.

Hall's bill did not address ethical or legal issues surrounding acts by terminally ill patients to end their lives. It only barred the use of taxpayer dollars to subsidize or promote such acts. Specifically, it prohibited Medicare, Medicaid, military and federal employee health care plans from paying for doctors to help terminally ill patients end their lives.

The bill did not affect a patient's right to reject or discontinue medical treatment. Nor did it affect funding for treatment to alleviate pain or discomfort.

States that legalized assisted suicide would be free to fund it or to allow patients to pay for it themselves. Doctors who assisted at a suicide would not be in jeopardy of losing Medicare, Medicaid or other forms of federal reimbursement for other services performed. For these reasons, the bill's impact was expected to be limited.

(Any attempt by Congress to ban assisted suicide outright was likely to run into constitutional problems based on the 10th Amendment, which gave to states all powers not explicitly delegated to the federal government.)

Critics said the likelihood of a judge forcing the federal government to pay for suicides was at best remote. They said the legislation fixed a problem that did not exist (federal funding) and did not address a problem that did exist (suicide). "In short, this bill prohibits absolutely nothing," said Sherrod Brown of Ohio, ranking Democrat on the House Commerce Subcommittee on Health and Environment.

At the time of the bill's passage, the Supreme Court was considering, in *Vacco v. Quill* and *Washington v. Glucksberg*, whether Americans had a right to assisted suicide. The court ruled the week of June 23 that states could bar assisted suicide and that individuals did not have a constitutional right to end their lives.

House Committee Action

Work on HR 1003 began in the House Commerce Committee's Subcommittee on Health and Environment, which approved it by voice vote March 13.

Henry A. Waxman, D-Calif., called the measure "redundant, a mere restatement of the status quo," saying such use of federal funds was already illegal. But Hall called on members to be "proactive," saying he introduced the legislation in response to court rulings in favor of assisted suicide. In one case, a Palm Beach County, Fla., judge ruled in January that a doctor could not be prosecuted for administering a fatal dose of drugs to a dying AIDS patient. The case was headed for the Florida Supreme Court.

In another case, the 9th Circuit Court of Appeals in February threw out a suit challenging a ballot initiative passed by Oregon voters in 1994 that made assisted suicide legal. That paved the way for the law to go into effect, making Oregon the only state with legalized assisted suicide. Oregon voters reaffirmed their assisted suicide law in November 1997.

Oregon's Medicaid director was quoted in news reports as saying that under the 1994 law, physician-assisted suicides could be covered under government-funded health plans. Hall said his bill would prevent that from happening.

The panel adopted, 15-10, an amendment by Chairman Michael Bilirakis, R-Fla., to authorize a one-year General Accounting Office study of end-of-life care and ways to reduce the suicide rate among the terminally ill. The amendment authorized grants for medical schools and other health care training facilities to teach medical professionals to address pain, depression and other issues to help prevent suicides.

Bilirakis' amendment replaced a proposal by Brown that would have required medical schools that received federal funding to provide training for medical students in pain management, disability awareness and treatment for depression. Brown's amendment also would have allowed the secretary of Health and Human Services (HHS) to award research grants aimed at reducing the rate of suicide, including assisted suicide.

Tom Coburn, R-Okla., a physician, said Brown's proposal would allow the government to dictate medical school curricula. "Let the professional organizations do that," he said.

Commerce Committee Backs Bill

The full House Commerce Committee approved the bill, 45-2, on March 20 (H Rept 105-46, Part 1).

Proponents said the measure would put Congress' views on record and write into law what was only a policy at HHS and other health care agencies.

Democrats argued the bill missed an opportunity to address why people committed suicide in the first place. "The only purpose of this bill is to make a statement," Waxman said. "We're not entering into a discussion" on why people would want to kill themselves.

Two attempts by Democrats to add provisions addressing care for the terminally ill, the depressed, those in chronic pain and others who might consider suicide were rejected.

Brown proposed linking about $100 million in federal funding to a requirement that medical schools develop curricula that included the care of patients who might be in danger of killing themselves. It was rejected, 17-24.

Anna G. Eshoo, D-Calif., proposed developing national guidelines for caring for the terminally ill. Her amendment was rejected 22-25.

The two lawmakers argued that their proposals would do more to prevent people from killing themselves than the underlying bill. Opponents of the Brown and Eshoo proposals said they would create new federal mandates on hospitals and medical schools. They also feared that the amendments could inject controversy into a bill that had bipartisan support. "Let's send a simple bill to a simple Congress," said Hall, the one Democrat who opposed the amendments.

Ways and Means Panel Gives OK

The House Ways and Means Subcommittee on Health gave voice vote approval March 18 to the portions of the bill affecting Medicare. Subcommittee Chairman Bill Thomas, R-Calif., pushed the provisions through with little dissent or discussion. The full Ways and Means panel never acted on it.

House/Senate Floor Action

The House on April 10 overwhelmingly endorsed HR 1003. The tally was 398-16, with all the dissenting votes coming from Democrats. *(Vote 75, p. H-24)*

Before the bill reached the floor, language was added allowing the HHS secretary to award grants to study the care of the terminally ill with an eye toward reducing suicides.

Jim McDermott, D-Wash., a psychiatrist and one of the bill's chief critics, argued that suicide was not a well-defined term for someone who was terminally ill and not interested in pursuing options to extend life. For this reason, he said, the bill could have unintended consequences. A better way of reducing suicide, he said, would be through greater use of Medicare for psychiatric care.

Senate Clears Bill

The Senate cleared HR 1003 on April 16 by a vote of 99-0. *(Vote 44, p. S-10)*

The closest thing to controversy during the floor debate came from two non-binding amendments by Paul Wellstone, D-Minn. His amendments were "sense of the Senate" resolutions to restore certain benefits taken away in the 1996 welfare overhaul (PL 104-193). Wellstone later withdrew them. Bill supporter John Ashcroft, R-Mo., said the amendments would force a House-Senate conference on the bill, instead of sending it straight to the president. ■

House Panel Approves Hemophiliac HIV Bill

The House Judiciary Committee gave voice vote approval Oct. 29 to a bill that would set up a $750 million fund to compensate hemophiliacs infected with HIV. The measure (HR 1023) proposed to make $100,000 available to each hemophiliac who was infected with HIV from tainted blood products between 1982 and 1987, the early years of the AIDS outbreak. HIV is the virus that causes AIDS.

Supporters said they knew the money would not do much to ease the pain, but said it might make life a little easier for some. The payments would be made to affected individuals, their spouses, children or parents. "These families have been both financially and emotionally devastated," said Judiciary Committee Chairman Henry J. Hyde, R-Ill.

In the early 1980s, about half the nation's 16,000 hemophiliacs — people with a blood-clotting disorder —were infected with the AIDS virus. More than 2,500 had died. The bill, sponsored by Porter J. Goss, R-Fla., was named for Ricky Ray, a 15-year-old Florida boy who died in 1992.

Bill supporters said the government failed to notify the public during the early 1980s, when it became clear that some of the blood supply was tainted. Subsequently, the nation's blood supply became subject to stringent testing. Hyde said the bill was a "humanitarian response" but not an admission of guilt by the government.

The committee approved by voice vote a substitute amendment by Hyde that lowered the proposed payment to each party from $125,000 to $100,000 and eliminated a provision that would have extended payments to others infected with HIV from tainted blood during the same period. ■

$13 Billion in Welfare Cuts Restored

President Clinton succeeded in changing some elements of the 1996 welfare overhaul act that had drawn sharp criticism from social welfare groups and from the president himself. The changes were negotiated as part of the bipartisan 1997 balanced-budget deal and enacted in the spending portion (HR 2015 — PL 105-33) of the budget-reconciliation package. *(Spending reconciliation, p. 2-47)*

The House adopted the conference report on the reconciliation bill, 346-85, on July 30. The Senate cleared the bill, 85-15, on July 31, and Clinton signed it into law Aug. 5. *(House vote 345, p. H-104; Senate vote 209, p. S-36)*

The modifications did not affect the central features of the 1996 welfare overhaul law (PL 104-193), which ended the federal guarantee of cash welfare to all eligible low-income mothers and children, set limits on eligibility for welfare, and gave the states broad new authority over their welfare programs.

However, Congress agreed to restore about $13 billion that had been cut from welfare related programs. While Clinton did not get everything he wanted — he had no luck in restoring most of the cuts in eligibility or allotments for food stamps, for example — he was able to restore key benefits for legal immigrants, get more help for welfare recipients joining the labor force and provide some additional money for the food stamp program.

Clinton had objected to the cuts in the food stamp program and to the denial of government services to legal immigrants even as he signed the 1996 overhaul. He said those changes were irrelevant to the legislation's main goal of moving welfare recipients into the work force. But they were at the heart of the law's savings, which were estimated at $54.6 billion over six years.

It was for that reason that the changes were embedded in the wide-ranging budget deal that fulfilled the Republicans' goal of reducing taxes and producing a balanced budget by 2002, while containing enough additional cuts to offset the welfare modifications.

The following were among the main changes to the welfare law made in the budget-reconciliation bill:

- **SSI.** In the most protracted struggle, Clinton and other Democrats ensured that all legal immigrants who were receiving Supplemental Security Income (SSI) and related Medicaid benefits on Aug. 22, 1996, the date the welfare overhaul was signed, would remain eligible. SSI provided cash to low-income individuals who were aged and/or disabled.

In addition, legal immigrants who were in the country on that date and later became disabled would be eligible for SSI and Medicaid benefits. Without the change, all non-citizens would have been removed from the SSI rolls on Oct. 1, 1997.

- **Medicaid.** The bill assured that Medicaid coverage would continue for disabled children who lost SSI benefits because of changes in the welfare law that tightened the definition of childhood disability.
- **Welfare-to-work.** A $3 billion fund was created to help states move long-term welfare recipients into the work force, targeted to areas with many such recipients and high poverty rates.
- **Food stamps.** The bill provided an additional $1.5 billion over five years for food stamps and for employment and training for people who might otherwise have lost their eligibility under the welfare overhaul law.

Democrats also blocked several Republican initiatives. Most notably, Clinton thwarted attempts by House Republicans to overturn a Labor Department directive that applied a wide variety of federal labor laws to welfare recipients who were required to work. Labor unions had strongly urged Clinton to buck Republicans on this issue.

The House GOP tried and failed to add language that would allow states that supplemented their federal SSI payments to reduce their support below existing levels. And Democrats blocked an attempt by Republicans to allow private companies to run state Medicaid and food stamp programs.

Background

The 1996 welfare overhaul bill had gained bipartisan approval from Congress after Clinton announced he would sign it despite his objections to provisions cutting the food stamp program and denying various federal benefits to legal aliens. *(1996 Almanac, p. 6-3)*

The landmark law ended the 61-year-old guarantee of federal welfare checks to all eligible low-income mothers and children. Instead, federal welfare funds were sent to the states in lump sums known as block grants, giving states almost complete control over eligibility and benefits.

It was the first time the federal government had transformed a major individual entitlement program into a block grant to the states. However, the law did impose some federal restrictions on use of the funds. Among the most prominent: welfare recipients were required to work within two years of receiving benefits, and they were limited to five years of aid.

However, the $54.6 billion in savings attributed to the bill did not come from ending federal welfare benefits. Most of it came from the two areas Clinton found most troubling.

About $23.3 billion came from scaling back food stamp benefits by cutting individual allotments and making other adjustments.

The other major savings came from denying an array of federal benefits, including food stamps and SSI, to most legal immigrants, including those who were already in the United States when the law was signed on Aug. 22, 1996. The benefits were to be cut off after one year, on Aug. 22, 1997.

Besides the food stamp and immigration provisions, the welfare act also made it harder for disabled children to qualify for federal aid, reorganized federal child-care assistance programs and toughened enforcement of child-support orders.

Clinton signed the bill despite a last-ditch appeal from liberals, but he registered his own objections and promised to seek changes. "I think it can be easily fixed," he said. As Clinton campaigned for re-election in the fall of 1996, he said a second term would put him in a position to correct the legislation's flaws.

While continued GOP control of Congress made any wide-ranging changes unlikely, the administration believed Republicans could be persuaded to relent on some of the welfare savings as part of a larger, bipartisan deal to balance the budget by 2002.

Clinton's Request

Clinton pressed the issue in his Feb. 4 State of the Union address. He stressed overturning the ban on aid to legal immigrants. "To do otherwise is simply unworthy of a great nation of immigrants," he said. He also called for $3.6 billion to help welfare recipients enter the work force. "No one can walk out of this chamber with a clear conscience unless you are prepared to finish the job," he said. *(Text, p. D-17)*

Clinton got more specific in his fiscal 1998 budget, submitted to Congress on Feb. 6. He asked lawmakers to restore about $18 billion of the savings expected under the welfare law. In addition, he sought $3.6 billion to help welfare recipients enter the work force. Specifically, he proposed to:

- **Legal immigrants.** Allow legal immigrants who became disabled after entering the country to receive SSI and Medicaid benefits, and provide Medicaid to legal immigrant children of poor families. Clinton also proposed making refugees and those granted asylum eligible for federal benefits for seven years instead of five. Cost: $14.6 billion.
- **Medicaid.** Allow disabled children to continue receiving Medicaid if they lost their SSI because of changes in the definition of childhood disability under the welfare law. Cost: $300 million.
- **Food stamps.** Ease the law's impact on families that received food stamps and had either high housing costs or vehicles valued above a certain level. Clinton wanted to provide more jobs for able-bodied childless adults and allow them to receive six months of food stamps out of every 12 months, instead of three months in every 36 months. Cost: $3.1 billion.
- **Welfare to work.** Provide $3 billion to help states and cities provide subsidies and other incentives to businesses to hire welfare recipients, and $552 million to allow employers to claim a 50 percent tax credit on the first $10,000 a year of wages, for up to two years, for each long-term welfare recipient they hired.

Republicans Warn Against Changes

Republican leaders cautioned against reopening the welfare law, saying it could end up being unraveled on many fronts. They were particularly concerned that the National Governors' Association (NGA) was about to recommend that legal immigrants remain eligible for federal aid.

Although the NGA generally supported the 1996 welfare overhaul, governors in states most affected by immigration, including Republican George E. Pataki of New York, were becoming increasingly concerned about the prospect of having the states provide for immigrants who were denied federal aid.

The NGA had not previously taken a position on the immigration provisions, but it was drafting a statement saying that immigrants "should not be barred" from SSI and food stamps if they were in the country legally when the law was signed.

Speaking at the NGA's annual meeting in Washington on Feb. 3, Senate Majority Leader Trent Lott, R-Miss., persuaded the 32 Republican governors — some of whom had played a significant role in drafting the welfare law — to support a more general statement. The draft was changed so that it urged Congress and the administration to "meet the needs of aged and disabled legal immigrants who cannot naturalize and whose benefits may be affected." The statement said the welfare bill need not be reopened.

GOP Gives Ground in Budget Deal

But Republicans began to give some ground as bipartisan talks began on balancing the budget. Clinton insisted that any budget deal had to restore some of the welfare cuts.

In addition, many lawmakers, especially those with large immigrant populations in their states, realized that legal immigrants who were disabled and who had paid taxes for up to 10 years, could be left with no means of support. Sen. Alfonse M. D'Amato, R-N.Y., who had endorsed the welfare overhaul, heaped scorn on colleagues who resisted efforts to restore the benefits. "Let them try living with no money and being disabled," he said.

To give Congress and Clinton more time to settle the matter, the SSI benefits were extended through Sept. 30, 1997, as part of the supplemental fiscal 1997 appropriations bill (HR 1871 — PL 105-18) signed into law June 12.

The final budget deal, which was announced May 2 and quickly translated into a congressional budget resolution (H Con Res 84 — H Rept 105-116), called for:

- **Legal immigrants.** $9.7 billion over five years to restore SSI and Medicaid benefits to about two-thirds of the 500,000 legal immigrants who were scheduled to lose them. Under the agreement, legal immigrants would be eligible for SSI if they: were receiving SSI as of Aug. 22, 1996, based on a disability; were receiving SSI as of Aug. 22, 1996, based on being elderly and could requalify for the aid based on a disability; or were in the United States as of Aug. 22, 1996, and later became disabled. Disabled legal immigrants who entered the country after Aug. 22, 1996, but before June 1, 1997, would also be eligible for the benefits.

As under the welfare law, all other legal immigrants who entered after Aug. 22, 1996, would be barred from receiving Medicaid benefits for five years, and would be ineligible for SSI until they became citizens.

- **Food stamps.** $1.5 billion in additional funds over five years so states could exempt up to 15 percent of their food stamp beneficiaries from work requirements under the welfare law.
- **Welfare-to-work.** $3 billion for state welfare-to-work activities.

The budget resolution was only a blueprint, however. The important part lay ahead, as lawmakers began crafting two huge reconciliation bills to carry out the terms of the agreement. Work on the welfare-related provisions fell under the jurisdiction of several committees: Ways and Means, and Education and the Workforce in the House, and the Finance Committee in the Senate. The food stamp provisions were handled separately by the House and Senate Agriculture committees.

House Ways and Means Committee

In what was seen as the first major break with the bipartisan budget deal, the House Ways and Means Committee proposed restoring SSI benefits to those legal immigrants who were receiving them when the welfare overhaul was enacted, whether they qualified because they were disabled or simply because they were elderly. But legal immigrants who were in the country but not on the rolls on Aug. 22, 1996, would not be eligible — even if they later became disabled.

The proposal was the centerpiece of the GOP-drafted Ways and Means package, which was estimated to cost $10 billion over five years. Other elements included:

- **Medicaid.** Restoration of Medicaid coverage to those legal immigrants who lost such benefits as a result of losing SSI coverage.
- **State supplements.** Repeal of a requirement that states that supplemented their federal SSI payments continue providing at least the same level of support as before. Republicans said Gov. Pete Wilson, R-Calif., and other governors wanted the requirement dropped. About 40 states supplemented SSI benefits with state funds.
- **Welfare-to-work.** $3 billion in grants over three years to help states and localities assist welfare recipients in finding jobs.

But in a move that was sharply criticized by Democrats, Republicans also included language that would allow states to pay less than the minimum wage to welfare recipients who were required to work in government or nonprofit jobs as a condition of receiving their welfare benefits. Under the provision, states could count the recipients' welfare, food stamps, Medicaid, child care and housing benefits as part of their compensation.

The provision would effectively reverse an administration directive that required states to pay the minimum wage to working welfare recipients. *(Minimum wage, p. 6-34)*

Plan Gets Partisan OK in Subcommittee

Republicans on the panel's Human Resources Subcommittee, who had drawn up the draft, endorsed the plan June 5 over vehement Democratic objections. The vote was 8-3.

The legislation was severely criticized by Democrats, including Vice President Al Gore and Senate Minority Leader Tom Daschle, D-S.D., who called it an "extraordinary revocation" of the budget blueprint painstakingly negotiated by the Clinton administration and congressional Republicans. The Clinton administration said about 75,000 fewer legal immigrants would qualify for SSI by 2002 under this revision.

"Your leadership agreed to it," Sander M. Levin of Michigan, the subcommittee's ranking Democrat, said of the budget deal, "It signed on the dotted line. No ifs, ands or buts."

Subcommittee Chairman E. Clay Shaw Jr., R-Fla., argued that his approach was more practical because it would not involve a complicated re-examination of whether elderly immigrants already on SSI also qualified as disabled and should be allowed to continue. "Our proposal improves upon the budget agreement and is completely consistent with the spirit of the agreement," he maintained.

Shaw also noted that the Ways and Means Committee had never felt bound by language written into a budget resolution.

Further angering most Democrats, the panel adopted, 7-4, an amendment by Jim McCrery, R-La., to deny SSI benefits for immigrants whose sponsors made $40,000 or more a year.

Shaw had included similar language in his original plan, but decided it was not practical. No sponsor had ever been required to support an immigrant for more than three or five years. The McCrery plan would effectively require those sponsors making more than $40,000 to support people indefinitely. Shaw also concluded that the plan would be difficult to administer and, according to the Congressional Budget Office (CBO), would not reduce spending significantly.

But McCrery argued that it would establish an important principle. "At a time we are cutting back on programs for citizens," he said, "it doesn't seem right that we would compel the citizen to pay taxes for these non-citizens [with sponsors]."

Other portions of the GOP proposal also created partisan rancor, with Democrats failing in their attempts to soften Shaw's plan. The subcommittee rejected, 4-7, an attempt by Pete Stark, D-Calif., to strike the proposal that states be allowed to pay less than the minimum wage to workfare beneficiaries. A proposal by Robert T. Matsui, D-Calif., to require that states continue their existing level of support to SSI recipients was rejected, 4-8.

Full Committee Endorses Measure

The full Ways and Means Committee approved the draft legislation June 10 by a largely party-line vote of 21-18, after defeating most Democratic attempts to amend it.

Republicans did make one change aimed at mitigating criticism that they were being too harsh on legal immigrants: They dropped McCrery's proposal to bar immigrants whose sponsors made $40,000 or more a year from receiving SSI benefits.

But an attempt by Xavier Becerra, D-Calif., to extend SSI benefits to legal immigrants who were in the country in August 1996 and later became disabled failed, 19-20. Becerra called Shaw's version "a breach of faith" from the bipartisan budget agreement.

Democrats argued that Republicans could accommodate Becerra's amendment, projected to cost $2.4 billion over five years, because the welfare-related features of the reconciliation bill would cost about $2.3 billion less than the budget resolution anticipated. "Now you have the resources to meet that agreement," Levin said. "Meet it. Meet it. Or else you're going to face horror stories."

But Shaw countered that his language was necessary to help control welfare-related costs.

Nancy L. Johnson of Connecticut, one of three Republicans who voted for Becerra's amendment, defended Shaw's original approach. She said it was preferable to removing elderly SSI beneficiaries from the rolls and making them reapply if they became disabled. She blamed Clinton for that approach, approved as part of the budget deal, calling it "appalling."

In addition to Johnson, Republicans Mac Collins of Georgia and Bill Thomas of California voted for Becerra's amendment.

Stark repeated his effort to ensure that workfare participants were covered by minimum wage laws and other workplace protections. Otherwise, he said, the legislation would create an "underclass." But Shaw noted that the minimum wage exemption only applied to workfare participants in public and nonprofit jobs, which he said were intended as a safety net, not full-time employment. The amendment failed, 16-22.

In other action, the committee:

➤ Approved, 20-17, an amendment by Barbara B. Kennelly, D-Conn., to exempt teenage mothers from the requirement that no more than 30 percent of those who counted toward a state's work participation standard be engaged in educational pursuits.

➤ Rejected, 16-23, an amendment by Matsui to require states that supplemented their federal SSI payments to maintain their existing level of support.

➤ Rejected, 16-19, an amendment by John Tanner, D-Tenn., to pay a performance bonus to states that were most successful in moving welfare recipients into the work force.

➤ Rejected, 16-21, an amendment by Stark to strike a requirement in the bill that no more than 30 percent of those who counted toward a state's work participation standard be engaged in educational pursuits.

House Education and the Workforce Committee

The House Education and the Workforce Committee approved several welfare-related provisions June 12 as part of its reconciliation package. The vote was 24-20.

The committee approved the creation of a $3 billion fund to help move welfare recipients into the work force, though it differed somewhat on the financing mechanism. While the Ways and Means version proposed to distribute half the money by formula and half by competitive grants, the Education Committee opted mainly for distributing the money by formula.

The committee also proposed exempting workfare recipients from wage laws and other work force protections. Chairman Bill Goodling, R-Pa., said that treating all welfare recipients as full-fledged employees would undercut the effectiveness of the 1996 welfare law.

Clinton Decision Spurs Minimum Wage Dispute

The dispute over whether welfare recipients should be guaranteed the minimum wage was set off May 22, when the Labor Department released guidelines applying a wide variety of federal labor laws to recipients who were required to work under the 1996 welfare overhaul law (PL 104-193).

The directive said most recipients would be subject to the Fair Labor Standards Act, which set federal minimum wage, overtime pay, child labor and record-keeping requirements. In addition, they would be covered by the Occupational Safety and Health Act, unemployment insurance measures and such anti-discrimination laws as the Civil Rights Act and the Americans with Disabilities Act.

House Republicans vowed to fight the decision, saying it would undercut a central feature of the 1996 overhaul, which required welfare recipients to work within two years of receiving benefits and made states responsible for ensuring that an increasing percentage of their welfare caseload was engaged in work activities.

Republicans said Clinton's directive would make it too expensive for states to subsidize jobs for welfare recipients who could not otherwise find work. "I think we're in the process of not only undoing welfare reform, but destroying the incentive of getting people into the labor market," said Phil Gramm, R-Texas, who blamed Clinton's stance on the sway of labor interests.

Democrats, however, insisted that determining how welfare recipients were treated in the workplace was a matter of principle not subject to compromise. "People who move from welfare to work who are employees should be treated as employees and not as second-class citizens," said Sander M. Levin, D-Mich.

The last big welfare law, enacted in 1988 (PL 100-485), had established more limited work requirements for welfare recipients and generally gave these so-called workfare participants fewer protections and benefits than applied to other employees. *(1988 Almanac, p. 349)*

The stakes became much higher with enactment of the 1996 overhaul, which established work requirements for virtually all welfare recipients. However, the 1996 law was largely silent on these issues. *(1996 Almanac, p. 6-3)*

"It was assumed that the previous distinction in statutes and case law between workfare and employment would continue to be recognized," said E. Clay Shaw Jr., R-Fla., chairman of the House Ways and Means Subcommittee on Human Resources.

House GOP Fails To Enact Limits

House Republicans sought to counter the Labor Department directive through language added to the spending portion (HR 2015) of the year's budget-reconciliation package.

Two House committees — Ways and Means and Education and the Workforce — approved provisions to exempt welfare recipients in government or nonprofit jobs from the federal minimum wage law. They initially proposed that states be allowed to count the value of Medicaid, child care and housing benefits as part of the compensation. (The directive already said food stamps could be considered compensation in certain circumstances.) Republicans later modified the provision so that only food stamps and cash welfare benefits could be counted.

When the provisions were dropped in conference at the insistence of the Senate and White House, Shaw said he would mark up a separate bill to overturn some of the administration's guidelines. But the effort never got off the ground.

Meeting in Las Vegas, Republican and Democratic leaders of the National Governors Association appealed July 30 to Congress and the White House to revise the administration directive. The governors indicated that they could accept the minimum wage requirements, but objected to giving welfare recipients other benefits, such as unemployment insurance.

House Speaker Newt Gingrich, R-Ga., later pledged to vigorously fight the administration over how to treat welfare recipients who were required to work.

"The Clinton administration, working with the unions and the bureaucrats and the liberals, is trying to undermine and destroy welfare reform," Gingrich said Aug. 22 at the Midwest Republican Leadership Conference in Indianapolis. "And we should make it a major national issue." Gingrich said he intended to make this "a major part of our September and October legislative agenda."

Despite the guidelines, it was still unclear exactly which protections and benefits would apply to welfare recipients. For example, the Treasury Department had not yet clarified under what circumstances Social Security would apply. Also, the guidelines said that unemployment coverage would depend on how an "employee" was defined under state laws, and that welfare recipients could be exempt while serving in "work training" programs.

William L. Clay, D-Mo., said the bill's treatment of welfare recipients "reminds me of slavery." An amendment by Clay to strike the minimum wage language was defeated, 19-25. An attempt by Lynn Woolsey, D-Calif., to add more worker protections for welfare recipients failed June 12, 15-20.

Senate Finance Committee

The Senate Finance Committee approved its welfare-related provisions June 18 by a vote of 20-0. Avoiding the partisanship that had accompanied the bill in the House, the committee bypassed one contentious topic and struck a compromise on another.

Overall, the thrust was generally similar to the proposals moving in the House. The Senate plan called for allocating $3 billion over three years to help states move long-term welfare recipients into the work force. And it proposed restoring SSI benefits to legal immigrants who were on the rolls when Clinton signed the 1996 welfare bill.

However, at the behest of Chairman William V. Roth Jr., R-Del., the Finance panel took no position on whether to exempt workfare beneficiaries from minimum wage laws.

The panel did approve by voice vote an amendment by Don Nickles, R-Okla., to clarify that welfare recipients could earn less than the minimum wage if they had been penalized by a state for not complying with the welfare law.

Roth also sought middle ground in the battle over which legal immigrants would regain access to SSI benefits. Like the

House bill, Roth's plan would allow legal immigrants who were collecting SSI by Aug. 22, 1996, to remain eligible for the aid. But it also allowed for legal immigrants who were in the country at that time and later became disabled to qualify for the aid if they applied by Sept. 30, 1997.

Office of Management and Budget Director Franklin D. Raines said that while the Finance Committee's plan was better than the House version, "it still fails to provide sufficient assistance for the most vulnerable individuals."

Roth directly contradicted the Clinton administration's wishes on another issue, proposing that Texas be allowed to hire private companies to run its Medicaid, food stamp and child nutrition programs. The Clinton administration had recently turned down Texas' request for a waiver that would allow it to do so.

After some parliamentary maneuvering, however, Roth agreed to drop provisions that would have enabled other states to apply for such demonstration projects.

Raines said that while certain functions, such as computer systems, could be contracted out to private entities, matters such as determining who was eligible for these social services ought to be handled by the government.

Kent Conrad, D-N.D., objected to the provision, saying it would amount to giving Texas a "blank check" and prompt other states to seek similar waivers. But Phil Gramm, R-Texas, argued that the money Texas would save from contracting out these services would enable the state to cover more children in Medicaid.

The provision was similar to one approved by the House Agriculture Committee as part of its food stamp proposals.

In other action, the Finance Committee:

➤ Approved, 11-9, an amendment by John D. Rockefeller IV, D-W.Va., to ensure that welfare recipients who benefited from a new welfare-to-work block grant would not displace existing workers.

➤ Approved, by voice vote, an amendment by Carol Moseley-Braun, D-Ill., to exempt teenage parents from the 1996 law's requirement that only 20 percent of a state's caseload could be enrolled in school and still count toward the state's work participation standard.

➤ Approved, 13-7, an amendment by Bob Graham, D-Fla., to continue to give the administration some flexibility in sanctioning states that fell short of the work requirements for welfare recipients. The welfare law let the secretary of Health and Human Services deny a state "not more than" 5 percent of its welfare block grant the first year, rising annually to a maximum of 21 percent.

Roth had proposed removing the phrase "not more than," to ensure that the maximum penalties would be imposed. But Graham said the sanctions should include room for "common sense and judgment."

➤ Approved, by voice vote, an amendment by D'Amato requiring that states applying for the welfare-to-work block grant spend at least 75 percent of the state money they previously spent on welfare programs. Roth's draft would have required them to spend 80 percent.

House/Senate Agriculture Committees

The House and Senate Agriculture committees endorsed a plan to allocate about $1.5 billion in new spending over five years for food stamps, employment and training for people who might otherwise have lost their eligibility under the new welfare law.

As in the budget agreement, the money was to go largely toward easing the effects of the 1996 welfare law on able-bodied, childless people who could not find jobs in time to comply with the law's new work requirements. About $580 million was to be spent on people who would be granted this new hardship exemption. The other $920 million would be designated for increased funding for food stamps and the existing food stamp employment and training programs.

The Senate Agriculture Committee approved the provisions, 16-1, on June 10. Jesse Helms, R-N.C., cast the lone "no" vote by proxy.

The House Agriculture Committee approved virtually the same provisions by voice vote June 12. The panel added a provision that would allow any state to hire private businesses to determine eligibility for food stamps, rather than relying on state agencies to do the work. The amendment was adopted, 24-19, mostly along party lines. Larry Combest, R-Texas, said it would save $10 million monthly in his home state.

The committee defeated, 13-30, an amendment by Charles W. Stenholm, D-Texas, that would have capped federal spending on food stamp administration and diverted the savings to an array of agricultural programs.

House/Senate Floor Action

The House and Senate took up the committee-approved welfare and food stamp provisions as part of their respective versions of the huge budget-reconciliation spending-cut bill. The House passed its bill (HR 2015 — H Rept 105-149) on June 25 by a vote of 270-162. The Senate passed its version (S 947) by a vote of 73-27 the same day. *(House vote 241, p. H-76; Senate vote 130, p. S-24)*

Both chambers made changes to the welfare-related provisions during floor action.

The most significant was a Senate amendment by Frank R. Lautenberg, D-N.J., to make legal immigrants who were in the United States as of Aug. 22, 1996, eligible for SSI regardless of when they became disabled. The Senate adopted the change June 25 by voice vote and with virtually no discussion. The amendment reflected the bipartisan budget accord.

Also in the Senate, Conrad successfully invoked a budget point of order against the proposal to allow private companies to run Medicaid, food stamp and child nutrition programs. The section was removed on the grounds that it would not significantly affect the budget deficit.

In the House, Republicans modified their minimum wage provision slightly. As part of the leadership's rule governing floor debate on the bill, the provision was altered so that only cash welfare benefits and food stamps could be counted toward compensation.

Conference/Final Action

Democrats ultimately prevailed on many of the welfare-related provision in the bill.

• **Legal immigrants.** At Clinton's insistence, the final bill followed the Senate version, restoring SSI and Medicaid benefits for legal immigrants who were on the rolls Aug. 22, 1996, as well as for those who were in the country on that date and later became disabled.

Clinton had indicated in a June 20 letter to John M. Spratt Jr., D-S.C., ranking member of the House Budget Committee, that he would veto a bill that did not include this provision.

• **Welfare-to-work fund.** A fund worth $3 billion was created to help states place long-term welfare recipients into the work force. The grants were to be administered by the Labor Department and distributed in fiscal 1998 and 1999. Seventy-five percent of the money would be distributed by formula and 25 percent through competitive grants. The money would be targeted to areas with high poverty rates and long-term welfare recipients.

• **Medicaid.** Medicaid benefits were continued for disabled children who lost their SSI benefits because of changes in SSI eligibility contained in the welfare overhaul law.

• **Food stamps.** The bill increased spending by a total of $1.5 billion over five years for food stamp, employment and training programs. States were allowed to exempt from work requirements up to 15 percent of able-bodied food stamp recipients between the ages of 18 and 50 who did not have dependents.

• **Minimum wage.** To the dismay of House Republicans, conferees dropped the proposal to allow states to pay welfare recipients in workfare slots less than the federal minimum wage.

• **State supplements.** The conference agreement did not include the House provision that would have allowed states that supplemented federal SSI benefits to reduce their effort.

• **Privatization.** The final bill did not include the House provision to allow private companies to determine eligibility for food stamps and Medicaid. Clinton prevailed in persuading lawmakers to drop the House provision, which would have let any state do so. ■

Adoption Bill Stresses Child's Safety

President Clinton signed legislation Nov. 19 designed to hasten the adoption of children in foster care. The Adoption and Safe Families Act (HR 867 — PL 105-89) changed existing law to give more emphasis to protecting children's safety and less to trying to reunite them with troubled families. It also gave states a financial incentive to find permanent adoptive parents for children in foster care.

"We know that foster parents provide safe and caring families for children," Clinton said. "But the children should not be trapped in them forever, especially when there are open arms waiting to welcome them into permanent homes."

Clinton said the legislation was consistent with his goal, announced in December 1996, of doubling the number of foster care children who were adopted or otherwise permanently placed in homes by 2002. There were 27,000 such placements in 1996. About a half-million children were in foster care, including many who had been there for two years or more.

The legislation was a recognition of the unintended consequences of the 1980 Child Welfare Act (PL 96-272), which required that states make a "reasonable effort" to reunite a child's natural family before allowing the child to be permanently adopted. Those efforts had contributed to an increase in the amount of time children spent in foster care, as states tried, often in vain, to reunite their families.

"The 'reasonable effort' provision has become a barrier to finding permanent, loving homes for children in foster care," said Rep. Dave Camp, R-Mich., who cosponsored the House version of the bill with Barbara B. Kennelly, D-Conn.

The final bill, worked out in informal negotiations with the Senate, gave states considerable leeway in determining what those efforts were. It made the child's health and safety the paramount factors.

• **State flexibility.** The legislation specified that states were not required to try to reunite a family if a court had determined that the child had been subjected to "aggravated circumstances," such as abandonment, torture, chronic abuse and sexual abuse, or when the parent had killed or assaulted another child.

"This is really the first time where federal legislation has made it clear in fact that the safety and health of children becomes the predominant national policy," said Sen. John D. Rockefeller IV, D-W.Va.

• **Hastening adoption proceedings.** States were required to terminate parental rights and begin adoption proceedings once a child had been in foster care for 15 out of the preceding 22 months. The bill also required states to hold earlier and more frequent hearings to track children after they entered the foster care system. The child was entitled to a hearing within 12 months, reduced from 18 months under existing law.

Foster parents were given a greater say in all proceedings, on the assumption that they, more than the biological parents or a state employee, were in a position to understand the child's best interests.

• **Criminal records checks.** States were required to run criminal records checks on any prospective foster or adoptive parents. Their application would be denied if they had had a felony conviction for child abuse or neglect, spousal abuse, crimes against children or violent crimes. States could opt out of this provision, but only by action of the governor or state legislature.

• **Special needs.** States were also required to provide health insurance for adopted children with special needs or disabilities in cases where the state determined the child would not have been adopted without medical assistance.

• **Financial incentives to states.** The legislation also gave states a financial incentive to get children out of foster care. A state would receive $4,000 for each adoption of a foster child that exceeded its previous annual level, or, in the case of fiscal 1998, the average of fiscal 1995-1997. For children with disabilities, the figure would rise to $6,000.

Total federal payments for these incentive adoptions were authorized at $20 million a year for five years beginning in fiscal 1999. The funding was in addition to the existing federal payments to states for placing children in foster care. The Congressional Budget Office estimated that the legislation would cost nothing — or result in savings — because the federal government would spend less on foster care.

• **Out-of-state adoption.** The bill also sought to encourage adoptions by prohibiting states from postponing or denying a suitable out-of-state adoption in order to find an in-state placement.

BOXSCORE

Adoption of Foster Children — HR 867. The bill gave states financial incentives and more flexibility to find permanent homes for children in foster care.

Report: H Rept 105-77.

KEY ACTION

April 30 — House passed HR 867, 416-5.

Nov. 8 — Senate passed HR 867, revised, by voice vote.

Nov. 13 — House passed compromise version of HR 867, 406-7; **Senate** cleared the bill by voice vote.

Nov. 19 — President signed HR 867— PL 105-89.

• **Safe families program.** In a section added by the Senate, the bill reauthorized and revised a program designed to keep troubled families together and give early help to children at risk of being put in foster care. The family preservation program — created as part of the 1993 budget-reconciliation law (PL 103-66) — was renamed the Promoting Safe and Stable Families program. *(1993 Almanac, p. 377)*

The program's mission was revised so that it could also be used to promote adoptions and to help reunify families for up to 15 months after a child was removed from the home. The program was authorized for $875 million over three years.

Background

Passage of HR 867 reflected widespread awareness that past efforts at moving children beyond foster care had not worked as intended.

Foster care was initially envisioned as a way to provide interim homes for children who were neglected by their natural families. The care was meant to be temporary and to result in the children either going home or being placed with adoptive parents. But the number of children in foster care had nearly doubled since 1983 as states struggled with the often insurmountable task of reuniting broken families.

The response, which had bipartisan support, was to legislate a shift in federal policy, giving first priority to the needs of the child in foster care, rather than to the troubled family from which the child came. "The big thing this bill does is swing the pendulum of government concern back in the direction of the children," said Rep. E. Clay Shaw Jr., R-Fla., chairman of the Human Resources Subcommittee.

Though child welfare advocates supported the bill, they warned that it still did not give states the resources they needed to deal with huge caseloads of foster children. Children in foster care were often harder to place than other children: They were often older, and many adoptive parents wanted to adopt babies; also, prospective parents were often wary of adopting children who were neglected during their formative years.

The 1980 legislation that had since come under such criticism had started out with many of the same goals as HR 867. When it was signed into law, President Jimmy Carter said it held "the promise of dramatically improving [children's] lives." *(1980 Almanac, p. 417)*

Congressional interest in promoting adoptions was demonstrated in 1996, when lawmakers provided adoptive parents a $5,000-per-child tax credit as part of a bill reducing taxes for small business and increasing the minimum wage (PL 104-188). *(1996 Almanac, pp. 2-34, 5-34)*

Legislative Action

HR 867 had an effortless journey through the House, beginning in the Ways and Means Subcommittee on Human Resources, which approved it by voice vote April 16. The full Ways and Means Committee approved it by voice vote April 23 (H Rept 105-77).

The original House bill differed from the final version in several respects. The requirement for states to terminate parental rights in the House version applied to children under age 10 who had been in foster care for 18 of the preceding 24 months. Criminal records checks on prospective foster and adoptive parents were to be optional for states.

The House passed the bill, unchanged, on April 30 by a vote of 416-5. *(Vote 96, p. H-32)*

Only a few family preservation advocates and critics of federal power opposed the measure. Rep. Ron Paul, R-Texas, said adoption policy should be left to the states. "Unfortunately for this country, few members of the 105th Congress have received word the era of big government is over."

After lingering for months, the legislation moved swiftly at the end of the session. The Senate gave voice vote approval Nov. 8 both to HR 867 and to an amendment by Larry E. Craig, R-Idaho, and John H. Chafee, R-R.I., that contained revisions to the earlier, House-passed version. Among the changes, the Senate amendment tightened requirements on screening foster and permanent adoptive parents, and added language to aid out-of-state adoptions. The Senate also attached the section reauthorizing the family preservation act.

Members worked out the relatively minor differences between the two versions of the bill in the waning days of the session without formally convening a conference committee.

The House then approved an omnibus amendment that reflected the compromise, and passed the bill, 406-7, on Nov. 13. The Senate accepted this latest version by voice vote later that day, clearing the measure for Clinton. *(Vote 635, p. H-188)* ■

Other Bills Related to Welfare

Congress cleared legislation placing new restrictions on various benefits to illegal immigrants and to prison inmates. An attempt to streamline adoption proceedings for American Indian children got no further than a Senate committee.

Adoption of American Indians

The Senate Indian Affairs Committee gave voice vote approval July 30 to a bill aimed at hastening the process for adopting American Indian children, but the measure went no further in the first session.

The legislation (S 569 — S Rept 105-156), sponsored by John McCain, R-Ariz., sought to create some certainty in the adoption process, which had been called into question by a few high-profile cases in which tribes attempted to intervene after children were placed with adoptive families. American Indians, concerned about the viability of their culture, often argued that children should remain in the tribe rather than be adopted by those who were not Indians.

Under the bill, tribes would be notified of all voluntary adoption proceedings involving children of those tribes. Existing law required notification only for children who were put up for adoption because of abuse or neglect.

The bill also proposed to limit how and when a tribe could intervene in an adoption proceeding. Any waiver of tribal rights would be considered final. A tribe seeking to intervene would have to prove that the child was eligible to become a member of the tribe.

The bill was considered a compromise between adoption-rights advocates and tribal leaders. Some Christian groups were concerned that the language might make adoption more difficult and less attractive to the biological mother. Abortion foes also feared the bill would encourage Indian women to abort their fetuses.

Most tribal groups supported the bill, but they remained wary of time limits on their opportunity to intervene. A similar measure had passed the Senate in 1996 but did not make it to the House floor. *(1996 Almanac, p. 6-27)*

Inmate Benefits

Under a provision of the budget-reconciliation bill (HR 2015 — PL 105-33), enacted Aug. 5, states were required to verify that prisoners were not receiving food stamps or being counted as part of a household that received them.

The legislation required states to set up systems, or use the Social Security Administration system, to gather the information. The requirement was to take effect one year after the bill was enacted, although the secretary of Agriculture could determine that "extraordinary circumstances" made it impractical for a state to obtain such information.

The House had passed similar requirements in a separate bill (HR 1000 — H Rept 105-43). Sponsored by Robert W. Goodlatte, R-Va., the bill originated in the House Agriculture Committee and passed in the House on April 8 by a vote of 409-0. *(Vote 73, p. H-24)*

The House also passed a bill by voice vote April 29 denying Social Security benefits to prisoners. That measure (HR 1048 — H Rept 105-78, Part 1) specified that Social Security benefits were to be denied to prisoners and to people found "guilty but insane" who were in institutions. (Existing law denied Social Security benefits to anyone who was to be imprisoned for more than a year.) Prison inmates also would be prohibited from receiving disability benefits under the bill.

The measure specified that welfare recipients who were charged with a drug-related crime could be denied benefits but only if they were charged after enactment of the welfare law (PL 104-193) on Aug. 22, 1996.

The House Ways and Means Committee approved the bill, sponsored by E. Clay Shaw Jr., R-Fla., on April 23 by a vote of 33-0. The panel approved non-binding language calling on the government to treat certain immigrant members of the Hmong tribe of Southeast Asia as U.S. military veterans in order to continue their eligibility for welfare. Recipients had worked with U.S. military and intelligence groups during the Vietnam War.

Relocation Aid

A bill signed into law Nov. 21 (S 1258 — PL 105-117) restricted relocation assistance to illegal aliens who were displaced by federally funded projects, such as construction of a highway. It amended the 1970 Uniform Relocation Assistance and Real Property Acquisition Policies Act (PL 91-646).

The legislation was prompted by a report in the San Diego Union-Tribune that an alleged illegal alien, displaced from her public housing complex, received $12,000 from the Department of Housing and Urban Development, while other displaced tenants received only $400 in relocation aid.

The bill "will remove one more magnet which draws illegal aliens to our country and ensure that our limited taxpayers' dollars are focused to our citizens who need help most," said Randy "Duke" Cunningham, R-Calif.

S 1258, introduced by Robert F. Bennett, R-Utah, was approved by the Senate Environment and Public Works Committee on Oct. 29. The Senate passed it by voice vote Nov. 8. The House cleared the bill by voice vote the following day.

The House had passed a similar bill (HR 849 — H Rept 105-147) on July 8 by a vote of 399-0. The House version, sponsored by Ron Packard, R-Calif., originated in the Transportation and Infrastructure Committee, which approved it by voice vote June 11. *(Vote 246, p. H-80)*

The bill proposed allowing the government to make exceptions in cases of extreme hardship and required that the Transportation Department ensure that the provisions were imposed in a non-discriminatory fashion. ■

Satcher's Surgeon General Nomination Postponed

The Senate postponed until 1998 a floor vote on the nomination of David Satcher to be surgeon general, despite what had looked like a smooth path toward confirmation.

Senate Majority Leader Trent Lott, R-Miss., said some senators wanted time for floor debate to discuss Satcher's position on several issues, including his opposition to a proposed ban on a particular abortion technique that opponents called a "partial birth" abortion. Lott said scheduling such floor time was difficult in the end-of-session rush of legislation.

"I assume his nomination will be confirmed but done after the first of the year," Lott said.

Satcher, 56, a physician, had served as director of the Centers for Disease Control and Prevention (CDC) since 1993. Prior to that, he had been president of Meharry Medical College in Nashville, Tenn.

The job of surgeon general, the nation's top health spokesman, had been vacant since 1994, when Joycelyn Elders was fired for controversial remarks on sexuality. Clinton's initial choice to replace her, Henry Foster, had been derailed by questions about the number of abortions he had performed. *(1995 Almanac, p. 7-26)*

The Senate Labor and Human Resources Committee recommended Satcher's nomination to the full Senate on Oct. 22, but five committee Republicans voted "no" because of Satcher's opposition to banning the so-called partial-birth abortion procedure. The vote was 12-5.

Republican Daniel R. Coats of Indiana led the opposition, saying he was disappointed that Satcher had chosen to support Clinton's opposition to banning the controversial abortion procedure.

He also expressed concern about Satcher's support for several AIDS studies that the CDC and the National Institutes of Health had conducted on pregnant, HIV-positive women in Africa, Asia and the Caribbean. In the studies, some women were given AZT, a relatively expensive drug that had been shown to reduce the transfer of HIV from mother to child, and others were given placebos. Also, some women were instructed to breast feed their babies — an activity believed to transfer AIDS — and some were told to use formula.

Coats said both sets of women should have been treated the same, and he compared the studies with those the U.S. Public Health Service conducted, beginning in 1932, to determine the effects of untreated syphilis in Tuskegee, Ala.

Edward M. Kennedy, D-Mass., said Coats' comparison was misplaced because the Tuskegee men were never told they had the disease or offered treatment, even when penicillin was discovered as a cure in the 1940s. Tennessee Republican Bill Frist, a physician and supporter of Satcher, defended the AIDS studies, saying they met international ethics standards.

John W. Warner, R-Va., said that while he sympathized with Coats, he would vote for Satcher because "I was deeply impressed with this man's commitment." Besides Warner and Frist, Republicans Susan Collins of Maine and committee Chairman James M. Jeffords of Vermont voted for Satcher, as did all panel Democrats. ■

CQ

Chapter 7

EDUCATION, HOUSING, LABOR & VETERANS

EDUCATION

Lawmakers Strike Compromise On Disabled Students Bill

States gain modest flexibility in disciplining disabled students; state funding formula also modified

A bill to reauthorize and revise the main federal education program for disabled students became law June 4 (HR 5 — PL 105-17), after backers crafted a compromise that sidestepped the feuding that had killed an earlier effort in 1996.

The 22-year-old Individuals with Disabilities Education Act (IDEA) had long been praised for guaranteeing access to free public education for disabled children nationwide, and any attempt to change it evoked strong emotions on all sides.

Critics complained that the program had become too costly, bureaucratic and overly protective of disabled students. Advocates of IDEA countered that the protections were needed to ensure that disabled children were not arbitrarily denied an education.

An attempt to reauthorize the disabilities law died in the 104th Congress after it became caught up in disputes over controversial GOP proposals to rewrite the law's federal funding formula and give schools more leeway to discipline disabled students. *(1996 Almanac, p. 7-16)*

To head off a repeat of that experience, the two key congressional committees — House Education and the Workforce and Senate Labor and Human Resources — adopted a consensus measure that had been worked out in closed-door negotiations by key staffers, Education Department officials, and interest groups.

The House passed the bill without change May 13, and the Senate cleared it unaltered, but only after killing a controversial amendment that would have given local officials more discretion in disciplining disabled students. Adoption of the amendment would have sent the bill to a House-Senate conference, potentially reopening the delicate negotiations.

The final bill gave states slightly more flexibility to discipline disabled students, although states still could not cut off educational services to them. The funding formula continued to stress the number of disabled children in a state, although a portion of it could reflect the state's overall number of school age children and its poverty rates.

BOXSCORE

IDEA Reauthorization — HR 5 (S 717). The bill revised and reauthorized the Individuals with Disabilities Education Act (IDEA), the main federal education program for children with disabilities.

Reports: H Rept 105-95, S Rept 105-17.

KEY ACTION

May 13 — House passed HR 5, 420-3.

May 14 — Senate cleared the bill, 98-1.

June 4 — President signed HR 5 — PL 105-17.

Bill Highlights

The bill contained major provisions to:

• **Discipline.** Allow schools to discipline disruptive disabled students for behavior not related to their disability in the same manner as they disciplined children without disabilities. Schools could automatically remove a disabled child from the regular classroom for up to 45 days for bringing a weapon or illegal drugs to school. Prior law allowed a 45-day removal from the classroom, but only for bringing a gun to school; otherwise, a school could not suspend, expel or change the placement of a disabled student for more than 10 days without the parents' consent or a court order.

The bill allowed a hearing officer rather than a court to determine whether disabled students could be moved to another classroom or another school to prevent them from endangering themselves or others. States were permitted to require that a disabled student's disciplinary record accompany the student to a new school. As under prior law, states could not end educational services to disabled students, even in extreme cases.

• **Funding formulas.** Retain existing funding formulas — which allocated federal money according to the number of disabled children in a school district — until appropriations reached $4.9 billion. (The fiscal 1997 appropriation was $4 billion.) Funds appropriated beyond $4.9 billion were to be allocated under a new formula based on a combination of school-age population (85 percent) and district poverty rates (15 percent).

Previously, funds had been distributed solely on the basis of the number of disabled children. Critics argued that this encouraged states to "over-identify" children as disabled in order to collect more money.

No state could receive less money under the new formula than it received the year the formula took effect.

• **Local contribution.** Require local school districts to contribute at least as much funding to the program as they had the previous year, until appropriations reached $4.1 billion. After that, school districts could use up to 20 percent of the increase in federal funding to supplant local money.

• **Attorneys' fees.** No longer require school districts to pay the fees of attorneys who represented the parents of disabled students in meetings that involved the student's individualized education plan, unless the meetings were under a court or administrative order.

Background

First enacted in 1975 as the Education for All Handicapped Children Act (PL 94-142), IDEA guaranteed the right of disabled children to a free education, and required that disabled students be in "the least restrictive environment." Unlike most civil rights legislation, IDEA also provided some federal funds to help carry out its mandates. Advocates for the disabled were proud of the program — which benefited an estimated 5.4 million disabled children nationwide — and cautious about making substantive changes. *(1975 Almanac, p. 651)*

But educators as well as some lawmakers, Republicans in particular, had seized on the need to reauthorize parts of the program as a chance to make sweeping changes. They were particularly interested in giving local school districts more flexibility to reduce costs and to discipline unruly disabled students.

In 1996, the House passed an IDEA reauthorization bill that would have distributed funds based mainly on a state's school-age population, rather than on the number of disabled children. Also, in cases where misconduct was unrelated to a student's disability, the bill would have allowed schools to apply the same disciplinary procedures to disabled students as to others, including expulsion without services.

Though the 1996 bill incorporated many suggestions made by a broad coalition representing disabled children and the general education community, advocates for disabled children still harbored reservations. The House passed the bill by voice vote, but Democrats cautioned that they would seek changes in conference.

In the Senate, the Labor and Human Resources Committee approved a somewhat narrower bill that said that if misconduct was not related to a student's disability, schools could employ the same disciplinary procedures they used for other students, including expulsion. But unless weapons or drugs were involved, the school would still be required to provide educational services.

Some GOP conservatives thought the Senate bill did not go far enough on discipline or in helping schools reduce the costs of special education. Republican leaders had little interest in a protracted debate, and the bill never came to the floor. *(1996 Almanac, p. 7-16)*

Committee Action

As the 105th Congress began, two committee chairmen — James M. Jeffords, R-Vt., of the Senate Labor and Human Resources Committee and Bill Goodling, R-Pa., of the House Education and the Workforce Committee — introduced bills (S 216, HR 5) that were virtually identical to those considered the year before.

However, at the urging of top Republican leaders, Goodling and Jeffords agreed to put their proposals aside and let staff members try to devise a new bill with more universal appeal.

Beginning in February, a group of congressional educational aides and officials from the Education Department quietly searched for a consensus. The negotiations were led by David Hoppe, the chief of staff to Senate Majority Leader Trent Lott, R-Miss., and the father of a child with Down's syndrome. The negotiators also worked closely with advocates for the disabled and for the public schools.

On May 7, the House Committee on Education and the Workforce and the Senate Labor and Human Resources Committee took up virtually identical versions of the resulting bill and approved them by voice vote (HR 5 — H Rept 105-95, S 717 — S Rept 105-17).

The Clinton administration and congressional leaders touted the speedy action as a triumph of bipartisanship. "This is a great example of Congress at its best," said Frank Riggs, R-Calif., at a joint news conference May 7. Lott and Education Secretary Richard W. Riley also attended the news conference.

House/Senate Floor Action

The House passed the bill May 13 by an overwhelming vote of 420-3, after taking it up under expedited procedures that precluded amendments. *(Vote 124, p. H-40)*

William L. Clay, Mo., the ranking Democrat on the Education and the Workforce Committee, called the measure "a truly remarkable example of what we can accomplish when we work together." Goodling agreed, saying, "I have never seen this happen in the 20 years I've been here."

The Senate cleared the bill the next day by a vote of 98-1, but the near-unanimous approval belied the difficult time Jeffords had fending off potential changes. *(Vote 66, p. S-14)*

Senate Turns Back Amendments

Jeffords had urged his colleagues not to offer amendments that could undo the compromise. "If they're identical, there is no chance of this falling apart," he said of the House and Senate bills. But not all senators saw it that way. Robert C. Smith, R-N.H., said in a May 13 floor speech that he objected to bringing HR 5 to the floor as a "locked-up agreement," with amendments discouraged.

Before the bill was passed, Jeffords turned back three amendments. The closest call came when 37 Republicans and 11 Democrats voted for an amendment that would have gutted the bill's delicately balanced provision on how much leeway to give school officials to discipline disabled students. The amendment, offered by Slade Gorton, R-Wash., would have left it up to each state or local school district to set its own discipline rules for disabled children. It was tabled (killed), 51-48. *(Vote 64, p. S-14)*

Gorton and other critics argued that though the bill offered local officials more flexibility to punish disabled students than did existing law, it would still leave a "double standard" for disabled pupils vs. other children and could lead to dangerous situations.

"Where there is a clear-cut example of behavior that is incompatible with a decent learning environment, the schools have to be able to take some action," said Christopher S. Bond., R-Mo.

Jeffords opposed the amendment because it threatened the compromise, and because he did not want to allow states and school districts to set their own policies. "This would create chaos," he said.

The second amendment, offered by Smith, would have required a court, when ordering a school district to pay attorneys' fees incurred by parents involved in IDEA disputes, to consider the impact such awards would have on the education of all children in the district. Smith and others argued that school districts spent too much money settling disputes between school districts and parents of disabled children. The Senate voted to table (kill) Smith's amendment, 68-31. *(Vote 65, p. S-14)*

Judd Gregg, R-N.H., offered, then withdrew, an amendment to add language to the bill to increase federal contributions to IDEA funding over seven years, including $4.16 billion in fiscal 1998 and $5.6 billion in fiscal 1999. The bill did not set authorization levels for federal contributions, leaving the issue to appropriators.

Gregg and other lawmakers complained that Congress had not lived up to the pledge made when the IDEA was created to provide 40 percent of its funding. The $4 billion appropriated in fiscal 1997 paid for less than 9 percent of the program. ■

Tax Incentives Enacted For Higher Education

A $35 billion package of tax breaks for higher education was enacted as part of budget-reconciliation legislation signed by President Clinton on Aug. 5 (HR 2014 — PL 105-34).

The education incentives — including credits and penalty-free withdrawals from individual retirement accounts (IRAs) — were a high priority for Clinton, who made them a condition for agreeing to the twin bills that made up the massive reconciliation legislation.

Republican leaders had agreed in May to include "roughly" $35 billion over five years in tax breaks to help middle-income families pay postsecondary education costs. But the nature and exact amount of the cuts remained a hot topic through the summer as the White House and Congress negotiated the terms of the tax- and spending-cut bills that made up the reconciliation package. *(Budget deal, p. 2-18)*

In the end, while Republicans shaped some of the details, Clinton met his goal with a five-year set of education tax breaks that totaled $35 billion. The House and Senate versions of the bill had called for $31 billion and $33 billion, respectively. The final bill also leaned heavily toward tax credits, favored by Clinton, rather than IRAs, which Democrats said would be used mainly by better-off taxpayers.

Notably absent from the final legislation was a GOP-sponsored provision that would have allowed parents to use special education savings accounts to finance their children's elementary and high school education at private schools. Clinton said that initiative would harm public education and vowed to veto the entire tax package if it were included. *(Tax reconciliation, p. 2-30; provisions, p. 2-39)*

House Republicans subsequently passed the proposal as a separate bill (HR 2646), but Democrats blocked action in the Senate. *(GOP school proposals, p. 7-6)*

Education Provisions in the Tax Bill

Two new tax credits — known as the HOPE credit and the lifetime learning credit — accounted for most of the $35 billion in education tax cuts. Together, they were projected to cost $31.6 billion over five years and $76 billion over 10 years. Both took effect Dec. 31, 1997.

In any year, for each student, an eligible taxpayer could choose among three options: the HOPE credit, the lifetime learning credit or money withdrawn tax-free from an education savings account.

The following is a summary of those and other education provisions in the bill:

- **HOPE credit.** Parents could claim a non-refundable tax credit of up to $1,500 for the first two years of postsecondary education for each student. The credit applied to tuition and fees, but not to the purchase of books or the cost of student activities. Starting in 2002, it was to be indexed for inflation.

Taxpayers were eligible for the full credit if their adjusted gross incomes were less than $40,000 for single filers and $80,000 for joint filers. The credit was phased out completely for individuals with $50,000 in adjusted gross income and joint filers making $100,000.

Clinton had called for such a credit, saying it would cover the costs of attending a typical community college. Similar proposals were included in the House and Senate versions of the tax-reconciliation bill.

- **Lifetime learning credit.** The bill also created a non-refundable lifetime learning credit for students in their last two years of college and in graduate school. Taxpayers could claim up to $1,000 per student each year through 2002, rising to $2,000 after 2002. Taxpayers were eligible for the full credit if their adjusted gross incomes were less than $40,000 for single filers and $80,000 for joint filers.

This was a Clinton initiative. Neither the House nor Senate versions of the tax bill included such a proposal.

- **IRA withdrawals.** Beginning in 1998, penalty-free withdrawals could be made from IRAs to pay for postsecondary, vocational and graduate education. Both Clinton and the Republicans had called for such a provision, though Clinton had wanted to restrict the penalty-free withdrawals to families with adjusted gross incomes under $100,000. The estimated cost of the provision was $812 million over five years and $1.7 billion over 10 years.
- **Education savings account.** Taxpayers could make after-tax contributions of up to $500 a year for each child under age 18 to a new education savings account. The account had to be created exclusively for paying the costs of higher education. The principal and interest could be withdrawn tax-free at any time to help pay for a child's college or graduate schooling.

The accounts could be used by virtually all taxpayers: The adjusted gross income limit was $95,000 for single filers and $150,000 for joint filers. The estimated cost: $3.9 billion over five years and $14.2 billion over 10 years.

- **Employer-provided education assistance.** The bill extended for three years a provision in existing law that allowed an employee to exclude from his or her taxable income $5,250 of employer-provided undergraduate education benefits. The estimated cost: $1.2 billion.
- **Student loan deduction.** Beginning in 1998, taxpayers could deduct up to $1,000 in interest payments on student loans, rising to $2,500 in 2001. Individual taxpayers with adjusted gross incomes of up to $40,000 would be eligible for the deduction, as would couples with incomes of up to $60,000. The estimated cost: $690 million over five years and $2.4 billion over 10 years.
- **Prepaid tuition programs.** Beginning in 1998, the existing deduction for state-sponsored prepaid tuition programs and state savings programs would be expanded to include the costs of room and board. The estimated cost: $533 million over five years and $1.5 billion over 10 years.

Background

In his Feb. 4 State of the Union address, Clinton outlined a series of tax breaks as part of a broader plan to boost higher education. On June 30, as the tax-reconciliation bill moved to the conference stage, he released a revised tax cut plan that added a so-called Kidsave IRA. *(Text, p. D-17)*

Clinton aimed his education cuts almost entirely at middle- and lower-income taxpayers by focusing on credits and deductions to offset the cost of tuition.

Clinton's main proposals were:

- **Hope credit.** A "Hope Scholarship" tax credit of $1,500 per student for two years, with the second year contingent on the student earning a B average. Clinton wanted the credit limited to families with gross adjusted incomes of up to $80,000 a year and phased out for those earning more than $100,000.
- **Deduction.** A tax deduction of up to $5,000, rising eventually to $10,000, to offset the cost of post secondary education and training. The deduction, which was not tied to an IRA, was to be available for families with adjusted gross incomes of less than $80,000, phasing out for those earning up to $100,000.

• **IRAs.** Penalty-free IRA withdrawals for postsecondary education for families with adjusted gross incomes of up to $100,000.

• **Kidsave.** A new IRA. Families receiving the new $500-per-child tax credit being created under the bill could put the funds into a so-called Kidsave account, along with $500 of their own money. The interest and principal could be withdrawn tax-free if the money was used for the child's education, the purchase of the child's first home or the taxpayer's retirement.

Clinton wanted to make the child credit partially refundable, meaning that families too poor to owe taxes could receive some or all of the money as a check.

Legislative Action

In contrast to Clinton's emphasis on credits and deductions, Republicans proposed devoting nearly one-third of the education tax cuts to IRAs. Democrats argued that lower-income taxpayers typically did not have enough money to save in an IRA.

The House and Senate passed somewhat different versions of the GOP education tax plan.

House Action

The House version of the tax bill, written in the Ways and Means Committee, included $31 billion in education tax breaks. The panel approved the overall proposal June 13 on a straight party-line vote of 22-16. The full House passed the tax bill (HR 2014 — H Rept 105-148) June 26 by a 253-179 vote. *(Vote 245, p. H-78)*

The House bill included the non-refundable HOPE credit of up to $1,500 per student for tuition and books in each of the first two years of college. The income thresholds were the same as in Clinton's plan.

As an alternative, under the House plan, parents could deduct up to $10,000 per year for each student from a new education investment account, similar to an IRA, or from a qualified pre-paid tuition program, as long as the money was used to pay for undergraduate education. Eligible expenses would include tuition, room and board.

Under the House bill, parents could put up to $5,000 a year per student into such an investment account, with a lifetime limit of $50,000 for each student. In addition, money could be withdrawn from a traditional IRA without penalty if it was used for higher education expenses, including tuition, books, room and board.

The House bill also included a small, non-refundable credit of up to $150 for extra costs, such as tutoring, for elementary and secondary school children.

Senate Action

The Senate tax-reconciliation provisions — drawn up by the Finance Committee and modified on the Senate floor — called for $33 billion in education incentives over five years. The Finance Committee approved the bill (S 949 — S Rept 105-33) in a bipartisan vote of 18-2 on June 19. The full Senate passed HR 2014, 80-18, on June 27 after substituting the text of S 949. *(Vote 160, p. S-28)*

The Senate plan contained incentives similar to those in the House bill, including an almost identical HOPE credit.

Like the House bill, the Senate measure also offered a tax break for money withdrawn from a special education savings account or a prepaid tuition program for education expenses. But instead of allowing a $10,000 per year deduction, the Senate opted to make the withdrawals tax free. The money could be used for undergraduate or graduate student expenses, including tuition, books, room and board.

Under the Senate bill, taxpayers could contribute up to $2,000 per year for each student, plus money from the child tax credit, into the new education IRA. (The Senate bill would have required taxpayers receiving the separate child credit to put a like amount into an education IRA.)

During floor action, the Senate agreed to a controversial amendment by Paul Coverdell, R-Ga., that would have allowed tax-free withdrawals from an education IRA to pay tuition for elementary and secondary students at parochial and private schools. The amendment was adopted June 27 by a vote of 58-42. *(Vote 150, p. S-27)*

Final Agreement

On July 19, as Republicans met among themselves to work out a joint House-Senate proposal on the overall tax bill to take to the White House, Clinton sent a letter to Senate Majority Leader Trent Lott, R-Miss., laying out his tax priorities. High among them, he wanted most of the GOP education proposals replaced with his own, which were targeted more at middle- and lower-income families.

Also, at the last minute, the administration threatened to veto the entire bill over Coverdell's amendment. The Senate had voted for the provision, and GOP leaders said they were not willing to abandon it unless Clinton put the veto threat in writing — which he did in a brief letter to Gingrich saying he "would veto any tax package that would undermine public education by providing tax benefits for private and parochial school expenses."

Republican negotiators, intent on avoiding a showdown with the White House, abandoned the provision — at the same time lambasting the president. Gingrich said Clinton once again had "chosen to place the interests of the powerful teachers' union bosses over those of America's schoolchildren."

The Speaker called the Coverdell amendment "a commonsense way to give parents the financial freedom to choose the best school for their children without taking a penny from the public school system," adding that he would work "to see that Sen. Coverdell's legislation becomes law, thereby ensuring every American child will receive a quality education." ■

Private School Aid Bills Blocked by Critics

Republican attempts to assist families in sending their children to private schools, particularly at the elementary and secondary level, met with defeat in the first session of the 105th Congress.

A bill to allow families to use tax-free education savings accounts to defray private or public school costs was dropped for the year after supporters in the Senate failed twice to limit debate on the measure. On Nov. 4, the day of the second Senate cloture vote, the House defeated a separate bill that would have allowed low-income families to use federal vouchers to send their children to private schools.

Education Savings Accounts

The House passed a bill (HR 2646) in October to allow parents, grandparents or scholarship sponsors to contribute up to $2,500 a year to a special education savings account. Both interest and principal could have been withdrawn tax-free to pay for any aspect of private or public school education, from kindergarten through college.

Republicans argued that the bill would give middle-class parents a helping hand. "This bill is one of the best things, in my opinion, to happen to education," said Ways and Means Chairman Bill Archer, R-Texas, the plan's sponsor. Social conservative organizations such as the Christian Coalition backed the plan, saying it would help families put a stronger emphasis on education.

But Democrats assailed the proposal as tilted toward affluent Americans who could afford to set aside several thousand dollars a year. "This only helps one class of people — upper-income constituents who live in the suburbs and send their children to private schools," said Martin Frost, D-Texas.

The plan was estimated to cost $2.6 billion over five years, after which the $2,500 limit would drop to $500 annually.

The bill would have expanded on a provision in the tax portion of the budget-reconciliation package (HR 2014 — PL 105-34) that allowed parents to put away up to $500 per child per year for higher education expenses in savings accounts similar to Individual Retirement Accounts (IRAs). The tax bill also allowed penalty-free withdrawals from all IRAs for undergraduate, graduate and vocational education expenses.

The Senate version of the tax-reconciliation bill would have gone further, allowing parents to use the accounts to pay costs of private or public education for elementary and secondary school children. President Clinton forced Republicans to drop that proposal, threatening to veto the entire reconciliation bill if it were included. *(Education tax breaks, p. 7-5)*

A Partisan OK From Ways and Means

Archer's separate education savings account bill began in the House Ways and Means Committee, which narrowly approved it Oct. 9 by a vote of 19-17 (H Rept 105-332).

The action followed a partisan debate over whether the plan would help low-income families. The Joint Committee on Taxation estimated that more than 14 million households would take advantage of the accounts, with benefits going mostly to families with adjusted gross incomes of $50,000 to $75,000 a year.

But Democrats argued that few parents could afford to set aside that much money. "For the average person in this country, it doesn't mean two hoots because they don't have the money to put in," said Gerald D. Kleczka, D-Wis.

John Ensign, R-Nev., put the onus on low-income people, saying they could afford to invest if they gave up a pack of cigarettes every day. "Most poor people who don't seem to be able to save money — a lot of them smoke," he said. "It is possible to scrimp and save if you want to take advantage of these education IRAs."

House Passes the Bill

The House passed the bill, 230-198, on Oct. 23, despite a veto threat from the administration. The day before the vote, Education Secretary Richard W. Riley said he would advise Clinton to reject the bill. Although Republicans appeared to lack the votes in both chambers to override a veto, they were hoping to make education an issue in the 1998 elections. *(Vote 524, p. H-160)*

The House rejected, 199-224, a Democratic substitute by Charles B. Rangel, D-N.Y., that instead would have enabled schools to raise more money for construction and other needs with bonds. *(Vote 523, p. H-160)*

The partisan floor debate focused on the conflicting estimates of who would benefit from the tax break. Bill supporters cited the Joint Tax estimates that 70 percent of the savings would go to families with adjusted gross annual incomes of $75,000 or less. Individuals with incomes of more than $110,000 would not be eligible for the accounts.

But the Treasury Department released an estimate that the wealthiest 20 percent of families would get nearly 70 percent of the benefits. Lower-income residents would receive only a marginal tax benefit — as little as $1 a year — because they did not pay much in taxes anyway, administration officials said.

Democrats Block Senate Action

In the Senate, Republicans tried twice to limit debate and bring the bill to a floor vote, but they were blocked by Democrats who complained that they had not been given a chance to amend the measure.

The first attempt to invoke cloture failed Oct. 30 by a vote of 56-41, four votes short of the 60 votes needed. *(Vote 288, p. S-50)*

Republicans, led by Paul Coverdell of Georgia, the bill's prime Senate backer, argued that two out of three people polled in a national survey supported the bill because it "gives them freedom to save and choose."

Democrats said they opposed the cloture motion to protect their right to offer amendments and because the Senate had held no hearings on the bill. They originally intended to defeat the motion to protest inaction on a stalled campaign finance reform bill (S 25). An agreement was reached Oct. 30 on the campaign finance bill, but that came after the deadline for offering amendments to HR 2646. *(Campaign finance bill, 1-26)*

Carol Moseley-Braun, D-Ill., raised the strongest objections to proceeding, saying hearings and committee action were necessary to fix what she called flaws in the measure. "This will benefit only the wealthy," she said.

Republicans tried again Nov. 4. This time the vote was 56-44, still four votes short of the 60 needed to move the bill toward passage. *(Vote 291, p. S-50)*

Minority Leader Tom Daschle, D-S.D., said Democrats blocked the measure because they were not permitted to offer amendments. Majority Leader Trent Lott, R-Miss., said he would seek action again in the second session. Coverdell said supporters would send the measure to the Finance Committee, where amendments could be considered.

School Vouchers

The House on Nov. 4 rejected a GOP proposal to provide vouchers — known as HELP (Helping Empower Low-Income Parents) scholarships — to low-income families that wanted to send their children to private school. The vote was 191-228. *(Vote 569, p. H-172)*

During the impassioned floor debate on the bill (HR 2746), Speaker Newt Gingrich, R-Ga., Majority Leader Dick Armey, R-Texas, and other Republicans argued that it was vital for low-income school children to find alternatives to poorly performing public schools.

The measure lost because 35 Republicans voted against it, while only four Democrats supported it. Sponsors had bypassed committee action on the bill, apparently out of concern that they lacked the votes for approval in the Education and the Workforce Committee.

The legislation, sponsored by Frank Riggs, R-Calif., chairman of the panel's Subcommittee on Early Childhood, Youth and Families, would have allowed states to use money from Title VI of the Elementary and Secondary Education Act to provide scholarships to low-income families to send their children to private schools, including religious schools.

The bill would have allowed states to reserve up to 25 percent of their Title VI funds for public and private school choice programs authorized by state law. States and local school districts received $310 million in Title VI money in fiscal 1997.

The scholarships were to be limited to students from families with incomes below 185 percent of the federal poverty level. Based on the poverty level in 1996 — the latest year available — the maximum family income for a scholarship would have been $29,435. The scholarships would have covered between 60 percent and 100 percent of per-pupil expenditures in the applicant's school district.

Democrats derided the legislation as an attempt to drain funds from public schools and said it would help relatively few low-income students. The Office of Management and Budget released a statement Oct. 30 saying that Clinton's senior advisers would recommend that he veto the bill.

William L. Clay of Missouri, the Education Committee's ranking Democrat, said the bill showed "Republicans' contempt for the masses" and represented "an outrageous abandonment of civil rights."

Matthew G. Martinez of California, ranking Democrat on the Early Childhood subcommittee, described it as "the extreme right's modern version of white flight from our cities. Just like we abandoned the poor parts of our cities . . . this bill will leave our public schools in ruin in search of a panacea for just a few."

Riggs responded that he deplored "the use of the race card and race baiting."

Republicans tried to cast the issue as a matter of choice, saying that students from poor families ought to be able to exercise some of the same education options as the well-to-do. Riggs said there were many Democrats who had "contempt for the fundamental right of parents to choose, who do not believe that we need improvement through education."

Gingrich added, "The only people in America without choice are the poorest children in the poorest neighborhoods who are trapped by the bureaucracies and the unions and exploited against their will."

Democrats sought to goad Republicans by contrasting GOP remarks supporting educational opportunities for the poor with their votes in the 104th Congress to refashion the federal school lunch program into a state block grant and to restrain spending on Head Start.

In the end, it was the opposition of the 35 Republicans, many of them moderates, that caused the bill's defeat. Marge Roukema, R-N.J., was one of the defectors. "Ultimately," she said, "these vouchers will result in gutting the public school system" by shifting money from public schools to private schools. ■

Private Lenders Get Bigger Role In Student Loan Consolidation

Legislation aimed at making it easier for students to consolidate their loans was enacted as part of the fiscal 1998 appropriations bill for the departments of Labor, Health and Human Services (HHS) and Education. President Clinton signed the bill into law Nov. 13 (HR 2264 — PL 105-78). The proposal had advanced in separate bills in both chambers before being rolled into the spending measure in conference.

Many students received loans from several sources and later combined them to obtain more favorable financing terms or simplify their payments. Previously, however, students with direct loans from the government were not permitted to consolidate their loans through private lenders under the guaranteed student loan program.

The bill allowed them to do so, and to retain the favorable interest rate subsidy they got through the direct loan program. The change was effective through Sept. 30, 1998.

The measure was a response to the Department of Education's difficulty in consolidating direct loans. The department's contractor had announced that it had a backlog of more than 80,000 borrowers trying to refinance multiple student loans into a single direct loan from the federal government. The department blamed computer problems and said the backlog would be eliminated by Dec. 1, 1997. However, Republicans remained skeptical.

Background

Under the traditional guaranteed student loan program, created in 1965, the federal government guaranteed student loans issued by private banks or other financial institutions. If a student defaulted, the loan was paid off by a state guarantee agency, which was eventually reimbursed by the federal government.

Under the direct loan program, created in 1993 as part of that year's budget-reconciliation law (PL 103-66), students could apply for loans directly to the government through their schools, bypassing the banks altogether. Students dealt with one entity for the life of that loan and had several repayment options, including one that tied payments to their income. *(1993 Almanac, p. 410)*

Borrowers who had taken out both guaranteed and direct student loans could combine their debt only by going to the government and obtaining a direct consolidated student loan. They could not combine both types of loans into a new guaranteed loan from a private lender.

Supporters argued that the direct loan program would lower interest rates for students and save the government money by cutting federal subsidies to banks. The direct student loan rate was generally capped at 8.25 percent.

Republicans doubted from the outset whether the government could handle student loans more efficiently than the guaranteed student loan market, and they seized on the Education Department's problems with consolidating loans as proof of the program's overall shortcomings.

Legislative Summary

The consolidation plan began in the House as a separate bill (HR 2535), introduced Sept. 24 by California Republican Howard P. "Buck" McKeon. Moving with uncommon bipartisanship and speed, the House Education and the Workforce Committee approved the measure Oct. 1 by a vote of 43-0 (H Rept 105-322).

"My legislation provides an immediate solution for students now, in the short term, rather than making them wait months for the department and its contractor to straighten things out," said McKeon, who chaired the panel's Subcommittee on Postsecondary Education, Training and Life-Long Learning.

"I had a hard time believing that the department, with all of its long-standing management problems, could get its act together and efficiently manage this program," said committee Chairman Bill Goodling, R-Pa. "My concern then and my concern now is that when the department drops the ball, it is students who get bounced around."

William L. Clay of Missouri, the panel's ranking Democrat,

objected to plans to pay the $25 million cost of the legislation out of the Education Department's administrative budget. "How can we ask the direct lending program to perform superbly while we cut administrative funding to the bone?" he asked. Clay also said it was unclear whether private lenders would refinance any of the direct loans.

Robert E. Andrews, D-N.J., defended the direct loan program, noting that it had provided aid to 2.1 million students in the 1996-97 academic year and was expected to benefit 2.8 million students in 1997-98. "I don't want the very real and significant problem that 85,000 students have encountered . . . to overshadow the fact that several million students have successfully obtained a student loan," he said.

McKeon said the legislation was not a prelude to a GOP attempt to abolish the direct loan program when the committee considered reauthorizing higher education programs early in 1998. "I don't like it," he said. "But I'm a realist. There's no way to kill direct loans. The president would veto it if we got the votes."

McKeon and Dale E. Kildee of Michigan, the subcommittee's ranking Democrat, both said after the markup that under a truce reached earlier in the year, they had agreed that they would not try to eliminate either the direct loan or the guaranteed loan program.

"There will be competition between the two programs," Kildee said. "But legislatively, we don't intend to make any significant changes."

The committee approved by voice vote an amendment by McKeon to clarify that the measure would cover all applications received after the legislation was enacted.

The panel also gave voice vote approval to an amendment by Clay and Kildee to ensure that those who received the new HOPE Scholarship would not have their Pell grants or other student financial aid reduced as a consequence.

The HOPE Scholarship was enacted as part of the tax portion of the 1997 budget-reconciliation bill (PL 105-34). It gave parents of students in the first two years of postsecondary education a tax credit of 100 percent on the first $1,000 of tuition and fees, and 50 percent on the second $1,000 of tuition and fees. *(Education tax breaks, p. 7-5)*

The panel's rapid handling of the legislation — the markup lasted about half an hour — and the widespread support it garnered were so unusual that Goodling took note of it. "Let the record show it was unanimous," he said after the vote. "Let it happen more often."

The House passed the bill by voice vote Oct. 21 despite administration objections.

The Clinton administration released a statement the day of the vote saying it opposed the legislation for several reasons. Among them: that it would not help those who could not get or did not want a guaranteed student loan, and that the $25 million to help pay for the legislation would come from the Education Department's administrative budget for student loans.

Senate Committee Approves Bill

The Senate Labor and Human Resources Committee gave voice vote approval to a companion bill on Oct. 22 (S 1294 — S Rept 105-122). The Senate panel's ranking Democrat, Edward M. Kennedy of Massachusetts, signaled that he would try to change the bill.

"It makes no sense to solve the consolidation problem by weakening the department's ability" to process loans, Kennedy said. But panel Chairman James M. Jeffords, R-Vt., said the situation would improve if Education Department officials "get their act together more quickly." ■

Other Legislation Related To Education

The House passed bills to assist charter schools and improve literacy among children, but the Senate did not take up either measure. In separate action, plans to save money in student loan programs were included in the 1997 budget-reconciliation package.

Charter Schools

The House passed a bill (HR 2616) to nearly double the amount of federal money available to charter schools, targeting the increase to states that gave charter schools significant autonomy and met other conditions. The Senate did not act on the measure in the first session.

The measure, sponsored by Republican Rep. Frank Riggs, of California, proposed authorizing $100 million in fiscal 1998 and undetermined amounts in fiscal years 1999 through 2002, for the federal charter schools program. The money was aimed primarily at helping to offset the start-up costs of such schools.

The bill also specified that funds in excess of $51 million — the amount appropriated for charter schools in fiscal 1997 — be distributed to states whose charter school laws met certain criteria. The proposal favored states that:

➤ Provided charter schools a high degree of autonomy over their budgets and expenditures.

➤ Increased the number of charter schools from year to year.

➤ Required periodic reviews to determine whether each charter school was meeting the academic performance requirements and goals set out in the school's charter.

Under the appropriations bill for the departments of Labor, Health and Human Services and Education, signed Nov. 13 (HR 2264 — PL 105-78), Congress agreed to provide $80 million for charter schools in fiscal 1998. Up to $29 million was to be directed by HR 2616 if that bill was enacted.

At the time, there were more than 500 charter schools nationwide. These were public schools established under state law that operated outside the usual school district rules and bureaucracy. Like traditional public schools, charter schools were nonsectarian, did not charge tuition, and had to follow federal education and civil rights statutes.

While state laws varied widely, the academic performance of the school's students was almost always a condition for measuring a charter school's success and determining whether its charter should continue.

In 1994, Congress agreed to authorize $15 million in fiscal 1995, and such sums as might be necessary in fiscal years 1996 through 1999, for the costs of starting charter schools. The Clinton administration requested $100 million for fiscal 1998. *(1994 Almanac, p. 395)*

Legislative Summary

The charter schools bill began in the House Committee on Education and the Workforce, which approved it Oct. 9 by a vote of 24-8 (H Rept 105-321). The panel rejected, 16-19, an amendment by Matthew G. Martinez, D-Calif., to require local school districts that applied for charter schools to outline how they would comply with the Individuals with

Disabilities Education Act (IDEA), which guaranteed a free, appropriate education to all students with disabilities.

The House passed the bill Nov. 7 by a vote of 367-57, after Martinez won voice vote approval for his IDEA amendment. *(Vote 611, p. H-182)*

Members defeated, 164-260, an amendment by John F. Tierney, D-Mass., that would have deleted the provisions that gave priority for part of the funding to states that met specific conditions. *(Vote 610, p. H-182)*

After passing the House, the bill was referred to the Senate Labor and Human Resources Committee.

Children's Literacy

Hoping to boost the country's literacy rate, the House on Nov. 8 passed a bill (HR 2614) aimed at upgrading the skills of teachers who taught reading and stimulating the development of more high-quality family literacy programs. The measure, based loosely on a proposal by President Clinton known as "America Reads," was approved by voice vote. The Senate did not take it up.

The bill, sponsored by Bill Goodling, R-Pa., chairman of the House Education and the Workforce Committee, proposed authorizing $260 million annually for three years for the program beginning in fiscal 1998, with the aim of having all children reading by the end of third grade.

The money would be distributed to states for use in creating and expanding reading and literacy partnerships between state and local officials. The partnerships would include in-service training for teachers and the use of reading tutors in before- and after-school programs for students needing help.

The bill also included support for family programs involving interactive literacy activities between parents and their children. These programs were intended to give extra support to children of illiterate parents.

The Education Department could also issue grants for Even Start programs, which were aimed at helping all children start school with the same educational skills.

The Education and the Workforce Committee approved the bill by voice vote Oct. 22 (H Rept 105-348), after Goodling postponed action for two weeks to protest Clinton's insistence on moving forward with his separate voluntary national student testing program.

After passing the House, the bill was referred to the Senate Labor and Human Resources Committee.

The fiscal 1998 appropriations bill for the departments of Labor, Health and Human Services, and Education provided $210 million in advance fiscal 1999 funding for the literacy initiative, pending completion of an authorization bill. The Clinton administration had requested $260 million in fiscal 1998. *(Appropriations, p. 9-50)*

Student Loan Cutbacks

Congress agreed to trim federal student loan programs for an estimated savings of $1.8 billion over five years. The changes were enacted as part of the spending-cuts portion of the 1997 budget-reconciliation package (HR 2015 — PL 105-33), signed into law Aug. 5.

The following are the main provisions:

➤ The agencies that guaranteed student loans were required to return $1 billion in reserve funds to the federal government in fiscal 2002. The amount was about half of what the agencies held in reserve as of Sept. 30, 1996.

➤ The bill reduced funds provided to the secretary of Education for administrative expenses associated with the direct and guaranteed student loan programs, for an estimated savings of about $600 million over five years.

➤ The bill eliminated the $10 loan-origination fee that the federal government paid to schools or agencies for each direct student loan that they made. The fiscal 1996 and 1997 appropriations bills for the Department of Education had prohibited the payment of this fee. The change was expected to save about $160 million over five years.

➤ As part of the bill, Congress repealed the 1917 Smith-Hughes Act (PL 64-347), which created the Federal Board of Vocational Education and provided federal aid to support the teaching of agriculture, industrial arts and home economics in public schools. States had received a small amount of vocational education funding each year under the law.

Legislative Summary

The student loan savings were crafted by the House and Senate authorizing committees responsible for education programs.

In the House, the Education and the Workforce Committee approved the proposals, 24-20, over strong Democratic opposition June 12 as part of its contribution to the budget-reconciliation bill.

Robert E. Andrews, D-N.J., tried to strike language requiring that guarantee agencies be paid an administrative cost allowance at a rate of 0.85 percent of new loan volume. He said the allowance should be based more on actual costs. His amendment failed, 21-24.

Andrews also offered an amendment to reduce the initial loan fees for students. As an offset, he proposed cutting back the amount the federal government reimbursed lenders on defaulted loans and reducing the amount guarantee agencies could collect on defaulted loans. It also failed on a 21-24 vote.

In the Senate, the Labor and Human Resources Committee approved similar student loan provisions June 11 by a vote of 17-1. Paul Wellstone, D-Minn., was the lone dissenter.

The committee rejected, 8-10, an amendment by Christopher J. Dodd, D-Conn., that would have eliminated the 0.85 percent administrative cost allowance for guarantee agencies.

The panel gave voice vote approval to an amendment by Tom Harkin, D-Iowa, to permit a guarantee agency to use earnings to limit student loan defaults.

The panel defeated, 8-10, an amendment by Edward M. Kennedy of Massachusetts, the committee's ranking Democrat, to reduce the initial loan fees for students in exchange for reducing insurance payments made to guarantee agencies on defaulted loans and payments to guarantee agencies for collecting defaults. ■

Herman Wins Labor Post Despite Controversy

Nearly six months after being nominated to become secretary of Labor, Alexis Herman easily won Senate confirmation April 30 on a bipartisan vote of 85-13. A majority of the chamber's Republicans joined 43 of 45 Democrats to ensure Herman's confirmation. Two Democrats were absent. *(Vote 54, p. S-12)*

Herman's nomination was initially jeopardized because of questions about her involvement in White House fundraising activities. It later became a bargaining chip in an escalating dispute between the Clinton administration and Senate GOP leaders over administration plans to give priority to unionized companies in federal construction projects.

The Senate Labor and Human Resources Committee had recommended Herman's confirmation by voice vote April 10.

Delay Over Fundraising Questions

Herman testified before the Labor panel March 18, after a delay of several months prompted by questions about whether she had inappropriately mixed politics with governing while serving as director of the White House Office of Public Liaison during President Clinton's first term.

After her testimony, committee Chairman James M. Jeffords, R-Vt., praised Herman for her knowledge of labor issues, which stemmed from stints as a union organizer and as director of the Labor Department's Women's Bureau during the Carter administration.

Herman, an African-American, was greeted at the hearing by a supportive, standing-room-only audience that included prominent blacks such as Children's Defense Fund President Marian Wright Edelman; NAACP President Kweisi Mfume, a former Democratic House member from Maryland (1987-96); newly confirmed Transportation Secretary Rodney Slater; and more than a dozen members of the Congressional Black Caucus.

Recalling the failed nominations of African-American law professor Lani Guinier in 1993 to head the Justice Department's civil rights division and of black physician Henry W. Foster Jr. in 1995 to be surgeon general, many of those on hand came to demonstrate their support for Herman. *(1993 Almanac, p. 307; 1995 Almanac, p. 7-26)*

In more than four hours of testimony, Herman responded to questions about her management philosophy, her activities in the Clinton White House, her experiences in the Labor Department in the 1970s and her work as a private consultant on diversity before she returned to government in 1993.

Few panel members delved deeply into allegations about Herman's involvement in White House political fundraising, the topic that initially threatened to derail the nomination.

Before the hearing, however, Herman was asked by the Labor panel to respond to written questions about her tenure as director of the Office of Public Liaison. At the hearing, Jeffords pointedly criticized the White House for alleged fundraising improprieties. "I am troubled by the culture that gives rise to so many missteps," Jeffords said. "I think the Office of Public Liaison made mistakes. And I think the nominee made some mistakes."

Herman was also questioned before the hearing about her role in a White House "coffee" for more than a dozen bankers that was attended by Clinton, former Democratic National Committee Co-chairman Don Fowler and Comptroller of the Currency Eugene Ludwig. Clinton had since conceded that Ludwig should not have been included in the coffee, because as comptroller he had direct regulatory control over the bankers.

Herman, whose job as director of Public Liaison often forced her to walk a fine line between politics and governing, had said she did not attend that event, nor was she aware that Ludwig would be there.

Herman reluctantly said at the hearing that administration officials had apparently made some mistakes.

While declining to embrace most Republican proposals, Herman did say she would support consolidating the nation's job training programs and establishing one-stop career centers in each state that could link job-seekers and displaced workers to employers and retraining programs in their region.

Labor Dispute Stalls Vote

Senate Republicans, including Majority Leader Trent Lott, R-Miss., and Majority Whip Don Nickles, R-Okla., further delayed Herman's confirmation, using it as leverage on the labor issue. They wanted Clinton to abandon plans to issue an executive order urging federal agencies to sign non-binding "project agreements" aimed at giving priority to unionized companies when awarding contracts on large, long-term projects such as dam construction.

GOP leaders argued that such an order would amount to a political payoff to organized labor for its support of Democratic candidates in the 1996 elections.

Senate Democrats responded the week of April 28 by refusing to allow other legislation — specifically, a bill (S 543) to shield volunteers from liability lawsuits — to reach the floor until Herman's confirmation was allowed to proceed. Two cloture votes aimed at moving the liability bill to the floor failed. *(Volunteer protection, p. 5-17)*

In search of a compromise, Nichols began negotiating with the White House on April 29.

Clinton agreed that instead of an executive order, he would issue a "presidential memorandum" that would have the same effect, except that it would expire when Clinton left office. An executive order would have remained in effect until a future president chose to rescind it.

After reaching the compromise, both sides claimed victory and Herman's confirmation was quickly approved.

"Ms. Herman's career has been filled with many firsts," said Jeffords, who pointed out that she would be the first African-American woman to serve as Labor secretary.

Democrats, including the Labor panel's ranking member, Edward M. Kennedy of Massachusetts, said the White House lost nothing in the compromise. "It was a mistake for the Republican leadership to hold [Herman's] nomination hostage on a separate labor issue," Kennedy said. "President Clinton gave up nothing substantial. The compromise on that issue is entirely satisfactory." ■

Senate Overwhelmingly Endorses Cuomo as HUD Secretary

The Senate confirmed Andrew M. Cuomo as secretary of the Department of Housing and Urban Development (HUD) on Jan. 29 by a vote of 99-0. *(Vote 3, p. S-2)*

Cuomo, son of former Democratic New York Gov. Mario M. Cuomo, got a warm welcome from the Senate Banking, Housing and Urban Affairs Committee at his Jan. 22 confirmation hearing, drawing bipartisan praise for his experience and commitment to making housing affordable, particularly for the poor and elderly.

Cuomo had previously been assistant HUD secretary for community planning and development for four years. As secretary, he succeeded Henry G. Cisneros, who returned to the private sector.

Banking panel members did make clear that their kind words for Cuomo did not extend to the department itself, which many conservative Republicans considered to be a bloated and poorly run bureaucracy. Cuomo was warned that the agency would go through tough times in an era of shrinking resources and growing needs.

"HUD has failed," said North Carolina Republican Sen. Lauch Faircloth. "In many instances, it's lost sight of its mission. Management is the problem. HUD has become a massive Washington bureaucracy."

Faircloth, who had introduced legislation in the 104th Congress aimed at eliminating the department, said the agency had too many programs and too many people.

Richard C. Shelby, R-Ala., said HUD had serious problems with its public and subsidized housing programs, which he said threatened to nearly consume the department's budget within a five-year period. "HUD has problems, both financially and operationally," said Shelby, adding that "the answer is not more money."

In response to such concerns, Cuomo said he was committed to continue streamlining efforts initiated by Cisneros, while also finding ways to meet the housing needs of low-income families and senior citizens. "We have to balance the budget and meet our responsibilities," he said. "We have to do both. I don't think the two are mutually inconsistent."

Cuomo said that under Clinton administration plans to reduce the size and scope of government, HUD was slated to have a work force of about 7,500 employees by 2000, nearly 30 percent smaller than in 1997. He said such a scenario would force the agency to become more efficient and would necessitate innovative thinking about how to do more with less. One strategy Cuomo said he would pursue was to have fewer people in Washington, while deploying more personnel to field offices around the country.

In public housing, Cuomo said he would seek to transfer more authority to the states and communities when local authorities were doing a good job. When public housing authorities were failing, however, Cuomo said he intended to do whatever was necessary to improve them.

Cuomo also pledged to overhaul the so-called Section 8 program, which consisted of roughly 8,500 privately owned, federally subsidized, low-income housing projects. Many of the apartment owners were collecting far more from the department in subsidies than they could collect in rent from ordinary tenants. ■

No Consensus on Housing Overhaul

For the second time in as many years, Republican plans to overhaul New Deal-era housing laws stalled in Congress as the House and Senate failed to agree on how far to go in rewriting public and subsidized housing programs.

As they had in 1996, both chambers passed their own prescriptions to heal the nation's public and subsidized housing (HR 2, S 462). Although the House bill was more far-reaching, the two measures had much in common.

Both prescribed shifting more decision-making on rents and tenants to local authorities. Both sought to pave the way for the working poor to return to public housing, though the House bill went much further. And both proposed to consolidate federal funding for public housing and low-income rental assistance into block grants to local authorities.

But the same disagreements that had killed similar legislation in 1996 resurfaced. Some were key to the bill, such as how much housing to reserve for those with very low incomes. Others were largely symbolic, such as whether to repeal the landmark New Deal law that established the framework for the existing public housing policies. *(1996 Almanac, p. 7-21)*

BOXSCORE

Public Housing Overhaul — HR 2, S 462. The bills proposed to rewrite New Deal-era housing laws in an effort to consolidate federal public and subsidized housing programs and shift primary responsibility to state and local authorities.

Reports: H Rept 105-76, Parts 1 and 2; S Rept 105-21

KEY ACTION

May 14 — House passed HR 2, 293-132.

Sept. 26 — Senate passed S 462 by voice vote.

Background

During the 1970s and 1980s, federal housing policy was an ideological battleground between congressional Democrats who wanted the government to provide more low-income housing and Republicans who wanted to get government out of the housing business. Democrats focused on tying the hands of federal bureaucrats, who, under President Ronald Reagan, had been permitting housing authorities to tear down public housing without any plans for replacing it. But the resulting restrictions, coupled with a lack of funds, often meant that dilapidated projects were kept in place.

The political dynamics changed dramatically in 1994 when Democrats, with encouragement from the Clinton administration, joined Republicans in embracing legislation to give state and local officials more control over housing programs. The House passed a housing reauthorization bill that sought to give local authorities more say over how to spend money to aid the homeless and more flexibility when selling or demolishing public housing units. The Senate Banking Committee approved a similar bill, but the measure died in the crush of end-of-session business. *(1994 Almanac, p. 408)*

The Republican takeover of Congress in 1995 pushed congressional thinking even further. Republicans included the Department of Housing and Urban Development (HUD) among the federal agencies they hoped to eliminate. Sen. Lauch Faircloth, R-N.C., and then-Rep. Sam Brownback, R-Kan., introduced bills (S 1145, HR 2198) to abolish HUD, but they never got off the ground.

That was due in large part to the Clinton administration's willingness to remake the troubled department — and to the unwillingness of moderate Republicans to eliminate a department that oversaw 1.25 million units housing about 3 million people.

HUD Secretary Henry G. Cisneros and, later, his successor, Andrew M. Cuomo, proposed dramatic staffing cuts and organizational changes to the department. They also recognized that if housing programs were to survive in increasingly tight budget years, they would have to have more flexible rules; many Republicans in Congress agreed.

Key Republican committee chairmen — Rep. Rick A. Lazio of New York and Sen. Connie Mack of Florida, who chaired the House and Senate Banking subcommittees responsible for housing — introduced bills in both the 104th and 105th Congresses to loosen many requirements on housing authorities in an effort to improve the cash flow of housing projects.

While Lazio, Mack and the Clinton administration agreed

on the general parameters of a housing overhaul, they did not always agree on the specifics. For example, as the House debated Lazio's measure in April 1997, Cuomo held a press conference criticizing the bill for seeking to direct scarce resources to the working poor instead of to the extremely poor — those living at or below 30 percent of a community's median income. "It's either public housing or the street," he said. "There's no place else for them to live."

Cuomo also touted an administration bill (HR 1447), which would have retained the 1937 U.S. Housing Act and combined numerous housing programs into two funding streams — one for capital expenditures, such as construction or major renovations to existing projects, and a second for operating expenses of local housing authorities. It also sought to give local agencies more flexibility by allowing well-managed authorities to operate with minimal federal regulation. Less well-run agencies would have been closely monitored by HUD. Poorly run, or "troubled" agencies, would have been given one year to improve or face a takeover by HUD or a receiver.

House Committee

Lazio's measure (HR 2) provoked sharp partisan rhetoric in a House Banking and Financial Services Committee markup that began April 15 and ended April 23. The panel approved the bill, 28-19, mostly along party lines (H Rept 105-76). Only two Democrats, Gary L. Ackerman of New York and Ken Bentsen of Texas, voted for the bill. Republican Ron Paul of Texas voted against it.

Republicans praised HR 2 as a blueprint for moving people off government dependency and into self-sufficiency. "This legislation is an opportunity for renewal," Lazio said. "That is the main mission of this legislation."

But Democrats such as Barney Frank of Massachusetts said the bill was too prescriptive and would fail to protect those with extremely low incomes. Frank predicted that if enacted, the measure would lead to increased homelessness nationwide. "This is part of a march away from compassion," Frank said. "This bill will drive housing authorities into doing less and less for poor people."

The bill proposed to repeal the U.S. Housing Act of 1937, deregulate public housing and rental assistance programs, and increase community control over such programs. The bill included provisions to:

- **Local control.** Shift more control and decision-making responsibilities from the federal government to local housing authorities, and allow housing authorities to create alternative programs to complement existing initiatives.
- **Rent flexibility.** Revise the so-called Brooke Amendment, which limited rent for public housing tenants to 30 percent of their adjusted income. Under that system, the rent automatically increased when the tenant earned more money, providing a disincentive to work. The bill would allow local housing agencies to offer tenants a choice between paying 30 percent of their income in rent as they did under existing law, or paying a presumably lower flat rent that they could negotiate with the housing authority.
- **Community service.** Require that unemployed, able-bodied public housing tenants who were not on welfare perform eight hours a month of community service. Welfare recipients were already subject to work requirements.
- **Failed housing authorities.** Require the federal government to move quickly to assume control of dysfunctional housing authorities by direct takeover or by placing such agencies in receivership.

A Contentious Markup

After an opening day devoted mostly to members' introductory remarks, the panel began the markup in earnest April 16 by wading into the thorny and divisive issue of income targeting — determining whether public housing ought to be reserved for the poorest of the poor, or whether people of marginally more means should be eligible.

Existing law required that about 75 percent of tenants in public housing projects earn no more than 30 percent of the median income in their local area. The vast majority of such tenants were unemployed and received public assistance such as welfare or Social Security disability benefits.

The bill proposed to alter the ratio by requiring that 65 percent of new tenants be from the so-called working poor — those who held jobs but lived at or below the poverty line. The remaining 35 percent of new residents would be those earning no more than 30 percent of the median income.

Republicans contended that increasing the percentage of working poor residents in public housing through such income mixing or "income targeting" would improve the culture in troubled housing projects and ultimately reduce incidents of crime and the presence of gangs and drugs.

"This is not so much about housing as it is about poverty," Lazio said. "Let's make sure that the environment we have is a healthy environment."

But Democrats such as Joseph P. Kennedy II of Massachusetts, the subcommittee's ranking member, said such income mixing would pit poor people against each other. "It is a devastating housing policy change," Kennedy said. "I don't believe for one minute that we should adopt housing policy in this committee that would essentially turn our back" on the poor.

Kennedy tried unsuccessfully April 16 to amend the bill's income targeting provisions. He proposed that at least 40 percent of new public housing tenants have incomes at 30 percent or less of an area's median income, and that no less than 90 percent of new residents have incomes at or below 60 percent of the median income. His proposal was defeated, 25-26.

The panel also rejected more than a dozen Democratic amendments aimed at softening what Democrats saw as harsh treatment of tenants under the bill. For example, the committee:

- Rejected, 19-26, an amendment by Jesse L. Jackson Jr. of Illinois that would have removed the proposed community service requirements.
- Rejected, 14-26, an amendment by Jackson to delete language allowing public housing tenants to be evicted if they failed to comply with community service requirements.
- Rejected, 17-23, a Jackson proposal to define the bill's work, job training and educational requirements as an unfunded federal mandate and to require the government to pay for it.
- Defeated, 15-27, an amendment by Melvin Watt of North Carolina to remove the community service requirements.
- Defeated, 13-24, an amendment by Frank to make the work, job training and education requirements optional and to place them under the purview of local housing authorities.

The panel also:

- Defeated, 17-24, an amendment by Maxine Waters, D-Calif., and Carolyn Cheeks Kilpatrick, D-Mich., that would have retained existing law permitting tenants suspected of non-criminal infractions to appear before housing review boards made up of their peers before being evicted from housing projects.
- Accepted by voice vote an amendment by Waters to require housing authorities to collect demographic data

about poor people — those whose incomes did not exceed 30 percent of the median — who failed to receive housing assistance.

➤ Rejected, 16-22, an amendment by Democrat Nydia M. Velázquez of New York that would have set minimum rents at public housing projects at zero to $25 a month instead of the $25 to $50 a month in the bill. The amendment also would have allowed "hardship cases" — those who could not afford to pay any rent — to be determined by HUD, not by local housing authorities.

➤ Defeated, 19-20, a proposal by Waters to require that when new housing units were constructed on land previously owned or occupied by a public housing authority, at least one-third of the units be reserved for low-income families.

Following fierce debate over desirable income levels for new public housing tenants and mandatory work requirements for the unemployed, the panel recessed April 17.

Democrats Keep Up the Attack

The committee reconvened the following week. Members waded through more than a dozen amendments April 23, defeating several Democratic proposals aimed at the heart of the bill. The panel:

➤ Defeated, 19-29, a Kennedy amendment that would have eliminated the new Home Rule Flexible Grant proposed in the bill. Under the initiative, localities would apply for federal block grants to be drawn from the housing dollars allocated to a community. With HUD's approval, such money could be used to develop housing initiatives that could compete with or complement existing programs. Republicans said this would foster cooperation between local governments and housing authorities.

➤ Rejected, 14-27, an amendment by Luis V. Gutierrez, D-Ill., that would have deleted a provision authorizing HUD to increase income eligibility levels to allow more communities — in some cases, better-off communities — to receive money under the Community Development Block Grant program and the HOME initiative. The block grant provided funds to localities for affordable housing and urban renewal. HOME provided funds to encourage home ownership in low-income areas.

➤ Rejected, 19-26, a proposal by Bruce F. Vento, D-Minn., to eliminate a provision that would permit HUD to impose sanctions on dysfunctional housing authorities by withholding Community Development Block Grant money.

➤ Defeated by voice vote an amendment by Vento that would have replaced the proposed public housing accreditation board, which would approve the operations of local housing agencies, with a less powerful performance evaluation board to assist HUD in monitoring local housing agencies.

The panel also:

➤ Approved by voice vote an amendment by Vento to extend the Community Partnerships Against Crime program from one year to five years, ending in fiscal 2002. The program provided funds to housing authorities to pay for security measures such as fences, security guards and increased police presence.

➤ Approved by voice vote an amendment by Lazio, Kennedy, Banking Committee Chairman Jim Leach, R-Iowa, and ranking committee Democrat Henry B. Gonzalez of Texas to authorize HUD to retain unspent funds from the Section 8 subsidized housing program to pay for Section 8 contracts or renewals. Under existing law, such funds could be reallocated for other purposes.

➤ Approved by voice vote an amendment by Michael N. Castle, R-Del., to give housing authorities access to state and local registries of sex offenders. Such lists could be used to screen adult applicants for public housing assistance.

➤ Approved by voice vote an amendment by Watt stipulating that HUD would not establish national occupancy standards for public housing. Watt said he grew up in a household with more than two people per bedroom, and he "turned out OK."

House Floor Action

Bill sponsors, who had spent more than a week shepherding the measure through committee, faced a similar task when the bill came to the House floor. The chamber began considering HR 2 on April 30 but did not pass it until May 14. The vote was 293-132, with 71 Democrats joining 222 Republicans to support the legislation. *(Vote 127, p. H-42)*

Bill sponsors were relieved, elated — and anxious for the Senate to move on its bill. "We're going to negotiate earlier, and I'm very confident we're going to resolve our differences and get a good bill the president will sign," Lazio said.

Getting Off to a Slow Start

In their opening remarks April 30, Republican supporters said the bill would usher in a new era of improved public housing by granting more authority to local agencies. "For the sake of decent standards of housing for the poor, more local discretion is needed," Lazio said. "Single dimension, lowest income housing simply has not worked."

Bill supporters also said that decentralizing public housing would allow local agencies to accept a higher percentage of the working poor.

Democrats argued that some of the measure's provisions were too prescriptive — Republican talk of deregulation notwithstanding — and that it would discriminate against the extremely poor by denying them access to housing in favor of those who were slightly better off.

As the debate opened, the administration offered its assessment, saying it supported many of the bill's objectives and provisions as well as the "determination to enact long overdue program reforms." But it added that unless several provisions were amended, it would oppose the legislation

Specifically, the White House opposed the income-eligibility level in the House bill, instead favoring the existing requirement that 75 percent of public housing residents earn 30 percent or less of an area's median income.

The administration also said the minimum rent for public housing and subsidized rental units should be $25 per month, rather than the bill's range of $25 to $50 per month. And it opposed a proposal to create a Housing Evaluation and Accreditation Board.

Democrats Fight Work Mandate

During two days of debate April 30 and May 1, House members considered a handful of the more than 20 proposed amendments to HR 2.

Democrats took particular exception to the proposed community service requirements. "This is not a work requirement," said Watt. "Work implies compensation. This is a volunteer mandate. We should not be doing this."

But Republicans, including Banking Committee Chairman Leach, said the work requirement was reasonable. "This is work for benefit," Leach said. "Housing is part of the compensation."

Democrats made a variety of attempts to eliminate the requirement, all of them unsuccessful. Watt moved to block consideration of the bill on the basis that the community service provisions would impose an unfunded mandate on the localities that had to administer them. The House voted, 237-183, to consider the bill, rejecting Watt's point of order. *(Vote 99, p. H-32)*

Members rejected, 160-251, an attempt by Jackson to eliminate a provision requiring housing authorities to evict tenants who failed to meet the community service requirement. *(Vote 100, p. H-34)*

Jackson failed, 181-216, with an amendment to exempt from the community service requirement single parents, grandparents or spouses who were the primary caregivers for children ages 6 or younger, senior citizens or the disabled. *(Vote 102, p. H-34)*

The House also defeated, 153-252, a proposal by Dave Weldon, R-Fla., to exempt 20 percent of the people that would have been exempted under Jackson's amendment. *(Vote 101, p. H-34)*

'Self-Sufficiency' or Targeting the Poor?

Deliberations over the so-called self-sufficiency provisions continued to dominate the debate when floor action continued the week of May 5.

Republicans defended HR 2 as a vehicle that could offer local housing officials more flexibility in providing services while also helping low-income people break their dependency on government programs. "It is a valid mission. It is an appropriate mission," Lazio said. "The most cost-effective thing we can do is move people to self-sufficiency." Added Richard H. Baker, R-La., "Public housing is not expected to be a retirement home. It's expected to be transitional housing."

But Democrats contended that the bill would penalize low-income people for being poor and result in more homeless among the neediest citizens. "This is not an American concept," Watt said. "It is a way of simply singling out the poor."

Two Democratic attempts to alter the mandatory community service provisions consumed a majority of the chamber's time. The first, by Watt, would have required that public housing residents who participated in the community service program be paid at least the prevailing minimum wage. It was rejected May 6 by a vote of 140-286. *(Vote 103, p. H-36)*

Democrats argued that requiring people to work without pay was equivalent to involuntary servitude, which was outlawed by the 13th Amendment. "If you want to raise their esteem," said Watt, "pay them for the work you're requiring." But Leach said the community service requirement was aimed at encouraging greater community involvement. "This is leadership of, by and for the poor," he said. "This is not inappropriate."

The second amendment, rejected 168-253, was a proposal by Frank to make the community service requirement optional. The amendment also would have made optional a requirement in the bill that certain tenants sign agreements with their housing authorities establishing a target date for moving out of public housing. *(Vote 104, p. H-36)*

In other action, the House:

➤ Approved by voice vote an amendment by Lazio that, among other things, would prohibit anyone classified as a "sexually violent predator" from receiving public housing assistance.

➤ Approved by voice vote an amendment by Sheila Jackson-Lee, D-Texas, to encourage, but not require, contractors working in public housing projects to employ residents of such communities in some capacity.

➤ Defeated by voice vote a proposal by Kennedy to increase from $2.5 billion to $3.7 billion the measure's annual authorization for capital grants and from $2.9 billion to $3.2 billion the bill's fiscal 1998 authorization for operating grants.

Debate Winds Down

As the floor action went into a third week May 13, the focus was once again on the community service provisions, though much of the earlier acrimony had petered out.

Kennedy tried unsuccessfully to require that owners of public rental units perform the same eight hours of community service that the bill expected of tenants. It was defeated, 87-341. *(Vote 122, p. H-40)*

On May 14, Kennedy tried unsuccessfully to win House support for a substitute amendment that, like the bill, would have consolidated public housing programs into two block grants and required local housing authorities to submit a management plan to HUD. Unlike the bill, however, the Kennedy amendment would have reserved 75 percent of tenant housing vouchers for families with incomes below 30 percent of the area's median income and would have denied vouchers to those earning more than 50 percent of an area's median income.

The substitute also would have established minimum rents of zero to $25 a month, compared with $25 to $50 in the bill, with exemptions for legal immigrants who lost their welfare benefits. Local housing authorities would have been allowed to adopt any minimum rent within the acceptable range.

The House rejected the Kennedy substitute amendment, 163-261. Kennedy also failed, on a voice vote, to send the bill back to committee. *(Vote 126, p. H-40)*

In other action on the bill May 13, the House:

➤ Approved by voice vote an amendment by Edolphus Towns, D-N.Y., to require HUD to include in its performance standards for a housing authority whether it had identified and tried to eradicate pest problems, such as cockroach infestations.

➤ Rejected an amendment by Kennedy to require that 75 percent of housing vouchers be given to families with incomes below 30 percent of the area's median income. The vote was 162-260. *(Vote 119, p. H-40)*

➤ Rejected an attempt by Kennedy to strike a provision of the bill allowing low-income housing programs developed and administered by local governments to be eligible for federal public housing funds. The vote was 153-270. *(Vote 120, p. H-40)*

➤ Rejected an amendment by Danny K. Davis, D-Ill., to allow HUD, when it took over or replaced the management of a troubled public housing authority, to exempt tenants and families that received rental assistance from the community service work requirements in the bill. The amendment failed, 145-282. *(Vote 123, p. H-40)*

Senate Committee

In contrast to the House's tortured consideration of HR 2, the Senate Banking, Housing and Urban Affairs Committee marked up its version of the bill quickly and quietly May 8, garnering an 18-0 vote (S 462 — S Rept 105-21).

Senate Republicans, including Banking Chairman Alfonse M. D'Amato of New York, said the legislation would dramatically improve the operation of local housing authorities while increasing the livability of many housing projects. "Public housing tenants have every right . . . to live in a safe and secure environment," D'Amato said. "These housing reforms will help clean up public housing, making it safe for our elderly, our hard-working families and our children."

Paul S. Sarbanes of Maryland, the panel's ranking Democrat, said that while the bill would do much to improve public housing, many aspects of the existing program already worked well. "In many communities, you cannot distinguish between public housing and the private housing which surrounds it," he said.

Like its House counterpart, the Senate bill proposed granting more control to local housing authorities and requiring more community involvement by housing residents.

It included a requirement that able-bodied adults residing in public housing perform at least eight hours of community service; residents could also fulfill the requirement by taking literacy or job training courses.

Despite the similarities, however, the Senate bill was much less sweeping. For example, it proposed to amend, not repeal, the 1937 United States Housing Act, and it did not call for the same rent flexibility as the House bill.

The Banking Committee made only a few changes. It agreed by voice vote to an amendment by Jack Reed, D-R.I., to allow local authorities to reduce rents for tenants whose welfare benefits were cut as a result of the 1996 welfare overhaul law (PL 104-193).

Members defeated, by voice vote, a proposal by Robert F. Bennett, R-Utah, to strike language requiring that public housing agencies permit tenants to own pets. Federal laws permitted pets under certain conditions.

After the committee's easy approval of the bill, Mack declared the legislation's prospects to be "much better than they were last year."

Senate Floor Action

Despite the bill's smooth ride in committee, Mack faced significant challenges in finding the right formula to ensure such easy passage on the floor. The Senate did not take up the bill until Sept. 26, when it passed it by voice vote with little fanfare and no discussion.

In the interim, Mack and his staff worked with Democrats to forge a bill that senators would easily accept. Mack and his staff were also distracted by an ongoing disagreement with Leach and Lazio over whether to include a fix for the Section 8 subsidized housing program in the appropriations measure to fund HUD, veterans programs and 17 independent agencies (HR 2158). *(Appropriations, p. 9-77)*

Among the most controversial issues in the housing bill was the proposal to give public housing authorities more incentives to attract the working poor to public housing, thereby creating a greater mix of incomes in public and subsidized housing. According to the Senate Banking Committee, under the existing system, the average public housing resident made less than 20 percent of median area income.

Democrats argued that increasing rents and loosening other requirements would prompt local authorities to evict their poorest residents and replace them with tenants who could pay more. Mack agreed to compromise, increasing the percentage of housing vouchers his bill would set aside for those with very low incomes under the Section 8 program.

Under the agreement, which the Senate adopted as part of a manager's amendment to the bill, housing authorities would have to distribute no less than 65 percent of the vouchers — up from 50 percent in the original bill — to the very poor. Mack also agreed to add a requirement that at least 90 percent of the vouchers go to people who earned less than 60 percent of an area's median income. Remaining vouchers could go to people who made 80 percent or less.

The bill's income requirements for public and Section 8 subsidized housing were also changed. At least 40 percent of units would have to be occupied by the very poor. At least 70 percent — down from 75 percent — would have to be occupied by those who made no more than 60 percent of the median income, and the remainder could go to those who made no more than 80 percent.

Final Action

In the end, time got away from Lazio and Mack. With less than a month left before adjournment, they met a handful of times to discuss their major disagreements, but neither chamber appointed conferees and formal negotiations never began.

Major conflicts included:

- **Community service.** The provisions in both bills requiring able-bodied adults in public housing to perform eight hours of community service a month. This was largely a philosophical difference between Republicans and Democrats.
- **Rent flexibility.** The House proposal to change the so-called Brooke Amendment, which prevented housing authorities from charging tenants more than 30 percent of their monthly incomes for rent. The House bill proposed that tenants be required to choose between that system or a flat rent set by local authorities. Minimum rents would be set from $25 per month to $50 per month except in cases of "severe financial hardship."

The Senate bill proposed allowing authorities to charge less than 30 percent of income for rent, but not more.

- **Penalties.** A House proposal that HUD be allowed to withhold coveted Community Development Block Grant funds from cities deemed to have "substantially contributed" to the troubled status of their housing authorities. The Senate bill contained no such provision.

Those issues were expected to face increasing scrutiny in 1998 as GOP leaders in both chambers increased pressure to enact a public housing overhaul measure to complement the welfare reform law enacted in 1996. ■

House Panel Votes To Overhaul Programs for Homeless

With a major bill to overhaul the public housing system stalled, leaders of the House Banking and Financial Services Committee pushed ahead on a smaller bill (HR 217) that focused on transforming federal programs for the homeless.

The bill, part of GOP plans to reorganize the Department of Housing and Urban Development (HUD), sought to merge seven programs into block grants. States, localities, territorial governments and others who served the homeless would be encouraged to use the grants to devise long-term solutions to homelessness, particularly by building permanent housing rather than shelters.

Other federal departments would be urged to assume the cost of support services for the homeless, such as drug treatment or mental health counseling. "All those services cannot come out of the HUD budget," said Rick A. Lazio, R-N.Y., chairman of the Banking and Financial Services Subcommittee on Housing and Community Opportunity. "Our first charge," he said, "is to provide safe, healthy housing for those people who otherwise have no other route to go."

Funding for homeless assistance programs had declined 25 percent since 1995. Like the larger public housing measure (HR 2, S 462), which both chambers passed earlier in the year, the bill for the homeless aimed to reshape the shrinking pie by sending money directly to those providing the services. *(Housing overhaul, p. 7-12)*

Lazio wanted to direct HUD money at brick and mortar

projects, and to limit what providers could spend on emergency shelters and social services. Under the bill, such services were to be identified and funded by a new Interagency Council on the Homeless, to include representatives from HUD and the departments of Health and Human Services, Labor, Education, Veterans Affairs and Agriculture. The council could issue its own block grants to local providers, if it used available funds in existing programs.

Lazio said the approach was ground-breaking, but Democrats John J. LaFalce of New York and Bruce F. Vento of Minnesota said it probably would not work. Others argued that bill sponsors were focusing too blindly on their goal of constructing more permanent housing, at the cost of other services.

Committee Markup

The Banking Committee approved Lazio's measure (H Rept 105-407) by voice vote Nov. 5 with broad support from Democrats. But several GOP conservatives signaled dissatisfaction with the measure.

Five Republicans — Bob Barr of Georgia, Ron Paul of Texas, Ed Royce of California, and Jim Ryun and Vince Snowbarger of Kansas — voted against a substitute by Lazio that made several changes sought by Democrats and retained authorization levels that conservatives said were too high. The five-year measure would authorize $1 billion annually for homeless programs through fiscal 2002. Lazio's amendment was approved, 35-5.

Minutes earlier, the committee defeated, 10-26, an amendment by Ryun that would have cut the annual authorization to $850 million, a level slightly higher than the amount appropriated for fiscal 1998. Ryun said the committee should stick to figures that would help balance the budget, but Lazio and Banking Committee Chairman Jim Leach, R-Iowa, said $1 billion was appropriate for new block grants.

Democrats argued that Leach and Lazio were not bold enough in urging higher appropriations for housing programs. Bernard Sanders, I-Vt., offered an amendment to increase the authorization to $1.6 billion. Said Barney Frank, D-Mass.: "What we should be doing in the authorization bill is appealing to the conscience of the country."

But Lazio countered that "when we pick a number out that is clearly unrealistic ... we become less credible and are more likely to be ignored." The committee defeated Sanders' amendment, 14-18.

Sanders, Donald Manzullo, R-Ill., and Jesse L. Jackson Jr., D-Ill., won voice vote approval for an amendment intended to reduce the emphasis on permanent housing. It removed a bill provision that would have barred providers from using more than 15 percent of their block grant on emergency shelters.

The committee also accepted an amendment by Jackson, Sanders, Luis V. Gutierrez, D-Ill., and Lucille Roybal-Allard, D-Calif., to increase from 30 percent to 35 percent the portion of block grants that providers could spend on support services, such as drug treatment, without matching each federal dollar.

The panel adopted by voice vote an amendment by Vento to allow those providing rooms for the homeless to continue to operate as part of the Section 8 subsidized housing program. A Democratic staff member said this would allow contracts with such facilities to be renewed in coming years. The bill, she said, had not been clear on the issue. ■

HUD Cost Reductions Made Permanent

Congress gave permanent status to three changes in housing law that had been reducing costs at the Department of Housing and Urban Development (HUD) since they were enacted in 1996. The permanent provisions were included in the spending portion of the 1997 budget-reconciliation package, signed into law Aug. 5 (HR 2015 — PL 105-33). They were projected to save $1.8 billion over five years.

The provisions had initially been enacted as part of the fiscal 1996 appropriations bill (PL 104-134) for HUD and the Department of Veterans Affairs (VA).

The changes affected the following areas:

- **Foreclosure relief limits.** The bill eliminated a HUD program that provided up to three years of foreclosure relief for borrowers who had defaulted on their federal home mortgages but who showed some potential for resuming payments. Lawmakers said the federal losses from this program were too great.

To minimize the losses but still provide some foreclosure relief, the bill allowed the Federal Housing Administration (FHA) and HUD to grant up to 12 months of relief from mortgage payments. In exchange for the government assuming the cost of those payments, lenders would be required to alter the terms of the loan, at least on a short-term basis, to make it easier for the borrower to pay.

- **Section 8 rent increases.** The bill also prohibited annual market-based increases in the federal subsidies paid to owners of Section 8 housing units if the rents the owners were charging exceeded HUD's fair market rent for that housing area.

Under the Section 8 program, low-income tenants paid a certain percentage of their income in rent, and the federal government made up the difference through subsidies to the property owner. Prior to enactment of this provision, owners of subsidized units received annual subsidy increases to keep up with any increases in local rents and to account for maintenance costs of vacated apartments.

Under the bill, rent increases had to reflect actual increases in operating costs rather than inflation in the housing market. Landlords could increase rents only if they demonstrated that the increases would not make the unit's rent higher than the rent for a similar unsubsidized unit. Owners of new or recently renovated units could adjust rents for inflation only if their units did not exceed the fair market rents for their area.

These changes were effective in fiscal 1999.

- **Section 8 subsidy reductions.** Finally, the bill reduced annual subsidy increases by 1 percentage point for owners of Section 8 properties that had no tenant turnover since the last annual increase. However, the Annual Adjustment Factor, the formula on which the federal government based rent increases, could not be reduced to less than 1 percent, so landlords could increase rents at least that much. The changes were to take effect in fiscal 1999.

Legislative Action

The provisions originated in the House Banking and Financial Services Committee and the Senate Banking, Housing and Urban Affairs Committee, both of which were charged with producing savings for the reconciliation bill.

The House committee went first, working swiftly along bipartisan lines June 11 to approve a five-year, $1.8 billion package of housing-related savings. The Senate Banking panel followed June 18, voting 18-0 in favor of a set of proposals projected to save $2 billion over five years.

Both committees got much of their savings from the proposed reductions in Section 8 rental housing subsidies. Both also included the limits on FHA foreclosure relief. But in a departure from the House bill, the Senate committee added so-called mark-to-market provisions for Section 8 housing. In fiscal 1998, the plan was projected to reduce the costs of renewing expiring Section 8 contracts by $500 million.

Crafted by Housing Subcommittee Chairman Connie Mack, R-Fla., the mark-to-market proposal called for subsidized Section 8 rent to be reduced to comparable rates in an area for non-subsidized housing, or to 90 percent of fair market rents if comparable properties did not exist. Comparable rates would be the rents charged in the neighborhood; fair market rents would the average for a specific area. State and local housing finance agencies, rather than HUD, would restructure the contracts.

The proposal also called for restructuring Section 8 mortgage debt insured by the FHA to reduce the number of expected defaults.

When House and Senate conferees on the housing section of the budget bill met the week of July 14, they were unable to reach agreement on the mark-to-market provisions, which were dropped at the insistence of House Banking Committee members.

A Second Try at Revamping Section 8

Subsequently, at the request of the Senate Banking Committee, Senate appropriators agreed to include Mack's mark-to-market plan in their version of the VA-HUD appropriations bill (S 1034). House appropriators had not included it in their version, and when the measure went to conference, the provision became one of the chief stumbling blocks.

The dispute was not among the appropriators, but between House and Senate authorizers. House Banking Committee Chairman Jim Leach, R-Iowa, and Rick A. Lazio, R-N.Y., chairman of the panel's Housing and Community Opportunity Subcommittee, opposed putting the provisions in the spending bill. They disagreed with some of the details, and they feared such a move would reduce momentum to enact a big public housing overhaul bill (HR 2) that had passed the House in May. The Senate passed a companion measure (S 462) on Sept. 26. *(Housing overhaul, p. 7-12)*

House Speaker Newt Gingrich, R-Ga., and the appropriators eventually stepped in, brokering a compromise that retained the bulk of Mack's proposal but added a few House ideas for implementing the changes. Under the final agreement, HUD was allowed to restructure the FHA-insured mortgages of multifamily properties where above-market-rate Section 8 rental assistance contracts were used, with the aim of cutting the federal subsidy costs, reducing the likelihood of FHA loan defaults, and ensuring the continued use of such properties for low-income housing. ■

No Agreement on Training Bills

Proponents of revamping the nation's uncoordinated and sometimes problematic mix of federal job training and vocational education programs moved bills in both chambers but failed to work out their differences before Congress adjourned for the year.

The House passed separate bills on job training (HR 1385) and vocational education (HR 1853). The job training bill called for consolidating more than 60 job training and adult education programs into three state block grants. The vocational education bill proposed reauthorizing and revamping vocational and technical education programs, in part by changing funding formulas to give somewhat less consideration to poverty rates and more to reaching people between ages 15 and 24, the general target group for such programs.

The Senate took a different tack, with Republicans and Democrats negotiating a compromise bill (S 1186) that covered both areas. Under the measure, crafted by Mike DeWine, R-Ohio, states would be able to create unified plans that encompassed job training, adult education and vocational education programs. The bill also proposed the creation of "one-stop" customer service centers to coordinate job training, career counseling and other employment services. The bill proposed retaining existing funding formulas while giving funding priority to states with successful consolidated programs.

BOXSCORE

Job Training, Vocational Education — HR 1385, HR 1853, S 1186. The bills aimed to revamp and consolidate a wide range of federal job training, vocational education and adult education programs.

Reports: H Rept 105-93 (HR 1385), H Rept 105-177 (HR 1853), S Rept 105-109.

KEY ACTION

May 16 — House passed HR 1385, 343-60.

July 22 — House passed HR 1853, 414-12.

Sept. 24 — Senate Labor and Human Resources Committee approved S 1186 by voice vote.

The DeWine bill drew broad bipartisan support and won easy approval Sept. 24 from the Labor and Human Resources Committee, but it subsequently drew opposition from various corners and went no further in the first session.

Some vocational education groups expressed concern that their programs would be given short shrift if they were combined with job training. Conservatives worried that the bill might contain educational mandates that were too stringent.

Background

Revamping federal job training and vocational educations programs was a priority for Republicans, but their initial efforts collapsed in the 104th Congress. House and Senate Republicans produced a conference report on a consolidation bill in July 1996, but they had not a single Democratic supporter. Sen. Edward M. Kennedy, D-Mass., one of the measure's early sponsors, vowed the revised bill would never get out of the Senate. The secretaries of Labor and Education quickly recommended a veto. Neither chamber considered the report, and the job training bill died at the end of the session.

The 1996 bill proposed to consolidate about 100 disparate job training and education programs into a single block grant, then turn the funds over to state and local governments.

The legislation had seemed a sure thing in late 1995, after versions sailed through both chambers with backing from the White House. But a full legislative plate prevented staff members from beginning work on a final bill until February 1996, and major differences between the House and Senate versions prolonged their efforts.

The delay gave time for opposition to arise. Conservative groups charged that the bill would set up unelected, Big Brother-like boards to oversee local labor markets while forcing children to choose career paths at a young age. Labor unions and business groups grew concerned that the bill would not provide sufficient funding for block grants.

In an effort to allay some of the conservative criticisms, Republican conferees included provisions to weaken a proposed national employment database, repeal a 1994 law (PL 103-239) backed by Clinton that helped high school seniors ease into the work force, and give federal officials less authority over federally funded local projects. That, in turn, brought firm opposition from the administration. *(1996 Almanac, p. 7-11)*

House Job Training Bill

The 1997 House job training bill (HR 1385), sponsored by Howard P. "Buck" McKeon, R-Calif., called for consolidating more than 50 federal job training and adult education programs into three state block grants to be overseen by the governors and state legislatures. Funding levels were left to appropriators.

The proposed grants were:

- **Job training.** An Adult Employment and Training Opportunities Grant for disadvantaged adults and dislocated workers who were chronically unemployed or who had lost their jobs as a result of economic shifts or corporate downsizing.
- **At-risk youths.** A Disadvantaged Youth Employment and Training Opportunities Grant for at-risk, low-income teenagers and young adults, including high school dropouts.
- **Adult literacy.** An Adult Education and Literacy Grant to assist low-income people to obtain the skills necessary to become employed, particularly those attempting to make the transition from public assistance to the work force.

Unlike the 1996 bill, HR 1385 did not deal with in-school vocational education programs. Instead, it focused on streamlining services for disadvantaged youths who in most cases already had dropped out of school.

Most programs for youths under the Job Training Partnership Act would be folded into the state block grants. However, federal administration would be retrained for the Job Corps, a residential vocational education and training program that served disadvantaged youths between ages 16 and 24.

The bill also included a three-year reauthorization for the Vocational Rehabilitation Act, which provided training and rehabilitation money to states for the mentally and physically disabled. Democrats were pleased that, unlike the 1996 version, the bill did not seek to turn vocational rehabilitation programs into a block grant. However, Democrats and representatives of the disabled strongly favored a five-year reauthorization.

House Subcommittee Action

The job-training bill began in the House Education and the Workforce Subcommittee on Postsecondary Education, Training and Life-Long Learning, which approved it by voice vote April 24.

Republicans, led by sponsor and subcommittee Chairman McKeon, said the bill would streamline the existing maze of job training and education programs and make services more accessible to those who needed them.

"Our current patchwork of federal programs is not the answer," McKeon said. He said that among other things, the bill would "result in enhanced services provided to welfare recipients who must make the transition from welfare to work."

But Democrats, including Dale E. Kildee of Michigan, the subcommittee's ranking member, said the bill was far from perfect and that much work remained to ensure that participants did not get lost in the transition.

During the 30-minute markup, panel members gave voice vote approval to a handful of amendments, including proposals:

- By John E. Peterson, R-Pa., to allow local training facilities and skill centers to offer job training and vocational services to people who were already working. The services would be provided during off-hours and on a fee basis.
- By Kildee, stipulating that no more than 10 percent of a state's job training money could be used for administration at the state level.
- By McKeon, making technical changes to the bill, including a provision aimed at giving disabled people more control over the selection and administration of their vocational rehabilitation and training programs.

Full Committee Markup

The full House Committee on Education and the Workforce approved the bill by voice vote April 30 (H Rept 105-93).

Democrats' chief concern was ensuring that the block grant money would be directed to the neediest areas. Overall, though, Democrats supported the bill, saying it was an improvement over the 1996 version.

For example, they liked the proposal to authorize separate grants for dislocated workers, rather than lumping them with funding for other grants as proposed in 1996. The earlier provision had prompted strong opposition from Democrats, who argued that dislocated workers could lose out under that kind of system. "This legislation represents a step in the right direction," Kildee said. "[It's] not perfect, but compromises never are."

The bill also had the qualified support of the Clinton administration.

- **Governors' powers.** The committee agreed to an amendment that would allow state legislatures to decide how to distribute the money from the block grants. The bill originally would have given that power to governors.

The 20-15 vote in favor of the amendment appeared to take committee Chairman Bill Goodling, R-Pa., by surprise. Goodling wanted governors to have the ultimate power to distribute the money. Seven Republicans voted for the amendment, which was sponsored by liberal Democrat Lynn Woolsey of California and conservative Republican Bob Schaffer of Colorado.

Woolsey argued that the ultimate decision to distribute the funds should not be left to one person and that state legislatures were less likely than governors to be influenced by politics.

Frank Riggs, R-Calif., who voted against the amendment, countered that governors and other state officials should not be left out of the process. Another opponent, Michael N. Castle, R-Del., argued that Congress should not "micro-manage" how states distributed the money.

- **Other changes.** Members also agreed by voice vote to a

series of amendments by McKeon including proposals to:

➤ Require that local work force development boards, to be created under the bill, provide public information about their membership and activities. The boards, to be made up of local business leaders, school officials and community activists, among others, would be charged with submitting a work force development plan for an area. McKeon's amendment also required that a local board's plan be made available to the public before it was submitted to the state.

➤ Make "displaced homemakers" eligible for job training programs under the bill. Displaced homemakers could include widows or others who were suddenly forced to find work when they no longer could afford to stay home.

House Passage

With strong Democratic support, the House passed the job training bill May 16 by a lopsided vote of 343-60. The bill drew support from 187 Democrats and 155 Republicans. Defections came among Republican social conservatives who expressed concern that aspects of the bill were too intrusive into people's personal lives. *(Vote 138, p. H-46)*

During nearly four hours of floor debate, the House gave voice vote approval to an amendment by Lindsey Graham, R-S.C., stipulating that parents and their children who were schooled at home would not be required to participate in any of the bill's programs.

The House rejected an effort by Major R. Owens, D-N.Y., to require states to sponsor a summer youth program independent of the program for disadvantaged youth contained in the bill. The amendment failed, 168-238. *(Vote 137, p. H-46)*

House Vocational Education Bill

The second House bill (HR 1853) focused on reauthorizing and revising the Carl D. Perkins Vocational and Applied Technology Education Act of 1990 (PL 101-392), which provided funds to states for vocational and technical training. The law had expired at the end of 1996, although Congress continued appropriating funds for the program, including $1.1 billion in fiscal 1997. *(1990 Almanac, p. 619)*

Under the bill, Congress would authorize $1.3 billion in fiscal 1998 and unspecified funds through 2002 for secondary and postsecondary school programs. The bill also proposed revamping both the formula used to distribute federal money to the states and the formula that guided how states allocated their funds to schools.

The proposed changes in the federal formula aimed to give more money to states based on their populations between ages 15 and 24, the group considered most likely to seek vocational and technical education. Fifty percent of the funds would be based on each state's population between ages 15 and 19, and 50 percent would be based on the population between ages 20 and 24. The per capita income in the state would have a bearing on the calculation.

Under existing law, 50 percent of the allotment of grant money was based on the population between ages 15 and 19, 20 percent on the population between ages 19 and 24, and 15 percent on the population between ages 25 and 65.

More controversial were the proposed changes in how states distributed the funds. Under existing law, 70 percent of the state distribution was based on the number of children in the Title I remedial education program for low-income students, 20 percent on the number enrolled in education programs for disabled students, and 10 percent on the general school enrollment.

The bill proposed changing that formula beginning in fiscal 1999, so that 50 percent of the money would be distributed based on each state's population between ages 15 and 19, and 50 percent on the number of children in that age group living in poverty.

States would have to distribute 90 percent of the federal money they received to schools, compared with 75 percent under existing law. The remaining 8 percent would be for state activities and 2 percent for administrative costs. Forcing states to distribute a higher percentage of their federal funds to schools was a favorite theme of Goodling's. "If we are going to see true change occur in vocational-technical education, it is going to come from the local level, and that is where our money should be," he said.

The bill contained two provisions that could benefit rural schools. One would enable states to set aside 10 percent of their grant for rural districts. The other would lower the minimum grant for secondary and postsecondary programs, enabling more small schools to qualify.

Subcommittee Action

The House Education and the Workforce Subcommittee on Early Childhood, Youth and Families approved the vocational education bill by voice vote June 12.

The subcommittee approved, also by voice vote, a package of amendments by Chairman Riggs aimed at reducing from 50 percent to 20 percent the amount of money a state could withhold from schools based on poor graduation rates.

The en bloc amendments also maintained the so-called tech-prep program as a separate entity to ensure that it was properly funded. The tech-prep program allowed a student to start a vocational training program in the last two years of high school and complete it during two years at a community college or postsecondary technical school.

The subcommittee's ranking Democrat, Matthew G. Martinez of California, sought to change the percentage of state funds going to localities from 90 percent to 85 percent, but he agreed to withdraw his amendment in the interests of moving the bill along.

Full Committee Markup

The full Education and the Workforce Committee approved the bill (H Rept 105-177) June 25 in a party-line vote of 20-18, after attempts to reach a bipartisan agreement collapsed.

Democrats opposed the bill primarily because of the requirement that states give less consideration to poverty rates when distributing the money than under existing law. They said the change would punish inner cities.

Republicans, they charged, were trying to rewrite the program to help suburban and rural schools at the expense of urban ones. Republicans responded that they were willing to compromise on many issues but that Democrats had adopted a take-it-or-leave-it attitude and refused to budge.

The panel approved by voice vote an amendment by Goodling making mostly minor changes to the subcommittee-approved bill.

The committee rejected several Democratic amendments, including proposals by:

➤ Martinez, to base some of the state distribution formula on existing law and some on a ratio of 60 percent for poverty rates and 40 percent for population. It lost, 16-22.

➤ Martinez, to substitute a Democratic proposal that, among other things, would have changed the GOP state distribution formula. It lost, 18-19.

➤ Donald M. Payne, D-N.J., to strike the allowable 10 percent set aside for rural areas. It lost, 16-20.

➤ Carolyn McCarthy, D-N.Y., to reduce the minimum grant for secondary schools from $15,000 to $10,000, instead of the bill's proposed $7,500. It failed by voice vote.

House Passage

After narrowly defeating an effort to ensure funding for training programs that were targeted at women, the House voted overwhelmingly July 22 to pass the bill. The tally was 414-12. *(Vote 289, p. H-90)*

Floor debate on the bill began July 17, following last-minute negotiations that resolved the major source of disagreement, the formula by which states would distribute grant funds to the schools

Under the compromise — sponsored by Goodling and adopted by voice vote — state-to-school district funding would be based in fiscal 1998 on the existing formula, which gave 70 percent of its weight to the number of low-income children, 20 percent to the number of disabled students, and 10 percent to enrollment in vocational programs. After that, the formula would gradually shift to a system based on poverty and population until fiscal 2002, when funding would be based 60 percent on poverty and 40 percent on population.

The compromise was to apply to funding at fiscal 1997 levels, about $1.1 billion. Funding above that level would be distributed on the 60 percent poverty to 40 percent population ratio starting in fiscal 1998.

Although the two parties were able to resolve their dispute over the funding formula, a separate disagreement over gender equity forced the leadership to postpone final action on the bill until July 22.

The dispute came over a dogged attempt by Patsy T. Mink, D-Hawaii, other Democratic women and Maryland Republican Constance A. Morella to ensure the continuation of existing funding levels for programs for displaced homemakers, pregnant women and single parents. Goodling and most other Republicans were determined to remove laws that mandated funding to serve certain populations, including one requiring that 10.5 percent of funding to go to vocational training for displaced homemakers, pregnant women and single parents.

"We can't take a little set-aside here and a little set-aside there," Goodling said. Morella responded that without the set-aside, some localities would drop their programs. Mink said lawmakers should remember that the programs served many who aimed to get off welfare, as they were required to do under the 1996 welfare law (PL 104-193). *(1996 Almanac, p. 6-3)*

When the House resumed debate July 22, Mink and her colleagues again pressed their amendment, which was rejected, 207-214. Unwilling to give up, Mink tried to send the bill back to the committee with instructions to add the language, but the House reaffirmed its earlier vote, defeating the motion, 207-220. *(Votes 286, 288, p. H-90)*

Democrats argued that the Mink amendment would guarantee existing services. Delegate Eleanor Holmes Norton, D-D.C., said it was in the government's interest to train these women. "These are the women most likely to cost the government the most," she said. But Goodling and other panel Republicans said the amendment would interfere with the bill's effort to give states and local governments wider latitude in spending their education money. "It is not a welfare program. It is an education bill," Goodling said.

The House also defeated, 189-230, a proposal by Joseph P. Kennedy II, D-Mass., to allow school districts to hire employees to coordinate vocational programs with the needs of local employers. Goodling said the bill would already allow such hiring without specifically mentioning work force coordinators. He said such specific mandates could cost the bill votes. *(Vote 287, p. H-90)*

Combined Senate Bill

The Senate Labor and Human Resources Committee easily approved its combined job training and vocational education bill (S 1186 — S Rept 105-109) by voice vote Sept. 24.

However, Labor Committee Chairman James M. Jeffords, R-Vt., a bill cosponsor, warned that combining the two House bills, then melding the House and Senate versions might prove too difficult in 1997. He said lawmakers were more committed to clearing appropriations bills and adjourning.

The bipartisan bill — cosponsored by liberal Democrats Edward M. Kennedy of Massachusetts and Paul Wellstone of Minnesota — proposed to consolidate state job training, vocational education and adult education programs, with specific funding streams for each area. States at the time had separate programs in each category. "One-stop" customer service centers would coordinate training, counseling and other employment services, giving job-seekers a central point of entry.

The legislation also proposed creating "individual training accounts" to give job seekers more autonomy in choosing training programs, and it called for giving state and local governments greater discretion in designing their training systems.

Programs would be evaluated according to such factors as graduation rate, job placement and wage increases, with evaluations made during the first six months and year at work.

Supporters said the bill would erase the confusion that came with an array of programs providing job training to low-income people, high school drop-outs and displaced workers. Jeffords said passage was critical to the success of the 1996 welfare overhaul law. "Welfare reform has no hope of success unless individuals have the appropriate education and training to compete in the work force," he said.

Although the measure had wide bipartisan support, some issues remained unresolved. Kennedy said he wanted safeguards to guarantee that states did not ignore "substantive requirements" dealing with job training and vocational and adult education. He said language in the existing bill was "overly broad" and had "provoked serious concern from a wide range of people," adding that the bill should clarify that state officials could not move money appropriated for one program into another.

Kennedy won voice vote approval for an amendment to move up by two years the date for allowing states to enact their own laws governing areas similar to those in the federal legislation. The new date was July 1, 1997, rather than July 1, 1999, as written in the bill. Kennedy said his amendment was crafted to avoid having states enact their own legislation to circumvent federal law.

John W. Warner, R-Va., offered an amendment, approved by voice vote, to establish a 21st Century Workforce Commission, made up of representatives from education, government and industry, to prepare a report on the work force during the age of information technology.

Bill sponsor DeWine said he was willing to accommodate concerns and "fine-tune" the legislation, but added: "We're not going to completely rewrite this bill." ■

Democrats Block Comp Time Bill

A key item on the Republican labor agenda — allowing employees to choose between compensatory time off and overtime pay — remained dormant after Senate Democrats blocked it in June, convinced that the legislation could be used to erode employee rights guaranteed by the Fair Labor Standards Act.

Republicans argued that the labor law was outdated and should be amended to provide maximum workplace flexibility. They said the comp time bill would give employees more control over their lives and their work schedules. Democrats responded that the bill would leave too much power in the hands of employers, who could coerce workers into accepting time off instead of money or discriminate against those who insisted on one form of compensation over the other.

The House bill (HR 1), which narrowly passed in March, sought to allow employers to give private sector employees the option of being paid at one-and-a-half times their hourly rate for hours worked beyond the traditional 40-hour work week, or taking compensatory time off figured at the same rate. To be eligible for compensatory time off under the bill, employees would have to have worked a minimum of 1,000 hours in the previous 12 months.

In the Senate, Democrats blocked floor action on a broader bill (S 4) crafted by the Labor Committee and cited by Majority Leader Trent Lott, R-Miss., as one of the Republicans' top legislative priorities for the year. The bill also sought to give employees a choice between overtime pay or compensatory time off. It proposed replacing the 40-hour week with an 80-hour, two-week period in which employees could work more than 40 hours one week and fewer hours the next.

Although President Clinton had embraced the concept of giving workers more time off to attend to pressing family and personal needs, he threatened to veto the bills moving through both chambers. The legislation was strongly endorsed by prominent business groups such as the National Federation of Independent Business and the U.S. Chamber of Commerce.

BOXSCORE

Overtime Pay — HR 1, S 4. The bills proposed amending the Fair Labor Standards Act to permit employers to offer a choice between compensatory time off and overtime pay.

Reports: H Rept 105-21, S Rept 105-11.

KEY ACTION

March 19 — House passed HR 1, 222-210.

June 4 — Senate failed to limit debate, 51-47 (60 votes needed).

Background

Over the strong objections of organized labor and many Democrats, the House passed a bill in July 1996 to allow nonunion employees to choose compensatory time off instead of overtime pay. But across the Capitol, where the minority had more clout, Senate Democrats blocked an attempt by Lott to bring a compensatory time bill up for consideration. *(1996 Almanac, p. 7-10)*

The crux of the dispute was whether the bill would allow employers to coerce workers into accepting compensatory time instead of time-and-a-half pay for work beyond 40 hours a week. Republicans said the bill would let workers determine whether to accept time or pay; Democrats said it did not have enough protections against subtle coercion.

Under the 1938 Fair Labor Standards Act, employers were required to compensate most work beyond a 40-hour work week at a rate of one-and-a-half times a worker's hourly wage. In 1985, the law was amended to allow federal, state and local government employees to be compensated with time off instead of overtime wages. Employees who were considered professionals were exempt from federal wage-and-hour laws.

House Committee

HR 1 began in the House Education and the Workforce Committee, which approved it, 23-17, on March 5 in a vote that fell largely along party lines (H Rept 105-21). The bill was sponsored by Cass Ballenger, R-N.C.

The committee rejected nine Democratic amendments, most of them aimed at protecting low-income workers from being coerced into accepting one type of compensation over another. The defeated amendments included proposals by:

➤ Ranking Democrat William L. Clay of Missouri, who sought to expand the 1993 Family and Medical Leave Act (PL 103-3) by providing workers with an additional 24 hours of unpaid leave each year. Under the proposal, rejected 14-25, employees could have used the time at their children's schools to serve as teachers' aides or to attend conferences. *(1993 Almanac, p. 389)*

➤ George Miller of California, to penalize businesses that tried to discriminate against workers who chose to receive one form of compensation over another. It was rejected, 15-25.

➤ Major R. Owens of New York, to exempt workers from the comp time bill if they earned less than two-and-a-half times the minimum wage. It was rejected, 15-25.

➤ Lynn Woolsey of California, to require employers to give workers comp time for any activities covered under the Family and Medical Leave Act, including caring for an elderly relative or a sick child. It was rejected, 16-25.

➤ Donald M. Payne of New Jersey, to exempt from the law migrant workers, temporary employees and garment industry workers. It was rejected, 15-26.

House Floor Action

The House passed HR 1 on March 19 by a vote of 222-210, bringing Republicans closer to a potential showdown with the White House. *(Vote 59, p. H-20)*

During more than five hours of frequently impassioned floor debate, Republicans contended that the bill would give working families more opportunities to attend to personal affairs or spend time with school-age children. "For some families, time is as important as money," said Deborah Pryce, R-Ohio. "Why would Washington stand in the way?"

But Democrats argued that the attempt to amend the Fair Labor Standards Act would put workers at a serious disadvantage. They said workers potentially could be coerced by employers into accepting one form of compensation rather than the other, and that they could be subject to discrimination or harassment for not complying with the employers' wishes.

Delegate Eleanor Holmes Norton, D-D.C., defended the

1938 labor law as "one of the great statutes of the 20th century," saying, "It ranks right up there with the civil rights legislation of the 1960s."

During the floor debate, members:

➤ Approved, 408-19, an amendment by Bill Goodling, R-Pa., chairman of the Education and the Workforce Committee, to limit eligibility for comp time to employees who had worked a minimum of 1,000 hours in the previous 12 months. The amendment also sought to reduce from 240 hours per year to 160 hours the time that could be accrued, or "banked," by workers, who could then take the time off later or redeem it for cash. *(Vote 55, p. H-18)*

➤ Approved, 390-36, an amendment by Allen Boyd, D-Fla., to sunset the comp time law in the private sector five years after enactment, allowing sufficient time to determine how well it worked. *(Vote 56, p. H-18)*

➤ Rejected, 182-237, a proposal by Owens to exempt workers who earned less than 250 percent of the minimum wage, $4.75 an hour at the time, from the comp time provisions, allowing them to receive only overtime pay for working more than 40 hours. *(Vote 57, p. H-18)*

➤ Rejected, 193-237, a substitute amendment by Miller with numerous protections for workers, including a prohibition against employers directly or indirectly soliciting employees to take comp time instead of overtime pay, and an exemption from the bill for employees who worked less than 35 hours per week. *(Vote 58, p. H-18)*

Senate Committee

After a markup that stretched over several weeks, the Senate Labor and Human Resources Committee approved its own comp time bill (S 4 — S Rept 105-11) on March 18 in a party-line vote of 10-8. The action came a day before the House passed its bill.

S 4 proposed amending existing labor law to permit private sector employers to give workers the option of being compensated with pay at time-and-a-half their hourly wages, or time off calculated at the same rate when they worked more than 40 hours in a week. The bill also included a plan to allow businesses to offer workers "flex-time" schedules. For example, employees could put in 50 hours one week and 30 hours the next without triggering overtime pay or adversely affecting other benefits, such as pensions or health insurance coverage.

Like their House counterparts, Senate Republicans believed the bill would give workers more control over their work schedules; they said existing labor laws had to be updated to reflect a changing society. "Many of these [laws] date from the 1930s when the world was much different," said Labor panel Chairman James M. Jeffords, R-Vt. "My feeling is it's time to change those rules."

But Senate Democrats said that unless the bill was amended to provide more protections for workers, they would strenuously oppose it when it reached the floor. They were particularly upset by the proposal to allow workers to put in 50 hours one week and 30 hours in a second without triggering overtime pay or adversely affecting other employee benefits such as health insurance.

Noting that public sector employees had such options, Mike DeWine, R-Ohio, said the bill would give workers more control over their work schedules. "This has not been a problem" in the public sector, he said. "It's voluntary. The employee doesn't have to enter this."

But Democrats such as ranking member Edward M. Kennedy of Massachusetts strenuously opposed the bill, arguing it could lead to discrimination, coercion and abuse by unscrupulous businesses that would prefer workers to take one form of compensation or the other. "The employers supporting this bill want to pay their workers less," Kennedy said. "This is the real story."

Democrats, who said they also wanted to give working families more flexibility in their work schedules, generally preferred to expand the 1993 Family and Medical Leave Act to allow employees to take up to 24 hours of additional unpaid time off annually for such purposes as attending parent-teacher conferences or serving as a teacher's aide.

Republicans, however, said expanding family leave would not go far enough to address workers' needs.

The Family and Medical Leave Act required employers of 50 or more workers to provide employees with up to 12 weeks of unpaid leave for the birth of a child or the illness of a close family member.

Amendments Considered

During debate on the bill March 13, the Senate committee:

➤ Approved, 10-8, along party lines, an amendment by DeWine to clarify that employee acceptance of comp time would be voluntary and permissible only after mutual agreement by workers and employers.

➤ Rejected, 8-10, along party lines, an amendment by Paul Wellstone, D-Minn., to ensure that employees could take compensatory time for any of the reasons covered under the family leave act, provided their absence would not cause "substantial and grievous injury to the operation of the employer."

Before the final vote March 18, the panel rejected, 8-10, a series of Democratic amendments, including proposals:

➤ By Christopher J. Dodd of Connecticut to expand the 1993 family leave act to make it applicable to businesses with as few as 25 workers, down from the existing threshold of 50.

➤ By Patty Murray of Washington to amend the family leave act to permit workers to take up to 24 hours of unpaid leave annually to attend parent-teacher conferences or serve as teachers' aides.

➤ By Wellstone to exempt seasonal employees and garment workers from coverage under the comp time legislation.

➤ By Kennedy to prohibit employers from discriminating against workers or forcing them to accept one form of compensation instead of another.

Senate Floor Action

The bill reached the Senate floor, but Democrats twice blocked efforts to limit debate and bring it to a vote. GOP leaders then pulled the measure for the year.

The first attempt to invoke cloture, thereby limiting debate and moving to final passage on the bill, failed May 15 by a vote of 53-47. A three-fifths majority (60 votes) was required. Two Republicans joined all 45 Democrats in voting against the motion. *(Vote 68, p. S-14)*

The Republicans — Alfonse M. D'Amato of New York and Arlen Specter of Pennsylvania — represented heavily unionized states and were up for re-election in 1998.

Republican leaders did not indicate at the time whether they would abandon S 4, try again for cloture, or begin negotiating with Democrats on a bill that could pass. A GOP aide said the vote was viewed as an initial test of support and did not mean the end of Republican efforts to pass a compensatory time bill.

The second and last attempt to close debate on the bill failed June 4 by a vote of 51-47, with three Republicans joining 44 Democrats in opposing cloture. Democrat Jack Reed of Rhode Island and Republican Jeffords of Vermont did not vote. *(Vote 93, p. S-18)*

The Republican "no" votes came from D'Amato, Specter, and Ben Nighthorse Campbell of Colorado, who was also up for re-election in 1998. Campbell had a record of backing labor unions; in 1996, for example, he voted for the minimum wage increase after voting against the Republican alternative. *(1996 Almanac, p. 7-3)*

Senior Republican leadership aides indicated that most GOP senators were not willing to work out the compromises that would be needed to enact the legislation; they preferred to use it as a political issue to skewer Democrats as being against flexibility in the workplace. ■

GOP Sharpens Focus on Teamsters

Republicans once again turned a spotlight on the International Brotherhood of Teamsters, but their focus was no longer on the union's Mafia ties, as it had been in the 1980s. Instead, Republicans were taking a close look at the role of the federal government.

At issue was the 1996 Teamsters election, which was court monitored, federally funded under a consent decree and subsequently invalidated because of funding irregularities involving the re-election campaign of union President Ron Carey. The federal government had spent $17.6 million to oversee the election, yet it had been unable to keep it free of fraud. Republicans insisted that taxpayers should not have to pay for a second election in less than a year.

Republicans on the House Education and the Workforce Subcommittee on Oversight and Investigations held hearings on the issue in October and agreed in November to hire staff for a full-fledged investigation.

Meanwhile, Congress barred the use of federal funds to conduct a rerun. The language was included in the spending bills for the departments of Labor, Health and Human Services (HHS), and Education (PL 105-78), signed Nov. 13, and for the departments of Commerce, Justice and State (PL 105-119), signed Nov. 26.

Background

Congress laid much of the groundwork for government intervention into the unions in the 1940s and 1950s, including passage of the 1959 Landrum-Griffin Act (PL 86-257), which broadened government jurisdiction over labor disputes, in part by making misappropriation of union funds a crime. *(1959 Almanac, p. 156)*

From the 1950s through much of the 1980s, Mafia influence in the Teamsters union was pervasive, largely because the trucking-dominated union was key to moving Mafia contraband across the country. Of five men who served as Teamsters presidents, three went to prison and a fourth died before beginning a sentence for embezzlement and racketeering. Congress held years of hearings, led by Sen. John L. McClellan, D-Ark. (1943-77), into union corruption. In the Kennedy years, Attorney General Robert F. Kennedy aggressively investigated Teamsters President Jimmy Hoffa.

In 1988, the Reagan administration sued the Teamsters under racketeering laws.

In 1989, under President George Bush, the Teamsters and the Justice Department reached an agreement that was ratified as a consent decree by the U.S. District Court of Southern New York. The decree specified that the union would conduct general elections for its officers in 1991; while the union would pay for the election, the federal government would oversee it. If the government chose to oversee the 1996 election, it would pay for "supervision."

Republicans charged during the October 1997 hearings that "supervision" did not mean paying for everything from printing ballots to overseeing local chapter elections to tabulating results. But Michael H. Holland, a Chicago labor lawyer who served as court-appointed overseer in the 1991 contest, said that the court had interpreted the term broadly.

Milwaukee attorney Barbara Zack Quindel, the court-appointed overseer for the 1996 contest, was given a broad range of duties, including reviewing all contributions to Carey, who had been hailed as a reformer, and James P. Hoffa, the son of the former Teamsters president, who were vying for control of the 1.4 million-member union.

The candidates were required to report their contributions quarterly; Quindel testified that she did not notice irregularities until the last filing, in December 1996, when the ballots for the contest had already been mailed to members. Carey was declared the winner Dec. 14, with 237,028 votes compared with Hoffa's 221,110. Both spent about $3 million on their campaigns.

After receiving the final campaign report, Quindel began to investigate several suspicious donations to Carey's campaign. Law enforcement officials simultaneously began looking into allegations that Carey officials had funneled illegal contributions into the campaign and had approached the Democratic National Committee about funneling contributions through the party that Carey could not take legally. In exchange, the Teamsters would contribute to the Democratic Party.

On Aug. 22, 1997, Quindel ruled that the 1996 election had been invalid, saying illegal contributions might have helped Carey win. The U.S. District Court of Southern New York, which had jurisdiction over the consent decree, subsequently agreed.

A month later, three Carey loyalists — campaign manager Jere Nash, direct mail specialist Martin Davis and telemarketer Michael Ansara — pleaded guilty to criminal conspiracy for their part in the financing schemes. Ansara had also pleaded guilty earlier to another count of conspiracy.

House Hearings

In hearings held Oct. 14-15, Republican members of the Education and the Workforce Oversight and Investigations Subcommittee argued that taxpayers should not bear the cost of a new election. "I think you're going to have a hard row to hoe if you're going to try to squeeze more money from this Congress," said Van Hilleary, R-Tenn.

Though panel Democrats joined Republicans in condemning the acts that invalidated the 1996 balloting, they warned that the government risked renewed Mafia influence in the union if it went too far in reducing its oversight.

Privately, Democrats questioned GOP motives for the hearings, which offered Republicans a chance to pelt their political opponents. In the 1995-96 election cycle, the Teamsters' political action committee (PAC), under Carey's direction, contributed about $2.5 million to Democratic candidates, leading all other PACs, according to the non-partisan Center for Responsive Politics. It gave about $106,000 to Republicans.

Requiring the Teamsters to pay the estimated $20 million cost of supervising the next election could also seriously affect the union's financial health. "They don't have the money. . . . It will be difficult for them to help their political allies," said Richard Hurd, professor of labor studies at Cornell University's school of Industrial and Labor Relations.

At the hearings, Republicans said taxpayers should not foot the bill for another Teamsters election because federal funding of the earlier one had not prevented corruption. They said the government had a legitimate role in monitoring the election, but questioned the government's decision to pay for it.

Besides investigating fundraising irregularities, the panel focused on how the Carey campaign conducted itself within the union. Five Teamsters testified that they had been physically attacked when they spoke against the Carey team or had been intimidated into giving tacit support to Carey.

For example, Barbara L. Dusina, a Tampa union organizer, said she had been pressured to contribute to Carey's campaign and gave $50 a month for nine months. "There was an unspoken message that if any staff person did not contribute, they would be unemployed after a Carey victory," Dusina said.

But Thomas Geoghegan, a Chicago attorney who had represented unions, including the Teamsters, as well as union dissidents, said the group's stories paled in comparison to past practices, which sometimes included murder to silence dissidents. "There was an atmosphere of darkness in the union that is gone now," he said. "The bone-chilling fear is gone."

That did not satisfy Republicans. "I'm delighted we've gone beyond killing somebody," said Charlie Norwood, R-Ga.

In a letter to subcommittee Chairman Peter Hoekstra, R-Mich., Carey said that anyone who said he feared retaliation was "not telling the truth."

Panel Launches Probe

On Nov. 5, the House Education and the Workforce Committee approved a contract retaining Washington lawyers Joseph E. diGenova and Victoria Toensing to help the Subcommittee on Oversight and Investigations probe the 1996 Teamsters' election. Under the contract, approved by voice vote, the lawyers — both former prosecutors and veterans of congressional investigations — were to receive $150,000 for a six-month probe. DiGenova was a former U.S. attorney in the District of Columbia, and Toensing, his wife, was formerly chief counsel to the Senate Intelligence Committee. They shared a private law practice.

Panel Democrats questioned the necessity of a committee investigation. "The proper thing for us to do would be to let the prosecutors do their job," said Robert E. Andrews, D-N.J. And, in a sign of the tensions brewing over the investigation, Democrats subsequently charged that the lawyers had serious conflicts of interest. Specifically, they said diGenova and Toensing should not be allowed to:

➤ Lobby members of Congress while under contract with the Subcommittee on Oversight and Investigations.

➤ Keep other lobbying clients while under contract to the subcommittee. The firm lobbied for three clients: the American Hospital Association, which had member hospitals with Teamsters contracts; American Rice Inc.; and Computer Integrated Specialists Inc.

➤ Represent Dan Burton, R-Ind., chairman of the House Government Reform and Oversight Committee, in an ongoing criminal investigation for allegedly "shaking down" a lobbyist from Pakistan for a campaign contribution. Burton had already subpoenaed records from the Teamsters in his own panel's campaign fundraising investigation.

"Of all the lawyers in Washington, why did they get someone laden, so heavily laden with conflict?" asked William L. Clay of Missouri, the ranking Democrat on the Education and the Workforce Committee.

"This is an act of a Johnny-come-lately," Toensing said of Clay's charges. "What did he want us to do, shut down our firm for six months?"

"We went through this backwards and forwards," Hoekstra said in response to Clay's charges. Toensing and diGenova were recommended by members of both parties for their thoroughness and fairness, he said. Their clients were reviewed for any possible conflict of interest. "They are top-flight people," Hoekstra said. "If there was a conflict, they would tell us first. They would not do anything to tarnish their reputations."

Ethics experts said conflicts of interest were common in Washington, and that the diGenova-Toensing contract did not

GOP Begins Labor Probe

House Republicans launched a $1.4 million study of labor law, workplace regulations and union activity in an effort to raise the profile of the GOP labor agenda. The initiative, by the Oversight and Investigations subcommittee of the House Education and the Workforce Committee, was quickly labeled by Democrats as an attempt to punish big labor for its support of Democrats in the 1996 elections.

The investigation was expected to delve into issues such as the use of union dues for political activities and allegations of corruption in setting federal wage standards under the Davis-Bacon law, which required federal contractors to pay locally prevailing wages generally interpreted as union scale.

Peter Hoekstra, R-Mich., who chaired the investigatory subcommittee, acknowledged that labor practices would be a target, but said workplace issues would be studied as well. "A lot of people are looking at this as a get-the-unions campaign, and it most definitely is not that," said Jon Brandt, Hoekstra's spokesman.

Brandt said the probe would look at broad issues such as labor-management relations in the 1990s, workplace conditions, and federal programs that affected employers and the workplace. He said it would include a review of programs run by the Department of Labor as well as the department's "spending habits."

The House Oversight Committee on July 8 awarded $1.4 million to the subcommittee, dipping into a $7.9 million reserve fund created earlier in the year to beef up congressional oversight of programs created during 40 years of Democratic rule on Capitol Hill.

Oversight Committee Democrats charged that Republicans were looking for ways to retaliate against the unions for their aggressive attacks on the GOP during the 1996 elections, when Republicans were hit with negative ads as part of a $35 million, union-financed campaign.

appear to violate any laws governing lawyers. If it violated any rules it was the rule of appearance, said Stanley Brand, a former counsel to the House.

No Federal Aid for Rerun

Pressing their objections to funding another Teamsters election, Republicans succeeded in including a provision in the Labor-HHS spending bill barring such an expenditure.

Both chambers had voted to restrict the funding in their initial versions of the bill, although the House language was tougher.

The Senate acted first, agreeing Sept. 11 to an amendment by Majority Whip Don Nickles, R-Okla., to prevent the Labor or Justice departments from paying for another Teamsters election. However, if the president certified that the union could not afford to finance the election, the Teamsters would be allowed to take out a federal loan at customary interest rates. The vote on the amendment to S 1061 was 58-42. *(Vote 233, p. S-39)*

The proviso was prompted by Quindel's Aug. 22 call to overturn the 1996 union election and hold a new vote because of the funding irregularities in Carey's campaign.

Pro-labor Democrats such as Massachusetts Sen. Edward M. Kennedy said Congress had no right to interfere with the consent order. "It's an outrage to ask Congress to abdicate our responsibility to help in eliminating corruption in this union," Kennedy said.

Kennedy and other Democrats also charged that Nickles was trying to interfere in the pending court case. Although Quindel had invalidated the election, the Southern District Court of New York had not yet ruled on how the rerun should proceed.

But Nickles said his amendment only addressed a situation that the consent decree did not — who should pay for the new election. "Taxpayers shouldn't have to pay for the Teamsters election twice," he said. "It's not the taxpayers' fault that there was fraud."

Nickles also questioned whether the Democrats were being unduly influenced by union campaign contributions. "Look at all the money that the Teamsters have given," he said. "The Democrats are just trying to give them a $22 million gift."

On Sept. 16, the House amended its version of the Labor-HHS spending bill (HR 2264) to ban any federal funds from being used to pay the expenses of an election officer appointed by a court to oversee a new Teamsters election. The amendment, by Hoekstra, was adopted 225-195, largely along party lines. *(Vote 399, p. H-122)*

When the bill reached conference, House and Senate negotiators accepted the stronger Senate language. The White House opposed both versions. *(Appropriations, p. 9-50)*

Hoekstra also succeeded in adding the ban to the Commerce-Justice-State spending bill in the House (HR 2267), and it was included in the final version. Hoekstra's amendment was adopted Sept. 26 by a vote of 213-189. *(Vote 459, p. H-140)*

Carey Disqualified

On Nov. 17, Quindel's successor, former U.S. District Judge Kenneth Conboy, ruled that Carey would not be allowed to participate in a rerun of the 1996 election. In his ruling, Conboy said Carey "tolerated and engaged in extensive rules violations" to infuse his campaign with cash and to stave off a strong challenge by Hoffa. Carey denied the charges.

Conboy disclosed that the Carey campaign had channeled $735,000 in dues to outside groups that then funneled the money into Carey's re-election fund. The report also detailed schemes in which the Carey camp raised funds from employers and officials at other unions, both of whom were prohibited from donating to Teamsters campaigns under the 1989 consent decree. In addition, the report detailed a scheme to swap donations to the Democratic National Committee for donations to Carey.

Conboy also called for an investigation into Hoffa's campaign finances. Hoffa maintained that investigators would find nothing wrong.

In both the 1991 and 1996 elections, Carey had been championed by reformers who believed his efforts to rid the union of graft and corruption would help revitalize the labor movement. Unlike past Teamsters leaders, Carey eschewed elaborate spending. He sold the union's limousines and two private jets and put more than 70 locals into trusteeships because of corruption.

Teamsters campaign contributions were also under investigation by a federal grand jury in New York. ■

Partisan Bickering Stalls OSHA Bills

The Senate Labor and Human Resources Committee added another item Oct. 22 to the stack of labor-related bills awaiting final action in 1998, while showing how far apart Republicans and Democrats remained on labor issues.

By a 10-8 party-line vote, the panel approved a bill (S 1237) aimed at reining in the Occupational Safety and Health Administration (OSHA) — an agency that business groups and congressional conservatives had long targeted as too confrontational and that most Democrats regarded as essential for ensuring workers' safety. The measure went no further, and there was no action on an identical House bill (HR 2579).

The legislation proposed to shift OSHA's focus from enforcing workplace health and safety laws to working with employers to fix problems, often without fining companies for those problems. It proposed giving employers several other directions to turn for advice, including using private and state consultants to determine whether they met OSHA requirements.

Debate on the bill, sponsored by Michael B. Enzi, R-Wyo., divided along party lines, despite Enzi's solicitation of Democratic views before introducing the bill, and his participation in more than 100 meetings with interested business and labor organizations.

As Enzi, other Republicans and some conservative House Democrats saw it, the main problem with OSHA was that it acted as a law enforcer instead of a teacher. The bill included provisions to limit the types of violations that triggered citations and to allow employers two years of freedom from citations if private consultants certified that their workplace met OSHA standards.

Democrats did not disagree with all of these proposals. Vice President Al Gore, in his 1993 report on revamping the federal government, recommended that OSHA encourage

Major Provisions of OSHA Bills

The Senate and House bills (S 1237, HR 2579) to revamp the Occupational Safety and Health Administration (OSHA) contained provisions to:

● **Employer citations.** Exempt employers from OSHA citations unless they knew they were violating safety rules or would have known with "reasonable diligence." The bill sought to prevent OSHA from citing employers if a violation occurred because employees were not following work rules, provided the employer had "adequately communicated" the rules to workers, who were properly trained and equipped. OSHA also could not cite employers if they demonstrated that employees were protected by "alternate methods" equal to or exceeding the rule at issue.

Under the bill, OSHA inspectors would be allowed to issue warnings instead of citations. When assessing civil penalties, the Occupational Safety and Health Review Commission would be required to give "due consideration" to factors such as employer size and history, and the severity of injuries that could have resulted from the violation.

● **Third-party assessments.** Create a program to allow employers to contract with a consultant accredited by the Labor Department to determine whether their workplace met OSHA requirements. If the consultant approved the workplace or if the employer made changes to bring the workplace up to code, the consultant was to issue a certificate of compliance. The certificate would exempt the employer for two years from civil penalties, unless the employer did not make "good faith" efforts to remain in compliance or workplace conditions underwent "fundamental change." Records related to the consultant's work could not be admitted in a court of law or administrative proceeding against the employer.

● **State assessments.** Require OSHA to enter into contracts with states to act as consultants. OSHA would reimburse 90 percent of state costs. The bill also required that no less than 15 percent of OSHA's annual appropriation be spent on education, consultation and "outreach efforts."

● **Safety teams.** Allow employers to create teams of appointed managers and employees to address workplace safety and health issues.

● **Investigating complaints.** Allow OSHA to decline to investigate complaints that the Labor secretary determined were not related to employee safety and health. At the time, OSHA had to review all employee complaints.

● **Scientific review.** Send proposed safety and health standards issued by the Labor secretary through an independent board established by the National Academy of Sciences.

The board would compare the proposal and scientific literature on the subject and could recommend changes to the secretary. If the secretary changed the proposal, it would have to be resubmitted to the board, which could again suggest changes. When the final standard was published in the Federal Register, the board's findings would be published with it.

● **Drug testing.** Allow employers to test employees for drug or alcohol use and allow OSHA to require such tests when investigating work-related fatalities or serious injuries, unless state law prohibited it.

● **Employee citations.** Allow OSHA to cite and fine employees who it believed violated safety and health rules regarding personal protective equipment. ■

employers to hire consultants to improve their worksites.

But Democrats generally opposed the incentives Republicans wanted to give employers for hiring such consultants. Jack Reed, D-R.I., said two years of protection from civil OSHA penalties would allow employers to "write a check and buy themselves two years of immunity."

Enzi said he would try to work out differences between Republicans and Democrats, but he defended his plans to change OSHA. "If you keep on doing what you've always been doing, you're going to end up with what you've got, and that's not acceptable," he said.

Background

Since its creation in 1970 as a division of the Labor Department, OSHA had been a thorn in the side of many employers and a prime target of Republicans and some conservative Democrats. The agency had the job of enforcing workplace health and safety laws and promulgating regulations. But it had only one inspector for every 3,000 worksites and could only inspect each site every 167 years on average, according to the House Small Business Committee, whose chairman, James M. Talent, R-Mo., sponsored the House bill.

Conservatives said when OSHA did inspect sites, it often used a "gotcha" approach. Instead of striving to understand a workplace's broad problems, they said, under-trained and over-burdened inspectors often looked for the easiest infractions to catch — usually those related to paperwork. That, conservatives said, caused widespread frustration among employers and did not fix workplace problems.

According to the Small Business Committee, seven of the most common 10 OSHA citations in fiscal 1994 were for missing paperwork, from record keeping to container labeling.

Still, bills to rein in the agency had died in committee in the Senate in 1996 and in subcommittee in the House. Related attempts in the 102nd and 103rd Congresses also were unsuccessful. *(1996 Almanac, p. 7-11)*

In drafting his 1997 bill, Enzi dropped several highly contentious provisions that had been included in the 1996 version, including a plan to limit OSHA to responding to employee complaints, rather than initiating its own investigations. Democrats lavishly praised Enzi's efforts. Ranking Democrat Edward M. Kennedy of Massachusetts said that in his 30 years on the committee he had seldom seen anything so "remarkable." But the compliments stopped there.

In a written statement to the Labor and Human Resources Committee, Kennedy said Enzi's bill "does many things that would undermine advances that have taken decades to achieve." And Paul Wellstone, D-Minn., Kennedy's frequent partner in jousting with panel Republicans, vowed that the bill "will not pass on the floor."

Committee Action

During the Oct. 22 markup, Democrats offered six amendments, all of which were rejected. Many addressed provisions in the bill that Labor Secretary Alexis Herman warned, in a letter to the committee, would prompt her to recommend that President Clinton veto the bill.

The committee adopted by voice vote an Enzi amendment making several changes, including a stipulation that a bill provision allowing employers to test workers for drug and alcohol use would not pre-empt state laws.

The panel rejected Democratic proposals to:

➤ Change the third-party consulting provisions, removing the two-year immunity clause and replacing it with a 50 percent discount on fines. The amendment, by Reed, was defeated in an 8-10 party-line vote.

➤ Alter another provision that Democrats found particularly egregious — one that would allow employers to create worker-management teams to address workplace health and safety issues. The amendment, by Patty Murray, D-Wash., was rejected, 7-11, with Jeff Bingaman, D-N.M., joining Republicans in voting against it.

Murray decried the provision as an attempt to implement a portion of the controversial TEAM Act (S 295), which would amend the 1935 National Labor Relations Act to make clear that businesses could establish management-worker groups to address such issues as quality, productivity and safety. The TEAM bill had stalled in the Senate in March under vociferous Democratic opposition. *(Workplace teams, this page)*

Murray's amendment would have required that the safety teams be composed equally of members appointed by employers and employees. In unionized workplaces, unions could name employee members. Where no unions existed, employees could elect their representatives.

Enzi said that in his many discussions with business and labor groups, no one was interested in such a complicated system.

➤ Prevent employers from firing workers who filed health or safety complaints. The proposal, by Wellstone, was rejected 8-9.

➤ Give official status to the OSHA office on construction safety, and require construction companies to make sure a "competent person" was at a construction site at all times to oversee a safety plan. The amendment, by Christopher J. Dodd, D-Conn., was defeated 8-10.

➤ Increase criminal penalties for company owners or managers who willfully violated health or safety standards, causing the death of an employee. The offense would have become a felony instead of a misdemeanor, carrying a prison sentence of up to 10 years and fines of up to $250,000. The amendment also would have made it a misdemeanor to willfully violate health and safety laws and maim an employee. The proposal, by Reed, was rejected 8-10.

➤ Allow OSHA to inspect and report on fatal accidents at farms employing fewer than 10 people. The amendment, offered by Reed, was rejected 8-10. ■

Other Labor-Related Measures Considered in 1997

A bill to ease regulations on employee-management teams in the workplace languished in the first session. On another front, Congress made several changes in pension rules.

Workplace Teams

A Republican effort to allow businesses to set up groups of workers and managers to address workplace issues stalled in the Senate in March under vociferous Democratic opposition. The so-called TEAM Act (S 295) proposed to amend the 1935 Labor Relations Act to allow the formation of worker-management groups to address such issues as productivity, quality control and workplace safety.

Republicans said the changes would promote innovation and give U.S. employers an edge in the global marketplace. "Rather than look backwards at the workplace of the 1930s, we should look forward to the 21st century," said Labor panel Chairman James M. Jeffords, R-Vt. "The law needs to be fixed."

Democrats, however, said the bill would undermine the rights of workers to unionize and bargain collectively. President Clinton, who vetoed a similar bill in 1996, again threatened to reject such a measure. *(1996 Almanac, p. 7-9)*

The Senate Labor and Human Resources Committee approved the bill March 5 on a 10-8 party-line vote. The action came after nearly 10 hours of debate that stretched over three meetings in two weeks. It also came over the strenuous objections of the panel's Democrats, who angrily charged that Republicans were trying to get back at organized labor for its efforts to unseat GOP members during the 1996 election.

"You can't wait to go after labor. You can't wait to go after working people in this country," said Minnesota Democrat Paul Wellstone, who joined others in predicting a messy floor fight. "We get the message, and when it gets to the floor, we are going to take this on."

Jeffords said that many employers who wanted to establish workplace teams were afraid to do so for fear of violating the law. Likening such a threat to a sword hanging over the heads of employers, Jeffords said the vast majority of businesses were interested in improving their performance, not taking advantage of their workers.

Before voting to report the bill to the floor, the panel rejected amendments by:

➤ Wellstone, to amend the National Labor Relations Act to allow the National Labor Relations Board (NLRB) to take any action it deemed necessary against employers found violating workers' rights to unionize. The proposal, defeated 7-11, also would have required the NLRB to issue orders barring businesses from repeating the violations for five years.

➤ Ranking Democrat Edward M. Kennedy of Massachusetts, to protect workers who participated in workplace teams from losing their rights to bargain collectively or to unionize. Kennedy contended that workers could be deemed supervisors or management as a result of their involvement in a worker-management group. The proposal was rejected, 8-10.

During earlier markup sessions Feb. 26 and Feb. 28, the committee rejected, 8-10, along strict party lines, five amendments offered by Kennedy. He proposed to:

➤ Extend the types of issues that workplace groups could discuss to include work organization, processes and the use of new technology.

➤ Make the TEAM Act inapplicable in workplaces where union organizing efforts were under way.

➤ Give union representatives the right to attend meetings called by employers and address workers gathered at such events.

➤ Give workers fired for union organizing the right to back pay equivalent to triple their salary, as well as attorneys' fees.

➤ Require the NLRB to provide injunctive relief when it was determined that an employee had been fired for union organizing.

Pension Changes

Congress addressed several pension issues as part of the tax cut bill (PL 105-34), signed Aug. 5 as part of the 1997 budget-reconciliation package. *(Tax reconciliation, p. 2-30)*

Changes in the new law included:

• **IRAs for homemakers.** A change in rules for traditional individual retirement accounts (IRAs) to provide more retirement protection for women who did not work outside the home. Under prior law, if a husband had a traditional pension plan at work and the couple's income exceeded $40,000, a wife who stayed at home could not make a $2,000 tax-deductible contribution to an IRA. In essence, a homemaker had no tax incentive to establish an IRA.

The new provision, sponsored by Sens. Judd Gregg,

R-N.H., and Bob Graham, D-Fla., allowed a stay-at-home spouse to contribute to an IRA even if a partner had an employer-sponsored plan at work.

• **Pension portability.** A provision assuring that a qualified retirement plan would not lose tax advantages if it accepted rollover contributions from a previous employer's plan that turned out to be tainted, or disqualified for tax breaks. The provision was part of a broader pension overhaul proposal by Graham and Sen. Charles E. Grassley, R-Iowa. Another item from their overhaul plan, a provision repealing a requirement that businesses file a report with the Labor Department when they made major changes in their pension plans, was also included in the tax bill.

• **Cash-out payments.** An increase in the amount in an employee's pension fund that would trigger an involuntary cash-out of benefits. Previously, an individual was required to take the money out in a lump sum if the pension plan was worth $3,500 or less. If it was worth more, payments were made periodically (usually monthly), resulting in more paperwork and responsibility for employers maintaining the accounts. The legislation increased the cash-out payment to $5,000.

• **401(k) plans.** A provision by Sen. Barbara Boxer, D-Calif., to prevent employers from requiring employees to place more than 10 percent of their 401(k) contributions into company stock or assets, unless the employee agreed. The provision came in response to the bankruptcy of Color Tile Inc., a Fort Worth, Texas, company that had 774 stores in 48 states. Eighty-three percent of the company's 401(k) assets had been invested in Color Tile itself. The failure nearly wiped out many employees' retirement savings. The provision was to go into effect in 1999.

Conferees on the tax bill dropped a provision, sponsored by Sen. Carol Moseley-Braun, D-Ill., that would have required workers with 401(k) plans who wanted to cash out their benefits to get permission from their spouses when deciding whether to withdraw the money in a lump sum or to receive periodic payments. Existing law required the consent of a spouse only on distributions from traditional pension plans that provided automatic survivor benefits.

Moseley-Braun argued that the increased variety in pension plans had exceeded the protections and that it was only fair to extend the consent requirement to 401(k) plans. She said the protection was needed by homemakers.

Employers and their representatives lobbied furiously to persuade negotiators to drop the provision, contending it would increase their paperwork and harm working women who would have to get their husbands' permission for access to their own money. "From the standpoint of women, it offers little support and does substantial harm," said Mark Ugoretz, president of the ERISA Industry Committee, a group representing employer benefits plans. Though they succeeded, employer groups said they expected the issue to return. ■

Vets Programs Modified, Health Needs Targeted

On Nov. 1, President Clinton signed into law a measure (S 714 — PL 105-114) that reauthorized and modified several veterans programs. Among its provisions, the bill changed the way the Department of Veterans Affairs (VA) handled sexual harassment and other discrimination claims, and directed the department to create a project targeting the health care needs of veterans of the 1991 Persian Gulf War.

Other provisions extended and streamlined laws under which the VA provided care to homeless veterans and veterans who suffered from chronic mental illness.

• **Sexual harassment.** The measure incorporated provisions, though in watered down form, of a previously passed House bill (HR 1703 — H Rept 105-292) dealing with sexual harassment and other discrimination claims.

Originally, the House bill would have required the department to hire well-trained employment law experts with no direct ties to the VA to investigate complaints. It also would have required that final rulings in discrimination cases be made by an independent administrative law judge rather than by a VA employee.

HR 1703 was approved in that form by the House Veterans' Affairs Committee on Sept. 30. The House passed the bill by voice vote under suspension of the rules Oct. 6.

But at the request of the VA, the legislation was changed before it was added to S 714. The final version still required the VA to establish new employment complaint resolution procedures, but no longer required that the matter be handled completely independent of the department. As enacted, it required the VA to establish a quasi-independent Office of Employment Discrimination Complaint Adjudication and contract with a private entity to assess the VA's handling of such complaints.

• **Gulf war veterans.** The omnibus bill also included a House passed measure (HR 2206) authorizing $5 million to establish a pilot project at 10 VA hospitals to serve veterans of the Persian Gulf War who suffered from undiagnosed illnesses. The program, to begin July 1, 1998, was subject to annual appropriations.

The hospitals were required to test new approaches to treating gulf war illnesses and improve existing treatments to help veterans cope. The bill required that a peer-review panel and the VA secretary approve the sites and the plans before funding was disbursed to ensure that the program was competitive. The VA supported the initiative, though some officials claimed it might be unnecessary because Persian Gulf War veterans already were being treated within accepted medical standards.

This section of the bill also rewrote existing law to make all veterans who served in the gulf war eligible for immediate VA care. Previously, services were offered only to veterans whose illnesses could be linked to exposure to toxic or hazardous compounds. The VA supported the change.

HR 2206 was approved Sept. 11 by the House Veterans' Affairs Committee (H Rept 105-293), and passed the House Oct. 6 by voice vote under suspension of the rules.

Some lawmakers also had contemplated liberalizing the rules governing disability compensation payment for Gulf War veterans with undiagnosed illnesses, such as chronic fatigue, skin rashes and joint aches. Veterans had been eligible for disability benefits for such undiagnosed illnesses, but only if they proved that their symptoms had appeared within two years of their return from the 1991 war.

Veterans' advocates, including lawmakers from both parties, said the two-year window had allowed the VA to deny benefits to a majority of gulf war veterans who had filed claims. They said many veterans became ill after the deadline.

But Clinton headed off possible action by Congress, announcing March 7 that the administration would issue new rules to expand from two years to 10 years the window of opportunity for veterans to file disability claims.

Legislative Action on S 714

The Senate Veterans' Affairs Committee approved the original version of S 714 (S Rept 105-123), without the sexual harassment or gulf war provisions, by voice vote Oct. 7. The Senate passed the bill by voice vote Nov. 5.

On Nov. 9, the House passed the bill by voice vote, but only after adding provisions from several other bills, including the sexual harassment and VA provisions. The changes had been worked out in advance by the House and Senate Veterans' Affairs panels.

The Senate concurred with the House changes by voice vote Nov. 10, clearing the bill for the president.

COLA

Veterans received a routine inflation adjustment in their benefits under a separate bill signed into law Nov. 19 (HR 2367 — PL 105-98).

The 2.1 percent increase, which was effective Dec. 1, was based on inflation as measured by the Consumer Price Index and was equal to adjustments made for Social Security recipients. Amounts were rounded down to the nearest dollar in compliance with the balanced-budget package, saving roughly $391 million over five years. *(Spending reconciliation bill highlights, p. 2-52)*

The cost of living increase affected roughly 2.2 million veterans with service-connected injuries. It also increased dependency and indemnity compensation paid to about 300,000 survivors of veterans who had died from service-connected injuries.

The bill began in the House Veterans' Affairs Subcommittee on Benefits, which approved it Aug. 4. The full Veterans' Affairs Committee followed suit Sept. 11. The House passed the measure Oct. 31, and the Senate cleared it Nov. 5. All were on voice votes.

Denial of Burial Rights

Veterans convicted of capital crimes became ineligible for burial with military honors under a bill signed into law Nov. 21 (S 923 — PL 105-116). The bill prohibited the "performance of military honors upon death" for veterans who had been sentenced to death or life imprisonment for a federal capital crime, or sentenced to death or life imprisonment without parole for a state capital crime.

Previously, veterans remained eligible for military burial and other benefits even if they had committed offenses such as murder that were punishable by death under federal law.

The legislation was prompted by the conviction of Army veteran Timothy McVeigh in the April 1995 bombing of a federal building in Oklahoma City that killed 168 people. The final bill was considerably narrower than the version initially passed by the Senate.

The bill, sponsored by Arlen Specter, R-Pa., and Robert G. Torricelli, D-N.J., initially proposed to deny all veterans' benefits, not just burial rights, to persons convicted of federal capital offenses. The Senate passed the bill in that form June 18 by a vote of 98-0. *(Vote 106, p. S-20)*

Specter called the terrorist attack in Oklahoma "the most heinous criminal act in the history of the United States," and said he was "surprised to learn" that McVeigh could claim veterans' benefits under existing law.

Senate Majority Whip Don Nickles, R-Okla., noted, "There is a forfeiture of veterans' benefits for a lot of crimes: mutiny, sedition . . . rebellion, insurrection, and advocating the overthrow of the government. But there is not for a federal capital offense."

Under S 923, a veteran who committed such an offense would forfeit all benefits, including aid for education, employment, disabilities and dependents. The bill did not apply to veterans whose capital crimes were committed under state laws.

The measure was then sent to the House, where the Veterans' Affairs Committee revised it to apply only to military burials. Veterans groups had complained that the original Senate version would unfairly penalize the families of such veterans.

The committee approved the revised bill (H Rept 105- 319) by voice vote Sept. 11, after debating a move to expand its scope to cover those convicted in state court. Spencer Bachus, R-Ala., offered the amendment, arguing that only a small percentage of capital cases were tried in federal court. Bachus cited the case of Army veteran Henry Francis Hays, a Ku Klux Klan member executed in Alabama June 7 after being convicted of murder in a state court for hanging a black child. Hays was buried with military honors.

But the VA said including state crimes would make the provision difficult to administer. Bachus eventually withdrew his amendment after committee Chairman Bob Stump, R-Ariz., assured him that his concerns would be considered before House floor debate.

The House passed S 923 by voice vote Oct. 31 after adopting a substitute amendment that denied military burials to veterans convicted of murder in state capital cases, as well as those convicted of federal capital crimes. The Senate concurred with the House-passed version by voice vote Nov. 10.

Disability Appeals

It became easier for veterans to appeal rulings on disability benefits under a bill signed into law Nov. 21 (HR 1090 — PL 105-111). Previous law gave the Department of Veterans Affairs (VA) discretion to review only those appeals it found to have merit. HR 1090 required the department to review any appeal claiming that the VA had made "clear and unmistakable error," so long as the appeal was properly filed.

The VA opposed the legislation, arguing that it would add to an already lengthy backlog of cases and could potentially reopen cases dating back to the 1930s. Veterans' advocates countered that no veteran should be denied benefits because of a VA error.

The House Veterans' Affairs Committee approved the bill March 20 (H Rept 105-52) and the House passed it April 16. The Senate cleared the bill Nov. 10; its Veterans' Affairs Committee had approved a similar measure Oct. 7. All the tallies were by voice vote.

Health Insurance Payments

Under the budget-reconciliation bill (PL 105-33) that President Clinton signed Aug. 5, the Department of Veterans Affairs (VA) gained the authority to keep the money it received from private insurance companies for treating veterans. The VA had been trying for years to gain this authority. Previously, the money had gone into the general Treasury.

If the change had been made outside the budget-reconciliation process, lawmakers would have had to offset the cost to the Treasury — about $600 million annually — by cutting other veterans programs. Adding it to reconciliation allowed greater flexibility in finding offsets.

In separate action, the House Veterans' Affairs Committee approved a bill (HR 1362 — H Rept 105-186, Part 1) to allow the VA to keep some of the payments it received from Medicare for treating elderly veterans. The bill proposed setting up a three-year pilot program to test the idea, known as Medicare subvention, at up to 12 VA medical facilities. Under existing law, the VA had to relinquish most of what it took in from Medicare and other outside insurers to the general Treasury.

The committee approved the bill by voice vote May 21. The panel's Health Subcommittee had approved it May 15, also by voice vote. The legislation went no further in the first session.

Initially, the bill would have allowed the pilot to involve as many as 30 hospitals. But to head off criticism about a possible drain on Medicare, the health insurance program for the elderly and disabled, the panel's Health Subcommittee adopted an amendment limiting the test to 12 facilities.

The full Veterans' Affairs panel approved another amendment that would allow the VA to enter into managed care agreements to provide health care for some veterans participating in the pilot program. Under such an agreement, the VA could receive a flat payment from Medicare and become the sole health care provider for a veteran. Otherwise, the VA would bill Medicare on a fee-for-service basis for specific services.

The bill capped the amount the VA could recover from Medicare each year at $50 million. Of that total, only $10 million could be billed for services provided to a veteran enrolled in a managed care agreement.

Job Preference

As in previous years, the House easily passed a bill to expand a hiring and job retention preference for veterans in the federal work force, but the measure saw no action in the Senate.

The bill (HR 240) proposed extending the policy, known as veterans' preference, to most non-political jobs in the federal government. Under existing law, it was applied only to certain executive branch agencies.

Under the measure, veterans who believed they had not been properly considered for federal jobs could sue in federal court after exhausting Labor Department appeals. The bill also sought to give veterans extra advantages during government layoffs.

The preference program, among other things, gave eligible veterans extra points on competitive civil service hiring exams and required agencies to keep veterans over non-veterans when eliminating positions. It also gave veterans more time to learn a new job if theirs was eliminated. The preference generally applied to those who had served in combat or became disabled while in the military.

Bill sponsor John L. Mica, R-Fla., contended that veterans' preference was often ignored or evaded and that the legislation was necessary to protect veterans against what he viewed as an "anti-veteran culture" within the federal bureaucracy.

The measure was similar to legislation introduced by Mica in the 104th Congress, which passed the House both as a free-standing measure and as an amendment to a Senate bill. The Senate did not consider either version. *(1996 Almanac, p. 7-15)*

Mica changed the legislation slightly in 1997, in part to appease postal workers who objected to provisions in the 1996 version.

The new bill contained a provision stipulating that veterans' preference could not interfere with the hiring procedures outlined by the Postal Service and its union under a collective bargaining agreement. Some postal workers had feared that the preference could lead to the hiring of unqualified veterans without a postal service background.

Mica added a second provision to make it a "prohibited personnel practice" for managers to knowingly evade veterans' preference. Such a violation could lead to firing, suspension or a $1,000 fine.

At a hearing Feb. 26, James B. King, director of the Office of Personnel Management, told the Government Reform and Oversight Civil Service Subcommittee that he supported the bill's goals. King asked, though, that it include a 90-day phase-in period for agencies to adjust their layoff procedures to give veterans extra advantages. The legislation, for example, would give veterans 150 days to learn a new job if theirs was eliminated, compared with 90 days for other employees.

The bill began in the Civil Service Subcommittee, which Mica chaired; the panel approved the measure on Feb. 26. The full committee followed suit March 12 (H Rept 105-40, Part 1). The House passed the measure April 9. All tallies were by voice vote.

Budget Cuts

Congress shaved about $2.7 billion from mandatory veterans spending over five years as part of the deficit-reducing budget-reconciliation bill that President Clinton signed on Aug 5 (PL 105-33). *(Spending reconciliation, p. 2-47)*

About $1 billion of the savings came from giving the VA new means to recover health care costs from private insurers and renewing the department's authority to charge co-payments for prescription drugs, hospital stays and other services. Another $391 million came from rounding down to the nearest dollar the annual inflation adjustment to veterans' benefits. *(Health insurance payments, p. 7-30)*

The Senate Veterans' Affairs panel approved the provisions, 11-0, on June 12. The House Veterans' Affairs panel approved a nearly identical plan the same day, 18-4. ■

Togo West Is Confirmed As VA Secretary

President Clinton on Dec. 2 formally announced his choice of Army Secretary Togo D. West Jr. to head the Department of Veterans' Affairs (VA). Clinton said he would send the nomination to the Senate when Congress reconvened in 1998. Meanwhile, he said, West would serve as acting VA secretary.

"Togo West's entire life has been dedicated to excellence and commitment, from his experience as an Army officer to his work in the Ford and Carter administrations, to his outstanding work as secretary of the Army," Clinton said. "He has always understood the special responsibility we owe to our men and women in uniform, both during and after their years of service."

West promised to protect government services for the nation's 25 million veterans, calling the programs "part of the effort to repay that debt, to keep the promise America has made to her veterans."

West was nominated to succeed former VA Secretary Jesse Brown, who resigned in July.

The nomination of West, secretary of the Army since 1993,

had been expected for several weeks before Clinton's announcement. Some veterans' organizations had expressed reservations, citing West's lack of experience in areas such as veterans' benefits. West said he would work to forge a relationship with veterans' groups and with Congress to "seek and do what is right for our veterans."

In the weeks before his appointment, West was the center of a spurt of interest in the way exceptions were granted for the interment of people who would not normally be accorded burial at Arlington National Cemetery. For several days, congressional Republicans jumped on suggestions that burial plots were awarded to Democratic Party donors. But the criticisms died down after West made public a list of all the waivers that he had granted during the Clinton administration and explained the basis for each exemption.

West, 55, a longtime Pentagon lawyer and lobbyist for the Northrop Corp., held engineering and law degrees from Washington's Howard University. If confirmed, West would be the third African American in the Clinton Cabinet, joining Transportation Secretary Rodney Slater and Labor Secretary Alexis Herman.

Gober's Name Withdrawn

Deputy VA secretary Hershel W. Gober had filled in as acting secretary following Brown's resignation and for a time was considered the likely successor. But Clinton withdrew the nomination at Gober's request Oct. 24, amid reports of sexual harassment allegations and questions about how the VA had investigated the case. Gober said he could best serve the administration by remaining in the post of deputy secretary.

News reports had surfaced a month before that Gober and his wife, VA general counsel Mary Lou Keener, racked up thousands of dollars in unjustified travel expenses to attend conferences and meetings, including a 1994 trip to finalize a lease on a VA building in Paris. Meanwhile, the Associated Press, quoting three anonymous officials, reported allegations of sexual harassment by Gober at the VA.

Senate Veterans' Affairs Committee Chairman Arlen Specter, R-Pa., had postponed a confirmation hearing, saying he wanted more information. Specter said Gober's withdrawal averted "what might have been a contentious hearing."

Gober, a longtime ally of the president, had been director of veterans affairs in Arkansas when Clinton was governor. ■

CQ

Chapter 8

DEFENSE & FOREIGN POLICY

DEFENSE AUTHORIZATION

Clinton Signs Defense Bill Despite Veto Threat

Congress adds $2.6 billion to Pentagon budget request, rebuffs Clinton on maintenance depots

House and Senate negotiators deadlocked for months over the fiscal 1998 defense authorization bill, not because of an inability to agree on money or bombers or missile defense, but because they could not resolve a parochial feud over Air Force maintenance depots.

Only the fear of being marginalized in the congressional debate over military policy drove conferees to an agreement on the $268.3 billion bill (HR 1119), which was sent to the White House on Nov. 6, nearly four months after it had gone to conference.

Despite his misgivings over the maintenance depot provisions and the overall spending level, which was $2.6 billion more than he had requested, President Clinton signed the bill into law Nov. 18 (PL 105-85).

Although the spending authority provided by the bill had largely been superseded by the fiscal 1998 defense appropriations bill already signed into law (PL 105-56), the Pentagon still was eager to have the authorization. For one thing, it gave military personnel a 2.8 percent pay increase in fiscal 1998, instead of the 2.3 percent government-wide pay raise they otherwise would have received, and it substantially increased bonuses for pilots who chose to stay in the service. *(Appropriations, p. 9-17)*

BOXSCORE

Fiscal 1998 Defense Authorization — HR 1119 (S 936). The bill authorized $268.3 billion for defense activities, $2.6 billion more than requested.

Reports: H Rept 105-132, S Rept 105-29; conference report, H Rept 105-340.

KEY ACTION

June 25 — House passed HR 1119, 304-120.

July 11 — Senate passed HR 1119 by voice vote after substituting the text of S 936, which had passed, 94-4.

Oct. 28 — House adopted the conference report, 286-123.

Nov. 6 — Senate cleared the bill, 90-10.

Nov. 18 — President signed HR 1119 — PL 105-85.

• **Maintenance depots.** On the issue of maintenance depots, the final bill contained provisions aimed at steering Air Force maintenance work to three government-owned depots and away from private contractors using depots in California and Texas that the government was leaving.

In an effort to save thousands of jobs in those key electoral states, Clinton in 1995 had announced a "privatization-in-place" policy under which contractors could bid for maintenance work they would perform using the depots scheduled to be shut down. That brought angry protests from lawmakers representing the three remaining Air Force depots, located in Georgia, Oklahoma and Utah.

The dispute over the depots helped sink a request by the administration that the bill authorize two more rounds of base closings — in 1999 and 2001.

• **B-2.** The final bill also denied proponents of the B-2 stealth bomber, built to evade detection and pierce Soviet air defenses, what may have been their final chance to buy more of the big planes than the 21 already paid for.

Led by Reps. Duncan Hunter, R-Calif., and Norm Dicks, D-Wash., whose states included B-2 factories, the House added $331 million to the bill to keep open some parts of the B-2 production network that were closing down, with a view toward buying at least nine more bombers in future budgets. But that effort was blocked by adamant opposition not only in the Senate and the Clinton administration, but among senior Air Force leaders, who insisted that future budgets could not absorb more of the planes. The B-2s cost more than $750 million apiece.

Ultimately, the bill included $331 million for the B-2, but the Pentagon was given a free hand to decide whether to use the money to gear up for buying additional planes or to repair and upgrade the B-2s already in service.

• **Bosnia.** On the issue of U.S. troops in Bosnia, which had lain dormant for most of the year, the bill called for U.S. operations to end June 30, 1998, the last deadline that had been set by Clinton. (Clinton subsequently announced that he had agreed in principle to keep U.S. forces in Bosnia, as part of a NATO-led peacekeeping force, beyond June 30. He did not set a new deadline.)

• **Abortion.** The defense bill continued the existing ban on female service members or military dependents obtaining privately funded abortions in U.S. military hospitals overseas unless the case involved rape, incest or danger to the life of the woman.

Such privately funded abortions had been allowed from 1973 until 1988 on grounds that abortions were illegal in some countries where U.S. forces were stationed, while in other countries local medical services were below par.

Late in his second term, President Ronald Reagan barred the practice. Clinton overturned the ban as one of his first acts after taking office in 1993. Republicans reinstated the ban after taking control of Congress in 1995, including it in the fiscal 1996 defense authorization bill. *(1995 Almanac, p. 9-3)*

Background

For four years, Republican defense experts had criticized Clinton's defense requests as inadequate to keep the military

Defense Authorization

Following are the major amounts in the fiscal 1998 defense authorization bill (HR 1119 —PL 105-85). The amounts are in millions of dollars; the totals may not add because of rounding.

	Clinton Request	House Bill	Senate Bill	Conference Agreement
Procurement	$42,883.0	$46,595.9	$47,028.1	$45,773.8
Research and development	35,934.5	37,273.7	36,957.0	36,537.0
Operations and maintenance	93,195.7	92,616.2	93,292.9	93,794.2
Personnel	69,473.8	69,539.8	69,245.0	69,470.5
Military construction	4,714.8	5,187.9	5,299.2	5,351.2
Family housing	3,668.4	3,935.9	3,783.1	3,822.5
Other military programs	2,169.4	2,154.6	1,488.4	2,032.3
Total, Defense Department	252,039.5	257,304.0	257,093.7	256,781.5
Energy Department, defense-related programs	13,615.1	10,969.4	11,221.9	11,520.3
Other non-military programs	42.0	—	—	—
Total authorization	$265,696.6	$268,273.4	$268,315.6	$268,301.8

SOURCES: House National Security Committee, Senate Armed Services Committee

services tuned to a high state of readiness and to carry out the overseas missions the president had assigned.

Some of those complaints were taking on a tone of frustrated resignation. GOP defense hawks had been unable to arouse public support for budget increases, given statements by senior military leaders that Clinton's budgets were adequate, albeit only barely so. "We cannot help the administration if the administration does not want help," lamented House National Security Committee Chairman Floyd D. Spence, R-S.C.

At the same time, the absence of a GOP consensus on defense policy for the post Cold War era, except for a commitment to anti-missile defense, left Republicans unable to frame an alternative of their own.

Republicans Criticize Clinton Budget

On Feb. 12, Defense Secretary William S. Cohen came to Capitol Hill to begin the formal debate on Clinton's $265.7 billion fiscal 1998 defense request, appearing before the House National Security Committee and the Senate Armed Services Committee.

Committee members of both parties were particularly unhappy that, once again, the administration was deferring a long-promised upturn in the budget for weapons procurement, which had declined about 70 percent in inflation-adjusted terms since 1985.

In 1996, Clinton had projected a $45.5 billion procurement request for fiscal 1998; his actual request was $42.9 billion. On paper, however, the administration remained committed to reaching, by fiscal 2001, the $60 billion procurement budget that Joint Chiefs of Staff Chairman Gen. John M. Shalikashvili had wanted to reach in fiscal 1998.

"We keep putting it off to some date in the future," Spence fumed. "How are we going to turn that budget up?" Shalikashvili, who retired at the end of September, said he was encouraged that his $60 billion target at least had become widely accepted as a goal.

Though the draw-down in active-duty military personnel begun a decade earlier was to have been all but completed in fiscal 1997, the president's budget request assumed a further reduction of 21,000 from the Navy and Air Force. A senior Pentagon official said the services had decided on the additional cuts to gain more money for weapons modernization.

Clinton's projected fiscal 1998 manpower ceiling of 1.43 million was about 14,000 below his planned manpower floor and conflicted with House-sponsored provisions in each of the two previous defense authorization bills barring the Defense Department from going below the planned personnel level.

The active-duty military had been cut by about one-third from its post-Vietnam War peak of 2.17 million.

The $93.2 billion request for operations and maintenance in fiscal 1998 was $5.1 billion higher than Clinton had projected in 1996. That cost increase, in turn, was largely to blame for the continuing slippage in the administration's often-promised upturn in Pentagon procurement funding.

Clinton's budget request continued the Pentagon's enthusiastic investment in the information revolution as a core element of future combat capability. Each of the services hoped to link not only its major weapons, but its supply units and, in the Army's case, even individual soldiers to an electronic web to provide "battlefield awareness" — a commonly shared map of friendly and enemy units that would allow U.S. commanders to strike the enemy at its weakest points.

Assessing Pentagon Needs

During the hearings, Hunter predicted that Congress would again add funds to Clinton's budget request. Noting that the budget had been written before Cohen, a Republican, took over at the Pentagon, Hunter said he hoped the new secretary would weigh in with "a dramatic increase in modernization and other areas."

Those hopes hinged on two long-term assessments of U.S. defense policy to be released during the year: the Pentagon's in-house Quadrennial Defense Review and the work of the congressionally mandated National Defense Panel. *(Assessments, p. 8-19)*

Cohen told the House National Security Committee on May 12 that he wanted the defense review's recommendations to be driven by strategic considerations, rather than by assumptions about the size of the defense budget, and that he did not foresee any "massive increases in the defense budget." "Many of the American people do not see [any] identifiable threat on the horizon," Cohen said.

Cohen's recommendations, announced May 19 and rooted in the Quadrennial Review, were to retain most of the Pentagon's existing forces, missions and strategies and to modernize the military with money cut from defense programs traditionally held sacred on Capitol Hill: military bases, civilian maintenance and administrative jobs, and the National Guard and reserves.

Budget Deal Sets Limit

Although defense hawks were dissatisfied with Clinton's budget request, they were constrained by their own leaders' commitment to eliminating the deficit.

Congressional leaders reached a budget agreement with the White House in May that included a fiscal 1998 ceiling of $268 billion for defense. The agreement, which aimed to balance the budget by 2002, was written into the fiscal 1998 budget resolution (H Con Res 84 — H Rept 105-116) that passed both chambers with bipartisan support in June. The defense total was $2.6 billion above what Clinton requested in February, but that increase was a relative pittance compared with the $11 billion that the defense committees had added to Clinton's fiscal 1997 defense budget request. *(Budget deal, p. 2-18)*

Republican defense experts contended that the resulting Pentagon budget would be too tight to allow the military to stay in fighting trim and modernize its arsenal while maintaining the high pace of overseas deployments that Clinton had approved.

"It's an impossible situation," said Curt Weldon, R-Pa., chairman of the House National Security Committee's Military Research and Development Subcommittee. "We have a president with an internationalist foreign policy and an isolationist defense budget."

House Committee

In a marathon session that stretched into the early morning hours of June 12, the House National Security Committee approved its version of the defense bill (HR 1119 — H Rept 105-132) after rejecting Cohen's plan to shut down additional military bases in order to pay for new weaponry. The Committee bill, approved 51-3, called for a total of $268 billion for defense in fiscal 1998.

• **Base closings/maintenance depots.** The bill ignored Cohen's recommendations that Congress authorize two additional rounds of base-closings — a key element of the Quadrennial Defense Review — and that it eliminate a requirement that at least 60 percent of depot maintenance — major overhauls of ships, planes, engines, and other items — be carried out by Pentagon-owned facilities.

Not only were base closings politically unpalatable, but many lawmakers complained that Clinton had manipulated the 1995 round for political gain. *(1995 Almanac, p. 9-19; 1996 Almanac, p. 8-19)*

At issue were two large Air Force maintenance depots — McClellan Air Logistics Center in Sacramento, Calif., and Kelly Air Logistics Center in San Antonio, Texas — targeted for closure in the 1995 round. It was widely believed on Capitol Hill that Clinton had interfered by announcing that, while the Air Force would pull out of the two bases, thousands of jobs at the two sites would be saved by having private contractors take them over.

The sharpest criticism came from members from Utah, Oklahoma and Georgia, where workers at the Air Force's three remaining depots had anticipated picking up the work from the California and Texas sites. They were backed by others, adamant that they would approve no further base closures until Clinton backed down on this issue and closed the McClellan and Kelly depots.

The committee included a provision to bar the assignment of any Air Force maintenance work to private contractors operating the California or Texas sites.

On the ratio of public to private maintenance work, the bill contained a provision making the application of the 60 percent requirement more restrictive.

• **Mixed-gender training/abortion.** The committee avoided a potentially explosive debate when Roscoe G. Bartlett, R-Md., dropped plans to offer an amendment to prohibit mixed-gender basic training. Bartlett contended that the Army's policy since 1994 of training male and female recruits together had seriously eroded the quality of recruit training and endangered combat readiness.

Senior military leaders opposed Bartlett's proposal. Gen. William Hartzog, commanding general of the Army's Training and Doctrine Command, told a Senate Armed Services subcommittee that "gender-integrated training is not broken."

Jane Harman, D-Calif., Bartlett's leading adversary, condemned the amendment, which Bartlett had offered and then withdrawn in the Military Personnel Subcommittee, as a step toward, "the rolling back of rights for women."

The committee rejected, 22-33, an amendment by Harman to repeal a law barring female service members or dependents overseas from obtaining abortions in U.S. military hospitals, even if they were paid for privately.

• **Shipbuilding.** The committee rejected, 24-29, a proposal by Herbert H. Bateman, R-Va., to add $345 million to begin buying components of a nuclear-powered aircraft carrier slated to replace the oil-fueled *Kitty Hawk* in 2008, when that ship would be 47 years old.

The Navy was planning to request an initial chunk of money to buy the ship's nuclear reactors and other key components in the fiscal 2000 budget, with the lion's share of the vessel's $5.2 billion price tag to be included in the fiscal 2002 request.

For months, however, Newport News Shipbuilding and Dry Dock in Bateman's district — the only company building nuclear-powered carriers and the largest private employer in Virginia — had been lobbying Congress to begin funding the ship in fiscal 1998. The company promised that the advance funding would reduce the total price of the vessel to $4.6 billion, a savings of $600 million.

The committee also approved a $2.6 billion request for the first of a new class of nuclear-powered submarines but moved to block the Navy's plan to have two commercial shipyards — Newport News and Bath Iron Works — team up to build the subs. The bill retained an earlier plan to have the two yards compete for the contracts.

• **B-2 bomber and air combat.** Clinton had requested $22 million to continue shutting down the production line for the giant, radar-evading B-2 bomber. The committee decided to add $331 million more, for a total of $353 million, and use the funds to restart production and purchase components for new planes.

The committee also agreed to authorize $1.3 billion to buy as many as 12 F/A-18 "E" and "F" model planes — enlarged versions of the F/A-18 "C" and "D" planes then in service.

The Navy requested $2.1 billion for the F/A-18 E and F, but Hunter, who chaired the Military Procurement Subcommittee, had slashed that to $1.3 billion to buy only four of those craft and 20 of the smaller, cheaper F/A-18 C and D models. Hunter contended that future defense budgets could not pay for all three of the Pentagon's fighter jet development programs.

After the Navy and prime contractor McDonnell Douglas launched a vigorous lobbying effort to restore funding for the F/A-18 E and F planes, H. James Saxton, R-N.J., offered an amendment in the full committee to use Hunter's $1.3 billion to buy nine older models and seven newer ones. The committee rejected Saxton's proposal, 21-34. It then approved, by voice vote, a proposal by James M. Talent, R-Mo., to spend the entire $1.3 billion to buy up to 12 of the F/A-18 E and F planes.

The measure authorized the $2.1 billion requested to continue developing the Air Force's F-22 fighter and cut $31 million from the $924 million requested to develop the Joint Strike Fighter, slated to replace jets of 1970s vintage beginning in 2008.

• **Missile defense.** House authorizers added hundreds of

Republicans Add $653 Million . . .

Although much of the steam had gone out of the Republican crusade for a national defense shield against ballistic missiles, President Clinton accepted Congress' addition of $653 million to the $3.4 billion he had requested for anti-missile defenses in his fiscal 1998 Pentagon budget. Clinton had asked for some of the extra money himself after his budget was sent to Congress in early February.

Republicans on the Senate Armed Services Committee tried to go further, requiring development and deployment of such a system by 2003, but the full Senate did not act on the measure (S 7). In the House, GOP leaders did not even attempt to pass a separate bill.

Clinton said he wanted design of a defense system to move forward but would hold off on a decision to actually put a missile defense in place until at least 2000, when the overseas threat would be reassessed. In any case, the system envisioned by both sides could fend off only a handful of incoming missiles.

In his February budget, Clinton requested $3.43 billion for anti-missile research and procurement, including $504 million for nationwide missile defense, $556 million for the Army's Theater High-Altitude Area Defense (THAAD) and $195 million for the Navy's "Upper Tier" system. Both the Army and Navy systems had limited regional coverage.

Subsequently, the administration asked for another $474 million for the nationwide defense program and cut $203 million from the Army request. Those changes brought Clinton's overall request to $3.7 billion.

The fiscal 1998 defense authorization bill (HR 1119 — PL 105-85) approved a total of $4.08 billion for missile defense — $653 million more than Clinton requested in February, but only $382 million more than the amended request. In addition to authorizing $978 million — the revised request — for nationwide defense, the bill approved $406 million for THAAD ($53 million more than the revised request) and $345 million for the Navy's Upper Tier missile (an additional $150 million).

The companion defense appropriations bill (HR 2266 — PL 105-56) provided a total of $4.18 billion for anti-missile programs, including $978 million for nationwide defense, $406 million for THAAD and $410 million for Upper Tier.

Senate Armed Services Committee Bill

The Senate Armed Services Committee tried to push the debate further, approving S 7 (S Rept 105-15) on April 24 by a party-line vote of 10-8. The bill was introduced by Majority Leader Trent Lott, R-Miss., and cosponsored by Armed Services Chairman Strom Thurmond, R-S.C., and 27 other Republicans. In addition to requiring development and deployment by 2003, it would have directed the president to seek changes in the 1972 Anti-ballistic Missile (ABM) Treaty.

S 7 called for negotiations with Russia to liberalize the treaty's stringent limits on anti-missile defenses for U.S. or Russian territory. If no agreement was reached within a year of enactment, the president would have been required to consult with the Senate on whether the United States should withdraw from the treaty.

millions of dollars to accelerate development of several anti-missile defense programs. But they did not seek to force deployment of a nationwide defense by 2003, a requirement that Clinton had strongly resisted and cited as grounds for vetoing the defense authorization bill in 1995. *(1995 Almanac, p. 9-3)*

• **Troop strength.** The House bill also included a provision barring any troop cuts below the levels set by the Pentagon's so-called bottom up review, conducted in 1993.

House Floor Action

The House passed the $268.3 billion defense authorization bill June 25 by a vote of 304-120. *(Vote 236, p. H-76)*

Lawmakers rejected, 89-322, a proposal by Bernard Sanders, I-Vt., that would have cut the authorization by 5 percent — a reduction of $13.4 billion. "The United States is spending many times more than all our so-called enemies," Sanders said. "When is enough enough?" *(Vote 214, p. H-70)*

But National Security Committee members responded that their recommended additions to Clinton's budget request were only a down payment on making up what the Pentagon itself described as a $15 billion annual shortfall in the weapons procurement budget.

The House did, however, agree to an amendment calling on the president to make a greater effort to get allied countries to pay a larger share of the cost of stationing U.S. forces on their territory. The proposal, cosponsored by Christopher Shays, R-Conn., and Barney Frank, D-Mass., was approved by voice vote.

The House also agreed, 405-14, to an amendment by Spence calling for broad cuts in Pentagon staff and procurement offices. *(Vote 215, p. H-70)*

Major Amendments

• **Bosnia mission.** The House challenged the administration on Bosnia, voting by a ratio of nearly 2-to-1 to end the deployment of U.S. troops in that country by June 30, 1998 — Clinton's announced deadline for a pullout.

It was the first significant congressional action on the subject since Clinton announced, shortly after his re-election, that U.S. forces, numbering about 8,000 in mid-1997, would remain in the Balkans through June 1998 — 18 months later than he had stipulated when he dispatched the troops to Bosnia in late 1995.

Lawmakers opposed to the continuing deployment argued that the mission, estimated to cost $7.3 billion through fiscal 1998, was draining money from combat readiness and that the White House had hinted the troops would remain longer than forecast.

Some supporters of a funding cutoff contended that there was no real prospect for establishing peace in a region torn by ethnic hatred, while others said U.S. withdrawal would force European governments to shoulder the peacekeeping burden.

Steve Buyer, R-Ind., offered an amendment to require a pullout by June 30, 1998. But Van Hilleary, R-Tenn., speaking for a group of lawmakers who wanted to repudiate Clinton's own deadline, offered a substitute setting the deadline at Dec. 31, 1997, with a proviso that Clinton could ask Congress to approve a six-month extension to June 30, 1998.

After rejecting Hilleary's substitute, 196-231, the House

. . . For Anti-Missile Defense

Background

In the 14 years since President Ronald Reagan launched his effort to develop a nationwide missile defense — officially the Strategic Defense Initiative (SDI) and derisively nicknamed "Star Wars" by its critics — most Republicans had taken the view that missile defenses should be fielded as quickly as was technically possible.

They argued that ballistic missiles, possibly armed with chemical or biological weapons, were, or soon would be, in the hands of rogue states. Such states, they warned, might well disregard the horrible logic of deterrence that kept U.S.-Soviet relations eerily stable for decades even though each country had thousands of nuclear missile warheads aimed at the other.

Republicans tried unsuccessfully to arouse public interest in the issue during Clinton's first term. Late in 1995, Clinton vetoed the first version of the annual defense authorization bill because it would have required a nationwide anti-missile defense by 2003. The veto was sustained, and there was no public outcry. *(1995 Almanac, p. 9-3)*

A House GOP effort in 1996 to pass a separate bill embodying the 2003 deadline collapsed when higher-than-anticipated estimates of the program's cost spooked budget-minded GOP deficit hawks. Senate action was blocked that year by a Democratic filibuster. An attempt to make it an issue in the 1996 presidential campaign fizzled. *(1996 Almanac, p. 8-13)*

Although the call for an anti-missile defense gained little political traction outside the ranks of Republican activists, the party's leading defense specialists remained passionately committed to the effort, albeit as a ground-based system rather than the space-based defense envisioned by Reagan.

The administration put more emphasis on trying to head off potential missile threats by diplomatic means, including arms control agreements. In particular, White House officials contended that missile defense programs should not unnecessarily disrupt the 1972 ABM Treaty, which imposed stringent limits on the deployment of missile defenses protecting either U.S. or Russian territory.

Administration officials said the treaty remained vital, reassuring Russia that its nuclear deterrent against the United States was still effective. Such reassurance was essential if the Russian legislature (the Duma) was to ratify the pending START II treaty slashing the number of U.S. and Russian nuclear warheads on long-range weapons. *(1996 Almanac, p. 8-17)*

Republicans complained that Democrats' deference to the ABM Treaty was a prescription for inaction or worse. They said it had led the Clinton administration to soft-pedal evidence of emerging missile threats. Although the treaty did not limit theater defenses, GOP critics insisted that the Pentagon had "dumbed down" THAAD and other theater defenses lest they be so capable that they might duplicate the role of a national missile defense system and thus circumvent the treaty's limits.

adopted Buyer's amendment, 278-148. Only two Republicans voted against the amendment, while 57 Democrats supported Buyer. *(Vote 233, p. H-74; Vote 234, p. H-76)*

• **B-2 bomber.** The B-2 debate turned on the money that the National Security Committee had added to the budget request as a down payment on buying nine more of the bombers in future years.

An amendment to block the plan was offered by Ronald V. Dellums of California, the committee's ranking Democrat, Budget Committee Chairman John R. Kasich, R-Ohio, and Mark Foley, R-Fla. It would have restored the requested authorization of $22 million to shut down B-2 production, while sweetening the deal by earmarking the additional $331 million to buy equipment for National Guard and reserve units.

Citing an estimate by the Congressional Budget Office (CBO), Dellums and his allies contended it would cost $27 billion to buy the nine additional planes and operate them for 20 years, money that would have to be squeezed out of other programs. Kasich argued that existing bombers could strike heavily defended targets with accurate, "standoff" guided missiles fired from beyond the reach of enemy anti-aircraft defenses.

But Spence said the Pentagon's public opposition to additional B-2s was the result of White House political pressure. He argued that events had vindicated past congressional initiatives forced on a reluctant Pentagon, such the use of nuclear power for warships.

In deciding whether to err on the side of building too many B-2s or too few, Speaker Newt Gingrich, R-Ga., declared in a rare floor speech, "I would rather be wrong [on the side of] too good a defense, with too good an airplane saving too many Americans."

The Dellums-Kasich amendment was rejected 209-216. *(Vote 228, p. H-74)*

• **Abortion.** In a vote that nearly duplicated one taken in 1996, the House on June 19 rejected, 196-224, Harman's amendment to repeal the law barring female members of the armed services or female dependents overseas from obtaining abortions in U.S. military hospitals, even if the procedures were paid for privately. *(Vote 217, p. H-70)*

Hunter conceded that existing law treated military women differently than other women. But he argued: "We have our [military] people focused on a high standard of duty, honor, country, and that involves a higher standard, sometimes, than the rest of the country."

Nancy L. Johnson, R-Conn., disputed that argument. "It is not a higher standard to deny service men and women the same rights as the citizens they defend," she said.

• **Maintenance depots.** The House rejected, 145-278, an attempt by Terry Everett, R-Ala., to strike the provision barring Air Force maintenance contracts with private firms at depots in Texas and California. *(Vote 229, p. H-74)*

Everett and his allies insisted that the issue was how to get the best deal for the Air Force on the work that had been slated for Sacramento and San Antonio.

Henry Bonilla, R-Texas, whose district included San Antonio, defended the administration's plan to have the three remaining Air Force depots bid for maintenance work against private companies that would use facilities and personnel from the two depots being shut down. "What is more American than having competition out there to bid for business?" he demanded.

But James V. Hansen, R-Utah, whose district included a depot that had hoped to pick up work when the others were shut down, insisted that the issue was Clinton's violation of the spirit, if not the letter, of the base closing law. "Can the president hide his politically motivated job program behind the shield of privatization and trick enough of us to look the other way?"

• **Nunn-Lugar.** For the second year, the House rejected, by a narrow margin, an effort to use the so-called Nunn-Lugar program as a lever on Russian policy. The program — named for its sponsors, former Sen. Sam Nunn, D-Ga. (1972-97) and Sen. Richard G. Lugar, R-Ind.— was aimed at helping former Soviet states dismantle their nuclear and chemical warfare arsenals.

The Clinton administration requested $382 million for the program. The committee version of the bill offered $285 million, of which $181 million was earmarked for Russia.

Dana Rohrabacher, R-Calif., proposed cutting off the funds for Russia if that country sold any SS-N-22 anti-ship cruise missiles to China. The missiles had a range of 60 miles and flew at twice the speed of sound only a few yards above the water, making them hard to intercept. Rohrabacher and his allies warned that the Russian-built missiles in China's arsenal might pose a grave threat to a U.S. fleet defending Taiwan. The danger would be more widespread, they said, if China, in turn, transferred the missiles to other countries hostile to the United States.

Opponents of the amendment contended that the reduction in former Soviet weaponry fostered by the Nunn-Lugar funding more than offset the increased threat from the cruise missiles. Above all, they emphasized, the Nunn-Lugar program should not be lumped into the politically unpopular category of foreign aid.

On June 11, the House had adopted an amendment by Rohrabacher to the fiscal 1998-99 State Department authorization bill (HR 1757) to bar foreign aid to Russia if it transferred the missiles to China. *(State Department authorization, p. 8-32)*

The House approved Rohrabacher's amendment to the defense bill June 23 by a preliminary vote of 215-206. That result was overturned, however, on June 25 when the House rejected the amendment, 204-219. *(Vote 230, p. H-74; vote 235, p. H-76)*

Other Amendments

In other action on the bill, the House:

➤ Adopted, 417-0, an amendment by Buyer requiring the departments of Defense and Veterans Affairs to conduct clinical trials of treatment for the various illnesses being reported by veterans of the 1991 Persian Gulf War and to develop a plan to provide medical care for those veterans. *(Vote 227, p. H-74)*

➤ Adopted, 416-0, an amendment by Spencer Bachus, R-Ala., to prohibit military burial for any veteran convicted of a capital crime and sentenced to death or life imprisonment. Members were concerned that Timothy McVeigh, convicted of the 1995 bombing of a federal office building in Oklahoma City that killed 168 people, might be eligible for a military burial if he was executed. McVeigh had served in the Persian Gulf. Bachus said he was more concerned that a Ku Klux Klan member, executed in June for a brutal, racially motivated murder, was buried with military honors in Mobile National Cemetery. *(Vote 225, p. H-72)*

➤ Adopted, 332-88, an amendment by Spence and Dellums requiring approval by the secretaries of State, Defense, Commerce and Energy and the director of the Arms Control and Disarmament Agency of any sale of high-powered supercomputers to a country suspected of fostering the spread of nuclear weapons. *(Vote 216, p. H-70)*

➤ Adopted, 290-100, an amendment by Weldon requiring that Clinton certify to Congress whether it was possible to verify his frequent assertion that Russian missiles were no longer aimed at the United States. Weldon and others contended that Clinton's repetition of the claim had eroded public support for larger defense budgets. *(Vote 223, p. H-72)*

➤ Adopted, 269-119, a proposal by James A. Traficant, Jr., D-Ohio, to authorize the deployment of up to 10,000 military personnel to guard U.S. borders against terrorists, drug smugglers and illegal immigrants. *(Vote 224, p. H-72)*

Senate Committee

The Senate Armed Services Committee approved its version of the $268 billion defense bill (S 936 — S Rept 105-29) by voice vote on June 18. The measure included provisions to slightly reduce the size of the Army and restrict Pentagon use of private contractors for maintenance work. Senate authorizers joined their House counterparts in rejecting the idea of additional base closings.

However, the Senate bill was sharply at odds with the version approved the same day by the House committee over B-2 production, the timetable for funding a new aircraft carrier and the number of Aegis destroyers to be funded in fiscal 19981

• **Maintenance depots.** Like the House, the Senate committee included a provision intended to bar the assignment of any Air Force maintenance work to private contractors operating former military depots in California and Texas.

The panel rejected by voice vote an attempt by senior Democrat Carl Levin of Michigan to eliminate the outright prohibition on privatizing overhaul work at the former Kelly and McClellan Air Force bases. Levin's amendment would have allowed the Pentagon to carry out its plan of conducting a competition between the existing depots and contractors to determine whether any work would be assigned to the Texas and California facilities under private management.

However, the Senate bill included a proposal, not in the House version, to lower from 60 percent to 50 percent the amount of maintenance that would have to be performed in government-owned depots.

• **Base closings.** The committee came within a single vote of approving Cohen's request for two additional rounds of base closings. An amendment to that effect, cosponsored by Levin, Charles S. Robb, D-Va., and Republicans Daniel R. Coats of Indiana and John McCain of Arizona, was rejected by a tie vote of 9-9.

• **B-2 bomber.** Disagreeing with House authorizers, the Senate committee included a provision specifically barring production of additional B-2 planes.

• **Shipbuilding.** With Virginia Republican John W. Warner chairing the Seapower Subcommittee, the Senate bill included the addition of $345 million to start buying components of a new aircraft carrier to be built by the Newport News Shipbuilding and Dry Dock. An amendment by Levin to require that the contractor guarantee its promise that the advance funding would reduce the total price to $4.6 billion was rejected, 11-7.

Senate authorizers also approved $3.5 billion for four Aegis destroyers, rather than the $2.8 billion requested in February for three of the ships. The destroyers were built by two shipyards: Bath Iron Works, a subsidiary of General Dynamics, located in Cohen's home state of Maine, and a Litton

B-2 Supporters Win Consolation Prize

Congress agreed to provide extra funds for the giant B-2 stealth bomber in fiscal 1998, but the money was unlikely to be used to buy more of the radar-evading planes. Indeed, it looked more like a consolation prize for the tenacious advocates of a larger B-2 fleet.

The defense authorization bill (PL 105-85) allowed the Pentagon to spend an additional $331 million on the program. The appropriations bill (PL 105-56) actually provided $157 million. *(Defense authorization, p. 8-3; appropriations, p. 9-17)*

However, Congress gave the president a free hand to use the money as a down payment on additional bombers — or to spend it for repairs and upgrades to the 21 B-2s already funded. No one doubted that President Clinton would choose the latter.

Clinton, Defense Secretary William S. Cohen and the top leadership of the Air Force all were adamantly opposed to buying additional B-2s. In fact, the administration had warned that Clinton would veto any effort to provide funds for additional B-2 production.

The B-2 debate did not seem to turn on a dispute over the adequacy of the B-2s that were entering service. The Air Force insisted the planes were having no more than routine "teething troubles" of the sort encountered by any new, complex weapon. Stung by news reports that rainstorms might strip away the plane's radar eluding qualities, the Air Force staged a vigorous public relations counterattack, flying reporters and TV camera crews to Whiteman Air Force Base in Missouri, where they were given unprecedented access to the bombers and their crews.

Like most other defense acquisition issues, the debate was dominated by the assumption that all budget battles for years to come would be zero-sum games: Adding anything would mean cutting something else of equal cost.

"What's working in our favor is that it's a very good airplane, and it does a job nothing else does," contended California Democrat Jane Harman, a leading House supporter of the add-on. "But the fact of a balanced-budget environment works against us," she added ruefully.

Arguments for Enlarging the B-2 Fleet

The plane's capacity for long-range precision attacks was the heart of proponents' arguments for buying more B-2s.

Many of the most prominent advocates, such as Reps. Duncan Hunter, R-Calif., and Norm Dicks, D-Wash., had a parochial interest in the program — a base or a subcontractor in their district. But the case for additional B-2s was also vigorously argued by defense analysts with no obvious dog in the fight, including analysts at the RAND Corp. and Andrew Krepinevich of the Center for Strategic and Budgetary Assessments, who had a record of iconoclastic thinking on defense issues.

Proponents of a larger B-2 fleet contended that the plane offered a uniquely valuable combination of three qualities:

➤ The range to strike almost anywhere on the globe from bases in the United States — with midair refueling — an advantage that loomed larger as the network of U.S. bases overseas shrank.

➤ A large payload of precision-guided bombs: 16 rather than the F-117's two. Moreover, with the B-2's ground-mapping radar and a newly developed bomb that carried dozens of "smart" anti-tank warheads, a few of the planes could decimate an armored division attacking a distant U.S. ally, according to studies by RAND.

➤ Most important, the stealthiness that would allow the plane to overfly targets defended by sophisticated, radar-guided anti-aircraft missiles, like the Russian SA-10, that were widely available in the global arms bazaar. To safely attack such a target, Hunter and others contended, a non-stealthy bomber would have to be accompanied by a panoply of supporting planes, including some to jam enemy radars, and fighters to fend off enemy aircraft.

Arguments Against More B-2s

Not only was the executive branch opposed, but so were many congressional defense specialists who saw the proposal as a threat to the budgets of other programs more important to them.

While lauding the B-2's in hand, the Air Force argued that it could not buy additional bombers without short-changing other programs, such as production of the F-22 fighter slated to begin in 1999. The Air Force put the total price for nine more copies of the B-2 at $13.5 billion (proponents assumed it was about 50 percent less). "The tradeoff does not warrant the acquisition of additional B-2s," said Gen. Michael E. Ryan, Clinton's nominee to become Air Force chief of staff.

B-2 critics argued that there was no need to fly over heavily defended targets that could be attacked by long-range cruise missiles, which were, themselves, stealthy. And the Pentagon maintained that, for any given amount of money, U.S. combat power in distant theaters would get more of a boost from the purchase of additional smart bombs to be carried by existing, non-stealthy planes than from the purchase of additional B-2s.

Assuming that the money would have to be siphoned away from other forces, the Pentagon raised two additional objections: The B-2 could not perform many of the jobs done by the weapons it would displace, such as the F-22's mission of sweeping the skies of enemy fighters. Also, some forces would have to be retired immediately in order to free funds for B-2s that would not enter service for years.

Hunter, Dicks, Krepinevich and others countered that the official Pentagon view assumed that U.S. forces — including short-range combat jets — would have access to nearby bases from which to strike enemy forces, as in the 1990-91 conflict in the Persian Gulf, when U.S. combat power was gradually built up in the web of bases that had been constructed in Saudi Arabia over the preceding decade.

Reading the lessons of that war, they argued, a future U.S. adversary would try to pre-empt such a nearby U.S. buildup, either by seizing potential bases at the outset of hostilities or by rendering them unusable with chemical or biological weapons: "None of those countries are going to make the same mistake Saddam made," Dicks warned. "There'd be an effort to 'lock out' the United States."

But even some of the strongest backers of buying more B-2s conceded that, in the post-Cold War world, they could not generate public support for a fight because public interest in defense issues was low. "All of a sudden, there isn't the same urgency," Dicks said.

Industries facility in the home state of Senate Majority Leader Trent Lott, R-Miss.

Lott had protested bitterly when the contract for a new class of amphibious landing ships went to a consortium including the Maine company, rather than one that included the Mississippi firm. Subsequently, Cohen announced an acceleration in the construction schedule for destroyers that would send more work to the Litton shipyard in Pascagoula, Miss.

Like the House committee, Senate authorizers approved the $2.6 billion requested for the first of a new class of nuclear-powered submarines.

• **Personnel.** The Senate committee decided to take a running start at the Quadrennial Review's call for modest additional reductions in active-duty military personnel, cutting the Army by about 10,000 troops below the level included in Clinton's budget request.

Senate Floor Action

The Senate passed S 936 on July 11 by a vote of 94-4, after dealing a blow to the Clinton administration's proposal to close more military bases. The Senate then substituted the text of its bill for the House measure (HR 1119) and formally passed that bill by voice vote. *(Vote 173, p. S-31)*

• **Base closings.** Faced with the prospect of authorizing additional rounds of base closures in 1999 and 2001, the Senate voted instead to study how much had been saved by the four rounds in 1989, 1991, 1993 and 1995.

McCain, Levin, Coats and Robb offered an amendment to authorize new closures under the rules enacted to govern the four earlier rounds — a commission designed to insulate the process from political influence.

But the Senate approved a substitute offered by Byron L. Dorgan, D-N.D., requiring the Pentagon to report to Congress on the cost and savings of the previous closures and recommend whether further base closings were needed. Support for the amendment was fueled in part by the contention that Clinton had meddled in the 1995 round for political reasons. But the lopsided vote — Dorgan's amendment was approved 66-33 — reflected a much broader skepticism. Both Lott and Minority Leader Tom Daschle, D-S.D., cosponsored the amendment; 22 other Democrats broke ranks with the White House to join them. *(Vote 165, p. S-29)*

Dorgan and others cited reports by the General Accounting Office (GAO) and CBO that the estimated savings from the previous base-closing rounds could not be verified.

Lott reinforced that argument with a more elemental appeal to his colleagues' fears that their states might lose jobs in future base-closing rounds. He handed out a list of 144 facilities in 35 states and two territories that had been considered for closure in one of the four previous rounds but had escaped the ax. "Think of what you have already been through," Lott said. "Do you want to go through that again?"

• **Bosnia mission.** Only a few senators debated an amendment dealing with the continued deployment of U.S. troops in Bosnia as part of a NATO-led peacekeeping force.

The language that was ultimately approved by voice vote merely expressed an opinion that U.S. troops should be withdrawn on the date Clinton had already set. Administration officials warned that the president would veto any effort to write the date into law.

• **Computer exports.** By a vote of 72-27, the Senate gutted an amendment that would have tightened government controls on the export of relatively sophisticated computers to certain countries, including China. *(Vote 166, p. S-30)*

The underlying issue was where to strike a balance between the U.S. computer industry's interest in growth markets overseas and the risk that sophisticated computers might help unfriendly states or terrorists to develop nuclear weapons or ballistic missiles that could threaten U.S. security.

Foreign countries were ranked in four tiers, depending on such risks. Exports were banned to "tier four" countries such as Iran and North Korea. Exports to "tier three" nations such as China and Russia depended on the computer's power, measured in millions of theoretical operations per second (MTOPS).

The Senate debate was sparked by several recent cases in which computers sold under those terms wound up in the hands of Russian or Chinese military organizations.

An amendment by Thad Cochran, R-Miss., and Richard J. Durbin, D-Ill., would have required Commerce Department approval for any sale to a "tier three" country of a 2,000-7,000 MTOPS computer. Under existing law, such sales were allowed without government approval. Industry groups and the Clinton administration vehemently opposed the amendment.

Cochran argued that computer manufacturers, eager for sales in a cutthroat marketplace, could not be expected to determine whether civilian or commercial entities among their potential customers were, in fact, fronts for military forces.

But Republican Rod Grams of Minnesota and Democrat Barbara Boxer of California insisted that the type of computers Cochran was trying to restrict were widely available from non-U.S. manufacturers, who would quickly snap up any potential U.S. sales that were delayed by Cochran's requirement for government approval.

The Senate substituted for the Cochran language a proposal by Grams requiring a GAO study of the national security risks posed by the sale of certain types of computers. It then adopted the gutted Cochran amendment by voice vote.

Other Amendments

In action on other amendments, the Senate:

➤ Adopted, by voice vote, a proposal by Lugar to increase by $135 million the amount to be authorized for Nunn-Lugar and related programs intended to help former Soviet states dispose of nuclear and other weapons. The amendment proposed to increase the authorization to $668 million, the amount requested.

➤ Adopted, by voice vote, an amendment by Levin to lock in the $600 million savings promised by Newport News if the Navy began purchasing parts for a new nuclear-powered aircraft carrier ahead of schedule.

➤ Rejected, 43-56, a proposal by Jeff Bingaman, D-N.M., to authorize the $29 million requested by the administration instead of the $147 million recommended by the Armed Services Committee to develop a space-based anti-missile laser. *(Vote 171, p. S-31)*

➤ Rejected, 19-79, a proposal by Russell D. Feingold, D-Wis., to require the Pentagon to select for cancellation one of three fighter planes under development or just entering production. *(Vote 172, p. S-31)*

➤ Rejected, 48-51, an attempt by Patty Murray, D-Wash., to repeal the law barring female service members or dependents from obtaining privately funded abortions in U.S. military hospitals overseas. *(Vote 167, p. S-30)*

➤ Tabled (killed), 83-16, an amendment by Charles E. Grassley, R-Iowa, and Boxer to limit to $200,000 the annual compensation for any executive that a company could charge to a Pentagon contract. *(Vote 170, p. S-30)*

➤ Tabled (killed), 58-41, an amendment by Paul Wellstone, D-Minn., to authorize the Defense secretary to transfer $400 million to the Department of Veterans Affairs. *(Vote 168, p. S-30)*

➤ Tabled (killed), 65-33, a Wellstone amendment to authorize the Defense secretary to transfer $5 million to the Agriculture Department to fund a school breakfast program. *(Vote 162, p. S-29)*

➤ Rejected, 46-53, an attempt by Slade Gorton, R-Wash., to require the Navy to set aside a decision to give the mothballed battleship *Missouri* to Honolulu and, instead, hold a new competition among cities bidding for the ship. *(Vote 163, p. S-29)*

Conference/Final Action

Lawmakers broke the logjam created by the dispute over maintenance depots Oct. 23 and completed work on the conference report for the $268.3 billion bill (H Rept 105-340).

The House agreed to the conference report Oct. 28 by a vote of 286-123. The Senate adopted the report Nov. 6 by a vote of 90-10, clearing the measure for the White House. *(House vote 534, p. H-164; Senate vote 296, p. S-51)*

In signing the bill Nov. 18, Clinton reiterated his concerns over the spending level and the language on maintenance depots, but he said the Pentagon had indicated it could conduct fair competition in the future between public and private maintenance facilities.

Clinton also vowed to seek legislation in 1998 to overturn provisions in the bill that would tighten controls on the export of super-computers to certain countries, including Israel, Russia and China.

Cuts to Clinton Programs

As usual, the conferees sliced several billion dollars from Clinton's budget, giving themselves leeway to add money for programs they favored without breaching the ceiling set by the budget resolution.

For instance, they cut nearly $1.5 billion they said was available because of outdated assumptions underlying the budget request. Included in that figure were cuts of:

➤ $655 million because lower-than-anticipated inflation meant lower prices.

➤ $460 million because when fiscal 1998 began Oct. 1, there were fewer military personnel and civilian employees than anticipated.

➤ $375 million because the dollar's growing strength against certain foreign currencies meant that U.S. forces stationed in those countries would pay less for locally purchased goods and services.

The conferees also slashed $2.3 billion that the administration had requested for novel management approaches to defense programs within the Energy Department.

One of the new proposals would have funded construction projects all at once, rather than in one-year increments. The other would have authorized $1 billion to privatize the cleanup of toxic and hazardous waste at nuclear weapons plants. The conferees approved only $224 million of that request.

Hot-Button Issues

Conferees reached the following agreements on a series of controversial issues:

• **Maintenance depots.** At the insistence of lawmakers representing the three remaining Air Force depots, in Georgia, Oklahoma and Utah, the conference report required private companies using the two closed depots to include in their bids the market cost of the facilities, thus nullifying any price advantage over the government depots, which were required to "charge" the Air Force a high enough price to cover their own costs.

At the same time, they accepted the Senate provision reducing the proportion of heavy maintenance work that had to be done at government depots from 60 percent to 50 percent, thereby helping the private companies. Another provision expanded the definition of "depot maintenance," thus enlarging the pool of work from which the government depots were guaranteed the smaller share.

• **B-2 bomber.** The conference report tracked the defense appropriations bill (HR 2266), giving the president discretion to use $331.2 million either to purchase additional B-2 bombers or to modify and repair the existing fleet of 21 of the stealth aircraft.

• **Bosnia mission.** The final bill implicitly acknowledged that Congress could not block Clinton from continuing the U.S. mission in Bosnia. While it barred the use of funds for U.S. operations in Bosnia after June 30, 1998, it allowed the president to waive that prohibition if he notified Congress at least 45 days in advance of the deadline and provided them with a strategic rationale for his decision along with a projection of the size, duration, mission, cost and "exit strategy" of the extended deployment.

The conference report also expressed the sense of Congress that European members of NATO, whose troops outnumbered U.S. forces in Bosnia and made up the bulk of the 32,000 peacekeepers, should provide all ground combat troops after June. Major European allies insisted they would pull their troops out of Bosnia if U.S. ground forces were withdrawn, in which case the brutal civil war almost certainly would reignite.

The issue had lain dormant for most of the year, but it reemerged during an unusually candid meeting between Clinton and about 30 lawmakers Nov. 4, just as the Senate was preparing to take up the conference report on the defense bill. Secretary of State Madeleine K. Albright told reporters the next day that "a consensus is forming" for a U.S. presence in Bosnia beyond the June 30, 1998, deadline. Several lawmakers, however, said the president needed to make a stronger case for extending the deadline.

• **Mixed-gender training.** In the wake of scandals and reports of sexual harassment in the services, particularly in training, the bill created a congressional commission to review the adequacy of recruit training and the services' policies on whether male and female recruits should train together. The Marine Corps was the only branch that still segregated the sexes in training.

The bill also included a provision intended to raise the standards for drill sergeants, including requiring psychological screening of all prospective drill sergeants.

• **Computer exports.** The conferees agreed to give the secretaries of State, Defense, Commerce and Energy and the director of the Arms Control and Disarmament Agency 10 days to review and decide whether to require an export license for any such sale to a country suspected of fostering the spread of nuclear weapons. The president could change the definition of computers covered by the requirement.

Conference Report Highlights

• **Personnel.** As requested, the conferees approved a ceiling of 1.43 million for the active-duty military, nearly 21,000 fewer than in fiscal 1997. But they rejected a House-passed provision that would have suspended for one year a program that allowed service members to retire, with a reduced pension, after only 15 years of service instead of the usual 20. This was part of an unsuccessful effort by the House to freeze the active-duty level.

The conferees approved a Guard and reserve of about

895,000, slightly smaller than had been requested. The most important element of the change was a cut of 5,000 from the Army National Guard, resulting in an authorized force of 362,000 instead of the 367,000 requested. The reduction, expected to save $22 million, was intended as a first step toward cuts recommended by the Pentagon's Quadrennial Review.

Lobbyists for the National Guard complained that the conferees did not make a similar reduction in the Army's active-duty manpower ceiling recommended in the review.

Supporters of the National Guard were dealt another blow when the conferees rejected a Senate-passed proposal to add a four-star general to the Joint Chiefs of Staff to represent the Guard and reserves. The White House and the Pentagon strongly opposed the proposal, saying it would violate the 1986 law (PL 99-433) that reorganized the military's high command. Instead, the conferees approved the appointment of two-star generals to advise the Joint Chiefs — one representing the services' reserve components and the other representing the Guard.

Though disappointed, the private National Guard Association of the United States expressed satisfaction that debate on the issue had alerted members of Congress to the Guard's needs. While Clinton requested $969 million for Guard and reserve equipment, the conferees added another $1.2 billion for a total of $2.2 billion.

In addition to authorizing the 2.8 percent increase in basic pay for military personnel that Clinton requested, the final bill consolidated several housing and food allowance programs to boost total compensation.

For example, service personnel not living in barracks or on ships had been reimbursed for part of their food and housing by a complex set of cash allowances. The conference report consolidated those payments into a housing allowance indexed to local housing costs and a "subsistence" allowance indexed to food costs.

The conference report included provisions intended to tighten the services' screening of prospective recruits' medical fitness. It also directed the secretary of Defense to provide incentives for recruits to improve their physical fitness before they enlisted.

The conferees also approved two provisions intended to cut costs by reducing the number of military and civilian employees in administrative jobs. One required a 25 percent reduction over the following five years in the number of people assigned to headquarters units — a cut of about 12,500 personnel — while the other required a reduction in fiscal 1998 of 25,000 employees from the number assigned to acquisition jobs, though the secretary of Defense could soften the cut to 10,000.

• **Ground combat.** Conferees approved without change the funding requests for several Army programs to upgrade existing weapons and develop others from scratch. All were to be linked in a web of digital communications that would give tank commanders, helicopter pilots and individual soldiers a shared map of the battlefield.

The final bill authorized $595 million to upgrade M-1 tanks with larger cannon, night-vision equipment and digital links; $512 million to equip missile-armed Apache helicopters with the Longbow target-finding radar; and $282 million to continue developing the new, smaller Comanche armed helicopter.

It added to Clinton's budget $209 million for Army and Marine Corps trucks, ranging in size from jeep-like "Humvees" to huge low-boy tractor-trailers designed to carry 70-ton tanks.

• **Air combat.** The final bill made only minor changes in the budget request for all three of a new generation of combat jets slated to enter service over the next decade, providing:

• $2.2 billion to gear up for production in 1999 of the Air Force's F-22 fighter.

• $2.1 billion to buy 20 of the Navy's F/A-18 E and F jets.

• $946 million to continue developing the Joint Strike Fighter.

The conferees also authorized funds beyond those requested to buy more of the fighters already in production:

• $226 million for five Air Force F-15s, an increase of two planes ($67 million) over the request.

• $66 million for three smaller F-16s that were not requested.

• **Naval forces.** Though the administration initially asked for $2.7 billion for three Navy destroyers built in Maine and Mississippi, senior administration officials had agreed with Lott months earlier to accept an additional $720 million for a fourth ship. The conference report authorized the entire $3.4 billion.

It also authorized the $2.3 billion requested for the first of a new class of submarines and the $1.6 billion requested to give the 22-year-old aircraft carrier *Nimitz* a three-year overhaul.

The bill added to the budget request down payments on two ships — $100 million for an amphibious landing transport to be built in Louisiana and $16 million for an oceanographic research ship to be built in Mississippi.

To begin work on the nuclear-powered aircraft carrier that would be built at Newport News in Virginia, the conferees approved only $50 million instead of the $345 million that carrier supporters had sought.

While the administration requested $90 million to begin designing a new, smaller and cheaper carrier, the conferees reduced that to $12 million while adding $17 million to perfect new technologies for the *Nimitz* class.

The final bill included only $35 million of the $150 million the Pentagon had requested to develop a so-called arsenal ship, a highly automated vessel with a small crew and hundreds of guided missiles. (The Navy canceled the project late in October, partly for want of congressional support.)

The conference report added $115 million to the $132 million requested to develop and begin deploying the Navy's "cooperative engagement system" — a digital communications network intended to link the radar of all the ships and planes in a fleet.

As requested, the conferees approved $1.9 billion for nine C-17 wide-body cargo jets. They also approved the $581 million requested to buy two additional cargo ships intended to carry tanks and other heavy combat equipment for Army units headed to distant trouble spots.

• **Pentagon purchasing.** The conferees accepted, with minor changes, a Senate provision increasing from $250,000 to $340,000 the amount a defense contractor could charge the Pentagon for salaries of its top five executives.

They also agreed to a House-passed provision making permanent a section of the fiscal 1997 defense appropriations bill (PL 104-208) that limited Pentagon reimbursement to contractors for the cost of mergers — $1 for every $2 the Pentagon saved because the merger lowered prices.

In addition, the bill repealed a law requiring that all weapons contracts include warranties. The GAO reported that the warranties cost $271 million annually and provided little return.

Another provision required the Pentagon to ensure that, by the start of fiscal 2001, 90 percent of all purchases of less than $2,500 be made by government credit card. The credit card procedure was intended to replace time-consuming red tape for routine purchases, such as office supplies. But mid-level managers had been slower to adopt the new streamlined procedures than its proponents had hoped. ■

Senate Ratifies Chemical Arms Pact

The Senate on April 24 ratified the 1993 Chemical Weapons Convention — a treaty banning the development, production, sale, use or stockpiling of chemical weapons — by a vote of 74-26, meeting the constitutional requirement for a two-thirds majority.

However, Congress adjourned for the year without completing action on separate legislation (HR 2709, S 610) to implement the agreement by requiring U.S. chemical companies to report on their activities and submit to international inspection. The Senate version of the bill also proposed to make the U.S. government liable for damages if a company's trade secrets were compromised by an inspection.

The Senate passed the implementation bill by voice vote May 23. The House put off considering it until the final days of the session, when GOP leaders linked it to legislation, opposed by the Clinton administration, to impose economic sanctions on Russian companies that aided Iran in its quest for ballistic missile technology. The House passed the combined bill Nov. 12, but the Senate did not act on it before adjourning for the year.

Senate approval of the chemical weapons ban (S Res 75) was a big win for President Clinton, who had faced determined opposition from GOP conservatives, but the victory came at a hefty price in concessions on collateral issues. The Senate added to the resolution 28 "understandings," which had been negotiated between Foreign Relations Committee Chairman Jesse Helms, R-N.C., and senior panel Democrat Joseph R. Biden Jr. of Delaware, limiting the treaty's reach.

Biden and other treaty supporters managed to defeat five additional provisions backed by Helms that they said would render the Chemical Weapons Convention useless.

The treaty fight also gave Majority Leader Trent Lott, R-Miss., an opportunity to demonstrate his leadership skills. While he helped win key agreements from the Clinton administration in return for putting the treaty on the Senate agenda, his role in forcing the measure to a vote damaged his relations with the hard-right faction of the Senate GOP.

As a part of the deal with Helms and Lott, the Clinton administration agreed to restructure the nation's foreign policy agencies, a top Helms goal. Clinton also agreed to submit to the Senate as treaty amendments the changes he had negotiated with Russia to the 1972 Anti-Ballistic Missile (ABM) Treaty and the 1990 Conventional Forces in Europe Treaty.

Although the restructuring plan was later included in the fiscal 1998 foreign operations appropriations bill (HR 2159), it was ultimately dropped at the insistence of House GOP conservatives angry over a decision by their leadership to drop abortion restrictions on family planning funds opposed by the Clinton administration. *(Appropriations, p. 9-37)*

Background

The chemical weapons treaty, signed in 1993, was designed to outlaw the development, production, transfer, stockpiling or use of chemical weapons for the battlefield. Negotiated by the Reagan and Bush administrations, the pact was signed by President George Bush shortly before he left office. *(Treaty, p. 8-14; 1993 Almanac, p. 474; 1994 Almanac, p. 437)*

The Senate Foreign Relations Committee approved a resolution ratifying the treaty in April 1996, and a floor vote was scheduled for September of that year. But the Clinton administration asked for a deferral at the last minute after a vigorous campaign by Helms, Sen. Jon Kyl, R-Ariz., and other GOP conservatives made it doubtful that the resolution of approval would pass by the two-thirds majority required for a treaty. *(1996 Almanac, p. 8-14)*

The biggest factor in derailing the treaty was the last-minute opposition of beleaguered GOP presidential candidate and former majority leader Bob Dole of Kansas, who spelled out his objections in a Sept. 11 letter to Lott. A number of uncommitted Republican senators then rallied around Dole.

The critics also got a boost from the unexpected intervention of the National Federation of Independent Business (NFIB). The potent small-business lobby warned that the treaty's reporting and inspection requirements might burden its 600,000 members.

The NFIB, most of whose members employed 10 or fewer people, was an energetic and effective opponent of government regulation and reporting mandates. But its opposition came as a surprise to treaty proponents because the pact had been vigorously supported from the outset by the Chemical Manufacturers Association, whose members expected to bear the brunt of the treaty's reporting and inspection requirements.

In a Sept. 9, 1996, letter to Lott, NFIB vice president for federal government relations Dan Danner expressed "serious concern" over the treaty's impact on small businesses that were consumers of regulated chemicals. "The [treaty] will continue to bury small businesses in paperwork and regulation," he said, citing estimates by the Commerce Department and by the since-defunct congressional Office of Technology Assessment.

However, the group later changed its stance, concluding in 1997 that the treaty posed no such risk. Danner said his letter had been "mischaracterized" as a statement that the powerful lobby opposed the treaty rather than what it actually was, an expression of concern. "There was a good deal of confusion about what kind of businesses . . . could be included," he said.

On the basis of information received subsequently — some of it in a meeting with William A. Reinsch, under secretary of Commerce for export administration — the federation concluded that the brunt of the treaty's data reporting impact would fall on large chemical companies, Danner said. Accordingly, he said, NFIB was taking no position on the treaty. "We just do not see enough of an impact," he said.

Preliminary Jockeying

Helms began the 1997 bidding on getting the chemical weapons treaty to the Senate floor with a Jan. 29 letter to Lott. Before the Senate considered the pact, Helms insisted, it should act first on Republican foreign policy priorities that had been blocked by the Clinton administration. Those items included bills to reorganize and reduce the U.S. foreign affairs bureaucracy, compel a similar reorganization of the United Nations and mandate deployment of anti-missile defenses for U.S. territory.

Helms also said that before the Senate acted on the chemical treaty, the administration should agree to seek Senate approval of modifications it was negotiating to the ABM Treaty and another treaty reducing conventional armed forces in Europe.

The 1993 Chemical Weapons Treaty

The Chemical Weapons Convention, signed in 1993, banned the use of chemical weapons in combat under all circumstances, including as a means of retaliation against chemical attack. Though the Geneva Protocol of 1925 banned the use of chemical weapons, many countries that ratified that pact nevertheless reserved the right to retaliate in kind if they were subjected to a chemical attack.

The 1993 treaty also prohibited the development, production, purchase or stockpiling of chemical weapons for battlefield use. It did not outlaw "riot-control agents" — non-lethal irritants such as tear gas — for domestic use in law enforcement. It did, however, prohibit use of such chemicals in combat against enemy troops.

The pact prohibited any signatory from helping any other state — whether or not it had signed the treaty — to engage in any of the prohibited activities. It also required signatory countries both to cut off the sale of certain chemicals to countries that did not sign and to enact criminal penalties against private citizens who attempted to frustrate the treaty's aims.

Each signatory country was to report to a newly created monitoring agency — the Organization for the Prohibition of Chemical Weapons — any chemical weapons in its possession, any transfers of chemical weapons into or out of its territory, and any facilities on its territory that had been or could have been used to produce chemical weapons.

This organization and the 41-nation Executive Council that governed it were established once the treaty went into force April 29.

Verification Procedures

To check on compliance, agency inspectors were empowered to periodically inspect declared chemical weapons sites and industrial facilities with a significant potential for producing chemical weapons.

The treaty took into account the fact that many chemicals used in commercial manufacturing also could be used to manufacture chemical weapons. The severity of the treaty's restrictions and the intrusiveness of verification procedures for any such facility varied with the degree to which its chemical products could be used for prohibited purposes and with the volume of such chemicals used annually by each plant.

Accordingly, the treaty recognized four broad categories of potentially weapons-related chemicals, three of which were listed in "schedules" annexed to the treaty:

➤ Schedule 1 included existing chemical warfare agents — nerve gases such as Sarin and blister agents such as mustard gas — as well as certain extremely toxic chemicals with very limited commercial utility. Facilities which processed 100 grams or more of these chemicals were subject to routine inspection.

➤ Schedule 2 included chemicals that could be used either as weapons or as the ingredients to make weapons but which also had some commercial uses, ranging from agricultural pesticides to the production of ballpoint pens. Depending on the specific chemical, companies would have to report on the use of more than some threshold amount, varying from 1 kilogram to 1 metric ton. Regular inspections of a plant would be triggered by the processing of from 10 kilograms to 10 metric tons of these chemicals.

➤ Schedule 3 included several other chemicals that had been used either as weapons or as weapons ingredients, but that also were used in large volume for commercial purposes. Plants handling more than 30 metric tons of these substances were to file data on the amount used. Facilities which used more than 200 metric tons were subject to routine inspection.

Other factories that produced certain types of organic chemicals were subject to reporting requirements if they produced more than 30 metric tons annually of compounds containing phosphorus, sulfur or fluorine or more than 200 metric tons of other chemicals. The threshold for routine inspections was production of more than 200 tons of any of these chemicals.

In addition, any signatory could request on short notice a "challenge inspection" by the international agency of any site in any other country. However, the request could be denied if three-quarters of the 41 countries on the agency's Executive Council deemed it frivolous, abusive or aimed at activities beyond the treaty's scope.

The inspectors were allowed to sample production lines, effluents and soil for evidence of prohibited activities. To protect military or commercial proprietary secrets, officials at a challenged facility were allowed to turn off computers and shroud sensitive instrument displays.

Even then, Helms said, the starting point for resuming consideration of the chemical weapons treaty should be a series of reservations he had drafted in April 1996, some of which had been rejected by his own Foreign Relations Committee. The reservations included language that was seen as effectively ruling out U.S. approval of the treaty.

For instance, one of Helms' requirements would have held U.S. ratification in abeyance until the treaty was ratified by pariah states, including Libya, Iraq, Syria and North Korea, all of which were suspected of having chemical weapons but none of which was likely to sign the treaty.

In his Feb. 4 State of the Union address, Clinton called for the Senate to approve the treaty by April 29, the date on which the agreement was to become legally binding. Unless the United States ratified the pact by then, he warned, U.S. officials would play no role in the international inspection agency that was to be established to monitor compliance. Clinton also maintained that the treaty would make U.S. troops safer from chemical attack and make it more difficult for terrorists to acquire chemical weapons. (*Text, p. D-17*)

Lott Assures Democrats of Floor Vote

Backers of the treaty claimed a tactical victory March 20 when Lott assured them he planned to bring the pact before the Senate following the two-week spring recess. "It is not my intent to stonewall or delay on this," Lott said.

That fell short of Democrats' desire for a firm agreement to vote before April 29, but such an explicit commitment would have brought Lott into a head-on collision with Helms.

Minority Leader Tom Daschle, D-S.D., said Lott had given him "adequate reason to be confident that we will take this [treaty] up in a time that will accord with ratification by the

28th of April." Senior Armed Services Committee Democrat Carl Levin of Michigan expressed more bluntly his reasons for accepting Lott's assurances: "He's putting his leadership on the line ... That's serious."

Daschle and other Democrats had earlier threatened to block Senate action on any other matter, including a resolution on the Mexican government's role in fighting drug-trafficking, unless Lott guaranteed a vote on the treaty before April 29. Lott bristled at the threat, insisting he was trying to broker a compromise between Helms and the administration. "If they jerk me around on this, I might change my attitude," he had told reporters March 20. Daschle quickly dropped his threat to block the Mexico vote.

Senate Hearings

Helms kicked off hearings on the Chemical Weapons Convention April 8, with three former Defense secretaries who were opposed to the treaty — James R. Schlesinger, who served under Presidents Richard M. Nixon and Gerald R. Ford; Donald H. Rumsfeld, who served in the Ford administration; and Caspar W. Weinberger, from the Reagan years. Their sentiments were echoed by a letter from a fourth former Pentagon chief, Dick Cheney, who served in the Bush administration.

Hammering at the fact that some pariah nations were not party to the treaty, Rumsfeld warned that the pact might "disarm democratic, friendly, non-aggressive nations that either do not have chemical weapons or, if they have them, would be most unlikely to use them against us, while it will not effectively apply to totalitarian, enemy and aggressive nations that would be most likely to use them against the U.S. and its allies."

The critics also contended that the treaty's vaunted verification procedures — including snap inspections by international teams at chemical manufacturing or storage sites in any signatory country — would be intrusive enough to put the trade secrets of U.S. companies at risk. At the same time, they argued that the inspection system could not catch cheaters, because the manufacture of chemical weapons was relatively easy.

"You cannot verify the production of chemical weapons, because any plant that can be used for the production of permitted chemicals can be used for the production of prohibited chemicals," Richard N. Perle, an assistant secretary of Defense in the Reagan administration, told the panel April 9.

Indeed, the critics maintained, the treaty was worse than useless. By collaborating in the international agency that would be set up to verify the treaty, they said, the United States would expose to other governments critical information about how it obtained and analyzed intelligence, thus helping them work out methods to evade U.S. detection. "We would be educating the very countries we are trying to stop," Perle warned.

Moreover, they argued, some of the treaty's provisions would undermine existing efforts to limit the spread of chemical weapons technology. Under Article X, which required signatories to provide chemical defense assistance to other countries that complied with the treaty, critics said the United States would have to turn over to hostile governments the Pentagon's anti-chemical defensive technologies, making it easier for those countries to nullify the defenses and thus threaten U.S. troops.

The critics also argued that Article XI of the treaty would outlaw existing agreements among chemical exporting nations to coordinate their export controls, the better to prevent rogue regimes or criminals from acquiring chemical weapons technology.

Supporters Present Their Case

The case for the treaty was argued on April 8 by Secretary of State Madeleine K. Albright and on April 9 by a panel of former national security officials, including retired Lt. Gen. Brent Scowcroft, national security adviser under Bush.

The proponents' point of departure was that the United States had decided to dispose of its own chemical weapons and that approving the treaty as it was would give Washington a useful, if limited, tool for leverage on other governments to do the same.

"The United States is going out of the chemical weapons business," Scowcroft reminded the panel. "The Chemical Weapons Convention will enter into force whether or not the United States ratifies it. We're not dealing with a bunch of putty here that we can mold as we want."

Even with some notorious chemical weapons users outside the treaty, Scowcroft argued, the fact that more than 160 countries had signed the pact created powerful international pressure against chemical weapons. "The very fact that you've mobilized world opinion does put pressure on the holdouts," he told the panel. "If they do things that are wrong, it's easier to call attention to it."

As for the treaty's net effect on U.S. intelligence, retired Adm. Elmo Zumwalt, a former chief of naval operations who was a member of the president's Foreign Intelligence Advisory Board, insisted that the gains would outweigh any losses. "However less than perfect it might be, the opportunity to inspect will give us additional information," he said.

The administration and treaty supporters insisted that the critics were misreading Articles X and XI. The former provision, they said, did not require the United States to provide any assistance other than medical antidotes, and the latter was consistent with existing chemical export control agreements.

Agreement to Vote

On April 10, Lott outlined elements of a deal to bring the treaty to the floor:

The Senate would begin debate the week of April 14 on a separate bill (S 495) by Kyl that would enact as U.S. law some provisions of the Chemical Weapons Convention. Kyl's bill was designed to provide political cover for Republicans who wanted to oppose the treaty but were leery of being seen as voting against a pact billed as banning poison gas.

The Senate would then turn to the resolution approving ratification of the treaty. Lott said this would happen the week of April 21. Democrats were pressing for the debate on the resolution to begin about April 16 with a final vote on the resolution of approval by April 24.

There would be about 15 hours of general debate on the treaty-approval resolution, including a closed session during which the Senate could discuss classified information.

In addition to adopting more than 20 "understandings" — modifications to the approval resolution — on which compromise language had been reached, the Senate would debate and vote on a small number of understandings that treaty supporters vehemently opposed.

The agreement for a final Senate vote on the treaty followed weeks of arduous negotiations. Helms and Biden had managed to reach accord on 28 out of the 33 amendments, or understandings, that Helms had included in the resolution of approval. Some of them perceptibly reduced the treaty's im-

Sen. Helms' Opposition to Treaty . . .

Negotiations on the ground rules for Senate debate on the Chemical Weapons Convention focused, in part, on 33 "understandings" that Senate Foreign Relations Committee Chairman Jesse Helms, R-N.C, wanted attached to the resolution (S 75) ratifying the pact. Helms, ranking committee Democrat Joseph R. Biden Jr. of Delaware, and the White House reached agreement on 28 of these provisos.

While the understandings did not amend the treaty itself — something prohibited by the treaty's own terms — they declared the U.S. interpretation of some treaty provisions and, in some cases, imposed legally binding obligations on U.S. officials.

Use of Tear Gas

One particularly thorny issue only settled near the end of the bargaining focused on the extent to which the treaty restricted use by military forces of tear gas and other, nonlethal riot-control agents. The treaty recognized a distinction between such irritants and chemical weapons. However, it barred the use of riot-control agents as weapons of war.

Early in the negotiations that led to the treaty, the Ford administration had defined this distinction in Executive Order 11850. The order cited four examples of circumstances in which the use of tear gas should be permissible under the treaty, for the sake of avoiding unnecessary loss of life: to subdue rioting enemy POWs, to protect supply convoys from riots and guerrilla attack, to help rescue a U.S. pilot from enemy troops or a POW from behind enemy lines and to incapacitate civilians being used as human shields by enemy troops.

In 1994, the Clinton administration revised the policy, concluding that the treaty would ban the use of tear gas in two of the four illustrative cases: rescuing a downed pilot and dealing with "human shield" tactics. The Joint Chiefs of Staff said that while they preferred the earlier interpretation, they still supported the treaty.

The administration ultimately accepted an understanding that reiterated the Ford administration interpretation that the treaty would not bar the use of tear gas in any of the four cases.

Snap Inspection Warrants

A second contentious issue on which Helms and the treaty's supporters reached agreement late in the game was the extent to which U.S. courts could protect companies targeted for surprise inspection by the international organization set up to verify the treaty.

While most of the verification provisions focused on designated military or industrial sites, the treaty also allowed any country to request a "challenge inspection" of any site, to be conducted on five days notice.

To trigger such an inspection, a country did not immediately need to identify the specific site to be inspected and needed to identify in only general terms the basis for requesting the inspection. The inspection then would occur unless three-fourths of the members of the verification organization's 41-country executive committee decided within 12 hours that the request was frivolous.

Treaty opponents argued that this procedure would lend itself to industrial espionage conducted under color of verifying compliance with the chemical weapons ban. Moreover, they argued, it would make a mockery of a U.S. company's right, under the Fourth Amendment to the Constitution, to freedom from "unreasonable searches and seizures."

At U.S. insistence, the treaty also included a provision requiring that inspections in any country be conducted in accord with that country's constitutional protections on searches and seizures. The treaty allowed officials at a challenged site to hide any equipment or information they deemed sensitive.

But Biden, Helms and the administration went further and agreed to an understanding that barred challenge inspections of privately owned facilities unless either the targeted company did not object or the U.S. government secured a criminal search warrant. To obtain such a warrant, the government would have to present evidence showing "probable cause" to believe that the treaty was being violated at a specific site, to which the search would be limited.

Other Compromises

Three other provisions agreed on in the final days of the negotiations provided that:

- **Analyzing samples.** Chemical samples collected from U.S. sites by treaty inspectors could only be analyzed in U.S. laboratories. This was in answer to the critics' argument that samples collected to verify that a factory was not making forbidden chemicals could also be used, in violation of the treaty, to ferret out military or commercial secrets.

pact on U.S. sovereignty. *(Understandings, this page)*

As part of his price for agreeing to a floor vote on the treaty, Helms insisted that the Senate first vote individually on each of the remaining five amendments. Clinton denounced the proposals at an April 18 news conference as "killer amendments" that would "prevent our participating in the treaty." But they highlighted key facets of the conservatives' case against the treaty, such as the fact that some rogue states known to possess chemical weapons were not party to the pact.

For all the conservative political capital invested in the anti-treaty effort thus far, a substantial number of Republican senators remained publicly undecided. Significantly, this group included several freshmen as well as Lott, whose ultimate decision was expected to carry great weight with other undecideds.

With momentum building toward the Senate debate on the treaty, both sides maneuvered for advantage.

On April 17, the Senate passed Kyl's bill, 53-44, which proposed incorporating some of the chemical weapons treaty's provisions into U.S. law. Though the measure had little chance of enactment, some treaty supporters worried that Republicans who voted for it might find it easier to oppose the treaty. *(Vote 45, p. S-10)*

The same day, Clinton signed off on a plan to consolidate several foreign affairs agencies. While Helms' aides insisted there was no quid-pro-quo, the deal was reported after Helms dropped his objection to the April 24 date for a vote on the chemical weapons pact.

. . . Results in Attached 'Understandings'

• **Waiver of immunity.** If an employee of the international verification organization were to compromise secret information gained as a result of an inspection, the president would demand that the employee's treaty-guaranteed immunity from U.S. legal jurisdiction be waived. Until the organization waived that immunity, the United States would withhold 50 percent of its annual payment to the organization.

• **U.S. payments.** The annual U.S. payment to the treaty organization would be limited to $25 million, unless Congress approved a presidential request for a higher payment.

Less Controversial Provisions

Many of the remaining understandings were relatively noncontroversial.

• **Congressional leverage.** Several of the understandings were intended to give Congress leverage over executive branch actions related to compliance with the treaty. These included requirements that the president report to Congress:

• Any violations of the pact.

• Any questions raised concerning compliance with the treaty.

• The treaty's effect on the U.S. policy of not using nuclear weapons to retaliate for a chemical attack by any state not armed with nuclear weapons.

• The preparedness of U.S. forces to carry out their mission, even in the face of a chemical weapons attack.

• Any proposed additions to the lists of chemicals for which the treaty mandated routine inspections.

• Procedures adopted to protect U.S. intelligence agencies from damage in case information they passed on to the international verification organization was leaked.

• The treaty's impact on legitimate U.S. chemical, biotechnical and pharmaceutical industries.

• **Treaty amendments.** Another of the understandings required a Senate vote on any proposed amendment to the treaty considered by the international organization. Such approval required a two-thirds majority.

• **Limiting U.S. financial obligations.** Other agreed-upon understandings sought to keep a rein on the U.S. share of the cost of the treaty's verification organization. These sections:

• Stipulated that U.S. payments to the organization be made only to the extent they were authorized and appropriated by Congress.

• Declared that the United States should not lose its vote in the treaty organization if it fell behind in its assessed payments because of congressional action.

• Mandated the creation within the treaty organization of an independent audit and oversight office.

• Ruled out in advance any proposal by Russia to make its approval of the treaty subject to U.S. financial aid to cover the cost of disposing of Russia's massive chemical weapons stockpile.

• Required that the United States not bear an excessive share of the cost of research projects aimed at improving the treaty's verification efforts.

• **Senate prerogatives.** Another set of compromise provisions affirmed various Senate prerogatives in approving treaties, including understandings that:

• Declared the sense of the Senate that U.S. negotiators should not include in future treaties a provision like the one in the Chemical Weapons Convention that prohibited countries from ratifying the pact with "reservations" that specifically repudiated certain provisions.

• Affirmed as a matter of principle that the Senate had the right to approve the treaty with reservations, even though it chose not to do so.

• Declared that the U.S. government could enter into an international arms control agreement only by treaty, requiring approval by a two-thirds majority of the Senate.

• Declared that, in interpreting the text of the treaty, the U.S. government was bound by the authoritative interpretations the executive branch provided to the Senate.

• **Other understandings.** The agreed-upon understandings also included provisos affirming that:

• The U.S. Constitution had primacy over the treaty.

• The treaty would not have prevented the March 1995 terrorist attack on Tokyo subways using nerve gas.

• A Pentagon agency should be given legal authority to help public and private U.S. facilities subjected to international inspection.

• **Incineration.** In addition, the administration agreed to a requirement that the United States, which planned to dispose of its chemical weapons by incineration, reserve the right to use alternative methods. The incineration plan was vehemently opposed by environmental activists.

Senate Approval

The Senate approved the treaty April 24 with seven votes to spare. A majority of Republicans (29 of 55) joined a solid phalanx of 45 Democrats to produce the 74-26 vote for S Res 75, the resolution of ratification. But first, the Senate rejected, by heavy margins, the five contested understandings attached by Helms. *(Vote 51, S-11)*

Biden said the Senate had rejected conservative demands that the United States rely on its own resources, rather than on multinational negotiations, to guard its interests. "The United States Senate said, 'We are going to be engaged in the world,' " Biden declared. "Any other decision . . . would have said that the neo-isolationists were on the rise, that the internationalists were on the run."

Lott's support was grudging. "The country is marginally better off with it than without it," he told the Senate. Lott voted for the five contested amendments. "If I had my way," he told reporters, "I'd like to see parts of this renegotiated. I'm not a big fan of this treaty."

On the morning of the vote, Lott had wrung one final concession from Clinton — a letter in which the president promised that the United States would withdraw from the treaty if two contentious sections of the pact ever allowed unfriendly nations to acquire chemical weapons or compromised U.S. security.

Lott's support for the treaty enraged conservative activists, who charged that the pact would compromise U.S.

sovereignty as well as military and trade secrets even as it fostered the spread of chemical weapons.

In a news conference April 25, a group of treaty opponents denounced Lott's vote for the treaty as a sellout of conservative principles. Frank J. Gaffney Jr., director of the Center for Security Policy and one of the chemical treaty's leading opponents, called Lott not a majority leader, but the "Senate majority compromiser."

Lott tried to parlay the attacks into political leverage on Clinton. "I'm going to take a lot of flak for it," he told reporters. "Now we're going to see if the president is going to show similar courage against his base."

Though Helms lost his battle to prevent ratification, he demonstrated that he could use the power of his chairmanship not simply to obstruct action indefinitely — he had been nicknamed "Senator No" in the past — but to extract important concessions.

The Five Killer Amendments

When the Senate began debate April 23, it gave voice vote approval to the 28 provisos that Helms and Biden had agreed on. The following day, the Senate adopted amendments by Biden deleting the remaining five Helms provisos, all opposed by the White House. But treaty supporters had to make some concessions of their own to get there.

The following were the five contested items:

- **Treaty renegotiation.** The language emphasized most strongly by treaty opponents would have barred ratification until the treaty was renegotiated to revise two sections: Article X, which allowed signatories to obtain anti-chemical defense technology, and Article XI, which affirmed the right of nations to conduct international trade in chemicals. The Senate deleted it by a vote of 66-34. *(Vote 50, p. S-11)*

Treaty critics argued that the articles would have the unintended effect of helping rogue nations to circumvent export controls and obtain advanced chemical weapons, while learning how to circumvent U.S. anti-chemical defenses.

Treaty supporters dismissed the argument as a willful misreading of the treaty, but they had agreed to two understandings, which Helms accepted. One stated that the requirement to provide defensive aid could be met by providing medical antidotes. The other stated that the United States and all other major chemical exporters agreed that the treaty was consistent with the Australia Group, the voluntary consortium through which these countries regulated chemical exports to potential bad actors.

Lott and some other Republicans, including Slade Gorton of Washington, said that was not enough. So on the morning of the Senate vote, Clinton sent Lott the letter promising to withdraw from the treaty if Articles X and XI were used to abet proliferation of chemical weapons.

- **Ratification by pariah states.** A second Helms proviso would have barred formal U.S. ratification until the pact was ratified by several countries hostile to U.S. interests and known to have chemical weapons. It was deleted, 71-29. *(Vote 46, p. S-11)*
- **Russian compliance.** Another would have barred U.S. ratification until Russia ratified and complied with two older chemical weapons agreements. The amendment was deleted, 66-34.*(Vote 47, p. S-11)*
- **Detection of violations.** A fourth amendment would have required the president to certify that U.S. intelligence agencies had "high confidence" that they could detect within a year if a country acquired a metric ton or more of a chemical weapons agent, and that U.S. agencies also could detect a pattern of minor violations over time.

The administration conceded that it could not meet that standard but insisted that the treaty would be valuable even if it could only be policed to the less exacting standard U.S. agencies said they could meet: that they could detect a systematic effort by an adversary to equip its army to wage chemical warfare. The language was deleted by a vote of 66-34. *(Vote 48, p. S-11)*

- **Barring certain inspectors.** The fifth disputed amendment would have required the president to bar from inspections on U.S. territory employees of the international verification agency who were nationals of China or certain other countries that had violated U.S. policy against nuclear proliferation. It was deleted, 56-44. *(Vote 49, p. S-11)*

Twenty-four Republicans voted to keep all five of the contested understandings and then voted against the resolution of ratification. They included veteran hard-liners such as Helms and Kyl, as well as four freshmen: Wayne Allard of Colorado, Sam Brownback of Kansas, Tim Hutchinson of Arkansas and Jeff Sessions of Alabama.

However, 20 Republicans voted to remove all the Helms provisions, or all but the one barring inspectors from rogue states, and for adoption of the resolution. They included party centrists such as Richard G. Lugar of Indiana and Ted Stevens of Alaska, as well as solid conservatives such as Daniel R. Coats of Indiana and Thad Cochran of Mississippi.

Implementation Legislation

The Senate on May 23 passed legislation to implement the Chemical Weapons Convention. The bill (S 610), which passed by voice vote, had won approval the previous day from the Senate Judiciary Committee, also by voice vote.

The measure contained provisions authorizing the president to issue regulations applying the treaty's chemical weapons prohibitions to anyone within the territory of the United States and to U.S. citizens anywhere in the world. The bill also included creation of a legal framework for the international inspections intended to verify compliance.

The framework included procedures by which inspectors could apply for search warrants to inspect private facilities. As part of its resolution approving the treaty, the Senate had insisted that before inspectors could enter a private factory or other facility, they would either have to have the owner's consent or obtain a criminal search warrant from a federal judge by showing "probable cause" that the treaty was being violated.

S 610 included language barring the government from requiring, as a condition of any contract, that a company agree to any request for an international inspection pursuant to the treaty. It also included a Republican-backed provision making it clear that Mace and pepper spray packaged for individual self-defense were not covered by the treaty's restrictions on "riot-control agents" such as tear gas.

Another provision, dropped during the May 22 committee markup, would have excluded from the country any inspector known by the government to have been a member of a terrorist group.

The requirement would not have been inconsistent with the treaty, which allowed any country to bar any inspector. But opponents argued that the proposed language would have required the president to divulge sensitive intelligence information by identifying some terrorists. They also complained that it might require the exclusion of inspectors who were members of erstwhile terrorist groups such as the African National Congress, which had become South Africa's ruling political party.

Committee Republicans and the Clinton administration also agreed on a compromise provision governing the right of companies to sue the U.S. government for damages resulting from the loss of trade secrets as a result of treaty inspections.

As passed, if the company established a prima facie case for its complaint, the government would have the burden of proving that the treaty inspection was not responsible for any damage suffered by the firm.

Bill Caught Up in Unrelated Fight

Moments before Congress adjourned on Nov. 13, Senate Democrats blocked floor consideration of a House-passed bill (HR 2709) that included the treaty implementation provisions. The primary purpose of HR 2709 was to impose tough economic sanctions against overseas companies and research institutes — mainly Russian — that were helping Iran develop ballistic missiles. The sanctions bill was strongly opposed by the Clinton administration, and proponents had attached the chemical weapons provisions to it in an attempt to shield it from a threatened veto. *(Sanctions, p. 8-42)*

The House had passed the combined bill by voice vote late on the night of Nov. 12. The White House said that measure was too rigid and would derail delicate negotiations with the Russian government aimed at ending the flow of lethal technology to Iran. ■

Hill Receives Military Report Cards

Defense specialists in Congress received two reports during the year assessing the nation's long-term defense needs.

Defense Secretary William S. Cohen went before the Senate Armed Services Committee and the House National Security Committee May 20 and May 21 to present recommendations from the Pentagon's Quadrennial Defense Review, a six-month assessment of future defense needs and plans. The second report, issued Dec. 1, came from a commission of defense specialists that had been set up by Congress to review the Pentagon study.

Meanwhile, in an effort to find more money for weapons modernization, Cohen announced a series of plans Nov. 10 that were aimed at making Pentagon operations cheaper and more agile.

Quadrennial Defense Review

The Pentagon's own review concluded that it was necessary to retain most of the existing forces, missions and strategies, and to modernize the military with money cut from defense programs traditionally held sacred on Capitol Hill — military bases, civilian maintenance and administrative jobs, and the National Guard and reserves.

The study reaffirmed the main elements of President Clinton's defense program, including the goal of being able to fight and win two major wars in widely separated regions but overlapping in time — for example, in the Persian Gulf and on the Korean peninsula.

But Cohen also reaffirmed the conclusion, reached nearly two years before by Joint Chiefs of Staff Chairman Gen. John M. Shalikashvili, that to fund necessary high-tech weapons, the Pentagon's annual procurement budget would have to reach $60 billion, a climb of some $15 billion.

Cohen told the committees that it would be too risky to make major cuts in force structure — the number of combat divisions, warships and fighter squadrons — or in plans to buy high-tech weaponry. He exhorted Congress instead to bolster the combat forces that made up the Pentagon's "teeth" by trimming the size of its administrative "tail."

The review recommended shifting about $15 billion a year from personnel and operating costs to procurement — the lion's share of which would come from a new round of base closings, a push to contract out administrative functions to private companies, and additional cuts in the National Guard and reserves.

Cohen and his top aides contended that the Pentagon had cut its overall size and its operating force by about one-third in the past decade while reducing the number of bases by only 18 percent.

In presenting the plan to the defense committees, Cohen acknowledged that Congress would have the final say, but he insisted there was no way to evade the choice between modernizing the combat forces and keeping the existing infrastructure. "All the easy choices have been made," Cohen said.

Some defense policy analysts complained that the defense review was merely a bureaucratic effort to preserve the status quo, and that the Pentagon had squandered an opportunity to radically reorganize its forces at a time when the country was relatively free of any major, imminent threat.

But the outside critics' objections did not appear to resonate with the two defense committees. Indeed, the most significant challenge to Cohen's plan came from House Republicans who complained that the defense review would inhibit public debate on the size of the defense budget because Cohen had insisted that its recommendations conform to defense budgets of no more than $250 billion, plus inflation.

The defense review's privatization recommendations followed the logic used by many large corporations — "focusing on what they do best, and let others do the rest," in the words of Deputy Defense Secretary John White. The argument was that the Pentagon would pay less for, say, civilian security services if it contracted with a firm that specialized in those services, partly because the department would benefit from competitive market pressures to keep costs down and partly because personnel cuts or relocations to achieve greater efficiencies would be less subject to political obstruction.

Missions and Forces

The Pentagon study said that U.S. forces not only had to be large enough to win two wars, they had to be able to continue the policy of deploying about 100,000 personnel in both Europe and the western Pacific.

The review also assumed that U.S. forces would continue to be deployed on peacekeeping missions, international training exercises and other non-war missions with about the same frequency and in about the same numbers as had been the recent norm.

Many Republicans had complained that Clinton had frittered away combat-readiness by sending units off on time-consuming missions peripheral to their combat assignments. But the facts of life were that the services kept picking up these assignments, so they were factored into the review.

Defense Department's Long-Range Plan . . .

The following is a summary of the weapons systems discussed in the Quadrennial Defense Review:

• **F-22.** Intended to succeed the F-15 as the Air Force's premier air-to-air combat plane, the F-22 had a radar-evading "stealthy" design and the ability to travel much farther at supersonic speed than the jets that were in service. The review called for reducing the total number purchased for this mission from the planned 438 aircraft to 339. Since the plane could carry precision-guided "smart bombs," additional F-22s might be purchased to replace ground attack versions of the F-15 and the F-117 "stealth" jets expected to wear out around 2015.

Some critics of the F-22 had contended that, although the F-15's basic design dated from the late 1960s, in the hands of highly skilled U.S. pilots and equipped with updated missiles and combat electronics, it should outclass any competing fighter for more than a decade, until the cheaper Joint Strike Fighter neared production.

But the Pentagon argued that the Joint Strike Fighter relied on technology that would be developed as part of the F-22 program. Moreover, it insisted, absolute U.S. control of the skies over any battlefield was too important to risk, partly because much of the Pentagon's battlefield intelligence was gathered by a handful of large, electronics-packed airplanes, designed as airliners, that would be sitting ducks for any enemy fighter.

• **F/A-18E/F.** The "E" and "F" models of the Navy's F/A-18 were enlarged variants of the F/A-18 "C" and "D" models then in service; the E and C were single-seat planes, while the F and D were two-seaters. The new version could fly farther and carry more weapons while absorbing the jarring impact of a carrier landing.

The Navy also touted the new version's higher "bring-back" capacity — its ability to land safely back on its ship still carrying munitions that had not been used on a mission. Navy planes assigned to peacekeeping missions were likely to carry precision-guided munitions that they probably would not drop but that would be too expensive simply to jettison.

The defense review proposed buying 548 of the new planes instead of 1,000. Defense Secretary William S. Cohen said the Navy might buy more than 548, depending in part on the progress of the Joint Strike Fighter. The plan was to begin production of the Navy's version of the joint fighter in 2008, but if the new plane had technical problems or if its price climbed too high, Cohen said, the Navy might buy as many as 237 additional F/A-18Es and Fs in lieu of some of the planned joint fighters.

The Pentagon also might buy additional F/A-18Es and Fs to replace its 1970s-vintage EA-6B radar jamming planes.

• **Joint Strike Fighter.** Two contractors offering different designs were competing to build three versions of the Joint Strike Fighter beginning late in the following decade — an Air Force version to replace 1970s-vintage F-16s; a Navy version, beefed up to take the shock of catapult launches and carrier landings, which would replace early-model F/A-18s; and a vertical takeoff version to replace the Harrier "jump jets" flown by the Marines and the British Navy. The defense review proposed reducing the total projected production run from 2,978 to 2,852, partly because of planned efficiencies in managing the inventory of planes being overhauled.

• **B-2 bombers.** The Pentagon weighed the pluses and minuses of scrapping some existing forces to pay for a larger fleet of B-2 "stealth" bombers, but it reaffirmed an earlier decision not to buy more of the planes beyond the 21 already funded.

Defense officials conceded that additional B-2s would make it easier to blunt a tank-led invasion of some distant ally in the first few days of a war, before most U.S. forces could reach the scene. And, since the big, radar-evading planes could fly directly over their targets with near impunity, they could drop guided, but unpowered, bombs that were much cheaper than the "standoff" guided missiles that non-stealthy planes would have to fire at the same targets from outside the range of anti-aircraft defenses.

However, the additional B-2s would be less versatile than some of the forces that would have to be sacrificed to pay for them.

The recommendation was to cut the active-duty force by 60,000 members, to 1.36 million, with most of the reductions coming out of the administrative "tail" rather than the combat "teeth" and with very little change in the number of major combat units. The Army would retain 10 divisions, and the Navy would keep its 12 aircraft carriers while slightly trimming the number of surface ships and submarines. The Marine Corps would retain three division-sized expeditionary forces, and the Air Force would keep 12 of its 13 active-duty fighter wings.

The planned Guard and reserve force would be cut by an additional 55,000 to a total of 835,000. Civilian Pentagon employment would drop by 80,000 to 640,000.

The decision to retain 10 Army divisions appeared to reflect a decision that "boots on the ground" remained a uniquely potent pledge of U.S. support.

On the other hand, Maj. Gen. Charles Link, the Air Force's chief contact with the review process, said May 22 that the review had convinced many Pentagon officials that modern planes with precision-guided weapons could play a larger role than many had assumed in blunting an invasion of an ally.

The review included a firm endorsement of every major weapons program under way at the time, though quantities would be more limited.

Some critics had argued that the Pentagon's chronic budget shortfall could be corrected, in large part, by canceling one or more of the new generation of weapons still on the drawing board or entering production. Key targets were the three fighter jet programs on which the Air Force, Navy and Marine Corps planned to spend more than $300 billion.

But the review concluded that canceling any of those programs — the Air Force F-22, the Navy F/A-18E and F, or the tri-service Joint Strike Fighter — "was not considered prudent given the warfighting risk of such a decision and the significant adverse impact it would have on technology development and the defense industrial base." *(Weapons, this page)*

Defense Review Panel

On Dec. 1, the blue-ribbon commission set up by Congress to review the quadrennial defense study and offer its own recommendations, issued its report. The panel's conclusion: The Pentagon should spend less money fine-tuning its existing forces and more on the weapons and tactics the nation might need in the coming 20 years.

Created under the fiscal 1997 defense authorization bill (PL 104-201), the nine-member panel was headed by Philip A. Odeen, president and CEO of BDM International Corp., a defense consulting and research firm. Odeen had held key positions in the Defense Department and on the National Security

. . . Highlights Major Weapons Programs

They could not dissuade potential troublemakers by lingering near a vulnerable ally in a long-term show of force. Nor could they carry the sheer weight of bombs that could be dropped by the existing fleet of B-52s, once enemy air defenses were quashed. Moreover, there would be a lag of nearly a decade between the time the Pentagon scrapped existing forces to buy the additional B-2s and the time the new planes were in service.

● **JSTARS.** The Joint Surveillance and Target Attack Radar System (JSTARS) was a Boeing jetliner with radar that could spot tank columns and other ground targets more than 100 miles away. The review called for buying only 13 of these planes instead of 19 as had been planned. If U.S. forces ever had to fight the two overlapping regional wars they were supposed to be able to win, some of the smaller JSTARS fleet would have to be moved from the first war to the second, once it began. The reduction in U.S.-owned aircraft would be offset if NATO accepted a U.S. offer to sell six JSTARS to the alliance. The review also called for studying the use of long-range, radar-equipped drones as a supplement.

● **V-22 Osprey.** The review called for reducing the number of Osprey tilt-rotor aircraft — hybrid airplane/helicopters the Marines planned to use to haul combat troops ashore from their transport ships. But that smaller fleet would be purchased more quickly than had been planned to replace the Marines' fleet of superannuated transport helicopters.

Both because one Osprey would be more capable than one of the existing helicopters and because the Marines intended to streamline their aircraft maintenance operations, they expected to buy 360 Ospreys instead of the 425 planned earlier. The smaller purchase, combined with a faster and thus more efficient production rate, was expected to save $3 billion.

● **Warships.** To sustain the existing pattern of routine carrier deployments in the western Pacific, the Arabian Sea and the Mediterranean, the review called for maintaining the force of 11 active duty aircraft carriers plus a 12th ship manned partly by reservists, which normally would be used for pilot training. To that end, it reaffirmed the plan to fund another nuclear-powered carrier in 2002 to replace the oil-powered Kitty Hawk, slated for retirement in 2008 after 47 years of service.

The review called for reducing the planned number of surface warships from 128 to 116, with no reduction in plans to fund three Aegis destroyers to be built in Mississippi and Maine.

It called for reducing the number of attack submarines from 52 to 50, but retained plans to buy an average of three or four new subs every two years, with the work to be shared by companies in Virginia and Connecticut.

● **Army digitization.** The review called for adding $1 billion to accelerate the Army's plan to equip its combat divisions with digital communications links so that all the units in a force would share a common map of the battlefield, showing the location of all friendly forces and identified enemies. The review also backed production of the only new major Army weapons under development, the Comanche "stealth" helicopter and the Crusader self-propelled cannon, which would be able to move faster and shoot farther than the mobile guns then in service.

● **Anti-missile defense.** The review delayed by two years, from 2004 to 2006, the planned date for full-scale deployment of the Army's Theater High-Altitude Area Defense (THAAD), an anti-missile system designed to protect units in the field against missiles that had been fired upward of 1,000 miles. THAAD prototypes had missed their targets in all of the four test intercepts that had been attempted.

The review also concluded that the Pentagon's effort to develop a thin anti-missile defense for U.S. territory that could be deployed by 2003 was badly underfunded. It called for doubling the total national missile defense budget for fiscal 1998-2003, from $2.3 billion to $4.6 billion. "Even with additional funds, [it] will remain a program with very high schedule and technical risk," the review concluded.

Council staff. The other eight members were retired senior military officers or veteran defense policy analysts.

The commission warned that Pentagon plans to improve the armored divisions and fighter squadrons that swept aside their Iraqi opponents in the 1991 Gulf War would be less relevant against threats that could develop in the next two decades. "We can assume that our enemies and future adversaries have learned from the Gulf War," the report said. "They are unlikely to confront us conventionally. . . . They will look for ways to match their strengths against our weaknesses."

To cope with such threats, the commission recommended developing forces that could be sent more quickly to distant trouble spots and, once there, be less vulnerable to chemical or biological weapons. The panel also recommended that the Pentagon devote more effort to preparing for attacks on U.S. territory, including terrorist strikes using nuclear, chemical and biological weapons.

To the dismay of conservatives pressing for the early deployment of a nationwide defense against ballistic missiles, however, the panel endorsed the administration's plan to develop such a defense but defer deployment until it seemed warranted by a specific threat.

The commission called for spending $5 billion to $10 billion annually for the proposed new forces. Acknowledging that the defense budget was unlikely to increase, it recommended getting the money by closing additional military bases and relying on private contractors rather than federal employees and military personnel for administrative and maintenance work.

Without such cutbacks in overhead costs, the panel warned, the Pentagon would have to cancel major weapons programs or disband some of its forces to pay for the needed transition. "If the only result of this is an active debate on these issues . . . we'll feel like our goals were achieved," Odeen told reporters Dec. 1.

The panel took exception to the Clinton administration's emphasis on being able to quickly win two major regional wars several weeks apart in distant locations such as the Persian Gulf and the Korean peninsula.

The commission conceded that U.S. forces had to remain capable of dealing with major conflicts in Korea and the Persian Gulf, but it contended that existing forces were up to that task.

And it warned that the two-war scenario was counterproductive for the long run, since it gave the services a rationale for spending money to beef up for traditional wars that were unlikely to happen, rather than developing the equipment and methods that would be needed to face the non-traditional threats that were likely to confront the country in the future.

In the future, the panel warned, U.S. forces destined for

overseas trouble spots would have to be ready in much less time than the six months it took to assemble the Gulf War force. And because prospective adversaries were likely to acquire ballistic missiles and cruise missiles carrying lethal chemical or biological warheads, the commission said, U.S. forces could not be dependent on the sprawling, vulnerable type of airfields, seaports and supply depots used in Saudi Arabia.

The commission acknowledged that the services were considering the types of changes it recommended, but it said the financial follow-through was too skimpy. "While they have these very clear ideas in mind [and] they talk a lot about them, we don't see much investment going on to make those changes," said Odeen.

The advisory panel called on the services to conduct large-scale exercises to test some of their novel concepts and to push ahead with those that showed promise.

Accelerating Modernization Plans

For example, the panel urged the Army to accelerate its two-stage plan for modernization over the following two decades.

The Army was planning initially to equip existing forces with new and upgraded weapons that incorporated digital communications links over which all the tank commanders, helicopter pilots and infantry commanders in a unit, for instance, could share a common battlefield map locating friendly and enemy forces.

Then, late in the next decade, the Army planned to begin a transition from that modernized force to a radically redesigned force that would consist of smaller, more agile combat units equipped with weapons that would be much lighter and more easily transported.

The panel wanted the Army to move more quickly. Odeen suggested this could be done by upgrading only half the Army's 10 combat divisions — those already stationed overseas and those in the United States that would be in the first wave deployed abroad to meet a crisis. That was consistent with the Odeen panel's view that the Pentagon should reduce the number of heavy, tank-equipped U.S.-based units, since they would take too long to deploy to a distant crisis.

Under Odeen's approach, the Army could spend more money developing the new force, because it would reduce the number of M-1 tanks to be upgraded as well as cut back the planned production of the Comanche helicopter and Crusader mobile cannon, the two highest-priority weapons programs in the Army's budget.

The panel took a similar approach on the Navy's modernization plans. On the one hand, it praised the service for exploring ways to concentrate power against a target by electronically linking widely dispersed ships and planes. On the other hand, it said the Navy was retarding its progress toward that goal by planning to spend more than $5 billion to build one last mammoth aircraft carrier of the *Nimitz* class.

The commission recommended that the Navy drop plans to build the additional ship, which was scheduled to enter service in about a decade, and instead develop two new types of less expensive ships: a smaller aircraft carrier and an "arsenal ship" intended to carry hundreds of cruise missiles and a very small crew.

As for combat aircraft, the National Defense Panel questioned plans by the Air Force, Navy and Marine Corps to acquire, by 2020, thousands of relatively short-range combat jets that could strike an enemy only from nearby bases that would be vulnerable to missile attacks using chemical or biological warheads.

The panel also decried the absence of any plans to expand the Pentagon's force of long-range attack aircraft.

Advocates of the B-2 stealth bomber had used this line of argument in their losing battle to buy more of the big, radar-evading planes than the 21 already funded. However, Odeen and other panel members insisted they were not specifically recommending that approach. Long-range aerial strikes could also be conducted, for instance, by planes much cheaper than the B-2 that could launch swarms of long-range, stealthy cruise missiles.

Cohen's Plan for Cutting Costs

Cohen's plan to cut costs at the Pentagon, announced Nov. 10, relied heavily on two more rounds of military base closings, an idea Congress had rejected earlier in the year. It also included proposals to make Pentagon operations cheaper and more agile by streamlining the Defense Department's organization and simplifying its purchasing. If fully implemented, the package promised to reduce operating costs by $6 billion a year, providing more money for weapons modernization.

Another Call for New Base Closings

Nearly half the anticipated savings — $2.8 billion — was to come from two more rounds of base closings that would require legislative authorization. Congress had brushed aside Cohen's proposal for new rounds of base closings in 1999 and 2001 as part of the fiscal 1998 defense authorization bill (HR 1119 — PL 105-85). *(Defense authorization, p. 8-3)*

Cohen's new plan put off the dates until 2001 and 2005, making it potentially more palatable by giving states time to absorb the economic impact of closures and deferring any new base closure decisions until after Clinton left office.

Congress had rejected Cohen's earlier base-closing proposal, in part, because many members felt that Clinton meddled improperly in the last base-closing round in 1995 by privatizing two Air Force maintenance depots in California and Texas that were supposed to be shut, thus saving jobs in the vote-rich states.

At his Nov. 10 news conference, Cohen acknowledged that the administration would have to sell Congress on the need to dispose of additional military installations. He said he hoped to do that partly by highlighting communities that had attracted more jobs than they had before by privately developing former military bases.

Ironically, Cohen needed legislation to authorize more base closings because of procedural hurdles he sponsored as a House member from Maine in the 1970s intent on squelching a Pentagon plan to close Loring Air Force Base in Limestone, Maine. *(1977 Almanac, p. 337)*

Outsourcing and Streamlining

Apart from the base closings, most of Cohen's streamlining could be accomplished without legislation, for an annual savings of about $3.2 billion.

However, more than three-quarters of that amount — $2.5 billion — was to come from another proposal likely to draw congressional opposition: allowing private contractors to bid against Pentagon agencies over the following five years in such areas as payroll management, personnel services, leased property management and drug testing.

About 2,000 such competitions had been held from 1979 to 1994, with government agencies and private firms each winning about half. According to the Defense Department, annual operating costs for the jobs were cut by 31 percent, for an annual savings of $1.5 billion.

But members of Congress representing significant numbers of federal employees typically opposed contracting out large numbers of jobs, warning that once the federal government lost its trained work force, the private company that won the competition had great leverage to raise its price for renewing the contract.

Cohen's Pentagon streamlining plan also included the following initiatives:

➤ A paper-free electronic procurement system for major weapons contracts by Jan. 1, 2000.

➤ Use of government credit cards, rather than laborious formal contracts, for 90 percent of all purchases of less than $2,500, about half of all Pentagon purchases.

➤ A halt to volume printing of all department-wide regulations by July 1998, making the regulations available only through the Internet or CD-ROMs.

➤ Private supply of utilities for military installations, where practical.

➤ Permanent legislative authority to use loans and other guarantees to induce private firms to build and manage housing for military families.

➤ Elimination of 30,000 out of 141,000 military and civilian jobs in administrative offices and headquarters. ■

NATO Expansion Forges Ahead

In a foreign policy triumph for President Clinton, the 16-member NATO alliance agreed July 8 to open its doors to three former members of the Warsaw Pact. With that momentous step, the U.S. debate over expanding the alliance shifted from the corridors of diplomacy and academic think tanks to the bare-knuckle world of domestic politics.

The decision to invite Poland, Hungary and the Czech Republic to join the alliance by 1999 required amending the 1949 North Atlantic Treaty. For Clinton, that created the formidable task of securing a two-thirds majority in the Senate. The administration said it planned to send the amendment to the Senate in early 1998 and hoped for a vote as early as March.

The early signs were generally encouraging for the administration. A number of leading senators, including Majority Leader Trent Lott, R-Miss., an unabashed supporter of a larger NATO, predicted that the enlargement plan would win the requisite majority.

For the most part, however, the decision to expand the alliance attracted surprisingly little initial attention on Capitol Hill and even less among the public at large. "I just don't hear a lot about it," said Democratic Sen. Paul Wellstone of Minnesota.

The plan appeared to gain momentum in the fall from a series of hearings in which the Senate Foreign Relations and Appropriations committees heard from top administration officials, former administration officials and leading defense experts outside the government.

However, Clinton's biggest challenge was expected to be selling an American public that was largely indifferent to international involvement on a policy that would commit the United States to send troops to defend Warsaw or Budapest, in the same way it was committed to defend Paris or London.

The expansion would extend to the new members of the alliance the "all for one" mutual defense pledge embodied in Article V of the 1949 treaty, which bound each member of NATO to regard an attack on any other member as an attack on itself. *(Treaty excerpts, p. 8-24)*

Background

NATO leaders agreed to extend the invitation to the three former Soviet satellites at their July summit in Madrid. *(Background, 1949 Almanac, p. 343)*

In opting to invite just three new members, as Clinton had insisted, the NATO allies rejected the approach backed by France and other European nations that had wanted to also extend invitations to Romania and Slovenia.

French President Jacques Chirac had argued that admitting those two nations would bring needed stability to the Balkans. But Clinton, with a strong assist from British Prime Minister Tony Blair, succeeded in limiting the initial round of invitees to three.

If the enlargement plan was ratified — amending the 1949 treaty required approval by the legislatures of all 16 NATO members, then by the prospective members themselves — Poland, Hungary and the Czech Republic would be admitted in time for the 50th anniversary of the alliance in April 1999. Romania, Slovenia and other nations passed over in the first round could reapply then, but the allies made no promises about further admissions.

Clinton called the decision to admit the three countries "a very great day," not just for the United States and its allies, but also "for the cause of freedom in the aftermath of the Cold War." He and other proponents argued that the expansion would provide a path toward a more united, democratic and prosperous Europe.

The president conceded that the decision was not risk-free, but at a news conference July 9 he contended that bringing the former Soviet bloc nations under NATO's defense umbrella was a "pretty good gamble." In the half-century history of the alliance, he said, "no NATO nation has ever been attacked, not once."

To sell the concept at home, the administration launched a campaign quarterbacked by Jeremy Rosner, who joined the State Department from the Carnegie Endowment for International Peace, where he had been analyzing NATO issues since leaving Clinton's National Security Council staff in 1994.

For its part, Congress had spent little time on the issue, although the Madrid decision had been widely anticipated. Since July 1994, when Clinton told the Polish legislature that the question of NATO's expansion was "not if, but when," and the start of the 105th Congress, there had been only one committee hearing dedicated to the issue — on June 20, 1996, by the House International Relations Committee. With a Senate vote not expected before 1998, Congress had been content to provide non-binding expressions of general support and modest amounts of financial aid to help aspiring states meet NATO's membership criteria.

Laying Out the Pros and Cons

The only serious U.S. opposition prior to the Madrid summit came from an ideologically diverse group of nearly 50 former government officials and foreign policy scholars, including former Democratic Sen. Sam Nunn of Georgia (1972-97) and Reagan administration arms control negotiator Paul Nitze.

In a letter to Clinton in June, the group called the enlarge-

NATO Treaty Excerpts

The following excerpts from the North Atlantic Treaty, signed April 4, 1949, in Washington, include requirements for mutual defense and the method for adding new members:

Article 2

The Parties will contribute toward the further development of peaceful and friendly international relations by strengthening their free institutions, by bringing about a better understanding of the principles upon which these institutions are founded, and by promoting conditions of stability and well-being. They will seek to eliminate conflict in their international economic policies and will encourage economic collaboration between any or all of them.

Article 5

The Parties agree that an armed attack against one or more of them in Europe or North America* shall be considered an attack against them all and consequently they agree that, if such an armed attack occurs, each of them, in exercise of the right of individual or collective self-defence recognised by Article 51 of the Charter of the United Nations, will assist the Party or Parties so attacked by taking forthwith, individually and in concert with the other Parties, such action as it deems necessary, including the use of armed force, to restore and maintain the security of the North Atlantic area ...

Article 10

The Parties may, by unanimous agreement, invite any other European State in a position to further the principles of this Treaty and to contribute to the security of the North Atlantic area to accede to this Treaty ...

Article 11

This Treaty shall be ratified and its provisions carried out by the Parties in accordance with their respective constitutional processes ...

** The area was later expanded with the addition of Turkey, Greece, Spain and West Germany.*

ment of NATO "a policy error of historic proportions" and warned that expanding the alliance would create new divisions in Europe, inflict huge financial costs on the United States and sow resentment in Russia.

Several senators also raised similar concerns, though no opposition had coalesced. "Before the United States supports the expansion of NATO, one question must be answered — what will be the cost to American taxpayers," said Sen. Tom Harkin, D-Iowa. "For too long, American taxpayers have been stuck with the tab for the defense of our allies."

Kay Bailey Hutchison, R-Texas, widely regarded as the leading Senate critic of expanding NATO, sent her own letter to Clinton in June, signed by 19 of her colleagues, posing sharp questions over the costs and commitments that would be borne by the United States in an expanded NATO. But Hutchison seemed more skeptical than hostile to the proposal. "I am not an opponent," she said later. "NATO expansion can be positive if it is done thoughtfully."

The administration argued that the NATO security umbrella needed to extend eastward, not to meet any specific military threat, but to fill a power vacuum in Central Europe.

"We are dealing with a new NATO," said Secretary of State Madeleine K. Albright. "And the new NATO is there to deal with problems of instability, and those are the ones that we see as the major problems facing all of us as we enter the 21st century."

Senate Foreign Relations Committee Chairman Jesse Helms, R-N.C., agreed that NATO should be expanded, but not for the reasons cited by Albright and Clinton. The primary rationale for expanding NATO, Helms wrote in an article in the European edition of The Wall Street Journal, "must be to hedge against the possible return of a nationalistic or imperialist Russia."

For the blue-ribbon panel of academics and experts that signed the blunt letter to Clinton in June, both arguments missed the mark. They insisted there was no power void in Europe and that any threat from a revanchist Russia was a long way off.

They argued that expanding NATO was likely to make Russia more — not less — of a potential threat. Expansion "will strengthen non-democratic opposition" in Russia and "undercut those who favor reform and cooperation with the West," their letter said.

While the arguments for and against the expansion of NATO had yet to be fully aired in Congress, both chambers had, since 1994, cast non-binding votes in favor of expanding the alliance. Congress also had authorized military aid to several Eastern European nations to prepare them for the eventual transition to NATO. *(1996 Almanac, p. 8-15)*

Those votes — largely related to the desire by both parties to court voters of Eastern European descent — seemed likely to make it difficult for senators to reverse their positions.

In 1997, both the House and Senate passed statements of support for the eventual admission of Romania and the three Baltic nations — Latvia, Lithuania and Estonia — to NATO. The provisions were included in a State Department authorization bill (HR 1757) that remained hung up in conference when the session ended. However, concern over the possible budgetary impact of NATO expansion led Congress to include language in both the defense authorization bill (HR 1119) and the defense appropriations bill (HR 2266) requiring detailed estimates of the cost to the United States. *(State Department authorization, p. 8-32)*

On April 22, Lott appointed 28 senators to a new, bipartisan NATO Observer Group, "to represent the diversity of views in the Senate . . . and to provide a focal point for addressing NATO issues that may cut across committee jurisdictions."

Committee Hearings

The first hearing of the year on NATO expansion, held April 23 by the Senate Armed Services Committee, featured a rare joint appearance on Capitol Hill by Secretary of State Albright and Defense Secretary William S. Cohen.

Additional hearings were held in the fall by the Foreign Relations and Appropriations committees, as lawmakers began preparing for the debate that was anticipated in the spring of 1998.

In a Sept. 17 letter to Albright, Helms offered his help in securing Senate ratification of NATO enlargement, but said the administration would have to set forth a military rationale, secure a promise from other NATO members to share the cost and outline Russia's role in NATO decision-making.

Senate Armed Services Committee

Albright and Cohen told the Senate Armed Services Committee on April 23 that enlarging NATO would reduce the threat of political instability and the risk of future warfare in Eastern Europe. "If there were a major threat to the peace and security of this region, it is already likely that we would choose to act," Albright said. "The point of enlargement is to deter such a threat from ever arising."

Committee members expressed some skepticism. Jeff Bingaman, D-N.M., said that including Poland and other former Soviet allies in NATO might strengthen the hand of militarists and nationalists in Russian domestic politics. John W. Warner, R-Va., warned that the public was in no mood to support new, expensive military commitments overseas. "I do not think America wants to foot that bill," he said.

Cohen replied that, by the administration's estimate, enlarging NATO would cost $25 billion to $37 billion over 13 years, with the United States' share amounting to only about $200 million annually. "Yes, it's going to be difficult to persuade the American people that we have to prepare to defeat an enemy which they can't really see," Cohen acknowledged. "Instability is the enemy. Ethnic rivalries are the enemy. . . . To the extent that we can reduce and eliminate them [by expanding the alliance], that redounds to our vital national security interest."

Senate Foreign Relations Committee

The cost of enlarging the alliance — in particular the U.S. share — and the risk of a Russian backlash if former Soviet satellites joined Moscow's one-time nemesis, emerged as key issues in October, when the Senate Foreign Relations Committee heard from Albright and from policy experts on both sides of the issue.

Albright told the committee Oct. 7 that admitting Poland, Hungary and the Czech Republic to the alliance was strategically advantageous, militarily practical and morally imperative, even though Europe faced no serious military threat at the time. "We do not know what other dangers may arise 10, 20 or even 50 years from now," Albright said. "We do know that . . . it will be in our interest to have a vigorous and larger alliance with those European democracies that share our values and our determination to defend them."

But two leading proponents of expansion, Richard G. Lugar, R-Ind., and Joseph R. Biden Jr., D-Del., warned that the administration had to justify the goal of keeping the United States deeply involved in managing the security of prosperous European nations. "The thing I hear my colleagues say is, 'Damn it, Joe, why can't *they* do it?'" Biden said after the Oct. 7 session.

In the second session, Oct. 9, critics of expansion insisted that the issue was not whether the United States should remain engaged with Europe but whether adding the three countries to a military alliance was the best way to foster their fledgling democratic institutions and market-based economies.

"What Eastern European countries most want and most need is a form of membership in the Western community that provides support for growing economic, social and political structures," argued veteran arms control negotiator Jonathan Dean.

Jeane J. Kirkpatrick, former U.S. representative to the United Nations, articulated the basic strategic argument for expansion, namely that U.S. interests were so deeply entrenched in Europe that U.S. forces would become involved in any major conflict that broke out on the continent, whether or not they were required by a formal treaty commitment. "The United States cannot be indifferent to a tragedy in the heart of the civilization of which we are part," she said.

Former White House national security adviser Zbigniew Brzezinski told the Senate panel Oct. 9 that a poll by the Pew Research Center, conducted Sept. 4-11, indicated broad support for the basic proposition that Europe's security was essential to America's.

The poll showed support for expansion outweighing opposition 63 percent to 18 percent. However, the poll also found a very low level of public awareness about the proposal: Only 10 percent could name even one of the three potential NATO members.

On the question of how the expansion would affect Russia, Johns Hopkins University professor Michael Mandelbaum told the committee Oct. 9: "The only coherent reason for expanding NATO is to contain Russia," a goal which, he said, was "at best premature and at worst counterproductive" if it provoked hostility from Moscow instead of deterring it.

Under Secretary of State Thomas R. Pickering, a career diplomat and ambassador to Moscow in 1993-96, assured the committee Oct. 30 that including Poland, Hungary and the Czech Republic in NATO would neither undermine pro-democracy political reformers in Russia nor goad Moscow into dangerous countermoves.

Pickering acknowledged that Russian leaders strongly opposed NATO's expansion to include the three former Soviet satellites. But he noted that, since the expansion effort had hit its stride, Russian President Boris Yeltsin had strengthened the hand of liberals in his own government and made progress toward wrapping up several arms control agreements that had been stalled by foreign policy hard-liners in the Duma, Russia's legislature. "This track record does not support the hypothesis that Russian reform or reformers and security cooperation will inevitably suffer as a result of NATO enlargement," he said.

Other witnesses told the panel that knitting the three countries securely into NATO would boost the prospects of Russia's democrats by eliminating the temptation for Moscow to strong-arm erstwhile client states and thus keep the country's political leaders focused on the need for internal reform.

At a subsequent hearing, held Oct. 30, Jack F. Matlock Jr., the U.S. ambassador in Moscow when the Soviet Union disintegrated in 1991, warned that NATO expansion might be "a profound strategic blunder."

Expressing a view shared by many other Russian affairs specialists, Matlock warned that NATO's incorporation of the three new members would alienate Russian leaders, who would see it as evidence that they still were viewed by Washington as potential enemies who could be pushed around. As a result, Matlock predicted, Russian officials would be less prone to cooperate on critical issues such as preventing terrorists from obtaining nuclear, chemical or biological weapons from the huge former Soviet arsenal.

Matlock also challenged the administration's premise that NATO had to expand eastward to fill a geopolitical vacuum that otherwise would tempt Russian meddling and make the three countries politically unstable. "This is a very stable part of Europe," he protested, adding that the countries' fledgling market economies and democratic political systems would be better served if they were admitted to the European Union.

But Pickering and other specialists insisted that NATO had to take seriously the possibility that, as Russia regained its economic footing, it might resume its historical effort to control weaker neighbors.

"St. Petersburg is closer to New York than it is to Vladivostok, and Vladivostok is closer to Seattle than it is to Moscow," former Secretary of State Henry A. Kissinger rumbled, "So they should not feel claustrophobic, but they do."

Although Kissinger wholeheartedly urged Senate approval of NATO expansion, he complained that the Clinton administration had gone too far in trying to mollify Russia's objections. In particular, he said that the Founding Act — an agreement for formal consultations between Russia and NATO —

would give Russia too much influence over NATO's internal deliberations.

Albright had assured the Senate committee Oct. 7 that the consultative arrangements would give Moscow "a voice, not a veto" in NATO's decisions. Kissinger said he accepted Albright's explanation, but he feared the wall between NATO's internal discussions and its deliberations with Russia would break down over time, because NATO officials would be thrown into daily contact with their Russian counterparts.

He recommended that the Senate stipulate in its resolution approving the NATO treaty changes that NATO's councils take primacy over the arrangements for consultation between NATO and Russia.

Senate Appropriations Committee

In appearances before the Senate Appropriations Committee Oct. 21, Cohen and Albright attempted to reassure senators on the cost of NATO expansion. They said the initial estimates, made before the alliance invited the three countries to join, might be too high. Cohen said the NATO allies were compiling new figures.

(Although Cohen had said in April that the expansion would cost $25 billion to $37 billion over 13 years, other sources had put the bill higher. The Congressional Budget Office said enlargement could cost up to $125 billion.)

"It now appears as we examine the assets and infrastructure of our new allies . . . that the commonly funded cost of integrating their armed forces will turn out to be lower than we estimated in February," Albright said.

Cohen said the initial estimate factored in four countries, not three, joining the alliance. In addition, he said the new members' forces were better prepared than was first thought and would not be as expensive to upgrade.

The General Accounting Office weighed in at an Oct. 23 hearing. Henry L. Hinton Jr., an assistant comptroller general, testified that while NATO planners would have cost estimates in December for the military requirements of new members, broader decisions about the alliance, its strategy and its budget would not be finished until June.

"Until this has been done," Hinton said, "the implications for the U.S. contributions to NATO's common budgets will be unclear."

Appropriations Committee Chairman Ted Stevens, R-Alaska, expressed concern that expanding NATO would divert money away from modernizing U.S. forces and from U.S. commitments in other regions such as Asia. Despite assurances from the administration, Stevens and others questioned whether some NATO members would pay their fair share for expanding the alliance.

Administration officials, however, stressed that protecting Central Europe from future threats far outweighed the initial cost of enlarging NATO. "If we are to avoid the tragedies of this century in the next one, then we must embrace the lessons that we've learned at such great cost to achieve the peace that we owe our children and their children," said Gen. Henry H. Shelton, chairman of the Joint Chiefs of Staff.

"One of those lessons," Shelton said, "is that peace is based on closer ties politically, economically and militarily, and NATO enlargement serves these ends very well."

Dale Bumpers, D-Ark., who indicated he would most likely support NATO enlargement despite strong misgivings, challenged Albright and Cohen's claims that NATO expansion did not pose a threat to Russia. "If the Russians feel threatened enough, I think history shows that they will penalize their efforts to build a vibrant economy in favor of building their military forces back up," he said.

Albright, however, said that rejecting NATO expansion would strengthen "extremists in Russia" and show that Russia had a "voice over what the United States and our allies would like to do in Central and Eastern Europe." ■

U.S. Refuses To Sign Land Mine Ban

Though a majority in the Senate expressed support for banning anti-personnel land mines, President Clinton said Sept. 17 that the United States would not sign a treaty to outlaw them. Canada had led negotiations on the treaty, which began in September in Oslo, Norway, and concluded December in Ottawa.

The United States, which joined the international negotiations belatedly, tried unsuccessfully to win two exemptions from the general ban — one to allow the use of anti-personnel mines in Korea, the other to allow the United States to continue packaging anti-personnel mines with its anti-tank mines, to make it harder for enemy troops to remove the anti-tank mines.

In hopes of putting pressure on Clinton to sign the mine ban treaty, Reps. Jack Quinn, R-N.Y., and Lane Evans, D-Ill., introduced a bill (HR 2459) Sept. 11 to unilaterally ban new U.S. deployments of anti-personnel mines beginning in 2000. The bill would have allowed the president to waive the ban in the case of anti-personnel mines in Korea. The House took no action on the measure.

Companion legislation (S 896) introduced in the Senate by Patrick J. Leahy, D-Vt., and Chuck Hagel, R-Neb., with 55 other Senators , also saw no action.

In December, the group that led the battle to outlaw anti-personnel land mines, the International Campaign to Ban Landmines and its coordinator Jody Williams, were awarded the Nobel Peace Prize for 1997.

Background

For five years, Leahy, Evans and an alliance of the Vietnam Veterans of America Foundation and other groups had fought to promote a ban on anti-personnel mines because of the toll they took on non-combatants, often years after the end of the war in which the mines were sown. *(1996 Almanac, p. 8-18)*

Leahy and his allies, including private international organizations such as the International Red Cross, argued that the relatively inexpensive mines were particularly heinous because of their indiscriminate harm to civilians. The U.S. government estimated that some 100 million mines were scattered around 64 countries, where they killed and maimed more than 25,000 persons annually.

"Land mines do have some marginal military value," Leahy acknowledged at a June 12 news conference. "But the damage done . . . far outweighs whatever small benefits they add to our enormous and unsurpassed military arsenal."

Images of thousands of children maimed by land mines mobilized public interest as no other defense issue had in recent years, especially given the publicity generated by such international figures as Diana, Princess of Wales, before her death.

Proponents of an outright ban on anti-personal mines included such prominent military figures as retired Army Gen. H. Norman Schwarzkopf, commander in chief of allied forces in the Persian Gulf War.

The Army vehemently opposed such a ban. However, 15 Republicans, including well-known defense hawks such as Hagel, twice wounded by land mines in Vietnam, and John McCain of Arizona, signed onto the mine ban legislation. Cosponsors included six senators who saw combat in Vietnam.

In addition, the nation's Roman Catholic bishops embraced the bill. "In our missions and relief projects, we've seen the dead and maimed children, the land and villages abandoned," Bishop James W. Malone said June 12. Banning anti-personnel mines was "an urgent moral priority for the Catholic Church," he said.

Clinton had announced in a 1994 U.N. speech the goal of "eventual elimination" of anti-personnel mines. However, when the U.N. Conference on Disarmament began talks on a treaty to that end, the U.S. held that the pact should exempt mines equipped to self-destruct after an interval of hours or days.

On May 16, 1996, Clinton called for negotiating a ban "as soon as possible," with the proviso that any agreement allow the use of all types of anti-personnel mines in Korea and of "smart," self-destructing mines anywhere.

The administration announced that about 3 million of the 4 million "dumb" anti-personnel mines in U.S. stockpiles would be disposed of by 1999, leaving slightly more than 1 million for training and for deployment in Korea, in case of war. Clinton also ordered the Pentagon to accelerate the search for alternatives that would eliminate the need for exceptions to a ban.

Canada and other countries, frustrated by the slow pace of the U.N. talks, decided to try to fashion a treaty on their own. At a meeting in Ottawa in October 1996, Canadian Foreign Minister Lloyd Axworthy set a deadline for this "fast track" approach, announcing that Canada would host a conference to conclude a mine-ban treaty by the end of the year. The Canadian initiative was backed by 74 countries.

U.S. Rejects Treaty

In January 1997, the Clinton administration announced that it preferred to negotiate a worldwide ban through the U.N. Committee on Disarmament. Leahy and his allies argued that the U.N. committee's rule requiring that such an accord have unanimous approval was likely to make it impossible to agree on an effective ban any time in the near future.

Finally, in the fall, the administration abandoned the slow-moving U.N. talks. White House officials announced Aug. 18 that they would meet with representatives of more than 100 other countries in Oslo on Sept. 1 for three weeks of talks to work out a land mine treaty.

However, U.S. negotiators continued to press for two exceptions to the ban.

In the case of Korea, the United States insisted that the treaty allow the use of anti-personnel mines by the 37,000 U.S. personnel who stood guard with 550,000 South Koreans against a North Korean army of 900,000 that was within artillery range of Seoul, the capital of South Korea.

The other exception was for the use of anti-personnel mines in so-called mixed systems — artillery shells or aerial bombs containing both anti-tank and anti-personnel mines to keep enemy troops from eliminating the anti-tank mines. The anti-personnel mines in the U.S. mixed systems were smart mines that automatically disarmed after a short period.

Administration officials said they also planned to increase Pentagon spending for mine-clearing equipment and to help countries infested with mines.

The Clinton team's approach was vehemently rejected by many of the humanitarian and religious groups in the United States and abroad that had brought the anti-personnel mine ban to the center of the diplomatic arena. Critics contended that the exemptions Clinton wanted could end up unraveling the treaty. "The poor countries won't give up 'dumb' mines if we don't give up 'smart' mines," said Caleb Rossiter, director of Demilitarization for Democracy, a pro-ban organization.

The International Committee of the Red Cross, in an Aug. 26 statement, said "a total and immediate prohibition on the use of all anti-personnel mines is essential for the effectiveness and credibility of the treaty."

Clinton, however, stuck with Pentagon leaders on the issue, and the brass invoked combat necessity and the safety of U.S. troops as the basis for exempting Korea and the anti-tank mine packages from a total ban.

"If it were so simple as 'land mines or children,' it would be easy," said Robert L. Cowles, director of the Pentagon's Office of De-Mining and Anti-Personnel Land Mine Policy. "What the president has to balance is humanitarian concerns, international responsibilities and the obligation to protect our men and women in uniform."

In his Aug. 18 announcement, Clinton did indicate a significant shift in administration policy. As a result of its review of alternatives to anti-personnel mines ordered in May 1996, the U.S. dropped its demand that self-destructing mines outside Korea be exempt from the ban. Thus, the Pentagon agreed to scrap more than 8 million smart anti-personnel mines.

Citing unnamed Pentagon sources, ban proponents said this would leave only 1 million "packages," each containing a mix of anti-tank mines and the self-destructing anti-personnel mines intended to protect them.

Clinton Administration Wins No Changes in Oslo

Having belatedly taken a seat at the Oslo conference, the Clinton administration won none of the concessions it wanted in a final agreement.

Congressional supporters of a global land mine ban stepped up pressure on the White House Sept. 11 by introducing a bill to unilaterally ban new U.S. deployments of anti-personnel mines beginning in 2000. The measure had upward of 130 cosponsors.

Even as the lines of political confrontation seemed to harden, however, National Security Council staffer Robert G. Bell, the top White House aide on arms control issues, predicted that an agreement could still be reached.

"Faced with a fundamental choice [between] a treaty that the United States signs, that puts the United States on a specific glide path toward [eventually eliminating] all U.S. anti-personnel land mines . . . versus, on the other hand, a . . . simpler treaty that's available sooner but has large gaps in its coverage," Bell said Sept. 5, "a majority of the states now in Oslo would choose the former."

In Oslo, South African Ambassador J. Selibi, who chaired the negotiating conference, said he would not hold a roll call vote on the final draft. That meant the Clinton administration did not have to formally oppose the treaty.

U.S. Won't Sign Treaty

On Sept. 17, Clinton announced that the United States would not sign the treaty because it did not include U.S.-proposed exemptions principally affecting the Korean peninsula.

Although he endorsed the treaty's goal, Clinton insisted that mines remained essential to the safety of U.S. troops in circumstances in which they would not threaten innocent civilians: "There is a line that I simply cannot cross, and that line is the safety and security of our men and women in uniform," he said.

Clinton ordered the Pentagon to develop alternatives that would allow it to dispense with the use of anti-personnel mines after 2003, except in Korea for another three years. His order did not affect mixed systems. ■

Conventional Forces Treaty Amendment Approved

The Senate agreed unanimously May 14 to allow Russia to keep more weapons on its Baltic and Caucasian frontiers under the 1990 Conventional Forces in Europe (CFE) Treaty. The CFE Treaty amendment, which increased the numbers of tanks, cannons and other heavy weaponry Russia was allowed to deploy, was approved 100-0. *(Vote 67, p. S-14)*

However, the unanimous vote masked a controversy over an unrelated provision that Republicans insisted be included in the resolution of approval. The provision was related to the separate 1972 U.S.-Soviet treaty limiting anti-ballistic missile (ABM) defenses.

Russia Wins Shift in Arms Limits

The 1990 CFE Treaty limited Soviet deployments in the flank areas of the Baltic and Caucasian frontiers to prevent Moscow from intimidating its NATO neighbors — Norway to the northwest and Turkey to the southwest — with tanks and artillery pieces that it was required to withdraw from East Germany under the pact.

When the Soviet Union dissolved, its CFE weapons limits, including the special limits in the flank regions, were parceled out among the successor nations. Since the flank regions cut through parts of Russia and Ukraine, the two countries divided the weapons limits set for those areas.

Starting in 1994, however, both countries demanded changes in the agreement. Ukraine complained that it would have to build new bases in northern Ukraine to house forces then stationed in the south, where they were inside the flank region. Russia complained that it was allowed too few weapons in its turbulent territory north of the newly independent Caucasian republics of Georgia and Azerbaijan, a requirement it flatly refused to meet.

In May 1996, the 30 countries participating in the CFE Treaty, including the United States, agreed to amend the treaty to allow Russia to keep more weapons on the flank but also allow more inspections to guard against any threatening buildup.

Outlining the proposed "flanks agreement" during a Foreign Relations Committee hearing April 29, administration officials met some skeptical questions from senators of both parties who complained that the revision could make it easier for Russia to intimidate former Soviet states and satellites.

Gordon H. Smith, R-Ore., called the amendment "an acceptable first step" in adapting the CFE Treaty to the post-Soviet era. But he objected to "the embarrassing spectacle of Western concessions in the face of Russian arms control violations."

Under Secretary of Defense Walter Slocombe said the real choice was either "the new rules or . . . a breakdown of the flank part of the CFE, and probably a breakdown of the whole agreement."

Although the treaty amendment turned out to be relatively non-controversial, a May 15 deadline for approving it gave Republicans leverage to press Clinton to accept, as a rider on the resolution of approval, the unrelated provision regarding the ABM Treaty.

GOP Gets Concession on ABM Treaty

The Senate Foreign Relations Committee approved the CFE Treaty amendment May 8 on a 17-0 vote. But one of the 14 conditions accompanying the resolution of ratification required the president to obtain Senate approval for a proposed agreement to make former Soviet republics parties to the separate 1972 ABM Treaty.

The White House had maintained that the president had the power to decide, without Senate approval, which former Soviet republics inherited the Soviet obligations under the ABM pact. Belarus, Ukraine and Kazakhstan, as well as Russia, were expected to be recognized as parties to the pact as legal successors to the defunct Soviet Union.

But conservatives, who saw the ABM Treaty as an obstacle to deployment of a nationwide anti-missile defense system, insisted that "multilateralizing" the pact to include four former Soviet states, rather than just Russia, would make it harder to negotiate a more liberal limit on anti-missile systems. They contended that that amounted to a significant change in the treaty, which should be presented to the Senate as an amendment to the pact, requiring approval by a two-thirds majority.

The Clinton administration and leading Senate Democrats opposed the provision but accepted it at the last minute. ■

Test Ban Treaty Submitted For Senate Ratification

President Clinton officially sent the Comprehensive Test Ban Treaty to the Senate on Sept. 22, setting the stage for a showdown over whether to ban nuclear testing worldwide. But a Senate ratification vote on what Clinton called "the longest-sought, hardest-fought prize in the history of arms control" was not expected until well into 1998. With conservative foes already mobilized, it was clear that the White House would have to expend considerable capital if it was to muster the two-thirds vote needed for ratification.

Submitting the treaty one year after he became the first of 146 world leaders to sign it, Clinton declared he would push to see the treaty enter into force "as soon as possible." *(1996 Almanac, p. 8-17)*

But Joseph R. Biden Jr. of Delaware, ranking Democrat on the Senate Foreign Relations Committee and the administration's point man on arms control, said he was "not confident of anything right now." Biden said Committee Chairman Jesse Helms, R-N.C., was "agnostic to against" the treaty, though he gave assurances that he would not bottle the treaty up indefinitely. The chairman's caveat: "I recommend that you do not hold your breath."

Conservatives raised serious questions about the impact of a test ban on the long-term effectiveness of the nation's nuclear arsenal. And a wide assortment of committees moved to assert oversight jurisdiction — including Foreign Relations; Armed Services; the Government Affairs Subcommittee on International Security, Proliferation and Federal Services; and the Energy and Water Development Appropriations Subcommittee.

Moreover, some of the most ardent and influential allies in

the battle to ban nuclear tests — such as Mark O. Hatfield, R-Ore., Sam Nunn, D-Ga., and Jim Exon, D-Neb. — had retired. Moderate senators who had lent pivotal support to other arms control treaties — such as Richard G. Lugar, R-Ind., and John McCain, R-Ariz. — had voted against test ban-related legislation as recently as 1992. McCain said he would withhold judgment and give the administration a chance to make its case, but he made it clear the White House had some convincing to do. Lugar described himself as "undecided and skeptical."

"This will be big, and it will be a very important debate for the future of the country," said Sen. Jon Kyl, R-Ariz., an ardent opponent of the test ban, who had led the unsuccessful battle against the Chemical Weapons Convention. *(Chemical weapons, 8-13)*

Clinton Pushes High-Tech Alternatives

For two years Clinton had been setting the groundwork to counter the claim that agreeing to a global test ban was tantamount to unilateral nuclear disarmament. The Department of Energy was constructing a dazzling array of facilities designed to replace explosive testing with scientific and computational simulators.

The cost of Clinton's "science-based stockpile stewardship" initiative was estimated by the Congressional Budget Office to be $61 billion through 2010. Among the projects planned or under construction were:

➤ The National Ignition Facility, the world's most powerful laser, a $1.2 billion project under construction at the Lawrence Livermore National Laboratory in California. The aim was to create miniature thermonuclear explosions in a lab.

➤ The $199 million Dual-Axis Radiographic Hydrotest Facility, a high-explosives project at the Los Alamos National Laboratory in New Mexico designed to model the initial implosion of a nuclear warhead.

➤ A giant atom smasher at Los Alamos to help scientists analyze a warhead's nuclear materials, and another one to create tritium, a vital component of hydrogen warheads.

➤ A multi-laboratory effort to create supercomputers hundreds of times more powerful than the largest in existence. The computational component, known as the Accelerated Strategic Computing Initiative, was to take data created by other scientific experiments and combine them to model the effects of aging on existing nuclear weapons.

Much of the money for these projects was going to New Mexico's two nuclear weapons labs, the Los Alamos and Sandia facilities. Program critics said such lavish support was in part designed to sway one potentially powerful ally: New Mexico's Republican Sen. Pete V. Domenici. Domenici had given qualified support to the test ban treaty, but only if the stockpile stewardship program unfolded with maximum effect.

But treaty opponents remained unconvinced that all the high-tech gadgetry would suffice in ensuring the existing arsenal was safe and reliable, and that weapons scientists could design weapons for a modern arsenal.

"If Domenici's jujitsu would actually ensure we would have a stockpile that's [as] safe and reliable as we have now, more power to him," said Frank J. Gaffney Jr., a Reagan administration official who led the charge against Clinton-era arms control accords. "But the problem is, it won't work." ■

Other Defense-Related Legislation

Procedures and rules within the Pentagon and the armed forces came under scrutiny on several fronts in 1997.

Capitol Hill Postings

The Defense Department routinely violated its rules governing assignment of military officers and civilian employees to work on Capitol Hill, according to a report by Pentagon Inspector General Eleanor Hill that was circulated to congressional offices July 16.

Although the rules allowed officers to work only on committee staffs, many had been assigned to the offices of individual members. Few of these assignments had been approved by an assistant secretary of Defense, as was required. Hill's report did not address the question of whether officers detailed to Congress had improperly worked on partisan political tasks, as critics alleged.

Hill's investigation was sparked in 1996 by retiring Rep. Patricia Schroeder, D-Colo., who cited published reports that House Speaker Newt Gingrich, R-Ga., had used officers assigned to his staff for partisan work, a charge Gingrich denied. Sen. Charles E. Grassley, R-Iowa, also called for a probe, insisting that it cover the role of military detailees throughout Congress.

Pornography Ban

A federal district judge in New York ruled Jan. 22 that legislation enacted in 1996 barring the sale or rental of sexually explicit magazines or videos on military bases was unconstitutional. The ban, a provision of the fiscal 1997 defense authorization bill (PL 104-201), had been sponsored by Rep. Roscoe G. Bartlett, R-Md. *(1996 Almanac, p. 8-3)*

The ruling by U.S. District Judge Shira A. Scheindlin came in a suit against the Defense Department by Bob Guccione, the publisher of Penthouse magazine, and others. "In the context of our long and rich First Amendment tradition," the judge wrote, "it becomes clear that sexually explicit material cannot be banned from sale or rental at military exchanges merely because it is offensive."

The conservative Family Research Council called the judge's ruling "a miscarriage of justice." Retired Lt. Col. Robert Maginnis, director of the council's military readiness project, said, "News that the military must continue selling woman-demeaning smut sends the wrong message to traumatized women who understand the direct association between exposure to pornography and sexual misconduct."

Sexual Harassment

Responding to studies that found widespread sexual harassment in the Army, senior Army leaders on Sept. 11 announced an "action plan" aimed at requiring more careful screening of prospective drill instructors and other soldiers who had contact with new recruits. Also, recruits' basic training curriculum was to be expanded from eight to nine weeks, with the additional time allocated for instruction in ethics and moral values.

The plan also called for more extensive training of all Army leaders in human relations, in order to "eliminate all forms of harassment and discrimination, and develop a culture in which people treat one another with dignity and respect."

The action followed a 10-month review by a panel of senior Army officers and civilians, which concluded that sexual harassment was occurring "throughout the Army, crossing gender, rank and racial lines," and that job discrimination was even more pervasive.

The Army acted based on the panel's report and a separate study conducted by the Army's inspector general. Many of the problems diagnosed by those reports, as well as several of the remedial steps, paralleled findings and recommendations of a three-member task force of the House National Security Committee, led by Steve Buyer, R-Ind.

In a joint statement, Buyer, Tillie Fowler, R-Fla., and Jane Harman, D-Calif., commended Army leaders for an "exhaustive effort" to get to the roots of the service's sexual misconduct problem.

Army Secretary Togo D. West Jr. insisted that the stronger emphasis on ensuring that all personnel received proper respect did not mean that the service had "suddenly gone all warm and fuzzy." He said ensuring mutual respect among all ranks was vital to fostering the cohesion and esprit de corps that was critical to a unit's combat capability.

West had chartered the two studies in late 1996 after incidents were disclosed in which drill sergeants at some training bases raped and sexually abused enlisted women under their command.

Based on a survey of Army personnel who were neither recruits nor trainers, the senior review panel reported that 80 percent of Army men surveyed and 84 percent of women reported having experienced sexually inappropriate behavior — ranging from assault to obnoxious humor — within the previous year. But only 7 percent of the men and 22 percent of the women reported having experienced sexual harassment. The corresponding figures for recruits were similar.

"Inappropriate behaviors are commonplace throughout the Army," the panel concluded, adding: "Soldiers seem to accept such behaviors as a normal part of Army life."

West and Army Chief of Staff Gen. Dennis L. Reimer concurred with the review panel's conclusion that a considerable share of the responsibility for this state of affairs lay with an Army leadership that had become lax about the importance of emphasizing respectful treatment of all soldiers. "Passive leadership has allowed sexual harassment to persist; active leadership can bring about change to eradicate it," the panel concluded. ■

Cohen Wins Speedy Approval As New Defense Secretary

William S. Cohen — former Republican senator from Maine and member of the Senate Armed Services Committee — won near-effortless approval to serve as the new secretary of Defense in the second Clinton administration. Cohen was questioned by his former colleagues on the Armed Services Committee, approved 18-0, and then confirmed by the full Senate without dissent — all in one day.

The 99-0 floor vote Jan. 22 came after a brief debate in which senators lauded their just-retired colleague as a thoughtful and independent-minded voice for bipartisanship in defense policy. Cohen, the only Republican to join the Clinton Cabinet, was sworn in Jan. 24. *(Vote 2, p. S-2)*

During his confirmation hearing, Cohen forcefully assured the Armed Services Committee that U.S. ground troops would not remain in Bosnia beyond the deadline of mid-1998. A member of the committee for his entire 18-year Senate career (1980-97), Cohen had criticized President Clinton in 1996 for not seeking congressional approval before he extended the Bosnia mission beyond the initial deadline of December 1996.

Reaffirming a view that he and other Clinton critics had often expressed, Cohen told the Jan. 22 hearing that an arbitrary deadline was not an adequate substitute for an "exit strategy" — a plan detailing how U.S. forces would disengage from a risky deployment.

But in the Bosnia case, Cohen argued, such a deadline would prod European governments into preparing to assume the entire Bosnia peacekeeping mission once the U.S. involvement came to an end. "This is a signal, and a very strong message to our European friends," he said. "We are not going to be there" after mid-summer of 1998. "It was principally a European problem to be solved," he added, "and it's time for them to assume responsibility."

Cohen also said that one of his first actions as secretary would be to visit European capitals to drive home this message.

Cohen had been critical of Clinton on many policy issues, including when to build a national anti-missile defense system. Though one of the Senate's most liberal Republicans on domestic issues, Cohen's record on defense questions was solidly in the GOP mainstream.

But he assured the committee that he could work effectively within the Clinton team. "My record is one of bridging differences — not papering them over, but building consensus behind reasonable and responsible compromises," he said. "Uniformity of opinion within an administration is not an imperative, or even an ideal to be sought."

Use of U.S. Troops Abroad

Cohen emphasized during the hearing that he was predisposed to be cautious in recommending the use of military forces abroad. But he also argued that there were cases in which such deployments might be justified, even though vital U.S. interests were not immediately jeopardized.

Such cases might arise, he said, if a crisis of less-than-vital importance had the potential to become a more serious threat. Bosnia was such a case, Cohen said. "If the war was allowed to continue to spread . . . if it involved Greece or Turkey, we might very well find that we had a vital national security interest that had been threatened and be required to respond with a much greater force," he said.

Cohen also said there were circumstances under which it was appropriate to use U.S. forces to alleviate humanitarian crises overseas if, for instance, lives were threatened on so large a scale that civilian agencies could not cope.

But he said that U.S. troops should be committed to such situations only if a careful analysis concluded that the benefits to the United States likely would exceed the cost. He also emphasized that before troops were deployed abroad on any mission, the president should consult with Congress in an effort to secure its endorsement.

He said he believed such consultation was constitutionally required, though he acknowledged that the point was disputed. He also conceded that the War Powers Resolution, which was intended to require congressional approval of deployments likely to involve U.S. forces in combat, was practically moot, since no president of either party had conceded its constitutionality, and Congress had never forced a court test of the issue.

But aside from the constitutional issue, Cohen argued that it would be politically prudent for a president to seek congressional approval of risky overseas troop deployments to shore up the national commitment to the mission against the domestic opposition that likely would arise if U.S. forces began to incur casualties. It was essential, he maintained, "that once we commit forces to a region of hostilities and danger, that . . . when the going gets tough, we're still there. Otherwise," he warned, "we will affect our credibility for years to come."

Missile Defense, Chemical Arms

Cohen had severely criticized Clinton for vetoing a defense authorization bill in 1995 over a GOP-backed provision intended to accelerate deployment of a nationwide defense against ballistic missiles. But in the Jan. 22 hearing, he said he was satisfied that subsequent changes in the administration's anti-missile defense program, including an increase in its projected budget, would meet many of his demands. *(1995 Almanac, p. 9-3)*

He also strongly endorsed the treaty banning chemical weapons that the Senate had shelved the previous fall after strong Republican opposition surfaced. Noting that the United States was slated to dismantle its own chemical weapons arsenal by 2004, Cohen said it made sense to approve the pact so that its inspection rules, intended to make it harder for countries to maintain hidden chemical arsenals, would go into force, and also to ensure that U.S. officials would be part of the treaty's international inspection team. *(Chemical weapons, p. 8-13)* ■

Other Defense, Foreign Policy Appointments

In addition to confirming William S. Cohen as secretary of Defense, the Senate endorsed President Clinton's choices to fill several other key military and civilian defense posts in 1997.

Gen. Shelton Confirmed To Head Joint Chiefs

Gen. Henry H. Shelton won voice vote approval from the Senate on Sept. 16 to succeed Gen. John M. Shalikashvili as chairman of the Joint Chiefs of Staff. Shalikashvili's term concluded at the end of September.

The Armed Services Committee had approved the nomination Sept. 9, following a hearing in which members of both parties lauded the 33-year Army veteran.

Shelton became the third Army officer in a row to serve in the top Pentagon spot and the first chairman whose military career was rooted in the special forces — elite units trained for missions of clandestine reconnaissance, guerrilla warfare and quasi-political dealings with foreign military forces and local populations.

He had served exclusively with special forces and light infantry, with no assignments to the Europe-oriented armored units that dominated the Army between the end of the Vietnam War and the collapse of the Soviet Union. His experience in the top ranks was heavily weighted toward combat assignments rather than staff offices. In the 14 years since he was promoted to colonel, he had been stationed in Washington, D.C., for only two years.

In 1991, Shelton helped lead a massive helicopter-borne assault far behind enemy lines to seal off a possible escape route for Iraqi forces in Kuwait. Three years later, he commanded U.S. forces entering Haiti, quickly shifting the operation from a combat assault to a peaceful occupation when negotiations with the ruling military junta produced a last-minute agreement. At the time Clinton tapped him for chairman, he was commander in chief of all special forces.

During the confirmation hearing, Georgia Democrat Max Cleland, himself a wounded Vietnam War veteran, called Shelton "the right man at the right time for the right job." Cleland said Shelton's background and experience would be useful in dealing with threats to U.S. security from terrorists, rogue states and drug cartels.

Although there was no controversy over the selection of Shelton, Senate action on the nomination was delayed for several days by Oregon Democrat Ron Wyden, who demanded that the Air Force reopen its investigation of the 1996 crash of a C-130 cargo plane in Oregon that killed 10 people. Wyden lifted his objection after the Air Force agreed to set up a special investigative panel.

Clinton initially offered the chairmanship to Air Force Gen. Joseph W. Ralston, the vice chairman of the Joint Chiefs. Ralston withdrew from consideration after it was disclosed that he had been involved in an adulterous affair in the early 1980s.

Gen. Clark Takes Top Europe Post

The Senate confirmed Army Gen. Wesley K. Clark, a specialist in armored combat with experience in field command, diplomacy and Washington policy-making, as the next commander in chief of U.S. forces in Europe. Clark was approved by voice vote July 9.

The 52-year-old Clark succeeded Gen. George Joulwan, who was retiring. Clark also succeeded Joulwan as NATO's top military commander, or Supreme Allied Commander, Europe. The alliance post, which required unanimous approval by NATO members, had always been held by a U.S. officer.

Clark's aptitude for high-level domestic and international politics and his ability to speak Russian were expected to serve him well in the NATO post, where the agenda would be topped by efforts to bring Eastern European countries into the alliance while remaining on good working terms with Russia, which bitterly opposed NATO's planned enlargement.

At the same time, NATO's next military chief could have to superintend the retrenchment, and possible withdrawal, of alliance military forces in Bosnia, where they were policing the Dayton peace accords.

Before taking the new post, Clark was commander in chief of the U.S. Southern Command, which ran U.S. military operations in Latin America south of Mexico. In 1995, he was the senior Pentagon member of the U.S. team led by former Assistant Secretary of State Richard C. Holbrooke that negotiated the Bosnia peace accords in Dayton, Ohio.

He was the top-rated cadet in his West Point graduating class of 1966 and then spent two years at Oxford University as a Rhodes Scholar, finishing the year Clinton arrived. Reportedly, the two men were only casually acquainted, until recently.

A wounded and decorated veteran of Vietnam, Clark had moved up a ladder of command assignments, commanding in turn a tank battalion, a brigade and, in 1992-94, the First Cavalry Division. Along the way, he also held key positions in the Army's combat training program.

But in other assignments, Clark was exposed to domestic and international politics while still a relatively junior officer. As a White House fellow in 1975-76, he worked for the director of the Office of Management and Budget, a position similar to one held a few years earlier by another polished and politically savvy young officer — Colin L. Powell Jr. In 1978-79, Clark got a crash course in NATO political and military issues while serving as an assistant to then-

European Commander Gen. Alexander M. Haig Jr.

In 1994, Clark became the chief strategic planner for the Joint Staff — in effect, the chief long-range planner for then-Joint Chiefs of Staff Chairman Gen. John M. Shalikashvili. In that capacity, Clark participated in the Dayton peace negotiations.

Deputy Secretary Slot Filled by Hamre

The Senate confirmed veteran congressional defense staffer John J. Hamre as deputy secretary of Defense by voice vote July 24. The vote came after Iowa Republican Charles E. Grassley, who had strongly criticized the nomination, announced he would not oppose it, after Hamre agreed to change a contract payment procedure which, according to the Pentagon's inspector general, was illegal.

Hamre, who had been under secretary of Defense and comptroller since 1993, succeeded John P. White in the Pentagon's second-ranking civilian job.

A cheerful bear of a man well over 6 feet tall, the 47-year-old Hamre had parlayed technical expertise, political savvy and self-deprecating wit into a gilt-edged reputation in most quarters on Capitol Hill over a career spanning nearly two decades.

Hamre joined the Congressional Budget Office in 1978 as a defense analyst, eventually becoming deputy director of the agency's division dealing with defense and foreign policy issues. In 1984, he joined the Senate Armed Services Committee staff, quickly establishing himself as an influential adviser to Georgia Democrat Sam Nunn (1972-1997) on weapons and budget issues. He also served as the committee's liaison to the Appropriations Committee.

When he became under secretary late in 1993, Hamre was the first Pentagon comptroller to supervise the Program Analysis and Evaluation organization, thus making him overseer of both budget and weapons issues. He emerged quickly as a key member of the department's civilian leadership.

William J. Perry, who became Defense secretary early in 1994, capitalized on Hamre's grasp of budget detail and his reservoir of good will in Congress by having the comptroller join Perry and Joint Chiefs of Staff Chairman Gen. John M. Shalikashvili as a third witness before congressional committees.

Hamre had played a key role in efforts to streamline Pentagon management, for example by reducing the number of accounting offices from 333 to 21. He occasionally highlighted his effort to reform the dozens of separate payroll systems by recounting the frequency with which the existing systems made mistakes in senior officials' monthly paychecks.

In May, Defense Secretary William S. Cohen named Hamre chairman of a high-level task force to make recommendations by the end of the year on additional reforms in Defense Department management.

Grassley, a frequent critic of Pentagon financial management, launched his attack on Hamre's nomination in late January. At issue was the handling of so-called progress payments doled out to contractors over the course of a contract. Citing reports by the Pentagon's inspector general, Grassley complained that departmental purchasing officials routinely violated the law when they made progress payments on contracts that were funded from more than one appropriation. Specifically, he said, officials were short-circuiting the congressional appropriations process by making payments out of appropriations accounts without ensuring that they matched the particular piece of work for which payment was being made.

In a July 22 meeting with Grassley and senior members of the Armed Services Committee, Hamre agreed to changes in the management of progress payments. ■

State Department Authorization Stalls

A two-year, $12 billion State Department authorization bill (HR 1757) that included key initiatives from both President Clinton and congressional Republicans fell victim to a dispute between Congress and the White House over abortion restrictions on international family planning aid.

The centerpiece of the bill was a plan negotiated by Senate Foreign Relations Committee Chairman Jesse Helms, R-N.C., and Joseph R. Biden Jr. of Delaware, the panel's ranking Democrat, to pay off $819 million in U.S. debts to the United Nations in return for sweeping U.N. management reforms.

The bill also included a restructuring of part of the nation's foreign policy apparatus that Clinton had agreed to in April. Though modest compared to his original proposal, the changes were a top a priority for Helms. The plan called for merging two agencies — the U.S. Information Agency (USIA) and the Arms Control and Disarmament Agency (ACDA) into the State Department. Portions of the Agency for International Development (AID), which ran the nation's foreign aid programs, would also be folded into State.

With the Helms-Biden deal in place, the bill sailed through the Senate in June. But when it came time to reconcile it with a version passed by the House, the momentum collapsed.

The House and Senate versions differed significantly in a number of areas — for example, the House bill included a more modest foreign affairs reorganization provision and no payment plan for U.N. debts. But the biggest dispute was over a House effort to bar aid to international family planning groups that promoted, performed or supported abortion. The provision had been added to the bill on the House floor by Christopher H. Smith, R-N.J.

Though Helms was a strong proponent of the anti-abortion policy, he desperately wanted the issue removed from the authorization measure and dealt with elsewhere. Any bill that included the restriction had an uncertain fate in the Senate and was sure to draw a presidential veto.

But House Republicans were adamant. "The House will not give in on this issue, period," said Republican Whip Tom DeLay of Texas.

An attempt by Smith to include similar abortion language in the fiscal 1998 foreign operations appropriations bill (HR 2159), had stalled that measure as well, and negotiations over the two bills became intertwined. *(Appropriations, p. 9-37)*

GOP conservatives were willing to go along with the U.N. payments, the State Department reorganization plan and a special $3.5 billion appropriation for the International Monetary Fund (IMF) sought by Clinton — but only if the president accepted the abortion restrictions on international family planning aid.

Clinton refused, and when the GOP leadership was forced

to compromise on the abortion provision in the foreign operations spending bill, rank-and-file conservatives refused to concede on the U.N. money, the State Department reorganization and the IMF funds. As a result, the authorization bill collapsed.

BOXSCORE

Fiscal 1998-99 State Department Authorization — HR 1757 (S 903, HR 1486). The legislation included provisions to authorize about $12 billion for the State Department and related agencies over two years, pay $819 million in debts to the United Nations, and restructure the U.S. foreign policy apparatus.

Reports: H Rept 105-94 (HR 1486), S Rept 105-28.

KEY ACTION

June 11 — House passed HR 1757 by voice vote.

June 17 — Senate passed HR 1757, 90-5, after substituting the text of S 903.

Background

The disputed abortion provision was an attempt to reinstitute the so-called Mexico City policy. Formulated by the Reagan administration in 1984 and continued by the Bush administration, the policy barred aid to groups that practiced or advocated abortion, even if they used their own money to do so. (Since 1973, U.S. law had outlawed direct funding of overseas abortions.)

One of Clinton's first acts as president in January 1993 was to overturn the policy. Since then, Republicans had sought to reinstate the ban legislatively, stepping up their efforts when they took control of Congress in 1995. Smith, who led the anti-abortion forces in the House, argued that providing U.S. funding to such groups simply allowed them to use their own money to perform or promote the use of abortion. *(1993 Almanac, p. 348).*

The Helms-Biden Breakthrough

The abortion deadlock scuttled an agreement between Helms and Biden that essentially would have given Clinton the U.N. money he wanted, while giving Helms at least a partial restructuring of foreign policy agencies.

- **U.N. Debts.** The Clinton administration had been trying for several years to persuade Congress to pay off U.S. debts to the United Nations, but lawmakers had resisted, insisting that the organization must first put its financial house in order.

The total amount owed had long been a matter of some dispute, largely because the State Department and the United Nations used different formulas for calculating the debts.

The U.N. said the United States owed $1.3 billion, while the administration put the debt at about $1 billion. The administration then subtracted another $106 million for what it said were U.N. debts to the United States for providing support for U.N. peacekeeping missions and for other debts that the United States had essentially renounced. Helms used different assumptions but arrived at the same bottom line.

Most of the U.S. debt payment was ultimately to go toward repaying nations, such as Great Britain and France, that had supplied troops for U.N. peacekeeping missions, including the operation in Bosnia.

Under the plan negotiated by Helms and Biden, the United States would pay the $819 million, but only if the United Nations cut its staff, slashed its budget and took a number of other actions, including reducing the U.S. share of its budget from 25 percent to 20 percent.

- **Reorganization.** Helms had been crusading to reorganize and downsize the foreign affairs bureaucracy since 1995, when he took over as chairman of the Senate Foreign Relations Committee. Initially, he tried to fold the three independent agencies, including all of AID, into the State Department, a plan that was flatly rejected by the administration. Helms later modified his proposal to require the consolidation of only one of the agencies with State, but Clinton still rejected it, vetoing a revised State Department authorization bill in April 1996. *(1995 Almanac, p. 10-3; 1996 Almanac, p. 9-3)*

With a greater spirit of negotiation prevailing in 1997, an inter-agency team of administration officials worked to come up with a reorganization plan that Clinton could endorse. On April 17, Clinton signed off on a proposal that went much further than the measure he had rejected in 1996. Under the plan:

- **ACDA.** The arms control agency — a relatively small organization with an annual budget of about $40 million would be merged with the State Department over the next year. The agency's director would become under secretary of State for arms control.
- **USIA.** The information agency — a larger outfit with an annual budget of about $1 billion — would be consolidated with the State Department over a two-year period.
- **AID.** The huge foreign aid agency, a prime target of Helms' downsizing efforts, would remain independent. AID's budget was about $3.4 billion a year. The agency's administrator would report to the secretary of State, and many of its administrative functions would be combined with the department.

The administration cautioned against expecting any significant financial savings or personnel downsizing from the plan, saying its main goal was to eliminate longstanding managerial and administrative redundancies.

The administration's change of course was the result of a variety of factors, including Vice President Al Gore's longstanding determination to "reinvent government" and Secretary of State Madeleine K. Albright's desire to reshape the nation's foreign policy apparatus to meet post-Cold War challenges.

But Clinton also clearly wanted to extend an olive branch to Helms. The president's decision came on the same day that Helms agreed to let a long-stalled chemical weapons treaty reach the Senate floor. Both sides denied there was an explicit linkage between the two developments. *(Chemical weapons, p. 8-13)*

House Subcommittee

On April 10, the House International Relations Subcommittee on International Operations and Human Rights gave voice vote approval to a two-year, $12.6 billion version of the bill (HR 1253). Smith, who chaired the subcommittee, said the measure would fund "99 percent" of the spending level requested by the administration for the State Department, ACDA and other foreign policy operations.

However, the legislation was essentially silent on two major subjects — the U.S. debts to the U.N. and the reorganization of the foreign affairs bureaucracy. Smith said he hoped the bill would eventually serve as the vehicle for compromises on those issues, both of which were tied up in negotiations with the White House.

And, while the bill was drafted to garner bipartisan support, it contained provisions the administration was certain to oppose, including $100 million over the following two fiscal years to move the U.S. Embassy in Israel from Tel Aviv to Jerusalem and a requirement that all U.S. government publications identify Jerusalem as Israel's capital.

Clinton had allowed a bill requiring that the U.S. Embassy be moved to Jerusalem by mid-1999 to become law (PL 104-45) without his signature in 1995, but the administration had yet to start constructing a new embassy. *(1995 Almanac, p. 10-23)*

The State Department bill also specified $20 million for a program to combat child labor abroad and included a proposal to authorize the secretary of State to eliminate convicted felons from the ranks of State Department employees.

House Full Committee

The full House International Relations Committee gave voice vote approval May 6 to a broader version of the bill (HR 1486 — H Rept 105-94) that combined the subcommittee provisions with a two-year authorization of foreign aid programs. That brought the bill's total to $32.4 billion — $16.4 billion in fiscal 1998 and $16 billion in fiscal 1999. Most of that, about $20.1 billion, was for foreign assistance.

Benjamin A. Gilman, R-N.Y., the committee chairman, saw the combined package as offering the best hope for getting a foreign aid authorization bill enacted for the first time since 1985. Gilman also assiduously courted the administration and panel Democrats. The result was a high degree of bipartisanship that contrasted sharply with the previous Congress, when Gilman and other committee Republicans rammed through a partisan bill slashing funds for international programs and challenging Clinton's foreign policy.

Before approving the bill, the committee gave voice vote approval to an amendment by Gilman adding $357 million over two fiscal years, bringing the fiscal 1998 level for international programs to within about $100 million of Clinton's request.

The sharpest debate during the markup, which began April 30, came on an issue that had divided Congress for years — whether to provide aid to the United Nations Population Fund. Smith had included a provision in the bill barring any funds for the U.N. agency unless it terminated all activities in China, whose government had been widely condemned for its policies of forced abortion and sterilization.

Tom Campbell, R-Calif., offered an amendment to strike Smith's provision, arguing that the population fund had largely pulled out of China.

Smith disputed that assertion, but Campbell prevailed. Three other Republicans supported the amendment, which the committee adopted 23-16. The amendment authorized $25 million each in fiscal years 1998 and 1999 for the U.N. group but barred the agency from expending any funds in China. It also included other conditions on use of the money.

Other Committee Amendments

In action on other amendments, the panel:

➤ Adopted by voice vote a proposal by Gary L. Ackerman, D-N.Y., to modify the bill's restrictions on United Nations Development Program activities in Myanmar (formerly Burma). The bill would have given pro-democracy dissidents in Myanmar the authority to decide which projects were funded by the U.N. agency. The amendment changed that to require only that those groups be consulted on the projects.

➤ Adopted by voice vote language by Ileana Ros-Lehtinen, R-Fla., a passionate critic of Fidel Castro's regime, to require that the administration submit quarterly reports on its implementation of a 1996 law (PL 104-114) imposing stiff sanctions on nations investing in Cuba. *(1996 Almanac p. 9-6)*

➤ Adopted, 19-15, a proposal by Ackerman to eliminate a section of the bill prohibiting aid to countries that supported U.S. positions in the U.N. General Assembly less than 25 percent of the time. Ackerman said the provision, inserted by Bill Goodling, R-Pa., would affect four countries — Cuba, North Korea, India and Syria — but that its impact would be felt only by India because it was the only U.S. aid recipient in the group.

➤ Adopted, 24-18, a proposal by Lee H. Hamilton, D-Ind., to end the annual drug certification process, which had been embroiled in controversy since Clinton certified Mexico as cooperating in the war on drugs, despite compelling evidence to the contrary

➤ Adopted, by voice vote, an amendment by Dana Rohrabacher, R-Calif., to bar U.S. aid to Russia unless it called off a proposed sale of advanced missiles to China. The panel agreed, 22-14, to a modification by Henry J. Hyde, R-Ill., that would allow the president to waive the restriction in the national security interest.

➤ Rejected, 13-28, an amendment by Mark Sanford, R-S.C., that would have cut the bill's funding by about $220 million in each of the two fiscal years. An earlier Sanford amendment aimed at reducing funding by nearly $3 billion in each of the two fiscal years, fell 12-29.

➤ Rejected, 21-23, an amendment by Cynthia A. McKinney, D-Ga., that would have established a "code of conduct" for U.S. arms transfers to foreign governments.

➤ Rejected, 9-32, a proposal by Campbell to reduce aid to Egypt and Israel by $2.5 million and boost funding for development aid to poor nations in Africa and elsewhere.

The bill also included provisions requiring that the administration establish a special envoy with ambassadorial rank for Tibet, which had been occupied by China for decades. If enacted, such a provision was certain to provoke outrage from Beijing.

Another provision proposed capping annual aid to Russia at $95 million — approximately the same level provided in fiscal 1997 — if Moscow followed through with plans to provide nuclear technology to Iran and Cuba. The administration had requested about $242 million for Russia in fiscal 1998.

House Floor Action

In an unusual move, House Republican leaders jettisoned the committee-approved bill in favor of a hastily drafted measure (HR 1757) designed to draw support from conservative Republicans. The new, $12.2 billion bill included the committee provisions on the State Department and related agencies, but it dropped nearly all the foreign aid authorization. The House passed HR 1757 by voice vote June 11.

The House also passed a second bill (HR 1758) endorsing the expansion of NATO to include the emerging democracies of Central and Eastern Europe. The text, approved on a routine voice vote, was added to HR 1757, once that bill had passed. *(NATO, p. 8-23)*

The centerpiece of HR 1757 was language directing a major reorganization of the foreign policy agencies along the lines agreed to by the Clinton administration. An amendment offered by Hamilton, which would have provided the president with broader latitude in carrying out the consolidation plan, failed, 202-224. *(Vote 160, p. H-54)*

The bill still did not include authorization for back payments to the United Nations.

It did contain many of the foreign policy provisions from the committee bill, including $100 million over two years to move the U.S. embassy in Israel to Jerusalem and the requirement that government publications refer to Jerusalem as the capital of Israel. It also proposed reducing funding for the International Atomic Energy Agency by the amount it spent to support nuclear programs in Cuba.

Setback for Authorizers

The move by GOP leaders to scuttle the committee-approved bill — a decision enforced by the Rules Committee during a contentious session on June 3 — was a rebuke of Gilman's leadership and drew heavy criticism from Democrats. Hamilton called it "an insult to the House International Relations Committee."

But Republicans insisted that the original bill faced certain defeat, largely because it was too generous to the administration. "It was obvious this would never pass the House," Rules Committee Chairman Gerald B.H. Solomon, R-N.Y., said of Gilman's bill.

The action, which marked another in a string of setbacks for the International Relations Committee, came at the behest of senior members of the House Appropriations Committee, who used blunt language in demanding that GOP leaders completely restructure the bill.

In a letter to Speaker Newt Gingrich, R-Ga., and other GOP leaders, Robert L. Livingston, R-La., the Appropriations Committee chairman, and Sonny Callahan, R-Ala., who chaired the Foreign Operations Subcommittee, charged that the International Relations Committee had essentially punted to the appropriators a number of tough policy issues, such as whether to attach conditions to aid for Ukraine and whether to authorize funds for the beleaguered Overseas Private Investment Corporation.

"We will do our job," the letter said. "We expect the authorizers to do theirs."

In addition, Callahan and Livingston objected to the high spending levels in the bill. "It is a near carbon copy of the administration request," they wrote.

Abortion Debate

In a reprise of struggles from previous years, Smith once again proposed banning all funding for international organizations that used their own funds to promote or perform abortions.

Campbell and James C. Greenwood, R-Pa., offered a substitute amendment that would have eliminated Smith's restrictions. They said the funding ban would result in the elimination of family planning programs in poor, overpopulated nations. Their alternative failed, 200-218. The House then adopted Smith's amendment, 232-189. Administration officials warned that it would provoke a presidential veto. *(Votes 167, 168, p. H-56)*

Other Amendments

In action on other amendments, the House:

➤ Defeated a proposal by Ron Paul, R-Texas, to require the United States to withdraw from the United Nations. Paul's amendment was rejected by an overwhelming vote of 54-369. But several senior Republicans, including DeLay and Dan Burton of Indiana, chairman of the Government Reform and Oversight Committee, supported the proposal. *(Vote 163, p. H-54)*

➤ Defeated, 176-244, a proposal by Cliff Stearns, R-Fla., to make Congress, rather than the secretary of State, responsible for deciding whether the United Nations had implemented management reforms. *(Vote 164, p. H-54)*

➤ Agreed to restrict funding to TV Marti, which beamed programs to Cuba. David E. Skaggs, D-Colo., argued for cutting off the funds, saying that because of jamming by the Cuban government, few people in that country saw the broadcasts.

Lincoln Diaz-Balart, R-Fla., offered a perfecting amendment to cut off funding for TV Marti, but only if the president certified that continuing the program was not in the national interest. Diaz-Balart's amendment carried on a 271-155 vote, and the revised amendment was then adopted by voice vote. *(Vote 159, p. H-52)*

➤ Adopted, 244-184, an amendment by Rohrabacher to restrict aid to Russia in an attempt to block Moscow's proposed transfer of SS-N-22 missiles to China. *(Vote 200, p. H-66)*

The latter stages of the House debate on the bill were dominated by a spat over a minor provision dealing with Cuba. On June 4, Jose E. Serrano, D-N.Y., a sharp critic of U.S. policy toward Cuba, had slipped in an amendment ordering the State Department to compile quarterly reports on complaints by the Cuban government against the actions of U.S. citizens.

Serrano's proposal was a tit-for-tat response to Ros-Lehtinen's amendment requiring that the administration file quarterly reports on its implementation of the 1996 Cuba sanctions law.

Ros-Lehtinen said she would demand a roll-call vote on Serrano's amendment, which had initially been approved by voice vote. But Serrano, who had fought with Ros-Lehtinen and other anti-Castro lawmakers in the past, decided to up the ante. He demanded roll-call votes on 21 other previously adopted amendments, tying up the House for hours. Only one vote was reversed — on Serrano's own amendment. It was defeated 141-287. *(Vote 191, p. H-62)*

Senate Committee

On June 12, the Senate Foreign Relations Committee approved a $12 billion, two-year State Department authorization bill (S 903 — S Rept 105-28), which included the deal struck by Helms and Biden on paying off most U.S. debts to the United Nations. The bill also included Helms' plan to consolidate foreign affairs agencies, which was still somewhat stronger than the plan agreed to by Clinton. The bill was approved by a vote of 14-4.

The dramatic breakthrough achieved by Helms and Biden after lengthy negotiations overshadowed House passage of HR 1757 the previous day.

Repaying U.N. Debts

The Helms-Biden agreement provided for payment over the following three years of $819 million in back debts to the United Nations, but only if that organization took a number of actions, including reducing the U.S. share of its budget from 25 percent to 20 percent. The world body would have to accept the $819 million as payment in full. It also would have to agree to implement a "negative growth budget" and permit Congress' General Accounting Office to audit its programs.

Responding to longstanding conservative fears that the United Nations represented a threat to U.S. sovereignty, the bill asserted "the supremacy of the United States Constitution" and prohibited the U.N. from establishing a standing army.

During the markup, Helms and Biden stood together against critics of the U.N. plan, led by Indiana Republican Richard G. Lugar, who contended that the United States had an obligation to pay its debts fully to the organization without imposing conditions. Failing to do so, he said, would weaken the U.N. and strain relations with U.S. allies in Europe.

Lugar proposed to authorize the $819 million in payments, with "no strings attached," over two years instead of three. But with the administration supporting the Helms-Biden plan, he acknowledged that his was a "Don Quixote effort." The committee tabled (killed) Lugar's amendment, 12-6.

U.N. Secretary-General Kofi Annan told a press briefing at the organization's New York headquarters that he hoped the plan would be changed, adding that "as far as positions of principle are concerned, I am 100 percent with Sen. Lugar." Other officials said privately that it would be enormously difficult to persuade the U.N. General Assembly, where there had long been considerable anti-American sentiment, to roll back the U.S. share of the budget from 25 percent to 20 percent.

Reorganization Plan

The second major issue debated by the committee was the proposed reorganization of the foreign affairs bureaucracy.

Like the House bill, S 903 proposed consolidating the arms control agency and USIA, along with parts of AID, into the State Department. But it went further by seeking to fold more of AID into State and requiring that foreign aid be funded through the State Department rather than through AID. The House bill adhered more closely to Clinton's approach.

Paul S. Sarbanes, D-Md., attempted to strike the reorganization section, saying it would impose a detailed organizational blueprint on the administration. Biden broke with many of his fellow Democrats in opposing the amendment. "This is a package," Biden said of the bill.

For his part, Helms, a harsh critic of AID and foreign aid generally, regretted that the consolidation plan didn't go further. "If I had my way, we would abolish AID entirely and start all over again," he said.

Sarbanes' amendment was rejected, 4-14.

Senate Floor Action

The Senate passed HR 1757 by a vote of 90-5 on June 17, after substituting the text of its two-year, $12 billion State Department authorization bill (S 903). *(Vote 105, p. S-20)*

Passage was virtually assured once Helms, a fierce critic of the United Nations, gave his seal of approval, making the bill palatable for other GOP conservatives, many of whom were normally leery of voting any funds for the United Nations. The only "no" votes came from Democrats Sarbanes, Jeff Bingaman of New Mexico, Robert C. Byrd of West Virginia, Tom Harkin of Iowa and Paul Wellstone of Minnesota.

The only challenge to the U.N. provision came from Lugar, who found himself in the unenviable position of trying to derail an initiative backed by leading conservatives, Biden and the administration. Lugar echoed the criticisms he raised during the committee markup, charging that the bill would force the U.N. into humiliating concessions and would fall far short of fully funding the U.S. debts to that organization.

As expected, Lugar's amendment was easily defeated, 25-73. *(Vote 102, p. S-20)*

Biden and Helms also teamed up to quash an amendment by Russell D. Feingold, D-Wis., to put U.S.-government broadcasting operations, such as Radio Free Europe and the recently established Radio Free Asia, into the State Department, along with USIA. The proposal was rejected, 21-74. *(Vote 104, p. S-20)*

The Senate adopted, 98-0, a noncontroversial amendment by Mike DeWine, R-Ohio, to bar Haitians involved in political violence at home from entering the United States. It also approved, 96-0, a nonbinding amendment by Robert F. Bennett, R-Utah, urging Clinton to sanction China for its sale of missile technology to Iran. *(Votes 101, 103, p. S-20)*

As the bill headed into conference, the big question was whether Helms' imprimatur would be sufficient to win over the many hard-core U.N. opponents in the House.

Conference

Four months after the sweeping State Department authorization bill went to conference, Congress adjourned for the year with no agreement on the legislation. It remained stalled over provisions on abortion and family planning attached to the House version.

The conference opened in late July and resumed when lawmakers returned from the August recess. But conferees could not find a way past the stubborn abortion dispute, which was also paralyzing work on the foreign operations spending bill.

The provision created an odd situation in which abortion foes such as Helms and House appropriator Callahan each struggled to get the issue attached to someone else's bill.

Faced with little progress in breaking the deadlock, Helms and Biden met with Senate Majority Leader Trent Lott, R-Miss., seeking his help in persuading Gingrich to find some compromise with Smith. The Senate also pressed Gilman to craft a solution.

But the House Republican leadership and a majority of GOP members made it clear they did not intend to budge on either bill. In a closed-door meeting Oct. 6 in the Speaker's office, Callahan and Livingston were outnumbered by about 20 GOP lawmakers who refused to drop the issue from the spending bill.

The next day, the House voted 233-194 to instruct appropriations conferees to insist on the restrictions on international family planning assistance. DeLay and Majority Leader Dick Armey, R-Texas, spoke in favor of the motion. In a clear signal of his support, Gingrich broke with the House custom of the Speaker abstaining from votes to cast his ballot for the motion. *(Vote 496, p. H-150)*

"We will not back down. We will not back away. And we just dare the Senate to stop us in our quest," said DeLay.

On Oct. 8, the House voted 236-190 for a motion by Callahan to instruct House conferees on the authorization bill to insist on the abortion restrictions. *(Vote 506, p. H-154)*

Unwilling to see their agreement collapse, Helms and Biden persuaded appropriators to include major elements of it in a compromise version of the foreign operations bill circulated Nov. 5. The proposal included language worked out by Helms, Biden and Albright to consolidate the foreign policy agencies, and it would have set in motion the payment of $819 million in U.S. debts to the United Nations in exchange for reforms by the world body.

But, in a new twist, the compromise was rejected by moderate House Republicans who opposed the abortion language or saw no point in guaranteeing a White House veto.

In the final days of the session, GOP leaders dropped the abortion language in order to get the spending bill enacted. Forced to back down, conservative House Republicans then rejected the plan to repay U.N. debts and reorganize the foreign policy apparatus.

"This was one time where the administration and Senate worked together," Helms said the week of Oct. 6 in bemoaning the intractable situation. "It's just defeating. But this too will pass." ■

China Critics Lose on Trade Vote

The House handed the Clinton administration and a powerful array of business interests a lopsided victory June 24 as it voted to extend China's trade status for another year.

There was never much doubt that China would retain its most-favored-nation (MFN) status, which had been renewed annually since 1980. But China's opponents — a coalition of conservative Republicans and liberal Democrats — had hoped for a close vote to register their dissatisfaction with Beijing's actions in areas ranging from weapons proliferation and trade to Taiwan and human rights.

Under MFN, Chinese goods entering the United States received the same low tariffs as imports from nearly every other nation.

The annual debate over China's MFN trade status featured several new elements in 1997. Many lawmakers were disturbed by allegations that China had tried to buy political influence in the 1996 U.S. elections, and several leading religious conservatives, alarmed by the alleged mistreatment of missionaries in China, joined the campaign against renewing MFN. *(Campaign finance probe, p. 1-20)*

But despite the persistent uneasiness over the state of Sino-American relations, a solid majority in the House felt that China was too large and too economically important to isolate. Supporters of unfettered trade with China contended that revoking MFN would not only harm U.S. businesses but also devastate the economy of Hong Kong, which reverted to Chinese sovereignty July 1. *(Hong Kong, this page)*

China's critics, particularly those in the House, vowed that the MFN vote would not be the last word, and they held true to their promise in the waning days of the session when the House approved nine bills on China-related issues. *(China bills, p. 8-38)*

Background

President Clinton kicked off the annual debate over U.S. policy toward China on May 19, announcing that he would once again renew Beijing's MFN trading status.

A diverse coalition of China critics, including religious groups, conservatives, human rights activists and labor unions, launched a campaign to overturn the decision but conceded it would be an uphill battle.

The opponents faced a tight timetable imposed by the Jackson-Vanik amendment to the 1974 Trade Act (PL 93-618), which governed the MFN debate on China and required both chambers to act within 90 days of the president's announcement. In addition, even if they mustered the votes necessary in both houses for a resolution disapproving MFN, they still would have needed a two-thirds majority to override a veto. *(1974 Almanac, p. 555)*

The administration, along with an alliance of business groups and congressional supporters, fought hard to make sure China retained its MFN status.

"We believe it's the best way to integrate China further into the family of nations and to secure our interests and ideals," Clinton told a group of business leaders May 19. Ending China's MFN status, he argued, "would cut off our contact with the Chinese people and undermine our influence with the Chinese government."

Opponents of MFN denounced the president's decision. "It is time to stop holding our policy hostage to the profits of a few exporting elites at the expense of most products made in America," said California Democrat Nancy Pelosi, who again joined forces with Virginia Republican Frank R. Wolf in leading the fight against MFN in the House.

For Gary L. Bauer of the Family Research Council and his allies among conservative Christians, and for neoconservative opinion leaders such as William Kristol, defeating MFN took on elements of a crusade. Before the House vote, the conservative Christian Coalition announced it would include MFN in its annual congressional "score card" used to grade lawmakers before elections.

House Action

The House Ways and Means Committee on June 18 overwhelmingly backed Clinton's decision to renew MFN for China. The committee sent a proposal to overturn China's trade status (H J Res 79 — H Rept 105-140) to the floor, but voted 34-5 to recommend it be defeated.

Some committee members said there was much to be angry with China about, but that U.S. businesses and strategic interests would suffer if normal trading relations were cut off. Chairman Bill Archer, R-Texas, said ending MFN would cost the U.S. bargaining power on human rights and other issues with China.

Jim Bunning, R-Ky., adamantly disagreed, arguing that in 16 years bargaining power had wrought little. Bunning was the only Republican to vote in favor of ending MFN. He was joined by four Democrats.

U.S.-Hong Kong Trade Ties

Hong Kong was allowed to maintain separate economic and trade offices in the United States after it reverted to Chinese control, under a bill that President Clinton signed into law June 27 (S 342 — PL 105-22). The bill was enacted on the eve of the transfer, which took place July 1.

The measure prevented Hong Kong trade offices in the United States from coming under the control of the Chinese Embassy in Washington. It also ensured that, following the reversion, Hong Kong civil servants working in those offices would be accorded the same status as officials with international organizations.

The trade office provisions were originally part of a broader bill (HR 750), which also would have authorized the president to reconsider the special status that Hong Kong enjoyed in a variety of areas, including trade and law enforcement, if China moved to restrict Hong Kong's autonomy. The House passed that bill March 11 by a vote of 416-1, with Ron Paul, R-Texas, casting the only dissenting vote. It had been approved by the International Relations Committee on March 6. *(Vote 38, p. H-14)*

On May 20, the Senate passed a narrower bill, S 342, which focused on the economic and trade offices. The bill passed on a voice vote after no debate. The House accepted that version June 17, also by voice vote, clearing it for the president.

House Floor Vote

The House handily rejected the resolution on June 24, defeating it by a vote of 173-259. Although the outcome disappointed MFN opponents, they did get 32 votes more than they had in 1996, when an identical resolution garnered 141 votes. The resolution needed approval from both chambers to take effect, so House rejection eliminated the need for Senate action. *(Vote 231, p. H-74)*

Of the 32 votes that the opponents picked up, only 14 came from Republicans. Overall, only 79 Republicans supported the resolution to cut off China's trade status, while 147 members opposed it.

The bitterness of the debate was underscored by Dana Rohrabacher, R-Calif., who said after the vote, "My hands are clean. I have not been shaking hands with butchers."

The outcome buoyed administration officials, who had been concerned by the defection of high-profile Republicans, including Budget Committee Chairman John R. Kasich of Ohio, from the pro-MFN camp.

Speaker Newt Gingrich, R-Ga., had flirted with the idea of extending MFN for only three to six months, so that Congress would be able to assess China's governance of Hong Kong. But Hong Kong Gov. Chris Patten essentially nixed that approach, warning in a letter to Gingrich in May that cutting off China's MFN status would "jeopardize rather than reinforce Hong Kong's way of life."

Democrats, too, were divided. Minority Leader Richard A. Gephardt of Missouri, a potential presidential candidate in 2000, joined conservatives in opposing the MFN extension. In an emotional floor speech, he said the United States had a moral obligation to look past China's immense economic potential and focus on its suppression of political and religious liberties. "This country is not just about business," Gephardt said. "This country is about an idea, a moral belief that every human being in the world is created with liberty and freedom."

Still, a strong majority of both parties agreed with the administration. "Washing our hands of China is simply irresponsible," said Majority Whip Tom DeLay, R-Texas. "Let us not impose a false isolation on China that diminishes our influence and hurts the very people we want to help." ■

Other China Bills Wait in Wings

Unable to end China's most-favored-nation (MFN) trade status with the United States, a coalition of conservative Republicans and liberal Democrats managed to express their frustration with Beijing on a variety of fronts by passing a series of nine bills in the House assailing the communist regime.

The bills, all of which passed by overwhelming majorities, attacked China's human rights record, its weapons and military technology sales to countries that supported terrorism, its treatment of religious minorities, its support of compulsory abortion and its antagonistic relationship with Taiwan.

However, the votes did not come until late in the session — the House leadership agreed to delay them to avoid upstaging the planned October summit between President Clinton and Chinese President Jiang Zemin. That scheduling decision left little time for Senate action before Congress adjourned. The Senate did not take up any of the bills. *(Jiang visit, p. 8-39)*

Legislative Summary

Even as the House began its annual debate on China's trade status, Speaker Newt Gingrich, R-Ga., was searching for an alternative way for Congress to express its views. He asked a pair of senior Republicans — David Dreier of California and John Edward Porter of Illinois — to review other avenues. Porter said he thought the MFN debate had become "a legislative dead-end." *(China MFN, p. 8-37)*

The group's proposal, later expanded, included increased broadcasts by Radio Free Asia to China, more funding for the National Endowment for Democracy's programs in China, and authorization for the State Department to deny visas to Chinese officials responsible for human rights violations or illicit arms transfers.

The House International Relations Committee marked up five of the bills, and the Ways and Means Committee reported a sixth. The other three bills went directly to the floor.

It took the International Relations Committee three days of contentious debate Sept. 26 and Sept. 29-30 to finish work on its five bills. Several Republicans and Democrats expressed strong reservations about the measures and about the committee's haste in pushing them through. Doug Bereuter, R-Neb., chairman of the Asia and the Pacific Subcommittee, was openly angry.

The bills comprised proposals to deny visas to Chinese officials who suppressed religion, increase the number of human rights monitors in China, authorize more funds for Radio Free Asia, punish China for missile sales to Iran and push development of a missile defense system to protect Taiwan.

The bills were ready by the beginning of October, but the administration pressured the House GOP leadership into delaying any floor action until after Jiang's visit.

Christopher H. Smith, R-N.J., an outspoken critic of the Chinese government, expressed dismay with the delay. "These bills represent the barest minimum of what we should be doing" about human rights abuses, he said. He was joined in his objections by three Democrats — House Minority Leader Richard A. Gephardt of Missouri, Democratic Whip David E. Bonior of Michigan and Nancy Pelosi of California. The three sent a letter to Clinton on Oct. 14 saying that Congress' voice on relations with China should not be stifled in advance of the summit.

The Clinton administration opposed six of the bills, considering them unnecessary or disruptive of its delicate diplomacy with China.

Floor Action

The House passed the nine bills in action that spanned five days, Nov. 5-9.

Lee H. Hamilton of Indiana, the ranking Democrat on the House International Relations Committee, was a lone voice arguing the administration's position. "I do not believe it serves American interests today to paint China, with all of its faults and with all of the concerns we have about its conduct, as a second evil empire," Hamilton said at the start of the House debate.

Several factors contributed to the lopsided support for the package. The summit meeting between Clinton and Jiang had

Jiang Zemin Visit Changes Few Minds

Chinese President Jiang Zemin paid a visit to Capitol Hill on Oct. 30, following two days of summit meetings with President Clinton. Jiang met with 55 members of the House and Senate, including all the members of the leadership except for House Republican Whip Tom DeLay, R-Texas, who stayed away to protest China's treatment of religious minorities.

Jiang's visit failed to dissuade members of Congress who were antagonistic toward Beijing, nor did it change the opinions of those who favored stronger ties between the two countries.

During his meeting with lawmakers in the wood-paneled Mansfield Room, Jiang appealed for restraint by the United States and particularly by Congress. "Practice over the years has shown that whenever the two sides observe the basic principles of mutual respect for sovereignty, territorial integrity, non-interference in each other's internal affairs, equality and mutual benefit . . . our bilateral relations develop smoothly," Jiang said.

But lawmakers peppered Jiang with pointed questions on everything from religious persecution to compulsory abortion. Rep. Christopher H. Smith, R-N.J., an outspoken critic of China's human rights record, said compulsory abortions were declared a crime against humanity at the Nuremberg War Crimes trials and "it is no less a crime in China today."

Several members asked for the release of political prisoners and called for China to stop jamming Radio Free Asia. Others asked about recent reports that Chinese prisoners were killed so their organs could be sold on the black market. Jiang denied that was the case.

Under pressure from the administration, House leaders had postponed floor consideration of a package of bills assailing the Chinese government and its policies. The bills subsequently passed by overwhelming margins. *(China bills, p. 8-38)*

Sentiment in the Senate was far less antagonistic. "It is essential to integrate and not isolate this strategic nation, but to do so in a manner that preserves our interests," said Joseph I. Lieberman, D-Conn., sponsor of a bill (S 1303) aimed at promoting China's integration into the world economic community.

Chuck Hagel, R-Neb., a cosponsor of Lieberman's bill, said the anti-China approach of the House bills was "not only punitive. It's not constructive, meaningful or comprehensive."

On the day of Jiang's arrival in Washington, Senate Finance Committee Chairman William V. Roth Jr., R-Del., introduced legislation to grant China permanent most-favored-nation trading status. "A China more fully immersed in global capitalism is more likely to behave in ways compatible with American interests and international norms," Roth said.

But senators remained wary of China's promises, particularly on nuclear non-proliferation and the export of technology to Iran and Pakistan. The high point of the summit had been an agreement by Clinton to certify that China was in compliance with the 1985 nuclear cooperation agreement. The administration received assurances that Beijing would stop selling technology to countries such as Iran and Pakistan that were trying to develop nuclear weapons. *(1985 Almanac, p. 110)*

Some in the Senate were sharply critical of the step. "The history of the administration's non-proliferation policy is littered with broken promises and worthless pledges," Republican Senator Jesse Helms of North Carolina, chairman of the Senate Foreign Relations Committee, said in advance of the summit.

Joseph R. Biden Jr. of Delaware, the ranking Democrat on the Foreign Relations Committee, said the agreement was only the first step, and Congress would have the final say on financing of any nuclear projects by the Export-Import Bank and the granting of export licenses.

Helms and Richard C. Shelby, R-Ala., chairman of the Senate Select Committee on Intelligence, said in an Oct. 27 letter to Clinton that they wanted to review all written texts of any nuclear agreements, all intelligence reports and data on Chinese proliferation since Jan. 1, 1986, as well as any intelligence on Chinese diversion of U.S. technology.

---

ended Oct. 30, so the votes did not threaten to upstage it. The Senate was considered unlikely to act on the legislation before adjournment, which made it a free vote. And a number of the bills were merely non-binding resolutions that lacked the force of law.

All that combined to give members a relatively painless way to send a message on human rights, weapons sales and Taiwan, while continuing to support MFN for China.

The Nine House Bills

The following is a summary of the nine bills that were passed by the House.

• **Human rights/nuclear sales to China.** A bill that drew little opposition in committee — a proposal to fund more personnel to monitor human rights in China (HR 2358 — H Rept 105-305) — became the vehicle for a floor amendment aimed at the centerpiece of the U.S.-China summit, an agreement to allow the sale of U.S. nuclear equipment to China in exchange for assurances from Beijing that it would discontinue its export of technology that enabled countries such as Iran and Pakistan to develop missiles and other weapons.

Clinton's agreement to certify that China was in compliance with the 1985 nuclear cooperation agreement cleared the way for companies such as Westinghouse Electric Corp. to sell nuclear-related products to China.

As initially approved Sept. 29 by the International Relations Committee, the bill would simply have authorized $2.2 million in fiscal 1998 and in fiscal 1999 for additional human rights monitors. The monitors were to be stationed at the U.S. Embassy in Beijing and at consulates in Guangzhou, Shanghai, Shenyang, Chengdu and Hong Kong. The bill also included a non-binding resolution calling for an end to the harvesting of bodily organs from Chinese prisoners for sale on the black market. The administration opposed the measure.

But when the bill reached the floor, International Relations Committee Chairman Benjamin A. Gilman, R-N.Y., and

Edward J. Markey, D-Mass., offered an amendment to revise the law (PL 99-183) implementing the nuclear cooperation agreement.

Under that law, no transfer to China of nuclear materials or components could take place until Congress had been in continuous session for 30 days after the president had certified that China was complying with nuclear non-proliferation statutues. The amendment would give Congress 120 days, rather than 30, to review the certification. *(1985 Almanac, p. 110)*

The House adopted the amendment, 394-29, then passed the bill Nov. 5 by a vote of 416-5. *(Votes 579, 580, p. H-174)*

• **Visa ban.** The most controversial bill (HR 967 — H Rept 105-309, Part 1) was a proposal to deny U.S. visas to Chinese officials who headed government-created religious organizations or who implemented policies that persecuted religious minorities. Exceptions would be made for heads of state and cabinet-level ministers, and the president would have the authority to waive any admission denial.

The International Relations Committee considered the bill on three separate days before approving it. When the panel first took it up Sept. 26, members voted 14-11 in favor of an amendment by Tom Campbell, R-Calif., that eliminated the bill's findings on religious persecution in China, a significant portion of the bill. A second amendment by Campbell that would have eliminated a prohibition on providing travel expenses for Chinese officials who headed the religious groups failed on a tie vote of 14-14.

Bill opponent Lee H. Hamilton of Indiana, ranking Democrat on the committee, raised the possibility that China could retaliate by restricting travel by U.S. religious leaders such as the Rev. Billy Graham. The administration opposed the bill.

At its next markup session Sept 29, the committee rejected the bill by a vote of 14-17. At the last minute, Gilman changed his vote to "no," which allowed him to bring up the legislation the next day for another vote. On Sept. 30, the committee approved the bill, 22-18.

The House passed the bill Nov. 6 by a vote of 366-54. *(Vote 595, p. H-178)*

• **Taiwan defense.** Under another bill that prompted fierce debate (HR 2386 — H Rept 105-308, Part 1), the secretary of Defense would be required to study the feasibility of constructing a theater ballistic missile defense that could protect Taiwan. The secretary would have to report by July 1, 1998, on the results of the study and a description of any existing U.S. ballistic missiles defense system that could be transferred to Taiwan in accordance with the Taiwan Relations Act (PL 96-8).

The bill expressed the sense of Congress that the president — if requested by Taiwan and in accordance with the results of the study — should transfer to Taiwan appropriate defense articles or services under the foreign military sales program for the purpose of operating a local-area ballistic missile defense system.

It also expressed the sense of Congress that Taiwan should be included in any missile defense cooperation in the Asia-Pacific region. The administration opposed the bill.

Hamilton argued that the legislation was illogical because it sought to ensure that Taiwan would get the missile defense system before the study had determined how to build it. In addition, he noted, the United States still had not developed theater ballistic missile defense for its own protection.

Lawmakers also wrangled over language in the bill suggesting that provisions of the Taiwan Relations Act, the 1979 law that provided U.S. security assurances to the island, took precedence over the 1982 joint communiqué between the United States and China that limited arms sales to Taiwan. *(1979 Almanac, p. 99; 1982 Almanac, p. 140)*

After much debate, the panel eliminated the language from the bill. It then approved the measure by voice vote.

The House passed the bill Nov. 6 by a vote of 301-116. *(Vote 601, p. H-180)*

• **Iran missiles.** The House passed a resolution urging the president to impose sanctions on China for transferring C-802 cruise missiles to Iran in violation of the 1992 Iran-Iraq Arms Non-Proliferation Act. The resolution (H Res 188 — H Rept 105-304) won voice vote approval from the International Relations Committee Sept. 29; the House adopted it Nov. 6 by a vote of 414-8. *(Vote 592, p. H-178)*

The non-proliferation provisions, enacted as part of the fiscal 1993 defense authorization bill (PL 103-160), required the president to apply sanctions to companies and countries that provided Iran or Iraq with strategic weapons, including the C-802 missile. The mandatory sanctions included a one-year suspension of U.S. aid to the offending country and a two-year ban on the company that made the weapons.

The bill also urged the president to take similar action against Russian companies that dealt with Iran.

In 1996, Chinese companies delivered more than 60 of the missiles to Iran for use by its navy.

• **Prison labor.** Another bill (HR 2195 — H Rept 105-366, Part 1) proposed authorizing $2 million for the U.S. Customs Service and the State Department in fiscal 1999 to enforce a 62-year-old ban on importing products made with prison labor and to hire more personnel to monitor imports. The bill also would give Customs and the State Department one year to submit a report detailing China's use of prison labor in manufacturing products for export and the U.S. government's progress in stemming such imports. China operated and maintained a forced-labor camp system known as Laogai.

The bill received voice vote approval from the Ways and Means Committee on Oct. 1. The House passed it Nov. 5, 419-2. *(Vote 582, p. H-174)*

• **Forced abortions.** Another bill (HR 2570), passed 415-1 on Nov. 6, condemned the actions of most Chinese officials involved in compulsory abortion or sterilization. It proposed that they be denied visas for entry into the United States. The administration opposed the bill; it did not go through a committee. *(Vote 598, p. H-178)*

• **Loan subsidies.** Also on Nov. 6, the House voted 354-59 in favor of a bill (HR 2605) that would direct the president to instruct U.S. officials at international financial organizations such as the World Bank and the International Monetary Fund to oppose below-market loans for China. The administration opposed the bill; it was not marked up in committee. *(Vote 605, p. H-180)*

• **Military products.** A bill (HR 2647), passed 408-10 on Nov. 7, proposed that the president be authorized to monitor, restrict, seize the assets of and ban companies in the United States associated with China's army. The secretary of Defense would be directed to compile a list of individuals working for these companies who were operating directly or indirectly in the United States. The administration opposed the bill; it was not marked up in committee. *(Vote 614, p. H-184)*

• **Radio Free Asia.** The last of the nine bills (HR 2232 — H Rept 105-303) proposed to authorize $30 million in fiscal 1998 and $22 million in fiscal 1999 for Radio Free Asia, a non-government outlet that broadcast in seven Asian languages and English. The House passed the bill, 401-21, on Nov. 9. The International Relations committee had approved the measure by voice vote Sept. 29. *(Vote 623, p. H-186)* ■

House Shelves Persecution Bill

Legislation aimed at punishing foreign regimes for persecuting citizens because of their religious beliefs garnered initial support across the political spectrum. But, the momentum quickly dissipated as lawmakers of both parties, including some of Congress' strongest human rights activists, took a closer look at the complex issues involved.

As a result, the bill (HR 2431, S 772) got no further than a House subcommittee in the first session. It also underwent several revisions as sponsors tried to ease members' concerns.

House and Senate GOP leaders had indicated an intent to pass a bill on religious persecution before the end of the year; the powerful Christian Coalition made it its top legislative priority, and various religious groups and human rights organizations embraced the effort.

However, when the details of the bill — first introduced May 20 as HR 1685, then revised and reintroduced Sept. 8 as HR 2431 — were laid out, it became evident to many lawmakers that translating a high-minded gesture supporting the right to worship into workable legislation that could pass Congress was a problem.

"The consequences were not clear when they put it in," Doug Bereuter, R-Neb., chairman of the House International Relations Subcommittee on Asia and the Pacific, said of the bill. "It stems from an ideological rather than a practical standpoint," said Amo Houghton, R-N.Y., a member of the International Relations Committee. "If it were up to me, I'd kill the whole bill."

Background

As introduced by Rep. Frank R. Wolf, R-Va., and Sen. Arlen Specter, R-Pa., in September, the legislation called for creating a White House Office of Religious Persecution Monitoring, whose director would determine whether a foreign government carried out, supported or failed to stop religious persecution. Such a determination would trigger automatic sanctions, including a ban on exports, a prohibition on all non-humanitarian aid, U.S. opposition to loans by multilateral development banks or the International Monetary Fund, and a denial of visas to those identified as persecutors. The president could waive the sanctions if he decided they were a threat to U.S. national security.

The bill also proposed to increase the importance of religious persecution as a criterion for granting asylum in the United States, giving such asylum-seekers the same status as ethnic minorities, human rights activists in Cuba and forced-labor conscripts.

Heading the list of countries for immediate scrutiny would be China, Vietnam, Sudan, Cuba, Morocco, Saudi Arabia, Pakistan, North Korea, Indonesia, Egypt and Laos. The religious persecution monitor's task would be to determine whether those countries were persecuting or allowing the persecution of Roman Catholics, evangelical Protestant Christians, non-Muslims and moderate Muslims.

Widespread Misgivings

During two days of hearings by the International Relations Committee the week of Sept. 8, proponents of the legislation described widespread religious persecution, from China's brutal treatment of Tibetan monks to the atrocities of Sudan's ongoing civil war between a Muslim-dominated government and Christians and animists. The witnesses said that bold action by Congress was imperative.

But while the hearings brought condemnation of regimes that imposed such suffering, there were misgivings on many fronts about the prospect of threatening allies with possible sanctions, especially countries where the rites and order of a predominant religion were distinctly different from the Judeo-Christian tradition in the United States.

Lawmakers from both parties raised questions about the effects on ordinary Americans of sanctioning oil-rich Saudi Arabia, the potential increase in immigration from those seeking asylum based on religious persecution, and the wisdom of cutting off multilateral bank loans aimed at assisting a country's economic development.

Bereuter and Tom Lantos, D-Calif., who had sponsored an earlier version of the bill, questioned the idea of establishing a White House office disconnected from the State Department and National Security Council. "What we do on human rights policy in general cannot be divorced from what we do in foreign policy," Bereuter said.

Lantos, an outspoken human rights activist, heralded the purpose of the legislation, but criticized the bill for giving a higher priority to religious persecution at the expense of other human rights, entrusting a White House office with determining whether a country would be sanctioned, and imposing automatic sanctions, which he described as "a one-size-fits-all policy."

The Clinton administration, which objected strongly to the legislation, opposed creating a White House office separate from the foreign policy apparatus.

Committee Democrats and the administration also expressed concern about the limited presidential authority to waive the sanctions and about what Secretary of State Madeleine K. Albright called "an artificial hierarchy of human rights," in which one class of persecuted people would be given precedence over others.

In addition, the bill threatened to highlight a growing divide within the Republican Party between social conservatives, such as the Christian Coalition, one of the bill's principal supporters, and economic conservatives, such as USA Engage, a business-backed lobbying group that was one of the bill's main opponents. The proposed economic sanctions created uneasiness within the influential business community, although most corporate leaders refrained from public comment.

House Subcommittee Action

The House International Relations Subcommittee on International Operations and Human Rights approved the bill by voice vote Sept. 18.

Subcommittee Chairman Christopher H. Smith, R-N.J., took a small step toward addressing some of the concerns voiced by members. The version of the bill he brought to the subcommittee markup expanded the list of denominations subject to religious persecution to include Jews, Muslims and Hindus as well as Christians. There had been some criticism that the bill focused only on persecuted Christians.

The original bill would have imposed immediate and harsh sanctions on Sudan, and precluded any attempt by the president to lift the penalties. The substitute proposed giving the president the power to waive the sanctions based on threats to U.S. national security, the same authority he was granted for other potentially sanctioned countries.

The subcommittee also approved, by voice vote, an amendment to permit the United States to continue humanitarian assistance as well as "development assistance which directly benefits the poor in the poorest countries" and was not administered by the government of a sanctioned country.

At the request of Dana Rohrabacher, R-Calif., the substitute bill also expanded its criticism of China to include the communist country's reported persecution of the Uyghur, a predominantly Muslim ethnic group in the formerly independent republic of East Turkistan.

Still outstanding, and beyond the jurisdiction of the International Relations Committee, was the provision to increase the importance of religious persecution as a criterion for granting asylum in the United States. The House Judiciary Committee was responsible for determining whether and how to alter the provision.

Bereuter remained wary of the legislation. "We have no jurisdiction over the most controversial provision," he said, adding that the bill overall "is much more complicated and potentially more difficult. And not all religious groups are firmly behind it."

Committee Action Postponed

In the face of growing opposition from all sides, the full International Relations Committee postponed action on the bill while the sponsors set out to draft compromise language. The committee did not mark up the bill in 1997.

An Oct. 10 draft of a revised bill proposed putting the monitoring office in the State Department rather than the White House, expanding the president's power to waive the penalties, and broadening the definition of religious groups subject to persecution. The original bill had emphasized the persecution of Christians. The revised bill still included automatic sanctions for countries that the sponsors believed should come under immediate scrutiny: China, Vietnam, Sudan, Cuba, Morocco, Saudi Arabia, Pakistan, North Korea, Indonesia, Egypt and Laos.

While reaction among religious groups was mixed, the changes did attract the support of the Union of American Hebrew Congregations and the Central Conference of American Rabbis, both of which had initially expressed concern over the legislation.

In the Senate, a Religious Persecution Task Force, headed by James M. Inhofe, R-Okla., analyzed the various legislative proposals and described the Wolf-Specter bill as a "starting point" with "some aspects that could be problematic."

Specifically, the task force said the success of targeted economic sanctions had been mixed because "they tend to be too weak and waiveable by the president." Also, the task force said that while giving victims of religious persecution a higher priority for admission to the United States as refugees or in granting asylum was a solution for 2 million Soviet Jews during the Cold War, it "may not be the solution for 50 million Chinese Christians today."

Other Action

In separate action, the Senate on Nov. 8 gave voice vote approval to a non-binding resolution expressing its concern over a new law in Russia discriminating against religious minorities. The resolution (S Con Res 58) assailed the law, which Russian President Boris Yeltsin signed Sept. 26, as a violation of international norms, treaties to which Russia was a signatory and the Russian constitution. The resolution also recommended that President Clinton explain to Yeltsin that the law could seriously harm U.S.-Russia relations.

Lawmakers angered by the religion law took a stronger step to punish Russia in the fiscal 1998 foreign operations spending bill (HR 2159 — PL 105-118). The bill, signed into law Nov. 26, included a provision prohibiting aid to Russia if it implemented the law. In an unusual move, Congress gave Clinton no authority to waive the sanctions.

In other action, the House defeated a non-binding resolution (H Con Res 22) that would have criticized Germany for its treatment of religious minorities, particularly members of the Church of Scientology. The vote was 101-318 on Nov. 9. The German government praised the defeat of the measure and objected to claims that individuals were being persecuted because of their religious affiliation. "This shows that reason has prevailed," German Foreign Minister Klaus Kinkel said in Bonn on Nov. 10. *(Vote 625, p. H-186)* ■

Tug of War Over Trade Sanctions

As they had for decades, lawmakers looked to trade and other economic sanctions as the weapon of choice when trying to change the behavior of foreign governments. And, like his predecessors, President Clinton resisted congressional mandates on trade and foreign policy, arguing that the administration had to retain the flexibility to fine-tune relations with other countries.

Cuba

On Jan. 3 and again on July 16, President Clinton signed six-month waivers of a statute permitting lawsuits against foreign companies that invested in Cuba. Congressional critics of Fidel Castro charged that Clinton's actions amounted to an indefinite suspension of a key provision of the 1996 Helms-Burton Cuba sanctions law (PL 104-114) designed to increase economic pressure on the Castro regime.

"He has rendered it to meaningless nothingness," said Senate Foreign Relations Committee Chairman Jesse Helms, R-N.C., a co-author of the 1996 law with Rep. Dan Burton, R-Ind.

The provision allowed U.S. nationals whose Cuban property had been confiscated by Castro's government to sue foreign companies that owned or benefited from that property. But at Clinton's behest, it also granted the president authority to block any litigation for six-month periods. Clinton's July 16 waiver marked the third time he had used that authority.

Other provisions of the Helms-Burton law codified the ongoing U.S. economic embargo against Cuba and denied entry into the United States of executives of foreign companies that possessed Cuban property that had been expropriated from U.S. nationals. *(1996 Almanac, p. 9-6)*

Stuart E. Eizenstat, the president's special representative for promoting democracy in Cuba, argued in January that the law had been successful in pressuring European and Latin American governments to take a harder line against the Castro regime, even though Clinton had not allowed the lawsuits provision to take effect. Eizenstat said the president would continue suspending the right to file suit "as long as our friends and allies continue their stepped-up efforts to promote democracy in Cuba."

Angered by the administration's handling of the sanctions law, Helms wrote a July 16 letter to Clinton, saying it was "increasingly obvious" that the administration had decided not to enforce the limitation on foreign businesses, since only two companies, Sherritt of Canada and Grupo Domos of Mexico, had been hit with sanctions. Clinton replied in an Aug. 14 letter that the administration continued to enforce the visa provision and was working with the European Union on the question of investments in Cuba.

Helms responded Oct. 3 with a letter to Secretary of State Madeleine K. Albright requesting that she provide his committee with "all memoranda, cables, minutes, electronic mail messages, telefaxes or other documents," including classified material, relating to the 1996 law. "Since the president failed to address my questions about enforcement of the Libertad Act, we are obliged to find out for ourselves whether this U.S. law is indeed being applied vigorously," he wrote.

Iran

Moments before Congress adjourned Nov. 13, Senate Democrats blocked floor consideration of a House bill (HR 2709) aimed at imposing tough economic sanctions on overseas companies and research institutes, mainly Russian, that were helping Iran develop ballistic missiles.

The Clinton administration strongly objected to the bill, saying it was too rigid and would derail delicate negotiations with the Russian government aimed at ending the flow of lethal technology to Iran. Hoping to force President Clinton to sign the bill anyway, the House had attached a separate bill (S 610) needed to implement the recently ratified chemical weapons treaty. But the White House warned that Clinton would still veto the Iran bill. *(Chemical weapons, p. 8-13)*

Like a similar Senate bill (S 1311), the House measure stemmed from congressional anger over widespread, credible reports that Russian state-owned companies had transferred high-strength metals, other exotic materials and technical assistance that Iran was using to extend the range of its Scud missiles far enough to threaten Israel and U.S. forces in the Middle East.

Bill supporters argued that the Clinton administration was unwilling to challenge Russia and enforce existing sanctions aimed at punishing those who dealt with Iran. "An incremental approach to this issue or reliance on friendly persuasion does not appear to be achieving any demonstrable result," said International Relations Committee Chairman Benjamin A. Gilman, R-N.Y.

Both the House and Senate versions of the legislation contained provisions to require the administration to publish periodic reports identifying companies or research institutes that, according to "credible reports," had transferred, or attempted to transfer, prohibited missile-related technology to Iran since August 1995. That was the date Russia joined the Missile Technology Control Regime, an international pact to prevent the proliferation of ballistic missile technology.

Specific economic sanctions, including a prohibition on any U.S. economic assistance, would be levied for at least two years against any organization violating the ban.

HR 2709 included a provision allowing the president to waive the required sanctions on national security grounds. The Senate bill had no such waiver.

The House bill had the support of more than 100 members, including Speaker Newt Gingrich, R-Ga., and Minority Leader Richard A. Gephardt, D-Mo. Three-fourths of the Senate, including Senate Majority Leader Trent Lott, R-Miss., and Minority Leader Tom Daschle, D-S.D., endorsed S 1311.

A key administration objection to both bills was that the sanctions would be triggered by "credible information" of a violation. Other laws that used economic sanctions to discourage weapons proliferation required sanctions only if a "preponderance of the evidence" indicated a violation.

In advance of the House markup, Secretary of State Madeleine K. Albright sent a letter to Lee H. Hamilton of Indiana, ranking Democrat on the International Relations Committee, saying she would recommend a veto. She said the proposed sanctions were "too inflexible, applying equally to minor transfers that have minimal effects on Iran's efforts to acquire ballistic missile capabilities and to transfers of serious items like missile guidance systems."

Sanction opponents also contended that the bill was unfair because it would not require that the leadership of an organization be found to have "knowingly" engaged in prohibited activity and because the bill was retroactive. They said an organization that had made prohibited transfers to Iran in the past would have no incentive to abstain from them in the future, since sanctions would be mandatory if its past deeds became known.

But the opponents failed to sway many in Congress. "They've been too slow to take action," Sen. Jon Kyl., R-Ariz., said of the administration. "There is a mountain of intelligence data that cannot be ignored. Iran is getting closer [to developing ballistic missiles]. We can't kick the can down the road another six months."

House Passes Bill; Senate Stops It

The House International Relations Committee approved the legislation by voice vote Oct. 24 (H Rept 105-375).

In its report, the committee said it wrote a deliberately low standard of evidence into the bill because the Clinton administration had interpreted the more demanding standard so strictly that it did not apply sanctions in cases in which Congress intended that they be imposed. "This legislation would be unnecessary if the executive branch were willing to comply with existing law governing missile technology controls," said Doug Bereuter, R-Neb.

The full House passed the bill by voice vote the night of Nov. 12, after attaching the text of S 610, the Senate bill to implement the Chemical Weapons Convention. Until such implementing legislation was enacted, the United States was in violation of the chemical weapons pact, and bill supporters were hoping that the linkage would be enough to counter the threatened veto of HR 2709.

However, the Office of Management and Budget said Nov. 7 that Clinton's top advisers would urge him to veto the sanctions bill with or without the add-on.

Lott tried to bring the bill up shortly before the session's end, but Democrats, heeding Clinton's veto threat, blocked it.

Myanmar

President Clinton announced April 22 that he was imposing a ban on new U.S. investments in Myanmar, formerly known as Burma, because of that Southeast Asian nation's continuing political repression and involvement in the illegal drug trade.

The action was taken under a provision of the fiscal 1997 omnibus appropriations law (PL 104-208) that allowed the president to ban new private U.S. investment in the event of "large-scale repression of or violence against" the democratic opposition in Myanmar. *(1996 Almanac, p. 10-51)*

Mitch McConnell, R-Ky., chairman of the Senate Foreign

Operations Appropriations Subcommittee, and Daniel Patrick Moynihan of New York, ranking Democrat on the Senate Finance Committee, called a joint news conference to express support for Clinton's move. However, McConnell also said he thought the administration was "trying to stay ahead of the curve" to avoid having Congress add tougher sanctions legislatively.

McConnell was hoping to codify the investment sanctions and apply them retroactively, essentially forcing all U.S. investors out of Myanmar. However, his legislation never got off the ground.

Although few U.S. companies were interested in investing in Myanmar, given the country's years of self-imposed isolation, a handful of oil companies, led by Unocal Corp., had mounted an aggressive and ultimately successful campaign in 1996 to limit the scope of the sanctions.

Unocal, which was part of an international consortium developing a billion-dollar natural gas pipeline in the Andaman Sea off Myanmar's coast, hired well-known Washington lobbyist Tom C. Korologos to help make its case. As the Senate moved to a showdown in July 1996 on an amendment by McConnell to impose an immediate ban on all U.S. investment in Myanmar, Unocal executives arrived in force to press for key changes.

They succeeded, as the Senate rejected McConnell's amendment in favor of a more modest package of sanctions proposed by Maine Republican William S. Cohen (who subsequently became secretary of Defense) and California Democrat Dianne Feinstein.

The Cohen-Feinstein amendment softened McConnell's proposal by granting the president the authority to impose sanctions, but not requiring that he use it. Equally important from Unocal's perspective, the amendment only applied to future investments while "grandfathering" existing projects. As a result of that provision, Unocal avoided having to sell its stake in the gas pipeline when Clinton imposed the sanctions in April 1997.

The oil companies had since turned to fighting a spate of local laws enacted by 13 cities and counties and the state of Massachusetts to bar their governments from buying from companies operating in Myanmar. The European Union was so troubled by these local sanction statutes that it filed a formal complaint at the World Trade Organization charging that the Massachusetts law violated the WTO's rules on government purchasing.

Terrorism

The House passed a relatively non-controversial bill to further limit U.S. trade with countries that supported terrorism. Similar language was included in the Senate-passed version of the State Department authorization bill (HR 1757), but that measure remained stalled at the close of the session.

HR 748 was designed to prohibit exceptions to a 1996 law (PL 104-132) that barred financial transactions between U.S. citizens and companies and countries that supported terrorism. The State Department listed Cuba, Libya, North Korea, Iran, Iraq, Syria and Sudan as terrorist sponsoring countries.

The 1996 law included an exception designed to exempt routine diplomatic transactions. But bill sponsor Bill McCollum, R-Fla., argued that the Treasury Department had broadened that exemption to create "a loophole big enough to drive a car bomb through."

HR 748 would eliminate the executive branch's right to make exceptions to these regulations, as the White House had done with Syria and Sudan. McCollum said the bill would allow exceptions only for cases of "routine diplomatic activity," such as when a visiting Syrian diplomat paid for a cab ride to the United Nations building.

The bill began in the House Judiciary Subcommittee on Crime, which approved it by voice vote June 12; the full committee followed suit June 18 (H Rept 105-141). Although the bill drew some opposition on the floor, the House passed it handily July 8, by a vote of 377-33. *(Vote 249, p. H-80)*

Lee H. Hamilton of Indiana, ranking Democrat on the International Relations Committee, said he and the Clinton administration believed the measure would go too far in ending financial transactions. He said it also could harm the Middle East peace process by strengthening sanctions against Syria, a key player in the region.

Hamilton said the bill should give the president authority to waive the prohibition when the national interest was at stake. McCollum said the measure would not affect the peace process but said he would work with Hamilton and the administration to settle their differences. ■

Senate Sidesteps Decertification Of Mexico's Anti-Drug Effort

After a series of high-profile debates, Congress decided not to overturn President Clinton's certification of Mexico as an ally in the fight against narcotics. Sidestepping a confrontation with the president and the Mexican government, the Senate on March 20 voted overwhelmingly in favor of a carefully negotiated substitute amendment that simply mandated a six-month review of Mexico's anti-narcotics efforts.

The action effectively eliminated any possibility that Congress would overturn Clinton's Feb. 28 certification of Mexican anti-drug cooperation, which had touched off a storm of protest on Capitol Hill.

As was the case in the 1995 showdown over Clinton's deployment of U.S. troops to Bosnia and the 1995 debate over the administration's economic bailout of Mexico, the Senate was far less inclined than the House to seriously challenge the president's certification decision. *(1995 Almanac, pp. 10-10, 10-16)*

Mexican counter-narcotics efforts came under scrutiny in early 1997 because the country's leading anti-drug agent, Gen. Jesus Gutierrez Rebollo, was fired and arrested after Mexican officials discovered that he was accepting bribes from one of the nation's largest drug cartels.

After weeks of debate and dispute over whether to decertify Mexico as an ally, the March 20 Senate vote was somewhat anti-climactic. By 94-5, the Senate adopted a bipartisan amendment that had received the blessing of Secretary of State Madeleine K. Albright and other senior administration officials. The Senate then adopted the underlying resolution (HJ Res 58) by voice vote. *(Vote 35, p. S-8)*

The resolution, which was the product of intense negotiations, required the president to report to Congress by Sept. 1 on whether Mexico had made "significant and demonstrable progress" in several areas, including dismantling drug cartels, improving relations with U.S. law enforcement agencies and implementing money-laundering laws.

However, in a major concession to the White House, the bipartisan group that crafted the measure — led by Republicans Paul Coverdell of Georgia and Kay Bailey Hutchison of Texas, and Democrat Dianne Feinstein of California — dropped a demand that Congress be permitted to vote to accept or reject the administration's findings.

In numerous briefings with lawmakers, senior administration officials had made the argument that taking a hard line would inflame nationalism in Mexico, triggering a backlash that would undermine bilateral efforts to crack down on the drug trade. "There was increasing recognition of the consequences of decertification," said John McCain, R-Ariz. "Anybody who knows Mexico knows there would be an anti-American backlash."

Others, however, argued that any step short of decertification would permit the United States and Mexico to continue a "silent conspiracy" in which both nations falsely claimed that progress was being achieved in the drug war. "Mexico pretends to be interdicting narcotics," said Robert G. Torricelli, D-N.J. "We pretend to believe them."

The Senate's action presented House leaders with a dilemma. On March 13, the House had voted 251-175 in favor of a tougher version of H J Res 58 (H Rept 105-10). Sponsored by Deputy Republican Whip Dennis Hastert of Illinois, it would have given Mexico 90 days to drastically upgrade its anti-drug cooperation with the United States or face the stigma of decertification. *(Vote 48, p. H-16)*

In order to send the president a Mexico resolution, the House would almost certainly have had to accept the Senate's version, which passed by a much wider margin than the House proposal. But acceding to the Senate version would have represented a cave-in by House leaders. Consequently, although Hastert and other senior Republicans wanted a conference with the Senate, no such meeting took place and the issue was never resurrected. ■

Diplomatic Immunity

The Senate passed a bill (S 759) by voice vote Nov. 8 to require that the State Department provide Congress with an annual report on the number of individuals in the United States with diplomatic immunity who were believed to have committed serious criminal offenses. A serious criminal offense was defined as any felony under federal, state or local law, as well as driving under the influence or reckless driving.

The bill stemmed from a Jan. 3 incident in Washington in which a 16-year-old Maryland girl was killed in an accident involving a diplomat from Georgia, Gueorgui Makharadze, who later pleaded guilty to involuntary manslaughter and aggravated assault.

The House expressed its feelings on the issue June 11, when it adopted, 386-42, an amendment to the State Department authorization bill requiring the department to keep such records. The State Department bill (HR 1757) was stalled at the end of the session. *(Vote 184, p. H-60)* ■

Helms Blocks Weld's Ambassador Bid

After an unprecedented, high stakes showdown with Senate Foreign Relations Committee Chairman Jesse Helms, R-N.C., that lasted through the summer, former Massachusetts Gov. William F. Weld on Sept. 15 gave up on his effort to become U.S. ambassador to Mexico.

Helms had opposed Weld's nomination from the start, saying the moderate Republican's record on drugs was too weak for an ambassador to Mexico. Weld did little to improve his chances, going out of his way to attack Helms and his control over the committee process.

The imbroglio, which provided a kind of summertime political theater in Washington, raised questions about the power of a single chairman to block a nomination, but in the end it had little fallout.

"The ultimate power of chairmen, in general, may make people think twice," said Delaware Sen. Joseph R. Biden Jr., the ranking Democrat on the panel. "But no hard feelings."

The bemused reaction in the Senate stemmed in large part from Weld's handling of the nomination. Tapped by President Clinton in April, Weld came out swinging rhetorically and never let up on either the conservative Helms or venerable Senate rules.

Open Warfare From the Outset

Helms opposed Weld's nomination from the outset, telling a television interviewer June 3 that the former governor was not "ambassador quality" and that he would block the nomination.

The drama deepened July 15 as the governor convened a news conference in Boston in which he urged Clinton not to give in to what he said was Helms' "ideological extortion." Weld claimed his nomination had "everything to do with the future of the Republican Party."

Weld's broadside surprised some senators, who said that attacking Helms only caused the senator to dig in further. "It's possible [Weld] must have given up on his prospects," said John McCain, R-Ariz. "Why else would he lash out at the chairman?"

But Biden suggested that Weld had little to lose. "He probably made a decision he was already in trouble with Helms," Biden said.

Moderate Republican Olympia J. Snowe of Maine said flatly, "He [Weld] should apologize."

In response, Helms released a statement charging, "Gov. Weld's record on drugs makes him unqualified for the post." The statement slammed Weld for supporting the medicinal use of marijuana and policies to supply needles to heroin addicts and criticized Weld's record in gaining drug convictions when he was a U.S. attorney.

Despite the growing flap, Clinton proceeded July 23 to formally nominate Weld for the Mexico post. Weld surprised the political world, announcing that he would resign the next day as governor so he could lobby full time for his confirmation. On a visit to the Capitol on July 31, he was told by Senate Majority Leader Trent Lott, R-Miss., that he should take another post "or look for work."

Helms Unbending on Hearing

Helms steadfastly refused to hold a confirmation hearing for Weld, despite the demands by a majority of his committee. However, on Sept. 5, four senior members of the committee — led by the No. 2 Republican, Richard G. Lugar of Indiana — filed a petition under a little-used Senate rule requesting a special session. Joining Lugar were Biden, John Kerry, D-Mass., and Gordon H. Smith, R-Ore.

"I have neither endorsed Gov. Weld nor indicated how I would vote on his nomination," Lugar said. "But I do believe that it is important for the Senate and for our system of governance that we have a hearing."

Helms responded that he would schedule a meeting Sept. 12, but "the Weld nomination will not be on the agenda." Helms used the half-hour meeting to attack his critics, singling out Lugar and Biden in particular, and arguing that they had thwarted numerous nominations.

"The distinguished senator from Indiana decided to challenge my authority as a committee chairman and, by implication, challenge the authority of all other committee chairmen, now and in the future," Helms said. "I have felt obliged to state this morning, in detail, for the record, the true facts."

With Weld and his wife, Susan, watching from the back of the committee room, Helms also made it clear that he would continue to block the nomination. However, he indicated in an Aug. 1 letter to Clinton, which was released at the hearing, that he would consider the moderate Republican for another diplomatic post.

At the same time, Helms did little to hide his animosity toward Weld. "Mr. Weld appears to be threatening that unless his nomination to Mexico is moved, he will begin a war within the Republican Party. Let him try," Helms said.

In his letter to Clinton, Helms said Weld was a "radical" in his support of medicinal use of marijuana, and that his outspoken support for its legalization was sufficient grounds to disqualify him. "You deserve a better nominee, and the nation needs an ambassador in Mexico with a proven record as a drug fighter," Helms wrote.

Following the hearing, Lott issued a statement that reiterated his request a day earlier that Clinton withdraw the nomination. "The heavy-handed and personally negative campaign waged by Mr. Weld for that position has demonstrated the need for a more able and more astute appointee to that post," Lott said.

The president declined to back down. "My position is the man should have a hearing," Clinton said.

And Weld continued his sharp attacks on Helms. "It seemed that the senator was set to show that the Senate is a despotic institution," he said. "People out there on Main Street are not going to understand. That's where the appeal stands at this point."

To emphasize the president's support, Weld and his wife went from the Capitol to the White House and had a brief chat with Clinton. White House aides said Clinton would call Lott to plead for Senate action.

But on Sept. 13, Lott phoned Clinton, indicating that a prolonged fight with Helms could spill into other foreign policy issues. "We need the chairman's cooperation, if not outright support" on other issues, Lott said Sept. 15.

Weld said he, too, feared that his nomination would have a detrimental effect on the working relationship between Congress and the White House, particularly in the area of free trade.

Weld Delivers Parting Shot

Unbowed to the end, Weld used the announcement of his withdrawal Sept. 15 to deliver an impudent statement, titled "How I Spent My Summer Vacation." Speaking in the White House briefing room, he assailed Helms, the Senate and Washington.

He recalled how he decided to resign as governor and pursue his confirmation full time: "So in July I left Boston, and I came down here, and I said, 'I want a fair hearing.' And I met lots of people who are experts in the way that government in Washington works, and they said, 'We can't just have a hearing. First you have to go on bended knee, and you have to kiss a lot of rings.' Well, my mother and father taught me that I'm no better than anybody else, but also that I'm no worse. So I said I wouldn't go on bended knee and I wouldn't kiss anything," Weld said.

Weld's approach throughout the process left several Republican chairmen and a good number of senior Democrats, who would not admit it publicly, secretly rooting for Helms. "I have the feeling the softness of the support of the Weld nomination is a manifestation that was happening behind the scenes," said Robert F. Bennett, R-Utah.

"It's not demeaning to pay a courtesy call," said McCain. "Committee chairmen, whether Helms or [someone else], deserve the respect of a courtesy call."

Ensuring a good relationship with Helms was clearly a priority for the White House, evidenced by the tempered comments of White House spokesman Mike McCurry following Weld's flippant announcement.

"We, throughout this process, have said that while we were fighting hard for Gov. Weld, we hoped that we were fighting fair and square. And we hope the chairman will recognize that and that we can continue to do the business that we need to do together as a country to advance America's interest in the world," McCurry said. ■

Albright Wins Endorsement As Secretary of State

Madeleine K. Albright was confirmed Jan. 22 as the nation's first female secretary of State, on a 99-0 Senate vote. West Virginia Democrat John D. Rockefeller IV, traveling in Japan, was the only senator not voting. *(Vote 1, p. S-2)*

For the most part, the floor debate was a reprise of Albright's smooth confirmation hearing Jan. 8 before the Senate Foreign Relations Committee. The committee approved her nomination Jan. 20, Inauguration Day, on an 18-0 vote. Foreign Relations Committee Chairman Jesse Helms, R-N.C., warmly praised Albright, who was previously U.S. representative to the United Nations. "She's a strong lady," Helms said. "She's a courageous lady."

During her day-long appearance before the committee Jan. 8, Albright received only rave reviews. However, Helms and his GOP colleagues made it clear that, while they were were taken with Albright as a messenger, they were less impressed with her message. Helms said his support for Albright "should in no way be misconstrued as an endorsement of the Clinton foreign policy."

Helms slammed Clinton's policies toward Haiti, Iraq and Cuba and charged that the administration in general had been "too often vacillating and insecure."

Albright was able to turn the hearing's only unscripted moment — a protest against U.S. policy toward Iraq by members of a left-wing religious group — to her advantage by using it to launch an off-the-cuff attack on Iraqi leader Saddam Hussein. Albright's deft handling of the incident confirmed her reputation as an effective, if sometimes unpredictable, advocate for U.S. interests abroad. On that count, she represented a dramatic contrast to the cautious, lawyerly Warren Christopher, who had resigned after serving as secretary of State in the first Clinton administration.

"I have been known for my plain-speaking," she told the panel. "I'm going to tell it like it is."

On the major international issues facing the United States — Russia and China, Bosnia and the Middle East — Albright indicated she would closely follow the course set by Christopher.

One of her biggest challenges, however, seemed likely to come at home in trying to convince an uninterested public of the need for global engagement and in trying to sell a skeptical Congress on the administration's overseas initiatives. During the hearing, Albright began making the case for increased funding for foreign aid and other international programs and for the Senate to approve a treaty banning the development and deployment of chemical weapons, issues on which the administration faced tough fights. *(Chemical weapons, p. 8-13)*

The 59-year-old Albright had no difficulty winning over the committee, which seemed eager to make history by confirming a woman as the nation's top diplomat. But she earned plaudits for her record as well as for her gender.

Helms expressed admiration for her lead role in denying a second term for U.N. Secretary-General Boutros Boutros-Ghali of Egypt, who had become something of a bogeyman to GOP critics of the United Nations. Albright helped orchestrate Boutros-Ghali's ouster and his replacement by Kofi Annan of Ghana, the administration's choice for the post. She also won accolades for bluntly criticizing some of the world's harshest dictatorships, including Cuba, Myanmar (formerly Burma) and Saddam Hussein's regime in Iraq.

While Albright was cautious in her policy pronouncements, she pledged to work with the committee on a plan to reorganize the foreign affairs bureaucracy, a cherished goal of Helms.

Richardson Named to U.N. Post

Bill Richardson won unanimous Senate approval Feb. 11 to become the new U.S. representative to the United Nations. The vote on Richardson, who had served more than 14 years as a Democratic representative from New Mexico, was 100-0. The Senate Foreign Relations Committee had approved his nomination earlier that day on an 18-0 vote. Richardson replaced Madeleine K. Albright, who resigned to become secretary of State. *(Vote 9, p. S-3)*

During the brief committee debate, Foreign Relations Chairman Jesse Helms, R-N.C., and other Republicans warned that congressional approval of a Clinton administration request for more than $1 billion to clear U.S. debts to the U.N. would hinge on the world body implementing major reforms. ■

Pete Peterson Confirmed As Envoy to Vietnam

Former Rep. Pete Peterson, D-Fla., who spent more than six years as a prisoner of war in Vietnam, headed back to Hanoi as the first U.S. ambassador to that country since the United States normalized relations with its former adversary in 1995.

The Senate approved Peterson's nomination by voice vote April 10, after a delay of nearly a year. The Foreign Relations Committee gave its approval March 4 by voice vote.

Peterson had been imprisoned and tortured by the North Vietnamese after his Air Force fighter-bomber was shot down in 1966. He was subsequently elected to the House, where he served from 1990 until he retired in 1997.

President Clinton nominated Peterson for the ambassadorship in May 1996, but the Foreign Relations Committee refused to act on his nomination that year, because Peterson ran afoul of a rarely-invoked constitutional provision barring lawmakers from serving in offices created during their terms.

The nomination was further delayed by Robert C. Smith, R-N.H., a leading critic of Clinton's decision to restore diplomatic ties with Vietnam. Smith wanted the White House to agree to consult with the intelligence community before declaring that Hanoi was fully cooperating in the search for clues to the fate of servicemen still listed as missing from the Vietnam War.

Smith removed his hold after receiving written assurances that the president would consult with a variety of defense and intelligence officials in determining whether Vietnam was cooperating to the fullest extent.

John Kerry, D-Mass., who helped lead a Senate investigation into cases of missing servicemen, said Peterson's presence in Hanoi would "enhance our credibility and greatly facilitate our ability to get those answers."

At a confirmation hearing before the Senate Foreign Relations Committee on Feb. 13, Craig Thomas, R-Wyo., said that as a former prisoner of war in Vietnam, Peterson was "exceptionally qualified for the position." Thomas chaired the Subcommittee on East Asian and Pacific Affairs.

But Thomas took a swipe at the administration's 1995 decision to normalize relations with Vietnam, charging that Hanoi was dragging its feet in providing information on the U.S. servicemen who were still listed as missing in action.

In addition, Thomas and other GOP lawmakers raised concerns that the administration's Vietnam policy might have been influenced by financial contributions made to Democrats from the Riady family of Indonesia, which had been at the center of a controversy over Democratic fundraising practices in the 1996 campaign. *(Campaign finance, p. 1-20)*

John McCain, R-Ariz., who had helped lead congressional efforts in behalf of normalizing relations with Hanoi, tried to put to rest speculation that campaign contributions played a role. "Let me say as strongly as I can that this rumor is entirely unsubstantiated by fact," McCain told the committee. McCain, too, had been a prisoner of war in Vietnam.

Other Ambassadors Confirmed

Several other key diplomatic posts were also filled:

- **Foley.** The Senate on Oct. 27 approved the nomination of former House Speaker Thomas S. Foley, D-Wash. (1965-95), to serve as U.S. ambassador to Japan. The vote was 91-0. *(Vote 281, p. S-48)*

Foley, who served for 15 terms in the House and was Speaker from 1989 to 1995, replaced former ambassador and onetime Vice President Walter F. Mondale, who left the ambassadorship in December 1996.

The Senate Foreign Relations Committee had approved his nomination by voice vote Oct. 8, following a hearing Sept. 24 in which members praised Foley but criticized the Clinton administration for leaving the ambassadorship open for more than nine months after Mondale's departure.

- **Fowler.** The Senate on Oct. 27 also confirmed former Sen. Wyche Fowler Jr., D-Ga. (House 1977-87, Senate 1987-93), as ambassador to Saudi Arabia. The vote was 90-0. *(Vote 280, p. S-48)*

The Senate Foreign Relations Committee had approved the nomination Oct. 8 by voice vote, after John Ashcroft, R-Mo., lifted a hold on the posting. Ashcroft wanted the administration to answer questions on U.S.-Saudi relations. Fowler had been in Saudi Arabia since August 1996, when Clinton appointed him while Congress was in recess.

- **Foglietta.** The Senate on Oct. 21 confirmed by voice vote the selection of Rep. Thomas M. Foglietta, D-Pa., to serve as U.S. ambassador to Italy. Foglietta, 68, had served in the House since 1981, where he represented the state's 1st District and fought hard to save Philadelphia's naval shipyard.
- **Boggs.** Former Rep. Corrine Claiborne "Lindy" Boggs, D-La., was confirmed by voice vote Oct. 9 as ambassador to the Vatican. Boggs had represented Louisiana's 2nd District from 1973 to 1991. ■

Intelligence Bottom Line Disclosed

After weeks of delay, Congress on Nov. 7 cleared a bill authorizing the activities of the Central Intelligence Agency, the National Reconnaissance Office and other intelligence-related organizations for fiscal 1998. President Clinton signed the measure into law Nov. 20 (S 858 — PL 105-107).

But the biggest news on intelligence funding came from outside Congress. Prompted by a lawsuit, Director of Central Intelligence George J. Tenet ended years of secrecy Oct. 15 by making public the total amount spent on intelligence — $26.6 billion in fiscal 1997. Reports of the level of spending had been around $30 billion until the Clinton administration's announcement.

BOXSCORE

Fiscal 1998 Intelligence Authorization — S 858 (HR 1775). The bill authorized an estimated $27 billion for the Central Intelligence Agency, the National Reconnaissance Office and other intelligence agencies.

Reports: S Rept 105-24, H Rept 105-135, Part 1; conference report, H Rept 105-350.

KEY ACTION

June 19 — Senate passed S 858, 98-1.

July 9 — House passed HR 1775 by voice vote.

July 17 — House passed S 858 by voice vote, after substituting the text of HR 1775.

Nov. 6 — Senate adopted the conference report by voice vote.

Nov. 7 — House cleared the bill, 385-36.

Nov. 20 — President signed S 858 — PL 105-107.

Background

The effort to reduce secrecy — the classification of documents and secrecy about funding — came from several fronts in 1997.

After a two-year study, a congressional commission led by Sen. Daniel Patrick Moynihan, D-N.Y., issued a report March 4 concluding that the government kept too many secrets, and that legislation was needed to rein in the practice.

Though secrecy was "an essential component of an effective national security, we have gone overboard," said Rep. Lee H. Hamilton, D-Ind., a commission member. "Information has been classified often not to protect national security," he said, "but to protect national security officials from embarrassment and inquiry."

The 12-member Commission on Protecting and Reducing Government Secrecy recommended legislation to set government-wide standards for classifying documents when there was a "demonstrable need" to protect the material, a timetable for declassifying documents and a National Declassification Center, probably at the National Archives, to coordinate the process.

According to the commission's report, 83 percent of all classified documents were generated by the Defense Department and the Central Intelligence Agency.

But even as the report was announced, members acknowledged that enacting such a law would be difficult, since government secrecy was historically the prerogative of the president, as commander in chief. Clinton had set his own guidelines for classifying documents in an executive order in April 1995.

Deputy White House Chief of Staff John D. Podesta, a member of the Moynihan commission, said Congress had to ensure that any legislation on secrecy "doesn't impinge on the president's authority to carry out national security."

Congress took no action on the report in 1997.

Lawsuit Demands Budget Total

On May 19, the Federation of American Scientists filed a lawsuit against the CIA demanding disclosure of the total amount spent annually on intelligence programs.

The organization noted that Clinton had issued a statement in 1996 authorizing Congress to make public the total appropriation for intelligence activities. The group also pointed to testimony before the Senate Intelligence Committee in 1996 by then-Director of Central Intelligence John M. Deutch, who said disclosing the overall budget figure would "not, in itself, harm intelligence activities."

The suit, filed in U.S. District Court in Washington, D.C., claimed the CIA was violating the Freedom of Information Act by refusing to disclose the overall budget figure.

"There is a mythology at work that this is sensitive. I don't think it can be taken at face value," said Steven Aftergood, director of the federation's project on government secrecy. "What's really going on is an attempt to insulate intelligence policy from the political process."

Although several blue-ribbon commissions had studied intelligence operations and recommended that the overall budget figure be disclosed, Congress continued to resist efforts to release the number. The House in 1996 rejected an amendment offered by John Conyers Jr., D-Mich., to the fiscal 1997 intelligence authorization bill (PL 104-293) to make public the total intelligence budget figure. Conyers introduced legislation in 1997 (HR 753) to require the disclosure of the total amount spent on intelligence-related activities. *(1996 Almanac, p. 9-16)*

The CIA had no comment on the lawsuit. Tenet, then acting director, had indicated previously that he could support making the total budget figure public as long as it did not lead to disclosure of the amount spent on specific activities. But Senate Intelligence Committee Chairman Richard C. Shelby, R-Ala., said he was concerned that such further disclosure was exactly what would happen if the overall budget figure was made public.

House Action

The House Intelligence Committee approved a draft fiscal 1998 intelligence reauthorization bill, later introduced as HR 1775 (H Rept 105-135, Part 1), in a closed-door session June 5. The vote was not made public.

The funding levels were classified, but the authorization was assumed at the time to be about $30 billion. According to C.W. "Bill" Young, R-Fla., who chaired the House Appropriations subcommittee with jurisdiction over intelligence agencies, Clinton had requested an $800 million increase over fiscal 1997.

The legislation stressed the importance of human intelligence — as opposed to electronic or other forms of acquiring information — which was reflected in an increase in funding for that component of intelligence-gathering, according to ranking panel Democrat Norm Dicks of Washington. Dicks said the panel also wanted to improve the analysis and dissemination of intelligence.

Committee Chairman Porter J. Goss, R-Fla., said he was putting emphasis on the intelligence community's "eyes and ears around the world." Goss, a former CIA agent, was in his first year as chairman of the panel.

In its report, the committee expressed a number of concerns over such areas as the analysis of intelligence. The report said intelligence analysts suffered from a lack of in-depth expertise and language skills, and the bill included authorization for a pilot program that would allow the intelligence community to seek advice from former employees, outside experts and linguists. The bill also called for greater emphasis on the processing, analysis and dissemination of intelligence and on long-term planning.

House Rejects Efforts To Cut Spending

The House passed the intelligence bill by voice vote July 9 after rebuffing two efforts to cut spending across the board.

Dicks said the legislation provided a 1.7 percent increase over the amount authorized by Congress for fiscal 1997 and was 0.7 percent above Clinton's fiscal 1998 request.

The House rejected, 142-289, an amendment by Independent Bernard Sanders of Vermont to cut intelligence funding based on fiscal 1997 levels by 5 percent. Lawmakers also defeated, 182-238, an attempt by Barney Frank, D-Mass., to reduce intelligence spending to the level requested by Clinton. *(Vote 253, p. H-80; vote 255, p. H-82)*

"If we are serious about deficit reduction, we cannot only go after working people and low-income people. We also have to have the courage to go after the intelligence community," Sanders said. But Goss defended the bill, saying: "Just because the Cold War is over does not make this world more safe."

Members also defeated, 192-237, an amendment by Conyers to make public the total amount spent on intelligence activities. *(Vote 254, p. H-82)*

Though Democrats on the committee said they supported the measure, Dicks expressed concern about a provision in the bill that would abolish the 3-year-old Defense Airborne Reconnaissance Office, created to coordinate airborne reconnaissance among the services. Goss said he was concerned that the agency did not have an adequate management system; Dicks said the committee acted too hastily.

The Senate Intelligence Committee had affirmed its support for the reconnaissance office, and the Clinton administration opposed its elimination.

Senate Action

The Senate Intelligence Committee approved its version of the intelligence authorization, later introduced as S 858 (S Rept 105-24), by voice vote in a closed session June 4.

Again, the funding level was assumed to be about $30 billion. Lawmakers provided few details after the markup. However, the panel members did not take any major steps toward reorganizing the intelligence community as they had attempted to do in the fiscal 1997 authorization bill. There were "no significant reorganization efforts," said the panel's vice chairman, Bob Kerrey, D-Neb.

In its report, the Intelligence Committee expressed deep concern over the handling and use of intelligence information by the intelligence community and the Pentagon during the Persian Gulf War. Of particular concern was the dissemination of information about a chemical weapons depot in Iraq and the possible exposure of U.S. troops to poisonous gas when they blew up the depot in 1991.

The bill required that the director of Central Intelligence submit a report identifying actions taken to improve cooperation between defense and intelligence officials and to enhance the handling and use of intelligence information before, during and after battle.

Among the few details revealed about funding priorities was a reduction of $75 million in spending on the Outrider unmanned aerial vehicle, used for surveillance and reconnaissance. The committee report noted that it had received testimony indicating "serious difficulty" with the program.

The report cited development problems with another unmanned aerial vehicle, Dark Star. The bill cut $20 million from the program and reduced the number of vehicles to be purchased.

The bill added $1.6 million to the administration's request for open-source collection, analysis and production of intelligence.

Senate Backs Whistleblower Provision

The Senate passed the bill, 98-1, on June 19, despite a veto threat from the White House over an attempt by the committee to protect whistleblowers. Democrat Tom Harkin of Iowa cast the lone "no" vote because the spending total was not made public. *(Vote 109, p. S-21)*

An amendment by Robert G. Torricelli, D-N.J., calling for disclosure of the spending total stirred the only controversy on the Senate floor. The Senate had included a provision in the previous year's reauthorization bill requiring that the total be disclosed, but the language was stripped from the bill in conference.

"This is a national policy to conceal the gross expenditures for the Central Intelligence Agency [but a policy] that has lost its rationale," Torricelli said.

But opponents argued that revealing the bottom line would allow adversaries to track U.S. funding for intelligence programs and adjust their own spending accordingly. They also maintained that releasing the budget number would lead to calls for revealing more funding details. "How do you defend that number without getting into the details," said Intelligence Committee member Jon Kyl, R-Ariz. "This is a slippery slope." The amendment was rejected on a 43-56 vote. *(Vote 108, p. S-21)*

What upset the administration, however, was a provision to require the president to make clear to federal employees or contractors that it was not illegal for them to disclose classified information to a member of Congress if the information showed evidence of criminal wrongdoing, if a false statement had been made to Congress or if there was evidence of a gross waste of funds or abuse of authority.

The provision stemmed from concern over a letter sent in late 1996 by the director of Central Intelligence to the State Department admonishing an employee who revealed to Torricelli classified information linking a CIA informant to two murders in Guatemala. *(1995 Almanac, p. 10-26)*

The Senate committee said in its report that it was concerned that this move and other statements by executive branch officials would signal to federal employees that "there are no circumstances" under which they could disclose evidence of wrongdoing involving classified information. "We simply intend it to preserve the ability of Congress to perform oversight, which cannot be done without information," said Kerrey.

The administration, however, said the provision was unconstitutional and could prompt a veto. A statement from the Office of Management and Budget said the provision was "clearly contrary to the Supreme Court's explicit recognition of the president's constitutional authority to protect national security and other privileged information."

The administration also expressed concern about some of the budgetary priorities in the bill.

Both Kerrey and Intelligence Committee Chairman Shelby said they believed the whistleblower issue could be worked out — "as long as it doesn't change the substance of what we're doing," Shelby added.

Shelby provided few specifics about the bill, except to say that it included "additional resources" to counter terrorism, nuclear proliferation, narcotics trafficking and foreign intelligence, as well as for covert action, research and development.

The bill also called for improvements in getting information to the families of U.S. nationals murdered or kidnapped overseas. It directed the secretary of State to identify all relevant information about such incidents and provide this information to the families, as long as it did not jeopardize national security.

Conference

House and Senate conferees agreed Sept. 16 on a compromise version of the bill (H Rept 105-350), after dropping the controversial whistleblower provision.

The closed-door meeting was dominated by discussion of the Senate provision. Senate Intelligence Committee members said the language was necessary to help them do their jobs, but the administration's veto threat was persuasive.

The conferees also rejected the provision in the House bill that would have abolished the Defense Airborne Reconnaissance Office. They instead deferred to the defense authorization bill, which sought to scale back the agency.

The final bill included the language directing the secretary of State to provide as much information as possible to families of Americans abused, tortured, kidnapped or killed overseas, as long as the disclosure did not jeopardize national security or an ongoing criminal investigation.

Another provision required the directors of Central Intelligence and the FBI to report on China's intelligence activities directed against or affecting the United States.

House, Senate Give Final Approval

After weeks of delay, the Senate adopted the conference report Nov. 6 by voice vote. The House cleared the bill the following day by a vote of 385-36. *(Vote 607, p. H-182)*

Although the legislation was generally non-controversial, Intelligence committee leaders in both chambers had agreed to hold it back while differences were worked out on the separate defense authorization bill (HR 1119), which traditionally moved first.

Since both measures authorized funding for some military-related intelligence activities, defense authorizers were concerned that moving the intelligence bill first might undermine support for the defense legislation, which had stalled for months in a dispute over Air Force maintenance depots. *(Defense authorization, p. 8-3)*

The funding level in the fiscal 1998 intelligence bill remained classified. But by that point, the Federation of American Scientists lawsuit had prompted Tenet to reveal that $26.6 billion had been spent on intelligence in fiscal 1997. Dicks said the conference report authorized 1.4 percent more than in fiscal 1997, which translated into nearly $27 billion. Tenet said decisions on disclosing spending totals in the future would be made on a case-by-case basis. ■

Tenet Wins CIA After Lake Pulls Out

The Senate on July 10 confirmed George J. Tenet as director of Central Intelligence, four months after he was nominated and nearly eight months after the job fell vacant. Tenet, 44, was confirmed by voice vote with little debate. Air Force Lt. Gen. John A. Gordon was confirmed as deputy director of Central Intelligence on Oct. 27, also by voice vote. *(Gordon, p. 8-52)*

President Clinton had announced selection of Tenet on March 19, after his first pick, former National Security advisor Tony Lake, abruptly withdrew his nomination. Lake's nomination had become caught up in partisan controversy over White House and Democratic fundraising practices.

Tenet's nomination was warmly received by the Senate Intelligence Committee, which regarded him as one of its own. Tenet had served as staff director for the committee from 1988 to 1993. After leaving the committee staff, he went to the National Security Council (NSC), where he worked as Lake's senior director for intelligence. He left that position in 1995 to become deputy director of Central Intelligence. He had been serving as acting director of Central Intelligence since December 1997, when John M. Deutch resigned from the intelligence community's top post.

Lake Withdraws

Clinton was forced to select a new nominee after Lake asked the president March 17 to withdraw his nomination. In a letter to Clinton, Lake complained that the nomination process had become a "political football in a game with constantly moving goalposts."

Lake's surprise decision came after three days of testimony, March 11-13, before the Senate Intelligence Committee. An additional round of hearings was scheduled for March 18-20. Lake's confirmation hearings had been postponed twice.

During the first week of hearings, questions for Lake included:

➤ His role in a 1994 decision by the Clinton administration to give tacit approval to the shipment of arms from Iran to the Muslim-dominated Bosnian government.

➤ Why he was not informed by his staffers about an FBI briefing detailing an alleged plan by the Chinese government to influence U.S. elections.

➤ Whether he could provide objective intelligence information, given his role in helping to formulate foreign policy.

Revelations that might have caused further problems for Lake broke March 17 when The Wall Street Journal reported allegations that Donald Fowler, former chairman of the Democratic National Committee (DNC), had attempted to persuade NSC officials to change a recommendation that controversial businessman Roger Tamraz, a heavy donor to the party, not be invited to White House meetings. *(Campaign finance investigation, p. 1-20)*

The story alleged that Fowler arranged to have a favorable CIA report on Tamraz sent to the NSC. Despite warnings against it, Tamraz was permitted to attend some White House events, the Journal reported.

The allegations raised questions about why Lake's subordinates did not bring the matter to his attention. The story also highlighted concern about the potential interference of politics at the CIA. In a March 17 statement, Tenet called the allegations "extremely serious" and said he had asked the CIA's inspector general to investigate.

Senate Intelligence Committee Vice Chairman Bob Kerrey, D-Neb., who had been expected to support Lake, expressed deep concern about the allegations raised in the Journal's story and said Lake's failure to ensure that NSC staff members would bring such a matter to his attention was a "potentially disqualifying mistake."

Kerrey said he communicated his concern to Lake and to the White House on March 17, leading to speculation that the potential loss of Kerrey's support added to Lake's decision to withdraw.

It was the second time a Clinton nominee had bowed out of consideration for the intelligence job. In 1995, retired Air Force Gen. Michael P.C. Carns withdrew after being picked to succeed R. James Woolsey as director of Central Intelligence. Carns was forced to step aside amid revelations that he had broken immigration laws when he brought a Filipino domestic worker to the United States. *(1995 Almanac, p. 10-28)*

Although Lake said he believed he had the votes to be confirmed, he said he was concerned that his nomination would be subjected to an "endless" series of delays, particularly in light of the allegations concerning the DNC, and continuing demands that all members of the Intelligence Committee be given access to a detailed FBI file on Lake.

Intelligence Committee Chairman Richard C. Shelby of Alabama and other GOP conservatives had been demanding access to the complete FBI file, not just the summary given to Shelby and Kerrey. A more detailed file was provided to the two committee leaders on March 14.

As a result, Lake said in his letter to Clinton, he did not believe the committee would vote on his nomination until after Easter (March 30). And even then, he said he expected that a floor vote would be continually delayed for as long as Clinton's "political opponents can do so."

"I have gone through the past three months and more with patience and, I hope, dignity. But I have lost the former and could lose the latter as this political circus continues indefinitely," Lake wrote.

Lake's view was shared by some members of the committee. Richard H. Bryan, D-Nev., said he agreed that the committee had to ask tough questions. But, he said, "it's pretty clear the strategy here is a partisan one to postpone any reasonable prospect for a vote."

Shelby denied there was any intent to delay the hearings, saying his goal was a fair but "rigorous" examination of the nominee. He indicated he also would like access to the complete FBI file on Tenet, according to The Washington Post.

Congressional Democrats and White House officials accused Senate Republicans of politicizing the confirmation process and waging personal attacks against Lake's integrity. At a March 18 briefing, White House Press Secretary Mike McCurry said the confirmation process Lake went through was "inexcusably flawed." During a news conference later that day, Clinton declared that "the cycle of political destruction must end."

Senate Minority Leader Tom Daschle, D-S.D., said the hearings amounted to "character assassination," and he called on the committee to apologize to Lake.

During a news conference with Shelby, Kerrey said, "I do think that . . . the process was not fair." In particular, he cited the demands for the complete FBI file on Lake, as well as Shelby's desire to subpoena NSC staff members to testify under oath.

Kerrey also criticized those who had made "innuendos" that Lake had broken the law in the Iran-Bosnia matter. A Justice Department investigation into whether Lake and other administration officials made false statements to a House committee found Lake did not commit any criminal wrongdoing.

Even some Republicans criticized the way in which Lake's nomination was handled. Richard G. Lugar, R-Ind., an Intelligence Committee member, described the confirmation process for Lake as "another example of Borking," a reference to the rough time Democrats gave Robert H. Bork before defeating his nomination to the Supreme Court in 1987. *(1987 Almanac, p. 271)*

Other Republicans argued that the process worked exactly as it was supposed to. "The process worked. In the end, he didn't stand up," said Phil Gramm, R-Texas, who threatened to keep Lake's nomination from coming to the floor if senators were not given access to the nominee's FBI file. "He was the wrong person for the wrong job."

Added Jon Kyl, R-Ariz., "This is a tough job. I didn't think the hearings were that tough at all."

Former Sen. David L. Boren, D-Okla., who chaired the Intelligence Committee from 1987 to 1993, said, "I do think there's legitimate room for people to question whether he was the right fit at CIA." But he added that Lake also had the misfortune of being ensnared by the controversy over White House and Democratic fundraising practices.

Tenet Nominated

Moving quickly to avoid further political controversy, Clinton on March 19 picked acting director Tenet for the post. Clinton appeared to be opting for a safe choice in Tenet, who had been easily confirmed by the Senate in 1995 as deputy director of Central Intelligence. Clinton noted that Tenet was well-known and well-respected in the Senate, and the nomination was met with praise by senators on both sides of the aisle. *(1995 Almanac, p. 10-28)*

"I have known George Tenet for several years and believe him to be a man of integrity and professionalism," said Shelby. "I will ensure that Mr. Tenet is given a fair and thorough examination."

Tenet called his nomination a "bittersweet moment." "I had hoped to serve with my good friend Tony Lake, as his deputy," Tenet told a news conference. Lake had said he would keep Tenet on if confirmed and reportedly recommended him as director when he told Clinton he was withdrawing his nomination.

Senate Confirmation Hearings

Tenet received a generally favorable reception from the Senate Intelligence Committee during a confirmation hearing May 6. He met with the panel behind closed doors May 7 to discuss classified issues.

Tenet promised the committee he would provide the "strong, stable and consistent" leadership needed to meet future threats to U.S. security.

Tenet was introduced at the May 6 hearing by Boren, his former boss. "If there is anything we need right now in terms of the directorship of the CIA . . . [it] is to have a director who is strong enough and independent enough, if necessary, to walk right in to the president of the United States or the chair of this committee . . . and say, 'You may

Gordon Named Deputy

The Senate on Oct. 27 confirmed Air Force Lt. Gen. John A. Gordon to be deputy director of Central Intelligence. The action was by voice vote. Gordon succeeded George J. Tenet, who was promoted by Clinton to be director of Central Intelligence. Gordon was a nearly 30-year veteran of the Air Force.

The Senate Intelligence Committee approved Gordon's nomination by voice vote on Oct. 8.

Gordon had served as Tenet's chief adviser on military affairs since September 1996. Tenet announced July 21 that President Clinton would nominate Gordon to the No. 2 position.

Before joining the CIA, Gordon served as special assistant to the Air Force chief of staff for long-range planning. Gordon, who joined the Air Force in 1968, served during the Bush administration on the National Security Council, specializing in defense and arms control issues.

not want to hear this, or I know you don't want to hear this, but you are going to hear it anyway' — to have that kind of force of character," Boren said. "I have not one doubt in my mind that George Tenet would deliver that kind of message to any of you if you needed to hear it in the interest of this country."

Although the committee spent little time probing the questions of administration policy and Democratic fundraising that had dominated Lake's appearance before the panel, Tenet was asked about allegations that the DNC had had contact with the CIA.

Tenet said he was never asked to meet with any political official while he worked at the NSC. Tenet added that "it is absolutely inappropriate for any political organization to believe that they can have access to anybody inside of my building [the CIA], period."

He also denied an allegation that he leaked to the news media the name of a CIA informant linked to two murders in Guatemala.

Neither issue generated any follow-up questions by senators.

Tenet Spells Out Views on Intelligence

Senators spent more time delving into Tenet's views on how, if confirmed, he would lead the nation's intelligence community, which included the CIA and several other intelligence agencies, most of which were part of the Defense Department.

"Ultimately, leadership at this moment means closing the door on the Cold War and embracing the challenges and opportunities of a new era," Tenet said.

Among the biggest threats facing the United States was terrorism. According to a State Department report, while the number of terrorist acts worldwide fell in 1996, the death toll from such incidents rose compared with years past.

"The fact is that the activity worldwide at this moment in time is unprecedented and the threat to U.S. interests is enormously high," Tenet told the committee.

Tenet was asked by several senators what reforms he believed still needed to be undertaken in the wake of the Aldrich H. Ames spy scandal, one of the most devastating in the CIA's history. *(1994 Almanac, p. 463)*

While noting that he intended to continue implementing reforms put in place under Deutch, Tenet said several important steps already had been made to beef up the agency's counter-intelligence efforts. In particular, he noted that he had been working with FBI Director Louis J. Freeh to improve cooperation with law enforcement authorities. He also said people within the agency's clandestine service understood that their work was subject to more oversight, that there was "greater transparency" to their activities.

"I think we are well down the road of getting much, much better here," Tenet said. "But the nature of our business is [that] I could never tell you we're risk-free on the espionage front."

At the same time, Tenet strongly defended the clandestine service and said that reports of severe morale problems were overstated.

Tenet also was asked if the CIA's intelligence gathering had suffered under a policy, instituted under Deutch, that required agents to balance an informant's intelligence value against any evidence of past criminal activity or human rights abuse. The agency reportedly had "scrubbed" its ranks of informants in recent years, dropping many either because they were not considered of value or because they had an unsavory past.

Tenet said he did not believe this effort impeded the agency's information collecting abilities. If anything, he said, it "has freed our officers up from continuing to deal with people who had very little value to the United States or to our intelligence service."

On other issues, Tenet said the intelligence community was shifting its commitment from larger spy satellites to smaller ones."We're going smaller, and there's no turning back from that decision," he said.

Tenet acknowledged the need for the intelligence community to increase its efforts to recruit officers who spoke a variety of languages and who had the "state of the art technical skills" needed to tackle the most difficult targets. "As vital as sophisticated technology is to our work, intelligence is primarily a human endeavor," he said.

Some senators did question Tenet about the CIA's failure to adequately notify military authorities before and after the Persian Gulf War about an Iraqi chemical weapons site that U.S. troops blew up in 1991. The CIA revealed in April that the agency was aware of the site in 1984 — much earlier than was previously acknowledged.

Tenet said he did not believe anyone at the CIA "was engaged in a conspiracy or somehow wanted to deny people access to information."

Later, in noting the ongoing effort to determine the cause of the Gulf War syndrome — a variety of symptoms and illnesses that had afflicted veterans of that war — Sen. Bryan said, "It just seems to me that somebody ought to have said, you know, maybe this doesn't have anything to do with it, but we probably should let people know that there were chemical weapons that were in there."

Tenet acknowledged that the information should have been revealed sooner. But, he said, "We're committed to doing all we can to get it all out."

Action Delayed During Probe of Finances

The committee was prepared to move Tenet's confirmation forward, but it waited for clearance from the Justice Department, which had been investigating Tenet's finances. Shelby announced the panel's decision after a May 14 closed-door session with Tenet, during which the panel's members were briefed by the Justice Department on the inquiry.

The Justice Department was investigating Tenet's failure to disclose until 1994 his partial ownership of telephone stock and real estate in Greece, property Tenet inherited after his father died in 1983, according to a White House official. His financial disclosure statement showed that along with some family members, he owned condominiums in Athens worth between $250,000 and $500,000, as well as stock in some U.S. telephone companies.

Tenet apparently was unaware of the holdings until 1994, when his brother discovered them in a safe deposit box. Tenet, who at the time was working for the NSC, informed White House ethics officials about the matter and was told to recuse himself from any matters connected to the holdings, the official said.

The department's investigation was to determine whether an independent counsel was necessary to pursue the matter. As deputy director of Central Intelligence, Tenet was covered by the independent counsel law.

Shelby and Kerrey made it clear they did not believe the investigation, requested by the White House, would hurt Tenet's prospects for confirmation. Shelby said Tenet was "a good, solid nominee," a feeling he said was "just about unanimous on the committee on both sides of the aisle."

Tenet Cleared, Confirmed

After receiving word from the Justice Department that Tenet had been cleared, the committee voted 19-0 to recommend his confirmation. The vote took place in a closed-door session July 10. Hours later, the Senate confirmed Tenet by voice vote.

In a letter to Shelby and Kerrey, acting Deputy Attorney General Seth P. Waxman said that Attorney General Janet Reno had decided against seeking an independent counsel based on the department's investigation. The department has "determined that there are no reasonable grounds to believe that further investigation is warranted," Waxman said.

Tenet said in a statement that he was "deeply honored" to be confirmed for the post. He also pledged to "deliver intelligence that is clear, objective and does not pull punches."

"I wish we could've done it earlier," Shelby said after the committee's vote. ■

CQ

Chapter 9

APPROPRIATIONS

OVERVIEW

All 13 Fiscal 1998 Bills Enacted Though Policy Disputes Persist

Republicans clear all bills for first time since taking control of Congress; Clinton uses line-item veto on nine

Abandoning the take-it-or-leave-it strategy that triggered two government shutdowns and hurt Republicans during their first two years in power, GOP leaders succeeded in getting all 13 regular appropriations bills enacted before adjourning for the year. Even so, disputes over partisan policy riders stalled work on four of the fiscal 1998 bills until November, requiring a string of six temporary appropriations bills, or continuing resolutions, to keep the government operating in the interim. The last two spending bills were cleared Nov. 13, the final day of the session.

Earlier in the year, Republicans staged an ill-conceived showdown with the White House over a fiscal 1997 supplemental appropriations bill (HR 1469) that seemed to signal they had learned little from their disastrous confrontations with Clinton in 1995-96. Despite repeated White House veto threats, GOP leaders in June tried to force the president to accept two controversial policy riders by attaching them to the must-pass supplemental, which contained badly needed disaster aid for victims of flooding in the Upper Midwest.

They gambled that Clinton would not dare to follow through on his veto threat, or that if he did, he would pay a high political price. That turned out to be a serious miscalculation. Clinton vetoed the bill as soon as he received it, and the public directed its anger at congressional Republicans for delaying the aid. In the end, they were forced to strip the riders and send Clinton a clean bill, which he signed.

The 13 Regular Bills

Work on the fiscal 1998 spending bills went into high gear in September, following a summer spent largely on completing a pair of massive budget-reconciliation bills. Just four of the 13 spending bills cleared by Sept. 30, the end of fiscal 1997, with a fifth completed the next day. By the end of October, four more of the bills had gone to the president. *(Budget-reconciliation, p. 2-27)*

That left four bills that had been snagged all along over controversial policy issues — foreign operations (abortion and family planning); District of Columbia (vouchers for private schooling); Labor, Health and Human Services and Education (national student testing); and Commerce, Justice, State (census sampling).

With the exception of Clinton's plan for voluntary national student testing, each of the issues had been hashed out before — mostly to the dissatisfaction of conservatives. But the conservatives refused to knuckle under, to the dismay of House Appropriations Committee Chairman Robert L. Livingston, R-La., who was determined to avoid having to bundle unfinished spending measures into a year-end omnibus appropriations bill. Twice before, Clinton had used such circumstances to maximize his leverage and force Republicans to accede to his priorities.

This time, the two sides essentially fought to a draw. Clinton had to delay his national voluntary testing plan, which was under attack from conservatives worried it would mean federal intrusion into local school systems, and from black and Hispanic lawmakers who said it would further stigmatize schools in low-income areas.

The student voucher plan, aimed at sending 2,000 low-income D.C. children to private or suburban schools, was scuttled by the Senate. On the census, the president was allowed to go forward with his plan to use statistical sampling in addition to traditional methods, but Republicans won the right to an expedited court challenge of the procedure.

House conservatives also backed down from their insistence on a provision that would have banned funds for family planning groups that promoted, performed or advocated abortion abroad even if they used their own money. But the victory cost Clinton two other key priorities — a plan to pay off back debts to the United Nations and a proposed $3.5 billion commitment to help underwrite an International Monetary Fund program to deal with global financial crises. In addition, the cherished plans of Senate Foreign Relations Committee Chairman Jesse Helms, R-N.C., to restructure foreign policy agencies and revamp the United Nations (HR 1757) were stalled by the same imbroglio over abortion.

Line-Item Veto

In perhaps the most historically significant development of the year on the appropriations front, Clinton used the new line-item veto (PL 104-130) for the first time to trim individual items in nine of the spending bills. *(Line-item veto, p. 2-63)*

The first appropriations bill to arrive on his desk was the $9.2 million military construction bill. Declaring that "the old rules have, in fact, changed," Clinton struck 38 projects totaling $287 million from the measure, provoking an angry bipartisan backlash in Congress. After that, he used the new power with relative caution. When it came to the huge, $247.7 billion defense appropriations bill, for example, he vetoed just 13 mostly marginal programs or research projects worth a total of $144 million.

While Congress had given the president the line-item veto, lawmakers were quick to try to limit its use. Although the White House acknowledged using faulty data in selecting some of the vetoed military construction projects and offered to work out a compromise, lawmakers instead cleared a bill (HR 2631) to restore all 38 projects. It met with a veto from Clinton, but the margins in both chambers were sufficient to ensure an override in the second session.

Lawmakers did not try to overturn any of the other line-item vetoes, but the administration backed down on the one item cut from the Treasury-Postal Service bill after the National Treasury Employees Union went to court. ■

Appropriations Mileposts

105th Congress – First Session

Bill	House Passed	Senate Passed	House Final *	Senate Final *	Signed	Story
Agriculture (HR 2160 — PL 105-86)	7/24/97	7/24/97	10/6/97	10/29/97	11/18/97	p. 9-5
Commerce, Justice, State, Judiciary (HR 2267 — PL 105-119)	9/30/97	7/29/97	11/13/97	11/13/97	11/26/97	p. 9-11
Defense (HR 2266 — PL 105-56)	7/29/97	7/15/97	9/25/97	9/25/97	10/8/97	p. 9-17
District of Columbia (HR 2607 — PL 105-100)	10/9/97	11/9/97	11/12/97	11/13/97	11/19/97	p. 9-27
Energy and Water Development (HR 2203 — PL 105-62)	7/25/97	7/16/97	9/30/97	9/30/97	10/13/97	p. 9-31
Foreign Operations (HR 2159 — PL 105-118)	9/4/97	7/17/97	11/13/97	11/13/97	11/26/97	p. 9-37
Interior (HR 2107 — PL 105-83)	7/15/97	9/18/97	10/24/97	10/28/97	11/14/97	p. 9-44
Labor, Health and Human Services, Education (HR 2264 — PL 105-78)	9/17/97	9/11/97	11/7/97	11/8//97	11/13/97	p. 9-50
Legislative Branch (HR 2209 — PL 105-55)	7/28/97	7/16/97	9/24/97	9/24/97	10/7/97	p. 9-58
Military Construction (HR 2016 — PL 105-45)	7/8/97	7/22/97	9/16/97	9/17/97	9/30/97	p. 9-61
Transportation (HR 2169 — PL 105-66)	7/23/97	7/30/97	10/9/97	10/9/97	10/27/97	p. 9-66
Treasury, Postal Service, General Government (HR 2378 — PL 105-61)	9/17/97	7/22/97	9/30/97	10/1/97	10/10/97	p. 9-71
VA-HUD-Independent Agencies (HR 2158 — PL 105-65)	7/16/97	7/22/97	10/8/97	10/9/97	10/27/97	p. 9-77
FY97 Supplemental Appropriations						
(HR 1469)	5/15/97	5/16/97	6/5/97	6/5/97	vetoed 6/9/97	p. 9-84
(HR 1871— PL 105-18)	6/12/97	6/12/97			6/12/97	p. 9-84

**Conference report adopted*

FDA Reform Slows Agriculture Bill

Congress cleared a $49.7 billion fiscal 1998 spending bill for agriculture, rural development and nutrition programs on Oct. 29. The measure, which President Clinton signed into law Nov. 18 (HR 2160 — PL 105-86), was $2.6 billion less than the administration had requested.

More than 70 percent of the money in the bill was designated for mandatory spending programs, such as food stamps and farm subsidies. Among other things, the measure included $25 billion for the food stamp program, $34 million to curb smoking among teenagers, and $188 million for commissions to the insurance companies and agents that administered federal crop insurance policies.

The bill's overall funding level was about $4 billion less than was appropriated for fiscal 1997. The reduction in funding was due in large part to changes made as a result of the 1996 welfare overhaul law (PL 104-193). *(1996 Almanac, p. 6-3)*

The annual bill got off to its typical quick start, passing both chambers in July and attracting little controversy itself. But GOP leaders delayed final action out of concern that early enactment might remove the urgency of separate legislation (S 830) to overhaul the Food and Drug Administration (FDA). The FDA was funded through the agriculture spending bill. *(FDA overhaul, p. 6-18)*

Congressional leaders allowed the agriculture appropriations bill to proceed to the president's desk only after the FDA bill had made considerable progress through conference in late October. In the end, the agriculture bill was enacted more than three months later than the fiscal 1997 measure had been the previous year.

The major issues on the spending bill itself were resolved far earlier in the process.

Agriculture appropriators spent much of their time on tobacco-related provisions. Both the House and the Senate rejected efforts to cut federal support for crop insurance and non-insured crop disaster assistance for tobacco growers.

Tobacco foes had more success on a second front, increasing funding for an FDA program aimed at curbing underage smoking. The final bill included $34 million, the amount requested by Clinton to expand the initiative nationwide.

Another dispute concerned commissions for insurance agents who administered crop insurance policies. House Democrats argued that the commissions were too high compared with those paid in other fields. The final version of the bill included $188 million for the program, $14 million less than the Senate's version, for the commissions.

Two days after signing the bill, Clinton utilized his line-item veto authority Nov. 20 to delete projects worth $1.9 million from the law. Among the items targeted were $600,000 for a new poisonous plants laboratory for the Agriculture Research Service in Logan, Utah, and $250,000 for a research grant to the University of Alaska to develop high-protein cattle feed.

BOXSCORE

Fiscal 1998 Agriculture Appropriations — HR 2160 (S 1033). The bill appropriated $49.7 billion for federal agriculture and nutrition programs.

Reports: H Rept 105-178, S Rept 105-51; conference report, H Rept 105-252.

KEY ACTION

July 24 — House passed HR 2160, 392-32.

July 24 — Senate passed S 1033, 99-0. (On Sept. 4, the Senate passed HR 2160 by voice vote after substituting text of S 1033.)

Oct. 6 — House adopted the conference report, 399-18.

Oct. 29 — Senate cleared the bill by voice vote.

Nov. 18 — President signed HR 2160 — PL 105-86.

Nov. 20 — President used the line-item veto to delete items from PL 105-86.

House Subcommittee

With little controversy, the House Appropriations Subcommittee on Agriculture, Rural Development, FDA and Related Agencies gave voice vote approval June 25 to a $49.4 billion draft that provided for few funding increases. The bill was later introduced as HR 2160.

The subcommittee was allocated $13.7 billion in discretionary spending for fiscal 1998, with the rest of the bill devoted to mandatory programs over which the appropriators had no direct control. On its face, the discretionary total appeared to be a large increase over the $12.9 billion appropriated the previous year. But subcommittee Chairman Joe Skeen, R-N.M., said the number was deceptive.

Skeen said the amount spent on discretionary programs in fiscal 1997 was actually $13.5 billion, because lawmakers had effectively used unspent mandatory funds for discretionary programs. For example, the Appropriations Committee applied $345 million from inflationary savings in the food stamps program toward discretionary accounts. Changes forced by the welfare law prevented the committee from taking advantage of such savings for fiscal 1998.

"We have very few increases in this bill," Skeen said. "The majority of items are frozen at last year's level or reduced."

The subcommittee bill put more emphasis on nutrition and on food and health safety than in the previous year. Among the accounts slated for an increase was the Women, Infants and Children (WIC) nutritional program, which got a $118.2 million boost over the fiscal 1997 level of $3.7 billion. This was in addition to the $76 million in funding for the program included in the fiscal 1997 supplemental appropriations bill (PL 105-18). Despite the increase, the WIC total still fell well short of the $4.1 billion requested by Clinton. *(Supplemental, p. 9-84)*

The panel also proposed to boost funding for rural housing by $67 million over fiscal 1997 levels to $1.1 billion, and increase spending for meat and poultry inspections by $15.7 million, to $589.7 million.

Underage Use of Tobacco

The subcommittee's version of the spending bill also called for a $23.2 million increase, to $944 million, for the FDA. The total included $15.3 million to expand FDA initiatives aimed at curbing tobacco use by underage consumers, through such means as requiring retailers to check the identification of purchasers to ensure they were at least 18.

The administration had requested $34 million for the initiative, $29 million more than was appropriated for fiscal 1997.

The FDA's tobacco regulations spurred one of the few debates during the subcommittee markup. Some Democrats expressed concern about report language proposed by Tom Latham, R-Iowa. Latham wanted to call on the FDA to ensure

Fiscal 1998 Agriculture Spending

(in thousands of dollars)

	Fiscal 1997 Appropriation	Fiscal 1998 Clinton Request	House Bill	Senate Bill	Conference Report
Agriculture Programs					
Crop insurance	$ 1,785,013	$1,584,135	$ 1,584,135	$ 1,584,135	$ 1,584,135
Agricultural Research Service	785,926	786,097	784,059	807,100	825,235
Commodity Credit Corporation	1,500,000	783,507	783,507	783,507	783,507
Farm Service Agency	748,540	746,889	704,553	703,209	703,209
Food safety and inspection	574,000	591,209	589,263	590,614	589,263
Cooperative State Research					
Extension Service	426,273	417,811	415,110	423,322	423,376
Research and education	421,504	422,342	421,223	427,526	431,410
Buildings and facilities	61,591	0	0	0	0
Animal and plant inspection	438,109	431,691	427,444	441,383	430,482
Other	977,058	1,179,970	1,166,139	1,162,535	1,161,820
Loan authorizations	*3,080,724*	*2,831,828*	*2,852,114*	*2,940,653*	*2,940,653*
Subtotal	**$ 7,718,014**	**$ 6,943,651**	**$ 6,875,433**	**$ 6,923,331**	**$ 6,932,437**
Conservation Programs					
Conservation operations	619,742	722,268	610,000	729,880	633,231
Watershed and flood prevention	101,036	40,000	101,036	40,000	101,036
Other	49,776	59,727	48,395	55,718	55,585
Subtotal	**$ 770,554**	**$ 821,995**	**$ 759,431**	**$ 825,598**	**$ 789,852**
Rural Economic and Community Development Programs					
Rural Housing Service	1,217,481	1,304,840	1,241,589	1,252,535	1,254,848
Rural Utilities Service	680,853	125,701	698,541	117,035	118,407
Other	105,422	750,018	101,038	709,285	714,813
Loan authorizations	*5,280,263*	*5,869,832*	*5,874,527*	*5,295,153*	*6,024,527*
Subtotal	**$ 2,003,756**	**$ 2,180,559**	**$ 2,041,168**	**$ 2,078,855**	**$ 2,088,068**
Domestic Food Programs					
Food stamp program	27,618,029	27,551,479	25,140,479	26,051,479	25,140,479
Child nutrition programs	8,653,297	7,782,766	7,766,966	7,769,066	7,767,816
Women, Infants and Children	3,805,807	4,108,000	3,924,000	3,927,600	3,924,000
Other	413,832	380,725	391,747	397,938	390,338
Subtotal	**$ 40,490,965**	**$ 39,822,970**	**$ 37,223,192**	**$ 38,146,083**	**$ 37,222,633**
Foreign Assistance and Related Programs					
PL 480 — Food for Progress	1,067,774	967,000	1,056,768	1,066,107	1,063,054
Program level	*1,107,305*	*990,149*	*1,105,048*	*1,114,530*	*1,111,508*
CCC export loan program	394,125	531,521	531,366	531,366	531,366
Loan guarantees	*5,500,000*	*5,500,000*	*5,500,000*	*5,500,000*	*5,500,000*
Foreign Agricultural Service	131,295	146,549	131,295	132,367	131,295
Subtotal	**$ 1,593,194**	**$ 1,645,070**	**$ 1,719,429**	**$ 1,729,840**	**$ 1,725,715**
Related Agencies					
Food and Drug Administration					
Appropriations	887,615	820,116	920,145	942,251	925,145
New proposed user fees	*0*	*131,643*	*0*	*0*	*0*
Other	65,391	67,829	64,829	67,829	65,829
Subtotal	**$ 953,006**	**$ 887,945**	**$ 984,974**	**$ 1,010,080**	**$ 990,974**
Emergency Appropriations					
PL 105-18	272,000	0	0	0	0
Other	88,000	0	0	0	0
Subtotal	**$ 360,000**	**$ 0**	**$ 0**	**$ 0**	**$ 0**
GRAND TOTAL					
New budget authority	**$ 53,889,489**	**$ 52,302,190**	**$ 49,603,627**	**$ 50,713,787**	**$ 49,749,679**
Loan authorizations	*13,860,987*	*14,201,660*	*14,226,641*	*13,735,806*	*14,465,180*

SOURCE: House Appropriations Committee

that it did not duplicate or waste financial resources on efforts that the Department of Health and Human Services' Substance Abuse and Mental Health Services Administration was already undertaking to curb underage tobacco use.

Opponents of the language argued it would curtail the FDA's ability to enforce regulations aimed at reducing smoking by underage youths. David R. Obey of Wisconsin, the ranking Democrat on the full Appropriations Committee, said Latham's proposal appeared to "play right into the hands of the tobacco companies."

Latham said his goal was simply to ensure that all the money appropriated for the FDA's regulations went toward reducing tobacco use by youths. He agreed to withdraw the proposed report language and to work on a more widely acceptable version.

Other Subcommittee Changes

Among those programs targeted for reductions from fiscal 1997 levels was the Farm Service Agency, which administered the major farm subsidy programs. Under the subcommittee's bill, the agency's funding was to be cut by $44 million, to $704 million.

The panel also adjusted to changes wrought by the sweeping 1996 farm bill (PL 104-127). That law dropped the designation of crop insurance as a mandatory spending program, which meant the subcommittee had to obligate money for the program out of discretionary funds. *(1996 Almanac, p. 3-15)*

Appropriators provided $152 million for crop insurance, much of it paid for by limiting to $270 million the amount in the bill for the Export Enhancement Program. The export program provided "bonuses" in the form of commodities or certificates redeemable for commodities to lower the net price of U.S. agriculture exports and improve their competitiveness on world markets. The program had been authorized at $500 million in fiscal 1998.

However, the subcommittee rejected, 1-11, an attempt by Latham to shift another $70 million from the export program to increase the commissions for agents administering crop insurance policies from the 24 percent included in the subcommittee's bill to 28 percent.

House Full Committee

The full House Appropriations Committee approved the $49.4 billion spending bill by voice vote July 9 (H Rept 105-178).

Despite recent acknowledgement by tobacco companies of the negative health effects of their products, the committee rejected by voice vote an amendment, offered by Nita M. Lowey, D-N.Y., to bar the federal government from subsidizing crop insurance or crop disaster assistance for tobacco farmers.

Lowey and other Democrats argued that it was hypocritical for the government to campaign for reduced tobacco use by Americans while providing support to tobacco farmers. "Given what we know about the health effects of tobacco, given the millions of dollars that we spend on preventing tobacco use, we have no business encouraging the growth of this product," Lowey said.

But lawmakers from tobacco-growing states said the amendment would do little to curb tobacco use and instead would unfairly penalize small farmers. "This is not Philip Morris" that would be affected by the amendment, said Harold Rogers, R-Ky., referring to the giant tobacco-products corporation. "If you want to take on tobacco, go after the real issue. This is an anti-small farmer amendment."

Other Amendments

The panel did approve a handful of amendments, including one by Skeen adding $9 million to the $15.3 million already in the bill for the FDA's initiatives on underage tobacco use.

The extra money was part of an en bloc amendment by Skeen that cut the amount proposed for the Export Enhancement Program from $270 million to $205 million. The amendment also added $36 million for commissions to agents who administered federal crop insurance policies, bringing the total to $188 million.

That move, however, drew fire from Obey, who noted that the Agriculture Department had said it needed only $152 million for the commissions. Obey, who opposed the spending bill, took a populist approach, saying the government should not increase subsidies for insurance agents "while we are in the process of grinding down support programs for farmers."

The committee adopted, 28-21, a proposal by George Nethercutt, R-Wash., to eliminate two positions in the Agriculture Department's Farm Service Agency: the deputy administrator and assistant deputy administrator for farm programs.

Nethercutt acted after the officials holding those positions declined to reverse a decision to accept only 22 percent of about 1 million acres that Washington farmers wanted to enroll in the Conservation Reserve Program, which paid farmers to idle environmentally sensitive land. "Something must be done to remedy incompetence," Nethercutt said.

The subcommittee's ranking Democrat, Marcy Kaptur of Ohio, and others argued that Nethercutt was setting a bad precedent and that Congress should not micromanage the Agriculture Department.

House Floor Action

The House passed the bill July 24 by a vote of 392-32, after a week of partisan squabbling over a procedural dispute unrelated to the bill itself. As passed, the bill called for $49.6 billion in appropriations. *(Vote 321, p. H-98)*

Agriculture spending bills generally enjoyed wide bipartisan support, and the fiscal 1998 bill was expected to be no different. House appropriators were so confident that the bill would not generate major controversy that they did not seek a rule to restrict the floor debate.

That provided an opening for many Democrats to vent their anger about House GOP actions that had nothing to do with the agriculture bill. Democrats were upset about the rule for debate on a separate measure — the foreign operations spending bill (HR 2159) — and took out their frustration by jamming up work on the agriculture bill with numerous demands for votes on procedural motions. "We were the instrument" for Democratic protests, said Skeen.

Republicans responded by passing a rule that limited the number of procedural motions and the time allowed for debate on amendments to the agriculture bill — a move that sparked further complaints by House Democrats that the rule was too restrictive.

Once the dust settled, few changes were made to the substance of the bill. Appropriators managed to rebuff several attempts to add controversial amendments on issues such as tobacco, sugar and peanuts.

The following major amendments were considered during the floor debate:

- **Tobacco subsidies.** Tobacco proved to be the most contentious issue. Lawmakers seeking to ban federal crop insurance and disaster aid for tobacco farmers hoped to seize momentum from a $368.5 billion legal settlement between state attorneys general and the tobacco industry announced June 20. Instead, they not only saw their effort to end the programs defeated, 209-216, but they lost ground from the previous year, when a similar amendment fell just two votes short. *(Vote 310, p. H-96; tobacco, p. 3-3)*

- **Underage smoking.** Tobacco industry foes were also defeated on a second front — an attempt to increase spending for FDA efforts to reduce underage tobacco use.

Senate appropriators had included $24 million for the program, compared with Clinton's request of $34 million. Martin T. Meehan, D-Mass., attempted to boost the amount by $10 million, offsetting the increase with a $14 million cut in the bill's $188 million allotment for crop insurance commissions. His amendment was rejected, 177-248. *(Vote 309, p. H-94)*

- **Sugar.** Members rejected, 175-253, an amendment by Charles E. Schumer, D-N.Y., and Dan Miller, R-Fla., to eliminate the non-recourse loan program for sugar. Non-recourse loans allowed growers who were unable to sell their sugar at the price established by the federal government to pay off their loans by forfeiting their sugar crop to the Agriculture Department. *(Vote 312, p. H-96)*

Miller said the federal government restricted the import of sugar and kept the price high so it would not lose money on the program, which he argued artificially inflated the price of sugar and forced consumers to pay higher prices for sugar and for products made with it.

Opponents disputed the assertion that consumers paid more. They also argued that there was no guarantee that sugar companies or manufacturers who used the sugar in other products would pass price reductions on to consumers.

- **Peanuts.** An attack on the peanut price-support program met with a similar fate. Mark W. Neumann, R-Wis., and Paul E. Kanjorski, D-Pa., sought to bar the use of funds in the bill to operate the peanut price-support program at a loan level greater than $550 per ton for the 1998 crop of peanuts grown under the government's quota system. That would have been a reduction of $60 a ton from the existing minimum price. The amendment was defeated, 185-242. *(Vote 314, p. H-96)*

- **Market Access Program.** The House also rejected attempts to cut funding for the Market Access Program, which provided grants to U.S. businesses to advertise their agricultural products overseas.

Schumer and Steve Chabot, R-Ohio, tried to eliminate the funding, but backers countered that the program had been reformed and was still necessary to help companies compete against foreign competitors who received government subsidies. The amendment was rejected, 150-277. *(Vote 316, p. H-96)*

- **WIC/insurance commissions.** Efforts to increase funding for nutrition programs by cutting the commissions paid to insurance agents also failed. Obey sought to boost spending for the WIC nutrition program by $23.7 million over the $3.9 billion funding in the bill. He wanted to pay for the extra funding by cutting spending for crop insurance commissions from $188 million to $152 million. The amendment was defeated, 195-230. *(Vote 308, p. H-94)*

Obey argued that the extra money was needed to ensure that the WIC program had the necessary carry-over funding to cover reimbursements that it would have to pay after the end of fiscal year 1998. He also maintained that the crop insurance program was being funded at a level much higher than the Agriculture Department said it would need.

Skeen and others argued, however, that WIC was already receiving an $118 million increase in the bill over fiscal 1997, an amount that would allow the program to maintain its existing caseload.

- **Discrimination office.** Lawmakers agreed by voice vote to an amendment by Albert R. Wynn, D-Md., to add $1.5 million for efforts to combat discrimination in agriculture programs by establishing an investigative unit within the Agriculture Department.

Senate Committee

The Senate Appropriations Committee approved its version of the bill (S 1033 — S Rept 105-51) July 17 by a vote of 28-0. Two days earlier, the Subcommittee on Agriculture, Rural Development and Related Agencies had approved the measure by voice vote.

The committee's draft bill recommended $50.6 billion for agriculture and nutrition programs in fiscal 1998, about $1 billion more than the House version. Of the total, $13.8 billion was for discretionary programs, $290 million more than in fiscal 1997.

The bill included $38 billion for a variety of domestic food assistance programs, $3.5 billion for low-income housing programs, and $822 million for conservation programs. Rural community advancement programs received about $638 million in the draft bill.

Tobacco issues dominated the Senate markups. Rather than provide $34 million, as requested, for FDA efforts to reduce underage tobacco use, the Senate chose to freeze spending at the fiscal 1997 level of $4.9 million.

Agriculture Subcommittee Chairman Thad Cochran, R-Miss., said additional funding for the initiative could come from the $368.5 billion the tobacco companies agreed to pay in their settlement with state attorneys general. "We have made the assumption that there will be funds forthcoming from the tobacco companies that will be available to help pay the costs of programs like this," Cochran said.

Tom Harkin, D-Iowa, proposed to increase funding for the FDA program to $34 million, paying for it by changing an existing 1 percent marketing assessment split between tobacco companies and tobacco farmers, to 2.1 percent, to be paid entirely by tobacco companies. But Harkin ended up withdrawing the amendment at the suggestion of members from both sides of the aisle who said it was too complex to approve without more study.

In other action, the committee approved by voice vote an amendment that, among other things, increased the bill's funding for low-income rental assistance by $17 million and for water and waste loans in the Rural Community Advancement Program by $5.8 million. The money was added after Senate appropriators increased the discretionary spending allocation for the agriculture bill by $20 million.

Senate Floor Action

Unencumbered by the extraneous issues that had bogged down the House bill, the Senate passed its $50.7 billion measure July 24 by a vote of 99-0. Like the House, which passed its bill the same day, the Senate successfully resisted efforts to attach controversial amendments related to tobacco and other issues. *(Vote 201, p. S-35)*

Anti-Tobacco Amendments Blocked

Once again, tobacco issues dominated the debate. An amendment, by Richard J. Durbin, D-Ill., to end federal support for tobacco crop insurance was tabled (killed), 53-47. "The Durbin amendment does not hit the tobacco companies," said Democrat Wendell H. Ford of Kentucky. "What it will do is ensure that tobacco farmers will slowly but surely go out of business." *(Vote 196, p. S-34)*

Ford offered a modification, tabled along with Durbin's amendment, that would have made broad changes to the crop insurance program by prohibiting farmers with more than 400 acres of farmable land from receiving crop insurance support.

The anti-tobacco forces also were defeated in their efforts to increase spending for the FDA's program on tobacco use by minors. A proposal by Harkin to provide the full $34 million requested by the administration was tabled (killed), 52-48. *(Vote 198, p. S-35)*

Harkin again proposed to pay for the increase by boosting the marketing assessment on the sale of tobacco and requiring the tobacco companies to pay the whole amount.

North Carolina Republican Jesse Helms countered by offering an amendment to increase the tax on ethanol, a corn-based product key to Iowa farmers, by 3 cents a gallon. He proposed using the money to establish a trust fund for anti-smoking efforts. The Senate tabled Helms' amendment, 76-24, before voting to kill Harkin's amendment. *(Vote 197, p. S-35)*

Other Amendments

The Senate also considered the following amendments:

- **Market Access Program.** Richard H. Bryan, D-Nev., revived an amendment he had offered in 1996 to reduce funding for the Market Access Program from $90 million to $70 million and prohibit participation by foreign companies, but it was tabled (killed), 59-40. *(Vote 199, p. S-35)*

"I believe this is corporate welfare in its worst form," Bryan said in support of his amendment. But backers of the marketing program countered that it had already been reformed and was still necessary to help American companies compete against foreign companies that received government subsidies.

- **Nutrition programs/insurance commissions.** Paul Wellstone, D-Minn., looked to the crop insurance commissions in an effort to find $5 million to restore funding for school breakfast outreach efforts and startup grants. "Clearly, this amendment speaks to priorities," Wellstone said. "Surely, we can find $5 million." But his amendment, which would have reduced funding for the commissions from $202 million to $197 million, was tabled (killed), 54-45. *(Vote 200, p. S-35)*
- **Discrimination office.** Like the House, Senate lawmakers agreed to add funding for efforts to combat discrimination in agriculture programs by re-establishing an investigative unit within the Agriculture Department.

Surprise Reversal on Tobacco

Tobacco foes scored an unexpected win Sept. 3 when the Senate reversed itself and voted to include the full $34 million requested for FDA efforts against underage smoking.

To pave the way for a House-Senate conference, Senate leaders had moved to pass HR 2160 after substituting the text of its own bill. Harkin took advantage of the procedural step to force a vote on a revamped version of his tobacco amendment. On Sept. 3, more than 20 senators reversed themselves, rejecting a motion to table the amendment by a vote of 28-70. The Senate then adopted the amendment by voice vote. *(Vote 212, p. S-37)*

Supporters of the increased FDA funding said they hoped the lopsided victory would strengthen their hand in conference. House Democrats added to the pressure by winning approval, 299-125, the same day for a non-binding motion instructing House conferees to agree to the Senate's position. The House-passed bill contained $24 million for the program. *(Vote 353, p. H-106)*

Harkin and others attributed part of the turnaround in the Senate to a change in the way he proposed to raise the extra $29 million for the FDA. Instead of increasing the marketing assessment paid by tobacco companies, he proposed to shift $29 million to the FDA from funds for computer equipment at the Agriculture Department.

Harkin also said he believed that pressure by anti-tobacco groups and publicity during the August recess over a $50 billion tax break for tobacco companies included in the recently enacted tax-reconciliation bill prompted some senators to change their votes. The tax break was subsequently repealed.

Conference/Final Action

House and Senate negotiators reached agreement Sept. 17 on a $49.7 billion compromise spending bill (H Rept 105-252). But it took the two chambers several additional weeks to clear the measure for the president, as its fate became entangled with progress of legislation to overhaul the FDA. The House adopted the conference report on the agriculture bill Oct. 6 by a vote of 399-18. The Senate cleared the bill by voice vote more than three weeks later, on Oct. 29. *(House vote 491, p. H-150)*

Overall, the final bill included $146 million more than the House version and $964 million less than the Senate measure. The large difference with the Senate bill was due mainly to an agreement to provide $100 million in contingency reserve funding for the food stamp program, compared with the $1 billion in the Senate-passed bill.

While the conference report was generally non-controversial, the leadership of both chambers held it up out of concern about its potential impact on the FDA overhaul legislation.

Republicans had deliberately linked the FDA overhaul to reauthorization of the popular Prescription Drug User Fee Act, a Clinton administration priority, to gain White House support for the broader bill. So GOP leaders became worried when the White House's Office of Management and Budget said that language in the agriculture spending bill could serve as a one-year reauthorization of the drug user fees.

House Republicans delayed taking up the conference report until progress was made on the FDA overhaul. After the House adopted the conference report Oct. 6, Lott delayed Senate action to allow the FDA conferees to finish their work.

The following were among the main issues resolved by the conferees:

- **Underage smoking.** With both chambers in agreement, lawmakers easily agreed to provide the $34 million that Clinton had requested for the FDA's anti-smoking program.
- **Crop insurance commissions.** The conference agreement included about $253 million for the Agriculture Department's Risk Management Agency, which managed federal crop insurance activities. Of that amount, $188 million was for commissions to insurance agents and companies — the same as in the House bill; the Senate had included $202 million. House Democrats argued that even $188 million was too generous, but the best they could do was to hold funding at the lower House level. The administration had requested $152 million.
- **Food and nutrition.** The agreement included a total of $37.2 billion for several domestic nutrition programs, including the House funding level of $25.1 billion for the food stamp program, about $2 million less than the administration's request and what was provided in fiscal 1997.

WIC received $3.9 billion, $118 million more than the previous fiscal year but $260 million less than the administration's request.

- **Export subsidies.** Conferees agreed to cap expenditures for the Export Enhancement Program at $150 million, compared with $205 million provided in the House bill.
- **Conservation programs.** One of the only issues to engage conversation during the brief conference meeting regarded funding for the Natural Resources Conservation Service, which provided conservation technical assistance to individuals, communities, watershed groups and tribal governments, as well as government agencies.

Patrick J. Leahy, D-Vt., said he was worried because the conservation service "keeps being downsized." The conferees provided $789 million for it, $20 million more than it received in fiscal 1997 but about $30 million less than the president requested.

- **Research.** Conferees provided $745 million for research through the Agricultural Research Service, about $20 million more than the House included in its bill and $7 million more than the Senate proposed. The bill also included $431 million for research and education activities in the Cooperative State Research, Education and Extension Service, about $10 million more than the House had provided and $4 million more than the Senate's version.

Line-Item Veto

Using what was considered a particularly light touch, Clinton on Nov. 20 announced that he was canceling five projects totaling $1.9 million from the $49.7 billion agriculture spending act. Clinton said the administration had not requested any of these projects, although House Appropriations Committee aides noted that most of the projects funded through the annual spending bill were not formally requested. *(Line-item veto, p. 2-63)*

The items cancelled under the line-item veto law were:

➤ $190,000 for two research projects at Ohio State University in the district of Republican Rep. Deborah Pryce. Clinton said there were other federal resources that the university could pursue for the projects.

➤ $900,000 to renovate an insect research laboratory in the district of Rep. Bennie Thompson, D-Miss.

➤ $600,000 to plan and design a new building for a poisonous plants laboratory for the Agriculture Research Service in Logan, Utah, represented by Republican Rep. James V. Hansen.

➤ $250,000 for a research grant to the University of Alaska to support research on high energy and high protein feeds for Alaska dairy cattle. ■

Census 2000 Dispute Slows CJS Bill

The $31.8 billion fiscal 1998 funding bill for the departments of Commerce, Justice and State and the federal judiciary was the last major piece of legislation to clear in the first session. While the principal holdup was language on how the 2000 census was to be conducted, other issues caused problems as well, including whether to split the mammoth 9th Judicial Circuit and whether the Justice Department should pay the legal fees of people it prosecuted unsuccessfully. The Senate cleared the bill Nov. 13, the last day of the session, and President Clinton signed it into law Nov. 26 (HR 2267 — PL 105-119).

The bill's primary focus was crime fighting, drug interdiction and apprehension of illegal immigrants — none of which was controversial. The Justice Department received $17.5 billion for fiscal 1998, $1 billion more than the previous year. The increase went largely to the Immigration and Naturalization Service (INS) to carry out provisions of the 1996 immigration law (PL 104-208), including adding 1,000 border agents.

The Commerce Department received $4.3 billion, a $450 million increase over fiscal 1997, with much of the extra funding devoted to the decennial census in 2000.

For the State Department, the bill included just over $4 billion, a slight increase over fiscal 1997. Of the total, $1.2 billion was for international organizations and peacekeeping.

Just clearing the bill was an accomplishment. Equivalent bills for fiscal 1996 and 1997 were so controversial that they never passed as free-standing bills, and had to be lumped into omnibus spending measures. *(1996 Almanac, p. 10-9)*

Final action on the fiscal 1998 bill got tangled up with a late-session push by the administration to win passage of fast-track trade legislation (HR 2621). The White House tried to use the census language as leverage to pick up Republican votes for fast track. In the end, the spending bill allowed the Census Bureau to proceed with "dress rehearsals" of the 2000 census in three sites, using controversial statistical sampling techniques in two and a traditional head count in the third. The bill also provided for an expedited judicial review for any court cases challenging the constitutionality of sampling. The compromise did not go over well with many Democrats, who wanted Clinton to take a harder line.

A proposal to split the 9th Circuit, which included nine Western states and two Pacific territories, was replaced in the final bill by a study of the issue. A proposal to force the Justice Department to pay the legal fees of people it prosecuted but failed to convict was modified to apply only in limited circumstances.

BOXSCORE

Fiscal 1998 Appropriations for Commerce, Justice, State and the Federal Judiciary — HR 2267 (S 1022). The bill appropriated $31.8 billion, more than half of it for law enforcement programs.

Reports: H Rept 105-207, S Rept 105-48; conference report, H Rept 105-405.

KEY ACTION

July 29 — Senate passed S 1022, 99-0.

Sept. 30 — House passed HR 2267, 227-199. **Senate** passed HR 2267 by voice vote Oct. 1, after inserting text of S 1022.

Nov. 13 — House adopted the conference report, 282-110. **Senate** cleared HR 2267 by voice vote.

Nov. 26 — President signed HR 2267— PL 105-119.

Dec. 2 — President used the line-item veto to delete a provision from PL 105-119.

Dispute Over Census Techniques

The 2000 census was the thorniest issue in the bill. Democrats and the Clinton administration wanted to use statistical sampling, a form of supplemental population count advocated by the Census Bureau and statisticians to reach the millions of people missed in the 1990 census. The proposal was strongly opposed by Republicans, who wanted the decennial head count to proceed the old-fashioned way, by reaching every home in the country.

The bureau planned to use traditional means — mail, telephone, personal contact — to reach about 90 percent of the population. But it wanted to count others — mostly people who did not speak English or did not trust census takers — by extrapolating from the hard data obtained in the traditional count.

Republicans argued that this amounted to funny math. "The Clinton administration is on the verge of creating a virtual America with virtual people," said Rep. Bob Barr, R-Ga. Critics also charged that sampling violated the constitutional requirement for "actual Enumeration . . . in such manner as [Congress] shall by law direct."

Democrats cited numerous scientific studies to argue that sampling would yield a more complete and accurate count. "They can do a better job than they did 10 years ago if they use statistical sampling," said Minority Leader Richard A. Gephardt, D-Mo.

They maintained that Republicans did not want a full count because it could result in more Democratic congressional and legislative districts, and because it would likely mean more federal money for areas served by Democrats. Those most likely to be missed in an attempt to physically contact everyone were African-Americans, Hispanics and American Indians, who tended to live in Democratic districts.

Some Republicans said they might be willing to experiment with sampling if they did not fear that the administration would use sampling for its own benefit — as they maintain it used a 1996 naturalization campaign to register new voters who presumably would support Democrats.

House Subcommittee

The House Commerce, Justice, State and Judiciary Appropriations Subcommittee approved a $31.2 billion version of the bill by voice vote July 10.

The panel steered clear of any policy decision on the prickly census issue, agreeing to provide money to start on either a full count or on sampling. It recommended $382 million for the census, $27 million more than the administration requested. Of that, $100 million would be available immediately. The remainder would await an agreement between the administration and Congress on how the census should proceed. "We're punting the ball to the authorizing committee," said Chairman Harold Rogers, R-Ky.

Fiscal 1998 Commerce-Justice-State Spending

(In thousands of dollars)

	Fiscal 1997 Appropriation	Fiscal 1998 Clinton Request	House Bill	Senate Bill	Final Bill
Department of Justice					
State and local law enforcement	$3,817,150	$3,697,855	$4,435,150	$4,046,150	$4,354,900
Other Office of Justice programs	325,255	432,354	434,175	596,590	445,275
Legal activities	2,508,760	2,645,395	2,509,471	2,510,800	2,509,673
Organized-crime drug enforcement	359,430	294,967	294,967	294,967	294,967
Federal Bureau of Investigation	2,837,610	3,089,675	2,974,571	3,075,395	2,974,548
Drug Enforcement Administration	1,001,194	1,087,562	1,130,000	1,090,882	1,135,378
Immigration and Naturalization Service	3,089,774	3,652,175	3,583,548	3,422,315	3,803,234
Offsetting fees	–975,774	–1,194,630	–1,215,191	–1,198,659	–1,461,183
Federal prison system	3,189,240	3,244,610	3,108,910	3,206,868	3,102,910
Other	272,364	314,058	299,290	232,682	302,758
TOTAL, Justice Department	**$16,425,003**	**$17,264,021**	**$17,554,891**	**$17,277,990**	**$17,462,460**
Related Agencies					
EEOC	239,740	246,000	239,740	242,000	242,000
Legal Services Corporation	283,000	340,000	250,000	300,000	283,000
The Judiciary					
Supreme Court	29,957	33,275	32,678	35,073	32,645
Courts of Appeals, district courts	3,100,390	3,463,774	3,292,458	3,336,362	3,286,031
Administrative Office of the U.S. Courts	49,450	54,108	52,000	53,843	52,000
Other	82,312	87,739	87,680	94,449	92,959
TOTAL, Judiciary	**$3,262,109**	**$3,638,896**	**$3,464,816**	**$3,519,727**	**$3,463,635**
Department of Commerce					
National Institute of Standards and Technology	581,000	692,544	686,544	603,892	677,852
National Oceanic and Atmospheric Administration	1,929,763	5,463,606	1,850,392	2,101,555	2,002,139
Census Bureau	345,500	661,182	686,625	658,782	693,091
Telecommunications and Information Admin.	51,740	54,074	55,340	63,064	57,550
International Trade Administration	270,000	271,636	279,500	280,736	283,066
Patent and Trademark Office	61,252	27,000	22,000	27,000	27,000
Economic Development Administration	425,736	343,028	361,000	272,028	361,028
Other	198,229	251,697	226,230	228,886	213,679
TOTAL, Commerce Department	**$3,863,220**	**$7,764,767**	**$4,167,631**	**$4,235,943**	**$4,315,405**
Related Agencies					
Federal Communications Commission (net)	35,556	56,556	24,556	23,426	23,991
Federal Trade Commission	27,025	28,000	19,000	28,000	18,500
Maritime Administration	159,900	161,400	138,950	137,000	138,825
Securities and Exchange Commission	37,778	35,889	33,477	35,889	33,477
Small Business Administration	852,417	700,635	728,237	708,632	716,132
Department of State					
Administration of Foreign Affairs	2,679,874	2,879,796	2,709,306	2,807,982	2,773,743
International organizations and conferences	1,244,400	1,313,941	1,241,452	1,157,329	1,211,515
Other	49,992	53,162	51,933	49,222	51,992
TOTAL, State Department	**$3,974,266**	**$4,246,899**	**$4,002,691**	**$4,014,533**	**$4,037,250**
Related Agencies					
Arms Control and Disarmament Agency	41,500	46,200	41,500	32,613	41,500
International broadcasting (USIA)	1,059,410	1,077,788	1,091,928	1,087,527	1,100,858
Other, rescissions	–$30,764	$ 50,886	$29,076	$10,275	–$60,126
GRAND TOTAL	**$30,230,160**	**$35,657,937**	**$31,786,493**	**$31,653,555**	**$31,816,907**
Crime trust fund	*$4,525,000*	*$5,238,000*	*$5,258,750*	*$5,224,822*	*$5,225,000*

SOURCE: House Appropriations Committee

The measure included healthy funding increases for the Justice Department, while other departments fought to stay even. Attorney General Janet Reno had seen her department's budget double since she took office in 1993. "If I had any concerns," said ranking subcommittee Democrat Alan B. Mollohan of West Virginia, "frankly they would be that this is too far slanted in that direction."

The bill included about $3 billion for the FBI, an increase of $137 million over fiscal 1997, and $1.1 billion for the Drug Enforcement Administration (DEA), a $129 million increase. The INS, seen by Republicans as vital but poorly run, got $3.6 billion, including offsetting fees. That was nearly $500 million more than in fiscal 1997. The bill also proposed giving the attorney general greater power to fire INS employees.

Clinton's cops-on-the-beat program was funded at the fiscal 1997 level of $1.4 billion, but the bill also included $523 million in law enforcement block grants. Republicans saw their block grant program as more flexible than Clinton's approach.

Appropriators sought to avoid past problems by funding programs — albeit at levels below what Clinton requested — that Republicans previously had tried to eliminate. The Legal Services Corporation, which provided legal counsel to the poor, was slated to get $141 million, far below Clinton's request for $340 million and about half what the agency got in fiscal 1997, but a starting point. The Advanced Technology Program, which helped private companies develop new technologies, was substantially cut.

The bill included $100 million for an initial payment to cover back U.S. dues to the United Nations. As in the census issue, appropriators put aside the larger question of what the total debt settlement should be.

House Full Committee

The bill emerged from the full Appropriations Committee largely as it arrived. The committee approved it by voice vote July 22 (H Rept 105-207). The one significant addition was an unusual proposal that members of Congress and their staffs be fully reimbursed for lawyers' fees should they be unsuccessfully prosecuted by the Justice Department.

The language, offered by John P. Murtha, D-Pa., was motivated by the experience of Murtha's Republican colleague from Pennsylvania, Joseph M. McDade. McDade had been the subject of a long and expensive investigation leading to an indictment on corruption charges, and ultimately to an acquittal. *(1996 Almanac, p. 1-35)*

The amendment was written to cover any member of Congress or employee paid by the House or Senate and to apply to all Justice Department prosecutions pertaining to a member's or employee's official duties. Reimbursement would be required if the charges were dropped, the individual were acquitted or a conviction were reversed on appeal. Though it would not be retroactive to include McDade, who was a member of the Appropriations panel, McDade argued that it was necessary because without it the Justice Department could mount open-ended, even politically motivated prosecutions with few consequences. After a speech on the issue, McDade received a standing ovation, followed by unanimous voice vote support for the Murtha amendment.

Murtha said his amendment was not so much about McDade as about "the independence of Congress." He said he wanted to reaffirm the constitutional separation of powers. "I'm trying to show that the House can set its own rules," he said. "The House of Representatives is a separate entity, and the Justice Department can't interpret the rules to suit themselves."

Although he supported the amendment, David R. Obey of Wisconsin, the committee's ranking Democrat, warned that it could open Congress to criticism that it was creating its own special privileges. Only two years earlier, Congress had made a point of applying to itself those labor laws that it imposed on others. *(1995 Almanac, p. 1-31)*

Democrats had no success in modifying the bill's controversial language on the upcoming census. Mollohan offered an amendment that would have allowed the entire $382 million census allocation to be spent in fiscal 1998, on the understanding that nothing would be spent on "irreversible" plans for sampling. Sampling would not have been banned in ensuing years. A three-member board would have overseen sampling to make sure it was not manipulated. The amendment was defeated, 25-33, along party lines.

House Floor Action

After weeks of delay and a contentious floor debate spread over four days, the House passed its $31.8 billion bill Sept. 30 by a vote of 227-199. To get the measure through, managers had to defeat opposition from Democrats over the census provisions, while preventing rebellions in their own left and right flanks. *(Vote 476, p. H-144)*

The bill began its fitful journey in the full House Sept. 24-26. On Sept. 25, members removed one item that had drawn a veto threat — a proposed 50 percent cut to the Legal Services Corporation — while adding another, a revised version of Murtha's Justice Department reimbursement proposal. Further distancing itself from the White House, the House also made the bill's census language more restrictive.

- **Legal Services.** The amendment to restore funding for Legal Services was offered by Mollohan and Jon D. Fox, R-Pa. The committee bill would have funded the agency at $141 million, a 50 percent cut from fiscal 1997. The Mollohan-Fox amendment, which restored $109 million, was adopted, 246-176. *(Vote 449, p. H-136)*
- **Reimbursement for legal fees.** Henry J. Hyde, R-Ill., proposed that the Justice Department be required to reimburse anyone who was the subject of a federal criminal proceeding that did not end in a conviction and for which the department could not show "substantial justification." It was adopted, 340-84. *(Vote 443, p. H-134)*

Hyde made the difficult-to-resist argument that Congress should not create a special benefit for itself that did not apply to the general public. At the same time, he argued that the original reimbursement provision was too broad. While he proposed to expand reimbursement to everyone, his amendment would apply only if the Justice Department could not justify its case. "I'm for law and order," Hyde said. "I'm for sending people to jail. I'm for the Justice Department prosecuting people. But not if they don't have substantial justification."

Opponents argued that the language could have sweeping implications that had not been fully considered. David E. Skaggs, D-Colo., questioned why Hyde, who chaired the Judiciary Committee, had not previously introduced freestanding legislation. The administration issued a statement saying that the provision would have a "profound and harmful impact" on the federal criminal justice system. It said the language "would create a monetary incentive for criminal defense attorneys to generate additional litigation in cases in which prosecutors have in good faith brought sound charges."

- **Census sampling.** The census issue dominated the final day of debate on the bill, with Mollohan and Christopher

Shays, R-Conn., offering an amendment to allow the use of sampling in the 2000 census.

As approved by the committee, HR 2267 would have fenced off all but $100 million of the $382 million appropriation for the upcoming census until a law was enacted laying out how the census should proceed. But on Sept. 23, the House Rules Committee changed the language to say that all the funds could be spent, but none could be used on sampling until the Supreme Court ruled on the constitutionality of the method.

Democrats argued that the Supreme Court was unlikely to rule on the matter in time to use sampling in the 2000 census. Even if it heard a case, they argued, the court could decline to rule on the matter; the court generally did not issue advisory opinions on issues pending before Congress. In fact, the court might not be able to find anyone with "standing" to sue over the matter until after the census had taken place.

Mollohan's amendment would have allowed preliminary work on sampling as long as no "irreversible" decisions were made to go in that direction. Several moderate Republicans from areas likely to be aided by sampling expressed sympathy, while several Democrats from areas that could be hurt indicated reservations. But both groups were under pressure to vote with their party. In the end, just nine Democrats and three Republicans crossed party lines on Mollohan's amendment, which was rejected, 197-228. *(Vote 475, p. H-144)*

"The issue is whether we spend more than $4 billion on a census that abandons, for the first time in our history, an actual head count, before we know whether such a thing is prudent and constitutional," said Rogers in advance of the debate.

Democrats charged that the GOP's guiding interest in fighting sampling was to undercount people who would likely yield more Democratic congressional and legislative districts. They said the language requiring the Supreme Court to rule on sampling was a ruse.

Senate Committee

Taking much the same route as their House colleagues, members of the Senate Appropriations Committee approved a $31.6 billion version of the spending bill July 15 by a vote of 28-0 (S 1022 — S Rept 105-48). The panel's Commerce, Justice, State Subcommittee had approved the measure by voice vote July 11.

The bill included $354 million to begin hiring staff for a full census count, and left room for preliminary work on sampling as long as no "irreversible plans or preparations" were made.

The measure included $3.1 billion for the FBI, $1.1 billion for the DEA and $3.4 billion for the INS, including offsetting fees. Like the House version, the bill included $1.4 billion for the cops-on-the-beat program; it also provided for $503 million in law enforcement block grants, slightly less than the House bill.

Senate appropriators agreed to provide $100 million for an initial payment to cover back U.S. dues to the United Nations.

The Senate bill also included a proposal to extend a State Department policy known as 245(i). The policy allowed illegal immigrants who were in line to become legal through family or employment sponsorship to get permanent-resident visas within the United States after paying a $1,000 fine. The program was set to expire Sept. 30. Without the extension, hundreds of thousands of immigrants feared being caught in a Catch-22: They would have to leave the country to get a permanent visa, or green card. But, under the 1996 immigration law (PL 104-208), they would be unable to re-enter the United States once they left.

The extension was not included in the House bill, and it was fiercely opposed by some lawmakers in that chamber who took a hard line on illegal immigration. *(Immigration, p. 5-11)*

Amendment Seeks To Split 9th Circuit

Before giving its approval, the full committee waded into a controversy over what to do about the huge 9th Judicial Circuit based in San Francisco. Roughly twice the size of other circuits, the 9th covered California, Oregon, Washington, Montana, Idaho, Nevada, Arizona, Alaska, Hawaii, Guam and the Northern Mariana Islands. It included appellate and lower courts. *(9th Circuit, p. 5-18)*

Mountain state Republicans had long sought to form a separate circuit for their region, arguing that the 9th was dominated by liberal California judges who did not understand the needs of their resource-rich states. Democrats, by contrast, were leery of putting much of the nation's timbering and mining interests under the jurisdiction of a new, conservative circuit.

The committee approved by voice vote an amendment by Judd Gregg, R-N.H., that called for severing California and the two Pacific territories from the other states. Under the proposal, Oregon, Washington, Montana, Idaho, Arizona and Alaska would become a separate circuit. Nevada and Hawaii could choose either circuit.

Senate Floor Action

Rushing to clear the decks for consideration of separate budget and tax bills before the August recess, the Senate passed its $31.6 billion Commerce, Justice, State spending bill July 29 — a full two months before the House completed work on its version. The vote was 99-0. *(Vote 206, p. S-36)*

About four dozen amendments were rolled into an en bloc package July 29 and approved by voice vote. One of the provisions struck language in the bill that Paul S. Sarbanes, D-Md., said could be interpreted to require a withdrawal from the United Nations under certain conditions. Another, by Paul Wellstone, D-Minn., said that in cases of domestic abuse, a husband's income could not be used to disqualify his wife from being represented by Legal Services.

The most controversial debate on the bill took place July 24, when members defeated an attempt by Dianne Feinstein, D-Calif., to drop the proposal to split up the 9th Judicial Circuit. Feinstein proposed instead to commission a study of the configuration of the 11 regional circuits. Her amendment was defeated on a straight party-line vote of 45-55. *(Vote 204, p. S-35)*

Feinstein called the proposed split "arbitrary, political and gerrymandered." She argued that the amendment would short-circuit the legislative process because it had not gone through the Judiciary Committee and had never been the subject of hearings. She said most judges and bar associations in the affected areas opposed dividing the circuit, and that their views had not been taken into consideration. "If you're going to split the 9th Circuit, do [it with] due diligence, consult the judges, do the studies," she said.

Republicans, particularly those from the states that would constitute a new 12th Circuit, said the split had been under study since 1973, and that several bills had been debated since then. The legislation had been stymied for several reasons, including opposition from the California delegation and from 9th Circuit judges. *(1996 Almanac, p. 5-46)*

"We have studied this matter to death," said Ted Stevens, R-Alaska, chairman of the Appropriations Committee. "Every year we hear the same thing from the largest delegation in the House and the two senators from California."

Initially, both of Hawaii's Democratic senators, Daniel K. Akaka and Daniel K. Inouye, crossed party lines to oppose the Feinstein amendment and support the split. No Hawaiian had been appointed an appellate judge in 13 years. The language in the bill guaranteed that each state in a circuit would have at least one sitting appellate judge. Both later changed their votes, however.

The same day, the Senate defeated a proposal to bar companies with annual revenues of $2.5 billion or more from getting grants under the Advanced Technology Program. Sam Brownback, R-Kan., said the program had become a corporate welfare handout for companies with enough money to do their own research. His amendment was defeated, 42-57. *(Vote 202, p. S-35)*

Richard G. Lugar, R-Ind., succeeded in restoring funds for the National Endowment for Democracy, which promoted democracy abroad. The funds had been eliminated in the committee bill. The Senate gave voice vote approval to a proposal by Lugar to transfer $30 million from a State Department account to the endowment. An attempt to table (kill) his amendment was defeated, 27-72. *(Vote 203, p. S-35)*

Conference/Final Action

It took another six weeks after the House passed its version of the bill Sept. 30 for House and Senate conferees to reconcile their differences. The conference report (H Rept 105-405) was filed Nov. 13, the final day of the session. Shortly after 10 p.m., in its last recorded vote of the year, the House adopted the report, 282-110. Earlier in the evening, the Senate had agreed by voice vote to approve the report and automatically send the bill to the president upon House action. *(Vote 640, p. H-190)*

Census Plan Cobbled Together

Until the end, the biggest stumbling block continued to be the census dispute. Clinton favored the more tolerant Senate language on sampling, but he was hamstrung because he was also using the sampling provision as leverage to try to pick up GOP votes on the fast-track trade bill. That infuriated a number of Democrats. "There's a lot of heartburn over the fact that the White House is negotiating the census in order to get votes for fast track," said Mollohan.

Incensed by the administration's stance, among other things, Obey used the first formal conference session Nov. 7 to announce plans to draw out the proceedings — and delay congressional adjournment — by offering numerous amendments to major and minor provisions. To underscore his annoyance, Obey, a fast-track opponent, offered amendments to reduce or eliminate funding for key administration goals. He proposed eliminating a $100 million appropriation for United Nations arrearages and cutting a weather satellite program championed by Vice President Al Gore. "If the administration wants the conference to respect their high-priority language, they have an obligation to get us census language," Obey said.

In the end, conferees took a split-the-difference approach. The final bill provided $390 million in fiscal 1998 for preparatory work on the census, and allowed the Census Bureau to conduct a "dress rehearsal" in the spring of 1998 to compare sampling and traditional techniques. The plan was to use sampling in Sacramento, Calif., and at an Indian reservation in Wisconsin, and to use a traditional head count in Columbia, S.C. An eight-member Census Monitoring Board, to be made up of four Democrats and four Republicans, was created to observe and monitor both the dress rehearsal and the implementation of the 2000 census.

The bill provided for expedited court review, which would allow any challenge to the use of sampling to go to a three-judge panel and then directly to the Supreme Court. Virtually anyone in the country would be able to a bring suit. However, since the Supreme Court generally granted standing only to parties that claimed to be aggrieved, it was unlikely that the court would hear a case before the 2000 census had occurred. Democrats were worried that a three-judge panel somewhere in the country could issue an injunction that could stop the dress rehearsal.

Other Disagreements Resolved

Other controversies settled in conference included:

- **245(i).** Conferees agreed to a compromise under which most future permanent visas would be issued only in an immigrant's home country, but anyone in the United States who submitted an application by Jan. 14, 1998, could get one here.

For immigrants seeking a green card through an employer, there were two significant exceptions. They would not need a pending green card application by Jan. 14, just a pending application for Labor Department certification that they possessed a job skill in high demand. Such a certificate was already a prerequisite for applying for an employment-based green card. Also, any skilled immigrant who fell into the status of an illegal alien for less than six months while waiting for paperwork (for example, if his or her temporary visa expired) could get a permanent visa in the United States.

- **Justice prosecutions.** The final bill required the federal government to reimburse the legal fees of those it criminally prosecuted and did not convict — but only if the suit was "vexatious, frivolous, or in bad faith." That was a much higher threshold than Hyde had proposed. The House version would have required reimbursement if the Justice Department could not show that it had had "substantial justification" to prosecute.
- **9th Judicial Circuit.** Senate Republicans lost their battle to split the massive circuit and had to settle instead for the creation of a five-person commission to study the composition and caseloads of all 11 circuit courts.
- **Legal Services Corporation.** The bill funded Legal Services at the fiscal 1997 level of $283 million. It also included language requiring publicly funded attorneys to disclose their fees.

Major Funding Highlights

The following are among the other major elements of the final bill:

- **FBI.** $3 billion for the FBI, a $136 million increase over fiscal 1997.
- **DEA.** $1.1 billion for the DEA, a $134 million increase over the previous year.
- **Cops-on-the-beat.** $1.4 billion for Clinton's Community Oriented Policing Service programs, the same as in fiscal 1997.
- **Violence Against Women.** $271 million for a program that encouraged police to make arrests in domestic violence cases and provided funding to prosecute such cases.
- **Juvenile crime.** $250 million for a new block grant program aimed at fighting juvenile crime. Earlier efforts in both chambers to authorize such a program had stalled (HR 3, S 10). The block grants, added in the House, were for law enforcement and improvements to the juvenile justice system.

Sen. Joseph R. Biden Jr. of Delaware, ranking Democrat on the Judiciary Youth Violence Subcommittee, expressed disappointment during floor debate on the conference report that none of the money would go to preventative programs. However, he said he was pleased that the final bill dropped an earlier requirement that states try more juveniles as adults to qualify for the federal funding. The bill required only that a state certify that it was actively considering such changes.

- **INS.** $3.8 billion for the INS, $713 million more than in fiscal 1997. The total included funding for 1,000 new border control agents and 2,564 more detention cells.
- **NIST.** $678 million for the National Institute of Standards and Technology, equal to the president's request and $97 million more than the previous year. The amount had been agreed upon during the balanced-budget negotiations. For the previous two years, House appropriators had tried to drastically cut funding for NIST accounts, particularly the Advanced Technology Program. The bill appropriated $193 million for the program and limited new grant awards to $82 million in fiscal 1998.
- **NOAA.** $2 billion for the National Oceanic and Atmospheric Administration, a slight reduction from the previous year.
- **International organizations and peacekeeping.** $956 million for U.S. payments to international organizations (including $54 million for arrearages to the United Nations) and $256 million for international peacekeeping operations.
- **USIA.** $1.1 billion for the United States Information Agency, including $35 million to support broadcasting to China.
- **Judiciary.** $3.5 billion for operating the federal court system, including a cost of living increase for judges.

Line-Item Veto

Clinton used his line-item veto authority Dec. 2 to cancel a single, $5 million project in the Commerce, Justice and State spending law. The project had been inserted into the conference report at the urging of Sen. Conrad Burns, R-Mont. The money was designated for research at Montana State University into environmentally friendly building products and technologies.

The White House said it was unnecessary and that it had not been "peer reviewed" by experts in the field of environmental technologies. Officials also pointed out that the money would come through the auspices of the NIST, which was not designed as an open-ended grant-making foundation.

Burns contended that the White House was not using a consistent rationale for deciding which projects to veto, noting that Clinton left untouched a $3.8 million NIST grant to Texas Tech University for research into storm-proof-building technologies. ■

Congress Backs Off on B-2, Bosnia

President Clinton signed the fiscal 1998 defense appropriations bill (HR 2266 — PL 105-56) into law Oct. 8, after forcing his congressional adversaries to back down on provisions aimed at restarting production of the B-2 stealth bomber and barring U.S. peacekeepers in Bosnia after June 30, 1998.

The final bill provided $247.7 billion for defense programs ranging from salaries and maintenance, to research and weapons procurement. The total was about $3.8 billion more than Clinton had requested in his Feb. 6 budget.

Combined with funds provided in two other appropriations bills — the military construction bill (HR 2016) and the defense sections of the energy and water measure (HR 2203) — it brought overall defense spending to $268 billion, the amount allowed under the bipartisan budget agreement reached by Clinton and Congress in the spring.

The conference report on the bill included a June 30, 1998, cutoff of funding for troops in Bosnia but gave the president authority to waive the ban if he sent Congress a detailed report on the reasons for doing so and the estimated size, duration and cost of the continued deployment. The House had voted for a firm cutoff of funds on June 30.

Clinton also faced down House defense appropriators over a provision intended to restart production of the B-2 stealth bomber. The conference report provided a total of $331 million for B-2 related procurement — $157 million more than requested — but left the president free to spend that money to upgrade and repair the 21 B-2s previously funded.

The bill also included $2.3 billion for the first of a new class of nuclear-powered submarines, and authorized the two commercial shipyards that built nuclear subs for the Navy to collaborate on construction of the new class. The authorization was included in the appropriations bill because the companion defense authorization bill (HR 1119) was stalled. It did not clear until Nov. 6. *(Defense authorization, p. 8-3)*

Six days after signing the bill, Clinton on Oct. 14 used his line-item veto authority to strike 13 projects for a savings of $144 million. *(Defense veto, pp. 9-20, 9-24)*

BOXSCORE

Fiscal 1998 Defense Appropriations — HR 2266 (S 1005). The bill provided $247.7 billion for Defense Department programs, $3.8 billion more than requested.

Reports: H Rept 105-206, S Rept 105-45; conference report, 105-265.

KEY ACTION

July 15 — Senate passed S 1005, 94-4.

July 29 — House passed HR 2266, 322-105; the **Senate** passed HR 2266 by voice vote, amended with the text of S 1005.

Sept. 25 — House adopted the conference report, 356-65; the **Senate** cleared the bill, 93-5.

Oct. 8 — President signed HR 2266 — PL 105-56.

Oct. 14 — President used line-item veto to cancel 13 projects.

Background

In his fiscal 1998 budget, submitted Feb. 6, Clinton requested $243.9 billion for programs covered by the defense appropriations bill — $1.5 billion less than Congress had appropriated for fiscal 1997.

Administration officials acknowledged that the Pentagon budget was a place-holder while two long-range reviews of U.S. defense requirements were conducted. The two studies — the Pentagon's internal Quadrennial Defense Review, and a legislatively chartered review by a National Defense Panel of outside experts — were slated for completion later in the year. *(Assessments, p. 8-19)*

Meanwhile, the fiscal 1998 budget was based on the goal, adopted by Clinton in 1993, of a force that could win two major regional wars breaking out several weeks apart in areas far from each other and from the United States. *(Clinton defense budget, p. 2-8)*

On Capitol Hill, the president's budget was received by defense appropriators who were strong advocates for more defense spending. They had ardently promoted the hefty increases Congress made in Clinton's defense budgets in 1995 and 1996, most of which were allocated to procurement priorities set by the services. This time, however, they were constrained by the fact that Republican leaders were making deficit reduction the top priority.

The bipartisan balanced-budget agreement reached in May, and embodied in Congress' fiscal 1998 budget resolution (H Con Res 84), put a ceiling of $268 billion on the overall defense budget. Most of that was for the Pentagon, with smaller amounts reserved for the military construction and energy and water bills.

In deciding how to allocate the Pentagon funds, the appropriations committees worked closely with the authorizers — the House National Security and Senate Armed Services committees — which had established themselves as arbiters of defense policy. In each chamber, the committees had long-since worked out methods of getting along, accommodating each other's top priorities so that the appropriations bills typically conformed to the authorizing legislation in most important respects.

Senate Committee

The Senate Appropriations Committee was the first to act, approving a $246.9 billion defense appropriations bill (S 1005 — S Rept 105-45) July 10 that largely mirrored the Senate's version of the defense authorization bill (S 936). The spending bill, approved by voice vote, was a $3.2 billion increase over Clinton's request. Like the authorization bill, it sought to accelerate some weapons programs without challenging Clinton's basic defense plan.

The panel added $440 million for two additional C-17 wide-body cargo jets, for a total of 11 of the big planes. Clinton had requested, and the Armed Services Committee had approved, nine of the planes for a total of $1.9 billion.

Ted Stevens, R-Alaska, who chaired both the Senate Appropriations Committee and its Defense subcommittee, contended that the Pentagon could save money in the long-run if it bought the C-17s at a faster rate.

The most significant cut in the bill, compared with the Senate authorization measure, was a reduction of $65 million in the $292 million requested for Trident II submarine-launched ballistic missiles. That would buy only five of the seven mis-

Defense Spending

(in thousands of dollars)

	Fiscal 1997 Appropriation	Fiscal 1998 Clinton Request	House Bill	Senate Bill	Conference Report
Personnel					
Army	$ 20,633,998	$ 20,492,257	$ 20,445,381	$ 20,426,457	$ 20,452,057
Navy	16,986,976	16,501,118	16,504,911	16,508,218	16,493,518
Marines	6,111,728	6,147,599	6,141,635	6,148,899	6,137,899
Air Force	17,069,490	17,154,556	17,044,874	17,206,056	17,102,120
National Guard, reserves	9,214,308	9,116,232	9,206,393	9,394,041	9,284,911
Subtotal	**$ 70,016,500**	**$ 69,411,762**	**$ 69,343,194**	**$ 69,683,671**	**$ 69,470,505**
Operations and Maintenance					
Army	$ 17,519,340	$ 17,049,484	$ 17,078,218	$ 16,913,473	$ 16,754,306
Navy	20,061,961	21,508,130	21,779,365	21,576,419	21,617,766
Marines	2,254,119	2,301,345	2,598,032	2,328,535	2,372,635
Air Force	17,263,193	18,817,785	18,740,167	18,592,385	18,492,883
Defense agencies	10,044,200	10,390,938	10,053,956	10,399,638	10,639,740
National Guard and reserves	8,582,539	9,012,539	9,196,469	9,248,882	9,310,912
Environmental restoration	1,314,016	1,263,937	1,263,937	1,296,937	1,296,937
Humanitarian assistance	49,000	80,130	55,557	40,130	47,130
Former Soviet threat reduction	327,900	382,200	284,700	382,200	382,200
Overseas contingencies	1,140,157	1,467,500	1,855,400	1,889,000	1,884,000
Barracks improvements	600,000	—	—	100,000	360,000
Other	6,797	6,952	6,952	6,952	6,952
Subtotal	**$ 79,163,222**	**$ 82,280,940**	**$ 82,912,753**	**$ 82,774,551**	**$ 82,895,461**
By transfer	*$ 150,000*	*$ 150,000*	*$ 150,000*	*$ 150,000*	*$ 150,000*
Procurement					
Army	$ 8,160,221	$ 6,619,249	$ 7,211,754	$ 7,512,883	$ 7,123,765
Navy	17,388,227	17,688,713	19,065,298	19,139,385	19,414,980
Marines	569,073	374,306	491,198	440,106	482,398
Air Force	14,939,958	15,207,825	15,711,043	15,856,625	15,866,628
National Guard and reserves	780,000	—	850,000	653,000	653,000
Defense agencies	1,978,005	1,695,085	2,186,669	1,753,285	2,106,444
Subtotal	**$ 43,815,484**	**$ 41,585,178**	**$ 45,515,962**	**$ 45,355,284**	**$ 45,647,215**
Research, development and testing					
Army	$ 5,062,763	$ 4,510,843	$ 4,686,427	$ 4,984,083	$ 5,156,507
Navy	8,208,946	7,611,022	7,907,837	7,532,846	8,115,686
Air Force	14,499,606	14,451,379	14,313,456	14,127,873	14,507,804
Other	9,669,806	9,361,247	9,810,204	9,891,256	10,111,327
Subtotal	**$ 37,441,121**	**$ 35,934,491**	**$ 36,717,924**	**$ 36,536,058**	**$ 37,891,324**
Other programs					
General provisions	$ –788,047	$ 103,000	$ –422,400	$ –663,500	$ –2,418,900
Revolving and management funds	2,375,902	2,163,378	2,171,878	1,388,078	2,046,900
Chemical agents destruction	758,447	620,700	595,700	609,700	600,700
Drug interdiction	807,800	652,582	713,082	691,482	712,882
Inspector general	139,157	138,380	142,980	135,380	138,380
Defense Health program	10,207,308	10,301,650	10,309,750	10,317,675	10,369,075
Subtotal	**$ 13,500,567**	**$ 13,979,690**	**$ 13,510,990**	**$ 12,478,815**	**$ 11,449,037**
Related agencies					
CIA retirement, disability	$ 196,400	$ 196,900	$ 196,900	$ 196,900	$ 196,900
Intelligence community management	129,164	122,580	125,580	122,580	121,080
Other	15,100	12,000	12,000	37,000	37,000
Subtotal	**$ 340,664**	**$ 331,480**	**$ 334,480**	**$ 356,480**	**$ 354,980**
TOTAL	**$ 244,277,558**	**$ 243,523,541**	**$ 248,335,303**	**$ 247,184,859**	**$ 247,708,522**
Other rescissions, adjustments	–1,887,832	400,000	—	—	—
GRAND TOTAL	**$ 242,389,726**	**$ 243,923,541**	**$ 248,335,303**	**$ 247,184,859**	**$ 247,708,522**

SOURCE: Senate and House Appropriations Committees

siles requested and approved by the authorization bill.

Among the Appropriations Committee's additions to Clinton's defense request were:

➤ $380 million for maintenance of facilities.

➤ $600 million for aircraft overhauls — $300 million apiece for the Navy and Air Force.

➤ $345 million to begin buying components for a nuclear-powered aircraft carrier slated for inclusion in the fiscal 2002 budget.

➤ $720 million for a fourth Navy destroyer equipped with the Aegis anti-aircraft system, in addition to the $2.7 billion requested and approved by the Armed Services Committee for three of the ships.

➤ $175 million for breast cancer research.

Major Provisions of the Senate Bill

● **Personnel.** The bill included $69.7 billion for military pay and benefits. That was expected to support an active duty force of 1.42 million, nearly 10,000 fewer than Clinton requested, and a reserve and National Guard force of 892,509, slightly more than Clinton sought. As requested, the bill provided for a 2.8 percent military pay raise.

In addition to approving most of the 21,000-member cut in active-duty personnel that Clinton requested, the bill proposed to reduce the Army by an additional 10,000, to a total of 485,000. This was to be a first step toward Army personnel cuts recommended in May in the Pentagon's Quadrennial Defense Review.

Senate appropriators did not include any of the additional cuts recommended for the politically well-connected National Guard and reserve forces. In fact, they added $203 million to the amount requested for Guard training.

● **Operations and maintenance.** The $82.7 billion included in the bill for day-to-day Defense Department operations included several large additions and cuts that had become routine.

For instance, the appropriators cut $368 million from Clinton's budget request because there were fewer civilians on the Pentagon payroll than was assumed. They also trimmed $221 million because the dollar had gained strength against some foreign currencies and U.S. forces stationed in those countries would pay less than was budgeted for locally purchased supplies and services.

On the other side of the ledger, large additions included $360 million for major overhauls of ships, planes and other items of equipment and $389 million for repair and maintenance of facilities.

Senate appropriators added $26 million to the amount requested for special forces — Army Green Berets, Navy SEALS and other unconventional warfare units. The increase was to offset a shortfall in the budget request that resulted from a late increase in the price of certain maintenance and support work performed for those forces by other Pentagon agencies.

To clean up toxic and hazardous waste at current and former military bases, the bill included $1.3 billion, $33 million more than Clinton requested.

● **Missile defense.** The Appropriations Committee proposed slowing production of Trident II submarine-launched missiles on the grounds that future arms control agreements might render additional missiles unnecessary.

For an array of anti-missile defense programs, the bill included slightly more than $4 billion, roughly the same as the Senate-passed authorization bill. The total included:

• $978 million to develop a system to protect U.S. territory against a limited number of attacking missiles. This included $504 million requested by Clinton in February and an additional $474 million requested in May.

• $353 million of the $556 million requested for the Army's Theater High-Altitude Area Defense system (THAAD), a long-range system intended to protect U.S. combat forces or overseas allies, but which had failed to hit its target in several tests.

• $275 million, $80 million more than was requested, for a long-range "theater-wide" defense version of the Navy's Standard antiaircraft missile.

• $148 million, instead of the $30 million requested, to continue developing a space-based anti-missile laser.

● **Ground combat.** The bill proposed adding $58 million to the total of $361 million requested for six programs to develop or buy components of an Army plan to link battlefield units in a digital network.

The bill also included:

• $282 million, as requested, to develop the Comanche armed helicopter, which would have a radar-evading stealth design. The Army considered the Comanche the linchpin of its future, digitized force.

• $512 million to equip existing Apache attack helicopters with Longbow radar units and digital communications.

• $595 million to upgrade M-1 tanks with larger cannon, digital links and improved electronics for fighting at night.

The appropriators also added $62 million to the $126 million requested to buy Bradley armored troop carriers with digital communications; and $247 million to the $285 million requested to buy Army trucks, ranging in size from Jeep-like "Humvees" to huge low-boy tractor-trailers designed to carry 70-ton tanks.

● **Air combat.** The bill proposed cutting $294 million from the $2.1 billion requested to continue developing the Air Force's F-22 fighter and to gear up to build the first two production-line planes in fiscal 1999.

The bill also included:

• $2.1 billion, as requested, to buy 20 enlarged "E" and "F" model F/A-18s, which the Navy planned to use as both a fighter and a bomber.

• $959 million, $28 million more than the administration requested, to continue developing the Joint Strike Fighter, intended to be built in different versions for the Navy, Air Force and Marine Corps.

• $260 million for six Air Force F-15s, instead of the $159 million requested for three of the planes.

• $107 million of the $203 million requested to develop a radar-evading, air-launched, guided missile with a range of more than 100 miles, which would allow U.S. pilots to attack heavily defended ground targets from a safe distance.

● **Naval warfare.** The Senate's versions of the authorization and appropriations bills were in agreement on major shipbuilding projects, recommending:

• $3.4 billion for four destroyers equipped with the Aegis anti-aircraft system. The ships would be built in Bath, Maine, by General Dynamics and in Pascagoula, Miss., by Litton Industries. The administration had requested three ships for a cost of $2.7 billion in February.

• $2.3 billion for the first of a new class of attack submarine, plus $285 million for components to be used in future ships of this type, both amounts as requested.

• $1.6 billion, as requested, for a three-year overhaul to refuel and modernize the nuclear-powered aircraft carrier *Nimitz*, commissioned in 1975.

• $345 million for components to be used in a new carrier, to be built by Newport News Shipbuilding and Dry Dock near Norfolk, Va. Initial funding for components had not been scheduled until 2000, with the bulk of the money slated for in-

Clinton Uses Delicate Touch With Veto Scalpel

Still smarting from Congress' outrage over the 38 projects he eliminated from the fiscal 1998 military construction bill, President Clinton used his line-item veto sparingly on the $247.7 billion defense appropriations bill (HR 2266 — PL 105-56). Acting on Oct. 14, he cancelled just 13 items totaling $144 million.

The White House initially complained that Congress had added 750 unrequested projects totaling $11 billion to the bill. In the end, Clinton vetoed less than 2 percent of those items, most of them research or science projects. "I think what I did today was responsible and quite restrained," he said. *(Text, p. D-42)*

The vetoed projects reflected a post-Cold War world of shrinking defense budgets and the difficulty many members of Congress had in letting go of popular but costly weapons. *(Vetoed projects, p. 9-24)*

For instance, the president struck $39 million that Congress had appropriated for the Blackbird spy plane retired by the Air Force but revived by Congress. Satellites had been doing most of the work.

Clinton also vetoed $37.5 million in research for a system to shoot down satellites (he had tried to end the program since 1993) and $30 million for the Clementine program to track and intercept asteroids in space. The program had its origins in President Ronald Reagan's Strategic Defense Initiative of the 1980s that envisioned a space-based defense against missiles.

Those two cuts, plus Clinton's veto of $10 million for an Air Force space plane, drew an angry response from former Reagan administration Pentagon official Frank J. Gaffney Jr. "Mr. Clinton has terminated technology development programs whose unavailability as deployed capabilities may prove disastrous in future conflicts," said a statement from the conservative Center for Security Policy, headed by Gaffney.

The White House said Clinton's decisions were based on a list of items that were deemed vital to national security and requested in the president's budget and long-range defense plans.

Five of the 13 projects vetoed were in neither the House nor the Senate versions of the defense spending bill but were added during the final negotiations. Pentagon spokesman Kenneth Bacon said they appeared in the conference report "as if by immaculate conception."

Hefty Projects Spared

Among the items Clinton left in the bill were $529 million for nine Lockheed C-130J cargo transport planes, eight more than the Pentagon sought; a $720 million down payment on a new Navy destroyer; $100 million toward construction of a new amphibious assault ship; and $250,000 for the development of two cruise ships for a company serving the Hawaiian islands.

In sparing those projects, the administration won friends and influence among congressional leaders.

The cargo transport planes were to be built at a plant in Marietta, Ga., near the district of House Speaker Newt Gingrich, R-Ga. The Navy destroyer was to be built in Pascagoula, Miss., the home of Senate Majority Leader Trent Lott, and the assault ship in Louisiana, home of Republican Robert L. Livingston, chairman of the House Appropriations Committee.

In a scathing Oct. 16 letter to Clinton accusing the president of playing politics with the line-item veto, Sen. John McCain, R-Ariz., zeroed in on the cruise-ship project as an example of "pork barrel" spending that should have been vetoed. The project had been written into the bill by Sen. Daniel K. Inouye of Hawaii, the influential ranking Democrat on the Senate Defense Appropriations Subcommittee.

"I fail to see," McCain wrote, "how a $250,000 earmark of funds to transfer commercial shipbuilding technology to the Navy, coupled with language creating a 30-year monopoly for a cruise line in Hawaii, contributes in any way to national security."

Defending the decision to spare the project, Deputy Defense Secretary John Hamre said that while the program was "not a defense issue at all," the military was interested in promoting construction of commercial vessels in U.S. shipyards.

McCain also complained that Clinton had failed to veto $15 million in the defense bill for electric vehicle research, $4 million for the Army's National Automotive Center in Detroit and $100,000 to preserve a Revolutionary War gunboat found in Lake Champlain.

---

clusion in the fiscal 2002 budget.

Appropriators added $36 million to install a new communications system in carrier-borne Hawkeye radar planes. The system was supposed to network all the radar in a task force so that any ship or plane could fire a missile at a target detected by any other unit.

The appropriators also sliced $83 million from the $150 million requested to develop an experimental "arsenal ship" intended to carry hundreds of missile launchers, a very small crew and a minimum of the sophisticated electronic gear.

- **Air and sea transport.** In addition to the $2.3 billion to buy 11 of the C-17 wide-body cargo jets, the bill included $627 million to buy seven V-22 Ospreys — hybrid airplane/helicopters used by the Marines as troop carriers. Clinton requested $472 million for five Ospreys, and the Senate authorization bill recommended $562 million for six of the craft.

The appropriations bill, like the authorization measure, proposed deleting the $581 million requested for two large cargo ships and the $70 million requested for components to be used in a third ship scheduled for inclusion in the fiscal 1999 budget.

The appropriations bill also omitted $190 million that the administration requested for two Boeing 757 jetliners to replace elderly Boeing 707s used by senior U.S. officials traveling abroad. The committee argued that the Air Force should adhere to its earlier plan to lease the two planes.

Senate Floor Action

The Senate passed its $247.2 billion version of the defense bill July 15 by a vote of 94-4, adding $3.3 billion to Clinton's budget request. *(Vote 176, p. S-31)*

Two days of desultory debate seemed to vindicate the judgment of Stevens that senators had little taste for lengthy consideration after having spent the better part of a week on the companion defense authorization bill. The low-key debate was particularly striking because the defense funding bill provided one of the few opportunities for Congress to assert itself on controversial national security issues.

Floor Amendments

Among the amendments considered during floor debate were the following:

- **NATO enlargement.** The Senate adopted by voice vote an amendment to require the secretary of Defense to report to Congress by Oct. 1 on the anticipated cost to the United States of admitting Poland, Hungary and the Czech Republic to NATO and on the U.S. troop commitments that would be required. The proposal was offered by Stevens and Daniel K. Inouye of Hawaii, the senior Democrat on the Defense Appropriations Subcommittee.

The Senate also adopted by voice vote an amendment by Dianne Feinstein, D-Calif., expressing the sense of Congress that admitting the three countries to the alliance should not increase the U.S. share of NATO's costs.

The Pentagon said the expansion was expected to cost the United States about $2 billion over the following decade, but other estimates were much higher.

- **Bosnia.** Kay Bailey Hutchison, R-Texas, and other critics of the use of U.S. troops in Bosnia warned that NATO's action July 10 seizing alleged war criminals in Bosnia for the first time, smacked of "mission creep" — taking on a new role without adequate consideration of the increased risks.

The Senate gave voice vote approval to an amendment by Hutchison expressing the sense of the Senate that the administration "should consult closely and in a timely manner" with Congress about the involvement of NATO forces in efforts to apprehend war criminals in Bosnia.

- **Hawaii cruises.** McCain tried to eliminate from the bill a complex section written by Inouye and apparently designed to benefit a U.S.-flag cruise ship line operating only among the Hawaiian Islands — American Hawaii Cruises, owned by American Classic Voyages Co. of Chicago.

McCain dropped his amendment when Inouye agreed to language stipulating that none of the funds provided by the bill would actually be used to build a cruise ship.

- **Other amendments.** In other action on the bill, the Senate:

➤ Rejected, 15-83, a proposal by Tom Harkin, D-Iowa, to bar the Pentagon from reimbursing defense contractors for the cost of corporate mergers. *(Vote 175, p. S-31)*

➤ Approved, by voice vote, an amendment by Stevens restoring $60 million that the committee had cut from the administration's $382.2 million request for the so-called Nunn-Lugar program. Named for its sponsors, former Sen. Sam Nunn, D-Ga. (1972-97), and Sen Richard G. Lugar, R-Ind., the program was aimed at helping former Soviet states dismantle their nuclear and chemical warfare arsenals.

➤ Agreed by voice vote to a McCain amendment to allow the secretary of Defense to waive various "Buy American" provisions in the bill.

House Committee

Disregarding threats of a presidential veto, the House Appropriations Committee on July 22 gave voice vote approval to a $248.3 billion appropriations bill (HR 2266 — H Rept 105-206) that set a firm deadline for the withdrawal of U.S. troops from Bosnia and lay the groundwork for buying more B-2 stealth bombers.

The Bosnia provision, which the House had also added to the companion defense authorization bill (HR 1119) in June, proposed to bar the use of funds for U.S. ground troops in Bosnia after June 30, 1998. That was the date Clinton himself had set for removing U.S. troops from the war-torn country, where they served as the backbone of a NATO-led peacekeeping force, but the administration vehemently opposed locking it in by law.

House appropriators added $331 million to Clinton's budget for stepped-up B-2 production — buying components and gearing up subcontractors in preparation for buying nine more bombers, in addition to the 21 planes previously authorized.

The bill included $4.4 billion more than Clinton requested for basic defense programs. The increase was partially offset by proposed cuts in Clinton's request for defense-related Energy Department programs.

As usual, the bill closely tracked the House version of the defense authorization bill, with most of the added funding going to weapons development and production programs.

One of the few dramatic departures from the authorization bill was the inclusion of the $2.1 billion requested for 20 F/A-18 E and F model Navy combat jets. The House version of the authorization bill approved only $1.35 billion for the planes.

The committee rejected, by voice vote, four amendments offered by ranking Democrat David R. Obey of Wisconsin to:

- Eliminate the $331 million in added spending for B-2 production.
- Cut $1 billion from the $2.1 billion in the bill for the Air Force's F-22 fighter, delaying production for five years.
- Cut $107 million from the $179 million the committee added to buy three midair refueling tanker versions of the C-130 Hercules cargo plane.
- Bar the use of funds to promote the transfer of high-tech weapons, such as front-line combat jets, to Latin America. U.S. policy had barred such transfers since 1977, but Obey said U.S. weapons manufacturers were mounting a "strong drive" to overturn the policy.

Other Highlights of the House Bill

- **Personnel.** The House bill proposed to fund an active-duty military of 1.43 million, as requested by Clinton, a reduction of about 21,000 from the fiscal 1997 level. It included a $185 million cut from the budget to conform with a proposal in the House authorization bill to suspend for one year authority for service members to retire after 15 years of active-duty, instead of the 20 years usually required. (The provision was dropped in the final authorization bill.)
- **Operations and maintenance.** The $83 billion included in the bill for operations and maintenance included several large increases in accounts that typically benefitted from congressional largess. Among these were additions of $925 million, on top of the $4.1 billion Clinton requested, for maintenance of facilities and $473 million, in addition to the $6.3 billion requested, for overhauls of ships, planes and other equipment.

The committee also added funds the administration had belatedly acknowledged were needed but had not included in the February budget request. These included $622 million for Navy and Air Force flight operations, in addition to the $15 billion requested, and $274 million for health care for military service members, retirees and dependents, in addition to the $10 billion requested.

The committee proposed cutting $97.5 million from the $382.2 million requested for the Nunn-Lugar program.

- **Ground and air combat.** The committee added $175 million to modernize Army scout helicopters with new target-finding electronics and anti-tank missiles. But to continue de-

Defense Spending Bill Highlights

The following are major elements of the fiscal 1998 defense appropriations bill (HR 2266 — PL 105-56), signed into law Oct. 8:

• **Personnel and operations.** The final bill provided for an active-duty force of 1.43 million members, about 21,000 fewer than the fiscal 1997 level and essentially the number Clinton requested.

Conferees dropped a Senate initiative that would have cut an additional 10,000 members from the Army, at an estimated savings of $266 million. Also rejected was a House initiative that would have suspended for one year a program under which service members were allowed to retire, with a reduced pension, after only 15 years of active-duty service instead of the usual 20.

For reserve and National Guard forces, the conference report set a personnel level of nearly 893,000, nearly 1,000 members more than the budget assumed.

The conferees added $369 million to the $6.3 billion Clinton requested for major overhauls of ships, aircraft and vehicles. They also added $725 million to the $4.1 million that was sought to repair and maintain facilities.

Acknowledging a miscalculation in its February budget request, the administration had requested an additional $622 million to cover the cost of Navy and Air Force flight operations. The conference committee approved the added request, but covered the cost of this and other readiness-related add-ons by levying a 1.5 percent across-the-board reduction in all procurement and research programs covered by the bill.

About $30 million was added to cover the cost of moving Army battalions to the huge computer-monitored, mock-combat range at Fort Irwin, in California's Mojave Desert.

More than $100 million was set aside to cover the personnel and operating costs of keeping intact some aerial units Pentagon budget-writers wanted to downsize or eliminate, including:

• $57 million to keep in service all 94 remaining B-52 bombers, including $10 million for modifications.

• $25.2 million to prevent a cutback in the size of Air National Guard and Air Force Reserve C-130 squadrons.

• $1 million to keep operating a squadron of C-130 "hurricane hunters" based at Keesler Air Force Base in Mississippi. Repeated Air Force efforts to slough off this mission on some other agency had been stymied by Gulf Coast legislators.

• $30 million to continue operating a few SR-71 long-range, high-speed spy planes, which were retired by the Air Force in 1990 and put back into service by orders of Congress.

• **Missiles and anti-missile defenses.** Conferees accepted the Senate proposal to slow the production of Trident II submarine-launched, nuclear-armed missiles, to allow for the possibility that future arms control agreements might render additional missiles superfluous. The bill provided $227 million for five missiles, a reduction of $65 million (two missiles) from the request.

Overall, conferees added less than $300 million to Clinton's request for anti-missile defense programs.

The president's February budget included slightly more than $3.4 billion, including $504 million to develop a system intended to protect U.S. territory against a handful of missiles that might be acquired surreptitiously by a rogue state. In May, as a result of the Pentagon's Quadrennial Review, the administration requested an additional $474 million for the national territory defense. Conferees approved the entire $978 million for nationwide defense.

Among the major changes the conferees made to the anti-missile programs were approval of:

• $406 million of the $556 million requested for the Army's Theater High-Altitude Area Defense (THAAD).

• $410 million instead of the $195 million requested for a long-range "theater-wide" anti-missile version of the Navy's ship-launched Standard missile.

• $98 million to continue development of a laser-armed anti-missile satellite.

• **Ground, air combat.** The bill included the $157 million requested by the Army for continued development of a digital communications network.

Also approved without change were funds requested for several major weapons programs in which these digital links were to be embedded, including: $595 million to upgrade M-1 tanks with digital

veloping the new radar-evading Comanche scout helicopter, the bill included only the $282 million requested, without the additional $40 million approved by the authorization bill.

The appropriators also were more restrained in adding funds to the Army's budget for combat vehicles to be turned over to the National Guard — an additional $115 million to upgrade early model Bradley troop carriers and $96 million for 36 self-propelled artillery pieces and the same number of armored ammunition carriers.

In addition to supporting the administration's request for the F/A-18 E and F, House appropriators agreed to fund the other two major combat jet programs at the levels requested: $2.1 billion for the Air Force's F-22 and $931 million for the Joint Strike Fighter.

The bill sought to kill an Air Force-led program to develop a Joint Air-to-Surface Standoff Missile — a stealth weapon that a plane could launch from beyond the reach of enemy anti-aircraft defenses.

• **Naval forces.** The committee added more than $400 million to various Navy programs to accelerate the development and deployment of defenses against anti-ship cruise missiles and to adapt destroyers to shoot down ballistic missiles with ranges upwards of several hundred miles.

Nearly half that amount — $199 million — was added to the $139 million requested for the "cooperative engagement capability," a system to network all the radar in a widely dispersed fleet so any ship or plane could fire a missile at a target detected by any other ship or plane.

In its report, the Appropriations Committee contended that the Navy was unwisely cutting budgetary corners by overhauling its nuclear-powered aircraft carriers and building new destroyers without adding essential anti-missile defenses. Accordingly, it approved the $1.6 billion requested for a three-year overhaul of the carrier *Nimitz*, but with a net addition of $13 million to incorporate some of the self-defense equipment.

Similarly, the appropriators approved the $2.7 billion that Clinton requested for three destroyers equipped with the Aegis anti-aircraft system, and they added $30 million to provide the cooperative engagement and anti-ballistic missile capabilities.

They also proposed to block the Navy's plan to sign a multi-year contract for 12 destroyers unless at least four of them included the anti-ballistic missile capability.

House Floor Action

Moving closer to a showdown with the Senate and Clinton on the B-2 bomber, the House passed its $248.3 billion appropriations bill July 29 after rejecting an attempt to eliminate links, a larger cannon and improved night-vision equipment; $324 million to continue developing the Crusader mobile cannon; $512 million to equip missile-armed Apache helicopters with the Longbow target-finding radar; and $282 million to continue development of the Comanche "scout" helicopter.

Conferees rejected a House initiative that would have added $157 million to continue upgrading existing Kiowa scout helicopters with new, target-finding electronics.

The final bill included $627 million for seven V-22 Ospreys, a hybrid airplane/helicopter the Marine Corps planned to use as a troop carrier, an increase of $155 million and two aircraft above Clinton's request.

The Army got an additional $210 million for upgraded Bradley troop carriers, mobile cannon and armor-plated ammunition carriers, all of them designated for the National Guard. This was in addition to the $653 million added to the bill to procure other equipment for National Guard and reserve units.

The final bill provided a total of $331 million for B-2 related procurement — $157 million more than requested — but left the president free to spend that money to upgrade and repair the 21 B-2s previously funded. The House had fought to add $331 million to begin gearing up production of nine more of the radar-evading stealth bombers.

With minor changes, the conferees approved the amounts requested for all three of a new generation of combat jets slated to enter service over the following decade, providing:

- $2.1 billion to gear up for production in 1999 of the Air Force's F-22 fighter.
- $2.1 billion to buy 20 F/A-18 "E" and "F" model planes, larger versions of the F/A-18s that were being used as both fighters and bombers.
- $957 million to continue developing the Joint Strike Fighter, slated to replace Navy, Marine Corps and Air Force jets of 1970s-vintage beginning in 2008.

The conferees managed to find additional funds to continue production of two Air Force fighters already in service:

- $226 million for five F-15s built in St. Louis by McDonnell Douglas — $67 million and two planes more than requested.
- $83 million for three additional Fort Worth-built Lockheed Martin F-16s. None were requested.

● **Naval warfare and transport.** Conferees agreed to provide the $2.7 billion requested for three Navy destroyers to be built by commercial shipyards in Maine and Mississippi, and they added $720 million for a fourth ship, to be built in Mississippi. The Pentagon had agreed to the fourth ship after Senate Majority Leader Trent Lott, R-Miss., objected when a team of companies that included the Mississippi yard — a Litton Industries facility in Pascagoula — lost a competition to build a fleet of amphibious transport ships, known as LPDs.

The bill included $2.3 billion for the first of a new class of nuclear-powered submarines and authorized the two commercial shipyards that built nuclear subs for the Navy to collaborate on construction of the new class.

The bill also included the $1.6 billion requested for a three-year overhaul and nuclear refueling of the carrier USS *Nimitz*, commissioned in 1975.

Conferees approved only $50 million of the $345 million the Senate had added to begin buying components for a new aircraft carrier to be built by Newport News Shipbuilding and Dry Dock near Norfolk, Va. The Pentagon had not scheduled initial funding for the components until 2002, with the bulk of the money slated for inclusion in the fiscal 2002 budget.

The conferees approved $213 million instead of the $139 million requested for the Navy's "cooperative engagement capability" — the fleet's counterpart to the Army's digital network links.

The final bill included the $1.9 billion requested to buy nine C-17 wide-body cargo jets, dropping the Senate proposal to buy two more.

Under prodding from Army Chief of Staff Gen. Dennis L. Reimer, the conference approved $650 million for two large, high-speed cargo ships intended to carry tanks and other heavy combat equipment for Army units deploying to distant trouble spots.

● **Other provisions.** About $75 million was cut from the bill to reflect anticipated savings from a provision in the defense authorization bill that would no longer require services to purchase a warranty for every weapon they buy.

About $10.4 billion — slightly more than was requested — was set aside for the Pentagon's health care system. This included $13 million to continue operating the armed services' medical school in Bethesda, Md., a perennial target of budget cutters. ■

---

the money added in committee to resume production of the stealth bomber. The bill passed by a vote of 322-105. *(Vote 338, p. H-102)*

The amendment to strike the extra $331 million in B-2 funding was offered by Obey, who proposed using most of the money for deficit reduction, with small amounts going to accelerate the upgrade of midair refueling tankers with new engines and to pay for breast cancer research. The proposal was rejected, 200-222. *(Vote 336, p. H-102)*

On the broader question of defense funding, the House rejected, 137-290, an amendment cosponsored by Christopher Shays, R-Conn., and Barney Frank, D-Mass., that would have cut the bill's overall spending by $3.9 billion, essentially freezing it at the fiscal 1997 level. *(Vote 337, p. H-102)*

The House rejected by voice vote an amendment by Jerrold Nadler, D-N.Y., designed to delay production of the Air Force's F-22 fighter for seven years. Nadler's amendment would have cut $420 million from the $2.1 billion in the bill for F-22 development.

The Air Force argued that the new plane, with its stealth design, was essential if U.S. pilots in future wars were to have a technological edge. But Nadler cited an analysis by the General Accounting Office (GAO), concluding that the F-15 would beat all comers at least through 2010, thus allowing the slowdown he proposed for the F-22.

Other Amendments Adopted

The House also gave voice vote approval to amendments:

➤ By Peter A. DeFazio, D-Ore., to increase by $15 million a medical research program run cooperatively by the Defense Department and the Department of Veterans Affairs.

➤ By Bernard Sanders, I-Vt., to double, to $4 million, the amount for the "Starbase" program under which National Guard members tutored youth in the fourth, fifth and sixth grades in math, technology and the importance of staying off drugs.

➤ By James A. Traficant Jr., D-Ohio, providing that no funds in the bill would be used to cover the cost of NATO expansion except as authorized by law.

➤ By Joseph P. Kennedy II, D-Mass., providing that blood samples taken from all military personnel be used only for purposes specified by existing Pentagon policy, which included identification of human remains and investigation of a crime.

➤ By Gerald B.H. Solomon, R-N.Y., to bar Pentagon contracts with any firm that had not complied with an existing law requiring companies to report on their hiring of veterans, particularly disabled veterans and those who served during the Vietnam War.

➤ By Tom Coburn, R-Okla., prohibiting the use of any funds in the bill for "Man and the Biosphere," an environmen-

Vetoed Provisions

President Clinton used his line-item veto sparingly on the fiscal 1998 Defense appropriations bill (PL 105-56), eliminating mostly marginal programs or research projects worth a total of $144 million. The following are the vetoed items:

- **SR-71 Blackbird.** Clinton vetoed $39 million for the ultra-fast, high-altitude spy plane, echoing the Air Force's finding a decade before that there was no military requirement for the Blackbird.

The Air Force had retired the spy planes in 1990, a quarter-century after they first flew, relying instead on satellites and other intelligence methods. After the 1991 war with Iraq, however, U.S. commanders complained that they had not received timely intelligence, and Congress ordered the Air Force in 1994 to put three Blackbirds back in service.

The plane's congressional fans, including veteran Senate appropriator Robert C. Byrd, D-W.Va., wanted Blackbirds to fly until unmanned reconnaissance planes became operational. Between fiscal 1995 and fiscal 1997, Congress appropriated $165 million to put Blackbirds in the air again. Two craft began flying operational missions again in January.

- **Fuel cell energy.** The White House cut $6 million for an Army project to study "molten carbonate fuel cell technology"as a clean source of energy, saying the project would not significantly contribute to U.S. military capability. The emerging technology converted fuels such as natural gas and coal into electricity.

"There are several projects included in the bill related to the same technology," said Clinton budget director Franklin D. Raines. "The ones that had a military application have been retained." The administration also said the Army project was better suited for the Energy Department, which had responsibility for alternative energy research.

- **Medical research.** Clinton vetoed two medical research projects that would have received Army research and development funds. He cut a $3 million periscopic surgery project, saying the Pentagon already funded microsurgery programs with specific military applications. He also cut a $4 million project for research on proton beam cancer therapy, to be conducted at Loma Linda University Medical Center in Southern California. The treatment allowed for precision radiation therapy on localized tumors and had been used to treat prostate, brain and eye cancers.

- **Sonar/acoustics.** Clinton vetoed a pair of $3 million Navy research projects aimed at sounding out the underwater depths.

The first would have done further research on a metal alloy, Terfenol-D, for high-power sonar systems. The high-tech alloy was one-third the weight of the metal being used in Navy sonar systems but achieved the same underwater sounding power. The new work was slated to be performed in part by the National Center of Excellence in Metal Working Technology, in Johnstown, Pa.

The second project would have continued research on use of a commercially available air gun to produce underwater acoustic signals. The gun could be useful for tracking submarines, Raines said, but would be valuable only in shallow waters, "where there is no current requirement for such capability."

- **Military space plane.** Clinton held back $10 million for research that was to have been launched on a military space plane. The funds would have gone toward hypersonic technology research, much of which would have occurred at the Air Force's Phillips Laboratory at Kirtland Air Force Base in Albuquerque, N.M. Clinton said development of reusable launch vehicles fell under the purview of NASA, not the Pentagon. According to the space plane program office at Phillips, however, the project funding was in the Air Force's fiscal 1999 budget.

- **Toxic chemicals.** Clinton cut $2 million in the bill for research on toxic chemicals aimed at determining how much cleanup was sufficient at military bases. The administration said the work would duplicate ongoing Pentagon research. The research was to be carried out at the Institute of Environmental and Human Health near Lubbock, Texas, and would have examined cleanup efforts at Brooks Air Force Base in San Antonio.

- **Rural Techlink.** Also cut was $1 million included in the bill for Techlink, a public-private partnership in Bozeman, Mont., to help funnel Pentagon-developed technologies into the private sector. The money would have helped companies in Montana, Idaho, Wyoming, South Dakota and North Dakota in developing commercial outlets for defense research.

Techlink had started a year and a half earlier, mostly with funding from NASA, to help the states' businesses build on the space agency's technology research. The vetoed money would have doubled Techlink's budget and broadened its coverage to some 80 defense labs, according to Peter Perna, Techlink's executive director. "This would have directly supported the Pentagon's dual-use strategy," he said. The Clinton administration said the Techlink funds would not contribute significantly to U.S. military capability.

- **Clementine II/ASAT.** Two of the most expensive items on Clinton's hit list were Star Wars-type programs with broader policy implications.

The first, known as Clementine II ($30 million), would have continued research on intercepting asteroids in space. The other, known as ASAT, for anti-satellite weapons program ($37.5 million), would have funded an experiment to prove the feasibility of destroying enemy satellites with land-based weapons. The original Clementine mapped the surface of the moon in 1994 but malfunctioned before it could go on to the asteroid Geographos. The new Clementine was to send probes to photograph and collide with asteroids.

Supporters of the project, mostly in the Senate, said Clementine would help research a defense against asteroids colliding with Earth. They had kept the project going over objections from the administration, which contended that the project was actually aimed at testing space-based missile defenses that could be illegal under a 1972 missile treaty.

The anti-satellite program had been continued by the Bush administration and Congress over Pentagon objections, but Congress went along when Clinton zeroed out the program in 1993. When the GOP took over on Capitol Hill in 1995, $30 million was earmarked for ASAT, followed by $50 million in 1996.

Clinton's Arms Control Adviser Robert G. Bell said there were effective anti-satellite alternatives, other than blowing them up in orbit. "We are confident that alternatives exist," he said, "including destroying ground stations linked to the satellite or jamming the links themselves."

- **Gallo Center.** Clinton vetoed $4 million for the Gallo Center for Environmental Technologies in New Jersey. Named after former Rep. Dean Gallo, R-N.J., and located at Picatinny Arsenal, the center researched ways to make, store and destroy ammunition without creating environmentally hazardous byproducts. Clinton said his budget included money for environmental technology research and that the Army saw no merit in the Gallo Center funds.

- **Optical correlators.** Also vetoed was $1.5 million for Air Force research on optical correlator technology, aimed at permitting clearer target recognition for precision guided bombs. It also had medical and commercial uses, including fingerprint scanning. About $4 million remained in the bill for Navy research into the technology. Clinton said the Air Force research would not add significantly to U.S. military capability.

tal research project with international links that some social conservatives viewed as potentially infringing on private property rights and local land-use decisions.

Conference/Final Action

House and Senate conferees agreed Sept. 19 on a $247.7 billion compromise bill (HR 2266 — PL 105-265), adding $3.8 billion to Clinton's request but dropping provisions Clinton strongly opposed. *(Highlights, p. 9-22)*

The House adopted the conference report Sept. 25 by a vote of 356-65. The Senate cleared the bill later the same day, 93-5. *(House vote 442, p. H-134; Senate vote 258, p. S-43)*

- **B-2.** The final bill included a total of $331 billion for B-2 related spending, $157 million above the president's request, but it did not require him to spend the money to begin buying additional planes, as the House had wanted.

The administration had warned that, if it came to a showdown, Clinton would either veto the entire Defense appropriations bill or use his line-item veto authority to knock out the money for new B-2s.

- **Bosnia.** The bill required that funds for deployment of U.S. peacekeepers in Bosnia be cut off after June 30, 1998, but it allowed Clinton to waive that limit if he told Congress in advance why he planned to leave troops in the war-torn Balkan country and for how long.

In the brief debate that preceded the Senate's adoption of the conference report, some members decried the deepening involvement of U.S. troops in efforts to rebuild the Bosnian state. "We are drifting into a political commitment that we do not understand," warned Hutchison, an outspoken opponent of the Bosnia deployment.

White House national security adviser Samuel R. Berger had used a Sept. 23 speech at Georgetown University to build a forceful case for continued U.S. involvement in Bosnia. Without it, he said, "Bosnia will almost certainly slide back into conflict, potentially leading to a wider war in southeastern Europe."

Conferees Rearrange Some Funding

Tight budget limits squeezed out some proposals for additional spending. The conferees dropped a House attempt to add funds to arm and upgrade some Army Kiowa scout helicopters, a program Congress had kept alive for years over Pentagon objections. They also dropped the $419 million Senate proposal to buy two more C-17 cargo jets than the nine Clinton had sought (and for which the conferees approved $2 billion).

The conferees also approved only $50 million of the $345 million the Senate had added to begin work on a $5 billion aircraft carrier.

But, as they did each year, the defense appropriators carved funds out of Clinton's budget to give themselves room to squeeze more congressional initiatives within the defense spending limits set by the budget resolution.

They cut more than $1.3 billion that they said was either superfluous or amounted to an unmanageably large increase over the prior year's appropriation for a given program. This included cuts made possible when contractors offered the Pentagon a lower price on an item than the budget had anticipated or because inflation proved to be less than estimated when the budget was drawn up.

About $425 million of the $1.3 billion in cuts was based on indications that the Pentagon would have fewer military personnel and civilian employees on its payroll at the start of fiscal 1998 than the budget assumed.

Another such reduction reflected the dollar's growing strength against some foreign currencies — a change that allowed U.S. forces stationed in those countries to pay less for locally purchased goods and services.

The administration had amended its own budget in February by trimming $261 million to reflect advantageous currency fluctuations. The conferees not only accepted the administration's adjustment but cut an additional $100 million for the same reason.

Also targeted for cuts were several programs that congressional budget experts routinely assumed could safely be whittled down without risk to the Pentagon's essential missions. Such cuts added up to more than $500 million, including savings achieved by eliminating $300 million for consultants, $72 million for federally sponsored think tanks such as the RAND Corp., $90 million for data processing systems and $78 million for official travel.

The defense conferees cut more than $300 million that they attributed to initial steps toward efficiencies outlined in the Pentagon's Quadrennial Defense Review of future defense plans, unveiled in May. These reductions were intended to slim down administrative headquarters and reduce the number of training exercises called by the Joint Chiefs of Staff. The Pentagon review warned that some units were giving up too much of the time they needed to hone their basic combat skills in order to participate in joint exercises with foreign forces — exercises that were conducted as much for diplomatic effect as for military purposes.

Aiming at Clinton

Reprising what had become a stock feature of the annual congressional defense debate, the Republican majority also made a point of trimming a handful of relatively small programs that were among Clinton's signature Pentagon initiatives. In this category, conferees approved:

- $125 million of the $225 million requested to develop "dual-use" technologies that would have both military and commercial application.
- $20 million of the $48 million requested to encourage incorporation of commercial technologies in military development programs.
- $81 million of the $121 million requested for fast-track development programs intended to translate promising technologies quickly into deployed weapons, leap-frogging the usual prolonged gestation process.
- $47 million of the $80 million requested for overseas humanitarian missions.

As late as the day the conference report was filed with the House, administration officials were demanding that conferees reopen some of these issues to give Clinton more of what he wanted, but their demands were refused.

Conferees accommodated Clinton on one politically charged program: They approved the entire $382 million requested for the Nunn-Lugar program.

Funds for Favored Projects

As always, the conferees funded some congressional initiatives that were blessed with particularly influential patrons, for example:

- As they had for years, conferees added money to buy C-130 Hercules cargo planes that were not requested by the administration. This year, the add-on came to $479 million for eight of the planes, which were built in a Marietta, Ga., plant just a short distance from the district of House Speaker Newt Gingrich.
- In addition to the $2.7 billion requested for three Navy

destroyers to be built by commercial shipyards in Maine and Mississippi, the conferees approved $720 million for a fourth ship, to be built in Lott's home state of Mississippi.

➤ Conferees also added $16 million as a down payment on an oceanographic research ship to be built by Trinity Marine in Moss Point, Miss., and $100 million to begin work on a second amphibious transport ship, known as an LPD, to be built by Avondale Shipyard in New Orleans, just outside the district of House Appropriations Committee Chairman Robert L. Livingston, R-La.

➤ Stevens got, among other things, $5 million for a Fairbanks landfill. Inouye got $35 million — instead of the $10 million Clinton requested and the House had approved — to continue removing unexploded bombs from Kaho'olawe, a Hawaiian island that was used as a Navy target range.

Likewise, the conferees accepted Inouye's provision that apparently would grant a U.S.-flag cruise line operating only in Hawaii a monopoly on business among the state's islands. ■

Congress Clears D.C. Bill on Final Day

Congress gave final approval to the fiscal 1998 District of Columbia appropriations bill Nov. 13, ending a battle over a school voucher provision that had stalled the measure until the last day of the session. President Clinton signed the $855 million bill into law Nov. 19 (HR 2607 — PL 105-100).

The bill's enactment followed a yearlong tug-of-war over how much money to appropriate for the District and how much authority to give it to run its government.

It also followed weeks of jockeying over extraneous provisions, the most contentious of which were the school voucher plan for poor children and a proposal to allow certain immigrants from Central America and the former Soviet republics to avoid immediate deportation. In the end, most of the add-ons, with the exception of the immigration provisions, were stripped from the bill.

Meanwhile, Congress watched as the District's public schools opened three weeks late because they were in disrepair, and the District of Columbia Control Board assumed even greater power over running the nation's capital, authority granted by Congress to get the District on a sound financial footing. *(D.C. overhaul, p. 3-10)*

BOXSCORE

Fiscal 1998 District of Columbia Appropriations — HR 2607 (S 1156). The bill appropriated $855 million for the District, most of it for federal agencies that were assuming responsibility for much of the city's services. It also approved a $4.97 billion local D.C. budget.

Reports: H Rept 105-298, S Rept 105-75.

KEY ACTION

Oct. 9 — House passed HR 2607, 203-202.

Nov. 9 — Senate passed HR 2607, revised, by voice vote.

Nov. 12 — House accepted Senate revisions, with an amendment, by voice vote.

Nov. 13 — Senate cleared the bill by voice vote.

Nov. 19 — President signed HR 2607 — PL 105-100.

Implementing an Overhaul Plan

At the request of congressional leaders, appropriators delayed getting started on the D.C. spending bill until authorizers could work out a plan to revamp the federal relationship with the nation's capital. The overhaul plan was enacted Aug. 5 as part of the budget-reconciliation package (HR 2015 — PL 105-33).

The reconciliation bill instituted management reforms and shifted several expensive city services —including the underfunded city employee pension plan and the prison and court systems — to the federal government in exchange for ending the annual federal payment to the city.

The federal government had traditionally provided an annual payment to partially reimburse the District for the property taxes it was unable to collect from the many federal and non-taxable entities based there. The payment had totaled $660 million in each of the three previous fiscal years. The reconciliation bill called for a one-time federal contribution of $190 million to the city in fiscal 1998.

In addition, the budget-reconciliation bill stripped the D.C. mayor, Democrat Marion S. Barry Jr., of much of his power. Under the bill, Barry retained control of only four minor departments.

The federally appointed control board was given final authority to choose the heads of nine other city departments, including mammoths such as public works and human services. Barry could still nominate the department heads who, under the reconciliation law, had to resign and either be replaced or reconfirmed.

The appropriations bill implemented many of those changes. It provided a total of $855 million in federal funds for the District, $136 million more than the fiscal 1997 level and $78 million more than Clinton had requested.

Of the total, only $190 million went directly to the city. The remaining $665 million went to the agencies and trustees charged with assuming responsibility for courts, prisons and other city services.

The bill also approved a $4.97 billion D.C. budget, which included local revenue as well as the federal funds. Under the Home Rule Act, the District could not spend money — either from the federal government or from local taxpayers — without a congressional appropriation.

The legislation included two funding limitations that had become standard for D.C. spending bills. It prohibited the use of any public funds, federal or local, for abortions in the District, except to save the life of the woman or in cases of rape or incest. It also barred the use of funds to implement the Domestic Partners Act, a 1992 city ordinance that allowed unmarried partners of city workers the same benefits as spouses.

The bill also contained language clarifying a portion of the overhaul plan that had upset city officials and activists. It ensured that the D.C. City Council would have a say in the mayor's appointments to head the nine city departments. Under the overhaul plan, the federally created control board would have been the only body that could accept or reject the appointments. The bill gave the council power to reject a candidate.

School Vouchers

For much of the session, GOP leaders steadfastly insisted that the measure would include their school voucher proposal. Under the plan, 2,000 poor D.C. children would get vouchers worth up to $3,200 apiece to attend private or parochial schools, or to go to public schools outside the city. Another 2,000 D.C. public school students would get $500 vouchers for tutoring.

The push was led by by House Majority Leader Dick Armey, R-Texas, with strong backing from Speaker Newt Gingrich, R-Ga. Critics said the vouchers were not enough to send children to most private schools in the area, but Armey said his staff had identified plenty of spots in mostly parochial schools.

GOP leaders argued that the vouchers would give low-income, inner-city families the same opportunities to seek a better education for their children that were available to richer families. Republicans hoped the voucher idea would provide them with a means to chip away at Democratic strongholds in minority communities and highlight Democratic ties to teachers' unions. They saw the District as offering fertile ground for testing their urban policy ideas.

Clinton and congressional Democrats vociferously op-

Fiscal 1998 D.C. Spending

(in thousands of dollars)

	Clinton Request	House Bill	Senate Bill	Final Bill
Total Federal Funds	$ 777,000	$ 827,500	$ 848,000	$ 855,000
Total D.C. budget	4,764,023	4,962,705	4,962,967	4,972,567

SOURCE: House Appropriations Committee

posed the voucher proposal, as they had two years earlier when Republicans tried to attach a similar plan to the D.C. spending bill, only to drop it five months later. *(1995 Almanac, p. 11-30)*

Opponents argued that, in the words of D.C. City Councilman Kevin Chavous, vouchers would create two school systems — "one for the haves and one for the have-nots." Chavous and other foes said vouchers would allow the best students to go elsewhere, leaving public schools underfunded and with troubled student bodies.

As in 1995, the House included the proposal in its fiscal 1998 bill, while Senate appropriators did not. An attempt to attach a voucher plan on the Senate floor failed in the face of a threatened Democratic filibuster. The leadership finally dropped the plan in an effort to produce a bill that could clear the Senate.

Senate Committee

The Senate Appropriations Committee actually started first, approving its version of the bill Sept. 9 by a vote of 27-1 (S 1156 — S Rept 105-75).

Members from both parties praised D.C. Subcommittee Chairman Lauch Faircloth, R-N.C., for producing a compromise bill that would implement the already enacted decisions to reassert Congress' power over District affairs. Only Richard C. Shelby, R-Ala., voted against it.

Faircloth worked with Democrats and city officials to ensure minimal opposition, at least in his chamber. Of House plans to do more, Faircloth said: "Before we start looking for new problems, let's solve some of those that we already have."

The bill called for an appropriation of $820 million in federal funds for the District. That included a $190 million federal contribution to the city, $30 million of which was directed to repaying part of the city's $500 million debt.

In addition to the federal payment, the bill included $630 million for federal agencies charged with taking over city functions. The change was expected to give the city about $200 million more to spend than it had anticipated when first writing its budget. The Senate bill required that at least $160 million of that go to pay down the city's debt. The rest would have to go to infrastructure improvements and management changes.

In addition to approving the city's $4.97 billion overall budget, the bill included a provision clarifying that the City Council would have a say on the mayor's appointments to head nine major city departments.

The bill also included a prohibition on any public funding for abortions in the District, and an injunction on the domestic partners ordinance.

Senate Floor Action

The Senate began debate on its version of the D.C. spending bill Sept. 24, but it was clear from the outset that the going would be rough. The biggest problems came over attempts to insert the voucher provision and to protect certain groups of immigrants from deportation.

• **Vouchers.** The school voucher amendment, offered by Daniel R. Coats, R-Ind., was identical to the House version. It had been introduced as separate legislation (S 847) by Coats and Joseph I. Lieberman, D-Conn.

Faircloth supported the concept of school vouchers, but he was committed to keeping the spending bill free of controversial amendments that might slow final action.

After hours of debate on the issue, the Senate effectively killed the voucher proposal Sept. 30, when it fell two votes short of the 60 necessary to block a filibuster by Edward M. Kennedy, D-Mass. The vote was 58-41. Four Democrats — Mary L. Landrieu and John B. Breaux, both of Louisiana, Daniel Patrick Moynihan of New York and Lieberman — joined 54 Republicans in favor of curbing debate and putting the proposal to a straightforward "yes" or "no" vote. John H. Chafee of Rhode Island was the only Republican voting "no." *(Vote 260, p. S-44)*

Before the cloture vote, Armey vowed that even if Senate Republicans lost, the final D.C. spending bill would contain the school voucher language. "I intend for it to come out of conference with it in it," Armey said. "I do intend it to be in the bill when it goes to the president."

Clinton denounced the school voucher idea but did not explicitly threaten to veto the bill, as administration officials had suggested he would. He did, however, come close to such a threat. "I call upon Congress to challenge our public schools, to change our public schools, but not walk away from them," he said at the White House. "I will veto any legislation that damages our commitment to public education and to higher standards."

• **Immigrants.** With the fight over vouchers apparently put off until conference, the Senate turned to another controversial issue — this one unrelated to the District of Columbia. Joined by Kennedy, Florida's two senators — Republican Connie Mack and Democrat Bob Graham — sought to allow 316,000 Central Americans who were granted temporary protection from deportation in the 1980s during civil strife in El Salvador and Nicaragua to continue to follow expiring immigration laws that would make it easier for them to remain in the United States. *(Immigration, p. 5-11)*

Mack was hospitalized twice during the debate, further slowing action on the bill. Finally, on Oct. 8, the Senate agreed to cut off debate on the immigration amendment, which was then adopted overwhelmingly. Both votes were 99-1. Robert C. Byrd, D-W.Va., cast the lone "no" vote, to protest that the amendment was unrelated to the underlying appropriations bill. *(Votes 268, 269, p. S-45)*

The immigration debate was not over, however. Carol Moseley-Braun, D-Ill., stalled further action on the D.C. bill, arguing that the provisions should be expanded to include more than 10,000 Haitians who entered the country by the early 1990s. The Black Caucus argued that the Haitians should receive the same protection as Central Americans, but Republicans said they only wanted to cover those who had fled communism.

• **Other Senate amendments.** Before work on the bill bogged down over immigration, the Senate made some other changes:

• **Senate 'holds.'** Ron Wyden, D-Ore., won voice vote approval Oct. 1 for an amendment requiring that senators who put "holds" on bills and nominations have their names published in the Congressional Record. Senators routinely blocked legislation by telling the leadership privately that they were putting a hold on it. "The Senate is not going to suffer if a little sunshine comes in," Wyden said.

Majority Leader Trent Lott, R-Miss., said he opposed putting the proposed Senate rule change on an appropriations bill. He said the Wyden language would be better considered as a separate bill at the beginning of a session of Congress.

• **Alcohol.** On Sept. 30, the Senate agreed by a vote of 69-27 to an amendment by Byrd to require that more alcohol and beverage control inspectors be hired for the District, and to bar alcohol billboards from being placed near schools. *(Vote 263, p. S-44)*

House Committee

The House District of Columbia Appropriations Subcommittee approved its draft of the spending bill, 6-3, on Sept. 17, after Democrats indicated they would save their fire for the full committee. The bill was later introduced as HR 2607.

Despite pleas from Appropriations Committee Chairman Robert L. Livingston, R-La., that they avoid controversial riders to the spending bills, Gingrich and House D.C. Appropriations Subcommittee Chairman Charles H. Taylor, R-N.C., included the school voucher provisions, projected to cost $7 million in fiscal 1998.

The subcommittee draft provided for a total of $825.5 million in federal funding for fiscal 1998. The amount included a direct contribution of $180 million to the city, with most of the remaining $617 million earmarked for transferring control of the District's costly prison, court and pension systems to the federal government.

Like the Senate bill, the House measure included provisions to prohibit public funding for abortions in the District and block the domestic partners ordinance.

The panel included a slew of other provisions, many of them at odds with the Senate version of the bill, which had been approved a week earlier by the Senate Appropriations Committee.

Among them were proposals to:

➤ Cut the city's own $4.47 billion budget by $300 million to allow for up to $200 million in tax cuts and retire part of the city's $500 million short-term debt. Taylor argued that tax and debt relief were vital to the city's financial health.

➤ Require that all city employees live in the District within a year of the bill's enactment.

➤ Cap punitive damages in medical liability cases in the District at $250,000.

➤ Eliminate funding for the University of the District of Columbia's law school if it failed to get accreditation in January 1998.

➤ Put a statutory cap on welfare spending in the city.

➤ Eliminate the property tax exemption for the National Education Association.

➤ Reopen Pennsylvania Avenue near the White House to traffic and end helicopter tours over Washington. The section of Pennsylvania Avenue had been closed in 1995 for security.

➤ Allow D.C. school officials to save money on construction and repair projects by waiving Davis-Bacon laws, which required contractors to pay an area's prevailing wages for construction and repair projects.

Full Committee Drops Some Provisions

The full Appropriations Committee approved the D.C. spending bill Sept. 29 on a 23-18 party-line vote (H Rept 105-298).

Though Democrats argued strongly against the vouchers — and a host of other legislative riders in the bill — the committee rejected their attempt to remove the provisions by substituting the Senate bill for the text of the House bill. The amendment, offered by James P. Moran, D-Va., was defeated 19-23.

Republicans did agree to remove some controversial provisions. The committee gave voice vote approval to an amendment by Taylor dropping his plan to cut the city's budget by $300 million to pay for tax cuts and debt reduction. As amended, the bill required that the city set aside at least $200 million for deficit reduction, but only required that it cut taxes if revenues came in higher than expected. Taylor also agreed to remove requirements that all city employees live in the District and that the city cut its staffing levels by 10 percent.

House Floor Action

With the voucher plan still intact, the bill squeaked through the House by a single vote Oct. 9, but only after GOP leaders held the tallying open for an extra 20 minutes. The final vote was 203-202. *(Vote 513, p. H-156)*

In their effort to win Democratic support, Republicans had paid too little attention to the GOP count and neglected to stop 12 Republicans from leaving town. With lawmakers missing, Republican leaders were forced to comb the halls for any available member.

Democrats, not a single one of whom voted for the bill, protested that 37 minutes were allowed for the roll call, which originally was set for 17 minutes.

Democratic Opposition

During the floor debate, Democrats again tried and failed to remove many of the legislative riders, particularly the voucher provision.

Democrats charged that the riders abrogated the Home Rule charter granted the city in 1975 after years of racially charged deliberations. "The issue here is not whether some of those political judgments should be arrived at," said David R. Obey of Wisconsin, the ranking Democrat on the Appropriations Committee. "The question is, 'Who should arrive at those judgments?'"

Democrat Eleanor Holmes Norton, the District's non-voting delegate to Congress, shouted, "Show some respect for me and the people I represent."

But Republicans retorted that Democrats were defending a failed system, particularly in their opposition to the voucher provision. "The minority party had their way in developing this city and this city's schools," said Anne M. Northup, R-Ky., "and we have an entirely broken system."

Moran tried again to replace the House language with the text of the relatively rider-free Senate bill, but he was defeated, 197-212, on a mostly party-line vote. *(Vote 512, p. H-156)*

Democrats did succeed in removing the Davis-Bacon waiver. An amendment by Martin Olav Sabo, D-Minn., to strike the provision was adopted, 234-188. *(Vote 511, p. H-156)*

Stripped-Down Bill

Shortly after the bill's near defeat in the House, and against the backdrop of on-and-off Senate floor action on the measure, Republican leaders decided to assume control. Their plan was to strip out all the riders but the voucher provision to try to set up a social policy showdown with Clinton.

Clinton's aides had said he would veto any measure that contained the voucher plan, although GOP leaders and the White House considered a proposal that would have written the $7 million voucher plan in such a way that Clinton could have nullified it with the line-item veto.

But GOP leaders re-examined their plans as they realized the difficulty of finding House support. Most Democrats would not vote for the bill because it contained the vouchers, and many conservatives were likely to oppose it because it did not include Taylor's legislative mandates. In the end, they agreed to drop the voucher plan.

With vouchers and the other mandates gone, GOP leaders had one final problem to tackle — the immigration amendment. They held fast against extending the protection to the Haitians but expanded the provision to allow some Nicaraguans and Cubans to become permanent residents and to protect from deportation those who had come to the United States from communist Latin American or Eastern European countries by the early 1990s.

Moseley-Braun agreed to drop her objection when the administration assured her that it would not deport the Haitians until Congress had had a chance to act separately on their fate.

With the exception of the immigration provision, the abortion ban and the domestic partners language, the final D.C. bill was what city officials had requested.

In accordance with the overhaul plan, it provided $190 million directly to the city — the amount in the Senate bill but $10 million more than the House had approved. It doled out the rest of the federal funds ($665 million) to agencies and trustees charged with assuming responsibility for the courts, and prisons and other city services.

Final Action

The Senate first passed the revised version of HR 2607 by voice vote Nov. 9. The House took it up Nov. 12 and passed it by voice vote after making a few changes, several of which had been requested by city officials and the control board overseeing the city's finances. Among them: provisions easing the creation of charter schools in the District and a $7 million increase in funding for the U.S. Park Police.

The Senate accepted the changes and cleared the bill by voice vote Nov. 13. ■

Water, Weapons Get More Funds

Under the firm hand of Sen. Pete V. Domenici, R-N.M., the House and Senate agreed on a generous, $21.2 billion energy and water spending plan for fiscal 1998. The final bill managed to satisfy the House's taste for politically popular water projects while also providing additional funding for energy and nuclear weapons programs favored in the Senate.

The total was $1.9 billion less than President Clinton requested and about $160 million less than was appropriated for fiscal 1997. Clinton signed the bill into law Oct. 13 (HR 2203 — PL 105-62).

Three-fourths of the funds — $15.9 billion — went to the Energy Department, largely for defense-related weapons activities. The remainder was devoted primarily to water projects built and maintained by two agencies — the Army Corps of Engineers ($4.1 billion) and the Interior Department's Bureau of Reclamation ($870 million).

BOXSCORE

Fiscal 1998 Energy and Water Development Appropriations — HR 2203 (S 1004). The $21.2 billion bill funded nuclear weapons programs, energy research and popular water projects.

Reports: H Rept 105-190, S Rept 105-44; conference report, H Rept 105-271.

KEY ACTION

July 16 — Senate passed S 1004, 99-0.

July 25 — House passed HR 2203, 418-7.

July 28 — Senate passed HR 2203 by prior agreement, after substituting the text of S 1004.

Sept. 30 — House adopted the conference report, 404-17. **Senate** cleared the bill, 99-0.

Oct. 13 — President signed HR 2203 — PL 105-62.

Oct. 17 — President used the line-item veto to delete provisions from PL 105-62.

New Faces, Old Conflicts

The Energy and Water Appropriations subcommittees in both chambers had new faces in key places in 1997. The House panel had a new chairman, Joseph M. McDade, R-Pa., and a new ranking Democrat, Vic Fazio of California. The Senate panel had a new ranking Democrat, Harry Reid of Nevada.

But the two subcommittees ended up following very traditional paths. The proceedings were dominated by Domenici, chairman of the Senate subcommittee and the sole surviving veteran at the helm. Senate appropriators produced a $21.2 billion version of the bill (S 1004) that included about $800 million more than their House counterparts for nuclear weapons programs. The $20.4 billion House version (HR 2203) proposed spending about $400 million more than the Senate on water projects.

To bridge the gap, Domenici used his clout as chairman of the Senate Budget Committee to get extra spending allocated to both subcommittees. That enabled the House and Senate appropriators to accommodate each other's priorities without sacrificing their own.

The move helped increase appropriations for nuclear weapons research, development and cleanup in the final bill to $11.5 billion, nearly $200 million above the fiscal 1997 level. The amount was still nearly $2.1 billion less than Clinton requested. Much of the difference resulted from a decision to provide just $200 million out of the $1 billion requested by Clinton to privatize the Energy Department's nuclear environmental management programs.

The nearly $5 billion in the final bill for water projects was more than either chamber had mustered. The Senate's original level was $4.5 billion and the House's $4.9 billion.

McDade and Fazio also left their own marks on the bill. McDade succeeded in cutting $36 million from the $106 million requested for the Tennessee Valley Authority (TVA) and inserting legislative language ensuring that the fiscal 1998 appropriation would be the last for the giant federally owned power utility. The attack on TVA, which had been sacrosanct since the Depression, left no doubt that decades of subcommittee domination by Democrat Tom Bevill of Alabama (1967-97) and Republican John T. Myers of Indiana (1967-97) were over. Both men retired at the end of the 104th Congress. *(TVA, p. 4-24)*

Once the bill was signed into law, Clinton exercised his line-item veto authority Oct. 17, striking eight projects worth $19.3 million.

Senate Committee

The Senate went first on the bill, with the Appropriations Subcommittee on Energy and Water Development approving a $21.2 billion draft July 8 by voice vote. The full committee followed suit two days later, July 10, also by voice vote (S 1004 — S Rept 105-44). The bill's total was $1.9 billion less than the administration's request, but $184 million above the amount provided in fiscal 1997.

As in the past, the bill reflected the strong support among Senate appropriators for Energy Department nuclear weapons programs. That support was led by Domenici, whose state was home to two major nuclear weapons laboratories — Los Alamos National Laboratory and Sandia National Laboratories.

Senate appropriators agreed to a total of $11.8 billion for defense-related nuclear activities, up from $11.3 billion the previous year. Domenici said that still fell short of the amount needed to ensure the safety and reliability of the nuclear arsenal.

- **Nuclear weapons.** Of the $11.8 billion, $4.3 billion was designated for nuclear weapons research, development and production, an increase of $300 million above Clinton's request and about $390 million more than was provided in fiscal 1997. Nuclear stockpile stewardship programs, the primary source of funds for nuclear weapons research, accounted for about $1.3 billion of that. Nuclear stockpile management, which paid for nuclear weapons production, was slated to receive $1.9 billion.

The $4.3 billion exceeded the annual average during the Cold War by $600 million, according to the Brookings Institution's Nuclear Weapons Cost Study Project. Much of the money was directed to the two nuclear weapons laboratories in New Mexico.

However, only Sen. Dale Bumpers, D-Ark., decried what he called a "staggering increase" in defense spending. Bumpers was particularly miffed after Domenici denied his request for $350,000 to decommission a defunct nuclear reactor in Arkansas.

The year before, over Bumpers' objections, Domenici had successfully increased funds for weapons activities from the

Energy-Water Development Spending

(in thousands of dollars)

	Fiscal 1997 Appropriation	Fiscal 1998 Clinton Request	House Bill	Senate Bill	Conference Report
Army Corps of Engineers (Defense Department)					
General construction	$ 1,081,942	$ 1,062,470	$ 1,475,892	$ 1,284,266	$1,473,373
Operation and maintenance	1,866,015*	1,618,000	1,726,955	1,661,203	1,740,025
Mississippi River flood control	330,374*	266,000	285,450	289,000	296,212
Flood control and coastal emergencies	425,000*	14,000	14,000	10,000	4,000
Other	403,872	410,000	527,260	418,065	550,804
TOTAL, Defense Department	**$ 4,107,203***	**$ 3,370,470**	**$ 4,029,557**	**$ 3,662,534**	**$ 4,064,414**
Interior Department					
Bureau of Reclamation					
Construction	394,056	0	0	0	0
Operation and maintenance	275,231*	0	0	0	0
Water and related resources	0	651,552	651,931	688,379	694,348
California Bay-Delta ecosystem restoration	0	143,300	120,000	50,000	85,000
Other	113,461	97,213	97,213	91,113	91,113
Subtotal, Bureau of Reclamation	**$ 782,748***	**$ 892,065**	**$ 869,144**	**$ 829,492**	**$ 870,461**
Central Utah project completion	43,627	41,153	41,153	41,153	41,153
TOTAL, Interior Department	**$ 826,375***	**$ 933,218**	**$ 910,297**	**$ 870,645**	**$ 911,614**
Energy Department					
Energy supply, research and development	2,699,728	2,999,497	880,730	953,915	906,807
Atomic energy defense					
Weapons activities	3,911,198	3,576,255	3,943,442	4,302,450	4,146,692
Defense environmental cleanup	5,459,304	5,052,499	5,263,270	5,311,974	4,429,438
Defense nuclear waste disposal	200,000	190,000	190,000	190,000	190,000
Defense environmental privatization	160,000	1,006,000	0	343,000	200,000
Defense facilities closure projects	0	0	0	0	890,800
Other defense activities	1,605,733	1,605,981	1,580,504	1,637,981	1,666,008
Defense asset acquisition	0	2,166,859	0	0	0
Subtotal, atomic energy defense	**$11,336,235**	**$13,597,594**	**$10,977,216**	**$11,785,405**	**$11,522,938**
Uranium supply and enrichment (net)	1,000	0	0	0	0
Decontamination and decommissioning	200,200	248,788	220,200	230,000	220,200
General science and other research	996,000	875,910	2,207,632	2,084,567	2,235,708
Civilian nuclear waste disposal	182,000	190,000	160,000	160,000	160,000
Departmental administration	89,633	101,274	83,393	89,517	87,417
Power Marketing Administration	228,769	237,121	228,445	243,621	240,945
Other	23,853	183,331	525,119	843,719	524,559
TOTAL, Energy Department	**$15,757,418**	**$18,433,515**	**$15,282,735**	**$16,390,744**	**$15,898,574**
Independent Agencies					
Appalachian Regional Commission	160,000	165,000	160,000	160,000	170,000
Nuclear Regulatory Commission	471,800	476,500	462,700	476,500	468,000
Revenues	– 457,300	– 457,500	– 446,700	– 457,500	– 450,000
Tennessee Valley Authority	106,000	106,000	0	86,000	70,000
Other	18,531	20,700	18,400	20,700	19,600
TOTAL, Independent Agencies	**$ 299,031**	**$ 310,700**	**$ 194,400**	**$ 285,700**	**$ 277,600**
GRAND TOTAL	**$20,990,027***	**$23,047,903**	**$20,416,989**	**$21,209,623**	**$21,152,202**

**Includes emergency appropriations*

SOURCE: House Appropriations Committee

White House's $3.7 billion request to $3.9 billion, arguing that top Energy Department officials had told him they would need $4 billion a year to maintain the nuclear stockpile. *(1996 Almanac, p. 10-42)*

Ranking Democrat Reid came to Domenici's defense during the full committee markup July 10, saying the money was needed to fund the president's expensive effort to replace explosive nuclear weapons testing with scientific simulators. "The chairman has followed to a 'T' what the president has wanted," Reid said. "This is not a program we dreamed up ourselves."

However, Domenici declined one administration request that would have benefited the New Mexico weapons labs greatly. To reassure conservatives that he was firmly behind plans by the weapons labs to develop alternatives to nuclear testing, Clinton requested $1 billion to cover the full cost of constructing those projects over the following decade. But Senate appropriators balked at the long-term plan and included funding only for the activities planned for fiscal 1998.

• **Environmental cleanup.** The subcommittee provided $5.26 million for environmental restoration and waste management related to nuclear weapons programs.

But it pared back the Energy Department's proposal to radically change the way nuclear weapons sites were cleaned up. Under the administration's privatization plan, the department proposed to bid out cleanup contracts with a fixed total price, with any final differences serving as an incentive or penalty to the private company. The agency sought $1 billion for the privatization initiative; the Senate bill included $300 million.

• **Water projects.** Domenici conceded that his draft could not accommodate the flood of requests for new water projects that members had lodged with the subcommittee, triggered by an unusually generous, $3.8 billion flood-control, navigation and dredging authorization bill (PL 104-303) that had been signed into law the previous year. *(1996 Almanac, p. 4-16)*

The Senate bill allocated $3.5 billion for Army Corps of Engineers water projects, about $100 million more than the administration's request, and $830 million for the Interior Department's Bureau of Reclamation, about $60 million less than requested. Domenici said the corps' budget had been stretched to the point that existing water projects were falling behind schedule and costs were actually rising. "Something is going to have to change," he said.

For a politically sensitive program to restore the Sacramento-San Joaquin Delta in California, the bill recommended $50 million. Clinton had requested $143 million.

• **Next Generation Internet.** The appropriators also refused to fund the administration's $25 million Next Generation Internet project. The initiative was intended to assist universities and the Energy Department's national laboratories in developing new switching, software and wiring to dramatically increase the speed of the existing Internet, which itself was largely started by federal funds. Sensitive to charges of "corporate welfare," GOP leaders decided that the job was best left to the private sector.

Senate Floor Action

The Senate passed the $21.2 billion bill July 16 by a vote of 99-0. Senators largely followed the appropriators' lead, and there were few controversies on the floor. *(Vote 179, p. S-32)*

Bumpers challenged Domenici to justify the extra spending on nuclear weapons programs. "I am within my right and, as a matter of fact, my duty to raise the question of why we are spending this much money when you consider the fact that there is no Soviet Union," Bumpers said. "They do not exist anymore, and so far as I know, they do not represent a nuclear threat to this country." But Bumpers ultimately withdrew an amendment to cut those funds by $258 million, saying he was "tired of jousting at windmills."

The Clinton administration also objected to the increase, saying the money would come out of its plan to privatize environmental cleanup activities.

The only other conflict involved Ben Nighthorse Campbell, R-Colo., who successfully diverted an attack on the controversial Animas-La Plata water project in southwest Colorado. The issue pitted Ute Indians against environmentalists and fiscal conservatives.

The project was favored by many Utes, who saw it as the fulfillment of a government promise made more than a century before to ensure water supplies to the Southern Ute Reservation, near Durango along the New Mexico border. But environmentalists decried it as ecologically damaging, and budget hawks labeled it a waste of taxpayers' money.

Russell D. Feingold, D-Wis., and Sam Brownback, R-Kan., offered an amendment to retain the $6 million in the bill for the project in fiscal 1998 but prohibit funds from being spent on construction until a scaled-down plan had been authorized. Ute tribal leaders and project supporters in Congress had unveiled a compromise plan July 8 intended to lower the project's cost from $744 million to $290 million, increase the proportion of water that would go to the Utes, and reduce the amount that would be diverted from the Animas River.

But Campbell spoke passionately of unemployment, teen suicides and fetal alcohol syndrome on the reservations of the West, and the Senate voted 56-42 to table (kill) the Feingold-Brownback amendment. *(Vote 177, p. S-31)*

House Committee Action

The House Energy and Water Development Appropriations Subcommittee gave voice vote approval July 11 to a $20.4 billion version of the bill, $2.6 billion less than the amount requested by the administration. Placing themselves on a collision course with the Senate over spending priorities, the panel agreed to channel significantly less money to the Energy Department and substantially more to water projects.

• **Nuclear weapons.** In sharp contrast to their Senate counterparts, House appropriators provided slightly less than $11 billion for nuclear defense activities, compared with $11.8 billion in the Senate bill.

The total included $3.9 billion for weapons research, development and production, compared with $4.3 billion in the Senate bill. It also included $5.3 billion for weapons-related environmental cleanup, slightly more than the Senate.

Like the Senate, House appropriators agreed to fund only one year of the administration's 10-year program to replace nuclear testing. McDade said he did not want to give the administration a decade-long blank check on nuclear weapons policy.

• **Defense-related cleanup.** The House bill gutted the Clinton administration's $1 billion effort to privatize much of the Energy Department's environmental cleanup program, providing just $102 million. Without the full $1 billion, Office of Management and Budget (OMB) Director Franklin D. Raines contended, the department would be forced to use traditional cleanup contracts that would be more expensive in the long run.

• **Non-defense environmental cleanup.** The draft bill

called for transferring much of the Energy Department's non-defense environmental cleanup responsibilities to the Corps of Engineers, a provision that the White House strongly opposed.

- **Water projects.** In his first year as subcommittee chairman, McDade was careful to give members what they wanted: funding for highly visible water projects in their districts. McDade "has long been one of the most popular members of this institution," said ranking Democrat Fazio, "and I can only say when this bill passes, he will be even more so."

The bill included $4.9 billion for water projects — $4 billion for the Corps of Engineers, an increase of $550 million over the president's request, and another $870 million for Interior's Bureau of Reclamation, slightly below the amount requested.

Fazio flexed his muscles and squeezed out $120 million for the California Bay-Delta ecosystem restoration project which was dear to his home state.

- **TVA.** For decades, the TVA had received federal funding for its non-power functions, such as flood control, navigation and environmental programs. Critics said the subsidies were distorting prices and giving unfair advantage to federal power agencies. Moreover, lawmakers in the Northeast and Midwest were increasingly frustrated that their regions were the only ones not benefiting from federally generated, low-cost electricity.

TVA supporters countered that other utilities were not expected to maintain waterways, protect stretches of wilderness and protect their customers from floods the way TVA did. If the federal subsidy to maintain those functions were eliminated, they argued, some other federal agency such as the Corps of Engineers would simply have to step in to perform them.

The TVA itself asked to have its subsidies ended in fiscal 1999, but the subcommittee bill opted to end them a year early, zeroing out the administration's $106 million TVA request.

- **Next Generation Internet.** Like the Senate bill, the House draft included no funding for the president's Next Generation Internet program.

Full Committee Endorses Bill

On July 17, the full House Appropriations Committee gave voice vote approval to a $20.4 billion version of the bill (H Rept 105-190) that continued to direct substantially more money to water projects and less to the Energy Department.

The proposed elimination of TVA funding received substantial attention during the markup. An attempt by TVA supporter Zach Wamp, R-Tenn., to restore $85 million for the power agency might have attracted some Democratic support. But Wamp overreached, proposing to take the money from the $120 million that Fazio had secured for the Sacramento-San Joaquin Delta water project. Fazio had the weight of a united California delegation behind him.

Wamp humorously tried to conjure the spirit of staunch TVA protectors Bevill and Myers. "Tom Bevill, where are you? Tom? John?" Wamp deadpanned as his amendment to restore funding to the TVA failed by a lopsided vote of 9-34.

House Floor Action

After a late-night debate that began July 24 and went past midnight, the House easily passed the $20.4 billion bill July 25 by a vote of 418-7. Other than shucking off three amendments, the bill faced almost no controversy. *(Vote 329, p. H-100)*

The few significant policy changes drew scattered expressions of concern on the House floor but no amendments to alter them. Edward Whitfield, R-Ky., was the only lawmaker to express concern about the funding cutoff proposed for the TVA.

James M. Talent, R-Mo., echoed the White House's concern about shifting the Energy Department's non-defense environmental cleanup responsibilities to the Army Corps of Engineers, asking whether cleanups of Cold War-era wastes that were finally showing progress might not be set back by the transfer. But Talent did not challenge the policy change.

Only a few efforts were made to alter the bill, and they followed a familiar path, with appropriations subcommittee members successfully beating them back.

- **Appalachian Regional Commission.** Scott L. Klug, R-Wis., again mounted what he called his "sometimes valiant and quixotic fight" against the Appalachian Regional Commission, proposing to strike $90 million from the agency's funding, thus eliminating its road-building program. Klug cited an assortment of alleged misuses of commission money, from the $750,000 he said went to the Carolina Panthers' football stadium in Charlotte, N.C., to the $1.2 million he said helped establish the National Track and Field Hall of Fame.

But a bipartisan contingent from the Appalachian region routed Klug, appealing to colleagues to maintain support for one of the poorest regions of the country. The House agreed and rejected the amendment July 25, 97-328. *(Vote 326, p. H-100)*

- **Animas-La Plata project.** The bill included no funding for the Colorado project, but $8.2 million of unspent money remained in the program's accounts. Tom Petri, R-Wis., and Peter A. DeFazio, D-Ore., who opposed the project on budgetary and environmental grounds, tried to prohibit the use of those funds to buy land or begin construction until Congress authorized plans to scale back the project.

In a parliamentary maneuver that caught Petri off guard, Fazio amended the Petri-DeFazio amendment to allow spending on any activity related to a 1988 congressional settlement with the Utes. Fazio's amendment passed, 223-201. *(Vote 328, p. H-100)*

- **Pyroprocessing.** Nuclear power opponent Edward J. Markey, D-Mass., tried to eliminate $33 million in the bill for an obscure Energy Department program known as pyroprocessing. The project, conducted at the agency's Argonne National Laboratory in Illinois and Idaho, aimed to separate the plutonium and uranium from spent nuclear fuel.

Markey said the project was wasteful and dangerous and could spread technology that would help rogue nations and terrorists obtain atomic weapons. "Then we would reap the whirlwind," he said in an impassioned, late-night speech to a virtually empty chamber.

But a bipartisan coalition from the Energy and Water Subcommittee, Illinois and Idaho said the program posed no risk of nuclear proliferation and was vital to solving the nation's nuclear waste disposal problem. They prevailed, defeating Markey's amendment, 134-290. *(Vote 327, p. H-100)*

Conference/Final Action

House and Senate conferees reached agreement Sept. 24 on a $21.2 billion compromise bill (H Rept 105-271) that provided the TVA with a final year of funding. The agreement significantly increased funding for nuclear weapons research and cleanup accounts over House-passed levels, while adding to the House's allotment for politically popular water projects.

The House adopted the conference report Sept. 30 by an overwhelming vote of 404-17 following a few minutes of low-key debate, mainly over the conferees' decision to shift responsibility for civilian radioactive waste cleanups from the Department of Energy to the Army Corps of Engineers. *(Vote 468, p. H-142)*

Hours later, the Senate voted 99-0, to clear the conference report, sending the bill to the White House for a grudging presidential signature. *(Vote 262, p. S-44)*

The final bill provided $15.9 billion for the Energy Department, 14 percent less than Clinton's $18.4 billion request. The difference was deceptive, however, since Congress provided only fiscal 1998 funding rather than the additional advanced budget authority that Clinton had requested.

Funding for the department's defense activities reached $11.5 billion — up from fiscal 1997's $11.3 billion level and the House's $11 billion, but down from the $11.8 billion in the Senate-passed bill.

While philosophical issues proved nettlesome, Domenici eased the funding problems considerably. He got House appropriators to shift $600 million from the Defense Appropriations Subcommittee to Energy and Water to increase that panel's nuclear defense allotment, and he arranged $183 million more in budget authority for the Senate's water accounts.

Conferees allocated $4.1 billion of the Energy Department money for core nuclear weapons research, development and production activities. That was $203 million more than the House figure, but $156 million less than approved by the Senate. Domenici accepted the lower figure only after private negotiations with the White House, where administration officials promised to request $4.5 billion for nuclear weapons activities in fiscal 1999.

The Bureau of Reclamation and the Army Corps of Engineers received $4.9 billion for water projects, compared with the Senate's original level of $4.5 billion and the House's $4.9 billion. Clinton requested $4.3 billion. Salted into the final bill were what OMB Director Raines said were "numerous unrequested and low-priority" water projects. Raines had urged conferees to purge the items in a letter Sept. 11.

Conference Highlights

Following are details on major elements of the compromise bill.

- **TVA.** The federal subsidy for the TVA survived another year — shriveled but intact. Conferees included $70 million for the agency's non-power functions, $36 million less than the president requested and $16 million less than the Senate had approved. However, an unyielding House contingent won explicit legislative language ensuring that the subsidy would be the agency's last.
- **Animas-La Plata project**. In a decision that disappointed environmentalists and budget hawks, the conferees designated $6 million for the Animas-La Plata water project in southwestern Colorado. Because the project was to fulfill treaty obligations to the Ute Indian tribes, lawmakers found it difficult to kill.
- **Defense-related cleanup.** Nuclear defense cleanup, a priority for Senate conferees, many of whom represented states with nuclear weapons laboratories or production sites, got $5.5 billion, about halfway between the House and Senate levels and about $540 million less than the White House had requested.

What evoked more strenuous objection from the White House, however, was the decision to include just $200 million for the effort to privatize the cleanup of nuclear weapons sites. The House had zeroed out the request; the Senate approved $343 million.

- **Non-defense environmental cleanup.** In his first conference as chairman of the House subcommittee, McDade held remarkably firm. Surprisingly, he gained backing from Domenici for his efforts to shift responsibility for civilian nuclear cleanups from the Energy Department to the Army Corps of Engineers, even though Reid called the proposal "one of the most ridiculous instances of bad government I've ever seen." The administration protested the move, saying the cleanups were finally making headway.

But House conferees, with Domenici's support, insisted the Army could do a better job. McDade complained that the Energy Department had completed just 50 percent of the job after spending 17 years and $585 million. On a roll call tally, Senate conferees voted against the change, 5-9, but in a closed-door session, Domenici and McDade prevailed.

- **Sacramento-San Joaquin Delta water project.** Splitting their differences, conferees agreed to provide $85 million for the California Bay-Delta ecosystem restoration project.
- **Energy research and development.** Conferees also split the difference on the Energy Department's energy supply, research and development accounts, allocating $907 million, more than the House's $881 million and less than the Senate's $954 million. The accounts covered programs for solar and renewable energy; nuclear energy; fusion energy; and environment, safety and health programs.

Solar and renewable energy, once a *bête noire* for budget hawks, received $346 million under the conference agreement, up from the House's $329 million allotment, the Senate's $301 million, and even the Clinton administration's request for $345 million. The bill included $243 million for nuclear energy programs (but no money for the advanced light water reactor program), and $232 million for fusion energy research and development.

- **Nuclear waste disposal.** The final bill provided a total of $350 million for disposing of nuclear waste.

That included $160 million appropriated from the Nuclear Waste Disposal Fund, consisting of fees paid by utilities with nuclear power plants, to develop facilities for safely disposing of spent nuclear fuel and high-level radioactive waste. The Energy Department was required by law to begin accepting spent nuclear fuel from utilities in 1998, but a permanent disposal site would not be available by then. Lawmakers were still locked in a battle over use of the Yucca Mountain site in Nevada. *(Yucca Mountain, p. 4-20)*

The total also included $190 million for the Defense Nuclear Waste Disposal account, which paid for costs associated with disposing of waste from nuclear weapons programs.

Line-Item Veto

Four days after signing the $21.2 billion bill into law, Clinton used his line-item veto authority Oct. 17 to excise eight projects worth $19.3 million. He struck five water projects, in Alaska, Indiana, Mississippi, Virginia and Pennsylvania, plus two Energy Department research programs and a science project at the Bureau of Reclamation.

The list hardly touched the 423 unrequested water projects in the law worth $817 million. But it did hit some of the most powerful members of Congress, among them Senate Majority Leader Trent Lott, R-Miss., and Senate Appropriations Committee Chairman Ted Stevens, R-Alaska.

"I tried to show deference to Congress' role in the appropriations process," Clinton said. "Nevertheless, I feel strongly that my administration should look for opportunities to save taxpayer dollars."

However, members tended to be especially sensitive about water projects, which provided an infusion of jobs and money into local economies, and the projects that Clinton did strike elicited expressions of outrage. "They just arbitrarily pull these things out of thin air over there," said Charles E. Brimmer, chief of staff for Peter J. Visclosky, D-Ind., a member of the Energy and Water Development Appropriations Subcommittee who lost a water project in his district. The vetoed water projects were:

➤ $1.9 million to dredge a section of Sardis Lake in northern Mississippi for a private marina and convention center.

➤ $800,000 to dredge the growing shoals in the Chena River, clearing a deeper route for a tourist boat plying the waters through Fairbanks, Alaska.

➤ $6 million to deepen the Allegheny River for tour boats traveling to a riverfront park in Kittanning, Pa.

➤ $3.5 million to dredge Lake George in Hobart, Ind., to head off spring flooding and help a waterfront economic development project.

➤ $800,000 for a flood control project to remove silt and debris from Neabsco Creek in Woodbridge, Va.

In addition, Clinton struck:

➤ $1 million for the Energy Department's Oak Ridge National Laboratory in Tennessee, to develop high-voltage power lines spanning long distances between power poles.

➤ $4 million to license a canister to store, transport and dispose of high-level nuclear waste from commercial power reactors.

➤ $1.3 million to complete work on a Bureau of Reclamation effort to use a technique developed by the mining industry to extract copper from hard-to-reach geological formations. ■

Foreign Aid: GOP Relents on Abortion

For the third consecutive year, a dispute over abortion restrictions on international family planning funds delayed completion of the foreign operations spending bill until the final days of the session, when a compromise was reached. President Clinton signed the fiscal 1998 bill Nov. 26 (HR 2159 — PL 105-118).

The $13.2 billion bill was significantly smaller than the $16.9 billion that Clinton had requested for foreign aid and related programs, but $800 million more than was appropriated for fiscal 1997. Under the bill, Israel received its customary $3.1 billion in U.S. aid, and Egypt got $2.1 billion. The bill also included $225 million in assistance to Jordan. The former states of the Soviet Union received $770 million, a reduction of $130 million from the amount requested.

But it was the dispute over abortion, not dollars, that nearly sank the bill. At issue was a House-passed provision, sponsored by Christopher H. Smith, R-N.J., barring funds for family planning groups that promoted, performed or advocated abortions abroad, even if they used their own money. The proposed ban faced strong opposition in the Senate, and the Clinton administration warned that the president would veto any bill that included it.

With appropriators from both chambers unable to resolve the seemingly intractable controversy, the Republican leadership finally stepped in during the last weeks of the session. Their solution was to strip away the restrictions, fund international family planning groups at the fiscal 1997 level of $385 million and provide the money at a rate of 8 percent per month. That cleared the way for final passage Nov. 13, the day Congress adjourned.

The decision to yield to the White House came at a price, however. Conservative House Republicans, forced to compromise on the family planning provision, blocked three unrelated items sought by the administration and Senate Republicans: payment of most U.S. debts to the United Nations, $3.5 billion for the International Monetary Fund (IMF) and consolidation of some foreign policy agencies.

The money for the IMF had been included in the Senate version of the bill but was not approved by the House. The U.N. money and reorganization plan were part of a State Department reauthorization measure (HR 1757), which became entangled in the negotiations over foreign aid abortion restrictions. *(State Department authorization, p. 8-32)*

The abortion language even became a bargaining chip in Clinton's unsuccessful effort to secure votes for legislation giving him fast-track trade authority. *(Fast track, p. 2-85)*

BOXSCORE

Fiscal 1998 Foreign Operations Appropriations — HR 2159 (S 955). The bill provided $13.2 billion for foreign aid and related programs, but omitted $3.5 billion requested for the International Monetary Fund.

Reports: H Rept 105-176, S Rept 105-35; conference report, H Rept 105-401.

KEY ACTION

July 17 — Senate passed S 955, 91-8.

Sept. 4 — House passed HR 2159, 375-49.

Sept. 5 — Senate passed HR 2159 by prior agreement, substituting the text of S 955.

Nov. 13 — House adopted the conference report, 333-76; **Senate** cleared the bill by voice vote.

Nov. 26 — President signed HR 2159 — PL 105-118.

Background

Secretary of State Madeleine K. Albright kicked off the White House campaign to boost funding for international affairs during her confirmation hearing Jan. 8. *(Albright, p. 8-46)*

The foreign operations budget, which funded foreign aid, U.S. contributions to the United Nations and multilateral banks, State Department salaries and other overseas activities, had been stagnant in recent years. Albright said the budget constraints had hamstrung diplomacy and undermined U.S. global credibility.

In his budget request, Clinton not only sought to increase spending for foreign operations generally. He also asked for $3.5 billion to underwrite the U.S. share of a new IMF loan account aimed at preventing massive currency fluctuations. While the size of the commitment raised eyebrows in the House and Senate, it was actually a swap of assets with the IMF, backed by the IMF's gold reserves. The administration said the $3.5 billion appropriation would entail no new outlays — actual spending — and would not add to the deficit.

Though the goal of increasing funds for overseas programs attracted some bipartisan interest, neither foreign aid nor international organizations were popular with the conservative Republicans who controlled Congress. And with Clinton and Republicans intent on balancing the budget, foreign operations were considered expendable.

Abortion Restrictions

An issue that would seem to have little to do with foreign aid — abortion — had delayed the foreign operations bill each year since 1995.

Since 1973, U.S. law had outlawed direct funding of overseas abortions. But Smith, who led the anti-abortion forces in the House, argued that U.S. funding for organizations such as the International Planned Parenthood Federation of London, allowed those groups to use their own money to perform or promote the use of abortion.

Smith again vowed to stand firm behind his proposal to reinstitute the so-called Mexico City policy barring U.S. funds for groups that practiced or advocated abortion, even with their own money. The policy, formulated by the Reagan administration in 1984 and continued by the Bush administration, was named for the site of a world conference on population. Clinton rescinded the policy as one of his first acts on taking office in 1993.

The administration and other opponents said Smith's amendments would block funding for groups that provided badly need family planning programs in developing countries, leading to more — not fewer — abortions in those countries.

A similar provision by Smith had held up final action on the fiscal 1996 foreign operations bill until January 1996, five months into the fiscal year. The appropriators finally agreed to punt the dispute to the authorizers, reducing funds for family planning programs by 35 percent from the previous year's level unless a separate bill authorizing those programs was enacted by July 1. That did not occur. *(1995 Almanac, p. 11-40; 1996 Almanac, p. 10-19)*

Fiscal 1998 Foreign Aid Spending

(in thousands of dollars)

	Fiscal 1997 Appropriation	Fiscal 1998 Clinton Request	House Bill	Senate Bill	Conference Report
Multilateral Aid					
World Bank					
Global Environment Facility	$ 35,000	$ 100,000	$ 35,000	$ 60,000	$ 47,500
International Development Association	700,000	1,034,504	606,000	1,034,504	1,034,504
International Finance Corporation	6,656	—	—	—	—
Inter-American Development Bank	35,611	46,446	46,446	46,446	46,446
Limitation on callable capital	*(1,503,719)*	*(1,503,719)*	*(1,503,719)*	*(1,503,719)*	*(1,503,719)*
Enterprise for the Americas	27,500	30,000	—	30,000	30,000
North American Development Bank	56,000	56,500	56,500	56,500	56,500
Asian Development Bank	113,222	163,222	113,222	163,222	163,222
African Development Fund	—	50,000	50,000	—	45,000
European Development Bank	11,916	35,779	35,779	35,779	35,779
International Monetary Fund	—	3,528,000	—	3,521,000	—
Other	169,950	365,000	194,000	277,000	192,000
TOTAL, Multilateral aid	**$ 1,155,855**	**$ 5,409,450**	**$ 1,136,946**	**$ 5,224,446**	**$ 1,650,949**
Bilateral Aid					
Agency for International Development (AID)					
Development assistance	1,181,500	998,000	1,167,000	1,793,093	1,210,000
Africa development aid	—	700,000	—	—	—
International disaster aid	190,000	190,000	190,000	195,000	190,000
AID operating expenses	470,750	473,000	468,750	473,000	473,000
Debt restructuring	27,000	34,000	27,000	34,000	27,000
Economic Support Fund	2,343,000	2,497,600	2,375,000	2,541,150	2,400,000
Assistance for Eastern Europe	475,000	492,000	470,000	485,000	485,000
Assistance for ex-Soviet states	625,000	900,000	625,000	800,000	770,000
International fund for Ireland	19,600	—	19,600	—	19,600
Other	685,326	84,255	734,255	84,255	734,255
Subtotal, AID	**$ 6,017,176**	**$ 6,368,855**	**$ 6,076,605**	**$ 6,405,498**	**$ 6,308,855**
State Department					
International narcotics control	213,000	230,000	230,000	216,200	230,000
Migration and refugee aid	650,000	650,000	650,000	650,000	650,000
Anti-terrorism assistance	—	19,000	—	—	—
Other	206,000	65,000	173,000	179,000	188,000
Subtotal, State Department	**$ 1,069,000**	**$ 964,000**	**$ 1,053,000**	**$ 1,045,200**	**$ 1,068,000**
Peace Corps	208,000	222,000	222,000	206,000	222,000
Other	—	36,000	31,500	—	—
TOTAL, bilateral aid	**$ 7,294,176**	**$ 7,590,855**	**$ 7,383,105**	**$ 7,656,698**	**$ 7,598,855**
Bilateral Military Aid (appropriated to the president)					
Foreign military financing (grants)	3,224,000	3,274,250	3,259,250	3,308,950	3,296,550
Foreign military loans	*(540,000)*	*(699,500)*	*(657,000)*	*(759,500)*	*(657,000)*
Loan subsidy	60,000	66,000	60,000	74,000	60,000
International military education and training	43,475	50,000	50,000	47,000	50,000
Special defense acquisition fund (offsetting collections)	– 166,000	– 106,000	–106,000	–106,000	–106,000
Peacekeeping operations	65,000	90,000	77,500	75,000	77,500
TOTAL, military aid	**$ 3,226,475**	**$ 3,374,250**	**$ 3,340,750**	**$ 3,398,950**	**$ 3,378,050**
Export Assistance					
Export-Import Bank	714,614	629,614	629,614	695,614	680,614
Trade and Development Agency	40,000	43,000	40,000	43,000	41,500
Overseas Private Investment Corporation (loan levels)	(1,440,000)	(1,933,000)	—	(1,933,000)	(1,933,000)
Subsidy/offsets	– 120,000	– 159,000	–219,000	–159,000	–159,000
TOTAL, export assistance	**$ 634,614**	**$ 513,614**	**$ 450,614**	**$ 579,614**	**$ 583,114**
GRAND TOTAL	**$ 12,311,120**	**$ 16,888,169**	**$ 12,311,415**	**$ 16,859,708**	**$ 13,190,968**

SOURCE: House and Senate Appropriations committees

In a last-minute deal on the fiscal 1997 foreign operations bill, Republicans agreed to let the money go without restrictions provided it would not be spent until July 1, unless both the House and Senate voted to release it earlier, which they did. *(Family planning, p. 9-40; 1996 Almanac, p. 10-48)*

Senate Committee

The Senate Appropriations Subcommittee on Foreign Operations approved a draft fiscal 1998 foreign aid spending bill, subsequently introduced as S 955, by voice vote June 18.

The draft provided the administration with about everything it sought. It recommended $16.9 billion in new budget authority for fiscal 1998, including the one-time $3.5 billion appropriation for the IMF. It included $13.2 billion for all other programs, an increase of $933 million from fiscal 1997 and just $116 million below Clinton's request.

However, subcommittee Chairman Mitch McConnell, R-Ky., stirred a furor by eliminating a longstanding provision earmarking a minimum of $2.1 billion in military and economic aid for Egypt. He said the action was intended to signal U.S. disfavor with Egypt's failure to live up to its 1979 peace agreement with Israel.

McConnell also saw Egypt as a source of funding to boost aid to Jordan. His bill included a new guarantee of $250 million in military and economic aid for that country, which he said had faced considerable risks for backing the Middle East peace process.

McConnell said his overarching goal was to use foreign aid to support nations that helped advance U.S. interests and to penalize those that did not. But Albright and several of McConnell's GOP colleagues, including Appropriations Committee Chairman Ted Stevens, R-Alaska, said that striking the earmark for Egypt would signal an erosion of U.S. support for a key U.S. ally. Stevens quickly delayed a full committee markup of the bill.

Aside from striking the Egypt earmark, the Senate bill contained few surprises. As approved by the subcommittee, it proposed to:

➤ Retain the popular earmark of $3.1 billion in economic and military assistance for Israel, for decades the largest recipient of U.S. foreign assistance.

➤ Provide $800 million in aid for Russia and the former Soviet republics, $100 million less than the amount requested. The aid to Russia would be barred unless Moscow scrapped its nuclear cooperation agreement with Iran.

At least $225 million out of the total was set aside for Ukraine, with the stipulation that about $100 million be held out until the Ukrainian government cracked down on corruption and ended harassment of U.S. firms. Another $100 million was set aside for Georgia.

➤ Include $950 million for the International Development Association (IDA), the World Bank affiliate that provided interest-free loans to the poorest countries, on the condition that that institution lift procurement restrictions against U.S. firms. The amount was $85 million less than Clinton requested but sufficient to clear most of the $235 million U.S. debt to the organization.

The bill set aside $95 million in aid for Armenia, despite reports of that country's growing military cooperation with Russia. But the subcommittee also adopted an amendment opening a huge loophole in the 5-year-old ban on direct U.S. assistance to oil-rich Azerbaijan, Armenia's bitter rival. The ban was imposed to pressure Azerbaijan to end its economic blockade of Armenia.

The amendment — offered by Democrats Patrick J. Leahy of Vermont and Robert C. Byrd of West Virginia and backed by U.S. oil companies — proposed permitting the Overseas Private Investment Corporation (OPIC), the Export-Import Bank, and the Trade and Development Agency to provide loans and credits to U.S. companies operating in Azerbaijan.

Full Committee Restores Egypt Earmark

The full Appropriations Committee approved the bill June 24 by a 27-1 vote (S Rept 105-35). But first, reflecting an agreement worked out by McConnell and Stevens, the panel agreed by voice vote to restore the traditional $2.1 billion earmark for Egypt and have the modification occur in the form of a chairman's amendment to be offered during floor debate on the bill.

Senate Floor Action

With surprisingly little controversy, the Senate passed the $16.9 billion bill July 17 by a vote of 91-8. *(Vote 185, p. S-32)*

• **Narcotics certification.** The only major foreign policy debate was over an amendment offered by John McCain, R-Ariz., and Christopher J. Dodd, D-Conn., to suspend the annual narcotics certification process for foreign countries for two years and develop a multilateral approach to stemming the spread of illicit drugs.

There was widespread frustration with the existing process. Established under a 1986 law (PL 99-570), it provided that nations considered sources or conduits for illicit drugs could lose some U.S. aid if they were considered uncooperative in the drug war.

The question of scrapping the certification process had been vigorously debated since February, when Clinton determined that Mexico had cooperated fully, despite incidents highlighting the failure of Mexico's counter-narcotics efforts, including the arrest of the nation's drug czar, Gen. Jesus Gutierrez Rebollo, on narcotics-related charges. *(Mexico, p. 8-44)*

McCain and Dodd said the Mexico situation underscored the need for a new approach, but most senators were reluctant to scrap the existing process, and the amendment was defeated 38-60. *(Vote 182, p. S-32)*

• **Aid to Russia.** The Senate adopted, 95-4, an amendment by GOP freshman Gordon H. Smith of Oregon to cut off aid to the Russian government if it enacted a pending plan that Smith said would result in discrimination against religious minorities. *(Vote 178, p. S-31)*

With less fanfare, the Senate agreed by voice vote to expand the bill's prohibition on aid to Russia if that country aided Iran's nuclear development program, to include selling ballistic missiles to Iran.

• **China MFN.** The Senate also weighed in on the question of trade relations with China, although the House had resolved that issue June 24 when it voted overwhelmingly to reject a resolution denying Beijing most-favored-nation (MFN) trade status. By law, such a resolution could take effect only if it was approved by both chambers. *(China MFN, p. 8-37)*

But Tim Hutchinson, R-Ark., a fierce critic of China, offered a non-binding amendment to cut off MFN. His proposal was defeated 22-77. *(Vote 184, p. S-32)*

House Committee

Clinton administration efforts to increase foreign aid spending ran into a formidable obstacle in the House: Alabama Republican Sonny Callahan, chairman of the Appropriations Subcommittee on Foreign Operations. Callahan was di-

Fiscal 1997 Family Planning Funds Released

Congress handed the Clinton administration an unusual victory in February, when both the House and Senate voted to release $385 million in previously appropriated international family planning aid without abortion restrictions.

The administration and abortion rights supporters in Congress succeeded in shifting the debate to the necessity of family planning in developing countries and away from the emotionally charged issue of abortion. The funding was part of the fiscal 1997 foreign operations appropriations bill.

While passage of the resolution (H J Res 36) did not increase the aggregate amount of money available for family planning, it made the funds available sooner. It meant that the administration had $123 million more to spend on such activities during fiscal 1997.

Clinton signed the measure into law Feb. 28 (PL 105-3), and the funds became available March 1. Had the bill failed, the disbursement would have been delayed until July 1.

Background

Since 1973, U.S. law had prohibited the government from directly paying for abortions overseas. But anti-abortion forces in Congress also opposed aiding overseas family planning groups that used non-U.S. money to advocate or perform abortions. *(1973 Almanac, p. 832)*

The battle in recent years had revolved around efforts by abortion opponents to reinstate the so-called Mexico City policy of the Reagan and Bush administrations, which denied U.S. funds to population planning groups that performed or advocated abortions, even if the groups used only their own money for the procedure. The Mexico City policy had remained in effect until January 1993, when newly elected President Clinton signed an executive memorandum revoking it.

Efforts to restore the restrictions stalled action on the fiscal 1997 foreign operations bill, making it one of six appropriations bills folded into an omnibus spending measure (PL 104-208) enacted Sept. 30, 1996. Under the intricate deal that allowed the bill to clear, Republican leaders agreed to drop the abortion restrictions they had been pushing. In return, the White House agreed to severe funding limitations. *(1996 Almanac, p. 10-48)*

The bill provided $79 million less than the president requested for international family planning activities. (Overall funding for such activities had declined from $548 million in fiscal 1995 to $385 million in fiscal 1997.) In addition, the money would not be available until July 1, 1997, and the administration was barred from spending more than 8 percent of the funds, about $31 million, a month.

The deal also required the president to report to Congress by Feb. 1, 1997, on the impact of the delay in releasing family planning funds. If he found that the limitation was having a negative effect on population programs, funds could be released beginning March 1 — but only if Congress approved the release by a joint resolution of approval no later than Feb. 28.

On Jan. 31, 1997, Clinton reported that 17 of 95 overseas programs might have to shut down, and that the reduced funding would result in "increased unintended pregnancies, more abortions, higher numbers of maternal and infant deaths and, of course, more births." Those findings automatically triggered a congressional vote on a resolution to begin releasing the funds March 1.

Legislative Action

The House passed the resolution Feb. 13 by a vote of 220-209, with 44 Republicans joining 175 Democrats and one Independent in favor. The Senate passed the measure, 53-46, on Feb. 25, clearing it for the president. *(House vote 22, p. H-8; Senate vote 13, p. S-4)*

The vote was a rare defeat in the House for abortion opponents, who had mounted an intensive campaign to kill the measure because it included no abortion restrictions.

Their setback was only partly ameliorated by the chance to cast a vote on a separate bill (HR 581), sponsored by Christopher H. Smith, R-N.J., to deny funds to overseas groups that used private money to perform or promote abortions. That bill passed, 231-194, but the Senate did not take it up. *(Vote 23, p. H-8)*

During the House debate, supporters of the resolution declared repeatedly that the vote was about family planning in developing countries — not about abortion. Opponents made the opposite argument. "Make no mistake about it," said Smith, "the consequence of approving Mr. Clinton's resolution is a fat payday for abortion providers."

Both sides expected the Senate vote to be much closer. Patrick J. Leahy, D-Vt., who managed the floor debate, said Vice President Al Gore was available if needed to cast a tie-breaking vote. But the measure passed by a relatively comfortable seven-vote margin, with 11 Republicans, including a number of abortion opponents, such as John W. Warner of Virginia and Gordon H. Smith of Oregon, supporting it.

Those senators were under considerable pressure because a number of anti-abortion and conservative religious organizations had portrayed the vote as the first major test on abortion in the new Congress. But Sen. Smith and other Republicans who backed the resolution seemed persuaded by arguments by the administration and family planning advocates that holding up the money would lead to a rise in unwanted pregnancies and, consequently, an increase in abortions. "To me, it's a good pro-life vote," Smith said afterward.

ametrically opposed to increases in foreign aid — not only because he personally disliked sending taxpayer dollars abroad, but also because he believed he would have an impossible task selling the House on more foreign assistance.

Callahan's draft bill, later introduced as HR 2159, won voice vote approval from his subcommittee June 25. It recommended $12.3 billion in foreign aid for fiscal 1998, about $4.5 billion less than Clinton requested and $200 million less than the $12.5 billion that was allocated to his subcommittee under the fiscal 1998 budget resolution (H Con Res 84).

Most of the difference between the bill and the administration's request resulted from the subcommittee's unwillingness to provide the $3.5 billion for the IMF or to pay $315 million in U.S. debts to other international financial institutions.

Some aspects of Callahan's approach, however, worked to the administration's advantage. A staunch supporter of presidential prerogatives, Callahan fought to keep his bill free of spending earmarks and policy prescriptions.

House Initiatives

In addition to dropping the IMF money, the subcommittee recommended a number of other changes to Clinton's request that differed from proposals in the Senate's bill.

- **IDA.** The subcommittee proposed cutting to $606 million the administration's request of $1 billion for the IDA, the primary source for loans to the world's poorest nations. The Senate bill included $950 million.
- **OPIC.** The House bill included no funds for OPIC programs, which stood to get $60 million under the Senate version. Although Callahan was a strong supporter of the agency, he wanted the International Relations Committee to first approve legislation authorizing OPIC. He hoped to avoid a floor fight on the future of the agency, which had come under attack as a prime example of "corporate welfare."
- **Armenia, Azerbaijan, Turkey.** The House panel struck its own delicate balance among the competing interests of Armenia, Azerbaijan and Turkey. Under the draft, U.S. humanitarian groups could begin operating in the disputed province of Nagorno-Karabakh, a predominantly Armenian enclave within Azerbaijan. That was a victory for the Armenian lobby.

Like the Senate version, the bill permitted aid for prodemocracy programs in Azerbaijan. Finally, it proposed $40 million in economic aid for Turkey, a historic adversary of Armenia, though half would go to the Turkish government and half to humanitarian and pro-democracy programs run by private U.S. aid groups.

- **Russia.** The subcommittee recommended $625 million of the $900 million requested for the former Soviet republics, compared with $800 million in the Senate bill.

Full Committee Approves Bill

The bill sailed through the full House Appropriations Committee with a minimum of controversy, winning voice vote approval July 9 (H Rept 105-176).

The markup was punctuated by a spirited debate over the U.S. Army School of the Americas, which trained Latin American military officers at Fort Benning, Ga. The school had come under fire for human rights abuses committed by several of its graduates, including former Panamanian leader Manuel Noriega.

The school was financed mainly through the defense budget, but Esteban E. Torres, D-Calif., proposed barring the use of funds in the bill's $50 million military training account to send Latin American officers to the school. His amendment was narrowly defeated, 21-23.

Reflecting the frustration building in Congress over recent actions by the Palestinian Authority, the committee report accompanying the bill directed the administration to submit a detailed assessment of Palestinian compliance with the peace agreement with Israel.

House Floor Action

The House passed its $12.3 billion foreign operations bill by a vote of 375-49 on Sept. 4. The strong bipartisan support, however, belied an inevitable stalemate with the Senate over an amendment barring aid to family planning groups that used their own money to subsidize abortion overseas. *(Vote 364, p. H-110)*

The House had begun considering the bill in July, but the dispute over abortion and family planning delayed action on key amendments until after the August recess.

On Sept. 4, members approved, 234-191, Smith's amendment barring the aid except in cases of rape, incest or danger to the life of the woman. The amendment also barred funding for any foreign organization that lobbied for or against abortion, and for the U.N. Population Fund unless it ceased all activities in China. *(Vote 363, p. H-110)*

Before voting on Smith's amendment, the House narrowly rejected a bipartisan substitute offered by Nancy Pelosi, D-Calif., and Benjamin A. Gilman, R-N.Y. The substitute, defeated 210-218, would have allowed funding for groups that did not "promote abortion as a method of family planning," even if they actually performed abortions. *(Vote 362, p. H-110)*

Pelosi and other supporters argued that in an imperfect world, the approach would allow family planning groups to provide contraceptives to women in underdeveloped countries and to prevent second and third abortions.

Other Floor Action

The House took the following acton on other amendments:

- **Palestinian aid.** On July 30, the day a pair of suicide bombings killed 15 people in a Jerusalem market, the House adopted, by voice vote, an amendment by H. James Saxton, R-N.J., to suspend aid to the Palestinian Authority for three months.
- **OPIC.** Members soundly rejected an attempt to cut funding for OPIC. The amendment by Budget Committee Chairman John R. Kasich, R-Ohio, who had assembled an ideologically diverse coalition to oppose OPIC and other trade development agencies, was defeated 156-272. *(Vote 346, p. H-104)*
- **Aid to India.** Despite published reports about close ties between Dan Burton, R-Ind., and Pakistan, the lawmaker pressed ahead with an amendment to cut funding for Pakistan's fierce rival, India, from $56 million to $42 million. It failed, 82-342. *(Vote 356, p. H-108)*
- **Africa aid.** The House adopted, 273-150, an amendment by Tom Campbell, R-Calif., to increase the amount in the bill for the African Development Fund by $25 million, raising the total to $50 million, the amount requested by the administration. *(Vote 357, p. H-108)*
- **Cuba.** Members approved yet another provision targeting the Cuban dictatorship of Fidel Castro. Robert Menendez, D-N.J., the son of Cuban immigrants, sponsored an amendment, adopted by voice vote, to bar funding for the International Atomic Energy Agency's programs in Cuba.
- **Cambodia.** Members adopted, also by voice vote, an amendment by Dana Rohrabacher, R-Calif., to bar all aid, including loans from multilateral development institutions such as the World Bank, for Cambodia's new regime.
- **Trophy hunting.** The House rejected, 159-267, an amendment by Jon D. Fox, R-Pa., and George Miller, D-Calif., that would have prohibited development assistance funds from directly supporting or promoting trophy hunting, or the international commercial trade in elephant ivory, elephant hides or rhinoceros horns. Fox contended that some foreign organizations were using U.S. funds to lobby Congress to promote the ivory trade and to weaken the foreign species provision of the Endangered Species Act. *(Vote 359, p. H-108)*

Conference/Final Action

House and Senate negotiators met Oct. 28 and in less than three hours ironed out virtually all their differences. Still left on the table, however, was the intractable dispute over abortion, which was turned over to the Republican leadership to resolve. "Every year this has been our stickiest and most difficult problem," said McConnell. With it went the question of funding the IMF special account.

For the remaining foreign aid programs, the conferees agreed to $13.2 billion after working out compromises on significant stumbling blocks such as aid to Jordan and assistance for the former states of the Soviet Union.

• **Israel and Jordan.** Angered by Israel's refusal to guarantee that it would contribute toward aid to Jordan, members of the House Appropriations Committee had put a hold on $75 million that Israel was scheduled to receive from the United States under the just-expired continuing resolution (H J Res 94 — PL 105-46). The resolution provided stop-gap funding for departments whose regular funding was covered by the unfinished appropriations bills.

But once Israel indicated that it would pay its $50 million portion — a guarantee in the form of a letter to the committee from the Israeli ambassador — the hold was lifted and the conferees were able to meet and agree on the aid package. The bill provided $225 million in assistance to Jordan, including the $50 million contribution from Israel and $50 million from Egypt. Israel received its customary $3.1 billion in U.S. assistance and Egypt $2.1 billion.

• **Former Soviet states.** Negotiators trimmed Clinton's request for the former states of the Soviet Union by $130 million, leaving $770 million. They reserved $250 million of the money for the troubled Southern Caucasus region, including $52.5 million to promote peace between Armenia and its neighbors, among them Azerbaijan.

The bill banned direct government-to-government economic aid to Azerbaijan, but it exempted political risk insurance provided by OPIC to U.S. companies investing in that country. Trade and Development Agency funds for feasibility studies and other economic development efforts were also permitted.

Reps. John Edward Porter, R-Ill., and Joe Knollenberg, R-Mich., won approval for an amendment that increased the amount earmarked for Georgia from $87.5 million to $92.5 million and for Armenia from $82.5 million to $87.5 million.

The conference report urged the Export-Import Bank to suspend all transactions with Gazprom, the largely state-owned Russian company, which was helping Iran in a $2 billion project to develop offshore natural gas deposits.

The bill also withheld 50 percent of the aid to Russia unless it ended its practice of sharing sensitive military technology with Iran, a provision the president could waive. In addition, conferees agreed on a version of a provision sponsored by Sen. Smith barring aid to Russia if it implemented recently passed laws discriminating against religious minorities.

• **Turkey, Greece.** The agreement provided a total of $105 million in loans to Greece and $150 million in loans to Turkey.

• **Pakistan.** Sen. Tom Harkin, D-Iowa, had little success in persuading the conferees to lift a ban on aid for military education and training in Pakistan. Pelosi, ranking Democrat on the House Foreign Operations subcommittee, argued that in light of Pakistan's nuclear weapons program, any attempt to end the prohibition should be opposed. Harkin's amendment failed on a voice vote.

The House conferees initially rejected, 5-9, an amendment sponsored by Stevens to provide $8.5 million in loan guarantees to help companies trying to develop the Russian Far East. But after a break in the conference, the vote was reversed and lawmakers agreed to $7.5 million in credit authority.

• **Cambodia.** The bill included language similar to the House bill prohibiting any funds from being made directly available to the Cambodian government, except for election monitoring, humanitarian aid, and de-mining activities.

• **North Korea.** The agreement included $30 million as requested to purchase and ship fuel oil to North Korea as part of a 1994 agreement intended to reduce that country's need for nuclear power plants.

• **Palestinians.** Conferees barred aid to the Palestinian Authority in the West Bank and Gaza unless the president determined that providing the money was in the interest of U.S. national security.

• **Development aid.** The final bill appropriated $1.2 billion for general development assistance, such as agriculture, rural development and basic education programs. In addition, it provided $650 million for a child survival and disease fund created under the fiscal 1997 spending bill.

• **International financial institutions.** The final bill appropriated $1.5 billion for international financial institutions, $3.6 billion less than Clinton requested. Most of the difference resulted from the decision not to provide the $3.5 million requested for the IMF.

The bill total included the full $1 billion requested for the IDA, pending a Treasury Department certification that the agency had lifted procurement restrictions against U.S. companies.

GOP Moderates Spurn Abortion Deal

After weeks of delay, and with the pressure to adjourn increasing, Republican leaders circulated a proposed compromise on the abortion dispute Nov. 5. However, two moderate House Republicans, Porter and Rodney Frelinghuysen of New Jersey, refused to sign the conference report, objecting to the attempt to write the ban on family planning aid into law. Their defiance left the House one signature shy of the number necessary to send the conference report to the floor.

All the Senate Republicans signed the conference report, but Democratic conferees from both chambers would have no part of the compromise. "I don't know of any Democrat who would sign the conference report," said David R. Obey of Wisconsin, ranking Democrat on the House Appropriations Committee.

Several House conservatives threatened to withhold support for legislation giving Clinton "fast track" authority to negotiate trade agreements unless he accepted their compromise on abortion. "I think there are about 15 to 16 conservatives who are not going to give them a vote [on fast-track] unless they get that resolved," said Tom Coburn, R-Okla.

The leadership essentially proposed to codify the restrictions on funding for international family planning groups, including the ban on lobbying. The president could have waived the restrictions on groups that performed abortion, but if he chose to exercise that authority, no more than $356 million could be provided in any fiscal year for family planning.

"We wouldn't want to put that language into present law," said Frelinghuysen.

Porter, a proponent of abortion rights and family planning, also opposed the compromise on principle, saying he saw no purpose in forcing a veto rather than negotiating a compromise with the White House.

Although the administration probably would have found the family planning provision difficult, if not impossible, to accept, the GOP leadership tried to make the package more appealing by including some provisions long sought by the White House.

For instance, they planned to add large chunks of the fiscal 1998-99 State Department authorization bill (HR 1757), which had languished in conference since July because of a similar House-passed provision on abortion and family planning.

Desperate to see their legislation enacted, Helms and Joseph R. Biden Jr. of Delaware, the ranking Democrat on the Senate Foreign Relations Committee, had pushed for weeks to include parts of the authorization bill in an appropriations measure. The language would have consolidated into the State Department two independent agencies — the Arms Control and Disarmament Agency and the United States Information Agency — along with parts of the Agency for International Development.

Helms, who spearheaded the consolidation effort, had worked closely with Albright and Biden on the final language.

The revised foreign operations bill also would have set in motion the payment of $819 million in U.S. debts to the United Nations in exchange for reforms by the world body, and provided the $3.5 billion requested for the IMF.

Republicans Agree To Drop Abortion Restrictions

With the date for adjournment looming, GOP leaders finally yielded to Clinton and approved overseas family planning aid without abortion restrictions, but they were forced to accede to conservative demands by denying the White House money for the IMF. Also denied was $926 million for a portion of the U.S. debts to the U.N. and for reorganizing the foreign policy agencies.

The final bill provided $385 million for family planning organizations, $58 million below the administration's request but the same as the fiscal 1997 level. The money was to be distributed at a rate of 8 percent a month, with no restrictive language.

Final Action

The conference report (H Rept 105-401) was finally filed Nov. 12. The House adopted it, 333-76, early on the morning of Nov. 13. The Senate cleared the bill by voice vote later that day. *(Vote 631, p. H-188)*

Pleas by Treasury Secretary Robert E. Rubin and Secretary of State Albright to relent on the IMF and U.N. funding proved unsuccessful. "No give. No give," said Coburn. "If we don't get something similar [on abortion restrictions], no IMF, no U.N. money, no reorganization."

"These issues should have been solved. We could have solved them. We offered two or three different compromises," said Gingrich. "[The administration's] position was remarkably rigid."

Within GOP ranks, however, there remained misgivings about adjourning without providing the money for the IMF and United Nations. "The intricacies of single-issue group politics is bedeviling our foreign policy at this time and jeopardizing the national interests of the United States," said House Banking and Financial Services Committee Chairman Jim Leach, R-Iowa, a moderate on abortion.

In the waning hours of the session, a Republican attempt to bundle the remaining spending bills together with the IMF and U.N. money, State Department reorganization and a version of the restriction on family planning aid was abandoned in the face of strong Democratic opposition and the possibility of a defeat in the House. ■

Interior Bill Dodges Controversies

The $13.8 billion fiscal 1998 Interior appropriations bill lived up to its reputation as one of the most contentious of the 13 annual spending measures. The bill dodged one controversy after another before congressional negotiators and the White House finally reached agreement on enough items to push a final version through. President Clinton signed it into law Nov. 14 (HR 2107 — PL 105-83).

Nearly half the bill, $6.6 billion, went to the Interior Department. Other major accounts included the Agriculture Department's Forest Service, which received $2.5 billion; various Energy Department programs, which got $1 billion; and Indian health programs at the Department of Health and Human Services (HHS), which received at $2.1 billion.

Throughout the late spring and early summer, congressional action on the bill was dominated by a debate over the future of the National Endowment for the Arts (NEA), which made grants to local opera companies, dance troupes, folk musicians and other artists. Although NEA funding was but a fraction of the appropriations bill, a philosophical battle over whether it should exist nearly sank the legislation in the House.

House conservatives, who saw the NEA as a money-waster and sponsor of objectionable art projects, held fast to a promise the Republican leadership had made in 1995 to zero out the agency by fiscal 1998. After some of the fiercest fighting of the appropriations season, House GOP leaders overcame the opposition of most Democrats and some moderate Republicans to push through its version of the spending bill with no funding for the agency.

The Senate, where the NEA had stronger, more bipartisan support, approved $100 million for the agency, almost equal to fiscal 1997 spending. As expected, the House-Senate conference hewed closely to the Senate position, providing $98 million. Clinton had requested $136 million. House conservatives were unhappy, but they could not generate the votes necessary to block the money.

Negotiators on the final bill faced another challenge in bridging a gap over $700 million for acquisition of environmentally sensitive property that was included in the Senate version of the bill. The House, which had not approved the funding, eventually relented, but House and Senate authorizers held up the bill for weeks trying to win oversight over how the money would be dispensed.

After signing the bill, Clinton deleted $6.2 million worth of projects, including a $5.2 million provision that would have transferred federal mineral rights to the state of Montana.

BOXSCORE

Fiscal 1998 Interior Appropriations — HR 2107. The bill provided $13.8 billion to fund the Interior Department and related agencies.

Reports: H Rept 105-163, S Rept 105-56; conference report, H Rept 105-337.

KEY ACTION

July 15 — House passed HR 2107, 238-192.

Sept. 18 — Senate passed HR 2107, revised, 93-3.

Oct. 24 — House adopted the conference report, 233-171.

Oct. 28 — Senate cleared the bill, 84-14.

Nov. 14 — President signed HR 2107— PL 105-83.

Nov. 20 — President used the line-item veto to delete provisions of PL 105-83.

House Subcommittee

The House Appropriations Interior Subcommittee approved a $13 billion version of the bill, later introduced as HR 2107, by voice vote June 17. The draft contained a number of controversial provisions, including an intended phaseout of federal arts funding and the rejection of a major Clinton administration environmental initiative.

The bill's total, which was in line with the panel's $13.1 billion allocation, was about $100 million less than Clinton had requested and about $550 million less than the $13.5 billion appropriated for fiscal 1997.

However, the Interior panel had a considerably easier time than it did the previous year, when Chairman Ralph Regula, R-Ohio, had to fight to get more money designated for his bill; he initially had been allocated only $11.4 billion. The difference in 1997 was due in part to the bipartisan budget agreement reached in May, which provided Interior and most of the other subcommittees with more money for fiscal 1998 than had been anticipated. *(Budget deal, p. 2-18; 1996 Almanac, p. 10-12)*

Many of the bill's high-profile accounts reflected the improved bottom line. The subcommittee recommended $1.6 billion for the National Park Service, $150 million more than in fiscal 1997; $1.1 billion for the Bureau of Land Management, a $38 million increase; and $725 million for the Fish and Wildlife Service, a $73 million increase.

The Forest Service also fared well, with a proposed $2.6 billion appropriation, $280 million more than the president requested. The $1.7 billion proposed for the Bureau of Indian Affairs, however, was $48 million less than the administration's request.

- **Land purchases.** The Interior Subcommittee did break with the White House in one instance, rejecting an administration request for $700 million to purchase certain environmentally sensitive lands. The $700 million had been included in the bipartisan budget deal, with $315 million of it intended for two environmentally sensitive properties in Montana and California. Regula said the balance of the request was for undetermined purchases — presumably included as a sweetener to other members whose districts might benefit from an infusion of federal money.

The land-purchase issue had arisen during the 1996 presidential campaign, when the White House, eager to fortify its environmental credentials, moved quickly to buy the properties.

One of the deals, announced Aug. 12, 1996, involved the New World Mine in Montana, which posed a pollution threat to Yellowstone National Park downstream in Wyoming. The other, unveiled Sept. 28, 1996, involved 7,500 acres of Northern California forest known as the Headwaters, which harbored prized ancient redwoods.

Regula's decision to exclude the projects was aimed at avoiding expensive land purchases that Congress would be financially responsible for maintaining. Regula said he opposed spending such an amount on new land, and tried to focus the committee on a backlog of maintenance projects at

Fiscal 1998 Interior Spending

(In thousands of dollars)

	Fiscal 1997 Appropriation	Fiscal 1998 Clinton Request	House Bill	Senate Bill	Conference Report
Interior Department					
Bureau of Land Management					
Management of lands & resources	$ 575,664	$ 587,495	$ 581,591	$ 578,851	$ 583,270
Wildland fire management	352,042	280,103	280,103	282,728	280,103
Payments in lieu of taxes	113,500	101,500	113,500	124,000	120,000
Other	154,442	152,441	153,344	152,744	152,544
Subtotal	**$ 1,195,648**	**$ 1,121,539**	**$ 1,128,583**	**$ 1,138,323**	**$ 1,135,917**
Fish and Wildlife Service					
Resource management	526,047	561,614	591,042	585,064	594,842
Construction	59,256	35,921	40,256	42,053	45,006
Land acquisition	44,479	44,560	53,000	57,292	62,632
Other	40,814	45,828	40,828	44,307	42,907
Subtotal	**$ 670,596**	**$ 687,923**	**$ 725,126**	**$ 728,716**	**$ 745,387**
National Park Service					
Operations	1,154,611	1,220,325	1,232,325	1,250,429	1,233,664
Construction	182,744	150,000	148,391	173,444	214,901
Land acquisition, state aid	53,915	70,900	129,000	126,690	143,290
Other	44,588	157,675	54,346	55,096	55,071
Subtotal	**$ 1,435,858**	**$ 1,598,900**	**$ 1,564,062**	**$ 1,605,659**	**$ 1,646,926**
Bureau of Indian Affairs					
Operation of Indian programs	1,443,502	1,542,305	1,526,815	1,529,024	1,528,588
Construction	100,531	125,118	110,751	125,051	125,051
Claim settlements, payments to Indians	69,241	59,352	41,352	43,352	43,352
Other	5,000	5,004	5,000	5,000	5,000
Subtotal	**$ 1,618,274**	**$ 1,731,779**	**$ 1,683,918**	**$ 1,702,427**	**$ 1,701,991**
Department offices	240,020	246,225	239,953	242,677	241,195
Geological Survey	740,051	745,388	755,795	758,160	759,160
Minerals Management Service	163,395	164,040	145,739	141,840	143,639
Surface Mining Reclamation	271,757	271,057	275,061	275,061	273,061
TOTAL, Interior Department	**$ 6,335,599**	**$ 6,566,851**	**$ 6,518,192**	**$ 6,592,863**	**$ 6,647,276**
Forest Service (Agriculture Department)					
National forest system	1,278,176	1,325,672	1,364,480	1,337,045	1,348,377
Wildland fire management	1,080,016	514,311	591,715	582,715	584,707
Forest and rangeland research	179,786	179,781	187,644	188,644	187,944
Reconstruction and construction	180,184	146,084	154,522	155,669	166,045
State and private forestry	155,461	156,408	157,922	162,668	161,237
Other	45,941	46,339	178,282	54,458	58,258
TOTAL, Forest Service	**$ 2,919,564**	**$ 2,368,595**	**$ 2,634,565**	**$ 2,481,199**	**$ 2,506,568**
Energy Department					
Energy conservation	569,762	707,700	644,766	629,357	611,723
Fossil energy research and development	364,704	346,408	313,153	363,969	362,403
Naval and Oil Shale Petroleum Reserves	143,786	117,000	115,000	107,000	107,000
Clean-coal technology (rescissions/deferrals)	–140,000	–286,000	–101,000	–101,000	–101,000
Other	53,845	273,025	68,025	64,025	68,025
TOTAL, Energy Department	**$ 992,097**	**$ 1,158,133**	**$ 1,039,944**	**$ 1,063,351**	**$ 1,048,151**
Other Related Agencies					
Indian Health Service	2,054,000	2,122,000	2,086,318	2,126,736	2,098,612
Indian education	61,000	0	0	0	0
Smithsonian Institution	371,342	428,407	388,407	402,558	402,258
National Endowment for the Humanities	110,000	136,000	110,000	110,700	110,700
National Endowment for the Arts	99,494	136,000	0	100,060	98,000
Other agencies	184,747	183,960	175,403	178,883	178,873
Emergency Appropriations (PL 105-18)	386,592	0	0	0	0
Priority land acquisitions	0	700,000	0	700,000	699,000
GRAND TOTAL	**$ 13,514,435**	**$ 13,799,946**	**$ 12,952,829**	**$ 13,756,350**	**$ 13,789,438**

SOURCE: House Appropriations Committee

land management agencies, totaling billions of dollars. Buying more land, he said, would further strain strapped agency maintenance budgets.

In addition, some conservative members opposed expanding federal land ownership and saw such purchases as fiscally imprudent.

The panel rejected, 5-6, a proposal by David R. Obey of Wisconsin, the ranking Democrat on the full committee, to include $65 million for the mine purchase. "I think there is a crucial issue at stake here in terms of Yellowstone," said Obey, warning that the issue would not go away. "I want to see who has guts enough to stand up on the floor and object to this."

• **NEA funding.** Tension over NEA funding had been building for months. Under pressure from the House Republican leadership and rank-and-file GOP conservatives, the subcommittee included $10 million for the agency, down from $99.5 million in fiscal 1997.

Regula agreed to drop language calling for the agency's elimination, but that move was largely moot, since the $10 million was intended to cover shutdown costs and could be used for little else.

The panel rejected, 5-6, an amendment by Sidney R. Yates of Illinois, the senior Democrat on the subcommittee, that would have restored funding for the arts agency to $99.5 million.

NEA opponents argued that federal arts funding was an unnecessary subsidy for private sector activities and that the money often went to arts projects of questionable taste and dubious artistic merit. Regula said the subcommittee's action was in accord with GOP leaders' 1995 agreement to eliminate the NEA by the end of fiscal 1998. The entire House Republican leadership had gone on record in recent months in favor of eliminating the agency. *(1995 Almanac, p. 11-48)*

But NEA proponents said the agency provided much-needed seed money for cash-strapped arts organizations, particularly in small towns across America. They also asserted that although the agency made some mistakes, its overall mission was sound. Among the proponents were some Republicans, mainly moderates, who said they intended to press their case and wanted a vote to restore the NEA funding on the floor.

The subcommittee draft included $110 million for the NEA's sister agency, the National Endowment for the Humanities (NEH) — equal to fiscal 1997 spending but $26 million less than the president wanted.

• **Forest road construction.** The draft included $89.1 million for a controversial Forest Service road construction account. Although it was a $3.7 million decrease from fiscal 1997, the item still brought objections from a bipartisan coalition of environmentalists and deficit hawks, who said such road funding would subsidize loggers and encourage road building harmful to the ecosystem.

Proponents of the road construction countered that the money would be used for basic maintenance and activities needed to protect the environment. The committee said the funds would be used to build just eight additional miles of roads. Other money not spent on new construction would go to reconstruction, engineering support and transportation planning. The Appropriations Committee estimated that more roads would be closed or decommissioned than built.

• **Park fees.** Among other provisions, the bill proposed changing the National Park Service's fee collection system to allow most parks that collected fees to keep 80 percent of the money, and send the other 20 percent to a fund for smaller cash-strapped parks. For years, park service officials had argued that entrance and other fees should be put back into the parks themselves, rather than being sent to the Treasury. By taking the money out of the parks, they said, the system provided little incentive for park managers to put a high priority on collecting fees.

The provision would also affect fee collections at many national wildlife refuges and national forests. It was estimated that the proposal would raise $400 million over the following three years.

House Full Committee

The $13 billion fiscal 1998 Interior spending bill departed the House Appropriations Committee on June 26 much as it had arrived. The committee approved the measure by voice vote (H Rept 105-163).

The lack of major revisions to the subcommittee draft set the stage for showdown votes on the House floor over the future of federal arts funding, federal purchase of environmentally sensitive land and construction of logging roads in federal forests.

• **NEA funding.** By far the biggest debate came on an unsuccessful attempt by Yates to undo the bill's substantial cut in funding for the NEA. Yates' amendment, rejected on a 28-31 vote that largely followed party lines, would have restored funding to the fiscal 1997 level of $99.5 million. "We do less for the arts than any other industrial country in the word," lamented Norm Dicks, D-Wash. "It's embarrassing."

• **Land purchases.** Democrats also took aim at Regula's decision to eliminate the $700 million requested for land purchases. The panel rejected, 21-31, an amendment by Obey to add $250 million to acquire the Northern California Headwaters forest and $65 million for the New World Mine site in Montana.

House Floor Action

The House passed the $13 billion spending bill July 15 by a vote of 238-192, but only after a series of heated battles that began with adoption of the rule governing floor action. *(Vote 275, p. H-86)*

The issue of arts funding dominated the three-day House debate on the bill. In the end, members not only blocked efforts to salvage funding for the NEA, but also eliminated the $10 million approved by the Appropriations Committee to shut down the agency.

Rule Seals NEA's Fate in House

The fate of the NEA was essentially written into the rule, which squeaked by in a dramatic 217-216 vote July 10. Fifteen Republicans and all but five of the Democrats who voted opposed the rule. *(Vote 259, p. H-82)*

A nearly unified Democratic Party and a band of Republicans, most of them Northeastern moderates, had demanded an up-or-down vote on the NEA. But the GOP leadership balked, instead crafting a rule guaranteed to block such an amendment. (The rule effectively barred the NEA funding on the grounds that the agency's authorization had expired.)

There was no shortage of reasons why the leadership prevailed on the rules vote. But in the final hours, the outcome turned on a single question: Would enough Republicans rally behind their leaders in what they had portrayed as a test of their ability to govern?

Twenty-eight Republicans had signed a June 26 letter to Speaker Newt Gingrich, R-Ga., calling for continued NEA funding. Behind the scenes, some conservatives acknowledged they did not have the votes and would lose the rule unless something was done.

Eventually, a way out appeared in the form of a proposal by Vernon J. Ehlers, R-Mich., to terminate the NEA but provide $80 million directly to the states in arts and education grants. The leadership wrote the rule in a way that guaranteed floor consideration of Ehlers' amendment.

Democrats charged that Republican leaders had embraced the Ehlers amendment purely as political cover to attract moderate and conservative support for the rule. "What's going on here is Operation Cover Your Tail," said Obey. Livid, Democrats joined July 11 with GOP conservatives and moderates — many of whom had voted for the rule — to defeat Ehlers' amendment, 155-271. *(Vote 266, p. H-84)*

Philip M. Crane, R-Ill., then raised a point of order striking even the $10 million in shutdown costs for the NEA included in the bill.

Other Amendments

Among the other amendments that enlivened the three days of floor debate were the following:

- **Land purchases.** An attempt July 10 by George Miller, D-Calif., to add the $700 million requested by the administration to acquire environmentally sensitive lands was blocked on procedural grounds.
- **Timber roads**. John Edward Porter, R-Ill., offered an amendment to slash $41.5 million from the $89.1 million in the bill for road construction in national forests, and to nearly eliminate the $50 million credit in the bill for timber companies that built such roads. Porter and others argued that the funding was a subsidy to timber companies to build environmentally destructive roads on federal land.

But lawmakers from Western and rural districts said the cuts would hurt the economies of rural communities. Dicks, who backed the roads program, managed to pre-empt Porter, modifying the amendment to reduce the funding for roads by $5.6 million and cut the credit by $25 million. The House adopted Dick's modification July 10 by a vote of 211-209. It then adopted the revised Porter amendment, 246-179. *(Votes 262, 263, p. H-84)*

- **NEH funding.** The House on July 15 rejected an amendment by Steve Chabot, R-Ohio, to eliminate funding for the National Endowment for the Humanities. The vote was 96-328. *(Vote 270, p. H-86)*
- **Biosphere.** Members on July 15 adopted an amendment by Tom Coburn, R-Okla., to prohibit funding for U.S. participation in two United Nations-sponsored international programs designed to recognize and preserve culturally and environmentally sensitive areas, known as World Heritage sites and biosphere reserves, including several dozen on U.S. soil. The vote was 222-203. *(Vote 273, p. H-86)*

Coburn and others argued that the programs had not been authorized by U.S. law. Supporters of the programs countered that they were worthwhile and clearly delineated by law and regulations. The House subsequently passed a bill to sharply curtail U.S. participation in the programs, but the Senate took no action on it. *(U.N. lands designation, p. 4-18)*

- **Tribal issues.** The House on July 15 rejected, 208-216, an amendment by Ernest Istook, R-Okla., that would have made it much harder for Indian tribes to buy and place in trust land outside reservations. *(Vote 272, p. H-86)*

Istook argued that the existing practice — which allowed tribal-run businesses on such land while shielding them from sales taxes — deprived states of revenue and gave the tribes a price advantage. His amendment would have required the federal government to purchase the land before it could be placed in trust.

- **Energy issues.** Members agreed by voice vote July 10 to a proposal by David E. Skaggs, D-Colo., to increase funding for energy efficiency and conservation programs by $8 million.

An amendment by Scott L. Klug, R-Wis., to reduce funding for the clean coal technology program by $292 million was rejected July 11, 173-243. Also defeated that day, 175-246, was an amendment by Ed Royce, R-Calif., to reduce fossil energy research by $21 million. *(Votes 264, 265, p. H-84)*

- **Nude beaches.** The House on July 15 adopted, 396-25, an amendment by Dave Weldon, R-Fla., to bar funding to designate the Canaveral National Seashore in Florida as a "clothing optional area." *(Vote 274, p. H-86)*
- **Deficit reduction.** Also adopted on July 15, by a vote of 314-109, was a "lockbox" amendment by Michael D. Crapo, R-Idaho, that would require conferees to designate any spending cuts in the bill for deficit reduction, rather than shifting the money to other accounts in the bill. *(Vote 271, p. H-86)*

Senate Subcommittee

As the Senate version of the bill began to take shape, it became clear that the two chambers were headed toward a clash in conference. The Senate Appropriations Interior Subcommittee approved a $13.8 version of the bill July 18 by voice vote. The panel included two major items that were not in the House-passed bill — the $700 million requested for land acquisition and $100 million for the NEA.

On many other items, the differences were much less significant. The Senate draft included $1.6 billion for the Interior Department's National Park Service, $33 million more than the House bill; $1.1 billion for the Bureau of Land Management, $8 million more than the House; and $2.5 billion for the Agriculture Department's Forest Service, $140 million less than the House bill.

- **Land purchases.** Of the $700 million in the subcommittee bill for land acquisitions, $315 million was designated for the New World Mine in Montana and the Headwaters forest in California, $100 million was set aside to match state funds for land acquisition, and $285 million was for unspecified projects. Subcommittee Chairman Slade Gorton, R-Wash., said the money would be provided subject to a project list developed by appropriators and negotiated between the White House and Congress. He also offered two caveats: The $315 million for Headwaters and the New World site was still subject to an authorization bill, and while he intended to abide by the budget agreement, he would not feel bound by it if he concluded that the administration was not living up to its end of the bargain.
- **NEA.** At the subcommittee markup, full Appropriations Committee Chairman Ted Stevens, R-Alaska, a supporter of funding for the NEA, announced he was working on a compromise that might pick up support in the House. "I recognize that when we go to conference, we're going to have a very bitter battle on that," added Senate subcommittee member Robert F. Bennett, R-Utah, another supporter of the arts agency.

Not every senator welcomed the chamber's role as guardian of the NEA. Conservatives, such as Jesse Helms, R-N.C., joined their House counterparts in portraying the agency as a waste of money and the source of objectionable arts projects.

But since 1995, when Republicans won a majority in Congress, most pressure to eliminate the NEA had come from the House. In the Senate, the agency counted among its allies not only liberals such as Edward M. Kennedy, D-Mass., but also conservatives such as Bennett.

● **Mining.** Harry Reid, D-Nev., won voice vote approval for an amendment requiring that the Interior secretary consult with governors before changing the rules for mining activities.

Reid complained that Interior Secretary Bruce Babbitt was trying to change the way mineral exploration was managed on public lands and was moving forward without proper consultation with Western governors. "He wants to do it his way or no way," said Reid.

Reid maintained that Babbitt was attempting to change the 1872 law governing mining activities through the federal rule-making process, after being stymied by the Senate during the early years of the Clinton presidency in his attempts to overhaul the law. *(Background, 1994 Almanac, p. 236)*

Dale Bumpers, D-Ark., a longtime critic of the 1872 law as a sweetheart deal for mining companies, took issue with Reid. "To say that governors are being ignored is a real stretch," said Bumpers. "I don't think the secretary would deny a call from any governor in the country."

● **Indian financial information**. Also included in the subcommittee draft bill was a provision directing the Bureau of Indian Affairs to ask for business income statements from tribes around the country. Gorton, a consistent critic of the bureau, said the provision would not mandate means testing for the tribes, although the gathering of financial information could be a precursor to such a shift. Critics said some tribes were better off than others because they ran profitable businesses and should not be entitled to as much federal money.

But Pete V. Domenici, R-N.M., said he did not like the way the study was structured in the bill. An aide said Domenici was worried that Gorton would look only at one side of the equation, ignoring the federal government's obligation to the tribes through treaties and other agreements.

● **Escalante National Monument.** The committee report accompanying the bill called for the Bureau of Land Management to issue a detailed budget for the controversial Escalante National Monument in Utah by Oct. 1 and required the bureau to work with local officials in developing a management plan. The monument had been established by Clinton in 1996.

Senate Full Committee

The full Senate Appropriations Committee approved the revised bill July 22 by a vote of 28-0 (HR 2107 — S Rept 105-56), generally following the subcommittee's lead with a few significant exceptions. In particular, the committee attached new provisions on American Indians and endangered grizzly bears that placed new obstacles in the bill's path.

● **Tribal immunity.** The committee-approved bill included a provision, authored by Gorton, to open federal courthouse doors to civil litigation against tribal governments. The language sparked opposition in the Senate and provoked the ire of the White House, which was concerned that it would open tribes to a rash of federal lawsuits.

Under existing law, tribes were for the most part immune from civil suits in federal courts. Gorton proposed to lift tribal immunity, allowing litigants to file civil suits including property rights claims against Indian tribes. He contended the issue was one of fairness, and that litigants who had legitimate claims against a tribe should not be denied access to federal courts. "It's a genuine waiver of sovereign immunity," Gorton said.

In a July 22 letter to the committee, the White House Office of Management and Budget (OMB) said the provision would open tribes to costly litigation, thus depleting their financial resources. "The proposed categorical waiver . . . would undermine the ability of tribes to perform government functions and jeopardize their solvency," said OMB.

Senate Indian Affairs Committee Chairman Ben Nighthorse Campbell, R-Colo., who also served on the Appropriations Committee, argued that the provision would allow litigants to "prey on the most vulnerable tribes" by filing costly lawsuits.

● **Grizzly bear habitat.** Environmental groups objected to an amendment by Larry E. Craig, R-Idaho, and Conrad Burns, R-Mont., approved by voice vote, to bar introducing grizzly bears in Idaho and Montana. The grizzly bear was listed as a threatened species under the Endangered Species Act.

Craig said his amendment was based on his contention that the bears would face problems adjusting to their new habitat and would cause troubles for ranchers and other local residents in the states. Environmental groups countered that Craig was seeking to undermine an agreement on bear reintroduction worked out by the timber industry, labor groups and local citizens.

Senate Floor Action

After slogging through a week of debate, the Senate on Sept. 18 passed its $13.8 billion version of HR 2107 by a vote of 93-3. As the Senate considered the bill, controversies over federal arts funding, Indian rights and logging roads began to fade, and the bill's outlook suddenly appeared far sunnier. *(Vote 251, p. S-42)*

● **NEA funding.** Discussions about the future of the federal arts endowment dominated the floor debate. A handful of amendments surfaced: Some senators favored eliminating arts funding outright; others favored a proposal to privatize the agency, while others supported sending arts money directly to states in lump sum payments and putting limits on the amount individual states could receive.

But in the end, the NEA supporters took the day and none of the amendments were approved. For agency proponents, the Senate's actions solidified the endowment's standing and sent a clear message to the House.

The Senate on Sept 17 and Sept 18:

➤ Defeated, 23-77, an amendment by Helms and John Ashcroft, R-Mo., to eliminate the agency and all federal arts funding outright. *(Vote 241, p. S-41)*

➤ Defeated, 37-62, an amendment by Tim Hutchinson, R-Ark., that would have eliminated the NEA, but sent arts funding to the states in lump sum payments based on a per capita formula. Each state would have received at least a $500,000 basic grant. *(Vote 245, p. S-41)*

➤ Defeated, 26-73, an amendment by Spencer Abraham, R-Mich., that called for phasing out NEA funding over three years and privatizing the agency. *(Vote 244, p. S-41)*

➤ Rejected, 39-61, a proposal by Kay Bailey Hutchison, R-Texas, to retain the agency but send 75 percent of the money to the states in lump sum payments, reserve 5 percent for administrative costs and spend the remainder on national grants to major ballet, opera and other arts groups. *(Vote 246, p. S-41)*

● **American Indian provisions.** Gorton agreed to drop his two provisions dealing with American Indians. In return Campbell agreed to hold hearings on the issue of tribal immunity the following year and perhaps consider legislation. Gorton also asked the General Accounting Office to prepare a report by June 1, 1998, on the distribution of funds by the Bureau of Indian Affairs, including "any inequities" in the allocation of funds to tribal governments.

● **Timber roads.** The Senate defeated, 49-51, an amendment by Richard H. Bryan, D-Nev., to reduce funding for Forest Service road construction by $10 million. *(Vote 243, p. S-41)*

Conference/Final Action

Negotiators reached agreement on a $13.8 billion fiscal 1998 Interior spending bill Oct. 22 (H Rept 105-337). Overcoming objections from some environmental groups, the House adopted the conference report Oct. 24 by a vote of 233-171; the Senate followed suit Oct. 28 by a lopsided vote of 84-14. *(House vote 531, p. H-162; Senate vote 283, p. S-49)*

In the weeks preceding the votes, major environmental groups and their mostly Democratic allies in the House and Senate took new aim at the measure, citing provisions funding logging roads in federal forests, renewing exports of timber grown on federal land and preventing the Forest Service from revising management plans for national forests.

The groups hoped to use their influence with the Clinton White House to prompt a veto of the bill. But there was much in the bill the administration favored, such as funding for the NEA and for land acquisitions, and the environmental groups were unsuccessful.

Conference Decisions

The following were among the principal decisions made by the conferees:

• **NEA**. The NEA survived the conference intact. Lawmakers provided the arts agency with $98 million, slightly less than the $100 million included in the Senate version, but a far cry from the zero funding in the House bill.

At Regula's the urging, however, the conference agreed to a number of new conditions, including:

➤ An increase in the amount of money that would be sent directly to the states from 35 percent to 40 percent.

➤ A 15 percent flexible cap on the amount of money that could be sent to any one state. A number of senators had objected that, under the existing system, a handful of states received the bulk of the money. New York, for example, received about 20 percent.

➤ No limits on money for touring theater, ballet and opera companies and other arts groups with a national focus.

Appropriators also agreed to provisions aimed at ensuring that education was a focus of grants and allowing NEA to raise money privately.

• **Land purchases.** As the appropriators neared completion of the conference report, House and Senate authorizers weighed in, arguing that the president should not have the right to spend money on the proposed land acquisitions without proper oversight from the House Resources and Senate Energy and Natural Resources committees.

In the end, the bill appropriated $699 million for land acquisition and maintenance, including $315 million for the New World Mine in Montana and Headwaters forest in California. The remainder of the funding was to be used for projects by the four land management agencies: the National Park Service, the Fish and Wildlife Service, the Bureau of Land Management and the Forest Service.

To satisfy the authorizers, the administration agreed to make the appropriations subject to a host of conditions. For the Headwater's forest deal, for example, the state of California would first have to fulfill its promise to provide $130 million toward the purchase price. An appraisal would also have to be conducted. The conference report directed that funds be used to compensate for tax losses due to the Headwaters purchase, and to repair a highway in Montana leading to Yellowstone park. It also delayed the release of the funds to provide congressional authorizing committees opportunities to review the matters.

• **Timber roads.** The agreement provided $88 million for Forest Service timber road construction. The final bill did not include provisions in both the House and Senate bills that would have capped the agency's "purchaser road credits" program, whereby timber companies built roads into national forests for logging purposes and, in return, received credits against the amounts they owed the federal government for timber sales. Instead, the agreement directed the Interior Department to continue managing the program as it had in fiscal 1997, when the program was capped at $50 million.

• **Parks upkeep/Alaskan marine research.** The agreement included a Senate provision to establish an $800 million fund for marine research in Alaska and for upkeep of national parks, forests, wildlife refuges and Bureau of Land Management land. The money was to come from Alaska oil lease revenues that were awarded to the Treasury in 1997. Under the provision, backed by Sen. John McCain, R-Ariz., $50 million in interest from the fund could be appropriated in fiscal 1999.

• **Mining.** Like the Senate-passed bill, the conference report required the Interior secretary to consult with governors before proceeding to change rules for mining activities.

• **Recreational fee.** Like the House bill, the conference agreement permitted parks and other public lands to keep 100 percent of the funds they collected under a fee-collection demonstration program.

• **Other provisions.** Negotiators resolved several other differences between the two chambers' bills. They dropped the House "lockbox" provision that would have required them to use any spending cuts exclusively for deficit reduction. The conference agreement included House language prohibiting funding for U.S. participation in the new U.N. land preservation programs, as well as Senate language barring the introduction of grizzly bears in Idaho and Montana. The bill also included the House provision barring funding for a nude beach in Florida.

Line-Item Veto

On Nov. 20, Clinton struck $6.2 million from the $13.8 billion spending bill. The biggest chunk, $5.2 million, came from a provision that would have transferred mineral rights to the state of Montana from the federal government. The provision was part of the purchase of the New World Mine in Montana. The president said the move would have set a costly precedent. Clinton also cut $1 million from the bill for construction of a dam in Mississippi to create a recreational lake on Forest Service land. ■

Testing Plan Nearly Sinks Labor Bill

For the first time in three years, Congress cleared a stand-alone spending bill for the departments of Labor, Health and Human Services (HHS) and Education. To get that far, the bill had to survive repeated attacks from House conservatives and protracted negotiations over a White House proposal for voluntary national testing of elementary school students. The Senate cleared the bill Nov. 8, and President Clinton signed it into law Nov. 13 (HR 2264 — PL 105-78).

The fiscal 1998 appropriations included $80.4 billion in discretionary spending — $5.7 billion more than in fiscal 1997 and $273 million more than Clinton requested. When combined with mandatory spending, the bill totaled $276.9 billion. It was the largest of the 13 annual appropriations bills, and the largest source of domestic discretionary spending.

The bill contained a number of policy provisions, some of them hotly contested, including plans to:

➤ Ban field testing or implementation of Clinton's national student testing proposal in fiscal 1998.

➤ Bar the use of federal funds to pay for a court-ordered Teamsters election.

➤ Place a six-month moratorium on federal funding of needle exchange programs aimed at slowing the spread of the AIDS virus.

➤ Repeal a potential $50 billion tax break for tobacco companies that was tucked into the tax-reconciliation bill.

➤ Extend existing prohibitions against federally funded abortions to managed care plans offered under Medicaid.

BOXSCORE

Fiscal 1998 Labor-HHS-Education Appropriations — HR 2264 (S 1061). The bill provided $276.9 billion — $80.4 billion of it discretionary spending — for the departments of Labor, Health and Human Services, and Education.

Reports: H Rept 105-205, S Rept 105-58; conference report, H Rept 105-390.

KEY ACTION

Sept. 11 — Senate passed S 1061, 92-8.

Sept. 17 — House passed HR 2264, 346-80; **Senate** passed HR 2264 by voice vote after substituting the text of S 1061.

Nov. 7 — House agreed to the conference report, 352-65.

Nov. 8 — Senate cleared the bill, 91-4

Nov. 13 — President signed HR 2264 — PL 105-78.

In the 104th Congress, partisan wrangling over Labor-HHS spending contributed to the government shutdown in the winter of 1995-96. The fiscal 1996 bill was ultimately enacted as part of a larger omnibus spending package. The fiscal 1997 bill, too, was folded into an omnibus measure. *(1995 Almanac, p. 11-55; 1996 Almanac, p. 10-59)*

By contrast, the fiscal 1998 bill got off to a fairly smooth start thanks in part to a relatively generous funding allocation by House appropriators, who gave the Labor-HHS Subcommittee an increase of more than $5 billion in discretionary spending compared with fiscal 1997. Appropriators hoped to win House passage of the bill before the August congressional recess, but threats from conservatives to offer more than 100 amendments forced the leadership to postpone action until September.

It took the House three weeks of on and off debate to pass its bill. Conservatives ended up losing more battles than they won, but claimed they were less interested in the outcome than in waging the fight. Their biggest victory came when they teamed up with Bill Goodling, R-Pa., chairman of the House Education and the Workforce Committee, to win House approval for an amendment to prohibit the administration from developing voluntary reading and math tests. However, the amendment was modified significantly before the bill was enacted.

On the other side of the Capitol, the Senate Appropriations Committee approved its version of the bill with less fanfare, as did the full Senate.

Background: National Testing

In his Feb. 4 State of the Union Message, Clinton proposed a voluntary national program to administer annual tests to fourth-graders in reading and eighth-graders in math. The exams were to be based on two existing tests — the National Assessment of Educational Progress (NAEP) and the Third International Mathematics and Science Study (TIMSS). Those tests, however, surveyed only a random sample of students; no student was tested on all items. By contrast, the president proposed tests that would allow evaluation of individual students, as well as school districts and states. Clinton contended the new tests would help assess how schools and students were faring and encourage better performance.

The administration initially drew criticism for insisting that it could develop the tests without congressional approval and for giving the project to the Education Department instead of an independent entity. Clinton eventually changed his mind, reaching a compromise with the Senate to let the National Assessment Governing Board, an independent entity that formed policy guidelines for the NAEP, oversee development of the tests.

The House, however, voted to ban funding for the tests in fiscal 1998. "We already have plenty of testing," said Goodling, who led the opposition. "Why have another measurement instrument to tell us what we already know?" He said he would rather send the money directly to classrooms.

Goodling received strong backing from a coalition of 11 conservative groups, including the Christian Coalition and Family Research Council. "We believe national testing will lead to an unwarranted national curriculum, stifling local control of education at the level of textbooks and teachers," they wrote in a July 29 letter to Republican House leaders. The testing proposal was also opposed by black and Hispanic members who contended that the tests would further stigmatize schools in low-income areas, and that what those schools needed was additional resources, not additional tests.

The stalemate stalled the House-Senate conference on the bill until Nov. 5, when Clinton and Goodling agreed to a compromise. The final deal gave the assessment board authority over the tests, prohibited any trial runs of the tests during fiscal 1998 and directed the National Academy of Sciences to study the tests while they were being developed. The academy was also to examine whether existing commercially available tests and state tests could be correlated and used as a substitute for new national tests.

Fiscal 1998 Labor-HHS-Education Spending

(in thousands of dollars)

	Fiscal 1997 Appropriation	Fiscal 1998 Clinton Request	House Bill	Senate Bill	Final Bill
Labor Department					
Training and employment services	$4,715,903	$5,295,318	$5,141,601	$5,260,053	$5,238,226
Trade adjustment, allowances	324,500	349,000	349,000	349,000	349,000
Unemployment insurance (advance)	373,000	392,000	392,000	392,000	392,000
Trust fund	*3,142,476*	*3,431,476*	*3,305,476*	*3,288,476*	*3,322,476*
Black lung disability	1,007,982	1,007,000	1,007,000	1,007,000	1,007,000
Occupational Safety & Health	324,955	347,805	336,205	336,205	336,480
Other	1,993,382	2,031,730	2,000,039	2,018,557	2,012,421
Total, Labor Department	**$8,739,722**	**$9,422,853**	**$9,225,845**	**$9,362,815**	**$9,335,127**
Health and Human Services					
Public Health					
Health resources and services	3,404,567	3,266,479	3,607,068	3,449,071	3,618,137
Ryan White AIDS program	*996,252*	*1,036,252*	*1,168,252*	*1,077,252*	*1,150,200*
Disease control	2,302,168	2,315,795	2,395,737	2,368,113	2,378,552
National Institutes of Health	12,740,843	13,078,203	13,505,294	13,692,844	13,647,843
Substance abuse/mental health	2,121,512	2,155,943	2,151,943	2,126,643	2,146,743
Health care financing					
Medicaid grants to states	103,367,016	104,383,650	104,383,650	104,455,650	104,455,650
Medicare and other Medicaid	60,079,000	63,581,000	63,581,000	63,581,000	60,904,000
Public Welfare					
Family support payments (AFDC)*	9,600,000	0	0	0	0
Low-income home energy assistance	1,000,000	1,000,000	1,000,000	1,200,000	1,100,000
Refugee assistance	412,076	392,332	415,000	392,332	415,000
Community services block grants	489,600	414,720	489,600	492,600	490,600
Child care block grant	953,762	1,000,000	937,000	963,120	1,002,672
Social Services block grants	2,500,000	2,380,000	2,245,000	2,245,000	2,299,000
Head Start	3,980,546	4,305,000	4,305,000	4,305,000	4,355,000
Programs for the aging	830,131	838,168	815,270	894,074	865,050
Foster care, adoption assistance	4,445,031	4,311,000	4,311,000	4,311,000	4,311,000
Other, including advances	1,900,652	–2,601,494	–2,578,195	–2,586,702	–2,548,695
Total, HHS	**$210,126,904**	**$200,820,796**	**$201,564,367**	**$201,889,745**	**$199,440,552**
Education Department					
Elementary and Secondary Education					
Goals 2000	491,000	620,000	387,165	530,000	491,000
Compensatory education (Title 1)	7,779,573	8,077,266	8,204,217	7,807,349	8,021,827
Impact aid	730,000	658,000	796,000	794,500	808,000
School improvement	1,425,618	1,299,222	1,507,388	1,542,293	1,538,188
Bilingual, immigrant education	261,700	354,000	354,000	354,000	354,000
Special education	4,035,979	4,210,000	4,428,647	4,958,073	4,810,646
Higher Education					
Pell grants, student financial aid	5,919,000	7,635,000	7,438,000	6,910,334	7,344,934
Guaranteed student loans	46,482	47,688	47,688	46,482	46,482
Higher education grants	879,048	1,035,292	909,893	929,752	946,738
Vocational, adult education	1,486,517	1,565,966	1,506,975	1,487,698	1,507,698
Rehabilitation services	2,509,428	2,583,376	2,589,176	2,591,286	2,591,195
Libraries	136,369	136,369	142,000	146,369	146,340
Education research	293,126	390,658	423,252	323,190	431,438
Other	2,964,138	3,456,657	3,409,788	3,545,377	3,467,570
Total, Education Department	**$28,957,978**	**$32,069,494**	**$32,144,189**	**$31,966,703**	**$32,506,056**
Domestic Volunteer Service Programs	213,849	260,300	227,547	232,604	256,604
Corporation for Public Broadcasting	250,000	325,000	300,000	300,000	300,000
Supplemental Security Income	19,547,010	16,380,000	16,380,000	16,417,525	16,370,000
Other related agencies	10,862,892	9,828,540	9,807,344	9,798,220	9,805,436
GRAND TOTAL **	**$287,231,140**	**$279,295,129**	**$279,180,156**	**$278,849,779**	**$276,890,064**
Trust Funds	*$11,713,312*	*$12,166,342*	*$11,843,060*	*$11,901,983*	*$11,873,485*

* *This and related programs were replaced by Temporary Assistance for Needy Families, at unspecified funding levels for fiscal 1998.*

** *Includes scorekeeping adjustments – fiscal 1997: $8,532,785; Clinton request: $10,188,146; House: $9,530,864; Senate:$8,957,667; final: $8,876,289.*

SOURCE: House and Senate Appropriations committees

House Subcommittee

A divided House Appropriations subcommittee approved a draft of the fiscal 1998 Labor-HHS spending bill by voice vote July 15.

The panel set funding for the overall bill at $279 billion, including $80 billion in discretionary funds — those over which appropriators had direct control. The measure called for ending more than 20 programs in the education and health departments, all funded at $50 million or less. It also maintained the so-called Hyde Amendment, named for its author, Rep. Henry J. Hyde, R-Ill., which barred federal funding for abortions except in cases of rape, incest or to save the woman's life.

Appropriations Committee Chairman Robert L. Livingston, R-La., warned members against adding extraneous legislative riders to the bill. "We've got a shot at getting a bill this time because you have acted in a solid bipartisan fashion," he told the subcommittee. Livingston said the "extremely narrow majorities" backing the draft bill could erode if it were loaded with items that too many members found objectionable. Subcommittee Chairman John Edward Porter, R-Ill., also urged members to resist legislative add-ons.

David R. Obey of Wisconsin, ranking Democrat on both the full Appropriations Committee and the Labor-HHS Subcommittee, said he was "not crazy about" the bill, but could support it if no major changes were made.

The panel proposed funding some education and job training programs at the levels requested by Clinton, while reducing funding for others that Republican leaders considered ineffective.

For example, appropriators met Clinton's requests for $1.1 billion for the Job Corps employment training program and $4.3 billion for the Head Start program for disadvantaged preschoolers. They also agreed to increase the maximum Pell grants award to $3,000, up from $2,700, as Clinton requested.

However, the subcommittee cut funding for Clinton's Goals 2000 education initiative to $475 million from $491 million the previous year. Clinton had asked for $620 million.

The panel allocated more money than Clinton requested for several health programs, including an extra $427 million for the National Institutes of Health (NIH), bringing the total to $13.5 billion. Funding for disease prevention programs at the Centers for Disease Control and Prevention (CDC) was increased to $2.4 billion, $68 million more than Clinton requested. Funding for the Ryan White AIDS health services program was increased by $172 million, to $1.2 billion.

The panel cut back on some of the funding requested for labor programs. For example, federal and state enforcement programs under the Occupational Safety and Health Administration (OSHA) were allocated $9.2 million less than the $214 million Clinton requested. Funding for the National Labor Relations Board (NLRB) was put at $175 million, the same level as in fiscal 1997 but $11 million less than requested.

By voice vote, the subcommittee rejected an amendment by Jay Dickey, R-Ark., to transfer $26.2 million from the NLRB to a fund for historically black colleges and universities. Dickey contended that the NLRB was "out of control" and its lawyers were harassing small businesses. Obey argued that Dickey's amendment would hurt the board's ability to protect workers.

Henry Bonilla, R-Texas, said he was pleased with a compromise regarding OSHA and ergonomics regulations. Bonilla wanted to stop OSHA from issuing regulations to protect workers from repetitive-motion injuries. The draft prohibited the agency from issuing a proposed or final standard on ergonomics for one year, though it did not include a Bonilla proposal to require the National Academy of Sciences to review scientific research on repetitive injuries and issue a report before OSHA could issue a regulation.

House Full Committee

The full House Appropriations Committee approved the bill by voice vote July 22. The draft, later introduced as HR 2264 (H Rept 105-205), included $80 billion in discretionary spending — nearly $5.3 billion more than in fiscal 1997, but $110 million less than Clinton requested.

Parental Consent

The biggest controversy in the full committee concerned an amendment by Ernest Istook, R-Okla., to require parental consent before minors could receive family planning services from federally funded clinics. Istook argued that it was morally wrong for minors to receive such sensitive aid as birth control and family planning assistance without parental involvement. The heated debate focused in part on a recent case in Crystal Lake, Ill., in which a schoolteacher allegedly had sex with an underage teenager for 18 months, driving her to the county health department for birth control injections without her parents' knowledge.

Subcommittee Chairman Porter described the issue as a "very complex matter" that should not be decided by appropriators. "Confidential access to family planning services is critical," said Porter, who often clashed with anti-abortion activists in his own party. He said requiring parental consent would cause some teenagers to delay or avoid necessary family planning services, resulting in more pregnancies and more sexually transmitted diseases.

Obey warned that controversial amendments such as Istook's would prompt Democratic opposition to the bill and a veto.

"Without bipartisan support, this bill will not pass," Livingston admonished, enunciating each word for emphasis and alluding to the prospect of repeating the partial government shutdowns in late 1995 and early 1996 that had backfired on Republicans.

Conservatives, however, refused to give up. "There are certain things that we must stand and fight for," said Mark W. Neumann, R-Wis., "even if it means a bill is not going to pass or a bill might be vetoed, and it means that we would have to wind up in some sort of a 'government shutdown.' "

Porter then trumped Istook's amendment with a substitute requiring that clinics encourage family participation, essentially reflecting existing law. It also required that clinics counsel minors to resist attempts to engage them in sexual activities. The committee approved the substitute, 30-27, effectively killing Istook's amendment. Eight Republicans joined a majority of Democrats in supporting the substitute; three Democrats joined most Republicans in opposing it.

Abortion Funding

Frank R. Wolf, R-Va., proposed extending the traditional prohibitions contained in the Hyde Amendment against federally funded abortions to managed care plans offered under Medicaid. Wolf said about 40 percent of Medicaid beneficiaries received their health care coverage through managed care systems. Because the federal government paid part of the premiums for these benefit packages, rather than reimbursing providers for specific medical services, the existing prohibition was difficult to enforce.

Wolf offered his amendment at Hyde's request. But Porter and others objected that it could be interpreted to restrict abortion services funded by states, local governments or private entities. Wolf eventually withdrew the amendment; he and Hyde were promised a chance to offer the language on the floor if a compromise could not be reached beforehand.

House Floor Action

After a lengthy debate that stretched on for eight days over a three-week period, the House passed the bill Sept. 17 by a vote of 346-80. By then, the Senate had already passed its version. *(Vote 402, p. H-122)*

House floor debate was dominated by a group of GOP conservatives who claimed the bill reflected Democratic spending priorities more than those of the Republicans. The group included Mark Souder, David M. McIntosh and John Hostettler, all of Indiana, Tom Coburn of Oklahoma, and Joel Hefley of Colorado. They drew up more than 100 amendments and threatened to debate them over several weeks unless the GOP leadership agreed to help them gain House approval for at least a half dozen or so revisions. Their favorite targets for cuts included OSHA, the NLRB, family planning programs and the Goals 2000 program championed by Clinton to help states develop education standards.

While their efforts routinely won the support of more than two-thirds of House Republicans, they still lost far more amendments than they won. "It's incremental change," McIntosh said. "But it's a significant move to show that Congress really is more conservative than this bill reflected."

Speaker Newt Gingrich, R-Ga., who was particularly sensitive to his party's conservative faction following an aborted attempt to overthrow him in July, did not try to quash the conservatives' efforts to remake the bill.

But Porter resisted most of the amendments and questioned the conservatives' goals. "We do not have a parliamentary system here," he said. "Our job is not to find where the center of the party is, but where the center of the Congress is, as representatives of the American people." Livingston, too, tried to hold the line. He appealed to the bill's opponents to "calm the tenor of their vehemence" and said Republicans could only demonstrate their ability to govern as a majority party if they could "produce a reasonable bill with as little rancor as possible."

But conservatives showed little inclination to go quietly. Souder said the bill was "at the heart of the differences between the two parties on how we are going to govern, and differences in our own party as to what the role of the federal government should be."

Conservatives Win Some Changes

The first time the conservatives' priorities were put to a test, they fell far short, though some subsequent amendments picked up support.

• **Wage-and-hour enforcement.** On Sept. 5, the House rejected, 167-260, a McIntosh amendment to shift $4.3 million from the Labor Department's wage-and-hour enforcement program to the special education program for disabled children. McIntosh said the amendment would "take funds away from the Washington bureaucracy and give them to our local schools." Democrats replied that enforcing wage-and-hour laws and funding special education were both worth supporting. "These are false choices you are asking people to make," said Rosa DeLauro, D-Conn. *(Vote 367, p. H-112)*

• **Family planning.** In a replay of the committee markup, the House conducted a heated debate on an amendment by Istook and Donald Manzullo, R-Ill., to require federally funded family planning clinics to give five days' notice to the parents of minors before distributing contraceptives to the youths.

As in committee, their plan was trumped by a substitute offered by Porter and Michael N. Castle, R-Del., to encourage family participation and provide counseling to minors on how to resist being coerced into sexual activities. The Castle substitute was approved, 220-201, on Sept. 9. The Istook amendment, as amended by Castle, was then adopted, 254-169. *(Votes 378, 379, p. H-114)*

"If you do things to make sexual activity by teens easier, there will be more sexual activity," warned Istook, "there will be more out-of-wedlock births, and there will be more abortions, too." Porter disagreed, saying that requiring parental notification would essentially prevent teens of dysfunctional families from getting "the kinds of services that prevent pregnancies, help to prevent sexually transmitted diseases, and in the end help to prevent abortions."

• **Needle exchange.** By a vote of 266-158, the House on Sept. 11 approved an amendment by Dennis Hastert, R-Ill., to ban the use of federal funds to establish a needle exchange program for users of illegal drugs. The bill would have permitted the distribution of sterile needles to illegal drug users if the HHS secretary determined that such programs were effective in preventing the spread of the AIDS-causing HIV virus and that they did not encourage the use of illegal drugs. *(Vote 391, p. H-118)*

• **Abortion funding.** The House on Sept. 11 also adopted, 270-150, an amendment by Hyde to extend the general prohibition against federally funded abortions to managed care providers under Medicaid. Specifically, the amendment proposed barring the use of funds in the bill to pay for any abortion, or to pay for health benefits coverage offered by a managed care provider or organization that included coverage of abortion. These prohibitions would not apply in cases of rape or incest, or if an abortion was necessary to save the life of the woman. *(Vote 388, p. H-116)*

• **National testing.** An amendment by Goodling to ban the use of funds in fiscal 1998 to develop the national tests proposed by Clinton was adopted Sept. 16 by a vote of 295-125. The amendment was supported by virtually every Republican, as well as by most members of the black and Hispanic caucuses. "Standardized testing has a negative, disparate impact on poor and minority students," said Rubén Hinojosa, D-Texas. "Equal opportunity in testing cannot be achieved given unequal education opportunity." *(Vote 398, p. H-120)*

Even some supporters of national testing voted for Goodling's amendment to show their opposition to the way the administration had handled it. "Unfortunately," said Castle, "this proposal has been poorly managed and executed, and consequently has not gained adequate support."

Members who supported national testing dismissed arguments that it represented a federal intrusion. "We are talking about the very basic skills needed to survive in America today, reading and math," said Bill Pascrell Jr., D-N.J. "National testing will provide us with a better picture of where we need to better target our resources."

Clinton later issued a statement indicating his resolve to proceed with the tests. "The same old forces that have resisted education reform over the past decade came together to defeat high national standards in the basics," he said. Goodling and Porter said they were determined to have the House prevail on the matter. "There is no compromise," Goodling said.

• **Teamsters election.** Also on Sept. 16, the House approved an amendment, by Peter Hoekstra, R-Mich., to ban the use of federal funds to pay the expenses of any election officer appointed by a court to oversee a new Teamsters election. The vote, largely along party lines, was 225-195. *(Vote 399, p. H-122)*

Under a 1989 consent agreement between the federal government and the Teamsters, the government agreed to supervise the 1991 and 1996 Teamsters presidential elections. The federal government spent at least $20 million overseeing the 1996 balloting. But in August 1997, a court-appointed election overseer invalidated the election, in which Teamsters President Ron Carey defeated challenger James P. Hoffa, because of questionable financing related to Carey's campaign. *(Teamsters, p. 7-24)*

• **Tobacco settlement credit.** Nita M. Lowey, D-N.Y., won voice vote approval Sept. 17 for an amendment to repeal a controversial $50 billion tax break for the tobacco industry that was included at the last minute in the tax reconciliation bill (PL 105-34). The tax bill specified that revenues raised from a 15-cent-per-pack increase in the tobacco tax would be subtracted from the amount the companies would pay under a proposed national settlement of ongoing tobacco litigation. The effect would be to reduce from $368.5 billion to $318.5 billion the amount the companies would have to pay over 25 years. *(Tobacco deal, p. 3-3)*

Additional Amendments Considered

The House approved a number of amendments by voice vote, including proposals by:

➤ John E. Peterson, R-Pa., to increase funding for vocational and adult education by $20 million and decrease the Goals 2000 program by the same amount.

➤ Tim Roemer, D-Ind., to increase funding for charter schools by $25 million and reduce the technology literacy challenge program by the same amount.

➤ Lindsey Graham, R-S.C., to increase funding for special education for disabled students by $55 million and decrease Goals 2000 by the same amount.

➤ Frank Riggs, R-Calif., to change the name of a new $200 million program to help schools improve performance from "whole school reform" to "comprehensive school reform." Conservatives wanted assurances that the program would not be related to a controversial education curriculum known as "whole language." The amendment also specified that the money was to be used to meet state performance standards.

The House rejected a number of amendments offered by conservatives, including proposals to:

➤ Increase funding for vocational and adult education by $11.3 million and reduce OSHA funding by the same amount. The proposal, by Roy Blunt, R-Mo., was rejected, 160-237. *(Vote 369, p. H-112)*

➤ Increase funding by $11.3 million for programs for students with disabilities and reduce OSHA funding by same amount. The amendment, by Charlie Norwood, R-Ga., was defeated, 157-240. *(Vote 370, p. H-112)*

➤ Increase funding for the State AIDS Drug Assistance Program by $34.8 million, taking the funds from various HHS accounts, including $22.6 million from refugee and entrant assistance. The amendment, by Coburn, was rejected, 141-282. *(Vote 377, p. H-114)*

➤ Increase funding by $18 million for Impact Aid, a program benefiting districts that educated children of military personnel and children who lived on Indian lands or in federally subsidized low-income housing. The proposal, by J.D. Hayworth, R-Ariz., would have reduced NLRB salaries and expenses by the same amount. It was defeated, 170-253. *(Vote 385, p. H-116)*

➤ Eliminate the $300 million advance fiscal 2000 funding in the bill for the Corporation for Public Broadcasting (CPB). The proposal, by Philip M. Crane, R-Ill., was rejected, 78-345. *(Vote 390, p. H-118)*

Senate Committee

The Senate Appropriations Committee approved its version of the spending bill (S 1061 — S Rept 105-58) on July 24 by a vote of 28-0. The panel's Labor-HHS Subcommittee had approved the measure two days earlier, also by voice vote. The bill — which called for about $79.7 billion in discretionary spending — evoked relatively little discussion at either markup.

The subcommittee added language to bar OSHA from issuing mandatory regulations on repetitive-motion injuries for one year. The amendment, by Judd Gregg, R-N.H., was approved by voice vote. In the full committee, appropriators gave voice vote approval to an omnibus amendment by subcommittee Chairman Arlen Specter, R-Pa., making several small funding changes.

Like their House counterparts, Senate appropriators allocated more money than Clinton requested for many health programs. The bill included $13.7 billion for the NIH, $2.4 billion for the CDC and $1.1 billion for the Ryan White AIDS program. Like the House bill, S 1061 included $4.3 billion as requested for Head Start, and denied a request for $21 million to promote adoptions.

Senate appropriators approved $530 million for the Goals 2000 program, more than in the House bill but still well below the $620 million requested by Clinton. Like their House counterparts, they proposed to delay the availability of the $260 million the administration sought to start a literacy initiative until fiscal 1999 — and only then if authorizing legislation were enacted by April 1, 1998. Also like their House colleagues, Senate appropriators rejected a $250 million request for a new training program geared to youths in high poverty areas. Instead, they proposed creating a demonstration program along those lines, setting aside additional money in fiscal 1999 only if the program was authorized.

Senate Floor Action

The Senate passed the bill Sept. 11 by a vote of 92-8, after adopting a compromise on Clinton's national testing proposal and making several other controversial changes. Once the House had acted Sept. 17, the Senate took up HR 2264, amended it to reflect its own bill, and passed it by voice vote. *(Vote 235, p. S-39)*

Education Block Grants

In a surprise move, the Senate on Sept. 11 agreed to a proposal by Slade Gorton, R-Wash., to give local school districts complete control over most federal elementary and secondary aid programs for one year. The Gorton amendment was adopted by voice vote, after a motion to table (kill) it was narrowly rejected, 49-51. *(Vote 232, p. S-39)*

The amendment called for creating two block grants worth a total of about $12 billion. School districts would be assured of receiving at least as much federal money as they would get without the amendment.

The first block grant, worth about $7 billion according to Gorton, would encompass the existing Title I program, the largest source of federal elementary and secondary aid. The funding formula would also be changed, and districts would gain wide latitude in using the money. The second block grant, worth about $5 billion, would cover a wide array of existing programs, including bilingual and immigrant education, education technology, the Goals 2000 program, safe and drug-free schools, professional development and 50 percent of the funding for vocational and adult education.

The biggest program excluded from the proposed block grants was special education assistance under the Individuals with Disabilities Education Act (IDEA).

Gorton said his amendment would let school districts set their own education policies and save what he described as about 15 percent in administrative expenses. "Distribute the money directly to the school districts that are providing education and let them spend it as they will," he said.

Democrats, shocked by Senate approval of the amendment, scrambled to respond. "There will be no requirements on how this money is to be spent — none whatsoever," said Tom Harkin of Iowa, ranking Democrat on the Labor-HHS Subcommittee. "They can take the money and build a swimming pool."

The Education Department said the amendment would prevent it from developing the national voluntary tests, an assertion Gorton denied. White House spokesman Mike McCurry described Gorton's amendment as "a back-door attempt to abolish the Department of Education." Education Secretary Richard W. Riley termed it "unacceptable."

Adoption of the amendment also provoked some opposition from House Republicans, including Labor-HHS Subcommittee Chairman Porter. Raising the money at one level of government and spending it at another without strings attached sounded "very much akin to revenue sharing, which everyone condemned," he said.

National Student Testing

In an unusual maneuver, the Senate temporarily suspended voting on a proposal by Gregg and Daniel R. Coats, R-Ind., to prohibit the administration from developing voluntary national reading and math tests so that the Labor-HHS Appropriations Subcommittee could hold a hearing Sept. 4.

"Our proposal for voluntary national tests is not revolutionary," Education Secretary Riley told the panel. "Voluntary national tests, linked to high standards, will give parents and teachers a much clearer, more realistic picture of how their children are actually doing." However, Goodling testified that the administration was misguided in developing the tests without explicit congressional approval. "Let's slow it down so that they don't make the mistake," he said. "Get us involved."

Gregg indicated that his opposition to the tests was less vehement than Goodling's. He said he wanted to ensure that the tests dealt only with basic reading and math skills and would not lead to "the slippery slope of moving down the road of a national curriculum."

After negotiating at length with Senate Democrats and administration officials, Gregg modified his amendment to allow development of the tests as long as oversight was shifted from the Education Department to the National Assessment Governing Board. The board would also be required to review any existing contracts and could modify or terminate them. The board's composition would be changed to assure bipartisanship and to focus on local and state officials. The Senate adopted the amendment Sept. 11 by a vote of 87-13. *(Vote 234, p. S-39)*

Porter and Goodling said they would resist the Senate's language on the tests. And Obey acknowledged that "the administration has a lot of work to do" to tame House opposition.

Teamsters Election

The Senate also adopted an amendment by Majority Whip Don Nickles, R-Okla., to require that the Teamsters union reimburse the government for the cost of rerunning the 1996 election. The amendment was approved Sept. 11 by a vote of 58-42. *(Vote 233, p. S-39)*

Under the amendment, the Labor and Justice departments would be barred from paying for the rerun unless the president certified that the union could not afford to finance it. In that case, the union could take out a federal loan at customary interest rates. Nickles and his supporters argued that the government should not pay for a new election when the first was declared invalid because of fraud.

A court-appointed overseer had recommended a new election, although the Southern District Court of New York, which oversaw the consent order, had yet to rule on it. As a result, many Democrats and two high-ranking Republicans — Appropriations Committee Chairman Ted Stevens of Alaska and Labor-HHS Subcommittee Chairman Specter — argued that the amendment would unfairly interfere in a pending court matter.

Edward M. Kennedy, D-Mass., tried to amend Nickles' proposal to prevent it from changing the 1989 consent agreement. Kennedy charged that Nickles and his supporters were reneging on the 1989 agreement and trying to punish the Teamsters for victories in a recent strike against United Parcel Service. He called it a "basic, fundamental assault" on the union.

Nickles countered that his amendment only addressed a situation that the compact did not — who should pay for the new election. "Taxpayers shouldn't have to pay for the Teamsters election twice," he said. "It's not the taxpayers' fault that there was fraud." The amendment was tabled (killed), 56-42. *(Vote 217, p. S-37)*

Fetal Tissue Research

An amendment to fund research related to Parkinson's disease, a degenerative disorder, touched off a contentious debate on the use of fetal tissue in research.

John McCain, R-Ariz., and Paul Wellstone, D-Minn., won approval to provide a total of $100 million in fiscal 1998 for up to 10 centers named after former Rep. Morris K. Udall, D-Ariz. (1961-1991) and devoted to research on Parkinson's disease. The proposal was adopted 95-3. *(Vote 214, p. S-37)*

The amendment prompted another by Coats to ban federal funding for research using aborted fetuses. Coats wanted to prevent research that used human fetal tissues, cells or organs from an embryo or dead fetus obtained during or after an induced abortion. His amendment did not apply to human fetal tissues, cells or organs obtained from a miscarriage or a pregnancy outside the womb. Coats argued that without his amendment, the legislation could encourage more abortions.

Kennedy argued that fetal tissue research was "a medical and not a moral issue," and that it was being used to treat and better understand diseases such as Parkinson's. He said there were "extensive safeguards built into the law and regulations to assure that there is no link between the decision to have an abortion and the decision to allow fetal tissue research to be conducted." Coats' amendment was defeated, 38-60. *(Vote 215, p. S-37)*

Other Amendments

The Senate voted on a number of other issues as well.

- **Tobacco credit.** After some parliamentary maneuvering, the Senate on Sept. 10 adopted an amendment by Richard J.

Durbin, D-Ill., to repeal the $50 billion tax break for the tobacco industry included in the balanced-budget tax law. The vote was 95-3. *(Vote 227, p. S-38)*

- **Abortion funding.** Senators approved, by voice vote, an amendment by John Ashcroft, R-Mo., to extend the traditional prohibitions against federally funded abortions to managed care plans offered under Medicaid.
- **Other amendments.** In other action, the Senate:
  - Defeated, 25-74, an amendment by Jon Kyl, R-Ariz., that would have increased funding for Pell grants by $528 million. Opponents said they objected to Kyl's plan to offset the money by decreasing aid to the Low-Income Home Energy Assistance Program (LIHEAP), which provided energy assistance to low-income people. *(Vote 213, p. S-37)*
  - Approved, 97-0, an amendment by Alfonse M. D'Amato, R-N.Y., to increase funding for programs under the Older Americans' Act by $40 million, to a total of $894 million. The programs provided home and community-based assistance, such as Meals on Wheels, to the elderly. The additional funds were to come from the administrative budgets of the Labor, HHS and Education departments. *(Vote 216, p. S-37)*

Conference/Final Action

Protracted negotiations over Clinton's plan for national testing delayed final action on the bill for more than a month. The House wanted to ban the funding in fiscal 1998; the Senate was willing to compromise with the administration to let the tests go forward under the authority of the independent National Assessment Governing Board.

House and Senate negotiators thought they had reached a compromise Oct. 30. But the House GOP leadership backed away from it, deferring to conservatives who insisted the proposal would not go far enough in blocking the tests. The stalemate was finally broken Nov. 5 in a White House meeting between key protagonists Clinton and Goodling. The conference report (H Rept 105-390) was filed Nov. 7, and the House adopted it the same day by a vote of 352-65. The Senate cleared the bill Nov. 8 by a vote of 91-4. *(House vote 615, p. H-184; Senate vote 298, p. S-51)*

The final bill provided $32.8 billion in discretionary spending for HHS, a 7 percent increase over fiscal 1997. Discretionary spending for the Education Department was set at $29.6 billion, a 10.5 percent increase; the Labor Department got $10.7 billion, a 4.4 percent increase.

Initial Testing Compromise Rejected

The initial compromise reached Oct. 30 allowed for continued development of the national tests under the National Assessment Governing Board, but prohibited the tests from being disseminated or administered without specific congressional authorization. The agreement also required that the tests be evaluated by the National Academy of Sciences. A motion to insist on the House position was rejected, 9-6, by House conferees, with the three highest-ranking Republicans joining Democrats to defeat it.

With the deal finally in place, conferees concluded their work early that evening, prompting Livingston to declare, "We have satisfied as many people as we can." Of the bill's fate, he said, "We're going to pass it — with great difficulty — but we're going to pass it." But the ink was barely dry when the House GOP leadership backed away in the face of a barrage of criticism from conservatives. "If we have to reopen the conference, we will," said House Majority Whip Tom DeLay, R-Texas.

Complicating the situation, the White House was unhappy with the compromise because it would not let the tests proceed unfettered.

At a special meeting of House Republicans on Oct. 31, Goodling argued for a revised plan that would stop any trial runs from being conducted unless two-thirds of the nation's governors gave their approval. Goodling said he was not concerned with Clinton's reaction to his suggestion. "I don't think anything we do will satisfy the White House," he said

For Goodling, the biggest problem with the compromise was that, while it would bar Clinton from administering the tests, it would allow the tests to be developed and to undergo trial runs in fiscal 1998. Goodling said the administration had not planned to begin administering the tests until the spring of 1999, anyway. By then, he said, proponents would have built momentum and the program would have moved inexorably forward, probably with appropriators' support.

The appropriators warned that reopening the deal was dangerous. Obey said he would seek to open negotiations on the entire conference agreement if the testing issue was revisited. "The Republican leadership was with us two days ago and now they're off it," he said. "This Congress will not end until the Republican leadership learns to say no to a few rejectionist members."

But the appropriators saved their most pointed comments for members of their own party. Obey warned Clinton not to veto the bill over the testing issue. "I think this is a reasonable compromise," he said. "If this bill gets vetoed, I will support an override, and I will support eliminating all ability to develop tests." Similarly, Livingston urged Goodling to embrace the compromise, saying, "He ought not snatch defeat from the jaws of victory."

But the compromise also came under bipartisan attack in the Senate. John Ashcroft, R-Mo., said 37 GOP senators wanted a complete ban on national testing along the lines of the House position. Ashcroft called the compromise "a sorry capitulation to a president who wants to move power out of the hands of parents and school boards, and into the hands of Washington bureaucrats." Meanwhile, Jeff Bingaman, D-N.M., said 37 Democratic senators opposed the compromise because it would not let the tests be fully administered. He said they would support a veto. "If the issue is truly about local control," he said, "then let's let local school districts decide whether they want this test or not."

A Cease-Fire on Testing

After the initial testing compromise fell apart, further negotiations finally yielded a plan acceptable to most parties Nov. 7. Like the initial agreement, it gave the National Assessment Governing Board authority over the national tests. But — in what Goodling viewed as a key concession — the new agreement also prohibited any trial runs of the tests during fiscal 1998. In addition, it required the National Academy of Sciences to examine whether existing commercially available tests and state tests could be correlated and used as a substitute for a new national test. It set deadlines of June 15 for an interim report, and Sept. 1 for a final report.

Clinton and Goodling reached an agreement in principle on the compromise Nov. 5, though it took two more days to work out the deal. Clinton said he told Goodling his concern was to have "some sort of clearly accepted standard of excellence that all our children would be expected to meet in reading and math." Goodling said the key concession he won was to prohibit trial runs of the tests through September 1998. The administration had planned to begin the trial runs in March, in hopes that it would be able to fully administer the tests in 1999. "If you do that," Goodling said of the trial runs, "you've lost the battle." The best course, Goodling said, was for Congress to further address the testing issue when it reauthorized the assessment board in 1998. "The bill is in our court," he said.

To appease black and Hispanic critics, the agreement instructed the assessment board to determine whether the tests accounted for the needs of students who were disadvantaged, disabled or had limited proficiency in English. Rep. Maxine Waters, D-Calif., chairman of the Congressional Black Caucus, said caucus members wanted assurances that the tests could not be used to prevent students from being promoted if their scores did not measure up. They also wanted more resources devoted to schools in low-income neighborhoods that tested poorly. Rep. Xavier Becerra, D-Calif., said Hispanics believed the reading test should be offered in Spanish as well as in English.

Other Key Issues Resolved

Other controversies resolved in conference included the following:

- **Needle exchange.** Conferees agreed to ban the use of federal funds to establish needle exchanges for users of illegal drugs until March 31, 1998. After that date, sterile needles could be exchanged for used ones if the HHS secretary determined that "such programs are effective in preventing the spread of HIV and do not encourage the use of illegal drugs." The House initially sought to ban federal funding for needle exchange programs; the Senate would have permitted it under certain conditions.
- **Teamsters election.** Conferees accepted House language banning the Labor Department from using funds to pay the expenses of any election officer appointed by a court to oversee a new Teamsters election. The Senate bill would have allowed the Teamsters to take out a federal loan at customary interest rates if the president certified that the union could not afford to pay for the election rerun. The Clinton administration opposed both versions.
- **Education block grants.** The conferees dropped the controversial Senate proposal to give local school districts complete control over most federal elementary and secondary aid programs for one year. The House bill had no such provision, and House conferees rejected the Senate's position, 6-9. Clinton had threatened to veto the bill if it included the plan. "When we get a Republican president, we're going to do it," Livingston assured Gorton, the amendment's sponsor.
- **Comprehensive school reform.** The final bill provided for a new $150 million program — called "comprehensive school reform" — to help schools improve their performance. The House had approved $200 million for the program; the Senate had no comparable provision.
- **Education infrastructure.** The bill did not provide any money for a new initiative that would fund school building repairs and related improvements. The Senate agreed to spend $100 million for that purpose; the House bill included no such provision.
- **Goals 2000.** Conferees provided $491 million, the same as in fiscal 1997, for the school reform program. The Senate had agreed to $530 million; the House bill contained $387 million. Clinton had requested $620 million.
- **Special education.** The final bill included about $4.8 billion for programs for disabled students, $775 million more than in fiscal 1997. The Senate had agreed to nearly $5 billion; the House bill contained $4.4 billion.
- **NIH.** Conferees agreed to provide $13.6 billion for the NIH, a $907 million increase over fiscal 1997. The total was $142.5 million more than the House bill, but $45 million less than the Senate bill.
- **Student loan consolidation.** The final bill included legislation (HR 2535) to make it easier to consolidate direct student loans. The measure, passed separately by the House on Oct. 21, allowed students to consolidate their loans from the government through private lenders under the guaranteed student loan program. *(Student loans, p. 7-8)*
- **Tobacco credit repeal.** The final bill included the provision contained in both the House and Senate versions repealing the $50 billion tax break offered to the tobacco companies under the tax-reconciliation bill. ■

Legislative Funds Get Slim Increase

Under pressure to show self-discipline in its own spending, Congress agreed to operate with only a slight increase in funding for fiscal 1998. The $2.25 billion legislative branch appropriations bill, cleared Sept. 24, was a 2 percent increase over the $2.17 billion provided in fiscal 1997. President Clinton signed the bill into law Oct. 7 (HR 2209 — PL 105-55).

HR 2209 was one of only four fiscal 1998 spending bills to escape Clinton's line-item veto pen. Congress and the White House traditionally allowed each other to write their own budgets.

The legislative branch bill funded members' personal offices, Capitol buildings and adjacent office complexes and several legislative branch operations, including the Library of Congress, the Congressional Budget Office, the General Accounting Office (GAO), the Government Printing Office, the Capitol police and the Architect of the Capitol. It did not cover lawmakers' salaries or committees' budgets.

Although legislative branch funding represented only a tiny slice of the total federal budget, the bill became a lightning rod for political feuds — particularly in the House — some of them springing from spending items in the bill, others wholly unrelated.

For one thing, it served as a symbolic battleground for a band of fiscally conservative House Republicans, who saw it as a test of their leaders' commitment to shrinking government and an important signal to the American public of Congress' budget-cutting sincerity.

The group fought to freeze legislative branch spending at the fiscal 1997 level, saying they had won such a commitment from House Speaker Newt Gingrich, R-Ga., in exchange for their vote May 1 to increase funds for a number of House committees. The 11 rebellious Republicans had joined with Democrats to vote down an earlier version of the committee funding resolution in defiance of GOP leaders. *(Committee funds, p. 1-16)*

For their part, House Democrats used the bill to raise a host of thorny issues, from the disputed election of Loretta Sanchez, D-Calif., to a pending, $1.4 million study of union activities and a proposed $600,000 expansion of the Joint Committee on Taxation.

The legislation took on no such added meaning in the Senate, where a more generous version sailed through committee and floor action on workmanlike voice votes.

The two major disputes that cropped up in the bill were resolved in conference. House and Senate conferees scaled back a request by the tax-writing committees for a big boost in staffing for the Joint Committee on Taxation.

The other disagreement was over funding for the GAO, the investigatory arm of Congress. The House agreed to boost the agency's spending as a compromise with Senate appropriators who argued that the GAO had already been cut to the bone.

BOXSCORE

Fiscal 1998 Legislative Branch Appropriations — HR 2209 (S 1019). The $2.25 billion bill funded members' offices, congressional buildings and related agencies such as the General Accounting Office and the Congressional Budget Office.

Reports: H Rept 105-196, S Rept 105-47; conference report, H Rept 105-254.

KEY ACTION

July 16 — Senate passed S 1019 by voice vote.

July 28 — House passed HR 2209, 214-203.

July 29 — Senate, under a previous agreement, automatically passed HR 2209, after substituting text of S 1019.

Sept. 24 — House adopted the conference report on HR 2209, 309-106; **Senate** cleared the bill, 90-10.

Oct. 7 — President signed HR 2209 — PL 105-55.

House Appropriations Legislative Branch Subcommittee Chairman James T. Walsh, R-N.Y., stressed that although the bill was a slight increase over fiscal 1997, it was true to the principles adopted by Republicans when they swept to power in the 104th Congress and began their quest to halt the expansion of the federal government.

He noted that total spending in the bill was at or below the levels of the bills passed in 1994 and 1995. "So the downsizing program begun in the 104th Congress is still intact," Walsh said.

Congress had cleared a $2.37 billion fiscal 1995 legislative branch appropriations bill in 1994. Appropriators reduced that to $2.18 billion the following year, cutting it by another $20 million in fiscal 1997. *(1994 Almanac, p. 524; 1995 Almanac, p. 11-61.)*

House Committee Action

Hoping to mollify the GOP hardliners, the House Appropriations Legislative Branch Subcommittee recommended a slight decrease in spending for congressional operations for fiscal 1997. The draft bill, approved by voice vote June 24, recommended $1.71 billion, $9 million less than the comparable amount for the previous year. (The measure did not include appropriations for Senate operations, which were customarily added by that chamber.)

Walsh said the bill would provide $143 million less in spending than the president's budget request, and would cut 309 full-time positions. Since Republicans came to power in 1995, Congress has trimmed roughly 3,800 staff positions in the legislative branch, he said.

Walsh said the fiscal conservatives "got better than a freeze; they got a cut." "I think we are moving in the right direction," said Matt Salmon, R-Ariz., one of the 11 rebels. "We're being heard, and that's good."

Other provisions in the bill included:

➤ $47.4 million for the 2.8 percent cost of living pay increase provided for in Clinton's budget. The COLA did not apply to members of Congress.

➤ $1.5 million for the first phase of the rehabilitation of the leaky Capitol dome.

➤ Funding for 85 full-time positions at the GAO, which had been unfilled because of earlier budget cuts.

Lawmakers had already transferred $33.5 million for rehabilitation of the Botanic Garden Conservatory from the legislative branch appropriations bill to a supplemental appropriations bill providing relief to victims of Midwest flooding. That bill was passed by Congress and signed into law June 12. If that money had remained in the legislative bill, the subcommittee would have had to make offsetting cuts to show it was holding the line on spending.

Democrats objected to a proposal in the draft bill to boost the number of full-time employees at the Joint Committee on Taxation from 61 to 73. Subcommittee Republicans had included the extra salary money in deference to two influential committee chairmen — Bill Archer, R-Texas, of the House Ways and Means Committee and William V. Roth Jr., R-Del., of the Senate Finance Committee — who said they needed the expertise as they tried to rewrite U.S. tax law.

That was precisely why Democrats, led by David R. Obey of Wisconsin, the ranking member of the full House Appropriations Committee, objected. "I don't see why we should be funding these little empires," Obey told the subcommittee in criticism reminiscent of GOP complaints when Democrats controlled the House.

Full committee Chairman Robert L. Livingston, R-La, said the disagreement would have to be resolved by the House leadership before the bill reached the floor. With the rebel Republicans threatening to break away, Livingston assumed he would need Democratic votes on the floor, and that meant dealing with Obey's objections.

Legislative Branch Spending

(In millions of dollars; totals may not add due to rounding.)

	Clinton Request	House Bill	Senate Bill	Final Bill
Congressional Operations				
House of Representatives	$ 752.4	$ 708.7	$ 708.7	$ 708.7
Senate	487.9	—	460.6	461.1
Joint Items	92.3	86.8	91.9	86.7
Office of Compliance	2.6	2.5	2.6	2.5
Congressional Budget Office	25.0	24.8	25.0	24.8
Architect of the Capitol	173.9	111.0	167.5	164.7
Congressional Research Service	66.8	64.6	65.1	64.6
Government Printing Office (congressional printing and binding)	84.0	70.7	82.3	70.7
SUBTOTAL	**$ 1,684.9**	**$ 1,069.1**	**$ 1,603.8**	**$ 1,583.7**
Related Agencies				
Botanic Garden	$ 11.7	$ 1.8	$ 3.2	$ 3.0
Library of Congress (except CRS)	$ 290.4	$ 277.7	$ 286.2	$ 281.8
Architect of the Capitol (library buildings and grounds)	15.8	10.1	14.7	11.6
Government Printing Office (Superintendent of Documents)	30.5	29.3	29.1	29.1
General Accounting Office	361.4	323.5	346.8	339.5
SUBTOTAL	**$ 709.7**	**$ 642.3**	**$ 680.0**	**$ 665.0**
GRAND TOTAL	**$ 2,394.6**	**$ 1,711.4**	**$ 2,283.8**	**$ 2,248.7**

SOURCE: Senate Appropriations Committee

Full Committee Modifies Bill

The full Appropriations Committee fought for about two hours July 17 before voting 29-24 along party lines to approve the $1.7 billion bill (H Rept 105-196).

House Democrats used the measure as a platform to protest a nine-month-old investigation into California Republican Robert K. Dornan's claims of vote fraud in the 1996 election he lost to Sanchez. Democrats charged that the inquiry, conducted by a House Oversight Committee task force, had become a political witch hunt that unfairly targeted Hispanic voters in California's 46th District. *(Sanchez, p. 1-19)*

Steny H. Hoyer, D-Md., proposed reimbursing the Immigration and Naturalization Service for costs incurred by the investigation, but his amendment was rejected 24-29.

The committee rejected, 24-28, an attempt by Vic Fazio, D-Calif., to eliminate the proposed funding for 12 extra staff members at the Joint Committee on Taxation. Fazio claimed Joint Tax had swerved from its non-partisan roots to become an advocacy arm for House Ways and Means Committee Chairman Archer. Under pressure from Democrats, however, Republicans scaled back their plan, instead seeking money for five new committee aides.

Democrats also objected to Republican plans to disburse $1.4 million from a special congressional fund to pay for an investigation of labor union activity. The fund was established in 1996 to bolster the oversight role of House committees. *(Labor probe, p. 7-25)*

House Floor Action

The House passed the bill on a close, 214-203, vote July 28, with all but one Democrat— James A. Traficant Jr. of Ohio — voting no. Seven Republicans also voted against the bill: Tom Coburn of Oklahoma, John Ensign of Nevada, Rick Hill of Montana, Kenny Hulshof of Missouri, Ron Paul of Texas, Mark Sanford of South Carolina, and Linda Smith of Washington. *(Vote 335, p. H-102)*

Although Walsh had hoped for bipartisan support, Democrats were angry because the Rules Committee, controlled by the GOP leadership, had barred them from offering amendments challenging the Sanchez election investigation and the planned labor union probe. Democrats used their floor time to air these issues, and they announced their intent to oppose the bill.

The Democrats claimed one small victory: Fazio was allowed to offer an amendment to stop Republicans from adding five full-time aides to the Joint Tax staff. "Our precious committee resources should not be going to highly politicized staff operations that will merely be used to advance a partisan agenda," Fazio said.

Walsh noted that Republicans had already reduced the staff expansion from 12 to five positions in deference to objections from Democrats and a few cost-conscious Republicans. The amendment failed, 199-213, and the funding for the extra staff remained in the bill. *(Vote 332, p. H-102)*

Senate Action

While House appropriators were wrangling over various partisan issues, the Senate Appropriations Committee on July 15 approved its own version of the bill, 27-0, with only minimal debate. The measure (S 1019 — S Rept 105-47) provided $1.5 billion, nearly $52 million more than senators had approved the previous year. Most of the increase was aimed at giving staff members a cost of living adjustment.

The Senate approved the bill by voice vote July 16. Appropriations bills were supposed to start in the House, but

HR 2209 was still in committee. So the Senate agreed that whenever the House bill arrived, it would be considered passed with all but the provisions on the House's own budget replaced with the Senate's language. That occurred July 29.

Conference/Final Action

House and Senate conferees completed work on the measure Sept. 1, agreeing to appropriate $2.25 billion for legislative branch operations (H Rept 105-254).

Senate Legislative Branch Appropriations Subcommittee Chairman Robert F. Bennett, R-Utah, said the Senate version of the bill called for $71 million more in spending than the House version. As a compromise, the Senate agreed to come down $50 million and the House came up $21 million, he said. "I'm going to hear about that, quite frankly," said Walsh, speaking of his deficit hawks.

Most of the additional funds agreed to by House conferees to reach a deal with the Senate were for the GAO, which had been treated more generously by the Senate. The GAO got $339 million in the conference agreement, about $16 million more than in the House version.

The conference agreement provided $708.7 million for House operations, compared with $684 million in fiscal 1997. It provided $513 million for Senate operations, over the $481.5 million the Senate spent the previous year.

Although Democrats had earlier threatened to tie up the bill to call attention to their protests over the Sanchez and union inquiries, they dropped those issues in conference.

The conferees agreed to add two-and-a-half staff positions to the Joint Tax Committee, down from the 12 new staff members Republicans had initially requested, a number later reduced to five.

Final House, Senate Votes

The House adopted the conference agreement Sept. 24 by a vote of 309-106, with the support of 158 Republicans and 150 Democrats. The dozen or so lawmakers who had been clamoring for a freeze voted against the bill. The Senate cleared the bill the same day, 90-10. *(House vote 432, p. H-132; Senate vote 257, p. S-43)*

Even in the final debate, there were a few protests. In the House, Democrats led by George Miller of California, raised the issue of Congress' reluctance to take up campaign finance legislation. "Somehow we are able to deal with those provisions of law that deal with the paper clips, the pencils, the paper, the notebooks, and everything else," Miller said. "But what we are not able to deal with is the issue of how we fund our campaigns."

During brief discussion of the bill in the Senate, Republican John McCain of Arizona complained that while the appropriators had managed to avoid the wasteful spending he said was found in other spending measures, the bill nonetheless had some questionable items, including $100,000 to design a new subway from the Capitol to the Russell Senate Office building. ■

Construction Bill Tests Line-Item Veto

The fiscal 1998 spending bill for military construction faced little opposition, drew overwhelming support in both chambers and was the first of the 13 regular appropriations bills to be cleared by Congress. President Clinton signed it into law Sept. 30 (HR 2016 — PL 105-45), making it the only one of the 13 to be enacted before the start of the new fiscal year.

The low profile was typical of the annual military construction bill, which was devoted to construction and repair projects at military bases in almost all 50 states, including National Guard and Reserve installations.

But HR 2016 contained funding for a number of projects that had not been requested by the Pentagon. That, together with the fact that it was the first spending bill to arrive on the president's desk, earned it another first: It was the first fiscal 1998 appropriations bill to become a target for Clinton's newly acquired line-item veto powers. On Oct. 6, Clinton "cancelled" 38 individual items in the bill totaling $287 million.

Using procedures laid out in the line-item veto law, lawmakers attempted to restore all 38 projects by clearing a separate bill (HR 2631) disapproving the president's actions. Clinton, in turn, vetoed the disapproval bill. His action, on Nov. 13, did not leave time for an override attempt in the first session, but a successful override was expected when lawmakers returned in 1998.

BOXSCORE

Fiscal 1998 Military Construction Appropriations — HR 2016. The $9.2 billion bill included funding for family housing, construction at U.S. bases, base-closing costs and a share of NATO infrastructure costs.

Reports: H Rept 105-150, S Rept 105-52; conference report, H Rept 105-247.

KEY ACTION

July 8 — House passed HR 2016, 395-14.

July 22 — Senate passed HR 2016, amended, 98-2.

Sept. 16 — House adopted the conference report, 413-12.

Sept. 17 — Senate cleared the bill, 97-3.

Sept. 30 — President signed HR 2016 — PL 105-45.

Oct. 6 — President cancelled 38 projects in PL 105-45.

Nov. 8 — House passed disapproval bill (HR 2631), 352-64.

Nov. 9 — Senate cleared HR 2631 by voice vote.

Nov. 13 — President vetoed HR 2631.

Spending Bill Highlights

As cleared, the military construction bill provided $9.2 billion in fiscal 1998 for military infrastructure costs at home and abroad — $800 million more than the administration requested, but $610 million less than was appropriated for fiscal 1997. The bill paid for on-base housing for the nation's military forces, as well as for day care and medical centers. It also covered the U.S. share of NATO infrastructure investment and the costs associated with base closures, such as environmental cleanup.

- **Family housing.** The bill's largest single account was $3.9 billion for family housing, approximately $203 million more than Clinton wanted. Bill sponsors in both chambers consistently spoke of the need to improve the "quality of life" for soldiers and sailors in order to retain their services.
- **Military construction.** HR 2016 also funded non-NATO military construction projects to the tune of $3.2 billion, $554 million more than the administration requested. Within that account, National Guard and Reserves construction received $461 million, a jump of $288 million above the level sought by the Pentagon.
- **NATO.** The bill provided $153 million for NATO infrastructure, $23 million less than the president wanted.
- **Base closures.** Appropriators followed the administration's request in providing $2.1 billion for base-closure costs, bringing to $17.8 billion the total cost for base closing since the first commission met.

The bill never took more than 15 minutes to mark up at the subcommittee or committee levels, drew no germane amendments, and faced only scattered opposition from deficit hawks, such as Sen. John McCain, R-Ariz., who called for Clinton to use his line-item veto authority to trim unrequested spending.

In addition to the unrequested projects, the administration objected to the lack of full funding for a variety of its priorities, including NATO investment and strategic fuel-storage planning and construction. The White House also unsuccessfully sought language to accelerate its plans to privatize portions of the military housing stock.

House Committee

The bill began in the House Appropriations Military Construction Subcommittee, which approved it June 18 by voice vote. In an amiable markup that lasted barely 15 minutes, ranking subcommittee Democrat W.G. "Bill" Hefner of North Carolina praised Chairman Ron Packard, R-Calif., for "having done the best you could with what we have."

Much of the increase over Clinton's request came in the area of family housing and so-called quality-of-life improvements, such as day care centers and medical facilities, considered necessary to maintain morale among the all-volunteer forces. The subcommittee draft included $3.9 billion for family housing programs, $278 million more than the Pentagon requested.

"The bulk of the bill addresses quality-of-life issues," said panel member Steny H. Hoyer, D-Md. "Obviously there's no opposition to quality of life."

Many of those quality-of-life projects had been requested by members, rather than by the Pentagon, but Packard said they all had been previously authorized or included in the House version of the fiscal 1998 defense authorization bill (HR 1119 — H Rept 105-132).

The spending bill included $752 million for barracks, $110 million more than the Pentagon requested, in part to implement a new "1 plus 1" barracks arrangement in which two enlisted personnel would live in private quarters but share a bathroom.

The bill contained $3 billion for construction and repair of barracks, roads, utilities, hospitals, schools and day care centers, $500 million more than the administration request.

Appropriators included $2.1 billion for base closure costs, as requested.

The bill offered $166.3 million for the U.S. share of NATO

Military Construction Spending

(In thousands of dollars)

	Clinton Request	House Bill	Senate Bill	Conference Report
Military Construction				
Army	$595,277	$721,027	$652,046	$714,377
Navy	540,106	685,306	605,756	683,666
Air Force	495,782	662,305	662,305	701,855
Defense agencies	673,633	613,333	690,889	646,342
Barracks repairs	—	—	—	—
National Guard and Reserves	172,886	327,808	568,749	460,533
NATO infrastructure	176,300	166,300	152,600	152,600
Subtotal	$2,653,984	$3,176,079	$3,332,345	$3,359,373
Family Housing				
Army	1,291,937	1,351,068	1,317,037	1,337,868
Navy	1,255,437	1,385,682	1,339,123	1,370,336
Air Force	1,083,362	1,171,643	1,126,867	1,125,943
Defense agencies	37,674	37,674	37,674	37,674
Homeowners Assistance Fund	—	—	—	—
Housing Improvement Fund	—	—	—	—
Subtotal	$3,668,410	$3,946,067	$3,820,701	$3,871,821
Base Realignment and Closure				
Part II — 1991 round	116,754	116,754	116,754	116,754
Part III — 1993 round	768,702	768,702	768,702	768,702
Part IV — 1995 round	1,175,398	1,175,398	1,175,398	1,175,398
Total	**$8,383,248**	**$9,183,000**	**$9,213,900**	**$9,292,048**
Revised economic assumptions	—	—	–31,000	–108,800
GRAND TOTAL	**$8,383,248**	**$9,183,000**	**$9,182,900**	**$9,183,248**

SOURCE: House and Senate Appropriations committees.

infrastructure costs, $10 million below the administration request. It contained no funds for the enlargement of NATO or the Partnership for Peace, and it required notification of Congress prior to construction of any new overseas installations.

In its report, the committee renewed complaints about the military's "crumbling infrastructure." It warned that the Defense Department was acting, in effect, like a homeowner who waited until the roof caved in before making any repairs.

The report also directed the Army National Guard Bureau to take a more active role in setting priorities for Guard construction projects.

It directed the Army to report to Congress by Dec. 15 about its plans to build an Army history museum in Virginia. The House had voted to block funding for the museum in June 1995, but some members were worried that the Army was pursuing the project using non-appropriated funds. *(1995 Almanac, p. 11-66)*

Packard said the subcommittee draft contained no major policy changes.

Quick Endorsement by Full Committee

The full Appropriations Committee approved the bill by voice vote June 24 in a markup that lasted less than 10 minutes (H Rept 105-150). The $9.2 billion measure attracted no amendments and drew tributes rather than debate from committee members.

The White House was not as enthusiastic. In a letter to the committee the day before the markup, Franklin D. Raines, director of the White House's Office of Management and Budget (OMB), took exception to 94 projects in the bill that it said had not been requested.

In a time of declining spending, the military construction bill remained a place where lawmakers could reward their districts with earmarked spending. Raines complained that more than $200 million would go toward "low priority items that are not in [the Defense Department's] long-range plans."

The bill contained $107 million, including $27.7 million in unrequested projects, for the Camp Pendleton Marine Corps Base and Air Station in Packard's district — the most funding for any facility in the bill.

The Army's Fort Bragg, just outside the North Carolina district of ranking subcommittee Democrat Hefner, was slated to receive $39.4 million, $17.7 million of which was unrequested. Nearby Pope Air Force Base was to receive $20.7 million, $12.3 million of which was unrequested.

House Floor Action

The House passed the $9.2 billion spending measure July 8 by a lopsided vote of 395-14. *(Vote 250, p. H-80)*

Base closure decisions sparked the sharpest disagreement on the floor. Bill McCollum, R-Fla., offered an amendment to prevent the Navy's Nuclear Power Propulsion Training Center from moving from Orlando, Fla., to Charleston, S.C., as ordered by the 1995 commission.

McCollum argued that the costs of moving would outweigh any savings from closing the facility in his district in the near term. But Packard raised a point of order that McCollum was trying to legislate on a spending bill, and Packard was sustained.

With more than half the military's housing stock classified as aged or otherwise substandard, several House members sought to answer administration complaints about some of the bill's earmarked projects. They contended that improved housing, day care centers and medical facilities were necessary to retain military volunteers. "Improving quality of life for those who serve in the armed forces, and for their families, is critical," said John W. Olver, D-Mass.

Senate Committee

The Senate Appropriations Committee approved a slightly different version of the $9.2 billion bill July 17 (S Rept 105-52). The panel approved HR 2016 and two other appropriations bills en bloc by a vote of 28-0.

The Senate measure contained $100,000 less than the House version in new funding for fiscal 1998, but $800 million more than the Clinton administration requested. Among the major additions to the budget request were $393 million for reserve and National Guard facilities, $152 million for family housing, and $68 million for medical care facilities.

The committee cut $69 million from the combined total of $474 million requested by the administration for construction at specific sites overseas and the U.S. contribution to NATO's fund for infrastructure facilities such as pipelines.

In their report, Senate appropriators questioned the administration's decision to devote nearly a quarter of the military construction budget request to overseas projects, and instructed the Pentagon to lease or share facilities with host nations where possible.

The committee also instructed the Defense Department to report by Oct. 15 on the demand for new NATO infrastructure if Poland, Hungary and the Czech Republic joined the alliance.

The panel did not object to all new overseas facilities. It approved $37 million requested for storage facilities in the Persian Gulf state of Qatar for U.S. Army heavy equipment. The idea was that the brigade's U.S.-based personnel could be flown quickly to the scene in a crisis. But the committee proposed withholding $10 million of the amount until the Pentagon provided a progress report on reaching an agreement with Qatar to share the cost of the new facility, as that country's government had agreed to do.

In its report, the committee endorsed in principle the policy of making the air base at Aviano, Italy, near Venice, a hub of U.S. fighter plane strength for southern Europe. But it complained that the Air Force had not nailed down with the Italian government a long-term lease on the base, and ordered a report on progress toward that goal.

Senate Floor Action

The measure continued its nearly trouble-free course July 22, easily passing the Senate by a vote of 98-2. *(Vote 192, p. S-34)*

The White House objected to 103 unrequested projects in the Senate bill. Military Construction Appropriations Subcommittee Chairman Conrad Burns, R-Mont., and Patty Murray of Washington, the subcommittee's ranking Democrat, defended the projects as necessary for maintaining quality of life for soldiers and sailors and their families.

Spouses "overwhelmingly tell me how difficult it is to stay in service with a lack of day care centers, medical centers" and other facilities, Murray said. The measure would boost the budget request for medical facilities by $68 million, to $209 million.

But McCain attacked several unrequested projects, maintaining that the reason these "low-priority" items were being funded was to "provide economic benefit to certain states." After McCain spoke, Appropriations Chairman Ted Stevens, R-Alaska, could be heard chiding him on the floor in good-natured tones, saying that some of the spending McCain objected to was for Alaska. Among the items McCain questioned were $1.4 million for refrigeration at an ice skating rink and $300,000 for a car wash at Fort Wainwright, Alaska.

McCain and fellow Arizona Republican Jon Kyl were the only senators to oppose HR 2016.

The Senate bill recommended $71 million less than the House version for active-duty military construction and $125 million less for family housing. The Senate, though, wanted to spend $569 million — $241 million more than the House — on National Guard and Reserve construction. "Let's face it. The regular service structure is downsizing," Burns said. "They're moving more to the Guard, and we have to have the buildings in place."

Conference/Final Action

House and Senate appropriators took less than 10 minutes on Sept. 9 to reconcile their differences on the military construction bill. "I am not aware of anyone at this point who is unhappy with the bill," said Packard.

The bottom lines of the House and Senate versions of HR 2016 differed by only $100,000. But conferees had to reconcile about 200 differing projects that would have cost a combined $1.6 billion, according to Packard. The House and Senate appropriators essentially split the difference when it came to totaling the major funding accounts.

The final version (H Rept 105-247) contained $3.9 billion in new funding for family housing accounts, including day care centers and medical facilities — about $74 million less than the House version, but some $51 million more than the Senate's.

National Guard and Reserve construction accounts got $460 million, about $132 million more than the House would have provided but $109 million less than the Senate wanted. The overall amount provided for military construction was $3.2 billion, about $31 million more than sought by the House and $125 million below the Senate's version.

The conference report included $2.1 billion for costs associated with base closures and realignments, as both the House and Senate agreed. But Burns used the conference as an occasion to offer a warning about the Pentagon's desire for two more rounds of base closures.

"We have spent much more money on environmental cleanup than was estimated or expected," Burns said. "Before we start another BRAC [Base Realignment and Closure Commission], we ought to reassess our environmental cleanup and how that impacts the rest of our military construction."

Final House, Senate Approval

The military construction bill became the first of the fiscal 1998 spending measures to be cleared for the president. The House adopted the conference report Sept. 16 by a lopsided vote of 413-12. The Senate cleared by the bill the next day, 97-3. *(House vote 394, p. H-120; Senate vote 240, p. S-41)*

Line-Item Veto

Declaring that "the old rules have, in fact, changed," Clinton on Oct. 6 used his powers under the 1996 line-item veto law (PL 104-130) to strike 38 military construction projects totaling $287 million from the bill. Among the excised projects were a $7.7 million ammunition supply and oil facility at Fort Bliss, Texas, and a $6.9 million launch pad renovation at the White Sands Missile Range in New Mexico. *(Vetoed projects, p. 9-64; line-item veto, p. 2-63)*

Clinton avoided picking and choosing from among political friends and enemies, simply signing one of several option papers presented by OMB analysts. Clinton loyalists such as Hoyer and Senate Minority Leader Tom Daschle, D-S.D., felt the lash of the vetoes, as did several senior appropriators such as Sen. Robert C. Byrd, D-W.Va., Rep. John P. Murtha, D-Pa., and Sen. Pete V. Domenici, R-N.M.

Clinton said he had made "tough calls involving real money and hard choices," but he pointedly did not describe the projects as wasteful or unnecessary. For one thing, 32 of the 38 projects he struck down were included in long-range Pentagon plans. He said he struck projects that met three criteria: They were not requested in his fiscal 1998 budget; there had not been enough design work done on them to ensure that construction could begin in 1998; and they would not "substantially improve the quality of life of military service members and their families." *(Text, p. D-43)*

The vetoes set off a furor in Congress. Members were genuinely stunned to find military construction projects in

Vetoed Provisions

The following are the 38 projects that President Clinton struck from the fiscal 1998 military construction appropriations bill (PL 105-45), beginning with the eight most expensive ($10 million and above):

Most Expensive Projects

● **Norfolk Naval Shipyard, Portsmouth, Va.** $19.9 million to speed up refurbishment work due to begin after the turn of the century, including construction of a new high-tech maintenance wharf large enough to hold two *Arleigh-Burke* class destroyers.

● **Mayport Naval Station near Jacksonville, Fla.** $17.9 million for dredging work and pier improvements to make way for eight destroyers expected to make Mayport their home port by fiscal year 2000.

● **Fort Carson Rail Yard, Fort Carson, Colo.** $16 million for the first phase of an upgrade that included building a state-of-the-art trackside warehouse at the World War II-era rail yard.

● **Dyess Air Force Base, Abilene, Texas.** $10 million to start building a new operations facility for the 13th Bomb Squadron, an 800-member B-1B squadron scheduled to be moved to Dyess in 2000.

● **Camp Williams, Utah.** $12.7 million to build facilities for an Army Reserve maintenance shop that was moving from its existing location at Fort Douglas, in Salt Lake City, to Camp Williams in order to make room for part of the Olympic Village slated for construction for the 2002 Salt Lake winter games.

● **Coronado Naval Amphibious Base, San Diego.** $10.1 million for two new buildings for the EOD (Explosive Ordnance Disposal) Unit at Coronado, which was working out of nine crumbling buildings that did not conform to current fire and safety codes.

● **Kirtland Air Force Base, Albuquerque, N.M.** $14 million to replace a 1950s-era building that housed the Theater Air Command and Control Simulation Facility (TACCSF) — one of the military's most advanced combat simulators, which allowed missile crews, pilots, and command and control personnel to practice real world combat situations.

● **Johnstown, Pa.** $14 million to build a new training center and hangar to replace cramped and dilapidated quarters used by an air reserve unit, Marine Wing Support Squadron 474.

Other Canceled Projects

● **California: Fort Irwin.** $2.7 million for a new helicopter landing pad and radio relay rooms for the Live Fire Command and Control Facility.

● **California: Fort Irwin.** $8.5 million for a 24-bay wash facility for wheeled and tracked vehicles.

● **California: Marine Corps Reserve Center, Pasadena.** $6.7 million to demolish an old reserve center and build a new one for the 4th Light Anti-Air Defense Battalion.

● **Florida: Whiting Field.** $1.3 million to extend one runway and clear land for another to accommodate Beech MKII training aircraft due to arrive in fiscal 2002.

● **Georgia: Moody Air Force Base.** $6.8 million to build new support facilities for combat search and rescue and pararescue training operations relocating from Patrick Air Force Base in Florida.

● **Hawaii: Fort Derussey.** $9.5 million to provide new space for the Asian Pacific Center, which educated military and civilian officials on Asian-Pacific security issues.

● **Idaho: Mountain Home Air Force Base.** $9.2 million to build a new B-1B aviation electronics test and repair shop for the Air Expeditionary Wing.

● **Idaho: Mountain Home Air Force Base.** $3.8 million to build a new facility for planning, and to brief and critique combat crews at the F-15C Squadron Operations Facility.

● **Indiana: Crane Naval Surface Warfare Center.** $4.1 million for a new support facility for chemical and biological warfare detection devices aboard ships.

● **Indiana: Grissom Air Reserve Base.** $8.9 million to build a new civil engineer complex, which would include maintenance shops, storage and a roads and grounds facility.

● **Kansas: McConnell Air Force Base.** $2.9 million to build a transportation complex to include vehicle operations and parking facilities.

● **Kentucky: Fort Campbell.** $9.9 million for a vehicle maintenance shop and storage for a forward support battalion and a combat support hospital.

● **Kentucky: Fort Knox.** $7.2 million to modify a rifle range to new standards, with 28 firing lanes.

● **Maryland: St. Inigoes Naval Electronic Systems Engineering Activity.** $2.6 million to build more hangar space for maintenance of unmanned aircraft.

● **Montana: Malmstrom Air Force Base.** $4.5 million to update kitchen facilities and add storage space for the airmen's dining facility.

● **Nevada: Nellis Air Force Base.** $2.0 million to build a larger facility to inspect, assemble and test explosive munitions used by training aircraft.

● **New Mexico: White Sands Missile Range.** $6.9 million to repair launch facilities for the Patriot, Stinger, Chaparral and HAWK missiles, and for the Multiple Launch Rocket System and Army Tactical Missile Systems.

● **New York: Fort Drum.** $9.0 million to replace existing aerial target ranges.

● **New York: Niagara Falls International Airport.** $2.1 million to replace two older buildings that housed a readiness office and combat arms training.

● **North Carolina: Fort Bragg.** $7.9 million to construct part of a training complex for military operations in urban terrain, with 32 buildings, streets, parking and a bridge.

● **Pennsylvania: U.S. Army Reserve Center, Oakdale.** $6.0 million to build a new facility for training in communications security and medical systems.

● **South Carolina: Leesburg Training Site, Eastover.** $3.8 million to replace a 4,200-square-foot battle simulation center with a new one 11 times as large.

● **South Dakota: Rapid City.** $5.2 million to provide new support facilities for UH-1 and C-12 aircraft, used by the 1085th Medical Air Ambulance Company, including a hangar, classroom and maintenance facilities.

● **Tennessee: Arnold Air Force Base.** $9.9 million to replace an old air dryer facility and support another testing facility for the new F-22 and Joint Strike Fighter.

● **Texas: Fort Bliss.** $7.7 million to expand areas for ammunition and other storage, and to build an oil dispensing facility.

● **Texas: Laughlin Air Force Base.** $4.8 million to build new facilities for painting T-1A, T-37 and T-38 aircraft.

● **Virginia: Norfolk Naval Air Station.** $4.0 million to build a new air traffic control facility and radar tower.

● **Virginia: Yorktown Naval Weapons Station.** $3.3 million to build an earth-covered storage facility for Tomahawk missiles.

● **West Virginia: Camp Dawson.** $6.8 million to expand facilities including administrative, training, exercise and storage space for several Army National Guard units.

● **Wisconsin: Mitchell Air Reserve Station, Milwaukee.** $4.2 million to replace an older, smaller aerial port training facility. ■

their districts on the chopping block. Lawmakers also hoped to discourage the White House from making wide use of the line-item veto on other spending bills — particularly those for the Pentagon and for energy and water development, both of which were packed with unrequested congressional pet projects.

Among the most common complaints was the lack of advance notification, which would have allowed members to fight for cherished projects. "I was stunned," said Democratic Sen. Bob Graham of Florida, who watched his state lose two projects. "They didn't handle it right."

OMB subsequently acknowledged that some of the vetoes had been based on erroneous information. One of the criteria used for recommending projects for the veto list was the extent to which design work had been completed, to ensure that ground could actually be broken for the projects during fiscal 1998. The Army and the Air Force conceded mistakes on the status of numerous projects. For example, the Army reported that no design work had been done on a Fort Campbell, Ky., project, when in fact the design was 90 percent completed.

"I want to state up front that, unfortunately, some of the information we provided leading up to the veto was incorrect," Air Force Major Gen. George T. Stringer told the National Security Committee in a statement Oct. 22.

For their part, those involved in crafting the military construction bill insisted they had only included projects that met certain tests, such as being included in the annual defense authorization bill and being construction-ready by the end of the fiscal year. "We had scrubbed that bill probably better than any we had ever had, and the things that they said weren't ready to go, that just wasn't the case," said Hefner.

Longtime appropriators also asked what was so sacrosanct about the president's budget. "If any president assumes that an interpretation of the line-item veto is that only the president's projects are clearly good enough to spend money on, then I tell you we have a real war going," Domenici said.

Disapproval Bill Cleared, Vetoed

In a bipartisan show of support, the Senate Appropriations Committee voted, 25-2, on Oct. 23 to restore 34 of the 38 vetoed projects. By then, the White House had acknowledged making mistakes and was offering to negotiate a solution, but Chairman Stevens proceeded with the markup, saying no deal had been reached.

On Oct. 30, the Senate passed a revised version of the bill (S 1292) that aimed to restore 36 of the 38 vetoed projects. The vote was 69-30, giving sponsors a three-vote cushion over the two-thirds majority needed to override the president's promised veto. *(Vote 287, p. S-49)*

Sen. Charles S. Robb, D-Va., said he opposed the disapproval bill because passage would undermine the line-item veto law. "What credibility can supporters of the line-item veto authority have if we disapprove vetoes on the first appropriations bill right out of the gate?" he asked.

But supporters of the disapproval measure argued that it was in keeping with the spirit of the line-item veto law. Stevens, who sponsored the override attempt, went so far as to threaten that he would offer legislation to repeal the line-item veto if his bill failed to pass.

"I think this is exactly how the process is supposed to work," said Kay Bailey Hutchison, R-Texas. "Congress did not take away its right to disagree with the president."

The day of the Senate vote, the White House acknowledged it had used erroneous data as the basis for vetoing 18 of the 38 projects. Administration officials refused to say which items had been canceled in error, but the White House reiterated its offer to work with Congress on restoring the vetoed projects.

On Nov. 8, the House voted 352-64 in favor of a bill (HR 2631) to overturn all 38 of the line-item vetoes. To avoid convening a House-Senate conference to reconcile the differences, the Senate cleared the House bill by voice vote Nov. 9. *(House vote 617, p. H-184)*

"Make way for liberty!" crowed Byrd, who had led the fight against granting the president line-item veto power in 1996.

On Nov. 13, Clinton vetoed the disapproval bill, insisting the cancelled projects "would not substantially improve the quality of life of military service members and their families." With the session winding to a close, members did not have time to attempt an override, but the veto-proof majorities for the bill in both chambers indicated that an override attempt in the second session would be successful. ■

Highways Receive Record Funding

The fiscal 1998 transportation spending bill (HR 2169), cleared Oct. 9, provided record amounts for highways, highway safety, and transit.

Total spending was set at $42.2 billion, up from the fiscal 1997 level of $38.1 billion and the president's request of $40.2 billion. Virtually all transportation programs received substantial spending increases, particularly highways, which got $23.3 billion. Funding was also increased for the Coast Guard, the Federal Aviation Administration (FAA), mass transit, and highway safety programs.

One of the few programs that lost funding was Amtrak, the federally owned passenger rail corporation, which was cut by 8 percent (about $45 million). Appropriators assumed that additional funding would be available to Amtrak under the tax-reconciliation bill (PL 105-34), which included up to $2.3 billion over two years for the financially troubled railroad, pending the enactment of Amtrak reform legislation.

President Clinton signed the transportation bill into law Oct. 27 (PL 105-66). On Nov. 1, he used his line-item veto power to cancel three projects worth a total of $6.2 million. The vetoed projects comprised a railroad dock improvement project in Alaska, an emergency preparedness and response center in Alabama, and an electronic bulletin board for surplus transit equipment in Georgia.

The bill's ride through Congress was supposed to have been a smooth one. Transportation spending for fiscal 1998 was closely tied to a drive to reauthorize the nation's pre-eminent transportation law, the Intermodal Surface Transportation Efficiency Act (ISTEA). Both chambers felt pressure from the authorizers to be generous with highway funding, and both bodies heeded the call, producing similarly generous bills with similar priorities.

But behind the scenes, Richard C. Shelby, R-Ala., in his first year as chairman of the Senate Appropriations Subcommittee on Transportation, was quietly sowing the seeds of what would become one of the thorniest controversies of the appropriations season. Two provisions — slipped in largely to help his home state — nearly brought down the bill.

The first skewed bus subsidies heavily toward Alabama, infuriating House Transportation Appropriations Subcommittee Chairman Frank R. Wolf, R-Va., who called it "raw pork." The second challenged an 18-year-old statute that restricted access to Dallas' Love Field airport and thus limited competition to the much larger Dallas-Fort Worth airport. The change was also expected to result in lower air fares for Alabama.

The Dallas proposal angered Texas' two Republican senators, divided the state's delegation in the House, reopened old wounds in Dallas and Fort Worth, and challenged powerful American Airlines. But Shelby stood his ground, and in the end, House and Senate conferees broke a months-long stalemate by largely giving in to his demands.

BOXSCORE

Fiscal 1998 Transportation Appropriations — HR 2169 (S 1048). The $42.2 billion bill provided $13.1 billion in new budget authority and $29.1 billion in trust fund spending. It covered highway, mass transit, rail, aviation and other programs, as well as the Coast Guard.

Reports: H Rept 105-188, S Rept 105-55; conference report, H Rept 105-313.

KEY ACTION

July 23 — House passed HR 2169, 424-5.

July 30 — Senate passed HR 2169, 98-1, after substituting the text of S 1048.

Oct. 9 — House adopted the conference report, 401-21. **Senate** cleared HR 2169 by voice vote.

Oct. 27 — President signed HR 2169 — PL 105-66.

Nov. 1 — President used the line-item veto to delete provisions from PL 105-66.

House Subcommittee

Work on the bill began in the House Transportation Appropriations Subcommittee, which gave voice vote approval June 24 to a $42.5 billion version. The measure was almost equally generous to highway, aviation, rail and public transportation programs. Even members who were pushing for substantial increases in transportation spending expressed surprise at the figures that emerged from the subcommittee.

Highway programs, the biggest part of the bill, stood to gain the most. Spending for core highway programs — construction and repair of the interstate highway system and other primary and secondary roads and bridges — would increase by nearly 20 percent over fiscal 1997 levels, to $21.5 billion.

The proposed increase was fueled in part by early congressional skirmishing over efforts to reauthorize ISTEA. To placate states and regions that were fighting over access to federal highway money, House Transportation and Infrastructure Committee Chairman Bud Shuster, R-Pa., was insisting on massive spending increases. *(Highway bill, p. 3-18)*

Shuster provided a glimpse of the widespread House support for his position — and sent a signal to appropriators — May 21, when he nearly succeeded in adding billions of dollars more for infrastructure to the fiscal 1998 budget resolution (H Con Res 84). His amendment failed 214-216. *(Vote 147, p. H-48)*

"People respond to pressure," said a committee aide of the fiscal 1998 highway funding level offered by the appropriations subcommittee. "They saw the support for transportation funding in those budget votes."

Subcommittee chairman Wolf emphasized, however, that the bill steered clear of any policy language that might conflict with reauthorization efforts. "There are no major policy changes or time bombs," he said. "For surface transportation programs . . . the bill assumes current law and does not presuppose or judge the reauthorization."

Other transportation programs were also in line to benefit from the subcommittee's largess. Mass transit programs were slated to receive $4.8 billion, an increase of $456 million over fiscal 1997; the FAA got a $769 million funding increase, to $9.1 billion; and the Coast Guard got $3.9 billion, about $105 million above the fiscal 1997 level.

Wolf made it clear that his first priority was transportation safety. The subcommittee bill included funds for 500 additional air traffic controllers and 326 additional FAA staff members responsible for safety certification and regulation. In addition, $35 million was designated for training air traffic controllers and safety inspectors, and $153 million went toward 18 air safety initiatives, including airport security devices, alert systems to prevent runway collisions, and new

Fiscal 1998 Transportation Spending

(in thousands of dollars)

	Fiscal 1997 Appropriation	Fiscal 1998 Clinton Request	House Bill	Senate Bill	Conference Report
Transportation Department					
Office of the Secretary	$193,787	$ 83,085	$ 74,783	$ 81,477	$ 75,774
Payments to air carriers (from trust fund)	*25,900*	*0*	*0*	*0*	*0*
Coast Guard					
Operating expenses	2,321,325	2,440,000	2,408,000	2,435,400	2,415,400
Acquisition, construction, improvements	374,840	370,000	370,000	403,300	388,850
Retired pay	617,284	645,696	645,696	653,196	653,196
Other	163,090	455,000	458,000	167,535	459,000
Subtotal, Coast Guard	**$ 3,476,539**	**$ 3,910,696**	**$ 3,881,696**	**$ 3,659,431**	**$ 3,916,446**
Federal Aviation Administration					
Operations and offsetting collections	4,850,500	5,036,100	5,300,000	5,325,900	5,301,934
User fees appropriation	0	300,000	0	0	0
Facilities and equipment	1,793,500	1,875,000	1,875,000	1,889,005	1,875,477
Research, engineering, development	187,412	200,000	185,000	214,250	199,183
Airport and Airway Trust Fund limit	*1,460,000*	*1,000,000*	*1,700,000*	*1,700,000*	*1,700,000*
Subtotal, FAA	**$ 6,831,412**	**$ 7,411,100**	**$ 7,360,000**	**$ 7,429,155**	**$ 7,376,594**
Federal Highway Administration					
Direct spending	150,000	250,000	0	308,000	300,000
Highway Trust Fund limit	*18,773,036*	*20,270,000*	*21,585,325*	*21,884,300*	*21,584,825*
Trust fund exempt obligations	*2,024,410*	*1,510,571*	*1,660,226*	*1,390,600*	*1,390,570*
National Highway Traffic Safety Administration					
Direct spending	135,612	147,500	146,907	146,500	146,962
NHTSA Highway Trust Fund limit	*168,100*	*185,500*	*186,500*	*187,000*	*186,500*
Federal Railroad Administration					
Amtrak grants	587,950	789,450	543,000	344,000	543,000
Northeast Corridor improvement	175,000	0	250,000	273,450	250,000
Other	268,683	128,859	125,834	154,773	143,790
Subtotal, railroads	**$ 1,031,633**	**$ 918,309**	**$ 918,834**	**$ 772,223**	**$ 936,790**
Federal Transit Administration					
Formula grants					
Direct spending	490,000	0	290,000	190,000	240,000
Trust Fund grants and limit	*2,059,185*	*3,498,500*	*2,410,000*	*2,210,000*	*2,410,000*
Discretionary grants trust fund limit	*1,900,000*	*0*	*2,000,000*	*2,008,000*	*2,000,000*
Other	332,997	338,818	337,738	284,747	343,738
Subtotal, transit	**$ 822,997**	**$ 338,818**	**$ 627,738**	**$ 474,747**	**$ 583,738**
Emergency and other spending	1,060,155	44,179	101,673	110,850	124,003
Rescissions	–1,719,033	–38,600	0	–228,600	–450,600
TOTAL, Transportation Department	**$ 11,983,102**	**$ 13,065,087**	**$ 13,111,631**	**$ 12,753,783**	**$ 13,009,707**
Related Agencies, Commissions					
National Transportation Safety Board	42,407	47,000	47,000	50,700	49,371
Emergency spending	36,859	0	0	0	0
Other	5,940	3,640	3,640	3,640	3,640
GRAND TOTAL	**$ 12,068,308**	**$ 13,115,727**	**$ 13,162,271**	**$ 12,808,123**	**$ 13,062,718**
Total limitations and exempt obligations	*$ 26,010,631*	*$ 27,114,571*	*$ 29,342,051*	*$ 29,379,900*	*$ 29,121,895*

SOURCE: House Appropriations Committee

runway lighting systems. The National Highway Traffic Safety Administration was slated to receive $333 million, a 10 percent increase over fiscal 1997 levels.

Even Amtrak, a longtime GOP target, received a modest $30 million increase in federal funding over fiscal 1997, bringing its total to $793 million. However, most of the additional funds were reserved for improvements to Amtrak's Northeast Corridor. While appropriations for Amtrak capital expenditures would increase by $36.6 million over fiscal 1997, operating assistance would be cut by $81.5 million.

An attempt by Sonny Callahan, R-Ala., to eliminate the Amtrak money was rejected by voice vote.

Given traditional Republican antipathy to Amtrak, rail boosters were relatively pleased with the outcome. "They were significantly more supportive than they were last year," said Ross Capon, executive director of the National Association of Railroad Passengers. "When you couple that with the positive comments members from both sides of the aisle made [at the markup], this has got to be regarded as positive for Amtrak."

Amtrak supporters did express concern, however, that the total might not be enough to stave off the railroad's looming insolvency.

The bill also included a provision calling for an independent commission, patterned after the military base realignment and closure commission, to examine Amtrak's economic problems and recommend train routes to close or restructure — with the commission's recommendations to be approved or rejected in their totality. The railway had been forced for years to continue unprofitable, long-distance routes by members of Congress eager to maintain rail service to their districts and states.

Overall, the spending cuts the subcommittee included in the bill were generally for administrative offices within the Transportation Department, including total cuts of $145 million from administrative accounts of the Federal Highway Administration, Federal Transit Administration, FAA, and the Transportation secretary. The bill contained no money for special highway demonstration projects, long derided by critics as "pork barrel" spending.

Besides the failed attempt to strip Amtrak funding, the only other amendment voted on at the markup was one by Harold Rogers, R-Ky., who sought to double to 12 the number of radar systems funded by the bill for Coast Guard C-130 transport planes patrolling the Caribbean in search of drug smugglers. The amendment was defeated, 4-9.

House Full Committee

The full Appropriations Committee approved the fiscal 1998 transportation spending bill July 11 by voice vote (H Rept 105-188).

The measure prompted relatively little debate among committee members, who welcomed the proposed increases for highway, aviation, rail and public transportation programs. Only minor changes were made to the subcommittee draft as part of a manager's amendment by Wolf.

Democrats complimented Wolf for his efforts in devising a bipartisan bill, though they raised some concerns. Martin Olav Sabo of Minnesota, the subcommittee's ranking Democrat, noted that while the $200 million proposed for transit operating assistance grants was $200 million more than the administration had proposed, it was still $200 million less than existing funding. "I wish we could do more," he said.

Sabo also expressed disappointment with the Amtrak funding. David R. Obey of Wisconsin, the full committee's ranking Democrat, also expressed concern about Amtrak's operating expenses. But he was more upset with the FAA, citing what he said was the agency's "arrogance" in not responding to concerns of members of Congress. Obey indicated that he was considering offering on the House floor an amendment to reduce the agency's administrative account.

House Floor Action

After a brief debate, the House easily passed the $42.5 billion bill July 23 by a vote of 424-5. *(Vote 302, p. H-94)*

"This is not a perfect bill, but it is about as perfect as we can get it. If it were perfect, it would have some of the 15 things I requested," quipped Callahan.

What friction existed focused on Amtrak. Maryland Democrat Benjamin L. Cardin and other Amtrak supporters warned that the $283 million proposed for Amtrak operations — $61 million below Clinton's request — could force Amtrak to go bankrupt in 1998.

On a point of order, Transportation and Infrastructure Committee Chairman Shuster struck from the bill Wolf's proposal for a commission to recommend Amtrak routes that should be shut down. Shuster argued that the provisions amounted to legislating on an appropriations bill, adding that Amtrak needed fundamental change immediately and could not wait for a commission. He indicated that his committee was planning the following week to mark up a bill that would overhaul Amtrak operations more quickly, and said that he could not go along with Wolf's idea, noting that "the base-closure commission left a bad taste in a lot of mouths around here." *(Amtrak overhaul, p. 3-22)*

Never shy to use his clout on transportation issues, Shuster left his marks all over the House bill. He also raised points of order against — and thereby struck from the bill — provisions that would have:

➤ Rescinded $38.6 million in previously approved contract authority for the program that subsidized passenger air service to rural areas.

➤ Limited the communities for which air service subsidies could be provided.

➤ Provided a greater share of funding for FAA operations from the Airport and Airway Trust Fund, rather than from the general Treasury.

Senate Committee

On July 15, the Senate Appropriations Subcommittee on Transportation approved a version of the bill, subsequently introduced as S 1048, that called for even more highway funding than the House — a record $23.6 billion for fiscal 1998.

Like the House bill, the Senate draft reflected pressure from lawmakers eager to increase highway funding as they prepared to take up the ISTEA reauthorization later in the year. "Twenty-three [billion dollars in the Senate bill] is better than 21 [billion for core highway programs in the House]," said Shuster, who wanted to authorize $32 billion a year for highways. "I'm more pleased than I was, but I'm less pleased than I'd like to be."

Overall, the subcommittee's draft was generally compatible with the House bill. It proposed spending a total of $41.8 billion for transportation programs. In addition to the highway funds, the total included $9.1 billion for the FAA (equal to the House bill), and $333.5 million for the National Highway Traffic Safety Administration ($100,000 more than the House bill). Coast Guard funding was set at $3.7 billion ($200 million less than the House bill).

Breaking with tradition, Shelby marked his first year chairing the subcommittee by refusing to allocate money for "highway demonstration projects." In recent years, the House had refused to fund such projects, while the Senate continued to do so and usually prevailed in conference. Shelby sounded less than certain that the Senate ultimately would forgo such projects, however, saying repeatedly they were not in the bill "yet."

The one element of controversy during the subcommittee markup involved Amtrak operating assistance, for which Shelby had included $190 million — a severe cut from the fiscal 1997 level of $364.5 million. Amtrak had requested $387 million in operating assistance for fiscal 1998, and the House bill included $283 million. Pressure from rail supporters, especially those from the Northeast, spurred Shelby to increase funding to the House level.

That was not enough, however, for Frank R. Lautenberg of New Jersey, the panel's ranking Democrat, or for the Clinton administration. "If we shortchange the operating subsidy [for Amtrak], we are saying, 'Be prepared to shut the doors,'" Lautenberg said, referring to the railroad's chronic financial problems. In a letter to House Appropriations Chairman Livingston, Office of Management and Budget (OMB) Director Franklin D. Raines said $283 million would fall $61 million short of the amount needed to keep the trains running in fiscal 1998.

But Shelby noted that the Amtrak issue could become moot once the tax-reconciliation bill was finalized. The Senate version of the tax bill proposed setting up an Amtrak trust fund using a half cent from the existing federal gas tax, which could yield up to $650 million a year for Amtrak. (That provision was later dropped in conference.)

Shelby did not include Wolf's proposal to set up a commission on closing unprofitable train routes. Indeed, much of the pressure to continue such routes had been exerted by senators.

Full Committee Boosts Amtrak Funds

The Senate Appropriations Committee easily approved the bill July 22 by a vote of 28-0 (S Rept 105-55).

During the markup, a full-court press by Amtrak supporter succeeded in increasing operating assistance for the railroad to $344 million, the level requested by Clinton. The amendment, offered by Lautenberg, added $61 million to the subcommittee bill. It was approved by voice vote.

The committee also adopted several other amendments, none of which raised any objections. One, offered by Shelby, would later almost derail the measure in conference with the House. Adopted by voice vote, it proposed to modify restrictions on the types of aircraft that could operate to and from Love Field airfield in Dallas, Texas, to allow certain larger aircraft to use the airport.

Senate Floor Action

To bipartisan applause, the Senate easily passed a $42.2 billion version of the bill (HR 2169) July 30 by a vote of 98-1. Several non-controversial amendments were adopted by voice vote, and senators had little but praise for the measure. Before passage, the Senate substituted the text of its own bill. *(Vote 208, p. S-36)*

Lautenberg called the bill "the culmination of a very long and arduous effort to re-establish transportation" as a federal budget priority.

William V. Roth Jr., R-Del., an ardent passenger-rail supporter, cast the only "no" vote. Roth objected to the lack of funding for Amtrak capital expenditures. Instead, the measure relied on up to $2.3 billion in capital subsidies that Roth, as chairman of the Senate Finance Committee, had included in the reconciliation package. The money was to be released upon the enactment of unspecified Amtrak management reforms. *(Tax-reconciliation bill, p. 2-30)*

There were no attempts on the floor to insert pet highway "demonstration projects" in the bill.

Conference/Final Action

House and Senate negotiators reached a compromise on the bill Oct. 7 (H Rept 105-313), but only after breaking a logjam over provisions inserted by Shelby to help his state of Alabama. Both chambers adopted the conference report Oct. 9 — the House by a vote of 401-21, and the Senate later that day by voice vote. *(House vote 510, p. H-154)*

The conference report provided a total of $42.2 billion for transportation programs in fiscal 1998 — slightly less than both the House and Senate versions, but almost $5.1 billion more than fiscal 1997 spending, and $2 billion more than requested by the president. Of the total, $13.5 billion was in the form of direct appropriations, and $29.1 billion was to be provided from the aviation and highway trust funds. The measure also rescinded about $451 million in previously appropriated transportation funding.

The agreement significantly increased spending for almost all transportation programs. The $23.3 billion included for highways was an increase of $2.3 billion over fiscal 1997 levels and $1.2 billion more than requested.

No money was set aside for highway "demonstration" projects, although the bill did appropriate an additional $300 million to be used by the Appalachian Regional Commission towards completion of the Appalachian regional highway system. Funding for the program was usually included in the energy and water appropriations bill, and the fiscal 1998 energy and water measure (HR 2203) included $103 million for such highway work.

Major features of the bill included:

- **Amtrak.** $543 million for Amtrak, a cut of $45 million from fiscal 1997, but equal to the House-approved level. The report assumed that additional capital funding would be provided under the tax-reconciliation act once Amtrak reform legislation was enacted.

In addition, the agreement provided $250 million for improvements to Amtrak's Northeast Corridor, $75 million more than fiscal 1997 funding, and $50 million more than requested.

- **Mass transit.** $4.8 billion for mass transit programs, up $462 million from fiscal 1997. The total included $2.5 billion for formula grants — including $150 million for transit operating subsidies, a cut of $250 million from fiscal 1997. It also included $2 billion in discretionary grants — $800 million for subway and commuter-rail modernization, $800 million for new transit systems or extensions, and $400 million for buses and bus facilities.
- **FAA.** $7.4 billion for the FAA, up $545 million from fiscal 1997, and $1.7 billion for airport improvement grants, up $240 million. Included was $5.3 billion for FAA operations, an increase of $452 million, and $1.9 billion for the modernization of FAA facilities and equipment.
- **Coast Guard.** $3.9 billion for the Coast Guard, an increase of $140 million from fiscal 1997 funding. Of the total, $300 million was to be used for defense-related activities, and $354 million was for Coast Guard drug interdiction activities.
- **Transportation safety.** Significant increases in funding for transportation safety, including increases of 11 percent

for research by the National Highway Traffic Safety Administration, 8 percent for state truck safety grants, 16 percent for state and community traffic safety grants, 35 percent for drunk driving countermeasure grants, and 11 percent for rail safety activities.

Battle Over Shelby Provisions

The main problems in conference came over Shelby's add-ons.

• **Love Airfield.** For more than a year, fledgling Legend Airlines had been pushing to fly retrofitted jets out of Dallas' Love Field, a circumvention of a 1979 amendment by former House Speaker Jim Wright, D-Texas. The so-called Wright amendment, enacted to protect the newly built Dallas-Fort Worth Airport from competition, mandated that planes out of Love Field could fly only to the four states contiguous with Texas, unless they had 56 seats or less.

Legend had proposed flying larger, DC-9-type jets out of Love Field, but retrofitting them to include only 56 seats. The company hoped that plush, wide seats with extra leg room, carry-on space and cargo capacity would attract business travelers eager to fly out of Love Field, which was considerably closer to downtown Dallas than Dallas-Forth Worth Airport. But the Department of Transportation, siding with Fort Worth-based American Airlines, ruled in September that such a move would contradict congressional intent.

"You've got one airline that has created just about a monopoly in the Dallas-Fort Worth area," Shelby said. "It comes down to who's going to be for the people's interest and who's going to be for the special interests."

To Texans, it was not that simple. Kay Granger, R-Texas, who led the fight in the House against Shelby, said the battle was pitting the will of the local community against outside meddling from Washington. Love Field was in a residential setting, she said, and the area could not safely absorb more traffic in its skies. More important, said Sen. Kay Bailey Hutchison, R-Texas, whose husband was a bond counsel for the Dallas-Fort Worth Airport, competition would begin bleeding Dallas-Fort Worth of its 150,000 jobs, while hampering its role as a major hub for air travelers nationwide.

Through sheer tenacity, Shelby won a partial repeal of the Wright amendment, with conferees agreeing to override the department's decision and allow Legend to fly its retrofitted planes. Also under the conference agreement, any airline would be able to fly from Love Field not only to the four contiguous states around Texas, but also to Alabama, Mississippi and Kansas.

Shelby promised he would be back each year to expand that list until the entire amendment was repealed. Likewise, Hutchison vowed to fight on, hinting that legal action could be in the works.

• **Alabama bus subsidies.** The other sticking point came over federal bus subsidies. In the Senate's original version, Alabama would have received $39 million of the $434 million total, nearly 10 percent of all bus funding and $28 million more than the House had allocated. Under Shelby's terms, Alabama's allotment would have been exceeded only by New York's, despite the fact that none of Alabama's cities fell within the 26 largest bus systems listed by the American Public Transit Association.

Wolf, who objected strenuously, wrote to House Speaker Newt Gingrich, R-Ga., saying that, "the American people are sick of it, and it must come out before the bill moves." But Shelby was unapologetic, arguing that Alabama had not received a cent in bus funding for nearly a decade.

Eventually, conferees agreed to give Alabama a total of $25.5 million, putting the state behind only California, New York and Pennsylvania in total bus funding.

Line-Item Veto

On Nov. 1, Clinton used his line-item veto authority to cancel three projects worth just $6.2 million out of the $42.2 billion transportation bill, which by then had been enacted into law.

Nearly all of the dollar value came from just one project, a $5.3 million railroad dock improvement program in the home state of Senate Appropriations Committee Chairman Ted Stevens, R-Alaska. House and Senate conferees had instructed the Federal Railroad Administration to send the money directly to the city of Seward to rehabilitate a dock attached to the Alaska Railroad.

OMB spokesman Lawrence J. Haas objected that the railroad administration's job was to oversee safety, whereas Seward's project was primarily dedicated to economic development. The beneficiaries of the project would be the city of Seward, the state, private cargo haulers and passenger ships. Moreover, he said Congress had provided no independent analysis of the project's potential return on investment.

The other two vetoed projects were a transportation emergency preparedness and response center in Arab, Ala., and an electronic distribution center for surplus transit equipment in Georgia.

The $450,000 emergency center had been featured on the front page of The Washington Post in mid-October as an example of projects tucked deeply into spending bills to avoid the line-item veto radar. It turned out the project was to be in Shelby's home state.

Shelby's office said the area had been torn apart by 117 storms and tornadoes over the previous decade that had killed as many as 60 people. But Haas said the federal government had helped build an emergency preparedness center in Alabama just five years before that was designed to serve the entire state. A fixed disaster field office — rather than a mobile unit — would serve little purpose unless the storm or tornado struck very nearby. Moreover, Haas noted, such a disaster center lay far outside the Transportation Department's mission.

Finally, Clinton vetoed a $500,000 transit project in the district of Rep. Mac Collins, R-Ga., saying it was an unneeded corporate subsidy. The project, proposed by a small Georgia company, would have been an electronic bulletin board for transit authorities to swap surplus property nationwide. Haas said the White House was "unaware of any evidence of the merit or need of the service."

Many considered Clinton's treatment of the $42.2 billion transportation spending law remarkably light, considering its scope. Sen. John McCain, R-Ariz., a strong proponent of using the process to cut wasteful spending, had listed hundreds of millions of dollars in other projects that were specifically earmarked with funds that McCain said should have been left to the discretion of the secretary of Transportation. ■

Treasury Bill Goes Down to the Wire

Congress cleared the fiscal 1998 spending bill for the Treasury Department, Postal Service and general government in the early hours of the new fiscal year, after dropping a controversial Senate provision that would have blocked a scheduled cost-of-living pay increase for lawmakers. The Senate cleared the bill Oct. 1, and President Clinton signed it into law Oct. 10 (HR 2378 — PL 105-61).

The final bill totalled $25.6 billion, with more than half the funds ($12.9 billion) reserved for mandatory programs — primarily health and pension benefits for retired federal workers.

The remaining $12.7 billion was discretionary spending, over which appropriators exerted annual control. The Treasury Department got the biggest share of that — $11.4 billion — which included funding for the Internal Revenue Service (IRS), Customs Service and Secret Service.

The bill also funded executive office agencies and federal agencies such as the General Services Administration (GSA), the Federal Election Commission (FEC) and the Office of Personnel Management.

The annual Treasury-Postal bill typically attracted controversial amendments, in part because it funded general government functions such as employee salaries and benefits. It had barely squeaked by in the House in both 1995 and 1996, stalled by disputes over abortion and other issues. Congress failed to clear the fiscal 1997 version as a separate measure, instead rolling it into an omnibus appropriations package (PL 104-208). *(1996 Almanac, p. 10-80; 1995 Almanac, p. 11-77)*

BOXSCORE

Fiscal 1998 Treasury-Postal Service Appropriations — HR 2378 (S 1023). The $25.6 billion bill funded the Treasury Department, the Executive Office of the president, federal construction and federal retiree benefits.

Reports: H Rept 105-240, S Rept 105-49; conference report, H Rept 105-284.

KEY ACTION

July 22 — Senate passed S 1023, 99-0.

Sept. 17 — House passed HR 2378, 231-192. **Senate** passed HR 2378 by voice vote after substituting the text of S 1023.

Sept. 30 — House adopted the conference report, 220-207.

Oct. 1 — Senate cleared HR 2378, 55-45.

Oct. 10 — President signed the bill — PL 105-61.

Oct. 16 — President used line-item veto to delete one item in PL 105-61.

The most controversial issue to arise on the fiscal 1998 bill was whether to deny members of Congress a 2.3 percent cost of living pay adjustment (COLA) scheduled to take effect Jan. 1, 1998.

Although the Treasury-Postal bill did not fund members' pay, it had been used for several years as a vehicle for amendments blocking the pay increase.

Under existing law, members were entitled to an automatic adjustment in pay each year. But each year since fiscal 1993, members — skittish about giving themselves a raise at a time of tight federal budgets — had rejected the pay increase. They also had denied COLAs to federal judges during this period, drawing considerable fire from some members of the bench. General government employees, however, continued to receive their COLA increases.

Some members in both chambers said Congress should continue the salary freeze until it erased the federal deficit, which was unlikely to happen before 2002. "This is not the time to be giving Congress a pay increase, when the budget is still unbalanced," said Rep. Jon Christensen, R-Neb.

Unable for political reasons to launch a frontal assault against amendments to block the pay increase, House and Senate leaders took different tacks.

The House approach was to sit on the bill, blaming the lack of action on scheduling conflicts. The issue was so sensitive that House leaders met privately to discuss a strategy for handling it, but said almost nothing about it in public. "I don't talk congressional pay raise," House Appropriations Chairman Robert L. Livingston, R-La., said July 16.

In the end, House leaders managed to get the Treasury-Postal bill passed without an amendment to bar the COLA. The Senate, by contrast, followed the pattern of the recent past and added an anti-pay raise amendment when the bill came to the floor. Because the House had delayed its work for so long, the Senate acted first — a complete reversal of customary practice. In fact, the Senate passed its version of the bill July 22, the same day that House appropriators finally began their subcommittee markup.

The final bill was silent on the issue of members' pay, thereby permitting the scheduled pay increase to take effect in fiscal 1998. The change increased lawmakers' annual pay from $133,600 to $136,700. Top leaders made more.

Other key elements of the final bill included the following:

- **IRS funding.** Despite objections from conservative Republicans, the bill gave the IRS $7.8 billion, a 10 percent increase over the previous year.
- **Abortion.** The bill continued an existing ban on the use of federal employee health plans to pay for abortions, except in cases of rape or incest, or when the life of the woman would be endangered. The debate on abortion coverage for federal employees was an annual feature of the bill. The ban had been included from 1984 to 1993, but was lifted after Clinton took office in 1993. The ban was reinstituted in the fiscal 1996 bill.
- **White House political events.** The final bill included provisions intended to ensure that political and certain reimbursable non-political events held at the White House were paid for in advance or that the government was promptly reimbursed for the costs of such events. The bill required that sponsors of reimbursable political events at the White House pay the estimated costs in advance. It also required that the national committee of the president's party maintain $25,000 on deposit to pay for political events during each fiscal year. The White House was required to bill the party or sponsor for any excess costs within 60 days of the event, and to collect payment within 30 days. Amounts not paid within that period would be subject to interest and penalty charges.
- **Anti-drug campaign.** The measure provided $195 million to fund an administration plan to launch a national anti-drug media campaign.

Senate Committee

Tired of waiting for the House to act, the Senate Treasury and General Government Appropriations Subcommittee on

Fiscal 1998 Treasury-Postal Service Spending

(in thousands of dollars)

	Fiscal 1997 Appropriation	Fiscal 1998 Clinton Request	House Bill	Senate Bill	Conference Report
Treasury Department					
U.S. Customs Service					
Salaries and expenses	$ 1,549,585	$ 1,566,826	$ 1,526,078	$ 1,551,028	$ 1,522,165
Air and marine interdiction	83,363	92,758	97,258	92,758	92,758
Other	5,406	10,918	5,406	5,406	5,406
Subtotal, Customs	**$ 1,638,354**	**$ 1,670,502**	**$ 1,628,742**	**$ 1,649,192**	**$ 1,620,329**
Internal Revenue Service					
Processing tax returns, assistance	1,790,288	2,943,174	2,915,100	2,943,174	2,925,874
Tax law enforcement	4,104,211	3,153,722	3,108,300	3,153,722	3,142,822
Information systems	1,323,075	1,772,487	1,618,500	1,597,487	1,272,487
Earned-income compliance	—	107,105	—	—	138,000
Rescission	–174,447	—	–14,500	—	-32,000
Subtotal, IRS	**$ 7,043,127**	**$ 7,976,488**	**$ 7,627,400**	**$ 7,694,383**	**$ 7,772,183**
Bureau of Alcohol, Tobacco and Firearms	467,372	551,976	533,671	528,512	533,956
U.S. Secret Service	561,053	585,147	561,511	579,985	573,147
Bureau of the Public Debt	165,335	169,426	169,426	169,426	169,426
Financial Management Service	196,518	202,560	199,675	202,490	202,490
Other	422,737	614,419	468,150	492,813	506,953
TOTAL, Treasury Department	**$ 10,494,496**	**$ 11,770,518**	**$ 11,188,575**	**$ 11,315,801**	**$ 11,378,484**
Postal Service					
Postal subsidies	90,463	86,274	86,274	86,274	86,274
Non-funded liabilities	35,536	34,850	34,850	34,850	—
TOTAL, Postal Service	**$ 125,999**	**$ 121,124**	**$ 121,124**	**$ 121,124**	**$ 86,274**
Executive Office of the President					
President's compensation	250	250	250	250	250
White House Office	40,193	51,199	51,199	51,199	51,199
Executive residence	7,827	8,245	8,245	8,245	8,245
National Security Council	6,648	6,648	6,648	6,648	6,648
Office of Management and Budget	55,573	57,240	57,240	57,240	57,440
Office of National Drug Control Policy	35,838	36,016	43,516	36,016	35,016
Federal drug control programs	127,102	140,207	146,207	140,207	159,007
Other	149,910	216,120	245,120	185,420	251,120
TOTAL, Executive Office	**$ 423,341**	**$ 515,925**	**$ 558,425**	**$ 485,225**	**$ 568,925**
Independent Agencies					
General Services Administration					
Federal Buildings Fund	400,544	84,000	—	—	—
Limitation on use of revenues	*(5,555,544)*	*(4,969,934)*	*(4,835,934)*	*(4,885,934)*	*(4,835,934)*
Other	146,216	140,607	143,565	140,565	143,565
Subtotal, GSA	**$ 546,760**	**$ 224,607**	**$ 143,565**	**$ 140,565**	**$ 143,565**
Office of Personnel Management					
Annuitants, health benefits	4,059,000	4,338,000	4,338,000	4,338,000	4,338,000
Annuitants, life insurance	33,000	32,000	32,000	32,000	32,000
Civil Service retirement, disability	7,989,000	8,336,000	8,336,000	8,336,000	8,336,000
Salaries and expenses	88,246	86,310	86,310	86,310	86,310
Subtotal, OPM	**$ 12,169,246**	**$ 12,792,310**	**$ 12,792,310**	**$ 12,792,310**	**$ 12,792,310**
Federal Election Commission	28,165	34,216	34,550	29,000	31,650
National Archives	214,180	213,117	214,492	221,117	221,305
U.S. Tax Court	33,781	34,293	33,921	34,293	33,921
Other, scorekeeping adjustments	65,655	380,055	296,138	67,104	330,645
GRAND TOTAL	**$ 24,070,095**	**$ 26,086,165**	**$ 25,383,100**	**$ 25,481,850**	**$ 25,587,079**

SOURCE: Senate, House Appropriations committees

July 11 marked up and quickly gave voice vote approval to a draft Treasury-Postal spending bill that totalled $25 billion. The subcommittee's markup lasted about 10 minutes.

The draft, later introduced as S 1023, included about $12.3 billion in discretionary spending, along with $12.7 billion in mandatory spending for pensions, life insurance and health benefits for federal retirees.

Subcommittee Chairman Ben Nighthorse Campbell, R-Colo., said the bill contained $6.2 billion for law enforcement programs.

In many respects, the bill hewed closely to Clinton administration priorities. As requested by the administration, it called for a one-year moratorium on the construction of new government buildings. The GSA's building fund was low on money, due to inaccurate estimates of rent costs and construction completion dates.

The bill contained about $110 million for the first year of a new anti-drug media campaign by the White House's Office of National Drug Control Policy. That was $65 million less than the administration requested, but senior appropriators questioned whether the government should spend money buying air time for anti-drug advertisements when broadcasters already ran public service announcements at no charge. "If we provide a new cash cow for the media, why would they want to donate their time?" asked Campbell.

The measure also included millions of dollars for projects favored by appropriators, including $150,000 to help mark the centennial of the Gold Rush in the home state of Senate Appropriations Committee Chairman Ted Stevens, R-Alaska, and an additional $3 million in drug control money for the Rocky Mountain area, which included Campbell's home state of Colorado.

Other items were $2.5 million for a global trade and research program in Montana, home state of GOP appropriator Conrad Burns; $4 million for renovations to the Harry S Truman Library in Missouri, home state of Republican Christopher S. Bond; and $3 million to the Lyndon B. Johnson Presidential Library in Texas, home state of Republican Kay Bailey Hutchison.

On July 15, the full Senate Appropriations Committee approved the bill, 27-0, without voting on any contentious amendments (S Rept 105-49).

Senate Floor Action

The Senate began debate on S 1023 on July 17 and passed the measure July 22 by a vote of 99-0. *(Vote 191, p. S-34)*

As one of its first actions, the Senate agreed to an amendment blocking the scheduled 2.3 percent pay increase for members in 1998. The amendment, by Sam Brownback, R-Kan., was approved by voice vote July 17. The Senate subsequently gave voice vote approval to an amendment by Orrin G. Hatch, R-Utah, to ensure that federal judges would receive their pay adjustment.

Unlike his House counterparts, Stevens had moved the bill quickly, waiting until after the Brownback amendment was approved before taking to the floor to warn that the pay freeze could discourage talented politicians from running for Congress. "What will be the decision made by young people who are thinking of coming here?" he asked.

• **Abortion.** By a vote of 54-45, the Senate adopted an amendment by Mike DeWine, R-Ohio, to bar federal employee health plans from paying for abortions except in cases of rape or incest, or when the life of the woman was endangered. *(Vote 190, p. S-34)*

Abortion-rights supporters, such as Barbara Boxer, D-Calif., argued that it was bad policy to deny federal employees benefits available to employees in the private sector. But Majority Whip Don Nickles, R-Okla., said taxpayers should not be required to subsidize abortions.

• **Breast cancer.** Some of the sharpest debate came over an amendment by Dianne Feinstein, D-Calif., calling for the Postal Service to develop a special stamp to raise money for breast cancer research. The stamp would cost 1 cent above the prevailing first-class rate, with the additional penny paying for research and the cost of administration. The amendment was adopted by a vote of 83-17. *(Vote 186, p. S-33)*

Feinstein said such a stamp could raise $60 million a year if it accounted for 10 percent of the sales of all first-class stamps.

Stevens scoffed at such an estimate, saying the stamp would be unlikely to raise more than a couple of million dollars. He also said that neither Congress nor the Postal Service had the authority to issue such a stamp, since all rate increases were handled by the independent Postal Rate Commission. Furthermore, he warned that other groups would turn to stamps to raise money, diluting the focus on breast cancer research.

But Feinstein argued that breast cancer was such a health problem that Congress should do anything it could. "It's worth a try," she said. "When you do anything for the first time, you never know what it is going to do."

• **Other amendments.** By voice vote, the Senate adopted an amendment by Lauch Faircloth, R-N.C., and Richard C. Shelby, R-Ala., to bar game software from computers in federal offices. The amendment provided an exception for cases where it would be cost-prohibitive to remove the software.

Jeff Bingaman, D-N.M., won voice vote approval to remove language from the bill that would have restricted federal agencies from using energy conservation services, such as those offered by local utilities, on a sole-source basis. An attempt by Stevens to table (kill) Bingaman's amendment failed, 35-64. *(Vote 189, p. S-34)*

House Subcommittee

The House Appropriations Subcommittee on Treasury, Postal Service and General Government approved its version of the spending bill by voice vote July 22, just hours after the Senate passed S 1023. The subcommittee bill, later introduced as HR 2378, proposed spending $25.4 billion. The discretionary portion — $12.5 billion — was close to $34 million less than in the Senate version and $85 million less than the administration's request.

The bill included $60 million more than the Senate had approved for the new anti-drug media campaign. Like the Senate, the subcommittee proposed a one-year moratorium on the construction of new federal buildings, due to a shortfall in the GSA building account.

In a key difference with the Senate-passed bill, the House version was silent on members' pay, thus allowing for an automatic cost of living increase to take effect.

The following are among the other elements of the subcommittee-approved bill:

• **White House political events.** Reflecting GOP anger at Clinton's use of the White House for political activities, the draft bill sought to ensure that tax dollars did not subsidize political events. It required that political organizations pay in advance when they staged events at the White House. It also required the White House to develop a system for defining an event as political or non-political and set up a new appropriations account for executive mansion events.

"These are reasonable requirements for the executive residence to adhere to," said subcommittee Chairman Jim Kolbe, R-Ariz. He said he was proposing the new rules because Democratic organizations were taking eight months or longer to reimburse the Treasury after using federal dollars for political events at the White House, and administration officials had failed to answer questions on the issue.

The bill proposed establishing a $25,000 revolving fund, capitalized by the president's political party, to help cover "spontaneous" political events.

Subcommittee Democrats accepted the provisions, and the administration had no immediate comment. "I don't think the White House is pleased with it, but I think it is one that can work," said Steny H. Hoyer of Maryland, the subcommittee's ranking Democrat.

The panel rejected, 5-5, an amendment by Ernest Istook, R-Okla., that would have barred White House employees from receiving salary supplements from a political party.

• **Abortion.** The subcommittee approved, by voice vote, an amendment by full committee Chairman Livingston continuing the prohibition on the use of federal employees' insurance policies to cover abortions, except in cases of rape, incest or danger to the woman's life.

• **Cooperative purchasing.** The panel agreed, by voice vote, to an amendment by Anne M. Northup, R-Ky., to prevent state and local governments from using federal "supply schedules" when making purchases. The cooperative purchasing provisions of the Federal Acquisition Streamlining Act permitted state and local governments to buy goods at the lower discounted prices negotiated by the GSA for the federal government.

Lawmakers were concerned that allowing all governments to purchase goods at rates available to federal agencies could hurt small companies that relied on state and local government contracts.

• **Monitoring private organizations.** Istook was rebuffed when he proposed an amendment requiring the Office of Management and Budget (OMB) to study assigning special coding numbers to nonprofit and for-profit organizations that received federal grants. The provision was reminiscent of a 1995 attempt by Istook to impose sweeping restrictions on lobbying activities by groups that received federal grants. *(1995 Almanac, pp. 1-17, 11-81)*

The subcommittee rejected the amendment, 4-6, after Istook refused a request by Kolbe to amend the bill report instead. After losing his first amendment, Istook belatedly took Kolbe's advice and offered an amendment to put his proposal in the report, but he lost again, 5-5, with an exasperated Kolbe voting against him.

House Full Committee

The full House Appropriations Committee approved the bill July 31 by a vote of 42-5 (H Rept 105-240), after debating several controversial provisions.

• **Firearm imports.** By voice vote, the committee adopted an amendment by John P. Murtha, D-Pa., to allow the importation of certain surplus U.S. firearms. The amendment, which was backed by the National Rifle Association, was adopted after little debate; it was unclear whether all committee members understood its ramifications.

Murtha sought to ease the way for the importation of firearms, including M-1 Garand and M-1 carbine rifles, that the United States had given or sold at a discount since the 1950s to Cold War allies. It proposed to bar funding to any U.S. agency that tried to block applications to import such weapons. Under existing law, the State and Treasury departments had discretion to block import applications — and nearly always did.

The amendment also proposed to end a requirement that the allies repay the Pentagon if any of the nearly 3 million weapons shipped overseas were resold.

Although the U.S. gun industry had long fought for the right to import the firearms, Clinton administration officials warned that the M-1 carbines could be converted to automatic weapons and used by criminals. "The administration is concerned about a large number of relatively inexpensive weapons coming back into this country," said Raymond W. Kelly, Treasury's under secretary for enforcement.

• **FEC.** The bill proposed making the release of $4.2 million in computer funding for the FEC contingent on the enactment of legislation to restrict each FEC commissioner to a single, six-year term. Clinton would also be required to fill existing vacancies. The six-member commission had one GOP vacancy. Two other members remained on the board, although their terms had expired.

Republican appropriators made no secret of their disdain for the commission, claiming that it investigated comparatively minor infringements while overlooking major campaign violations. "The Federal Election Commission is an example of an agency that does no good whatsoever," said Livingston. In fact, Livingston said he would have preferred to close the FEC and make the Justice Department responsible for policing the campaign finance system. But, he said, "We're not going to go that far — yet."

OMB objected sharply to the provisions, saying they would place "unwarranted and intrusive limitations" on the FEC.

The committee rejected, 18-32, an amendment by Hoyer that would have sidestepped the issue by moving the computer funding into salaries and expenses, roughly meeting the FEC's budget request. Hoyer said the FEC needed additional staff for investigations and audits stemming from the 1996 elections.

But subcommittee chairman Kolbe said the FEC needed the computers more.

• **Abortion.** Appropriators rejected, 21-27, an amendment by Nita M. Lowey, D-N.Y., to delete the bill's prohibition on abortion coverage except in cases of rape and incest or if the life of the woman was in danger.

• **Overseas package delivery.** By a vote of 29-8, the committee agreed to an amendment by Northup to temporarily halt negotiations to expedite overseas customs handling of bulk parcels delivered by the Postal Service. The amendment proposed to ban the use of funds to expand the U.S. Postal Service's Global Package Link Service, a merchandise delivery service offered by the Postal Service for international delivery (and customs clearance) of retail merchandise sold by large volume catalog retailers or other retailers.

The Postal Service had agreements with three countries, including Japan, for such expedited handling and was negotiating for the service with several other countries, drawing objections from such competitors as United Parcel Service.

• **Other amendments.** The committee also:

➤ Rejected, 19-34, an amendment by Robert B. Aderholt, R-Ala., to require public disclosure of the methodology and data for federally funded research.

➤ Rejected, by voice vote, an amendment by Carrie P. Meek, D-Fla., to allow state and local governments to buy lifesaving drugs and data processing equipment at rates available to federal agencies. The bill instead included a controversial provision, opposed by the administration, to bar state and local governments from using federal supply schedules. The committee also rejected, by voice vote, a related amendment by James P. Moran, D-Va., to exempt only data processing equipment.

House Floor Action

After a debate that lasted only an hour, the House on Sept. 17 passed the Treasury-Postal bill by a vote of 231-192, over the opposition of Tom Coburn, R-Okla., and his anti-pay-raise allies. Hours later, the Senate passed HR 2378 by voice vote after substituting the text of S 1023. *(House vote 403, p. H-122)*

The House struck a number of controversial provisions on procedural grounds that did not require votes, and swiftly disposed of other amendments without recorded votes.

House leaders staved off a COLA amendment by relying on the tactics of speed and surprise to outflank Coburn and other conservatives. The vote on final passage came before Coburn could get back from his office in the Cannon building with an amendment to block the pay increase. "I ran back over here," said a disappointed Coburn, who arrived at the House floor minutes after debate on the Treasury measure was gaveled shut. "I'm sweating. . . . They scooped us."

The leadership strategy was prompted by private pleas from many members of both parties — especially veterans — who were weary of working without a raise. "These members have been four years without a raise and no adjustment for inflation," Majority Leader Dick Armey, R-Texas, said before the vote. "They all have families."

Armey and other leaders decided to bring up the bill under an "open rule," meaning a pay raise amendment would have been out of order under House rules that barred legislating on an appropriations bill.

But pay raise opponents could have tried to override the ruling of the chair. So as an insurance measure, House leaders also decided to take their opponents by surprise. After letting it be known that the appropriations bill for the departments of Commerce, Justice and State and the Judiciary (HR 2267) would be taken up on Sept. 17, they abruptly turned instead to the Treasury-Postal bill.

Pay raise opponents were caught off guard without any prepared amendment. Coburn learned that the bill was on the floor by accident, when he wandered by to drop off an amendment on the Commerce measure.

After hesitating on whether to challenge his leaders, Coburn said he rushed back to his office to copy the pay raise language that was added to the fiscal 1997 Treasury bill.

But he could not outsprint the leadership. In a scripted debate, members quickly disposed of amendments by voice vote and peaceably removed potentially contentious provisions that were non-germane to the bill.

After about 60 minutes — without a single word about the pay raise issue — debate was gaveled shut and the final vote began. The House had spent the equivalent of just one minute of debate for every $423 million in the bill. Leaders insisted that their swift consideration had nothing to do with the pay raise issue. "It was just non-controversial," Livingston maintained.

Several contentious provisions were stripped from the bill on the basis that they constituted legislating on an appropriations bill in violation of House rules. Among them was the proposal to allow the importation of certain surplus U.S. firearms, such as M-1 Garand and carbine rifles.

Similarly, members quickly removed the provision barring the Postal Service from expanding an expedited overseas delivery system.

And, after a surprisingly brief debate, members agreed by voice vote to continue the existing prohibition on abortion coverage by federal employees' health insurance plans.

Floor Amendments

By voice vote, the House approved amendments:

➤ By Rod R. Blagojevich, D-Ill., to increase by $1 million funding for the Bureau of Alcohol, Tobacco and Firearms to trace illegal guns owned by juvenile criminals.

➤ By Bernard Sanders, I-Vt., to ban the use of funds by the Customs Service to allow the importation of goods made by forced or indentured child labor.

➤ By John E. Sununu, R-N.H., to appropriate $200,000 to study the impact of new rules and regulations on small businesses.

➤ By Bob Filner, D-Calif., to bar the IRS from printing individuals' Social Security numbers on the outside of envelopes.

Conference

By the time conferees met on Sept. 29, staff had resolved all but one issue — members' pay. In a meeting that lasted only four minutes, conferees agreed to adopt the House position permitting the COLA to take effect.

On a 3-3 vote conducted mostly by proxies, Senate conferees failed to insist on retaining their provision to eliminate the fiscal 1998 pay raise. Stevens, Robert C. Byrd, D-W.Va., and Barbara A. Mikulski, D-Md., voted against the Senate provision, thereby supporting the pay increase.

Stevens said he saw no reason why lawmakers should forgo a cost of living adjustment for a fifth consecutive year. "The retired people have gotten them [cost of living raises in Social Security]; the military has gotten them," he said. "There's no reason not to get them."

In an unusual step, House leaders barred two conferees who opposed the pay raise — Istook and Northup — from negotiating over sections of the bill related to the salary issue.

Other Conference Decisions

The final bill (H Rept 105-284) totalled $25.6 billion — $202 million more than the House-passed bill, with $145 million of that increase going to the IRS. Compared with the Senate version, the final bill provided $103 million more, including $78 million more for the IRS.

Conferees agreed to:

- **White House political events.** Accept House provisions requiring that White House political events be prepaid by outside sources and that the federal government be promptly reimbursed for any excess costs of such events. The Senate bill had no comparable provisions.
- **Anti-drug campaign.** Provide $195 million to launch a national anti-drug media campaign, compared to $110 million in the Senate bill and $170 million approved by the House.
- **Cooperative purchasing.** Include a provision barring state and local governments from buying goods at discount rates through federal supply schedules.
- **IRS funding.** Provide $7.8 billion for the IRS, an increase of $729 million (10 percent) over fiscal 1997 but $204 million less than the administration's request. Final funding for the IRS was $145 million more than in the House bill, and $78 million more than the Senate had approved.

Final Action

The House adopted the conference report, 220-207, in a dramatic seesaw vote Sept. 30. The next day — the first of the new fiscal year — a deeply divided Senate cleared the bill, 55-45. *(House vote 474, p. H-144; Senate vote 264, p. S-44)*

Controversial provisions in the final bill required House GOP leaders to bring pressure on the rank and file to get the measure through. Some Democrats withheld their "yea" votes until the end of the balloting to pressure more Republicans to vote for the bill and thereby indirectly support a pay raise. During the debate, many newer members on both sides of the aisle objected sharply to the decision to drop the congressional pay freeze.

Conservatives criticized the 10 percent funding increase for the IRS, which had drawn fire in a series of high-profile hearings. "We as Republicans are going around the country right now criticizing the IRS, while we are increasing their dollars here," said Mark Souder, R-Ind. "There are many reasons why we are doing it, but nevertheless, it is rather an inconsistent message." *(IRS overhaul, p. 2-71)*

Souder and other conservatives also questioned a $67 million increase in the bill for the Bureau of Alcohol, Tobacco and Firearms.

And House members of both parties, including Thomas M. Davis III, R-Va., and Dennis J. Kucinich, D-Ohio, objected to the provision barring state and local governments from obtaining supplies at special discount prices available to federal agencies under supply schedules negotiated by the GSA.

But veteran appropriators defended the bill, saying lawmakers deserved the pay raise and arguing that the IRS increase was necessary in part to convert computers for use in the next century.

When the 15 minutes allowed for voting in the House ran out, the conference report was still 20 votes short, and more than 150 members had not yet voted. GOP leaders gradually closed the gap. "There was a lot of arm-twisting going on," said Matt Salmon, R-Ariz, who opposed the bill. In the end, 113 Democrats and 107 Republicans voted for the bill.

The only suspense in the Senate was triggered by Brownback, a pay-increase opponent who considered waging a filibuster. But Brownback said he lacked the 41 votes needed to sustain such a maneuver.

Line-Item Veto

Clinton used his line-item veto authority Oct. 16 to strike one item from the Treasury-Postal bill — a provision allowing longtime federal workers to switch retirement plans. Clinton said the proposal, which was added in conference by Stevens, was not requested, that it was "hastily conceived," and that conferees had included it without public debate. *(Text, p. D-42)*

The National Treasury Employees Union promptly filed suit to challenge the president's authority. The case was combined with two others, with oral arguments scheduled for Jan. 14, 1998, before Judge Thomas F. Hogan of the U.S. District Court for the District of Columbia.

Before the scheduled oral arguments, however, the Justice Department reached an agreement with the union in which it admitted that the president had exceeded his authority in striking the item. On Jan. 6, 1998, Judge Hogan signed a consent order invalidating Clinton's use of the line-item veto in this instance. The result of the consent decree was that the provision remained in the bill.

The restored pension change permitted about 1.1 million federal workers hired before 1983 to switch from the old Civil Service Retirement System to the Federal Employees Retirement System. It enabled veteran workers to take greater advantage of tax-deferred savings plans, and allowed widowed federal employees to receive higher Social Security survivors' payments.

In vetoing the $845 million provision, Clinton had said he was killing a "dollar amount of discretionary budget authority." But as Justice later conceded, no budget authority was involved. The veto instead would have effectively reduced federal revenues because workers who switched plans would contribute a smaller portion of their wages into the system. ■

VA-HUD Bill Revamps Housing Subsidies

For the second straight year, Republican appropriators in both chambers managed to keep the spending bill for veterans, housing, environmental and space programs free of the kind of controversial policy riders that had triggered a veto of the fiscal 1996 version.

Indeed, the fiscal 1998 VA-HUD spending bill seemed poised for quick enactment when initial versions passed the House and Senate in July. But a fight among Republicans over the troubled Section 8 subsidized housing program, and a host of last-minute demands from the administration, slowed progress on the legislation to a crawl. It was not signed into law until Oct. 27, nearly a month after the start of the new fiscal year (HR 2158 — PL 105-65).

The wide-ranging bill provided a total of $90.7 billion for the Department of Veterans Affairs (VA), the Department of Housing and Urban Development (HUD), and 17 independent agencies — including the Environmental Protection Agency (EPA), National Aeronautics and Space Administration (NASA), National Science Foundation (NSF), and Federal Emergency Management Agency (FEMA).

Most agencies fared better or about the same as they had the previous fiscal year. HUD was the biggest winner, garnering $23.7 billion in appropriations, an increase of $7.4 billion over fiscal 1997. Most of that increase was needed to renew thousands of Section 8 low-income rental housing subsidy contracts that were due to expire in fiscal 1998.

The EPA received $7.4 billion, an increase of more than $560 million over fiscal 1997, while NSF spending rose by $159 million to $3.4 billion. The AmeriCorps national service program, a high Clinton priority, got a $26 million increase to $429 million. The Community Development Financial Institutions program, which assisted financial institutions that operated in economically distressed and underserved communities, received $80 million, a $30 million increase, after being threatened with no funding because of allegations of mismanagement and favoritism in the program.

Most other agencies remained relatively even, though FEMA got just $830 million, $4.3 billion less than in fiscal 1997. However, most of the previous year's funding came from a supplemental spending bill (PL 105-18) enacted in June 1997 to deal with disasters across the nation. *(Supplemental, p. 9-84)*

The VA-HUD measure also terminated the federal Office of Consumer Affairs, which had received $1.5 million the previous year.

On Nov. 1, five days after signing the bill, Clinton used his line-item veto power to cancel seven projects worth $14 million. The vetoed projects included NASA telescopes in Arizona and Chile, a wastewater treatment project in Vermont, a new national cemetery in Oklahoma, a police training complex in Alabama, and a trade and development grant in Montana.

BOXSCORE

Fiscal 1998 VA-HUD Appropriations — HR 2158 (S 1034). The $90.7 billion bill funded the departments of Veterans Affairs (VA) and Housing and Urban Development (HUD), as well as agencies such as NASA and the Environmental Protection Agency.

Reports: H Rept 105-175, S Rept 105-53; conference report, 105-297.

KEY ACTION

July 16 — House passed HR 2158, 397-31.

July 22 — Senate passed HR 2158, revised, 99-1.

Oct. 8 — House adopted the conference report, 405-21.

Oct. 9 — Senate cleared the bill by voice vote.

Oct. 27 — President signed HR 2158 — PL 105-65.

Nov. 1 — President used the line-item veto to delete provisions from PL 105-65.

Background

The main hurdle for the fiscal 1998 VA-HUD appropriations bill was a disagreement among House and Senate authorizers over HUD's Section 8 housing subsidy program for low-income families, the elderly and the disabled.

Under Section 8, put in place by the Nixon administration, low-income tenants paid a certain percentage of their income in rent to participating landlords. In return, the federal government subsidized the rents, often at well above market rates, and guaranteed the landlord's mortgage. The government had entered into thousands of such contracts with landlords in the 1970s and 1980s.

The program covered an estimated 3 million units, providing housing for some 4 million people. Most Section 8 tenants lived on fixed incomes from sources such as Social Security, welfare or cash benefits provided to the low-income, aged, blind and disabled. Other tenants were classified as the so-called working poor, who had jobs but whose earnings were well below the poverty line.

The immediate problem facing Congress was the fact that nearly 3 million Section 8 contracts were due to expire over the following five years, 2 million of them in fiscal 1998. HUD estimated that renewing the contracts without reducing the subsidies would cost more than $9 billion in fiscal 1998 alone, a figure that both parties viewed as excessive.

Yet allowing the contracts to expire would substantially deplete housing supplies, especially for the elderly and disabled, and could cause many property owners to default on their mortgages. Such defaults could create an even more serious financial crisis because most Section 8 properties were insured by the Federal Housing Administration (FHA).

The congressional budget resolution (H Con Res 84) assumed full funding for all expiring Section 8 contracts in fiscal 1998 at a cost of $9.2 billion. But it also called for reducing the subsidies to bring rents more closely in line with similar, non-subsidized housing in an area.

The Senate included the loan restructuring in its version of 1997 budget-reconciliation bill (HR 2015), but House and Senate authorizers could not reach an agreement on the proposal, and the issue was punted to the appropriators.

House Subcommittee

The House Appropriations Subcommittee on VA, HUD, and Independent Agencies approved a $91.7 billion draft version of the bill, later introduced as HR 2158, by voice vote with little dissent June 25. The bill's bottom line was $5.8 billion more than the amount provided in fiscal 1997, and $666 million more than Clinton requested.

Debate was marked by bipartisan cooperation stemming

VA-HUD-Independent Agencies Spending

(in thousands of dollars)

	Fiscal 1997 Appropriation	Fiscal 1998 Clinton Request	House Bill	Senate Bill	Conference Report
Veterans Affairs					
Veterans benefits	$ 21,327,936	$ 21,704,389	$ 21,704,389	$ 21,704,389	$ 21,704,389
Compensation and pensions	*19,599,259*	*19,932,997*	*19,932,997*	*19,932,997*	*19,932,997*
Veterans Health Administration	17,336,654	17,253,380	17,359,006	17,354,000	17,404,256
Construction projects	425,858	245,800	336,100	259,100	352,900
Other	996,045	1,012,581	1,048,081	991,581	991,331
TOTAL, Veterans Affairs	**$ 40,086,493**	**$ 40,216,150**	**$ 40,447,576**	**$ 40,309,070**	**$ 40,452,876**
Housing and Urban Development					
HOME program	1,400,000	1,309,000	1,500,000	1,400,000	1,500,000
Housing preservation	5,750,000	0	0	0	0
Public housing capital fund	0	2,500,000	2,500,000	2,500,000	2,500,000
Public housing operating fund	0	2,900,000	2,900,000	2,900,000	2,900,000
Section 8 subsidized housing	4,640,000	10,676,000	10,393,000	10,119,000	9,373,000
Severely distressed public housing	550,000	524,000	524,000	550,000	550,000
Federal Housing Administration	185,470	196,305	196,305	196,305	201,305
Limitation on guaranteed loans	*127,400,000*	*127,400,000*	*127,400,000*	*127,400,000*	*127,400,000*
Ginnie Mae (receipts)	–218,000	–204,000	–204,000	–204,000	–204,000
Limitation on guaranteed loans	*110,000,000*	*130,000,000*	*130,000,000*	*130,000,000*	*130,000,000*
Homeless assistance	823,000	823,000	823,000	823,000	823,000
Community development grants	4,850,000	4,600,000	4,600,000	4,600,000	4,675,000
Other HUD accounts, including rescissions	–1,676,661	1,248,950	1,890,950	1,936,950	1,343,450
TOTAL, HUD	**$ 16,303,809**	**$ 24,573,255**	**$ 25,123,255**	**$ 24,821,255**	**$ 23,661,755**
NASA					
Human space flight	5,362,900	5,326,500	5,426,500	5,326,500	5,506,500
Science, aeronautics and technology	5,767,100	5,642,000	5,690,000	5,642,000	5,690,000
Mission support, other	2,579,200	2,531,500	2,531,500	2,521,500	2,451,500
TOTAL, NASA	**$ 13,709,200**	**$ 13,500,000**	**$ 13,648,000**	**$ 13,490,000**	**$ 13,648,000**
Environmental Protection Agency					
Abatement, control, programs, facilities	2,540,941	2,809,388	2,724,837	2,575,561	2,696,562
Superfund	1,348,245	2,042,848	1,454,058	1,353,359	1,453,359
State and tribal assistance grants	2,910,207	2,793,257	3,026,182	3,047,000	3,213,125
TOTAL, EPA	**$ 6,799,393**	**$ 7,645,493**	**$ 7,205,077**	**$ 6,975,920**	**$ 7,363,046**
Selected Independent Agencies					
Community Devel. Financial Institutions	50,000	125,000	125,000	0	80,000
Federal Emergency Management Agency	5,103,556	838,558	1,028,058	793,558	829,958
Disaster relief	*4,600,000*	*370,000*	*500,000*	*320,000*	*320,000*
Food and shelter program	*100,000*	*100,000*	*100,000*	*100,000*	*100,000*
National Science Foundation	3,270,000	3,367,000	3,486,826	3,377,000	3,429,000
Research	*2,432,000*	*2,514,700*	*2,537,526*	*2,524,700*	*2,545,700*
Education	*619,000*	*625,500*	*632,500*	*625,500*	*632,500*
Consumer Product Safety Commission	42,500	45,000	44,000	45,000	45,000
Selective Service System	22,930	23,919	23,413	23,413	23,413
Corporation for National Service	402,500	549,000	202,500	423,500	428,500
GRAND TOTAL	**$ 85,895,503**	**$ 90,990,338**	**$ 91,461,593**	**$ 90,367,535**	**$ 90,735,430**

SOURCE: House Appropriations Committee

from the substantial allocation the panel had received from the full Appropriations Committee, and from the absence of the kind of divisive policy riders that had driven a wedge between Republicans and Democrats in previous years. *(1995 Almanac, p. 11-83)*

Subcommittee chairman Jerry Lewis, R-Calif., easily convinced most members to refrain from offering amendments in hopes of working out any disagreements before the full committee considered the legislation.

However, the panel did adopt by voice vote an amendment by Carrie P. Meek, D-Fla., to transfer $195 million from excess reserves in Section 8 public housing accounts to the Section 202 elderly housing program.

The subcommittee also initially adopted, by voice vote, an amendment by Mark W. Neumann, R-Wis., that would have required the EPA to get a state's approval before it added a site to the superfund toxic-waste cleanup list. But David R. Obey of Wisconsin, ranking Democrat on the full committee, raised concerns about the potential impact on a Wisconsin superfund site, and consistent with the panel's comity, Lewis vitiated the vote, leaving the issue for the full committee. No one protested.

Major elements of the subcommittee bill included the following:

• **HUD.** $25.1 billion for HUD, $8.8 billion above fiscal 1997 funding and $550 million more than the administration's request.

The total included $9.2 billion for the renewal of Section 8 contracts, as stipulated in the budget resolution. However, Lewis criticized HUD for inconsistent reports on the amount of money in Section 8 reserve accounts, which public housing authorities were required to maintain. Reflecting his frustration, Lewis offered no opposition to Meek's amendment to cut the Section 8 reserves and transfer the money to housing for the elderly.

• **EPA.** $7.2 billion for EPA, 6 percent more than fiscal 1997 funding, but $413 million less than requested. The total included $1.5 billion for cleanup of superfund hazardous waste sites, $106 million more than in fiscal 1997, but $589 million less than Clinton sought.

• **Veterans.** $40.4 billion for the VA, including $21.7 billion for veterans benefits, and $17.3 billion for the Veterans Health Administration — $51 million less than fiscal 1997 funding. Lewis said another $468 million would probably be available for veterans' medical care once the Veterans' Affairs Committee completed work on authorizing legislation to allow the VA to keep, rather than turn over to the Treasury, money it received from health insurance claims filed for veterans at its hospitals, as called for in the budget resolution.

• **NASA.** $13.6 billion for NASA, $61 million less than in fiscal 1997, but an increase of $148 million over Clinton's request. Of that amount, $5.4 billion was for human space flight.

• **Science.** $3.5 billion for the National Science Foundation, 7 percent more than fiscal 1997 spending and $120 million more than the president requested.

• **AmeriCorps.** $403 million for AmeriCorps, Clinton's national service program, which offered stipends toward college tuition in exchange for community service. AmeriCorps was an annual target of congressional Republicans, who portrayed it as a costly, ineffective program that congressional investigators had concluded had difficulty in retaining participants and persuading some of its graduates to pursue educational opportunities. However, faced with a veto threat if the program was eliminated, the subcommittee agreed to continue the fiscal 1997 funding level, $147 million below the president's request.

• **FEMA.** $1.1 billion for FEMA, $250 million more than requested — including $60 million in unrequested funds to plan and construct a full-scale windstorm simulation center in Idaho.

• **Consumer affairs.** As it had the year before, the panel sought to abolish the Office of Consumer Affairs, which advised the president on consumer issues and for which the administration requested $1.8 million. Under Lewis' draft bill, responsibility for the office's Consumer Resource Handbook would be transferred to another federal agency. Appropriators had left the office unfunded in the fiscal 1997 VA-HUD bill, only to see it revived as part of the subsequently enacted omnibus spending bill (PL 104-208) at a cost of $1.5 million. Lewis said that would not happen again.

• **Community development banks.** The bill included $125 million for the Community Development Financial Institutions program — a $75 million increase over fiscal 1997 funding and equal to the level called for in the budget agreement. The program had been created in 1994 (PL 103-325) to increase lending to small businesses and other organizations in low-income rural and urban areas through grants and loans to community development banks, credit unions and other financial institutions. *(1994 Almanac, p. 100)*

However, the appropriators did little to hide their anger over management of the program, which was the subject of an internal Treasury Department investigation, following allegations of improper activities in the first round of grant awards in 1996, as well as published reports that early recipients included an Arkansas firm with ties to first lady Hillary Rodham Clinton.

In their report accompanying the bill, the appropriators urged the Inspector General to "expeditiously and aggressively" investigate the allegations. "The committee has recommended funding this program . . . for the obvious reason that guilt must first be proven before punishment is administered," the report said.

House Full Committee

The full Appropriations Committee approved the spending bill July 8 by voice vote, after rejecting attempts by GOP conservatives to eliminate Clinton's National Service program and limit the EPA's authority (H Rept 105-175). Lewis said he hoped to keep the bill clean of policy riders that might prompt a veto.

Todd Tiahrt, R-Kan., proposed eliminating AmeriCorps, using the bulk of the money for deficit reduction, and designating $50 million for research into illnesses suffered by veterans of the 1991 Persian Gulf War. Tiahrt was backed by defense hawk Norm Dicks, D-Wash.

Lewis reluctantly opposed the amendment, warning that it would attract a presidential veto, force the issue into end-of-session dealings on spending bills, and undermine the authority of the appropriators. Committee Chairman Robert L. Livingston, R-La., told GOP colleagues that if they wanted to make a political statement, the House floor was a better venue. Lewis subsequently offered a substitute, approved by voice vote, earmarking $20 million in veterans health spending for Gulf War research.

The committee rejected by voice vote a proposal by Neumann to provide an additional $579 million for VA health care, in case the department failed to receive $604 million in expected fiscal 1998 revenues from health insurance claims filed for veterans at VA hospitals, as stipulated in the budget resolution. Neumann feared that negotiators would abandon that plan in conference on the budget-reconciliation bill. But Lewis and Livingston warned against pre-empting the conferees and promised to address the issue in the conference on the VA-HUD bill if the reconciliation provision did not survive.

Neumann also reoffered his subcommittee proposal to require EPA to get a state governor's approval before adding superfund sites to the national priorities list. He argued that similar language was in the fiscal 1995 rescissions bill (PL 104-19) and the fiscal 1996 omnibus spending bill (PL 104-134), and should be included again.

But Obey said the restriction would prevent the EPA from designating the Fox River in Wisconsin as a superfund site, despite the presence of 11 million cubic yards of sediment containing polychlorinated biphenyls, or PCBs, a hazardous substance used in insulation. He offered a modification to Neumann's amendment, which would delay implementation of the requirement until April 1, 1998.

"I would not want to have any one man in any one state" override an EPA cleanup, said Obey. Other members also expressed concern about how the provision would affect their states, and they accepted Obey's amended version, 22-18 — then torpedoed the entire provision by a vote of 15-30.

House Floor Action

After two days of debate, the House passed a $91.5 billion version of the bill July 16 by an overwhelming vote of 397-31. But first, lawmakers delivered a severe hit to Clinton's National Service program, while abandoning an attempt to slash funding for the troubled community lending program. *(Vote 280, p. H-88)*

• **AmeriCorps.** The effort to eliminate AmeriCorps was again led by Tiahrt with a handful of other House Republicans. The money, Tiahrt argued, could be better used examining the causes of Gulf War-related illnesses. "Caring for veterans who fought for America's freedom and security is a necessary function of our federal government," Tiahrt said. "Paying healthy AmeriCorps volunteers is simply not."

Supporters of the program said three out of five AmeriCorps participants had completed 1,700 hours of service and nearly four out of five had earned education awards. They said the program had trained more than 300,000 volunteers who had tutored, rehabilitated houses, cleaned up neighborhoods and planted trees.

Christopher Shays, R-Conn., took umbrage at his colleagues' partisan attack on the program, created in 1993 with GOP support. "I hear people calling it the president's program, and yet the president worked very hard with Republicans to make it a bipartisan program," Shays said.

In a deal worked out between the majority and minority, Tiahrt agreed to cut AmeriCorps funding in the bill roughly in half, providing $203 million, while refraining from seeking a recorded vote that might force lawmakers to oppose additional money for veterans' health research. The amendment, adopted by voice vote July 15, proposed using a portion of the savings to increase funding for veterans medical research by $25 million, and to increase by $5 million the $20 million already earmarked in the bill to study the cause of illnesses suffered by veterans of the 1991 Persian Gulf War.

• **Community lending.** Mark Foley, R-Fla., sparked a lengthy debate with a proposal to reduce funding in the bill for community development financial institutions to the fiscal 1997 level of $50 million.

Republicans criticized the program for awarding $11 million in grants and loans without providing any documentation on why the recipients were selected. "Only in Washington would we be sitting here debating a 150 percent increase in funding for a program that is judged, by any objective standard, a monument to bureaucratic bungling and administrative inefficiency," said Foley.

Democrats argued that to freeze the funds while the program was under investigation would unfairly penalize distressed communities and jeopardize the balanced-budget agreement. "The administration and congressional leadership in fact agreed to this increase precisely because [the lending program] is a win-win for all parties involved," said Jesse L. Jackson Jr., D-Ill.

During more than two hours of floor debate, Jackson and Floyd H. Flake, D-N.Y., repeatedly sought out Foley and others in hopes of modifying the amendment. Foley offered a compromise: $125 million for the program pending an investigation, plus a program evaluation and uniform standards for awarding grants by Oct. 1, or the amount would be reduced to $50 million. But further talks failed over the question of who would conduct the investigation.

Foley finally withdrew his amendment after receiving promises from Lewis and ranking VA-HUD subcommittee Democrat Louis Stokes of Ohio, to discuss the issue with the administration before the bill went to conference.

• **FEMA.** Spirited debate also occurred over $60 million included in the bill for a windstorm simulation center in Idaho to provide information on the impact of hurricane-force conditions on buildings and other structures

Obey, who had expressed concern over the project in the subcommittee, recited a litany of problems: Clinton never requested the money; the project was unauthorized; the manufacturer, Lockheed Martin, was seeking a special contract to alleviate its cost overruns; and the $60 million was only a down payment on a $181 million project. Several members from hurricane-prone regions, including Meek, opposed Obey's effort, saying the research was necessary.

The House agreed, 322-110, to Obey's proposal to cut $60 million from FEMA and transfer $48 million of it to veterans' medical care. It then adopted, 244-187, an amendment offered by Stokes on Obey's behalf specifically deleting the $60 million earmark for the windstorm simulation center. *(Votes 276, 277, p. H-86)*

Other Amendments

In other action on the bill, the House:

➤ Approved by voice vote an amendment by Lewis to cut $174,000 from the budget of the National Science Foundation. Members were incensed that the NSF had provided $194,000 for a study on why people decided not to run for Congress.

➤ Rejected, 200-227, an attempt by F. James Sensenbrenner Jr., R-Wis., to cut $100 million added to the bill by the Appropriations Committee for NASA's Human Space Flight account for "Russian program assurance." The money was added to address space station program needs that resulted from delays by Russia in meeting its commitments to the space station project. NASA had announced April 9 that construction of the space station would be delayed until late 1998 because of Russia's inability to deliver a key component of the project on time. *(Vote 278, p. H-88)*

➤ Approved by voice vote an amendment by Gerald B. H. Solomon, R-N.Y., to ensure that the VA received at least $579 million of the estimated $604 million it expected to get in fiscal 1998 from health insurance claims filed for veterans at its hospitals.

➤ Approved by voice vote an amendment by Solomon to prohibit grants or contracts using VA-HUD money from going to universities or colleges that barred ROTC or military recruiters on campus.

➤ Approved by voice vote a proposal by Ken Bentsen, D-

Texas, to prohibit the use of EPA funds to implement rules that would allow the import into the United States of wastes containing hazardous levels of PCBs.

➤ Approved by voice vote an amendment by Lewis to increase funding for construction of veterans' cemeteries by $5.5 million, and to reduce funding for construction of state veterans' extended care facilities by an equal amount.

➤ Lastly, rejected, 193-235, a motion by Joseph P. Kennedy II, D-Mass., to send the bill back to committee with instructions to increase spending on various housing programs by $160 million. Kennedy, the ranking Democrat on the Banking Subcommittee on Housing and Community Opportunity, had not been present on the House floor earlier in the day when the housing title of the bill was being considered and consequently was unable under House rules to offer specific housing amendments. *(Vote 279, p. H-88)*

Senate Committee

The Senate VA-HUD Appropriations Subcommittee approved a $90.4 billion version of the bill by voice vote July 15. On July 17, the full committee concurred, 28-0 (S 1034 — S Rept 105-53). The bill's total was about $1 billion less than the House version.

The Senate measure was similar to the House bill in a number of areas, including proposals to:

➤ Increase Clinton's budget request for the VA to $40.3 billion from $40.2 billion.

➤ Reduce funding for the EPA to slightly less than $7 billion, compared with $7.6 billion in Clinton's budget.

➤ Abolish the Office of Consumer Affairs.

➤ Provide $9.2 billion in fiscal 1998 to deal with HUD's costly problem of renewing Section 8 subsidized housing contracts.

However, the Senate bill diverged from the House version in several areas, including Senate proposals to:

• **AmeriCorps.** Provide $403 million for the AmeriCorps program, equal to its fiscal 1997 funding. House appropriators initially agreed to that amount, but it was later cut in half.

• **Community development banks.** Zero out the Community Development Financial Institutions program, for which the House bill provided $125 million. In its report accompanying the bill, the committee requested an audit by the General Accounting Office (GAO), saying it was "deeply concerned with this program's track record of accountability with respect to previously appropriated funds."

• **Section 8.** Perhaps the most significant difference with the House bill was the inclusion in the Senate version of provisions to reduce rental subsidies for Section 8 housing.

The so-called mark-to-market proposal — crafted by Connie Mack, chairman of the Senate Banking, Housing and Urban Affairs Committee's Housing Subcommittee — sought to reduce the cost of renewing the Section 8 contracts, mostly by cutting subsidies to landlords who charged more-than-market rents. In fiscal 1998, it was expected to reduce renewal costs by $500 million.

Under Mack's plan, rents would be reduced to comparable rates in an area for non-subsidized housing, or to 90 percent of fair market rents if comparable properties did not exist. Comparable rates would be the rents charged in the neighborhood; fair market rents would be the average for a specific area. State and local housing finance agencies, rather than HUD, would restructure the contracts.

The proposal also called for restructuring Section 8 mortgage debt insured by the FHA to reduce the number of expected defaults. The provisions would sunset in 2001, by which time most Section 8 contracts would have been renewed, or would have lapsed.

The provisions had originally been included in the Senate-passed version of the budget-reconciliation bill (HR 2015). However, House and Senate conferees on the budget bill were unable to reach agreement on the plan the week of July 14, and they dropped it in the face of objections from members of the House Banking Committee. Members of the Senate Banking Committee then asked the appropriations panel to include it in the VA-HUD spending bill.

The Section 8 proposal had the support of VA-HUD Subcommittee Chairman Christopher S. Bond, R-Mo., and the strong backing of the Senate Banking panel.

Senate Floor Action

The Senate passed HR 2158 on July 22 by a lopsided vote of 99-1, after substituting the text of its own $90.4 billion bill. Only a handful of amendments were offered during less than a day of debate. *(Vote 194, p. S-34)*

Casting the sole dissenting vote was Jon Kyl, R-Ariz., who opposed the legislation because of its overall spending increase of about $4.5 billion over fiscal 1997 levels, the significant jump in HUD funding from $16.3 billion to $24.8 billion without offsetting reductions, and the $424 million allocated in the final bill to the AmeriCorps program.

As he had in years past, Dale Bumpers, D-Ark., sought to kill NASA's space station program, arguing that it had been beset by cost overruns that forced NASA to take money away from more worthy projects. He cited newly released information from the GAO, which found that since April 1996, cost overruns had more than tripled with schedule slippage increasing by nearly 50 percent.

"I've stood on this floor for six long years and said, 'Show me, tell me what are the achievements. . . . I've been met with a deafening roar of silence," said Bumpers.

But with photographs of a successful mission to Mars being beamed back to the United States almost daily, Bumpers had little chance of persuading his colleagues to terminate the space station. "This is not the time to abort the mission," said Bond.

Bumpers' amendment, which would have eliminated all space station funding except $600 million for close-down costs, was tabled (killed) by a vote of 69-31. *(Vote 193, p. S-34)*

Amendments adopted during the Senate debate — all of them by voice vote — included:

➤ A proposal by Barbara A. Mikulski of Maryland, the ranking Democrat on the VA-HUD subcommittee, to trim spending in the bill for veterans and housing in order to provide an additional funding for several programs. She proposed allocating an extra $25 million for empowerment zones, economically strapped areas that received help for job creation and training; an additional $20 million for the America Reads literacy program under AmeriCorps to support 1,300 tutors to help children learn to read; and $5 million for a pre-disaster mitigation program that would allow FEMA to help disaster-prone communities prepare for possible earthquakes or hurricanes.

➤ Four amendments by Bond, on behalf of several other senators, to allow the state of Florida to use certain funds for a wastewater treatment facility; to prohibit distribution of Native American Housing block grant funding to persons who violated program rules; to make funding available for NASA's Neutral Buoyancy Simulator; and to prohibit federal locality pay increases for employees who were transferred as a result of sexual harassment.

➤ Two amendments by Bumpers, to earmark NASA funds for a National Research Council report on the space station program; and to restore the authority of the VA to request waivers of certain visa requirements for foreign doctors working at VA hospitals.

➤ An amendment by Paul Wellstone, D-Minn., to require the Senate Veterans Affairs' Committee to hold hearings on proposals that would require the VA to provide medical care to veterans exposed to radiation in tests conducted by the military.

Conference/Final Action

House and Senate conferees reached agreement on a compromise bill Sept. 30, the final day of the fiscal year, following last-minute compromises on housing policy and on new funding concerns raised by the administration. The House agreed to the conference report Oct. 8 by a vote of 405-21, and the Senate cleared the bill the following day by voice vote. *(House vote 505, p. H-152)*

The conference agreement (H Rept 105-297) provided a total of $90.7 billion for veterans, housing, space, science, and environmental programs in fiscal 1998 — $4.8 billion more than fiscal 1997 spending, but $255 million less than requested by the president. Of the total, $68.6 billion, or about 76 percent, was for discretionary spending programs.

The conferees had originally hoped to start and finish work on the bill Sept. 26. As the meeting began, however, conference chairman Bond announced that White House Office of Management and Budget Director Franklin D. Raines had contacted him an hour before with a seven-page list of concerns that could prompt Clinton to veto the bill — a threat that annoyed members of both parties.

"We've really got to talk with our own White House about these new late passions that they have," said Mikulski. Democrats suggested postponing action so they could talk to the Clinton administration, while Republicans asked for a delay so they could continue to work out differences between members of House and Senate authorizing committees over the proposed reforms to the Section 8 program.

The conference reconvened Sept. 30. But while Bond and Lewis waited in the committee room, the real negotiations continued outside, where other lawmakers and staff worked feverishly to reach agreement on the housing and funding issues.

Differences Over Section 8 Reforms

The most pressing problem for the conference was the disagreement among Republican authorizers over whether to use the bill to revamp the expiring Section 8 contracts.

House and Senate Banking committee staff debated the details of revamping Section 8 subsidized housing contracts in the Capitol hallway just outside the conference meeting room. Their bosses — Mack and Rick A. Lazio, R-N.Y., chairman of the House Housing Subcommittee — had butted heads over Mack's "mark-to-market" proposal in the Senate version of the bill.

Lazio and House Banking Committee Chairman Jim Leach, R-Iowa, opposed including the provisions in the spending bill because they disagreed with some of the details and because they feared it would reduce momentum to enact a big public housing overhaul bill (HR 2) that had passed the House in May. The Senate passed a companion measure (S 462) on Sept. 26. *(Housing overhaul, p. 7-12)*

Speaker Newt Gingrich, R-Ga., and the appropriators eventually stepped in, brokering a compromise that retained the bulk of Mack's proposal but added a few House ideas for implementing the changes. Under the final agreement, HUD was allowed to restructure the FHA-insured mortgages of multifamily properties where above-market-rate Section 8 rental assistance contracts were used, with the aim of cutting the federal subsidy costs, reducing the likelihood of FHA loan defaults, and ensuring the continued use of such properties for low-income housing.

The agreement included a Lazio proposal to create a new independent office at HUD, the Office of Multifamily Housing Assistance Restructuring, to oversee the restructuring of the housing contracts and to update Congress on the program's progress. Actual restructuring of mortgages would be conducted by state or local housing finance agencies, or other capable entities, acting on behalf of HUD, and they would be encouraged to work with nonprofit groups and others interested in the project, as Lazio had wanted.

The restructuring was expected to result in fiscal 1998 savings of $562 million, which the conferees used to offset funding for other programs funded in the bill.

Meeting New White House Demands

Elsewhere on the Hill, House Democrats were on the phone with the White House, encouraging administration officials to drop objections to the bill in exchange for increased funding for the superfund toxic waste cleanup program, economic development programs, and the president's AmeriCorps program.

Ultimately, nearly all the programs mentioned by Clinton received a little more money than conferees had initially agreed to, but not as much as the administration wanted. And most of the new funding came with hard-to-meet requirements. The conferees agreed to add to the bill:

- **Superfund.** $650 million more for superfund — bringing the total to $2.2 billion. But the additional money would not be available until fiscal 1999, and then only if authorizing legislation was enacted by May 15, 1998.
- **Community development banks.** $6 million in addition to the $74 million agreed to by conferees for the Community Development Financial Institutions program, bringing the total to $80 million — $30 million more than the fiscal 1997 level.

The House had agreed to the president's request of $125 million, while the Senate provided no funding in response to allegations of mismanagement and favoritism in making grants under the program. That controversy had been largely resolved in August, however, after the two Treasury Department officials in charge of the program resigned and the department announced it was strengthening internal procedures and controls.

- **AmeriCorps.** $5 million more for the AmeriCorps program, bringing the total to $429 million — $26 million more than fiscal 1997 funding, but still $120 million less than Clinton requested. The extra $5 million could be used only for literacy programs.
- **'Brownfields.'** $25 million to create a demonstration project on community development within HUD to address administration concerns over insufficient funding to redevelop "brownfields" — environmentally damaged industrial areas. Conferees had originally included $86 million for brownfields cleanup under EPA. The additional $25 million came from cuts in the Community Development Block Grant program, which received $4.67 billion under the final legislation.
- **Other.** Other additions were:
  - $8 million in addition to the $11 million in the bill for economic development initiatives by the HUD secretary.

• $1 million for an "unforeseen contingency fund" at the White House. The fund usually was included in the Treasury-Postal Service appropriations bill but was omitted from the fiscal 1998 version (HR 2378).

The extra funds for AmeriCorps, community lending, HUD initiatives and the White House fund were offset by reducing the amount in the bill for empowerment zones by $20 million, leaving only $5 million for planning activities.

South Pole Station

After the various negotiations were seemingly complete, Bond and Lewis left the room briefly to discuss the proposals privately. They returned, however, to find another problem — Senate Appropriations Committee Chairman Ted Stevens, R-Alaska, was upset about a House provision to step up funding for a South Pole research station.

Stevens argued that the research could have been done at a Navy station in Point Barrow, Alaska, which had been closed, instead of at the National Science Foundation's South Pole site, which, he said, was "almost impossible to get to." Stevens asked: "How do I explain to my Eskimo people?"

Lewis was hesitant to give in, saying that the $115 million approved by the House to rebuild the South Pole station would address "long-term diplomatic concerns" with other countries conducting research there. He was also eager to move forward after resolving the other differences. But Stevens warned that the issue would not end there. "You go ahead and do it," he said, "but I'll rescind it next year." Finally, Bond stepped in and offered a successful compromise, cutting funds to rebuild the South Pole station to $70 million, with half the money withheld until Oct. 1, 1998.

Other Conference Decisions

While much of the conferees' attention was diverted by the Section 8 dispute and Clinton's new demands, members reached agreement with relative ease on other issues, including the following:

• **HUD.** $23.7 billion for HUD, an increase of $7.4 billion from fiscal 1997 levels. The total included $9.4 billion for Section 8 housing subsidy contracts, $8.2 billion of it allocated for the renewal of expiring contracts.

• **EPA.** $7.4 billion for EPA, an increase of 8 percent over fiscal 1997, but $282 million less than Clinton requested. The superfund account got $1.5 billion for fiscal 1998, as well as the $650 million advance appropriation for fiscal 1999, subject to authorization.

• **Veterans.** $40.5 billion for the VA, including $17.1 billion for medical care and the treatment of eligible beneficiaries. The bill also assumed the availability of $604 million from reimbursements from insurance companies for VA-provided medical care — resulting in a total of 4 percent more for VA medical care than was provided in fiscal 1997.

• **FEMA.** $830 million for FEMA, including $320 million for disaster relief activities.

• **NASA.** $13.7 billion for NASA, $180 million more than requested. The amount included $5.5 billion for NASA's human space flight activities, $2.4 billion of it for continued development of the international space station.

However, only $1.5 billion of the space station funds would be available before March 31, 1998; the remainder would be released once NASA provided a detailed report on the project's outlook and potential effect on other NASA programs.

• **Science.** $3.4 billion for the National Science Foundation, $159 million more than was provided in fiscal 1997.

• **Consumer affairs.** The bill included no funds for the Office of Consumer Affairs, thereby terminating it.

Line-Item Veto

On Nov. 1, Clinton used his line-item veto authority to cancel seven projects worth $14 million from the $90.7 billion measure, which by then had been enacted into law.

Clinton said he targeted projects not included in his budget request and those whose removal would not "impair any essential government functions" or "harm the national interest." While the seven vetoed projects constituted pocket change for the federal budget, members who championed them were stung by the loss.

"It wasn't pork," said Senate Assistant Majority Leader Don Nickles, R-Okla., who lost $900,000 to finish planning a new national cemetery at Fort Sill, Okla. "It was a project we worked on for 10 to 12 years." Combined with $500,000 in previously appropriated funds, the appropriation would have paid to complete the project's planning phase.

In his veto message, Clinton said the project was not necessary because the VA planned to open five new cemeteries in the next two years. Clinton said such expenditures on new veterans' cemeteries was "unprecedented since the Civil War." He said if the nation needed yet another cemetery, "several other sites would be higher priority than Fort Sill in terms of veterans served."

Most of the dollar value of the vetoes came from eliminating $10 million set aside to fund telescopes in Arizona and Chile as part of NASA's Origins project, which used ground- and space-based telescopes to search for planets capable of supporting life. Clinton said that the two projects would not add to NASA's knowledge and that the Arizona telescope, located at the University of Arizona, would duplicate work already being done at the NASA-funded Keck Observatory in Mauna Kea, Hawaii.

Clinton also vetoed $600,000 earmarked for a demonstration project in South Burlington, Vt., that used solar power to decompose municipal waste. The project, created in fiscal 1992 by Clinton ally Sen. Patrick J. Leahy, D-Vt., had received $7.2 million in federal funds since that time. Clinton cited an EPA report saying the project "does not appear to offer any economic advantages over conventional technologies."

The only state to lose two provisions was Alabama. Clinton removed $1 million earmarked for the state's Department of Environmental Management to build a central facility for the Water and Wastewater Institute in Montgomery, and $15,000 for a police training complex in Arab, a small town about 30 miles south of Huntsville.

Clinton also vetoed:

➤ A $1 million grant to the Carter County Chamber of Commerce in Montana for trade and development activities. Funding would have come from HUD's Community Development Block Grant program, which Clinton said should not be used for promotional and business outreach activities.

➤ $500,000 to extend water and sewer lines to a new industrial park in Ayr Township, Pa. The project, in GOP Rep. Bud Shuster's district, would have primarily benefited private entities, Clinton said. ■

GOP Backs Down on Disaster Aid Bill

Victories on Capitol Hill were rarely as lopsided as the one scored by President Clinton on June 12 when he signed an $8.9 billion emergency spending bill to provide disaster relief to 23 states and finance Pentagon peacekeeping operations (HR 1871 — PL 105-18).

Clinton had vetoed a virtually identical bill (HR 1469) just three days earlier over controversial policy provisions that Republicans had attached despite repeated White House warnings that they would draw a veto.

The supplemental was urgently needed to speed federal funds to areas in the Plains and Upper Midwest suffering from record spring floods. Particularly hard hit was Grand Forks, N.D, which was inundated by water from the swollen Red River.

House appropriators had worked quickly in late April to craft the measure, with the aim of clearing it before members left for the Memorial Day recess. But action stalled almost immediately, as GOP leaders maneuvered to attach legislative riders, gambling that they could either force Clinton to sign an expanded bill or reap the political gains if he vetoed it.

But with flood victims desperate for federal help and nightly newscasts highlighting the story, the GOP strategy backfired. Bogged down by disputes over unrelated provisions, lawmakers did not finish work on the bill until after the Memorial Day recess.

As promised, Clinton vetoed the measure June 9, blaming GOP leaders for weighing the bill down with "contentious issues totally unrelated to disaster assistance, needlessly delaying essential relief."

Clinton cited several provisions, including a proposal aimed at increasing Congress' leverage in future budget negotiations with the White House. It would have guaranteed continued funding to any agency whose regular appropriations bill had not become law by the Oct. 1 start of the fiscal year.

A second objectionable provision would have blocked the use of controversial sampling techniques during the 2000 census. Republicans disliked the sampling idea because it was expected to produce a higher count of Democratic-leaning citizens in inner cities.

Battered by the national media, losing in the polls and fighting among themselves, Republican leaders decided to cut their losses and send Clinton a clean flood aid bill that he would sign.

To underscore his victory, Clinton held a hastily scheduled signing ceremony June 12 in the Oval Office, during which he underlined his signature twice and then raised his clenched fist in the air.

"It doesn't get any better than this," said Sen. Christopher J. Dodd, D-Conn. "The only victory [Republicans] had was that it ended today rather than next week."

GOP leaders came away virtually empty-handed. Republicans across the political spectrum were upset with the way their leadership handled the episode, which was reminiscent of the appropriations battles of 1995, when voters blamed Republicans more than Clinton for temporarily shutting down parts of the federal government.

"It's another example, like the shutdown of the government, where people lose confidence in Republicans' ability to lead," said David M. McIntosh, R-Ind., a leader of the firebrand class of 1994. "I would hope that this is the last time that they paint themselves into a corner," said moderate Marge Roukema, R-N.J. "I would have thought they understood better by now."

The spending in the new bill was virtually identical to that in the earlier version, despite vows by GOP leaders that the price tag would shrink or that Clinton would be forced to accept at least some elements of the GOP agenda.

The bill channeled $5.6 billion in disaster aid to 35 states, including $3.3 billion for the Federal Emergency Management Agency (FEMA), $585 million for the Army Corps of Engineers and $650 million for emergency highway repairs.

It also replenished $1.7 billion in Pentagon accounts that had been tapped for the Bosnia peacekeeping mission and to enforce a no-fly zone over Iraq, and it provided $932 million in mandatory appropriations for veterans compensation and pensions required to finance a 2.9 percent cost of living increase.

The bill contained $8 billion in rescissions (cuts) in unspent budget authority — including $1.9 billion in military funding and $1.6 billion from federal transportation programs.

BOXSCORE

Fiscal 1997 Supplemental Appropriations — HR 1871, (HR 1469, S 672). The bill provided emergency disaster aid and reimbursed the Pentagon for peacekeeping operations.

Reports: H Rept 105-83, S Rept 105-16; conference report, H Rept 105-119.

KEY ACTION

May 8 — Senate passed S 672, 78-22.

May 15 — House passed HR 1469, 244-178.

May 16 — Senate passed HR 1469 by previous agreement, after substituting text of S 672.

June 5 — Senate adopted conference report on HR 1469, 67-31. **House** cleared HR 1469, 220-201.

June 9 — President vetoed HR 1469.

June 12 — House passed HR 1871, 348-74. **Senate** cleared the bill, 78-21.

June 12 — President signed

House Committee

House appropriators began assembling the bill in April, working from a White House request for $4.1 billion in supplemental funds not anticipated in the regular fiscal 1997 appropriations bills. Clinton sought $2 billion for disaster relief and $2.1 billion for defense, chiefly peacekeeping operations in Bosnia and enforcement of the no-fly zone over Iraq.

But the cost of the bill quickly swelled, thanks in large part to the growing toll from winter storms and unusually severe spring flooding across many parts of the country.

Initial drafting by nine House appropriations subcommittees the week of April 14 more than doubled the bill's bottom line to $8.2 billion. The defense portion remained about the same size, but the disaster relief portion grew substantially.

Full Appropriations Committee

The bill sailed through the full House Appropriations Committee by voice vote April 24, after members agreed to add another $200 million for flood relief to the Upper Midwest (HR 1469 — H Rept 105-83).

Clinton had asked the appropriators to add an extra $300 million, following a high-profile helicopter tour of the Red River valley. The formal request reached the committee just hours before the markup.

House Appropriations Chairman Robert L. Livingston, R-La., agreed to include $200 million of that, predicting that he would support another add-on once detailed estimates on the flood damage were available. But he denied the other $100 million, requested for Community Development Block Grants, saying the program was not typically used to render disaster aid. The panel adopted Livingston's amendment by voice vote.

As approved by the committee, the bill contained $5.5 billion in disaster assistance, about $3.6 billion of it dedicated to FEMA; $1.34 billion to help the Pentagon pay for the Bosnia peacekeeping mission; and $562 million to pay for enforcing the no-fly zone over Iraq.

The measure also included $753 million in new mandatory spending for veterans' compensation and pensions, due to a new cost of living adjustment and more claims than had been anticipated. The funding, requested by the administration, did not require an offset under budget rules.

In addition to the FEMA money, the disaster-related portion of the bill included:

➤ $650 million from the federal Highway Trust Fund to repair flood-damaged roads in the West, Midwest, Mid-Atlantic and northern plains states. Clinton had requested $291 million, but the committee said that was insufficient.

➤ $197 million for repairs to national parks, mostly for flood and storm damage during the winter at Yosemite National Park in California.

➤ $585 million for the Army Corps of Engineers to repair levees and other flood control projects, as well as for dredging to restore portions of the Mississippi and Ohio rivers to navigable depths.

The measure also contained a roster of spending cuts that Livingston claimed "fully offset" and "paid for" the new commitments.

However, the Congressional Budget Office (CBO) estimated that the bill would add $5.6 billion to the deficit through fiscal 2002, chiefly because many of the cuts would not produce budget savings in the short term. Others were bookkeeping changes that would not produce measurable savings.

For example, one of the main proposed offsets — redirecting $3.8 billion in unspent Department of Housing and Urban Development (HUD) budget authority for Section 8 subsidized housing programs — meant HUD would have to take the money out of fiscal 1998 funds. In effect, appropriators were borrowing from 1998 and future years to finance the flood aid. Clinton had requested a rescission of $250 million.

A more questionable offset was a plan to cancel $1.6 billion in Department of Transportation "contract authority" for airport, transit and rail modernization grants. The authority would allow the department to enter into contracts without having received an appropriation. However, it had already been capped by appropriators and was no longer expected to be spent. CBO did not credit the provision as generating any savings.

The Pentagon's portion of the bill was to be financed by cuts in about 60 programs and accounts ($993 million), as well as easier-to-produce savings generated from revised inflation rates, fluctuations in foreign currency exchanges and unobligated balances ($861 million). Military construction accounts produced $180 million in savings, mostly from revised inflation rates.

Amendments and Controversies

There was virtually universal agreement that the bill had to pass quickly, and Livingston struggled to keep it free of controversial policy riders that could slow its pace. Clinton kept up the pressure, meeting with weary flood victims and calling on Congress to resist the "irresistible temptation" to tack on unrelated legislation that would bog down the funding.

But the must-pass measure already carried several controversial provisions, and members used the markup to try to add more.

- **Offsets.** Citing the CBO estimates, Mark W. Neumann, R-Wis., proposed to lower the bill's price tag to $4.7 billion and provide additional spending cuts in a way that he said would guarantee the measure did not add to the deficit. Neumann offered a list of politically impossible cuts, such as wiping out aid to Russia and other former Soviet states, killing Clinton's AmeriCorps community service program, and zeroing out the Goals 2000 education program. His amendment was defeated by voice vote.
- **WIC.** Some of the most vigorous debate came on an amendment by ranking Democrat David R. Obey of Wisconsin to fully fund the administration's request for $76 million for the Women, Infants and Children (WIC) food voucher program. The committee bill included $38 million.

Obey said without the additional funding, states would have to drop as many as 200,000 pregnant women and children from the program. Republicans countered that the program typically failed to spend many times that amount by the end of each fiscal year. The panel defeated Obey's amendment, 24-28.

- **Endangered Species Act.** The committee adopted by voice vote an amendment by Joseph M. McDade, R-Pa., to waive regulations of the Endangered Species Act for repairs on flood-control projects that were carried out in response to an imminent threat to human lives and property. The projects had to be in counties that were declared federal disaster areas.

The effect would be to extend to all federal disaster areas a waiver policy that the U.S. Fish and Wildlife Service had implemented in February for 46 counties in California.

McDade's amendment replaced much broader language written by the Energy and Water Appropriations Subcommittee, which would have suspended the species protection act for flood-control projects nationwide whenever inspections revealed an imminent threat to the health and safety of nearby citizens. Environmentalists attacked that provision as a dangerous, overly broad exemption from environmental review.

By adopting McDade's amendment, the committee satisfied two leading critics of the flood-control exemptions: George Miller of California, the ranking Democrat on the House Resources Committee, and Sherwood Boehlert, R-N.Y. Both said they supported the panel's revision.

But the compromise drew catcalls from conservatives, including Resources Committee Chairman Don Young, R-Alaska, and Richard W. Pombo, R-Calif., who said that the change would not go far enough in exempting flood-control projects.

Pombo, other GOP conservatives and some Democrats said reviews under the Endangered Species Act were often so protracted that they delayed and discouraged basic maintenance of levees. Miller and Boehlert dismissed the connection and said the species law already allowed emergency repairs of levees.

But House GOP leaders were still worried that the provision would spark a floor fight reminiscent of earlier battles on the environment that damaged Republicans during the

104th Congress. So the day after the markup, the leadership said it would scrap the provision entirely.

• **Farmland protection.** The committee stopped just short of killing a second controversial environmental provision. The panel rejected, 22-26, an amendment by George Nethercutt, R-Wash., to drop a proposal to reduce from 19 million to 14 million the number of acres that could be enrolled in the Conservation Reserve Program in fiscal 1997. The program paid farmers to idle environmentally sensitive land.

House farm-program authorizers, including Bob Smith, R-Ore., and Charles W. Stenholm of Texas, the chairman and ranking Democrat on the Agriculture Committee respectively, strongly opposed the provision. Stenholm said appropriators had not vetted it with the authorizers.

• **Bosnia withdrawal.** Another potential controversy involved the funding for U.S. participation in the U.N. peacekeeping effort in Bosnia. Members of both parties, especially junior Republicans, were upset by the administration's failure to meet self-imposed deadlines to withdraw troops from Bosnia and wanted to force action before the administration's latest deadline of June 30, 1998.

Todd Tiahrt, R-Kan., offered an amendment to force the withdrawal by Sept. 30, 1997, but ultimately withdrew it, saying he did not want to start a fight that could delay disaster relief.

• **Automatic 'CR.'** Dan Miller, R-Fla., offered and then withdrew an amendment to automatically enact a stopgap continuing resolution, or CR, at 98 percent of prior year levels for any appropriations bill not enacted by the Oct. 1 start of the fiscal year. The amendment would have enabled Republicans to threaten to freeze spending at 1997 levels as a way to gain concessions from Clinton.

The "automatic CR" idea was widely backed in the Senate, and top House leaders such as Majority Leader Dick Armey, R-Texas, said that if the Senate included the provision in its version of the bill, the House would likely accept the language in conference.

Senate Committee

The Senate Appropriations Committee approved an $8.4 billion version of the emergency spending bill (S 672 — S Rept 105-16) April 30 after an unusually contentious markup.

Approval came on a 16-12 vote, with support from Democrats Byron L. Dorgan of North Dakota and Barbara Boxer of California, whose states had a huge stake in the bill. New Hampshire Republican Judd Gregg voted against the bill saying it had "too much money, too little offsets" — but only after he was sure it had enough votes to advance.

Unlike the House committee's bill, S 672 contained the automatic CR provision. The language drew extended attacks from Democrats and a direct veto threat from the White House, but Republicans insisted on retaining it. They saw it as a way of regaining the leverage they had lost the previous September, when Clinton used veto threats to extract last-minute concessions on spending and policy from Republicans anxious to get home and campaign and desperate to avoid being blamed for another government shutdown. *(1996 Almanac, p. 10-20)*

Robert C. Byrd, D-W.Va., led the effort to strike the automatic CR, arguing that it would render the Appropriations Committee impotent and risk "mindless cuts" in discretionary programs. His amendment was defeated, 13-15.

Not all Republicans favored the idea. Livingston argued that it would make it very difficult to bring the appropriations season to a close because there would be no hard and fast deadline. House Rules Committee Chairman Gerald B. H. Solomon, R-N.Y., said the change had the potential to cut the defense budget and make it virtually impossible to force deep cuts in programs that Republicans disliked, such as the National Endowment for the Arts.

In addition to the automatic CR language, the Senate bill contained a number of other unrelated provisions including two environmental proposals that attracted veto threats in their own right. The bill proposed to:

• **Endangered Species Act.** Exempt the operation and repair of flood control projects from parts of the Endangered Species Act. Environmentalists and the administration said the language, by Larry E. Craig, R-Idaho, was so broadly drafted as to waive the act in non-emergency situations and that it had the potential to threaten fish stocks and other species.

• **Roads on federal lands.** Make it easier for states and localities to build roads on federal lands, including wilderness areas. The language, by Appropriations Committee Chairman Ted Stevens, R-Alaska, was aimed at ending a longstanding controversy over how to resolve right-of-way claims on federal lands held by states and other parties.

But Stevens' proposal was vigorously opposed by environmentalists, who said it would open the door to more road building on federal property, upsetting delicate ecosystems and disturbing habitat. Interior Secretary Bruce Babbitt said the language would "effectively render the federal government powerless to prevent the conversion of footpaths, dog sled trails, Jeep tracks, ice roads and other primitive transportation routes into paved highways."

No similar provision existed in the House version of the measure.

Most Provisions Track House Bill

Nearly obscured in the heat of the debate was the substance of the much-needed bill. Similar to the House bill, it included $5.5 billion in emergency disaster relief, $3.5 billion of it for FEMA, and $1.8 billion to finance the Bosnia peacekeeping mission and enforce the no-fly zone in Iraq.

In addition to money for FEMA, disaster funding included:

• $100 million for Community Development Block Grants, mostly for the Upper Midwest.

• $650 million for highway repair projects.

• $390 million for Army Corps of Engineers levee repair projects.

• $161 million for Agriculture Department watershed and flood prevention efforts.

In addition, the bill included the following non-emergency spending:

• $58 million of the administration's $76 million request for additional WIC funds.

• $100 million as a down payment on $921 million in U.S. arrears to the United Nations due in 1999. The bill specified that the money could be released only if a separate authorization bill was enacted.

• $125 million for block grants to states to extend Supplemental Security Income (SSI) benefits for legal immigrants for two months beyond the Aug. 22 cutoff date set in the 1996 welfare overhaul law (PL 104-193). The extension would give budget negotiators additional time to work on the issue.

• $31 million for the District of Columbia to repair schools and raise police salaries by 10 percent.

• $753 million in new mandatory spending for veterans' compensation and pensions.

• $15 million for research on environmental risk factors tied to regional variations in the incidence of breast cancer.

The Senate bill also contained many of the same offsets proposed in the House bill: $1.8 billion from various defense programs and inflation and foreign exchange recalculations, $234 million less than the House; $1.6 billion in budget authority from various transportation trust funds that had already been capped; and $3.7 billion in unspent funds for HUD's Section 8 subsidized housing programs.

In an offset not identified by the House, the Senate proposed to rescind $365 million for a NASA wind-tunnel project.

Senate Floor Action

The Senate approved S 672 late on May 8 with the automatic CR provision in tact, though it delayed formal passage because the House had not yet acted on its own version. The vote was 78-22. *(Vote 63, p. S-13)*

Senators agreed by unanimous consent to insert the Senate text into HR 1469 once that measure had passed the House, pass the amended bill, and go to conference. That occurred on May 16. By longstanding tradition, the House acted first on spending bills.

In addition to the CR language, the Senate bill contained several legislative riders, along with non-emergency spending such as $933 million in new spending from the highway trust fund, and a few special-interest projects.

Senators from the Dakotas and Minnesota won a late-stage concession to shift $400 million from FEMA disaster relief programs into the more flexible Community Development Block Grant program, bringing that total to $500 million. That set up a conflict with the House, where Livingston specifically rejected block grant funding when the House committee crafted HR 1469.

Majority Leader Trent Lott, R-Miss., had moved to invoke cloture on the bill even though Democrats gave no signal that they would filibuster. Cloture was invoked May 7 on a 100-0 vote. The move forced senators to submit amendments early and made most of those filed non-germane. *(Vote 57, p. S-13)*

Battle Lines Drawn

• **Automatic CR.** The Clinton administration immediately renewed its veto threat, saying the automatic CR could force a spending freeze below the levels outlined in a just-announced bipartisan budget agreement. Minority Leader Tom Daschle, D-S.D., said he had the votes to sustain a veto. *(Budget deal, p. 2-18)*

The White House also claimed that Lott had promised during the budget talks to drop the automatic CR language. White House lobbyist John Hilley told an assembly of Democratic senators that Lott had specifically signed off on dropping the CR provision, provided that Democrats would agree not to not filibuster a stand-alone bill aimed at achieving the same goal (S 547).

Lott vehemently denied any such deal, insisting that he had said he would consider the idea only if the sponsors of the provision — Sens. Kay Bailey Hutchison, R-Texas, and John McCain, R-Ariz. — gave their approval. They did not.

Byrd renewed his effort to kill the automatic CR provision, saying it would put discretionary spending "on automatic pilot." But the Senate voted 55-45, along party lines, to retain it. *(Vote 61, p. S-13)*

Some Republicans barely hid their pleasure at placing Clinton in the uncomfortable position of vetoing the must-pass bill.

• **Roads on federal lands**. Another provision that had drawn a veto threat — Stevens' language to make it easier for states and localities to build roads on federal lands — also remained in the bill, though only by a slim margin. The Senate voted, 51-49, to table (kill) an amendment by Dale Bumpers, D-Ark. to strike the provision. *(Vote 59, p. S-13)*

• **Endangered Species Act.** Craig's proposal to exempt flood control projects from parts of the Endangered Species Act was significantly narrowed May 8 and was no longer controversial. Language worked out on a bipartisan basis and offered by Harry Reid, D-Nev., focused specifically on repairs needed to respond to an "imminent threat to human lives and property in 1996 and 1997." It was adopted by voice vote.

• **Census Bureau.** Ernest F. Hollings, D-S.C., succeeded in striking a provision from the committee-approved bill that would have barred the Census Bureau from developing a plan to use sampling techniques as part of the 2000 census. By voice vote the Senate adopted Hollings' amendment to replace the sampling ban with largely symbolic language to block any "irreversible plans" to use sampling.

Those opposing the use of sampling techniques argued that the Constitution required an actual count of the population, not a statistical estimate. Proponents contended that the use of such statistical techniques was necessary to assure an accurate count of minority populations, especially given the widely acknowledged undercount of such populations in the 1990 census.

The House bill did not address the issue.

Other Amendments Adopted

It took almost the entire week for the Senate to work through the bill. The following were among the amendments adopted during the floor action:

• **SSI**. The Senate agreed, 89-11, to extend SSI and Medicaid benefits for up to 500,000 disabled legal immigrants facing a cutoff on Aug. 22. The extension, proposed by Alfonse M. D'Amato, R-N.Y., replaced the committee-approved plan for a $125 million block grant to the states. The extension of existing benefits was expected to cost $240 million, financed by rescinding $585 million in budget authority from a welfare jobs training program that was freed up after states instead applied for block grants under the welfare system overhaul (PL 104-193). *(Vote 58, p. S-13)*

• **Community Development Block Grants.** Senators agreed to a proposal by Stevens to shift $400 million from FEMA funding into Community Development Block Grants. Senators from North and South Dakota and Minnesota lobbied hard for additional funding and lined up votes by bringing local officials from flood-stricken areas to meet with their colleagues.

• **Bosnia.** In a move more symbolic than substantive, the Senate adopted by voice vote an amendment by Russell D. Feingold, D-Wis., and modified by Hutchison to bar the use of money provided in the bill to support the Bosnia peacekeeping mission beyond June 30, 1998. Because the bill would support the mission only through Sept. 30, 1997, the amendment had no practical effect other than to express a sense of the Senate for an exit from Bosnia at a certain date.

• **Other amendments.** The Senate also adopted amendments by:

- Paul Wellstone, D-Minn., to strike a special-interest provision attached by Hollings for a 14-month patent extension on an anti-inflammatory drug known as Toradol, produced by pharmaceutical giant Hoffmann-La Roche Inc. Wellstone's amendment, approved by voice vote, paved the way for the development of a less expensive generic alternative.
- Rod Grams, R-Minn., and Tim Johnson, D-S.D., to ease certain banking regulations for disaster-area lenders. The change was adopted 98-0. *(Vote 56, p. S-13)*

Amendments Defeated

The magnitude of the tragedy in the Midwest obscured concerns among deficit hawks that the bill, while "offset" with reductions in budget authority, would still add close to $6 billion to the budget deficit over the following several years, at least as scored by CBO.

An amendment by Phil Gramm, R-Texas, to pay for the bill with across-the-board cuts in non-defense discretionary spending was tabled (killed) May 8, 62-38. Stevens estimated that affected programs would have been cut by 5 percent for the rest of fiscal 1997. *(Vote 62, p. S-13)*

In a battle that broke along regional rather than partisan lines, the Senate voted 54-46 to table (or kill) an amendment by John W. Warner, R-Va., that would have shifted tens of millions of dollars in highway funds to Southern and Midwestern states. *(Vote 60, p. S-13)*

Instead, the underlying bill appropriated $318 million in highway funds mostly to "donor" states — those that remitted more in gasoline taxes to the federal Highway Trust Fund than they got back. It also appropriated $475 million to recipient states, including Alaska and Northeastern states, as well as another $139 million that was not in dispute.

The money was expected to be an issue in conference, because the House version contained only $318 million.

An effort by McCain to drop several pet projects — including a $12.3 million parking garage at a Cleveland veterans hospital, $12.6 million to complete a Kentucky bridge project and $3.6 million for Utah to plan for the 2002 Winter Olympics — was killed by voice vote.

House Floor Action

Undeterred by the veto threats, the House approved its $8.4 billion bill May 15 on a 244-178 vote — after adding its own version of the automatic CR provision. *(Vote 136, p. H-44)*

House leaders had postponed floor action for two weeks, waiting to see whether the automatic CR rider would remain in the Senate bill. The delay had particularly angered Livingston, who said it put enactment of the disaster relief by Congress' self-imposed Memorial Day deadline in severe doubt.

House action was further stalled May 14 after 43 Republicans, upset over a variety of issues, joined almost all Democrats to kill the initial rule for floor debate (H Res 146). The rule, which failed 193-229, would have made several controversial amendments in order, including a plan to cut off funding for U.S. ground troops in Bosnia after June 30, 1998, and a proposal to replace most of the nearly 60 separate Pentagon rescissions in the bill with cuts in a single program that assisted former Soviet republics in dismantling their nuclear and chemical arsenals. *(Vote 125, p. H-40)*

After the initial rule was rejected, GOP leaders issued a new rule (H Res 149) that dropped the Bosnia and Soviet republics amendments and made other adjustments. On the second try, the rule passed, 269-152. *(Vote 130, p. H-42)*

Changes Made on the House Floor

When the bill came to the floor May 15, the House made several major changes.

- **Automatic CR.** Most important, by a 227-197 vote that required serious whipping by GOP leaders, members adopted the automatic CR amendment, which was offered by George W. Gekas, R-Pa. *(Vote 134, p. H-44)*

The language was inserted over protests from Livingston, who said it would involve "a dramatic shift of power between the legislative and executive branch." A sizable band of conservatives also balked at the language, complaining that it would not cut spending. The House provision sought to finance each program covered by an unfinished fiscal 1998 appropriations bill at 100 percent of its fiscal 1997 funding.

House leaders delayed the vote until they had prodded their troops back in line, and only 14 Republicans defected, including Livingston, who voted only after it was clear the amendment would prevail.

- **SSI.** The House also followed the Senate's example and inserted into the bill an extension through Sept. 30 of SSI and health care benefits for up to 500,000 legal immigrants who were otherwise set to lose them Aug. 22.
- **Transportation funding.** The most significant change to the underlying bill came on a series of points of order by Spencer Bachus, R-Ala., a member of the Transportation and Infrastructure Committee, that struck $1.6 billion in proposed rescissions in Department of Transportation "contract authority" for airport, transit and rail modernization grants. The vote was a victory for Transportation Committee Chairman Bud Shuster, R-Pa., in his ongoing turf battle with appropriators, but it also eliminated $1.6 billion in offsets for the spending in the bill.

In fact, as pointed out by deficit hawk Neumann, the committee-reported bill would add $5.8 billion to the deficit. Neumann tried twice to cut the bill's price tag, but he was decisively defeated. By a 100-324 vote, the House rejected a Neumann bid to cut $2.4 billion in advance 1998 funding for FEMA, rescind an unspecified $3.6 billion in 1997 appropriations and restore $3.8 billion in rescissions from the Section 8 subsidized housing program. *(Vote 132, p. H-44)*

After the $1.6 billion in Highway Trust Fund offsets was struck from the bill, Neumann lost, 115-305, a bid to reduce FEMA's appropriation by a corresponding amount. *(Vote 135, p. H-44)*

Livingston promised that, despite the loss of the $1.6 billion offset, "when this bill returns from conference, it will be fully funded."

- **WIC.** The House agreed, 338-89, to increase WIC funding in the bill to $76 million. The Agriculture Department said that without the additional $38 million, about 180,000 of the program's 7.4 million beneficiaries risked being cut from the program. The amendment was offered by Obey, the Democratic bill manager, on behalf of Marcy Kaptur, D-Ohio. *(Vote 131, p. H-42)*
- **Environmental provisions.** Leaders of the House Agriculture and Resources committees each raised points of order against provisions that touched on sensitive environmental issues.

Agriculture Committee Chairman Smith struck Walsh's proposal to cap at 14 million acres the amount of land that could be enrolled in the Conservation Reserve Program in fiscal 1997.

Resources Committee Chairman Young removed the language that would have allowed emergency repairs of flood-control projects without the delays he said could be caused by reviews required under the Endangered Species Act. Young said the provision did not go far enough; related Senate language was expected to prevail.

Conference/Veto

A conference to reconcile differences in the House and Senate versions of the bill began May 20, with Livingston expressing hope that the negotiations could be wrapped up that day.

However, given the short time available before the recess, it was virtually impossible — for logistical and political reasons — to clear the bill, get it vetoed and then quickly pass a cleaned-up bill for Clinton to sign.

Conferees might have been able to finish in time to get the measure to Clinton before leaving May 23 for the Memorial Day recess. But GOP leaders did not want to be out of town and miss the chance to react quickly when Clinton vetoed the bill. With pressure off to resolve the toughest issues, even some of the smaller ones resisted solution.

With the conference stalled, Livingston crafted a bare-bones bill that included $500 million for the Pentagon, $100 million for Community Development block grants, $225 million for FEMA, $20 million for WIC and $71 million for flood control projects. Gingrich supported Livingston, and the idea was fine with Senate leaders. But Armey and others in the House GOP leadership quashed the move.

Livingston went to the floor May 22 to try to pass the bill by unanimous consent, but the leadership refused to recognize him. The sometimes-combustible chairman was barely able to contain his fury.

"I thought we had it worked out to pass the emergency part of it," Lott commented later. "There were some people saying we ought to move parts of it and other people saying, 'No, if we do that, we won't get the rest of it.' "

In a show of dissatisfaction, the House then voted 67-278 to defeat an adjournment resolution (H Con Res 87) offered by Armey. Leading the revolt was an enraged Livingston, normally a GOP loyalist. *(Vote 155, p. H-50)*

The vote on adjournment did not block members from going home; it simply meant the House had to meet in pro forma session every three days until members returned June 3. But the image of leaving without having sent any aid to the 35 states eligible to benefit from the $8.4 billion spending bill hurt Republicans.

The fight over the disaster aid bill also spilled over to broader budget matters, foiling plans to wrap up work on the bipartisan budget resolution (H Con Res 84) and putting off work on the 13 annual spending bills for fiscal 1998.

Armey — chief among those blocking a slimmed-down stopgap supplemental — publicly apologized to representatives from the flood-ravaged Dakotas. Armey noted that there was $2 billion in the FEMA pipeline, and he insisted the delay in passing the supplemental would not harm relief efforts.

That assurance did not impress members whose constituents were desperate for a congressional response to the flood damage. "We have made a crucial mistake in putting politics and process in front of people," said South Dakota Republican John Thune.

Conferees Finish After Recess

Reconvening after their much-criticized Memorial Day break, House and Senate conferees quickly wrapped up their negotiations on the bill June 4. The conference report (H Rept 105-119) bore Republican signatures only; no Democratic conferee signed it.

The Senate adopted the conference report June 5 on a 67-31 vote; minutes later, the House cleared the bill for Clinton by a 220-201 vote more reflective of the bitterness that had engulfed the measure all along. *(Senate vote 95, p. S-18; House vote 169, p. H-56)*

Though the bill was headed for a certain veto, Republicans appeared to lack a concrete strategy for getting another bill signed into law. "The census language and anti-government shutdown language will be in the next bill," a defiant Lott told reporters, who was also pushing to cut the total spending.

The cleared bill provided a total of $8.9 billion in fiscal 1997 appropriations — including $5.4 billion in emergency disaster relief, $1.7 billion to repay the Pentagon for peacekeeping activities in Bosnia and the Iraqi no-fly zone, and $932 million in mandatory spending, mostly for veterans' benefits.

The disaster funds included $3.4 billion for FEMA; $500 million in Community Development Block Grants; $650 million for emergency highway repairs; and $585 million for various Army Corps of Engineers projects.

The bill also included an extension of SSI and Medicaid benefits for up to 500,000 legal immigrants through Sept. 30. Like the House and Senate bills, it provided $76 million for WIC, the amount the administration had requested.

In other decisions, conferees:

- **Roads on public land.** Dropped Stevens' proposal to allow Western states such as his to build roads on federal lands. Instead, Stevens inserted language to establish a commission, tilted toward Western interests, that would recommend a solution to the longstanding controversy. The resulting legislation would advance under fast-track rules and could not be filibustered in the Senate.
- **Census.** Defeated, 13-15, a motion by Hollings to insist on the Senate-passed language on the census. Republicans had to delay the vote to make sure Hutchison would switch her position and support the GOP line. She voted to support sampling in committee, but folded after pressure from top GOP leaders who told her the House could not pass the bill without their tougher language.
- **Highways.** Agreed to release $695 million in additional federal highway funding. So-called donor states that remitted more in gasoline taxes to the Highway Trust Fund than they got back would receive $318 million; "donee" states would receive $237 million, and another $140 million would go to states that did not receive their shares of funding due to a Treasury Department clerical error.
- **Transportation rescissions.** Restored the $1.6 billion in transportation trust fund rescissions that had been knocked out of the House bill after objections from Shuster.
- **Other decisions.** Conferees also agreed to:
  - Adopt the Senate amendment on deferring certain requirements of the Endangered Species Act for emergency flood control repairs, which was similar to the House-passed language.
  - Drop $31 million in Senate-backed assistance to the District of Columbia for a police pay raise and school repairs, after the House insisted on transferring authority over city contracts from the mayor to an independent chief financial official.
  - Modify House language that would have given the president authority to cut off aid earmarked for Ukraine by Sen. Mitch McConnell, R-Ky., in the fiscal 1997 foreign aid bill. Instead, the cutoff would only apply to aid that went directly to the Ukrainian government. The government was under attack for turning a blind eye to rampant corruption that was harming U.S. business interests.
  - Add $175 million in mandatory spending for veterans' compensation and pensions, bringing the total in the bill to $928 million.

Clinton's Veto Comes Quickly

As the week of June 9 opened, the rider-laden version of the bill remained at the Capitol, held back by Republican leaders who did not want to ship it to the White House until they had returned to Washington after the weekend. The bill was sent to Clinton the afternoon of June 9, and aides boasted that he vetoed it just 19 minutes after it arrived and immediately sent it back up Pennsylvania Avenue.

"The congressional majority — despite the obvious and urgent need to speed critical relief to people in the Dakotas, Minnesota, California and 29 other states ravaged by flooding and other natural disasters — has chosen to weigh down this legislation with a series of unacceptable provisions that it knows will draw my veto," Clinton wrote in his veto message. "The time has come to stop playing politics with the lives of Americans in need." *(Text, p. D-32)*

"I think we demonstrated we don't have the kind of clout we think we do when we think we're going to ram it down the president's throat," said Rep. Ray LaHood, R-Ill.

Regardless of the merits of the riders, the ploy by GOP leaders to force Clinton to swallow them as a condition for obtaining flood relief had backfired. In a poll by the Gallup Organization for CNN and USA Today, 55 percent of respondents blamed Republicans for delaying the disaster aid, compared with only 25 percent who blamed Clinton.

Republicans thought Clinton would pay a price for vetoing the bill, but there had been so many delays in getting the bill to the White House in the first place that the GOP's message was overwhelmed by criticism from flood victims. Assurances that recovery was "in the pipeline" were lost amid media images of thousands of people in North Dakota living in temporary shelters.

Although the FEMA did have about $1.5 billion remaining in its flood accounts, the delay in passing the bill held up $500 million in Community Development Block Grants needed to buy property and permit people to relocate out of flood plains.

Clean Bill

After vowing to keep up the fight, Republican leaders gave in June 12, clearing a bill stripped of virtually all controversial riders. The House passed the revised bill (HR 1871) June 12 on a 348-74 vote, with virtually the entire GOP leadership voting "no." The Senate cleared the bill, 78-21. *(House vote 203, p. H-66; Senate vote 100, p. S-19)*

The only remnant of the riders was language requiring the Commerce Department within 30 days to provide Congress with its plan for conducting the 2000 census, including its estimates of how accurate sampling would be.

The automatic CR language was to advance later in the summer as a free-standing measure. Daschle promised not to filibuster it.

Stevens agreed to drop the proposal for a commission to recommend a solution to the impasse over building roads on federal lands, and Babbitt promised to send a bill to Congress.

How the GOP Strategy Collapsed

Although Lott and others had talked about sending Clinton a slimmed-down bill that included the same objectionable riders, the GOP plan quickly crumbled. Only hours after the veto, before most top House leaders had even returned to the Capitol, Lott had already begun looking for a deal. He signaled that the census sampling language so eagerly sought by the House was not a priority.

Still, Lott was taking a tough line toward the White House: "They had thought somehow or other that they'd just veto this bill and we'd pop it right back," Lott said, with a snap of his fingers. "It ain't going to work that way, so what we need is for [the White House] to engage."

But Clinton and his aides refused to back down, and the pressure continued to build.

By Tuesday, June 10, the House was preparing to return Lott's favor. House leaders suddenly said they could accept the idea of moving the automatic CR as a stand-alone bill, provided Senate Democrats would not filibuster the move. Senate Republicans generally felt more strongly about the CR than did their House colleagues.

Meanwhile, anxiety was building among Republicans. Sen. Rod Grams of Minnesota., normally a party loyalist, wrote Lott and Daschle to ask that the riders be stripped from the bill. "We're getting pounded," said Rep. Fred Upton of Michigan, a leader of GOP moderates.

For their part, Democrats, especially in the Senate, remained relentlessly focused. Daschle tied up the Senate, saying nothing would pass until a second — and signable — flood aid measure came to the floor. Democratic senators spent an all-night vigil in Daschle's office June 10-11, working late-night talk radio programs and Internet "chat rooms" and winning a prime spot on NBC's "Today" program.

By Wednesday, June 11, Republicans were preparing to fold. Twenty moderates — enough to ensure a loss on the floor — signed a letter to Gingrich asking, in words contained in Clinton's veto message, for a "clean, unencumbered" measure.

Later, after a discussion on the Senate floor with Daschle, Lott declared that he had reached agreement to strip the automatic CR from the bill and move it as a stand-alone measure. The House's census language would be worked out between the House and the administration, Lott said.

Lott still insisted that the measure's price tag shrink below the total in the earlier bill, but House appropriators said no, insisting on the full amount of aid. And Daschle stood firm that disaster relief would not be cut by a dime. The House threatened to pass the bill and adjourn, dropping it in the Senate's lap with no alternative but to go along.

By June 12, the collapse was complete. Lott won nothing, despite an ambitious effort to showcase his dealmaking skills. He voted against the bill. Ironically, he had foreshadowed his own course the previous week when he dismissed Clinton's veto threat, saying of the president: "Sometimes you threaten things you don't actually do. Sometimes you are bluffing." ■

CQ

Chapter 10

POLITICAL REPORT

THE ELECTORATE

Suburbs Become Battleground As Campaigns Chase Votes

Fewer Americans consider themselves city or country dwellers, but Republicans no longer win suburbs by default

Two trends that had been discussed since the 1960s reached new heights of importance in the mid-1990s. One was the willingness of Southerners to embrace Republican candidates not only for president but for governor and for Congress. The other, at work nationwide, was the increasing political prominence of the suburbs.

Many observers noted that the top three leaders of the new Republican majority in the House in 1995 and again in 1997 were all from the South: Speaker Newt Gingrich of Georgia, Majority Leader Dick Armey of Texas and Majority Whip Tom DeLay of Texas. It was not as often noted that all three were from suburban districts: Gingrich from the suburbs of Atlanta, Armey from those of Dallas-Fort Worth and DeLay from the outer rim of sprawling metropolitan Houston.

The suburbs elected a plurality of the members of the House, more than either the cities or the rural districts, both of which had declined in number and influence in the previous three decades. It was the tendency of Republicans to win in these districts that, in tandem with the Republicanizing of Dixie, delivered control of the House to the GOP in 1994 and kept that control intact in 1996.

At the same time, the suburbs had become far less homogenous than they once were — economically, racially, ethnically and politically. As a result, it could be said that President Clinton was not only the first Democrat to carry the suburbs since 1964 (when Lyndon B. Johnson's landslide re-election dominated all demographics) but the first Democrat whose winning plurality was reliant on the suburbs. Other Democrats who won the White House in the 20th century depended on a coalition of big city voters — largely blue-collar ethnic voters and racial minorities — and traditional rural Democrats in the South and West who distrusted the GOP as the party of Wall Street and the banks. But Clinton won re-election in 1996 carrying the critical constituencies of the suburbs.

He won most of the congressional districts in which 60 percent or more of the people lived in suburbs (by the definition used by the Census Bureau). Even more remarkably, he won nine of the 10 states in which suburbanites consituted a majority of the statewide population. The only such state he lost was Utah, and even there he did better in 1996 than he had in 1992.

The heightened competitiveness in the suburbs was on display in other ways in 1997. New Jersey, the only state in the union in which all the congressional districts fit the 60 percent test of being suburban, experienced the closest and most interesting off-year election of 1997.

Republican Gov. Christine Todd Whitman narrowly won re-election with a plurality of the vote in New Jersey, holding off a challenge from a little-known Democratic state senator aided by several right-of-center third-party contestants.

Whitman had cut taxes and seen her state's economy thrive. She also had taken the moderate-to-liberal positions on social issues, such as abortion, that were often seen as the preferred view of the suburbs. But Whitman's difficulties highlighted the degree to which the suburbs remained independent, an unclaimed territory that could not be predicted with the reliability of urban or rural precincts.

In New Jersey, two issues of special interest to commuting suburbanites (car insurance rates and property taxes) dominated the debate. Similarly, in Virginia, a close gubernatorial race was broken open when one candidate, GOP Attorney General James S. Gilmore III, promised to repeal the personal property tax on cars and light trucks and went on to win. ■

How CQ Classifies Districts

Under the system used by Congressional Quarterly, districts are classified as urban when at least 60 percent of their residents live within central cities of a metropolitan area. They are defined as suburban when at least 60 percent of their residents live within a metropolitan area but outside a central city. Rural districts are those that have at least 60 percent of their residents living outside a metropolitan area (and outside towns with populations of 25,000 or more). Where none of the categories account for 60 percent, the district is designated as mixed.

By this definition, 37 percent of all districts were suburban, 35 percent were "mixed," 15 percent were urban and 13 percent were rural.

The chart below compares voting in the 1996 presidential election with the composition of the House at full strength in the summer of 1997. One rural House seat (Vermont) was held by an independent.

	Total Districts	'96 Presidential Clinton	/ Dole	'97 House Seats Dem.	/ GOP	House Democrats Lag Behind Clinton
Urban	67	61	6	58	9	-3
Suburban	160	105	55	68	92	-37
Rural	57	33	24	19	37	-14
Mixed	151	81	70	61	90	-20
TOTAL	**435**	**280**	**155**	**206**	**228**	**-74**

SOURCE: Congressional Quarterly

Suburbia: A Growing Political Force

No longer homogeneous or predictable, the suburbs had a newfound power in the 1990s to determine the nation's political direction. That power was on display in the 1996 elections, when the suburbs played a decisive role in choosing a Democratic president and a closely divided but Republican House.

Increasingly diverse — both in demographics and in political inclination — the suburbs bore little resemblance to the 1950s image of all-white, middle- and upper-middle class bedroom communities made up of rock-ribbed Republicans.

The sheer growth of the suburbs was part of the story. Roughly half the population of the United States lived in the suburbs in 1997 — and the percentage of suburbanites was even higher among registered voters.

Fourteen states had populations with suburban majorities, according to the 1990 census, including six of the largest: California, Florida, Michigan, New Jersey, Ohio and Pennsylvania.

Even when a relatively high 60 percent threshold was used to define a suburban district, there were more such districts in the 105th Congress than there were urban and rural districts combined. *(Defining suburbs, p. 10-5)*

As suburban areas grew, their residents became more diverse — and less wedded to a single party. In 1996, 13 of the 14 suburban-majority states voted for Clinton, Yet Republicans won a majority of congressional seats in seven of these states and tied for control in another. *(Suburban states, below)*

A Century of Growth

Suburban areas, and their role in national elections, were largely a 20th century phenomenon. For much of the country's history, elections were defined in terms of the city versus the countryside. But by the turn of the century, a third force — the suburbs — had begun developing along transportation routes that radiated out from the major cities.

The suburbs grew gradually during the first half of the century, then exploded after World War II, when the effects of planes, trains and automobiles reached a critical mass. The 1970 census showed, for the first time, that more people were living in the suburbs than in urban or rural areas.

Residents of those burgeoning post-war suburbs tended to reflect basic Republican characteristics — they were relatively affluent, well-educated, overwhelmingly white and often antipathetic to the neighboring urban center that was generally dominated by racial minorities and Democratic

As a result, for a generation after World War II, the suburbs were a cornerstone of GOP presidential victories — from Dwight D. Eisenhower to George Bush. During those years, the suburbs were also a major source of the party's strength in Congress.

Suburban areas continued to grow and spread in the 1980s and 1990s, but as they did, they also began to change. From 1950 to 1990, the population of Orange County, Calif., swelled more than tenfold, from 216,000 to more than 2.4 million. New York's Suffolk County grew nearly fivefold, from 276,000 to more than 1.3 million, and the population of Virginia's Fairfax County jumped more than eightfold, from less than 100,000 to more than 800,000.

The result was every possible variety of suburb — inner, outer, blue-collar, white-collar, minority, low-income, upper-income, high density, low density.

Democratic Inroads

While Republicans remained the party of the suburbs in Congress in the 1990s, they lost that distinction at the presidential level. Clinton established a beachhead in the suburbs in 1992, and then widened it in winning re-election in 1996. He rode the Democratic trend that had come with demographic changes, but he also exploited his relative youthfulness and the issues of interest to the generation that elected the nation's first Baby Boom president.

Of the nation's 28 largest suburban counties (those with a 1990 population of more than 500,000), Clinton carried 24 in 1996 — a level of suburban hegemony approaching that of Republicans Eisenhower, Richard M. Nixon and Ronald Reagan in their heyday.

Before Clinton, 17 of these suburban behemoths had not voted for a Democratic presidential candidate since the

Where the 'Burbs Are

State	Suburban% of Population	Electoral Vote	'96 Presidential Winner	Control of House Delegation
New Jersey	84.7%	15	Clinton (54%)	Republicans (7-6)
Maryland	74.7	10	Clinton (54%)	Split (4-4)
Rhode Island	64.9	4	Clinton (60%)	Democrats (2-0)
Florida	63.5	25	Clinton (48%)	Republicans (15-8)
Pennsylvania	60.3	23	Clinton (49%)	Democrats (11-10)
Connecticut	58.2	8	Clinton (53%)	Democrats (4-2)
California	57.2	54	Clinton (51%)	Democrats (29-23)
Massachusetts	56.2	12	Clinton (62%)	Democrats (10-0)
Michigan	56.1	18	Clinton (52%)	Democrats (10-6)
Delaware	55.6	3	Clinton (52%)	Republicans (1-0)
Utah	55.6	5	Dole (54%)	Republicans (3-0)
Washington	55.1	11	Clinton (50%)	Republicans (6-3)
Nevada	50.3	4	Clinton (44%)	Republicans (2-0)
Ohio	50.1	21	Clinton (47%)	Republicans (11-8)

SOURCE: 1990 Census

What Makes a Suburb a Suburb?

Defining what constituted a suburban congressional district could sometimes be tricky. Some measurements stressed land use or population density. Others, including the one preferred over the years by Congressional Quarterly, emphasized population.

The CQ standard was based on Metropolitan Statistical Areas (MSAs), with a suburb defined as a section inside a metropolitan area but outside its central city. Few districts, roughly 30 nationwide, had a population that was 100 percent suburban. Conversely, however, only about 20 districts nationwide could be said to have no suburban component at all.

These "suburb free" districts tended to be either in the Great Plains or in the heart of a big city such as New York. Only one state, Alaska, had no population that fit the CQ definition of a suburb based on Census Bureau data. (The Census Bureau itself did not release an official figure for suburban population.)

Suburban Districts Dominate

Under the CQ system, a suburban district was one that had at least 60 percent of its population living within a defined metropolitan area but outside a central city.

The suburban population could be exaggerated a bit by this terminology because metropolitan areas often extended deep into the countryside to include long-range commuters. The Washington metropolitan area, for instance, reached fully 50 miles west of the Potomac River, basically to the base of the Blue Ridge Mountains. But any rural elements that were included in the metropolitan population tended to be offset by the stringent 60 percent standard, which weeded more marginal districts out of the suburban category.

Altogether, 212 districts out of 435 nationwide had suburban majorities, and 160 met the CQ standard and were at least 60 percent suburban.

By either measurement, the number of suburban districts dwarfed the total for either the cities or rural areas, each of which had lost ground to the suburbs over the previous two decades. (Redistricting since 1993 had changed the lines in several states, although the number of suburban districts stayed roughly the same.)

The distribution of congressional seats had actually lagged behind the shifts in population. According to census data, by 1970 more people were living in the suburbs than in urban or rural areas. However, a CQ study in 1973 found the number of rural (92), suburban (88) and urban districts (78) to be roughly equal, with a plurality of districts classified as mixed (177). Since then, the number of suburban seats had nearly doubled, while the other three categories had each declined. A Congressional Research Service (CRS) analysis in 1993 found the breakdown of districts, by CQ definition, to be: suburban (160), urban (67), rural (57) and mixed (151).

Half the districts in California were at least 60 percent suburban. So were half of those in Michigan and nearly half in New York, as were more than 60 percent of the districts in Florida and Pennsylvania and all but one of the 13 districts in New Jersey. *(Suburban district growth, p. 10-8)*

Changing the Profile of the Big Cities

The growth of the suburban population, coupled with the ongoing exodus from the cities, had reversed the ratio of urban-suburban congressional seats in a number of major metropolitan areas.

In 1960, Philadelphia had six congressional districts entirely within its city limits, all represented by Democrats. There were three congressional districts outside the city limits, all represented by Republicans. In 1997, there were three city-based districts in Philadelphia (held by Democrats) and four in the immediate suburbs (held by Republicans).

In 1960, six Michigan congressional districts still included wards of Detroit, with three districts containing suburbs of the city. In 1997, there were still eight districts in the Detroit area, but only two were in the city (and both had some suburban territory attached). In New York, the loss of some population in the previous four decades meant the dramatic loss of congressional seats as the rest of the nation grew. Thus, the city's five boroughs went from having 22 seats in Congress to having just 12.

1960s. Seven of them were counties that Clinton had not won in 1992. *(Large suburban counties, p. 10-6)*

Many of the counties Clinton brought into the Democratic column in 1996 were synonymous with affluence, such as Fairfield County, Conn. (with upscale Greenwich and Darien); Oakland County, Mich.; and Lake County, Ill., which included many of the well-heeled, lakefront communities north of Chicago.

But in 1996, Clinton was also the first Democratic standard-bearer since Hubert H. Humphrey in 1968 to carry the blue-collar suburbs of Macomb County, Mich., and the first Democrat since Lyndon B. Johnson in 1964 to win New Jersey's Bergen County, extending from older, inner suburbs across the Hudson River from New York City to stylish enclaves such as Saddle River in the hills to the west.

Residents and Economy Changing

Such ticket-splitting — found in major suburban areas across the country — reflected the demographic and economic diversity that had accompanied the growth of the suburbs.

In devising a neighborhood classification system, the Claritas Corp., a marketing firm, came up with at least 10 categories of suburban neighborhoods, from "Blue Blood Estates" to the primarily Southern, primarily working-class suburbs of "Norma Rae-ville." Among the suburban classifications in between were the aging tract subdivisions of "Levittown, U.S.A.," and the exurban boom towns of the "New Homesteaders."

In general, the inner suburbs were no longer almost wholly white, a change that worked to the advantage of Clinton and other Democrats.

Prince George's County, Md., immediately to the east of Washington, D.C., for example, had become majority-black. Fairfax County, the linchpin of the Northern Virginia suburbs, was roughly one-quarter minority (closely divided between Asian-Americans, Hispanics and blacks).

Just as visibly, the minority population was steadily in-

Clinton's Suburban Breakthrough

For a generation after World War II, Republican dominance in the suburbs was integral to the party's success in winning presidential elections. And in the heyday of GOP presidential dominance, from the elections of 1968 through 1988, Republican standard-bearers carried a large majority of the nation's most populous suburban counties in every single election.

But President Clinton blunted the GOP victory formula in the 1990s by scoring major breakthroughs in the suburbs.

The chart below lists 28 counties with a 1990 population exceeding 500,000 that lacked a dominant urban center and were predominantly suburban in character. Democrat Walter F. Mondale carried only two of these counties in 1984 against Ronald Reagan; Michael S. Dukakis took only six of them in 1988 against George Bush.

But in 1992, Clinton won 18 of these suburban behemoths and in 1996 he swept 24. In most of these suburban counties, Clinton's 1996 vote share showed a larger increase from 1992 than the 6 percentage-point gain (from 43 percent to 49 percent) he registered nationally.

The vote percentages in the chart are based on official returns, with the change in the Clinton vote share from 1992 to 1996 based on whole percentage points.

County	# of Dem. Winners, 1968-88	1992 Winner	1996 Winner	Change in Clinton Vote Share
Contra Costa, Calif.	2 ('68, '88)	Clinton (51%)	Clinton (56%)	+5%
Orange, Calif.	0	Bush (44%)	Dole (52%)	+6%
Riverside, Calif.	0	Clinton (39%)	Dole (46%)	+4%
San Bernardino, Calif.	0	Clinton (39%)	Clinton (44%)	+5%
San Mateo, Calif.	2 ('68, '88)	Clinton (54%)	Clinton (61%)	+7%
Ventura, Calif.	0	Clinton (37%)	Clinton (44%)	+7%
Fairfield, Conn.	0	Bush (43%)	Clinton (49%)	+10%
Broward, Fla.	1 ('76)	Clinton (52%)	Clinton (64%)	+12%
De Kalb, Ga.	3 ('76, '80, '88)	Clinton (58%)	Clinton (67%)	+9%
Du Page, Ill.	0	Bush (48%)	Dole (51%)	+9%
Lake, Ill.	0	Bush (44%)	Clinton (46%)	+9%
Baltimore, Md.*	0	Clinton (44%)	Clinton (49%)	+4%
Montgomery, Md.	3 ('68, '76, '88)	Clinton (55%)	Clinton (59%)	+5%
Prince George's, Md.	4 ('76, '80, '84, '88)	Clinton (66%)	Clinton (74%)	+8%
Middlesex, Mass.	6 ('68-'88)	Clinton (50%)	Clinton (64%)	+14%
Macomb, Mich.	1 ('68)	Bush (42%)	Clinton (50%)	+13%
Oakland, Mich.	0	Bush (44%)	Clinton (48%)	+9%
St. Louis, Mo.*	0	Clinton (44%)	Clinton (49%)	+5%
Bergen, N.J.	0	Bush (44%)	Clinton (53%)	+11%
Middlesex, N.J.	2 ('68, '76)	Clinton (45%)	Clinton (56%)	+11%
Monmouth, N.J.	0	Bush (44%)	Clinton (48%)	+10%
Nassau, N.Y.	0	Clinton (46%)	Clinton (56%)	+10%
Suffolk, N.Y.	0	Bush (40%)	Clinton (52%)	+13%
Westchester, N.Y.	0	Clinton (49%)	Clinton (57%)	+8%
Bucks, Pa.	0	Clinton (39%)	Clinton (45%)	+6%
Delaware, Pa.	0	Clinton (42%)	Clinton (49%)	+7%
Montgomery, Pa.	0	Clinton (43%)	Clinton (49%)	+6%
Fairfax, Va.	0	Bush (44%)	Dole (48%)	+5%

** Does not include city of same name.*

creasing in that quintessential hotbed of Sun Belt Republicanism, Orange County, Calif. In one recent year, the most common surname among residents buying houses in the county was Nguyen.

The suburbs were also diversifying economically and socially. Their traditional role as bedroom communities was giving way as businesses and jobs moved to what author Joel Garreau described as "Edge Cities." Most suburban workers no longer commuted to a central city, but to workplaces sprouting up near the intersections of major interstate highways.

Variety Near the Capitol

Several variations of 1990s suburbia were evident within a short drive of the nation's capital. Immediately to the east of the city was the majority-black Maryland 4th District, the destination of much of the black exodus from the nation's capital. To the north, the Maryland 8th was the most affluent district in the country as measured by median family income.

To the west lay the three suburban districts of Northern Virginia. Taken together, they offered a microcosm of suburban terrain throughout the country.

Directly across the Potomac River from the capital were the inner suburbs of the Virginia 8th District — older, more ethnic, and more citified than the suburban jurisdictions farther to the west. The 8th was friendly turf for the Democrats, giving Clinton 55 percent of the vote in 1996 and easily re-electing Democratic Rep. James P. Moran.

Moran described the 8th as half urban and half suburban. "People who choose to live in a more urban setting accept a level of socio-interdependency and are more tolerant on social issues," said Moran. People who move farther out, he said, are often trying to "get away from [the perception] of crowding and crime."

Immediately to the west was the Virginia 11th, a new district formed as a result of the Old Dominion's population growth in the 1980s. Straddling the Washington Beltway, the district contained portions of both the inner and outer suburbs. The 11th was classic ticket-splitting country: In 1992, it voted Republican for president and Democratic for Congress; in 1996, it went

Democratic for president and Republican for Congress.

Though the 11th was pure suburban, with no urban or rural parts, it was hardly bland. The district's GOP Rep. Thomas M. Davis III, was an avid student of suburban politics, much of it coming from simply observing neighborhoods and their different housing patterns. Davis said his constituency was what Chicago used to be, "a series of small neighborhoods, each with their own little culture."

Farthest out from Washington was the Virginia 10th, extending from the outer suburbs into the mountains and valleys beyond. The land area was nearly nine times as large as the 8th and 11th districts combined, but most of the population was packed into the fast-growing outer suburbs of Loudoun, western Fairfax and western Prince William counties.

The outer suburbs were newer, more conservative and more homogeneously white than the suburbs closer to the city. Although the commuting distances were longer, the lower housing prices attracted younger families, who tended to vote Republican. "People are never more conservative politically than when they are a young family with kids," said Davis. "They tend to be protective of their kids and worried about their future."

All that made the 10th a GOP enclave. Voters there gave Republican presidential candidate Bob Dole 54 percent of the vote in 1996 and overwhelmingly re-elected veteran Republican Rep. Frank R. Wolf.

Wealth, the Suburbs and Ticket-Splitting

Affluence, the suburbs and Republicanism had long gone hand in hand. But 1996 saw an unusual degree of ticket-splitting in this corner of the electorate. Of the nation's 30 most affluent districts — a heavily suburban list — 23 voted for President Clinton in 1996; 20 elected Republican congressmen, with 13 of these districts voting Clinton for president, but Republican for the House.

The income data is based on an analysis by David C. Huckabee of the Congressional Research Service, using median family income figures from the 1990 census. An asterisk (*) indicates districts where lines had changed since the analysis was prepared in 1993. For a definition of suburban, urban and mixed districts, see box, p. 10-5.

District	Type	Median Family Income	Party	'96 Winner/ Presidential Vote
1) Md. 8	Suburb	$64,199	R	Clinton/(57%)
2) N.J. 11	Suburb	$63,574	R	Dole/(49%)
3) N.J. 12	Suburb	$62,034	R	Clinton/(48%)
4) N.Y. 3	Suburb	$61,611	R	Clinton/(53%)
5) Calif. 10	Suburb	$60,079	D	Clinton/(48%)
6) Va. 11	Suburb	$59,989	R	Clinton/(48%)
7) N.Y. 14	Urban	$59,953	D	Clinton/(70%)
8) Calif. 47	Suburb	$59,936	R	Dole/(54%)
9) N.J. 5	Suburb	$59,583	R	Dole/(47%)
10) Calif. 14	Suburb	$59,492	D	Clinton/(58%)
11) Va. 8	Suburb	$58,582	D	Clinton/(55%)
12) Ill. 10	Suburb	$58,407	R	Clinton/(50%)
13) N.Y. 5	Mixed	$57,915	D	Clinton/(60%)
14) N.J. 7	Suburb	$57,563	R	Clinton/(51%)
15) N.Y. 19	Suburb	$57,419	R	Clinton/(48%)
16) Calif. 24	Urban	$57,375	D	Clinton/(52%)
17) Calif. 15	Urban	$57,300	R	Clinton/(53%)
18) N.Y. 4	Suburb	$56,588	D	Clinton/(56%)
19) Calif. 36	Suburb	$56,567	D	Clinton/(47%)
20) Conn. 4	Mixed	$56,320	R	Clinton/(51%)
21) Mich. 11	Suburb	$56,234	R	Clinton/(46%)
22) Ill. 13	Suburb	$55,481	R	Dole/(50%)
23) Ga. 6*	Suburb	$55,056	R	Dole/(61%)
24) Calif. 29	Urban	$55,001	D	Clinton/(66%)
25) N.Y. 18	Suburb	$53,968	D	Clinton/(58%)
26) N.Y. 20	Suburb	$53,782	R	Clinton/(54%)
27) N.Y. 2	Suburb	$53,215	R	Clinton/(54%)
28) Ill. 8	Suburb	$53,105	R	Dole/(49%)
29) Pa. 13	Suburb	$52,778	R	Clinton/(50%)
30) Texas 3*	Suburb	$52,367	R	Dole/(59%)

New Political Agenda

As the economy and demographics of the suburbs changed, so did the concerns of suburban voters. "The issue agenda is now a more complex one," said Lee M. Miringoff, the director of the Marist College Institute for Public Opinion in New York.

Fiscal conservatism still resonated in the suburbs. But in the 1990s, cultural issues had also become important as the Republican Party veered right to embrace social conservatism. While this move won the GOP new adherents in some parts of the country, it was not a net plus in the suburbs. The party lost once-secure votes among educated working women, in particular, as a result of its hard-line stance on such issues as abortion.

At the same time, high-voltage topics such as crime took a different form. The law-and-order sentiment that ran rampant after the social unrest of the 1960s was being replaced in many affluent suburbs by a fear of guns. "The gun issue in suburban areas is far more potent an issue than abortion," said Paul M. Green, an Illinois political analyst at Governors State University.

The party's presidential standard-bearers in the 1990s, Bush and Dole, were less successful in this regard. Both took a tumble in the suburbs, where their age was viewed negatively by many younger voters. Bush was nearing 70 and Dole was over 70 at the time each ran against Clinton — creating the widest age gaps between the two major party nominees since the 1850s.

"You can never underestimate the generational appeal that Bill Clinton had versus Bob Dole," said Republican Davis. Clinton "was a Baby Boomer, and the suburbs are chock-full of Baby Boomers," he said.

Democrat Moran gave Clinton's record more credit for his victory in the suburbs in 1996. "Until Clinton, Ike was the top

A House in the Suburbs

In the quarter century after Richard M. Nixon was president, suburban population growth nearly doubled the number of congressional districts that could be called predominantly suburban.

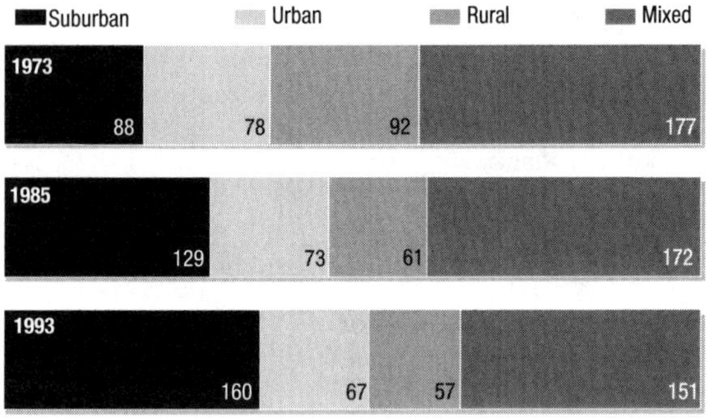

	Suburban	Urban	Rural	Mixed
1973	88	78	92	177
1985	129	73	61	172
1993	160	67	57	151

Change% Surburban **+82%** Urban **-14%** Rural **-38%** Mixed **-15%**

Source: Congressional Research Service, Congressional Quarterly

suburban president," said Moran. "I think Clinton is comparable in delivery for suburban voters."

To Moran, Eisenhower was the architect of the interstate highway system, expanded middle-class housing and promoted ideological balance in the political system, all of interest to suburban voters.

Under Clinton, said Moran, the suburban, high-tech economy had been booming with advances in global trade. There was a focus on suburban quality of life, from family medical leave to education tax credits. And there were no foreign wars. "If you don't draft anybody," said Moran, "you don't interfere with middle-class ambitions for their kids."

Yet Clinton's success did not mean that his party was about to gain the upper hand in the suburbs. Many suburbs that voted for Clinton in 1996 voted decisively for Republican gubernatorial, Senate and House candidates in 1994. "If the economy goes south on the Democrats, I think a lot of their suburban gains start to disappear," said Davis. "I think that the suburbs have always been subject to swings."

Although incomes varied widely within some districts, suburban constituencies were generally affluent. Among the 30 wealthiest districts in the country, 23 were suburban — including nine of the top 10. *(Wealthy suburbs, p. 10-7)*

Yet affluence was no longer synonymous with straight-ticket Republicanism. The two richest districts in the Washington, D.C., area were also the two most apt to split their tickets. Both Constance A. Morella's Maryland 8th and Davis' Virginia 11th voted to re-elect Clinton and their Republican House member in 1996.

In general, inner suburban districts, such as Moran's, that combined characteristics of suburbs and cities leaned Democratic in their voting. Outer suburban districts, such as Wolf's, that combined suburbs with rural, small-town America leaned Republican.

Yet many suburban voters shared some similar interests whether they lived near or far from the city. Throughout Northern Virginia, for example, issues that involved transportation, federal employees, and urban-suburban relations were of mutual concern.

In the end, said Davis, campaigns in the suburbs basically came down to each candidate selling himself. "People that are educated are not knee-jerk about voting for party," said Davis. "They tend to pick and choose candidates."

Many suburban congressmen displayed similar independence. In recent years, there had been no suburban caucus, and Wolf said there was no need for one. "I'm not a big caucus person," he said. "They tend to Balkanize Congress."

Power in Congress

Although they did not always identify themselves as suburban, the rise of the suburbs was reflected in the House leadership from both sides of the aisle.

The GOP leadership hailed from the fast-growing suburbs of the Sun Belt, where the party was dominant. House Speaker Newt Gingrich represented a district in the Atlanta suburbs. Majority Leader Dick Armey's constituency was anchored in the suburbs of Dallas; Majority Whip Tom DeLay's included suburbs of Houston.

Democratic leaders came from the suburbs of the Frost Belt, where the party had been able to hold its own in congressional voting. Minority Leader Richard A. Gephardt represented a district that lay predominantly in the St. Louis suburbs. Minority Whip David E. Bonior's constituency was centered in suburban Macomb County, outside Detroit, and Democratic Caucus Chairman Vic Fazio represented a California district that stretched north and west from the suburbs of Sacramento. ■

Cities Shrink, Still Aid Democrats

While America's cities continued to decline in population, they were far from being political backwaters. In fact, they were the cornerstone of the two Democratic presidential victories in the 1990s, and it was the party's near monopoly on urban seats that kept it within striking distance of regaining a majority in the House.

President Clinton carried 61 of the 67 urban congressional districts across the country in 1996; 58 of those districts elected Democrats to Congress. (As defined by Congressional Quarterly, an urban district was one in which at least 60 percent of the people lived within the central city of a defined metropolitan area.)

While Republicans had been able to break the Democratic hegemony in a number of cities at the mayoral level, in presidential and congressional voting, urban America was more decidedly Democratic than at any time since Franklin D. Roosevelt.

Yet fewer than one out of every six districts across the country was urban, a proportion expected to decline further through reapportionment and redistricting after 2000.

That meant Democrats also had to have a strong presence in another sector of the electorate if their huge advantage in the cities was to make a difference.

Clinton found such a niche with his breakthrough in the suburbs in the presidential elections of 1992 and 1996. But congressional Democrats still showed little vote-getting appeal beyond city limits. While they controlled more than 85 percent of the urban House seats in the 105th Congress, they held only 40 percent of those classified as suburban, rural or mixed. *(Suburbs, p. 10-4)*

Shifting Urban Population

In terms of population, cities hit their apogee around 1950. The census that year found that 56 percent of the population lived in metropolitan areas, 33 percent in central cities and 23 percent nearby in what would be regarded as the suburban portion.

The 1990 census showed the metropolitan population up to 77 percent, a surge composed entirely of growth in the suburbs, which had doubled in size to 46 percent of the national population. The urban share was down slightly to 31 percent.

The nearly static urban proportion of the population represented the countervailing effects of two competing trends: sharp population losses since 1950 in most of the older cities of the Frost Belt, largely offset by dramatic population growth in most of the newer urban centers of the Sun Belt.

In 1950, nine of the 10 largest cities lay in a swath extending from Boston to St. Louis, with Los Angeles the lone Sun Belt city to make the Top 10. In 1997, only four of the 10 were in the Frost Belt and six were in the Sun Belt. When states were categorized according to the proportion of their population living in central cities, Arizona topped the list (55 percent urban), followed by New York (48 percent urban), Texas (47 percent) and Alaska (41 percent). *(Geographic shift, below)*

Several factors contributed to the turnaround. Many of the cities of the South and West had swollen with the military spending of World War II and the Cold War.

Equally important was the success of the newer cities in legally annexing adjacent land, incorporating high-growth suburban territory within their city limits. It was nearly impossible to accomplish this in the older, more settled metropolitan areas where outlying communities had long been separately incorporated and highly vigilant about city encroachment.

The size of Houston jumped from 160 square miles in 1950 to 556 square miles in 1980, according to Columbia University political scientist Kenneth T. Jackson in his book, "The Crabgrass Frontier." In the same 30-year period, the area of Jacksonville, Fla., mushroomed from 30 square miles to 841 square miles (approaching the total land mass of Rhode Island).

Many of the Sun Belt cities also enjoyed a favorable business climate, unburdened by the transition away from a manufacturing economy that weighed down their Frost Belt counterparts. That transition had been debilitating for even the most economically diverse cities in the Northeast and Midwest. Chicago and Philadelphia had each lost roughly one-quarter of their population since 1950. Cleveland and Detroit had lost nearly one-half, and the once-prominent city of St. Louis had lost more than half its population since midcentury.

Actually, St. Louis, Boston and Buffalo, N.Y., had more people in 1900 than in the mid-1990s, and the populations of Pittsburgh, Cincinnati and Newark, N.J., were roughly the same as they had been at the turn of the century.

Congressional Seats Shift Too

As a result of these population shifts, there were more urban congressional districts in the Sun Belt states of the South and West (37) than in the Frost Belt states of the Northeast and Midwest (30).

By this method, New York still had a dozen con-

Sun Belt Rises; Frost Belt Melts

Six of the 10 largest cities in the United States were in the Sun Belt, according to 1994 population estimates from the Census Bureau. New York and Chicago still occupied first and third place, respectively. But like most cities across the Frost Belt, each had lost population since 1950, the time of peak population for many cities in the Northeast and Midwest.

In the chart below, each city's 1994 population rank is noted at left.

	1950	1994	Change, 1950-1994	
Frost Belt Cities				
1) New York	7,891,957	7,333,253	– 558,704	(-7.1%)
3) Chicago	3,620,962	2,731,743	– 889,219	(-24.6%)
5) Philadelphia	2,071,605	1,524,249	– 547,356	(-26.4%)
10) Detroit	1,849,568	992,038	– 857,530	(-46.4%)
Sun Belt Cities				
2) Los Angeles	1,970,358	3,448,613	+ 1,478,255	(+75.0%)
4) Houston	596,163	1,702,086	+ 1,105,923	(+185.5%)
6) San Diego	334,387	1,151,977	+ 817,590	(+244.5%)
7) Phoenix	106,818	1,048,949	+ 942,131	(+882.0%)
8) Dallas	434,462	1,022,830	+ 588,368	(+135.4%)
9) San Antonio	408,442	998,905	+ 590,463	(+144.6%)

Northern City Turnouts Down, Democratic Margins Up

Since Franklin D. Roosevelt's New Deal in the 1930s, major urban centers — especially those in the industrial Frost Belt — had been major players in the Democratic coalition. But at no time had urban America been more decidedly Democratic in its presidential voting than in 1996.

While fewer people voted in industrial-state urban centers in the 1990s than had done so at mid-century, Democratic pluralities in many of these cities had increased dramatically. The cities had largely lost their Republican base, while those who remained or moved in tended to be Democrats.

The chart below compares electoral data from the presidential election of 1952 with that of 1996 in a selected group of seven cities. The data are based on official results from both elections.

	Votes Cast (thousands)		City's Percentage of State Vote		Democratic Margin (thousands)	
	1952	1996	1952	1996	1952	1996
New York	3,411	1,961	48%	31%	359	1,173
Chicago	1,842	869	41	20	161	559
Philadelphia	959	533	21	12	160	328
Detroit	813	299	29	8	170	261
Boston	357	170	15	7	69	92
Baltimore	350	183	39	10	12	117
Milwaukee	307	208	19	9	9	88

SOURCE: America Votes

gressional seats, but Chicago was down to five, Philadelphia to three, Detroit to two and Boston and Baltimore to one each. Once-powerful Frost Belt cities such as St. Louis and Cleveland no longer had a seat they could truly call their own. Democratic Reps. Richard A. Gephardt and William L. Clay still called St. Louis home, but most of their constituents did not. So too in Ohio, where neither of the two Cleveland-area seats encompassed enough of the city to be considered urban.

Democrats Score Gains

Yet in presidential voting, the Democrats had managed to make more out of less. Their increasing domination of the Northern urban vote was all the more remarkable considering that the most recent Democratic presidents (Clinton, Jimmy Carter and Lyndon B. Johnson) had all been sons of the small-town South.

A case in point was Chicago, where the number of votes cast for president in 1996 was less than half the number cast in 1952 (down from more than 1.8 million to less than 900,000), yet the plurality for Clinton was more than three times as large as it was in 1952 for Illinois' native son Adlai E. Stevenson (up from about 160,000 to nearly 560,000).

The improved Democratic showing had a lot to do with the changing demographic mix in the cities. As whites left Chicago, the minority proportion of the city's population rose steadily. Chicago was less than 15 percent black in 1950; four decades later, it was nearly 40 percent black, and 20 percent of the population was Hispanic.

Chicago was hardly unique. A more variegated racial mix was a component of urban change in both the Frost and Sun belts. New York, for example, which was less than 10 percent black in 1950, was nearly 30 percent black in 1990 and 24 percent Hispanic. Detroit, 16 percent black in 1950, was more than three-quarters black at the last census. Los Angeles, which was 17 percent Hispanic in 1970 had grown to 40 percent Hispanic two decades later (the black population, at 14 percent, had fallen about 4 percentage points over the same period).

Nationally, minorities made up more than 40 percent of the population of central cities in 1990. And the urban slice of the electorate also tended to be disproportionately poorer than other sectors and more dependent on government help that the Democrats were traditionally more willing to offer.

According to a study by the Congressional Research Service in 1993, only nine of the 100 most affluent congressional districts in median family income were urban. Most of the urban districts were in the bottom half in terms of income.

But demographics alone did not account for the increased Democratic nature of the urban vote. Republicans had a lot to do with it as well, reinforcing the effects of population shifts with their own strategic decisions. When they moved rightward in the 1960s on social issues, shedding the "party of Lincoln" sobriquet to become the party of the suburbs and the South, they essentially conceded the cities in national races to the Democrats.

In 1996, the nation's three largest cities (New York, Los Angeles and Chicago) constituted just 5 percent of the national population and even a smaller percentage of the national turnout. But they provided more than 25 percent of Clinton's nationwide margin of victory: 2.1 million of the 8.2 million votes by which Clinton carried the popular vote.

Adding Clinton's pluralities in Philadelphia and Detroit, the cumulative margin he collected just in these five cities represented nearly one-third of his national victory margin. *(Northern city voting, above left)*

Trading Places

This degree of Democratic domination was a far cry from the beginning of the 20th century, when Republicans were widely viewed as the champions of the city against a Democratic Party still closely associated with the rural South. Democrats did not seriously compete for urban presidential votes until 1928, when they nominated Alfred E. Smith, a product of New York's Lower East Side.

They completed their political takeover of the cities in the following decade during the Depression, when FDR's New Dealers designed many of their programs to help working-class urban voters. *(Party shift, p. 10-11)*

Republicans, though, were able to remain fairly competitive in urban voting into the early 1960s. They were still numerous in many city neighborhoods, and the party had some appeal among blacks because it maintained its historic commitment to civil rights. But the GOP lost much of its remaining urban base in 1964, when it nominated conservative Arizona Sen. Barry M. Goldwater over New York Gov. Nelson A. Rockefeller and moved decidedly rightward on social issues.

In the 1990s, said Margaret M. Weir, a senior fellow in government studies at the Brookings Institution, the Republican conservative mainstream was widely viewed as "pretty anti-urban, anti-social spending, anti-mass transit and anti-infrastructure spending." To many city voters, she said, "Republicans stand for shrunken government."

The GOP made a modest bid to regain an urban toehold in 1996, choosing former Housing and Urban Development Secretary Jack F. Kemp as its vice presidential candidate. Kemp made well-publicized campaign forays into heavily black Harlem, south-central Los Angeles and Southside Chicago. Yet, the Republican presidential vote was even lower in many cities in 1996 than it had been in 1992.

Cities Lack Clout in Congress

The cities tended to have more impact on presidential elections than on congressional elections. Urban residents rarely enjoyed clout on Capitol Hill commensurate with their numbers.

Through much of the 20th century, cities were gerrymandered out of seats by rural-dominated state legislatures. By the time the Supreme Court finally made one-man, one-vote the law of the land in the 1960s, the cities were past their heyday.

Even in the years when Democrats were in control of Congress, power often rested with a conservative coalition of Republicans and Southern Democrats who were hardly sympathetic to urban interests. Vestiges of that alliance remained. "This is now a suburban country with a suburban government," said Richard Wade, a professor of urban history at the City University of New York. "Cities are more and more like Indian wards in the old days."

In the 1990s, urban House members were a minority within a minority party. Even though virtually all were Democrats, they constituted less than 30 percent of the House Democratic Caucus. And on critical votes that exposed fault lines within the party, the city members often found themselves on the losing side.

In a July 1996 vote on a controversial plan to dismantle the federal welfare program, 64 percent of non-urban Democrats voted in favor, 87 percent of urban Democrats voted against. The result was a 98-98 split among House Democrats on the conference report, although overwhelming Republican support for welfare reform ensured the bill's easy passage. *(1996 Almanac, pp. 6-3, H-124)*

Similarly, in the May 1997 vote to adopt the fiscal 1998 budget resolution, which included significant cuts in spending and taxes, 72 percent of non-urban Democrats voted in favor, 55 percent of urban Democrats voted against. Again with hefty Republican support, the measure passed. *(Budget resolution, p. 2-23; vote, p. H-56)*

GOP Inroads in Local Politics

Though urban America remained reliably Democratic in voting for president and Congress, a growing sense of social disintegration in the cities had led to some dramatic changes in the political order at the local level — changes that could presage a return to two-party voting in the metropolitan core.

Since 1980, four of the nation's largest cities — New York, Los Angeles, Chicago and Philadelphia — had had black mayors. But in 1997, none did. Part of that was due to demographics. None of the four was majority black. But there also seemed to have been a change in voter attitude in the cities, where race-based politics was seen as a frill when viewed against the long-standing backdrop of urban decay.

"Because of economic conditions, there are far more moderate politicians on the [urban] scene, black and white," said University of Maryland political scientist Ronald Walters.

All four cities had elected white mayors who campaigned on the need for government efficiency and law and order. In New York and Los Angeles, they were Republicans who proved popular in spite of the strongly Democratic terrain. Mayors Rudolph W. Giuliani and Richard Riordan won second terms in New York and Los Angeles, respectively, in 1997.

Other cities, including San Diego and Jersey City, N.J., had also elected Republican mayors despite their Democratic majorities.

But big-city Republicans were often somewhat removed from the GOP mainstream, and their triumphs were not universally applauded within the party. Giuliani and Riordan held their party at arm's length and presented themselves as clean, efficient agents of change. Riordan endorsed Democrat Dianne Feinstein for re-election to the Senate in 1994; Giuliani backed Democratic Gov. Mario M. Cuomo's unsuccessful 1994 re-election bid in New York.

"If [Giuliani] were in Congress, I suspect he would be in

From GOP to Democratic: Cities Shift Allegiance

In the early 1900s, Democrats were still identified with the rural South and much of urban America voted Republican. But that began to change as increasing numbers of city dwellers, arriving from Europe or from rural America, were organized politically by the Democratic Party. In 1928, the shift got its symbol when the Democratic presidential nomination went to a son of urban America, Alfred E. Smith from New York's Lower East Side. The transformation of cities into Democratic strongholds was cemented in the following decade by the Depression and by Franklin D. Roosevelt's New Deal, which directed much of its federal largess to the cities.

The chart below highlights results in a regional sampling of cities from five separate presidential elections over the course of the 20th century.

The elections featured are 1920, the first in which women were allowed to vote; 1928, when the Democrats ran Smith; 1936, when FDR won a landslide re-election victory based largely on his party's new-found urban appeal; 1960, when Democrat John F. Kennedy, a Boston Catholic, fashioned a narrow victory based largely on the strength of urban votes; and the 1996 election.

The party of the presidential winner in each of the five elections is indicated with "R" for Republican and "D" for Democratic. The percentage represents the Democratic share of the city's total vote in that particular election.

	1920	1928	1936	1960	1996
New York	R 27%	D 60%	D 73%	D 63%	D 77%
Philadelphia	R 22%	R 40%	D 61%	D 68%	D 77%
Baltimore	R 39%	R 48%	D 68%	D 64%	D 79%
New Orleans	D 65%	D 80%	D 91%	D 50%	D 76%
St. Louis	R 38%	D 52%	D 66%	D 67%	D 75%
Denver	R 33%	R 36%	D 65%	D 50%	D 62%
San Francisco	R 22%	D 49%	D 74%	D 58%	D 72%

the left wing of the Democratic Party," said David A. Bositis, senior political analyst at the Joint Center for Political and Economic Studies.

The electoral success of the Republican mayors was due less to "their political ideology than being linked to an agenda for change," said Rep. Earl Blumenauer, a Democrat who represented Portland, Ore. Urban issues are not party issues by nature, he said. "Local officials dealing with police and parks and people's backyards . . . can't afford to be gratuitously partisan."

Still, the willingness of voters in several big cities to back Republicans of any stripe for a major office was noteworthy and there were several reasons to think it could be an early sign that the era of almost automatic Democratic voting in the cities was coming to an end.

For one thing, the urban political machines that once routinely delivered votes for Democratic candidates were a thing of the past. Civil service reforms had reduced patronage in city halls, and modern election methods had made it harder to manufacture votes.

Just as important was the Democrats' own loss of interest in the cities and their problems. While Clinton was never expected to be another FDR, many urban advocates found his support of budget austerity and the 1996 welfare overhaul a bitter disappointment. "Clinton has been pretty indifferent to the cities," said Bositis.

Also, the era of expansive federal involvement in the cities was only a memory. No one spoke of returning to the grand scale of "urban renewal" of the 1950s, the Great Society of the 1960s or even Richard M. Nixon's revenue-sharing plans of the 1970s.

The trend in the 1980s and 1990s was to return authority and responsibility to state and local governments, a development that corresponded with some city voters' new willingness to judge individual Republican candidates on their own terms.

City-savvy Republicans had shown they could win when they united and turned out white voters. Where GOP politics were inclusive enough to appeal to middle-class minorities as well, their urban growth potential appeared considerable. The more that Democrats emulated Clinton, wooing the suburbs while taking the cities largely for granted, the more opportunity the GOP was likely to find downtown. ■

Rural Voter the Least Predictable

Nearly a century after it had lost its central role in national politics, rural America retained a unique place in the country's political psyche. That, and the fact that the rural vote was often up for grabs, allowed rural areas to retain some measure of political importance despite their decline in population and congressional representation.

While rural America was hardly monolithic in the late 20th century, its residents shared some characteristics. They were generally less affluent, more likely to be white and politically more conservative than the rest of the nation, particularly on social issues such as abortion and gun control.

Much of rural America tended to vote Republican, especially after the Democratic hold on the rural South was broken. In the 105th Congress, Republicans held nearly two-thirds of the districts in which at least 60 percent of the population lived outside a metropolitan area.

Yet rural America could be called the least predictable of the nation's demographic or geographic blocs. Unlike the cities, which for decades had voted overwhelmingly Democratic in federal elections, rural voters were willing to split ballots and make quick partisan turnarounds. In 1996, while most rural districts elected Republicans to the House, a clear majority of the rural districts also voted for President Clinton.

Rural discontent with the status quo had been a cornerstone of congressional upheaval throughout the nation's history, and that was the case in 1994, when Republicans gained control of Congress. From 1993 to 1997 the GOP picked up a net 15 House seats in rural America, including 11 in the South alone. Seats formerly held by such Democratic lions as Tom Bevill of Alabama, William H. Natcher of Kentucky, and Jamie L. Whitten and G. V. "Sonny" Montgomery of Mississippi had fallen to Republicans who were not likely to give them back soon.

Many of the Democrats who found success in rural America were traditional conservatives — Dixiecrats, or "Tory" Democrats in Texas, or "Pinto" Democrats elsewhere in the Southwest. In the 1990s, they were more likely to call themselves "Blue Dogs," a group dedicated to resisting leftward impulses within the House Democratic Caucus.

They were fiscally conservative and positioned to the right of the mainstream of their national party on social issues. But that did not make them functional Republicans. While most rural GOP House members drew ratings in 1996 from the liberal Americans for Democratic Action (ADA) that were in the single digits (on a 100-point scale), prominent Blue Dog Democrats such as Collin C. Peterson of Minnesota and Charles W. Stenholm of Texas had ADA scores in 1996 of at least 50 percent.

By and large, rural Democratic congressmen were in agreement with the Clinton administration much of the time. "My constituents are closer to this administration than most of them would even think on policy issues" such as health care, education and taxes, said Democratic Rep. Ted Strickland, who represented a rural district in southern Ohio. Problems with the administration, he said, tended to come on "socially divisive issues."

Losing Strength, Slowly

Through much of the 19th century, the United States was an agrarian nation. But in the 1900s, the country went through two transformations. Early in the century, the cities gained ascendancy over the countryside. That era gave way gradually after World War II, with the suburbs establishing hegemony. *(Suburbs, p. 10-4; cities, p. 10-9)*

Despite the change, rural America was able to maintain bastions of political might in malapportioned legislatures at both the state and national level. But that grip was weakened by population shifts and finally broken by the Supreme Court in the 1960s with its "one-person, one-vote" decision.

In the decades that followed, the demographic trends that forced the law to change accelerated. In 1997, nearly four out of every five Americans lived in cities or suburbs. Barely one out of five lived in small towns or the countryside, and the rural share of congressional seats was even smaller.

As recently as 1966, there had been 181 districts (or 42 percent of the entire House) with a population that was majority rural. But by 1993, that number was down to 77 districts (18 percent). Congressional Quarterly classified a district as rural only when at least 60 percent of its residents lived outside a metropolitan area and outside towns with populations of 25,000 or more. Using that definition, just 57 districts in the 105th Congress could be considered rural (13 percent of the House). *(Rural districts, this page)*

Geographically, most of the rural districts were in the South and Midwest (21 apiece), with the rest almost evenly split between the East (eight) and the West (seven).

Most were overwhelmingly white. The bulk of the rural districts had a non-Hispanic white population in excess of 90 percent. Only a handful were predominantly minority, and they were clustered in the Sun Belt — in the old Cotton Belt states and in areas of the Southwest where Latino immigrants had concentrated.

Economically, rural America was comparatively poor. According to a 1993 study by the Congressional Research Service, no rural district was ranked in the top 100 in terms of median family income (based on 1990 census data); only two districts (both in New England) were in the top 200. Most rural districts were among the bottom 100 in this measurement of personal affluence.

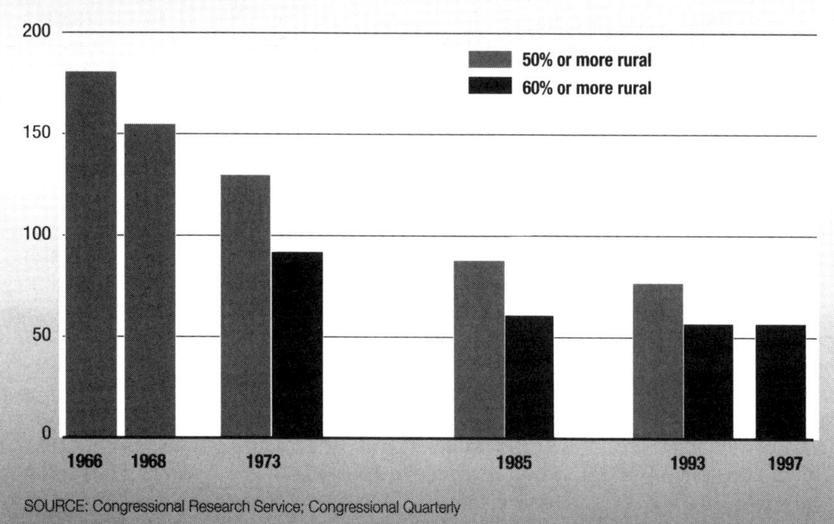

Their voting power in national elections had declined as well. According to 1996 population estimates, 13 states had a rural majority, a number that included the president's home state of Arkansas as well as Iowa, the traditional kick-off point for the quadrennial presidential nominating process. But this baker's dozen offered only 59 electoral votes to a presidential candidate fortunate enough to win them all. That was just five more electoral votes than were available in California alone.

In some large battleground states such as California, the rural vote was almost an afterthought. Only 3 percent of California's residents lived outside metro areas. In Massachusetts and New Jersey, the rural population was less than 5 percent. In Florida and New York, it was less than 10 percent, and it was less than 20 percent in Illinois, Michigan, Ohio, Pennsylvania and Texas. The non-metro population was even under 20 percent in the vast Western states of Arizona, Colorado and Nevada, where most residents lived in large metropolitan centers such as Phoenix, Denver and Las Vegas.

The Mystique of the Countryside

Voting power aside, however, rural America retained significance because its mystique refused to recede. Even as the nation became citified and suburbanized, national politicians tended to become more and more deliberate in their identification with small-town America.

President Dwight D. Eisenhower, a career military man who entered politics from an address in Manhattan, always insisted his hometown was Abilene, Kan. (which he had left while still a boy). President Richard M. Nixon harked back to a pre-suburban Whittier, Calif. Jimmy Carter went home to the farm at Plains, Ga., and Ronald Reagan shunned images of Hollywood for those of the Illinois towns of Dixon and Tampico.

As Clinton moved onto the national stage in 1992, it was as the candidate from "a place called Hope." The slogan struck an optimistic chord in a year when many voters thought the economy was mired in recession. But it also accented his roots in small-town Arkansas and linked him with traditional family values at a time when his personal character was already under attack.

Clinton underscored his identification with small-town America in the 1992 campaign with a series of bus trips across the rural heartland. On the eve of the 1996 Democratic convention, he made a well-publicized train trip that traversed rural Ohio and Michigan. As a consequence, while liberal Democrats such as George S. McGovern, Walter F. Mondale and Michael S. Dukakis were buried in the rural voting when they ran for president, Carter and Clinton made deep inroads into the rural electorate.

Carter more completely dominated the rural South in his successful run for the White House in 1976, but Clinton more deeply penetrated the rural vote in other parts of the country. In Illinois, for instance, he won more than two dozen downstate counties in 1992 that no Democratic presidential candidate had carried at least since Lyndon B. Johnson's landslide victory over Barry M. Goldwater in 1964. Clinton carried most of those counties again in 1996.

Reality is More Complex

Despite the imagery, in virtually every state the rural electorate was variegated. "It's difficult to talk about rural areas in the singular," says Republican consultant David Hill about his home state of Texas.

Paul M. Green, an Illinois political analyst at Governors State University, said Illinois' huge downstate area was divided into three different sectors by its major east-west interstate highways. South of Interstate 70, the land was not particularly prosperous and prisons were a basic growth industry. The area was populated by "traditional good old boy downstate Democrats," he said. "It's the only place in Illinois that thinks Clinton doesn't talk with an accent."

A bit to the north between Interstates 70 and 80, the soil was rich and deep. This area, described by Green as "the heart of Republican central Illinois," was for years the bailiwick of House Minority Leader Robert H. Michel.

North of Interstate 80, the rural areas were being eaten up by the westward expansion of the Chicago suburbs. "In our lifetime," said Green, "the suburbs will sprawl from Chicago to Rock Island [on the Iowa border]."

University of Akron political scientist John C. Green described a similar division within Ohio's rural sector. There is "Hoosier Ohio" and "Appalachian Ohio," he said. The latter, covering the southern part of the state, was not economically prosperous, depended on government aid and was apt to vote Democratic — especially if a Southerner such as Carter or Clinton headed the ticket.

"Hoosier Ohio," covering much of the central and northern parts of the state, was Republican corn country. "Farmers there are small-business people," said Green. "While Appalachian [Ohio] feels left behind," Hoosier Ohio is "more prosperous and feels integrated into the modern economy."

That distinction could be found throughout rural America: energetic, growing rural areas, and rural areas that were isolated and dying.

G. Terry Madonna, a political scientist at Millersville University in Pennsylvania, described less fortunate communities in the hills and hollows of that state. They seem "locked in time and space," he said, and there was little in-migration. "The values that exist there are the values that have been held [there] for generations," said Madonna. If time did not stand still, it at least moved far more slowly than elsewhere.

That often meant that political values such as populism and isolationism — including an aversion to foreign military adventures, treaties and trade agreements — endured across generations. The member of Congress for a given rural district might be a Democrat in one era, a Republican in another, but in either case he was likely to be a white male with a traditional family and a tendency to value the past.

Rural Volatility

Country values, with their emphasis on self-reliance and social conservatism, often worked to the political advantage of Republicans. But that was offset, at least in some rural areas, by a sense of unease with the economic status quo. Rural areas "lag behind the cities in income and tend toward populism, left and right," said Albert J. Menendez, the author of several books on religion and politics.

Gun clubs, veterans' organizations and evangelical churches were often abundant. "There's a higher percentage of religious orthodoxy in rural America," said Menendez. "It's a little more conservative, a little more intense." It provides, he added, "a sense of belonging."

But there was also a sense of uncertainty in many rural areas. Family farms, once the backbone of an agrarian economy, were giving way to agribusiness. Only a handful of congressional districts, all clustered in the Midwest, had as many as one resident in 10 actually living on a farm. Small towns increasingly needed a light industry or two to supply jobs, but their ability to attract them often depended on the adequacy of basic services — roads, schools, health care — that were uneven across rural America.

According to a study by Calvin L. Beale, a demographer with the Department of Agriculture, and Kenneth M. Johnson, a sociologist at Loyola University in Chicago, more than half the nation's roughly 2,300 rural counties (those without an urban center of 50,000 or more) lost population in the 1980s — but three-quarters of them showed population gains from 1990 to 1996.

The major gainers — at the opposite end of the spectrum from Madonna's isolated Pennsylvania communities — were counties with retirement or recreational facilities or those within proximity of a major population center.

Among the recreation-retirement counties experiencing robust growth in the affluent 1990s was Arkansas' Baxter County, on the Missouri state line. Baxter gained population in both the 1980s and 1990s. According to the 1990 census, nearly 30 percent of the county population was age 65 or older — more than double the national average. Baxter had lured not only retiring Arkansans content to live out their days in their home state, but an influx from Kansas City, St. Louis and other major metropolitan areas.

Any hope for a comeback in rural areas depended on communities such as these. Rural population growth based on retirees could have an unpredictable political effect, however, depending on which political concerns — Medicare, tax levels, property rights — motivated older voters in the future.

And there was no guarantee that such a rural rebound would continue. "We could still have reversals," said Agriculture Department demographer Beale. The seven-year phaseout of farm subsidies instituted by the 1996 farm bill was a major uncertainty. "What happens when there is a large corn crop or a large wheat crop and nobody to buy it?" asked Beale. Moreover, economic conditions had improved in major urban areas since the early 1990s, when much of the most recent movement to rural America had taken place.

Yet, Beale added, population centers had grown so large and congested that "a number of people are fed up with the pace and stress of metro living. Under any type of average economic conditions," he said, "we'll have more people moving out of metro areas for non-[metro] areas than are moving in."

That trend seemed likely to be encouraged in the computer age by the increasing ability of people to live where they wanted to, not where they had to. "There's more diversity out there [in rural America] than we have seen in the past," said Ohio's Green.

All of this meant the country cousin could be a growing force in the future. The trends were not likely to have much impact on the Electoral College any time soon. But new growth could sustain the vitality of rural America and preserve its political influence and aspirations — even as the agrarian myths of the past faded into memory. ■

GOP Holds Ground In 1997 Contests

Continuing their domination of elections held in the odd-numbered years of the 1990s, Republicans in 1997 won the bellwether gubernatorial races in Virginia and New Jersey, the mayoral races in New York and Los Angeles, and two of the three special elections held to fill congressional vacancies. Three other congressional vacancies remained at year's end. *(Membership changes, p. 1-8)*

Other political events in 1997 included the resignation of Arizona's Republican Gov. Fife Symington, who was convicted Sept. 3 on seven counts of fraud stemming from his career as a real estate developer. He was succeeded Sept. 8 by Jane Dee Hull, another Republican, who had been secretary of state.

Also in 1997, a trickle of judicial decisions, legislative actions and out-of-court settlements kept alive the process of redrawing congressional districts in several states.

But most of the big events took place Nov. 4, giving Republicans a chance to claim momentum going into the midterm elections of 1998. Democrats argued that the electoral outcomes of 1997 merely demonstrated voters' satisfaction with the status quo, much as the 1996 presidential and congressional elections had done.

One thing about the 1997 races was undeniable: The cataract of money spent by candidates, parties and independent organizations in the 1996 presidential and congressional cycle continued at full flow. "The conduct of fundraising continues pretty much unabashed, and candidates are continually looking for the same huge amounts of money to get their message out in the best way they can," said Greg D. Kubiak of the Center for Strategic and International Studies, a proponent of overhauling campaign finance laws.

Through much of 1997, the news was filled with stories about investigations into campaign finance practices. The Department of Justice was on the case, as were several Senate and House committees. Much of the attention was focused on the raising and spending of unregulated "soft money" — which was legally permitted for "party building" activities but not for conducting specific campaigns. *(Campaign finance investigation, p. 1-20)*

But despite months of embarrassing revelations, mostly about President Clinton and the Democrats, practical politicians were apparently taking one lesson to heart in 1997: Raise and spend as much soft money as you can. "In the [1996] cycle, issue ads and soft money flowed into the election at an unprecedented level, and that has continued with the races [of 1997], and it's a predictor for [1998]," said James A. Thurber, director of the Center for Congressional and Presidential Studies at American University in Washington.

In 1997, at least, the principal beneficiaries were Republicans. The Democratic Party, having been buffeted all year by the campaign finance hearings in the Senate, was strapped by debts and legal fees. By its own estimates, the Democratic National Committee (DNC) spent about $8 million more on legal fees in 1997 than it did in aiding its candidates.

While Democrats scratched together $1 million for their November contestants, Republicans pumped as much as $5 million into the gubernatorial contests and the special House election held in New York's Staten Island-based 13th District.

"It ought to be a lesson to the people who think that you can limit the amounts candidates spend," said Herbert E. Alexander, an expert on campaign finance at the University of Southern California. "Those spending limits turn out to be meaningless," he said. "What they do is limit what the candidates can spend, but they don't limit what outsiders can spend, including the parties as outsiders and surrogate spenders."

Republicans were quick to note that, while the Democratic Party was all but sidelined in 1997, Democratic candidates benefited from such "surrogate spenders" as labor unions. "Try to find out what the unions spent in [New York]," said House Speaker Newt Gingrich, R-Ga., on Nov. 5. "They won't tell you."

Thurber said the trend toward relying on outside money was making individual candidates less important to their own campaigns. "Ultimately, it undermines the ability of candidates to control their own destinies and agendas," he said.

Jim Nicholson, chairman of the Republican National Committee (RNC), acknowledged that situations could arise in which candidates were reduced to spectators while outside groups waged war with their own campaigns. ■

GOP's Whitman Wins By a Whisker In New Jersey Governor's Race

New Jersey Democrat Jim McGreevey, a state senator and mayor of Woodbridge Township, came within about 27,000 votes of unseating GOP Gov. Christine Todd Whitman Nov. 4. Her margin of victory was within about 600 votes of her margin in 1993, when she upset Democratic Gov. James J. Florio.

Whitman (R)	1,133,394	46.9%
McGreevey (D)	1,107,968	45.8

Whitman took 47 percent of the vote to McGreevey's 46 percent. Libertarian Murray Sabrin won 5 percent, while Conservative Party nominee Richard J. Pezzullo took nearly 1.5 percent. In the end, exit polls suggested Whitman survived because just enough conservatives decided to stick with her despite her views on abortion and other social issues.

Gubernatorial candidates in New Jersey received generous state matching funds if they agreed to limit their own campaign spending to $10 million. But that did not prevent the national parties and various outside groups from lending a hand. Clinton twice stumped the state for McGreevey, attending a fundraising dinner that netted $2 million for the DNC. And Republicans spent about $760,000 on an advertising campaign that attacked Democrats for high taxes in the pre-Whitman era.

Whitman did not have to devote much of her time to fundraising, as she easily raised the $2.3 million needed to qualify for the full amount of matching state funds (at a ratio of about 2-to-1). McGreevey, however, needed much of the year to reach the threshold and was still dividing his time between campaigning and fundraising in the fall. A flush state GOP had operatives in every county to identify likely voters and turn them out — getting its network in place months before the cash-starved Democrats could mount a comparable effort.

Whitman's victories in the affluent central counties were partially offset by McGreevey's totals in the key Democratic counties of Essex, Hudson and Camden, as well as his home county of Middlesex. But his margins were slimmer than those of winning Democrat Robert G. Torricelli in the 1996 Senate race. Had McGreevey matched Torricelli's percentages in these venues, he would have won.

Although McGreevey did a fair job of turning out party

support, he was unable to claim as many independent voters as early polls had suggested he might. Whitman, meanwhile, was able to cut the usual Republican gender gap to almost nil. While exit polls showed she did better among men than women — as Republican candidates nearly always did — the difference was reduced to 2 percentage points. (She took 48 percent of men's votes and 46 percent of women's.)

The election was mostly a referendum on Whitman, as could be expected when an incumbent was on the ballot against a little-known challenger. The only elected Republican woman governor in the nation and the only Republican to win a presidential, senatorial or gubernatorial vote in New Jersey since 1988, Whitman tried to highlight her successes, beginning with her 30 percent cut in income tax rates and the thriving state economy.

But she also was forced to admit that not all was well: "You've sent me a message," a contrite Whitman said in a late-season campaign ad. "Auto insurance and property taxes cost too much, and people are hurting. I've heard you loud and clear." ■

GOP's Gilmore Rides Car Tax Cut To Governorship in Virginia

Republican James S. Gilmore III, a former state attorney general, defeated Democratic Lt. Gov. Donald S. Beyer Jr. in the most expensive gubernatorial contest in the history of the commonwealth.

Gilmore (R)	969,062	55.8%
Beyer (D)	738,971	42.6

Gilmore had been elected attorney general in 1993, alongside his predecessor as governor, Republican George F. Allen. But Gilmore resigned early in 1997 to devote himself full time to his campaign. Allen was not eligible to succeed himself, as Virginia limited governors to a single term.

Gilmore spent $10 million, and was aided by $2 million in outside GOP money in winning 56 percent of the vote. Beyer spent $8 million to win 43 percent of the vote. Beyer enjoyed little monetary help from his national party, and had to borrow an estimated $400,000 to keep his campaign on the air in the final days. Beyer, a millionaire car dealer, proved unwilling to pump large sums of family money into the campaign as he had in earlier races.

Virginia turnout was the lowest of the modern era. The 48 percent initially reported contrasted with the 55 percent turnout in 1985, when flooding shut down many polling places.

But if the race failed to entice a majority of registered voters, it was nevertheless a big win for the GOP, marking the first time that Republicans had swept all the constitutional offices in Virginia — and the first time they had done so in any Southern state since Reconstruction.

Gilmore's appeal was simple, calling for the abolition of the personal property tax on cars and trucks. "This is an identifiable tax which is very much hated, and it cut across the major elements of Beyer's base," said Patrick McSweeney, former chairman of the Virginia GOP. By emphasizing the tax cut in his advertising, Gilmore was able to break open what had been a closely contested race through most of the year.

Gilmore even won in the populous Northern Virginia suburbs, Beyer's geographical base. Those communities, where many residents commuted to Washington, D.C., were home to some of the highest car tax rates in the Old Dominion. "If you hit a particular tax like that, you'll get a response," McSweeney said. "They'll worry about the spending cuts later." Beyer called Gilmore's plan irresponsible, but his complaints were undercut when he released a rival plan several weeks after attacking Gilmore's.

Beyer also failed in his efforts to tar Gilmore as an enemy of abortion rights and a tool of television evangelist Pat Robertson. Although he was anti-abortion, Gilmore had said he did not expect abortion to be an issue for his administration. And while Gilmore had accepted $100,000 for his two statewide campaigns from Robertson, the issue seemed to energize religious conservatives without arousing much interest among other voters. ■

Hull Holds Governor's Chair For Arizona Republicans

After preparing quietly and informally for 16 weeks while her predecessor was on trial for fraud, Republican Jane Dee Hull took the oath of office as the new governor of Arizona on Sept. 8.

Her predecessor, GOP Gov. Fife Symington, was convicted Sept. 3 of seven counts of fraud in connection with his career as a real estate developer. Hull, who had been the secretary of state (the second highest statewide office in Arizona), tried to reassure voters with the promise of a "seamless" transition.

Hull, 62, was the first woman to be Speaker of the Arizona House. She was also the second woman elevated to the Arizona governorship in the previous nine years. In both instances, the women succeeded sitting governors who were forced to resign in disgrace.

Rose Mofford, a Democrat, served as governor from 1988 to 1991, having taken the reins from Republican Evan Mecham. Mecham was impeached on charges of obstructing justice and illegally lending state money to his car dealership.

The charges against Symington stemmed from incidents in his career as a developer that predated his term in office. (He was acquitted of attempted extortion, the single count that arose from his official duties.) U.S. District Judge Roger Strand declared a mistrial on 11 other counts on which the jury deadlocked.

Symington won his first term as governor in 1991, beating Phoenix Mayor Terry Goddard in a runoff election. With the savings and loan debacle still fresh in voters' minds, Goddard attempted to link Symington, who had served as a director of Southwest Savings and Loan Association, to Charles H. Keating Jr., the leading figure in the S&L scandal, who had Arizona ties.

Goddard's charges failed to stick, but within months of Symington's inauguration the FBI launched an investigation into the failure of Southwest, which had invested heavily in Symington's Camelback Esplanade development. In 1990, Symington had signed a financial statement disclosing his net worth at $12 million. The next month, he was able to secure a $10 million loan to underwrite his downtown Phoenix Mercado development with a personal guarantee of repayment.

Symington was re-elected in 1994 with 53 percent of the vote and had long vowed that he would be acquitted in time to run again in 1998 — repeating this prediction even as his trial approached. But in fact the governor had been under a cloud during the whole of his second term. His inability to repay creditors had led him to declare bankruptcy in 1995, at which time he claimed nearly $25 million in debts. He was indicted on the criminal counts in June 1996. ■

Three States Hold Special Elections

Special elections were held in congressional districts in Texas (April 12), New Mexico (May 13) and New York (Nov. 4) following the death of one incumbent and the resignations of two others. The special elections yielded a net gain of one seat for the Republicans.

Texas — 28th

Texas state Rep. Ciro D. Rodriguez won a ticket to Washington April 12 with two-thirds of the vote in a runoff election in San Antonio. Rodriguez, 50, assumed the seat formerly held by Democrat Frank Tejeda, who died Jan. 30 of pneumonia following surgery and treatment for a brain tumor.

According to the official returns, Rodriguez received 19,992 votes to Juan Solis' 9,990. Both runoff contestants were Democrats, as was Tejeda.

Rodriguez (D)	19,992	67%
Solis (D)	9,990	33

Rodriguez, a 10-year veteran of the state Legislature who previously served 12 years on the Harlandale School Board, had the backing of most of the San Antonio Democratic establishment. He had dominated 14 rivals in the first round of voting in the March 15 special election, but his 46 percent share of the vote fell short of the majority required to win the seat outright.

Rodriguez was forced into a runoff with his nearest rival, former City Councilman Juan Solis, who had gotten 26.5 percent in the first round. Solis, who had resigned from the council to seek Tejeda's seat, immediately launched an aggressive runoff challenge to Rodriguez. Solis characterized himself as the true heir to Tejeda because he shared the former member's anti-abortion position (Rodriguez supported abortion rights).

Solis also campaigned for gun owners' rights and anti-crime measures and accused Rodriguez of being "a wild-eyed liberal." But Solis' best claim to the votes of conservatives and Tejeda admirers may have been the endorsements he received from some members of Tejeda's family.

Rodriguez countered Solis' claim to Tejeda's mystique by saying he had known the deceased incumbent since they went to high school and college together. He said he would go to Washington to fight for education and to protect Social Security and other programs.

The real test for Rodriguez had been in the March round. Under Texas election law, all special-election candidates appeared on one ballot regardless of party. If no one won a majority, the top two finishers, regardless of party, met in a runoff. Turnout also had been weak in the March vote; officials said only about 30,000 votes were cast. None of the also-ran candidates — seven Democrats, five Republicans and one independent — managed a double-digit percentage share of the vote. Best known among them was Mark Cude, a Republican businessman who had received 23 percent of the vote against Tejeda in 1996. Cude's 2,452 votes on March 15 put him in third place with 8 percent of the overall vote. Four other Republicans received less than 7 percent among them.

Rodriguez was the favorite because he was the best-known Democrat and had raised by far the most money (more than $250,000). Rodriguez also enjoyed the unanimous backing of the local labor council of the AFL-CIO. The union endorsement was considered especially useful in a low-turnout special election.

A former teacher and social worker, Rodriguez had been a familiar face in local politics since the 1970s. But becoming the front-runner for Tejeda's seat meant jumping an extra rung on the local ladder of political succession. His biggest break came in February, when state Sen. Frank Madla, who held the seat Tejeda once held in the state Senate, decided not to run for Congress. Madla subsequently endorsed Rodriguez, as did neighboring state Rep. John Longoria.

Tejeda had represented the district since its creation in the aftermath of the 1990 census, which gave Texas three new seats in Congress. State legislators then created the 28th expressly to be a Hispanic-majority district, stretching it for more than 250 miles so as to connect south San Antonio to counties on the Mexican border. The district was about three-fifths Hispanic in the 1990 census, and it usually voted heavily Democratic. President Clinton received more than 80 percent of the vote there in 1996.

New Mexico — 3rd

Republican Bill Redmond scored a head-turning, upset victory in New Mexico's heavily Democratic 3rd District May 13. The early favorite in the race, Democratic nominee Eric Serna, found himself dividing the district's usual Democratic vote with Carol Miller, the nominee of the Green Party, a rising force in state politics.

Redmond (R)	43,559	43.0%
Serna (D)	40,542	40.1
Miller (G)	17,101	16.9

Official returns showed Redmond with 43,559 votes (43 percent) to 40,542 (40 percent) for Serna, a member of the state Corporation Commission. The Green's Miller, a health care consultant, received 17,101 (17 percent), the Libertarian Party nominee Ed Nagel received 392 votes, Daniel Pearlman of the Reform Party (formed to support the presidential candidacy of Ross Perot) received 304 votes, and three write-in candidates wound up with 38 votes total.

Redmond, 43, succeeded former Democratic incumbent Bill Richardson, who was sworn in as the U.S. representative to the United Nations on Feb. 13. Richardson had held the seat since the district was created in 1982. He won his eighth term in 1996, collecting 67 percent of the vote against Redmond with no Green Party challenger. *(Richardson, p. 8-46)*

Redmond was sworn in May 20, giving House Republicans a 228-206 edge over Democrats, with one independent. Democrats held a 2-to-1 edge in registration over Republicans in the ethnically diverse and expansive 3rd District, so Serna initially had been the heavy favorite to succeed Richardson.

Serna, 47, raised more than $500,000 for the race, compared with about $250,000 for Redmond and $30,000 for Miller. But Serna's candidacy ran into a series of problems that led many in his own party to question his electability. A state co-chairman for the 1996 Clinton-Gore campaign, Serna had hoped to receive personal help from President Clinton as well as from Richardson, but neither man came to the state to campaign for him.

Democrats blamed Serna's loss on the Green Party's insistence on nominating a candidate of its own. Miller campaigned against Serna and clearly took votes away from him in several of the counties where Democrats had the greatest electoral

Ballot Initiatives

It was easy to sum up the fate of the ballot initiatives most people were following Nov. 4: They lost. As a rule, voters across the country said no to changes in their statutes and state constitutions, reflecting the satisfaction with the status quo that was evident in the high rates of re-election for incumbents.

In Houston, voters defeated a proposition that would have ended the city's affirmative action program in hiring and contracting. The 55 percent vote defending the program was attributed to strong turnout among minority voters and to the popularity of retiring Mayor Bob Lanier, who had fathered the program and opposed the proposition.

In Washington state, voters defeated separate efforts to restrict handgun sales, ban hiring discrimination against homosexuals and permit the medicinal use of marijuana and other drugs.

In Oregon, by a ratio of 3-to-2, voters refused to repeal the doctor-assisted suicide measure they had approved in 1994. In Colorado, voters rejected proposed increases in gasoline and telephone taxes to pay for transportation and communications improvements.

In Maine, voters said no to new restrictions on the clear-cutting of timber. In Ohio, the majority sided with labor in rejecting changes to the worker's compensation law. And in New York, by a ratio of 3-to-2, voters refused to call a convention to consider various amendments to the state Constitution.

advantage, including Santa Fe, the district's largest city. Miller ran a strong campaign and picked up endorsements from two of the state's largest newspapers, the Albuquerque Journal and Albuquerque Tribune. "I don't think there's any question that the Democratic candidate would have won had it been a two-person race," said Sen. Jeff Bingaman, who became the only Democrat in the state's delegation.

But several other factors also contributed to Redmond's upset. A strong last-minute push by Democrats to increase turnout was not enough to avert the usual downturn in participation in special elections: Less than 40 percent of the registered voters cast ballots — as compared with 66 percent in November.

University of New Mexico political scientist Chris Garcia also cited broad Democratic dissatisfaction with Serna. Although Serna had been positioning himself to succeed Richardson for years, a poll in the newspaper the Santa Fe New Mexican conducted in early May showed Serna with a 31 percent unfavorability rating among likely voters.

Some Democrats objected to the process by which Serna was nominated in March, when members of the state party's central committee selected him as their candidate. State election law called for the two parties to nominate special-election candidates with no primary.

Redmond renewed past allegations that state employees and people with business before the corporation commissioner were urged to buy jewelry from the Serna family's store. Serna also had been accused of using a car in a previous campaign that was provided by businessmen whose activities were regulated by the commission.

A lengthy article in a Santa Fe alternative newspaper that appeared shortly before the election — headlined "Eric Serna's Troubling Ethical History" — listed allegations of misdeeds involving Serna dating back to 1981. Serna dismissed all allegations against him as insignificant and attempted to portray Redmond as "a radical right-wing preacher who wants to impose his extreme values and social agenda on all of us."

But Redmond said such counter-attacks failed to take hold. "The cookie-cutter approach of the Democrats that I was an extremist just didn't work in this race," he said. "I'm an average middle-class citizen of northern New Mexico; my approach is common sense."

Redmond's campaign stressed his support for the House Republican agenda, including repeal of the ban on assault weapons and enactment of environmental laws to protect the rights of private property owners.

New York — 13th

In a special election scheduled to coincide with New York City's regular local election Nov. 4, Republican City Councilman Vito J. Fossella ran away from his Democrat opponent, state Rep. Eric N. Vitaliano, and claimed the Staten Island congressional seat vacated Aug. 1 by the resignation of Republican Rep. Susan Molinari. Molinari resigned to accept a job as an on-air personality with CBS-TV, appearing in a Saturday morning news and information program.

Fossella (R)	79,838	61.3%
Vitaliano (D)	50,373	38.7

The seat had been held by Molinari (1990-97) and her father, Guy V. Molinari (1981-90), who had become the Staten Island Borough President. The senior Molinari had helped move his daughter from the city council to Congress when he retired in 1990. Fossella held the same council seat when his chance at Congress came along seven years later.

The senior Molinari endorsed Fossella, referred to him as "my son," and discouraged other prospective candidates from running. The nominations of both parties were bestowed by votes of local party committees as no primary election was held.

Most polls had shown the Fossella-Vitaliano race to be tight until mid-October, when the Republican National Committee (RNC) weighed in with TV ads attacking Vitaliano for having supported state tax increases. The national GOP also spent heavily on mail and get-out-the-vote efforts in the district, which included all of Staten Island and portions of Brooklyn.

Fossella spent about $1 million on his own campaign, while Vitaliano raised about $250,000 less. The RNC spent about $1.5 million buying ads in the costly market of the nation's largest city. The regular limit on such a contribution from the national party would have been $63,620. But the far larger amount was legal because it paid for ads that attacked Fossella's opponent without mentioning Fossella by name or asking voters explicitly to vote for or against either candidate.

Fossella was also lifted by the landslide re-election victory of New York City's Republican mayor, Rudolph W. Giuliani, who received more than 80 percent of the vote on Staten Island. Giuliani, riding a wave of appreciation for an improved economy and lower violent crime rates, was one of many mayors re-elected Nov. 4. Throughout the campaign, Fossella's posters and other advertising featured the popular mayor's endorsement.

Anticipating a Republican year and a big vote, Vitaliano had offered himself to voters as a conservative who supported the death penalty and opposed abortion rights. He also tried to find a benefit in the help the RNC gave Fossella, saying it proved his opponent's lack of independence — specifically arguing that it made Speaker Newt Gingrich, R-Ga., an issue in the campaign. Vitaliano went after the Speaker with gusto, but Fossella sidestepped the issue easily. He was too much of a local product to be made a stalking horse, and his predecessor was widely viewed as having been at odds with the Speaker.

At the same time, Republicans were able to convince voters that Vitaliano's record in Albany of support for tax hikes and increased welfare spending did not match his rhetoric.

Both candidates focused often on local transportation issues, and both claimed credit for the closure of the Fresh Kills landfill. Each had sponsored legislation to shut the dump, Fossella in the City Council, Vitaliano in Albany. ■

Texas, North Carolina Maps Upheld by Federal Panels

Although the decade was nearing its end, the protracted process of drawing congressional districts based on the 1990 census continued to make news in 1997 in several states.

Long-running cases in Texas and North Carolina came to an apparent end in mid-September, leaving only one state, Virginia, still under court order to draw new district lines.

Black incumbents survived competitive primaries and general elections in other states in 1996, including Georgia and Florida, after their districts were redrawn to be less than half black. But in Louisiana, where a court challenge led to a remapping, the number of districts electing black representatives in 1996 slipped from two to one.

The new maps in Texas and North Carolina did not appear to endanger incumbent minority members. But the more difficult question for the future was whether non-incumbent black candidates would be able to win a first election in districts where blacks did not have a clear majority.

Also in 1997, new lines were drawn for one Long Island district by the New York legislature, and an agreement was reached that obviated a challenge to the lines in use in South Carolina. In Illinois, the decision of a three-judge panel to allow the oddly shaped majority-Hispanic 4th District was still standing at year's end, although there was a chance of a review by the Supreme Court.

Under guidelines set by the Supreme Court in a series of decisions since 1993, certain black-majority and Hispanic-majority districts were declared invalid. The high court ruled it unconstitutional to draw a district using race as the "predominant factor." *(1996 Almanac, p. 11-37; 1995 Almanac, p. 12-3; 1993 Almanac, p. 325)*

Following the Supreme Court's guidelines, panels of judges in each of the affected states had either redrawn the districts themselves, accepted the remapping done by state legislators or endorsed the outcome of private negotiations between the state and the plaintiffs who had challenged the old map in court.

Illinois

In Illinois, the Hispanic-majority 4th, held by Democrat Luis V. Gutierrez, was upheld in August for a second time by a three-judge panel. The Supreme Court in November 1996 had asked that panel to re-examine its first (March 1996) decision in light of the high court's intervening rulings in the Texas and North Carolina cases.

The court in Chicago reconsidered and again determined that the 4th did not violate the high court's guidelines. An appeal of that ruling to the Supreme Court was pending at the end of 1997.

New York

Also in August, the state of New York redrew six congressional districts that included parts of the New York City boroughs of Queens, Brooklyn and Manhattan. The new map was necessitated by a three-judge panel's decision earlier in the year that found the 12th District of Democratic Rep. Nydia M. Velázquez unconstitutional.

The panel had thrown out the district lines on Feb. 26, ruling that the 12th's serpentine design across three New York City boroughs rendered it an unconstitutional racial gerrymander. The district, which had been drawn to aggregate Hispanic votes, touched seven other congressional districts.

Under the new map, the Hispanic population of the 12th dropped from nearly 58 percent to about 45 percent.

Adjustments to the district, which Velázquez had won easily three times, necessitated changes to the districts of five other Democrats, all of whom had won their re-elections easily in 1996 in heavily Democratic districts.

North Carolina

In North Carolina, a three-judge panel on Sept. 15 upheld new district lines that had been drawn by the state legislature in March. The legislature had acted after a June 1996 Supreme Court ruling that the existing North Carolina 12th District, held by Democrat Melvin Watt, had been drawn with race as the predominant factor.

Under the new North Carolina plan, the controversial 12th District would still span much of the state to connect black voters in Charlotte to others in Greensboro and Winston-Salem. But the district would no longer reach all the way to Durham, and the black percentage of its population would drop from 57 percent to 46 percent.

The new map also had some potential effect on every other district in the state. The percentage of blacks would drop from 57 percent to 50 percent in the 1st District, home of the state's only other African-American member, Democratic Rep. Eva Clayton. However, all of the state's 12 House members — six Republicans and six Democrats — were expected to survive politically within the new lines.

The legislators' latest plan was approved by the Justice Department and by the panel of three federal judges that had struck down the previous map. No sooner had it gained all the necessary approvals, however, than it was challenged by one of the same plaintiffs who had sued to overturn the previous map, a law professor at Duke University. That appeal was still pending at year's end.

South Carolina

A lawsuit involving South Carolina's 6th District, held by Democrat James E. Clyburn, was settled Aug. 6. The district had been challenged by two white residents who said racial redistricting had violated their constitutional rights. The plaintiffs dropped their suit in exchange for the state's admission that, in an effort to create a district that was more than 60 percent black, state legislators drew the 6th to connect black voters in four cities.

While Clyburn's district covered much of the state and arched its back to avoid three counties around Charleston, it retained a logical shape. It was also the only black district in the state.

Texas

On Sept. 16, a federal panel in Texas upheld the lines it had drawn in 1996 for 13 districts in its largest metropolitan areas. One district in Dallas and two in Houston had been ruled unconstitutional, and 10 other districts had to be altered in the subsequent remapping. The Texas panel had also thrown out the results of primary and runoff elections held earlier in the year. Special elections and runoffs had to be held in all 13 affected districts.

The panel had then allowed a period of time for the state legislature to enact changes in the plan, which it did not.

Virginia

The one state that ended 1997 under a court order to draw new lines before the 1998 elections was Virginia. Democratic Rep. Robert C. Scott had won in that district since 1992 and was the only black House member from Virginia since Reconstruction.

On Feb. 7, a panel of three federal judges sitting in Richmond, Va., struck down the state's 3rd Congressional District. The panel had conducted a trial in September 1996 after several parties challenged the lines in use since 1992.

The existing 3rd, drawn to maximize the chances of electing a black representative, extended its arms to disparate parts of southeastern and eastern Virginia. About one-fourth of its population lived in the city of Richmond, at the end of one western-reaching arm, but Scott himself hailed from Newport News, at the district's most southeastern point.

The panel's Feb. 7 judgment applied the criteria from the Supreme Court's recent "predominant factor" cases. As a result, observers saw little or no chance that the panel would be overturned on appeal. Appeals of rulings by federal judicial panels handling redistricting matters went directly to the Supreme Court. The state of Virginia did appeal the Feb. 7 ruling but the Supreme Court refused to review it.

Gov. George F. Allen refused to call the legislature into special session in the fall of 1997, pushing the issue of new lines into 1998. Most observers expected relatively minor changes to be made to the 3rd by compromise agreement among the affected congressmen, the legislature and the governor. ■

CQ

Appendix A

GLOSSARY

Glossary of Congressional Terms

Act — The term for legislation once it has passed both chambers of Congress and has been signed by the president or passed over his veto, thus becoming law. Also used in parliamentary terminology for a bill that has been passed by one house and engrossed. *(Also see engrossed bill.)*

Adjournment sine die — Adjournment without a fixed day for reconvening — literally, "adjournment without a day." Usually used to connote the final adjournment of a session of Congress. A session can continue until noon Jan. 3 of the following year, when, under the 20th Amendment to the Constitution, it automatically terminates. Both chambers must agree to a concurrent resolution for either chamber to adjourn for more than three days.

Adjournment to a day certain — Adjournment under a motion or resolution that fixes the next time of meeting. Under the Constitution, neither chamber can adjourn for more than three days without the concurrence of the other. A session of Congress is not ended by adjournment to a day certain.

Amendment — A proposal by a member of Congress to alter the language, provisions or stipulations in a bill or in another amendment. An amendment usually is printed, debated and voted upon in the same manner as a bill.

Amendment in the nature of a substitute — Usually an amendment that seeks to replace the entire text of a bill by striking out everything after the enacting clause and inserting a new version of the bill. An amendment in the nature of a substitute can also refer to an amendment that replaces a large portion of the text of a bill.

Appeal — A member's challenge of a ruling or decision made by the presiding officer of the chamber. A senator can appeal to members of the Senate to override the decision. If carried by a majority vote, the appeal nullifies the chair's ruling. In the House, the decision of the Speaker traditionally has been final; seldom are there appeals to the members to reverse the Speaker's stand. To appeal a ruling is considered an attack on the Speaker.

Appropriations bill — A bill that gives legal authority to spend or obligate money from the Treasury. The Constitution disallows money to be drawn from the Treasury "but in Consequence of Appropriations made by Law."

By congressional custom, an appropriations bill originates in the House. It is not supposed to be considered by the full House or Senate until a related measure authorizing the funding is enacted. An appropriations bill grants the actual budget authority approved by the authorization bill, though not necessarily the full amount permissible under the authorization.

If the 13 regular appropriations bills are not enacted by the start of the fiscal year, Congress must pass a stopgap spending bill or the departments and agencies covered by the unfinished bills must shut down.

About half of all budget authority, notably that for Social Security and interest on the federal debt, does not require annual appropriations; those programs exist under permanent appropriations. *(Also see authorization bill, budget authority, budget process, supplemental appropriations bill.)*

Authorization bill — Basic, substantive legislation that establishes or continues the legal operation of a federal program or agency either indefinitely or for a specific period of time, or which sanctions a particular type of obligation or expenditure. Under the rules of both chambers, appropriations for a program or agency may not be considered until the program has been authorized, although this requirement is often waived.

An authorization sets the maximum amount of funds that can be given to a program or agency, although sometimes it merely authorizes "such sums as may be necessary." *(Also see backdoor spending authority.)*

Backdoor spending authority — Budget authority provided in legislation outside the normal appropriations process. The most common forms of backdoor spending are borrowing authority, contract authority, entitlements and loan guarantees that commit the government to payments of principal and interest on loans — such as guaranteed student loans — made by banks or other private lenders. Loan guarantees result in actual outlays only when there is a default by the borrower.

In some cases, such as interest on the public debt, a permanent appropriation is provided that becomes available without further action by Congress.

Bills — Most legislative proposals before Congress are in the form of bills and are designated according to the chamber in which they originate — HR in the House of Representatives or S in the Senate — and by a number assigned in the order in which they are introduced during the two-year period of a congressional term.

"Public bills" deal with general questions and become public laws if they are cleared by Congress and signed by the president. "Private bills" deal with individual matters, such as claims against the government, immigration and naturalization cases or land titles, and become private laws if approved and signed. *(Also see private bills, resolution.)*

Bills introduced — In both the House and Senate, any number of members may join in introducing a single bill or resolution. The first member listed is the sponsor of the bill, and all subsequent members listed are cosponsors.

Many bills are committee bills and are introduced under the name of the chairman of the committee or subcommittee. All appropriations bills fall into this category. A committee frequently holds hearings on a number of related bills and may agree to one of them or to an entirely new bill. *(Also see clean bill.)*

Bills referred — After a bill is introduced, it is referred to the committee or committees that have jurisdiction over the subject with which the bill is concerned. Under the standing rules of the House and Senate, bills are referred by the Speaker in the House and by the presiding officer in the Senate. In practice, the House and Senate parliamentarians act for these officials and refer the vast majority of bills. *(Also see discharge a committee.)*

Borrowing authority — Statutory authority that permits

a federal agency to incur obligations and make payments for specified purposes with borrowed money.

Budget — The document sent to Congress by the president early each year estimating government revenue and expenditures for the ensuing fiscal year.

Budget Act — The common name for the Congressional Budget and Impoundment Control Act of 1974, which established the current budget process and created the Congressional Budget Office. The act also put limits on presidential authority to spend appropriated money. It has undergone several major revisions since 1974. *(Also see budget process, impoundments.)*

Budget authority — Authority for federal agencies to enter into obligations that result in immediate or future outlays. The basic forms of budget authority are appropriations, contract authority and borrowing authority. Budget authority may be classified by (1) the period of availability (one-year, multiple-year or without a time limitation), (2) the timing of congressional action (current or permanent) or (3) the manner of determining the amount available (definite or indefinite). *(Also see appropriations, outlays.)*

Budget process — The annual budget process was created by the Congressional Budget and Impoundment Control Act of 1974, with a timetable that was modified in 1990. Under the law, the president must submit his proposed budget by the first Monday in February. Congress is supposed to complete an annual budget resolution by April 15, setting guidelines for congressional action on spending and tax measures.

Budget rules enacted in the 1990 Budget Enforcement Act and updated in 1993 and 1997 set caps on discretionary spending through fiscal 2002. The caps can be adjusted annually to account for changes in the economy and other limited factors. In addition, pay-as-you-go (PAYGO) rules require that any tax cut, new entitlement program or expansion of existing entitlement benefits be offset by an increase in taxes or a cut in entitlement spending.

The rules hold Congress harmless for budget-deficit increases that lawmakers do not explicitly cause — for example, increases due to a recession or to an expansion in the number of beneficiaries qualifying for existing entitlement programs, such as Medicare or food stamps.

If Congress exceeds the discretionary spending caps in its appropriations bills, the law requires an across-the-board cut — known as a sequester — in non-exempt discretionary spending accounts. If Congress violates the PAYGO rules, entitlement programs are subject to a sequester. Supplemental appropriations are subject to similar controls, with the proviso that if both Congress and the president agree, spending designated as an emergency can exceed the caps.

Budget resolution — A concurrent resolution that is passed by both chambers of Congress but does not require the president's signature. The measure sets a strict ceiling on discretionary budget authority, along with non-binding recommendations about how the spending should be allocated. The budget resolution may also contain "reconciliation instructions" requiring authorizing and tax-writing committees to propose changes in existing law to meet deficit-reduction goals. The Budget Committee in each chamber then bundles those proposals into a reconciliation bill and sends it to the floor. *(Also see reconciliation.)*

By request — A phrase used when a senator or representative introduces a bill at the request of an executive agency or private organization but does not necessarily endorse the legislation.

Calendar — An agenda or list of business awaiting possible action by each chamber. The House uses six legislative calendars. They are the Consent, Corrections, Discharge, House, Private and Union calendars. *(Also see individual listings.)*

In the Senate, all legislative matters reported from committee go on one calendar. They are listed there in the order in which committees report them or the Senate places them on the calendar, but they may be called up out of order by the majority leader, either by obtaining unanimous consent of the Senate or by a motion to call up a bill. The Senate also has one non-legislative calendar, which is used for treaties and nominations. *(Also see executive calendar.)*

Call of the calendar — Senate bills that are not brought up for debate by a motion, unanimous consent or a unanimous consent agreement are brought before the Senate for action when the calendar listing them is "called." Bills must be called in the order listed. Measures considered by this method usually are non-controversial, and debate on the bill and any proposed amendments is limited to five minutes for each senator.

Chamber — The meeting place for the membership of either the House or the Senate; also the membership of the House or Senate meeting as such.

Clean bill — Frequently after a committee has finished a major revision of a bill, one of the committee members, usually the chairman, will assemble the changes and what is left of the original bill into a new measure and introduce it as a "clean bill." The revised measure, which is given a new number, is referred back to the committee, which reports it to the floor for consideration. This often is a timesaver, as committee-recommended changes in a clean bill do not have to be considered and voted on by the chamber. Reporting a clean bill also protects committee amendments that could be subject to points of order concerning germaneness.

Clerk of the House — An officer of the House of Representatives who supervises its records and legislative business. Many former administrative duties were transferred in 1992 to a new position, the director of non-legislative and financial services.

Cloture — The process by which a filibuster can be ended in the Senate other than by unanimous consent. A motion for cloture can apply to any measure before the Senate, including a proposal to change the chamber's rules. A cloture motion requires the signatures of 16 senators to be introduced. To end a filibuster, the cloture motion must obtain the votes of three-fifths of the entire Senate membership (60 if there are no vacancies), except when the filibuster is against a proposal to amend the standing rules of the Senate and a two-thirds vote of senators present and voting is required.

The cloture request is put to a roll call vote one hour after the Senate meets on the second day following introduction of the motion. If approved, cloture limits each senator to one hour of debate. The bill or amendment in question comes to a final vote after 30 hours of consideration, including debate time and the time it takes to conduct roll calls, quorum calls and other procedural motions. *(Also see filibuster.)*

Committee — A division of the House or Senate that prepares legislation for action by the parent chamber or makes investigations as directed by the parent chamber.

There are several types of committees. Most standing committees are divided into subcommittees, which study legislation, hold hearings and report bills, with or without amendments, to the full committee. Only the full committee can report legislation for action by the House or Senate. *(Also see standing, oversight, select and special committees.)*

Committee of the Whole — The working title of what is formally "The Committee of the Whole House [of Representatives] on the State of the Union." The membership is composed of all House members sitting as a committee. Any 100 members who are present on the floor of the chamber to consider legislation comprise a quorum of the committee. Any legislation, however, must first have passed through the regular legislative or appropriations committee and have been placed on the calendar.

Technically, the Committee of the Whole considers only bills directly or indirectly appropriating money, authorizing appropriations or involving taxes or charges on the public. Because the Committee of the Whole need number only 100 representatives, a quorum is more readily attained and legislative business is expedited. Before 1971, members' positions were not individually recorded on votes taken in the Committee of the Whole.

When the full House resolves itself into the Committee of the Whole, it replaces the Speaker with a "chairman." A measure is debated and amendments may be proposed, with votes on amendments as needed. *(Also see five-minute rule.)*

When the committee completes its work on the measure, it dissolves itself by "rising." The Speaker returns, and the chairman of the Committee of the Whole reports to the House that the committee's work has been completed. At this time, members may demand a roll call vote on any amendment adopted in the Committee of the Whole. The final vote is on passage of the legislation.

In 1993 and 1994, the four delegates from the territories and the resident commissioner of Puerto Rico were allowed to vote on questions before the Committee of the Whole. If their votes were decisive in the outcome, however, the matter was automatically re-voted, with the delegates and resident commissioner ineligible. They could vote on final passage of bills or on separate votes demanded after the Committee of the Whole rises. This limited voting right was rescinded in 1995.

Committee veto — A requirement added to a few statutes directing that certain policy directives by an executive department or agency be reviewed by certain congressional committees before they are implemented. Under common practice, the government department or agency and the committees involved are expected to reach a consensus before the directives are carried out. *(Also see legislative veto.)*

Concurrent resolution — A concurrent resolution, designated H Con Res or S Con Res, must be adopted by both chambers, but it is not sent to the president for approval and, therefore, does not have the force of law. A concurrent resolution, for example, is used to fix the time for adjournment of a Congress. It is also used to express the sense of Congress on a foreign policy or domestic issue. The annual budget resolution is a concurrent resolution.

Conference — A meeting between representatives of the House and the Senate to reconcile differences between the two chambers on provisions of a bill. Members of the conference committee are appointed by the Speaker and the presiding officer of the Senate.

A majority of the conferees for each chamber must agree on a compromise, reflected in a "conference report" before the final bill can go back to both chambers for approval. When the conference report goes to the floor, it is difficult to amend. If it is not approved by both chambers, the bill may go back to conference under certain situations, or a new conference may be convened. Many rules and informal practices govern the conduct of conference committees.

Bills that are passed by both chambers with only minor differences need not be sent to conference. Either chamber may "concur" with the other's amendments, completing action on the legislation. Sometimes leaders of the committees of jurisdiction work out an informal compromise instead of having a formal conference. *(Also see custody of the papers.)*

Confirmations — *(See nominations.)*

Congressional Record — The daily, printed account of proceedings in both the House and Senate chambers, showing substantially verbatim debate, statements and a record of floor action. Highlights of legislative and committee action are given in a Daily Digest section of the Record, and members are entitled to have their extraneous remarks printed in an appendix known as "Extension of Remarks." Members may edit and revise remarks made on the floor during debate, although the House in 1995 limited members to technical or grammatical changes.

The Congressional Record provides a way to distinguish remarks spoken on the floor of the House and Senate from undelivered speeches. In the Senate, all speeches, articles and other matter that members insert in the Record without actually reading them on the floor are set off by large black dots, or bullets. However, a loophole allows a member to avoid the bulleting if he or she delivers any portion of the speech in person. In the House, undelivered speeches and other material are printed in a distinctive typeface. The record is also available in electronic form. *(Also see Journal.)*

Congressional terms of office — Terms normally begin on Jan. 3 of the year following a general election. Terms are two years for representatives and six years for senators. Representatives elected in special elections are sworn in for the remainder of a term. Under most state laws, a person may be appointed to fill a Senate vacancy and serve until a successor is elected; the successor serves until the end of the term applying to the vacant seat.

Consent Calendar — Members of the House may place on this calendar most bills on the Union or House Calendar that are considered non-controversial. Bills on the Consent Calendar normally are called on the first and third Mondays of each month. On the first occasion that a bill is called in this manner, consideration may be blocked by the objection of any member. The second time, if there are three objections, the bill is stricken from the Consent Calendar. If fewer than three members object, the bill is given immediate consideration.

A member may also postpone action on the bill by asking

that the measure be passed over "without prejudice." In that case, no objection is recorded against the bill and its status on the Consent Calendar remains unchanged. A bill stricken from the Consent Calendar remains on the Union or House Calendar. The Consent Calendar has seldom been used in recent years.

Continuing resolution — A joint resolution, cleared by Congress and signed by the president, to provide new budget authority for federal agencies and programs until the regular appropriations bills have been enacted. Also known as "CRs" or continuing appropriation, continuing resolutions are used to keep agencies operating when, as often happens, Congress fails to finish the regular appropriations process by the start of the new fiscal year.

The CR usually specifies a maximum rate at which an agency may incur obligations, based on the rate of the prior year, the president's budget request or an appropriations bill passed by either or both chambers of Congress but not yet enacted.

Contract authority — Budget authority contained in an authorization bill that permits the federal government to enter into contracts or other obligations for future payments from funds not yet appropriated by Congress. The assumption is that funds will be provided in a subsequent appropriations act. *(Also see budget authority.)*

Corrections Calendar, Corrections Day — A House calendar established in 1995 to speed consideration of bills aimed at eliminating burdensome or unnecessary regulations. Bills on the Corrections Calendar can be called up on the second and fourth Tuesday of each month, called Corrections Day. They are subject to one hour of debate without amendment, and require a three-fifths majority for passage. *(Also see calendar.)*

Correcting recorded votes — Rules prohibit members from changing their votes after the result has been announced. Occasionally, however, a member may announce hours, days or months after a vote has been taken that he or she was "incorrectly recorded." In the Senate, a request to change one's vote almost always receives unanimous consent, so long as it does not change the outcome. In the House, members are prohibited from changing votes if they were tallied by the electronic voting system.

Cosponsor — *(See bills introduced.)*

Current services estimates — Estimated budget authority and outlays for federal programs and operations for the forthcoming fiscal year based on continuation of existing levels of service without policy changes but with adjustments for inflation and for demographic changes that affect programs. These estimates, accompanied by the underlying economic and policy assumptions upon which they are based, are transmitted by the president to Congress when the budget is submitted.

Custody of the papers — To reconcile differences between the House and Senate versions of a bill, a conference may be arranged. The chamber with "custody of the papers" — the engrossed bill, engrossed amendments, messages of transmittal — is the only body empowered to request the conference. By custom, the chamber that asks for a conference is the last to act on the conference report.

Custody of the papers sometimes is manipulated to ensure that a particular chamber acts either first or last on the conference report. *(Also see conference.)*

Deferral — Executive branch action to defer, or delay, the spending of appropriated money. The 1974 Congressional Budget and Impoundment Control Act requires a special message from the president to Congress reporting a proposed deferral of spending. Deferrals may not extend beyond the end of the fiscal year in which the message is transmitted. A federal district court in 1986 struck down the president's authority to defer spending for policy reasons; the ruling was upheld by a federal appeals court in 1987. Congress can prohibit proposed deferrals by enacting a law doing so; most often, cancellations of proposed deferrals are included in appropriations bills. *(Also see rescission.)*

Dilatory motion — A motion made for the purpose of killing time and preventing action on a bill or amendment. House rules outlaw dilatory motions, but enforcement is largely within the discretion of the Speaker or chairman of the Committee of the Whole. The Senate does not have a rule barring dilatory motions except under cloture.

Discharge a committee — Occasionally, attempts are made to relieve a committee of jurisdiction over a bill that is before it. This is attempted more often in the House than in the Senate, and the procedure rarely is successful.

In the House, if a committee does not report a bill within 30 days after the measure is referred to it, any member may file a discharge motion. Once offered, the motion is treated as a petition needing the signatures of a majority of members (218 if there are no vacancies). After the required signatures have been obtained, there is a delay of seven days.

Thereafter, on the second and fourth Mondays of each month, except during the last six days of a session, any member who has signed the petition must be recognized, if he or she so desires, to move that the committee be discharged. Debate on the motion to discharge is limited to 20 minutes. If the motion is carried, consideration of the bill becomes a matter of high privilege.

If a resolution to consider a bill is held up in the Rules Committee for more than seven legislative days, any member may enter a motion to discharge the committee. The motion is handled like any other discharge petition in the House. Occasionally, to expedite non-controversial legislative business, a committee is discharged by unanimous consent of the House, and a petition is not required. In 1993, the signatures on pending discharge petitions — previously kept secret — were made a matter of public record. *(For Senate procedure, see discharge resolution.)*

Discharge Calendar — The House calendar to which motions to discharge committees are referred when they have the required number of signatures (218) and are awaiting floor action. *(Also see calendar.)*

Discharge petition — *(See discharge a committee.)*

Discharge resolution — In the Senate, a special motion that any senator may introduce to relieve a committee from consideration of a bill before it. The resolution can be called up for Senate approval or disapproval in the same manner as any other Senate business. *(For House procedure, see discharge a committee.)*

Discretionary spending caps — *(See budget process.)*

Division of a question for voting — A practice that is more common in the Senate but also used in the House whereby a member may demand a division of an amendment or a motion for purposes of voting. Where an amendment or motion can be divided, the individual parts are voted on separately when a member demands a division. This procedure occurs most often during the consideration of conference reports.

Division vote — *(See standing vote.)*

Enacting clause — Key phrase in bills beginning, "Be it enacted by the Senate and House of Representatives . . ." A successful motion to strike it from legislation kills the measure.

Engrossed bill — The final copy of a bill as passed by one chamber, with the text as amended by floor action and certified by the clerk of the House or the secretary of the Senate.

Enhanced rescission — Authority given to the president under the 1996 Legislative Line-Item Veto Act to cancel specific items in an enacted bill. Though the cancellation authority is meant primarily for appropriations bills, it can also be used on new entitlement spending and on certain targeted tax provisions. The president's decision takes effect automatically unless it is blocked by a special "disapproval bill" passed in identical form by both chambers. The president can veto a disapproval bill, requiring a two-thirds vote in each chamber to override him.

The authority is known as a legislative line-item veto to distinguish it from a true line-item veto. The latter, which would require a constitutional amendment, would allow the president to strike individual lines from an appropriations bill before signing it. *(Also see deferral.)*

Enrolled bill — The final copy of a bill that has been passed in identical form by both chambers. It is certified by an officer of the chamber of origin (clerk of the House or secretary of the Senate) and then sent on for the signatures of the House Speaker, the Senate president pro tempore and the president of the United States. An enrolled bill is printed on parchment.

Entitlement program — A federal program that guarantees a certain level of benefits to people or other entities who meet requirements set by law. Examples include Social Security and unemployment benefits. Some entitlements have permanent appropriations; others are funded under annual appropriations bills. In either case, it is mandatory for Congress to provide the money.

Executive Calendar — A non-legislative calendar in the Senate that lists presidential documents such as treaties and nominations. *(Also see calendar.)*

Executive document — A document, usually a treaty, sent to the Senate by the president for consideration or approval. Executive documents are referred to committee in the same manner as other measures. Unlike legislative documents, treaties do not die at the end of a Congress but remain "live" proposals until acted on by the Senate or withdrawn by the president.

Executive session — A meeting of a Senate or House committee (or occasionally of either chamber) that only its members may attend. Witnesses regularly appear at committee meetings in executive session — for example, Defense Department officials during presentations of classified defense information. Other members of Congress may be invited, but the public and news media are not allowed to attend.

Filibuster — A time-delaying tactic associated with the Senate and used by a minority in an effort to prevent a vote on a bill or amendment that probably would pass if voted upon directly. The most common method is to take advantage of the Senate's rules permitting unlimited debate, but other forms of parliamentary maneuvering may be used.

The stricter rules of the House make filibusters more difficult, but delaying tactics are employed occasionally through various procedural devices allowed by House rules. *(Also see cloture.)*

Fiscal year — Financial operations of the government are carried out in a 12-month fiscal year, beginning on Oct. 1 and ending on Sept. 30. The fiscal year carries the date of the calendar year in which it ends. (From fiscal 1844 to fiscal 1976, the fiscal year began July 1 and ended the following June 30.)

Five-minute rule — A debate-limiting rule of the House that is invoked when the House sits as the Committee of the Whole. Under the rule, a member offering an amendment and a member opposing it are each allowed to speak for five minutes. Debate is then closed. In practice, amendments regularly are debated for more than 10 minutes, with members gaining the floor by offering pro forma amendments or obtaining unanimous consent to speak longer than five minutes. *(Also see Committee of the Whole, hour rule, strike out the last word.)*

Floor manager — A member who has the task of steering legislation through floor debate and amendment to a final vote in the House or the Senate. Floor managers usually are chairmen or ranking members of the committee that reported the bill. Managers are responsible for apportioning the debate time granted to supporters of the bill. The ranking minority member of the committee normally apportions time for the minority party's participation in the debate.

Frank — A member's facsimile signature, which is used on envelopes in lieu of stamps for the member's official outgoing mail. The "franking privilege" is the right to send mail postage-free.

Germane — Pertaining to the subject matter of the measure at hand. All House amendments must be germane to the bill being considered. The Senate requires that amendments be germane when they are proposed to general appropriations bills or to bills being considered once cloture has been adopted or, frequently, when the Senate is proceeding under a unanimous consent agreement placing a time limit on consideration of a bill. The 1974 budget act also requires that amendments to concurrent budget resolutions be germane.

In the House, floor debate must be germane, and the first three hours of debate each day in the Senate must be germane to the pending business.

Gramm-Rudman-Hollings Deficit Reduction Act — *(See sequester.)*

Grandfather clause — A provision that exempts people

or other entities already engaged in an activity from rules or legislation affecting that activity.

Hearings — Committee sessions for taking testimony from witnesses. At hearings on legislation, witnesses usually include specialists, government officials and spokesmen for individuals or entities affected by the bill or bills under study. Hearings related to special investigations bring forth a variety of witnesses. Committees sometimes use their subpoena power to summon reluctant witnesses. The public and news media may attend open hearings but are barred from closed, or "executive," hearings. The vast majority of hearings are open to the public. *(Also see executive session.)*

Hold-harmless clause — A provision added to legislation to ensure that recipients of federal funds do not receive less in a future year than they did in the current year if a new formula for allocating funds authorized in the legislation would result in a reduction to the recipients. This clause has been used most often to soften the impact of sudden reductions in federal grants.

Hopper — Box on House clerk's desk into which members deposit bills and resolutions to introduce them.

Hour rule — A provision in the rules of the House that permits one hour of debate time for each member on amendments debated in the House of Representatives sitting as the House. Therefore, the House normally amends bills while sitting as the Committee of the Whole, where the five-minute rule on amendments operates.

House as in the Committee of the Whole — A procedure that can be used to expedite consideration of certain measures such as continuing resolutions and, when there is debate, private bills. The procedure can be invoked only with the unanimous consent of the House or a rule from the Rules Committee and has procedural elements of both the House sitting as the House of Representatives, such as the Speaker presiding and the previous question motion being in order, and the House sitting as the Committee of the Whole, with the five-minute rule being in order. *(See Committee of the Whole.)*

House Calendar — A listing for action by the House of public bills that do not directly or indirectly appropriate money or raise revenue. *(Also see calendar.)*

Immunity — The constitutional privilege of members of Congress to make verbal statements on the floor and in committee for which they cannot be sued or arrested for slander or libel. Also, freedom from arrest while traveling to or from sessions of Congress or on official business. Members in this status may only be arrested for treason, felonies or a breach of the peace, as defined by congressional manuals.

Joint committee — A committee composed of a specified number of members of both the House and Senate. A joint committee may be investigative or research-oriented, an example of the latter being the Joint Economic Committee. Others have housekeeping duties; examples include the joint committees on Printing and on the Library of Congress.

Joint resolution — Like a bill, a joint resolution, designated H J Res or S J Res, requires the approval of both chambers and the signature of the president, and has the force of law if approved. There is no practical difference between a bill and a joint resolution. A joint resolution generally is used to deal with a limited matter such as a single appropriation.

Joint resolutions are also used to propose amendments to the Constitution. In that case they require a two-thirds majority in both chambers. They do not require a presidential signature, but they must be ratified by three-fourths of the states to become a part of the Constitution. *(Also see concurrent resolution, resolution.)*

Journal — The official record of the proceedings of the House and Senate. The Journal records the actions taken in each chamber, but, unlike the Congressional Record, it does not include the substantially verbatim report of speeches, debates, statements and the like.

Law — An act of Congress that has been signed by the president or passed, over his veto, by Congress. Public bills, when signed, become public laws and are cited by the letters PL and a hyphenated number. The number before the hyphen corresponds to the Congress, and the one or more digits after the hyphen refer to the numerical sequence in which the president signed the bills during that Congress. Private bills, when signed, become private laws. *(Also see bills, private bills.)*

Legislative day — The "day" extending from the time either chamber meets after an adjournment until the time it next adjourns. Because the House normally adjourns from day to day, legislative days and calendar days usually coincide. But in the Senate, a legislative day may, and frequently does, extend over several calendar days. *(Also see recess.)*

Line-item veto — *(See enhanced rescission.)*

Loan guarantees — Loans to third parties for which the federal government guarantees the repayment of principal or interest, in whole or in part, to the lender in the event of default.

Lobby — A group seeking to influence the passage or defeat of legislation. Originally the term referred to people frequenting the lobbies or corridors of legislative chambers to speak to lawmakers.

The definition of a lobby and the activity of lobbying is a matter of differing interpretation. By some definitions, lobbying is limited to direct attempts to influence lawmakers through personal interviews and persuasion. Under other definitions, lobbying includes attempts at indirect, or "grassroots," influence, such as persuading members of a group to write or visit their district's representative and state's senators or attempting to create a climate of opinion favorable to a desired legislative goal.

The right to attempt to influence legislation is based on the First Amendment to the Constitution, which says Congress shall make no law abridging the right of the people "to petition the government for a redress of grievances."

Majority leader — Floor leader for the majority party in each chamber. In the Senate, in consultation with the minority leader, the majority leader directs the legislative schedule for the chamber. He or she is also his party's spokesperson and chief strategist. In the House, the majority leader is second to the Speaker in the majority party's leadership and serves as the party's legislative strategist. *(Also see Speaker, whip.)*

Manual — The official handbook in each chamber prescribing in detail its organization, procedures and operations.

Marking up a bill — Going through the contents of a piece of legislation in committee or subcommittee to, for example, consider the provisions, act on amendments to provisions and proposed revisions to the language, and insert new sections and phraseology. If the bill is extensively amended, the committee's version may be introduced as a separate (or "clean") bill, with a new number, before being considered by the full House or Senate. *(Also see clean bill.)*

Minority leader — Floor leader for the minority party in each chamber.

Morning hour — The time set aside at the beginning of each legislative day for the consideration of regular, routine business. The "hour" is of indefinite duration in the House, where it is rarely used. In the Senate, it is the first two hours of a session following an adjournment, as distinguished from a recess. The morning hour can be terminated earlier if the morning business has been completed.

Business includes such matters as messages from the president, communications from the heads of departments, messages from the House, the presentation of petitions, reports of standing and select committees and the introduction of bills and resolutions.

During the first hour of the morning hour in the Senate, no motion to proceed to the consideration of any bill on the calendar is in order except by unanimous consent. During the second hour, motions can be made but must be decided without debate. Senate committees may meet while the Senate conducts the morning hour.

Motion — In the House or Senate chamber, a request by a member to institute any one of a wide array of parliamentary actions. He or she "moves" for a certain procedure, such as the consideration of a measure. The precedence of motions, and whether they are debatable, is set forth in the House and Senate manuals.

Nominations — Presidential appointments to office subject to Senate confirmation. Although most nominations win quick Senate approval, some are controversial and become the topic of hearings and debate. Sometimes senators object to appointees for patronage reasons — for example, when a nomination to a local federal job is made without consulting the senators of the state concerned. In some situations a senator may object that the nominee is "personally obnoxious" to him. Usually other senators join in blocking such appointments out of courtesy to their colleagues. *(Also see senatorial courtesy.)*

One-minute speeches — Addresses by House members at the beginning of a legislative day. The speeches may cover any subject but are limited to one minute's duration.

Outlays — Actual spending that flows from the liquidation of budget authority. Outlays associated with appropriations bills and other legislation are estimates of future spending made by the Congressional Budget Office (CBO) and the White House's Office of Management and Budget (OMB). CBO's estimates govern bills for the purpose of congressional floor debate, while OMB's numbers govern when it comes to determining whether legislation exceeds spending caps.

Outlays in a given fiscal year may result from budget authority provided in the current year or in previous years. *(Also see budget authority, budget process.)*

Override a veto — If the president vetoes a bill and sends it back to Congress with his objections, Congress may try to override his veto and enact the bill into law. Neither chamber is required to attempt to override a veto. The override of a veto requires a recorded vote with a two-thirds majority of those present and voting in each chamber. The question put to each chamber is: "Shall the bill pass, the objections of the president to the contrary notwithstanding?" *(Also see pocket veto, veto.)*

Oversight committee — A congressional committee or designated subcommittee that is charged with general oversight of one or more federal agencies' programs and activities. Usually, the oversight panel for a particular agency is also the authorizing committee for that agency's programs and operations.

Pair — A voluntary, informal arrangement that two lawmakers, usually on opposite sides of an issue, make on recorded votes. In many cases the result is to subtract a vote from each side, with no effect on the outcome.

Pairs are not authorized in the rules of either chamber, are not counted in tabulating the final result and have no official standing. However, members pairing are identified in the Congressional Record, along with their positions on such votes, if known. A member who expects to be absent for a vote can pair with a member who plans to vote, with the latter agreeing to withhold his or her vote.

There are three types of pairs:

(1) A live pair involves a member who is present for a vote and another who is absent. The member in attendance votes and then withdraws the vote, announcing that he or she has a live pair with colleague "X" and stating how the two members would have voted, one in favor, the other opposed. A live pair may affect the outcome of a closely contested vote, since it subtracts one "yea" or one "nay" from the final tally. A live pair may cover one or several specific issues.

(2) A general pair, widely used in the House, does not entail any arrangement between two members and does not affect the vote. Members who expect to be absent notify the clerk that they wish to make a general pair. Each member then is paired with another desiring a pair, and their names are listed in the Congressional Record. The member may or may not be paired with another taking the opposite position, and no indication of how the members would have voted is given.

(3) A specific pair is similar to a general pair, except that the opposing stands of the two members are identified and printed in the Congressional Record.

Pay-as-you go (PAYGO) rules — *(See budget process.)*

Petition — A request or plea sent to one or both chambers from an organization or private citizens' group seeking support for particular legislation or favorable consideration of a matter not yet receiving congressional attention. Petitions are referred to appropriate committees. In the House, a petition signed by a majority of members (218) can discharge a bill from a committee. *(Also see discharge a committee.)*

Pocket veto — The act of the president in withholding his approval of a bill after Congress has adjourned. When Congress is in session, a bill becomes law without the president's signature if he does not act upon it within 10 days, excluding Sundays, from the time he receives it. But if Congress adjourns sine die within that 10-day period, the bill will die even if the president does not formally veto it.

The Supreme Court in 1986 agreed to decide whether the

president could pocket veto a bill during recesses and between sessions of the same Congress or only between Congresses. The justices in 1987 declared the case moot, however, because the bill in question was invalid once the case reached the court. *(Also see adjournment sine die, veto.)*

Point of order — An objection raised by a member that the chamber is departing from rules governing its conduct of business. The objector cites the rule violated, with the chair sustaining his or her objection if correctly made. Order is restored by the chair's suspending proceedings of the chamber until it conforms to the prescribed "order of business."

Both chambers have procedures for overcoming a point of order, either by vote or, what is most common in the House, by including language in the rule for floor consideration that waives a point of order against a given bill. *(Also see rules.)*

President of the Senate — Under the Constitution, the vice president of the United States presides over the Senate. In his absence, the president pro tempore, or a senator designated by the president pro tempore, presides over the chamber.

President pro tempore — The chief officer of the Senate in the absence of the vice president — literally, but loosely, the president for a time. The president pro tempore is elected by his fellow senators. Recent practice has been to elect the senator of the majority party with the longest period of continuous service.

Previous question — A motion for the previous question, when carried, has the effect of cutting off all debate, preventing the offering of further amendments and forcing a vote on the pending matter. In the House, a motion for the previous question is not permitted in the Committee of the Whole, unless a rule governing debate provides otherwise. The motion for the previous question is a debate-limiting device and is not in order in the Senate.

Printed amendment — A House rule guarantees five minutes of floor debate in support and five minutes in opposition, and no other debate time, on amendments printed in the Congressional Record at least one day prior to the amendment's consideration in the Committee of the Whole.

In the Senate, while amendments may be submitted for printing, they have no parliamentary standing or status. An amendment submitted for printing in the Senate, however, may be called up by any senator.

Private bill — A bill dealing with individual matters such as claims against the government, immigration or land titles. When a private bill is before the chamber, two members may block its consideration, thereby recommitting the bill to committee. The backers still have recourse, however. The measure can be put into an "omnibus claims bill" — several private bills rolled into one. As with any bill, no part of an omnibus claims bill may be deleted without a vote. When the private bill goes back to the House floor in this form, it can be deleted from the omnibus bill only by majority vote.

Private Calendar — The House calendar for private bills. The Private Calendar must be called on the first Tuesday of each month, and the Speaker may call it on the third Tuesday of each month as well. *(Also see calendar, private bill.)*

Privileged questions — The order in which bills, motions and other legislative measures are considered on the floor of the Senate and House is governed by strict priorities. A motion to table, for instance, is more privileged than a motion to recommit. Thus, if a member moves to recommit a bill to committee for further consideration, another member can supersede the first action by moving to table it, and a vote will occur first on the motion to table (or kill) the motion to recommit. A motion to adjourn is considered "of the highest privilege" and must be considered before virtually any other motion.

Pro forma amendment — *(See strike out the last word.)*

Public Laws — *(See law.)*

Questions of privilege — These are matters affecting members of Congress individually or collectively. Matters affecting the rights, safety, dignity and integrity of proceedings of the House or Senate as a whole are questions of privilege in both chambers.

Questions involving individual members are called questions of "personal privilege." A member rising to ask a question of personal privilege is given precedence over almost all other proceedings. For instance, if a member feels that he or she has been improperly impugned in comments by another member, he or she can immediately demand to be heard on the floor on a question of personal privilege. An annotation in the House rules points out that the privilege rests primarily on the Constitution, which gives members a conditional immunity from arrest and an unconditional freedom to speak in the House.

In 1993, the House changed its rules to allow the Speaker to delay for two legislative days the floor consideration of a question of the privileges of the House unless it is offered by the majority leader or minority leader.

Quorum — The number of members whose presence is necessary for the transaction of business. In the Senate and House, it is a majority of the membership. In the Committee of the Whole House, a quorum is 100. If a point of order is made that a quorum is not present, the only business that is in order is either a motion to adjourn or a motion to direct the sergeant-at-arms to request the attendance of absentees. In practice, however, both chambers conduct much of their business without a quorum present. *(Also see Committee of the Whole House.)*

Reading of bills — Traditional parliamentary procedure required bills to be read three times before they were passed. This custom is of little modern significance. Normally a bill is considered to have its first reading when it is introduced and printed, by title, in the Congressional Record. In the House, a bill's second reading comes when floor consideration begins. (The actual reading of a bill is most likely to occur at this point, if at all.) The second reading in the Senate is supposed to occur on the legislative day after the measure is introduced, but before it is referred to committee. The third reading (again, usually by title) takes place when floor action has been completed on amendments.

Recess — A recess, as distinguished from adjournment, does not end a legislative day and therefore does not interrupt unfinished business. (The rules in each chamber set forth certain matters to be taken up and disposed of at the beginning of each legislative day.) The House usually adjourns from day to day. The Senate often recesses, thus meeting on the same legislative day for several calendar days or even weeks at a time.

Recognition — The power of recognition of a member is lodged in the Speaker of the House and the presiding officer of the Senate. The presiding officer names the member to speak first when two or more members simultaneously request recognition. The order of recognition is governed by precedents and tradition for many situations. In the Senate, for instance, the majority leader has the right to be recognized first.

Recommit to committee — A motion, made on the floor after a bill has been debated, to return it to the committee that reported it. If approved, recommittal usually is considered a death blow to the bill. In the House, the right to offer a motion to recommit is guaranteed to the minority leader or someone he or she designates.

A motion to recommit may include instructions to the committee to report the bill again with specific amendments or by a certain date. Or the instructions may direct that a particular study be made, with no definite deadline for further action.

If the recommittal motion includes instructions to "report the bill back forthwith" and the motion is adopted, floor action on the bill continues with the changes directed by the instructions automatically incorporated into the bill; the committee does not actually reconsider the legislation.

Reconciliation — The 1974 budget act created a "reconciliation" procedure for bringing existing tax and spending laws into conformity with ceilings set in the congressional budget resolution. Under the procedure, the budget resolution sets specific deficit-reduction targets and instructs tax-writing and authorizing committees to propose changes in existing law to meet those targets. Those recommendations are consolidated without change by the Budget committees into an omnibus reconciliation bill, which then must be considered and approved by both chambers of Congress.

Special rules in the Senate limit debate on a reconciliation bill to 20 hours and bar extraneous or non-germane amendments. *(Also see budget resolution, sequester.)*

Reconsider a vote — Until it is disposed of, a motion to reconsider the vote by which an action was taken has the effect of putting the action in abeyance. In the Senate, the motion can be made only by a member who voted on the prevailing side of the original question or by a member who did not vote at all. In the House, it can be made only by a member on the prevailing side.

A common practice in the Senate after close votes on an issue is a motion to reconsider, followed by a motion to table the motion to reconsider. On this motion to table, senators vote as they voted on the original question, which allows the motion to table to prevail, assuming there are no switches. That closes the matter, and further motions to reconsider are not entertained.

In the House, as a routine precaution, a motion to reconsider usually is made every time a measure is passed. Such a motion almost always is tabled immediately, thus shutting off the possibility of future reconsideration except by unanimous consent.

Motions to reconsider must be entered in the Senate within the next two days the Senate is in session after the original vote has been taken. In the House, they must be entered either on the same day or on the next succeeding day the House is in session. Sometimes on a close vote, a member will switch his or her vote to be eligible to offer a motion to reconsider.

Recorded vote — A vote upon which each member's stand is individually made known. In the Senate, this is accomplished through a roll call of the entire membership, to which each senator on the floor must answer "yea," "nay" or "present." Since January 1973, the House has used an electronic voting system for recorded votes, including yea-and-nay votes formerly taken by roll calls.

When not required by the Constitution, a recorded vote can be obtained on questions in the House on the demand of one-fifth (44 members) of a quorum or one-fourth (25) of a quorum in the Committee of the Whole. Recorded votes are required in the House for appropriations, budget and tax bills. *(Also see yeas and nays.)*

Report — Both a verb and a noun as a congressional term. A committee that has been examining a bill referred to it by the parent chamber "reports" its findings and recommendations to the chamber when it completes consideration and returns the measure. The process is called "reporting" a bill. In some cases, a bill is reported without a written report.

A "report" is the document setting forth the committee's explanation of its action. Senate and House reports are numbered separately and are designated S Rept or H Rept. When a committee report is not unanimous, the dissenting committee members may file a statement of their views, called minority or dissenting views and referred to as a minority report. Members in disagreement with some provisions of a bill may file additional or supplementary views. Sometimes a bill is reported without a committee recommendation.

Legislative committees occasionally submit adverse reports. However, when a committee is opposed to a bill, it usually fails to report the bill at all. Some laws require that committee reports — favorable or adverse — be made.

Rescission — Cancellation of budget authority that was previously appropriated but has not yet been spent. *(Also see enhanced rescission.)*

Resolution — A "simple" resolution, designated H Res or S Res, deals with matters entirely within the prerogatives of a single chamber. It requires neither passage by the other chamber nor approval by the president, and it does not have the force of law. Most resolutions deal with the rules or procedures of one chamber. They are also used to express the sentiments of a single chamber, such as condolences to the family of a deceased member, or to comment on foreign policy or executive business. A simple resolution is the vehicle for a "rule" from the House Rules Committee. *(Also see concurrent and joint resolutions, rules.)*

Rider — An amendment, usually not germane, that its sponsor hopes to get through more easily by including it in other legislation. A rider becomes law if the bill to which it is attached is enacted. Amendments providing legislative directives in appropriations bills are examples of riders, though technically legislation is banned from appropriations bills.

The House, unlike the Senate, has a strict germaneness rule; thus, riders usually are Senate devices to get legislation enacted quickly or to bypass lengthy House consideration and, possibly, opposition.

Rules — Each chamber has a body of rules and precedents that govern the conduct of business. These rules deal with issues such as duties of officers, the order of business, admission to the floor, parliamentary procedures on handling amendments and voting, and jurisdictions of committees. They are normally changed only at the start of each Congress.

In the House, a rule may also be a resolution reported by the Rules Committee to govern the handling of a particular bill on the floor. The committee may report a rule, also called a special order, in the form of a simple resolution. If the House adopts the resolution, the temporary rule becomes as valid as any standing rule and lapses only after action has been completed on the measure to which it pertains.

The rule sets the time limit on general debate. It may also waive points of order against provisions of the bill in question such as non-germane language or against certain amendments expected on the floor. It may even forbid all amendments or all amendments except those proposed by the legislative committee that handled the bill. In this instance, it is known as a "closed" rule as opposed to an "open" rule, which puts no limitation on floor amendments, thus leaving the bill completely open to alteration by the adoption of germane amendments. *(Also see point of order.)*

Secretary of the Senate — Chief administrative officer of the Senate, responsible for overseeing the duties of Senate employees, educating Senate pages, administering oaths, overseeing the registration of lobbyists and handling other tasks necessary for the continuing operation of the Senate. *(Also see Clerk of the House.)*

Select or special committee — A committee set up for a special purpose and, usually, for a limited time by resolution of either the House or Senate. Most special committees are investigative and lack legislative authority: Legislation is not referred to them, and they cannot report bills to their parent chambers. The House in 1993 terminated its four select committees.

Senatorial courtesy — A general practice with no written rule — sometimes referred to as "the courtesy of the Senate" — applied to consideration of executive nominations. Generally, it means that nominations from a state are not to be confirmed unless they have been approved by the senators of the president's party of that state, with other senators following their colleagues' lead in the attitude they take toward consideration of such nominations. *(Also see nominations.)*

Sequester — Automatic, across-the-board spending cuts, generally triggered after the close of a session by a report issued by the Office of Management and Budget. Under the 1985 Gramm-Rudman anti-deficit law, modified in 1987, a year-end sequester was triggered if the deficit exceeded a preset maximum. However, the Budget Enforcement Act of 1990, updated in 1993 and 1997, effectively replaced that procedure through fiscal 2002.

Instead, if Congress exceeds an annual cap on discretionary budget authority or outlays, a sequester is triggered for all eligible discretionary spending to make up the difference. If Congress violates pay-as-you-go rules by allowing the net effect of legislated changes in mandatory spending and taxes to increase the deficit, a sequester is triggered for all non-exempt entitlement programs. Similar procedures apply to supplemental appropriations bills. *(Also see budget process.)*

Sine die — *(See adjournment sine die.)*

Speaker — The presiding officer of the House of Representatives, selected by his party caucus and formally elected by the whole House. While both parties nominate candidates, choice by the majority party is tantamount to election. In 1995, House rules were changed to limit the Speaker to four consecutive terms.

Special session — A session of Congress after it has adjourned sine die, completing its regular session. Special sessions are convened by the president.

Spending authority — The 1974 budget act defines spending authority as borrowing authority, contract authority and entitlement authority for which budget authority is not provided in advance by appropriation acts.

Sponsor — *(See bills introduced.)*

Standing committees — Committees that are permanently established by House and Senate rules. The standing committees of the House were reorganized in 1974, with some changes in jurisdictions and titles made when Republicans took control of the House in 1995. The last major realignment of Senate committees was in 1977. The standing committees are legislative committees: Legislation may be referred to them, and they may report bills and resolutions to their parent chambers.

Standing vote — A non-recorded vote used in both the House and Senate. (A standing vote is also called a division vote.) Members in favor of a proposal stand and are counted by the presiding officer. Then members opposed stand and are counted. There is no record of how individual members voted.

Statutes at large — A chronological arrangement of the laws enacted in each session of Congress. Though indexed, the laws are not arranged by subject matter, and there is no indication of how they changed previously enacted laws. *(Also see law, U.S. Code.)*

Strike from the Record — A member of the House who is offended by remarks made on the House floor may move that the offending words be "taken down" for the Speaker's cognizance and then expunged from the debate as published in the Congressional Record.

Strike out the last word — A motion whereby a House member is entitled to speak for five minutes on an amendment then being debated by the chamber. A member gains recognition from the chair by moving to "strike out the last word" of the amendment or section of the bill under consideration. The motion is pro forma, requires no vote and does not change the amendment being debated. *(Also see five-minute rule.)*

Substitute — A motion, amendment or entire bill introduced in place of the pending legislative business. Passage of the substitute kills the original measure by supplanting it. The substitute may also be amended. *(Also see amendment in the nature of a substitute.)*

Supplemental appropriations bill — Legislation appropriating funds after the regular annual appropriations bill for a federal department or agency has been enacted. Supplemental appropriations bills often arrive about halfway through the fiscal year, when needs that Congress and the president did not anticipate (or may not have wanted to fund) become pressing. In recent years, supplementals have been driven by spending to help victims of natural disasters and to carry out peacekeeping commitments.

Suspend the rules — A time-saving procedure for passing bills in the House. The wording of the motion, which may be made by any member recognized by the Speaker, is: "I move to suspend the rules and pass the bill . . ." A favorable vote by two-thirds of those present is required for passage. Debate is limited to 40 minutes, and no amendments from the floor are permitted. If a two-thirds favorable vote is not attained, the bill may be considered later under regular procedures. The suspension procedure is in order every Monday and Tuesday and is intended to be reserved for non-controversial bills.

Table a bill — Motions to table, or to "lay on the table," are used to block or kill amendments or other parliamentary questions. When approved, a tabling motion is considered the final disposition of that issue. One of the most widely used parliamentary procedures, the motion to table is not debatable, and adoption requires a simple majority vote.

In the Senate, however, different language sometimes is used. The motion may be worded to let a bill "lie on the table," perhaps for subsequent "picking up." This motion is more flexible, keeping the bill pending for later action, if desired. Tabling motions on amendments are effective debate-ending devices in the Senate.

Treaties — Executive proposals — in the form of resolutions of ratification — which must be submitted to the Senate for approval by two-thirds of the senators present. Treaties are normally sent to the Foreign Relations Committee for scrutiny before the Senate takes action. Foreign Relations has jurisdiction over all treaties, regardless of the subject matter. Treaties are read three times and debated on the floor in much the same manner as legislative proposals. After approval by the Senate, treaties are formally ratified by the president.

Trust funds — Funds collected and used by the federal government for carrying out specific purposes and programs according to terms of a trust agreement or statute such as the Social Security and unemployment compensation trust funds. Such funds are administered by the government in a fiduciary capacity and are not available for the general purposes of the government.

Unanimous consent — A procedure used to expedite floor action. Proceedings of the House or Senate and action on legislation often take place upon the unanimous consent of the chamber, whether or not a rule of the chamber is being violated. It is frequently used in a routine fashion, such as by a senator requesting the unanimous consent of the Senate to have specified members of his or her staff present on the floor during debate on a specific amendment. A single member's objection blocks a unanimous consent request.

Unanimous consent agreement — A device used in the Senate to expedite legislation. Much of the Senate's legislative business, dealing with both minor and controversial issues, is conducted through unanimous consent or unanimous consent agreements. On major legislation, such agreements usually are printed and transmitted to all senators in advance of floor debate. Once agreed to, they are binding on all members unless the Senate, by unanimous consent, agrees to modify them. An agreement may list the order in which various bills are to be considered; specify the length of time for debate on bills and contested amendments and when they are to be voted upon; and, frequently, require that all amendments introduced be germane to the bill under consideration.

In this regard, unanimous consent agreements are similar to the "rules" issued by the House Rules Committee for bills pending in the House.

Union Calendar — Bills that directly or indirectly appropriate money or raise revenue are placed on this House calendar according to the date they are reported from committee. *(Also see calendar.)*

U.S. Code — A consolidation and codification of the general and permanent laws of the United States arranged by subject under 50 titles, the first six dealing with general or political subjects, and the other 44 alphabetically arranged from agriculture to war. The U.S. Code is updated annually, and a new set of bound volumes is published every six years. *(Also see law, statutes at large.)*

Veto — Disapproval by the president of a bill or joint resolution (other than one proposing an amendment to the Constitution). When Congress is in session, the president must veto a bill within 10 days, excluding Sundays, after he has received it; otherwise, it becomes law without his signature. When the president vetoes a bill, he returns it to the chamber of origin along with a message stating his objections. *(Also see pocket veto, override a veto.)*

Voice vote — In either the House or Senate, members answer "aye" or "no" in chorus, and the presiding officer decides the result. The term is also used loosely to indicate action by unanimous consent or without objection. *(Also see yeas and nays.)*

Whip — In effect, the assistant majority or minority leader, in either the House or Senate. His or her job is to help marshal votes in support of party strategy and legislation.

Without objection — Used in lieu of a vote on non-controversial motions, amendments or bills that may be passed in either chamber if no member voices an objection.

Yeas and nays — The Constitution requires that yea-and-nay votes be taken and recorded when requested by one-fifth of the members present. In the House, the Speaker determines whether one-fifth of the members present requested a vote. In the Senate, practice requires only 11 members. The Constitution requires the yeas and nays on a veto override attempt. *(Also see recorded vote.)*

Yielding — When a member has been recognized to speak, no other member may speak unless he or she obtains permission from the member recognized. This permission is called yielding and usually is requested in the form, "Will the gentleman (or gentlelady) yield to me?" While this activity occasionally is seen in the Senate, the Senate has no rule or practice to parcel out time.

In the House, the floor manager of a bill usually apportions debate time by yielding specific amounts of time to members who have requested it. ■

CQ

Appendix B

CONGRESS AND ITS MEMBERS

The Legislative Process in Brief

(Parliamentary terms used below are defined in the glossary, p. A-3.)

Introduction of Bills

A House member (including the resident commissioner of Puerto Rico and non-voting delegates of the District of Columbia, Guam, the Virgin Islands and American Samoa) may introduce any one of several types of bills and resolutions by handing it to the clerk of the House or placing it in a box called the hopper.

A senator first gains recognition of the presiding officer to announce the introduction of a bill. If objection is offered by any senator, the introduction of the bill is postponed until the following day.

As the next step in either the House or Senate, the bill is numbered, referred to committee, labeled with the sponsor's name and sent to the Government Printing Office so that copies can be made for subsequent study and action. Senate bills may be sponsored jointly and carry several senators' names.

Until 1978, the House limited the number of members who could cosponsor any one bill; the ceiling was eliminated at the beginning of the 96th Congress.

A bill written in the executive branch and proposed as an administration measure usually is introduced by the chairman of the congressional committee that has jurisdiction over the subject or by the committee's senior member of the president's party.

Bills. Prefixed with HR in the House, S in the Senate, followed by a number. Used as the form for most legislation, whether general or special, public or private.

Joint Resolutions. Designated H J Res or S J Res. Subject to the same procedure as bills, with the exception of a joint resolution proposing an amendment to the Constitution. The latter must be approved by two-thirds of both houses and is thereupon sent directly to the administrator of general services for submission to the states for ratification instead of being presented to the president for approval.

Concurrent Resolutions. Designated H Con Res or S Con Res. Used for matters affecting the operations of both houses. These resolutions do not become law.

Resolutions. Designated H Res or S Res. Used for a matter concerning the operation of either house alone and adopted only by the chamber in which they originate.

Committee Action

With few exceptions, bills are referred to the appropriate standing committees. The job of referral formally is the responsibility of the Speaker of the House and the presiding officer of the Senate, but this task usually is carried out on their behalf by the parliamentarians of the House and Senate.

Precedent, statute and the jurisdictional mandates of the committees as set forth in the rules of the House and Senate determine which committees receive what kinds of bills. An exception is the referral of private bills, which are sent to whatever committee is designated by their sponsors. Bills technically are considered "read for the first time" when referred to House committees.

When a bill reaches a committee, it is placed on the committee's calendar. At that time the bill comes under the sharpest congressional focus. Its chances for passage are quickly determined; the great majority of bills fall by the legislative roadside.

Failure of a committee to act on a bill is equivalent to killing it; the measure can be withdrawn from the committee's purview only by a discharge petition signed by a majority of the House membership on House bills or by adoption of a special resolution in the Senate. Discharge attempts rarely succeed.

The first committee action taken on a bill usually is a request for comment on it by interested government agencies. The committee chairman may assign the bill to a subcommittee for study and hearings, or it may be considered by the full committee. Hearings may be public, closed (executive session) or both. After considering a bill, a subcommittee reports to the full committee its recommendations for action and any proposed amendments.

The full committee then votes on its recommendation to the House or Senate. This procedure is called "ordering a bill reported."

Occasionally a committee may order a bill reported unfavorably; most of the time a report, submitted by the committee chairman to the House or Senate, calls for favorable action on the measure since the committee can effectively "kill" a bill by simply not taking any action.

After the bill is reported, the committee chairman instructs the staff to prepare a written report. The report describes the bill's purposes and scope, explains the committee revisions, notes proposed changes in existing law and, usually, includes the views of the executive branch agencies consulted. Often committee members opposing a bill include dissenting views in the report.

Usually, the committee "marks up" or proposes amendments to the bill. If they are substantial and the measure is complicated, the committee may order a "clean bill" introduced, which will embody the proposed amendments. The original bill then is put aside and the clean bill, with a new number, is reported to the floor.

The chamber must approve, alter or reject the committee amendments before the bill itself can be put to a vote.

Floor Action

After a bill is reported back to the house where it originated, it is placed on the calendar.

Debate. A bill is brought to debate by varying procedures. If it is a routine measure, it may await the call of the calendar, although few measures win consideration this way. Otherwise, if it is urgent or important, it can be taken up in the Senate either by unanimous consent or by a majority vote. The majority leader, in consultation with the minority leader and others, schedules the bills that will be taken up for debate.

In the House, precedence is granted if a special rule is obtained from the Rules Committee. A request for a special rule usually is made by the chairman of the committee that favorably reported the bill, supported by the bill's sponsor and other committee members. The request, considered by the Rules Committee in the same way that other committees consider legislative measures, is in the form of a resolution providing for immediate consideration of the bill.

The Rules Committee reports the resolution to the House, where it is debated and voted upon in the same fashion as regular bills. If the Rules Committee should fail to report a rule requested by a committee, there are several ways to bring the bill to the House floor — under suspension of the rules, on Calendar Wednesday or by a discharge motion.

The resolutions providing special rules are important because they specify how long the bill may be debated and whether it may be amended from the floor. If floor amendments are banned, the bill is considered under a "closed rule," which usually allows only changes proposed by the committee that first reported the measure to the House, subject to chamber acceptance.

When a bill is debated under an "open rule," amendments may be offered from the floor. Committee amendments always are taken up first but may be changed, like all amendments up to the second degree; that is, an amendment to an amendment to an amendment is not in order.

Duration of debate in the House depends on whether the bill is under discussion by the House proper or before the House when it is sitting as the Committee of the Whole House on the State of the Union.

Sitting as the House, the amount of time for debate is determined by special rule or, if the measure is under consideration without a rule, an hour is allocated for each member.

The House considers almost all important bills within a parliamentary framework known as the Committee of the Whole. It is not a committee as the word usually is understood; it is the full House meeting under another name for the purpose of speeding action on legislation.

Technically, the House sits as the Committee of the Whole when it considers any tax measure or bill dealing with public appropriations. It can also resolve itself into the Committee of the Whole if a member moves to do so and the motion is carried. The Speaker appoints a member to serve as the chairman.

The rules of the House permit the Committee of the Whole to meet when a quorum of 100 members is present on the floor and to amend and act on bills, within certain time limitations. When the Committee of the Whole has acted, it "rises," the Speaker returns as the presiding officer of the House and the member appointed chairman of the Committee of the Whole reports the action of the committee and its recommendations.

In the Committee of the Whole, the amount of time agreed on for general debate is equally divided between proponents and opponents. At the end of general discussion, the bill is read section by section for amendment. Debate on an amendment is limited to five minutes for each side; this is called the "five-minute rule." In practice, amendments regularly are debated more than 10 minutes, with members gaining the floor by offering pro forma amendments or obtaining unanimous consent to speak longer than five minutes.

The Committee of the Whole cannot pass a bill; it reports the measure to the full House with whatever changes it has approved. The full House then may pass or reject the bill — or, on occasion, recommit the bill to committee. Amendments adopted in the Committee of the Whole may be put to a second vote in the full House.

In the 103rd Congress only, the delegates from the territories, the District of Columbia and the resident commissioner of Puerto Rico were allowed to vote in the Committee of the Whole. But any question decided by their votes had to be revoted by the House, without their participation.

Senate debate usually is unlimited. It can be halted only by unanimous consent or by "cloture," which requires a three-fifths majority of the entire Senate or, in the case of a proposed change in the Senate rules, a two-thirds vote.

Votes. Voting on bills may occur repeatedly before they are finally approved or rejected. The House votes on the rule for a bill and on various amendments to the bill. Voting on amendments often is a more illuminating test of a bill's support than is the final tally. Sometimes members approve final passage of bills after vigorously supporting amendments that, if adopted, would scuttle the legislation.

The Senate has three different methods of voting: an untabulated voice vote, a standing vote (called a division) and a recorded roll call, to which members answer "yea" or "nay" when their names are called.

The House also employs voice and standing votes, but since January 1973, yeas and nays have been recorded by an electronic voting device, eliminating the need for time-consuming roll calls.

Since 1971, one-fifth of a quorum can demand that the votes of individual members be recorded, thereby forcing them to take a public position on amendments to key bills.

After amendments to a bill have been voted upon, a vote may be taken on a motion to recommit the bill to committee. If carried, this vote removes the bill from the chamber's calendar and is usually a death blow to the bill — unless the motion carries specific instructions on how to change the bill; in that case, the bill is usually re-reported immediately with the instructed changes.

If the motion is unsuccessful, the bill then is "read for the third time." An actual reading usually is dispensed with. Until 1965, an opponent of a bill could delay this move by objecting and asking for a full reading of an engrossed (certified in final form) copy of the bill. After the "third reading," the vote on final passage is taken.

The final vote may be followed by a motion to reconsider, and this motion may be followed by a move to lay the motion on the table. Usually, those voting for the bill's passage vote for the tabling motion, thus safeguarding the final passage action. With that, the bill is formally passed by the chamber. While a motion to reconsider a Senate vote is pending on a bill, the measure cannot be sent to the House.

Action in Second House

After a bill is passed, it is sent to the other chamber. This body may then take one of several steps. It may pass the bill as is — accepting the other chamber's language. It may send the bill to committee for scrutiny or alteration, or reject the entire bill, advising the other house of its actions. Or it simply may ignore the bill submitted while it continues work on its own version of the proposed legislation. Frequently, one chamber may approve a version of a bill that is greatly at variance with the version passed by the other house, and then substitute its contents for the language of the other, retaining only the latter's bill number.

A provision of the Legislative Reorganization Act of 1970

permits a separate House vote on any non-germane amendment added by the Senate to a House-passed bill and requires a majority vote to retain the amendment. Previously, the House was forced to act on the bill as a whole; the only way to defeat the non-germane amendment was to reject the entire bill.

Often, the second chamber makes only minor changes. If these are readily agreed to by the other house, the bill then is sent to the president.

If the opposite chamber significantly alters the bill submitted to it, however, the measure usually is "sent to conference." The chamber that has possession of the "papers" (engrossed bill, engrossed amendments, messages of transmittal) requests a conference, and the other chamber must agree to it. If the second house does not agree, the bill dies.

Conference, Final Action

Conference. A conference reconciles the differences between House and Senate versions of a legislative bill. The conferees usually are senior members appointed by the presiding officers of the two houses, from the committees that managed the bills. Under this arrangement the conferees of one house have the duty of trying to maintain their chamber's position in the face of amending actions by the conferees (also referred to as "managers") of the other house.

The number of conferees from each chamber varies, depending upon the length or complexity of the bill involved. A majority vote controls the action of each group; a large representation does not give one chamber a voting advantage over the other.

Theoretically, conferees are not allowed to write new legislation in reconciling the two versions before them, but this curb sometimes is bypassed. Many bills have been put into acceptable compromise form only after new language was provided by the conferees.

The 1970 Reorganization Act attempted to tighten restrictions on conferees by forbidding them to introduce any language on a topic that neither chamber sent to conference or to modify any topic beyond the scope of the differing versions of the bill. But this is sometimes ignored.

Frequently, the ironing out of difficulties takes days or even weeks. As a conference proceeds, conferees reconcile differences between the versions. Generally, they grant concessions only insofar as they are sure that the chamber they represent will accept the compromises.

Occasionally, uncertainty over how either house will react, or the refusal of a chamber to back down on a disputed amendment, results in an impasse, and the bills die in conference even though each was approved by its sponsoring chamber.

Conferees may go back to their respective chambers for further instructions, when they report certain portions in disagreement. Then the chamber concerned can either "recede and concur" in the amendment of the other house or "insist on its amendment."

When the conferees have reached agreement, they prepare a conference report embodying their recommendations. The report, in document form, must be submitted to each house.

The conference report must be adopted by each house; adoption of the report is approval of the compromise bill. The chamber that asked for a conference yields to the other chamber the opportunity to vote first.

Final Steps. After a bill has been passed by both the House and Senate in identical form, all of the original papers are sent to the enrolling clerk of the chamber in which the bill originated. He then prepares an enrolled bill, which is printed on parchment paper.

When this bill has been certified as correct by the secretary of the Senate or the clerk of the House, depending on which chamber originated the bill, it is signed first (no matter whether it originated in the Senate or House) by the Speaker of the House and then by the presiding officer of the Senate. It is next sent to the White House to await action.

If the president approves the bill, he signs it, dates it and usually writes the word "approved" on the document. If he does not sign it within 10 days (Sundays excepted) and Congress is in session, the bill becomes law without his signature. Should Congress adjourn before the 10 days expire, and the president fails to sign the measure, it does not become law. This procedure is called the pocket veto.

A president vetoes a bill by refusing to sign it and, before the 10-day period expires, returning it to Congress with a message stating his reasons. The message is sent to the chamber that originated the bill. If no action is taken on the message, the bill dies.

Congress, however, can attempt to override the veto and enact the bill, "the objections of the president to the contrary notwithstanding." Overriding a veto requires a two-thirds vote of those present, who must number a quorum and must vote by roll call.

Debate can precede this vote, with motions permitted to lay the message on the table, postpone action on it or refer it to committee. If the president's veto is overridden in both houses, the bill becomes law. Otherwise, it is dead.

When bills are passed finally and signed, or passed over a veto, they are given law numbers in numerical order as they become law. There are two series of numbers, one for public laws and one for private laws, starting with the number "1" for each two-year term of Congress. They then are identified by law number and by Congress — for example, Private Law 1, 104th Congress (or Private Law 104-1); Public Law 208, 104th Congress (or PL 104-208). ■

Members of the 105th Congress, First Session . . .

(As of Nov. 13, 1997, when the first session of the 105th Congress adjourned sine die.)

Representatives
R 228; D 204; I 1; 2 vacancies

— A —

Abercrombie, Neil, D-Hawaii (1)
Ackerman, Gary L., D-N.Y. (5)
Aderholt, Robert B., R-Ala. (4)
Allen, Tom, D-Maine (1)
Andrews, Robert E., D-N.J. (1)
Archer, Bill, R-Texas (7)
Armey, Dick, R-Texas (26)

— B —

Bachus, Spencer, R-Ala. (6)
Baesler, Scotty, D-Ky. (6)
Baker, Richard H., R-La. (6)
Baldacci, John, D-Maine (2)
Ballenger, Cass, R-N.C. (10)
Barcia, James A., D-Mich. (5)
Barr, Bob, R-Ga. (7)
Barrett, Bill, R-Neb. (3)
Barrett, Thomas M., D-Wis. (5)
Bartlett, Roscoe G., R-Md. (6)
Barton, Joe L., R-Texas (6)
Bass, Charles, R-N.H. (2)
Bateman, Herbert H., R-Va. (1)
Becerra, Xavier, D-Calif. (30)
Bentsen, Ken, D-Texas (25)
Bereuter, Doug, R-Neb. (1)
Berman, Howard L., D-Calif. (26)
Berry, Marion, D-Ark. (1)
Bilbray, Brian P., R-Calif. (49)
Bilirakis, Michael, R-Fla. (9)
Bishop, Sanford D. Jr., D-Ga. (2)
Blagojevich, Rod R., D-Ill. (5)
Bliley, Thomas J. Jr., R-Va. (7)
Blumenauer, Earl, D-Ore. (3)
Blunt, Roy, R-Mo. (7)
Boehlert, Sherwood, R-N.Y. (23)
Boehner, John A., R-Ohio (8)
Bonilla, Henry, R-Texas (23)
Bonior, David E., D-Mich. (10)
Bono, Sonny, R-Calif. (44)
Borski, Robert A., D-Pa. (3)
Boswell, Leonard L., D-Iowa (3)
Boucher, Rick, D-Va. (9)
Boyd, Allen, D-Fla. (2)
Brady, Kevin, R-Texas (8)
Brown, Corrine, D-Fla. (3)
Brown, George E. Jr., D-Calif. (42)
Brown, Sherrod, D-Ohio (13)
Bryant, Ed, R-Tenn. (7)
Bunning, Jim, R-Ky. (4)
Burr, Richard M., R-N.C. (5)
Burton, Dan, R-Ind. (6)
Buyer, Steve, R-Ind. (5)

— C —

Callahan, Sonny, R-Ala. (1)
Calvert, Ken, R-Calif. (43)
Camp, Dave, R-Mich. (4)
Campbell, Tom, R-Calif. (15)
Canady, Charles T., R-Fla. (12)
Cannon, Christopher B., R-Utah (3)
Cardin, Benjamin L., D-Md. (3)
Carson, Julia, D-Ind. (10)
Castle, Michael N., R-Del. (AL)
Chabot, Steve, R-Ohio (1)
Chambliss, Saxby, R-Ga. (8)
Chenoweth, Helen, R-Idaho (1)
Christensen, Jon, R-Neb. (2)
Clay, William L., D-Mo. (1)
Clayton, Eva, D-N.C. (1)
Clement, Bob, D-Tenn. (5)
Clyburn, James E., D-S.C. (6)
Coble, Howard, R-N.C. (6)
Coburn, Tom, R-Okla. (2)
Collins, Mac, R-Ga. (3)
Combest, Larry, R-Texas (19)
Condit, Gary A., D-Calif. (18)
Conyers, John Jr., D-Mich. (14)
Cook, Merrill, R-Utah (2)
Cooksey, John, R-La. (5)
Costello, Jerry F., D-Ill. (12)
Cox, Christopher, R-Calif. (47)
Coyne, William J., D-Pa. (14)
Cramer, Robert E. "Bud", D-Ala. (5)
Crane, Philip M., R-Ill. (8)
Crapo, Michael D., R-Idaho (2)
Cubin, Barbara, R-Wyo. (AL)
Cummings, Elijah E., D-Md. (7)
Cunningham, Randy "Duke", R-Calif. (51)

— D —

Danner, Pat, D-Mo. (6)
Davis, Danny K., D-Ill. (7)
Davis, Jim, D-Fla. (11)
Davis, Thomas M. III, R-Va. (11)
Deal, Nathan, R-Ga. (9)
DeFazio, Peter A., D-Ore. (4)
DeGette, Diana, D-Colo. (1)
Delahunt, Bill, D-Mass. (10)
DeLauro, Rosa, D-Conn. (3)
DeLay, Tom, R-Texas (22)
Dellums, Ronald V., D-Calif. (9)
Deutsch, Peter, D-Fla. (20)
Diaz-Balart, Lincoln, R-Fla. (21)
Dickey, Jay, R-Ark. (4)
Dicks, Norm, D-Wash. (6)
Dingell, John D., D-Mich. (16)
Dixon, Julian C., D-Calif. (32)
Doggett, Lloyd, D-Texas (10)
Dooley, Cal, D-Calif. (20)
Doolittle, John T., R-Calif. (4)
Doyle, Mike, D-Pa. (18)
Dreier, David, R-Calif. (28)
Duncan, John J. "Jimmy" Jr., R-Tenn. (2)
Dunn, Jennifer, R-Wash. (8)

— E —

Edwards, Chet, D-Texas (11)
Ehlers, Vernon J., R-Mich. (3)
Ehrlich, Robert L. Jr., R-Md. (2)
Emerson, Jo Ann, R-Mo. (8)
Engel, Eliot L., D-N.Y. (17)
English, Phil, R-Pa. (21)
Ensign, John, R-Nev. (1)
Eshoo, Anna G., D-Calif. (14)
Etheridge, Bob, D-N.C. (2)
Evans, Lane, D-Ill. (17)
Everett, Terry, R-Ala. (2)
Ewing, Thomas W., R-Ill. (15)

— F —

Farr, Sam, D-Calif. (17)
Fattah, Chaka, D-Pa. (2)
Fawell, Harris W., R-Ill. (13)
Fazio, Vic, D-Calif. (3)
Filner, Bob, D-Calif. (50)
Flake, Floyd H., D-N.Y. (6)
Foley, Mark, R-Fla. (16)
Forbes, Michael P., R-N.Y. (1)
Ford, Harold E. Jr., D-Tenn. (9)
Fossella, Vito J., R-N.Y. (13)
Fowler, Tillie, R-Fla. (4)
Fox, Jon D., R-Pa. (13)
Frank, Barney, D-Mass. (4)
Franks, Bob, R-N.J. (7)
Frelinghuysen, Rodney, R-N.J. (11)
Frost, Martin, D-Texas (24)
Furse, Elizabeth, D-Ore. (1)

— G —

Gallegly, Elton, R-Calif. (23)
Ganske, Greg, R-Iowa (4)
Gejdenson, Sam, D-Conn. (2)
Gekas, George W., R-Pa. (17)
Gephardt, Richard A., D-Mo. (3)
Gibbons, Jim, R-Nev. (2)
Gilchrest, Wayne T., R-Md. (1)
Gillmor, Paul E., R-Ohio (5)
Gilman, Benjamin A., R-N.Y. (20)
Gingrich, Newt, R-Ga. (6)
Gonzalez, Henry B., D-Texas (20)
Goode, Virgil H. Jr., D-Va. (5)
Goodlatte, Robert W., R-Va. (6)
Goodling, Bill, R-Pa. (19)
Gordon, Bart, D-Tenn. (6)
Goss, Porter J., R-Fla. (14)
Graham, Lindsey, R-S.C. (3)
Granger, Kay, R-Texas (12)
Green, Gene, D-Texas (29)
Greenwood, James C., R-Pa. (8)
Gutierrez, Luis V., D-Ill. (4)
Gutknecht, Gil, R-Minn. (1)

— H —

Hall, Ralph M., D-Texas (4)
Hall, Tony P., D-Ohio (3)
Hamilton, Lee H., D-Ind. (9)
Hansen, James V., R-Utah (1)
Harman, Jane, D-Calif. (36)
Hastert, Dennis, R-Ill. (14)
Hastings, Alcee L., D-Fla. (23)
Hastings, Richard "Doc", R-Wash. (4)
Hayworth, J.D., R-Ariz. (6)
Hefley, Joel, R-Colo. (5)
Hefner, W.G. "Bill", D-N.C. (8)
Herger, Wally, R-Calif. (2)
Hill, Rick, R-Mont. (AL)
Hilleary, Van, R-Tenn. (4)
Hilliard, Earl F., D-Ala. (7)
Hinchey, Maurice D., D-N.Y. (26)
Hinojosa, Rubén, D-Texas (15)
Hobson, David L., R-Ohio (7)
Hoekstra, Peter, R-Mich. (2)
Holden, Tim, D-Pa. (6)
Hooley, Darlene, D-Ore. (5)
Horn, Steve, R-Calif. (38)
Hostettler, John, R-Ind. (8)
Houghton, Amo, R-N.Y. (31)
Hoyer, Steny H., D-Md. (5)
Hulshof, Kenny, R-Mo. (9)
Hunter, Duncan, R-Calif. (52)
Hutchinson, Asa, R-Ark. (3)
Hyde, Henry J., R-Ill. (6)

— I —

Inglis, Bob, R-S.C. (4)
Istook, Ernest, R-Okla. (5)

— J —

Jackson, Jesse Jr., D-Ill. (2)
Jackson-Lee, Sheila, D-Texas (18)
Jefferson, William J., D-La. (2)
Jenkins, Bill, R-Tenn. (1)
John, Chris, D-La. (7)
Johnson, Eddie Bernice, D-Texas (30)
Johnson, Jay W., D-Wis. (8)
Johnson, Nancy L., R-Conn. (6)
Johnson, Sam, R-Texas (3)
Jones, Walter B. Jr., R-N.C. (3)

— K —

Kanjorski, Paul E., D-Pa. (11)
Kaptur, Marcy, D-Ohio (9)
Kasich, John R., R-Ohio (12)
Kelly, Sue W., R-N.Y. (19)
Kennedy, Joseph P. II, D-Mass. (8)
Kennedy, Patrick J., D-R.I. (1)
Kennelly, Barbara B., D-Conn. (1)
Kildee, Dale E., D-Mich. (9)
Kilpatrick, Carolyn Cheeks, D-Mich. (15)
Kim, Jay C., R-Calif. (41)
Kind, Ron, D-Wis. (3)
King, Peter T., R-N.Y. (3)
Kingston, Jack, R-Ga. (1)
Kleczka, Gerald D., D-Wis. (4)
Klink, Ron, D-Pa. (4)
Klug, Scott L., R-Wis. (2)
Knollenberg, Joe, R-Mich. (11)
Kolbe, Jim, R-Ariz. (5)
Kucinich, Dennis J., D-Ohio (10)

— L —

LaFalce, John J., D-N.Y. (29)
LaHood, Ray, R-Ill. (18)
Lampson, Nick, D-Texas (9)
Lantos, Tom, D-Calif. (12)
Largent, Steve, R-Okla. (1)
Latham, Tom, R-Iowa (5)
LaTourette, Steven C., R-Ohio (19)
Lazio, Rick A., R-N.Y. (2)
Leach, Jim, R-Iowa (1)
Levin, Sander M., D-Mich. (12)
Lewis, Jerry, R-Calif. (40)
Lewis, John, D-Ga. (5)
Lewis, Ron, R-Ky. (2)
Linder, John, R-Ga. (11)
Lipinski, William O., D-Ill. (3)
Livingston, Robert L., R-La. (1)
LoBiondo, Frank A., R-N.J. (2)
Lofgren, Zoe, D-Calif. (16)
Lowey, Nita M., D-N.Y. (18)
Lucas, Frank D., R-Okla. (6)
Luther, William P. "Bill", D-Minn. (6)

— M —

Maloney, Carolyn B., D-N.Y. (14)
Maloney, Jim, D-Conn. (5)
Manton, Thomas J., D-N.Y. (7)
Manzullo, Donald, R-Ill. (16)
Markey, Edward J., D-Mass. (7)
Martinez, Matthew G., D-Calif. (31)
Mascara, Frank R., D-Pa. (20)
Matsui, Robert T., D-Calif. (5)
McCarthy, Carolyn, D-N.Y. (4)
McCarthy, Karen, D-Mo. (5)
McCollum, Bill, R-Fla. (8)
McCrery, Jim, R-La. (4)
McDade, Joseph M., R-Pa. (10)
McDermott, Jim, D-Wash. (7)
McGovern, Jim, D-Mass. (3)
McHale, Paul, D-Pa. (15)
McHugh, John M., R-N.Y. (24)
McInnis, Scott, R-Colo. (3)
McIntosh, David M., R-Ind. (2)
McIntyre, Mike, D-N.C. (7)
McKeon, Howard P. "Buck", R-Calif. (25)
McKinney, Cynthia A., D-Ga. (4)
McNulty, Michael R., D-N.Y. (21)
Meehan, Martin T., D-Mass. (5)
Meek, Carrie P., D-Fla. (17)
Menendez, Robert, D-N.J. (13)
Metcalf, Jack, R-Wash. (2)
Mica, John L., R-Fla. (7)
Millender-McDonald, Juanita, D-Calif. (37)
Miller, Dan, R-Fla. (13)
Miller, George, D-Calif. (7)
Minge, David, D-Minn. (2)
Mink, Patsy T., D-Hawaii (2)
Moakley, Joe, D-Mass. (9)
Mollohan, Alan B., D-W.Va. (1)
Moran, James P., D-Va. (8)
Moran, Jerry, R-Kan. (1)
Morella, Constance A., R-Md. (8)
Murtha, John P., D-Pa. (12)
Myrick, Sue, R-N.C. (9)

— N —

Nadler, Jerrold, D-N.Y. (8)
Neal, Richard E., D-Mass. (2)
Nethercutt, George, R-Wash. (5)
Neumann, Mark W., R-Wis. (1)
Ney, Bob, R-Ohio (18)
Northup, Anne M., R-Ky. (3)
Norwood, Charlie, R-Ga. (10)
Nussle, Jim, R-Iowa (2)

— O —

Oberstar, James L., D-Minn. (8)
Obey, David R., D-Wis. (7)
Olver, John W., D-Mass. (1)
Ortiz, Solomon P., D-Texas (27)
Owens, Major R., D-N.Y. (11)
Oxley, Michael G., R-Ohio (4)

— P —

Packard, Ron, R-Calif. (48)
Pallone, Frank Jr., D-N.J. (6)
Pappas, Michael, R-N.J. (12)
Parker, Mike, R-Miss. (4)
Pascrell, Bill Jr., D-N.J. (8)
Pastor, Ed, D-Ariz. (2)
Paul, Ron, R-Texas (14)
Paxon, Bill, R-N.Y. (27)
Payne, Donald M., D-N.J. (10)
Pease, Ed, R-Ind. (7)
Pelosi, Nancy, D-Calif. (8)
Peterson, Collin C., D-Minn. (7)
Peterson, John E., R-Pa. (5)
Petri, Tom, R-Wis. (6)
Pickering, Charles W. "Chip" Jr., R-Miss. (3)
Pickett, Owen B., D-Va. (2)
Pitts, Joseph R., R-Pa. (16)

. . . Governors, Justices, Cabinet Rank Officers

Pombo, Richard W., R-Calif. (11)
Pomeroy, Earl, D-N.D. (AL)
Porter, John Edward, R-Ill. (10)
Portman, Rob, R-Ohio (2)
Poshard, Glenn, D-Ill. (19)
Price, David E., D-N.C. (4)
Pryce, Deborah, R-Ohio (15)

— Q —

Quinn, Jack, R-N.Y. (30)

— R —

Radanovich, George P., R-Calif. (19)
Rahall, Nick J. II, D-W.Va. (3)
Ramstad, Jim, R-Minn. (3)
Rangel, Charles B., D-N.Y. (15)
Redmond, Bill, R-N.M. (3)
Regula, Ralph, R-Ohio (16)
Reyes, Silvestre, D-Texas (16)
Riggs, Frank, R-Calif. (1)
Riley, Bob, R-Ala. (3)
Rivers, Lynn, D-Mich. (13)
Rodriguez, Ciro D., D-Texas (28)
Roemer, Tim, D-Ind. (3)
Rogan, James E., R-Calif. (27)
Rogers, Harold, R-Ky. (5)
Rohrabacher, Dana, R-Calif. (45)
Ros-Lehtinen, Ileana, R-Fla. (18)
Rothman, Steven R., D-N.J. (9)
Roukema, Marge, R-N.J. (5)
Roybal-Allard, Lucille, D-Calif. (33)
Royce, Ed, R-Calif. (39)
Rush, Bobby L., D-Ill. (1)
Ryun, Jim, R-Kan. (2)

— S —

Sabo, Martin Olav, D-Minn. (5)
Salmon, Matt, R-Ariz. (1)
Sanchez, Loretta, D-Calif. (46)
Sanders, Bernard, I-Vt. (AL)
Sandlin, Max, D-Texas (1)
Sanford, Mark, R-S.C. (1)
Sawyer, Tom, D-Ohio (14)
Saxton, H. James, R-N.J. (3)
Scarborough, Joe, R-Fla. (1)
Schaefer, Dan, R-Colo. (6)
Schaffer, Bob, R-Colo. (4)
Schiff, Steven H., R-N.M. (1)
Schumer, Charles E., D-N.Y. (9)
Scott, Robert C., D-Va. (3)
Sensenbrenner, F. James Jr., R-Wis. (9)
Serrano, Jose E., D-N.Y. (16)
Sessions, Pete, R-Texas (5)
Shadegg, John, R-Ariz. (4)
Shaw, E. Clay Jr., R-Fla. (22)
Shays, Christopher, R-Conn. (4)
Sherman, Brad, D-Calif. (24)
Shimkus, John, R-Ill. (20)
Shuster, Bud, R-Pa. (9)
Sisisky, Norman, D-Va. (4)
Skaggs, David E., D-Colo. (2)
Skeen, Joe, R-N.M. (2)
Skelton, Ike, D-Mo. (4)
Slaughter, Louise M., D-N.Y. (28)
Smith, Adam, D-Wash. (9)
Smith, Bob, R-Ore. (2)
Smith, Christopher H., R-N.J. (4)
Smith, Lamar, R-Texas (21)
Smith, Linda, R-Wash. (3)
Smith, Nick, R-Mich. (7)
Snowbarger, Vince, R-Kan. (3)
Snyder, Vic, D-Ark. (2)
Solomon, Gerald B.H., R-N.Y. (22)
Souder, Mark, R-Ind. (4)
Spence, Floyd D., R-S.C. (2)
Spratt, John M. Jr., D-S.C. (5)
Stabenow, Debbie, D-Mich. (8)
Stark, Pete, D-Calif. (13)
Stearns, Cliff, R-Fla. (6)
Stenholm, Charles W., D-Texas (17)
Stokes, Louis, D-Ohio (11)
Strickland, Ted, D-Ohio (6)
Stump, Bob, R-Ariz. (3)
Stupak, Bart, D-Mich. (1)
Sununu, John E., R-N.H. (1)

— T —

Talent, James M., R-Mo. (2)
Tanner, John, D-Tenn. (8)
Tauscher, Ellen O., D-Calif. (10)
Tauzin, W.J. "Billy", R-La. (3)
Taylor, Charles H., R-N.C. (11)
Taylor, Gene, D-Miss. (5)
Thomas, Bill, R-Calif. (21)
Thompson, Bennie, D-Miss. (2)
Thornberry, William M. "Mac", R-Texas (13)
Thune, John, R-S.D. (AL)
Thurman, Karen L., D-Fla. (5)
Tiahrt, Todd, R-Kan. (4)
Tierney, John F., D-Mass. (6)
Torres, Esteban E., D-Calif. (34)
Towns, Edolphus, D-N.Y. (10)
Traficant, James A. Jr., D-Ohio (17)
Turner, Jim, D-Texas (2)

— U —

Upton, Fred, R-Mich. (6)

— V —

Velázquez, Nydia M., D-N.Y. (12)
Vento, Bruce F., D-Minn. (4)
Visclosky, Peter J., D-Ind. (1)

— W —

Walsh, James T., R-N.Y. (25)
Wamp, Zach, R-Tenn. (3)
Waters, Maxine, D-Calif. (35)
Watkins, Wes, R-Okla. (3)
Watt, Melvin, D-N.C. (12)
Watts, J.C., R-Okla. (4)
Waxman, Henry A., D-Calif. (29)
Weldon, Curt, R-Pa. (7)
Weldon, Dave, R-Fla. (15)
Weller, Jerry, R-Ill. (11)
Wexler, Robert, D-Fla. (19)
Weygand, Bob, D-R.I. (2)
White, Rick, R-Wash. (1)
Whitfield, Edward, R-Ky. (1)
Wicker, Roger, R-Miss. (1)
Wise, Bob, D-W.Va. (2)
Wolf, Frank R., R-Va. (10)
Woolsey, Lynn, D-Calif. (6)
Wynn, Albert R., D-Md. (4)

— Y —

Yates, Sidney R., D-Ill. (9)
Young, C.W. Bill, R-Fla. (10)
Young, Don, R-Alaska (AL)

Delegates

Christian-Green, Donna M., D-Virgin Is.
Faleomavaega, Eni F.H., D-Am. Samoa
Norton, Eleanor Holmes, D-D.C.
Romero-Barcelo, Carlos, D-P.R.
Underwood, Robert A., D-Guam

Senators
R 55; D 45

Abraham, Spencer, R-Mich.
Akaka, Daniel K., D-Hawaii
Allard, Wayne, R-Colo.
Ashcroft, John, R-Mo.
Baucus, Max, D-Mont.
Bennett, Robert F., R-Utah
Biden, Joseph R. Jr., D-Del.
Bingaman, Jeff, D-N.M.
Bond, Christopher S., R-Mo.
Boxer, Barbara, D-Calif.
Breaux, John B., D-La.
Brownback, Sam, R-Kan.
Bryan, Richard H., D-Nev.
Bumpers, Dale, D-Ark.
Burns, Conrad, R-Mont.
Byrd, Robert C., D-W.Va.
Campbell, Ben Nighthorse, R-Colo.
Chafee, John H., R-R.I.
Cleland, Max, D-Ga.
Coats, Daniel R., R-Ind.
Cochran, Thad, R-Miss.
Collins, Susan, R-Maine
Conrad, Kent, D-N.D.
Coverdell, Paul, R-Ga.
Craig, Larry E., R-Idaho
D'Amato, Alfonse M., R-N.Y.
Daschle, Tom, D-S.D.
DeWine, Mike, R-Ohio
Dodd, Christopher J., D-Conn.
Domenici, Pete V., R-N.M.
Dorgan, Byron L., D-N.D.
Durbin, Richard J., D-Ill.
Enzi, Michael B., R-Wyo.
Faircloth, Lauch, R-N.C.
Feingold, Russell D., D-Wis.
Feinstein, Dianne, D-Calif.
Ford, Wendell H., D-Ky.
Frist, Bill, R-Tenn.
Glenn, John, D-Ohio
Gorton, Slade, R-Wash.
Graham, Bob, D-Fla.
Gramm, Phil, R-Texas
Grams, Rod, R-Minn.
Grassley, Charles E., R-Iowa
Gregg, Judd, R-N.H.
Hagel, Chuck, R-Neb.
Harkin, Tom, D-Iowa
Hatch, Orrin G., R-Utah
Helms, Jesse, R-N.C.
Hollings, Ernest F., D-S.C.
Hutchinson, Tim, R-Ark.
Hutchison, Kay Bailey, R-Texas
Inhofe, James M., R-Okla.
Inouye, Daniel K., D-Hawaii
Jeffords, James M., R-Vt.
Johnson, Tim, D-S.D.
Kempthorne, Dirk, R-Idaho
Kennedy, Edward M., D-Mass.
Kerrey, Bob, D-Neb.
Kerry, John, D-Mass.
Kohl, Herb, D-Wis.
Kyl, Jon, R-Ariz.
Landrieu, Mary L., D-La.
Lautenberg, Frank R., D-N.J.
Leahy, Patrick J., D-Vt.
Levin, Carl, D-Mich.
Lieberman, Joseph I., D-Conn.
Lott, Trent, R-Miss.
Lugar, Richard G., R-Ind.
Mack, Connie, R-Fla.
McCain, John, R-Ariz.
McConnell, Mitch, R-Ky.
Mikulski, Barbara A., D-Md.
Moseley-Braun, Carol, D-Ill.
Moynihan, Daniel Patrick, D-N.Y.
Murkowski, Frank H., R-Alaska
Murray, Patty, D-Wash.
Nickles, Don, R-Okla.
Reed, Jack, D-R.I.
Reid, Harry, D-Nev.
Robb, Charles S., D-Va.
Roberts, Pat, R-Kan.
Rockefeller, John D. IV, D-W.Va.
Roth, William V. Jr., R-Del.
Santorum, Rick, R-Pa.
Sarbanes, Paul S., D-Md.
Sessions, Jeff, R-Ala.
Shelby, Richard C., R-Ala.
Smith, Gordon H., R-Ore.
Smith, Robert C., R-N.H.
Snowe, Olympia J., R-Maine
Specter, Arlen, R-Pa.
Stevens, Ted, R-Alaska
Thomas, Craig, R-Wyo.
Thompson, Fred, R-Tenn.
Thurmond, Strom, R-S.C.
Torricelli, Robert G., D-N.J.
Warner, John W., R-Va.
Wellstone, Paul, D-Minn.
Wyden, Ron, D-Ore.

Governors
R 32; D 17; I 1

Ala. — Fob James Jr., R
Alaska — Tony Knowles, D
Ariz. — Fife Symington, R
Ark. — Mike Huckabee, R
Calif. — Pete Wilson, R
Colo. — Roy Romer, D
Conn. — John G. Rowland, R
Del. — Thomas R. Carper, D
Fla. — Lawton Chiles, D
Ga. — Zell Miller, D
Hawaii — Benjamin J. Cayetano, D
Idaho — Phil Batt, R
Ill. — Jim Edgar, R
Ind. — Frank L. O'Bannon, D
Iowa — Terry E. Branstad, R
Kan. — Bill Graves, R
Ky. — Paul E. Patton, D
La. — Mike Foster, R
Maine — Angus King, I
Md. — Parris N. Glendening, D
Mass. — William F. Weld, R
Mich. — John Engler, R
Minn. — Arne Carlson, R
Miss. — Kirk Fordice, R
Mo. — Mel Carnahan, D
Mont. — Marc Racicot, R
Neb. — Ben Nelson, D
Nev. — Bob Miller, D
N.H. — Jeanne Shaheen, D
N.J. — Christine Todd Whitman, R
N.M. — Gary E. Johnson, R
N.Y. — George E. Pataki, R
N.C. — James B. Hunt Jr., D
N.D. — Edward T. Schafer, R
Ohio — George V. Voinovich, R
Okla. — Frank Keating, R
Ore. — John Kitzhaber, D
Pa. — Tom Ridge, R
R.I. — Lincoln C. Almond, R
S.C. — David Beasley, R
S.D. — William J. Janklow, R
Tenn. — Don Sundquist, R
Texas — George W. Bush, R
Utah — Michael O. Leavitt, R
Vt. — Howard Dean, D
Va. — George F. Allen, R
Wash. — Gary Locke, D
W.Va. — Cecil H. Underwood, R
Wis. — Tommy G. Thompson, R
Wyo. — Jim Geringer, R

Supreme Court

Rehnquist, William H. — Va., Chief Justice
Breyer, Stephen G. — Mass.
Ginsburg, Ruth Bader — N.Y.
Kennedy, Anthony M. — Calif.
O'Connor, Sandra Day — Ariz.
Scalia, Antonin — Va.
Souter, David H. — N.H.
Stevens, John Paul — Ill.
Thomas, Clarence — Ga.

Cabinet

Albright, Madeleine K. — State
Babbitt, Bruce — Interior
Brown, Jesse — Veterans Affairs
Cohen, William S. — Defense
Cuomo, Andrew M. — HUD
Daley, William M. — Commerce
Glickman, Dan — Agriculture
Herman, Alexis — Labor (nominee)
Peña, Federico F. — Energy (nominee)
Reno, Janet — Attorney General
Richardson, Bill — U.N. Representative
Riley, Richard W. — Education
Rubin, Robert E. — Treasury
Shalala, Donna E. — HHS
Slater, Rodney — Transportation
Other Executive Branch Officers
Gore, Al — Vice President
Barshefsky, Charlene — U.S. Trade Representative (nominee)
Berger, Samuel R. — National Security Adviser
Bowles, Erskine — Chief of Staff
Browner, Carol M. — EPA Administrator
Lake, Anthony — Director of Central Intelligence (nominee)
Raines, Franklin D. — OMB Director
Sperling, Gene — Chairman, National Economic Council
Yellen, Janet — Chairman, Council of Economic Advisers

Characteristics of Congress

Following is a compilation of information about individual members of the first session of the 105th Congress — their birth dates, occupations, and religion. Senate and House seniority lists begin on page B-18.

The average age of the members of the first session of the 105th Congress was 52.7, slightly higher than in the previous Congress. As in other years, the biggest single occupational group in Congress was lawyers. Business people and bankers in the House increased from a low of 118 in the 95th Congress to 181 in the 105th Congress, while in the same period the number of lawyers declined from 222 to 172. Roman Catholic members made up the largest religious group, followed by members of the Baptist, Methodist and Presbyterian faiths.

Senate — Birth Dates, Occupations, Religions

(As of Nov. 13, 1997, when the first session of the 105th Congress adjourned sine die.)

ALABAMA

Shelby (R) — May 6, 1934. Occupation: Lawyer. Religion: Presbyterian.

Sessions (R) — Dec. 24, 1946. Occupation: Lawyer. Religion: Methodist.

ALASKA

Stevens (R) — Nov. 18, 1923. Occupation: Lawyer. Religion: Episcopalian.

Murkowski (R) — March 28, 1933. Occupation: Banker. Religion: Roman Catholic.

ARIZONA

McCain (R) — Aug. 29, 1936. Occupation: Navy officer; Senate Navy liaison, beer distributor. Religion: Episcopalian.

Kyl (R) — April 25, 1942. Occupation: Lawyer. Religion: Presbyterian.

ARKANSAS

Bumpers (D) — Aug. 12, 1925. Occupation: Lawyer, farmer, hardware company executive. Religion: Methodist.

Hutchinson (R) — Aug. 11, 1949. Occupation: Minister, college instructor, radio station executive. Religion: Baptist.

CALIFORNIA

Feinstein (D) — June 22, 1933. Occupation: Public official. Religion: Jewish.

Boxer (D) — Nov. 11, 1940. Occupation: Congressional aide, journalist, stockbroker. Religion: Jewish.

COLORADO

Campbell (R) — April 13, 1933. Occupation: Jewelry designer, rancher; horse trainer, teacher. Religion: Unspecified.

Allard (R) — Dec. 2, 1943. Occupation: Veterinarian. Religion: Protestant.

CONNECTICUT

Dodd (D) — May 27, 1944. Occupation: Lawyer. Religion: Roman Catholic.

Lieberman (D) — Feb. 24, 1942. Occupation: Lawyer. Religion: Jewish.

DELAWARE

Roth (R) — July 22, 1921. Occupation: Lawyer. Religion: Episcopalian.

Biden (D) — Nov. 20, 1942. Occupation: Lawyer. Religion: Roman Catholic.

FLORIDA

Graham (D) — Nov. 9, 1936. Occupation: Real estate developer, cattle rancher. Religion: United Church of Christ.

Mack (R) — Oct. 29, 1940. Occupation: Banker. Religion: Roman Catholic.

GEORGIA

Coverdell (R) — Jan. 20, 1939. Occupation: Financial executive, Peace Corps director. Religion: Methodist.

Cleland (D) — Aug. 24, 1942. Occupation: White House official. Religion: Methodist.

HAWAII

Inouye (D) — Sept. 7, 1924. Occupation: Lawyer. Religion: Methodist.

Akaka (D) — Sept. 11, 1924. Occupation: Elementary school teacher and principal, state official. Religion: Congregationalist.

IDAHO

Craig (R) — July 20, 1945. Occupation: Farmer; rancher. Religion: Methodist.

Kempthorne (R) — Oct. 29, 1951. Occupation: Public affairs manager; securities representative, political consultant, building association executive. Religion: Methodist.

ILLINOIS

Moseley-Braun (D) — Aug. 16, 1947. Occupation: Lawyer. Religion: Roman Catholic.

Durbin (D) — Nov. 21, 1944. Occupation: Lawyer, congressional and legislative aide. Religion: Roman Catholic.

INDIANA

Lugar (R) — April 4, 1932. Occupation: Manufacturing executive, farm manager. Religion: Methodist.

Coats (R) — May 16, 1943. Occupation: Lawyer. Religion: Presbyterian.

IOWA

Grassley (R) — Sept. 17, 1933. Occupation: Farmer. Religion: Baptist.

Harkin (D) — Nov. 19, 1939. Occupation: Lawyer. Religion: Roman Catholic.

KANSAS

Brownback (R) — Sept. 12, 1956. Occupation: Teacher, lawyer, White House aide, broadcaster. Religion: Methodist.

Roberts (R) — April 20, 1936. Occupation: Journalist, congressional aide. Religion: Methodist.

KENTUCKY

Ford (D) — Sept. 8, 1924. Occupation: Insurance executive. Religion: Baptist.

McConnell (R) — Feb. 20, 1942. Occupation: Lawyer. Religion: Baptist.

LOUISIANA

Breaux (D) — March 1, 1944. Occupation: Lawyer. Religion: Roman Catholic.

Landrieu (D) — Nov. 23, 1955. Occupation: Real estate agent. Religion: Roman Catholic.

MAINE

Snowe (R) — Feb. 21, 1947. Occupation: Public official. Religion: Greek Orthodox.

Collins (R) — Dec. 7, 1952. Occupation: Business center director, state deputy treasurer, SBA official, state financial regulation commissioner, congressional aide. Religion: Roman Catholic.

MARYLAND

Sarbanes (D) — Feb. 3, 1933. Occupation: Lawyer. Religion: Greek Orthodox.

Mikulski (D) — July 20, 1936. Occupation: Social worker. Religion: Roman Catholic.

MASSACHUSETTS

Kennedy (D) — Feb. 22, 1932. Occupation: Lawyer. Religion: Roman Catholic.

Kerry (D) — Dec. 11, 1943. Occupation: Lawyer. Religion: Roman Catholic.

MICHIGAN

Levin (D) — June 28, 1934. Occupation: Lawyer. Religion: Jewish.

Abraham (R) — June 12, 1952. Occupation: Lawyer, congressional aide, vice presidential aide. Religion: Eastern Orthodox Christian.

MINNESOTA

Wellstone (D) — July 21, 1944. Occupation: Professor. Religion: Jewish.

Grams (R) — Feb. 4, 1948. Occupation: Contractor, television journalist. Religion: Lutheran.

MISSISSIPPI

Cochran (R) — Dec. 7, 1937. Occupation: Lawyer. Religion: Baptist.

Lott (R) — Oct. 9, 1941. Occupation: Lawyer. Religion: Baptist.

MISSOURI

Bond (R) — March 6, 1939. Occupation: Lawyer. Religion: Presbyterian.

Ashcroft (R) — May 9, 1942. Occupation: Lawyer. Religion: Assembly of God.

MONTANA

Baucus (D) — Dec. 11, 1941. Occupation: Lawyer. Religion: United Church of Christ.

Burns (R) — Jan. 25, 1935. Occupation: Radio and television broadcaster. Religion: Lutheran.

NEBRASKA

Kerrey (D) — Aug. 27, 1943. Occupation: Restaurateur. Religion: Congregationalist.

Hagel (R) — Oct. 4, 1946. Occupation: Investment bank executive, international business consultant, congressional aide. Religion: Episcopalian.

NEVADA

Reid (D) — Dec. 2, 1939. Occupation: Lawyer. Religion: Mormon.

Bryan (D) — July 16, 1937. Occupation: Lawyer. Religion: Episcopalian.

NEW HAMPSHIRE

Smith (R) — March 30, 1941. Occupation: Real estate broker, high school teacher. Religion: Roman Catholic.

Gregg (R) — Feb. 14, 1947. Occupation: Lawyer. Religion: Congregationalist.

NEW JERSEY

Lautenberg (D) — Jan. 23, 1924. Occupation: Computer firm executive. Religion: Jewish.

Torricelli (D) — Aug. 26, 1951. Occupation: Lawyer. Religion: Methodist.

NEW MEXICO

Domenici (R) — May 7, 1932. Occupation: Lawyer. Religion: Roman Catholic.

Bingaman (D) — Oct. 3, 1943. Occupation: Lawyer. Religion: Methodist.

NEW YORK

Moynihan (D) — March 16, 1927. Occupation: Professor, writer. Religion: Roman Catholic.

D'Amato (R) — Aug. 1, 1937. Occupation: Lawyer. Religion: Roman Catholic.

NORTH CAROLINA

Helms (R) — Oct. 18, 1921. Occupation: Journalist, broadcasting executive; banking executive, congressional aide. Religion: Baptist.

Faircloth (R) — Jan. 14, 1928. Occupation: Farm owner. Religion: Presbyterian.

NORTH DAKOTA

Conrad (D) — March 12, 1948. Occupation: Management and personnel director. Religion: Unitarian.

Dorgan (D) — May 14, 1942. Occupation: Public official. Religion: Lutheran.

OHIO

Glenn (D) — July 18, 1921. Occupation: Astronaut, soft drink company executive. Religion: Presbyterian.

DeWine (R) — Jan. 5, 1947. Occupation: Lawyer. Religion: Roman Catholic.

OKLAHOMA

Nickles (R) — Dec. 6, 1948. Occupation: Machine company executive. Religion: Roman Catholic.

Inhofe (R) — Nov. 17, 1934. Occupation: Real estate developer, insurance executive. Religion: Presbyterian.

OREGON

Wyden (D) — May 3, 1949. Occupation: Lawyer, professor. Religion: Jewish.

Smith (R) — May 25, 1952. Occupation: Frozen food company executive, lawyer. Religion: Mormon.

PENNSYLVANIA

Specter (R) — Feb. 12, 1930. Occupation: Lawyer, professor. Religion: Jewish.

Santorum (R) — May 10, 1958. Occupation: Lawyer, legislative aide. Religion: Roman Catholic.

RHODE ISLAND

Chafee (R) — Oct. 22, 1922. Occupation: Lawyer. Religion: Episcopalian.

Reed (D) — Nov. 12, 1949. Occupation: Lawyer. Religion: Roman Catholic.

SOUTH CAROLINA

Thurmond (R) — Dec. 5, 1902. Occupation: Lawyer, teacher; coach; education administrator. Religion: Baptist.

Hollings (D) — Jan. 1, 1922. Occupation: Lawyer. Religion: Lutheran.

SOUTH DAKOTA

Daschle (D) — Dec. 9, 1947. Occupation: Congressional aide. Religion: Roman Catholic.

Johnson (D) — Dec. 28, 1946. Occupation: Lawyer. Religion: Lutheran.

TENNESSEE

Thompson (R) — Aug. 19, 1942. Occupation: Lawyer, actor. Religion: Protestant.

Frist (R) — Feb. 22, 1952. Occupation: Surgeon. Religion: Presbyterian.

TEXAS

Gramm (R) — July 8, 1942. Occupation: Professor. Religion: Episcopalian.

Hutchison (R) — July 22, 1943. Occupation: Broadcast journalist, banking executive, candy manufacturer. Religion: Episcopalian.

UTAH

Hatch (R) — March 22, 1934. Occupation: Lawyer. Religion: Mormon.

Bennett (R) — Sept. 18, 1933. Occupation: Management consultant. Religion: Mormon.

VERMONT

Leahy (D) — March 31, 1940. Occupation: Lawyer. Religion: Roman Catholic.

Jeffords (R) — May 11, 1934. Occupation: Lawyer. Religion: Congregationalist.

VIRGINIA

Warner (R) — Feb. 18, 1927. Occupation: Lawyer, farmer. Religion: Episcopalian.

Robb (D) — June 26, 1939. Occupation: Lawyer. Religion: Episcopalian.

WASHINGTON

Gorton (R) — Jan. 8, 1928. Occupation: Lawyer. Religion: Episcopalian.

Murray (D) — Oct. 11, 1950. Occupation: Educator. Religion: Roman Catholic.

WEST VIRGINIA

Byrd (D) — Nov. 20, 1917. Occupation: Lawyer. Religion: Baptist.

Rockefeller (D) — June 18, 1937. Occupation: Public official. Religion: Presbyterian.

WISCONSIN

Kohl (D) — Feb. 7, 1935. Occupation: Businessman; professional basketball team owner. Religion: Jewish.

Feingold (D) — March 2, 1953. Occupation: Lawyer. Religion: Jewish.

WYOMING

Thomas (R) — Feb. 17, 1933. Occupation: Power company executive. Religion: Methodist.

Enzi (R) — Feb. 1, 1944. Occupation: Accountant, shoe store owner. Religion: Presbyterian.

House — Birth Dates, Occupations, Religions

(As of Nov. 13, 1997, when the first session of the 105th Congress adjourned sine die.)

ALABAMA

1 **Callahan (R)** — Sept. 11, 1932. Occupation: Moving and storage company executive. Religion: Roman Catholic.

2 **Everett (R)** — Feb. 15, 1937. Occupation: Newspaper executive, construction company owner, farm owner, real estate developer. Religion: Baptist.

3 **Riley (R)** — Oct. 3, 1944. Occupation: Auto dealer, trucking company executive, farmer. Religion: Baptist.

4 **Aderholt (R)** — July 22, 1965. Occupation: Municipal judge, lawyer, gubernatorial aide. Religion: Protestant.

5 **Cramer (D)** — Aug. 22, 1947. Occupation: Lawyer. Religion: Methodist.

6 **Bachus (R)** — Dec. 28, 1947. Occupation: Lawyer, manufacturer. Religion: Baptist.

7 **Hilliard (D)** — April 9, 1942. Occupation: Lawyer, insurance broker. Religion: Baptist.

ALASKA

AL **Young (R)** — June 9, 1933. Occupation: Elementary school teacher, riverboat captain. Religion: Episcopalian.

ARIZONA

1 **Salmon (R)** — Jan. 21, 1958. Occupation: Communications company executive. Religion: Mormon.

2 **Pastor (D)** — June 28, 1943. Occupation: Teacher, gubernatorial aide, public policy consultant. Religion: Roman Catholic.

3 **Stump (R)** — April 4, 1927. Occupation: Cotton farmer. Religion: Seventh-Day Adventist.

4 **Shadegg (R)** — Oct. 22, 1949. Occupation: Lawyer. Religion: Episcopalian.

5 **Kolbe (R)** — June 28, 1942. Occupation: Real estate consultant. Religion: Methodist.

6 **Hayworth (R)** — July 12, 1958. Occupation: Sports broadcaster, public relations consultant, insurance agent. Religion: Baptist.

ARKANSAS

1 **Berry (D)** — Aug. 27, 1942. Occupation: Farmer, White House aide. Religion: Methodist.

2 **Snyder (D)** — Sept. 27, 1947. Occupation: Physician, lawyer. Religion: Presbyterian.

3 **Hutchinson (R)** — Dec. 3, 1950. Occupation: Lawyer. Religion: Baptist.

4 **Dickey (R)** — Dec. 14, 1939. Occupation: Lawyer, restaurateur. Religion: Methodist.

CALIFORNIA

1 **Riggs (R)** — Sept. 5, 1950. Occupation: Police officer, real estate developer, educational software executive. Religion: Episcopalian.

2 **Herger (R)** — May 20, 1945. Occupation: Rancher, gas company executive. Religion: Mormon.

3 **Fazio (D)** — Oct. 11, 1942. Occupation: Journalist, congressional and legislative consultant. Religion: Episcopalian.

4 **Doolittle (R)** — Oct. 30, 1950. Occupation: Lawyer. Religion: Mormon.

5 **Matsui (D)** — Sept. 17, 1941. Occupation: Lawyer. Religion: Methodist.

6 **Woolsey (D)** — Nov. 3, 1937. Occupation: Personnel service owner. Religion: Presbyterian.

7 **Miller (D)** — May 17, 1945. Occupation: Lawyer, legislative aide. Religion: Roman Catholic.

8 **Pelosi (D)** — March 26, 1940. Occupation: Public relations consultant. Religion: Roman Catholic.

9 **Dellums (D)** — Nov. 24, 1935. Occupation: Psychiatric social worker. Religion: Protestant.

10 **Tauscher (D)** — Nov. 15, 1951. Occupation: Child care screening executive, marketing executive, investment banker. Religion: Roman Catholic.

11 **Pombo (R)** — Jan. 8, 1961. Occupation: Rancher. Religion: Roman Catholic.

12 **Lantos (D)** — Feb. 1, 1928. Occupation: Professor. Religion: Jewish.

13 **Stark (D)** — Nov. 11, 1931. Occupation: Banker. Religion: Unitarian.

14 **Eshoo (D)** — Dec. 13, 1942. Occupation: Legislative aide. Religion: Roman Catholic.

15 **Campbell (R)** — Aug. 14, 1952. Occupation: Professor of economics, federal official, lawyer. Religion: Roman Catholic.

16 **Lofgren (D)** — Dec. 21, 1947. Occupation: Lawyer, professor, congressional aide. Religion: Unspecified.

17 **Farr (D)** — July 4, 1941. Occupation: State legislative aide. Religion: Episcopalian.

18 **Condit (D)** — April 21, 1948. Occupation: Public official. Religion: Baptist.

19 **Radanovich (R)** — June 20, 1955. Occupation: Vintner, bank manager, carpenter. Religion: Roman Catholic.

20 **Dooley (D)** — Jan. 11, 1954. Occupation: Farmer. Religion: Protestant.

21 **Thomas (R)** — Dec. 6, 1941. Occupation: Professor. Religion: Baptist.

22 **Vacant** — Capps (D) died Oct. 28, 1997.
23 **Gallegly (R)** — March 7, 1944. Occupation: Real estate broker. Religion: Protestant.
24 **Sherman (D)** — Oct. 24, 1954. Occupation: Accountant, lawyer. Religion: Jewish.
25 **McKeon (R)** — Sept. 9, 1939. Occupation: Clothing store owner. Religion: Mormon.
26 **Berman (D)** — April 15, 1941. Occupation: Lawyer. Religion: Jewish.
27 **Rogan (R)** — Aug. 21, 1957. Occupation: Lawyer. Religion: Christian.
28 **Dreier (R)** — July 5, 1952. Occupation: Real estate manager and developer. Religion: Christian Scientist.
29 **Waxman (D)** — Sept. 12, 1939. Occupation: Lawyer. Religion: Jewish.
30 **Becerra (D)** — Jan. 26, 1958. Occupation: Lawyer. Religion: Roman Catholic.
31 **Martinez (D)** — Feb. 14, 1929. Occupation: Upholstery company owner. Religion: Roman Catholic.
32 **Dixon (D)** — Aug. 8, 1934. Occupation: Legislative aide, lawyer. Religion: Episcopalian.
33 **Roybal-Allard (D)** — June 12, 1941. Occupation: Nonprofit worker. Religion: Roman Catholic.
34 **Torres (D)** — Jan. 27, 1930. Occupation: International trade executive, autoworker; labor official. Religion: Unspecified.
35 **Waters (D)** — Aug. 15, 1938. Occupation: Head Start official. Religion: Christian.
36 **Harman (D)** — June 28, 1945. Occupation: Lawyer, White House aide, congressional aide. Religion: Jewish.
37 **Millender-McDonald (D)**— Sept. 7, 1938. Occupation: Teacher. Religion: Baptist.
38 **Horn (R)** — May 31, 1931. Occupation: Professor, college president. Religion: Protestant.
39 **Royce (R)** — Oct. 12, 1951. Occupation: Tax manager. Religion: Roman Catholic.
40 **Lewis (R)** — Oct. 21, 1934. Occupation: Insurance executive. Religion: Presbyterian.
41 **Kim (R)** — March 27, 1939. Occupation: Civil engineer. Religion: Methodist.
42 **Brown (D)** — March 6, 1920. Occupation: Management consultant, physicist. Religion: Methodist.
43 **Calvert (R)** — June 8, 1953. Occupation: Real estate executive. Religion: Protestant.
44 **Bono (R)** — Feb. 16, 1935. Occupation: Restaurateur, entertainer. Religion: Roman Catholic.
45 **Rohrabacher (R)** — June 21, 1947. Occupation: White House speechwriter, journalist. Religion: Baptist.
46 **Sanchez (D)** — Jan. 7, 1960. Occupation: Financial advisor, strategic management associate. Religion: Roman Catholic.
47 **Cox (R)** — Oct. 16, 1952. Occupation: White House counsel. Religion: Roman Catholic.
48 **Packard (R)** — Jan. 19, 1931. Occupation: Dentist. Religion: Mormon.
49 **Bilbray (R)** — Jan. 28, 1951. Occupation: Tax firm owner. Religion: Roman Catholic.
50 **Filner (D)** — Sept. 4, 1942. Occupation: Public official, college professor. Religion: Jewish.
51 **Cunningham (R)** — Dec. 8, 1941. Occupation: Computer software executive. Religion: Christian.
52 **Hunter (R)** — May 31, 1948. Occupation: Lawyer. Religion: Baptist.

COLORADO

1 **DeGette (D)** — July 29, 1957. Occupation: Lawyer. Religion: Presbyterian.
2 **Skaggs (D)** — Feb. 22, 1943. Occupation: Lawyer, congressional aide. Religion: Congregationalist.
3 **McInnis (R)** — May 9, 1953. Occupation: Lawyer. Religion: Roman Catholic.
4 **Schaffer (R)** — July 24, 1962. Occupation: Property manager, marketing executive, congressional aide. Religion: Roman Catholic.
5 **Hefley (R)** — April 18, 1935. Occupation: Community planner, management consultant. Religion: Presbyterian.
6 **Schaefer (R)** — Jan. 25, 1936. Occupation: Public relations consultant. Religion: Roman Catholic.

CONNECTICUT

1 **Kennelly (D)** — July 10, 1936. Occupation: Public official. Religion: Roman Catholic.
2 **Gejdenson (D)** — May 20, 1948. Occupation: Dairy farmer. Religion: Jewish.
3 **DeLauro (D)** — March 2, 1943. Occupation: Political activist. Religion: Roman Catholic.
4 **Shays (R)** — Oct. 18, 1945. Occupation: Real estate broker, public official. Religion: Christian Scientist.
5 **Maloney (D)** — Sept. 17, 1948. Occupation: Lawyer. Religion: Roman Catholic.
6 **Johnson (R)** — Jan. 5, 1935. Occupation: Civic leader. Religion: Unitarian.

DELAWARE

AL **Castle (R)** — July 2, 1939. Occupation: Lawyer. Religion: Roman Catholic.

FLORIDA

1 **Scarborough (R)** — April 9, 1963. Occupation: Lawyer. Religion: Baptist.
2 **Boyd (D)** — June 6, 1945. Occupation: Farmer. Religion: Methodist.
3 **Brown (D)** — Nov. 11, 1946. Occupation: College guidance counselor, travel agency owner. Religion: Baptist.
4 **Fowler (R)** — Dec. 23, 1942. Occupation: White House aide, congressional aide, lawyer. Religion: Episcopalian.
5 **Thurman (D)** — Jan. 12, 1951. Occupation: Teacher. Religion: Episcopalian.
6 **Stearns (R)** — April 16, 1941. Occupation: Hotel executive. Religion: Presbyterian.
7 **Mica (R)** — Jan. 27, 1943. Occupation: Government consultant. Religion: Episcopalian.
8 **McCollum (R)** — July 12, 1944. Occupation: Lawyer. Religion: Episcopalian.
9 **Bilirakis (R)** — July 16, 1930. Occupation: Lawyer, restaurateur. Religion: Greek Orthodox.
10 **Young (R)** — Dec. 16, 1930. Occupation: Insurance executive, public official. Religion: Methodist.
11 **Davis (D)** — Oct. 11, 1957. Occupation: Lawyer. Religion: Episcopalian.
12 **Canady (R)** — June 22, 1954. Occupation: Lawyer. Religion: Presbyterian.
13 **Miller (R)** — May 30, 1942. Occupation: Businessman. Religion: Episcopalian.
14 **Goss (R)** — Nov. 26, 1938. Occupation: Businessman, newspaper founder, CIA agent. Religion: Presbyterian.
15 **Weldon (R)** — Aug. 31, 1953. Occupation: Physician. Religion: Christian.
16 **Foley (R)** — Sept. 8, 1954. Occupation: Catering company founder, real estate broker, restaurant chain owner. Religion: Roman Catholic.
17 **Meek (D)** — April 29, 1926. Occupation: Educational administrator, teacher. Religion: Baptist.
18 **Ros-Lehtinen (R)** — July 15, 1952. Occupation: Teacher, private school administrator. Religion: Roman Catholic.
19 **Wexler (D)** — Jan. 2, 1961. Occupation: Lawyer. Religion: Jewish.
20 **Deutsch (D)** — April 1, 1957. Occupation: Lawyer, non-profit executive. Religion: Jewish.
21 **Diaz-Balart (R)** — Aug. 13, 1954. Occupation: Lawyer. Religion: Roman Catholic.

22 **Shaw (R)** — April 19, 1939. Occupation: Nurseryman, lawyer. Religion: Roman Catholic.

23 **Hastings (D)** — Sept. 5, 1936. Occupation: Lawyer. Religion: African Methodist Episcopal.

GEORGIA

1 **Kingston (R)** — April 24, 1955. Occupation: Insurance broker. Religion: Episcopalian.

2 **Bishop (D)** — Feb. 4, 1947. Occupation: Lawyer. Religion: Baptist.

3 **Collins (R)** — Oct. 15, 1944. Occupation: Trucking company owner. Religion: Methodist.

4 **McKinney (D)** — March 17, 1955. Occupation: Professor. Religion: Roman Catholic.

5 **Lewis (D)** — Feb. 21, 1940. Occupation: Civil rights activist. Religion: Baptist.

6 **Gingrich (R)** — June 17, 1943. Occupation: Professor. Religion: Baptist.

7 **Barr (R)** — Nov. 5, 1948. Occupation: Lawyer, CIA analyst. Religion: Methodist.

8 **Chambliss (R)** — Nov. 10, 1943. Occupation: Lawyer, hotel owner. Religion: Episcopalian.

9 **Deal (R)** — Aug. 25, 1942. Occupation: Lawyer. Religion: Baptist.

10 **Norwood (R)** — July 27, 1941. Occupation: Dentist. Religion: Methodist.

11 **Linder (R)** — Sept. 9, 1942. Occupation: Financial executive, dentist. Religion: Presbyterian.

HAWAII

1 **Abercrombie (D)** — June 26, 1938. Occupation: Educator. Religion: Unspecified.

2 **Mink (D)** — Dec. 6, 1927. Occupation: Lawyer. Religion: Protestant.

IDAHO

1 **Chenoweth (R)** — Jan. 27, 1938. Occupation: Public affairs and policy consultant, congressional aide. Religion: Christian.

2 **Crapo (R)** — May 20, 1951. Occupation: Lawyer. Religion: Mormon.

ILLINOIS

1 **Rush (D)** — Nov. 23, 1946. Occupation: Insurance broker, political aide. Religion: Protestant.

2 **Jackson (D)** — March 11, 1965. Occupation: Lawyer. Religion: Baptist.

3 **Lipinski (D)** — Dec. 22, 1937. Occupation: Parks supervisor. Religion: Roman Catholic.

4 **Gutierrez (D)** — Dec. 10, 1954. Occupation: Teacher, social worker. Religion: Roman Catholic.

5 **Blagojevich (D)** — Dec. 10, 1956. Occupation: Lawyer. Religion: Protestant.

6 **Hyde (R)** — April 18, 1924. Occupation: Lawyer. Religion: Roman Catholic.

7 **Davis (D)** — Sept. 6, 1941. Occupation: Healthcare consultant, teacher. Religion: Baptist.

8 **Crane (R)** — Nov. 3, 1930. Occupation: Professor, author, advertising executive. Religion: Protestant.

9 **Yates** (D) — Aug. 27, 1909. Occupation: Lawyer. Religion: Jewish.

10 **Porter (R)** — June 1, 1935. Occupation: Lawyer. Religion: Presbyterian.

11 **Weller (R)** — July 7, 1957. Occupation: Congressional aide, state and federal official, hog farmer, sales representative. Religion: Christian.

12 **Costello (D)** — Sept. 25, 1949. Occupation: Law enforcement official. Religion: Roman Catholic.

13 **Fawell (R)** — March 25, 1929. Occupation: Lawyer. Religion: Methodist.

14 **Hastert (R)** — Jan. 2, 1942. Occupation: Teacher, restaurateur. Religion: Protestant.

15 **Ewing (R)** — Sept. 19, 1935. Occupation: Lawyer. Religion: Methodist.

16 **Manzullo (R)** — March 24, 1944. Occupation: Lawyer. Religion: Baptist.

17 **Evans (D)** — Aug. 4, 1951. Occupation: Lawyer. Religion: Roman Catholic.

18 **LaHood (R)** — Dec. 6, 1945. Occupation: Congressional aide, teacher, youth bureau director, urban planning commission director. Religion: Roman Catholic.

19 **Poshard (D)** — Oct. 30, 1945. Occupation: Educator. Religion: Baptist.

20 **Shimkus (R)** — Feb. 21, 1958. Occupation: Teacher, Army officer. Religion: Lutheran.

INDIANA

1 **Visclosky (D)** — Aug. 13, 1949. Occupation: Lawyer. Religion: Roman Catholic.

2 **McIntosh (R)** — June 8, 1958. Occupation: Lawyer, White House aide, national security and public policy analyst. Religion: Episcopalian.

3 **Roemer (D)** — Oct. 30, 1956. Occupation: Congressional aide. Religion: Roman Catholic.

4 **Souder (R)** — July 18, 1950. Occupation: Congressional aide, general store owner. Religion: United Brethren in Christ.

5 **Buyer (R)** — Nov. 26, 1958. Occupation: Lawyer. Religion: Methodist.

6 **Burton (R)** — June 21, 1938. Occupation: Real estate and insurance agent. Religion: Protestant.

7 **Pease (R)** — May 22, 1951. Occupation: College administrator, lawyer. Religion: United Methodist.

8 **Hostettler (R)** — July 19, 1961. Occupation: Mechanical engineer. Religion: General Baptist.

9 **Hamilton (D)** — April 20, 1931. Occupation: Lawyer. Religion: Methodist.

10 **Carson (D)** — July 8, 1938. Occupation: Clothing store owner, human resource manager, congressional aide. Religion: Baptist.

IOWA

1 **Leach (R)** — Oct. 15, 1942. Occupation: Propane gas company executive, foreign service officer. Religion: Episcopalian.

2 **Nussle (R)** — June 27, 1960. Occupation: Lawyer. Religion: Lutheran.

3 **Boswell (D)** — Jan. 10, 1934. Occupation: Farmer. Religion: Reorganized Church of Jesus Christ of Latter Day Saints.

4 **Ganske (R)** — March 31, 1949. Occupation: Plastic surgeon. Religion: Roman Catholic.

5 **Latham (R)** — July 14, 1948. Occupation: Seed company executive, insurance agency marketing representative, insurance agent, bankteller. Religion: Lutheran.

KANSAS

1 **Moran (R)** — May 29, 1954. Occupation: Lawyer. Religion: Protestant.

2 **Ryun (R)** — April 29, 1947. Occupation: Motivational speaker, author, product consultant, olympic athlete. Religion: Presbyterian.

3 **Snowbarger (R)** — Sept. 16, 1949. Occupation: Lawyer, college instructor. Religion: Nazarene.

4 **Tiahrt (R)** — June 15, 1951. Occupation: College instructor, airline company manager. Religion: Assembly of God.

KENTUCKY

1 **Whitfield (R)** — May 25, 1943. Occupation: Lawyer, oil distributor, railroad executive. Religion: Presbyterian.

2 **Lewis (R)** — Sept. 14, 1946. Occupation: Bookstore owner, minister, public official. Religion: Baptist.

3 **Northup (R)** — Jan. 22, 1948. Occupation: Teacher. Religion: Roman Catholic.

4 **Bunning (R)** — Oct. 23, 1931. Occupation: Investment broker, sports agent, professional baseball player. Religion: Roman Catholic.

5 **Rogers (R)** — Dec. 31, 1937. Occupation: Lawyer. Religion: Baptist.
6 **Baesler (D)** — July 9, 1941. Occupation: Lawyer, farmer. Religion: Independent Christian.

LOUISIANA

1 **Livingston (R)** — April 30, 1943. Occupation: Lawyer. Religion: Episcopalian.
2 **Jefferson (D)** — March 14, 1947. Occupation: Lawyer. Religion: Baptist.
3 **Tauzin (R)** — June 14, 1943. Occupation: Lawyer. Religion: Roman Catholic.
4 **McCrery (R)** — Sept. 18, 1949. Occupation: Lawyer, congressional aide, government relations executive. Religion: Methodist.
5 **Cooksey (R)** — Aug. 20, 1941. Occupation: Physician. Religion: Methodist.
6 **Baker (R)** — May 22, 1948. Occupation: Real estate broker. Religion: Methodist.
7 **John (D)** — Jan. 5, 1960. Occupation: Transportation business owner. Religion: Roman Catholic.

MAINE

1 **Allen (D)** — April 16, 1945. Occupation: Policy consultant, lawyer, congressional aide. Religion: Protestant.
2 **Baldacci (D)** — Jan. 30, 1955. Occupation: Restaraunt owner. Religion: Roman Catholic.

MARYLAND

1 **Gilchrest (R)** — April 15, 1946. Occupation: High school teacher. Religion: Methodist.
2 **Ehrlich (R)** — Nov. 25, 1957. Occupation: Lawyer, football coach. Religion: Methodist.
3 **Cardin (D)** — Oct. 5, 1943. Occupation: Lawyer. Religion: Jewish.
4 **Wynn (D)** — Sept. 10, 1951. Occupation: Lawyer. Religion: Baptist.
5 **Hoyer (D)** — June 14, 1939. Occupation: Lawyer. Religion: Baptist.
6 **Bartlett (R)** — June 3, 1926. Occupation: Teacher, engineer. Religion: Seventh-Day Adventist.
7 **Cummings (D)** — Jan. 18, 1951. Occupation: Lawyer. Religion: Baptist.
8 **Morella (R)** — Feb. 12, 1931. Occupation: Professor. Religion: Roman Catholic.

MASSACHUSETTS

1 **Olver (D)** — Sept. 3, 1936. Occupation: Professor. Religion: Unspecified.
2 **Neal (D)** — Feb. 14, 1949. Occupation: Public official, college lecturer. Religion: Roman Catholic.
3 **McGovern (D)** — Nov. 20, 1959. Occupation: Congressional aide. Religion: Roman Catholic.
4 **Frank (D)** — March 31, 1940. Occupation: Lawyer. Religion: Jewish.
5 **Meehan (D)** — Dec. 30, 1956. Occupation: Lawyer. Religion: Roman Catholic.
6 **Tierney (D)** — Sept. 18, 1951. Occupation: Lawyer. Religion: Unspecified.
7 **Markey (D)** — July 11, 1946. Occupation: Lawyer. Religion: Roman Catholic.
8 **Kennedy (D)** — Sept. 24, 1952. Occupation: Energy company executive. Religion: Roman Catholic.
9 **Moakley (D)** — April 27, 1927. Occupation: Lawyer. Religion: Roman Catholic.
10 **Delahunt (D)** — July 18, 1941. Occupation: Lawyer. Religion: Roman Catholic.

MICHIGAN

1 **Stupak (D)** — Feb. 29, 1952. Occupation: Lawyer, state trooper, patrolman. Religion: Roman Catholic.
2 **Hoekstra (R)** — Oct. 30, 1953. Occupation: Furniture company executive. Religion: Christian Reformed Church.
3 **Ehlers (R)** — Feb. 6, 1934. Occupation: Professor, physicist. Religion: Christian Reformed Church.
4 **Camp (R)** — July 9, 1953. Occupation: Lawyer. Religion: Roman Catholic.
5 **Barcia (D)** — Feb. 25, 1952. Occupation: Congressional aide. Religion: Roman Catholic.
6 **Upton (R)** — April 23, 1953. Occupation: Congressional aide, budget analyst. Religion: Protestant.
7 **Smith (R)** — Nov. 5, 1934. Occupation: Dairy farmer. Religion: Congregationalist.
8 **Stabenow (D)** — April 29, 1950. Occupation: Leadership training consultant. Religion: United Methodist.
9 **Kildee (D)** — Sept. 16, 1929. Occupation: Teacher. Religion: Roman Catholic.
10 **Bonior (D)** — June 6, 1945. Occupation: Probation officer, adoption caseworker. Religion: Roman Catholic.
11 **Knollenberg (R)** — Nov. 28, 1933. Occupation: Insurance broker. Religion: Roman Catholic.
12 **Levin (D)** — Sept. 6, 1931. Occupation: Lawyer. Religion: Jewish.
13 **Rivers (D)** — Dec. 19, 1956. Occupation: Law clerk. Religion: Protestant.
14 **Conyers (D)** — May 16, 1929. Occupation: Lawyer. Religion: Baptist.
15 **Kilpatrick (D)** — June 25, 1945. Occupation: Teacher. Religion: Baptist.
16 **Dingell (D)** — July 8, 1926. Occupation: Lawyer. Religion: Roman Catholic.

MINNESOTA

1 **Gutknecht (R)** — March 20, 1951. Occupation: Real estate broker, school supplies salesman, auctioneer, computer software salesman. Religion: Roman Catholic.
2 **Minge (D)** — March 19, 1942. Occupation: Lawyer. Religion: Lutheran.
3 **Ramstad (R)** — May 6, 1946. Occupation: Lawyer, legislative aide. Religion: Protestant.
4 **Vento (D)** — Oct. 7, 1940. Occupation: Science teacher. Religion: Roman Catholic.
5 **Sabo (D)** — Feb. 28, 1938. Occupation: Public official. Religion: Lutheran.
6 **Luther (D)** — June 27, 1945. Occupation: Lawyer. Religion: Roman Catholic.
7 **Peterson (D)** — June 29, 1944. Occupation: Accountant. Religion: Lutheran.
8 **Oberstar (D)** — Sept. 10, 1934. Occupation: Language teacher, congressional aide. Religion: Roman Catholic.

MISSISSIPPI

1 **Wicker (R)** — July 5, 1951. Occupation: Lawyer, congressional aide. Religion: Southern Baptist.
2 **Thompson (D)** — Jan. 28, 1948. Occupation: Teacher. Religion: Methodist.
3 **Pickering (R)** — Aug. 10, 1963. Occupation: Congressional aide. Religion: Baptist.
4 **Parker (R)** — Oct. 31, 1949. Occupation: Funeral director. Religion: Presbyterian.
5 **Taylor (D)** — Sept. 17, 1953. Occupation: Sales representative. Religion: Roman Catholic.

MISSOURI

1 **Clay (D)** — April 30, 1931. Occupation: Real estate and insurance broker. Religion: Roman Catholic.
2 **Talent (R)** — Oct. 18, 1956. Occupation: Lawyer. Religion: Presbyterian.
3 **Gephardt (D)** — Jan. 31, 1941. Occupation: Lawyer. Religion: Baptist.
4 **Skelton (D)** — Dec. 20, 1931. Occupation: Lawyer. Religion: Christian Church.
5 **McCarthy (D)** — March 18, 1947. Occupation: Teacher. Religion: Roman Catholic.
6 **Danner (D)** — Jan. 13, 1934. Occupation: Congressional aide, federal official. Religion: Roman Catholic.

7 **Blunt (R)** — Jan. 10, 1950. Occupation: University president, teacher. Religion: Baptist.
8 **Emerson (R)** — Sept. 16, 1950. Occupation: Public affairs executive, lobbyist. Religion: Presbyterian.
9 **Hulshof (R)** — May 22, 1958. Occupation: Public defender, prosecuter, state assistant attorney general. Religion: Roman Catholic.

MONTANA

AL **Hill (R)** — Dec. 30, 1946. Occupation: Surety bonding and insurance company owner, insurance agent. Religion: Assembly of God.

NEBRASKA

1 **Bereuter (R)** — Oct. 6, 1939. Occupation: Urban planner, professor, state official. Religion: Lutheran.
2 **Christensen (R)** — Feb. 20, 1963. Occupation: Insurance agent, insurance marketing director, fertilizer holding company executive. Religion: Christian Missionary Alliance.
3 **Barrett (R)** — Feb. 9, 1929. Occupation: Real estate and insurance broker. Religion: Presbyterian.

NEVADA

1 **Ensign (R)** — March 25, 1958. Occupation: Veterinarian, casino manager. Religion: Christian.
2 **Gibbons (R)** — Dec. 16, 1944. Occupation: Airline pilot, lawyer, mining company owner, geologist. Religion: Protestant.

NEW HAMPSHIRE

1 **Sununu (R)** — Sept. 10, 1964. Occupation: Small business consultant, corporate financial officer, management consultant, design engineer. Religion: Roman Catholic.
2 **Bass (R)** — Jan. 8, 1952. Occupation: Congressional aide, architectural products executive. Religion: Episcopalian.

NEW JERSEY

1 **Andrews (D)** — Aug. 4, 1957. Occupation: Professor. Religion: Episcopalian.
2 **LoBiondo (R)** — May 12, 1946. Occupation: Trucking company operations manager. Religion: Roman Catholic.
3 **Saxton (R)** — Jan. 22, 1943. Occupation: Real estate broker, elementary school teacher. Religion: Methodist.
4 **Smith (R)** — March 4, 1953. Occupation: Sporting goods executive. Religion: Roman Catholic.
5 **Roukema (R)** — Sept. 19, 1929. Occupation: High school government and history teacher. Religion: Protestant.
6 **Pallone (D)** — Oct. 30, 1951. Occupation: Lawyer. Religion: Roman Catholic.
7 **Franks (R)** — Sept. 21, 1951. Occupation: Newspaper owner. Religion: Methodist.
8 **Pascrell (D)** — Jan. 27, 1937. Occupation: City official, teacher. Religion: Roman Catholic.
9 **Rothman (D)** — Oct. 14, 1952. Occupation: Lawyer. Religion: Jewish.
10 **Payne (D)** — July 16, 1934. Occupation: Community development executive. Religion: Baptist.
11 **Frelinghuysen (R)** — April 29, 1946. Occupation: Public official. Religion: Episcopalian.
12 **Pappas (R)** — Dec. 29, 1960. Occupation: Insurance agent. Religion: Christian.
13 **Menendez (D)** — Jan. 1, 1954. Occupation: Lawyer. Religion: Roman Catholic.

NEW MEXICO

1 **Schiff (R)** — March 18, 1947. Occupation: Lawyer. Religion: Jewish. S
2 **Skeen (R)** — June 30, 1927. Occupation: Sheep rancher, soil and water engineer, flying service operator. Religion: Roman Catholic.
3 **Redmond (R)** — Jan. 28, 1954. Occupation: Minister, teacher, businessman. Religion: Independent Christian.

NEW YORK

1 **Forbes (R)** — July 16, 1952. Occupation: Chamber of commerce manager. Religion: Roman Catholic.
2 **Lazio (R)** — March 13, 1958. Occupation: Lawyer. Religion: Roman Catholic.
3 **King (R)** — April 5, 1944. Occupation: Lawyer. Religion: Roman Catholic.
4 **McCarthy (D)** — Jan. 5, 1944. Occupation: Nurse. Religion: Roman Catholic.
5 **Ackerman (D)** — Nov. 19, 1942. Occupation: Teacher, publisher and editor, advertising executive. Religion: Jewish.
6 **Flake (D)** — Jan. 30, 1945. Occupation: Minister. Religion: African Methodist Episcopal.
7 **Manton (D)** — Nov. 3, 1932. Occupation: Lawyer. Religion: Roman Catholic.
8 **Nadler (D)** — June 13, 1947. Occupation: City official, lawyer. Religion: Jewish.
9 **Schumer (D)** — Nov. 23, 1950. Occupation: Lawyer. Religion: Jewish.
10 **Towns (D)** — July 21, 1934. Occupation: Professor, hospital administrator. Religion: Independent Baptist.
11 **Owens (D)** — June 28, 1936. Occupation: Librarian. Religion: Baptist.
12 **Velazquez (D)** — March 22, 1953. Occupation: Professor. Religion: Roman Catholic.
13 **Fossella (R)** — March 9, 1965. Occupation: Management consultant. Religion: Roman Catholic.
14 **Maloney (D)** — Feb. 19, 1948. Occupation: Legislative aide, teacher. Religion: Presbyterian.
15 **Rangel (D)** — June 11, 1930. Occupation: Lawyer. Religion: Roman Catholic.
16 **Serrano (D)** — Oct. 24, 1943. Occupation: Public official. Religion: Roman Catholic.
17 **Engel (D)** — Feb. 18, 1947. Occupation: Teacher; guidance counselor. Religion: Jewish.
18 **Lowey (D)** — July 5, 1937. Occupation: Public official. Religion: Jewish.
19 **Kelly (R)** — Sept. 26, 1936. Occupation: Professor; teacher, hospital administrative aide; medical researcher, retailer. Religion: Presbyterian.
20 **Gilman (R)** — Dec. 6, 1922. Occupation: Lawyer. Religion: Jewish.
21 **McNulty (D)** — Sept. 16, 1947. Occupation: Public official. Religion: Roman Catholic.
22 **Solomon (R)** — Aug. 14, 1930. Occupation: Insurance executive. Religion: Presbyterian.
23 **Boehlert (R)** — Sept. 28, 1936. Occupation: Congressional aide, public relations executive. Religion: Roman Catholic.
24 **McHugh (R)** — Sept. 29, 1948. Occupation: City official; legislative aide, insurance broker. Religion: Roman Catholic.
25 **Walsh (R)** — June 19, 1947. Occupation: Marketing executive, social worker. Religion: Roman Catholic.
26 **Hinchey (D)** — Oct. 27, 1938. Occupation: State employee. Religion: Roman Catholic.
27 **Paxon (R)** — April 29, 1954. Occupation: Public official. Religion: Roman Catholic.
28 **Slaughter (D)** — Aug. 14, 1929. Occupation: Market researcher, gubernatorial aide. Religion: Episcopalian.
29 **LaFalce (D)** — Oct. 6, 1939. Occupation: Lawyer. Religion: Roman Catholic.
30 **Quinn (R)** — April 13, 1951. Occupation: Teacher. Religion: Roman Catholic.
31 **Houghton (R)** — Aug. 7, 1926. Occupation: Glassworks company executive. Religion: Episcopalian.

NORTH CAROLINA

1 **Clayton (D)** — Sept. 16, 1934. Occupation: Consulting firm owner; nonprofit executive, state official, university official. Religion: Presbyterian.
2 **Etheridge (D)** — Aug. 7, 1941. Occupation: Hardware store owner, tobacco farmer. Religion: Presbyterian.
3 **Jones (R)** — Feb. 10, 1943. Occupation: Lighting company executive, insurance benefits company executive. Religion: Roman Catholic.

4 **Price (D)** — Aug. 17, 1940. Occupation: Professor. Religion: Baptist.
5 **Burr (R)** — Nov. 30, 1955. Occupation: Marketing manager. Religion: Presbyterian.
6 **Coble (R)** — March 18, 1931. Occupation: Lawyer, insurance claims supervisor. Religion: Presbyterian.
7 **McIntyre (D)** — Aug. 6, 1956. Occupation: Lawyer. Religion: Presbyterian.
8 **Hefner (D)** — April 11, 1930. Occupation: Broadcasting executive. Religion: Baptist.
9 **Myrick (R)** — Aug. 1, 1941. Occupation: Advertising executive. Religion: Evangelical Methodist.
10 **Ballenger (R)** — Dec. 6, 1926. Occupation: Plastics company executive. Religion: Episcopalian.
11 **Taylor (R)** — Jan. 23, 1941. Occupation: Tree farmer, banker. Religion: Baptist.
12 **Watt (D)** — Aug. 26, 1945. Occupation: Lawyer. Religion: Presbyterian.

NORTH DAKOTA

AL **Pomeroy (D)** — Sept. 2, 1952. Occupation: Lawyer. Religion: Presbyterian.

OHIO

1 **Chabot (R)** — Jan. 22, 1953. Occupation: Lawyer. Religion: Roman Catholic.
2 **Portman (R)** — Dec. 19, 1955. Occupation: Lawyer, White House aide; congressional aide. Religion: Methodist.
3 **Hall (D)** — Jan. 16, 1942. Occupation: Real estate broker. Religion: Presbyterian.
4 **Oxley (R)** — Feb. 11, 1944. Occupation: FBI agent, lawyer. Religion: Lutheran.
5 **Gillmor (R)** — Feb. 1, 1939. Occupation: Lawyer. Religion: Protestant.
6 **Strickland (D)** — Aug. 4, 1941. Occupation: Professor, psychologist. Religion: Methodist.
7 **Hobson (R)** — Oct. 17, 1936. Occupation: Financial executive. Religion: Methodist.
8 **Boehner (R)** — Nov. 17, 1949. Occupation: Plastics and packaging executive. Religion: Roman Catholic.
9 **Kaptur (D)** — June 17, 1946. Occupation: Urban planner; White House aide. Religion: Roman Catholic.
10 **Kucinich (D)** — Oct. 8, 1946. Occupation: Video producer, public power consultant. Religion: Roman Catholic.
11 **Stokes (D)** — Feb. 23, 1925. Occupation: Lawyer. Religion: African Methodist Episcopal Zion.
12 **Kasich (R)** — May 13, 1952. Occupation: Legislative aide. Religion: Christian.
13 **Brown (D)** — Nov. 9, 1952. Occupation: Teacher. Religion: Lutheran.
14 **Sawyer (D)** — Aug. 15, 1945. Occupation: Teacher. Religion: Presbyterian.
15 **Pryce (R)** — July 29, 1951. Occupation: Judge; lawyer. Religion: Presbyterian.
16 **Regula (R)** — Dec. 3, 1924. Occupation: Lawyer, businessman. Religion: Episcopalian.
17 **Traficant (D)** — May 8, 1941. Occupation: County drug program director, sheriff. Religion: Roman Catholic.
18 **Ney (R)** — July 5, 1954. Occupation: State health and education program manager, local safety director, educator. Religion: Roman Catholic.
19 **LaTourette (R)** — July 22, 1954. Occupation: Lawyer. Religion: Methodist.

OKLAHOMA

1 **Largent (R)** — Sept. 28, 1955. Occupation: Marketing consultant, professional football player. Religion: Protestant.
2 **Coburn (R)** — March 14, 1948. Occupation: Physician, optical firm manager. Religion: Baptist.
3 **Watkins (R)** — Dec. 15, 1938. Occupation: Communications executive, homebuilding contractor, economic developer. Religion: Presbyterian.
4 **Watts (R)** — Nov. 18, 1957. Occupation: Property management company owner, professional football player. Religion: Southern Baptist.
5 **Istook (R)** — Feb. 11, 1950. Occupation: Lawyer. Religion: Mormon.
6 **Lucas (R)** — Jan. 6, 1960. Occupation: Farmer; rancher. Religion: Baptist.

OREGON

1 **Furse (D)** — Oct. 13, 1936. Occupation: Community activist. Religion: Protestant.
2 **Smith (R)** — June 16, 1931. Occupation: Public relations firm owner, cattle rancher, businessman. Religion: Presbyterian.
3 **Blumenauer (D)** — Aug. 16, 1949. Occupation: Lawyer, public official. Religion: Unspecified.
4 **DeFazio (D)** — May 27, 1947. Occupation: Congressional aide. Religion: Roman Catholic.
5 **Hooley (D)** — April 4, 1939. Occupation: Teacher. Religion: Lutheran.

PENNSYLVANIA

1 **Vacant** — Foglietta (D) resigned Nov. 11, 1997.
2 **Fattah (D)** — Nov. 21, 1956. Occupation: Public official. Religion: Baptist.
3 **Borski (D)** — Oct. 20, 1948. Occupation: Stockbroker. Religion: Roman Catholic.
4 **Klink (D)** — Sept. 23, 1951. Occupation: Television journalist. Religion: United Church of Christ.
5 **Peterson (R)** — Dec. 25, 1938. Occupation: Supermarket owner. Religion: Methodist.
6 **Holden (D)** — March 5, 1957. Occupation: Sheriff. Religion: Roman Catholic.
7 **Weldon (R)** — July 22, 1947. Occupation: Teacher, consultant. Religion: Protestant.
8 **Greenwood (R)** — May 4, 1951. Occupation: State official. Religion: Presbyterian.
9 **Shuster (R)** — Jan. 23, 1932. Occupation: Computer industry executive. Religion: United Church of Christ.
10 **McDade (R)** — Sept. 29, 1931. Occupation: Lawyer. Religion: Roman Catholic.
11 **Kanjorski (D)** — April 2, 1937. Occupation: Lawyer. Religion: Roman Catholic.
12 **Murtha (D)** — June 17, 1932. Occupation: Car wash owner and operator. Religion: Roman Catholic.
13 **Fox (R)** — April 22, 1947. Occupation: Lawyer. Religion: Jewish.
14 **Coyne (D)** — Aug. 24, 1936. Occupation: Accountant. Religion: Roman Catholic.
15 **McHale (D)** — July 26, 1950. Occupation: Lawyer, adjunct professor. Religion: Roman Catholic.
16 **Pitts (R)** — Oct. 10, 1939. Occupation: Nursery owner, teacher. Religion: Protestant.
17 **Gekas (R)** — April 14, 1930. Occupation: Lawyer. Religion: Greek Orthodox.
18 **Doyle (D)** — Aug. 5, 1953. Occupation: Insurance company executive, state legislative aide. Religion: Roman Catholic.
19 **Goodling (R)** — Dec. 5, 1927. Occupation: Public school superintendent. Religion: Methodist.
20 **Mascara (D)** — Jan. 19, 1930. Occupation: Accountant. Religion: Roman Catholic.
21 **English (R)** — June 20, 1956. Occupation: State legislative aide. Religion: Roman Catholic.

RHODE ISLAND

1 **Kennedy (D)** — July 14, 1967. Occupation: Public official. Religion: Roman Catholic.
2 **Weygand (D)** — May 10, 1948. Occupation: Landscape architect, architectural firm executive. Religion: Roman Catholic.

SOUTH CAROLINA

1 **Sanford (R)** — May 28, 1960. Occupation: Real estate investor, investment banker. Religion: Episcopalian.
2 **Spence (R)** — April 9, 1928. Occupation: Lawyer. Religion: Lutheran.
3 **Graham (R)** — July 9, 1955. Occupation: Lawyer. Religion: Southern Baptist.
4 **Inglis (R)** — Oct. 11, 1959. Occupation: Lawyer. Religion: Presbyterian.
5 **Spratt (D)** — Nov. 1, 1942. Occupation: Lawyer. Religion: Presbyterian.
6 **Clyburn (D)** — July 21, 1940. Occupation: State official. Religion: African Methodist Episcopal.

SOUTH DAKOTA

AL **Thune (R)** — Jan. 7, 1961. Occupation: Municipal league executive, congressional aide. Religion: Protestant.

TENNESSEE

1 **Jenkins (R)** — Nov. 29, 1936. Occupation: Lawyer, farmer. Religion: Baptist.
2 **Duncan (R)** — July 21, 1947. Occupation: Judge; lawyer. Religion: Presbyterian.
3 **Wamp (R)** — Oct. 28, 1957. Occupation: Real estate broker. Religion: Baptist.
4 **Hilleary (R)** — June 20, 1959. Occupation: Textile industry executive. Religion: Presbyterian.
5 **Clement (D)** — Sept. 23, 1943. Occupation: College president, marketing, management and real estate executive. Religion: Methodist.
6 **Gordon (D)** — Jan. 24, 1949. Occupation: Lawyer. Religion: Methodist.
7 **Bryant (R)** — Sept. 7, 1948. Occupation: Lawyer. Religion: Protestant.
8 **Tanner (D)** — Sept. 22, 1944. Occupation: Lawyer, businessman. Religion: Disciples of Christ.
9 **Ford (D)** — May 11, 1970. Occupation: Law clerk. Religion: Baptist.

TEXAS

1 **Sandlin (D)** — Sept. 29, 1952. Occupation: Lawyer, county judge, fuel company executive. Religion: Baptist.
2 **Turner (D)** — Feb. 6, 1946. Occupation: Lawyer. Religion: Baptist.
3 **Johnson (R)** — Oct. 11, 1930. Occupation: Home builder. Religion: Methodist.
4 **Hall (D)** — May 3, 1923. Occupation: Lawyer, businessman. Religion: Methodist.
5 **Sessions (R)** — March 22, 1955. Occupation: Public policy analyst, phone company executive. Religion: United Methodist. .
6 **Barton (R)** — Sept. 15, 1949. Occupation: Engineering consultant. Religion: Methodist.
7 **Archer (R)** — March 22, 1928. Occupation: Lawyer, feed company executive. Religion: Roman Catholic.
8 **Brady (R)** — April 7, 1955. Occupation: Chamber of commerce executive. Religion: Roman Catholic.
9 **Lampson (D)** — Feb. 14, 1945. Occupation: Teacher, tax assessor. Religion: Roman Catholic.
10 **Doggett (D)** — Oct. 6, 1946. Occupation: Lawyer. Religion: Methodist.
11 **Edwards (D)** — Nov. 24, 1951. Occupation: Radio station executive. Religion: Methodist.
12 **Granger (R)** — Jan. 18, 1943. Occupation: Insurance agent. Religion: Methodist.
13 **Thornberry (R)** — July 15, 1958. Occupation: Lawyer, cattleman, State Department official, congressional aide. Religion: Presbyterian.
14 **Paul (R)** — Aug. 20, 1935. Occupation: Physician. Religion: Protestant.
15 **Hinojosa (D)** — Aug. 20, 1940. Occupation: Food processing executive. Religion: Roman Catholic.
16 **Reyes (D)** — Nov. 10, 1944. Occupation: U.S. Border Patrol agent. Religion: Roman Catholic.
17 **Stenholm (D)** — Oct. 26, 1938. Occupation: Cotton farmer. Religion: Lutheran.
18 **Jackson-Lee (D)** — Jan. 12, 1950. Occupation: Lawyer, congressional aide. Religion: Seventh-Day Adventist. Seniority: 148.
19 **Combest (R)** — March 20, 1945. Occupation: Farmer, congressional aide, electronics wholesaler. Religion: Methodist.
20 **Gonzalez (D)** — May 3, 1916. Occupation: Teacher, public relations consultant; translator. Religion: Roman Catholic.
21 **Smith (R)** — Nov. 19, 1947. Occupation: Lawyer, rancher. Religion: Christian Scientist.
22 **DeLay (R)** — April 8, 1947. Occupation: Pest control executive. Religion: Baptist.
23 **Bonilla (R)** — Jan. 2, 1954. Occupation: Television executive. Religion: Baptist.
24 **Frost (D)** — Jan. 1, 1942. Occupation: Lawyer. Religion: Jewish.
25 **Bentsen (D)** — June 3, 1959. Occupation: Investment banker, congressional aide. Religion: Presbyterian.
26 **Armey (R)** — July 7, 1940. Occupation: Economist. Religion: Presbyterian.
27 **Ortiz (D)** — June 3, 1937. Occupation: Law enforcement official. Religion: Methodist.
28 **Rodriquez (D)** — Dec. 9, 1946. Occupation: Legislator, educator, social worker. Religion: Roman Catholic.
29 **Green (D)** — Oct. 17, 1947. Occupation: Lawyer. Religion: Methodist.
30 **Johnson (D)** — Dec. 3, 1935. Occupation: Airport shop owner. Religion: Baptist.

UTAH

1 **Hansen (R)** — Aug. 14, 1932. Occupation: Insurance executive, developer. Religion: Mormon.
2 **Cook (R)** — May 6, 1946. Occupation: Explosives company executive, radio talk show host, management consultant. Religion: Mormon.
3 **Cannon (R)** — Oct. 20, 1950. Occupation: Venture capital executive, steel company executive, lawyer. Religion: Mormon.

VERMONT

AL **Sanders (I)** — Sept. 8, 1941. Occupation: Professor, free-lance writer. Religion: Jewish.

VIRGINIA

1 **Bateman (R)** — Aug. 7, 1928. Occupation: Lawyer. Religion: Protestant.
2 **Pickett (D)** — Aug. 31, 1930. Occupation: Lawyer, accountant. Religion: Baptist.
3 **Scott (D)** — April 30, 1947. Occupation: Lawyer. Religion: Episcopalian.
4 **Sisisky (D)** — June 9, 1927. Occupation: Beer and soft drink distributor. Religion: Jewish.
5 **Goode (D)** — Oct. 17, 1946. Occupation: Lawyer. Religion: Baptist.
6 **Goodlatte (R)** — Sept. 22, 1952. Occupation: Lawyer, congressional aide. Religion: Christian Scientist.
7 **Bliley (R)** — Jan. 28, 1932. Occupation: Funeral director. Religion: Roman Catholic.
8 **Moran (D)** — May 16, 1945. Occupation: Investment banker. Religion: Roman Catholic.
9 **Boucher (D)** — Aug. 1, 1946. Occupation: Lawyer. Religion: Methodist.
10 **Wolf (R)** — Jan. 30, 1939. Occupation: Lawyer. Religion: Presbyterian.
11 **Davis (R)** — Jan. 5, 1949. Occupation: Lawyer, professional services firm executive, state legislative aide. Religion: Christian Scientist.

WASHINGTON

1 **White (R)** — Nov. 6, 1953. Occupation: Lawyer, law clerk. Religion: Presbyterian.
2 **Metcalf (R)** — Nov. 30, 1927. Occupation: Teacher, bed and breakfast owner. Religion: Christian.
3 **Smith (R)** — July 16, 1950. Occupation: Tax preparation centers manager, tax consultant. Religion: Assembly of God.
4 **Hastings (R)** — Feb. 7, 1941. Occupation: Paper company executive. Religion: Roman Catholic.
5 **Nethercutt (R)** — Oct. 7, 1944. Occupation: Lawyer, congressional aide. Religion: Protestant.
6 **Dicks (D)** — Dec. 16, 1940. Occupation: Congressional aide. Religion: Lutheran.
7 **McDermott (D)** — Dec. 28, 1936. Occupation: Psychiatrist. Religion: Episcopalian.
8 **Dunn (R)** — July 29, 1941. Occupation: State party official. Religion: Episcopalian.
9 **Smith (D)** — June 15, 1965. Occupation: City prosecutor, lawyer. Religion: Christian.

WEST VIRGINIA

1 **Mollohan (D)** — May 14, 1943. Occupation: Lawyer. Religion: Baptist.
2 **Wise (D)** — Jan. 6, 1948. Occupation: Lawyer. Religion: Episcopalian.
3 **Rahall (D)** — May 20, 1949. Occupation: Broadcasting executive; travel agent. Religion: Presbyterian.

WISCONSIN

1 **Neumann (R)** — Feb. 27, 1954. Occupation: Home builder; real estate broker, teacher. Religion: Lutheran.
2 **Klug (R)** — Jan. 16, 1953. Occupation: Television journalist, business development and investment executive. Religion: Roman Catholic.
3 **Kind (D)** — March 16, 1963. Occupation: Lawyer. Religion: Lutheran.
4 **Kleczka (D)** — Nov. 26, 1943. Occupation: Accountant. Religion: Roman Catholic.
5 **Barrett (D)** — Dec. 8, 1953. Occupation: Lawyer. Religion: Roman Catholic.
6 **Petri (R)** — May 28, 1940. Occupation: Lawyer. Religion: Lutheran.
7 **Obey (D)** — Oct. 3, 1938. Occupation: Real estate broker. Religion: Roman Catholic.
8 **Johnson (D)** — Sept. 30, 1943. Occupation: Broadcast journalist. Religion: Presbyterian.
9 **Sensenbrenner (R)** — June 14, 1943. Occupation: Lawyer. Religion: Episcopalian.

WYOMING

AL **Cubin (R)** — Nov. 30, 1946. Occupation: Medical office manager, real estate agent, chemist. Religion: Episcopalian.

Seniority in the Senate

(As of Nov. 13, 1997, when the first session of the 105th Congress adjourned sine die.)

New committee assignments are made by order of seniority, as determined by the parties. Senate rank generally is determined by the official date service began. When a senator is appointed or elected to fill an unexpired term, the appointment, certification or swearing-in date determines rank. The parties have rules to set seniority for those sworn in on the same date. Generally, they rank prior Senate service first, followed by House and gubernatorial service. The GOP breaks ties by drawing lots; Democrats, by state population. Dates following senators' names refer to the beginning of their current service.

Republicans

1. Thurmond[1] — Nov. 7, 1956
2. Stevens — Dec. 24, 1968
3. Roth — Jan. 1, 1971
4. Domenici — Jan. 3, 1973
5. Helms — Jan. 3, 1973
6. Chafee (ex-governor) — Dec. 29, 1976
7. Hatch — Jan. 3, 1977
8. Lugar — Jan. 3, 1977
9. Cochran — Dec. 27, 1978
10. Warner — Jan. 2, 1979
11. Grassley (ex-representative, three House terms) — Jan. 3, 1981
12. D'Amato — Jan. 3, 1981
13. Murkowski — Jan. 3, 1981
14. Nickles — Jan. 3, 1981
15. Specter — Jan. 3, 1981
16. Gramm (ex-representative, three House terms) — Jan. 3, 1985
17. McConnell — Jan. 3, 1985
18. Shelby (ex-representative, four House terms)[2] — Jan. 6, 1987
19. McCain (ex-representative, two House terms) — Jan. 6, 1987
20. Bond (ex-governor) — Jan. 6, 1987
21. Gorton (ex-senator) — Jan. 3, 1989
22. Lott (ex-representative, eight House terms) — Jan. 3, 1989
23. Jeffords (ex-representative, seven House terms) — Jan. 3, 1989
24. Coats (ex-representative, four House terms) — Jan. 3, 1989
25. Mack (ex-representative, three House terms) — Jan. 3, 1989
26. Burns — Jan. 3, 1989
27. Craig (ex-representative, five House terms) — Jan. 3, 1991
28. Smith (ex-representative, three House terms) — Jan. 3, 1991
29. Gregg (ex-representative, four House terms, ex-governor) — Jan. 5, 1993
30. Campbell[3] (ex-representative, three House terms) — Jan. 5, 1993
31. Faircloth — Jan. 5, 1993
32. Bennett — Jan. 5, 1993
33. Kempthorne — Jan. 5, 1993
34. Coverdell — Jan. 5, 1993
35. Hutchison — June 14, 1993
36. Inhofe — Nov. 17, 1994
37. Thompson — Dec. 9, 1994
38. Snowe (ex-representative, eight House terms) — Jan. 4, 1995
39. Kyl (ex-representative, four House terms) — Jan. 4, 1995
40. DeWine (ex-representative, four House terms) — Jan. 4, 1995
41. Thomas (ex-representative, three House terms) — Jan. 4, 1995
42. Santorum (ex-representative, two House terms) — Jan. 4, 1995
43. Grams (ex-representative, one House term) — Jan. 4, 1995
44. Ashcroft (ex-governor) — Jan. 4, 1995
45. Frist — Jan. 4, 1995
46. Abraham — Jan. 4, 1995
47. Brownback (ex-representative, one House term) — Nov. 27, 1996
48. Roberts (ex-representative, eight House terms) — Jan. 7, 1997
49. Allard (ex-representative, three House terms) — Jan. 7, 1997
50. Hutchinson (ex-representative, two House terms) — Jan. 7, 1997
51. Collins — Jan. 7, 1997
52. Hagel — Jan. 7, 1997
53. Enzi — Jan. 7, 1997
54. Sessions — Jan. 7, 1997
55. Smith[4] — Jan. 7, 1997

Democrats

1. Byrd — Jan. 3, 1959
2. Kennedy — Nov. 7, 1962
3. Inouye — Jan. 3, 1963
4. Hollings — Nov. 9, 1966
5. Biden — Jan. 3, 1973
6. Glenn — Dec. 24, 1974
7. Ford — Dec. 28, 1974
8. Bumpers (ex-governor) — Jan. 3, 1975
9. Leahy — Jan. 3, 1975
10. Sarbanes (ex-representative, three House terms) — Jan. 3, 1977
11. Moynihan — Jan. 3, 1977
12. Baucus — Dec. 15, 1978
13. Levin — Jan. 3, 1979
14. Dodd — Jan. 3, 1981
15. Lautenberg — Dec. 27, 1982
16. Bingaman — Jan. 3, 1983
17. Kerry — Jan. 2, 1985
18. Harkin — Jan. 3, 1985
19. Rockefeller — Jan. 15, 1985
20. Breaux (ex-representative, eight House terms) — Jan. 6, 1987
21. Mikulski (ex-representative, five House terms) — Jan. 6, 1987
22. Daschle (ex-representative, four House terms) — Jan. 6, 1987
23. Reid (ex-representative, two House terms) — Jan. 6, 1987
24. Graham (ex-governor) — Jan. 6, 1987
25. Conrad — Jan. 6, 1987
26. Bryan (ex-governor) — Jan. 3, 1989
27. Robb (ex-governor) — Jan. 3, 1989
28. Kerrey (ex-governor) — Jan. 3, 1989
29. Kohl — Jan. 3, 1989
30. Lieberman — Jan. 3, 1989
31. Akaka — May 16, 1990
32. Wellstone — Jan. 3, 1991
33. Feinstein — Nov. 10, 1992
34. Dorgan — Dec. 15, 1992
35. Boxer (ex-representative, five House terms) — Jan. 5, 1993
36. Moseley-Braun — Jan. 5, 1993
37. Murray — Jan. 5, 1993
38. Feingold — Jan. 5, 1993
39. Wyden — Feb. 5, 1996
40. Durbin (ex-representative, seven House terms) — Jan. 7, 1997
41. Torricelli (ex-representative, seven House terms) — Jan. 7, 1997
42. Johnson (ex-representative, five House terms) — Jan. 7, 1997
43. Reed (ex-representative, three House terms) — Jan. 7, 1997
44. Cleland — Jan. 7, 1997
45. Landrieu — Jan. 7, 1997

[1] *Thurmond began his Senate service Nov. 7, 1956, as a Democrat. He switched parties Sept. 16, 1964. The GOP allowed his seniority to count from 1956.*
[2] *Shelby began Senate service Jan. 6, 1987, as a Democrat. He switched parties Nov. 9, 1994. The GOP allowed his seniority to count from 1987 and credited his House service as a Democrat.*
[3] *Campbell began Senate service Jan. 5, 1993, as a Democrat. He switched parties March 3, 1995. The GOP allowed his seniority to count from 1993 and credited his House service as a Democrat.*
[4] *The GOP did not give Robert C. Smith of New Hampshire credit for his service in 1990 because his predecessor stepped down voluntarily.*

Seniority in the House

(As of Nov. 13, 1997, when the first session of the 105th Congress adjourned sine die.)

For making committee assignments, both parties use the seniority system, although with slightly different rules.

House rank generally is determined according to the official date that the member began service, except when the members were elected to fill vacancies, in which instance the date of election determines rank.

For members who previously served in the House, the Republican Conference awards credit for the amount of time served. Democrats put such members at the head of the class for that year, starting with those with the longest consecutive service. However, they do not assign numbers. Unlike in the Senate, no credit is given for prior service as a senator or governor.

In the following list, the dates after members' names refer to the beginning of their current service (although the Republican Conference uses the date a Congress began, rather than the date of swearing-in).

Members designated with an asterisk * began service as Democrats, but later switched parties. The Republican Conference permitted their seniority to count from when they began service.

Republicans

1. McDade (Pa.) — Jan. 9, 1963
2. Crane (Ill.) — Nov. 25, 1969
3. Archer (Texas) — Jan. 21, 1971
4. Spence (S.C.) — Jan. 21, 1971
5. Young (Fla.) — Jan. 21, 1971
6. Gilman (N.Y.) — Jan. 3, 1973
7. Regula (Ohio) — Jan. 3, 1973
8. Shuster (Pa.) — Jan. 3, 1973
9. Young (Alaska) — March 6, 1973
10. Goodling (Pa.) — Jan. 14, 1975
11. Hyde (Ill.) — Jan. 14, 1975
12. Leach (Iowa) — Jan. 4, 1977
13. Stump (Ariz.) — Jan. 4, 1977 *
14. Livingston (La.) — Aug. 27, 1977
15. Bereuter (Neb.) — Jan. 15, 1979
16. Gingrich (Ga.) — Jan. 15, 1979
17. Lewis (Calif.) — Jan. 15, 1979
18. Sensenbrenner (Wis.) — Jan. 15, 1979
19. Solomon (N.Y.) — Jan. 15, 1979
20. Thomas (Calif.) — Jan. 15, 1979
21. Petri (Wis.) — April 3, 1979
22. Porter (Ill.) — Jan. 22, 1980
23. Tauzin (La.) — May 17, 1980 *
24. Bliley (Va.) — Jan. 5, 1981
25. Dreier (Calif.) — Jan. 5, 1981
26. Hansen (Utah) — Jan. 5, 1981
27. Hunter (Calif.) — Jan. 5, 1981
28. McCollum (Fla.) — Jan. 5, 1981
29. Rogers (Ky.) — Jan. 5, 1981
30. Roukema (N.J.) — Jan. 5, 1981
31. Shaw (Fla.) — Jan. 5, 1981
32. Skeen (N.M.) — Jan. 5, 1981
33. Smith (N.J.) — Jan. 5, 1981
34. Wolf (Va.) — Jan. 5, 1981
35. Oxley (Ohio) — June 25, 1981
36. Bateman (Va.) — Jan. 3, 1983
37. Bilirakis (Fla.) — Jan. 3, 1983
38. Boehlert (N.Y.) — Jan. 3, 1983
39. Burton (Ind.) — Jan. 3, 1983
40. Gekas (Pa.) — Jan. 3, 1983
41. Johnson (Conn.) — Jan. 3, 1983
42. Kasich (Ohio) — Jan. 3, 1983
43. Packard (Calif.) — Jan. 3, 1983
44. Schaefer (Colo.) — March 29, 1983
45. Saxton (N.J.) — Nov. 6, 1984
46. Watkins (Okla.) — (seven terms previously) — Jan. 7, 1997
47. Armey (Texas) — Jan. 3, 1985
48. Barton (Texas) — Jan. 3, 1985
49. Callahan (Ala.) — Jan. 3, 1985
50. Coble (N.C.) — Jan. 3, 1985
51. Combest (Texas) — Jan. 3, 1985
52. DeLay (Texas) — Jan. 3, 1985
53. Fawell (Ill.) — Jan. 3, 1985
54. Kolbe (Ariz.) — Jan. 3, 1985
55. Ballenger (N.C.) — Nov. 4, 1986
56. Smith (Ore.) — (six terms previously) — Jan. 7, 1997
57. Baker (La.) — Jan. 6, 1987
58. Bunning (Ky.) — Jan. 6, 1987
59. Gallegly (Calif.) — Jan. 6, 1987
60. Hastert (Ill.) — Jan. 6, 1987
61. Hefley (Colo.) — Jan. 6, 1987
62. Herger (Calif.) — Jan. 6, 1987
63. Houghton (N.Y.) — Jan. 6, 1987
64. Morella (Md.) — Jan. 6, 1987
65. Smith (Texas) — Jan. 6, 1987
66. Upton (Mich.) — Jan. 6, 1987
67. Weldon (Pa.) — Jan. 6, 1987
68. Shays (Conn.) — Aug. 18, 1987
69. McCrery (La.) — April 16, 1988
70. Duncan (Tenn.) — Nov. 9, 1988
71. Cox (Calif.) — Jan. 3, 1989
72. Gillmor (Ohio) — Jan. 3, 1989
73. Goss (Fla.) — Jan. 3, 1989
74. Parker (Miss.) — Jan. 3, 1989 *
75. Paxon (N.Y.) — Jan. 3, 1989
76. Rohrabacher (Calif.) — Jan. 3, 1989
77. Schiff (N.M.) — Jan. 3, 1989
78. Stearns (Fla.) — Jan. 3, 1989
79. Walsh (N.Y.) — Jan. 3, 1989
80. Ros-Lehtinen (Fla.) — Aug. 29, 1989
81. Paul (Texas) — (four terms previously) — Jan. 7, 1997
82. Barrett (Neb.) — Jan. 3, 1991
83. Boehner (Ohio) — Jan. 3, 1991
84. Camp (Mich.) — Jan. 3, 1991
85. Cunningham (Calif.) — Jan. 3, 1991
86. Doolittle (Calif.) — Jan. 3, 1991
87. Gilchrest (Md.) — Jan. 3, 1991
88. Hobson (Ohio) — Jan. 3, 1991
89. Klug (Wis.) — Jan. 3, 1991
90. Nussle (Iowa) — Jan. 3, 1991
91. Ramstad (Minn.) — Jan. 3, 1991
92. Taylor (N.C.) — Jan. 3, 1991
93. Johnson (Texas) — May 18, 1991
94. Ewing (Ill.) — July 2, 1991
95. Campbell (Calif.) (prior service 1989-93) — Dec. 12, 1995
96. Bachus (Ala.) — Jan. 5, 1993
97. Bartlett (Md.) — Jan. 5, 1993
98. Bonilla (Texas) — Jan. 5, 1993
99. Buyer (Ind.) — Jan. 5, 1993
100. Calvert (Calif.) — Jan. 5, 1993
101. Canady (Fla.) — Jan. 5, 1993
102. Castle (Del.) — Jan. 5, 1993
103. Collins (Ga.) — Jan. 5, 1993
104. Crapo (Idaho) — Jan. 5, 1993
105. Deal (Ga.) — Jan. 5, 1993 *
106. Diaz-Balart (Fla.) — Jan. 5, 1993
107. Dickey (Ark.) — Jan. 5, 1993
108. Dunn (Wash.) — Jan. 5, 1993
109. Everett (Ala.) — Jan. 5, 1993
110. Fowler (Fla.) — Jan. 5, 1993
111. Franks (N.J.) — Jan. 5, 1993
112. Goodlatte (Va.) — Jan. 5, 1993
113. Greenwood (Pa.) — Jan. 5, 1993
114. Hoekstra (Mich.) — Jan. 5, 1993
115. Horn (Calif.) — Jan. 5, 1993
116. Inglis (S.C.) — Jan. 5, 1993
117. Istook (Okla.) — Jan. 5, 1993
118. Kim (Calif.) — Jan. 5, 1993
119. King (N.Y.) — Jan. 5, 1993
120. Kingston (Ga.) — Jan. 5, 1993
121. Knollenberg (Mich.) — Jan. 5, 1993
122. Lazio (N.Y.) — Jan. 5, 1993
123. Linder (Ga.) — Jan. 5, 1993
124. McHugh (N.Y.) — Jan. 5, 1993
125. McInnis (Colo.) — Jan. 5, 1993
126. McKeon (Calif.) — Jan. 5, 1993
127. Manzullo (Ill.) — Jan. 5, 1993
128. Mica (Fla.) — Jan. 5, 1993
129. Miller (Fla.) — Jan. 5, 1993
130. Pombo (Calif.) — Jan. 5, 1993
131. Pryce (Ohio) — Jan. 5, 1993
132. Quinn (N.Y.) — Jan. 5, 1993
133. Royce (Calif.) — Jan. 5, 1993

134. Smith (Mich.) — Jan. 5, 1993
135. Talent (Mo.) — Jan. 5, 1993
136. Portman (Ohio) — May 4, 1993
137. Ehlers (Mich.) — Dec. 8, 1993
138. Lucas (Okla.) — May 10, 1994
139. Lewis (Ky.) — May 24, 1994
140. Largent (Okla.) — Nov. 29, 1994
141. Riggs (Calif.) (one term previously) — Jan. 4, 1995
142. Barr (Ga.) — Jan. 4, 1995
143. Bass (N.H.) — Jan. 4, 1995
144. Bilbray (Calif.) — Jan. 4, 1995
145. Bono (Calif.) — Jan. 4, 1995
146. Bryant (Tenn.) — Jan. 4, 1995
147. Burr (N.C.) — Jan. 4, 1995
148. Chabot (Ohio) — Jan. 4, 1995
149. Chambliss (Ga.) — Jan. 4, 1995
150. Chenoweth (Idaho) — Jan. 4, 1995
151. Christensen (Neb.) — Jan. 4, 1995
152. Coburn (Okla.) — Jan. 4, 1995
153. Cubin (Wyo.) — Jan. 4, 1995
154. Davis (Va.) — Jan. 4, 1995
155. Ehrlich (Md.) — Jan. 4, 1995
156. English (Pa.) — Jan. 4, 1995
157. Ensign (Nev.) — Jan. 4, 1995
158. Foley (Fla.) — Jan. 4, 1995
159. Forbes (N.Y.) — Jan. 4, 1995
160. Fox (Pa.) — Jan. 4, 1995
161. Frelinghuysen (N.J.) — Jan. 4, 1995
162. Ganske (Iowa) — Jan. 4, 1995
163. Graham (S.C.) — Jan. 4, 1995
164. Gutknecht (Minn.) — Jan. 4, 1995
165. Hastings (Wash.) — Jan. 4, 1995
166. Hayworth (Ariz.) — Jan. 4, 1995
167. Hilleary (Tenn.) — Jan. 4, 1995
168. Hostettler (Ind.) — Jan. 4, 1995
169. Jones (N.C.) — Jan. 4, 1995
170. Kelly (N.Y.) — Jan. 4, 1995
171. LaHood (Ill.) — Jan. 4, 1995
172. LaTourette (Ohio) — Jan. 4, 1994
173. Latham (Iowa) — Jan. 4, 1995
174. LoBiondo (N.J.) — Jan. 4, 1995
175. McIntosh (Ind.) — Jan. 4, 1995
176. Metcalf (Wash.) — Jan. 4, 1995
177. Myrick (N.C.) — Jan. 4, 1995
178. Nethercutt (Wash.) — Jan. 4, 1995
179. Neumann (Wis.) — Jan. 4, 1995
180. Ney (Ohio) — Jan. 4, 1995
181. Norwood (Ga.) — Jan. 4, 1995
182. Radanovich (Calif.) — Jan. 4, 1995
183. Salmon (Ariz.) — Jan. 4, 1995
184. Sanford (S.C.) — Jan. 4, 1995
185. Scarborough (Fla.) — Jan. 4, 1995
186. Shadegg (Ariz.) — Jan. 4, 1995
187. Smith (Wash.) — Jan. 4, 1995
188. Souder (Ind.) — Jan. 4, 1995
189. Thornberry (Texas) — Jan. 4, 1995
190. Tiahrt (Kan.) — Jan. 4, 1995
191. Wamp (Tenn.) — Jan. 4, 1995
192. Weldon (Fla.) — Jan. 4, 1995
193. Weller (Ill.) — Jan. 4, 1995
194. White (Wash.) — Jan. 4, 1995
195. Whitfield (Ky.) — Jan. 4, 1995
196. Wicker (Miss.) — Jan. 4, 1995
197. Watts (Okla.) — Jan. 9, 1995
198. Emerson (Mo.) — Jan. 7, 1997
199. Ryun (Kan.) — Nov. 6, 1996
200. Aderholt (Ala.) — Jan. 7, 1997
201. Blunt (Mo.) — Jan. 7, 1997
202. Cannon (Utah) — Jan. 7, 1997
203. Cook (Utah) — Jan. 7, 1997
204. Cooksey (La.) — Jan. 7, 1997
205. Gibbons (Nev.) — Jan. 7, 1997
206. Granger (Texas) — Jan. 7, 1997
207. Hill (Mont.) — Jan. 7, 1997
208. Hulshof (Mo.) — Jan. 7, 1997
209. Hutchinson (Ark.) — Jan. 7, 1997
210. Jenkins (Tenn.) — Jan. 7, 1997
211. Moran (Kan.) — Jan. 7, 1997
212. Northup (Ky.) — Jan. 7, 1997
213. Pappas (N.J.) — Jan. 7, 1997
214. Pease (Ind.) — Jan. 7, 1997
215. Peterson (Pa.) — Jan. 7, 1997
216. Pickering (Miss.) — Jan. 7, 1997
217. Pitts (Pa.) — Jan. 7, 1997
218. Riley (Ala.) — Jan. 7, 1997
219. Rogan (Calif.) — Jan. 7, 1997
220. Schaffer (Colo.) — Jan. 7, 1997
221. Sessions (Texas) — Jan. 7, 1997
222. Shimkus (Ill.) — Jan. 7, 1997
223. Snowbarger (Kan.) — Jan. 7, 1997
224. Sununu (N.H.) — Jan. 7, 1997
225. Thune (S.D.) — Jan. 7, 1997
226. Brady (Texas) — Jan. 7, 1997

Democrats

Dingell (Mich.) — Dec. 13, 1955
Gonzalez (Texas) — Nov. 4, 1961
Yates (Ill.) (seven terms previously) — Jan. 4, 1965
Conyers (Mich.) — Jan. 4, 1965
Hamilton (Ind.) — Jan. 4, 1965
Clay (Mo.) — Jan. 3, 1969
Stokes (Ohio) — Jan. 3, 1969
Obey (Wis.) — April 1, 1969
Dellums (Calif.) — Jan. 21, 1971
Rangel (N.Y.) — Jan. 21, 1971
Brown (Calif.) (four terms previously) — Jan. 3, 1973
Moakley (Mass.) — Jan. 3, 1973
Stark (Calif.) — Jan. 3, 1973
Murtha (Pa.) — Feb. 5, 1974
Hefner (N.C.) — Jan. 14, 1975
LaFalce (N.Y.) — Jan. 14, 1975
Miller (Calif.) — Jan. 14, 1975
Oberstar (Minn.) — Jan. 14, 1975
Waxman (Calif.) — Jan. 14, 1975
Markey (Mass.) — Nov. 2, 1976
Bonior (Mich.) — Jan. 4, 1977
Dicks (Wash.) — Jan. 4, 1977
Gephardt (Mo.) — Jan. 4, 1977
Kildee (Mich.) — Jan. 4, 1977
Rahall (W.Va.) — Jan. 4, 1977
Skelton (Mo.) — Jan. 4, 1977
Vento (Minn.) — Jan. 4, 1977
Dixon (Calif.) — Jan. 15, 1979
Fazio (Calif.) — Jan. 15, 1979
Frost (Texas) — Jan. 15, 1979
Hall (Ohio) — Jan. 15, 1979
Matsui (Calif.) — Jan. 15, 1979
Sabo (Minn.) — Jan. 15, 1979
Stenholm (Texas) — Jan. 15, 1979
Coyne (Pa.) — Jan. 5, 1981
Frank (Mass.) — Jan. 5, 1981
Gejdenson (Conn.) — Jan. 5, 1981
Hall (Texas) — Jan. 5, 1981
Lantos (Calif.) — Jan. 5, 1981
Schumer (N.Y.) — Jan. 5, 1981
Hoyer (Md.) — May 19, 1981
Kennelly (Conn.) — Jan. 12, 1982
Martinez (Calif.) — July 13, 1982
Berman (Calif.) — Jan. 3, 1983
Borski (Pa.) — Jan. 3, 1983
Boucher (Va.) — Jan. 3, 1983
Evans (Ill.) — Jan. 3, 1983
Kaptur (Ohio) — Jan. 3, 1983
Levin (Mich.) — Jan. 3, 1983
Lipinski (Ill.) — Jan. 3, 1983
Mollohan (W.Va.) — Jan. 3, 1983
Ortiz (Texas) — Jan. 3, 1983
Owens (N.Y.) — Jan. 3, 1983
Sisisky (Va.) — Jan. 3, 1983
Spratt (S.C.) — Jan. 3, 1983
Torres (Calif.) — Jan. 3, 1983
Towns (N.Y.) — Jan. 3, 1983
Wise (W.Va.) — Jan. 3, 1983
Ackerman (N.Y.) — March 1, 1983
Kleczka (Wis.) — April 3, 1984
Gordon (Tenn.) — Jan. 3, 1985
Kanjorski (Pa.) — Jan. 3, 1985
Manton (N.Y.) — Jan. 3, 1985
Traficant (Ohio) — Jan. 3, 1985
Visclosky (Ind.) — Jan. 3, 1985
Cardin (Md.) — Jan. 6, 1987
DeFazio (Ore.) — Jan. 6, 1987
Flake (N.Y.) — Jan. 6, 1987
Kennedy (Mass.) — Jan. 6, 1987
Lewis (Ga.) — Jan. 6, 1987
Pickett (Va.) — Jan. 6, 1987
Sawyer (Ohio) — Jan. 6, 1987
Skaggs (Colo.) — Jan. 6, 1987
Slaughter (N.Y.) — Jan. 6, 1987
Pelosi (Calif.) — June 2, 1987
Clement (Tenn.) — Jan. 19, 1988
Costello (Ill.) — Aug. 9, 1988
Pallone (N.J.) — Nov. 9, 1988
Engel (N.Y.) — Jan. 3, 1989
Lowey (N.Y.) — Jan. 3, 1989
McDermott (Wash.) — Jan. 3, 1989
McNulty (N.Y.) — Jan. 3, 1989
Neal (Mass.) — Jan. 3, 1989
Payne (N.J.) — Jan. 3, 1989
Poshard (Ill.) — Jan. 3, 1989
Tanner (Tenn.) — Jan. 3, 1989
Condit (Calif.) — Sept. 12, 1989
Taylor (Miss.) — Oct. 17, 1989

Serrano (N.Y.) — March 20, 1990
Mink (Hawaii) (six terms previously) — Sept. 22, 1990
Andrews (N.J.) — Nov. 7, 1990
Abercrombie (Hawaii) (one term previously) — Jan. 3, 1991
Cramer (Ala.) — Jan. 3, 1991
DeLauro (Conn.) — Jan. 3, 1991
Dooley (Calif.) — Jan. 3, 1991
Edwards (Texas) — Jan. 3, 1991
Jefferson (La.) — Jan. 3, 1991
Moran (Va.) — Jan. 3, 1991
Peterson (Minn.) — Jan. 3, 1991
Roemer (Ind.) — Jan. 3, 1991
Waters (Calif.) — Jan. 3, 1991
Olver (Mass.) — June 4, 1991
Pastor (Ariz.) — Sept. 24, 1991
Clayton (N.C.) — Nov. 4, 1992
Nadler (N.Y.) — Nov. 4, 1992
Baesler (Ky.) — Jan. 5, 1993
Barcia (Mich.) — Jan. 5, 1993
Barrett (Wis.) — Jan. 5, 1993
Becerra (Calif.) — Jan. 5, 1993
Bishop (Ga.) — Jan. 5, 1993
Brown (Fla.) — Jan. 5, 1993
Brown (Ohio) — Jan. 5, 1993
Clyburn (S.C.) — Jan. 5, 1993
Danner (Mo.) — Jan. 5, 1993
Deutsch (Fla.) — Jan. 5, 1993
Eshoo (Calif.) — Jan. 5, 1993
Filner (Calif.) — Jan. 5, 1993
Furse (Ore.) — Jan. 5, 1993
Green (Texas) — Jan. 5, 1993
Gutierrez (Ill.) — Jan. 5, 1993
Harman (Calif.) — Jan. 5, 1993
Hastings (Fla.) — Jan. 5, 1993
Hilliard (Ala.) — Jan. 5, 1993
Hinchey (N.Y.) — Jan. 5, 1993
Holden (Pa.) — Jan. 5, 1993
Johnson (Texas) — Jan. 5, 1993
Klink (Pa.) — Jan. 5, 1993
Maloney (N.Y.) — Jan. 5, 1993
McHale (Pa.) — Jan. 5, 1993
McKinney (Ga.) — Jan. 5, 1993
Meehan (Mass.) — Jan. 5, 1993
Meek (Fla.) — Jan. 5, 1993
Menendez (N.J.) — Jan. 5, 1993
Minge (Minn.) — Jan. 5, 1993
Pomeroy (N.D.) — Jan. 5, 1993
Roybal-Allard (Calif.) — Jan. 5, 1993
Rush (Ill.) — Jan. 5, 1993
Scott (Va.) — Jan. 5, 1993
Stupak (Mich.) — Jan. 5, 1993
Thurman (Fla.) — Jan. 5, 1993
Velázquez (N.Y.) — Jan. 5, 1993
Watt (N.C.) — Jan. 5, 1993
Woolsey (Calif.) — Jan. 5, 1993
Wynn (Md.) — Jan. 5, 1993
Thompson (Miss.) — April 13, 1993
Farr (Calif.) — June 8, 1993
Baldacci (Maine) — Jan. 4, 1995
Bentsen (Texas) — Jan. 4, 1995
Doggett (Texas) — Jan. 4, 1995
Doyle (Pa.) — Jan. 4, 1995
Fattah (Pa.) — Jan. 4, 1995
Jackson-Lee (Texas) — Jan. 4, 1995
Kennedy (R.I.) — Jan. 4, 1995
Lofgren (Calif.) — Jan. 4, 1995
Luther (Minn.) — Jan. 4, 1995
Mascara (Pa.) — Jan. 4, 1995
McCarthy (Mo.) — Jan. 4, 1995
Rivers (Mich.) — Jan. 4, 1995
Jackson (Ill.) — Dec. 12, 1995
Millender-McDonald (Calif.) — March 26, 1996
Cummings (Md.) — April 16, 1996
Blumenauer (Ore.) — May 21, 1996
Price (N.C.) (four terms previously) — Jan. 7, 1997
Strickland (Ohio) (one term previously) — Jan. 7, 1997
Allen (Maine) — Jan. 7, 1997
Berry (Ark.) — Jan. 7, 1997
Blagojevich (Ill.) — Jan. 7, 1997
Boswell (Iowa) — Jan. 7, 1997
Boyd (Fla.) — Jan. 7, 1997
Carson (Ind.) — Jan. 7, 1997
Davis (Ill.) — Jan. 7, 1997
Davis (Fla.) — Jan. 7, 1997
DeGette (Colo.) — Jan. 7, 1997
Delahunt (Mass.) — Jan. 7, 1997
Etheridge (N.C.) — Jan. 7, 1997
Ford (Tenn.) — Jan. 7, 1997
Goode (Va.) — Jan. 7, 1997
Hinojosa (Texas) — Jan. 7, 1997
Hooley (Ore.) — Jan. 7, 1997
John (La.) — Jan. 7, 1997
Johnson (Wis.) — Jan. 7, 1997
Kilpatrick (Mich.) — Jan. 7, 1997
Kind (Wis.) — Jan. 7, 1997
Kucinich (Ohio) — Jan. 7, 1997
Lampson (Texas) — Jan. 7, 1997
Maloney (Conn.) — Jan. 7, 1997
McCarthy (N.Y.) — Jan. 7, 1997
McGovern (Mass.) — Jan. 7, 1997
McIntyre (N.C.) — Jan. 7, 1997
Pascrell (N.J.) — Jan. 7, 1997
Reyes (Texas) — Jan. 7, 1997
Rothman (N.J.) — Jan. 7, 1997
Sanchez (Calif.) — Jan. 7, 1997
Sandlin (Texas) — Jan. 7, 1997
Sherman (Calif.) — Jan. 7, 1997
Smith (Wash.) — Jan. 7, 1997
Snyder (Ark.) — Jan. 7, 1997
Stabenow (Mich.) — Jan. 7, 1997
Tauscher (Calif.) — Jan. 7, 1997
Tierney (Mass.) — Jan. 7, 1997
Turner (Texas) — Jan. 7, 1997
Wexler (Fla.) — Jan. 7, 1997
Weygand (R.I.) — Jan. 7, 1997
Rodriquez (Texas) — April 17, 1997
Redmond (N.M.) — May 20, 1997
Fossella (N.Y.) — Nov. 5, 1997

Congressional Committees

PARTY

SENATE

HOUSE

JOINT

Key to the Listings

Order of lists: The guide begins with party committees; followed by Senate committees, listed alphabetically; then House committees; and joint committees. Committee and subcommittee rosters list Republicans on the left in roman type and Democrats on the right in *italics*. (Rep. Bernard Sanders of Vermont, an independent, is listed in **boldface**.) Freshmen are noted with a †. In the Senate, freshmen are those first elected in 1996.

The committee lists are arranged by seniority, as reported by each committee. Chairmen are listed first, regardless of seniority.

There are also lists of the committee assignments of each senator and House member *(pp. B-58, B-60)*, as well as a listing of the seniority rankings of all members by chamber and political party *(pp. B-18, B-19)*.

Party Committees

105th Congress, First Session

(Committees and subcommittees are subject to change during a session.)

Senate Republicans

President Pro Tempore . . . . Strom Thurmond, S.C.
Majority Leader . . . . Trent Lott, Miss.
Assistant Majority Leader . . . . Don Nickles, Fla.
Conference Chairman . . . . Connie Mack, Fla.
Conference Secretary . . . . Paul Coverdell, Ga.
Chief Deputy Whip . . . . Judd Gregg, N.H.

Deputy Whips . . . . Olympia Snowe, Maine
Spencer Abraham, Mich.
John Ashcroft, Mo.
Conrad Burns, Mont.
Daniel R. Coats, Ind.
Susan Collins, Maine
Chuck Hagel, Neb.
Kay Bailey Hutchison, Texas
Dirk Kempthorne, Idaho
Jon Kyl, Ariz.
Gordon H. Smith, Ore.

Policy Committee

Advises on party action and policy.

Larry E. Craig, Idaho, chairman

Committee on Committees

Makes Republican committee assignments.

Slade Gordon, chairman

National Republican Senatorial Committee

Campaign support committee for Republican senatorial candidates.

Mitch McDonnell, Ky., chairman

Senate Democrats

Senate President . . . . Vice President Al Gore
Minority Leader . . . . Tom Daschle, S.D.
Minority Whip . . . . Wendell H. Ford, Ky.
Conference Chairman . . . . Tom Daschle, S.D.
Conference Secretary . . . . Barbara A. Mikulski, Md.
Chief Deputy Whip . . . . John B. Breaux, La.
Assistant Floor Leader . . . . Byron L. Dorgan, N.D.
Deputy Whips . . . . Jeff Bingaman, N.M.
Joseph I. Lieberman, Conn.
Patty Murray, Wash.
Charles S. Robb, Va.

Policy Committee

An arm of the Democratic Caucus that advises on legislative priorities.

Tom Daschle, S.D., co-chairman
Harry Reid, Nev., co-chairman
Paul S. Sarbanes, Md., vice chairman
Charles S. Robb, Va., vice chairman
Patty Murray, Wash., vice chairman
John Glenn, Ohio, vice chairman

Jack Reed, R.I.
Max Cleland, Ga.
Carol Moseley-Braun, Ill.
Russell D. Feingold, Wis.
Bob Kerrey, Neb.
Ernest F. Hollings, S.C.
Dale Bumpers, Ark.
Daniel Patrick Moynihan, N.Y.
John D. Rockefeller IV, W.Va.
Daniel K. Akaka, Hawaii
Byron L. Dorgan, N.D.
Joseph I. Lieberman, Conn.
Paul Wellstone, Minn.
Dianne Feinstein, Calif.
Ron Wyden, Ore.
Robert G. Torricelli, N.J.
Wendell H. Ford, Ky., ex officio
Barbara A. Mikulski, Md. ex officio

Steering and Coordination Committee

Makes Democratic committee assignments.

John Kerry, Mass., chairman

Daniel K. Inouye, Hawaii
Robert C. Byrd, W.Va.
Edward M. Kennedy, Mass.
Joseph R. Biden Jr., Del.
Wendell H. Ford, Ky.
Patrick J. Leahy, Vt.
Christopher J. Dodd, Conn.
Tom Harkin, Iowa
Max Baucus, Mont.
Bob Graham, Fla.
Kent Conrad, N.D.
Carl Levin, Mich.
Richard H. Bryan, Nev.
Herb Kohl, Wis.
Barbara Boxer, Calif.
John B. Breaux, La.
Tom Daschle, S.D.
Frank R. Lautenberg, N.J.
Jeff Bingaman, N.M.

Technology and Communications Committee

Seeks to improve communications with the public about the Democratic Party and its policies.

John D. Rockefeller IV, W.Va., chairman

John Glenn, Ohio
Ernest F. Hollings, S.C.
Patty Murray, Wash.
Charles S. Robb, Va.
Jeff Bingaman, N.M.
Christopher J. Dodd, Conn.
Frank R. Lautenberg, N.J.
Kent Conrad, N.D.
Tom Daschle, S.D., ex officio
Wendell H. Ford, Ky., ex officio
Barbara A. Mikulski, Md., ex officio
John B. Breaux, La., ex officio

Democratic Senatorial Campaign Committee

Campaign support committee for Democratic senatorial candidates.

Bob Kerrey, Neb.; Robert G. Torricelli, N.J.; John D. Rockefeller IV, W. Va.; Max Baucus, Mont.; Tom Harkin, Iowa; Charles S. Robb, Va.; Kent Conrad, N.D.; Richard H. Bryan, Nev.; Jack Reed, R.I.; Edward M. Kennedy, Mass.; Paul Wellstone, Minn.; Dianne Feinstein, Calif.; Mary L. Landrieu, La.; Joseph I. Lieberman, Conn.; Richard J. Durbin, Ill.

House Republicans

Speaker of the House .... Newt Gingrich, Ga.
Majority Leader .... Dick Armey, Texas
Majority Whip .... Tom DeLay, Texas
Conference Chairman .... John A. Boehner, Ohio
Conference Vice Chairman .... Jennifer Dunn, Wash.
Conference Secretary............. Deborah Pryce, Ohio
Chief Deputy Whip .... Dennis Hastert, Ill.

Deputy Whips .... Cass Ballenger, N.C.
Jim Bunning, Ky.
Mac Collins, Ga.
Michael D. Crapo, Idaho
Barbara Cubin, Wyo.
John T. Doolittle, Calif.
Thomas W. Ewing, Ill.
Mark Foley, Fla.
Tillie Fowler, Fla.
Porter J. Goss, Fla.
Van Hilleary, Tenn.
Rick A. Lazio, N.Y.
Bob Ney, Ohio
W.J. "Billy" Tauzin, La.
Roger Wicker, Miss.

Assistant Whips:
Charles Bass, N.H.; Roy Blunt, Mo.; Henry Bonilla, Texas; Richard M. Burr, N.C.; Steve Buyer, Ind.; Sonny Callahan, Ala.; Dave Camp, Mich.; Randy "Duke" Cunningham, Calif.; Thomas M. Davis III, Va.; Nathan Deal, Ga.; Robert L. Ehrlich Jr., Md.; Jon D. Fox, Pa.; Bob Franks, N.J.; Paul E. Gillmor, Ohio; Robert W. Goodlatte, Va.; Lindsey Graham, S.C.; Kay Granger, Texas; J.D. Hayworth, Ariz.; David L. Hobson, Ohio; Bob Inglis, S.C.; Ernest Istook, Okla.; Sam Johnson, Texas; Sue W. Kelly, N.Y.; Jack Kingston, Ga.; Scott L. Klug, Wis.; Frank A. LoBiondo, N.J.; Frank D. Lucas, Okla.; Scott McInnis, Colo.; David M. McIntosh, Ind.; Howard P. "Buck" McKeon, Calif.; Dan Miller, Fla.; Michael Pappas, N.J.; Ed Pease, Ind.; Charles W. "Chip" Pickering Jr., Miss.; Joseph R. Pitts, Pa.; Richard W. Pombo, Calif.; Rob Portman, Ohio; George P. Radanovich, Calif.; Bob Riley, Ala.; James E. Rogan, Calif.; Ed Royce, Calif.; John Shadegg, Ariz.; Vince Snowbarger, Kan.; Mark Souder, Ind.; John Thune, S.D.; Todd Tiahrt, Kan.; James T. Walsh, N.Y.; Jerry Weller, Ill.

Steering Committee

Makes Republican committee assignments.

Newt Gingrich, Ga., chairman

Jennifer Dunn, Wash.
Dick Armey, Texas
Tom DeLay, Texas
John A. Boehner, Ohio
Christopher Cox, Calif.
John Linder, Ga.
Bill Paxon, N.Y.
Robert L. Livingston, La.
John R. Kasich, Ohio
Gerald B.H. Solomon, N.Y.
Bill Archer, Texas
David Dreier, Calif.
C.W. Bill Young, Fla.
Dennis Hastert, Ill.
Tom Latham, Iowa.
Bud Shuster, Pa.
John M. McHugh, N.Y.
Cass Ballenger, N.C.
Joe L. Barton, Texas
Bob Stump, Ariz.
Don Young, Alaska
Saxby Chambliss, Ga.
Lindsey Graham, S.C.
Roy Blunt, Mo.

Policy Committee

Advises on party action and policy.

Christopher Cox, Calif., chairman

Newt Gingrich, Ga.
Dick Armey, Texas
Tom DeLay, Texas
John A. Boehner, Ohio
Bill Paxon, N.Y
Jennifer Dunn, Wash.
John Linder, Ga.
David M. McIntosh, Ind.
Sue Myrick, N.C.
John Thune, S.D.
Gerald B.H. Solomon, N.Y.
Bill Archer, Texas
Robert L. Livingston, La.
John R. Kasich, Ohio
Thomas J. Bliley Jr., Va
Richard W. Pombo, Calif.
Todd Tiahrt, Kan.
Rob Portman, Ohio
Benjamin A. Gilman, N.Y.
Floyd D. Spence, S.C.
Tom Coburn, Okla.
Jack Metcalf, Wash.
Doug Bereuter, Neb.
Vacancy
Vacancy
Rick Hill, Mont.
Jim Gibbons, Nev.
Robert W. Goodlatte, Va.
Joe Knollenberg, Mich.
Ron Lewis, Ky.
Charles W. "Chip" Pickering Jr., Miss.

Bob Barr, Ga.
Nick Smith, Mich.
Frank Riggs, Calif.
Bob Schaffer, Colo.
John E. Sununu, N.H.
Cliff Stearns, Fla.
Curt Weldon, Pa.

National Republican Congressional Committee

Campaign support committee for Republican House candidates.

John Linder, Ga., chairman
Deborah Pryce, Ohio, vice chairman
Jim McCrery, La., vice chairman
Michael D. Crapo, Idaho, vice chairman
Ed Royce, Calif., Executive Committee chairman
Newt Gingrich, Ga., ex officio
Dick Armey, Texas, ex officio
Tom DeLay, Texas, ex officio
John A. Boehner, Ohio, ex officio
Jennifer Dunn, Wash., ex officio
Christopher Cox, Calif., ex officio

Bob Barr, Ga.
Charles Bass, N.H.
Sherwood Boehlert, N.Y.
Dave Camp, Mich.
Christopher B. Cannon, Utah
Jon Christensen, Neb.
Tom Coburn, Okla.
Thomas M. Davis III, Va.
John T. Doolittle, Calif.
Jo Ann Emerson, Mo.
John Ensign, Nev.
Thomas W. Ewing, Ill.
Mark Foley, Fla.
Bob Franks, N.J.
Gil Gutknecht, Minn.
Richard "Doc"Hastings, Wash.
David L. Hobson, Ohio
Ray LaHood, Ill.
Rick A. Lazio, N.Y.
Jerry Moran, Kan.
Sue Myrick, N.C.
Anne M. Northup, Ky.
Charles W. "Chip" Pickering Jr., Miss.
John Thune, S.D.
Jerry Weller, Ill.
Roger Wicker, Miss.

House Democrats

Minority Leader .... Richard A. Gephardt, Mo.
Minority Whip.................... David E. Bonior, Mich.
Caucus Chairman .... Vic Fazio, Calif.
Caucus Vice Chairman....... Barbara B. Kennelly, Conn.
Chief Deputy Whips.............. Rosa DeLauro, Conn.
Chet Edwards, Texas
John Lewis, Ga.
Robert Menendez, N.J.

Regional Whips (by region number):

1 .... Xavier Becerra, Calif.
2.............................. Nancy Pelosi, Calif.
3 .... Dale E. Kildee, Mich.
4 .... Peter J. Visclosky, Ind.
5 .... Norm Dicks, Wash.
6......................... Charles W. Stenholm, Texas
7 .... Gene Taylor, Miss.
8 .... Melvin Watt, N.C.
9 .... Frank Pallone Jr., N.J.
10 .... Sherrod Brown, Ohio
11 .... Gary L. Ackerman, N.Y.
12 .... Richard E. Neal, Mass.

Steering Committee

Makes Democratic committee assignments.

Richard A. Gephardt, Mo., co-chairman
Steny H. Hoyer, Md., co-chairman
Jose E. Serrano, N.Y., vice chairman
Maxine Waters, Calif., vice chairman

Richard A. Gephardt, Mo.
Steny H. Hoyer, Md.
Richard E. Neal, Mass.
David R. Obey, Wis.
Jose E. Serrano, N.Y.
Maxine Waters, Calif.
David E. Bonior, Mich.
Vic Fazio, Calif.
Barbara B. Kennelly, Conn.
Martin Frost, Texas
Rosa DeLauro, Conn.
Chet Edwards, Texas
John Lewis, Ga.
Xavier Becerra, Calif.
Nancy Pelosi, Calif.
Dale E. Kildee, Mich.
Peter J. Visclosky, Ind.
Norm Dicks, Wash.
Charles W. Stenholm, Texas
Gene Taylor, Miss.
Melvin Watt, N.C.
Frank Pallone Jr., N.J.
Sherrod Brown, Ohio
Gary L. Ackerman, N.Y.
John M. Spratt Jr., S.C.
Joe Moakley, Mass.
Charles B. Rangel, N.Y.
John D. Dingell, Mich.
Benjamin L. Cardin, Md.
Leonard L. Boswell, Iowa
Debbie Stabenow, Mich.
Tom Allen, Maine
Robert A. Borski, Pa.
Jane Harman, Calif.
William J. Jefferson, La.
William O. Lipinski, Ill.
Edward J. Markey, Mass.
Robert T. Matsui, Calif.
Jim McDermott, Wash.
John P. Murtha, Pa.
Ed Pastor, Ariz.
John Tanner, Tenn.
Henry A. Waxman, Calif.
Vacancy

Policy Committee

Studies and proposes legislation and makes public Democratic policy positions.

Democratic Congressional Campaign Committee

Campaign support committee for Democratic House candidates.

Martin Frost, Texas, chairman

Senate Committees
105th Congress, First Session

(Committees and subcommittees are subject to change during a session.)

Agriculture, Nutrition and Forestry

Republicans (10)
Richard G. Lugar, Ind., chairman
Jesse Helms, N.C.
Thad Cochran, Miss.
Mitch McConnell, Ky.
Paul Coverdell, Ga.
Rick Santorum, Pa.
Pat Roberts, Kan. †
Charles E. Grassley, Iowa
Phil Gramm, Texas
Larry E. Craig, Idaho

Democrats (8)
Tom Harkin, Iowa, ranking member
Patrick J. Leahy, Vt.
Kent Conrad, N.D.
Tom Daschle, S.D.
Max Baucus, Mont.
Bob Kerrey, Neb.
Tim Johnson, S.D. †
Mary L. Landrieu, La. †

† Denotes freshmen.

Jurisdiction: Agriculture in general; animal industry and diseases; crop insurance and soil conservation; farm credit and farm security; food from fresh waters; food stamp program; forestry in general; home economics; human nutrition; inspection of livestock, meat and agricultural products; pests and pesticides; plant industry, soils and agricultural engineering; rural development, rural electrification and watersheds; school nutrition programs. The chairman and ranking minority member are non-voting members ex officio of all subcommittees of which they are not regular members.

Forestry, Conservation and Rural Revitalization

Santorum, chairman

Grassley	*Conrad*
Coverdell	*Leahy*
Roberts†	*Daschle*
Craig	*Baucus*

Marketing, Inspection and Product Promotion

Coverdell, chairman

Helms	*Baucus*
Cochran	*Kerrey (Neb.)*
McConnell	*Landrieu †*

Production and Price Competitiveness

Roberts, chairman †

Cochran	*Kerrey (Neb.)*
Helms	*Daschle*
Grassley	*Johnson †*
Gramm	*Landrieu †*

Research, Nutrition and General Legislation

McConnell, chairman

Gramm	*Leahy*
Craig	*Conrad*
Santorum	*Johnson †*

Appropriations

Republicans (15)
Ted Stevens, Alaska, chairman
Thad Cochran, Miss.
Arlen Specter, Pa.
Pete V. Domenici, N.M.
Christopher S. Bond, Mo.
Slade Gorton, Wash.
Mitch McConnell, Ky.
Conrad Burns, Mont.
Richard C. Shelby, Ala.
Judd Gregg, N.H.
Robert F. Bennett, Utah
Ben Nighthorse Campbell, Colo.
Larry E. Craig, Idaho
Lauch Faircloth, N.C.
Kay Bailey Hutchison, Texas

Democrats (13)
Robert C. Byrd, W.Va., ranking member
Daniel K. Inouye, Hawaii
Ernest F. Hollings, S.C.
Patrick J. Leahy, Vt.
Dale Bumpers, Ark.
Frank R. Lautenberg, N.J.
Tom Harkin, Iowa
Barbara A. Mikulski, Md.
Harry Reid, Nev.
Herb Kohl, Wis.
Patty Murray, Wash.
Byron L. Dorgan, N.D
Barbara Boxer, Calif.

Jurisdiction: Appropriation of revenue; rescission of appropriations; new spending authority under the Congressional Budget Act. Chairman and ranking minority member are non-voting members ex officio of all subcommittees.

Agriculture, Rural Development and Related Agencies

Cochran, chairman

Specter	*Bumpers*
Bond	*Harkin*
Gorton	*Kohl*
McConnell	*Byrd*
Burns	*Leahy*

Commerce, Justice, State and Judiciary

Gregg, chairman

Stevens	*Hollings*
Domenici	*Inouye*
McConnell	*Bumpers*
Hutchison (Texas)	*Lautenberg*
Campbell	*Mikulski*

Defense

Stevens, chairman

Cochran	*Inouye*
Specter	*Hollings*
Domenici	*Byrd*
Bond	*Leahy*
McConnell	*Bumpers*
Shelby	*Lautenberg*
Gregg	*Harkin*
Hutchison (Texas)	*Dorgan*

District of Columbia

Faircloth, chairman

Hutchison (Texas)	*Boxer*

Energy and Water Development

Domenici, chairman

Cochran	*Reid*
Gorton	*Byrd*
McConnell	*Hollings*
Bennett	*Murray*
Burns	*Kohl*
Craig	*Dorgan*

Foreign Operations

McConnell, chairman

Specter	*Leahy*
Gregg	*Inouye*
Shelby	*Lautenberg*
Bennett	*Harkin*
Campbell	*Mikulski*
Stevens	*Murray*

Interior

Gorton, chairman

Stevens	*Byrd*
Cochran	*Leahy*
Domenici	*Bumpers*
Burns	*Hollings*
Bennett	*Reid*
Gregg	*Dorgan*
Campbell	*Boxer*

Labor, Health and Human Services and Education

Specter, chairman

Cochran	*Harkin*
Gorton	*Hollings*
Bond	*Inouye*
Gregg	*Bumpers*
Faircloth	*Reid*
Craig	*Kohl*
Hutchison (Texas)	*Murray*

Legislative Branch

Bennett, chairman

Stevens	*Dorgan*
Craig	*Boxer*

Military Construction

Burns, chairman

Hutchison (Texas)	*Murray*
Faircloth	*Reid*
Craig	*Inouye*

Transportation

Shelby, chairman

Domenici	*Lautenberg*
Specter	*Byrd*
Bond	*Mikulski*
Gorton	*Reid*
Bennett	*Kohl*
Faircloth	*Murray*

Treasury and General Government

Campbell, chairman

Shelby	*Kohl*
Faircloth	*Mikulski*

VA, HUD and Independent Agencies

Bond, chairman

Burns	*Mikulski*
Stevens	*Leahy*
Shelby	*Lautenberg*
Campbell	*Harkin*
Craig	*Boxer*

Armed Services

Republicans (10)	***Democrats (8)***
Strom Thurmond, S.C., chairman	*Carl Levin, Mich., ranking member*
John W. Warner, Va.	*Edward M. Kennedy, Mass.*
John McCain, Ariz.	*Jeff Bingaman, N.M.*
Daniel R. Coats, Ind.	*John Glenn, Ohio*
Robert C. Smith, N.H.	*Robert C. Byrd, W.Va.*
Dirk Kempthorne, Idaho	*Charles S. Robb, Va.*
James M. Inhofe, Okla.	*Joseph I. Lieberman, Conn.*
Rick Santorum, Pa.	*Max Cleland, Ga. †*
Olympia J. Snowe, Maine	
Pat Roberts, Kan. †	

† Denotes freshmen.

Jurisdiction: Defense and defense policy generally; aeronautical and space activities peculiar to or primarily associated with the development of weapons systems or military operations; maintenance and operation of the Panama Canal, including the Canal Zone; military research and development; national security aspects of nuclear energy; naval petroleum reserves (except Alaska); armed forces generally; Selective Service System; strategic and critical materials. The chairman and ranking minority member are non-voting members ex officio of all subcommittees of which they are not regular members.

Acquisition and Technology

Santorum, chairman

Smith (N.H.)	*Lieberman*
Snowe	*Kennedy*
Roberts †	*Bingaman*

Airland Forces

Coats, chairman

Warner	*Glenn*
Kempthorne	*Bingaman*
Inhofe	*Byrd*
Santorum	*Lieberman*
Roberts†	*Cleland †*

Personnel

Kempthorne, chairman

McCain	*Cleland†*
Coats	*Kennedy*
Snowe	*Robb*

Readiness

Inhofe, chairman

McCain	*Robb*
Coats	*Glenn*
Roberts †	*Cleland †*

Seapower

Warner, chairman

McCain	*Kennedy*
Smith (N.H.)	*Byrd*
Santorum	*Robb*
Snowe	*Lieberman*

Strategic Forces

Smith (N.H.), chairman

Warner	*Bingaman*
Kempthorne	*Glenn*
Inhofe	*Byrd*

Banking, Housing and Urban Affairs

Republicans (10)	***Democrats (8)***
Alfonse M. D'Amato, N.Y., chairman	*Paul S. Sarbanes, Md., ranking member*
Phil Gramm, Texas	*Christopher J. Dodd, Conn.*
Richard C. Shelby, Ala.	*John Kerry, Mass.*
Connie Mack, Fla.	*Richard H. Bryan, Nev.*
Lauch Faircloth, N.C.	*Barbara Boxer, Calif.*
Robert F. Bennett, Utah	*Carol Moseley-Braun, Ill.*
Rod Grams, Minn.	*Tim Johnson, S.D. †*
Wayne Allard, Colo. †	*Jack Reed, R.I. †*
Michael B. Enzi, Wyo. †	
Chuck Hagel, Neb. †	

† Denotes freshmen.

Jurisdiction: Banks, banking and financial institutions; price controls; deposit insurance; economic stabilization and growth; defense production; export and foreign trade promotion; export controls; federal monetary policy, including Federal Reserve System; financial aid to commerce and industry; issuance and redemption of notes; money and credit, including currency and coinage; nursing home construction; public and private housing, including veterans' housing; renegotiation of government contracts; urban development and mass transit; international economic policy. The chairman and ranking minority member are non-voting members ex officio of all subcommittees of which they are not regular members.

Financial Institutions and Regulatory Relief

Faircloth, chairman

Allard †	*Bryan*
Enzi †	*Johnson †*
Shelby	*Boxer*
Mack	*Moseley-Braun*
Grams	*Reed †*
Gramm	

Financial Services and Technology

Bennett, chairman

Hagel †	*Boxer*
Mack	*Kerry*
Grams	*Dodd*
Enzi †	*Johnson †*

Housing Opportunity and Community Development

Mack, chairman

Faircloth	*Kerry*
Enzi †	*Reed †*
Shelby	*Dodd*
Allard †	*Bryan*
Hagel †	*Moseley-Braun*

International Finance

Grams, chairman

Hagel†	*Moseley-Braun*
Gramm	*Boxer*
Bennett	*Reed †*

Securities

Gramm, chairman

Shelby	*Dodd*
Allard †	*Johnson †*
Bennett	*Kerry*
Faircloth	*Bryan*

Budget

Republicans (12)	***Democrats (10)***
Pete V. Domenici, N.M., chairman	*Frank R. Lautenberg, N.J., ranking member*
Charles E. Grassley, Iowa	*Ernest F. Hollings, S.C.*
Don Nickles, Okla.	*Kent Conrad, N.D.*
Phil Gramm, Texas	*Paul S. Sarbanes, Md.*
Christopher S. Bond, Mo.	*Barbara Boxer, Calif.*
Slade Gorton, Wash.	*Patty Murray, Wash.*
Judd Gregg, N.H.	*Ron Wyden, Ore.*
Olympia J. Snowe, Maine	*Russell D. Feingold, Wis.*
Spencer Abraham, Mich.	*Tim Johnson, S.D. †*
Bill Frist, Tenn.	*Richard J. Durbin, Ill.†*
Rod Grams, Minn.	
Gordon H. Smith, Ore. †	

Jurisdiction: Federal budget generally; concurrent budget resolutions; Congressional Budget Office.

† Denotes freshmen.
Budget has no subcommittees.

Commerce, Science and Transportation

Republicans (11)	***Democrats (9)***
John McCain, Ariz., chairman	*Ernest F. Hollings, S.C., ranking member*
Ted Stevens, Alaska	*Daniel K. Inouye, Hawaii*
Conrad Burns, Mont.	*Wendell H. Ford, Ky.*
Slade Gorton, Wash.	*John D. Rockefeller IV, W.Va.*
Trent Lott, Miss.	*John Kerry, Mass.*
Kay Bailey Hutchison, Texas	*John B. Breaux, La.*
Olympia J. Snowe, Maine	*Richard H. Bryan, Nev.*
John Ashcroft, Mo.	*Byron L. Dorgan, N.D.*
Bill Frist, Tenn.	*Ron Wyden, Ore.*
Spencer Abraham, Mich.	
Sam Brownback, Kan. †	

Jurisdiction: Interstate commerce and transportation generally; Coast Guard; coastal zone management; communications; highway safety; inland waterways, except construction; marine fisheries; Merchant Marine and navigation; non-military aeronautical and space sciences; oceans, weather and atmospheric activities; interoceanic canals generally; regulation of consumer products and services; science, engineering and technology research, development and policy; sports; standards and measurement; transportation and commerce aspects of outer continental shelf lands. Chairman and ranking minority member are non-voting members ex officio of all subcommittees of which they are not regular members.

Commerce, Science and Transportation Subcommittees listed on p. B-30

† Denotes freshmen.

Aviation

Gorton, chairman

Stevens	*Ford*
Burns	*Hollings*
Lott	*Inouye*
Hutchison (Texas)	*Bryan*
Ashcroft	*Rockefeller*
Frist	*Breaux*
Snowe	*Dorgan*
Brownback †	*Wyden*

Communications

Burns, chairman

Stevens	*Hollings*
Gorton	*Inouye*
Lott	*Ford*
Ashcroft	*Kerry (Mass.)*
Hutchison (Texas)	*Breaux*
Abraham	*Rockefeller*
Frist	*Dorgan*
Brownback †	*Wyden*

Consumer Affairs, Foreign Commerce and Tourism

Ashcroft, chairman

Gorton	*Breaux*
Abraham	*Ford*
Burns	*Bryan*
Brownback †	

Manufacturing and Competitiveness

Abraham, chairman

Snowe	*Bryan*
Ashcroft	*Hollings*
Frist	*Dorgan*
Brownback †	*Rockefeller*

Oceans and Fisheries

Snowe, chairman

Stevens	*Kerry (Mass.)*
Gorton	*Inouye*
Hutchison (Texas)	*Breaux*

Science, Technology and Space

Frist, chairman

Burns	*Rockefeller*
Hutchison (Texas)	*Kerry (Mass.)*
Stevens	*Bryan*
Abraham	*Dorgan*

Surface Transportation and Merchant Marine

Hutchison (Texas), chairman

Stevens	*Inouye*
Burns	*Breaux*
Snowe	*Dorgan*
Frist	*Bryan*
Abraham	*Wyden*
Ashcroft	

Energy and Natural Resources

Republicans (11)	***Democrats (9)***
Frank H. Murkowski, Alaska, chairman	*Dale Bumpers, Ark., ranking member*
Pete V. Domenici, N.M.	*Wendell H. Ford, Ky.*
Don Nickles, Okla.	*Jeff Bingaman, N.M.*
Larry E. Craig, Idaho	*Daniel K. Akaka, Hawaii*
Ben Nighthorse Campbell, Colo.	*Byron L. Dorgan, N.D.*
Craig Thomas, Wyo.	*Bob Graham, Fla.*
Jon Kyl, Ariz.	*Ron Wyden, Ore.*
Rod Grams, Minn.	*Tim Johnson, S.D. †*
Gordon H. Smith, Ore. †	*Mary L. Landrieu, La. †*
Slade Gorton, Wash.	
Conrad Burns, Mont.	

† Denotes freshmen.

Jurisdiction: Energy policy, regulation, conservation, research and development; coal; energy-related aspects of deep-water ports; hydroelectric power, irrigation and reclamation; mines, mining and minerals generally; national parks, recreation areas, wilderness areas, wild and scenic rivers, historic sites, military parks and battlefields; naval petroleum reserves in Alaska; non-military development of nuclear energy; oil and gas production and distribution; public lands and forests; solar energy systems; territorial possessions of the United States. The chairman and ranking minority member are non-voting members ex officio of all subcommittees of which they are not regular members.

Energy, Research, Development, Production and Regulation

Nickles, chairman

Domenici	*Ford*
Craig	*Bingaman*
Grams	*Graham*
Gorton	*Wyden*
Campbell	*Johnson †*
Smith (Ore.) †	*Landrieu †*

Forests and Public Land Management

Craig, chairman

Burns	*Dorgan*
Domenici	*Graham*
Thomas	*Wyden*
Kyl	*Johnson †*
Smith (Ore.) †	*Landrieu †*

National Parks, Historic Preservation and Recreation

Thomas, chairman

Campbell	*Bingaman*
Grams	*Akaka*
Nickles	*Graham*
Burns	*Landrieu †*

Water and Power

Kyl, chairman

Smith (Ore.) †	*Akaka*
Gorton	*Ford*
Campbell	*Dorgan*
Craig	*Wyden*

Environment and Public Works

Republicans (10)	**Democrats (8)**
John H. Chafee, R.I., chairman	*Max Baucus, Mont., ranking member*
John W. Warner, Va.	*Daniel Patrick Moynihan, N.Y.*
Robert C. Smith, N.H.	*Frank R. Lautenberg, N.J.*
Dirk Kempthorne, Idaho	*Harry Reid, Nev.*
James M. Inhofe, Okla.	*Bob Graham, Fla.*
Craig Thomas, Wyo.	*Joseph I. Lieberman, Conn.*
Christopher S. Bond, Mo.	*Barbara Boxer, Calif.*
Tim Hutchinson, Ark. †	*Ron Wyden, Ore.*
Wayne Allard, Colo. †	
Jeff Sessions, Ala. †	

† Denotes freshmen.

Jurisdiction: Environmental policy, research and development; air, water and noise pollution; construction and maintenance of highways; environmental aspects of outer continental shelf lands; environmental effects of toxic substances other than pesticides; fisheries and wildlife; flood control and improvements of rivers and harbors; non-military environmental regulation and control of nuclear energy; ocean dumping; public buildings and grounds; public works, bridges and dams; regional economic development; solid waste disposal and recycling; water resources. The chairman is a nonvoting member ex officio of all committees on which he is not a regular member.

Clean Air, Wetlands, Private Property and Nuclear Safety

Inhofe, chairman

Hutchinson (Ark.) †	*Graham*
Allard †	*Lieberman*
Sessions †	*Boxer*

Drinking Water, Fisheries and Wildlife

Kempthorne, chairman

Thomas	*Reid*
Bond	*Lautenberg*
Warner	*Lieberman*
Hutchinson (Ark.) †	*Wyden*

Superfund, Waste Control and Risk Assessment

Smith (N.H.), chairman

Warner	*Lautenberg*
Inhofe	*Moynihan*
Allard †	*Boxer*
Sessions †	*Graham*

Transportation and Infrastructure

Warner, chairman

Smith (N.H.)	*Baucus*
Kempthorne	*Moynihan*
Bond	*Reid*
Inhofe	*Graham*
Thomas	*Boxer*

Finance

Republicans (11)	***Democrats (9)***
William V. Roth Jr., Del., chairman	*Daniel Patrick Moynihan, N.Y., ranking member*
John H. Chafee, R.I.	*Max Baucus, Mont.*
Charles E. Grassley, Iowa	*John D. Rockefeller IV, W.Va.*
Orrin G. Hatch, Utah	*John B. Breaux, La.*
Alfonse M. D'Amato, N.Y.	*Kent Conrad, N.D.*
Frank H. Murkowski, Alaska	*Bob Graham, Fla.*
Don Nickles, Okla.	*Carol Moseley-Braun, Ill.*
Phil Gramm, Texas	*Richard H. Bryan, Nev.*
Trent Lott, Miss.	*Bob Kerrey, Neb.*
James M. Jeffords, Vt.	
Connie Mack, Fla.	

Jurisdiction: Revenue measures generally; taxes; tariffs and import quotas; reciprocal trade agreements; customs; revenue sharing; federal debt limit; Social Security; health programs financed by taxes or trust funds. Chairman and ranking minority member are non-voting members ex officio of all subcommittees of which they are not regular members.

Health Care

Gramm, chairman

Roth	*Rockefeller*
Chafee	*Baucus*
Grassley	*Conrad*
Hatch	*Graham*
D'Amato	*Moseley-Braun*
Nickles	*Bryan*
Jeffords	*Kerrey (Neb.)*

International Trade

Grassley, chairman

Roth	*Moynihan*
Chafee	*Baucus*
Hatch	*Rockefeller*
D'Amato	*Breaux*
Murkowski	*Conrad*
Gramm	*Graham*
Lott	*Moseley-Braun*
Mack	*Kerrey (Neb.)*

Long-Term Growth, Debt and Deficit Reduction

Mack, chairman

Murkowski	*Graham*
Lott	*Bryan*

Social Security and Family Policy

Chafee, chairman

Nickles	Breaux
Gramm	Moynihan
Jeffords	Rockefeller
	Moseley-Braun

Taxation and IRS Oversight

Nickles, chairman

Roth	*Baucus*
Grassley	*Moynihan*
Hatch	*Breaux*
D'Amato	*Conrad*
Murkowski	*Bryan*
Lott	*Kerrey (Neb.)*
Jeffords	
Mack	

Foreign Relations

Republicans (10)	***Democrats (8)***
Jesse Helms, N.C., chairman	*Joseph R. Biden Jr., Del., ranking member*
Richard G. Lugar, Ind.	*Paul S. Sarbanes, Md.*
Paul Coverdell, Ga.	*Christopher J. Dodd, Conn.*
Chuck Hagel, Neb. †	*John Kerry, Mass.*
Gordon H. Smith, Ore. †	*Charles S. Robb, Va.*
Craig Thomas, Wyo.	*Russell D. Feingold, Wis.*
John Ashcroft, Mo.	*Dianne Feinstein, Calif.*
Rod Grams, Minn.	*Paul Wellstone, Minn.*
Bill Frist, Tenn.	
Sam Brownback, Kan. †	

† Denotes freshmen.

Jurisdiction: Relations of the United States with foreign nations generally; treaties; foreign economic, military, technical and humanitarian assistance; foreign loans; diplomatic service; International Red Cross; international aspects of nuclear energy; International Monetary Fund; intervention abroad and declarations of war; foreign trade; national security; oceans and international environmental and scientific affairs; protection of U.S. citizens abroad; United Nations; World Bank and other development assistance organizations. The chairman and ranking minority member are non-voting members ex officio of all subcommittees of which they are not regular members.

African Affairs

Ashcroft, chairman

Grams	*Feingold*
Frist	*Sarbanes*

East Asian and Pacific Affairs

Thomas, chairman

Frist	*Kerry (Mass.)*
Lugar	*Robb*
Coverdell	*Feingold*
Hagel †	*Feinstein*

European Affairs

Smith (Ore.), chairman †

Lugar	*Biden*
Ashcroft	*Wellstone*
Hagel †	*Sarbanes*
Thomas	*Dodd*

International Economic Policy, Export and Trade Promotion

Hagel, chairman †

Thomas	*Sarbanes*
Frist	*Biden*
Coverdell	*Wellstone*

International Operations

Grams, chairman

Helms	*Feinstein*
Brownback†	*Dodd*
Smith (Ore.)†	*Kerry (Mass.)*

Near Eastern and South Asian Affairs

Brownback, chairman †

Smith (Ore.) †	*Robb*
Grams	*Feinstein*
Helms	*Wellstone*
Ashcroft	*Sarbanes*

Western Hemisphere, Peace Corps, Narcotics and Terrorism

Coverdell, chairman

Helms	*Dodd*
Lugar	*Kerry (Mass.)*
Brownback †	*Robb*

Governmental Affairs

Republicans (9)	***Democrats (7)***
Fred Thompson, Tenn., chairman	*John Glenn, Ohio, ranking member*
William V. Roth Jr., Del.	*Carl Levin, Mich.*
Ted Stevens, Alaska	*Joseph I. Lieberman, Conn.*
Susan Collins, Maine †	*Daniel K. Akaka, Hawaii*
Sam Brownback, Neb. †	*Richard J. Durbin, Ill. †*
Pete V. Domenici, N.M.	*Robert G. Torricelli, N.J. †*
Thad Cochran, Miss.	*Max Cleland, Ga. †*
Don Nickles, Okla.	
Arlen Specter, Pa.	

† Denotes freshmen.

Jurisdiction: Archives of the United States; budget and accounting measures; census and statistics; federal civil service; congressional organization; intergovernmental relations; government information; District of Columbia; organization and management of nuclear export policy; executive branch organization and reorganization; Postal Service; efficiency, economy and effectiveness of government. Chairman and ranking minority member are non-voting members ex officio of all subcommittees of which they are not regular members.

International Security, Proliferation and Federal Services

Cochran, chairman †

Stevens	*Levin*
Collins †	*Akaka*
Domenici	*Durbin †*
Nickles	*Torricelli †*
Specter	*Cleland †*

Investigations

Collins, chairman †

Roth	*Glenn*
Stevens	*Levin*
Brownback †	*Lieberman*
Domenici	*Akaka*
Cochran	*Durbin †*
Nickles	*Torricelli †*
Specter	*Cleland †*

Oversight of Government Management and the District of Columbia

Brownback, chairman

Roth	*Lieberman*
Specter	*Cleland †*

Indian Affairs

Republicans (8)

Ben Nighthorse Campbell, Colo., chairman
Frank H. Murkowski, Alaska
John McCain, Ariz.
Slade Gorton, Wash.
Pete V. Domenici, N.M.
Craig Thomas, Wyo.
Orrin G. Hatch, Utah
James M. Inhofe, Okla.

Democrats (6)

Daniel K. Inouye, Hawaii, ranking member
Kent Conrad, N.D.
Harry Reid, Nev.
Daniel K. Akaka, Hawaii
Paul Wellstone, Minn.
Byron L. Dorgan, N.D.

Jurisdiction: Problems and opportunities of Indians, including Indian land management and trust responsibilities, education, health, special services, loan programs and claims against the United States.

Indian Affairs has no subcommittees.

Judiciary

Republicans (10)

Orrin G. Hatch, Utah, chairman
Strom Thurmond, S.C.
Charles E. Grassley, Iowa
Arlen Specter, Pa.
Fred Thompson, Tenn.
Jon Kyl, Ariz.
Mike DeWine, Ohio
John Ashcroft, Mo.
Spencer Abraham, Mich.
Jeff Sessions, Ala. †

Democrats (8)

Patrick J. Leahy, Vt., ranking member
Edward M. Kennedy, Mass.
Joseph R. Biden Jr., Del.
Herb Kohl, Wis.
Dianne Feinstein, Calif.
Russell D. Feingold, Wis.
Richard J. Durbin, Ill. †
Robert G. Torricelli, N.J. †

† Denotes freshmen.

Jurisdiction: Civil and criminal judicial proceedings in general; penitentiaries; bankruptcy, mutiny, espionage and counterfeiting; civil liberties; constitutional amendments; apportionment of representatives; government information; immigration and naturalization; interstate compacts in general; claims against the United States; patents, copyrights and trademarks; monopolies and unlawful restraints of trade; holidays and celebrations. The chairman and ranking minority member are non-voting members ex officio of all subcommittees of which they are not regular members.

Administrative Oversight and the Courts

Grassley, chairman

Thurmond	*Durbin †*
Sessions †	*Feingold*
Kyl	*Kohl*

Antitrust, Business Rights and Competition

DeWine, chairman

Hatch	*Kohl*
Thurmond	*Torricelli †*
Specter	*Leahy*

Constitution, Federalism and Property Rights

Ashcroft, chairman

Hatch	*Feingold*
Abraham	*Kennedy*
Thurmond	*Torricelli †*
Thompson	

Immigration

Abraham, chairman

Grassley	*Kennedy*
Kyl	*Feinstein*
Specter	*Durbin †*

Technology, Terrorism and Government Information

Kyl, chairman

Hatch	*Feinstein*
Specter	*Biden*
Thompson	*Durbin †*

Youth Violence

Sessions, chairman †

Thompson	*Biden*
DeWine	*Torricelli †*
Ashcroft	*Kohl*
Grassley	*Feinstein*

Labor and Human Resources

Republicans (10)

James M. Jeffords, Vt., chairman
Daniel R. Coats, Ind.
Judd Gregg, N.H.
Bill Frist, Tenn.
Mike DeWine, Ohio
Michael B. Enzi, Wyo. †
Tim Hutchinson, Ark. †
Susan Collins, Maine †
John W. Warner, Va.
Mitch McConnell, Ky.

Democrats (8)

Edward M. Kennedy, Mass., ranking member
Christopher J. Dodd, Conn.
Tom Harkin, Iowa
Barbara A. Mikulski, Md.
Jeff Bingaman, N.M.
Paul Wellstone, Minn.
Patty Murray, Wash.
Jack Reed, R.I. †

† Denotes freshmen.

Jurisdiction: Education, labor, health and public welfare in general; aging; arts and humanities; biomedical research and development; child labor; convict labor; domestic activities of the Red Cross; equal employment opportunity; handicapped people; labor standards and statistics; mediation and arbitration of labor disputes; occupational safety and health; private pensions; public health; railway labor and retirement; regulation of foreign laborers; student loans; wages and hours; agricultural colleges; Gallaudet University; Howard University; St. Elizabeths Hospital in Washington, D.C. Chairman and ranking minority member are non-voting members ex officio of all subcommittees of which they are not regular members.

Aging

Gregg, chairman

Hutchinson (Ark.) †	*Mikulski*
Warner	*Murray*

Children and Families

Coats, chairman

Gregg	*Dodd*
Frist	*Bingaman*
Hutchinson (Ark.) †	*Wellstone*
Collins †	*Murray*
McConnell	*Reed †*

Employment and Training

DeWine, chairman

Jeffords	*Wellstone*
Enzi †	*Kennedy*
Warner	*Dodd*
McConnell	*Harkin*

Public Health and Safety

Frist, chairman

Jeffords	*Kennedy*
Coats	*Harkin*
DeWine	*Mikulski*
Enzi †	*Bingaman*
Collins †	*Reed †*

Rules and Administration

Republicans (9)

John W. Warner, Va., chairman
Jesse Helms, N.C.
Ted Stevens, Alaska
Mitch McConnell, Ky.
Thad Cochran, Miss.
Rick Santorum, Pa.
Don Nickles, Okla.
Trent Lott, Miss.
Kay Bailey Hutchison, Texas

Democrats (7)

Wendell H. Ford, Ky., ranking member
Robert C. Byrd, W.Va.
Daniel K. Inouye, Hawaii
Daniel Patrick Moynihan, N.Y.
Christopher J. Dodd, Conn.
Dianne Feinstein, Calif.
Robert G. Torricelli, N.J. †

† Denotes freshman.

Jurisdiction: Senate administration in general; corrupt practices; qualifications of senators; contested elections; federal elections in general; Government Printing Office; Congressional Record; meetings of Congress and attendance of members; presidential succession; the Capitol, congressional office buildings, the Library of Congress, the Smithsonian Institution and the Botanic Garden.

Rules and Administration has no subcommittees.

Select Ethics

Republicans (3)

Robert C. Smith, N.H., chairman
Pat Roberts, Kan. †
Jeff Sessions, Ala. †

Democrats (3)

Harry Reid, Nev., vice chairman
Patty Murray, Wash.
Kent Conrad, N.D.

Jurisdiction: Studies and investigates standards and conduct of Senate members and employees and may recommend remedial action.

Select Ethics has no subcommittees.

† Denotes freshmen

Select Intelligence

Republicans (10)

Richard C. Shelby, Ala., chairman
John H. Chafee, R.I.
Richard G. Lugar, Ind.
Mike DeWine, Ohio
Jon Kyl, Ariz.
James M. Inhofe, Okla.
Orrin G. Hatch, Utah
Pat Roberts, Kan. †
Wayne Allard, Colo. †
Daniel R. Coats, Ind.

Democrats (9)

Bob Kerrey, Neb., vice chairman
John Glenn, Ohio
Richard H. Bryan, Nev.
Bob Graham, Fla.
John Kerry, Mass.
Max Baucus, Mont.
Charles S. Robb, Va.
Frank R. Lautenberg, N.J.
Carl Levin, Mich.

Jurisdiction: Legislative and budgetary authority over the Central Intelligence Agency, the Defense Intelligence Agency, the National Security Agency and intelligence activities of the Federal Bureau of Investigation and other components of the federal intelligence community. The majority leader and minority leader are members ex officio of the committee.

Select Intelligence has no subcommittees.

† Denotes freshmen.

Small Business

Republicans (10)

Christopher S. Bond, Mo., chairman
Conrad Burns, Mont.
Paul Coverdell, Ga.
Dirk Kempthorne, Idaho
Robert F. Bennett, Utah
John W. Warner, Va.
Bill Frist, Tenn.
Olympia J. Snowe, Maine
Lauch Faircloth, N.C.
Mike Enzi, Wyo. †

Democrats (8)

John Kerry, Mass., ranking member
Dale Bumpers, Ark.
Carl Levin, Mich.
Tom Harkin, Iowa
Joseph I. Lieberman, Conn.
Paul Wellstone, Minn.
Max Cleland, Ga. †
Mary L. Landrieu, La. †

Jurisdiction: Problems of small business; Small Business Administration.

Small Business has no subcommittees.

† Denotes freshmen.

Special Aging

Republicans (10)

Charles E. Grassley, Iowa, chairman
James M. Jeffords, Vt.
Larry E. Craig, Idaho
Conrad Burns, Mont.
Richard C. Shelby, Ala.
Rick Santorum, Pa.
John W. Warner, Va.
Chuck Hagel, Neb. †
Susan Collins, Maine †
Michael B. Enzi, Wyo. †

Democrats (8)

John B. Breaux, La., ranking member
John Glenn, Ohio
Harry Reid, Nev.
Herb Kohl, Wis.
Russell D. Feingold, Wis.
Carol Moseley-Braun, Ill.
Ron Wyden, Ore.
Jack Reed, R.I. †

† Denotes freshmen.

Jurisdiction: Problems and opportunities of older people including health, income, employment, housing, and care and assistance. Reports findings and makes recommendations to the Senate, but cannot report legislation.

Special Aging has no subcommittees.

Veterans' Affairs

Republicans (7)

Arlen Specter, Pa., chairman
Strom Thurmond, S.C.
Frank H. Murkowski, Alaska
James M. Jeffords, Vt.
Ben Nighthorse Campbell, Colo.
Larry E. Craig, Idaho
Tim Hutchinson, Ark. †

Democrats (5)

John D. Rockefeller IV, W.Va., ranking member
Bob Graham, Fla.
Daniel K. Akaka, Hawaii
Paul Wellstone, Minn.
Patty Murray, Wash.

† Denotes freshman.

Jurisdiction: Veterans' measures in general; compensation; life insurance issued by the government on account of service in the armed forces; national cemeteries; pensions; readjustment benefits; veterans' hospitals, medical care and treatment; vocational rehabilitation and education.

Veterans' Affairs has no subcommittees.

House Committees

105th Congress, First Session

(Committees and subcommittees are subject to change during a session.)

Agriculture

Republicans (27)

Bob Smith, Ore., chairman †
Larry Combest, Texas
Bill Barrett, Neb.
John A. Boehner, Ohio
Thomas W. Ewing, Ill.
John T. Doolittle, Calif.
Robert W. Goodlatte, Va.
Richard W. Pombo, Calif.
Charles T. Canady, Fla.
Nick Smith, Mich.
Terry Everett, Ala.
Frank D. Lucas, Okla.
Ron Lewis, Ky.
Helen Chenoweth, Idaho
John Hostettler, Ind.
Ed Bryant, Tenn.
Mark Foley, Fla.
Saxby Chambliss, Ga.
Ray LaHood, Ill.
Jo Ann Emerson, Mo. †
Jerry Moran, Kan. †
Roy Blunt, Mo. †
Charles W. "Chip" Pickering Jr., Miss. †
Bob Schaffer, Colo. †
John Thune, S.D. †
Bill Jenkins, Tenn. †
John Cooksey, La. †

Democrats (23)

Charles W. Stenholm, Texas, ranking member
George E. Brown Jr., Calif.
Gary A. Condit, Calif.
Collin C. Peterson, Minn.
Cal Dooley, Calif.
Eva Clayton, N.C.
David Minge, Minn.
Earl F. Hilliard, Ala.
Earl Pomeroy, N.D.
Tim Holden, Pa.
Scotty Baesler, Ky.
Sanford D. Bishop Jr., Ga.
Bennie Thompson, Miss.
Sam Farr, Calif.
John Baldacci, Maine
Marion Berry, Ark. †
Virgil H. Goode Jr., Va. †
Mike McIntyre, N.C. †
Debbie Stabenow, Mich. †
Bob Etheridge, N.C. †
Chris John, La. †
Jay W. Johnson, Wis. †
Leonard L. Boswell, Iowa †

† Denotes freshmen.

Jurisdiction: Agriculture generally; forestry in general, and forest reserves other than those created from the public domain; adulteration of seeds, insect pests, and protection of birds and animals in forest reserves; agricultural and industrial chemistry; agricultural colleges and experiment stations; agricultural economics and research; agricultural education extension services; agricultural production and marketing and stabilization of prices of agricultural products, and commodities (not including distribution outside the United States); animal industry and diseases of animals; commodities exchanges; crop insurance and soil conservation; dairy industry; entomology and plant quarantine; extension of farm credit and farm security; inspection of livestock, poultry, meat products, seafood and seafood products; human nutrition and home economics; plant industry, soils and agricultural engineering; rural electrification; rural development; water conservation related to activities of the Department of Agriculture. The chairman and ranking minority member are voting members ex officio of all subcommittees of which they are not regular members.

Department Operations, Nutrition and Foreign Agriculture

Goodlatte, chairman

Ewing
Canady
Smith (Mich.)
Foley
LaHood
Thune †

Clayton
Thompson
Berry †
Brown (Calif.)
Bishop

Forestry, Resource Conservation and Research

Combest, chairman

Barrett (Neb.)
Doolittle
Pombo
Smith (Mich.)
Everett
Lucas
Lewis (Ky.)
Chenoweth
Hostettler
Chambliss
LaHood
Emerson †
Moran (Kan.) †
Pickering †
Schaffer, Bob †
Jenkins †
Cooksey †

Dooley
Brown (Calif.)
Farr
Stabenow †
John †
Peterson (Minn.)
Clayton
Minge
Hilliard
Pomeroy
Holden
Baesler
Baldacci
Berry †
Goode †

General Farm Commodities

Barrett (Neb.), chairman

Combest
Boehner
Lucas
Chambliss †
Emerson †
Moran (Kan.) †
Thune †
Cooksey †

Minge
Thompson
McIntyre †
Stabenow †
Etheridge †
John †
Johnson (Wis.) †

Livestock, Dairy and Poultry

Pombo, chairman

Boehner	*Peterson (Minn.)*
Goodlatte	*Hilliard*
Smith (Mich.)	*Holden*
Lucas	*Johnson (Wis.) †*
Lewis (Ky.)	*Condit*
Hostettler	*Dooley*
Blunt †	*Farr*
Pickering †	*Boswell †*
Jenkins †	

Risk Management and Specialty Crops

Ewing, chairman

Combest	*Condit*
Doolittle	*Baesler*
Pombo	*Bishop*
Smith (Mich.)	*Pomeroy*
Everett	*Baldacci*
Lewis (Ky.)	*Goode †*
Bryant	*McIntyre †*
Foley	*Etheridge †*
Chambliss	*Boswell †*
Moran (Kan.) †	

Appropriations

Republicans (34)	***Democrats (26)***
Robert L. Livingston, La., chairman	*David R. Obey, Wis., ranking member*
Joseph M. McDade, Pa.	*Sidney R. Yates, Ill.*
C.W. Bill Young, Fla.	*Louis Stokes, Ohio*
Ralph Regula, Ohio	*John P. Murtha, Pa.*
Jerry Lewis, Calif.	*Norm Dicks, Wash.*
John Edward Porter, Ill.	*Martin Olav Sabo, Minn.*
Harold Rogers, Ky.	*Julian C. Dixon, Calif.*
Joe Skeen, N.M.	*Vic Fazio, Calif.*
Frank R. Wolf, Va.	*W.G. "Bill" Hefner, N.C.*
Tom DeLay, Texas	*Steny H. Hoyer, Md.*
Jim Kolbe, Ariz.	*Alan B. Mollohan, W.Va.*
Ron Packard, Calif.	*Marcy Kaptur, Ohio*
Sonny Callahan, Ala.	*David E. Skaggs, Colo.*
James T. Walsh, N.Y.	*Nancy Pelosi, Calif.*
Charles H. Taylor, N.C.	*Peter J. Visclosky, Ind.*
David L. Hobson, Ohio	*Esteban E. Torres, Calif.*
Ernest Istook, Okla.	*Nita M. Lowey, N.Y.*
Henry Bonilla, Texas	*Jose E. Serrano, N.Y.*
Joe Knollenberg, Mich.	*Rosa DeLauro, Conn.*
Dan Miller, Fla.	*James P. Moran, Va.*
Jay Dickey, Ark.	*John W. Olver, Mass.*
Jack Kingston, Ga.	*Ed Pastor, Ariz.*
Mike Parker, Miss.	*Carrie P. Meek, Fla.*
Rodney Frelinghuysen, N.J.	*David E. Price, N.C. †*
Roger Wicker, Miss.	*Chet Edwards, Texas*
Michael P. Forbes, N.Y.	
George Nethercutt, Wash.	
Mark W. Neumann, Wis.	
Randy "Duke" Cunningham, Calif	
Todd Tiahrt, Kan.	
Zach Wamp, Tenn.	
Tom Latham, Iowa	
Anne M. Northup, Ky. †	
Robert B. Aderholt, Ala. †	

† Denotes freshmen.

Jurisdiction: Appropriation of the revenue for the support of the government; rescissions of appropriations contained in appropriation acts; transfers of unexpended balances; new spending authority under the Congressional Budget Act. The chairman and ranking minority member are voting members ex officio of all subcommittees of which they are not regular members.

Agriculture, Rural Development, FDA and Related Agencies

Skeen, chairman

Walsh	*Kaptur*
Dickey	*Fazio*
Kingston	*Serrano*
Nethercutt	*DeLauro*
Bonilla	
Latham	

Commerce, Justice, State and Judiciary

Rogers, chairman

Kolbe	*Mollohan*
Taylor (N.C.)	*Skaggs*
Regula	*Dixon*
Forbes	
Latham	

District of Columbia

Taylor (N.C.), chairman

Neumann	*Moran (Va.)*
Cunningham	*Sabo*
Tiahrt	*Dixon*
Northup †	
Aderholt †	

Energy and Water Development

McDade, chairman

Rogers	*Fazio*
Knollenberg	*Visclosky*
Frelinghuysen	*Edwards*

Parker	*Pastor*
Callahan	
Dickey	

Foreign Operations,Export Financing and Related Programs

Callahan, chairman

Porter	*Pelosi*
Wolf	*Yates*
Packard	*Lowey*
Knollenberg	*Torres*
Forbes	
Kingston	
Frelinghuysen	

Interior

Regula, chairman

McDade	*Yates*
Kolbe	*Murtha*
Skeen	*Dicks*
Taylor (N.C.)	*Skaggs*
Nethercutt	*Moran (Va.)*
Miller (Fla.)	
Wamp	

Labor, Health and Human Services, and Education

Porter, chairman

Young (Fla.)	*Obey*
Bonilla	*Stokes*
Istook	*Hoyer*
Miller (Fla.)	*Pelosi*
Dickey	*Lowey*
Wicker	*DeLauro*
Northup †	

Legislative Branch

Walsh, chairman

Young (Fla.)	*Serrano*
Cunningham	*Fazio*
Wamp	*Kaptur*
Latham	

Military Construction

Packard, chairman

Porter	*Hefner*
Hobson	*Olver*
Wicker	*Edwards*
Kingston	*Dicks*
Parker	*Hoyer*
Tiahrt	
Wamp	

National Security

Young (Fla.), chairman

McDade	*Murtha*
Lewis (Calif.)	*Dicks*
Skeen	*Hefner*
Hobson	*Sabo*
Bonilla	*Dixon*
Nethercutt	*Visclosky*
Istook	
Cunningham	

Transportation

Wolf, chairman

DeLay	*Sabo*
Regula	*Torres*
Rogers	*Olver*
Packard	*Pastor*
Callahan	
Tiahrt	
Aderholt †	

Treasury, Postal Service and General Government

Kolbe, chairman

Wolf	*Hoyer*
Istook	*Meek*
Forbes	*Price (N.C.) †*
Northup †	
Aderholt †	

Veterans Affairs, Housing and Urban Development and Independent Agencies

Lewis (Calif.), chairman

DeLay	*Stokes*
Walsh	*Mollohan*
Hobson	*Kaptur*
Knollenberg	*Meek*
Frelinghuysen	*Price(N.C.) †*
Neumann	
Wicker	

Banking and Financial Services

Republicans (29)

Jim Leach, Iowa, chairman
Bill McCollum, Fla. vice chairman
Marge Roukema, N.J.
Doug Bereuter, Neb.
Richard H. Baker, La.
Rick A. Lazio, N.Y.
Spencer Bachus, Ala.
Michael N. Castle, Del.
Peter T. King, N.Y.
Tom Campbell, Calif.
Ed Royce, Calif.
Frank D. Lucas, Okla.
Jack Metcalf, Wash.
Bob Ney, Ohio
Robert L. Ehrlich Jr., Md.
Bob Barr, Ga.
Jon D. Fox, Pa.
Sue W. Kelly, N.Y.
Ron Paul, Texas †
Dave Weldon, Fla.
Merrill Cook, Utah †
Vince Snowbarger, Kan. †
Jim Ryun, Kan. †
Bob Riley, Ala. †
Rick Hill, Mont. †
Pete Sessions, Texas †
Steven C. LaTourette, Ohio
2 vacancies

Democrats (24)

Henry B. Gonzalez, Texas, ranking member
John J. LaFalce, N.Y.
Bruce F. Vento, Minn.
Charles E. Schumer, N.Y.
Barney Frank, Mass.
Paul E. Kanjorski, Pa.
Joseph P. Kennedy II, Mass.
Floyd H. Flake, N.Y.
Maxine Waters, Calif.
Carolyn B. Maloney, N.Y.
Luis V. Gutierrez, Ill.
Lucille Roybal-Allard, Calif.
Thomas M. Barrett, Wis.
Nydia M. Velázquez, N.Y.
Melvin Watt, N.C.
Maurice D. Hinchey, N.Y.
Gary L. Ackerman, N.Y.
Ken Bentsen, Texas
Jesse L. Jackson Jr., Ill.
Cynthia A. McKinney, Ga.
Carolyn Cheeks Kilpatrick, Mich. †
Jim Maloney, Conn. †
Darlene Hooley, Ore. †
Julia Carson, Ind. †

Independent (1)

Bernard Sanders, Vt. *

† Denotes freshmen.

** Sanders accrues seniority among Democrats on the full committee and on subcommittees. He is ranked below Maxine Waters of California on the full committee. His position in subcommittee rankings is reflected in the listings.*

Jurisdiction: Banks and banking, including deposit insurance and federal monetary policy; bank capital markets activities generally; depository institution securities activities generally, including the activities of any affiliates, except for functional regulation under applicable securities laws not involving safety and soundness; economic stabilization, defense production, renegotiation, and control of the price of commodities, rents, and services; financial aid to commerce and industry (other than transportation); international finance; international financial and monetary organizations; money and credit, including currency and the issuance of notes and redemption thereof; gold and silver, including the coinage thereof; valuation and revaluation of the dollar; public and private housing; urban development. The chairman and ranking minority member are non-voting members ex officio of all subcommittees of which they are not regular members.

Capital Markets, Securities and Government-Sponsored Enterprises

Baker, chairman

Lucas	*Kanjorski*
Cook †	*Schumer*
Snowbarger †	*Flake*
Riley †	*Waters*
Hill †	*Gutierrez*
Sessions †	*Vento*
Lazio	*Roybal-Allard*
Bachus	*Barrett (Wis.)*
King	*Watt*
Campbell	*Ackerman*
1 vacancy	

Domestic and International Monetary Policy

Castle, chairman

Fox	*Flake*
LaTourette	*Frank*
Royce	*Kennedy (Mass.)*
Lucas	**Sanders**
Metcalf	*Kanjorski*
Ney	*Velázquez*
Barr	*Maloney (N.Y.)*
Paul †	*Hinchey*
Weldon (Fla.)	*Bentsen*
2 vacancies	*Jackson*

Financial Institutions and Consumer Credit

Roukema, chairman

McCollum	*Vento*
Bereuter	*LaFalce*
King	*Schumer*
Campbell	*Maloney (N.Y.)*
Royce	*Barrett (Wis.)*
Metcalf	*Watt*
Ehrlich	*Roybal-Allard*
Barr	*Ackerman*
Kelly	*Bentsen*
Paul †	*McKinney*
Weldon (Fla.)	*Kilpatrick †*
Ryun†	

General Oversight and Investigations

Bachus, chairman

Riley †	*Waters*
LaTourette	*McKinney*
King	*Kilpatrick †*
Ney	*Hooley †*
Vacancy	

Housing and Community Opportunity

Lazio, chairman

Ney
Roukema
Bereuter
Baker
Castle
Ehrlich
Fox
Kelly
Cook †
Hill †
Sessions †
Metcalf

Kennedy (Mass.)
Sanders
Gutierrez
Velázquez
Frank
Hinchey
Jackson
LaFalce
Maloney (Conn.) †
Hooley †
Carson †

Budget

Republicans (24)

John R. Kasich, Ohio, chairman
David L. Hobson, Ohio
Christopher Shays, Conn.
Wally Herger, Calif.
Jim Bunning, Ky.
Lamar Smith, Texas
Dan Miller, Fla.
Bob Franks, N.J.
Nick Smith, Mich.
Bob Inglis, S.C.
Jim Nussle, Iowa
Peter Hoekstra, Mich.
John Shadegg, Ariz.
George P. Radanovich, Calif.
Charles Bass, N.H.
Mark W. Neumann, Wis.
Mike Parker, Miss.
Robert L. Ehrlich Jr., Md.
Gil Gutknecht, Minn.
Van Hilleary, Tenn.
Kay Granger, Texas †
John E. Sununu, N.H. †
Joseph R. Pitts, Pa. †

Democrats (19)

John M. Spratt Jr., S.C., ranking member
Alan B. Mollohan, W.Va.
Jerry F. Costello, Ill.
Patsy T. Mink, Hawaii
Earl Pomeroy, N.D.
Lynn Woolsey, Calif.
Lucille Roybal-Allard, Calif.
Lynn Rivers, Mich.
Lloyd Doggett, Texas
Bennie Thompson, Miss.
Benjamin L. Cardin, Md.
David Minge, Minn.
Scotty Baesler, Ky.
Ken Bentsen, Texas
Jim Davis, Fla. †
Brad Sherman, Calif. †
Bob Weygand, R.I. †
Eva Clayton, N.C.
Vacancy

† Denotes freshmen.

Jurisdiction: Budget process generally; concurrent budget resolutions; measures relating to special controls over the federal budget; Congressional Budget Office.

House Budget has no subcommittees.

Commerce

Republicans (28)

Thomas J. Bliley Jr., Va., chairman
W.J. "Billy" Tauzin, La.
Michael G. Oxley, Ohio
Michael Bilirakis, Fla.
Dan Schaefer, Colo.
Joe L. Barton, Texas
Dennis Hastert, Ill.
Fred Upton, Mich.
Cliff Stearns, Fla.
Bill Paxon, N.Y.
Paul E. Gillmor, Ohio
Scott L. Klug, Wis.
James C. Greenwood, Pa.
Michael D. Crapo, Idaho
Christopher Cox, Calif.
Nathan Deal, Ga.
Steve Largent, Okla.
Richard M. Burr, N.C.
Brian P. Bilbray, Calif.
Edward Whitfield, Ky.
Greg Ganske, Iowa
Charlie Norwood, Ga.
Rick White, Wash.
Tom Coburn, Okla.
Rick A. Lazio, N.Y.
Barbara Cubin, Wyo.
James E. Rogan, Calif. †
John M. Shimkus, Ill. †

Democrats (23)

John D. Dingell, Mich., ranking member
Henry A. Waxman, Calif.
Edward J. Markey, Mass.
Ralph M. Hall, Texas
Rick Boucher, Va.
Thomas J. Manton, N.Y.
Edolphus Towns, N.Y.
Frank Pallone Jr., N.J.
Sherrod Brown, Ohio
Bart Gordon, Tenn.
Elizabeth Furse, Ore.
Peter Deutsch, Fla.
Bobby L. Rush, Ill.
Anna G. Eshoo, Calif.
Ron Klink, Pa.
Bart Stupak, Mich.
Eliot L. Engel, N.Y.
Tom Sawyer, Ohio
Albert R. Wynn, Md.
Gene Green, Texas
Karen McCarthy, Mo.
Ted Strickland, Ohio †
Diana DeGette, Colo. †

† Denotes freshmen.

Jurisdiction: Interstate and foreign commerce generally; biomedical research and development; consumer affairs and consumer protection; health and health facilities, except health care supported by payroll deductions; interstate energy compacts; measures relating to the exploration, production, storage, supply, marketing, pricing, and regulation of energy resources, including all fossil fuels, solar energy, and other unconventional or renewable energy resources; measures relating to the conservation of energy resources; measures relating to energy information generally; measures relating to (A) the generation and marketing of power (except by federally chartered or federal regional power marketing authorities), (B) the reliability and interstate transmission of, and ratemaking for, all power, and (C) the siting of generation facilities, except the installation of interconnections between government water power projects; measures relating to general management of the Department of Energy, and the management and all functions of the Federal Energy Regulatory Commission; national energy policy generally; public health and quarantine; regulation of the domestic nuclear energy industry, including regulation of research and development reactors and nuclear regulatory research; regulation of interstate and foreign communications; securities and exchanges; travel and tourism; nuclear and other energy, and nonmilitary nuclear energy and research and development, including the disposal of nuclear waste. The chairman and ranking minority member are voting members ex officio of all subcommittees of which they are not regular members.

Energy and Power

Schaefer, Dan, chairman

Crapo	*Hall (Texas)*
Bilirakis	*Furse*
Hastert	*Rush*
Upton	*McCarthy (Mo.)*
Stearns	*Wynn*
Paxon	*Markey*
Largent	*Boucher*
Burr	*Towns*
Whitfield	*Pallone*
Norwood	*Brown (Ohio)*
White	*Gordon*
Coburn	*Deutsch*
Rogan †	*Vacancy*
Shimkus †	

Finance and Hazardous Materials

Oxley, chairman

Tauzin	*Manton*
Paxon	*Stupak*
Gillmor	*Engel*
Klug	*Sawyer*
Greenwood	*Strickland †*
Crapo	*DeGette †*
Deal	*Markey*
Largent	*Hall (Texas)*
Bilbray	*Towns*
Ganske	*Pallone*
White	*Furse*
Lazio	*Vacancy*
Cubin	

Health and Environment

Bilirakis, chairman

Hastert	*Brown (Ohio)*
Barton	*Waxman*
Upton	*Towns*
Klug	*Pallone*
Greenwood	*Deutsch*
Deal	*Eshoo*
Burr	*Stupak*
Bilbray	*Green*
Whitfield	*Strickland †*
Ganske	*DeGette †*
Norwood	*Hall (Texas)*
Coburn	*Furse*
Lazio	*Vacancy*
Cubin	

Oversight and Investigations

Barton, chairman

Cox	*Klink*
Greenwood	*Waxman*
Crapo	*Deutsch*
Burr	*Stupak*
Bilbray	*Engel*
Ganske	*Sawyer*
Coburn	

Telecommunications, Trade and Consumer Protection

Tauzin, chairman

Oxley	*Markey*
Schaefer, Dan	*Boucher*
Barton	*Gordon*
Hastert	*Engel*
Upton	*Sawyer*
Stearns	*Manton*
Gillmor	*Rush*
Klug	*Eshoo*
Cox	*Klink*
Deal	*Wynn*
Largent	*Green*
White	*McCarthy (Mo.)*
Rogan †	*Shimkus †*

Education and The Workforce

Republicans (25)	***Democrats (20)***
Bill Goodling, Pa., chairman	*William L. Clay, Mo., ranking member*
Tom Petri, Wis.	*George Miller, Calif.*
Marge Roukema, N.J.	*Dale E. Kildee, Mich.*
Harris W. Fawell, Ill.	*Matthew G. Martinez, Calif.*
Cass Ballenger, N.C.	*Major R. Owens, N.Y.*
Bill Barrett, Neb.	*Donald M. Payne, N.J.*
Peter Hoekstra, Mich.	*Patsy T. Mink, Hawaii*
Howard P. "Buck" McKeon, Calif.	*Robert E. Andrews, N.J.*
Michael N. Castle, Del.	*Tim Roemer, Ind.*
Sam Johnson, Texas	*Robert C. Scott, Va.*
James M. Talent, Mo.	*Lynn Woolsey, Calif.*
James C. Greenwood, Pa.	*Carlos Romero-Barceló, Puerto Rico*
Joe Knollenberg, Mich.	*Chaka Fattah, Pa.*
Frank Riggs, Calif.	*Earl Blumenauer, Ore.*
Lindsey Graham, S.C.	*Rubén Hinojosa, Texas †*
Mark Souder, Ind.	*Carolyn McCarthy, N.Y. †*
David M. McIntosh, Ind.	*John F. Tierney, Mass. †*
Charlie Norwood, Ga.	*Ron Kind, Wis. †*
Ron Paul, Texas †	*Loretta Sanchez, Calif. †*
Bob Schaffer, Colo. †	*Harold E. Ford Jr., Tenn. †*
John E. Peterson, Pa. †	
Fred Upton, Mich.	
Nathan Deal, Ga.	
Van Hilleary, Tenn.	
Joe Scarborough, Fla.	

† Denotes freshmen.

Jurisdiction: Measures relating to education or labor generally; child labor; Columbia Institution for the Deaf, Dumb and Blind; Howard University; Freedmen's Hospital; convict labor and the entry of goods made by convicts into interstate commerce; food programs for children in schools; labor standards and statistics; mediation and arbitration of labor disputes; regulation or prevention of importation of foreign laborers under contract; U.S. Employees' Compensation Commission; vocational rehabilitation; wages and hours of labor; welfare of miners; work incentive programs. The chairman and ranking minority member are non-voting members ex officio of all subcommittees of which they are not regular members.

Early Childhood, Youth and Families

Riggs, chairman

Castle	*Martinez*
Johnson, Sam	*Miller (Calif.)*
Souder	*Scott*
Paul †	*Fattah*
Goodling	*Kildee*
Greenwood	*Owens*
McIntosh	*Payne*
Peterson (Pa.) †	*Mink*
Upton	*Roemer*
Hilleary	

Employer-Employee Relations

Fawell, chairman

Talent	*Payne*
Knollenberg	*Fattah*
Petri	*Hinojosa †*
Roukema	*McCarthy (N.Y.) †*
Ballenger	*Tierney †*
Goodling	

Oversight and Investigations

Hoekstra, chairman

Norwood	*Mink*
Hilleary	*Kind †*
Scarborough	*Sanchez †*
McKeon	*Ford †*
Fawell	

Postsecondary Education, Training and Life-Long Learning

McKeon, chairman

Goodling	*Kildee*
Petri	*Andrews*
Roukema	*Roemer*
Barrett (Neb.)	*Woolsey*
Greenwood	*Romero-Barceló*
Graham	*Blumenauer*
McIntosh	*Hinojosa †*
Schaffer, Bob †	*McCarthy (N.Y.) †*
Peterson (Pa.) †	*Tierney †*
Castle	*Kind †*
Riggs	*Sanchez †*
Souder	*Ford †*
Upton	
Deal	

Workforce Protections

Ballenger, chairman

Fawell	*Owens*
Barrett (Neb.)	*Miller (Calif.)*
Hoekstra	*Martinez*
Graham	*Andrews*
Paul †	*Woolsey*
Schaffer, Bob †	

Government Reform and Oversight

Republicans (24)

Dan Burton, Ind., chairman
Benjamin A. Gilman, N.Y.
Dennis Hastert, Ill.
Constance A. Morella, Md.
Christopher Shays, Conn.
Steven H. Schiff, N.M.
Christopher Cox, Calif.
Ileana Ros-Lehtinen, Fla.
John M. McHugh, N.Y.
Steve Horn, Calif.
John L. Mica, Fla.
Thomas M. Davis III, Va.
David M. McIntosh, Ind.
Mark Souder, Ind.
Joe Scarborough, Fla.
John Shadegg, Ariz.
Steven C. LaTourette, Ohio
Mark Sanford, S.C.
John E. Sununu, N.H. †
Pete Sessions, Texas †
Michael Pappas, N.J. †
Vince Snowbarger, Kan. †
Bob Barr, Ga.
Vacancy

Democrats (19)

Henry A. Waxman, Calif., ranking member
Tom Lantos, Calif.
Bob Wise, W.Va.
Major R. Owens, N.Y.
Edolphus Towns, N.Y.
Paul E. Kanjorski, Pa.
Gary A. Condit, Calif.
Carolyn B. Maloney, N.Y.
Thomas M. Barrett, Wis.
Eleanor Holmes Norton, D.C.
Chaka Fattah, Pa.
Tim Holden, Pa.
Elijah E. Cummings, Md.
Dennis J. Kucinich, Ohio †
Rod R. Blagojevich, Ill. †
Danny K. Davis, Ill. †
John F. Tierney, Mass. †
Jim Turner, Texas †
Tom Allen, Maine †

Independent (1)

Bernard Sanders, Vt.

† Denotes freshmen.

Jurisdiction: Civil service, including intergovernmental personnel; the status of officers and employees of the United States, including their compensation, classification, and retirement; measures relating to the municipal affairs of the District of Columbia in general, other than appropriations; federal paperwork reduction; government management and accounting measures, generally; holidays and celebrations; overall economy, efficiency and management of government operations and activities, including federal procurement; National Archives; population and demography generally, including the census; Postal Service generally, including the transportation of mail; public information and records; relationship of the federal government to the states and municipalities generally; reorganizations in the executive branch of the government. The chairman and ranking minority member are voting members ex officio of all subcommittees of which they are not regular members.

Civil Service

Mica, chairman

Pappas †	*Cummings*
Morella	*Norton*
Cox	
Sessions †	

District of Columbia

Davis (Va.), chairman

Morella	*Norton*
Ros-Lehtinen	*Allen †*
Horn	

Government Management, Information and Technology

Horn, chairman

Sessions †	*Maloney (N.Y.)*
Davis (Va.)	*Kanjorski*
Scarborough	*Owens*
Sanford	*Blagojevich †*
Sununu †	*Davis (Ill.) †*
Vacancy	

Human Resources

Shays, chairman

Snowbarger †	*Towns*
Gilman	*Kucinich*
McIntosh	*Allen †*
Souder	*Lantos*
Pappas †	**Sanders**
Schiff	*Barrett (Wis.)*

National Economic Growth, Natural Resources and Regulatory Affairs

McIntosh, chairman

Sununu †	*Sanders*
Hastert	*Tierney †*
Scarborough	*Turner †*
Shadegg	*Kanjorski*
LaTourette	*Condit*
Snowbarger †	*Kucinich †*
Barr	*Fattah*
Vacancy	

National Security, International Affairs and Criminal Justice

Hastert, chairman

Souder	*Barrett (Wis.)*
Shays	*Lantos*
Schiff	*Wise*
Ros-Lehtinen	*Condit*
McHugh	*Blagojevich †*
Mica	*Maloney (N.Y.)*
Shadegg	*Cummings*
LaTourette	*Turner †*
Barr	

Postal Service

McHugh, chairman

Sanford	*Fattah*
Gilman	*Owens*
LaTourette	*Davis (Ill.) †*
Sessions †	

House Oversight

Republicans (5)

Bill Thomas, Calif., chairman
Bob Ney, Ohio
John A. Boehner, Ohio
Vernon J. Ehlers, Mich.
Kay Granger, Texas †

Democrats (3)

Sam Gejdenson, Conn., ranking member
Steny H. Hoyer, Md.
Carolyn Cheeks Kilpatrick, Mich. †

† Denotes freshmen.

Jurisdiction: Accounts of the House generally; assignment of office space for members and committees; disposition of useless executive papers; matters relating to the election of the president, vice president, or members of Congress; corrupt practices; contested elections; credentials and qualifications; federal elections generally; appropriations from accounts for committee salaries and expenses (except for the Committee on Appropriations), House Information Systems, and allowances and expenses of members, House officers and administrative offices of the House; auditing and settling of all such accounts; expenditure of such accounts; employment of persons by the House, including clerks for members and committees, and reporters of debates; Library of Congress and the House Library; statuary and pictures; acceptance or purchase of works of art for the Capitol; the Botanic Garden; management of the Library of Congress; purchase of books and manuscripts; Smithsonian Institution and the incorporation of similar institutions; Franking Commission; printing and correction of the Congressional Record; services to the House, including the House restaurant, parking facilities and administration of the House office buildings and of the House wing of the Capitol; travel of members of the House; raising, reporting and use of campaign contributions for candidates for office of representative in the House of Representatives, of delegate, and of resident commissioner to the United States from Puerto Rico; compensation, retirement and other benefits of the members, officers, and employees of the Congress.

House Oversight has no subcommittees.

International Relations

Republicans (26)

Benjamin A. Gilman, N.Y., chairman
Bill Goodling, Pa.
Jim Leach, Iowa
Henry J. Hyde, Ill.
Doug Bereuter, Neb.
Christopher H. Smith, N.J.
Dan Burton, Ind.
Elton Gallegly, Calif.
Ileana Ros-Lehtinen, Fla.
Cass Ballenger, N.C.
Dana Rohrabacher, Calif.
Donald Manzullo, Ill.
Ed Royce, Calif.
Peter T. King, N.Y.
Jay C. Kim, Calif.
Steve Chabot, Ohio
Mark Sanford, S.C.
Matt Salmon, Ariz.
Amo Houghton, N.Y.
Tom Campbell, Calif.
Jon D. Fox, Pa.
John M. McHugh, N.Y.
Lindsey Graham, S.C. †
Roy Blunt, Mo. †
Jerry Moran, Kan. †
Kevin Brady, Texas †

Democrats (21)

Lee H. Hamilton, Ind., ranking member
Sam Gejdenson, Conn.
Tom Lantos, Calif.
Howard L. Berman, Calif.
Gary L. Ackerman, N.Y.
Eni F.H. Faleomavaega, Am. Samoa
Matthew G. Martinez, Calif.
Donald M. Payne, N.J.
Robert E. Andrews, N.J.
Robert Menendez, N.J.
Sherrod Brown, Ohio
Cynthia A. McKinney, Ga.
Alcee L. Hastings, Fla.
Pat Danner, Mo.
Earl F. Hilliard, Ala.
Brad Sherman, Calif. †
Robert Wexler, Fla. †
Dennis J. Kucinich, Ohio †
Steven R. Rothman, N.J. †
Bob Clement, Tenn.

† Denotes freshmen.

Jurisdiction: Relations of the United States with foreign nations generally; acquisition of land and buildings for embassies and legations in foreign countries; establishment of boundary lines between the United States and foreign nations; export controls, including nonproliferation of nuclear technology and nuclear hardware; foreign loans; international commodity agreements (other than those involving sugar), including all agreements for cooperation in the export of nuclear technology and nuclear hardware; international conferences and congresses; international education; intervention abroad and declarations of war; measures relating to the diplomatic service; measures to foster commercial intercourse with foreign nations and to safeguard American business interests abroad; measures relating to international economic policy; neutrality; protection of American citizens abroad and expatriation; American National Red Cross; trading with the enemy; U.N. organizations. The chairman and ranking minority member are non-voting members ex officio of all subcommittees of which they are not regular members.

Africa

Royce, chairman

Houghton
Chabot
Sanford
Campbell
McHugh

Menendez
Payne
Hastings (Fla.)
Kucinich †

Asia and the Pacific

Bereuter, chairman

Leach	*Berman*
Rohrabacher	*Faleomavaega*
King	*Andrews*
Kim	*Brown (Ohio)*
Salmon	*Martinez*
Fox	*Hastings (Fla.)*
McHugh	*Wexler †*
Manzullo	
Royce	

International Economic Policy and Trade

Ros-Lehtinen, chairman

Manzullo	*Gejdenson*
Chabot	*Danner*
Campbell	*Hilliard*
Graham	*Sherman †*
Blunt †	*Kucinich †*
Moran (Kan.) †	*Rothman †*
Brady †	*Clement*
Bereuter	*Lantos*
Rohrabacher	

International Operations and Human Rights

Smith (N.J.), chairman

Goodling	*Lantos*
Hyde	*McKinney*
Burton	*Ackerman*
Ballenger	*Faleomavaega*
King	*Payne*
Salmon	*Hilliard*
Graham	*Wexler †*
Ros-Lehtinen	

Western Hemisphere

Gallegly, chairman

Ballenger	*Ackerman*
Sanford	*Martinez*
Smith (N.J.)	*Andrews*
Burton	*Menendez*
Ros-Lehtinen	*McKinney*
Kim	*Sherman †*
Blunt †	
Brady †.	

Judiciary

Republicans (20)

Henry J. Hyde, Ill., chairman
F. James Sensenbrenner Jr., Wis.
Bill McCollum, Fla.
George W. Gekas, Pa.
Howard Coble, N.C.
Lamar Smith, Texas
Steven H. Schiff, N.M.
Elton Gallegly, Calif.
Charles T. Canady, Fla.
Bob Inglis, S.C.
Robert W. Goodlatte, Va.
Steve Buyer, Ind.
Sonny Bono, Calif.
Ed Bryant, Tenn.
Steve Chabot, Ohio
Bob Barr, Ga.
Bill Jenkins, Tenn. †
Asa Hutchinson, Ark. †
Ed Pease, Ind. †
Christopher B. Cannon, Utah †

Democrats (15)

John Conyers Jr., Mich., ranking member
Barney Frank, Mass.
Charles E. Schumer, N.Y.
Howard L. Berman, Calif.
Rick Boucher, Va.
Jerrold Nadler, N.Y.
Robert C. Scott, Va.
Melvin Watt, N.C.
Zoe Lofgren, Calif.
Sheila Jackson-Lee, Texas
Maxine Waters, Calif.
Martin T. Meehan, Mass.
Bill Delahunt, Mass. †
Robert Wexler, Fla. †
Steven R. Rothman, N.J. †

† Denotes freshmen.

Jurisdiction: The judiciary and judicial proceedings, civil and criminal; administrative practice and procedure; apportionment of representatives; bankruptcy, mutiny, espionage, and counterfeiting; civil liberties; constitutional amendments; federal courts and judges, and local courts in the territories and possessions; immigration and naturalization; interstate compacts, generally; measures relating to claims against the United States; meetings of Congress, attendance of members and their acceptance of incompatible offices; national penitentiaries; patents, the Patent Office, copyrights, and trademarks; presidential succession; protection of trade and commerce against unlawful restraints and monopolies; revision and codification of the Statutes of the United States; state and territorial boundaries; subversive activities affecting the internal security of the United States. The chairman and ranking minority member are non-voting members ex officio of all subcommittees of which they are not regular members.

Commercial and Administrative Law

Gekas, chairman

Schiff	*Nadler*
Smith (Texas)	*Jackson-Lee*
Inglis	*Meehan*
Bryant	*Delahunt †*
Chabot	

Constitution

Canady, chairman

Hyde	*Scott*
Inglis	*Waters*
Bryant	*Serrano*
Jenkins	*Conyers*
Goodlatte	*Nadler*
Barr	*Watt*
Hutchinson †	

Courts and Intellectual Property

Coble, chairman

Sensenbrenner	*Frank*
Gallegly	*Conyers*
Goodlatte	*Berman*
Bono	*Boucher*
Pease †	*Lofgren*
Cannon †	*Delahunt †*
McCollum	
Canady	

Crime

McCollum, chairman

Schiff	*Schumer*
Buyer	*Jackson-Lee*
Chabot	*Meehan*
Barr	*Wexler †*
Hutchinson †	*Rothman †*
Gekas	
Coble	

Immigration and Claims

Smith (Texas), chairman

Gallegly	*Watt*
Bono	*Schumer*
Jenkins †	*Berman*
Pease †	*Lofgren*
Cannon †	*Wexler †*
Bryant	

National Security

Republicans (30)

Floyd D. Spence, S.C., chairman
Bob Stump, Ariz.
Duncan Hunter, Calif.
John R. Kasich, Ohio
Herbert H. Bateman, Va.
James V. Hansen, Utah
Curt Weldon, Pa.
Joel Hefley, Colo.
H. James Saxton, N.J.
Steve Buyer, Ind.
Tillie Fowler, Fla.
John M. McHugh, N.Y.
James M. Talent, Mo.
Terry Everett, Ala.
Roscoe G. Bartlett, Md.
Howard P. "Buck" McKeon, Calif.
Ron Lewis, Ky.
J.C. Watts, Okla.
William M. "Mac" Thornberry, Texas
John Hostettler, Ind.
Saxby Chambliss, Ga.
Van Hilleary, Tenn.
Joe Scarborough, Fla.
Walter B. Jones Jr., N.C.
Lindsey Graham, S.C.
Sonny Bono, Calif.
Jim Ryun, Kan. †
Michael Pappas, N.J. †
Bob Riley, Ala. †
Jim Gibbons, Nev. †

Democrats (25)

Ronald V. Dellums, Calif., ranking member
Ike Skelton, Mo.
Norman Sisisky, Va.
John M. Spratt Jr., S.C.
Solomon P. Ortiz, Texas
Owen B. Pickett, Va.
Lane Evans, Ill.
Gene Taylor, Miss.
Neil Abercrombie, Hawaii
Martin T. Meehan, Mass.
Robert A. Underwood, Guam
Jane Harman, Calif.
Paul McHale, Pa.
Patrick J. Kennedy, R.I.
Rod R. Blagojevich, Ill. †
Silvestre Reyes, Texas †
Tom Allen, Maine †
Vic Snyder, Ark. †
Jim Turner, Texas †
Allen Boyd, Fla. †
Adam Smith, Wash. †
Loretta Sanchez, Calif. †
Jim Maloney, Conn. †
Mike McIntyre, N.C. †
Vacancy

† Denotes freshmen.

Jurisdiction: Common defense generally; Department of Defense generally, including the Departments of the Army, Navy, and Air Force generally; ammunition depots; forts; arsenals; Army, Navy and Air Force reservations and establishments; conservation, development and use of naval petroleum and oil shale reserves; interoceanic canals generally, including measures relating to the maintenance, operation, and administration of interoceanic canals; Merchant Marine Academy, and State Maritime Academies; military applications of nuclear energy; tactical intelligence and intelligence related activities of the Department of Defense; national security aspects of merchant marine, including financial assistance for the construction and operation of vessels, the maintenance of the U.S. shipbuilding and ship repair industrial base, cabotage, cargo preference and merchant marine officers and seamen as these matters relate to national security; pay, promotion, retirement, and other benefits and privileges of members of the armed forces; scientific research and development in support of the armed services; selective service; Size and composition of the Army, Navy, Marine Corps, and Air Force; soldiers' and sailors' homes; strategic and critical materials necessary for the common defense.

Military Installations and Facilities

Hefley, chairman

McHugh	*Ortiz*
Hostettler	*Sisisky*
Hilleary	*Abercrombie*
Scarborough	*Underwood*
Stump	*Reyes †*
Saxton	*Snyder †*
Buyer	*Boyd †*
Fowler	*Smith (Wash.) †*
Everett	

Military Personnel

Buyer, chairman

Talent	*Taylor (Miss.)*
Bartlett	*Skelton*
Lewis (Ky.)	*Pickett*
Watts	*Underwood*
Thornberry	*Harman*
Graham	*Kennedy (R.I.)*
Bono	*Maloney (Conn.) †*
Ryun †	

Military Procurement

Hunter, chairman

Spence	*Skelton*
Stump	*Dellums*
Hansen	*Spratt*
Saxton	*Evans*
Talent	*Blagojevich †*
Everett	*Allen †*
McKeon	*Snyder †*
Lewis (Ky.)	*Turner †*
Watts	*Boyd †*
Thornberry	*Smith (Wash.) †*
Graham	*Maloney (Conn.) †*
Bono	*McIntyre †*
Ryun †	
Pappas †	

Military Readiness

Bateman, chairman

Kasich	*Sisisky*
Fowler	*Ortiz*
Chambliss	*Pickett*
Jones	*Evans*
Riley †	*Taylor (Miss.)*
Gibbons †	*Meehan*
Hunter	*Underwood*
Hansen	*McHale*
Weldon (Pa.)	*Vacancy*
McKeon	

Military Research and Development

Weldon (Pa.), chairman

Bartlett	*Pickett*
Kasich	*Abercrombie*
Bateman	*Meehan*
Hefley	*Harman*
McHugh	*McHale*
Hostettler	*Kennedy (R.I.)*
Chambliss	*Blagojevich †*
Hilleary	*Reyes †*
Scarborough	*Allen †*
Jones	*Turner †*
Pappas †	*Sanchez †*
Riley †	
Gibbons †	

Merchant Marine

Bateman, chairman

Hunter	*Abercrombie*
Weldon (Pa.)	*Taylor*
Saxton	*Harman*
Scarborough	*Kennedy (R.I.)*
2 vacancies	*Allen †*
	Smith (Wash.) †

Morale, Welfare and Recreation

McHugh, chairman

Stump	*Meehan*
Bateman	*Sisisky*
Bartlett	*Ortiz*
Watts	*Pickett*
Chambliss	*Underwood*
Scarborough	*Sanchez*
Jones	

Resources

Republicans (27)	***Democrats (23)***
Don Young, Alaska, chairman	*George Miller, Calif., ranking member*
W.J. "Billy" Tauzin, La.	*Edward J. Markey, Mass.*
James V. Hansen, Utah	*Nick J. Rahall II, W.Va.*
H. James Saxton, N.J.	*Bruce F. Vento, Minn.*
Elton Gallegly, Calif.	*Dale E. Kildee, Mich.*
John J. "Jimmy" Duncan Jr., Tenn.	*Peter A. DeFazio, Ore.*
Joel Hefley, Colo.	*Eni F.H. Faleomavaega, Am. Samoa*
John T. Doolittle, Calif.	*Neil Abercrombie, Hawaii*
Wayne T. Gilchrest, Md.	*Solomon P. Ortiz, Texas*
Ken Calvert, Calif.	*Owen B. Pickett, Va.*
Richard W. Pombo, Calif.	*Frank Pallone Jr., N.J.*
Barbara Cubin, Wyo.	*Cal Dooley, Calif.*
Helen Chenoweth, Idaho	*Carlos Romero-Barceló, P.R.*
Linda Smith, Wash.	*Maurice D. Hinchey, N.Y.*
George P. Radanovich, Calif.	*Robert A. Underwood, Guam*
Walter B. Jones Jr., N.C.	*Sam Farr, Calif.*
William M. "Mac" Thornberry, Texas	*Patrick J. Kennedy, R.I.*
John Shadegg, Ariz.	*Adam Smith, Wash. †*
John Ensign, Nev.	*Bill Delahunt, Mass. †*
Bob Smith, Ore. †	*Chris John, La. †*
Christopher B. Cannon, Utah †	*Donna M. Christian-Green, V.I. †*
Kevin Brady, Texas †	*Nick Lampson, Texas †*
John E. Peterson, Pa. †	*Ron Kind, Wis. †*
Rick Hill, Mont. †	
Bob Schaffer, Colo. †	
Jim Gibbons, Nev. †	
Michael D. Crapo, Idaho	

† Denotes freshmen.

Jurisdiction: Public lands generally, including entry, easements, and grazing; mining interests generally; fisheries and wildlife, including research, restoration, refuges, and conservation; forest reserves and national parks created from the public domain; forfeiture of land grants and alien ownership, including alien ownership of mineral lands; Geological Survey; international fishing agreements; interstate compacts relating to apportionment of waters for irrigation purposes; irrigation and reclamation, including water supply for reclamation projects, and easements of public lands for irrigation projects, and acquisition of private lands when necessary to complete irrigation projects; measures relating to the care and management of Indians, including the care and allotment of Indian lands and general and special measures relating to claims which are paid out of Indian funds; measures relating generally to the insular possessions of the United States, except those affecting the revenue and appropriations; military parks and battlefields, national cemeteries administered by the secretary of the Interior, parks within the District of Columbia, and the erection of monuments to the memory of individuals; mineral land laws, claims and entries; mineral resources of the public lands; mining schools and experimental stations; marine affairs (including coastal zone management), except for measures relating to oil and other pollution of navigable waters; oceanography; petroleum conservation on the public lands and conservation of the radium supply in the United States; preservation of prehistoric ruins and objects of interest on the public domain; relations of the United States with the Indians and the Indian tribes; Trans-Alaska Oil Pipeline (except rate-making). The chairman and ranking minority member are non-voting members ex officio of all subcommittees of which they are not regular members.

Energy and Mineral Resources

Cubin, chairman

Tauzin	*Romero-Barceló*
Duncan	*Rahall*
Calvert	*Ortiz*
Thornberry	*Dooley*
Cannon †	*Kennedy (R.I.)*
Brady †	*John †*
Gibbons †	*Christian-Green †*

Fisheries Conservation, Wildlife and Oceans

Saxton, chairman

Tauzin	*Abercrombie*
Gilchrest	*Ortiz*
Jones	*Pallone*
Peterson (Pa.) †	*Farr*
Crapo	*Vacancy*

Forests and Forest Health

Chenoweth, chairman

Hansen	*Hinchey*
Doolittle	*Vento*
Radanovich	*Kildee*
Peterson (Pa.) †	*3 vacancies*
Hill †	
Schaffer, Bob †	

National Parks and Public Lands

Hansen, chairman

Gallegly	*Faleomavaega*
Duncan	*Markey*
Hefley	*Rahall*
Gilchrest	*Vento*
Pombo	*Kildee*
Chenoweth	*Pallone*
Smith (Wash.)	*Romero-Barceló*
Radanovich	*Hinchey*
Jones	*Underwood*
Shadegg	*Kennedy (R.I.)*
Ensign	*Delahunt †*
Smith (Ore.) †	*Christian-Green †*
Hill †	*Vacancy*
Gibbons †	

Water and Power

Doolittle, chairman

Calvert	*DeFazio*
Pombo	*Miller (Calif.)*
Chenoweth	*Pickett*
Smith (Wash.)	*Dooley*
Radanovich	*Farr*
Thornberry	*Smith (Wash.) †*
Shadegg	*4 vacancies*
Ensign	
Smith (Ore.) †	
Cannon †	
Crapo	

Rules

Republicans (9)

Gerald B.H. Solomon, N.Y., chairman
David Dreier, Calif.
Porter J. Goss, Fla.
John Linder, Ga.
Deborah Pryce, Ohio
Lincoln Diaz-Balart, Fla.
Scott McInnis, Colo.
Richard "Doc" Hastings, Wash.
Sue Myrick, N.C.

Democrats (4)

Joe Moakley, Mass., ranking member
Martin Frost, Texas
Tony P. Hall, Ohio
Louise M. Slaughter, N.Y.

Jurisdiction: Rules and joint rules (other than rules or joint rules relating to the Code of Official Conduct), and order of business of the House; recesses and final adjournments of Congress.

Legislative and Budget Process

Goss, chairman

Linder	*Frost*
Pryce (Ohio)	*Moakley*
Hastings (Wash.)	
Solomon	

Rules and Organization of the House

Dreier, chairman

Diaz-Balart	*Hall (Ohio)*
McInnis	*Slaughter*
Myrick	
Solomon	

Science

Republicans (25)

F. James Sensenbrenner Jr., Wis., chairman
Sherwood Boehlert, N.Y.
Harris W. Fawell, Ill.
Constance A. Morella, Md.
Curt Weldon, Pa.
Dana Rohrabacher, Calif.
Steven H. Schiff, N.M.
Joe L. Barton, Texas
Ken Calvert, Calif.
Roscoe G. Bartlett, Md.
Vernon J. Ehlers, Mich.
Dave Weldon, Fla.
Matt Salmon, Ariz.
Thomas M. Davis III, Va.
Gil Gutknecht, Minn.
Mark Foley, Fla.
Thomas W. Ewing, Ill.
Charles W. "Chip" Pickering Jr., Miss. †
Christopher B. Cannon, Utah †
Kevin Brady, Texas †
Merrill Cook, Utah †
Phil English, Pa.
George Nethercutt, Wash.
Tom Coburn, Okla.
Pete Sessions, Texas †

Democrats (21)

George E. Brown Jr., Calif., ranking member
Ralph M. Hall, Texas
Bart Gordon, Tenn.
James A. Traficant Jr., Ohio
Tim Roemer, Ind.
Robert E. "Bud" Cramer, Ala.
James A. Barcia, Mich.
Paul McHale, Pa.
Eddie Bernice Johnson, Texas
Alcee L. Hastings, Fla.
Lynn Rivers, Mich.
Zoe Lofgren, Calif.
Lloyd Doggett, Texas
Mike Doyle, Pa.
Sheila Jackson-Lee, Texas
William P. "Bill" Luther, Minn.
Debbie Stabenow, Mich. †
Bob Etheridge, N.C. †
Nick Lampson, Texas †
Darlene Hooley, Ore. †

† Denotes freshmen.

Jurisdiction: All energy research, development, and demonstration, and projects therefor, and all federally owned or operated nonmilitary energy laboratories; astronautical research and development, including resources, personnel, equipment, and facilities; civil aviation research and development; environmental research and development; marine research; measures relating to the commercial application of energy technology; National Institute of Standards and Technology, standardization of weights and measures and the metric system; National Aeronautics and Space Administration; National Space Council; National Science Foundation; National Weather Service; outer space, including exploration and control thereof; science scholarships; scientific research, development, and demonstration, and related projects. The chairman and ranking minority member are members ex officio of all subcommittees of which they are not regular members.

Basic Research

Schiff, chairman

Boehlert	*Barcia*
Morella	*Etheridge †*
Barton	*Rivers*
Gutknecht	*Jackson-Lee*
Ewing	*Luther*
Pickering †	*Brown (Calif.)*
Sessions †	
Sensenbrenner	

Energy and Environment

Calvert, chairman

Fawell	*Roemer*
Weldon (Pa.)	*McHale*
Rohrabacher	*Doyle*
Schiff	*Hooley †*
Ehlers	*Hall (Texas)*
Salmon	*Johnson, E.B.*
Foley	*Lofgren*
English	*Doggett*
Coburn	*Brown (Calif.)*
Sensenbrenner	

Space and Aeronautics

Rohrabacher, chairman

Barton	*Cramer*
Calvert	*Hall (Texas)*
Bartlett	*Traficant*
Weldon (Fla.)	*Hastings (Fla.)*
Salmon	*Jackson-Lee*
Davis (Va.)	*Luther*
Foley	*Lofgren*
Pickering †	*Lampson †*
Cannon †	*Gordon*
Brady †	*Brown (Calif.)*
Cook †	
Nethercutt	

Technology

Morella, chairman

Weldon (Pa.)	*Gordon*
Bartlett	*Johnson, E.B.*
Ehlers	*Rivers*
Davis (Va.)	*Doggett*
Gutknecht	*Stabenow †*
Ewing	*Barcia*
Cannon †	*McHale*
Brady †	*Doyle*
Cook †	*Brown (Calif.)*

Select Intelligence

Republicans (9)	***Democrats (7)***
Porter J. Goss, Fla., chairman	*Norm Dicks, Wash., ranking member*
C.W. Bill Young, Fla.	*Julian C. Dixon, Calif.*
Jerry Lewis, Calif.	*David E. Skaggs, Colo.*
Bud Shuster, Pa.	*Nancy Pelosi, Calif.*
Bill McCollum, Fla.	*Jane Harman, Calif.*
Michael N. Castle, Del.	*Ike Skelton, Mo.*
Sherwood Boehlert, N.Y.	*Sanford D. Bishop Jr., Ga.*
Charles Bass, N.H.	
Jim Gibbons, Nev. †	

† Denotes freshmen.

Jurisdiction: Legislative and budgetary authority over the National Security Agency and the director of central intelligence, the Defense Intelligence Agency, the National Security Agency, intelligence activities of the Federal Bureau of Investigation and other components of the federal intelligence community. The Speaker of the House and minority leader are non-voting members ex officio of the full committee.

Human Intelligence, Analysis and Counterintelligence

McCollum, chairman

Shuster	*Dixon*
Castle	*Skaggs*
Bass	*Pelosi*
	Bishop

Technical and Tactical Intelligence

Lewis (Calif.), chairman

Young (Fla.)	*Skaggs*
Boehlert	*Dicks*
Gibbons †	*Harman*
	Skelton

Small Business

Republicans (19)	***Democrats (16)***
James M. Talent, Mo., chairman	*John J. LaFalce, N.Y., ranking member*
Larry Combest, Texas	*Norman Sisisky, Va.*
Joel Hefley, Colo.	*Floyd H. Flake, N.Y.*
Donald Manzullo, Ill.	*Glenn Poshard, Ill.*
Roscoe G. Bartlett, Md.	*Nydia M. Velázquez, N.Y.*
Linda Smith, Wash.	*William P. "Bill" Luther, Minn.*
Frank A. LoBiondo, N.J.	*John Baldacci, Maine*
Sue W. Kelly, N.Y.	*Jesse Jackson Jr., Ill.*
Walter B. Jones Jr., N.C.	*Juanita Millender-McDonald, Calif.*
Mark E. Souder, Ind.	*Bob Weygand, R.I.*
Steve Chabot, Ohio	*Danny K. Davis, Ill. †*
Jim Ryun, Kan. †	*Allen Boyd, Fla. †*
Vince Snowbarger, Kan. †	*Carolyn McCarthy, N.Y. †*
Michael Pappas, N.J. †	*Bill Pascrell Jr., N.J. †*
Phil English, Pa.	*Virgil H. Goode Jr., Va. †*
David M. McIntosh, Ind.	*1 vacancy*
Jo Ann Emerson, Mo. †	
Rick Hill, Mont. †	
John E. Sununu, N.H. †	

† Denotes freshmen.

Jurisdiction: Assistance to and protection of small business, including financial aid, regulatory flexibility, and paperwork reduction; participation of small business enterprises in federal procurement and government contracts.

Empowerment

Souder, chairman

LoBiondo	*Velázquez*
Jones	*Flake*
Chabot	*Davis (Ill.) †*
English	*Pascrell †*
Smith (Wash.)	*Jackson*

Government Programs and Oversight

Bartlett, chairman

Combest	*Poshard*
Pappas †	*Jackson*
Smith (Wash.)	*Weygand †*
Hill †	*Boyd †*
Sununu †	*McCarthy (N.Y.) †*

Regulatory Reform and Paperwork Reduction

Kelly, chairman

Combest	*Luther*
Ryun †	*Sisisky*
McIntosh	*Goode †*
Emerson †	*Millender-McDonald*
Vacancy	*Boyd †*

Tax, Finance and Exports

Manzullo, chairman

Smith (Wash.)	*Baldacci*
Snowbarger †	*Millender-McDonald*
LoBiondo	*Weygand †*
Jones	*Davis (Ill.) †*
Vacancy	*McCarthy (N.Y.) †*

Standards of Official Conduct

Republicans (5)	***Democrats (5)***
James V. Hansen, Utah, chairman	*Howard L. Berman, Calif., ranking member*
Lamar Smith, Texas	*Martin Olav Sabo, Minn.*
Joel Hefley of Colo	*Chaka Fattah, Pa.*
Robert W. Goodlatte, Va.	*Ed Pastor, Ariz.*
Joe Knollenberg, Mich.	*Zoe Lofgren, Calif.*

Jurisdiction: Measures relating to the Code of Official Conduct. As required by the new House ethics rules, members who did not sit on the committee itself were named to a "pool" that would investigate charges of impropriety by their colleagues. Although rules allowed for a 20-member pool, only 19 members were named.

Ethics "Pool"

Herbert H. Bateman, Va.	*James E. Clyburn, S.C.*
Ed Bryant, Tenn.	*Mike Doyle, Pa.*
Nathan Deal, Ga.	*Chet Edwards, Texas*
Richard "Doc" Hastings, Wash.	*Ron Klink, Pa.*
Jim McCrery, La.	*John Lewis, Ga.*
Howard P. "Buck" McKeon, Calif.	*Carrie P. Meek, Fla.*
Dan Miller, Fla.	*Robert C. Scott, Va.*
Rob Portman, Ohio	*Bart Stupak, Mich.*
James M. Talent, Mo.	*John Tanner, Tenn.*
William M. "Mac" Thornberry, Texas	

Transportation and Infrastructure

Republicans (40)

Bud Shuster, Pa., chairman
Don Young, Alaska
Tom Petri, Wis.
Sherwood Boehlert, N.Y.
Herbert H. Bateman, Va.
Howard Coble, N.C.
John J. "Jimmy" Duncan Jr., Tenn.
Thomas W. Ewing, Ill.
Wayne T. Gilchrest, Md.
Jay C. Kim, Calif.
Steve Horn, Calif.
Bob Franks, N.J.
John L. Mica, Fla.
Jack Quinn, N.Y.
Tillie Fowler, Fla.
Vernon J. Ehlers, Mich.
Spencer Bachus, Ala.
Steven C. LaTourette, Ohio
Sue W. Kelly, N.Y.
Ray LaHood, Ill.
Richard H. Baker, La.
Frank Riggs, Calif.
Charles Bass, N.H.
Bob Ney, Ohio
Jack Metcalf, Wash.
Jo Ann Emerson, Mo. †
Ed Pease, Ind. †
Roy Blunt, Mo. †
Joseph R. Pitts, Pa. †
Asa Hutchinson, Ark. †
Merrill Cook, Utah †
John Cooksey, La. †
John Thune, S.D. †
Charles W. "Chip" Pickering Jr., Miss. †
Kay Granger, Texas †
Jon D. Fox, Pa.
Thomas M. Davis III, Va.
Frank A. LoBiondo, N.J.
J.C. Watts, Okla.

Democrats (33)

James L. Oberstar, Minn., ranking member
Nick J. Rahall II, W.Va.
Robert A. Borski, Pa.
William O. Lipinski, Ill.
Bob Wise, W.Va.
James A. Traficant Jr., Ohio
Peter A. DeFazio, Ore.
Bob Clement, Tenn.
Jerry F. Costello, Ill.
Glenn Poshard, Ill.
Robert E. "Bud" Cramer, Ala.
Eleanor Holmes Norton, D.C.
Jerrold Nadler, N.Y.
Pat Danner, Mo.
Robert Menendez, N.J.
James E. Clyburn, S.C.
Corrine Brown, Fla.
James A. Barcia, Mich.
Bob Filner, Calif.
Eddie Bernice Johnson, Texas
Frank R. Mascara, Pa.
Gene Taylor, Miss.
Juanita Millender-McDonald, Calif.
Elijah E. Cummings, Md.
Earl Blumenauer, Ore.
Max Sandlin, Texas †
Ellen O. Tauscher, Calif. †
Bill Pascrell Jr., N.J. †
Jay W. Johnson, Wis. †
Leonard L. Boswell, Iowa †
Jim McGovern, Mass. †
2 vacancies

† Denotes freshmen.

Jurisdiction: Coast Guard; federal management of emergencies and natural disasters; flood control and improvement of waterways; inspection of merchant marine vessels; navigation and related laws; rules and international arrangements to prevent collisions at sea; measures, other than appropriations, that relate to construction, maintenance and safety of roads; buildings and grounds of the Botanic Gardens, the Library of Congress and the Smithsonian Institution and other government buildings within the District of Columbia; post offices, customhouses, Federal courthouses, and merchant marine, except for national security aspects of merchant marine; pollution of navigable waters; bridges and dams, related transportation regulatory agencies; transportation, including civil aviation, railroads, water transportation, infrastructure, labor, and railroad retirement and unemployment (except revenue measures); water power. The chairman and ranking minority member are voting members ex officio of all subcommittees of which they are not regular members.

Aviation

Duncan, chairman

Blunt †	*Lipinski*
Ewing	*Boswell †*
Ehlers	*Poshard*
LaHood	*Rahall*
Bass	*Traficant*
Metcalf	*DeFazio*
Pease †	*Costello*
Pitts †	*Cramer*
Hutchinson †	*Danner*
Cook †	*Clyburn*
Cooksey †	*Brown (Fla.)*
Pickering †	*Johnson, E.B.*
Granger †	*Millender-McDonald*
	Cummings

Coast Guard and Maritime Transportation

Gilchrest, chairman

Pitts †	*Clement*
Young (Alaska)	*Johnson (Wis.) †*
Coble	*Vacancy*

Public BuildingsEconomic Development

Kim, chairman

Cooksey †	*Traficant*
Duncan	*Norton*
LaTourette	*2 vacancies*
Vacancy	

Surface Transportation

Petri, chairman

Pickering †	*Rahall*
Bateman	*DeFazio*
Coble	*Cramer*
Ewing	*Danner*
Horn	*Clyburn*
Franks	*Brown (Fla.)*
Mica	*Barcia*
Quinn	*Filner*
Fowler	*Johnson, E.B.*
Bachus	*Mascara*
LaTourette	*Millender-McDonald*
Kelly	*Costello*
LaHood	*Norton*
Baker	*Nadler*
Riggs	*Menendez*
Bass	*Taylor*

Ney	*Cummings*
Metcalf	*Sandlin †*
Emerson †	*Tauscher †*
Pease †	*Pascrell †*
Hutchinson †	*McGovern †*
Cook †	
Thune †	
Granger †	

Railroads

Vacant, chairman

Granger †	*Wise*
Boehlert	*Blumenauer*
Franks	*Borski*
Mica	*Lipinski*
Quinn	*Clement*
Fowler	*Nadler*
Bachus	*Filner*
Pitts †	*Sandlin †*

Water Resources and Environment

Boehlert, chairman

Thune †	*Borski*
Young (Alaska)	*Johnson (Wis.) †*
Petri	*Wise*
Bateman	*Menendez*
Gilchrest	*Barcia*
Kim	*Mascara*
Horn	*Taylor*
Franks	*Blumenauer*
Quinn	*Tauscher †*
Ehlers	*Pascrell †*
LaTourette	*Boswell †*
Kelly	*McGovern †*
Baker	*Rahall*
Riggs	*Vacancy*
Ney	
Emerson †	

Veteran's Affairs

Republicans (16)	***Democrats (13)***
Bob Stump, Ariz., chairman	*Lane Evans, Ill., ranking member*
Christopher H. Smith, N.J.	*Joseph P. Kennedy II, Mass.*
Michael Bilirakis, Fla.	*Bob Filner, Calif.*
Floyd D. Spence, S.C.	*Luis V. Gutierrez, Ill.*
Terry Everett, Ala.	*Sanford D. Bishop Jr., Ga.*
Steve Buyer, Ind.	*James E. Clyburn, S.C.*
Jack Quinn, N.Y.	*Corrine Brown, Fla.*
Spencer Bachus, Ala.	*Mike Doyle, Pa.*
Cliff Stearns, Fla.	*Frank R. Mascara, Pa.*
Dan Schaefer, Colo.	*Collin C. Peterson, Minn.*
Jerry Moran, Kan. †	*Julia Carson, Ind. †*
John Cooksey, La. †	*Silvestre Reyes, Texas †*
Asa Hutchinson, Ark. †	*Vic Snyder, Ark. †*
J.D. Hayworth, Ariz.	
Helen Chenoweth, Idaho	
Ray LaHood, Ill.	

† Denotes freshmen.

Jurisdiction: Veterans' measures generally; cemeteries of the United States in which veterans of any war or conflict are or may be buried, whether in the United States or abroad, except cemeteries administered by the secretary of the Interior; compensation, vocational rehabilitation, and education of veterans; life insurance issued by the government on account of service in the armed forces; pensions of all the wars of the United States, readjustment of servicemen to civil life; soldiers' and sailors' civil relief; veterans' hospitals, medical care and treatment of veterans.

Benefits

Quinn, chairman

Schaefer, Dan	*Filner*
Hayworth	*Mascara*
LaHood	*Reyes †*
Vacancy	*Bishop*

Health

Stearns, chairman

Smith (N.J.)	*Gutierrez*
Bilirakis	*Kennedy (Mass.)*
Bachus	*Brown (Fla.)*
Moran (Kan.) †	*Doyle*
Cooksey †	*Peterson (MInn.)*
Hutchison †	*Carson †*
Chenoweth	

Oversight and Investigations

Everett, chairman

Stump	*Bishop*
Spence	*Clyburn*
Buyer	*Snyder †*

Ways and Means

Republicans (23)	***Democrats (16)***
Bill Archer, Texas, chairman	*Charles B. Rangel, N.Y., ranking member*
Philip M. Crane, Ill.	*Pete Stark, Calif.*
Bill Thomas, Calif.	*Robert T. Matsui, Calif.*
E. Clay Shaw Jr., Fla.	*Barbara B. Kennelly, Conn.*
Nancy L. Johnson, Conn.	*William J. Coyne, Pa.*
Jim Bunning, Ky.	*Sander M. Levin, Mich.*
Amo Houghton, N.Y.	*Benjamin L. Cardin, Md.*
Wally Herger, Calif.	*Jim McDermott, Wash.*
Jim McCrery, La.	*Gerald D. Kleczka, Wis.*
Dave Camp, Mich.	*John Lewis, Ga.*
Jim Ramstad, Minn.	*Richard E. Neal, Mass.*
Jim Nussle, Iowa	*Michael R. McNulty, N.Y.*
Sam Johnson, Texas	*William J. Jefferson, La.*
Jennifer Dunn, Wash.	*John Tanner, Tenn.*
Mac Collins, Ga.	*Xavier Becerra, Calif.*
Rob Portman, Ohio	*Karen L. Thurman, Fla.*
Phil English, Pa.	
John Ensign, Nev.	
Jon Christensen, Neb.	
Wes Watkins, Okla. †	
J.D. Hayworth, Ariz.	
Jerry Weller, Ill.	
Kenny Hulshof, Mo. †	

† Denotes freshmen.

Jurisdiction: Revenue measures generally; reciprocal trade agreements; customs, collection districts, and ports of entry and delivery; revenue measures relating to the insular possessions; bonded debt of the United States; deposit of public moneys; transportation of dutiable goods; tax-exempt foundations and charitable trusts; national Social Security, except (A) health care and facilities programs that are supported from general revenues as opposed to payroll deductions and (B) work incentive programs. The chairman and ranking minority member are non-voting members ex officio of all subcommittees of which they are not regular members.

Health

Thomas, chairman

Johnson (Conn.)	*Stark*
McCrery	*Cardin*
Ensign	*Kleczka*
Christensen	*Lewis (Ga.)*
Crane	*Becerra*
Houghton	
Johnson, Sam	

Human Resources

Shaw, chairman

Camp	*Levin*
McCrery	*Stark*
Collins	*Matsui*
English	*Coyne*
Ensign	*McDermott*
Hayworth	
Watkins †	

Oversight

Johnson (Conn.), chairman

Portman	*Coyne*
Ramstad	*Kleczka*
Dunn	*McNulty*
English	*Tanner*
Watkins †	*Thurman*
Weller †	
Hulshof †	

Social Security

Bunning, chairman

Johnson, Sam	*Kennelly*
Collins	*Neal*
Portman	*Levin*
Christensen	*Jefferson*
Hayworth	*Tanner*
Weller †	
Hulshof †	

Trade

Crane, chairman

Thomas	*Matsui*
Shaw	*Rangel*
Houghton	*Neal*
Camp	*McDermott*
Ramstad	*McNulty*
Dunn	*Jefferson*
Herger	
Nussle	

Joint Committees

105th Congress, First Session

(Committees and subcommittees are subject to change during a session.)

Joint Economic Committee

HOUSE

H. James Saxton, N.J., chairman
Donald Manzullo, Ill.
Mark Sanford, S.C.
William M. "Mac" Thornberry, Texas
John T. Doolittle, Calif.
Jim McCrery, La.

Pete Stark, Calif., ranking member
Lee H. Hamilton, Ind.
Maurice D. Hinchey, N.Y.
Carolyn B. Maloney, N.Y.

SENATE

Connie Mack, Fla., vice chairman
William V. Roth Jr., Del.
Robert F. Bennett, Utah
Rod Grams, Minn.
Sam Brownback, Kan. †
Jeff Sessions, Ala. †

Jeff Bingaman, N.M.
Paul S. Sarbanes, Md.
Edward M. Kennedy, Mass.
Charles S. Robb, Va.

† Denotes freshmen.

Jurisdiction: Studies and investigates all recommendations in the president's annual Economic Report to Congress. Reports findings and recommendations to the House and Senate.

Joint Library Committee

HOUSE

John W. Warner, Va., chairman
Ted Stevens, Alaska
Thad Cochran, Miss.

Daniel Patrick Moynihan, N.Y.
Dianne Feinstein, Calif.

SENATE

Bill Thomas, Calif., vice chairman
Bob Ney, Ohio
Vernon J. Ehlers, Mich.

Carolyn Cheeks Kilpatrick, Mich., ranking member †
Sam Gejdenson, Conn.

† Denotes freshmen.

Jurisdiction: Management and expansion of the Library of Congress; receipt of gifts for the benefit of the library; development and maintenance of the Botanic Garden; placement of statues and other works of art in the Capitol.

Joint Printing Committee

HOUSE

John W. Warner, Va., chairman
Thad Cochran, Miss.
Mitch McConnell, Ky.

Wendell H. Ford, Ky., ranking member
Daniel K. Inouye, Hawaii

SENATE

Bill Thomas, Calif., vice chairman
Bob Ney, Ohio
Kay Granger, Texas †

Steny H. Hoyer, Md.
Sam Gejdenson, Conn.

† Denotes freshman.

Jurisdiction: Probes inefficiency and waste in the printing, binding and distribution of federal government publications. Oversees arrangement and style of the Congressional Record.

Joint Committee On Taxation

HOUSE

Bill Archer, Texas, chairman
Philip M. Crane, Ill.
Bill Thomas, Calif.

Charles B. Rangel, N.Y.
Pete Stark, Calif.

SENATE

William V. Roth Jr., Del., vice chairman
John H. Chafee, R.I.
Charles E. Grassley, Iowa

Daniel Patrick Moynihan, N.Y.
Max Baucus, Mont.

Jurisdiction: Operation, effects and administration of the federal system of internal revenue taxes; measures and methods for simplification of taxes.

Senate Committee Assignments

(Committees and subcommittees are subject to change during a session.)

Abraham: Commerce, Science & Transportation; Judiciary; Budget
Akaka: Energy & Natural Resources; Governmental Affairs; Indian Affairs; Veterans' Affairs
Allard: Environment & Public Works; Banking, Housing & Urban Affairs; Select Intelligence
Ashcroft: Commerce, Science & Transportation; Foreign Relations; Judiciary
Baucus: Agriculture, Nutrition & Forestry; Environment & Public Works (ranking member); Select Intelligence; Joint Taxation; Finance
Bennett: Appropriations; Joint Economic; Banking, Housing & Urban Affairs; Small Business
Biden: Foreign Relations (ranking member); Judiciary
Bingaman: Armed Services; Joint Economic (ranking member); Labor & Human Resources; Energy & Natural Resources
Bond: Appropriations; Budget; Small Business (chairman); Environment & Public Works
Boxer: Appropriations; Environment & Public Works; Budget; Banking, Housing & Urban Affairs
Breaux: Commerce, Science & Transportation; Special Aging (ranking member); Finance
Brownback: Commerce, Science & Transportation; Governmental Affairs; Foreign Relations; Joint Economic
Bryan: Commerce, Science & Transportation; Banking, Housing & Urban Affairs; Select Intelligence; Finance
Bumpers: Appropriations; Small Business; Energy & Natural Resources (ranking member)
Burns: Appropriations; Energy & Natural Resources; Commerce, Science & Transportation; Special Aging; Small Business
Byrd: Appropriations (ranking member); Armed Services; Rules & Administration
Campbell: Appropriations; Energy & Natural Resources; Veterans' Affairs; Indian Affairs (chairman)
Chafee: Environment & Public Works (chairman); Joint Taxation; Finance; Select Intelligence
Cleland: Armed Services; Governmental Affairs; Small Business
Coats: Armed Services; Select Intelligence; Labor & Human Resources
Cochran: Appropriations; Rules & Administration; Governmental Affairs; Agriculture, Nutrition & Forestry; Joint Printing
Collins: Governmental Affairs; Special Aging; Labor & Human Resources
Conrad: Agriculture, Nutrition & Forestry; Finance; Select Ethics; Indian Affairs; Budget
Coverdell: Agriculture, Nutrition & Forestry; Foreign Relations; Small Business
Craig: Appropriations; Energy & Natural Resources; Special Aging; Veterans' Affairs; Agriculture, Nutrition & Forestry
D'Amato: Banking, Housing & Urban Affairs (chairman); Finance
Daschle: Agriculture, Nutrition & Forestry
DeWine: Judiciary; Select Intelligence; Labor & Human Resources
Dodd: Foreign Relations; Labor & Human Resources; Rules & Administration; Banking, Housing & Urban Affairs
Domenici: Appropriations; Budget (chairman); Indian Affairs; Governmental Affairs; Energy & Natural Resources
Dorgan: Appropriations; Indian Affairs; Energy & Natural Resources; Commerce, Science & Transportation
Durbin: Judiciary; Budget; Governmental Affairs
Enzi: Banking, Housing & Urban Affairs; Small Business; Labor & Human Resources; Special Aging
Faircloth: Appropriations; Small Business; Banking, Housing & Urban Affairs
Feingold: Foreign Relations; Judiciary; Special Aging; Budget
Feinstein: Foreign Relations; Rules & Administration; Joint Library; Judiciary
Ford: Commerce, Science & Transportation; Energy & Natural Resources; Rules & Administration; Joint Printing (ranking member)
Frist: Commerce, Science & Transportation; Foreign Relations; Labor & Human Resources; Budget; Small Business
Glenn: Armed Services; Special Aging; Governmental Affairs (ranking member); Select Intelligence
Gorton: Appropriations; Budget; Indian Affairs; Energy & Natural Resources; Commerce, Science & Transportation
Graham: Environment & Public Works; Veterans' Affairs; Select Intelligence; Finance; Energy & Natural Resources
Gramm: Agriculture, Nutrition & Forestry; Budget; Finance; Banking, Housing & Urban Affairs
Grams: Foreign Relations; Joint Economic; Budget; Energy & Natural Resources; Banking, Housing & Urban Affairs
Grassley: Agriculture, Nutrition & Forestry; Special Aging (chairman); Joint Taxation; Budget; Finance; Judiciary
Gregg: Appropriations; Budget; Labor & Human Resources
Hagel: Foreign Relations; Banking, Housing & Urban Affairs; Special Aging
Harkin: Appropriations; Agriculture, Nutrition & Forestry (ranking member); Labor & Human Resources; Small Business
Hatch: Judiciary (chairman); Finance; Select Intelligence; Indian Affairs
Helms: Agriculture, Nutrition & Forestry; Foreign Relations (chairman); Rules & Administration
Hollings: Appropriations; Budget; Commerce, Science & Transportation (ranking member)
Hutchinson: Environment & Public Works; Labor & Human Resources; Veterans' Affairs
Hutchison: Appropriations; Commerce, Science & Transportation; Rules & Administration
Inhofe: Armed Services; Environment & Public Works; Select Intelligence; Indian Affairs; Joint Printing
Inouye: Appropriations; Rules & Administration; Indian Affairs (ranking member); Commerce, Science & Transportation
Jeffords: Finance; Veterans' Affairs; Labor & Human Resources (chairman); Special Aging
Johnson: Agriculture, Nutrition & Forestry; Banking, Housing & Urban Affairs; Budget; Energy & Natural Resources
Kempthorne: Armed Services; Small Business; Environment & Public Works
Kennedy: Armed Services; Joint Economic; Labor & Human Resources (ranking member); Judiciary
Kerrey: Agriculture, Nutrition & Forestry; Finance; Select Intelligence (ranking member)
Kerry: Commerce, Science & Transportation; Select Intelligence; Small Business (ranking member); Foreign Relations; Banking, Housing & Urban Affairs
Kohl: Appropriations; Special Aging; Judiciary
Kyl: Judiciary; Select Intelligence; Energy & Natural Resources
Landrieu: Agriculture, Nutrition & Forestry; Small Business; Energy & Natural Resources
Lautenberg: Appropriations; Budget (ranking member); Select Intelligence; Environment & Public Works

Leahy: Appropriations; Judiciary (ranking member); Agriculture, Nutrition & Forestry
Levin: Armed Services (ranking member); Small Business; Governmental Affairs; Select Intelligence
Lieberman: Armed Services; Environment & Public Works; Small Business; Governmental Affairs
Lott: Commerce, Science & Transportation; Rules & Administration; Finance
Lugar: Agriculture, Nutrition & Forestry (chairman); Select Intelligence; Foreign Relations
Mack: Banking, Housing & Urban Affairs; Joint Economic; Finance
McCain: Armed Services; Indian Affairs; Commerce, Science & Transportation (chairman)
McConnell: Appropriations; Rules & Administration; Labor & Human Resources; Agriculture; Joint Printing; Nutrition & Forestry
Mikulski: Appropriations; Labor & Human Resources
Moseley-Braun: Banking, Housing & Urban Affairs; Finance; Special Aging
Moynihan: Environment & Public Works; Finance (ranking member); Joint Taxation (ranking member); Rules & Administration; Joint Library (ranking member)
Murkowski: Energy & Natural Resources (chairman); Finance; Veterans' Affairs; Indian Affairs
Murray: Appropriations; Select Ethics; Labor & Human Resources; Veterans' Affairs; Budget
Nickles: Energy & Natural Resources; Rules & Administration; Budget; Governmental Affairs; Finance
Reed: Banking, Housing & Urban Affairs; Labor & Human Resources; Special Aging
Reid: Appropriations; Select Ethics (vice chairman); Special Aging; Indian Affairs; Environment & Public Works
Robb: Armed Services; Select Intelligence; Foreign Relations; Joint Economic
Roberts: Agriculture, Nutrition & Forestry; Armed Services; Select Intelligence; Select Ethics
Rockefeller: Commerce, Science & Transportation; Finance; Veterans' Affairs (ranking member)
Roth: Finance (chairman); Joint Taxation (vice chairman); Governmental Affairs; Joint Economic
Santorum: Agriculture, Nutrition & Forestry; Armed Services; Special Aging; Rules & Administration
Sarbanes: Foreign Relations; Joint Economic; Banking, Housing & Urban Affairs (ranking member); Budget
Sessions: Environment & Public Works; Judiciary; Select Ethics; Joint Economic
Shelby: Appropriations; Special Aging; Select Intelligence (chairman); Banking, Housing & Urban Affairs
Smith (Ore.): Foreign Relations; Budget; Energy & Natural Resources
Smith (N.H.): Armed Services; Select Ethics (chairman); Environment & Public Works
Snowe: Armed Services; Small Business; Budget; Commerce, Science & Transportation
Specter: Appropriations; Veterans' Affairs (chairman); Governmental Affairs; Judiciary
Stevens: Appropriations (chairman); Rules & Administration; Governmental Affairs; Commerce, Science & Transportation
Thomas: Environment & Public Works; Energy & Natural Resources; Foreign Relations; Indian Affairs
Thompson: Judiciary; Governmental Affairs (chairman)
Thurmond: Armed Services (chairman); Veterans' Affairs; Judiciary
Torricelli: Judiciary; Rules & Administration; Governmental Affairs
Warner: Armed Services; Environment & Public Works; Small Business; Special Aging; Rules & Administration (chairman); Joint Printing (chairman); Labor & Human Resources
Wellstone: Foreign Relations; Veterans' Affairs; Small Business; Indian Affairs; Labor & Human Resources
Wyden: Commerce, Science & Transportation; Special Aging; Budget; Energy & Natural Resources; Environment & Public Works

House Committee Assignments

(Committees and subcommittees are subject to change during a session.)

Abercrombie: National Security; Resources
Ackerman: Banking & Financial Services; International Relations
Aderholt: Appropriations
Allen: National Security; Government Reform & Oversight
Andrews: International Relations; Education & The Workforce
Archer: Ways & Means (chairman); Joint Taxation (chairman)
Bachus: Banking & Financial Services; Veterans' Affairs; Transportation & Infrastructure
Baesler: Agriculture; Budget
Baker: Banking & Financial Services; Transportation & Infrastructure
Baldacci: Agriculture; Small Business
Ballenger: International Relations; Education & The Workforce
Barcia: Transportation & Infrastructure; Science
Barr: Banking & Financial Services; Government Reform & Oversight; Judiciary
Barrett (Neb.): Agriculture; Education & The Workforce
Barrett (Wis.): Banking & Financial Services; Government Reform & Oversight
Bartlett: National Security; Science; Small Business
Barton: Science; Commerce
Bass: Budget; Transportation & Infrastructure; Select Intelligence
Bateman: National Security; Transportation & Infrastructure
Becerra: Ways & Means
Bentsen: Banking & Financial Services; Budget
Bereuter: Banking & Financial Services; International Relations
Berman: International Relations; Judiciary
Berry: Agriculture
Bilbray: Commerce
Bilirakis: Veterans' Affairs; Commerce
Bishop: Agriculture; Veterans' Affairs
Blagojevich: National Security; Government Reform & Oversight
Bliley: Commerce (chairman)
Blumenauer: Education & The Workforce
Blunt: Agriculture; International Relations; Transportation & Infrastructure
Boehlert: Transportation & Infrastructure; Select Intelligence; Science
Boehner: Agriculture; House Oversight
Bonilla: Appropriations
Bono: Judiciary; National Security
Borski: Transportation & Infrastructure
Boswell: Agriculture; Transportation & Infrastructure
Boucher: Judiciary; Commerce
Boyd: National Security; Small Business
Brady: International Relations; Resources; Science
Brown (Fla.): Transportation & Infrastructure; Veterans' Affairs
Brown (Calif.): Agriculture; Science (ranking member)
Brown (Ohio): International Relations; Commerce
Bryant: Agriculture; Judiciary
Bunning: Budget; Ways & Means
Burr: Commerce
Burton: International Relations; Government Reform & Oversight (chairman)
Buyer: Judiciary; Veterans' Affairs; National Security
Callahan: Appropriations
Calvert: Resources; Science
Camp: Ways & Means
Campbell: Banking & Financial Services; International Relations
Canady: Agriculture; Judiciary
Cannon: Judiciary; Resources; Science
Cardin: Budget; Ways & Means
Carson: Banking & Financial Services; Veterans' Affairs
Castle: Banking & Financial Services; Education & The Workforce; Select Intelligence
Chabot: International Relations; Judiciary; Small Business
Chambliss: Agriculture; National Security
Chenoweth: Agriculture; Resources; Veterans' Affairs
Christensen: Ways & Means
Christian-Green: Resources
Clay: Education & The Workforce (ranking member)
Clayton: Agriculture; Budget
Clement: International Relations; Transportation & Infrastructure
Clyburn: Transportation & Infrastructure; Veterans' Affairs
Coble: Judiciary; Transportation & Infrastructure
Coburn: Science; Commerce
Collins: Ways & Means
Combest: Agriculture; Small Business
Condit: Agriculture; Government Reform & Oversight
Conyers: Judiciary (ranking member)
Cook: Banking & Financial Services; Science; Transportation & Infrastructure
Cooksey: Agriculture; Veterans' Affairs; Transportation & Infrastructure
Costello: Budget; Transportation & Infrastructure
Cox: Government Reform & Oversight; Commerce
Coyne: Ways & Means
Cramer: Transportation & Infrastructure; Science
Crane: Ways & Means; Joint Taxation
Crapo: Resources; Commerce
Cubin: Resources; Commerce
Cummings: Transportation & Infrastructure; Government Reform & Oversight
Cunningham: Appropriations
Danner: International Relations; Transportation & Infrastructure
Davis (Ill.): Small Business; Government Reform & Oversight
Davis (Fla.): Budget
Davis (Va.): Transportation & Infrastructure; Science; Government Reform & Oversight
Deal: Commerce; Education & The Workforce
DeFazio: Resources; Transportation & Infrastructure
DeGette: Commerce
Delahunt: Judiciary; Resources
DeLauro: Appropriations
DeLay: Appropriations
Dellums: National Security (ranking member)
Deutsch: Commerce
Diaz-Balart: Rules
Dickey: Appropriations
Dicks: Appropriations; Select Intelligence (ranking member)
Dingell: Commerce (ranking member)
Dixon: Appropriations; Select Intelligence
Doggett: Budget; Science
Dooley: Agriculture; Resources
Doolittle: Agriculture; Joint Economic; Resources
Doyle: Veterans' Affairs; Science
Dreier: Rules
Duncan: Resources; Transportation & Infrastructure
Dunn: Ways & Means
Edwards: Appropriations
Ehlers: Transportation & Infrastructure; House Oversight; Science
Ehrlich: Banking & Financial Services; Budget
Emerson: Agriculture; Transportation & Infrastructure; Small Business

Engel: Commerce
English: Small Business; Ways & Means; Science
Ensign: Resources; Ways & Means
Eshoo: Commerce
Etheridge: Agriculture; Science
Evans: National Security; Veterans' Affairs (ranking member)
Everett: Agriculture; Veterans' Affairs; National Security
Ewing: Agriculture; Transportation & Infrastructure; Science
Faleomavaega: International Relations; Resources
Farr: Agriculture; Resources
Fattah: Government Reform & Oversight; Education & The Workforce
Fawell: Science; Education & The Workforce
Fazio: Appropriations
Filner: Transportation & Infrastructure; Veterans' Affairs
Flake: Banking & Financial Services; Small Business
Foley: Agriculture; Science
Forbes: Appropriations
Ford: Education & The Workforce
Fowler: National Security; Transportation & Infrastructure
Fox: Banking & Financial Services; International Relations; Transportation & Infrastructure
Frank: Banking & Financial Services; Judiciary
Franks: Budget; Transportation & Infrastructure
Frelinghuysen: Appropriations
Frost: Rules
Furse: Commerce
Gallegly: International Relations; Resources; Judiciary
Ganske: Commerce
Gejdenson: International Relations; House Oversight (ranking member)
Gekas: Judiciary
Gibbons: National Security; Select Intelligence; Resources
Gilchrest: Resources; Transportation & Infrastructure
Gillmor: Commerce
Gilman: International Relations (chairman); Government Reform & Oversight
Gonzalez: Banking & Financial Services (ranking member)
Goode: Agriculture; Small Business
Goodlatte: Agriculture; Judiciary
Goodling: International Relations; Education & The Workforce (chairman)
Gordon: Science; Commerce
Goss: Rules; Select Intelligence (chairman)
Graham: International Relations; Education & The Workforce; National Security
Granger: Budget; Transportation & Infrastructure; House Oversight
Green: Commerce
Greenwood: Commerce; Education & The Workforce
Gutierrez: Banking & Financial Services; Veterans' Affairs
Gutknecht: Budget; Science
Hall (Texas): Science; Commerce
Hall (Ohio): Rules
Hamilton: International Relations (ranking member); Joint Economic
Hansen: National Security; Resources
Harman: National Security; Select Intelligence
Hastert: Government Reform & Oversight; Commerce
Hastings (Fla.): International Relations; Science
Hastings (Wash.): Rules
Hayworth: Veterans' Affairs; Ways & Means
Hefley: National Security; Small Business; Resources
Hefner: Appropriations
Herger: Budget; Ways & Means
Hill: Banking & Financial Services; Small Business; Resources
Hilleary: Budget; National Security; Education & The Workforce
Hilliard: Agriculture; International Relations
Hinchey: Banking & Financial Services; Joint Economic; Resources
Hinojosa: Education & The Workforce
Hobson: Appropriations; Budget
Hoekstra: Budget; Education & The Workforce
Holden: Agriculture; Government Reform & Oversight
Hooley: Banking & Financial Services; Science
Horn: Transportation & Infrastructure; Government Reform & Oversight
Hostettler: Agriculture; National Security
Houghton: International Relations; Ways & Means
Hoyer: Appropriations; House Oversight
Hulshof: Ways & Means
Hunter: National Security
Hutchinson: Judiciary; Transportation & Infrastructure; Veterans' Affairs
Hyde: International Relations; Judiciary (chairman)
Inglis: Budget; Judiciary
Istook: Appropriations
Jackson: Banking & Financial Services; Small Business
Jackson-Lee: Judiciary; Science
Jefferson: Ways & Means
Jenkins: Agriculture; Judiciary
John: Agriculture; Resources
Johnson, E.B.: Transportation & Infrastructure; Science
Johnson (Wis.): Agriculture; Transportation & Infrastructure
Johnson (Conn.): Ways & Means
Johnson, Sam: Ways & Means; Education & The Workforce
Jones: National Security; Resources; Small Business
Kanjorski: Banking & Financial Services; Government Reform & Oversight
Kaptur: Appropriations
Kasich: Budget (chairman); National Security
Kelly: Banking & Financial Services; Transportation & Infrastructure; Small Business
Kennedy (Mass.): Banking & Financial Services; Veterans' Affairs
Kennedy (R.I.): National Security; Resources
Kennelly: Ways & Means
Kildee: Resources; Education & The Workforce
Kilpatrick: Banking & Financial Services; House Oversight
Kim: International Relations; Transportation & Infrastructure
Kind: Resources; Education & The Workforce
King: Banking & Financial Services; International Relations
Kingston: Appropriations
Kleczka: Ways & Means
Klink: Commerce
Klug: Commerce
Knollenberg: Appropriations; Education & The Workforce
Kolbe: Appropriations
Kucinich: International Relations; Government Reform & Oversight
LaFalce: Banking & Financial Services; Small Business (ranking member)
LaHood: Agriculture; Transportation & Infrastructure; Veterans' Affairs
Lampson: Resources; Science
Lantos: International Relations; Government Reform & Oversight
Largent: Commerce
Latham: Appropriations
LaTourette: Banking & Financial Services; Government Reform & Oversight; Transportation & Infrastructure
Lazio: Banking & Financial Services; Commerce
Leach: Banking & Financial Services (chairman); International Relations
Levin: Ways & Means
Lewis (Calif.): Appropriations; Select Intelligence
Lewis (Ga.): Ways & Means
Lewis (Ky.): Agriculture; National Security
Linder: Rules

Lipinski: Transportation & Infrastructure
Livingston: Appropriations (chairman)
LoBiondo: Small Business; Transportation & Infrastructure
Lofgren: Judiciary; Science
Lowey: Appropriations
Lucas: Agriculture; Banking & Financial Services
Luther: Small Business; Science
Maloney (N.Y.): Banking & Financial Services; Joint Economic; Government Reform & Oversight
Maloney (Conn.): Banking & Financial Services; National Security
Manton: Commerce
Manzullo: International Relations; Joint Economic; Small Business
Markey: Resources; Commerce
Martinez: International Relations; Education & The Workforce
Mascara: Transportation & Infrastructure; Veterans' Affairs
Matsui: Ways & Means
McCarthy (N.Y.): Small Business; Education & The Workforce
McCarthy (Mo.): Commerce
McCollum: Banking & Financial Services; Select Intelligence; Judiciary
McCrery: Ways & Means; Joint Economic
McDade: Appropriations
McDermott: Ways & Means
McGovern: Transportation & Infrastructure
McHale: National Security; Science
McHugh: International Relations; National Security; Government Reform & Oversight
McInnis: Rules
McIntosh: Small Business; Education & The Workforce; Government Reform & Oversight
McIntyre: Agriculture; National Security
McKeon: National Security; Education & The Workforce
McKinney: Banking & Financial Services; International Relations
McNulty: Ways & Means
Meehan: Judiciary; National Security
Meek: Appropriations
Menendez: International Relations; Transportation & Infrastructure
Metcalf: Banking & Financial Services; Transportation & Infrastructure
Mica: Transportation & Infrastructure; Government Reform & Oversight
Millender-McDonald: Small Business; Transportation & Infrastructure
Miller (Fla.): Appropriations; Budget
Miller (Calif.): Resources (ranking member); Education & The Workforce
Minge: Agriculture; Budget
Mink: Budget; Education & The Workforce
Moakley: Rules (ranking member)
Mollohan: Appropriations; Budget
Moran (Va.): Appropriations
Moran (Kan.): Agriculture; Veterans' Affairs; International Relations
Morella: Government Reform & Oversight; Science
Murtha: Appropriations
Myrick: Rules
Nadler: Judiciary; Transportation & Infrastructure
Neal: Ways & Means
Nethercutt: Appropriations; Science
Neumann: Appropriations; Budget
Ney: Banking & Financial Services; House Oversight; Transportation & Infrastructure
Northup: Appropriations
Norton: Transportation & Infrastructure; Government Reform & Oversight
Norwood: Commerce; Education & The Workforce
Nussle: Budget; Ways & Means
Oberstar: Transportation & Infrastructure (ranking member)
Obey: Appropriations (ranking member)
Olver: Appropriations
Ortiz: National Security; Resources
Owens: Government Reform & Oversight; Education & The Workforce
Oxley: Commerce
Packard: Appropriations
Pallone: Resources; Commerce
Pappas: National Security; Government Reform & Oversight; Small Business
Parker: Appropriations; Budget
Pascrell: Small Business; Transportation & Infrastructure
Pastor: Appropriations
Paul: Banking & Financial Services; Education & The Workforce
Paxon: Commerce
Payne: International Relations; Education & The Workforce
Pease: Judiciary; Transportation & Infrastructure
Pelosi: Appropriations; Select Intelligence
Peterson (Minn.): Agriculture; Veterans' Affairs
Peterson (Pa.): Resources; Education & The Workforce
Petri: Transportation & Infrastructure; Education & The Workforce
Pickering: Agriculture; Transportation & Infrastructure; Science
Pickett: National Security; Resources
Pitts: Budget; Transportation & Infrastructure
Pombo: Agriculture; Resources
Pomeroy: Agriculture; Budget
Porter: Appropriations
Portman: Ways & Means
Poshard: Small Business; Transportation & Infrastructure
Price: Appropriations
Pryce: Rules
Quinn: Transportation & Infrastructure; Veterans' Affairs
Radanovich: Budget; Resources
Rahall: Resources; Transportation & Infrastructure
Ramstad: Ways & Means
Rangel: Ways & Means (ranking member); Joint Taxation
Regula: Appropriations
Reyes: National Security; Veterans' Affairs
Riggs: Transportation & Infrastructure; Education & The Workforce
Riley: Banking & Financial Services; National Security
Rivers: Budget; Science
Roemer: Science; Education & The Workforce
Rogan: Commerce
Rogers: Appropriations
Rohrabacher: International Relations; Science
Romero-Barceló: Resources; Education & The Workforce
Ros-Lehtinen: International Relations; Government Reform & Oversight
Rothman: International Relations; Judiciary
Roukema: Banking & Financial Services; Education & The Workforce
Roybal-Allard: Banking & Financial Services; Budget
Royce: Banking & Financial Services; International Relations
Rush: Commerce
Ryun: Banking & Financial Services; National Security; Small Business
Sabo: Appropriations
Salmon: International Relations; Science
Sanchez: National Security; Education & The Workforce
Sanders: Banking & Financial Services; Government Reform & Oversight
Sandlin: Transportation & Infrastructure
Sanford: International Relations; Government Reform & Oversight; Joint Economic
Sawyer: Commerce
Saxton: National Security; Resources; Joint Economic (chairman)
Scarborough: National Security; Government Reform & Oversight; Education & The Workforce

Schaefer: Veterans' Affairs; Commerce
Schaffer: Agriculture; Resources; Education & The Workforce
Schiff: Judiciary; Science; Government Reform & Oversight
Schumer: Banking & Financial Services; Judiciary
Scott: Judiciary; Education & The Workforce
Sensenbrenner: Judiciary; Science (chairman)
Serrano: Appropriations
Sessions: Banking & Financial Services; Science; Government Reform & Oversight
Shadegg: Budget; Resources; Government Reform & Oversight
Shaw: Ways & Means
Shays: Budget; Government Reform & Oversight
Sherman: Budget; International Relations
Shimkus: Commerce
Shuster: Transportation & Infrastructure (chairman); Select Intelligence
Sisisky: National Security; Small Business
Skaggs: Appropriations; Select Intelligence
Skeen: Appropriations
Skelton: National Security; Small Business
Slaughter: Rules
Smith, Adam: National Security; Resources
Smith (Ore.): Agriculture (chairman); Resources
Smith (N.J.): International Relations; Veterans' Affairs
Smith (Texas): Budget; Judiciary
Smith, Linda: Resources; Small Business
Smith (Mich.): Agriculture; Budget
Snowbarger: Banking & Financial Services; Government Reform & Oversight; Small Business
Snyder: National Security; Veterans' Affairs
Solomon: Rules (chairman)
Souder: Small Business; Government Reform & Oversight; Education & The Workforce
Spence: National Security (chairman); Veterans' Affairs
Spratt: Budget (ranking member); National Security
Stabenow: Agriculture; Science
Stark: Ways & Means; Joint Taxation; Joint Economic
Stearns: Veterans' Affairs; Commerce
Stenholm: Agriculture (ranking member)
Stokes: Appropriations
Strickland: Commerce
Stump: National Security; Veterans' Affairs (chairman)
Stupak: Commerce
Sununu: Budget; Small Business; Government Reform & Oversight
Talent: National Security; Small Business (chairman); Education & The Workforce
Tanner: Ways & Means
Tauscher: Transportation & Infrastructure
Tauzin: Resources; Commerce
Taylor (N.C.): Appropriations
Taylor (Miss.): National Security; Transportation & Infrastructure
Thomas: Ways & Means; Joint Taxation; House Oversight (chairman)
Thompson: Agriculture; Budget
Thornberry: National Security; Joint Economic; Resources
Thune: Agriculture; Transportation & Infrastructure
Thurman: Ways & Means
Tiahrt: Appropriations
Tierney: Government Reform & Oversight; Education & The Workforce
Torres: Appropriations
Towns: Government Reform & Oversight; Commerce
Traficant: Transportation & Infrastructure; Science
Turner: National Security; Government Reform & Oversight
Underwood: National Security; Resources
Upton: Commerce; Education & The Workforce
Velázquez: Banking & Financial Services; Small Business
Vento: Banking & Financial Services; Resources
Visclosky: Appropriations
Walsh: Appropriations
Wamp: Appropriations
Waters: Banking & Financial Services; Judiciary
Watkins: Ways & Means
Watt: Banking & Financial Services; Judiciary
Watts: Banking & Financial Services; Transportation & Infrastructure; National Security
Waxman: Government Reform & Oversight (ranking member); Commerce
Weldon (Pa.): National Security; Science
Weldon (Fla.): Banking & Financial Services; Science
Weller: Ways & Means
Wexler: International Relations; Judiciary
Weygand: Budget; Small Business
White: Commerce
Whitfield: Commerce
Wicker: Appropriations
Wise: Transportation & Infrastructure; Government Reform & Oversight
Wolf: Appropriations
Woolsey: Budget; Education & The Workforce
Wynn: Commerce
Yates: Appropriations
Young (Fla.): Appropriations; Select Intelligence
Young (Alaska): Resources (chairman); Transportation & Infrastructure

CQ

VOTE STUDIES

PRESIDENTIAL SUPPORT

Clinton Finds Support on Hill Despite GOP's Vocal Attacks

President fared surprisingly well in 1997, given Republican control of Congress and his administration's ongoing political troubles

For Republicans, criticizing President Clinton became almost second nature. In 1997, they blasted the president for his dubious campaign fund-raising practices, his proposed clean air rules, his NATO expansion plans, his nominee for a sensitive civil rights post, even his choice of name for his puppy. A handful of House Republicans tried to launch impeachment proceedings against him.

But when it came time to stop talking and start voting, the GOP-led Congress, for the second consecutive year, handed Clinton more victories than defeats.

According to Congressional Quarterly's annual study of voting patterns in the House and Senate, the president prevailed on 53.6 percent of the roll call votes on which he staked out a clear position.

CQ VOTE STUDIES

By historical standards, Clinton's score was not all that impressive. Since 1953, when Dwight D. Eisenhower was inaugurated and CQ began analyzing voting patterns, five presidents had served at least five years. Only Richard M. Nixon's fifth-year score was lower than Clinton's — 50.6 percent — and at the time Nixon was mired in the morass of Watergate.

But considering Clinton's political handicaps, he acquitted himself well on Capitol Hill in 1997. Not only did he confront a Congress controlled by the opposition party, but his administration could barely get through a week without having to cope with the fallout from some real or alleged scandal.

Clinton's score declined only slightly from 1996, when he prevailed on 55.1 percent of roll calls on which he took a stand. By contrast, Ronald Reagan's success rating fell from 65.8 percent in 1984 to 59.9 percent in 1985, which seemed to cement his status as a lame duck. And Reagan, unlike Clinton, had the advantage of working with a Senate controlled by his own party.

Clinton's middling score demonstrated that both parties heeded the message delivered by voters in 1996, when they returned him to the White House and GOP majorities to the House and Senate. Turned off by the budget stalemate and government shutdowns — for which they overwhelmingly blamed Republicans — voters demanded that the two parties work together.

Clinton and Congress cooperated impressively on the budget, producing a plan to eliminate the federal deficit by 2002 while also cutting taxes. The sweeping agreement was disparaged by both liberals and conservatives, as well as by economists who claimed that the nation's thriving economy would have wiped out the deficit if the politicians had just left well enough alone.

But Clinton and GOP leaders basked in the glow from that accomplishment, which enabled both sides to claim credit for putting the nation on a path to its first balanced budget since 1969. And Clinton extracted significant concessions from Republicans, including new funding to expand health insurance for children.

Fast-Track Setback

Although Congress' legislative output beyond the budget bills was relatively slim in 1997, many of those other achievements also bore a bipartisan imprint. Both Clinton and Republican leaders took credit for bills to streamline the regulatory process of the Food and Drug Administration (S 830 — PL 105-115) and revamp adoption procedures (HR 867 — PL 105-89).

But late in the session, Clinton suffered a humiliating defeat when a revolt by House Democrats denied him the renewal of "fast track" trade negotiating authority. He asked GOP leaders to pull the plug on the legislation (HR 2621) before it came to a vote. Because CQ tabulates only the percentage of presidential roll call victories, that setback was not reflected in Clinton's score.

The fast-track debacle robbed some of the luster from the budget deal and exposed Clinton's shortcomings as a leader, according to several experts on the presidency.

"It was an important test and he failed," said George C. Edwards III, director of the Center for Presidential Studies at Texas A&M University. "It is an issue on which most presidents have prevailed."

Thinking Small?

Clinton kicked off the year with a State of the Union address in which he sketched out a grand vision "to make a nation and a world better than any we have ever known." But his proposals for achieving that lofty goal were modest, modeled on those of his re-election campaign. *(Text, p. D-17)*

The president called for a significant increase in spending for education, a program of voluntary national testing for elementary students, school uniforms and the restoration of welfare benefits to legal immigrants. He also urged quick action on a treaty outlawing chemical weapons (S Res 75) and set a July 4 deadline for enactment of campaign finance legislation (S 25), sponsored by Republican Sen. John McCain of Arizona and Democratic Sen. Russell D. Feingold of Wisconsin.

With the economy booming and the president enjoying favorable public approval ratings, many observers chided Clinton for putting forward what they regarded as an ex-

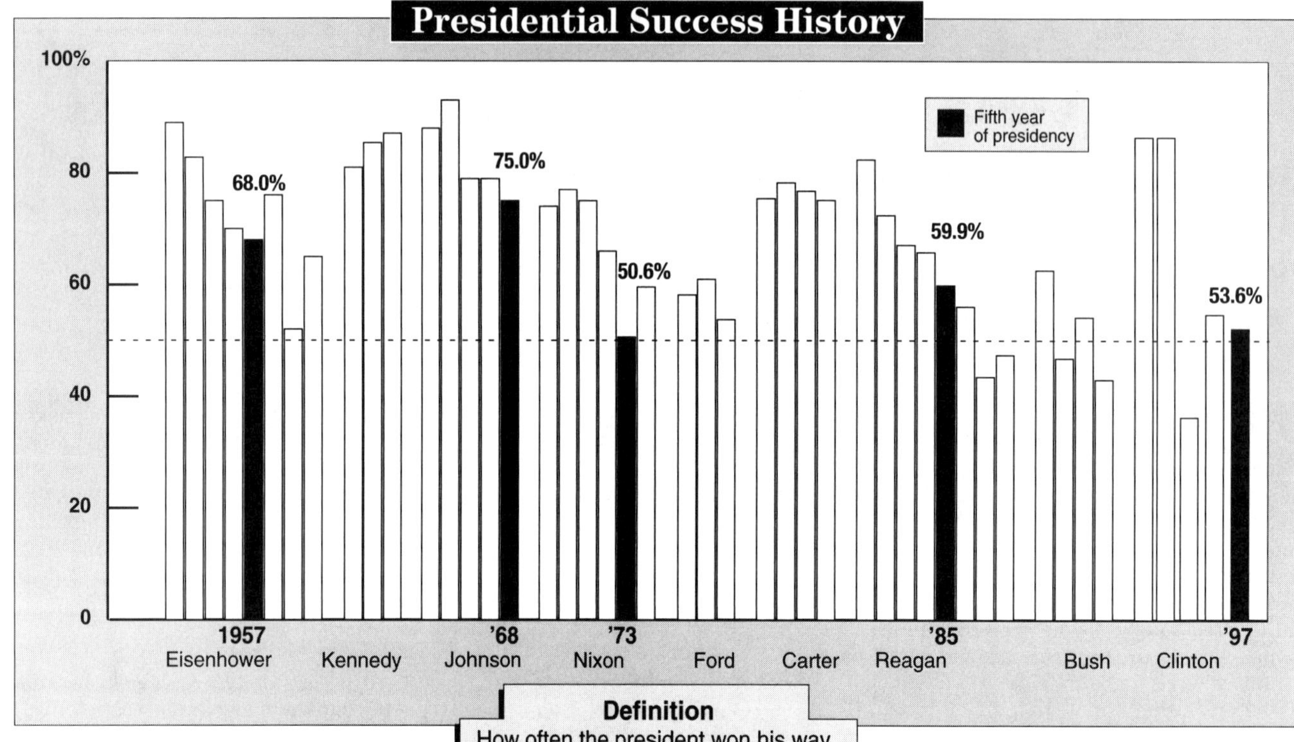

Definition

How often the president won his way on roll call votes on which he took a clear position.

1997 Data

Senate	45 victories 18 defeats
House	29 victories 46 defeats

Total Clinton success rate **53.6%**

cessively timid second-term agenda.

In a thinly disguised attack on Clinton, House Democratic Leader Richard A. Gephardt of Missouri took to task political leaders who were unwilling to take bold initiatives. "Too often, our leaders seem enamored with small ideas that nibble around the edges of big problems," Gephardt said.

Clinton bristled at such criticism. During a December interview with The New York Times, he made a point of stretching his pronunciation of the word "big" in describing his proposals.

But in putting together his program, Clinton was acutely aware of his political constraints. After his cherished health care initiative flamed out in 1994 without a direct floor vote, he was forced to think small, or at least smaller.

Clinton Wins Some, Loses Others

So how did the president do in 1997?

In April, he achieved an important victory when the Senate approved the chemical weapons treaty over the vociferous objections of Foreign Relations Committee Chairman Jesse Helms of North Carolina and other conservative Republicans. That was among Clinton's top foreign policy priorities.

Clinton scored another clear-cut triumph in June, when GOP leaders badly overreached in attempting to use an $8.9 billion disaster relief bill (HR 1871 — PL 105-18) as a vehicle for a pair of pet legislative proposals that the president staunchly opposed. The skirmish was a replay of the budget battles of the previous two years. Clinton hung tough and the Republicans caved, stripping out the disputed policy riders.

Congress filled a good portion of Clinton's legislative wish list when it passed a pair of budget-reconciliation bills (HR 2015 — PL 105-33, HR 2014 — PL 105-34). That legislation restored some welfare benefits for legal immigrants, funded his health initiative for children and provided increased funding for education.

For their part, Republicans fulfilled their longstanding goals of providing a $500-per-child tax credit for families and reducing tax rates on individual capital gains, the profits made on sales of assets such as stocks.

On the negative side of the ledger, the president suffered a series of stinging defeats in the session's contentious final days. The fast-track bill went down, and Congress refused to act on Clinton's request for new funding for the United Nations and the International Monetary Fund. Those foreign policy issues were to be rejoined in 1998, but the White House faced tough fights on all three matters.

Clinton's Independence Day deadline for passage of the McCain-Feingold bill came and went without any congressional action on the legislation. The bill eventually was blocked in the Senate by a GOP-led filibuster.

Clinton barely avoided being steamrolled by Republicans on the highly politicized issue of revamping the IRS. He belatedly backed a House bill (HR 2676) aimed at making the tax-collection agency more customer-friendly, but only after it became clear that it had overwhelming Democratic as well as Republican support. The administration won some modifications in the final bill, which the House approved on a 426-4 vote.

On education, the White House and the GOP fought to a draw. Congress boosted overall funding by about 12 percent in fiscal 1998, although much of the extra money went to GOP priorities rather than Clinton's.

The debate over Clinton's plan for voluntary national student testing exploded into one of the nastiest fights of the year, as an unlikely coalition of House Republicans and minority Democrats bitterly opposed the proposal. Under a

Leading Scorers: Clinton's Support, Opposition

Support indicates those who in 1997 voted most often for President Clinton's position; opposition shows those who most often voted against the president's position.

Scores are based on actual votes cast, and members are listed alphabetically when their scores are tied. Members who missed half or more of the votes are not listed.

Support

Senate

Republicans		Democrats	
Jeffords, Vt.	78%	Dodd, Conn.	94%
Snowe, Maine	78	Lieberman, Conn.	93
Collins, Maine	76	Bingaman, N.M.	92
Chafee, R.I.	75	Daschle, S.D.	92
Specter, Pa.	71	Durbin, Ill.	92
Stevens, Alaska	71	Mikulski, Md.	91
McCain, Ariz.	70	Akaka, Hawaii	90
Cochran, Miss.	68	Kohl, Wis.	90
Domenici, N.M.	67	Levin, Mich.	90
Gorton, Wash.	67	Boxer, Calif.	89
Warner, Va.	67	Bryan, Nev.	89
Campbell, Colo.	66	Feinstein, Calif.	89
Roth, Del.	65	Kerrey, Neb.	89
Smith, Ore.	65	Torricelli, N.J.	89

House

Republicans		Democrats	
Morella, Md.	73%	Skaggs, Colo.	93%
Houghton, N.Y.	60	Yates, Ill.	92
Johnson, Conn.	60	Brown, Calif.	90
Boehlert, N.Y.	59	Lofgren, Calif.	89
Castle, Del.	55	Eshoo, Calif.	88
Roukema, N.J.	55	Gonzalez, Texas	88
Shays, Conn.	55	Sawyer, Ohio	88
Kolbe, Ariz.	52	Capps, Calif.	87
Ramstad, Minn.	52	Furse, Ore.	87
Campbell, Calif.	51	Sabo, Minn.	87
		Becerra, Calif.	86
		Berman, Calif.	86
		Fattah, Pa.	86
		Waxman, Calif.	86

Opposition

Senate

Republicans		Democrats	
Faircloth, N.C.	59%	Hollings, S.C.	25%
Helms, N.C.	53	Ford, Ky.	21
Allard, Colo.	52	Breaux, La.	19
Inhofe, Okla.	51	Byrd, W.Va.	19
Ashcroft, Mo.	49	Conrad, N.D.	19
Enzi, Wyo.	49	Dorgan, N.D.	19
Smith, N.H.	49	Moynihan, N.Y.	18
Grams, Minn.	47	Wellstone, Minn.	17
Craig, Idaho	46		
Brownback, Kan.	44		
Coverdell, Ga.	44		
Gramm, Texas	44		
Lott, Miss.	44		
Sessions, Ala.	44		

House

Republicans		Democrats	
Istook, Okla.	82%	Hall, Texas	73%
Weldon, Fla.	81	Goode, Va.	71
Crapo, Idaho	80	Taylor, Miss.	67
Dickey, Ark.	80	Traficant, Ohio	64
Rohrabacher, Calif.	80	Danner, Mo.	58
Snowbarger, Kan.	80	Lipinski, Ill.	58
Barr, Ga.	79	McIntyre, N.C.	56
Hilleary, Tenn.	79	Barcia, Mich.	55
Stump, Ariz.	79	Skelton, Mo.	53
Paxon, N.Y.	78	Kaptur, Ohio	51
		Holden, Pa.	50
		Peterson, Minn.	49
		Cramer, Ala.	48
		John, La.	48

carefully crafted compromise, the administration could not begin conducting the tests until Oct. 1, 1998, although an independent board was permitted to continue developing the tests.

Some Caveats

The Congressional Quarterly study was based on the results of 138 roll call votes on which CQ's editors and reporters determined that the president had taken a clearly stated position. Of those, 75 votes were in the House and 63 in the Senate.

In the House, Clinton had 29 victories against 46 defeats, for a score of 38.7 percent. But he made up for that in the Senate, winning on 45 roll call votes and losing on only 18, to compile an eye-popping rating of 71.4 percent.

Those scores provide a statistical snapshot of Clinton's year on Capitol Hill and are useful in comparing the success of recent presidents. But important caveats apply.

For one thing, each roll call vote on which the president took a position was given equal weight. In the CQ survey, votes on the budget package counted as much as votes on relatively minor amendments to appropriations bills. There also were instances when a major presidential initiative was shelved without a roll call vote, as occurred on fast track.

Clinton's surprisingly high score in the Senate was inflated by the extraordinarily large number of Cabinet and judicial nominees who were confirmed on roll call votes — and the fact that more controversial nominees did not make it to the floor for votes.

While presidents traditionally filled a large number of Cabinet vacancies in the first year of their second terms, the nominees often were approved without a roll call. In 1985, the first year of Reagan's second term, only 17 presidential nominees required roll call votes.

In 1997, 29 roll call votes were held on 27 judicial, Cabinet and other nominees, all of whom were confirmed by lopsided majorities. Opponents in many cases had demanded the right to vote "no."

The other Senate votes included 17 on domestic policy issues, on which Clinton scored seven victories and 10 defeats;

seven on defense and foreign policy issues (two victories and five defeats); and 10 on economic affairs and trade (seven victories and three defeats). *(List of votes, p. C-15)*

The House votes included 37 on domestic policy issues, on which Clinton scored 15 victories and suffered 22 defeats; 22 on defense and foreign policy issues (four victories and 18 defeats); and 16 on economic affairs and trade issues (10 victories and six defeats). *(List of votes, p. C-16)*

The sharpest turnaround in any of those categories over the previous year came in the House on defense and foreign policy. In 1996, Clinton won on a majority of the defense and foreign policy votes, 10 to eight. Nearly a third of his 18 foreign policy defeats in 1997 came in the final days of the session on a series of bills challenging the administration's policy toward China on issues such as human rights and religious persecution.

Tale of Two Chambers

Clinton clearly had a good year in the Senate.

The Senate Republican leadership decided early that 1997 would be the year that the GOP proved it was capable of governing. On the budget and appropriations process, the order of the day was compromise, not confrontation, with the White House. "Last year was about proving that the system worked," said a senior Republican official.

Appropriations Committee Chairman Ted Stevens, R-Alaska, whisked through all 13 appropriations measures with barely a hitch. The spending bills largely were free of policy provisions opposed by the administration.

Of Clinton's 18 defeats in the Senate, none ranked as crippling. Three losses came on the campaign finance bill, and two others were on bipartisan legislation (HR 1122) to ban a second- and third-term abortion procedure that opponents called "partial birth" abortion. The Senate approved that bill in May on a 64-36 vote. But Clinton vetoed the legislation in October, and the margin by which the Senate passed the measure left proponents three votes short of the 67 needed to override the president.

For the most part, Senate Majority Leader Trent Lott, R-Miss., was not inclined to challenge Clinton. His cautious approach frustrated some conservatives, but Lott struggled against his own political constraints. Republicans held a 55-45 majority in the Senate, which made it relatively easy for Democrats to muster the 41 votes needed to sustain a filibuster.

"The minority in the Senate is in such a good position to prevent anything from happening that it forces the majority to make a deal prior to the floor vote," said Charles O. Jones, a political scientist at the University of Wisconsin—Madison.

In addition, Clinton had consistently moved in the GOP's direction, on matters ranging from the budget to IRS reform. Even though the battles over those issues were waged on the GOP's ideological turf, Clinton frequently was able to claim victory. "Many of the policies the president endorsed weren't his policies," said Texas Republican Sen. Phil Gramm.

Clinton fared much worse on roll calls in the House, where the majority tended to rule, and the minority — no matter how determined — usually was not in a position to block legislation.

Several of Clinton's defeats in the House came on issues that were important to the GOP's conservative base or its pro-business allies. The votes usually ended up as largely symbolic gestures, however, since the bills had very little chance of being acted on by the Senate.

That was the case in October, when the House approved little-noticed but far-reaching legislation aimed at strengthening the rights of private property owners (HR 1534). The proposal was staunchly opposed by the administration and many environmental groups. More than anything else, the vote was a testament to the lobbying clout of the National Association of Home Builders, which led an all-out campaign in behalf of the bill. That measure — like other environmental and lands bills championed by House conservatives — faced an uncertain fate in the Senate in 1998.

Stung by the concessions the GOP leadership made in the budget deal, House conservatives also sought to eliminate funding for the National Endowment for the Arts, even though it was obvious that the Senate was in no mood to go along.

Clinton's score also was reduced when the House, in the session's final days, approved those minor bills criticizing China. Normally, such proposals would be packaged together in a single omnibus bill. But the China bills were voted on separately, tagging Clinton with six defeats instead of one.

Few Surprises

In addition to analyzing the president's success on roll call votes, CQ also studied how often individual lawmakers supported his position, regardless of whether he prevailed.

There were few surprises in 1997. The average House Democrat supported Clinton 71 percent of the time, down slightly from 1996. The average Republican in the House backed the president 30 percent of the time, compared with 38 percent the year before.

As in recent years, the president's strongest GOP supporters tended to be moderates from the East Coast. Constance A. Morella of Maryland again took the top spot among Republican supporters of Clinton, voting with him 73 percent of the time.

Conservative Democrat Ralph M. Hall from Texas was the president's most consistent opponent from his own party, a title Hall had retained for several years. Hall opposed Clinton 73 percent of the time, which was the same score compiled by House Majority Whip Tom DeLay, R-Texas.

The presidential support scores of individual senators were higher than usual because of the large number of confirmation votes. As a result, the average Republican voted with Clinton 60 percent of the time. Even Majority Leader Lott supported him on the majority of votes, backing him 56 percent of the time.

Olympia J. Snowe of Maine and James M. Jeffords of Vermont backed Clinton most often among GOP senators, supporting him on 78 percent of votes.

A trio of conservative Democrats who often opposed the president over the years retired at the end of the 104th Congress: Sam Nunn of Georgia, J. Bennett Johnston of Louisiana and Howell Heflin of Alabama. With their departure, Ernest F. Hollings of South Carolina emerged as Clinton's leading Senate Democratic skeptic, voting against him 25 percent of the time.

Continuing Enigma

Throughout his presidency, Clinton's success ratings varied widely. In 1994, Clinton had an outstanding year as Democrats gave him victories on 86.4 percent of roll calls. Politically, however, the year could not have been worse, as Republicans used the fall elections to take control of the House and Senate for the first time in 40 years. In 1995, Clinton was left for dead politically, scoring 36.2 percent. In 1996 he engineered the biggest single-year comeback in the history of the CQ survey, winning on 55.1 percent of roll call votes. *(1994 Almanac, p. 3-C; 1995 Almanac, p. C-3; 1996 Almanac, p. C-3)*

That made it risky, if not foolhardy, to venture a guess as to how he would fare during the rest of his tenure. But there were some important points to keep in mind.

As they looked ahead to an election year, when the political atmosphere was certain to turn more partisan, Republicans in both chambers were eager to promote issues that would energize their conservative base. The idea of hanging some defeats on the president, even on bills that did not become law, was quite appealing to Republicans.

But Clinton was able to come up with small-but-popular initiatives that had kept Republicans on the defensive. Privately, they were concerned that Clinton might hit political pay dirt with his plan to make child care more affordable for working families, which he outlined in his State of the Union address in January 1998.

Clinton undoubtedly hoped to replicate the legislative success that Reagan achieved in 1986, the sixth year of his presidency. Reagan's support score fell from 59.9 percent to 56.1 percent. But it was an extraordinarily productive year, as Congress enacted a sweeping tax overhaul bill, a major rewrite of the nation's immigration law and an important environmental measure. *(1986 Almanac, p. 21-C)*

There was only one hitch. Reagan, like Clinton, discovered that legislative output did not necessarily translate into political success. That year, Republicans lost control of the Senate to Democrats. ■

Despite Drop in Partisan Votes, Bickering Continued in 1997

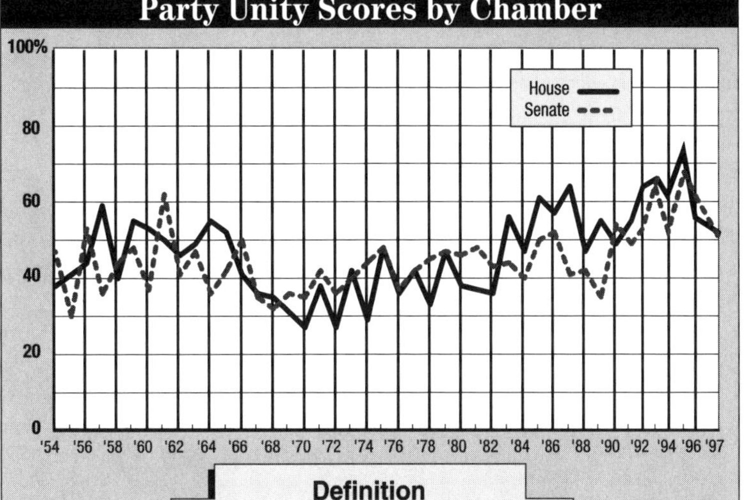

Definition

The percentage of recorded floor votes in each chamber on which a majority of one party voted against a majority of the other party.

1997 Data

	Partisan Votes	Total Votes	Percent
Senate	150	298	50.3%
House	319	633	50.4%

Partisan voting in 1997 was low by contemporary standards, but whether such a decline represented an improvement in the congressional situation depended on one's point of view. It was the classic question of whether the glass was half empty or half full.

In the House, a majority of Republicans voted against a majority of Democrats 50.4 percent of the time, according to an analysis of 1997 roll call votes compiled by Congressional Quarterly. In the Senate, the votes split that way by almost exactly the same proportion — 50.3 percent. It was a turnaround from 1995, when the parties split on 71.4 percent of votes.

"The House Republican leadership was interested in governing, and not simply playing opposition [to a Democratic White House]," said William F. Connelly Jr., a Washington and Lee University political scientist. "It's clear that they were more serious about policy than politics."

"That's good news," said Rep. Sherwood Boehlert, a moderate Republican from New York. "When all is said and done, the overwhelming majority of Americans are moderates who want to get things done."

But more ideologically ardent Republicans and Democrats expressed some fear that a rapprochement on issues such as balancing the budget and lowering tax rates — and overhauling the means of collecting taxes — threatened to homogenize the two parties.

"I certainly have a different point of view," said conservative Republican Rep. Tom Coburn of Oklahoma. "My point of view is one of disgust. . . . I don't think our leadership has the courage to make us take tough votes."

Coburn complained that the agreement that balanced the budget "blurs the lines with the Democrats." To try to sharpen those lines, Coburn in September helped to instigate a three-week series of largely unsuccessful attempts to amend a bill (HR 2264) to provide funding for the departments of Labor, Health and Human Services, and Education.

Rep. David E. Skaggs of Colorado, a senior Democrat on the Appropriations Committee, characterized that long series of votes as "a very shrewd tactic" on the part of House GOP leaders to let the more conservative members of their conference blow off steam. "We all have to go back to school on a regular basis to remember that this is not a parliamentary system, and the Constitution essentially drives a consensus approach to government in this country," he said.

Skaggs, along with many other Hill watchers, argued that because the House GOP held only an 11-seat majority, it had to attract significant Democratic support to ensure a working majority.

"What that drop [in partisan voting] probably reflects is that when it came to passage, they voted together and began to compromise," said Johns Hopkins University political scientist Joseph Cooper. "Their basic problem is that Clinton has the veto, so they can't get exactly what would be pleasing to their party."

Speaking of rifts within the GOP Conference that made unanimity nearly impossible, Republican Rep. Cass Ballenger of North Carolina likened his party's strategy of crafting legis-

Leading Scorers: Party Unity

Support indicates those who in 1997 most consistently voted with their party's majority against the other party; opposition shows how often members voted against their party's majority. Scores are based on votes cast; members are listed alphabetically when scores are tied. Members who missed half the votes are not listed.

Support

Senate — Republicans

Ashcroft, Mo.	99%	Thomas, Wyo.	98	Brownback, Kan.	96
Gramm, Texas	99	Craig, Idaho	97	Hutchinson, Ark.	95
Helms, N.C.	99	Faircloth, N.C.	97	Hutchison, Texas	95
Inhofe, Okla.	99	Grams, Minn.	97	Thurmond, S.C.	95
Kyl, Ariz.	99	Kempthorne, Idaho	97	Burns, Mont.	94
Sessions, Ala.	99	McConnell, Ky.	97	Lott, Miss.	94
Allard, Colo.	98	Nickles, Okla.	97		
Enzi, Wyo.	98	Smith, N.H.	97		

Senate — Democrats

Reed, R.I.	99%	Kerry, Mass.	97	Daschle, S.D.	92
Sarbanes, Md.	98	Wellstone, Minn.	96	Harkin, Iowa	92
Akaka, Hawaii	97	Levin, Mich.	95	Mikulski, Md.	92
Boxer, Calif.	97	Lautenberg, N.J.	94	Inouye, Hawaii	91
Durbin, Ill.	97	Murray, Wash.	93	Glenn, Ohio	90
Kennedy, Mass.	97	Bumpers, Ark.	92	Torricelli, N.J.	90

House — Republicans

Snowbarger, Kan.	99%	Cubin, Wyo.	97	Paxon, N.Y.	97
Barr, Ga.	98	Hayworth, Ariz.	97	Riley, Ala.	97
Hastings, Wash.	98	Herger, Calif.	97	Schaefer, Colo.	97
Ryun, Kan.	98	Istook, Okla.	97	Spence, S.C.	97
Solomon, N.Y.	98	Lewis, Ky.	97	Stump, Ariz.	97
Aderholt, Ala.	97	Lucas, Okla.	97	Tiahrt, Kan.	97
Baker, La.	97	McKeon, Calif.	97	Watkins, Okla.	97
Brady, Texas	97	Myrick, N.C.	97		

House — Democrats

Becerra, Calif.	99%	Vento, Minn.	98	Olver, Mass.	97
Furse, Ore.	99	Woolsey, Calif.	98	Payne, N.J.	97
DeGette, Colo.	98	Coyne, Pa.	97	Serrano, N.Y.	97
McDermott, Wash.	98	Hinchey, N.Y.	97	Waxman, Calif.	97
Roybal-Allard, Calif.	98	Lewis, Ga.	97	Yates, Ill.	97
Velázquez, N.Y.	98	Miller, Calif.	97		

Opposition

Senate — Republicans

Specter, Pa.	50%	Snowe, Maine	41	Collins, Maine	39
Jeffords, Vt.	47	Chafee, R.I.	39	D'Amato, N.Y.	33

Senate — Democrats

Breaux, La.	35%	Baucus, Mont.	27	Lieberman, Conn.	23
Graham, Fla.	29	Hollings, S.C.	26	Moynihan, N.Y.	22
Robb, Va.	29	Kohl, Wis.	26	Ford, Ky.	21
Bryan, Nev.	28	Landrieu, La.	23	Kerrey, Neb.	21

House — Republicans

Morella, Md.	42%	Johnson, Conn.	32	Boehlert, N.Y.	30
Shays, Conn.	34	Roukema, N.J.	31	Gilman, N.Y.	30

House — Democrats

Traficant, Ohio	77%	Stenholm, Texas	47	John, La.	40
Goode, Va.	62	McIntyre, N.C.	46	Barcia, Mich.	39
Hall, Texas	61	Cramer, Ala.	42	Danner, Mo.	39
Taylor, Miss.	55	Condit, Calif.	40	Peterson, Minn.	39

lation to win Democratic support to a game of bridge. "You gotta attract some cards from both sides," he said.

Appropriations bills were the vehicles for other disputes on contentious issues from abortion to school vouchers, but by and large the spending process was conducted in a bipartisan fashion in the wake of the budget agreement — particularly in the Senate, where Appropriations Chairman Ted Stevens, R-Alaska, blustered his bills through early, the old-fashioned way, by sharing the wealth with Democratic colleagues.

The percentage of roll call votes in which a majority of one party squared off against a majority of the other declined from 1996 by 12 percentage points in the Senate and by 6 percentage points in the House. It was the lowest percentage of partisan votes registered in the House since 1990, and the lowest score in a non-election year since 1981. (Partisan voting tended to decline in election years, as party leaders sought to avoid controversy and get matters in Congress finished and out of the way for members needing to hit the campaign trail.)

In the generally less combative Senate, the 1997 share of votes that split the parties was the lowest since 1991. But the percentage of partisan votes in both chambers was still fairly high by postwar standards.

And even though the proportion of partisan votes jumped around, the behavior of individual members showed there was virtually no overlap between the two parties.

On party-unity votes, Republicans succeeded in holding an average of 88 percent of their conference in line in the House, and 87 percent in the Senate. The Democrats stayed together on party-unity votes an average of 82 percent of the time in the House, and 85 percent in the Senate.

The strong unity among members of the respective caucuses meant that the outliers in both parties tended to come from their respective moderate wings, which in both cases was essentially a geographical definition.

The Republicans willing to split from party ranks most often hailed from the Northeast, the old "Eastern Establishment" province that once defined the party but had become the GOP's weakest arena. Similarly, the few remaining Democrats from the party's old, conservative Southern base were generally the most willing to walk over to the GOP side when the parties locked horns.

Labor Disagreements

Despite their meeting of minds on such matters as the budget, the parties agreed to disagree on labor, with Republicans loudly complaining that Democrats were lugging water for their sponsors from the union movement, and Democrats complaining about GOP attacks on workers.

"In spite of the fact they don't represent but 12 or 13 percent of the people, they spend their money and lobby just about better than anybody else," Ballenger, chairman of the Education and the Workforce Subcommittee on Employer-Employee Relations, said in grudging admiration of unions.

Yet despite the political heat generated by the stepped-up political activities of "Big Labor," the GOP in 1997 largely slowed its efforts, carried over from the 104th, to revise federal labor law. With about two dozen Republicans voting the wishes of a strong labor presence in their districts, GOP leaders were afraid to risk losses on labor issues, as they had in 1996 on a minimum-wage increase.

Excepting a plan to allow employers to offer their workers compensatory time off in lieu of overtime pay, Republicans barely touched issues that were anathema to the unions — at least on the floor. Even on the plan to extend so-called fast-track trade negotiating authority, House GOP leaders pulled the bill short of a vote once it became clear they could not supply the votes to make up for weak Democratic support.

Rep. David Dreier of California, a senior Republican on the Rules Committee, said the GOP wanted to be known as "governing conservatives," but he admitted some chagrin as potential 1998 Republican candidates complained they could hardly find any votes on which their Democratic opponents differed from their own positions.

House freshmen of both parties, in contrast to the GOP-dominated Class of 1994, were generally older, more experienced legislators inclined toward centrism and a pragmatic will toward final passage. Their inclinations also helped lower the partisan temperature from the 104th Congress.

"There's a perpetual tension between getting something done and being able to highlight the differences," said Rep. Tom Allen, a freshman Democrat from Maine. "Really, the two parties need to do both of those things: get something done, and make sure the public can understand the difference between the two sides."

But if the House was, on the whole, a more civil and cooperative place in 1997 than it had been in the two or three previous years, there were still plenty of areas of contention and skirmishes between the two caucuses.

Democrats angered by the investigation into the election of Rep. Loretta Sanchez, D-Calif., for instance, forced 15 votes to address the issue. And Democrats offered enough motions to adjourn or rise from the Committee of the Whole to account for more than 15 percent of the party-line votes.

But at the same time, other dilatory tactics, such as forcing roll call votes on suspension bills and approving the Journal, led to more than a third of the nonpartisan votes in 1997. Forcing roll calls ate up time, but most members from both parties voted "aye" on such matters.

In the Senate

A frustrated minority in the Senate had more effective tactics with which to express its will. Cloture motions were rejected 17 times in 1997; cloture was invoked just seven times.

On the 17 rejected motions, Senate Democrats cast 743 votes according to their leaders' wishes, against just nine votes cast the Republican way. Democrats thus were able to block final votes on issues from school vouchers to requiring unions to get members' approval for political expenditures.

Senate Democrats sometimes were able to bend enough Republican colleagues to their point of view to actually win votes, not just block GOP initiatives. For example, a united bloc of Democrats combined with a bare majority of Senate Republicans (29-26) to ensure the two-thirds adoption of the chemical weapons treaty over the strong objection of Foreign Relations Committee Chairman Jesse Helms, R-N.C.

A majority of Democrats beat a majority of Republicans on 46 of the 150 party-dividing Senate votes. By contrast, House Democrats triumphed on just 58 of their chamber's 319 disputed votes.

Still, in the Senate there was a perfect separation between individual members of the two parties. All Republicans were more prone to vote Republican than any Democrat. And all Democrats were more prone to vote Democratic than any Republican. The closest the parties came to meeting in that chamber came in the persons of John B. Breaux, D-La., and Arlen Specter, R-Pa. Breaux voted with his party a mere 65 percent of the time, while Specter nearly evenly divided his votes for and against his party.

The six lowest scoring Republicans all hailed from the Northeast, including New Yorker Alfonse M. D'Amato, whose party-support score plummeted from 87 percent in 1996 to 67 percent in 1997 — the biggest drop of any senator.

For Joel H. Silbey, a congressional historian at Cornell University in Ithaca, N.Y., the D'Amato case offered proof for his thesis that members felt more pressure to vote according to the whims of their districts and states than they did in eras of stronger party discipline, as in the early 1900s.

"You could use as a case study Al D'Amato," Silbey said. "His party-unity scores every six years are going to go down through the floor." D'Amato, who had made high-profile moves to dissociate himself from some GOP policies as he geared up for a 1998 re-election bid, also saw his party unity score fall just ahead of his 1992 effort. A Quinnipiac College poll conducted in December showed D'Amato's job approval rating had climbed to 46 percent from 32 percent in September 1996. ■

Trends Diminish Coalition's Clout

For much of the 20th century, being a conservative or a liberal in Congress did not necessarily translate into being a Republican or a Democrat — even after the New Deal aligned the parties basically along those lines.

Southern Democrats such as Reps. John Bell Williams of Mississippi (1947-68) and Joseph David Waggonner Jr. of Louisiana (1961-79) were as conservative as Republicans on almost all issues and more conservative than many on questions of race. Williams and Waggonner cast their votes when the powerful partnership between Southern Democrats and Republicans, known as the conservative coalition, was in its heyday, determining the outcome of a quarter of the votes Congress took.

In 1997, the picture was different. Republicans did not need Democratic votes to win and did not always try to get them. The conservative coalition appeared only 8.6 percent of the time in the first session of the 105th Congress. That figure was down slightly from 12 percent in 1996 and 11 percent in 1995. It was slightly higher than the tallies for 1994 and 1987, both of which came in at 8 percent, the smallest percentage of such votes since Congressional Quarterly started tracking them in the 1950s.

Though the political pairing occurred far less frequently than it did in previous decades, it still offered a statistical analysis of liberalism and conservatism in a particular Congress. For instance, conservative Reps. Roger Wicker of Mississippi and John Linder of Georgia ranked among the 16 Republicans in the House who voted with the coalition 100 percent of the time in 1997, while liberal Rep. Edward J. Markey, D-Mass., was among those who voted with it the least, at 5 percent.

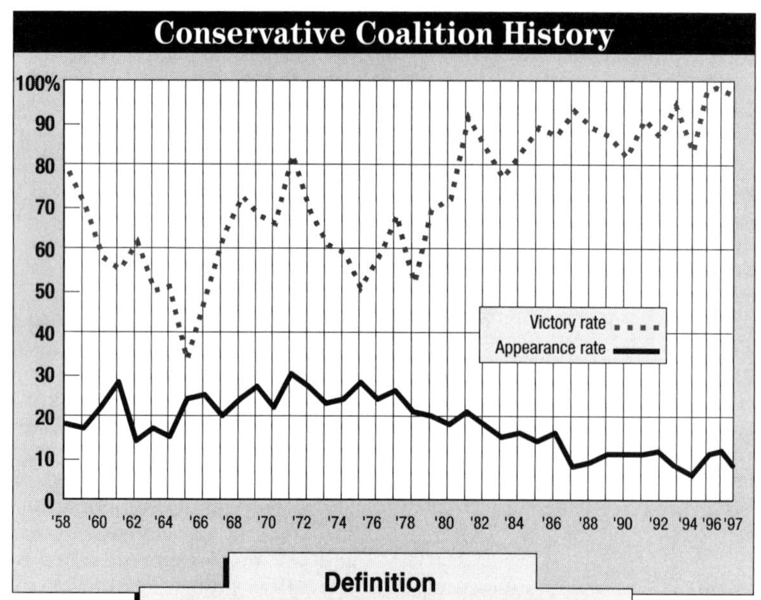

Definition

A voting bloc in the House and Senate consisting of a majority of Republicans and a majority of Southern Democrats, combined against a majority of Northern Democrats.

1997 Data

Senate	23 victories
	2 defeats
	25 appearances in 298 votes
House	55 victories
	0 defeats
	55 appearances in 633 votes

Total Congress appearance rate **8.6%**
Total Congress victory rate **97.5%**

But the infrequency of the coalition's appearance and its focus on parochial Southern interests meant it was no longer an accurate measure of conservatism throughout history. The only Southern Democrat to vote with the coalition 100 percent of the time in 1997 was Sen. John B. Breaux of Louisiana, hardly a Williams or Waggonner clone.

Contemporary conservative Democrats, "even though they are conservative relative to their party, are not conservative relative to Congress," said David W. Rohde, a political scientist at Michigan State University who studied the coalition. "There used to be Southern Democrats who were as conservative as Jesse Helms [R-N.C.]. John Breaux is not as conservative as Jesse Helms."

The reasons for this shift in Congress and the conservative coalition were numerous. Most white Southern Democrats had retired or their spots had been taken by Republicans or black Democrats. The issues before Congress were generally less charged than the 1960s and '70s staples of civil rights, social programs and the Vietnam War. And both political parties exercised greater control over their members, making it more difficult for mavericks.

Each of those three trends was manifest in 1997: the number of white Southern Democrats in Congress was a relatively small 42, party leaders compromised on (or set aside) many contentious measures before bringing them to the floor, and Democratic leaders reached out to appease their caucus of "Blue Dogs," as the alliance of conservative House Democrats was informally called, on the right.

As a result, the conservative coalition surfaced in only 25 of the Senate's 298 votes and 55 of the House's 633.

1997's Conservative Democrats

In previous conservative coalition tallies, Breaux had taken a back seat to more conservative Southern Democrats, such as Sens. Richard C. Shelby and Howell Heflin of Alabama, Sam Nunn of Georgia, and fellow Louisianan J. Bennett Johnston.

But as the 104th Congress began, Shelby joined the newly dominant Republican party, and as it came to an end, Nunn, Heflin and Johnston announced their retirements.

Democrats managed to retain Nunn's and Johnston's seats. Johnston's successor, Mary L. Landrieu, supported the conservative coalition 88 percent of the time in her freshman year, a similar rate to Johnston's 86 percent in 1996. But Max Cleland, who replaced Nunn, voted with the coalition only 72 percent of the time, far less than Nunn's 95 percent in 1996.

Breaux predicted that the new Southern Democrats "will become reflective of their predecessors. I think their constituencies dictate that." He explained his coalition voting score in a similar way. "My own state is moderate to conservative," he said. "I don't think people care so much if I'm voting with Democrats or with Republicans as that I am just voting a moderate to conservative line."

The coalition also lost consistent backers in the House as the 104th came to a close, but some were replaced with new members sympathetic to the cause.

Rep. Bill Brewster of Oklahoma, who supported the coalition 98 percent of the time in 1996, retired that year, as did high scoring Reps. Glen Browder of Alabama, G.V. "Sonny" Montgomery of Mississippi and Pete Geren of Texas. Republicans won all four of those seats.

The coalition's most consistent House Democratic supporter in 1996 — Virginia's Norman Sisisky — also topped the list in 1997, voting with the coalition 96 percent of the time. Three new Southern Democrats followed Sisisky in the rankings. Mike McIntyre of North Carolina and Chris John of Louisiana voted with the coalition 95 percent of the time, while Virgil H. Goode Jr. of Virginia voted with it 93 percent of the time.

But some Southern Democrats consistently opposed the coalition. They were, by and large, African Americans, including Georgians John Lewis and Cynthia A. McKinney, who voted against the coalition more than 80 percent of the time (not counting absences).

Those differences showed how the Democratic Party and the South had changed, said Charles Bullock, a political scientist at the University of Georgia.

Once a bastion of "Yellow Dog" Democrats, the South was represented largely by conservative Republicans. Democrats who held seats in the South tended to represent sizable minority constituencies. The only black congressman to consis-

Leading Scorers: Conservative Coalition

High scorers in support are those who in 1997 voted most often with the conservative coalition. Opposition figures are for those who voted most often against the coalition. Scores are based on votes cast, and members are listed alphabetically when scores are tied. Members who missed half the votes are not listed.

Support

Southern Democrats

Breaux, La.	100%	Graham, Fla.	80	Ford, Ky.	72
Landrieu, La.	88	Cleland, Ga.	72	Robb, Va.	72

Republicans

Cochran, Miss.	100%	Sessions, Ala.	100	Murkowski, Alaska	96
Craig, Idaho	100	Ashcroft, Mo.	96	Nickles, Okla.	96
Frist, Tenn.	100	Burns, Mont.	96	Shelby, Ala.	96
Inhofe, Okla.	100	Campbell, Colo.	96	Stevens, Alaska	96
Kempthorne, Idaho	100	Domenici, N.M.	96	Thompson, Tenn.	96
Lott, Miss.	100	Hagel, Neb.	96	Thurmond, S.C.	96
McConnell, Ky.	100	Helms, N.C.	96	Warner, Va.	96

Northern Democrats

Baucus, Mont.	72%	Conrad, N.D.	68	Feinstein, Calif.	56
Bryan, Nev.	68	Moynihan, N.Y.	64	Kohl, Wis.	56

Southern Democrats

Sisisky, Va.	96%	Cramer, Ala.	93	Pickett, Va.	93
John, La.	95	Goode, Va.	93	Ortiz, Texas	92
McIntyre, N.C.	95	Hall, Texas	93		

Republicans

Baker, La.	100%	LaHood, Ill.	100	Redmond, N.M.	100
Buyer, Ind.	100	Linder, Ga.	100	Solomon, N.Y.	100
Hastert, Ill.	100	McCrery, La.	100	Tauzin, La.	100
Hastings, Wash.	100	Mica, Fla.	100	Wicker, Miss.	100
Hunter, Calif.	100	Oxley, Ohio	100		
Hyde, Ill.	100	Packard, Calif.	100		

Northern Democrats

Barcia, Mich.	89%	Skelton, Mo.	83	Hamilton, Ind.	78
Traficant, Ohio	87	Holden, Pa.	80	Murtha, Pa.	78

Opposition

Southern Democrats

Bumpers, Ark.	72%	Hollings, S.C.	29

Republicans

Specter, Pa.	48%	D'Amato, N.Y.	36	Collins, Maine	32
Jeffords, Vt.	44	Chafee, R.I.	32	Snowe, Maine	32

Northern Democrats

Kennedy, Mass.	100%	Boxer, Calif.	88	Sarbanes, Md.	88
Wellstone, Minn.	100	Durbin, Ill.	88	Kerry, Mass.	84
Reed, R.I.	96	Murray, Wash.	88	Lautenberg, N.J.	84

Southern Democrats

Doggett, Texas	85%	McKinney, Ga.	82	Hastings, Fla.	69
Lewis, Ga.	83	Watt, N.C.	71	Clayton, N.C.	66

Republicans

Paul, Texas	51%	Morella, Md.	46	Ramstad, Minn.	35
Shays, Conn.	48	Campbell, Calif.	38	Klug, Wis.	32

Northern Democrats

Markey, Mass.	95%	Becerra, Calif.	94	Miller, Calif.	94
Stark, Calif.	95	Dellums, Calif.	94		
Velázquez, N.Y.	95	McDermott, Wash.	94		

tently vote with the coalition was Sanford D. Bishop Jr. of Georgia, at 73 percent in 1997.

The decline of white Southern Democrats had vastly changed the conservative coalition, Bullock said. For instance, the five Deep South states, once an incubator for very conservative Democrats among their 36 House seats, in 1997 was home to only four white Democrats: John M. Spratt Jr. of South Carolina, Robert E. "Bud" Cramer of Alabama, Gene Taylor of Mississippi and Chris John of Louisiana.

"White Southern Democrats are not quite the same as white Democrats from other areas," said Rep. David E. Price, D-N.C., a political scientist. "The different variations have some relevance, but just not like they used to."

Most of 1997's conservative to moderate Southern Democrats in the House had joined with like-minded party members in one of two groups — the more conservative Blue Dogs and the more centrist New Democrat Coalition. While both groups occasionally disagreed with the party line, Minority Leader Richard A. Gephardt of Missouri made sure their views were taken into account, said John Tanner of Tennessee, a member of both groups. As a result, Southern Democrats did not need to vote against their Northern party mates as much in 1997, he said.

"There's been consultation and an accommodation of the moderate and conservative wing, and, therefore, there will naturally be less voting against [the party] on the floor," Tanner said. "You've had input and said, 'Look, if you change it this way, we can live with it.' "

Another reason Democrats did not split as much was that most of the issues that came to the floor were not as politically dicey as those that surfaced decades before.

Coalition Issues

When the conservative coalition reached its apex in 1971, appearing 30 percent of the time and winning 83 percent of those votes, Congress and the nation were in the midst of a tumultuous policy debate. Among the votes facing members were an amendment to develop a uniform national policy on school busing, an amendment to cut off funds to U.S. forces in Indochina except for withdrawal and a bill to extend the draft for two years.

Southern Democrats and Republicans pulled together easily and quickly. The conservative coalition got its way on all three issues.

In contrast, the issues which drew the coalition together in 1997 seemed relatively minuscule, though the lack of weighty decisions was not so much a factor of the coalition as it was a factor of Congress itself.

In 1997, most controversies either ended in a compromise nearly everyone could support, such as the budget agreement, or did not come to the floor at all, such as affirmative action.

That fit into a trend that began in the mid-1980s of limiting voting opportunities on the floor, said Sarah Binder, a fellow in governmental studies at the Brookings Institution in Washington, D.C.

In 1997, the coalition surfaced most often in the House to assist in passing resources-related initiatives like a private property rights bill (HR 1534) or a bill to open a temporary storage site for nuclear waste at Yucca Mountain, Nev. (HR 1270), and in fending off defense cuts. In addition, the coalition converged to block abolition of the tobacco crop insurance and peanut quota programs and to fight increases in funding for anti-tobacco initiatives. All three votes came on the fiscal 1998 agriculture spending bill (HR 2160). Seven of the votes in which Southern Democrats split from Northern ones involved procedural motions that Democrats filed to gum up floor action.

In the Senate, the coalition appeared most often in 1997 on budgetary issues. On a proposed constitutional amendment to require balanced federal budgets, five Southern Democrats joined all 55 Republicans and six Northern Democrats to support the measure. But that was one short of the two-thirds majority, or 67 votes, needed for passage. The only other Senate defeat for the coalition came on a motion to table an amendment to the supplemental fiscal 1997 appropriations bill (S 672) that would have distributed highway improvement funds based on 1991 numbers. Though all eight Southern Democrats and 31 Republicans voted against the motion, it succeeded 54-46.

Overall, the coalition's success rate in the House and Senate continued to be high, 97.5 percent. ■

Voting Diligence at 45-Year High

Although the dean of the Democrats missed his first vote in 13 years, the Senate set a record for diligence in voting in 1997. The 98.7 percent participation rate was the highest recorded for either chamber in the 45 years that Congressional Quarterly has been tracking absences. Together, both chambers matched the all-time high of 96.5 percent set in 1995.

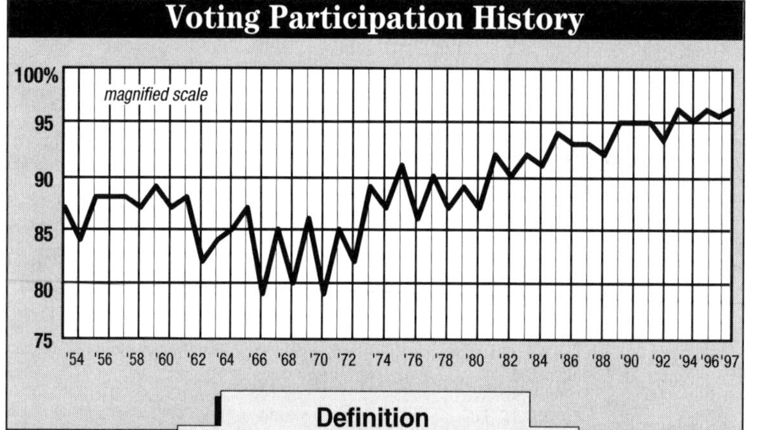

Definition

How often a member voted "yea" or "nay" on roll call votes on the floor of the House or Senate.

1997 Data

	Recorded Votes	Participation Rate
Senate	298	98.7%
House	633	96.3%
Total Congress	931	96.5%

The record capped a three-decade upsurge in voting in both chambers, as members (and their leaders) sought protection from accusations that they were not always on the job.

West Virginia Democratic Sen. Robert C. Byrd, the Senate's fiercest champion of tradition, missed his first vote since 1984 when he was felled by a stomach virus and missed a Sept. 16 vote to limit debate on the Food and Drug Administration overhaul bill.

The next-longest streak belonged to Charles E. Grassley, R-Iowa, who had not missed a vote since 1993. While that may have paled in comparison with Sen. William Proxmire, D-Wis., who voted in every roll call between 1966 and his retirement in 1988, and former Rep. William H. Natcher, D-Ky., whose voting streak spanned 40 years, younger members seemed to try to emulate them.

In 1997, 26 senators, including six freshmen, participated in all 298 roll call votes, while nine House members, five of them freshmen, made it to all 633 votes. Scores of other members missed only one or two votes.

South Carolina Republican Strom Thurmond, at 95 the oldest senator in history, missed only two of the 298 votes.

In the House, members voted 96.3 percent of the time, a number slightly higher than the previous year, and barely lower than the record 96.4 percent of 1995.

A 10-year House voting streak ended Oct. 22 for Christopher Shays, R-Conn., who was praying in the Capitol chapel when his uncharged beeper failed to warn him of a vote.

The House had more than twice as many roll call votes as in the Senate and 179 more than in the second session of the 104th Congress.

The increase in House votes was partly due to a flurry of procedural motions toward the end of the session. To protest an investigation into the 1996 victory of California Democrat Loretta Sanchez over Republican Robert K. Dornan and a standstill on campaign finance legislation, Democrats delayed floor action by introducing motions to adjourn and demanding recorded votes. "It was a pain," recalls Shays. "It was totally procedural and silly."

Members seemed well aware of predecessors who paid dearly for their absences.

In 1994, Sheila Jackson-Lee ousted incumbent Rep. Craig Washington of Texas in the Democratic primary. Washington, who had served since 1990, had one of the House's lowest voting participation rates. Jackson-Lee told voters that Washington, who also was a frequent absentee during his 10 years in the state House, was not paying enough attention to his constituents, an argument that struck a chord with Texas voters.

Rep. Jesse L. Jackson Jr., D-Ill., a sophomore who thus far had a perfect record since taking office, said he voted because it was important, adding that he "wouldn't want to be someone's poster child for what Democrats aren't doing."

Jackson routinely interrupted basketball games in the House gym to run upstairs and vote, and nearly missed his great-grandmother's funeral for a roll call. He said he wanted to hug a Republican who, as presiding officer, held the vote open for extra minutes so he could rush to the floor to cast a ballot.

"It's a bipartisan thing," said a Democratic leadership aide. "You don't want to trick anyone into missing a vote."

This year, even the lowest-scoring members missed relatively few votes. Barbara A. Mikulski, D-Md., with 92 percent, was at the bottom of the Senate list. The two Michigan senators, Republican Spencer Abraham and Democrat Carl Levin, held perfect scores for two years.

The House had 19 members with scores below 90 percent, but that included Bill Richardson, D-N.M., (35 percent) and Susan Molinari, R-N.Y., (79 percent) who resigned mid-session to take other jobs. Rep. Steven H. Schiff, R-N.M., (10 percent) spent most of the session undergoing treatment for skin cancer. ■

Congressional Quarterly's Voting Analyses

Since 1945, Congressional Quarterly has analyzed the voting behavior of members of Congress. The studies have become references for academics, journalists, politicians and students of how Congress behaves as an institution and how individual members vote. CQ's study of the key votes of 1997 begins on p. C-35.

Explanatory notes: In most charts of individual members' scores that follow, a member's score is calculated two ways: once based on all votes, regardless of whether the member voted; another time based only on the votes he or she actually cast. For consistency with previous years, graphs and breakdowns of chambers, parties and regions are based on the first set of scores. Lists of individual leaders are based on votes cast, not counting absences.

Scores are rounded off to the nearest percentage point, except that no score is rounded up to 100 percent.

Congressional Quarterly defines regions of the United States as follows: **East:** Conn., Del., Maine, Md., Mass., N.H., N.J., N.Y., Pa., R.I., Vt., W.Va. **West:** Alaska, Ariz., Calif., Colo., Hawaii, Idaho, Mont., Nev., N.M., Ore., Utah, Wash., Wyo. **South:** Ala., Ark., Fla., Ga., Ky., La., Miss., N.C., Okla., S.C., Tenn., Texas, Va. **Midwest:** Ill., Ind., Iowa, Kan., Mich., Minn., Mo., Neb., N.D., Ohio, S.D., Wis.

References to Northern Democrats and Northern Republicans include all members who do not represent the 13 Southern states, as defined by CQ.

Presidential Support Definitions

Congressional Quarterly determines presidential positions on congressional votes by examining the statements made by President Clinton or his authorized spokesmen. ***Support*** measures the percentage of the time members voted in accord with the position of the president. ***Opposition*** measures the percentage of the time members voted against the president's position. ***Success*** measures the percentage of the contested votes on which the president prevailed. Absences lowered parties' scores.

National Security vs. Domestic Issues

Following are 1997 presidential success scores broken down into domestic and national security issues, with national security including foreign policy and defense. Scores for 1996 are in parentheses:

	National Security		Domestic		Average	
Senate	58%	(58%)	75%	(57%)	71%	(58%)
House	18	(56)	47	(52)	39	(53)
Average	32	(57)	61	(55)	54	(55)

Average Scores

Scores for 1996 are in parentheses:

	Support			
	Republicans		Democrats	
Senate	60%	(37%)	85%	(83%)
House	30	(38)	71	(74)

	Opposition			
	Republicans		Democrats	
Senate	39%	(61%)	13%	(15%)
House	68	(59)	26	(21)

Regional Averages

Scores for 1996 are in parentheses:

Support

	East		West		South		Midwest	
Republicans								
Senate	66%	(46%)	60%	(36%)	56%	(33%)	58%	(35%)
House	39	(45)	28	(36)	27	(34)	31	(39)
Democrats								
Senate	84	(86)	87	(86)	83	(75)	86	(85)
House	73	(76)	77	(77)	66	(70)	69	(73)

Opposition

	East		West		South		Midwest	
Republicans								
Senate	31%	(52%)	39%	(62%)	42%	(65%)	41%	(62%)
House	60	(51)	68	(62)	71	(62)	68	(59)
Democrats								
Senate	12	(13)	12	(13)	17	(20)	13	(14)
House	24	(19)	20	(19)	31	(24)	28	(23)

Success Rate History

Average scores for both chambers of Congress:

Eisenhower	
1953	89.0%
1954	82.8
1955	75.0
1956	70.0
1957	68.0
1958	76.0
1959	52.0
1960	65.0

Kennedy	
1961	81.0%
1962	85.4
1963	87.1

Johnson	
1964	88.0%
1965	93.0
1966	79.0
1967	79.0
1968	75.0

Nixon	
1969	74.0%
1970	77.0
1971	75.0
1972	66.0
1973	50.6
1974	59.6

Ford	
1974	58.2%
1975	61.0
1976	53.8

Carter	
1977	75.4%
1978	78.3
1979	76.8
1980	75.1

Reagan	
1981	82.4%
1982	72.4
1983	67.1
1984	65.8
1985	59.9
1986	56.1
1987	43.5
1988	47.4

Bush	
1989	62.6%
1990	46.8
1991	54.2
1992	43.0

Clinton	
1993	86.4%
1994	86.4
1995	36.2
1996	55.1
1997	53.6

1997 Senate Presidential Position Votes

The following is a list of Senate votes in 1997 on which there was a clear presidential position, listed by roll call number with a brief description and categorized by topic. *(Definition, p. C-14)*

Domestic Policy

7 Victories

Vote Number	Description
66	Education
76	Tobacco policy
244	Arts funding
245	Arts funding
246*	Arts funding
266	Campaign finance (cloture)
274	Campaign finance (cloture)

10 Defeats

Vote Number	Description
40	Nuclear waste
42*	Nuclear waste
70	Abortion
71*	Abortion
149	Tobacco policy
167	Abortion
233	Teamsters election
267*	Campaign finance (cloture)
270	Campaign finance (cloture)
273	Campaign finance (cloture)

Nominations

29 Victories

Vote Number	Description
1	Madeleine K. Albright confirmation
2	William S. Cohen confirmation
3	Andrew M. Cuomo confirmation
4	William M. Daley confirmation
6	Rodney Slater confirmation
9	Bill Richardson confirmation
26	Charlene Barshefsky waiver
27	Charlene Barshefsky confirmation
30	Federico F. Peña confirmation
34	Merrick B. Garland confirmation
54	Alexis Herman confirmation
174	Joel I. Klein confirmation (cloture)
187	Joel I. Klein confirmation
188	Eric H. Holder Jr. confirmation
218	Henry Harold Kennedy Jr. confirmation
219	Frank M. Hull confirmation
236	Joseph F. Bataillon confirmation
237	Christopher Droney confirmation
238	Janet C. Hall confirmation
259	Katharine Sweeney Hayden confirmation
279	Algenon L. Marbley confirmation
280	Wyche Fowler Jr. confirmation
281	Thomas S. Foley confirmation
284	William E. Kennard confirmation
286	Charles J. Siragusa confirmation
290	Charles O. Rossotti confirmation
293	James S. Gwin confirmation
295	Ronald Lee Gilman confirmation
297	Christina A. Snyder confirmation

Defense and Foreign Policy

2 Victories

Vote Number	Description
13	Family planning
51*	Chemical weapons

5 Defeats

Vote Number	Description
45	Chemical weapons
109	Intelligence spending
178	Russia religious freedom
182	Drug certification
296	Defense spending

Economic Affairs and Trade

7 Victories

Vote Number	Description
24*	Balanced-budget amendment
25	Trade agreements
92*	Budget
96	Budget
100	Supplemental appropriations
209	Budget
211	Taxes

3 Defeats

Vote Number	Description
61†	Automatic continuing resolution
95	Supplemental appropriations
287*	Line-item veto

*Congressional Quarterly Key Vote (p. C-33)

Senate Success Rate

Victories	45
Defeats	18
Total	63
Success Rate	71.4%

1997 House Presidential Position Votes

The following is a list of House votes in 1997 on which there was a clear presidential position, listed by roll call number with a brief description and categorized by topic. *(Definition, p. C-14)*

Domestic Policy

15 Victories

Vote Number	Description
72	Housing
90	Space station
93	Property transfer
96	Adoption
124	Education
131	WIC funding
133	Immigrants' SSI
138	Job training
147*	Transportation
151	Dolphin-safe tuna
156	Wildlife refuges
266	Arts funding
272	Tribal lands
449†	Legal services
569*	School vouchers

22 Defeats

Vote Number	Description
23	Abortion
58	Overtime pay
59	Overtime pay
65*	Abortion
92	Agriculture policy
118	Juvenile crime
127*	Housing
168	Abortion
194	Abortion
217	Abortion
290	Horse preservation
363	Abortion
398	Education testing
443	Legal expenses
475	Census sampling
495	Monument designation
500	Abortion
513	District of Columbia
519*	Property rights
524	Education
557	Nuclear waste
598	Abortion

Defense and Foreign Policy

4 Victories

Vote Number	Description
22	Family planning
231	China MFN
233*	Bosnia policy
235	Russian missile transfer

18 Defeats

Vote Number	Description
46	Mexico drug policy
47	Mexico drug policy
48	Mexico drug policy
160	Agency consolidation
178	Russian missile transfer
228	B-2 bomber
229	Military depots
230	Russian missile transfer
234	Bosnia policy
336	B-2 bomber
338	Defense spending
504	U.N. land designation
534	Defense spending
580	China human rights
595	China religious persecution
601	Taiwan missile defense
605	China loans
614	China military companies

Economic Affairs and Trade

10 Victories

Vote Number	Description
27	Airline taxes
76	Tax browsing
78	Taxes
148*	Budget
166	Budget
203	Supplemental appropriations
293	Trademark law treaty
345	Budget
350	Taxes
577*	IRS overhaul

6 Defeats

Vote Number	Description
44	Budget
134	Automatic continuing resolution
136	Supplemental appropriations
169	Supplemental appropriations
245	Taxes
617	Line-item veto

**Congressional Quarterly Key Vote (p. C-38)*

House Success Rate

Victories	29
Defeats	46
Total	75
Success Rate	38.7%

	1	2	3
ALABAMA			
Sessions	56	43	56
Shelby	57	43	57
ALASKA			
Murkowski	59	38	61
Stevens	71	29	71
ARIZONA			
Kyl	57	43	57
McCain	68	29	70
ARKANSAS			
Hutchinson	59	40	60
Bumpers	86	14	86
CALIFORNIA			
Boxer	89	11	89
Feinstein	89	11	89
COLORADO			
Allard	48	52	48
Campbell	65	33	66
CONNECTICUT			
Dodd	92	6	94
Lieberman	90	6	93
DELAWARE			
Roth	62	33	65
Biden	76	14	84
FLORIDA			
Mack	57	38	60
Graham	84	16	84
GEORGIA			
Coverdell	56	44	56
Cleland	87	13	87
HAWAII			
Akaka	90	10	90
Inouye	83	13	87
IDAHO			
Craig	54	46	54
Kempthorne	59	41	59
ILLINOIS			
Durbin	92	8	92
Moseley-Braun	84	16	84
INDIANA			
Coats	54	41	57
Lugar	62	38	62
IOWA			
Grassley	60	40	60
Harkin	83	13	87
KANSAS			
Brownback	56	44	56
Roberts	59	41	59
KENTUCKY			
McConnell	59	41	59
Ford	78	21	79
LOUISIANA			
Breaux	81	19	81
Landrieu	87	13	87
MAINE			
Collins	76	24	76
Snowe	78	22	78
MARYLAND			
Mikulski	79	8	91
Sarbanes	87	13	87
MASSACHUSETTS			
Kennedy	84	11	88
Kerry	87	13	87
MICHIGAN			
Abraham	60	40	60
Levin	90	10	90
MINNESOTA			
Grams	52	46	53
Wellstone	83	17	83
MISSISSIPPI			
Cochran	67	32	68
Lott	56	44	56
MISSOURI			
Ashcroft	51	49	51
Bond	60	37	62
MONTANA			
Burns	54	41	57
Baucus	87	13	87
NEBRASKA			
Hagel	59	41	59
Kerrey	87	11	89
NEVADA			
Bryan	89	11	89
Reid	84	16	84
NEW HAMPSHIRE			
Gregg	63	37	63
Smith	51	49	51
NEW JERSEY			
Lautenberg	83	13	87
Torricelli	89	11	89
NEW MEXICO			
Domenici	67	33	67
Bingaman	92	8	92
NEW YORK			
D'Amato	54	37	60
Moynihan	81	17	82
NORTH CAROLINA			
Faircloth	38	54	41
Helms	44	51	47
NORTH DAKOTA			
Conrad	81	19	81
Dorgan	81	19	81
OHIO			
DeWine	62	38	62
Glenn	81	13	86
OKLAHOMA			
Inhofe	49	51	49
Nickles	59	41	59
OREGON			
Smith	65	35	65
Wyden	81	13	86
PENNSYLVANIA			
Santorum	60	38	61
Specter	71	29	71
RHODE ISLAND			
Chafee	73	24	75
Reed	86	14	86
SOUTH CAROLINA			
Thurmond	57	41	58
Hollings	75	25	75
SOUTH DAKOTA			
Daschle	90	8	92
Johnson	84	13	87
TENNESSEE			
Frist	59	41	59
Thompson	59	41	59

KEY

Democrats ***Republicans***

	1	2	3
TEXAS			
Gramm	56	44	56
Hutchison	62	37	63
UTAH			
Bennett	60	37	62
Hatch	63	37	63
VERMONT			
Jeffords	75	21	78
Leahy	87	13	87
VIRGINIA			
Warner	63	32	67
Robb	87	13	87
WASHINGTON			
Gorton	67	33	67
Murray	87	13	87
WEST VIRGINIA			
Byrd	81	19	81
Rockefeller	79	13	86
WISCONSIN			
Feingold	86	14	86
Kohl	90	10	90
WYOMING			
Enzi	51	49	51
Thomas	57	43	57

Presidential Support and Opposition: Senate

1. Clinton Support Score, 1997. Percentage of 63 recorded votes in 1997 on which President Clinton took a position and on which a senator voted "yea" or "nay" in agreement with the president's position. Failures to vote lowered both support and opposition scores.

2. Clinton Opposition Score, 1997. Percentage of 63 recorded votes in 1997 on which President Clinton took a position and on which a senator voted "yea" or "nay" in disagreement with the president's position. Failures to vote lowered both support and opposition scores.

3. Clinton Support Score, 1997. Percentage of 63 recorded votes in 1997 on which President Clinton took a position and on which a senator was present and voted "yea" or "nay" in agreement with the president's position. In this version of the study, absences were not counted; therefore, failures to vote did not lower support or opposition scores. Opposition scores, not listed here, are the inverse of the support score; i.e., the opposition score is equal to 100 percent minus the individual's support score.

Presidential Support and Opposition: House

1. Clinton Support Score, 1997. Percentage of 75 recorded votes in 1997 on which President Clinton took a position and on which a representative voted "yea" or "nay" in agreement with the president's position. Failures to vote lowered both support and opposition scores.

2. Clinton Opposition Score, 1997. Percentage of 75 recorded votes in 1997 on which President Clinton took a position and on which a representative voted "yea" or "nay" in disagreement with the president's position. Failures to vote lowered both support and opposition scores.

3. Clinton Support Score, 1997. Percentage of 75 recorded votes in 1997 on which President Clinton took a position and on which a representative was present and voted "yea" or "nay" in agreement with the president's position. In this version of the study, absences were not counted; therefore, failures to vote did not lower support or opposition scores. Opposition scores, not listed here, are the inverse of the support score; i.e., the opposition score is equal to 100 percent minus the individual's support score.

[1] *Walter Capps, D-Calif., died Oct. 28. He was eligible to vote on 64 presidential support votes.*

[2] *Newt Gingrich, R-Ga., as Speaker of the House, voted at his discretion on 23 presidential support votes in 1997.*

[3] *Bill Redmond, R-N.M., was sworn in May 20, replacing Bill Richardson, D-N.M., who resigned Feb. 13. Redmond was eligible for 50 presidential support votes in 1997. Richardson was eligible for no presidential support votes in 1997.*

[4] *Vito J. Fossella, R-N.Y., was sworn in Nov. 5, replacing Susan Molinari, R-N.Y., who resigned Aug. 1. Fossella was eligible for 8 presidential support votes in 1997. Molinari was eligible for 53 presidential support votes in 1997. Her support score was 40 percent; opposition score, 47 percent; support score adjusted for absences, 46 percent.*

[5] *Ciro D. Rodriguez, D-Texas, was sworn in April 17, replacing Frank Tejeda, D-Texas, who died on Jan. 30. Rodriguez was eligible for 62 presidential support votes in 1997. Tejeda was eligible for no presidential support votes in 1997.*

KEY

Democrats ***Republicans***
Independent

	1	2	3
ALABAMA			
1 *Callahan*	27	72	27
2 ***Everett***	27	73	27
3 ***Riley***	20	67	23
4 ***Aderholt***	24	76	24
5 Cramer	52	48	52
6 ***Bachus***	25	73	26
7 Hilliard	67	28	70
ALASKA			
AL *Young*	21	63	25
ARIZONA			
1 ***Salmon***	24	76	24
2 Pastor	79	20	80
3 ***Stump***	20	77	21
4 ***Shadegg***	24	75	24
5 ***Kolbe***	52	48	52
6 ***Hayworth***	29	71	29
ARKANSAS			
1 Berry	59	41	59
2 Snyder	84	16	84
3 ***Hutchinson***	27	73	27
4 ***Dickey***	20	80	20
CALIFORNIA			
1 ***Riggs***	33	67	33
2 ***Herger***	27	68	28
3 Fazio	81	19	81
4 ***Doolittle***	24	72	25
5 Matsui	72	24	75
6 Woolsey	80	19	81
7 Miller	75	19	80
8 Pelosi	77	19	81
9 Dellums	79	20	80
10 Tauscher	79	20	80
11 ***Pombo***	23	76	23
12 Lantos	69	17	80
13 Stark	72	23	76
14 Eshoo	87	12	88
15 ***Campbell***	51	49	51
16 Lofgren	88	11	89
17 Farr	73	15	83
18 Condit	53	45	54
19 ***Radanovich***	27	72	27
20 Dooley	75	24	76
21 ***Thomas***	35	65	35
22 Capps[1]	84	13	87
23 ***Gallegly***	29	69	30
24 Sherman	77	23	77
25 ***McKeon***	29	71	29
26 Berman	81	13	86
27 ***Rogan***	25	72	26
28 ***Dreier***	27	72	27
29 Waxman	85	13	86
30 Becerra	80	13	86
31 Martinez	72	24	75
32 Dixon	76	20	79
33 Roybal-Allard	83	16	84
34 Torres	73	19	80
35 Waters	75	25	75
36 Harman	71	28	72
37 Millender-McD.	81	19	81
38 ***Horn***	47	53	47
39 ***Royce***	24	76	24
40 ***Lewis***	33	61	35
41 ***Kim***	28	72	28
42 Brown	88	9	90
43 ***Calvert***	27	72	27
44 ***Bono***	33	67	33
45 ***Rohrabacher***	20	79	20
46 Sanchez	68	31	69
47 ***Cox***	23	67	25
48 ***Packard***	27	72	27
49 ***Bilbray***	35	63	36
50 Filner	72	23	76
51 ***Cunningham***	28	72	28
52 ***Hunter***	24	73	25
COLORADO			
1 DeGette	80	17	82
2 Skaggs	93	7	93
3 ***McInnis***	27	71	27
4 ***Schaffer***	28	72	28
5 ***Hefley***	25	75	25
6 ***Schaefer***	24	76	24
CONNECTICUT			
1 Kennelly	85	15	85
2 Gejdenson	83	16	84
3 DeLauro	83	16	84
4 ***Shays***	55	45	55
5 Maloney	68	32	68
6 ***Johnson***	60	40	60
DELAWARE			
AL ***Castle***	55	45	55
FLORIDA			
1 ***Scarborough***	23	77	23
2 Boyd	61	39	61
3 Brown	69	28	71
4 ***Fowler***	31	69	31
5 Thurman	79	21	79
6 ***Stearns***	25	75	25
7 ***Mica***	25	72	26
8 ***McCollum***	27	72	27
9 ***Bilirakis***	28	72	28
10 ***Young***	27	71	27
11 Davis	80	19	81
12 ***Canady***	29	71	29
13 ***Miller***	33	67	33
14 ***Goss***	31	69	31
15 ***Weldon***	19	77	19
16 ***Foley***	36	64	36
17 Meek	71	29	71
18 ***Ros-Lehtinen***	32	67	32
19 Wexler	76	20	79
20 Deutsch	75	21	78
21 ***Diaz-Balart***	29	65	31
22 ***Shaw***	36	64	36
23 Hastings	69	28	71
GEORGIA			
1 ***Kingston***	21	73	23
2 Bishop	57	41	58
3 ***Collins***	27	72	27
4 McKinney	72	16	82
5 Lewis	77	20	79
6 ***Gingrich***[2]	26	74	26
7 ***Barr***	21	79	21
8 ***Chambliss***	25	72	26
9 ***Deal***	23	77	23
10 ***Norwood***	24	76	24
11 ***Linder***	31	67	32
HAWAII			
1 Abercrombie	72	27	73
2 Mink	72	27	73
IDAHO			
1 ***Chenoweth***	24	76	24
2 ***Crapo***	20	79	20
ILLINOIS			
1 Rush	76	20	79
2 Jackson	79	21	79
3 Lipinski	40	55	42
4 Gutierrez	68	23	75
5 Blagojevich	80	17	82
6 ***Hyde***	28	71	28
7 Davis	76	23	77
8 ***Crane***	23	75	23
9 Yates	60	5	92
10 ***Porter***	47	49	49
11 ***Weller***	28	72	28
12 Costello	57	39	60
13 ***Fawell***	43	57	43
14 ***Hastert***	32	68	32
15 ***Ewing***	36	64	36
16 ***Manzullo***	23	76	23

	1	2	3
17 Evans	73	27	73
18 ***LaHood***	31	69	31
19 Poshard	60	40	60
20 ***Shimkus***	28	72	28
INDIANA			
1 Visclosky	65	33	66
2 ***McIntosh***	25	65	28
3 Roemer	55	45	55
4 ***Souder***	24	71	25
5 ***Buyer***	24	75	24
6 ***Burton***	25	73	26
7 ***Pease***	28	72	28
8 ***Hostettler***	25	75	25
9 Hamilton	71	29	71
10 Carson	72	16	82
IOWA			
1 ***Leach***	48	52	48
2 ***Nussle***	28	71	28
3 Boswell	73	27	73
4 ***Ganske***	32	68	32
5 ***Latham***	28	72	28
KANSAS			
1 ***Moran***	27	73	27
2 ***Ryun***	24	76	24
3 ***Snowbarger***	20	79	20
4 ***Tiahrt***	23	77	23
KENTUCKY			
1 ***Whitfield***	31	69	31
2 ***Lewis***	25	71	26
3 ***Northup***	25	75	25
4 ***Bunning***	27	72	27
5 ***Rogers***	27	73	27
6 Baesler	59	41	59
LOUISIANA			
1 ***Livingston***	32	68	32
2 Jefferson	61	24	72
3 ***Tauzin***	31	69	31
4 ***McCrery***	29	69	30
5 ***Cooksey***	28	71	28
6 ***Baker***	24	73	25
7 John	51	47	52
MAINE			
1 Allen	81	17	82
2 Baldacci	83	16	84
MARYLAND			
1 ***Gilchrest***	44	55	45
2 ***Ehrlich***	33	67	33
3 Cardin	83	17	83
4 Wynn	75	25	75
5 Hoyer	75	24	76
6 ***Bartlett***	27	73	27
7 Cummings	76	23	77
8 ***Morella***	73	27	73
MASSACHUSETTS			
1 Olver	80	20	80
2 Neal	75	20	79
3 McGovern	84	16	84
4 Frank	77	21	78
5 Meehan	81	17	82
6 Tierney	75	25	75
7 Markey	76	24	76
8 Kennedy	77	21	78
9 Moakley	69	29	70
10 Delahunt	76	24	76
MICHIGAN			
1 Stupak	71	29	71
2 ***Hoekstra***	27	69	28
3 ***Ehlers***	41	57	42
4 ***Camp***	32	68	32
5 Barcia	45	55	45
6 ***Upton***	37	63	37
7 ***Smith***	35	63	36
8 Stabenow	81	19	81
9 Kildee	63	37	63
10 Bonior	71	27	73
11 ***Knollenberg***	31	69	31
12 Levin	84	16	84
13 Rivers	83	17	83
14 Conyers	77	16	83
15 Kilpatrick	73	23	76
16 Dingell	77	19	81
MINNESOTA			
1 ***Gutknecht***	28	72	28
2 Minge	80	20	80
3 ***Ramstad***	52	48	52
4 Vento	84	16	84
5 Sabo	87	13	87
6 Luther	77	23	77
7 Peterson	51	49	51
8 Oberstar	63	36	64
MISSISSIPPI			
1 ***Wicker***	28	71	28
2 Thompson	68	29	70
3 ***Pickering***	21	71	23
4 ***Parker***	25	72	26
5 Taylor	33	67	33
MISSOURI			
1 Clay	75	19	80
2 ***Talent***	27	72	27
3 Gephardt	69	21	76
4 Skelton	43	48	47
5 McCarthy	81	17	82
6 Danner	41	56	42
7 ***Blunt***	24	72	25
8 ***Emerson***	27	73	27
9 ***Hulshof***	29	71	29
MONTANA			
AL ***Hill***	24	76	24
NEBRASKA			
1 ***Bereuter***	40	60	40
2 ***Christensen***	27	73	27
3 ***Barrett***	33	67	33
NEVADA			
1 ***Ensign***	28	67	30
2 ***Gibbons***	29	68	30
NEW HAMPSHIRE			
1 ***Sununu***	29	71	29
2 ***Bass***	39	61	39
NEW JERSEY			
1 Andrews	60	16	79
2 ***LoBiondo***	36	63	36
3 ***Saxton***	35	65	35
4 ***Smith***	36	63	36
5 ***Roukema***	55	44	55
6 Pallone	79	21	79
7 ***Franks***	45	55	45
8 Pascrell	68	32	68
9 Rothman	77	21	78
10 Payne	72	20	78
11 ***Frelinghuysen***	48	52	48
12 ***Pappas***	24	76	24
13 Menendez	75	24	76
NEW MEXICO			
1 ***Schiff***	7	7	50
2 ***Skeen***	32	68	32
3 ***Redmond***[3]	26	74	26
NEW YORK			
1 ***Forbes***	28	63	31
2 ***Lazio***	44	55	45
3 ***King***	32	67	32
4 McCarthy	69	29	70
5 Ackerman	79	17	82
6 Flake	64	20	76
7 Manton	56	36	61
8 Nadler	80	17	82
9 Schumer	69	15	83
10 Towns	67	23	75
11 Owens	75	24	76
12 Velázquez	76	19	80
13 ***Fossella***[4]	13	88	13
14 Maloney	77	19	81
15 Rangel	80	17	82
16 Serrano	80	20	80
17 Engel	71	21	77
18 Lowey	83	15	85
19 ***Kelly***	41	57	42
20 ***Gilman***	49	51	49
21 McNulty	65	32	67
22 ***Solomon***	24	76	24
23 ***Boehlert***	57	40	59
24 ***McHugh***	32	60	35
25 ***Walsh***	36	61	37
26 Hinchey	80	19	81
27 ***Paxon***	21	76	22
28 Slaughter	77	20	79
29 LaFalce	76	20	79
30 ***Quinn***	36	60	38
31 ***Houghton***	56	37	60
NORTH CAROLINA			
1 Clayton	71	24	75
2 Etheridge	63	32	66
3 ***Jones***	24	75	24
4 Price	73	23	76
5 ***Burr***	28	71	28
6 ***Coble***	24	76	24
7 McIntyre	43	53	44
8 Hefner	57	25	69
9 ***Myrick***	24	75	24
10 ***Ballenger***	27	69	28
11 ***Taylor***	27	69	28
12 Watt	77	23	77
NORTH DAKOTA			
AL Pomeroy	69	28	71
OHIO			
1 ***Chabot***	27	73	27
2 ***Portman***	31	68	31
3 Hall	63	35	64
4 ***Oxley***	35	64	35
5 ***Gillmor***	31	67	32
6 Strickland	69	29	70
7 ***Hobson***	33	67	33
8 ***Boehner***	25	72	26
9 Kaptur	45	47	49
10 Kucinich	65	35	65
11 Stokes	76	23	77
12 ***Kasich***	31	68	31
13 Brown	81	17	82
14 Sawyer	87	12	88
15 ***Pryce***	40	59	41
16 ***Regula***	39	61	39
17 Traficant	36	64	36
18 ***Ney***	33	65	34
19 ***LaTourette***	33	63	35
OKLAHOMA			
1 ***Largent***	23	77	23
2 ***Coburn***	23	72	24
3 ***Watkins***	24	68	26
4 ***Watts***	24	72	25
5 ***Istook***	17	77	18
6 ***Lucas***	29	71	29
OREGON			
1 Furse	83	12	87
2 ***Smith***	25	67	28
3 Blumenauer	80	17	82
4 DeFazio	67	32	68
5 Hooley	80	20	80
PENNSYLVANIA			
1 Foglietta	77	13	85
2 Fattah	85	13	86
3 Borski	60	39	61
4 Klink	60	39	61
5 ***Peterson***	28	71	28
6 Holden	49	49	50
7 ***Weldon***	36	61	37
8 ***Greenwood***	48	51	49
9 ***Shuster***	25	72	26
10 ***McDade***	31	64	32
11 Kanjorski	68	32	68
12 Murtha	64	35	65
13 ***Fox***	33	67	33
14 Coyne	83	17	83
15 McHale	68	32	68
16 ***Pitts***	28	72	28
17 ***Gekas***	29	71	29
18 Doyle	61	39	61
19 ***Goodling***	27	73	27
20 Mascara	61	39	61
21 ***English***	37	60	38
RHODE ISLAND			
1 Kennedy	76	23	77
2 Weygand	65	33	66
SOUTH CAROLINA			
1 ***Sanford***	24	75	24
2 ***Spence***	27	73	27
3 ***Graham***	25	75	25
4 ***Inglis***	24	75	24
5 Spratt	73	27	73
6 Clyburn	75	25	75
SOUTH DAKOTA			
AL ***Thune***	27	72	27
TENNESSEE			
1 ***Jenkins***	29	71	29
2 ***Duncan***	29	69	30
3 ***Wamp***	28	72	28
4 ***Hilleary***	20	77	21
5 Clement	64	32	67
6 Gordon	63	33	65
7 ***Bryant***	25	71	26
8 Tanner	59	40	59
9 Ford	79	20	80
TEXAS			
1 Sandlin	67	33	67
2 Turner	61	35	64
3 ***Johnson***	28	69	29
4 Hall	27	73	27
5 ***Sessions***	25	73	26
6 ***Barton***	24	72	25
7 ***Archer***	29	69	30
8 ***Brady***	28	71	28
9 Lampson	77	23	77
10 Doggett	79	19	81
11 Edwards	72	27	73
12 ***Granger***	29	71	29
13 ***Thornberry***	32	67	32
14 ***Paul***	40	59	41
15 Hinojosa	71	27	73
16 Reyes	69	28	71
17 Stenholm	52	47	53
18 Jackson-Lee	75	24	76
19 ***Combest***	29	71	29
20 Gonzalez	56	8	88
21 ***Smith***	31	68	31
22 ***DeLay***	27	73	27
23 ***Bonilla***	33	64	34
24 Frost	77	21	78
25 Bentsen	80	20	80
26 ***Armey***	25	75	25
27 Ortiz	55	43	56
28 Rodriguez[5]	74	26	74
29 Green	61	35	64
30 Johnson	79	21	79
UTAH			
1 ***Hansen***	27	71	27
2 ***Cook***	24	76	24
3 ***Cannon***	31	69	31
VERMONT			
AL Sanders	73	27	73
VIRGINIA			
1 ***Bateman***	35	64	35
2 Pickett	76	23	77
3 Scott	72	28	72
4 Sisisky	60	40	60
5 Goode	28	68	29
6 ***Goodlatte***	29	71	29
7 ***Bliley***	29	71	29
8 Moran	75	25	75
9 Boucher	72	23	76
10 ***Wolf***	28	71	28
11 ***Davis***	39	61	39
WASHINGTON			
1 ***White***	44	55	45
2 ***Metcalf***	24	76	24
3 ***Smith***	25	73	26
4 ***Hastings***	28	69	29
5 ***Nethercutt***	29	71	29
6 Dicks	77	21	78
7 McDermott	80	15	85
8 ***Dunn***	31	69	31
9 Smith	83	17	83
WEST VIRGINIA			
1 Mollohan	55	33	62
2 Wise	80	20	80
3 Rahall	61	39	61
WISCONSIN			
1 ***Neumann***	24	72	25
2 ***Klug***	41	56	42
3 Kind	79	21	79
4 Kleczka	64	35	65
5 Barrett	84	16	84
6 ***Petri***	29	71	29
7 Obey	69	28	71
8 Johnson	81	17	82
9 ***Sensenbrenner***	32	68	32
WYOMING			
AL ***Cubin***	21	59	27

Party Unity Definitions

Party unity votes. Recorded votes that split the parties, with a majority of voting Democrats opposing a majority of voting Republicans. Members who switched parties are accounted for.

Party unity support. Percentage of party unity votes on which members voted "yea" or "nay" *in agreement* with a majority of their party. Failures to vote lowered scores for chambers and parties.

Opposition to party. Percentage of party unity votes on which members voted "yea" or "nay" in disagreement with a majority of their party. Failures to vote lowered scores for chambers and parties.

Average Scores by Chamber

	1997		1996	
	Rep.	**Dem.**	**Rep.**	**Dem.**
Party Unity	88%	82%	87%	80%
Senate	87	85	89	84
House	88	82	87	80

	1997		1996	
	Rep.	**Dem.**	**Rep.**	**Dem.**
Opposition	9%	15%	10%	15%
Senate	12	14	9	14
House	9	15	10	15

Sectional Support, Opposition

SENATE	**Support**	**Opposition**
Northern Republicans	84%	15%
Southern Republicans	93	6
Northern Democrats	87	12
Southern Democrats	76	23

HOUSE	**Support**	**Opposition**
Northern Republicans	86%	11%
Southern Republicans	90	6
Northern Democrats	84	12
Southern Democrats	75	21

1997 Victories, Defeats

	Senate	**House**	**Total**
Republicans won, Democrats lost	104	261	365
Democrats won, Republicans lost	46	58	104

Unanimous Voting by Parties

The number of times each party voted unanimously on 1997 party unity votes. Scores for 1996 in parentheses:

	Senate	**House**	**Total**
Republicans voted unanimously	38 (47)	63 (32)	101 (79)
Democrats voted unanimously	35 (35)	11 (10)	46 (45)

Party Unity Average Scores

Average scores for each party in both chambers of Congress:

Year	**Republicans**	**Democrats**	**Year**	**Republicans**	**Democrats**
1962	68%	69%	1980	70%	68%
1963	72	71	1981	76	69
1964	69	67	1982	71	72
1965	70	69	1983	74	76
1966	67	61	1984	72	74
1967	71	66	1985	75	79
1968	63	57	1986	71	78
1969	62	62	1987	74	81
1970	59	57	1988	73	79
1971	66	62	1989	73	81
1972	64	57	1990	74	81
1973	68	68	1991	78	81
1974	62	63	1992	79	79
1975	70	69	1993	84	85
1976	66	65	1994	83	83
1977	70	67	1995	91	80
1978	67	64	1996	87	80
1979	72	69	1997	88	82

1997 Party Unity Votes

Following are the votes, by roll call number, on which a majority of Democrats voted against a majority of Republicans.

House

(319 of 633 "yea/nay" votes)

	57	91	127	169	230	272	315	360	409	470	498	529	566	618
2	58	98	129	177	233	273	318	362	410	471	499	530	567	620
3	59	99	130	178	234	275	320	363	411	472	500	534	568	621
4	60	100	134	179	235	277	322	367	412	474	501	536	569	622
5	61	101	136	183	236	278	324	368	413	475	502	537	570	628
6	62	102	137	185	238	279	325	369	428	476	503	538	574	630
7	63	103	140	187	239	281	327	370	429	477	504	541	578	632
21	64	104	141	188	240	282	328	373	430	478	506	545	581	633
22	65	106	144	189	241	283	332	377	444	479	511	546	583	634
23	67	108	146	191	242	284	333	378	445	481	512	547	584	636
31	69	109	147	194	243	286	334	379	446	482	513	548	587	638
41	70	111	149	200	244	287	335	385	447	483	514	549	588	639
42	71	113	151	210	245	288	336	386	449	484	515	553	589	
43	74	115	157	217	253	296	341	388	450	485	518	556	590	
44	78	117	158	219	254	303	342	389	451	486	519	558	593	
45	79	118	159	220	255	304	343	391	453	487	520	559	596	
46	82	119	160	221	258	305	346	392	454	488	522	560	599	
47	83	120	161	222	259	306	352	393	455	489	523	561	601	
48	85	121	162	223	260	308	353	398	456	493	524	562	602	
49	86	123	164	224	262	309	357	399	458	494	525	563	604	
51	87	125	167	228	263	310	358	403	459	495	527	564	610	
54	88	126	168	229	266	313	359	407	465	496	528	565	612	

Senate

(150 of 298 "yea/nay" votes)

7	19	37	49	68	81	98	118	129	143	156	183	223	247	270
8	20	38	50	69	83	99	119	130	144	158	190	224	248	272
10	21	39	52	70	85	108	120	131	145	159	196	225	249	273
12	22	40	53	71	87	111	121	132	146	161	198	229	252	274
13	23	41	59	72	88	112	122	133	147	162	200	232	253	275
14	24	42	60	73	89	113	124	134	149	163	202	233	254	277
15	31	45	61	76	91	114	125	137	150	167	204	242	260	278
16	32	46	62	77	93	115	126	139	151	168	212	243	264	282
17	33	47	64	79	94	116	127	140	153	171	215	245	266	288
18	36	48	65	80	97	117	128	142	154	177	217	246	267	291

Proportion of Partisan Roll Calls

How often a majority of Democrats voted against a majority of Republicans:

Year	House	Senate	Year	House	Senate	Year	House	Senate	Year	House	Senate
1954	38%	47%	1965	52%	42%	1976	36%	37%	1987	64%	41%
1955	41	30	1966	41	50	1977	42	42	1988	47	42
1956	44	53	1967	36	35	1978	33	45	1989	55	35
1957	59	36	1968	35	32	1979	47	47	1990	49	54
1958	40	44	1969	31	36	1980	38	46	1991	55	49
1959	55	48	1970	27	35	1981	37	48	1992	64	53
1960	53	37	1971	38	42	1982	36	43	1993	65	67
1961	50	62	1972	27	36	1983	56	44	1994	62	52
1962	46	41	1973	42	40	1984	47	40	1995	73	69
1963	49	47	1974	29	44	1985	61	50	1996	56	62
1964	55	36	1975	48	48	1986	57	52	1997	50	50

Party Unity and Party Opposition: House

1. Party Unity, 1997. Percentage of 319 party unity recorded votes in 1997 on which a representative voted "yea" or "nay" in agreement with a majority of his or her party. (Party unity roll calls are those on which a majority of voting Democrats opposed a majority of voting Republicans.) Failures to vote lowered both party unity and party opposition scores.

2. Party Opposition, 1997. Percentage of 319 party unity recorded votes in 1997 on which a representative voted "yea" or "nay" in disagreement with a majority of his or her party. Failures to vote lowered both party unity and party opposition scores.

3. Party Unity, 1997. Percentage of 319 party unity recorded votes in 1997 on which a representative was present and voted "yea" or "nay" in agreement with a majority of his or her party. In this version of the study, absences were not counted; therefore, failures to vote did not lower unity or opposition scores. Opposition scores, not listed here, are the inverse of the unity score; i.e., the opposition score is equal to 100 percent minus the individual's unity score.

[1] Walter Capps, D-Calif., died Oct. 28. He was eligible to vote on 266 party unity votes.

[2] Newt Gingrich, R-Ga., as Speaker of the House, voted at his discretion on 49 party unity votes in 1997.

[3] Bill Redmond, R-N.M,. was sworn in May 20, replacing Bill Richardson, D-N.M., who resigned Feb. 13. Redmond was eligible for 249 party unity votes in 1997. Richardson was eligible for seven party unity votes in 1997. His support score was 5 percent; opposition score, 7 percent; support score adjusted for absences, 100 percent.

[4] Vito J. Fossella, R-N.Y., was sworn in Nov. 5, replacing Susan Molinari, R-N.Y., who resigned Aug. 1. Fossella was eligible for 28 party unity votes in 1997. Molinari was eligible for 171 party unity votes in 1997. Her support score was 74 percent; opposition score, 9 percent; support score adjusted for absences, 89 percent.

[5] Thomas M. Foglietta, D-Pa., resigned Nov. 11. He was eligible for 621 votes.

[6] Ciro D. Rodriguez, D-Texas, was sworn in April 17, replacing Frank Tejeda, D-Texas, who died on Jan. 30. Rodriguez was eligible for 281 party unity votes in 1997. Tejeda was eligible for six party unity votes in 1997.

KEY

Democrats ***Republicans***
Independent

	1	2	3
ALABAMA			
1 ***Callahan***	90	7	93
2 ***Everett***	95	4	96
3 ***Riley***	87	3	97
4 ***Aderholt***	97	3	97
5 Cramer	58	42	58
6 ***Bachus***	93	6	94
7 Hilliard	83	8	91
ALASKA			
AL ***Young***	71	6	93
ARIZONA			
1 ***Salmon***	93	6	94
2 Pastor	86	13	87
3 ***Stump***	97	3	97
4 ***Shadegg***	94	4	96
5 ***Kolbe***	79	19	81
6 ***Hayworth***	97	3	97
ARKANSAS			
1 Berry	72	28	72
2 Snyder	87	13	87
3 ***Hutchinson***	93	6	94
4 ***Dickey***	91	6	94
CALIFORNIA			
1 ***Riggs***	89	8	91
2 ***Herger***	93	3	97
3 Fazio	89	10	90
4 ***Doolittle***	91	5	94
5 Matsui	89	8	92
6 Woolsey	96	2	98
7 Miller	90	3	97
8 Pelosi	91	4	96
9 Dellums	88	5	95
10 Tauscher	87	13	87
11 ***Pombo***	92	5	95
12 Lantos	87	6	94
13 Stark	82	3	96
14 Eshoo	91	8	92
15 ***Campbell***	75	25	75
16 Lofgren	92	8	92
17 Farr	85	7	93
18 Condit	60	39	60
19 ***Radanovich***	92	5	95
20 Dooley	75	23	77
21 ***Thomas***	88	10	90
22 Capps[1]	91	7	93
23 ***Gallegly***	88	7	93
24 Sherman	78	20	80
25 ***McKeon***	97	3	97
26 Berman	81	9	90
27 ***Rogan***	92	4	95
28 ***Dreier***	93	5	95
29 Waxman	92	3	97
30 Becerra	93	1	99
31 Martinez	80	14	85
32 Dixon	86	11	88
33 Roybal-Allard	98	2	98
34 Torres	87	3	96
35 Waters	92	6	94
36 Harman	79	17	83
37 Millender-McD.	94	5	95
38 ***Horn***	71	29	71
39 ***Royce***	90	8	91
40 ***Lewis***	83	12	87
41 ***Kim***	91	7	93
42 Brown	88	5	94
43 ***Calvert***	93	5	95
44 ***Bono***	91	5	94
45 ***Rohrabacher***	92	8	92
46 Sanchez	78	15	84
47 ***Cox***	87	6	94
48 ***Packard***	92	8	92
49 ***Bilbray***	87	13	87
50 Filner	93	5	95
51 ***Cunningham***	95	4	96
52 ***Hunter***	93	4	96
COLORADO			
1 DeGette	94	2	98
2 Skaggs	91	8	92
3 ***McInnis***	87	6	94
4 ***Schaffer***	93	7	93
5 ***Hefley***	94	5	95
6 ***Schaefer***	96	3	97
CONNECTICUT			
1 Kennelly	91	8	92
2 Gejdenson	93	6	94
3 DeLauro	96	4	96
4 ***Shays***	66	34	66
5 Maloney	84	15	85
6 ***Johnson***	67	32	68
DELAWARE			
AL ***Castle***	72	28	72
FLORIDA			
1 ***Scarborough***	87	8	91
2 Boyd	68	32	68
3 Brown	84	11	88
4 ***Fowler***	91	5	94
5 Thurman	84	16	84
6 ***Stearns***	93	5	95
7 ***Mica***	93	4	96
8 ***McCollum***	91	5	94
9 ***Bilirakis***	92	6	94
10 ***Young***	84	10	89
11 Davis	83	16	84
12 ***Canady***	93	5	95
13 ***Miller***	90	10	90
14 ***Goss***	90	6	94
15 ***Weldon***	87	4	96
16 ***Foley***	88	10	90
17 Meek	82	12	88
18 ***Ros-Lehtinen***	84	11	88
19 Wexler	84	9	90
20 Deutsch	82	11	88
21 ***Diaz-Balart***	82	12	87
22 ***Shaw***	87	13	87
23 Hastings	84	7	92
GEORGIA			
1 ***Kingston***	89	7	93
2 Bishop	75	23	77
3 ***Collins***	90	4	96
4 McKinney	83	9	90
5 Lewis	96	3	97
6 ***Gingrich***[2]	94	4	96
7 ***Barr***	97	2	98
8 ***Chambliss***	93	4	96
9 ***Deal***	96	4	96
10 ***Norwood***	93	4	96
11 ***Linder***	91	6	94
HAWAII			
1 Abercrombie	85	13	87
2 Mink	93	6	94
IDAHO			
1 ***Chenoweth***	90	7	93
2 ***Crapo***	93	6	94
ILLINOIS			
1 Rush	90	5	95
2 Jackson	95	5	95
3 Lipinski	59	34	64
4 Gutierrez	86	8	91
5 Blagojevich	87	10	89
6 ***Hyde***	89	9	91
7 Davis	92	5	95
8 ***Crane***	92	3	96
9 Yates	70	2	97
10 ***Porter***	73	23	76
11 ***Weller***	92	8	92
12 Costello	73	23	76
13 ***Fawell***	77	19	80
14 ***Hastert***	95	4	96

	1	2	3
15 ***Ewing***	91	7	93
16 ***Manzullo***	95	4	96
17 Evans	93	7	93
18 ***LaHood***	91	9	91
19 Poshard	76	24	76
20 ***Shimkus***	94	6	94
INDIANA			
1 Visclosky	80	18	81
2 ***McIntosh***	83	5	95
3 Roemer	68	31	69
4 ***Souder***	90	5	95
5 ***Buyer***	86	6	93
6 ***Burton***	92	5	95
7 ***Pease***	93	7	93
8 ***Hostettler***	96	4	96
9 Hamilton	70	30	70
10 Carson	84	7	92
IOWA			
1 ***Leach***	71	28	72
2 ***Nussle***	92	6	94
3 Boswell	72	28	72
4 ***Ganske***	86	12	88
5 ***Latham***	93	7	93
KANSAS			
1 ***Moran***	95	5	95
2 ***Ryun***	96	2	98
3 ***Snowbarger***	98	1	99
4 ***Tiahrt***	95	3	97
KENTUCKY			
1 ***Whitfield***	92	7	93
2 ***Lewis***	94	3	97
3 ***Northup***	92	8	92
4 ***Bunning***	93	5	95
5 ***Rogers***	91	8	92
6 Baesler	63	37	63
LOUISIANA			
1 ***Livingston***	88	10	90
2 Jefferson	83	10	89
3 ***Tauzin***	91	7	93
4 ***McCrery***	90	6	94
5 ***Cooksey***	90	5	95
6 ***Baker***	90	3	97
7 John	59	40	60
MAINE			
1 Allen	94	6	94
2 Baldacci	88	10	90
MARYLAND			
1 ***Gilchrest***	80	19	81
2 ***Ehrlich***	89	11	89
3 Cardin	85	15	85
4 Wynn	87	12	88
5 Hoyer	84	14	85
6 ***Bartlett***	96	4	96
7 Cummings	93	6	94
8 ***Morella***	57	41	58
MASSACHUSETTS			
1 Olver	96	3	97
2 Neal	89	8	92
3 McGovern	96	4	96
4 Frank	91	5	94
5 Meehan	92	4	95
6 Tierney	94	5	95
7 Markey	94	4	96
8 Kennedy	93	6	94
9 Moakley	87	9	91
10 Delahunt	92	6	94
MICHIGAN			
1 Stupak	82	16	83
2 ***Hoekstra***	90	8	92
3 ***Ehlers***	80	16	83
4 ***Camp***	92	8	92
5 Barcia	60	38	61
6 ***Upton***	83	17	83
7 ***Smith***	88	9	90
8 Stabenow	87	12	88
9 Kildee	77	23	77
10 Bonior	91	8	92
11 ***Knollenberg***	89	10	90
12 Levin	92	8	92
13 Rivers	89	11	89
14 Conyers	90	4	96
15 Kilpatrick	95	4	96
16 Dingell	83	13	86
MINNESOTA			
1 ***Gutknecht***	92	8	92

	1	2	3
2 Minge	77	23	77
3 ***Ramstad***	75	25	75
4 Vento	98	2	98
5 Sabo	92	8	92
6 Luther	83	17	83
7 Peterson	60	39	61
8 Oberstar	77	16	82
MISSISSIPPI			
1 ***Wicker***	94	5	95
2 Thompson	87	11	89
3 ***Pickering***	92	4	96
4 ***Parker***	91	6	94
5 Taylor	45	54	45
MISSOURI			
1 Clay	86	4	95
2 ***Talent***	94	5	95
3 Gephardt	80	8	91
4 Skelton	59	36	62
5 McCarthy	88	10	90
6 Danner	60	38	61
7 ***Blunt***	93	5	95
8 ***Emerson***	95	4	96
9 ***Hulshof***	93	7	93
MONTANA			
AL ***Hill***	94	6	94
NEBRASKA			
1 ***Bereuter***	84	13	87
2 ***Christensen***	93	5	95
3 ***Barrett***	88	8	92
NEVADA			
1 ***Ensign***	86	13	87
2 ***Gibbons***	88	8	92
NEW HAMPSHIRE			
1 ***Sununu***	95	5	95
2 ***Bass***	86	13	87
NEW JERSEY			
1 Andrews	77	8	90
2 ***LoBiondo***	83	17	83
3 ***Saxton***	84	15	85
4 ***Smith***	80	18	82
5 ***Roukema***	67	30	69
6 Pallone	89	8	92
7 ***Franks***	74	25	75
8 Pascrell	79	19	81
9 Rothman	87	12	88
10 Payne	87	3	97
11 ***Frelinghuysen***	78	22	78
12 ***Pappas***	91	9	91
13 Menendez	88	10	90
NEW MEXICO			
1 ***Schiff***	8	2	79
2 ***Skeen***	91	9	91
3 ***Redmond***[3]	94	5	95
NEW YORK			
1 ***Forbes***	63	24	72
2 ***Lazio***	76	20	79
3 ***King***	82	16	83
4 McCarthy	83	15	85
5 Ackerman	86	3	96
6 Flake	69	12	85
7 Manton	74	19	80
8 Nadler	93	3	96
9 Schumer	82	9	90
10 Towns	85	6	93
11 Owens	93	3	96
12 Velazquez	94	2	98
13 ***Fossella***[4]	100	0	100
14 Maloney	93	5	95
15 Rangel	91	4	96
16 Serrano	95	3	97
17 Engel	91	8	92
18 Lowey	92	5	95
19 ***Kelly***	79	20	80
20 ***Gilman***	69	30	70
21 McNulty	84	13	87
22 ***Solomon***	95	2	98
23 ***Boehlert***	69	30	70
24 ***McHugh***	83	13	86
25 ***Walsh***	85	13	87
26 Hinchey	94	3	97
27 ***Paxon***	97	3	97
28 Slaughter	92	4	96
29 LaFalce	82	13	86
30 ***Quinn***	80	17	83
31 ***Houghton***	64	25	72

	1	2	3
NORTH CAROLINA			
1 Clayton	88	6	94
2 Etheridge	78	19	80
3 ***Jones***	93	4	96
4 Price	84	14	86
5 ***Burr***	92	6	94
6 ***Coble***	93	6	94
7 McIntyre	53	46	54
8 Hefner	78	14	85
9 ***Myrick***	94	3	97
10 ***Ballenger***	90	4	95
11 ***Taylor***	85	5	95
12 Watt	94	6	94
NORTH DAKOTA			
AL Pomeroy	74	20	78
OHIO			
1 ***Chabot***	87	13	87
2 ***Portman***	88	9	90
3 Hall	68	27	72
4 ***Oxley***	82	10	89
5 ***Gillmor***	88	9	91
6 Strickland	82	17	83
7 ***Hobson***	90	10	90
8 ***Boehner***	93	4	96
9 Kaptur	73	19	79
10 Kucinich	80	19	81
11 Stokes	86	5	94
12 ***Kasich***	88	8	92
13 Brown	94	4	96
14 Sawyer	94	5	95
15 ***Pryce***	86	9	90
16 ***Regula***	86	14	86
17 Traficant	23	77	23
18 ***Ney***	89	9	91
19 ***LaTourette***	82	15	84
OKLAHOMA			
1 ***Largent***	88	7	93
2 ***Coburn***	85	6	93
3 ***Watkins***	93	3	97
4 ***Watts***	94	4	96
5 ***Istook***	93	3	97
6 ***Lucas***	97	3	97
OREGON			
1 Furse	92	1	99
2 ***Smith***	84	5	94
3 Blumenauer	88	7	93
4 DeFazio	88	10	90
5 Hooley	88	12	88
PENNSYLVANIA			
1 Foglietta[5]	72	5	94
2 Fattah	91	4	96
3 Borski	82	15	84
4 Klink	68	31	69
5 ***Peterson***	95	4	96
6 Holden	61	37	63
7 ***Weldon***	76	16	83
8 ***Greenwood***	76	21	79
9 ***Shuster***	89	7	93
10 ***McDade***	80	14	85
11 Kanjorski	78	22	78
12 Murtha	60	37	62
13 ***Fox***	81	19	81
14 Coyne	97	3	97
15 McHale	80	19	81
16 ***Pitts***	96	4	96
17 ***Gekas***	88	10	90
18 Doyle	67	32	68
19 ***Goodling***	90	8	91
20 Mascara	71	28	71
21 ***English***	85	14	86
RHODE ISLAND			
1 Kennedy	91	6	94
2 Weygand	84	13	86
SOUTH CAROLINA			
1 ***Sanford***	87	11	89
2 ***Spence***	96	3	97
3 ***Graham***	93	5	95
4 ***Inglis***	93	5	95
5 Spratt	81	17	83
6 Clyburn	87	11	89
SOUTH DAKOTA			
AL ***Thune***	95	5	95
TENNESSEE			
1 ***Jenkins***	93	6	94
2 ***Duncan***	89	10	90

	1	2	3
3 ***Wamp***	88	7	93
4 ***Hilleary***	95	4	96
5 Clement	71	25	74
6 Gordon	68	30	69
7 ***Bryant***	94	4	96
8 Tanner	66	33	66
9 Ford	91	7	93
TEXAS			
1 Sandlin	74	26	74
2 Turner	67	32	68
3 ***Johnson***	88	5	95
4 Hall	38	61	39
5 ***Sessions***	95	4	96
6 ***Barton***	86	8	92
7 ***Archer***	93	3	96
8 ***Brady***	96	3	97
9 Lampson	85	14	86
10 Doggett	91	8	92
11 Edwards	76	22	78
12 ***Granger***	91	5	95
13 ***Thornberry***	94	4	96
14 ***Paul***	80	19	81
15 Hinojosa	83	15	84
16 Reyes	77	19	80
17 Stenholm	52	46	53
18 Jackson-Lee	90	8	92
19 ***Combest***	94	4	96
20 Gonzalez	43	3	93
21 ***Smith***	92	6	94
22 ***DeLay***	94	3	96
23 ***Bonilla***	84	6	93
24 Frost	83	15	85
25 Bentsen	84	15	85
26 ***Armey***	94	4	96
27 Ortiz	61	35	64
28 Rodriguez[6]	87	13	87
29 Green	75	23	77
30 Johnson	88	11	89
UTAH			
1 ***Hansen***	91	4	96
2 ***Cook***	92	8	92
3 ***Cannon***	93	6	94
VERMONT			
AL Sanders	92	6	94
VIRGINIA			
1 ***Bateman***	87	12	88
2 Pickett	63	35	64
3 Scott	87	11	89
4 Sisisky	62	38	62
5 Goode	37	61	38
6 ***Goodlatte***	94	6	94
7 ***Bliley***	90	6	94
8 Moran	78	19	80
9 Boucher	76	17	82
10 ***Wolf***	87	11	88
11 ***Davis***	81	18	82
WASHINGTON			
1 ***White***	84	11	89
2 ***Metcalf***	86	11	88
3 ***Smith***	89	8	91
4 ***Hastings***	96	2	98
5 ***Nethercutt***	93	4	96
6 Dicks	78	18	81
7 McDermott	92	2	98
8 ***Dunn***	94	5	95
9 Smith	83	16	84
WEST VIRGINIA			
1 Mollohan	69	28	71
2 Wise	80	16	83
3 Rahall	71	27	72
WISCONSIN			
1 ***Neumann***	83	11	88
2 ***Klug***	78	18	81
3 Kind	89	11	89
4 Kleczka	79	19	81
5 Barrett	91	9	91
6 ***Petri***	83	16	84
7 Obey	88	10	90
8 Johnson	85	14	86
9 ***Sensenbrenner***	85	12	88
WYOMING			
AL ***Cubin***	75	3	97

	1	2	3
ALABAMA			
Sessions	99	1	99
Shelby	93	7	93
ALASKA			
Murkowski	91	7	93
Stevens	78	21	79
ARIZONA			
Kyl	98	1	99
McCain	83	15	84
ARKANSAS			
Hutchinson	92	5	95
Bumpers	92	8	92
CALIFORNIA			
Boxer	95	3	97
Feinstein	85	13	86
COLORADO			
Allard	98	2	98
Campbell	83	17	83
CONNECTICUT			
Dodd	87	13	87
Lieberman	76	23	77
DELAWARE			
Roth	79	20	80
Biden	81	18	82
FLORIDA			
Mack	86	11	88
Graham	71	29	71
GEORGIA			
Coverdell	93	7	93
Cleland	84	16	84
HAWAII			
Akaka	95	3	97
Inouye	85	9	91
IDAHO			
Craig	97	3	97
Kempthorne	96	3	97
ILLINOIS			
Durbin	96	3	97
Moseley-Braun	83	17	83
INDIANA			
Coats	83	12	87
Lugar	83	17	83
IOWA			
Grassley	91	9	91
Harkin	90	8	92
KANSAS			
Brownback	96	4	96
Roberts	87	10	90
KENTUCKY			
McConnell	97	3	97
Ford	79	21	79
LOUISIANA			
Breaux	65	35	65
Landrieu	76	23	77
MAINE			
Collins	61	39	61
Snowe	59	41	59
MARYLAND			
Mikulski	87	8	92
Sarbanes	97	2	98
MASSACHUSETTS			
Kennedy	96	3	97
Kerry	97	3	97
MICHIGAN			
Abraham	93	7	93
Levin	95	5	95
MINNESOTA			
Grams	94	3	97
Wellstone	91	4	96
MISSISSIPPI			
Cochran	81	18	82
Lott	94	6	94
MISSOURI			
Ashcroft	99	1	99
Bond	87	11	89
MONTANA			
Burns	92	6	94
Baucus	72	27	73
NEBRASKA			
Hagel	92	8	92
Kerrey	78	21	79
NEVADA			
Bryan	71	28	72
Reid	83	17	83
NEW HAMPSHIRE			
Gregg	87	13	87
Smith	97	3	97
NEW JERSEY			
Lautenberg	94	6	94
Torricelli	90	10	90
NEW MEXICO			
Domenici	84	15	85
Bingaman	87	11	88
NEW YORK			
D'Amato	67	33	67
Moynihan	77	22	78
NORTH CAROLINA			
Faircloth	95	3	97
Helms	98	1	99
NORTH DAKOTA			
Conrad	79	18	82
Dorgan	84	13	87
OHIO			
DeWine	81	19	81
Glenn	89	10	90
OKLAHOMA			
Inhofe	96	1	99
Nickles	97	3	97
OREGON			
Smith	83	17	83
Wyden	83	17	83
PENNSYLVANIA			
Santorum	90	9	91
Specter	50	49	50
RHODE ISLAND			
Chafee	60	39	61
Reed	98	1	99
SOUTH CAROLINA			
Thurmond	95	5	95
Hollings	72	25	74
SOUTH DAKOTA			
Daschle	91	8	92
Johnson	86	14	86
TENNESSEE			
Frist	89	11	89
Thompson	89	11	89
TEXAS			
Gramm	99	1	99
Hutchison	95	5	95
UTAH			
Bennett	85	13	87
Hatch	86	13	87
VERMONT			
Jeffords	51	46	53
Leahy	89	11	89
VIRGINIA			
Warner	88	11	89
Robb	71	29	71
WASHINGTON			
Gorton	83	17	83
Murray	93	7	93
WEST VIRGINIA			
Byrd	81	19	81
Rockefeller	83	11	88
WISCONSIN			
Feingold	86	14	86
Kohl	74	26	74
WYOMING			
Enzi	97	2	98
Thomas	98	2	98

KEY

Democrats ***Republicans***

Party Unity and Party Opposition: Senate

1. Party Unity, 1997. Percentage of 150 party unity recorded votes in 1997 on which a senator voted "yea" or "nay" in agreement with a majority of his or her party. (Party unity roll calls are those on which a majority of voting Democrats opposed a majority of voting Republicans.) Failures to vote lowered both party unity and party opposition scores.

2. Party Opposition, 1997. Percentage of 150 party unity recorded votes in 1997 on which a senator voted "yea" or "nay" in disagreement with a majority of his or her party. Failures to vote lowered both party unity and party opposition scores.

3. Party Unity, 1997. Percentage of 150 party unity recorded votes in 1997 on which a senator was present and voted "yea" or "nay" in agreement with a majority of his or her party. In this version of the study, absences were not counted; therefore, failures to vote did not lower unity or opposition scores. Opposition scores, not listed here, are the inverse of the unity score; i.e., the opposition score is equal to 100 percent minus the individual's unity score.

Conservative Coalition Definitions

Conservative coalition. As used in this study, "conservative coalition" means a voting alliance of Republicans and Southern Democrats against the Northern Democrats in Congress. This meaning, rather than any philosophic definition of the "conservative coalition" position, is the basis for CQ's selection of coalition votes.

Conservative coalition vote. Any vote in the Senate or the House on which a majority of voting Southern Democrats and a majority of voting Republicans opposed a majority of voting Northern Democrats. Votes on which there was an even division within the ranks of voting Northern Democrats, Southern Democrats or Republicans are not included.

Conservative coalition support score. Percentage of conservative coalition votes on which a member voted "yea" or "nay" *in agreement* with the position of the conservative coalition. Failures to vote, even if a member announced a stand, lower the score.

Conservative coalition opposition score. Percentage of conservative coalition votes on which a member voted "yea" or "nay" *in disagreement* with the position of the conservative coalition. Failures to vote, even if a member announced a stand, lower the score.

Average Scores

Scores for 1996 are in parentheses:

Coalition Support

	Southern Democrats	Republicans	Northern Democrats
Senate	73% (66)	87% (88)	32% (30)
House	63 (63)	86 (85)	33 (31)

Coalition Opposition

	Southern Democrats	Republicans	Northern Democrats
Senate	27% (30)	12% (10)	67% (69)
House	34 (30)	10 (12)	64 (65)

Regional Averages

Scores for 1996 are in parentheses:

Support

	East	West	South	Midwest
Republicans				
Senate	70% (79)	91% (88)	95% (93)	94% (89)
House	82 (74)	86 (89)	89 (91)	86 (81)
Democrats				
Senate	27% (27)	37% (37)	73% (66)	34% (27)
House	31 (29)	27 (28)	63 (63)	40 (35)

Opposition

	East	West	South	Midwest
Republicans				
Senate	30% (19)	9% (9)	5% (5)	15% (9)
House	16 (21)	9 (9)	7 (7)	12 (17)
Democrats				
Senate	72% (71)	65% (62)	27% (30)	62% (73)
House	66 (66)	69 (69)	34 (30)	57 (62)

Conservative Coalition History

Following is the percentage of the recorded votes for both chambers of Congress on which the coalition appeared and its percentage of victories:

Year	Appearances	Victories	Year	Appearances	Victories
1970	22%	66%	1984	16%	83%
1971	30	83	1985	14	89
1972	27	69	1986	16	87
1973	23	61	1987	8	93
1974	24	59	1988	9	89
1975	28	50	1989	11	87
1976	24	58	1990	11	82
1977	26	68	1991	11	91
1978	21	52	1992	12	87
1979	20	70	1993	9	94
1980	18	72	1994	8	82
1981	21	92	1995	11	98
1982	18	85	1996	12	99
1983	15	77	1997	9	98

1997 Conservative Coalition Votes

The following is a list of Senate votes, by roll call number, cast in 1997 on which a majority of Southern Democrats and a majority of Republicans voted against a majority of all other Democrats. *(Definition, p. C-25)*

55 House Victories

Vote No.	Description
31	Religious expression
35	Procedural motion
92	Farm programs
112	Juvenile crime
114	Juvenile crime
118	Juvenile crime
127*	Housing
146	Budget
151	Fishing programs
183	State Department
202	Flag desecration
221	Defense spending
223	Defense spending
229	Defense spending
236	Defense spending
253	Intelligence spending
260	Interior appropriations
271	Interior appropriations
304	Procedural motion
308	Agriculture appropriations
309	Agriculture appropriations
310	Agriculture appropriations
314	Agriculture appropriations
315	Agriculture appropriations
320	Procedural motion
322	Agriculture appropriations
327	Energy and water appropriations
328	Energy and water appropriations
336	Defense spending
337	Defense spending
338	Defense spending
359	Foreign operations appropriations
398	Labor-HHS appropriations
444	CJS appropriations
448	Procedural motion
453	Procedural motion
454	Procedural motion
481	Procedural motion
500	Abortion
518	Property rights
519*	Property rights
527	Interior appropriations
531	Interior appropriations
534	Defense spending
536	Nuclear waste
538	Education spending
546	Grazing fees
548	Grazing fees
550	Nuclear waste
553	Nuclear waste
556	Nuclear waste
557	Nuclear waste
586	Procedural motion
601	Taiwan
618	Agriculture programs

0 House Defeats

23 Senate Victories

Vote No.	Description
21	Balanced-budget constitutional amendment
69	Abortion
76	Budget
91	Budget
102	State Department
104	State Department
113*	Budget
114	Budget
115	Budget
123	Budget
130	Budget
131	Taxes
132	Taxes
137	Taxes
149	Taxes
158	Taxes
162	Defense spending
165	Defense spending
196	Agriculture appropriations
198	Agriculture appropriations
199	Agriculture appropriations
210	Taxes
229	Labor-HHS appropriations

2 Senate Defeats

Vote No.	Description
24*	Balanced-budget constitutional amendment
60	Supplemental appropriations

** Congressional Quarterly Key Vote, p. C-33*

House Victory Rate

Victories	55
Defeats	0
Total	55
Victory Rate	100%

Senate Victory Rate

Victories	23
Defeats	2
Total	25
Victory Rate	92%

KEY

Democrats ***Republicans***

	1	2	3
ALABAMA			
Sessions	100	0	100
Shelby	96	4	96
ALASKA			
Murkowski	96	4	96
Stevens	96	4	96
ARIZONA			
Kyl	88	12	88
McCain	76	24	76
ARKANSAS			
Hutchinson	92	8	92
Bumpers	28	72	28
CALIFORNIA			
Boxer	12	88	12
Feinstein	56	44	56
COLORADO			
Allard	92	8	92
Campbell	96	4	96
CONNECTICUT			
Dodd	40	60	40
Lieberman	52	48	52
DELAWARE			
Roth	88	12	88
Biden	48	48	50
FLORIDA			
Mack	88	12	88
Graham	80	20	80
GEORGIA			
Coverdell	92	8	92
Cleland	72	28	72
HAWAII			
Akaka	20	80	20
Inouye	44	52	46
IDAHO			
Craig	100	0	100
Kempthorne	96	0	100
ILLINOIS			
Durbin	12	88	12
Moseley-Braun	44	56	44
INDIANA			
Coats	76	20	79
Lugar	72	28	72
IOWA			
Grassley	84	16	84
Harkin	20	76	21
KANSAS			
Brownback	84	16	84
Roberts	80	4	95
KENTUCKY			
McConnell	100	0	100
Ford	72	28	72
LOUISIANA			
Breaux	100	0	100
Landrieu	88	12	88
MAINE			
Collins	68	32	68
Snowe	68	32	68
MARYLAND			
Mikulski	16	76	17
Sarbanes	12	88	12
MASSACHUSETTS			
Kennedy	0	100	0
Kerry	16	84	16
MICHIGAN			
Abraham	80	20	80
Levin	20	80	20
MINNESOTA			
Grams	88	12	88
Wellstone	0	100	0
MISSISSIPPI			
Cochran	100	0	100
Lott	100	0	100
MISSOURI			
Ashcroft	96	4	96
Bond	88	12	88
MONTANA			
Burns	96	4	96
Baucus	72	28	72
NEBRASKA			
Hagel	96	4	96
Kerrey	52	48	52
NEVADA			
Bryan	68	32	68
Reid	32	68	32
NEW HAMPSHIRE			
Gregg	72	28	72
Smith	84	16	84
NEW JERSEY			
Lautenberg	16	84	16
Torricelli	32	68	32
NEW MEXICO			
Domenici	96	4	96
Bingaman	28	68	29
NEW YORK			
D'Amato	64	36	64
Moynihan	64	36	64
NORTH CAROLINA			
Faircloth	88	12	88
Helms	96	4	96
NORTH DAKOTA			
Conrad	68	32	68
Dorgan	44	56	44
OHIO			
DeWine	76	24	76
Glenn	36	64	36
OKLAHOMA			
Inhofe	100	0	100
Nickles	96	4	96
OREGON			
Smith	84	16	84
Wyden	28	72	28
PENNSYLVANIA			
Santorum	84	16	84
Specter	52	48	52
RHODE ISLAND			
Chafee	68	32	68
Reed	4	96	4
SOUTH CAROLINA			
Thurmond	96	4	96
Hollings	68	28	71
SOUTH DAKOTA			
Daschle	36	56	39
Johnson	24	72	25
TENNESSEE			
Frist	100	0	100
Thompson	96	4	96
TEXAS			
Gramm	92	8	92
Hutchison	88	12	88
UTAH			
Bennett	88	12	88
Hatch	88	12	88
VERMONT			
Jeffords	56	44	56
Leahy	20	80	20
VIRGINIA			
Warner	96	4	96
Robb	72	28	72
WASHINGTON			
Gorton	84	16	84
Murray	12	88	12
WEST VIRGINIA			
Byrd	36	64	36
Rockefeller	28	72	28
WISCONSIN			
Feingold	28	72	28
Kohl	56	44	56
WYOMING			
Enzi	88	8	92
Thomas	88	12	88

Conservative Coalition Support and Opposition: Senate

1. Conservative Coalition Support, 1997. Percentage of 25 recorded votes in 1997 on which the conservative coalition appeared and on which a senator voted "yea" or "nay" in agreement with the position of the conservative coalition. Failures to vote lowered both support and opposition scores.

2. Conservative Coalition Opposition, 1997. Percentage of 25 recorded votes in 1997 on which the conservative coalition appeared and on which a senator voted "yea" or "nay" in disagreement with the position of the conservative coalition. Failures to vote lowered both support and opposition scores.

3. Conservative Coalition Support, 1997. Percentage of 25 recorded votes in 1997 on which the conservative coalition appeared and on which a senator was present and voted "yea" or "nay" in agreement with the position of the conservative coalition. In this version of the study, absences were not counted; therefore, failures to vote did not lower support or opposition scores. Opposition scores, not listed here, are the inverse of the support score; i.e., the opposition score is equal to 100 percent minus the individual's support score.

Conservative Coalition Support and Opposition: House

1. Conservative Coalition Support, 1997. Percentage of 55 recorded votes in 1997 on which the conservative coalition appeared and on which a representative voted "yea" or "nay" in agreement with the position of the conservative coalition. Failures to vote lowered both support and opposition scores.

2. Conservative Coalition Opposition, 1997. Percentage of 55 recorded votes in 1997 on which the conservative coalition appeared and on which a representative voted "yea" or "nay" in disagreement with the position of the conservative coalition. Failures to vote lowered both support and opposition scores.

3. Conservative Coalition Support, 1997. Percentage of 55 recorded votes in 1997 on which the conservative coalition appeared and on which a representative was present and voted "yea" or "nay" in agreement with the position of the conservative coalition. In this version of the study, absences were not counted; therefore, failures to vote did not lower support or opposition scores. Opposition scores, not listed here, are the inverse of the support score; i.e., the opposition score is equal to 100 percent minus the individual's support score.

[1]Walter Capps, D-Calif., died Oct. 28. He was eligible to vote on 43 conservative coalition votes.

[2]Newt Gingrich, R-Ga., as Speaker of the House, voted at his discretion on seven conservative coalition votes in 1997.

[3]Bill Redmond, R-N.M., was sworn in May 20, replacing Bill Richardson, D-N.M., who resigned Feb. 13. Redmond was eligible for 48 conservative coalition votes in 1997. Richardson was eligible for no conservative coalition votes in 1997.

[4]Vito J. Fossella, R-N.Y., was sworn in Nov. 5, replacing Susan Molinari, R-N.Y., who resigned Aug. 1. Fossella was eligible for three conservative coalition votes in 1997. Molinari was eligible for 31 conservative coalition votes in 1997. Her support score was 65 percent; opposition score, 3 percent; support score adjusted for absences, 95 percent.

[5]Ciro D. Rodriguez, D-Texas, was sworn in April 17, replacing Frank Tejeda, D-Texas, who died on Jan. 30. Rodriguez was eligible for 53 conservative coalition votes in 1997. Tejeda was eligible for no conservative coalition votes in 1997.

KEY

Democrats ***Republicans***
Independent

	1	2	3
ALABAMA			
1 ***Callahan***	91	5	94
2 ***Everett***	93	5	94
3 ***Riley***	89	4	96
4 ***Aderholt***	96	4	96
5 Cramer	93	7	93
6 ***Bachus***	91	9	91
7 Hilliard	44	55	44
ALASKA			
AL ***Young***	64	4	95
ARIZONA			
1 ***Salmon***	82	16	83
2 Pastor	49	51	49
3 ***Stump***	95	5	95
4 ***Shadegg***	91	9	91
5 ***Kolbe***	89	9	91
6 ***Hayworth***	91	9	91
ARKANSAS			
1 Berry	71	29	71
2 Snyder	51	49	51
3 ***Hutchinson***	89	11	89
4 ***Dickey***	87	9	91
CALIFORNIA			
1 ***Riggs***	85	15	85
2 ***Herger***	87	9	91
3 Fazio	45	51	47
4 ***Doolittle***	84	13	87
5 Matsui	36	60	38
6 Woolsey	13	85	13
7 Miller	5	84	6
8 Pelosi	7	84	8
9 Dellums	5	93	6
10 Tauscher	42	58	42
11 ***Pombo***	85	11	89
12 Lantos	20	73	22
13 Stark	4	71	5
14 Eshoo	13	85	13
15 ***Campbell***	62	38	62
16 Lofgren	20	80	20
17 Farr	29	67	30
18 Condit	69	31	69
19 ***Radanovich***	91	5	94
20 Dooley	73	25	74
21 ***Thomas***	96	2	98
22 Capps[1]	33	63	34
23 ***Gallegly***	87	9	91
24 Sherman	47	53	47
25 ***McKeon***	89	9	91
26 Berman	25	71	26
27 ***Rogan***	84	7	92
28 ***Dreier***	95	2	98
29 Waxman	7	91	7
30 Becerra	5	93	6
31 Martinez	47	44	52
32 Dixon	36	62	37
33 Roybal-Allard	13	85	13
34 Torres	16	78	17
35 Waters	18	78	19
36 Harman	51	47	52
37 Millender-McD.	22	78	22
38 ***Horn***	73	27	73
39 ***Royce***	76	24	76
40 ***Lewis***	96	4	96
41 ***Kim***	95	5	95
42 Brown	24	64	27
43 ***Calvert***	96	2	98
44 ***Bono***	89	7	92
45 ***Rohrabacher***	80	18	81
46 Sanchez	49	47	51
47 ***Cox***	84	11	88
48 ***Packard***	100	0	100
49 ***Bilbray***	87	13	87
50 Filner	11	84	12
51 ***Cunningham***	85	15	85
52 ***Hunter***	95	0	100
COLORADO			
1 DeGette	7	89	8
2 Skaggs	33	67	33
3 ***McInnis***	89	4	96
4 ***Schaffer***	91	7	93
5 ***Hefley***	93	7	93
6 ***Schaefer***	96	4	96
CONNECTICUT			
1 Kennelly	31	65	32
2 Gejdenson	31	67	31
3 DeLauro	22	76	22
4 ***Shays***	51	47	52
5 Maloney	53	47	53
6 ***Johnson***	78	22	78
DELAWARE			
AL ***Castle***	76	24	76
FLORIDA			
1 ***Scarborough***	80	13	86
2 Boyd	87	13	87
3 Brown	44	53	45
4 ***Fowler***	93	2	98
5 Thurman	53	47	53
6 ***Stearns***	93	7	93
7 ***Mica***	98	0	100
8 ***McCollum***	93	5	94
9 ***Bilirakis***	93	5	94
10 ***Young***	91	7	93
11 Davis	56	42	57
12 ***Canady***	95	4	96
13 ***Miller***	84	16	84
14 ***Goss***	85	11	89
15 ***Weldon***	75	7	91
16 ***Foley***	87	13	87
17 Meek	53	44	55
18 ***Ros-Lehtinen***	89	9	91
19 Wexler	44	49	47
20 Deutsch	40	55	42
21 ***Diaz-Balart***	87	4	96
22 ***Shaw***	93	7	93
23 Hastings	29	64	31
GEORGIA			
1 ***Kingston***	91	9	91
2 Bishop	73	27	73
3 ***Collins***	85	7	92
4 McKinney	16	73	18
5 Lewis	16	80	17
6 ***Gingrich***[2]	100	0	100
7 ***Barr***	93	7	93
8 ***Chambliss***	93	4	96
9 ***Deal***	93	7	93
10 ***Norwood***	91	7	93
11 ***Linder***	91	0	100
HAWAII			
1 Abercrombie	33	67	33
2 Mink	20	78	20
IDAHO			
1 ***Chenoweth***	82	9	90
2 ***Crapo***	96	4	96
ILLINOIS			
1 Rush	31	67	31
2 Jackson	15	85	15
3 Lipinski	65	29	69
4 Gutierrez	20	78	20
5 Blagojevich	42	56	43
6 ***Hyde***	95	0	100
7 Davis	18	82	18
8 ***Crane***	87	7	92
9 Yates	9	64	13
10 ***Porter***	75	22	77
11 ***Weller***	95	5	95
12 Costello	55	40	58
13 ***Fawell***	84	15	85
14 ***Hastert***	98	0	100

	1	2	3
15 *Ewing*	87	5	94
16 *Manzullo*	85	13	87
17 Evans	20	78	20
18 *LaHood*	98	0	100
19 Poshard	60	40	60
20 *Shimkus*	98	2	98
INDIANA			
1 Visclosky	56	44	56
2 *McIntosh*	71	7	91
3 Roemer	55	44	56
4 *Souder*	82	16	83
5 *Buyer*	89	0	100
6 *Burton*	93	7	93
7 *Pease*	87	13	87
8 *Hostettler*	89	11	89
9 Hamilton	76	22	78
10 Carson	24	69	25
IOWA			
1 *Leach*	69	24	75
2 *Nussle*	89	11	89
3 Boswell	75	25	75
4 *Ganske*	73	25	74
5 *Latham*	93	7	93
KANSAS			
1 *Moran*	91	9	91
2 *Ryun*	91	5	94
3 *Snowbarger*	89	7	92
4 *Tiahrt*	93	5	94
KENTUCKY			
1 *Whitfield*	93	5	94
2 *Lewis*	93	5	94
3 *Northup*	95	4	96
4 *Bunning*	96	4	96
5 *Rogers*	96	4	96
6 Baesler	82	16	83
LOUISIANA			
1 *Livingston*	91	5	94
2 Jefferson	45	53	46
3 *Tauzin*	95	0	100
4 *McCrery*	93	0	100
5 *Cooksey*	87	5	94
6 *Baker*	98	0	100
7 John	95	5	95
MAINE			
1 Allen	36	64	36
2 Baldacci	36	64	36
MARYLAND			
1 *Gilchrest*	87	11	89
2 *Ehrlich*	91	9	91
3 Cardin	45	55	45
4 Wynn	49	49	50
5 Hoyer	60	36	62
6 *Bartlett*	95	5	95
7 Cummings	22	73	23
8 *Morella*	53	45	54
MASSACHUSETTS			
1 Olver	13	87	13
2 Neal	18	78	19
3 McGovern	9	89	9
4 Frank	13	85	13
5 Meehan	16	84	16
6 Tierney	9	91	9
7 Markey	5	95	5
8 Kennedy	18	78	19
9 Moakley	16	80	17
10 Delahunt	9	91	9
MICHIGAN			
1 Stupak	35	64	35
2 *Hoekstra*	71	25	74
3 *Ehlers*	71	25	74
4 *Camp*	85	13	87
5 Barcia	85	11	89
6 *Upton*	78	22	78
7 *Smith*	82	15	85
8 Stabenow	45	53	46
9 Kildee	64	36	64
10 Bonior	20	76	21
11 *Knollenberg*	95	4	96
12 Levin	31	65	32
13 Rivers	25	75	25
14 Conyers	7	85	8
15 Kilpatrick	24	75	24
16 Dingell	42	49	46
MINNESOTA			
1 *Gutknecht*	91	9	91

	1	2	3
2 Minge	55	45	55
3 *Ramstad*	65	35	65
4 Vento	7	93	7
5 Sabo	24	76	24
6 Luther	35	65	35
7 Peterson	71	29	71
8 Oberstar	22	75	23
MISSISSIPPI			
1 *Wicker*	96	0	100
2 Thompson	56	44	56
3 *Pickering*	89	5	94
4 *Parker*	87	5	94
5 Taylor	75	25	75
MISSOURI			
1 Clay	16	75	18
2 *Talent*	82	16	83
3 Gephardt	24	65	27
4 Skelton	80	16	83
5 McCarthy	22	76	22
6 Danner	71	27	72
7 *Blunt*	93	4	96
8 *Emerson*	98	2	98
9 *Hulshof*	89	11	89
MONTANA			
AL *Hill*	91	7	93
NEBRASKA			
1 *Bereuter*	84	13	87
2 *Christensen*	84	15	85
3 *Barrett*	95	2	98
NEVADA			
1 *Ensign*	67	31	69
2 *Gibbons*	71	20	78
NEW HAMPSHIRE			
1 *Sununu*	85	15	85
2 *Bass*	82	18	82
NEW JERSEY			
1 Andrews	31	62	33
2 *LoBiondo*	73	27	73
3 *Saxton*	93	7	93
4 *Smith*	73	25	74
5 *Roukema*	75	25	75
6 Pallone	29	69	30
7 *Franks*	69	31	69
8 Pascrell	55	45	55
9 Rothman	49	51	49
10 Payne	9	80	10
11 *Frelinghuysen*	82	18	82
12 *Pappas*	85	15	85
13 Menendez	45	55	45
NEW MEXICO			
1 *Schiff*	0	0	0
2 *Skeen*	98	2	98
3 *Redmond*[6]	100	0	100
NEW YORK			
1 *Forbes*	69	20	78
2 *Lazio*	82	13	87
3 *King*	96	4	96
4 McCarthy	38	58	40
5 Ackerman	22	73	23
6 Flake	44	40	52
7 Manton	62	36	63
8 Nadler	11	84	12
9 Schumer	27	67	29
10 Towns	29	69	30
11 Owens	9	91	9
12 Velázquez	5	95	5
13 *Fossella*[4]	100	0	100
14 Maloney	24	73	25
15 Rangel	11	80	12
16 Serrano	11	87	11
17 Engel	24	73	25
18 Lowey	16	82	17
19 *Kelly*	71	24	75
20 *Gilman*	80	20	80
21 McNulty	22	76	22
22 *Solomon*	100	0	100
23 *Boehlert*	75	25	75
24 *McHugh*	93	5	94
25 *Walsh*	89	9	91
26 Hinchey	7	91	7
27 *Paxon*	95	4	96
28 Slaughter	15	84	15
29 LaFalce	22	73	23
30 *Quinn*	87	11	89
31 *Houghton*	80	9	90

	1	2	3
NORTH CAROLINA			
1 Clayton	33	64	34
2 Etheridge	82	18	82
3 *Jones*	95	5	95
4 Price	65	35	65
5 *Burr*	91	5	94
6 *Coble*	85	15	85
7 McIntyre	95	5	95
8 Hefner	60	31	66
9 *Myrick*	95	4	96
10 *Ballenger*	84	5	94
11 *Taylor*	85	2	98
12 Watt	29	71	29
NORTH DAKOTA			
AL Pomeroy	69	25	73
OHIO			
1 *Chabot*	73	25	74
2 *Portman*	78	20	80
3 Hall	60	40	60
4 *Oxley*	96	0	100
5 *Gillmor*	87	5	94
6 Strickland	44	49	47
7 *Hobson*	91	9	91
8 *Boehner*	95	2	98
9 Kaptur	42	51	45
10 Kucinich	31	69	31
11 Stokes	29	60	33
12 *Kasich*	76	22	78
13 Brown	15	84	15
14 Sawyer	33	67	33
15 *Pryce*	93	5	94
16 *Regula*	95	5	95
17 Traficant	87	13	87
18 *Ney*	91	5	94
19 *LaTourette*	91	7	93
OKLAHOMA			
1 *Largent*	84	9	90
2 *Coburn*	76	9	89
3 *Watkins*	95	2	98
4 *Watts*	89	9	91
5 *Istook*	95	4	96
6 *Lucas*	93	7	93
OREGON			
1 Furse	7	85	8
2 *Smith*	84	4	96
3 Blumenauer	18	76	19
4 DeFazio	15	85	15
5 Hooley	36	64	36
PENNSYLVANIA			
1 Foglietta	11	69	14
2 Fattah	13	85	13
3 Borski	40	58	41
4 Klink	69	31	69
5 *Peterson*	96	2	98
6 Holden	80	20	80
7 *Weldon*	75	13	85
8 *Greenwood*	71	22	76
9 *Shuster*	87	9	91
10 *McDade*	91	4	96
11 Kanjorski	44	56	44
12 Murtha	78	22	78
13 *Fox*	78	22	78
14 Coyne	13	87	13
15 McHale	55	45	55
16 *Pitts*	95	5	95
17 *Gekas*	95	4	96
18 Doyle	60	36	62
19 *Goodling*	85	15	85
20 Mascara	65	35	65
21 *English*	80	18	81
RHODE ISLAND			
1 Kennedy	22	76	22
2 Weygand	27	73	27
SOUTH CAROLINA			
1 *Sanford*	71	29	71
2 *Spence*	96	2	98
3 *Graham*	96	4	96
4 *Inglis*	91	9	91
5 Spratt	65	35	65
6 Clyburn	58	40	59
SOUTH DAKOTA			
AL *Thune*	98	2	98
TENNESSEE			
1 *Jenkins*	98	2	98
2 *Duncan*	73	25	74

	1	2	3
3 *Wamp*	87	9	91
4 *Hilleary*	89	9	91
5 Clement	75	25	75
6 Gordon	82	16	83
7 *Bryant*	91	9	91
8 Tanner	82	18	82
9 Ford	44	55	44
TEXAS			
1 Sandlin	85	11	89
2 Turner	85	15	85
3 *Johnson*	80	7	92
4 Hall	93	7	93
5 *Sessions*	93	7	93
6 *Barton*	80	9	90
7 *Archer*	85	5	94
8 *Brady*	93	7	93
9 Lampson	56	44	56
10 Doggett	15	85	15
11 Edwards	73	25	74
12 *Granger*	95	2	98
13 *Thornberry*	93	4	96
14 *Paul*	49	51	49
15 Hinojosa	78	20	80
16 Reyes	76	22	78
17 Stenholm	85	15	85
18 Jackson-Lee	35	60	37
19 *Combest*	95	5	95
20 Gonzalez	16	24	41
21 *Smith*	95	5	95
22 *DeLay*	91	7	93
23 *Bonilla*	85	7	92
24 Frost	71	27	72
25 Bentsen	62	38	62
26 *Armey*	93	4	96
27 Ortiz	89	7	92
28 Rodriguez[5]	58	42	58
29 Green	73	25	74
30 Johnson	53	47	53
UTAH			
1 *Hansen*	84	9	90
2 *Cook*	89	11	89
3 *Cannon*	89	9	91
VERMONT			
AL Sanders	13	84	13
VIRGINIA			
1 *Bateman*	95	2	98
2 Pickett	93	7	93
3 Scott	60	40	60
4 Sisisky	96	4	96
5 Goode	93	7	93
6 *Goodlatte*	93	7	93
7 *Bliley*	89	2	98
8 Moran	53	44	55
9 Boucher	58	36	62
10 *Wolf*	89	7	92
11 *Davis*	87	9	91
WASHINGTON			
1 *White*	93	7	93
2 *Metcalf*	89	11	89
3 *Smith*	91	9	91
4 *Hastings*	96	0	100
5 *Nethercutt*	95	2	98
6 Dicks	65	35	65
7 McDermott	5	93	6
8 *Dunn*	98	2	98
9 Smith	44	53	45
WEST VIRGINIA			
1 Mollohan	69	24	75
2 Wise	56	38	60
3 Rahall	53	40	57
WISCONSIN			
1 *Neumann*	69	25	73
2 *Klug*	65	31	68
3 Kind	33	67	33
4 Kleczka	38	58	40
5 Barrett	11	89	11
6 *Petri*	75	25	75
7 Obey	16	84	16
8 Johnson	49	51	49
9 *Sensenbrenner*	71	29	71
WYOMING			
AL *Cubin*	65	2	97

Voting Participation: House

1. Voting Participation, 1997. Percentage of 633 recorded votes in 1997 on which a representative voted "yea" or "nay."

2. Voting Participation, 1997. Percentage of 604 recorded votes in 1997 on which a representative voted "yea" or "nay." In this version of the study, 29 votes on approval of the House Journal were not included.

Absences due to illness. *Congressional Quarterly no longer designates members who missed votes due to illness. In the past, notations to that effect were based on official statements published in the Congressional Record, but these were found to be inconsistently used.*

Rounding. *Scores are rounded to the nearest percentage, except that no scores are rounded up to 100 percent. Members with a 100 percent score participated in all recorded votes for which they were eligible.*

Conflicts of interest. *Norman Sisisky, D-Va., declared that he voted present to avoid the appearance of a possible conflict of interest on vote 312, an amendment to cut sugar programs.*

[1] *Walter Capps, D-Calif., died Oct. 28. He was eligible for 525 votes.*

[2] *Newt Gingrich, R-Ga., as Speaker of the House, voted at his discretion on 61 votes in 1997.*

[3] *Bill Redmond, R-N.M., was sworn in May 20, replacing Bill Richardson, D-N.M., who resigned Feb. 13. Redmond was eligible for 496 votes in 1997. Richardson was eligible for 20 votes in 1997. His voting participation score was 35 percent; 32 percent not including Journal votes.*

[4] *Vito J. Fossella, R-N.Y., was sworn in Nov. 5, replacing Susan Molinari, R-N.Y., who resigned Aug. 1. Fossella was eligible for 64 votes in 1997. Molinari was eligible for 347 votes in 1997. Her voting participation score was 79 percent; 78 percent not including Journal votes.*

[5] *Thomas M. Foglietta, D-Pa., resigned Nov. 11. He was eligible for 621 votes.*

[6] *Ciro D. Rodriguez, D-Texas, was sworn in April 17, replacing Frank Tejeda, D-Texas, who died on Jan. 30. Rodriguez was eligible for 556 votes in 1997. Tejeda was eligible for eight votes in 1997. His voting participation score was 0 percent; 0 percent not including Journal votes.*

KEY

Democrats ***Republicans***
Independent

	1	2
ALABAMA		
1 ***Callahan***	97	97
2 ***Everett***	99	99
3 ***Riley***	88	88
4 ***Aderholt***	99	99
5 Cramer	99	99
6 ***Bachus***	99	99
7 Hilliard	93	93
ALASKA		
AL ***Young***	73	74
ARIZONA		
1 ***Salmon***	98	98
2 Pastor	99	99
3 ***Stump***	99	99
4 ***Shadegg***	98	98
5 ***Kolbe***	98	98
6 ***Hayworth***	99	99
ARKANSAS		
1 Berry	99	99
2 Snyder	99	99
3 ***Hutchinson***	98	98
4 ***Dickey***	98	98
CALIFORNIA		
1 ***Riggs***	95	96
2 ***Herger***	95	96
3 Fazio	98	99
4 ***Doolittle***	96	97
5 Matsui	97	97
6 Woolsey	96	97
7 Miller	92	92
8 Pelosi	93	93
9 Dellums	91	92
10 Tauscher	99	99
11 ***Pombo***	95	96
12 Lantos	92	92
13 Stark	86	86
14 Eshoo	97	97
15 ***Campbell***	99	99
16 Lofgren	99	99
17 Farr	91	91
18 Condit	99	99
19 ***Radanovich***	96	96
20 Dooley	98	98
21 ***Thomas***	98	98
22 ***Capps***[1]	98	98
23 ***Gallegly***	96	96
24 Sherman	98	98
25 ***McKeon***	99	99
26 Berman	91	91
27 ***Rogan***	96	96
28 ***Dreier***	98	98
29 Waxman	94	95
30 Becerra	93	94
31 Martinez	94	95
32 Dixon	95	97
33 Roybal-Allard	99	99
34 Torres	91	92
35 Waters	96	97
36 Harman	96	96
37 Millender-McD.	98	98
38 ***Horn***	99	99
39 ***Royce***	98	99
40 ***Lewis***	96	96
41 ***Kim***	99	99
42 Brown	93	94
43 ***Calvert***	98	99
44 ***Bono***	94	95
45 ***Rohrabacher***	99	99
46 Sanchez	95	95
47 ***Cox***	91	92
48 ***Packard***	99	99
49 ***Bilbray***	97	97
50 Filner	97	97
51 ***Cunningham***	99	99
52 ***Hunter***	94	94
COLORADO		
1 DeGette	96	96
2 Skaggs	98	99
3 ***McInnis***	94	94
4 ***Schaffer***	99	99
5 ***Hefley***	99	99
6 ***Schaefer***	99	99
CONNECTICUT		
1 Kennelly	99	99
2 Gejdenson	98	98
3 DeLauro	99	99
4 ***Shays***	99	99
5 Maloney	99	99
6 ***Johnson***	99	99
DELAWARE		
AL ***Castle***	99	99
FLORIDA		
1 ***Scarborough***	93	94
2 Boyd	99	99
3 Brown	94	95
4 ***Fowler***	97	97
5 Thurman	99	99
6 ***Stearns***	99	99
7 ***Mica***	96	96
8 ***McCollum***	97	96
9 ***Bilirakis***	99	99
10 ***Young***	94	95
11 Davis	98	99
12 ***Canady***	99	99
13 ***Miller***	99	99
14 ***Goss***	97	97
15 ***Weldon***	92	92
16 ***Foley***	98	98
17 Meek	94	94
18 ***Ros-Lehtinen***	95	95
19 Wexler	94	95
20 Deutsch	95	95
21 ***Diaz-Balart***	95	95
22 ***Shaw***	99	99
23 Hastings	90	90
GEORGIA		
1 ***Kingston***	98	98
2 Bishop	99	99
3 ***Collins***	95	96
4 McKinney	92	92
5 Lewis	98	98
6 ***Gingrich***[2]		
7 ***Barr***	98	98
8 ***Chambliss***	97	98
9 ***Deal***	99	99
10 ***Norwood***	97	97
11 ***Linder***	97	97
HAWAII		
1 Abercrombie	98	98
2 Mink	99	99
IDAHO		
1 ***Chenoweth***	96	96
2 ***Crapo***	98	99
ILLINOIS		
1 Rush	94	94
2 Jackson	100	100
3 Lipinski	92	93
4 Gutierrez	95	95
5 Blagojevich	98	98
6 ***Hyde***	97	98
7 Davis	98	98
8 ***Crane***	95	96
9 Yates	73	72
10 ***Porter***	96	97
11 ***Weller***	99	99
12 Costello	97	97
13 ***Fawell***	97	97
14 ***Hastert***	98	99

	1	2
15 ***Ewing***	98	98
16 ***Manzullo***	99	99
17 Evans	99	99
18 ***LaHood***	99	99
19 Poshard	99	99
20 ***Shimkus***	100	100
INDIANA		
1 Visclosky	98	98
2 ***McIntosh***	89	89
3 Roemer	98	99
4 ***Souder***	95	96
5 ***Buyer***	94	94
6 ***Burton***	97	97
7 ***Pease***	100	100
8 ***Hostettler***	98	98
9 Hamilton	99	99
10 Carson	87	87
IOWA		
1 ***Leach***	97	97
2 ***Nussle***	98	98
3 Boswell	99	99
4 ***Ganske***	99	99
5 ***Latham***	99	99
KANSAS		
1 ***Moran***	99	100
2 ***Ryun***	99	99
3 ***Snowbarger***	98	98
4 ***Tiahrt***	98	99
KENTUCKY		
1 ***Whitfield***	98	98
2 ***Lewis***	97	97
3 ***Northup***	99	99
4 ***Bunning***	98	98
5 ***Rogers***	99	99
6 Baesler	98	98
LOUISIANA		
1 ***Livingston***	97	98
2 Jefferson	92	92
3 ***Tauzin***	96	97
4 ***McCrery***	95	96
5 ***Cooksey***	93	94
6 ***Baker***	94	94
7 John	97	97
MAINE		
1 Allen	99	99
2 Baldacci	99	99
MARYLAND		
1 ***Gilchrest***	99	99
2 ***Ehrlich***	99	99
3 Cardin	98	98
4 Wynn	99	99
5 Hoyer	98	98
6 ***Bartlett***	99	99
7 Cummings	98	99
8 ***Morella***	97	98
MASSACHUSETTS		
1 Olver	99	99
2 Neal	95	95
3 McGovern	99	99
4 Frank	96	96
5 Meehan	96	96
6 Tierney	99	99
7 Markey	97	98
8 Kennedy	98	98
9 Moakley	97	97
10 Delahunt	98	98
MICHIGAN		
1 Stupak	98	99
2 ***Hoekstra***	97	97
3 ***Ehlers***	97	97
4 ***Camp***	99	99
5 Barcia	97	97
6 ***Upton***	99	99
7 ***Smith***	97	97
8 Stabenow	98	99
9 Kildee	100	100
10 Bonior	96	97
11 ***Knollenberg***	99	99
12 Levin	99	99
13 Rivers	100	100
14 Conyers	91	92
15 Kilpatrick	97	97
16 Dingell	95	96
MINNESOTA		
1 ***Gutknecht***	99	99

	1	2
2 Minge	99	99
3 ***Ramstad***	100	100
4 Vento	99	99
5 Sabo	99	99
6 Luther	99	99
7 Peterson	99	99
8 Oberstar	94	95
MISSISSIPPI		
1 ***Wicker***	99	99
2 Thompson	97	97
3 ***Pickering***	96	96
4 ***Parker***	96	96
5 Taylor	98	99
MISSOURI		
1 Clay	90	90
2 ***Talent***	98	98
3 Gephardt	87	87
4 Skelton	95	95
5 McCarthy	97	98
6 Danner	98	98
7 ***Blunt***	98	98
8 ***Emerson***	98	98
9 ***Hulshof***	99	99
MONTANA		
AL ***Hill***	99	99
NEBRASKA		
1 ***Bereuter***	98	98
2 ***Christensen***	99	99
3 ***Barrett***	97	97
NEVADA		
1 ***Ensign***	98	98
2 ***Gibbons***	96	96
NEW HAMPSHIRE		
1 ***Sununu***	99	99
2 ***Bass***	99	99
NEW JERSEY		
1 Andrews	86	87
2 ***LoBiondo***	99	99
3 ***Saxton***	98	99
4 ***Smith***	96	97
5 ***Roukema***	96	96
6 Pallone	97	97
7 ***Franks***	99	99
8 Pascrell	98	99
9 Rothman	97	97
10 Payne	92	92
11 ***Frelinghuysen***	99	99
12 ***Pappas***	100	100
13 Menendez	98	98
NEW MEXICO		
1 ***Schiff***	10	9
2 ***Skeen***	99	99
3 ***Redmond***[3]	99	97
NEW YORK		
1 ***Forbes***	88	88
2 ***Lazio***	97	97
3 ***King***	98	98
4 McCarthy	98	98
5 Ackerman	91	91
6 Flake	78	78
7 Manton	94	94
8 Nadler	95	95
9 Schumer	91	91
10 Towns	90	91
11 Owens	93	94
12 Velazquez	96	96
13 ***Fossella***[4]	100	100
14 Maloney	97	98
15 Rangel	92	92
16 Serrano	96	96
17 Engel	95	97
18 Lowey	95	95
19 ***Kelly***	98	98
20 ***Gilman***	98	98
21 McNulty	97	97
22 ***Solomon***	96	96
23 ***Boehlert***	99	99
24 ***McHugh***	97	97
25 ***Walsh***	98	99
26 Hinchey	95	96
27 ***Paxon***	99	99
28 Slaughter	95	96
29 LaFalce	96	97
30 ***Quinn***	96	96
31 ***Houghton***	91	91

	1	2
NORTH CAROLINA		
1 Clayton	95	96
2 Etheridge	98	98
3 ***Jones***	99	99
4 Price	99	99
5 ***Burr***	96	97
6 ***Coble***	98	98
7 McIntyre	98	98
8 Hefner	90	90
9 ***Myrick***	97	97
10 ***Ballenger***	95	95
11 ***Taylor***	89	89
12 Watt	99	99
NORTH DAKOTA		
AL Pomeroy	94	94
OHIO		
1 ***Chabot***	99	99
2 ***Portman***	97	97
3 Hall	95	95
4 ***Oxley***	94	94
5 ***Gillmor***	96	96
6 Strickland	98	98
7 ***Hobson***	99	99
8 ***Boehner***	98	98
9 Kaptur	91	92
10 Kucinich	99	99
11 Stokes	92	92
12 ***Kasich***	97	97
13 Brown	97	98
14 Sawyer	99	99
15 ***Pryce***	95	95
16 ***Regula***	99	100
17 Traficant	99	99
18 ***Ney***	98	98
19 ***LaTourette***	96	96
OKLAHOMA		
1 ***Largent***	94	94
2 ***Coburn***	92	92
3 ***Watkins***	95	95
4 ***Watts***	97	97
5 ***Istook***	95	96
6 ***Lucas***	99	99
OREGON		
1 Furse	92	92
2 ***Smith***	91	91
3 Blumenauer	95	95
4 DeFazio	97	97
5 Hooley	99	99
PENNSYLVANIA		
1 Foglietta[5]	73	74
2 Fattah	94	95
3 Borski	98	98
4 Klink	99	99
5 ***Peterson***	99	99
6 Holden	98	98
7 ***Weldon***	91	91
8 ***Greenwood***	96	96
9 ***Shuster***	96	96
10 ***McDade***	92	93
11 Kanjorski	99	99
12 Murtha	97	98
13 ***Fox***	99	99
14 Coyne	99	99
15 McHale	99	99
16 ***Pitts***	100	100
17 ***Gekas***	97	98
18 Doyle	99	99
19 ***Goodling***	98	98
20 Mascara	99	99
21 ***English***	98	98
RHODE ISLAND		
1 Kennedy	97	97
2 Weygand	97	97
SOUTH CAROLINA		
1 ***Sanford***	98	98
2 ***Spence***	99	99
3 ***Graham***	98	98
4 ***Inglis***	98	98
5 Spratt	97	97
6 Clyburn	98	98
SOUTH DAKOTA		
AL ***Thune***	99	99
TENNESSEE		
1 ***Jenkins***	99	99
2 ***Duncan***	99	99

	1	2
3 ***Wamp***	97	97
4 ***Hilleary***	99	99
5 Clement	97	97
6 Gordon	98	98
7 ***Bryant***	98	98
8 Tanner	98	99
9 Ford	98	99
TEXAS		
1 Sandlin	99	99
2 Turner	98	98
3 ***Johnson***	93	93
4 Hall	99	99
5 ***Sessions***	99	99
6 ***Barton***	93	93
7 ***Archer***	96	97
8 ***Brady***	99	99
9 Lampson	99	99
10 Doggett	99	99
11 Edwards	96	96
12 ***Granger***	96	96
13 ***Thornberry***	99	99
14 ***Paul***	98	98
15 Hinojosa	98	98
16 Reyes	94	95
17 Stenholm	98	98
18 Jackson-Lee	98	98
19 ***Combest***	98	98
20 Gonzalez	47	47
21 ***Smith***	97	97
22 ***DeLay***	98	98
23 ***Bonilla***	89	89
24 Frost	97	97
25 Bentsen	99	99
26 ***Armey***	97	98
27 Ortiz	97	97
28 Rodriguez[6]	99	99
29 Green	97	97
30 Johnson	99	99
UTAH		
1 ***Hansen***	96	96
2 ***Cook***	100	100
3 ***Cannon***	98	98
VERMONT		
AL Sanders	96	97
VIRGINIA		
1 ***Bateman***	98	98
2 Pickett	97	97
3 Scott	98	98
4 Sisisky	98	99
5 Goode	98	98
6 ***Goodlatte***	99	99
7 ***Bliley***	98	98
8 Moran	95	95
9 Boucher	93	93
10 ***Wolf***	98	98
11 ***Davis***	99	99
WASHINGTON		
1 ***White***	95	95
2 ***Metcalf***	97	97
3 ***Smith***	97	97
4 ***Hastings***	98	98
5 ***Nethercutt***	98	98
6 Dicks	97	98
7 McDermott	95	95
8 ***Dunn***	99	99
9 Smith	97	98
WEST VIRGINIA		
1 Mollohan	93	93
2 Wise	96	96
3 Rahall	98	98
WISCONSIN		
1 ***Neumann***	94	95
2 ***Klug***	96	96
3 Kind	99	99
4 Kleczka	98	99
5 Barrett	99	99
6 ***Petri***	99	99
7 Obey	97	97
8 Johnson	99	99
9 ***Sensenbrenner***	98	98
WYOMING		
AL ***Cubin***	78	78

	1	2
ALABAMA		
Sessions	99	99
Shelby	100	100
ALASKA		
Murkowski	97	97
Stevens	99	99
ARIZONA		
Kyl	99	99
McCain	98	98
ARKANSAS		
Hutchinson	98	98
Bumpers	100	100
CALIFORNIA		
Boxer	99	99
Feinstein	99	99
COLORADO		
Allard	100	100
Campbell	99	99
CONNECTICUT		
Dodd	98	98
Lieberman	99	99
DELAWARE		
Roth	98	98
Biden	96	96
FLORIDA		
Mack	98	98
Graham	99	99
GEORGIA		
Coverdell	100	100
Cleland	100	100
HAWAII		
Akaka	98	98
Inouye	95	95
IDAHO		
Craig	100	100
Kempthorne	99	99
ILLINOIS		
Durbin	99	99
Moseley-Braun	99	99
INDIANA		
Coats	96	96
Lugar	100	100

	1	2
IOWA		
Grassley	100	100
Harkin	95	95
KANSAS		
Brownback	100	100
Roberts	97	97
KENTUCKY		
McConnell	99	99
Ford	99	99
LOUISIANA		
Breaux	99	99
Landrieu	99	99
MAINE		
Collins	100	100
Snowe	100	100
MARYLAND		
Mikulski	92	92
Sarbanes	99	99
MASSACHUSETTS		
Kennedy	97	97
Kerry	99	99
MICHIGAN		
Abraham	100	100
Levin	100	100
MINNESOTA		
Grams	98	98
Wellstone	96	96
MISSISSIPPI		
Cochran	99	99
Lott	100	100
MISSOURI		
Ashcroft	99	99
Bond	99	99
MONTANA		
Burns	96	96
Baucus	99	99
NEBRASKA		
Hagel	100	100
Kerrey	99	99
NEVADA		
Bryan	99	99
Reid	99	99

	1	2
NEW HAMPSHIRE		
Gregg	99	99
Smith	100	100
NEW JERSEY		
Lautenberg	99	99
Torricelli	100	100
NEW MEXICO		
Domenici	99	99
Bingaman	96	96
NEW YORK		
D'Amato	97	97
Moynihan	99	99
NORTH CAROLINA		
Faircloth	96	96
Helms	98	98
NORTH DAKOTA		
Conrad	99	99
Dorgan	98	98
OHIO		
DeWine	100	100
Glenn	97	97
OKLAHOMA		
Inhofe	98	98
Nickles	100	100
OREGON		
Smith	99	99
Wyden	99	99
PENNSYLVANIA		
Santorum	99	99
Specter	99	99
RHODE ISLAND		
Chafee	98	98
Reed	99	99
SOUTH CAROLINA		
Thurmond	99	99
Hollings	97	97
SOUTH DAKOTA		
Daschle	97	97
Johnson	98	98
TENNESSEE		
Frist	100	100
Thompson	100	100

KEY

Democrats ***Republicans***

	1	2
TEXAS		
Gramm	100	100
Hutchison	99	99
UTAH		
Bennett	97	97
Hatch	99	99
VERMONT		
Jeffords	97	97
Leahy	98	98
VIRGINIA		
Warner	98	98
Robb	100	100
WASHINGTON		
Gorton	100	100
Murray	99	99
WEST VIRGINIA		
Byrd	99	99
Rockefeller	95	95
WISCONSIN		
Feingold	100	100
Kohl	100	100
WYOMING		
Enzi	99	99
Thomas	99	99

Voting Participation: Senate

1. Voting Participation, 1997. Percentage of 298 recorded votes in 1997 on which a senator voted "yea" or "nay."

2. Voting Participation, 1997. Percentage of 297 recorded votes in 1997 on which a senator voted "yea" or "nay." In this version of the study, one vote to instruct the sergeant at arms to request the attendance of absent senators is not included.

Absences due to illness. *Congressional Quarterly no longer designates members who missed votes due to illness. In the past, notations to that effect were based on official statements published in the Congressional Record, but these were found to be inconsistently used.*

Rounding. *Scores are rounded to nearest percentage, except that no scores are rounded up to 100 percent. Members with a 100 percent score participated in all recorded votes for which they were eligible.*

Conflicts of interest. *Christopher J. Dodd, D-Conn., declared that he voted present to avoid the appearance of a possible conflict of interest on votes 28, 29, 32 and 33, concerning investigations into the 1996 presidential elections, when he was general chairman of the Democratic National Party.*

John McCain, R-Ariz., declared that he voted present to avoid the appearance of a possible conflict of interest on votes 136 and 263, concerning taxation of alcohol.

Middle-of-the-Road Path Proves Much Smoother for GOP

It was a sobering lesson for Republicans still intent on forcing radical changes in the federal government. In 1997, just three years removed from the GOP revolution, what prevailed in Congress was legislation that could only be described as moderate.

Conservatives came close on several of the core issues they had championed since they captured control of Congress in 1994. But a review of the 27 key votes of 1997, as determined by the editors of Congressional Quarterly's Weekly Report, showed that on those priorities of the conservative agenda, the GOP rank and file failed to muster enough votes to overcome either bipartisan opposition or the prospect of a presidential veto.

The list of failed bills read like a manifesto for the GOP to galvanize a significant portion of its political base: legislation to provide private-school vouchers, eliminate the National Endowment for the Arts (NEA), ban a controversial abortion procedure, allow compensatory time off instead of overtime pay, and amend the Constitution to require a balanced federal budget. Pollsters called those "wedge issues."

What emerged instead from the first session of the 105th Congress was legislation that reflected a middle-of-the-road perspective, the centerpiece of which was the balanced-budget deal that aimed to eliminate the deficit by 2002 while cutting taxes and reordering federal spending priorities.

Central to the bipartisan climate that led to the budget package was the high-stakes cooperation between President Clinton and Senate Majority Leader Trent Lott, R-Miss. Their comity also ensured Senate passage April 24 of a historic treaty banning chemical weapons. Lott took considerable flak from his party's right for supporting the treaty, with some conservative pundits even questioning his patriotism. Unbowed, Lott then threw down the gauntlet to Clinton, calling on the president to stand up to the left wing of his own party to reach a compromise on the balanced-budget package.

Clinton accepted the challenge, and — despite the showdowns that had led to government shutdowns in 1995-1996 — the Republican-controlled Congress and Democratic White House had their budget agreement just nine days after the chemical weapons treaty vote. The blueprint of the deal, written into the fiscal 1998 budget resolution (H Con Res 84), passed in early June, setting the stage for much of the rest of the first session.

Another area where House Republicans won some successes through moderation was the environment. An attempt in May to waive the 1973 Endangered Species Act for flood control projects, a huge step back from earlier attempts to rewrite the law, was undercut by Democrats and moderate Republicans. But as the year went on, Westerners became more astute, demanding more leadership support and trying to build coalitions. In the fall, they were able to win House passage for relatively modest bills to revise federal grazing policy and to give property owners greater access to federal courts and greater clout with local zoning boards.

What follows is a review of CQ's key votes of 1997, a dozen from the Senate and 15 from the House. They appear in chronological order, first Senate and then House.

How CQ Picks Key Votes

Since 1945, Congressional Quarterly has selected a series of key votes on major issues of the year.

An issue is judged by the extent to which it represents:

- A matter of major controversy.
- A matter of presidential or political power.
- A matter of potentially great impact on the nation and lives of Americans.

For each group of related votes on an issue, one key vote usually is chosen — one that, in the opinion of CQ editors, was most important in determining the outcome.

Charts showing how each member of Congress voted on these issues can be found as follows:

Senate key votes 1-6 .... C-46
Senate key votes 7-12 .... C-47
House key votes 1-7 .... C-48
House key votes 8-15 .... C-50

Key SENATE Votes

1. Balanced-Budget Amendment

Working with a new and smaller cast, but one that followed the script that worked in 1995, Senate Democrats again scuttled a cornerstone of the Republican agenda: a constitutional amendment to require a balanced federal budget.

During the dramatic 1995 debate, then-Majority Leader Bob Dole, R-Kan., delayed the vote as he frantically tried to win over a wavering Democrat. In the end, he had to accept defeat on a 65-35 vote; 67 votes were required to prevail. *(1995 Almanac, p. 2-34)*

Still, Republicans entered the 1997 debate with high hopes. If every veteran of the 1995 vote remained consistent, and if every freshman elected in 1996 kept his or her campaign promise to support the amendment (S J Res 1), it would pass with 68 votes.

Fewer votes were considered "in play" than in 1995, when a half-dozen Democrats who had previously backed the amendment switched their votes. After three years of debating and voting on the issue, Senate veterans had their positions set in concrete. Consequently, the outcome hung on the votes of four freshman Democrats: Robert G. Torricelli of New Jersey and Tim Johnson of South Dakota, both of whom had voted for the amendment as members of the House; and Max Cleland of Georgia and Mary L. Landrieu of Louisiana, who had supported it in their campaigns.

It was a group over which Majority Leader Trent Lott, R-Miss., and his floor lieutenants had no control. And none among them was ready to show his or her hand early. From the beginning, the four freshmen held private meetings and advised one another on their thoughts about such a critical issue arising at the outset of their Senate careers.

Minority Leader Tom Daschle, D-S.D., held a series of one-on-one meetings with the newcomers, counseled them to avoid making any hasty decisions and gently cajoled them to change their minds. Robert C. Byrd, D-W.Va., and Daniel Patrick Moynihan, D-N.Y. — veteran opponents of the amendment — also sought out the freshmen to make their case.

By all accounts, Daschle was masterly, pressing the issue with a light but determined hand. "He wasn't pushy at all," said Torricelli. "He asked me only to consider the consequences of being the deciding vote to amend the Constitution."

Cleland was first off the fence, confirming Feb. 14 that he would vote for the amendment. But Johnson countered on Feb. 20, announcing that he would switch and vote against it. That left the fate of the amendment with Torricelli and Landrieu. If either switched, the amendment would die. Advertising campaigns, both pro and con, went on the air in selected states, but as before, they appeared to have no impact on the outcome.

After weeks of wavering, Landrieu announced Feb. 25 that she would vote for the amendment. She acknowledged that had it not been for her campaign promise, she would have opposed it.

That left it to Toricelli to be the deciding vote. On Feb. 26, he declared: "All doubts concerning amendments to the Constitution must be settled in leaving the genius of the Founding Fathers undisturbed."

By the time the vote arrived March 4, it had been drained of suspense. The only ripple of excitement came as the count, with time running down, stalled briefly at 66-33, a potentially winning two-thirds tally. But then Bob Kerrey, D-Neb., swept into the chamber, voted "no," and the amendment died, 66-34: R 55-0, D 11-34 (ND 6-31, SD 5-3). *(Senate key vote 1, p. C-46; balanced-budget amendment, p. 2-66)*

2. Yucca Mountain

In a victory for the nuclear power industry, the Senate on April 15 passed a bill (S 104) to create a temporary nuclear waste storage site in the Nevada desert. But the win was not big enough to beat a trump card held by the opponents, led by Nevada's two Democratic senators, Harry Reid and Richard H. Bryan. For, while the bill garnered two more votes than had a similar bill passed by the Senate in 1996, it was still two votes short of the two-thirds needed to override a promised veto. The vote was 65-34: R 53-2; D 12-32 (ND 8-28, SD 4-4). *(Senate key vote 2, p. C-46; Yucca Mountain, p. 4-20)*

President Clinton vowed to veto the temporary nuclear waste storage site proposal until a study was completed on the viability of Yucca Mountain to be the home of a permanent repository. The study was slated to be finished in 1998.

The bill would have required the temporary waste site to open in 2003. Frank H. Murkowski, R-Alaska, chairman of the Senate Energy and Natural Resources Committee, tried to attract support by adding a provision giving the president until March 1, 1999, to halt construction of the temporary storage site if he found that permanent storage was not viable at Yucca Mountain. The president and Congress would then have two years to approve an alternate site; if they failed, construction would begin automatically in Nevada.

Nuclear utilities argued the bill was needed to allow removal of the growing inventory of nuclear waste stored in 35 states. A 1982 law required the federal government to dispose of civilian nuclear waste starting Jan. 31, 1998.

Despite the deadline, the bill was opposed by 32 Democrats and two Republicans — Ben Nighthorse Campbell of Colorado and Daniel R. Coats of Indiana.

Supporters would have had a veto-proof margin if not for "no" votes cast by first-year Democrats Richard J. Durbin of Illinois and Mary L. Landrieu of Louisiana. Their Democratic predecessors, Paul Simon of Illinois and J. Bennett Johnston of Louisiana, backed the temporary storage site in 1996. Durbin cited concerns about nuclear waste transportation and environmental protection; Landrieu expressed sympathy for nuclear utilities but cited concern about unfinished plans for permanent storage.

Backers of the bill also picked up two votes they did not have in 1996. Environment and Public Works Committee Chairman John H. Chafee, R-R.I., switched his vote to "yes," citing improved environmental provisions in the 1997 bill. Ron Wyden, D-Ore., also switched from a "no" vote on the 1996 bill to a "yes" on S 104. *(1996 Almanac, p. 4-30)*

3. Chemical Weapons Treaty

The most vigorous attack on President Clinton's national security policy during the year was beaten back in April when the Senate approved a treaty banning chemical weapons after rejecting several amendments that would have weakened the pact. However, Clinton was able to win the fight only after making significant concessions to leading Republicans on other foreign policy matters.

At issue was the Chemical Weapons Convention, signed shortly before President George Bush left office in January 1993. The treaty banned the development, production, storage, use, sale or purchase of chemical weapons. Negotiated by the Bush and Reagan administrations with the active cooperation of major chemical manufacturing firms, the treaty was supported not only by most Democrats but also by many prominent members of the GOP foreign policy establishment.

Nevertheless, conservatives had held up ratification in 1996, saying the treaty would be ineffective in halting the spread of chemical weapons and that it would lull the country into a false sense of security. Critics also said the treaty's far-reaching system of international inspections was a threat to U.S. sovereignty and to U.S. companies' competitive secrets. *(1996 Almanac, p. 8-14)*

In January 1997, Clinton and his top aides launched a full-court press to secure Senate approval of the treaty by April 29, the date on which it was to take effect. Treaty supporters contended that public abhorrence of chemical weapons would provide the leverage needed to secure the necessary two-thirds majority if the Senate could be forced to vote on the pact.

Ultimately, Clinton got his vote, but he had to trade for it with Majority Leader Trent Lott, R-Miss., and with Foreign Relations Committee Chairman Jesse Helms, R-N.C., who opposed the treaty and had the power to keep it bottled up in his committee.

Helms was mollified partly by the administration's acceptance of a raft of proposed amendments to the resolution of approval (S Res 75). One of these required the treaty's international inspection teams to obtain a criminal search warrant from a U.S. judge if they wanted to inspect an American company's facility without its consent.

Helms also was persuaded not to obstruct Senate action by the administration's agreement to his long-standing goal of streamlining the foreign policy bureaucracy by consolidating the United States Information Agency, the Arms Control and Disarmament Agency and parts of the Agency for International Development into the State Department.

At Lott's insistence, the administration also agreed that modifications to existing arms control treaties, which were being negotiated with Russia, would be sent to the Senate as formal amendments to those treaties, requiring a two-thirds majority vote. This was advantageous to conservatives who were particularly opposed to proposed changes in the 1972 treaty limiting anti-ballistic missile (ABM) defenses.

However, the Senate did reject five other proposed changes, dubbed "killer amendments" by the administration. Although Lott supported all of them, he announced that he would support the treaty, albeit unenthusiastically. The Senate approved the resolution April 24 by a vote of 74-26: R 29-26; D 45-0 (ND 37-0; SD 8-0). *(Senate key vote 3, p. C-46; chemical weapons, p. 8-13)*

4. Compensatory Time Off

Less than a year after Senate Democrats blocked consideration of a key component in the GOP's labor agenda, Republican leaders took another run at moving legislation (S 4, HR 1) to allow employees to take compensatory time off instead of overtime pay.

The House had passed a version of the plan in July 1996 and again on March 19, 1997, and Senate leaders wanted to see if anything had changed in their chamber. Fifteen new members — nine Republicans and six Democrats — had joined the Senate. Mike DeWine, R-Ohio, acting on behalf of Republican bill sponsors, had agreed to sweeten the pot by, for example, amending the original measure to honor collective bargaining contracts.

The bill proposed to amend the 1938 Fair Labor Standards Act to allow private-sector hourly workers to take compensatory time in lieu of overtime pay and to work schedules other than the traditional 40-hour week. DeWine agreed to clarify that seasonal and temporary workers could not be offered the compensatory time option unless they worked at least 1,250 hours for an employer in a year.

Republicans said the measure would give workers who earned an hourly wage the same opportunities to take time off that salaried workers had.

But Democrats reiterated their charges that the bill would allow employers, not employees, to choose how workers would be compensated for extra work. They also objected to undoing the 40-hour work week, which they considered a sacred element of labor law. The bill allowed for an 80-hour, two-week work period in which employees could, for example, work 50 hours one week and 30 the next with no extra pay.

Democrats' arguments were buoyed by a veto threat from President Clinton and strong labor union opposition to the bill, reflecting the deep political chasm that existed between the two parties on labor issues. With the Democratic Party highly indebted to unions and Republicans' indebted to the business community, the comp-time bill was a measure on which neither party could afford to compromise.

On May 15, Republicans tried to limit debate on the bill and thereby block a Democratic filibuster, but Democrats formed a brick wall in opposition. The motion to invoke cloture failed 53-47: R 53-2; D 0-45 (ND 0-37, SD 0-8). A three-fifths majority, or 60 votes, was needed, so the motion failed by seven votes. *(Senate key vote 4, p. C-46; Comp time, p. 7-22)*

The Democrats were joined by two Republicans facing 1998 re-election contests in strong union states — Alfonse M. D'Amato of New York and Arlen Specter of Pennsylvania.

After a brief cooling-off period, Republicans made another attempt to move the bill, but they fared no better. In a June 4 cloture vote, they lost another GOP vote when Ben Nighthorse Campbell of Colorado joined D'Amato and Specter. James M. Jeffords, R-Vt., was absent. With the absence of one Democrat — Jack Reed of Rhode Island — the tally was 51-47, nine votes short.

5. Abortion Procedure Ban

Both sides were braced for a close outcome May 20, when the Senate voted on banning a controversial procedure that opponents termed "partial birth" abortion.

The Senate had passed a similar bill in December 1995 by a vote of 54-44, well short of the 67 votes needed to override a presidential veto. The shortfall only increased in September 1997, when the Senate sustained President Clinton's veto, 57-41. *(1995 Almanac, p. 7-30; 1996 Almanac, p. 6-43)*

However, the political environment surrounding the debate differed substantially in the 105th Congress. New concerns had arisen about how often the practice, carried out in the second or third trimester of pregnancy, was performed. Some newly elected Republicans brought additional support for banning the practice. And the American Medical Association announced it would support the ban, a move that prompted some senators to switch their votes and support the bill.

Bill supporters, mostly Republicans, argued that the type of abortion described in the legislation was a violent and unnecessary procedure that should be outlawed. Opponents countered that the measure was too narrowly drawn, and that women would be in jeopardy unless an exception were permitted to prevent serious injury to a woman's physical health.

The House already had passed the ban with a solid veto-proof majority, and Sen. Rick Santorum, R-Pa., the bill's sponsor, made what he termed "technical" changes to broaden support for the measure. Alterations included clarifying the definition of the procedure and reiterating that doctors would be shielded from criminal penalties if a life-threatening medical emergency forced them to use the procedure.

When the final count was taken May 20, supporters were still three votes short of the 67 needed for a veto override. However, their margin of victory had increased since December 1995. The vote was 64-36: R 51-4; D 13-32 (ND 9-28, SD 4-4). *(Senate key vote 5, p. C-46; abortion procedure ban, p. 6-12)*

Several Democrats, including Minority Leader Tom Daschle of South Dakota, Robert C. Byrd of West Virginia and Ernest F. Hollings of South Carolina, switched their votes to support, rather than oppose, the ban.

Adding to the drama was a floor speech by Daschle, who had tried unsuccessfully to alter the bill. Daschle, a Roman Catholic, challenged church officials — including those in his home state — for criticizing his attempts to find a middle ground on the issue. "Their harsh rhetoric and vitriolic characterizations . . . proved to be a consequential impediment to the decision I have made today," he said. "It was most instructive."

6. Budget Resolution

After the bitter budget wars that marked 1995 and 1996, the consensus-oriented Senate — never completely comfortable with the confrontational tactics of the House GOP vanguard — eagerly embraced the chance to produce a bipartisan budget in 1997.

Budget Committee Chairman Pete V. Domenici, R-N.M., was the chief player in early-stage talks with White House officials. A veteran of every big budget battle since he first became chairman of the committee in 1981, Domenici saw at the beginning of the year an economic and political landscape favorable for an agreement to achieve the first balanced budget in almost 30 years.

Getting toward balance represented a historic accomplishment, though the episode left veterans of prior deficit-reduction deals grasping for a little credit as well. The 1997 deal was made possible by the unpopular 1990 and 1993 budgets, which produced inflation-adjusted deficit savings that far exceeded those of the landmark 1997 pact.

And the magnitude of the deficit problem had been steadily shrinking. Congressional Budget Office "baseline" estimates of the 2002 deficit had shrunk from the $349 billion figure Republicans had worked from in 1995 to only $188 billion when the 1997 negotiations began in earnest.

Domenici, Budget Committee Staff Director G. William Hoagland, White House budget chief Franklin D. Raines and top administration lobbyist John L. Hilley commenced back-channel talks that produced the parameters of a deal and built up the more trusting atmosphere that was required to reach agreement.

Domenici held off writing the budget resolution until congressional Republicans and the White House had struck a deal, which traded long-term savings from Medicare and other programs for tax cuts and some short-term spending increases. Finally, on May 15, the agreement was ready, and Domenici moved swiftly to translate it into a budget resolution (H Con Res 84) and get it through the Senate. The measure came to the floor with a series of proposed amendments that allowed members to point out what they considered to be flaws in the agreement.

It fell to Majority Leader Trent Lott, R-Miss., to close the deal — and to sell it to his fellow conservatives.

It was an easy sell. Some conservative purists such as Phil Gramm, R-Texas, protested that the middle-of-the-road deal represented an abdication of core GOP values. But almost everybody else found the opportunity to vote for a balanced budget and the first major tax cut since the beginning of Ronald Reagan's presidency too alluring to pass up.

Despite scares over amendments to shift additional funding to highway projects (killed, 51-49) and a "deal-buster" that would have raised cigarette taxes to finance a children's health care initiative (killed 55-45), the budget resolution passed unscathed. The Senate adopted the measure May 23 by a vote of 78-22: R 41-14; D 37-8 (ND 31-6, SD 6-2). *(Senate key vote 6, p. C-46; budget resolution, p. 2-23)*

The bipartisanship witnessed during the debate on the budget resolution carried over into the crafting of the reconciliation bills required to implement the policy changes dictated by H Con Res 84. Despite extensive wrangling between the White House and Republicans, mostly over taxes, the mutual interest in enacting the budget deal kept Domenici and his House counterpart, John R. Kasich, R-Ohio, confident the deal would hold.

7. Medicare Means Testing

In a bold move to restructure Medicare, the federal health insurance program for the elderly and disabled, the Senate proposed requiring that some wealthier beneficiaries pay higher premiums for visits to their doctors.

Under existing law, beneficiaries paid 25 percent of the costs of Medicare Part B, which covered doctors' visits and other outpatient services. But in provisions written by the Finance Committee, the spending-cut portion of the Senate's reconciliation package (S 947) sought to introduce so-called means testing. The Senate bill proposed requiring individuals with at least $50,000 in adjusted gross annual incomes and couples with at least $75,000 to pay a larger share of their premiums. People with adjusted gross incomes of at least $100,000 and couples with incomes of at least $125,000 would pay the whole Part B premium.

Senate Budget Committee Chairman Pete V. Domenici, R-N.M., said linking premiums to income would raise about $4 billion and affect about 5 percent of Medicare's more than 38 million elderly and disabled beneficiaries.

Supporters, who included both Democrats and Republicans, argued the change was only fair, and that taxpayers should not help foot the bill for wealthier seniors. But opponents such as Edward M. Kennedy, D-Mass., said that requiring some seniors to pay more of their Part B premiums would be the first step toward making Medicare a welfare program rather than a federal entitlement program.

Kennedy fought to amend the means-testing provision. He tried to delay its onset by two years, having it begin in 2000 rather than 1998, but that proposal failed, 37-63. Kennedy did win a battle to make sure all senators had to abide by means testing. His amendment to require senators who earned more than $100,000 per year — as all of them did — to pay the full Part B premium, should the means-testing provision become law, passed by voice vote.

But Kennedy failed to remove means testing from the bill. He offered an amendment to do so, but Senate Finance Committee Chairman William V. Roth Jr., R-Del., moved to table, or kill, Kennedy's proposal on June 24. Roth's motion won on a vote of 70-30: R 49-6; D 21-24 (ND 15-22, SD 6-2). *(Senate key vote 7, p.C-47; Medicare, p. 6-3)*

The Senate's landmark vote to include means testing had little staying power, however. The idea did not have wide bipartisan support in the House and was not included in the budget deal (H Con Res 84) that Republicans, Democrats and the White House had agreed to in May. That fact brought opposition from the White House, although President Clinton had included means testing in his own failed 1993 health care overhaul plan. Opposition also came from the American Association of Retired Persons, a powerful lobbying group for senior citizens.

Those concerns, plus a shortage of House members to back the proposal, forced means testing out of the final package adopted by Senate and House conferees. Instead, the spending cut bill (PL 105-33) created a bipartisan commission to review Medicare's long-term solvency.

8. Arts Funding

The Senate once again demonstrated its strong support for the National Endowment for the Arts (NEA), defeating efforts to abolish — or even revamp — federal funding for the arts.

The issue was thrust to center stage largely because the House, in its version of the fiscal 1998 Interior appropriations bill (HR 2107), attempted to zero out the agency. House conservatives had won a promise from the leadership to try to eliminate the NEA, and the leadership lobbied hard for the no-funding position.

For the better part of the summer, senators and aides tried without success to find a compromise. Instead, when the Senate version of the Interior bill reached the floor, it was met with a host of NEA proposals, ranging from the outright elimination of federal arts funding to privatizing the NEA or restricting its funding options.

Arguably the most moderate attempt to revise the agency

was made by Kay Bailey Hutchison, R-Texas. Hutchison typified a small band of senators who supported federal arts funding but believed some changes were in order. Top on this group's list of complaints was that the arts agency directed too much money to a handful of states, such as New York, depriving others of badly needed resources. They also said it spent too much money on administrative costs in Washington; many senators clearly favored finding a way to put more money in the hands of their state and local arts organizations, without increasing the overall funding ceiling for the agency.

Hutchison's amendment proposed to retain the agency but send 75 percent of the funding directly to the states in lump sum payments. Of the remainder, 5 percent would be spent for administrative costs, and the rest on national grants to major ballet, opera and other arts groups. Hutchison also proposed limiting the amount of money that could go to an individual state to 6.6 percent.

Hutchison hoped her effort would catch fire with other moderates who supported the agency, firming up long-term backing for the NEA. Instead, the Senate soundly defeated Hutchison, as it did all other major amendments to revise the NEA. The Sept. 18 vote was 39-61: R 39-16; 0-45 (ND 0-37, SD 0-8). *(Senate key vote 8, p. C-47; appropriations, p. 9-44)*

In the end, the House conservatives had to back off. The final bill included $98 million for the NEA, roughly equal to the Senate level.

9. Campaign Finance

A burgeoning scandal over campaign finance abuses triggered a full-blown Senate investigation, a spate of other congressional probes and a seemingly endless stream of newspaper stories documenting massive abuses of — and flaws in — the nation's fundraising laws. But the intense furor over campaign finance did little to boost prospects for legislation intended to revamp the political fundraising system.

An unlikely pair of senators, Arizona Republican John McCain and Wisconsin Democrat Russell D. Feingold, sponsored a bill (S 25) aimed at closing what they said were two of the biggest fundraising loopholes. The bill sought to eliminate "soft money" — unregulated donations to parties rather than candidates — and place limits on independent, issue-oriented television advertisements that implicitly promoted candidates.

McCain and Feingold hoped that popular outrage over the fundraising scandals would enable them to overcome determined opposition, led by Senate Majority Leader Trent Lott, R-Miss., and Mitch McConnell, R-Ky.

But it was an uphill battle from the beginning. Although poll after poll showed that the vast majority of Americans were dissatisfied with the existing system, polls also showed that cynical voters did not expect Washington to change the rules.

Lott and McConnell said that the real problem lay with President Clinton and other Democrats who, they contended, were willing to ignore existing laws to finance their 1996 campaign. Not only were new laws not needed, they said, but the McCain-Feingold bill would trample on constitutionally protected freedom of political speech.

As the showdown approached in early October, it became clear that McCain and Feingold needed 60 votes to break an all but certain GOP-led filibuster. With commitments of support from all 45 Senate Democrats and four Republicans — McCain, Susan Collins of Maine, Fred Thompson of Tennessee and Arlen Specter of Pennsylvania — their magic number was 11 votes, all of which would have to come from Republicans.

The two men pulled out all the stops: McCain went on radio talk shows, cable news shows and network political chat shows to make the case for sweeping change in the campaign finance system. In an effort to widen support, McCain and Feingold scaled back their bill by dropping a controversial provision to provide free television time to candidates who voluntarily agreed to spending limits.

But their drive fell short, as Lott, McConnell and company were able to successfully filibuster the bill. On Oct. 7, the Senate rejected a motion to invoke cloture and thus limit debate on the bill. The vote was 53-47: R 8-47; D 45-0 (ND 37-0, SD 8-0). A vote of three-fifths of the Senate (60 votes) was required to invoke cloture. *(Senate key vote 9, p. C-47; campaign finance bill, p. 1-26)*

McCain and Feingold picked up no ground over their earlier effort to move the legislation. In June 1996, the Senate defeated a cloture motion on a more sweeping version of the McCain-Feingold bill on a 54-46 vote, with one more senator voting to end the filibuster than in 1997. Eight Republicans voted for cloture then, too; the key difference was that there were two more Democrats in the Senate at the time, one of whom voted for cloture and one against. *(1996 Almanac, p. 1-21)*

10. Line-Item Veto

The Senate wasted little time in expressing its disapproval of the way President Clinton used his newly acquired line-item veto authority. Three and a half weeks after Clinton first struck projects from an appropriations bill, better than two-thirds of the Senate voted to overturn his decision.

Led by Appropriations Chairman Ted Stevens, R-Alaska, senators vented their ire at Clinton's methodology in selecting 38 military construction projects, totaling $287 million, to cancel — especially after the White House conceded that it had based some of its decisions on faulty data. Clinton had signed the bill (HR 2016 — PL 105-45) on Sept. 30.

The congressional uproar forced Clinton to reassess his line-item veto strategy. He would not again try to excise as many projects from a single bill.

On Oct. 30, the day of the Senate vote, the White House released a letter admitting errors on numerous veto decisions and offering to work with appropriators to restore funding for affected projects. Stevens, however, repeatedly took to the floor to complain that the administration refused to specify which of its choices had been made in error.

Much of the floor debate on the disapproval bill (S 1292) centered on the question of how Clinton selected the items to veto, with a number of senators taking time to extol the virtues of canceled projects in their home states.

With passage clear, the one contentious question was whether supporters of the line-item veto (PL 104-130), which Congress had granted to the president in 1996, were obliged to accept his decisions as falling within the intent of the new law. *(1996 Almanac, p. 2-28)*

"What credibility can supporters of the line-item veto authority have if we disapprove vetoes on the first appropriations bill right out of the gate?" Charles S. Robb, D-Va., asked.

But supporters of the disapproval bill argued that it was in keeping with the spirit of the line-item veto law. "I think this is exactly how the process is supposed to work," said Kay Bailey Hutchison, R Texas. "Congress did not take away its right to disagree with the president."

Stevens went so far as to threaten to repeal the line-item

veto if his bill failed to pass.

The disapproval bill passed 69-30: R 42-12; D 27-18 (ND 24-13, SD 3-5). That gave sponsors a three-vote cushion over the two-thirds majority they would need to overcome Clinton's veto. *(Senate key vote 10, p. C-47; line-item veto, p. 2-63; appropriations, p. 9-61; vetoed provisions, p. 9-64)*

Although House appropriators initially signaled their disinterest in challenging the president, hinting they might instead try to restore the military construction funding through a supplemental appropriations bill, the Senate vote emboldened the House to pass a slightly different version of the disapproval bill (HR 2631), which the Senate then accepted. Although Clinton vetoed that bill Nov. 13, the veto-proof margins mustered in both chambers made it clear that he would ultimately be overridden.

11. Education Savings Accounts

Senate Democrats on Oct. 31 blocked a top Republican education priority: a bill to establish tax-free education savings accounts that could be used to defray private or public school costs. A GOP effort to invoke cloture, thereby limiting debate on the bill, failed by four votes.

Republicans originally tried to include a similar provision in the tax portion of the balanced-budget reconciliation package (HR 2014 — PL 105-34). But they withdrew it at the last moment when President Clinton, fearing that the measure would harm public schools, threatened to veto the whole tax bill if it were included. *(Private schooling, p. 7-6)*

Republicans blasted Clinton for yielding to opposition from teachers' unions and vowed to pass a free-standing measure over Clinton's objections. Under the subsequent legislation (HR 2646), sponsored by House Ways and Means Committee Chairman Bill Archer, R-Texas, parents would have been able to invest up to $2,500 a year in special accounts and use the principal and interest tax-free for education-related expenses. The accounts were to be structured somewhat like Individual Retirement Accounts.

The legislation advanced through Ways and Means and the House in October on closely contested votes. Senate supporters hoped to move it swiftly to Clinton's desk.

But most Democrats were in no mood to comply. They initially opposed the cloture motion as part of their protest over a stalled bill (S 25) on campaign finance revisions. But even when senators agreed Oct. 30 on how they would consider the campaign finance bill, Democrats still objected to the education measure on procedural grounds. Their arguments: No Senate hearings were held on it, and Democrats would be barred from offering a full range of amendments to it.

Paul Coverdell, R-Ga., chief Senate sponsor of the legislation, had hoped to attract bipartisan support, but only two Democrats voted for cloture — Robert G. Torricelli of New Jersey and Joseph I. Lieberman of Connecticut. On the other side, John H. Chafee of Rhode Island broke ranks with Republicans and voted against cloture. The cloture motion failed 56-41, four votes short of the 60 needed to move the bill toward passage: R 54-1; D 2-40 (ND 2-32, SD 0-8). *(Senate key vote 11, p. C-47)*

Coverdell tried again to invoke cloture Nov. 4, but still fell four votes short, 56-44.

12. 'Fast Track' Trade Authority

With time running out on the session, President Clinton made a desperate bid to regain "fast-track" authority to negotiate and get expedited review of trade agreements. When it appeared he was badly behind in the House, he turned to the Senate.

The Senate historically had favored free trade, and there was no doubt that that chamber could muster the majority required to pass the bill (S 1269). The only question was whether there would be enough votes to beat a promised filibuster by opponents such as Democrats Byron L. Dorgan of North Dakota and Ernest F. Hollings of South Carolina.

Under the Constitution, trade bills were required to originate in the House because they affected tariff revenues. But Senate Majority Leader Trent Lott, R-Miss., began the floor debate at the administration's request. The idea was that a big show of Senate support would give momentum to the troubled House effort.

The bill zipped out of the Finance Committee as expected Oct. 1, and Lott predicted from the outset that the votes were there to reach the 60-vote mark required to beat a filibuster. Dorgan, the most active of the opponents, cast the debate as a referendum on trade pacts such as the 1993 North American Free Trade Agreement (NAFTA). Dorgan criticized NAFTA for turning a $2 billion trade surplus with Mexico into a $16 billion deficit, and for accompanying job losses in certain manufacturing sectors.

Supporters countered that fast track was merely a procedural device and that any trade pact negotiated under fast-track rules could subsequently be rejected by Congress.

As Lott predicted, the Senate on Nov. 4 acted to invoke cloture on the motion to proceed to the bill by a surprisingly big vote of 69-31: R 43-12; D 26-19 (ND 20-17, SD 6-2). *(Senate key vote 12, p. C-47; fast track, p. 2-85)*

After invoking cloture, the Senate approved the motion to proceed the next day by a 68-31 vote. The Senate then turned to other business in the end-of-session crunch, and the bill was put on the back burner pending a vote in the House.

Despite the stakes, the debate never seemed to grip the Senate. With both sides viewing the vote as a foregone conclusion, the lobbying forces — labor unions in opposition and the business community in favor — focused their fire on the House.

Most House Democrats were dismissive of Clinton's request, and they were not swayed by the strong Senate vote. Republican leaders shelved the companion House bill in the early hours of Nov. 10.

Key **HOUSE** *Votes*

1. Election of Speaker

In a remarkable twist of history, Newt Gingrich, the upstart Georgian who led Republicans to a majority in Congress in 1995, found himself on the brink of ruin at the start of the 105th Congress.

Two years earlier, he had been the undisputed leader of the Republican Party and one of the country's most important politicians. But a series of tactical missteps in his first two years in power, some of them highly embarrassing for his party, coupled with doubts raised about his personal conduct by a House ethics investigation, led to a make-or-break vote for the Speaker on Jan. 7. What should have been a standard exercise — the ratification of the majority party's nominee for Speaker — instead turned into an intrigue-filled squeaker.

Although Gingrich still commanded the support of a large share of House Republicans, the November 1996 election had so narrowed the GOP advantage that he could withstand few defections. Republicans held only a 227-207 edge over the

Democrats. If all the Democrats and the House's one independent voted for Minority Leader Richard A. Gephardt, D-Mo., and 20 Republicans voted "present" or for someone other than Gingrich, then Gephardt would have become Speaker.

Some lawmakers, such as New York GOP Reps. Peter T. King and Michael P. Forbes, aired their doubts publicly, attracting the attention of the national media. But the biggest threat to Gingrich was a silent revolt among a loosely aligned group of disgruntled Republicans who held out as undecided votes, hoping to force him to step down.

The rebels had grown disillusioned with Gingrich, convinced that his usefulness as chief party visionary no longer made up for his abysmally low public approval ratings, frequent gaffes and often unpredictable leadership style. The unresolved issues of the ethics case only exacerbated their concerns.

Gingrich on Dec. 21, 1996, had admitted after two years of denials that he had failed to properly manage the financing of his political activities through charitable foundations. Gingrich also conceded that he gave the committee misleading information during the investigation. Yet the panel had not issued its final report or recommended a punishment, and would not do so until after the Speaker's election, leaving lawmakers partly in the dark as they prepared to vote.

Gingrich, long a scrappy political fighter, refused to capitulate. He instead brought all the considerable resources of his office to bear. He and his five top allies and their staffs worked telephones and fax machines throughout the Christmas season, waging a one-on-one campaign to put down the rebellion. Gingrich was aided by the heavy hitters of the House GOP: Majority Leader Dick Armey and Whip Tom DeLay, both of Texas; Conference Chairman John A. Boehner of Ohio; National Republican Congressional Committee Chairman John Linder, a homestate ally from Georgia; and Bill Paxon of New York, the chairman of the Speaker's planning group.

The uncertainty lasted right up to the day of the vote. When the time came, five Republicans voted "present" rather than back Gingrich, and four more voted for other, undeclared candidates of their choosing. Two voted for Jim Leach, R-Iowa; one for former House Minority Leader Robert H. Michel, R-Ill. (1957-95); and one for former Rep. Robert S. Walker, R-Pa. (1977-97).

Gingrich only narrowly prevailed with 216 votes to 205 votes for Gephardt, who, as expected, captured all of the Democratic votes: R 216-0; D 0-204 (ND 0-150, SD 0-54); I 0-1. *(House key vote 1, p. C-48; Gingrich, p. 1-11)*

2. Reprimand of Speaker

House Republicans hit a low point of their fledgling majority Jan. 21, when they cast an historic vote to punish Speaker Newt Gingrich, R-Ga., for rules violations. The overwhelming vote marked the first time a sitting Speaker had been sanctioned formally .

Gingrich was reprimanded for bringing discredit on the House with his ethical misconduct. He was also fined $300,000 for the costs to the House of sorting out his misleading statements to the ethics committee. The vote was 395-28, with five members voting present: R 196-26; D 198-2 (ND 147-0, SD 51-2); I 1-0. *(House key vote 2, p. C-48; Gingrich, p. 1-11)*

In a kind of plea bargain with the Committee on Standards of Official Conduct, the formal name of the ethics committee, Gingrich escaped the most serious charge — that he knowingly used charitable foundations to finance his political activities in the early 1990s, when he was plotting the Republican takeover of Congress. But he admitted that he failed to seek proper legal advice in using the tax-exempt groups for political ends.

In what turned out to be a more damaging admission, the Speaker also acknowledged misleading the committee during its probe, though he blamed his lawyer for submitting conflicting and false statements to investigators.

The Speaker's admissions, coming after two years of consistent denials of wrongdoing, caused chaos in Republican ranks. Many were stunned when the ethics committee, including its GOP members, recommended a harsh penalty and an unprecedented $300,000 fine. Some who had been lobbied hard to cast votes for Gingrich for Speaker felt hoodwinked when they saw the report by the panel and its special counsel, James M. Cole.

Although Republicans did not relish reprimanding their Speaker, which had the potential to reflect poorly on the party as a whole, most felt they could not contest the findings of the independent counsel and the bipartisan ethics committee. Only 26 Republicans voted against the sanctions.

Many of those who did vote "no" said they either did not want to set a precedent for fining members such extraordinary amounts or that they believed that the fine was simply too harsh a penalty. Two Southern Democrats also voted "no": Gene Taylor of Mississippi and Earl F. Hilliard of Alabama.

The ethics embarrassment reverberated throughout the year, and it was one of the events that presaged a midsummer attempt by a group of disgruntled Republicans along with some of Gingrich's allies to oust the Speaker.

Gingrich, once considered one of the country's most influential politicians, was, after the vote, a greatly diminished figure, no longer able to dictate the national agenda. At the same time, President Clinton, fresh from winning re-election, was making a political comeback. In the months following the vote, the talk was no longer of whether the president was "relevant," but of whether the House Speaker was.

3. Abortion Procedure Ban

Opponents of a second- and third-trimester abortion procedure found support from an unlikely source in their battle to enact legislation banning the practice.

Ron Fitzsimmons, executive director of the National Coalition of Abortion Providers, admitted in interviews that the procedure opponents called "partial-birth" abortion was performed more frequently than he had acknowledged in 1996, when Congress passed and President Clinton vetoed a similar measure. A significant part of abortion-rights advocates' defense of the procedure had rested on the assumption that it was rarely done. *(1996 Almanac, p. 6-43)*

The revelation gave abortion foes renewed zeal in their bid to enact HR 1122, which called for fines and up to two years in jail for physicians who performed such abortions.

Attempts by abortion-rights supporters to broaden the legislation to allow an exception to protect a woman's health were rejected. Under the bill, the procedure would be allowed only if needed to save the woman's life.

The final vote brought little surprise, with the chamber overwhelmingly supporting the ban by more than the two-thirds majority needed to override a presidential veto. The vote on passage was 295-136: R 218-8; D 77-127 (ND 51-99, SD 26-28); I 0-1. *(House key vote 3, p. C-48; abortion procedure ban, p. 6-12)*

Three members, apparently persuaded by the Fitzsimmons revelation, switched their votes from "no" in 1996 to "yes" in 1997. They were: Christopher Shays, R-Conn.; Rodney Frelinghuysen, R-N.J.; and Sue W. Kelly, R-N.Y. Peter J. Visclosky, D-Ind., also changed his vote to "yes," but he had changed his mind earlier, voting Sept. 19, 1996, to override Clinton's veto. Martin Frost, D-Texas, switched his vote to oppose the bill.

4. Endangered Species Act

After taking a licking on environmental issues in the 104th Congress, Western Republicans in the House pledged in the 105th to keep their bills narrowly focused and easy to explain. Gone from their must-do list were comprehensive bills to rewrite the 1973 Endangered Species Act, overhaul federal grazing policy or push a major rewrite of federal regulations.

The new incrementalism embraced by the Westerners got its first big test in early May on a bill (HR 478) to waive the Endangered Species Act for flood-control projects. Westerners wagered that they would win by portraying their bill as a targeted attempt to protect people from rising flood waters.

They tried to gain support by casting the bill as a choice between protecting people or safeguarding bugs and rodents under the species law. But the strategy did not pay off. The House on May 7 approved a narrowing amendment that altered the bill so much that supporters of HR 478 opted to pull it from the floor.

The vote on the amendment, offered by Sherwood Boehlert, R-N.Y., was 227-196: R 54-169; D 172-27 (ND 137-9, SD 35-18); I 1-0. *(House key vote 4, p. C-48; endangered species act, p. 4-7)*

Aftershocks from the vote reverberated for months. It worsened relations between many Westerners and Boehlert, a moderate who often allied himself with environmental groups. Westerners charged that Boehlert and many of the moderate Eastern House Republicans had sold them out on an issue of great importance to their constituents, and they vowed to seek payback. They also were displeased with the GOP leadership, which did little to bolster the prospects for the flood-control bill.

Determined to play hardball and demand leadership support, Westerners were ready by the fall to push through the House bills revising federal grazing policy, property rights and other statutes affecting Western lands.

This time, they got leadership backing. On a bill (HR 2493) to alter federal grazing policy, House Speaker Newt Gingrich, R-Ga., got actively involved to broker a compromise.

Typical of how transformational the May vote on the flood-control bill was for many Westerners was the reaction of George P. Radanovich, R-Calif., who said he became much more active on Western issues because of the defeat of the bill. "Our approach to this problem is going to be both a carrot and a stick," he said in October of Eastern Republican defections. "The stick may be we're just not going to be there for them on issues of importance."

5. Housing Overhaul

After failing to forge a consensus with the Senate in 1996 to overhaul the public housing system, House Republicans hoped to get an early start on a nearly identical plan in 1997. In late April, they resurrected legislation (HR 2) that proposed sweeping changes in the nation's public and subsidized housing laws. The bill aimed to give local authorities more leeway over eligibility and rents, and to generate a steadier cash flow for housing projects.

The House floor action on the measure recalled the debate on welfare overhaul legislation (PL 104-193) in the 104th Congress: Many members from both parties agreed that the system in question was broken, but they differed over how far to go to fix it. *(1996 Almanac, p. 6-3)*

The housing measure, like the welfare bill, proposed changing decades of social policy, sending block grants and authority for public and subsidized housing to local boards. To GOP leaders, it represented the next step in their plans to remake the nation's social programs, and they showed the priority they placed on the legislation by making it the second House bill introduced in the 105th Congress.

The bill included repeal of the 1937 law that set up the public housing system, and liberal Democrats feared that and other proposed changes would cut the social safety net for the nation's poorest people.

Unlike the tightly controlled consideration of the welfare measure, however, leaders allowed nearly unlimited debate on the housing bill, to explore it fully and to fill up what had been a sparse floor schedule. By issuing an "open rule" for floor consideration, the Rules Committee enabled any member to offer a germane amendment. Debate spanned seven days over three weeks.

The most vociferous arguments centered on a provision that would open public housing to the working poor. Democrats charged that Republicans were seeking to throw out the poorest tenants to make way for those who could afford to pay more. "It will fix public housing all right," said Joseph P. Kennedy II, D-Mass., ranking member on the Housing Subcommittee of the Banking and Financial Services Committee. "It fixes this problem by simply eliminating the poor from eligibility for this program."

But Republicans said that change, along with others, was needed to diversify public housing's clientele and to ensure that local authorities had the flexibility to make public housing a good place to live. "Single-dimension, lowest-income housing simply has not worked," said bill sponsor Rick A. Lazio, R-N.Y., chairman of the Housing Subcommittee.

Liberal Democrats also strongly objected to a provision to require able-bodied, unemployed tenants to perform eight hours of community service a month in exchange for their apartments. They said it was unfair because other recipients of federal aid were not required to perform similar service. Republicans said it was a small price to pay for housing.

Despite the vocal objections from liberals, however, more than a third of the House Democrats joined all but one Republican in voting for the bill May 14. These Democrats were mostly white conservatives and moderates from the South, the West and rural areas, who believed that more local flexibility might improve housing programs. The final tally was 293-132: R 222-1; D 71-130 (ND 43-104, SD 28-26); I 0-1. *(House key vote 5, p. C-48; housing overhaul, p. 7-12)*

6. Highway Funding

On its face, the amendment to the fiscal 1998 budget resolution (H Con Res 84) did not seem so telling. Offered by House Transportation and Infrastructure Committee Chairman Bud Shuster, R-Pa., it proposed to increase transportation spending under the just-completed balanced-budget deal by $12 billion over five years. Shuster proposed to offset fully the increase with a 0.39 percent across-the-board reduction in other discretionary accounts, coupled with a comparable scaling back of proposed tax cuts.

In fact, however, the vote taken in the early morning hours of May 21 was a struggle between the high-minded ideals of the Republican leadership and the emergent primal desires for money of an elected body politic. By the time it was over,

Shuster had lost, but his two-vote margin of defeat was a watershed in the still-brief history of Republican control of Congress: It was once again safe to spend money. Those desires would have to be placated.

Shuster and his sprawling committee had groused for weeks that the balanced-budget deal did not allow adequate funding for the nation's highways, roads, bridges and transit systems. While GOP leaders hailed the era of balanced budgets and fiscal restraint, Shuster was firing off an intemperate memo declaring, "The numbers . . . are UNACCEPTABLE." *(Budget resolution, p. 2-23; highway bill, p. 3-18)*

Under pressure, congressional budget writers agreed during the week of May 12 to provide an additional $1 billion for transportation, raising highway spending levels under the budget deal to about $22 billion by 2002, compared with the 1997 level of $20 billion. But that still was nowhere near the $32 billion Shuster was demanding.

Shuster's showdown with the leadership put the GOP rank and file in a difficult position. About 400 members had already come to the powerful chairman to request tens of billions of dollars for district projects. Even if, as Shuster insisted, there were no overt threats that requests would be denied if they failed to support the amendment, members perceived a threat.

At the same time, GOP leaders said Shuster's amendment would upset the delicate balance reached in the May budget deal, skew funding away from Republican priorities, and possibly bring down what many Republicans had come to Washington to produce: a balanced budget. The amendment would have reduced defense spending over five years by $6 billion, domestic programs by $5 billion and the proposed tax cut by about $1 billion.

Belatedly realizing the amendment's appeal, House Speaker Newt Gingrich, R-Ga., and the Clinton administration launched a frantic counteroffensive May 20, warning that Shuster's plan could open the floodgates for every chairman to request more money. The leadership called a closed-door conference at 10 p.m., at which Gingrich and Budget Committee Chairman John R. Kasich, R-Ohio, urged members to stand by the budget accord.

"Until he gets the entire federal budget spent on concrete and blacktop, I'm sure he won't be happy," House Republican Conference Chairman John A. Boehner of Ohio said of Shuster.

The late-night effort succeeded — barely. During the tense 3 a.m. vote, which seesawed back and forth, Gingrich fanned out to marshal support. The leadership held the vote open as they twisted just enough arms to defeat Shuster. The final vote was 214-216: R 58-168; D 155-48 (ND 118-32, SD 37-16); I 1-0. *(House key vote 6, p. C-48)*

7. Budget Resolution

After the standoffs that led to government shutdowns in 1995-1996, it was difficult to imagine congressional Republicans and President Clinton agreeing on a split-their-differences budget. But as compromises went, the 1997 budget deal proved relatively palatable to the overwhelming majority of the House.

A thriving economy that filled Treasury coffers with unexpected revenues made the task much easier and certainly more rewarding. The federal deficit could be eliminated even while taxes were being cut and spending boosted in certain areas. The result: A balanced budget that was seemingly pain free.

Also providing motivation to both sides was the 1996 election, which returned the incumbent president to office while retaining congressional control by the opposition party. It was seen as a clear mandate to work together.

Adoption of the budget resolution (H Con Res 84) was the first of many important junctures as Congress and the White House fleshed out the framework of the May 2 agreement. Later would come passage of the twin tax and spending cut bills (PL 105-34, PL 105-33) that traded long-term cuts in programs such as Medicare for GOP-inspired tax cuts and new spending for several Clinton priorities.

Despite having to compromise with the enemy, most Republicans embraced the deal, which met at least two of the chief criteria of the vetoed 1995 Republican budget: balance by 2002 and a sizable net tax cut, though only one-third the size of their earlier budget.

The budget resolution also had sweeping support among Democrats, though liberals and House Democratic Leader Richard A. Gephardt of Missouri attacked the deal as favoring the wealthy with tax cuts while cutting programs aimed at helping low-income families and the working poor. Gephardt's opposition was interpreted by many as an initial volley in a likely 2000 challenge to Vice President Al Gore for the Democratic presidential nomination.

For most Democrats, though, the prospect of voting for a balanced budget was too appealing to give up. Indeed, prevailing sentiment among both Republicans and Democrats was to embrace the budget as the best either side could get in a time of divided government. Also contributing to the big vote on final passage was the fact that the resolution served as a blueprint and did not contain the actual policy changes that would come later.

The House adopted the resolution by a vote of 333-99: R 201-26; D 132-72 (ND 90-60, SD 42-12); I 0-1. *(House key vote 7, p. C-48; budget resolution, p. 2-23)*

8. Bosnia Deadline

The House in June narrowly rejected a proposal to force the withdrawal of U.S. troops from Bosnia by the end of 1997. The vote highlighted both congressional opposition to the deployment and the difficulty critics faced in trying to overcome President Clinton's determination to see the Bosnia mission through.

The House had opposed sending U.S. forces to Bosnia ever since late 1995 when Clinton promised up to 20,000 troops to help enforce a peace agreement ending that country's brutal civil war. Even before the start of the November 1995 negotiations in Dayton, Ohio, that ultimately produced the agreement, the House adopted, by a 3-1 margin, a nonbinding resolution repudiating Clinton's troop pledge. *(1995 Almanac, p. 10-10)*

Once the Dayton agreement was signed, efforts in the Senate to block deployment of U.S. troops collapsed. Clinton had committed the country's credibility to the deal, which was to be guaranteed for one year by a NATO-led force of 60,000 troops, including the Americans. Even then, however, the House came within a few votes of passing a bill that would have denied funds for the mission.

On Nov. 15, 1996, a week after he was re-elected, Clinton announced that a smaller U.S. force would remain in Bosnia through June 1998 — 18 months after the Dec. 31, 1996, deadline he had promised a year earlier.

The first congressional challenge to this policy change came in June 1997, when the House took up the annual defense authorization bill.

Critics argued that the combat readiness of U.S. forces was being sapped to pay for the Bosnia operation, which was estimated to cost $7.3 billion through the end of fiscal 1997. Some opponents argued that the task of the peacekeeping force was hopeless, since there was no chance of re-creating the multiethnic Bosnian state envisaged by the Dayton agreement. Others argued for withdrawal of U.S. forces as a way to force European governments to shoulder the burden of keeping the peace with U.S. communications and intelligence support.

The Clinton administration, backed by many House Democrats, warned that a U.S. pullout from Bosnia would undermine the tenuous peace that had been established, since the other major participants in the peacekeeping force had made it clear their forces would leave if the Americans did.

In an effort to finesse that argument, Steve Buyer, R-Ind., offered an amendment to the fiscal 1998 defense authorization bill (HR 1119) requiring a pullout by June 30, 1998. Although that was the date Clinton himself had set for the end of the deployment, it was widely believed that the administration would break that deadline, just as it had broken its first one.

Van Hilleary, R-Tenn., and other Clinton opponents wanted a chance to go further, repudiating Clinton's policy outright. On June 24, Hilleary offered an amendment to force withdrawal of the troops by Dec. 31, 1997. It was rejected by a vote of 196-231: R 174-49; D 21-182 (ND 15-133; SD 6-49), I 1-0. *(House key vote 8, p. C-50; defense authorization, p. 8-3)*

The House subsequently adopted Buyer's provision, 278-148. A similar provision was included in the companion defense appropriations bill for fiscal 1998 (HR 2266).

The administration threatened to veto both the authorization and appropriations bills if they included a June 1998 deadline. Ultimately, both bills were enacted with provisions stipulating that Clinton could keep forces in Bosnia beyond the deadline if he first reported to Congress on the strategic rationale for his decision, along with estimates of the size, duration, cost, mission and exit strategy of the extended deployment.

9. Arts Funding

Conservative House Republicans had leaned hard on the GOP leadership to eliminate funding for the National Endowment for the Arts (NEA). The leadership complied, and the version of the $13 billion fiscal 1998 Interior appropriations bill (HR 2107) that was sent to the House floor included zero funding for the agency.

By all accounts, the one vote that would decide the fate of the NEA in the House was not on passage of the bill itself, or even on an individual amendment, but the much-anticipated vote on the rules that would govern the floor debate.

NEA supporters argued that the endowment provided crucial seed money to struggling arts organizations. The opposition said the federal government had no role to play in arts funding, and complained that the NEA funded lewd, pornographic and objectionable art.

A nearly unified Democratic Party and a band of Republicans, most of them Northeastern moderates, wanted the Republican leadership to allow an up-or-down vote on the agency. The leadership refused, choosing instead to live up to its 1995 promise to the conservatives to eliminate the agency in fiscal 1998.

So not only did the Interior bill include no funding for the agency, but the rule for debate did not allow an amendment on the issue. Supporters of the NEA said that the leadership realized it did not have the votes to sustain the zero funding position and had stacked the procedural deck against them. House Majority Whip Tom DeLay, R-Texas, made no secret of the fact that he considered the vote a crucial test of loyalty, and he lobbied hard to get the troops to support the rule.

In the days leading up to the vote, DeLay stepped up the arm-twisting. The outcome remained in doubt until the very end, and was decided by a single "yea" vote, cast by John M. McHugh, R-N.Y., in the closing minutes and only after the urgent pleas of the leadership.

Just five Democrats voted for the rule, and 15 Republicans broke ranks to oppose it. The July 10 tally was 217-216: R 212-15; D 5-200 (ND 2-148, SD 3-52); I 0-1. *(House key vote 9, p. C-50; appropriations, p. 9-44)*

A number of NEA supporters came to the leadership's side. Sherwood Boehlert, R-N.Y., supported funding for the agency but said he voted for the rule "for the leadership." Boehlert and other NEA supporters figured they could show their loyalty to the leadership and still win on NEA, since the Senate appeared likely to restore funding. In fact, the final bill included $98 million for the agency, just below the level included in the Senate version of the bill.

10. International Family Planning

Desperate for a compromise that would head off another protracted dispute over abortion and foreign aid programs, House Democrats and moderate Republicans proposed allowing overseas family planning groups to remain eligible for U.S. funds under some conditions, even if they performed abortions.

But their bipartisan amendment to the fiscal 1998 foreign operations spending bill (HR 2159) faltered in the face of continued support for a ban on aid to international family planning groups that used even their own money to subsidize abortions. The outcome assured a drawn-out fight with the Senate and the Clinton administration over the appropriations bill.

In his first week on the job in January 1993, President Clinton had rescinded the longstanding GOP policy barring funds for international groups that practiced or advocated abortion. It was one of several actions that Clinton, a supporter of abortion rights, took to reverse rules created during the Reagan and Bush eras. *(1993 Almanac, p. 348)*

Several Republicans in Congress sought to overturn Clinton's move legislatively, by attaching restrictive abortion provisions to must-pass spending bills. With the GOP takeover of the House in 1994, Christopher H. Smith, R-N.J., succeeded in attaching an amendment reinstituting the prohibition on family planning funds to the House version of the foreign operations spending bill.

In the final hours of each congressional session since then, House, Senate and State Department negotiators had been forced to come up with a compromise acceptable to the Senate, whose legislation did not include the restrictions, and the White House, which threatened a veto if the language was included.

The compromise on family planning in the fiscal 1997 version of the foreign operations bill permitted distribution of U.S. aid to international groups on July 1, 1998. Earlier distribution on March 1, 1998, was permitted, but only if both chambers passed a resolution by Feb. 28, 1998, agreeing to the early payment. Democratic leaders and the State Department won that battle by portraying the vote as an effort to promote family planning, not abortion, and warning that without the funds, family planning in Third World countries would be devastated. *(Family planning, p. 9-40)*

But Smith was not deterred. During the summer, he vexed

negotiators on a separate, fiscal 1998-99 State Department authorization bill (HR 1757) by attaching a version of the family planning amendment. *(State Department authorization, p. 8-32)*

In September, he turned his attention to the fiscal 1998 foreign operations spending bill.

The first hurdle was securing enough votes to defeat a bipartisan substitute offered by Nancy Pelosi, D-Calif.; Benjamin A. Gilman, R-N.Y.; and James C. Greenwood, R-Pa. The House Rules Committee tried to block their efforts, refusing to allow any substitute amendment to Smith's. Democratic women retaliated, delaying House action on unrelated legislation by requiring a string of roll call votes and forcing the Rules Committee to relent and permit the substitute measure to be offered.

The bipartisan amendment would have allowed U.S. aid to continue to go to organizations that did not promote abortion as a method of family planning. If those groups did provide abortions, they would have had to pay for those procedures from their own funds.

Smith criticized the substitute as purposely vague and argued that only his proposal addressed the problems with the White House policy. Greenwood countered that adopting the Smith amendment would lead to an intractable controversy and delay adjournment yet again.

The House rejected the Pelosi-Gilman-Greenwood substitute on Sept. 4 by a narrow margin, 210-218: R 38-185; D 171-33 (ND 125-26, SD 46-7); I 1-0. The House then easily adopted Smith's amendment banning the funds. *(House key vote 10, p. C-50; appropriations, p. 9-37)*

(Months later, in the final days of the session, House and Senate leaders and the administration produced a compromise that pleased neither side. Family planning groups received the same amount for fiscal 1998 as they had in fiscal 1997 — $385 million — but with no restrictions.)

11. Congressional Pay Raise

More than most bills, a pay raise for members of Congress required creative legislating. GOP House leaders proved their mettle by finessing a 2.3 percent pay increase through to passage, with thankful rank-and-file lawmakers suffering only a brief drubbing by hometown editorial writers.

The way they did it provided a how-to guide for congressional leaders in years to come.

Under a 1989 law, members of Congress were entitled to an automatic cost of living adjustment (COLA), which was intended to take the politics out of annual pay-raise debates. But each year since fiscal 1993, someone had introduced an amendment blocking the raise. The amendments were usually offered on the annual appropriations bill for the Treasury Department, Postal Service and other government operations. The amendment always passed, with lawmakers fearful of the political repercussions of voting against it.

This time, however, House leaders outwitted the perennial pay raise opponents. First, they brought the Treasury funding bill (HR 2378) to the floor Sept. 17 without warning and without sending it through the Rules Committee, where opponents typically introduced their amendment. Blindsided, the opposition had too little time to organize an effort on the floor, and the bill passed 231-192.

But the key vote came a week later.

Now organized and fully aware that the leaders were angling to allow the raise to go through, opponents led by Linda Smith, R-Wash., insisted on an up-or-down vote on the issue. The leadership at first balked, but then capitulated — sort of.

The leaders agreed to hold a roll call vote on a procedural motion on the Treasury funding bill as the House prepared to send it to conference, where differing House and Senate versions of the bill had yet to be resolved.

If the highly technical motion, called "ordering the previous question," passed, Smith under House rules would be barred from amending the bill with a COLA block. But if it failed, she could offer her amendment.

The motion prevailed, 229-199: R 114-110; D 115-88 (ND 88-62; SD 27-26); I 0-1. And Smith was unable to offer her amendment. *(House key vote 11, p. C-50; appropriations, p. 9-71; congressional pay raise, p. 1-30)*

The leaders in effect had given lawmakers a way to vote themselves a pay raise without appearing to do so. Those who voted for the motion could claim they were simply voting on a technical motion dealing with instructions to conferees, not a pay raise. The vote offered members crucial cover, a plausible way of obscuring their actual position on the issue.

The House vote was an important internal political victory for Speaker Newt Gingrich, R-Ga., and his leadership team. Mindful of their obligations to the rank-and-file members who elected them, they had managed to give lawmakers something they wanted with a minimal amount of political pain.

With the way paved for it by the House, the Senate on Oct. 1 followed suit by approving the conference report on the Treasury bill without a ban on the pay raise. The raise boosted lawmakers' $133,600 annual salary to $136,700. Action on the raise was followed by a spate of negative news stories and condemnations from newspaper editorial boards. Some of the sharpest criticism was of the purposefully cunning way House leaders handled the matter, and of the absence of a clear up-or-down vote. But the uproar was short-lived.

12. Private Property Rights

The nation's home builders got plenty of respect on Capitol Hill, but they had seldom flexed their lobbying clout. In 1997, they sought to change all that and focused intently on making a splash with legislation to provide new rights to property owners.

Republicans had long favored such legislation, and the House GOP had included a bill to expand the rights of private property owners in its list of priorities for the 104th Congress. But their earlier effort fell short, attacked by a coalition of Democrats, environmentalists and some local elected officials, as well as moderate Republicans, as an attempt gut key environmental laws. *(1996 Almanac, p. 3-3)*

The bills that failed in the 104th Congress, including one sponsored by then-Senate Majority Leader Bob Dole, R-Kan., were aimed at compensating owners for government actions that diminished property values.

Sponsors argued that federal regulators were imposing money-losing restrictions on property owners but offering no compensation. They said this flouted the Fifth Amendment, which barred the government from "taking" property without just compensation.

But environmentalists prevailed using the counterargument that requiring greater compensation would tie agencies in knots. Fiscal conservatives were concerned that the federal Treasury would be drained in the process.

In 1997, the 190,000-member National Association of Home Builders and their congressional allies decided on a different tack. They abandoned the compensation approach, focusing instead on a plan (HR 1534) to give property owners more power to get their proposals addressed by local zoning boards.

Republicans put the bill on the fast track in the fall, and it sailed easily through the House. The Oct. 22 vote was 248-178: R 193-30; D 55-147 (ND 25-124, SD 30-23); I 0-1. *(House key vote 12, p. C-50; property rights, p. 3-9)*

The final outcome was largely the result of a high-profile lobbying campaign by the home builders, who mobilized support with a small army of lobbyists and some last-minute hardball from Western lawmakers.

They also benefited by selling the bill as a narrow procedural change. Under existing law, developers first had to exhaust appeals to planning agency decisions in state courts and be denied compensation before a federal court would hear a Fifth Amendment takings claim. The process could stretch on for years, forcing average homeowners and developers into legal limbo. To address the situation, HR 1534 offered property owners the option of taking their case directly to a federal court after filing at least two appeals to a planning board decision.

Still, many in the opposition said the home builders had used their influence to pressure members into supporting a bill that few of them understood. Opponents said the bill would shake up local zoning matters, giving developers broad new powers to get zoning changes for oversized discount stores and seedy adult bookstores. Environmental groups said they would highlight the vote during the 1998 midterm elections.

13. Private School Vouchers

The House rejected a key element of the Republican education agenda Nov. 4 by defeating a bill (HR 2746) that would have enabled low-income families to use federal money to send their children to private schools.

Republicans pushed the proposal at least partly to distinguish their views on education from Democrats. They framed it as a way to enhance parental choices, especially among low-income families who were unable to flee poor-performing inner city schools.

Republicans initially hoped to rally a broad coalition behind the bill, which called for the creation of so-called HELP (Helping Empower Low-Income Parents) scholarships. They touted support from Rep. Floyd H. Flake, D-N.Y., an African-American minister, plus the strong backing of Speaker Newt Gingrich, R-Ga., and Majority Leader Dick Armey, R-Texas.

The legislation, sponsored by Frank Riggs, R-Calif., proposed allowing states to use money from Title VI of the Elementary and Secondary Education Act to help low-income families send their children to private schools, including religious schools. Under existing law, states and local school districts used Title VI money — $310 million in fiscal 1997 — for various public school programs. Under the bill, they could reserve up to 25 percent of their Title VI funds for public and private school choice programs authorized by state law.

But there were limits to the bill's appeal. In fact, the leadership bypassed committee action on the bill, apparently out of concern that it lacked the votes for approval in the Education and the Workforce Committee.

Republicans tried to cast the issue as a matter of choice, saying that students from poor families ought to have access to the same education opportunities as those enjoyed by the well-to-do.

Democrats derided the legislation as an attempt to drain funds from public schools and said it would help relatively few low-income students. William L. Clay of Missouri, the Education committee's ranking Democrat, said the bill "sends a clear and chilling signal that the Republicans have declared war on public education." The administration warned that a veto was likely.

In the end, however, it was the opposition of 35 Republicans, many of them moderates, that caused the bill's defeat. One of them, Marge Roukema, R-N.J., said, "Ultimately, these vouchers will result in gutting the public school system" by shifting money from public schools to private schools. The vote was 191-228: R 187-35; D 4-192 (ND 2-140, SD 2-52); I 0-1. *(House key vote 13, p. C-50; private schooling, p. 7-6)*

14. Caribbean Trade

What sponsors viewed as a non-controversial offer of equity to 26 small and friendly nations in the Caribbean turned virtually overnight into a showdown over U.S. trade policy. The unexpected result: House defeat of a bill (HR 2644) aimed at expanding trade preferences for key products from those countries. The vote on Nov. 4 was 182-234: R 136-83; D 46-150 (ND 32-111, SD 14-39); I 0-1. *(House key vote 14, p. C-50, Caribbean trade, p. 2-88)*

Part of the opposition was the result of pent-up frustration over the mixed results of the 1993 North American Free Trade Agreement (NAFTA). Part of it was parochial concern on the part of members with industries in their districts that competed with plants in the Caribbean. But a major part of the opposition was an effort by Democrats to send a signal to President Clinton as he pressed his down-to-the-wire bid to win "fast-track" trade negotiating authority.

Supporters of the bill argued that the 26 nations — which had been given special status under President Ronald Reagan's 1983 economic-development program known as the Caribbean Basin Initiative (PL 98-67) — had suffered since the passage of NAFTA, because Mexican exports were given even greater benefits. *(CBI, 1983 Almanac, p. 252; NAFTA, 1993 Almanac, p. 171)*

The bill had been around since 1995, and the Ways and Means Committee had voted in June to make it a provision of the tax bill (HR 2014) that was moving as part of the budget reconciliation package. No controversy emerged until conference, when it was dropped at the insistence of the Senate because no committee in that chamber had considered it.

House Ways and Means Chairman Bill Archer, R-Texas, introduced the bill again Oct. 9, and it was approved by the committee by voice vote the same day.

Its supporters did not expect it to draw the sort of opposition it did when it reached the floor Nov. 4. Some opponents argued that imports from the Caribbean countries had grown, not shrunk, since the passage of NAFTA and outpaced imports from Mexico in many sectors. Others argued that the expanded Caribbean benefits did not have as many safeguards attached as NAFTA did.

But the strongest objections came from lawmakers representing states that were home to textile industries. The imports that would have become eligible for duty-free treatment included textiles as well as finished apparel, footwear, handbags and luggage. "HR 2644 will have a greater impact on the U.S. apparel industry and U.S. apparel workers than NAFTA ever had," warned John M. Spratt Jr., D-S.C.

15. IRS Overhaul

Even the most fervent supporters of overhauling the management of the Internal Revenue Service were shocked at how swiftly the latest attack in the anti-tax movement took hold. By the time the vote was called, the outcome was preordained. The political firestorm around the IRS and its alleged abuse of taxpayers had rolled over any opposition in its path.

Congressional efforts to revamp the IRS began in June in the driest, most conventional of ways, with a sober, 190-page report issued by a bipartisan commission chaired by Sen. Bob Kerrey, D-Neb., and Rep. Rob Portman, R-Ohio. But by Nov. 5, when the House voted on an IRS restructuring bill (HR 2676), the issue had exploded. *(IRS overhaul, p. 2-71)*

Senate Finance Committee hearings into alleged IRS abuses in September had struck a nerve nationwide. Indeed, pollsters were hearing that the IRS was one of the very few issues out of Congress that resonated with voters.

When it came time to vote on a broad package to restructure IRS management, provide new rights for taxpayers and curb additions to the tax code, virtually no one on Capitol Hill — not even independent Bernard Sanders of Vermont — wanted to be seen defending the tax collector. The tally was 426-4: R 225-0; D 200-4 (ND 146-4, SD 54-0); I 1-0. *(House key vote 15, p. C-50)*

The only "no" votes came from Democrat Steny H. Hoyer of Maryland, who had numerous federal employees in his suburban Washington district, and three Ways and Means Committee Democrats: Jim McDermott of Washington and Robert T. Matsui and Pete Stark, both of California.

The administration and key House Democrats had initially opposed legislation unveiled by Kerrey and Portman to implement their commission's recommendations. They said the bills would give the private sector too much influence over the tax code, open the IRS to conflicts of interest and compromise the executive branch's authority on tax policy.

Ways and Means Committee Chairman Bill Archer, R-Texas, later added a provision shifting the burden of proof for malfeasance from the taxpayer to the IRS in tax court proceedings, a move decried by some accountants as an invitation for tax cheating and a prescription for a more intrusive IRS.

But voter sentiment was clearly against the Democrats. By the time the revised IRS bill reached the Ways and Means Committee, ranking Democrat Charles B. Rangel of New York and Minority Leader Richard A. Gephardt, D-Mo., had signed on. In an extraordinary bit of political theater, Treasury Secretary Robert E. Rubin was dispatched Oct. 21 to Capitol Hill to renounce his once-vociferous opposition, explain that he had won significant changes to the bill and declare his support. ■

SENATE KEY VOTES 1, 2, 3, 4, 5, 6

	1	2	3	4	5	6
ALABAMA						
Sessions	Y	Y	N	Y	Y	Y
Shelby	Y	Y	N	Y	Y	Y
ALASKA						
Murkowski	Y	Y	Y	Y	Y	Y
Stevens	Y	Y	Y	Y	Y	Y
ARIZONA						
Kyl	Y	Y	N	Y	Y	N
McCain	Y	Y	Y	Y	Y	Y
ARKANSAS						
Hutchinson	Y	Y	N	Y	Y	Y
Bumpers	N	N	Y	N	N	N
CALIFORNIA						
Boxer	N	N	Y	N	N	Y
Feinstein	N	N	Y	N	N	Y
COLORADO						
Allard	Y	Y	N	Y	Y	N
Campbell	Y	N	N	Y	Y	Y
CONNECTICUT						
Dodd	N	N	Y	N	N	Y
Lieberman	N	N	Y	N	N	Y
DELAWARE						
Roth	Y	Y	Y	Y	Y	Y
Biden	Y	N	Y	N	Y	Y
FLORIDA						
Mack	Y	Y	N	Y	Y	Y
Graham	Y	Y	Y	N	N	Y
GEORGIA						
Coverdell	Y	Y	N	Y	Y	Y
Cleland	Y	Y	Y	N	N	Y
HAWAII						
Akaka	N	N	Y	N	N	Y
Inouye	N	N	Y	N	N	Y
IDAHO						
Craig	Y	Y	N	Y	Y	Y
Kempthorne	Y	Y	N	Y	Y	Y
ILLINOIS						
Durbin	N	N	Y	N	N	Y
Moseley-Braun	Y	Y	Y	N	N	Y
INDIANA						
Coats	Y	N	Y	Y	Y	N
Lugar	Y	Y	Y	Y	Y	Y
IOWA						
Grassley	Y	Y	N	Y	Y	Y
Harkin	Y	Y	Y	N	N	Y
KANSAS						
Brownback	Y	Y	N	Y	Y	Y
Roberts	Y	Y	Y	Y	Y	Y
KENTUCKY						
McConnell	Y	Y	Y	Y	Y	Y
Ford	N	N	Y	N	Y	Y
LOUISIANA						
Breaux	Y	N	Y	N	Y	Y
Landrieu	Y	N	Y	N	Y	Y
MAINE						
Collins	Y	Y	Y	Y	N	Y
Snowe	Y	Y	Y	Y	N	Y
MARYLAND						
Mikulski	N	N	Y	N	N	Y
Sarbanes	N	N	Y	N	N	N
MASSACHUSETTS						
Kennedy	N	N	Y	N	N	N
Kerry	N	N	Y	N	N	N
MICHIGAN						
Abraham	Y	Y	Y	Y	Y	Y
Levin	N	Y	Y	N	N	Y
MINNESOTA						
Grams	Y	Y	N	Y	Y	N
Wellstone	N	N	Y	N	N	N
MISSISSIPPI						
Cochran	Y	Y	Y	Y	Y	Y
Lott	Y	Y	Y	Y	Y	Y
MISSOURI						
Ashcroft	Y	Y	N	Y	Y	N
Bond	Y	Y	N	Y	Y	Y
MONTANA						
Burns	Y	Y	N	Y	Y	Y
Baucus	Y	N	Y	N	N	Y
NEBRASKA						
Hagel	Y	Y	Y	Y	Y	Y
Kerrey	N	N	Y	N	N	Y
NEVADA						
Bryan	Y	N	Y	N	N	Y
Reid	N	N	Y	N	Y	Y
NEW HAMPSHIRE						
Gregg	Y	Y	Y	Y	Y	Y
Smith	Y	Y	N	Y	Y	N
NEW JERSEY						
Lautenberg	N	N	Y	N	N	Y
Torricelli	N	N	Y	N	N	Y
NEW MEXICO						
Domenici	Y	Y	Y	Y	Y	Y
Bingaman	N	N	Y	N	N	Y
NEW YORK						
D'Amato	Y	Y	Y	N	Y	Y
Moynihan	N	N	Y	N	Y	N
NORTH CAROLINA						
Faircloth	Y	Y	N	Y	Y	N
Helms	Y	Y	N	Y	Y	N
NORTH DAKOTA						
Conrad	N	N	Y	N	Y	Y
Dorgan	N	N	Y	N	Y	Y
OHIO						
DeWine	Y	Y	Y	Y	Y	Y
Glenn	N	N	Y	N	N	Y
OKLAHOMA						
Inhofe	Y	Y	N	Y	Y	N
Nickles	Y	Y	N	Y	Y	Y
OREGON						
Smith	Y	Y	Y	Y	Y	Y
Wyden	N	Y	Y	N	N	Y
PENNSYLVANIA						
Santorum	Y	Y	Y	Y	Y	Y
Specter	Y	Y	Y	N	Y	N
RHODE ISLAND						
Chafee	Y	Y	Y	Y	N	Y
Reed	N	N	Y	N	N	N
SOUTH CAROLINA						
Thurmond	Y	Y	N	Y	Y	Y
Hollings	N	Y	Y	N	Y	N
SOUTH DAKOTA						
Daschle	N	N	Y	N	Y	Y
Johnson	N	Y	Y	N	Y	Y
TENNESSEE						
Frist	Y	Y	Y	Y	Y	Y
Thompson	Y	Y	N	Y	Y	N
TEXAS						
Gramm	Y	Y	N	Y	Y	N
Hutchison	Y	Y	N	Y	Y	Y
UTAH						
Bennett	Y	Y	N	Y	Y	Y
Hatch	Y	Y	Y	Y	Y	Y
VERMONT						
Jeffords	Y	Y	Y	Y	N	Y
Leahy	N	Y	Y	N	Y	Y
VIRGINIA						
Warner	Y	Y	Y	Y	Y	Y
Robb	Y	Y	Y	N	N	Y
WASHINGTON						
Gorton	Y	Y	Y	Y	Y	Y
Murray	N	Y	Y	N	N	Y
WEST VIRGINIA						
Byrd	N	N	Y	N	Y	Y
Rockefeller	N	?	Y	N	N	Y
WISCONSIN						
Feingold	N	N	Y	N	N	Y
Kohl	Y	Y	Y	N	N	Y
WYOMING						
Enzi	Y	Y	Y	Y	Y	N
Thomas	Y	Y	Y	Y	Y	N

ND Northern Democrats SD Southern Democrats

Southern states - Ala., Ark., Fla., Ga., Ky., La., Miss., N.C., Okla., S.C., Tenn., Texas, Va.

KEY

- Y Voted for (yea).
- # Paired for.
- \+ Announced for.
- N Voted against (nay).
- X Paired against.
- – Announced against.
- P Voted "present."
- C Voted "present" to avoid possible conflict of interest.
- ? Did not vote or otherwise make a position known.

Democrats *Republicans*

Following are Senate votes from 1997 selected by Congressional Quarterly as key votes. Original vote number in parentheses.

1. S J Res 1. Balanced-Budget Constitutional Amendment/Passage. Passage of the joint resolution to propose a constitutional amendment to balance the budget by the year 2002 or two years after ratification by three-fourths of the states, whichever is later. Rejected 66-34: R 55-0; D 11-34 (ND 6-31, SD 5-3), March 4, 1997. A two-thirds majority vote of those present and voting (67 in this case) is required to pass a joint resolution proposing an amendment to the Constitution. A "nay" was a vote in support of the president's position. *(Senate vote 24)*

2. S 104. Interim Nuclear Waste Repository/Passage. Passage of the bill to establish an interim high-level nuclear waste repository at Yucca Mountain, Nevada. The bill gives the president until March 1, 1999, to halt construction at the temporary waste site if it is deemed unsuitable as a permanent repository. The president would then have 18 months to choose an alternate site, which Congress would have two years to approve. If an alternate is not agreed upon, construction would automatically begin at the Nevada site. Passed 65-34: R 53-2; D 12-32 (ND 8-28, SD 4-4), April 15, 1997. A "nay" was a vote in support of the president's position. *(Senate vote 42)*

3. S Res 75. Chemical Weapons Treaty/Adoption. Adoption of the resolution of ratification of the treaty to prohibit development, production, acquisition, stockpiling, transfer or use of chemical weapons. Adopted 74-26: R 29-26; D 45-0 (ND 37-0, SD 8-0), April 24, 1997. A two-thirds majority of those present and voting (67 in this case) is required for adoption of resolutions of ratification. A "yea" was a vote in support of the president's position. *(Senate vote 51)*

4. S 4. Compensatory Time, Flexible Credit/Cloture. Motion to invoke cloture (thus limiting debate) on the bill to amend the 1938 Fair Labor Standards Act to allow private-sector employees to choose compensatory time off or flexible hour programs instead of overtime pay. Motion rejected 53-47: R 53-2; D 0-45 (ND 0-37, SD 0-8), May 15, 1997. Three-fifths of the total Senate (60) is required to invoke cloture. *(Senate vote 68)*

5. HR 1122. Abortion Procedure Ban/Passage. Passage of the bill to impose penalties on doctors who perform certain abortion procedures, in which the person performing the abortion partially delivers the fetus before completing the abortion. An exception would be granted if the procedure was necessary to save the life of the woman. The bill was amended to clarify the definition of the procedure and to allow an accused doctor a hearing before a state medical board before trial. Passed 64-36: R 51-4; D 13-32 (ND 9-28, SD 4-4), May 20, 1997. A "nay" was a vote in support of the president's position. *(Senate vote 71)*

6. H Con Res 84. Fiscal 1998 Budget Resolution/Adoption. Adoption of the concurrent resolution to adopt a five-year budget plan that would balance the budget by 2002 by cutting projected spending by approximately $320 billion and cutting taxes by a net $85 billion. Projected spending cuts would include reductions of $115 billion in Medicare, $13.6 billion in Medicaid and $138 billion in discretionary spending. The resolution sets binding levels for the fiscal year ending Sept. 30, 1998: budget authority, $1,702.0 billion; outlays, $1,692.3 billion; revenues, $1,601.8 billion; deficit, $90.5 billion. Adopted 78-22: R 41-14; D 37-8 (ND 31-6, SD 6-2), May 23, 1997. (Before passage the Senate struck all after the enacting clause and inserted the text of S Con Res 27 as amended.) A "yea" was a vote in support of the president's position. *(Senate vote 92)*

SENATE KEY VOTES 7, 8, 9, 10, 11, 12

	7	8	9	10	11	12
ALABAMA						
Sessions	Y	Y	N	N	Y	Y
Shelby	Y	Y	N	Y	Y	N
ALASKA						
Murkowski	Y	Y	N	Y	Y	Y
Stevens	Y	N	N	Y	Y	N
ARIZONA						
Kyl	Y	Y	N	N	Y	Y
McCain	N	Y	Y	N	Y	Y
ARKANSAS						
Hutchinson	Y	Y	Y	N	Y	Y
Bumpers	Y	N	Y	N	N	Y
CALIFORNIA						
Boxer	N	N	Y	Y	N	N
Feinstein	Y	N	Y	Y	N	N
COLORADO						
Allard	Y	Y	N	Y	Y	Y
Campbell	Y	N	N	Y	Y	N
CONNECTICUT						
Dodd	Y	N	Y	N	N	Y
Lieberman	Y	N	Y	N	Y	Y
DELAWARE						
Roth	Y	N	N	Y	Y	Y
Biden	N	N	Y	Y	N	Y
FLORIDA						
Mack	Y	Y	N	Y	Y	Y
Graham	Y	N	Y	Y	N	Y
GEORGIA						
Coverdell	N	Y	N	Y	Y	Y
Cleland	N	N	Y	Y	N	Y
HAWAII						
Akaka	N	N	Y	Y	N	Y
Inouye	N	N	Y	Y	N	Y
IDAHO						
Craig	Y	Y	N	Y	Y	Y
Kempthorne	Y	Y	N	Y	Y	Y
ILLINOIS						
Durbin	N	N	Y	N	N	N
Moseley-Braun	N	N	Y	Y	N	N
INDIANA						
Coats	Y	Y	N	?	Y	Y
Lugar	Y	Y	N	Y	Y	Y

	7	8	9	10	11	12
IOWA						
Grassley	Y	Y	N	N	Y	Y
Harkin	Y	N	Y	Y	N	N
KANSAS						
Brownback	Y	Y	N	Y	Y	Y
Roberts	Y	Y	N	Y	Y	Y
KENTUCKY						
McConnell	Y	Y	N	Y	Y	Y
Ford	N	N	Y	Y	N	N
LOUISIANA						
Breaux	Y	N	Y	N	N	Y
Landrieu	Y	N	Y	N	N	Y
MAINE						
Collins	Y	N	Y	Y	Y	Y
Snowe	N	N	Y	Y	Y	N
MARYLAND						
Mikulski	N	N	Y	Y	N	N
Sarbanes	N	N	Y	Y	N	N
MASSACHUSETTS						
Kennedy	N	N	Y	Y	N	N
Kerry	Y	N	Y	N	N	Y
MICHIGAN						
Abraham	N	Y	N	N	Y	Y
Levin	Y	N	Y	Y	N	N
MINNESOTA						
Grams	Y	Y	N	N	Y	Y
Wellstone	N	N	Y	N	-	N
MISSISSIPPI						
Cochran	Y	N	N	Y	Y	Y
Lott	Y	Y	N	Y	Y	Y
MISSOURI						
Ashcroft	Y	Y	N	N	Y	Y
Bond	Y	Y	N	Y	Y	Y
MONTANA						
Burns	Y	Y	N	Y	Y	N
Baucus	Y	N	Y	Y	-	Y
NEBRASKA						
Hagel	Y	Y	N	Y	Y	Y
Kerrey	Y	N	Y	N	N	Y
NEVADA						
Bryan	Y	N	Y	N	N	Y
Reid	N	N	Y	Y	N	N

	7	8	9	10	11	12
NEW HAMPSHIRE						
Gregg	Y	Y	N	Y	Y	Y
Smith	Y	Y	N	Y	Y	N
NEW JERSEY						
Lautenberg	N	N	Y	Y	N	Y
Torricelli	N	N	Y	Y	Y	N
NEW MEXICO						
Domenici	Y	N	N	Y	Y	Y
Bingaman	Y	N	Y	Y	N	Y
NEW YORK						
D'Amato	N	N	N	Y	Y	Y
Moynihan	Y	N	Y	Y	N	Y
NORTH CAROLINA						
Faircloth	Y	Y	N	Y	Y	N
Helms	Y	Y	N	Y	Y	Y
NORTH DAKOTA						
Conrad	Y	N	Y	N	N	N
Dorgan	N	N	Y	Y	N	N
OHIO						
DeWine	Y	Y	N	Y	Y	Y
Glenn	Y	N	Y	Y	N	Y
OKLAHOMA						
Inhofe	Y	Y	N	Y	Y	N
Nickles	Y	Y	N	N	Y	Y
OREGON						
Smith	Y	N	N	Y	Y	Y
Wyden	N	N	Y	N	N	Y
PENNSYLVANIA						
Santorum	Y	Y	N	Y	Y	N
Specter	N	N	Y	Y	Y	N
RHODE ISLAND						
Chafee	Y	N	Y	Y	N	Y
Reed	N	N	Y	Y	N	N
SOUTH CAROLINA						
Thurmond	Y	Y	N	N	Y	N
Hollings	Y	N	Y	N	N	N
SOUTH DAKOTA						
Daschle	N	N	Y	N	N	Y
Johnson	N	N	Y	N	N	Y
TENNESSEE						
Frist	Y	Y	N	Y	Y	Y
Thompson	Y	Y	Y	Y	Y	Y

KEY

Y Voted for (yea).
\# Paired for.
\+ Announced for.
N Voted against (nay).
X Paired against.
\- Announced against.
P Voted "present."
C Voted "present" to avoid possible conflict of interest.
? Did not vote or otherwise make a position known.

Democrats ***Republicans***

	7	8	9	10	11	12
TEXAS						
Gramm	Y	Y	N	N	Y	Y
Hutchison	Y	Y	N	Y	Y	Y
UTAH						
Bennett	Y	N	N	Y	Y	Y
Hatch	Y	N	N	Y	Y	Y
VERMONT						
Jeffords	Y	N	Y	Y	Y	Y
Leahy	N	N	Y	Y	N	Y
VIRGINIA						
Warner	Y	N	N	Y	Y	Y
Robb	Y	N	Y	N	N	Y
WASHINGTON						
Gorton	Y	N	N	Y	Y	Y
Murray	N	N	Y	Y	N	Y
WEST VIRGINIA						
Byrd	N	N	Y	Y	N	N
Rockefeller	N	N	Y	Y	?	Y
WISCONSIN						
Feingold	Y	N	Y	N	N	N
Kohl	Y	N	Y	N	N	Y
WYOMING						
Enzi	Y	Y	N	Y	Y	N
Thomas	Y	Y	N	N	Y	Y

ND Northern Democrats SD Southern Democrats

Southern states - Ala., Ark., Fla., Ga., Ky., La., Miss., N.C., Okla., S.C., Tenn., Texas, Va.

7. S 947. Fiscal 1998 Budget Reconciliation — Spending/Medicare Means Testing. Roth, R-Del., motion to table (kill) the Kennedy, D-Mass., amendment to strike the section that introduces a means-based formula to determine insurance premiums under Medicare Part B. Motion agreed to 70-30: R 49-6; D 21-24 (ND 15-22, SD 6-2), June 24, 1997. *(Senate vote 113)*

8. HR 2107. Fiscal 1998 Interior Appropriations/NEA Funding. Hutchison, R-Texas, amendment to establish a $100 million state block grant program for the arts. The National Endowment for the Arts would be allowed to earmark 25 percent of the funds for major arts organizations. Rejected 39-61: R 39-16; D 0-45 (ND 0-37, SD 0-8), Sept. 18, 1997. A "nay" was a vote in support of the president's position. *(Senate vote 246)*

9. S 25. Campaign Finance Overhaul/Cloture. Motion to invoke cloture (thus limiting debate) on the bill to revise financing of federal political campaigns. Motion rejected 53-47: R 8-47; D 45-0 (ND 37-0, SD 8-0), Oct. 7, 1997. Three-fifths of the total Senate (60) is required to invoke cloture. A "yea" was a vote in support of the president's position. *(Senate vote 267)*

10. S 1292. Line-Item Veto Disapproval/Passage. Passage of the bill to disapprove President Clinton's line-item vetoes of 36 projects, totaling $287 million, in the fiscal 1998 military construction appropriations bill (HR 2016 — PL 105-45). Passed 69-30: R 42-12; D 27-18 (ND 24-13, SD 3-5), Oct. 30, 1997. A "nay" was a vote in support of the president's position. *(Senate vote 287)*

11. HR 2646. Education Savings Accounts/Cloture. Motion to invoke cloture (thus limiting debate) on the bill allowing parents to invest up to $2,500 annually in savings accounts designated for education-related expenses. Withdrawals of both principal and interest from such accounts could be made without incurring tax liability. Motion rejected 56-41: R 54-1; D 2-40 (ND 2-32, SD 0-8), Oct. 31, 1997. Three-fifths of the total Senate (60) is required to invoke cloture. *(Senate vote 288)*

12. S 1269. Fast Track/Cloture. Motion to invoke cloture (thus limiting debate) on the motion to proceed to the bill allowing the president to submit bills implementing trade pacts to Congress under expedited review procedures requiring up-or-down votes without amendments. Motion agreed to 69-31: R 43-12; D 26-19 (ND 20-17, SD 6-2), Nov. 4, 1997. Three-fifths of the total Senate (60) is required to invoke cloture. *(Senate vote 292)*

HOUSE KEY VOTES 1, 2, 3, 4, 5, 6, 7

Following are House votes from 1997 selected by Congressional Quarterly as key votes. Original vote number in parentheses.

1. Election of the Speaker. Nomination of Newt Gingrich, R-Ga., and Richard A. Gephardt, D-Mo., for Speaker of the House of Representatives for the 105th Congress. Gingrich elected 216-205, with four Republican votes cast for others: R 216-0; D 0-204 (ND 0-150, SD 0-54); I 0-1, Jan. 7, 1997. A "Y" on the chart represents a vote for Gingrich; an "N" represents a vote for Gephardt, except where footnoted. *(House vote 3)*

2. H Res 31. Reprimand of Rep. Newt Gingrich/Adoption. Adoption of the resolution to adopt the Jan. 17, 1997, report of the ethics committee recommending that Speaker Newt Gingrich, R-Ga., be reprimanded and that he pay $300,000 to the House. Adopted 395-28: R 196-26; D 198-2 (ND 147-0, SD 51-2); I 1-0, Jan. 21, 1997. *(House vote 8)*

3. HR 1122. Abortion Procedure Ban/Passage. Passage of the bill to impose penalties on doctors who perform certain abortion procedures, in which the person performing the abortion partially delivers the fetus before completing the abortion. An exception would be granted if the procedure was necessary to save the life of the woman. Passed 295-136: R 218-8; D 77-127 (ND 51-99, SD 26-28); I 0-1, March 20, 1997. A "nay" was a vote in support of the president's position. *(House vote 65)*

4. HR 478. Endangered Species Act Flood Waivers/Project Exemption Limitation. Boehlert, R-N.Y., substitute amendment to provide waivers of the Endangered Species Act consultation regulations for repair or replacement of flood control facilities in counties declared federal disaster areas through 1998 and waive the requirements for any project to repair a flood control facility that presents a substantial threat to human lives and property. Adopted 227-196: R 54-169; D 172-27 (ND 137-9, SD 35-18); I 1-0, May 7, 1997. *(House vote 108)*

5. HR 2. Public Housing System Overhaul/Passage. Passage of the bill to replace federal low-income housing programs with block grants to local authorities, eliminate most federal regulations affecting low-income housing assistance, and change tenant income, employment, and eligibility requirements. Passed 293-132: R 222-1; D 71-130 (ND 43-104, SD 28-26); I 0-1, May 14, 1997. A "nay" was a vote in support of the president's position. *(House vote 127)*

6. H Con Res 84. Fiscal 1998 Budget Resolution/Shuster Substitute. Shuster, R-Pa., substitute amendment to balance the budget by 2002 by increasing outlays for federal highway and mass transit programs to $137 billion, offset by an across-the-board reduction of 0.39 percent in discretionary spending and tax cuts to be phased in over four years, beginning in fiscal 1999. Rejected 214-216: R 58-168; D 155-48 (ND 118-32, SD 37-16); I 1-0, May 21, 1997 (in the session that began and the Congressional Record dated May 20). A "nay" was a vote in support of the president's position. *(House vote 147)*

7. H Con Res 84. Fiscal 1998 Budget Resolution/Adoption. Adoption of the concurrent resolution to adopt a five-year budget plan that would balance the budget by 2002 by cutting projected spending by approximately $280 billion and cutting taxes by $85 billion, for a net deficit reduction of $204.3 billion. Projected spending cuts would include reductions of $115 billion in Medicare, $13.6 billion in Medicaid and approximately $140 billion in discretionary spending. The resolution sets binding levels for the fiscal year ending Sept. 30, 1998: budget authority, $1,702.2 billion; outlays, $1,692.2 billion; revenues, $1,601.8 billion; deficit, $90.4 billion. Adopted 333-99: R 201-26; D 132-72 (ND 90-60, SD 42-12); I 0-1, May 21, 1997 (in the session that began and the Congressional Record dated May 20). A "yea" was a vote in support of the president's position. *(House vote 148)*

[1] *On key vote 1, voted for Rep. Jim Leach, R-Iowa.*
[2] *Newt Gingrich, R-Ga., as Speaker of the House, voted at his discretion.*
[3] *On key vote 1, voted for Rep. Robert H. Michel, R-Ill. (1957-1995)*
[4] *Bill Richardson, D-N.M., resigned Feb. 13. He was eligible to vote on key votes 1 and 2. Bill Redmond, R-N.M,. was sworn in May 20. He was eligible to vote on key votes 6-15.*
[5] *On key vote 1, voted for Rep. Jim Leach, R-Iowa.*
[6] *Frank Tejeda, D-Texas, died on Jan. 30. He was eligible to vote on key votes 1 and 2. Ciro D. Rodriguez, D-Texas, was sworn in April 17. He was eligible for key votes 4-15.*
[7] *On key vote 1, voted for Rep. Robert S. Walker, R-Pa. (1977-1997)*

KEY

- Y Voted for (yea).
- # Paired for.
- \+ Announced for.
- N Voted against (nay).
- X Paired against.
- – Announced against.
- P Voted "present."
- C Voted "present" to avoid possible conflict of interest.
- ? Did not vote or otherwise make a position known.

Democrats ***Republicans***
Independent

	1	2	3	4	5	6	7
ALABAMA							
1 ***Callahan***	Y	N	Y	N	Y	N	Y
2 ***Everett***	Y	Y	Y	N	Y	N	Y
3 ***Riley***	Y	Y	Y	N	Y	N	Y
4 ***Aderholt***	Y	Y	Y	N	Y	N	Y
5 Cramer	N	Y	Y	N	Y	Y	Y
6 ***Bachus***	Y	Y	Y	N	Y	Y	Y
7 Hilliard	N	N	N	Y	N	Y	N
ALASKA							
AL ***Young***	Y	N	Y	N	Y	Y	Y
ARIZONA							
1 ***Salmon***	Y	Y	Y	N	Y	N	N
2 Pastor	N	Y	N	Y	N	Y	Y
3 ***Stump***	Y	N	Y	N	Y	N	Y
4 ***Shadegg***	Y	Y	Y	N	Y	N	N
5 ***Kolbe***	Y	?	N	N	Y	N	Y
6 ***Hayworth***	Y	Y	Y	N	Y	N	Y
ARKANSAS							
1 Berry	N	Y	Y	N	Y	Y	Y
2 Snyder	N	Y	N	Y	Y	N	Y
3 ***Hutchinson***	Y	Y	Y	N	Y	Y	Y
4 ***Dickey***	Y	Y	Y	N	Y	Y	Y
CALIFORNIA							
1 ***Riggs***	Y	Y	Y	N	Y	Y	Y
2 ***Herger***	Y	N	Y	N	Y	N	Y
3 Fazio	N	Y	N	Y	N	N	Y
4 ***Doolittle***	Y	N	Y	N	Y	N	Y
5 Matsui	N	Y	N	Y	Y	Y	Y
6 Woolsey	N	Y	N	Y	N	Y	Y
7 Miller	N	Y	N	Y	N	Y	N
8 Pelosi	N	Y	N	Y	N	Y	N
9 Dellums	N	Y	N	Y	N	Y	N
10 Tauscher	N	Y	N	Y	Y	Y	Y
11 ***Pombo***	Y	Y	Y	N	Y	N	N
12 Lantos	N	Y	N	Y	N	Y	Y
13 Stark	N	Y	N	Y	N	Y	N
14 Eshoo	N	Y	N	Y	N	Y	Y
15 ***Campbell***[1]	N	Y	N	N	Y	N	Y
16 Lofgren	N	Y	N	Y	N	Y	Y
17 Farr	N	Y	N	Y	N	Y	Y
18 Condit	N	Y	Y	N	Y	N	Y
19 ***Radanovich***	Y	Y	Y	N	Y	N	Y
20 Dooley	N	Y	N	N	Y	N	Y
21 ***Thomas***	Y	Y	Y	N	Y	N	Y
22 Capps	N	Y	N	Y	Y	Y	Y
23 ***Gallegly***	Y	Y	Y	N	Y	Y	Y
24 Sherman	N	Y	N	Y	Y	N	Y
25 ***McKeon***	Y	N	Y	N	Y	N	Y
26 Berman	N	Y	N	Y	N	N	Y
27 ***Rogan***	Y	Y	Y	N	Y	N	Y
28 ***Dreier***	Y	Y	Y	N	Y	N	Y
29 Waxman	N	Y	N	Y	N	N	N
30 Becerra	N	Y	N	+	N	Y	N
31 Martinez	N	Y	Y	Y	N	Y	Y
32 Dixon	N	Y	N	Y	N	Y	N
33 Roybal-Allard	N	Y	N	Y	N	Y	N
34 Torres	N	Y	N	Y	N	Y	Y
35 Waters	N	P	N	Y	N	Y	N
36 Harman	N	Y	N	Y	Y	N	Y
37 Millender-McD.	N	Y	N	Y	N	Y	N
38 ***Horn***	Y	Y	N	Y	Y	Y	Y
39 ***Royce***	Y	Y	Y	N	Y	N	Y
40 ***Lewis***	Y	N	Y	N	Y	Y	Y
41 ***Kim***	Y	Y	Y	N	Y	Y	Y
42 Brown	N	Y	N	Y	N	Y	N
43 ***Calvert***	Y	Y	Y	N	Y	N	Y
44 ***Bono***	Y	Y	Y	N	Y	N	Y
45 ***Rohrabacher***	Y	Y	Y	N	Y	N	N
46 Sanchez	N	Y	N	Y	Y	Y	Y
47 ***Cox***	Y	Y	Y	N	Y	N	N
48 ***Packard***	Y	N	Y	N	Y	N	Y
49 ***Bilbray***	Y	Y	Y	N	Y	N	Y
50 Filner	N	Y	N	#	N	Y	N
51 ***Cunningham***	Y	Y	Y	N	Y	N	Y
52 ***Hunter***	Y	N	Y	N	Y	N	N
COLORADO							
1 DeGette	N	Y	N	Y	N	Y	N
2 Skaggs	N	Y	N	Y	N	N	Y
3 ***McInnis***	Y	Y	Y	N	Y	N	Y
4 ***Schaffer***	Y	Y	Y	N	Y	N	Y
5 ***Hefley***	Y	Y	Y	N	Y	N	Y
6 ***Schaefer***	Y	Y	Y	N	Y	Y	Y
CONNECTICUT							
1 Kennelly	N	Y	N	Y	N	Y	Y
2 Gejdenson	N	Y	N	Y	N	Y	Y
3 DeLauro	N	Y	N	Y	N	Y	Y
4 ***Shays***	Y	Y	Y	Y	Y	N	Y
5 Maloney	N	Y	Y	Y	N	Y	Y
6 ***Johnson***	Y	Y	N	Y	Y	N	Y
DELAWARE							
AL ***Castle***	Y	Y	Y	Y	Y	N	Y
FLORIDA							
1 ***Scarborough***	Y	Y	Y	N	Y	N	N
2 Boyd	N	Y	Y	N	Y	N	Y
3 Brown	N	Y	N	Y	N	Y	N
4 ***Fowler***	Y	Y	Y	N	Y	N	Y
5 Thurman	N	Y	N	Y	N	N	Y
6 ***Stearns***	Y	Y	Y	N	Y	N	Y
7 ***Mica***	Y	N	Y	N	Y	Y	Y
8 ***McCollum***	Y	Y	Y	N	Y	N	N
9 ***Bilirakis***	Y	Y	Y	N	Y	N	Y
10 ***Young***	Y	Y	Y	N	Y	N	Y
11 Davis	N	Y	Y	Y	Y	N	Y
12 ***Canady***	Y	Y	Y	N	Y	N	Y
13 ***Miller***	Y	Y	Y	N	Y	N	Y
14 ***Goss***	Y	Y	Y	Y	Y	N	Y
15 ***Weldon***	Y	Y	Y	N	Y	N	N
16 ***Foley***	Y	Y	Y	X	Y	N	Y
17 Meek	N	Y	N	Y	N	Y	N
18 ***Ros-Lehtinen***	Y	Y	Y	Y	Y	N	Y
19 Wexler	N	Y	N	Y	Y	Y	Y
20 Deutsch	N	Y	N	Y	Y	Y	Y
21 ***Diaz-Balart***	Y	Y	Y	Y	Y	N	Y
22 ***Shaw***	Y	Y	Y	N	Y	N	Y
23 Hastings	N	P	N	Y	N	Y	N
GEORGIA							
1 ***Kingston***	Y	Y	Y	Y	Y	N	Y
2 Bishop	N	Y	N	N	N	Y	Y
3 ***Collins***	Y	Y	Y	N	Y	N	Y
4 McKinney	N	Y	N	?	N	Y	Y
5 Lewis	N	Y	N	Y	N	Y	N
6 ***Gingrich***[2]			Y			N	Y
7 ***Barr***	Y	N	Y	N	Y	N	Y
8 ***Chambliss***	Y	Y	Y	N	Y	N	Y
9 ***Deal***	Y	Y	Y	N	Y	N	Y
10 ***Norwood***	Y	Y	Y	N	Y	N	Y
11 ***Linder***	Y	Y	Y	N	Y	N	Y
HAWAII							
1 Abercrombie	N	P	N	Y	N	Y	Y
2 Mink	N	Y	N	Y	N	Y	N
IDAHO							
1 ***Chenoweth***	Y	Y	Y	N	Y	N	N
2 ***Crapo***	Y	Y	Y	N	Y	N	N
ILLINOIS							
1 Rush	N	Y	N	Y	N	Y	N
2 Jackson	N	Y	N	Y	N	Y	N
3 Lipinski	N	Y	Y	Y	Y	Y	N
4 Gutierrez	N	Y	N	Y	N	N	N
5 Blagojevich	N	Y	N	Y	Y	Y	Y
6 ***Hyde***	Y	Y	Y	N	Y	N	N
7 Davis	N	Y	N	Y	N	Y	N
8 ***Crane***	Y	Y	Y	N	Y	N	N
9 Yates	N	Y	N	Y	N	?	X
10 ***Porter***	Y	Y	Y	Y	Y	N	Y
11 ***Weller***	Y	Y	Y	Y	Y	N	Y
12 Costello	N	Y	Y	Y	N	Y	Y
13 ***Fawell***	Y	Y	Y	Y	Y	N	Y
14 ***Hastert***	Y	Y	Y	N	Y	N	Y

ND Northern Democrats SD Southern Democrats

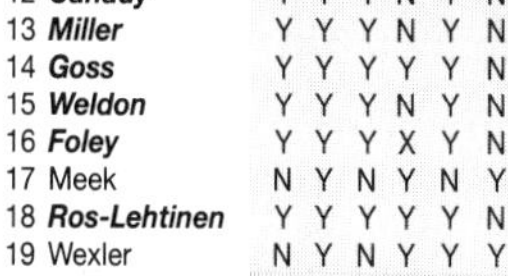

	1	2	3	4	5	6	7
15 ***Ewing***	Y	Y	Y	N	Y	N	Y
16 ***Manzullo***	Y	Y	Y	N	Y	Y	Y
17 Evans	N	Y	N	Y	N	N	N
18 ***LaHood***	Y	Y	Y	Y	Y	Y	Y
19 Poshard	N	Y	Y	Y	N	Y	Y
20 ***Shimkus***	Y	Y	Y	N	Y	N	Y
INDIANA							
1 Visclosky	N	Y	Y	Y	Y	Y	Y
2 ***McIntosh***	Y	Y	Y	N	Y	N	N
3 Roemer	N	Y	Y	Y	Y	Y	Y
4 ***Souder***	Y	Y	Y	N	Y	N	Y
5 ***Buyer***	Y	N	Y	N	Y	Y	Y
6 ***Burton***	Y	N	Y	N	Y	N	Y
7 ***Pease***	Y	Y	Y	N	Y	Y	Y
8 ***Hostettler***	P	Y	Y	N	Y	Y	Y
9 Hamilton	N	Y	Y	Y	Y	Y	Y
10 Carson	?	?	N	Y	N	Y	Y
IOWA							
1 ***Leach***[3]	N	Y	Y	Y	Y	N	Y
2 ***Nussle***	Y	Y	Y	N	Y	N	Y
3 Boswell	N	Y	Y	N	N	Y	Y
4 ***Ganske***	Y	Y	Y	N	Y	N	N
5 ***Latham***	Y	Y	Y	N	Y	N	Y
KANSAS							
1 ***Moran***	Y	Y	Y	N	Y	Y	Y
2 ***Ryun***	Y	Y	Y	N	Y	N	Y
3 ***Snowbarger***	Y	Y	Y	N	Y	N	Y
4 ***Tiahrt***	Y	Y	Y	N	Y	N	Y
KENTUCKY							
1 ***Whitfield***	Y	Y	Y	N	Y	N	Y
2 ***Lewis***	Y	Y	Y	N	Y	N	Y
3 ***Northup***	Y	Y	Y	N	Y	Y	Y
4 ***Bunning***	Y	Y	Y	N	Y	N	Y
5 ***Rogers***	Y	Y	Y	N	Y	N	Y
6 Baesler	N	Y	Y	N	Y	Y	Y
LOUISIANA							
1 ***Livingston***	Y	N	Y	N	Y	N	Y
2 Jefferson	N	Y	Y	N	N	?	?
3 ***Tauzin***	Y	+	Y	N	Y	N	Y
4 ***McCrery***	Y	Y	Y	N	Y	N	Y
5 ***Cooksey***	Y	Y	Y	N	Y	Y	Y
6 ***Baker***	Y	Y	Y	N	Y	Y	Y
7 John	N	Y	Y	N	Y	Y	Y
MAINE							
1 Allen	N	Y	N	Y	N	N	Y
2 Baldacci	N	Y	N	Y	N	N	Y
MARYLAND							
1 ***Gilchrest***	Y	Y	Y	Y	Y	N	Y
2 ***Ehrlich***	Y	Y	Y	N	Y	N	Y
3 Cardin	N	Y	N	Y	Y	N	Y
4 Wynn	N	Y	N	Y	N	Y	Y
5 Hoyer	N	Y	N	Y	N	N	Y
6 ***Bartlett***	Y	N	Y	N	Y	N	Y
7 Cummings	N	Y	N	Y	N	Y	Y
8 ***Morella***	P	Y	N	Y	Y	N	Y
MASSACHUSETTS							
1 Olver	N	Y	N	Y	N	Y	N
2 Neal	N	Y	Y	Y	N	Y	Y
3 McGovern	N	Y	N	Y	N	Y	N
4 Frank	N	Y	N	Y	N	Y	N
5 Meehan	N	Y	N	Y	N	Y	Y
6 Tierney	N	Y	N	Y	N	Y	N
7 Markey	N	Y	N	Y	N	Y	N
8 Kennedy	N	Y	N	Y	N	Y	N
9 Moakley	N	Y	Y	Y	N	Y	N
10 Delahunt	N	Y	N	+	N	Y	N
MICHIGAN							
1 Stupak	N	Y	Y	Y	N	Y	Y
2 ***Hoekstra***	Y	Y	Y	N	Y	N	Y
3 ***Ehlers***	Y	Y	Y	N	Y	Y	Y
4 ***Camp***	Y	Y	Y	N	Y	Y	Y
5 Barcia	N	Y	Y	Y	Y	Y	Y
6 ***Upton***	Y	Y	Y	Y	Y	Y	Y
7 ***Smith***	Y	Y	Y	Y	Y	N	Y
8 Stabenow	N	Y	N	Y	Y	Y	Y
9 Kildee	N	Y	Y	Y	N	Y	Y
10 Bonior	N	Y	Y	Y	N	Y	Y
11 ***Knollenberg***	Y	Y	Y	N	Y	N	Y
12 Levin	N	Y	N	Y	N	Y	Y
13 Rivers	N	Y	N	Y	N	Y	Y
14 Conyers	N	P	N	Y	N	N	N
15 Kilpatrick	N	Y	N	Y	N	Y	N
16 Dingell	N	Y	Y	Y	N	Y	Y
MINNESOTA							
1 ***Gutknecht***	Y	Y	Y	N	Y	N	Y

	1	2	3	4	5	6	7
2 Minge	N	Y	Y	Y	Y	N	Y
3 ***Ramstad***	Y	Y	Y	Y	Y	N	Y
4 Vento	N	Y	N	Y	N	Y	Y
5 Sabo	N	Y	N	Y	N	N	Y
6 Luther	N	Y	N	Y	Y	Y	Y
7 Peterson	N	Y	Y	N	Y	Y	Y
8 Oberstar	N	Y	Y	Y	N	Y	N
MISSISSIPPI							
1 ***Wicker***	Y	N	Y	N	Y	N	Y
2 Thompson	N	Y	N	Y	N	Y	N
3 ***Pickering***	Y	Y	Y	N	Y	N	Y
4 ***Parker***	Y	Y	Y	N	Y	N	Y
5 Taylor	N	N	Y	N	Y	N	Y
MISSOURI							
1 Clay	N	Y	N	?	N	Y	N
2 ***Talent***	Y	Y	Y	N	Y	N	Y
3 Gephardt	P	Y	Y	Y	N	Y	N
4 Skelton	N	Y	Y	N	?	N	Y
5 McCarthy	N	Y	N	Y	Y	Y	Y
6 Danner	N	Y	Y	N	Y	Y	Y
7 ***Blunt***	Y	Y	Y	N	Y	Y	Y
8 ***Emerson***	Y	Y	Y	N	Y	Y	Y
9 ***Hulshof***	Y	Y	Y	N	Y	N	Y
MONTANA							
AL ***Hill***	Y	Y	Y	N	Y	Y	N
NEBRASKA							
1 ***Bereuter***	Y	Y	Y	N	Y	Y	Y
2 ***Christensen***	Y	Y	Y	N	Y	N	Y
3 ***Barrett***	Y	Y	Y	N	Y	N	Y
NEVADA							
1 ***Ensign***	Y	Y	Y	N	Y	+	Y
2 ***Gibbons***	Y	Y	Y	N	Y	N	Y
NEW HAMPSHIRE							
1 ***Sununu***	Y	Y	Y	Y	Y	N	Y
2 ***Bass***	Y	Y	Y	Y	Y	Y	Y
NEW JERSEY							
1 Andrews	N	Y	N	?	?	Y	Y
2 ***LoBiondo***	Y	Y	Y	Y	Y	Y	Y
3 ***Saxton***	Y	Y	Y	Y	Y	N	Y
4 ***Smith***	Y	Y	Y	Y	Y	Y	Y
5 ***Roukema***	Y	Y	Y	Y	Y	N	Y
6 Pallone	N	Y	N	Y	N	Y	Y
7 ***Franks***	Y	Y	Y	Y	Y	Y	Y
8 Pascrell	N	Y	Y	Y	Y	Y	Y
9 Rothman	N	Y	N	Y	N	Y	Y
10 Payne	N	Y	N	Y	N	Y	N
11 ***Frelinghuysen***	Y	Y	Y	Y	Y	N	Y
12 ***Pappas***	Y	Y	Y	Y	Y	N	Y
13 Menendez	N	Y	N	Y	N	Y	Y
NEW MEXICO							
1 ***Schiff***	Y	Y	Y	?	?	?	#
2 ***Skeen***	Y	Y	Y	N	Y	N	Y
3 Redmond[4]						N	Y
NEW YORK							
1 ***Forbes***[5]	N	Y	Y	Y	Y	Y	Y
2 ***Lazio***	Y	Y	Y	Y	Y	N	Y
3 ***King***	Y	N	Y	N	Y	Y	N
4 McCarthy	N	Y	N	Y	Y	Y	Y
5 Ackerman	N	Y	N	Y	Y	Y	Y
6 Flake	N	Y	Y	Y	?	Y	Y
7 Manton	N	Y	Y	Y	Y	Y	Y
8 Nadler	N	Y	N	Y	N	Y	N
9 Schumer	N	Y	N	Y	N	Y	Y
10 Towns	N	Y	N	Y	N	Y	N
11 Owens	N	Y	N	Y	N	Y	N
12 Velazquez	N	Y	N	Y	N	Y	N
13 ***Molinari***	Y	Y	Y	N	Y	Y	Y
14 Maloney	N	Y	N	Y	N	Y	Y
15 Rangel	N	Y	N	Y	N	Y	N
16 Serrano	N	Y	N	Y	N	Y	N
17 Engel	N	Y	N	Y	N	Y	N
18 Lowey	N	Y	N	Y	Y	Y	Y
19 ***Kelly***	Y	Y	Y	Y	Y	Y	Y
20 ***Gilman***	Y	Y	N	Y	Y	N	Y
21 McNulty	N	Y	Y	Y	N	N	N
22 ***Solomon***	Y	N	Y	N	Y	N	Y
23 ***Boehlert***	Y	Y	N	Y	Y	Y	Y
24 ***McHugh***	Y	Y	Y	N	Y	N	Y
25 ***Walsh***	Y	Y	Y	Y	Y	N	Y
26 Hinchey	N	Y	N	Y	N	Y	N
27 ***Paxon***	Y	Y	Y	N	Y	N	Y
28 Slaughter	N	Y	N	Y	N	Y	N
29 LaFalce	N	Y	Y	Y	N	Y	Y
30 ***Quinn***	Y	Y	Y	Y	Y	Y	Y
31 ***Houghton***	Y	Y	Y	Y	Y	Y	Y

	1	2	3	4	5	6	7
NORTH CAROLINA							
1 Clayton	N	Y	N	Y	N	Y	Y
2 Etheridge	N	Y	Y	Y	N	Y	Y
3 ***Jones***	Y	Y	Y	N	Y	N	Y
4 Price	N	Y	N	Y	N	Y	Y
5 ***Burr***	Y	Y	Y	N	Y	N	Y
6 ***Coble***	Y	Y	Y	N	Y	Y	Y
7 McIntyre	N	Y	Y	Y	Y	Y	Y
8 Hefner	N	Y	Y	Y	?	Y	Y
9 ***Myrick***	Y	N	Y	N	Y	N	Y
10 ***Ballenger***	Y	Y	Y	N	Y	N	Y
11 ***Taylor***	Y	N	Y	N	Y	N	Y
12 Watt	N	Y	N	Y	N	Y	N
NORTH DAKOTA							
AL Pomeroy	N	Y	Y	N	Y	N	Y
OHIO							
1 ***Chabot***	Y	Y	Y	N	Y	N	Y
2 ***Portman***	Y	Y	Y	N	Y	N	Y
3 Hall	N	Y	Y	Y	N	N	Y
4 ***Oxley***	Y	Y	+	N	Y	N	Y
5 ***Gillmor***	Y	Y	Y	Y	Y	Y	Y
6 Strickland	N	Y	Y	Y	Y	Y	Y
7 ***Hobson***	Y	Y	Y	Y	Y	N	Y
8 ***Boehner***	Y	Y	Y	N	Y	N	Y
9 Kaptur	N	Y	?	Y	Y	Y	N
10 Kucinich	N	Y	Y	Y	N	N	N
11 Stokes	N	Y	N	Y	N	Y	N
12 ***Kasich***	Y	Y	Y	N	+	N	Y
13 Brown	N	Y	N	Y	N	N	N
14 Sawyer	N	Y	N	Y	N	N	Y
15 ***Pryce***	Y	Y	Y	N	Y	N	Y
16 ***Regula***	Y	Y	Y	N	Y	N	Y
17 Traficant	N	Y	N	Y	Y	Y	N
18 ***Ney***	Y	Y	Y	N	Y	N	Y
19 ***LaTourette***	Y	Y	Y	Y	Y	Y	Y
OKLAHOMA							
1 ***Largent***	Y	Y	Y	N	Y	N	N
2 ***Coburn***	Y	N	Y	N	Y	N	N
3 ***Watkins***	Y	Y	Y	N	?	N	Y
4 ***Watts***	Y	+	Y	N	Y	N	Y
5 ***Istook***	Y	Y	Y	N	Y	N	N
6 ***Lucas***	Y	Y	Y	N	Y	N	Y
OREGON							
1 Furse	N	Y	N	Y	Y	Y	Y
2 ***Smith***	Y	Y	Y	N	Y	N	Y
3 Blumenauer	N	Y	N	Y	N	Y	N
4 DeFazio	N	Y	N	Y	N	Y	N
5 Hooley	N	Y	N	Y	Y	Y	Y
PENNSYLVANIA							
1 Foglietta	N	Y	Y	Y	N	N	Y
2 Fattah	N	Y	N	Y	N	Y	Y
3 Borski	N	Y	Y	Y	N	Y	N
4 Klink	N	Y	Y	Y	Y	Y	Y
5 ***Peterson***	Y	Y	Y	N	Y	Y	Y
6 Holden	N	Y	Y	N	Y	Y	Y
7 ***Weldon***	Y	Y	Y	Y	Y	Y	Y
8 ***Greenwood***	Y	Y	N	Y	Y	Y	Y
9 ***Shuster***	Y	Y	Y	N	Y	Y	N
10 ***McDade***	Y	Y	Y	Y	Y	Y	Y
11 Kanjorski	N	Y	Y	Y	N	Y	N
12 Murtha	N	Y	Y	Y	Y	N	Y
13 ***Fox***	Y	Y	Y	Y	Y	Y	Y
14 Coyne	N	Y	N	Y	N	Y	N
15 McHale	N	Y	Y	Y	Y	Y	Y
16 ***Pitts***	Y	Y	Y	N	Y	Y	Y
17 ***Gekas***	Y	Y	Y	N	Y	Y	Y
18 Doyle	N	Y	Y	Y	Y	Y	Y
19 ***Goodling***	Y	Y	Y	N	Y	N	Y
20 Mascara	N	Y	Y	Y	Y	Y	Y
21 ***English***	Y	Y	Y	Y	Y	Y	Y
RHODE ISLAND							
1 Kennedy	N	Y	Y	Y	N	N	N
2 Weygand	N	Y	Y	Y	N	N	N
SOUTH CAROLINA							
1 ***Sanford***	Y	Y	Y	Y	Y	N	N
2 ***Spence***	Y	Y	Y	N	Y	N	Y
3 ***Graham***	Y	Y	Y	N	Y	N	Y
4 ***Inglis***	Y	Y	Y	N	Y	N	Y
5 Spratt	N	Y	Y	Y	N	N	Y
6 Clyburn	N	Y	N	Y	N	Y	N
SOUTH DAKOTA							
AL ***Thune***	Y	Y	Y	N	Y	Y	Y
TENNESSEE							
1 ***Jenkins***	Y	Y	Y	N	Y	N	Y
2 ***Duncan***	Y	Y	Y	N	Y	Y	Y

	1	2	3	4	5	6	7
3 ***Wamp***	Y	Y	Y	N	Y	N	Y
4 ***Hilleary***	Y	Y	Y	N	Y	N	Y
5 Clement	N	Y	Y	Y	N	Y	Y
6 Gordon	N	Y	Y	Y	N	Y	Y
7 ***Bryant***	Y	Y	Y	N	Y	N	Y
8 Tanner	N	Y	Y	Y	Y	Y	Y
9 Ford	N	Y	N	Y	Y	Y	Y
TEXAS							
1 Sandlin	N	Y	Y	N	Y	Y	Y
2 Turner	N	Y	Y	N	Y	Y	Y
3 ***Johnson, Sam***	+	N	Y	N	Y	N	Y
4 Hall	N	Y	Y	N	Y	N	Y
5 ***Sessions***	Y	N	Y	N	Y	N	Y
6 ***Barton***	Y	N	Y	?	Y	N	N
7 ***Archer***	Y	Y	Y	N	Y	N	Y
8 ***Brady***	Y	Y	Y	N	Y	N	Y
9 Lampson	N	Y	Y	Y	Y	Y	Y
10 Doggett	N	Y	N	Y	Y	Y	Y
11 Edwards	N	Y	N	N	Y	N	Y
12 ***Granger***	Y	?	Y	N	Y	N	Y
13 ***Thornberry***	Y	Y	Y	N	Y	N	Y
14 ***Paul***	Y	Y	Y	N	N	N	N
15 Hinojosa	N	Y	Y	Y	N	Y	Y
16 Reyes	N	Y	Y	?	Y	N	Y
17 Stenholm	N	Y	Y	N	Y	N	Y
18 Jackson-Lee	N	Y	N	Y	N	N	N
19 ***Combest***	Y	Y	Y	N	Y	Y	Y
20 Gonzalez	N	Y	N	Y	N	Y	Y
21 ***Smith***	Y	N	Y	N	Y	N	Y
22 ***DeLay***	Y	N	Y	N	Y	N	Y
23 ***Bonilla***	Y	Y	Y	N	Y	N	Y
24 Frost	N	Y	N	Y	N	Y	Y
25 Bentsen	N	Y	N	Y	Y	N	Y
26 ***Armey***	Y	Y	Y	N	Y	N	Y
27 Ortiz	N	Y	N	Y	Y	Y	Y
28 Rodriguez[6]					N	N	Y
29 Green	N	Y	N	Y	Y	Y	Y
30 Johnson, E.B.	N	Y	N	Y	N	Y	N
UTAH							
1 ***Hansen***	Y	Y	Y	N	Y	N	Y
2 ***Cook***	Y	Y	Y	N	Y	Y	Y
3 ***Cannon***	Y	Y	Y	N	Y	N	Y
VERMONT							
AL *Sanders*	N	Y	N	Y	N	Y	N
VIRGINIA							
1 ***Bateman***	Y	Y	Y	N	Y	N	Y
2 Pickett	N	Y	N	N	Y	N	Y
3 Scott	N	Y	N	Y	N	Y	N
4 Sisisky	N	Y	Y	N	Y	N	Y
5 Goode	N	Y	Y	N	Y	Y	Y
6 ***Goodlatte***	Y	Y	Y	N	Y	N	Y
7 ***Bliley***	Y	Y	Y	N	Y	N	Y
8 Moran	N	Y	Y	Y	Y	N	Y
9 Boucher	N	Y	N	Y	N	?	N
10 ***Wolf***	P	Y	Y	Y	Y	N	Y
11 ***Davis***	Y	Y	Y	Y	Y	N	Y
WASHINGTON							
1 ***White***	Y	Y	Y	Y	Y	N	Y
2 ***Metcalf***	Y	Y	Y	Y	Y	Y	Y
3 ***Smith, Linda***[7]	N	Y	Y	Y	Y	Y	Y
4 ***Hastings***	Y	Y	Y	N	Y	N	Y
5 ***Nethercutt***	Y	Y	Y	N	Y	N	Y
6 Dicks	N	Y	N	Y	Y	N	Y
7 McDermott	N	P	N	Y	Y	Y	N
8 ***Dunn***	Y	Y	Y	N	Y	N	Y
9 Smith, Adam	N	Y	N	Y	Y	N	Y
WEST VIRGINIA							
1 Mollohan	N	Y	Y	Y	N	Y	N
2 Wise	N	Y	N	Y	Y	Y	Y
3 Rahall	N	Y	Y	Y	N	Y	N
WISCONSIN							
1 ***Neumann***	P	Y	Y	Y	Y	N	Y
2 ***Klug***	P	Y	Y	Y	Y	N	N
3 Kind	N	Y	Y	Y	Y	Y	Y
4 Kleczka	N	Y	Y	Y	–	Y	Y
5 Barrett	N	Y	Y	Y	N	N	Y
6 ***Petri***	Y	Y	Y	Y	Y	Y	Y
7 Obey	N	Y	Y	Y	N	N	N
8 Johnson	N	Y	Y	Y	N	Y	Y
9 ***Sensenbrenner***	Y	Y	Y	Y	Y	N	Y
WYOMING							
AL ***Cubin***	Y	Y	Y	N	Y	N	N

Southern states - Ala., Ark., Fla., Ga., Ky., La., Miss., N.C., Okla., S.C., Tenn., Texas, Va.

HOUSE KEY VOTES 8, 9, 10, 11, 12, 13, 14, 15

8. HR 1119. Fiscal 1998 Defense Authorization/Bosnia Troop Withdrawal Substitute. Hilleary, R-Tenn., substitute amendment to the Buyer, R-Ind., amendment to prohibit the obligation of funds for ground deployment of U.S. troops in Bosnia after Dec. 31, 1997, unless the president submits a report to Congress requesting an extension of funding. The Hilleary amendment would require the extension to be approved by a joint resolution of Congress and would permit deployment for an additional 180 days or until June 30, 1998. Rejected 196-231: R 174-49; D 21-182 (ND 15-133, SD 6-49); I 1-0, June 24, 1997. A "nay" was a vote in support of the president's position. *(House vote 233)*

9. HR 2107. Fiscal 1998 Interior Appropriations/Rule. Adoption of the rule (H Res 181) to provide for House floor consideration of the bill to provide $13 billion in new budget authority for the Department of the Interior and related agencies for fiscal 1998. The rule did not waive a point of order against the $10 million of funding in the bill for the National Endowment for the Arts because its authorization had expired. Adopted 217-216: R 212-15; D 5-200 (ND 2-148, SD 3-52); I 0-1, July 10, 1997. *(House vote 259)*

10. HR 2159. Fiscal 1998 Foreign Operations Appropriations/Overseas Abortion Funding. Gilman, R-N.Y., amendment to the Smith, R-N.J., amendment to allow organizations that do not promote abortion as a method of family planning but use their own funds to perform abortions to remain eligible for international family planning funding. The amendment also would prohibit funding for lobbying for or against abortion, and for the U.N. Population Fund unless the president certifies that the organization has ceased all activity in China. Rejected 210-218: R 38-185; D 171-33 (ND 125-26, SD 46-7); I 1-0, Sept. 4, 1997. *(House vote 362)*

11. HR 2378. Fiscal 1998 Treasury-Postal Service Appropriations/Previous Question. Hoyer, D-Md., motion to order the previous question (thus ending debate and the possibility of amendment) on the Hoyer motion to instruct conferees to increase funding for the Exploited Child Unit of the National Center for Missing and Exploited Children. A "nay" vote would have allowed Smith, R-Wash., to offer an amendment to block a cost of living adjustment for members of Congress. Motion agreed to 229-199: R 114-110; D 115-88 (ND 88-62, SD 27-26); I 0-1, Sept. 24, 1997. *(House vote 435)*

12. HR 1534. Private Property Rights/Passage. Passage of the bill to establish guidelines for allowing private property owners to appeal local, state and federal land use decisions in federal courts. The bill would require federal courts to consider all cases qualifying as "takings" under the Fifth Amendment to the Constitution. Passed 248-178: R 193-30; D 55-147 (ND 25-124, SD 30-23); I 0-1, Oct. 22, 1997. A "nay" was a vote in support of the president's position. *(House vote 519)*

13. HR 2746. Private School Vouchers/Passage. Passage of the bill to authorize states to use certain federal elementary and secondary education funds to provide scholarships to low-income families to send their children to public, private or religious schools. Rejected 191-228: R 187-35; D 4-192 (ND 2-140, SD 2-52); I 0-1, Nov. 4, 1997. A "nay" was a vote in support of the president's position. *(House vote 569)*

14. HR 2644. Caribbean and Central American Trade/Passage. Crane, R-Ill., motion to suspend the rules and pass the bill to provide Caribbean and Central American countries duty-free trade benefits on certain products similar to those accorded to Mexico under the North American Free Trade Agreement. Motion rejected 182-234: R 136-83; D 46-150 (ND 32-111, SD 14-39); I 0-1, Nov. 4, 1997. *(House vote 570)*

15. HR 2676. Internal Revenue Service Overhaul/Passage. Passage of the bill to restructure the management of the Internal Revenue Service by establishing an oversight board to oversee the agency's operations. The bill would shift the burden of proof from the taxpayer to the IRS in cases before the U.S. Tax Court. Passed 426-4: R 225-0; D 200-4 (ND 146-4, SD 54-0); I 1-0, Nov. 5, 1997. A "yea" was a vote in support of the president's position. *(House vote 577)*

[1]*Walter Capps, D-Calif., died Oct. 28.*
[2]*Newt Gingrich, R-Ga., as Speaker of the House, voted at his discretion.*
[3]*Susan Molinari, R-N.Y., resigned Aug. 1. She was eligible to vote on key votes 1-9. Vito J. Fossella, R-N.Y., was sworn in Nov. 5. He was eligible to vote on key vote 15.*

KEY

- Y Voted for (yea).
- # Paired for.
- \+ Announced for.
- N Voted against (nay).
- X Paired against.
- – Announced against.
- P Voted "present."
- C Voted "present" to avoid possible conflict of interest.
- ? Did not vote or otherwise make a position known.

Democrats ***Republicans***
Independent

	8	9	10	11	12	13	14	15
ALABAMA								
1 ***Callahan***	N	Y	N	Y	Y	Y	Y	Y
2 ***Everett***	Y	Y	N	N	Y	Y	N	Y
3 ***Riley***	Y	Y	N	N	Y	#	#	+
4 ***Aderholt***	Y	Y	N	N	Y	Y	N	Y
5 Cramer	N	N	Y	N	Y	N	N	Y
6 ***Bachus***	Y	Y	N	Y	Y	Y	Y	Y
7 Hilliard	N	N	Y	Y	Y	N	N	Y
ALASKA								
AL ***Young***	Y	Y	N	Y	Y	Y	N	Y
ARIZONA								
1 ***Salmon***	Y	Y	N	N	Y	Y	Y	Y
2 Pastor	N	N	Y	N	N	N	Y	Y
3 ***Stump***	Y	Y	N	N	Y	Y	Y	Y
4 ***Shadegg***	Y	Y	N	N	Y	Y	Y	Y
5 ***Kolbe***	N	Y	Y	Y	Y	Y	Y	Y
6 ***Hayworth***	Y	Y	N	N	Y	Y	Y	Y
ARKANSAS								
1 Berry	Y	N	Y	N	Y	N	Y	Y
2 Snyder	N	N	Y	N	N	N	N	Y
3 ***Hutchinson***	Y	Y	N	N	Y	N	N	Y
4 ***Dickey***	Y	Y	N	Y	Y	Y	N	Y
CALIFORNIA								
1 ***Riggs***	Y	Y	N	N	Y	Y	N	Y
2 ***Herger***	Y	Y	N	N	Y	Y	Y	Y
3 Fazio	N	N	Y	Y	Y	N	Y	Y
4 ***Doolittle***	Y	Y	N	Y	Y	Y	N	Y
5 Matsui	N	N	Y	Y	N	N	Y	N
6 Woolsey	N	N	Y	Y	N	N	N	Y
7 Miller	N	N	Y	Y	N	N	N	Y
8 Pelosi	N	N	Y	Y	N	N	Y	Y
9 Dellums	N	N	Y	Y	N	N	N	Y
10 Tauscher	N	N	Y	N	N	N	N	Y
11 ***Pombo***	Y	Y	N	Y	Y	Y	N	Y
12 Lantos	N	N	Y	Y	?	N	N	Y
13 Stark	N	N	Y	Y	N	N	N	N
14 Eshoo	N	N	Y	Y	N	N	Y	Y
15 ***Campbell***	Y	Y	Y	Y	Y	Y	Y	Y
16 Lofgren	N	N	Y	N	N	N	N	Y
17 Farr	N	N	Y	Y	N	N	N	Y
18 Condit	Y	Y	Y	Y	Y	N	N	Y
19 ***Radanovich***	Y	Y	N	N	Y	Y	N	Y
20 Dooley	N	N	Y	Y	Y	N	Y	Y
21 ***Thomas***	Y	Y	Y	Y	Y	Y	Y	Y
22 Capps[1]	N	N	Y	N	N			
23 ***Gallegly***	Y	Y	N	Y	Y	Y	N	Y
24 Sherman	N	N	Y	N	N	N	N	Y
25 ***McKeon***	Y	Y	N	Y	Y	Y	Y	Y
26 Berman	N	N	Y	Y	N	N	Y	Y
27 ***Rogan***	Y	Y	N	N	Y	Y	Y	Y
28 ***Dreier***	Y	Y	N	Y	Y	Y	Y	Y
29 Waxman	N	N	Y	Y	N	N	N	Y
30 Becerra	N	N	Y	Y	N	N	N	Y
31 Martinez	N	N	Y	Y	Y	N	N	Y
32 Dixon	N	N	Y	Y	N	N	Y	Y
33 Roybal-Allard	N	N	Y	Y	N	N	N	Y
34 Torres	?	N	Y	Y	N	N	N	Y
35 Waters	N	N	Y	Y	N	N	N	Y
36 Harman	N	N	Y	Y	Y	N	N	Y
37 Millender-McD.	N	N	Y	Y	N	N	N	Y
38 ***Horn***	Y	N	Y	Y	N	N	Y	Y
39 ***Royce***	Y	Y	N	N	Y	Y	N	Y
40 ***Lewis***	N	Y	Y	Y	Y	Y	Y	Y
41 ***Kim***	Y	Y	N	Y	Y	Y	Y	Y
42 Brown	N	N	Y	Y	N	N	N	Y
43 ***Calvert***	Y	Y	N	Y	Y	Y	Y	Y
44 ***Bono***	N	Y	N	Y	Y	Y	N	Y
45 ***Rohrabacher***	Y	Y	N	Y	Y	Y	N	Y
46 Sanchez	N	N	Y	N	Y	N	Y	Y
47 ***Cox***	?	Y	N	Y	Y	Y	Y	Y
48 ***Packard***	Y	Y	N	Y	Y	Y	Y	Y
49 ***Bilbray***	Y	Y	Y	Y	N	Y	Y	Y
50 Filner	Y	N	Y	Y	N	N	N	Y
51 ***Cunningham***	Y	Y	N	Y	Y	Y	Y	Y
52 ***Hunter***	N	Y	N	?	Y	Y	N	Y
COLORADO								
1 DeGette	N	N	Y	N	N	N	N	Y
2 Skaggs	N	N	Y	Y	N	N	Y	Y
3 ***McInnis***	Y	Y	N	N	Y	Y	N	Y
4 ***Schaffer***	Y	Y	N	N	Y	Y	N	Y
5 ***Hefley***	Y	Y	N	Y	Y	Y	N	Y
6 ***Schaefer***	Y	Y	N	Y	Y	Y	N	Y
CONNECTICUT								
1 Kennelly	N	N	Y	N	N	N	Y	Y
2 Gejdenson	N	N	Y	N	N	N	N	Y
3 DeLauro	N	N	Y	N	N	N	N	Y
4 ***Shays***	Y	Y	Y	N	N	Y	Y	Y
5 Maloney	N	N	Y	N	N	N	N	Y
6 ***Johnson***	Y	Y	Y	N	N	N	Y	Y
DELAWARE								
AL ***Castle***	N	N	Y	Y	N	N	Y	Y
FLORIDA								
1 ***Scarborough***	Y	Y	N	N	Y	Y	N	Y
2 Boyd	Y	N	Y	N	Y	N	N	Y
3 Brown	N	N	Y	Y	N	N	N	Y
4 ***Fowler***	Y	Y	Y	Y	Y	Y	Y	Y
5 Thurman	N	N	Y	N	N	N	N	Y
6 ***Stearns***	Y	Y	N	N	Y	Y	N	Y
7 ***Mica***	Y	Y	N	N	Y	Y	N	Y
8 ***McCollum***	Y	Y	N	Y	Y	Y	Y	Y
9 ***Bilirakis***	Y	Y	N	Y	Y	Y	N	Y
10 ***Young***	N	Y	N	Y	Y	Y	N	Y
11 Davis	N	N	Y	N	N	N	Y	Y
12 ***Canady***	Y	Y	N	N	Y	Y	N	Y
13 ***Miller***	Y	Y	N	Y	Y	Y	Y	Y
14 ***Goss***	Y	Y	N	Y	N	Y	Y	Y
15 ***Weldon***	+	Y	N	Y	Y	Y	Y	Y
16 ***Foley***	Y	Y	Y	Y	Y	Y	Y	Y
17 Meek	N	N	Y	Y	N	N	N	Y
18 ***Ros-Lehtinen***	Y	Y	N	Y	Y	Y	N	Y
19 Wexler	N	N	Y	Y	N	N	Y	Y
20 Deutsch	N	N	Y	N	Y	N	Y	Y
21 ***Diaz-Balart***	Y	Y	N	Y	Y	Y	N	Y
22 ***Shaw***	N	Y	Y	Y	Y	Y	Y	Y
23 Hastings	N	N	Y	?	N	N	N	Y
GEORGIA								
1 ***Kingston***	Y	Y	N	Y	Y	Y	N	Y
2 Bishop	N	N	Y	Y	Y	N	N	Y
3 ***Collins***	Y	Y	N	Y	Y	N	Y	Y
4 McKinney	N	N	Y	N	N	N	Y	Y
5 Lewis	N	N	Y	Y	N	N	N	Y
6 ***Gingrich***[2]		Y		Y	Y	Y		Y
7 ***Barr***	Y	Y	N	Y	Y	Y	N	Y
8 ***Chambliss***	Y	Y	N	N	?	Y	N	Y
9 ***Deal***	Y	Y	N	Y	Y	Y	N	Y
10 ***Norwood***	Y	Y	N	N	Y	Y	N	Y
11 ***Linder***	N	Y	N	Y	Y	Y	Y	Y
HAWAII								
1 Abercrombie	N	N	Y	N	N	N	N	Y
2 Mink	Y	N	Y	N	N	N	N	Y
IDAHO								
1 ***Chenoweth***	Y	Y	N	N	Y	Y	N	Y
2 ***Crapo***	Y	Y	N	Y	Y	Y	N	Y
ILLINOIS								
1 Rush	N	N	Y	Y	N	N	N	Y
2 Jackson	N	N	Y	Y	N	N	N	Y
3 Lipinski	Y	N	N	Y	N	Y	N	Y
4 Gutierrez	N	N	Y	N	N	N	N	Y
5 Blagojevich	N	N	Y	N	N	N	N	Y
6 ***Hyde***	N	Y	N	Y	Y	Y	Y	Y
7 Davis	N	N	Y	N	N	N	N	Y
8 ***Crane***	Y	Y	N	Y	Y	Y	Y	Y
9 Yates	?	N	Y	Y	N	N	N	Y
10 ***Porter***	N	Y	Y	Y	N	X	#	Y
11 ***Weller***	Y	Y	N	N	Y	Y	Y	Y
12 Costello	N	N	N	N	N	N	N	Y
13 ***Fawell***	N	Y	Y	Y	N	N	?	Y
14 ***Hastert***	Y	Y	N	Y	Y	Y	Y	Y

ND Northern Democrats SD Southern Democrats

	8	9	10	11	12	13	14	15
15 ***Ewing***	Y	Y	N	Y	N	Y	Y	Y
16 ***Manzullo***	Y	Y	N	N	Y	Y	Y	Y
17 Evans	Y	N	Y	N	N	N	N	Y
18 ***LaHood***	Y	Y	N	Y	Y	N	Y	Y
19 Poshard	N	N	N	N	N	N	N	Y
20 ***Shimkus***	Y	Y	N	N	Y	Y	Y	Y
INDIANA								
1 Visclosky	N	N	Y	N	N	N	N	Y
2 ***McIntosh***	Y	Y	N	N	?	Y	Y	Y
3 Roemer	N	N	N	N	Y	N	Y	Y
4 ***Souder***	Y	Y	N	N	Y	Y	N	Y
5 ***Buyer***	N	Y	N	Y	Y	Y	Y	Y
6 ***Burton***	Y	Y	N	Y	Y	Y	N	Y
7 ***Pease***	Y	Y	N	N	Y	Y	Y	Y
8 ***Hostettler***	N	Y	N	N	Y	Y	Y	Y
9 Hamilton	N	N	Y	N	Y	N	Y	Y
10 Carson	N	N	Y	N	N	N	N	Y
IOWA								
1 ***Leach***	N	N	Y	N	Y	N	Y	Y
2 ***Nussle***	Y	Y	N	N	Y	Y	Y	Y
3 Boswell	N	N	Y	N	Y	N	N	Y
4 ***Ganske***	Y	Y	N	Y	N	Y	Y	Y
5 ***Latham***	Y	Y	N	Y	Y	Y	Y	Y
KANSAS								
1 ***Moran***	Y	Y	N	N	Y	N	Y	Y
2 ***Ryun***	Y	Y	N	N	Y	Y	Y	Y
3 ***Snowbarger***	Y	Y	N	N	Y	Y	Y	Y
4 ***Tiahrt***	Y	Y	N	N	Y	Y	N	Y
KENTUCKY								
1 ***Whitfield***	Y	Y	N	N	Y	Y	N	Y
2 ***Lewis***	Y	Y	N	N	Y	Y	N	Y
3 ***Northup***	Y	Y	N	N	Y	Y	N	Y
4 ***Bunning***	Y	Y	N	N	Y	Y	N	Y
5 ***Rogers***	Y	Y	N	Y	Y	Y	N	Y
6 Baesler	N	N	Y	N	Y	N	N	Y
LOUISIANA								
1 ***Livingston***	N	Y	N	Y	Y	Y	Y	Y
2 Jefferson	N	N	Y	Y	Y	N	Y	Y
3 ***Tauzin***	Y	Y	N	Y	Y	Y	N	Y
4 ***McCrery***	Y	Y	N	Y	Y	Y	Y	Y
5 ***Cooksey***	Y	Y	N	N	Y	Y	X	Y
6 ***Baker***	Y	Y	N	N	Y	Y	Y	Y
7 John	Y	N	N	N	Y	Y	N	Y
MAINE								
1 Allen	N	N	Y	N	N	N	N	Y
2 Baldacci	N	N	Y	N	Y	N	N	Y
MARYLAND								
1 ***Gilchrest***	Y	Y	Y	Y	N	Y	Y	Y
2 ***Ehrlich***	Y	Y	Y	Y	Y	Y	Y	Y
3 Cardin	N	N	Y	Y	N	N	N	Y
4 Wynn	N	N	Y	Y	N	N	Y	Y
5 Hoyer	N	N	Y	Y	Y	N	Y	N
6 ***Bartlett***	Y	Y	N	N	Y	Y	N	Y
7 Cummings	N	N	Y	Y	N	N	Y	Y
8 ***Morella***	N	N	Y	Y	N	N	Y	Y
MASSACHUSETTS								
1 Olver	N	N	Y	Y	N	N	N	Y
2 Neal	Y	N	Y	Y	N	N	N	Y
3 McGovern	N	N	Y	N	N	N	N	Y
4 Frank	Y	N	Y	Y	N	N	N	Y
5 Meehan	N	N	Y	N	N	N	Y	Y
6 Tierney	Y	N	Y	N	N	N	N	Y
7 Markey	Y	N	Y	Y	N	N	N	Y
8 Kennedy	N	N	Y	Y	N	N	Y	Y
9 Moakley	N	N	Y	Y	N	N	N	Y
10 Delahunt	N	N	Y	Y	N	N	N	Y
MICHIGAN								
1 Stupak	N	N	N	Y	N	N	N	Y
2 ***Hoekstra***	Y	Y	N	Y	Y	Y	Y	Y
3 ***Ehlers***	N	Y	N	Y	N	Y	Y	Y
4 ***Camp***	Y	Y	N	Y	Y	Y	Y	Y
5 Barcia	Y	N	N	N	Y	N	N	Y
6 ***Upton***	Y	Y	Y	Y	Y	Y	Y	Y
7 ***Smith***	N	Y	N	N	Y	Y	N	Y
8 Stabenow	N	N	Y	N	N	N	N	Y
9 Kildee	N	N	N	N	N	N	N	Y
10 Bonior	N	N	Y	Y	N	N	N	Y
11 ***Knollenberg***	N	Y	N	Y	Y	Y	Y	Y
12 Levin	N	N	Y	Y	N	N	N	Y
13 Rivers	N	N	Y	N	N	N	N	Y
14 Conyers	N	N	Y	Y	N	N	N	Y
15 Kilpatrick	N	N	Y	N	N	N	N	Y
16 Dingell	N	N	Y	Y	N	N	N	Y
MINNESOTA								
1 ***Gutknecht***	Y	Y	N	N	Y	Y	N	Y

	8	9	10	11	12	13	14	15
2 Minge	N	N	Y	N	N	N	Y	Y
3 ***Ramstad***	Y	N	Y	N	N	N	Y	Y
4 Vento	N	N	Y	Y	N	N	N	Y
5 Sabo	N	N	Y	Y	N	N	N	Y
6 Luther	N	N	Y	N	N	N	Y	Y
7 Peterson	Y	N	N	N	Y	N	Y	Y
8 Oberstar	N	N	N	Y	N	N	N	Y
MISSISSIPPI								
1 ***Wicker***	N	Y	N	Y	Y	Y	Y	Y
2 Thompson	N	N	Y	Y	Y	N	N	Y
3 ***Pickering***	Y	Y	N	Y	Y	Y	Y	Y
4 ***Parker***	Y	Y	N	Y	Y	Y	N	Y
5 Taylor	N	Y	N	N	Y	N	N	Y
MISSOURI								
1 Clay	N	N	Y	Y	N	N	N	Y
2 ***Talent***	Y	Y	N	N	Y	Y	Y	Y
3 Gephardt	N	N	Y	Y	N	N	N	Y
4 Skelton	N	N	N	N	Y	N	N	Y
5 McCarthy	N	N	Y	N	N	N	Y	Y
6 Danner	Y	N	Y	N	Y	N	N	Y
7 ***Blunt***	N	Y	N	Y	Y	N	Y	Y
8 ***Emerson***	N	Y	N	N	Y	Y	Y	Y
9 ***Hulshof***	Y	Y	N	N	Y	Y	Y	Y
MONTANA								
AL ***Hill***	Y	Y	N	N	Y	Y	Y	Y
NEBRASKA								
1 ***Bereuter***	Y	Y	N	N	N	N	Y	Y
2 ***Christensen***	Y	Y	N	N	Y	Y	Y	Y
3 ***Barrett***	Y	Y	N	N	Y	N	Y	Y
NEVADA								
1 ***Ensign***	Y	Y	N	N	Y	Y	N	Y
2 ***Gibbons***	Y	Y	Y	N	Y	Y	N	Y
NEW HAMPSHIRE								
1 ***Sununu***	Y	Y	N	N	Y	Y	Y	Y
2 ***Bass***	Y	Y	Y	N	N	Y	Y	Y
NEW JERSEY								
1 Andrews	N	N	Y	N	N	N	N	Y
2 ***LoBiondo***	Y	N	N	N	Y	N	N	Y
3 ***Saxton***	Y	N	N	Y	N	N	N	Y
4 ***Smith***	N	Y	N	Y	N	N	N	Y
5 ***Roukema***	Y	N	Y	N	N	N	Y	Y
6 Pallone	N	N	Y	Y	N	N	N	Y
7 ***Franks***	Y	N	Y	N	Y	Y	N	Y
8 Pascrell	N	N	Y	N	Y	N	N	Y
9 Rothman	N	N	Y	N	Y	N	N	Y
10 Payne	N	N	Y	Y	N	?	?	Y
11 ***Frelinghuysen***	N	Y	Y	Y	N	N	Y	Y
12 ***Pappas***	Y	Y	N	N	Y	Y	Y	Y
13 Menendez	N	N	Y	Y	N	?	?	Y
NEW MEXICO								
1 ***Schiff***	?	?	?	?	?	?	?	?
2 ***Skeen***	N	Y	Y	Y	Y	Y	Y	Y
3 ***Redmond***	N	Y	N	N	Y	Y	Y	Y
NEW YORK								
1 ***Forbes***	Y	N	N	N	N	Y	N	Y
2 ***Lazio***	N	N	Y	Y	N	Y	Y	Y
3 ***King***	N	Y	N	Y	Y	Y	Y	Y
4 McCarthy	N	N	Y	Y	N	N	N	Y
5 Ackerman	N	N	Y	Y	N	?	?	Y
6 Flake	N	N	Y	N	N	Y	Y	Y
7 Manton	N	N	N	Y	N	N	N	Y
8 Nadler	N	N	Y	Y	N	N	N	Y
9 Schumer	?	N	Y	N	N	N	Y	Y
10 Towns	N	N	Y	Y	N	?	Y	Y
11 Owens	N	N	Y	Y	N	N	N	Y
12 Velazquez	N	N	Y	Y	N	N	N	Y
13 ***Fossella***[3]								Y
14 Maloney	N	N	Y	Y	N	N	N	Y
15 Rangel	N	N	Y	Y	N	N	N	Y
16 Serrano	Y	N	Y	Y	N	N	N	Y
17 Engel	N	N	Y	Y	N	N	N	Y
18 Lowey	N	N	Y	Y	N	N	N	Y
19 ***Kelly***	Y	N	Y	N	N	Y	Y	Y
20 ***Gilman***	N	Y	Y	Y	N	N	Y	Y
21 McNulty	N	N	Y	Y	N	?	?	Y
22 ***Solomon***	Y	Y	N	Y	Y	Y	N	Y
23 ***Boehlert***	N	Y	Y	Y	N	N	N	Y
24 ***McHugh***	N	Y	Y	Y	N	N	N	Y
25 ***Walsh***	Y	Y	N	N	N	Y	N	Y
26 Hinchey	N	N	Y	Y	N	N	N	Y
27 ***Paxon***	Y	Y	N	Y	Y	Y	Y	Y
28 Slaughter	N	–	Y	N	N	–	–	Y
29 LaFalce	N	N	Y	Y	N	N	N	Y
30 ***Quinn***	N	N	N	Y	Y	N	N	Y
31 ***Houghton***	N	N	Y	Y	Y	N	Y	Y

	8	9	10	11	12	13	14	15
NORTH CAROLINA								
1 Clayton	N	N	Y	Y	N	N	N	Y
2 Etheridge	N	N	Y	N	Y	N	N	Y
3 ***Jones***	Y	Y	N	N	Y	Y	Y	Y
4 Price	N	N	Y	N	N	N	N	Y
5 ***Burr***	Y	Y	N	N	Y	N	Y	Y
6 ***Coble***	Y	Y	N	Y	Y	Y	Y	Y
7 McIntyre	N	N	N	N	Y	N	N	Y
8 Hefner	N	N	Y	Y	N	N	N	Y
9 ***Myrick***	Y	Y	N	N	Y	Y	N	Y
10 ***Ballenger***	Y	Y	N	Y	Y	Y	Y	Y
11 ***Taylor***	Y	Y	N	Y	Y	Y	Y	Y
12 Watt	N	N	Y	Y	N	N	N	Y
NORTH DAKOTA								
AL Pomeroy	N	N	Y	N	N	N	N	Y
OHIO								
1 ***Chabot***	Y	Y	N	N	Y	Y	Y	Y
2 ***Portman***	Y	Y	N	N	N	Y	Y	Y
3 Hall	N	N	N	Y	Y	N	Y	Y
4 ***Oxley***	N	Y	N	Y	Y	Y	Y	Y
5 ***Gillmor***	N	Y	N	N	Y	Y	Y	Y
6 Strickland	N	N	Y	N	?	N	N	Y
7 ***Hobson***	Y	Y	Y	Y	Y	Y	Y	Y
8 ***Boehner***	N	Y	N	Y	Y	Y	N	Y
9 Kaptur	N	N	N	N	N	N	N	Y
10 Kucinich	N	N	N	N	N	N	N	Y
11 Stokes	N	N	Y	Y	N	N	N	Y
12 ***Kasich***	Y	Y	N	N	Y	Y	Y	Y
13 Brown	N	N	Y	Y	N	N	N	Y
14 Sawyer	N	N	Y	Y	N	N	N	Y
15 ***Pryce***	Y	Y	+	Y	Y	Y	Y	Y
16 ***Regula***	N	Y	Y	Y	Y	N	Y	Y
17 Traficant	Y	Y	N	N	Y	N	N	Y
18 ***Ney***	Y	Y	N	Y	Y	N	Y	Y
19 ***LaTourette***	Y	Y	N	Y	Y	Y	Y	Y
OKLAHOMA								
1 ***Largent***	Y	Y	N	N	Y	Y	Y	Y
2 ***Coburn***	Y	Y	N	N	Y	?	?	Y
3 ***Watkins***	Y	Y	N	N	Y	Y	Y	Y
4 ***Watts***	Y	Y	N	N	Y	Y	Y	Y
5 ***Istook***	Y	Y	N	N	Y	Y	N	Y
6 ***Lucas***	Y	Y	N	N	Y	Y	N	Y
OREGON								
1 Furse	N	N	Y	Y	N	N	N	Y
2 ***Smith***	Y	Y	N	Y	Y	Y	N	Y
3 Blumenauer	N	N	Y	Y	Y	N	Y	Y
4 DeFazio	Y	N	Y	N	N	N	N	Y
5 Hooley	N	N	Y	N	N	N	N	Y
PENNSYLVANIA								
1 Foglietta	N	N	Y	?	N	?	?	Y
2 Fattah	N	N	Y	Y	N	N	Y	Y
3 Borski	N	N	N	Y	N	N	N	Y
4 Klink	N	N	N	Y	N	N	N	Y
5 ***Peterson***	Y	Y	N	N	Y	Y	N	Y
6 Holden	N	N	N	N	Y	?	N	Y
7 ***Weldon***	N	Y	N	Y	Y	Y	N	Y
8 ***Greenwood***	N	Y	Y	Y	N	Y	Y	Y
9 ***Shuster***	Y	Y	N	Y	Y	Y	N	Y
10 ***McDade***	Y	Y	N	Y	Y	N	N	Y
11 Kanjorski	N	N	N	Y	N	N	N	Y
12 Murtha	N	N	N	Y	Y	N	N	Y
13 ***Fox***	N	Y	N	N	Y	Y	N	Y
14 Coyne	N	N	Y	Y	N	N	N	Y
15 McHale	N	N	Y	N	N	N	N	Y
16 ***Pitts***	Y	Y	N	N	Y	Y	Y	Y
17 ***Gekas***	Y	Y	N	N	Y	Y	N	Y
18 Doyle	N	N	N	Y	Y	N	N	Y
19 ***Goodling***	Y	Y	N	N	Y	Y	N	Y
20 Mascara	N	N	N	N	Y	N	N	Y
21 ***English***	Y	Y	N	N	Y	N	Y	Y
RHODE ISLAND								
1 Kennedy	N	N	Y	N	N	N	N	Y
2 Weygand	N	N	N	N	Y	N	N	Y
SOUTH CAROLINA								
1 ***Sanford***	Y	Y	N	N	N	Y	Y	Y
2 ***Spence***	Y	Y	N	Y	Y	Y	N	Y
3 ***Graham***	Y	Y	N	N	Y	Y	N	Y
4 ***Inglis***	Y	Y	N	N	Y	Y	N	Y
5 Spratt	N	N	Y	Y	N	N	N	Y
6 Clyburn	N	N	Y	Y	N	N	N	Y
SOUTH DAKOTA								
AL ***Thune***	Y	Y	N	N	Y	N	Y	Y
TENNESSEE								
1 ***Jenkins***	Y	Y	N	N	Y	N	N	Y
2 ***Duncan***	Y	Y	N	N	Y	Y	N	Y

	8	9	10	11	12	13	14	15
3 ***Wamp***	Y	Y	N	N	Y	Y	N	Y
4 ***Hilleary***	Y	Y	N	N	Y	Y	N	Y
5 Clement	N	N	Y	Y	Y	N	Y	Y
6 Gordon	N	N	Y	N	Y	N	N	Y
7 ***Bryant***	+	Y	N	N	Y	Y	Y	Y
8 Tanner	N	N	Y	Y	Y	N	Y	Y
9 Ford	N	N	Y	N	Y	N	N	Y
TEXAS								
1 Sandlin	N	N	Y	N	Y	N	N	Y
2 Turner	N	N	Y	N	Y	N	N	Y
3 ***Johnson, Sam***	Y	Y	N	Y	Y	Y	Y	Y
4 Hall	Y	Y	N	N	Y	Y	N	Y
5 ***Sessions***	Y	Y	N	N	Y	Y	Y	Y
6 ***Barton***	Y	Y	N	Y	Y	Y	Y	Y
7 ***Archer***	Y	Y	N	Y	Y	Y	Y	Y
8 ***Brady***	Y	Y	N	N	Y	Y	Y	Y
9 Lampson	N	N	Y	N	N	N	N	Y
10 Doggett	N	N	Y	Y	N	N	N	Y
11 Edwards	N	N	Y	Y	Y	N	?	Y
12 ***Granger***	Y	Y	N	N	Y	Y	Y	Y
13 ***Thornberry***	Y	Y	N	N	Y	Y	Y	Y
14 ***Paul***	Y	Y	N	N	Y	Y	N	Y
15 Hinojosa	N	N	Y	N	Y	N	N	Y
16 Reyes	N	N	Y	N	N	N	N	Y
17 Stenholm	N	Y	N	N	Y	N	Y	Y
18 Jackson-Lee	N	N	Y	Y	–	N	Y	Y
19 ***Combest***	Y	Y	N	N	Y	Y	Y	Y
20 Gonzalez	N	N	?	?	?	?	?	?
21 ***Smith***	N	Y	N	Y	Y	Y	Y	Y
22 ***DeLay***	Y	Y	N	Y	Y	Y	Y	Y
23 ***Bonilla***	Y	Y	N	?	Y	Y	Y	Y
24 Frost	N	N	Y	Y	Y	N	N	Y
25 Bentsen	N	N	Y	Y	N	N	Y	Y
26 ***Armey***	N	Y	N	Y	Y	Y	Y	Y
27 Ortiz	N	N	N	Y	Y	N	N	Y
28 Rodriguez	N	N	Y	N	N	N	N	Y
29 Green	Y	N	Y	N	N	N	N	Y
30 Johnson, E.B.	N	N	Y	Y	N	N	Y	Y
UTAH								
1 ***Hansen***	Y	Y	N	Y	Y	Y	N	Y
2 ***Cook***	Y	N	N	N	Y	Y	N	Y
3 ***Cannon***	Y	Y	N	N	Y	N	Y	Y
VERMONT								
AL *Sanders*	Y	N	Y	N	N	N	N	Y
VIRGINIA								
1 ***Bateman***	N	Y	N	Y	Y	Y	Y	Y
2 Pickett	N	N	Y	Y	Y	N	Y	Y
3 Scott	N	N	Y	Y	Y	N	N	Y
4 Sisisky	N	N	Y	Y	Y	N	N	Y
5 Goode	Y	N	N	N	Y	N	N	Y
6 ***Goodlatte***	Y	Y	N	Y	Y	N	Y	Y
7 ***Bliley***	N	Y	N	Y	Y	Y	Y	Y
8 Moran	N	N	Y	Y	N	N	N	Y
9 Boucher	N	N	?	Y	N	N	N	Y
10 ***Wolf***	N	Y	N	Y	Y	Y	N	Y
11 ***Davis***	N	Y	Y	Y	Y	N	Y	Y
WASHINGTON								
1 ***White***	N	Y	Y	N	Y	Y	Y	Y
2 ***Metcalf***	Y	Y	N	N	Y	Y	N	Y
3 ***Smith, Linda***	Y	Y	N	N	Y	Y	N	Y
4 ***Hastings***	Y	Y	N	Y	Y	Y	Y	Y
5 ***Nethercutt***	Y	Y	N	N	Y	Y	Y	Y
6 Dicks	N	N	Y	Y	N	N	Y	Y
7 McDermott	N	N	Y	Y	N	N	Y	N
8 ***Dunn***	Y	Y	Y	Y	Y	Y	Y	Y
9 Smith, Adam	N	N	Y	N	N	N	N	Y
WEST VIRGINIA								
1 Mollohan	N	N	N	Y	N	N	N	Y
2 Wise	N	N	Y	N	N	N	?	Y
3 Rahall	N	N	N	Y	N	N	N	Y
WISCONSIN								
1 ***Neumann***	Y	Y	–	N	Y	Y	N	Y
2 ***Klug***	Y	Y	Y	Y	N	N	Y	Y
3 Kind	N	N	Y	Y	N	N	N	Y
4 Kleczka	N	N	Y	Y	N	N	N	Y
5 Barrett	N	N	Y	N	N	N	N	Y
6 ***Petri***	Y	Y	N	N	Y	Y	Y	Y
7 Obey	N	N	Y	Y	N	N	N	Y
8 Johnson	N	N	Y	N	N	N	N	Y
9 ***Sensenbrenner***	Y	Y	N	N	Y	Y	Y	Y
WYOMING								
AL ***Cubin***	Y	Y	N	N	?	?	?	?

Southern states - Ala., Ark., Fla., Ga., Ky., La., Miss., N.C., Okla., S.C., Tenn., Texas, Va.

CQ

Appendix D

TEXTS

SPEAKER'S RE-ELECTION

Gingrich Sets Inclusive Tone, Attacks Drugs, Ignorance

Following is The Associated Press text of the speech given by House Speaker Newt Gingrich, R-Ga., after his re-election to the speakership on Jan. 7:

Gingrich: Let me say to those who voted for me, from the bottom of my heart, thank you. To those who voted for someone else, I hope that I can work with you in such a way that you feel that I am capable of being Speaker of the whole House and representing everyone.

To the freshmen and their families and all the young people who are here today, you are part of a wonderful experience. Just as in less than two weeks we will welcome the president for an inaugural, we here in the legislative branch also celebrate a remarkable moment which the entire world watches; a time when an entire nation voluntarily decides how to govern itself and does so in such a manner that there is a sense among the entire country that freedom is secure and that every citizen can participate.

This is the 105th time we've done this as a country — every two years. The first one actually did not occur until April the 1st, 1789, because while everyone was supposed to show up in March for the brand new Congress, they couldn't find a quorum. And then they all came together. And there are wonderful stories by people who were there written in their diaries and their letters about the fact that they were just folks from all over, of many different backgrounds. Back then they would all have been male and they would all have been white and they would all have been property holders.

Today we have extended democracy and freedom to levels that the Founding Fathers could not have imagined. And any citizen anywhere on the planet watching through C-SPAN and through the networks and seeing this room and its diversity can appreciate the degree to which America opens its doors and its hearts to all people of all backgrounds to have a better future.

In addition to the elected members, we are very fortunate to have a professional staff on both sides of the aisle and a professional staff serving on a nonpartisan basis. And let me say that I think that Robin Carle stood well as the clerk of the House in representing all of us in establishing the dignity.

And I thought that in the interchanges between she and Chairman [Vic] Fazio [D-Calif.] that the world could see legitimate partisanship engaged in legitimacy — legitimately, exactly the way it should be; in a professional, in a courteous, in a firm way on both sides. And I think that's part of what we have to teach the world.

In just a few moments, my dear friend John [D.] Dingell [D-Mich.], who represents a tradition in his district, who has fought all these years for all that he believes in, who in the last Congress served so ably in helping pass the telecommunications bill, is going to swear me in. And I am going to ask — then I will have a chance to swear you in. But before that, if I might, I'd say to my dear friend — let me say my wife is here and my mother and my relatives.

And two years ago, they were here with my father. He is not here today, as I think all of you know. He was an infantryman. He served this country. He believed in honor, duty, country.

Let me say to the entire House that two years ago, when I became the first Republican Speaker in 40 years, to the degree I was too brash, too self-confident or too pushy, I apologize. To whatever degree, in any way, that I brought controversy or inappropriate attention to the House, I apologize.

It is my intention to do everything I can to work with every member of this Congress. And I would just say, as with telecommunication in Congressman Dingell's case, on welfare reform, on line item veto, on telecommunications reform, on steps towards a balanced budget, again and again we found a bipartisan majority willing to pass significant legislation, willing to work together.

There's much work to be done. I've asked Chairman Henry [J.] Hyde [R-Ill.] of the Judiciary Committee to look at the issue of judicial activism. He has agreed to hold hearings looking at that issue.

I think all of us should focus on increasing American jobs through world sales. And I have asked Chairman [Bill] Archer [R-Texas] to look at the whole issue of taxation and how it affects American job creation.

I've also asked the Ways and Means Committee to look at oversight on NAFTA, on the World Trade Organization, because the fact is, we have to move the legislative branch into the information age. If there are going to be continuing bodies around the world, then Chairman [Benjamin A.] Gilman [R-N.Y.] in International Relations and Chairman Archer and others have to get in the habit, I think, of a kind of aggressive oversight, reporting to the nation on whether or not our interests are being protected.

I've also asked Chairman Archer to prepare a series of hearings looking at the entire issue of how we revise the entire tax code; whether we go towards a flat tax or whether we replace the income tax with a sales tax, or what we do; but to begin a process that, frankly, may take four to six years, but is the right direction for the right reason.

Finally, I've asked Chairman [Floyd D.] Spence [R-S.C.] on the National Security Committee, both to look at the issue of national missile defense and to look at the question of military reform.

And let me say to all of my friends on both sides of the aisle, we have every opportunity through reform to shrink the Pentagon to a triangle; we have every opportunity to apply the lessons of downsizing, the lessons of the information age. And just because something is in uniform doesn't mean it has to be saluted, but instead, we should be getting every penny for our taxpayers, and we in the Congress should be looking at long-term contracting as one way to dramatically lower the cost of defense.

But I want to talk about one other area. And here I just want to say there's something more than legislation. Each of us is a leader back home. And I want to just talk very briefly about three topics, and it's about these children and their America, children on both sides of the aisle, children from all backgrounds in every state.

I think we have to ask the question, as leaders, beyond legislation: How do we continue to create one nation under God, indivisible, with liberty and justice for all? I believe most Americans, whether native-born or immigrant, still desire for us to be one nation. So let me briefly talk about three areas that I think are vital.

Let me say first, I think — I'm going to talk just for a second about race, drugs and ignorance. First, let me ask all you: Do we not need to rethink our whole approach to race? And let me draw the parallel to Dick Fosbury. He was a high jumper. In the 1968 Olympics in Mexico City, he developed an entire new approach which is now used by everyone. Yet for six years, the U.S. Olympic Committee rejected it.

My point is very simple. I don't believe any rational American can be comfortable with where we are on the issue of race. And I think all of us ought to take on the challenge as leaders, beyond legislation, beyond our normal jobs, of asking some new questions in some new ways. After all, what does race mean when, if based on merit alone, ethnic Asians would make up a clear majority at the University of California at Berkeley? What does race mean when colleges recruit minorities in the name of inclusiveness and diversity and then segregate them in their own dormitories? What does race mean when many Americans cannot fill out their census forms because they're an amalgam of races? And furthermore, if those of us who are conservative say that bureaucracy and compulsion is not the answer, then what are we going to say to a child born in a poor neighborhood with a broken home and no one to help them rise, who has no organic contact to prosperity and has no organic contact to a better future?

Now, I mentioned this in passing two years ago, and one of the failures that I would take some of the responsibility for is that we did not follow up. But I want to put it right on the table today that every one of us, as a leader, has an obligation to reach out beyond party and beyond ideology and, as Americans, to say, "One of the highest values we're going to spend the next two years on is openly dealing with the challenge of meaning that when we say in our declaration that we are endowed by our Creator with certain unalienable rights, including life, liberty and the pursuit of happiness, that every child in every neighborhood, of every background, is endowed by God.

"And every time America fails to meet that, we are failing to meet God's test for the country we should be."

Let me say second about drugs; I think we have to redefine and rethink our approach to drugs. One of my close friends had her 19-year-old sister overdose, and her 19-year-old sister today is in a coma and celebrated her 20th birthday in that coma. Drugs aren't statistics. As Charlie Rangel [D-N.Y.] told me at breakfast just two years ago, drugs are real human beings being destroyed. Drugs are real violence. If we did not have drugs in this country, the amount of spouse abuse, the amount of child abuse, the amount of violence would drop dramatically. And so I want to suggest that we should take seriously reaching across all barriers and establishing an all-out effort.

You know, the Columbia University Center for Addiction and Substance Abuse has done a fascinating study. The center found that one of the best predictors of whether a child will stay free of drugs is whether he or she practices a religion. Joe Califano, Lyndon Johnson's former adviser and Jimmy Carter's secretary of Health and Human Services [formerly Health, Education and Welfare], says that religion is part of the solution to our drug problems and to drug treatment itself. Alcoholics Anonymous refers to a "higher power." I don't know what all the answers are. But I do know that if we love these children, in addition to fighting racism and reaching out to every child, we need to decide that we are prepared to have the equivalent of an abolitionist movement against drugs and to do what it takes so that none of these children end up in a coma celebrating their birthday or end up dead.

Lastly, we need to pay closer attention to a word you don't hear much anymore: ignorance. Traditionally, ignorance ranked with pestilence, hunger, war as abominations upon humanity. But in recent years, the word ignorance has been cleaned up and refined into some aspect of educational failure. I mean by ignorance something deeper. It's not about geography in the third grade. It's about learning the work ethic. It's about learning to be a citizen. It's about learning to save. It's about all the things that make us functional. It's about the things that allow virtually everybody in this room to get up each morning and have a good life.

There are too many places in America where people are born into dysfunction, educated into dysfunction and live in dysfunction, and we should find a way to reach out in this modern era and use every tool at our fingertips, from computers to television to radio to personal volunteerism, so that every family that today happens to be dysfunctional has a chance within the next few years to learn to be functional.

And I think we should take ignorance as serious a problem as drugs or race.

We in the Congress have one place; we have an obligation beyond any other, and that's this city. And I want to commend [Delegate] Eleanor Holmes Norton [D-D.C.] for the leadership she has shown and the courage she has shown day after day and week after week. She and Tom Davis [R-Va.] and Jim Walsh [R-N.Y.] worked their hearts out over the last two years, and I believe it is fair to say that in some ways, we have begun to make progress. It is not easy. It has to be done carefully. It cannot violate the right of the citizens of this city. But let's be candid; first, this is our national capital. We have a unique obligation on both sides of the aisle, to care about Washington, because we are today to Washington what a state government would be back home to your town. We have an unusual obligation to Washington.

Second, it is our national capital. And people looked at me as though I'd lost my mind a year and a half ago when I met with [Washington, D.C.] Mayor [Marion S.] Barry and I said, "You know, our vision ought to be the finest capital city in the world." And that ought to be our vision.

And furthermore, if we're going to talk honestly about race and we're going to talk honestly about drugs and we're going to talk honestly about ignorance, we owe it to every citizen of this District, every child in this District, to have a decent chance to grow up and go to a school that succeeds, in a neighborhood that is drug-free and safe, with an expectation of getting a job in a community that actually cares about them and provides a better future. And we should take on as a capital — as a Congress, our responsibilities to the District of Columbia, and we should do it proudly. And we should not be ashamed to go back home and say, "You're darn right we're helping our national capital because we want you to visit it with pride, and we want you to know that you can say to anyone anywhere in the world: Come to America and visit Washington, it is a great city."

Let me close with this final thought — and I appreciate my friend John [Dingell] standing there. And I apologize for having drawn you forward, particularly since you're standing on one foot.

But this has been a very difficult time. And to those who agonized and ended up voting for me, I thank you. Some of this difficulty, frankly, I brought on myself. We will deal with that in more detail later. And I apologize to the House and the country for having done so. Some of it is part of the natural process of partisan competition.

This morning, a very dear friend of mine said that he was going to pray to God that I would win today, and I asked him not to. I asked him to pray to God that whatever happens is what God wants, and then we would try to understand it and learn from it.

Let me put that forward in the same thing for all of us as we approach the next two years. I was really struck about a month ago when I walked down to the Lincoln Memorial and I read the Second Inaugural, which is short enough to be on the wall. And 12 times in that inaugural, Lincoln refers to God. I went back and read Washington's first inaugural, which is replete with reference to America existing within God's framework. I read Jefferson's first inaugural — since he's often described as a Deist — which refers to the importance and the power of Providence. All of you can visit the Jefferson Memorial where he says — around the top it is inscribed —"I have sworn upon the altar of God Almighty eternal hostility against all forms of tyranny over the minds of men."

We have much to be proud of as Americans.

This is a great and a wonderful system. We have much to be ashamed of as Americans; from drug addiction to spouse and child abuse; to children living in ignorance and poverty surrounded by the greatest, wealthiest nation in the world; to a political system that clearly has to be overhauled from the ground up if it is going to be worthy of the respect we want and cherish.

I would just suggest to all of you that until we learn in a non-sectarian way — not Baptist, not Catholic, not Jewish — in a non-sectarian way — until we learn to re-establish the authority that we are endowed by our Creator, that we owe it to our Creator, and that we need to seek divine guidance in what we are doing, we are not going to solve this country's problems. In that spirit, with your prayers and help, I will seek to be worthy of being Speaker of the House, and I will seek to work with every member sent by their constituents to represent them in the United States Congress.

And I now call on my dear friend, the senior member of the House and a wonderful person, John Dingell. I am ready to take the oath of office, and I ask the dean of the House of Representatives, the Honorable John Dingell of Michigan, to administer the oath.

Dingell: Would the gentleman from Georgia please raise his right hand?

Do you solemnly swear that you will support and defend the Constitution of the United States against all enemies foreign and domestic, and that you will bear true faith and allegiance to the same, and that you take this obligation freely without any mental reservation or purpose of evasion, and that you will well and faithfully discharge the duties of the office on which you are about to enter, so help you God?

Gingrich: I do. ■

ETHICS

Excerpts of Findings In Gingrich Case

Following are excerpts of the report, released Jan. 17, 1997, issued by special counsel James M. Cole about the alleged ethics violations of House Speaker Newt Gingrich, R-Ga. The excerpts include the summary of the House ethics subcommittee's findings and the analysis and conclusion of the charges:

C. SUMMARY OF THE SUBCOMMITTEE'S FACTUAL FINDINGS

The Subcommittee found that in regard to two projects, Mr. Gingrich engaged in activity involving 501(c)(3) organizations that was substantially motivated by partisan, political goals. The Subcommittee also found that Mr. Gingrich provided the Committee with material information about one of those projects that was inaccurate, incomplete, and unreliable.

1. AOW/ACTV

The first project was a television program called the American Opportunities Workshop (AOW). It took place in May 1990. The idea for this project came from Mr. Gingrich and he was principally responsible for developing its message. AOW involved broadcasting a television program on the subject of various governmental issues. Mr. Gingrich hoped that this program would help create a "citizens' movement." Workshops were set up throughout the country where people could gather to watch the program and be recruited for the citizens' movement. While the program was educational, the citizens' movement was also considered a tool to recruit non-voters and people who were apolitical to the Republican Party. The program was deliberately free of any references to Republicans or partisan politics because Mr. Gingrich believed such references would dissuade the target audience of non-voters from becoming involved.

AOW started out as a project of GOPAC, a political action committee dedicated to, among other things, achieving Republican control of the United States House of Representatives.

Its methods for accomplishing this goal included the development and articulation of a political message and the dissemination of that message as widely as possible. One such avenue of dissemination was AOW. The program, however, consumed a substantial portion of GOPAC's revenues. Because of the expense, Mr. Gingrich and others at GOPAC decided to transfer the project to a 501(c)(3) organization in order to attract tax-deductible funding. The 501(c)(3) organization chosen was the Abraham Lincoln Opportunity Foundation (ALOF).

ALOF was dormant at the time and was revived to sponsor AOW's successor, American Citizens' Television (ACTV). ALOF operated out of GOPAC's offices. Virtually all its officers and employers were simultaneously GOPAC officers or employees. ACTV had the same educational aspects and partisan, political goals as AOW. The principal difference between the two was that ACTV used approximately $260,000 in tax-deductible contributions to fund its operations. ACTV broadcast three television programs in 1990 and then ceased operations. The last program was funded by a 501(c)(4) organization because the show's content was deemed to be too political for a 501(c)(3) organization.

2. Renewing American Civilization

The second project utilizing 501(c)(3) organizations involved a college course taught by Mr. Gingrich called Renewing American Civilization. Mr. Gingrich developed the course as a subset to and tool of a larger political and cultural movement also called Renewing American Civilization. The goal of this movement, as stated by Mr. Gingrich, was the replacement of the "welfare state" with an "opportunity society." A primary means of achieving this goal was the development of the movement's message and the dissemination of that message as widely as possible. Mr. Gingrich intended that a "Republican majority" would be the heart of the movement and that the movement would "professionalize" House Republicans. A method for achieving these goals was to use the movement's message to "attract voters, resources, and candidates." According to Mr. Gingrich, the course was, among other things, a primary and essential means to develop and disseminate the message of the movement.

The core message of the movement and the course was that the welfare state had failed, that it could not be repaired but had to be replaced, and that it had to be replaced with an opportunity society based on what Mr. Gingrich called the "Five Pillars of American Civilization." These were: 1) personal strength; 2) entrepreneurial free enterprise; 3) the spirit of invention; 4) quality as defined by Edwards Deming; and 5) the lessons of American history. The message also concentrated on three substantive areas. These were: 1) jobs and economic growth; 2) health; and 3) saving the inner city.

This message was also Mr. Gingrich's main campaign theme in 1993 and 1994 and Mr. Gingrich sought to have Republican candidates adopt the Renewing American Civilization message in their campaigns. In the context of political campaigns, Mr. Gingrich used the term "welfare state" as a negative label for Democrats and the term "opportunity society" as a positive label for Republicans.

As General Chairman of GOPAC, Mr. Gingrich decided that GOPAC would use Renewing American Civilization as its political message and theme during 1993-1994. GOPAC, however, was having financial difficulties and could not afford to disseminate its political messages as it had in past years. GOPAC had a number of roles in regard to the course. For example, GOPAC personnel helped develop, manage, promote, and raise funds for the course.

GOPAC Charter Members helped develop the idea to teach the course as a means for communicating GOPAC's message. GOPAC Charter Members at Charter Meetings helped develop the content of the course. GOPAC was "better off" as a result of the nationwide dissemination of the Renewing American Civilization message via the course in that the message GOPAC had adopted and determined to be the one that would help it achieve its goals was broadcast widely and at no cost to GOPAC.

The course was taught at Kennesaw State College (KSC) in 1993 and at Reinhardt College in 1994 and 1995. Each course consisted of ten lectures and each lecture consisted of approximately four hours of classroom instruction, for a total of forty hours. Mr. Gingrich taught twenty hours of each course and his co-teacher, or occasionally a guest lecturer, taught twenty hours. Students from each of the colleges as well as people who were not students attended the lectures. Mr. Gingrich's 20-hour portion of the course was taped and distributed to remote sites, referred to as "site hosts," via satellite, videotape and cable television. As with AOW/ACTV, Renewing American Civilization involved setting up workshops around the country where people could gather to watch the course. While the course was educational, Mr. Gingrich intended that the workshops would be, among other things, a recruiting tool for GOPAC and the Republican Party.

The major costs for the Renewing American Civilization course were for dissemination of the lectures. This expense was primarily paid for by tax-deductible contributions made to the 501(c)(3) organizations that sponsored the course. Over the three years the course was broadcast, approximately $1.2 million was spent on the project. The Kennesaw State College Foundation (KSCF) sponsored the course the first year. All funds raised were turned over to KSCF and dedicated exclusively for the use of the Renewing American Civilization course.

KSCF did not, however, manage the course and its role was limited to depositing donations into its bank account and paying bills from that account that were presented to it by the Dean of the KSC Business School. KSCF contracted with the Washington Policy Group, Inc. (WPG) to manage and raise funds for the course's development, production and distribution. Jeffrey Eisenach, GOPAC's Executive Director from June 1991 to June 1993, was the president and sole owner of WPG. WPG and Mr. Eisenach played similar roles with respect to AOW/ACTV.

When the contract between WPG and KSCF ended in the fall of 1993, the Progress and Freedom Foundation (PFF) assumed the role WPG had with the course at the same rate of compensation. Mr. Eisenach was PFF's founder and president. Shortly after PFF took over the management of the course, the Georgia Board of Regents passed a resolution prohibiting any elected official from teaching at a Georgia state educational institution. This was the culmination of a controversy that had arisen around the course at KSC. A group of KSC faculty had objected to the course being taught on the campus because of a belief that it was an effort to use the college to disseminate a political message. Because of the Board of Regents' decision and the controversy, it was decided that the course would be moved to a private college.

The course was moved to Reinhardt for the 1994 and 1995 sessions. While there, PFF assumed full responsibility for the course. PFF no longer received payments to run the course but, instead, took in all contributions to the course and paid all the bills, including paying Reinhardt for the use of the college's video production facilities. All funds for the course were raised by and expended by PFF under its tax-exempt status.

3. Failure to Seek Legal Advice

Under the Internal Revenue Code, a 501(c)(3) organization must be operated exclusively for exempt purposes. The presence of a single non-exempt purpose, if more than insubstantial in nature, will destroy the exemption regardless of the number or importance of truly exempt purposes. Conferring a benefit on private interests is a non-exempt purpose. Under the Internal Revenue Code, a 501(c)(3) organization is also prohibited from intervening in a political campaign or providing any support to a political action committee. These prohibitions reflect congressional concerns that taxpayer funds not be used to subsidize political activity.

During the Preliminary Inquiry, the Subcommittee consulted with an expert in the law of tax-exempt organizations and read materials on the subject. Mr. Gingrich's activities on behalf of AOW/ACTV and Renewing American Civilization, as well as the activities of others on behalf of those projects done with Mr. Gingrich's knowledge and approval, were reviewed by the expert. The expert concluded that those activities violated the status of the organizations under section 501(c)(3) in that, among other things, those activities were intended to confer more than insubstantial benefits on GOPAC, Mr. Gingrich, and Republican entities and candidates, and provided support to GOPAC.

At Mr. Gingrich's request, the Subcommittee also heard from tax counsel retained by Mr. Gingrich for the purposes of the Preliminary Inquiry. While that counsel is an experienced tax attorney with a sterling reputation, he has less experience in dealing with tax-exempt organizations law than does the expert retained by the Subcommittee. According to Mr. Gingrich's tax counsel, the type of activity involved in the AOW/ACTV and Renewing American Civilization projects would not violate the status of the relevant organizations under section 501(c)(3). He opined that once it was determined that an activity was "educational," as defined by the IRS, and did not have the effect of benefiting a private interest, it did not violate the private benefit prohibition. In the view of Mr. Gingrich's tax counsel, motivation on the part of an organization's principals and agents is irrelevant. Further, he opined that a 501(c)(3) organization does not violate the private benefit prohibition or political campaign prohibition through close association with or support of a political action committee unless it specifically calls for the election or defeat of an identifiable political candidate.

Both the Subcommittee's tax expert and Mr. Gingrich's tax counsel, however, agreed that had Mr. Gingrich sought their advice before embarking on activities of the type involved in AOW/ACTV and the Renewing American Civilization course, each of them would have advised Mr. Gingrich not to use a 501(c)(3) organization as he had in regard to those activities. The Subcommittee's tax expert said that doing so would violate 501(c)(3). During his appearance before the Subcommittee, Mr. Gingrich's tax counsel said that he would not have recommended the use of 501(c)(3) organizations to sponsor the course because the combination of politics and 501(c)(3) organizations is an "explosive mix" almost certain to draw the attention of the IRS.

Based on the evidence, it was clear that Mr. Gingrich intended that the AOW/ACTV and Renewing American Civilization projects have substantial partisan, political purposes. In addition, he was aware that political activities in the context of 501(c)(3) organizations were problematic. Prior to embarking on these projects, Mr. Gingrich had been involved with another organization that had direct experience with the private benefit prohibition in a political context, the American Campaign Academy. In a 1989 Tax Court opinion issued less than a year before Mr. Gingrich set the AOW/ACTV project into motion, the Academy was denied its exemption under 501(c)(3) because, although educational, it conferred an impermissible private benefit on Republican candidates and entities. Close associates of Mr. Gingrich were principals in the American Campaign Academy, Mr. Gingrich taught at the Academy, and Mr. Gingrich had been briefed at the time on the tax controversy surrounding the Academy. In addition, Mr. Gingrich stated publicly that he was taking a very aggressive approach to the use of 501(c)(3) organizations in regard to, at least, the Renewing American Civilization course.

Taking into account Mr. Gingrich's background, experience, and sophistication with respect to tax-exempt organizations, and his status as a Member of Congress obligated to maintain high ethical standards, the Subcommittee concluded that Mr. Gingrich should have known to seek appropriate legal advice to ensure that his conduct in regard to the AOW/ACTV and Renewing American Civilization projects was in compliance with 501(c)(3). Had he sought and followed such advice — after having set out all the relevant facts, circumstances, plans, and goals described above — 501(c)(3) organizations would not have been used to sponsor Mr. Gingrich's ACTV and Renewing American Civilization projects.

4. Mr. Gingrich's Statements to the Committee

In responding to the complaints filed against him concerning the Renewing American Civilization course, Mr. Gingrich submitted several letters to the Committee. His first letter, dated October 4, 1994, did not address the tax issues raised in Mr. Jones' complaint, but rather responded to the part of the complaint concerning unofficial use of official resources.

In it Mr. Gingrich stated that GOPAC, among other organizations, paid people to work on the course. After this response, the Committee wrote Mr. Gingrich and asked him specifically to address issues related to whether the course had a partisan, political aspect to it and, if so, whether it was appropriate for a 501(c)(3) organization to be used to sponsor the course. The Committee also specifically asked whether GOPAC had any relationship to the course. Mr. Gingrich's letter in response, dated December 8, 1994, was prepared by his attorney, but it was read, approved, and signed by Mr. Gingrich. It stated that the course had no partisan, political aspects to it, that his motivation for teaching the course was not political, and that GOPAC neither was involved in nor received any benefit from any aspect of the course. In his testimony before the Subcommittee, Mr. Gingrich admitted that these statements were not true.

When the amended complaint was filed with the Committee in January 1995, Mr. Gingrich's attorney responded to the complaint on behalf of Mr. Gingrich in a letter dated March 27, 1995. His attorney addressed all the issues in the amended complaint, including the issues related to the Renewing American Civilization course. The letter was signed by Mr. Gingrich's attorney, but Mr. Gingrich reviewed and approved it prior to its being delivered to the Committee. In an interview with Mr. Cole, Mr. Gingrich stated that if he had seen anything inaccurate in the letter he would have instructed his attorney to correct it. Similar to the December 8, 1994, letter, the March 27, 1995, letter stated that the course had no partisan, political aspects to it, that Mr. Gingrich's motivation for teaching the course was not political, and that GOPAC had no involvement in nor received any benefit from any aspect of the course. In his testimony before the Subcommittee, Mr. Gingrich admitted that these statements were not true.

The goal of the letters was to have the complaints dismissed. Of the people involved in drafting or editing the letters, or reviewing them for accuracy, only Mr. Gingrich had personal knowledge of the facts contained in the letters regarding the course. The facts in the letters that were inaccurate, incomplete, and unreliable were material to the Committee's determination on how to proceed with the tax questions contained in the complaints.

D. STATEMENT OF ALLEGED VIOLATION

On December 21, 1996, the Subcommittee issued a Statement of Alleged Violation (SAV) stating that Mr. Gingrich had engaged in conduct that did not reflect creditably on the House of Representatives in that by failing to seek and follow legal advice, Mr. Gingrich failed to take appropriate steps to ensure that activities with respect to the AOW/ACTV project and the Renewing American Civilization project were in accordance with section 501(c)(3); and that on or about December 8, 1994, and on or about March 27, 1995, information was transmitted to the Committee by and on behalf of Mr. Gingrich that was material to matters under consideration by the Committee, which information, as Mr. Gingrich should have known, was inaccurate, incomplete, and unreliable.

On December 21, 1996, Mr. Gingrich filed an answer with the Subcommittee admitting to this violation of House Rules.

IX. Analysis and Conclusion

A. Tax Issues

In reviewing the evidence concerning both the AOW/ACTV project and the Renewing American Civilization project, certain patterns became apparent. In both instances, GOPAC had initiated the use of the messages as part of its political program to build a Republican majority in Congress. In both instances there was an effort to have the material appear to be nonpartisan on its face, yet serve as a partisan, political message for the purpose of building the Republican Party.

Under the "methodology test" set out by the Internal Revenue Service, both projects qualified as educational. However, they both had substantial partisan, political aspects. Both were initiated as political projects and both were motivated, at least in part, by political goals.

The other striking similarity is that, in both situations, GOPAC was in need of a new source of funding for the projects and turned to a 501(c)(3) organization for that purpose.

Once the projects had been established at the 501(c)(3) organizations, however, the same people continued to manage it as had done so at GOPAC, the same message was used as when it was at GOPAC, and the dissemination of the message was directed toward the same goal as when the project was at GOPAC — building the Republican Party. The only significant difference was that the activity was funded by a 501(c)(3) organization.

This was not a situation where one entity develops a message through a course or a television program for purely educational purposes and then an entirely separate entity independently decides to adopt that message for partisan, political purposes. Rather, this was a coordinated effort to have the 501(c)(3) organization help in achieving a partisan, political goal. In both instances the idea to develop the message and disseminate it for partisan, political use came first. The use of the 501(c)(3) came second as a source of funding.

This factual analysis was accepted by all Members of the Subcommittee and the Special Counsel. However, there was a difference of opinion as to the result under 501(c)(3) when applying the law to these facts. Ms. Roady, the Subcommittee's tax expert, was of the opinion that the facts presented a clear violation of 501(c)(3) because the evidence showed that the activities were intended to benefit Mr. Gingrich, GOPAC, and other Republican candidates and entities. Mr. Holden, Mr. Gingrich's tax attorney, disagreed. He found that the course was nonpartisan in its content, and even though he assumed that the motivation for disseminating it involved partisan, political goals, he did not find a sufficiently narrow targeting of the dissemination to conclude that it was a private benefit to anyone.

Some Members of the Subcommittee and the Special Counsel agreed with Ms. Roady and concluded that there was a clear violation of 501(c)(3) with respect to AOW/ACTV and Renewing American Civilization. Other Members of the Subcommittee were troubled by reaching this conclusion and believed that the facts of this case presented a unique situation that had not previously been addressed by the legal authorities.

As such, they did not feel comfortable supplanting the functions of the Internal Revenue Service or the Tax Court in rendering a ruling on what they believed to be an unsettled area of the law.

B. STATEMENTS MADE TO THE COMMITTEE

The letters Mr. Gingrich submitted to the Committee concerning the Renewing American Civilization complaint were very troubling to the Subcommittee. They contained definitive statements about facts that went to the heart of the issues placed before the Committee. In the case of the December 8, 1994, letter, it was in response to a direct request from the Committee for specific information relating to the partisan, political nature of the course and GOPAC's involvement in it.

Both letters were efforts by Mr. Gingrich to have the Committee dismiss the complaints without further inquiry. In such situations, the Committee does and should place great reliance on the statements of Members. The letters were prepared by Mr. Gingrich's lawyers.

After the Subcommittee deposed the lawyers, the reasons for the statements being in the letters was not made any clearer. The lawyers did not conduct any independent factual research.

Looking at the information the lawyers used to write the letters, the Subcommittee was unable to find any factual basis for the inaccurate statements contained therein. A number of exhibits attached to the complaint were fax transmittal sheets from GOPAC.

While this did not on its face establish anything more than GOPAC's fax machine having been used for the project, it certainly should have put the attorneys on notice that there was some relationship between the course and GOPAC that should have been examined before saying that GOPAC had absolutely no involvement in the course.

The lawyers said they relied on Mr. Gingrich and his staff to ensure that the letters were accurate; however, none of Mr. Gingrich's staff had sufficient knowledge to be able to verify the accuracy of the facts. While Mr. Gaylord and Mr. Eisenach did have sufficient knowledge to verify many of the facts, they were not asked to do so. The only person who reviewed the letters for accuracy, with sufficient knowledge to verify those facts, was Mr. Gingrich.

The Subcommittee considered the relevance of the reference to GOPAC in Mr. Gingrich's first letter to the Committee dated October 4, 1994. In that letter he stated that GOPAC was one of the entities that paid people to work on the course. Some Members of the Subcommittee believed that this was evidence of lack of intent to deceive the Committee on Mr. Gingrich's part because if he had planned to hide GOPAC's involvement, he would not have made such an inconsistent statement in the subsequent letters. Other Members of the Subcommittee and the Special Counsel appreciated this point, but believed the first letter was of little value. The statement in that letter was only directed to establishing that Mr. Gingrich had not used congressional resources in developing the course.

The first letter made no attempt to address the tax issues, even though it was a prominent feature of the complaint. When the Committee specifically focused Mr. Gingrich's attention on that issue and questions concerning GOPAC's involvement in the course, his response was not accurate.

During his testimony before the Subcommittee, Mr. Gingrich stated that he did not intend to mislead the Committee and apologized for his conduct. This statement was a relevant consideration for some Members of the Subcommittee, but not for others.

The Subcommittee concluded that because these inaccurate statements were provided to the Committee, this matter was not resolved as expeditiously as it could have been. This caused a controversy over the matter to arise and last for a substantial period of time, it disrupted the operations of the House, and it cost the House a substantial amount of money in order to determine the facts.

C. STATEMENT OF ALLEGED VIOLATION

Based on the information described above, the Special Counsel proposed a Statement of Alleged Violations (SAV) to the Subcommittee on December 12, 1996. The SAV contained three counts:

1) Mr. Gingrich's activities on behalf of ALOF in regard to AOW/ACTV, and the activities of others in that regard with his knowledge and approval, constituted a violation of ALOF's status under section 501(c)(3);

2) Mr. Gingrich's activities on behalf of Kennesaw State College Foundation, the Progress and Freedom Foundation, and Reinhardt College in regard to the Renewing American Civilization course, and the activities of others in that regard with his knowledge and approval, constituted a violation of those organizations' status under section 501(c)(3); and

3) Mr. Gingrich had provided information to the Committee, directly or through counsel, that was material to matters under consideration by the Committee, which Mr. Gingrich knew or should have known was inaccurate, incomplete, and unreliable.

1. Deliberations on the Tax Counts

There was a difference of opinion regarding whether to issue the SAV as drafted on the tax counts. Concern was expressed about deciding this tax issue in the context of an ethics proceeding. This led the discussion to the question of the appropriate focus for the Subcommittee. A consensus began to build around the view that the proper focus was on the conduct of the Member, rather than a resolution of issues of tax law. From the beginning of the Preliminary Inquiry, there was a desire on the part of each of the Members to find a way to reach a unanimous conclusion in this matter. The Members felt it was important to confirm the bipartisan nature of the ethics process.

The discussion turned to what steps Mr. Gingrich had taken in regard to these two projects to ensure they were done in accord with the provisions of 501(c)(3). In particular, the Subcommittee was concerned with the fact that:

1) Mr. Gingrich had been "very well aware" of the American Campaign Academy case prior to embarking [on this] project;

2) he had been involved with 501(c)(3) organizations to a sufficient degree to know that politics and tax-deductible contributions are, as his tax counsel said, an "explosive mix";

3) he was clearly involved in a project that had significant partisan, political goals, and he had taken an aggressive approach to the tax laws in regard to both AOW/ACTV; and

4) Renewing American Civilization projects. Even Mr. Gingrich's own tax lawyer told the Subcommittee that if Mr. Gingrich had come to him before embarking on these projects, he would have advised him to not use a 501(c)(3) organization for the dissemination of AOW/ACTV or Renewing American Civilization.

Had Mr. Gingrich sought and followed this advice, he would not have used the 501(c)(3) organizations, would not have had his projects subsidized by taxpayer funds, and would not have created this controversy that has caused significant disruption to the House. The Subcommittee concluded that there were significant and substantial warning signals to Mr. Gingrich that he should have heeded prior to embarking on these projects. Despite these warnings, Mr. Gingrich did not seek any legal advice to ensure his conduct conformed with the provisions of 501(c)(3).

In looking at this conduct in light of all the facts and circumstances, the Subcommittee was faced with a disturbing choice. Either Mr. Gingrich did not seek legal advice because he was aware that it would not have permitted him to use a 501(c)(3) organization for his projects, or he was reckless in not taking care that, as a Member of Congress, he made sure that his conduct conformed with the law in an area where he had ample warning that his intended course of action was fraught with legal peril.

The Subcommittee decided that regardless of the resolution of the 501(c)(3) tax question, Mr. Gingrich's conduct in this regard was improper, did not reflect creditably on the House, and was deserving of sanction.

2. Deliberations Concerning the Letters

The Subcommittee's deliberation concerning the letters provided to the Committee centered on the question of whether Mr. Gingrich intentionally submitted inaccurate information. There was a belief that the record developed before the Subcommittee was not conclusive on this point. The Special Counsel suggested that a good argument could be made, based on the record, that Mr. Gingrich did act intentionally, however it would be difficult to establish that with a high degree of certainty.

The culmination of the evidence on this topic again left the Subcommittee with a disturbing choice. Either Mr. Gingrich intentionally made misrepresentations to the Committee, or he was again reckless in the way he provided information to the Committee concerning a very important matter.

The standard applicable to the Subcommittee's deliberations was whether there is reason to believe that Mr. Gingrich had acted as charged in this count of the SAV. All felt that this standard had been met in regard to the allegation that Mr. Gingrich "knew" that the information he provided to the Committee was inaccurate.

However, there was considerable discussion to the effect that if Mr. Gingrich wanted to admit to submitting information to the Committee that he "should have known" was inaccurate, the Subcommittee would consider deleting the allegation that he knew the information was inaccurate.

The Members were of the opinion that if there were to be a final adjudication of the matter, taking into account the higher standard of proof that is involved at that level, "should have known" was an appropriate framing of the charge in light of all the facts and circumstances.

3. Discussions with Mr. Gingrich's Counsel and Recommended Sanction

On December 13, 1996, the Subcommittee issued an SAV charging Mr. Gingrich with three counts of violations of House Rules. Two counts concerned the failure to seek legal advice in regard to the 501(c)(3) projects, and one count concerned providing the Committee with information which he knew or should have known was inaccurate.

At the time the Subcommittee voted this SAV, the Members discussed the matter among themselves and reached a consensus that it would be in the best interests of the House for the matter to be resolved without going through a disciplinary hearing. It was estimated that such a hearing could take up to three months to complete and would not begin for several months.

Because of this, it was anticipated that the House would have to deal with this matter for another six months. Even though the Subcommittee Members felt that it would be advantageous to the House to avoid a disciplinary hearing, they all were committed to the proposition that any resolution of the matter had to reflect adequately the seriousness of the offenses.

To this end, the Subcommittee Members discussed and agreed upon a recommended sanction that was fair in light of the conduct reflected in this matter, but explicitly recognized that the full Committee would make the ultimate decision as to the recommendation to the full House as to the appropriate sanction.

In determining what the appropriate sanction should be in this matter, the Subcommittee and Special Counsel considered the seriousness of the conduct, the level of care exercised by Mr. Gingrich, the disruption caused to the House by the conduct, the cost to the House in having to pay for an extensive investigation, and the repetitive nature of the conduct.

As is noted above, the Subcommittee was faced with troubling choices in each of the areas covered by the Statement of Alleged Violation. Either Mr. Gingrich's conduct in regard to the 501(c)(3) organizations and the letters he submitted to the Committee was intentional or it was reckless. Neither choice reflects creditably on the House.

While the Subcommittee was notable to reach a comfortable conclusion on these issues, the fact that the choice was presented is a factor in determining the appropriate sanction. In addition, the violation does not represent only a single instance of reckless conduct.

Rather, over a number of years and in a number of situations, Mr. Gingrich showed a disregard and lack of respect for the standards of conduct that applied to his activities.

Under the Rules of the Committee, a reprimand is the appropriate sanction for a serious violation of House Rules and a censure is appropriate for a more serious violation of

House Rules. *Rule 20(g), Rules of the Committee on Standards of Official Conduct.*

It was the opinion of the Subcommittee that this matter fell somewhere in between. Accordingly, the Subcommittee and the Special Counsel recommend that the appropriate sanction should be a reprimand and a payment reimbursing the House for some of the costs of the investigation in the amount of $300,000.

Mr. Gingrich has agreed that this is the appropriate sanction in this matter.

Beginning on December 15, 1996, Mr. Gingrich's counsel and the Special Counsel began discussions directed toward resolving the matter without a disciplinary hearing. The discussions lasted through December 20, 1996.

At that time an understanding was reached by both Mr. Gingrich and the Subcommittee concerning this matter. That understanding was put on the record on December 21, 1996 by Mr. Cole [as] follows:

Mr. Cole: The subcommittee has had an opportunity to review the facts in this case, and has had extensive discussion about the appropriate resolution of this matter.

Mr. Cardin: If I might just add here to your next understanding, the Members of the subcommittee, prior to the adoption of the Statement of Alleged Violation, were concerned that the nonpartisan deliberations of the subcommittee continue beyond the findings of the subcommittee. Considering the record of the full Ethics Committee in the 104th Congress and the partisan environment in the full House, the Members of the subcommittee felt that it was important to exercise bipartisan leadership beyond the workings of the subcommittee.

Mr. Cole: It was the opinion of the Members of the subcommittee and the Special Counsel, that based on the facts of this case as they are currently known, the appropriate sanction for the conduct described in the original Statement of Alleged Violations is a reprimand and the payment of $300,000 toward the cost of the preliminary inquiry.

In light of this opinion, the subcommittee Members and the Special Counsel intend to recommend to the full committee that this be the sanction recommended by the full committee to the House. The Members also intend to support this as the sanction in the committee and on the Floor of the House.

However, if new facts are developed or brought to the attention of the Members of the subcommittee, they are free to change their opinions.

The Subcommittee, through its counsel, has communicated this to Mr. Gingrich, through his counsel. Mr. Gingrich has agreed that if the subcommittee will amend the Statement of Alleged Violations to be one count, instead of three counts, however, still including all of the conduct described in the original Statement of Alleged Violations, and will allow the addition of some language which reflects aspects of the record in this matter concerning the involvement of Mr. Gingrich's counsel in the preparation of the letters described in the original Count 3 of the Statement of Alleged Violations,[88] he will admit to the entire Statement of Alleged Violation and agree to the view of the subcommittee Members and the Special Counsel as to the appropriate sanction.

In light of Mr. Gingrich's admission to the Statement of Alleged Violation, the subcommittee is of the view that the rules of the committee will not require that an adjudicatory hearing take place; however, a sanction hearing will need to be held under the rules.

The subcommittee and Mr. Gingrich desire to have the sanction hearing concluded as expeditiously as possible, but it is understood that this will not take place at the expense of orderly procedure and a full and fair opportunity for the full committee to be informed of any information necessary for each Member of the full committee to be able to make a decision at the sanction hearing.

After the subcommittee has voted a new Statement of Alleged Violation, Mr. Gingrich will file his answer admitting to it. The subcommittee will seek the permission of the full committee to release the Statement of Alleged Violation, Mr. Gingrich's answer, and a brief press release which has been approved by Mr. Gingrich's counsel. At the same time, Mr. Gingrich will release a brief press release that has been approved by the subcommittee's Special Counsel.

Both the subcommittee and Mr. Gingrich agree that no public comment should be made about this matter while it is still pending. This includes having surrogates sent out to comment on the matter and attempt to mischaracterize it.

Accordingly, beyond the press statements described above, neither Mr. Gingrich nor any Member of the subcommittee may make any further public comment. Mr. Gingrich understands that if he violates this provision, the subcommittee will have the option of reinstating the original Statement of Alleged Violations and allowing Mr. Gingrich an opportunity to withdraw his answer.

And I should note that it is the intention of the subcommittee that "public comments" refers to press statements; that, obviously, we are free and Mr. Gingrich is free to have private conversations with Members of Congress about these matters.[89]

After the Subcommittee voted to issue the substitute SAV, the Special Counsel called Mr. Gingrich's counsel and read to him what was put on the record concerning this matter. Mr. Gingrich's counsel then delivered to the Subcommittee Mr. Gingrich's answer admitting to the Statement of Alleged Violation.

D. POST-DECEMBER 21, 1996, ACTIVITY

Following the release of this Statement of Alleged Violation, numerous press accounts appeared concerning this matter. In the opinion of the Subcommittee Members and the Special Counsel, a number of the press accounts indicated that Mr. Gingrich had violated the agreement concerning statements about the matter. Mr. Gingrich's counsel was notified of the Subcommittee's concerns and the Subcommittee met to consider what action to take in light of this apparent violation. The Subcommittee determined that it would not nullify the agreement.

While there was serious concern about whether Mr. Gingrich had complied with the agreement, the Subcommittee was of the opinion that the best interests of the House still lay in resolving the matter without a disciplinary hearing and with the recommended sanction that its Members had previously determined was appropriate. However, Mr. Gingrich's counsel was informed that the Subcommittee believed a violation of the agreement had occurred and retained the right to withdraw from the agreement with appropriate notice to Mr. Gingrich. To date no such notice has been given.

FOOTNOTES

[88]:These changes included the removal of the word "knew" from the original Count 3, making the charge read that Mr. Gingrich "should have known" the information was inaccurate.

[89]:It was also agreed that in the private conversations Mr. Gingrich was not to disclose the terms of the agreement with the Subcommittee. ■

INAUGURAL ADDRESS

Clinton Outlines His Vision For a New Century

Following is the Jan. 20 text of President Clinton's second inaugural speech, provided by the Federal Document Clearing House:

President Clinton: My fellow citizens, at this last presidential inauguration of the 20th century, let us lift our eyes toward the challenges that await us in the next century.

It is our great good fortune that time and chance have put us not only at the edge of a new century in a new millennium, but on the edge of a bright new prospect in human affairs: a moment that will define our course and our character for decades to come.

We must keep our old democracy forever young.

Guided by the ancient vision of a promised land, let us set our sights upon a land of new promise.

The promise of America was born in the 18th century out of the bold conviction that we are all created equal. It was extended and preserved in the 19th century, when our nation spread across the continent, saved the union and abolished the awful scourge of slavery.

Then, in turmoil and triumph, that promise exploded on to the world stage to make this the American Century — and what a century it has been.

America became the world's mightiest industrial power, saved the world from tyranny in two world wars and a long Cold War, and time and again reached out across the globe to millions who, like us, longed for the blessings of liberty.

Along the way, Americans produced a great middle class and security in old age; built unrivaled centers of learning and opened public schools to all; split the atom and explored the heavens; invented the computer and the microchip; and deepened the wellspring of justice by making a revolution in civil rights for African-Americans and all minorities, and extending the circle of citizenship, opportunity and dignity to women.

Now, for the third time, a new century is upon us and another time to choose. We began the 19th century with a choice to spread our nation from coast to coast.

We began the 20th century with a choice to harness the industrial revolution to our values of free enterprise, conservation and human decency. Those choices made all the difference.

At the dawn of the 21st century, a free people must now choose to shape the forces of the Information Age and the global society; to unleash the limitless potential of all our people; and, yes, to form a more perfect union.

When last we gathered, our march to this new future seemed less certain than it does today. We vowed then to set a clear course to renew our nation.

In these four years, we have been touched by tragedy, exhilarated by challenge, strengthened by achievement.

America stands alone as the world's indispensable nation. Once again, our economy is the strongest on earth. Once again, we are building stronger families, thriving communities, better educational opportunities, a cleaner environment.

Problems that once seemed destined to deepen now bend to our efforts. Our streets are safer and record numbers of our fellow citizens have moved from welfare to work.

And once again, we have resolved for our time a great debate over the role of government. Today, we can declare government is not the problem and government is not the solution. We, the American people, we are the solution.

Our Founders understood that well and gave us a democracy strong enough to endure for centuries, flexible enough to face our common challenges and advance our common dreams in each new day.

The Role of Government

As times change, so government must change. We need a new government for a new century: humble enough not to try to solve all our problems for us, but strong enough to give us the tools to solve our problems for ourselves; a government that is smaller, lives within its means and does more with less.

Yet, where it can stand up for our values and interests around the world, and where it can give Americans the power to make a real difference in their everyday lives, government should do more, not less.

The preeminent mission of our new government is to give all Americans an opportunity — not a guarantee — but a real opportunity to build better lives.

Beyond that, my fellow citizens, the future is up to us. Our Founders taught us that the preservation of our liberty and our union depends upon responsible citizenship, and we need a new sense of responsibility for our new century.

There is work to do, work that government alone cannot do: teaching children to read, hiring people off welfare rolls, coming out from behind locked doors and shuttered windows to help reclaim our streets from drugs and gangs and crime, taking time out of our own lives to serve others.

Each and every one of us in our own way must assume personal responsibility, not only for ourselves and our families, but for our neighbors and our nation.

Our greatest responsibility is to embrace a new spirit of community for a new century. For any one of us to succeed, we must succeed as one America. The challenge of our past remains the challenge of our future.

Will we be one nation, one people, with one common destiny — or not?

Will we all come together or come apart?

The divide of race has been America's constant curse, and each new wave of immigrants gives new targets to old prejudices. Prejudice and contempt cloaked in the pretense of religious or political convictions are no different.

These forces have nearly destroyed our nation in the past. They plague us still. They fuel the fanaticism of terror. And they torment the lives of millions in fractured nations all around the world.

These obsessions cripple both those who hate and, of course, those who are hated, robbing both of what they might become. We cannot, we will not succumb to the dark impulses that lurk in the far regions of the soul everywhere. We shall overcome them.

And we shall replace them with a generous spirit of a people who feel at home with one another.

Our rich texture of racial, religious and political diversity will be a godsend in the 21st century. Great rewards will come to those who can live together, learn together, work together, forge new ties that bind together.

The Shape of an Era To Come

As this new era approaches, we can already see its broad outlines.

Ten years ago, the Internet was the mystical province of physicists. Today, it is a commonplace encyclopedia for millions of school children.

Scientists now are decoding the blueprint of human life. Cures for our most feared illnesses seem close at hand. The world is no longer divided into two hostile camps.

Instead, now we are building bonds with nations that once were our adversaries. Growing connections of commerce and culture give us a chance to lift the fortunes and spirits of people the world over.

And for the very first time in all of history, more people on this planet live under democracy than dictatorship.

My fellow Americans, as we look back at this remarkable century, we may ask, can we hope not just to follow, but even to surpass the achievements of the 20th century in America and to avoid the awful bloodshed that stained its legacy?

To that question, every American here

and every American in our land today must answer a resounding yes.

'A New Land of Promise'

This is the heart of our task. With a new vision of government, a new sense of responsibility, a new spirit of community, we will sustain America's journey. The promise we sought in a new land, we will find again in a land of new promise.

In this new land, education will be every citizen's most prized possession. Our schools will have the highest standards in the world, igniting the spark of possibility in the eyes of every girl and every boy. And the doors of higher education will be opened to all.

The knowledge and power of the Information Age will be within reach not just of the few but of every classroom, every library, every child.

Parents and children will have time not only to work but to read and play together. And the plans they make at their kitchen table will be those of a better home, a better job, the certain chance to go college.

Our streets will echo again with the laughter of our children, because no one will try to shoot them or sell them drugs anymore.

Everyone who can work will work, with today's permanent underclass part of tomorrow's growing middle class.

New miracles of medicine at last will reach not only those who can claim care now but the children and hard-working families too long denied.

We will stand mighty for peace and freedom, and maintain a strong defense against terror and destruction. Our children will sleep free from the threat of nuclear, chemical or biological weapons.

Ports and airports, farms and factories will thrive with trade and innovation and ideas. And the world's greatest democracy will lead a whole world of democracies.

Our land of new promise will be a nation that meets its obligations; a nation that balances its budget, but never loses the balance of its values; a nation where . . . a nation where our grandparents have secure retirement and health care, and their grandchildren know we have made the reforms necessary to sustain those benefits for their time; a nation that fortifies the world's most productive economy, even as it protects the great natural bounty of our water, air and majestic land.

And in this land of new promise, we will have reformed our politics so that the voice of the people will always speak louder than the din of narrow interests, regaining the participation and deserving the trust of all Americans.

Fellow citizens, let us build that America: a nation ever moving forward toward realizing the full potential of all its citizens. Prosperity and power—yes, they are important, and we must maintain them. But let us never forget the greatest progress we have made and the greatest progress we have yet to make is in the human heart.

In the end, all the world's wealth and a thousand armies are no match for the strength and decency of the human spirit.

Evoking King's Dream

Thirty-four years ago, the man whose life we celebrate today spoke to us down there at the other end of this mall in words that moved the conscience of a nation. Like a prophet of old, he told of his dream that one day America would rise up and treat all its citizens as equals before the law and in the heart.

Martin Luther King's dream was the American Dream. His quest is our quest: the ceaseless striving to live out our true creed. Our history has been built on such dreams and labors. And by our dreams and labors, we will redeem the promise of America in the 21st century.

To that effort, I pledge all my strength and every power of my office. I ask the members of Congress here to join in that pledge.

The American people returned to office a president of one party and a Congress of another. Surely, they did not do this to advance the politics of petty bickering and extreme partisanship they plainly deplore.

No. They call on us instead to be repairers of the breach and to move on with America's mission. America demands and deserves big things from us, and nothing big ever came from being small.

Let us remember the timeless wisdom of Cardinal Bernardin when facing the end of his own life.

He said it is wrong to waste the precious gift of time on acrimony and division.

Fellow citizens, we must not waste the precious gift of this time, for all of us are on that same journey of our lives. And our journey, too, will come to an end. But the journey of our America must go on.

And so, my fellow Americans, we must be strong, for there is much to dare. The demands of our time are great, and they are different. Let us meet them with faith and courage, with patience and a grateful, happy heart.

Let us shape the hope of this day into the noblest chapter in our history. Yes, let us build our bridge . . . a bridge wide enough and strong enough for every American to cross over to a blessed land of new promise.

May those generations whose faces we cannot yet see — whose names we may never know — say of us here that we led our beloved land into a new century with the American dream alive for all her children, with the American promise of a more perfect union a reality for all her people, with America's bright flame of freedom spreading throughout all the world.

From the height of this place and the summit of this century, let us go forth.

May God strengthen our hands for the good work ahead and always, always bless our America. ■

ETHICS

Excerpts of Counsel Report In Gingrich Ethics Case

Following are excerpts of the report, filed Jan. 16, 1997, by J. Randolph Evans and Ed Bethune, the counsels for House Speaker Newt Gingrich, R-Ga., in the ethics case against the Speaker:

This is the Report of Counsel for the Respondent Speaker Newt Gingrich. This Report is being submitted in connection with the Sanction Hearing specified in Rule 20 of the Rules of the Committee on Standards of Official Conduct ("Rules") regarding written submissions by counsel. The Report is subject to two limitations. First, the Report has been prepared without the access to all of the information collected by the Investigative Subcommittee. Respondent was limited to certain exhibits made available by the Committee; selected transcripts made available by the Committee; and public documents. Second, Respondent has not been afforded the opportunity to conduct discovery or otherwise develop information relating to the matter before the Committee.

Overview

On December 21, 1996, the Investigative Subcommittee issued a Statement of Alleged Violation. The Statement was the product of an investigation by the Investigative Subcommittee and Special Counsel. It is important to note that the process was one-sided: witnesses were not subject to cross-examination; documents were not subject to pertinency or admissibility standards; and traditional rules establishing standards for admissibility, pertinency and reliability of evidence were not applied. Respondent was not permitted to participate in the examination of witnesses or documents.

Also on December 21, 1996, Respondent submitted an Answer admitting the alleged violation. Pursuant to Rule 19(c) of the Rules, Respondent's admission relieved the Committee of determining through an adjudicatory subcommittee at a Disciplinary Hearing whether the single count in the Statement of Alleged Violation was proven by clear and convincing evidence. At such a Disciplinary Hearing, Respondent would have been afforded the opportunity to cross-examine witnesses, challenge documents and obtain discovery.

With the Statement of Alleged Violation and the Answer, the next process contemplated by the Rules is a Sanction Hearing pursuant to Rule 20. This process does not entail a trial on the merits of the alleged violation. Instead, the process is limited to determining the appropriate sanction, if any, for the violation.

This Report is submitted for that purpose. This is not a report in response to the Special Counsel's Report. It does not contain a fact by fact, argument by argument response to the Special Counsel's Report. Respondent does not accept as true the asserted factual statements and characterizations thereof beyond the facts contained in the Statement of Alleged Violation admitted by Respondent's Answer. It is relatively easy for an attorney, such as the Special Counsel, to piece together testimony and documents, free from the tests of cross-examination, hearsay limits and other evidentiary standards to assure accuracy, and free from the boundaries of reality, to reach virtually any conclusion through clinical forensic reconstruction. This Report is designed to put the facts before the Committee in the context of the real world so that the Committee can determine the appropriate sanction, if any, for the violation, in the absence of an adversary process.

Let there be no mistake, Respondent has accepted the Investigative Subcommittee's Statement of Alleged Violation. In doing so, Respondent has accepted the facts contained therein. This does not mean, however, that Respondent accepts as true those asserted facts not contained in the Statement of Alleged Violation. To assist the Committee in its decision-making process, attached hereto as Appendix A is a timeline of the events relating to the Renewing American Civilization course. This Report is submitted to place the general body of facts in the context of reality as opposed to a version of the facts viewed with hindsight that could only exist in a laboratory free from the dynamics of the real world. For assistance in placing the facts in context, please see Appendix B.

Scope of Hearing

There have been a myriad of charges and allegations made against Respondent. With the exception of the single violation contained in the Statement of Alleged Violation, those charges and allegations are untrue and groundless. The only violation before this Committee for purposes of determining the appropriate sanction, if any, is the violation contained in the Statement of Alleged Violation. The Statement of Alleged Violation describes conduct which violates Rule 43(1) of the Rules of the Committee on Standards of Official Conduct. Rule 43(1) provides as follows:

A Member, officer, or employee of the House of Representatives shall conduct himself at all times in a manner which shall reflect creditably on the House of Representatives. Rules of the Committee on Standards of Official Conduct, Rule 43, clause 1.

Paragraph 52 of the Statement of Alleged Violation contains the only violation found, and states that: [R]egardless of the resolution of whether the activities described in paragraphs 2 through 41 constitute a violation of section 501(c)(3) of the Internal Revenue Code, **by failing to seek and follow legal advice** described in paragraphs 15 and 40, **Mr. Gingrich failed to take appropriate steps to ensure that the activities . . . were in accordance with section 501(c)(3)** of the Internal Revenue Code; and on or about March 27, 1995, and on or about December 8, 1994, **information was transmitted to the Committee by and on behalf of Mr. Gingrich that was material to matters under consideration by the Committee, which information, as Mr. Gingrich should have known, was inaccurate, incomplete, and unreliable.**

Statement of Alleged Violation, 52, p. 22 (emphasis added).

The standard relating to the adoption of a Statement is contained in Rule 17(d) of the Rules of the Committee on Standards of Official Conduct and provides: Upon completion to the Preliminary Inquiry, an investigative subcommittee, by majority vote of its members, may adopt a Statement of Alleged Violation if it determines that there is **reason to believe** that a violation has occurred. (emphasis added). Rules of the Committee on Standards of Official Conduct, Rule 17(d).

Given the false information which has been disseminated regarding the violation, it is important to note that the Investigative Subcommittee: **did not** charge Respondent with any violation of U.S. tax law; **did not** charge Respondent with intending to deceive the Committee; **did not** charge Respondent with illegal activities or criminal tax violations; and **did not** charge Respondent with money laundering.

Indeed, based on the standard applied by the Investigative Subcommittee, there is **no reason to believe** that any such allegations are true. All statements to the contrary are not only false, but maliciously false, as established by the language of the Statement of Alleged Violation.

The Real World

In the real world, Members of Congress necessarily confront many issues incidental to their multiple responsibilities. Chapter 9 of the House Ethics Manual itself addresses "Involvement With Official and Unofficial Organizations." On page 307, the House Ethics Manual states: "Members and employees of the House need to distinguish carefully between official and unofficial activities when they interact with private organizations."

Also in the real world, Members interact with a variety of organizations. Some are political action committees; some are charitable organizations (Section 501(c)(3) entities); and others are lobbying organizations (Section 501(c)(4) entities). It is neither illegal nor inappropriate for Members to participate as directors, officers or trustees of these political action committees, charitable organizations and lobbying organizations. According to The Exempt Organization Tax Review, "a review of Members' 1988 financial disclosure forms . . . showed that 51 Senators and 146 House Members were founders, officers or directors of tax-exempt organizations." See, Exhibit A: The Exempt Organization Tax Review, Dec.-Jan. 1990, p. 680. Indeed, "five candidates in the 1988 presidential contest had tax-exempt groups ostensibly doing research and educational activities in the months preceding their campaigns." Id.

The Internal Revenue Service specifically contemplated such structures. As described by the IRS: A number of IRC 501(c)(3) organizations have related IRC 501(c)(4) organizations that conduct political campaign activities, usually through a PAC (an IRC 527(f) separate segregated fund). So long as the organizations are kept separate (with appropriate record keeping and fair market reimbursement for facilities and services), the activities of the IRC 501(c)(4) organizations or of the PAC will not jeopardize the IRC 501(c)(3) organization's exempt status. 1992 IRS CPE, at 439.

In addition, it is not unusual that the political action committees, charitable organizations and lobbying organizations share the same address and operate out of the same offices. For example, the National Organization of Women (a section 501(c)(4)), National Organization of Women Foundation Inc. (a section 501(c)(3)), and the National Organization of Women Political Action Committee (a political action committee) all list as their address 1000 16th St. NW 700, Washington, D.C. For a further listing of multiple, affiliated Political Action Committees/Section 501(c)(3) entities/Section 501 (c)(4) entities sharing the same address, see Exhibit B and Appendix D.

Finally, it is common for these multiple-entity organizations to engage simultaneously in activities that have political implications. For example, the Sierra Club operates a section 501(c)(3) entity designated as Sierra Club Fund; a section 501(c)(4) entity designated as Sierra Club; a political action committee designated as Sierra Club Committee on Political Education; and a section 501(c)(3) entity designated as Sierra Club Legal Defense Fund. All of the entities list as their address 730 Polk Street, San Francisco, CA. The Internet home page of Sierra Club reflects its broad-ranging purposes, including those which are political. The home page states as follows:

The Sierra Club has played an increasingly active role in elections in recent years. Candidates who can be counted on to preserve the environment can count on our support — in the form of endorsements, contributions, publicity, and volunteer support. Candidates who try to deceive the public by supporting efforts to eliminate or weaken our basic environment safeguards will be called to account for their actions. In 1996, concerned citizens have the opportunity to reverse the tide of the last election. We have no choice, as the 21st century nears, but to send to Washington elected officials who have a genuine commitment to preserving and protecting the Earth. With your help, the 1996 elections can set a new course for our nation. . . .

"Failing To Seek and Follow" Legal Advice

The Statement of Alleged Violation alleges that, "by failing to seek and follow the legal advice" of tax counsel to ensure that the activities described in the Statement of Alleged Violation "were in accordance with section 501(c)(3) of the Internal Revenue Code," Respondent's conduct constituted a violation of Rule 43(1) of the Rules of the United States House of Representatives. (S.A.V., 52-53). It is important to note that, contrary to the statements of some, the Investigative Subcommittee did not find that Respondent's activities violated federal tax law or caused the tax-exempt organizations to violate their tax exempt status. The fact is that a violation of law may not, in and of itself, be a violation of the Code of Official Conduct. As noted on page 12 of the Ethics Manual, "[d]uring the floor debate preceding the adoption of the Code, Representative Price of Illinois, Chairman of the Select Committee on Standards of Official Conduct, rejected the notion that violations of the law are simultaneous violations of the Code. . . . "

Certainly, a knowing violation of law could constitute conduct that did not reflect creditably on the House of Representatives in violation of Rule 43(1). Here, there has been no finding of a knowing violation of law. In fact, such a finding would be directly contradicted by the findings in the Statement of Alleged Violation itself.

The Statement of Alleged Violation notes that tax counsel retained by the Investigative Subcommittee and tax counsel retained by Respondent disagree regarding whether the activities at issue constitute a violation of the tax-exempt organizations' section 501(c)(3) status. The only clear conclusion from the findings and the testimony before the Investigative Subcommittee is that there is no clear answer. In the absence of a clear answer, there could be no knowing violation of law.

Although there appears to be no precedent for it, the issue then becomes whether there is a violation when a Member is actually aware that the law is unsettled, but nonetheless proceeds with the activity with knowledge that a public controversy may ensue, resulting in discredit to the House of Representatives. In this case, the hindsight conclusions of the tax counsel who appeared before the Investigative Subcommittee are that any counsel presented with the facts alleged in the Statement of Alleged Violation "would have advised that it not be conducted under the auspices of an organization exempt from taxation under section 501(c)(3) of the Internal Revenue Code." (S.A.V., 15, 40). After two years of public controversy driven largely by interests totally unrelated to the tax-exempt status of the organizations, the tax attorney's position is a relatively obvious conclusion for attorneys operating with the benefit of hindsight. Respondent's conduct must, however, be evaluated in the real world, real time context of what was the generally accepted practice in 1993 when the course was established.

The use of Charitable Funds in Support of Nonpartisan Political Education was an Accepted Practice in 1992 and 1993

First, the Respondent's activities were not inconsistent with clear federal tax law in the opinion of all tax practitioners at the relevant time. The practice in the real world at the time was that the conduct engaged in by Respondent was in accord with the conduct of many well-advised contemporary charitable educational entities, the comment of legal scholars, and the practice of other Members of Congress.

Nonprofit organizations, to qualify for tax-exempt status, must satisfy the basic criteria established by section 501(c)(3) of the Internal Revenue Code ("IRC" or "the Code"), regulations promulgated thereunder, judicial interpretation of the law and its regulations, Internal Revenue Service ("IRS") Revenue Rulings, IRS Letter Rulings, tax notices, and the various other means such as IRS press releases and announcements by which citizens can attempt to anticipate IRS interpretation of their conduct under the law.

Section 501(C)(3)and the Regulations Promulgated Thereunder

In essence, section 501(c)(3) of the Internal Revenue Code provides that entities must satisfy several basic criteria to qualify for exempt status. First, the entity must be "organized and operated exclusively for" one or more of several enumerated charitable, religious or educational purposes; second, "no part" of the net earnings of the entity may inure to the benefit of any private shareholder or individual; third, "no substantial part of the activities" of that entity may be "carrying on propaganda, or otherwise attempting to influence legislation"; and fourth, the entity must not "participate in or intervene in . . . , any political campaign on behalf of (or in opposition to) any candidate for public office." IRC ss 501(c)(3).

The legislative history of the campaign intervention rule reflects the difficulties practitioners have encountered in applying these provisions. This provision of the Code was added to the federal tax law when then-Senator Lyndon B. Johnson offered the provision by way of a floor amendment to the Revenue Act of 1954 without congressional hearings out of concern that funds provided by a charitable foundation had been used to finance the campaign of a primary opponent. B. Hopkins, The Law of Tax-Exempt Organizations, p. 327 (6th ed. 1992); Lobbying and Political Activities of Tax-Exempt Organizations: Hearings before the Subcommittee on Oversight of the House Committee on Ways and Means, 100th Cong., 1st Sess. 19-20, 423 (1987) (Statements of Bruce Hopkins, Baker & Hostetler and the United States Catholic Conference). In offering the amendment, Senator Johnson stated that the purpose of the amendment was to "den[y] tax exempt status to not only those people who influence legislation but also to those who intervene in any public campaign on behalf of any candidate for any public office." 100 Cong. Rec. 9604 (1954).

Section 1.501(c)(3)-1 of the Income Tax Regulations ("the Regulations") marked a retreat from the "exclusively for" language of section 501(c)(3) by providing that "lain organization will be regarded as 'operated exclusively' for one or more exempt purposes only if it engages primarily in activities which accomplish one or more of such exempt purposes specified in section 501 (c)(3). An organization will not be so regarded if more than an insubstantial part of its activities is not in furtherance of an exempt purpose." 26 C.F.R. 1.501(c)(3)-1(c)(1). Thus, contrary to the language of section 501(c)(3), the IRS has indicated that conduct not consistent with articulated exempt purposes will not jeopardize exempt status as long as such conduct constitutes only an "insubstantial part" of its overall activities. Id.

The Regulations further provide that an entity will not be regarded as being operated exclusively for exempt purposes if it satisfies the IRS' definition of an "action" organization. 26 C.F.R. 1.501(c)(3)-1(c)(3). An "action" organization is defined as one that devotes "a substantial part of its activities [to] attempting to influence legislation by propaganda or otherwise." 26 C.F.R. 1.501(c)(3)-1 (c)(3)(ii). Likewise, "lain organization is an 'action' organization if it participates or intervenes, directly or indirectly, in any political campaign on behalf of or in opposition to any candidate for public office." 26 C.F.R. 1.501(c)(3)-1(c)(3)(iii). . . .

Dec. 8, 1994, March 27, 1995, Letters

As background, it is important to note that the Respondent has been proactive, as opposed to reactive, with the Committee in connection with the Renewing American Civilization course and any potential ethics issues which it might present. Respondent has waived attorney-client privileges, produced thousands of documents and met with the Investigative Subcommittee at its convenience. The proactive involvement began with his letter dated May 12, 1993, in which he specifically inquired if "the committee [had] any concerns about this project." Then, in June of 1993, Respondent, Jeffrey Eisenach, Annette Meeks and Linda Nave met with then Committee counsel David J. McCarthy. (See Letter of Speaker Gingrich to Reps. Goss and Cardin, October 31, 1996, with attachments (including Letter of David J. McCarthy to Rep. Hobson, December 1, 1994)). During the course of that meeting, Mr. McCarthy recalls that:

The discussion eventually turned to fundraising for the course. Jeff Eisenach began to volunteer details of how he contemplated fundraising, and I interrupted his explanation with a question, "are you on the House payroll?" When he answered that he was not, never had been, and did not ever expect to be, I shifted the focus of the discussion by explaining that I was not interested in what Eisenach was planning to do, I was only interested in what Mr. Gingrich and any House employees were going to do. . . .

Then Mr. Gingrich again brought up Eisenach and asked whether he should not get the Committee's written advice that Eisenach would be permitted to engage in the fundraising. His concern seemed to be that Eisenach's identity with GOPAC, along with his fundraising for the course through the college foundation, could open him to criticism that the motivation for the course was political. I replied that, in my judgment, Mr. Gingrich should not ask the Committee to pass on the activity of Eisenach.

First, I explained that because Eisenach was not a Member, officer or employee of the House, his activity was really outside of the Committee's jurisdiction. Secondly, I told him that, to my knowledge of tax law, the issue of whether the contributions in support of the course would keep their tax- deductible status would turn not on who did the fundraising but on how the funds were spent, and that the educational nature of the course spoke for itself. I told him that I was aware of no law or IRS regulation that would prevent Eisenach from raising charitable contributions, even at the same time that he was raising political contributions. In any event, I advised him, I expected the Committee to stick by its advisory opinion in the Ethics Manual and not get into second-guessing the IRS on its determination of tax-exempt status.

I also felt that because the Committee's written answer might decline to offer advice on Eisenach fundraising activity — it being outside the Committee's purview — he might be just as well off not to raise the question in his letter. My experience was that Members found it annoying when the Committee in a written advisory opinion would explicitly decline to answer a question. I believe that there was some brief discussion about Eisenach leaving GOPAC, in any event, to focus on the course fundraising. (Letter of David J. McCarthy to Rep. David Hobson, December 1, 1994, at 1-2).

The significance of these passages from McCarthy's letter is twofold. First, they demonstrate that Respondent expressly referenced GOPAC and the involvement of Eisenach in course fundraising in his consultations with Committee counsel. Secondly, these passages explain that Respondent did not make reference to GOPAC involvement in the course in his letter of July 21, 1993, providing additional information to Representative McDermott as Committee Chairman on the **express advice of Committee counsel.** (See Letter to Rep. Jim McDermott, July 21, 1993; see also, Letter from Committee to Speaker Gingrich, October 31, 1994, at 2).

Then, on September 7, 1994, Ben Jones, Respondent's electoral opponent, filed his first ethics complaint against Respondent. Respondent's initial responsive submission to the Committee dated October 4, 1994, prepared by a member of Respondent's staff, expressly refers to GOPAC's involvement in the course. In particular, the letter states:

I would like to make it **abundantly clear** that those who were paid for course preparation were paid by either the Kennesaw State Foundation [sic], the Progress and Freedom Foundation or GOPAC. . . . Those persons paid by one of the aforementioned groups include: Dr. Jeffrey Eisenach, Mike DuGally, Jana Rogers, Patty Stechschultez [sic], Pamla Prochnow, Dr. Steve Hanser, Joe Gaylord and Nancy Desmond. (Letter to Rep. Jim McDermott, October 4, 1994, at 2). (Emphasis added.)

As the above-quoted passage indicates, Respondent expressly referred in correspondence with the Committee to the involvement of GOPAC in the course and the use of GOPAC funds to pay individuals for course preparation. Indeed, there is no question that the Committee was aware of involvement by GOPAC. This knowledge was confirmed in the Committee's letter dated October 31, 1994, to Respondent. Significantly, the Committee's letter notes that Respondent's October 4, 1994, letter "sufficiently answered most of the allegations raised in Mr. Jones' complaint."

Eliminating any issue regarding the Committee's awareness of GOPAC's involvement, however, the Committee's October 31, 1994, letter went on to state: "A number of documents reflect the involvement of GOPAC and GOPAC employees in developing and raising funds for the course."

The letter continues: "in addition to the above, various other documents related to the course were sent out on GOPAC letterhead, were sent from GOPAC's fax machine, used GOPAC's address as a place to mail materials related to the course, and referred to registration materials being included in GOPAC Farmteam mailings." In all, the Committee's October 31, 1994, letter makes reference to GOPAC no less than 46 times and cites extensive documentation referring to GOPAC. (See, Letter from Committee to Speaker Gingrich, October 31, 1994). Interestingly, from the original complaint to the October 31, 1994, Committee correspondence, GOPAC is mentioned by name 92 times in correspondence to and from the Committee.

Dec. 8, 1994, Letter

As reflected above, the Committee's request for information was dated October 31, 1994. On November 8, 1994, election day, Republicans captured a majority of seats in the U.S. House of Representatives. The process of transition began immediately. In the context of these events Respondent retained counsel on November 15, 1994, to represent him in connection with the ethics investigation.

Counsel began preparation of the response. An associate was assigned to prepare an initial draft of the response. The attorneys coordinated their efforts with a member of Respondent's staff. Subsequently, the December 8, 1994, letter was presented to Respondent for review and signature. It does not appear that there was any communication between the attorneys and the Respondent until after December 8, 1994.

Regarding the response, Respondent testified that he would have turned and said "I want this done . . . "(Gingrich Tr., 11/13/96, at p. 28). Respondent testified that, in November, "we, in effect, had decided to go from [the staff member] being in charge to [the staff member] coordinating with the law firm and the law firm being in charge." Respondent testified that it was his understanding that the law firm was primarily responsible for drafting the December 8th letter. (Gingrich Tr. 11/13/96, at 28).

The firm partner recalls that his role and that of his firm in the preparation of the December 1994 letter was to prepare a response working with the staff member. (Baran Tr. at 6-7). The partner assigned responsibility for preparing an initial draft to an associate at the firm. (Baran Tr. at 9-10; Mehlman Tr. at 15). The associate testified that in preparing the draft response to the October 31, 1994, letter, he relied upon "various correspondence" between Respondent and the Committee including the October 4, 1994 letter, the course book, a pamphlet on the course, and the Jones' complaint with exhibits and the videotapes of the course. (Mehlman Tr. at 15-16). The associate further testified that it was his understanding that he did not need to go beyond these materials in drafting the response. (Mehlman Tr. at 19). The associate testified that, in preparing the draft, he never contacted anyone at GOPAC (Mehlman Tr. at 18, 28), nor did he contact Dr. Eisenach (Mehlman Tr. at 28) or Respondent (Mehlman Tr. at 27) to confirm any of the information contained in the December 8, 1994, letter. The associate then met with the partner to review the draft and some editorial changes were made. (Mehlman Tr. at 18).

The partner testified that his review was limited to the October 31, 1994, letter from the Committee, the Jones Complaint with exhibits and telephone conversations, and that otherwise "[he] didn't have any other independent factual gathering." (Baran Tr, at 13). The partner further indicated that he had no contact with the Kennesaw State College Foundation (KSCF), Kennesaw State College or Reinhardt College in preparing the December 8th letter. (Baran Tr. at 18). The partner further testified that his first contact with Respondent during this time period was on December 9, 1994, and that he had no recollection of having discussed the letter at all and that he had no contact with Respondent concerning the matter prior to that time. (Baran Tr. at 18, 33).

Turning then to the involvement of Respondent and his staff in the December 8, 1994, letter, the partner indicated that the letter "eventually went from our office to [the staff member.]." (Baran Tr. at 14). Respondent's testimony confirms that it was his understanding that the law firm would be responsible for preparing the response in coordination with his staff member. (Gingrich Tr., 11/13/96, at 28). Respondent indicated that, in assigning this task, "[the staff member] would have been acting with my authority to conduct what we thought at the time was a thorough investigation." (Gingrich Tr., 11/13/96, at 15-16). However, the testimony makes apparent that the staff member believed that the partner attorney was checking the factual basis of the statements for accuracy while the partner attorney was under the misimpression that the staff member was doing so. This miscommunication extended not only to the research into the factual bases for the statements but to the communication of these findings to Respondent. As noted above, the partner attorney testified that he did not discuss the contents of the letter with Respondent prior to submission. (Baran Tr. at 18, 33). Nor does Respondent recall such a meeting. (Gingrich Tr., 11/13/96, at 30). Nor apparently did anyone on Respondent's staff confirm the facts contained in the letter with Respondent prior to its submission in any systematic fashion. The staff member's recollection is that she did not even see Respondent during the signing process, but forwarded the letter to Respondent for signature through the executive assistant. (Meeks Tr. at 76-77).

March 27, 1995, Letter

Turning then to the letter to the Committee of March 27, 1995, similar miscues appear to have resulted in inaccuracies in statements made to the Committee. Again the attorneys had responsibility for the preparation of the submission on Respondent's behalf, and on this occasion, the responsibility for the initial drafting fell to the associate as well as to a more senior associate. The senior associate testified that, in drafting the facts section of the March 27 response, he relied upon the October 4 letter, the attachments to the amended complaint, the original Jones complaint and its exhibits, the December 8 letter, all of the exhibits included with the March 27 submission and conversations with the Respondent's staff member. (Toner Tr. at 19, 29-30, 34).

The senior associate further indicated that he made no contact with anyone at GOPAC, the Progress & Freedom Foundation, Reinhardt College, Kennesaw State College or the Kennesaw State College Foundation in preparing the March 27, 1995, letter. (Toner Tr. at 19-20; 26-27; see also, Baran Tr. at 27 (no contact with GOPAC)). The junior associate similarly testified that he had relied upon the correspondence and materials he had from the December 8 submission as well as having reviewed other responses by the senior associate and the partner. (Mehlman Tr. at 38).

Both associates indicated that they were not personally aware of efforts to check the factual accuracy of the March 27, 1995, submission. (Toner Tr. at 38-39; Mehlman Tr. at 53). The senior associate testified that he was similarly unaware of any contacts with people outside the firm, other than Respondent's staff member, to confirm the factual basis for statements contained in the submission (Toner Tr. at 56), and that he was not aware of any changes made to the document based on comments from anyone associated with the Respondent. (Toner Tr. at 60-61). The junior associate indicated that he did not recall contacting any outside persons to confirm such facts. (Mehlman Tr. at 38). The partner additionally confirmed that, while he reviewed the drafts and edits with the associate, he did not recall making any outside inquiries of anyone regarding the Renewing American Civilization course with one possible exception. (Baran Tr. at 28).

Asked if he was aware of any additional factual inquiry done in preparation for the March 27, 1995, submission in addition to that previously done for the December 8, 1994, submission, the partner replied: "Factual inquiry — none that I recall — no." (Baran Tr. at 30-31). The partner's testimony was that after drafting and editing the March 27, 1995, document "at some point we would have sent a draft that we felt comfortable with over to the Speaker's office." (Baran Tr. at 28). The partner testified that he did not recall any discussions with the Respondent prior to the submission of the March 27, 1995, letter over the partner's signature. (Baran Tr. at 32). The firm's billing records reflect that the submission was filed on March 27, 1995, at 6:05 and delivered to Tony Blankley of Respondent's staff at 6:35 that same evening. (WFP 00224).

The purpose of this extended review of the testimony offered in this proceeding regarding the process of preparing these submissions to the Committee is not an attempt to shift the ultimate responsibility for submitting these statements from Respondent to others, but only to demonstrate that the testimony of record in this matter clearly supports the conclusion that any inaccuracies contained in these submissions were the result of regrettable errors rather than of any intent to mislead this Committee. In their testimony before this Committee, the staff members as well as the attorneys repeatedly testified that they were never told, directly or indirectly, by Respondent, or anyone on his behalf, to provide anything other than accurate information to the Committee.

Mr. Goss. For the record, you may want to respond to this. I will try and make it as clearly as I can. Do you have any personal knowledge of whether the Speaker either directly or through his attorney Mr. Baran deliberately provided anything other than accurate, reliable or complete information to this committee regarding his response related to the complaints with regard to the letters that we have talked about today?

The Witness. Do I have any knowledge that any of the information was false? Is that the question?

Mr. Goss. Was deliberately provided, that was other than accurate, reliable or complete.

The Witness. No.

Mr. Goss. Do you know if Mr. Gingrich at any time tried to forward or intended to forward to us incomplete, inaccurate or unreliable information?

The Witness. If I may editorialize on my answer for a second, we really — in the two replies that I was involved in, we really, in our estimation, tried to comply as fully, completely, honestly, straight forward, and promptly as we were able.

Mr. Schiff. The question is did Mr. Gingrich ever suggest to you in any way, shape, or form, that you do other than that?

The Witness. Oh, goodness, no. (Meeks Tr. at 85-86).

Mr. Goss. Do you have any knowledge that Mr. Gingrich was aware that any of the information contained in the letters that we have talked about at the time that those letters were submitted were incomplete, misleading, or inaccurate?

The Witness. No. (Baran Tr. at 60).

Mr. Schiff. Could I ask you two questions on that; actually, I may be leaping ahead, but a general question? Was there anything told to you that you heard either directly or indirectly, that indicated that it was the purpose of either the Speaker or of Mr. Baran or of anyone else connected with this case, to deceive this committee and to provide anything but accurate information?

The Witness. No.

Mr. Schiff. Your assumption, then, is you are supposed to put together a correct statement of the facts and submit it to us?

The Witness. Absolutely. (Toner Tr. at 28).

Representative Goss summarized the testimony on this point most succinctly, observing:

Mr. Goss. Okay. I have only one little thought. We seem to have gotten into a situation where we know we have some information that is not everything we desired it to be, and we are trying to track down why and how we got into that position. It seems that Mr. Gingrich was relying on you [Baran] and some other people to do the December 8th letter, or his December 8th letter was given to somebody else and they were supplemented by your firm, and your firm in turn, by your testimony, you were relying pretty much on what that individual, who would be Ms. Meeks, was doing and you were just checking for legalities rather than substance, would be sort of the way I read you testimony, and therefore the problem started on December 8th was further compounded on March 27th on that letter because you used some of the material from the December 8th letter. Is that correct?

The Witness [the partner attorney]: Yes. I would agree with that characterization. (Baran Tr. at 59).

Respondent's own testimony before this Committee similarly endorses this version of events:

. . . After reviewing my testimony, my counsel's testimony, and the testimony of his two associates, the ball appears to have been dropped between my staff and my counsel regarding the investigation and verification of the responses submitted to the committee.

As I testified, I erroneously, it turns out, relied on others to verify the accuracy of the statements and responses. This did not happen. As my counsel's testimony indicates, there was no detailed discussion with me regarding the submissions before they were sent to the committee. Nonetheless, I bear responsibility for them, and I again apologize to the committee for what was an inadvertent and embarrassing breakdown. (Gingrich Tr., 12/10/96, at 5-6).

Upon realizing that errors were made, Speaker Gingrich has openly and publicly accepted responsibility for these errors and has offered his sincere apologies to this Committee and the House.

Notwithstanding these circumstances, the bottom line is that inaccurate, incomplete and unreliable information was submitted to the Committee. There are no circumstances which can justify the submission of inaccurate, incomplete or unreliable information to the Committee. The information submitted was submitted on Respondent's behalf. Respondent has accepted full responsibility.

Respectfully submitted, this 16th day of January, 1997. ■

J. Randolph Evans
Arnall, Golden & Gregory, L.L.P.
2800 One Atlantic Center
1201 W. Peachtree Street
Atlanta, Georgia 30309
Counsel for Respondent

Ed Bethune
Bracewell & Patterson, L.L.P.
2000 K Street, N.W.
Suite 500
Washington, D.C. 20006-1872
Co-Counsel for Respondent

STATE OF THE UNION ADDRESS

Clinton Focuses on Education, Working With GOP on Budget

Following is a transcript of President Clinton's State of the Union address on Feb. 4, as provided by The Associated Press:

President Clinton: Thank you. Thank you very much.

Mr. Speaker, Mr. Vice President, members of the 105th Congress, distinguished guests, my fellow Americans:

I think I should start by saying thanks for inviting me back.

I come before you tonight with a challenge as great as any in our peacetime history — and a plan of action to meet that challenge, to prepare our people for the bold new world of the 21st century.

We have much to be thankful for. With four years of growth, we have won back the basic strength of our economy. With crime and welfare rolls declining, we are winning back our optimism, the enduring faith that we can master any difficulty. With the Cold War receding and global commerce at record levels, we are helping to win an unrivaled peace and prosperity all across the world.

My fellow Americans, the state of our union is strong, but now we must rise to the decisive moment, to make a nation and a world better than any we have ever known.

The new promise of the global economy, the Information Age, unimagined new work, life-enhancing technology — all these are ours to seize. That is our honor and our challenge. We must be shapers of events, not observers, for if we do not act, the moment will pass and we will lose the best possibilities of our future.

We face no imminent threat, but we do have an enemy. The enemy of our time is inaction.

So tonight I issue a call to action — action by this Congress, action by our states, by our people to prepare America for the 21st century; action to keep our economy and our democracy strong and working for all our people; action to strengthen education and harness the forces of technology and science; action to build stronger families and stronger communities and a safer environment; action to keep America the world's strongest force for peace, freedom and prosperity; and above all, action to build a more perfect union here at home.

The spirit we bring to our work will make all the difference.

We must be committed to the pursuit of opportunity for all Americans, responsibility from all Americans in a community of all Americans. And we must be committed to a new kind of government: not to solve all our problems for us, but to give our people — all our people — the tools they need to make the most of their own lives. And we must work together.

The people of this nation elected us all. They want us to be partners, not partisans. They put us all right here in the same boat. They gave us all oars, and they told us to row. Now, here is the direction I believe we should take.

Balanced Budget

First, we must move quickly to complete the unfinished business of our country: to balance the budget, renew our democracy and finish the job of welfare reform.

Over the last four years, we have brought new economic growth by investing in our people, expanding our exports, cutting our deficits, creating over 11 million new jobs, a four-year record.

Now we must keep our economy the strongest in the world. We here tonight have an historic opportunity. Let this Congress be the Congress that finally balances the budget. Thank you.

In two days I will propose a detailed plan to balance the budget by 2002. This plan will balance the budget and invest in our people while protecting Medicare, Medicaid, education and the environment. It will balance the budget and build on the vice president's efforts to make our government work better — even as it costs less.

It will balance the budget and provide middle-class tax relief to pay for education and health care, to help to raise a child, to buy and sell a home.

Balancing the budget requires only your vote and my signature. It does not require us to rewrite our Constitution. I believe, I believe it is both unnecessary, unwise to adopt a balanced-budget amendment that could cripple our country in time of economic crisis and force unwanted results such as judges halting Social Security checks or increasing taxes.

Let us at least agree we should not pass any measure, no measure should be passed that threatens Social Security. We don't need, whatever your view on that, we all must concede we don't need a constitutional amendment, we need action. Whatever our differences, we should balance the budget now, and then, for the long-term health of our society, we must agree to a bipartisan process to preserve Social Security and reform Medicare for the long run, so that these fundamental programs will be as strong for our children as they are for our parents.

And let me say something that's not in my script tonight. I know this is not going to be easy. But I really believe one of the reasons the American people gave me a second term was to take the tough decisions in the next four years that will carry our country through the next 50 years. I know it is easier for me than for you to say or do. But another reason I was elected is to support all of you, without regard to party, to give you what is necessary to join in these decisions. We owe it to our country and to our future.

Campaign Finance Reform

Our second piece of unfinished business requires us to commit ourselves tonight, before the eyes of America, to finally enacting bipartisan campaign finance reform.

Now, Senators [John] McCain [R-Ariz.] and [Russell D.] Feingold [D-Wis.], Representatives [Christopher] Shays [R-Conn.] and [Martin T.] Meehan [D-Mass.] have reached across party lines here to craft tough and fair reform. Their proposal would curb spending, reduce the role of special interests, create a level playing field between challengers and incumbents, and ban contributions from non-citizens, all corporate sources, and the other large soft-money contributions that both parties receive.

You know and I know that this can be delayed, and you know and I know that delay will mean the death of reform.

So let's set our own deadline. Let's work together to write bipartisan campaign finance reform into law and pass McCain-Feingold by the day we celebrate the birth of our democracy, July the 4th.

From Welfare to Work

There is a third piece of unfinished business. Over the last four years, we moved a record two and a quarter million people off the welfare roles. Then last year Congress enacted landmark welfare reform legislation demanding that all able-bodied recipients assume the responsibility of moving from welfare to work. Now each and every one of us has to fulfill our responsibility, indeed our moral obligation, to make sure that people who now must work can work. And now we must act to meet a new goal: 2 million more people off the welfare rolls by the year 2000.

Here is my plan: tax credits and other incentives for businesses that hire people off welfare; incentives for job placement firms in states to create more jobs for welfare recipients; training, transportation and child care to help people go to work.

Now I challenge every state — turn those welfare checks into private sector paychecks. I challenge every religious congregation, every community nonprofit, every business to hire someone off welfare. And I'd like to say especially to every employer in our country who ever criticized the old welfare system, you can't blame that old system anymore; we have torn it down. Now, do your part. Give someone on welfare the chance to go to work.

Tonight I am pleased to announce that five major corporations — Sprint, Monsanto, UPS, Burger King and United Airlines — will be the first to join in a new national effort to marshal America's businesses large and small to create jobs so that people can move from welfare to work.

We passed welfare reform. All of you know I believe we were right to do it. But no one can walk out of this chamber with a clear conscience unless you are prepared to finish the job.

And we must join together to do something else, too, something both Republican and Democratic governors have asked us to do: to restore basic health and disability benefits when misfortune strikes immigrants who came to this country legally, who work hard, pay taxes and obey the law. To do otherwise is simply unworthy of a great nation of immigrants.

Education

Now, looking ahead, the greatest step of all, the high threshold to the future we must now cross, and my No. 1 priority for the next four years, is to ensure that all Americans have the best education in the world. Thank you.

Let's work together to meet these three goals: every 8-year-old must be able to read, every 12-year-old must be able to log on to the Internet, every 18-year-old must be able to go to college and every adult American must be able to keep on learning for a lifetime.

My balanced budget makes an unprecedented commitment to these goals — $51 billion next year — but far more than money is required. I have a plan, a call to action for American education based on these 10 principles:

First, a national crusade for education standards — not federal government standards, but national standards, representing what all our students must know to succeed in the knowledge economy of the 21st century. Every state and school must shape the curriculum to reflect these standards and train teachers to lift students up to them. To help schools meet the standards and measure their progress, we will lead an effort over the next two years to develop national tests of student achievement in reading and math.

Tonight I issue a challenge to the nation. Every state should adopt high national standards, and by 1999, every state should test every fourth-grader in reading and every eighth-grader in math to make sure these standards are met.

Raising standards will not be easy, and some of our children will not be able to meet them at first. The point is not to put our children down, but to lift them up. Good tests will show us who needs help, what changes in teaching to make, and which schools need to improve. They can help us end social promotion, for no child should move from grade school to junior high or junior high to high school until he or she is ready.

Last month our secretary of Education, Dick Riley, and I visited northern Illinois, where eighth-grade students from 20 school districts, in a project aptly called First in the World, took the third International Math and Science Study.

That's a test that reflects the world-class standards our children must meet for the new era. And those students in Illinois tied for first in the world in science and came in second in math. Two of them, Kristen Tanner and Chris Getsla, are here tonight along with their teacher, Sue Winski. They're up there with the first lady, and they prove that when we aim high and challenge our students, they will be the best in the world. Let's give them a hand. Stand up, please.

Second, to have the best schools, we must have the best teachers. Most of us in this chamber would not be here tonight without the help of those teachers. I know that I wouldn't be here.

For years many of our educators, led by North Carolina's [Democratic] governor, Jim Hunt, and the National Board for Professional Teaching Standards, have worked very hard to establish nationally accepted credentials for excellence in teaching.

Just 500 of these teachers have been certified since 1995. My budget will enable 100,000 more to seek national certification as master teachers. We should reward and recognize our best teachers. And as we reward them, we should quickly and fairly remove those few who don't measure up, and we should challenge more of our finest young people to consider teaching as a career.

Third, we must do more to help all our children read. Forty percent — 40 percent — of our 8-year-olds cannot read on their own. That's why we have just launched the America Reads initiative, to build a citizen army of 1 million volunteer tutors to make sure every child can read independently by the end of the 3rd grade. We will use thousands of AmeriCorps volunteers to mobilize this citizen army. We want at least 100,000 college students to help.

And tonight I'm pleased that 60 college presidents have answered my call, pledging that thousands of their work-study students will serve for one year as reading tutors.

This is also a challenge to every teacher and every principal.

You must use these tutors to help your students read. And it is especially a challenge to our parents. You must read with your children every night.

This leads to the fourth principle: Learning begins in the first days of life. Scientists are now discovering how young children develop emotionally and intellectually from their very first days and how important it is for parents to begin immediately talking, singing, even reading to their infants. The first lady has spent years writing about this issue, studying it. And she and I are going to convene a White House conference on early learning and the brain this spring to explore how parents and educators can best use these startling new findings.

We already know we should start teaching children before they start school. That's why this balanced budget expands Head Start to 1 million children by 2002. And that is why the vice president and Mrs. Gore will host their annual family conference this June on what we can do to make sure that parents are an active part of their children's learning all the way through school.

They've done a great deal to highlight the importance of family in our life, and now they're turning their attention to getting more parents involved in their children's learning all the way through school. I thank you, Mr. Vice President, and I thank you especially, Tipper, for what you're doing.

Fifth, every state should give parents the power to choose the right public school for their children. Their right to choose will foster competition and innovation that can make public schools better. We should also make it possible for more parents and teachers to start charter schools, schools that set and meet the highest standards and exist only as long as they do.

Our plan will help America to create 3,000 of these charter schools by the next century, nearly seven times as there are in the country today, so that parents will have even more choices in sending their children to the best schools.

Sixth, character education must be taught in our schools. We must teach our children to be good citizens. And we must continue to promote order and discipline; supporting communities that introduce school uniforms, impose curfews, enforce truancy laws, remove disruptive students from the classroom, and have zero tolerance for guns and drugs in schools.

Seventh, we cannot expect our children to raise themselves up in schools that are literally falling down. With the student population at an all-time high, and record numbers of school buildings falling into disrepair, this has now become a serious national concern. Therefore, my budget includes a new initiative: $5 billion to help communities finance $20 billion in school construction over the next four years.

Eighth, we must make the 13th and 14th years of education — at least two years of college — just as universal in America by the 21st century as a high school education is today, and we must open the doors of college to all Americans.

To do that, I propose America's Hope Scholarship, based on Georgia's pioneering program — two years of a $1,500 tax credit for college tuition, enough to pay for the typical community college. I also propose a tax deduction of up to $10,000 a year for all tuition after high school, an expanded IRA you can withdraw from tax free for education, and the largest increase in Pell grant scholarships in 20 years.

Now this plan will give most families the ability to pay no taxes on money they save for college tuition. I ask you to pass it and give every American who works hard the chance to go to college.

Ninth, in the 21st century we must expand the frontiers of learning across a lifetime. All our people, of whatever age, must have the chance to learn new skills.

Most Americans live near a community college. The roads that take them there can be paths to a better future. My GI bill for America's workers will transform the confusing tangle of federal training programs into a simple skill grant to go directly into eligible workers' hands.

For too long this bill has been sitting on that desk there, without action. I ask you to pass it now. Let's give more of our workers the ability to learn and to earn for a lifetime.

Tenth, we must bring the power of the Information Age into all our schools.

Last year, I challenged America to connect every classroom and library to the Internet by the year 2000, so that for the first time in our history, children in the most isolated rural town, the most comfortable suburbs, the poorest inner-city schools will have the same access to the same universe of knowledge.

That is my plan — a call to action for American education. Some may say that it is unusual for a president to pay this kind of attention to education. Some may say it is simply because the president and his wonderful wife have been obsessed with this subject for more years than they can recall. That is not what is driving these proposals. We must understand the significance of this endeavor.

One of the greatest sources of our strength throughout the Cold War was a bipartisan foreign policy. Because our future was at stake, politics stopped at the water's edge. Now I ask you, and I ask all our nation's governors, I ask parents, teachers and citizens all across America, for a new nonpartisan commitment to education, because education is a critical national security issue for our future and politics must stop at the schoolhouse door.

Harnessing Technology

To prepare America for the 21st century, we must harness the powerful forces of science and technology to benefit all Americans. This is the first State of the Union carried live in video over the Internet, but we've only begun to spread the benefits of a technology revolution that should become the modern birthright of every citizen.

Our effort to connect every classroom is just the beginning. Now we should connect every hospital to the Internet so that doctors can instantly share data about their patients with the best specialists in the field.

And I challenge the private sector tonight to start by connecting every children's hospital as soon as possible so that a child in bed can stay in touch with school, family and friends. A sick child need no longer be a child alone.

We must build the second generation of the Internet so that our leading universities and national laboratories can communicate in speeds a thousand times faster than today to develop new medical treatments, new sources of energy, new ways of working together. But we cannot stop there.

As the Internet becomes our new town square, a computer in every home — a teacher of all subjects, a connection to all cultures— this will no longer be a dream, but a necessity. And over the next decade, that must be our goal.

We must continue to explore the heavens, pressing on with the Mars probes and the International Space Station, both of which will have practical applications for our everyday living.

We must speed the remarkable advances in medical science. The human genome project is now decoding the genetic mysteries of life. American scientists have discovered genes linked to breast cancer and ovarian cancer and medication that stops a stroke in progress and begins to reverse its effects, and treatments that dramatically lengthen the lives of people with HIV and AIDS.

Since I took office, funding for AIDS research at the National Institutes of Health has increased dramatically to $1.5 billion. With new resources, NIH will now become the most powerful discovery engine for an AIDS vaccine, working with other scientists, to finally end the threat of AIDS. Remember that every year, every year we move up the discovery of an AIDS vaccine we'll save millions of lives around the world. We must reinforce our commitment to medical science.

To prepare America for the 21st century, we must build stronger families. Over the past four years, the Family and Medical Leave Law has helped millions of Americans to take time off to be with their families.

With new pressures on people and the way they work and live, I believe we must expand family leave so that workers can take time off for teacher conferences and a child's medical checkup. We should pass flex time so workers can choose to be paid for overtime in income or trade it in for time off to be with their families.

We must continue, step by step, to give more families access to affordable quality health care. Forty million Americans still lack health insurance. Ten million children still lack health insurance. Eighty percent of them have working parents who pay taxes. That is wrong.

My balanced budget will extend health coverage to up to 5 million of those children. Since nearly half of all children who lose their insurance do so because their parents lose or change a job, my budget will also ensure that people who temporarily lose their jobs can still afford to keep their health insurance. No child should be without a doctor just because a parent is without a job.

My Medicare plan modernizes Medicare, increases the life of the trust fund to 10 years, provides support for respite care for the many families with loved ones afflicted with Alzheimer's, and, for the first time, it would fully pay for annual mammograms.

Just as we ended drive-through deliveries of babies last year, we must now end the dangerous and demeaning practice of forcing women home from the hospital only hours after a mastectomy.

I ask your support for bipartisan legislation to guarantee that a woman can stay in the hospital for 48 hours after a mastectomy. With us tonight is Dr. Kristen Zarfos, a Connecticut surgeon whose outrage at this practice spurred a national movement and inspired this legislation. I'd like her to stand so we can thank her for her efforts. Dr. Zarfos, thank you.

In the last four years, we have increased child support collections by 50 percent. Now we should go further and do better by making it a felony for any parent to cross a state line in an attempt to flee from this, his or her most sacred obligation.

Finally, we must also protect our children by standing firm in our determination to ban the advertising and marketing of cigarettes that endanger their lives.

Building Stronger Communities

To prepare America for the 21st century, we must build stronger communities. We should start with safe streets. Serious crime has dropped five years in a row. The key has been community policing. We must finish the job of putting 100,000 community police on the streets of the United States.

We should pass the Victims' Rights Amendment to the Constitution, and I ask you to mount a full-scale assault on juvenile crime, with legislation that declares war on gangs with new prosecutors and tougher penalties, extends the Brady bill so violent teen criminals will not be able to buy handguns, requires child safety locks on handguns to prevent unauthorized use, and helps to keep our schools open after hours, on weekends and in the summer so our young people will have someplace to go and something to say yes to.

This balanced budget includes the largest anti-drug effort ever — to stop drugs at their source; punish those who push them; and teach our young people that drugs are wrong, drugs are illegal, and drugs will kill them. I hope you will support it.

Our growing economy has helped to revive poor urban and rural neighborhoods, but we must do more to empower them to create the conditions in which all families can flourish and to create jobs through investment by business and loans by banks.

We should double the number of empowerment zones. They've already brought so much hope to communities like Detroit, where the unemployment rate has been cut in half in four years. We should restore contaminated urban land and buildings to constructive use. We should expand the network of community development banks.

And together, we must pledge tonight that we will use this empowerment approach, including private sector tax incentives, to renew our capital city so that Washington is a great place to work and live — and once again the proud face America shows the world.

We must protect our environment in every community. In the last four years, we cleaned up 250 toxic waste sites, as many as in the previous 12. Now we should clean up 500 more so that our children grow up next to parks, not poison. I urge you to pass my proposal to make big polluters live by a simple rule: If you pollute our environment, you should pay to clean it up.

In the last four years, we strengthened our nation's safe food and clean drinking water laws; we protected some of America's rarest, most beautiful land in Utah's Red Rocks region; created three new national parks in the California desert; and began to restore the Florida Everglades.

Now we must be as vigilant with our rivers as we are with our lands. Tonight I announce that this year I will designate 10 American Heritage Rivers to help communities alongside them revitalize their waterfronts and clean up pollution in the rivers, proving once again that we can grow the economy as we protect the environment.

We must also protect our global environment, working to ban the worst toxic chemicals and to reduce the greenhouse gases that challenge our health even as they change our climate.

Now, we all know that in all of our communities some of our children simply don't have what they need to grow and learn in their own homes or schools or neighborhoods. And that means the rest of us must do more, for they are our children, too. That's why [former] President [George] Bush, General Colin Powell [former chairman of the Joint Chiefs of Staff], former Housing Secretary Henry Cisneros will join the vice president and me to lead the President's Summit of Service in Philadelphia in April.

Our national service program, AmeriCorps, has already helped 70,000 young people to work their way through college as they serve America. Now we intend to mobilize millions of Americans to serve in thousands of ways. Citizen service is an American responsibility which all Americans should embrace. And I ask your support for that endeavor.

I'd like to make just one last point about our national community. Our economy is measured in numbers and statistics. And it's very important. But the enduring worth of our nation lies in our shared values and our soaring spirit. So instead of cutting back on our modest efforts to support the arts and humanities, I believe we should stand by them and challenge our artists, musicians and writers, challenge our museums, libraries and theaters.

We should challenge all Americans in the arts and humanities to join with their fellow citizens to make the year 2000 a national celebration of the American spirit in every community, a celebration of our common culture in the century that is past and in the new one to come in a new millennium so that we can remain the world's beacon not only of liberty but of creativity long after the fireworks have faded.

World Leadership

To prepare America for the 21st century, we must master the forces of change in the world and keep American leadership strong and sure for an uncharted time.

Fifty years ago, a farsighted America led in creating the institutions that secured victory in the Cold War and built a growing world economy. As a result, today more people than ever embrace our ideals and share our interests. Already we have dismantled many of the blocks and barriers that divided our parents' world. For the first time, more people live under democracy than dictatorship, including every nation in our own hemisphere but one, and its day, too, will come.

Now we stand at another moment of change and choice, and another time to be farsighted, to bring America 50 more years of security and prosperity.

In this endeavor, our first task is to help to build for the very first time an undivided, democratic Europe. When Europe is stable, prosperous, and at peace, America is more secure.

To that end, we must expand NATO by 1999, so that countries that were once our adversaries can become our allies. At the special NATO summit this summer, that is what we will begin to do. We must strengthen NATO's Partnership for Peace with nonmember allies. And we must build a stable partnership between NATO and a democratic Russia.

An expanded NATO is good for America, and a Europe in which all democracies define their future not in terms of what they can do to each other, but in terms of what they can do together for the good of all — that kind of Europe is good for America.

Second, America must look to the East no less than to the West.

Our security demands it. Americans fought three wars in Asia in this century.

Our prosperity requires it. More than 2 million American jobs depend upon trade with Asia. There, too, we are helping to shape an Asian Pacific community of cooperation, not conflict.

But let our progress there not mask the peril that remains. Together with South Korea, we must advance peace talks with North Korea and bridge the Cold War's last divide. And I call on Congress to fund our share of the agreement under which North Korea must continue to freeze and then dismantle its nuclear weapons program.

We must pursue a deeper dialogue with China for the sake of our interests and our ideals. An isolated China is not good for America. A China playing its proper role in the world is. I will go to China, and I have invited China's president to come here, not because we agree on everything, but because engaging China is the best way to work on our common challenges, like ending nuclear testing, and to deal frankly with our fundamental differences, like human rights.

The American people must prosper in the global economy. We've worked hard to tear down trade barriers abroad so that we can create good jobs at home. I'm proud to say that today America is once again the most competitive nation and the No. 1 exporter in the world.

Now we must act to expand our exports, especially to Asia and Latin America, two of the fastest-growing regions on earth, or be left behind as these emerging economies forge new ties with other nations. That is why we need the authority now to conclude new trade agreements that open markets to our goods and services even as we preserve our values.

We need not shrink from the challenge of the global economy. After all, we have the best workers and the best products. In a truly open market, we can out-compete anyone, anywhere on earth.

But this is about more than economics. By expanding trade, we can advance the cause of freedom and democracy around the world. There is no better example of this truth than Latin America, where democracy and open markets are on the march together. That is why I will visit there in the spring to reinforce our important ties.

We should all be proud that America led the effort to rescue our neighbor, Mexico, from its economic crisis. And we should all be proud that last month Mexico repaid the United States, three full years ahead of schedule, with half a billion-dollar profit to us.

America must continue to be an unrelenting force for peace. From the Middle East to Haiti, from Northern Ireland to Africa, taking reasonable risks for peace keeps us from being drawn into far more costly conflicts later. With American leadership, the killing has stopped in Bosnia. Now the habits of peace must take hold.

The new NATO force will allow reconstruction and reconciliation to accelerate. Tonight I ask Congress to continue its strong support of our troops. They are doing a remarkable job there for America, and America must do right by them.

Fifth, we must move strongly against new threats to our security. In the past four years, we agreed to ban — we led the way to a worldwide agreement to ban nuclear testing.

With Russia, we dramatically cut nuclear arsenals and we stopped targeting each other's citizens. We are acting to prevent nuclear materials from falling into the wrong hands, and to rid the world of land mines.

We are working with other nations with renewed intensity to fight drug traffickers and to stop terrorists before they act and hold them fully accountable if they do.

Now we must rise to a new test of leadership — ratifying the Chemical Weapons Convention. Make no mistake about it, it will make our troops safer from chemical attack. It will help us to fight terrorism. We have no more important obligations, especially in the wake of what we now know about the Gulf War.

This treaty has been bipartisan from the beginning, supported by Republican and Democratic administrations, and Republican and Democratic members of Congress, and already approved by 68 nations. But if we do not act by April the 29th, when this convention goes into force — with or without us — we will lose the chance to have Americans leading and enforcing this effort. Together we must make the Chemical Weapons Convention law so that at last we can begin to outlaw poisoned gas from the earth.

Finally, we must have the tools to meet all these challenges. We must maintain a strong and ready military. We must increase funding for weapons modernization by the year 2000. And we must take good care of our men and women in uniform. They are the world's finest.

We must also renew our commitment to America's diplomacy and pay our debts and dues to international financial institutions like the World Bank — and to a reforming United Nations. Every dollar — every dollar we devote to preventing conflicts, to promoting democracy, to stopping the spread of disease and starvation brings a sure return in security and savings. Yet international affairs spending today is just 1 percent of the federal budget, a small fraction of what America invested in diplomacy to choose leadership over escapism at the start of the Cold War.

If America is to continue to lead the world, we here who lead America simply must find the will to pay our way. A farsighted America moved the world to a better place over these last 50 years. And so it can be for another 50 years. But a shortsighted America will soon find its words falling on deaf ears all around the world.

Almost exactly 50 years ago in the first winter of the Cold War, President [Harry S] Truman stood before a Republican Congress and called upon our country to meet its responsibilities of leadership. This was his warning. He said, "If we falter, we may endanger the peace of the world, and we shall surely endanger the welfare of this nation."

That Congress, led by Republicans like Senator Arthur Vandenberg [of Michigan], answered President Truman's call. Together, they made the commitments that strengthened our country for 50 years. Now let us do the same. Let us do what it takes to remain the indispensable nation, to keep America strong, secure and prosperous for another 50 years.

Strength Through Diversity

In the end, more than anything else, our world leadership grows out of the power of our example here at home, out of our ability to remain strong as one America.

All over the world people are being torn asunder by racial, ethnic and religious conflicts that fuel fanaticism and terror. We are the world's most diverse democracy, and the world looks to us to show that it is possible to live and advance together across those kinds of differences. America has always been a nation of immigrants.

From the start, a steady stream of people in search of freedom and opportunity have left their own lands to make this land their home. We started as an experiment in democracy fueled by Europeans. We have grown into an experiment in democratic diversity fueled by openness and promise.

My fellow Americans, we must never, ever believe that our diversity is a weakness; it is our greatest strength.

Americans speak every language, know every country. People on every continent can look to us and see the reflection of their own great potential, and they always will, as long as we strive to give all our citizens, whatever their background, an opportunity to achieve their own greatness.

We're not there yet. We still see evidence of a biting bigotry and intolerance in ugly words and awful violence, in burned churches and bombed buildings. We must fight against this in our country and in our hearts.

Just a few days before my second inauguration, one of our country's best-known pastors, Reverend Robert Schuller, suggested that I read Isaiah 58:12. Here's what it says: "Thou shalt raise up the foundations of many generations, and thou shalt be called the repairer of the breach, the restorer of paths to dwell in."

I placed my hand on that verse when I took the oath of office, on behalf of all Americans, for no matter what our differences in our faiths, our backgrounds, our politics, we must all be repairers of the breach.

I want to say a word about two other Americans who show us how. Congressman Frank Tejeda [D-Texas] was buried yesterday, a proud American whose family came from Mexico. He was only 51 years old. He was awarded the Silver Star, the Bronze Star and the Purple Heart fighting for his country in Vietnam. And he went on to serve Texas and America fighting for our future here in this chamber.

We are grateful for his service and honored that his mother, Lillie Tejeda, and his sister, Mary Alice, have come from Texas to be with us here tonight. And we welcome you. Thank you.

Gary Locke, the newly elected governor of Washington state, is the first Chinese-American governor in the history of our country. He's the proud son of two of the millions of Asian-American immigrants who strengthened America with their hard work, family values and good citizenship.

He represents the future we can all achieve. Thank you, governor, for being here. Please stand up.

Reverend Schuller, Congressman Tejeda, Governor Locke, along with Kristen Tanner and Chris Getsla, Sue Winski and Dr. Kristen Zarfos — they're all Americans from different roots whose lives reflect the best of what we can become when we are one America.

We may not share a common past, but we surely do share a common future. Building one America is our most important mission, the foundation for many generations of every other strength we must build for this new century. Money cannot buy it, power cannot compel it, technology cannot create it. It can only come from the human spirit.

America is far more than a place; it is an idea — the most powerful idea in the history of nations, and all of us in this chamber, we are now the bearers of that idea, leading a great people into a new world.

A child born tonight will have almost no memory of the 20th century. Everything that child will know about America will be because of what we do now to build a new century. We don't have a moment to waste.

Tomorrow there will be just over 1,000 days until the year 2000. One thousand days to prepare our people. One thousand days to work together. One thousand days to build a bridge to a land of new promise.

My fellow Americans, we have work to do. Let us seize those days and the century.

Thank you. God bless you. And God bless America. ■

REPUBLICAN RESPONSE

Watts Asks Voters To Demand Balanced-Budget Amendment

Following is The Associated Press transcript of the Republican response to President Clinton's Feb. 4 State of the Union address, delivered by Rep. J.C. Watts of Oklahoma:

Good evening. My name is J.C. Watts Jr. I'm the Republican congressman from the 4th District of Oklahoma, and I've been asked to speak to the American people in response to the president's address this evening.

Before I get into my presentation, I want to send condolences to the Tejeda family on behalf of the 105th Congress. Frank was a friend, he was a wonderful spirit, and he will be surely missed.

I don't intend to take a lot of your time. It's late, and there has been a lot of talk already this evening, but I want to tell you a little bit about where I'm from.

I grew up in Oklahoma. My district includes the towns of Midwest City, Norman, Lawton, Walters, Waurika and Duncan, just to name a few. We raise cattle back home, we grow some cotton and wheat, peanuts, and we drill for oil.

We've got Tinker and Altus Air Force bases nearby, and we have the Army post at Fort Sill. The University of Oklahoma is there. That's where I went to school. I played a little football and graduated with a degree in journalism. I tell you all this because I want you to know that the district I'm blessed to represent is as diverse as America itself.

It's the kind of place reporters usually call the heartland. And they're right. In so many ways it is America's heart.

I'm going to try to use my words tonight and my time not to confuse issues but to clarify them; not to obscure my philosophy and my party's, but to illuminate it, because the way I see it the purpose of politics is to lead, not to mislead.

Those of us who have been sent to Washington have a moral responsibility to offer more than poll-tested phrases and winning smiles. We must offer a serious vision. We must share our intentions. We must make our plans clear. That's my job tonight: to tell you what we believe, what the Republican Party believes, and what we will work for.

We believe first of all that the state of this union really isn't determined in Washington, D.C. It never has been, and it never will be. But for a long time the federal government has been grabbing too much power and too much authority over all of the people. And it is those people, it is all of us, who decide the real state of the union.

Doc Benson in Oklahoma City decides the state of the union. He runs a nonprofit called the Education and Employment Ministry, where he believes that you restore men and women by restoring their dreams and finding them a job.

Freddy Garcia is the state of the union also. Freddy was a drug addict in San Antonio, Texas. Now he has a ministry helping people get off drugs. His Victory Fellowship has success rates that the social scientists can only dream of.

I saw the state of the union last week in Marlow, Okla. A bunch of us met at the elementary school where we ate beef brisket and baked beans, and the Chamber of Commerce recognized the Farm Family of the Year. The McCarleys won, and their kids were oh, so proud.

The strength of America is not in Washington, the strength of America is at home in lives well lived in the land of faith and family. The strength of America is not on Wall Street but on Main Street, not in big business but in small businesses with local owners and workers. It's not in Congress, it's in the city hall. And I pray Republicans and Democrats both understand this. We shouldn't just say it, we should live it.

And so we have made it our mission to limit the claims and demands of Washington; to limit its call for more power, more authority and more taxes. Our mission is to return power to your home, to where mothers and fathers can exercise it according to their beliefs.

So let me tell you three actions the Republicans will take in the coming year.

First, we can help our country by bringing back the knowledge, the ancient wisdom, that we're nothing without our spiritual, traditional and family values. The Republicans will take action to give those values a bigger place in solving America's problems. After all, our values are more important to our future than any so-called bureaucratic breakthrough. Think about your life and how you built it.

I didn't get my values from Washington. I got my values from my parents, from Buddy and Helen Watts, in Eufaula, Okla. I got my values growing up in a poor black neighborhood on the east side of the railroad tracks, where money was scarce but dreams were plentiful and love was all around. I got my values from a strong family, a strong church and a strong neighborhood.

I wasn't raised to be Republican or Democrat. My parents just taught by example. They taught me and my brothers and sisters that, if you lived under their roof, you were going to work. They taught us, if you made a mistake, as we all do, you've got to own up to it, you call it what it is, and you try to turn it around. They taught us, if you spend more money than you make, you're on a sure road to disaster.

I was taught to respect everyone for the simple reason that we're all God's children. I was taught, in the words of Dr. Martin Luther King Jr., and from my uncle, Wade Watts, to judge a man not by the color of his skin, but by the content of his character. And I was taught that character does count, and that character is simply doing what's right when nobody's looking.

My parents also taught me I could do anything if I applied myself and understood sacrifice and commitment.

Now if you agree with those things my parents taught me and that I'm trying to teach my children, then, friends, we have common ground.

It is the Republican Party that has been trying to return these values to government, and it hasn't been easy, because for a long time the government has acted as if it didn't have any common sense.

Here's an example: For the past 30 years our nation's spent $5 trillion trying to erase poverty, and the result, as you know, is that we didn't get rid of it at all. In fact, we spread it. We destroyed the self-esteem of millions of people, grinding them down in a welfare system that penalizes moms for wanting to marry the father of their children, and penalizes mom for wanting to save money. Friends, that's not right.

Last year, the Republican Congress moved to reform the welfare system, and for the first time in my lifetime, we're helping people climb the ladder of economic opportunity.

Let me tell you the next step.

A number of my colleagues and I, my Republican colleagues and I, are working on a package called The American Community Renewal Act. It seeks to return government to the side of the institutions that hold communities together: faith, family, hard work, strong neighborhoods. This will help rebuild low-income communities through their own moral renewal and giving them economic opportunity. It also recognizes that faith-based institutions contribute to the healing of our nation's problems.

So our first priority is to bring values back and give them pride of place in our moral and economic renewal. And in the next few weeks we will be visiting a number of communities to highlight the accomplishments of active faith-based organizations.

The second thing Republicans will do is face a problem that demands immediate attention. We must get our government's financial affairs in order. The biggest step in that direction is an amendment to the U.S. Constitution that demands that the federal government balance its books.

We are more than $5 trillion in debt. This year we will spend $330 billion on interest payments alone on the national debt. And you know what? Not one dime of that $330 billion will go to strengthen Medicare, Medicaid. Not one dime of it will go to find a cure for cancer or fight drugs and crime. And worse yet, not one dime will go toward learning, making the classrooms a centerpiece of our education.

Over $5 trillion worth of national debt is more than financially irresponsible. Friends, it's immoral, because someone is going to have to pay the piper. And you know who it's going to be? It's going to be our kids and our grandkids.

The American family is already overtaxed. Right now, the average family spends about half of every dollar they earn in some type of government tax or government fee.

Consider a 5-year-old child today. If things continue as they are, by the time they're 25 they'll pay about 84 cents of every dollar they make in some government tax or government fee. Friends, that's more than a shame, it's a scandal.

The balanced-budget amendment will force the government to change its ways permanently.

No longer will the president or Congress be able to spend money we don't have on benefits our children will never see.

In a few weeks, we will vote on that amendment. Republicans can't pass it on our own; it takes a two-thirds majority. So we need Democrat votes and we need your help. We need you to write or call your representatives and senators and tell them to pass the balanced-budget amendment now.

And here's the good news. A balanced budget will lower your house payment, lower your car payment, lower your student loan payments. The savings could be as much as $1,500 a year. Well, to some up here in Washington, $1,500 may not be much; however, it's a new washer and dryer, it's a home computer, or money toward a much-needed second car for a hard-working family.

And by the way, don't believe all those dire warnings about the amendment wrecking Social Security. That's just not true. I encourage all of us in Congress — Republicans and Democrats — to appeal to people's intelligence and not to their fears.

President Clinton was right on target tonight. He said people want bipartisanship. I believe they do. But they want the kind of bipartisanship that results in progress. They don't want phony compromise; they don't want the kind of weak, back-scratching, go-along-to-get-along bipartisanship that allows lawmakers to feel good but gets bad results.

There are some striking examples of cooperation this past year. When Republicans led the effort to reform welfare, President Clinton opposed it at first, but eventually, after we passed it, he bowed to the will of the people and signed it. We applaud the president's embrace of reform. And, Mr. President, from the bottom of my heart, we are pleased to continue this bipartisan effort.

And there was a promise of bipartisanship tonight when the president signaled his interest in tax relief.

Working Americans need real tax relief, not just targeted tax cuts to help one group at the expense of another. We all pay too much in taxes.

I hope the president shares this belief with us and works with us to bring desperately needed tax relief to America's working families. And we must work together — Democrats and Republicans — to win the twin wars against drugs and ignorance. The war on drugs can and will be won in large measure by making sure that every child in America can walk to school safely, sit in a classroom where the teacher can really help them learn.

Third, and finally, I want to say a few words about the Republican vision of how we can continue to make this one nation under God, indivisible with liberty and justice for all.

You know, I'm just old enough to remember the Jim Crow brand of discrimination. I've seen issues of race hurt human beings and hurt our entire nation. Too often when we talk about racial healing, we make the old assumption that government can heal the racial divide.

In my lifetime there have been some great and good laws that took some evil and ignorant laws off the books, so legislation has its place. But friends, we're at a point now where we have to ask ourselves some questions, and I ask you — if legislation is the answer to the racial divide in our nation, then why in God's name in our time has the division grown? Why is the healing we long for so far from reality? Why does it seem that the more laws we pass, the less love we have?

The fact is our problems can't be solved by legislation alone. Surely we have learned from our long, difficult journey a great truth: government can't ease all pain. We must deal with the heart of man.

Republicans and Democrats — red, yellow, black and white — have to understand that we must individually, all of us, accept our share of responsibility. We must decide as we stand on the edge of the new age if we will be captives of the past. America must be a place where all of us — red, yellow, brown, black and white — in some way feel a part of the American Dream. It does not happen by dividing us into racial groups. It does not happen by trying to turn rich against poor or by using the politics of fear. It does not happen by reducing our values to the lowest common denominator. And, friends, it does not happen by asking Americans to accept what's immoral and wrong in the name of tolerance.

We must make our mark on the future as a people who care — care for our families, for one another, for our neighbors, for all the beautiful children. We must make our mark as people who share and help each other in need. We must be a people who dare, dare to take responsibility for our hatreds and fears and ask God to heal us from within.

And we must be a people of prayer, a people who pray as if the strength of our nation depended on it, because it does. When you come right down to it, that's our vision and our agenda.

All over the country I've often told the story of a boy and his father. The father was trying to get some work done, and the boy wanted the daddy's attention, but the father was busy at his desk with so much to do. To occupy the boy, this father gave his son a pencil and a paper and said, "Here, son, go draw the family." Two minutes later, he was back with a picture, all stick figures. So the dad, trying to buy some more time, said, "Here, go draw the dog." Two minutes later, he comes back with another stick figure.

Now the father was exasperated. He looked around, he saw a magazine, and he remembered that he had seen a picture of the world in this magazine. In what he thought was a stroke of genius, the father tore out the picture and tore it into 20 different pieces, and he said, "Here, son. Go put the world back together."

And you know what happened? Five minutes later the little Michelangelo was back, saying, "Daddy, look what I've done." The father looked, and he said, "Son, how did you do it so quickly? How did you put the world back together so quickly?"And the little boy answered, "Dad, it was easy. There was a picture of a man on the back of the map, on the back of the world. And once I put the man back together, the world fell into place."

And friends, this is our agenda: to put our men and women back together, to put ourselves back together, and, in that way, get our country back together.

I am reminded of the final words of President John Kennedy's inaugural address. He said this: "Let us go forth to lead the land we love, knowing that here on Earth, God's work truly must be our own." I say amen to that.

Thank you for your graciousness in listening to me so late in the evening. God bless you, and God bless our children. And thank you very much. ■

VICE PRESIDENTIAL NEWS CONFERENCE

Gore Discusses Fundraising, His Role in the Campaign

Following is a transcript of a March 3 news conference in which Vice President Al Gore discussed his role in Democratic fundraising:

GORE: Good afternoon. Thank you all for coming. Mike was out here a little bit earlier and I noticed you had a number of questions for him about my role in the campaign, so I thought it would be a good idea for me to come down and answer your questions.

I want to make a short opening statement, and then I'll be happy to take your questions.

First of all, I want to spell out the facts of my role in the campaign. First of all, to state the obvious, I was a candidate for re-election in the campaign. I worked very hard for the re-election of President Clinton and myself. I'm very proud that I was able to be effective in helping to re-elect President Clinton. And I was very proud that I was able to also in — as part of that effort — to help raise campaign funds.

Everything that I did I understood to be lawful. I attended campaign — traditional campaign fundraising events as a principal speaker in many locations all around the country. The vast majority of the campaign funds that I've been given credit for raising came in that form.

I also made telephone calls to ask people to host events and to ask people to make lawful contributions to the campaign.

On a few occasions, I made some telephone calls from my office in the White House using a DNC [Democratic National Committee] credit card. I was advised there was nothing wrong with that practice.

The Hatch Act has a specific provision saying that, while federal employees are prohibited from requesting campaign contributions, the president and the vice president are not covered by that act because, obviously, we are candidates.

The separate question of whether or not campaign contributions can be asked for from somebody who is in a federal office or in a room that is used for official business is part of a law that was intended to prohibit putting pressure on federal employees and soliciting from federal employees.

I've never solicited a contribution from any federal employee, nor would I. Nor did I ever ask for a campaign contribution from anyone who was in a government office or on federal property.

Now all of the charges related to telephone calls were made to the Democratic National Committee. There were a few occasions which I made such calls. The first was in December of 1995. As we continue our review of this, we have found the first session in December of 1995. There were a few other sessions during which I made telephone calls in the spring of 1996.

My counsel — Charles Burson is my counsel here — my counsel advises me that there is no controlling legal authority or case that says that there was any violation of law whatsoever in the manner in which I asked people to contribute to our re-election campaign.

I have decided to adopt a policy of not making any such calls ever again, notwithstanding the fact that they are charged to the Democratic National Committee as a matter of policy. We're continuing our review of this matter and I think the entire episode constitutes further reasons why there should be campaign finance reform.

The president and I strongly support campaign finance reform, and we hope it is adopted.

Now . . . Helen?

. . . are you saying that there — that you never did any fundraising from a government office or building or . . .

I never asked for a campaign contribution from anyone who was in a government office. I never did anything that I thought was wrong.

If there had been a shred of doubt in my mind that anything I did was a violation of law, I assure you I would not have done that. And my counsel advises me, let me repeat, that there is no controlling legal authority that says that any of these activities violated any law.

Mr. Vice President, but given the fact that you now have changed your policy, I'm sure you can understand the appearance, whether or not it was technically legal, the appearance wasn't very good, and that one of these people you apparently solicited told Bob Woodward and The Washington Post that it amounted to, in his opinion, at least, a shakedown — that when you were soliciting funds from him, given his nature of his business, you were shaking him down.

Well, I cannot explain to you what some anonymous source wants to say. I can tell you this, that I never, ever said or did anything that would have given rise to a feeling like that on the part of someone who was asked to support our campaign. I never did that, and I never would do that.

There's a memo from the White House counsel written in 1995 that very simply says, no solicitation can be made from the White House — no phone calls, no mail. How can you say that that was OK for you to do it?

That memo, authored by former White House Counsel Ab Mikva, was addressed to White House employees other than the president and vice president. All White House employees, just like all other federal employees, are prohibited from asking for campaign contributions. There is an exemption for the president and vice president.

But that particular memo was not designed to address either the president or the vice president, because there is a different section of law that applies to the president and vice president as candidates, as opposed to the White House staff.

So you're saying that you were exempt from any proscriptions, from raising money right there in the White House. That was OK for you to do?

That particular — No, no. No, no. I'd never ask anyone in the White House for a campaign contribution.

You sat in the White House. You called people and asked them for contributions.

Well, let me — I stated the fax situation earlier.

And I described it in some detail. I never have asked a federal employee for a contribution, never would, never will. I have never asked anyone in the White House or on federal property for a campaign contribution.

Now — and all calls that I made were charged to the Democratic National Committee. I was advised there was nothing wrong with that. My counsel tells me there is no controlling legal authority that says was any violation of any law. Yes?

Mr. Vice President, excuse me, there was a little discrepancy in the Buddhist temple. Can you clear that up? I mean, because certain statements were made, denied, and then actually accepted.

Well, that's a separate matter and I've dealt with it, and I don't really want to go back into that now.

We can come back to it at the end of this if you want to.

Making a Difference

You said that there were only a few instances where you did . . .

Correct.

. . . ask people for money. Could you say why in those instances you did? Were you told that you would make the difference? Or was it for a particular sum? Did someone in the campaign say, "We need you to close this"? Can you explain the circumstances under which you . . .

I participated in meetings of our top campaign advisers where it became clear that, in order to achieve the president's goals of getting a balanced budget, passing these measures to protect Medicare and Medicaid and education and the environment and so forth, that the DNC needed a larger budget to put advertisements on television.

And I volunteered to raise — to help in the effort to raise money for the Democratic National Committee.

Outside Calls

Mr. Vice President, I'm confused on one point. I've heard what you said. And as picayune as it may seem, there seems to be conflict over whether or not you're saying the law allows you, as vice president, to sit in your office and to use a federal phone credit card or not, to make a call to someone outside. You're saying that the law does allow you to be in, basically, federal property and use federal property, although it's being reimbursed to some degree, that that — that is OK?

As a matter of policy, I decided that I'm not going to do that. As a matter of law, there is no — according to my counsel — there is no controlling legal authority, no case ever brought, ever decided that says that is a violation of law.

The intent of the statute — let me repeat — was to prevent a supervisor from talking to a federal employee and saying, "We want you to contribute money." I've never done that.

Secondly, I have never asked anyone who was on federal property or in the White House for a campaign contribution.

But you're . . .

A follow-up here and then I'll go to you.

But if you're in the clear on it, then why shift policy, if you're in the clear on that?

Well, because it's aroused a great deal of concern and comment, and it's not — it's not something that I want to continue if it's going to raise this kind of concern.

Just to follow up on that, are you basically then admitting that you made a mistake or made mistakes?

No.

What I am saying — I mean implicit in the decision to change the policy and say I'm not going to make such calls again is an acknowledgement that if — you know — if I had realized in advance that this would cause such concern, then I wouldn't have done it in the first place.

But let me repeat — I understood what I did to be legal and appropriate. I felt like I was doing the right thing. I am proud that I was able to do a lot of effective work to help re-elect Bill Clinton and keep this country moving in the right direction.

I'll spare you the rhetoric about the results of what we have been able to do, but I want you to know that I'm very proud to be a part of that effort.

Soft Money

What is your position on the — on the elimination of soft money from campaigns?

Oh, I favor — I favor the so-called McCain-Feingold bill which would do that. The president and I strongly favor campaign finance reform legislation that would accomplish that objective, and we hope that it will pass.

Vice President Gore, there has been a lot written about your impregnable reputation for a — for being above the fray and for being ethically someone who really hasn't been questioned on these issues. Does this shatter that, and does it hurt you for the year 2000?

Well, on the second part of it, I'm — I've told you before that I'm not focused on a political campaign in the future. I'm focused on doing everything I can to help this president be the best president he's capable of being and to move this country in the right direction. And he's doing a terrific job. I'm very proud to be a part of his team.

On the first part of the question, I'll say again, I never did anything that I felt was wrong, much less illegal. And again, I am advised that there is no controlling legal authority that says this was in violation of law.

That Uncomfortable Feeling

Vice President Gore, did you feel any discomfort at all as you called these individuals and asked them for donations? And did you ask for specific amounts of money when you spoke with them?

Yes, I did. On the first part of your question — you know, I served eight years in the House and eight years in the Senate, and I was used to calling people to ask them to help with the campaign.

I introduced legislation some years ago to call for complete public financing of campaigns and to prevent the contributions that are now legal, over and above, the public financing of the presidential campaigns.

The legislation that I sponsored and supported did not have enough support to pass. I still favor that legislation, but it didn't pass. There's probably even less support for it now.

So we have a system of campaign finance here in the United States that says candidates who are running for office ought to go out and ask people to contribute to their campaigns and to have fundraisers. And so I was used to doing that as a candidate for the House, as a candidate for the Senate.

I would be surprised if all — if all 100 members of the United States Senate and all 435 — well, there are probably some House members who don't, because they have safe seats and don't raise any money. But I would be surprised if all senators and most all House members did not, as a matter of routine, call people up and ask them to hold fundraisers and ask them to help raise money.

That is the standard way that we finance campaigns. So I was used to that. Does it make one uncomfortable to do that? Why, sure. But if you believe in what you're doing, in balancing the budget and moving this country forward, and you know that the only way you can be successful in achieving the agenda you believe is right for the country, is to play by the rules as they exist and raise campaign funds, then you do that.

And typically, what happens to members of the House and Senate is they'll put it off and put it off until the election year comes and then the people helping them will say, you've got to devote time to raise money. And they say, oh, I hate this, I don't want to do it. And then they get into it and they start making the calls and they raise the money.

I'm exactly the same way.

In the Year 2000

Mr. Vice President, if there's nothing coy about the year 2000, anyone who expects to run for president in 2000 has to start very early thinking about money. Predecessors of yours have started PACs, political action committees or fundraising arms.

What are you going to do between now and 19 . . .

I've made no decision about that whatsoever. And I really am focused on my work as vice president and doing everything I can to help this president.

If the time comes when I become a candidate, I'll be glad to answer such questions and talk about such matters at that time. But we're not there yet.

So you're going to raise no money at all? You will raise no money at all for a political action committee or anything else that would . . .

I have not set up a political action committee and I've made no decision to do so. Whether I will in the future or not, I really haven't decided.

Inaccurate Impressions

Mr. Vice President — something that I'm just a little confused about. You said there was only just a handful of incidents when you used the White House.

Correct.

So we can assume the preponderance of calls were made from the DNC or your residence? Is that . . .

No, no, there were a handful of incidents, period.

Oh, these are the only incidents that you raised money, period.

That's correct. I went to the DNC on one occasion in, I believe, October of 1994 to help raise money for the party. You know, the impression was created that I went out and raised all this money and then they talked about me calling people on the telephone, and the two things were put together to give the impression that I raised all this money by calling people on the telephone.

So you're saying . . .

That is not an accurate impression. Most all of the money for the campaign that I'm given credit for raising came in the form of traditional events where I was the main speaker at fundraising events.

There were a few occasions, as I said at the very outset, where I did make telephone calls and I have described those.

But that was the minor part of what I did in raising funds.

. . . anybody calling you a solicitor-in-chief. Could we get clear on this? . . . Is there something . . .

I never heard such a phrase. I never heard such a phrase until I read it in the paper.

Mr. Vice President, you said that the president and vice president were covered under the Hatch Act and that part — in that way, you two were different.

Yes.

But the other part of the statute seems to set up federal buildings as a sanctuary from fundraising. Were you unaware of that part of the statute?

No, I was not. And let me repeat — I never asked for a contribution from anyone who was in a federal building. And all of the calls that I made were charged to the DNC. I was advised that was proper. In reviewing the matter, my counsel advises me there's no case. There's no controlling legal authority that says that violated the law.

Well, then the question — is it possible that the absence of case law on this means that reasonable people could differ about what parts of the statute mean, applied to different activities in which you may have taken part at different times?

Well, that's not a question for me to determine. I'm advised that it is — that there is no case or no controlling legal authority that says it is a violation of the law. And I never did anything that I felt was wrong, much less a violation of the law.

Mr. Vice President, also, did you know about — did the president know about any of these calls you made? Did you discuss it? Did he ever ask you to make any calls? Was he aware of your . . .

No, he never asked me to make calls. I'm sure that he was aware that I was helping to raise funds for the campaign. It's — well, I won't comment on what other vice presidents have or have not done.

But I don't think it is surprising to people that when a president and vice president are running for re-election that the vice president helps to raise funds for the campaign.

And anybody who wants to create the impression that that is something brand new in American politics, I would invite to take another look at that question.

Mr. Vice President, when the Clinton-Gore election agreed to take public funds, it also agreed to spending caps. And yet you're referring to the DNC's soft money operation as "our campaign." Doesn't this operation show that, as a practical matter, there was no distinction between the Clinton-Gore campaign and the DNC's soft money operation?

No, there was a clear distinction. There was a separate message. There were separate legal requirements. It was — it was separate in most all respects.

Now, the fact that the agenda supported by the Democratic National Committee's advertisements was similar to and overlapping with the agenda that was being pressed by the incumbent Democratic president should not be surprising.

And again, it's hardly unique in American political history for an incumbent president to be supported by the political party of which he is the titular head. That is commonplace.

Mr. Vice President, was there any particular urgency to the calls the few occasions that you did make calls from the White House. Were they — could not have waited until you were in a setting away from your office in the White House?

Well, first of all, as I said before, I was advised there was nothing wrong with it.

So the question did not occur in that form. So there was not a sense of urgency in that sense.

We felt, as we were preparing for our campaign, a general sense that, you know, we wanted to make sure that we had the ability to compete.

Let me remind you that the — our opponents raised over all, I believe, what, 40 percent more than we did? And so we knew that they had a big head start and that they had a huge collection of resources, so we felt that — we felt the need to move on with it.

To follow up on that, you also could have made these very same calls from somewhere else?

One more, and then I'm going to have to go.

You have said that this is not unique in American politics, but judging from the comments of your predecessors, it would appear that direct solicitation by the vice president had not been done in the past. Were you aware of that?

No.

And also the fact that the president himself refused to make these phone calls. Were you aware of that, and why did you think perhaps a different sort of standard applied to you?

No, I was not aware of the latter. On the first part of your question, what I said was not unique was the practice of incumbent vice presidents running for re-election, going out to help raise money for the campaign and for the political party of which they were a part.

And I will leave it to you all to determine whether that's totally unique or not. I'm not — I don't want to get into what any other vice president has done. I'm proud of what I did.

I do not feel like I did anything wrong, much less illegal. I — I am proud to have done everything I possibly could to help support the re-election of this president and to help move his agenda forward. It is helping this country.

Our economy is roaring. Inflation is low. Crime is down. Investments in education and protecting the environment are going up.

Social trends are favorable. Economic trends are favorable. We are moving in the right direction.

Let me tell you. One of the principal reasons we are is that we have a president and a group of people who are proud to support his efforts, who are willing to go out there every day and fight hard, sometimes against powerful odds, to make sure that we pass this agenda and move forward. And I am very proud to continue to play a role in that.

Thank you very much. ■

CAMPAIGN FINANCE

Attorney General Details Reasons For Rejecting Call for Counsel

Following is the full text of Attorney General Janet Reno's letter, released April 14, to Senate Judiciary Committee Chairman Orrin G. Hatch, R-Utah, explaining her office's decision not to appoint an independent counsel to investigate White House and Democratic campaign fund-raising:

Dear Mr. Chairman:

On March 13, 1997, you and nine other majority party members of the Committee on the Judiciary of the United States Senate wrote to me requesting the appointment of an independent counsel to investigate possible fundraising violations in connection with the 1996 campaign. You made that request pursuant to a provision of the Independent Counsel Act, 28 U.S.C. Section 592(g)(1), which provides that "a majority of majority party members (of the Committee on the Judiciary) . . . may request in writing that the Attorney General apply for the appointment of an independent counsel." The act requires me to respond within 30 days, setting forth the reasons for my decision on each of the matters with respect to which your request is made. 28 U.S.C. Section 592(g)(2).

I am writing to inform you that I have not initiated a "preliminary investigation" (as that term is defined in the Independent Counsel Act) of any of the matters mentioned in your letter. Rather, as you know, matters relating to campaign financing in the 1996 Federal elections have been under active investigation since November by a task force of career Justice Department prosecutors and Federal Bureau of Investigation [FBI] agents. This task force is pursuing the investigation vigorously and diligently, and it will continue to do so. I can assure you that I have given your views and your arguments careful thought, but at this time, I am unable to agree, based on the facts and the law, that an independent counsel should be appointed to handle this investigation.

1. The Independent Counsel Act

In order to explain my reasons, I would like to outline briefly the relevant provisions of the Independent Counsel Act. The Act can be invoked in two circumstances that are relevant here:

First, if there are sufficient allegations (as further described below) of criminal activity by a covered person, defined as the President and Vice President, cabinet officers, certain other enumerated high Federal officials, or certain specified officers of the President's election campaign (not party officials), see 28 U.S.C. Section 591(b), I must seek appointment of an independent counsel.

Second, if there are sufficient allegations of criminal activity by a person other than a covered person, and I determine that "an investigation or prosecution of (that) person by the Department of Justice may result in a personal, financial or political conflict of interest," see 28 U.S.C. Section 591(c)(1), I may seek appointment of an independent counsel.

In either case, I must follow a two-step process to determine whether the allegations are sufficient. First I must determine whether the allegations are sufficiently specific and credible to constitute grounds to investigate whether an individual may have violated Federal criminal law. 28 U.S.C. Section 591(d). If so, the Department commences a "preliminary investigation" for up to 90 days (which can be extended an additional 60 days upon a showing of good cause). 28 U.S.C. Section 592(a). If, at the conclusion of this "preliminary investigation," I determine further investigation of the matters is warranted, I must seek an independent counsel.

Certain important features of the Act are critical to my decision in this case:

First, the Act sets forth the only circumstances in which I may seek an independent counsel pursuant to its provisions. I may not invoke its procedures unless the statutory requirements are met.

Second, the Act does not permit or require me to commence a preliminary investigation unless there is specific and credible evidence that a crime may have been committed. In your letter, you suggest that it is not the responsibility of the Department of Justice to determine whether a particular set of facts suggests a potential Federal crime, but that such legal determinations should be left to an independent counsel. I do not agree. Under the Independent Counsel Act, it is the Department's obligation to determine in the first instance whether particular conduct potentially falls within the scope of a particular criminal statute such that criminal investigation is warranted. If it is our conclusion that the alleged conduct is not criminal, then there is no basis for appointment of an independent counsel, because there would be no specific and credible allegation of a violation of criminal law. See 28 U.S.C. Section 592(a)(1).

Third, there is an important difference between the mandatory and discretionary provisions of the Act. Once I have received specific and credible allegations of criminal conduct by a covered person, I must commence a preliminary investigation and, if further investigation is warranted at the end of the preliminary investigation, seek appointment of an independent counsel. If, on the other hand, I receive specific and credible evidence that a person not covered by the mandatory provisions of the Act has committed a crime, and I determine that a conflict of interest exists with respect to the investigation of that person, I may but need not commence a preliminary investigation pursuant to the provisions of the Act. This provision gives me the flexibility to decide whether, overall, the national interest would be best served by appointment of an independent counsel in such a case, or whether it would be better for the Department of Justice to continue a vigorous investigation of the matter.

Fourth, even this discretionary provision is not available unless I find a conflict of interest of the sort contemplated by the Act. The Congress has made it very clear that this provision should be invoked only in certain narrow circumstances. Under the Act, I must conclude that there is a potential for an actual conflict of interest, rather than merely an appearance of a conflict of interest. The Congress expressly adopted this higher standard to ensure that the provision would not be invoked unnecessarily. See 128 Cong. Rec. H 9507 (daily ed. Dec. 13, 1982) (statement of Rep. Hall.) Moreover, I must find that there is a potential for such an actual conflict with respect to the investigation of a particular person, not merely with respect to the overall matter. Indeed, when the Act was reauthorized in 1994, Congress considered a proposal for a more flexible standard for invoking the discretionary clause, which would have permitted its use to refer any "matter" to an Independent Counsel when the purposes of the Act would be served. Congress rejected this suggestion, explaining that such a standard would "substantially lower the threshold for use of the general discretionary provision." H.R. Conf. Rep. No. 511, 103rd Cong., 2nd Sess. 9 (1994).

2. Covered Persons: The Mandatory Provisions of the Act.

Let me now turn to the specific allegations in your letter. You assert that there are "new questions of possible wrongdoing by senior White House officials themselves," and you identify a number of particular types of conduct in support of this claim. While all of the specific issues you mention are under review or active investigation by the task force, at this time we have no specific, credible evidence that any covered White House official may have committed a

Federal crime in respect to any of these issues. Nevertheless, I will discuss separately each area that you raise.

Fundraising on Federal Property.

First, you suggest that "federal officials may have illegally solicited and/or received contributions on federal property." The conduct you describe could be a violation of 18 U.S.C. Section 607. We are aware of a number of allegations of this sort; all are being evaluated, and where appropriate, investigations have been commenced. The Department takes allegations of political fundraising by Federal employees on Federal property seriously, and in appropriate cases would not hesitate to prosecute such matters. Indeed, the Public Integrity Section, which is overseeing the work of the campaign financing task force, recently obtained a number of guilty pleas from individuals who were soliciting and accepting political contributions within the Department of Agriculture.

The analysis of a potential section 607 violation is a fact-specific inquiry. A number of different factors must be considered when reviewing allegations that this law may have been violated:

First, the law specifically applies only to contributions as technically defined by the Federal Election Campaign Act (FECA) funds commonly referred to as "hard money." The statute originally applied broadly to any political fundraising, but in 1979, over the objection of the Department of Justice, Congress narrowed the scope of section 607 to render it applicable only to FECA contributions. Before concluding that section 607 may have been violated, we must have evidence that a particular solicitation involved a "contribution" within the definition of the FECA.

Second, there are private areas of the White House that, as a general rule, fall outside the scope of the statute, because of the statutory requirement that the particular solicitation occur in an area "occupied in the discharge of official duties." 3 Op. Off. Legal Counsel 31 (1979). The distinction recognizes that while the Federal Government provides a residence to the president, similar to the housing that it might provide to foreign service officers, this residence is still the personal home of an individual within which restrictions that might validly apply to the Federal workplace should not be imposed. Before we can conclude that section 607 may have been violated, we must have evidence that fundraising took place in locations covered by the provisions of the statute.

With respect to coordinated media advertisements by political parties (an area that has received much attention of late), the proper characterization of a particular expenditure depends not on the degree of coordination, but rather on the content of the message. Indeed, just last year the FEC [Federal Election Commission] and the Department of Justice took this position in a brief filed before the Supreme Court, in a case decided on other grounds. See generally, Brief for the Respondent, *Colorado Republican Federal Campaign Committee v. FEC*, (S. Ct. No. 95-489) at 2-3, 18 n.15, 23-24. In this connection, the FEC has concluded that party media advertisements that focus on "national legislative activity" and that do not contain an "electioneering message" may be financed, in part, using "soft" money, i.e., money that does not comply with FECA's contribution limits. FEC Advisory Op. 1995-25, 2 Fed. Elec. Camp. Fin. Guide (CCH) Paragraph 6162, at 12, 109-12,110 (August 24, 1995); FEC Advisory Op. 1985-14, 2 Fed. Elec. Camp. Fin. Guide (CCH) Paragraph 5819, at 11,185-11,186 (May 30, 1985). Moreover, such advertisements are not subject to any applicable limitations on coordinated expenditures by the party on behalf of its candidates. AO 1985-14 at 11-185-11,186.

We recognize that there are allegations that both presidential candidates and both national political parties engaged in a concerted effort to take full advantage of every funding option available to them under the law, to craft advertisements that took advantage of the lesser regulation quantities of soft political funding to finance these ventures. However, at the present time, we lack specific and credible evidence suggesting that these activities violated the FECA. Moreover, even assuming that, after a thorough investigation, the FEC were to conclude that regulatory violations occurred, we presently lack specific and credible evidence suggesting that any covered person participated in any such violations.

3. Conflict of Interest: The Discretionary Provisions of the Act.

In urging me to conclude that the investigation poses the type of potential conflict of interest contemplated by the Act, you rely heavily on my testimony before the Senate Committee on Government Affairs in 1993 in support of reauthorization of the Independent Counsel Act. I stand by those views and continue to support the overall concept underlying the Act. My decisions pursuant to the Act have been, I believe, fully consistent with those views.

The remarks you quote from my testimony should be interpreted within the context of the statutory language I was discussing. When, for example, I referred to the need for the Act to deal with the inherent conflict of interest when the Department of Justice investigates "high-level Executive Branch officials," I was referring to persons covered under the mandatory provisions of the Act. With respect to the conflict of interest provision, my testimony expressed the conviction that the Act "would in no way pre-empt this Department's authority to investigate public corruption," and that the Department was clearly capable of "vigorous investigation of wrongdoing by public officials, whatever allegiance or stripes they may wear. I will vigorously defend and continue this tradition." While I endorsed the concept of the discretionary clause to deal with unforeseeable situations, I strongly emphasized that "it is part of the Attorney General's job to make difficult decisions in tough cases. I have no intention of abdicating that responsibility."

These principles continue to guide my decision making today.

These are times when reliance on the discretionary clause is appropriate, and indeed, as you point out, I have done so myself on a few occasions. However, in each of those cases, I considered the particular factual context in which the allegations against those persons arose and the history of the matter. Moreover, even after finding the existence of a potential conflict, I must consider whether under all the circumstances discretionary appointment of an independent counsel is appropriate. In each case, therefore, the final decision has been an exercise of my discretion, as provided for under the act.

I have undertaken the same examination here. Based on the facts as we know them now, I have not concluded that any conflict of interest would ensue from our vigorous and thorough investigation of the allegations contained in your letter.

Your letter relies upon press reports, certain documents and various public statements which you assert demonstrate that "officials at the highest level of the White House were involved in formulating, coordinating and implementing the Democratic National Committee's (DNC's) Fundraising efforts for the 1996 presidential campaign." You suggest that a thorough investigation of "fundraising improprieties" will therefore necessarily include an inquiry into the "knowledge and/or complicity of very senior White House officials," and that the Department of Justice would therefore have a conflict of interest investigating these allegations.

To the extent that "improprieties" comprise crimes, they are being thoroughly investigated by the agents and prosecutors assigned to the task force. Should that investigation develop at any time specific and credible evidence that any covered person may have committed a crime, the Act will be triggered, and I will fulfill my responsibilities under the Act. In addition, should that investigation develop specific and credible evidence that a crime may have been committed by a "very senior" White House official who is not covered by the Act, I will decide whether investigation of that person by the Department might result in a conflict of interest, and, if so, whether the discretionary clause should be invoked. Until then, however, the mere fact that employees of the White House and the DNC worked closely together in the course of President Clinton's re-election campaign does not warrant appointment of an independent counsel. As I have stated above, the Department has a long history of investigating allegations of criminal activity by high-ranking Government officials without fear or favor, and will do so in this case.

I also do not accept the suggestion that there will be widespread public distrust of the actions and conclusions of the Department if it continues to investigate this matter, creating a conflict of interest warranting the appointment of an independent counsel. First, unless I find that the investigation of a particular person against whom specific and credible allegations have been made would pose a conflict, I have no authority to utilize the procedures of the Act. Moreover, I have confidence that the career professionals in the Department will investigate this matter in a fashion that will satisfy the American people that justice has been done.

Finally, even were I to determine that a conflict of interest of the sort contemplated by the statute exists in this case, and as noted above I do not find such a conflict at this time, there would be a number of weighty considerations that I would have to consider in determining whether to exercise my discretion to seek an independent counsel at this time. Because invocation of the conflict of interest provision is discretionary, it would still be my responsibility in that circumstance to weigh all the factors and determine whether appointment of an independent counsel would best serve the national interest. If in the future this investigation reveals evidence indicating that a conflict of interest exists, these factors will continue to weigh heavily in my evaluation of whether or not to invoke the discretionary provisions of the Act.

I assure you, once again, that allegations of violations of Federal criminal law with respect to campaign financing in the course of the 1996 Federal elections will be thoroughly investigated and, if appropriate, prosecuted. At this point it appears to me that that task should be performed by the Department of Justice and its career investigators and prosecutors. I want to emphasize, however, that the task force continues to receive new information (much has been discovered even since I received your letter), and I will continue to monitor the investigation closely in light of my responsibilities under the Independent Counsel Act. Should future developments make it appropriate to invoke the procedures of the Act, I will do so without hesitation. ■

Sincerely,
JANET RENO

ETHICS

'I Have a Moral Obligation to Pay . . . Out of Personal Funds'

Following is the Federal News Service transcript of the April 17 remarks by House Speaker Newt Gingrich, R-Ga., about how he plans to resolve his ethics settlement:

SPEAKER GINGRICH: I am standing here in the people's House at the center of freedom, and it's clear to me that for America to be healthy, our House of Representatives must be healthy. The Speaker of the House has a unique responsibility in this regard.

When I became Speaker of the House, it was the most moving day I could have imagined. It was the culmination of a dream. Little did I know that only two years later I would go through a very painful time. During my first two years as Speaker, 81 charges were filed against me. Of the 81 charges, 80 were found not to have merit and were dismissed as virtually meaningless.

But the American public might wonder what kind of man has 81 charges brought against him.

Under our system of government, attacks and charges can be brought with impunity against congressmen, sometimes with or without foundation.

Some of these charges involved a college course I taught about renewing American civilization. I am a college teacher by background. After years of teaching, it never occurred to me that teaching a college course about American civilization and the core values that have made our country successful could become an issue. However, as a precaution, I received the Ethics Committee's approval in advance for teaching the course, and I accepted no payment for teaching the course. Nonetheless, the course became embroiled in controversy.

But the most significant problem surfaced not from teaching the course but from answering the Ethics Committee's inquiries. Before the 1994 election, the committee asked questions and I submitted a letter in response. The committee agreed that this letter was accurate. Later, I hired a law firm to assist me in answering additional questions coming from the committee.

A letter developed by the law firm became the heart of the problem. I signed that letter, and it became the basis for a later, longer letter signed by an attorney. I was deeply saddened to learn almost two years later that these letters were inaccurate and misleading.

While the letters were developed and drafted by my former attorneys, I bear the full responsibility for them, and I accept that responsibility. Those letters should not have been submitted. The members of the ethics committee should never have to worry about the quality and accuracy of information that that committee receives.

Mainly because these two letters contradicted my own earlier and correct letter, the ethics committee spent a great deal of time and money to figure out exactly what happened. For this time and effort, for which I am deeply sorry and deeply regret, I have agreed to reimburse the American taxpayers $300,000 for legal expenses and cost incurred by the committee in its investigation. It was the opinion of the committee, and my own opinion, that had accurate information been submitted in those two letters, the investigation would have ended much sooner with less cost to the taxpayer.

It was not based on violation of any law or for the misuse of charitable contributions. There was no finding by the committee that I purposely tried to deceive anyone.

To me, it simply seemed wrong to ask the taxpayers to pay for an investigation that should have been unnecessary. That is why I voluntarily agreed to reimburse the taxpayers. Never before in history had a member of Congress agreed to be responsible for the cost of an investigation conducted by a committee of the House.

This $300,000 reimbursement is not a fine, as some have asserted. The settlement itself, and the report of the Select Committee on Ethics, makes it clear that it is a reimbursement of legal expenses and costs only.

The committee, and its special counsel, did not stipulate how the reimbursement should be paid.

One option is to pay completely with campaign funds. As a matter of law, the attorneys tell me, there is little question that my campaign has the legal authority under existing law and committee rules to pay the reimbursement.

The second option is to pay by means of a legal defense fund. The committee has previously determined that members may set up such a fund.

A third option is to sue the law firm and apply the proceeds to the reimbursement.

And the fourth option is to pay completely with personal funds.

As we considered these options, we sought to do what was right for the House as it relates to future precedents and for re-establishing the trust of the American people in this vital institution.

My campaign could have paid the entire amount, and it would have been legal and within past precedents of the House. Yet, on reflection, it was clear that many Americans would have regarded this as another example of politics as usual and of avoiding responsibility.

A lawsuit against the lawyers who prepared the two documents is a future possibility for me as a citizen, but that option could take years in court.

A legal trust fund was, in many ways, the most appealing. There is more than adequate precedent for such a fund. Many friends from across the entire country had called to offer contributions. Many of my colleagues on both sides of the aisle felt that this was the safest approach.

Yet, on reflection, it was clear that a legal trust fund would simply lead to a new controversy over my role. I have a higher responsibility as Speaker to do the right thing in the right way and to serve responsibly.

I also must consider what the personal payment precedent would mean to this House as an institution. Many of you in this chamber — on both sides of the aisle — have raised serious concerns, citing the fear that a personal payment will establish a precedent that could financially ruin members who are assessed costs incurred — incurred by special counsels.

In the current environment, who could feel safe? There should be no precedent that penalizes the spouses and children of our members. But that is what this option could effectively do. And this is something we must address.

Yet the question still remains: What is the right decision for me and my wife personally, for my family, for this institution, and for the American people?

Marianne and I have spent hours and hours discussing these options. She's here today, and let me just say that I have never been prouder of Marianne than over the last few months.

Her ability to endure the press scrutiny, to live beyond the attacks, to enjoy life despite hostilities, has been a remarkable thing to observe and a wonderful thing to participate in.

But she always came back to the same key question: What is the right thing to do for the right principles?

Through the difficult days and weeks as we reviewed the options, it was the courage of her counsel which always led me to do my best.

Marianne and I decided whatever the consequences, we had to do what was best, what was right morally and spiritually. We had to put into perspective how our lives had been torn apart by the weight of this decision. We had to take into account the negative feelings that Americans have about government, Congress and scandals. We had to take into account the responsibility that the Speaker of the House has to [adhere to] a higher standard. And that is why we came to the conclusion, of our own choice without being forced, that I have a moral obligation to pay the $300,000 out of personal funds; that any other step would simply be seen as one more politician shirking his duty and one more example of failing to do the right thing. Therefore, as a person of limited means, I have arranged to borrow the money from Bob Dole, a close personal friend of impeccable integrity. And I will personally pay it back. The taxpayers will be fully reimbursed. The agreement will be completely honored. The integrity of the House ethics process will have been protected. This is my duty as Speaker, and I will do it personally.

I will also ask the House to pass a resolution affirming that this is a voluntary action on my part, and that it will establish no precedent for any other member in the future. It is vital that we not go down the road of destroying middle-class members by establishing any personal burden in a non-judicial system.

It is important to put decisions about politics and government in perspective. This past year, I've experienced some personal losses. I lost my father, and my mother lost her husband of 50 years. My mother, due to serious health problems, is being forced to move into assisted living. My mother has lost her home, her husband, and her life as she knew it.

This week, before making this decision, I visited my mother in her hospital in Harrisburg. And I should say she's now out, and is in the assisted living facility. I asked her how she could handle these setbacks with such a positive attitude. She said "Newtie" — she still calls me that, I don't think I'm ever going to get to "Mr. Speaker" with my mother — she says "Newtie, you just have to get on with life."

Coming back from Harrisburg, I realized that she gave me strength, and had made me realize that for Marianne and myself, moving on with our lives in the right way by doing the right thing was our most important goal.

Let me make clear, we endure the difficulties and the pain of the current political process because we believe renewing America is the great challenge for our generation. I said on the day I became Speaker for the second time that we should focus on the challenges of race, drugs, ignorance and faith.

Over the past few months, I have met with Americans of all backgrounds and all races as we discussed new approaches and new solutions. I am convinced that we can enter the 21st century with a renewed America of remarkable power and ability. This is a great country filled with good people. We do have the capacity to reform welfare and help every citizen move from welfare to work. We do have the potential to help our poorest citizens move from poverty to prosperity. We do have the potential to replace quotas with friendship, and set-asides with volunteerism. We can reach out to every American child of every ethnic background in every neighborhood and help them achieve their Creator's endowed unalienable right to pursue happiness. We can't guarantee happiness, but we can guarantee the right to pursue.

Recently, I had a chance to have breakfast with the fine young men and women of the 2nd Infantry Division in Korea, where my father had served. Today South Korea is free and prosperous because young Americans for 47 years have risked their lives in alliance with young Koreans. I was reminded on that morning that freedom depends on courage and integrity; that honor, duty, country is not just a motto, it is a way of life.

We in this House must live every day in that tradition. We have much to do to clean up our political and governmental processes. We have much to do to communicate with our citizens and with those around the world who believe in freedom and yearn for freedom.

Everywhere I went recently — in Hong Kong, Beijing, Shanghai, Taipei, Seoul and Tokyo — people talked about freedom of speech, free elections, the rule of law, an independent judiciary, the right to own private property, and the right to pursue happiness through free markets.

We in this House are role models. People all over the world watch us and study us. When we fall short, they lose hope. When we fail, they despair. To the degree I have made mistakes, they have been errors of implementation but never of intent.

This House is at the center of freedom and it deserves from all of us a commitment to be worthy of that honor. Today I am doing what I can to personally live up to that calling and that standard. I hope my colleagues will join me in that quest.

May God bless this House, and may God bless America. Thank you. ■

VETO MESSAGE

President Details Rejection Of Supplemental Bill

Following is a Federal News Service transcript of President Clinton's June 9 veto of the fiscal 1997 supplemental disaster relief bill (HR 1469):

TO THE HOUSE OF REPRESENTATIVES: I am returning herewith without my approval HR 1469, the "Supplemental Appropriations and Rescissions Act, FY 1997." The congressional majority — despite the obvious and urgent need to speed critical relief to people in the Dakotas, Minnesota, California, and 29 other states ravaged by flooding and other natural disasters — has chosen to weigh down this legislation with a series of unacceptable provisions that it knows will draw my veto. The time has come to stop playing politics with the lives of Americans in need and to send me a clean, unencumbered disaster relief bill that I can and will sign the moment it reaches my desk.

On March 19, 1997, I sent the Congress a request for emergency disaster assistance and urged the Congress to approve it promptly. Both the House and Senate Appropriations Committees acted expeditiously to approve the legislation. The core of this bill, appropriately, provides $5.8 billion of much-needed help to people in hard-hit states and, in addition, contains $1.8 billion for the Department of Defense related to our peacekeeping efforts in Bosnia and Southwest Asia [Persian Gulf area]. Regrettably, the Republican leadership chose to include contentious issues totally unrelated to disaster assistance, needlessly delaying essential relief.

The bill contains a provision that would create an automatic continuing resolution for all of fiscal year 1998. While the goal of ensuring that the government does not shut down again is a worthy one, this provision is ill-advised. The issue here is not about shutting down the government. Last month, I reached agreement with the bipartisan leadership of Congress on a plan to balance the budget by 2002. That agreement is the right way to finish the job of putting our fiscal house in order, consistent with our values and principles. Putting the government's finances on automatic pilot is not.

The backbone of the bipartisan budget agreement is the plan to balance the budget while providing funds for critical investments in education, the environment and other priorities. The automatic continuing resolution would provide resources for fiscal year 1998 that are $18 billion below the level contained in the bipartisan budget agreement, threatening such investments in our future. For example: College aid would be reduced by $1.7 billion, eliminating nearly 375,000 students from the Pell Grant program; the number of women, infants and children receiving food and other services through WIC would be cut by an average of 500,000 per month; up to 56,000 fewer children would participate in Head Start; the number of border patrol and FBI agents would be reduced, as would the number of air traffic controllers; and our goal of cleaning up 900 superfund sites by the year 2000 could not be accomplished.

The bill also contains a provision that would permanently prohibit the Department of Commerce from using statistical sampling techniques in the 2000 decennial census for the purpose of apportioning Representatives in Congress among the States. Without sampling, the cost of the decennial census will increase as its accuracy, especially with regard to minorities and groups that are traditionally undercounted, decreases substantially. The National Academy of Sciences and other experts have recommended the use of statistical sampling for the 2000 decennial census.

The Department of Justice, under the Carter and Bush administrations and during my administration, has issued three opinions regarding the constitutionality and legality of sampling in the decennial census. All three opinions concluded that the Constitution and relevant statutes permit the use of sampling in the decennial census. Federal courts that have addressed the issue have held that the Constitution and federal statutes allow sampling.

The enrolled bill contains an objectionable provision that would promote the conversion of certain claimed rights of way into paved highways across sensitive national parks, public lands and military installations. Under the provision, a 13-member commission would study the issue and provide recommendations to resolve outstanding Revised Statute (R.S.) 2477 claims. R.S. 2477 was enacted in 1866 to grant rights of way for the construction of highways over public lands not already reserved for public uses. It was repealed in 1976, subject to "valid, existing rights."

This provision in the enrolled bill is objectionable because it is cumbersome, flawed, and duplicates the extensive public hearings conducted by the Department of the Interior over the last four years. In addition, the proposed commission excludes the secretary of Defense, but military installations are among the federal properties that would be affected by the recommendations of the commission. Furthermore, there is no assurance that the proposed commission would provide a balanced representation of views or proper public participation. Under the provision, the secretary of the Interior can disapprove the commission's recommendations, preventing their submission to the Congress under "fast-track" procedures in the House and Senate. I believe — and my administration has stated — that a better approach would be for Interior to submit a legislative proposal to the Congress within 180 days to clarify R.S. 2477 claim issues permanently, with full congressional and public consideration. The enrolled bill contains an objectionable provision that funds the Commission for the Advancement of Federal Law Enforcement. I agree with the Fraternal Order of Police and other national law enforcement organizations that certain activities of the commission, such as evaluating the handling of specific investigative cases, could interfere with federal law enforcement policy and operations. This type of oversight is most properly the role of Congress, not an unelected review board. If external views about law enforcement programs are needed, a better approach would be to fund the National Commission to Support Law Enforcement.

I also object to two other items in the bill. One reduces funding for the Ounce of Prevention Council by roughly one-third. This reduction would substantially diminish the work of the council in coordinating crime prevention efforts at the federal level and assisting community efforts to make their neighborhoods safer. The council is in the process of awarding $1.8 million for grants to prevent youth substance abuse and of evaluating its existing grant programs. The council has received over 300 applications from communities and community-based organizations from all across the country for these grants. In addition, the bill reduces funding for the Department of Defense Dual-Use Applications Program. That program helps to develop technologies used and tested by the cost-conscious commercial sector and to incorporate them into military systems. Reducing funding for this program would result in higher costs for future defense systems. The projects selected in this year's competition will save the Department of Defense an estimated $3 billion.

Finally, by including extraneous issues in this bill, the Republican leadership has also delayed necessary funding for maintaining military readiness. The secretary of Defense has written the Congress detailing the potential disruption of military training.

I urge the Congress to remove these extraneous provisions and to send me a straightforward disaster relief bill that I can sign promptly, so that we can help hard-hit American families and businesses as they struggle to rebuild. Americans in need should not have to endure further delay. ■

WILLIAM J. CLINTON
THE WHITE HOUSE
June 9, 1997

BUDGET

President Clinton Announces 'A Principled Compromise'

The following is a Federal News Service text of President Clinton's July 29 remarks on the balanced-budget agreement:

PRESIDENT CLINTON: Good afternoon.

Ladies and gentlemen, we have the pleasure of announcing today an historic agreement that will benefit generations of Americans. Last night,we reached agreement with Congress on detailed legislation to balance the budget in a way that honors our values, invests in our people, and cuts taxes for middle-class families. After decades of deficits, we have put America's fiscal house in order again. Thank you. Thank you. Above all, we are investing in education, America's most important priority. I am particularly pleased that the first balanced budget in a generation is also the best education budget in a generation and the best for future generations.

This agreement meets my goal of balancing the budget in a way that honors our values, invests in our people, and prepares America for the 21st century. It is very, very good for our country. It's a victory for every parent who wants a good education for their children, for every child in a poor household who needs health care, for every immigrant struggling to make it here, for every family working to build a secure future. It is the best investment we can make in America's future.

Let me underscore the magnitude of this achievement. Four-and-a-half years ago, when this administration took office, America's budget deficit was $290 billion and rising. We put in place a comprehensive economic strategy to cut the deficit and invest in our people. The budget plan adopted in 1993 made a large contribution to today's conditions in America: a strong economy, low inflation and a deficit that has already shrunk by more than 80 percent. The budget agreement that we announce today would not be possible had it not been for the tough vote taken in 1993 to set us on the right path.

And just as important, it will give our people the tools to reap the rewards of economic growth. Let me mention just a few of the details of this plan.

First, at the heart of this balanced budget is the historic investment in education, the most significant increase in education funding in more than 30 years. It includes $35 billion in tax relief to help families pay for college and training, the largest investment in higher education since the G.I. bill 50 years ago. It will give every American who needs it a Hope scholarship to pay for the first two years of college. It gives tax relief for all four years of college, and for education throughout a lifetime.

The overall budget agreement also includes the largest increase in Pell grant scholarships for deserving students in three decades, funds our "America Reads" challenge, helps to connect all our schools and libraries to the Internet by the year 2000.

As the spending bills move forward in weeks to come, we will work to see that they reflect this agreement. I am pleased that this legislation will give communities substantial tax cuts to help to build and modernize our schools. All across America, I have challenged our people to make sure that every 8-year-old can read, every 12-year-old can log on to the Internet, every 18-year-old can go to college, every adult can keep learning for a lifetime. This balanced budget makes unprecedented progress toward those goals.

Second, this is a balanced budget that strengthens our families by extending health insurance coverage to up to 5 million children. By investing fully $24 billion, we will be able to provide quality medical care for these children, everything from regular checkups to major surgery. I want to thank all of the people in the Congress and among my fellow Democrats here who worked so hard on the health care issue.

But I especially want to say thanks to Sen. Kennedy, Sen. Rockefeller, and to the first lady for what they have done over these years to help us to reach this important day. We want every child in America to grow up healthy and strong, and this investment takes a major step toward that goal.

I'm also pleased that Congress agreed to pay for the children's health care in part with the new 15-cents-a-pack tax on cigarettes. Not only will this new revenue help to pay for health care, it will help prevent children from taking up smoking in the first place.

Third, this is a balanced budget that provides modest tax relief to the middle class, helping families to raise their children, buy and sell a home, save for their retirement with expanded IRAs, and send their children to college. We fought very hard to make sure this tax cut helped a wide range of middle-class parents, all those who are working hard to raise their children, pay their taxes, and be good citizens. And the agreement does just that.

Fourth, this is a balanced budget that will help us finish the job of welfare reform, providing $3 billion to move welfare recipients to private-sector jobs, keeping our promise made last year to provide $12 billion to restore disability and health benefits for 350,000 legal immigrants. And as the vice president will describe, it will double the number of empowerment zones to bring the spark of private enterprise to our hardest-pressed neighborhoods.

Finally, this is a balanced budget that honors our commitment to our parents by extending the Medicare Trust Fund for a decade, and to the next generation by continuing our commitment to the environment, to protect our air, our land, our water, to clean up the worst toxic waste sites in the nation.

And we achieve all these goals while eliminating the budget deficit by 2002. We are determined never again to repeat the mistakes of the past, when we mortgaged our economy to reckless policies. This budget reforms and cuts yesterday's government so that we can help provide our people the means to meet the challenges of tomorrow.

Let me thank the negotiators for the administration, who did a superb job; all the Democratic lawmakers here; and indeed all the members of Congress who worked hard on this legislation.

I also want to say a special word of appreciation to Sen. Lott and Speaker Gingrich, to Sen. Domenici and Congressman Kasich, and to their committee chairs, who worked with us across the lines of substantial philosophical and practical differences to reach a good faith agreement that is an honorable and principled compromise.

And especially let me thank Sens. Daschle and Lautenberg, Congressman Spratt and Congressman Rangel for their leadership.

This agreement is a monument to the efforts that people . . . can make when they put aside partisan interests to work together for the common good and our common future. It reflects the values and aspirations of all Americans, and I hope and expect it will marshal strong majorities of both parties in both houses.

This summer we had an historic opportunity to strengthen America for the 21st century, and we have seized it. Now our nation can move forward stronger, more vibrant, more united than ever. For that I am profoundly grateful.

Now I'd like to ask the vice president to come forward. And let me thank you all again for this great, great day. ■

WILLIAM J. CLINTON
THE WHITE HOUSE
June 29, 1997

BUDGET

GOP Leaders Extol Tax Cuts, Other Budget Deal Features

Following is a transcript of remarks made July 29 by Senate Majority Leader Trent Lott, R-Miss.; House Speaker Newt Gingrich, R-Ga.; Sens. William V. Roth Jr., R-Del., and Pete V. Domenici, R-N.M.; and Reps. Bill Archer, R-Texas, and John R. Kasich, R-Ohio, on the balanced-budget agreement:

GINGRICH: Let me just say that we are delighted to be here to celebrate a great victory for all of these young people and for the country they will someday inherit and lead.

We believe that by balancing the budget, by saving Medicare and by cutting taxes that we truly create an opportunity for them to grow up in an America which is stronger, which has more jobs, which has more take-home pay, that we give their parents a chance to have more money at home to spend on their family because we believe that parents are more important than bureaucrats in raising children.

And we give these young people a chance to go on to school, to have a better education, then once they leave school to have a better chance at a better job with better take-home pay, and finally, that as they save and work all their lives, that they will have a tax code that encourages savings. It encourages job creation. And it gives them a better chance for a future which then allows them, when they retire, to be in a Medicare system which has real choices and uses the best medicine available in their lifetime.

Those are the kind of changes these two bills involve. It is a great victory for all Americans. It is a bipartisan victory. We join the president in working together to truly create a better future for all of us and our children.

And I yield to Sen. Lott without whose help this would have been impossible.

LOTT: Thank you, Mr. Speaker. Thank you, Mr. Speaker, and thanks to all of you. It's an exciting time to be here this afternoon, especially with all these young people, all these parents here. You represent what we've been working on all year long.

Today we celebrate the beginning of a new era of freedom. We have joined the president and we have come to an agreement that will lead us to less Washington spending, to tax relief for working Americans, to security for our senior citizens and less dependency on the government, more responsibility and opportunity for individuals, communities and states.

This truly is a great moment. We made a decision earlier this year that we're going to work together to get this victory for the American people. And that's what it's really about.

It's not about partisan politics. It's not about who's president or who's in the Congress. It's about returning the government to the people.

We have accomplished this with this agreement that we entered into last night, and that we're going to pass through the Congress during the next two days.

Thank you very much for being here and joining us in this celebration for the American people.

DOMENICI: . . . Well, look, I want to just say that I've been working at a balanced budget for two decades now, and — so I'm kind of overwhelmed. But I think it's time that we in the Congress who claim we're the adult leaders of America, pay our own bills, and not pass the bills on to our children to be paid.

We believe that those who work hard and follow the laws, and do what they can for their country and their family ought to pay less taxes and ought to keep more of their money, because they can make better decisions than we can. And that's what we've done here. Hard-working, middle-income Americans get a tax break for a change.

And then, we're concerned about our families now and our families in the future, and so we've taken care of our senior citizens. We've made Medicare solvent for a decade, we've given seniors options so that they will have better health care, and it will cost less. So, all in all, this bipartisan effort is what the American people expect of those who claim to be leaders of this country. We are proud to join with the president, who is not of our party, to join hands and say, "American people, we heard you.

You wanted us to work together, we have, and now the American people have a victory, not Republicans and not Democrats, all Americans win today."

KASICH: This agreement — this agreement, and make no mistake about it — begins the era that recognizes the limits of government.

You see, what this agreement is all about, with our tax cuts that put power in people's pockets, with the Medicare choices that our senior citizens will have from their homes, with the relaxed rules that are going to be designed from Washington to give the governors the ability to administer a program for the poor and the disabled; what this is about, is transferring power, money and influence from this city, where it's been for 50 years, back into the hands of every hard-working American and every young person, you see, because what this is all about is not about the power of government; the future is about the power of each and every one of you here today.

Eight years ago, in 1989, I had a dream that we could balance the federal budget and let people keep more of what they earn. There are a lot of young people here today, and I'm here to tell you, live your dreams, fight for your dreams, stand with integrity; and at the end of the day, not only will you win, but those who watch you will win, and our country will win. God bless America.

ARCHER: This tax bill is good for America. It provides relief to more than 40 million middle-income families with children. It cuts capital gains taxes so we can increase and retain savings and create jobs. And it tells young people that education is not only a goal but that we, through the tax code, will help reduce the cost of it.

It is a victory for all Americans, and you've already heard that what we do is we provide power back to the people so that they can spend their own money instead of taxing people and bringing the money to Washington to try to solve their problems. A $500-per-child tax credit that includes teenagers, covers middle-income working moms and dads, capital gains relief, with a drop to 20 percent and 18 percent for long-term holdings.

Deep and immediate debt tax relief. An increase in the health insurance deduction for the self-employed to 100 percent. Tax relief for education.

And on and on and on.

And while doing it, we close tax loopholes equal to $10 billion so there are no special tax benefits to people that the rest don't get in that category.

This is a superb bill for America. It lets people keep their money, increases growth and job opportunity, and it's just the beginning. You ain't seen nothing yet.

ROTH: We indeed have a lot to celebrate today. Today we are reversing the decades-old trend of bigger government, bigger taxes, and bigger spending. These bills would not be possible without the leadership of the Republican Party.

Balancing the budget and cutting taxes are Republican ideas — make no mistake about that. We can be proud that we are carrying out these ideas in a bipartisan manner. We have found that Republican common sense ideas do have allies on the Democratic side.

In the past year, we have begun to tear down the walls of partisanship and to work with our Democratic colleagues to make common sense reforms for America. Common sense ideas have created common ground between the part[ies], and this common ground has given us a major tax cut, a balanced budget for the American people. And let me re-emphasize, rescore: Make no mistake about it, this is merely a beginning. ■

VETO MESSAGE

Clinton Details Reasons for Using New Veto Power on Three Items

Following is the Federal News Service transcript of the Aug. 11 remarks by President Clinton at the White House when he vetoed provisions from the tax bill:

PRESIDENT CLINTON: Last week we took historic action to put America's economic house in order when I signed into law the first balanced budget in a generation, one that honors our values, invests in our people, prepares our nation for the 21st century. It includes the largest increase in college aid since the G.I. Bill; the largest increase in children's health since the creation of Medicaid over 30 years ago; tax cuts that are the equivalent of a thousand-dollar raise in take-home pay for the average family with two children; and much more that is good for America.

The new balanced-budget law also offers the first opportunity to use a powerful new tool to protect taxpayers, the line-item veto, a tool designed to fight against waste and unjustifiable expenditures, to ensure government works for the public interest, not the private interests.

In the past, good legislation could be cluttered up with unjustifiable or wasteful spending or tax provisions, leaving the president no choice but to sign or veto the overall legislation. With the line-item veto, the president can sign an overall bill into law, but cancel a particular spending project or a particular tax break that benefits only a handful of individuals or companies.

Forty-three governors throughout our nation already have the line-item veto power. Last year, I signed the federal line-item veto into law. Last month, the United States Supreme Court, on procedural grounds, rejected a challenge to this authority.

No other state in the nation would be given this provision, and it is unfair to the rest of our nation's taxpayers to ask them to subsidize it.

Finally, I will cancel a provision that, though well-intended, is poorly designed. This provision would have allowed a very limited number of agribusinesses to avoid paying capital gains taxes, possibly forever, on the sales of certain assets to farmers' cooperatives. And it could have benefited not only traditional farm co-ops but giant organizations which do not need, and should not trigger, the law's benefits.

Because I strongly support family farmers, farm cooperatives and the acquisition of production facilities by co-ops, this was a very difficult decision for me. And I intend to work with Congressmen [Charles W.] Stenholm [D-Texas] and [Kenny] Hulshof [R-Mo.], and Senators [Tom] Daschle [D-S.D.], [Byron L.] Dorgan [D-N.D.] and [Kent] Conrad [D-N.D.], and other interested members of the Congress to redesign this effort so that it is better targeted and not susceptible to abuse.

The actions I take today will save the American people hundreds of millions of dollars over the next 10 years and send a signal that the Washington rules have changed for good, and for the good of the American people. From now on, presidents will be able to say no to wasteful spending or tax loopholes even as they say yes to vital legislation.

Special interests will not be able to play the old game of slipping a provision into a massive bill in the hope that no one will notice. For the first time, the president is exercising the power to prevent that from happening.

The first balanced budget in a generation is now also the first budget in American history to be strengthened by the line-item veto, and that will strengthen our country.

And now I want to go and sign these provisions.

The Only 'Pork'?

QUESTION: Mr. President, is that the only pork you find in that budget?

CLINTON: I think that my staff is going to brief you about it, but let me say that they have — that the relevant Cabinet and staff members have gone over this quite extensively.

Keep in mind, the primary use of the line-item veto overwhelmingly was meant to be in the appropriations process, which has not even started yet. I don't have the first appropriations bill.

There are only a few spending items in this balanced budget that are part of the so-called entitlements process, so that — for example, you had the . . . New York Medicaid provision there, on provider taxes.

With regard to the taxes, there were some 79 items certified to me, but that was only because of their size; that is, the number of people affected by it. Of those 79, 30 or more were actually recommendations by the Treasury Department to fix flaws in the present laws or to ease the transitions in the tax laws. And another dozen or more were put in by Congress, by agreement with the Treasury Department, to fix procedural problems in the law. Then there were a number of others that I . . . I agreed were good policy.

So these are the ones that I think — and then there were several others that I might have line-item vetoed, but they were plainly part of the understandings reached with Congress as a part of the budget process.

So these seemed to me to be the ones on — after being briefed by my staff, that both involved significant amounts of money and met the three criteria that I mentioned. And I — I believe it was the appropriate thing to do.

Surviving the Challenge

Q: Were these the most glaring examples of why you were given this power and therefore they might hold up better in a court challenge?

CLINTON: Well, I wouldn't say that. I expect the most glaring examples to come up in the appropriations process, at least if the past is any prologue. Now, it may be that the use of the line-item veto here will mean that it won't have to be used as much in the appropriations process and that would please me greatly. But I think it's important that the American people understand that when the line-item veto was given to the president, the primary assumption was that it would take out special projects that were typically funded in big bills and those are those big appropriations bills, none of which has come to me yet.

But I do believe that this should withstand court challenge because the process by which the matters were reviewed, at least, was a very careful, exhaustive process and I received input from people all over the country that had interest in it to my Cabinet and staff members. But we worked very hard on this and, well, since I told you after my press conference on Thursday [Aug. 7] that I would be meeting with my staff and I had meetings and conversations in each since then before finally making these decisions.

Symbolism of Veto

Q: It sounds as though between the deliberations among your staff and the talk about the court challenge and the difficulty finding items in this particular tax and spending legislation that you decided to act now largely for symbolic reasons instead of . . .

CLINTON: No, I wouldn't say that. I think these three things are appropriate. But I just want to point out that the — that I think that when the Congress sort of thought, for example, 79 tax items, assuming, people will say, well, maybe you ought to veto 76 of them and I think it's important to recognize if there never were 79 candidates for a line-item veto there. The Congress is required — the Joint Tax Committee is required by law to certify to the president all the tax items that benefit fewer than a hundred people. And there were — the vast majority of those were either put in by the Treasury Department, or by the congressional committees with the support of the Treasury Department, to actually clean up procedural problems in the law so that the numbers were smaller.

Then there were a number of things that, as I said, I might well have line-item vetoed, but they were part of the overall budget process, and they did a lot of good for the American people. And I have to honor the agreements that were made in the process of it. So these things, I hope, will be both real and symbolic in the sense that I am hopeful that this will work out pretty much the way it did when I was governor; that is, when you know the president is prepared to use the line-item veto, that tends to operate as a deterrent against the most egregious kinds of projects that would otherwise not be funded.

So it would suit me if, after a while, the use of the veto became quite rare because there was a disciplined agreement not to have projects that ought not to be funded in the first place.

A Constitutional Question

Q: Sir, could you tell me where in the Constitution the president is given this kind of power that hasn't been exerted until now?

CLINTON: Well, the power is given by legislation. The real question is, does the Constitution permit or forbid the Congress to give the president this kind of power? I believe that, since — if you look at the fact that 43 states have this — the power for the governor — and it has been upheld in state after state after state, the provisions of most state constitutions are similar to the provisions of the federal Constitution in the general allocation of executive authority and legislative authority.

So I think it is an implicit thing, as long as the legislature has the right to override the executive, then, for the legislature to allow the executive to make reasoned judgments about particular items in these omnibus bills I do not believe is an unconstitutional delegation of the legislature's authority to the president.

So they — keep in mind — they can override this. If they decide that they think I am wrong, they can — if — and two-thirds of them agree — they can override this.

A Question of Appropriations

Q: Mr. President, Senator [John] McCain [R-Ariz.] sent you a note last week, saying you ought to consider putting off a line-item veto until you get the appropriations bills, on the grounds that it may be a blow to the spirit of cooperation that produced the tax cut and the balanced-budget bills in the first place. Did you give that any consideration?

CLINTON: Absolutely.

And when Senator McCain came to see me about the campaign-finance issue and our common support for his legislation, we talked about it a little bit. As I have already said to you that one of the reasons that we have decided on a relatively small number is I didn't want to touch anything that I thought where there was even a question that it might have been part of the negotiating process and a cooperative spirit with Congress. But if — you know, if you look at these three things, they present three entirely different problems, but I think all three are outside the scope of the budget negotiating process, and all three are the kinds of things that the line-item veto was meant for. The first, the avoidance of federal taxation in an inappropriate way; the second, giving a break to one state in a way that would immediately disadvantage several others and potentially disadvantage all the other states; and the third, as I said, I believe a very worthy goal, having incentives for farmers co-ops to buy integrated — to integrate with production facilities, in a way that is over broad and could lead to the total avoidance of taxation under circumstances which are inappropriate, which would require a more disciplined fix. I think those are the kinds of things that the line-item veto was meant to deal with in these contexts.

Now, when you get to the appropriations process, it will be somewhat more straightforward, you know: Should this project be built or not; should this road be built or not; should this money be given to this agency or not for this program? And I think that those are the things where typically it's in use at the state level.

But in the context of taxes and the entitlements, I thought each of these three things presented a representative case where the veto was intended to be used.

Thank you. ■

TOBACCO SETTLEMENT

Clinton Details Five Key Elements For Teen Smoking Legislation

Following is the White House transcript of President Clinton's Sept. 17 remarks about the tobacco settlement:

PRESIDENT CLINTON: Thank you very much. Mr. Vice President [Al Gore], Secretary [Donna E.] Shalala, Secretary [Dan] Glickman, thank you for your work. Thank you, domestic policy adviser Bruce Reed. I'd like to say a special word of thanks to [former Food and Drug Administration Commissioner] David Kessler for the work he did — historic work he did at the FDA when he was here. Thank you, Dr. [C. Everett] Koop [former surgeon general], and members of the public community who are here. To members of Congress, the attorneys general, the representatives of plaintiffs in the private litigation — and we have one of the injured parties here representing all of the them. We thank all of them for coming today.

This is a time of prosperity and hope and optimism for America, with our economy improving, making progress on our social problems, our efforts to lead the world to a more prosperous and peaceful future making headway. But I think we all know that this country still has some significant challenges, especially in the health field. And if we think about what we want America to be like in the 21st century, the health of our people and especially the health of our children must be paramount in our thinking, in our vision, and in our efforts.

That's why, a year ago, I worked with the FDA and we launched this nationwide effort to protect our children from the dangers of tobacco by reducing youth access to tobacco products, by preventing companies from advertising to our children.

The purpose of the FDA rule was to reduce youth smoking by 50 percent within seven years. Earlier this year, a federal judge in North Carolina said that the FDA has the authority to regulate tobacco products to protect the health of our children. There have also been other examples of litigation progress, as you know, brought by private plaintiffs and by the attorneys general. Now, these victories for public health drove the tobacco companies to the bargaining table. They extracted concessions that would have been literally unthinkable just a short time ago.

I want to say a special word of thanks to the attorneys general and the other parties who worked hard to negotiate this settlement. Everyone knows we would not be here had it not been for their foresight, their determination, and their relentless efforts.

Now we have this unprecedented opportunity to enact comprehensive tobacco legislation, working with all the parties involved — the members of Congress, the attorneys general, the representatives of injured parties, the public health community, the tobacco farmers and others. We have moved from confrontation and denial and inertia to the brink of action on behalf of our children, and that is all to the good.

Today I want to challenge Congress to build on this historic opportunity by passing sweeping tobacco legislation that has one goal in mind: the dramatic reduction of teen smoking. In the coming weeks I will invite congressional leaders from both parties to the White House to launch a bipartisan effort to enact such legislation.

There are five key elements that must be at the heart of any national tobacco legislation. Reducing teen smoking has always been America's bottom line. It must be the industry's bottom line. That is why I believe the first thing any tobacco legislation must include is a comprehensive plan to reduce teen smoking, including tough penalties. These penalties should be non-tax-deductible, uncapped, and escalating to give the tobacco industry the strongest possible incentive to stop targeting children as new customers.

Pricing

One of the surest ways of reducing youth smoking is to increase the price of cigarettes. Today I call for a combination of industry payments and penalties to increase the price of cigarettes.

Today I call for a combination of industry payments and penalties to increase the price of cigarettes by up to a dollar and a half a pack over the next decade, as needed, to meet our youth reduction targets. And I call upon the House to follow the lead of the United States Senate and repeal the provision giving the tobacco industry a $50 billion tax credit.

FDA Regulation

Second, any legislation must affirm the full authority of the FDA to regulate tobacco products. I believe the FDA's jurisdiction over tobacco products must be as strong and effective as its authority over drugs and devices. In particular, legislation cannot impose any special procedural hurdles on the FDA's regulation of tobacco products.

Industry Accountability

Third, effective legislation must include measures to hold the industry accountable, especially in any efforts to market products to children, while insisting on changes in the way it does business. I ask the industry again to make a voluntary commitment to stop advertising to children. And I call upon Congress to pass legislation providing for broad document disclosure so that the public can learn everything the tobacco companies know about the health effects of their products and their attempts to market to our children.

Additional Health Goals

Fourth, federal tobacco legislation must aim not only to reduce youth smoking, but to meet other health goals as well. These include the reduction of second-hand smoke, the expansion of smoking prevention and cessation programs, the strengthening of international efforts to control tobacco, and the provision of funds for medical research and other important health objectives. We must build on the bipartisan agreement to fund children's health care in the recent balanced budget.

Protection of Tobacco Farmers

And finally, any tobacco legislation must protect tobacco farmers and their communities. We know that tobacco farmers are honest, hard-working people, most of whom live and work on small, family-owned farms. In some states, entire communities rely on income from the tobacco crop. Any legislation must protect these farmers, their families and their communities from loss of income.

Let me say in closing, I want to thank the Vice President, especially, who cares so passionately about this issue. He's played a key role in our efforts to protect our children from the dangers of tobacco. I've asked him to take the lead in building broad bipartisan support around the country for our plan. I also want to thank Secretary Shalala, Secretary Glickman and Bruce Reed, and all those who work so hard on our administration's analysis of the proposed settlement and where we are.

And finally, let me say again, we wouldn't be here if it weren't for all the people in this room and the countless others they represent around the country. To me, this is not about money. It is not about how much money we can extract from the tobacco industry. It is about fulfilling our duties as parents and responsible adults to protect our children and to build the future of this country. We are doing everything we can in this administration to give parents the tools they need to raise their children, but parents have to be our partners as well. If this is not just about money, we have to recognize that even beyond the tobacco companies and all of us in this room, every parent in America has a responsibility to talk to their children about the dangers of tobacco, illegal drugs, and other things that can hurt them. We know if we have strong parental responsibility here, they can make a great deal of difference in protecting our children as well.

If we take responsibility, if we pass this legislation, if we do what we should here, if the tobacco industry will work with us, if other members of Congress in both parties will work with us, we will have gone a very long way toward creating the state of health for our children that will make America an even greater nation in the new century.

Thank you.

Chances for Adoption

Q: Mr. President, what are the chances of the Congress adopting your policy? And why is the industry so conspicuously absent?

CLINTON: Well, first of all, I was encouraged by some of the comments that were made by some industry representatives. I think that they know that they have to have federal legislation. They have an interest in that as well. And I would hope that they would be willing to work with us. But we cannot have the FDA crippled here, and we have to have real and meaningful penalties if the targets for youth smoking are not met. And so I feel very good about that.

I think the Congress — I think it's highly likely that they will take action. When they take action depends, I think, upon when they can work through the issues for themselves and how they decide how to divide up the work among the committees. But it's not too soon to start. We could have hearings on this fairly soon, and I would hope to work with the Congress to develop a bill that would embody these principles.

Future Liability

Q: Mr. President, you haven't said what you're willing to agree to for the tobacco industry. Are you willing to agree to immunity from future liability?

CLINTON: Well, I don't think they've asked for future liability, I think they've asked for immunity from liability for past suits. And the question there would be, what are they willing to agree to. They need to come and meet with us. We need to discuss it, and we need to see whether we can embody these five principles. These are the things I'm interested in.

To me, I'll say again, this is not primarily about money. This is about changing the behavior of the United States, both the behavior of the tobacco companies, the behavior of the American people, the future behavior of our children. I'm trying to create an environment here with these five principles that I believe would achieve that. And if they want to be our partners in it, I think we can get there. And I hope they will be.

Q: Are you willing to put your prestige on the line to ensure that this becomes law?

CLINTON: Well, I think my personal prestige on this has been on the line for more than a year now. (Laughter.) There for a while, I thought more than my prestige was on the line. (Laughter.) You know, for a person involved in public life in Washington today, personal prestige may be an oxymoron. (Laughter.) But at least you still have your neck most days.

Tobacco Farmers

Q: What do you say to the people . . . to protect the well-being of tobacco farmers — sounds like you're going to take away their livelihood?

CLINTON: Well, there are a number of things which can be done, and I don't want to get into the details. Secretary Glickman can talk about it. But we have had farmers in various sectors in our agriculture society facing constricted incomes before, and we have done things which helped them. There was a — for example, I remember a few years ago something that affected dairy farmers in my state. There was a massive buyout program for dairy farmers, and in a lot of states like Arkansas, there were any number of small farmers that were having a very difficult time who had a chance to start their life on a different basis.

I don't want to minimize this. Tobacco has a very high return per acre. So it's not a simple thing. You can't just say to a tobacco farmer to go plant soybeans, even if the soil will hold them. This is, from an agricultural point of view, economically complex. But, nonetheless, we have a responsibility to these people. They haven't done anything wrong. They haven't done anything illegal. They're good, hard-working, tax-paying citizens, and they have not caused this problem. And we cannot let them, their families or their communities just be crippled and broken by this. And I don't think any member of the public health community wants to do that. And the Agricultural Department and I am personally very committed to this part -- to me, this is one of the five things we have to do.

We're trying to change America and make everybody whole. And they deserve a chance to have their lives and be made whole and go on with the future as well, and I'm determined to see that they're a part of this.

Public Relations of the Deal

Q: What do you say to the attorneys who thought this was a good deal and very proudly proclaimed it?

CLINTON: Well, first of all, they were a part of all these ongoing reviews. Everybody was heard in this review process. And, secondly, they all recognize, too, that this agreement has to be ratified by Congress. The tobacco companies recognize that. That means that all of us who are part of that process are, in effect, parties to this case, too. And that's the way you need to look at this. We're building on their deal. We're not rejecting their agreement, we're building on it. We're not rejecting what the attorneys general did, we're building on it. Look, if it hadn't been for what they did, we wouldn't be here.

I realize that there were two great things that started this. One is what Dr. Kessler and what we did at the FDA, and the fact that our administration was the first one ever willing to take this on. The other was the actions by the attorneys general and the private lawsuits that got the disclosure of the documents that created a . . . change in the public attitude and the public efforts here.

And then long before that, there were the efforts of all of these people here from the public health community who have been telling us all this for years. And they had the public primed for it. Then, the lawsuits brought about the disclosures and then the FDA was moving. Those three things together, I think — and, of course, now there have been a lot of congressional hearings. Rep. [Henry A.] Waxman [D-Calif.] had a full head of hair when he came to Congress before he started — (Laughter.) And so I think you've got to give — to me, we're building on this progress, and that's the way you have to look at this. We are trying to do the best thing for the country in a way that is consistent with the agreement they made. We're building on the agreement. Were not tearing it down, we're building on it. And I think we can get legislation that will reflect it.

Thank you. ■

PRESIDENTIAL ADDRESS TO U.N.

Clinton Calls for 'New Era' of Peace And Economic Opportunity

Following is the White House transcript of President Clinton's Sept. 22 address to the United Nations:

PRESIDENT CLINTON: Mr. President [Hennadiy Vdovenko], Mr. Secretary General [Kofi Annan], distinguished guests: Five years ago, when I first addressed this Assembly, the Cold War had only just ended and the transition to a new era was beginning. Now, together, we are making that historic transition.

Behind us we leave a century full of humanity's capacity for the worst and its genius for the best. Before us, at the dawn of a new millennium, we can envision a new era that escapes the 20th century's darkest moments, fulfills its most brilliant possibilities and crosses frontiers yet unimagined.

We are off to a promising start. For the first time in history, more than half the people represented in this Assembly freely choose their own governments. Free markets are growing, spreading individual opportunity and national well-being. Early in the 21st century, more than 20 of this Assembly's members, home to half the Earth's population, will lift themselves from the ranks of low-income nations.

Powerful forces are bringing us closer together, profoundly changing the way we work and live and relate to each other. Every day, millions of our citizens on every continent use laptops and satellites to send information, products and money across the planet in seconds. Bit by bit, the information age is chipping away at the barriers — economic, political and social — that once kept people locked in and ideas locked out. Science is unraveling mysteries in the tiniest of human genes and the vast cosmos.

Never in the course of human history have we had a greater opportunity to make our people healthier and wiser, to protect our planet from decay and abuse, to reap the benefits of free markets without abandoning the social contract and its concern for the common good. Yet today's possibilities are not tomorrow's guarantees. We have work to do.

The forces of global integration are a great tide, inexorably wearing away the established order of things. But we must decide what will be left in its wake. People fear change when they feel its burdens but not its benefits. They are susceptible to misguided protectionism, to the poisoned appeals of extreme nationalism, and ethnic, racial and religious hatred. New global environmental challenges require us to find ways to work together without damaging legitimate aspirations for progress. We're all vulnerable to the reckless acts of rogue states and to an unholy axis of terrorists, drug traffickers and international criminals. These 21st-century predators feed on the very free flow of information and ideas and people we cherish. They abuse the vast power of technology to build black markets for weapons, to compromise law enforcement with huge bribes of illicit cash, to launder money with the keystroke of a computer. These forces are our enemies. We must face them together because no one can defeat them alone.

New Strategy of Security

To seize the opportunities and move against the threats of this new global era, we need a new strategy of security. Over the past five years, nations have begun to put that strategy in place through a new network of institutions and arrangements with distinct missions but a common purpose — to secure and strengthen the gains of democracy and free markets while turning back their enemies.

We see this strategy taking place on every continent — expanded military alliances like NATO, its Partnership for Peace, its partnerships with a democratic Russia and a democratic Ukraine; free-trade arrangements like the WTO [World Trade Organization] and the Global Information Technology Agreement; and the move toward free-trade areas by nations in the Americas, the Asia-Pacific region and elsewhere around the world; strong arms control regimes like the Chemical Weapons Convention and the Nonproliferation Treaty; multinational coalitions with zero tolerance for terrorism, corruption, crime and drug trafficking; binding international commitments to protect the environment and safeguard human rights.

Through this web of institutions and arrangements, nations are now setting the international ground rules for the 21st century, laying a foundation for security and prosperity for those who live within them, while isolating those who challenge them from the outside. This system will develop and endure only if those who follow the rules of peace and freedom fully reap their rewards. Only then will our people believe that they have a stake in supporting and shaping the emerging international system.

Core Missions

The United Nations must play a leading role in this effort, filling in the fault lines of the new global era. The core missions it has pursued during its first half-century will be just as relevant during the next half-century: the pursuit of peace and security, promoting human rights and moving people from poverty to dignity and prosperity through sustainable development.

Conceived in the caldron of war, the United Nations' first task must remain the pursuit of peace and security. For 50 years the U.N. has helped prevent world war and nuclear holocaust. Unfortunately, conflicts between nations and within nations had endured. From 1945 until today, they have cost 20 million lives. Just since the end of the Cold War, each year there have been more than 30 armed conflicts in which more than a thousand people have lost their lives, including, of course, a quarter of a million killed in the former Yugoslavia and more than half a million in Rwanda. Millions of personal tragedies the world over are a warning that we dare not be complacent or indifferent. Trouble in a far corner can become a plague on everyone's house.

People the world over cheered the hopeful developments in Northern Ireland, grieved over the innocent loss of life and the stalling of the peace process in the Middle East and longed for a resolution of the differences on the Korean Peninsula, or between Greece and Turkey, or between the great nations of India and Pakistan as they celebrate the 50th anniversaries of their birth.

The United Nations continues to keep many nations away from bloodshed: in El Salvador and Mozambique, in Haiti and Namibia, in Cyprus and in Bosnia, where so much remains to be done but can still be done because the bloodshed has ended.

The record of service of the United Nations has left a legacy of sacrifice. Just last week, we lost some of our finest sons and daughters in a crash of a U.N. helicopter in Bosnia. Five were Americans, five were Germans, one Polish and one British; all citizens of the world we are trying to make, each a selfless servant of peace. And the world is poorer for their passing.

At this very moment, the United Nations is keeping the peace in 16 countries, often in partnership with regional organizations like NATO, the OAS [Organization of American States], ASEAN [Association of Southeast Asian Nations] and ECOWAS [Economic Community of West African States], avoiding wider conflicts and even greater suffering. Our shared commitment to more realistic peacekeeping training for U.N. troops, a stronger role for civilian police, better integration between military and civilian agencies — all these will help the United Nations to meet these missions in the years ahead.

At the same time, we must improve the U.N.'s capabilities, after a conflict ends, to help peace become self-sustaining. The U.N. cannot build nations, but it can help nations to build themselves by fostering legitimate institutions of government, monitoring elections and laying a strong foundation for economic reconstruction.

This week, the Security Council will hold an unprecedented ministerial meeting on African security, which our secretary of State is proud to chair, and which President [Robert] Mugabe, chairman of the Organization of African Unity, will address. It will highlight the role the United Nations can and should play in preventing conflict on a continent where amazing progress toward demo-cracy and development is occurring alongside still too much discord, disease and distress.

In the 21st century, our security will be challenged increasingly by interconnected groups that traffic in terror, organized crime and drug smuggling. Already these international crime and drug syndicates drain up to $750 billion a year from legitimate economies. That sum exceeds the combined GNP of more than half the nations in this room. These groups threaten to undermine confidence in fragile new democracies and market economies that so many of you are working so hard to see endure.

Two years ago I called upon all the members of this Assembly to join in the fight against these forces. I applaud the U.N.'s recent resolution calling on its members to join the major international antiterrorism conventions, making clear the emerging international consensus that terrorism is always a crime and never a justifiable political act. As more countries sign on, terrorists will have fewer places to run or hide.

I also applaud the steps that members are taking to implement the declaration on crime and public security that the United States proposed two years ago, calling for increased cooperation to strengthen every citizen's right to basic safety, through cooperation on extradition and asset forfeiture, shutting down gray markets for guns and false documents, attacking corruption and bringing higher standards to law enforcement in new democracies.

The spread of these global criminal syndicates also has made all the more urgent our common quest to eliminate weapons of mass destruction. We cannot allow them to fall or to remain in the wrong hands. Here, too, the United Nations must lead, and it has, from UNSCOM [U.N. Special Commission] in Iraq to the International Atomic Energy Agency, now the most expansive global system ever devised to police arms control agreements.

When we met here last year, I was honored to be the first of 146 leaders to sign the Comprehensive Test Ban Treaty [CTBT], our commitment to end all nuclear tests for all time — the longest-sought, hardest-fought prize in the history of arms control. It will help to prevent the nuclear powers from developing more advanced and more dangerous weapons. It will limit the possibilities for other states to acquire such devices.

I am pleased to announce that today I am sending this crucial treaty to the United States Senate for ratification. Our common goal should be to enter the CTBT into force as soon as possible, and I ask for all of you to support that goal.

Defending Human Rights

The United Nations' second core mission must be to defend and extend universal human rights and to help democracy's remarkable gains endure. Fifty years ago the U.N.'s Universal Declaration of Human Rights stated the international community's conviction that people everywhere have the right to be treated with dignity, to give voice to their opinions, to choose their leaders; that these rights are universal — not American rights, not Western rights, not rights for the developed world only, but rights inherent in the humanity of people everywhere.

Over the past decade, these rights have become a reality for more people than ever — from Asia to Africa, from Europe to the Americas. In a world that links rich and poor, North and South, city and countryside, in an electronic network of shared images in real time, the more these universal rights take hold, the more people who do not enjoy them will demand them.

Armed with photocopiers and fax machines, e-mail and the Internet, supported by an increasingly important community of non-governmental organizations, they will make their demands known, spreading the spirit of freedom, which as the history of the last 10 years has shown us, ultimately will prevail.

The United Nations must be prepared to respond, not only by setting standards but by implementing them. To deter abuses, we should strengthen the U.N.'s field operations and early warning systems. To strengthen democratic institutions, the best guarantors of human rights, we must pursue programs to help new legal, parliamentary and electoral institutions get off the ground. To punish those responsible for crimes against humanity and to promote justice so that peace endures, we must maintain our strong support for the U.N.'s war crime tribunals and truth commissions. And before the century ends, we should establish a permanent international court to prosecute the most serious violations of humanitarian law.

The United States welcomes the Secretary General's efforts to strengthen the role of human rights within the U.N. system and his splendid choice of Mary Robinson as the new High Commissioner. We will work hard to make sure that she has the support she needs to carry out her mandate.

Finally, the United Nations has a special responsibility to make sure that as the global economy creates greater wealth, it does not produce growing disparities between the haves and have-nots, or threaten the global environment — our common home.

Progress is not yet everyone's partner. More than half the world's people are two days' walk from a telephone, literally disconnected from the global economy. Tens of millions lack the education, the training, the skills they need to make the most of their God-given abilities.

The men and women of the United Nations have expertise across the entire range of humanitarian and development activities. Every day they are making a difference. We see it in nourished bodies of once-starving children, in the full lives of those immunized against disease, in the bright eyes of children exposed to education through the rich storehouse of human knowledge, in refugees cared for and returned to their homes, in the health of rivers and lakes restored.

The United Nations must focus even more on shifting resources from handouts to hand-ups, on giving people the tools they need to make the most of their own destinies. Spreading ideas in education and technology, the true wealth of nations, is the best way to give people a chance to succeed.

And the United Nations must continue to lead in ensuring that today's progress does not come at tomorrow's expense. When the nations of the world gather again next December in Kyoto from the U.N. Climate Change Conference, all of us, developed and developing nations, must seize the opportunity to turn back the clock on greenhouse gas emissions so that we can leave a healthy planet to our children.

In these efforts, the U.N. no longer can and no longer need go it alone. Innovative partnerships with the private sector, NGOs [non-government organizations] and the international financial institutions can leverage its effectiveness many times over. Last week, a truly visionary American, Ted Turner, made a remarkable donation to strengthen the U.N.'s development and humanitarian programs. His gesture highlights the potential for partnership between the U.N. and the private sector in contributions of time, resources and expertise. And I hope more will follow his lead.

In this area and others, the Secretary General is aggressively pursuing the most far-reaching reform of the United Nations in its history — not to make the U.N. smaller as an end in itself, but to make it better. The United States strongly supports his leadership. We should pass the Secretary General's reform agenda this session.

U.N. Dues

On every previous occasion I have addressed this assembly, the issue of our country's dues has brought the commitment of the United States to the United Nations into question. The United States was a founder of the U.N. We are proud to be its host. We believe in its ideals. We continue to be, as we have been, its largest contributor. We are committed to seeing the United Nations succeed in the 21st century.

This year, for the first time since I have been president, we have an opportunity to put the questions of debts and dues behind us once and for all, and to put the United Nations on a sounder financial footing for the future. I have made it a priority to work with our Congress on comprehensive legislation that would allow us to pay off the bulk of our arrears and assure full financing of America's assessment in the years ahead. Our Congress' actions to solve this problem reflects a strong bipartisan commitment to the United Nations and to America's role within it.

At the same time, we look to member states to adopt a more equitable scale of assessment. Let me say that we also strongly support expanding the Security Council to give more countries a voice in the most important work of the U.N. In more equitably sharing responsibility for its successes, we can make the U.N. stronger and more democratic than it is today. I ask the General Assembly to act on these proposals this year so that we can move forward together.

At the dawn of a new century, so full of hope, but not free of peril, more than ever we need a United Nations where people of reason can work through shared problems and take action to combat them, where nations of good will can join in the struggle for freedom and prosperity, where we can shape a future of peace and progress and the preservation of our planet.

We have the knowledge, we have the intelligence, we have the energy, we have the resources for the work before us. We are building the necessary networks of cooperation. The great question remaining is whether we have the vision and the heart necessary to imagine a future that is different from the past, necessary to free ourselves from destructive patterns of relations with each other and within our own nations and live a future that is different.

A new century and a new millennium is upon us. We are literally present at the future, and it is the great gift that is our obligation to leave our children.

Thank you very much. ■

VETO MESSAGE

Clinton Outlines Reasons For Defense Veto Items

Following is the text of President Clinton's statement accompanying his Oct. 14 line-item veto of portions of the defense appropriations bill (HR 2266 — 105-56):

Over the past four and a half years, my administration has worked hard to cut the deficit and to ensure that our tax dollars are used wisely, carefully, and effectively. We have reduced the deficit by 85 percent even before enacting the historic balanced-budget legislation this past summer.

The line-item veto gives the president an important tool to save taxpayers money, avoid unnecessary government spending, and ensure that the national interest prevails over narrow interests. It will enable America to continue the fiscal discipline that has helped create our strong economic expansion. And by allowing a president to sign important legislation while canceling projects that do not meet important national goals, it will change the way Washington works.

America must — and will — continue to have the world's strongest military. We have an obligation to manage our defense budget with both national security and fiscal responsibility in mind. Every penny of our defense dollars should be used to sustain and strengthen the best-trained, the best-equipped, and the best-prepared armed forces in the world.

Today, for the third time, I am using the line-item veto to cancel 13 projects inserted by Congress into the Department of Defense's appropriations bill.

These cancellations will save the American taxpayer $144 million. This use of the line-item veto will help ensure that we focus on the projects that will best secure our strength in the years to come.

I canceled the projects because they were not requested in my Fiscal year 1998 budget, and because either they were not contained in our Future Years Defense Program or the Department of Defense determined that they would not make a significant contribution to U.S. military capability. In two cases, I canceled items that had broader policy implications for longstanding U.S. national security policy. I have been assured by the Secretary of Defense that none of the cancellations would undercut our national security or adversely affect the readiness of our forces or their operations in defense of our Nation.

As I said last week, I will continue to scrutinize other appropriation bills, using appropriate criteria in each instance, and I will exercise the line-item veto when warranted. ■

WILLIAM J. CLINTON
THE WHITE HOUSE
Oct. 14, 1997

VETO MESSAGE

Federal Retirement Provision Draws Line-Item Pen

Following is the text of a statement by President Clinton accompanying his line-item veto of provisions of the Treasury-Postal appropriations bill (HR 2378 — PL 105-61) on Oct. 16. Clinton's veto message, addressed to the leaders of Congress was brief:

In accordance with the Line Item Veto Act, I hereby cancel the dollar amount of discretionary budget authority, as specified in the attached report, contained in the Treasury and General Government Appropriations Act, 1998. I have determined that the cancellation of this amount will reduce the federal budget deficit, will not impair any essential government functions and will not harm the national interest. This letter, together with its attachment, constitutes a special message under section 1022 of the Congressional Budget and Impoundment Control Act of 1974, as amended.

CLINTON: I have used my line-item veto authority today to cancel a provision of the 1998 Treasury and General Government Appropriations Act that provides an open season for certain federal employees to switch retirement systems.

This line-item veto will save $854 million over five years by preventing a hastily conceived, undebated provision from becoming law. In addition, my action will keep agencies from having to reallocate another $1.3 billion in limited discretionary resources to pay higher retirement benefits, rather than spend it on other priorities such as pay increases, or essential agency needs.

I did not propose this provision in my 1998 budget, it was not the subject of public hearings and it was not considered by either the House or the Senate. Instead, it was added at the end of the legislative process, in a House-Senate conference committee. I believe that by canceling this provision, I am using my line-item veto authority in an appropriate manner.

I am committed to ensuring that the federal government can recruit and retain the quality individuals we need to administer federal programs. I will work with Congress to ensure that our federal civil servants are compensated fairly for the essential work they do for the American people. ■

WILLIAM J. CLINTON
THE WHITE HOUSE
Oct. 16, 1997

VETO MESSAGE

Clinton: Cuts Won't Harm Nation's Defense

Following are excerpts of remarks made by President Clinton just before he used his line-item veto authority Oct. 6 on provisions in the military construction bill (HR 2016 — PL 105-45). Clinton's veto message, addressed to Congress, was brief:

In accordance with the Line Item Veto Act, I hereby cancel the dollar amounts of discretionary budget authority, as specified in the attached reports, contained in the Military Construction Appropriations Act 1998. I have determined that the cancellation of these amounts will reduce the Federal budget deficit, will not impair any essential Government functions, and will not harm the national interest.

CLINTON: Good afternoon. Today we take another step on the long journey to bring fiscal discipline to Washington.

Over the past four-and-a-half years, we've worked hard to cut the deficit and to ensure that our tax dollars are used wisely, carefully and effectively. We have reduced the deficit by 85 percent even before the balanced-budget legislation passed. The balanced budget I signed into law this summer will extend our fiscal discipline well into the next century, keeping our economy strong.

But to follow through on the balanced budget, government must continue to live within its means, within the framework established in the agreement. The line-item veto, which all presidents of both parties had sought for more than a century, gives the president a vital new tool to ensure that our tax dollars are well spent, to stand up for the national interests over narrow interests.

Six days ago, I signed into law the Military Construction Appropriations Act, a $9.2 billion measure that is vital to our national defense. Today I'm using the line-item veto to cancel 38 projects inserted into that bill by the Congress that were not requested by the military, cannot make a contribution to our national defense in the coming year, and will not immediately benefit the quality of life and well-being of our men and women in uniform.

The use of the line-item veto saves taxpayers nearly $290 million and makes clear that the old rules have, in fact, changed.

I want to stress that I have retained most of the projects that were added by Congress to my own spending request. Congress plays a vital role in this process, and its judgment is entitled to respect and deference. Many of the projects I have chosen to cancel have merit, but should be considered in the future. This is simply the wrong time.

The projects I have canceled are all over the country, in the districts of lawmakers of both parties. These are tough calls involving real money and hard choices. I canceled the projects that met three neutral and objective criteria:

First, the Department of Defense concluded that these projects were not a priority at this time, after conducting its own rigorous, massive planning process. Judgments about our defense needs made by military professionals must continue to be the basis of our national defense budgeting.

Second, the projects I am canceling do not make an immediate contribution to the housing, education, recreation, child care, health or religious life of our men and women in uniform. Our fighting forces and their families make extraordinary sacrifices for us, and I have a longstanding commitment to improve their living conditions. I have, therefore, left untouched a number of extra projects not requested this year because they fulfill that commitment in enhancing the quality of life of our men and women in the service.

Third, I am canceling projects that would not have been built in fiscal year 1998 in any event; projects where the Department of Defense has not yet even done design work. In short, whether they're meritorious or not, they will not be built in the coming year in any event.

In canceling these projects, I was determined to do nothing that would undercut our national security. Every penny of our defense dollars should be used to maintain and improve the world's strongest system of national defense.

Also, under the balanced budget, however, we have the added obligation, again I say, to ensure that taxpayer funds are expended wisely. The use of the line-item veto here will ensure that we focus on those projects that will best secure our strength in the years to come. . . .

Thank you. ■

VETO MESSAGE

President Repeats Objections To Abortion Measure

Following is the text of President Clinton's Oct. 10 veto of the bill (HR 1122) to ban a certain kind of abortion procedure:

TO THE HOUSE OF REPRESENTATIVES:

I am returning herewith without my approval HR 1122, which would prohibit doctors from performing a certain kind of abortion. I am returning HR 1122 for exactly the same reasons I returned an earlier substantially identical version of this bill, HR 1833, last year. My veto message of April 10, 1996, fully explains my reasons for returning that bill and applies to HR 1122 as well. HR 1122 is a bill that is consistent neither with the Constitution nor sound public policy.

As I have stated on many occasions, I support the decision in *Roe v. Wade* protecting a woman's right to choose. Consistent with that decision, I have long opposed late-term abortions, and I continue to do so except in those instances necessary to save the life of a woman or prevent serious harm to her health. Unfortunately, HR 1122 does not contain an exception to the measure's ban that will adequately protect the lives and health of the small group of women in tragic circumstances who need an abortion performed at a late stage of pregnancy to avert death or serious injury.

I have asked the Congress repeatedly, for almost two years, to send me legislation that includes a limited exception for the small number of compelling cases where use of this procedure is necessary to avoid serious health consequences. When governor of Arkansas, I signed a bill into law that barred third-trimester abortions, with an appropriate exception for life or health. I would do so again, but only if the bill contains an exception for the rare cases where a woman faces death or serious injury. I believe the Congress should work in a bipartisan manner to fashion such legislation. ■

WILLIAM J. CLINTON
THE WHITE HOUSE
Oct. 10, 1997

TRADE AUTHORITY

Clinton Says He Is Still Confident Of Fast Track's Ultimate Passage

Following is a Federal News Service transcript of President Clinton's Nov. 10 remarks about fast track trade authority:

PRESIDENT CLINTON: Good morning.

Ladies and gentlemen, as you know, we have postponed the vote in the House of Representatives on renewing fast-track authority to strengthen our ability to expand exports through new agreements. I am disappointed, of course, that this step was necessary, because we worked very hard and we are very close to having the requisite number of votes. But early this morning, it became clear to me that, if the matter were taken to a vote, there was a substantial chance that we would not get the votes necessary to pass the bill.

Let me begin by saying a profound word of thanks to Speaker [Newt] Gingrich [R-Ga.], and to the leadership team in the House, who worked with us on this; and on the Democratic side, to Reps. [Vic] Fazio [D-Calif.] and [Robert T.] Matsui [D-Calif.], and the others who were helping them. This was a partnership for the national interest, and I am very grateful for what they are doing.

I think most of you know what happened. We have been having a big debate in our party for several years on the question of trade and its role in our economic future. Even though we clearly have a majority of the Democratic mayors and governors, and we had a majority in the Senate, we don't have a majority in the House who agree with the position that I have taken. We worked hard to overcome their objections, and we didn't succeed. And because we didn't have more Democratic votes, we then had to get a bigger share of the Republican vote. Now that brought into play the controversy over international family planning and the so-called Mexico City language. Had we been able to resolve that, I think we could have gotten enough votes on the Republican side, to go with the Democrats' votes we had, to pass the bill. Clearly, I think we could have. But we simply were not able to do that.

And I say that without undue criticism of anyone. The people who took the position that they could not give their votes to the fast-track legislation believe very deeply, in principle, that we should change our family-planning funding. I, on the other hand, believe that it would have been wrong for me to mix the two issues and to compromise what I believe in principle. And in the end, this matter could not go forward because of that disagreement.

But what we're going to do now is to regroup a little bit and find a way to succeed. And I think we'll be able to do that.

I also know, from my extensive work now in the House, that there are a large number of House members who are interested in trying to find some constructive resolution of this matter. And I think we may well be able to do that.

I expect that we will successfully press forward with this issue in this Congress, and at the appropriate time. So I'm — I'm not particularly concerned about the long run. I think we'll be able to prevail.

Today, let me say again, I think it's important that all of us do more to make the case. This country is in good shape. We have 13-and-a-half million more jobs. We have a 4.7 percent unemployment rate. We know that a third of that growth has come from trade. We know that the countries that are willing to enter into agreements with us in the kinds of areas of agreement that we need to push on a regional and worldwide basis will lower barriers more in other countries than they will in our country.

But we also know that the benefits of trade are often not seen as directly tied to trade when a plant expands or a new contract is signed. And whenever a plant closes down, generally it's easy to tie it to trade, whether trade had anything to do with it or not. So we have a — we have some more work to do. But on balance, based on where we are now, I'm quite optimistic that we will ultimately prevail in this Congress.

And I'm very pleased, again, with the good partnership that we had with Speaker Gingrich and the House leadership team and with the Democrats who helped us. And so we're just going to go forward.

I think it's clear to everybody that America's leadership in the world depends upon America's continuing economic leadership. And this, therefore, has to be only a temporary obstacle, because in the end we always find out a way to do what's right for America, to maintain our leadership and maintain our economic growth. ■

CQ

Appendix E

PUBLIC LAWS

Public Laws

PL 105-1 (H J Res 25) Make technical corrections to the Omnibus Consolidated Appropriations Act of 1997 (PL 104-208). Introduced by LIVINGSTON, R-La., Jan. 9, 1997. House passed Jan. 9. Senate passed Jan. 21. President signed Feb. 3, 1997.

PL 105-2 (HR 668) Amend the Internal Revenue Code of 1986 to reinstate the Airport and Airway Trust Fund excise taxes. Introduced by ARCHER, R-Texas, Feb. 11, 1997. House Ways and Means reported Feb. 13 (H Rept 105-5). House passed, under suspension of the rules, Feb. 26. Senate passed Feb. 27. President signed Feb. 28, 1997.

PL 105-3 (H J Res 36) Approve the presidential finding that the limitation on obligations imposed by section 518A(a) of the Foreign Operations Export Financing and Related Programs Appropriations Act of 1997, is having a negative impact on the proper functioning of the population planning program. Introduced by ARMEY, R-Texas, Feb. 4, 1997. House appropriations discharged Feb. 10. House passed Feb. 13. Senate passed Feb. 25. President signed Feb. 28, 1997.

PL 105-4 (HR 499) Designate the facility of the United States Postal Service under construction at 7411 Barlite Blvd. in San Antonio, Texas, as the "Frank M. Tejeda Post Office Building." Introduced by BONILLA, R-Texas, Feb. 4, 1997. House passed, under suspension of the rules, Feb. 5. Senate passed Feb. 26. President signed March 3, 1997.

PL 105-5 (S J Res 5) Wave certain provisions of the Trade Act of 1974 relating to the appointment of the United States Trade Representative. Introduced by ROTH, R-Del., Jan. 21, 1997. Senate Finance reported Feb. 3 (no written report). Senate passed March 5. House passed, under suspension of the rules, March 11. President signed March 17, 1997.

PL 105-6 (HR 924) Amend Title 18, U.S. Code, to give further assurance to victims of crime of their right to attend and observe the trials of those accused of the crime. Introduced by McCOLLUM, R-Fla., March 5, 1997. House Judiciary reported, amended, March 17 (H Rept 105-28). House passed, as amended, under suspension of the rules, March 18. Senate passed March 19. President signed March 19, 1997.

PL 105-7 (HR 514) Permit the waiver of District of Columbia residency requirements for certain employees of the Office of the Inspector General of the District of Columbia. Introduced by DAVIS, R-Va., Feb. 4, 1997. House Government Reform and Oversight reported, amended, March 17 (H Rept 105-29). House passed, as amended, under suspension of the rules, March 18. Senate passed March 20. President signed March 25, 1997.

PL 105-8 (S 410) Extend the effective date of the Investment Advisers Supervision Coordination Act. Introduced by D'AMATO, R-N.Y., March 6, 1997. Senate passed March 12. House passed March 18. President signed March 31, 1997.

PL 105-9 (HR 412) Approve a settlement agreement between the Bureau of Reclamation and the Oroville-Tonasket Irrigation District. Introduced by HASTINGS, R-Wash., Jan. 9, 1997. House Resources reported, amended, March 10 (H Rept 105-8). House passed, amended, March 18. Senate passed April 8. President signed April 14, 1997.

PL 105-10 (HR 785) Designate the J. Phil Campbell Sr. Natural Resource Conservation Center. Introduced by NORWOOD, R-Ga., Feb. 13, 1997. House Agriculture reported March 20 (H Rept 105-36). House passed, under suspension of the rules, April 8. Senate passed April 10. President signed April 24, 1997.

PL 105-11 (HR 1225) Make a technical correction to Title 28, U.S. Code, relating to jurisdiction for lawsuits against terrorist states. Introduced by HYDE, R-Ill., April 8, 1997. House Judiciary reported April 10 (H Rept 105-48). House passed, under suspension of the rules, April 15. Senate passed April 24. President signed April 25, 1997.

PL 105-12 (HR 1003) Clarify federal law with respect to restricting the use of federal funds in support of assisted suicide. Introduced by HALL, D-Texas, March 11, 1997. House Commerce reported, amended, April 8 (H Rept 105-46, Part 1). House passed, as amended, under suspension of the rules, April 10. Senate passed April 16. President signed April 18, 1997.

PL 105-13 (HR 1001) Extend the term of appointment of certain members of the Prospective Payment Assessment Commission and the Physician Payment Review Commission. Introduced by THOMAS, R-Calif., March 10, 1997. House Ways and Means reported April 10 (H Rept 105-49, Part 1). House Commerce reported April 14 (H Rept 105-49, Part 2). House passed, under suspension of the rules, April 15. Senate passed April 30. President signed May 14, 1997.

PL 105-14 (S 305) Authorize the president to award a gold medal on behalf of the Congress to Francis Albert "Frank" Sinatra in recognition of his outstanding and enduring contributions through his entertainment career and humanitarian activities. Introduced by D'AMATO, R-N.Y., Feb. 12, 1997. Senate passed Feb. 26. House passed April 29. President signed May 14, 1997.

PL 105-15 (HR 968) Amend Title XVIII and XIX of the Social Security Act to permit a waiver of the prohibition of offering nurse aide training and competency evaluation programs in certain nursing facilities. Introduced by EHRLICH, R-Md., March 6, 1997. House Ways and Means reported, amended, March 13 (H Rept 105-23, Part 1). House Commerce reported, amended, March 18 (H Rept 105-23, Part 2). House passed, amended, April 8. Senate passed April 30. President signed May 15, 1997.

PL 105-16 (HR 1650) Authorize the president to award a gold medal on behalf of the Congress to Mother Teresa of Calcutta in recognition of her outstanding and enduring contributions through humanitarian and charitable activities. Introduced by CHRISTENSEN, R-Neb., May 16, 1997. House passed, under suspension of the rules, May 20. Senate passed May 21. President signed June 2, 1997.

PL 105-17 (HR 5) Amend the Individuals with Disabilities Education Act to reauthorize and make improvements to that

Act. Introduced by GOODLING, R-Pa., Jan. 7, 1997. House Education and the Workforce reported, amended, May 13 (H Rept 105-95). House passed as amended, under suspension of the rules, May 13. Senate passed May 14. President signed June 4, 1997.

PL 105-18 (HR 1871) Make emergency supplemental appropriations for recovery from natural disasters, and for overseas peacekeeping efforts, including those in Bosnia, for the fiscal year ending Sept. 30, 1997. Introduced by LIVINGSTON, R-La., June 12, 1997. House Appropriations and Budget discharged. House passed June 12. Senate passed June 12. President signed June 12, 1997.

PL 105-19 (S 543) Provide certain protections to volunteers, nonprofit organizations and governmental entities in lawsuits based on the activities of volunteers. Introduced by COVERDELL, R-Ga., April 9, 1997. Senate passed, amended, May 1. House Judiciary discharged. House passed, with amendment, May 21. Senate agreed to House amendment May 21. President signed June 18, 1997.

PL 105-20 (HR 956) Amend the National Narcotics Leadership Act of 1988 to establish and encourage local communities that first demonstrate a comprehensive, long-term commitment to reduce substance abuse among youth. Introduced by PORTMAN, R-Ohio, March 5, 1997. House Government Reform and Oversight reported, amended, May 20 (H Rept 105-105, Part 1). House Commerce discharged. House passed as amended, under suspension of the rules, May 22. Senate passed June 18. President signed June 27, 1997.

PL 105-21 (H J Res 32) Consent to certain amendments enacted by the legislature of the state of Hawaii to the Hawaiian Homes Commission Act of 1920. Introduced by ABERCROMBIE, D-Hawaii, Jan. 21, 1997. House Resources reported March 11 (H Rept 105-16). House passed, under suspension of the rules, March 11. Senate Energy and Natural Resources reported May 16 (S Rept 105-19). Senate passed June 12. President signed June 27, 1997.

PL 105-22 (S 342) Extend certain privileges, exemptions and immunities to Hong Kong Economic and Trade Offices. Introduced by THOMAS, R-Wyo., Feb. 24, 1997. Senate Foreign Relations reported May 8 (no written report). Senate passed May 20. House passed, under suspension of the rules, June 17. President signed June 27, 1997.

PL 105-23 (HR 363) Amend section 2118 of the Energy Policy Act of 1992 to extend the Electric and Magnetic Fields Research and Public Information Dissemination Program. Introduced by TOWNS, D-N.Y., Jan. 7, 1997. House Commerce reported, amended, April 21 (H Rept 105-60, Part 1). House Science reported, amended, April 21 (H Rept 105-60, Part 2). House passed, as amended, under suspension of the rules, April 29. Senate Energy and Natural Resources reported June 12 (S Rept 105-27). Senate passed June 20. President signed July 3, 1997.

PL 105-24 (HR 1306) Amend the Federal Deposit Insurance Act to clarify the applicability of host state laws to any branch in such state of an out-of-state bank. Introduced by ROUKEMA, R-N.J., April 10, 1997. House passed, amended, under suspension of the rules, May 21. Senate passed with amendments June 12. House agreed to Senate amendments June 24. President signed July 3, 1997.

PL 105-25 (HR 1553) Amend the President John F. Kennedy Assassination Records Collection Act of 1992 to extend the authorization of the Assassination Records Review Board until Sept. 30, 1998. Introduced by BURTON, R-Ind., May 8, 1997. House Government Reform and Oversight reported June 19 (H Rept 105-138, Part 1). House Judiciary discharged. House passed, under suspension of the rules, June 23. Senate passed June 25. President signed July 3, 1997.

PL 105-26 (HR 1902) Immunize donations made in the form of charitable gift annuities and charitable remainder trusts from the antitrust laws and state laws similar to the antitrust laws. Introduced by HYDE, R-Ill., June 17, 1997. House Judiciary reported June 23 (H Rept 105-146). House passed, under suspension of the rules, June 23. Senate passed June 24. President signed July 3, 1997.

PL 105-27 (HR 173) Amend the Federal Property and Administrative Services Act of 1949 to authorize donation of surplus federal law enforcement canines to their handlers. Introduced by GALLEGLY, R-Calif., Jan. 7, 1997. House passed, amended, under suspension of the rules, April 16. Senate Governmental Affairs reported June 26 (no written report). Senate passed June 27. President signed July 18, 1997.

PL 105-28 (HR 649) Amend sections of the Department of Energy Organization Act that are obsolete or inconsistent with other statutes and to repeal a related section of the Federal Energy Administration Act of 1974. Introduced by SCHAEFER, R-Colo., Feb. 6, 1997. House Commerce reported June 11 (H Rept 105-11). House passed, under suspension of the rules, March 11. Senate Energy and Natural Resources reported March 12 (S Rept 105-26). Senate passed June 27. President signed July 18, 1997.

PL 105-29 (S J Res 29) Direct the secretary of the Interior to design and construct a permanent addition to the Franklin D. Roosevelt Memorial in Washington, D.C. Introduced by INOUYE, D-Hawaii, May 1, 1997. Senate passed May 1. House Resources reported July 8 (H Rept 105-167). House passed, under suspension of the rules, July 8. President signed July 24, 1997.

PL 105-30 (HR 1901) Clarify that the protections of the Federal Tort Claims Act apply to the members and personnel of the National Gambling Impact Study Commission. Introduced by HYDE, R-Ill., June 17, 1997. House Judiciary reported June 23 (H Rept 105-145). House passed, under suspension of the rules, June 23. Senate passed July 9. President signed July 25, 1997.

PL 105-31 (HR 2018) Waive temporarily the Medicaid enrollment composition rule for the Better Health Plan of Amherst, N.Y. Introduced by PAXON, R-N.Y., June 24, 1997. House Commerce reported, amended, July 8 (H Rept 105-165). House passed, as amended, under suspension of the rules, July 8. Senate passed July 11. President signed July 25, 1997.

PL 105-32 (H J Res 90) Waive certain enrollment requirements with respect to two specified bills of the 105th Congress. Introduced by DIAZ-BALART, R-Fla., July 31, 1997. House passed July 31. Senate passed July 31. President signed Aug. 1, 1997.

PL 105-33 (HR 2015) Provide for reconciliation pursuant to subsections (b)(1) and (c) of section 105 of the concurrent resolution on the budget for fiscal year 1998 (H Con Res 84) to balance the federal budget. Introduced by KASICH, R-Ohio, June 23, 1997. House Budget reported June 24 (H Rept 105-149). House passed, amended, June 25. Senate passed, with amendment, June 25. Conference report filed in the House July 29 (H Rept 105-217). House agreed to conference report July 30. Senate cleared July 31. President signed Aug. 5, 1997.

PL 105-34 (HR 2014) Provide for reconciliation pursuant to subsections (b)(2) and (d) of section 105 of the concurrent resolution on the budget for fiscal year 1998 (H Con Res 84) to reduce taxes. Introduced by KASICH, R-Ohio, June 23, 1997. House Budget reported June 24 (H Rept 105-148). House passed, amended, June 26. Senate passed, with amendment, June 27. Conference report filed in the House July 30 (H Rept 105-220). House agreed to conference report July 31. Senate cleared July 31. President signed Aug. 5, 1997.

PL 105-35 (HR 1226) Amend the Internal Revenue Code of 1986 to prevent the unauthorized inspection of tax returns or tax return information. Introduced by ARCHER, R-Texas, April 8, 1997. House Ways and Means reported, amended, April 14 (H Rept 105-51). House passed, as amended, under suspension of the rules, April 15. Senate passed July 23. President signed Aug. 5, 1997.

PL 105-36 (HR 709) Reauthorize and amend the National Geologic Mapping Act of 1992. Introduced by CUBIN, R-Wyo., Feb. 12, 1997. House Resources reported, amended, March 11 (H Rept 105-17). House passed, as amended, under suspension of the rules, March 11. Senate Energy and Natural Resources discharged. Senate passed July 23. President signed Aug. 5, 1997.

PL 105-37 (S 430) Amend the Act of June 20, 1910, to protect the permanent trust funds of the state of New Mexico from erosion due to inflation and modify the basis on which distributions are made from those funds. Introduced by DOMENICI, R-N.M., March 12, 1997. Energy and Natural Resources reported May 15 (S Rept 105-18). Senate passed May 21. House passed, under suspension of the rules, July 28. President signed Aug. 7, 1997.

PL 105-38 (S 670) Amend the Immigration and Nationality Technical Corrections Act of 1994 to eliminate the special transition rule for issuance of a certificate of citizenship for certain children born outside the United States. Introduced by ABRAHAM, R-Mich., April 30, 1997. Senate Judiciary reported May 8 (no written report). Senate passed May 14. House Judiciary discharged. House passed July 28. President signed Aug. 8, 1997.

PL 105-39 (HR 1198) Direct the secretary of the Interior to convey certain land to Grants Pass, Ore. Introduced by SMITH, R-Ore., March 20, 1997. House Resources reported, amended, July 8 (H Rept 105-166). House passed, amended, under suspension of the rules, July 8. Senate Energy and Natural Resources reported July 30 (no written report). Senate passed July 31. President signed Aug. 11, 1997.

PL 105-40 (HR 1944) Provide for a land exchange involving the Warner Canyon Ski Area and other land in Oregon. Introduced by SMITH, R-Ore., June 17, 1997. House Resources reported July 21 (H Rept 105-193). House passed, under suspension of the rules, July 22. Senate Energy and Natural Resources reported July 30 (no written report). Senate passed July 31. President signed Aug. 11, 1997.

PL 105-41 (HR 1585) Allow postal patrons to contribute to funding for breast cancer research through the voluntary purchase of certain specially issued U.S. postage stamps. Introduced by MOLINARI, R-N.Y., May 13, 1997. House passed, amended, under suspension of the rules, July 22. Senate passed July 24. President signed Aug. 13, 1997.

PL 105-42 (HR 408) Amend the Marine Mammal Protection Act of 1972 to support the International Dolphin Conservation Program in the eastern tropical Pacific Ocean. Introduced by GILCHREST, R-Md., Jan. 9, 1997. House Resources reported, amended, April 24 (H Rept 105-74, Part 1). House Ways and Means reported May 1 (H Rept 105-74, Part 2). House passed, amended, May 21. Senate Commerce, Science and Transportation discharged. Senate passed, with amendment, July 30. House agreed to Senate amendment July 31. President signed Aug. 15, 1997.

PL 105-43 (HR 1866) Continue favorable treatment for need-based educational aid under the antitrust laws. Introduced by SMITH, R-Texas, June 11, 1997. House Judiciary reported June 23 (H Rept 105-144). House passed, under suspension of the rules, June 23. Senate passed, with amendment, July 30. House agreed to Senate amendment, under suspension of the rules, Sept. 8. President signed Sept. 17, 1997.

PL 105-44 (HR 63) Designate the reservoir created by Trinity Dam in the Central Valley project in California as "Trinity Lake." Introduced by HERGER, R-Calif., Jan. 7, 1997. House Resources reported March 10 (H Rept 105-9). House passed, under suspension of the rules, March 11. Senate Energy and Natural Resources reported Sept. 2 (S Rept 105-70). Senate passed Sept. 16. President signed Sept. 30, 1997.

PL 105-45 (HR 2016) Make appropriations for military construction, family housing and base realignment and closure for the Department of Defense for the fiscal year ending Sept. 30, 1998. Introduced by PACKARD, R-Calif., June 24, 1997. House Appropriations reported June 24 (H Rept 105-150). House passed July 8. Senate Appropriations reported, amended, July 17 (S Rept 105-52). Senate passed, with amendments, July 22. Conference report filed in the House Sept. 9 (H Rept 105-247). House agreed to conference report Sept. 16. Senate cleared Sept. 17. President signed Sept. 30, 1997. President exercised line-item-veto authority (H Doc 105-147), Oct. 6, 1997.

PL 105-46 (H J Res 94) A joint resolution making continuing appropriations for fiscal year 1998. Introduced by LIVINGSTON, R-La., Sept. 26, 1997. House Appropriations discharged. House passed Sept. 29. Senate passed Sept. 30. President signed Sept. 30, 1997.

PL 105-47 (S 910) Authorize appropriations for carrying out the Earthquake Hazards Reduction Act of 1977 for fiscal years 1998 and 1999. Introduced by FRIST, R-Tenn.,

June 16, 1997. Senate Commerce, Science and Transportation reported, amended, July 30 (S Rept 105-59). Senate passed, amended, July 31. House passed, under suspension of the rules, Sept. 16. President signed Oct. 1, 1997.

PL 105-48 (S 1211) Provide permanent authority for the administration of au pair programs. Introduced by HELMS, R-N.C., Sept. 24. Senate Foreign Relations reported Sept. 24 (no written report). Senate passed Sept. 25. House passed, under suspension of the rules, Sept. 29. President signed Oct. 1, 1997.

PL 105-49 (HR 111) Authorize the secretary of Agriculture to convey a parcel of unused agricultural land in Dos Palos, Calif., to the Dos Palos Ag Boosters for use as a farm school. Introduced by CONDIT, D-Calif., Jan. 7, 1997. House Agriculture reported March 20 (H Rept 105-34). House passed, amended, under suspension of the rules, April 16. Senate Agriculture, Nutrition, and Forestry discharged. Senate passed Sept. 23. President signed Oct. 6, 1997.

PL 105-50 (HR 680) Amend the Federal Property and Administrative Services Act of 1949 to authorize the transfer to states of surplus personal property for donation to nonprofit providers of necessaries to impoverished families and individuals. Introduced by HAMILTON, D-Ind., Feb. 11, 1997. House passed, amended, under suspension of the rules April 29. Senate Governmental Affairs reported June 26 (no written report). Senate passed, with amendments, July 9. House agreed to Senate amendments Sept. 18. President signed Oct. 6, 1997.

PL 105-51 (HR 2248) Authorize the president to award a gold medal on behalf of the Congress to Ecumenical Patriarch Bartholomew in recognition of his outstanding and enduring contributions toward religious understanding and peace. Introduced by LEACH, R-Iowa, July 24, 1997. House Banking and Financial Services discharged. House passed Sept. 17. Senate passed Sept. 24. President signed Oct. 6, 1997.

PL 105-52 (HR 2443) Designate the federal building at 601 Fourth Street, N.W., in the District of Columbia, as the “Federal Bureau of Investigation, Washington Field Office Memorial Building,” in honor of William H. Christian Jr., Martha Dixon Martinez, Michael J. Miller, Anthony Palmisano and Edwin R. Woodriffe. Introduced by NORTON, D-D.C., Sept. 9, 1997. House Transportation and Infrastructure discharged. House passed Sept. 18. Senate Environment and Public Works reported Sept. 24 (no written report). Senate passed Sept. 24. President signed Oct. 6, 1997.

PL 105-53 (S 996) Provide for the authorization of appropriations in each fiscal year for arbitration in U.S. district courts. Introduced by GRASSLEY, R-Iowa, July 8, 1997. Senate Judiciary discharged. Senate passed, amended, July 31. House passed, with amendments, under suspension of the rules, Sept. 23. Senate agreed to House amendments Sept. 30. President signed Oct. 6, 1997.

PL 105-54 (S 1198) Amend the Immigration and Nationality Act to extend the special immigrant religious worker program; to amend the Illegal Immigration Reform and Immigrant Responsibility Act of 1996 to extend the deadline for designation of an effective date for paperwork changes in the employer sanctions program; and to require the secretary of State to waive or reduce the fee for application and issuance of a non-immigrant visa for aliens coming to the United States for certain charitable purposes. Introduced by ABRAHAM, R-Mich., Sept. 18. Senate passed, amended, Sept. 18. House passed, with amendments, under suspension of the rules, Oct. 1. Senate agreed to House amendments Oct. 1. President signed Oct. 6, 1997.

PL 105-55 (HR 2209) Make appropriations for the legislative branch for the fiscal year ending Sept. 30, 1998. Introduced by WALSH, R-N.Y., July 22. House Appropriations reported July 22 (H Rept 105-196). House passed, amended, July 28. Senate passed, with amendment, July 29. Conference report filed in the House Sept. 18 (H Rept 105-254). House agreed to conference report Sept. 24. Senate agreed to conference report Sept. 24. President signed Oct. 7, 1997.

PL 105-56 (HR 2266) Make appropriations for the Department of Defense for the fiscal year ending Sept. 30, 1998. Introduced by YOUNG, R-Fla., July 25, 1997. House Appropriations reported July 25 (H Rept 105-206). House passed, amended, July 29. Senate passed, with amendment, July 29. Conference report filed in the House Sept. 23 (H Rept 105-265). House agreed to conference report Sept. 25. Senate agreed to conference report Sept. 25. President signed Oct. 8, 1997. President exercised line-item veto authority (H Doc 105-155), Oct. 14, 1997.

PL 105-57 (HR 1420) Amend the National Wildlife Refuge System Administration Act of 1966 to improve the management of the National Wildlife Refuge System. Introduced by YOUNG, R-Alaska, April 23, 1997. House Resources reported April 23 (H Rept 105-106). House passed, amended, under suspension of the rules June 3. Senate passed, with amendments, Sept. 10. House agreed to Senate amendments, under suspension of the rules, Sept. 23. President signed Oct. 9, 1997.

PL 105-58 (S 871) To establish the Oklahoma City National Memorial as a unit of the National Park System and to designate the Oklahoma City Memorial Trust. Introduced by NICKLES, R-Okla., June 10, 1997. Senate Energy and Natural Resources reported July 30 (S Rept 105-71). Senate passed July 31. House passed, with amendment, under suspension of the rules, Sept. 23. Senate agreed to House amendment Sept. 25. President signed Oct. 9, 1997.

PL 105-59 (HR 394) Provide for the release of the reversionary interest held by the United States in certain property located in the county of Iosco, Mich. Introduced by BARCIA, D-Mich., Jan. 9, 1997. House Agriculture reported March 20 (H Rept 105-35). House passed, under suspension of the rules, April 8. Senate Agriculture, Nutrition, and Forestry discharged. Senate passed, Sept. 30. President signed Oct. 10, 1997.

PL 105-60 (HR 1948) Provide for the exchange of lands within Admiralty Island National Monument. Introduced by YOUNG, R-Alaska, June 17, 1997. House Resources reported, amended, Sept. 23 (H Rept 105-261). House passed, amended, under suspension of the rules, Sept. 23. Senate passed Sept. 30. President signed Oct. 10, 1997.

PL 105-61 (HR 2378) Make appropriations for the Treasury Department, the Postal Service, the Executive Office of the President, and certain independent agencies, for the fiscal year ending Sept. 30, 1998. Introduced by KOLBE, R-Ariz., Sept. 3, 1997. House Appropriations reported draft bill Aug. 5 (H Rept 105-240, Parts 1, 2 and 3). House passed, amended, Sept. 17. Senate passed, with amendment, Sept. 17. Conference report filed in the House Sept. 29 (H Rept 105-284). House agreed to conference report Sept. 30. Senate agreed to conference report Oct. 1. President signed Oct. 10, 1997. President exercised line-item veto authority (H Doc 105-156), Oct. 16, 1997.

PL 105-62 (HR 2203) Make appropriations for energy and water development for the fiscal year ending Sept. 30, 1998. Introduced by McDADE, R-Pa., July 21, 1997. House Appropriations reported July 21 (H Rept 105-190). House passed, amended, July 25. Senate passed, with amendment, July 28. Conference report filed in the House Sept. 26 (H Rept 105-271). House agreed to conference report Sept. 30. Senate agreed to conference report Sept. 30. President signed Oct. 13, 1997. President exercised line-item-veto authority (H Doc 105-157), Oct. 16, 1997.

PL 105-63 (S 1000) To designate the U.S. courthouse at 500 State Ave. in Kansas City, Kan., as the "Robert J. Dole United States Courthouse." Introduced by ROBERTS, R-Kan., July 10, 1997. Senate Environment and Public Works reported July 24 (no written report). Senate passed July 25. House passed, under suspension of the rules, Sept. 23. President signed Oct. 22, 1997.

PL 105-64 (H J Res 97) Make further continuing appropriations for the fiscal year 1998. Introduced by LIVINGSTON, R-La., Oct. 21, 1997. House passed Oct. 22. Senate passed Oct. 23. President signed Oct. 23, 1997.

PL 105-65 (HR 2158) Make appropriations for the Departments of Veterans Affairs and Housing and Urban Development, and for various independent agencies, commissions, corporations and offices for the fiscal year ending Sept. 30, 1998. Introduced by LEWIS, R-Calif., July 11, 1997. House Appropriations reported July 11 (H Rept 105-175). House passed, amended, July 16. Senate passed, with amendment, July 22. Conference report filed in the House Oct. 6 (H Rept 105-297). House agreed to conference report Oct. 8. Senate agreed to conference report Oct. 9. President signed Oct. 27, 1997. President exercised line-item veto authority (H Doc 105-167), Nov. 1, 1997.

PL 105-66 (HR 2169) Make appropriations for the Department of Transportation and related agencies for the fiscal year ending Sept. 30, 1998. Introduced by WOLF, R-Va., July 16, 1997. House Appropriations reported July 16 (H Rept 105-188). House passed, amended, July 23. Senate passed, with amendment, July 30. Conference report filed in the House Oct. 7 (H Rept 105-313). House agreed to conference report Oct. 9. Senate agreed to conference report Oct. 9. President signed Oct. 27, 1997. President exercised line-item veto authority (H Doc 105-168), Nov. 1, 1997.

PL 105-67 (H J Res 75) A joint resolution to confer status as an honorary veteran of the U.S. Armed Forces on Leslie Townes "Bob" Hope. Introduced by STUMP, R-Ariz., April 30, 1997. House Veterans' Affairs reported June 3 (H Rept 105-109). House passed, under suspension of the rules, June 3. Senate Veterans' Affairs reported Sept. 4 (no written report). Senate passed Sept. 9. President signed Oct. 30, 1997.

PL 105-68 (H J Res 101) A joint resolution making further continuing appropriations for the fiscal year 1998. Introduced by LIVINGSTON, R-La., Nov. 7, 1997. House Appropriations discharged. House passed Nov. 7. Senate passed Nov. 7. President signed Nov. 7, 1997.

PL 105-69 (H J Res 104) A joint resolution making further continuing appropriations for the fiscal year 1998. Introduced by LIVINGSTON, R-La., Nov. 9, 1997. House Appropriations discharged. House passed Nov. 9. Senate passed Nov. 9. President signed Nov. 9, 1997.

PL 105-70 (HR 2013) Designate the facility of the U.S. Postal Service located at 551 Kingstown Road in South Kingstown, R.I., as the "David B. Champagne Post Office Building." Introduced by WEYGAND, D-R.I., June 23, 1997. House passed, under suspension of the rules, Oct. 21. Senate passed Oct. 24. President signed Nov. 10, 1997.

PL 105-71 (H J Res 105) A joint resolution making further continuing appropriations for the fiscal year 1998. Introduced by LIVINGSTON, R-La., Nov. 10, 1997. House Appropriations discharged. House passed Nov. 10 (legislative day of Nov. 9). Senate passed Nov. 10. President signed Nov. 10, 1997.

PL 105-72 (S 1227) Amend Title I of the Employee Retirement Income Security Act of 1974 to clarify treatment of investment managers under such title. Introduced by JEFFORDS, R-Vt., Sept. 26, 1997. Senate passed Sept. 26. House passed, under suspension of the rules, Oct. 28. President signed Nov. 10, 1997.

PL 105-73 (HR 2464) Amend the Immigration and Nationality Act to exempt internationally adopted children under age 10 from the immunization requirement. Introduced by McCOLLUM, R-Fla., Sept. 11, 1997. House Judiciary reported, amended, Oct. 1 (H Rept 105-289). House passed, amended, under suspension of the rules, Oct. 21. Senate passed Nov. 4. President signed Nov. 12, 1997.

PL 105-74 (S 587) Require the secretary of the Interior to exchange certain lands located in Hinsdale County, Colo. Introduced by CAMPBELL, R-Colo., April 16, 1997. Senate Energy and Natural Resources reported, amended, Oct. 6 (S Rept 105-96). Senate passed, amended, Oct. 9. House passed, under suspension of the rules, Nov. 4. President signed Nov. 12, 1997.

PL 105-75 (S 588) Provide for the expansion of the Eagles Nest Wilderness within the Arapaho National Forest and the White River National Forest, Colo., to include land known as the Slate Creek Addition. Introduced by CAMPBELL, R-Colo., April 16, 1997. Senate Energy and Natural Resources reported, amended, Oct. 6 (S Rept 105-97). Senate passed, amended, Oct. 9. House passed, under suspension of the rules, Nov. 4. President signed Nov. 12, 1997.

PL 105-76 (S 589) Provide for a boundary adjustment and land conveyance involving the Raggeds Wilderness, White River National Forest, Colo., to correct the effects of earlier erroneous land surveys. Introduced by CAMP-

BELL, R-Colo., April 16, 1997. Senate Energy and Natural Resources reported, amended, Oct. 6 (S Rept 105-98). Senate passed, amended, Oct. 9. House passed, under suspension of the rules, Nov. 4. President signed Nov. 12, 1997.

PL 105-77 (S 591) Transfer the Dillon Ranger District in the Arapaho National Forest to the White River National Forest in Colorado. Introduced by CAMPBELL, R-Colo., April 16, 1997. Senate Energy and Natural Resources reported, amended, Oct. 6 (S Rept 105-99). Senate passed, amended, Oct. 9. House passed, under suspension of the rules, Nov. 4. President signed Nov. 12, 1997.

PL 105-78 (HR 2264) Make appropriations for the departments of Labor, Health and Human Services, and Education, and related agencies for the fiscal year ending Sept. 30, 1998. Introduced by PORTER, R-Ill., July 25, 1997. House Appropriations reported July 25 (H Rept 105-205). House passed, amended, Sept. 17. Senate passed, with amendment, Sept. 17. Conference report filed in the House Nov. 7 (H Rept 105-390). House agreed to conference report Nov. 7. Senate cleared Nov. 8. President signed Nov. 13, 1997.

PL 105-79 (HR 79) Provide for the conveyance of certain land in the Six Rivers National Forest in California for the benefit of the Hoopa Valley Tribe. Introduced by RIGGS, R-Calif., Jan. 7, 1997. House Resources reported, amended, June 3 (H Rept 105-110). House passed, amended, under suspension of the rules, June 3. Senate Indian Affairs reported Oct. 29 (S Rept 105-117). Senate passed Nov. 4. President signed Nov. 13, 1997.

PL 105-80 (HR 672) Make technical amendments to certain provisions of Title 17, U.S. Code. Introduced by COBLE, R-N.C., Feb. 11, 1997. House Judiciary reported, amended, March 17 (H Rept 105-25). House passed, amended, under suspension of the rules, March 18. Senate Judiciary discharged. Senate passed, with amendments, Oct. 30. House agreed to Senate amendments, under suspension of the rules, Nov. 4. President signed Nov. 13, 1997.

PL 105-81 (HR 708) Require the secretary of the Interior to conduct a study concerning grazing use of certain land within and adjacent to Grand Teton National Park, Wyo., and to extend temporarily certain grazing privileges. Introduced by CUBIN, R-Wyo., Feb. 12, 1997. House Resources reported, amended, Oct. 6 (H Rept 105-300). House passed, amended, under suspension of the rules, Oct. 21. Senate passed Nov. 4. President signed Nov. 13, 1997.

PL 105-82 (S 931) Designate the Marjory Stoneman Douglas Wilderness and the Ernest F. Coe Visitor Center. Introduced by GRAHAM, D-Fla., June 18, 1997. Senate Energy and Natural Resources reported Sept. 2 (S Rept 105-68). Senate passed Sept. 16. House passed, under suspension of the rules, Nov. 4. President signed Nov. 13, 1997.

PL 105-83 (HR 2107) Make appropriations for the Department of the Interior and related agencies for the fiscal year ending Sept. 30, 1998. Introduced by REGULA, R-Ohio, July 1, 1997. House Appropriations reported July 1 (H Rept 105-163). House passed, amended, July 15. Senate Appropriations reported, amended, July 22 (S Rept 105-56). Senate passed, with amendments, Sept. 18. Conference report filed in the House Oct. 22 (H Rept 105-337). House agreed to conference report Oct. 24. Senate agreed to conference report Oct. 28. President signed Nov. 14, 1997.

PL 105-84 (H J Res 106) A joint resolution making further continuing appropriations for the fiscal year 1998. Introduced by LIVINGSTON, R-La., Nov. 13, 1997. House Appropriations discharged. House passed Nov. 13. Senate passed Nov. 13. President signed Nov. 14, 1997.

PL 105-85 (HR 1119) Authorize appropriations for fiscal year 1998 for military activities of the Department of Defense, and to prescribe military personnel strengths for fiscal years 1998 and 1999. Introduced by SPENCE, R-S.C., March 19, 1997. House National Security reported, amended, June 16 (H Rept 105-132). House passed, amended, June 25. Senate passed, with amendments, July 11. Conference report filed in the House Oct. 23 (H Rept 105-340). House agreed to conference report Oct. 28. Senate agreed to conference report Nov. 6. President signed Nov. 18, 1997.

PL 105-86 (HR 2160) Make appropriations for Agriculture, Rural Development, Food and Drug Administration, and related agencies programs for the fiscal year ending Sept. 30, 1998. Introduced by SKEEN, R-N.M., July 14, 1997. House Appropriations reported July 14 (H Rept 105-178). House passed, amended, July 24. Senate passed, with amendment, Sept. 3. Conference report filed in the House Sept. 17 (H Rept 105-252). House agreed to conference report Oct. 6. Senate agreed to conference report Oct. 29. President signed Nov. 18, 1997.

PL 105-87 (HR 282) Designate the U.S. Post Office building located at 153 East 110th St. in New York as the "Oscar Garcia Rivera Post Office Building." Introduced by SERRANO, D-N.Y., Jan. 7, 1997. House passed, under suspension of the rules, Oct. 21. Senate Governmental Affairs reported Nov. 6 (no written report). Senate passed Nov. 9. President signed Nov. 19, 1997.

PL 105-88 (HR 681) Designate the U.S. Post Office building at 313 East Broadway in Glendale, Calif., as the "Carlos J. Moorhead Post Office Building." Introduced by HYDE, R-Ill., Feb. 11, 1997. House passed, under suspension of the rules, Oct. 21. Senate Governmental Affairs reported Nov. 6 (no written report). Senate passed Nov. 9. President signed Nov. 19, 1997.

PL 105-89 (HR 867) Promote the adoption of children in foster care. Introduced by CAMP, R-Mich., Feb. 27, 1997. House Ways and Means reported, amended, April 28 (H Rept 105-77). House passed, amended, April 30. Senate passed, with amendment, Nov. 8. House agreed to Senate amendment, with amendment, pursuant to H Res 327 Nov. 13. Senate agreed to House amendment to Senate amendment Nov. 13. President signed Nov. 19, 1997.

PL 105-90 (HR 1057) Designate the building in Indianapolis that houses the operations of the Circle City Station Post Office as the "Andrew Jacobs, Jr. Post Office Building." Introduced by BURTON, R-Ind., March 13, 1997. House passed, under suspension of the rules, June 17. Senate Governmental Affairs discharged. Senate passed Nov. 9. President signed Nov. 19, 1997.

PL 105-91 (HR 1058) Designate the facility of the U.S. Postal Service under construction at 150 West Margaret Drive in Terre Haute, Ind., as the "John T. Myers Post Office Building." Introduced by BURTON, R-Ind., March 13, 1997. House passed, under suspension of the rules, June 17. Senate Governmental Affairs discharged. Senate passed Nov. 9. President signed Nov. 19, 1997.

PL 105-92 (HR 1377) Amend Title I of the Employee Retirement Income Security Act of 1974 to encourage retirement income savings. Introduced by FAWELL, R-Ill., April 17, 1997. House Education and the Workforce reported, amended, May 20 (H Rept 105-104). House passed, amended, under suspension of the rules, May 21. Senate Labor and Human Resources discharged. Senate passed, with amendment, Nov. 7. House agreed to Senate amendment, under suspension of the rules, Nov. 9. President signed Nov. 19, 1997.

PL 105-93 (HR 1479) Designate the federal building and U.S. Courthouse at 300 Northeast First Avenue in Miami as the "David W. Dyer Federal Courthouse." Introduced by HASTINGS, D-Fla., April 29, 1997. House Transportation and Infrastructure reported, amended, July 31 (H Rept 105-227). House passed, amended, under suspension of the rules, Oct. 29. Senate Environment and Public Works discharged. Senate passed Nov. 9. President signed Nov. 19, 1997.

PL 105-94 (HR 1484) Redesignate the Dublin Federal Courthouse building in Dublin, Ga., as the "J. Roy Rowland Federal Courthouse." Introduced by NORWOOD, R-Ga., April 29, 1997. House Transportation and Infrastructure reported, amended, July 31 (H Rept 105-226). House passed, amended, under suspension of the rules, Oct. 29. Senate Environment and Public Works discharged. Senate passed Nov. 9. President signed Nov. 19, 1997.

PL 105-95 (HR 1747) Amend the John F. Kennedy Center Act to authorize the design and construction of additions to the parking garage and certain site improvements. Introduced by SHUSTER, R-Pa., May 22, 1997. House Transportation and Infrastructure reported, amended, June 12 (H Rept 105-130). House passed, amended, under suspension of the rules, June 17. Senate passed Nov. 7. President signed Nov. 19, 1997.

PL 105-96 (HR 1787) Assist in the conservation of Asian elephants by supporting and providing financial resources for the conservation programs of nations within the range of Asian elephants and projects of persons with demonstrated expertise in the conservation of Asian elephants. Introduced by SAXTON, R-N.J., June 4, 1997. House Resources reported, amended, Sept. 23 (H Rept 105-266, Part 1). House International Relations discharged. House passed, amended, under suspension of the rules, Oct. 21. Senate Environment and Public Works reported Nov. 7 (no written report). Senate passed Nov. 8. President signed Nov. 19, 1997.

PL 105-97 (HR 2129) Designate the U.S. Post Office located at 150 North 3rd St. in Steubenville, Ohio, as the "Douglas Applegate Post Office." Introduced by TRAFICANT, D-Ohio, July 9, 1997. House passed, under suspension of the rules, Oct. 21. Senate Governmental Affairs reported Nov. 6 (no written report). Senate passed Nov. 9. President signed Nov. 19, 1997.

PL 105-98 (HR 2367) Increase, effective Dec. 1, 1997, the rates of compensation for veterans with service-connected disabilities and the rates of dependency and indemnity compensation for the survivors of certain disabled veterans. Introduced by STUMP, R-Ariz., July 31, 1997. House Veterans' Affairs reported Oct. 9 (H Rept 105-320). House passed, amended, Oct. 31. Senate passed Nov. 5. President signed Nov. 19, 1997.

PL 105-99 (HR 2564) Designate the U.S. Post Office located at 450 North Centre St. in Pottsville, Pa., as the "Peter J. McCloskey Postal Facility." Introduced by HOLDEN, D-Pa., Sept. 26, 1997. House passed, under suspension of the rules, Oct. 21. Senate Governmental Affairs reported Nov. 6 (no written report). Senate passed Nov. 9. President signed Nov. 19, 1997.

PL 105-100 (HR 2607) Make appropriations for the government of the District of Columbia and other activities chargeable in whole or in part against the revenues of said District for the fiscal year ending Sept. 30, 1998. Introduced by TAYLOR, R-N.C., Oct. 6, 1997. House Appropriations reported Oct. 6 (H Rept 105-298). House passed, amended, Oct. 9. Senate passed, with amendments, Nov. 9. House agreed to the Senate amendment to the text, with an amendment, and disagreed to the Senate amendment to the title, Nov. 12. Senate receded from its amendment to the title Nov. 13. Senate agreed to the House amendment to the Senate amendment to the text Nov. 13. President signed Nov. 19, 1997.

PL 105-101 (S 813) Amend chapter 91 of Title 18, U.S. Code, to provide criminal penalties for theft and willful vandalism at national cemeteries. Introduced by THURMOND, R-S.C., May 23, 1997. Senate Judiciary reported, amended, Oct. 23 (no written report). Senate passed, amended, Nov. 4. House passed, under suspension of the rules, Nov. 8. President signed Nov. 19, 1997.

PL 105-102 (HR 1086) Codify without substantive change laws related to transportation and to improve the U.S. Code. Introduced by HYDE, R-Ill., March 17, 1997. House Judiciary reported, amended, June 25 (H Rept 105-153). House passed, amended, under suspension of the rules, July 8. Senate Judiciary reported Sept. 18 (no written report). Senate passed Nov. 8. President signed Nov. 20, 1997.

PL 105-103 (HR 2813) Waive time limitations specified by law in order to allow the Medal of Honor to be awarded to Robert R. Ingram of Jacksonville, Fla., for acts of valor while a Navy Hospital Corpsman in the republic of Vietnam during the Vietnam conflict. Introduced by FOWLER, R-Fla., Nov. 4, 1997. House passed, under suspension of the rules, Nov. 8. Senate passed Nov. 10. President signed Nov. 20, 1997.

PL 105-104 (H J Res 91) A joint resolution granting the consent of Congress to the Apalachicola-Chattahoochee-Flint River Basin Compact. Introduced by BARR, R-Ga., July 31, 1997. House Judiciary reported, amended, Oct. 31 (H Rept 105-369). House passed, amended, under suspension of the rules, Nov. 4. Senate passed Nov. 7. President signed Nov. 20, 1997.

PL 105-105 (H J Res 92) A joint resolution granting the consent of Congress to the Alabama-Coosa-Tallapoosa River Basin Compact. Introduced by CALLAHAN, R-Ala., July 31, 1997. House Judiciary reported Oct. 31 (H Rept 105-370). House passed, amended, under suspension of the rules, Nov. 4. Senate passed Nov. 7. President signed Nov. 20, 1997.

PL 105-106 (S 669) Provide for the acquisition of the Plains Railroad Depot at the Jimmy Carter National Historic Site. Introduced by COVERDELL, R-Ga., April 30, 1997. Senate Energy and Natural Resources reported June 26 (S Rept 105-39). Senate passed July 11. House passed, under suspension of the rules, Nov. 9. President signed Nov. 20, 1997.

PL 105-107 (S 858) Authorize appropriations for fiscal year 1998 for intelligence and intelligence-related activities of the federal government, the Community Management Account and the Central Intelligence Agency Retirement and Disability System. Introduced by SHELBY, R-Ala., June 9, 1997. Senate Intelligence reported June 9 (S Rept 105-24). Senate Armed Services reported June 18 (no written report). Senate passed, amended, June 19. House passed with amendment July 17. Conference report filed in the House Oct. 28 (H Rept 105-350). Senate agreed to conference report Nov. 6. House agreed to conference report Nov. 7. President signed Nov. 20, 1997.

PL 105-108 (S 1231) Authorize appropriations for fiscal years 1998 and 1999 for the U.S. Fire Administration. Introduced by FRIST, R-Tenn., Sept. 26, 1997. Senate Commerce, Science and Transportation reported Oct. 30 (S Rept 105-124). Senate passed Nov. 4. House passed, under suspension of the rules, Nov. 9. President signed Nov. 20, 1997.

PL 105-109 (S 1347) Permit the city of Cleveland to convey certain lands that the United States conveyed to the city. Introduced by GLENN, D-Ohio, Oct. 30, 1997. Senate Commerce, Science and Transportation discharged. Senate passed Nov. 8. House passed, under suspension of the rules, Nov. 9. President signed Nov. 20, 1997.

PL 105-110 (S 1377) Amend the act incorporating the American Legion to make a technical correction. Introduced by HATCH, R-Utah, Nov. 5, 1997. Senate passed Nov. 5. House passed, under suspension of the rules, Nov. 8. President signed Nov. 20, 1997.

PL 105-111 (HR 1090) Amend Title 38, U.S Code, to allow revision of veterans-benefits decisions based on clear and unmistakable error. Introduced by EVANS, D-Ill., March 18, 1997. House Veterans' Affairs reported April 14 (H Rept 105-52). House passed, under suspension of the rules, April 16. Senate Veterans' Affairs discharged. Senate passed Nov. 10. President signed Nov. 21, 1997.

PL 105-112 (HR 1840) Provide a law enforcement exception to the prohibition on the advertising of certain electronic devices. Introduced by McCOLLUM, R-Fla., June 10, 1997. House Judiciary reported June 26 (H Rept 105-162). House passed, under suspension of the rules, July 8. Senate Judiciary discharged. Senate passed Nov. 10. President signed Nov. 21, 1997.

PL 105-113 (HR 2366) Transfer to the secretary of Agriculture the authority to conduct the census of agriculture. Introduced by STENHOLM, D-Texas, July 31, 1997. House Agriculture reported Oct. 2 (H Rept 105-296, Part 1). House passed, under suspension of the rules, Oct. 21. Senate Governmental Affairs reported Nov. 7 (S Rept 105-141). Senate passed Nov. 10. President signed Nov. 21, 1997.

PL 105-114 (S 714) Extend and improve the Native American Veteran Housing Loan Pilot Program of the Department of Veterans Affairs, to extend certain authorities of the secretary of Veterans Affairs relating to services for homeless veterans, and to extend certain other authorities of the secretary. Introduced by AKAKA, D-Hawaii, May 7, 1997. Senate Veterans' Affairs reported, amended, Oct. 30 (S Rept 105-123). Senate passed, amended, Nov. 5. House passed, with amendments, under suspension of the rules, Nov. 9. Senate agreed to House amendments Nov. 10. President signed Nov. 21, 1997.

PL 105-115 (S 830) Amend the Federal Food, Drug, and Cosmetic Act and the Public Health Service Act to improve the regulation of food, drugs, devices and biological products. Introduced by JEFFORDS, R-Vt., June 5, 1997. Senate Labor and Human Resources reported, amended, July 1 (S Rept 105-43). Senate passed, amended, Sept. 24. House passed, with amendments, Oct. 7. Conference report filed in the House Nov. 9 (H Rept 105-399). Senate agreed to conference report Nov. 9. House agreed to conference report, under suspension of the rules, Nov. 9. President signed Nov. 21, 1997.

PL 105-116 (S 923) Amend Title 38, U.S. Code, to prohibit interment or memorialization in certain cemeteries of persons committing federal or state capital crimes. Introduced by SPECTER, R-Pa., June 17, 1997. Senate Veterans' Affairs discharged. Senate passed, amended, June 18. House Veterans' Affairs reported, with amendments, Oct. 9 (H Rept 105-319). House passed, with amendments, Oct. 31. Senate agreed to House amendments Nov. 10. President signed Nov. 21, 1997.

PL 105-117 (S 1258) Amend the Uniform Relocation Assistance and Real Property Acquisition Policies Act of 1970 to prohibit an alien who is not lawfully present in the United States from receiving assistance under that Act. Introduced by BENNETT, R-Utah, Oct. 6, 1997. Senate Environment and Public Works reported, amended, Nov. 4 (no written report). Senate passed, amended, Nov. 8. House passed, under suspension of the rules, Nov. 9. President signed Nov. 21, 1997.

PL 105-118 (HR 2159) Make appropriations for foreign operations, export financing and related programs for the fiscal year ending Sept. 30, 1998. Introduced by CALLAHAN, R-Ala., July 14, 1997. House Appropriations reported July 14 (H Rept 105-176). House passed, amended, Sept. 4. Senate passed, with amendment, Sept. 5. Conference report filed in the House Nov. 12 (H Rept 105-401). House agreed to conference report Nov. 13 (legislative day of Nov. 12), 1997. Senate agreed to conference report Nov. 13. President signed Nov. 26, 1997.

PL 105-119 (HR 2267) Make appropriations for the departments of Commerce, Justice, and State, the Judiciary and related agencies for the fiscal year ending Sept. 30, 1998. Introduced by ROGERS, R-Ky., July 25, 1997. House Appropriations reported July 25 (H Rept 105-207). House passed, amended, Sept. 30. Senate passed, with amendment, Oct. 1. Conference report filed in the House Nov. 13 (H Rept 105-405). House agreed to conference report Nov. 13. Senate agreed to conference report Nov. 13. President signed Nov. 26, 1997. President exercised line-item-veto authority, Dec. 2, 1997.

PL 105-120 (H J Res 103) A joint resolution waiving certain enrollment requirements with respect to certain specified bills of the 105th Congress. Introduced by ARMEY, R-Texas, Nov. 8, 1997. House Oversight discharged. House passed Nov. 10 (legislative day of Nov. 9). Senate passed Nov. 13. President signed Nov. 26, 1997.

PL 105-121 (S 1026) Reauthorize the Export-Import Bank of the United States. Introduced by GRAMS, R-Minn., July 17, 1997. Senate Banking, Housing, and Urban Affairs reported, amended, Sept. 10 (S Rept 105-76). Senate passed, amended, Sept. 16. House passed, with amendment, Oct. 6. Conference report filed in the House Nov. 7 (H Rept 105-392). Senate agreed to conference report Nov. 8. House agreed to conference report, under suspension of the rules, Nov. 9. President signed Nov. 26, 1997.

PL 105-122 (S 819) Designate the U.S. Courthouse at 200 South Washington St. in Alexandria, Va., as the "Martin V.B. Bostetter Jr. United States Courthouse." Introduced by WARNER, R-Va., June 2, 1997. Senate Environment and Public Works reported June 5 (no written report). Senate passed June 12. House passed, under suspension of the rules, Nov. 13. President signed Dec. 1, 1997.

PL 105-123 (S 833) Designate the federal building courthouse at Public Square and Superior Avenue in Cleveland as the "Howard M. Metzenbaum United States Courthouse." Introduced by LAUTENBERG, D-N.J., June 5, 1997. Senate Environment and Public Works reported June 26 (no written report). Senate passed July 25. House passed, under suspension of the rules, Nov. 13. President signed Dec. 1, 1997.

PL 105-124 (S 1228) Provide for a 10-year circulating commemorative coin program to commemorate each of the 50 states. Introduced by CHAFEE, R-R.I., Sept. 26, 1997. Senate Banking, Housing, and Urban Affairs reported, amended, Oct. 31 (S Rept 105-130). Senate passed, amended, Nov. 9. House passed, under suspension of the rules, Nov. 13. President signed Dec. 1, 1997.

PL 105-125 (S 1354) Amend the Communications Act of 1934 to provide for the designation of common carriers not subject to the jurisdiction of a state commission as eligible telecommunications carriers. Introduced by McCAIN, R-Ariz., Oct. 31, 1997. Senate Commerce, Science and Transportation reported Nov. 8 (no written report). Senate passed Nov. 9. House passed, under suspension of the rules, Nov. 13. President signed Dec. 1, 1997.

PL 105-126 (S 1378) Extend the authorization of use of official mail in the location and recovery of missing children. Introduced by WARNER, R-Va., Nov. 5, 1997. Senate passed Nov. 5. House passed, under suspension of the rules, Nov. 12. President signed Dec. 1, 1997.

PL 105-127 (S 1417) Provide for the design, construction, furnishing and equipping of a Center for Performing Arts within the complex known as the New Mexico Hispanic Cultural Center. Introduced by DOMENICI, R-N.M., Nov. 7, 1997. Senate passed Nov. 7. House passed, under suspension of the rules, Nov. 13. President signed Dec. 1, 1997.

PL 105-128 (S 1505) Make technical and conforming amendments to the Museum and Library Services. Introduced by JEFFORDS, R-Vt., Nov. 9, 1997. Senate passed Nov. 9. House passed, under suspension of the rules, Nov. 13. President signed Dec. 1, 1997.

PL 105-129 (S 1507) Amend the National Defense Authorization Act for fiscal year 1998 to make certain technical corrections. Introduced by THURMOND, R-S.C., Nov. 9, 1997. Senate passed Nov. 9. House passed, under suspension of the rules, Nov. 12. President signed Dec. 1, 1997.

PL 105-130 (S 1519) Provide a six-month extension of highway, highway safety and transit programs pending enactment of a law reauthorizing the Intermodal Surface Transportation Efficiency Act of 1991. Introduced by BOND, R-Mo., Nov. 10, 1997. Senate passed Nov. 10. House passed, under suspension of the rules, Nov. 12. President signed Dec. 1, 1997.

PL 105-131 (HR 1254) Designate the U.S. Post Office building located at 1919 West Bennett Street in Springfield, Mo., as the "John N. Griesemer Post Office Building." Introduced by BLUNT, R-Mo., April 9, 1997. House passed, amended, under suspension of the rules, Sept. 16. Senate Governmental Affairs discharged. Senate passed Nov. 13. President signed Dec. 2, 1997.

PL 105-132 (S 156) Provide certain benefits of the Pick-Sloan Missouri River Basin program to the Lower Brule Sioux Tribe. Introduced by DASCHLE, D-S.D., Jan. 21, 1997. Senate Energy and Natural Resources discharged. Senate Indian Affairs reported Nov. 8 (S Rept 105-146). Senate passed, amended, Nov. 9. House Resources discharged. House passed Nov. 13. President signed Dec. 2, 1997.

PL 105-133 (S 476) Provide for the establishment of not less than 2,500 Boys and Girls Clubs of America facilities by the year 2000. Introduced by HATCH, R-Utah, March 19, 1997. Senate Judiciary reported May 1 (no written report). Senate passed May 15. House Judiciary discharged. House passed, with amendment, Nov. 13. Senate agreed to House amendment Nov. 13. President signed Dec. 2, 1997.

PL 105-134 (S 738) Reform the statutes relating to Amtrak, and to authorize appropriations for Amtrak. Introduced by HUTCHISON, R-Texas, May 14, 1997. Senate Commerce, Science and Transportation reported, amended, Sept. 24 (S Rept 105-85). Senate passed, amended, Nov. 7. House passed, with amendment, under suspension of the rules, Nov. 13. Senate agreed to House amendment Nov. 13. President signed Dec. 2, 1997.

PL 105-135 (S 1139) Reauthorize the programs of the Small Business Administration. Introduced by BOND, R-Mo., Aug. 19, 1997. Senate Small Business reported Aug. 19 (S Rept 105-62). Senate passed, amended, Sept. 9. House passed, with amendments, Sept. 29. Senate agreed to House amendment, with amendment, Oct. 31. House agreed to Senate amendment to House amendment, under suspension of the rules, Nov. 9. President signed Dec. 2, 1997.

PL 105-136 (S 1161) Amend the Immigration and Nationality Act to authorize appropriations for refugee and entrant assistance for fiscal years 1998 and 1999. Introduced by ABRAHAM, R-Mich., Sept. 10, 1997. Senate passed Sept. 10. House failed to pass, under suspension of the rules, Oct. 1 (two-thirds required). House passed, under suspension of the rules, Nov. 13. President signed Dec. 2, 1997.

PL 105-137 (S 1193) Amend chapter 443 of Title 49, U.S. Code, to extend the authorization of the aviation insurance program. Introduced by GORTON, R-Wash., Sept. 18, 1997. Senate Commerce, Science and Transportation reported, amended, Nov. 6 (S Rept 105-140). Senate passed, amended, Nov. 8. House passed Nov. 13. President signed Dec. 2, 1997.

PL 105-138 (S 1559) Provide for the design, construction, furnishing and equipping of a Center for Historically Black Heritage within Florida A&M University. Introduced by MACK, R-Fla., Nov. 13, 1997. Senate passed Nov. 13. House passed Nov. 13. President signed Dec. 2, 1997.

PL 105-139 (S 1565) Make technical corrections to the Nicaraguan Adjustment and Central American Relief Act. Introduced by ABRAHAM, R-Mich., Nov. 13, 1997. Senate passed Nov. 13. House passed Nov. 13. President signed Dec. 2, 1997.

PL 105-140 (S J Res 39) Provide for the convening of the second session of the 105th Congress. Introduced by LOTT, R-Miss., Nov. 13, 1997. Senate passed Nov. 13. House passed Nov. 13. President signed Dec. 2, 1997.

PL 105-141 (HR 1493) Require the attorney general to establish a program in local prisons to identify, prior to arraignment, criminal aliens and aliens who are unlawfully present in the United States. Introduced by GALLEGLY, R-Calif., April 30, 1997. House Judiciary reported, amended, Oct. 23 (H Rept 105-338). House passed, under suspension of the rules, Nov. 4. Senate Judiciary discharged. Senate passed Nov. 13. President signed Dec. 5, 1997.

PL 105-142 (HR 2626) Clarify the Pilot Records Improvement Act of 1996. Introduced by DUNCAN, R-Tenn., Oct. 7, 1997. House Transportation and Infrastructure reported, amended, Oct. 31 (H Rept 105-372). House passed, amended, under suspension of the rules, Nov. 9. Senate passed Nov. 13. President signed Dec. 5, 1997.

PL 105-143 (HR 1604) Provide for the division, use and distribution of judgment funds of the Ottawa and Chippewa Indians of Michigan pursuant to dockets numbered 18-E, 58, 364 and 18-R before the Indian Claims Commission. Introduced by KILDEE, D-Mich., May 14, 1997. House Resources reported, amended Oct. 28 (H Rept 105-352). House passed, amended, under suspension of the rules, Nov. 4. Senate passed, with amendments, Nov. 9. House agreed to Senate amendments Nos. 1-60, 62 and 63 and disagreed to Senate amendment No. 61, under suspension of the rules Nov. 13. Senate receded from its amendment No. 61 Nov. 13. President signed Dec. 15, 1997.

PL 105-144 (HR 2979) Authorize acquisition of certain real property for the Library of Congress. Introduced by THOMAS, R-Calif., Nov. 9, 1997. House passed, amended, under suspension of the rules. Nov. 12. Senate passed Nov. 13. President signed Dec. 15, 1997.

PL 105-145 (H J Res 95) Grant the consent of Congress to the Chickasaw Trail Economic Development Compact. Introduced by BRYANT, R-Tenn., Oct. 6, 1997. House Judiciary reported Nov. 7 (H Rept 105-389). House passed, under suspension of the rules, Nov. 12. Senate passed Nov. 13. President signed Dec. 15, 1997.

PL 105-146 (HR 1658) Reauthorize and amend the Atlantic Striped Bass Conservation Act and related laws. Introduced by SAXTON, R-N.J., May 16, 1997. House Resources reported, amended, July 8 (H Rept 105-169). House passed, amended, under suspension of the rules, July 8. Senate Commerce, Science and Transportation reported, with amendments, Nov. 8 (S Rept 105-149). Senate passed, with amendments, Nov. 10. House agreed to Senate amendments, under suspension of the rules, Nov. 13. President signed Dec. 16, 1997.

PL 105-147 (HR 2265) Amend the provisions of Titles 17 and 18, U.S. Code, to provide greater copyright protection by amending criminal copyright infringement provisions. Introduced by GOODLATTE, R-Va., July 25, 1997. House Judiciary reported, amended, Oct. 23 (H Rept 105-339). House passed, amended, under suspension of the rules, Nov. 4. Senate Judiciary discharged. Senate passed Nov. 13. President signed Dec. 16, 1997.

PL 105-148 (HR 2476) Amend Title 49, U.S. Code, to require the National Transportation Safety Board and individual foreign air carriers to address the needs of families of passengers involved in aircraft accidents involving foreign air carriers. Introduced by UNDERWOOD, D-Guam, Sept. 15, 1997. House Transportation and Infrastructure reported, amended, Oct. 31 (H Rept 105-371). House passed, amended, under suspension of the rules, Nov. 9. Senate passed Nov. 13. President signed Dec. 16, 1997.

PL 105-149 (HR 3025) Amend the federal charter for Group Hospitalization and Medical Services, Inc. Introduced by DAVIS, R-Va., Nov. 12, 1997. House passed, under suspension of the rules, Nov. 13. Senate passed Nov. 13. President signed Dec. 16, 1997.

PL 105-150 (HR 3034) Amend section 13031 of the Consolidated Omnibus Budget Reconciliation Act of 1985, relating to customs user fees, to allow the use of such fees to provide for customs inspection personnel in connection with the arrival of passengers in Florida. Introduced by SHAW, R-Fla., Nov. 12, 1997. House passed, under suspension of the rules, Nov. 13. Senate passed Nov. 13. President signed Dec. 16.

PL 105-151(H J Res 96) Grant the consent and approval of Congress for Maryland, Virginia and the District of Columbia to amend the Washington Metropolitan Area Transit Regulation Compact. Introduced by DAVIS, R-Va., Oct. 9, 1997. House Judiciary reported Nov. 8 (H Rept 105-396). House passed, under suspension of the rules, Nov. 12. Senate passed Nov. 13. President signed Dec. 16, 1997.

PL 105-152 (HR 2796) Authorize the reimbursement of members of the Army deployed to Europe in support of operations in Bosnia for certain out-of-pocket expenses incurred by the members during the period beginning on Oct. 1, 1996, and ending on May 31, 1997. Introduced by CLAYTON, D-N.C., Nov. 4, 1997. House passed, amended, under suspension of the rules, Nov. 13. Senate passed Nov. 13. President signed Dec. 17, 1997.

PL 105-153 (HR 2977) Amend the Federal Advisory Committee Act to clarify public disclosure requirements that are applicable to the National Academy of Sciences and the National Academy of Public Administration. Introduced by HORN, R-Calif., Nov. 9, 1997. House passed, under suspension of the rules, Nov. 10 (legislative day of Nov. 9). Senate passed Nov. 13. President signed Dec. 17, 1997. ■

CQ

Appendix H

HOUSE ROLL CALL VOTES

HOUSE VOTES 2, 3, 4, 5, 6 *

* **2. Election of the Speaker/Motion to Table.** Boehner, R-Ohio, motion to table (kill) the Fazio, D-Calif., motion to appeal the Clerk's ruling that the motion to elect the speaker of the House was of higher privilege than a motion to postpone the election. Motion agreed to 222-210: R- 222-4; D 0-205 (ND 0-151, SD 0-54); I 0-1, Jan. 7, 1997.

3. Election of the Speaker. Nomination of Newt Gingrich, R-Ga., and Richard A. Gephardt, D-Mo., for Speaker of the House of Representatives for the 105th Congress. Gingrich elected 216-205, with four Republican votes cast for other names: R 216-0; D 0-204 (ND 0-150, SD 0-54); I 0-1, Jan. 7, 1997. A "Y" on the chart represents a vote for Gingrich; an "N" represents a vote for Gephardt, except where footnoted. A majority of the votes cast for a person by name (213 in this case) is needed for election. All members-elect are eligible to vote on the election for the Speaker.

4. H Res 5. Rules of the House/Previous Question. Solomon, R-N.Y., motion to order the previous question (thus ending debate and the possibility of amendment) on the resolution containing the House rules for the 105th Congress, which extends the rules of the House for the 104th Congress except for certain changes recommended by the Republican Conference. Motion agreed to 221-202: R 221-0; D 0-201 (ND 0-148, SD 0-53); I 0-1, Jan. 7, 1997.

5. H Res 5. Rules of the House/Motion to Commit. McDermott, D-Wash., motion to commit the resolution to a select committee composed of the majority and minority leaders with instructions to report it back to the House with an amendment to allow the ethics committee to submit its report regarding the ethics inquiry into Newt Gingrich, R-Ga., after Jan. 21, 1997. Motion rejected 205-223: R 2-223; D 202-0 (ND 148-0, SD 54-0); I 1-0, Jan. 7 1997.

6. H Res 5. Rules of the House/Adoption. Adoption of the resolution to adopt House rules for the 105th Congress, which extends the rules for the 104th Congress except for certain changes recommended by the Republican Conference. The resolution includes a rule that requires the Speaker to develop a system of drug testing for the House, and a rule extending the tenure of the current ethics committee until the House acts on the committee's report regarding Speaker Newt Gingrich, R-Ga., or until Jan. 21, 1997, whichever is earlier. Adopted 226-202: R 223-2; D 3-199 (ND 1-147, SD 2-52); I 0-1, Jan. 7, 1997.

** NOTE: The first session of the 105th Congress began with Vote 1, a quorum call. CQ does not include quroum calls in its vote charts.*

[1] *On Vote 3, voted for Rep. Jim Leach, R-Iowa.*

[2] *On Vote 3, voted for Rep. Robert H. Michel, R-Ill. (1957-95).*

[3] *Jo Ann Emerson, Mo., was elected on Nov. 5, 1996, as an independent. She registered as a Republican with the Clerk of the House on Jan. 7, 1997, too late for her independent designation to be changed on that date in the House Clerk's tallies.*

[4] *On Vote 3, voted for Rep. Jim Leach, R-Iowa.*

[5] *On Vote 3, voted for Rep. Robert S. Walker, R-Pa. (1977-97).*

KEY

Y Voted for (yea).
\# Paired for.
\+ Announced for.
N Voted against (nay).
X Paired against.
\- Announced against.
P Voted "present."
C Voted "present" to avoid possible conflict of interest.
? Did not vote or otherwise make a position known.

Democrats ***Republicans***
Independent

	2	3	4	5	6
ALABAMA					
1 ***Callahan***	Y	Y	Y	N	Y
2 ***Everett***	Y	Y	Y	N	Y
3 ***Riley***	Y	Y	Y	N	Y
4 ***Aderholt***	Y	Y	Y	N	Y
5 Cramer	N	N	N	Y	N
6 ***Bachus***	Y	Y	Y	N	Y
7 Hilliard	N	N	N	Y	N
ALASKA					
AL ***Young***	Y	Y	Y	N	Y
ARIZONA					
1 ***Salmon***	Y	Y	Y	N	Y
2 Pastor	N	N	N	Y	N
3 ***Stump***	Y	Y	Y	N	Y
4 ***Shadegg***	Y	Y	Y	N	Y
5 ***Kolbe***	Y	Y	Y	N	Y
6 ***Hayworth***	Y	Y	Y	N	Y
ARKANSAS					
1 Berry	N	N	N	Y	N
2 Snyder	N	N	N	Y	N
3 ***Hutchinson***	Y	Y	Y	N	Y
4 ***Dickey***	Y	Y	Y	N	Y
CALIFORNIA					
1 ***Riggs***	Y	Y	Y	N	Y
2 ***Herger***	Y	Y	Y	N	Y
3 Fazio	N	N	N	Y	N
4 ***Doolittle***	Y	Y	Y	N	Y
5 Matsui	N	N	N	Y	N
6 Woolsey	N	N	N	Y	N
7 Miller	N	N	N	Y	N
8 Pelosi	N	N	N	Y	N
9 Dellums	N	N	N	Y	N
10 Tauscher	N	N	N	Y	N
11 ***Pombo***	Y	Y	Y	N	Y
12 Lantos	N	N	N	Y	N
13 Stark	N	N	N	Y	N
14 Eshoo	N	N	N	Y	N
15 ***Campbell***[1]	Y	N	Y	N	N
16 Lofgren	N	N	N	Y	N
17 Farr	N	N	N	Y	N
18 Condit	N	N	?	?	N
19 ***Radanovich***	Y	Y	Y	N	Y
20 Dooley	N	N	N	Y	N
21 ***Thomas***	Y	Y	Y	N	Y
22 Capps	N	N	N	Y	N
23 ***Gallegly***	Y	Y	Y	N	Y
24 Sherman	N	N	N	Y	N
25 ***McKeon***	Y	Y	Y	N	Y
26 Berman	N	N	N	Y	N
27 ***Rogan***	Y	Y	Y	N	Y
28 ***Dreier***	Y	Y	Y	N	Y
29 Waxman	N	N	N	Y	N
30 Becerra	N	N	N	Y	N
31 Martinez	N	N	N	Y	N
32 Dixon	N	N	N	Y	N
33 Roybal-Allard	N	N	N	Y	N
34 Torres	N	N	?	?	?
35 Waters	N	N	N	Y	N
36 Harman	N	N	N	Y	N
37 Millender-McD.	N	N	N	Y	N
38 ***Horn***	Y	Y	Y	N	Y
39 ***Royce***	Y	Y	Y	N	Y
40 ***Lewis***	Y	Y	Y	N	Y
41 ***Kim***	Y	Y	Y	N	Y
42 Brown	N	N	N	Y	N
43 ***Calvert***	Y	Y	Y	N	Y
44 ***Bono***	Y	Y	Y	N	Y
45 ***Rohrabacher***	Y	Y	Y	N	Y
46 Sanchez	N	N	N	Y	N
47 ***Cox***	Y	Y	Y	N	Y
48 ***Packard***	Y	Y	Y	N	Y
49 ***Bilbray***	Y	Y	Y	N	Y
50 Filner	N	N	N	Y	N
51 ***Cunningham***	Y	Y	Y	N	Y
52 ***Hunter***	Y	Y	Y	N	Y
COLORADO					
1 DeGette	N	N	N	Y	N
2 Skaggs	N	N	N	Y	N
3 ***McInnis***	Y	Y	Y	N	?
4 ***Schaffer***	Y	Y	Y	N	Y
5 ***Hefley***	Y	Y	Y	N	Y
6 ***Schaefer***	Y	Y	Y	N	Y
CONNECTICUT					
1 Kennelly	N	N	N	Y	N
2 Gejdenson	N	N	N	Y	N
3 DeLauro	N	N	N	Y	N
4 ***Shays***	Y	Y	Y	N	Y
5 Maloney	N	N	N	Y	N
6 ***Johnson***	Y	Y	Y	N	Y
DELAWARE					
AL ***Castle***	Y	Y	Y	N	Y
FLORIDA					
1 ***Scarborough***	Y	Y	Y	N	Y
2 Boyd	N	N	N	Y	N
3 Brown	N	N	?	Y	N
4 ***Fowler***	Y	Y	Y	N	Y
5 Thurman	N	N	N	Y	N
6 ***Stearns***	Y	Y	Y	N	Y
7 ***Mica***	Y	Y	Y	N	Y
8 ***McCollum***	Y	Y	Y	N	Y
9 ***Bilirakis***	Y	Y	Y	N	Y
10 ***Young***	Y	Y	Y	N	Y
11 Davis	N	N	N	Y	N
12 ***Canady***	Y	Y	Y	N	Y
13 ***Miller***	Y	Y	Y	N	Y
14 ***Goss***	Y	Y	Y	Y	Y
15 ***Weldon***	Y	Y	Y	N	Y
16 ***Foley***	Y	Y	Y	N	Y
17 Meek	N	N	N	Y	N
18 ***Ros-Lehtinen***	Y	Y	Y	N	Y
19 Wexler	N	N	N	Y	N
20 Deutsch	N	N	N	Y	N
21 ***Diaz-Balart***	Y	Y	Y	N	Y
22 ***Shaw***	Y	Y	Y	N	Y
23 Hastings	N	N	N	Y	N
GEORGIA					
1 ***Kingston***	Y	Y	Y	N	Y
2 Bishop	N	N	N	Y	N
3 ***Collins***	Y	Y	Y	N	Y
4 McKinney	N	N	N	Y	N
5 Lewis	N	N	N	Y	N
6 ***Gingrich***	Y	?	Y		
7 ***Barr***	Y	Y	Y	N	Y
8 ***Chambliss***	Y	Y	Y	N	Y
9 ***Deal***	Y	Y	Y	N	Y
10 ***Norwood***	Y	Y	Y	N	Y
11 ***Linder***	Y	Y	Y	N	Y
HAWAII					
1 Abercrombie	N	N	N	Y	N
2 Mink	N	N	N	Y	N
IDAHO					
1 ***Chenoweth***	Y	Y	Y	N	Y
2 ***Crapo***	Y	Y	Y	N	Y
ILLINOIS					
1 Rush	N	N	N	Y	N
2 Jackson	N	N	N	Y	N
3 Lipinski	N	N	N	Y	N
4 Gutierrez	N	N	N	?	N
5 Blagojevich	N	N	?	Y	N
6 ***Hyde***	Y	Y	Y	N	Y
7 Davis	N	N	N	Y	N
8 ***Crane***	Y	Y	Y	N	Y
9 Yates	N	N	N	Y	N
10 ***Porter***	Y	Y	Y	N	Y
11 ***Weller***	Y	Y	?	N	Y
12 Costello	N	N	N	Y	N
13 ***Fawell***	Y	Y	Y	N	Y
14 ***Hastert***	Y	Y	Y	N	Y

ND Northern Democrats SD Southern Democrats

	2	3	4	5	6
15 ***Ewing***	Y	Y	Y	N	Y
16 ***Manzullo***	Y	Y	Y	N	Y
17 Evans	N	N	N	Y	N
18 ***LaHood***	Y	Y	Y	N	Y
19 Poshard	N	N	N	Y	N
20 ***Shimkus***	Y	Y	Y	N	Y
INDIANA					
1 Visclosky	N	N	N	Y	N
2 ***McIntosh***	Y	Y	Y	N	Y
3 Roemer	N	N	N	Y	N
4 ***Souder***	Y	Y	Y	N	Y
5 ***Buyer***	Y	Y	Y	N	Y
6 ***Burton***	Y	Y	Y	N	Y
7 ***Pease***	Y	Y	Y	N	Y
8 ***Hostettler***	Y	P	Y	N	Y
9 Hamilton	N	N	N	Y	N
10 Carson	?	?	?	?	?
IOWA					
1 ***Leach*** [2]	Y	N	Y	N	Y
2 ***Nussle***	Y	Y	Y	N	Y
3 Boswell	N	N	N	Y	N
4 ***Ganske***	Y	Y	Y	N	Y
5 ***Latham***	Y	Y	Y	N	Y
KANSAS					
1 ***Moran***	Y	Y	Y	N	Y
2 ***Ryun***	Y	Y	Y	N	Y
3 ***Snowbarger***	Y	Y	Y	N	Y
4 ***Tiahrt***	Y	Y	Y	N	Y
KENTUCKY					
1 ***Whitfield***	Y	Y	Y	N	Y
2 ***Lewis***	Y	Y	Y	N	Y
3 ***Northup***	Y	Y	Y	N	Y
4 ***Bunning***	Y	Y	Y	N	Y
5 ***Rogers***	Y	Y	Y	N	Y
6 Baesler	N	N	N	Y	N
LOUISIANA					
1 ***Livingston***	Y	Y	Y	N	Y
2 Jefferson	N	N	N	Y	N
3 ***Tauzin***	Y	Y	Y	N	Y
4 ***McCrery***	Y	Y	Y	N	Y
5 ***Cooksey***	Y	Y	?	N	Y
6 ***Baker***	Y	Y	Y	N	Y
7 John	N	N	N	Y	N
MAINE					
1 Allen	N	N	N	Y	N
2 Baldacci	N	N	N	Y	N
MARYLAND					
1 ***Gilchrest***	Y	Y	Y	N	Y
2 ***Ehrlich***	Y	Y	Y	N	Y
3 Cardin	N	N	N	Y	N
4 Wynn	N	N	N	Y	N
5 Hoyer	N	N	N	Y	N
6 ***Bartlett***	Y	Y	Y	N	Y
7 Cummings	N	N	N	Y	N
8 ***Morella***	N	P	Y	N	Y
MASSACHUSETTS					
1 Olver	N	N	N	Y	N
2 Neal	N	N	N	Y	N
3 McGovern	N	N	N	Y	N
4 Frank	N	N	N	Y	N
5 Meehan	N	N	N	Y	N
6 Tierney	N	N	N	Y	N
7 Markey	N	N	N	Y	N
8 Kennedy	N	N	N	Y	N
9 Moakley	N	N	N	Y	N
10 Delahunt	N	N	N	Y	N
MICHIGAN					
1 Stupak	N	N	N	Y	N
2 ***Hoekstra***	Y	Y	Y	N	Y
3 ***Ehlers***	Y	Y	Y	N	Y
4 ***Camp***	Y	Y	Y	N	Y
5 Barcia	N	N	N	Y	N
6 ***Upton***	Y	Y	Y	N	Y
7 ***Smith***	Y	Y	Y	N	Y
8 Stabenow	N	N	N	Y	?
9 Kildee	N	N	N	Y	N
10 Bonior	N	N	N	Y	N
11 ***Knollenberg***	Y	Y	Y	N	Y
12 Levin	N	N	N	Y	N
13 Rivers	N	N	N	Y	N
14 Conyers	N	N	N	Y	N
15 Kilpatrick	N	N	N	Y	N
16 Dingell	N	N	N	Y	N
MINNESOTA					
1 ***Gutknecht***	Y	Y	Y	N	Y

	2	3	4	5	6
2 Minge	N	N	N	Y	N
3 ***Ramstad***	Y	Y	Y	N	Y
4 Vento	N	N	N	Y	N
5 Sabo	N	N	N	Y	N
6 Luther	N	N	N	Y	N
7 Peterson	N	N	N	Y	N
8 Oberstar	N	N	N	Y	N
MISSISSIPPI					
1 ***Wicker***	Y	Y	Y	N	Y
2 Thompson	N	N	N	Y	N
3 ***Pickering***	Y	Y	Y	N	Y
4 ***Parker***	Y	Y	Y	N	Y
5 Taylor	N	N	N	Y	N
MISSOURI					
1 Clay	N	N	N	Y	N
2 ***Talent***	Y	Y	Y	N	Y
3 Gephardt	N	P	N	Y	N
4 Skelton	N	N	N	Y	N
5 McCarthy	N	N	N	Y	N
6 Danner	N	N	N	Y	N
7 ***Blunt***	Y	Y	Y	N	Y
8 ***Emerson*** [3]	Y	Y	Y	N	Y
9 ***Hulshof***	Y	Y	Y	N	Y
MONTANA					
AL ***Hill***	Y	Y	Y	N	Y
NEBRASKA					
1 ***Bereuter***	Y	Y	Y	N	Y
2 ***Christensen***	Y	Y	Y	N	Y
3 ***Barrett***	Y	Y	?	N	Y
NEVADA					
1 ***Ensign***	Y	Y	Y	N	Y
2 ***Gibbons***	Y	Y	Y	N	Y
NEW HAMPSHIRE					
1 ***Sununu***	Y	Y	Y	N	Y
2 ***Bass***	Y	Y	Y	N	Y
NEW JERSEY					
1 Andrews	N	N	N	Y	N
2 ***LoBiondo***	Y	Y	Y	N	Y
3 ***Saxton***	Y	Y	Y	N	Y
4 ***Smith***	Y	Y	Y	N	Y
5 ***Roukema***	Y	Y	Y	N	Y
6 Pallone	N	N	N	Y	N
7 ***Franks***	Y	Y	Y	N	Y
8 Pascrell	N	N	N	Y	N
9 Rothman	N	N	N	Y	N
10 Payne	N	N	N	Y	N
11 ***Frelinghuysen***	Y	Y	Y	N	Y
12 ***Pappas***	Y	Y	Y	N	Y
13 Menendez	N	N	N	Y	N
NEW MEXICO					
1 ***Schiff***	Y	Y	Y	Y	Y
2 ***Skeen***	Y	Y	Y	N	Y
3 Richardson	N	N	N	Y	?
NEW YORK					
1 ***Forbes*** [4]	N	N	Y	N	Y
2 ***Lazio***	Y	Y	Y	N	Y
3 ***King***	Y	Y	Y	N	Y
4 McCarthy	N	N	N	Y	N
5 Ackerman	N	N	N	Y	N
6 Flake	N	N	N	Y	N
7 Manton	N	N	N	Y	N
8 Nadler	N	N	N	Y	N
9 Schumer	N	N	N	Y	N
10 Towns	N	N	N	Y	N
11 Owens	N	N	N	Y	N
12 Velázquez	N	N	N	Y	N
13 ***Molinari***	Y	Y	Y	N	Y
14 Maloney	N	N	N	Y	N
15 Rangel	N	N	N	Y	N
16 Serrano	N	N	N	Y	N
17 Engel	N	N	N	Y	N
18 Lowey	N	N	N	Y	N
19 ***Kelly***	Y	Y	Y	N	Y
20 ***Gilman***	Y	Y	Y	N	Y
21 McNulty	N	N	N	Y	N
22 ***Solomon***	Y	Y	Y	N	Y
23 ***Boehlert***	Y	Y	Y	N	Y
24 ***McHugh***	Y	Y	Y	N	Y
25 ***Walsh***	Y	Y	Y	N	Y
26 Hinchey	N	N	N	Y	N
27 ***Paxon***	Y	Y	Y	N	Y
28 Slaughter	N	N	N	Y	N
29 LaFalce	N	N	N	Y	N
30 ***Quinn***	Y	Y	Y	N	Y

	2	3	4	5	6
31 ***Houghton***	Y	Y	Y	N	Y
NORTH CAROLINA					
1 Clayton	N	N	N	Y	N
2 Etheridge	N	N	N	Y	N
3 ***Jones***	Y	Y	Y	N	Y
4 Price	N	N	N	Y	N
5 ***Burr***	Y	Y	Y	N	Y
6 ***Coble***	Y	Y	Y	N	Y
7 McIntyre	N	N	N	Y	N
8 Hefner	N	N	N	Y	N
9 ***Myrick***	Y	Y	Y	N	Y
10 ***Ballenger***	Y	Y	Y	N	Y
11 ***Taylor***	Y	Y	Y	N	Y
12 Watt	N	N	N	Y	N
NORTH DAKOTA					
AL Pomeroy	N	N	N	Y	N
OHIO					
1 ***Chabot***	Y	Y	Y	N	Y
2 ***Portman***	Y	Y	Y	N	Y
3 Hall	N	N	N	Y	N
4 ***Oxley***	Y	Y	Y	N	Y
5 ***Gillmor***	Y	Y	Y	N	Y
6 Strickland	N	N	N	Y	N
7 ***Hobson***	Y	Y	Y	N	Y
8 ***Boehner***	Y	Y	Y	N	Y
9 Kaptur	N	N	N	Y	N
10 Kucinich	N	N	N	Y	N
11 Stokes	N	N	N	Y	N
12 ***Kasich***	Y	Y	Y	N	Y
13 Brown	N	N	N	Y	N
14 Sawyer	N	N	N	Y	N
15 ***Pryce***	Y	Y	Y	N	Y
16 ***Regula***	Y	Y	Y	N	Y
17 Traficant	N	N	N	Y	Y
18 ***Ney***	Y	Y	Y	N	Y
19 ***LaTourette***	Y	Y	Y	N	Y
OKLAHOMA					
1 ***Largent***	Y	Y	Y	N	Y
2 ***Coburn***	Y	Y	Y	N	Y
3 ***Watkins***	Y	Y	Y	N	Y
4 ***Watts***	Y	Y	Y	N	Y
5 ***Istook***	Y	Y	Y	N	Y
6 ***Lucas***	Y	Y	Y	N	Y
OREGON					
1 Furse	N	N	N	Y	N
2 ***Smith***	Y	Y	Y	N	Y
3 Blumenauer	N	N	N	Y	N
4 DeFazio	N	N	N	Y	N
5 Hooley	N	N	N	Y	N
PENNSYLVANIA					
1 Foglietta	N	N	N	Y	N
2 Fattah	N	N	N	Y	N
3 Borski	N	N	N	Y	N
4 Klink	N	N	N	Y	N
5 ***Peterson***	Y	Y	?	N	Y
6 Holden	N	N	N	Y	N
7 ***Weldon***	Y	Y	Y	N	Y
8 ***Greenwood***	Y	Y	Y	N	Y
9 ***Shuster***	Y	Y	Y	N	Y
10 ***McDade***	Y	Y	Y	N	Y
11 Kanjorski	N	N	N	Y	N
12 Murtha	N	N	N	Y	N
13 ***Fox***	Y	Y	Y	N	Y
14 Coyne	N	N	N	Y	N
15 McHale	N	N	N	Y	N
16 ***Pitts***	Y	Y	Y	N	Y
17 ***Gekas***	Y	Y	Y	N	Y
18 Doyle	N	N	N	Y	N
19 ***Goodling***	Y	Y	Y	N	Y
20 Mascara	N	N	N	Y	N
21 ***English***	Y	Y	Y	N	Y
RHODE ISLAND					
1 Kennedy	N	N	N	Y	N
2 Weygand	N	N	N	Y	N
SOUTH CAROLINA					
1 ***Sanford***	N	Y	?	?	Y
2 ***Spence***	Y	Y	Y	N	Y
3 ***Graham***	Y	Y	Y	N	Y
4 ***Inglis***	Y	Y	Y	N	Y
5 Spratt	N	N	N	Y	N
6 Clyburn	N	N	N	Y	N
SOUTH DAKOTA					
AL ***Thune***	Y	Y	Y	N	Y

	2	3	4	5	6
TENNESSEE					
1 ***Jenkins***	Y	Y	Y	N	Y
2 ***Duncan***	Y	Y	Y	N	Y
3 ***Wamp***	Y	Y	Y	N	Y
4 ***Hilleary***	Y	Y	Y	N	Y
5 Clement	N	N	N	Y	N
6 Gordon	N	N	N	Y	N
7 ***Bryant***	Y	Y	Y	N	Y
8 Tanner	N	N	N	Y	N
9 Ford	N	N	N	Y	N
TEXAS					
1 Sandlin	N	N	N	Y	N
2 Turner	N	N	N	Y	N
3 ***Johnson, Sam***	?	+	Y	N	Y
4 Hall	N	N	N	Y	Y
5 ***Sessions***	Y	Y	Y	N	Y
6 ***Barton***	Y	Y	Y	N	Y
7 ***Archer***	Y	Y	Y	N	Y
8 ***Brady***	Y	Y	?	N	Y
9 Lampson	N	N	N	Y	N
10 Doggett	N	N	N	Y	N
11 Edwards	N	N	N	Y	N
12 ***Granger***	Y	Y	Y	N	Y
13 ***Thornberry***	Y	Y	Y	N	Y
14 ***Paul***	Y	Y	Y	N	N
15 Hinojosa	N	N	N	Y	N
16 Reyes	N	N	N	Y	N
17 Stenholm	N	N	N	Y	N
18 Jackson-Lee	N	N	N	Y	N
19 ***Combest***	Y	Y	Y	N	Y
20 Gonzalez	N	N	N	Y	N
21 ***Smith***	Y	Y	Y	N	Y
22 ***DeLay***	Y	Y	Y	N	Y
23 ***Bonilla***	Y	Y	Y	N	Y
24 Frost	N	N	N	Y	N
25 Bentsen	N	N	N	Y	N
26 ***Armey***	Y	Y	Y	N	Y
27 Ortiz	N	N	N	Y	N
28 Tejeda	?	?	?	?	?
29 Green	N	N	N	Y	N
30 Johnson, E.B.	N	N	N	Y	N
UTAH					
1 ***Hansen***	Y	Y	Y	N	Y
2 ***Cook***	Y	Y	Y	N	Y
3 ***Cannon***	Y	Y	Y	N	Y
VERMONT					
AL *Sanders*	N	N	N	Y	N
VIRGINIA					
1 ***Bateman***	Y	Y	Y	N	Y
2 Pickett	N	N	N	Y	N
3 Scott	N	N	N	Y	N
4 Sisisky	N	N	N	Y	N
5 Goode	N	N	N	Y	Y
6 ***Goodlatte***	Y	Y	Y	N	Y
7 ***Bliley***	Y	Y	Y	N	Y
8 Moran	N	N	N	Y	N
9 Boucher	N	N	N	Y	N
10 ***Wolf***	Y	P	Y	N	Y
11 ***Davis***	Y	Y	Y	N	Y
WASHINGTON					
1 ***White***	Y	Y	Y	N	Y
2 ***Metcalf***	Y	Y	Y	N	Y
3 ***Smith, Linda*** [5]	N	N	Y	N	Y
4 ***Hastings***	Y	Y	Y	N	Y
5 ***Nethercutt***	Y	Y	Y	N	Y
6 Dicks	N	N	N	Y	N
7 McDermott	N	N	N	Y	N
8 ***Dunn***	Y	Y	Y	N	Y
9 Smith, Adam	N	N	N	Y	N
WEST VIRGINIA					
1 Mollohan	N	N	N	Y	N
2 Wise	N	N	N	Y	N
3 Rahall	N	N	N	Y	N
WISCONSIN					
1 ***Neumann***	Y	P	Y	N	Y
2 ***Klug***	Y	P	Y	N	Y
3 Kind	N	N	N	Y	N
4 Kleczka	N	N	N	Y	N
5 Barrett	N	N	N	Y	N
6 ***Petri***	Y	Y	Y	N	Y
7 Obey	N	N	N	Y	N
8 Johnson	N	N	N	Y	N
9 ***Sensenbrenner***	Y	Y	Y	N	Y
WYOMING					
AL ***Cubin***	Y	Y	Y	N	Y

Southern states - Ala., Ark., Fla., Ga., Ky., La., Miss., N.C., Okla., S.C., Tenn., Texas, Va.

HOUSE VOTES 7, 8, 9, 10

7. S Con Res 3. Recess Schedule/Adoption. Adoption of the concurrent resolution to establish the House and Senate recess or adjournment schedules during January and February 1997. Adopted 222-198: R 219-0; D 3-197 (ND 1-145, SD 2-52); I 0-1, Jan. 7, 1997.

8. H Res 31. Reprimand of Rep. Newt Gingrich/Adoption. Adoption of the resolution to adopt the Jan. 17, 1997, report of the ethics committee recommending that Speaker Newt Gingrich, R-Ga., be reprimanded for bringing discredit upon the House by failing to seek legal advice regarding the use of tax-exempt foundations for political purposes, and for providing inaccurate information to the House ethics subcommittee investigating the case. The committee also recommended that the Speaker pay $300,000 to the House to cover some of the committee costs incurred while attempting to reconcile conflicting statements made by Gingrich. Adopted 395-28: R 196-26; D 198-2 (ND 147-0, SD 51-2); I 1-0, Jan. 21, 1997.

9. HR 499. Frank M. Tejeda Post Office/Passage. McHugh, R-N.Y., motion to suspend the rules and pass the bill to designate the Frank M. Tejeda Post Office in San Antonio, Texas. Motion agreed to 400-0: R 211-0; D 188-0 (ND 136-0, SD 52-0); I 1-0, Feb. 5, 1997. A two-thirds majority of those present and voting (267 in this case) is required under suspension of the rules.

10. Procedural Motion/Journal. Approval of the House Journal of Tuesday, Feb. 4, 1997. Approved 376-28: R 203-10; D 172-18 (ND 126-12, SD 46-6); I 1-0, Feb. 5, 1997.

[1] *Rep. Frank M. Tejeda, D-Texas, died Jan. 30, 1997.*

KEY

- Y Voted for (yea).
- # Paired for.
- + Announced for.
- N Voted against (nay).
- X Paired against.
- – Announced against.
- P Voted "present."
- C Voted "present" to avoid possible conflict of interest.
- ? Did not vote or otherwise make a position known.

Democrats ***Republicans***
Independent

	7	8	9	10
ALABAMA				
1 ***Callahan***	Y	N	Y	Y
2 ***Everett***	Y	Y	Y	Y
3 ***Riley***	Y	Y	Y	Y
4 ***Aderholt***	Y	Y	Y	Y
5 Cramer	N	Y	Y	Y
6 ***Bachus***	Y	Y	Y	Y
7 Hilliard	N	N	Y	N
ALASKA				
AL ***Young***	Y	N	Y	Y
ARIZONA				
1 ***Salmon***	Y	Y	Y	Y
2 Pastor	N	Y	Y	Y
3 ***Stump***	Y	N	Y	Y
4 ***Shadegg***	Y	Y	Y	Y
5 ***Kolbe***	Y	?	Y	Y
6 ***Hayworth***	Y	Y	Y	Y
ARKANSAS				
1 Berry	N	Y	Y	Y
2 Snyder	N	Y	Y	Y
3 ***Hutchinson***	Y	Y	Y	Y
4 ***Dickey***	Y	Y	Y	Y
CALIFORNIA				
1 ***Riggs***	Y	Y	Y	Y
2 ***Herger***	Y	N	Y	Y
3 Fazio	N	Y	Y	Y
4 ***Doolittle***	Y	N	Y	Y
5 Matsui	N	Y	Y	Y
6 Woolsey	N	Y	Y	Y
7 Miller	N	Y	Y	N
8 Pelosi	N	Y	Y	Y
9 Dellums	N	Y	Y	Y
10 Tauscher	N	Y	Y	Y
11 ***Pombo***	Y	Y	?	?
12 Lantos	N	Y	Y	Y
13 Stark	N	Y	Y	N
14 Eshoo	N	Y	Y	Y
15 ***Campbell***	Y	Y	Y	Y
16 Lofgren	N	Y	Y	Y
17 Farr	N	Y	Y	Y
18 Condit	N	Y	Y	Y
19 ***Radanovich***	Y	Y	Y	Y
20 Dooley	N	Y	Y	Y
21 ***Thomas***	Y	Y	Y	Y
22 Capps	N	Y	Y	Y
23 ***Gallegly***	Y	Y	Y	Y
24 Sherman	N	Y	Y	Y
25 ***McKeon***	Y	N	Y	Y
26 Berman	N	Y	Y	Y
27 ***Rogan***	Y	Y	Y	Y
28 ***Dreier***	Y	Y	Y	Y
29 Waxman	N	Y	Y	Y
30 Becerra	N	Y	Y	Y
31 Martinez	N	Y	Y	Y
32 Dixon	N	Y	Y	Y
33 Roybal-Allard	N	Y	Y	Y
34 Torres	?	Y	Y	Y
35 Waters	N	P	Y	N
36 Harman	N	Y	Y	Y
37 Millender-McD.	N	Y	Y	Y
38 ***Horn***	Y	Y	Y	Y
39 ***Royce***	Y	Y	Y	Y
40 ***Lewis***	Y	N	Y	Y

	7	8	9	10
41 ***Kim***	Y	Y	Y	Y
42 Brown	N	Y	Y	Y
43 ***Calvert***	Y	Y	Y	Y
44 ***Bono***	Y	Y	Y	Y
45 ***Rohrabacher***	Y	Y	Y	Y
46 Sanchez	N	Y	Y	Y
47 ***Cox***	Y	Y	Y	Y
48 ***Packard***	Y	N	Y	Y
49 ***Bilbray***	Y	Y	Y	Y
50 Filner	N	Y	Y	N
51 ***Cunningham***	Y	Y	Y	Y
52 ***Hunter***	Y	N	Y	Y
COLORADO				
1 DeGette	N	Y	Y	Y
2 Skaggs	N	Y	Y	Y
3 ***McInnis***	?	Y	Y	Y
4 ***Schaffer***	Y	Y	Y	Y
5 ***Hefley***	Y	Y	Y	N
6 ***Schaefer***	Y	Y	Y	Y
CONNECTICUT				
1 Kennelly	N	Y	Y	Y
2 Gejdenson	N	Y	?	?
3 DeLauro	N	Y	Y	Y
4 ***Shays***	Y	Y	Y	Y
5 Maloney	N	Y	Y	Y
6 ***Johnson***	Y	Y	Y	Y
DELAWARE				
AL ***Castle***	Y	Y	Y	Y
FLORIDA				
1 ***Scarborough***	Y	Y	Y	Y
2 Boyd	N	Y	Y	Y
3 Brown	N	Y	Y	Y
4 ***Fowler***	Y	Y	Y	Y
5 Thurman	N	Y	Y	Y
6 ***Stearns***	Y	Y	Y	Y
7 ***Mica***	Y	N	Y	Y
8 ***McCollum***	Y	Y	Y	Y
9 ***Bilirakis***	Y	Y	Y	Y
10 ***Young***	?	Y	?	?
11 Davis	N	Y	Y	Y
12 ***Canady***	Y	Y	Y	Y
13 ***Miller***	Y	Y	Y	Y
14 ***Goss***	Y	Y	Y	Y
15 ***Weldon***	Y	Y	Y	Y
16 ***Foley***	Y	Y	Y	Y
17 Meek	N	Y	Y	Y
18 ***Ros-Lehtinen***	?	Y	Y	Y
19 Wexler	N	Y	Y	Y
20 Deutsch	N	Y	Y	Y
21 ***Diaz-Balart***	Y	Y	Y	Y
22 ***Shaw***	Y	Y	Y	Y
23 Hastings	N	P	Y	N
GEORGIA				
1 ***Kingston***	Y	Y	Y	Y
2 Bishop	N	Y	Y	Y
3 ***Collins***	Y	Y	Y	Y
4 McKinney	N	Y	Y	Y
5 Lewis	N	Y	Y	N
6 ***Gingrich***				
7 ***Barr***	Y	N	Y	Y
8 ***Chambliss***	Y	Y	Y	Y
9 ***Deal***	Y	Y	Y	Y
10 ***Norwood***	Y	Y	?	?
11 ***Linder***	Y	Y	?	?
HAWAII				
1 Abercrombie	N	P	Y	N
2 Mink	N	Y	Y	Y
IDAHO				
1 ***Chenoweth***	Y	Y	?	?
2 ***Crapo***	Y	Y	+	Y
ILLINOIS				
1 Rush	N	Y	Y	Y
2 Jackson	N	Y	Y	Y
3 Lipinski	N	Y	Y	Y
4 Gutierrez	N	Y	Y	Y
5 Blagojevich	N	Y	Y	Y
6 ***Hyde***	Y	Y	Y	Y
7 Davis	N	Y	Y	Y
8 ***Crane***	Y	Y	Y	Y
9 Yates	?	Y	Y	N
10 ***Porter***	Y	Y	Y	Y
11 ***Weller***	Y	Y	Y	N
12 Costello	N	Y	Y	Y
13 ***Fawell***	Y	Y	Y	Y
14 ***Hastert***	Y	Y	Y	Y

ND Northern Democrats SD Southern Democrats

	7	8	9	10
15 ***Ewing***	Y	Y	Y	Y
16 ***Manzullo***	Y	Y	Y	Y
17 Evans	N	Y	Y	Y
18 ***LaHood***	Y	Y	Y	Y
19 Poshard	N	Y	Y	Y
20 ***Shimkus***	Y	Y	Y	Y
INDIANA				
1 Visclosky	N	Y	Y	N
2 ***McIntosh***	Y	Y	Y	Y
3 Roemer	N	Y	+	+
4 ***Souder***	Y	Y	Y	Y
5 ***Buyer***	Y	N	Y	Y
6 ***Burton***	Y	N	Y	Y
7 ***Pease***	Y	Y	Y	Y
8 ***Hostettler***	Y	Y	?	Y
9 Hamilton	N	Y	Y	Y
10 Carson	?	?	?	?
IOWA				
1 ***Leach***	Y	Y	Y	Y
2 ***Nussle***	Y	Y	Y	Y
3 Boswell	N	Y	Y	Y
4 ***Ganske***	Y	Y	Y	Y
5 ***Latham***	Y	Y	Y	Y
KANSAS				
1 ***Moran***	Y	Y	Y	Y
2 ***Ryun***	Y	Y	Y	Y
3 ***Snowbarger***	Y	Y	Y	Y
4 ***Tiahrt***	Y	Y	Y	Y
KENTUCKY				
1 ***Whitfield***	Y	Y	Y	Y
2 ***Lewis***	Y	Y	Y	Y
3 ***Northup***	Y	Y	Y	Y
4 ***Bunning***	Y	Y	Y	Y
5 ***Rogers***	Y	Y	Y	Y
6 Baesler	N	Y	Y	Y
LOUISIANA				
1 ***Livingston***	Y	N	Y	Y
2 Jefferson	N	Y	Y	?
3 ***Tauzin***	Y	+	Y	Y
4 ***McCrery***	Y	Y	Y	Y
5 ***Cooksey***	Y	Y	?	?
6 ***Baker***	Y	Y	Y	Y
7 John	N	Y	Y	Y
MAINE				
1 Allen	N	Y	Y	Y
2 Baldacci	N	Y	Y	Y
MARYLAND				
1 ***Gilchrest***	Y	Y	Y	Y
2 ***Ehrlich***	Y	Y	Y	Y
3 Cardin	N	Y	Y	Y
4 Wynn	N	Y	Y	Y
5 Hoyer	N	Y	?	?
6 ***Bartlett***	Y	N	Y	Y
7 Cummings	N	Y	?	?
8 ***Morella***	Y	Y	Y	Y
MASSACHUSETTS				
1 Olver	N	Y	Y	Y
2 Neal	N	Y	Y	Y
3 McGovern	N	Y	Y	Y
4 Frank	N	Y	Y	Y
5 Meehan	N	Y	Y	Y
6 Tierney	N	Y	Y	Y
7 Markey	N	Y	Y	Y
8 Kennedy	N	Y	Y	Y
9 Moakley	N	Y	Y	Y
10 Delahunt	N	Y	Y	Y
MICHIGAN				
1 Stupak	N	Y	Y	Y
2 ***Hoekstra***	?	Y	Y	Y
3 ***Ehlers***	Y	Y	Y	Y
4 ***Camp***	Y	Y	Y	Y
5 Barcia	N	Y	Y	Y
6 ***Upton***	Y	Y	Y	Y
7 ***Smith***	Y	Y	Y	Y
8 Stabenow	N	Y	Y	Y
9 Kildee	N	Y	Y	Y
10 Bonior	N	Y	Y	Y
11 ***Knollenberg***	Y	Y	Y	Y
12 Levin	N	Y	Y	Y
13 Rivers	N	Y	Y	Y
14 Conyers	N	P	Y	Y
15 Kilpatrick	N	Y	Y	Y
16 Dingell	N	Y	Y	Y
MINNESOTA				
1 ***Gutknecht***	Y	Y	Y	N

	7	8	9	10
2 Minge	N	Y	Y	Y
3 ***Ramstad***	Y	Y	Y	N
4 Vento	N	Y	Y	Y
5 Sabo	N	Y	Y	N
6 Luther	N	Y	Y	Y
7 Peterson	N	Y	Y	Y
8 Oberstar	N	Y	Y	N
MISSISSIPPI				
1 ***Wicker***	Y	N	Y	N
2 Thompson	N	Y	Y	N
3 ***Pickering***	Y	Y	Y	Y
4 ***Parker***	Y	Y	Y	Y
5 Taylor	N	N	Y	N
MISSOURI				
1 Clay	N	Y	?	?
2 ***Talent***	Y	Y	Y	Y
3 Gephardt	N	Y	Y	Y
4 Skelton	N	Y	+	Y
5 McCarthy	N	Y	Y	Y
6 Danner	N	Y	Y	Y
7 ***Blunt***	Y	Y	?	Y
8 ***Emerson***	Y	Y	Y	Y
9 ***Hulshof***	Y	Y	Y	Y
MONTANA				
AL ***Hill***	Y	Y	?	Y
NEBRASKA				
1 ***Bereuter***	Y	Y	Y	Y
2 ***Christensen***	Y	Y	Y	Y
3 ***Barrett***	Y	Y	?	?
NEVADA				
1 ***Ensign***	Y	Y	Y	N
2 ***Gibbons***	Y	Y	Y	N
NEW HAMPSHIRE				
1 ***Sununu***	Y	Y	Y	?
2 ***Bass***	Y	Y	Y	Y
NEW JERSEY				
1 Andrews	N	Y	Y	Y
2 ***LoBiondo***	Y	Y	Y	Y
3 ***Saxton***	Y	Y	Y	Y
4 ***Smith***	?	Y	Y	Y
5 ***Roukema***	Y	Y	Y	Y
6 Pallone	N	Y	Y	Y
7 ***Franks***	Y	Y	Y	Y
8 Pascrell	N	Y	Y	N
9 Rothman	N	Y	Y	Y
10 Payne	N	Y	Y	Y
11 ***Frelinghuysen***	Y	Y	Y	Y
12 ***Pappas***	Y	Y	Y	Y
13 Menendez	N	Y	Y	Y
NEW MEXICO				
1 ***Schiff***	Y	Y	Y	Y
2 ***Skeen***	Y	Y	Y	Y
3 Richardson	?	Y	Y	Y
NEW YORK				
1 ***Forbes***	Y	Y	Y	Y
2 ***Lazio***	Y	Y	+	Y
3 ***King***	Y	N	Y	Y
4 McCarthy	N	Y	Y	Y
5 Ackerman	N	Y	Y	Y
6 Flake	N	Y	Y	Y
7 Manton	N	Y	Y	Y
8 Nadler	N	Y	Y	Y
9 Schumer	N	Y	Y	Y
10 Towns	N	Y	?	?
11 Owens	N	Y	Y	Y
12 Velázquez	N	Y	Y	Y
13 ***Molinari***	Y	Y	Y	Y
14 Maloney	N	Y	Y	Y
15 Rangel	?	Y	Y	Y
16 Serrano	N	Y	Y	Y
17 Engel	N	Y	Y	Y
18 Lowey	N	Y	Y	Y
19 ***Kelly***	Y	Y	Y	Y
20 ***Gilman***	Y	Y	Y	Y
21 McNulty	N	Y	Y	Y
22 ***Solomon***	Y	N	Y	Y
23 ***Boehlert***	Y	Y	Y	Y
24 ***McHugh***	Y	Y	Y	Y
25 ***Walsh***	Y	Y	Y	Y
26 Hinchey	N	Y	Y	Y
27 ***Paxon***	Y	Y	Y	Y
28 Slaughter	N	Y	Y	Y
29 LaFalce	N	Y	Y	Y
30 ***Quinn***	Y	Y	Y	Y

	7	8	9	10
31 ***Houghton***	Y	Y	Y	Y
NORTH CAROLINA				
1 Clayton	N	Y	Y	Y
2 Etheridge	N	Y	Y	Y
3 ***Jones***	Y	Y	Y	Y
4 Price	N	Y	Y	Y
5 ***Burr***	Y	Y	Y	Y
6 ***Coble***	Y	Y	Y	Y
7 McIntyre	N	Y	Y	Y
8 Hefner	N	Y	Y	Y
9 ***Myrick***	Y	N	Y	Y
10 ***Ballenger***	Y	Y	Y	Y
11 ***Taylor***	Y	N	Y	?
12 Watt	N	Y	Y	Y
NORTH DAKOTA				
AL Pomeroy	N	Y	Y	Y
OHIO				
1 ***Chabot***	Y	Y	Y	Y
2 ***Portman***	Y	Y	Y	Y
3 Hall	N	Y	Y	Y
4 ***Oxley***	Y	Y	Y	Y
5 ***Gillmor***	Y	Y	Y	N
6 Strickland	N	Y	Y	Y
7 ***Hobson***	Y	Y	Y	Y
8 ***Boehner***	Y	Y	Y	Y
9 Kaptur	N	Y	Y	Y
10 Kucinich	N	Y	Y	Y
11 Stokes	?	Y	Y	Y
12 ***Kasich***	Y	Y	Y	Y
13 Brown	N	Y	?	?
14 Sawyer	N	Y	Y	Y
15 ***Pryce***	Y	Y	Y	Y
16 ***Regula***	Y	Y	Y	Y
17 Traficant	N	Y	?	?
18 ***Ney***	Y	Y	Y	Y
19 ***LaTourette***	Y	Y	Y	Y
OKLAHOMA				
1 ***Largent***	Y	Y	?	?
2 ***Coburn***	Y	N	Y	?
3 ***Watkins***	Y	Y	?	Y
4 ***Watts***	Y	+	Y	N
5 ***Istook***	Y	Y	Y	?
6 ***Lucas***	Y	Y	Y	Y
OREGON				
1 Furse	N	Y	?	Y
2 ***Smith***	?	Y	Y	Y
3 Blumenauer	N	Y	Y	Y
4 DeFazio	N	Y	Y	N
5 Hooley	N	Y	Y	Y
PENNSYLVANIA				
1 Foglietta	N	Y	?	?
2 Fattah	N	Y	Y	Y
3 Borski	N	Y	Y	N
4 Klink	N	Y	Y	Y
5 ***Peterson***	Y	Y	Y	Y
6 Holden	N	Y	Y	Y
7 ***Weldon***	?	Y	Y	Y
8 ***Greenwood***	Y	Y	Y	Y
9 ***Shuster***	Y	Y	Y	Y
10 ***McDade***	Y	Y	?	?
11 Kanjorski	N	Y	Y	Y
12 Murtha	Y	Y	Y	Y
13 ***Fox***	Y	Y	Y	Y
14 Coyne	N	Y	Y	Y
15 McHale	N	Y	Y	Y
16 ***Pitts***	Y	Y	Y	Y
17 ***Gekas***	Y	Y	Y	Y
18 Doyle	N	Y	?	?
19 ***Goodling***	Y	Y	Y	Y
20 Mascara	N	Y	Y	Y
21 ***English***	Y	Y	Y	N
RHODE ISLAND				
1 Kennedy	N	Y	Y	Y
2 Weygand	N	Y	Y	Y
SOUTH CAROLINA				
1 ***Sanford***	Y	Y	Y	Y
2 ***Spence***	Y	Y	Y	Y
3 ***Graham***	Y	Y	Y	Y
4 ***Inglis***	Y	Y	Y	Y
5 Spratt	N	Y	Y	Y
6 Clyburn	N	Y	Y	Y
SOUTH DAKOTA				
AL ***Thune***	Y	Y	Y	Y

	7	8	9	10
TENNESSEE				
1 ***Jenkins***	Y	Y	Y	Y
2 ***Duncan***	Y	Y	Y	Y
3 ***Wamp***	Y	Y	Y	Y
4 ***Hilleary***	Y	Y	Y	Y
5 Clement	N	Y	?	?
6 Gordon	N	Y	Y	Y
7 ***Bryant***	Y	Y	Y	Y
8 Tanner	N	Y	Y	Y
9 Ford	N	Y	Y	Y
TEXAS				
1 Sandlin	N	Y	Y	Y
2 Turner	N	Y	+	Y
3 ***Johnson, Sam***	Y	N	Y	Y
4 Hall	Y	Y	Y	Y
5 ***Sessions***	Y	N	Y	Y
6 ***Barton***	Y	N	Y	Y
7 ***Archer***	Y	Y	Y	Y
8 ***Brady***	Y	Y	Y	Y
9 Lampson	N	Y	Y	Y
10 Doggett	N	Y	Y	Y
11 Edwards	N	Y	Y	Y
12 ***Granger***	Y	?	Y	Y
13 ***Thornberry***	Y	Y	Y	Y
14 ***Paul***	Y	Y	Y	Y
15 Hinojosa	N	Y	Y	Y
16 Reyes	N	Y	Y	Y
17 Stenholm	N	Y	Y	Y
18 Jackson-Lee	N	Y	Y	Y
19 ***Combest***	Y	Y	Y	Y
20 Gonzalez	N	Y	Y	Y
21 ***Smith***	Y	N	Y	Y
22 ***DeLay***	Y	N	Y	Y
23 ***Bonilla***	Y	Y	Y	Y
24 Frost	N	Y	Y	Y
25 Bentsen	N	Y	Y	Y
26 ***Armey***	Y	Y	Y	Y
27 Ortiz	N	Y	Y	Y
28 Tejeda[1]	?	?		
29 Green	N	Y	Y	Y
30 Johnson, E.B.	N	Y	Y	Y
UTAH				
1 ***Hansen***	Y	Y	Y	Y
2 ***Cook***	Y	Y	Y	Y
3 ***Cannon***	Y	Y	Y	Y
VERMONT				
AL *Sanders*	N	Y	Y	Y
VIRGINIA				
1 ***Bateman***	Y	Y	Y	Y
2 Pickett	N	Y	Y	N
3 Scott	N	Y	Y	Y
4 Sisisky	N	Y	Y	Y
5 Goode	N	Y	Y	Y
6 ***Goodlatte***	Y	Y	Y	Y
7 ***Bliley***	Y	Y	Y	Y
8 Moran	N	Y	Y	Y
9 Boucher	Y	Y	Y	Y
10 ***Wolf***	Y	Y	Y	Y
11 ***Davis***	Y	Y	Y	Y
WASHINGTON				
1 ***White***	Y	Y	Y	Y
2 ***Metcalf***	Y	Y	Y	Y
3 ***Smith, Linda***	Y	Y	Y	Y
4 ***Hastings***	Y	Y	Y	Y
5 ***Nethercutt***	Y	Y	Y	Y
6 Dicks	N	Y	Y	Y
7 McDermott	N	P	Y	Y
8 ***Dunn***	Y	Y	Y	Y
9 Smith, Adam	N	Y	?	?
WEST VIRGINIA				
1 Mollohan	N	Y	Y	Y
2 Wise	N	Y	Y	Y
3 Rahall	N	Y	Y	Y
WISCONSIN				
1 ***Neumann***	Y	Y	Y	Y
2 ***Klug***	Y	Y	Y	Y
3 Kind	N	Y	Y	Y
4 Kleczka	N	Y	Y	Y
5 Barrett	N	Y	?	?
6 ***Petri***	Y	Y	Y	Y
7 Obey	N	Y	?	?
8 Johnson	N	Y	Y	Y
9 ***Sensenbrenner***	Y	Y	Y	Y
WYOMING				
AL ***Cubin***	Y	Y	Y	Y

Southern states - Ala., Ark., Fla., Ga., Ky., La., Miss., N.C., Okla., S.C., Tenn., Texas, Va.

HOUSE VOTES 11, 12, 13, 14, 15, 16, 17, 18

11. H J Res 2. Term Limit Constitutional Amendment/Arkansas Substitute. Hutchinson, R-Ark., substitute amendment to impose a six-year lifetime limit on House members and a 12-year limit on senators. The amendment proposed the exact language used in an Arkansas ballot initiative instructing its delegation on how to vote to avoid a ballot notation in future elections. Rejected 85-341: R 67-157; D 18-183 (ND 13-134, SD 5-49); I 0-1, Feb. 12, 1997.

12. H J Res 2. Term Limit Constitutional Amendment/Colorado Substitute. McInnis, R-Colo., substitute amendment to impose a six-year lifetime limit on House members and a 12-year limit on senators. The amendment proposed the exact language used in a Colorado ballot initiative instructing its delegation on how to vote to avoid a ballot notation in future elections. Rejected 87-339: R 70-154; D 17-184 (ND 13-135, SD 4-49); I 0-1, Feb. 12, 1997.

13. H J Res 2. Term Limit Constitutional Amendment/Idaho Substitute. Crapo, R-Idaho, substitute amendment to impose a six-year lifetime limit on House members and a 12-year limit for senators. The amendment proposed the exact language used in an Idaho ballot initiative instructing its delegation on how to vote to avoid a ballot notation in future elections. Rejected 85-339: R 67-157; D 18-181 (ND 13-134, SD 5-47); I 0-1, Feb. 12, 1997.

14. H J Res 2. Term Limit Constitutional Amendment/Missouri Substitute. Blunt, R-Mo., substitute amendment to impose a six-year lifetime limit on House members and a 12-year limit on senators, and allow states to enact longer or shorter term limits. The amendment proposed the exact language used in a Missouri ballot initiative instructing its delegation on how to vote to avoid a ballot notation in future elections. Rejected 72-353: R 54-168; D 18-184 (ND 12-136, SD 6-48); I 0-1, Feb. 12, 1997.

15. H J Res 2. Term Limit Constitutional Amendment/Nebraska Substitute. Christensen, R-Neb., substitute amendment to impose a six-year lifetime limit on House members and a 12-year limit on senators. The amendment proposed the exact language used in a Nebraska ballot initiative instructing its delegation on how to vote to avoid a ballot notation in future elections. Rejected 83-342: R 66-156; D 17-185 (ND 13-135, SD 4-50); I 0-1, Feb. 12, 1997.

16. H J Res 2. Term Limit Constitutional Amendment/Nevada Substitute. Ensign, R-Nev., substitute amendment to impose a six-year lifetime limit on House members and a 12-year limit on senators. The amendment proposed the exact language used in a Colorado ballot initiative instructing its delegation on how to vote to avoid a ballot notation in future elections. Rejected 85-339: R 68-153; D 17-185 (ND 12-136, SD 5-49); I 0-1, Feb. 12, 1997.

17. H J Res 2. Term Limit Constitutional Amendment/South Dakota Substitute. Thune, R-S.D., substitute amendment to impose a six-year lifetime limit on House members and a 12-year limit on senators. The amendment proposed the exact language used in a South Dakota ballot initiative instructing its delegation on how to vote to avoid a ballot notation in future elections. Rejected 83-342: R 66-157; D 17-184 (ND 13-134, SD 4-50); I 0-1, Feb. 12, 1997.

18. H J Res 2. Term Limit Constitutional Amendment/Consecutive-Year Limit. Fowler, R-Fla., substitute amendment to impose a limit of eight consecutive years on House members and a limit of 12 consecutive years on senators. Rejected 91-335: R 72-151; D 19-183 (ND 13-135, SD 6-48); I 0-1, Feb. 12, 1997.

KEY

- Y Voted for (yea).
- # Paired for.
- + Announced for.
- N Voted against (nay).
- X Paired against.
- – Announced against.
- P Voted "present."
- C Voted "present" to avoid possible conflict of interest.
- ? Did not vote or otherwise make a position known.

Democrats ***Republicans***
Independent

	11	12	13	14	15	16	17	18
ALABAMA								
1 ***Callahan***	N	N	N	N	N	N	N	Y
2 ***Everett***	N	N	N	N	N	N	N	N
3 ***Riley***	Y	Y	Y	N	Y	Y	Y	Y
4 ***Aderholt***	N	N	N	N	N	N	N	N
5 Cramer	Y	Y	Y	Y	Y	Y	Y	Y
6 ***Bachus***	N	N	N	N	N	N	N	N
7 Hilliard	N	N	N	N	N	N	N	N
ALASKA								
AL ***Young***	?	?	?	?	?	?	?	?
ARIZONA								
1 ***Salmon***	Y	Y	Y	Y	Y	Y	Y	N
2 Pastor	N	N	N	N	N	N	N	N
3 ***Stump***	N	N	N	N	N	N	N	N
4 ***Shadegg***	Y	Y	Y	Y	Y	Y	Y	Y
5 ***Kolbe***	N	N	N	N	N	N	N	N
6 ***Hayworth***	N	N	N	N	N	N	N	N
ARKANSAS								
1 Berry	N	N	N	N	N	N	N	N
2 Snyder	N	N	N	N	N	N	N	N
3 ***Hutchinson***	Y	N	N	N	N	N	N	N
4 ***Dickey***	Y	Y	Y	N	Y	Y	Y	N
CALIFORNIA								
1 ***Riggs***	N	N	Y	N	N	N	N	Y
2 ***Herger***	Y	Y	Y	Y	Y	Y	Y	Y
3 Fazio	N	N	N	N	N	N	N	N
4 ***Doolittle***	N	N	N	N	N	N	N	N
5 Matsui	N	N	N	N	N	N	N	N
6 Woolsey	N	N	N	N	N	N	N	N
7 Miller	N	N	N	N	N	N	N	N
8 Pelosi	N	N	N	N	N	N	?	N
9 Dellums	N	N	N	N	N	N	N	N
10 Tauscher	N	N	N	N	N	N	N	N
11 ***Pombo***	N	N	N	N	N	N	N	N
12 Lantos	N	N	N	N	N	N	N	N
13 Stark	N	N	N	N	N	N	N	N
14 Eshoo	N	N	N	N	N	N	N	N
15 ***Campbell***	N	N	N	N	N	N	N	N
16 Lofgren	N	N	N	N	N	N	N	N
17 Farr	N	N	N	N	N	N	N	N
18 Condit	Y	Y	Y	Y	Y	Y	Y	Y
19 ***Radanovich***	N	N	N	N	N	Y	Y	Y
20 Dooley	N	N	N	N	N	N	N	N
21 ***Thomas***	N	N	N	N	N	N	N	N
22 Capps	N	N	N	N	N	N	N	N
23 ***Gallegly***	N	N	N	N	N	N	N	N
24 Sherman	N	N	N	N	N	N	N	Y
25 ***McKeon***	N	N	N	N	N	N	N	N
26 Berman	N	N	N	N	N	N	N	N
27 ***Rogan***	N	N	N	N	N	N	N	N
28 ***Dreier***	N	N	N	N	N	N	N	N
29 Waxman	N	N	N	N	N	N	N	N
30 Becerra	N	N	N	N	N	N	N	N
31 Martinez	N	N	N	N	N	N	N	N
32 Dixon	N	N	N	N	N	N	N	N
33 Roybal-Allard	N	N	N	N	N	N	N	N
34 Torres	N	N	N	N	N	N	N	N
35 Waters	N	N	N	N	N	N	N	N
36 Harman	Y	Y	Y	Y	Y	Y	Y	Y
37 Millender-McD.	N	N	N	N	N	N	N	N
38 ***Horn***	N	N	N	N	N	N	N	N
39 ***Royce***	Y	Y	Y	Y	Y	Y	Y	Y
40 ***Lewis***	N	N	N	N	N	N	N	N
41 ***Kim***	Y	Y	Y	Y	Y	Y	Y	Y
42 Brown	N	N	N	N	N	N	N	N
43 ***Calvert***	N	N	N	N	N	N	N	N
44 ***Bono***	Y	Y	Y	Y	+	Y	Y	Y
45 ***Rohrabacher***	Y	Y	Y	Y	Y	Y	Y	Y
46 Sanchez	N	N	N	N	N	N	N	N
47 ***Cox***	N	N	N	N	N	N	N	N
48 ***Packard***	N	N	N	N	N	N	N	N
49 ***Bilbray***	Y	Y	Y	Y	Y	Y	Y	Y
50 Filner	N	N	N	N	N	N	N	N
51 ***Cunningham***	N	N	N	N	N	N	N	N
52 ***Hunter***	N	N	N	N	N	N	N	N
COLORADO								
1 DeGette	N	N	N	N	N	N	N	N
2 Skaggs	N	N	N	N	N	N	N	N
3 ***McInnis***	N	Y	N	N	N	N	N	N
4 ***Schaffer***	N	Y	N	N	N	N	N	N
5 ***Hefley***	N	Y	N	N	N	N	N	N
6 ***Schaefer***	N	Y	N	N	N	N	N	N
CONNECTICUT								
1 Kennelly	N	N	N	N	N	N	N	N
2 Gejdenson	N	N	N	N	N	N	N	N
3 DeLauro	N	N	N	N	N	N	N	N
4 ***Shays***	N	N	N	N	N	N	N	N
5 Maloney	Y	Y	Y	Y	Y	Y	Y	Y
6 ***Johnson***	N	N	N	N	N	N	N	N
DELAWARE								
AL ***Castle***	N	N	N	N	N	N	N	N
FLORIDA								
1 ***Scarborough***	?	?	?	?	?	?	?	?
2 Boyd	N	N	N	N	N	N	N	N
3 Brown	N	N	N	N	N	N	N	N
4 ***Fowler***	N	N	N	N	N	N	N	Y
5 Thurman	N	N	N	N	N	N	N	N
6 ***Stearns***	N	N	N	N	N	N	N	N
7 ***Mica***	N	N	N	N	N	N	N	N
8 ***McCollum***	N	N	N	N	N	N	N	N
9 ***Bilirakis***	N	N	N	N	N	N	N	Y
10 ***Young***	N	N	N	N	N	N	N	Y
11 Davis	N	N	N	N	N	N	N	N
12 ***Canady***	N	N	N	N	N	N	N	Y
13 ***Miller***	N	N	N	N	N	N	N	N
14 ***Goss***	Y	Y	Y	Y	Y	Y	Y	Y
15 ***Weldon***	Y	Y	Y	N	Y	Y	Y	Y
16 ***Foley***	N	N	N	N	N	N	N	Y
17 Meek	N	N	?	N	N	N	N	N
18 ***Ros-Lehtinen***	N	N	N	N	N	N	N	Y
19 Wexler	N	N	?	N	N	N	N	N
20 Deutsch	Y	Y	Y	Y	Y	Y	Y	Y
21 ***Diaz-Balart***	N	N	N	N	N	N	N	N
22 ***Shaw***	N	N	N	N	N	N	N	Y
23 Hastings	N	N	N	N	N	N	N	N
GEORGIA								
1 ***Kingston***	N	N	N	N	N	N	N	N
2 Bishop	N	N	N	N	N	N	N	N
3 ***Collins***	N	N	N	N	N	N	N	N
4 McKinney	N	N	N	N	N	N	N	N
5 Lewis	N	N	N	N	N	N	N	N
6 ***Gingrich***								
7 ***Barr***	N	N	N	N	N	N	N	N
8 ***Chambliss***	N	N	N	N	N	N	N	N
9 ***Deal***	N	N	N	N	N	N	N	N
10 ***Norwood***	N	N	N	N	N	N	N	Y
11 ***Linder***	N	N	N	N	N	N	N	N
HAWAII								
1 Abercrombie	N	N	N	N	N	N	N	N
2 Mink	N	N	N	N	N	N	N	N
IDAHO								
1 ***Chenoweth***	Y	Y	Y	N	Y	Y	Y	N
2 ***Crapo***	Y	Y	Y	N	Y	Y	Y	N
ILLINOIS								
1 Rush	N	N	N	N	N	N	N	N
2 Jackson	N	N	N	N	N	N	N	N
3 Lipinski	N	N	N	N	N	N	N	N
4 Gutierrez	N	N	N	N	N	N	N	N
5 Blagojevich	N	N	N	N	N	N	N	Y
6 ***Hyde***	N	N	N	N	N	N	N	N
7 Davis	N	N	N	N	N	N	N	N
8 ***Crane***	Y	Y	Y	Y	Y	Y	Y	Y
9 Yates	N	N	N	N	N	N	N	N
10 ***Porter***	N	N	N	N	N	N	N	N
11 ***Weller***	N	N	N	N	N	N	N	N
12 Costello	N	N	N	N	N	N	N	N
13 ***Fawell***	N	N	N	N	N	N	N	N
14 ***Hastert***	N	N	N	N	N	N	N	N
15 ***Ewing***	N	N	N	N	N	N	N	N

ND Northern Democrats SD Southern Democrats

	11	12	13	14	15	16	17	18
16 ***Manzullo***	N	N	N	N	N	N	N	N
17 Evans	N	N	N	N	N	N	N	N
18 ***LaHood***	N	N	N	N	N	N	N	N
19 Poshard	N	N	N	N	N	N	N	N
20 ***Shimkus***	N	N	N	N	N	N	N	N
INDIANA								
1 Visclosky	N	N	N	N	N	N	N	N
2 ***McIntosh***	Y	Y	Y	Y	Y	Y	Y	N
3 Roemer	N	N	N	N	N	N	N	N
4 ***Souder***	N	N	N	N	N	N	N	N
5 ***Buyer***	N	N	N	N	N	N	N	N
6 ***Burton***	N	N	N	N	N	N	N	N
7 ***Pease***	N	N	N	N	N	N	N	N
8 ***Hostettler***	N	N	N	N	N	N	N	N
9 Hamilton	N	N	N	N	N	N	N	N
10 Carson	?	?	?	?	?	?	?	?
IOWA								
1 ***Leach***	N	N	N	N	N	N	N	N
2 ***Nussle***	N	N	N	N	N	N	N	N
3 Boswell	N	N	N	N	N	N	N	N
4 ***Ganske***	Y	Y	Y	Y	Y	Y	Y	Y
5 ***Latham***	N	N	N	N	N	N	N	N
KANSAS								
1 ***Moran***	N	N	N	N	N	N	N	N
2 ***Ryun***	N	N	N	N	N	N	N	N
3 ***Snowbarger***	N	N	N	N	N	N	N	N
4 ***Tiahrt***	N	N	N	N	N	N	N	N
KENTUCKY								
1 ***Whitfield***	Y	Y	Y	Y	Y	Y	Y	Y
2 ***Lewis***	Y	Y	Y	Y	Y	Y	Y	Y
3 ***Northup***	N	N	N	N	N	N	N	N
4 ***Bunning***	N	N	N	N	N	N	N	N
5 ***Rogers***	N	N	N	N	N	N	N	N
6 Baesler	N	N	N	N	N	N	N	N
LOUISIANA								
1 ***Livingston***	N	N	N	N	N	N	N	N
2 Jefferson	N	N	N	N	N	N	N	N
3 ***Tauzin***	Y	Y	Y	N	Y	Y	Y	N
4 ***McCrery***	Y	Y	Y	N	Y	Y	Y	N
5 ***Cooksey***	Y	Y	Y	Y	Y	Y	Y	Y
6 ***Baker***	N	N	N	N	N	N	N	N
7 John	N	N	N	N	N	N	N	Y
MAINE								
1 Allen	N	N	N	N	N	N	N	N
2 Baldacci	Y	Y	Y	Y	Y	Y	Y	N
MARYLAND								
1 ***Gilchrest***	N	N	N	N	N	N	N	N
2 ***Ehrlich***	N	N	N	N	N	N	N	N
3 Cardin	N	N	N	N	N	N	N	N
4 Wynn	N	N	N	N	N	N	N	N
5 Hoyer	N	N	N	N	N	N	N	N
6 ***Bartlett***	Y	Y	Y	Y	Y	Y	Y	Y
7 Cummings	N	N	N	N	N	N	N	N
8 ***Morella***	N	N	N	N	N	N	N	N
MASSACHUSETTS								
1 Olver	N	N	N	N	N	N	N	N
2 Neal	N	N	N	N	N	N	N	N
3 McGovern	N	N	N	N	N	N	N	N
4 Frank	N	N	N	N	N	N	N	N
5 Meehan	Y	Y	Y	Y	Y	Y	Y	Y
6 Tierney	N	N	N	N	N	N	N	N
7 Markey	N	N	N	N	N	N	N	N
8 Kennedy	N	N	N	N	N	N	N	N
9 Moakley	N	N	N	N	N	N	N	N
10 Delahunt	N	N	N	N	N	N	N	N
MICHIGAN								
1 Stupak	N	N	N	N	N	N	N	N
2 ***Hoekstra***	N	N	N	N	N	N	N	N
3 ***Ehlers***	N	N	N	N	N	N	N	N
4 ***Camp***	N	N	N	N	N	N	N	N
5 Barcia	Y	Y	Y	Y	Y	Y	Y	Y
6 ***Upton***	N	N	N	N	N	N	N	N
7 ***Smith***	Y	Y	Y	Y	Y	Y	Y	Y
8 Stabenow	N	N	N	N	N	N	N	N
9 Kildee	N	N	N	N	N	N	N	N
10 Bonior	N	N	N	N	N	N	N	N
11 ***Knollenberg***	N	N	N	N	N	N	N	N
12 Levin	N	N	N	N	N	N	N	N
13 Rivers	N	N	N	N	N	N	N	N
14 Conyers	N	N	N	N	N	N	N	N
15 Kilpatrick	N	N	N	N	N	N	N	N
16 Dingell	N	N	N	N	N	N	N	N
MINNESOTA								
1 ***Gutknecht***	N	N	N	N	N	N	N	N
2 Minge	Y	Y	Y	Y	Y	Y	Y	Y

	11	12	13	14	15	16	17	18
3 ***Ramstad***	N	N	N	N	N	N	N	N
4 Vento	N	N	N	N	N	N	N	N
5 Sabo	N	N	N	N	N	N	N	N
6 Luther	N	N	N	N	N	N	N	N
7 Peterson	Y	Y	Y	Y	Y	Y	Y	Y
8 Oberstar	N	N	N	N	N	N	N	N
MISSISSIPPI								
1 ***Wicker***	N	N	N	N	N	N	N	N
2 Thompson	N	N	N	N	N	N	N	N
3 ***Pickering***	N	N	N	–	N	N	N	N
4 ***Parker***	N	N	N	N	N	N	N	N
5 Taylor	N	N	N	N	N	N	N	N
MISSOURI								
1 Clay	?	?	?	?	?	?	?	?
2 ***Talent***	Y	Y	Y	Y	Y	Y	Y	Y
3 Gephardt	N	N	N	N	N	N	N	N
4 Skelton	N	N	N	N	N	N	N	N
5 McCarthy	Y	Y	Y	Y	Y	Y	Y	N
6 Danner	Y	Y	Y	Y	Y	Y	Y	Y
7 ***Blunt***	Y	Y	Y	Y	Y	Y	Y	Y
8 ***Emerson***	Y	Y	Y	Y	Y	Y	Y	Y
9 ***Hulshof***	N	N	N	N	N	N	N	N
MONTANA								
AL ***Hill***	Y	Y	Y	Y	Y	Y	Y	N
NEBRASKA								
1 ***Bereuter***	N	N	N	N	N	N	N	N
2 ***Christensen***	Y	Y	Y	N	Y	Y	Y	N
3 ***Barrett***	N	N	N	N	N	N	N	N
NEVADA								
1 ***Ensign***	Y	Y	Y	Y	Y	Y	Y	Y
2 ***Gibbons***	Y	Y	Y	Y	Y	Y	Y	Y
NEW HAMPSHIRE								
1 ***Sununu***	N	N	N	N	N	N	N	N
2 ***Bass***	Y	Y	Y	Y	Y	Y	N	Y
NEW JERSEY								
1 Andrews	N	N	N	N	N	N	N	N
2 ***LoBiondo***	Y	Y	Y	Y	Y	Y	Y	Y
3 ***Saxton***	N	N	N	N	N	N	N	N
4 ***Smith***	N	N	N	–	–	–	N	N
5 ***Roukema***	N	N	N	N	N	N	N	N
6 Pallone	N	N	N	N	N	N	N	N
7 ***Franks***	Y	Y	Y	Y	Y	Y	Y	Y
8 Pascrell	N	N	N	N	N	N	N	N
9 Rothman	N	N	N	N	N	N	N	N
10 Payne	N	N	N	N	N	N	N	N
11 ***Frelinghuysen***	N	N	N	N	N	N	N	N
12 ***Pappas***	N	N	N	N	N	N	N	N
13 Menendez	N	N	N	N	N	N	N	N
NEW MEXICO								
1 ***Schiff***	N	N	N	N	N	N	N	N
2 ***Skeen***	N	N	N	N	N	N	N	N
3 Richardson	?	?	?	?	?	?	?	?
NEW YORK								
1 ***Forbes***	Y	Y	Y	Y	Y	Y	Y	Y
2 ***Lazio***	N	N	N	N	N	N	N	N
3 ***King***	N	N	N	N	N	N	N	N
4 McCarthy	N	N	N	N	N	N	N	N
5 Ackerman	N	N	N	N	N	N	N	N
6 Flake	N	N	N	N	N	N	N	N
7 Manton	N	N	N	N	N	N	N	N
8 Nadler	N	N	N	N	N	N	N	N
9 Schumer	N	N	N	N	N	N	N	N
10 Towns	N	N	?	N	N	N	N	N
11 Owens	N	N	N	N	N	N	N	N
12 Velázquez	N	N	N	N	N	N	N	N
13 ***Molinari***	N	N	N	N	N	N	N	N
14 Maloney	N	N	N	N	N	N	N	N
15 Rangel	N	N	N	N	N	N	N	N
16 Serrano	N	N	N	N	N	N	N	N
17 Engel	N	N	N	N	N	N	N	N
18 Lowey	N	N	N	N	N	N	N	N
19 ***Kelly***	N	N	N	N	N	N	N	N
20 ***Gilman***	N	N	N	N	N	N	N	N
21 McNulty	Y	Y	Y	Y	Y	Y	Y	Y
22 ***Solomon***	N	N	N	N	N	N	N	N
23 ***Boehlert***	N	N	N	N	N	N	N	N
24 ***McHugh***	N	N	N	N	N	N	N	N
25 ***Walsh***	N	N	N	N	N	N	N	N
26 Hinchey	N	N	N	N	N	N	N	N
27 ***Paxon***	N	N	N	N	N	N	N	N
28 Slaughter	N	N	N	N	N	N	N	N
29 LaFalce	N	N	N	N	N	N	N	N
30 ***Quinn***	N	N	N	N	N	N	N	N
31 ***Houghton***	N	N	N	N	N	N	N	N

	11	12	13	14	15	16	17	18
NORTH CAROLINA								
1 Clayton	N	N	N	N	N	N	N	N
2 Etheridge	N	N	N	N	N	N	N	N
3 ***Jones***	Y	Y	Y	Y	Y	Y	Y	Y
4 Price	N	N	N	N	N	N	N	N
5 ***Burr***	Y	Y	Y	Y	Y	Y	Y	Y
6 ***Coble***	Y	Y	Y	Y	Y	Y	Y	Y
7 McIntyre	N	N	N	N	N	N	N	N
8 Hefner	N	N	N	N	N	N	N	N
9 ***Myrick***	Y	Y	Y	Y	Y	Y	Y	Y
10 ***Ballenger***	N	N	N	N	N	N	N	N
11 ***Taylor***	N	N	N	N	N	?	N	Y
12 Watt	N	N	N	N	N	N	N	N
NORTH DAKOTA								
AL Pomeroy	N	N	N	N	N	N	N	N
OHIO								
1 ***Chabot***	Y	Y	Y	Y	Y	Y	Y	Y
2 ***Portman***	N	N	N	N	N	N	N	N
3 Hall	N	N	N	N	N	N	N	N
4 ***Oxley***	N	N	N	N	N	N	N	N
5 ***Gillmor***	Y	Y	Y	Y	Y	Y	Y	Y
6 Strickland	N	N	N	N	N	N	N	N
7 ***Hobson***	N	N	N	N	N	N	N	N
8 ***Boehner***	N	N	N	N	N	N	N	N
9 Kaptur	N	N	N	N	N	N	N	N
10 Kucinich	N	N	N	N	N	N	N	N
11 Stokes	N	N	N	N	N	N	N	N
12 ***Kasich***	N	N	N	N	N	N	N	N
13 Brown	N	N	N	N	N	N	N	N
14 Sawyer	N	N	N	N	N	N	N	N
15 ***Pryce***	N	N	N	N	N	N	N	Y
16 ***Regula***	N	N	N	N	N	N	N	N
17 Traficant	N	N	N	N	N	N	N	Y
18 ***Ney***	Y	Y	Y	Y	Y	Y	Y	Y
19 ***LaTourette***	N	N	N	N	N	?	N	Y
OKLAHOMA								
1 ***Largent***	Y	Y	Y	Y	Y	Y	Y	Y
2 ***Coburn***	Y	Y	Y	Y	Y	Y	Y	Y
3 ***Watkins***	N	N	N	N	N	N	N	N
4 ***Watts***	Y	Y	Y	Y	Y	Y	Y	N
5 ***Istook***	N	N	N	N	N	N	N	N
6 ***Lucas***	Y	Y	Y	N	Y	Y	Y	Y
OREGON								
1 Furse	Y	Y	Y	N	Y	Y	Y	Y
2 ***Smith***	N	N	N	N	N	N	N	N
3 Blumenauer	N	N	N	N	N	N	N	N
4 DeFazio	Y	Y	Y	Y	Y	Y	Y	N
5 Hooley	N	N	N	N	N	N	N	N
PENNSYLVANIA								
1 Foglietta	N	N	N	N	N	N	N	N
2 Fattah	N	N	N	N	N	N	N	N
3 Borski	N	N	N	N	N	N	N	N
4 Klink	N	N	N	N	N	N	N	N
5 ***Peterson***	N	N	N	N	N	N	N	N
6 Holden	N	N	N	N	N	N	N	N
7 ***Weldon***	N	N	N	N	N	N	N	N
8 ***Greenwood***	N	N	N	N	N	N	N	N
9 ***Shuster***	N	N	N	N	N	N	N	N
10 ***McDade***	N	N	N	N	N	N	N	N
11 Kanjorski	?	N	N	N	N	N	N	N
12 Murtha	N	N	N	N	N	N	N	N
13 ***Fox***	Y	Y	Y	Y	Y	Y	Y	Y
14 Coyne	N	N	N	N	N	N	N	N
15 McHale	N	N	N	N	N	N	N	N
16 ***Pitts***	N	N	N	N	N	N	N	N
17 ***Gekas***	N	N	N	N	N	N	N	N
18 Doyle	N	N	N	N	N	N	N	N
19 ***Goodling***	N	N	N	N	N	N	?	N
20 Mascara	N	N	N	N	N	N	N	N
21 ***English***	N	N	N	N	Y	Y	N	Y
RHODE ISLAND								
1 Kennedy	N	N	N	N	N	N	N	N
2 Weygand	N	N	N	N	N	N	N	N
SOUTH CAROLINA								
1 ***Sanford***	Y	Y	Y	Y	Y	Y	Y	Y
2 ***Spence***	Y	N	N	N	N	N	N	N
3 ***Graham***	Y	Y	Y	Y	Y	Y	Y	Y
4 ***Inglis***	Y	Y	Y	Y	Y	Y	Y	N
5 Spratt	N	?	N	N	N	N	N	N
6 Clyburn	N	N	N	N	N	N	N	N
SOUTH DAKOTA								
AL ***Thune***	Y	Y	Y	N	Y	Y	Y	N
TENNESSEE								
1 ***Jenkins***	N	N	N	N	N	N	N	N
2 ***Duncan***	N	N	N	N	N	N	N	?

	11	12	13	14	15	16	17	
3 ***Wamp***	Y	Y	Y	Y	Y	Y	Y	Y
4 ***Hilleary***	Y	Y	Y	Y	Y	Y	Y	Y
5 Clement	N	N	N	Y	N	N	N	N
6 Gordon	Y	N	N	N	N	N	N	N
7 ***Bryant***	Y	Y	Y	Y	Y	Y	Y	Y
8 Tanner	N	N	N	N	N	N	N	N
9 Ford	N	N	N	N	N	N	N	N
TEXAS								
1 Sandlin	N	N	N	N	N	N	N	N
2 Turner	N	N	N	N	N	N	N	N
3 ***Johnson, Sam***	N	N	N	N	N	N	N	N
4 Hall	Y	Y	Y	Y	Y	Y	Y	Y
5 ***Sessions***	N	N	N	N	N	N	N	N
6 ***Barton***	N	N	N	N	N	N	N	N
7 ***Archer***	N	N	N	N	N	N	N	N
8 ***Brady***	N	N	N	N	N	N	N	N
9 Lampson	N	N	N	N	N	N	N	N
10 Doggett	N	N	N	N	N	N	N	N
11 Edwards	N	N	N	N	N	N	N	N
12 ***Granger***	N	N	N	N	N	N	N	N
13 ***Thornberry***	Y	Y	Y	Y	Y	Y	Y	Y
14 ***Paul***	Y	Y	Y	Y	Y	Y	Y	Y
15 Hinojosa	N	N	N	N	N	N	N	N
16 Reyes	N	N	Y	N	N	N	N	Y
17 Stenholm	N	N	N	N	N	N	N	N
18 Jackson-Lee	N	N	N	Y	N	N	N	N
19 ***Combest***	Y	Y	Y	Y	Y	Y	Y	Y
20 Gonzalez	N	N	N	N	N	N	N	N
21 ***Smith***	N	N	N	N	N	N	N	N
22 ***DeLay***	N	N	N	N	N	N	N	N
23 ***Bonilla***	N	N	N	N	N	N	N	Y
24 Frost	N	N	N	N	N	N	N	N
25 Bentsen	N	N	N	N	N	N	N	N
26 ***Armey***	Y	Y	Y	Y	Y	Y	Y	Y
27 Ortiz	N	N	N	N	N	N	N	N
27 Ortiz	N	N	N	N	N	N	N	N
28 Vacant								
30 Johnson, E.B.	N	N	N	N	N	N	N	N
UTAH								
1 ***Hansen***	N	N	N	N	N	N	N	N
2 ***Cook***	Y	Y	Y	Y	Y	Y	Y	Y
3 ***Cannon***	Y	Y	Y	Y	Y	Y	Y	Y
VERMONT								
AL *Sanders*	N	N	N	N	N	N	N	N
VIRGINIA								
1 ***Bateman***	N	N	N	N	N	N	N	N
2 Pickett	N	N	N	N	N	N	N	N
3 Scott	N	N	N	N	N	N	N	N
4 Sisisky	N	N	N	N	N	N	N	N
5 Goode	Y	Y	Y	Y	Y	Y	Y	Y
6 ***Goodlatte***	N	N	N	N	N	N	N	N
7 ***Bliley***	N	N	N	N	N	N	N	N
8 Moran	N	N	N	N	N	N	N	N
9 Boucher	N	N	N	N	N	N	N	N
10 ***Wolf***	N	N	N	N	N	N	N	N
11 ***Davis***	N	N	N	N	N	Y	Y	Y
WASHINGTON								
1 ***White***	N	N	Y	N	N	N	N	Y
2 ***Metcalf***	Y	Y	Y	Y	Y	Y	Y	Y
3 ***Smith, Linda***	N	N	N	N	N	N	N	Y
4 ***Hastings***	N	N	N	N	N	N	N	N
5 ***Nethercutt***	N	N	N	N	N	N	N	Y
6 Dicks	N	N	N	N	N	N	N	N
7 McDermott	N	N	N	N	N	N	N	N
8 ***Dunn***	Y	Y	Y	Y	Y	Y	Y	Y
9 Smith, Adam	N	N	N	N	N	N	N	N
WEST VIRGINIA								
1 Mollohan	N	N	N	N	N	N	N	N
2 Wise	N	N	N	N	N	N	N	N
3 Rahall	N	N	N	N	N	N	N	N
WISCONSIN								
1 ***Neumann***	Y	Y	Y	Y	Y	Y	Y	Y
2 ***Klug***	Y	Y	Y	Y	Y	Y	Y	Y
3 Kind	N	N	N	N	N	N	N	N
4 Kleczka	N	N	N	N	N	N	N	N
5 Barrett	N	N	N	N	N	N	N	N
6 ***Petri***	N	Y	N	N	Y	N	N	N
7 Obey	?	?	?	?	?	?	?	?
8 Johnson	N	N	N	N	N	N	N	N
9 ***Sensenbrenner***	N	N	N	N	N	N	N	N
WYOMING								
AL ***Cubin***	Y	Y	Y	N	Y	Y	Y	Y

Southern states - Ala., Ark., Fla., Ga., Ky., La., Miss., N.C., Okla., S.C., Tenn., Texas, Va.

HOUSE VOTES 19, 20, 21, 22, 23

19. H J Res 2. Term Limit Constitutional Amendment/State Discretion. Scott, D-Va., substitute amendment to impose a 12-year lifetime limit on House members and senators and to allow states to enact shorter limits. Rejected 97-329: R 73-151; D 24-177 (ND 16-131, SD 8-46); I 0-1, Feb. 12, 1997.

20. H J Res 2. Term Limit Constitutional Amendment/Retroactivity. Barton, R-Texas, substitute amendment to apply a 12-year lifetime cap on congressional terms retroactively. Rejected 152-274: R 71-152; D 81-121 (ND 54-94, SD 27-27); I 0-1, Feb. 12, 1997.

21. H J Res 2. Term Limit Constitutional Amendment/Passage. Passage of the joint resolution to propose a constitutional amendment to impose a 12-year lifetime limit on congressional service in each chamber. Rejected 217-211: R 180-45; D 37-165 (ND 25-123, SD 12-42); I 0-1, Feb. 12, 1997. A two-thirds majority vote of those present and voting (286 in this case) is required to pass a joint resolution proposing an amendment to the Constitution.

22. H J Res 36. International Family Planning Funds Early Release/Passage. Adoption of the joint resolution to authorize the early release of $385 million for international family planning activities beginning on March 1. Passed 220-209: R 44-182; D 175-27 (ND 128-20, SD 47-7); I 1-0, Feb. 13, 1997. A "yea" was a vote in support of the president's position.

23. HR 581. International Family Planning Funds/Passage. Passage of the bill to release early $385 million of appropriated funds for international family planning on March 1 and bar funding for family planning organizations that use private funds to perform or promote the use of abortion. Passed 231-194: R 194-30; D 37-163 (ND 28-118, SD 9-45); I 0-1, Feb. 13, 1997. A "nay" was a vote in support of the president's position.

[1] *Bill Richardson, D-N.M., resigned Feb. 13, 1997. The last vote for which he was eligible was vote 21.*

KEY

- Y Voted for (yea).
- # Paired for.
- + Announced for.
- N Voted against (nay).
- X Paired against.
- – Announced against.
- P Voted "present."
- C Voted "present" to avoid possible conflict of interest.
- ? Did not vote or otherwise make a position known.

Democrats ***Republicans***
Independent

	19	20	21	22	23
ALABAMA					
1 ***Callahan***	N	N	Y	N	Y
2 ***Everett***	N	N	Y	N	Y
3 ***Riley***	N	N	Y	N	Y
4 ***Aderholt***	N	N	Y	N	Y
5 Cramer	Y	Y	Y	Y	Y
6 ***Bachus***	N	N	Y	N	Y
7 Hilliard	N	N	N	Y	N
ALASKA					
AL ***Young***	?	?	?	?	?
ARIZONA					
1 ***Salmon***	Y	N	Y	N	Y
2 Pastor	N	N	N	Y	N
3 ***Stump***	N	N	Y	N	Y
4 ***Shadegg***	Y	Y	Y	N	Y
5 ***Kolbe***	N	N	Y	Y	N
6 ***Hayworth***	Y	N	Y	N	Y
ARKANSAS					
1 Berry	N	N	Y	Y	Y
2 Snyder	N	N	N	Y	N
3 ***Hutchinson***	N	N	N	N	Y
4 ***Dickey***	N	N	N	N	Y
CALIFORNIA					
1 ***Riggs***	Y	N	Y	N	Y
2 ***Herger***	Y	N	Y	N	Y
3 Fazio	N	N	N	Y	N
4 ***Doolittle***	N	N	Y	N	Y
5 Matsui	N	N	N	Y	N
6 Woolsey	N	N	N	Y	N
7 Miller	N	N	N	Y	N
8 Pelosi	N	N	N	Y	N
9 Dellums	N	N	N	Y	N
10 Tauscher	N	N	N	Y	N
11 ***Pombo***	N	N	Y	N	Y
12 Lantos	N	Y	N	Y	N
13 Stark	N	N	N	Y	N
14 Eshoo	N	Y	Y	Y	N
15 ***Campbell***	N	Y	Y	Y	N
16 Lofgren	N	Y	N	Y	N
17 Farr	N	Y	N	Y	N
18 Condit	Y	Y	Y	Y	N
19 ***Radanovich***	Y	Y	Y	N	Y
20 Dooley	N	N	N	Y	N
21 ***Thomas***	N	N	Y	Y	N
22 Capps	N	N	N	Y	N
23 ***Gallegly***	N	N	Y	N	Y
24 Sherman	Y	Y	Y	Y	N
25 ***McKeon***	Y	N	Y	N	Y
26 Berman	N	Y	N	Y	N
27 ***Rogan***	Y	Y	Y	N	Y
28 ***Dreier***	N	N	N	N	Y
29 Waxman	N	Y	N	Y	N
30 Becerra	N	N	N	Y	N
31 Martinez	N	N	N	Y	N
32 Dixon	N	N	N	Y	N
33 Roybal-Allard	N	N	N	Y	N
34 Torres	N	N	N	Y	N
35 Waters	N	N	N	Y	N
36 Harman	Y	Y	Y	Y	N
37 Millender-McD.	N	N	N	Y	N
38 ***Horn***	N	N	Y	Y	N
39 ***Royce***	Y	Y	Y	N	Y
40 ***Lewis***	N	N	N	Y	Y
41 ***Kim***	Y	Y	Y	N	Y
42 Brown	N	N	N	Y	N
43 ***Calvert***	Y	Y	Y	N	Y
44 ***Bono***	N	N	Y	N	Y
45 ***Rohrabacher***	Y	N	Y	N	Y
46 Sanchez	N	Y	N	Y	N
47 ***Cox***	N	Y	Y	N	Y
48 ***Packard***	N	N	Y	N	Y
49 ***Bilbray***	Y	Y	Y	Y	Y
50 Filner	N	N	N	Y	N
51 ***Cunningham***	N	Y	Y	N	Y
52 ***Hunter***	N	N	N	N	Y
COLORADO					
1 DeGette	N	N	N	Y	N
2 Skaggs	N	N	N	Y	N
3 ***McInnis***	N	N	N	N	Y
4 ***Schaffer***	N	N	N	N	Y
5 ***Hefley***	N	N	Y	N	Y
6 ***Schaefer***	N	N	N	N	Y
CONNECTICUT					
1 Kennelly	N	N	N	Y	N
2 Gejdenson	N	N	N	Y	N
3 DeLauro	N	N	N	Y	N
4 ***Shays***	N	N	N	Y	N
5 Maloney	Y	Y	Y	Y	N
6 ***Johnson***	N	N	N	Y	N
DELAWARE					
AL ***Castle***	N	N	Y	Y	N
FLORIDA					
1 ***Scarborough***	?	?	?	N	Y
2 Boyd	N	N	N	Y	N
3 Brown	N	N	N	Y	N
4 ***Fowler***	Y	N	Y	Y	Y
5 Thurman	N	Y	N	Y	N
6 ***Stearns***	N	Y	Y	N	Y
7 ***Mica***	N	N	Y	N	Y
8 ***McCollum***	N	N	Y	N	Y
9 ***Bilirakis***	Y	N	Y	N	Y
10 ***Young***	Y	N	Y	N	Y
11 Davis	N	Y	N	Y	N
12 ***Canady***	Y	N	Y	N	Y
13 ***Miller***	N	N	Y	Y	Y
14 ***Goss***	Y	N	Y	N	Y
15 ***Weldon***	N	Y	Y	N	Y
16 ***Foley***	N	N	Y	Y	Y
17 Meek	N	N	N	Y	N
18 ***Ros-Lehtinen***	N	N	Y	N	Y
19 Wexler	N	Y	Y	Y	N
20 Deutsch	Y	Y	Y	Y	N
21 ***Diaz-Balart***	N	N	Y	N	Y
22 ***Shaw***	N	N	Y	Y	Y
23 Hastings	N	N	N	Y	N
GEORGIA					
1 ***Kingston***	N	N	Y	N	Y
2 Bishop	N	N	N	Y	N
3 ***Collins***	N	N	Y	N	Y
4 McKinney	N	N	N	Y	N
5 Lewis	N	N	N	Y	N
6 ***Gingrich***			Y	N	
7 ***Barr***	N	N	Y	N	Y
8 ***Chambliss***	N	N	Y	N	Y
9 ***Deal***	Y	Y	Y	N	Y
10 ***Norwood***	N	N	Y	N	Y
11 ***Linder***	N	N	Y	N	Y
HAWAII					
1 Abercrombie	N	N	N	Y	N
2 Mink	N	N	N	Y	?
IDAHO					
1 ***Chenoweth***	N	N	N	N	Y
2 ***Crapo***	N	N	N	N	Y
ILLINOIS					
1 Rush	N	N	N	Y	N
2 Jackson	N	N	N	Y	N
3 Lipinski	N	N	N	N	Y
4 Gutierrez	N	Y	N	Y	N
5 Blagojevich	Y	Y	Y	Y	N
6 ***Hyde***	N	N	N	N	Y
7 Davis	N	N	N	Y	N
8 ***Crane***	Y	Y	Y	N	Y
9 Yates	N	N	N	Y	N
10 ***Porter***	N	N	N	Y	Y
11 ***Weller***	Y	Y	Y	N	Y
12 Costello	N	N	N	N	Y
13 ***Fawell***	N	N	N	Y	N
14 ***Hastert***	N	N	Y	N	Y

ND Northern Democrats SD Southern Democrats

	19	20	21	22	23
15 ***Ewing***	N	N	Y	N	Y
16 ***Manzullo***	Y	Y	Y	N	Y
17 Evans	N	N	N	Y	N
18 ***LaHood***	N	N	Y	N	Y
19 Poshard	Y	Y	Y	N	Y
20 ***Shimkus***	N	Y	Y	N	Y
INDIANA					
1 Visclosky	N	N	N	Y	N
2 ***McIntosh***	Y	Y	Y	N	Y
3 Roemer	N	N	N	N	Y
4 ***Souder***	N	Y	Y	N	Y
5 ***Buyer***	N	N	Y	N	Y
6 ***Burton***	N	N	Y	N	Y
7 ***Pease***	N	N	Y	N	Y
8 ***Hostettler***	N	N	N	N	Y
9 Hamilton	N	N	N	Y	Y
10 Carson	?	?	?	?	X
IOWA					
1 ***Leach***	N	N	Y	Y	N
2 ***Nussle***	N	N	Y	N	+
3 Boswell	N	Y	Y	Y	N
4 ***Ganske***	Y	Y	Y	Y	Y
5 ***Latham***	N	N	Y	N	Y
KANSAS					
1 ***Moran***	N	Y	Y	N	Y
2 ***Ryun***	N	N	Y	N	Y
3 ***Snowbarger***	N	N	Y	N	Y
4 ***Tiahrt***	Y	Y	Y	N	Y
KENTUCKY					
1 ***Whitfield***	Y	Y	Y	N	Y
2 ***Lewis***	Y	Y	Y	N	Y
3 ***Northup***	N	N	N	N	Y
4 ***Bunning***	N	N	Y	N	Y
5 ***Rogers***	N	N	N	N	Y
6 Baesler	N	N	N	Y	N
LOUISIANA					
1 ***Livingston***	N	N	N	N	Y
2 Jefferson	N	N	N	Y	N
3 ***Tauzin***	N	N	Y	N	Y
4 ***McCrery***	N	Y	Y	N	Y
5 ***Cooksey***	Y	Y	Y	N	Y
6 ***Baker***	N	N	Y	N	Y
7 John	N	N	Y	N	Y
MAINE					
1 Allen	N	N	N	Y	N
2 Baldacci	N	N	N	Y	N
MARYLAND					
1 ***Gilchrest***	N	N	Y	Y	N
2 ***Ehrlich***	N	N	N	Y	Y
3 Cardin	N	N	N	Y	N
4 Wynn	N	N	N	Y	N
5 Hoyer	N	Y	N	Y	N
6 ***Bartlett***	Y	Y	Y	N	Y
7 Cummings	N	N	N	Y	N
8 ***Morella***	N	N	N	Y	N
MASSACHUSETTS					
1 Olver	N	Y	N	Y	N
2 Neal	N	Y	N	Y	N
3 McGovern	N	N	N	Y	N
4 Frank	N	Y	N	Y	N
5 Meehan	Y	Y	Y	Y	N
6 Tierney	N	Y	N	Y	N
7 Markey	N	Y	N	Y	N
8 Kennedy	N	N	N	Y	N
9 Moakley	N	Y	N	Y	Y
10 Delahunt	N	Y	N	Y	N
MICHIGAN					
1 Stupak	N	Y	N	N	Y
2 ***Hoekstra***	N	Y	Y	N	Y
3 ***Ehlers***	N	Y	Y	N	Y
4 ***Camp***	N	N	Y	N	Y
5 Barcia	Y	Y	Y	N	Y
6 ***Upton***	N	Y	Y	Y	N
7 ***Smith***	Y	Y	Y	N	Y
8 Stabenow	N	N	N	Y	N
9 Kildee	N	N	N	N	Y
10 Bonior	N	Y	N	Y	Y
11 ***Knollenberg***	N	N	Y	N	Y
12 Levin	N	N	N	Y	N
13 Rivers	N	N	N	Y	N
14 Conyers	N	N	N	Y	N
15 Kilpatrick	N	Y	N	Y	N
16 Dingell	N	Y	N	Y	N
MINNESOTA					
1 ***Gutknecht***	N	N	Y	N	Y
2 Minge	Y	Y	Y	Y	N
3 ***Ramstad***	Y	N	Y	Y	N
4 Vento	N	N	N	Y	N
5 Sabo	N	Y	N	Y	N
6 Luther	Y	Y	Y	Y	N
7 Peterson	Y	Y	Y	N	Y
8 Oberstar	N	N	N	N	Y
MISSISSIPPI					
1 ***Wicker***	N	N	N	N	Y
2 Thompson	N	N	N	Y	N
3 ***Pickering***	N	N	N	N	Y
4 ***Parker***	N	N	N	N	Y
5 Taylor	N	Y	N	N	Y
MISSOURI					
1 Clay	?	?	?	?	?
2 ***Talent***	Y	Y	Y	N	Y
3 Gephardt	N	N	N	Y	N
4 Skelton	N	N	N	N	Y
5 McCarthy	N	N	N	Y	N
6 Danner	Y	Y	Y	Y	Y
7 ***Blunt***	N	N	N	N	Y
8 ***Emerson***	Y	Y	Y	N	Y
9 ***Hulshof***	N	N	Y	N	Y
MONTANA					
AL ***Hill***	Y	Y	Y	N	Y
NEBRASKA					
1 ***Bereuter***	N	N	Y	Y	Y
2 ***Christensen***	N	N	N	N	Y
3 ***Barrett***	N	N	Y	N	Y
NEVADA					
1 ***Ensign***	Y	Y	Y	N	Y
2 ***Gibbons***	Y	Y	Y	Y	Y
NEW HAMPSHIRE					
1 ***Sununu***	N	N	Y	N	Y
2 ***Bass***	N	N	Y	Y	N
NEW JERSEY					
1 Andrews	N	N	N	Y	N
2 ***LoBiondo***	Y	Y	Y	N	Y
3 ***Saxton***	N	N	Y	N	Y
4 ***Smith***	N	N	N	N	Y
5 ***Roukema***	N	N	N	Y	N
6 Pallone	N	N	N	Y	N
7 ***Franks***	Y	Y	Y	Y	N
8 Pascrell	N	Y	Y	Y	N
9 Rothman	N	N	N	Y	N
10 Payne	N	N	N	Y	N
11 ***Frelinghuysen***	N	N	Y	Y	N
12 ***Pappas***	N	N	N	N	Y
13 Menendez	N	N	N	Y	N
NEW MEXICO					
1 ***Schiff***	Y	Y	Y	Y	N
2 ***Skeen***	N	N	N	N	Y
3 Richardson[1]	?	?	?		
NEW YORK					
1 ***Forbes***	Y	Y	Y	N	Y
2 ***Lazio***	Y	N	Y	Y	N
3 ***King***	N	N	N	N	Y
4 McCarthy	N	N	N	Y	N
5 Ackerman	N	N	N	Y	N
6 Flake	N	N	N	Y	N
7 Manton	N	N	N	N	Y
8 Nadler	N	N	N	Y	N
9 Schumer	N	N	N	Y	N
10 Towns	N	Y	N	Y	N
11 Owens	N	N	N	Y	N
12 Velázquez	N	N	N	Y	N
13 ***Molinari***	N	N	N	Y	N
14 Maloney	N	N	N	Y	N
15 Rangel	?	N	N	Y	N
16 Serrano	N	N	N	Y	N
17 Engel	N	Y	N	Y	N
18 Lowey	N	N	N	Y	N
19 ***Kelly***	N	N	Y	Y	N
20 ***Gilman***	N	N	N	Y	N
21 McNulty	Y	Y	Y	Y	Y
22 ***Solomon***	N	?	Y	N	Y
23 ***Boehlert***	N	N	N	Y	N
24 ***McHugh***	N	Y	N	N	Y
25 ***Walsh***	N	N	Y	N	Y
26 Hinchey	N	Y	N	Y	N
27 ***Paxon***	N	N	Y	N	Y
28 Slaughter	N	Y	N	Y	N
29 LaFalce	N	Y	N	N	#
30 ***Quinn***	N	N	Y	N	Y
31 ***Houghton***	N	N	Y	Y	N
NORTH CAROLINA					
1 Clayton	N	N	N	Y	N
2 Etheridge	Y	Y	N	Y	N
3 ***Jones***	Y	Y	Y	N	Y
4 Price	N	N	N	Y	N
5 ***Burr***	Y	Y	Y	N	Y
6 ***Coble***	N	Y	Y	N	Y
7 McIntyre	N	Y	Y	N	Y
8 Hefner	N	Y	N	Y	N
9 ***Myrick***	Y	Y	Y	N	Y
10 ***Ballenger***	N	N	Y	N	Y
11 ***Taylor***	N	Y	Y	N	Y
12 Watt	N	N	N	Y	N
NORTH DAKOTA					
AL Pomeroy	N	Y	N	Y	N
OHIO					
1 ***Chabot***	Y	Y	Y	N	Y
2 ***Portman***	N	N	Y	N	Y
3 Hall	N	Y	N	Y	Y
4 ***Oxley***	N	N	N	N	Y
5 ***Gillmor***	Y	N	Y	N	Y
6 Strickland	N	N	N	Y	N
7 ***Hobson***	N	N	Y	Y	N
8 ***Boehner***	N	N	Y	N	Y
9 Kaptur	N	N	N	Y	N
10 Kucinich	N	N	N	N	Y
11 Stokes	N	N	N	Y	N
12 ***Kasich***	N	N	Y	N	Y
13 Brown	N	Y	Y	Y	N
14 Sawyer	N	N	N	Y	N
15 ***Pryce***	Y	Y	Y	Y	N
16 ***Regula***	N	N	Y	Y	Y
17 Traficant	N	N	Y	N	N
18 ***Ney***	Y	Y	Y	N	Y
19 ***LaTourette***	N	Y	Y	N	Y
OKLAHOMA					
1 ***Largent***	Y	Y	Y	N	Y
2 ***Coburn***	Y	Y	Y	N	Y
3 ***Watkins***	N	N	Y	N	Y
4 ***Watts***	N	N	Y	N	Y
5 ***Istook***	N	N	Y	N	Y
6 ***Lucas***	N	N	Y	N	Y
OREGON					
1 Furse	Y	Y	Y	Y	N
2 ***Smith***	N	N	Y	N	Y
3 Blumenauer	N	Y	N	Y	N
4 DeFazio	Y	N	Y	Y	N
5 Hooley	N	N	N	Y	N
PENNSYLVANIA					
1 Foglietta	N	N	N	Y	N
2 Fattah	N	Y	N	Y	N
3 Borski	N	N	N	Y	Y
4 Klink	N	N	N	Y	Y
5 ***Peterson***	N	N	Y	N	Y
6 Holden	N	Y	Y	N	Y
7 ***Weldon***	N	N	Y	N	Y
8 ***Greenwood***	N	N	Y	Y	N
9 ***Shuster***	N	N	Y	N	Y
10 ***McDade***	N	N	N	N	Y
11 Kanjorski	N	N	N	Y	Y
12 Murtha	N	N	N	Y	Y
13 ***Fox***	Y	Y	Y	Y	Y
14 Coyne	N	N	N	Y	N
15 McHale	N	N	N	Y	N
16 ***Pitts***	N	N	Y	N	Y
17 ***Gekas***	N	Y	Y	Y	Y
18 Doyle	N	N	Y	N	Y
19 ***Goodling***	N	N	Y	N	Y
20 Mascara	N	N	Y	N	Y
21 ***English***	Y	N	Y	N	Y
RHODE ISLAND					
1 Kennedy	N	N	N	Y	N
2 Weygand	N	N	N	N	Y
SOUTH CAROLINA					
1 ***Sanford***	Y	Y	Y	N	Y
2 ***Spence***	N	N	Y	N	Y
3 ***Graham***	Y	Y	Y	N	Y
4 ***Inglis***	Y	N	Y	N	Y
5 Spratt	N	Y	N	Y	N
6 Clyburn	N	Y	N	Y	N
SOUTH DAKOTA					
AL ***Thune***	N	N	N	N	Y
TENNESSEE					
1 ***Jenkins***	N	N	Y	N	Y
2 ***Duncan***	N	N	N	N	Y
3 ***Wamp***	Y	N	Y	N	Y
4 ***Hilleary***	Y	N	Y	N	Y
5 Clement	N	N	N	Y	N
6 Gordon	Y	N	Y	Y	N
7 ***Bryant***	Y	Y	Y	N	Y
8 Tanner	N	Y	N	Y	N
9 Ford	N	N	N	Y	N
TEXAS					
1 Sandlin	N	Y	N	Y	N
2 Turner	N	Y	Y	Y	N
3 ***Johnson, Sam***	N	N	Y	N	Y
4 Hall	Y	Y	Y	N	Y
5 ***Sessions***	N	N	Y	N	Y
6 ***Barton***	Y	Y	Y	N	Y
7 ***Archer***	N	N	N	N	Y
8 ***Brady***	Y	Y	Y	N	Y
9 Lampson	N	Y	N	Y	N
10 Doggett	N	Y	N	Y	N
11 Edwards	N	N	N	Y	N
12 ***Granger***	N	N	Y	N	Y
13 ***Thornberry***	Y	Y	Y	N	Y
14 ***Paul***	Y	Y	Y	N	N
15 Hinojosa	N	N	Y	Y	N
16 Reyes	N	Y	Y	Y	N
17 Stenholm	N	N	N	N	Y
18 Jackson-Lee	N	Y	N	Y	N
19 ***Combest***	Y	Y	Y	N	Y
20 Gonzalez	N	N	N	Y	N
21 ***Smith***	N	N	Y	N	Y
22 ***DeLay***	N	Y	N	N	Y
23 ***Bonilla***	N	Y	Y	N	Y
24 Frost	N	N	N	Y	N
25 Bentsen	N	Y	N	Y	N
26 ***Armey***	Y	Y	Y	N	Y
27 Ortiz	N	N	N	N	Y
28 Vacant					
29 Green	N	Y	N	Y	N
30 Johnson, E.B.	N	Y	N	Y	N
UTAH					
1 ***Hansen***	N	N	Y	N	Y
2 ***Cook***	Y	Y	Y	N	Y
3 ***Cannon***	Y	Y	Y	N	Y
VERMONT					
AL *Sanders*	N	N	N	Y	N
VIRGINIA					
1 ***Bateman***	N	N	N	N	Y
2 Pickett	N	N	N	Y	N
3 Scott	Y	Y	N	Y	N
4 Sisisky	N	Y	N	Y	N
5 Goode	Y	Y	Y	N	Y
6 ***Goodlatte***	Y	N	Y	N	Y
7 ***Bliley***	N	N	N	N	Y
8 Moran	Y	Y	N	Y	N
9 Boucher	N	Y	N	Y	N
10 ***Wolf***	N	N	Y	N	Y
11 ***Davis***	Y	Y	Y	Y	Y
WASHINGTON					
1 ***White***	Y	N	Y	N	N
2 ***Metcalf***	Y	N	Y	N	Y
3 ***Smith, Linda***	Y	N	Y	N	Y
4 ***Hastings***	N	N	Y	N	Y
5 ***Nethercutt***	N	N	Y	N	Y
6 Dicks	N	N	N	Y	N
7 McDermott	N	N	N	Y	N
8 ***Dunn***	Y	N	Y	Y	Y
9 Smith, Adam	N	Y	Y	Y	N
WEST VIRGINIA					
1 Mollohan	N	N	N	N	Y
2 Wise	N	Y	N	Y	N
3 Rahall	N	N	N	N	Y
WISCONSIN					
1 ***Neumann***	Y	Y	Y	N	Y
2 ***Klug***	N	Y	Y	Y	N
3 Kind	Y	Y	Y	Y	N
4 Kleczka	N	Y	N	Y	N
5 Barrett	N	Y	N	Y	N
6 ***Petri***	N	Y	N	N	Y
7 Obey	?	?	?	?	?
8 Johnson	N	N	N	Y	N
9 ***Sensenbrenner***	N	Y	N	N	Y
WYOMING					
AL ***Cubin***	N	N	Y	N	Y

Southern states - Ala., Ark., Fla., Ga., Ky., La., Miss., N.C., Okla., S.C., Tenn., Texas, Va.

HOUSE VOTES 24, 25, 26, 27, 28

24. Procedural Motion/Journal. Approval of the House Journal of Tuesday, Feb. 25, 1997. Approved 378-36: R 206-11; D 171-25 (ND 125-19, SD 46-6); I 1-0, Feb. 26, 1997.

25. HR 624. Armored Car Guard Gun Licenses/Passage. Tauzin, R-La., motion to suspend the rules and pass the bill to require states to legally recognize a weapons license obtained by an armored car guard in another state. Motion agreed to 416-0: R 219-0; D 196-0 (ND 144-0, SD 52-0); I 1-0, Feb. 26, 1997. A two-thirds majority of those present and voting (278 in this case) is required for passage under suspension of the rules.

26. HR 497. District of Columbia Health Provider Charter Repeal/Passage. Davis, R-Va., motion to suspend the rules and pass the bill to repeal the federal charter of Group Hospitalization and Medical Services Inc., and authorize the insurance plan to become a nonprofit corporation in the District of Columbia. Motion agreed to 417-0: R 219-0; D 197-0 (ND 144-0, SD 53-0); I 1-0, Feb. 26, 1997. A two-thirds majority of those present and voting (278 in this case) is required for passage under suspension of the rules.

27. HR 668. Airline Tax Reinstatement/Passage. Archer, R-Texas, motion to suspend the rules and pass the bill to reinstate the federal aviation excise taxes through Sept. 30, 1997. Motion agreed to 347-73: R 158-64; D 188-9 (ND 138-6, SD 50-3); I 1-0, Feb. 26, 1997. A two-thirds majority of those present and voting (280 in this case) is required for passage under suspension of the rules. A "yea" was a vote in support of the president's position.

28. Procedural Motion/Journal. Approval of the House Journal of Wednesday, Feb. 26, 1997. Approved 332-38: R189-11; D 143-27 (ND 103-19, SD 40-8); I 0-0, Feb. 27, 1997.

KEY

Y	Voted for (yea).
#	Paired for.
+	Announced for.
N	Voted against (nay).
X	Paired against.
–	Announced against.
P	Voted "present."
C	Voted "present" to avoid possible conflict of interest.
?	Did not vote or otherwise make a position known.

Democrats ***Republicans***
Independent

	24	25	26	27	28
ALABAMA					
1 ***Callahan***	Y	Y	Y	Y	Y
2 ***Everett***	Y	Y	Y	Y	Y
3 ***Riley***	Y	Y	Y	N	Y
4 ***Aderholt***	Y	Y	Y	N	Y
5 Cramer	Y	Y	Y	Y	Y
6 ***Bachus***	Y	Y	Y	Y	Y
7 Hilliard	N	Y	Y	N	?
ALASKA					
AL ***Young***	Y	Y	Y	N	Y
ARIZONA					
1 ***Salmon***	Y	Y	Y	N	Y
2 Pastor	Y	Y	Y	Y	Y
3 ***Stump***	Y	Y	Y	N	Y
4 ***Shadegg***	Y	Y	Y	N	Y
5 ***Kolbe***	Y	Y	Y	Y	Y
6 ***Hayworth***	Y	Y	Y	Y	Y
ARKANSAS					
1 Berry	Y	Y	Y	Y	Y
2 Snyder	Y	Y	Y	Y	Y
3 ***Hutchinson***	Y	Y	?	Y	Y
4 ***Dickey***	Y	Y	Y	N	Y
CALIFORNIA					
1 ***Riggs***	Y	Y	Y	Y	Y
2 ***Herger***	Y	Y	Y	Y	Y
3 Fazio	N	Y	Y	Y	N
4 ***Doolittle***	?	?	?	?	?
5 Matsui	Y	Y	Y	Y	Y
6 Woolsey	Y	Y	Y	Y	Y
7 Miller	N	Y	Y	Y	Y
8 Pelosi	Y	Y	Y	Y	Y
9 Dellums	Y	Y	Y	Y	?
10 Tauscher	Y	Y	Y	Y	Y
11 ***Pombo***	N	Y	Y	N	N
12 Lantos	?	?	?	?	Y
13 Stark	Y	Y	Y	Y	?
14 Eshoo	Y	Y	?	Y	Y
15 ***Campbell***	Y	Y	Y	Y	Y
16 Lofgren	Y	Y	Y	Y	Y
17 Farr	Y	Y	Y	Y	Y
18 Condit	Y	Y	Y	N	?
19 ***Radanovich***	Y	Y	Y	Y	Y
20 Dooley	Y	Y	Y	Y	Y
21 ***Thomas***	Y	Y	Y	Y	Y
22 Capps	Y	Y	Y	Y	Y
23 ***Gallegly***	Y	Y	Y	Y	Y
24 Sherman	Y	Y	Y	Y	Y
25 ***McKeon***	Y	Y	Y	Y	Y
26 Berman	Y	Y	Y	Y	Y
27 ***Rogan***	Y	Y	Y	N	Y
28 ***Dreier***	Y	Y	Y	N	Y
29 Waxman	Y	Y	Y	Y	Y
30 Becerra	Y	Y	Y	Y	Y
31 Martinez	Y	Y	Y	Y	?
32 Dixon	Y	Y	Y	Y	Y
33 Roybal-Allard	Y	Y	Y	Y	Y
34 Torres	Y	Y	Y	Y	Y
35 Waters	N	Y	Y	Y	N
36 Harman	Y	Y	Y	Y	Y
37 Millender-McD.	N	Y	Y	Y	Y
38 ***Horn***	Y	Y	Y	Y	Y
39 ***Royce***	Y	Y	Y	N	Y
40 ***Lewis***	Y	Y	Y	Y	Y
41 ***Kim***	Y	Y	Y	Y	Y
42 Brown	N	Y	Y	Y	N
43 ***Calvert***	Y	Y	Y	Y	?
44 ***Bono***	Y	?	Y	Y	?
45 ***Rohrabacher***	Y	Y	Y	N	Y
46 Sanchez	Y	Y	Y	N	Y
47 ***Cox***	Y	Y	Y	?	?
48 ***Packard***	Y	Y	Y	Y	Y
49 ***Bilbray***	Y	Y	Y	Y	Y
50 Filner	N	Y	Y	Y	N
51 ***Cunningham***	Y	Y	Y	Y	Y
52 ***Hunter***	Y	Y	Y	N	Y
COLORADO					
1 DeGette	Y	Y	Y	Y	Y
2 Skaggs	Y	Y	Y	Y	Y
3 ***McInnis***	Y	?	Y	Y	Y
4 ***Schaffer***	Y	Y	Y	N	Y
5 ***Hefley***	N	Y	Y	N	N
6 ***Schaefer***	Y	Y	Y	N	Y
CONNECTICUT					
1 Kennelly	Y	Y	Y	Y	Y
2 Gejdenson	Y	Y	Y	Y	Y
3 DeLauro	Y	Y	Y	Y	Y
4 ***Shays***	Y	Y	Y	Y	Y
5 Maloney	Y	Y	Y	N	Y
6 ***Johnson***	Y	Y	Y	Y	Y
DELAWARE					
AL ***Castle***	Y	Y	Y	Y	Y
FLORIDA					
1 ***Scarborough***	Y	Y	Y	N	Y
2 Boyd	Y	Y	Y	Y	Y
3 Brown	Y	Y	Y	Y	Y
4 ***Fowler***	Y	Y	Y	Y	Y
5 Thurman	Y	Y	Y	Y	Y
6 ***Stearns***	N	Y	Y	N	Y
7 ***Mica***	Y	Y	Y	N	Y
8 ***McCollum***	Y	Y	Y	Y	Y
9 ***Bilirakis***	?	Y	Y	Y	Y
10 ***Young***	Y	Y	Y	N	Y
11 Davis	Y	Y	Y	Y	?
12 ***Canady***	Y	Y	Y	Y	Y
13 ***Miller***	Y	Y	Y	Y	Y
14 ***Goss***	Y	Y	Y	Y	Y
15 ***Weldon***	Y	Y	Y	Y	Y
16 ***Foley***	Y	Y	?	Y	Y
17 Meek	Y	Y	Y	Y	Y
18 ***Ros-Lehtinen***	Y	Y	Y	Y	?
19 Wexler	Y	Y	Y	Y	Y
20 Deutsch	Y	Y	Y	Y	?
21 ***Diaz-Balart***	Y	Y	Y	Y	Y
22 ***Shaw***	Y	Y	Y	Y	Y
23 Hastings	N	Y	Y	Y	Y
GEORGIA					
1 ***Kingston***	Y	Y	Y	N	Y
2 Bishop	Y	Y	Y	Y	Y
3 ***Collins***	Y	Y	Y	Y	Y
4 McKinney	Y	Y	Y	Y	?
5 Lewis	N	Y	Y	Y	N
6 ***Gingrich***					
7 ***Barr***	Y	Y	Y	N	Y
8 ***Chambliss***	Y	Y	Y	Y	Y
9 ***Deal***	Y	Y	Y	N	?
10 ***Norwood***	Y	Y	Y	N	Y
11 ***Linder***	?	Y	Y	Y	?
HAWAII					
1 Abercrombie	N	Y	Y	Y	N
2 Mink	Y	Y	Y	Y	Y
IDAHO					
1 ***Chenoweth***	N	Y	Y	N	Y
2 ***Crapo***	Y	Y	Y	N	Y
ILLINOIS					
1 Rush	N	Y	Y	Y	N
2 Jackson	Y	Y	Y	Y	Y
3 Lipinski	Y	Y	Y	Y	?
4 Gutierrez	N	Y	Y	Y	Y
5 Blagojevich	Y	Y	Y	Y	Y
6 ***Hyde***	Y	Y	Y	Y	Y
7 Davis	Y	Y	Y	Y	?
8 ***Crane***	N	Y	Y	Y	Y
9 Yates	N	Y	Y	Y	Y
10 ***Porter***	Y	Y	Y	Y	Y
11 ***Weller***	N	Y	Y	Y	N
12 Costello	Y	Y	Y	Y	N
13 ***Fawell***	Y	Y	Y	Y	Y
14 ***Hastert***	Y	Y	Y	Y	Y

ND Northern Democrats SD Southern Democrats

	24	25	26	27	28
15 ***Ewing***	Y	Y	Y	Y	Y
16 ***Manzullo***	Y	Y	Y	Y	Y
17 Evans	Y	Y	Y	Y	Y
18 ***LaHood***	Y	Y	Y	Y	?
19 Poshard	Y	Y	Y	Y	Y
20 ***Shimkus***	Y	Y	Y	N	Y
INDIANA					
1 Visclosky	N	Y	Y	Y	N
2 ***McIntosh***	Y	Y	Y	N	Y
3 Roemer	Y	Y	Y	N	Y
4 ***Souder***	Y	Y	Y	N	Y
5 ***Buyer***	?	Y	Y	Y	Y
6 ***Burton***	Y	Y	Y	N	Y
7 ***Pease***	Y	Y	Y	Y	Y
8 ***Hostettler***	?	Y	Y	N	Y
9 Hamilton	Y	Y	Y	Y	Y
10 Carson	?	?	?	?	?
IOWA					
1 ***Leach***	Y	Y	Y	Y	Y
2 ***Nussle***	Y	Y	Y	Y	N
3 Boswell	Y	Y	Y	Y	Y
4 ***Ganske***	Y	Y	Y	Y	Y
5 ***Latham***	Y	Y	Y	Y	?
KANSAS					
1 ***Moran***	Y	Y	Y	Y	Y
2 ***Ryun***	Y	Y	Y	N	Y
3 ***Snowbarger***	Y	Y	Y	N	Y
4 ***Tiahrt***	Y	Y	Y	N	?
KENTUCKY					
1 ***Whitfield***	Y	Y	Y	Y	Y
2 ***Lewis***	Y	Y	Y	Y	Y
3 ***Northup***	Y	Y	Y	Y	Y
4 ***Bunning***	Y	Y	Y	Y	Y
5 ***Rogers***	Y	Y	Y	Y	Y
6 Baesler	Y	Y	Y	Y	Y
LOUISIANA					
1 ***Livingston***	Y	Y	Y	Y	Y
2 Jefferson	Y	Y	Y	Y	Y
3 ***Tauzin***	Y	Y	Y	N	Y
4 ***McCrery***	Y	Y	Y	Y	Y
5 ***Cooksey***	Y	?	?	N	Y
6 ***Baker***	Y	Y	Y	Y	Y
7 John	Y	Y	Y	Y	Y
MAINE					
1 Allen	Y	Y	Y	Y	Y
2 Baldacci	Y	Y	Y	Y	Y
MARYLAND					
1 ***Gilchrest***	Y	Y	Y	Y	Y
2 ***Ehrlich***	Y	Y	Y	Y	Y
3 Cardin	Y	Y	Y	Y	Y
4 Wynn	Y	Y	Y	Y	Y
5 Hoyer	Y	Y	Y	Y	Y
6 ***Bartlett***	Y	Y	Y	Y	Y
7 Cummings	Y	Y	Y	Y	Y
8 ***Morella***	?	?	?	Y	Y
MASSACHUSETTS					
1 Olver	Y	Y	Y	Y	Y
2 Neal	Y	Y	Y	Y	Y
3 McGovern	Y	Y	Y	Y	Y
4 Frank	Y	Y	Y	Y	Y
5 Meehan	Y	Y	Y	Y	Y
6 Tierney	Y	Y	Y	Y	Y
7 Markey	Y	Y	Y	Y	Y
8 Kennedy	Y	Y	Y	Y	Y
9 Moakley	Y	Y	Y	Y	?
10 Delahunt	Y	Y	Y	Y	Y
MICHIGAN					
1 Stupak	Y	Y	Y	Y	Y
2 ***Hoekstra***	Y	Y	?	N	Y
3 ***Ehlers***	Y	Y	Y	Y	Y
4 ***Camp***	Y	Y	Y	Y	Y
5 Barcia	Y	Y	Y	Y	Y
6 ***Upton***	Y	Y	Y	N	Y
7 ***Smith***	Y	Y	?	X	?
8 Stabenow	Y	Y	Y	Y	Y
9 Kildee	Y	Y	Y	Y	Y
10 Bonior	Y	Y	Y	Y	N
11 ***Knollenberg***	Y	Y	Y	Y	Y
12 Levin	Y	Y	Y	Y	Y
13 Rivers	Y	Y	Y	Y	Y
14 Conyers	Y	Y	Y	Y	Y
15 Kilpatrick	Y	Y	Y	Y	Y
16 Dingell	Y	Y	Y	?	Y

	24	25	26	27	28
MINNESOTA					
1 ***Gutknecht***	N	Y	Y	Y	N
2 Minge	Y	Y	Y	Y	Y
3 ***Ramstad***	N	Y	Y	Y	N
4 Vento	Y	Y	Y	Y	Y
5 Sabo	N	Y	Y	Y	N
6 Luther	Y	Y	Y	Y	Y
7 Peterson	Y	Y	Y	Y	Y
8 Oberstar	N	Y	Y	Y	N
MISSISSIPPI					
1 ***Wicker***	Y	Y	Y	Y	N
2 Thompson	N	Y	Y	Y	N
3 ***Pickering***	Y	Y	Y	N	Y
4 ***Parker***	Y	Y	Y	N	N
5 Taylor	?	?	Y	N	N
MISSOURI					
1 Clay	?	?	?	?	?
2 ***Talent***	Y	Y	Y	N	?
3 Gephardt	N	Y	Y	Y	N
4 Skelton	Y	Y	Y	Y	Y
5 McCarthy	+	+	Y	Y	Y
6 Danner	?	?	?	#	?
7 ***Blunt***	Y	Y	Y	Y	Y
8 ***Emerson***	Y	Y	Y	Y	Y
9 ***Hulshof***	Y	Y	Y	Y	N
MONTANA					
AL ***Hill***	Y	Y	Y	N	Y
NEBRASKA					
1 ***Bereuter***	Y	Y	Y	Y	Y
2 ***Christensen***	Y	Y	Y	Y	Y
3 ***Barrett***	Y	Y	Y	Y	Y
NEVADA					
1 ***Ensign***	N	Y	Y	Y	N
2 ***Gibbons***	Y	Y	Y	N	Y
NEW HAMPSHIRE					
1 ***Sununu***	Y	Y	Y	Y	Y
2 ***Bass***	Y	Y	Y	Y	Y
NEW JERSEY					
1 Andrews	Y	Y	Y	N	?
2 ***LoBiondo***	Y	Y	Y	Y	Y
3 ***Saxton***	Y	Y	Y	Y	Y
4 ***Smith***	Y	Y	Y	Y	Y
5 ***Roukema***	Y	Y	Y	Y	Y
6 Pallone	Y	Y	Y	Y	Y
7 ***Franks***	Y	Y	Y	Y	Y
8 Pascrell	N	Y	Y	Y	N
9 Rothman	Y	Y	Y	Y	Y
10 Payne	Y	Y	Y	Y	?
11 ***Frelinghuysen***	Y	Y	Y	Y	Y
12 ***Pappas***	Y	Y	Y	N	Y
13 Menendez	N	Y	Y	Y	N
NEW MEXICO					
1 ***Schiff***	Y	Y	Y	N	?
2 ***Skeen***	Y	Y	Y	Y	Y
3 Vacant					
NEW YORK					
1 ***Forbes***	Y	Y	Y	N	?
2 ***Lazio***	Y	Y	Y	Y	Y
3 ***King***	Y	Y	Y	Y	Y
4 McCarthy	Y	Y	Y	Y	Y
5 Ackerman	Y	Y	Y	Y	?
6 Flake	Y	Y	Y	Y	Y
7 Manton	Y	Y	Y	Y	Y
8 Nadler	Y	Y	Y	Y	?
9 Schumer	Y	Y	Y	Y	Y
10 Towns	Y	Y	Y	Y	Y
11 Owens	Y	Y	Y	Y	Y
12 Velázquez	Y	Y	Y	Y	?
13 ***Molinari***	Y	Y	Y	Y	?
14 Maloney	Y	Y	Y	Y	N
15 Rangel	Y	Y	Y	Y	?
16 Serrano	Y	Y	Y	Y	Y
17 Engel	+	+	+	+	+
18 Lowey	Y	Y	Y	Y	Y
19 ***Kelly***	Y	Y	Y	Y	Y
20 ***Gilman***	Y	Y	Y	N	Y
21 McNulty	Y	Y	Y	Y	?
22 ***Solomon***	Y	Y	Y	Y	Y
23 ***Boehlert***	Y	Y	Y	Y	Y
24 ***McHugh***	Y	Y	Y	Y	Y
25 ***Walsh***	Y	Y	Y	Y	Y
26 Hinchey	Y	Y	Y	Y	N
27 ***Paxon***	Y	Y	Y	Y	Y
28 Slaughter	Y	Y	Y	Y	Y

	24	25	26	27	28
29 LaFalce	Y	Y	Y	Y	?
30 ***Quinn***	Y	Y	Y	Y	Y
31 ***Houghton***	Y	Y	Y	Y	Y
NORTH CAROLINA					
1 Clayton	Y	Y	Y	Y	Y
2 Etheridge	Y	Y	Y	Y	Y
3 ***Jones***	Y	Y	Y	N	Y
4 Price	Y	Y	Y	Y	Y
5 ***Burr***	Y	Y	Y	Y	Y
6 ***Coble***	Y	Y	Y	Y	Y
7 McIntyre	Y	Y	Y	Y	Y
8 Hefner	Y	Y	Y	Y	?
9 ***Myrick***	Y	Y	Y	N	Y
10 ***Ballenger***	Y	Y	Y	Y	Y
11 ***Taylor***	Y	Y	Y	N	Y
12 Watt	Y	Y	Y	Y	Y
NORTH DAKOTA					
AL Pomeroy	Y	Y	Y	Y	Y
OHIO					
1 ***Chabot***	Y	Y	Y	N	Y
2 ***Portman***	Y	Y	Y	Y	?
3 Hall	Y	Y	Y	Y	Y
4 ***Oxley***	Y	Y	Y	Y	Y
5 ***Gillmor***	N	Y	Y	Y	Y
6 Strickland	Y	Y	Y	Y	Y
7 ***Hobson***	Y	Y	Y	Y	Y
8 ***Boehner***	Y	Y	Y	Y	Y
9 Kaptur	?	?	?	?	?
10 Kucinich	N	Y	Y	N	N
11 Stokes	Y	Y	Y	Y	?
12 ***Kasich***	Y	Y	Y	N	Y
13 Brown	Y	Y	Y	Y	?
14 Sawyer	Y	Y	Y	Y	Y
15 ***Pryce***	Y	Y	Y	Y	?
16 ***Regula***	Y	Y	Y	Y	P
17 Traficant	Y	Y	Y	Y	Y
18 ***Ney***	Y	Y	Y	Y	Y
19 ***LaTourette***	Y	?	Y	Y	Y
OKLAHOMA					
1 ***Largent***	?	Y	Y	N	Y
2 ***Coburn***	Y	Y	Y	N	Y
3 ***Watkins***	Y	Y	Y	Y	Y
4 ***Watts***	Y	Y	Y	Y	Y
5 ***Istook***	Y	Y	Y	Y	?
6 ***Lucas***	Y	Y	Y	Y	?
OREGON					
1 Furse	Y	Y	Y	Y	Y
2 ***Smith***	?	?	?	?	?
3 Blumenauer	Y	Y	Y	Y	Y
4 DeFazio	N	Y	Y	Y	N
5 Hooley	Y	Y	Y	Y	Y
PENNSYLVANIA					
1 Foglietta	Y	Y	Y	Y	N
2 Fattah	Y	Y	Y	Y	?
3 Borski	N	Y	Y	Y	N
4 Klink	Y	Y	Y	Y	?
5 ***Peterson***	Y	Y	Y	Y	?
6 Holden	Y	Y	Y	Y	Y
7 ***Weldon***	Y	Y	Y	Y	Y
8 ***Greenwood***	Y	Y	Y	Y	Y
9 ***Shuster***	Y	Y	Y	Y	Y
10 ***McDade***	Y	Y	Y	Y	Y
11 Kanjorski	Y	Y	Y	Y	Y
12 Murtha	Y	Y	Y	Y	Y
13 ***Fox***	Y	Y	Y	Y	Y
14 Coyne	Y	Y	Y	Y	?
15 McHale	Y	Y	Y	Y	Y
16 ***Pitts***	Y	Y	Y	Y	Y
17 ***Gekas***	Y	Y	Y	Y	Y
18 Doyle	Y	Y	Y	Y	?
19 ***Goodling***	Y	Y	Y	Y	Y
20 Mascara	Y	Y	Y	Y	Y
21 ***English***	N	Y	Y	Y	N
RHODE ISLAND					
1 Kennedy	Y	Y	Y	Y	Y
2 Weygand	Y	Y	Y	Y	?
SOUTH CAROLINA					
1 ***Sanford***	Y	Y	Y	N	Y
2 ***Spence***	Y	Y	Y	Y	Y
3 ***Graham***	Y	Y	Y	N	Y
4 ***Inglis***	Y	Y	Y	Y	?
5 Spratt	Y	Y	Y	Y	Y
6 Clyburn	N	Y	Y	Y	N
SOUTH DAKOTA					
AL ***Thune***	Y	Y	Y	Y	Y

	24	25	26	27	28
TENNESSEE					
1 ***Jenkins***	Y	Y	Y	Y	Y
2 ***Duncan***	Y	Y	Y	Y	Y
3 ***Wamp***	Y	Y	Y	Y	Y
4 ***Hilleary***	Y	Y	Y	N	Y
5 Clement	Y	Y	Y	Y	Y
6 Gordon	Y	Y	Y	Y	Y
7 ***Bryant***	Y	Y	Y	Y	?
8 Tanner	Y	Y	Y	Y	Y
9 Ford	Y	Y	Y	Y	Y
TEXAS					
1 Sandlin	Y	Y	Y	Y	Y
2 Turner	Y	Y	Y	Y	Y
3 ***Johnson, Sam***	Y	Y	Y	Y	Y
4 Hall	Y	Y	Y	N	Y
5 ***Sessions***	Y	Y	Y	Y	Y
6 ***Barton***	Y	Y	Y	Y	Y
7 ***Archer***	Y	Y	Y	Y	?
8 ***Brady***	Y	Y	Y	Y	Y
9 Lampson	Y	Y	Y	Y	Y
10 Doggett	Y	Y	Y	Y	Y
11 Edwards	Y	Y	Y	Y	Y
12 ***Granger***	Y	Y	Y	Y	Y
13 ***Thornberry***	Y	Y	Y	N	Y
14 ***Paul***	Y	Y	Y	N	Y
15 Hinojosa	Y	Y	Y	Y	Y
16 Reyes	?	?	?	#	?
17 Stenholm	Y	Y	Y	Y	N
18 Jackson-Lee	Y	Y	Y	Y	Y
19 ***Combest***	Y	Y	Y	Y	?
20 Gonzalez	Y	Y	Y	Y	Y
21 ***Smith***	Y	Y	Y	Y	Y
22 ***DeLay***	Y	Y	Y	Y	Y
23 ***Bonilla***	Y	Y	Y	Y	Y
24 Frost	Y	Y	Y	Y	Y
25 Bentsen	Y	Y	Y	Y	Y
26 ***Armey***	Y	Y	Y	Y	Y
27 Ortiz	Y	Y	Y	Y	Y
28 Vacant					
29 Green	Y	Y	Y	Y	N
30 Johnson, E.B.	Y	Y	Y	Y	N
UTAH					
1 ***Hansen***	Y	Y	Y	Y	Y
2 ***Cook***	Y	Y	Y	Y	Y
3 ***Cannon***	Y	Y	Y	N	Y
VERMONT					
AL *Sanders*	Y	Y	Y	Y	?
VIRGINIA					
1 ***Bateman***	Y	Y	Y	Y	Y
2 Pickett	N	Y	Y	Y	N
3 Scott	Y	Y	Y	Y	Y
4 Sisisky	Y	Y	Y	Y	Y
5 Goode	Y	Y	Y	Y	Y
6 ***Goodlatte***	Y	Y	Y	Y	Y
7 ***Bliley***	Y	Y	Y	Y	Y
8 Moran	Y	Y	Y	Y	Y
9 Boucher	Y	Y	Y	Y	Y
10 ***Wolf***	Y	Y	Y	Y	Y
11 ***Davis***	Y	Y	Y	Y	Y
WASHINGTON					
1 ***White***	?	Y	Y	Y	Y
2 ***Metcalf***	Y	Y	Y	Y	Y
3 ***Smith, Linda***	Y	Y	Y	Y	Y
4 ***Hastings***	Y	Y	Y	Y	Y
5 ***Nethercutt***	Y	Y	Y	Y	Y
6 Dicks	Y	Y	Y	Y	Y
7 McDermott	Y	Y	Y	Y	Y
8 ***Dunn***	Y	Y	Y	Y	Y
9 Smith, Adam	Y	Y	Y	Y	Y
WEST VIRGINIA					
1 Mollohan	Y	Y	Y	Y	Y
2 Wise	Y	Y	Y	Y	Y
3 Rahall	Y	Y	Y	Y	Y
WISCONSIN					
1 ***Neumann***	Y	Y	Y	N	Y
2 ***Klug***	Y	Y	Y	N	Y
3 Kind	Y	Y	Y	Y	Y
4 Kleczka	Y	Y	Y	Y	?
5 Barrett	Y	Y	Y	Y	Y
6 ***Petri***	Y	Y	Y	Y	Y
7 Obey	Y	Y	Y	Y	P
8 Johnson	Y	Y	Y	Y	Y
9 ***Sensenbrenner***	Y	Y	Y	N	Y
WYOMING					
AL ***Cubin***	Y	Y	Y	N	Y

Southern states - Ala., Ark., Fla., Ga., Ky., La., Miss., N.C., Okla., S.C., Tenn., Texas, Va.

HOUSE VOTES 29, 30, 31, 32, 33, 34, 35

29. H Con Res 17. Congratulate Guatemala on Peace Process/Adoption. Gilman, R-N.Y., motion to suspend the rules and adopt the concurrent resolution to congratulate the people of Guatemala on the success of recent negotiations to establish a peace process for Guatemala. Motion agreed to 416-0: R 218-0; D 197-0 (ND 144-0, SD 53-0); I 1-0, March 5, 1997. A two-thirds majority of those present and voting (278 in this case) is required for adoption under suspension of the rules.

30. H Con Res 18. Congratulate Nicaragua on Elections/Adoption. Gilman, R-N.Y., motion to suspend the rules and adopt the concurrent resolution to congratulate the people of Nicaragua on the success of their democratic elections. Motion agreed to 417-0: R 218-0; D 198-0 (ND 144-0, SD 54-0); I 1-0, March 5, 1997. A two-thirds majority of those present and voting (278 in this case) is required for adoption under suspension of the rules.

31. H Con Res 31. Public Display of the Ten Commandments/Adoption. Canady, R-Fla., motion to suspend the rules and adopt the concurrent resolution to express the sense of Congress that the public display of the Ten Commandments in government buildings should be permitted. Motion agreed to 295-125: R 216-4; D 79-120 (ND 48-97, SD 31-23); I 0-1, March 5, 1997. A two-thirds majority of those present and voting (280 in this case) is required for adoption under suspension of the rules.

32. Procedural Motion/Adjourn. Miller, D-Calif., motion to adjourn. Motion rejected 75-293: R 2-196; D 73-97 (ND 56-64, SD 17-33); I 0-0, March 6, 1997.

33. Procedural Motion/Journal. Approval of the House Journal of Wednesday, March 5, 1997. Approved 355-43: R 206-11; D 148-32 (ND 106-22, SD 42-10); I 1-0, March 6, 1997.

34. HR 513. D.C. City Council Contract Review/Passage. Davis, R-Va., motion to suspend the rules and pass the bill to exempt certain contracts entered into by the District of Columbia government from review by the D.C. City Council. Motion agreed to 390-7: R 212-6; D 177-1 (ND 124-1, SD 53-0); I 1-0, March 6, 1997. A two-thirds majority of those present and voting (265 in this case) is required for passage under suspension of the rules.

35. Procedural Motion/Adjourn. Miller, D-Calif., motion to adjourn. Motion rejected 84-312: R 7-211; D 77-100 (ND 65-61, SD 12-39); I 0-1, March 6, 1997.

KEY

Y	Voted for (yea).
#	Paired for.
+	Announced for.
N	Voted against (nay).
X	Paired against.
–	Announced against.
P	Voted "present."
C	Voted "present" to avoid possible conflict of interest.
?	Did not vote or otherwise make a position known.

Democrats ***Republicans***
Independent

	29	30	31	32	33	34	35
ALABAMA							
1 ***Callahan***	Y	Y	Y	N	Y	Y	N
2 ***Everett***	Y	Y	Y	N	Y	Y	N
3 ***Riley***	Y	Y	Y	N	Y	Y	N
4 ***Aderholt***	Y	Y	Y	N	Y	Y	N
5 Cramer	Y	Y	Y	N	Y	Y	N
6 ***Bachus***	Y	Y	Y	N	Y	Y	N
7 Hilliard	Y	Y	N	N	N	Y	N
ALASKA							
AL ***Young***	Y	Y	Y	?	Y	Y	N
ARIZONA							
1 ***Salmon***	Y	Y	Y	N	Y	Y	N
2 Pastor	Y	Y	N	N	Y	Y	N
3 ***Stump***	Y	Y	Y	N	Y	N	N
4 ***Shadegg***	Y	Y	Y	N	Y	Y	N
5 ***Kolbe***	Y	Y	Y	N	Y	Y	N
6 ***Hayworth***	Y	Y	Y	N	Y	Y	N
ARKANSAS							
1 Berry	Y	Y	Y	N	Y	Y	N
2 Snyder	Y	Y	N	N	Y	Y	N
3 ***Hutchinson***	Y	Y	Y	?	Y	Y	N
4 ***Dickey***	Y	Y	Y	N	Y	Y	N
CALIFORNIA							
1 ***Riggs***	Y	Y	Y	?	Y	Y	N
2 ***Herger***	Y	Y	Y	?	Y	Y	N
3 Fazio	Y	Y	N	Y	Y	Y	Y
4 ***Doolittle***	Y	Y	Y	N	Y	Y	N
5 Matsui	Y	Y	N	Y	Y	Y	Y
6 Woolsey	Y	Y	N	N	Y	Y	N
7 Miller	Y	Y	N	Y	N	Y	Y
8 Pelosi	Y	Y	N	Y	Y	Y	Y
9 Dellums	Y	Y	N	Y	Y	Y	Y
10 Tauscher	Y	Y	N	Y	Y	Y	Y
11 ***Pombo***	Y	Y	Y	N	N	Y	N
12 Lantos	?	?	?	Y	Y	Y	Y
13 Stark	Y	Y	N	Y	Y	Y	Y
14 Eshoo	Y	Y	Y	Y	Y	Y	Y
15 ***Campbell***	Y	Y	Y	N	Y	Y	N
16 Lofgren	Y	Y	N	?	Y	Y	N
17 Farr	Y	Y	Y	Y	Y	Y	Y
18 Condit	Y	Y	Y	N	Y	Y	N
19 ***Radanovich***	Y	Y	Y	N	Y	Y	N
20 Dooley	Y	Y	N	N	Y	Y	N
21 ***Thomas***	Y	Y	Y	N	Y	Y	N
22 Capps	Y	Y	Y	N	Y	Y	Y
23 ***Gallegly***	Y	Y	Y	?	?	?	?
24 Sherman	Y	Y	N	N	Y	Y	Y
25 ***McKeon***	Y	Y	Y	N	?	?	?
26 Berman	Y	Y	N	Y	Y	Y	N
27 ***Rogan***	Y	Y	Y	N	Y	Y	N
28 ***Dreier***	?	?	?	?	?	?	?
29 Waxman	Y	Y	N	N	Y	Y	N
30 Becerra	Y	Y	N	Y	Y	Y	N
31 Martinez	Y	Y	N	Y	Y	Y	Y
32 Dixon	Y	Y	N	N	Y	Y	Y
33 Roybal-Allard	Y	Y	N	?	Y	Y	N
34 Torres	Y	Y	N	Y	Y	Y	Y
35 Waters	Y	Y	N	Y	N	?	Y
36 Harman	Y	Y	N	Y	Y	Y	Y
37 Millender-McD.	Y	Y	N	Y	Y	Y	Y
38 ***Horn***	Y	Y	N	N	Y	Y	N
39 ***Royce***	Y	Y	Y	N	Y	Y	N
40 ***Lewis***	Y	Y	Y	N	Y	Y	N
41 ***Kim***	Y	Y	Y	N	Y	Y	N
42 Brown	?	?	N	Y	N	Y	Y
43 ***Calvert***	Y	Y	Y	N	Y	Y	N
44 ***Bono***	Y	Y	Y	N	Y	Y	N
45 ***Rohrabacher***	Y	Y	Y	?	Y	Y	N
46 Sanchez	Y	Y	Y	–	+	+	+
47 ***Cox***	Y	Y	Y	N	Y	Y	N
48 ***Packard***	Y	Y	Y	N	Y	Y	N
49 ***Bilbray***	Y	Y	Y	N	Y	Y	N
50 Filner	Y	Y	Y	Y	N	Y	Y
51 ***Cunningham***	Y	Y	Y	N	Y	Y	N
52 ***Hunter***	Y	Y	Y	N	Y	Y	N
COLORADO							
1 DeGette	Y	Y	N	Y	Y	Y	Y
2 Skaggs	Y	Y	N	N	?	?	N
3 ***McInnis***	Y	Y	Y	N	Y	Y	N
4 ***Schaffer***	Y	Y	Y	N	Y	N	N
5 ***Hefley***	Y	Y	Y	N	N	Y	N
6 ***Schaefer***	Y	Y	Y	N	Y	N	N
CONNECTICUT							
1 Kennelly	Y	Y	N	Y	N	Y	Y
2 Gejdenson	Y	Y	N	Y	Y	Y	Y
3 DeLauro	Y	Y	N	Y	Y	Y	Y
4 ***Shays***	Y	Y	Y	N	Y	Y	N
5 Maloney	Y	Y	Y	Y	Y	Y	Y
6 ***Johnson***	Y	Y	Y	?	Y	Y	N
DELAWARE							
AL ***Castle***	Y	Y	Y	N	Y	Y	N
FLORIDA							
1 ***Scarborough***	Y	Y	Y	N	Y	Y	N
2 Boyd	Y	Y	Y	N	Y	Y	N
3 Brown	Y	Y	N	N	Y	Y	N
4 ***Fowler***	Y	Y	Y	N	Y	Y	N
5 Thurman	Y	Y	N	N	Y	Y	N
6 ***Stearns***	Y	Y	Y	N	Y	N	N
7 ***Mica***	Y	Y	Y	N	Y	Y	N
8 ***McCollum***	Y	Y	Y	N	Y	Y	N
9 ***Bilirakis***	Y	Y	Y	N	Y	Y	N
10 ***Young***	Y	Y	Y	?	Y	Y	N
11 Davis	Y	Y	Y	N	?	Y	N
12 ***Canady***	Y	Y	Y	?	Y	Y	N
13 ***Miller***	Y	Y	Y	N	Y	Y	N
14 ***Goss***	Y	Y	Y	N	Y	Y	N
15 ***Weldon***	Y	Y	Y	N	Y	?	N
16 ***Foley***	Y	Y	Y	N	Y	Y	N
17 Meek	Y	Y	N	N	Y	Y	N
18 ***Ros-Lehtinen***	Y	Y	Y	N	Y	Y	N
19 Wexler	Y	Y	N	Y	Y	Y	Y
20 Deutsch	Y	Y	N	Y	Y	Y	Y
21 ***Diaz-Balart***	Y	Y	Y	N	Y	Y	?
22 ***Shaw***	Y	Y	Y	N	Y	Y	N
23 Hastings	Y	Y	N	Y	Y	Y	Y
GEORGIA							
1 ***Kingston***	Y	Y	Y	N	Y	Y	N
2 Bishop	Y	Y	Y	N	Y	Y	N
3 ***Collins***	Y	Y	Y	N	Y	Y	N
4 McKinney	Y	Y	N	N	Y	Y	N
5 Lewis	Y	Y	N	N	N	Y	N
6 ***Gingrich***							
7 ***Barr***	P	P	Y	N	Y	Y	N
8 ***Chambliss***	Y	Y	Y	N	Y	Y	N
9 ***Deal***	Y	Y	Y	N	Y	Y	N
10 ***Norwood***	Y	Y	Y	N	Y	Y	N
11 ***Linder***	Y	Y	Y	N	Y	Y	N
HAWAII							
1 Abercrombie	Y	Y	N	Y	N	Y	Y
2 Mink	Y	Y	N	Y	Y	Y	Y
IDAHO							
1 ***Chenoweth***	Y	P	Y	N	Y	Y	N
2 ***Crapo***	Y	Y	Y	N	Y	Y	N
ILLINOIS							
1 Rush	Y	Y	Y	N	Y	Y	N
2 Jackson	Y	Y	N	N	Y	Y	N
3 Lipinski	Y	Y	Y	Y	Y	Y	N
4 Gutierrez	Y	Y	N	N	N	Y	N
5 Blagojevich	Y	Y	Y	Y	Y	Y	?
6 ***Hyde***	Y	Y	Y	N	Y	Y	N
7 Davis	Y	Y	N	N	Y	Y	N
8 ***Crane***	Y	Y	Y	N	Y	Y	N
9 Yates	Y	Y	N	Y	Y	Y	Y
10 ***Porter***	Y	Y	?	N	Y	Y	N
11 ***Weller***	Y	Y	Y	N	N	N	Y
12 Costello	Y	Y	Y	N	Y	Y	N
13 ***Fawell***	Y	Y	Y	N	Y	Y	N
14 ***Hastert***	Y	Y	Y	N	Y	Y	N

ND Northern Democrats SD Southern Democrats

	29	30	31	32	33	34	35
15 *Ewing*	Y	Y	Y	N	?	Y	N
16 *Manzullo*	Y	Y	Y	N	Y	Y	N
17 Evans	Y	Y	N	Y	Y	Y	N
18 *LaHood*	Y	Y	Y	N	Y	Y	N
19 Poshard	Y	Y	Y	N	Y	Y	N
20 *Shimkus*	Y	Y	Y	N	Y	Y	N
INDIANA							
1 Visclosky	Y	Y	Y	N	N	Y	N
2 *McIntosh*	Y	Y	Y	N	N	Y	N
3 Roemer	Y	Y	Y	N	Y	Y	N
4 *Souder*	Y	Y	Y	N	Y	Y	N
5 *Buyer*	Y	Y	Y	N	Y	Y	N
6 *Burton*	Y	Y	Y	N	Y	Y	N
7 *Pease*	Y	Y	Y	N	Y	Y	N
8 *Hostettler*	Y	Y	Y	N	Y	Y	N
9 Hamilton	Y	Y	Y	N	Y	Y	N
10 Carson	?	?	?	N	Y	Y	Y
IOWA							
1 *Leach*	Y	Y	Y	N	Y	Y	N
2 *Nussle*	Y	Y	Y	Y	N	Y	Y
3 Boswell	Y	Y	N	N	Y	Y	N
4 *Ganske*	Y	Y	Y	?	Y	Y	N
5 *Latham*	Y	Y	Y	N	Y	Y	N
KANSAS							
1 *Moran*	Y	Y	Y	N	Y	Y	N
2 *Ryun*	Y	Y	Y	N	Y	Y	N
3 *Snowbarger*	Y	Y	Y	N	Y	Y	N
4 *Tiahrt*	Y	Y	Y	N	Y	Y	N
KENTUCKY							
1 *Whitfield*	Y	Y	Y	N	Y	Y	N
2 *Lewis*	Y	Y	Y	N	Y	Y	N
3 *Northup*	Y	Y	Y	N	Y	Y	N
4 *Bunning*	Y	Y	Y	N	Y	Y	N
5 *Rogers*	Y	Y	Y	N	Y	Y	N
6 Baesler	Y	Y	Y	?	?	?	?
LOUISIANA							
1 *Livingston*	Y	Y	Y	N	Y	Y	N
2 Jefferson	Y	Y	N	Y	Y	Y	Y
3 *Tauzin*	Y	Y	Y	?	Y	Y	N
4 *McCrery*	Y	Y	Y	?	Y	Y	N
5 *Cooksey*	+	+	+	N	Y	Y	N
6 *Baker*	Y	Y	Y	N	Y	Y	N
7 John	Y	Y	Y	Y	Y	Y	Y
MAINE							
1 Allen	Y	Y	Y	Y	Y	Y	N
2 Baldacci	Y	Y	N	N	N	Y	N
MARYLAND							
1 *Gilchrest*	Y	Y	Y	N	Y	Y	N
2 *Ehrlich*	Y	Y	Y	N	Y	Y	N
3 Cardin	Y	Y	Y	N	Y	Y	N
4 Wynn	Y	Y	Y	N	Y	Y	Y
5 Hoyer	Y	Y	Y	Y	Y	Y	N
6 *Bartlett*	Y	Y	Y	N	Y	Y	N
7 Cummings	Y	Y	N	N	Y	Y	N
8 *Morella*	Y	Y	N	N	Y	Y	N
MASSACHUSETTS							
1 Olver	Y	Y	N	Y	Y	Y	Y
2 Neal	Y	Y	N	Y	Y	Y	Y
3 McGovern	Y	Y	N	?	?	?	?
4 Frank	Y	Y	N	Y	Y	Y	Y
5 Meehan	Y	Y	N	Y	Y	Y	Y
6 Tierney	Y	Y	N	Y	Y	Y	Y
7 Markey	Y	Y	N	N	Y	Y	Y
8 Kennedy	Y	Y	N	Y	Y	Y	Y
9 Moakley	Y	Y	N	N	Y	Y	Y
10 Delahunt	Y	Y	N	?	Y	Y	Y
MICHIGAN							
1 Stupak	Y	Y	Y	?	?	?	?
2 *Hoekstra*	Y	Y	Y	?	?	?	?
3 *Ehlers*	Y	Y	Y	N	Y	Y	N
4 *Camp*	Y	Y	Y	?	?	?	?
5 Barcia	Y	Y	Y	?	?	?	?
6 *Upton*	Y	Y	Y	N	Y	Y	N
7 *Smith*	Y	Y	Y	N	Y	Y	N
8 Stabenow	Y	Y	Y	–	+	+	–
9 Kildee	Y	Y	Y	N	Y	Y	N
10 Bonior	Y	Y	N	N	N	Y	N
11 *Knollenberg*	Y	Y	Y	N	Y	Y	N
12 Levin	Y	Y	N	–	+	+	–
13 Rivers	Y	Y	N	N	Y	Y	N
14 Conyers	Y	Y	N	?	?	?	?
15 Kilpatrick	Y	Y	N	?	?	?	?
16 Dingell	Y	Y	N	?	?	?	?

	29	30	31	32	33	34	35
MINNESOTA							
1 *Gutknecht*	Y	Y	Y	N	Y	Y	N
2 Minge	Y	Y	Y	N	Y	Y	N
3 *Ramstad*	Y	Y	Y	N	N	Y	N
4 Vento	Y	Y	N	N	Y	Y	Y
5 Sabo	Y	Y	N	N	N	Y	Y
6 Luther	Y	Y	N	N	Y	Y	N
7 Peterson	Y	Y	Y	N	Y	Y	N
8 Oberstar	Y	Y	N	N	N	Y	Y
MISSISSIPPI							
1 *Wicker*	Y	Y	Y	N	Y	Y	N
2 Thompson	Y	Y	N	Y	N	Y	N
3 *Pickering*	Y	Y	Y	N	Y	Y	N
4 *Parker*	?	?	?	N	Y	Y	Y
5 Taylor	Y	Y	Y	Y	N	Y	Y
MISSOURI							
1 Clay	Y	Y	N	N	N	Y	Y
2 *Talent*	Y	Y	Y	N	Y	Y	N
3 Gephardt	Y	Y	N	Y	N	Y	?
4 Skelton	Y	Y	Y	N	Y	Y	N
5 McCarthy	Y	Y	N	–	+	+	–
6 Danner	Y	Y	Y	N	Y	Y	N
7 *Blunt*	Y	Y	Y	?	Y	Y	N
8 *Emerson*	Y	Y	Y	N	Y	Y	N
9 *Hulshof*	Y	Y	Y	N	N	Y	N
MONTANA							
AL *Hill*	Y	Y	Y	N	Y	Y	N
NEBRASKA							
1 *Bereuter*	Y	Y	Y	N	Y	Y	N
2 *Christensen*	Y	Y	Y	N	Y	Y	N
3 *Barrett*	Y	Y	Y	N	Y	Y	N
NEVADA							
1 *Ensign*	Y	Y	Y	N	N	Y	N
2 *Gibbons*	Y	Y	Y	N	N	Y	N
NEW HAMPSHIRE							
1 *Sununu*	Y	Y	Y	N	Y	Y	N
2 *Bass*	Y	Y	Y	?	Y	Y	N
NEW JERSEY							
1 Andrews	Y	Y	N	Y	Y	Y	N
2 *LoBiondo*	Y	Y	Y	N	Y	Y	N
3 *Saxton*	Y	Y	Y	N	Y	Y	N
4 *Smith*	Y	Y	Y	N	Y	Y	N
5 *Roukema*	Y	Y	Y	N	Y	Y	N
6 Pallone	Y	Y	N	Y	Y	Y	Y
7 *Franks*	Y	Y	Y	N	Y	Y	N
8 Pascrell	Y	Y	N	N	N	Y	N
9 Rothman	Y	Y	N	Y	Y	Y	N
10 Payne	Y	Y	N	Y	Y	Y	N
11 *Frelinghuysen*	Y	Y	Y	N	Y	Y	Y
12 *Pappas*	Y	Y	Y	N	Y	Y	N
13 Menendez	Y	Y	N	N	N	Y	N
NEW MEXICO							
1 *Schiff*	?	?	?	?	?	?	?
2 *Skeen*	Y	Y	Y	N	Y	Y	N
3 Vacant							
NEW YORK							
1 *Forbes*	Y	Y	Y	N	Y	Y	N
2 *Lazio*	Y	Y	Y	N	Y	Y	N
3 *King*	Y	Y	Y	N	Y	Y	N
4 McCarthy	Y	Y	N	N	Y	Y	Y
5 Ackerman	Y	Y	N	?	?	?	?
6 Flake	Y	Y	Y	?	?	?	?
7 Manton	Y	Y	Y	N	Y	Y	N
8 Nadler	?	?	?	?	?	?	?
9 Schumer	Y	Y	N	?	?	?	?
10 Towns	Y	Y	Y	Y	?	?	N
11 Owens	Y	Y	N	Y	Y	Y	Y
12 Velázquez	Y	Y	N	N	N	Y	N
13 *Molinari*	Y	Y	Y	?	Y	Y	N
14 Maloney	Y	Y	N	?	?	?	?
15 Rangel	Y	Y	N	?	Y	?	N
16 Serrano	Y	Y	N	?	Y	Y	?
17 Engel	Y	Y	N	?	?	?	?
18 Lowey	Y	Y	N	N	Y	Y	Y
19 *Kelly*	Y	Y	Y	N	Y	Y	N
20 *Gilman*	Y	Y	N	N	Y	Y	N
21 McNulty	Y	Y	N	?	?	?	?
22 *Solomon*	Y	Y	Y	N	Y	Y	N
23 *Boehlert*	Y	Y	N	N	Y	Y	N
24 *McHugh*	Y	Y	Y	N	Y	Y	N
25 *Walsh*	Y	Y	Y	N	Y	Y	N
26 Hinchey	Y	Y	N	?	?	?	?
27 *Paxon*	Y	Y	Y	?	Y	Y	N
28 Slaughter	Y	Y	N	Y	Y	Y	Y

	29	30	31	32	33	34	35
29 LaFalce	Y	Y	Y	N	Y	Y	N
30 *Quinn*	Y	Y	Y	N	Y	Y	N
31 *Houghton*	Y	Y	Y	?	Y	Y	N
NORTH CAROLINA							
1 Clayton	Y	Y	N	N	Y	Y	N
2 Etheridge	Y	Y	Y	N	Y	Y	N
3 *Jones*	Y	Y	Y	N	Y	Y	N
4 Price	Y	Y	Y	Y	Y	Y	N
5 *Burr*	Y	Y	Y	?	Y	Y	N
6 *Coble*	Y	Y	Y	N	Y	Y	N
7 McIntyre	Y	Y	Y	N	Y	Y	N
8 Hefner	Y	Y	Y	Y	Y	Y	N
9 *Myrick*	Y	Y	Y	N	?	Y	N
10 *Ballenger*	Y	Y	Y	N	Y	Y	N
11 *Taylor*	Y	Y	Y	N	Y	Y	N
12 Watt	Y	Y	N	Y	N	Y	Y
NORTH DAKOTA							
AL Pomeroy	Y	Y	Y	?	?	?	N
OHIO							
1 *Chabot*	?	?	?	N	Y	Y	N
2 *Portman*	Y	Y	Y	N	Y	Y	N
3 Hall	Y	Y	Y	?	Y	Y	Y
4 *Oxley*	Y	Y	Y	N	Y	Y	N
5 *Gillmor*	Y	Y	Y	N	Y	Y	N
6 Strickland	+	+	–	+	+	+	+
7 *Hobson*	Y	Y	Y	N	Y	Y	N
8 *Boehner*	Y	Y	Y	N	Y	Y	N
9 Kaptur	Y	Y	N	Y	Y	Y	Y
10 Kucinich	Y	Y	N	N	N	N	N
11 Stokes	Y	Y	N	N	Y	Y	N
12 *Kasich*	Y	Y	Y	N	Y	Y	N
13 Brown	Y	Y	Y	Y	Y	Y	Y
14 Sawyer	Y	Y	N	N	Y	Y	N
15 *Pryce*	Y	Y	Y	N	Y	Y	N
16 *Regula*	Y	Y	Y	N	Y	Y	N
17 Traficant	Y	Y	Y	N	Y	Y	Y
18 *Ney*	Y	Y	Y	N	N	Y	N
19 *LaTourette*	Y	Y	Y	?	Y	Y	N
OKLAHOMA							
1 *Largent*	Y	Y	Y	N	Y	Y	N
2 *Coburn*	Y	Y	Y	N	Y	Y	N
3 *Watkins*	Y	Y	Y	N	Y	Y	N
4 *Watts*	Y	Y	Y	N	Y	Y	N
5 *Istook*	Y	Y	Y	N	Y	Y	N
6 *Lucas*	Y	Y	Y	N	Y	Y	N
OREGON							
1 Furse	Y	Y	N	?	?	?	?
2 *Smith*	Y	Y	Y	N	Y	Y	N
3 Blumenauer	Y	Y	N	N	Y	Y	Y
4 DeFazio	Y	Y	N	?	N	Y	Y
5 Hooley	Y	Y	Y	Y	Y	Y	Y
PENNSYLVANIA							
1 Foglietta	Y	Y	N	?	N	Y	Y
2 Fattah	Y	Y	N	N	Y	Y	Y
3 Borski	Y	Y	Y	N	N	Y	Y
4 Klink	Y	Y	Y	N	Y	Y	N
5 *Peterson*	Y	Y	Y	N	Y	Y	N
6 Holden	Y	Y	Y	N	Y	Y	N
7 *Weldon*	Y	Y	Y	N	Y	Y	N
8 *Greenwood*	Y	Y	Y	N	Y	Y	Y
9 *Shuster*	Y	Y	Y	?	?	?	?
10 *McDade*	Y	Y	Y	N	Y	Y	Y
11 Kanjorski	Y	Y	Y	N	Y	Y	Y
12 Murtha	Y	Y	Y	N	Y	Y	Y
13 *Fox*	Y	Y	Y	N	Y	Y	N
14 Coyne	Y	Y	N	N	Y	Y	N
15 McHale	Y	Y	Y	N	Y	Y	N
16 *Pitts*	Y	Y	Y	N	Y	Y	N
17 *Gekas*	Y	Y	Y	Y	Y	Y	Y
18 Doyle	Y	Y	Y	N	Y	Y	N
19 *Goodling*	Y	Y	Y	N	Y	Y	N
20 Mascara	Y	Y	Y	N	Y	Y	N
21 *English*	Y	Y	Y	N	N	Y	N
RHODE ISLAND							
1 Kennedy	Y	Y	N	Y	Y	Y	Y
2 Weygand	Y	Y	N	Y	Y	Y	Y
SOUTH CAROLINA							
1 *Sanford*	Y	Y	Y	N	Y	Y	N
2 *Spence*	Y	Y	Y	N	Y	Y	N
3 *Graham*	Y	Y	Y	N	Y	Y	N
4 *Inglis*	Y	Y	Y	N	Y	Y	N
5 Spratt	Y	Y	Y	N	Y	Y	N
6 Clyburn	?	Y	Y	Y	N	Y	?

	29	30	31	32	33	34	35
SOUTH DAKOTA							
AL *Thune*	Y	Y	Y	N	Y	Y	N
TENNESSEE							
1 *Jenkins*	Y	Y	Y	N	Y	Y	N
2 *Duncan*	Y	Y	Y	N	Y	Y	N
3 *Wamp*	Y	Y	Y	N	Y	Y	N
4 *Hilleary*	Y	Y	Y	N	Y	Y	N
5 Clement	Y	Y	Y	N	Y	Y	N
6 Gordon	Y	Y	Y	N	Y	Y	N
7 *Bryant*	Y	Y	Y	N	Y	Y	N
8 Tanner	Y	Y	Y	N	Y	Y	N
9 Ford	Y	Y	Y	Y	Y	Y	Y
TEXAS							
1 Sandlin	Y	Y	Y	Y	Y	Y	Y
2 Turner	Y	Y	Y	N	Y	Y	Y
3 *Johnson, Sam*	Y	Y	Y	N	Y	Y	N
4 Hall	Y	Y	Y	N	Y	Y	N
5 *Sessions*	Y	Y	Y	N	Y	Y	N
6 *Barton*	Y	Y	Y	N	Y	Y	N
7 *Archer*	Y	Y	Y	?	Y	Y	N
8 *Brady*	Y	Y	Y	?	Y	Y	N
9 Lampson	Y	Y	Y	N	Y	Y	N
10 Doggett	Y	Y	N	Y	Y	Y	Y
11 Edwards	Y	Y	N	N	Y	Y	N
12 *Granger*	Y	Y	Y	N	Y	Y	N
13 *Thornberry*	Y	Y	Y	N	Y	Y	N
14 *Paul*	P	P	Y	N	Y	N	N
15 Hinojosa	Y	Y	Y	Y	Y	Y	N
16 Reyes	Y	Y	Y	Y	Y	Y	N
17 Stenholm	Y	Y	Y	N	Y	Y	N
18 Jackson-Lee	Y	Y	N	N	Y	Y	N
19 *Combest*	Y	Y	Y	N	Y	Y	N
20 Gonzalez	Y	Y	N	?	Y	Y	N
21 *Smith*	Y	Y	Y	N	Y	Y	N
22 *DeLay*	?	Y	Y	N	Y	Y	N
23 *Bonilla*	Y	Y	Y	N	Y	Y	N
24 Frost	Y	Y	N	Y	Y	Y	?
25 Bentsen	Y	Y	N	?	Y	Y	N
26 *Armey*	Y	Y	Y	N	Y	Y	N
27 Ortiz	Y	Y	Y	N	Y	Y	N
28 Vacant							
29 Green	Y	Y	Y	N	N	Y	N
30 Johnson, E.B.	Y	Y	N	N	N	Y	Y
UTAH							
1 *Hansen*	Y	Y	Y	N	Y	Y	N
2 *Cook*	Y	Y	Y	N	Y	Y	N
3 *Cannon*	Y	Y	Y	N	Y	Y	N
VERMONT							
AL Sanders	Y	Y	N	?	Y	Y	N
VIRGINIA							
1 *Bateman*	Y	Y	Y	N	Y	Y	N
2 Pickett	Y	Y	N	N	N	Y	N
3 Scott	Y	Y	N	N	N	Y	N
4 Sisisky	Y	Y	Y	N	Y	Y	N
5 Goode	Y	Y	Y	N	Y	Y	N
6 *Goodlatte*	Y	Y	Y	N	Y	Y	N
7 *Bliley*	Y	Y	Y	N	Y	Y	N
8 Moran	Y	Y	Y	N	Y	Y	N
9 Boucher	Y	Y	Y	?	Y	Y	N
10 *Wolf*	Y	Y	Y	N	Y	Y	N
11 *Davis*	Y	Y	Y	N	Y	Y	N
WASHINGTON							
1 *White*	Y	Y	Y	N	Y	Y	N
2 *Metcalf*	Y	Y	Y	N	Y	Y	N
3 *Smith, Linda*	Y	Y	Y	N	Y	Y	N
4 *Hastings*	Y	Y	Y	?	Y	Y	N
5 *Nethercutt*	Y	Y	Y	N	Y	Y	N
6 Dicks	Y	Y	N	Y	Y	Y	Y
7 McDermott	Y	Y	N	Y	N	Y	Y
8 *Dunn*	Y	Y	Y	?	Y	Y	N
9 Smith, Adam	Y	Y	N	Y	Y	Y	?
WEST VIRGINIA							
1 Mollohan	Y	Y	Y	N	Y	Y	N
2 Wise	?	?	?	?	Y	Y	N
3 Rahall	+	+	+	N	Y	Y	N
WISCONSIN							
1 *Neumann*	Y	Y	Y	N	Y	Y	N
2 *Klug*	Y	Y	Y	N	Y	Y	N
3 Kind	Y	Y	N	N	Y	Y	N
4 Kleczka	Y	Y	N	?	Y	Y	N
5 Barrett	Y	Y	Y	Y	Y	Y	N
6 *Petri*	Y	Y	Y	N	Y	Y	N
7 Obey	Y	Y	Y	N	Y	P	N
8 Johnson	Y	Y	Y	Y	Y	Y	Y
9 *Sensenbrenner*	Y	Y	Y	N	Y	Y	N
WYOMING							
AL *Cubin*	Y	Y	Y	N	Y	Y	N

Southern states - Ala., Ark., Fla., Ga., Ky., La., Miss., N.C., Okla., S.C., Tenn., Texas, Va.

HOUSE VOTES 36, 37, 38, 39, 40, 41, 42, 43

36. H Con Res 16. Improved Living Standards for South Asians/Adoption. Gilman, R-N.Y., motion to suspend the rules and adopt the concurrent resolution to congratulate the governments of Bangladesh, India and Nepal for cooperating to improve the living standards of people living in the Ganges and Brahmaputra River Basin. Motion agreed to 415-1: R 222-1; D 192-0 (ND 139-0, SD 53-0); I 1-0, March 11, 1997. A two-thirds majority of those present and voting (278 in this case) is required for adoption under suspension of the rules.

37. H Res 68. Reaffirm U.S.-Japan Security Treaty/Adoption. Bereuter, R-Neb., motion to suspend the rules and adopt the resolution to express the sense of the House that the Treaty of Mutual Cooperation and Security between the United States and Japan remains vital to the security interests of both nations, as well as other countries in the Asia-Pacific region. Motion agreed to 403-16: R 213-10; D 189-6 (ND 136-5, SD 53-1); I 1-0, March 11, 1997. A two-thirds majority of those present and voting (280 in this case) is required for adoption under suspension of the rules.

38. HR 750. Hong Kong Autonomy/Passage. Bereuter, R-Neb., motion to suspend the rules and pass the bill to reaffirm support for the autonomy of Hong Kong and establish guidelines under which the president may modify the application of U.S. law with respect to Hong Kong. Motion agreed to 416-1: R 220-1; D 195-0 (ND 141-0, SD 54-0); I 1-0, March 11, 1997. A two-thirds majority of those present and voting (278 in this case) is required for passage under suspension of the rules.

39. Procedural Motion/Journal. Approval of the House Journal of Tuesday, March 11, 1997. Approved 370-44: R 208-11; D 162-33 (ND 116-26, SD 46-7); I 0-0, March 12, 1997.

40. Procedural Motion/Adjourn. Bonior, D-Mich., motion to adjourn. Motion rejected 26-392: R 0-220; D 26-171 (ND 24-119, SD 2-52); I 0-1, March 12, 1997.

41. H Res 89. Request New Balanced Budget From President/Previous Question. Solomon, R-N.Y., motion to order the previous question (thus ending debate and the possibility of amendment) on adoption of the rule (H Res 90) to provide for House floor consideration of the resolution to request the president to submit to the House by April 7 a new budget plan for fiscal 1998 that will balance the federal budget by fiscal 2002 using Congressional Budget Office economic assumptions. Motion agreed to 226-200: R 225-0; D 1-199 (ND 1-145, SD 0-54); I 0-1, March 12, 1997.

42. H Res 89. Request New Balanced Budget From President/Rule. Adoption of the rule (H Res 90) to provide for House floor consideration of the resolution to request the president to submit to the House by April 7 a new budget plan for fiscal 1998 that will balance the federal budget by fiscal 2002 using Congressional Budget Office economic assumptions. Adopted 226-202: R 225-0; D 1-201 (ND 1-147, SD 0-54); I 0-1, March 12, 1997.

43. H Res 89. Request New Balanced Budget From President/Recommit. Spratt, D-S.C., motion to recommit the resolution to the Budget Committee with instructions to report it back with an amendment to request the Budget Committee to report a budget plan for fiscal 1998 that will balance the federal budget by fiscal 2002 in sufficient time to adhere to the statutory budget resolution deadline of April 15, under the Congressional Budget Act of 1974. Motion rejected 202-225: R 0-224; D 201-1 (ND 148-0, SD 53-1); I 1-0, March 12, 1997.

KEY

- Y Voted for (yea).
- # Paired for.
- \+ Announced for.
- N Voted against (nay).
- X Paired against.
- – Announced against.
- P Voted "present."
- C Voted "present" to avoid possible conflict of interest.
- ? Did not vote or otherwise make a position known.

Democrats ***Republicans***
Independent

	36	37	38	39	40	41	42	43
ALABAMA								
1 ***Callahan***	Y	Y	Y	Y	N	Y	Y	N
2 ***Everett***	Y	Y	Y	N	N	Y	Y	N
3 ***Riley***	Y	Y	Y	Y	N	Y	Y	N
4 ***Aderholt***	Y	Y	Y	Y	N	Y	Y	N
5 Cramer	Y	Y	Y	Y	N	N	N	Y
6 ***Bachus***	Y	Y	Y	Y	N	Y	Y	N
7 Hilliard	Y	Y	Y	N	N	N	N	Y
ALASKA								
AL ***Young***	Y	Y	Y	Y	N	Y	Y	N
ARIZONA								
1 ***Salmon***	Y	Y	Y	Y	N	Y	Y	N
2 Pastor	Y	Y	Y	Y	N	N	N	Y
3 ***Stump***	Y	Y	Y	Y	N	Y	Y	N
4 ***Shadegg***	Y	Y	Y	Y	N	Y	Y	N
5 ***Kolbe***	Y	Y	Y	Y	N	Y	Y	N
6 ***Hayworth***	Y	Y	Y	Y	N	Y	Y	N
ARKANSAS								
1 Berry	Y	Y	Y	Y	Y	N	N	Y
2 Snyder	Y	Y	Y	Y	N	N	N	Y
3 ***Hutchinson***	Y	Y	Y	Y	N	Y	Y	N
4 ***Dickey***	Y	Y	Y	Y	N	Y	Y	N
CALIFORNIA								
1 ***Riggs***	Y	Y	Y	Y	?	Y	Y	N
2 ***Herger***	Y	Y	Y	Y	N	Y	?	N
3 Fazio	Y	Y	Y	N	Y	N	N	Y
4 ***Doolittle***	Y	Y	Y	Y	N	Y	Y	N
5 Matsui	Y	Y	Y	Y	N	N	N	Y
6 Woolsey	Y	Y	Y	Y	N	N	N	Y
7 Miller	Y	Y	Y	N	Y	N	N	Y
8 Pelosi	Y	Y	Y	Y	Y	N	N	Y
9 Dellums	Y	Y	Y	Y	N	N	N	Y
10 Tauscher	Y	Y	Y	Y	N	N	N	Y
11 ***Pombo***	Y	Y	Y	N	N	Y	Y	N
12 Lantos	Y	Y	Y	Y	N	N	N	Y
13 Stark	Y	Y	Y	Y	N	N	N	Y
14 Eshoo	Y	Y	Y	Y	Y	N	N	Y
15 ***Campbell***	Y	Y	Y	Y	N	Y	Y	N
16 Lofgren	Y	Y	Y	Y	N	N	N	Y
17 Farr	Y	Y	Y	Y	N	N	N	Y
18 Condit	Y	Y	Y	N	N	N	N	Y
19 ***Radanovich***	Y	Y	Y	Y	N	Y	Y	N
20 Dooley	Y	Y	Y	Y	N	N	N	Y
21 ***Thomas***	Y	Y	Y	Y	N	Y	Y	N
22 Capps	Y	Y	Y	Y	N	N	N	Y
23 ***Gallegly***	Y	Y	Y	Y	N	Y	Y	N
24 Sherman	Y	Y	Y	N	N	N	N	Y
25 ***McKeon***	Y	N	Y	Y	N	Y	Y	N
26 Berman	Y	Y	Y	Y	N	N	N	Y
27 ***Rogan***	Y	Y	Y	Y	N	Y	Y	N
28 ***Dreier***	Y	Y	Y	Y	N	Y	Y	N
29 Waxman	Y	Y	Y	Y	N	N	N	Y
30 Becerra	Y	Y	Y	Y	N	N	N	Y
31 Martinez	Y	Y	Y	N	Y	N	N	Y
32 Dixon	Y	Y	Y	?	N	?	?	?
33 Roybal-Allard	Y	Y	Y	Y	N	N	N	Y
34 Torres	Y	Y	Y	?	?	?	?	Y
35 Waters	Y	Y	Y	Y	N	N	N	Y
36 Harman	Y	Y	Y	Y	N	N	N	Y
37 Millender-McD.	?	?	?	Y	N	N	N	Y
38 ***Horn***	Y	Y	Y	Y	N	Y	Y	N
39 ***Royce***	Y	Y	Y	Y	N	Y	Y	N
40 ***Lewis***	Y	Y	Y	Y	N	Y	Y	N
41 ***Kim***	Y	Y	Y	Y	N	Y	Y	N
42 Brown	Y	Y	Y	N	?	N	N	Y
43 ***Calvert***	Y	Y	Y	Y	N	Y	Y	N
44 ***Bono***	Y	Y	Y	Y	N	Y	Y	N
45 ***Rohrabacher***	Y	Y	Y	Y	N	Y	Y	N
46 Sanchez	Y	Y	Y	Y	N	N	N	Y
47 ***Cox***	Y	Y	Y	Y	N	Y	Y	N
48 ***Packard***	Y	Y	Y	Y	N	Y	Y	N
49 ***Bilbray***	Y	N	Y	Y	N	Y	Y	N
50 Filner	Y	Y	Y	N	Y	N	N	Y
51 ***Cunningham***	Y	Y	Y	Y	N	Y	Y	N
52 ***Hunter***	Y	N	Y	Y	N	Y	Y	N
COLORADO								
1 DeGette	Y	Y	Y	Y	N	N	N	Y
2 Skaggs	Y	Y	Y	Y	N	N	N	Y
3 ***McInnis***	Y	Y	Y	Y	N	Y	Y	N
4 ***Schaffer***	Y	Y	Y	Y	N	Y	Y	N
5 ***Hefley***	Y	Y	Y	N	N	Y	Y	N
6 ***Schaefer***	Y	N	Y	Y	N	Y	Y	N
CONNECTICUT								
1 Kennelly	Y	Y	Y	Y	N	N	N	Y
2 Gejdenson	?	Y	Y	Y	N	N	N	Y
3 DeLauro	Y	Y	Y	Y	N	N	N	Y
4 ***Shays***	Y	Y	Y	Y	N	Y	Y	N
5 Maloney	Y	Y	Y	Y	N	N	N	Y
6 ***Johnson***	Y	Y	Y	Y	N	Y	Y	N
DELAWARE								
AL ***Castle***	Y	Y	Y	Y	N	Y	Y	N
FLORIDA								
1 ***Scarborough***	Y	N	Y	Y	N	Y	Y	N
2 Boyd	Y	Y	Y	Y	N	N	N	Y
3 Brown	Y	Y	Y	Y	N	N	N	Y
4 ***Fowler***	Y	N	Y	Y	N	Y	Y	N
5 Thurman	Y	Y	Y	Y	N	N	N	Y
6 ***Stearns***	Y	Y	Y	Y	N	Y	Y	N
7 ***Mica***	Y	Y	Y	Y	N	Y	Y	N
8 ***McCollum***	Y	Y	Y	Y	N	Y	Y	N
9 ***Bilirakis***	Y	Y	Y	Y	N	Y	Y	N
10 ***Young***	Y	Y	Y	Y	N	Y	Y	N
11 Davis	Y	Y	Y	Y	N	N	N	Y
12 ***Canady***	Y	Y	Y	Y	N	Y	Y	N
13 ***Miller***	Y	Y	Y	Y	N	Y	Y	N
14 ***Goss***	Y	Y	Y	Y	N	Y	Y	N
15 ***Weldon***	Y	Y	Y	Y	N	Y	Y	N
16 ***Foley***	Y	Y	Y	Y	N	Y	Y	N
17 Meek	Y	Y	Y	Y	N	N	N	Y
18 ***Ros-Lehtinen***	Y	Y	Y	Y	N	Y	Y	N
19 Wexler	Y	Y	Y	Y	N	N	N	Y
20 Deutsch	Y	Y	Y	Y	N	N	N	Y
21 ***Diaz-Balart***	Y	Y	Y	Y	N	Y	Y	N
22 ***Shaw***	Y	Y	Y	Y	N	Y	Y	N
23 Hastings	Y	Y	Y	Y	N	N	N	Y
GEORGIA								
1 ***Kingston***	Y	Y	Y	Y	N	Y	Y	N
2 Bishop	Y	Y	Y	Y	N	N	N	Y
3 ***Collins***	Y	Y	Y	Y	N	Y	Y	N
4 McKinney	Y	Y	Y	Y	N	N	N	Y
5 Lewis	Y	Y	Y	?	N	N	N	Y
6 ***Gingrich***								
7 ***Barr***	Y	Y	Y	Y	N	Y	Y	N
8 ***Chambliss***	Y	Y	Y	Y	N	Y	Y	N
9 ***Deal***	Y	Y	Y	Y	N	Y	Y	N
10 ***Norwood***	Y	Y	Y	Y	N	Y	Y	N
11 ***Linder***	Y	Y	Y	?	N	Y	Y	N
HAWAII								
1 Abercrombie	Y	Y	Y	N	N	N	N	Y
2 Mink	Y	Y	Y	Y	Y	N	N	Y
IDAHO								
1 ***Chenoweth***	Y	Y	Y	Y	N	Y	Y	N
2 ***Crapo***	Y	Y	Y	Y	N	Y	Y	N
ILLINOIS								
1 Rush	?	?	?	?	N	N	N	Y
2 Jackson	Y	Y	Y	Y	N	N	N	Y
3 Lipinski	Y	Y	Y	Y	N	N	N	Y
4 Gutierrez	Y	Y	Y	Y	N	N	N	Y
5 Blagojevich	Y	Y	Y	Y	N	N	N	Y
6 ***Hyde***	Y	Y	Y	Y	N	Y	Y	N
7 Davis	Y	Y	Y	Y	N	N	N	Y
8 ***Crane***	Y	Y	Y	Y	N	Y	Y	N
9 Yates	Y	N	Y	Y	N	N	N	Y
10 ***Porter***	Y	Y	Y	Y	N	Y	Y	N
11 ***Weller***	Y	Y	Y	N	N	Y	Y	N
12 Costello	Y	Y	Y	Y	N	N	N	Y
13 ***Fawell***	Y	Y	Y	Y	N	Y	Y	N
14 ***Hastert***	Y	Y	Y	Y	N	Y	Y	N

ND Northern Democrats SD Southern Democrats

	36	37	38	39	40	41	42	43
15 ***Ewing***	Y	Y	Y	Y	N	Y	Y	N
16 ***Manzullo***	Y	Y	Y	Y	N	Y	Y	N
17 Evans	Y	Y	Y	Y	N	N	N	Y
18 ***LaHood***	Y	Y	Y	Y	N	Y	Y	N
19 Poshard	Y	Y	Y	Y	N	N	N	Y
20 ***Shimkus***	Y	Y	Y	Y	N	Y	Y	N
INDIANA								
1 Visclosky	Y	Y	Y	N	N	N	N	Y
2 ***McIntosh***	Y	Y	Y	Y	N	Y	Y	N
3 Roemer	Y	Y	Y	Y	N	N	N	Y
4 ***Souder***	Y	N	Y	Y	N	Y	Y	?
5 ***Buyer***	Y	N	Y	Y	N	Y	Y	N
6 ***Burton***	Y	Y	Y	Y	N	Y	Y	N
7 ***Pease***	Y	Y	Y	Y	N	Y	Y	N
8 ***Hostettler***	Y	Y	Y	Y	N	Y	Y	N
9 Hamilton	Y	Y	Y	Y	N	N	N	Y
10 Carson	?	?	?	Y	N	N	N	Y
IOWA								
1 ***Leach***	Y	Y	Y	Y	N	Y	Y	N
2 ***Nussle***	Y	Y	Y	?	N	Y	Y	N
3 Boswell	Y	Y	Y	Y	N	N	N	Y
4 ***Ganske***	Y	Y	Y	Y	N	Y	Y	N
5 ***Latham***	Y	Y	Y	Y	N	Y	Y	N
KANSAS								
1 ***Moran***	Y	Y	Y	Y	N	Y	Y	N
2 ***Ryun***	Y	Y	Y	Y	N	Y	Y	N
3 ***Snowbarger***	Y	Y	Y	Y	N	Y	Y	N
4 ***Tiahrt***	Y	Y	Y	Y	N	Y	Y	N
KENTUCKY								
1 ***Whitfield***	Y	Y	Y	Y	N	Y	Y	N
2 ***Lewis***	Y	Y	Y	Y	N	Y	Y	N
3 ***Northup***	Y	Y	Y	Y	N	Y	Y	N
4 ***Bunning***	Y	Y	Y	Y	N	Y	Y	N
5 ***Rogers***	Y	Y	Y	Y	N	Y	Y	N
6 Baesler	Y	Y	Y	Y	N	N	N	Y
LOUISIANA								
1 ***Livingston***	Y	Y	Y	Y	N	Y	Y	?
2 Jefferson	Y	Y	Y	Y	N	N	N	Y
3 ***Tauzin***	Y	Y	Y	Y	N	Y	Y	N
4 ***McCrery***	Y	Y	Y	Y	N	Y	Y	N
5 ***Cooksey***	Y	Y	Y	?	?	Y	Y	N
6 ***Baker***	Y	Y	Y	Y	N	Y	Y	N
7 John	Y	Y	Y	Y	N	N	N	Y
MAINE								
1 Allen	Y	Y	Y	Y	N	N	N	Y
2 Baldacci	Y	Y	Y	Y	N	N	N	Y
MARYLAND								
1 ***Gilchrest***	Y	Y	Y	Y	N	Y	Y	N
2 ***Ehrlich***	Y	Y	Y	Y	N	Y	Y	N
3 Cardin	Y	Y	Y	Y	N	N	N	Y
4 Wynn	Y	Y	Y	Y	Y	N	N	Y
5 Hoyer	Y	Y	Y	Y	N	N	N	Y
6 ***Bartlett***	Y	Y	Y	Y	N	Y	Y	N
7 Cummings	Y	Y	Y	Y	N	N	N	Y
8 ***Morella***	Y	Y	Y	Y	N	Y	Y	N
MASSACHUSETTS								
1 Olver	Y	Y	Y	?	Y	N	N	Y
2 Neal	Y	Y	Y	Y	Y	N	N	Y
3 McGovern	Y	Y	Y	N	Y	N	N	Y
4 Frank	Y	N	Y	Y	Y	N	N	Y
5 Meehan	Y	Y	Y	Y	N	N	N	Y
6 Tierney	Y	Y	Y	Y	N	N	N	Y
7 Markey	Y	Y	Y	Y	N	N	N	Y
8 Kennedy	Y	Y	Y	Y	N	N	N	Y
9 Moakley	Y	Y	Y	Y	N	N	N	Y
10 Delahunt	Y	Y	Y	Y	Y	N	N	Y
MICHIGAN								
1 Stupak	Y	Y	Y	Y	N	N	N	Y
2 ***Hoekstra***	Y	Y	Y	Y	N	Y	Y	N
3 ***Ehlers***	Y	Y	Y	Y	N	Y	Y	N
4 ***Camp***	Y	Y	Y	Y	N	Y	Y	N
5 Barcia	Y	Y	Y	Y	N	N	N	Y
6 ***Upton***	Y	Y	Y	Y	N	Y	Y	N
7 ***Smith***	Y	Y	Y	Y	N	Y	Y	N
8 Stabenow	Y	Y	Y	Y	N	N	N	Y
9 Kildee	Y	Y	Y	Y	N	N	N	Y
10 Bonior	Y	Y	Y	N	N	N	N	Y
11 ***Knollenberg***	Y	Y	Y	Y	N	Y	Y	N
12 Levin	Y	Y	Y	Y	N	N	N	Y
13 Rivers	Y	Y	Y	Y	N	N	N	Y
14 Conyers	Y	Y	Y	Y	Y	N	N	Y
15 Kilpatrick	Y	Y	Y	Y	N	N	N	Y
16 Dingell	Y	Y	Y	Y	Y	?	N	Y
MINNESOTA								
1 ***Gutknecht***	Y	Y	Y	N	N	Y	Y	N
2 Minge	Y	Y	Y	Y	N	N	N	Y
3 ***Ramstad***	Y	Y	Y	N	N	Y	Y	N
4 Vento	Y	Y	Y	N	N	N	N	Y
5 Sabo	Y	Y	Y	N	Y	N	N	Y
6 Luther	Y	Y	Y	Y	N	N	N	Y
7 Peterson	Y	Y	Y	Y	N	N	N	Y
8 Oberstar	Y	Y	Y	N	N	N	N	Y
MISSISSIPPI								
1 ***Wicker***	Y	Y	Y	Y	N	Y	Y	N
2 Thompson	Y	Y	Y	N	N	N	N	Y
3 ***Pickering***	Y	Y	Y	Y	N	Y	Y	N
4 ***Parker***	Y	Y	Y	Y	N	Y	Y	N
5 Taylor	Y	N	Y	N	N	N	N	Y
MISSOURI								
1 Clay	Y	Y	Y	N	N	N	N	Y
2 ***Talent***	Y	Y	Y	Y	N	Y	Y	N
3 Gephardt	?	?	?	N	Y	N	N	Y
4 Skelton	Y	Y	Y	Y	N	N	N	Y
5 McCarthy	+	Y	Y	Y	N	N	N	Y
6 Danner	Y	N	Y	Y	N	N	N	Y
7 ***Blunt***	Y	Y	Y	Y	N	Y	Y	N
8 ***Emerson***	Y	Y	Y	Y	N	Y	Y	N
9 ***Hulshof***	Y	Y	Y	Y	N	Y	Y	N
MONTANA								
AL ***Hill***	Y	Y	Y	Y	N	Y	Y	N
NEBRASKA								
1 ***Bereuter***	Y	Y	Y	Y	N	Y	Y	N
2 ***Christensen***	Y	Y	Y	Y	N	Y	Y	N
3 ***Barrett***	Y	Y	Y	Y	N	Y	Y	N
NEVADA								
1 ***Ensign***	Y	Y	Y	N	N	Y	Y	N
2 ***Gibbons***	Y	Y	Y	N	N	Y	Y	N
NEW HAMPSHIRE								
1 ***Sununu***	Y	Y	Y	Y	N	Y	Y	N
2 ***Bass***	Y	Y	Y	Y	N	Y	Y	N
NEW JERSEY								
1 Andrews	?	?	?	Y	N	N	N	?
2 ***LoBiondo***	Y	Y	Y	Y	N	Y	Y	N
3 ***Saxton***	Y	Y	Y	Y	N	Y	Y	N
4 ***Smith***	Y	Y	Y	Y	N	Y	Y	N
5 ***Roukema***	?	?	?	?	N	Y	Y	N
6 Pallone	Y	Y	Y	N	N	N	N	Y
7 ***Franks***	Y	Y	Y	Y	N	Y	Y	N
8 Pascrell	Y	Y	Y	N	N	N	N	Y
9 Rothman	Y	Y	Y	Y	N	N	N	Y
10 Payne	Y	Y	Y	?	N	N	N	Y
11 ***Frelinghuysen***	Y	Y	Y	Y	N	Y	Y	N
12 ***Pappas***	Y	Y	Y	Y	N	Y	Y	N
13 Menendez	Y	Y	Y	?	N	N	N	Y
NEW MEXICO								
1 ***Schiff***	Y	Y	Y	Y	N	Y	Y	N
2 ***Skeen***	Y	Y	Y	Y	N	Y	Y	N
3 Vacant								
NEW YORK								
1 ***Forbes***	Y	Y	Y	Y	N	Y	Y	N
2 ***Lazio***	Y	Y	Y	Y	N	Y	Y	N
3 ***King***	Y	Y	Y	Y	N	Y	Y	N
4 McCarthy	Y	Y	Y	Y	N	N	N	Y
5 Ackerman	Y	Y	Y	?	?	N	N	Y
6 Flake	?	?	?	Y	N	N	N	Y
7 Manton	Y	Y	Y	Y	N	N	N	Y
8 Nadler	Y	Y	Y	Y	N	N	N	Y
9 Schumer	Y	Y	Y	Y	N	N	N	Y
10 Towns	?	?	?	Y	Y	N	N	Y
11 Owens	?	?	?	?	Y	N	N	Y
12 Velázquez	Y	Y	Y	N	N	N	N	Y
13 ***Molinari***	Y	Y	Y	?	N	Y	Y	N
14 Maloney	Y	Y	Y	N	N	N	N	Y
15 Rangel	Y	Y	Y	Y	N	N	N	Y
16 Serrano	Y	Y	Y	Y	N	N	N	Y
17 Engel	Y	Y	Y	Y	N	N	N	Y
18 Lowey	Y	Y	Y	Y	N	N	N	Y
19 ***Kelly***	Y	Y	Y	Y	N	Y	Y	N
20 ***Gilman***	Y	Y	Y	Y	N	Y	Y	N
21 McNulty	Y	Y	Y	Y	N	N	N	Y
22 ***Solomon***	Y	Y	Y	Y	N	Y	Y	N
23 ***Boehlert***	Y	Y	Y	Y	N	Y	Y	N
24 ***McHugh***	Y	Y	Y	Y	N	Y	Y	N
25 ***Walsh***	Y	Y	Y	Y	N	Y	Y	N
26 Hinchey	Y	Y	Y	N	N	N	N	Y
27 ***Paxon***	Y	Y	Y	Y	N	Y	Y	N
28 Slaughter	Y	Y	Y	Y	N	N	N	Y
29 LaFalce	Y	Y	Y	Y	N	N	N	Y
30 ***Quinn***	Y	Y	Y	Y	?	Y	Y	N
31 ***Houghton***	Y	Y	Y	Y	N	Y	Y	N
NORTH CAROLINA								
1 Clayton	Y	Y	Y	Y	N	N	N	Y
2 Etheridge	Y	Y	Y	Y	N	N	N	Y
3 ***Jones***	Y	Y	Y	Y	N	Y	Y	N
4 Price	Y	Y	Y	Y	N	N	N	Y
5 ***Burr***	Y	Y	Y	Y	N	Y	Y	N
6 ***Coble***	?	?	?	?	?	?	?	N
7 McIntyre	Y	Y	Y	Y	N	N	N	Y
8 Hefner	Y	Y	Y	Y	N	N	N	Y
9 ***Myrick***	Y	Y	Y	Y	N	Y	Y	N
10 ***Ballenger***	Y	Y	Y	Y	?	Y	Y	N
11 ***Taylor***	Y	Y	Y	Y	N	Y	Y	N
12 Watt	Y	Y	Y	Y	N	N	N	Y
NORTH DAKOTA								
AL Pomeroy	Y	Y	Y	Y	?	N	N	Y
OHIO								
1 ***Chabot***	Y	Y	Y	Y	N	Y	Y	N
2 ***Portman***	Y	Y	Y	Y	N	Y	Y	N
3 Hall	Y	Y	Y	Y	?	N	N	Y
4 ***Oxley***	Y	Y	Y	Y	N	Y	Y	N
5 ***Gillmor***	Y	Y	Y	Y	N	Y	Y	N
6 Strickland	Y	Y	Y	Y	Y	N	N	Y
7 ***Hobson***	Y	Y	Y	Y	N	Y	Y	N
8 ***Boehner***	Y	Y	Y	Y	N	Y	Y	N
9 Kaptur	?	?	?	?	?	?	?	?
10 Kucinich	Y	Y	Y	N	N	N	N	Y
11 Stokes	Y	Y	Y	Y	N	N	N	Y
12 ***Kasich***	Y	Y	Y	Y	N	Y	Y	N
13 Brown	Y	Y	Y	Y	Y	N	N	Y
14 Sawyer	Y	Y	Y	Y	N	N	N	Y
15 ***Pryce***	Y	Y	+	Y	N	Y	Y	N
16 ***Regula***	Y	Y	Y	Y	N	Y	Y	N
17 Traficant	Y	N	Y	Y	N	Y	Y	Y
18 ***Ney***	Y	Y	Y	Y	N	Y	Y	N
19 ***LaTourette***	Y	Y	Y	Y	N	Y	Y	N
OKLAHOMA								
1 ***Largent***	?	?	?	Y	N	Y	Y	N
2 ***Coburn***	Y	Y	Y	Y	N	Y	Y	N
3 ***Watkins***	Y	Y	Y	Y	N	Y	Y	N
4 ***Watts***	Y	Y	Y	N	N	Y	Y	N
5 ***Istook***	Y	Y	Y	Y	N	Y	Y	N
6 ***Lucas***	Y	Y	Y	Y	N	Y	Y	N
OREGON								
1 Furse	?	?	?	Y	N	N	N	Y
2 ***Smith***	Y	Y	Y	Y	N	Y	Y	N
3 Blumenauer	Y	Y	Y	Y	N	N	N	Y
4 DeFazio	Y	N	Y	N	Y	N	N	Y
5 Hooley	Y	Y	Y	Y	N	N	N	Y
PENNSYLVANIA								
1 Foglietta	Y	Y	Y	N	N	N	N	Y
2 Fattah	Y	Y	Y	Y	N	N	N	Y
3 Borski	Y	Y	Y	N	N	N	N	Y
4 Klink	Y	Y	Y	Y	N	N	N	Y
5 ***Peterson***	Y	Y	Y	Y	N	Y	Y	N
6 Holden	Y	Y	Y	Y	N	N	N	Y
7 ***Weldon***	Y	Y	Y	Y	N	Y	Y	N
8 ***Greenwood***	Y	Y	?	?	N	Y	Y	N
9 ***Shuster***	Y	Y	Y	Y	N	Y	Y	N
10 ***McDade***	Y	Y	Y	Y	N	Y	Y	N
11 Kanjorski	Y	Y	Y	Y	N	N	N	Y
12 Murtha	Y	Y	Y	Y	N	N	N	Y
13 ***Fox***	Y	Y	Y	Y	N	Y	Y	N
14 Coyne	Y	Y	Y	Y	N	N	N	Y
15 McHale	Y	Y	Y	Y	N	N	N	Y
16 ***Pitts***	Y	Y	Y	Y	N	Y	Y	N
17 ***Gekas***	Y	Y	Y	Y	N	Y	Y	N
18 Doyle	Y	Y	Y	Y	N	N	N	Y
19 ***Goodling***	Y	Y	Y	Y	N	Y	Y	N
20 Mascara	Y	Y	Y	Y	N	N	N	Y
21 ***English***	Y	Y	Y	N	N	Y	Y	N
RHODE ISLAND								
1 Kennedy	Y	Y	Y	Y	Y	?	N	Y
2 Weygand	Y	Y	Y	Y	?	N	N	Y
SOUTH CAROLINA								
1 ***Sanford***	Y	Y	Y	Y	N	Y	Y	N
2 ***Spence***	Y	N	Y	Y	N	Y	Y	N
3 ***Graham***	Y	Y	Y	Y	N	Y	Y	N
4 ***Inglis***	Y	Y	Y	Y	N	Y	Y	N
5 Spratt	Y	Y	Y	Y	N	N	N	Y
6 Clyburn	?	Y	Y	N	N	N	N	Y
SOUTH DAKOTA								
AL ***Thune***	Y	Y	Y	Y	N	Y	Y	N
TENNESSEE								
1 ***Jenkins***	Y	Y	Y	Y	N	Y	Y	N
2 ***Duncan***	Y	Y	Y	Y	N	Y	Y	N
3 ***Wamp***	Y	Y	Y	Y	N	Y	Y	N
4 ***Hilleary***	Y	Y	Y	Y	N	Y	Y	N
5 Clement	Y	Y	Y	Y	N	N	N	Y
6 Gordon	Y	Y	Y	Y	N	N	N	Y
7 ***Bryant***	Y	Y	Y	Y	N	Y	Y	N
8 Tanner	Y	Y	Y	Y	N	N	N	Y
9 Ford	Y	Y	Y	Y	N	N	N	Y
TEXAS								
1 Sandlin	Y	Y	Y	Y	Y	N	N	Y
2 Turner	Y	Y	Y	Y	N	N	N	Y
3 ***Johnson, Sam***	Y	Y	Y	Y	N	Y	Y	N
4 Hall	Y	Y	Y	Y	N	N	N	Y
5 ***Sessions***	Y	Y	Y	Y	N	Y	Y	N
6 ***Barton***	Y	Y	Y	Y	N	Y	Y	N
7 ***Archer***	Y	Y	Y	Y	N	Y	Y	N
8 ***Brady***	Y	Y	Y	Y	N	Y	Y	N
9 Lampson	Y	Y	Y	Y	N	N	N	Y
10 Doggett	Y	Y	Y	Y	N	N	N	Y
11 Edwards	Y	Y	Y	Y	N	N	N	Y
12 ***Granger***	Y	Y	Y	Y	N	Y	Y	N
13 ***Thornberry***	Y	Y	Y	Y	N	Y	Y	N
14 ***Paul***	N	N	N	Y	N	Y	Y	N
15 Hinojosa	Y	Y	Y	Y	N	N	N	Y
16 Reyes	Y	Y	Y	Y	N	N	N	Y
17 Stenholm	Y	Y	Y	N	N	N	N	Y
18 Jackson-Lee	Y	Y	Y	Y	N	N	N	Y
19 ***Combest***	Y	Y	Y	Y	N	Y	Y	N
20 Gonzalez	Y	Y	Y	Y	N	N	N	Y
21 ***Smith***	Y	Y	Y	Y	N	Y	Y	N
22 ***DeLay***	Y	Y	Y	Y	N	Y	Y	N
23 ***Bonilla***	Y	Y	Y	Y	N	Y	Y	N
24 Frost	Y	Y	Y	Y	N	N	N	Y
25 Bentsen	Y	Y	Y	Y	N	N	N	Y
26 ***Armey***	Y	Y	Y	Y	N	Y	Y	N
27 Ortiz	Y	Y	Y	Y	N	N	N	Y
28 Vacant								
29 Green	Y	Y	Y	N	N	N	N	Y
30 Johnson, E.B.	Y	Y	Y	Y	N	N	N	Y
UTAH								
1 ***Hansen***	Y	Y	Y	Y	N	Y	Y	N
2 ***Cook***	Y	Y	Y	Y	N	Y	Y	N
3 ***Cannon***	Y	Y	Y	Y	N	Y	Y	N
VERMONT								
AL *Sanders*	Y	Y	Y	?	N	N	N	Y
VIRGINIA								
1 ***Bateman***	Y	Y	Y	Y	N	Y	Y	N
2 Pickett	Y	Y	Y	N	N	N	N	Y
3 Scott	Y	Y	Y	Y	N	N	N	Y
4 Sisisky	Y	Y	Y	Y	N	N	N	Y
5 Goode	Y	Y	Y	Y	N	N	N	N
6 ***Goodlatte***	Y	Y	Y	Y	N	Y	Y	N
7 ***Bliley***	Y	Y	Y	Y	N	Y	Y	N
8 Moran	Y	Y	Y	Y	N	N	N	Y
9 Boucher	Y	Y	Y	Y	N	N	N	Y
10 ***Wolf***	Y	Y	Y	N	N	Y	Y	N
11 ***Davis***	Y	Y	Y	Y	N	Y	Y	N
WASHINGTON								
1 ***White***	Y	Y	Y	Y	N	Y	Y	N
2 ***Metcalf***	Y	Y	Y	Y	N	Y	Y	N
3 ***Smith, Linda***	Y	Y	Y	Y	N	Y	Y	N
4 ***Hastings***	Y	Y	Y	Y	N	Y	Y	N
5 ***Nethercutt***	Y	Y	Y	Y	N	Y	Y	N
6 Dicks	Y	Y	Y	Y	N	N	N	Y
7 McDermott	Y	Y	Y	N	Y	N	N	Y
8 ***Dunn***	Y	Y	Y	Y	N	Y	Y	N
9 Smith, Adam	Y	Y	Y	Y	N	N	N	Y
WEST VIRGINIA								
1 Mollohan	Y	Y	Y	Y	?	N	N	Y
2 Wise	Y	Y	Y	Y	N	N	N	Y
3 Rahall	Y	Y	Y	Y	N	N	N	Y
WISCONSIN								
1 ***Neumann***	Y	Y	Y	Y	N	Y	Y	N
2 ***Klug***	Y	Y	Y	Y	N	Y	Y	N
3 Kind	Y	Y	Y	Y	N	N	N	Y
4 Kleczka	Y	Y	Y	Y	N	N	N	Y
5 Barrett	Y	Y	Y	Y	N	N	N	Y
6 ***Petri***	Y	Y	Y	Y	N	Y	Y	N
7 Obey	Y	Y	Y	Y	N	N	N	Y
8 Johnson	Y	Y	Y	Y	N	N	N	Y
9 ***Sensenbrenner***	Y	Y	Y	Y	?	Y	Y	N
WYOMING								
AL ***Cubin***	Y	Y	Y	Y	N	Y	Y	N

Southern states - Ala., Ark., Fla., Ga., Ky., La., Miss., N.C., Okla., S.C., Tenn., Texas, Va.

HOUSE VOTES 44, 45, 46, 47, 48, 49, 50

44. H Res 89. Request New Balanced Budget from President/Adoption. Adoption of the resolution to request the president to submit to the House by April 7 a new budget plan for fiscal 1998 that will balance the federal budget by fiscal 2002 using Congressional Budget Office economic assumptions. Adopted 231-197: R 223-2; D 8-194 (ND 3-145, SD 5-49); I 0-1, March 12, 1997. A "nay" was a vote in support of the president's position.

45. H J Res 58. Reverse Mexico Anti-Drug Certification/Rule. Adoption of the rule (H Res 95) to provide for House floor consideration of the joint resolution to reverse the president's certification of Mexico as fully cooperating in the fight against drug smuggling. Adopted 213-209: R 209-13; D 4-195 (ND 1-148, SD 3-47); I 0-1, March 13, 1997.

46. H J Res 58. Reverse Mexico Anti-Drug Certification/Conditional Delay. Hastert, R-Ill., amendment to the Gilman, R-N.Y., substitute amendment to delay decertification of Mexico for 90 days unless the president certifies to Congress that he has obtained reliable assurances that Mexico will meet certain criteria. Adopted 212-205: R 205-19; D 7-185 (ND 3-140, SD 4-45); I 0-1, March 13, 1997. A "nay" was a vote in support of the president's position.

47. H J Res 58. Reverse Mexico Anti-Drug Certification/National Security Waiver. Gilman, R-N.Y., substitute amendment to reverse the president's certification of Mexico but allow a one-year waiver on national security grounds. Adopted 229-195: R 204-21; D 24-174 (ND 13-135, SD 11-39); I 1-0, March 13, 1997. A "nay" was a vote in support of the president's position.

48. H J Res 58. Reverse Mexico Anti-Drug Certification/Passage. Passage of the joint resolution to reverse the president's certification of Mexico but allow a one-year waiver on national security grounds. The joint resolution delays decertification for 90 days unless the president certifies to Congress that he has obtained reliable assurances that Mexico will meet certain criteria related to fighting drug smuggling. Passed 251-175: R 204-21; D 46-154 (ND 27-123, SD 19-31); I 1-0, March 13, 1997. A "nay" was a vote in support of the president's position.

49. HR 852. Electronic Filing of Federal Forms/Previous Question. Myrick, R-N.C., motion to order the previous question (thus ending debate and the possibility of amendment) on adoption of the rule (H Res 88) to provide for floor consideration of the bill to require federal agencies to provide businesses and the public with the option of filing information with the government by electronic means. Motion agreed to 219-187: R 216-0; D 3-186 (ND 1-140, SD 2-46); I 0-1, March 13, 1997.

50. HR 852. Electronic Filing of Federal Forms/Passage. Passage of the bill to require federal agencies to provide businesses and the public with the option of filing information with the government by electronic means. Passed 395-0: R 207-0; D 187-0 (ND 140-0, SD 47-0); I 1-0, March 13, 1997.

KEY

- Y Voted for (yea).
- # Paired for.
- + Announced for.
- N Voted against (nay).
- X Paired against.
- – Announced against.
- P Voted "present."
- C Voted "present" to avoid possible conflict of interest.
- ? Did not vote or otherwise make a position known.

Democrats ***Republicans*** *Independent*

	44	45	46	47	48	49	50
ALABAMA							
1 ***Callahan***	Y	Y	Y	Y	Y	Y	?
2 ***Everett***	Y	Y	Y	Y	Y	Y	?
3 ***Riley***	Y	Y	Y	Y	Y	Y	Y
4 ***Aderholt***	Y	Y	Y	Y	Y	Y	Y
5 Cramer	Y	N	N	Y	Y	N	Y
6 ***Bachus***	Y	Y	Y	Y	Y	Y	Y
7 Hilliard	N	N	N	N	N	N	Y
ALASKA							
AL ***Young***	Y	Y	Y	Y	Y	Y	Y
ARIZONA							
1 ***Salmon***	Y	Y	Y	Y	Y	Y	Y
2 Pastor	N	N	Y	Y	N	N	Y
3 ***Stump***	Y	Y	Y	Y	Y	Y	Y
4 ***Shadegg***	Y	N	Y	Y	N	Y	Y
5 ***Kolbe***	Y	N	Y	Y	N	Y	Y
6 ***Hayworth***	Y	Y	Y	Y	Y	Y	Y
ARKANSAS							
1 Berry	N	N	N	N	N	N	Y
2 Snyder	N	N	N	N	N	N	Y
3 ***Hutchinson***	Y	+	Y	Y	Y	Y	Y
4 ***Dickey***	Y	Y	Y	Y	Y	Y	Y
CALIFORNIA							
1 ***Riggs***	Y	Y	Y	Y	Y	Y	Y
2 ***Herger***	Y	Y	Y	Y	Y	Y	Y
3 Fazio	N	N	N	N	N	N	Y
4 ***Doolittle***	Y	Y	Y	Y	Y	Y	Y
5 Matsui	N	N	N	N	N	N	Y
6 Woolsey	N	N	N	N	N	N	Y
7 Miller	N	N	N	N	N	N	Y
8 Pelosi	N	N	N	N	N	N	Y
9 Dellums	N	N	N	?	N	N	Y
10 Tauscher	N	N	N	N	N	N	Y
11 ***Pombo***	Y	Y	Y	Y	Y	Y	Y
12 Lantos	N	N	N	N	N	N	Y
13 Stark	N	N	N	N	Y	N	Y
14 Eshoo	N	N	N	N	N	N	Y
15 ***Campbell***	Y	Y	N	Y	Y	Y	Y
16 Lofgren	N	N	P	N	N	N	Y
17 Farr	N	N	N	N	N	N	Y
18 Condit	Y	N	N	N	Y	N	Y
19 ***Radanovich***	Y	Y	Y	Y	Y	Y	Y
20 Dooley	N	N	N	N	N	N	Y
21 ***Thomas***	Y	Y	Y	Y	Y	Y	Y
22 Capps	N	N	N	N	N	N	Y
23 ***Gallegly***	Y	Y	Y	Y	Y	?	?
24 Sherman	N	N	N	N	N	N	Y
25 ***McKeon***	Y	Y	Y	Y	Y	Y	Y
26 Berman	N	N	N	N	N	?	?
27 ***Rogan***	Y	Y	Y	Y	Y	Y	Y
28 ***Dreier***	Y	Y	Y	Y	N	Y	Y
29 Waxman	N	N	N	N	N	N	Y
30 Becerra	N	N	P	N	N	N	?
31 Martinez	N	N	N	N	N	N	Y
32 Dixon	?	N	N	N	N	N	Y
33 Roybal-Allard	N	N	P	N	N	N	Y
34 Torres	N	N	P	N	N	N	Y
35 Waters	N	N	N	N	N	N	Y
36 Harman	N	N	N	?	Y	N	Y
37 Millender-McD.	N	N	N	N	N	N	Y
38 ***Horn***	Y	Y	Y	Y	Y	Y	Y
39 ***Royce***	Y	Y	Y	Y	Y	Y	Y
40 ***Lewis***	Y	Y	Y	Y	Y	Y	Y
41 ***Kim***	Y	Y	Y	Y	Y	Y	Y
42 Brown	N	N	N	N	N	N	?
43 ***Calvert***	Y	Y	Y	Y	Y	Y	Y
44 ***Bono***	Y	N	Y	Y	Y	Y	Y
45 ***Rohrabacher***	Y	Y	Y	Y	Y	Y	Y
46 Sanchez	N	N	P	N	N	N	+
47 ***Cox***	Y	?	Y	Y	Y	Y	Y
48 ***Packard***	Y	Y	Y	Y	Y	Y	Y
49 ***Bilbray***	Y	N	Y	N	N	Y	Y
50 Filner	N	N	P	N	N	N	Y
51 ***Cunningham***	Y	Y	Y	Y	Y	Y	Y
52 ***Hunter***	Y	Y	N	N	Y	Y	Y
COLORADO							
1 DeGette	N	N	N	N	N	N	Y
2 Skaggs	N	N	N	N	N	N	Y
3 ***McInnis***	Y	Y	Y	Y	Y	Y	Y
4 ***Schaffer***	Y	Y	Y	N	Y	Y	Y
5 ***Hefley***	Y	Y	N	N	Y	Y	Y
6 ***Schaefer***	Y	Y	Y	N	Y	?	?
CONNECTICUT							
1 Kennelly	N	N	N	N	N	N	Y
2 Gejdenson	N	N	N	N	N	N	Y
3 DeLauro	N	N	N	N	N	N	Y
4 ***Shays***	Y	Y	Y	N	N	Y	Y
5 Maloney	N	N	N	N	N	N	Y
6 ***Johnson***	Y	N	N	N	N	Y	?
DELAWARE							
AL ***Castle***	Y	Y	Y	Y	Y	Y	Y
FLORIDA							
1 ***Scarborough***	Y	Y	N	N	Y	Y	Y
2 Boyd	N	N	N	N	Y	N	Y
3 Brown	N	N	N	N	Y	N	Y
4 ***Fowler***	Y	Y	Y	Y	Y	Y	Y
5 Thurman	N	N	N	N	Y	N	Y
6 ***Stearns***	Y	N	Y	Y	Y	Y	Y
7 ***Mica***	Y	N	N	Y	Y	Y	Y
8 ***McCollum***	Y	Y	Y	Y	Y	Y	Y
9 ***Bilirakis***	Y	Y	Y	Y	Y	Y	Y
10 ***Young***	Y	Y	Y	Y	Y	?	?
11 Davis	N	N	N	Y	Y	N	Y
12 ***Canady***	Y	Y	Y	Y	Y	Y	Y
13 ***Miller***	Y	Y	Y	Y	Y	Y	Y
14 ***Goss***	Y	Y	Y	Y	Y	Y	Y
15 ***Weldon***	Y	Y	Y	Y	Y	Y	Y
16 ***Foley***	Y	Y	Y	Y	Y	Y	Y
17 Meek	N	Y	N	N	Y	N	Y
18 ***Ros-Lehtinen***	Y	Y	Y	Y	Y	Y	+
19 Wexler	N	N	N	N	N	N	Y
20 Deutsch	N	N	N	N	N	N	Y
21 ***Diaz-Balart***	Y	Y	Y	Y	Y	Y	Y
22 ***Shaw***	Y	Y	N	Y	Y	Y	Y
23 Hastings	N	N	N	N	Y	N	Y
GEORGIA							
1 ***Kingston***	Y	?	?	?	?	?	?
2 Bishop	Y	N	N	N	N	N	Y
3 ***Collins***	Y	Y	Y	Y	Y	Y	Y
4 McKinney	N	Y	Y	Y	Y	N	Y
5 Lewis	N	N	N	N	N	N	Y
6 ***Gingrich***			Y	Y	Y		
7 ***Barr***	Y	Y	Y	Y	Y	Y	Y
8 ***Chambliss***	Y	Y	Y	Y	Y	Y	Y
9 ***Deal***	Y	Y	Y	Y	Y	Y	Y
10 ***Norwood***	Y	Y	Y	Y	Y	Y	Y
11 ***Linder***	Y	Y	Y	Y	Y	Y	Y
HAWAII							
1 Abercrombie	N	N	N	N	N	N	Y
2 Mink	N	N	N	N	N	N	Y
IDAHO							
1 ***Chenoweth***	Y	Y	N	Y	Y	Y	Y
2 ***Crapo***	Y	Y	Y	Y	Y	Y	Y
ILLINOIS							
1 Rush	N	N	N	N	N	N	Y
2 Jackson	N	N	N	N	N	N	Y
3 Lipinski	N	N	N	Y	Y	N	Y
4 Gutierrez	N	N	P	N	N	?	Y
5 Blagojevich	N	N	N	N	N	N	Y
6 ***Hyde***	Y	Y	Y	Y	Y	Y	?
7 Davis	N	N	N	N	N	N	Y
8 ***Crane***	Y	Y	Y	Y	Y	Y	Y
9 Yates	N	N	N	N	N	N	Y
10 ***Porter***	Y	Y	Y	Y	Y	Y	Y
11 ***Weller***	Y	Y	Y	Y	Y	Y	Y
12 Costello	N	N	N	N	Y	?	Y
13 ***Fawell***	Y	Y	Y	Y	Y	Y	Y
14 ***Hastert***	Y	Y	Y	Y	Y	Y	Y

ND Northern Democrats SD Southern Democrats

	44	45	46	47	48	49	50
15 ***Ewing***	Y	Y	Y	Y	Y	Y	Y
16 ***Manzullo***	Y	Y	Y	Y	Y	Y	Y
17 Evans	N	N	N	N	Y	N	Y
18 ***LaHood***	Y	Y	Y	Y	Y	Y	Y
19 Poshard	N	N	N	Y	Y	N	Y
20 ***Shimkus***	Y	Y	Y	Y	Y	Y	Y
INDIANA							
1 Visclosky	Y	N	N	N	Y	N	Y
2 ***McIntosh***	Y	Y	Y	N	Y	Y	Y
3 Roemer	N	N	N	Y	Y	N	Y
4 ***Souder***	?	Y	Y	Y	Y	Y	Y
5 ***Buyer***	Y	Y	Y	Y	Y	Y	Y
6 ***Burton***	Y	Y	Y	Y	Y	Y	Y
7 ***Pease***	Y	Y	Y	Y	Y	Y	Y
8 ***Hostettler***	Y	Y	Y	Y	Y	Y	Y
9 Hamilton	N	N	N	N	N	N	Y
10 Carson	N	N	N	N	N	?	Y
IOWA							
1 ***Leach***	Y	Y	Y	Y	Y	?	Y
2 ***Nussle***	N	Y	Y	Y	Y	Y	Y
3 Boswell	N	N	N	N	N	N	Y
4 ***Ganske***	Y	Y	Y	Y	Y	Y	Y
5 ***Latham***	Y	Y	Y	Y	Y	Y	Y
KANSAS							
1 ***Moran***	Y	Y	Y	Y	Y	Y	Y
2 ***Ryun***	Y	Y	Y	Y	Y	Y	?
3 ***Snowbarger***	Y	Y	Y	Y	Y	Y	Y
4 ***Tiahrt***	Y	Y	Y	Y	Y	Y	Y
KENTUCKY							
1 ***Whitfield***	Y	Y	Y	Y	Y	Y	Y
2 ***Lewis***	Y	Y	Y	Y	Y	Y	Y
3 ***Northup***	Y	Y	Y	Y	Y	Y	Y
4 ***Bunning***	Y	Y	Y	Y	Y	Y	Y
5 ***Rogers***	Y	Y	Y	Y	Y	Y	Y
6 Baesler	N	N	N	Y	Y	N	Y
LOUISIANA							
1 ***Livingston***	Y	Y	Y	Y	Y	Y	Y
2 Jefferson	N	N	N	N	N	N	Y
3 ***Tauzin***	Y	Y	Y	Y	Y	Y	Y
4 ***McCrery***	Y	Y	Y	Y	Y	Y	?
5 ***Cooksey***	Y	?	Y	Y	Y	Y	Y
6 ***Baker***	Y	Y	Y	Y	Y	?	?
7 John	N	N	N	N	N	?	?
MAINE							
1 Allen	N	N	N	N	N	N	Y
2 Baldacci	N	N	N	N	N	N	Y
MARYLAND							
1 ***Gilchrest***	Y	Y	Y	Y	N	Y	Y
2 ***Ehrlich***	Y	Y	Y	Y	Y	Y	Y
3 Cardin	N	N	N	N	N	N	Y
4 Wynn	N	N	N	N	N	N	Y
5 Hoyer	N	N	N	N	N	N	Y
6 ***Bartlett***	Y	Y	Y	Y	Y	Y	Y
7 Cummings	N	N	N	N	N	N	Y
8 ***Morella***	Y	Y	N	N	N	Y	Y
MASSACHUSETTS							
1 Olver	N	N	N	N	N	N	Y
2 Neal	N	N	N	N	Y	N	Y
3 McGovern	N	N	N	N	N	N	Y
4 Frank	N	N	N	N	N	N	Y
5 Meehan	N	N	N	N	N	?	?
6 Tierney	N	N	N	N	N	N	Y
7 Markey	N	N	N	N	Y	N	Y
8 Kennedy	N	N	N	N	N	N	Y
9 Moakley	N	N	N	N	N	N	Y
10 Delahunt	N	?	N	Y	Y	N	Y
MICHIGAN							
1 Stupak	N	N	N	N	N	N	Y
2 ***Hoekstra***	Y	Y	Y	Y	Y	Y	Y
3 ***Ehlers***	Y	Y	Y	Y	N	Y	Y
4 ***Camp***	Y	Y	Y	Y	Y	Y	Y
5 Barcia	N	N	N	N	Y	N	Y
6 ***Upton***	Y	N	Y	Y	Y	Y	Y
7 ***Smith***	Y	Y	Y	Y	Y	Y	Y
8 Stabenow	N	N	N	N	N	N	Y
9 Kildee	N	N	N	N	Y	N	Y
10 Bonior	N	N	N	N	N	N	Y
11 ***Knollenberg***	Y	Y	Y	Y	Y	Y	Y
12 Levin	N	N	N	N	N	N	Y
13 Rivers	N	N	N	N	N	N	Y
14 Conyers	N	N	N	N	?	N	Y
15 Kilpatrick	N	N	N	N	N	N	Y
16 Dingell	N	N	N	N	N	N	Y

	44	45	46	47	48	49	50
MINNESOTA							
1 ***Gutknecht***	Y	Y	Y	Y	Y	Y	Y
2 Minge	N	N	N	N	N	N	Y
3 ***Ramstad***	Y	Y	Y	Y	Y	Y	Y
4 Vento	N	N	N	N	N	N	Y
5 Sabo	N	N	N	N	N	N	Y
6 Luther	N	N	N	N	N	N	Y
7 Peterson	Y	N	N	N	Y	N	Y
8 Oberstar	N	N	N	N	N	N	Y
MISSISSIPPI							
1 ***Wicker***	Y	Y	Y	Y	Y	Y	Y
2 Thompson	N	N	N	N	N	N	Y
3 ***Pickering***	Y	Y	Y	Y	Y	Y	Y
4 ***Parker***	Y	Y	Y	N	N	Y	Y
5 Taylor	Y	N	Y	Y	Y	N	Y
MISSOURI							
1 Clay	N	N	N	N	N	?	?
2 ***Talent***	Y	Y	Y	Y	Y	Y	Y
3 Gephardt	N	N	N	N	N	N	Y
4 Skelton	N	N	N	N	Y	N	Y
5 McCarthy	N	N	N	N	N	–	+
6 Danner	N	N	Y	Y	Y	N	Y
7 ***Blunt***	Y	Y	Y	Y	Y	Y	Y
8 ***Emerson***	Y	Y	Y	Y	Y	Y	Y
9 ***Hulshof***	Y	Y	Y	Y	Y	Y	Y
MONTANA							
AL ***Hill***	Y	Y	Y	Y	Y	Y	Y
NEBRASKA							
1 ***Bereuter***	Y	Y	Y	Y	Y	Y	Y
2 ***Christensen***	Y	Y	Y	Y	Y	Y	Y
3 ***Barrett***	Y	Y	Y	Y	Y	Y	Y
NEVADA							
1 ***Ensign***	Y	Y	N	N	Y	Y	Y
2 ***Gibbons***	Y	Y	Y	Y	Y	Y	Y
NEW HAMPSHIRE							
1 ***Sununu***	Y	Y	Y	Y	Y	Y	Y
2 ***Bass***	Y	Y	Y	Y	Y	Y	Y
NEW JERSEY							
1 Andrews	?	N	N	N	N	N	Y
2 ***LoBiondo***	Y	Y	Y	Y	Y	Y	Y
3 ***Saxton***	Y	Y	Y	Y	Y	Y	Y
4 ***Smith***	Y	Y	Y	Y	Y	Y	Y
5 ***Roukema***	Y	Y	N	Y	Y	?	?
6 Pallone	N	N	N	N	N	N	Y
7 ***Franks***	Y	Y	Y	Y	Y	Y	Y
8 Pascrell	N	N	N	N	Y	N	Y
9 Rothman	N	N	N	N	N	N	Y
10 Payne	N	N	N	?	N	N	Y
11 ***Frelinghuysen***	Y	Y	Y	Y	Y	Y	Y
12 ***Pappas***	Y	Y	Y	Y	Y	Y	Y
13 Menendez	N	N	N	N	N	N	Y
NEW MEXICO							
1 ***Schiff***	Y	N	N	Y	N	Y	Y
2 ***Skeen***	Y	Y	Y	Y	Y	Y	Y
3 Vacant							
NEW YORK							
1 ***Forbes***	Y	Y	Y	Y	Y	Y	Y
2 ***Lazio***	Y	Y	Y	Y	Y	Y	Y
3 ***King***	Y	Y	N	N	Y	Y	Y
4 McCarthy	N	N	N	N	N	N	Y
5 Ackerman	N	N	N	N	N	N	Y
6 Flake	N	N	N	N	N	N	Y
7 Manton	N	N	N	N	N	?	?
8 Nadler	N	N	N	N	N	N	Y
9 Schumer	N	N	N	N	N	N	Y
10 Towns	N	N	N	N	N	N	Y
11 Owens	N	N	N	N	N	N	Y
12 Velázquez	N	N	P	N	N	N	Y
13 ***Molinari***	Y	Y	Y	Y	Y	Y	Y
14 Maloney	N	N	N	N	N	N	Y
15 Rangel	N	N	N	N	N	N	Y
16 Serrano	N	N	N	N	N	N	Y
17 Engel	N	N	N	N	N	N	Y
18 Lowey	N	N	N	N	N	N	Y
19 ***Kelly***	Y	Y	Y	Y	Y	Y	Y
20 ***Gilman***	Y	Y	Y	Y	Y	Y	Y
21 McNulty	N	N	N	N	Y	N	Y
22 ***Solomon***	Y	Y	Y	Y	Y	Y	Y
23 ***Boehlert***	Y	Y	Y	Y	Y	Y	Y
24 ***McHugh***	Y	Y	?	?	?	?	?
25 ***Walsh***	Y	Y	Y	Y	Y	Y	Y
26 Hinchey	N	N	N	N	N	N	Y
27 ***Paxon***	Y	Y	Y	Y	Y	Y	Y
28 Slaughter	N	N	N	N	Y	N	Y

	44	45	46	47	48	49	50
29 LaFalce	N	N	N	N	N	N	Y
30 ***Quinn***	Y	Y	Y	Y	Y	Y	Y
31 ***Houghton***	Y	Y	Y	Y	N	Y	Y
NORTH CAROLINA							
1 Clayton	N	?	?	?	?	?	?
2 Etheridge	N	?	?	?	?	?	?
3 ***Jones***	Y	Y	Y	Y	Y	Y	Y
4 Price	N	?	?	?	?	?	?
5 ***Burr***	Y	Y	Y	Y	Y	Y	Y
6 ***Coble***	Y	Y	Y	Y	Y	Y	Y
7 McIntyre	N	?	?	?	?	?	?
8 Hefner	N	N	N	N	Y	N	Y
9 ***Myrick***	Y	Y	Y	Y	Y	Y	Y
10 ***Ballenger***	Y	Y	Y	Y	Y	Y	Y
11 ***Taylor***	Y	Y	Y	Y	Y	Y	Y
12 Watt	N	N	N	N	N	N	Y
NORTH DAKOTA							
AL Pomeroy	N	N	N	N	N	N	Y
OHIO							
1 ***Chabot***	Y	Y	Y	Y	Y	Y	Y
2 ***Portman***	Y	Y	Y	Y	Y	Y	Y
3 Hall	N	N	N	N	N	N	Y
4 ***Oxley***	Y	Y	Y	N	N	Y	Y
5 ***Gillmor***	Y	Y	Y	N	N	Y	Y
6 Strickland	N	N	N	N	N	N	Y
7 ***Hobson***	Y	Y	Y	Y	Y	Y	Y
8 ***Boehner***	Y	Y	Y	Y	Y	Y	Y
9 Kaptur	?	?	N	Y	Y	N	Y
10 Kucinich	N	N	N	Y	Y	N	Y
11 Stokes	N	N	N	N	N	N	Y
12 ***Kasich***	Y	Y	Y	Y	Y	Y	Y
13 Brown	N	N	N	N	N	N	Y
14 Sawyer	N	N	N	N	N	N	Y
15 ***Pryce***	Y	Y	Y	Y	Y	Y	Y
16 ***Regula***	Y	Y	Y	Y	Y	Y	Y
17 Traficant	N	Y	Y	Y	Y	N	Y
18 ***Ney***	Y	Y	Y	Y	Y	Y	Y
19 ***LaTourette***	Y	Y	Y	Y	Y	Y	Y
OKLAHOMA							
1 ***Largent***	Y	Y	Y	Y	Y	Y	?
2 ***Coburn***	N	Y	Y	Y	N	Y	Y
3 ***Watkins***	Y	Y	Y	Y	Y	Y	Y
4 ***Watts***	Y	Y	–	N	Y	Y	Y
5 ***Istook***	Y	Y	Y	Y	Y	Y	Y
6 ***Lucas***	Y	Y	Y	Y	Y	Y	Y
OREGON							
1 Furse	N	N	N	N	N	N	Y
2 ***Smith***	Y	Y	Y	Y	Y	Y	Y
3 Blumenauer	N	N	N	N	N	Y	?
4 DeFazio	N	N	N	Y	Y	N	Y
5 Hooley	N	N	N	N	N	N	Y
PENNSYLVANIA							
1 Foglietta	N	N	N	N	N	?	Y
2 Fattah	N	N	N	N	N	N	Y
3 Borski	N	N	N	N	N	N	Y
4 Klink	N	N	N	N	N	N	Y
5 ***Peterson***	Y	Y	Y	Y	Y	Y	Y
6 Holden	N	N	N	Y	Y	N	Y
7 ***Weldon***	Y	Y	N	Y	Y	Y	Y
8 ***Greenwood***	Y	Y	Y	Y	Y	Y	Y
9 ***Shuster***	Y	Y	Y	Y	Y	Y	Y
10 ***McDade***	Y	Y	Y	Y	Y	Y	Y
11 Kanjorski	N	N	N	N	N	N	Y
12 Murtha	N	N	N	N	N	N	Y
13 ***Fox***	Y	Y	Y	Y	Y	Y	Y
14 Coyne	N	N	N	N	N	N	Y
15 McHale	N	N	N	Y	Y	N	Y
16 ***Pitts***	Y	Y	Y	Y	Y	Y	Y
17 ***Gekas***	Y	Y	Y	Y	Y	Y	Y
18 Doyle	N	N	N	N	N	N	Y
19 ***Goodling***	Y	Y	Y	Y	Y	Y	Y
20 Mascara	N	N	N	N	N	N	Y
21 ***English***	Y	Y	N	Y	Y	Y	Y
RHODE ISLAND							
1 Kennedy	N	N	N	N	N	N	Y
2 Weygand	N	N	N	N	N	N	Y
SOUTH CAROLINA							
1 ***Sanford***	Y	Y	Y	Y	Y	Y	Y
2 ***Spence***	Y	Y	Y	Y	Y	Y	Y
3 ***Graham***	Y	Y	Y	Y	Y	Y	Y
4 ***Inglis***	Y	Y	Y	Y	Y	Y	Y
5 Spratt	N	N	N	N	Y	N	Y
6 Clyburn	N	N	N	N	N	N	Y

	44	45	46	47	48	49	50
SOUTH DAKOTA							
AL ***Thune***	Y	Y	Y	Y	Y	Y	Y
TENNESSEE							
1 ***Jenkins***	Y	Y	Y	Y	Y	Y	Y
2 ***Duncan***	Y	Y	Y	Y	Y	Y	Y
3 ***Wamp***	Y	Y	Y	Y	Y	Y	Y
4 ***Hilleary***	Y	Y	Y	Y	Y	Y	Y
5 Clement	N	N	N	Y	Y	N	Y
6 Gordon	N	N	N	Y	Y	N	Y
7 ***Bryant***	Y	Y	Y	Y	Y	Y	Y
8 Tanner	N	N	N	Y	Y	N	Y
9 Ford	N	N	N	N	N	N	Y
TEXAS							
1 Sandlin	N	N	N	N	N	N	Y
2 Turner	N	N	N	N	N	N	Y
3 ***Johnson, Sam***	Y	N	Y	Y	Y	Y	Y
4 Hall	Y	Y	Y	N	Y	Y	Y
5 ***Sessions***	Y	Y	Y	Y	Y	Y	Y
6 ***Barton***	Y	N	N	N	N	?	?
7 ***Archer***	Y	Y	Y	Y	Y	Y	Y
8 ***Brady***	Y	Y	Y	Y	N	Y	Y
9 Lampson	N	N	N	N	N	N	Y
10 Doggett	N	N	N	N	N	N	Y
11 Edwards	N	N	N	N	N	N	Y
12 ***Granger***	Y	Y	Y	Y	Y	Y	Y
13 ***Thornberry***	Y	Y	Y	N	N	Y	Y
14 ***Paul***	Y	N	N	N	N	Y	Y
15 Hinojosa	N	N	N	N	N	N	Y
16 Reyes	N	N	N	N	N	N	Y
17 Stenholm	N	N	N	N	N	N	Y
18 Jackson-Lee	N	N	N	N	N	N	Y
19 ***Combest***	Y	Y	N	Y	Y	Y	Y
20 Gonzalez	N	N	N	N	N	N	Y
21 ***Smith***	Y	Y	Y	Y	Y	?	?
22 ***DeLay***	Y	Y	Y	Y	Y	Y	Y
23 ***Bonilla***	Y	N	N	N	N	Y	Y
24 Frost	N	N	N	N	N	N	Y
25 Bentsen	N	N	N	N	N	N	Y
26 ***Armey***	Y	Y	Y	Y	Y	Y	Y
27 Ortiz	N	N	P	N	N	?	?
28 Vacant							
29 Green	N	N	N	N	N	N	Y
30 Johnson, E.B.	N	N	N	N	N	N	Y
UTAH							
1 ***Hansen***	Y	Y	Y	Y	Y	Y	Y
2 ***Cook***	Y	Y	Y	Y	Y	Y	Y
3 ***Cannon***	Y	Y	Y	N	N	Y	Y
VERMONT							
AL *Sanders*	N	N	N	Y	Y	N	Y
VIRGINIA							
1 ***Bateman***	Y	Y	Y	Y	Y	Y	Y
2 Pickett	N	N	N	N	N	N	Y
3 Scott	N	N	N	N	N	N	Y
4 Sisisky	N	N	N	Y	Y	N	Y
5 Goode	Y	N	N	Y	Y	N	Y
6 ***Goodlatte***	Y	Y	Y	Y	Y	Y	Y
7 ***Bliley***	Y	Y	Y	Y	Y	Y	Y
8 Moran	N	N	N	Y	Y	N	Y
9 Boucher	N	N	Y	N	N	Y	?
10 ***Wolf***	Y	Y	Y	Y	Y	Y	Y
11 ***Davis***	Y	Y	Y	Y	Y	Y	Y
WASHINGTON							
1 ***White***	Y	Y	Y	Y	Y	Y	Y
2 ***Metcalf***	Y	Y	Y	Y	Y	Y	Y
3 ***Smith, Linda***	Y	Y	Y	Y	Y	Y	Y
4 ***Hastings***	Y	Y	Y	Y	Y	Y	Y
5 ***Nethercutt***	Y	Y	Y	Y	Y	Y	+
6 Dicks	N	N	N	N	N	?	?
7 McDermott	N	N	N	N	N	N	Y
8 ***Dunn***	Y	Y	Y	Y	Y	Y	Y
9 Smith, Adam	N	N	N	Y	Y	N	?
WEST VIRGINIA							
1 Mollohan	N	N	N	N	N	N	Y
2 Wise	N	N	N	N	N	N	Y
3 Rahall	N	N	N	N	N	N	Y
WISCONSIN							
1 ***Neumann***	Y	Y	Y	Y	Y	Y	Y
2 ***Klug***	Y	Y	Y	Y	Y	Y	?
3 Kind	N	N	N	N	N	N	Y
4 Kleczka	N	N	N	N	N	N	Y
5 Barrett	N	N	N	N	N	N	Y
6 ***Petri***	Y	Y	Y	Y	Y	Y	Y
7 Obey	N	N	N	N	N	N	Y
8 Johnson	N	N	N	N	N	N	Y
9 ***Sensenbrenner***	Y	Y	Y	Y	Y	Y	Y
WYOMING							
AL ***Cubin***	Y	Y	Y	Y	Y	Y	Y

Southern states - Ala., Ark., Fla., Ga., Ky., La., Miss., N.C., Okla., S.C., Tenn., Texas, Va.

HOUSE VOTES 51, 52, 53, 54, 55, 56, 57, 58

51. HR 412. Oroville-Tonasket Claim Settlement/Independent Appraisal. Miller, D-Calif., amendment to require the Oroville-Tonasket Irrigation district in the state of Washington to pay the federal government fair market value, determined by an independent appraisal panel, to obtain title to the irrigation system. Rejected 195-232: R 22-202; D 172-30 (ND 133-16, SD 39-14); I 1-0, March 18, 1997. (HR 412 subsequently was passed by voice vote.)

52. HR 924. Crime Victim Rights/Passage. McCollum, R-Fla., motion to suspend the rules and pass the bill to prevent federal judges from barring crime victims and their families from attending the trials of those accused of the crime and testifying in the sentencing phase. Motion agreed to 418-9: R 224-0; D 193-9 (ND 145-4, SD 48-5); I 1-0, March 18, 1997. A two-thirds majority of those present and voting (285 in this case) is required for passage under suspension of the rules.

53. HR 672. Copyright Technical Amendments/Passage. Coble, R-N.C., motion to suspend the rules and pass the bill to make technical amendments to certain provisions of the U.S. Copyright Act (Title 17, U.S. Code). Motion agreed to 424-2: R 222-1; D 201-1 (ND 148-1, SD 53-0); I 1-0, March 18, 1997. A two-thirds majority of those present and voting (284 in this case) is required for passage under suspension of the rules.

54. HR 1. Overtime Pay/Rule. Adoption of the rule (H Res 99) to provide for House floor consideration of the bill to allow private-sector employers to offer workers the choice of taking one and one-half hours of compensatory time instead of cash wages for overtime pay. Adopted 229-195: R 222-2; D 7-192 (ND 2-143, SD 5-49); I 0-1, March 19, 1997.

55. HR 1. Overtime Pay/Eligibility Requirements, Limits. Goodling, R-Pa., amendment to require that an employee work at least 1,000 hours during a period of continuous employment within the last year before the employee would be eligible for compensatory time, and reduce the maximum number of hours of compensatory time that an employee may accrue from 240 to 160 hours. Adopted 408-19: R 217-7; D 190-12 (ND 139-10, SD 51-2); I 1-0, March 19, 1997.

56. HR 1. Overtime Pay/Five-Year Sunset. Boyd, D-Fla., amendment to sunset the bill's compensatory time provisions in five years. Adopted 390-36: R 192-33; D 197-3 (ND 144-3, SD 53-0); I 1-0, March 19, 1997.

57. HR 1. Overtime Pay/Low-Wage Employee Exemption. Owens, D-N.Y., amendment to exempt from the bill's compensatory time provisions employees who earn less than two-and-a-half times the minimum wage. Rejected 182-237: R 6-216: D 175-21 (ND 135-10, SD 40-11); I 1-0, March 19, 1997.

58. HR 1. Overtime Pay/Democratic Substitute. Miller, D-Calif., substitute amendment to allow private-sector employees the choice of taking one and one-half hours of compensatory time instead of cash wages for overtime pay, but apply eligibility restrictions for certain employees, disallow employers from conditioning benefits or overtime pay on an employee's decision to reject compensatory time and require employers who offer compensatory time to provide employees 24 hours of unpaid leave yearly to participate in a child's education activities or medical appointments. Rejected 193-237: R 3-223; D 189-14 (ND 143-6, SD 46-8); I 1-0, March 19, 1997. A "yea" was a vote in support of the president's position.

KEY

- Y Voted for (yea).
- # Paired for.
- + Announced for.
- N Voted against (nay).
- X Paired against.
- – Announced against.
- P Voted "present."
- C Voted "present" to avoid possible conflict of interest.
- ? Did not vote or otherwise make a position known.

Democrats ***Republicans*** *Independent*

	51	52	53	54	55	56	57	58
ALABAMA								
1 ***Callahan***	N	Y	Y	Y	Y	Y	N	N
2 ***Everett***	N	Y	Y	Y	Y	Y	N	N
3 ***Riley***	N	Y	Y	Y	Y	Y	N	N
4 ***Aderholt***	N	Y	Y	Y	Y	Y	N	N
5 Cramer	N	Y	Y	N	Y	Y	Y	Y
6 ***Bachus***	N	Y	Y	Y	Y	Y	Y	N
7 Hilliard	Y	N	Y	N	Y	Y	Y	Y
ALASKA								
AL ***Young***	N	Y	Y	Y	Y	Y	N	N
ARIZONA								
1 ***Salmon***	N	Y	Y	Y	Y	N	N	N
2 Pastor	Y	Y	Y	N	Y	Y	Y	Y
3 ***Stump***	N	Y	Y	Y	Y	Y	?	N
4 ***Shadegg***	N	Y	Y	Y	Y	N	N	N
5 ***Kolbe***	N	Y	Y	Y	Y	Y	N	N
6 ***Hayworth***	N	Y	Y	Y	Y	Y	N	N
ARKANSAS								
1 Berry	N	Y	Y	N	Y	Y	Y	N
2 Snyder	N	Y	Y	N	Y	Y	Y	Y
3 ***Hutchinson***	N	Y	Y	Y	Y	Y	N	N
4 ***Dickey***	N	Y	Y	Y	Y	Y	N	N
CALIFORNIA								
1 ***Riggs***	N	Y	Y	Y	Y	Y	N	N
2 ***Herger***	N	Y	Y	Y	N	N	N	N
3 Fazio	N	Y	Y	N	Y	+	Y	Y
4 ***Doolittle***	N	Y	Y	Y	Y	Y	N	N
5 Matsui	Y	Y	Y	N	Y	Y	?	Y
6 Woolsey	Y	Y	Y	N	Y	Y	Y	Y
7 Miller	Y	Y	Y	N	Y	Y	Y	Y
8 Pelosi	Y	Y	Y	N	Y	Y	Y	Y
9 Dellums	Y	Y	Y	N	Y	Y	Y	Y
10 Tauscher	Y	Y	Y	N	Y	Y	Y	Y
11 ***Pombo***	N	Y	Y	Y	Y	Y	N	N
12 Lantos	Y	Y	Y	N	Y	Y	Y	Y
13 Stark	Y	Y	Y	?	Y	Y	Y	Y
14 Eshoo	?	Y	Y	N	Y	Y	Y	Y
15 ***Campbell***	Y	Y	Y	Y	N	N	N	N
16 Lofgren	Y	Y	Y	N	Y	Y	Y	Y
17 Farr	Y	?	Y	N	Y	Y	Y	Y
18 Condit	N	Y	Y	N	Y	Y	N	Y
19 ***Radanovich***	N	Y	Y	Y	Y	Y	N	N
20 Dooley	N	Y	Y	Y	Y	Y	N	N
21 ***Thomas***	N	Y	Y	Y	Y	Y	N	N
22 Capps	Y	Y	Y	N	Y	Y	Y	Y
23 ***Gallegly***	N	Y	Y	Y	Y	Y	N	N
24 Sherman	Y	Y	Y	N	Y	Y	Y	Y
25 ***McKeon***	N	Y	Y	Y	Y	Y	N	N
26 Berman	Y	Y	Y	N	Y	Y	Y	Y
27 ***Rogan***	N	Y	Y	Y	+	Y	N	N
28 ***Dreier***	N	Y	Y	Y	Y	Y	N	N
29 Waxman	Y	Y	Y	N	Y	Y	Y	Y
30 Becerra	Y	Y	Y	N	Y	Y	Y	Y
31 Martinez	Y	Y	Y	N	Y	Y	Y	Y
32 Dixon	Y	Y	Y	N	Y	Y	Y	Y
33 Roybal-Allard	Y	Y	Y	N	Y	Y	Y	Y
34 Torres	Y	Y	Y	?	Y	Y	Y	Y
35 Waters	Y	N	Y	N	Y	Y	Y	Y
36 Harman	Y	Y	Y	N	Y	Y	N	Y
37 Millender-McD.	Y	Y	Y	N	Y	Y	Y	Y
38 ***Horn***	N	Y	Y	Y	Y	Y	Y	N
39 ***Royce***	Y	Y	Y	Y	Y	N	N	N
40 ***Lewis***	N	Y	Y	Y	Y	Y	N	N
41 ***Kim***	N	Y	Y	Y	Y	Y	N	N
42 Brown	Y	Y	Y	N	Y	Y	Y	Y
43 ***Calvert***	N	Y	Y	?	Y	Y	N	N
44 ***Bono***	N	Y	Y	Y	Y	Y	N	N
45 ***Rohrabacher***	N	Y	Y	Y	Y	N	N	N
46 Sanchez	Y	Y	Y	?	Y	Y	Y	Y
47 ***Cox***	N	Y	Y	Y	Y	Y	N	N
48 ***Packard***	N	Y	Y	Y	Y	Y	N	N
49 ***Bilbray***	N	Y	Y	Y	Y	Y	N	N
50 Filner	Y	Y	Y	N	Y	Y	Y	Y
51 ***Cunningham***	N	Y	Y	Y	Y	Y	N	N
52 ***Hunter***	N	Y	Y	Y	N	Y	N	N
COLORADO								
1 DeGette	Y	Y	Y	N	Y	Y	Y	Y
2 Skaggs	Y	Y	Y	?	Y	Y	Y	Y
3 ***McInnis***	N	Y	Y	Y	Y	Y	N	N
4 ***Schaffer***	N	Y	Y	Y	N	Y	N	N
5 ***Hefley***	N	Y	Y	Y	N	N	N	N
6 ***Schaefer***	N	Y	Y	Y	Y	Y	N	N
CONNECTICUT								
1 Kennelly	Y	Y	Y	N	Y	Y	Y	Y
2 Gejdenson	Y	Y	Y	N	Y	Y	Y	Y
3 DeLauro	Y	Y	Y	N	Y	Y	Y	Y
4 ***Shays***	Y	Y	Y	Y	Y	N	N	N
5 Maloney	Y	Y	Y	N	Y	Y	Y	Y
6 ***Johnson***	Y	Y	Y	Y	Y	Y	N	N
DELAWARE								
AL ***Castle***	Y	Y	Y	Y	Y	Y	N	N
FLORIDA								
1 ***Scarborough***	N	Y	Y	Y	Y	N	N	N
2 Boyd	N	Y	Y	Y	Y	Y	N	Y
3 Brown	Y	Y	Y	N	Y	Y	Y	Y
4 ***Fowler***	N	Y	Y	Y	Y	Y	N	N
5 Thurman	Y	Y	Y	N	Y	Y	Y	Y
6 ***Stearns***	N	Y	Y	Y	Y	Y	N	N
7 ***Mica***	N	Y	Y	Y	Y	Y	N	N
8 ***McCollum***	N	Y	Y	Y	Y	Y	N	N
9 ***Bilirakis***	N	Y	Y	Y	Y	Y	N	N
10 ***Young***	N	Y	Y	Y	Y	Y	N	N
11 Davis	Y	Y	Y	N	Y	Y	Y	Y
12 ***Canady***	N	Y	Y	Y	Y	Y	N	N
13 ***Miller***	N	Y	Y	Y	Y	Y	N	N
14 ***Goss***	N	Y	Y	Y	Y	Y	N	N
15 ***Weldon***	N	Y	Y	Y	Y	Y	N	N
16 ***Foley***	N	Y	Y	Y	Y	Y	N	N
17 Meek	Y	N	Y	N	Y	Y	Y	Y
18 ***Ros-Lehtinen***	N	Y	Y	Y	Y	Y	N	N
19 Wexler	Y	Y	Y	N	Y	Y	Y	Y
20 Deutsch	Y	Y	Y	N	Y	Y	Y	Y
21 ***Diaz-Balart***	N	Y	Y	Y	Y	Y	N	N
22 ***Shaw***	N	Y	Y	Y	Y	Y	N	N
23 Hastings	Y	N	Y	N	Y	Y	Y	Y
GEORGIA								
1 ***Kingston***	N	Y	Y	Y	Y	N	N	N
2 Bishop	N	Y	Y	N	Y	Y	Y	Y
3 ***Collins***	N	Y	Y	Y	Y	Y	N	N
4 McKinney	Y	Y	Y	N	N	Y	Y	N
5 Lewis	Y	Y	Y	N	Y	Y	Y	Y
6 ***Gingrich***								
7 ***Barr***	N	Y	Y	Y	Y	N	N	N
8 ***Chambliss***	N	Y	Y	Y	Y	Y	N	N
9 ***Deal***	N	Y	Y	Y	Y	Y	N	N
10 ***Norwood***	N	Y	Y	Y	Y	Y	N	N
11 ***Linder***	N	Y	Y	Y	Y	Y	N	N
HAWAII								
1 Abercrombie	Y	Y	Y	N	Y	Y	Y	Y
2 Mink	Y	Y	Y	N	Y	Y	Y	Y
IDAHO								
1 ***Chenoweth***	N	Y	Y	Y	Y	Y	N	N
2 ***Crapo***	N	Y	Y	Y	Y	Y	N	N
ILLINOIS								
1 Rush	Y	Y	Y	N	N	Y	Y	Y
2 Jackson	Y	N	Y	N	Y	Y	Y	Y
3 Lipinski	Y	Y	Y	N	Y	Y	Y	Y
4 Gutierrez	Y	Y	Y	N	Y	Y	Y	Y
5 Blagojevich	Y	Y	Y	N	Y	Y	Y	Y
6 ***Hyde***	N	Y	Y	Y	Y	Y	N	N
7 Davis	Y	Y	Y	N	N	Y	Y	Y
8 ***Crane***	N	Y	Y	Y	Y	Y	N	N
9 Yates	Y	Y	Y	N	Y	Y	Y	Y
10 ***Porter***	Y	Y	Y	Y	Y	Y	N	N
11 ***Weller***	Y	Y	Y	Y	Y	Y	N	N
12 Costello	Y	Y	Y	N	Y	Y	Y	Y
13 ***Fawell***	Y	Y	Y	Y	Y	Y	N	N
14 ***Hastert***	N	Y	Y	Y	Y	Y	N	N

ND Northern Democrats SD Southern Democrats

	51	52	53	54	55	56	57	58
15 ***Ewing***	N	Y	Y	Y	Y	Y	N	N
16 ***Manzullo***	N	Y	Y	Y	Y	Y	N	N
17 Evans	Y	Y	Y	N	Y	Y	Y	Y
18 ***LaHood***	N	Y	Y	Y	Y	Y	N	N
19 Poshard	Y	Y	Y	N	Y	Y	Y	Y
20 ***Shimkus***	N	Y	Y	Y	Y	Y	N	N
INDIANA								
1 Visclosky	Y	Y	Y	N	Y	Y	Y	N
2 ***McIntosh***	N	Y	Y	Y	Y	N	N	N
3 Roemer	N	Y	Y	N	Y	Y	N	Y
4 ***Souder***	N	Y	Y	Y	Y	Y	N	N
5 ***Buyer***	N	Y	Y	Y	Y	Y	N	N
6 ***Burton***	N	Y	Y	Y	Y	Y	N	N
7 ***Pease***	N	Y	Y	Y	Y	N	N	N
8 ***Hostettler***	N	Y	Y	Y	Y	N	N	N
9 Hamilton	N	Y	Y	N	Y	Y	Y	Y
10 Carson	Y	Y	Y	N	?	Y	Y	Y
IOWA								
1 ***Leach***	N	Y	Y	Y	Y	Y	N	N
2 ***Nussle***	N	Y	Y	Y	Y	Y	N	N
3 Boswell	Y	Y	Y	N	Y	Y	Y	Y
4 ***Ganske***	N	Y	?	Y	Y	Y	N	N
5 ***Latham***	N	Y	Y	Y	Y	Y	N	N
KANSAS								
1 ***Moran***	N	Y	Y	Y	Y	Y	N	N
2 ***Ryun***	N	Y	Y	Y	Y	Y	N	N
3 ***Snowbarger***	N	Y	Y	Y	Y	Y	N	N
4 ***Tiahrt***	N	Y	Y	Y	Y	Y	N	N
KENTUCKY								
1 ***Whitfield***	N	Y	Y	Y	Y	Y	N	N
2 ***Lewis***	N	Y	Y	Y	Y	Y	N	N
3 ***Northup***	N	Y	Y	Y	Y	N	N	N
4 ***Bunning***	N	Y	Y	Y	Y	Y	N	N
5 ***Rogers***	N	Y	Y	Y	Y	Y	N	N
6 Baesler	Y	Y	Y	N	Y	Y	Y	N
LOUISIANA								
1 ***Livingston***	N	Y	Y	Y	Y	Y	N	N
2 Jefferson	Y	Y	Y	N	Y	Y	Y	Y
3 ***Tauzin***	?	?	?	Y	Y	Y	N	N
4 ***McCrery***	N	Y	Y	Y	Y	Y	N	N
5 ***Cooksey***	N	Y	Y	Y	Y	Y	N	N
6 ***Baker***	N	Y	Y	Y	Y	Y	N	N
7 John	N	Y	Y	Y	Y	Y	Y	Y
MAINE								
1 Allen	Y	Y	Y	N	Y	Y	Y	Y
2 Baldacci	Y	Y	Y	N	Y	Y	Y	Y
MARYLAND								
1 ***Gilchrest***	N	Y	Y	Y	Y	N	–	N
2 ***Ehrlich***	N	Y	Y	Y	Y	Y	N	N
3 Cardin	Y	Y	Y	N	Y	Y	N	Y
4 Wynn	Y	Y	Y	N	Y	Y	Y	Y
5 Hoyer	Y	Y	Y	N	Y	Y	Y	Y
6 ***Bartlett***	N	Y	Y	Y	Y	N	N	N
7 Cummings	Y	Y	Y	N	Y	Y	Y	Y
8 ***Morella***	Y	Y	Y	Y	Y	Y	N	Y
MASSACHUSETTS								
1 Olver	Y	Y	Y	N	Y	Y	Y	Y
2 Neal	Y	Y	Y	N	N	Y	Y	Y
3 McGovern	Y	Y	Y	N	Y	Y	Y	Y
4 Frank	Y	Y	Y	N	Y	Y	Y	?
5 Meehan	Y	Y	Y	N	Y	Y	Y	Y
6 Tierney	Y	Y	Y	N	Y	Y	Y	Y
7 Markey	Y	Y	Y	N	Y	Y	Y	Y
8 Kennedy	Y	Y	Y	N	Y	Y	Y	Y
9 Moakley	Y	Y	Y	N	Y	Y	Y	Y
10 Delahunt	Y	N	Y	N	N	Y	Y	Y
MICHIGAN								
1 Stupak	Y	Y	Y	N	Y	Y	Y	Y
2 ***Hoekstra***	Y	Y	Y	Y	Y	Y	N	N
3 ***Ehlers***	N	Y	Y	Y	Y	N	N	N
4 ***Camp***	N	Y	Y	Y	Y	Y	N	N
5 Barcia	Y	Y	Y	?	Y	Y	Y	Y
6 ***Upton***	N	Y	Y	Y	Y	Y	N	N
7 ***Smith***	Y	Y	Y	Y	Y	Y	N	N
8 Stabenow	Y	Y	Y	N	Y	Y	Y	Y
9 Kildee	Y	Y	Y	N	Y	Y	Y	Y
10 Bonior	Y	Y	Y	N	Y	Y	Y	Y
11 ***Knollenberg***	N	Y	Y	Y	Y	Y	N	N
12 Levin	Y	Y	Y	N	Y	Y	Y	Y
13 Rivers	Y	Y	Y	N	Y	Y	Y	Y
14 Conyers	Y	Y	Y	N	Y	Y	Y	Y
15 Kilpatrick	Y	Y	Y	N	Y	Y	Y	Y
16 Dingell	Y	Y	Y	N	Y	Y	?	Y
MINNESOTA								
1 ***Gutknecht***	N	Y	Y	Y	Y	Y	N	N
2 Minge	Y	Y	Y	N	Y	Y	Y	Y

	51	52	53	54	55	56	57	58
3 ***Ramstad***	Y	Y	Y	Y	Y	Y	N	N
4 Vento	Y	Y	Y	N	Y	Y	Y	Y
5 Sabo	Y	Y	Y	N	Y	Y	Y	Y
6 Luther	Y	Y	Y	N	Y	Y	Y	Y
7 Peterson	N	Y	Y	Y	Y	Y	Y	Y
8 Oberstar	Y	Y	Y	N	Y	Y	?	Y
MISSISSIPPI								
1 ***Wicker***	N	Y	Y	Y	Y	Y	N	N
2 Thompson	Y	Y	Y	N	Y	Y	Y	Y
3 ***Pickering***	N	Y	Y	Y	Y	Y	N	N
4 ***Parker***	N	Y	Y	Y	Y	Y	N	N
5 Taylor	Y	Y	Y	N	Y	Y	N	N
MISSOURI								
1 Clay	Y	N	Y	N	Y	Y	Y	Y
2 ***Talent***	N	Y	Y	Y	Y	Y	N	N
3 Gephardt	Y	Y	Y	N	Y	?	?	N
4 Skelton	N	Y	Y	N	Y	Y	Y	Y
5 McCarthy	Y	Y	Y	N	Y	Y	Y	Y
6 Danner	N	Y	Y	N	Y	Y	Y	Y
7 ***Blunt***	N	Y	Y	Y	Y	Y	N	N
8 ***Emerson***	N	Y	Y	Y	Y	Y	N	N
9 ***Hulshof***	N	Y	Y	Y	Y	Y	N	N
MONTANA								
AL ***Hill***	N	Y	Y	Y	Y	Y	N	N
NEBRASKA								
1 ***Bereuter***	N	Y	Y	Y	Y	Y	N	N
2 ***Christensen***	N	Y	Y	Y	Y	Y	N	N
3 ***Barrett***	N	Y	Y	Y	Y	Y	N	N
NEVADA								
1 ***Ensign***	N	Y	Y	Y	Y	Y	N	N
2 ***Gibbons***	N	Y	Y	Y	Y	Y	N	N
NEW HAMPSHIRE								
1 ***Sununu***	N	Y	Y	Y	Y	Y	N	N
2 ***Bass***	N	Y	Y	Y	Y	Y	N	N
NEW JERSEY								
1 Andrews	Y	Y	Y	N	Y	Y	Y	Y
2 ***LoBiondo***	Y	Y	Y	Y	Y	Y	N	N
3 ***Saxton***	N	Y	Y	Y	Y	Y	N	N
4 ***Smith***	N	Y	Y	Y	Y	Y	N	N
5 ***Roukema***	Y	Y	Y	Y	Y	Y	N	N
6 Pallone	Y	Y	Y	N	Y	Y	Y	Y
7 ***Franks***	Y	Y	Y	N	Y	Y	N	N
8 Pascrell	Y	Y	Y	N	Y	Y	Y	Y
9 Rothman	Y	Y	Y	N	Y	Y	Y	Y
10 Payne	Y	Y	Y	N	Y	Y	Y	Y
11 ***Frelinghuysen***	N	Y	Y	Y	Y	Y	N	N
12 ***Pappas***	N	Y	Y	Y	Y	Y	N	N
13 Menendez	Y	Y	Y	N	Y	Y	Y	Y
NEW MEXICO								
1 ***Schiff***	N	Y	Y	Y	Y	Y	N	N
2 ***Skeen***	N	Y	Y	Y	Y	Y	N	N
3 Vacant								
NEW YORK								
1 ***Forbes***	Y	Y	Y	Y	N	N	N	N
2 ***Lazio***	N	Y	Y	N	Y	Y	Y	Y
3 ***King***	N	Y	Y	Y	Y	Y	N	N
4 McCarthy	N	Y	Y	N	Y	Y	Y	Y
5 Ackerman	Y	Y	Y	N	Y	Y	Y	Y
6 Flake	Y	Y	Y	N	Y	Y	Y	Y
7 Manton	Y	Y	Y	N	Y	Y	Y	Y
8 Nadler	Y	Y	Y	N	Y	Y	Y	Y
9 Schumer	Y	Y	Y	N	Y	Y	Y	Y
10 Towns	Y	Y	Y	N	N	Y	Y	Y
11 Owens	Y	Y	Y	N	N	Y	Y	N
12 Velázquez	Y	Y	Y	N	N	Y	Y	Y
13 ***Molinari***	N	Y	Y	Y	Y	Y	N	N
14 Maloney	Y	Y	Y	N	Y	Y	Y	Y
15 Rangel	Y	Y	Y	N	Y	Y	N	Y
16 Serrano	Y	Y	Y	N	Y	Y	Y	Y
17 Engel	Y	Y	Y	N	Y	Y	Y	Y
18 Lowey	Y	Y	Y	N	Y	Y	Y	Y
19 ***Kelly***	N	Y	Y	Y	Y	Y	N	N
20 ***Gilman***	Y	Y	Y	Y	Y	Y	N	N
21 McNulty	Y	Y	Y	N	Y	Y	Y	Y
22 ***Solomon***	N	Y	Y	Y	Y	Y	N	N
23 ***Boehlert***	Y	Y	Y	Y	Y	Y	N	N
24 ***McHugh***	N	Y	Y	Y	Y	Y	N	N
25 ***Walsh***	Y	Y	Y	Y	Y	Y	N	N
26 Hinchey	Y	Y	Y	N	Y	Y	Y	Y
27 ***Paxon***	N	Y	Y	Y	Y	Y	N	N
28 Slaughter	Y	Y	?	N	Y	Y	Y	Y
29 LaFalce	Y	Y	Y	N	Y	Y	?	Y
30 ***Quinn***	N	Y	Y	Y	Y	Y	N	N
31 ***Houghton***	N	Y	Y	Y	Y	Y	N	N

	51	52	53	54	55	56	57	58
NORTH CAROLINA								
1 Clayton	Y	Y	Y	N	Y	Y	Y	Y
2 Etheridge	Y	Y	Y	N	Y	Y	Y	Y
3 ***Jones***	N	Y	Y	Y	Y	Y	N	N
4 Price	Y	Y	Y	N	Y	Y	?	Y
5 ***Burr***	N	Y	Y	Y	Y	Y	N	N
6 ***Coble***	N	Y	Y	Y	Y	Y	N	N
7 McIntyre	N	Y	Y	N	Y	Y	N	Y
8 Hefner	Y	Y	Y	N	Y	Y	Y	Y
9 ***Myrick***	N	Y	Y	Y	Y	Y	N	N
10 ***Ballenger***	N	Y	Y	Y	Y	Y	N	N
11 ***Taylor***	N	Y	Y	Y	?	Y	N	N
12 Watt	Y	N	Y	N	N	Y	Y	Y
NORTH DAKOTA								
AL Pomeroy	N	Y	Y	N	Y	Y	Y	Y
OHIO								
1 ***Chabot***	N	Y	Y	Y	Y	Y	N	N
2 ***Portman***	N	Y	Y	Y	Y	Y	N	N
3 Hall	Y	Y	Y	N	Y	Y	Y	Y
4 ***Oxley***	N	Y	Y	Y	Y	Y	N	N
5 ***Gillmor***	N	Y	Y	Y	Y	Y	N	N
6 Strickland	N	Y	Y	N	N	N	N	N
7 ***Hobson***	N	Y	Y	Y	Y	Y	N	N
8 ***Boehner***	N	Y	Y	Y	Y	N	N	N
9 Kaptur	#	?	?	?	?	?	?	?
10 Kucinich	Y	Y	N	N	N	N	Y	N
11 Stokes	Y	Y	Y	N	Y	Y	Y	Y
12 ***Kasich***	Y	Y	Y	Y	Y	?	?	N
13 Brown	Y	Y	Y	N	Y	Y	Y	Y
14 Sawyer	Y	Y	Y	N	Y	Y	Y	Y
15 ***Pryce***	N	Y	Y	Y	Y	Y	N	N
16 ***Regula***	N	Y	Y	Y	Y	Y	N	N
17 Traficant	N	Y	Y	N	Y	Y	Y	Y
18 ***Ney***	N	Y	Y	Y	Y	Y	N	N
19 ***LaTourette***	N	Y	Y	Y	Y	Y	N	N
OKLAHOMA								
1 ***Largent***	N	Y	Y	Y	Y	Y	Y	N
2 ***Coburn***	N	Y	Y	Y	Y	Y	N	N
3 ***Watkins***	N	Y	Y	Y	Y	Y	N	N
4 ***Watts***	N	Y	Y	Y	Y	Y	N	N
5 ***Istook***	X	Y	Y	Y	Y	Y	N	N
6 ***Lucas***	N	Y	Y	Y	Y	Y	N	N
OREGON								
1 Furse	Y	Y	Y	N	Y	Y	Y	Y
2 ***Smith***	N	Y	Y	Y	Y	Y	N	N
3 Blumenauer	Y	Y	Y	N	Y	Y	Y	Y
4 DeFazio	Y	Y	Y	N	Y	Y	Y	Y
5 Hooley	Y	Y	Y	N	Y	Y	Y	Y
PENNSYLVANIA								
1 Foglietta	Y	Y	Y	N	Y	Y	Y	Y
2 Fattah	Y	Y	Y	N	Y	Y	Y	Y
3 Borski	Y	Y	Y	N	Y	Y	Y	Y
4 Klink	N	Y	Y	N	N	Y	Y	Y
5 ***Peterson***	N	Y	Y	Y	Y	Y	N	N
6 Holden	Y	Y	Y	N	Y	Y	Y	Y
7 ***Weldon***	Y	Y	Y	Y	Y	Y	N	N
8 ***Greenwood***	N	Y	Y	Y	Y	Y	N	N
9 ***Shuster***	N	Y	Y	?	Y	Y	N	N
10 ***McDade***	N	Y	Y	Y	Y	Y	Y	N
11 Kanjorski	Y	Y	Y	N	Y	?	Y	Y
12 Murtha	Y	Y	Y	N	Y	Y	Y	Y
13 ***Fox***	N	Y	Y	Y	Y	Y	N	N
14 Coyne	Y	Y	Y	N	Y	Y	Y	Y
15 McHale	Y	Y	Y	N	Y	Y	Y	Y
16 ***Pitts***	N	Y	Y	Y	Y	Y	N	N
17 ***Gekas***	N	Y	Y	Y	Y	Y	N	N
18 Doyle	Y	Y	Y	N	Y	Y	Y	Y
19 ***Goodling***	N	Y	Y	Y	Y	Y	N	N
20 Mascara	Y	Y	Y	N	Y	Y	Y	Y
21 ***English***	N	Y	Y	Y	Y	Y	?	Y
RHODE ISLAND								
1 Kennedy	Y	Y	Y	N	Y	Y	Y	Y
2 Weygand	Y	Y	Y	N	Y	Y	Y	Y
SOUTH CAROLINA								
1 ***Sanford***	N	Y	Y	Y	Y	Y	N	N
2 ***Spence***	N	Y	Y	Y	Y	Y	N	N
3 ***Graham***	N	Y	Y	Y	Y	Y	N	N
4 ***Inglis***	N	Y	Y	Y	Y	Y	N	N
5 Spratt	Y	Y	Y	N	?	?	?	Y
6 Clyburn	Y	Y	Y	N	Y	Y	Y	Y
SOUTH DAKOTA								
AL ***Thune***	N	Y	Y	Y	Y	Y	N	N

	51	52	53	54	55	56	57	
TENNESSEE								
1 ***Jenkins***	N	Y	Y	Y	Y	Y	N	N
2 ***Duncan***	N	Y	Y	Y	Y	Y	N	N
3 ***Wamp***	N	Y	Y	Y	Y	Y	N	N
4 ***Hilleary***	N	Y	Y	Y	Y	Y	N	N
5 Clement	Y	Y	Y	N	Y	Y	?	Y
6 Gordon	Y	Y	Y	N	Y	Y	N	Y
7 ***Bryant***	N	Y	Y	Y	Y	Y	N	N
8 Tanner	Y	Y	Y	N	Y	Y	N	Y
9 Ford	Y	Y	Y	N	Y	Y	Y	Y
TEXAS								
1 Sandlin	Y	Y	Y	N	Y	Y	Y	Y
2 Turner	?	?	?	N	Y	Y	Y	Y
3 ***Johnson, Sam***	N	Y	Y	Y	Y	N	N	N
4 Hall	N	Y	Y	Y	Y	Y	N	N
5 ***Sessions***	N	Y	Y	Y	Y	Y	N	N
6 ***Barton***	N	Y	N	Y	Y	Y	N	N
7 ***Archer***	N	Y	Y	Y	Y	Y	N	N
8 ***Brady***	N	Y	Y	Y	Y	N	N	N
9 Lampson	Y	Y	Y	N	Y	Y	Y	Y
10 Doggett	Y	Y	Y	N	Y	Y	Y	Y
11 Edwards	Y	Y	Y	N	Y	Y	Y	Y
12 ***Granger***	N	?	?	Y	Y	N	N	N
13 ***Thornberry***	N	Y	Y	Y	Y	N	N	N
14 ***Paul***	N	Y	Y	Y	N	N	N	N
15 Hinojosa	Y	Y	Y	N	Y	Y	Y	Y
16 Reyes	Y	Y	Y	N	Y	Y	Y	Y
17 Stenholm	N	Y	Y	Y	Y	Y	N	N
18 Jackson-Lee	Y	Y	Y	N	Y	Y	Y	Y
19 ***Combest***	N	Y	Y	Y	Y	Y	N	N
20 Gonzalez	Y	Y	Y	N	Y	Y	Y	Y
21 ***Smith***	N	Y	Y	Y	Y	N	N	N
22 ***DeLay***	N	Y	Y	Y	Y	N	N	N
23 ***Bonilla***	N	Y	Y	Y	Y	N	N	N
24 Frost	Y	Y	Y	N	Y	Y	Y	Y
25 Bentsen	Y	Y	Y	N	Y	Y	N	Y
26 ***Armey***	N	Y	Y	Y	Y	Y	N	N
27 Ortiz	N	Y	Y	N	Y	Y	Y	Y
28 Vacant								
29 Green	Y	Y	Y	N	Y	Y	Y	Y
30 Johnson, E.B.	Y	Y	Y	N	Y	Y	Y	Y
UTAH								
1 ***Hansen***	N	Y	Y	Y	Y	Y	N	N
2 ***Cook***	N	Y	Y	Y	Y	Y	N	N
3 ***Cannon***	N	Y	Y	Y	Y	Y	N	N
VERMONT								
AL *Sanders*	Y	Y	Y	N	Y	Y	Y	Y
VIRGINIA								
1 ***Bateman***	N	Y	Y	Y	Y	Y	N	N
2 Pickett	N	Y	Y	N	Y	Y	N	Y
3 Scott	Y	N	Y	N	Y	Y	Y	Y
4 Sisisky	N	Y	Y	N	Y	Y	N	N
5 Goode	N	Y	Y	Y	Y	Y	N	N
6 ***Goodlatte***	N	Y	Y	Y	Y	Y	N	N
7 ***Bliley***	N	Y	Y	Y	Y	N	N	N
8 Moran	Y	Y	Y	N	Y	Y	Y	Y
9 Boucher	N	Y	Y	N	Y	Y	Y	Y
10 ***Wolf***	N	Y	Y	Y	Y	Y	N	N
11 ***Davis***	N	Y	Y	Y	Y	N	N	N
WASHINGTON								
1 ***White***	N	Y	Y	Y	Y	Y	N	N
2 ***Metcalf***	N	Y	Y	Y	Y	Y	Y	N
3 ***Smith, Linda***	N	Y	Y	Y	Y	Y	N	N
4 ***Hastings***	N	Y	Y	Y	Y	N	N	N
5 ***Nethercutt***	N	Y	Y	Y	Y	Y	N	N
6 Dicks	N	Y	Y	N	Y	Y	Y	Y
7 McDermott	N	Y	Y	N	Y	N	Y	Y
8 ***Dunn***	N	Y	Y	Y	Y	Y	N	N
9 Smith, Adam	N	Y	Y	N	Y	Y	N	Y
WEST VIRGINIA								
1 Mollohan	Y	Y	Y	N	Y	Y	N	Y
2 Wise	Y	Y	Y	N	Y	Y	Y	Y
3 Rahall	Y	Y	Y	N	Y	Y	Y	Y
WISCONSIN								
1 ***Neumann***	N	Y	Y	Y	Y	Y	N	N
2 ***Klug***	Y	Y	Y	Y	Y	Y	N	N
3 Kind	Y	Y	Y	N	Y	Y	N	Y
4 Kleczka	Y	Y	Y	N	Y	Y	Y	Y
5 Barrett	Y	Y	Y	N	Y	Y	Y	Y
6 ***Petri***	N	Y	Y	Y	Y	N	N	N
7 Obey	Y	Y	Y	N	Y	Y	Y	Y
8 Johnson	Y	Y	Y	N	Y	Y	Y	Y
9 ***Sensenbrenner***	N	Y	Y	Y	Y	N	N	N
WYOMING								
AL ***Cubin***	N	Y	Y	Y	Y	Y	N	N

Southern states - Ala., Ark., Fla., Ga., Ky., La., Miss., N.C., Okla., S.C., Tenn., Texas, Va.

HOUSE VOTES 59, 60, 61, 62, 63, 64, 65, 67 *

59. HR 1. Overtime Pay/Passage. Passage of the bill to allow private-sector employees the choice of taking one and one-half hours of compensatory time instead of cash wages for overtime pay. Passed 222-210: R 209-18: D 13-191 (ND 4-146, SD 9-45); I 0-1, March 19, 1997. A "nay" was a vote in support of the president's position.

60. Procedural Motion/Adjourn. Obey, D-Wis., motion to adjourn. Motion rejected 183-221: R 0-213; D 182-8 (ND 135-5, SC 47-3); I 1-0, March 20, 1997.

61. HR 1122. Abortion Procedure Ban/Previous Question. Myrick, R-N.C., motion to order the previous question (thus ending debate and the possibility of amendment) on adoption of the rule (H Res 100) to provide for House floor consideration of the bill to impose penalties on doctors who perform certain abortion procedures, in which the person performing the abortion partially delivers the fetus before completing the abortion. An exception would be granted where the procedure was necessary to save the life of the woman. Motion agreed to 243-184: R 211-12; D 32-171 (ND 22-127, SD 10-44); I 0-1, March 20, 1997.

62. HR 1122. Abortion Procedure Ban/Rule. Adoption of the rule (H Res 100) to provide for House floor consideration of the bill to impose penalties on doctors who perform certain abortion procedures, in which the person performing the abortion partially delivers the fetus before completing the abortion. An exception would be granted where the procedure was necessary to save the life of the woman. Adopted 247-175: R 204-15; D 43-159 (ND 28-120, SD 15-39); I 0-1, March 20, 1997.

63. HR 1122. Abortion Procedure Ban/Motion To Table Appeal. Canady, R-Fla., motion to table (kill) the Hoyer, D-Md., motion to appeal the chair's ruling that the Hoyer motion to recommit the bill with instructions to report it back with a substitute amendment to impose civil penalties on doctors who perform an abortion after the fetus has become viable, with exceptions where the procedure was necessary to save the life or avert serious adverse health consequences of the woman, was out of order. Motion agreed to 265-165: R 220-5; D 45-159 (ND 31-119, SD 14-40); I 1-0, March 20, 1997.

64. HR 1122. Abortion Procedure Ban/Recommit. Frank, D-Mass., motion to recommit the bill to the Judiciary Committee with instructions to report it back with an amendment to add an exception where the procedure was necessary to avert serious adverse physical health consequences to the woman. Motion rejected 149-282: (R 16-210; D 132-72 (ND 96-54, SD 36-18); I 1-0, March 20, 1997.

65. HR 1122. Abortion Procedure Ban/Passage. Passage of the bill to impose penalties on doctors who perform certain abortion procedures, in which the person performing the abortion partially delivers the fetus before completing the abortion. An exception would be granted where the procedure was necessary to save the life of the woman. Passed 295-136: R 218-8; D 77-127 (ND 51-99, SD 26-28); I 0-1, March 20, 1997. A "nay" was a vote in support of the president's position.

*** 67. H Res 91. House Committee Funding/Rule.** Adoption of the rule (H Res 101) to provide for House floor consideration of the resolution to authorize $178.3 billion in 1997-98 for the operation of House committees. The 1997-98 level is a 14 percent increase from the 1995-96 level, including funds to be used for an investigation by the Government Reform and Oversight Committee of Democratic fundraising activities in the 1996 election. Rejected 210-213: R 210-11; D 0-201 (ND 0-147, SD 0-54); I 0-1, March 20, 1997.

** Omitted votes are quorum calls. CQ does not include quorum calls in its vote charts.*

KEY

- Y Voted for (yea).
- # Paired for.
- \+ Announced for.
- N Voted against (nay).
- X Paired against.
- – Announced against.
- P Voted "present."
- C Voted "present" to avoid possible conflict of interest.
- ? Did not vote or otherwise make a position known.

Democrats ***Republicans***
Independent

	59	60	61	62	63	64	65	67
ALABAMA								
1 ***Callahan***	Y	N	Y	?	Y	N	Y	Y
2 ***Everett***	Y	N	Y	Y	Y	N	Y	Y
3 ***Riley***	Y	N	Y	Y	Y	N	Y	Y
4 ***Aderholt***	Y	N	Y	Y	Y	N	Y	Y
5 Cramer	N	?	N	Y	Y	N	Y	N
6 ***Bachus***	N	N	Y	Y	Y	N	Y	Y
7 Hilliard	N	Y	N	N	N	Y	N	N
ALASKA								
AL ***Young***	N	?	Y	Y	Y	N	Y	Y
ARIZONA								
1 ***Salmon***	Y	N	Y	Y	Y	N	Y	N
2 Pastor	N	Y	N	N	N	Y	N	N
3 ***Stump***	Y	N	Y	Y	Y	N	Y	Y
4 ***Shadegg***	Y	N	Y	Y	Y	N	Y	Y
5 ***Kolbe***	Y	N	Y	N	Y	Y	N	Y
6 ***Hayworth***	Y	N	Y	Y	Y	N	Y	Y
ARKANSAS								
1 Berry	N	Y	N	N	N	N	Y	N
2 Snyder	N	N	N	N	N	Y	N	N
3 ***Hutchinson***	Y	N	Y	Y	Y	N	Y	Y
4 ***Dickey***	Y	N	Y	Y	Y	N	Y	Y
CALIFORNIA								
1 ***Riggs***	Y	?	Y	Y	Y	N	Y	Y
2 ***Herger***	Y	?	Y	Y	Y	N	Y	Y
3 Fazio	N	Y	N	N	N	N	N	N
4 ***Doolittle***	Y	N	Y	Y	Y	N	Y	Y
5 Matsui	N	Y	N	N	N	Y	N	N
6 Woolsey	N	Y	N	N	N	Y	N	N
7 Miller	N	Y	N	N	N	Y	N	N
8 Pelosi	N	Y	N	N	N	N	N	N
9 Dellums	N	Y	N	N	N	Y	N	N
10 Tauscher	N	Y	N	N	N	N	N	N
11 ***Pombo***	Y	N	Y	Y	Y	N	Y	Y
12 Lantos	N	Y	N	N	N	Y	N	N
13 Stark	N	?	N	N	N	Y	N	N
14 Eshoo	N	Y	N	N	N	Y	N	N
15 ***Campbell***	Y	N	N	N	Y	Y	N	Y
16 Lofgren	N	Y	N	N	N	N	N	N
17 Farr	N	Y	N	N	N	N	N	N
18 Condit	N	Y	N	N	N	N	Y	N
19 ***Radanovich***	Y	?	Y	Y	Y	N	Y	Y
20 Dooley	Y	Y	N	N	N	Y	N	N
21 ***Thomas***	Y	N	Y	Y	Y	N	Y	Y
22 Capps	N	Y	N	N	N	Y	N	N
23 ***Gallegly***	Y	N	Y	Y	Y	N	Y	Y
24 Sherman	N	Y	N	N	N	Y	N	N
25 ***McKeon***	Y	N	Y	Y	Y	N	Y	Y
26 Berman	N	Y	N	N	N	Y	N	N
27 ***Rogan***	Y	N	Y	Y	Y	N	Y	Y
28 ***Dreier***	Y	N	Y	Y	Y	N	Y	Y
29 Waxman	N	Y	N	?	N	N	N	N
30 Becerra	N	Y	N	N	N	Y	N	N
31 Martinez	N	Y	N	N	N	N	Y	N
32 Dixon	N	Y	N	N	N	Y	N	N
33 Roybal-Allard	N	Y	N	N	N	Y	N	N
34 Torres	N	Y	N	?	N	Y	N	N
35 Waters	N	Y	N	N	N	Y	N	N
36 Harman	Y	Y	N	N	N	N	N	N
37 Millender-McD.	N	Y	N	N	N	Y	N	N
38 ***Horn***	N	N	Y	N	Y	Y	N	Y
39 ***Royce***	Y	N	Y	Y	Y	N	Y	Y
40 ***Lewis***	Y	N	?	Y	Y	N	Y	Y
41 ***Kim***	Y	N	Y	Y	Y	N	Y	Y
42 Brown	N	Y	?	N	N	Y	N	N
43 ***Calvert***	Y	N	Y	Y	Y	N	Y	Y
44 ***Bono***	Y	N	Y	?	Y	N	Y	Y
45 ***Rohrabacher***	Y	N	Y	Y	Y	N	Y	Y
46 Sanchez	N	Y	N	N	N	Y	N	N
47 ***Cox***	Y	N	Y	Y	Y	N	Y	Y
48 ***Packard***	Y	N	Y	Y	Y	N	Y	Y
49 ***Bilbray***	Y	N	Y	Y	Y	N	Y	Y
50 Filner	N	Y	N	N	N	Y	N	N
51 ***Cunningham***	Y	N	Y	Y	Y	N	Y	Y
52 ***Hunter***	Y	N	Y	Y	Y	N	Y	Y
COLORADO								
1 DeGette	N	Y	N	N	N	N	N	N
2 Skaggs	N	Y	N	N	N	Y	N	N
3 ***McInnis***	Y	N	Y	Y	Y	N	Y	Y
4 ***Schaffer***	Y	N	Y	Y	Y	N	Y	Y
5 ***Hefley***	Y	N	Y	Y	Y	N	Y	Y
6 ***Schaefer***	Y	N	Y	Y	Y	N	Y	Y
CONNECTICUT								
1 Kennelly	N	Y	N	N	N	Y	N	N
2 Gejdenson	N	Y	N	N	N	Y	N	N
3 DeLauro	N	Y	N	N	N	Y	N	N
4 ***Shays***	Y	N	N	N	N	Y	Y	Y
5 Maloney	N	Y	N	N	N	Y	Y	N
6 ***Johnson***	Y	N	N	N	N	Y	N	Y
DELAWARE								
AL ***Castle***	Y	N	N	N	Y	Y	Y	Y
FLORIDA								
1 ***Scarborough***	Y	N	Y	Y	Y	N	Y	N
2 Boyd	Y	Y	N	N	N	Y	Y	N
3 Brown	N	Y	N	N	N	Y	N	N
4 ***Fowler***	Y	N	Y	Y	Y	N	Y	Y
5 Thurman	N	Y	N	N	N	Y	N	N
6 ***Stearns***	Y	N	Y	Y	Y	N	Y	Y
7 ***Mica***	Y	N	Y	Y	Y	N	Y	Y
8 ***McCollum***	Y	N	Y	Y	Y	N	Y	Y
9 ***Bilirakis***	Y	N	Y	Y	Y	N	Y	Y
10 ***Young***	Y	N	?	Y	Y	N	Y	Y
11 Davis	N	Y	N	N	N	Y	Y	N
12 ***Canady***	Y	N	Y	Y	Y	N	Y	Y
13 ***Miller***	Y	N	Y	Y	Y	N	Y	Y
14 ***Goss***	Y	N	Y	Y	Y	N	Y	Y
15 ***Weldon***	Y	N	Y	Y	Y	N	Y	Y
16 ***Foley***	Y	N	Y	Y	Y	N	Y	Y
17 Meek	N	Y	N	N	N	Y	N	N
18 ***Ros-Lehtinen***	Y	N	Y	Y	Y	N	Y	Y
19 Wexler	N	Y	N	N	N	N	N	N
20 Deutsch	N	Y	N	N	Y	Y	N	N
21 ***Diaz-Balart***	N	N	Y	Y	Y	N	Y	Y
22 ***Shaw***	Y	N	Y	Y	Y	N	Y	Y
23 Hastings	N	Y	N	N	N	Y	N	N
GEORGIA								
1 ***Kingston***	Y	N	Y	Y	Y	N	Y	Y
2 Bishop	N	Y	N	N	N	Y	N	N
3 ***Collins***	Y	N	Y	Y	Y	N	Y	Y
4 McKinney	N	Y	N	N	N	Y	N	N
5 Lewis	N	Y	N	N	N	Y	N	N
6 ***Gingrich***	Y					N	Y	Y
7 ***Barr***	Y	N	Y	Y	Y	N	Y	Y
8 ***Chambliss***	Y	N	Y	Y	Y	N	Y	Y
9 ***Deal***	Y	N	Y	Y	Y	N	Y	Y
10 ***Norwood***	Y	N	Y	Y	Y	N	Y	Y
11 ***Linder***	Y	N	Y	Y	Y	N	Y	Y
HAWAII								
1 Abercrombie	N	Y	N	N	N	N	N	N
2 Mink	N	Y	N	N	N	N	N	N
IDAHO								
1 ***Chenoweth***	Y	N	Y	Y	Y	N	Y	Y
2 ***Crapo***	Y	N	Y	Y	Y	N	Y	Y
ILLINOIS								
1 Rush	N	Y	N	N	N	Y	N	N
2 Jackson	N	Y	N	N	N	Y	N	N
3 Lipinski	N	Y	Y	Y	Y	N	Y	N
4 Gutierrez	N	Y	N	N	N	N	N	N
5 Blagojevich	N	?	N	N	N	Y	N	N
6 ***Hyde***	Y	N	Y	Y	Y	N	Y	Y
7 Davis	N	?	N	N	N	Y	N	N
8 ***Crane***	Y	?	Y	Y	Y	N	Y	Y
9 Yates	N	Y	N	N	N	Y	N	N
10 ***Porter***	Y	N	Y	Y	Y	N	Y	Y
11 ***Weller***	N	N	Y	Y	Y	N	Y	Y
12 Costello	N	Y	Y	Y	Y	N	Y	N
13 ***Fawell***	Y	N	Y	Y	Y	N	Y	Y
14 ***Hastert***	Y	N	Y	Y	Y	N	Y	Y

ND Northern Democrats SD Southern Democrats

	59	60	61	62	63	64	65	67
15 *Ewing*	Y	N	Y	Y	Y	N	Y	Y
16 *Manzullo*	Y	N	Y	Y	Y	N	Y	Y
17 Evans	N	Y	N	N	N	Y	N	N
18 *LaHood*	Y	N	Y	Y	Y	N	Y	Y
19 Poshard	N	Y	Y	Y	Y	N	Y	N
20 *Shimkus*	N	N	Y	Y	Y	N	Y	Y
INDIANA								
1 Visclosky	N	Y	N	N	N	N	Y	N
2 *McIntosh*	Y	?	Y	+	Y	N	Y	Y
3 Roemer	N	Y	Y	Y	Y	N	Y	N
4 *Souder*	Y	N	Y	Y	Y	N	Y	N
5 *Buyer*	Y	N	Y	Y	Y	N	Y	Y
6 *Burton*	Y	N	Y	?	Y	N	Y	Y
7 *Pease*	Y	N	Y	Y	Y	N	Y	Y
8 *Hostettler*	Y	N	Y	Y	Y	N	Y	Y
9 Hamilton	N	Y	Y	Y	Y	N	Y	N
10 Carson	N	Y	N	N	N	Y	N	N
IOWA								
1 *Leach*	Y	N	Y	Y	Y	N	Y	Y
2 *Nussle*	Y	N	Y	Y	Y	N	Y	Y
3 Boswell	N	Y	N	N	N	N	Y	N
4 *Ganske*	Y	N	Y	Y	Y	N	Y	Y
5 *Latham*	Y	N	Y	Y	Y	N	Y	Y
KANSAS								
1 *Moran*	Y	N	Y	Y	Y	N	Y	Y
2 *Ryun*	Y	N	Y	Y	Y	N	Y	Y
3 *Snowbarger*	Y	N	Y	Y	Y	N	Y	Y
4 *Tiahrt*	Y	N	Y	Y	Y	N	Y	Y
KENTUCKY								
1 *Whitfield*	Y	N	Y	Y	Y	N	Y	Y
2 *Lewis*	Y	N	Y	Y	Y	N	Y	Y
3 *Northup*	Y	N	Y	Y	Y	N	Y	Y
4 *Bunning*	Y	N	Y	Y	Y	N	Y	Y
5 *Rogers*	Y	N	Y	Y	Y	N	Y	Y
6 Baesler	N	Y	Y	Y	Y	N	Y	N
LOUISIANA								
1 *Livingston*	Y	N	Y	Y	Y	N	Y	Y
2 Jefferson	N	Y	N	Y	N	Y	Y	N
3 *Tauzin*	Y	N	Y	Y	Y	N	Y	Y
4 *McCrery*	Y	?	Y	Y	Y	N	Y	Y
5 *Cooksey*	Y	N	Y	Y	Y	N	Y	Y
6 *Baker*	Y	N	Y	Y	Y	N	Y	Y
7 John	Y	Y	Y	Y	Y	N	Y	N
MAINE								
1 Allen	N	Y	N	N	N	N	N	N
2 Baldacci	N	Y	N	N	N	Y	N	N
MARYLAND								
1 *Gilchrest*	Y	N	Y	Y	Y	Y	Y	Y
2 *Ehrlich*	Y	N	Y	Y	Y	N	Y	Y
3 Cardin	N	Y	N	N	N	Y	N	N
4 Wynn	N	Y	N	N	N	Y	N	N
5 Hoyer	N	Y	N	N	N	Y	N	N
6 *Bartlett*	Y	N	Y	Y	Y	N	Y	Y
7 Cummings	N	Y	N	N	N	Y	N	N
8 *Morella*	Y	N	N	N	N	Y	N	Y
MASSACHUSETTS								
1 Olver	N	Y	N	N	N	Y	N	N
2 Neal	N	Y	N	N	Y	Y	N	N
3 McGovern	N	Y	N	N	N	Y	N	N
4 Frank	N	Y	N	N	N	Y	N	N
5 Meehan	N	Y	N	N	N	Y	N	N
6 Tierney	N	Y	N	N	N	Y	N	N
7 Markey	N	Y	N	N	N	Y	N	N
8 Kennedy	N	Y	N	N	N	Y	N	?
9 Moakley	N	Y	N	N	Y	Y	Y	N
10 Delahunt	N	Y	N	N	N	Y	N	N
MICHIGAN								
1 Stupak	N	Y	Y	Y	Y	N	Y	N
2 *Hoekstra*	Y	N	Y	Y	Y	N	Y	Y
3 *Ehlers*	Y	N	Y	Y	Y	N	Y	Y
4 *Camp*	Y	N	Y	Y	Y	N	Y	Y
5 Barcia	N	Y	Y	Y	Y	N	Y	N
6 *Upton*	Y	N	Y	Y	Y	N	Y	Y
7 *Smith*	Y	N	Y	Y	Y	N	Y	Y
8 Stabenow	N	Y	N	N	N	Y	N	N
9 Kildee	N	Y	Y	Y	Y	N	Y	N
10 Bonior	N	Y	N	N	N	Y	N	N
11 *Knollenberg*	Y	N	Y	Y	Y	N	Y	Y
12 Levin	N	Y	N	N	N	Y	N	N
13 Rivers	N	Y	N	N	N	Y	N	N
14 Conyers	N	Y	N	N	N	Y	N	N
15 Kilpatrick	N	Y	N	N	N	Y	N	N
16 Dingell	N	Y	N	Y	N	N	Y	N
MINNESOTA								
1 *Gutknecht*	Y	N	Y	Y	Y	N	Y	Y
2 Minge	Y	Y	N	N	N	Y	Y	N

	59	60	61	62	63	64	65	67
3 *Ramstad*	Y	N	N	N	Y	Y	Y	Y
4 Vento	N	Y	N	N	N	Y	N	N
5 Sabo	N	Y	N	N	N	Y	N	N
6 Luther	N	Y	N	N	N	Y	N	N
7 Peterson	Y	Y	Y	Y	Y	N	Y	N
8 Oberstar	N	N	Y	Y	Y	N	Y	N
MISSISSIPPI								
1 *Wicker*	Y	N	Y	Y	Y	N	Y	Y
2 Thompson	N	Y	N	N	N	Y	N	N
3 *Pickering*	Y	N	Y	Y	Y	N	Y	Y
4 *Parker*	Y	N	Y	Y	Y	N	Y	Y
5 Taylor	Y	N	Y	Y	Y	N	Y	N
MISSOURI								
1 Clay	N	?	N	N	N	Y	N	N
2 *Talent*	Y	?	Y	Y	Y	N	Y	Y
3 Gephardt	N	Y	N	N	N	Y	Y	N
4 Skelton	N	Y	Y	Y	Y	N	Y	N
5 McCarthy	N	Y	N	N	N	Y	N	N
6 Danner	N	Y	N	Y	Y	N	Y	N
7 *Blunt*	Y	N	Y	Y	Y	N	Y	Y
8 *Emerson*	Y	N	Y	Y	Y	N	Y	Y
9 *Hulshof*	Y	N	Y	Y	Y	N	Y	Y
MONTANA								
AL *Hill*	Y	N	Y	Y	Y	N	Y	Y
NEBRASKA								
1 *Bereuter*	Y	N	Y	Y	Y	N	Y	Y
2 *Christensen*	Y	N	Y	Y	Y	N	Y	Y
3 *Barrett*	Y	N	Y	Y	Y	N	Y	Y
NEVADA								
1 *Ensign*	Y	N	Y	Y	Y	N	Y	Y
2 *Gibbons*	Y	N	Y	Y	Y	N	Y	Y
NEW HAMPSHIRE								
1 *Sununu*	Y	N	Y	Y	Y	N	Y	Y
2 *Bass*	Y	N	Y	Y	Y	N	Y	Y
NEW JERSEY								
1 Andrews	N	Y	N	N	N	Y	N	?
2 *LoBiondo*	N	N	Y	Y	Y	N	Y	Y
3 *Saxton*	Y	?	Y	Y	Y	N	Y	Y
4 *Smith*	N	N	Y	Y	Y	N	Y	Y
5 *Roukema*	Y	N	Y	Y	Y	N	Y	Y
6 Pallone	N	Y	N	N	N	Y	N	N
7 *Franks*	Y	?	Y	Y	Y	N	Y	Y
8 Pascrell	N	Y	N	Y	N	N	Y	N
9 Rothman	N	Y	N	N	N	Y	N	N
10 Payne	N	Y	N	N	N	Y	N	N
11 *Frelinghuysen*	Y	N	N	N	Y	Y	Y	Y
12 *Pappas*	Y	N	Y	Y	Y	N	Y	Y
13 Menendez	N	Y	N	N	N	Y	N	N
NEW MEXICO								
1 *Schiff*	N	N	Y	Y	Y	N	Y	Y
2 *Skeen*	Y	N	Y	Y	Y	N	Y	Y
3 Vacant								
NEW YORK								
1 *Forbes*	N	?	Y	Y	Y	N	Y	Y
2 *Lazio*	Y	N	Y	N	Y	N	Y	Y
3 *King*	N	N	Y	Y	Y	N	Y	Y
4 McCarthy	N	Y	N	N	N	Y	N	N
5 Ackerman	N	Y	N	N	N	Y	N	N
6 Flake	N	?	N	N	N	Y	Y	?
7 Manton	N	Y	N	N	Y	N	Y	N
8 Nadler	N	Y	N	N	N	N	N	N
9 Schumer	N	Y	N	N	N	N	N	N
10 Towns	N	Y	N	N	N	Y	N	N
11 Owens	N	Y	N	N	N	N	N	N
12 Velázquez	N	Y	N	N	N	N	N	N
13 *Molinari*	Y	N	N	N	Y	N	Y	Y
14 Maloney	N	Y	N	N	N	N	N	N
15 Rangel	N	?	N	N	N	Y	N	N
16 Serrano	N	Y	N	N	N	Y	N	N
17 Engel	N	Y	N	N	N	Y	N	N
18 Lowey	N	Y	N	N	N	N	N	N
19 *Kelly*	Y	N	Y	Y	Y	Y	Y	Y
20 *Gilman*	N	N	N	N	Y	Y	N	Y
21 McNulty	N	Y	Y	Y	Y	N	Y	N
22 *Solomon*	Y	N	Y	Y	Y	N	Y	Y
23 *Boehlert*	N	N	N	N	N	Y	N	Y
24 *McHugh*	N	N	Y	Y	Y	N	Y	Y
25 *Walsh*	Y	N	Y	Y	Y	N	Y	Y
26 Hinchey	N	?	N	N	N	Y	N	N
27 *Paxon*	Y	N	Y	Y	Y	N	Y	Y
28 Slaughter	N	Y	N	N	N	N	N	N
29 LaFalce	N	Y	N	N	Y	N	Y	N
30 *Quinn*	N	N	Y	Y	Y	N	Y	Y
31 *Houghton*	Y	N	Y	Y	Y	Y	Y	Y

	59	60	61	62	63	64	65	67
NORTH CAROLINA								
1 Clayton	N	Y	N	N	N	Y	N	N
2 Etheridge	N	Y	N	N	N	Y	Y	N
3 *Jones*	Y	N	Y	Y	Y	N	Y	Y
4 Price	N	Y	N	N	N	Y	N	N
5 *Burr*	Y	N	Y	Y	Y	N	Y	Y
6 *Coble*	Y	N	Y	Y	Y	N	Y	Y
7 McIntyre	Y	Y	Y	Y	Y	N	Y	N
8 Hefner	N	Y	N	Y	N	N	Y	N
9 *Myrick*	Y	N	Y	Y	Y	N	Y	Y
10 *Ballenger*	Y	N	Y	Y	Y	N	Y	Y
11 *Taylor*	Y	N	Y	Y	Y	N	Y	Y
12 Watt	N	Y	N	N	N	Y	N	N
NORTH DAKOTA								
AL Pomeroy	N	Y	N	N	N	Y	Y	N
OHIO								
1 *Chabot*	Y	N	Y	Y	Y	N	Y	N
2 *Portman*	Y	N	Y	Y	Y	N	Y	Y
3 Hall	N	Y	Y	Y	Y	N	Y	N
4 *Oxley*	Y	?	?	?	?	?	+	+
5 *Gillmor*	Y	N	Y	Y	Y	N	Y	?
6 Strickland	N	Y	N	N	N	Y	Y	N
7 *Hobson*	Y	N	Y	Y	Y	N	Y	Y
8 *Boehner*	Y	N	Y	Y	Y	N	Y	Y
9 Kaptur	?	?	?	?	?	?	?	?
10 Kucinich	N	Y	N	Y	Y	N	Y	N
11 Stokes	N	?	N	N	N	Y	N	N
12 *Kasich*	Y	N	Y	Y	Y	N	Y	?
13 Brown	N	Y	N	N	N	Y	N	N
14 Sawyer	N	Y	N	N	N	Y	N	N
15 *Pryce*	Y	N	Y	Y	Y	N	Y	Y
16 *Regula*	Y	N	Y	Y	Y	N	Y	Y
17 Traficant	N	N	Y	Y	Y	N	Y	N
18 *Ney*	Y	N	Y	Y	Y	N	Y	Y
19 *LaTourette*	Y	N	Y	Y	Y	N	Y	Y
OKLAHOMA								
1 *Largent*	Y	N	Y	Y	Y	N	Y	N
2 *Coburn*	Y	N	Y	Y	Y	N	Y	N
3 *Watkins*	Y	N	Y	Y	Y	N	Y	Y
4 *Watts*	Y	N	Y	Y	Y	N	Y	Y
5 *Istook*	Y	N	Y	Y	Y	N	Y	Y
6 *Lucas*	Y	N	Y	Y	Y	N	Y	Y
OREGON								
1 Furse	N	Y	N	N	N	Y	N	N
2 *Smith*	Y	N	Y	Y	Y	N	Y	Y
3 Blumenauer	N	Y	N	N	N	Y	N	N
4 DeFazio	N	Y	N	N	N	Y	N	N
5 Hooley	N	Y	N	N	N	Y	N	N
PENNSYLVANIA								
1 Foglietta	N	Y	N	N	N	N	Y	N
2 Fattah	N	?	N	N	N	Y	N	N
3 Borski	N	Y	N	Y	Y	N	Y	N
4 Klink	N	Y	Y	Y	Y	N	Y	N
5 *Peterson*	Y	N	Y	Y	Y	N	Y	Y
6 Holden	N	Y	Y	Y	Y	N	Y	N
7 *Weldon*	Y	N	Y	Y	Y	N	Y	Y
8 *Greenwood*	Y	N	N	N	N	Y	N	Y
9 *Shuster*	Y	N	Y	Y	Y	N	Y	Y
10 *McDade*	N	N	Y	Y	Y	N	Y	Y
11 Kanjorski	N	Y	Y	Y	Y	N	Y	N
12 Murtha	N	Y	Y	Y	Y	N	Y	N
13 *Fox*	Y	N	Y	Y	Y	N	Y	Y
14 Coyne	N	Y	N	N	N	Y	N	N
15 McHale	N	Y	N	N	N	N	Y	N
16 *Pitts*	Y	N	Y	Y	Y	N	Y	Y
17 *Gekas*	Y	N	Y	Y	Y	N	Y	Y
18 Doyle	N	Y	Y	Y	Y	N	Y	N
19 *Goodling*	Y	N	Y	Y	Y	N	Y	Y
20 Mascara	N	Y	Y	Y	Y	N	Y	N
21 *English*	N	N	Y	Y	Y	N	Y	Y
RHODE ISLAND								
1 Kennedy	N	Y	N	N	N	Y	Y	N
2 Weygand	N	?	N	N	Y	N	Y	N
SOUTH CAROLINA								
1 *Sanford*	Y	N	Y	Y	Y	N	Y	N
2 *Spence*	Y	N	Y	Y	Y	N	Y	Y
3 *Graham*	Y	N	Y	Y	Y	N	Y	N
4 *Inglis*	Y	N	Y	Y	Y	N	Y	N
5 Spratt	N	Y	N	N	N	Y	Y	N
6 Clyburn	N	Y	N	N	N	Y	N	N
SOUTH DAKOTA								
AL *Thune*	Y	N	Y	Y	Y	N	Y	Y

	59	60	61	62	63	64	65	
TENNESSEE								
1 *Jenkins*	Y	N	Y	Y	Y	N	Y	Y
2 *Duncan*	Y	N	Y	Y	Y	N	Y	Y
3 *Wamp*	Y	N	Y	Y	Y	N	Y	Y
4 *Hilleary*	Y	N	Y	+	Y	N	Y	Y
5 Clement	N	?	Y	Y	Y	N	Y	N
6 Gordon	N	Y	N	Y	Y	N	Y	N
7 *Bryant*	Y	N	Y	Y	Y	N	Y	Y
8 Tanner	Y	Y	N	N	N	N	Y	N
9 Ford	N	Y	N	N	N	Y	N	N
TEXAS								
1 Sandlin	N	Y	N	N	N	Y	Y	N
2 Turner	N	?	Y	Y	Y	N	Y	N
3 *Johnson, Sam*	Y	N	Y	Y	Y	N	Y	Y
4 Hall	Y	N	Y	Y	Y	N	Y	N
5 *Sessions*	Y	N	Y	Y	Y	N	Y	Y
6 *Barton*	Y	N	Y	Y	Y	N	Y	Y
7 *Archer*	Y	N	Y	Y	Y	N	Y	Y
8 *Brady*	Y	N	Y	Y	Y	N	Y	Y
9 Lampson	N	Y	N	N	N	Y	Y	N
10 Doggett	N	Y	N	N	N	Y	N	N
11 Edwards	N	Y	N	N	N	Y	N	N
12 *Granger*	Y	N	Y	Y	Y	N	Y	Y
13 *Thornberry*	Y	N	Y	Y	Y	N	Y	Y
14 *Paul*	Y	N	Y	Y	Y	N	Y	Y
15 Hinojosa	N	Y	N	N	N	Y	Y	N
16 Reyes	N	Y	N	N	N	Y	Y	N
17 Stenholm	Y	?	Y	Y	Y	N	Y	N
18 Jackson-Lee	N	Y	N	N	N	Y	N	N
19 *Combest*	Y	N	Y	Y	Y	N	Y	Y
20 Gonzalez	N	Y	N	N	N	Y	Y	N
21 *Smith*	Y	N	Y	Y	Y	N	Y	?
22 *DeLay*	Y	N	Y	Y	Y	N	Y	Y
23 *Bonilla*	Y	N	Y	Y	Y	N	Y	Y
24 Frost	N	Y	N	N	N	Y	N	N
25 Bentsen	N	Y	N	N	N	Y	N	N
26 *Armey*	Y	N	Y	Y	Y	N	Y	Y
27 Ortiz	N	Y	Y	Y	Y	N	Y	N
28 Vacant								
29 Green	N	Y	N	N	N	Y	N	N
30 Johnson, E.B.	N	Y	N	N	N	Y	N	N
UTAH								
1 *Hansen*	Y	N	Y	Y	Y	N	Y	Y
2 *Cook*	Y	N	Y	Y	Y	N	Y	Y
3 *Cannon*	Y	N	Y	Y	Y	N	Y	Y
VERMONT								
AL *Sanders*	N	Y	N	N	N	Y	N	N
VIRGINIA								
1 *Bateman*	Y	N	Y	Y	Y	N	Y	Y
2 Pickett	Y	Y	N	N	N	N	N	N
3 Scott	N	Y	N	N	N	Y	N	N
4 Sisisky	N	Y	N	Y	Y	N	Y	N
5 Goode	Y	Y	Y	Y	Y	N	Y	N
6 *Goodlatte*	Y	N	Y	Y	Y	N	Y	Y
7 *Bliley*	Y	N	Y	Y	Y	N	Y	Y
8 Moran	N	Y	N	N	N	Y	Y	N
9 Boucher	N	Y	N	N	N	Y	N	N
10 *Wolf*	Y	N	Y	Y	Y	N	Y	Y
11 *Davis*	Y	N	Y	Y	Y	N	Y	Y
WASHINGTON								
1 *White*	Y	N	Y	Y	Y	N	Y	Y
2 *Metcalf*	N	N	Y	Y	Y	N	Y	Y
3 *Smith, Linda*	Y	N	Y	?	Y	N	Y	?
4 *Hastings*	Y	N	Y	Y	Y	N	Y	Y
5 *Nethercutt*	Y	N	Y	Y	Y	N	Y	Y
6 Dicks	N	Y	N	N	N	Y	N	N
7 McDermott	N	Y	N	N	N	Y	N	N
8 *Dunn*	Y	N	Y	Y	Y	N	Y	Y
9 Smith, Adam	N	Y	N	N	N	Y	N	N
WEST VIRGINIA								
1 Mollohan	N	N	Y	Y	Y	N	Y	N
2 Wise	N	Y	N	N	N	Y	N	N
3 Rahall	N	N	Y	Y	Y	N	Y	N
WISCONSIN								
1 *Neumann*	Y	N	Y	Y	Y	N	Y	N
2 *Klug*	Y	?	N	N	Y	Y	Y	Y
3 Kind	N	Y	N	N	N	Y	Y	N
4 Kleczka	N	N	N	Y	N	Y	Y	N
5 Barrett	N	Y	N	N	N	Y	Y	N
6 *Petri*	Y	N	Y	Y	Y	N	Y	Y
7 Obey	N	Y	N	N	Y	Y	Y	N
8 Johnson	N	Y	N	N	N	Y	Y	N
9 *Sensenbrenner*	Y	N	Y	Y	Y	N	Y	?
WYOMING								
AL *Cubin*	Y	N	Y	Y	Y	N	Y	Y

Southern states - Ala., Ark., Fla., Ga., Ky., La., Miss., N.C., Okla., S.C., Tenn., Texas, Va.

HOUSE VOTES 68, 69, 70, 71

68. Procedural Motion/Journal. Approval of the House Journal of Thursday, March 20, 1997. Approved 328-49: R 190-15; D 137-34 (ND 100-27, SD 37-7); I 1-0, March 21, 1997.

69. H Res 91. House Committee Funding/Rule. Adoption of the rule (H Res 105) to provide for House floor consideration of the resolution to authorize temporary funding at current levels for the operations of House committees from April 1, 1997, through May 2, 1997, except the Government Reform and Oversight Committee, which is authorized $20 million for the 105th Congress. The resolution authorizes a $7.9 million reserve fund that would be allocated by the House Oversight Committee to meet currently unanticipated committee needs. Adopted 218-179: R 217-0; D 1-178 (ND 1-132, SD 0-46); I 0-1, March 21, 1997.

70. H Res 91. House Committee Funding/Recommit. Gejdenson, D-Conn., motion to recommit the resolution to the House Oversight Committee with instructions to report it back with an amendment to authorize temporary funding at current levels for the operations of House committees from April 1, 1997, through May 2, 1997, including the Government Reform and Oversight Committee, and remove authorization for a $7.9 million reserve fund that would be allocated by the House Oversight Committee to meet currently unanticipated committee needs. Motion rejected 176-214: R 1-213; D 174-1 (ND 131-1, SD 43-0); I 1-0, March 21, 1997.

71. H Res 91. House Committee Funding/Adoption. Adoption of the resolution to authorize temporary funding at current levels for the operations of House committees from April 1, 1997, through May 2, 1997, except the Government Reform and Oversight Committee, which is authorized $20 million for the 105th Congress. The resolution authorizes a $7.9 million reserve fund that would be allocated by the House Oversight Committee to meet currently unanticipated committee needs. Adopted 213-179: R 211-3; D 2-175 (ND 1-132, SD 1-43); I 0-1, March 21, 1997.

KEY

- Y Voted for (yea).
- # Paired for.
- \+ Announced for.
- N Voted against (nay).
- X Paired against.
- \- Announced against.
- P Voted "present."
- C Voted "present" to avoid possible conflict of interest.
- ? Did not vote or otherwise make a position known.

Democrats **Republicans**
Independent

	68	69	70	71
ALABAMA				
1 **Callahan**	Y	Y	N	Y
2 **Everett**	Y	Y	N	?
3 **Riley**	Y	Y	N	Y
4 **Aderholt**	Y	Y	N	Y
5 Cramer	Y	N	Y	N
6 **Bachus**	Y	Y	N	Y
7 Hilliard	N	N	Y	N
ALASKA				
AL **Young**	Y	Y	N	Y
ARIZONA				
1 **Salmon**	Y	Y	N	Y
2 Pastor	Y	N	Y	N
3 **Stump**	Y	Y	N	Y
4 **Shadegg**	Y	Y	N	Y
5 **Kolbe**	Y	Y	N	Y
6 **Hayworth**	Y	Y	N	Y
ARKANSAS				
1 Berry	Y	N	Y	N
2 Snyder	Y	N	Y	N
3 **Hutchinson**	Y	Y	N	Y
4 **Dickey**	N	Y	N	Y
CALIFORNIA				
1 **Riggs**	?	Y	-	Y
2 **Herger**	?	Y	N	Y
3 Fazio	N	N	Y	N
4 **Doolittle**	Y	Y	N	Y
5 Matsui	Y	N	Y	N
6 Woolsey	Y	N	Y	N
7 Miller	N	N	Y	N
8 Pelosi	?	?	?	?
9 Dellums	Y	N	Y	N
10 Tauscher	Y	N	Y	N
11 **Pombo**	Y	Y	N	Y
12 Lantos	Y	N	Y	N
13 Stark	?	?	?	?
14 Eshoo	Y	N	Y	N
15 **Campbell**	Y	Y	N	Y
16 Lofgren	Y	N	Y	N
17 Farr	Y	N	Y	N
18 Condit	Y	N	Y	N
19 **Radanovich**	Y	Y	N	Y
20 Dooley	Y	N	Y	N
21 **Thomas**	Y	Y	N	Y
22 Capps	Y	N	Y	N
23 **Gallegly**	Y	Y	N	Y
24 Sherman	Y	N	Y	N
25 **McKeon**	Y	Y	N	Y
26 Berman	?	?	?	?
27 **Rogan**	Y	Y	N	Y
28 **Dreier**	Y	Y	N	Y
29 Waxman	Y	N	Y	N
30 Becerra	?	N	Y	N
31 Martinez	Y	N	Y	N
32 Dixon	?	N	Y	N
33 Roybal-Allard	Y	N	Y	N
34 Torres	?	?	?	?
35 Waters	Y	N	Y	?
36 Harman	Y	N	Y	N
37 Millender-McD.	Y	N	Y	N
38 **Horn**	Y	Y	N	Y
39 **Royce**	Y	Y	N	Y
40 **Lewis**	Y	Y	N	Y

	68	69	70	71
41 **Kim**	Y	Y	N	Y
42 Brown	N	N	Y	N
43 **Calvert**	Y	Y	N	Y
44 **Bono**	Y	Y	N	Y
45 **Rohrabacher**	Y	Y	N	Y
46 Sanchez	Y	N	Y	N
47 **Cox**	?	Y	N	Y
48 **Packard**	Y	Y	N	Y
49 **Bilbray**	P	Y	N	Y
50 Filner	N	N	Y	N
51 **Cunningham**	Y	Y	N	Y
52 **Hunter**	Y	Y	N	Y
COLORADO				
1 DeGette	Y	N	Y	N
2 Skaggs	N	N	Y	N
3 **McInnis**	?	Y	N	Y
4 **Schaffer**	Y	Y	N	Y
5 **Hefley**	N	Y	N	Y
6 **Schaefer**	Y	Y	N	Y
CONNECTICUT				
1 Kennelly	Y	N	Y	N
2 Gejdenson	Y	N	Y	N
3 DeLauro	Y	N	Y	N
4 **Shays**	Y	Y	N	Y
5 Maloney	Y	N	Y	N
6 **Johnson**	Y	Y	N	Y
DELAWARE				
AL **Castle**	Y	Y	N	Y
FLORIDA				
1 **Scarborough**	Y	Y	N	Y
2 Boyd	Y	N	Y	N
3 Brown	?	N	Y	N
4 **Fowler**	Y	Y	N	Y
5 Thurman	Y	N	Y	N
6 **Stearns**	?	Y	N	Y
7 **Mica**	Y	Y	N	Y
8 **McCollum**	Y	Y	N	Y
9 **Bilirakis**	Y	Y	N	Y
10 **Young**	Y	Y	N	Y
11 Davis	Y	N	Y	N
12 **Canady**	Y	Y	N	Y
13 **Miller**	Y	Y	N	Y
14 **Goss**	Y	Y	N	Y
15 **Weldon**	Y	Y	N	Y
16 **Foley**	+	Y	N	Y
17 Meek	Y	N	Y	N
18 **Ros-Lehtinen**	Y	Y	N	Y
19 Wexler	?	?	?	?
20 Deutsch	Y	N	?	X
21 **Diaz-Balart**	Y	Y	N	Y
22 **Shaw**	Y	Y	N	Y
23 Hastings	?	?	?	?
GEORGIA				
1 **Kingston**	Y	Y	N	Y
2 Bishop	Y	?	?	?
3 **Collins**	?	Y	N	Y
4 McKinney	Y	N	Y	N
5 Lewis	Y	N	Y	N
6 **Gingrich**				
7 **Barr**	Y	Y	N	Y
8 **Chambliss**	Y	Y	N	Y
9 **Deal**	Y	Y	N	Y
10 **Norwood**	Y	Y	?	?
11 **Linder**	Y	Y	N	Y
HAWAII				
1 Abercrombie	N	N	Y	N
2 Mink	Y	N	Y	N
IDAHO				
1 **Chenoweth**	Y	Y	N	Y
2 **Crapo**	Y	Y	N	Y
ILLINOIS				
1 Rush	N	N	Y	N
2 Jackson	Y	N	Y	N
3 Lipinski	?	?	?	?
4 Gutierrez	?	?	?	?
5 Blagojevich	Y	N	Y	N
6 **Hyde**	Y	Y	N	Y
7 Davis	Y	N	Y	N
8 **Crane**	?	Y	N	Y
9 Yates	N	N	Y	N
10 **Porter**	Y	Y	N	Y
11 **Weller**	N	Y	N	Y
12 Costello	Y	N	Y	N
13 **Fawell**	N	Y	N	Y
14 **Hastert**	Y	Y	N	Y

ND Northern Democrats SD Southern Democrats

	68	69	70	71
15 ***Ewing***	Y	Y	N	Y
16 ***Manzullo***	Y	Y	N	Y
17 Evans	Y	N	Y	N
18 ***LaHood***	Y	Y	N	Y
19 Poshard	Y	N	Y	N
20 ***Shimkus***	Y	Y	N	Y
INDIANA				
1 Visclosky	N	N	Y	N
2 ***McIntosh***	?	Y	N	Y
3 Roemer	Y	N	Y	N
4 ***Souder***	Y	Y	N	Y
5 ***Buyer***	?	?	?	?
6 ***Burton***	Y	Y	N	Y
7 ***Pease***	Y	Y	N	Y
8 ***Hostettler***	Y	Y	N	Y
9 Hamilton	Y	N	Y	N
10 Carson	Y	N	Y	N
IOWA				
1 ***Leach***	Y	Y	N	Y
2 ***Nussle***	Y	Y	N	Y
3 Boswell	Y	N	Y	N
4 ***Ganske***	Y	Y	N	Y
5 ***Latham***	Y	Y	N	Y
KANSAS				
1 ***Moran***	Y	Y	N	Y
2 ***Ryun***	Y	Y	N	Y
3 ***Snowbarger***	Y	Y	N	Y
4 ***Tiahrt***	Y	Y	N	Y
KENTUCKY				
1 ***Whitfield***	Y	Y	N	Y
2 ***Lewis***	Y	Y	N	Y
3 ***Northup***	Y	Y	N	Y
4 ***Bunning***	Y	Y	?	#
5 ***Rogers***	Y	Y	N	Y
6 Baesler	Y	N	Y	Y
LOUISIANA				
1 ***Livingston***	Y	Y	N	Y
2 Jefferson	Y	N	Y	N
3 ***Tauzin***	Y	Y	N	Y
4 ***McCrery***	Y	Y	N	Y
5 ***Cooksey***	Y	Y	N	Y
6 ***Baker***	Y	Y	N	Y
7 John	Y	N	Y	N
MAINE				
1 Allen	Y	N	Y	N
2 Baldacci	Y	N	Y	N
MARYLAND				
1 ***Gilchrest***	Y	Y	N	Y
2 ***Ehrlich***	Y	Y	N	Y
3 Cardin	Y	N	Y	N
4 Wynn	Y	N	Y	N
5 Hoyer	Y	N	Y	N
6 ***Bartlett***	Y	Y	N	Y
7 Cummings	?	N	Y	N
8 ***Morella***	Y	Y	N	Y
MASSACHUSETTS				
1 Olver	Y	N	Y	N
2 Neal	N	N	Y	N
3 McGovern	Y	N	Y	N
4 Frank	?	?	?	?
5 Meehan	?	?	?	?
6 Tierney	Y	N	Y	N
7 Markey	Y	N	Y	N
8 Kennedy	Y	N	Y	N
9 Moakley	Y	N	Y	N
10 Delahunt	Y	N	Y	N
MICHIGAN				
1 Stupak	Y	N	Y	N
2 ***Hoekstra***	Y	Y	N	Y
3 ***Ehlers***	Y	Y	N	Y
4 ***Camp***	Y	Y	N	Y
5 Barcia	Y	N	?	N
6 ***Upton***	Y	Y	N	Y
7 ***Smith***	Y	Y	N	Y
8 Stabenow	Y	N	Y	N
9 Kildee	Y	N	Y	N
10 Bonior	Y	N	Y	N
11 ***Knollenberg***	Y	Y	N	Y
12 Levin	Y	N	Y	N
13 Rivers	Y	N	Y	N
14 Conyers	?	?	?	?
15 Kilpatrick	Y	N	Y	N
16 Dingell	Y	N	Y	N
MINNESOTA				
1 ***Gutknecht***	N	Y	N	Y
2 Minge	Y	N	Y	N
3 ***Ramstad***	N	Y	N	Y
4 Vento	N	N	Y	N
5 Sabo	N	N	Y	N
6 Luther	Y	N	Y	N
7 Peterson	Y	N	Y	N
8 Oberstar	N	N	Y	N
MISSISSIPPI				
1 ***Wicker***	N	Y	N	Y
2 Thompson	N	N	Y	N
3 ***Pickering***	Y	Y	N	Y
4 ***Parker***	Y	Y	N	Y
5 Taylor	N	N	Y	N
MISSOURI				
1 Clay	N	N	Y	N
2 ***Talent***	Y	Y	N	Y
3 Gephardt	Y	N	Y	N
4 Skelton	Y	N	Y	N
5 McCarthy	Y	N	Y	N
6 Danner	Y	N	Y	N
7 ***Blunt***	Y	Y	N	Y
8 ***Emerson***	Y	Y	N	Y
9 ***Hulshof***	Y	Y	N	Y
MONTANA				
AL ***Hill***	Y	Y	N	N
NEBRASKA				
1 ***Bereuter***	Y	Y	N	Y
2 ***Christensen***	Y	Y	N	Y
3 ***Barrett***	Y	Y	N	Y
NEVADA				
1 ***Ensign***	N	Y	N	Y
2 ***Gibbons***	Y	Y	N	Y
NEW HAMPSHIRE				
1 ***Sununu***	Y	Y	N	Y
2 ***Bass***	Y	Y	N	Y
NEW JERSEY				
1 Andrews	?	?	?	?
2 ***LoBiondo***	N	Y	N	Y
3 ***Saxton***	Y	Y	N	Y
4 ***Smith***	?	Y	N	Y
5 ***Roukema***	Y	Y	N	N
6 Pallone	Y	N	Y	N
7 ***Franks***	?	?	?	?
8 Pascrell	?	?	?	?
9 Rothman	?	?	?	?
10 Payne	Y	N	Y	N
11 ***Frelinghuysen***	Y	Y	N	Y
12 ***Pappas***	Y	Y	N	Y
13 Menendez	N	N	Y	N
NEW MEXICO				
1 ***Schiff***	Y	Y	N	Y
2 ***Skeen***	Y	Y	N	Y
3 Vacant				
NEW YORK				
1 ***Forbes***	?	?	?	?
2 ***Lazio***	Y	Y	N	Y
3 ***King***	N	Y	N	Y
4 McCarthy	Y	N	Y	N
5 Ackerman	Y	N	Y	N
6 Flake	?	?	?	?
7 Manton	Y	N	Y	N
8 Nadler	?	?	Y	N
9 Schumer	Y	N	Y	N
10 Towns	?	N	Y	N
11 Owens	?	?	?	?
12 Velázquez	?	?	?	?
13 ***Molinari***	Y	Y	N	Y
14 Maloney	N	N	Y	N
15 Rangel	Y	N	Y	N
16 Serrano	Y	N	Y	N
17 Engel	?	N	Y	N
18 Lowey	Y	N	Y	N
19 ***Kelly***	Y	Y	N	Y
20 ***Gilman***	Y	Y	N	Y
21 McNulty	Y	N	Y	N
22 ***Solomon***	Y	Y	N	Y
23 ***Boehlert***	Y	Y	N	Y
24 ***McHugh***	Y	Y	N	Y
25 ***Walsh***	Y	Y	N	Y
26 Hinchey	N	N	Y	N
27 ***Paxon***	Y	Y	N	Y
28 Slaughter	N	N	?	N
29 LaFalce	N	N	Y	N
30 ***Quinn***	Y	Y	N	Y
31 ***Houghton***	Y	Y	N	Y
NORTH CAROLINA				
1 Clayton	Y	N	Y	N
2 Etheridge	Y	N	Y	N
3 ***Jones***	N	Y	N	Y
4 Price	Y	N	Y	N
5 ***Burr***	Y	Y	N	Y
6 ***Coble***	Y	Y	N	Y
7 McIntyre	Y	N	Y	N
8 Hefner	Y	N	?	N
9 ***Myrick***	Y	Y	N	Y
10 ***Ballenger***	Y	Y	N	Y
11 ***Taylor***	Y	Y	N	Y
12 Watt	N	N	Y	N
NORTH DAKOTA				
AL Pomeroy	Y	N	Y	N
OHIO				
1 ***Chabot***	Y	Y	N	Y
2 ***Portman***	Y	Y	N	Y
3 Hall	Y	N	Y	N
4 ***Oxley***	?	?	?	#
5 ***Gillmor***	Y	Y	N	Y
6 Strickland	N	N	Y	N
7 ***Hobson***	Y	Y	N	Y
8 ***Boehner***	Y	Y	N	Y
9 Kaptur	?	?	?	X
10 Kucinich	N	N	Y	N
11 Stokes	Y	N	Y	N
12 ***Kasich***	?	?	?	?
13 Brown	N	N	Y	N
14 Sawyer	Y	N	Y	N
15 ***Pryce***	Y	Y	N	Y
16 ***Regula***	Y	Y	N	Y
17 Traficant	Y	Y	N	Y
18 ***Ney***	Y	Y	N	Y
19 ***LaTourette***	Y	Y	N	Y
OKLAHOMA				
1 ***Largent***	Y	Y	N	Y
2 ***Coburn***	Y	Y	N	Y
3 ***Watkins***	Y	Y	N	Y
4 ***Watts***	N	Y	N	Y
5 ***Istook***	Y	Y	N	Y
6 ***Lucas***	Y	Y	N	Y
OREGON				
1 Furse	N	N	Y	N
2 ***Smith***	Y	Y	N	Y
3 Blumenauer	?	?	?	?
4 DeFazio	N	N	Y	N
5 Hooley	N	N	Y	N
PENNSYLVANIA				
1 Foglietta	Y	N	Y	N
2 Fattah	Y	N	Y	N
3 Borski	N	N	Y	N
4 Klink	Y	N	Y	N
5 ***Peterson***	Y	Y	N	Y
6 Holden	Y	N	Y	N
7 ***Weldon***	Y	Y	N	Y
8 ***Greenwood***	Y	Y	N	Y
9 ***Shuster***	Y	Y	N	Y
10 ***McDade***	Y	Y	N	Y
11 Kanjorski	Y	N	Y	N
12 Murtha	Y	N	Y	N
13 ***Fox***	Y	Y	N	Y
14 Coyne	Y	N	Y	N
15 McHale	Y	N	Y	N
16 ***Pitts***	Y	Y	N	Y
17 ***Gekas***	Y	Y	N	Y
18 Doyle	Y	N	Y	N
19 ***Goodling***	Y	Y	N	Y
20 Mascara	Y	N	Y	N
21 ***English***	N	Y	N	Y
RHODE ISLAND				
1 Kennedy	Y	N	Y	N
2 Weygand	Y	N	Y	N
SOUTH CAROLINA				
1 ***Sanford***	Y	Y	N	Y
2 ***Spence***	Y	Y	N	Y
3 ***Graham***	Y	Y	N	Y
4 ***Inglis***	Y	Y	N	Y
5 Spratt	Y	N	?	?
6 Clyburn	?	?	?	?
SOUTH DAKOTA				
AL ***Thune***	N	Y	N	Y
TENNESSEE				
1 ***Jenkins***	Y	Y	N	Y
2 ***Duncan***	Y	Y	N	Y
3 ***Wamp***	N	Y	N	Y
4 ***Hilleary***	Y	Y	N	Y
5 Clement	Y	N	Y	N
6 Gordon	?	N	Y	N
7 ***Bryant***	Y	Y	N	Y
8 Tanner	Y	N	Y	N
9 Ford	?	N	Y	N
TEXAS				
1 Sandlin	Y	N	Y	N
2 Turner	Y	N	Y	N
3 ***Johnson, Sam***	Y	Y	N	Y
4 Hall	Y	N	Y	N
5 ***Sessions***	Y	Y	N	Y
6 ***Barton***	Y	Y	N	Y
7 ***Archer***	Y	Y	N	Y
8 ***Brady***	Y	Y	N	Y
9 Lampson	Y	N	Y	N
10 Doggett	Y	N	Y	N
11 Edwards	Y	N	Y	N
12 ***Granger***	Y	Y	N	Y
13 ***Thornberry***	?	?	?	?
14 ***Paul***	Y	Y	N	Y
15 Hinojosa	Y	N	Y	N
16 Reyes	Y	N	Y	N
17 Stenholm	Y	N	Y	N
18 Jackson-Lee	N	N	Y	N
19 ***Combest***	Y	Y	N	Y
20 Gonzalez	?	N	Y	N
21 ***Smith***	?	?	?	?
22 ***DeLay***	Y	Y	N	Y
23 ***Bonilla***	Y	Y	N	Y
24 Frost	Y	N	Y	N
25 Bentsen	Y	N	Y	N
26 ***Armey***	Y	Y	N	Y
27 Ortiz	Y	N	Y	N
28 Vacant				
29 Green	?	?	?	?
30 Johnson, E.B.	N	N	Y	N
UTAH				
1 ***Hansen***	Y	Y	N	Y
2 ***Cook***	Y	Y	N	Y
3 ***Cannon***	Y	Y	N	Y
VERMONT				
AL *Sanders*	Y	N	Y	N
VIRGINIA				
1 ***Bateman***	Y	Y	N	Y
2 Pickett	N	?	?	?
3 Scott	?	?	?	?
4 Sisisky	Y	N	Y	N
5 Goode	Y	N	Y	N
6 ***Goodlatte***	Y	Y	N	Y
7 ***Bliley***	Y	Y	N	Y
8 Moran	Y	N	Y	N
9 Boucher	?	?	?	?
10 ***Wolf***	Y	Y	N	Y
11 ***Davis***	Y	Y	N	Y
WASHINGTON				
1 ***White***	Y	Y	N	Y
2 ***Metcalf***	Y	Y	N	Y
3 ***Smith, Linda***	?	?	?	?
4 ***Hastings***	Y	Y	N	Y
5 ***Nethercutt***	Y	Y	N	Y
6 Dicks	Y	N	Y	N
7 McDermott	N	N	Y	N
8 ***Dunn***	Y	Y	N	Y
9 Smith, Adam	Y	N	Y	N
WEST VIRGINIA				
1 Mollohan	Y	N	Y	N
2 Wise	Y	N	Y	N
3 Rahall	Y	N	Y	N
WISCONSIN				
1 ***Neumann***	Y	Y	Y	N
2 ***Klug***	?	Y	N	Y
3 Kind	Y	N	Y	N
4 Kleczka	?	N	Y	N
5 Barrett	Y	N	Y	N
6 ***Petri***	Y	Y	N	Y
7 Obey	Y	N	Y	N
8 Johnson	Y	N	Y	N
9 ***Sensenbrenner***	?	?	?	?
WYOMING				
AL ***Cubin***	Y	Y	N	Y

Southern states - Ala., Ark., Fla., Ga., Ky., La., Miss., N.C., Okla., S.C., Tenn., Texas, Va.

HOUSE VOTES 72, 73, 74, 75

72. HR 28. Rural Rental Housing Loan Guarantee/Passage. Lazio, R-N.Y., motion to suspend the rules and pass the bill to authorize permanently the Rural Multifamily Rental Housing Loan Guarantee Program, which guarantees rural rental housing loans made by private lenders to families with low and moderate incomes. Motion agreed to 397-14: R 207-14; D 189-0 (ND 137-0, SD 52-0); I 1-0, April 8, 1997. A two-thirds majority of those present and voting (274 in this case) is required for passage under suspension of the rules. A "yea" was a vote in support of the president's position.

73. HR 1000. Food Stamp Benefits to Prisoners/Passage. Smith, R-Ore., motion to suspend the rules and pass the bill to require states to verify that prisoners in any penal facility are not counted as household members when determining eligibility for food stamp benefits. Motion agreed to 409-0: R 220-0; D 188-0 (ND 136-0, SD 52-0); I 1-0, April 8, 1997. A two-thirds majority of those present and voting (273 in this case) is required for passage under suspension of the rules.

74. H Res 107. Expedited Floor Procedures/Previous Question. Dreier, R-Calif., motion to order the previous question (thus ending debate and the possibility of amendment) on adoption of the resolution to permit House floor consideration of bills under suspension of the rules on Wednesday, April 9 or on Thursday, April 10. Motion agreed to 213-196: R 213-0; D 0-195 (ND 0-144, SD 0-51); I 0-1, April 9, 1997.

75. HR 1003. Assisted Suicide Funding Ban/Passage. Bliley, R-Va., motion to suspend the rules and pass the bill to prohibit the use of federal funds for assisted suicide, euthanasia and mercy killing. Motion agreed to 398-16: R 216-0; D 181-16 (ND 130-14, SD 51-2); I 1-0, April 10, 1997. A two-thirds majority of those present and voting (276 in this case) is required for passage under suspension of the rules.

KEY

- Y Voted for (yea).
- # Paired for.
- + Announced for.
- N Voted against (nay).
- X Paired against.
- – Announced against.
- P Voted "present."
- C Voted "present" to avoid possible conflict of interest.
- ? Did not vote or otherwise make a position known.

Democrats ***Republicans***
Independent

	72	73	74	75
ALABAMA				
1 ***Callahan***	Y	Y	Y	Y
2 ***Everett***	Y	Y	Y	Y
3 ***Riley***	Y	Y	Y	Y
4 ***Aderholt***	Y	Y	Y	Y
5 Cramer	Y	Y	N	Y
6 ***Bachus***	Y	Y	Y	Y
7 Hilliard	Y	Y	N	Y
ALASKA				
AL ***Young***	Y	Y	?	Y
ARIZONA				
1 ***Salmon***	N	Y	Y	Y
2 Pastor	Y	Y	N	Y
3 ***Stump***	N	Y	Y	Y
4 ***Shadegg***	Y	Y	Y	Y
5 ***Kolbe***	Y	Y	Y	Y
6 ***Hayworth***	Y	Y	Y	Y
ARKANSAS				
1 Berry	Y	Y	N	Y
2 Snyder	Y	Y	N	Y
3 ***Hutchinson***	Y	Y	Y	Y
4 ***Dickey***	Y	Y	Y	?
CALIFORNIA				
1 ***Riggs***	Y	Y	Y	Y
2 ***Herger***	Y	Y	Y	Y
3 Fazio	Y	Y	N	Y
4 ***Doolittle***	Y	Y	?	?
5 Matsui	Y	Y	N	Y
6 Woolsey	Y	Y	N	Y
7 Miller	Y	Y	N	N
8 Pelosi	Y	Y	N	Y
9 Dellums	Y	Y	N	N
10 Tauscher	Y	Y	N	Y
11 ***Pombo***	Y	Y	Y	Y
12 Lantos	Y	Y	N	Y
13 Stark	?	?	?	N
14 Eshoo	Y	Y	N	Y
15 ***Campbell***	Y	Y	Y	Y
16 Lofgren	Y	Y	N	Y
17 Farr	Y	Y	N	Y
18 Condit	Y	Y	N	Y
19 ***Radanovich***	Y	Y	Y	+
20 Dooley	Y	Y	N	Y
21 ***Thomas***	Y	Y	Y	Y
22 Capps	Y	Y	N	+
23 ***Gallegly***	Y	Y	Y	Y
24 Sherman	Y	Y	N	Y
25 ***McKeon***	Y	Y	Y	Y
26 Berman	Y	?	N	Y
27 ***Rogan***	Y	Y	Y	Y
28 ***Dreier***	Y	Y	Y	Y
29 Waxman	Y	Y	N	N
30 Becerra	Y	Y	?	N
31 Martinez	Y	Y	N	Y
32 Dixon	Y	Y	N	Y
33 Roybal-Allard	Y	Y	N	Y
34 Torres	?	Y	N	Y
35 Waters	Y	Y	N	N
36 Harman	Y	Y	N	Y
37 Millender-McD.	Y	Y	N	Y
38 ***Horn***	Y	Y	Y	Y
39 ***Royce***	N	Y	Y	Y
40 ***Lewis***	Y	Y	Y	Y
41 ***Kim***	Y	Y	Y	Y
42 Brown	Y	Y	N	Y
43 ***Calvert***	Y	Y	Y	Y
44 ***Bono***	Y	Y	Y	+
45 ***Rohrabacher***	N	Y	Y	Y
46 Sanchez	Y	Y	N	Y
47 ***Cox***	Y	Y	Y	Y
48 ***Packard***	Y	Y	Y	Y
49 ***Bilbray***	Y	Y	Y	Y
50 Filner	?	?	?	?
51 ***Cunningham***	Y	Y	Y	Y
52 ***Hunter***	Y	Y	Y	Y
COLORADO				
1 DeGette	Y	Y	N	N
2 Skaggs	Y	Y	N	Y
3 ***McInnis***	Y	Y	Y	Y
4 ***Schaffer***	Y	Y	Y	+
5 ***Hefley***	Y	Y	Y	Y
6 ***Schaefer***	Y	Y	Y	Y
CONNECTICUT				
1 Kennelly	Y	Y	N	Y
2 Gejdenson	Y	Y	N	Y
3 DeLauro	Y	Y	N	Y
4 ***Shays***	Y	Y	Y	Y
5 Maloney	Y	Y	N	Y
6 ***Johnson***	Y	Y	Y	Y
DELAWARE				
AL ***Castle***	Y	Y	Y	Y
FLORIDA				
1 ***Scarborough***	N	Y	Y	?
2 Boyd	Y	Y	?	Y
3 Brown	Y	Y	N	Y
4 ***Fowler***	Y	Y	Y	Y
5 Thurman	Y	Y	N	Y
6 ***Stearns***	Y	Y	Y	Y
7 ***Mica***	Y	Y	Y	Y
8 ***McCollum***	Y	Y	Y	Y
9 ***Bilirakis***	Y	Y	Y	Y
10 ***Young***	Y	Y	Y	Y
11 Davis	Y	Y	N	Y
12 ***Canady***	Y	Y	Y	Y
13 ***Miller***	Y	Y	Y	Y
14 ***Goss***	Y	Y	Y	Y
15 ***Weldon***	Y	Y	Y	Y
16 ***Foley***	Y	Y	Y	Y
17 Meek	Y	Y	N	Y
18 ***Ros-Lehtinen***	Y	Y	Y	Y
19 Wexler	Y	Y	N	Y
20 Deutsch	Y	Y	N	Y
21 ***Diaz-Balart***	Y	Y	Y	Y
22 ***Shaw***	Y	Y	Y	Y
23 Hastings	Y	Y	N	Y
GEORGIA				
1 ***Kingston***	Y	Y	Y	Y
2 Bishop	Y	Y	?	Y
3 ***Collins***	Y	Y	Y	Y
4 McKinney	Y	Y	N	N
5 Lewis	Y	Y	N	Y
6 ***Gingrich***				
7 ***Barr***	Y	Y	?	Y
8 ***Chambliss***	Y	Y	?	Y
9 ***Deal***	Y	Y	Y	Y
10 ***Norwood***	Y	Y	Y	Y
11 ***Linder***	Y	Y	Y	Y
HAWAII				
1 Abercrombie	Y	Y	N	Y
2 Mink	Y	Y	N	Y
IDAHO				
1 ***Chenoweth***	Y	Y	Y	Y
2 ***Crapo***	Y	Y	Y	Y
ILLINOIS				
1 Rush	Y	Y	N	Y
2 Jackson	Y	Y	N	N
3 Lipinski	Y	Y	N	Y
4 Gutierrez	?	?	N	Y
5 Blagojevich	Y	Y	N	Y
6 ***Hyde***	Y	Y	Y	Y
7 Davis	Y	Y	N	Y
8 ***Crane***	Y	Y	Y	Y
9 Yates	Y	Y	N	N
10 ***Porter***	Y	Y	?	?
11 ***Weller***	Y	Y	Y	Y
12 Costello	Y	Y	N	Y
13 ***Fawell***	Y	Y	?	Y
14 ***Hastert***	Y	Y	Y	Y
15 ***Ewing***	Y	Y	Y	Y

ND Northern Democrats SD Southern Democrats

	72	73	74	75
16 ***Manzullo***	N	Y	Y	Y
17 Evans	Y	Y	N	Y
18 ***LaHood***	Y	Y	Y	Y
19 Poshard	Y	Y	N	Y
20 ***Shimkus***	Y	Y	Y	Y
INDIANA				
1 Visclosky	Y	Y	N	Y
2 ***McIntosh***	Y	Y	Y	Y
3 Roemer	Y	Y	N	Y
4 ***Souder***	N	Y	Y	Y
5 ***Buyer***	Y	Y	Y	Y
6 ***Burton***	Y	Y	Y	Y
7 ***Pease***	Y	Y	Y	Y
8 ***Hostettler***	N	Y	Y	Y
9 Hamilton	Y	Y	N	Y
10 Carson	?	?	?	?
IOWA				
1 ***Leach***	Y	Y	Y	Y
2 ***Nussle***	Y	Y	Y	Y
3 Boswell	Y	Y	N	Y
4 ***Ganske***	Y	Y	Y	Y
5 ***Latham***	Y	Y	Y	Y
KANSAS				
1 ***Moran***	Y	Y	Y	Y
2 ***Ryun***	Y	Y	?	Y
3 ***Snowbarger***	Y	Y	Y	Y
4 ***Tiahrt***	Y	Y	Y	Y
KENTUCKY				
1 ***Whitfield***	Y	Y	Y	Y
2 ***Lewis***	Y	Y	Y	Y
3 ***Northup***	Y	Y	Y	Y
4 ***Bunning***	Y	Y	Y	Y
5 ***Rogers***	Y	Y	Y	Y
6 Baesler	Y	Y	N	Y
LOUISIANA				
1 ***Livingston***	Y	Y	Y	Y
2 Jefferson	Y	Y	N	Y
3 ***Tauzin***	Y	Y	Y	Y
4 ***McCrery***	Y	Y	Y	Y
5 ***Cooksey***	Y	Y	Y	Y
6 ***Baker***	Y	Y	Y	Y
7 John	Y	Y	N	Y
MAINE				
1 Allen	Y	Y	N	Y
2 Baldacci	Y	Y	N	Y
MARYLAND				
1 ***Gilchrest***	Y	Y	Y	Y
2 ***Ehrlich***	Y	Y	Y	Y
3 Cardin	Y	Y	N	Y
4 Wynn	Y	Y	N	Y
5 Hoyer	Y	Y	N	Y
6 ***Bartlett***	Y	Y	Y	Y
7 Cummings	Y	Y	N	Y
8 ***Morella***	Y	Y	Y	Y
MASSACHUSETTS				
1 Olver	Y	Y	N	Y
2 Neal	Y	Y	N	Y
3 McGovern	Y	Y	N	Y
4 Frank	Y	Y	N	N
5 Meehan	Y	Y	N	Y
6 Tierney	Y	Y	N	Y
7 Markey	Y	Y	N	Y
8 Kennedy	Y	Y	N	Y
9 Moakley	Y	Y	N	?
10 Delahunt	Y	Y	N	Y
MICHIGAN				
1 Stupak	Y	Y	N	Y
2 ***Hoekstra***	N	Y	Y	Y
3 ***Ehlers***	Y	+	Y	Y
4 ***Camp***	Y	Y	Y	Y
5 Barcia	Y	Y	N	Y
6 ***Upton***	Y	Y	Y	Y
7 ***Smith***	Y	Y	Y	Y
8 Stabenow	Y	Y	N	Y
9 Kildee	Y	Y	N	Y
10 Bonior	Y	Y	N	Y
11 ***Knollenberg***	Y	Y	Y	Y
12 Levin	Y	Y	N	Y
13 Rivers	Y	Y	N	Y
14 Conyers	Y	Y	N	N
15 Kilpatrick	+	+	N	N
16 Dingell	Y	Y	N	Y
MINNESOTA				
1 ***Gutknecht***	Y	Y	Y	Y
2 Minge	Y	Y	N	Y

	72	73	74	75
3 ***Ramstad***	Y	Y	Y	Y
4 Vento	Y	Y	N	Y
5 Sabo	Y	Y	N	Y
6 Luther	Y	Y	N	Y
7 Peterson	Y	Y	?	?
8 Oberstar	Y	Y	N	Y
MISSISSIPPI				
1 ***Wicker***	Y	Y	Y	Y
2 Thompson	Y	Y	N	Y
3 ***Pickering***	Y	Y	Y	Y
4 ***Parker***	Y	Y	Y	Y
5 Taylor	Y	Y	N	Y
MISSOURI				
1 Clay	Y	Y	N	Y
2 ***Talent***	Y	Y	Y	Y
3 Gephardt	Y	Y	N	Y
4 Skelton	Y	Y	N	Y
5 McCarthy	Y	Y	N	Y
6 Danner	Y	Y	N	Y
7 ***Blunt***	Y	Y	Y	Y
8 ***Emerson***	Y	Y	Y	Y
9 ***Hulshof***	Y	Y	Y	Y
MONTANA				
AL ***Hill***	Y	Y	Y	Y
NEBRASKA				
1 ***Bereuter***	Y	Y	Y	Y
2 ***Christensen***	Y	Y	Y	Y
3 ***Barrett***	Y	Y	Y	Y
NEVADA				
1 ***Ensign***	Y	Y	Y	Y
2 ***Gibbons***	Y	Y	Y	Y
NEW HAMPSHIRE				
1 ***Sununu***	Y	Y	Y	Y
2 ***Bass***	Y	Y	Y	Y
NEW JERSEY				
1 Andrews	?	?	?	Y
2 ***LoBiondo***	Y	Y	Y	Y
3 ***Saxton***	Y	Y	Y	Y
4 ***Smith***	Y	Y	Y	Y
5 ***Roukema***	Y	Y	Y	Y
6 Pallone	Y	Y	N	Y
7 ***Franks***	Y	Y	Y	Y
8 Pascrell	Y	Y	N	Y
9 Rothman	Y	Y	N	Y
10 Payne	Y	Y	N	Y
11 ***Frelinghuysen***	Y	Y	Y	Y
12 ***Pappas***	Y	Y	Y	Y
13 Menendez	Y	Y	N	Y
NEW MEXICO				
1 ***Schiff***	?	?	?	?
2 ***Skeen***	Y	Y	Y	Y
3 Vacant				
NEW YORK				
1 ***Forbes***	Y	Y	Y	Y
2 ***Lazio***	Y	Y	Y	Y
3 ***King***	Y	Y	Y	Y
4 McCarthy	?	?	?	Y
5 Ackerman	Y	Y	N	Y
6 Flake	Y	Y	N	Y
7 Manton	Y	Y	N	Y
8 Nadler	Y	Y	N	N
9 Schumer	Y	Y	N	Y
10 Towns	?	?	N	Y
11 Owens	Y	Y	N	Y
12 Velázquez	?	?	N	Y
13 ***Molinari***	Y	Y	Y	Y
14 Maloney	Y	Y	N	Y
15 Rangel	Y	Y	N	Y
16 Serrano	Y	Y	N	Y
17 Engel	Y	Y	N	Y
18 Lowey	Y	Y	N	Y
19 ***Kelly***	Y	Y	Y	Y
20 ***Gilman***	Y	Y	Y	Y
21 McNulty	Y	Y	N	Y
22 ***Solomon***	Y	Y	Y	Y
23 ***Boehlert***	Y	Y	Y	Y
24 ***McHugh***	Y	Y	Y	Y
25 ***Walsh***	Y	Y	Y	Y
26 Hinchey	?	?	N	Y
27 ***Paxon***	Y	Y	Y	Y
28 Slaughter	Y	Y	N	Y
29 LaFalce	Y	Y	N	Y
30 ***Quinn***	Y	Y	Y	Y
31 ***Houghton***	Y	Y	Y	Y

	72	73	74	75
NORTH CAROLINA				
1 Clayton	Y	Y	N	Y
2 Etheridge	+	+	N	Y
3 ***Jones***	Y	Y	Y	Y
4 Price	Y	Y	N	Y
5 ***Burr***	Y	Y	Y	Y
6 ***Coble***	Y	Y	Y	Y
7 McIntyre	Y	Y	N	Y
8 Hefner	?	?	?	?
9 ***Myrick***	Y	Y	Y	Y
10 ***Ballenger***	+	+	+	+
11 ***Taylor***	Y	Y	Y	Y
12 Watt	Y	Y	N	Y
NORTH DAKOTA				
AL Pomeroy	+	+	N	?
OHIO				
1 ***Chabot***	Y	Y	Y	Y
2 ***Portman***	Y	Y	Y	Y
3 Hall	?	?	N	Y
4 ***Oxley***	Y	Y	Y	Y
5 ***Gillmor***	Y	Y	Y	Y
6 Strickland	Y	Y	N	Y
7 ***Hobson***	Y	Y	Y	Y
8 ***Boehner***	Y	Y	Y	Y
9 Kaptur	?	?	N	Y
10 Kucinich	Y	Y	N	Y
11 Stokes	Y	Y	N	Y
12 ***Kasich***	Y	Y	Y	Y
13 Brown	Y	Y	N	Y
14 Sawyer	Y	Y	N	Y
15 ***Pryce***	Y	Y	Y	Y
16 ***Regula***	Y	Y	Y	Y
17 Traficant	Y	Y	N	Y
18 ***Ney***	Y	Y	Y	Y
19 ***LaTourette***	Y	Y	Y	Y
OKLAHOMA				
1 ***Largent***	Y	Y	Y	Y
2 ***Coburn***	N	Y	Y	Y
3 ***Watkins***	Y	Y	Y	Y
4 ***Watts***	?	?	?	?
5 ***Istook***	?	?	?	Y
6 ***Lucas***	Y	Y	Y	Y
OREGON				
1 Furse	Y	Y	N	Y
2 ***Smith***	Y	Y	Y	Y
3 Blumenauer	Y	Y	N	Y
4 DeFazio	Y	Y	N	Y
5 Hooley	Y	Y	N	Y
PENNSYLVANIA				
1 Foglietta	Y	Y	N	Y
2 Fattah	Y	Y	N	Y
3 Borski	Y	Y	N	Y
4 Klink	Y	Y	N	Y
5 ***Peterson***	Y	Y	Y	Y
6 Holden	Y	Y	N	Y
7 ***Weldon***	Y	Y	Y	Y
8 ***Greenwood***	Y	Y	Y	Y
9 ***Shuster***	Y	Y	Y	Y
10 ***McDade***	Y	Y	Y	Y
11 Kanjorski	Y	Y	N	Y
12 Murtha	Y	Y	N	Y
13 ***Fox***	Y	Y	Y	Y
14 Coyne	Y	Y	N	Y
15 McHale	Y	Y	N	Y
16 ***Pitts***	Y	Y	Y	Y
17 ***Gekas***	Y	Y	Y	Y
18 Doyle	Y	Y	N	Y
19 ***Goodling***	Y	Y	Y	Y
20 Mascara	Y	Y	N	Y
21 ***English***	Y	Y	Y	Y
RHODE ISLAND				
1 Kennedy	Y	Y	N	Y
2 Weygand	Y	Y	N	Y
SOUTH CAROLINA				
1 ***Sanford***	N	Y	Y	Y
2 ***Spence***	Y	Y	Y	Y
3 ***Graham***	Y	Y	Y	Y
4 ***Inglis***	Y	Y	Y	Y
5 Spratt	Y	Y	N	Y
6 Clyburn	Y	Y	N	Y
SOUTH DAKOTA				
AL ***Thune***	Y	Y	Y	Y
TENNESSEE				
1 ***Jenkins***	Y	Y	Y	Y
2 ***Duncan***	Y	Y	Y	Y

	72	73	74	75
3 ***Wamp***	Y	Y	Y	Y
4 ***Hilleary***	Y	Y	Y	Y
5 Clement	Y	Y	N	Y
6 Gordon	Y	Y	N	Y
7 ***Bryant***	?	?	Y	Y
8 Tanner	Y	Y	N	Y
9 Ford	Y	Y	N	Y
TEXAS				
1 Sandlin	Y	Y	N	Y
2 Turner	Y	Y	N	Y
3 ***Johnson, Sam***	Y	Y	Y	Y
4 Hall	Y	Y	N	Y
5 ***Sessions***	Y	Y	Y	Y
6 ***Barton***	Y	Y	?	Y
7 ***Archer***	Y	Y	Y	Y
8 ***Brady***	Y	Y	Y	Y
9 Lampson	Y	Y	N	Y
10 Doggett	Y	Y	N	Y
11 Edwards	Y	Y	N	Y
12 ***Granger***	Y	Y	?	Y
13 ***Thornberry***	Y	Y	Y	Y
14 ***Paul***	N	Y	Y	Y
15 Hinojosa	Y	Y	N	Y
16 Reyes	Y	Y	N	Y
17 Stenholm	Y	Y	N	Y
18 Jackson-Lee	Y	Y	N	Y
19 ***Combest***	Y	Y	Y	Y
20 Gonzalez	Y	Y	N	Y
21 ***Smith***	Y	Y	Y	Y
22 ***DeLay***	Y	Y	Y	Y
23 ***Bonilla***	Y	Y	Y	Y
24 Frost	Y	Y	N	Y
25 Bentsen	Y	Y	N	Y
26 ***Armey***	Y	Y	Y	Y
27 Ortiz	Y	Y	N	Y
28 Vacant				
29 Green	Y	Y	N	Y
30 Johnson, E.B.	Y	Y	N	Y
UTAH				
1 ***Hansen***	Y	Y	Y	Y
2 ***Cook***	Y	Y	Y	Y
3 ***Cannon***	Y	Y	Y	Y
VERMONT				
AL *Sanders*	Y	Y	N	Y
VIRGINIA				
1 ***Bateman***	Y	Y	Y	Y
2 Pickett	Y	Y	N	Y
3 Scott	Y	Y	N	N
4 Sisisky	Y	Y	N	Y
5 Goode	Y	Y	N	Y
6 ***Goodlatte***	Y	Y	Y	Y
7 ***Bliley***	Y	Y	Y	Y
8 Moran	Y	Y	N	Y
9 Boucher	Y	Y	N	Y
10 ***Wolf***	Y	Y	Y	Y
11 ***Davis***	Y	Y	Y	Y
WASHINGTON				
1 ***White***	Y	Y	Y	Y
2 ***Metcalf***	Y	Y	Y	Y
3 ***Smith, Linda***	Y	Y	Y	Y
4 ***Hastings***	Y	Y	Y	Y
5 ***Nethercutt***	Y	Y	Y	Y
6 Dicks	Y	Y	N	Y
7 McDermott	Y	Y	N	N
8 ***Dunn***	Y	Y	Y	Y
9 Smith, Adam	Y	Y	N	Y
WEST VIRGINIA				
1 Mollohan	Y	?	N	?
2 Wise	Y	Y	N	Y
3 Rahall	Y	Y	N	Y
WISCONSIN				
1 ***Neumann***	N	Y	Y	Y
2 ***Klug***	Y	Y	Y	Y
3 Kind	Y	Y	N	Y
4 Kleczka	Y	Y	N	Y
5 Barrett	Y	Y	N	Y
6 ***Petri***	Y	Y	Y	Y
7 Obey	Y	Y	N	Y
8 Johnson	Y	Y	N	Y
9 ***Sensenbrenner***	N	Y	Y	Y
WYOMING				
AL ***Cubin***	Y	Y	Y	Y

Southern states - Ala., Ark., Fla., Ga., Ky., La., Miss., N.C., Okla., S.C., Tenn., Texas, Va.

HOUSE VOTES 76, 77, 78, 79, 80

76. HR 1226. Tax Return Browsing/Passage. Archer, R-Texas, motion to suspend the rules and pass the bill to make it unlawful for federal employees and others to inspect any tax return or return information without authorization. Violators could be subject to a $1,000 fine and up to one year in prison. In addition, federal officers and employees could be dismissed from employment. Motion agreed to 412-0: R 219-0; D 192-0 (ND 139-0, SD 53-0); I 1-0, April 15, 1997. A two-thirds majority of those present and voting (275 in this case) is required for passage under suspension of the rules. A "yea" was a vote in support of the president's position.

77. H Res 109. Family Tax Relief/Adoption. Archer, R-Texas, motion to suspend the rules and adopt the resolution to express the sense of the House that Congress and the president should work together to enact permanent tax relief for American families. Motion agreed to 412-0: R 219-0; D 192-0 (ND 139-0, SD 53-0); I 1-0, April 15, 1997. A two-thirds majority of those present and voting (275 in this case) is required for adoption under suspension of the rules.

78. H J Res 62. Tax Limitation Constitutional Amendment/Passage. Passage of the joint resolution proposing a constitutional amendment requiring a two-thirds majority vote in both the House and Senate in order to raise taxes. Rejected 233-190: R 208-15; D 25-174 (ND 14-131, SD 11-43); I 0-1, April 15, 1997. A two-thirds majority of those present and voting (282 in this case) is required to pass a joint resolution proposing an amendment to the Constitution. A "nay" was a vote in support of the president's position.

79. H Res 112. Expedited Floor Procedures/Previous Question. Dreier, R-Calif., motion to order the previous question (thus ending debate and the possibility of amendment) on adoption of the resolution to permit House floor consideration of bills under suspension of the rules on Wednesday, April 16. Motion agreed to 223-199: R 222-0; D 1-198 (ND 0-145, SD 1-53); I 0-1, April 16, 1997.

80. HR 607. Private Mortgage Insurance Cancellation/Passage. Leach, R-Iowa, motion to suspend the rules and pass the bill to require mortgage lenders to automatically cancel future private mortgage insurance when homeowners' equity reaches 25 percent of the purchase price and require lenders to provide written disclosure of consumer cancellation rights. Motion agreed to 421-7: R 218-7; D 202-0 (ND 148-0, SD 54-0); I 1-0, April 16, 1997. A two-thirds majority of those present and voting (286 in this case) is required for passage under suspension of the rules.

KEY

- Y Voted for (yea).
- # Paired for.
- + Announced for.
- N Voted against (nay).
- X Paired against.
- – Announced against.
- P Voted "present."
- C Voted "present" to avoid possible conflict of interest.
- ? Did not vote or otherwise make a position known.

Democrats ***Republicans***
Independent

	76	77	78	79	80
ALABAMA					
1 ***Callahan***	Y	Y	Y	Y	Y
2 ***Everett***	Y	Y	Y	Y	Y
3 ***Riley***	Y	Y	Y	Y	Y
4 ***Aderholt***	Y	Y	Y	Y	Y
5 Cramer	Y	Y	Y	N	Y
6 ***Bachus***	Y	Y	Y	Y	Y
7 Hilliard	Y	Y	N	N	Y
ALASKA					
AL ***Young***	Y	Y	Y	Y	Y
ARIZONA					
1 ***Salmon***	Y	Y	Y	Y	Y
2 Pastor	Y	Y	N	N	Y
3 ***Stump***	Y	Y	Y	Y	Y
4 ***Shadegg***	Y	Y	Y	Y	Y
5 ***Kolbe***	Y	Y	Y	Y	Y
6 ***Hayworth***	Y	Y	Y	Y	Y
ARKANSAS					
1 Berry	Y	Y	Y	N	Y
2 Snyder	Y	Y	N	N	Y
3 ***Hutchinson***	Y	Y	Y	Y	Y
4 ***Dickey***	Y	Y	Y	Y	Y
CALIFORNIA					
1 ***Riggs***	Y	Y	Y	Y	Y
2 ***Herger***	Y	Y	Y	Y	Y
3 Fazio	Y	Y	N	N	Y
4 ***Doolittle***	Y	Y	Y	Y	N
5 Matsui	Y	Y	N	N	Y
6 Woolsey	Y	Y	N	N	Y
7 Miller	Y	Y	N	N	Y
8 Pelosi	Y	Y	N	?	?
9 Dellums	Y	Y	N	N	Y
10 Tauscher	Y	Y	N	N	Y
11 ***Pombo***	Y	Y	Y	Y	Y
12 Lantos	Y	Y	N	N	Y
13 Stark	Y	Y	N	N	Y
14 Eshoo	Y	Y	N	N	Y
15 ***Campbell***	Y	Y	N	Y	N
16 Lofgren	Y	Y	N	N	Y
17 Farr	Y	Y	N	N	Y
18 Condit	Y	Y	Y	N	Y
19 ***Radanovich***	Y	Y	Y	Y	Y
20 Dooley	Y	Y	N	N	Y
21 ***Thomas***	Y	Y	Y	Y	Y
22 Capps	Y	Y	N	N	Y
23 ***Gallegly***	Y	Y	Y	Y	Y
24 Sherman	Y	Y	Y	N	Y
25 ***McKeon***	Y	Y	Y	Y	Y
26 Berman	Y	Y	N	N	Y
27 ***Rogan***	Y	Y	Y	Y	Y
28 ***Dreier***	Y	Y	Y	Y	Y
29 Waxman	Y	Y	N	?	Y
30 Becerra	Y	Y	N	N	Y
31 Martinez	Y	Y	N	N	Y
32 Dixon	Y	Y	N	N	Y
33 Roybal-Allard	Y	Y	N	N	Y
34 Torres	Y	Y	N	N	Y
35 Waters	Y	Y	N	N	Y
36 Harman	Y	Y	Y	N	Y
37 Millender-McD.	Y	Y	N	N	Y
38 ***Horn***	Y	Y	Y	Y	Y
39 ***Royce***	Y	Y	Y	Y	Y
40 ***Lewis***	Y	Y	?	Y	Y
41 ***Kim***	Y	Y	Y	Y	Y
42 Brown	Y	Y	N	N	Y
43 ***Calvert***	Y	Y	Y	Y	Y
44 ***Bono***	Y	Y	Y	Y	Y
45 ***Rohrabacher***	Y	Y	Y	Y	Y
46 Sanchez	Y	Y	Y	N	Y
47 ***Cox***	Y	Y	Y	Y	Y
48 ***Packard***	Y	Y	Y	Y	Y
49 ***Bilbray***	+	+	Y	Y	Y
50 Filner	Y	Y	N	N	Y
51 ***Cunningham***	Y	Y	Y	Y	Y
52 ***Hunter***	Y	Y	Y	Y	Y
COLORADO					
1 DeGette	Y	Y	N	N	Y
2 Skaggs	Y	Y	N	N	Y
3 ***McInnis***	Y	Y	Y	Y	Y
4 ***Schaffer***	Y	Y	Y	Y	Y
5 ***Hefley***	Y	Y	Y	Y	Y
6 ***Schaefer***	Y	Y	Y	Y	Y
CONNECTICUT					
1 Kennelly	Y	Y	N	N	Y
2 Gejdenson	Y	Y	N	N	Y
3 DeLauro	Y	Y	N	N	Y
4 ***Shays***	Y	Y	Y	Y	Y
5 Maloney	Y	Y	Y	N	Y
6 ***Johnson***	Y	Y	N	Y	Y
DELAWARE					
AL ***Castle***	Y	Y	Y	Y	Y
FLORIDA					
1 ***Scarborough***	Y	Y	Y	Y	N
2 Boyd	Y	Y	N	N	Y
3 Brown	Y	Y	N	N	Y
4 ***Fowler***	Y	Y	Y	Y	Y
5 Thurman	Y	Y	N	N	Y
6 ***Stearns***	Y	Y	Y	Y	Y
7 ***Mica***	Y	Y	Y	Y	Y
8 ***McCollum***	Y	Y	Y	Y	Y
9 ***Bilirakis***	Y	Y	Y	Y	Y
10 ***Young***	Y	Y	N	Y	Y
11 Davis	Y	Y	N	N	Y
12 ***Canady***	Y	Y	Y	Y	Y
13 ***Miller***	Y	Y	Y	Y	Y
14 ***Goss***	Y	Y	Y	Y	Y
15 ***Weldon***	Y	Y	Y	Y	Y
16 ***Foley***	Y	Y	Y	Y	Y
17 Meek	Y	Y	N	N	Y
18 ***Ros-Lehtinen***	Y	Y	Y	Y	Y
19 Wexler	?	Y	N	N	Y
20 Deutsch	Y	Y	N	N	Y
21 ***Diaz-Balart***	Y	Y	Y	Y	Y
22 ***Shaw***	Y	Y	N	Y	Y
23 Hastings	Y	Y	N	N	Y
GEORGIA					
1 ***Kingston***	Y	Y	Y	Y	Y
2 Bishop	Y	Y	N	N	Y
3 ***Collins***	Y	Y	Y	Y	Y
4 McKinney	Y	Y	N	N	Y
5 Lewis	Y	Y	N	N	Y
6 ***Gingrich***					
7 ***Barr***	Y	Y	Y	Y	Y
8 ***Chambliss***	Y	Y	Y	Y	Y
9 ***Deal***	Y	Y	Y	Y	Y
10 ***Norwood***	Y	Y	Y	Y	Y
11 ***Linder***	Y	Y	Y	Y	Y
HAWAII					
1 Abercrombie	Y	Y	N	N	Y
2 Mink	Y	Y	N	N	Y
IDAHO					
1 ***Chenoweth***	Y	Y	Y	Y	Y
2 ***Crapo***	Y	Y	Y	Y	Y
ILLINOIS					
1 Rush	Y	Y	N	N	Y
2 Jackson	Y	Y	N	N	Y
3 Lipinski	Y	Y	N	N	Y
4 Gutierrez	Y	Y	N	N	Y
5 Blagojevich	Y	Y	N	N	Y
6 ***Hyde***	Y	Y	Y	Y	Y
7 Davis	Y	Y	N	N	Y
8 ***Crane***	Y	Y	Y	Y	N
9 Yates	Y	Y	N	N	Y
10 ***Porter***	Y	Y	N	Y	Y
11 ***Weller***	Y	Y	Y	Y	Y
12 Costello	?	?	?	?	?
13 ***Fawell***	Y	Y	Y	Y	Y
14 ***Hastert***	Y	Y	Y	Y	Y
15 ***Ewing***	Y	Y	Y	Y	Y

ND Northern Democrats SD Southern Democrats

	76	77	78	79	80
16 ***Manzullo***	Y	Y	Y	Y	Y
17 Evans	Y	Y	N	N	Y
18 ***LaHood***	Y	Y	Y	Y	Y
19 Poshard	Y	Y	N	N	Y
20 ***Shimkus***	Y	Y	Y	Y	Y
INDIANA					
1 Visclosky	Y	Y	N	N	Y
2 ***McIntosh***	Y	Y	Y	Y	Y
3 Roemer	Y	Y	Y	N	Y
4 ***Souder***	?	?	Y	Y	Y
5 ***Buyer***	Y	Y	Y	Y	Y
6 ***Burton***	Y	Y	Y	Y	Y
7 ***Pease***	Y	Y	Y	Y	Y
8 ***Hostettler***	Y	Y	N	Y	Y
9 Hamilton	Y	Y	N	N	Y
10 Carson	?	?	N	N	Y
IOWA					
1 ***Leach***	Y	Y	Y	Y	Y
2 ***Nussle***	Y	Y	Y	Y	Y
3 Boswell	Y	Y	N	N	Y
4 ***Ganske***	Y	Y	Y	Y	Y
5 ***Latham***	Y	Y	Y	Y	Y
KANSAS					
1 ***Moran***	Y	Y	Y	Y	Y
2 ***Ryun***	Y	Y	Y	Y	Y
3 ***Snowbarger***	Y	Y	Y	Y	Y
4 ***Tiahrt***	Y	Y	Y	Y	Y
KENTUCKY					
1 ***Whitfield***	Y	Y	Y	Y	Y
2 ***Lewis***	Y	Y	Y	Y	Y
3 ***Northup***	Y	Y	Y	Y	Y
4 ***Bunning***	Y	Y	Y	Y	Y
5 ***Rogers***	Y	Y	Y	Y	Y
6 Baesler	Y	Y	N	N	Y
LOUISIANA					
1 ***Livingston***	Y	Y	Y	Y	Y
2 Jefferson	Y	Y	N	N	Y
3 ***Tauzin***	Y	Y	Y	Y	Y
4 ***McCrery***	Y	Y	Y	Y	Y
5 ***Cooksey***	Y	Y	Y	Y	Y
6 ***Baker***	Y	Y	Y	Y	Y
7 John	Y	Y	Y	N	Y
MAINE					
1 Allen	Y	Y	N	N	Y
2 Baldacci	Y	Y	N	N	Y
MARYLAND					
1 ***Gilchrest***	Y	Y	?	Y	Y
2 ***Ehrlich***	Y	Y	Y	Y	Y
3 Cardin	Y	Y	N	N	Y
4 Wynn	Y	Y	N	N	Y
5 Hoyer	Y	Y	N	N	Y
6 ***Bartlett***	Y	Y	Y	Y	Y
7 Cummings	Y	Y	N	N	Y
8 ***Morella***	Y	Y	N	Y	Y
MASSACHUSETTS					
1 Olver	Y	Y	N	N	Y
2 Neal	Y	Y	N	N	Y
3 McGovern	Y	Y	N	N	Y
4 Frank	Y	Y	N	N	Y
5 Meehan	Y	Y	N	N	Y
6 Tierney	Y	Y	N	N	Y
7 Markey	Y	Y	N	?	Y
8 Kennedy	Y	Y	N	N	Y
9 Moakley	Y	Y	N	N	Y
10 Delahunt	Y	?	N	N	Y
MICHIGAN					
1 Stupak	Y	Y	N	N	Y
2 ***Hoekstra***	Y	Y	Y	Y	Y
3 ***Ehlers***	Y	Y	Y	Y	Y
4 ***Camp***	Y	Y	Y	Y	Y
5 Barcia	Y	Y	Y	N	Y
6 ***Upton***	Y	Y	Y	Y	Y
7 ***Smith***	Y	Y	Y	Y	Y
8 Stabenow	Y	Y	N	N	Y
9 Kildee	Y	Y	N	N	Y
10 Bonior	Y	Y	N	N	Y
11 ***Knollenberg***	Y	Y	Y	Y	Y
12 Levin	Y	Y	N	N	Y
13 Rivers	Y	Y	N	N	Y
14 Conyers	?	Y	N	N	Y
15 Kilpatrick	+	+	N	N	Y
16 Dingell	Y	Y	N	N	?
MINNESOTA					
1 ***Gutknecht***	Y	Y	Y	Y	Y
2 Minge	Y	Y	N	N	Y

	76	77	78	79	80
3 ***Ramstad***	Y	Y	Y	Y	Y
4 Vento	Y	Y	N	N	Y
5 Sabo	Y	Y	N	N	Y
6 Luther	Y	Y	N	N	Y
7 Peterson	Y	Y	Y	N	Y
8 Oberstar	Y	Y	N	N	Y
MISSISSIPPI					
1 ***Wicker***	Y	Y	Y	Y	Y
2 Thompson	Y	Y	N	N	Y
3 ***Pickering***	Y	Y	Y	Y	Y
4 ***Parker***	Y	Y	Y	Y	Y
5 Taylor	Y	Y	Y	N	Y
MISSOURI					
1 Clay	Y	Y	N	N	Y
2 ***Talent***	Y	Y	Y	Y	Y
3 Gephardt	Y	Y	N	N	Y
4 Skelton	Y	Y	Y	N	Y
5 McCarthy	Y	Y	N	N	Y
6 Danner	?	?	Y	N	Y
7 ***Blunt***	Y	Y	Y	Y	Y
8 ***Emerson***	Y	Y	Y	Y	Y
9 ***Hulshof***	Y	Y	Y	Y	Y
MONTANA					
AL ***Hill***	Y	Y	N	Y	N
NEBRASKA					
1 ***Bereuter***	Y	Y	N	Y	Y
2 ***Christensen***	Y	Y	Y	Y	Y
3 ***Barrett***	Y	Y	Y	Y	Y
NEVADA					
1 ***Ensign***	Y	Y	Y	Y	Y
2 ***Gibbons***	Y	Y	Y	Y	Y
NEW HAMPSHIRE					
1 ***Sununu***	Y	Y	Y	Y	Y
2 ***Bass***	Y	Y	Y	Y	Y
NEW JERSEY					
1 Andrews	Y	Y	Y	N	Y
2 ***LoBiondo***	Y	Y	Y	Y	Y
3 ***Saxton***	Y	Y	Y	Y	Y
4 ***Smith***	Y	Y	Y	Y	Y
5 ***Roukema***	Y	Y	N	Y	Y
6 Pallone	Y	Y	Y	N	Y
7 ***Franks***	Y	Y	Y	Y	Y
8 Pascrell	Y	Y	N	N	Y
9 Rothman	Y	Y	N	N	Y
10 Payne	Y	Y	?	N	Y
11 ***Frelinghuysen***	Y	Y	Y	Y	Y
12 ***Pappas***	Y	Y	Y	Y	Y
13 Menendez	Y	Y	N	N	Y
NEW MEXICO					
1 ***Schiff***	?	?	?	?	?
2 ***Skeen***	Y	?	Y	Y	Y
3 Vacant					
NEW YORK					
1 ***Forbes***	Y	Y	Y	Y	Y
2 ***Lazio***	Y	Y	Y	Y	Y
3 ***King***	?	?	Y	Y	Y
4 McCarthy	Y	Y	Y	N	Y
5 Ackerman	Y	Y	N	?	Y
6 Flake	?	?	?	N	Y
7 Manton	?	?	?	N	Y
8 Nadler	Y	Y	N	N	Y
9 Schumer	Y	Y	N	N	Y
10 Towns	?	?	?	N	Y
11 Owens	?	?	N	N	Y
12 Velázquez	Y	Y	N	N	Y
13 ***Molinari***	Y	Y	Y	Y	Y
14 Maloney	Y	Y	N	N	Y
15 Rangel	?	?	N	N	Y
16 Serrano	Y	Y	N	N	Y
17 Engel	Y	Y	N	N	Y
18 Lowey	?	?	?	N	Y
19 ***Kelly***	Y	Y	Y	Y	Y
20 ***Gilman***	Y	Y	Y	Y	Y
21 McNulty	Y	Y	N	N	Y
22 ***Solomon***	Y	Y	Y	Y	Y
23 ***Boehlert***	Y	Y	N	Y	Y
24 ***McHugh***	Y	Y	Y	Y	Y
25 ***Walsh***	Y	Y	N	Y	Y
26 Hinchey	Y	Y	N	N	Y
27 ***Paxon***	Y	Y	Y	Y	Y
28 Slaughter	Y	Y	N	N	Y
29 LaFalce	Y	Y	N	N	Y
30 ***Quinn***	Y	Y	Y	Y	Y
31 ***Houghton***	Y	Y	N	Y	Y

	76	77	78	79	80
NORTH CAROLINA					
1 Clayton	Y	Y	N	N	Y
2 Etheridge	Y	Y	Y	N	Y
3 ***Jones***	Y	Y	Y	Y	Y
4 Price	Y	Y	N	N	Y
5 ***Burr***	Y	Y	Y	Y	Y
6 ***Coble***	Y	Y	Y	Y	Y
7 McIntyre	Y	Y	Y	N	Y
8 Hefner	Y	Y	N	N	Y
9 ***Myrick***	Y	Y	Y	Y	Y
10 ***Ballenger***	Y	Y	Y	Y	Y
11 ***Taylor***	Y	Y	Y	Y	Y
12 Watt	Y	Y	N	N	Y
NORTH DAKOTA					
AL Pomeroy	Y	Y	N	N	Y
OHIO					
1 ***Chabot***	Y	Y	Y	Y	Y
2 ***Portman***	Y	Y	Y	Y	Y
3 Hall	Y	Y	N	N	Y
4 ***Oxley***	Y	Y	Y	Y	Y
5 ***Gillmor***	Y	Y	N	Y	Y
6 Strickland	Y	Y	N	N	Y
7 ***Hobson***	Y	Y	Y	Y	Y
8 ***Boehner***	Y	Y	Y	Y	Y
9 Kaptur	Y	Y	N	N	Y
10 Kucinich	Y	Y	N	N	Y
11 Stokes	Y	Y	N	N	Y
12 ***Kasich***	Y	Y	Y	Y	Y
13 Brown	Y	Y	N	N	Y
14 Sawyer	?	?	N	N	Y
15 ***Pryce***	Y	Y	Y	Y	Y
16 ***Regula***	Y	Y	Y	Y	Y
17 Traficant	Y	Y	Y	N	Y
18 ***Ney***	Y	Y	Y	Y	Y
19 ***LaTourette***	Y	Y	Y	Y	Y
OKLAHOMA					
1 ***Largent***	Y	Y	Y	Y	Y
2 ***Coburn***	Y	Y	Y	Y	Y
3 ***Watkins***	Y	Y	Y	Y	Y
4 ***Watts***	Y	Y	Y	Y	Y
5 ***Istook***	?	?	Y	?	Y
6 ***Lucas***	Y	Y	Y	Y	Y
OREGON					
1 Furse	Y	Y	N	N	Y
2 ***Smith***	Y	Y	Y	Y	Y
3 Blumenauer	Y	Y	N	N	Y
4 DeFazio	Y	Y	N	N	Y
5 Hooley	Y	Y	N	N	Y
PENNSYLVANIA					
1 Foglietta	Y	Y	N	N	Y
2 Fattah	Y	Y	N	?	Y
3 Borski	Y	Y	N	N	Y
4 Klink	Y	Y	N	N	Y
5 ***Peterson***	Y	Y	Y	Y	Y
6 Holden	Y	Y	N	N	Y
7 ***Weldon***	Y	Y	Y	Y	Y
8 ***Greenwood***	Y	Y	Y	Y	Y
9 ***Shuster***	Y	Y	Y	Y	Y
10 ***McDade***	Y	Y	Y	Y	Y
11 Kanjorski	Y	Y	N	N	Y
12 Murtha	Y	Y	N	N	Y
13 ***Fox***	Y	Y	Y	Y	Y
14 Coyne	Y	Y	N	N	Y
15 McHale	Y	Y	N	N	Y
16 ***Pitts***	Y	Y	Y	Y	Y
17 ***Gekas***	Y	Y	Y	?	Y
18 Doyle	Y	Y	N	N	Y
19 ***Goodling***	Y	Y	Y	Y	Y
20 Mascara	Y	Y	N	N	Y
21 ***English***	Y	Y	Y	Y	Y
RHODE ISLAND					
1 Kennedy	Y	Y	N	N	Y
2 Weygand	Y	Y	N	N	Y
SOUTH CAROLINA					
1 ***Sanford***	Y	Y	Y	Y	Y
2 ***Spence***	Y	Y	Y	Y	Y
3 ***Graham***	Y	Y	Y	Y	Y
4 ***Inglis***	?	Y	Y	Y	Y
5 Spratt	Y	Y	N	N	Y
6 Clyburn	Y	Y	N	N	Y
SOUTH DAKOTA					
AL ***Thune***	Y	Y	Y	Y	Y
TENNESSEE					
1 ***Jenkins***	Y	Y	Y	Y	Y
2 ***Duncan***	Y	Y	Y	Y	Y

	76	77	78	79	80
3 ***Wamp***	Y	Y	Y	Y	Y
4 ***Hilleary***	+	Y	Y	Y	Y
5 Clement	Y	Y	N	N	Y
6 Gordon	Y	Y	Y	N	Y
7 ***Bryant***	Y	Y	Y	Y	Y
8 Tanner	Y	Y	N	N	Y
9 Ford	Y	Y	N	N	Y
TEXAS					
1 Sandlin	Y	?	Y	N	Y
2 Turner	Y	Y	N	N	Y
3 ***Johnson, Sam***	Y	Y	Y	Y	Y
4 Hall	Y	Y	Y	Y	Y
5 ***Sessions***	Y	Y	Y	Y	Y
6 ***Barton***	Y	Y	Y	Y	Y
7 ***Archer***	Y	Y	Y	Y	Y
8 ***Brady***	Y	Y	Y	Y	Y
9 Lampson	Y	Y	N	N	Y
10 Doggett	Y	Y	N	N	Y
11 Edwards	Y	Y	N	N	Y
12 ***Granger***	Y	Y	Y	Y	Y
13 ***Thornberry***	Y	Y	Y	Y	Y
14 ***Paul***	Y	Y	Y	Y	N
15 Hinojosa	Y	Y	N	N	Y
16 Reyes	Y	Y	N	N	Y
17 Stenholm	Y	Y	N	N	Y
18 Jackson-Lee	Y	Y	N	N	Y
19 ***Combest***	Y	Y	Y	Y	Y
20 Gonzalez	Y	Y	N	N	Y
21 ***Smith***	Y	?	Y	Y	Y
22 ***DeLay***	Y	Y	Y	Y	N
23 ***Bonilla***	Y	Y	Y	Y	Y
24 Frost	Y	Y	N	N	Y
25 Bentsen	Y	Y	N	N	Y
26 ***Armey***	Y	Y	Y	Y	Y
27 Ortiz	Y	Y	N	N	Y
28 Vacant					
29 Green	Y	Y	Y	N	Y
30 Johnson, E.B.	Y	Y	N	N	Y
UTAH					
1 ***Hansen***	Y	Y	Y	Y	Y
2 ***Cook***	Y	Y	Y	Y	Y
3 ***Cannon***	Y	Y	Y	Y	Y
VERMONT					
AL *Sanders*	Y	Y	N	N	Y
VIRGINIA					
1 ***Bateman***	Y	Y	N	Y	Y
2 Pickett	Y	Y	N	N	Y
3 Scott	Y	Y	N	N	Y
4 Sisisky	Y	Y	N	N	Y
5 Goode	Y	Y	Y	N	Y
6 ***Goodlatte***	Y	Y	Y	Y	Y
7 ***Bliley***	Y	Y	Y	Y	Y
8 Moran	Y	Y	N	N	Y
9 Boucher	Y	Y	N	N	Y
10 ***Wolf***	Y	Y	Y	Y	Y
11 ***Davis***	Y	Y	Y	Y	Y
WASHINGTON					
1 ***White***	Y	Y	Y	?	Y
2 ***Metcalf***	Y	Y	Y	Y	Y
3 ***Smith, Linda***	Y	Y	Y	Y	Y
4 ***Hastings***	Y	Y	Y	Y	Y
5 ***Nethercutt***	Y	Y	Y	Y	Y
6 Dicks	Y	Y	N	N	Y
7 McDermott	Y	Y	N	N	Y
8 ***Dunn***	Y	Y	Y	Y	Y
9 Smith, Adam	Y	Y	N	N	Y
WEST VIRGINIA					
1 Mollohan	Y	Y	N	N	Y
2 Wise	Y	Y	N	N	Y
3 Rahall	Y	Y	N	N	Y
WISCONSIN					
1 ***Neumann***	Y	Y	Y	Y	Y
2 ***Klug***	Y	Y	Y	Y	Y
3 Kind	Y	Y	N	N	Y
4 Kleczka	Y	Y	N	N	Y
5 Barrett	Y	Y	N	N	Y
6 ***Petri***	Y	Y	Y	Y	Y
7 Obey	Y	Y	N	N	Y
8 Johnson	Y	Y	N	N	Y
9 ***Sensenbrenner***	Y	Y	Y	Y	Y
WYOMING					
AL ***Cubin***	Y	Y	Y	Y	Y

Southern states - Ala., Ark., Fla., Ga., Ky., La., Miss., N.C., Okla., S.C., Tenn., Texas, Va.

HOUSE VOTES 81, 82, 83, 84, 85

81. H Con Res 61. Honor Jackie Robinson/Adoption. Horn, R-Calif., motion to suspend the rules and adopt the concurrent resolution to honor the achievements of Jackie Robinson, who broke the color barrier in major league baseball in 1947. Motion agreed to 427-0: R 225-0; D 201-0 (ND 147-0, SD 54-0); I 1-0, April 16, 1997. A two-thirds majority of those present and voting (285 in this case) is required for adoption under suspension of the rules.

82. Procedural Motion/Striking Words. Question of striking the words of John Lewis, D-Ga. Agreed to strike words 227-190: R 221-0; D 6-189 (ND 6-135, SD 0-54); I 0-1, April 17, 1997.

83. Procedural Motion/Permission to Speak. Solomon, R-N.Y., motion to table the Doggett, D-Texas, motion to allow John Lewis, D-Ga., to proceed in order after his words were stricken from the Congressional Record. Under the rules of the House, a member whose words are taken down for an improper reference loses the privilege of debate for the rest of the day unless the House allows him to proceed. Motion agreed to 223-199: R 222-0; D 1-198 (ND 1-145, SD 0-53); I 0-1, April 17, 1997.

84. Procedural Motion/Journal. Approval of the House Journal of Wednesday, April 16, 1997. Approved 317-100: R 212-7; D 104-93 (ND 74-69, SD 30-24); I 1-0, April 17, 1997.

85. HR 400. Patent System Overhaul/Patent Term Restoration. Rohrabacher, R-Calif., substitute amendment to establish specific circumstances under which a patent may be published and establish a patent term at 17 years from the date the patent is granted, or 20 years from the date on which the patent was filed. Rejected 178-227: R 123-89; D 54-138 (ND 46-92, SD 8-46); I 1-0, April 17, 1997.

[1] *Ciro D. Rodriguez, D-Texas, was sworn in April 17, replacing the late Frank Tejeda, D. The first vote for which he was eligible was vote 85.*

KEY

- Y Voted for (yea).
- # Paired for.
- \+ Announced for.
- N Voted against (nay).
- X Paired against.
- – Announced against.
- P Voted "present."
- C Voted "present" to avoid possible conflict of interest.
- ? Did not vote or otherwise make a position known.

Democrats ***Republicans***
Independent

	81	82	83	84	85
ALABAMA					
1 ***Callahan***	Y	Y	Y	N	?
2 ***Everett***	Y	Y	Y	Y	Y
3 ***Riley***	Y	Y	Y	Y	Y
4 ***Aderholt***	Y	Y	Y	Y	N
5 Cramer	Y	N	N	Y	Y
6 ***Bachus***	Y	Y	Y	Y	Y
7 Hilliard	Y	N	N	N	N
ALASKA					
AL ***Young***	Y	Y	Y	Y	Y
ARIZONA					
1 ***Salmon***	Y	Y	Y	Y	Y
2 Pastor	Y	N	N	Y	N
3 ***Stump***	Y	Y	Y	Y	Y
4 ***Shadegg***	Y	Y	Y	Y	Y
5 ***Kolbe***	Y	Y	Y	Y	N
6 ***Hayworth***	Y	Y	Y	Y	Y
ARKANSAS					
1 Berry	Y	N	N	N	N
2 Snyder	Y	N	N	Y	Y
3 ***Hutchinson***	Y	Y	Y	Y	Y
4 ***Dickey***	Y	Y	Y	Y	N
CALIFORNIA					
1 ***Riggs***	Y	Y	Y	Y	Y
2 ***Herger***	Y	Y	Y	Y	Y
3 Fazio	Y	N	N	N	N
4 ***Doolittle***	Y	Y	Y	Y	Y
5 Matsui	Y	N	N	Y	N
6 Woolsey	Y	N	N	Y	N
7 Miller	Y	N	N	N	Y
8 Pelosi	?	N	N	Y	N
9 Dellums	Y	N	N	N	Y
10 Tauscher	Y	N	N	N	N
11 ***Pombo***	Y	Y	Y	Y	Y
12 Lantos	Y	N	N	N	N
13 Stark	Y	N	N	N	N
14 Eshoo	Y	N	N	?	N
15 ***Campbell***	Y	Y	Y	Y	Y
16 Lofgren	Y	N	N	Y	N
17 Farr	Y	N	?	?	N
18 Condit	Y	N	N	Y	Y
19 ***Radanovich***	Y	Y	Y	Y	Y
20 Dooley	Y	N	N	Y	N
21 ***Thomas***	Y	Y	Y	Y	Y
22 Capps	Y	N	N	Y	N
23 ***Gallegly***	Y	Y	Y	Y	Y
24 Sherman	Y	N	N	N	Y
25 ***McKeon***	Y	Y	Y	Y	Y
26 Berman	Y	P	N	Y	N
27 ***Rogan***	Y	Y	Y	Y	N
28 ***Dreier***	Y	Y	Y	Y	?
29 Waxman	Y	N	N	Y	N
30 Becerra	Y	N	N	?	N
31 Martinez	Y	N	N	Y	Y
32 Dixon	Y	N	N	Y	Y
33 Roybal-Allard	Y	N	N	Y	N
34 Torres	Y	N	N	Y	N
35 Waters	Y	N	N	Y	Y
36 Harman	Y	?	?	Y	?
37 Millender-McD.	Y	N	N	N	?
38 ***Horn***	Y	Y	Y	Y	N
39 ***Royce***	Y	Y	Y	Y	Y
40 ***Lewis***	Y	Y	Y	Y	Y
41 ***Kim***	Y	Y	Y	Y	Y
42 Brown	Y	N	N	?	N
43 ***Calvert***	Y	Y	Y	Y	Y
44 ***Bono***	Y	Y	Y	?	Y
45 ***Rohrabacher***	Y	Y	Y	Y	Y
46 Sanchez	Y	N	N	N	N
47 ***Cox***	Y	Y	Y	Y	Y
48 ***Packard***	Y	Y	Y	Y	N
49 ***Bilbray***	Y	Y	Y	Y	N
50 Filner	Y	N	N	N	Y
51 ***Cunningham***	Y	Y	Y	Y	Y
52 ***Hunter***	Y	Y	Y	Y	Y
COLORADO					
1 DeGette	Y	N	N	N	–
2 Skaggs	Y	Y	N	N	N
3 ***McInnis***	Y	Y	Y	Y	Y
4 ***Schaffer***	Y	Y	Y	Y	Y
5 ***Hefley***	Y	Y	Y	N	Y
6 ***Schaefer***	Y	Y	Y	Y	#
CONNECTICUT					
1 Kennelly	Y	N	N	N	N
2 Gejdenson	Y	N	N	Y	N
3 DeLauro	Y	N	N	N	N
4 ***Shays***	Y	Y	Y	Y	N
5 Maloney	Y	N	N	Y	Y
6 ***Johnson***	Y	Y	Y	Y	N
DELAWARE					
AL ***Castle***	Y	Y	Y	Y	N
FLORIDA					
1 ***Scarborough***	Y	Y	Y	Y	Y
2 Boyd	Y	N	N	Y	N
3 Brown	Y	N	N	Y	N
4 ***Fowler***	Y	Y	Y	Y	Y
5 Thurman	Y	N	N	Y	N
6 ***Stearns***	Y	Y	Y	Y	Y
7 ***Mica***	Y	Y	Y	Y	Y
8 ***McCollum***	Y	Y	Y	Y	N
9 ***Bilirakis***	Y	Y	Y	Y	Y
10 ***Young***	Y	Y	Y	Y	N
11 Davis	Y	N	N	N	N
12 ***Canady***	Y	Y	Y	Y	N
13 ***Miller***	Y	Y	Y	Y	Y
14 ***Goss***	Y	Y	Y	Y	Y
15 ***Weldon***	Y	Y	Y	Y	N
16 ***Foley***	Y	Y	Y	Y	Y
17 Meek	Y	N	N	N	N
18 ***Ros-Lehtinen***	Y	Y	Y	Y	Y
19 Wexler	Y	N	N	N	N
20 Deutsch	Y	N	N	N	N
21 ***Diaz-Balart***	Y	Y	Y	Y	Y
22 ***Shaw***	Y	Y	Y	Y	N
23 Hastings	Y	N	N	N	N
GEORGIA					
1 ***Kingston***	Y	Y	Y	Y	Y
2 Bishop	Y	N	N	N	N
3 ***Collins***	Y	Y	Y	Y	Y
4 McKinney	Y	N	N	Y	Y
5 Lewis	Y	N	N	N	N
6 ***Gingrich***					
7 ***Barr***	Y	Y	Y	Y	Y
8 ***Chambliss***	Y	Y	Y	Y	Y
9 ***Deal***	Y	Y	Y	Y	Y
10 ***Norwood***	Y	Y	Y	Y	Y
11 ***Linder***	Y	Y	Y	Y	N
HAWAII					
1 Abercrombie	Y	N	N	N	Y
2 Mink	?	N	N	Y	Y
IDAHO					
1 ***Chenoweth***	Y	Y	Y	Y	Y
2 ***Crapo***	Y	Y	Y	Y	Y
ILLINOIS					
1 Rush	Y	N	N	N	N
2 Jackson	Y	N	N	N	Y
3 Lipinski	Y	N	N	N	Y
4 Gutierrez	Y	N	N	N	N
5 Blagojevich	Y	N	N	Y	N
6 ***Hyde***	Y	Y	Y	Y	N
7 Davis	Y	?	N	Y	N
8 ***Crane***	Y	?	?	?	?
9 Yates	Y	N	N	N	N
10 ***Porter***	Y	Y	Y	Y	N
11 ***Weller***	Y	Y	Y	N	N
12 Costello	?	?	?	?	?
13 ***Fawell***	Y	Y	Y	Y	N
14 ***Hastert***	Y	Y	Y	Y	N
15 ***Ewing***	Y	Y	Y	?	N

ND Northern Democrats SD Southern Democrats

	81	82	83	84	85
16 ***Manzullo***	Y	Y	Y	Y	Y
17 Evans	Y	N	N	Y	N
18 ***LaHood***	Y	Y	Y	Y	Y
19 Poshard	Y	N	N	N	Y
20 ***Shimkus***	Y	Y	Y	Y	N
INDIANA					
1 Visclosky	Y	N	N	N	N
2 ***McIntosh***	Y	Y	Y	Y	Y
3 Roemer	Y	N	N	N	N
4 ***Souder***	Y	Y	Y	Y	Y
5 ***Buyer***	Y	Y	Y	N	N
6 ***Burton***	Y	Y	Y	Y	Y
7 ***Pease***	Y	Y	Y	Y	N
8 ***Hostettler***	Y	Y	Y	Y	Y
9 Hamilton	Y	N	N	Y	N
10 Carson	Y	N	N	Y	N
IOWA					
1 ***Leach***	Y	Y	Y	Y	Y
2 ***Nussle***	Y	Y	Y	Y	N
3 Boswell	Y	N	N	Y	N
4 ***Ganske***	Y	Y	Y	Y	N
5 ***Latham***	Y	Y	Y	Y	N
KANSAS					
1 ***Moran***	Y	Y	Y	Y	Y
2 ***Ryun***	Y	Y	Y	Y	Y
3 ***Snowbarger***	Y	Y	Y	Y	Y
4 ***Tiahrt***	Y	Y	Y	Y	Y
KENTUCKY					
1 ***Whitfield***	Y	?	Y	Y	Y
2 ***Lewis***	Y	Y	Y	Y	Y
3 ***Northup***	Y	Y	Y	Y	N
4 ***Bunning***	Y	Y	Y	Y	?
5 ***Rogers***	Y	Y	Y	Y	N
6 Baesler	Y	N	N	Y	N
LOUISIANA					
1 ***Livingston***	Y	Y	Y	Y	Y
2 Jefferson	Y	N	?	N	N
3 ***Tauzin***	Y	Y	Y	Y	N
4 ***McCrery***	Y	Y	Y	Y	?
5 ***Cooksey***	Y	Y	Y	Y	Y
6 ***Baker***	Y	Y	Y	Y	?
7 John	Y	N	N	Y	N
MAINE					
1 Allen	Y	?	N	Y	N
2 Baldacci	Y	N	N	N	Y
MARYLAND					
1 ***Gilchrest***	Y	Y	Y	Y	N
2 ***Ehrlich***	Y	Y	Y	Y	N
3 Cardin	Y	P	N	Y	Y
4 Wynn	Y	N	N	Y	N
5 Hoyer	Y	N	N	N	Y
6 ***Bartlett***	Y	Y	Y	Y	Y
7 Cummings	Y	N	N	Y	N
8 ***Morella***	Y	?	?	?	N
MASSACHUSETTS					
1 Olver	Y	N	N	N	Y
2 Neal	Y	N	N	N	N
3 McGovern	Y	N	N	N	N
4 Frank	Y	N	N	N	N
5 Meehan	Y	N	N	N	N
6 Tierney	Y	?	?	?	N
7 Markey	Y	N	N	N	N
8 Kennedy	Y	N	N	Y	N
9 Moakley	Y	N	N	Y	N
10 Delahunt	Y	N	N	N	N
MICHIGAN					
1 Stupak	Y	N	N	N	N
2 ***Hoekstra***	Y	Y	Y	Y	N
3 ***Ehlers***	Y	Y	Y	Y	N
4 ***Camp***	Y	Y	Y	Y	N
5 Barcia	Y	N	N	N	Y
6 ***Upton***	Y	Y	Y	Y	N
7 ***Smith***	Y	Y	Y	Y	Y
8 Stabenow	Y	N	N	N	N
9 Kildee	Y	N	N	Y	Y
10 Bonior	Y	N	N	N	Y
11 ***Knollenberg***	Y	Y	Y	Y	N
12 Levin	Y	N	N	N	N
13 Rivers	Y	N	N	N	Y
14 Conyers	Y	N	N	Y	N
15 Kilpatrick	Y	N	N	N	N
16 Dingell	?	N	N	Y	N
MINNESOTA					
1 ***Gutknecht***	Y	Y	Y	Y	N
2 Minge	Y	Y	N	Y	N

	81	82	83	84	85
3 ***Ramstad***	Y	Y	Y	N	N
4 Vento	Y	N	N	Y	N
5 Sabo	Y	N	N	?	N
6 Luther	Y	Y	N	Y	N
7 Peterson	Y	N	N	Y	N
8 Oberstar	Y	N	N	N	Y
MISSISSIPPI					
1 ***Wicker***	Y	Y	Y	Y	N
2 Thompson	Y	N	N	N	N
3 ***Pickering***	Y	Y	Y	Y	Y
4 ***Parker***	Y	Y	Y	Y	Y
5 Taylor	Y	N	N	N	N
MISSOURI					
1 Clay	Y	N	N	N	?
2 ***Talent***	Y	Y	Y	Y	Y
3 Gephardt	Y	N	N	N	Y
4 Skelton	Y	N	N	Y	N
5 McCarthy	Y	N	N	Y	N
6 Danner	Y	N	N	Y	Y
7 ***Blunt***	Y	Y	Y	Y	N
8 ***Emerson***	Y	Y	Y	Y	Y
9 ***Hulshof***	Y	Y	Y	Y	Y
MONTANA					
AL ***Hill***	Y	Y	Y	Y	Y
NEBRASKA					
1 ***Bereuter***	Y	Y	Y	Y	Y
2 ***Christensen***	Y	Y	Y	Y	Y
3 ***Barrett***	Y	Y	Y	Y	–
NEVADA					
1 ***Ensign***	Y	Y	Y	N	Y
2 ***Gibbons***	Y	Y	Y	Y	Y
NEW HAMPSHIRE					
1 ***Sununu***	Y	Y	Y	Y	Y
2 ***Bass***	Y	Y	Y	Y	N
NEW JERSEY					
1 Andrews	Y	?	?	?	?
2 ***LoBiondo***	Y	Y	Y	Y	Y
3 ***Saxton***	Y	Y	Y	Y	Y
4 ***Smith***	Y	Y	Y	Y	Y
5 ***Roukema***	Y	Y	Y	Y	N
6 Pallone	Y	N	N	N	Y
7 ***Franks***	Y	Y	Y	Y	N
8 Pascrell	Y	N	N	N	Y
9 Rothman	Y	N	N	Y	N
10 Payne	Y	N	N	N	Y
11 ***Frelinghuysen***	Y	Y	Y	Y	N
12 ***Pappas***	Y	Y	Y	Y	Y
13 Menendez	Y	N	N	N	Y
NEW MEXICO					
1 ***Schiff***	?	?	?	?	?
2 ***Skeen***	Y	Y	Y	Y	N
3 Vacant					
NEW YORK					
1 ***Forbes***	Y	Y	Y	Y	Y
2 ***Lazio***	Y	Y	Y	Y	Y
3 ***King***	Y	Y	Y	Y	Y
4 McCarthy	Y	N	N	N	Y
5 Ackerman	Y	N	N	N	N
6 Flake	Y	N	N	N	?
7 Manton	Y	N	N	Y	N
8 Nadler	Y	N	N	Y	N
9 Schumer	Y	N	N	Y	N
10 Towns	Y	N	N	Y	?
11 Owens	Y	?	N	N	N
12 Velázquez	Y	N	N	N	N
13 ***Molinari***	Y	Y	Y	Y	Y
14 Maloney	Y	N	N	N	N
15 Rangel	Y	N	N	Y	N
16 Serrano	Y	N	N	Y	N
17 Engel	Y	N	N	N	N
18 Lowey	Y	N	N	Y	N
19 ***Kelly***	Y	Y	Y	Y	N
20 ***Gilman***	Y	Y	Y	Y	N
21 McNulty	Y	N	N	N	Y
22 ***Solomon***	Y	Y	Y	Y	Y
23 ***Boehlert***	Y	Y	Y	Y	N
24 ***McHugh***	Y	Y	Y	Y	Y
25 ***Walsh***	Y	Y	Y	Y	Y
26 Hinchey	Y	N	N	N	?
27 ***Paxon***	Y	Y	Y	Y	N
28 Slaughter	Y	N	N	N	N
29 LaFalce	Y	N	N	N	N
30 ***Quinn***	Y	Y	Y	Y	N
31 ***Houghton***	Y	Y	Y	Y	N

	81	82	83	84	85
NORTH CAROLINA					
1 Clayton	Y	N	N	Y	Y
2 Etheridge	Y	N	N	Y	–
3 ***Jones***	Y	Y	Y	Y	Y
4 Price	Y	N	N	Y	N
5 ***Burr***	Y	Y	Y	Y	N
6 ***Coble***	Y	Y	Y	Y	N
7 McIntyre	Y	N	N	Y	Y
8 Hefner	Y	N	N	Y	N
9 ***Myrick***	Y	Y	Y	Y	Y
10 ***Ballenger***	Y	Y	Y	Y	Y
11 ***Taylor***	Y	Y	Y	Y	Y
12 Watt	Y	N	N	N	N
NORTH DAKOTA					
AL Pomeroy	Y	N	N	N	N
OHIO					
1 ***Chabot***	Y	Y	Y	Y	N
2 ***Portman***	Y	Y	Y	Y	N
3 Hall	Y	Y	N	Y	N
4 ***Oxley***	Y	Y	Y	Y	N
5 ***Gillmor***	Y	Y	Y	Y	Y
6 Strickland	Y	N	N	N	Y
7 ***Hobson***	Y	Y	Y	Y	N
8 ***Boehner***	Y	Y	Y	Y	N
9 Kaptur	Y	N	N	Y	Y
10 Kucinich	Y	N	N	N	Y
11 Stokes	Y	N	N	Y	N
12 ***Kasich***	Y	Y	Y	Y	N
13 Brown	Y	N	N	N	Y
14 Sawyer	Y	P	N	Y	N
15 ***Pryce***	Y	Y	Y	Y	N
16 ***Regula***	Y	Y	Y	Y	Y
17 Traficant	Y	Y	Y	Y	Y
18 ***Ney***	Y	Y	Y	Y	Y
19 ***LaTourette***	Y	Y	Y	Y	Y
OKLAHOMA					
1 ***Largent***	Y	Y	Y	Y	Y
2 ***Coburn***	Y	Y	Y	Y	Y
3 ***Watkins***	Y	Y	Y	Y	N
4 ***Watts***	Y	Y	Y	Y	Y
5 ***Istook***	Y	?	?	?	Y
6 ***Lucas***	Y	Y	Y	Y	Y
OREGON					
1 Furse	Y	N	N	N	N
2 ***Smith***	Y	Y	Y	Y	N
3 Blumenauer	Y	N	N	Y	?
4 DeFazio	Y	N	N	N	N
5 Hooley	Y	N	N	Y	N
PENNSYLVANIA					
1 Foglietta	Y	N	N	N	?
2 Fattah	Y	N	N	N	N
3 Borski	Y	N	N	N	?
4 Klink	Y	N	N	Y	Y
5 ***Peterson***	Y	Y	Y	Y	N
6 Holden	Y	N	N	Y	N
7 ***Weldon***	Y	Y	Y	Y	N
8 ***Greenwood***	Y	Y	Y	Y	N
9 ***Shuster***	Y	Y	Y	Y	N
10 ***McDade***	Y	Y	Y	Y	Y
11 Kanjorski	Y	N	N	N	N
12 Murtha	Y	N	N	Y	Y
13 ***Fox***	Y	Y	Y	Y	N
14 Coyne	Y	N	N	Y	Y
15 McHale	Y	N	N	Y	N
16 ***Pitts***	Y	Y	Y	Y	N
17 ***Gekas***	Y	Y	Y	?	N
18 Doyle	Y	N	N	Y	Y
19 ***Goodling***	Y	Y	Y	Y	Y
20 Mascara	Y	N	N	Y	Y
21 ***English***	Y	Y	Y	N	Y
RHODE ISLAND					
1 Kennedy	Y	N	N	N	N
2 Weygand	Y	N	N	Y	Y
SOUTH CAROLINA					
1 ***Sanford***	Y	Y	Y	Y	Y
2 ***Spence***	Y	Y	Y	Y	Y
3 ***Graham***	Y	Y	Y	Y	Y
4 ***Inglis***	Y	Y	Y	Y	N
5 Spratt	Y	N	N	Y	N
6 Clyburn	Y	N	N	N	N
SOUTH DAKOTA					
AL ***Thune***	Y	Y	Y	Y	Y
TENNESSEE					
1 ***Jenkins***	Y	Y	Y	Y	N
2 ***Duncan***	Y	Y	Y	Y	Y

	81	82	83	84	85
3 ***Wamp***	Y	Y	Y	Y	Y
4 ***Hilleary***	Y	Y	Y	Y	Y
5 Clement	Y	N	N	Y	N
6 Gordon	Y	N	N	Y	N
7 ***Bryant***	Y	Y	Y	Y	N
8 Tanner	Y	N	N	Y	N
9 Ford	Y	N	N	N	N
TEXAS					
1 Sandlin	Y	N	N	Y	N
2 Turner	Y	N	N	Y	N
3 ***Johnson, Sam***	Y	Y	Y	Y	?
4 Hall	Y	N	N	Y	N
5 ***Sessions***	Y	Y	Y	Y	Y
6 ***Barton***	Y	Y	Y	Y	?
7 ***Archer***	Y	Y	Y	Y	N
8 ***Brady***	Y	Y	Y	Y	N
9 Lampson	Y	N	N	N	N
10 Doggett	Y	N	N	N	N
11 Edwards	Y	N	N	N	N
12 ***Granger***	Y	Y	Y	Y	N
13 ***Thornberry***	Y	Y	Y	Y	Y
14 ***Paul***	Y	Y	Y	Y	Y
15 Hinojosa	Y	N	N	Y	N
16 Reyes	Y	N	N	Y	N
17 Stenholm	Y	N	N	Y	N
18 Jackson-Lee	Y	N	N	N	Y
19 ***Combest***	Y	Y	Y	Y	Y
20 Gonzalez	Y	N	N	Y	N
21 ***Smith***	Y	Y	Y	Y	N
22 ***DeLay***	Y	Y	Y	Y	N
23 ***Bonilla***	Y	Y	Y	Y	Y
24 Frost	Y	N	N	N	N
25 Bentsen	Y	N	N	Y	N
26 ***Armey***	Y	Y	Y	Y	N
27 Ortiz	Y	N	N	Y	Y
28 Rodriguez[1]					N
29 Green	Y	N	N	N	N
30 Johnson, E.B.	Y	N	N	N	N
UTAH					
1 ***Hansen***	Y	Y	Y	Y	Y
2 ***Cook***	Y	Y	Y	Y	Y
3 ***Cannon***	Y	Y	Y	Y	N
VERMONT					
AL *Sanders*	Y	N	N	Y	Y
VIRGINIA					
1 ***Bateman***	Y	Y	Y	Y	N
2 Pickett	Y	N	N	N	N
3 Scott	Y	N	N	Y	N
4 Sisisky	Y	N	N	Y	N
5 Goode	Y	N	N	N	Y
6 ***Goodlatte***	Y	Y	Y	Y	N
7 ***Bliley***	Y	Y	Y	Y	N
8 Moran	Y	N	N	Y	N
9 Boucher	Y	N	N	Y	N
10 ***Wolf***	Y	Y	Y	Y	N
11 ***Davis***	Y	Y	Y	Y	N
WASHINGTON					
1 ***White***	Y	Y	Y	Y	N
2 ***Metcalf***	Y	Y	Y	Y	Y
3 ***Smith, Linda***	Y	Y	Y	Y	Y
4 ***Hastings***	Y	Y	Y	Y	Y
5 ***Nethercutt***	Y	Y	Y	Y	N
6 Dicks	Y	N	N	Y	–
7 McDermott	Y	N	N	N	N
8 ***Dunn***	Y	Y	Y	Y	X
9 Smith, Adam	Y	N	N	Y	N
WEST VIRGINIA					
1 Mollohan	Y	N	N	Y	N
2 Wise	Y	N	N	Y	N
3 Rahall	Y	N	N	Y	N
WISCONSIN					
1 ***Neumann***	Y	Y	Y	Y	Y
2 ***Klug***	Y	Y	Y	Y	?
3 Kind	Y	Y	N	Y	N
4 Kleczka	Y	N	N	Y	Y
5 Barrett	Y	N	N	Y	Y
6 ***Petri***	Y	Y	Y	Y	Y
7 Obey	Y	N	N	Y	Y
8 Johnson	Y	N	N	N	N
9 ***Sensenbrenner***	Y	Y	Y	Y	?
WYOMING					
AL ***Cubin***	Y	Y	Y	Y	Y

Southern states - Ala., Ark., Fla., Ga., Ky., La., Miss., N.C., Okla., S.C., Tenn., Texas, Va.

HOUSE VOTES 86, 87, 88, 89, 90, 91

86. HR 400. Patent System Overhaul/Prior Use Claim Limitation. Campbell, R-Calif., amendment to limit prior use claims on newly patented items to the scope and volume agreed to before the patent is issued. Rejected 185-224: R 114-100; D 70-124 (ND 57-84, SD 13-40); I 1-0, April 23, 1997.

87. HR 400. Patent System Overhaul/Publication Limitation. Campbell, R-Calif., amendment to limit publication of information on all patent applications until after there have been two substantive Patent and Trademark Office actions relating to the issuance of a patent. Rejected 167-242: R 113-100; D 53-142 (ND 43-99, SD 10-43); I 1-0, April 23, 1997.

88. HR 400. Patent System Overhaul/Publication Exceptions. Kaptur, D-Ohio, amendment to prohibit the Patent and Trademark Office from publishing the patent applications of small businesses, universities and individual investors until the patent is granted and establish specific circumstances under which other patent applications may be published. Adopted 220-193: R 129-87; D 90-106 (ND 67-76, SD 23-30); I 1-0, April 23, 1997.

89. HR 400. Patent System Overhaul/Patent and Trademark Office Operations. Hunter, R-Calif., amendment to require that all patent examination and search duties be performed within the United States by federal employees; require patent examiners to spend 5 percent of their time yearly in examiner training; exempt the Patent and Trademark Office from federally mandated full-time employee requirements; and establish an incentive program to retain examiners. Rejected 133-280: R 85-131; D 47-149 (ND 40-103, SD 7-46); I 1-0, April 23, 1997.

90. HR 1275. Civilian Space Authorization/Space Station Termination. Roemer, D-Ind., amendment to terminate the space station by eliminating the $2.1 billion authorization in fiscal 1998 and 1999 for the program and authorize $500 million in fiscal 1998 for project termination costs. Rejected 112-305: R 45-174; D 66-131 (ND 62-84, SD 4-47); I 1-0, April 24, 1997. A "nay" was a vote in support of the president's position.

91. HR 1275. Civilian Space Authorization/Minority Research Programs. Jackson-Lee, D-Texas, amendment to increase NASA minority research and education program funding by $8.1 million in fiscal 1998 for minority institutions other than historically black colleges and universities. Rejected 186-226: R 16-201; D 169-25 (ND 126-16, SD 43-9); I 1-0, April 24, 1997.

KEY

- Y Voted for (yea).
- # Paired for.
- + Announced for.
- N Voted against (nay).
- X Paired against.
- – Announced against.
- P Voted "present."
- C Voted "present" to avoid possible conflict of interest.
- ? Did not vote or otherwise make a position known.

Democrats ***Republicans***
Independent

	86	87	88	89	90	91
ALABAMA						
1 ***Callahan***	N	N	N	N	N	N
2 ***Everett***	Y	Y	Y	Y	N	N
3 ***Riley***	Y	Y	Y	Y	N	N
4 ***Aderholt***	N	N	Y	N	N	N
5 Cramer	N	N	Y	N	N	N
6 ***Bachus***	Y	Y	Y	Y	N	N
7 Hilliard	N	N	Y	N	N	Y
ALASKA						
AL ***Young***	N	N	Y	Y	N	N
ARIZONA						
1 ***Salmon***	Y	Y	Y	Y	N	N
2 Pastor	N	N	N	N	N	Y
3 ***Stump***	Y	Y	Y	Y	N	N
4 ***Shadegg***	Y	N	Y	N	N	N
5 ***Kolbe***	N	N	N	N	N	N
6 ***Hayworth***	Y	Y	Y	Y	N	N
ARKANSAS						
1 Berry	N	N	N	N	Y	Y
2 Snyder	N	N	N	N	N	Y
3 ***Hutchinson***	N	Y	Y	N	N	N
4 ***Dickey***	N	N	Y	N	N	N
CALIFORNIA						
1 ***Riggs***	N	Y	Y	N	N	N
2 ***Herger***	Y	Y	Y	Y	Y	N
3 Fazio	N	N	N	N	N	Y
4 ***Doolittle***	Y	Y	Y	Y	N	N
5 Matsui	N	N	N	N	N	Y
6 Woolsey	N	N	Y	N	Y	Y
7 Miller	N	N	Y	Y	Y	Y
8 Pelosi	N	N	Y	N	Y	Y
9 Dellums	Y	Y	Y	N	Y	Y
10 Tauscher	Y	N	N	N	N	Y
11 ***Pombo***	Y	Y	Y	Y	N	N
12 Lantos	N	N	N	N	N	Y
13 Stark	Y	Y	Y	Y	Y	Y
14 Eshoo	N	N	N	N	N	Y
15 ***Campbell***	Y	Y	Y	Y	N	N
16 Lofgren	N	N	N	N	N	Y
17 Farr	N	N	N	N	N	Y
18 Condit	Y	Y	Y	Y	N	?
19 ***Radanovich***	Y	N	Y	Y	N	N
20 Dooley	N	N	N	N	N	Y
21 ***Thomas***	N	N	N	N	N	N
22 Capps	N	N	N	N	N	Y
23 ***Gallegly***	Y	Y	Y	Y	N	N
24 Sherman	N	N	N	N	N	N
25 ***McKeon***	Y	Y	Y	Y	N	N
26 Berman	N	N	N	N	N	Y
27 ***Rogan***	N	N	N	N	N	N
28 ***Dreier***	N	N	N	N	N	N
29 Waxman	N	N	N	N	Y	Y
30 Becerra	N	N	N	N	N	Y
31 Martinez	Y	Y	Y	Y	N	Y
32 Dixon	Y	Y	Y	N	N	Y
33 Roybal-Allard	Y	N	N	N	N	Y
34 Torres	N	N	Y	N	N	Y
35 Waters	Y	Y	Y	Y	N	Y
36 Harman	N	N	Y	N	N	Y
37 Millender-McD.	N	N	Y	N	N	Y
38 ***Horn***	N	N	N	N	N	N
39 ***Royce***	Y	Y	Y	Y	N	N
40 ***Lewis***	N	Y	N	N	N	N
41 ***Kim***	Y	N	Y	N	N	N
42 Brown	N	N	N	N	N	Y
43 ***Calvert***	Y	Y	Y	Y	N	N
44 ***Bono***	Y	Y	Y	Y	N	N
45 ***Rohrabacher***	Y	Y	Y	Y	N	N
46 Sanchez	Y	N	N	N	N	Y
47 ***Cox***	Y	Y	Y	N	N	N
48 ***Packard***	N	N	N	N	N	N
49 ***Bilbray***	Y	N	Y	Y	Y	N
50 Filner	Y	Y	Y	Y	N	Y
51 ***Cunningham***	Y	Y	N	N	Y	N
52 ***Hunter***	Y	Y	Y	Y	N	N
COLORADO						
1 DeGette	N	N	N	N	N	Y
2 Skaggs	N	N	N	N	N	Y
3 ***McInnis***	Y	Y	Y	Y	Y	N
4 ***Schaffer***	Y	Y	Y	Y	Y	N
5 ***Hefley***	Y	Y	Y	Y	N	N
6 ***Schaefer***	Y	Y	Y	Y	N	N
CONNECTICUT						
1 Kennelly	N	N	N	N	N	Y
2 Gejdenson	N	N	Y	N	N	Y
3 DeLauro	N	N	Y	N	N	Y
4 ***Shays***	N	N	N	N	Y	Y
5 Maloney	Y	N	N	N	N	Y
6 ***Johnson***	N	N	N	N	N	N
DELAWARE						
AL ***Castle***	N	N	N	N	N	N
FLORIDA						
1 ***Scarborough***	Y	Y	Y	Y	N	N
2 Boyd	N	N	Y	N	N	N
3 Brown	Y	N	Y	N	N	Y
4 ***Fowler***	Y	N	Y	N	N	N
5 Thurman	Y	Y	N	N	N	Y
6 ***Stearns***	Y	N	Y	N	N	N
7 ***Mica***	Y	Y	Y	Y	N	N
8 ***McCollum***	Y	N	N	N	N	N
9 ***Bilirakis***	Y	Y	Y	Y	N	N
10 ***Young***	N	N	N	N	N	N
11 Davis	N	N	N	N	N	Y
12 ***Canady***	N	N	N	N	N	N
13 ***Miller***	Y	Y	Y	N	N	N
14 ***Goss***	Y	Y	Y	Y	N	N
15 ***Weldon***	Y	Y	N	Y	N	N
16 ***Foley***	Y	Y	Y	Y	N	Y
17 Meek	N	N	Y	N	N	Y
18 ***Ros-Lehtinen***	Y	Y	Y	Y	N	Y
19 Wexler	N	N	N	N	N	N
20 Deutsch	#	?	X	?	N	Y
21 ***Diaz-Balart***	?	?	?	?	N	Y
22 ***Shaw***	N	N	N	N	N	N
23 Hastings	N	N	N	N	N	Y
GEORGIA						
1 ***Kingston***	X	?	X	X	Y	N
2 Bishop	N	N	Y	N	?	Y
3 ***Collins***	?	?	Y	N	N	N
4 McKinney	Y	Y	Y	Y	N	Y
5 Lewis	N	N	N	N	N	Y
6 ***Gingrich***						
7 ***Barr***	Y	Y	Y	Y	N	N
8 ***Chambliss***	N	N	N	N	N	N
9 ***Deal***	N	Y	Y	N	N	N
10 ***Norwood***	Y	Y	Y	Y	N	N
11 ***Linder***	N	N	N	N	N	N
HAWAII						
1 Abercrombie	Y	Y	Y	Y	N	Y
2 Mink	Y	Y	Y	Y	Y	Y
IDAHO						
1 ***Chenoweth***	Y	Y	Y	Y	N	N
2 ***Crapo***	Y	Y	Y	Y	N	N
ILLINOIS						
1 Rush	?	?	?	?	N	Y
2 Jackson	N	N	N	N	N	Y
3 Lipinski	Y	Y	Y	Y	Y	N
4 Gutierrez	Y	Y	Y	Y	Y	Y
5 Blagojevich	N	N	N	N	Y	Y
6 ***Hyde***	N	N	N	N	N	N
7 Davis	N	N	N	N	N	Y
8 ***Crane***	N	N	N	N	N	N
9 Yates	?	?	?	?	?	?
10 ***Porter***	Y	N	Y	N	?	?
11 ***Weller***	N	Y	Y	Y	N	N
12 Costello	Y	Y	Y	N	Y	Y
13 ***Fawell***	N	N	N	N	N	N
14 ***Hastert***	N	Y	Y	N	N	N

ND Northern Democrats SD Southern Democrats

	86	87	88	89	90	91
15 *Ewing*	N	Y	Y	Y	N	N
16 *Manzullo*	Y	Y	Y	Y	+	X
17 Evans	N	N	N	N	Y	Y
18 *LaHood*	Y	Y	Y	N	N	N
19 Poshard	Y	Y	Y	N	Y	Y
20 *Shimkus*	N	N	N	N	N	N
INDIANA						
1 Visclosky	N	N	N	N	Y	Y
2 *McIntosh*	Y	N	Y	N	N	N
3 Roemer	N	N	N	N	Y	Y
4 *Souder*	N	N	N	N	N	N
5 *Buyer*	N	N	N	N	N	N
6 *Burton*	N	N	N	Y	N	N
7 *Pease*	N	N	N	N	N	N
8 *Hostettler*	N	N	Y	Y	N	N
9 Hamilton	N	N	N	N	Y	Y
10 Carson	N	N	N	N	Y	Y
IOWA						
1 *Leach*	Y	Y	Y	N	Y	N
2 *Nussle*	N	N	N	N	Y	?
3 Boswell	N	N	N	N	N	Y
4 *Ganske*	N	N	N	N	Y	N
5 *Latham*	N	N	N	N	Y	N
KANSAS						
1 *Moran*	Y	Y	Y	Y	N	N
2 *Ryun*	Y	Y	Y	Y	N	N
3 *Snowbarger*	Y	Y	Y	Y	N	N
4 *Tiahrt*	Y	Y	Y	Y	N	N
KENTUCKY						
1 *Whitfield*	N	Y	Y	Y	N	N
2 *Lewis*	Y	Y	Y	Y	N	N
3 *Northup*	N	N	N	N	N	N
4 *Bunning*	N	N	N	N	N	N
5 *Rogers*	N	N	N	N	N	N
6 Baesler	N	N	N	N	N	N
LOUISIANA						
1 *Livingston*	Y	Y	Y	N	N	N
2 Jefferson	N	N	Y	N	N	Y
3 *Tauzin*	N	N	Y	N	N	N
4 *McCrery*	N	Y	Y	N	N	?
5 *Cooksey*	Y	Y	N	N	N	N
6 *Baker*	Y	Y	Y	Y	N	N
7 John	N	N	N	N	N	Y
MAINE						
1 Allen	N	N	N	N	N	Y
2 Baldacci	Y	Y	Y	Y	N	Y
MARYLAND						
1 *Gilchrest*	N	N	N	N	N	N
2 *Ehrlich*	N	N	N	N	N	N
3 Cardin	N	Y	Y	N	N	N
4 Wynn	N	N	Y	N	N	Y
5 Hoyer	Y	Y	Y	Y	N	Y
6 *Bartlett*	Y	Y	Y	Y	N	N
7 Cummings	?	N	N	N	N	Y
8 *Morella*	N	N	N	N	N	N
MASSACHUSETTS						
1 Olver	Y	Y	Y	Y	Y	Y
2 Neal	N	N	N	N	N	Y
3 McGovern	Y	N	Y	N	N	Y
4 Frank	Y	N	N	N	Y	Y
5 Meehan	N	N	N	N	Y	Y
6 Tierney	N	N	N	N	Y	Y
7 Markey	N	N	N	N	Y	Y
8 Kennedy	Y	N	N	N	Y	Y
9 Moakley	N	N	N	N	Y	Y
10 Delahunt	N	N	N	N	Y	Y
MICHIGAN						
1 Stupak	Y	Y	Y	N	Y	N
2 *Hoekstra*	?	?	?	?	?	?
3 *Ehlers*	Y	N	N	N	N	N
4 *Camp*	Y	N	N	N	Y	N
5 Barcia	Y	Y	Y	Y	N	N
6 *Upton*	Y	N	Y	N	Y	N
7 *Smith*	Y	Y	Y	Y	N	N
8 Stabenow	N	N	Y	N	N	Y
9 Kildee	Y	Y	Y	Y	N	Y
10 Bonior	Y	Y	Y	Y	N	Y
11 *Knollenberg*	N	N	N	N	N	N
12 Levin	N	N	Y	N	Y	Y
13 Rivers	Y	Y	Y	Y	Y	Y
14 Conyers	N	N	N	N	Y	Y
15 Kilpatrick	?	?	?	?	N	Y
16 Dingell	N	N	N	N	Y	N
MINNESOTA						
1 *Gutknecht*	N	N	N	N	N	N
2 Minge	N	N	N	N	Y	Y
3 *Ramstad*	N	N	N	N	Y	N
4 Vento	N	N	N	N	Y	Y
5 Sabo	N	N	N	N	N	Y
6 Luther	N	N	N	N	Y	Y
7 Peterson	N	N	N	N	Y	N
8 Oberstar	Y	Y	Y	Y	Y	Y
MISSISSIPPI						
1 *Wicker*	N	N	Y	N	N	N
2 Thompson	N	N	Y	N	N	Y
3 *Pickering*	Y	Y	Y	N	N	N
4 *Parker*	Y	Y	Y	N	N	N
5 Taylor	?	?	?	?	N	N
MISSOURI						
1 Clay	N	N	Y	N	N	?
2 *Talent*	Y	Y	Y	Y	N	N
3 Gephardt	Y	Y	Y	Y	N	Y
4 Skelton	N	N	N	Y	N	Y
5 McCarthy	N	N	N	N	Y	N
6 Danner	Y	Y	Y	Y	Y	N
7 *Blunt*	N	N	N	N	N	N
8 *Emerson*	Y	Y	Y	Y	N	N
9 *Hulshof*	Y	Y	Y	Y	N	N
MONTANA						
AL *Hill*	Y	Y	Y	Y	N	N
NEBRASKA						
1 *Bereuter*	Y	Y	Y	N	Y	N
2 *Christensen*	Y	Y	Y	N	Y	N
3 *Barrett*	N	N	N	N	N	N
NEVADA						
1 *Ensign*	Y	Y	Y	Y	Y	Y
2 *Gibbons*	Y	Y	N	Y	N	N
NEW HAMPSHIRE						
1 *Sununu*	N	Y	Y	N	N	N
2 *Bass*	Y	Y	N	N	Y	N
NEW JERSEY						
1 Andrews	?	?	?	?	?	?
2 *LoBiondo*	Y	Y	Y	Y	Y	N
3 *Saxton*	Y	Y	Y	Y	N	N
4 *Smith*	Y	Y	Y	Y	N	N
5 *Roukema*	N	N	N	N	Y	N
6 Pallone	Y	Y	Y	Y	Y	Y
7 *Franks*	N	N	Y	N	Y	N
8 Pascrell	Y	Y	Y	Y	N	Y
9 Rothman	N	N	N	N	N	Y
10 Payne	N	N	Y	N	N	Y
11 *Frelinghuysen*	N	N	N	N	N	N
12 *Pappas*	Y	Y	Y	Y	N	N
13 Menendez	Y	N	Y	N	N	Y
NEW MEXICO						
1 *Schiff*	?	?	?	?	?	?
2 *Skeen*	N	N	N	N	N	N
3 Vacant						
NEW YORK						
1 *Forbes*	Y	Y	Y	Y	N	Y
2 *Lazio*	N	Y	Y	N	Y	Y
3 *King*	Y	Y	Y	Y	N	N
4 McCarthy	Y	Y	Y	Y	N	Y
5 Ackerman	N	N	N	N	N	Y
6 Flake	N	N	N	N	N	Y
7 Manton	N	N	N	N	N	Y
8 Nadler	N	N	N	N	Y	Y
9 Schumer	N	N	N	N	Y	Y
10 Towns	X	?	?	?	X	#
11 Owens	Y	N	Y	N	Y	Y
12 Velázquez	?	?	#	?	#	#
13 *Molinari*	Y	Y	Y	N	Y	N
14 Maloney	N	N	N	N	Y	Y
15 Rangel	Y	N	Y	N	N	Y
16 Serrano	N	N	N	N	N	Y
17 Engel	Y	N	N	N	N	Y
18 Lowey	N	N	N	N	Y	Y
19 *Kelly*	N	N	N	N	N	N
20 *Gilman*	N	N	N	N	N	Y
21 McNulty	Y	Y	Y	Y	Y	Y
22 *Solomon*	Y	Y	Y	Y	Y	N
23 *Boehlert*	N	N	N	N	N	N
24 *McHugh*	Y	Y	Y	Y	Y	N
25 *Walsh*	Y	Y	Y	Y	N	N
26 Hinchey	N	N	N	N	N	Y
27 *Paxon*	N	N	N	N	Y	N
28 Slaughter	N	N	N	N	N	Y
29 LaFalce	N	N	N	N	Y	Y
30 *Quinn*	N	N	N	N	N	Y
31 *Houghton*	N	N	N	N	N	Y
NORTH CAROLINA						
1 Clayton	Y	Y	Y	N	N	Y
2 Etheridge	N	N	N	N	N	Y
3 *Jones*	Y	Y	Y	Y	N	N
4 Price	N	N	N	N	N	Y
5 *Burr*	N	N	N	N	N	N
6 *Coble*	N	N	N	N	Y	N
7 McIntyre	Y	Y	Y	N	N	Y
8 Hefner	N	N	N	N	?	?
9 *Myrick*	Y	Y	Y	Y	Y	?
10 *Ballenger*	+	+	+	+	N	N
11 *Taylor*	?	?	?	?	N	N
12 Watt	Y	Y	Y	N	N	Y
NORTH DAKOTA						
AL Pomeroy	Y	N	Y	Y	Y	N
OHIO						
1 *Chabot*	N	N	N	N	Y	N
2 *Portman*	N	N	N	N	Y	N
3 Hall	N	N	Y	N	N	?
4 *Oxley*	N	N	N	N	N	N
5 *Gillmor*	Y	N	Y	N	N	N
6 Strickland	Y	Y	Y	N	Y	N
7 *Hobson*	Y	Y	N	N	N	N
8 *Boehner*	N	N	N	N	N	N
9 Kaptur	Y	Y	Y	Y	Y	Y
10 Kucinich	Y	Y	Y	Y	N	Y
11 Stokes	N	N	N	N	N	Y
12 *Kasich*	N	N	N	N	N	N
13 Brown	Y	Y	Y	Y	Y	Y
14 Sawyer	N	N	N	N	N	Y
15 *Pryce*	N	N	N	N	N	N
16 *Regula*	Y	Y	Y	Y	N	N
17 Traficant	Y	Y	Y	Y	N	Y
18 *Ney*	Y	Y	Y	Y	N	N
19 *LaTourette*	Y	Y	Y	Y	N	N
OKLAHOMA						
1 *Largent*	Y	Y	Y	Y	Y	N
2 *Coburn*	Y	Y	Y	Y	Y	N
3 *Watkins*	Y	N	N	N	Y	N
4 *Watts*	Y	Y	Y	Y	Y	Y
5 *Istook*	Y	Y	Y	Y	N	N
6 *Lucas*	Y	Y	Y	Y	N	N
OREGON						
1 Furse	?	?	?	?	?	?
2 *Smith*	X	X	X	-	?	?
3 Blumenauer	Y	N	N	N	Y	Y
4 DeFazio	Y	Y	Y	Y	Y	?
5 Hooley	N	N	N	N	N	Y
PENNSYLVANIA						
1 Foglietta	N	N	N	N	Y	Y
2 Fattah	N	N	Y	N	Y	Y
3 Borski	N	N	N	N	N	Y
4 Klink	Y	Y	Y	Y	N	Y
5 *Peterson*	N	N	Y	N	N	N
6 Holden	N	Y	Y	Y	Y	N
7 *Weldon*	N	N	Y	N	?	N
8 *Greenwood*	N	N	N	N	N	N
9 *Shuster*	N	N	N	N	Y	N
10 *McDade*	Y	Y	Y	N	N	Y
11 Kanjorski	Y	Y	Y	Y	Y	N
12 Murtha	Y	N	Y	N	N	N
13 *Fox*	N	N	Y	N	N	Y
14 Coyne	Y	N	N	N	Y	Y
15 McHale	N	N	Y	Y	N	N
16 *Pitts*	N	N	N	N	N	Y
17 *Gekas*	N	?	N	N	N	N
18 Doyle	Y	Y	Y	Y	Y	N
19 *Goodling*	N	N	N	Y	N	N
20 Mascara	Y	Y	Y	Y	N	Y
21 *English*	N	Y	Y	Y	N	N
RHODE ISLAND						
1 Kennedy	N	N	N	N	N	Y
2 Weygand	Y	N	Y	N	N	Y
SOUTH CAROLINA						
1 *Sanford*	#	#	#	?	Y	N
2 *Spence*	N	N	Y	Y	N	N
3 *Graham*	Y	Y	Y	Y	N	N
4 *Inglis*	?	?	?	?	Y	N
5 Spratt	N	N	Y	N	N	Y
6 Clyburn	N	N	Y	N	N	Y
SOUTH DAKOTA						
AL *Thune*	Y	Y	Y	N	N	N
TENNESSEE						
1 *Jenkins*	N	N	N	N	N	N
2 *Duncan*	Y	Y	Y	N	Y	N
3 *Wamp*	Y	Y	Y	Y	Y	Y
4 *Hilleary*	Y	Y	Y	N	Y	N
5 Clement	Y	Y	N	Y	-	+
6 Gordon	Y	N	Y	N	N	Y
7 *Bryant*	?	?	N	N	N	N
8 Tanner	N	N	N	N	?	?
9 Ford	N	N	N	N	N	Y
TEXAS						
1 Sandlin	N	N	N	N	N	Y
2 Turner	N	N	N	N	N	Y
3 *Johnson, Sam*	N	N	N	N	N	N
4 Hall	N	Y	Y	Y	N	Y
5 *Sessions*	N	Y	Y	Y	N	N
6 *Barton*	N	N	N	N	N	Y
7 *Archer*	N	Y	Y	N	N	N
8 *Brady*	N	N	Y	N	N	N
9 Lampson	N	N	N	N	N	Y
10 Doggett	N	N	N	N	N	Y
11 Edwards	N	N	N	N	N	Y
12 *Granger*	N	N	N	N	N	N
13 *Thornberry*	Y	Y	Y	N	N	N
14 *Paul*	Y	Y	Y	N	Y	N
15 Hinojosa	N	N	N	N	Y	Y
16 Reyes	N	N	N	N	N	Y
17 Stenholm	N	N	Y	N	N	Y
18 Jackson-Lee	Y	N	Y	N	Y	Y
19 *Combest*	Y	Y	Y	Y	N	N
20 Gonzalez	N	N	N	N	N	Y
21 *Smith*	N	N	N	N	N	N
22 *DeLay*	N	Y	Y	N	N	N
23 *Bonilla*	Y	Y	Y	N	N	N
24 Frost	N	N	N	N	N	Y
25 Bentsen	N	N	N	N	N	Y
26 *Armey*	N	N	N	N	N	N
27 Ortiz	Y	Y	Y	Y	N	Y
28 Rodriguez	N	N	Y	N	N	Y
29 Green	Y	Y	Y	N	N	Y
30 Johnson, E.B.	Y	N	N	N	N	Y
UTAH						
1 *Hansen*	Y	Y	Y	Y	N	N
2 *Cook*	Y	Y	Y	N	N	N
3 *Cannon*	N	N	N	N	N	N
VERMONT						
AL *Sanders*	Y	Y	Y	Y	Y	Y
VIRGINIA						
1 *Bateman*	N	N	N	N	N	N
2 Pickett	N	N	N	N	N	N
3 Scott	N	N	N	N	N	Y
4 Sisisky	N	N	N	N	N	N
5 Goode	Y	Y	Y	Y	Y	Y
6 *Goodlatte*	N	N	N	N	Y	N
7 *Bliley*	N	N	N	N	N	N
8 Moran	N	N	Y	Y	Y	N
9 Boucher	N	N	N	N	N	N
10 *Wolf*	Y	N	N	N	N	N
11 *Davis*	Y	N	N	N	N	N
WASHINGTON						
1 *White*	N	N	N	N	N	N
2 *Metcalf*	Y	Y	Y	Y	N	N
3 *Smith, Linda*	Y	Y	Y	Y	N	N
4 *Hastings*	Y	Y	Y	N	N	N
5 *Nethercutt*	N	N	Y	N	N	N
6 Dicks	N	N	N	N	N	Y
7 McDermott	N	N	N	N	N	Y
8 *Dunn*	N	N	N	N	N	N
9 Smith, Adam	N	N	N	N	N	Y
WEST VIRGINIA						
1 Mollohan	N	N	N	N	N	Y
2 Wise	?	?	?	?	N	Y
3 Rahall	+	+	Y	Y	N	Y
WISCONSIN						
1 *Neumann*	Y	Y	Y	Y	Y	N
2 *Klug*	Y	N	N	N	Y	N
3 Kind	N	N	N	N	Y	Y
4 Kleczka	Y	Y	Y	Y	Y	Y
5 Barrett	Y	Y	Y	N	Y	Y
6 *Petri*	Y	Y	Y	Y	N	N
7 Obey	Y	Y	Y	Y	Y	Y
8 Johnson	N	N	N	N	N	Y
9 *Sensenbrenner*	N	Y	Y	N	N	N
WYOMING						
AL *Cubin*	#	?	#	#	?	X

Southern states - Ala., Ark., Fla., Ga., Ky., La., Miss., N.C., Okla., S.C., Tenn., Texas, Va.

HOUSE VOTES 92, 93, 94, 95, 96, 97, 98, 99

92. HR 1342. Conservation Reserve Program Extension/Passage. Smith, R-Ore., motion to suspend the rules and pass the bill to allow certain farmers to remain enrolled in the Conservation Reserve Program for one additional year while the Department of Agriculture evaluates their bids for new 10-year contracts. Motion agreed to 325-92: R 213-8; D 112-83 (ND 71-72, SD 41-1); I 0-1, April 29, 1997. A two-thirds majority of those present and voting (278 in this case) is required for passage under suspension of the rules. A "nay" was a vote in support of the president's position.

93. HR 680. Surplus Federal Property Transfer/Passage. Horn, R-Calif., motion to suspend the rules and pass the bill to allow surplus federal property to be transferred to nonprofit organizations that assist low-income individuals and families. Motion agreed to 418-0: R 222-0; D 195-0 (ND 143-0, SD 52-0); I 1-0, April 29, 1997. A two-thirds majority of those present and voting (279 in this case) is required for passage under suspension of the rules. A "yea" was a vote in support of the president's position.

94. HR 363. Electric and Magnetic Fields Research Reauthorization/Passage. Schaefer, R-Colo., motion to suspend the rules and pass the bill to authorize $46 million in fiscal 1998 for the Department of Energy's Electric and Magnetic Fields Research and Public Information Dissemination Program. Motion agreed to 387-35: R 189-34; D 197-1 (ND 144-1, SD 53-0); I 1-0, April 29, 1997. A two-thirds majority of those present and voting (282 in this case) is required for passage under suspension of the rules.

95. HR 1271. Federal Aviation Administration Research Authorization/Passage. Passage of the bill to authorize $672 million through fiscal 2000 for the Federal Aviation Administration's research, engineering, and development programs. Passed 414-7: R 216-7; D 197-0 (ND 145-0, SD 52-0); I 1-0, April 29, 1997.

96. HR 867. Foster Children Adoption/Passage. Passage of the bill to require states to pursue adoptions for children who have been in foster care for 18 months or more, give states more discretion to permanently remove foster children from abusive homes, and provide financial incentives for states that increase adoptions from the foster care system. Passed 416-5: R 217-4; D 198-1 (ND 147-1, SD 51-0); I 1-0, April 30, 1997. A "yea" was a vote in support of the president's position.

97. Procedural Motion/Journal. Approval of the House Journal of Wednesday, April 30, 1997. Approved 343-42: R 192-11; D 151-31 (ND 108-24, SD 43-7); I 0-0, May 1, 1997.

98. H Res 129. House Committee Funding/Adoption. Adoption of the resolution to authorize $149.9 million in 1997-98 for the operation of most House committees. The 1997-98 level is 5.4 percent higher than the 1995-96 level. Adopted 262-157: R 210-9; D 52-147 (ND 41-103, SD 11-44); I 0-1, May 1, 1997.

99. HR 2. Public Housing System Overhaul/Question of Consideration. Question of whether the House should consider the committee substitute amendment to replace federal low-income housing programs with block grants to local authorities, eliminate most federal regulations affecting low-income housing assistance, and change tenant income, employment and eligibility requirements. A parliamentary point of order had been raised that the committee substitute amendment violated the unfunded mandates law (PL 104-4). Agreed to consider 237-183: R 223-0; D 14-182 (ND 7-136, SD 7-46); I 0-1, May 1, 1997.

KEY

- Y Voted for (yea).
- # Paired for.
- + Announced for.
- N Voted against (nay).
- X Paired against.
- – Announced against.
- P Voted "present."
- C Voted "present" to avoid possible conflict of interest.
- ? Did not vote or otherwise make a position known.

Democrats ***Republicans***
Independent

	92	93	94	95	96	97	98	99
ALABAMA								
1 ***Callahan***	Y	Y	Y	Y	Y	Y	Y	Y
2 ***Everett***	Y	Y	Y	Y	Y	Y	Y	Y
3 ***Riley***	Y	Y	Y	Y	Y	Y	Y	Y
4 ***Aderholt***	Y	Y	Y	Y	Y	Y	Y	Y
5 Cramer	Y	Y	Y	Y	Y	Y	N	Y
6 ***Bachus***	Y	Y	Y	Y	Y	Y	Y	Y
7 Hilliard	Y	Y	Y	Y	Y	N	N	N
ALASKA								
AL ***Young***	Y	Y	Y	Y	Y	?	Y	Y
ARIZONA								
1 ***Salmon***	Y	Y	N	Y	Y	Y	Y	Y
2 Pastor	N	Y	Y	Y	Y	Y	N	N
3 ***Stump***	Y	Y	N	Y	?	Y	Y	Y
4 ***Shadegg***	Y	Y	N	Y	Y	Y	Y	Y
5 ***Kolbe***	Y	Y	Y	Y	Y	Y	Y	Y
6 ***Hayworth***	Y	Y	Y	Y	Y	Y	Y	Y
ARKANSAS								
1 Berry	Y	Y	Y	Y	Y	Y	N	Y
2 Snyder	Y	Y	Y	Y	Y	Y	N	N
3 ***Hutchinson***	Y	Y	Y	Y	Y	?	Y	Y
4 ***Dickey***	Y	Y	Y	Y	Y	Y	N	Y
CALIFORNIA								
1 ***Riggs***	Y	Y	Y	Y	Y	?	Y	Y
2 ***Herger***	?	?	?	?	?	?	?	?
3 Fazio	N	Y	Y	Y	Y	N	Y	N
4 ***Doolittle***	Y	Y	Y	Y	Y	Y	Y	Y
5 Matsui	?	?	?	?	Y	Y	N	N
6 Woolsey	Y	Y	Y	Y	Y	Y	N	N
7 Miller	N	Y	Y	Y	Y	Y	Y	N
8 Pelosi	N	Y	Y	Y	Y	Y	N	N
9 Dellums	N	Y	Y	Y	Y	Y	Y	N
10 Tauscher	Y	Y	Y	Y	Y	Y	N	N
11 ***Pombo***	Y	Y	Y	Y	Y	N	?	Y
12 Lantos	?	?	?	?	Y	Y	N	N
13 Stark	N	Y	Y	Y	Y	N	N	N
14 Eshoo	N	Y	Y	Y	Y	Y	Y	N
15 ***Campbell***	Y	Y	Y	Y	N	Y	Y	Y
16 Lofgren	N	Y	Y	Y	Y	Y	N	N
17 Farr	Y	Y	Y	Y	Y	Y	Y	N
18 Condit	Y	Y	Y	Y	Y	?	N	N
19 ***Radanovich***	Y	Y	Y	Y	Y	Y	Y	Y
20 Dooley	N	Y	Y	Y	Y	N	N	N
21 ***Thomas***	Y	Y	Y	Y	Y	Y	Y	Y
22 Capps	+	+	Y	Y	Y	N	N	N
23 ***Gallegly***	?	Y	Y	Y	Y	Y	Y	Y
24 Sherman	N	Y	Y	Y	Y	Y	N	N
25 ***McKeon***	Y	Y	Y	Y	Y	Y	Y	Y
26 Berman	?	?	Y	Y	Y	Y	Y	N
27 ***Rogan***	Y	Y	Y	Y	Y	Y	Y	Y
28 ***Dreier***	Y	Y	Y	Y	Y	Y	Y	Y
29 Waxman	N	Y	Y	Y	Y	Y	N	N
30 Becerra	N	Y	Y	Y	Y	Y	–	N
31 Martinez	Y	Y	Y	Y	Y	Y	Y	N
32 Dixon	N	Y	Y	Y	Y	Y	N	N
33 Roybal-Allard	N	Y	Y	Y	Y	Y	N	N
34 Torres	N	Y	Y	Y	Y	?	N	N
35 Waters	N	Y	Y	Y	Y	N	N	N
36 Harman	N	Y	Y	Y	Y	Y	N	N
37 Millender-McD.	N	Y	Y	Y	Y	Y	N	N
38 ***Horn***	Y	Y	Y	Y	Y	Y	Y	Y
39 ***Royce***	Y	Y	N	N	Y	Y	Y	Y
40 ***Lewis***	N	Y	Y	Y	Y	Y	?	Y
41 ***Kim***	Y	Y	Y	Y	Y	Y	Y	Y
42 Brown	Y	Y	Y	Y	Y	N	Y	N
43 ***Calvert***	Y	Y	Y	Y	Y	Y	Y	Y
44 ***Bono***	Y	Y	Y	Y	Y	+	Y	Y
45 ***Rohrabacher***	Y	Y	N	Y	Y	Y	Y	Y
46 Sanchez	N	Y	Y	Y	Y	Y	N	N
47 ***Cox***	Y	Y	N	Y	Y	Y	Y	Y
48 ***Packard***	Y	Y	Y	Y	Y	Y	Y	Y
49 ***Bilbray***	Y	Y	Y	Y	Y	Y	Y	Y
50 Filner	N	Y	Y	Y	Y	N	N	N
51 ***Cunningham***	Y	Y	Y	Y	Y	Y	Y	Y
52 ***Hunter***	Y	Y	Y	Y	Y	Y	Y	Y
COLORADO								
1 DeGette	Y	Y	Y	Y	Y	Y	N	N
2 Skaggs	Y	Y	Y	Y	Y	Y	N	N
3 ***McInnis***	Y	Y	Y	Y	Y	Y	Y	Y
4 ***Schaffer***	Y	Y	N	N	Y	Y	Y	Y
5 ***Hefley***	Y	Y	N	Y	Y	N	Y	Y
6 ***Schaefer***	Y	Y	Y	Y	Y	Y	Y	Y
CONNECTICUT								
1 Kennelly	N	Y	Y	Y	Y	Y	N	N
2 Gejdenson	N	Y	Y	Y	Y	Y	Y	N
3 DeLauro	N	Y	Y	Y	Y	N	N	N
4 ***Shays***	Y	Y	Y	Y	Y	Y	Y	Y
5 Maloney	N	Y	Y	Y	Y	Y	N	N
6 ***Johnson***	Y	Y	Y	Y	Y	Y	Y	Y
DELAWARE								
AL ***Castle***	Y	Y	Y	Y	Y	Y	Y	Y
FLORIDA								
1 ***Scarborough***	Y	Y	N	Y	Y	Y	Y	Y
2 Boyd	Y	Y	Y	Y	Y	Y	N	N
3 Brown	N	Y	Y	Y	Y	Y	N	N
4 ***Fowler***	Y	Y	Y	Y	Y	Y	Y	Y
5 Thurman	N	Y	Y	Y	Y	Y	N	N
6 ***Stearns***	Y	Y	Y	Y	Y	Y	Y	Y
7 ***Mica***	Y	Y	Y	Y	Y	Y	Y	Y
8 ***McCollum***	Y	Y	Y	Y	Y	Y	Y	Y
9 ***Bilirakis***	Y	Y	Y	Y	Y	Y	Y	Y
10 ***Young***	Y	Y	Y	Y	Y	Y	Y	Y
11 Davis	Y	Y	Y	Y	Y	Y	N	N
12 ***Canady***	Y	Y	Y	Y	Y	Y	Y	Y
13 ***Miller***	Y	Y	Y	Y	Y	?	Y	Y
14 ***Goss***	Y	Y	Y	Y	Y	Y	Y	Y
15 ***Weldon***	Y	Y	Y	Y	Y	Y	Y	Y
16 ***Foley***	Y	Y	N	Y	Y	Y	Y	Y
17 Meek	Y	Y	Y	Y	Y	Y	N	N
18 ***Ros-Lehtinen***	Y	Y	Y	Y	Y	Y	Y	Y
19 Wexler	Y	Y	Y	Y	?	?	N	Y
20 Deutsch	N	Y	Y	Y	Y	Y	N	N
21 ***Diaz-Balart***	Y	Y	Y	Y	Y	Y	Y	Y
22 ***Shaw***	Y	Y	Y	Y	Y	Y	Y	Y
23 Hastings	Y	Y	Y	Y	Y	Y	N	N
GEORGIA								
1 ***Kingston***	Y	Y	N	Y	Y	Y	Y	Y
2 Bishop	Y	Y	Y	Y	Y	Y	N	N
3 ***Collins***	Y	Y	N	Y	Y	Y	Y	Y
4 McKinney	?	?	Y	Y	Y	Y	N	N
5 Lewis	N	Y	Y	Y	?	N	N	N
6 ***Gingrich***								
7 ***Barr***	Y	Y	Y	Y	Y	Y	Y	Y
8 ***Chambliss***	Y	Y	Y	Y	Y	Y	Y	Y
9 ***Deal***	Y	Y	Y	Y	Y	Y	Y	Y
10 ***Norwood***	Y	Y	N	Y	Y	Y	Y	Y
11 ***Linder***	Y	Y	N	Y	Y	Y	Y	Y
HAWAII								
1 Abercrombie	Y	Y	Y	Y	Y	N	N	N
2 Mink	Y	Y	Y	Y	N	?	N	N
IDAHO								
1 ***Chenoweth***	Y	Y	Y	Y	Y	N	Y	Y
2 ***Crapo***	Y	Y	Y	Y	Y	Y	Y	Y
ILLINOIS								
1 Rush	Y	Y	Y	Y	Y	Y	N	N
2 Jackson	N	Y	Y	Y	Y	Y	N	N
3 Lipinski	Y	Y	Y	Y	Y	Y	Y	N
4 Gutierrez	Y	Y	Y	Y	Y	N	N	N
5 Blagojevich	Y	Y	Y	Y	Y	Y	N	N
6 ***Hyde***	Y	Y	Y	Y	Y	Y	Y	Y
7 Davis	N	Y	Y	Y	Y	?	?	?
8 ***Crane***	Y	Y	Y	Y	Y	?	Y	Y
9 Yates	?	?	?	?	Y	?	?	N
10 ***Porter***	Y	Y	Y	Y	?	?	Y	Y
11 ***Weller***	Y	Y	Y	Y	Y	N	Y	Y
12 Costello	Y	Y	Y	Y	Y	N	Y	N
13 ***Fawell***	Y	Y	Y	Y	Y	Y	Y	Y
14 ***Hastert***	Y	Y	Y	Y	Y	Y	Y	Y
15 ***Ewing***	Y	Y	Y	Y	Y	Y	Y	Y

ND Northern Democrats SD Southern Democrats

	92	93	94	95	96	97	98	99
16 ***Manzullo***	Y	Y	N	Y	N	Y	Y	Y
17 Evans	Y	Y	Y	Y	Y	Y	Y	N
18 ***LaHood***	Y	Y	Y	Y	Y	Y	Y	Y
19 Poshard	Y	Y	Y	Y	Y	Y	N	N
20 ***Shimkus***	Y	Y	Y	Y	Y	Y	Y	Y
INDIANA								
1 Visclosky	N	Y	Y	Y	Y	N	Y	N
2 ***McIntosh***	Y	Y	Y	Y	N	?	N	Y
3 Roemer	Y	Y	Y	Y	Y	Y	Y	N
4 ***Souder***	Y	Y	N	Y	Y	?	Y	Y
5 ***Buyer***	Y	Y	Y	Y	Y	Y	Y	Y
6 ***Burton***	Y	Y	Y	Y	Y	?	Y	Y
7 ***Pease***	Y	Y	Y	Y	Y	Y	Y	Y
8 ***Hostettler***	Y	Y	Y	Y	Y	Y	Y	Y
9 Hamilton	Y	Y	Y	Y	Y	Y	Y	N
10 Carson	N	Y	Y	Y	Y	Y	N	N
IOWA								
1 ***Leach***	Y	Y	Y	Y	Y	Y	Y	Y
2 ***Nussle***	Y	Y	Y	Y	Y	?	Y	Y
3 Boswell	Y	Y	Y	Y	Y	Y	N	N
4 ***Ganske***	Y	Y	Y	Y	Y	Y	Y	Y
5 ***Latham***	Y	Y	Y	Y	Y	?	Y	Y
KANSAS								
1 ***Moran***	Y	Y	Y	Y	Y	?	N	Y
2 ***Ryun***	Y	Y	Y	Y	Y	Y	Y	Y
3 ***Snowbarger***	Y	Y	N	Y	Y	Y	Y	Y
4 ***Tiahrt***	Y	Y	N	Y	Y	Y	N	Y
KENTUCKY								
1 ***Whitfield***	Y	Y	Y	Y	Y	Y	Y	Y
2 ***Lewis***	Y	Y	Y	Y	Y	Y	Y	Y
3 ***Northup***	Y	Y	Y	Y	Y	?	Y	Y
4 ***Bunning***	Y	Y	Y	Y	Y	Y	Y	Y
5 ***Rogers***	Y	Y	Y	Y	Y	Y	Y	Y
6 Baesler	Y	Y	Y	Y	Y	?	Y	?
LOUISIANA								
1 ***Livingston***	N	Y	Y	Y	Y	?	Y	Y
2 Jefferson	Y	Y	Y	Y	Y	Y	N	N
3 ***Tauzin***	Y	Y	Y	Y	Y	Y	Y	Y
4 ***McCrery***	Y	Y	Y	Y	Y	Y	Y	Y
5 ***Cooksey***	Y	Y	Y	Y	Y	Y	Y	Y
6 ***Baker***	Y	Y	Y	Y	Y	Y	Y	Y
7 John	Y	Y	Y	Y	?	Y	Y	N
MAINE								
1 Allen	Y	Y	Y	Y	?	Y	N	N
2 Baldacci	Y	Y	Y	Y	Y	Y	N	N
MARYLAND								
1 ***Gilchrest***	Y	Y	Y	Y	Y	Y	Y	Y
2 ***Ehrlich***	Y	Y	Y	Y	Y	?	Y	Y
3 Cardin	N	Y	Y	Y	Y	?	N	N
4 Wynn	Y	Y	Y	Y	Y	Y	N	N
5 Hoyer	Y	Y	Y	Y	Y	Y	Y	N
6 ***Bartlett***	Y	Y	Y	Y	Y	?	Y	Y
7 Cummings	Y	Y	Y	Y	Y	Y	N	N
8 ***Morella***	Y	Y	Y	Y	Y	Y	Y	Y
MASSACHUSETTS								
1 Olver	Y	Y	Y	Y	Y	Y	N	?
2 Neal	N	Y	Y	Y	Y	Y	N	N
3 McGovern	N	Y	Y	Y	Y	N	N	N
4 Frank	N	Y	Y	Y	Y	Y	N	N
5 Meehan	N	Y	Y	Y	Y	Y	N	N
6 Tierney	N	Y	Y	Y	Y	?	N	N
7 Markey	N	Y	Y	Y	Y	Y	N	N
8 Kennedy	N	Y	Y	Y	Y	Y	N	N
9 Moakley	N	Y	Y	Y	Y	Y	N	N
10 Delahunt	N	Y	Y	Y	Y	Y	N	N
MICHIGAN								
1 Stupak	Y	Y	Y	Y	Y	?	?	?
2 ***Hoekstra***	?	?	?	?	Y	Y	Y	Y
3 ***Ehlers***	Y	Y	N	Y	Y	Y	Y	Y
4 ***Camp***	Y	Y	Y	Y	Y	Y	Y	Y
5 Barcia	Y	Y	Y	Y	Y	Y	Y	Y
6 ***Upton***	Y	Y	Y	Y	Y	Y	Y	Y
7 ***Smith***	Y	Y	Y	Y	Y	Y	Y	Y
8 Stabenow	N	Y	Y	Y	Y	Y	N	N
9 Kildee	Y	Y	Y	Y	Y	Y	Y	N
10 Bonior	N	Y	Y	Y	?	Y	N	N
11 ***Knollenberg***	Y	Y	Y	Y	Y	Y	Y	Y
12 Levin	N	Y	Y	Y	Y	Y	N	N
13 Rivers	N	Y	Y	Y	Y	Y	N	N
14 Conyers	N	Y	Y	Y	Y	?	?	N
15 Kilpatrick	N	Y	Y	Y	Y	N	Y	N
16 Dingell	Y	Y	Y	Y	Y	N	Y	N
MINNESOTA								
1 ***Gutknecht***	Y	Y	Y	Y	Y	Y	Y	Y
2 Minge	Y	Y	Y	Y	Y	Y	N	N

	92	93	94	95	96	97	98	99
3 ***Ramstad***	Y	Y	Y	Y	Y	N	Y	Y
4 Vento	N	Y	Y	Y	Y	Y	N	N
5 Sabo	Y	Y	Y	Y	Y	N	Y	N
6 Luther	Y	Y	Y	Y	Y	Y	N	N
7 Peterson	Y	Y	Y	Y	Y	Y	N	N
8 Oberstar	Y	Y	Y	Y	Y	?	Y	N
MISSISSIPPI								
1 ***Wicker***	Y	Y	Y	Y	Y	Y	Y	Y
2 Thompson	Y	Y	Y	Y	Y	N	N	N
3 ***Pickering***	Y	Y	Y	Y	Y	Y	Y	Y
4 ***Parker***	Y	Y	Y	Y	Y	Y	Y	Y
5 Taylor	N	Y	Y	Y	Y	N	N	N
MISSOURI								
1 Clay	N	Y	Y	Y	Y	N	Y	N
2 ***Talent***	Y	Y	N	Y	Y	Y	Y	Y
3 Gephardt	N	Y	Y	Y	Y	N	N	N
4 Skelton	Y	Y	Y	Y	Y	Y	Y	N
5 McCarthy	N	Y	Y	Y	Y	Y	N	N
6 Danner	Y	Y	Y	Y	Y	Y	N	N
7 ***Blunt***	Y	Y	N	N	Y	Y	Y	Y
8 ***Emerson***	Y	Y	Y	Y	Y	Y	N	Y
9 ***Hulshof***	Y	Y	N	N	Y	N	N	Y
MONTANA								
AL ***Hill***	Y	Y	Y	Y	Y	Y	Y	Y
NEBRASKA								
1 ***Bereuter***	Y	Y	Y	Y	Y	Y	Y	Y
2 ***Christensen***	Y	Y	Y	Y	Y	Y	Y	Y
3 ***Barrett***	Y	Y	Y	Y	Y	+	Y	Y
NEVADA								
1 ***Ensign***	P	?	N	Y	Y	N	Y	Y
2 ***Gibbons***	Y	Y	Y	Y	Y	Y	Y	Y
NEW HAMPSHIRE								
1 ***Sununu***	Y	Y	Y	Y	Y	Y	Y	Y
2 ***Bass***	Y	Y	Y	Y	Y	Y	Y	Y
NEW JERSEY								
1 Andrews	?	?	?	?	Y	?	?	?
2 ***LoBiondo***	Y	Y	Y	Y	Y	N	Y	Y
3 ***Saxton***	Y	Y	Y	Y	Y	Y	Y	Y
4 ***Smith***	Y	Y	Y	Y	Y	Y	Y	Y
5 ***Roukema***	Y	Y	Y	Y	Y	Y	Y	Y
6 Pallone	N	Y	Y	Y	Y	N	N	N
7 ***Franks***	Y	Y	Y	Y	Y	Y	Y	Y
8 Pascrell	Y	Y	Y	Y	Y	?	?	?
9 Rothman	Y	Y	Y	Y	Y	Y	N	N
10 Payne	N	Y	Y	Y	Y	Y	N	N
11 ***Frelinghuysen***	Y	Y	Y	Y	Y	Y	Y	Y
12 ***Pappas***	Y	Y	N	Y	Y	Y	N	Y
13 Menendez	Y	Y	Y	Y	Y	Y	N	N
NEW MEXICO								
1 ***Schiff***	?	?	?	?	?	?	?	?
2 ***Skeen***	N	Y	Y	Y	Y	Y	Y	Y
3 Vacant								
NEW YORK								
1 ***Forbes***	Y	Y	Y	Y	Y	?	Y	Y
2 ***Lazio***	Y	Y	Y	Y	Y	Y	Y	Y
3 ***King***	Y	Y	Y	Y	Y	Y	Y	Y
4 McCarthy	Y	Y	Y	Y	Y	Y	N	Y
5 Ackerman	Y	Y	Y	Y	Y	Y	N	N
6 Flake	N	Y	Y	Y	Y	Y	N	N
7 Manton	Y	Y	Y	Y	Y	Y	N	N
8 Nadler	N	Y	Y	Y	Y	?	N	N
9 Schumer	N	Y	Y	Y	Y	Y	N	N
10 Towns	Y	Y	Y	Y	Y	Y	N	N
11 Owens	N	Y	Y	Y	Y	Y	N	N
12 Velázquez	N	Y	Y	Y	Y	Y	N	N
13 ***Molinari***	Y	Y	Y	Y	Y	Y	Y	Y
14 Maloney	N	Y	Y	Y	Y	?	N	N
15 Rangel	N	Y	Y	Y	Y	Y	N	N
16 Serrano	N	Y	Y	Y	Y	Y	N	N
17 Engel	–	+	+	+	+	+	N	Y
18 Lowey	N	Y	Y	Y	Y	Y	N	N
19 ***Kelly***	Y	Y	Y	Y	Y	Y	Y	Y
20 ***Gilman***	Y	Y	Y	Y	Y	Y	Y	Y
21 McNulty	Y	Y	Y	Y	Y	Y	Y	N
22 ***Solomon***	Y	Y	N	Y	Y	Y	Y	Y
23 ***Boehlert***	Y	Y	Y	Y	Y	Y	Y	Y
24 ***McHugh***	Y	Y	Y	Y	Y	Y	Y	Y
25 ***Walsh***	N	Y	Y	Y	Y	Y	Y	Y
26 Hinchey	N	Y	Y	Y	Y	N	N	N
27 ***Paxon***	Y	Y	Y	Y	Y	Y	Y	Y
28 Slaughter	Y	Y	Y	Y	Y	Y	N	N
29 LaFalce	Y	Y	Y	Y	Y	Y	Y	N
30 ***Quinn***	Y	Y	Y	Y	Y	Y	Y	Y
31 ***Houghton***	Y	Y	Y	Y	Y	Y	Y	Y

	92	93	94	95	96	97	98	99
NORTH CAROLINA								
1 Clayton	Y	Y	Y	Y	Y	?	N	N
2 Etheridge	Y	Y	Y	Y	Y	Y	N	N
3 ***Jones***	Y	Y	N	Y	Y	Y	Y	Y
4 Price	Y	Y	Y	Y	Y	Y	N	N
5 ***Burr***	Y	Y	Y	Y	Y	Y	Y	Y
6 ***Coble***	Y	Y	N	Y	Y	Y	Y	Y
7 McIntyre	Y	Y	Y	Y	Y	Y	N	N
8 Hefner	?	?	?	?	Y	Y	N	N
9 ***Myrick***	Y	Y	Y	Y	Y	Y	?	Y
10 ***Ballenger***	Y	Y	Y	Y	Y	Y	Y	Y
11 ***Taylor***	Y	Y	Y	Y	Y	Y	Y	Y
12 Watt	N	Y	Y	Y	Y	?	N	N
NORTH DAKOTA								
AL Pomeroy	Y	Y	Y	Y	Y	Y	Y	N
OHIO								
1 ***Chabot***	Y	Y	Y	Y	Y	Y	Y	Y
2 ***Portman***	Y	Y	Y	Y	Y	Y	Y	Y
3 Hall	N	Y	Y	Y	Y	Y	N	N
4 ***Oxley***	Y	Y	Y	Y	Y	Y	?	Y
5 ***Gillmor***	Y	Y	Y	Y	Y	N	Y	Y
6 Strickland	N	Y	Y	Y	Y	Y	N	N
7 ***Hobson***	Y	Y	Y	Y	Y	Y	Y	Y
8 ***Boehner***	Y	Y	Y	Y	Y	Y	Y	Y
9 Kaptur	N	Y	Y	Y	Y	?	N	?
10 Kucinich	N	Y	Y	Y	Y	N	N	N
11 Stokes	Y	Y	Y	Y	Y	Y	N	N
12 ***Kasich***	Y	Y	Y	Y	Y	Y	Y	Y
13 Brown	N	Y	Y	Y	Y	Y	N	N
14 Sawyer	Y	Y	Y	Y	Y	Y	N	N
15 ***Pryce***	Y	Y	Y	Y	Y	Y	Y	Y
16 ***Regula***	Y	Y	Y	Y	Y	Y	Y	Y
17 Traficant	Y	Y	Y	Y	Y	Y	Y	Y
18 ***Ney***	Y	Y	Y	Y	Y	Y	Y	Y
19 ***LaTourette***	Y	Y	Y	Y	Y	Y	Y	Y
OKLAHOMA								
1 ***Largent***	Y	Y	Y	Y	Y	Y	Y	Y
2 ***Coburn***	Y	Y	Y	Y	Y	Y	Y	Y
3 ***Watkins***	Y	Y	Y	Y	Y	Y	Y	Y
4 ***Watts***	Y	Y	N	Y	Y	Y	Y	Y
5 ***Istook***	Y	Y	Y	Y	Y	?	?	?
6 ***Lucas***	Y	Y	Y	Y	Y	Y	Y	Y
OREGON								
1 Furse	Y	Y	Y	Y	Y	N	N	N
2 ***Smith***	Y	Y	Y	Y	Y	Y	Y	Y
3 Blumenauer	Y	Y	Y	Y	Y	Y	N	N
4 DeFazio	Y	Y	Y	Y	Y	?	N	?
5 Hooley	Y	Y	Y	Y	Y	Y	N	N
PENNSYLVANIA								
1 Foglietta	N	Y	Y	Y	Y	?	N	N
2 Fattah	N	Y	Y	Y	Y	?	?	N
3 Borski	Y	Y	Y	Y	Y	N	Y	N
4 Klink	Y	Y	Y	Y	Y	Y	Y	Y
5 ***Peterson***	Y	Y	Y	Y	Y	Y	Y	Y
6 Holden	Y	Y	Y	Y	Y	Y	N	Y
7 ***Weldon***	Y	Y	Y	Y	Y	Y	Y	Y
8 ***Greenwood***	Y	Y	Y	Y	Y	Y	Y	Y
9 ***Shuster***	Y	Y	Y	Y	Y	Y	Y	Y
10 ***McDade***	Y	Y	Y	Y	Y	Y	Y	Y
11 Kanjorski	Y	Y	Y	Y	Y	Y	N	N
12 Murtha	Y	Y	Y	Y	Y	Y	Y	N
13 ***Fox***	Y	Y	Y	Y	Y	N	Y	Y
14 Coyne	N	Y	Y	Y	Y	Y	N	N
15 McHale	Y	Y	Y	Y	Y	Y	Y	N
16 ***Pitts***	Y	Y	Y	Y	Y	Y	Y	Y
17 ***Gekas***	Y	Y	Y	Y	Y	Y	Y	Y
18 Doyle	Y	Y	Y	Y	Y	Y	N	Y
19 ***Goodling***	Y	Y	Y	Y	Y	Y	Y	Y
20 Mascara	Y	Y	Y	Y	Y	Y	N	N
21 ***English***	Y	Y	Y	Y	+	N	Y	Y
RHODE ISLAND								
1 Kennedy	Y	Y	Y	Y	Y	Y	N	–
2 Weygand	N	Y	Y	Y	Y	Y	N	N
SOUTH CAROLINA								
1 ***Sanford***	Y	Y	N	N	Y	Y	Y	Y
2 ***Spence***	Y	Y	Y	Y	Y	Y	Y	Y
3 ***Graham***	Y	Y	Y	Y	Y	Y	Y	Y
4 ***Inglis***	Y	Y	Y	Y	Y	Y	Y	Y
5 Spratt	Y	Y	Y	?	Y	Y	Y	N
6 Clyburn	Y	Y	Y	Y	Y	N	N	N
SOUTH DAKOTA								
AL ***Thune***	Y	Y	Y	Y	Y	Y	Y	Y
TENNESSEE								
1 ***Jenkins***	Y	Y	Y	Y	Y	Y	Y	Y
2 ***Duncan***	Y	Y	N	Y	Y	Y	Y	Y

	92	93	94	95	96	97	98	
3 ***Wamp***	Y	Y	Y	Y	Y	Y	Y	Y
4 ***Hilleary***	Y	Y	Y	Y	Y	Y	Y	Y
5 Clement	N	Y	Y	Y	Y	Y	N	N
6 Gordon	N	Y	Y	Y	Y	Y	N	N
7 ***Bryant***	Y	Y	Y	Y	Y	Y	Y	Y
8 Tanner	Y	Y	Y	Y	Y	Y	N	N
9 Ford	N	Y	Y	Y	Y	Y	N	N
TEXAS								
1 Sandlin	Y	Y	Y	Y	Y	Y	N	N
2 Turner	Y	Y	Y	Y	Y	Y	N	Y
3 ***Johnson, Sam***	N	Y	N	Y	Y	Y	Y	Y
4 Hall	Y	Y	Y	Y	Y	Y	Y	N
5 ***Sessions***	Y	Y	Y	Y	Y	Y	Y	Y
6 ***Barton***	Y	Y	Y	Y	Y	Y	Y	Y
7 ***Archer***	N	Y	Y	Y	Y	Y	Y	Y
8 ***Brady***	Y	Y	Y	Y	Y	Y	Y	Y
9 Lampson	Y	Y	Y	Y	Y	Y	N	N
10 Doggett	Y	Y	Y	Y	Y	Y	Y	N
11 Edwards	Y	Y	Y	Y	Y	Y	N	N
12 ***Granger***	Y	Y	Y	Y	Y	Y	Y	Y
13 ***Thornberry***	Y	Y	Y	Y	Y	Y	Y	Y
14 ***Paul***	Y	Y	N	N	N	Y	N	Y
15 Hinojosa	Y	Y	Y	Y	Y	Y	N	N
16 Reyes	Y	Y	Y	Y	Y	Y	N	N
17 Stenholm	Y	Y	Y	Y	Y	Y	Y	?
18 Jackson-Lee	Y	Y	Y	Y	Y	Y	N	N
19 ***Combest***	Y	Y	Y	Y	Y	Y	Y	Y
20 Gonzalez	Y	Y	Y	Y	Y	?	Y	N
21 ***Smith***	Y	Y	Y	Y	Y	Y	Y	Y
22 ***DeLay***	N	Y	Y	Y	Y	Y	Y	Y
23 ***Bonilla***	Y	Y	Y	Y	Y	Y	Y	Y
24 Frost	Y	Y	Y	Y	Y	Y	N	N
25 Bentsen	Y	Y	Y	Y	Y	Y	N	N
26 ***Armey***	Y	Y	Y	Y	Y	Y	Y	Y
27 Ortiz	Y	Y	Y	Y	Y	Y	N	N
28 Rodriguez	Y	Y	Y	Y	Y	Y	N	N
29 Green	+	+	+	+	+	N	N	Y
30 Johnson, E.B.	Y	Y	Y	Y	Y	Y	N	N
UTAH								
1 ***Hansen***	Y	Y	Y	Y	Y	Y	Y	Y
2 ***Cook***	Y	Y	Y	Y	Y	Y	Y	Y
3 ***Cannon***	Y	Y	N	Y	Y	Y	Y	Y
VERMONT								
AL *Sanders*	N	Y	Y	Y	Y	?	N	N
VIRGINIA								
1 ***Bateman***	Y	Y	Y	Y	Y	Y	Y	Y
2 Pickett	Y	Y	Y	Y	Y	N	Y	N
3 Scott	Y	Y	Y	Y	Y	Y	Y	N
4 Sisisky	Y	Y	Y	Y	Y	Y	Y	N
5 Goode	Y	Y	Y	Y	Y	Y	N	Y
6 ***Goodlatte***	Y	Y	Y	Y	Y	Y	Y	Y
7 ***Bliley***	Y	Y	Y	Y	Y	Y	Y	Y
8 Moran	N	Y	Y	Y	Y	Y	N	Y
9 Boucher	N	Y	Y	Y	Y	Y	Y	N
10 ***Wolf***	Y	Y	Y	Y	Y	?	Y	Y
11 ***Davis***	N	Y	Y	Y	Y	Y	Y	Y
WASHINGTON								
1 ***White***	Y	Y	Y	Y	Y	Y	Y	Y
2 ***Metcalf***	Y	Y	Y	Y	Y	Y	Y	Y
3 ***Smith, Linda***	Y	Y	Y	Y	Y	Y	Y	Y
4 ***Hastings***	Y	Y	Y	Y	Y	Y	Y	Y
5 ***Nethercutt***	Y	Y	Y	Y	Y	Y	Y	Y
6 Dicks	Y	Y	Y	Y	Y	Y	Y	N
7 McDermott	N	Y	Y	Y	Y	N	N	N
8 ***Dunn***	Y	Y	Y	Y	Y	Y	Y	Y
9 Smith, Adam	Y	Y	Y	Y	Y	Y	N	N
WEST VIRGINIA								
1 Mollohan	?	?	?	?	Y	Y	Y	N
2 Wise	Y	Y	Y	Y	Y	Y	Y	N
3 Rahall	Y	Y	Y	Y	Y	Y	Y	N
WISCONSIN								
1 ***Neumann***	Y	Y	N	N	Y	Y	N	Y
2 ***Klug***	Y	Y	Y	Y	Y	Y	Y	Y
3 Kind	N	Y	Y	Y	Y	Y	N	N
4 Kleczka	Y	Y	Y	Y	Y	Y	N	N
5 Barrett	N	Y	Y	Y	Y	Y	N	N
6 ***Petri***	Y	Y	Y	Y	Y	Y	Y	Y
7 Obey	Y	Y	Y	Y	Y	Y	Y	N
8 Johnson	Y	Y	N	Y	Y	Y	N	N
9 ***Sensenbrenner***	Y	Y	Y	Y	Y	Y	Y	Y
WYOMING								
AL ***Cubin***	Y	Y	Y	Y	Y	Y	Y	Y

Southern states - Ala., Ark., Fla., Ga., Ky., La., Miss., N.C., Okla., S.C., Tenn., Texas, Va.

HOUSE VOTES 100, 101, 102

100. HR 2. Public Housing System Overhaul/Eviction. Jackson, D-Ill., amendment to restrict public housing authorities from evicting residents who fail to meet the eight-hour per month community service requirement. Rejected 160-251: R 6-207; D 153-44 (ND 117-26, SD 36-18); I 1-0, May 1, 1997.

101. HR 2. Public Housing System Overhaul/Community Service Exemption Cap. Weldon, R-Fla., amendment to the Jackson, D-Ill., amendment to limit the number of exemptions from the eight-hour per month community service requirement to no more than 20 percent of the total number of families served by a public housing program. The Jackson amendment would exempt single parents of young dependent children and primary caregivers of senior citizens and disabled persons from the requirement. Rejected 153-252: R 138-71; D 15-180 (ND 4-137, SD 11-43); I 0-1, May 1, 1997.

102. HR 2. Public Housing System Overhaul/Community Service Exemption. Jackson, D-Ill., amendment to exempt single parents of young dependent children and primary caregivers of senior citizens and disabled persons from the eight-hour per month community service requirement. Rejected 181-216: R 13-189; D 167-27 (ND 127-14, SD 40-13); I 1-0, May 1, 1997.

KEY

- Y Voted for (yea).
- # Paired for.
- \+ Announced for.
- N Voted against (nay).
- X Paired against.
- \- Announced against.
- P Voted "present."
- C Voted "present" to avoid possible conflict of interest.
- ? Did not vote or otherwise make a position known.

Democrats ***Republicans*** *Independent*

	100	101	102
ALABAMA			
1 ***Callahan***	N	Y	?
2 ***Everett***	N	Y	N
3 ***Riley***	N	N	N
4 ***Aderholt***	N	Y	N
5 Cramer	N	Y	N
6 ***Bachus***	N	N	N
7 Hilliard	Y	N	Y
ALASKA			
AL ***Young***	N	Y	N
ARIZONA			
1 ***Salmon***	N	Y	N
2 Pastor	Y	N	Y
3 ***Stump***	N	Y	N
4 ***Shadegg***	N	Y	N
5 ***Kolbe***	N	Y	N
6 ***Hayworth***	N	Y	N
ARKANSAS			
1 Berry	Y	N	Y
2 Snyder	Y	N	Y
3 ***Hutchinson***	N	Y	N
4 ***Dickey***	N	Y	N
CALIFORNIA			
1 ***Riggs***	N	Y	N
2 ***Herger***	?	?	?
3 Fazio	Y	N	Y
4 ***Doolittle***	N	N	N
5 Matsui	Y	N	Y
6 Woolsey	Y	N	Y
7 Miller	Y	N	Y
8 Pelosi	Y	N	Y
9 Dellums	Y	N	Y
10 Tauscher	N	N	N
11 ***Pombo***	N	N	N
12 Lantos	Y	N	Y
13 Stark	Y	N	Y
14 Eshoo	Y	N	Y
15 ***Campbell***	Y	N	Y
16 Lofgren	Y	N	Y
17 Farr	Y	N	Y
18 Condit	N	N	N
19 ***Radanovich***	N	N	N
20 Dooley	N	N	Y
21 ***Thomas***	N	Y	N
22 Capps	Y	N	Y
23 ***Gallegly***	N	?	?
24 Sherman	N	Y	N
25 ***McKeon***	N	Y	N
26 Berman	Y	N	Y
27 ***Rogan***	N	Y	N
28 ***Dreier***	N	Y	N
29 Waxman	Y	N	Y
30 Becerra	Y	N	Y
31 Martinez	Y	N	Y
32 Dixon	Y	N	Y
33 Roybal-Allard	Y	N	Y
34 Torres	Y	N	Y
35 Waters	Y	N	Y
36 Harman	N	N	Y
37 Millender-McD.	Y	N	Y
38 ***Horn***	N	Y	N
39 ***Royce***	N	Y	N
40 ***Lewis***	N	N	N
41 ***Kim***	N	Y	N
42 Brown	Y	N	Y
43 ***Calvert***	N	Y	N
44 ***Bono***	N	Y	N
45 ***Rohrabacher***	N	N	N
46 Sanchez	N	N	N
47 ***Cox***	N	N	N
48 ***Packard***	N	Y	N
49 ***Bilbray***	N	Y	N
50 Filner	Y	N	Y
51 ***Cunningham***	N	Y	N
52 ***Hunter***	N	N	N
COLORADO			
1 DeGette	Y	N	Y
2 Skaggs	Y	N	Y
3 ***McInnis***	N	Y	?
4 ***Schaffer***	N	Y	N
5 ***Hefley***	N	N	N
6 ***Schaefer***	N	Y	N
CONNECTICUT			
1 Kennelly	Y	N	Y
2 Gejdenson	Y	N	Y
3 DeLauro	Y	N	Y
4 ***Shays***	N	Y	N
5 Maloney	N	N	Y
6 ***Johnson***	N	Y	N
DELAWARE			
AL ***Castle***	N	N	N
FLORIDA			
1 ***Scarborough***	N	N	N
2 Boyd	N	N	N
3 Brown	Y	N	Y
4 ***Fowler***	N	Y	N
5 Thurman	Y	Y	Y
6 ***Stearns***	N	Y	N
7 ***Mica***	N	Y	N
8 ***McCollum***	N	Y	N
9 ***Bilirakis***	N	Y	N
10 ***Young***	N	N	N
11 Davis	Y	N	Y
12 ***Canady***	N	Y	N
13 ***Miller***	N	Y	N
14 ***Goss***	N	Y	N
15 ***Weldon***	N	Y	N
16 ***Foley***	N	Y	N
17 Meek	Y	N	Y
18 ***Ros-Lehtinen***	Y	Y	+
19 Wexler	Y	N	Y
20 Deutsch	N	N	Y
21 ***Diaz-Balart***	Y	Y	Y
22 ***Shaw***	N	Y	N
23 Hastings	Y	N	Y
GEORGIA			
1 ***Kingston***	N	Y	N
2 Bishop	Y	N	Y
3 ***Collins***	N	Y	N
4 McKinney	Y	N	Y
5 Lewis	Y	N	Y
6 ***Gingrich***			
7 ***Barr***	N	Y	N
8 ***Chambliss***	N	Y	N
9 ***Deal***	N	Y	N
10 ***Norwood***	N	Y	N
11 ***Linder***	N	N	N
HAWAII			
1 Abercrombie	Y	N	Y
2 Mink	Y	N	Y
IDAHO			
1 ***Chenoweth***	N	N	N
2 ***Crapo***	N	N	N
ILLINOIS			
1 Rush	Y	N	Y
2 Jackson	Y	N	Y
3 Lipinski	Y	N	Y
4 Gutierrez	Y	N	Y
5 Blagojevich	N	N	Y
6 ***Hyde***	?	?	?
7 Davis	?	?	?
8 ***Crane***	N	Y	N
9 Yates	Y	N	Y
10 ***Porter***	N	Y	N
11 ***Weller***	N	Y	N
12 Costello	Y	N	Y
13 ***Fawell***	N	Y	N
14 ***Hastert***	N	Y	N
15 ***Ewing***	N	Y	N

ND Northern Democrats SD Southern Democrats

	100	101	102
16 ***Manzullo***	N	N	N
17 Evans	Y	N	Y
18 ***LaHood***	N	N	Y
19 Poshard	Y	N	Y
20 ***Shimkus***	N	Y	N
INDIANA			
1 Visclosky	Y	N	Y
2 ***McIntosh***	N	Y	N
3 Roemer	Y	N	Y
4 ***Souder***	N	Y	N
5 ***Buyer***	?	?	?
6 ***Burton***	N	Y	N
7 ***Pease***	N	Y	N
8 ***Hostettler***	N	Y	N
9 Hamilton	Y	N	Y
10 Carson	Y	N	Y
IOWA			
1 ***Leach***	N	Y	N
2 ***Nussle***	N	N	N
3 Boswell	N	N	Y
4 ***Ganske***	N	N	N
5 ***Latham***	N	Y	N
KANSAS			
1 ***Moran***	N	N	N
2 ***Ryun***	N	Y	N
3 ***Snowbarger***	N	Y	N
4 ***Tiahrt***	N	N	N
KENTUCKY			
1 ***Whitfield***	N	Y	Y
2 ***Lewis***	N	Y	N
3 ***Northup***	N	N	N
4 ***Bunning***	N	N	?
5 ***Rogers***	N	Y	N
6 Baesler	N	N	N
LOUISIANA			
1 ***Livingston***	N	N	N
2 Jefferson	Y	N	Y
3 ***Tauzin***	N	Y	N
4 ***McCrery***	N	Y	N
5 ***Cooksey***	N	Y	N
6 ***Baker***	?	?	?
7 John	N	N	N
MAINE			
1 Allen	Y	N	Y
2 Baldacci	Y	N	Y
MARYLAND			
1 ***Gilchrest***	N	Y	N
2 ***Ehrlich***	N	N	N
3 Cardin	Y	N	Y
4 Wynn	Y	N	Y
5 Hoyer	Y	N	Y
6 ***Bartlett***	N	N	N
7 Cummings	Y	N	Y
8 ***Morella***	Y	N	N
MASSACHUSETTS			
1 Olver	Y	N	Y
2 Neal	Y	N	Y
3 McGovern	Y	N	Y
4 Frank	Y	N	Y
5 Meehan	Y	N	Y
6 Tierney	Y	N	Y
7 Markey	Y	N	Y
8 Kennedy	Y	N	Y
9 Moakley	Y	N	Y
10 Delahunt	Y	N	Y
MICHIGAN			
1 Stupak	?	?	?
2 ***Hoekstra***	N	Y	N
3 ***Ehlers***	N	Y	N
4 ***Camp***	N	Y	N
5 Barcia	N	N	N
6 ***Upton***	N	Y	N
7 ***Smith***	N	N	N
8 Stabenow	N	N	Y
9 Kildee	Y	N	Y
10 Bonior	Y	N	Y
11 ***Knollenberg***	N	N	N
12 Levin	Y	N	Y
13 Rivers	Y	N	Y
14 Conyers	Y	N	Y
15 Kilpatrick	Y	N	Y
16 Dingell	N	N	Y
MINNESOTA			
1 ***Gutknecht***	N	Y	N
2 Minge	Y	N	Y

	100	101	102
3 ***Ramstad***	N	Y	N
4 Vento	Y	N	Y
5 Sabo	Y	N	Y
6 Luther	N	N	Y
7 Peterson	N	N	N
8 Oberstar	?	?	?
MISSISSIPPI			
1 ***Wicker***	N	Y	N
2 Thompson	Y	N	Y
3 ***Pickering***	N	Y	N
4 ***Parker***	N	Y	?
5 Taylor	N	Y	N
MISSOURI			
1 Clay	Y	N	Y
2 ***Talent***	N	N	N
3 Gephardt	Y	N	Y
4 Skelton	Y	N	Y
5 McCarthy	Y	N	Y
6 Danner	N	?	?
7 ***Blunt***	N	Y	N
8 ***Emerson***	N	Y	N
9 ***Hulshof***	N	Y	N
MONTANA			
AL ***Hill***	N	Y	N
NEBRASKA			
1 ***Bereuter***	N	N	N
2 ***Christensen***	N	Y	–
3 ***Barrett***	N	Y	N
NEVADA			
1 ***Ensign***	N	N	N
2 ***Gibbons***	N	Y	N
NEW HAMPSHIRE			
1 ***Sununu***	N	Y	N
2 ***Bass***	N	N	N
NEW JERSEY			
1 Andrews	?	?	?
2 ***LoBiondo***	N	N	Y
3 ***Saxton***	N	Y	N
4 ***Smith***	N	Y	Y
5 ***Roukema***	N	N	N
6 Pallone	Y	N	Y
7 ***Franks***	N	N	Y
8 Pascrell	Y	N	N
9 Rothman	Y	N	Y
10 Payne	Y	N	Y
11 ***Frelinghuysen***	N	Y	N
12 ***Pappas***	N	N	N
13 Menendez	Y	N	Y
NEW MEXICO			
1 ***Schiff***	?	?	?
2 ***Skeen***	N	N	N
3 Vacant			
NEW YORK			
1 ***Forbes***	Y	N	Y
2 ***Lazio***	N	Y	N
3 ***King***	N	N	N
4 McCarthy	Y	N	Y
5 Ackerman	Y	N	Y
6 Flake	Y	N	Y
7 Manton	#	X	#
8 Nadler	Y	N	Y
9 Schumer	Y	N	Y
10 Towns	Y	Y	Y
11 Owens	Y	N	Y
12 Velázquez	Y	N	Y
13 ***Molinari***	N	Y	N
14 Maloney	Y	N	Y
15 Rangel	Y	N	Y
16 Serrano	Y	N	Y
17 Engel	Y	N	Y
18 Lowey	Y	N	Y
19 ***Kelly***	N	Y	N
20 ***Gilman***	N	Y	N
21 McNulty	Y	N	Y
22 ***Solomon***	N	N	N
23 ***Boehlert***	N	N	N
24 ***McHugh***	N	Y	Y
25 ***Walsh***	?	?	?
26 Hinchey	Y	N	Y
27 ***Paxon***	N	Y	N
28 Slaughter	Y	N	Y
29 LaFalce	+	–	+
30 ***Quinn***	N	Y	Y
31 ***Houghton***	N	Y	N

	100	101	102
NORTH CAROLINA			
1 Clayton	Y	N	Y
2 Etheridge	Y	N	Y
3 ***Jones***	N	Y	N
4 Price	Y	N	Y
5 ***Burr***	N	Y	N
6 ***Coble***	N	Y	N
7 McIntyre	Y	N	Y
8 Hefner	Y	N	Y
9 ***Myrick***	N	N	N
10 ***Ballenger***	N	N	N
11 ***Taylor***	N	N	N
12 Watt	Y	N	Y
NORTH DAKOTA			
AL Pomeroy	N	N	Y
OHIO			
1 ***Chabot***	N	N	N
2 ***Portman***	N	Y	N
3 Hall	Y	N	Y
4 ***Oxley***	N	Y	N
5 ***Gillmor***	N	Y	N
6 Strickland	N	N	N
7 ***Hobson***	N	N	N
8 ***Boehner***	N	N	N
9 Kaptur	N	N	Y
10 Kucinich	Y	N	Y
11 Stokes	Y	N	Y
12 ***Kasich***	N	?	N
13 Brown	Y	?	Y
14 Sawyer	Y	N	Y
15 ***Pryce***	N	Y	N
16 ***Regula***	N	N	N
17 Traficant	N	N	N
18 ***Ney***	N	Y	N
19 ***LaTourette***	Y	N	Y
OKLAHOMA			
1 ***Largent***	?	?	?
2 ***Coburn***	?	?	?
3 ***Watkins***	N	Y	N
4 ***Watts***	N	N	Y
5 ***Istook***	N	N	N
6 ***Lucas***	N	Y	N
OREGON			
1 Furse	Y	N	Y
2 ***Smith***	N	Y	N
3 Blumenauer	Y	N	#
4 DeFazio	?	?	?
5 Hooley	Y	N	Y
PENNSYLVANIA			
1 Foglietta	Y	N	Y
2 Fattah	Y	N	Y
3 Borski	Y	N	Y
4 Klink	N	N	N
5 ***Peterson***	N	Y	N
6 Holden	N	N	N
7 ***Weldon***	N	Y	N
8 ***Greenwood***	?	#	X
9 ***Shuster***	N	Y	N
10 ***McDade***	N	N	N
11 Kanjorski	N	N	Y
12 Murtha	N	N	Y
13 ***Fox***	N	N	N
14 Coyne	Y	N	Y
15 McHale	N	Y	N
16 ***Pitts***	N	Y	N
17 ***Gekas***	N	N	N
18 Doyle	N	N	N
19 ***Goodling***	N	N	N
20 Mascara	Y	N	Y
21 ***English***	N	N	N
RHODE ISLAND			
1 Kennedy	Y	N	Y
2 Weygand	Y	N	Y
SOUTH CAROLINA			
1 ***Sanford***	N	Y	N
2 ***Spence***	N	Y	N
3 ***Graham***	N	N	N
4 ***Inglis***	N	N	N
5 Spratt	N	N	Y
6 Clyburn	Y	N	?
SOUTH DAKOTA			
AL ***Thune***	N	N	N
TENNESSEE			
1 ***Jenkins***	N	N	N
2 ***Duncan***	N	Y	N

	100	101	102
3 ***Wamp***	N	Y	?
4 ***Hilleary***	N	Y	N
5 Clement	N	N	N
6 Gordon	N	N	N
7 ***Bryant***	N	Y	N
8 Tanner	N	N	N
9 Ford	Y	N	Y
TEXAS			
1 Sandlin	Y	N	Y
2 Turner	N	N	Y
3 ***Johnson, Sam***	N	?	?
4 Hall	N	Y	N
5 ***Sessions***	N	Y	N
6 ***Barton***	?	?	?
7 ***Archer***	N	Y	N
8 ***Brady***	N	Y	N
9 Lampson	Y	N	Y
10 Doggett	Y	Y	Y
11 Edwards	N	Y	Y
12 ***Granger***	N	Y	N
13 ***Thornberry***	N	Y	N
14 ***Paul***	N	Y	N
15 Hinojosa	Y	N	Y
16 Reyes	Y	N	Y
17 Stenholm	N	Y	N
18 Jackson-Lee	Y	N	Y
19 ***Combest***	N	Y	N
20 Gonzalez	Y	N	Y
21 ***Smith***	N	Y	N
22 ***DeLay***	?	?	?
23 ***Bonilla***	?	?	?
24 Frost	Y	N	Y
25 Bentsen	Y	N	Y
26 ***Armey***	N	Y	N
27 Ortiz	X	?	X
28 Rodriguez	Y	N	Y
29 Green	Y	Y	Y
30 Johnson, E.B.	Y	N	Y
UTAH			
1 ***Hansen***	N	Y	N
2 ***Cook***	N	N	N
3 ***Cannon***	N	Y	N
VERMONT			
AL *Sanders*	Y	N	Y
VIRGINIA			
1 ***Bateman***	N	Y	?
2 Pickett	N	N	N
3 Scott	Y	N	Y
4 Sisisky	N	Y	N
5 Goode	N	Y	N
6 ***Goodlatte***	N	Y	N
7 ***Bliley***	N	N	N
8 Moran	N	N	Y
9 Boucher	Y	Y	Y
10 ***Wolf***	N	N	Y
11 ***Davis***	N	N	N
WASHINGTON			
1 ***White***	N	N	N
2 ***Metcalf***	N	N	N
3 ***Smith, Linda***	N	Y	N
4 ***Hastings***	N	Y	N
5 ***Nethercutt***	N	Y	N
6 Dicks	?	?	?
7 McDermott	Y	N	Y
8 ***Dunn***	N	N	N
9 Smith, Adam	N	Y	N
WEST VIRGINIA			
1 Mollohan	Y	N	Y
2 Wise	Y	N	Y
3 Rahall	Y	N	Y
WISCONSIN			
1 ***Neumann***	N	N	N
2 ***Klug***	?	?	?
3 Kind	Y	N	Y
4 Kleczka	Y	N	Y
5 Barrett	Y	N	Y
6 ***Petri***	N	Y	N
7 Obey	Y	N	Y
8 Johnson	Y	N	Y
9 ***Sensenbrenner***	N	?	?
WYOMING			
AL ***Cubin***	N	Y	N

Southern states - Ala., Ark., Fla., Ga., Ky., La., Miss., N.C., Okla., S.C., Tenn., Texas, Va.

HOUSE VOTES 103, 104, 105, 106, 107, 108, 109, 110

103. HR 2. Public Housing System Overhaul/Community Service Compensation. Watt, D-N.C., amendment to compensate public housing residents who are required to perform eight hours per month community service at a rate not less than the minimum wage. Rejected 140-286: R 1-223; D 138-63 (ND 105-42, SD 33-21); I 1-0, May 6, 1997.

104. HR 2. Public Housing System Overhaul/Self-Sufficiency Contracts. Frank, D-Mass., amendment to make self-sufficiency contracts, under which tenants must set a target date for moving out of public housing and agree to do eight hours of community service each month, optional rather than mandatory. Rejected 168-253: R 3-217; D 164-36 (ND 126-20, SD 38-16); I 1-0, May 6, 1997.

105. H Res 93. Consumer Price Index Adjustments/Adoption. Souder, R-Ind., motion to suspend the rules and adopt the resolution to express the sense of the House that changes in methodology used to determine the Consumer Price Index should be made only by the Bureau of Labor Statistics. Adopted 399-16: R 212-7; D 186-9 (ND 136-6, SD 50-3); I 1-0, May 7, 1997. A two-thirds majority of those present and voting (277 in this case) is required for adoption under suspension of the rules.

106. HR 2. Public Housing System Overhaul/Tenant Rents. Frank, D-Mass., amendment to strike the provision of the bill that requires local housing authorities to allow public housing residents to choose between a flat-rate rent based on the rental value of the unit and rent based on the resident's income, thus limiting tenant rents to no more than 30 percent of adjusted family income. Rejected 172-252: R 0-225; D 171-27 (ND 130-15, SD 41-12); I 1-0, May 7, 1997.

107. HR 478. Endangered Species Act Flood Waivers/Rule. Adoption of the rule (H Res 142) to provide House floor consideration of the bill to exempt government agencies reconstructing, operating, maintaining or repairing flood control projects, facilities, or structures from review under the Endangered Species Act. Adopted 415-8: R 221-0; D 193-8 (ND 139-8, SD 54-0); I 1-0, May 7, 1997.

108. HR 478. Endangered Species Act Flood Waivers/Project Exemption Limitation. Boehlert, R-N.Y., substitute amendment to provide waivers of the Endangered Species Act consultation regulations for repair or replacement of flood control facilities in counties declared federal disaster areas through 1998 and waive the requirements for any project to repair a flood control facility that presents a substantial threat to human lives and property. Adopted 227-196: R 54-169; D 172-27 (ND 137-9, SD 35-18); I 1-0, May 7, 1997.

109. HR 3. Juvenile Crime/Rule. Adoption of the rule (H Res 143) to provide House floor consideration of the bill to make it easier for federal authorities to prosecute and try as adults juveniles who commit federal violent crimes or federal drug-trafficking offenses and authorize $1.5 billion in financial incentives for state and local authorities to treat as adults juveniles charged with serious crimes. Adopted 252-159: R 218-1; D 34-157 (ND 16-122, SD 18-35); I 0-1, May 7, 1997.

110. Procedural Motion/Journal. Approval of the House Journal of Wednesday, May 7, 1997. Approved 350-56: R 186-24; D 163-32 (ND 123-21, SD 40-11); I 1-0, May 8, 1997.

KEY

- Y Voted for (yea).
- # Paired for.
- \+ Announced for.
- N Voted against (nay).
- X Paired against.
- \- Announced against.
- P Voted "present."
- C Voted "present" to avoid possible conflict of interest.
- ? Did not vote or otherwise make a position known.

Democrats ***Republicans***
Independent

	103	104	105	106	107	108	109	110
ALABAMA								
1 ***Callahan***	N	N	Y	N	Y	N	Y	Y
2 ***Everett***	N	N	Y	N	Y	N	Y	Y
3 ***Riley***	N	N	Y	N	Y	N	Y	Y
4 ***Aderholt***	N	N	?	N	Y	N	Y	Y
5 Cramer	N	N	Y	N	Y	N	Y	Y
6 ***Bachus***	N	N	Y	N	Y	N	Y	Y
7 Hilliard	Y	Y	Y	Y	Y	Y	N	N
ALASKA								
AL ***Young***	N	N	Y	N	Y	N	Y	Y
ARIZONA								
1 ***Salmon***	N	N	Y	N	Y	N	Y	N
2 Pastor	Y	Y	Y	Y	Y	Y	N	Y
3 ***Stump***	N	N	Y	N	Y	N	Y	Y
4 ***Shadegg***	N	N	Y	N	Y	N	Y	Y
5 ***Kolbe***	?	?	?	N	Y	N	Y	Y
6 ***Hayworth***	N	N	Y	N	Y	N	Y	Y
ARKANSAS								
1 Berry	N	Y	Y	Y	Y	N	Y	N
2 Snyder	Y	Y	Y	Y	Y	Y	N	Y
3 ***Hutchinson***	N	N	Y	N	Y	N	Y	Y
4 ***Dickey***	N	N	Y	N	Y	N	Y	Y
CALIFORNIA								
1 ***Riggs***	N	N	Y	N	Y	N	Y	?
2 ***Herger***	N	N	Y	N	Y	N	Y	?
3 Fazio	Y	Y	Y	Y	Y	Y	N	Y
4 ***Doolittle***	N	N	Y	N	Y	N	Y	?
5 Matsui	Y	Y	Y	Y	Y	Y	N	Y
6 Woolsey	Y	Y	Y	Y	Y	Y	N	Y
7 Miller	Y	Y	Y	Y	Y	Y	N	Y
8 Pelosi	Y	Y	Y	Y	Y	Y	?	Y
9 Dellums	Y	Y	Y	Y	Y	Y	N	Y
10 Tauscher	N	N	Y	Y	Y	Y	N	Y
11 ***Pombo***	N	N	Y	N	Y	N	?	Y
12 Lantos	Y	Y	Y	Y	Y	Y	N	Y
13 Stark	Y	?	Y	Y	Y	Y	?	Y
14 Eshoo	Y	Y	Y	Y	Y	Y	N	Y
15 ***Campbell***	N	Y	N	N	Y	N	Y	Y
16 Lofgren	Y	Y	Y	N	Y	Y	N	Y
17 Farr	Y	Y	Y	Y	Y	Y	N	Y
18 Condit	N	N	Y	N	Y	N	N	Y
19 ***Radanovich***	N	N	Y	N	Y	N	Y	Y
20 Dooley	N	N	Y	N	Y	N	?	Y
21 ***Thomas***	N	N	Y	N	Y	N	Y	Y
22 Capps	Y	Y	Y	Y	Y	Y	N	Y
23 ***Gallegly***	N	N	Y	N	Y	N	Y	Y
24 Sherman	N	N	Y	N	Y	Y	Y	Y
25 ***McKeon***	N	N	Y	N	Y	N	Y	Y
26 Berman	Y	Y	Y	Y	Y	Y	?	Y
27 ***Rogan***	N	N	Y	N	Y	N	Y	Y
28 ***Dreier***	N	N	Y	N	Y	N	Y	Y
29 Waxman	?	?	Y	Y	Y	Y	N	Y
30 Becerra	+	+	?	?	?	+	-	Y
31 Martinez	Y	Y	Y	Y	Y	Y	?	Y
32 Dixon	Y	Y	Y	Y	Y	Y	N	?
33 Roybal-Allard	Y	Y	Y	Y	Y	Y	N	Y
34 Torres	Y	Y	Y	Y	Y	Y	N	Y
35 Waters	Y	Y	N	Y	Y	Y	N	Y
36 Harman	N	Y	Y	N	Y	Y	?	Y
37 Millender-McD.	Y	Y	Y	Y	Y	Y	N	Y
38 ***Horn***	N	N	Y	N	Y	Y	Y	Y
39 ***Royce***	N	N	Y	N	Y	N	Y	Y
40 ***Lewis***	N	N	Y	N	Y	N	Y	N
41 ***Kim***	N	N	Y	N	Y	N	Y	Y
42 Brown	Y	Y	Y	Y	Y	Y	N	?
43 ***Calvert***	N	N	Y	N	Y	N	Y	Y
44 ***Bono***	N	N	Y	N	Y	N	Y	Y
45 ***Rohrabacher***	N	N	Y	N	Y	N	Y	Y
46 Sanchez	N	N	Y	Y	Y	Y	N	Y
47 ***Cox***	N	?	Y	N	?	N	Y	?
48 ***Packard***	N	N	Y	N	Y	N	Y	Y
49 ***Bilbray***	N	N	Y	N	Y	N	Y	Y
50 Filner	Y	Y	Y	Y	N	#	-	?
51 ***Cunningham***	N	N	Y	N	Y	N	Y	Y
52 ***Hunter***	N	N	?	N	Y	N	Y	Y
COLORADO								
1 DeGette	Y	Y	Y	Y	Y	Y	N	Y
2 Skaggs	Y	Y	Y	Y	Y	Y	N	Y
3 ***McInnis***	N	N	Y	N	Y	N	Y	Y
4 ***Schaffer***	N	N	Y	N	Y	N	Y	Y
5 ***Hefley***	N	N	Y	N	Y	N	Y	N
6 ***Schaefer***	N	N	Y	N	Y	N	Y	Y
CONNECTICUT								
1 Kennelly	N	Y	Y	Y	Y	Y	N	Y
2 Gejdenson	Y	Y	Y	Y	?	Y	N	Y
3 DeLauro	Y	Y	Y	Y	Y	Y	N	Y
4 ***Shays***	N	N	Y	N	Y	Y	Y	Y
5 Maloney	N	Y	Y	Y	Y	Y	N	Y
6 ***Johnson***	N	N	Y	N	Y	Y	Y	Y
DELAWARE								
AL ***Castle***	N	N	Y	N	Y	Y	Y	Y
FLORIDA								
1 ***Scarborough***	N	N	Y	N	Y	N	Y	Y
2 Boyd	N	N	Y	N	Y	N	Y	Y
3 Brown	Y	Y	Y	Y	Y	Y	N	Y
4 ***Fowler***	N	N	Y	N	Y	N	Y	Y
5 Thurman	Y	Y	Y	Y	Y	Y	N	Y
6 ***Stearns***	N	N	Y	N	Y	N	Y	Y
7 ***Mica***	N	N	Y	N	Y	N	Y	Y
8 ***McCollum***	N	N	Y	N	Y	N	Y	Y
9 ***Bilirakis***	N	N	Y	N	Y	N	Y	Y
10 ***Young***	N	?	Y	N	Y	N	Y	Y
11 Davis	Y	Y	Y	Y	Y	Y	Y	?
12 ***Canady***	N	N	Y	N	Y	N	Y	Y
13 ***Miller***	N	N	Y	N	Y	N	Y	Y
14 ***Goss***	N	N	Y	N	Y	Y	Y	Y
15 ***Weldon***	N	N	Y	N	Y	N	Y	Y
16 ***Foley***	N	N	Y	N	Y	X	Y	Y
17 Meek	Y	Y	Y	Y	Y	Y	N	Y
18 ***Ros-Lehtinen***	N	N	Y	N	Y	Y	Y	Y
19 Wexler	Y	Y	Y	Y	Y	Y	N	?
20 Deutsch	N	N	Y	Y	Y	Y	N	Y
21 ***Diaz-Balart***	N	N	Y	N	Y	Y	Y	Y
22 ***Shaw***	N	N	Y	N	Y	N	Y	Y
23 Hastings	Y	Y	Y	Y	Y	Y	N	Y
GEORGIA								
1 ***Kingston***	N	N	Y	N	Y	Y	Y	Y
2 Bishop	Y	Y	Y	Y	Y	N	N	Y
3 ***Collins***	N	?	Y	N	Y	N	Y	N
4 McKinney	Y	Y	Y	Y	Y	?	?	?
5 Lewis	Y	Y	Y	Y	Y	Y	N	N
6 ***Gingrich***								
7 ***Barr***	N	N	N	N	Y	N	Y	Y
8 ***Chambliss***	N	N	Y	N	Y	N	Y	?
9 ***Deal***	N	N	Y	N	Y	N	Y	Y
10 ***Norwood***	N	N	Y	N	Y	N	Y	Y
11 ***Linder***	N	N	Y	N	Y	N	?	Y
HAWAII								
1 Abercrombie	Y	Y	Y	Y	Y	Y	N	N
2 Mink	Y	Y	Y	Y	Y	Y	N	Y
IDAHO								
1 ***Chenoweth***	N	N	Y	N	Y	N	Y	Y
2 ***Crapo***	N	N	Y	N	Y	N	Y	Y
ILLINOIS								
1 Rush	Y	Y	Y	Y	Y	Y	N	Y
2 Jackson	Y	Y	Y	Y	Y	Y	N	Y
3 Lipinski	Y	Y	Y	N	Y	Y	N	Y
4 Gutierrez	Y	Y	?	?	Y	Y	N	N
5 Blagojevich	N	Y	Y	Y	Y	Y	N	Y
6 ***Hyde***	N	N	Y	N	Y	N	Y	Y
7 Davis	Y	Y	Y	Y	Y	Y	N	Y
8 ***Crane***	N	N	Y	N	Y	N	Y	Y
9 Yates	Y	Y	Y	Y	Y	Y	?	Y
10 ***Porter***	N	N	Y	N	Y	Y	Y	?
11 ***Weller***	N	N	Y	N	Y	Y	Y	N
12 Costello	Y	Y	Y	Y	Y	Y	N	N
13 ***Fawell***	N	N	Y	N	Y	Y	Y	Y
14 ***Hastert***	N	N	Y	N	Y	N	Y	Y
15 ***Ewing***	N	N	Y	N	Y	N	Y	Y

ND Northern Democrats SD Southern Democrats

	103	104	105	106	107	108	109	110
16 ***Manzullo***	N	N	Y	N	Y	N	Y	Y
17 Evans	Y	Y	Y	Y	Y	Y	N	Y
18 ***LaHood***	N	N	Y	N	Y	Y	Y	Y
19 Poshard	Y	Y	Y	Y	Y	Y	N	N
20 ***Shimkus***	N	N	Y	N	Y	N	Y	Y
INDIANA								
1 Visclosky	N	Y	N	Y	Y	Y	N	N
2 ***McIntosh***	N	N	Y	N	Y	N	Y	Y
3 Roemer	N	Y	Y	N	Y	Y	Y	Y
4 ***Souder***	N	N	Y	N	Y	N	Y	?
5 ***Buyer***	N	N	Y	N	Y	N	Y	Y
6 ***Burton***	N	N	Y	N	Y	N	Y	Y
7 ***Pease***	N	N	Y	N	Y	N	Y	Y
8 ***Hostettler***	N	N	Y	N	Y	N	Y	Y
9 Hamilton	Y	Y	Y	Y	Y	Y	N	Y
10 Carson	Y	Y	Y	Y	Y	Y	N	Y
IOWA								
1 ***Leach***	N	N	Y	N	Y	Y	Y	Y
2 ***Nussle***	N	N	Y	N	Y	N	Y	N
3 Boswell	N	Y	N	Y	Y	N	N	Y
4 ***Ganske***	N	N	Y	N	Y	N	Y	Y
5 ***Latham***	N	N	Y	N	Y	N	Y	Y
KANSAS								
1 ***Moran***	N	N	Y	N	Y	N	Y	Y
2 ***Ryun***	N	N	Y	N	Y	N	Y	Y
3 ***Snowbarger***	N	?	Y	N	Y	N	Y	Y
4 ***Tiahrt***	N	N	Y	N	Y	N	Y	Y
KENTUCKY								
1 ***Whitfield***	N	Y	Y	N	Y	N	Y	Y
2 ***Lewis***	N	N	Y	N	Y	N	Y	Y
3 ***Northup***	N	N	Y	N	Y	N	Y	Y
4 ***Bunning***	N	N	Y	N	Y	N	Y	Y
5 ***Rogers***	N	N	Y	N	Y	N	Y	Y
6 Baesler	N	N	Y	N	Y	N	Y	Y
LOUISIANA								
1 ***Livingston***	N	N	Y	N	Y	N	Y	?
2 Jefferson	Y	Y	Y	Y	Y	N	N	Y
3 ***Tauzin***	N	N	Y	N	Y	N	?	Y
4 ***McCrery***	N	N	Y	N	Y	N	Y	Y
5 ***Cooksey***	N	N	Y	N	Y	N	Y	Y
6 ***Baker***	N	N	Y	N	Y	N	Y	Y
7 John	N	Y	Y	N	Y	N	Y	Y
MAINE								
1 Allen	Y	Y	+	Y	Y	Y	N	Y
2 Baldacci	Y	Y	Y	Y	Y	Y	N	Y
MARYLAND								
1 ***Gilchrest***	N	N	Y	N	Y	Y	Y	Y
2 ***Ehrlich***	N	N	Y	N	Y	N	?	Y
3 Cardin	N	Y	Y	N	Y	Y	N	Y
4 Wynn	Y	Y	Y	Y	Y	Y	N	Y
5 Hoyer	Y	Y	Y	Y	Y	Y	N	Y
6 ***Bartlett***	N	N	Y	N	Y	N	Y	Y
7 Cummings	Y	Y	Y	Y	Y	Y	N	Y
8 ***Morella***	N	N	Y	N	Y	Y	Y	Y
MASSACHUSETTS								
1 Olver	Y	Y	Y	Y	Y	Y	N	Y
2 Neal	Y	Y	Y	Y	Y	Y	N	Y
3 McGovern	Y	Y	Y	Y	Y	Y	N	Y
4 Frank	Y	Y	Y	Y	Y	Y	N	Y
5 Meehan	Y	Y	Y	Y	Y	Y	N	Y
6 Tierney	Y	Y	Y	Y	Y	Y	N	Y
7 Markey	Y	Y	Y	Y	Y	Y	N	Y
8 Kennedy	Y	Y	Y	Y	Y	Y	N	Y
9 Moakley	Y	Y	Y	Y	Y	Y	N	Y
10 Delahunt	Y	Y	Y	Y	Y	+	N	Y
MICHIGAN								
1 Stupak	Y	Y	Y	Y	Y	Y	N	N
2 ***Hoekstra***	N	N	Y	N	Y	N	Y	Y
3 ***Ehlers***	N	N	Y	N	Y	Y	Y	Y
4 ***Camp***	N	N	Y	N	Y	N	Y	Y
5 Barcia	Y	Y	Y	Y	Y	Y	N	Y
6 ***Upton***	N	N	Y	N	Y	Y	Y	Y
7 ***Smith***	N	N	Y	N	Y	Y	Y	Y
8 Stabenow	N	Y	Y	Y	N	Y	N	Y
9 Kildee	Y	Y	Y	Y	Y	Y	N	Y
10 Bonior	Y	Y	Y	Y	Y	Y	N	Y
11 ***Knollenberg***	N	N	Y	N	Y	N	Y	Y
12 Levin	Y	N	Y	Y	Y	Y	N	Y
13 Rivers	Y	Y	Y	Y	Y	Y	N	Y
14 Conyers	Y	Y	Y	Y	Y	Y	N	Y
15 Kilpatrick	Y	Y	Y	Y	Y	Y	N	Y
16 Dingell	Y	N	Y	Y	Y	Y	Y	Y
MINNESOTA								
1 ***Gutknecht***	N	N	Y	N	Y	N	Y	N
2 Minge	N	Y	N	N	Y	Y	N	Y

	103	104	105	106	107	108	109	110
3 ***Ramstad***	N	N	Y	N	Y	Y	Y	N
4 Vento	Y	Y	Y	Y	N	Y	N	Y
5 Sabo	Y	Y	Y	Y	Y	Y	N	N
6 Luther	N	N	Y	Y	Y	Y	N	Y
7 Peterson	N	N	Y	N	Y	N	Y	Y
8 Oberstar	Y	Y	Y	Y	Y	Y	N	N
MISSISSIPPI								
1 ***Wicker***	N	N	Y	N	Y	N	Y	N
2 Thompson	Y	Y	Y	Y	Y	Y	N	N
3 ***Pickering***	N	N	Y	N	Y	N	Y	Y
4 ***Parker***	N	N	Y	N	Y	N	Y	Y
5 Taylor	N	N	N	N	Y	N	N	N
MISSOURI								
1 Clay	?	?	?	?	?	?	?	?
2 ***Talent***	N	N	Y	N	Y	N	?	Y
3 Gephardt	Y	Y	Y	Y	Y	Y	?	N
4 Skelton	Y	Y	Y	N	Y	N	Y	Y
5 McCarthy	Y	Y	Y	Y	Y	Y	Y	Y
6 Danner	N	N	Y	N	Y	N	Y	Y
7 ***Blunt***	N	N	Y	N	?	N	Y	?
8 ***Emerson***	N	N	Y	N	Y	N	Y	Y
9 ***Hulshof***	N	N	Y	N	Y	N	Y	N
MONTANA								
AL ***Hill***	N	N	Y	N	Y	N	Y	N
NEBRASKA								
1 ***Bereuter***	N	N	Y	N	Y	N	Y	Y
2 ***Christensen***	N	N	Y	N	Y	N	Y	Y
3 ***Barrett***	N	N	Y	N	Y	N	Y	Y
NEVADA								
1 ***Ensign***	N	N	Y	N	Y	N	Y	N
2 ***Gibbons***	N	N	Y	N	Y	N	Y	N
NEW HAMPSHIRE								
1 ***Sununu***	N	N	Y	N	Y	Y	Y	Y
2 ***Bass***	N	N	Y	N	Y	Y	Y	Y
NEW JERSEY								
1 Andrews	?	?	?	?	?	?	?	?
2 ***LoBiondo***	N	N	Y	N	Y	Y	Y	N
3 ***Saxton***	N	N	Y	N	Y	Y	Y	Y
4 ***Smith***	N	N	Y	N	Y	Y	Y	Y
5 ***Roukema***	N	N	Y	N	Y	Y	N	Y
6 Pallone	Y	Y	Y	Y	Y	Y	N	N
7 ***Franks***	N	N	Y	N	Y	Y	Y	Y
8 Pascrell	N	Y	Y	Y	Y	Y	N	N
9 Rothman	N	Y	Y	Y	Y	Y	N	Y
10 Payne	Y	Y	Y	Y	Y	Y	N	Y
11 ***Frelinghuysen***	N	N	Y	N	Y	Y	Y	Y
12 ***Pappas***	N	N	Y	N	Y	Y	Y	Y
13 Menendez	Y	Y	Y	Y	Y	Y	N	N
NEW MEXICO								
1 ***Schiff***	?	?	?	?	?	?	?	?
2 ***Skeen***	N	N	Y	N	Y	N	Y	Y
3 Vacant								
NEW YORK								
1 ***Forbes***	Y	N	N	N	Y	Y	Y	N
2 ***Lazio***	N	N	Y	N	Y	Y	Y	Y
3 ***King***	N	N	N	N	Y	N	Y	Y
4 McCarthy	N	Y	Y	Y	Y	Y	N	Y
5 Ackerman	Y	Y	Y	N	Y	Y	N	Y
6 Flake	Y	Y	Y	Y	Y	Y	N	Y
7 Manton	N	N	?	Y	Y	Y	N	Y
8 Nadler	Y	Y	Y	Y	Y	Y	N	Y
9 Schumer	N	Y	Y	Y	Y	Y	N	Y
10 Towns	Y	Y	Y	Y	Y	Y	N	Y
11 Owens	Y	Y	N	Y	Y	Y	N	Y
12 Velázquez	Y	Y	Y	Y	Y	Y	N	N
13 ***Molinari***	N	N	Y	N	Y	N	Y	Y
14 Maloney	Y	Y	Y	Y	Y	Y	N	Y
15 Rangel	Y	Y	?	Y	Y	Y	N	Y
16 Serrano	Y	Y	Y	Y	Y	Y	N	Y
17 Engel	Y	Y	Y	Y	Y	Y	N	+
18 Lowey	Y	Y	Y	Y	Y	Y	N	Y
19 ***Kelly***	N	N	Y	N	Y	Y	Y	Y
20 ***Gilman***	N	N	Y	N	Y	Y	Y	Y
21 McNulty	Y	Y	Y	Y	N	Y	N	N
22 ***Solomon***	N	N	Y	N	Y	N	Y	Y
23 ***Boehlert***	N	N	Y	N	Y	Y	Y	Y
24 ***McHugh***	N	N	Y	N	Y	N	Y	Y
25 ***Walsh***	N	N	Y	N	Y	Y	Y	Y
26 Hinchey	Y	Y	Y	Y	N	Y	N	Y
27 ***Paxon***	N	N	Y	N	Y	N	Y	Y
28 Slaughter	Y	Y	Y	Y	Y	Y	N	N
29 LaFalce	Y	Y	Y	Y	Y	Y	N	N
30 ***Quinn***	N	N	Y	N	Y	Y	Y	Y
31 ***Houghton***	N	N	Y	N	Y	Y	Y	Y

	103	104	105	106	107	108	109	110
NORTH CAROLINA								
1 Clayton	Y	Y	Y	Y	Y	Y	N	Y
2 Etheridge	Y	Y	Y	Y	Y	Y	N	Y
3 ***Jones***	N	N	Y	N	Y	N	Y	Y
4 Price	Y	Y	Y	Y	Y	Y	N	Y
5 ***Burr***	N	N	Y	N	?	N	Y	Y
6 ***Coble***	N	N	Y	N	Y	N	Y	Y
7 McIntyre	N	N	Y	Y	Y	Y	N	Y
8 Hefner	Y	Y	Y	Y	Y	Y	N	?
9 ***Myrick***	N	N	Y	N	Y	N	Y	Y
10 ***Ballenger***	N	N	Y	N	Y	N	Y	Y
11 ***Taylor***	N	N	N	N	?	N	Y	Y
12 Watt	Y	Y	Y	Y	Y	Y	N	N
NORTH DAKOTA								
AL Pomeroy	Y	N	Y	Y	Y	N	N	Y
OHIO								
1 ***Chabot***	N	N	Y	N	Y	N	Y	Y
2 ***Portman***	N	N	Y	N	Y	N	Y	Y
3 Hall	N	N	Y	Y	Y	Y	N	Y
4 ***Oxley***	N	N	Y	N	Y	N	Y	Y
5 ***Gillmor***	N	N	Y	N	Y	Y	Y	Y
6 Strickland	N	Y	Y	Y	Y	Y	N	Y
7 ***Hobson***	N	N	Y	N	Y	Y	Y	Y
8 ***Boehner***	N	N	Y	N	Y	N	Y	Y
9 Kaptur	Y	Y	?	?	Y	Y	N	Y
10 Kucinich	Y	Y	Y	Y	Y	Y	N	N
11 Stokes	Y	Y	Y	Y	Y	Y	N	Y
12 ***Kasich***	N	N	Y	N	Y	N	Y	?
13 Brown	Y	Y	+	Y	Y	Y	N	Y
14 Sawyer	Y	Y	Y	Y	Y	Y	N	Y
15 ***Pryce***	N	N	Y	N	Y	N	Y	N
16 ***Regula***	N	N	Y	N	Y	N	Y	Y
17 Traficant	N	N	Y	N	Y	N	Y	Y
18 ***Ney***	N	N	Y	N	Y	N	Y	Y
19 ***LaTourette***	N	N	Y	N	Y	Y	Y	Y
OKLAHOMA								
1 ***Largent***	N	N	Y	N	Y	N	Y	Y
2 ***Coburn***	N	N	Y	N	Y	N	Y	Y
3 ***Watkins***	N	N	Y	N	Y	N	Y	Y
4 ***Watts***	N	N	Y	N	Y	N	Y	N
5 ***Istook***	N	N	Y	N	Y	N	Y	Y
6 ***Lucas***	N	N	Y	N	Y	N	Y	Y
OREGON								
1 Furse	Y	Y	Y	Y	N	Y	N	Y
2 ***Smith***	N	N	Y	N	Y	N	Y	Y
3 Blumenauer	N	Y	N	Y	Y	Y	N	Y
4 DeFazio	N	Y	Y	?	N	Y	N	N
5 Hooley	Y	Y	Y	Y	Y	Y	N	Y
PENNSYLVANIA								
1 Foglietta	Y	Y	Y	Y	Y	Y	N	Y
2 Fattah	Y	Y	Y	Y	Y	Y	N	Y
3 Borski	N	Y	Y	Y	Y	Y	N	N
4 Klink	N	N	Y	Y	Y	Y	Y	Y
5 ***Peterson***	N	N	Y	N	Y	N	Y	Y
6 Holden	N	N	Y	Y	Y	N	Y	Y
7 ***Weldon***	N	N	Y	N	Y	Y	Y	Y
8 ***Greenwood***	N	N	Y	N	Y	Y	?	Y
9 ***Shuster***	N	N	Y	N	Y	N	Y	Y
10 ***McDade***	N	N	N	N	Y	Y	Y	Y
11 Kanjorski	N	Y	Y	Y	Y	Y	Y	Y
12 Murtha	N	N	Y	Y	Y	Y	Y	Y
13 ***Fox***	N	Y	Y	N	Y	Y	Y	N
14 Coyne	Y	Y	Y	Y	Y	Y	N	Y
15 McHale	N	N	Y	Y	Y	Y	N	Y
16 ***Pitts***	N	N	Y	N	Y	N	Y	Y
17 ***Gekas***	N	N	Y	N	Y	N	Y	Y
18 Doyle	N	N	Y	Y	Y	Y	Y	?
19 ***Goodling***	N	N	Y	N	Y	N	Y	Y
20 Mascara	N	N	Y	Y	Y	Y	Y	Y
21 ***English***	N	N	Y	N	Y	Y	Y	N
RHODE ISLAND								
1 Kennedy	Y	Y	Y	Y	N	Y	N	N
2 Weygand	N	Y	Y	Y	Y	Y	N	Y
SOUTH CAROLINA								
1 ***Sanford***	N	N	Y	N	Y	Y	Y	Y
2 ***Spence***	N	N	Y	N	Y	N	Y	Y
3 ***Graham***	N	N	Y	N	Y	N	Y	Y
4 ***Inglis***	N	N	Y	N	Y	N	Y	Y
5 Spratt	N	Y	Y	Y	Y	Y	N	Y
6 Clyburn	Y	Y	Y	Y	Y	Y	N	N
SOUTH DAKOTA								
AL ***Thune***	N	N	Y	N	Y	N	Y	N
TENNESSEE								
1 ***Jenkins***	N	N	Y	N	Y	N	Y	+
2 ***Duncan***	N	N	Y	N	Y	N	Y	Y

	103	104	105	106	107	108	109	
3 ***Wamp***	N	N	Y	N	Y	N	Y	N
4 ***Hilleary***	N	N	Y	N	Y	N	Y	N
5 Clement	N	N	N	Y	Y	Y	N	Y
6 Gordon	N	N	Y	Y	Y	Y	Y	Y
7 ***Bryant***	N	N	Y	N	Y	N	Y	Y
8 Tanner	N	N	Y	N	Y	Y	Y	Y
9 Ford	Y	Y	Y	Y	Y	Y	N	Y
TEXAS								
1 Sandlin	Y	Y	Y	Y	Y	N	Y	Y
2 Turner	N	N	Y	Y	Y	N	Y	Y
3 ***Johnson, Sam***	N	N	Y	N	Y	N	Y	Y
4 Hall	N	N	N	N	Y	N	Y	Y
5 ***Sessions***	N	N	+	N	Y	N	Y	?
6 ***Barton***	N	N	Y	N	Y	?	Y	Y
7 ***Archer***	N	N	?	N	Y	N	Y	Y
8 ***Brady***	N	N	Y	N	Y	N	Y	Y
9 Lampson	Y	Y	Y	Y	Y	Y	N	Y
10 Doggett	N	Y	Y	Y	Y	Y	N	Y
11 Edwards	Y	Y	+	+	Y	N	N	Y
12 ***Granger***	N	N	Y	N	Y	N	Y	?
13 ***Thornberry***	N	N	Y	N	Y	N	Y	Y
14 ***Paul***	N	N	N	N	Y	N	Y	Y
15 Hinojosa	Y	Y	Y	Y	Y	Y	N	Y
16 Reyes	?	?	?	?	?	?	N	Y
17 Stenholm	N	N	N	N	Y	N	Y	Y
18 Jackson-Lee	Y	Y	Y	Y	Y	Y	N	N
19 ***Combest***	N	N	Y	N	Y	N	Y	Y
20 Gonzalez	Y	Y	Y	Y	Y	Y	N	Y
21 ***Smith***	N	N	Y	N	Y	N	Y	Y
22 ***DeLay***	N	N	Y	N	Y	N	Y	Y
23 ***Bonilla***	N	N	Y	N	Y	N	Y	Y
24 Frost	Y	Y	Y	Y	Y	Y	N	Y
25 Bentsen	Y	Y	Y	Y	Y	Y	N	Y
26 ***Armey***	N	N	Y	N	Y	N	Y	Y
27 Ortiz	N	N	Y	Y	Y	N	Y	Y
28 Rodriguez	Y	Y	Y	Y	Y	N	N	Y
29 Green	Y	N	Y	Y	Y	Y	Y	N
30 Johnson, E.B.	Y	Y	Y	Y	Y	Y	N	N
UTAH								
1 ***Hansen***	N	N	Y	N	Y	N	Y	N
2 ***Cook***	N	N	Y	N	Y	N	Y	Y
3 ***Cannon***	N	N	Y	N	Y	N	Y	Y
VERMONT								
AL *Sanders*	Y	Y	Y	Y	Y	Y	N	Y
VIRGINIA								
1 ***Bateman***	N	N	Y	N	Y	N	Y	Y
2 Pickett	N	Y	Y	N	Y	N	Y	N
3 Scott	Y	Y	Y	Y	Y	Y	N	Y
4 Sisisky	N	Y	Y	N	Y	N	Y	Y
5 Goode	N	N	Y	N	Y	N	Y	Y
6 ***Goodlatte***	N	N	Y	N	Y	N	Y	Y
7 ***Bliley***	N	N	Y	N	Y	N	Y	Y
8 Moran	N	N	Y	N	Y	Y	Y	Y
9 Boucher	Y	Y	Y	Y	Y	Y	?	Y
10 ***Wolf***	N	N	Y	N	Y	Y	Y	?
11 ***Davis***	N	N	Y	N	Y	Y	Y	Y
WASHINGTON								
1 ***White***	N	N	Y	N	Y	Y	Y	?
2 ***Metcalf***	N	N	?	N	Y	Y	Y	Y
3 ***Smith, Linda***	N	N	Y	N	Y	Y	Y	Y
4 ***Hastings***	N	N	Y	N	Y	N	Y	Y
5 ***Nethercutt***	N	N	Y	N	Y	N	Y	Y
6 Dicks	N	Y	Y	Y	Y	Y	?	Y
7 McDermott	Y	Y	Y	Y	Y	Y	N	N
8 ***Dunn***	N	N	Y	N	Y	N	Y	Y
9 Smith, Adam	N	Y	Y	Y	Y	Y	Y	Y
WEST VIRGINIA								
1 Mollohan	Y	Y	Y	Y	Y	Y	Y	Y
2 Wise	Y	Y	Y	Y	Y	Y	N	Y
3 Rahall	Y	Y	Y	Y	Y	Y	N	Y
WISCONSIN								
1 ***Neumann***	N	N	Y	N	Y	Y	Y	Y
2 ***Klug***	N	N	Y	N	Y	Y	Y	Y
3 Kind	Y	Y	Y	Y	Y	Y	N	Y
4 Kleczka	N	Y	Y	Y	Y	Y	N	Y
5 Barrett	Y	Y	Y	Y	Y	Y	N	Y
6 ***Petri***	N	N	Y	N	Y	Y	Y	Y
7 Obey	N	Y	Y	Y	Y	Y	N	Y
8 Johnson	N	Y	Y	Y	Y	Y	N	Y
9 ***Sensenbrenner***	N	N	Y	N	Y	Y	Y	Y
WYOMING								
AL ***Cubin***	N	N	Y	N	Y	N	Y	N

Southern states - Ala., Ark., Fla., Ga., Ky., La., Miss., N.C., Okla., S.C., Tenn., Texas, Va.

HOUSE VOTES 111, 112, 113, 114, 115, 116, 117, 118

111. HR 3. Juvenile Crime/Prevention Grants. Stupak, D-Mich., substitute amendment to authorize $1.5 billion in discretionary grants to local communities for juvenile crime prevention programs and construction of juvenile incarceration facilities. The amendment would require localities to use at least 60 percent of grant funds for prevention and early intervention programs. Rejected 200-224: R 5-218; D 194-6 (ND 145-2, SD 49-4); I 1-0, May 8, 1997.

112. HR 3. Juvenile Crime/Drug Conspiracy Prosecution. Waters, D-Calif., amendment to delete the provision that would require juveniles who are charged with conspiracy to commit drug crimes to be prosecuted as adults. Rejected 100-320: R 2-217; D 97-103 (ND 79-68, SD 18-35); I 1-0, May 8, 1997.

113. HR 3. Juvenile Crime/Young Juvenile Prosecution. Conyers, D-Mich., amendment to delete the provision that would permit prosecution of 13-year-olds as adults. Rejected 129-288: R 7-211; D 121-77 (ND 93-52, SD 28-25); I 1-0, May 8, 1997.

114. HR 3. Juvenile Crime/Prison Funding. Scott, D-Va., amendment to delete the provision that would allow states to use juvenile crime block grant funds to build, operate or expand juvenile prisons and detention centers. Rejected 101-321: R 3-218; D 97-103 (ND 79-68, SD 18-35); I 1-0, May 8, 1997.

115. HR 3. Juvenile Crime/Prevention Programs. Lofgren, D-Calif., amendment to require 50 percent of the juvenile crime block grant funds to be used for juvenile crime prevention programs. Rejected 191-227: R 6-213; D 184-14 (ND 141-5, SD 43-9); I 1-0, May 8, 1997.

116. HR 3. Juvenile Crime/Sex Offender Notification. Dunn, R-Wash., amendment to require states to submit a plan to the Justice Department describing the process by which parents will be notified whenever a convicted juvenile sex offender is enrolled in an elementary or secondary school in order to be eligible for certain funding. Adopted 398-21: R 216-4; D 181-17 (ND 133-14, SD 48-3); I 1-0, May 8, 1997.

117. HR 3. Juvenile Crime/Recommit. Conyers, D-Mich., motion to recommit the bill to the Judiciary Committee with instructions to report it back with an amendment to eliminate the bill's conditions for states to receive juvenile crime block grant funds and give states more discretion to use the funds for prevention programs. Motion rejected 174-243: R 2-216; D 171-27 (ND 130-15, SD 41-12); I 1-0, May 8, 1997.

118. HR 3. Juvenile Crime/Passage. Passage of the bill to make it easier for federal authorities to prosecute juveniles who commit federal violent crimes or federal drug-trafficking offenses as adults and authorize $1.5 billion in financial incentives through fiscal 2000 for state and local authorities to prosecute juveniles charged with serious crimes as adults. Passed 286-132: R 209-9; D 77-122 (ND 43-103, SD 34-19); I 0-1, May 8, 1997. A "nay" was a vote in support of the president's position.

KEY

- Y Voted for (yea).
- # Paired for.
- + Announced for.
- N Voted against (nay).
- X Paired against.
- – Announced against.
- P Voted "present."
- C Voted "present" to avoid possible conflict of interest.
- ? Did not vote or otherwise make a position known.

Democrats ***Republicans***
Independent

	111	112	113	114	115	116	117	118
ALABAMA								
1 ***Callahan***	N	N	N	N	N	Y	N	Y
2 ***Everett***	N	N	N	N	N	Y	N	Y
3 ***Riley***	N	N	N	N	N	Y	N	Y
4 ***Aderholt***	N	N	N	N	N	Y	N	Y
5 Cramer	N	N	N	N	N	Y	N	Y
6 ***Bachus***	N	N	N	N	N	Y	N	Y
7 Hilliard	Y	Y	Y	Y	Y	Y	Y	N
ALASKA								
AL ***Young***	N	N	N	N	N	Y	N	Y
ARIZONA								
1 ***Salmon***	N	N	N	N	N	Y	N	Y
2 Pastor	Y	N	Y	Y	Y	Y	Y	N
3 ***Stump***	N	N	N	N	N	Y	N	Y
4 ***Shadegg***	N	N	N	N	N	Y	N	N
5 ***Kolbe***	N	N	N	N	N	Y	N	Y
6 ***Hayworth***	N	N	N	N	N	Y	N	Y
ARKANSAS								
1 Berry	Y	N	Y	Y	Y	Y	N	N
2 Snyder	Y	N	Y	N	N	Y	Y	N
3 ***Hutchinson***	N	N	N	N	N	Y	N	Y
4 ***Dickey***	N	N	N	N	N	Y	N	Y
CALIFORNIA								
1 ***Riggs***	N	N	N	N	N	Y	N	Y
2 ***Herger***	N	N	N	N	N	Y	N	Y
3 Fazio	Y	Y	Y	N	Y	Y	Y	N
4 ***Doolittle***	N	N	N	N	N	Y	N	Y
5 Matsui	Y	Y	N	N	Y	Y	?	N
6 Woolsey	Y	Y	Y	Y	Y	Y	Y	N
7 Miller	Y	Y	Y	Y	Y	Y	Y	N
8 Pelosi	Y	Y	Y	Y	Y	Y	Y	N
9 Dellums	Y	Y	Y	Y	Y	Y	Y	N
10 Tauscher	Y	N	N	N	Y	Y	Y	Y
11 ***Pombo***	N	N	N	N	N	Y	N	Y
12 Lantos	Y	Y	Y	Y	Y	Y	Y	N
13 Stark	Y	Y	Y	Y	Y	N	Y	N
14 Eshoo	Y	N	Y	Y	Y	Y	Y	N
15 ***Campbell***	Y	N	N	N	N	N	N	N
16 Lofgren	Y	Y	Y	Y	Y	Y	Y	N
17 Farr	Y	Y	Y	Y	Y	Y	Y	N
18 Condit	Y	N	N	N	Y	Y	Y	Y
19 ***Radanovich***	N	N	N	N	N	Y	N	Y
20 Dooley	Y	N	N	N	Y	Y	Y	Y
21 ***Thomas***	N	N	N	N	N	Y	N	Y
22 Capps	Y	Y	Y	N	Y	+	Y	N
23 ***Gallegly***	N	N	N	N	N	Y	N	Y
24 Sherman	Y	N	N	N	Y	Y	Y	Y
25 ***McKeon***	N	N	N	N	N	Y	N	Y
26 Berman	Y	N	Y	N	Y	Y	Y	N
27 ***Rogan***	N	N	N	N	N	Y	N	Y
28 ***Dreier***	N	N	N	N	N	Y	N	Y
29 Waxman	Y	Y	Y	Y	Y	Y	Y	N
30 Becerra	Y	Y	Y	Y	Y	N	Y	N
31 Martinez	Y	Y	Y	Y	Y	Y	Y	N
32 Dixon	Y	Y	Y	N	Y	Y	Y	N
33 Roybal-Allard	Y	Y	Y	Y	Y	Y	Y	N
34 Torres	Y	N	Y	Y	Y	Y	Y	N
35 Waters	Y	Y	Y	Y	Y	N	Y	N
36 Harman	Y	N	N	N	Y	Y	Y	Y
37 Millender-McD.	Y	Y	Y	Y	Y	Y	Y	N
38 ***Horn***	N	N	N	N	N	Y	N	Y
39 ***Royce***	N	N	N	N	N	Y	N	Y
40 ***Lewis***	?	N	N	N	N	Y	N	Y
41 ***Kim***	N	N	N	N	N	Y	N	Y
42 Brown	Y	Y	Y	Y	Y	Y	Y	N
43 ***Calvert***	N	N	N	N	N	Y	X	#
44 ***Bono***	N	N	N	N	N	Y	N	Y
45 ***Rohrabacher***	N	Y	N	N	N	Y	N	Y
46 Sanchez	Y	?	?	N	Y	Y	Y	Y
47 ***Cox***	N	N	N	N	?	Y	N	Y
48 ***Packard***	N	N	N	N	N	Y	N	Y
49 ***Bilbray***	N	N	N	N	N	Y	N	Y
50 Filner	?	#	#	#	#	?	#	X
51 ***Cunningham***	N	N	N	N	N	Y	N	Y
52 ***Hunter***	N	N	N	N	N	Y	N	Y
COLORADO								
1 DeGette	Y	Y	Y	Y	Y	Y	Y	N
2 Skaggs	Y	N	Y	Y	Y	Y	Y	N
3 ***McInnis***	N	N	N	N	N	Y	N	Y
4 ***Schaffer***	N	N	N	N	N	Y	N	N
5 ***Hefley***	N	N	N	N	N	Y	N	Y
6 ***Schaefer***	N	N	N	N	N	Y	N	Y
CONNECTICUT								
1 Kennelly	Y	Y	Y	Y	Y	Y	Y	N
2 Gejdenson	Y	Y	Y	Y	Y	Y	Y	N
3 DeLauro	Y	N	N	N	Y	Y	Y	Y
4 ***Shays***	N	N	N	N	Y	Y	Y	Y
5 Maloney	Y	N	N	N	Y	Y	Y	Y
6 ***Johnson***	N	N	N	N	+	Y	N	Y
DELAWARE								
AL ***Castle***	N	N	N	N	Y	Y	N	Y
FLORIDA								
1 ***Scarborough***	N	X	?	N	N	Y	N	Y
2 Boyd	Y	N	N	N	Y	Y	Y	Y
3 Brown	Y	Y	Y	Y	Y	Y	Y	N
4 ***Fowler***	N	N	N	N	N	Y	N	Y
5 Thurman	Y	Y	Y	Y	Y	Y	Y	N
6 ***Stearns***	N	N	N	N	N	Y	N	Y
7 ***Mica***	N	N	N	N	N	Y	N	Y
8 ***McCollum***	N	N	N	N	N	Y	N	Y
9 ***Bilirakis***	N	N	N	N	N	Y	N	Y
10 ***Young***	N	N	N	N	N	Y	N	Y
11 Davis	Y	N	Y	N	Y	Y	Y	Y
12 ***Canady***	N	N	N	N	N	Y	N	Y
13 ***Miller***	N	N	N	N	N	Y	N	Y
14 ***Goss***	N	N	N	N	N	Y	N	Y
15 ***Weldon***	N	N	N	N	N	Y	N	Y
16 ***Foley***	N	N	N	N	N	Y	N	Y
17 Meek	Y	Y	Y	Y	Y	Y	Y	N
18 ***Ros-Lehtinen***	N	N	N	N	N	Y	N	Y
19 Wexler	Y	N	N	N	Y	Y	Y	Y
20 Deutsch	Y	N	N	N	Y	Y	Y	Y
21 ***Diaz-Balart***	N	X	X	X	X	?	?	#
22 ***Shaw***	N	N	N	N	N	Y	N	Y
23 Hastings	Y	Y	Y	Y	Y	N	Y	N
GEORGIA								
1 ***Kingston***	N	N	N	N	N	Y	N	Y
2 Bishop	Y	Y	Y	Y	Y	Y	Y	Y
3 ***Collins***	N	N	N	N	N	Y	N	Y
4 McKinney	?	#	?	?	?	?	?	?
5 Lewis	Y	Y	Y	Y	Y	Y	Y	N
6 ***Gingrich***								
7 ***Barr***	N	N	?	N	N	Y	N	Y
8 ***Chambliss***	N	N	N	N	N	Y	N	Y
9 ***Deal***	N	N	N	N	N	Y	N	Y
10 ***Norwood***	N	N	N	N	N	Y	N	Y
11 ***Linder***	N	N	N	N	N	Y	N	Y
HAWAII								
1 Abercrombie	P	Y	Y	N	N	Y	N	Y
2 Mink	Y	Y	Y	Y	Y	Y	Y	N
IDAHO								
1 ***Chenoweth***	N	N	N	N	N	Y	N	Y
2 ***Crapo***	N	N	N	N	N	Y	N	Y
ILLINOIS								
1 Rush	Y	Y	Y	Y	Y	Y	Y	N
2 Jackson	Y	Y	Y	Y	Y	Y	Y	N
3 Lipinski	Y	N	N	N	Y	Y	N	Y
4 Gutierrez	Y	Y	Y	Y	Y	Y	?	?
5 Blagojevich	Y	N	N	N	?	Y	Y	N
6 ***Hyde***	N	N	N	N	N	Y	N	Y
7 Davis	Y	Y	Y	Y	Y	Y	Y	N
8 ***Crane***	N	N	N	N	N	Y	N	Y
9 Yates	Y	Y	Y	Y	Y	N	Y	N
10 ***Porter***	N	N	N	N	N	Y	N	Y
11 ***Weller***	N	N	N	N	N	Y	N	Y
12 Costello	?	?	?	?	?	?	?	?
13 ***Fawell***	N	N	N	N	N	?	N	Y
14 ***Hastert***	N	N	N	N	N	Y	N	Y
15 ***Ewing***	N	N	N	N	N	Y	N	Y

ND Northern Democrats SD Southern Democrats

	111	112	113	114	115	116	117	118
16 ***Manzullo***	N	N	N	N	N	Y	N	Y
17 Evans	Y	Y	Y	Y	Y	Y	Y	N
18 ***LaHood***	N	N	N	N	N	Y	N	Y
19 Poshard	Y	N	N	N	Y	Y	Y	Y
20 ***Shimkus***	N	N	N	N	N	Y	N	Y
INDIANA								
1 Visclosky	Y	N	Y	N	Y	Y	Y	N
2 ***McIntosh***	N	N	N	N	N	Y	N	Y
3 Roemer	Y	N	N	N	Y	Y	Y	Y
4 ***Souder***	N	N	N	N	N	Y	N	Y
5 ***Buyer***	N	N	Y	N	?	N	N	Y
6 ***Burton***	N	N	N	N	N	Y	N	Y
7 ***Pease***	N	N	N	N	N	Y	N	Y
8 ***Hostettler***	N	N	N	N	N	Y	N	N
9 Hamilton	Y	N	N	N	N	Y	Y	Y
10 Carson	Y	Y	Y	Y	Y	Y	Y	N
IOWA								
1 ***Leach***	N	N	N	N	N	Y	N	Y
2 ***Nussle***	N	N	N	N	N	Y	N	Y
3 Boswell	Y	N	N	N	Y	Y	N	Y
4 ***Ganske***	N	N	N	N	N	Y	N	Y
5 ***Latham***	N	N	N	N	N	Y	N	Y
KANSAS								
1 ***Moran***	N	N	N	N	N	Y	N	Y
2 ***Ryun***	N	N	N	N	N	Y	N	Y
3 ***Snowbarger***	N	N	N	N	N	Y	N	Y
4 ***Tiahrt***	N	N	N	N	N	Y	N	Y
KENTUCKY								
1 ***Whitfield***	N	N	N	N	N	Y	N	Y
2 ***Lewis***	N	N	N	N	N	Y	N	Y
3 ***Northup***	N	N	N	–	N	Y	N	Y
4 ***Bunning***	N	N	N	N	N	Y	N	Y
5 ***Rogers***	N	N	N	N	N	Y	N	Y
6 Baesler	N	N	N	N	N	Y	N	Y
LOUISIANA								
1 ***Livingston***	N	N	N	N	N	Y	N	Y
2 Jefferson	Y	Y	Y	Y	Y	Y	Y	N
3 ***Tauzin***	N	N	N	N	N	Y	N	Y
4 ***McCrery***	N	N	N	N	N	Y	?	?
5 ***Cooksey***	N	N	N	N	N	Y	N	Y
6 ***Baker***	N	N	N	N	N	Y	N	Y
7 John	Y	N	N	N	Y	Y	Y	Y
MAINE								
1 Allen	Y	Y	Y	N	Y	Y	Y	N
2 Baldacci	Y	Y	N	N	Y	Y	Y	N
MARYLAND								
1 ***Gilchrest***	N	N	N	N	N	Y	N	Y
2 ***Ehrlich***	N	N	N	N	N	Y	N	Y
3 Cardin	Y	N	N	N	Y	Y	Y	N
4 Wynn	Y	Y	Y	Y	Y	Y	Y	N
5 Hoyer	Y	N	N	N	Y	Y	Y	N
6 ***Bartlett***	N	N	N	N	N	Y	N	Y
7 Cummings	Y	Y	Y	Y	Y	Y	Y	N
8 ***Morella***	Y	Y	N	N	Y	Y	Y	N
MASSACHUSETTS								
1 Olver	Y	Y	Y	Y	Y	Y	Y	N
2 Neal	Y	N	Y	Y	Y	Y	Y	N
3 McGovern	Y	Y	Y	Y	Y	Y	Y	N
4 Frank	Y	Y	?	N	Y	Y	Y	N
5 Meehan	Y	N	Y	N	Y	Y	Y	N
6 Tierney	Y	N	Y	Y	Y	Y	Y	N
7 Markey	Y	Y	Y	N	Y	Y	Y	N
8 Kennedy	Y	N	Y	N	Y	Y	Y	N
9 Moakley	Y	Y	Y	Y	Y	Y	+	X
10 Delahunt	Y	Y	Y	Y	Y	Y	Y	N
MICHIGAN								
1 Stupak	Y	N	Y	Y	Y	Y	Y	N
2 ***Hoekstra***	N	N	N	N	N	Y	N	Y
3 ***Ehlers***	Y	N	Y	Y	N	Y	N	N
4 ***Camp***	N	N	N	N	N	Y	N	Y
5 Barcia	Y	N	N	N	N	Y	N	Y
6 ***Upton***	N	N	N	N	N	Y	N	Y
7 ***Smith***	N	N	N	N	N	Y	N	Y
8 Stabenow	Y	Y	Y	N	Y	Y	Y	Y
9 Kildee	Y	N	N	N	Y	Y	Y	Y
10 Bonior	Y	Y	Y	Y	Y	Y	Y	N
11 ***Knollenberg***	N	N	N	N	N	Y	N	Y
12 Levin	Y	N	N	N	Y	Y	Y	N
13 Rivers	Y	N	Y	N	Y	Y	Y	N
14 Conyers	Y	Y	Y	Y	Y	N	Y	N
15 Kilpatrick	Y	Y	Y	Y	Y	Y	Y	N
16 Dingell	Y	N	N	N	Y	N	Y	Y
MINNESOTA								
1 ***Gutknecht***	N	N	N	N	N	Y	N	Y
2 Minge	Y	Y	Y	N	Y	Y	Y	N

	111	112	113	114	115	116	117	118
3 ***Ramstad***	N	N	N	N	N	Y	N	Y
4 Vento	Y	Y	Y	Y	Y	Y	Y	N
5 Sabo	Y	Y	Y	Y	Y	N	Y	N
6 Luther	Y	N	N	N	Y	Y	Y	Y
7 Peterson	N	N	N	N	Y	Y	Y	Y
8 Oberstar	Y	Y	Y	Y	Y	Y	Y	N
MISSISSIPPI								
1 ***Wicker***	N	N	N	N	N	Y	N	Y
2 Thompson	Y	Y	Y	Y	Y	Y	Y	N
3 ***Pickering***	–	–	–	–	–	+	–	+
4 ***Parker***	N	N	N	N	N	Y	N	Y
5 Taylor	N	N	N	N	N	Y	N	Y
MISSOURI								
1 Clay	?	?	?	?	?	?	?	?
2 ***Talent***	N	N	N	N	N	Y	N	Y
3 Gephardt	Y	Y	Y	Y	Y	Y	Y	N
4 Skelton	Y	N	N	N	Y	Y	Y	Y
5 McCarthy	Y	N	Y	Y	Y	Y	Y	N
6 Danner	Y	N	N	N	N	Y	N	Y
7 ***Blunt***	N	N	N	N	N	Y	N	Y
8 ***Emerson***	N	N	N	N	N	Y	N	Y
9 ***Hulshof***	N	N	N	N	N	Y	N	Y
MONTANA								
AL ***Hill***	N	N	N	N	N	Y	N	Y
NEBRASKA								
1 ***Bereuter***	N	N	N	N	N	Y	N	Y
2 ***Christensen***	N	N	N	N	N	Y	N	Y
3 ***Barrett***	N	N	N	N	N	Y	N	Y
NEVADA								
1 ***Ensign***	Y	N	N	Y	Y	Y	N	Y
2 ***Gibbons***	N	N	N	N	N	Y	N	Y
NEW HAMPSHIRE								
1 ***Sununu***	N	N	N	N	N	Y	N	Y
2 ***Bass***	N	N	N	N	N	Y	N	Y
NEW JERSEY								
1 Andrews	Y	N	N	N	Y	Y	Y	Y
2 ***LoBiondo***	N	N	N	N	N	Y	N	Y
3 ***Saxton***	N	N	N	N	N	Y	N	Y
4 ***Smith***	N	N	N	N	N	Y	N	Y
5 ***Roukema***	N	N	Y	N	N	Y	N	Y
6 Pallone	Y	Y	N	N	Y	Y	Y	N
7 ***Franks***	N	N	Y	N	N	Y	N	Y
8 Pascrell	Y	N	N	N	Y	Y	N	Y
9 Rothman	Y	Y	N	N	Y	Y	Y	Y
10 Payne	Y	Y	Y	Y	Y	Y	Y	N
11 ***Frelinghuysen***	N	N	N	N	N	Y	N	Y
12 ***Pappas***	N	N	N	N	N	Y	N	Y
13 Menendez	Y	N	N	N	Y	Y	Y	N
NEW MEXICO								
1 ***Schiff***	?	?	?	?	?	?	?	?
2 ***Skeen***	N	N	N	N	N	Y	N	Y
3 Vacant								
NEW YORK								
1 ***Forbes***	N	N	N	N	N	Y	N	Y
2 ***Lazio***	N	N	N	N	N	Y	N	Y
3 ***King***	N	N	N	N	N	Y	N	Y
4 McCarthy	Y	N	N	Y	Y	Y	Y	N
5 Ackerman	Y	N	Y	Y	Y	Y	Y	N
6 Flake	Y	Y	Y	Y	Y	Y	Y	N
7 Manton	Y	N	N	N	Y	Y	Y	Y
8 Nadler	Y	Y	?	N	Y	Y	Y	N
9 Schumer	Y	N	N	N	Y	Y	Y	N
10 Towns	Y	Y	Y	Y	Y	N	Y	N
11 Owens	Y	Y	Y	Y	Y	Y	Y	N
12 Velázquez	Y	Y	Y	Y	Y	Y	Y	N
13 ***Molinari***	N	N	N	N	N	Y	N	Y
14 Maloney	Y	Y	Y	N	Y	Y	Y	Y
15 Rangel	Y	Y	Y	Y	Y	N	Y	N
16 Serrano	Y	Y	Y	Y	Y	Y	Y	N
17 Engel	Y	N	N	N	Y	Y	Y	Y
18 Lowey	Y	N	N	N	Y	Y	Y	Y
19 ***Kelly***	N	N	N	N	N	Y	N	Y
20 ***Gilman***	N	N	N	N	N	N	N	Y
21 McNulty	Y	N	Y	Y	Y	Y	Y	Y
22 ***Solomon***	N	N	N	N	N	Y	N	Y
23 ***Boehlert***	N	N	N	N	N	Y	N	Y
24 ***McHugh***	N	N	N	N	N	Y	N	Y
25 ***Walsh***	N	N	N	N	N	Y	N	Y
26 Hinchey	Y	Y	Y	Y	Y	N	Y	N
27 ***Paxon***	N	N	N	N	N	?	?	?
28 Slaughter	Y	Y	Y	Y	Y	Y	Y	N
29 LaFalce	Y	N	Y	Y	Y	Y	Y	N
30 ***Quinn***	N	N	N	N	Y	Y	N	Y
31 ***Houghton***	N	N	N	N	N	Y	N	Y

	111	112	113	114	115	116	117	118
NORTH CAROLINA								
1 Clayton	Y	Y	Y	Y	Y	Y	Y	N
2 Etheridge	Y	N	N	N	Y	Y	Y	Y
3 ***Jones***	N	N	N	N	N	Y	N	Y
4 Price	Y	N	Y	N	Y	Y	Y	Y
5 ***Burr***	N	N	N	N	N	Y	N	Y
6 ***Coble***	N	N	N	N	N	Y	N	Y
7 McIntyre	Y	N	N	N	Y	Y	Y	Y
8 Hefner	?	?	?	?	?	?	?	?
9 ***Myrick***	N	N	N	N	N	Y	N	Y
10 ***Ballenger***	N	N	N	N	N	Y	N	Y
11 ***Taylor***	N	N	N	N	N	Y	N	Y
12 Watt	Y	Y	Y	Y	Y	N	N	N
NORTH DAKOTA								
AL Pomeroy	Y	N	Y	N	Y	Y	Y	N
OHIO								
1 ***Chabot***	N	N	N	N	N	Y	N	Y
2 ***Portman***	N	N	N	N	N	Y	N	Y
3 Hall	Y	N	N	N	Y	Y	Y	Y
4 ***Oxley***	N	N	N	N	N	Y	N	Y
5 ***Gillmor***	N	N	N	N	N	Y	N	Y
6 Strickland	Y	N	Y	N	Y	Y	Y	N
7 ***Hobson***	N	N	N	N	N	Y	N	Y
8 ***Boehner***	N	N	N	N	N	Y	N	Y
9 Kaptur	Y	N	N	?	Y	Y	Y	Y
10 Kucinich	Y	N	N	N	Y	Y	Y	Y
11 Stokes	Y	Y	Y	Y	Y	N	Y	N
12 ***Kasich***	N	N	N	N	N	?	N	Y
13 Brown	Y	N	Y	Y	Y	Y	Y	N
14 Sawyer	Y	N	Y	Y	Y	Y	Y	N
15 ***Pryce***	N	N	N	N	N	Y	N	Y
16 ***Regula***	N	N	N	N	N	Y	N	Y
17 Traficant	N	N	N	N	N	Y	N	Y
18 ***Ney***	N	N	N	N	N	Y	N	Y
19 ***LaTourette***	N	N	N	N	N	Y	N	Y
OKLAHOMA								
1 ***Largent***	N	N	N	N	N	Y	N	Y
2 ***Coburn***	N	N	N	N	N	Y	N	Y
3 ***Watkins***	N	N	N	N	N	Y	N	Y
4 ***Watts***	N	?	Y	N	N	Y	N	Y
5 ***Istook***	N	N	N	N	N	Y	?	Y
6 ***Lucas***	N	N	N	N	N	Y	N	Y
OREGON								
1 Furse	Y	Y	Y	Y	Y	Y	Y	N
2 ***Smith***	N	N	N	N	N	Y	N	Y
3 Blumenauer	Y	Y	Y	Y	Y	Y	Y	N
4 DeFazio	Y	Y	Y	Y	Y	Y	Y	N
5 Hooley	Y	N	N	Y	+	Y	Y	Y
PENNSYLVANIA								
1 Foglietta	Y	Y	Y	Y	Y	N	Y	N
2 Fattah	Y	Y	Y	Y	Y	N	Y	N
3 Borski	Y	Y	N	N	Y	Y	Y	Y
4 Klink	Y	N	N	Y	Y	Y	N	N
5 ***Peterson***	N	–	N	N	N	Y	N	Y
6 Holden	Y	N	N	N	Y	Y	N	Y
7 ***Weldon***	N	N	N	N	N	Y	N	Y
8 ***Greenwood***	N	N	N	N	N	N	N	Y
9 ***Shuster***	N	N	N	N	N	Y	N	Y
10 ***McDade***	N	N	N	N	N	Y	N	Y
11 Kanjorski	Y	N	N	Y	Y	Y	N	N
12 Murtha	Y	N	N	N	Y	Y	N	N
13 ***Fox***	N	N	N	N	N	Y	N	Y
14 Coyne	Y	Y	Y	Y	Y	Y	Y	N
15 McHale	Y	N	N	N	Y	Y	Y	Y
16 ***Pitts***	N	N	N	N	N	Y	N	Y
17 ***Gekas***	N	N	N	N	N	Y	N	Y
18 Doyle	Y	N	N	N	Y	Y	N	N
19 ***Goodling***	N	N	N	Y	Y	Y	N	Y
20 Mascara	Y	N	N	N	Y	Y	N	N
21 ***English***	N	N	N	N	N	Y	N	+
RHODE ISLAND								
1 Kennedy	Y	Y	Y	Y	Y	Y	Y	N
2 Weygand	Y	Y	Y	N	Y	Y	Y	N
SOUTH CAROLINA								
1 ***Sanford***	N	N	N	N	N	Y	N	N
2 ***Spence***	N	N	N	N	N	Y	N	Y
3 ***Graham***	N	N	N	N	N	Y	N	Y
4 ***Inglis***	N	N	N	N	N	Y	N	Y
5 Spratt	Y	N	Y	N	Y	?	Y	Y
6 Clyburn	Y	Y	Y	Y	Y	Y	Y	N
SOUTH DAKOTA								
AL ***Thune***	N	N	N	N	N	Y	N	Y
TENNESSEE								
1 ***Jenkins***	N	N	N	N	N	Y	N	Y
2 ***Duncan***	N	N	Y	N	N	Y	N	Y

	111	112	113	114	115	116	117	
3 ***Wamp***	N	N	N	N	N	Y	N	Y
4 ***Hilleary***	N	N	N	N	N	Y	N	Y
5 Clement	Y	N	N	N	N	Y	N	Y
6 Gordon	Y	N	N	N	N	Y	N	Y
7 ***Bryant***	N	N	N	N	N	Y	N	Y
8 Tanner	Y	N	N	N	N	Y	N	Y
9 Ford	Y	Y	Y	Y	Y	Y	Y	N
TEXAS								
1 Sandlin	Y	N	Y	N	Y	Y	Y	Y
2 Turner	Y	N	N	N	Y	Y	Y	Y
3 ***Johnson, Sam***	N	N	N	?	N	Y	N	Y
4 Hall	Y	N	N	N	Y	Y	Y	Y
5 ***Sessions***	N	N	N	N	N	Y	N	Y
6 ***Barton***	N	N	N	N	N	Y	N	Y
7 ***Archer***	N	N	N	N	?	Y	N	Y
8 ***Brady***	N	N	N	N	N	Y	N	Y
9 Lampson	Y	N	Y	N	Y	Y	Y	Y
10 Doggett	Y	N	Y	N	Y	Y	Y	N
11 Edwards	Y	N	N	N	Y	Y	Y	Y
12 ***Granger***	N	N	N	N	N	Y	N	Y
13 ***Thornberry***	N	N	N	N	N	Y	N	Y
14 ***Paul***	N	N	N	N	N	Y	N	N
15 Hinojosa	Y	Y	Y	Y	Y	Y	Y	Y
16 Reyes	Y	N	N	N	Y	Y	Y	Y
17 Stenholm	Y	N	N	N	Y	Y	Y	Y
18 Jackson-Lee	Y	Y	Y	Y	Y	Y	Y	N
19 ***Combest***	N	N	N	N	N	Y	N	Y
20 Gonzalez	Y	Y	Y	N	Y	Y	Y	N
21 ***Smith***	N	N	N	N	N	Y	N	Y
22 ***DeLay***	N	N	?	N	N	Y	N	Y
23 ***Bonilla***	N	N	N	N	N	Y	N	Y
24 Frost	Y	N	N	N	Y	Y	Y	Y
25 Bentsen	Y	N	N	N	Y	Y	Y	Y
26 ***Armey***	N	N	N	N	N	Y	N	Y
27 Ortiz	Y	N	N	N	Y	Y	N	Y
28 Rodriguez	Y	N	N	N	Y	Y	Y	Y
29 Green	Y	N	N	N	Y	Y	N	Y
30 Johnson, E.B.	Y	Y	Y	Y	Y	Y	Y	N
UTAH								
1 ***Hansen***	N	N	–	N	N	Y	N	Y
2 ***Cook***	N	N	N	N	N	Y	N	Y
3 ***Cannon***	N	N	N	N	N	Y	N	N
VERMONT								
AL *Sanders*	Y	Y	Y	Y	Y	Y	Y	N
VIRGINIA								
1 ***Bateman***	N	N	N	N	N	Y	N	Y
2 Pickett	Y	N	Y	N	N	Y	N	Y
3 Scott	Y	Y	Y	Y	Y	N	Y	N
4 Sisisky	Y	N	N	N	Y	Y	Y	Y
5 Goode	N	N	N	N	N	Y	N	Y
6 ***Goodlatte***	N	N	N	N	N	Y	N	Y
7 ***Bliley***	N	?	?	N	N	Y	N	Y
8 Moran	Y	N	Y	N	Y	Y	Y	Y
9 Boucher	Y	N	N	N	?	?	Y	Y
10 ***Wolf***	N	N	N	N	N	Y	N	Y
11 ***Davis***	N	N	N	N	N	Y	N	Y
WASHINGTON								
1 ***White***	N	N	N	N	N	Y	N	Y
2 ***Metcalf***	N	N	N	N	N	Y	N	Y
3 ***Smith, Linda***	N	N	N	N	N	Y	N	Y
4 ***Hastings***	N	N	N	N	N	Y	?	?
5 ***Nethercutt***	N	N	N	N	N	Y	N	Y
6 Dicks	Y	N	N	N	Y	Y	Y	Y
7 McDermott	Y	Y	Y	Y	Y	N	Y	N
8 ***Dunn***	N	N	N	N	N	Y	N	Y
9 Smith, Adam	Y	N	N	N	Y	Y	N	Y
WEST VIRGINIA								
1 Mollohan	Y	Y	Y	Y	Y	Y	Y	N
2 Wise	Y	N	Y	N	Y	Y	Y	N
3 Rahall	Y	Y	Y	N	Y	Y	N	N
WISCONSIN								
1 ***Neumann***	N	N	N	N	N	Y	N	Y
2 ***Klug***	N	N	N	N	N	Y	N	Y
3 Kind	Y	N	N	N	Y	Y	Y	Y
4 Kleczka	Y	N	N	Y	Y	Y	Y	Y
5 Barrett	Y	Y	Y	Y	Y	Y	Y	N
6 ***Petri***	Y	N	Y	N	N	Y	N	Y
7 Obey	Y	Y	Y	Y	Y	Y	Y	N
8 Johnson	Y	Y	Y	Y	Y	Y	Y	Y
9 ***Sensenbrenner***	N	N	N	N	N	Y	N	Y
WYOMING								
AL ***Cubin***	N	N	N	N	N	Y	N	Y

Southern states - Ala., Ark., Fla., Ga., Ky., La., Miss., N.C., Okla., S.C., Tenn., Texas, Va.

HOUSE VOTES 119, 120, 121, 122, 123, 124, 125, 126

119. HR 2. Public Housing System Overhaul/Rental Vouchers. Kennedy, D-Mass., amendment to require 75 percent of choice-based rental vouchers issued annually to be given to families with incomes below 30 percent of area median income, with all such assistance reserved for those making less than 50 percent of median income. Rejected 162-260: R 0-222; D 161-38 (ND 119-26, SD 42-12); I 1-0, May 13, 1997.

120. HR 2. Public Housing System Overhaul/Government Grants. Kennedy, D-Mass., amendment to strike provisions under which local governments could receive federal assistance to administer their own flexible low-income housing programs, and receive all the federal public housing funding that would otherwise be provided to the local housing authority. Rejected 153-270: R 3-219; D 149-51 (ND 119-27, SD 30-24); I 1-0, May 13, 1997.

121. HR 2. Public Housing System Overhaul/Housing Board. Vento, D-Minn., amendment to strike bill provisions to create a Housing Evaluation and Accreditation Board to evaluate the performance of local housing authorities. Rejected 200-228: R 3-221; D 196-7 (ND 144-5, SD 52-2); I 1-0, May 13, 1997.

122. HR 2. Public Housing System Overhaul/Community Service. Kennedy, D-Mass., amendment to require landlords of and investors in Section 8 housing to perform eight hours of community service each month. Rejected 87-341: R 1-223; D 85-118 (ND 66-83, SD 19-35); I 1-0, May 13, 1997.

123. HR 2. Public Housing System Overhaul/Tenant Exemptions. Davis, D-Ill., amendment to allow the Department of Housing and Urban Development, when it takes over or replaces the management of a troubled public housing authority, to exempt public housing tenants from the eight-hours-per-month community service requirement and some other requirements. Rejected 145-282: R 2-221; D 142-61 (ND 115-34, SD 27-27); I 1-0, May 13, 1997.

124. HR 5. Individuals with Disabilities Education Act Reauthorization/Passage. Goodling, R-Pa., motion to suspend the rules and pass the bill to authorize such sums as necessary for the Individuals with Disabilities Education Act, allow schools more flexibility to discipline disabled students and change the program's grant funding formula once the annual total appropriation exceeds $4.9 billion. Passed 420-3: R 221-3; D 198-0 (ND 144-0, SD 54-0); I 1-0, May 13, 1997. A two-thirds majority of those present and voting (282 in this case) is required for passage under suspension of the rules. A "yea" was a vote in support of the president's position.

125. HR 1469. Supplemental Fiscal 1997 Appropriations/Rule. Adoption of the rule (H Res 146) to provide for House floor consideration of the bill to provide $8.4 billion in additional funds for fiscal 1997, including $5.6 billion in emergency disaster aid for flood-stricken regions and $2.0 billion to finance military peacekeeping operations in Bosnia and the Middle East. Rejected 193-229: R 180-43; D 13-185 (ND 9-135, SD 4-50); I 0-1, May 14, 1997.

126. HR 2. Public Housing System Overhaul/Kennedy Substitute. Kennedy, D-Mass., substitute amendment to consolidate public housing programs into two grant programs, require local housing authorities to establish minimum rents with exceptions, and target public housing assistance so that 40 percent of available public housing units each year would be reserved for families with income below 30 percent of area median income. Rejected 163-261: R 0-222; D 162-39 (ND 127-20, SD 35-19); I 1-0, May 14, 1997.

KEY

Y Voted for (yea).
\# Paired for.
\+ Announced for.
N Voted against (nay).
X Paired against.
– Announced against.
P Voted "present."
C Voted "present" to avoid possible conflict of interest.
? Did not vote or otherwise make a position known.

Democrats ***Republicans*** *Independent*

	119	120	121	122	123	124	125	126
ALABAMA								
1 ***Callahan***	N	N	N	N	N	Y	Y	N
2 ***Everett***	N	N	N	N	N	Y	Y	N
3 ***Riley***	N	N	N	N	N	Y	Y	N
4 ***Aderholt***	N	N	N	N	N	Y	Y	N
5 Cramer	N	N	Y	N	N	Y	N	N
6 ***Bachus***	N	N	Y	N	N	Y	Y	N
7 Hilliard	Y	Y	Y	Y	Y	Y	N	Y
ALASKA								
AL ***Young***	?	?	?	?	?	?	Y	N
ARIZONA								
1 ***Salmon***	N	N	N	N	N	Y	Y	N
2 Pastor	Y	Y	Y	Y	Y	?	N	Y
3 ***Stump***	N	N	N	N	N	Y	Y	N
4 ***Shadegg***	N	N	N	N	N	Y	Y	N
5 ***Kolbe***	N	N	N	N	N	Y	N	N
6 ***Hayworth***	N	N	N	N	N	Y	Y	N
ARKANSAS								
1 Berry	Y	Y	Y	N	Y	Y	Y	Y
2 Snyder	Y	N	Y	N	Y	Y	N	Y
3 ***Hutchinson***	N	N	N	N	N	Y	N	N
4 ***Dickey***	N	N	N	N	N	Y	Y	N
CALIFORNIA								
1 ***Riggs***	N	N	N	N	N	Y	Y	N
2 ***Herger***	N	N	N	N	N	Y	Y	N
3 Fazio	Y	Y	Y	N	N	Y	N	Y
4 ***Doolittle***	N	N	N	N	N	Y	N	N
5 Matsui	Y	N	Y	N	N	Y	N	Y
6 Woolsey	Y	Y	Y	N	Y	Y	N	Y
7 Miller	Y	Y	Y	N	Y	Y	N	Y
8 Pelosi	Y	Y	Y	Y	Y	Y	N	Y
9 Dellums	Y	Y	Y	Y	Y	Y	N	Y
10 Tauscher	Y	N	Y	N	N	Y	N	N
11 ***Pombo***	N	N	N	N	N	Y	N	N
12 Lantos	Y	Y	Y	Y	Y	Y	N	Y
13 Stark	Y	Y	Y	Y	Y	Y	?	Y
14 Eshoo	Y	Y	Y	N	Y	Y	N	Y
15 ***Campbell***	N	N	N	N	Y	Y	Y	N
16 Lofgren	N	N	Y	N	Y	Y	N	N
17 Farr	Y	Y	Y	N	Y	Y	N	Y
18 Condit	N	N	N	N	N	Y	N	N
19 ***Radanovich***	N	N	N	N	N	Y	N	N
20 Dooley	N	N	Y	N	N	Y	N	N
21 ***Thomas***	N	N	N	N	N	Y	Y	N
22 Capps	Y	Y	Y	N	Y	Y	N	Y
23 ***Gallegly***	N	N	N	N	N	Y	Y	N
24 Sherman	N	N	N	N	N	Y	N	N
25 ***McKeon***	N	N	N	N	N	Y	Y	N
26 Berman	Y	Y	Y	N	N	Y	N	Y
27 ***Rogan***	N	N	N	N	N	Y	N	N
28 ***Dreier***	N	N	N	N	N	Y	Y	N
29 Waxman	Y	Y	Y	N	Y	Y	N	Y
30 Becerra	Y	Y	Y	Y	Y	?	N	Y
31 Martinez	Y	Y	Y	Y	Y	Y	N	Y
32 Dixon	Y	Y	Y	N	N	Y	N	Y
33 Roybal-Allard	Y	Y	Y	Y	Y	Y	N	Y
34 Torres	Y	Y	Y	Y	Y	Y	N	Y
35 Waters	Y	Y	Y	Y	Y	Y	N	Y
36 Harman	Y	Y	Y	N	Y	Y	N	Y
37 Millender-McD.	Y	Y	Y	Y	Y	Y	N	Y
38 ***Horn***	N	N	N	N	N	Y	Y	N
39 ***Royce***	N	N	N	N	N	Y	Y	N
40 ***Lewis***	N	N	N	N	N	Y	Y	N
41 ***Kim***	N	N	N	N	N	Y	Y	N
42 Brown	Y	Y	Y	N	Y	Y	N	Y
43 ***Calvert***	N	N	N	N	N	Y	Y	N
44 ***Bono***	N	N	N	N	N	Y	Y	N
45 ***Rohrabacher***	N	N	N	N	N	Y	Y	N
46 Sanchez	Y	Y	Y	Y	N	Y	N	N
47 ***Cox***	N	N	N	N	N	Y	Y	N
48 ***Packard***	N	N	N	N	N	Y	Y	N
49 ***Bilbray***	N	N	N	N	N	Y	Y	N
50 Filner	Y	Y	Y	Y	Y	Y	N	Y
51 ***Cunningham***	N	N	N	N	N	Y	Y	N
52 ***Hunter***	N	N	N	N	N	Y	Y	N
COLORADO								
1 DeGette	Y	Y	Y	Y	Y	Y	?	Y
2 Skaggs	Y	Y	Y	N	Y	Y	N	Y
3 ***McInnis***	N	N	N	N	N	Y	Y	N
4 ***Schaffer***	N	N	N	N	N	Y	Y	N
5 ***Hefley***	N	N	Y	N	N	Y	Y	N
6 ***Schaefer***	N	N	N	N	N	Y	Y	N
CONNECTICUT								
1 Kennelly	Y	Y	Y	N	Y	Y	N	Y
2 Gejdenson	Y	Y	Y	Y	Y	Y	N	Y
3 DeLauro	Y	Y	Y	N	Y	Y	N	Y
4 ***Shays***	N	N	N	N	N	Y	N	N
5 Maloney	Y	Y	Y	N	Y	Y	N	Y
6 ***Johnson***	N	Y	N	N	N	Y	Y	N
DELAWARE								
AL ***Castle***	N	N	N	N	N	Y	N	N
FLORIDA								
1 ***Scarborough***	N	N	N	N	N	Y	Y	N
2 Boyd	Y	N	Y	N	N	Y	N	N
3 Brown	Y	Y	Y	Y	Y	Y	N	Y
4 ***Fowler***	N	N	N	N	N	Y	Y	N
5 Thurman	Y	Y	Y	N	Y	Y	N	Y
6 ***Stearns***	N	N	N	N	N	Y	Y	N
7 ***Mica***	N	N	N	N	N	Y	Y	N
8 ***McCollum***	N	N	N	N	N	Y	Y	N
9 ***Bilirakis***	N	N	N	N	N	Y	Y	N
10 ***Young***	N	N	N	N	N	Y	Y	N
11 Davis	Y	N	Y	N	Y	Y	N	Y
12 ***Canady***	N	N	N	N	N	Y	Y	N
13 ***Miller***	N	N	N	N	N	Y	Y	N
14 ***Goss***	N	N	N	N	N	Y	Y	N
15 ***Weldon***	N	N	N	N	N	Y	Y	N
16 ***Foley***	N	N	N	N	N	Y	Y	N
17 Meek	Y	Y	Y	Y	Y	Y	Y	Y
18 ***Ros-Lehtinen***	N	N	N	N	N	Y	Y	N
19 Wexler	Y	Y	Y	N	N	Y	N	Y
20 Deutsch	Y	Y	Y	N	N	Y	N	Y
21 ***Diaz-Balart***	N	N	N	N	N	Y	Y	N
22 ***Shaw***	N	N	N	N	N	Y	Y	N
23 Hastings	Y	Y	Y	N	N	Y	N	Y
GEORGIA								
1 ***Kingston***	–	–	N	N	N	Y	N	N
2 Bishop	Y	Y	Y	Y	Y	Y	N	Y
3 ***Collins***	N	N	N	N	N	Y	N	N
4 McKinney	Y	Y	Y	Y	Y	Y	N	Y
5 Lewis	Y	Y	Y	Y	Y	Y	N	Y
6 ***Gingrich***	S	S	S	S	S	S	S	S
7 ***Barr***	N	N	N	N	N	Y	N	N
8 ***Chambliss***	N	N	N	N	N	Y	N	N
9 ***Deal***	N	N	N	N	N	Y	N	N
10 ***Norwood***	N	N	N	N	N	Y	N	N
11 ***Linder***	N	N	N	N	N	Y	Y	N
HAWAII								
1 Abercrombie	+	N	Y	Y	Y	Y	N	Y
2 Mink	Y	N	Y	Y	Y	Y	N	Y
IDAHO								
1 ***Chenoweth***	N	N	N	N	N	Y	N	N
2 ***Crapo***	N	N	N	N	N	Y	Y	?
ILLINOIS								
1 Rush	?	?	?	?	?	?	N	Y
2 Jackson	Y	Y	Y	Y	Y	Y	N	Y
3 Lipinski	N	N	Y	N	Y	Y	N	N
4 Gutierrez	Y	Y	Y	Y	Y	?	Y	Y
5 Blagojevich	?	?	Y	Y	N	?	N	Y
6 ***Hyde***	N	N	N	N	N	Y	Y	N
7 Davis	Y	Y	Y	Y	Y	Y	N	Y
8 ***Crane***	N	N	N	N	N	Y	Y	N
9 Yates	Y	Y	Y	Y	Y	Y	N	Y
10 ***Porter***	N	N	N	N	N	Y	Y	N
11 ***Weller***	N	N	N	N	N	Y	Y	N
12 Costello	Y	Y	Y	N	Y	Y	N	Y
13 ***Fawell***	N	N	N	N	N	Y	Y	N
14 ***Hastert***	N	N	N	N	N	Y	Y	N

ND Northern Democrats SD Southern Democrats

	119	120	121	122	123	124	125	126
15 ***Ewing***	N	N	N	N	N	Y	Y	N
16 ***Manzullo***	N	N	N	N	N	Y	Y	N
17 Evans	Y	Y	Y	Y	Y	Y	N	Y
18 ***LaHood***	N	N	N	N	N	N	Y	N
19 Poshard	Y	Y	Y	N	Y	Y	N	Y
20 ***Shimkus***	N	N	N	N	N	Y	Y	N
INDIANA								
1 Visclosky	N	N	N	Y	N	Y	N	Y
2 ***McIntosh***	N	N	N	N	N	Y	N	N
3 Roemer	N	N	Y	N	Y	Y	N	Y
4 ***Souder***	N	N	N	N	N	Y	N	N
5 ***Buyer***	N	N	N	N	N	Y	?	N
6 ***Burton***	N	N	N	N	N	Y	Y	N
7 ***Pease***	N	N	N	N	N	Y	Y	N
8 ***Hostettler***	N	N	N	N	N	Y	Y	N
9 Hamilton	Y	N	Y	N	Y	Y	N	Y
10 Carson	Y	Y	Y	Y	Y	Y	N	Y
IOWA								
1 ***Leach***	N	N	N	N	N	Y	Y	N
2 ***Nussle***	N	N	N	N	N	Y	Y	N
3 Boswell	N	Y	Y	N	N	Y	N	Y
4 ***Ganske***	N	N	N	N	N	Y	Y	N
5 ***Latham***	N	N	N	N	N	Y	Y	N
KANSAS								
1 ***Moran***	N	N	N	N	N	Y	Y	N
2 ***Ryun***	N	N	N	N	N	Y	Y	N
3 ***Snowbarger***	N	N	N	N	N	Y	Y	N
4 ***Tiahrt***	N	N	N	N	N	Y	N	N
KENTUCKY								
1 ***Whitfield***	N	N	N	N	N	Y	Y	N
2 ***Lewis***	N	N	N	N	N	Y	Y	N
3 ***Northup***	N	Y	N	N	Y	Y	Y	N
4 ***Bunning***	N	N	N	N	N	Y	Y	N
5 ***Rogers***	N	N	N	N	N	Y	Y	N
6 Baesler	N	N	Y	N	N	Y	N	N
LOUISIANA								
1 ***Livingston***	N	N	N	N	N	Y	Y	N
2 Jefferson	Y	Y	Y	Y	Y	Y	N	Y
3 ***Tauzin***	N	N	N	N	N	Y	Y	N
4 ***McCrery***	N	N	N	N	N	Y	Y	N
5 ***Cooksey***	N	N	N	N	N	Y	N	N
6 ***Baker***	N	N	N	N	N	Y	Y	N
7 John	Y	N	Y	N	N	Y	N	N
MAINE								
1 Allen	Y	Y	Y	Y	Y	Y	N	Y
2 Baldacci	Y	Y	Y	N	Y	Y	N	Y
MARYLAND								
1 ***Gilchrest***	N	N	N	N	N	Y	Y	N
2 ***Ehrlich***	N	N	N	N	N	Y	N	N
3 Cardin	Y	N	Y	N	N	Y	N	Y
4 Wynn	N	N	Y	Y	Y	Y	Y	Y
5 Hoyer	Y	Y	Y	N	N	Y	N	Y
6 ***Bartlett***	N	N	N	N	N	Y	Y	N
7 Cummings	Y	Y	Y	Y	Y	Y	N	Y
8 ***Morella***	N	N	N	N	N	Y	Y	N
MASSACHUSETTS								
1 Olver	Y	Y	Y	Y	Y	Y	Y	Y
2 Neal	Y	Y	Y	Y	Y	Y	N	Y
3 McGovern	Y	Y	Y	Y	Y	Y	N	Y
4 Frank	Y	Y	Y	Y	Y	Y	N	Y
5 Meehan	Y	Y	Y	Y	Y	Y	N	Y
6 Tierney	Y	Y	Y	Y	Y	Y	N	Y
7 Markey	Y	Y	Y	Y	Y	Y	N	Y
8 Kennedy	Y	Y	Y	Y	Y	Y	N	Y
9 Moakley	Y	Y	Y	Y	Y	Y	N	Y
10 Delahunt	Y	Y	Y	Y	Y	Y	N	Y
MICHIGAN								
1 Stupak	N	Y	Y	Y	N	Y	N	Y
2 ***Hoekstra***	N	N	N	N	N	Y	Y	N
3 ***Ehlers***	N	N	N	N	N	Y	Y	N
4 ***Camp***	N	N	N	N	N	Y	N	N
5 Barcia	Y	Y	Y	N	Y	Y	Y	Y
6 ***Upton***	N	N	N	N	N	Y	N	N
7 ***Smith***	N	N	N	N	N	Y	Y	-
8 Stabenow	N	Y	Y	N	Y	Y	N	N
9 Kildee	Y	Y	Y	N	Y	Y	N	Y
10 Bonior	Y	Y	Y	Y	Y	Y	N	Y
11 ***Knollenberg***	N	N	N	N	N	Y	Y	N
12 Levin	Y	Y	Y	N	N	Y	N	Y
13 Rivers	Y	Y	Y	N	Y	Y	N	Y
14 Conyers	?	Y	Y	Y	Y	Y	N	Y
15 Kilpatrick	Y	Y	Y	Y	Y	Y	N	Y
16 Dingell	Y	Y	Y	N	N	Y	Y	Y
MINNESOTA								
1 ***Gutknecht***	N	N	N	N	N	Y	N	N
2 Minge	Y	N	Y	N	N	Y	Y	Y

	119	120	121	122	123	124	125	126
3 ***Ramstad***	N	N	N	N	N	Y	Y	N
4 Vento	Y	Y	Y	Y	Y	Y	N	Y
5 Sabo	Y	N	Y	N	Y	Y	N	Y
6 Luther	Y	N	N	N	N	Y	N	N
7 Peterson	N	N	Y	N	N	Y	Y	N
8 Oberstar	Y	Y	Y	Y	N	Y	N	Y
MISSISSIPPI								
1 ***Wicker***	N	N	N	N	N	Y	N	N
2 Thompson	Y	Y	Y	Y	Y	Y	N	Y
3 ***Pickering***	N	N	N	N	N	Y	N	N
4 ***Parker***	N	N	N	N	N	Y	N	N
5 Taylor	N	N	Y	N	N	Y	N	N
MISSOURI								
1 Clay	Y	Y	Y	Y	Y	Y	N	Y
2 ***Talent***	N	N	N	N	N	Y	Y	N
3 Gephardt	Y	Y	Y	N	Y	Y	N	Y
4 Skelton	?	?	?	?	?	?	?	?
5 McCarthy	Y	N	Y	N	Y	Y	N	Y
6 Danner	N	N	Y	N	N	Y	N	N
7 ***Blunt***	N	N	N	N	N	Y	N	N
8 ***Emerson***	N	N	N	N	N	Y	Y	N
9 ***Hulshof***	N	N	N	N	N	Y	N	N
MONTANA								
AL ***Hill***	N	N	N	N	N	Y	N	N
NEBRASKA								
1 ***Bereuter***	N	N	N	N	N	Y	Y	N
2 ***Christensen***	N	N	N	N	N	Y	N	N
3 ***Barrett***	N	N	N	N	N	Y	Y	N
NEVADA								
1 ***Ensign***	N	Y	N	N	N	Y	Y	N
2 ***Gibbons***	N	N	N	N	N	Y	Y	N
NEW HAMPSHIRE								
1 ***Sununu***	N	N	N	N	N	Y	Y	N
2 ***Bass***	N	N	N	N	N	Y	N	N
NEW JERSEY								
1 Andrews	Y	Y	Y	N	Y	Y	?	?
2 ***LoBiondo***	N	N	N	N	N	Y	Y	N
3 ***Saxton***	N	N	N	N	N	Y	Y	N
4 ***Smith***	N	N	N	N	N	Y	Y	N
5 ***Roukema***	N	N	N	N	N	Y	Y	N
6 Pallone	Y	Y	Y	N	Y	Y	N	Y
7 ***Franks***	N	N	N	N	N	Y	Y	N
8 Pascrell	Y	Y	Y	N	N	Y	N	Y
9 Rothman	Y	Y	Y	N	Y	Y	N	Y
10 Payne	Y	Y	Y	Y	Y	Y	N	Y
11 ***Frelinghuysen***	N	N	N	N	N	Y	Y	N
12 ***Pappas***	N	N	N	N	N	Y	N	N
13 Menendez	Y	Y	Y	N	Y	Y	N	Y
NEW MEXICO								
1 ***Schiff***	?	?	?	?	?	?	?	?
2 ***Skeen***	N	N	N	N	N	Y	Y	N
3 Vacant								
NEW YORK								
1 ***Forbes***	N	N	N	N	N	Y	Y	N
2 ***Lazio***	N	N	N	N	N	Y	Y	N
3 ***King***	N	N	N	N	N	Y	N	N
4 McCarthy	N	Y	Y	N	Y	Y	N	Y
5 Ackerman	Y	Y	Y	N	Y	Y	N	Y
6 Flake	Y	Y	Y	Y	Y	Y	?	?
7 Manton	N	Y	Y	N	N	Y	N	N
8 Nadler	Y	Y	Y	N	Y	Y	N	Y
9 Schumer	N	Y	Y	N	Y	?	N	Y
10 Towns	Y	Y	Y	Y	Y	Y	N	Y
11 Owens	Y	Y	Y	Y	Y	Y	N	Y
12 Velázquez	Y	Y	Y	Y	Y	Y	N	Y
13 ***Molinari***	N	N	N	N	N	Y	Y	N
14 Maloney	Y	Y	Y	N	Y	Y	N	Y
15 Rangel	Y	?	Y	Y	Y	Y	N	Y
16 Serrano	Y	Y	Y	Y	Y	Y	N	Y
17 Engel	Y	Y	Y	N	Y	Y	N	Y
18 Lowey	N	Y	Y	N	Y	Y	N	Y
19 ***Kelly***	N	N	N	N	N	Y	Y	N
20 ***Gilman***	N	N	N	N	N	Y	Y	N
21 McNulty	Y	Y	Y	N	Y	Y	N	Y
22 ***Solomon***	N	N	N	N	N	Y	Y	N
23 ***Boehlert***	N	N	N	N	N	Y	Y	N
24 ***McHugh***	N	N	N	N	N	Y	Y	N
25 ***Walsh***	N	N	N	N	N	Y	Y	N
26 Hinchey	?	?	Y	Y	Y	Y	N	Y
27 ***Paxon***	N	N	N	N	N	Y	Y	N
28 Slaughter	Y	Y	Y	Y	Y	Y	N	Y
29 LaFalce	Y	Y	Y	N	Y	Y	N	Y
30 ***Quinn***	N	N	N	N	N	Y	Y	N
31 ***Houghton***	N	N	N	N	N	Y	Y	N

	119	120	121	122	123	124	125	126
NORTH CAROLINA								
1 Clayton	Y	Y	Y	Y	Y	Y	N	Y
2 Etheridge	N	Y	Y	N	N	Y	N	Y
3 ***Jones***	N	N	N	N	N	Y	N	N
4 Price	N	Y	Y	N	Y	Y	N	Y
5 ***Burr***	N	N	N	N	N	Y	Y	N
6 ***Coble***	N	N	N	N	N	Y	Y	N
7 McIntyre	Y	Y	Y	N	N	Y	Y	Y
8 Hefner	?	?	?	?	?	?	?	?
9 ***Myrick***	N	N	N	N	N	Y	Y	N
10 ***Ballenger***	N	N	N	N	N	Y	Y	N
11 ***Taylor***	?	?	N	N	N	Y	Y	N
12 Watt	Y	Y	Y	N	Y	Y	N	Y
NORTH DAKOTA								
AL Pomeroy	Y	Y	Y	Y	N	Y	Y	Y
OHIO								
1 ***Chabot***	N	N	N	N	N	Y	Y	N
2 ***Portman***	N	N	N	N	N	Y	Y	N
3 Hall	Y	Y	Y	N	Y	Y	N	Y
4 ***Oxley***	N	N	N	N	N	Y	Y	N
5 ***Gillmor***	N	N	N	N	N	Y	Y	N
6 Strickland	Y	N	Y	Y	Y	Y	N	Y
7 ***Hobson***	N	N	N	N	N	Y	Y	N
8 ***Boehner***	N	N	N	N	N	Y	Y	N
9 Kaptur	N	Y	Y	N	N	Y	N	N
10 Kucinich	Y	Y	Y	Y	Y	Y	N	Y
11 Stokes	Y	Y	Y	Y	Y	Y	N	Y
12 ***Kasich***	N	N	N	N	N	Y	Y	N
13 Brown	Y	Y	Y	Y	Y	Y	N	Y
14 Sawyer	Y	Y	Y	N	Y	Y	N	Y
15 ***Pryce***	N	N	N	N	N	Y	Y	N
16 ***Regula***	N	N	N	N	N	Y	Y	N
17 Traficant	N	N	Y	N	N	Y	Y	N
18 ***Ney***	N	N	N	N	N	Y	Y	N
19 ***LaTourette***	N	N	N	N	N	Y	Y	N
OKLAHOMA								
1 ***Largent***	N	N	N	N	N	Y	Y	N
2 ***Coburn***	N	N	N	N	N	Y	Y	N
3 ***Watkins***	N	N	N	N	N	Y	Y	?
4 ***Watts***	N	N	N	N	N	Y	Y	N
5 ***Istook***	N	N	N	N	N	Y	Y	N
6 ***Lucas***	N	N	N	N	N	Y	Y	N
OREGON								
1 Furse	Y	Y	Y	Y	Y	Y	N	Y
2 ***Smith***	N	N	N	N	N	Y	Y	N
3 Blumenauer	Y	Y	Y	Y	Y	Y	N	Y
4 DeFazio	Y	N	Y	N	Y	Y	N	Y
5 Hooley	Y	Y	Y	N	Y	Y	N	Y
PENNSYLVANIA								
1 Foglietta	Y	Y	Y	Y	Y	Y	N	Y
2 Fattah	Y	Y	Y	Y	Y	Y	N	?
3 Borski	Y	Y	Y	N	Y	Y	N	Y
4 Klink	N	Y	Y	N	Y	Y	N	N
5 ***Peterson***	N	N	N	N	N	Y	Y	N
6 Holden	N	Y	Y	N	N	Y	?	N
7 ***Weldon***	N	N	N	N	N	Y	N	N
8 ***Greenwood***	N	N	N	N	N	Y	Y	N
9 ***Shuster***	N	N	N	N	N	Y	Y	N
10 ***McDade***	N	N	N	N	N	Y	Y	N
11 Kanjorski	Y	Y	Y	N	N	Y	N	Y
12 Murtha	N	N	Y	N	Y	Y	N	N
13 ***Fox***	N	N	N	N	N	Y	Y	N
14 Coyne	Y	Y	Y	Y	Y	Y	N	Y
15 McHale	Y	N	Y	N	Y	Y	?	Y
16 ***Pitts***	N	N	N	N	N	Y	N	N
17 ***Gekas***	N	N	N	N	?	Y	Y	N
18 Doyle	N	Y	N	N	Y	Y	N	N
19 ***Goodling***	N	N	N	N	N	Y	Y	N
20 Mascara	N	Y	N	N	N	Y	N	N
21 ***English***	N	N	N	N	N	Y	Y	N
RHODE ISLAND								
1 Kennedy	Y	Y	Y	Y	Y	Y	N	Y
2 Weygand	Y	Y	Y	N	Y	Y	N	Y
SOUTH CAROLINA								
1 ***Sanford***	N	N	N	N	N	Y	Y	N
2 ***Spence***	N	N	N	N	N	Y	Y	N
3 ***Graham***	N	N	N	N	N	Y	Y	N
4 ***Inglis***	N	N	N	N	N	Y	Y	N
5 Spratt	Y	Y	Y	N	N	Y	N	Y
6 Clyburn	Y	Y	Y	Y	Y	Y	N	Y
SOUTH DAKOTA								
AL ***Thune***	N	N	N	N	N	Y	Y	N

	119	120	121	122	123	124	125	
TENNESSEE								
1 ***Jenkins***	N	N	N	N	N	Y	Y	N
2 ***Duncan***	N	N	N	Y	N	Y	Y	N
3 ***Wamp***	N	N	N	N	N	Y	Y	N
4 ***Hilleary***	N	N	N	N	N	Y	N	N
5 Clement	Y	Y	Y	N	N	Y	N	Y
6 Gordon	Y	N	Y	N	N	Y	N	N
7 ***Bryant***	N	N	N	N	N	Y	Y	N
8 Tanner	Y	N	Y	N	N	Y	N	N
9 Ford	Y	Y	Y	Y	Y	Y	N	Y
TEXAS								
1 Sandlin	Y	N	Y	N	Y	Y	N	N
2 Turner	Y	N	Y	N	N	Y	N	N
3 ***Johnson, Sam***	N	N	N	N	N	Y	Y	N
4 Hall	N	N	Y	N	N	Y	N	N
5 ***Sessions***	N	N	N	N	N	Y	N	N
6 ***Barton***	N	N	N	N	N	Y	Y	N
7 ***Archer***	N	N	N	N	N	Y	Y	N
8 ***Brady***	N	N	N	N	N	Y	N	N
9 Lampson	Y	N	Y	N	N	Y	N	Y
10 Doggett	Y	N	N	N	N	Y	N	N
11 Edwards	Y	N	N	Y	N	Y	N	N
12 ***Granger***	N	N	N	N	N	Y	N	N
13 ***Thornberry***	N	N	N	N	N	Y	Y	N
14 ***Paul***	N	N	N	N	N	N	Y	N
15 Hinojosa	Y	N	Y	Y	Y	Y	N	Y
16 Reyes	Y	Y	Y	N	Y	Y	N	N
17 Stenholm	N	N	Y	N	N	Y	N	N
18 Jackson-Lee	Y	Y	Y	Y	Y	Y	N	Y
19 ***Combest***	N	N	N	N	N	Y	Y	N
20 Gonzalez	Y	Y	Y	Y	Y	Y	N	Y
21 ***Smith***	N	N	N	N	N	Y	Y	N
22 ***DeLay***	N	N	N	N	N	Y	N	N
23 ***Bonilla***	N	N	N	N	N	Y	Y	N
24 Frost	Y	Y	Y	N	Y	Y	N	Y
25 Bentsen	Y	N	Y	N	Y	Y	N	Y
26 ***Armey***	N	N	N	N	N	Y	Y	N
27 Ortiz	N	Y	Y	N	N	Y	N	N
28 Rodriguez	Y	Y	Y	Y	Y	Y	N	Y
29 Green	Y	N	Y	Y	N	Y	N	Y
30 Johnson, E.B.	Y	Y	Y	Y	Y	Y	N	Y
UTAH								
1 ***Hansen***	N	N	N	N	N	Y	Y	N
2 ***Cook***	N	N	N	N	N	Y	Y	N
3 ***Cannon***	N	N	N	N	N	Y	?	N
VERMONT								
AL *Sanders*	Y	Y	Y	Y	Y	Y	N	Y
VIRGINIA								
1 ***Bateman***	N	N	N	N	N	N	Y	N
2 Pickett	N	N	Y	N	N	Y	N	N
3 Scott	Y	Y	Y	Y	Y	Y	N	Y
4 Sisisky	N	N	Y	N	N	Y	N	N
5 Goode	N	N	Y	N	N	Y	Y	N
6 ***Goodlatte***	N	N	N	N	N	Y	Y	N
7 ***Bliley***	N	N	N	N	N	Y	Y	N
8 Moran	N	N	Y	N	N	Y	N	N
9 Boucher	Y	N	Y	N	N	Y	N	Y
10 ***Wolf***	N	N	N	N	N	Y	Y	N
11 ***Davis***	N	N	N	N	N	Y	Y	N
WASHINGTON								
1 ***White***	N	N	N	N	N	Y	Y	N
2 ***Metcalf***	N	N	N	N	N	Y	Y	N
3 ***Smith, Linda***	N	N	Y	N	N	Y	Y	N
4 ***Hastings***	N	N	N	N	N	Y	Y	N
5 ***Nethercutt***	N	N	N	N	N	Y	Y	N
6 Dicks	Y	N	Y	N	Y	Y	N	Y
7 McDermott	Y	Y	Y	N	Y	Y	N	Y
8 ***Dunn***	N	N	N	N	N	Y	Y	N
9 Smith, Adam	N	Y	Y	N	N	Y	N	N
WEST VIRGINIA								
1 Mollohan	Y	Y	Y	N	Y	Y	N	Y
2 Wise	N	N	Y	N	Y	Y	N	Y
3 Rahall	Y	Y	Y	Y	Y	Y	N	Y
WISCONSIN								
1 ***Neumann***	N	N	N	N	N	Y	Y	N
2 ***Klug***	N	N	N	N	N	Y	Y	N
3 Kind	Y	Y	Y	N	Y	Y	N	Y
4 Kleczka	Y	Y	Y	Y	Y	Y	N	Y
5 Barrett	Y	Y	Y	N	Y	Y	N	Y
6 ***Petri***	N	N	N	N	N	Y	Y	N
7 Obey	Y	Y	Y	N	Y	Y	N	Y
8 Johnson	Y	Y	Y	N	Y	Y	N	Y
9 ***Sensenbrenner***	N	N	N	N	N	Y	Y	N
WYOMING								
AL ***Cubin***	N	N	N	N	N	Y	N	N

Southern states - Ala., Ark., Fla., Ga., Ky., La., Miss., N.C., Okla., S.C., Tenn., Texas, Va.

HOUSE VOTES 127, 128, 129, 130, 131

127. HR 2. Public Housing System Overhaul/Passage. Passage of the bill to replace federal low-income housing programs with block grants to local authorities, eliminate most federal regulations affecting low-income housing assistance, and change tenant income, employment and eligibility requirements. Passed 293-132: R 222-1; D 71-130 (ND 43-104, SD 28-26); I 0-1, May 14, 1997. A "nay" was a vote in support of the president's position.

128. Procedural Motion/Journal. Approval of the House Journal of Wednesday, May 14, 1997. Approved 334-62: R 186-21; D 148-41 (ND 107-32, SD 41-9); I 0-0, May 15, 1997.

129. HR 1469. Fiscal 1997 Supplemental Appropriations/ Previous Question. Solomon, R-N.Y., motion to order the previous question (thus ending debate and the possibility of amendment) on adoption of the rule (H Res 149) to provide for House floor consideration of the bill to provide $8.4 billion in additional funds for fiscal 1997, including $5.5 billion in emergency disaster aid for flood-stricken regions and $2.0 billion to finance military peacekeeping operations in Bosnia and the Middle East. Motion agreed to 228-196: R 220-2; D 8-193 (ND 7-140, SD 1-53); I 0-1, May 15, 1997.

130. HR 1469. Fiscal 1997 Supplemental Appropriations/ Rule. Adoption of the rule (H Res 149) to provide for House floor consideration of the bill to provide $8.4 billion in additional funds for fiscal 1997, including $5.5 billion in emergency disaster aid for flood-stricken regions and $2.0 billion to finance military peacekeeping operations in Bosnia and the Middle East. Adopted 269-152: 215-8; D 54-143 (ND 37-106, SD 17-37); I 0-1, May 15, 1997.

131. HR 1469. Fiscal 1997 Supplemental Appropriations/ Women, Infants and Children Program. Obey, D-Wis., amendment to add an additional $38 million in funding for the Special Supplemental Food Program for Women, Infants and Children, increasing the total appropriation to $76 million, the amount requested by the administration. Adopted 338-89: R 134-89; D 203-0 (ND 149-0, SD 54-0); I 1-0, May 15, 1997. A "yea" was a vote in support of the president's position.

KEY

- Y Voted for (yea).
- \# Paired for.
- \+ Announced for.
- N Voted against (nay).
- X Paired against.
- \- Announced against.
- P Voted "present."
- C Voted "present" to avoid possible conflict of interest.
- ? Did not vote or otherwise make a position known.

Democrats ***Republicans***
Independent

	127	128	129	130	131
ALABAMA					
1 ***Callahan***	Y	Y	Y	Y	N
2 ***Everett***	Y	Y	Y	Y	Y
3 ***Riley***	Y	Y	Y	Y	Y
4 ***Aderholt***	Y	Y	Y	Y	Y
5 Cramer	Y	Y	N	Y	Y
6 ***Bachus***	Y	Y	Y	Y	Y
7 Hilliard	N	N	N	N	Y
ALASKA					
AL ***Young***	Y	?	Y	Y	Y
ARIZONA					
1 ***Salmon***	Y	?	Y	Y	Y
2 Pastor	N	N	N	N	Y
3 ***Stump***	Y	Y	Y	Y	N
4 ***Shadegg***	Y	Y	Y	Y	N
5 ***Kolbe***	Y	Y	Y	Y	Y
6 ***Hayworth***	Y	Y	Y	Y	Y
ARKANSAS					
1 Berry	Y	N	N	Y	Y
2 Snyder	Y	Y	N	N	Y
3 ***Hutchinson***	Y	Y	?	Y	Y
4 ***Dickey***	Y	Y	Y	Y	N
CALIFORNIA					
1 ***Riggs***	Y	Y	Y	Y	Y
2 ***Herger***	Y	Y	Y	Y	N
3 Fazio	N	N	N	N	Y
4 ***Doolittle***	Y	Y	Y	Y	N
5 Matsui	Y	Y	N	Y	Y
6 Woolsey	N	Y	N	N	Y
7 Miller	N	?	N	N	Y
8 Pelosi	N	Y	N	N	Y
9 Dellums	N	?	N	N	Y
10 Tauscher	Y	Y	N	N	Y
11 ***Pombo***	Y	N	Y	Y	N
12 Lantos	N	Y	N	Y	Y
13 Stark	N	?	N	N	Y
14 Eshoo	N	Y	N	N	Y
15 ***Campbell***	Y	Y	Y	Y	Y
16 Lofgren	N	Y	N	N	Y
17 Farr	N	Y	N	N	Y
18 Condit	Y	Y	N	Y	Y
19 ***Radanovich***	Y	Y	Y	Y	N
20 Dooley	Y	Y	N	N	Y
21 ***Thomas***	Y	Y	Y	Y	Y
22 Capps	Y	Y	N	N	Y
23 ***Gallegly***	Y	Y	Y	Y	Y
24 Sherman	Y	Y	N	N	Y
25 ***McKeon***	Y	Y	Y	Y	N
26 Berman	N	Y	?	?	Y
27 ***Rogan***	Y	Y	Y	Y	Y
28 ***Dreier***	Y	Y	Y	Y	N
29 Waxman	N	Y	N	N	Y
30 Becerra	N	N	N	N	Y
31 Martinez	N	Y	N	N	Y
32 Dixon	N	?	N	Y	Y
33 Roybal-Allard	N	Y	N	N	Y
34 Torres	N	Y	N	N	Y
35 Waters	N	Y	N	Y	Y
36 Harman	Y	Y	N	Y	Y
37 Millender-McD.	N	Y	N	N	Y
38 ***Horn***	Y	Y	Y	Y	Y
39 ***Royce***	Y	Y	Y	Y	N
40 ***Lewis***	Y	Y	Y	Y	N
41 ***Kim***	Y	Y	Y	Y	Y
42 Brown	N	N	?	?	Y
43 ***Calvert***	Y	?	Y	Y	N
44 ***Bono***	Y	Y	Y	Y	Y
45 ***Rohrabacher***	Y	Y	Y	Y	N
46 Sanchez	Y	Y	N	Y	Y
47 ***Cox***	Y	Y	Y	Y	N
48 ***Packard***	Y	Y	Y	Y	N
49 ***Bilbray***	Y	Y	Y	Y	Y
50 Filner	N	N	N	N	Y
51 ***Cunningham***	Y	Y	Y	Y	Y
52 ***Hunter***	Y	Y	Y	Y	N
COLORADO					
1 DeGette	N	Y	N	N	Y
2 Skaggs	N	Y	N	N	Y
3 ***McInnis***	Y	Y	Y	Y	N
4 ***Schaffer***	Y	N	Y	Y	N
5 ***Hefley***	Y	N	Y	Y	N
6 ***Schaefer***	Y	?	Y	Y	Y
CONNECTICUT					
1 Kennelly	N	Y	N	N	Y
2 Gejdenson	N	Y	N	N	Y
3 DeLauro	N	Y	N	N	Y
4 ***Shays***	Y	Y	Y	N	Y
5 Maloney	N	Y	N	N	Y
6 ***Johnson***	Y	?	Y	Y	Y
DELAWARE					
AL ***Castle***	Y	Y	Y	Y	Y
FLORIDA					
1 ***Scarborough***	Y	Y	Y	Y	N
2 Boyd	Y	Y	N	Y	Y
3 Brown	N	Y	N	N	Y
4 ***Fowler***	Y	Y	Y	Y	Y
5 Thurman	N	Y	N	N	Y
6 ***Stearns***	Y	N	Y	N	Y
7 ***Mica***	Y	+	+	+	+
8 ***McCollum***	Y	Y	Y	Y	Y
9 ***Bilirakis***	Y	Y	Y	Y	Y
10 ***Young***	Y	?	Y	Y	Y
11 Davis	Y	Y	N	N	Y
12 ***Canady***	Y	Y	Y	Y	Y
13 ***Miller***	Y	Y	Y	Y	N
14 ***Goss***	Y	Y	Y	Y	Y
15 ***Weldon***	Y	Y	Y	Y	N
16 ***Foley***	Y	Y	Y	Y	Y
17 Meek	N	Y	N	Y	Y
18 ***Ros-Lehtinen***	Y	Y	Y	Y	Y
19 Wexler	Y	Y	N	N	Y
20 Deutsch	Y	Y	N	N	Y
21 ***Diaz-Balart***	Y	Y	Y	Y	Y
22 ***Shaw***	Y	Y	Y	Y	Y
23 Hastings	N	Y	N	N	Y
GEORGIA					
1 ***Kingston***	Y	Y	N	N	N
2 Bishop	N	N	N	Y	Y
3 ***Collins***	Y	Y	Y	N	N
4 McKinney	N	Y	N	N	Y
5 Lewis	N	N	N	N	Y
6 ***Gingrich***					
7 ***Barr***	Y	Y	Y	Y	N
8 ***Chambliss***	Y	Y	Y	Y	Y
9 ***Deal***	Y	Y	Y	N	N
10 ***Norwood***	Y	Y	Y	N	N
11 ***Linder***	Y	?	Y	Y	N
HAWAII					
1 Abercrombie	N	N	N	N	Y
2 Mink	N	Y	N	N	Y
IDAHO					
1 ***Chenoweth***	Y	N	Y	Y	N
2 ***Crapo***	Y	Y	Y	Y	N
ILLINOIS					
1 Rush	N	N	N	N	Y
2 Jackson	N	Y	N	N	Y
3 Lipinski	Y	N	N	N	Y
4 Gutierrez	N	Y	N	Y	Y
5 Blagojevich	Y	Y	N	N	Y
6 ***Hyde***	Y	Y	Y	Y	Y
7 Davis	N	Y	N	N	Y
8 ***Crane***	Y	Y	Y	Y	N
9 Yates	N	?	N	N	Y
10 ***Porter***	Y	?	Y	Y	Y
11 ***Weller***	Y	N	Y	Y	Y
12 Costello	N	N	N	N	Y
13 ***Fawell***	Y	Y	Y	Y	Y
14 ***Hastert***	Y	Y	Y	Y	Y

ND Northern Democrats SD Southern Democrats

	127	128	129	130	131
15 ***Ewing***	Y	Y	Y	Y	Y
16 ***Manzullo***	Y	Y	Y	Y	N
17 Evans	N	Y	N	N	Y
18 ***LaHood***	Y	Y	Y	Y	Y
19 Poshard	N	N	N	N	Y
20 ***Shimkus***	Y	Y	Y	Y	Y
INDIANA					
1 Visclosky	Y	N	N	N	Y
2 ***McIntosh***	Y	Y	Y	Y	N
3 Roemer	Y	Y	N	Y	Y
4 ***Souder***	Y	?	Y	Y	Y
5 ***Buyer***	Y	Y	Y	Y	N
6 ***Burton***	Y	Y	Y	Y	N
7 ***Pease***	Y	Y	Y	Y	Y
8 ***Hostettler***	Y	Y	Y	Y	Y
9 Hamilton	Y	Y	N	Y	Y
10 Carson	N	Y	N	N	Y
IOWA					
1 ***Leach***	Y	Y	Y	Y	Y
2 ***Nussle***	Y	N	Y	Y	N
3 Boswell	N	Y	N	Y	Y
4 ***Ganske***	Y	Y	Y	Y	Y
5 ***Latham***	Y	Y	Y	N	Y
KANSAS					
1 ***Moran***	Y	Y	Y	Y	Y
2 ***Ryun***	Y	Y	Y	Y	N
3 ***Snowbarger***	Y	Y	Y	Y	N
4 ***Tiahrt***	Y	N	Y	Y	N
KENTUCKY					
1 ***Whitfield***	Y	Y	Y	Y	Y
2 ***Lewis***	Y	Y	Y	Y	Y
3 ***Northup***	Y	Y	Y	Y	N
4 ***Bunning***	Y	Y	Y	Y	Y
5 ***Rogers***	Y	Y	Y	Y	Y
6 Baesler	Y	Y	N	N	Y
LOUISIANA					
1 ***Livingston***	Y	Y	Y	Y	N
2 Jefferson	N	?	N	N	Y
3 ***Tauzin***	Y	?	Y	Y	Y
4 ***McCrery***	Y	?	Y	Y	N
5 ***Cooksey***	Y	Y	Y	Y	Y
6 ***Baker***	Y	Y	Y	Y	N
7 John	Y	Y	N	N	Y
MAINE					
1 Allen	N	Y	N	N	Y
2 Baldacci	N	Y	N	N	Y
MARYLAND					
1 ***Gilchrest***	Y	Y	Y	Y	Y
2 ***Ehrlich***	Y	Y	Y	Y	N
3 Cardin	Y	Y	N	N	Y
4 Wynn	N	Y	Y	Y	Y
5 Hoyer	N	Y	N	N	Y
6 ***Bartlett***	Y	Y	Y	Y	Y
7 Cummings	N	Y	N	N	Y
8 ***Morella***	Y	Y	Y	Y	Y
MASSACHUSETTS					
1 Olver	N	N	N	N	Y
2 Neal	N	Y	N	N	Y
3 McGovern	N	Y	N	N	Y
4 Frank	N	Y	N	N	Y
5 Meehan	N	Y	N	N	Y
6 Tierney	N	Y	N	N	Y
7 Markey	N	Y	N	N	Y
8 Kennedy	N	Y	N	N	Y
9 Moakley	N	Y	N	N	Y
10 Delahunt	N	Y	N	N	Y
MICHIGAN					
1 Stupak	N	N	N	N	Y
2 ***Hoekstra***	Y	Y	Y	Y	N
3 ***Ehlers***	Y	Y	Y	Y	Y
4 ***Camp***	Y	Y	Y	Y	Y
5 Barcia	Y	Y	N	Y	Y
6 ***Upton***	Y	Y	Y	Y	Y
7 ***Smith***	Y	Y	Y	Y	Y
8 Stabenow	Y	Y	N	N	Y
9 Kildee	N	Y	N	N	Y
10 Bonior	N	N	N	N	Y
11 ***Knollenberg***	Y	Y	Y	Y	N
12 Levin	N	Y	N	N	Y
13 Rivers	N	Y	N	N	Y
14 Conyers	N	Y	N	N	Y
15 Kilpatrick	N	Y	N	N	Y
16 Dingell	N	Y	Y	Y	Y
MINNESOTA					
1 ***Gutknecht***	Y	N	Y	Y	N
2 Minge	Y	Y	Y	Y	Y
3 ***Ramstad***	Y	N	Y	Y	Y
4 Vento	N	N	N	N	Y
5 Sabo	N	N	N	Y	Y
6 Luther	Y	Y	N	Y	Y
7 Peterson	Y	Y	Y	?	Y
8 Oberstar	N	N	N	N	Y
MISSISSIPPI					
1 ***Wicker***	Y	Y	Y	Y	N
2 Thompson	N	?	N	N	Y
3 ***Pickering***	Y	Y	Y	Y	N
4 ***Parker***	Y	Y	Y	Y	N
5 Taylor	Y	N	N	Y	Y
MISSOURI					
1 Clay	N	N	N	Y	Y
2 ***Talent***	Y	?	Y	Y	N
3 Gephardt	N	N	N	N	Y
4 Skelton	?	?	?	?	?
5 McCarthy	Y	Y	N	Y	Y
6 Danner	Y	Y	N	Y	Y
7 ***Blunt***	Y	Y	Y	Y	N
8 ***Emerson***	Y	Y	Y	Y	Y
9 ***Hulshof***	Y	N	Y	Y	Y
MONTANA					
AL ***Hill***	Y	Y	Y	Y	Y
NEBRASKA					
1 ***Bereuter***	Y	Y	Y	Y	Y
2 ***Christensen***	Y	Y	Y	Y	Y
3 ***Barrett***	Y	Y	Y	Y	Y
NEVADA					
1 ***Ensign***	Y	N	Y	Y	Y
2 ***Gibbons***	Y	N	Y	Y	Y
NEW HAMPSHIRE					
1 ***Sununu***	Y	Y	Y	Y	Y
2 ***Bass***	Y	Y	Y	Y	Y
NEW JERSEY					
1 Andrews	?	?	?	?	?
2 ***LoBiondo***	Y	N	Y	Y	Y
3 ***Saxton***	Y	Y	Y	Y	Y
4 ***Smith***	Y	Y	Y	Y	Y
5 ***Roukema***	Y	Y	Y	Y	Y
6 Pallone	N	N	N	N	Y
7 ***Franks***	Y	Y	Y	Y	Y
8 Pascrell	Y	N	N	N	Y
9 Rothman	N	N	N	N	Y
10 Payne	N	Y	N	N	Y
11 ***Frelinghuysen***	Y	Y	Y	Y	Y
12 ***Pappas***	Y	Y	Y	Y	Y
13 Menendez	N	Y	N	N	Y
NEW MEXICO					
1 ***Schiff***	?	?	?	?	?
2 ***Skeen***	Y	Y	Y	Y	N
3 Vacant					
NEW YORK					
1 ***Forbes***	Y	Y	Y	Y	Y
2 ***Lazio***	Y	Y	Y	Y	Y
3 ***King***	Y	Y	Y	Y	Y
4 McCarthy	Y	Y	N	N	Y
5 Ackerman	Y	Y	N	N	Y
6 Flake	?	Y	N	N	Y
7 Manton	Y	Y	N	N	Y
8 Nadler	N	Y	N	N	Y
9 Schumer	N	Y	N	N	Y
10 Towns	N	?	N	Y	Y
11 Owens	N	Y	N	N	Y
12 Velázquez	N	N	N	N	Y
13 ***Molinari***	Y	Y	Y	Y	Y
14 Maloney	N	Y	N	N	Y
15 Rangel	N	Y	N	N	Y
16 Serrano	N	Y	N	N	Y
17 Engel	N	+	N	N	Y
18 Lowey	Y	Y	N	N	Y
19 ***Kelly***	Y	Y	Y	Y	Y
20 ***Gilman***	Y	Y	Y	Y	Y
21 McNulty	N	N	N	N	Y
22 ***Solomon***	Y	N	Y	Y	Y
23 ***Boehlert***	Y	Y	Y	Y	Y
24 ***McHugh***	Y	Y	N	N	Y
25 ***Walsh***	Y	Y	Y	Y	Y
26 Hinchey	N	N	N	N	Y
27 ***Paxon***	Y	Y	Y	Y	N
28 Slaughter	N	N	N	N	Y
29 LaFalce	N	Y	N	Y	Y
30 ***Quinn***	Y	Y	Y	Y	Y
31 ***Houghton***	Y	Y	Y	Y	N
NORTH CAROLINA					
1 Clayton	N	Y	N	Y	Y
2 Etheridge	N	Y	N	N	Y
3 ***Jones***	Y	Y	Y	Y	Y
4 Price	N	Y	N	Y	Y
5 ***Burr***	Y	Y	Y	Y	N
6 ***Coble***	Y	Y	Y	Y	N
7 McIntyre	Y	Y	N	Y	Y
8 Hefner	?	?	?	?	?
9 ***Myrick***	Y	Y	Y	Y	Y
10 ***Ballenger***	Y	Y	Y	Y	N
11 ***Taylor***	Y	Y	Y	Y	N
12 Watt	N	Y	N	N	Y
NORTH DAKOTA					
AL Pomeroy	Y	Y	Y	Y	Y
OHIO					
1 ***Chabot***	Y	Y	Y	Y	N
2 ***Portman***	Y	Y	Y	Y	Y
3 Hall	N	?	N	Y	Y
4 ***Oxley***	Y	Y	Y	Y	N
5 ***Gillmor***	Y	Y	Y	Y	Y
6 Strickland	Y	N	N	Y	Y
7 ***Hobson***	Y	Y	Y	Y	Y
8 ***Boehner***	Y	Y	Y	Y	N
9 Kaptur	Y	Y	N	?	Y
10 Kucinich	N	N	N	?	Y
11 Stokes	N	Y	N	N	Y
12 ***Kasich***	+	Y	Y	Y	Y
13 Brown	N	N	N	N	Y
14 Sawyer	N	Y	N	N	Y
15 ***Pryce***	Y	Y	Y	Y	Y
16 ***Regula***	Y	Y	Y	Y	Y
17 Traficant	Y	Y	Y	Y	Y
18 ***Ney***	Y	Y	Y	Y	Y
19 ***LaTourette***	Y	?	Y	Y	Y
OKLAHOMA					
1 ***Largent***	Y	Y	Y	Y	N
2 ***Coburn***	Y	Y	Y	Y	N
3 ***Watkins***	?	?	?	?	?
4 ***Watts***	Y	N	Y	Y	Y
5 ***Istook***	Y	Y	Y	Y	N
6 ***Lucas***	Y	Y	Y	Y	Y
OREGON					
1 Furse	Y	Y	N	N	Y
2 ***Smith***	Y	Y	Y	Y	N
3 Blumenauer	N	Y	N	–	Y
4 DeFazio	N	N	N	N	Y
5 Hooley	Y	Y	N	N	Y
PENNSYLVANIA					
1 Foglietta	N	N	N	N	Y
2 Fattah	N	?	N	N	Y
3 Borski	N	N	N	Y	Y
4 Klink	Y	Y	N	N	Y
5 ***Peterson***	Y	Y	Y	Y	Y
6 Holden	Y	Y	N	Y	Y
7 ***Weldon***	Y	Y	Y	Y	Y
8 ***Greenwood***	Y	Y	Y	Y	Y
9 ***Shuster***	Y	Y	Y	Y	Y
10 ***McDade***	Y	?	Y	Y	Y
11 Kanjorski	N	Y	N	Y	Y
12 Murtha	Y	Y	N	Y	Y
13 ***Fox***	Y	N	Y	Y	Y
14 Coyne	N	Y	N	N	Y
15 McHale	Y	Y	N	N	Y
16 ***Pitts***	Y	Y	Y	Y	Y
17 ***Gekas***	Y	Y	Y	Y	Y
18 Doyle	Y	Y	N	Y	Y
19 ***Goodling***	Y	Y	Y	Y	N
20 Mascara	Y	Y	N	Y	Y
21 ***English***	Y	N	Y	Y	Y
RHODE ISLAND					
1 Kennedy	N	Y	N	Y	Y
2 Weygand	N	Y	N	N	Y
SOUTH CAROLINA					
1 ***Sanford***	Y	Y	Y	Y	N
2 ***Spence***	Y	Y	Y	Y	Y
3 ***Graham***	Y	Y	Y	Y	N
4 ***Inglis***	Y	Y	Y	Y	N
5 Spratt	N	Y	N	Y	Y
6 Clyburn	N	N	N	N	Y
SOUTH DAKOTA					
AL ***Thune***	Y	N	Y	Y	Y
TENNESSEE					
1 ***Jenkins***	Y	Y	Y	Y	Y
2 ***Duncan***	Y	Y	Y	Y	Y
3 ***Wamp***	Y	N	Y	Y	Y
4 ***Hilleary***	Y	N	Y	Y	N
5 Clement	N	Y	N	N	Y
6 Gordon	N	?	N	Y	Y
7 ***Bryant***	Y	Y	Y	Y	Y
8 Tanner	Y	Y	N	N	Y
9 Ford	Y	Y	N	N	Y
TEXAS					
1 Sandlin	Y	Y	N	N	Y
2 Turner	Y	Y	N	Y	Y
3 ***Johnson, Sam***	Y	Y	Y	Y	N
4 Hall	Y	Y	N	N	Y
5 ***Sessions***	Y	Y	Y	Y	Y
6 ***Barton***	Y	Y	Y	Y	N
7 ***Archer***	Y	?	Y	Y	N
8 ***Brady***	Y	Y	Y	Y	N
9 Lampson	Y	Y	N	N	Y
10 Doggett	Y	Y	N	N	Y
11 Edwards	Y	Y	N	N	Y
12 ***Granger***	Y	Y	Y	Y	Y
13 ***Thornberry***	Y	Y	Y	Y	N
14 ***Paul***	N	Y	Y	Y	Y
15 Hinojosa	N	Y	N	N	Y
16 Reyes	Y	Y	N	N	Y
17 Stenholm	Y	Y	N	Y	Y
18 Jackson-Lee	N	Y	N	N	Y
19 ***Combest***	Y	Y	Y	Y	N
20 Gonzalez	N	?	N	N	Y
21 ***Smith***	Y	?	Y	Y	Y
22 ***DeLay***	Y	Y	Y	Y	N
23 ***Bonilla***	Y	Y	Y	Y	N
24 Frost	N	Y	N	N	Y
25 Bentsen	Y	Y	N	N	Y
26 ***Armey***	Y	Y	Y	Y	N
27 Ortiz	Y	Y	N	N	Y
28 Rodriguez	N	Y	N	N	Y
29 Green	Y	N	N	N	Y
30 Johnson, E.B.	N	Y	N	N	Y
UTAH					
1 ***Hansen***	Y	Y	Y	Y	N
2 ***Cook***	Y	Y	Y	Y	Y
3 ***Cannon***	Y	Y	Y	Y	Y
VERMONT					
AL *Sanders*	N	?	N	N	Y
VIRGINIA					
1 ***Bateman***	Y	Y	Y	Y	N
2 Pickett	Y	N	N	N	Y
3 Scott	N	N	N	Y	Y
4 Sisisky	Y	Y	N	Y	Y
5 Goode	Y	Y	N	Y	Y
6 ***Goodlatte***	Y	Y	Y	Y	N
7 ***Bliley***	Y	Y	Y	Y	N
8 Moran	Y	Y	Y	Y	Y
9 Boucher	N	Y	N	N	Y
10 ***Wolf***	Y	Y	Y	Y	Y
11 ***Davis***	Y	Y	Y	Y	Y
WASHINGTON					
1 ***White***	Y	Y	Y	Y	Y
2 ***Metcalf***	Y	Y	Y	Y	N
3 ***Smith, Linda***	Y	Y	Y	Y	Y
4 ***Hastings***	Y	Y	Y	Y	N
5 ***Nethercutt***	Y	Y	Y	Y	N
6 Dicks	Y	Y	N	Y	Y
7 McDermott	Y	N	N	N	Y
8 ***Dunn***	Y	Y	Y	Y	Y
9 Smith, Adam	Y	?	N	N	Y
WEST VIRGINIA					
1 Mollohan	N	Y	N	N	Y
2 Wise	Y	Y	N	Y	Y
3 Rahall	N	Y	N	Y	Y
WISCONSIN					
1 ***Neumann***	Y	Y	Y	Y	N
2 ***Klug***	Y	Y	Y	Y	Y
3 Kind	Y	Y	N	N	Y
4 Kleczka	–	Y	Y	Y	Y
5 Barrett	N	Y	N	N	Y
6 ***Petri***	Y	Y	Y	Y	Y
7 Obey	N	Y	N	N	Y
8 Johnson	N	Y	N	N	Y
9 ***Sensenbrenner***	Y	Y	Y	Y	Y
WYOMING					
AL ***Cubin***	Y	Y	Y	Y	Y

Southern states - Ala., Ark., Fla., Ga., Ky., La., Miss., N.C., Okla., S.C., Tenn., Texas, Va.

HOUSE VOTES 132, 133, 134, 135, 136

132. HR 1469. Fiscal 1997 Supplemental Appropriations/ Spending Reductions. Neumann, R-Wis., amendment to strike $2.4 million in advance fiscal 1998 funding for the Federal Emergency Management Agency, rescind $3.6 billion in undefined fiscal 1997 budget authority and restore $3.8 billion in rescissions from the Section 8 assisted housing program. Rejected 100-324: R 98-122; D 2-201 (ND 2-147, SD 0-54); I 0-1, May 15, 1997.

133. HR 1469. Fiscal 1997 Supplemental Appropriations/ SSI Payment Extension. Diaz-Balart, R-Fla., amendment to postpone the scheduled termination of Supplemental Security Income (SSI) payments to legal immigrants until the end of fiscal 1997. Under the 1996 welfare system overhaul (PL 104-193), such payments to legal immigrants would end on Aug. 22. Adopted 345-74: R 149-71; D 195-3 (ND 145-0, SD 50-3); I 1-0, May 15, 1997. A "yea" was a vote in support of the president's position.

134. HR 1469. Fiscal 1997 Supplemental Appropriations/ Automatic Continuing Resolution. Gekas, R-Pa., amendment to automatically provide funding for federal programs that lack appropriations authority at the start of fiscal 1998 at 100 percent of their fiscal 1997 levels until fiscal 1998 appropriations are enacted. Adopted 227-197: R 210-14; D 17-182 (ND 9-138, SD 8-44); I 0-1, May 15, 1997. A "nay" was a vote in support of the president's position.

135. HR 1469. Fiscal 1997 Supplemental Appropriations/ FEMA Spending Reduction. Neumann, R-Wis., amendment to strike $1.7 billion in advance fiscal 1998 funding for the Federal Emergency Management Agency (FEMA), reducing the FEMA disaster relief appropriation to $1.9 billion. Rejected 115-305: R 108-113; D 7-191 (ND 2-143, SD 5-48); I 0-1, May 15, 1997.

136. HR 1469. Fiscal 1997 Supplemental Appropriations/ Passage. Passage of the bill to provide $8.4 billion in additional funds for fiscal 1997, including $5.5 billion in emergency disaster aid for flood-stricken regions and $2.0 billion to finance military peacekeeping operations in Bosnia and the Middle East. Passed 244-178: R 175-46; D 69-131 (ND 45-102, SD 24-29); I 0-1, May 15, 1997. A "nay" was a vote in support of the president's position.

KEY

- Y Voted for (yea).
- # Paired for.
- + Announced for.
- N Voted against (nay).
- X Paired against.
- – Announced against.
- P Voted "present."
- C Voted "present" to avoid possible conflict of interest.
- ? Did not vote or otherwise make a position known.

Democrats ***Republicans***
Independent

	132	133	134	135	136
ALABAMA					
1 ***Callahan***	N	Y	N	N	Y
2 ***Everett***	N	N	Y	N	Y
3 ***Riley***	N	N	Y	N	Y
4 ***Aderholt***	N	N	N	Y	Y
5 Cramer	N	Y	N	N	N
6 ***Bachus***	Y	N	Y	N	Y
7 Hilliard	N	Y	N	N	N
ALASKA					
AL ***Young***	Y	Y	Y	N	Y
ARIZONA					
1 ***Salmon***	Y	Y	Y	Y	N
2 Pastor	N	Y	N	N	N
3 ***Stump***	Y	N	Y	Y	Y
4 ***Shadegg***	Y	N	Y	Y	N
5 ***Kolbe***	N	Y	Y	N	Y
6 ***Hayworth***	N	Y	Y	N	Y
ARKANSAS					
1 Berry	N	Y	N	N	Y
2 Snyder	N	Y	N	N	Y
3 ***Hutchinson***	N	N	Y	N	Y
4 ***Dickey***	N	N	Y	N	Y
CALIFORNIA					
1 ***Riggs***	N	Y	Y	N	Y
2 ***Herger***	N	N	Y	Y	Y
3 Fazio	N	Y	N	N	Y
4 ***Doolittle***	Y	Y	Y	Y	Y
5 Matsui	N	Y	N	N	Y
6 Woolsey	N	Y	N	N	Y
7 Miller	N	Y	N	N	N
8 Pelosi	N	Y	N	N	N
9 Dellums	N	Y	N	N	N
10 Tauscher	N	Y	N	N	Y
11 ***Pombo***	N	Y	Y	Y	Y
12 Lantos	N	Y	N	N	Y
13 Stark	N	Y	N	N	N
14 Eshoo	N	Y	N	N	N
15 ***Campbell***	Y	Y	Y	Y	N
16 Lofgren	N	Y	N	N	Y
17 Farr	N	Y	N	N	N
18 Condit	N	?	N	Y	Y
19 ***Radanovich***	Y	Y	Y	?	Y
20 Dooley	N	Y	N	N	N
21 ***Thomas***	N	Y	Y	N	Y
22 Capps	N	Y	N	N	Y
23 ***Gallegly***	N	Y	Y	N	Y
24 Sherman	N	Y	Y	N	Y
25 ***McKeon***	N	Y	Y	N	Y
26 Berman	N	Y	N	?	N
27 ***Rogan***	N	Y	Y	N	Y
28 ***Dreier***	N	Y	Y	N	Y
29 Waxman	N	Y	N	N	N
30 Becerra	N	Y	N	N	N
31 Martinez	N	Y	N	N	N
32 Dixon	N	Y	N	N	N
33 Roybal-Allard	N	Y	N	N	N
34 Torres	N	Y	N	N	N
35 Waters	N	Y	N	N	N
36 Harman	N	Y	N	N	Y
37 Millender-McD.	N	Y	N	N	N
38 ***Horn***	N	Y	Y	N	Y
39 ***Royce***	Y	N	Y	Y	N
40 ***Lewis***	N	Y	N	N	Y

	132	133	134	135	136
41 ***Kim***	N	Y	Y	N	Y
42 Brown	N	Y	N	N	N
43 ***Calvert***	N	Y	Y	N	Y
44 ***Bono***	N	Y	Y	N	Y
45 ***Rohrabacher***	Y	N	Y	Y	N
46 Sanchez	N	Y	N	N	Y
47 ***Cox***	?	Y	Y	Y	N
48 ***Packard***	N	N	N	N	Y
49 ***Bilbray***	N	Y	Y	N	Y
50 Filner	N	Y	N	N	N
51 ***Cunningham***	N	Y	Y	N	Y
52 ***Hunter***	N	Y	Y	Y	Y
COLORADO					
1 DeGette	N	Y	N	N	N
2 Skaggs	N	Y	N	N	N
3 ***McInnis***	Y	Y	Y	Y	N
4 ***Schaffer***	Y	N	Y	Y	N
5 ***Hefley***	Y	N	Y	Y	Y
6 ***Schaefer***	Y	N	Y	Y	Y
CONNECTICUT					
1 Kennelly	N	Y	N	N	N
2 Gejdenson	N	Y	N	N	N
3 DeLauro	N	Y	N	N	N
4 ***Shays***	Y	Y	Y	Y	N
5 Maloney	N	Y	N	N	N
6 ***Johnson***	N	Y	Y	N	Y
DELAWARE					
AL ***Castle***	Y	Y	Y	Y	N
FLORIDA					
1 ***Scarborough***	Y	N	Y	Y	N
2 Boyd	N	Y	N	N	Y
3 Brown	N	Y	N	N	N
4 ***Fowler***	N	Y	Y	N	Y
5 Thurman	N	Y	N	N	Y
6 ***Stearns***	Y	Y	Y	Y	N
7 ***Mica***	?	Y	Y	Y	N
8 ***McCollum***	N	Y	Y	Y	Y
9 ***Bilirakis***	N	Y	Y	N	Y
10 ***Young***	N	Y	Y	N	Y
11 Davis	N	Y	N	N	N
12 ***Canady***	N	Y	Y	N	Y
13 ***Miller***	Y	N	Y	Y	Y
14 ***Goss***	N	Y	Y	Y	Y
15 ***Weldon***	Y	Y	Y	Y	Y
16 ***Foley***	Y	Y	Y	Y	Y
17 Meek	N	Y	N	N	Y
18 ***Ros-Lehtinen***	N	Y	Y	N	Y
19 Wexler	N	Y	N	N	Y
20 Deutsch	N	Y	N	N	N
21 ***Diaz-Balart***	N	Y	Y	N	Y
22 ***Shaw***	N	Y	Y	N	Y
23 Hastings	N	Y	N	N	Y
GEORGIA					
1 ***Kingston***	Y	N	Y	Y	N
2 Bishop	N	Y	Y	N	Y
3 ***Collins***	Y	N	Y	Y	N
4 McKinney	N	Y	N	N	N
5 Lewis	N	Y	N	N	N
6 ***Gingrich***			Y		
7 ***Barr***	Y	N	Y	Y	Y
8 ***Chambliss***	N	N	Y	Y	Y
9 ***Deal***	Y	N	Y	Y	N
10 ***Norwood***	Y	N	Y	Y	N
11 ***Linder***	Y	Y	Y	Y	Y
HAWAII					
1 Abercrombie	N	Y	N	N	Y
2 Mink	N	Y	N	N	N
IDAHO					
1 ***Chenoweth***	?	Y	Y	N	N
2 ***Crapo***	Y	?	Y	N	Y
ILLINOIS					
1 Rush	N	Y	N	N	N
2 Jackson	N	Y	N	N	N
3 Lipinski	Y	Y	Y	N	Y
4 Gutierrez	N	Y	N	N	Y
5 Blagojevich	N	Y	N	N	N
6 ***Hyde***	N	Y	Y	N	Y
7 Davis	N	Y	N	N	N
8 ***Crane***	Y	Y	Y	Y	Y
9 Yates	N	Y	N	?	?
10 ***Porter***	N	Y	Y	Y	Y
11 ***Weller***	N	Y	Y	N	Y
12 Costello	N	Y	N	N	N
13 ***Fawell***	N	Y	Y	Y	Y
14 ***Hastert***	N	Y	Y	Y	Y
15 ***Ewing***	Y	Y	Y	Y	Y

ND Northern Democrats SD Southern Democrats

	132	133	134	135	136
16 ***Manzullo***	Y	Y	Y	Y	Y
17 Evans	N	Y	N	N	N
18 ***LaHood***	N	Y	Y	N	Y
19 Poshard	N	Y	N	N	N
20 ***Shimkus***	N	Y	Y	Y	Y
INDIANA					
1 Visclosky	N	Y	N	N	N
2 ***McIntosh***	Y	Y	Y	Y	N
3 Roemer	N	Y	N	N	Y
4 ***Souder***	Y	Y	Y	Y	P
5 ***Buyer***	N	N	Y	N	Y
6 ***Burton***	Y	N	Y	Y	N
7 ***Pease***	N	Y	Y	N	Y
8 ***Hostettler***	Y	N	Y	Y	Y
9 Hamilton	N	Y	N	N	Y
10 Carson	N	Y	N	N	N
IOWA					
1 ***Leach***	Y	Y	Y	N	Y
2 ***Nussle***	Y	N	Y	Y	N
3 Boswell	N	Y	N	N	N
4 ***Ganske***	Y	N	Y	Y	Y
5 ***Latham***	N	N	Y	N	Y
KANSAS					
1 ***Moran***	Y	Y	Y	Y	Y
2 ***Ryun***	Y	N	Y	Y	N
3 ***Snowbarger***	Y	N	Y	Y	Y
4 ***Tiahrt***	Y	N	Y	Y	N
KENTUCKY					
1 ***Whitfield***	N	Y	Y	N	Y
2 ***Lewis***	N	Y	Y	N	Y
3 ***Northup***	N	Y	Y	N	Y
4 ***Bunning***	N	Y	Y	Y	Y
5 ***Rogers***	N	N	N	N	Y
6 Baesler	N	Y	N	N	Y
LOUISIANA					
1 ***Livingston***	N	Y	N	N	Y
2 Jefferson	N	?	?	?	?
3 ***Tauzin***	N	Y	Y	N	Y
4 ***McCrery***	N	Y	Y	N	Y
5 ***Cooksey***	N	Y	Y	N	Y
6 ***Baker***	N	Y	Y	N	Y
7 John	N	Y	N	N	N
MAINE					
1 Allen	N	Y	N	N	N
2 Baldacci	N	Y	N	N	N
MARYLAND					
1 ***Gilchrest***	N	Y	Y	N	Y
2 ***Ehrlich***	N	Y	Y	Y	Y
3 Cardin	N	Y	Y	N	Y
4 Wynn	N	Y	Y	N	Y
5 Hoyer	N	Y	Y	N	Y
6 ***Bartlett***	Y	Y	Y	Y	Y
7 Cummings	N	Y	Y	N	Y
8 ***Morella***	N	Y	Y	N	Y
MASSACHUSETTS					
1 Olver	N	Y	N	N	N
2 Neal	N	Y	N	N	N
3 McGovern	N	Y	N	N	N
4 Frank	N	Y	N	N	N
5 Meehan	Y	Y	N	Y	N
6 Tierney	N	Y	N	N	N
7 Markey	N	Y	N	N	N
8 Kennedy	N	Y	N	N	Y
9 Moakley	N	Y	N	N	N
10 Delahunt	N	Y	N	N	N
MICHIGAN					
1 Stupak	N	Y	N	N	N
2 ***Hoekstra***	Y	Y	Y	Y	N
3 ***Ehlers***	N	Y	Y	Y	N
4 ***Camp***	Y	Y	Y	Y	Y
5 Barcia	N	Y	N	N	Y
6 ***Upton***	Y	Y	Y	Y	N
7 ***Smith***	Y	+	Y	Y	N
8 Stabenow	N	Y	N	N	Y
9 Kildee	N	Y	N	N	N
10 Bonior	N	Y	N	N	N
11 ***Knollenberg***	N	Y	N	N	Y
12 Levin	N	Y	N	N	N
13 Rivers	N	Y	N	N	N
14 Conyers	N	Y	N	?	N
15 Kilpatrick	N	Y	N	N	N
16 Dingell	N	Y	N	N	Y
MINNESOTA					
1 ***Gutknecht***	Y	N	Y	Y	Y
2 Minge	N	Y	N	N	Y

	132	133	134	135	136
3 ***Ramstad***	N	Y	N	N	Y
4 Vento	N	Y	N	N	Y
5 Sabo	N	Y	N	N	Y
6 Luther	N	Y	N	N	Y
7 Peterson	N	Y	N	N	Y
8 Oberstar	N	Y	N	N	Y
MISSISSIPPI					
1 ***Wicker***	N	Y	Y	N	Y
2 Thompson	N	Y	N	N	N
3 ***Pickering***	Y	N	Y	N	Y
4 ***Parker***	N	N	Y	N	Y
5 Taylor	N	N	Y	N	Y
MISSOURI					
1 Clay	N	Y	N	N	N
2 ***Talent***	Y	Y	Y	Y	Y
3 Gephardt	N	Y	N	N	N
4 Skelton	?	?	?	?	?
5 McCarthy	N	Y	N	N	N
6 Danner	N	Y	N	N	Y
7 ***Blunt***	N	N	Y	Y	Y
8 ***Emerson***	N	N	Y	N	Y
9 ***Hulshof***	Y	N	Y	Y	N
MONTANA					
AL ***Hill***	Y	Y	Y	Y	Y
NEBRASKA					
1 ***Bereuter***	N	N	Y	Y	Y
2 ***Christensen***	Y	N	Y	Y	Y
3 ***Barrett***	N	Y	N	N	Y
NEVADA					
1 ***Ensign***	Y	Y	Y	Y	Y
2 ***Gibbons***	N	Y	Y	N	Y
NEW HAMPSHIRE					
1 ***Sununu***	Y	N	Y	Y	Y
2 ***Bass***	Y	N	Y	Y	N
NEW JERSEY					
1 Andrews	?	?	?	?	?
2 ***LoBiondo***	N	Y	Y	N	Y
3 ***Saxton***	N	Y	Y	N	Y
4 ***Smith***	N	Y	Y	N	Y
5 ***Roukema***	N	Y	Y	N	Y
6 Pallone	N	Y	N	N	N
7 ***Franks***	Y	Y	Y	Y	Y
8 Pascrell	N	Y	N	N	N
9 Rothman	N	Y	N	N	N
10 Payne	N	Y	N	N	N
11 ***Frelinghuysen***	N	Y	Y	N	Y
12 ***Pappas***	N	Y	Y	Y	Y
13 Menendez	N	Y	N	N	N
NEW MEXICO					
1 ***Schiff***	?	?	?	?	?
2 ***Skeen***	N	Y	Y	N	Y
3 Vacant					
NEW YORK					
1 ***Forbes***	N	Y	Y	N	Y
2 ***Lazio***	Y	Y	Y	N	Y
3 ***King***	N	Y	Y	N	Y
4 McCarthy	N	Y	Y	N	Y
5 Ackerman	N	Y	N	N	N
6 Flake	N	Y	N	N	N
7 Manton	N	?	?	?	?
8 Nadler	N	Y	N	N	Y
9 Schumer	N	Y	N	N	N
10 Towns	N	Y	N	N	N
11 Owens	N	Y	N	N	N
12 Velázquez	N	+	N	N	N
13 ***Molinari***	?	?	?	?	?
14 Maloney	N	Y	N	N	N
15 Rangel	N	Y	N	N	N
16 Serrano	N	Y	N	N	N
17 Engel	N	Y	N	N	N
18 Lowey	N	Y	N	N	N
19 ***Kelly***	N	Y	Y	N	Y
20 ***Gilman***	N	Y	Y	N	Y
21 McNulty	N	Y	N	N	N
22 ***Solomon***	Y	N	Y	Y	N
23 ***Boehlert***	N	Y	Y	N	?
24 ***McHugh***	N	Y	Y	N	Y
25 ***Walsh***	N	Y	Y	N	Y
26 Hinchey	N	Y	N	N	N
27 ***Paxon***	Y	N	Y	N	Y
28 Slaughter	N	Y	N	N	N
29 LaFalce	N	Y	N	N	N
30 ***Quinn***	N	Y	Y	N	Y
31 ***Houghton***	N	Y	N	N	Y

	132	133	134	135	136
NORTH CAROLINA					
1 Clayton	N	Y	N	N	Y
2 Etheridge	N	Y	N	N	Y
3 ***Jones***	Y	N	Y	Y	N
4 Price	N	Y	N	N	Y
5 ***Burr***	Y	N	Y	Y	N
6 ***Coble***	Y	N	Y	Y	N
7 McIntyre	N	Y	N	N	Y
8 Hefner	?	?	?	?	?
9 ***Myrick***	Y	Y	Y	Y	Y
10 ***Ballenger***	Y	Y	Y	Y	Y
11 ***Taylor***	Y	Y	Y	Y	Y
12 Watt	N	Y	N	Y	Y
NORTH DAKOTA					
AL Pomeroy	N	Y	N	N	Y
OHIO					
1 ***Chabot***	Y	N	Y	Y	Y
2 ***Portman***	Y	Y	Y	N	Y
3 Hall	N	Y	N	N	Y
4 ***Oxley***	N	Y	Y	N	Y
5 ***Gillmor***	N	Y	Y	N	Y
6 Strickland	N	Y	N	N	Y
7 ***Hobson***	N	Y	Y	N	Y
8 ***Boehner***	N	N	Y	N	Y
9 Kaptur	N	Y	N	N	Y
10 Kucinich	N	Y	N	N	N
11 Stokes	N	Y	N	N	N
12 ***Kasich***	Y	Y	Y	Y	Y
13 Brown	N	Y	N	N	N
14 Sawyer	N	Y	N	N	N
15 ***Pryce***	N	Y	Y	N	Y
16 ***Regula***	N	Y	Y	N	Y
17 Traficant	N	Y	Y	N	Y
18 ***Ney***	N	Y	Y	N	Y
19 ***LaTourette***	N	Y	Y	N	Y
OKLAHOMA					
1 ***Largent***	Y	N	Y	Y	N
2 ***Coburn***	Y	N	Y	Y	N
3 ***Watkins***	?	?	?	?	?
4 ***Watts***	Y	Y	Y	Y	Y
5 ***Istook***	Y	–	Y	Y	Y
6 ***Lucas***	N	Y	Y	N	Y
OREGON					
1 Furse	N	Y	N	N	N
2 ***Smith***	N	Y	Y	?	Y
3 Blumenauer	N	Y	N	N	N
4 DeFazio	N	Y	N	N	N
5 Hooley	N	Y	N	N	Y
PENNSYLVANIA					
1 Foglietta	N	Y	N	N	N
2 Fattah	N	Y	N	N	N
3 Borski	N	Y	N	N	N
4 Klink	N	Y	N	N	N
5 ***Peterson***	N	Y	Y	N	Y
6 Holden	N	Y	N	N	Y
7 ***Weldon***	N	Y	Y	N	Y
8 ***Greenwood***	N	Y	Y	N	Y
9 ***Shuster***	N	N	Y	N	Y
10 ***McDade***	N	Y	Y	N	Y
11 Kanjorski	N	Y	N	N	N
12 Murtha	N	Y	N	N	N
13 ***Fox***	N	Y	Y	N	Y
14 Coyne	N	Y	N	N	N
15 McHale	N	Y	N	N	Y
16 ***Pitts***	N	Y	Y	N	Y
17 ***Gekas***	Y	Y	Y	N	Y
18 Doyle	N	Y	N	N	N
19 ***Goodling***	N	Y	Y	Y	Y
20 Mascara	N	Y	N	N	N
21 ***English***	Y	Y	Y	N	Y
RHODE ISLAND					
1 Kennedy	N	Y	N	N	N
2 Weygand	N	Y	N	N	N
SOUTH CAROLINA					
1 ***Sanford***	Y	N	Y	Y	N
2 ***Spence***	N	Y	Y	N	Y
3 ***Graham***	Y	N	Y	Y	N
4 ***Inglis***	Y	N	Y	Y	N
5 Spratt	N	Y	N	N	Y
6 Clyburn	N	Y	N	N	N
SOUTH DAKOTA					
AL ***Thune***	N	N	N	N	Y
TENNESSEE					
1 ***Jenkins***	N	Y	Y	N	Y
2 ***Duncan***	Y	Y	Y	Y	N

	132	133	134	135	136
3 ***Wamp***	N	Y	N	N	Y
4 ***Hilleary***	Y	N	Y	Y	N
5 Clement	N	Y	N	N	Y
6 Gordon	N	Y	Y	N	Y
7 ***Bryant***	Y	N	Y	Y	Y
8 Tanner	N	Y	N	N	Y
9 Ford	N	Y	N	N	N
TEXAS					
1 Sandlin	N	Y	N	N	N
2 Turner	N	Y	N	N	N
3 ***Johnson, Sam***	Y	N	Y	Y	Y
4 Hall	N	N	Y	Y	Y
5 ***Sessions***	Y	N	Y	Y	Y
6 ***Barton***	Y	N	Y	Y	Y
7 ***Archer***	N	Y	Y	Y	Y
8 ***Brady***	Y	N	Y	Y	Y
9 Lampson	N	Y	N	N	N
10 Doggett	N	Y	Y	Y	N
11 Edwards	N	Y	N	N	N
12 ***Granger***	N	Y	Y	N	Y
13 ***Thornberry***	Y	Y	Y	Y	Y
14 ***Paul***	Y	N	N	Y	N
15 Hinojosa	N	Y	–	N	N
16 Reyes	N	Y	N	N	Y
17 Stenholm	N	Y	Y	Y	N
18 Jackson-Lee	N	Y	N	N	N
19 ***Combest***	N	N	Y	Y	Y
20 Gonzalez	N	Y	N	N	N
21 ***Smith***	N	Y	Y	N	Y
22 ***DeLay***	Y	N	Y	N	Y
23 ***Bonilla***	N	Y	Y	N	Y
24 Frost	N	Y	N	N	N
25 Bentsen	N	Y	N	N	N
26 ***Armey***	Y	N	Y	Y	Y
27 Ortiz	N	Y	N	N	Y
28 Rodriguez	N	Y	N	N	N
29 Green	N	Y	N	N	N
30 Johnson, E.B.	N	Y	N	N	N
UTAH					
1 ***Hansen***	N	N	Y	N	Y
2 ***Cook***	N	Y	Y	N	Y
3 ***Cannon***	Y	N	Y	Y	Y
VERMONT					
AL *Sanders*	N	Y	N	N	N
VIRGINIA					
1 ***Bateman***	N	Y	Y	N	Y
2 Pickett	N	Y	N	N	Y
3 Scott	N	Y	N	N	N
4 Sisisky	N	Y	N	N	Y
5 Goode	N	N	Y	Y	Y
6 ***Goodlatte***	N	Y	Y	N	Y
7 ***Bliley***	Y	Y	Y	N	Y
8 Moran	N	Y	Y	N	Y
9 Boucher	N	Y	N	N	N
10 ***Wolf***	N	Y	Y	N	Y
11 ***Davis***	N	Y	Y	N	Y
WASHINGTON					
1 ***White***	Y	Y	Y	Y	Y
2 ***Metcalf***	Y	Y	Y	Y	Y
3 ***Smith, Linda***	N	Y	Y	N	Y
4 ***Hastings***	N	Y	Y	Y	Y
5 ***Nethercutt***	N	Y	N	N	Y
6 Dicks	N	Y	N	N	N
7 McDermott	N	Y	N	N	N
8 ***Dunn***	N	Y	Y	N	Y
9 Smith, Adam	N	Y	N	N	Y
WEST VIRGINIA					
1 Mollohan	N	?	?	N	N
2 Wise	N	Y	N	N	Y
3 Rahall	N	Y	N	N	Y
WISCONSIN					
1 ***Neumann***	Y	Y	Y	Y	N
2 ***Klug***	Y	Y	Y	Y	N
3 Kind	N	Y	N	N	N
4 Kleczka	N	Y	Y	N	Y
5 Barrett	N	Y	N	N	N
6 ***Petri***	Y	N	Y	Y	N
7 Obey	N	Y	N	N	N
8 Johnson	N	Y	N	N	N
9 ***Sensenbrenner***	Y	N	Y	Y	N
WYOMING					
AL ***Cubin***	Y	Y	Y	Y	N

Southern states - Ala., Ark., Fla., Ga., Ky., La., Miss., N.C., Okla., S.C., Tenn., Texas, Va.

HOUSE VOTES 137, 138, 139, 140, 141, 142

137. HR 1385. Job Training Program Consolidation/Summer Youth Employment. Owens, D-N.Y., amendment to separate the summer youth employment program from the bill's disadvantaged youth block grant program in order to require a separate appropriation for the program as in current law. Rejected 168-238: R 3-211; D 164-27 (ND 123-15, SD 41-12); I 1-0; May 16, 1997.

138. H 1385. Job Training Program Consolidation/Passage. Passage of the bill to consolidate 60 existing federal employment, job training and adult literacy programs into three block grant programs to the states. Passed 343-60: R 155-56; D 187-4 (ND 137-1, SD 50-3); I 1-0, May 16, 1997. A "yea" was a vote in support of the president's position.

139. Procedural Motion/Journal. Approval of the House Journal of Monday, May 19, 1997. Approved 311-44: R 176-13; D 135-31 (ND 98-21, SD 37-10); I 0-0, May 20, 1997.

140. H Con Res 84. Fiscal 1998 Budget Resolution/Previous Question. Solomon, R-N.Y., motion to order the previous question (thus ending debate and the possibility of amendment) on adoption of the rule (H Res 152) to provide for House floor consideration of the resolution to adopt a five-year budget plan that would balance the budget by fiscal 2002 and set binding budget levels for the fiscal year ending Sept. 30, 1998. Motion agreed to 220-200: R 218-4; D 2-196 (ND 2-144, SD 0-52); I 0-0, May 20, 1997.

141. H Con Res 84. Fiscal 1998 Budget Resolution/Rule. Adoption of the rule (H Res 152) to provide for House floor consideration of the resolution to adopt a five-year budget plan that would balance the budget by fiscal 2002 and set binding budget levels for the fiscal year ending Sept. 30, 1998. Adopted 278-142: R 212-8; D 66-134 (ND 53-94, SD 13-40); I 0-0, May 20, 1997.

142. S Con Res 26. Congressional Ceremony for Mother Teresa/Adoption. Thomas, R-Calif., motion to suspend the rules and adopt the concurrent resolution to permit the use of the Capitol Rotunda for a congressional ceremony to honor Mother Teresa on June 5. Adopted 415-0: R 218-0; D 197-0 (ND 145-0, SD 52-0); I 0-0, May 20, 1997. A two-thirds majority of those present and voting (277 in this case) is required for adoption under suspension of the rules.

[1] *Bill Redmond, R-N.M., was sworn in May 20, replacing Democrat Bill Richardson, who resigned Feb. 13 to become U.N. representative. The first vote for which Redmond was eligible was vote 140.*

KEY

- Y Voted for (yea).
- # Paired for.
- + Announced for.
- N Voted against (nay).
- X Paired against.
- – Announced against.
- P Voted "present."
- C Voted "present" to avoid possible conflict of interest.
- ? Did not vote or otherwise make a position known.

Democrats ***Republicans***
Independent

	137	138	139	140	141	142
ALABAMA						
1 ***Callahan***	N	N	Y	Y	Y	Y
2 ***Everett***	N	N	Y	Y	Y	Y
3 ***Riley***	N	N	Y	Y	Y	Y
4 ***Aderholt***	N	N	Y	Y	Y	Y
5 Cramer	N	Y	Y	N	N	Y
6 ***Bachus***	N	Y	Y	Y	Y	Y
7 Hilliard	Y	Y	N	N	N	Y
ALASKA						
AL ***Young***	N	Y	Y	Y	Y	Y
ARIZONA						
1 ***Salmon***	N	N	Y	Y	Y	Y
2 Pastor	Y	Y	Y	N	Y	Y
3 ***Stump***	N	N	Y	Y	Y	Y
4 ***Shadegg***	N	N	Y	Y	Y	Y
5 ***Kolbe***	N	Y	Y	Y	Y	Y
6 ***Hayworth***	N	N	Y	Y	Y	Y
ARKANSAS						
1 Berry	Y	Y	N	N	N	Y
2 Snyder	Y	Y	Y	N	Y	Y
3 ***Hutchinson***	N	N	Y	Y	Y	Y
4 ***Dickey***	N	N	Y	Y	Y	Y
CALIFORNIA						
1 ***Riggs***	N	Y	?	Y	N	Y
2 ***Herger***	N	Y	Y	Y	Y	Y
3 Fazio	Y	Y	N	N	N	Y
4 ***Doolittle***	N	N	Y	Y	Y	Y
5 Matsui	Y	Y	Y	N	N	Y
6 Woolsey	Y	Y	?	?	?	?
7 Miller	?	?	N	N	N	Y
8 Pelosi	Y	Y	Y	N	N	Y
9 Dellums	Y	Y	Y	N	Y	Y
10 Tauscher	Y	Y	Y	N	N	Y
11 ***Pombo***	N	N	N	Y	Y	Y
12 Lantos	Y	Y	?	N	N	Y
13 Stark	Y	Y	N	N	N	Y
14 Eshoo	Y	Y	Y	N	Y	Y
15 ***Campbell***	N	N	Y	N	N	Y
16 Lofgren	N	Y	Y	N	N	Y
17 Farr	Y	Y	Y	N	N	Y
18 Condit	N	Y	Y	N	N	Y
19 ***Radanovich***	N	N	Y	Y	Y	Y
20 Dooley	Y	Y	Y	N	N	Y
21 ***Thomas***	N	Y	Y	Y	Y	Y
22 Capps	Y	Y	Y	N	Y	Y
23 ***Gallegly***	N	Y	Y	Y	Y	Y
24 Sherman	N	Y	Y	N	Y	Y
25 ***McKeon***	N	Y	Y	Y	Y	Y
26 Berman	Y	Y	Y	N	N	Y
27 ***Rogan***	N	N	?	Y	Y	Y
28 ***Dreier***	N	Y	Y	Y	Y	Y
29 Waxman	Y	Y	?	?	?	?
30 Becerra	Y	Y	Y	N	N	Y
31 Martinez	Y	Y	?	N	N	Y
32 Dixon	Y	Y	Y	N	Y	Y
33 Roybal-Allard	Y	Y	Y	N	N	Y
34 Torres	Y	Y	Y	N	N	Y
35 Waters	Y	Y	?	N	Y	?
36 Harman	Y	Y	Y	N	N	Y
37 Millender-McD.	Y	Y	Y	N	Y	Y
38 ***Horn***	N	Y	Y	Y	Y	Y
39 ***Royce***	N	N	Y	Y	Y	Y
40 ***Lewis***	N	Y	Y	Y	Y	Y
41 ***Kim***	N	Y	Y	Y	Y	Y
42 Brown	Y	Y	?	N	N	Y
43 ***Calvert***	N	Y	?	Y	Y	Y
44 ***Bono***	N	Y	+	Y	Y	Y
45 ***Rohrabacher***	N	Y	Y	Y	Y	Y
46 Sanchez	Y	Y	Y	N	N	Y
47 ***Cox***	N	N	Y	Y	Y	Y
48 ***Packard***	N	+	Y	Y	Y	Y
49 ***Bilbray***	N	Y	?	?	?	?
50 Filner	Y	Y	N	N	N	Y
51 ***Cunningham***	N	Y	Y	Y	Y	Y
52 ***Hunter***	N	Y	?	Y	Y	Y
COLORADO						
1 DeGette	?	?	Y	N	N	Y
2 Skaggs	Y	Y	Y	N	N	Y
3 ***McInnis***	N	Y	?	Y	Y	Y
4 ***Schaffer***	N	Y	N	N	Y	Y
5 ***Hefley***	N	N	N	Y	Y	Y
6 ***Schaefer***	N	N	Y	Y	Y	Y
CONNECTICUT						
1 Kennelly	Y	Y	?	N	Y	Y
2 Gejdenson	Y	Y	Y	N	Y	Y
3 DeLauro	Y	Y	Y	N	N	Y
4 ***Shays***	N	Y	Y	Y	Y	Y
5 Maloney	Y	Y	Y	Y	N	Y
6 ***Johnson***	N	Y	Y	Y	Y	Y
DELAWARE						
AL ***Castle***	N	Y	Y	Y	Y	Y
FLORIDA						
1 ***Scarborough***	N	N	Y	Y	Y	Y
2 Boyd	N	Y	Y	N	N	Y
3 Brown	Y	Y	?	?	?	?
4 ***Fowler***	N	Y	+	+	+	Y
5 Thurman	Y	Y	Y	N	N	Y
6 ***Stearns***	N	N	Y	Y	N	Y
7 ***Mica***	N	Y	Y	Y	Y	Y
8 ***McCollum***	N	Y	Y	Y	Y	Y
9 ***Bilirakis***	N	Y	?	Y	Y	Y
10 ***Young***	?	?	Y	Y	Y	Y
11 Davis	Y	Y	Y	N	N	Y
12 ***Canady***	N	Y	Y	Y	Y	Y
13 ***Miller***	N	Y	Y	Y	Y	Y
14 ***Goss***	N	N	Y	Y	Y	Y
15 ***Weldon***	N	N	Y	Y	Y	Y
16 ***Foley***	N	Y	Y	Y	Y	Y
17 Meek	Y	Y	Y	N	N	Y
18 ***Ros-Lehtinen***	N	Y	?	Y	Y	Y
19 Wexler	Y	Y	Y	N	N	Y
20 Deutsch	Y	Y	Y	N	N	Y
21 ***Diaz-Balart***	N	Y	Y	Y	Y	Y
22 ***Shaw***	N	Y	Y	Y	Y	Y
23 Hastings	Y	Y	N	N	N	Y
GEORGIA						
1 ***Kingston***	Y	N	Y	Y	Y	Y
2 Bishop	Y	Y	Y	N	N	Y
3 ***Collins***	N	N	Y	Y	Y	Y
4 McKinney	Y	Y	Y	N	N	Y
5 Lewis	Y	Y	N	N	N	Y
6 ***Gingrich***						
7 ***Barr***	N	N	Y	Y	Y	?
8 ***Chambliss***	N	Y	?	Y	Y	Y
9 ***Deal***	N	Y	Y	Y	Y	Y
10 ***Norwood***	N	Y	Y	Y	Y	Y
11 ***Linder***	N	Y	Y	Y	Y	Y
HAWAII						
1 Abercrombie	Y	Y	N	N	Y	Y
2 Mink	Y	Y	Y	N	Y	Y
IDAHO						
1 ***Chenoweth***	N	N	Y	Y	Y	Y
2 ***Crapo***	N	N	Y	Y	Y	Y
ILLINOIS						
1 Rush	Y	Y	Y	N	N	Y
2 Jackson	Y	Y	Y	N	N	Y
3 Lipinski	N	Y	N	N	N	Y
4 Gutierrez	?	?	?	N	Y	Y
5 Blagojevich	Y	Y	Y	N	N	Y
6 ***Hyde***	N	N	Y	Y	Y	Y
7 Davis	Y	N	?	N	N	Y
8 ***Crane***	N	N	Y	Y	Y	Y
9 Yates	Y	Y	Y	N	N	Y
10 ***Porter***	N	Y	Y	Y	Y	Y
11 ***Weller***	N	Y	N	Y	Y	Y
12 Costello	Y	Y	Y	N	N	Y
13 ***Fawell***	N	Y	Y	Y	Y	Y
14 ***Hastert***	N	Y	?	?	?	?
15 ***Ewing***	N	Y	Y	Y	Y	Y

ND Northern Democrats SD Southern Democrats

	137	138	139	140	141	142
16 ***Manzullo***	N	N	Y	Y	Y	Y
17 Evans	Y	Y	Y	N	N	Y
18 ***LaHood***	N	N	Y	Y	Y	Y
19 Poshard	Y	Y	N	N	N	Y
20 ***Shimkus***	N	Y	Y	Y	Y	Y
INDIANA						
1 Visclosky	Y	Y	?	N	N	Y
2 ***McIntosh***	N	Y	Y	Y	Y	Y
3 Roemer	N	Y	Y	N	Y	Y
4 ***Souder***	N	Y	?	Y	Y	Y
5 ***Buyer***	?	Y	Y	Y	Y	Y
6 ***Burton***	N	N	Y	Y	Y	?
7 ***Pease***	N	Y	Y	Y	Y	Y
8 ***Hostettler***	N	N	?	Y	Y	Y
9 Hamilton	N	Y	Y	N	Y	Y
10 Carson	Y	Y	?	N	N	Y
IOWA						
1 ***Leach***	N	Y	Y	Y	Y	Y
2 ***Nussle***	N	Y	Y	Y	N	Y
3 Boswell	Y	Y	Y	N	Y	Y
4 ***Ganske***	N	Y	Y	Y	Y	Y
5 ***Latham***	N	Y	Y	Y	Y	Y
KANSAS						
1 ***Moran***	N	Y	Y	Y	Y	Y
2 ***Ryun***	N	Y	Y	Y	Y	Y
3 ***Snowbarger***	N	Y	Y	Y	Y	Y
4 ***Tiahrt***	N	Y	?	Y	Y	Y
KENTUCKY						
1 ***Whitfield***	N	Y	Y	Y	Y	Y
2 ***Lewis***	N	N	Y	Y	Y	Y
3 ***Northup***	N	Y	Y	Y	Y	Y
4 ***Bunning***	N	Y	Y	Y	Y	Y
5 ***Rogers***	N	Y	Y	Y	Y	Y
6 Baesler	N	Y	Y	N	N	Y
LOUISIANA						
1 ***Livingston***	N	Y	?	Y	Y	Y
2 Jefferson	?	?	?	?	?	?
3 ***Tauzin***	N	Y	Y	Y	Y	Y
4 ***McCrery***	N	Y	Y	Y	Y	Y
5 ***Cooksey***	N	Y	Y	Y	Y	Y
6 ***Baker***	N	?	Y	Y	Y	Y
7 John	N	Y	Y	N	N	Y
MAINE						
1 Allen	Y	Y	Y	N	N	Y
2 Baldacci	Y	Y	Y	N	Y	Y
MARYLAND						
1 ***Gilchrest***	N	Y	Y	Y	Y	Y
2 ***Ehrlich***	N	Y	?	Y	Y	Y
3 Cardin	Y	Y	Y	N	Y	Y
4 Wynn	Y	Y	Y	N	Y	Y
5 Hoyer	N	Y	Y	N	Y	Y
6 ***Bartlett***	N	Y	Y	Y	Y	Y
7 Cummings	Y	Y	Y	N	N	Y
8 ***Morella***	N	Y	Y	Y	Y	Y
MASSACHUSETTS						
1 Olver	Y	Y	Y	N	N	Y
2 Neal	Y	Y	Y	N	N	Y
3 McGovern	Y	Y	Y	N	Y	Y
4 Frank	Y	Y	Y	N	N	?
5 Meehan	Y	Y	Y	N	N	Y
6 Tierney	Y	Y	Y	N	N	Y
7 Markey	Y	Y	?	N	N	Y
8 Kennedy	Y	Y	?	N	Y	Y
9 Moakley	Y	Y	Y	N	Y	Y
10 Delahunt	Y	Y	Y	N	N	Y
MICHIGAN						
1 Stupak	Y	Y	N	N	N	Y
2 ***Hoekstra***	N	Y	Y	Y	Y	Y
3 ***Ehlers***	N	Y	Y	Y	Y	Y
4 ***Camp***	N	Y	Y	Y	Y	Y
5 Barcia	Y	Y	Y	N	Y	Y
6 ***Upton***	N	Y	Y	Y	Y	Y
7 ***Smith***	N	Y	Y	Y	Y	Y
8 Stabenow	Y	Y	Y	N	Y	Y
9 Kildee	Y	Y	Y	N	N	Y
10 Bonior	Y	Y	?	N	N	Y
11 ***Knollenberg***	N	Y	Y	Y	Y	Y
12 Levin	Y	Y	Y	N	Y	Y
13 Rivers	Y	Y	Y	N	N	Y
14 Conyers	Y	Y	?	N	N	Y
15 Kilpatrick	Y	Y	Y	N	N	Y
16 Dingell	Y	Y	Y	N	N	Y
MINNESOTA						
1 ***Gutknecht***	N	Y	N	Y	Y	Y
2 Minge	N	Y	Y	N	N	Y

	137	138	139	140	141	142
3 ***Ramstad***	N	Y	N	Y	Y	Y
4 Vento	Y	Y	Y	N	Y	Y
5 Sabo	N	Y	?	N	Y	Y
6 Luther	Y	Y	Y	N	N	Y
7 Peterson	N	Y	Y	N	N	Y
8 Oberstar	N	Y	N	N	Y	Y
MISSISSIPPI						
1 ***Wicker***	X	?	Y	Y	Y	?
2 Thompson	Y	Y	N	N	N	Y
3 ***Pickering***	N	Y	Y	Y	Y	Y
4 ***Parker***	N	Y	?	Y	Y	Y
5 Taylor	N	N	?	N	N	Y
MISSOURI						
1 Clay	Y	Y	N	N	N	Y
2 ***Talent***	N	N	Y	Y	Y	Y
3 Gephardt	?	?	N	N	N	Y
4 Skelton	?	?	Y	N	N	Y
5 McCarthy	Y	Y	Y	N	N	Y
6 Danner	N	Y	Y	N	N	Y
7 ***Blunt***	N	Y	?	Y	Y	Y
8 ***Emerson***	N	N	Y	Y	Y	Y
9 ***Hulshof***	N	N	N	Y	Y	Y
MONTANA						
AL ***Hill***	N	Y	N	N	N	Y
NEBRASKA						
1 ***Bereuter***	N	Y	Y	Y	Y	Y
2 ***Christensen***	N	Y	Y	Y	Y	Y
3 ***Barrett***	N	Y	Y	Y	Y	Y
NEVADA						
1 ***Ensign***	Y	Y	N	Y	Y	Y
2 ***Gibbons***	N	Y	Y	Y	Y	Y
NEW HAMPSHIRE						
1 ***Sununu***	N	Y	Y	Y	Y	Y
2 ***Bass***	N	Y	Y	Y	Y	Y
NEW JERSEY						
1 Andrews	?	?	Y	N	Y	Y
2 ***LoBiondo***	–	+	N	Y	Y	Y
3 ***Saxton***	N	Y	Y	Y	Y	Y
4 ***Smith***	N	Y	Y	Y	Y	Y
5 ***Roukema***	N	Y	Y	Y	Y	Y
6 Pallone	Y	Y	N	N	Y	Y
7 ***Franks***	N	Y	Y	Y	Y	Y
8 Pascrell	N	Y	N	N	Y	Y
9 Rothman	Y	Y	Y	N	Y	Y
10 Payne	Y	Y	?	N	N	Y
11 ***Frelinghuysen***	N	Y	Y	Y	Y	Y
12 ***Pappas***	N	N	Y	Y	Y	Y
13 Menendez	Y	Y	?	N	Y	Y
NEW MEXICO						
1 ***Schiff***	?	?	?	?	?	?
2 ***Skeen***	N	Y	Y	Y	Y	Y
3 ***Redmond*** [1]				Y	Y	Y
NEW YORK						
1 ***Forbes***	N	Y	?	Y	Y	Y
2 ***Lazio***	N	Y	?	Y	Y	Y
3 ***King***	N	N	Y	Y	Y	Y
4 McCarthy	Y	Y	Y	N	Y	Y
5 Ackerman	?	?	?	?	?	?
6 Flake	?	?	Y	N	N	Y
7 Manton	?	?	?	N	N	Y
8 Nadler	Y	Y	Y	N	N	Y
9 Schumer	?	Y	?	?	N	Y
10 Towns	#	?	?	N	N	Y
11 Owens	Y	Y	Y	N	N	Y
12 Velázquez	Y	Y	?	N	N	Y
13 ***Molinari***	?	?	Y	Y	Y	Y
14 Maloney	Y	Y	N	N	N	Y
15 Rangel	Y	Y	?	N	N	Y
16 Serrano	Y	Y	?	N	Y	Y
17 Engel	Y	Y	Y	N	N	Y
18 Lowey	Y	Y	Y	N	N	Y
19 ***Kelly***	N	Y	Y	Y	Y	Y
20 ***Gilman***	N	Y	Y	Y	Y	Y
21 McNulty	Y	Y	N	N	N	Y
22 ***Solomon***	N	N	Y	Y	Y	Y
23 ***Boehlert***	?	?	Y	Y	Y	Y
24 ***McHugh***	N	Y	Y	Y	Y	Y
25 ***Walsh***	N	Y	Y	Y	Y	Y
26 Hinchey	Y	Y	?	–	–	?
27 ***Paxon***	N	Y	Y	Y	Y	Y
28 Slaughter	Y	Y	Y	N	N	Y
29 LaFalce	Y	Y	N	N	N	Y
30 ***Quinn***	#	?	Y	Y	Y	Y
31 ***Houghton***	N	Y	Y	Y	Y	Y

	137	138	139	140	141	142
NORTH CAROLINA						
1 Clayton	Y	Y	Y	N	N	Y
2 Etheridge	Y	Y	Y	N	Y	Y
3 ***Jones***	N	N	?	Y	Y	Y
4 Price	Y	Y	?	N	N	Y
5 ***Burr***	N	Y	?	Y	Y	Y
6 ***Coble***	N	N	Y	Y	Y	Y
7 McIntyre	Y	Y	Y	N	N	Y
8 Hefner	?	?	N	N	Y	Y
9 ***Myrick***	N	Y	Y	Y	Y	Y
10 ***Ballenger***	–	+	Y	Y	Y	Y
11 ***Taylor***	N	Y	Y	Y	Y	Y
12 Watt	Y	Y	Y	N	N	Y
NORTH DAKOTA						
AL Pomeroy	N	Y	Y	N	Y	Y
OHIO						
1 ***Chabot***	N	Y	Y	Y	Y	Y
2 ***Portman***	N	Y	?	Y	Y	Y
3 Hall	Y	Y	Y	Y	Y	Y
4 ***Oxley***	N	Y	Y	Y	Y	Y
5 ***Gillmor***	?	?	Y	Y	Y	Y
6 Strickland	Y	Y	Y	N	Y	Y
7 ***Hobson***	N	Y	Y	Y	Y	Y
8 ***Boehner***	N	Y	Y	Y	Y	Y
9 Kaptur	Y	Y	Y	N	N	Y
10 Kucinich	Y	Y	N	N	N	Y
11 Stokes	Y	Y	Y	N	Y	Y
12 ***Kasich***	N	Y	Y	Y	Y	Y
13 Brown	?	?	Y	N	N	Y
14 Sawyer	Y	Y	Y	N	N	Y
15 ***Pryce***	N	Y	Y	Y	Y	Y
16 ***Regula***	N	Y	Y	Y	Y	Y
17 Traficant	Y	Y	Y	Y	Y	Y
18 ***Ney***	N	Y	Y	Y	Y	Y
19 ***LaTourette***	Y	Y	Y	Y	Y	Y
OKLAHOMA						
1 ***Largent***	N	Y	?	Y	Y	Y
2 ***Coburn***	N	Y	Y	Y	?	Y
3 ***Watkins***	?	?	Y	Y	Y	Y
4 ***Watts***	X	?	N	Y	Y	Y
5 ***Istook***	N	?	?	Y	N	Y
6 ***Lucas***	N	Y	Y	Y	Y	Y
OREGON						
1 Furse	Y	Y	Y	N	N	Y
2 ***Smith***	N	Y	Y	Y	Y	Y
3 Blumenauer	Y	Y	Y	N	N	Y
4 DeFazio	Y	Y	N	N	N	Y
5 Hooley	Y	Y	Y	N	Y	Y
PENNSYLVANIA						
1 Foglietta	Y	Y	?	N	N	Y
2 Fattah	Y	Y	N	N	N	Y
3 Borski	Y	Y	N	N	Y	Y
4 Klink	Y	?	Y	N	N	Y
5 ***Peterson***	N	Y	?	Y	Y	Y
6 Holden	Y	Y	?	N	Y	Y
7 ***Weldon***	N	Y	Y	Y	Y	Y
8 ***Greenwood***	N	Y	?	Y	Y	Y
9 ***Shuster***	N	Y	Y	Y	Y	Y
10 ***McDade***	N	Y	Y	Y	Y	Y
11 Kanjorski	Y	Y	Y	N	N	Y
12 Murtha	?	?	Y	N	Y	Y
13 ***Fox***	N	Y	Y	Y	Y	Y
14 Coyne	Y	Y	?	N	N	Y
15 McHale	Y	Y	Y	N	N	Y
16 ***Pitts***	N	Y	Y	Y	Y	Y
17 ***Gekas***	N	Y	Y	Y	Y	Y
18 Doyle	Y	Y	?	N	Y	Y
19 ***Goodling***	N	Y	?	Y	Y	Y
20 Mascara	Y	Y	Y	N	Y	Y
21 ***English***	N	Y	N	Y	Y	Y
RHODE ISLAND						
1 Kennedy	Y	Y	?	N	N	Y
2 Weygand	Y	Y	Y	N	Y	Y
SOUTH CAROLINA						
1 ***Sanford***	N	N	?	Y	Y	Y
2 ***Spence***	N	Y	Y	Y	Y	Y
3 ***Graham***	N	Y	?	Y	Y	Y
4 ***Inglis***	N	Y	Y	Y	Y	Y
5 Spratt	Y	Y	Y	N	Y	?
6 Clyburn	Y	Y	N	N	Y	Y
SOUTH DAKOTA						
AL ***Thune***	N	N	Y	Y	Y	Y
TENNESSEE						
1 ***Jenkins***	N	Y	Y	Y	?	Y
2 ***Duncan***	N	N	Y	Y	Y	Y

	137	138	139	140	141	142
3 ***Wamp***	N	N	Y	Y	N	Y
4 ***Hilleary***	N	Y	N	Y	Y	Y
5 Clement	Y	Y	Y	N	Y	Y
6 Gordon	Y	Y	Y	N	N	Y
7 ***Bryant***	N	Y	Y	Y	Y	Y
8 Tanner	N	Y	Y	N	N	Y
9 Ford	Y	Y	Y	N	N	Y
TEXAS						
1 Sandlin	Y	Y	Y	N	N	Y
2 Turner	N	Y	Y	N	N	Y
3 ***Johnson, Sam***	N	Y	Y	Y	Y	Y
4 Hall	N	N	Y	N	N	Y
5 ***Sessions***	N	N	Y	Y	Y	Y
6 ***Barton***	N	?	Y	N	N	?
7 ***Archer***	N	Y	Y	Y	Y	Y
8 ***Brady***	N	Y	Y	Y	Y	Y
9 Lampson	Y	Y	?	N	Y	Y
10 Doggett	Y	Y	Y	N	N	Y
11 Edwards	Y	Y	Y	N	N	Y
12 ***Granger***	N	Y	Y	Y	Y	?
13 ***Thornberry***	N	Y	Y	Y	Y	Y
14 ***Paul***	N	N	Y	Y	Y	Y
15 Hinojosa	Y	Y	Y	N	N	Y
16 Reyes	Y	Y	Y	N	N	Y
17 Stenholm	N	Y	Y	N	N	Y
18 Jackson-Lee	Y	Y	?	N	N	Y
19 ***Combest***	N	Y	Y	Y	Y	Y
20 Gonzalez	Y	Y	Y	N	Y	Y
21 ***Smith***	N	Y	Y	Y	Y	Y
22 ***DeLay***	N	Y	?	Y	Y	Y
23 ***Bonilla***	N	Y	Y	Y	Y	Y
24 Frost	Y	Y	?	N	Y	Y
25 Bentsen	Y	Y	Y	N	Y	Y
26 ***Armey***	N	Y	Y	Y	Y	Y
27 Ortiz	Y	Y	Y	N	Y	Y
28 Rodriguez	Y	Y	?	N	Y	Y
29 Green	Y	Y	N	N	N	Y
30 Johnson, E.B.	Y	Y	N	N	N	Y
UTAH						
1 ***Hansen***	N	Y	Y	Y	Y	Y
2 ***Cook***	N	N	Y	Y	Y	Y
3 ***Cannon***	N	N	Y	Y	Y	Y
VERMONT						
AL *Sanders*	Y	Y	?	?	?	?
VIRGINIA						
1 ***Bateman***	N	Y	Y	Y	Y	Y
2 Pickett	Y	Y	N	N	N	Y
3 Scott	Y	Y	Y	N	N	Y
4 Sisisky	N	Y	Y	N	N	Y
5 Goode	N	N	Y	N	N	Y
6 ***Goodlatte***	N	Y	Y	Y	Y	Y
7 ***Bliley***	N	Y	Y	Y	Y	Y
8 Moran	Y	Y	Y	?	Y	Y
9 Boucher	N	Y	Y	N	N	Y
10 ***Wolf***	N	Y	Y	Y	Y	Y
11 ***Davis***	N	Y	Y	Y	Y	Y
WASHINGTON						
1 ***White***	N	Y	?	?	?	?
2 ***Metcalf***	N	N	Y	Y	Y	Y
3 ***Smith, Linda***	N	N	?	Y	Y	Y
4 ***Hastings***	N	Y	Y	Y	Y	Y
5 ***Nethercutt***	N	Y	?	Y	Y	Y
6 Dicks	Y	Y	Y	N	Y	Y
7 McDermott	Y	Y	N	N	N	Y
8 ***Dunn***	N	Y	Y	Y	Y	Y
9 Smith, Adam	N	Y	Y	N	Y	Y
WEST VIRGINIA						
1 Mollohan	Y	Y	Y	N	Y	Y
2 Wise	Y	Y	?	N	Y	Y
3 Rahall	Y	Y	Y	N	Y	Y
WISCONSIN						
1 ***Neumann***	N	N	?	Y	Y	Y
2 ***Klug***	N	Y	Y	Y	Y	Y
3 Kind	Y	Y	Y	N	N	Y
4 Kleczka	Y	Y	Y	N	Y	Y
5 Barrett	Y	Y	Y	N	N	Y
6 ***Petri***	N	N	Y	Y	Y	Y
7 Obey	Y	Y	Y	N	N	Y
8 Johnson	Y	Y	Y	N	N	Y
9 ***Sensenbrenner***	N	N	Y	Y	Y	Y
WYOMING						
AL ***Cubin***	N	Y	Y	Y	Y	Y

Southern states - Ala., Ark., Fla., Ga., Ky., La., Miss., N.C., Okla., S.C., Tenn., Texas, Va.

HOUSE VOTES 143, 144, 145, 146, 147, 148

143. H Con Res 84. Fiscal 1998 Budget Resolution/ Congressional Black Caucus Substitute. Waters, D-Calif., substitute amendment to balance the budget by 2002 by cutting defense spending by $189.9 billion and increasing revenues by $195 billion by closing corporate tax loopholes. The substitute does not include any tax cuts and maintains Medicaid funding at current levels. Rejected 72-358: R 0-227; D 71-131 (ND 54-95, SD 17-36); I 1-0, May 21, 1997 (in the session that began and the Congressional Record dated May 20).

144. H Con Res 84. Fiscal 1998 Budget Resolution/ Conservative Action Team Substitute. Doolittle, R-Calif., substitute amendment to balance the budget by 2002 by cutting non-defense discretionary spending to levels requested in the president's fiscal 1997 budget, allowing an increase in net tax cuts to $192.5 billion over five years from $85 billion. The substitute would allow a point of order to be raised against any legislation that would cause total outlays to exceed total receipts in fiscal 2002 and in subsequent years. Rejected 119-313: R 117-110; D 2-202 (ND 0-150, SD 2-52); I 0-1, May 21, 1997 (in the session that began and the Congressional Record dated May 20).

145. H Con Res 84. Fiscal 1998 Budget Resolution/Brown Substitute. Brown, D-Calif., substitute amendment to balance the budget by 2002 by reducing total spending by $220 billion over five years, limiting defense spending to fiscal 1997 levels while providing increased spending in science, energy, environment, transportation, education and training, and law enforcement. The substitute would eliminate the tax cuts in the resolution, make no net change to Medicaid spending, and incorporate proposals from the budget resolution to yield a $115 billion reduction in Medicare spending. Rejected 91-339: R 0-226; D 90-113 (ND 71-78, SD 19-35); I 1-0, May 21, 1997 (in the session that began and the Congressional Record dated May 20).

146. H Con Res 84. Fiscal 1998 Budget Resolution/Kennedy Substitute. Kennedy, D-Mass., substitute amendment to balance the budget by 2002 by limiting net tax cuts to $60 billion over five years, cutting defense spending by $20 billion over five years, and increasing domestic spending by $64 billion over five years for health, education, transportation, housing, science and economic development. The substitute would reduce the growth of Medicare by $97 billion and would restore $8.7 billion in Medicaid spending to provide additional benefits and increase hospital reimbursements. Rejected 123-306: R 0-225; D 122-81 (ND 103-46, SD 19-35); I 1-0, May 21, 1997 (in the session that began and the Congressional Record dated May 20).

147. H Con Res 84. Fiscal 1998 Budget Resolution/Shuster Substitute. Shuster, R-Pa., substitute amendment to balance the budget by 2002 by increasing outlays for federal highway and mass transit programs to $137 billion, offset by an across-the-board reduction of 0.0039 percent in discretionary spending and tax cuts to be phased in over four years, beginning in fiscal 1999. Rejected 214-216: R 58-168; D 155-48 (ND 118-32, SD 37-16); I 1-0, May 21, 1997 (in the session that began and the Congressional Record dated May 20). A "nay" was a vote in support of the president's position.

148. H Con Res 84. Fiscal 1998 Budget Resolution/Adoption. Adoption of the concurrent resolution to adopt a five-year budget plan that would balance the budget by 2002 by cutting projected spending by approximately $280 billion and cutting taxes by $85 billion, for a net deficit reduction of $204.3 billion. Projected spending cuts would include reductions of $115 billion in Medicare, $13.6 billion in Medicaid and approximately $140 billion in discretionary spending. The plan calls for additional funds to provide health insurance to currently uninsured children and to restore Supplemental Security Income and Medicaid benefits for some legal immigrants scheduled to lose their benefits under the 1996 welfare system overhaul (PL 104-193). The resolution sets binding levels for the fiscal year ending Sept. 30, 1998: budget authority, $1,702.2 billion; outlays, $1,692.2 billion; revenues, $1,601.8 billion; deficit, $90.4 billion. Adopted 333-99: R 201-26; D 132-72 (ND 90-60, SD 42-12); I 0-1, May 21, 1997 (in the session that began and the Congressional Record dated May 20). A "yea" was a vote in support of the president's position.

KEY

Y Voted for (yea).
\# Paired for.
\+ Announced for.
N Voted against (nay).
X Paired against.
\- Announced against.
P Voted "present."
C Voted "present" to avoid possible conflict of interest.
? Did not vote or otherwise make a position known.

Democrats ***Republicans***
Independent

	143	144	145	146	147	148
ALABAMA						
1 ***Callahan***	N	Y	N	N	N	Y
2 ***Everett***	N	Y	N	N	N	Y
3 ***Riley***	N	Y	N	N	N	Y
4 ***Aderholt***	N	Y	N	N	N	Y
5 Cramer	N	N	N	N	Y	Y
6 ***Bachus***	N	Y	N	N	Y	Y
7 Hilliard	Y	N	Y	N	Y	N
ALASKA						
AL ***Young***	N	Y	N	N	Y	Y
ARIZONA						
1 ***Salmon***	N	Y	N	N	N	N
2 Pastor	Y	N	Y	Y	Y	Y
3 ***Stump***	N	Y	N	N	N	Y
4 ***Shadegg***	N	Y	N	N	N	N
5 ***Kolbe***	N	N	N	N	N	Y
6 ***Hayworth***	N	Y	N	N	N	Y
ARKANSAS						
1 Berry	N	N	N	N	Y	Y
2 Snyder	N	N	N	N	N	Y
3 ***Hutchinson***	N	Y	N	N	Y	Y
4 ***Dickey***	N	Y	N	N	Y	Y
CALIFORNIA						
1 ***Riggs***	N	N	N	N	Y	Y
2 ***Herger***	N	Y	N	N	N	Y
3 Fazio	N	N	N	N	N	Y
4 ***Doolittle***	N	Y	N	N	N	Y
5 Matsui	N	N	Y	Y	Y	Y
6 Woolsey	Y	N	Y	Y	Y	Y
7 Miller	Y	N	Y	Y	Y	N
8 Pelosi	Y	N	Y	Y	Y	N
9 Dellums	Y	N	Y	Y	Y	N
10 Tauscher	N	N	N	N	Y	Y
11 ***Pombo***	N	Y	N	N	N	N
12 Lantos	N	N	N	Y	Y	Y
13 Stark	Y	N	Y	Y	Y	N
14 Eshoo	N	N	N	N	Y	Y
15 ***Campbell***	N	N	N	N	N	Y
16 Lofgren	N	N	Y	Y	Y	Y
17 Farr	N	N	Y	Y	Y	Y
18 Condit	N	N	N	N	N	Y
19 ***Radanovich***	N	N	N	N	N	Y
20 Dooley	N	N	N	N	N	Y
21 ***Thomas***	N	N	N	N	N	Y
22 Capps	N	N	N	Y	Y	Y
23 ***Gallegly***	N	N	N	N	Y	Y
24 Sherman	N	N	N	N	N	Y
25 ***McKeon***	N	Y	N	N	N	Y
26 Berman	N	N	Y	Y	N	Y
27 ***Rogan***	N	N	N	N	N	Y
28 ***Dreier***	N	Y	N	N	N	Y
29 Waxman	Y	N	Y	Y	N	N
30 Becerra	Y	N	Y	Y	Y	N
31 Martinez	Y	N	Y	Y	Y	Y
32 Dixon	Y	N	Y	Y	Y	N
33 Roybal-Allard	Y	N	Y	Y	Y	N
34 Torres	Y	N	Y	Y	Y	Y
35 Waters	Y	N	Y	N	Y	N
36 Harman	N	N	N	N	N	Y
37 Millender-McD.	Y	N	Y	Y	Y	N
38 ***Horn***	N	N	N	N	Y	Y
39 ***Royce***	N	Y	N	N	N	Y
40 ***Lewis***	N	Y	N	N	Y	Y
41 ***Kim***	N	N	N	N	Y	Y
42 Brown	Y	N	Y	Y	Y	N
43 ***Calvert***	N	Y	N	N	N	Y
44 ***Bono***	N	N	N	N	N	Y
45 ***Rohrabacher***	N	Y	N	N	N	N
46 Sanchez	N	N	N	N	Y	Y
47 ***Cox***	N	Y	N	N	N	N
48 ***Packard***	N	N	N	N	N	Y
49 ***Bilbray***	N	N	N	N	N	Y
50 Filner	Y	N	Y	Y	Y	N
51 ***Cunningham***	N	Y	N	N	N	Y
52 ***Hunter***	N	Y	N	N	N	N
COLORADO						
1 DeGette	N	N	N	Y	Y	N
2 Skaggs	N	N	Y	Y	N	Y
3 ***McInnis***	N	N	N	N	N	Y
4 ***Schaffer***	N	Y	N	N	N	Y
5 ***Hefley***	N	Y	N	N	N	Y
6 ***Schaefer***	N	Y	N	N	Y	Y
CONNECTICUT						
1 Kennelly	N	N	N	Y	Y	Y
2 Gejdenson	N	N	N	Y	Y	Y
3 DeLauro	N	N	N	Y	Y	Y
4 ***Shays***	N	N	N	N	N	Y
5 Maloney	N	N	N	N	Y	Y
6 ***Johnson***	N	N	N	N	N	Y
DELAWARE						
AL ***Castle***	N	N	N	N	N	Y
FLORIDA						
1 ***Scarborough***	N	Y	N	N	N	N
2 Boyd	N	N	N	N	N	Y
3 Brown	Y	N	Y	Y	Y	N
4 ***Fowler***	N	Y	N	N	N	Y
5 Thurman	N	N	N	Y	N	Y
6 ***Stearns***	N	Y	N	N	N	Y
7 ***Mica***	N	Y	N	N	Y	Y
8 ***McCollum***	N	Y	N	N	N	N
9 ***Bilirakis***	N	N	N	N	N	Y
10 ***Young***	N	N	N	N	N	Y
11 Davis	N	N	N	N	N	Y
12 ***Canady***	N	Y	N	N	N	Y
13 ***Miller***	N	Y	N	N	N	Y
14 ***Goss***	N	Y	N	N	N	Y
15 ***Weldon***	N	N	N	N	N	N
16 ***Foley***	N	Y	N	N	N	Y
17 Meek	Y	N	Y	N	Y	N
18 ***Ros-Lehtinen***	N	N	N	N	N	Y
19 Wexler	N	N	N	Y	Y	Y
20 Deutsch	N	N	N	Y	Y	Y
21 ***Diaz-Balart***	N	N	N	N	N	Y
22 ***Shaw***	N	N	N	N	N	Y
23 Hastings	Y	N	Y	Y	Y	N
GEORGIA						
1 ***Kingston***	N	Y	N	N	N	Y
2 Bishop	P	N	N	N	Y	Y
3 ***Collins***	N	N	N	N	N	Y
4 McKinney	Y	N	Y	Y	Y	Y
5 Lewis	Y	N	Y	Y	Y	N
6 ***Gingrich***	N	N	N	N	N	Y
7 ***Barr***	N	Y	N	N	N	Y
8 ***Chambliss***	N	N	N	N	N	Y
9 ***Deal***	N	Y	N	N	N	Y
10 ***Norwood***	N	Y	N	N	N	Y
11 ***Linder***	N	N	N	N	N	Y
HAWAII						
1 Abercrombie	N	N	N	N	Y	Y
2 Mink	Y	N	Y	Y	Y	N
IDAHO						
1 ***Chenoweth***	N	Y	N	N	N	N
2 ***Crapo***	N	Y	N	N	N	N
ILLINOIS						
1 Rush	Y	N	Y	Y	Y	N
2 Jackson	Y	N	Y	Y	Y	N
3 Lipinski	Y	N	N	Y	Y	N
4 Gutierrez	Y	N	N	Y	N	N
5 Blagojevich	N	N	Y	Y	Y	Y
6 ***Hyde***	N	N	N	N	N	N
7 Davis	Y	N	Y	Y	Y	N
8 ***Crane***	N	Y	N	N	N	N
9 Yates	?	?	?	?	?	X
10 ***Porter***	N	N	N	N	N	Y
11 ***Weller***	N	N	N	N	N	Y
12 Costello	N	N	N	Y	Y	Y
13 ***Fawell***	N	N	N	N	N	Y
14 ***Hastert***	N	N	N	N	N	Y
15 ***Ewing***	N	Y	N	N	N	Y

ND Northern Democrats SD Southern Democrats

	143	144	145	146	147	148
16 ***Manzullo***	N	Y	N	N	Y	Y
17 Evans	N	N	N	Y	N	N
18 ***LaHood***	N	N	N	N	Y	Y
19 Poshard	N	N	N	Y	Y	Y
20 ***Shimkus***	N	N	N	N	N	Y
INDIANA						
1 Visclosky	N	N	N	N	Y	Y
2 ***McIntosh***	N	Y	N	?	N	N
3 Roemer	N	N	N	N	Y	Y
4 ***Souder***	N	Y	N	N	N	Y
5 ***Buyer***	N	Y	N	N	Y	Y
6 ***Burton***	N	Y	N	N	N	Y
7 ***Pease***	N	Y	N	N	Y	Y
8 ***Hostettler***	N	Y	N	N	Y	Y
9 Hamilton	N	N	Y	Y	Y	Y
10 Carson	Y	N	Y	Y	Y	Y
IOWA						
1 ***Leach***	N	N	N	N	N	Y
2 ***Nussle***	N	N	N	N	N	Y
3 Boswell	N	N	N	N	Y	Y
4 ***Ganske***	N	N	N	N	N	N
5 ***Latham***	N	N	N	N	N	Y
KANSAS						
1 ***Moran***	N	Y	N	N	Y	Y
2 ***Ryun***	N	Y	N	N	N	Y
3 ***Snowbarger***	N	Y	N	N	N	Y
4 ***Tiahrt***	N	Y	N	N	N	Y
KENTUCKY						
1 ***Whitfield***	N	Y	N	N	N	Y
2 ***Lewis***	N	Y	N	N	N	Y
3 ***Northup***	N	N	N	N	Y	Y
4 ***Bunning***	N	N	N	N	N	Y
5 ***Rogers***	N	N	N	N	N	Y
6 Baesler	N	N	N	N	Y	Y
LOUISIANA						
1 ***Livingston***	N	N	N	N	N	Y
2 Jefferson	?	?	?	?	?	?
3 ***Tauzin***	N	N	N	N	N	Y
4 ***McCrery***	N	N	N	N	N	Y
5 ***Cooksey***	N	N	N	N	Y	Y
6 ***Baker***	N	N	N	N	Y	Y
7 John	N	N	N	N	Y	Y
MAINE						
1 Allen	N	N	N	N	N	Y
2 Baldacci	N	N	N	N	N	Y
MARYLAND						
1 ***Gilchrest***	N	N	N	N	N	Y
2 ***Ehrlich***	N	N	N	N	N	Y
3 Cardin	N	N	N	Y	N	Y
4 Wynn	Y	N	Y	Y	Y	Y
5 Hoyer	N	N	N	N	N	Y
6 ***Bartlett***	N	Y	N	N	N	Y
7 Cummings	Y	N	Y	N	Y	Y
8 ***Morella***	N	N	N	N	N	Y
MASSACHUSETTS						
1 Olver	Y	N	Y	Y	Y	N
2 Neal	N	N	N	Y	Y	Y
3 McGovern	Y	N	Y	Y	Y	N
4 Frank	Y	N	Y	Y	Y	N
5 Meehan	N	N	?	Y	Y	Y
6 Tierney	Y	N	Y	Y	Y	N
7 Markey	Y	N	Y	Y	Y	N
8 Kennedy	N	N	N	Y	Y	N
9 Moakley	Y	N	Y	Y	Y	N
10 Delahunt	Y	N	N	Y	Y	N
MICHIGAN						
1 Stupak	N	N	N	Y	Y	Y
2 ***Hoekstra***	N	Y	N	N	N	Y
3 ***Ehlers***	N	N	N	N	Y	Y
4 ***Camp***	N	Y	N	N	Y	Y
5 Barcia	N	N	Y	N	Y	Y
6 ***Upton***	N	Y	N	N	Y	Y
7 ***Smith***	N	Y	N	N	N	Y
8 Stabenow	N	N	N	N	Y	Y
9 Kildee	N	N	N	N	Y	Y
10 Bonior	Y	N	Y	Y	Y	Y
11 ***Knollenberg***	N	N	N	N	N	Y
12 Levin	N	N	N	N	Y	Y
13 Rivers	N	N	Y	Y	Y	Y
14 Conyers	?	N	Y	Y	N	N
15 Kilpatrick	Y	N	Y	N	Y	N
16 Dingell	N	N	N	N	Y	Y
MINNESOTA						
1 ***Gutknecht***	N	N	N	N	N	Y
2 Minge	N	N	N	N	N	Y

	143	144	145	146	147	148
3 ***Ramstad***	N	N	N	N	N	Y
4 Vento	N	N	Y	Y	Y	Y
5 Sabo	N	N	N	N	N	Y
6 Luther	N	N	N	N	N	Y
7 Peterson	N	N	N	N	Y	Y
8 Oberstar	Y	N	Y	Y	Y	N
MISSISSIPPI						
1 ***Wicker***	N	N	N	N	N	Y
2 Thompson	Y	N	Y	N	Y	N
3 ***Pickering***	N	Y	N	N	N	Y
4 ***Parker***	N	N	N	N	N	Y
5 Taylor	N	N	N	N	N	Y
MISSOURI						
1 Clay	Y	N	Y	N	Y	N
2 ***Talent***	N	Y	?	?	N	Y
3 Gephardt	N	N	Y	Y	Y	N
4 Skelton	N	N	N	N	N	Y
5 McCarthy	N	N	N	N	Y	Y
6 Danner	N	N	N	N	Y	Y
7 ***Blunt***	N	Y	N	N	Y	Y
8 ***Emerson***	N	N	N	N	Y	Y
9 ***Hulshof***	N	N	N	N	N	Y
MONTANA						
AL ***Hill***	N	Y	N	N	Y	N
NEBRASKA						
1 ***Bereuter***	N	N	N	N	Y	Y
2 ***Christensen***	N	Y	N	N	N	Y
3 ***Barrett***	N	N	N	N	N	Y
NEVADA						
1 ***Ensign***	N	Y	N	N	+	Y
2 ***Gibbons***	N	Y	N	N	N	Y
NEW HAMPSHIRE						
1 ***Sununu***	N	N	N	N	N	Y
2 ***Bass***	N	N	N	N	Y	Y
NEW JERSEY						
1 Andrews	N	N	N	N	Y	Y
2 ***LoBiondo***	N	N	N	N	Y	Y
3 ***Saxton***	N	N	N	N	N	Y
4 ***Smith***	N	N	N	N	Y	Y
5 ***Roukema***	N	N	N	N	N	Y
6 Pallone	N	N	N	Y	Y	Y
7 ***Franks***	N	N	N	N	Y	Y
8 Pascrell	N	N	N	N	Y	Y
9 Rothman	N	N	N	Y	Y	Y
10 Payne	Y	N	Y	Y	Y	N
11 ***Frelinghuysen***	N	N	N	N	N	Y
12 ***Pappas***	N	Y	N	N	N	Y
13 Menendez	N	N	N	Y	Y	Y
NEW MEXICO						
1 ***Schiff***	?	?	?	?	?	#
2 ***Skeen***	N	N	N	N	N	Y
3 ***Redmond***	N	Y	N	N	N	Y
NEW YORK						
1 ***Forbes***	N	Y	N	N	Y	Y
2 ***Lazio***	N	N	N	N	N	Y
3 ***King***	N	N	N	N	Y	N
4 McCarthy	N	N	N	Y	Y	Y
5 Ackerman	N	N	N	Y	Y	Y
6 Flake	Y	N	N	Y	Y	Y
7 Manton	N	N	N	Y	Y	Y
8 Nadler	Y	N	Y	Y	Y	N
9 Schumer	N	N	N	Y	Y	Y
10 Towns	Y	N	Y	Y	Y	N
11 Owens	Y	N	Y	Y	Y	N
12 Velázquez	Y	N	Y	Y	Y	N
13 ***Molinari***	N	N	N	N	Y	Y
14 Maloney	N	N	N	Y	Y	Y
15 Rangel	Y	N	Y	Y	Y	N
16 Serrano	Y	N	Y	Y	Y	N
17 Engel	Y	N	Y	Y	Y	N
18 Lowey	N	N	N	Y	Y	Y
19 ***Kelly***	N	N	N	N	Y	Y
20 ***Gilman***	N	N	N	N	N	Y
21 McNulty	N	N	Y	Y	N	N
22 ***Solomon***	N	Y	N	N	N	Y
23 ***Boehlert***	N	N	N	N	Y	Y
24 ***McHugh***	N	N	N	N	N	Y
25 ***Walsh***	N	N	N	N	N	Y
26 Hinchey	Y	N	Y	Y	Y	N
27 ***Paxon***	N	Y	N	N	N	Y
28 Slaughter	Y	N	Y	Y	Y	N
29 LaFalce	N	N	Y	Y	Y	Y
30 ***Quinn***	N	N	N	N	Y	Y
31 ***Houghton***	N	N	N	N	Y	Y

	143	144	145	146	147	148
NORTH CAROLINA						
1 Clayton	Y	N	Y	Y	Y	Y
2 Etheridge	N	N	Y	Y	Y	Y
3 ***Jones***	N	Y	N	N	N	Y
4 Price	N	N	N	N	Y	Y
5 ***Burr***	N	Y	N	N	N	Y
6 ***Coble***	N	Y	N	N	Y	Y
7 McIntyre	N	N	N	N	Y	Y
8 Hefner	N	N	Y	Y	Y	Y
9 ***Myrick***	N	Y	N	N	N	Y
10 ***Ballenger***	N	Y	N	N	N	Y
11 ***Taylor***	N	Y	N	N	N	Y
12 Watt	Y	N	Y	Y	Y	N
NORTH DAKOTA						
AL Pomeroy	N	N	N	?	N	Y
OHIO						
1 ***Chabot***	N	Y	N	N	N	Y
2 ***Portman***	N	N	N	N	N	Y
3 Hall	N	N	N	N	N	Y
4 ***Oxley***	N	N	N	N	N	Y
5 ***Gillmor***	N	Y	N	N	Y	Y
6 Strickland	N	N	N	Y	Y	Y
7 ***Hobson***	N	N	N	N	N	Y
8 ***Boehner***	N	Y	N	N	N	Y
9 Kaptur	N	N	N	Y	Y	N
10 Kucinich	N	N	N	N	N	N
11 Stokes	Y	N	Y	Y	Y	N
12 ***Kasich***	N	N	N	N	N	Y
13 Brown	N	N	N	Y	N	N
14 Sawyer	N	N	N	Y	N	Y
15 ***Pryce***	N	N	N	N	N	Y
16 ***Regula***	N	N	N	N	N	Y
17 Traficant	N	N	N	N	Y	N
18 ***Ney***	N	N	N	N	N	Y
19 ***LaTourette***	N	N	N	N	Y	Y
OKLAHOMA						
1 ***Largent***	N	Y	N	N	N	N
2 ***Coburn***	N	Y	N	N	N	N
3 ***Watkins***	N	N	N	N	N	Y
4 ***Watts***	N	Y	N	N	N	Y
5 ***Istook***	N	Y	N	N	N	N
6 ***Lucas***	N	N	N	N	N	Y
OREGON						
1 Furse	Y	N	Y	Y	Y	Y
2 ***Smith***	N	N	N	N	N	Y
3 Blumenauer	N	N	Y	N	Y	N
4 DeFazio	N	N	N	N	Y	N
5 Hooley	N	N	N	Y	Y	Y
PENNSYLVANIA						
1 Foglietta	Y	N	Y	Y	N	Y
2 Fattah	Y	N	Y	Y	Y	Y
3 Borski	N	N	N	Y	Y	N
4 Klink	N	N	Y	Y	Y	Y
5 ***Peterson***	N	Y	N	N	Y	Y
6 Holden	N	N	N	Y	Y	Y
7 ***Weldon***	N	N	N	N	Y	Y
8 ***Greenwood***	N	N	N	N	Y	Y
9 ***Shuster***	N	Y	N	N	Y	N
10 ***McDade***	N	N	N	N	Y	Y
11 Kanjorski	N	N	Y	Y	Y	N
12 Murtha	N	N	N	N	N	Y
13 ***Fox***	N	N	N	N	Y	Y
14 Coyne	Y	N	Y	Y	Y	N
15 McHale	N	N	N	N	Y	Y
16 ***Pitts***	N	Y	N	N	Y	Y
17 ***Gekas***	N	Y	N	N	Y	Y
18 Doyle	N	N	Y	N	Y	Y
19 ***Goodling***	N	N	N	N	N	Y
20 Mascara	N	N	N	Y	Y	Y
21 ***English***	N	N	N	N	Y	Y
RHODE ISLAND						
1 Kennedy	N	N	N	Y	N	N
2 Weygand	N	N	N	Y	N	N
SOUTH CAROLINA						
1 ***Sanford***	N	N	N	N	N	N
2 ***Spence***	N	N	N	N	N	Y
3 ***Graham***	N	Y	N	N	N	Y
4 ***Inglis***	N	Y	N	N	N	Y
5 Spratt	N	N	N	N	N	Y
6 Clyburn	Y	N	Y	N	Y	N
SOUTH DAKOTA						
AL ***Thune***	N	Y	N	N	Y	Y
TENNESSEE						
1 ***Jenkins***	N	N	N	N	N	Y
2 ***Duncan***	N	Y	N	N	Y	Y

	143	144	145	146	147	148
3 ***Wamp***	N	Y	N	N	N	Y
4 ***Hilleary***	N	Y	N	N	N	Y
5 Clement	N	N	N	N	Y	Y
6 Gordon	N	N	N	N	Y	Y
7 ***Bryant***	N	Y	N	N	N	Y
8 Tanner	N	N	N	N	Y	Y
9 Ford	Y	N	Y	N	Y	Y
TEXAS						
1 Sandlin	N	N	N	N	Y	Y
2 Turner	Y	N	N	N	Y	Y
3 ***Johnson, Sam***	N	Y	N	N	N	Y
4 Hall	N	Y	N	N	N	Y
5 ***Sessions***	N	Y	N	N	N	Y
6 ***Barton***	N	Y	N	N	N	N
7 ***Archer***	N	N	N	N	N	Y
8 ***Brady***	N	Y	N	N	N	Y
9 Lampson	N	N	N	N	Y	Y
10 Doggett	N	N	Y	N	Y	Y
11 Edwards	N	N	N	N	N	Y
12 ***Granger***	N	N	N	N	N	Y
13 ***Thornberry***	N	Y	N	N	N	Y
14 ***Paul***	N	Y	N	N	N	N
15 Hinojosa	N	N	N	N	Y	Y
16 Reyes	N	N	N	N	N	Y
17 Stenholm	N	N	N	N	N	Y
18 Jackson-Lee	Y	N	Y	Y	N	N
19 ***Combest***	N	Y	N	N	Y	Y
20 Gonzalez	Y	N	N	Y	Y	Y
21 ***Smith***	N	Y	N	N	N	Y
22 ***DeLay***	N	N	N	N	N	Y
23 ***Bonilla***	N	Y	N	N	N	Y
24 Frost	N	N	N	N	Y	Y
25 Bentsen	N	N	N	Y	N	Y
26 ***Armey***	N	N	N	N	N	Y
27 Ortiz	N	N	N	N	Y	Y
28 Rodriguez	N	N	N	Y	N	Y
29 Green	N	N	Y	Y	Y	Y
30 Johnson, E.B.	Y	N	Y	Y	Y	N
UTAH						
1 ***Hansen***	N	Y	N	N	N	Y
2 ***Cook***	N	N	N	N	Y	Y
3 ***Cannon***	N	Y	N	N	N	Y
VERMONT						
AL *Sanders*	Y	N	Y	Y	Y	N
VIRGINIA						
1 ***Bateman***	N	N	N	N	N	Y
2 Pickett	N	N	N	N	N	Y
3 Scott	Y	N	Y	Y	Y	N
4 Sisisky	N	N	N	N	N	Y
5 Goode	N	Y	N	N	Y	Y
6 ***Goodlatte***	N	Y	N	N	N	Y
7 ***Bliley***	N	N	N	N	N	Y
8 Moran	Y	N	Y	Y	N	Y
9 Boucher	N	N	N	N	?	N
10 ***Wolf***	N	N	N	N	N	Y
11 ***Davis***	N	N	N	N	Y	Y
WASHINGTON						
1 ***White***	N	N	N	N	N	Y
2 ***Metcalf***	N	N	N	N	Y	Y
3 ***Smith, Linda***	N	N	N	N	Y	Y
4 ***Hastings***	N	Y	N	N	N	Y
5 ***Nethercutt***	N	Y	N	N	N	Y
6 Dicks	N	N	N	N	N	Y
7 McDermott	Y	N	Y	Y	Y	N
8 ***Dunn***	N	Y	N	N	N	Y
9 Smith, Adam	N	N	N	N	N	Y
WEST VIRGINIA						
1 Mollohan	N	N	N	Y	Y	N
2 Wise	N	N	Y	Y	Y	Y
3 Rahall	N	N	N	Y	Y	N
WISCONSIN						
1 ***Neumann***	N	Y	N	N	N	Y
2 ***Klug***	N	N	N	N	N	N
3 Kind	N	N	Y	N	Y	Y
4 Kleczka	N	N	N	N	Y	Y
5 Barrett	Y	N	Y	Y	N	Y
6 ***Petri***	N	Y	N	N	Y	Y
7 Obey	N	N	Y	Y	N	N
8 Johnson	N	N	N	Y	Y	Y
9 ***Sensenbrenner***	N	Y	N	N	N	Y
WYOMING						
AL ***Cubin***	N	Y	N	N	N	N

Southern states - Ala., Ark., Fla., Ga., Ky., La., Miss., N.C., Okla., S.C., Tenn., Texas, Va.

HOUSE VOTES 149, 150, 151, 152, 153, 154, 155

149. HR 408. Dolphin-Safe Tuna/Previous Question. Hastings, R-Wash., motion to order the previous question (thus ending debate and the possibility of amendment) on adoption of the rule (H Res 153) to provide House floor consideration of the bill to end the existing tuna import embargo against Latin America and to permit tuna caught with purse seine nets to be labeled as dolphin-safe as long as no dolphins were observed being killed when the tuna was caught. Motion agreed to 226-203: R 223-1; D 3-201 (ND 2-148, SD 1-53); I 0-1, May 21, 1997.

150. HR 911. Volunteer Liability Limitation/Passage. Inglis, R-S.C., motion to suspend the rules and pass the bill to limit the liability of volunteers in most cases if they are acting within the scope of their responsibilities and are not engaging in criminal or negligent behavior. The bill would allow states to opt out of the program if their own laws are deemed adequate. Motion agreed to 390-35: R 217-4; D 172-31 (ND 129-21, SD 43-10); I 1-0, May 21, 1997. A two-thirds majority of those present and voting (284 in this case) is required for passage under suspension of the rules.

151. HR 408. Dolphin-Safe Tuna/Passage. Passage of the bill to end the existing tuna import embargo against Latin America and to permit tuna caught with purse seine nets to be labeled as dolphin-safe as long as no dolphins were observed being killed when the tuna was caught. Passed 262-166: R 204-19; D 58-146 (ND 30-120, SD 28-26); I 0-1, May 21, 1997. A "yea" was a vote in support of the president's position.

152. Procedural Motion/Adjourn. Moakley, D-Mass., motion to adjourn. Motion rejected 80-339: R 1-218; D 78-121 (ND 61-86, SD 17-35); I 1-0, May 22, 1997.

153. HR 956. Community Drug Prevention Program/Passage. Portman, R-Ohio, motion to suspend the rules and pass the bill to authorize $144 billion through fiscal 2002 to establish a program to support local communities in the development and implementation of comprehensive drug prevention programs, redirecting funds from existing federal drug-control programs. Passed 420-1: R 217-1; D 202-0 (ND 149-0, SD 53-0); I 1-0, May 22, 1997. A two-thirds majority of those present and voting (281 in this case) is required for passage under suspension of the rules.

154. Procedural Motion/Journal. Approval of the House Journal of Wednesday, May 21, 1997. Approved 352-65: R 201-16; D 150-49 (ND 109-38, SD 41-11); I 1-0, May 22, 1997.

155. Adjournment Resolution/Adoption. Adoption of the concurrent resolution to allow the adjournment of the House and the Senate until June 3 and June 2, respectively. Rejected 67-278: R 67-104; D 0-173 (ND 0-128, SD 0-45); I 0-1, May 22, 1997.

KEY

- Y Voted for (yea).
- \# Paired for.
- \+ Announced for.
- N Voted against (nay).
- X Paired against.
- – Announced against.
- P Voted "present."
- C Voted "present" to avoid possible conflict of interest.
- ? Did not vote or otherwise make a position known.

Democrats ***Republicans***
Independent

	149	150	151	152	153	154	155
ALABAMA							
1 ***Callahan***	Y	Y	Y	N	Y	Y	N
2 ***Everett***	Y	Y	Y	N	Y	Y	N
3 ***Riley***	Y	Y	Y	N	Y	Y	N
4 ***Aderholt***	Y	Y	Y	N	Y	Y	N
5 Cramer	N	Y	Y	N	Y	Y	N
6 ***Bachus***	Y	Y	Y	N	Y	Y	N
7 Hilliard	N	N	N	Y	Y	N	N
ALASKA							
AL ***Young***	Y	Y	Y	N	Y	Y	Y
ARIZONA							
1 ***Salmon***	Y	Y	Y	N	Y	Y	?
2 Pastor	N	Y	Y	N	Y	Y	N
3 ***Stump***	Y	Y	Y	N	Y	Y	Y
4 ***Shadegg***	Y	Y	Y	N	Y	Y	?
5 ***Kolbe***	Y	Y	Y	N	Y	Y	?
6 ***Hayworth***	Y	Y	Y	N	Y	Y	N
ARKANSAS							
1 Berry	N	Y	Y	N	Y	Y	N
2 Snyder	N	Y	Y	N	Y	Y	N
3 ***Hutchinson***	Y	Y	Y	N	Y	Y	N
4 ***Dickey***	Y	Y	Y	N	Y	Y	Y
CALIFORNIA							
1 ***Riggs***	Y	Y	Y	N	Y	Y	N
2 ***Herger***	Y	Y	Y	N	Y	Y	N
3 Fazio	N	Y	N	N	Y	N	N
4 ***Doolittle***	Y	Y	Y	N	Y	Y	N
5 Matsui	N	Y	Y	N	Y	Y	N
6 Woolsey	N	Y	N	Y	Y	Y	N
7 Miller	N	Y	N	Y	Y	N	N
8 Pelosi	N	Y	N	?	Y	?	N
9 Dellums	N	Y	N	N	Y	Y	N
10 Tauscher	N	N	N	N	Y	Y	N
11 ***Pombo***	Y	N	Y	N	Y	N	N
12 Lantos	N	Y	N	Y	Y	Y	N
13 Stark	N	Y	N	N	Y	N	?
14 Eshoo	N	Y	N	N	Y	Y	N
15 ***Campbell***	Y	Y	N	N	Y	Y	Y
16 Lofgren	N	N	N	N	Y	Y	N
17 Farr	N	Y	N	N	Y	N	N
18 Condit	N	Y	N	N	Y	Y	N
19 ***Radanovich***	Y	Y	?	N	Y	Y	Y
20 Dooley	N	Y	Y	N	Y	Y	?
21 ***Thomas***	Y	Y	Y	N	Y	Y	N
22 Capps	N	Y	N	N	Y	Y	N
23 ***Gallegly***	Y	Y	Y	N	Y	Y	N
24 Sherman	N	Y	N	N	Y	Y	N
25 ***McKeon***	Y	Y	Y	N	Y	Y	Y
26 Berman	N	N	N	N	Y	Y	?
27 ***Rogan***	Y	Y	Y	N	Y	Y	Y
28 ***Dreier***	Y	Y	Y	N	Y	Y	N
29 Waxman	N	Y	N	Y	Y	Y	?
30 Becerra	N	N	N	?	Y	N	N
31 Martinez	N	Y	N	N	Y	Y	N
32 Dixon	N	Y	N	Y	Y	Y	N
33 Roybal-Allard	N	N	N	Y	Y	Y	N
34 Torres	N	Y	N	?	Y	Y	N
35 Waters	N	N	N	Y	Y	Y	N
36 Harman	N	Y	N	N	Y	Y	N
37 Millender-McD.	N	Y	N	Y	Y	Y	N
38 ***Horn***	Y	Y	N	N	Y	Y	Y
39 ***Royce***	Y	Y	Y	N	Y	Y	Y
40 ***Lewis***	Y	Y	Y	N	Y	Y	?
41 ***Kim***	Y	Y	Y	N	Y	Y	N
42 Brown	N	N	N	Y	Y	N	N
43 ***Calvert***	Y	Y	Y	N	Y	Y	?
44 ***Bono***	Y	Y	Y	N	Y	Y	N
45 ***Rohrabacher***	Y	Y	Y	N	Y	Y	Y
46 Sanchez	N	Y	N	N	Y	Y	N
47 ***Cox***	Y	Y	Y	N	Y	Y	N
48 ***Packard***	Y	Y	Y	N	Y	Y	?
49 ***Bilbray***	Y	Y	Y	N	Y	Y	Y
50 Filner	N	N	N	Y	Y	N	N
51 ***Cunningham***	Y	Y	Y	N	Y	Y	?
52 ***Hunter***	?	?	Y	?	Y	Y	Y
COLORADO							
1 DeGette	N	Y	N	Y	Y	Y	N
2 Skaggs	N	Y	Y	N	Y	Y	N
3 ***McInnis***	Y	Y	Y	N	Y	Y	Y
4 ***Schaffer***	Y	Y	Y	N	Y	Y	N
5 ***Hefley***	Y	Y	Y	N	Y	N	Y
6 ***Schaefer***	Y	Y	Y	N	Y	Y	Y
CONNECTICUT							
1 Kennelly	N	Y	N	N	Y	Y	N
2 Gejdenson	N	Y	N	Y	Y	N	?
3 DeLauro	N	Y	N	Y	Y	N	N
4 ***Shays***	Y	Y	N	N	Y	Y	N
5 Maloney	N	Y	N	Y	Y	Y	N
6 ***Johnson***	Y	Y	Y	N	Y	Y	N
DELAWARE							
AL ***Castle***	Y	Y	Y	N	Y	Y	?
FLORIDA							
1 ***Scarborough***	Y	Y	Y	N	Y	Y	N
2 Boyd	N	Y	Y	N	Y	Y	N
3 Brown	N	Y	N	Y	Y	Y	N
4 ***Fowler***	Y	Y	Y	N	Y	Y	?
5 Thurman	N	Y	N	N	Y	Y	N
6 ***Stearns***	Y	Y	Y	N	Y	Y	N
7 ***Mica***	Y	Y	Y	N	Y	Y	?
8 ***McCollum***	Y	Y	Y	N	Y	Y	?
9 ***Bilirakis***	Y	Y	N	N	Y	Y	?
10 ***Young***	Y	Y	N	N	Y	Y	?
11 Davis	N	Y	Y	N	Y	Y	N
12 ***Canady***	Y	Y	Y	N	Y	Y	?
13 ***Miller***	Y	Y	Y	N	Y	Y	Y
14 ***Goss***	Y	Y	Y	N	Y	Y	N
15 ***Weldon***	Y	Y	Y	N	Y	Y	N
16 ***Foley***	Y	Y	Y	N	Y	Y	?
17 Meek	N	N	N	Y	Y	Y	N
18 ***Ros-Lehtinen***	Y	Y	Y	N	Y	Y	?
19 Wexler	N	Y	N	Y	Y	Y	?
20 Deutsch	N	N	N	?	?	?	?
21 ***Diaz-Balart***	Y	Y	Y	N	Y	Y	?
22 ***Shaw***	Y	Y	Y	N	Y	Y	N
23 Hastings	N	N	N	Y	Y	N	N
GEORGIA							
1 ***Kingston***	Y	Y	Y	N	Y	Y	?
2 Bishop	N	Y	N	Y	Y	Y	N
3 ***Collins***	Y	Y	Y	N	Y	Y	Y
4 McKinney	N	Y	N	N	Y	Y	N
5 Lewis	?	?	–	Y	Y	N	N
6 ***Gingrich***							
7 ***Barr***	Y	Y	Y	N	Y	Y	Y
8 ***Chambliss***	Y	Y	Y	N	Y	Y	N
9 ***Deal***	Y	Y	N	N	Y	?	?
10 ***Norwood***	Y	Y	Y	N	?	Y	N
11 ***Linder***	Y	Y	Y	N	Y	Y	Y
HAWAII							
1 Abercrombie	N	Y	N	N	Y	N	N
2 Mink	N	Y	N	Y	Y	Y	N
IDAHO							
1 ***Chenoweth***	Y	Y	Y	N	Y	Y	N
2 ***Crapo***	Y	Y	Y	N	Y	Y	Y
ILLINOIS							
1 Rush	N	Y	N	N	Y	Y	?
2 Jackson	N	N	N	N	Y	Y	N
3 Lipinski	N	Y	N	N	Y	Y	?
4 Gutierrez	N	Y	N	Y	Y	N	N
5 Blagojevich	N	Y	N	N	Y	Y	N
6 ***Hyde***	Y	Y	?	N	Y	Y	N
7 Davis	N	N	N	Y	Y	Y	N
8 ***Crane***	Y	Y	Y	N	Y	Y	Y
9 Yates	N	Y	N	Y	Y	Y	?
10 ***Porter***	Y	Y	Y	N	Y	Y	N
11 ***Weller***	Y	Y	N	N	Y	N	?
12 Costello	N	Y	N	N	Y	N	N
13 ***Fawell***	Y	Y	Y	N	Y	Y	N
14 ***Hastert***	Y	Y	Y	N	Y	Y	Y
15 ***Ewing***	Y	Y	Y	N	Y	Y	N

ND Northern Democrats SD Southern Democrats

	149	150	151	152	153	154	155
16 ***Manzullo***	Y	N	Y	N	Y	Y	N
17 Evans	N	Y	N	N	Y	Y	N
18 ***LaHood***	Y	Y	Y	N	Y	Y	N
19 Poshard	N	Y	N	N	Y	N	N
20 ***Shimkus***	Y	Y	Y	N	Y	Y	N
INDIANA							
1 Visclosky	N	Y	N	N	Y	Y	N
2 ***McIntosh***	Y	Y	N	N	Y	Y	?
3 Roemer	N	Y	Y	N	Y	Y	N
4 ***Souder***	Y	Y	Y	N	Y	Y	Y
5 ***Buyer***	Y	Y	Y	N	Y	Y	Y
6 ***Burton***	Y	Y	Y	N	+	Y	Y
7 ***Pease***	Y	Y	N	N	Y	Y	N
8 ***Hostettler***	Y	Y	Y	N	Y	Y	Y
9 Hamilton	N	Y	Y	N	Y	Y	N
10 Carson	N	Y	N	Y	Y	Y	N
IOWA							
1 ***Leach***	Y	Y	Y	N	Y	Y	?
2 ***Nussle***	Y	Y	Y	N	Y	Y	N
3 Boswell	N	Y	Y	N	Y	Y	N
4 ***Ganske***	Y	Y	Y	N	Y	Y	N
5 ***Latham***	Y	Y	Y	N	Y	Y	N
KANSAS							
1 ***Moran***	Y	Y	Y	N	Y	Y	N
2 ***Ryun***	Y	Y	Y	N	Y	Y	N
3 ***Snowbarger***	?	?	?	?	?	?	?
4 ***Tiahrt***	Y	Y	Y	N	Y	Y	Y
KENTUCKY							
1 ***Whitfield***	Y	Y	Y	N	Y	Y	N
2 ***Lewis***	Y	Y	Y	N	Y	Y	N
3 ***Northup***	Y	Y	Y	N	Y	Y	N
4 ***Bunning***	Y	Y	Y	N	Y	Y	?
5 ***Rogers***	Y	Y	Y	N	Y	Y	N
6 Baesler	N	Y	N	N	Y	Y	?
LOUISIANA							
1 ***Livingston***	Y	Y	Y	N	Y	Y	N
2 Jefferson	N	N	N	Y	Y	Y	N
3 ***Tauzin***	Y	Y	Y	N	Y	Y	N
4 ***McCrery***	Y	Y	Y	?	Y	Y	N
5 ***Cooksey***	Y	Y	Y	N	Y	?	?
6 ***Baker***	Y	Y	Y	N	Y	Y	?
7 John	N	Y	Y	Y	Y	Y	?
MAINE							
1 Allen	N	Y	N	Y	+	Y	N
2 Baldacci	N	Y	N	N	Y	Y	N
MARYLAND							
1 ***Gilchrest***	Y	Y	Y	N	Y	Y	Y
2 ***Ehrlich***	Y	Y	Y	N	Y	Y	Y
3 Cardin	N	Y	Y	N	Y	Y	?
4 Wynn	N	Y	N	N	Y	Y	N
5 Hoyer	N	Y	Y	N	Y	Y	N
6 ***Bartlett***	Y	Y	Y	N	Y	Y	Y
7 Cummings	N	Y	N	N	Y	Y	N
8 ***Morella***	Y	Y	Y	N	Y	?	Y
MASSACHUSETTS							
1 Olver	N	Y	N	N	Y	N	N
2 Neal	N	Y	N	Y	Y	Y	N
3 McGovern	N	Y	N	Y	Y	Y	N
4 Frank	N	Y	N	Y	Y	Y	N
5 Meehan	N	Y	N	N	Y	Y	N
6 Tierney	N	N	N	Y	Y	Y	?
7 Markey	N	N	N	Y	Y	Y	N
8 Kennedy	N	Y	N	Y	Y	Y	N
9 Moakley	N	Y	N	Y	Y	Y	N
10 Delahunt	N	N	N	Y	Y	Y	N
MICHIGAN							
1 Stupak	N	Y	N	N	Y	N	N
2 ***Hoekstra***	Y	Y	Y	N	Y	Y	N
3 ***Ehlers***	Y	Y	Y	N	Y	Y	N
4 ***Camp***	Y	Y	Y	N	Y	Y	Y
5 Barcia	N	Y	N	N	Y	Y	N
6 ***Upton***	Y	Y	Y	N	Y	Y	N
7 ***Smith***	Y	Y	Y	N	Y	Y	N
8 Stabenow	N	Y	N	Y	Y	N	N
9 Kildee	N	Y	N	Y	Y	Y	N
10 Bonior	N	Y	N	Y	Y	N	?
11 ***Knollenberg***	Y	Y	Y	N	Y	Y	Y
12 Levin	N	Y	N	Y	Y	Y	N
13 Rivers	N	Y	N	N	Y	Y	N
14 Conyers	N	N	N	Y	Y	Y	?
15 Kilpatrick	N	Y	N	Y	Y	Y	?
16 Dingell	N	Y	Y	Y	Y	Y	N
MINNESOTA							
1 ***Gutknecht***	Y	Y	Y	N	Y	Y	?
2 Minge	N	Y	Y	N	Y	Y	N

	149	150	151	152	153	154	155
3 ***Ramstad***	Y	Y	Y	N	Y	N	N
4 Vento	N	Y	N	N	Y	Y	?
5 Sabo	N	Y	N	N	Y	N	N
6 Luther	N	Y	N	N	Y	?	N
7 Peterson	Y	Y	Y	N	Y	Y	N
8 Oberstar	N	N	N	N	Y	N	N
MISSISSIPPI							
1 ***Wicker***	Y	Y	Y	N	Y	N	N
2 Thompson	N	Y	N	?	?	?	?
3 ***Pickering***	Y	Y	Y	N	Y	Y	N
4 ***Parker***	Y	Y	Y	N	Y	Y	N
5 Taylor	N	Y	N	N	Y	N	N
MISSOURI							
1 Clay	N	Y	N	Y	Y	N	N
2 ***Talent***	Y	Y	Y	N	Y	Y	Y
3 Gephardt	N	Y	N	N	Y	N	N
4 Skelton	N	Y	Y	N	Y	Y	?
5 McCarthy	N	Y	N	N	Y	Y	N
6 Danner	N	Y	Y	N	Y	Y	N
7 ***Blunt***	Y	Y	Y	N	Y	Y	N
8 ***Emerson***	Y	Y	Y	N	Y	Y	N
9 ***Hulshof***	Y	Y	Y	N	Y	N	N
MONTANA							
AL ***Hill***	Y	Y	Y	N	Y	Y	N
NEBRASKA							
1 ***Bereuter***	Y	Y	Y	N	Y	Y	N
2 ***Christensen***	Y	Y	Y	N	Y	Y	N
3 ***Barrett***	Y	Y	Y	N	Y	Y	N
NEVADA							
1 ***Ensign***	Y	Y	Y	N	Y	N	N
2 ***Gibbons***	Y	Y	Y	N	Y	N	N
NEW HAMPSHIRE							
1 ***Sununu***	Y	Y	Y	N	Y	Y	N
2 ***Bass***	Y	Y	Y	N	Y	Y	Y
NEW JERSEY							
1 Andrews	?	?	?	?	?	?	?
2 ***LoBiondo***	Y	Y	Y	N	Y	N	?
3 ***Saxton***	Y	Y	Y	N	Y	Y	Y
4 ***Smith***	Y	Y	Y	N	Y	Y	N
5 ***Roukema***	Y	Y	Y	N	Y	Y	N
6 Pallone	N	Y	N	Y	Y	N	N
7 ***Franks***	Y	Y	N	N	Y	Y	N
8 Pascrell	N	Y	N	Y	Y	N	N
9 Rothman	N	Y	N	N	Y	Y	?
10 Payne	N	Y	N	Y	Y	Y	N
11 ***Frelinghuysen***	Y	Y	Y	N	Y	Y	?
12 ***Pappas***	Y	Y	Y	N	Y	Y	N
13 Menendez	N	Y	N	N	Y	N	N
NEW MEXICO							
1 ***Schiff***	?	?	?	?	?	?	?
2 ***Skeen***	Y	Y	Y	N	Y	Y	N
3 ***Redmond***	Y	Y	Y	N	Y	N	N
NEW YORK							
1 ***Forbes***	N	Y	N	N	Y	N	N
2 ***Lazio***	Y	Y	Y	N	Y	Y	?
3 ***King***	Y	Y	Y	N	Y	Y	?
4 McCarthy	N	Y	N	Y	Y	Y	N
5 Ackerman	N	Y	N	Y	Y	Y	?
6 Flake	N	Y	N	Y	Y	Y	?
7 Manton	N	Y	Y	Y	Y	Y	N
8 Nadler	N	N	N	Y	Y	Y	N
9 Schumer	N	Y	N	N	Y	Y	N
10 Towns	N	Y	N	Y	Y	Y	N
11 Owens	N	Y	N	Y	Y	Y	N
12 Velázquez	N	Y	N	N	Y	Y	?
13 ***Molinari***	Y	Y	Y	N	Y	Y	Y
14 Maloney	N	Y	N	Y	Y	Y	N
15 Rangel	N	N	Y	Y	Y	Y	N
16 Serrano	N	Y	N	N	Y	Y	N
17 Engel	N	Y	N	N	Y	Y	N
18 Lowey	N	Y	N	N	Y	Y	N
19 ***Kelly***	Y	Y	Y	N	Y	Y	N
20 ***Gilman***	Y	Y	Y	N	Y	Y	N
21 McNulty	N	Y	N	Y	Y	N	N
22 ***Solomon***	Y	Y	Y	N	Y	Y	Y
23 ***Boehlert***	Y	Y	Y	N	Y	Y	N
24 ***McHugh***	Y	Y	Y	?	?	?	?
25 ***Walsh***	Y	Y	Y	N	Y	Y	N
26 Hinchey	N	Y	N	Y	Y	N	N
27 ***Paxon***	Y	Y	Y	N	Y	Y	Y
28 Slaughter	N	Y	N	Y	Y	?	N
29 LaFalce	N	N	Y	N	Y	Y	N
30 ***Quinn***	Y	Y	Y	Y	Y	Y	?
31 ***Houghton***	Y	Y	Y	N	Y	Y	?

	149	150	151	152	153	154	155
NORTH CAROLINA							
1 Clayton	N	N	N	N	Y	Y	N
2 Etheridge	N	Y	Y	N	Y	Y	N
3 ***Jones***	Y	Y	Y	N	Y	Y	N
4 Price	N	Y	Y	N	Y	Y	N
5 ***Burr***	Y	Y	Y	N	Y	Y	Y
6 ***Coble***	Y	N	Y	N	Y	Y	Y
7 McIntyre	N	?	Y	N	Y	Y	N
8 Hefner	N	Y	Y	?	Y	N	N
9 ***Myrick***	Y	Y	Y	N	Y	Y	Y
10 ***Ballenger***	Y	Y	Y	N	Y	Y	?
11 ***Taylor***	Y	Y	Y	N	Y	Y	?
12 Watt	N	N	N	Y	Y	N	N
NORTH DAKOTA							
AL Pomeroy	N	Y	Y	N	Y	Y	N
OHIO							
1 ***Chabot***	Y	Y	N	N	Y	Y	N
2 ***Portman***	Y	Y	Y	N	Y	Y	N
3 Hall	N	Y	Y	N	Y	Y	N
4 ***Oxley***	Y	Y	Y	N	+	+	?
5 ***Gillmor***	Y	Y	Y	N	Y	Y	Y
6 Strickland	N	Y	N	N	Y	N	N
7 ***Hobson***	Y	Y	Y	N	Y	Y	?
8 ***Boehner***	Y	Y	Y	N	Y	Y	N
9 Kaptur	N	Y	N	Y	Y	Y	?
10 Kucinich	N	N	N	N	Y	N	N
11 Stokes	N	Y	N	Y	Y	Y	N
12 ***Kasich***	Y	Y	Y	N	Y	Y	Y
13 Brown	N	Y	N	Y	Y	N	N
14 Sawyer	N	Y	Y	N	Y	Y	N
15 ***Pryce***	Y	Y	Y	N	Y	Y	N
16 ***Regula***	Y	Y	Y	N	Y	Y	N
17 Traficant	Y	Y	Y	N	Y	Y	N
18 ***Ney***	Y	Y	Y	N	Y	Y	N
19 ***LaTourette***	Y	Y	Y	N	Y	Y	Y
OKLAHOMA							
1 ***Largent***	Y	Y	Y	N	?	?	?
2 ***Coburn***	Y	Y	Y	N	Y	Y	?
3 ***Watkins***	Y	Y	Y	N	Y	Y	N
4 ***Watts***	Y	?	Y	N	Y	N	N
5 ***Istook***	Y	Y	Y	?	?	?	?
6 ***Lucas***	Y	Y	Y	N	Y	Y	?
OREGON							
1 Furse	N	Y	N	N	Y	N	N
2 ***Smith***	Y	Y	Y	N	Y	Y	Y
3 Blumenauer	N	Y	N	N	Y	Y	N
4 DeFazio	N	Y	N	Y	Y	N	N
5 Hooley	N	Y	Y	N	Y	Y	N
PENNSYLVANIA							
1 Foglietta	N	Y	N	Y	Y	N	?
2 Fattah	N	N	N	Y	Y	N	?
3 Borski	N	Y	N	N	Y	N	N
4 Klink	N	Y	N	Y	Y	Y	N
5 ***Peterson***	Y	Y	Y	N	Y	Y	Y
6 Holden	N	Y	N	N	Y	Y	N
7 ***Weldon***	Y	?	Y	N	Y	Y	?
8 ***Greenwood***	Y	?	Y	N	Y	Y	?
9 ***Shuster***	Y	Y	Y	N	Y	Y	?
10 ***McDade***	Y	Y	Y	N	Y	Y	?
11 Kanjorski	N	Y	Y	Y	Y	Y	N
12 Murtha	N	Y	N	N	Y	Y	N
13 ***Fox***	Y	Y	Y	N	Y	Y	?
14 Coyne	N	Y	N	Y	Y	Y	N
15 McHale	N	Y	N	N	Y	Y	N
16 ***Pitts***	Y	Y	Y	N	Y	Y	Y
17 ***Gekas***	Y	Y	Y	N	Y	Y	Y
18 Doyle	N	Y	N	N	Y	Y	N
19 ***Goodling***	Y	Y	Y	N	Y	Y	Y
20 Mascara	N	Y	N	N	Y	Y	N
21 ***English***	Y	Y	Y	N	Y	N	Y
RHODE ISLAND							
1 Kennedy	N	Y	N	Y	Y	N	N
2 Weygand	N	Y	N	Y	Y	Y	N
SOUTH CAROLINA							
1 ***Sanford***	Y	Y	N	N	Y	Y	Y
2 ***Spence***	Y	Y	Y	N	Y	Y	N
3 ***Graham***	Y	Y	Y	N	Y	Y	Y
4 ***Inglis***	Y	Y	Y	N	Y	Y	Y
5 Spratt	N	Y	N	N	Y	Y	N
6 Clyburn	N	Y	N	Y	Y	N	N
SOUTH DAKOTA							
AL ***Thune***	Y	Y	Y	N	Y	Y	N
TENNESSEE							
1 ***Jenkins***	Y	Y	Y	N	Y	Y	N
2 ***Duncan***	Y	Y	Y	N	Y	Y	?

	149	150	151	152	153	154	155
3 ***Wamp***	Y	Y	Y	N	Y	N	N
4 ***Hilleary***	Y	Y	Y	N	Y	N	N
5 Clement	N	Y	Y	N	Y	Y	N
6 Gordon	N	Y	Y	N	Y	Y	?
7 ***Bryant***	Y	Y	Y	N	Y	Y	N
8 Tanner	N	Y	Y	N	Y	Y	N
9 Ford	N	Y	N	Y	Y	?	N
TEXAS							
1 Sandlin	N	N	Y	N	Y	Y	N
2 Turner	N	Y	Y	N	Y	Y	N
3 ***Johnson, Sam***	Y	Y	Y	N	Y	Y	Y
4 Hall	Y	Y	Y	N	Y	Y	N
5 ***Sessions***	Y	Y	N	N	Y	N	N
6 ***Barton***	Y	Y	N	N	Y	Y	?
7 ***Archer***	Y	Y	Y	N	Y	Y	Y
8 ***Brady***	Y	Y	Y	N	Y	Y	Y
9 Lampson	N	Y	N	Y	Y	Y	N
10 Doggett	N	N	N	Y	Y	Y	N
11 Edwards	N	Y	Y	N	Y	Y	N
12 ***Granger***	Y	Y	Y	N	Y	Y	?
13 ***Thornberry***	Y	Y	Y	N	Y	Y	Y
14 ***Paul***	Y	N	N	N	N	Y	?
15 Hinojosa	N	Y	Y	N	Y	Y	N
16 Reyes	N	Y	Y	N	Y	Y	N
17 Stenholm	N	Y	Y	Y	Y	Y	N
18 Jackson-Lee	N	Y	N	N	Y	Y	?
19 ***Combest***	Y	Y	Y	N	Y	Y	Y
20 Gonzalez	N	Y	Y	N	Y	Y	N
21 ***Smith***	Y	Y	Y	N	Y	Y	?
22 ***DeLay***	Y	Y	Y	N	Y	Y	?
23 ***Bonilla***	Y	Y	Y	N	Y	Y	Y
24 Frost	N	Y	Y	Y	Y	Y	N
25 Bentsen	N	Y	N	N	Y	Y	N
26 ***Armey***	Y	Y	Y	N	Y	Y	Y
27 Ortiz	N	Y	Y	N	Y	Y	N
28 Rodriguez	N	Y	Y	N	Y	N	N
29 Green	N	Y	Y	N	Y	N	?
30 Johnson, E.B.	N	Y	Y	Y	Y	N	N
UTAH							
1 ***Hansen***	Y	Y	Y	N	Y	Y	Y
2 ***Cook***	Y	Y	Y	N	Y	Y	Y
3 ***Cannon***	Y	Y	Y	?	?	?	?
VERMONT							
AL *Sanders*	N	Y	N	Y	Y	Y	N
VIRGINIA							
1 ***Bateman***	Y	Y	Y	N	Y	Y	N
2 Pickett	N	Y	Y	N	Y	N	?
3 Scott	N	N	N	N	Y	Y	N
4 Sisisky	N	Y	N	N	Y	Y	N
5 Goode	N	Y	Y	N	Y	Y	N
6 ***Goodlatte***	Y	Y	Y	N	Y	Y	N
7 ***Bliley***	Y	Y	Y	N	Y	Y	Y
8 Moran	N	Y	N	N	Y	Y	N
9 Boucher	N	Y	N	N	Y	Y	?
10 ***Wolf***	Y	Y	Y	N	Y	Y	Y
11 ***Davis***	Y	Y	Y	N	Y	Y	Y
WASHINGTON							
1 ***White***	Y	Y	Y	?	Y	Y	N
2 ***Metcalf***	Y	Y	N	N	Y	Y	?
3 ***Smith, Linda***	Y	Y	Y	N	Y	Y	N
4 ***Hastings***	Y	Y	Y	N	Y	Y	N
5 ***Nethercutt***	Y	Y	Y	N	Y	Y	N
6 Dicks	N	Y	Y	N	Y	Y	N
7 McDermott	N	Y	N	Y	Y	N	N
8 ***Dunn***	Y	Y	Y	N	Y	Y	N
9 Smith, Adam	N	Y	Y	N	Y	Y	N
WEST VIRGINIA							
1 Mollohan	N	N	Y	N	Y	Y	N
2 Wise	N	Y	N	N	Y	Y	N
3 Rahall	N	Y	N	N	Y	Y	N
WISCONSIN							
1 ***Neumann***	Y	Y	N	N	Y	Y	Y
2 ***Klug***	Y	Y	N	N	Y	Y	N
3 Kind	N	Y	N	N	Y	Y	N
4 Kleczka	N	Y	N	N	Y	Y	N
5 Barrett	N	Y	N	N	Y	Y	N
6 ***Petri***	Y	Y	Y	N	Y	Y	N
7 Obey	N	Y	N	N	Y	Y	N
8 Johnson	N	Y	Y	N	Y	N	N
9 ***Sensenbrenner***	Y	Y	Y	N	Y	Y	Y
WYOMING							
AL ***Cubin***	Y	Y	Y	N	Y	Y	N

Southern states - Ala., Ark., Fla., Ga., Ky., La., Miss., N.C., Okla., S.C., Tenn., Texas, Va.

HOUSE VOTES 156, 157,158, 159

156. HR 1420. Wildlife Refuges/Passage. Young, R-Alaska, motion to suspend the rules and pass the bill to establish a mission of conservation for the National Wildlife Refuge System and allow public recreational use of a refuge only when the use is compatible with the conservation and established purpose of an individual refuge. Motion agreed to 407-1: R 213-1; D 193-0 (ND 142-0, SD 51-0); I 1-0, June 3, 1997. A two-thirds majority of those present and voting (272 in this case) is required for passage under suspension of the rules. A "yea" was a vote in support of the president's position.

157. HR 1757. Fiscal 1998-99 State Department Authorization/Previous Question. Diaz-Balart, R-Fla., motion to order the previous question (thus ending debate and the possibility of amendment) on adoption of the rule (H Res 159) to provide House floor consideration of the bill to authorize $6.1 billion in both fiscal 1998 and fiscal 1999 for the State Department and related agencies and to merge the functions of the U.S. Information Agency, the International Development Cooperation Agency, the Arms Control and Disarmament Agency and certain functions of the Agency for International Development into the State Department. The rule also provides for House floor consideration of the bill (HR 1758) to specify U.S. policy toward the North Atlantic Treaty Organization. Motion agreed to 219-204: R 219-4; D 0-199 (ND 0-148, SD 0-51); I 0-1, June 4, 1997.

158. HR 1757. Fiscal 1998-99 State Department Authorization/Rule. Adoption of the rule (H Res 159) to provide House floor consideration of the bill to authorize $6.1 billion in both fiscal 1998 and fiscal 1999 for the State Department and related agencies and to merge the functions of the U.S. Information Agency, the International Development Cooperation Agency, the Arms Control and Disarmament Agency and certain functions of the Agency for International Development into the State Department. The rule also provides for House floor consideration of the bill (HR 1758) to specify U.S. policy toward the North Atlantic Treaty Organization. Adopted 221-200: R 220-2; D 1-197 (ND 1-146, SD 0-51); I 0-1, June 4, 1997.

159. HR 1757. Fiscal 1998-99 State Department Authorization/TV Marti. Diaz-Balart, R-Fla., amendment to the Skaggs, D-Colo., amendment to discontinue funding for TV Marti broadcasts to Cuba after Sept. 30, 1997, only if the president certifies that continued funding is not in the national interest. The original amendment would have terminated funding on that date. Adopted 271-155: R 207-18; D 64-136 (ND 39-107, SD 25-29); I 0-1, June 4, 1997. (Subsequently, the Skaggs amendment was adopted by voice vote.)

KEY

- Y Voted for (yea).
- # Paired for.
- + Announced for.
- N Voted against (nay).
- X Paired against.
- – Announced against.
- P Voted "present."
- C Voted "present" to avoid possible conflict of interest.
- ? Did not vote or otherwise make a position known.

Democrats ***Republicans***
Independent

	156	157	158	159
ALABAMA				
1 ***Callahan***	Y	Y	Y	Y
2 ***Everett***	Y	Y	Y	Y
3 ***Riley***	Y	Y	Y	Y
4 ***Aderholt***	Y	Y	Y	Y
5 Cramer	Y	N	N	N
6 ***Bachus***	?	Y	Y	Y
7 Hilliard	Y	?	?	N
ALASKA				
AL ***Young***	Y	Y	Y	Y
ARIZONA				
1 ***Salmon***	Y	Y	Y	Y
2 Pastor	Y	N	N	Y
3 ***Stump***	?	Y	Y	Y
4 ***Shadegg***	Y	Y	Y	Y
5 ***Kolbe***	Y	Y	Y	Y
6 ***Hayworth***	Y	Y	Y	Y
ARKANSAS				
1 Berry	Y	N	N	Y
2 Snyder	Y	N	N	Y
3 ***Hutchinson***	Y	Y	Y	Y
4 ***Dickey***	Y	Y	Y	Y
CALIFORNIA				
1 ***Riggs***	Y	Y	Y	Y
2 ***Herger***	Y	Y	Y	Y
3 Fazio	Y	N	N	?
4 ***Doolittle***	Y	Y	Y	Y
5 Matsui	Y	N	N	N
6 Woolsey	Y	N	N	N
7 Miller	Y	N	N	N
8 Pelosi	Y	N	N	N
9 Dellums	Y	N	N	N
10 Tauscher	Y	N	N	N
11 ***Pombo***	Y	Y	Y	Y
12 Lantos	?	?	?	?
13 Stark	Y	N	N	N
14 Eshoo	Y	N	N	N
15 ***Campbell***	Y	Y	Y	Y
16 Lofgren	Y	N	N	N
17 Farr	?	?	?	?
18 Condit	Y	N	N	Y
19 ***Radanovich***	Y	Y	Y	Y
20 Dooley	Y	N	N	N
21 ***Thomas***	Y	Y	Y	Y
22 Capps	Y	N	N	N
23 ***Gallegly***	Y	Y	Y	Y
24 Sherman	Y	N	N	Y
25 ***McKeon***	Y	Y	Y	Y
26 Berman	Y	N	N	N
27 ***Rogan***	Y	Y	Y	Y
28 ***Dreier***	Y	Y	Y	Y
29 Waxman	Y	N	N	N
30 Becerra	Y	N	N	N
31 Martinez	Y	N	N	N
32 Dixon	?	N	N	N
33 Roybal-Allard	Y	N	N	N
34 Torres	Y	N	N	N
35 Waters	Y	N	N	N
36 Harman	Y	N	N	N
37 Millender-McD.	Y	N	N	N
38 ***Horn***	Y	Y	Y	Y
39 ***Royce***	Y	Y	Y	Y
40 ***Lewis***	?	?	?	Y
41 ***Kim***	Y	Y	Y	Y
42 Brown	Y	N	N	N
43 ***Calvert***	Y	Y	Y	Y
44 ***Bono***	Y	Y	Y	Y
45 ***Rohrabacher***	?	Y	Y	Y
46 Sanchez	Y	N	N	N
47 ***Cox***	Y	Y	Y	Y
48 ***Packard***	Y	Y	Y	Y
49 ***Bilbray***	?	Y	Y	Y
50 Filner	Y	N	N	N
51 ***Cunningham***	Y	Y	Y	Y
52 ***Hunter***	?	Y	Y	Y
COLORADO				
1 DeGette	Y	N	N	N
2 Skaggs	Y	N	N	N
3 ***McInnis***	Y	Y	Y	Y
4 ***Schaffer***	Y	Y	Y	Y
5 ***Hefley***	Y	Y	Y	Y
6 ***Schaefer***	Y	Y	Y	Y
CONNECTICUT				
1 Kennelly	Y	N	N	N
2 Gejdenson	Y	N	N	N
3 DeLauro	Y	N	N	N
4 ***Shays***	Y	Y	Y	Y
5 Maloney	Y	N	N	N
6 ***Johnson***	Y	Y	Y	Y
DELAWARE				
AL ***Castle***	Y	Y	Y	Y
FLORIDA				
1 ***Scarborough***	Y	Y	Y	Y
2 Boyd	Y	N	N	Y
3 Brown	Y	N	N	Y
4 ***Fowler***	Y	Y	Y	Y
5 Thurman	Y	N	N	N
6 ***Stearns***	Y	Y	Y	Y
7 ***Mica***	Y	Y	Y	Y
8 ***McCollum***	Y	Y	Y	Y
9 ***Bilirakis***	Y	Y	Y	Y
10 ***Young***	Y	Y	Y	Y
11 Davis	Y	N	N	Y
12 ***Canady***	Y	Y	Y	Y
13 ***Miller***	Y	Y	Y	Y
14 ***Goss***	Y	Y	Y	Y
15 ***Weldon***	Y	Y	Y	Y
16 ***Foley***	Y	Y	Y	Y
17 Meek	Y	N	N	Y
18 ***Ros-Lehtinen***	Y	Y	Y	Y
19 Wexler	Y	N	N	Y
20 Deutsch	Y	N	N	Y
21 ***Diaz-Balart***	Y	Y	Y	Y
22 ***Shaw***	Y	Y	Y	Y
23 Hastings	Y	N	N	Y
GEORGIA				
1 ***Kingston***	Y	Y	Y	Y
2 Bishop	Y	N	N	Y
3 ***Collins***	Y	Y	Y	Y
4 McKinney	Y	N	N	N
5 Lewis	Y	N	N	N
6 ***Gingrich***				
7 ***Barr***	Y	Y	Y	Y
8 ***Chambliss***	Y	Y	Y	Y
9 ***Deal***	Y	Y	Y	N
10 ***Norwood***	Y	Y	Y	Y
11 ***Linder***	Y	Y	Y	Y
HAWAII				
1 Abercrombie	Y	N	N	N
2 Mink	Y	N	N	N
IDAHO				
1 ***Chenoweth***	Y	Y	Y	Y
2 ***Crapo***	Y	Y	Y	Y
ILLINOIS				
1 Rush	Y	N	N	N
2 Jackson	Y	N	N	N
3 Lipinski	Y	N	N	Y
4 Gutierrez	Y	N	N	Y
5 Blagojevich	?	N	N	Y
6 ***Hyde***	Y	Y	Y	Y
7 Davis	Y	N	N	Y
8 ***Crane***	Y	Y	Y	Y
9 Yates	Y	N	?	N
10 ***Porter***	Y	Y	Y	Y
11 ***Weller***	Y	Y	Y	Y
12 Costello	Y	N	N	N
13 ***Fawell***	Y	Y	Y	Y
14 ***Hastert***	Y	Y	Y	Y
15 ***Ewing***	Y	Y	Y	Y

ND Northern Democrats SD Southern Democrats

	156	157	158	159
16 ***Manzullo***	Y	Y	Y	Y
17 Evans	Y	N	N	N
18 ***LaHood***	Y	Y	Y	Y
19 Poshard	Y	N	N	N
20 ***Shimkus***	Y	Y	Y	N
INDIANA				
1 Visclosky	Y	N	N	N
2 ***McIntosh***	Y	Y	Y	Y
3 Roemer	Y	N	N	N
4 ***Souder***	Y	Y	Y	Y
5 ***Buyer***	Y	Y	Y	Y
6 ***Burton***	Y	Y	Y	Y
7 ***Pease***	Y	Y	Y	Y
8 ***Hostettler***	Y	Y	Y	Y
9 Hamilton	Y	N	N	N
10 Carson	Y	N	N	N
IOWA				
1 ***Leach***	Y	N	Y	Y
2 ***Nussle***	Y	Y	Y	Y
3 Boswell	Y	N	Y	Y
4 ***Ganske***	Y	Y	Y	N
5 ***Latham***	Y	Y	Y	Y
KANSAS				
1 ***Moran***	Y	Y	Y	Y
2 ***Ryun***	Y	Y	Y	Y
3 ***Snowbarger***	Y	Y	Y	Y
4 ***Tiahrt***	Y	Y	Y	Y
KENTUCKY				
1 ***Whitfield***	Y	Y	Y	N
2 ***Lewis***	Y	Y	Y	Y
3 ***Northup***	Y	Y	Y	Y
4 ***Bunning***	Y	Y	Y	Y
5 ***Rogers***	Y	Y	Y	Y
6 Baesler	Y	N	N	N
LOUISIANA				
1 ***Livingston***	Y	Y	Y	Y
2 Jefferson	Y	?	?	?
3 ***Tauzin***	Y	Y	Y	Y
4 ***McCrery***	Y	Y	Y	Y
5 ***Cooksey***	Y	Y	Y	Y
6 ***Baker***	Y	Y	Y	Y
7 John	Y	N	N	Y
MAINE				
1 Allen	Y	N	N	N
2 Baldacci	Y	N	N	N
MARYLAND				
1 ***Gilchrest***	Y	Y	Y	Y
2 ***Ehrlich***	Y	Y	Y	Y
3 Cardin	Y	N	N	N
4 Wynn	Y	N	N	Y
5 Hoyer	Y	N	N	Y
6 ***Bartlett***	Y	Y	Y	N
7 Cummings	Y	N	N	N
8 ***Morella***	Y	Y	Y	N
MASSACHUSETTS				
1 Olver	Y	N	N	N
2 Neal	Y	N	N	N
3 McGovern	Y	N	N	N
4 Frank	Y	N	N	N
5 Meehan	Y	N	N	N
6 Tierney	Y	N	N	N
7 Markey	Y	N	N	N
8 Kennedy	Y	N	N	N
9 Moakley	Y	N	N	N
10 Delahunt	Y	N	N	N
MICHIGAN				
1 Stupak	Y	N	N	Y
2 ***Hoekstra***	Y	Y	Y	N
3 ***Ehlers***	Y	Y	Y	Y
4 ***Camp***	Y	Y	Y	Y
5 Barcia	Y	N	N	N
6 ***Upton***	Y	Y	Y	N
7 ***Smith***	Y	Y	Y	Y
8 Stabenow	Y	N	N	Y
9 Kildee	Y	N	N	N
10 Bonior	Y	N	N	N
11 ***Knollenberg***	Y	Y	Y	Y
12 Levin	Y	N	N	Y
13 Rivers	Y	N	N	N
14 Conyers	Y	N	N	N
15 Kilpatrick	Y	N	N	N
16 Dingell	Y	N	N	N
MINNESOTA				
1 ***Gutknecht***	Y	N	N	Y
2 Minge	Y	N	N	N

	156	157	158	159
3 ***Ramstad***	Y	N	Y	Y
4 Vento	Y	N	N	N
5 Sabo	Y	N	N	N
6 Luther	Y	N	N	N
7 Peterson	Y	N	N	Y
8 Oberstar	Y	N	N	N
MISSISSIPPI				
1 ***Wicker***	Y	Y	Y	Y
2 Thompson	?	N	N	N
3 ***Pickering***	+	+	+	+
4 ***Parker***	Y	Y	Y	N
5 Taylor	Y	N	N	N
MISSOURI				
1 Clay	Y	N	N	N
2 ***Talent***	Y	Y	Y	Y
3 Gephardt	Y	N	N	Y
4 Skelton	Y	N	N	Y
5 McCarthy	Y	N	N	N
6 Danner	Y	N	N	N
7 ***Blunt***	Y	Y	Y	Y
8 ***Emerson***	Y	Y	Y	Y
9 ***Hulshof***	Y	Y	Y	Y
MONTANA				
AL ***Hill***	Y	Y	Y	Y
NEBRASKA				
1 ***Bereuter***	Y	Y	Y	Y
2 ***Christensen***	Y	Y	Y	N
3 ***Barrett***	Y	Y	Y	Y
NEVADA				
1 ***Ensign***	?	Y	Y	Y
2 ***Gibbons***	Y	Y	Y	Y
NEW HAMPSHIRE				
1 ***Sununu***	Y	Y	Y	Y
2 ***Bass***	Y	Y	Y	Y
NEW JERSEY				
1 Andrews	?	?	?	?
2 ***LoBiondo***	Y	Y	Y	Y
3 ***Saxton***	Y	Y	Y	Y
4 ***Smith***	Y	Y	Y	Y
5 ***Roukema***	Y	Y	Y	Y
6 Pallone	Y	N	N	Y
7 ***Franks***	Y	Y	Y	Y
8 Pascrell	Y	N	N	Y
9 Rothman	Y	N	N	Y
10 Payne	?	N	N	N
11 ***Frelinghuysen***	Y	Y	Y	Y
12 ***Pappas***	Y	Y	Y	Y
13 Menendez	Y	N	N	Y
NEW MEXICO				
1 ***Schiff***	?	?	?	?
2 ***Skeen***	Y	Y	Y	Y
3 ***Redmond***	Y	Y	Y	Y
NEW YORK				
1 ***Forbes***	Y	Y	Y	Y
2 ***Lazio***	Y	Y	Y	Y
3 ***King***	Y	Y	Y	Y
4 McCarthy	Y	N	N	Y
5 Ackerman	Y	N	N	Y
6 Flake	Y	N	N	N
7 Manton	Y	N	N	Y
8 Nadler	Y	N	N	N
9 Schumer	Y	N	N	N
10 Towns	Y	N	N	N
11 Owens	Y	N	N	N
12 Velázquez	Y	N	N	N
13 ***Molinari***	Y	Y	Y	Y
14 Maloney	Y	N	N	Y
15 Rangel	Y	N	N	N
16 Serrano	Y	N	N	N
17 Engel	Y	N	N	Y
18 Lowey	Y	N	N	N
19 ***Kelly***	Y	Y	Y	Y
20 ***Gilman***	Y	Y	Y	Y
21 McNulty	Y	N	N	Y
22 ***Solomon***	Y	Y	Y	Y
23 ***Boehlert***	Y	Y	Y	N
24 ***McHugh***	Y	Y	Y	Y
25 ***Walsh***	Y	Y	Y	Y
26 Hinchey	Y	N	N	N
27 ***Paxon***	Y	Y	Y	Y
28 Slaughter	Y	N	N	N
29 LaFalce	Y	N	N	N
30 ***Quinn***	Y	Y	Y	Y
31 ***Houghton***	Y	Y	Y	Y

	156	157	158	159
NORTH CAROLINA				
1 Clayton	?	?	?	N
2 Etheridge	Y	N	N	N
3 ***Jones***	Y	Y	Y	Y
4 Price	Y	N	N	N
5 ***Burr***	Y	Y	Y	Y
6 ***Coble***	Y	Y	Y	N
7 McIntyre	Y	N	N	N
8 Hefner	Y	?	?	N
9 ***Myrick***	Y	Y	Y	Y
10 ***Ballenger***	Y	Y	Y	Y
11 ***Taylor***	Y	Y	Y	Y
12 Watt	Y	N	N	N
NORTH DAKOTA				
AL Pomeroy	Y	N	N	?
OHIO				
1 ***Chabot***	Y	Y	Y	Y
2 ***Portman***	Y	Y	Y	Y
3 Hall	Y	N	N	Y
4 ***Oxley***	Y	Y	Y	Y
5 ***Gillmor***	Y	Y	Y	Y
6 Strickland	Y	N	N	Y
7 ***Hobson***	Y	Y	Y	Y
8 ***Boehner***	Y	Y	Y	Y
9 Kaptur	Y	N	N	Y
10 Kucinich	Y	N	N	Y
11 Stokes	Y	N	N	N
12 ***Kasich***	Y	Y	Y	Y
13 Brown	Y	N	N	N
14 Sawyer	Y	N	N	N
15 ***Pryce***	Y	Y	Y	Y
16 ***Regula***	Y	Y	Y	N
17 Traficant	Y	N	N	Y
18 ***Ney***	Y	Y	Y	Y
19 ***LaTourette***	Y	Y	Y	Y
OKLAHOMA				
1 ***Largent***	Y	Y	Y	Y
2 ***Coburn***	Y	Y	Y	Y
3 ***Watkins***	Y	Y	Y	Y
4 ***Watts***	Y	Y	Y	Y
5 ***Istook***	Y	Y	Y	Y
6 ***Lucas***	Y	Y	Y	Y
OREGON				
1 Furse	?	N	N	N
2 ***Smith***	Y	Y	Y	Y
3 Blumenauer	Y	N	N	N
4 DeFazio	?	N	N	N
5 Hooley	Y	N	N	N
PENNSYLVANIA				
1 Foglietta	Y	N	N	N
2 Fattah	Y	N	N	N
3 Borski	Y	N	N	N
4 Klink	Y	N	N	Y
5 ***Peterson***	Y	Y	Y	Y
6 Holden	Y	N	N	Y
7 ***Weldon***	Y	Y	Y	Y
8 ***Greenwood***	Y	Y	Y	Y
9 ***Shuster***	Y	Y	Y	N
10 ***McDade***	Y	?	?	Y
11 Kanjorski	Y	N	N	N
12 Murtha	Y	N	N	Y
13 ***Fox***	Y	Y	Y	Y
14 Coyne	Y	N	N	Y
15 McHale	Y	N	N	N
16 ***Pitts***	Y	Y	Y	Y
17 ***Gekas***	Y	Y	Y	Y
18 Doyle	Y	N	N	Y
19 ***Goodling***	Y	Y	Y	Y
20 Mascara	Y	N	N	Y
21 ***English***	Y	Y	Y	Y
RHODE ISLAND				
1 Kennedy	Y	N	N	Y
2 Weygand	Y	N	N	N
SOUTH CAROLINA				
1 ***Sanford***	+	Y	Y	Y
2 ***Spence***	Y	Y	Y	Y
3 ***Graham***	Y	Y	Y	Y
4 ***Inglis***	Y	Y	Y	Y
5 Spratt	Y	N	N	Y
6 Clyburn	Y	N	N	N
SOUTH DAKOTA				
AL ***Thune***	Y	N	N	Y
TENNESSEE				
1 ***Jenkins***	Y	Y	Y	Y
2 ***Duncan***	Y	Y	Y	Y

	156	157	158	159
3 ***Wamp***	Y	Y	Y	Y
4 ***Hilleary***	?	Y	Y	Y
5 Clement	Y	N	N	Y
6 Gordon	Y	N	N	Y
7 ***Bryant***	Y	Y	Y	Y
8 Tanner	Y	N	N	N
9 Ford	+	N	N	Y
TEXAS				
1 Sandlin	Y	N	N	N
2 Turner	Y	N	N	N
3 ***Johnson, Sam***	Y	Y	Y	Y
4 Hall	Y	N	N	N
5 ***Sessions***	Y	Y	Y	Y
6 ***Barton***	?	Y	Y	Y
7 ***Archer***	Y	Y	Y	Y
8 ***Brady***	Y	Y	Y	Y
9 Lampson	Y	N	N	N
10 Doggett	?	N	N	N
11 Edwards	Y	N	N	Y
12 ***Granger***	Y	Y	Y	Y
13 ***Thornberry***	Y	Y	Y	Y
14 ***Paul***	N	Y	Y	N
15 Hinojosa	Y	N	N	Y
16 Reyes	Y	N	N	Y
17 Stenholm	Y	N	N	N
18 Jackson-Lee	Y	N	N	Y
19 ***Combest***	Y	Y	Y	Y
20 Gonzalez	Y	N	N	N
21 ***Smith***	Y	Y	Y	Y
22 ***DeLay***	Y	Y	Y	Y
23 ***Bonilla***	Y	Y	Y	Y
24 Frost	Y	N	N	Y
25 Bentsen	Y	N	N	Y
26 ***Armey***	Y	Y	Y	Y
27 Ortiz	Y	N	N	Y
28 Rodriguez	Y	N	N	N
29 Green	Y	N	N	Y
30 Johnson, E.B.	Y	N	N	Y
UTAH				
1 ***Hansen***	Y	Y	Y	Y
2 ***Cook***	Y	Y	Y	Y
3 ***Cannon***	Y	Y	Y	Y
VERMONT				
AL *Sanders*	Y	N	N	N
VIRGINIA				
1 ***Bateman***	Y	Y	Y	Y
2 Pickett	Y	N	N	N
3 Scott	Y	N	N	N
4 Sisisky	Y	N	N	Y
5 Goode	Y	N	N	N
6 ***Goodlatte***	Y	Y	Y	Y
7 ***Bliley***	Y	Y	Y	Y
8 Moran	Y	N	N	N
9 Boucher	Y	N	N	N
10 ***Wolf***	Y	Y	Y	Y
11 ***Davis***	Y	Y	Y	Y
WASHINGTON				
1 ***White***	Y	Y	Y	Y
2 ***Metcalf***	Y	Y	Y	Y
3 ***Smith, Linda***	?	Y	Y	Y
4 ***Hastings***	Y	Y	Y	Y
5 ***Nethercutt***	Y	Y	Y	Y
6 Dicks	?	N	N	N
7 McDermott	Y	N	N	N
8 ***Dunn***	Y	Y	?	Y
9 Smith, Adam	Y	N	N	N
WEST VIRGINIA				
1 Mollohan	Y	N	N	N
2 Wise	Y	N	N	Y
3 Rahall	Y	N	N	N
WISCONSIN				
1 ***Neumann***	Y	Y	Y	N
2 ***Klug***	Y	Y	Y	Y
3 Kind	Y	N	N	N
4 Kleczka	Y	N	N	N
5 Barrett	Y	N	N	N
6 ***Petri***	Y	Y	Y	N
7 Obey	Y	N	N	N
8 Johnson	Y	N	N	N
9 ***Sensenbrenner***	Y	Y	Y	N
WYOMING				
AL ***Cubin***	Y	Y	Y	Y

Southern states - Ala., Ark., Fla., Ga., Ky., La., Miss., N.C., Okla., S.C., Tenn., Texas, Va.

HOUSE VOTES 160, 161, 162, 163, 164

160. HR 1757. Fiscal 1998-99 State Department Authorization/Foreign Affairs Agency Consolidation. Hamilton, D-Ind., amendment to require the president to submit a proposal to Congress to consolidate foreign affairs agencies within 120 days of the bill's enactment and allow Congress to disapprove the plan under expedited procedures within 120 days of the proposal's submission. Rejected 202-224: R 3-222; D 198-2 (ND 145-1, SD 53-1); I 1-0, June 4, 1997. A "yea" was a vote in support of the president's position.

161. HR 1757. Fiscal 1998-99 State Department Authorization/Surplus Overseas Property. Bachus, R-Ala., amendment to require the State Department to submit annual reports to Congress on overseas surplus properties for sale and to earmark sale proceeds for deficit reduction. Adopted 277-146: R 197-25; D 80-120 (ND 54-93, SD 26-27); I 0-1, June 4, 1997.

162. HR 1757. Fiscal 1998-99 State Department Authorization/Employee Due Process. Goss, R-Fla., amendment to strike bill provisions that require the State Department inspector general to inform any department employee who is the likely subject or target of a criminal investigation of their due process rights. Adopted 214-211: R 212-12; D 2-198 (ND 2-145, SD 0-53); I 0-1, June 4, 1997.

163. HR 1757. Fiscal 1998-99 State Department Authorization/U.N. Withdrawal. Paul, R-Texas, amendment to require the United States to withdraw from the United Nations and close the U.S. Mission there. The amendment would prohibit the appropriation of funds for any contributions to the United Nations and the participation of U.S. military personnel in any U.N. military or peacekeeping operation. Rejected 54-369: R 52-171; D 2-197 (ND 0-146, SD 2-51); I 0-1, June 4, 1997.

164. HR 1757. Fiscal 1998-99 State Department Authorization/U.N. Contributions. Stearns, R-Fla., amendment to allow Congress, rather than the secretary of State, to decide whether to withhold 20 percent of the U.S. contribution to the United Nations if it were determined that the world body had failed to implement consensus-based decision-making procedures on budget matters to assure that sufficient attention was paid to the views of the United States and other major contributors. Rejected 176-244: R 167-56; D 9-187 (ND 4-140, SD 5-47); I 0-1, June 4, 1997.

KEY

- Y Voted for (yea).
- # Paired for.
- + Announced for.
- N Voted against (nay).
- X Paired against.
- – Announced against.
- P Voted "present."
- C Voted "present" to avoid possible conflict of interest.
- ? Did not vote or otherwise make a position known.

Democrats ***Republicans***
Independent

	160	161	162	163	164
ALABAMA					
1 ***Callahan***	N	Y	Y	N	Y
2 ***Everett***	N	Y	Y	Y	Y
3 ***Riley***	N	Y	Y	Y	Y
4 ***Aderholt***	N	Y	Y	Y	Y
5 Cramer	Y	Y	N	N	Y
6 ***Bachus***	N	Y	Y	N	Y
7 Hilliard	Y	N	N	N	N
ALASKA					
AL ***Young***	N	N	Y	Y	Y
ARIZONA					
1 ***Salmon***	N	Y	Y	Y	Y
2 Pastor	Y	Y	N	N	N
3 ***Stump***	N	Y	Y	Y	Y
4 ***Shadegg***	N	Y	Y	Y	Y
5 ***Kolbe***	N	N	Y	N	N
6 ***Hayworth***	N	Y	Y	N	Y
ARKANSAS					
1 Berry	Y	Y	N	N	N
2 Snyder	Y	N	N	N	N
3 ***Hutchinson***	N	Y	Y	N	Y
4 ***Dickey***	N	Y	Y	Y	Y
CALIFORNIA					
1 ***Riggs***	N	Y	Y	N	N
2 ***Herger***	N	Y	Y	N	Y
3 Fazio	Y	N	N	N	N
4 ***Doolittle***	N	Y	Y	Y	Y
5 Matsui	Y	N	N	N	N
6 Woolsey	Y	N	N	N	N
7 Miller	Y	N	N	N	N
8 Pelosi	Y	N	N	N	N
9 Dellums	Y	N	N	N	N
10 Tauscher	Y	Y	N	N	N
11 ***Pombo***	N	Y	Y	Y	Y
12 Lantos	?	?	?	?	?
13 Stark	Y	N	N	N	N
14 Eshoo	Y	Y	Y	N	N
15 ***Campbell***	N	Y	Y	N	Y
16 Lofgren	Y	N	N	N	N
17 Farr	?	?	?	?	?
18 Condit	Y	Y	N	N	Y
19 ***Radanovich***	N	Y	N	N	Y
20 Dooley	Y	N	N	N	N
21 ***Thomas***	N	Y	Y	N	N
22 Capps	Y	N	N	N	N
23 ***Gallegly***	N	Y	Y	N	Y
24 Sherman	Y	N	N	N	N
25 ***McKeon***	N	Y	Y	N	Y
26 Berman	Y	N	N	–	N
27 ***Rogan***	N	Y	Y	N	Y
28 ***Dreier***	N	Y	Y	N	Y
29 Waxman	Y	N	N	N	N
30 Becerra	?	N	N	N	N
31 Martinez	?	N	N	N	N
32 Dixon	Y	N	N	N	N
33 Roybal-Allard	Y	N	N	N	N
34 Torres	Y	N	N	N	N
35 Waters	Y	N	N	N	?
36 Harman	Y	Y	N	N	N
37 Millender-McD.	Y	N	N	N	N
38 ***Horn***	N	Y	Y	N	N
39 ***Royce***	N	?	Y	?	Y
40 ***Lewis***	N	Y	Y	N	N
41 ***Kim***	N	Y	Y	N	Y
42 Brown	Y	N	N	N	N
43 ***Calvert***	N	Y	Y	N	Y
44 ***Bono***	N	Y	Y	N	Y
45 ***Rohrabacher***	N	Y	Y	Y	Y
46 Sanchez	Y	Y	N	N	N
47 ***Cox***	N	Y	Y	N	Y
48 ***Packard***	N	Y	Y	N	N
49 ***Bilbray***	N	Y	Y	N	Y
50 Filner	Y	N	N	N	N
51 ***Cunningham***	N	Y	Y	Y	Y
52 ***Hunter***	N	N	Y	Y	Y
COLORADO					
1 DeGette	Y	N	N	N	N
2 Skaggs	Y	N	N	N	N
3 ***McInnis***	N	Y	Y	N	Y
4 ***Schaffer***	N	Y	Y	Y	Y
5 ***Hefley***	N	Y	Y	Y	Y
6 ***Schaefer***	N	Y	Y	Y	Y
CONNECTICUT					
1 Kennelly	Y	N	N	N	N
2 Gejdenson	Y	N	N	N	N
3 DeLauro	Y	N	N	N	N
4 ***Shays***	N	Y	Y	N	N
5 Maloney	Y	N	N	N	N
6 ***Johnson***	N	Y	Y	N	N
DELAWARE					
AL ***Castle***	N	N	Y	N	N
FLORIDA					
1 ***Scarborough***	N	Y	Y	Y	Y
2 Boyd	Y	Y	N	N	N
3 Brown	Y	N	N	N	N
4 ***Fowler***	N	Y	Y	N	Y
5 Thurman	Y	Y	N	N	N
6 ***Stearns***	N	Y	Y	N	Y
7 ***Mica***	N	Y	Y	N	Y
8 ***McCollum***	N	Y	Y	N	Y
9 ***Bilirakis***	N	Y	Y	N	Y
10 ***Young***	N	Y	Y	N	Y
11 Davis	Y	N	N	N	N
12 ***Canady***	N	Y	Y	N	Y
13 ***Miller***	N	Y	Y	N	Y
14 ***Goss***	N	Y	Y	N	Y
15 ***Weldon***	N	Y	Y	Y	Y
16 ***Foley***	N	Y	Y	Y	Y
17 Meek	Y	N	N	N	N
18 ***Ros-Lehtinen***	N	Y	Y	Y	Y
19 Wexler	Y	N	N	N	N
20 Deutsch	Y	N	N	N	N
21 ***Diaz-Balart***	N	Y	Y	N	Y
22 ***Shaw***	N	Y	Y	N	N
23 Hastings	Y	N	N	N	N
GEORGIA					
1 ***Kingston***	N	Y	Y	Y	Y
2 Bishop	Y	Y	N	N	N
3 ***Collins***	N	Y	Y	N	Y
4 McKinney	Y	N	N	N	N
5 Lewis	Y	N	N	N	N
6 ***Gingrich***					
7 ***Barr***	N	Y	Y	Y	Y
8 ***Chambliss***	N	Y	Y	N	Y
9 ***Deal***	N	Y	Y	N	Y
10 ***Norwood***	N	Y	Y	N	Y
11 ***Linder***	N	Y	Y	Y	Y
HAWAII					
1 Abercrombie	Y	Y	N	N	?
2 Mink	Y	N	N	N	N
IDAHO					
1 ***Chenoweth***	N	Y	Y	Y	Y
2 ***Crapo***	N	Y	Y	Y	Y
ILLINOIS					
1 Rush	Y	N	N	N	N
2 Jackson	Y	N	N	N	N
3 Lipinski	Y	Y	N	N	N
4 Gutierrez	Y	N	N	N	N
5 Blagojevich	Y	N	N	N	N
6 ***Hyde***	N	Y	Y	N	N
7 Davis	Y	N	N	N	N
8 ***Crane***	N	Y	Y	Y	Y
9 Yates	Y	N	N	N	N
10 ***Porter***	N	N	Y	N	N
11 ***Weller***	N	Y	Y	N	Y
12 Costello	Y	Y	N	N	N
13 ***Fawell***	N	Y	Y	N	N
14 ***Hastert***	N	Y	Y	N	Y
15 ***Ewing***	N	Y	Y	N	Y

ND Northern Democrats SD Southern Democrats

	160	161	162	163	164
16 ***Manzullo***	N	Y	N	Y	Y
17 Evans	Y	Y	N	N	N
18 ***LaHood***	N	N	Y	N	N
19 Poshard	Y	Y	N	N	N
20 ***Shimkus***	N	Y	Y	N	Y
INDIANA					
1 Visclosky	Y	N	N	N	N
2 ***McIntosh***	N	Y	Y	Y	?
3 Roemer	Y	Y	N	N	N
4 ***Souder***	N	Y	Y	N	Y
5 ***Buyer***	N	?	?	?	?
6 ***Burton***	N	N	Y	Y	Y
7 ***Pease***	N	Y	Y	N	Y
8 ***Hostettler***	N	Y	N	N	Y
9 Hamilton	Y	N	N	N	N
10 Carson	Y	Y	N	N	N
IOWA					
1 ***Leach***	Y	N	Y	N	N
2 ***Nussle***	N	Y	Y	N	Y
3 Boswell	Y	Y	N	N	N
4 ***Ganske***	N	Y	Y	N	N
5 ***Latham***	N	Y	Y	N	N
KANSAS					
1 ***Moran***	N	Y	Y	Y	Y
2 ***Ryun***	N	Y	Y	Y	Y
3 ***Snowbarger***	N	Y	Y	N	Y
4 ***Tiahrt***	N	Y	Y	N	Y
KENTUCKY					
1 ***Whitfield***	N	Y	Y	N	Y
2 ***Lewis***	N	Y	Y	N	Y
3 ***Northup***	N	Y	Y	N	N
4 ***Bunning***	N	Y	Y	N	Y
5 ***Rogers***	N	N	Y	N	N
6 Baesler	Y	Y	N	N	N
LOUISIANA					
1 ***Livingston***	N	Y	Y	N	N
2 Jefferson	?	?	?	?	?
3 ***Tauzin***	N	Y	Y	N	Y
4 ***McCrery***	N	Y	Y	N	N
5 ***Cooksey***	N	Y	Y	N	Y
6 ***Baker***	N	Y	Y	N	Y
7 John	Y	Y	N	N	N
MAINE					
1 Allen	Y	N	N	N	N
2 Baldacci	Y	Y	N	N	N
MARYLAND					
1 ***Gilchrest***	N	N	Y	N	N
2 ***Ehrlich***	N	Y	N	N	Y
3 Cardin	Y	N	N	N	N
4 Wynn	Y	N	N	N	N
5 Hoyer	Y	N	N	N	N
6 ***Bartlett***	N	Y	Y	Y	Y
7 Cummings	Y	Y	N	N	N
8 ***Morella***	Y	N	Y	N	N
MASSACHUSETTS					
1 Olver	Y	N	N	N	N
2 Neal	Y	Y	N	N	N
3 McGovern	Y	N	N	N	N
4 Frank	Y	Y	N	N	N
5 Meehan	Y	Y	N	N	N
6 Tierney	Y	Y	N	N	N
7 Markey	Y	N	N	N	N
8 Kennedy	Y	N	N	N	N
9 Moakley	Y	N	N	N	N
10 Delahunt	Y	N	N	N	N
MICHIGAN					
1 Stupak	Y	Y	N	N	N
2 ***Hoekstra***	N	Y	Y	N	Y
3 ***Ehlers***	N	Y	Y	N	N
4 ***Camp***	N	Y	Y	N	Y
5 Barcia	Y	Y	N	N	Y
6 ***Upton***	N	Y	Y	N	Y
7 ***Smith***	N	N	Y	N	Y
8 Stabenow	Y	Y	N	N	N
9 Kildee	Y	Y	N	N	N
10 Bonior	Y	N	N	N	N
11 ***Knollenberg***	N	Y	Y	N	N
12 Levin	Y	N	N	N	N
13 Rivers	Y	Y	N	N	N
14 Conyers	Y	N	N	N	N
15 Kilpatrick	Y	N	N	N	N
16 Dingell	Y	N	N	N	?
MINNESOTA					
1 ***Gutknecht***	N	Y	Y	N	Y
2 Minge	Y	Y	N	N	N

	160	161	162	163	164
3 ***Ramstad***	N	Y	Y	N	N
4 Vento	Y	N	N	N	N
5 Sabo	Y	N	N	N	N
6 Luther	Y	Y	N	N	N
7 Peterson	Y	Y	N	N	Y
8 Oberstar	Y	N	N	N	N
MISSISSIPPI					
1 ***Wicker***	N	Y	N	N	Y
2 Thompson	Y	N	N	N	N
3 ***Pickering***	+	+	+	−	−
4 ***Parker***	N	Y	Y	N	Y
5 Taylor	Y	Y	N	Y	Y
MISSOURI					
1 Clay	Y	N	N	N	N
2 ***Talent***	N	Y	Y	N	Y
3 Gephardt	Y	N	N	N	N
4 Skelton	Y	Y	N	N	N
5 McCarthy	Y	Y	N	N	N
6 Danner	Y	Y	N	N	N
7 ***Blunt***	N	Y	Y	N	Y
8 ***Emerson***	N	Y	Y	N	Y
9 ***Hulshof***	N	Y	Y	Y	Y
MONTANA					
AL ***Hill***	N	Y	Y	N	Y
NEBRASKA					
1 ***Bereuter***	N	N	Y	N	Y
2 ***Christensen***	N	Y	Y	N	Y
3 ***Barrett***	N	Y	Y	N	N
NEVADA					
1 ***Ensign***	N	Y	Y	Y	Y
2 ***Gibbons***	N	Y	Y	Y	Y
NEW HAMPSHIRE					
1 ***Sununu***	N	Y	Y	N	Y
2 ***Bass***	N	Y	Y	N	Y
NEW JERSEY					
1 Andrews	?	?	?	?	?
2 ***LoBiondo***	N	Y	Y	N	Y
3 ***Saxton***	N	Y	Y	N	N
4 ***Smith***	N	N	N	N	Y
5 ***Roukema***	N	Y	Y	N	N
6 Pallone	Y	N	N	N	N
7 ***Franks***	N	Y	Y	N	Y
8 Pascrell	Y	Y	N	N	N
9 Rothman	Y	Y	N	N	N
10 Payne	Y	N	N	N	N
11 ***Frelinghuysen***	N	Y	Y	N	N
12 ***Pappas***	N	Y	Y	N	Y
13 Menendez	Y	N	N	N	N
NEW MEXICO					
1 ***Schiff***	?	?	?	?	?
2 ***Skeen***	N	Y	Y	N	N
3 ***Redmond***	N	Y	Y	N	Y
NEW YORK					
1 ***Forbes***	N	Y	N	N	N
2 ***Lazio***	N	N	Y	N	N
3 ***King***	N	Y	Y	N	N
4 McCarthy	Y	Y	N	N	N
5 Ackerman	Y	N	N	N	N
6 Flake	Y	N	N	N	N
7 Manton	Y	N	N	N	N
8 Nadler	Y	N	N	N	N
9 Schumer	Y	Y	N	N	N
10 Towns	Y	N	N	N	N
11 Owens	Y	N	N	N	N
12 Velázquez	Y	N	N	N	N
13 ***Molinari***	N	Y	Y	N	N
14 Maloney	Y	Y	N	N	N
15 Rangel	Y	N	N	N	N
16 Serrano	Y	N	N	N	N
17 Engel	Y	N	N	N	N
18 Lowey	Y	N	N	N	N
19 ***Kelly***	N	Y	Y	N	Y
20 ***Gilman***	N	N	Y	N	N
21 McNulty	Y	N	N	N	N
22 ***Solomon***	N	Y	Y	Y	Y
23 ***Boehlert***	N	N	Y	N	N
24 ***McHugh***	N	Y	Y	N	N
25 ***Walsh***	N	Y	Y	N	N
26 Hinchey	Y	N	N	N	N
27 ***Paxon***	N	Y	Y	N	Y
28 Slaughter	Y	N	N	N	N
29 LaFalce	Y	N	N	N	N
30 ***Quinn***	N	Y	N	N	N
31 ***Houghton***	N	N	N	N	N

	160	161	162	163	164
NORTH CAROLINA					
1 Clayton	Y	N	N	N	N
2 Etheridge	Y	Y	N	N	N
3 ***Jones***	N	Y	Y	Y	Y
4 Price	Y	Y	N	N	N
5 ***Burr***	N	Y	Y	N	Y
6 ***Coble***	N	Y	Y	N	Y
7 McIntyre	Y	Y	N	N	N
8 Hefner	Y	Y	N	N	N
9 ***Myrick***	N	Y	Y	N	Y
10 ***Ballenger***	N	Y	Y	N	Y
11 ***Taylor***	N	N	Y	N	Y
12 Watt	Y	N	N	N	N
NORTH DAKOTA					
AL Pomeroy	Y	N	N	N	N
OHIO					
1 ***Chabot***	N	Y	Y	N	N
2 ***Portman***	N	Y	Y	N	N
3 Hall	Y	N	N	N	N
4 ***Oxley***	N	N	Y	N	Y
5 ***Gillmor***	N	N	Y	N	N
6 Strickland	Y	Y	N	N	N
7 ***Hobson***	N	Y	Y	N	Y
8 ***Boehner***	N	Y	Y	N	Y
9 Kaptur	Y	Y	N	N	N
10 Kucinich	Y	N	N	N	N
11 Stokes	Y	N	N	N	N
12 ***Kasich***	N	Y	Y	N	Y
13 Brown	Y	N	N	N	N
14 Sawyer	Y	N	N	N	N
15 ***Pryce***	N	Y	Y	N	N
16 ***Regula***	N	N	Y	N	N
17 Traficant	N	Y	Y	N	Y
18 ***Ney***	N	Y	Y	Y	Y
19 ***LaTourette***	N	Y	Y	N	N
OKLAHOMA					
1 ***Largent***	N	Y	Y	Y	Y
2 ***Coburn***	N	Y	Y	Y	Y
3 ***Watkins***	N	?	Y	N	Y
4 ***Watts***	N	Y	Y	N	Y
5 ***Istook***	N	Y	Y	Y	Y
6 ***Lucas***	N	Y	Y	Y	Y
OREGON					
1 Furse	Y	N	N	N	N
2 ***Smith***	N	Y	Y	N	Y
3 Blumenauer	Y	N	N	N	N
4 DeFazio	Y	Y	N	N	N
5 Hooley	Y	Y	N	N	N
PENNSYLVANIA					
1 Foglietta	Y	N	N	N	N
2 Fattah	Y	?	?	?	?
3 Borski	Y	N	N	N	N
4 Klink	Y	Y	N	N	N
5 ***Peterson***	N	Y	Y	N	Y
6 Holden	Y	Y	N	N	N
7 ***Weldon***	N	Y	Y	N	Y
8 ***Greenwood***	N	Y	Y	N	N
9 ***Shuster***	N	Y	Y	N	Y
10 ***McDade***	N	Y	Y	N	N
11 Kanjorski	Y	Y	N	N	N
12 Murtha	Y	N	N	N	N
13 ***Fox***	N	Y	Y	N	Y
14 Coyne	Y	N	N	N	N
15 McHale	Y	Y	N	N	N
16 ***Pitts***	N	Y	Y	N	Y
17 ***Gekas***	N	N	Y	N	Y
18 Doyle	Y	Y	N	N	N
19 ***Goodling***	N	Y	Y	N	Y
20 Mascara	Y	Y	N	N	N
21 ***English***	N	Y	Y	N	Y
RHODE ISLAND					
1 Kennedy	Y	Y	N	N	N
2 Weygand	Y	Y	N	N	N
SOUTH CAROLINA					
1 ***Sanford***	N	Y	Y	N	N
2 ***Spence***	N	Y	Y	N	Y
3 ***Graham***	N	Y	N	N	Y
4 ***Inglis***	N	Y	Y	N	Y
5 Spratt	Y	N	N	N	N
6 Clyburn	Y	N	N	N	N
SOUTH DAKOTA					
AL ***Thune***	N	Y	Y	N	Y
TENNESSEE					
1 ***Jenkins***	N	Y	Y	N	Y
2 ***Duncan***	N	Y	Y	Y	Y

	160	161	162	163	164
3 ***Wamp***	N	Y	Y	Y	Y
4 ***Hilleary***	N	Y	Y	N	Y
5 Clement	Y	N	N	N	N
6 Gordon	Y	Y	N	N	N
7 ***Bryant***	N	Y	Y	N	Y
8 Tanner	Y	Y	N	N	N
9 Ford	Y	N	N	N	N
TEXAS					
1 Sandlin	Y	Y	N	N	N
2 Turner	Y	Y	N	N	N
3 ***Johnson, Sam***	N	Y	Y	Y	Y
4 Hall	N	Y	N	Y	Y
5 ***Sessions***	N	Y	Y	Y	Y
6 ***Barton***	N	Y	Y	N	Y
7 ***Archer***	N	Y	Y	N	Y
8 ***Brady***	N	Y	Y	N	Y
9 Lampson	Y	Y	N	N	N
10 Doggett	Y	Y	N	N	N
11 Edwards	Y	Y	N	N	Y
12 ***Granger***	N	Y	Y	N	N
13 ***Thornberry***	N	Y	Y	N	Y
14 ***Paul***	N	Y	Y	Y	Y
15 Hinojosa	Y	N	N	N	N
16 Reyes	Y	N	N	N	N
17 Stenholm	Y	Y	N	N	Y
18 Jackson-Lee	Y	N	N	N	N
19 ***Combest***	N	Y	Y	Y	Y
20 Gonzalez	Y	N	N	N	N
21 ***Smith***	N	Y	Y	N	Y
22 ***DeLay***	N	Y	Y	Y	Y
23 ***Bonilla***	N	Y	Y	Y	N
24 Frost	Y	N	N	N	N
25 Bentsen	Y	N	N	N	N
26 ***Armey***	N	N	Y	N	Y
27 Ortiz	Y	Y	N	N	?
28 Rodriguez	Y	Y	N	N	N
29 Green	Y	Y	N	N	N
30 Johnson, E.B.	Y	N	N	N	N
UTAH					
1 ***Hansen***	N	Y	Y	N	Y
2 ***Cook***	N	Y	Y	N	Y
3 ***Cannon***	N	Y	Y	N	Y
VERMONT					
AL *Sanders*	Y	N	N	N	N
VIRGINIA					
1 ***Bateman***	N	N	Y	N	N
2 Pickett	Y	Y	N	N	N
3 Scott	Y	N	N	N	N
4 Sisisky	Y	Y	N	N	N
5 Goode	Y	?	?	?	?
6 ***Goodlatte***	N	Y	Y	N	Y
7 ***Bliley***	N	Y	Y	N	Y
8 Moran	Y	N	N	N	N
9 Boucher	Y	N	N	N	N
10 ***Wolf***	N	Y	Y	N	Y
11 ***Davis***	Y	Y	N	N	N
WASHINGTON					
1 ***White***	N	Y	Y	N	N
2 ***Metcalf***	N	Y	Y	N	Y
3 ***Smith, Linda***	N	Y	Y	N	Y
4 ***Hastings***	N	Y	Y	N	Y
5 ***Nethercutt***	N	Y	Y	Y	Y
6 Dicks	Y	N	N	N	N
7 McDermott	Y	N	N	N	N
8 ***Dunn***	N	Y	Y	N	Y
9 Smith, Adam	Y	N	N	N	N
WEST VIRGINIA					
1 Mollohan	Y	N	N	N	N
2 Wise	Y	N	N	N	N
3 Rahall	Y	N	N	N	N
WISCONSIN					
1 ***Neumann***	N	Y	Y	N	Y
2 ***Klug***	N	Y	Y	N	Y
3 Kind	Y	Y	N	N	N
4 Kleczka	Y	Y	N	N	N
5 Barrett	Y	Y	N	N	N
6 ***Petri***	N	Y	Y	N	N
7 Obey	Y	Y	N	N	N
8 Johnson	Y	Y	N	N	N
9 ***Sensenbrenner***	N	Y	Y	N	Y
WYOMING					
AL ***Cubin***	N	Y	Y	Y	Y

Southern states - Ala., Ark., Fla., Ga., Ky., La., Miss., N.C., Okla., S.C., Tenn., Texas, Va.

HOUSE VOTES 165, 166, 167, 168, 169

165. H Con Res 84. Fiscal 1998 Budget Resolution/Rule. Adoption of the rule (H Res 160) to waive all points of order against and provide for House floor consideration of the conference report on the concurrent resolution to adopt a five-year budget plan that would balance the budget by fiscal 2002 and set binding budget levels for the fiscal year ending Sept. 30, 1998. Adopted 373-47: R 220-0; D 153-46 (ND 109-39, SD 44-7); I 0-1, June 5, 1997.

166. H Con Res 84. Fiscal 1998 Budget Resolution/Conference Report. Adoption of the conference report on the concurrent resolution to adopt a five-year budget plan that would balance the budget by fiscal 2002 by cutting projected spending by approximately $322 billion, adding or restoring $32.7 billion in priority spending and cutting taxes by a net of $85 billion, for a net deficit reduction of $204.3 billion. Projected spending cuts would include reductions of $115 billion in Medicare, $13.6 billion in Medicaid and approximately $139 billion in discretionary spending. The plan calls for additional spending to provide health insurance to currently uninsured children and to restore Supplemental Security Income and Medicaid benefits eliminated under the 1996 welfare system overhaul (PL 104-193). The resolution sets binding levels for the fiscal year ending Sept. 30, 1998: budget authority, $1,703.8 trillion; outlays, $1,692.3 trillion; revenues, $1,601.8 trillion; deficit, $90.5 billion. Adopted 327-97: R 198-26; D 129-70 (ND 86-62, SD 43-8); I 0-1, June 5, 1997. A "yea" was a vote in support of the president's position.

167. HR 1757. Fiscal 1998-99 State Department Authorization/Overseas Abortion Funding. Campbell, R-Calif., amendment to the Smith, R-N.J., amendment to prohibit only the direct use of funds to pay for abortions or abortion counseling in any foreign country, except in cases of rape, incest or where the life of the mother is endangered. The amendment would also prohibit funding for lobbying for or against abortion and impose a dollar-for-dollar reduction in funding to the U.N. Population Fund for any amount it spends on future program activities in China. Rejected 200-218: R 37-182; D 162-36 (ND 118-30, SD 44-6); I 1-0, June 5, 1997.

168. HR 1757. Fiscal 1998-99 State Department Authorization/International Family Planning Funding Restrictions. Smith, R-N.J., amendment to prohibit funding to any private, nongovernmental or multilateral organization that directly or indirectly performs abortions in a foreign country, except in cases of rape, incest or when the life of the mother is endangered. The amendment would prohibit funding for any foreign organization that lobbies for or against abortion and funding for the U.N. Population Fund unless the organization ceases all activities in China. Adopted 232-189: R 192-30; D 40-158 (ND 32-115, SD 8-43); I 0-1, June 5, 1997. A "nay" was a vote in support of the president's position.

169. HR 1469. Supplemental Fiscal 1997 Appropriations/Conference Report. Adoption of the conference report on the bill to provide about $8.6 billion in additional funds for fiscal 1997, including about $5.4 billion in emergency disaster aid for the flood-stricken Northwest and $1.9 billion to finance military peacekeeping operations in Bosnia and the Middle East. The bill also includes provisions that automatically provide funding for federal programs that lack appropriations authority at the start of fiscal 1998 at 100 percent of their fiscal 1997 levels until fiscal 1998 appropriations are enacted and prohibits the Census Bureau from using statistical sampling in calculating the national population in 2000. Adopted 220-201: R 188-35; D 32-165 (ND 22-125, SD 10-40); I 0-1, June 5, 1997. A "nay" was a vote in support of the president's position.

KEY

- Y Voted for (yea).
- # Paired for.
- + Announced for.
- N Voted against (nay).
- X Paired against.
- – Announced against.
- P Voted "present."
- C Voted "present" to avoid possible conflict of interest.
- ? Did not vote or otherwise make a position known.

Democrats ***Republicans*** *Independent*

	165	166	167	168	169
ALABAMA					
1 ***Callahan***	Y	Y	N	Y	Y
2 ***Everett***	Y	Y	N	Y	Y
3 ***Riley***	Y	Y	N	Y	Y
4 ***Aderholt***	Y	Y	N	Y	Y
5 Cramer	Y	Y	Y	Y	N
6 ***Bachus***	Y	Y	N	Y	Y
7 Hilliard	N	N	Y	N	N
ALASKA					
AL ***Young***	Y	Y	N	Y	Y
ARIZONA					
1 ***Salmon***	Y	N	N	Y	N
2 Pastor	Y	Y	Y	N	N
3 ***Stump***	Y	Y	N	Y	Y
4 ***Shadegg***	Y	N	N	Y	N
5 ***Kolbe***	Y	Y	Y	N	Y
6 ***Hayworth***	Y	Y	N	Y	Y
ARKANSAS					
1 Berry	Y	Y	Y	Y	Y
2 Snyder	Y	Y	Y	N	N
3 ***Hutchinson***	Y	Y	N	Y	Y
4 ***Dickey***	Y	Y	N	Y	Y
CALIFORNIA					
1 ***Riggs***	Y	Y	N	Y	Y
2 ***Herger***	Y	Y	N	Y	Y
3 Fazio	Y	Y	Y	N	Y
4 ***Doolittle***	Y	Y	N	Y	Y
5 Matsui	Y	Y	Y	?	Y
6 Woolsey	Y	Y	Y	N	N
7 Miller	N	N	Y	N	N
8 Pelosi	N	N	Y	N	N
9 Dellums	N	N	Y	N	N
10 Tauscher	Y	Y	Y	N	Y
11 ***Pombo***	Y	N	N	Y	Y
12 Lantos	?	?	?	?	?
13 Stark	N	N	Y	N	N
14 Eshoo	Y	Y	Y	N	N
15 ***Campbell***	Y	Y	Y	N	N
16 Lofgren	Y	Y	Y	N	N
17 Farr	?	?	?	?	?
18 Condit	Y	Y	Y	N	Y
19 ***Radanovich***	Y	Y	N	Y	Y
20 Dooley	Y	Y	Y	N	N
21 ***Thomas***	Y	Y	Y	N	Y
22 Capps	Y	Y	Y	N	Y
23 ***Gallegly***	Y	Y	N	Y	Y
24 Sherman	Y	Y	Y	N	N
25 ***McKeon***	Y	Y	N	Y	Y
26 Berman	Y	Y	Y	N	N
27 ***Rogan***	Y	Y	N	Y	Y
28 ***Dreier***	Y	Y	N	Y	Y
29 Waxman	Y	N	Y	N	N
30 Becerra	N	N	Y	N	N
31 Martinez	N	Y	N	N	N
32 Dixon	Y	N	Y	N	N
33 Roybal-Allard	Y	N	Y	N	N
34 Torres	N	N	Y	N	N
35 Waters	N	N	Y	N	N
36 Harman	Y	Y	Y	N	N
37 Millender-McD.	Y	N	Y	N	N
38 ***Horn***	Y	Y	Y	N	Y
39 ***Royce***	Y	Y	N	Y	Y
40 ***Lewis***	Y	Y	N	Y	Y
41 ***Kim***	Y	Y	N	Y	Y
42 Brown	Y	N	Y	N	N
43 ***Calvert***	Y	Y	N	Y	Y
44 ***Bono***	Y	Y	N	Y	Y
45 ***Rohrabacher***	Y	N	N	Y	N
46 Sanchez	Y	Y	Y	N	N
47 ***Cox***	Y	N	N	Y	N
48 ***Packard***	Y	Y	N	Y	Y
49 ***Bilbray***	Y	Y	Y	N	Y
50 Filner	N	N	Y	N	N
51 ***Cunningham***	Y	Y	N	Y	Y
52 ***Hunter***	Y	N	N	Y	Y
COLORADO					
1 DeGette	Y	N	Y	N	N
2 Skaggs	Y	Y	Y	N	N
3 ***McInnis***	Y	Y	N	Y	N
4 ***Schaffer***	Y	Y	N	Y	N
5 ***Hefley***	Y	Y	N	Y	N
6 ***Schaefer***	Y	Y	N	Y	N
CONNECTICUT					
1 Kennelly	Y	Y	Y	N	N
2 Gejdenson	Y	Y	Y	N	N
3 DeLauro	Y	Y	Y	N	N
4 ***Shays***	Y	Y	Y	N	N
5 Maloney	Y	Y	Y	N	N
6 ***Johnson***	?	Y	Y	N	Y
DELAWARE					
AL ***Castle***	Y	Y	Y	N	N
FLORIDA					
1 ***Scarborough***	Y	N	N	Y	N
2 Boyd	Y	Y	Y	N	N
3 Brown	N	N	Y	N	N
4 ***Fowler***	Y	Y	Y	Y	Y
5 Thurman	Y	Y	Y	N	N
6 ***Stearns***	Y	N	N	Y	N
7 ***Mica***	Y	Y	N	Y	N
8 ***McCollum***	Y	N	N	Y	Y
9 ***Bilirakis***	Y	Y	N	Y	Y
10 ***Young***	Y	Y	N	Y	Y
11 Davis	Y	Y	+	N	N
12 ***Canady***	Y	Y	N	Y	Y
13 ***Miller***	Y	Y	N	Y	N
14 ***Goss***	Y	Y	N	Y	Y
15 ***Weldon***	Y	N	N	Y	Y
16 ***Foley***	Y	Y	Y	Y	Y
17 Meek	?	Y	Y	N	Y
18 ***Ros-Lehtinen***	Y	Y	N	Y	Y
19 Wexler	Y	Y	Y	N	N
20 Deutsch	Y	?	?	?	?
21 ***Diaz-Balart***	Y	+	–	+	+
22 ***Shaw***	Y	Y	Y	Y	Y
23 Hastings	N	N	Y	N	N
GEORGIA					
1 ***Kingston***	Y	Y	N	Y	N
2 Bishop	Y	Y	Y	N	N
3 ***Collins***	Y	Y	N	Y	N
4 McKinney	Y	Y	Y	N	?
5 Lewis	N	N	Y	N	N
6 ***Gingrich***					
7 ***Barr***	Y	Y	N	Y	Y
8 ***Chambliss***	Y	Y	N	Y	Y
9 ***Deal***	Y	Y	N	Y	N
10 ***Norwood***	Y	Y	N	Y	N
11 ***Linder***	Y	Y	N	Y	Y
HAWAII					
1 Abercrombie	Y	Y	Y	N	N
2 Mink	N	N	Y	N	N
IDAHO					
1 ***Chenoweth***	Y	N	N	Y	Y
2 ***Crapo***	Y	N	N	Y	Y
ILLINOIS					
1 Rush	N	N	Y	N	N
2 Jackson	Y	N	Y	N	N
3 Lipinski	N	N	N	Y	N
4 Gutierrez	Y	N	Y	N	N
5 Blagojevich	Y	Y	Y	N	N
6 ***Hyde***	Y	N	N	Y	Y
7 Davis	Y	N	N	N	N
8 ***Crane***	Y	N	N	Y	Y
9 Yates	N	N	Y	N	N
10 ***Porter***	Y	Y	Y	N	Y
11 ***Weller***	Y	Y	N	Y	Y
12 Costello	Y	Y	N	Y	N
13 ***Fawell***	Y	Y	Y	N	Y
14 ***Hastert***	Y	Y	N	Y	Y
15 ***Ewing***	Y	Y	N	Y	Y

ND Northern Democrats SD Southern Democrats

	165	166	167	168	169
16 ***Manzullo***	Y	Y	N	Y	Y
17 Evans	Y	N	Y	N	N
18 ***LaHood***	Y	Y	N	Y	Y
19 Poshard	Y	Y	N	Y	N
20 ***Shimkus***	Y	Y	N	Y	Y
INDIANA					
1 Visclosky	N	Y	Y	N	N
2 ***McIntosh***	Y	Y	?	Y	Y
3 Roemer	Y	Y	N	Y	Y
4 ***Souder***	?	Y	N	Y	Y
5 ***Buyer***	Y	Y	N	Y	Y
6 ***Burton***	Y	Y	?	Y	Y
7 ***Pease***	Y	Y	N	Y	Y
8 ***Hostettler***	Y	Y	N	Y	Y
9 Hamilton	Y	Y	Y	Y	Y
10 Carson	Y	Y	Y	N	N
IOWA					
1 ***Leach***	Y	Y	Y	N	Y
2 ***Nussle***	Y	Y	?	Y	Y
3 Boswell	Y	Y	Y	N	N
4 ***Ganske***	Y	N	N	Y	Y
5 ***Latham***	Y	Y	N	Y	Y
KANSAS					
1 ***Moran***	Y	Y	N	Y	Y
2 ***Ryun***	Y	Y	N	Y	Y
3 ***Snowbarger***	Y	Y	N	Y	Y
4 ***Tiahrt***	Y	Y	N	Y	Y
KENTUCKY					
1 ***Whitfield***	Y	Y	N	Y	Y
2 ***Lewis***	Y	Y	N	Y	Y
3 ***Northup***	Y	Y	N	Y	Y
4 ***Bunning***	Y	Y	N	Y	Y
5 ***Rogers***	Y	Y	N	Y	Y
6 Baesler	Y	Y	Y	N	Y
LOUISIANA					
1 ***Livingston***	Y	Y	N	Y	Y
2 Jefferson	?	X	?	?	?
3 ***Tauzin***	Y	Y	N	Y	Y
4 ***McCrery***	Y	Y	N	Y	Y
5 ***Cooksey***	Y	Y	N	Y	Y
6 ***Baker***	Y	Y	N	Y	Y
7 John	Y	Y	N	Y	N
MAINE					
1 Allen	Y	Y	Y	N	N
2 Baldacci	Y	Y	Y	N	N
MARYLAND					
1 ***Gilchrest***	Y	Y	Y	N	Y
2 ***Ehrlich***	Y	Y	Y	N	Y
3 Cardin	Y	Y	Y	N	N
4 Wynn	Y	Y	Y	N	N
5 Hoyer	Y	Y	Y	N	N
6 ***Bartlett***	Y	Y	N	Y	Y
7 Cummings	Y	Y	Y	N	N
8 ***Morella***	Y	Y	Y	N	Y
MASSACHUSETTS					
1 Olver	N	N	Y	N	N
2 Neal	Y	Y	Y	N	N
3 McGovern	Y	N	Y	N	N
4 Frank	Y	N	Y	N	N
5 Meehan	Y	Y	Y	N	N
6 Tierney	N	N	Y	N	N
7 Markey	N	N	Y	N	N
8 Kennedy	N	N	Y	N	N
9 Moakley	Y	N	Y	Y	N
10 Delahunt	Y	N	Y	N	N
MICHIGAN					
1 Stupak	Y	Y	N	Y	N
2 ***Hoekstra***	Y	Y	N	Y	N
3 ***Ehlers***	Y	Y	N	Y	Y
4 ***Camp***	Y	Y	N	Y	Y
5 Barcia	Y	Y	N	Y	Y
6 ***Upton***	Y	Y	Y	N	N
7 ***Smith***	Y	Y	–	Y	N
8 Stabenow	Y	Y	Y	N	N
9 Kildee	Y	Y	N	Y	N
10 Bonior	N	Y	N	Y	N
11 ***Knollenberg***	Y	Y	N	Y	Y
12 Levin	Y	Y	Y	N	N
13 Rivers	Y	Y	Y	N	N
14 Conyers	N	N	N	N	N
15 Kilpatrick	N	N	Y	N	N
16 Dingell	Y	Y	Y	N	Y
MINNESOTA					
1 ***Gutknecht***	Y	Y	N	Y	Y
2 Minge	Y	Y	Y	N	Y

	165	166	167	168	169
3 ***Ramstad***	Y	Y	Y	N	Y
4 Vento	Y	Y	Y	N	N
5 Sabo	Y	Y	Y	N	N
6 Luther	Y	Y	Y	N	Y
7 Peterson	Y	Y	N	Y	Y
8 Oberstar	N	N	N	Y	N
MISSISSIPPI					
1 ***Wicker***	Y	Y	N	Y	Y
2 Thompson	N	N	Y	N	N
3 ***Pickering***	+	+	–	+	+
4 ***Parker***	Y	Y	N	Y	Y
5 Taylor	Y	Y	N	Y	Y
MISSOURI					
1 Clay	N	N	Y	N	N
2 ***Talent***	Y	Y	N	Y	Y
3 Gephardt	Y	N	Y	N	N
4 Skelton	Y	Y	N	Y	Y
5 McCarthy	Y	Y	Y	N	N
6 Danner	Y	Y	Y	Y	Y
7 ***Blunt***	Y	Y	N	Y	Y
8 ***Emerson***	Y	Y	N	Y	Y
9 ***Hulshof***	Y	Y	N	Y	N
MONTANA					
AL ***Hill***	Y	N	N	Y	Y
NEBRASKA					
1 ***Bereuter***	Y	Y	N	Y	Y
2 ***Christensen***	Y	Y	N	Y	Y
3 ***Barrett***	Y	Y	N	Y	Y
NEVADA					
1 ***Ensign***	Y	Y	N	Y	Y
2 ***Gibbons***	Y	Y	Y	Y	Y
NEW HAMPSHIRE					
1 ***Sununu***	Y	Y	N	Y	Y
2 ***Bass***	Y	Y	Y	N	N
NEW JERSEY					
1 Andrews	?	?	?	?	?
2 ***LoBiondo***	Y	Y	N	Y	Y
3 ***Saxton***	Y	Y	N	Y	Y
4 ***Smith***	Y	Y	N	Y	Y
5 ***Roukema***	Y	Y	Y	N	N
6 Pallone	Y	Y	Y	N	N
7 ***Franks***	Y	Y	Y	N	Y
8 Pascrell	Y	Y	Y	N	N
9 Rothman	Y	Y	Y	N	N
10 Payne	N	N	Y	N	N
11 ***Frelinghuysen***	Y	Y	Y	N	Y
12 ***Pappas***	Y	Y	N	Y	Y
13 Menendez	Y	Y	Y	N	N
NEW MEXICO					
1 ***Schiff***	?	?	?	?	?
2 ***Skeen***	Y	Y	N	Y	Y
3 ***Redmond***	Y	Y	N	Y	Y
NEW YORK					
1 ***Forbes***	Y	Y	N	Y	Y
2 ***Lazio***	Y	Y	Y	N	Y
3 ***King***	Y	N	N	Y	Y
4 McCarthy	N	Y	Y	N	Y
5 Ackerman	Y	Y	Y	N	N
6 Flake	Y	Y	Y	N	N
7 Manton	Y	Y	N	Y	N
8 Nadler	N	N	Y	N	N
9 Schumer	Y	Y	Y	N	?
10 Towns	Y	N	Y	N	N
11 Owens	N	N	Y	N	N
12 Velázquez	N	N	Y	N	N
13 ***Molinari***	Y	Y	Y	Y	Y
14 Maloney	Y	Y	Y	N	N
15 Rangel	N	N	Y	N	N
16 Serrano	Y	N	Y	N	N
17 Engel	Y	N	Y	N	N
18 Lowey	Y	Y	Y	N	N
19 ***Kelly***	Y	Y	Y	N	Y
20 ***Gilman***	Y	Y	Y	N	Y
21 McNulty	N	N	Y	N	N
22 ***Solomon***	Y	Y	N	Y	Y
23 ***Boehlert***	Y	Y	Y	N	Y
24 ***McHugh***	Y	Y	N	Y	Y
25 ***Walsh***	Y	Y	N	Y	Y
26 Hinchey	Y	N	Y	N	N
27 ***Paxon***	Y	Y	N	Y	Y
28 Slaughter	Y	N	Y	N	N
29 LaFalce	Y	Y	N	Y	N
30 ***Quinn***	Y	Y	N	Y	Y
31 ***Houghton***	Y	Y	Y	N	Y

	165	166	167	168	169
NORTH CAROLINA					
1 Clayton	Y	Y	Y	N	N
2 Etheridge	Y	Y	Y	N	N
3 ***Jones***	Y	Y	N	Y	N
4 Price	Y	Y	Y	N	N
5 ***Burr***	Y	Y	N	Y	N
6 ***Coble***	Y	Y	N	Y	Y
7 McIntyre	Y	Y	N	Y	Y
8 Hefner	Y	Y	Y	N	N
9 ***Myrick***	Y	Y	N	Y	Y
10 ***Ballenger***	Y	Y	N	Y	Y
11 ***Taylor***	Y	Y	N	Y	Y
12 Watt	N	N	Y	N	N
NORTH DAKOTA					
AL Pomeroy	Y	Y	Y	N	Y
OHIO					
1 ***Chabot***	Y	Y	N	Y	Y
2 ***Portman***	Y	Y	N	Y	Y
3 Hall	Y	Y	N	Y	N
4 ***Oxley***	Y	Y	N	Y	Y
5 ***Gillmor***	Y	Y	N	Y	Y
6 Strickland	Y	Y	Y	N	Y
7 ***Hobson***	Y	Y	Y	N	Y
8 ***Boehner***	Y	Y	N	Y	Y
9 Kaptur	Y	N	N	Y	N
10 Kucinich	N	N	N	Y	N
11 Stokes	N	N	Y	N	N
12 ***Kasich***	Y	Y	N	Y	Y
13 Brown	Y	N	Y	N	N
14 Sawyer	Y	Y	Y	N	N
15 ***Pryce***	Y	Y	Y	N	Y
16 ***Regula***	Y	Y	Y	Y	Y
17 Traficant	Y	N	N	Y	Y
18 ***Ney***	Y	Y	N	Y	Y
19 ***LaTourette***	Y	Y	N	Y	Y
OKLAHOMA					
1 ***Largent***	Y	N	N	Y	N
2 ***Coburn***	Y	N	N	Y	N
3 ***Watkins***	Y	Y	N	Y	Y
4 ***Watts***	Y	Y	N	Y	Y
5 ***Istook***	?	N	N	Y	Y
6 ***Lucas***	Y	Y	N	Y	Y
OREGON					
1 Furse	Y	Y	Y	N	N
2 ***Smith***	Y	Y	N	Y	Y
3 Blumenauer	Y	N	Y	N	N
4 DeFazio	N	N	Y	N	N
5 Hooley	Y	Y	Y	N	Y
PENNSYLVANIA					
1 Foglietta	Y	Y	Y	N	N
2 Fattah	Y	Y	Y	N	N
3 Borski	N	N	N	Y	N
4 Klink	Y	N	N	Y	N
5 ***Peterson***	Y	Y	N	+	Y
6 Holden	Y	Y	N	Y	N
7 ***Weldon***	Y	Y	N	Y	Y
8 ***Greenwood***	?	Y	Y	N	Y
9 ***Shuster***	Y	N	N	Y	Y
10 ***McDade***	Y	Y	N	Y	Y
11 Kanjorski	N	N	N	Y	N
12 Murtha	Y	Y	N	Y	N
13 ***Fox***	Y	Y	N	Y	Y
14 Coyne	Y	N	Y	N	N
15 McHale	Y	Y	Y	N	Y
16 ***Pitts***	Y	Y	N	Y	Y
17 ***Gekas***	Y	Y	N	Y	Y
18 Doyle	Y	Y	N	Y	N
19 ***Goodling***	Y	Y	N	Y	Y
20 Mascara	Y	Y	N	Y	N
21 ***English***	Y	Y	N	Y	Y
RHODE ISLAND					
1 Kennedy	N	N	Y	N	N
2 Weygand	Y	N	N	Y	N
SOUTH CAROLINA					
1 ***Sanford***	Y	N	N	Y	N
2 ***Spence***	Y	Y	N	Y	Y
3 ***Graham***	Y	Y	N	Y	Y
4 ***Inglis***	Y	Y	N	Y	N
5 Spratt	Y	Y	Y	N	N
6 Clyburn	Y	Y	Y	N	N
SOUTH DAKOTA					
AL ***Thune***	Y	Y	N	Y	Y
TENNESSEE					
1 ***Jenkins***	Y	Y	N	Y	Y
2 ***Duncan***	Y	Y	N	Y	Y

	165	166	167	168	169
3 ***Wamp***	Y	Y	N	Y	Y
4 ***Hilleary***	Y	Y	N	Y	Y
5 Clement	Y	Y	Y	N	N
6 Gordon	Y	Y	Y	N	Y
7 ***Bryant***	Y	Y	N	Y	Y
8 Tanner	Y	Y	Y	N	Y
9 Ford	Y	Y	Y	N	N
TEXAS					
1 Sandlin	Y	Y	Y	N	N
2 Turner	?	#	?	?	X
3 ***Johnson, Sam***	Y	Y	N	Y	Y
4 Hall	Y	Y	N	Y	Y
5 ***Sessions***	Y	Y	N	Y	Y
6 ***Barton***	?	N	N	Y	Y
7 ***Archer***	Y	Y	N	Y	?
8 ***Brady***	Y	Y	N	Y	Y
9 Lampson	N	Y	Y	N	N
10 Doggett	Y	Y	Y	N	N
11 Edwards	Y	Y	Y	N	N
12 ***Granger***	Y	Y	N	Y	Y
13 ***Thornberry***	Y	Y	N	Y	Y
14 ***Paul***	Y	N	N	Y	N
15 Hinojosa	Y	Y	Y	N	N
16 Reyes	Y	Y	Y	N	Y
17 Stenholm	Y	Y	N	Y	N
18 Jackson-Lee	Y	Y	Y	N	N
19 ***Combest***	Y	Y	N	Y	Y
20 Gonzalez	Y	Y	Y	N	N
21 ***Smith***	Y	Y	N	Y	Y
22 ***DeLay***	Y	Y	N	Y	Y
23 ***Bonilla***	Y	Y	N	Y	Y
24 Frost	Y	Y	Y	N	N
25 Bentsen	Y	Y	Y	N	N
26 ***Armey***	Y	Y	N	Y	Y
27 Ortiz	Y	Y	N	Y	Y
28 Rodriguez	Y	Y	Y	N	N
29 Green	Y	Y	Y	N	N
30 Johnson, E.B.	Y	Y	Y	N	N
UTAH					
1 ***Hansen***	Y	Y	N	Y	Y
2 ***Cook***	Y	Y	N	Y	Y
3 ***Cannon***	Y	Y	N	Y	Y
VERMONT					
AL *Sanders*	N	N	Y	N	N
VIRGINIA					
1 ***Bateman***	Y	Y	N	Y	Y
2 Pickett	Y	Y	Y	N	N
3 Scott	Y	N	Y	N	N
4 Sisisky	Y	Y	Y	N	N
5 Goode	?	?	?	?	#
6 ***Goodlatte***	Y	Y	N	Y	Y
7 ***Bliley***	Y	Y	N	Y	Y
8 Moran	Y	Y	Y	N	N
9 Boucher	Y	N	Y	N	N
10 ***Wolf***	Y	Y	N	Y	Y
11 ***Davis***	Y	Y	Y	N	Y
WASHINGTON					
1 ***White***	Y	Y	Y	?	Y
2 ***Metcalf***	Y	Y	N	Y	Y
3 ***Smith, Linda***	Y	Y	N	Y	Y
4 ***Hastings***	Y	Y	N	Y	Y
5 ***Nethercutt***	Y	Y	N	Y	Y
6 Dicks	Y	Y	Y	N	N
7 McDermott	N	N	Y	N	N
8 ***Dunn***	Y	Y	N	Y	Y
9 Smith, Adam	Y	Y	Y	N	N
WEST VIRGINIA					
1 Mollohan	Y	N	N	Y	N
2 Wise	Y	Y	Y	N	N
3 Rahall	N	N	N	Y	Y
WISCONSIN					
1 ***Neumann***	Y	Y	?	Y	N
2 ***Klug***	Y	N	Y	N	N
3 Kind	Y	Y	Y	N	N
4 Kleczka	Y	Y	Y	Y	Y
5 Barrett	Y	Y	Y	N	N
6 ***Petri***	Y	Y	N	Y	Y
7 Obey	N	N	Y	Y	N
8 Johnson	Y	Y	Y	N	N
9 ***Sensenbrenner***	Y	Y	N	Y	N
WYOMING					
AL ***Cubin***	Y	N	N	Y	Y

Southern states - Ala., Ark., Fla., Ga., Ky., La., Miss., N.C., Okla., S.C., Tenn., Texas, Va.

HOUSE VOTES 170, 171, 172, 173, 174, 175, 176, 177

170. HR 1757. Fiscal 1998-99 State Department Authorization/U.N. Headquarters. Stearns, R-Fla., amendment to express the sense of Congress that the United Nations should study whether the United Nations should relocate its headquarters and become a part-time body. Rejected 108-315: R 103-118; D 5-196 (ND 0-146, SD 5-50); I 0-1, June 10, 1997.

171. HR 1757. Fiscal 1998-99 State Department Authorization/Sudan Sanctions. Scarborough, R-Fla., amendment to apply the financial transaction restrictions contained in the Anti-Terrorism and Effective Death Penalty Act (PL 104-132) to Sudan and cease diplomatic relations with the country unless the president certifies that Sudan has ceased supporting terrorism. Adopted 415-9: R 221-2; D 193-7 (ND 139-6, SD 54-1); I 1-0, June 10, 1997.

172. HR 1757. Fiscal 1998-99 State Department Authorization/Syria Sanctions. Engel, D-N.Y., amendment to express the sense of Congress that the United States should consider applying sanctions to Syria identical to those currently enforced against Iran and Libya if Syria does not change policies supporting terrorism. Adopted 410-15: R 221-2; D 188-13 (ND 135-11, SD 53-2); I 1-0, June 10, 1997.

173. HR 1757. Fiscal 1998-99 State Department Authorization/Kashmiri Hostage Release. Nethercutt, R-Wash., amendment to express the sense of Congress that the militant organization Al-Faran should immediately release U.S. citizen Donald Hutchings and three Western Europeans being held hostage in northwest India. Adopted 425-0: R 222-0; D 202-0 (ND 147-0, SD 55-0); I 1-0, June 10, 1997.

174. HR 1757. Fiscal 1998-99 State Department Authorization/Libya Assistance. Ney, R-Ohio, amendment to prohibit foreign assistance to any country that assists Libya in circumventing U.N. sanctions. Adopted 426-0: R 224-0; D 201-0 (ND 146-0, SD 55-0); I 1-0, June 10, 1997.

175. HR 1757. Fiscal 1998-99 State Department Authorization/Cuban Cigars. Miller, D-Calif., amendment, as amended, to express the sense of Congress that the U.S. government should permit the sale of Cuban cigars in the United States, but not until the government of Cuba frees all political prisoners, legalizes all political activity and agrees to hold free elections. Adopted 375-49: R 217-6; D 157-43 (ND 107-38, SD 50-5); I 1-0, June 10, 1997.

176. H Con Res 60. Jerusalem Reunification/Adoption. Gilman, R-N.Y., motion to suspend the rules and adopt the concurrent resolution to express the sense of Congress that Jerusalem must remain an undivided city where ethnic and religious rights are tolerated and to call upon the president and secretary of State to publicly affirm that Jerusalem must remain the undivided capital of Israel. Motion agreed to 406-17: R 219-3; D 186-14 (ND 135-11, SD 51-3); I 1-0, June 10, 1997. A two-thirds majority of those present and voting (282 in this case) is required for adoption under suspension of the rules.

177. HR 1469. Supplemental Fiscal 1997 Appropriations/Motion To Refer Veto Message. McDade, R-Pa., motion to order the previous question (thus ending debate and the possibility of amendment) on the motion to refer President Clinton's June 9 veto message of the bill to the Appropriations Committee. The bill would provide about $8.6 billion in additional funds for fiscal 1997, including about $5.6 billion in emergency disaster aid for 35 states and $1.9 billion to finance military peacekeeping in Bosnia and the Middle East. The bill also includes provisions that automatically provide funding for federal programs that lack appropriations authority at the start of fiscal 1998 at 100 percent of their fiscal 1997 levels until fiscal 1998 appropriations are enacted and that prohibit the Census Bureau from using statistical sampling in calculating the national population in 2000. Motion agreed to 216-205: R 216-5; D 0-199 (ND 0-145, SD 0-54); I 0-1, June 10, 1997. (Subsequently, the motion to refer was adopted by voice vote.)

KEY

- Y Voted for (yea).
- # Paired for.
- + Announced for.
- N Voted against (nay).
- X Paired against.
- – Announced against.
- P Voted "present."
- C Voted "present" to avoid possible conflict of interest.
- ? Did not vote or otherwise make a position known.

Democrats ***Republicans***
Independent

	170	171	172	173	174	175	176	177
ALABAMA								
1 ***Callahan***	Y	Y	Y	Y	Y	Y	Y	Y
2 ***Everett***	Y	Y	Y	Y	Y	Y	Y	Y
3 ***Riley***	Y	Y	Y	Y	Y	Y	Y	Y
4 ***Aderholt***	Y	Y	Y	Y	Y	Y	Y	Y
5 Cramer	Y	Y	Y	Y	Y	Y	Y	N
6 ***Bachus***	Y	Y	Y	Y	Y	Y	Y	Y
7 Hilliard	N	Y	Y	Y	Y	Y	Y	N
ALASKA								
AL ***Young***	Y	Y	Y	Y	Y	Y	Y	Y
ARIZONA								
1 ***Salmon***	?	?	?	?	Y	Y	Y	Y
2 Pastor	N	Y	Y	Y	Y	Y	Y	N
3 ***Stump***	Y	Y	Y	Y	Y	Y	Y	Y
4 ***Shadegg***	Y	Y	Y	Y	Y	Y	Y	Y
5 ***Kolbe***	N	Y	Y	Y	Y	Y	Y	Y
6 ***Hayworth***	Y	Y	Y	Y	Y	Y	Y	Y
ARKANSAS								
1 Berry	N	Y	Y	Y	Y	Y	Y	N
2 Snyder	N	Y	Y	Y	Y	N	Y	N
3 ***Hutchinson***	Y	Y	Y	Y	Y	Y	Y	Y
4 ***Dickey***	N	Y	Y	Y	Y	Y	Y	Y
CALIFORNIA								
1 ***Riggs***	–	Y	Y	Y	Y	Y	Y	Y
2 ***Herger***	N	Y	Y	Y	Y	Y	Y	Y
3 Fazio	N	Y	Y	Y	Y	Y	Y	N
4 ***Doolittle***	Y	Y	Y	Y	Y	Y	Y	Y
5 Matsui	N	Y	Y	Y	Y	Y	Y	N
6 Woolsey	N	Y	Y	Y	Y	Y	Y	N
7 Miller	N	Y	Y	Y	Y	Y	Y	N
8 Pelosi	N	Y	Y	Y	Y	Y	?	N
9 Dellums	N	Y	Y	Y	Y	N	N	N
10 Tauscher	N	Y	Y	Y	Y	Y	Y	N
11 ***Pombo***	Y	Y	Y	Y	Y	Y	Y	Y
12 Lantos	N	Y	Y	Y	Y	Y	Y	N
13 Stark	N	Y	Y	Y	Y	Y	Y	N
14 Eshoo	N	Y	Y	Y	Y	Y	Y	N
15 ***Campbell***	Y	N	Y	Y	Y	Y	Y	Y
16 Lofgren	N	Y	Y	Y	Y	Y	Y	N
17 Farr	?	?	?	?	?	?	?	?
18 Condit	N	Y	Y	Y	Y	Y	Y	N
19 ***Radanovich***	Y	Y	Y	Y	Y	?	Y	Y
20 Dooley	N	Y	Y	Y	Y	N	Y	N
21 ***Thomas***	N	Y	Y	Y	Y	Y	Y	Y
22 Capps	N	Y	Y	Y	Y	Y	Y	N
23 ***Gallegly***	N	Y	Y	Y	Y	Y	Y	Y
24 Sherman	N	Y	Y	Y	Y	Y	Y	N
25 ***McKeon***	Y	Y	Y	Y	Y	Y	Y	Y
26 Berman	N	Y	Y	Y	Y	Y	Y	N
27 ***Rogan***	Y	Y	Y	Y	Y	Y	Y	Y
28 ***Dreier***	Y	Y	Y	Y	Y	Y	Y	Y
29 Waxman	N	Y	Y	Y	Y	N	Y	N
30 Becerra	N	Y	Y	Y	Y	N	Y	?
31 Martinez	N	Y	Y	Y	Y	Y	Y	N
32 Dixon	N	Y	Y	Y	Y	Y	Y	N
33 Roybal-Allard	N	Y	Y	Y	Y	Y	Y	N
34 Torres	N	Y	Y	Y	Y	N	Y	N
35 Waters	N	Y	N	Y	Y	N	Y	N
36 Harman	N	N	Y	Y	Y	Y	Y	N
37 Millender-McD.	N	Y	Y	Y	Y	Y	Y	N
38 ***Horn***	N	Y	Y	Y	Y	Y	Y	Y
39 ***Royce***	Y	Y	Y	Y	Y	Y	Y	Y
40 ***Lewis***	N	Y	Y	Y	Y	Y	Y	Y
41 ***Kim***	N	Y	Y	Y	Y	Y	Y	Y
42 Brown	N	Y	Y	Y	Y	Y	Y	N
43 ***Calvert***	N	Y	Y	Y	Y	Y	Y	Y
44 ***Bono***	Y	Y	Y	Y	Y	Y	Y	Y
45 ***Rohrabacher***	Y	Y	Y	Y	Y	Y	Y	Y
46 Sanchez	N	Y	Y	Y	Y	Y	Y	N
47 ***Cox***	Y	Y	Y	Y	Y	Y	Y	Y
48 ***Packard***	N	Y	Y	Y	Y	Y	Y	?
49 ***Bilbray***	Y	Y	Y	Y	Y	Y	Y	Y
50 Filner	N	Y	Y	Y	Y	Y	Y	N
51 ***Cunningham***	Y	Y	Y	Y	Y	Y	Y	Y
52 ***Hunter***	Y	Y	Y	Y	Y	Y	Y	Y
COLORADO								
1 DeGette	N	Y	Y	Y	Y	N	Y	N
2 Skaggs	N	Y	Y	Y	Y	N	Y	N
3 ***McInnis***	Y	Y	Y	Y	Y	Y	Y	Y
4 ***Schaffer***	Y	Y	Y	Y	Y	Y	Y	Y
5 ***Hefley***	Y	Y	Y	Y	Y	Y	Y	Y
6 ***Schaefer***	Y	Y	Y	Y	Y	Y	Y	Y
CONNECTICUT								
1 Kennelly	N	Y	Y	Y	Y	Y	Y	N
2 Gejdenson	N	Y	Y	Y	Y	Y	Y	N
3 DeLauro	N	Y	Y	Y	Y	Y	Y	N
4 ***Shays***	N	Y	Y	Y	Y	Y	Y	Y
5 Maloney	N	Y	Y	Y	Y	Y	Y	N
6 ***Johnson***	N	Y	Y	Y	Y	Y	Y	Y
DELAWARE								
AL ***Castle***	N	Y	Y	Y	Y	N	Y	Y
FLORIDA								
1 ***Scarborough***	Y	Y	Y	Y	Y	Y	Y	Y
2 Boyd	N	Y	Y	Y	Y	Y	Y	N
3 Brown	N	Y	Y	Y	Y	Y	Y	N
4 ***Fowler***	Y	Y	Y	Y	Y	Y	Y	Y
5 Thurman	N	Y	Y	Y	Y	Y	Y	N
6 ***Stearns***	Y	Y	Y	Y	Y	Y	Y	Y
7 ***Mica***	N	Y	Y	Y	Y	Y	Y	Y
8 ***McCollum***	N	Y	Y	Y	Y	Y	Y	Y
9 ***Bilirakis***	N	Y	Y	Y	Y	Y	Y	Y
10 ***Young***	N	Y	Y	Y	Y	Y	Y	Y
11 Davis	N	Y	Y	Y	Y	Y	Y	N
12 ***Canady***	N	Y	Y	Y	Y	Y	Y	Y
13 ***Miller***	N	Y	Y	Y	Y	Y	Y	Y
14 ***Goss***	N	Y	Y	Y	Y	Y	Y	Y
15 ***Weldon***	Y	Y	Y	Y	Y	Y	Y	Y
16 ***Foley***	Y	Y	Y	Y	Y	Y	Y	Y
17 Meek	N	Y	Y	Y	Y	Y	Y	N
18 ***Ros-Lehtinen***	N	Y	Y	Y	Y	Y	Y	Y
19 Wexler	N	Y	Y	Y	Y	Y	Y	N
20 Deutsch	N	Y	Y	Y	Y	Y	Y	N
21 ***Diaz-Balart***	N	Y	Y	Y	Y	Y	Y	Y
22 ***Shaw***	N	Y	Y	Y	Y	Y	Y	Y
23 Hastings	N	Y	Y	Y	Y	Y	Y	N
GEORGIA								
1 ***Kingston***	Y	Y	Y	Y	Y	Y	Y	Y
2 Bishop	N	Y	Y	Y	Y	Y	Y	N
3 ***Collins***	Y	Y	Y	Y	Y	Y	Y	Y
4 McKinney	N	Y	Y	Y	Y	Y	Y	N
5 Lewis	N	Y	Y	Y	Y	N	Y	N
6 ***Gingrich***								
7 ***Barr***	Y	Y	Y	Y	Y	Y	Y	Y
8 ***Chambliss***	Y	Y	Y	Y	Y	Y	Y	Y
9 ***Deal***	Y	Y	Y	Y	Y	Y	Y	Y
10 ***Norwood***	Y	Y	Y	Y	Y	Y	Y	Y
11 ***Linder***	N	Y	Y	Y	Y	Y	Y	Y
HAWAII								
1 Abercrombie	N	Y	Y	Y	Y	N	Y	N
2 Mink	N	Y	Y	Y	Y	N	Y	N
IDAHO								
1 ***Chenoweth***	Y	Y	Y	Y	Y	Y	Y	Y
2 ***Crapo***	Y	Y	Y	Y	Y	Y	Y	Y
ILLINOIS								
1 Rush	N	Y	?	Y	Y	Y	Y	N
2 Jackson	N	Y	Y	Y	Y	N	Y	N
3 Lipinski	N	Y	Y	Y	Y	Y	Y	N
4 Gutierrez	N	Y	Y	Y	Y	Y	Y	N
5 Blagojevich	N	Y	Y	Y	Y	Y	Y	N
6 ***Hyde***	N	Y	Y	Y	Y	Y	Y	Y
7 Davis	N	Y	Y	Y	Y	Y	Y	N
8 ***Crane***	Y	Y	Y	Y	Y	Y	Y	Y
9 Yates	N	Y	Y	Y	Y	Y	Y	N
10 ***Porter***	N	Y	Y	Y	Y	Y	Y	Y
11 ***Weller***	Y	Y	Y	Y	Y	Y	Y	Y
12 Costello	N	Y	Y	Y	Y	Y	Y	N
13 ***Fawell***	N	Y	Y	Y	Y	Y	Y	?
14 ***Hastert***	N	Y	Y	Y	Y	Y	Y	Y
15 ***Ewing***	N	Y	Y	Y	Y	Y	Y	Y

ND Northern Democrats SD Southern Democrats

	170	171	172	173	174	175	176	177
16 ***Manzullo***	Y	Y	Y	Y	Y	Y	Y	Y
17 Evans	N	Y	Y	Y	Y	Y	Y	N
18 ***LaHood***	N	Y	N	Y	Y	Y	Y	Y
19 Poshard	N	Y	Y	Y	Y	Y	Y	N
20 ***Shimkus***	Y	Y	Y	Y	Y	Y	Y	Y
INDIANA								
1 Visclosky	N	Y	Y	Y	Y	Y	Y	N
2 ***McIntosh***	Y	Y	Y	Y	Y	Y	Y	Y
3 Roemer	N	Y	Y	Y	Y	Y	Y	N
4 ***Souder***	Y	Y	Y	Y	Y	Y	Y	Y
5 ***Buyer***	N	Y	Y	Y	Y	Y	Y	Y
6 ***Burton***	Y	Y	Y	Y	Y	Y	Y	Y
7 ***Pease***	N	Y	Y	Y	Y	Y	Y	Y
8 ***Hostettler***	Y	Y	Y	Y	Y	Y	Y	Y
9 Hamilton	N	Y	N	Y	Y	Y	N	N
10 Carson	N	Y	Y	Y	Y	Y	Y	N
IOWA								
1 ***Leach***	N	Y	Y	Y	Y	Y	Y	N
2 ***Nussle***	Y	Y	Y	Y	Y	Y	Y	Y
3 Boswell	N	Y	Y	Y	Y	Y	Y	N
4 ***Ganske***	N	Y	Y	Y	Y	Y	Y	Y
5 ***Latham***	N	Y	Y	Y	Y	Y	Y	Y
KANSAS								
1 ***Moran***	Y	Y	Y	Y	Y	Y	Y	Y
2 ***Ryun***	Y	Y	Y	Y	Y	Y	Y	Y
3 ***Snowbarger***	N	Y	Y	Y	Y	Y	Y	Y
4 ***Tiahrt***	Y	Y	Y	Y	Y	Y	Y	Y
KENTUCKY								
1 ***Whitfield***	Y	Y	Y	Y	Y	Y	Y	Y
2 ***Lewis***	Y	Y	Y	Y	Y	Y	Y	Y
3 ***Northup***	N	Y	Y	Y	Y	Y	+	Y
4 ***Bunning***	N	Y	Y	Y	Y	Y	Y	Y
5 ***Rogers***	N	Y	Y	Y	Y	Y	Y	Y
6 Baesler	N	Y	Y	Y	Y	Y	Y	N
LOUISIANA								
1 ***Livingston***	N	Y	?	?	Y	Y	?	Y
2 Jefferson	N	Y	Y	Y	Y	Y	Y	N
3 ***Tauzin***	N	Y	Y	Y	Y	Y	Y	?
4 ***McCrery***	N	Y	Y	Y	Y	Y	Y	Y
5 ***Cooksey***	Y	Y	Y	Y	Y	Y	Y	Y
6 ***Baker***	N	Y	Y	Y	Y	Y	Y	Y
7 John	N	Y	N	Y	Y	Y	Y	N
MAINE								
1 Allen	N	Y	Y	Y	Y	Y	Y	N
2 Baldacci	N	Y	Y	Y	Y	Y	Y	N
MARYLAND								
1 ***Gilchrest***	N	Y	Y	Y	Y	Y	Y	Y
2 ***Ehrlich***	N	Y	Y	Y	Y	Y	Y	Y
3 Cardin	N	Y	Y	Y	Y	Y	Y	N
4 Wynn	N	Y	Y	Y	Y	Y	Y	N
5 Hoyer	N	Y	Y	Y	Y	Y	Y	N
6 ***Bartlett***	Y	Y	Y	Y	Y	Y	Y	Y
7 Cummings	N	Y	Y	Y	Y	Y	Y	N
8 ***Morella***	N	Y	Y	Y	Y	Y	Y	Y
MASSACHUSETTS								
1 Olver	N	Y	Y	Y	Y	Y	Y	N
2 Neal	N	Y	Y	Y	Y	?	Y	N
3 McGovern	N	Y	Y	Y	Y	N	Y	N
4 Frank	N	Y	Y	Y	Y	N	Y	N
5 Meehan	N	Y	Y	Y	Y	Y	Y	N
6 Tierney	N	Y	Y	Y	Y	N	Y	N
7 Markey	N	Y	Y	Y	Y	N	Y	N
8 Kennedy	N	Y	Y	Y	Y	Y	Y	N
9 Moakley	N	Y	Y	Y	Y	N	Y	N
10 Delahunt	N	Y	Y	Y	Y	Y	Y	N
MICHIGAN								
1 Stupak	N	Y	Y	Y	Y	Y	Y	N
2 ***Hoekstra***	N	Y	Y	Y	Y	Y	Y	Y
3 ***Ehlers***	N	Y	Y	Y	Y	N	Y	Y
4 ***Camp***	N	Y	Y	Y	Y	Y	Y	Y
5 Barcia	N	Y	Y	Y	Y	Y	Y	?
6 ***Upton***	N	Y	Y	Y	Y	Y	Y	Y
7 ***Smith***	Y	Y	Y	Y	Y	N	Y	Y
8 Stabenow	N	Y	Y	Y	Y	Y	Y	N
9 Kildee	N	Y	Y	Y	Y	Y	Y	N
10 Bonior	N	Y	N	Y	Y	Y	N	N
11 ***Knollenberg***	N	Y	Y	Y	Y	Y	Y	Y
12 Levin	N	Y	Y	Y	Y	Y	Y	N
13 Rivers	N	Y	Y	Y	Y	Y	Y	N
14 Conyers	N	N	N	Y	Y	N	N	N
15 Kilpatrick	N	Y	Y	Y	Y	Y	Y	N
16 Dingell	N	Y	Y	Y	Y	Y	N	N
MINNESOTA								
1 ***Gutknecht***	Y	Y	Y	Y	Y	Y	Y	Y
2 Minge	N	Y	N	Y	Y	N	N	N

	170	171	172	173	174	175	176	177
3 ***Ramstad***	N	Y	Y	Y	Y	Y	Y	N
4 Vento	N	Y	Y	Y	Y	Y	Y	N
5 Sabo	N	Y	N	Y	Y	N	Y	N
6 Luther	N	Y	Y	Y	Y	Y	Y	N
7 Peterson	N	Y	Y	Y	Y	Y	Y	N
8 Oberstar	N	Y	Y	Y	Y	N	Y	N
MISSISSIPPI								
1 ***Wicker***	N	Y	Y	Y	Y	Y	Y	Y
2 Thompson	N	Y	Y	Y	Y	Y	Y	N
3 ***Pickering***	N	Y	Y	Y	Y	Y	Y	Y
4 ***Parker***	N	Y	Y	Y	Y	Y	Y	Y
5 Taylor	Y	Y	Y	Y	Y	Y	Y	N
MISSOURI								
1 Clay	N	Y	Y	Y	Y	N	Y	N
2 ***Talent***	N	Y	Y	Y	Y	Y	Y	Y
3 Gephardt	N	Y	Y	Y	Y	Y	Y	N
4 Skelton	N	Y	Y	Y	Y	Y	Y	N
5 McCarthy	N	Y	Y	Y	Y	Y	Y	N
6 Danner	N	Y	Y	Y	Y	Y	Y	N
7 ***Blunt***	N	Y	Y	Y	Y	Y	Y	Y
8 ***Emerson***	Y	Y	Y	Y	Y	Y	Y	N
9 ***Hulshof***	Y	Y	Y	Y	Y	Y	Y	Y
MONTANA								
AL ***Hill***	Y	Y	Y	Y	Y	Y	Y	Y
NEBRASKA								
1 ***Bereuter***	N	Y	Y	Y	Y	Y	Y	Y
2 ***Christensen***	Y	Y	Y	Y	Y	Y	Y	Y
3 ***Barrett***	N	Y	Y	Y	Y	Y	Y	Y
NEVADA								
1 ***Ensign***	Y	Y	Y	Y	Y	Y	Y	Y
2 ***Gibbons***	Y	Y	Y	Y	Y	Y	Y	Y
NEW HAMPSHIRE								
1 ***Sununu***	N	Y	Y	Y	Y	Y	N	Y
2 ***Bass***	N	Y	Y	Y	Y	Y	Y	Y
NEW JERSEY								
1 Andrews	N	Y	Y	Y	Y	Y	Y	N
2 ***LoBiondo***	N	Y	Y	Y	Y	Y	Y	Y
3 ***Saxton***	N	Y	Y	Y	Y	Y	Y	Y
4 ***Smith***	N	Y	Y	Y	Y	Y	Y	Y
5 ***Roukema***	N	Y	Y	Y	Y	Y	Y	N
6 Pallone	N	Y	Y	Y	Y	Y	Y	N
7 ***Franks***	N	Y	Y	Y	Y	Y	Y	Y
8 Pascrell	N	Y	Y	Y	Y	Y	Y	N
9 Rothman	?	?	?	?	?	?	Y	N
10 Payne	N	Y	Y	Y	Y	Y	Y	N
11 ***Frelinghuysen***	N	Y	Y	Y	Y	Y	Y	Y
12 ***Pappas***	N	Y	Y	Y	Y	Y	Y	Y
13 Menendez	N	Y	Y	Y	Y	Y	Y	N
NEW MEXICO								
1 ***Schiff***	?	?	?	?	?	?	?	?
2 ***Skeen***	N	Y	Y	Y	Y	Y	Y	Y
3 ***Redmond***	N	Y	Y	Y	Y	Y	Y	Y
NEW YORK								
1 ***Forbes***	N	Y	Y	Y	Y	Y	Y	Y
2 ***Lazio***	N	Y	Y	Y	Y	Y	Y	Y
3 ***King***	N	Y	Y	Y	Y	Y	Y	Y
4 McCarthy	N	Y	Y	Y	Y	Y	Y	N
5 Ackerman	N	Y	Y	Y	Y	Y	Y	N
6 Flake	?	?	?	?	?	?	?	?
7 Manton	N	Y	Y	Y	Y	Y	Y	N
8 Nadler	N	Y	Y	Y	Y	N	Y	N
9 Schumer	N	Y	Y	Y	?	?	?	?
10 Towns	N	Y	Y	Y	Y	N	Y	N
11 Owens	N	?	Y	Y	Y	Y	Y	N
12 Velázquez	N	Y	Y	Y	Y	N	Y	N
13 ***Molinari***	?	?	?	?	?	?	?	?
14 Maloney	N	Y	Y	Y	Y	Y	Y	N
15 Rangel	N	Y	Y	Y	Y	N	Y	N
16 Serrano	N	Y	Y	Y	Y	N	Y	N
17 Engel	N	Y	Y	Y	Y	Y	Y	N
18 Lowey	N	Y	Y	Y	Y	Y	Y	N
19 ***Kelly***	N	Y	Y	Y	Y	Y	Y	Y
20 ***Gilman***	N	Y	Y	Y	Y	Y	Y	Y
21 McNulty	N	Y	Y	Y	Y	Y	Y	N
22 ***Solomon***	Y	Y	Y	Y	Y	Y	Y	Y
23 ***Boehlert***	N	Y	Y	Y	Y	Y	Y	Y
24 ***McHugh***	N	Y	Y	Y	Y	Y	Y	Y
25 ***Walsh***	N	Y	Y	Y	Y	Y	Y	Y
26 Hinchey	N	N	Y	Y	Y	N	Y	N
27 ***Paxon***	Y	Y	Y	Y	Y	Y	Y	Y
28 Slaughter	N	Y	Y	Y	Y	Y	Y	N
29 LaFalce	N	N	N	Y	Y	Y	Y	N
30 ***Quinn***	N	Y	Y	Y	Y	Y	Y	Y
31 ***Houghton***	N	Y	Y	Y	Y	Y	Y	Y

	170	171	172	173	174	175	176	177
NORTH CAROLINA								
1 Clayton	N	Y	Y	Y	Y	Y	N	N
2 Etheridge	N	Y	Y	Y	Y	Y	Y	N
3 ***Jones***	Y	Y	Y	Y	Y	Y	Y	Y
4 Price	N	Y	Y	Y	Y	Y	Y	N
5 ***Burr***	Y	Y	Y	Y	Y	Y	Y	Y
6 ***Coble***	Y	Y	Y	Y	Y	Y	Y	Y
7 McIntyre	N	Y	Y	Y	Y	Y	Y	N
8 Hefner	N	Y	Y	Y	Y	Y	Y	N
9 ***Myrick***	N	Y	Y	Y	Y	Y	Y	Y
10 ***Ballenger***	N	Y	Y	Y	Y	Y	Y	Y
11 ***Taylor***	Y	Y	Y	Y	Y	Y	Y	Y
12 Watt	N	N	Y	Y	Y	N	N	N
NORTH DAKOTA								
AL Pomeroy	N	Y	Y	Y	Y	Y	Y	N
OHIO								
1 ***Chabot***	N	Y	Y	Y	Y	Y	Y	Y
2 ***Portman***	N	Y	Y	Y	Y	Y	Y	Y
3 Hall	N	?	?	?	?	?	Y	N
4 ***Oxley***	N	Y	Y	Y	Y	Y	Y	Y
5 ***Gillmor***	N	Y	Y	Y	Y	Y	Y	Y
6 Strickland	N	Y	Y	Y	Y	Y	Y	N
7 ***Hobson***	N	Y	Y	Y	Y	Y	Y	Y
8 ***Boehner***	N	Y	Y	Y	Y	Y	Y	Y
9 Kaptur	N	Y	Y	Y	Y	Y	Y	N
10 Kucinich	N	N	N	Y	Y	N	N	N
11 Stokes	N	Y	Y	Y	Y	Y	Y	N
12 ***Kasich***	?	Y	Y	Y	Y	Y	Y	Y
13 Brown	N	Y	Y	Y	Y	Y	Y	N
14 Sawyer	N	Y	Y	Y	Y	Y	Y	N
15 ***Pryce***	?	Y	Y	Y	Y	Y	Y	Y
16 ***Regula***	Y	Y	Y	Y	Y	Y	Y	Y
17 Traficant	N	Y	Y	Y	Y	Y	N	N
18 ***Ney***	N	Y	Y	Y	Y	Y	Y	Y
19 ***LaTourette***	N	Y	Y	Y	Y	Y	Y	Y
OKLAHOMA								
1 ***Largent***	Y	Y	Y	Y	Y	Y	Y	Y
2 ***Coburn***	N	Y	Y	Y	Y	Y	Y	Y
3 ***Watkins***	Y	Y	Y	Y	Y	N	Y	Y
4 ***Watts***	Y	Y	Y	Y	Y	Y	Y	Y
5 ***Istook***	Y	Y	Y	Y	Y	Y	Y	Y
6 ***Lucas***	Y	Y	Y	Y	Y	N	Y	Y
OREGON								
1 Furse	N	Y	Y	Y	Y	N	Y	N
2 ***Smith***	N	Y	Y	Y	Y	Y	Y	Y
3 Blumenauer	N	Y	Y	Y	Y	Y	?	N
4 DeFazio	N	Y	Y	Y	Y	N	Y	N
5 Hooley	N	Y	Y	Y	Y	Y	Y	N
PENNSYLVANIA								
1 Foglietta	?	Y	Y	Y	Y	N	Y	N
2 Fattah	N	Y	Y	Y	Y	Y	Y	?
3 Borski	?	?	Y	Y	Y	Y	Y	N
4 Klink	N	Y	Y	Y	Y	Y	Y	N
5 ***Peterson***	N	Y	Y	Y	Y	Y	Y	Y
6 Holden	N	Y	Y	Y	Y	N	Y	N
7 ***Weldon***	N	Y	Y	Y	Y	Y	Y	Y
8 ***Greenwood***	N	Y	Y	Y	Y	Y	Y	Y
9 ***Shuster***	Y	Y	Y	Y	Y	Y	Y	Y
10 ***McDade***	N	Y	Y	Y	Y	Y	Y	Y
11 Kanjorski	N	Y	Y	Y	Y	N	Y	N
12 Murtha	N	Y	Y	Y	Y	N	Y	N
13 ***Fox***	N	Y	Y	Y	Y	Y	Y	Y
14 Coyne	N	Y	Y	Y	Y	N	Y	N
15 McHale	N	Y	Y	Y	Y	N	Y	N
16 ***Pitts***	N	Y	Y	Y	Y	Y	Y	Y
17 ***Gekas***	Y	Y	Y	Y	Y	Y	Y	Y
18 Doyle	N	Y	Y	Y	Y	Y	Y	N
19 ***Goodling***	Y	Y	Y	Y	Y	Y	Y	Y
20 Mascara	N	Y	Y	Y	Y	Y	Y	N
21 ***English***	N	Y	Y	Y	Y	Y	Y	Y
RHODE ISLAND								
1 Kennedy	N	Y	Y	Y	Y	Y	Y	N
2 Weygand	N	Y	Y	Y	Y	Y	Y	N
SOUTH CAROLINA								
1 ***Sanford***	Y	Y	Y	Y	Y	Y	Y	Y
2 ***Spence***	Y	Y	Y	Y	Y	Y	Y	Y
3 ***Graham***	N	Y	Y	Y	Y	Y	Y	Y
4 ***Inglis***	N	Y	Y	Y	Y	Y	Y	Y
5 Spratt	N	Y	Y	Y	Y	Y	Y	N
6 Clyburn	N	Y	Y	Y	Y	Y	Y	N
SOUTH DAKOTA								
AL ***Thune***	Y	?	Y	Y	Y	Y	Y	N
TENNESSEE								
1 ***Jenkins***	N	Y	Y	Y	Y	Y	Y	Y
2 ***Duncan***	Y	Y	Y	Y	Y	Y	Y	Y

	170	171	172	173	174	175	176	
3 ***Wamp***	Y	Y	Y	Y	Y	Y	Y	Y
4 ***Hilleary***	Y	Y	Y	Y	Y	Y	Y	Y
5 Clement	N	Y	Y	Y	Y	Y	Y	N
6 Gordon	N	Y	Y	Y	Y	Y	Y	N
7 ***Bryant***	N	Y	Y	Y	Y	Y	Y	Y
8 Tanner	N	Y	Y	Y	Y	Y	Y	N
9 Ford	N	Y	Y	Y	Y	Y	Y	N
TEXAS								
1 Sandlin	N	Y	Y	Y	Y	Y	Y	N
2 Turner	N	Y	Y	Y	Y	Y	Y	N
3 ***Johnson, Sam***	N	Y	Y	Y	Y	Y	Y	Y
4 Hall	Y	Y	N	Y	Y	Y	Y	N
5 ***Sessions***	Y	Y	Y	Y	Y	Y	Y	Y
6 ***Barton***	Y	Y	Y	Y	Y	Y	Y	Y
7 ***Archer***	N	Y	Y	Y	Y	Y	Y	Y
8 ***Brady***	Y	Y	Y	Y	Y	Y	Y	Y
9 Lampson	N	Y	Y	Y	Y	Y	Y	N
10 Doggett	N	Y	Y	Y	Y	Y	Y	N
11 Edwards	N	Y	Y	Y	Y	Y	Y	N
12 ***Granger***	N	Y	Y	Y	Y	Y	Y	Y
13 ***Thornberry***	Y	Y	Y	Y	Y	Y	Y	Y
14 ***Paul***	Y	N	N	P	Y	Y	N	Y
15 Hinojosa	N	Y	Y	Y	Y	N	Y	N
16 Reyes	N	Y	Y	Y	Y	Y	Y	N
17 Stenholm	N	Y	Y	Y	Y	Y	Y	N
18 Jackson-Lee	N	Y	Y	Y	Y	Y	Y	N
19 ***Combest***	Y	Y	Y	Y	Y	Y	Y	Y
20 Gonzalez	N	Y	Y	Y	Y	Y	Y	N
21 ***Smith***	N	Y	Y	Y	Y	Y	Y	Y
22 ***DeLay***	Y	Y	Y	Y	Y	Y	Y	Y
23 ***Bonilla***	N	Y	Y	Y	Y	Y	Y	Y
24 Frost	N	Y	Y	Y	Y	Y	Y	N
25 Bentsen	N	Y	Y	Y	Y	Y	Y	N
26 ***Armey***	N	Y	Y	Y	Y	Y	Y	Y
27 Ortiz	N	Y	Y	Y	Y	Y	Y	N
28 Rodriguez	N	Y	Y	Y	Y	Y	Y	N
29 Green	Y	Y	Y	Y	Y	Y	Y	N
30 Johnson, E.B.	N	Y	Y	Y	Y	N	Y	N
UTAH								
1 ***Hansen***	Y	Y	Y	Y	Y	Y	Y	Y
2 ***Cook***	N	Y	Y	Y	Y	Y	Y	Y
3 ***Cannon***	N	Y	Y	Y	Y	Y	Y	Y
VERMONT								
AL *Sanders*	N	Y	Y	Y	Y	Y	Y	N
VIRGINIA								
1 ***Bateman***	N	Y	Y	Y	Y	Y	P	Y
2 Pickett	N	Y	Y	Y	Y	Y	?	N
3 Scott	N	Y	Y	Y	Y	Y	Y	N
4 Sisisky	N	Y	Y	Y	Y	Y	Y	N
5 Goode	Y	Y	Y	Y	Y	Y	Y	N
6 ***Goodlatte***	Y	Y	Y	Y	Y	Y	Y	Y
7 ***Bliley***	N	Y	Y	Y	Y	Y	Y	Y
8 Moran	N	Y	Y	Y	Y	Y	N	N
9 Boucher	N	Y	Y	Y	Y	Y	Y	?
10 ***Wolf***	N	Y	Y	Y	?	?	Y	Y
11 ***Davis***	N	Y	Y	Y	Y	Y	Y	Y
WASHINGTON								
1 ***White***	N	Y	Y	Y	Y	Y	Y	Y
2 ***Metcalf***	Y	Y	Y	Y	Y	Y	Y	?
3 ***Smith, Linda***	Y	Y	Y	Y	Y	Y	Y	Y
4 ***Hastings***	Y	Y	Y	Y	Y	Y	Y	Y
5 ***Nethercutt***	N	Y	Y	Y	Y	N	Y	Y
6 Dicks	N	Y	Y	Y	Y	Y	Y	N
7 McDermott	N	Y	N	Y	Y	N	N	N
8 ***Dunn***	Y	Y	Y	Y	Y	Y	Y	Y
9 Smith, Adam	N	Y	Y	Y	Y	Y	Y	N
WEST VIRGINIA								
1 Mollohan	N	Y	Y	Y	Y	Y	Y	N
2 Wise	N	Y	Y	Y	Y	Y	Y	N
3 Rahall	N	N	N	Y	Y	Y	N	N
WISCONSIN								
1 ***Neumann***	Y	Y	Y	Y	Y	Y	Y	Y
2 ***Klug***	Y	Y	Y	Y	Y	Y	Y	Y
3 Kind	N	Y	Y	Y	Y	Y	Y	N
4 Kleczka	N	Y	Y	Y	Y	N	Y	N
5 Barrett	N	Y	Y	Y	Y	Y	Y	N
6 ***Petri***	N	Y	Y	Y	Y	Y	N	Y
7 Obey	N	Y	N	Y	Y	Y	N	N
8 Johnson	N	Y	Y	Y	Y	Y	Y	N
9 ***Sensenbrenner***	Y	Y	Y	Y	Y	Y	Y	Y
WYOMING								
AL ***Cubin***	Y	Y	Y	Y	Y	Y	Y	Y

Southern states - Ala., Ark., Fla., Ga., Ky., La., Miss., N.C., Okla., S.C., Tenn., Texas, Va.

HOUSE VOTES 178, 179, 180, 181, 182, 183, 184, 185

178. HR 1757. Fiscal 1998-99 State Department Authorization/Russian Missile Transfer. Rohrabacher, R-Calif., amendment to prohibit the payment of $95 million in foreign assistance currently designated for Russia in fiscal 1998 and 1999 if Russia transfers an SS-N-22 missile system to China. Adopted 225-190: R 181-37; D 43-153 (ND 29-114, SD 14-39); I 1-0, June 11, 1997. A "nay" was a vote in support of the president's position.

179. HR 1757. Fiscal 1998-99 State Department Authorization/Funding Cut. Sanford, R-S.C., amendment to reduce the authorized spending levels in the bill in fiscal 1998 and 1999 to the amount appropriated in fiscal 1997, a reduction of approximately $265 million in each fiscal year. Rejected 163-261: R 146-74; D 17-186 (ND 10-138, SD 7-48); I 0-1, June 11, 1997.

180. HR 1757. Fiscal 1998-99 State Department Authorization/Agency Consolidation. Separate vote at the request of Serrano, D-N.Y., on the Gilman, R-N.Y., amendment adopted by voice vote in the Committee of the Whole to require the president to submit a proposal to Congress to consolidate foreign affairs agencies within 60 days of the bill's enactment and require the abolition of the Arms Control and Disarmament Agency and the U.S. Information Agency by Oct. 1, 1998, consolidating their functions into the State Department by no later than Oct. 1, 1999. Adopted 420-6: R 217-6; D 202-0 (ND 147-0, SD 55-0); I 1-0, June 11, 1997.

181. HR 1757. Fiscal 1998-99 State Department Authorization/Passport Information Services. Separate vote at the request of Serrano, D-N.Y., on the Gilman, R-N.Y., amendment adopted June 4 by voice vote in the Committee of the Whole to strike the bill's designation of $5 million for passport information services and require that such information be provided for a fee, as in current law. Adopted 422-0: R 222-0; D 199-0 (ND 145-0, SD 54-0); I 1-0, June 11, 1997.

182. HR 1757. Fiscal 1998-99 State Department Authorization/Radio Free Asia. Separate vote at the request of Serrano, D-N.Y., on the Smith, R-N.J., amendment adopted June 4 by voice vote in the Committee of the Whole to increase funding for Radio Free Asia by $40 million. Adopted 354-72: R 209-14; D 145-57 (ND 97-50, SD 48-7); I 0-1, June 11, 1997.

183. HR 1757. Fiscal 1998-99 State Department Authorization/TV Marti. Separate vote at the request of Serrano, D-N.Y., on the Skaggs, D-Colo., amendment adopted June 4 in the Committee of the Whole (vote 159) to discontinue funding for TV Marti broadcasts to Cuba after Sept. 30, 1997, only if the president certifies that continued funding is not in the national interest. Adopted 279-149: R 204-19; D 75-129 (ND 46-103, SD 29-26); I 0-1, June 11, 1997.

184. HR 1757. Fiscal 1998-99 State Department Authorization/Diplomatic Immunity. Separate vote at the request of Serrano, D-N.Y., on the Hefley, R-Colo., amendment adopted June 4 by voice vote in the Committee of the Whole to require the State Department to maintain records of incidents involving those with diplomatic immunity who are believed to have committed serious crimes. Adopted 386-42: R 224-0; D 162-41 (ND 115-33, SD 47-8); I 0-1, June 11, 1997.

185. HR 1757. Fiscal 1998-99 State Department Authorization/Surplus Overseas Property. Separate vote at the request of Serrano, D-N.Y., on the Bachus, R-Ala., amendment adopted June 4 in the Committee of the Whole (vote 161) to require the State Department to submit annual reports to Congress on overseas surplus properties for sale and designate sale proceeds for deficit reduction. Adopted 283-146: R 203-21; D 80-124 (ND 54-95, SD 26-29); I 0-1, June 11, 1997.

KEY

- Y Voted for (yea).
- # Paired for.
- \+ Announced for.
- N Voted against (nay).
- X Paired against.
- – Announced against.
- P Voted "present."
- C Voted "present" to avoid possible conflict of interest.
- ? Did not vote or otherwise make a position known.

Democrats ***Republicans***
Independent

	178	179	180	181	182	183	184	185
ALABAMA								
1 ***Callahan***	Y	N	Y	Y	Y	Y	Y	Y
2 ***Everett***	Y	Y	Y	Y	Y	Y	Y	Y
3 ***Riley***	Y	Y	Y	Y	Y	Y	Y	Y
4 ***Aderholt***	Y	Y	Y	Y	Y	Y	Y	Y
5 Cramer	Y	Y	Y	Y	Y	N	Y	Y
6 ***Bachus***	Y	Y	Y	Y	Y	Y	Y	Y
7 Hilliard	N	N	Y	Y	Y	N	Y	N
ALASKA								
AL ***Young***	Y	Y	Y	Y	Y	Y	Y	Y
ARIZONA								
1 ***Salmon***	Y	Y	Y	Y	Y	Y	Y	Y
2 Pastor	N	N	Y	Y	Y	Y	Y	Y
3 ***Stump***	Y	Y	Y	Y	Y	Y	Y	Y
4 ***Shadegg***	Y	Y	Y	Y	Y	Y	Y	Y
5 ***Kolbe***	N	N	Y	Y	Y	Y	Y	N
6 ***Hayworth***	Y	Y	Y	Y	Y	Y	Y	Y
ARKANSAS								
1 Berry	N	N	Y	Y	Y	N	Y	Y
2 Snyder	N	N	Y	Y	Y	Y	N	N
3 ***Hutchinson***	Y	Y	Y	Y	Y	Y	Y	Y
4 ***Dickey***	Y	Y	Y	Y	Y	Y	Y	Y
CALIFORNIA								
1 ***Riggs***	Y	Y	Y	Y	Y	Y	Y	Y
2 ***Herger***	Y	Y	Y	Y	Y	Y	Y	Y
3 Fazio	N	N	Y	Y	Y	Y	Y	N
4 ***Doolittle***	?	Y	Y	Y	Y	Y	Y	Y
5 Matsui	N	N	Y	Y	Y	N	Y	N
6 Woolsey	N	N	Y	Y	Y	N	N	N
7 Miller	Y	N	Y	Y	N	N	Y	N
8 Pelosi	Y	N	Y	?	Y	Y	Y	N
9 Dellums	N	N	Y	Y	N	N	N	N
10 Tauscher	N	N	Y	Y	Y	N	Y	Y
11 ***Pombo***	Y	Y	Y	Y	N	Y	Y	Y
12 Lantos	N	N	Y	Y	Y	Y	Y	N
13 Stark	Y	N	?	Y	?	N	Y	N
14 Eshoo	N	N	Y	Y	Y	N	Y	Y
15 ***Campbell***	Y	Y	Y	Y	Y	Y	Y	Y
16 Lofgren	N	N	Y	Y	Y	N	Y	N
17 Farr	?	?	?	?	?	?	?	?
18 Condit	Y	Y	Y	Y	N	N	Y	Y
19 ***Radanovich***	Y	Y	Y	Y	Y	Y	Y	Y
20 Dooley	N	N	Y	Y	N	N	Y	N
21 ***Thomas***	Y	N	Y	Y	Y	Y	Y	Y
22 Capps	N	N	Y	Y	Y	N	Y	N
23 ***Gallegly***	Y	N	Y	Y	Y	Y	Y	Y
24 Sherman	N	N	Y	Y	Y	Y	Y	N
25 ***McKeon***	Y	Y	Y	Y	Y	Y	Y	Y
26 Berman	N	N	Y	Y	Y	N	N	N
27 ***Rogan***	Y	Y	Y	Y	Y	Y	Y	Y
28 ***Dreier***	Y	Y	Y	Y	Y	Y	Y	Y
29 Waxman	N	N	Y	Y	Y	N	N	N
30 Becerra	N	N	Y	Y	N	N	N	N
31 Martinez	N	N	Y	Y	N	N	N	N
32 Dixon	N	N	Y	Y	Y	N	N	N
33 Roybal-Allard	N	N	Y	Y	Y	N	N	N
34 Torres	N	N	Y	Y	N	N	Y	N
35 Waters	N	N	Y	Y	N	N	N	N
36 Harman	N	Y	Y	Y	Y	N	Y	Y
37 Millender-McD.	N	N	Y	Y	N	N	N	N
38 ***Horn***	N	N	Y	?	Y	Y	Y	N
39 ***Royce***	Y	Y	N	Y	Y	Y	Y	Y
40 ***Lewis***	N	N	Y	Y	Y	Y	Y	Y
41 ***Kim***	Y	Y	Y	Y	Y	Y	Y	Y
42 Brown	N	N	Y	Y	N	N	N	N
43 ***Calvert***	Y	N	Y	Y	Y	Y	Y	Y
44 ***Bono***	Y	Y	Y	Y	Y	Y	Y	Y
45 ***Rohrabacher***	Y	Y	N	Y	Y	Y	Y	Y
46 Sanchez	N	N	Y	Y	Y	N	Y	Y
47 ***Cox***	Y	Y	N	Y	Y	Y	Y	Y
48 ***Packard***	Y	N	Y	Y	Y	Y	Y	Y
49 ***Bilbray***	Y	N	Y	Y	Y	N	Y	Y
50 Filner	N	N	Y	Y	N	N	P	N
51 ***Cunningham***	Y	Y	Y	Y	Y	Y	Y	Y
52 ***Hunter***	Y	Y	Y	Y	Y	Y	Y	Y
COLORADO								
1 DeGette	N	N	Y	Y	Y	N	Y	N
2 Skaggs	N	N	Y	Y	Y	N	Y	N
3 ***McInnis***	Y	N	Y	Y	Y	Y	Y	Y
4 ***Schaffer***	Y	Y	Y	Y	Y	Y	Y	Y
5 ***Hefley***	Y	Y	Y	Y	Y	Y	Y	Y
6 ***Schaefer***	Y	Y	Y	Y	Y	Y	Y	Y
CONNECTICUT								
1 Kennelly	N	N	Y	Y	Y	N	Y	N
2 Gejdenson	N	N	Y	Y	N	N	Y	N
3 DeLauro	N	N	Y	Y	Y	N	Y	N
4 ***Shays***	Y	Y	Y	Y	Y	Y	Y	Y
5 Maloney	N	N	Y	Y	Y	Y	Y	Y
6 ***Johnson***	N	N	Y	Y	Y	Y	Y	N
DELAWARE								
AL ***Castle***	Y	Y	Y	Y	Y	Y	Y	N
FLORIDA								
1 ***Scarborough***	Y	?	N	Y	Y	Y	Y	Y
2 Boyd	Y	N	Y	Y	Y	Y	Y	N
3 Brown	N	N	Y	Y	Y	Y	Y	N
4 ***Fowler***	Y	Y	Y	Y	Y	Y	Y	Y
5 Thurman	Y	N	Y	Y	Y	N	Y	Y
6 ***Stearns***	Y	Y	Y	Y	Y	Y	Y	Y
7 ***Mica***	Y	Y	Y	Y	Y	Y	Y	Y
8 ***McCollum***	Y	N	Y	Y	Y	Y	Y	Y
9 ***Bilirakis***	N	Y	Y	Y	Y	Y	Y	Y
10 ***Young***	Y	Y	Y	Y	Y	Y	Y	Y
11 Davis	N	N	Y	Y	Y	Y	Y	N
12 ***Canady***	Y	N	Y	Y	Y	Y	Y	Y
13 ***Miller***	N	Y	Y	Y	Y	Y	Y	Y
14 ***Goss***	N	N	Y	Y	Y	Y	Y	Y
15 ***Weldon***	Y	Y	Y	Y	?	Y	Y	Y
16 ***Foley***	Y	Y	Y	Y	Y	Y	Y	Y
17 Meek	N	N	Y	Y	Y	Y	N	N
18 ***Ros-Lehtinen***	Y	N	Y	Y	Y	Y	Y	Y
19 Wexler	N	N	Y	Y	Y	Y	Y	N
20 Deutsch	N	N	Y	Y	Y	Y	Y	N
21 ***Diaz-Balart***	Y	N	Y	Y	Y	Y	Y	Y
22 ***Shaw***	Y	Y	Y	Y	Y	Y	Y	Y
23 Hastings	N	N	Y	Y	Y	Y	N	N
GEORGIA								
1 ***Kingston***	Y	Y	Y	Y	N	Y	Y	Y
2 Bishop	N	N	Y	Y	Y	Y	Y	Y
3 ***Collins***	Y	Y	Y	Y	Y	Y	Y	Y
4 McKinney	Y	N	Y	Y	Y	N	N	N
5 Lewis	N	N	Y	Y	N	N	N	N
6 ***Gingrich***								
7 ***Barr***	Y	Y	Y	Y	Y	Y	Y	Y
8 ***Chambliss***	Y	Y	Y	Y	Y	Y	Y	Y
9 ***Deal***	Y	Y	N	Y	Y	N	Y	Y
10 ***Norwood***	Y	Y	Y	Y	Y	Y	Y	Y
11 ***Linder***	?	N	Y	Y	Y	Y	Y	Y
HAWAII								
1 Abercrombie	Y	N	Y	Y	Y	N	Y	Y
2 Mink	N	N	Y	Y	Y	N	N	N
IDAHO								
1 ***Chenoweth***	Y	Y	Y	Y	Y	Y	Y	Y
2 ***Crapo***	Y	Y	Y	Y	Y	Y	Y	Y
ILLINOIS								
1 Rush	N	N	Y	Y	N	N	N	N
2 Jackson	N	N	Y	Y	N	N	Y	N
3 Lipinski	Y	N	Y	Y	Y	Y	Y	Y
4 Gutierrez	?	N	Y	Y	Y	Y	Y	N
5 Blagojevich	N	N	Y	Y	Y	Y	Y	N
6 ***Hyde***	N	Y	Y	Y	Y	Y	Y	Y
7 Davis	–	N	Y	Y	N	N	Y	N
8 ***Crane***	?	Y	Y	Y	Y	Y	Y	Y
9 Yates	N	N	Y	Y	N	N	Y	N
10 ***Porter***	N	N	Y	?	Y	Y	Y	Y
11 ***Weller***	Y	N	Y	Y	Y	Y	Y	Y
12 Costello	Y	N	Y	Y	Y	N	Y	Y
13 ***Fawell***	Y	N	Y	Y	Y	Y	Y	Y
14 ***Hastert***	Y	Y	Y	Y	Y	Y	Y	Y
15 ***Ewing***	N	N	Y	Y	Y	Y	Y	Y

ND Northern Democrats SD Southern Democrats

	178	179	180	181	182	183	184	185
16 ***Manzullo***	Y	Y	Y	Y	Y	Y	Y	Y
17 Evans	N	N	Y	Y	N	N	Y	Y
18 ***LaHood***	N	N	Y	Y	Y	Y	Y	N
19 Poshard	Y	N	Y	Y	Y	N	Y	Y
20 ***Shimkus***	Y	N	Y	Y	Y	Y	Y	Y
INDIANA								
1 Visclosky	N	N	+	+	Y	N	N	N
2 ***McIntosh***	Y	Y	Y	Y	Y	Y	Y	Y
3 Roemer	N	Y	Y	Y	Y	N	Y	Y
4 ***Souder***	Y	Y	Y	Y	Y	Y	Y	Y
5 ***Buyer***	Y	N	Y	Y	Y	Y	Y	Y
6 ***Burton***	Y	Y	Y	Y	Y	Y	Y	Y
7 ***Pease***	Y	Y	Y	Y	Y	Y	Y	Y
8 ***Hostettler***	Y	Y	Y	Y	Y	Y	Y	Y
9 Hamilton	N	N	Y	Y	Y	N	N	N
10 Carson	N	N	Y	Y	Y	Y	Y	Y
IOWA								
1 ***Leach***	Y	N	Y	Y	Y	Y	Y	N
2 ***Nussle***	Y	Y	Y	Y	Y	Y	Y	Y
3 Boswell	N	Y	Y	Y	Y	Y	Y	Y
4 ***Ganske***	N	Y	Y	Y	N	N	Y	Y
5 ***Latham***	Y	N	Y	Y	Y	Y	Y	Y
KANSAS								
1 ***Moran***	Y	Y	Y	Y	Y	Y	Y	Y
2 ***Ryun***	Y	Y	Y	Y	Y	Y	Y	Y
3 ***Snowbarger***	Y	Y	Y	Y	Y	Y	Y	Y
4 ***Tiahrt***	Y	Y	Y	Y	Y	Y	Y	Y
KENTUCKY								
1 ***Whitfield***	Y	Y	Y	Y	Y	N	Y	Y
2 ***Lewis***	Y	Y	Y	Y	Y	Y	Y	Y
3 ***Northup***	Y	N	Y	Y	Y	Y	Y	Y
4 ***Bunning***	Y	Y	Y	Y	Y	Y	Y	Y
5 ***Rogers***	Y	N	Y	Y	Y	Y	Y	N
6 Baesler	N	N	Y	Y	Y	N	Y	Y
LOUISIANA								
1 ***Livingston***	Y	N	Y	Y	Y	Y	Y	Y
2 Jefferson	N	N	Y	Y	Y	N	Y	N
3 ***Tauzin***	Y	Y	Y	Y	Y	Y	Y	Y
4 ***McCrery***	Y	N	Y	Y	Y	Y	Y	Y
5 ***Cooksey***	Y	N	Y	Y	Y	Y	Y	Y
6 ***Baker***	Y	Y	Y	Y	Y	Y	Y	Y
7 John	N	N	Y	Y	Y	Y	Y	Y
MAINE								
1 Allen	N	N	Y	Y	Y	N	Y	N
2 Baldacci	N	N	Y	Y	Y	N	Y	Y
MARYLAND								
1 ***Gilchrest***	Y	N	Y	Y	Y	Y	Y	Y
2 ***Ehrlich***	N	N	Y	Y	Y	Y	Y	Y
3 Cardin	Y	N	Y	Y	Y	Y	Y	N
4 Wynn	Y	N	Y	Y	Y	Y	Y	N
5 Hoyer	N	N	Y	Y	Y	Y	Y	N
6 ***Bartlett***	Y	Y	Y	Y	Y	N	Y	Y
7 Cummings	N	N	Y	Y	N	N	Y	Y
8 ***Morella***	N	N	Y	Y	Y	Y	Y	N
MASSACHUSETTS								
1 Olver	N	N	Y	Y	N	N	Y	N
2 Neal	Y	N	Y	Y	Y	N	Y	Y
3 McGovern	N	N	Y	Y	Y	Y	N	N
4 Frank	N	N	Y	Y	N	N	Y	Y
5 Meehan	Y	N	Y	Y	N	N	Y	N
6 Tierney	Y	N	Y	Y	N	N	N	Y
7 Markey	Y	N	Y	Y	Y	N	Y	N
8 Kennedy	N	N	Y	Y	Y	N	Y	N
9 Moakley	N	N	Y	Y	Y	N	Y	N
10 Delahunt	N	N	Y	Y	Y	N	Y	N
MICHIGAN								
1 Stupak	N	N	Y	Y	Y	Y	Y	N
2 ***Hoekstra***	Y	Y	Y	Y	N	N	Y	Y
3 ***Ehlers***	Y	N	Y	Y	Y	Y	Y	Y
4 ***Camp***	Y	Y	Y	Y	Y	Y	Y	Y
5 Barcia	Y	N	Y	Y	Y	Y	Y	Y
6 ***Upton***	Y	Y	Y	Y	Y	N	Y	Y
7 ***Smith***	N	?	Y	Y	Y	Y	Y	N
8 Stabenow	N	N	Y	Y	Y	Y	Y	Y
9 Kildee	N	N	Y	Y	Y	N	Y	Y
10 Bonior	N	N	Y	Y	Y	N	N	N
11 ***Knollenberg***	N	N	Y	Y	Y	Y	Y	Y
12 Levin	N	N	Y	Y	Y	Y	Y	N
13 Rivers	Y	N	Y	Y	N	N	Y	Y
14 Conyers	N	N	Y	Y	N	N	Y	N
15 Kilpatrick	N	N	Y	Y	N	N	Y	N
16 Dingell	N	N	Y	Y	N	N	N	N
MINNESOTA								
1 ***Gutknecht***	Y	Y	Y	Y	Y	Y	Y	Y
2 Minge	N	N	Y	Y	N	N	Y	Y

	178	179	180	181	182	183	184	185
3 ***Ramstad***	Y	Y	Y	Y	Y	Y	Y	Y
4 Vento	N	N	Y	Y	N	N	Y	Y
5 Sabo	N	N	Y	Y	N	N	Y	N
6 Luther	Y	Y	Y	Y	N	N	Y	Y
7 Peterson	Y	N	Y	Y	Y	Y	Y	Y
8 Oberstar	N	N	Y	Y	Y	N	Y	N
MISSISSIPPI								
1 ***Wicker***	Y	Y	Y	Y	Y	Y	Y	Y
2 Thompson	N	N	Y	Y	Y	N	Y	N
3 ***Pickering***	Y	Y	Y	Y	Y	Y	Y	Y
4 ***Parker***	Y	Y	Y	Y	N	N	Y	Y
5 Taylor	Y	Y	Y	Y	Y	N	Y	Y
MISSOURI								
1 Clay	N	N	Y	Y	N	N	N	N
2 ***Talent***	Y	Y	Y	Y	Y	Y	Y	Y
3 Gephardt	N	N	Y	Y	Y	Y	Y	N
4 Skelton	Y	N	Y	Y	Y	Y	Y	Y
5 McCarthy	N	Y	Y	Y	N	N	Y	Y
6 Danner	Y	Y	Y	Y	N	N	Y	Y
7 ***Blunt***	Y	Y	Y	Y	Y	Y	Y	Y
8 ***Emerson***	Y	Y	Y	Y	Y	Y	Y	Y
9 ***Hulshof***	Y	Y	Y	Y	Y	Y	Y	Y
MONTANA								
AL ***Hill***	Y	Y	Y	Y	Y	Y	Y	Y
NEBRASKA								
1 ***Bereuter***	N	N	Y	Y	Y	Y	Y	N
2 ***Christensen***	Y	Y	Y	Y	Y	N	Y	Y
3 ***Barrett***	Y	Y	Y	Y	Y	N	Y	Y
NEVADA								
1 ***Ensign***	Y	Y	Y	Y	Y	Y	Y	Y
2 ***Gibbons***	Y	Y	Y	Y	Y	Y	Y	Y
NEW HAMPSHIRE								
1 ***Sununu***	Y	Y	Y	Y	Y	Y	Y	Y
2 ***Bass***	N	Y	Y	Y	Y	Y	Y	Y
NEW JERSEY								
1 Andrews	N	Y	Y	Y	Y	Y	Y	Y
2 ***LoBiondo***	Y	N	Y	Y	Y	Y	Y	Y
3 ***Saxton***	Y	N	Y	Y	Y	Y	Y	Y
4 ***Smith***	N	N	Y	Y	Y	Y	Y	N
5 ***Roukema***	N	N	Y	Y	Y	Y	Y	N
6 Pallone	N	N	Y	Y	Y	Y	Y	N
7 ***Franks***	Y	N	Y	Y	Y	Y	Y	Y
8 Pascrell	N	N	Y	Y	Y	Y	Y	Y
9 Rothman	N	N	Y	Y	Y	Y	Y	Y
10 Payne	N	N	Y	Y	N	N	N	N
11 ***Frelinghuysen***	N	N	Y	Y	Y	Y	Y	Y
12 ***Pappas***	Y	N	Y	Y	Y	Y	Y	Y
13 Menendez	N	N	Y	Y	Y	Y	Y	N
NEW MEXICO								
1 ***Schiff***	?	?	?	?	?	?	?	?
2 ***Skeen***	Y	N	Y	Y	Y	Y	Y	Y
3 ***Redmond***	Y	N	Y	Y	Y	Y	Y	Y
NEW YORK								
1 ***Forbes***	+	−	+	+	+	+	+	+
2 ***Lazio***	Y	N	Y	Y	Y	Y	Y	N
3 ***King***	N	N	Y	Y	Y	Y	Y	N
4 McCarthy	N	N	Y	Y	Y	Y	Y	Y
5 Ackerman	N	N	Y	Y	Y	Y	Y	N
6 Flake	?	?	?	?	?	?	?	?
7 Manton	N	N	Y	Y	Y	Y	Y	N
8 Nadler	N	N	Y	Y	Y	N	Y	N
9 Schumer	?	N	Y	Y	Y	N	Y	Y
10 Towns	N	?	Y	Y	Y	N	N	N
11 Owens	N	N	Y	Y	N	N	N	N
12 Velázquez	N	N	Y	Y	N	N	N	N
13 ***Molinari***	?	?	?	?	?	?	?	?
14 Maloney	N	N	Y	Y	Y	Y	Y	Y
15 Rangel	N	N	Y	Y	?	N	Y	N
16 Serrano	N	N	Y	Y	N	N	N	N
17 Engel	?	N	Y	Y	Y	Y	Y	N
18 Lowey	N	N	Y	Y	Y	N	Y	N
19 ***Kelly***	Y	N	Y	Y	Y	Y	Y	Y
20 ***Gilman***	N	N	Y	Y	Y	Y	Y	N
21 McNulty	?	N	Y	Y	Y	Y	Y	N
22 ***Solomon***	Y	Y	Y	Y	Y	Y	Y	Y
23 ***Boehlert***	N	N	Y	Y	Y	N	Y	N
24 ***McHugh***	Y	N	Y	Y	Y	Y	Y	Y
25 ***Walsh***	?	N	Y	Y	Y	Y	Y	Y
26 Hinchey	Y	N	Y	?	N	N	Y	N
27 ***Paxon***	Y	Y	Y	Y	Y	Y	Y	Y
28 Slaughter	N	N	Y	Y	N	N	Y	N
29 LaFalce	N	N	Y	Y	Y	N	Y	N
30 ***Quinn***	Y	N	Y	Y	Y	Y	Y	Y
31 ***Houghton***	N	N	Y	Y	Y	Y	Y	N

	178	179	180	181	182	183	184	185
NORTH CAROLINA								
1 Clayton	N	N	Y	Y	Y	Y	N	N
2 Etheridge	N	N	Y	Y	Y	Y	Y	Y
3 ***Jones***	Y	Y	Y	Y	Y	Y	Y	Y
4 Price	N	N	Y	Y	Y	N	Y	Y
5 ***Burr***	Y	Y	Y	Y	Y	Y	Y	Y
6 ***Coble***	Y	Y	Y	Y	N	N	Y	Y
7 McIntyre	Y	N	Y	Y	Y	N	Y	Y
8 Hefner	N	N	Y	Y	Y	N	Y	Y
9 ***Myrick***	Y	Y	Y	Y	Y	Y	Y	Y
10 ***Ballenger***	N	Y	Y	Y	Y	Y	Y	Y
11 ***Taylor***	N	N	Y	Y	Y	Y	Y	Y
12 Watt	N	N	Y	Y	N	N	N	N
NORTH DAKOTA								
AL Pomeroy	N	N	Y	Y	Y	N	Y	N
OHIO								
1 ***Chabot***	Y	Y	Y	Y	N	Y	Y	Y
2 ***Portman***	Y	Y	Y	Y	Y	Y	Y	Y
3 Hall	N	N	Y	Y	Y	N	Y	N
4 ***Oxley***	N	N	Y	Y	Y	Y	Y	Y
5 ***Gillmor***	Y	N	Y	Y	Y	Y	Y	Y
6 Strickland	N	N	Y	Y	Y	Y	Y	Y
7 ***Hobson***	Y	N	Y	Y	Y	Y	Y	Y
8 ***Boehner***	?	Y	Y	Y	Y	Y	Y	Y
9 Kaptur	Y	N	Y	Y	Y	Y	Y	Y
10 Kucinich	N	N	Y	Y	Y	Y	Y	N
11 Stokes	N	N	Y	Y	N	N	N	N
12 ***Kasich***	Y	N	Y	Y	Y	Y	Y	Y
13 Brown	N	N	Y	Y	Y	Y	Y	N
14 Sawyer	N	N	Y	Y	Y	N	Y	N
15 ***Pryce***	Y	Y	Y	Y	Y	Y	Y	Y
16 ***Regula***	N	N	Y	Y	Y	Y	Y	N
17 Traficant	Y	Y	Y	Y	Y	Y	Y	Y
18 ***Ney***	Y	Y	Y	Y	Y	Y	Y	Y
19 ***LaTourette***	Y	N	Y	Y	Y	Y	Y	Y
OKLAHOMA								
1 ***Largent***	Y	Y	Y	Y	Y	Y	Y	Y
2 ***Coburn***	Y	Y	Y	Y	Y	Y	Y	Y
3 ***Watkins***	Y	Y	Y	Y	Y	Y	Y	Y
4 ***Watts***	Y	N	Y	Y	Y	Y	Y	Y
5 ***Istook***	Y	Y	Y	Y	Y	Y	Y	Y
6 ***Lucas***	Y	Y	Y	Y	Y	Y	Y	Y
OREGON								
1 Furse	N	N	Y	Y	Y	N	Y	N
2 ***Smith***	N	N	Y	Y	Y	Y	Y	Y
3 Blumenauer	N	N	Y	Y	Y	N	Y	N
4 DeFazio	Y	Y	Y	Y	N	N	Y	N
5 Hooley	N	N	Y	Y	Y	N	Y	Y
PENNSYLVANIA								
1 Foglietta	N	N	Y	Y	N	N	N	N
2 Fattah	N	N	Y	Y	N	N	N	N
3 Borski	N	N	Y	Y	Y	N	N	N
4 Klink	N	N	Y	Y	Y	Y	Y	Y
5 ***Peterson***	Y	Y	Y	Y	Y	Y	Y	Y
6 Holden	Y	N	Y	Y	Y	Y	Y	Y
7 ***Weldon***	N	Y	Y	Y	Y	Y	Y	Y
8 ***Greenwood***	Y	?	Y	Y	Y	Y	Y	Y
9 ***Shuster***	Y	Y	Y	Y	N	N	Y	Y
10 ***McDade***	N	N	Y	Y	Y	Y	Y	Y
11 Kanjorski	N	N	Y	Y	N	N	Y	Y
12 Murtha	N	N	Y	Y	Y	Y	N	N
13 ***Fox***	Y	N	Y	Y	Y	Y	Y	Y
14 Coyne	N	N	Y	Y	Y	Y	Y	N
15 McHale	Y	N	Y	Y	Y	N	Y	Y
16 ***Pitts***	Y	N	Y	Y	Y	Y	Y	Y
17 ***Gekas***	N	Y	Y	Y	Y	Y	Y	Y
18 Doyle	N	N	Y	Y	Y	Y	Y	Y
19 ***Goodling***	Y	Y	Y	Y	N	Y	Y	Y
20 Mascara	Y	N	Y	Y	Y	Y	Y	Y
21 ***English***	Y	Y	Y	Y	Y	Y	Y	Y
RHODE ISLAND								
1 Kennedy	N	N	Y	Y	Y	Y	Y	Y
2 Weygand	N	N	Y	Y	Y	N	Y	Y
SOUTH CAROLINA								
1 ***Sanford***	Y	Y	Y	Y	N	Y	Y	Y
2 ***Spence***	Y	Y	Y	Y	Y	Y	Y	Y
3 ***Graham***	N	Y	Y	Y	Y	Y	Y	Y
4 ***Inglis***	Y	Y	Y	Y	Y	Y	Y	Y
5 Spratt	N	N	Y	Y	Y	Y	Y	N
6 Clyburn	N	N	Y	Y	Y	Y	Y	N
SOUTH DAKOTA								
AL ***Thune***	Y	Y	Y	Y	Y	Y	Y	Y
TENNESSEE								
1 ***Jenkins***	Y	Y	Y	Y	Y	Y	Y	Y
2 ***Duncan***	Y	Y	Y	Y	N	Y	Y	Y

	178	179	180	181	182	183	184	
3 ***Wamp***	Y	Y	Y	Y	Y	Y	Y	Y
4 ***Hilleary***	Y	Y	Y	Y	Y	Y	Y	Y
5 Clement	Y	N	Y	Y	N	Y	Y	N
6 Gordon	Y	N	Y	Y	Y	Y	Y	Y
7 ***Bryant***	Y	Y	Y	Y	Y	Y	Y	Y
8 Tanner	Y	Y	Y	Y	Y	N	Y	Y
9 Ford	N	N	Y	Y	Y	Y	Y	N
TEXAS								
1 Sandlin	N	N	Y	?	Y	N	Y	Y
2 Turner	Y	N	Y	Y	Y	N	Y	Y
3 ***Johnson, Sam***	Y	Y	Y	Y	Y	Y	Y	N
4 Hall	Y	Y	Y	Y	Y	N	Y	Y
5 ***Sessions***	Y	Y	Y	Y	Y	Y	Y	Y
6 ***Barton***	Y	Y	Y	Y	Y	Y	Y	Y
7 ***Archer***	Y	Y	Y	Y	Y	?	Y	Y
8 ***Brady***	Y	Y	Y	Y	Y	Y	Y	Y
9 Lampson	N	N	Y	Y	Y	Y	Y	Y
10 Doggett	Y	Y	Y	Y	Y	N	Y	Y
11 Edwards	N	N	Y	Y	Y	Y	Y	Y
12 ***Granger***	Y	Y	Y	Y	Y	Y	Y	Y
13 ***Thornberry***	Y	Y	Y	Y	Y	Y	Y	Y
14 ***Paul***	Y	Y	Y	Y	N	N	Y	Y
15 Hinojosa	N	N	Y	Y	N	Y	Y	N
16 Reyes	N	N	Y	Y	Y	Y	Y	N
17 Stenholm	?	Y	Y	Y	Y	N	Y	Y
18 Jackson-Lee	N	N	Y	Y	Y	Y	N	N
19 ***Combest***	Y	Y	Y	Y	Y	Y	Y	Y
20 Gonzalez	?	N	Y	Y	Y	N	Y	N
21 ***Smith***	?	?	?	Y	Y	Y	Y	Y
22 ***DeLay***	Y	Y	Y	Y	Y	N	Y	Y
23 ***Bonilla***	Y	N	Y	Y	N	Y	Y	Y
24 Frost	N	N	Y	Y	Y	Y	Y	N
25 Bentsen	N	N	Y	Y	Y	Y	Y	N
26 ***Armey***	Y	Y	Y	Y	Y	N	Y	N
27 Ortiz	N	N	Y	Y	Y	Y	Y	Y
28 Rodriguez	N	N	Y	Y	N	N	Y	N
29 Green	Y	N	Y	Y	Y	Y	Y	Y
30 Johnson, E.B.	N	N	Y	Y	Y	Y	Y	N
UTAH								
1 ***Hansen***	Y	Y	Y	Y	Y	Y	Y	Y
2 ***Cook***	Y	Y	Y	Y	Y	Y	Y	Y
3 ***Cannon***	Y	Y	N	Y	Y	Y	Y	Y
VERMONT								
AL *Sanders*	Y	N	Y	Y	N	N	N	N
VIRGINIA								
1 ***Bateman***	N	N	Y	Y	Y	Y	Y	Y
2 Pickett	N	N	Y	Y	Y	Y	Y	Y
3 Scott	N	N	Y	Y	Y	N	Y	Y
4 Sisisky	N	N	Y	Y	Y	Y	Y	Y
5 Goode	Y	Y	Y	Y	N	N	Y	Y
6 ***Goodlatte***	Y	Y	Y	Y	Y	Y	Y	Y
7 ***Bliley***	N	N	Y	Y	Y	Y	Y	Y
8 Moran	N	N	Y	Y	Y	N	Y	N
9 Boucher	N	N	Y	Y	N	N	Y	N
10 ***Wolf***	Y	N	Y	Y	Y	Y	Y	Y
11 ***Davis***	Y	N	Y	Y	Y	Y	Y	Y
WASHINGTON								
1 ***White***	N	Y	Y	Y	Y	Y	Y	Y
2 ***Metcalf***	Y	N	Y	Y	Y	Y	Y	Y
3 ***Smith, Linda***	Y	Y	Y	Y	Y	Y	Y	Y
4 ***Hastings***	Y	Y	Y	Y	Y	Y	Y	Y
5 ***Nethercutt***	Y	Y	Y	Y	Y	Y	Y	Y
6 Dicks	N	N	Y	Y	Y	N	Y	N
7 McDermott	N	N	Y	Y	N	N	N	N
8 ***Dunn***	Y	N	Y	Y	Y	Y	Y	Y
9 Smith, Adam	N	N	Y	Y	Y	N	Y	N
WEST VIRGINIA								
1 Mollohan	?	N	Y	Y	N	N	Y	N
2 Wise	N	N	Y	?	Y	N	Y	N
3 Rahall	N	N	Y	Y	Y	Y	N	N
WISCONSIN								
1 ***Neumann***	Y	Y	Y	Y	Y	N	Y	Y
2 ***Klug***	Y	Y	Y	Y	Y	Y	Y	Y
3 Kind	N	N	Y	Y	Y	N	Y	Y
4 Kleczka	Y	N	Y	Y	N	N	Y	Y
5 Barrett	Y	N	Y	Y	N	N	N	Y
6 ***Petri***	Y	Y	Y	Y	Y	N	Y	Y
7 Obey	N	N	Y	Y	N	N	N	Y
8 Johnson	N	N	Y	Y	Y	Y	Y	Y
9 ***Sensenbrenner***	Y	Y	Y	Y	N	N	Y	Y
WYOMING								
AL ***Cubin***	Y	Y	Y	Y	Y	Y	Y	Y

Southern states - Ala., Ark., Fla., Ga., Ky., La., Miss., N.C., Okla., S.C., Tenn., Texas, Va.

HOUSE VOTES 186, 187, 188, 189, 190, 191, 192, 193

186. HR 1757. Fiscal 1998-99 State Department Authorization/Foreign Service. Separate vote requested by Serrano, D-N.Y., on the Gilman, R-N.Y., amendment adopted June 4 by voice vote in the Committee of the Whole to authorize certain employees in U.S. embassies to carry out certain consular functions, to change the authorized strength of the Foreign Service and to disallow the extradition of people against their will to a country where they may be subject to torture. Adopted 428-0: R 223-0; D 204-0 (ND 149-0, SD 55-0); I 1-0, June 11, 1997.

187. HR 1757. Fiscal 1998-99 State Department Authorization/Employee Due Process. Separate vote at the request of Serrano, D-N.Y., on the Goss, R-Fla., amendment adopted June 4 in the Committee of the Whole (vote 162) to strike bill provisions that require the State Department inspector general to inform any department employee who is the likely subject or target of a criminal investigation of their due process rights. Adopted 226-201: R 221-1; D 5-199 (ND 3-146, SD 2-53); I 0-1, June 11, 1997.

188. HR 1757. Fiscal 1998-99 State Department Authorization/World Heritage Programs. Separate vote at the request of Serrano, D-N.Y., on the Coburn, R-Okla., amendment adopted June 4 by voice vote in the Committee of the Whole to prohibit funding for the World Heritage Program or the Man and Biosphere Program administered by the U.N. Educational, Scientific and Cultural Organization. Adopted 222-202: R 203-19; D 19-182 (ND 8-138, SD 11-44); I 0-1, June 11, 1997.

189. HR 1757. Fiscal 1998-99 State Department Authorization/Peru and various other countries. Separate vote requested by Serrano, D-N.Y., on the Gilman, R-N.Y., amendment adopted June 4 by voice vote in the Committee of the Whole to urge Peru to respect the rights of prisoners and expedite legal procedures, to establish special envoys to promote mutual disarmament talks throughout the world and to make funds available for the programs of the Cuban Liberty and Democratic Solidarity Act of 1996 (PL 104-114). Adopted 292-135: R 101-123; D 190-12 (ND 142-5, SD 48-7); I 1-0, June 11, 1997.

190. HR 1757. Fiscal 1998-99 State Department Authorization/Humanitarian Aid Delivery. Separate vote at the request of Serrano, D-N.Y., on the Smith, R-N.J., amendment adopted June 4 by voice vote in the Committee of the Whole to require the president to report to Congress on any border closure or economic or commercial blockade by any newly independent state of the former Soviet Union that impedes the delivery of U.S. humanitarian assistance. Adopted 425-0: R 222-0; D 202-0 (ND 147-0, SD 55-0); I 1-0, June 11, 1997.

191. HR 1757. Fiscal 1998-99 State Department Authorization/Cuban Complaint Report. Separate vote at the request of Serrano, D-N.Y., on the Serrano amendment adopted June 4 by voice vote in the Committee of the Whole to require the president to submit to Congress quarterly reports on the number of complaints against the United States by the Cuban government. Rejected 141-287: R 0-223; D 140-64 (ND 107-42, SD 33-22); I 1-0, June 11, 1997.

192. HR 1757. Fiscal 1998-99 State Department Authorization/Ukraine. Separate vote at the request of Serrano, D-N.Y., on the Fox, R-Pa., amendment adopted June 4 by voice vote in the Committee of the Whole to express the sense of Congress that Ukraine should receive at least $225 million annually in aid in fiscal 1998 and 1999 and that the government should be commended for its decision to relinquish nuclear weapons. Adopted 415-12: R 221-3; D 193-9 (ND 138-9, SD 55-0); I 1-0, June 11, 1997.

193. HR 1757. Fiscal 1998-99 State Department Authorization/Child and Spousal Support Obligations. Separate vote at the request of Serrano, D-N.Y., on the Lazio, R-N.Y., amendment adopted June 4 by voice vote in the Committee of the Whole to express the sense of Congress that U.N. personnel should comply with child- and spousal-support orders issued by U.S. federal, state and local courts and that payments to the United Nations should be prohibited if it does not actively enforce such a policy. Adopted 387-38: R 220-2; D 167-35 (ND 119-29, SD 48-6); I 0-1, June 11, 1997.

KEY

Y Voted for (yea).
\# Paired for.
\+ Announced for.
N Voted against (nay).
X Paired against.
– Announced against.
P Voted "present."
C Voted "present" to avoid possible conflict of interest.
? Did not vote or otherwise make a position known.

Democrats ***Republicans***
Independent

	186	187	188	189	190	191	192	193
ALABAMA								
1 ***Callahan***	Y	Y	Y	Y	Y	N	Y	Y
2 ***Everett***	Y	Y	Y	N	Y	N	Y	Y
3 ***Riley***	Y	Y	Y	N	Y	N	Y	Y
4 ***Aderholt***	Y	Y	Y	N	Y	N	Y	Y
5 Cramer	Y	N	N	Y	Y	N	Y	Y
6 ***Bachus***	Y	Y	?	Y	Y	N	Y	Y
7 Hilliard	Y	N	N	N	Y	Y	Y	N
ALASKA								
AL ***Young***	Y	Y	Y	N	Y	N	Y	Y
ARIZONA								
1 ***Salmon***	Y	Y	Y	Y	Y	N	Y	Y
2 Pastor	Y	N	N	Y	Y	Y	N	Y
3 ***Stump***	Y	Y	Y	N	Y	N	Y	Y
4 ***Shadegg***	Y	Y	Y	N	Y	N	Y	Y
5 ***Kolbe***	Y	Y	N	Y	Y	N	Y	Y
6 ***Hayworth***	Y	Y	Y	N	Y	N	Y	Y
ARKANSAS								
1 Berry	Y	N	Y	Y	Y	Y	Y	Y
2 Snyder	Y	N	N	Y	Y	Y	Y	Y
3 ***Hutchinson***	Y	Y	Y	N	Y	N	Y	Y
4 ***Dickey***	Y	Y	Y	N	Y	N	Y	Y
CALIFORNIA								
1 ***Riggs***	Y	+	Y	Y	Y	N	Y	Y
2 ***Herger***	Y	Y	Y	N	Y	N	Y	Y
3 Fazio	Y	N	N	Y	Y	Y	Y	Y
4 ***Doolittle***	Y	Y	Y	N	Y	N	Y	Y
5 Matsui	Y	N	N	Y	Y	Y	Y	Y
6 Woolsey	Y	N	N	Y	Y	Y	Y	Y
7 Miller	Y	N	N	Y	Y	Y	Y	N
8 Pelosi	Y	N	N	Y	Y	Y	Y	Y
9 Dellums	Y	N	N	Y	Y	Y	Y	N
10 Tauscher	Y	N	N	Y	Y	Y	Y	Y
11 ***Pombo***	Y	Y	Y	N	Y	N	Y	Y
12 Lantos	Y	N	N	Y	Y	Y	Y	Y
13 Stark	Y	N	N	Y	Y	Y	Y	Y
14 Eshoo	Y	N	N	Y	Y	Y	Y	N
15 ***Campbell***	Y	Y	Y	Y	Y	N	Y	N
16 Lofgren	Y	N	N	Y	Y	Y	Y	Y
17 Farr	?	?	?	?	?	?	?	?
18 Condit	Y	N	Y	Y	Y	Y	Y	Y
19 ***Radanovich***	Y	Y	Y	N	Y	N	Y	Y
20 Dooley	Y	N	N	Y	Y	Y	Y	N
21 ***Thomas***	Y	Y	Y	Y	?	N	Y	Y
22 Capps	Y	N	N	Y	Y	Y	Y	N
23 ***Gallegly***	Y	Y	Y	N	Y	N	Y	Y
24 Sherman	Y	N	N	Y	Y	N	Y	Y
25 ***McKeon***	Y	Y	Y	N	Y	N	Y	Y
26 Berman	Y	N	N	Y	?	N	Y	N
27 ***Rogan***	Y	Y	Y	N	Y	N	Y	Y
28 ***Dreier***	Y	Y	Y	Y	Y	N	Y	Y
29 Waxman	Y	N	N	Y	Y	Y	Y	Y
30 Becerra	Y	N	N	Y	Y	Y	N	N
31 Martinez	Y	N	?	?	Y	Y	Y	Y
32 Dixon	Y	N	N	Y	Y	Y	Y	Y
33 Roybal-Allard	Y	N	N	Y	Y	Y	Y	N
34 Torres	Y	N	N	Y	Y	Y	Y	Y
35 Waters	Y	N	N	N	Y	Y	Y	N
36 Harman	Y	N	N	Y	Y	Y	Y	Y
37 Millender-McD.	Y	N	N	Y	Y	Y	Y	Y
38 ***Horn***	Y	Y	N	Y	Y	N	Y	Y
39 ***Royce***	Y	Y	Y	N	Y	?	Y	Y
40 ***Lewis***	Y	Y	Y	N	Y	N	Y	Y
41 ***Kim***	Y	Y	Y	Y	Y	N	Y	Y
42 Brown	Y	N	N	N	Y	Y	Y	N
43 ***Calvert***	Y	Y	Y	Y	Y	N	Y	Y
44 ***Bono***	Y	Y	Y	N	Y	N	Y	Y
45 ***Rohrabacher***	Y	Y	Y	N	Y	N	Y	Y
46 Sanchez	Y	N	N	Y	Y	Y	Y	Y
47 ***Cox***	?	Y	Y	Y	Y	N	Y	Y
48 ***Packard***	Y	Y	Y	Y	Y	N	Y	Y
49 ***Bilbray***	Y	Y	Y	N	Y	N	Y	Y
50 Filner	Y	N	N	Y	Y	Y	N	N
51 ***Cunningham***	Y	Y	Y	Y	Y	N	Y	Y
52 ***Hunter***	Y	?	Y	N	Y	N	Y	Y
COLORADO								
1 DeGette	Y	N	N	Y	Y	Y	Y	Y
2 Skaggs	Y	N	N	N	Y	Y	Y	N
3 ***McInnis***	Y	Y	Y	Y	Y	N	Y	Y
4 ***Schaffer***	Y	Y	Y	Y	Y	N	Y	Y
5 ***Hefley***	Y	Y	Y	N	Y	N	Y	Y
6 ***Schaefer***	Y	Y	Y	Y	Y	N	Y	Y
CONNECTICUT								
1 Kennelly	Y	N	N	Y	Y	Y	Y	Y
2 Gejdenson	Y	N	N	Y	Y	Y	Y	Y
3 DeLauro	Y	N	N	Y	Y	Y	Y	Y
4 ***Shays***	Y	Y	Y	Y	Y	N	Y	Y
5 Maloney	Y	N	N	Y	Y	N	Y	Y
6 ***Johnson***	Y	Y	Y	Y	Y	N	Y	Y
DELAWARE								
AL ***Castle***	Y	Y	N	N	Y	N	Y	Y
FLORIDA								
1 ***Scarborough***	Y	Y	Y	N	Y	N	Y	Y
2 Boyd	Y	N	N	Y	Y	N	Y	Y
3 Brown	Y	N	N	N	Y	N	Y	Y
4 ***Fowler***	Y	Y	Y	Y	Y	N	Y	Y
5 Thurman	Y	N	N	Y	Y	N	Y	Y
6 ***Stearns***	Y	Y	Y	Y	Y	N	Y	Y
7 ***Mica***	Y	Y	Y	N	Y	N	Y	Y
8 ***McCollum***	Y	Y	Y	Y	Y	N	Y	Y
9 ***Bilirakis***	Y	Y	Y	Y	Y	N	Y	Y
10 ***Young***	Y	Y	Y	Y	Y	N	Y	Y
11 Davis	Y	N	N	Y	Y	N	Y	N
12 ***Canady***	Y	Y	Y	N	Y	N	Y	Y
13 ***Miller***	Y	Y	Y	Y	Y	N	Y	Y
14 ***Goss***	Y	Y	Y	Y	Y	N	Y	Y
15 ***Weldon***	Y	Y	Y	Y	Y	N	Y	Y
16 ***Foley***	Y	Y	Y	Y	Y	N	Y	Y
17 Meek	Y	N	N	N	Y	Y	Y	Y
18 ***Ros-Lehtinen***	Y	Y	Y	Y	Y	N	Y	Y
19 Wexler	Y	N	N	Y	Y	N	Y	Y
20 Deutsch	Y	N	N	Y	Y	N	Y	Y
21 ***Diaz-Balart***	Y	Y	Y	Y	Y	N	Y	Y
22 ***Shaw***	Y	Y	Y	Y	Y	N	Y	Y
23 Hastings	Y	N	N	N	Y	Y	Y	Y
GEORGIA								
1 ***Kingston***	Y	Y	Y	N	Y	N	Y	Y
2 Bishop	Y	N	N	Y	Y	Y	Y	Y
3 ***Collins***	Y	Y	Y	N	Y	N	Y	Y
4 McKinney	Y	N	N	Y	Y	Y	Y	Y
5 Lewis	Y	N	N	Y	Y	Y	Y	Y
6 ***Gingrich***								
7 ***Barr***	Y	Y	Y	N	Y	N	Y	Y
8 ***Chambliss***	Y	Y	Y	N	Y	N	Y	Y
9 ***Deal***	Y	Y	Y	N	Y	N	Y	Y
10 ***Norwood***	Y	Y	Y	N	Y	N	Y	Y
11 ***Linder***	Y	Y	Y	Y	Y	N	Y	Y
HAWAII								
1 Abercrombie	Y	N	N	Y	Y	Y	Y	Y
2 Mink	Y	N	N	Y	Y	Y	Y	Y
IDAHO								
1 ***Chenoweth***	Y	Y	Y	Y	Y	N	Y	Y
2 ***Crapo***	Y	Y	Y	Y	Y	N	Y	Y
ILLINOIS								
1 Rush	Y	N	N	Y	Y	Y	Y	Y
2 Jackson	Y	N	N	Y	Y	Y	Y	N
3 Lipinski	Y	N	N	Y	Y	N	Y	Y
4 Gutierrez	Y	N	N	Y	Y	N	Y	Y
5 Blagojevich	Y	N	Y	Y	Y	N	Y	Y
6 ***Hyde***	Y	Y	Y	N	Y	N	Y	Y
7 Davis	Y	N	N	Y	Y	Y	Y	Y
8 ***Crane***	Y	Y	Y	N	Y	N	Y	Y
9 Yates	Y	N	N	Y	Y	Y	Y	Y
10 ***Porter***	Y	Y	N	Y	Y	N	Y	Y
11 ***Weller***	Y	Y	Y	N	Y	N	Y	Y
12 Costello	Y	N	N	Y	Y	Y	Y	Y
13 ***Fawell***	Y	Y	N	Y	Y	N	Y	Y
14 ***Hastert***	Y	Y	Y	N	Y	N	Y	Y
15 ***Ewing***	Y	Y	Y	Y	Y	N	Y	Y

ND Northern Democrats SD Southern Democrats

	186	187	188	189	190	191	192	193
16 ***Manzullo***	Y	Y	Y	Y	Y	N	Y	Y
17 Evans	Y	N	N	Y	Y	Y	Y	Y
18 ***LaHood***	Y	Y	Y	Y	Y	N	Y	Y
19 Poshard	Y	N	N	Y	Y	Y	Y	Y
20 ***Shimkus***	Y	Y	Y	N	Y	N	Y	Y
INDIANA								
1 Visclosky	Y	N	N	Y	Y	Y	Y	Y
2 ***McIntosh***	Y	Y	Y	N	Y	N	Y	?
3 Roemer	Y	N	N	Y	Y	Y	Y	Y
4 ***Souder***	Y	Y	Y	N	Y	N	Y	Y
5 ***Buyer***	Y	Y	Y	N	Y	N	N	Y
6 ***Burton***	Y	Y	Y	N	Y	N	Y	Y
7 ***Pease***	Y	Y	Y	Y	Y	N	N	Y
8 ***Hostettler***	Y	Y	Y	N	Y	N	Y	Y
9 Hamilton	Y	N	N	Y	Y	Y	N	N
10 Carson	Y	N	N	Y	Y	Y	Y	N
IOWA								
1 ***Leach***	Y	Y	N	Y	Y	N	Y	Y
2 ***Nussle***	Y	Y	Y	N	Y	N	Y	Y
3 Boswell	Y	N	N	Y	Y	Y	Y	Y
4 ***Ganske***	Y	Y	Y	Y	Y	N	Y	Y
5 ***Latham***	Y	Y	Y	Y	Y	N	Y	Y
KANSAS								
1 ***Moran***	Y	Y	Y	N	Y	N	Y	Y
2 ***Ryun***	Y	Y	Y	N	Y	N	Y	Y
3 ***Snowbarger***	Y	Y	Y	N	Y	N	Y	Y
4 ***Tiahrt***	Y	Y	Y	N	Y	N	Y	Y
KENTUCKY								
1 ***Whitfield***	Y	Y	Y	N	Y	N	Y	Y
2 ***Lewis***	Y	Y	Y	N	Y	N	Y	Y
3 ***Northup***	Y	Y	Y	Y	Y	N	Y	Y
4 ***Bunning***	Y	Y	Y	Y	Y	N	Y	Y
5 ***Rogers***	Y	Y	Y	N	Y	N	Y	Y
6 Baesler	Y	N	Y	Y	Y	Y	Y	Y
LOUISIANA								
1 ***Livingston***	Y	Y	Y	Y	Y	N	Y	Y
2 Jefferson	Y	N	N	N	Y	Y	Y	Y
3 ***Tauzin***	Y	Y	Y	Y	Y	N	Y	Y
4 ***McCrery***	Y	Y	Y	N	Y	N	Y	Y
5 ***Cooksey***	Y	Y	Y	N	Y	N	Y	Y
6 ***Baker***	Y	Y	Y	N	Y	N	Y	Y
7 John	Y	N	N	Y	Y	Y	Y	Y
MAINE								
1 Allen	Y	N	N	Y	Y	Y	Y	Y
2 Baldacci	Y	N	N	Y	Y	Y	Y	Y
MARYLAND								
1 ***Gilchrest***	Y	Y	N	Y	Y	N	Y	Y
2 ***Ehrlich***	Y	Y	Y	N	Y	N	Y	Y
3 Cardin	Y	N	N	Y	Y	N	Y	Y
4 Wynn	Y	N	N	Y	Y	Y	Y	Y
5 Hoyer	Y	N	N	Y	Y	Y	Y	Y
6 ***Bartlett***	Y	Y	Y	N	Y	N	Y	Y
7 Cummings	Y	N	N	Y	Y	Y	Y	Y
8 ***Morella***	Y	Y	N	Y	Y	N	Y	Y
MASSACHUSETTS								
1 Olver	Y	N	N	Y	Y	Y	Y	N
2 Neal	Y	N	N	Y	Y	Y	Y	Y
3 McGovern	Y	N	N	Y	Y	Y	Y	Y
4 Frank	Y	N	N	Y	Y	Y	Y	Y
5 Meehan	Y	N	N	Y	Y	Y	Y	Y
6 Tierney	Y	N	N	Y	Y	Y	Y	Y
7 Markey	Y	N	N	Y	Y	Y	Y	Y
8 Kennedy	Y	N	N	Y	Y	N	Y	Y
9 Moakley	Y	N	N	Y	Y	Y	Y	Y
10 Delahunt	Y	N	Y	Y	Y	Y	Y	Y
MICHIGAN								
1 Stupak	Y	N	N	Y	Y	N	Y	Y
2 ***Hoekstra***	Y	Y	Y	N	Y	N	Y	Y
3 ***Ehlers***	Y	Y	N	N	Y	N	Y	Y
4 ***Camp***	Y	Y	Y	N	Y	N	Y	Y
5 Barcia	Y	Y	Y	Y	Y	N	Y	Y
6 ***Upton***	Y	Y	Y	Y	Y	N	Y	Y
7 ***Smith***	Y	Y	Y	N	Y	N	Y	Y
8 Stabenow	Y	N	N	Y	Y	Y	Y	Y
9 Kildee	Y	N	N	Y	Y	N	Y	Y
10 Bonior	Y	N	N	Y	Y	Y	Y	N
11 ***Knollenberg***	Y	Y	Y	N	Y	N	Y	Y
12 Levin	Y	N	N	Y	Y	N	Y	Y
13 Rivers	Y	N	N	Y	Y	Y	Y	N
14 Conyers	Y	N	N	Y	Y	Y	Y	N
15 Kilpatrick	Y	N	N	Y	Y	Y	Y	N
16 Dingell	Y	N	N	Y	Y	Y	Y	N
MINNESOTA								
1 ***Gutknecht***	Y	Y	Y	N	Y	N	Y	Y
2 Minge	Y	N	N	Y	Y	Y	Y	Y

	186	187	188	189	190	191	192	193
3 ***Ramstad***	Y	Y	N	Y	Y	N	Y	Y
4 Vento	Y	N	N	Y	Y	Y	Y	Y
5 Sabo	Y	N	N	Y	Y	Y	Y	Y
6 Luther	Y	N	N	Y	Y	Y	Y	Y
7 Peterson	Y	N	Y	Y	Y	N	?	Y
8 Oberstar	Y	N	N	Y	Y	Y	Y	Y
MISSISSIPPI								
1 ***Wicker***	Y	Y	Y	N	Y	N	Y	Y
2 Thompson	Y	N	N	N	Y	Y	Y	Y
3 ***Pickering***	Y	Y	Y	Y	Y	N	Y	Y
4 ***Parker***	Y	Y	Y	N	Y	N	Y	Y
5 Taylor	Y	N	Y	Y	Y	Y	Y	Y
MISSOURI								
1 Clay	Y	N	N	N	Y	Y	Y	Y
2 ***Talent***	Y	Y	Y	N	Y	N	Y	Y
3 Gephardt	Y	N	N	Y	Y	N	Y	Y
4 Skelton	Y	N	N	Y	Y	N	Y	Y
5 McCarthy	Y	N	N	Y	Y	N	Y	Y
6 Danner	Y	N	Y	Y	Y	N	Y	Y
7 ***Blunt***	Y	Y	Y	N	Y	N	Y	Y
8 ***Emerson***	Y	Y	Y	N	Y	N	Y	Y
9 ***Hulshof***	Y	Y	Y	N	Y	N	Y	Y
MONTANA								
AL ***Hill***	Y	Y	Y	N	Y	N	Y	Y
NEBRASKA								
1 ***Bereuter***	Y	Y	N	Y	Y	N	Y	Y
2 ***Christensen***	Y	Y	Y	Y	Y	N	Y	Y
3 ***Barrett***	Y	Y	Y	N	Y	N	Y	Y
NEVADA								
1 ***Ensign***	Y	Y	Y	Y	Y	N	Y	Y
2 ***Gibbons***	Y	Y	Y	Y	Y	N	Y	Y
NEW HAMPSHIRE								
1 ***Sununu***	Y	Y	Y	Y	Y	N	Y	Y
2 ***Bass***	Y	Y	Y	Y	Y	N	Y	Y
NEW JERSEY								
1 Andrews	Y	N	N	Y	Y	N	Y	Y
2 ***LoBiondo***	Y	Y	Y	Y	Y	N	Y	Y
3 ***Saxton***	Y	Y	N	N	Y	N	Y	Y
4 ***Smith***	Y	N	Y	Y	Y	N	Y	Y
5 ***Roukema***	Y	Y	N	Y	Y	N	Y	Y
6 Pallone	Y	N	N	Y	Y	N	Y	Y
7 ***Franks***	Y	Y	N	Y	Y	N	Y	Y
8 Pascrell	Y	N	N	Y	Y	N	Y	Y
9 Rothman	Y	N	N	Y	Y	N	Y	Y
10 Payne	Y	N	N	N	Y	Y	Y	N
11 ***Frelinghuysen***	Y	Y	N	Y	Y	N	Y	Y
12 ***Pappas***	Y	Y	Y	N	Y	N	Y	Y
13 Menendez	Y	N	N	Y	Y	N	Y	Y
NEW MEXICO								
1 ***Schiff***	?	?	?	?	?	?	?	?
2 ***Skeen***	Y	Y	Y	Y	Y	N	Y	Y
3 ***Redmond***	Y	Y	Y	N	Y	N	Y	Y
NEW YORK								
1 ***Forbes***	+	-	+	+	+	-	+	+
2 ***Lazio***	Y	Y	N	Y	Y	N	Y	Y
3 ***King***	Y	Y	Y	Y	Y	N	Y	Y
4 McCarthy	Y	N	N	Y	Y	N	Y	Y
5 Ackerman	Y	N	?	Y	Y	Y	Y	Y
6 Flake	?	?	?	?	?	?	?	?
7 Manton	Y	N	N	Y	Y	N	Y	Y
8 Nadler	Y	N	N	Y	Y	Y	Y	Y
9 Schumer	Y	N	N	Y	Y	Y	Y	Y
10 Towns	Y	N	N	Y	Y	Y	Y	Y
11 Owens	Y	N	N	Y	Y	Y	Y	Y
12 Velázquez	Y	N	N	Y	Y	Y	Y	N
13 ***Molinari***	?	?	?	?	?	?	?	?
14 Maloney	Y	N	N	Y	Y	Y	Y	Y
15 Rangel	Y	N	?	Y	Y	Y	Y	Y
16 Serrano	Y	N	N	Y	Y	Y	Y	Y
17 Engel	Y	N	N	Y	Y	N	Y	Y
18 Lowey	Y	N	N	Y	Y	Y	Y	Y
19 ***Kelly***	Y	Y	Y	N	Y	N	Y	Y
20 ***Gilman***	Y	Y	Y	Y	Y	N	Y	Y
21 McNulty	Y	N	N	Y	Y	N	Y	Y
22 ***Solomon***	Y	Y	Y	N	Y	N	Y	Y
23 ***Boehlert***	Y	Y	Y	Y	Y	N	Y	Y
24 ***McHugh***	Y	Y	Y	Y	Y	N	Y	Y
25 ***Walsh***	Y	Y	Y	Y	Y	N	Y	Y
26 Hinchey	Y	N	N	Y	Y	Y	Y	Y
27 ***Paxon***	Y	Y	Y	N	Y	N	Y	Y
28 Slaughter	Y	N	N	Y	Y	Y	Y	Y
29 LaFalce	Y	N	N	Y	Y	Y	Y	Y
30 ***Quinn***	Y	Y	Y	Y	Y	N	Y	Y
31 ***Houghton***	Y	Y	Y	Y	Y	N	Y	Y

	186	187	188	189	190	191	192	193
NORTH CAROLINA								
1 Clayton	Y	N	N	Y	Y	Y	Y	Y
2 Etheridge	Y	N	N	Y	Y	Y	Y	Y
3 ***Jones***	Y	Y	Y	N	Y	N	Y	Y
4 Price	Y	N	N	Y	Y	Y	Y	Y
5 ***Burr***	Y	Y	Y	N	Y	N	Y	Y
6 ***Coble***	Y	Y	Y	N	Y	N	Y	Y
7 McIntyre	Y	N	Y	Y	Y	N	Y	Y
8 Hefner	Y	N	N	Y	Y	Y	Y	Y
9 ***Myrick***	Y	Y	Y	N	Y	N	Y	Y
10 ***Ballenger***	Y	Y	Y	N	Y	N	Y	Y
11 ***Taylor***	Y	Y	Y	Y	Y	N	Y	Y
12 Watt	Y	N	N	Y	Y	Y	Y	N
NORTH DAKOTA								
AL Pomeroy	Y	N	N	Y	Y	N	Y	Y
OHIO								
1 ***Chabot***	Y	Y	Y	Y	Y	N	Y	Y
2 ***Portman***	Y	Y	Y	Y	Y	N	Y	Y
3 Hall	Y	N	N	Y	Y	Y	Y	Y
4 ***Oxley***	Y	Y	Y	Y	Y	N	Y	Y
5 ***Gillmor***	Y	Y	Y	Y	Y	N	Y	Y
6 Strickland	Y	N	N	Y	Y	N	Y	Y
7 ***Hobson***	Y	Y	Y	N	Y	N	Y	Y
8 ***Boehner***	Y	Y	Y	N	Y	N	Y	Y
9 Kaptur	Y	N	N	Y	Y	N	Y	Y
10 Kucinich	Y	N	N	Y	Y	Y	Y	Y
11 Stokes	Y	N	N	Y	Y	Y	Y	Y
12 ***Kasich***	Y	Y	Y	Y	Y	N	Y	Y
13 Brown	Y	N	N	Y	Y	Y	Y	Y
14 Sawyer	Y	N	N	Y	Y	Y	Y	Y
15 ***Pryce***	Y	Y	Y	N	Y	N	Y	Y
16 ***Regula***	Y	Y	Y	Y	Y	N	Y	Y
17 Traficant	Y	Y	Y	Y	Y	N	Y	Y
18 ***Ney***	Y	Y	Y	Y	Y	N	Y	Y
19 ***LaTourette***	Y	Y	Y	Y	Y	N	Y	Y
OKLAHOMA								
1 ***Largent***	Y	Y	?	N	Y	N	Y	Y
2 ***Coburn***	Y	Y	Y	N	Y	N	Y	Y
3 ***Watkins***	Y	Y	Y	N	Y	N	Y	Y
4 ***Watts***	Y	Y	Y	N	Y	N	Y	Y
5 ***Istook***	Y	Y	Y	N	Y	N	Y	Y
6 ***Lucas***	Y	Y	Y	N	Y	N	Y	Y
OREGON								
1 Furse	Y	N	N	Y	Y	Y	Y	N
2 ***Smith***	Y	Y	Y	N	Y	N	Y	Y
3 Blumenauer	Y	N	N	Y	Y	Y	Y	Y
4 DeFazio	Y	N	N	P	P	Y	N	Y
5 Hooley	Y	N	N	Y	Y	Y	Y	Y
PENNSYLVANIA								
1 Foglietta	Y	N	N	Y	Y	Y	Y	N
2 Fattah	Y	N	N	Y	Y	Y	Y	Y
3 Borski	Y	N	N	Y	Y	N	Y	Y
4 Klink	Y	N	N	Y	Y	Y	Y	Y
5 ***Peterson***	Y	Y	Y	N	Y	N	Y	Y
6 Holden	Y	N	N	Y	Y	N	Y	Y
7 ***Weldon***	Y	Y	Y	N	Y	N	Y	Y
8 ***Greenwood***	Y	Y	Y	Y	Y	N	Y	Y
9 ***Shuster***	Y	Y	Y	N	Y	N	Y	Y
10 ***McDade***	Y	Y	Y	N	Y	N	Y	Y
11 Kanjorski	Y	N	N	Y	Y	Y	N	Y
12 Murtha	Y	N	N	Y	Y	N	Y	Y
13 ***Fox***	Y	Y	Y	Y	Y	N	Y	Y
14 Coyne	Y	N	N	Y	Y	Y	Y	Y
15 McHale	Y	N	N	Y	Y	Y	Y	Y
16 ***Pitts***	Y	Y	Y	N	Y	N	Y	Y
17 ***Gekas***	Y	Y	Y	N	Y	N	Y	Y
18 Doyle	Y	N	N	Y	Y	N	Y	Y
19 ***Goodling***	Y	Y	Y	Y	Y	N	Y	?
20 Mascara	Y	N	N	Y	Y	N	Y	Y
21 ***English***	Y	Y	N	N	Y	N	Y	Y
RHODE ISLAND								
1 Kennedy	Y	N	N	Y	Y	N	Y	Y
2 Weygand	Y	N	N	Y	Y	Y	Y	Y
SOUTH CAROLINA								
1 ***Sanford***	Y	Y	Y	N	Y	N	Y	Y
2 ***Spence***	Y	Y	Y	N	Y	N	Y	Y
3 ***Graham***	Y	Y	Y	N	Y	N	Y	Y
4 ***Inglis***	Y	Y	Y	Y	Y	N	Y	Y
5 Spratt	Y	N	N	Y	Y	N	Y	Y
6 Clyburn	Y	N	N	Y	Y	Y	Y	Y
SOUTH DAKOTA								
AL ***Thune***	Y	Y	Y	Y	Y	N	Y	Y
TENNESSEE								
1 ***Jenkins***	Y	Y	Y	N	Y	N	Y	Y
2 ***Duncan***	Y	Y	Y	Y	Y	N	Y	Y

	186	187	188	189	190	191	192	
3 ***Wamp***	Y	Y	Y	N	Y	N	Y	Y
4 ***Hilleary***	Y	Y	Y	N	Y	N	Y	Y
5 Clement	Y	N	N	Y	Y	Y	Y	N
6 Gordon	Y	N	N	Y	Y	N	Y	Y
7 ***Bryant***	Y	Y	Y	Y	Y	N	Y	Y
8 Tanner	Y	N	N	Y	Y	N	Y	Y
9 Ford	Y	N	N	Y	Y	Y	Y	Y
TEXAS								
1 Sandlin	Y	N	N	Y	Y	N	Y	Y
2 Turner	Y	N	Y	Y	Y	Y	Y	Y
3 ***Johnson, Sam***	Y	Y	Y	N	Y	N	Y	Y
4 Hall	Y	Y	Y	Y	Y	Y	Y	Y
5 ***Sessions***	Y	Y	Y	Y	Y	N	Y	Y
6 ***Barton***	Y	Y	Y	N	Y	N	Y	Y
7 ***Archer***	Y	Y	Y	N	Y	N	Y	Y
8 ***Brady***	Y	Y	Y	N	Y	N	Y	Y
9 Lampson	Y	N	Y	Y	Y	N	Y	Y
10 Doggett	Y	N	N	Y	Y	Y	Y	?
11 Edwards	Y	N	N	Y	Y	N	Y	Y
12 ***Granger***	Y	Y	Y	N	Y	N	Y	Y
13 ***Thornberry***	Y	Y	Y	N	Y	N	Y	Y
14 ***Paul***	Y	Y	Y	N	Y	N	N	N
15 Hinojosa	Y	N	N	Y	Y	N	Y	Y
16 Reyes	Y	N	N	Y	Y	N	Y	Y
17 Stenholm	Y	N	Y	Y	Y	Y	Y	Y
18 Jackson-Lee	Y	N	N	Y	Y	Y	Y	Y
19 ***Combest***	Y	Y	Y	Y	Y	N	Y	Y
20 Gonzalez	Y	N	N	Y	Y	Y	Y	Y
21 ***Smith***	Y	Y	Y	Y	Y	N	Y	Y
22 ***DeLay***	Y	Y	Y	N	Y	N	Y	Y
23 ***Bonilla***	Y	Y	Y	N	Y	N	Y	Y
24 Frost	Y	N	N	Y	Y	Y	Y	Y
25 Bentsen	Y	N	N	Y	Y	N	Y	Y
26 ***Armey***	Y	Y	Y	N	?	N	Y	Y
27 Ortiz	Y	N	N	Y	Y	N	Y	Y
28 Rodriguez	Y	N	N	Y	Y	Y	Y	Y
29 Green	Y	N	Y	Y	Y	N	Y	Y
30 Johnson, E.B.	Y	N	N	Y	Y	Y	Y	N
UTAH								
1 ***Hansen***	Y	Y	Y	N	Y	N	Y	Y
2 ***Cook***	Y	Y	Y	N	Y	N	Y	Y
3 ***Cannon***	Y	Y	Y	N	Y	N	Y	Y
VERMONT								
AL *Sanders*	Y	N	N	Y	Y	Y	Y	N
VIRGINIA								
1 ***Bateman***	Y	Y	Y	N	Y	N	Y	Y
2 Pickett	Y	N	N	Y	Y	N	Y	Y
3 Scott	Y	N	Y	Y	Y	Y	Y	N
4 Sisisky	Y	N	N	Y	Y	N	Y	Y
5 Goode	Y	N	Y	N	Y	N	Y	Y
6 ***Goodlatte***	Y	Y	Y	Y	Y	N	Y	Y
7 ***Bliley***	Y	Y	Y	N	Y	N	Y	Y
8 Moran	Y	Y	N	Y	Y	Y	Y	Y
9 Boucher	Y	N	N	Y	Y	Y	Y	Y
10 ***Wolf***	Y	Y	Y	Y	Y	N	Y	Y
11 ***Davis***	Y	Y	N	Y	Y	N	Y	Y
WASHINGTON								
1 ***White***	Y	Y	Y	Y	Y	N	Y	Y
2 ***Metcalf***	Y	Y	Y	Y	Y	N	Y	Y
3 ***Smith, Linda***	Y	Y	Y	Y	Y	N	Y	Y
4 ***Hastings***	Y	Y	Y	N	Y	N	Y	Y
5 ***Nethercutt***	Y	Y	Y	Y	Y	N	Y	Y
6 Dicks	Y	Y	N	Y	Y	Y	Y	Y
7 McDermott	Y	N	N	Y	Y	Y	N	N
8 ***Dunn***	Y	Y	Y	N	Y	N	Y	Y
9 Smith, Adam	Y	N	N	Y	Y	N	Y	Y
WEST VIRGINIA								
1 Mollohan	Y	N	N	Y	Y	N	?	?
2 Wise	Y	N	N	Y	Y	N	Y	Y
3 Rahall	Y	N	N	Y	Y	N	N	N
WISCONSIN								
1 ***Neumann***	Y	Y	Y	Y	Y	N	Y	Y
2 ***Klug***	Y	Y	N	N	Y	N	Y	Y
3 Kind	Y	N	N	Y	Y	N	Y	Y
4 Kleczka	Y	N	Y	Y	Y	Y	Y	Y
5 Barrett	Y	N	N	Y	Y	Y	Y	Y
6 ***Petri***	Y	Y	Y	Y	Y	N	Y	Y
7 Obey	Y	N	N	Y	Y	Y	N	N
8 Johnson	Y	N	N	Y	Y	N	Y	N
9 ***Sensenbrenner***	Y	Y	Y	N	Y	N	Y	Y
WYOMING								
AL ***Cubin***	Y	Y	Y	Y	Y	N	Y	Y

Southern states - Ala., Ark., Fla., Ga., Ky., La., Miss., N.C., Okla., S.C., Tenn., Texas, Va.

HOUSE VOTES 194, 195, 196, 197, 198

194. HR 1757. Fiscal 1998-99 State Department Authorization/International Family Planning Funding Restrictions. Separate vote at the request of Serrano, D-N.Y., on the Smith, R-N.J., amendment adopted June 5 in the Committee of the Whole (vote 168) to prohibit funding to any private, non-governmental or multilateral organization that directly or indirectly performs abortions in a foreign country, except in cases of rape, incest or when the life of the mother is endangered. The amendment would prohibit funding for any foreign organization that lobbies for or against abortion and funding for the U.N. Population Fund unless the organization ceases all activities in China. Adopted 234-193: R 193-31; D 41-161 (ND 32-115, SD 9-46); I 0-1, June 11, 1997. A "nay" was a vote in support of the president's position.

195. HR 1757. Fiscal 1998-99 State Department Authorization/Sudan Sanctions. Separate vote at the request of Serrano, D-N.Y., on the Scarborough, R-Fla., amendment adopted June 10 in the Committee of the Whole (vote 171) to apply the financial transaction restrictions contained in the Anti-Terrorism and Effective Death Penalty Act (PL 104-132) to Sudan and cease diplomatic relations with the country unless the president certifies that Sudan has ceased supporting terrorism. Adopted 410-12: R 217-2; D 192-10 (ND 138-9, SD 54-1); I 1-0, June 11, 1997.

196. HR 1757. Fiscal 1998-99 State Department Authorization/Kashmiri Hostage Release. Separate vote at the request of Serrano, D-N.Y., on the Nethercutt, R-Wash., amendment adopted June 10 in the Committee of the Whole (vote 173) to express the sense of Congress that the militant organization Al-Faran should immediately release U.S. citizen Donald Hutchings and three Western Europeans being held hostage in northwest India. Adopted 423-0: R 221-0; D 201-0 (ND 146-0, SD 55-0); I 1-0, June 11, 1997.

197. HR 1757. Fiscal 1998-99 State Department Authorization/Cuban Cigars. Separate vote at the request of Serrano, D-N.Y., on the Miller, D-Calif., amendment, as amended, adopted June 10 in the Committee of the Whole (vote 175) to express the sense of Congress that the U.S. government should permit the sale of Cuban cigars in the United States, but not until the government of Cuba frees all political prisoners, legalizes all political activity and agrees to hold free and fair elections. Adopted 366-59: R 215-7; D 151-51 (ND 105-42, SD 46-9); I 0-1, June 11, 1997.

198. HR 1757. Fiscal 1998-99 State Department Authorization/Romania NATO Assistance. Separate vote requested by Serrano, D-N.Y., on the Fox, R-Pa., amendment adopted June 10 by voice vote in the Committee of the Whole to designate Romania as eligible for assistance under the NATO Participation Act of 1994 (PL 103-447). Adopted 417-10: R 219-3; D 197-7 (ND 143-6, SD 54-1); I 1-0, June 11, 1997.

KEY

- Y Voted for (yea).
- # Paired for.
- + Announced for.
- N Voted against (nay).
- X Paired against.
- – Announced against.
- P Voted "present."
- C Voted "present" to avoid possible conflict of interest.
- ? Did not vote or otherwise make a position known.

Democrats **_Republicans_**
Independent

	194	195	196	197	198
ALABAMA					
1 ***Callahan***	Y	Y	Y	Y	Y
2 ***Everett***	Y	Y	Y	Y	Y
3 ***Riley***	Y	Y	Y	Y	Y
4 ***Aderholt***	Y	Y	Y	Y	Y
5 Cramer	Y	Y	Y	Y	Y
6 ***Bachus***	Y	Y	Y	Y	Y
7 Hilliard	N	Y	Y	N	Y
ALASKA					
AL ***Young***	Y	?	Y	N	Y
ARIZONA					
1 ***Salmon***	Y	Y	Y	Y	Y
2 Pastor	N	Y	Y	Y	Y
3 ***Stump***	Y	Y	Y	Y	Y
4 ***Shadegg***	Y	Y	Y	Y	Y
5 ***Kolbe***	N	Y	Y	Y	Y
6 ***Hayworth***	Y	Y	Y	Y	Y
ARKANSAS					
1 Berry	Y	Y	Y	Y	Y
2 Snyder	N	Y	Y	N	Y
3 ***Hutchinson***	Y	Y	Y	Y	Y
4 ***Dickey***	Y	Y	Y	Y	Y
CALIFORNIA					
1 ***Riggs***	Y	Y	Y	Y	Y
2 ***Herger***	Y	Y	Y	Y	Y
3 Fazio	N	Y	Y	Y	Y
4 ***Doolittle***	Y	Y	Y	Y	Y
5 Matsui	N	Y	Y	Y	Y
6 Woolsey	N	Y	Y	Y	Y
7 Miller	N	Y	Y	Y	Y
8 Pelosi	?	?	?	Y	Y
9 Dellums	N	Y	Y	N	Y
10 Tauscher	N	Y	Y	Y	Y
11 ***Pombo***	Y	Y	Y	Y	Y
12 Lantos	N	Y	Y	Y	Y
13 Stark	N	N	Y	Y	Y
14 Eshoo	N	Y	Y	Y	Y
15 ***Campbell***	N	N	Y	Y	Y
16 Lofgren	N	Y	Y	Y	Y
17 Farr	?	?	?	?	?
18 Condit	N	Y	Y	Y	N
19 ***Radanovich***	Y	Y	Y	Y	?
20 Dooley	N	Y	Y	N	Y
21 ***Thomas***	N	Y	Y	Y	Y
22 Capps	N	Y	Y	Y	Y
23 ***Gallegly***	Y	Y	Y	Y	Y
24 Sherman	N	Y	Y	Y	Y
25 ***McKeon***	Y	Y	Y	Y	Y
26 Berman	N	Y	Y	Y	Y
27 ***Rogan***	Y	Y	Y	Y	Y
28 ***Dreier***	Y	Y	Y	Y	Y
29 Waxman	N	Y	Y	N	Y
30 Becerra	N	Y	Y	N	Y
31 Martinez	N	Y	Y	Y	Y
32 Dixon	N	Y	Y	Y	Y
33 Roybal-Allard	N	Y	Y	N	Y
34 Torres	N	Y	Y	Y	Y
35 Waters	N	Y	Y	N	Y
36 Harman	N	N	Y	Y	Y
37 Millender-McD.	N	Y	Y	Y	Y
38 ***Horn***	N	Y	Y	Y	Y
39 ***Royce***	Y	Y	Y	Y	Y
40 ***Lewis***	Y	Y	Y	Y	Y
41 ***Kim***	Y	Y	Y	Y	Y
42 Brown	N	Y	Y	N	Y
43 ***Calvert***	Y	Y	Y	Y	Y
44 ***Bono***	Y	Y	Y	Y	Y
45 ***Rohrabacher***	Y	Y	Y	Y	Y
46 Sanchez	N	Y	Y	Y	Y
47 ***Cox***	Y	Y	Y	Y	Y
48 ***Packard***	Y	Y	Y	Y	Y
49 ***Bilbray***	N	Y	Y	Y	Y
50 Filner	N	Y	Y	Y	Y
51 ***Cunningham***	Y	Y	Y	Y	Y
52 ***Hunter***	Y	Y	Y	?	Y
COLORADO					
1 DeGette	N	Y	Y	N	Y
2 Skaggs	N	Y	?	N	Y
3 ***McInnis***	Y	Y	Y	Y	Y
4 ***Schaffer***	Y	Y	Y	Y	Y
5 ***Hefley***	Y	Y	Y	Y	N
6 ***Schaefer***	Y	Y	Y	Y	Y
CONNECTICUT					
1 Kennelly	N	Y	Y	Y	Y
2 Gejdenson	N	Y	Y	Y	Y
3 DeLauro	N	Y	Y	Y	Y
4 ***Shays***	N	Y	Y	Y	Y
5 Maloney	N	Y	Y	Y	Y
6 ***Johnson***	N	Y	Y	Y	Y
DELAWARE					
AL ***Castle***	N	Y	Y	N	Y
FLORIDA					
1 ***Scarborough***	Y	Y	Y	Y	Y
2 Boyd	N	Y	Y	Y	Y
3 Brown	N	Y	Y	Y	Y
4 ***Fowler***	Y	Y	Y	Y	Y
5 Thurman	N	Y	Y	Y	Y
6 ***Stearns***	Y	Y	Y	Y	Y
7 ***Mica***	Y	Y	Y	Y	Y
8 ***McCollum***	Y	Y	Y	Y	Y
9 ***Bilirakis***	Y	Y	Y	Y	Y
10 ***Young***	Y	Y	Y	Y	Y
11 Davis	N	Y	Y	Y	Y
12 ***Canady***	Y	Y	Y	Y	Y
13 ***Miller***	Y	Y	Y	Y	Y
14 ***Goss***	Y	Y	Y	Y	Y
15 ***Weldon***	Y	Y	Y	Y	Y
16 ***Foley***	Y	Y	Y	Y	Y
17 Meek	N	Y	Y	N	Y
18 ***Ros-Lehtinen***	Y	Y	Y	Y	Y
19 Wexler	N	Y	Y	Y	Y
20 Deutsch	N	Y	Y	Y	Y
21 ***Diaz-Balart***	Y	Y	Y	Y	Y
22 ***Shaw***	Y	Y	Y	Y	Y
23 Hastings	N	Y	Y	Y	Y
GEORGIA					
1 ***Kingston***	Y	Y	Y	Y	Y
2 Bishop	N	Y	Y	Y	Y
3 ***Collins***	Y	Y	Y	Y	Y
4 McKinney	N	Y	Y	N	Y
5 Lewis	N	Y	Y	N	Y
6 ***Gingrich***					
7 ***Barr***	Y	Y	Y	Y	Y
8 ***Chambliss***	Y	Y	Y	Y	Y
9 ***Deal***	Y	Y	Y	Y	Y
10 ***Norwood***	Y	Y	Y	Y	Y
11 ***Linder***	Y	Y	Y	Y	Y
HAWAII					
1 Abercrombie	N	Y	Y	N	Y
2 Mink	N	Y	Y	N	Y
IDAHO					
1 ***Chenoweth***	Y	Y	Y	Y	Y
2 ***Crapo***	Y	Y	Y	Y	Y
ILLINOIS					
1 Rush	N	Y	Y	N	Y
2 Jackson	N	Y	Y	N	Y
3 Lipinski	Y	Y	Y	Y	Y
4 Gutierrez	N	Y	Y	Y	Y
5 Blagojevich	N	Y	Y	Y	Y
6 ***Hyde***	Y	Y	Y	Y	Y
7 Davis	N	Y	Y	N	Y
8 ***Crane***	Y	Y	Y	Y	Y
9 Yates	N	Y	Y	Y	N
10 ***Porter***	N	Y	Y	Y	Y
11 ***Weller***	Y	Y	Y	Y	Y
12 Costello	Y	Y	Y	Y	Y
13 ***Fawell***	N	Y	Y	Y	Y
14 ***Hastert***	Y	Y	Y	Y	Y

ND Northern Democrats SD Southern Democrats

	194	195	196	197	198
15 ***Ewing***	Y	Y	Y	Y	Y
16 ***Manzullo***	Y	Y	Y	Y	Y
17 Evans	N	Y	Y	Y	Y
18 ***LaHood***	Y	Y	Y	Y	Y
19 Poshard	Y	Y	Y	Y	Y
20 ***Shimkus***	Y	Y	Y	Y	Y
INDIANA					
1 Visclosky	N	Y	Y	N	Y
2 ***McIntosh***	Y	Y	Y	Y	Y
3 Roemer	Y	Y	Y	Y	Y
4 ***Souder***	Y	Y	Y	Y	Y
5 ***Buyer***	Y	Y	Y	Y	Y
6 ***Burton***	Y	Y	Y	Y	Y
7 ***Pease***	Y	Y	Y	Y	Y
8 ***Hostettler***	Y	Y	Y	Y	Y
9 Hamilton	Y	Y	Y	Y	Y
10 Carson	N	Y	Y	Y	Y
IOWA					
1 ***Leach***	N	Y	Y	Y	Y
2 ***Nussle***	Y	Y	Y	Y	Y
3 Boswell	N	Y	Y	Y	Y
4 ***Ganske***	Y	Y	Y	Y	Y
5 ***Latham***	Y	Y	Y	Y	Y
KANSAS					
1 ***Moran***	Y	Y	Y	Y	Y
2 ***Ryun***	Y	Y	Y	Y	Y
3 ***Snowbarger***	Y	Y	Y	Y	Y
4 ***Tiahrt***	Y	Y	Y	Y	Y
KENTUCKY					
1 ***Whitfield***	Y	Y	Y	Y	Y
2 ***Lewis***	Y	Y	Y	Y	Y
3 ***Northup***	Y	Y	Y	Y	Y
4 ***Bunning***	Y	Y	Y	Y	Y
5 ***Rogers***	Y	Y	Y	Y	Y
6 Baesler	N	Y	Y	Y	Y
LOUISIANA					
1 ***Livingston***	Y	Y	Y	Y	Y
2 Jefferson	N	Y	Y	N	Y
3 ***Tauzin***	Y	Y	Y	Y	Y
4 ***McCrery***	Y	Y	Y	Y	Y
5 ***Cooksey***	Y	Y	Y	Y	Y
6 ***Baker***	Y	Y	Y	Y	Y
7 John	Y	Y	Y	Y	Y
MAINE					
1 Allen	N	Y	Y	Y	Y
2 Baldacci	N	Y	Y	Y	Y
MARYLAND					
1 ***Gilchrest***	N	Y	Y	Y	Y
2 ***Ehrlich***	N	Y	Y	Y	Y
3 Cardin	N	Y	Y	Y	Y
4 Wynn	N	Y	Y	Y	Y
5 Hoyer	N	Y	Y	Y	Y
6 ***Bartlett***	Y	Y	Y	Y	Y
7 Cummings	N	Y	Y	Y	Y
8 ***Morella***	N	Y	Y	Y	Y
MASSACHUSETTS					
1 Olver	N	Y	Y	Y	Y
2 Neal	N	Y	Y	Y	Y
3 McGovern	N	Y	Y	N	Y
4 Frank	N	Y	Y	Y	Y
5 Meehan	N	Y	Y	?	Y
6 Tierney	N	Y	Y	N	Y
7 Markey	N	Y	Y	Y	Y
8 Kennedy	N	Y	Y	Y	Y
9 Moakley	Y	Y	Y	N	Y
10 Delahunt	N	Y	Y	N	Y
MICHIGAN					
1 Stupak	Y	Y	Y	Y	Y
2 ***Hoekstra***	Y	Y	Y	Y	Y
3 ***Ehlers***	Y	Y	Y	N	Y
4 ***Camp***	Y	Y	Y	Y	Y
5 Barcia	Y	Y	Y	Y	Y
6 ***Upton***	N	Y	Y	Y	Y
7 ***Smith***	Y	Y	Y	N	Y
8 Stabenow	N	Y	Y	Y	Y
9 Kildee	Y	Y	Y	Y	Y
10 Bonior	Y	Y	Y	Y	Y
11 ***Knollenberg***	Y	Y	Y	Y	Y
12 Levin	N	Y	Y	Y	Y
13 Rivers	N	Y	Y	Y	Y
14 Conyers	N	N	Y	N	N
15 Kilpatrick	N	Y	Y	N	Y
16 Dingell	Y	Y	Y	Y	Y
MINNESOTA					
1 ***Gutknecht***	Y	Y	Y	Y	Y

	194	195	196	197	198
2 Minge	N	Y	Y	N	Y
3 ***Ramstad***	N	Y	Y	Y	Y
4 Vento	N	Y	Y	Y	Y
5 Sabo	N	Y	Y	N	N
6 Luther	N	Y	Y	Y	Y
7 Peterson	Y	Y	Y	Y	Y
8 Oberstar	Y	Y	Y	Y	Y
MISSISSIPPI					
1 ***Wicker***	Y	Y	Y	Y	Y
2 Thompson	N	Y	Y	Y	Y
3 ***Pickering***	Y	Y	Y	Y	Y
4 ***Parker***	Y	Y	Y	Y	Y
5 Taylor	Y	Y	Y	Y	Y
MISSOURI					
1 Clay	N	Y	Y	N	Y
2 ***Talent***	Y	Y	Y	Y	Y
3 Gephardt	N	Y	Y	Y	Y
4 Skelton	Y	Y	Y	Y	Y
5 McCarthy	N	Y	Y	Y	Y
6 Danner	Y	Y	Y	Y	N
7 ***Blunt***	Y	Y	Y	Y	Y
8 ***Emerson***	Y	Y	Y	?	?
9 ***Hulshof***	Y	Y	Y	Y	Y
MONTANA					
AL ***Hill***	Y	Y	Y	Y	Y
NEBRASKA					
1 ***Bereuter***	Y	Y	Y	Y	Y
2 ***Christensen***	Y	Y	Y	Y	Y
3 ***Barrett***	Y	Y	Y	Y	Y
NEVADA					
1 ***Ensign***	Y	Y	Y	Y	Y
2 ***Gibbons***	Y	Y	Y	Y	Y
NEW HAMPSHIRE					
1 ***Sununu***	Y	Y	Y	Y	Y
2 ***Bass***	N	Y	Y	Y	Y
NEW JERSEY					
1 Andrews	N	Y	Y	Y	Y
2 ***LoBiondo***	Y	Y	Y	Y	Y
3 ***Saxton***	Y	Y	Y	Y	Y
4 ***Smith***	Y	Y	Y	Y	Y
5 ***Roukema***	N	Y	Y	Y	Y
6 Pallone	N	Y	Y	Y	Y
7 ***Franks***	N	Y	Y	Y	Y
8 Pascrell	N	Y	Y	Y	Y
9 Rothman	N	Y	Y	Y	Y
10 Payne	N	Y	Y	N	Y
11 ***Frelinghuysen***	N	Y	Y	Y	Y
12 ***Pappas***	Y	Y	Y	Y	Y
13 Menendez	N	Y	Y	Y	Y
NEW MEXICO					
1 ***Schiff***	?	?	?	?	?
2 ***Skeen***	Y	Y	Y	Y	Y
3 ***Redmond***	Y	Y	Y	Y	Y
NEW YORK					
1 ***Forbes***	+	+	+	+	+
2 ***Lazio***	N	Y	Y	Y	Y
3 ***King***	Y	Y	Y	Y	Y
4 McCarthy	N	Y	Y	Y	Y
5 Ackerman	N	Y	Y	Y	Y
6 Flake	?	?	?	?	?
7 Manton	Y	Y	Y	Y	Y
8 Nadler	N	Y	Y	N	Y
9 Schumer	N	Y	Y	Y	Y
10 Towns	N	Y	Y	Y	Y
11 Owens	N	Y	Y	Y	Y
12 Velázquez	N	Y	Y	N	Y
13 ***Molinari***	?	?	?	?	?
14 Maloney	N	Y	Y	Y	Y
15 Rangel	N	Y	Y	N	Y
16 Serrano	N	Y	Y	N	Y
17 Engel	N	Y	Y	Y	Y
18 Lowey	N	Y	Y	Y	Y
19 ***Kelly***	N	Y	Y	Y	Y
20 ***Gilman***	N	Y	Y	Y	Y
21 McNulty	N	Y	Y	Y	Y
22 ***Solomon***	Y	Y	Y	Y	Y
23 ***Boehlert***	N	Y	Y	Y	Y
24 ***McHugh***	Y	Y	Y	Y	Y
25 ***Walsh***	Y	Y	Y	Y	Y
26 Hinchey	N	N	Y	N	Y
27 ***Paxon***	Y	Y	Y	Y	Y
28 Slaughter	N	Y	Y	Y	Y
29 LaFalce	Y	N	Y	Y	Y
30 ***Quinn***	Y	Y	Y	Y	Y

	194	195	196	197	198
31 ***Houghton***	N	Y	Y	Y	Y
NORTH CAROLINA					
1 Clayton	N	Y	Y	N	Y
2 Etheridge	N	Y	Y	Y	Y
3 ***Jones***	Y	Y	Y	Y	Y
4 Price	N	Y	Y	Y	Y
5 ***Burr***	Y	Y	Y	Y	Y
6 ***Coble***	Y	Y	Y	Y	Y
7 McIntyre	Y	Y	Y	Y	Y
8 Hefner	N	Y	Y	Y	Y
9 ***Myrick***	Y	Y	Y	Y	Y
10 ***Ballenger***	Y	Y	Y	Y	Y
11 ***Taylor***	Y	?	Y	Y	Y
12 Watt	N	N	Y	N	N
NORTH DAKOTA					
AL Pomeroy	N	Y	Y	Y	Y
OHIO					
1 ***Chabot***	Y	Y	Y	Y	Y
2 ***Portman***	Y	Y	Y	Y	Y
3 Hall	Y	Y	Y	Y	Y
4 ***Oxley***	Y	Y	Y	Y	Y
5 ***Gillmor***	Y	Y	Y	Y	Y
6 Strickland	N	Y	Y	Y	Y
7 ***Hobson***	N	Y	Y	Y	Y
8 ***Boehner***	Y	Y	Y	Y	Y
9 Kaptur	Y	Y	Y	Y	Y
10 Kucinich	Y	N	Y	N	Y
11 Stokes	N	Y	Y	N	Y
12 ***Kasich***	Y	Y	Y	Y	Y
13 Brown	N	Y	Y	Y	Y
14 Sawyer	N	Y	Y	Y	Y
15 ***Pryce***	N	Y	Y	Y	Y
16 ***Regula***	Y	Y	Y	Y	Y
17 Traficant	Y	Y	Y	Y	Y
18 ***Ney***	Y	Y	Y	Y	Y
19 ***LaTourette***	Y	Y	Y	Y	Y
OKLAHOMA					
1 ***Largent***	Y	Y	Y	Y	Y
2 ***Coburn***	Y	Y	Y	Y	Y
3 ***Watkins***	Y	Y	Y	N	Y
4 ***Watts***	Y	Y	Y	Y	Y
5 ***Istook***	Y	Y	Y	Y	Y
6 ***Lucas***	Y	Y	Y	N	Y
OREGON					
1 Furse	N	Y	Y	N	Y
2 ***Smith***	Y	Y	Y	Y	Y
3 Blumenauer	N	Y	Y	Y	Y
4 DeFazio	N	N	Y	N	Y
5 Hooley	N	Y	Y	Y	Y
PENNSYLVANIA					
1 Foglietta	N	Y	Y	N	Y
2 Fattah	N	Y	Y	N	Y
3 Borski	Y	Y	Y	Y	Y
4 Klink	Y	Y	Y	Y	Y
5 ***Peterson***	Y	Y	Y	Y	Y
6 Holden	Y	Y	Y	N	Y
7 ***Weldon***	Y	Y	Y	Y	Y
8 ***Greenwood***	N	?	Y	Y	Y
9 ***Shuster***	Y	Y	Y	Y	Y
10 ***McDade***	Y	Y	Y	Y	Y
11 Kanjorski	Y	Y	Y	N	Y
12 Murtha	Y	Y	Y	N	Y
13 ***Fox***	Y	?	Y	Y	Y
14 Coyne	N	Y	Y	N	Y
15 McHale	N	Y	Y	N	Y
16 ***Pitts***	Y	Y	Y	Y	Y
17 ***Gekas***	Y	Y	Y	Y	Y
18 Doyle	Y	Y	Y	Y	Y
19 ***Goodling***	Y	Y	Y	Y	Y
20 Mascara	Y	Y	Y	Y	Y
21 ***English***	Y	Y	Y	Y	Y
RHODE ISLAND					
1 Kennedy	N	Y	Y	Y	Y
2 Weygand	Y	Y	Y	Y	Y
SOUTH CAROLINA					
1 ***Sanford***	Y	Y	Y	Y	Y
2 ***Spence***	Y	Y	Y	Y	Y
3 ***Graham***	Y	Y	Y	Y	Y
4 ***Inglis***	Y	Y	Y	Y	Y
5 Spratt	N	Y	Y	Y	Y
6 Clyburn	N	Y	Y	Y	Y
SOUTH DAKOTA					
AL ***Thune***	Y	Y	Y	Y	Y

	194	195	196	197	198
TENNESSEE					
1 ***Jenkins***	Y	Y	Y	Y	Y
2 ***Duncan***	Y	Y	Y	Y	N
3 ***Wamp***	Y	Y	Y	Y	Y
4 ***Hilleary***	Y	Y	Y	Y	Y
5 Clement	N	Y	Y	Y	Y
6 Gordon	N	Y	Y	Y	Y
7 ***Bryant***	Y	Y	Y	Y	Y
8 Tanner	N	Y	Y	Y	Y
9 Ford	N	Y	Y	Y	Y
TEXAS					
1 Sandlin	N	Y	Y	Y	Y
2 Turner	N	Y	Y	Y	Y
3 ***Johnson, Sam***	Y	Y	Y	Y	Y
4 Hall	Y	Y	Y	Y	Y
5 ***Sessions***	Y	Y	Y	Y	Y
6 ***Barton***	Y	Y	Y	Y	Y
7 ***Archer***	Y	Y	Y	Y	Y
8 ***Brady***	Y	Y	Y	Y	Y
9 Lampson	N	Y	Y	Y	Y
10 Doggett	N	Y	Y	Y	Y
11 Edwards	N	Y	Y	Y	Y
12 ***Granger***	Y	Y	Y	Y	Y
13 ***Thornberry***	Y	Y	Y	Y	Y
14 ***Paul***	Y	N	Y	Y	N
15 Hinojosa	N	Y	Y	Y	Y
16 Reyes	N	Y	Y	Y	Y
17 Stenholm	Y	Y	Y	Y	Y
18 Jackson-Lee	N	Y	Y	Y	Y
19 ***Combest***	Y	Y	Y	Y	Y
20 Gonzalez	N	Y	Y	Y	Y
21 ***Smith***	Y	Y	Y	Y	Y
22 ***DeLay***	Y	Y	Y	Y	Y
23 ***Bonilla***	Y	Y	Y	Y	Y
24 Frost	N	Y	Y	Y	Y
25 Bentsen	N	Y	Y	Y	Y
26 ***Armey***	Y	?	?	Y	Y
27 Ortiz	Y	Y	Y	Y	Y
28 Rodriguez	N	Y	Y	Y	Y
29 Green	N	Y	Y	Y	Y
30 Johnson, E.B.	N	Y	Y	N	Y
UTAH					
1 ***Hansen***	Y	Y	Y	Y	Y
2 ***Cook***	Y	Y	Y	Y	Y
3 ***Cannon***	Y	Y	Y	Y	Y
VERMONT					
AL *Sanders*	N	Y	Y	N	Y
VIRGINIA					
1 ***Bateman***	Y	Y	Y	Y	Y
2 Pickett	N	Y	Y	Y	Y
3 Scott	N	Y	Y	Y	Y
4 Sisisky	N	Y	Y	Y	Y
5 Goode	Y	Y	Y	Y	Y
6 ***Goodlatte***	Y	Y	Y	Y	Y
7 ***Bliley***	Y	Y	Y	Y	Y
8 Moran	N	Y	Y	Y	Y
9 Boucher	N	Y	Y	Y	Y
10 ***Wolf***	Y	Y	Y	Y	Y
11 ***Davis***	N	Y	Y	Y	Y
WASHINGTON					
1 ***White***	N	Y	Y	Y	Y
2 ***Metcalf***	Y	Y	?	Y	Y
3 ***Smith, Linda***	Y	Y	Y	Y	Y
4 ***Hastings***	Y	Y	Y	Y	Y
5 ***Nethercutt***	Y	Y	Y	N	Y
6 Dicks	N	Y	Y	Y	Y
7 McDermott	N	N	Y	Y	Y
8 ***Dunn***	Y	Y	?	Y	Y
9 Smith, Adam	N	Y	Y	Y	Y
WEST VIRGINIA					
1 Mollohan	?	?	?	?	Y
2 Wise	N	Y	Y	Y	Y
3 Rahall	Y	N	Y	Y	Y
WISCONSIN					
1 ***Neumann***	Y	Y	Y	Y	Y
2 ***Klug***	N	Y	Y	Y	Y
3 Kind	N	Y	Y	Y	Y
4 Kleczka	Y	Y	Y	N	Y
5 Barrett	N	Y	Y	Y	Y
6 ***Petri***	Y	Y	Y	Y	Y
7 Obey	Y	Y	Y	Y	N
8 Johnson	N	Y	Y	Y	Y
9 ***Sensenbrenner***	Y	Y	Y	Y	Y
WYOMING					
AL ***Cubin***	Y	Y	Y	Y	Y

Southern states - Ala., Ark., Fla., Ga., Ky., La., Miss., N.C., Okla., S.C., Tenn., Texas, Va.

HOUSE VOTES 199, 200, 201, 202, 203

199. HR 1757. Fiscal 1998-99 State Department Authorization/Libya Assistance. Separate vote at the request of Serrano, D-N.Y., on the Ney, R-Ohio, amendment adopted June 10 in the Committee of the Whole (vote 174) to prohibit foreign assistance to any country that assists Libya in circumventing U.N. sanctions. Adopted 427-0: R 224-0; D 202-0 (ND 147-0, SD 55-0); I 1-0, June 11, 1997.

200. HR 1757. Fiscal 1998-99 State Department Authorization/Russian Missile Transfer. Separate vote at the request of Serrano, D-N.Y., on the Rohrabacher, R-Calif., amendment adopted earlier in the day in the Committee of the Whole (vote 178) to prohibit the transfer of $95 million in foreign assistance currently designated for Russia in fiscal 1998 and 1999 if Russia transfers an SS-N-22 missile system to China. Adopted 244-184: R 196-27; D 47-157 (ND 30-119, SD 17-38); I 1-0, June 11, 1997.

201. HR 1757. Fiscal 1998-99 State Department Authorization/Palestinian Executions. Separate vote at the request of Serrano, D-N.Y., on the Paxon, R-N.Y., amendment adopted June 10 by voice vote in the Committee of the Whole to express the sense of Congress condemning the Palestinian Authority for its policy and practice of executing Palestinians who engage in land sales to Jews. Adopted 425-0: R 222-0; D 202-0 (ND 147-0, SD 55-0); I 1-0, June 11, 1997.

202. H J Res 54. Flag Desecration/Passage. Passage of the joint resolution to propose a constitutional amendment to allow Congress to prohibit physical desecration of the U.S. flag. Passed 310-114: R 210-13; D 100-100 (ND 60-86, SD 40-14); I 0-1, June 12, 1997. A two-thirds majority of those present and voting (283 in this case) is required to pass a joint resolution proposing an amendment to the Constitution.

203. HR 1871. Fiscal 1997 Supplemental Appropriations/Passage. Passage of the bill to provide about $8.6 billion in additional funds for fiscal 1997, including about $5.6 billion in emergency disaster aid for 35 states and $1.9 billion to finance military peacekeeping operations in Bosnia and the Middle East. Passed 348-74: R 150-73; D 197-1 (ND 143-0, SD 54-1); I 1-0, June 12, 1997. A "yea" was a vote in support of the president's position.

KEY

- Y Voted for (yea).
- # Paired for.
- + Announced for.
- N Voted against (nay).
- X Paired against.
- – Announced against.
- P Voted "present."
- C Voted "present" to avoid possible conflict of interest.
- ? Did not vote or otherwise make a position known.

Democrats **_Republicans_**
Independent

	199	200	201	202	203
ALABAMA					
1 ***Callahan***	Y	Y	Y	Y	N
2 ***Everett***	Y	Y	Y	Y	Y
3 ***Riley***	Y	Y	Y	Y	N
4 ***Aderholt***	Y	Y	Y	Y	Y
5 Cramer	Y	Y	Y	Y	Y
6 ***Bachus***	Y	Y	Y	Y	Y
7 Hilliard	Y	N	Y	Y	Y
ALASKA					
AL ***Young***	Y	Y	Y	Y	Y
ARIZONA					
1 ***Salmon***	Y	Y	Y	Y	N
2 Pastor	Y	N	Y	N	Y
3 ***Stump***	Y	Y	Y	Y	Y
4 ***Shadegg***	Y	Y	Y	N	N
5 ***Kolbe***	Y	N	Y	N	Y
6 ***Hayworth***	Y	Y	Y	Y	Y
ARKANSAS					
1 Berry	Y	N	Y	Y	Y
2 Snyder	Y	N	Y	N	Y
3 ***Hutchinson***	Y	Y	Y	Y	Y
4 ***Dickey***	Y	Y	Y	Y	Y
CALIFORNIA					
1 ***Riggs***	Y	Y	Y	Y	Y
2 ***Herger***	Y	Y	Y	Y	Y
3 Fazio	Y	N	Y	N	Y
4 ***Doolittle***	Y	Y	Y	Y	Y
5 Matsui	Y	N	Y	N	Y
6 Woolsey	Y	N	Y	N	Y
7 Miller	Y	Y	Y	?	?
8 Pelosi	Y	Y	Y	N	?
9 Dellums	Y	N	Y	N	Y
10 Tauscher	Y	N	Y	N	Y
11 ***Pombo***	Y	Y	Y	Y	Y
12 Lantos	Y	N	Y	Y	Y
13 Stark	Y	N	Y	N	Y
14 Eshoo	Y	N	Y	N	Y
15 ***Campbell***	Y	Y	Y	Y	N
16 Lofgren	Y	N	Y	N	Y
17 Farr	?	?	?	?	?
18 Condit	Y	Y	Y	Y	Y
19 ***Radanovich***	Y	Y	Y	Y	Y
20 Dooley	Y	N	Y	Y	Y
21 ***Thomas***	Y	Y	Y	Y	Y
22 Capps	Y	N	Y	#	Y
23 ***Gallegly***	Y	Y	Y	Y	Y
24 Sherman	Y	N	Y	Y	Y
25 ***McKeon***	Y	Y	Y	Y	Y
26 Berman	Y	N	Y	N	Y
27 ***Rogan***	Y	Y	Y	Y	Y
28 ***Dreier***	Y	Y	Y	Y	Y
29 Waxman	Y	N	Y	N	Y
30 Becerra	Y	N	Y	N	Y
31 Martinez	Y	N	Y	Y	?
32 Dixon	Y	N	Y	N	Y
33 Roybal-Allard	Y	N	Y	N	Y
34 Torres	Y	N	Y	Y	Y
35 Waters	?	N	Y	N	Y
36 Harman	Y	N	Y	Y	Y
37 Millender-McD.	Y	N	Y	N	Y
38 ***Horn***	Y	N	Y	Y	Y
39 ***Royce***	Y	Y	Y	Y	N
40 ***Lewis***	Y	N	Y	Y	Y
41 ***Kim***	Y	Y	Y	Y	Y
42 Brown	Y	N	Y	N	Y
43 ***Calvert***	Y	Y	Y	Y	Y
44 ***Bono***	Y	Y	Y	Y	Y
45 ***Rohrabacher***	Y	Y	Y	Y	N
46 Sanchez	Y	N	Y	Y	Y
47 ***Cox***	Y	Y	Y	Y	N
48 ***Packard***	Y	Y	Y	Y	Y
49 ***Bilbray***	Y	Y	Y	Y	N
50 Filner	Y	N	Y	N	Y
51 ***Cunningham***	Y	Y	Y	Y	Y
52 ***Hunter***	Y	Y	Y	Y	N
COLORADO					
1 DeGette	Y	N	Y	N	Y
2 Skaggs	Y	N	Y	N	Y
3 ***McInnis***	Y	Y	Y	Y	N
4 ***Schaffer***	Y	Y	Y	Y	N
5 ***Hefley***	Y	Y	Y	Y	N
6 ***Schaefer***	Y	Y	Y	Y	N
CONNECTICUT					
1 Kennelly	Y	N	Y	Y	Y
2 Gejdenson	Y	N	Y	N	Y
3 DeLauro	Y	N	Y	N	Y
4 ***Shays***	Y	N	Y	N	N
5 Maloney	Y	N	Y	Y	Y
6 ***Johnson***	Y	Y	Y	Y	Y
DELAWARE					
AL ***Castle***	Y	Y	Y	Y	Y
FLORIDA					
1 ***Scarborough***	Y	Y	Y	Y	N
2 Boyd	Y	Y	Y	Y	Y
3 Brown	Y	N	Y	+	Y
4 ***Fowler***	Y	Y	Y	Y	Y
5 Thurman	Y	Y	Y	Y	Y
6 ***Stearns***	Y	Y	Y	Y	N
7 ***Mica***	Y	Y	Y	Y	N
8 ***McCollum***	Y	Y	Y	Y	Y
9 ***Bilirakis***	Y	N	Y	Y	Y
10 ***Young***	Y	Y	Y	Y	Y
11 Davis	Y	N	Y	Y	Y
12 ***Canady***	Y	Y	Y	Y	Y
13 ***Miller***	Y	Y	Y	Y	N
14 ***Goss***	Y	N	Y	Y	Y
15 ***Weldon***	Y	Y	Y	Y	N
16 ***Foley***	Y	Y	Y	Y	Y
17 Meek	Y	N	Y	N	Y
18 ***Ros-Lehtinen***	Y	Y	Y	Y	Y
19 Wexler	Y	N	Y	Y	Y
20 Deutsch	Y	N	Y	Y	Y
21 ***Diaz-Balart***	Y	Y	Y	Y	Y
22 ***Shaw***	Y	Y	Y	N	Y
23 Hastings	Y	N	Y	N	Y
GEORGIA					
1 ***Kingston***	Y	Y	Y	Y	N
2 Bishop	Y	N	Y	Y	Y
3 ***Collins***	Y	Y	Y	Y	N
4 McKinney	Y	Y	Y	N	Y
5 Lewis	Y	N	Y	N	Y
6 ***Gingrich***					
7 ***Barr***	Y	Y	Y	Y	N
8 ***Chambliss***	Y	Y	Y	Y	N
9 ***Deal***	Y	Y	Y	Y	N
10 ***Norwood***	Y	Y	Y	Y	N
11 ***Linder***	Y	Y	Y	Y	Y
HAWAII					
1 Abercrombie	Y	Y	Y	N	Y
2 Mink	Y	N	Y	N	Y
IDAHO					
1 ***Chenoweth***	Y	Y	Y	Y	Y
2 ***Crapo***	Y	Y	Y	Y	Y
ILLINOIS					
1 Rush	Y	N	Y	X	?
2 Jackson	Y	N	Y	N	Y
3 Lipinski	Y	Y	Y	Y	Y
4 Gutierrez	Y	Y	Y	Y	Y
5 Blagojevich	Y	N	Y	Y	Y
6 ***Hyde***	Y	Y	Y	Y	Y
7 Davis	Y	N	Y	N	Y
8 ***Crane***	Y	Y	Y	Y	N
9 Yates	Y	N	Y	N	Y
10 ***Porter***	Y	N	Y	N	Y
11 ***Weller***	Y	Y	Y	Y	Y
12 Costello	Y	Y	Y	Y	Y
13 ***Fawell***	Y	Y	Y	Y	Y
14 ***Hastert***	Y	Y	Y	Y	N

ND Northern Democrats SD Southern Democrats

	199	200	201	202	203
15 ***Ewing***	Y	Y	Y	Y	Y
16 ***Manzullo***	Y	Y	Y	Y	Y
17 Evans	Y	N	Y	N	Y
18 ***LaHood***	Y	N	Y	Y	Y
19 Poshard	Y	Y	Y	N	Y
20 ***Shimkus***	Y	Y	Y	Y	Y
INDIANA					
1 Visclosky	Y	N	Y	N	Y
2 ***McIntosh***	Y	Y	?	Y	N
3 Roemer	Y	N	Y	Y	Y
4 ***Souder***	Y	Y	Y	Y	P
5 ***Buyer***	Y	Y	Y	Y	N
6 ***Burton***	Y	Y	Y	Y	N
7 ***Pease***	Y	Y	Y	Y	N
8 ***Hostettler***	Y	Y	Y	Y	Y
9 Hamilton	Y	N	Y	Y	Y
10 Carson	Y	N	Y	Y	Y
IOWA					
1 ***Leach***	Y	Y	Y	N	Y
2 ***Nussle***	Y	Y	Y	Y	N
3 Boswell	Y	N	Y	Y	Y
4 ***Ganske***	Y	Y	Y	Y	Y
5 ***Latham***	Y	Y	Y	Y	Y
KANSAS					
1 ***Moran***	Y	Y	Y	Y	Y
2 ***Ryun***	Y	Y	Y	Y	N
3 ***Snowbarger***	Y	Y	Y	Y	N
4 ***Tiahrt***	Y	Y	Y	Y	N
KENTUCKY					
1 ***Whitfield***	Y	Y	Y	Y	Y
2 ***Lewis***	Y	Y	Y	Y	Y
3 ***Northup***	Y	Y	Y	Y	Y
4 ***Bunning***	Y	Y	Y	Y	Y
5 ***Rogers***	Y	Y	Y	Y	Y
6 Baesler	Y	N	Y	Y	Y
LOUISIANA					
1 ***Livingston***	Y	Y	Y	Y	Y
2 Jefferson	Y	Y	Y	Y	Y
3 ***Tauzin***	Y	Y	Y	Y	Y
4 ***McCrery***	Y	Y	Y	?	Y
5 ***Cooksey***	Y	Y	Y	Y	Y
6 ***Baker***	Y	Y	Y	Y	Y
7 John	Y	N	Y	Y	Y
MAINE					
1 Allen	Y	N	Y	N	Y
2 Baldacci	Y	N	Y	Y	Y
MARYLAND					
1 ***Gilchrest***	Y	Y	Y	N	Y
2 ***Ehrlich***	Y	N	Y	Y	Y
3 Cardin	Y	Y	Y	N	Y
4 Wynn	Y	Y	Y	Y	Y
5 Hoyer	Y	N	Y	N	Y
6 ***Bartlett***	Y	Y	Y	Y	N
7 Cummings	Y	N	Y	N	Y
8 ***Morella***	Y	N	Y	Y	Y
MASSACHUSETTS					
1 Olver	Y	N	Y	N	Y
2 Neal	Y	Y	Y	Y	Y
3 McGovern	Y	N	Y	Y	Y
4 Frank	Y	N	Y	N	Y
5 Meehan	Y	Y	Y	N	Y
6 Tierney	Y	Y	Y	N	Y
7 Markey	Y	Y	Y	N	Y
8 Kennedy	Y	N	Y	Y	Y
9 Moakley	Y	N	Y	Y	Y
10 Delahunt	Y	N	Y	Y	Y
MICHIGAN					
1 Stupak	Y	N	Y	Y	Y
2 ***Hoekstra***	Y	Y	Y	N	N
3 ***Ehlers***	Y	Y	Y	N	Y
4 ***Camp***	Y	Y	Y	Y	Y
5 Barcia	Y	Y	Y	Y	Y
6 ***Upton***	Y	Y	Y	Y	N
7 ***Smith***	Y	N	Y	+	N
8 Stabenow	Y	N	Y	Y	Y
9 Kildee	Y	Y	Y	Y	Y
10 Bonior	?	N	P	N	Y
11 ***Knollenberg***	Y	N	Y	Y	Y
12 Levin	Y	N	Y	N	Y
13 Rivers	Y	Y	Y	N	Y
14 Conyers	Y	N	Y	N	Y
15 Kilpatrick	Y	N	Y	N	Y
16 Dingell	Y	N	Y	N	Y
MINNESOTA					
1 ***Gutknecht***	Y	Y	Y	Y	Y

	199	200	201	202	203
2 Minge	Y	N	Y	N	Y
3 ***Ramstad***	Y	Y	Y	Y	Y
4 Vento	Y	N	Y	N	Y
5 Sabo	Y	N	Y	N	Y
6 Luther	Y	Y	Y	Y	Y
7 Peterson	Y	N	Y	Y	Y
8 Oberstar	Y	N	Y	N	Y
MISSISSIPPI					
1 ***Wicker***	Y	Y	Y	Y	Y
2 Thompson	Y	N	Y	Y	Y
3 ***Pickering***	Y	Y	Y	Y	Y
4 ***Parker***	Y	Y	Y	Y	Y
5 Taylor	Y	Y	Y	Y	Y
MISSOURI					
1 Clay	Y	N	Y	N	Y
2 ***Talent***	Y	Y	Y	Y	Y
3 Gephardt	Y	N	Y	Y	Y
4 Skelton	Y	Y	Y	Y	Y
5 McCarthy	Y	N	Y	Y	Y
6 Danner	Y	Y	Y	Y	Y
7 ***Blunt***	Y	Y	Y	Y	Y
8 ***Emerson***	Y	Y	Y	Y	Y
9 ***Hulshof***	Y	Y	Y	Y	N
MONTANA					
AL ***Hill***	Y	Y	Y	Y	Y
NEBRASKA					
1 ***Bereuter***	Y	N	Y	Y	Y
2 ***Christensen***	Y	Y	Y	Y	N
3 ***Barrett***	Y	Y	Y	Y	Y
NEVADA					
1 ***Ensign***	Y	Y	Y	Y	Y
2 ***Gibbons***	Y	Y	Y	Y	Y
NEW HAMPSHIRE					
1 ***Sununu***	Y	Y	Y	Y	Y
2 ***Bass***	Y	N	Y	Y	N
NEW JERSEY					
1 Andrews	Y	N	Y	Y	Y
2 ***LoBiondo***	Y	Y	Y	Y	Y
3 ***Saxton***	Y	Y	Y	Y	Y
4 ***Smith***	Y	N	Y	Y	Y
5 ***Roukema***	Y	N	Y	Y	Y
6 Pallone	Y	N	Y	Y	Y
7 ***Franks***	Y	Y	Y	Y	Y
8 Pascrell	Y	N	Y	Y	Y
9 Rothman	Y	N	Y	Y	Y
10 Payne	Y	N	Y	N	Y
11 ***Frelinghuysen***	Y	N	Y	Y	Y
12 ***Pappas***	Y	Y	Y	Y	Y
13 Menendez	Y	N	Y	Y	Y
NEW MEXICO					
1 ***Schiff***	?	?	?	?	?
2 ***Skeen***	Y	Y	Y	Y	Y
3 ***Redmond***	Y	Y	Y	Y	Y
NEW YORK					
1 ***Forbes***	+	+	+	#	+
2 ***Lazio***	Y	?	Y	Y	Y
3 ***King***	Y	N	Y	Y	Y
4 McCarthy	Y	N	Y	Y	Y
5 Ackerman	Y	N	Y	N	Y
6 Flake	?	?	?	?	?
7 Manton	Y	N	Y	Y	Y
8 Nadler	Y	N	Y	N	Y
9 Schumer	Y	N	Y	N	Y
10 Towns	Y	N	Y	Y	Y
11 Owens	Y	N	Y	N	Y
12 Velázquez	Y	N	Y	N	Y
13 ***Molinari***	?	?	?	Y	Y
14 Maloney	Y	N	Y	N	Y
15 Rangel	Y	N	Y	N	Y
16 Serrano	Y	N	Y	N	Y
17 Engel	Y	N	Y	N	Y
18 Lowey	Y	N	Y	N	Y
19 ***Kelly***	Y	Y	Y	Y	Y
20 ***Gilman***	Y	N	Y	Y	Y
21 McNulty	Y	N	Y	Y	Y
22 ***Solomon***	Y	Y	Y	Y	Y
23 ***Boehlert***	Y	N	Y	Y	Y
24 ***McHugh***	Y	Y	Y	Y	Y
25 ***Walsh***	Y	Y	Y	Y	Y
26 Hinchey	Y	Y	Y	N	Y
27 ***Paxon***	Y	Y	Y	Y	N
28 Slaughter	Y	N	Y	N	Y
29 LaFalce	Y	N	Y	N	?
30 ***Quinn***	Y	Y	Y	Y	Y

	199	200	201	202	203
31 ***Houghton***	Y	Y	Y	Y	Y
NORTH CAROLINA					
1 Clayton	Y	N	Y	N	Y
2 Etheridge	Y	N	Y	Y	Y
3 ***Jones***	Y	Y	Y	Y	N
4 Price	Y	N	Y	N	Y
5 ***Burr***	Y	Y	Y	Y	N
6 ***Coble***	Y	Y	Y	Y	Y
7 McIntyre	Y	Y	Y	Y	Y
8 Hefner	Y	N	Y	Y	Y
9 ***Myrick***	Y	Y	Y	Y	N
10 ***Ballenger***	Y	Y	Y	Y	Y
11 ***Taylor***	Y	N	Y	Y	Y
12 Watt	Y	N	Y	N	Y
NORTH DAKOTA					
AL Pomeroy	Y	N	Y	Y	Y
OHIO					
1 ***Chabot***	Y	Y	Y	Y	Y
2 ***Portman***	Y	Y	Y	Y	Y
3 Hall	Y	N	Y	N	Y
4 ***Oxley***	Y	Y	Y	Y	Y
5 ***Gillmor***	Y	Y	Y	Y	Y
6 Strickland	Y	N	Y	Y	Y
7 ***Hobson***	Y	Y	Y	Y	Y
8 ***Boehner***	Y	Y	Y	Y	N
9 Kaptur	Y	Y	Y	Y	Y
10 Kucinich	Y	N	Y	Y	Y
11 Stokes	Y	N	Y	N	Y
12 ***Kasich***	Y	Y	Y	Y	Y
13 Brown	Y	N	Y	Y	Y
14 Sawyer	Y	N	Y	N	Y
15 ***Pryce***	Y	Y	Y	Y	Y
16 ***Regula***	Y	N	Y	Y	Y
17 Traficant	Y	Y	Y	Y	Y
18 ***Ney***	Y	Y	Y	Y	Y
19 ***LaTourette***	Y	Y	Y	Y	Y
OKLAHOMA					
1 ***Largent***	Y	Y	Y	Y	N
2 ***Coburn***	Y	Y	Y	Y	N
3 ***Watkins***	Y	Y	Y	Y	Y
4 ***Watts***	Y	Y	Y	Y	Y
5 ***Istook***	Y	Y	Y	Y	N
6 ***Lucas***	Y	Y	Y	Y	Y
OREGON					
1 Furse	Y	N	Y	N	Y
2 ***Smith***	Y	Y	Y	Y	Y
3 Blumenauer	Y	N	Y	N	Y
4 DeFazio	Y	Y	Y	N	Y
5 Hooley	Y	N	Y	N	Y
PENNSYLVANIA					
1 Foglietta	Y	N	Y	N	Y
2 Fattah	Y	Y	Y	N	Y
3 Borski	Y	N	Y	N	Y
4 Klink	Y	N	Y	N	Y
5 ***Peterson***	Y	Y	Y	Y	Y
6 Holden	Y	Y	Y	Y	Y
7 ***Weldon***	Y	N	Y	Y	Y
8 ***Greenwood***	Y	Y	Y	N	Y
9 ***Shuster***	Y	Y	Y	Y	Y
10 ***McDade***	Y	N	Y	Y	?
11 Kanjorski	Y	N	Y	Y	Y
12 Murtha	Y	N	Y	Y	Y
13 ***Fox***	Y	Y	Y	Y	Y
14 Coyne	Y	N	Y	N	Y
15 McHale	Y	Y	Y	N	Y
16 ***Pitts***	Y	Y	Y	Y	Y
17 ***Gekas***	Y	N	Y	Y	Y
18 Doyle	Y	N	Y	Y	Y
19 ***Goodling***	Y	Y	Y	Y	N
20 Mascara	Y	Y	Y	Y	Y
21 ***English***	Y	Y	Y	Y	Y
RHODE ISLAND					
1 Kennedy	Y	N	Y	N	Y
2 Weygand	Y	N	Y	N	Y
SOUTH CAROLINA					
1 ***Sanford***	Y	Y	Y	Y	N
2 ***Spence***	Y	Y	Y	Y	Y
3 ***Graham***	Y	Y	Y	Y	N
4 ***Inglis***	Y	Y	Y	Y	N
5 Spratt	Y	Y	Y	Y	Y
6 Clyburn	Y	N	Y	Y	Y
SOUTH DAKOTA					
AL ***Thune***	Y	Y	Y	Y	Y

	199	200	201	202	203
TENNESSEE					
1 ***Jenkins***	Y	Y	Y	Y	Y
2 ***Duncan***	Y	Y	Y	Y	N
3 ***Wamp***	Y	Y	Y	Y	Y
4 ***Hilleary***	Y	Y	Y	Y	N
5 Clement	Y	Y	Y	Y	Y
6 Gordon	Y	Y	Y	Y	Y
7 ***Bryant***	Y	Y	Y	Y	Y
8 Tanner	Y	Y	Y	N	Y
9 Ford	Y	N	Y	Y	Y
TEXAS					
1 Sandlin	Y	N	Y	Y	Y
2 Turner	Y	Y	Y	Y	Y
3 ***Johnson, Sam***	Y	Y	Y	Y	N
4 Hall	Y	Y	Y	Y	Y
5 ***Sessions***	Y	Y	Y	Y	N
6 ***Barton***	Y	Y	Y	Y	N
7 ***Archer***	Y	Y	Y	Y	N
8 ***Brady***	Y	Y	Y	Y	N
9 Lampson	Y	N	Y	Y	Y
10 Doggett	Y	Y	Y	N	Y
11 Edwards	Y	N	Y	Y	Y
12 ***Granger***	Y	Y	Y	Y	Y
13 ***Thornberry***	Y	Y	Y	Y	N
14 ***Paul***	Y	Y	P	N	N
15 Hinojosa	Y	N	Y	Y	Y
16 Reyes	Y	N	Y	Y	Y
17 Stenholm	Y	Y	Y	Y	N
18 Jackson-Lee	Y	N	Y	N	Y
19 ***Combest***	Y	Y	Y	Y	N
20 Gonzalez	Y	N	Y	N	Y
21 ***Smith***	Y	Y	Y	Y	Y
22 ***DeLay***	Y	Y	Y	Y	N
23 ***Bonilla***	Y	Y	Y	Y	N
24 Frost	Y	N	Y	Y	Y
25 Bentsen	Y	N	Y	Y	Y
26 ***Armey***	Y	Y	Y	Y	N
27 Ortiz	Y	N	Y	Y	Y
28 Rodriguez	Y	N	Y	Y	Y
29 Green	Y	Y	Y	Y	Y
30 Johnson, E.B.	Y	N	Y	Y	Y
UTAH					
1 ***Hansen***	Y	Y	Y	Y	Y
2 ***Cook***	Y	Y	Y	Y	Y
3 ***Cannon***	Y	Y	Y	Y	N
VERMONT					
AL *Sanders*	Y	Y	Y	N	Y
VIRGINIA					
1 ***Bateman***	Y	Y	Y	Y	Y
2 Pickett	Y	N	Y	Y	Y
3 Scott	Y	N	Y	N	Y
4 Sisisky	Y	N	Y	Y	Y
5 Goode	Y	Y	Y	Y	Y
6 ***Goodlatte***	Y	Y	Y	Y	Y
7 ***Bliley***	Y	N	Y	Y	Y
8 Moran	Y	N	Y	Y	Y
9 Boucher	Y	N	Y	N	Y
10 ***Wolf***	Y	Y	Y	Y	Y
11 ***Davis***	Y	Y	Y	Y	Y
WASHINGTON					
1 ***White***	Y	N	Y	N	Y
2 ***Metcalf***	Y	Y	Y	Y	Y
3 ***Smith, Linda***	Y	Y	Y	Y	Y
4 ***Hastings***	Y	Y	Y	Y	Y
5 ***Nethercutt***	Y	Y	Y	Y	Y
6 Dicks	Y	N	Y	N	Y
7 McDermott	Y	N	Y	N	?
8 ***Dunn***	Y	Y	Y	Y	Y
9 Smith, Adam	Y	N	Y	Y	Y
WEST VIRGINIA					
1 Mollohan	Y	N	Y	Y	Y
2 Wise	Y	N	Y	Y	Y
3 Rahall	Y	N	P	Y	Y
WISCONSIN					
1 ***Neumann***	Y	Y	Y	Y	N
2 ***Klug***	Y	Y	Y	Y	N
3 Kind	Y	N	Y	N	Y
4 Kleczka	Y	Y	Y	N	Y
5 Barrett	Y	Y	Y	N	Y
6 ***Petri***	Y	Y	Y	N	N
7 Obey	Y	N	Y	N	Y
8 Johnson	Y	N	Y	Y	Y
9 ***Sensenbrenner***	Y	Y	Y	Y	N
WYOMING					
AL ***Cubin***	Y	Y	Y	Y	Y

Southern states - Ala., Ark., Fla., Ga., Ky., La., Miss., N.C., Okla., S.C., Tenn., Texas, Va.

HOUSE VOTES 204, 205, 206, 207, 208, 209, 210, 211

204. HR 1057. Andrew Jacobs Jr. Post Office/Passage. McHugh, R-N.Y., motion to suspend the rules and pass the bill to designate the Andrew Jacobs Jr. Post Office in Indianapolis. Motion agreed to 413-0: R 217-0; D 195-0 (ND 143-0, SD 52-0); I 1-0, June 17, 1997. A two-thirds majority of those present and voting (276 in this case) is required for passage under suspension of the rules.

205. HR 1058. John T. Myers Post Office/Passage. McHugh, R-N.Y., motion to suspend the rules and pass the bill to designate the John T. Myers Post Office in Terre Haute, Ind.. Motion agreed to 416-0: R 218-0; D 197-0 (ND 145-0, SD 52-0); I 1-0, June 17, 1997. A two-thirds majority of those present and voting (278 in this case) is required for passage under suspension of the rules.

206. HR 985. Eagles Nest Wilderness Expansion/Passage. Chenoweth, R-Idaho, motion to suspend the rules and pass the bill to authorize the addition of a 160-acre tract of land to the Eagles Nest Wilderness in Colorado if the tract is acquired by the U.S. Forest Service before Dec. 31, 2000. Motion agreed to 412-4: R 215-4; D 196-0 (ND 144-0, SD 52-0); I 1-0, June 17, 1997. A two-thirds majority of those present and voting (278 in this case) is required for passage under suspension of the rules.

207. H J Res 56. End of Slavery Celebration/Passage. Pappas, R-N.J., motion to suspend the rules and pass the joint resolution to express the sense of Congress that the celebration of the end of slavery in the United States is an important part of the country's heritage. Motion agreed to 419-0: R 219-0; D 199-0 (ND 146-0, SD 53-0); I 1-0, June 17, 1997. A two-thirds majority of those present and voting (280 in this case) is required for passage under suspension of the rules.

208. HR 437. National Sea Grant College Program/Passage. Passage of the bill to authorize $166.2 million through fiscal 2000 for the National Sea Grant College program and to modify the program to streamline the grant process and require peer review of proposed projects. Passed 422-3: R 219-2; D 202-1 (ND 148-0, SD 54-1); I 1-0, June 18, 1997.

209. Procedural Motion/Journal. Approval of the House Journal of Tuesday, June 17, 1997. Approved 366-50: R 192-22; D 173-28 (ND 127-20, SD 46-8); I 1-0, June 18, 1997.

210. Procedural Motion/Adjourn. Frank, D-Mass., motion to adjourn. Motion rejected 123-282: R 2-212; D 120-70 (ND 89-47, SD 31-23); I 1-0, June 19, 1997.

211. Procedural Motion/Adjourn. Forbes, R-N.Y., motion to adjourn. Motion rejected 27-389: R 4-218; D 23-170 (ND 20-118, SD 3-52); I 0-1, June 19, 1997.

KEY

Y Voted for (yea).
\# Paired for.
\+ Announced for.
N Voted against (nay).
X Paired against.
– Announced against.
P Voted "present."
C Voted "present" to avoid possible conflict of interest.
? Did not vote or otherwise make a position known.

Democrats ***Republicans***
Independent

	204	205	206	207	208	209	210	211
ALABAMA								
1 ***Callahan***	?	?	?	?	Y	Y	N	N
2 ***Everett***	Y	Y	Y	Y	Y	Y	N	N
3 ***Riley***	Y	Y	Y	Y	Y	Y	N	Y
4 ***Aderholt***	Y	Y	Y	Y	Y	Y	N	N
5 Cramer	Y	Y	Y	Y	Y	Y	N	N
6 ***Bachus***	Y	Y	Y	Y	Y	Y	N	N
7 Hilliard	Y	Y	Y	Y	Y	N	N	N
ALASKA								
AL ***Young***	Y	Y	Y	Y	Y	Y	?	N
ARIZONA								
1 ***Salmon***	Y	Y	Y	Y	Y	Y	?	N
2 Pastor	Y	Y	Y	Y	Y	Y	Y	Y
3 ***Stump***	Y	Y	N	Y	Y	Y	N	N
4 ***Shadegg***	Y	Y	Y	Y	Y	Y	N	N
5 ***Kolbe***	Y	Y	Y	Y	Y	Y	N	N
6 ***Hayworth***	Y	Y	Y	Y	Y	Y	N	N
ARKANSAS								
1 Berry	Y	Y	Y	Y	Y	Y	Y	N
2 Snyder	Y	Y	Y	Y	Y	Y	Y	N
3 ***Hutchinson***	Y	Y	Y	Y	Y	Y	N	N
4 ***Dickey***	Y	Y	Y	Y	Y	Y	N	N
CALIFORNIA								
1 ***Riggs***	Y	Y	Y	Y	Y	Y	N	N
2 ***Herger***	Y	Y	Y	Y	Y	Y	N	N
3 Fazio	Y	Y	Y	Y	Y	N	Y	N
4 ***Doolittle***	Y	Y	Y	Y	Y	Y	N	N
5 Matsui	Y	Y	Y	Y	Y	Y	Y	N
6 Woolsey	+	+	+	Y	Y	Y	Y	N
7 Miller	?	?	?	?	?	?	?	?
8 Pelosi	Y	Y	Y	Y	Y	Y	Y	N
9 Dellums	Y	Y	Y	Y	Y	Y	Y	N
10 Tauscher	Y	Y	Y	Y	Y	Y	Y	N
11 ***Pombo***	?	?	?	?	?	?	?	?
12 Lantos	Y	Y	Y	Y	Y	Y	Y	N
13 Stark	Y	Y	Y	Y	Y	Y	Y	Y
14 Eshoo	Y	Y	Y	Y	Y	Y	Y	N
15 ***Campbell***	Y	Y	Y	Y	Y	Y	N	N
16 Lofgren	Y	Y	Y	Y	Y	Y	N	N
17 Farr	Y	Y	Y	Y	Y	Y	Y	Y
18 Condit	Y	Y	Y	Y	Y	Y	Y	Y
19 ***Radanovich***	Y	Y	Y	Y	Y	Y	N	N
20 Dooley	Y	Y	Y	Y	Y	Y	N	N
21 ***Thomas***	Y	Y	Y	Y	Y	Y	N	N
22 Capps	?	Y	Y	Y	Y	Y	Y	N
23 ***Gallegly***	Y	Y	Y	Y	Y	Y	N	N
24 Sherman	Y	Y	Y	Y	Y	Y	N	N
25 ***McKeon***	Y	Y	Y	Y	Y	Y	N	N
26 Berman	Y	Y	Y	Y	Y	Y	Y	N
27 ***Rogan***	Y	Y	Y	Y	Y	Y	N	N
28 ***Dreier***	Y	Y	Y	Y	Y	Y	N	N
29 Waxman	Y	Y	Y	Y	Y	Y	Y	Y
30 Becerra	Y	Y	Y	Y	Y	Y	Y	N
31 Martinez	Y	Y	Y	Y	Y	Y	Y	N
32 Dixon	Y	Y	Y	Y	Y	Y	?	N
33 Roybal-Allard	Y	Y	Y	Y	Y	Y	Y	N
34 Torres	Y	Y	Y	Y	Y	Y	Y	N
35 Waters	Y	Y	Y	Y	Y	N	Y	N
36 Harman	Y	Y	Y	Y	Y	Y	N	N
37 Millender-McD.	Y	Y	Y	Y	Y	Y	Y	Y
38 ***Horn***	Y	Y	Y	Y	Y	Y	N	N
39 ***Royce***	Y	Y	Y	Y	Y	Y	?	N
40 ***Lewis***	Y	Y	Y	Y	Y	?	N	N
41 ***Kim***	Y	Y	Y	Y	Y	Y	N	N
42 Brown	Y	Y	Y	Y	Y	N	?	Y
43 ***Calvert***	Y	Y	Y	Y	Y	Y	N	N
44 ***Bono***	Y	Y	Y	Y	Y	Y	?	N
45 ***Rohrabacher***	Y	Y	Y	Y	Y	Y	N	N
46 Sanchez	Y	Y	Y	Y	Y	Y	Y	N
47 ***Cox***	Y	Y	Y	Y	Y	Y	N	N
48 ***Packard***	Y	Y	Y	Y	Y	Y	N	N
49 ***Bilbray***	Y	Y	?	?	Y	Y	N	N
50 Filner	Y	Y	Y	Y	Y	N	Y	Y
51 ***Cunningham***	Y	Y	Y	Y	Y	Y	N	N
52 ***Hunter***	Y	Y	Y	Y	Y	Y	N	N
COLORADO								
1 DeGette	Y	Y	Y	Y	Y	Y	?	?
2 Skaggs	Y	Y	Y	Y	Y	Y	Y	N
3 ***McInnis***	Y	Y	Y	Y	Y	Y	N	N
4 ***Schaffer***	Y	Y	Y	Y	Y	N	N	N
5 ***Hefley***	Y	Y	Y	Y	N	N	N	N
6 ***Schaefer***	Y	Y	Y	Y	Y	Y	N	N
CONNECTICUT								
1 Kennelly	Y	Y	Y	Y	Y	Y	Y	N
2 Gejdenson	Y	Y	Y	Y	Y	Y	Y	N
3 DeLauro	Y	Y	Y	Y	Y	Y	Y	N
4 ***Shays***	Y	Y	Y	Y	Y	Y	N	N
5 Maloney	Y	Y	Y	Y	Y	Y	Y	N
6 ***Johnson***	Y	Y	Y	Y	Y	Y	N	N
DELAWARE								
AL ***Castle***	Y	Y	Y	Y	Y	Y	N	N
FLORIDA								
1 ***Scarborough***	Y	Y	Y	Y	Y	Y	N	N
2 Boyd	Y	Y	Y	Y	Y	Y	N	N
3 Brown	Y	Y	Y	Y	Y	Y	Y	N
4 ***Fowler***	Y	Y	Y	Y	Y	Y	N	Y
5 Thurman	Y	Y	Y	Y	Y	Y	N	N
6 ***Stearns***	Y	Y	Y	Y	Y	N	N	N
7 ***Mica***	+	+	+	+	Y	Y	N	N
8 ***McCollum***	Y	Y	Y	Y	Y	Y	N	N
9 ***Bilirakis***	Y	Y	Y	Y	Y	Y	N	N
10 ***Young***	Y	Y	Y	Y	Y	Y	N	N
11 Davis	Y	Y	Y	Y	Y	Y	N	N
12 ***Canady***	Y	Y	Y	Y	Y	Y	N	N
13 ***Miller***	Y	Y	Y	Y	Y	Y	N	N
14 ***Goss***	Y	Y	Y	Y	Y	Y	N	N
15 ***Weldon***	Y	Y	Y	Y	Y	Y	N	N
16 ***Foley***	Y	Y	Y	Y	Y	Y	N	N
17 Meek	Y	Y	Y	Y	Y	Y	Y	N
18 ***Ros-Lehtinen***	+	+	+	+	Y	Y	N	N
19 Wexler	Y	Y	Y	Y	Y	Y	Y	N
20 Deutsch	+	+	Y	Y	Y	Y	N	N
21 ***Diaz-Balart***	?	Y	Y	Y	Y	Y	?	N
22 ***Shaw***	Y	Y	Y	Y	Y	Y	N	N
23 Hastings	Y	Y	Y	Y	Y	N	Y	Y
GEORGIA								
1 ***Kingston***	Y	Y	Y	Y	Y	Y	N	N
2 Bishop	Y	Y	Y	Y	Y	Y	Y	N
3 ***Collins***	Y	Y	Y	Y	Y	Y	N	N
4 McKinney	Y	Y	Y	Y	Y	Y	N	N
5 Lewis	Y	Y	Y	Y	Y	N	Y	N
6 ***Gingrich***								
7 ***Barr***	Y	Y	Y	Y	Y	Y	N	N
8 ***Chambliss***	Y	Y	Y	Y	Y	Y	N	N
9 ***Deal***	Y	Y	Y	Y	Y	Y	N	N
10 ***Norwood***	Y	Y	Y	Y	Y	Y	N	N
11 ***Linder***	Y	Y	Y	Y	Y	Y	N	N
HAWAII								
1 Abercrombie	Y	Y	Y	Y	Y	N	N	N
2 Mink	Y	Y	Y	Y	Y	Y	Y	Y
IDAHO								
1 ***Chenoweth***	Y	Y	Y	Y	Y	N	N	N
2 ***Crapo***	Y	Y	Y	Y	Y	Y	N	N
ILLINOIS								
1 Rush	Y	Y	Y	Y	Y	Y	Y	N
2 Jackson	Y	Y	Y	Y	Y	Y	N	N
3 Lipinski	?	?	?	?	?	?	?	?
4 Gutierrez	Y	Y	Y	Y	Y	Y	N	N
5 Blagojevich	Y	Y	Y	Y	Y	Y	N	N
6 ***Hyde***	Y	Y	Y	Y	Y	Y	N	N
7 Davis	Y	Y	Y	Y	Y	N	Y	N
8 ***Crane***	Y	Y	Y	Y	Y	Y	?	N
9 Yates	Y	Y	Y	Y	Y	Y	N	N
10 ***Porter***	Y	Y	Y	Y	Y	Y	N	N
11 ***Weller***	Y	Y	Y	Y	Y	N	N	N
12 Costello	Y	Y	Y	Y	Y	Y	N	N
13 ***Fawell***	Y	Y	Y	Y	Y	?	N	N
14 ***Hastert***	Y	Y	Y	Y	Y	Y	N	N
15 ***Ewing***	Y	Y	Y	Y	Y	Y	N	N

ND Northern Democrats SD Southern Democrats

	204	205	206	207	208	209	210	211
16 ***Manzullo***	Y	Y	Y	Y	Y	Y	N	N
17 Evans	Y	Y	Y	Y	Y	Y	Y	N
18 ***LaHood***	Y	Y	Y	+	Y	Y	N	N
19 Poshard	Y	Y	Y	Y	Y	N	N	N
20 ***Shimkus***	Y	Y	Y	Y	Y	Y	N	N
INDIANA								
1 Visclosky	Y	Y	Y	Y	Y	Y	N	N
2 ***McIntosh***	Y	Y	Y	Y	Y	Y	N	N
3 Roemer	Y	Y	Y	Y	Y	Y	N	N
4 ***Souder***	Y	Y	Y	Y	Y	Y	N	N
5 ***Buyer***	Y	Y	Y	Y	Y	Y	N	N
6 ***Burton***	Y	Y	Y	Y	Y	Y	N	N
7 ***Pease***	Y	Y	Y	Y	Y	Y	N	N
8 ***Hostettler***	Y	Y	Y	Y	Y	Y	N	N
9 Hamilton	Y	Y	Y	Y	Y	Y	N	N
10 Carson	Y	Y	Y	Y	Y	Y	Y	N
IOWA								
1 ***Leach***	Y	Y	Y	Y	Y	Y	N	N
2 ***Nussle***	Y	Y	Y	Y	Y	Y	N	N
3 Boswell	Y	Y	Y	Y	Y	Y	N	N
4 ***Ganske***	Y	Y	Y	Y	Y	Y	N	N
5 ***Latham***	Y	Y	Y	Y	Y	Y	N	N
KANSAS								
1 ***Moran***	Y	Y	Y	Y	Y	Y	N	N
2 ***Ryun***	Y	Y	Y	Y	Y	Y	N	N
3 ***Snowbarger***	Y	Y	Y	Y	Y	Y	N	N
4 ***Tiahrt***	Y	Y	Y	Y	Y	N	N	N
KENTUCKY								
1 ***Whitfield***	Y	Y	Y	Y	Y	Y	N	N
2 ***Lewis***	Y	Y	Y	Y	Y	Y	N	N
3 ***Northup***	Y	Y	Y	Y	Y	Y	N	N
4 ***Bunning***	Y	Y	Y	Y	Y	Y	N	N
5 ***Rogers***	Y	Y	Y	Y	Y	Y	N	N
6 Baesler	Y	Y	Y	Y	Y	Y	N	N
LOUISIANA								
1 ***Livingston***	Y	Y	Y	Y	Y	Y	N	N
2 Jefferson	?	?	?	?	Y	Y	Y	N
3 ***Tauzin***	Y	Y	Y	Y	Y	Y	N	N
4 ***McCrery***	Y	Y	Y	Y	Y	Y	N	N
5 ***Cooksey***	Y	Y	Y	Y	Y	Y	N	N
6 ***Baker***	Y	Y	Y	Y	Y	Y	N	N
7 John	Y	Y	Y	Y	Y	Y	Y	Y
MAINE								
1 Allen	Y	Y	Y	Y	Y	Y	N	N
2 Baldacci	Y	Y	Y	Y	Y	Y	N	N
MARYLAND								
1 ***Gilchrest***	Y	Y	Y	Y	Y	Y	N	N
2 ***Ehrlich***	Y	Y	Y	Y	Y	Y	N	N
3 Cardin	?	?	?	?	Y	Y	N	N
4 Wynn	Y	Y	Y	Y	Y	Y	Y	N
5 Hoyer	Y	Y	Y	Y	Y	Y	Y	N
6 ***Bartlett***	Y	Y	Y	Y	Y	Y	N	N
7 Cummings	Y	Y	Y	Y	Y	Y	N	N
8 ***Morella***	Y	Y	Y	Y	Y	Y	N	N
MASSACHUSETTS								
1 Olver	Y	Y	Y	Y	Y	Y	Y	N
2 Neal	Y	Y	Y	Y	Y	Y	Y	N
3 McGovern	Y	Y	Y	Y	Y	Y	Y	N
4 Frank	Y	Y	Y	Y	Y	Y	Y	N
5 Meehan	Y	Y	Y	Y	Y	Y	?	N
6 Tierney	Y	Y	Y	Y	Y	Y	Y	N
7 Markey	Y	Y	Y	Y	Y	Y	Y	?
8 Kennedy	Y	Y	Y	Y	Y	Y	Y	N
9 Moakley	Y	Y	Y	Y	Y	Y	Y	N
10 Delahunt	Y	Y	Y	Y	Y	Y	Y	N
MICHIGAN								
1 Stupak	Y	Y	Y	Y	Y	N	Y	N
2 ***Hoekstra***	Y	Y	Y	Y	Y	Y	N	N
3 ***Ehlers***	Y	Y	Y	Y	Y	Y	N	N
4 ***Camp***	Y	Y	Y	Y	Y	Y	?	N
5 Barcia	Y	Y	Y	Y	Y	Y	Y	N
6 ***Upton***	Y	Y	Y	Y	Y	Y	N	N
7 ***Smith***	Y	Y	Y	Y	+	Y	N	N
8 Stabenow	Y	Y	Y	Y	Y	Y	Y	N
9 Kildee	Y	Y	Y	Y	Y	Y	N	N
10 Bonior	Y	Y	Y	Y	Y	Y	Y	N
11 ***Knollenberg***	Y	Y	Y	Y	Y	Y	N	N
12 Levin	Y	Y	Y	Y	Y	Y	Y	N
13 Rivers	Y	Y	Y	Y	Y	Y	N	N
14 Conyers	Y	Y	Y	Y	Y	Y	Y	Y
15 Kilpatrick	Y	Y	Y	Y	Y	Y	Y	N
16 Dingell	Y	Y	Y	Y	Y	Y	Y	Y
MINNESOTA								
1 ***Gutknecht***	Y	Y	Y	Y	Y	Y	N	N
2 Minge	Y	Y	Y	Y	Y	Y	N	N

	204	205	206	207	208	209	210	211
3 ***Ramstad***	Y	Y	Y	Y	Y	N	N	N
4 Vento	Y	Y	Y	Y	Y	Y	Y	N
5 Sabo	Y	Y	Y	Y	Y	N	N	N
6 Luther	Y	Y	Y	Y	Y	Y	N	N
7 Peterson	Y	Y	Y	Y	Y	Y	N	N
8 Oberstar	Y	Y	Y	Y	Y	N	?	Y
MISSISSIPPI								
1 ***Wicker***	Y	Y	Y	Y	Y	Y	N	N
2 Thompson	Y	Y	Y	Y	Y	N	Y	N
3 ***Pickering***	Y	Y	Y	Y	Y	Y	N	N
4 ***Parker***	Y	Y	Y	Y	Y	Y	N	N
5 Taylor	Y	Y	Y	Y	N	N	N	N
MISSOURI								
1 Clay	Y	Y	Y	Y	Y	N	Y	N
2 ***Talent***	Y	Y	Y	Y	Y	Y	N	N
3 Gephardt	Y	Y	Y	Y	Y	N	Y	?
4 Skelton	Y	Y	Y	Y	Y	Y	N	N
5 McCarthy	Y	Y	Y	Y	Y	Y	Y	N
6 Danner	Y	Y	Y	Y	Y	Y	N	N
7 ***Blunt***	Y	Y	Y	Y	Y	Y	N	N
8 ***Emerson***	Y	Y	Y	Y	Y	Y	N	N
9 ***Hulshof***	Y	Y	Y	Y	Y	N	N	N
MONTANA								
AL ***Hill***	Y	Y	Y	Y	Y	?	N	N
NEBRASKA								
1 ***Bereuter***	Y	Y	Y	Y	Y	Y	N	N
2 ***Christensen***	Y	Y	Y	Y	Y	Y	N	N
3 ***Barrett***	Y	Y	Y	Y	Y	Y	N	N
NEVADA								
1 ***Ensign***	?	Y	Y	Y	Y	N	N	N
2 ***Gibbons***	Y	Y	Y	Y	Y	N	N	N
NEW HAMPSHIRE								
1 ***Sununu***	Y	Y	Y	Y	Y	N	N	N
2 ***Bass***	Y	Y	Y	Y	Y	Y	N	N
NEW JERSEY								
1 Andrews	Y	Y	Y	Y	?	?	Y	N
2 ***LoBiondo***	Y	Y	Y	Y	Y	N	N	N
3 ***Saxton***	Y	Y	Y	Y	Y	Y	N	N
4 ***Smith***	Y	Y	Y	Y	?	?	N	N
5 ***Roukema***	Y	Y	Y	Y	Y	Y	N	N
6 Pallone	Y	Y	Y	Y	Y	Y	Y	N
7 ***Franks***	Y	Y	Y	Y	Y	Y	N	N
8 Pascrell	Y	Y	Y	Y	Y	N	N	N
9 Rothman	Y	Y	Y	Y	Y	Y	N	N
10 Payne	Y	Y	Y	Y	Y	Y	Y	N
11 ***Frelinghuysen***	Y	Y	Y	Y	Y	Y	N	N
12 ***Pappas***	Y	Y	Y	Y	Y	Y	N	N
13 Menendez	Y	Y	Y	Y	Y	Y	N	N
NEW MEXICO								
1 ***Schiff***	?	?	?	?	?	?	?	?
2 ***Skeen***	Y	Y	Y	Y	Y	Y	N	N
3 ***Redmond***	Y	Y	Y	Y	Y	Y	N	N
NEW YORK								
1 ***Forbes***	Y	Y	Y	Y	Y	Y	Y	Y
2 ***Lazio***	Y	Y	Y	Y	Y	Y	N	N
3 ***King***	Y	Y	Y	Y	Y	Y	N	Y
4 McCarthy	Y	Y	Y	Y	Y	Y	N	Y
5 Ackerman	Y	Y	Y	Y	Y	Y	Y	Y
6 Flake	Y	Y	?	Y	Y	Y	?	?
7 Manton	Y	Y	Y	Y	Y	Y	?	?
8 Nadler	Y	Y	Y	Y	Y	Y	Y	N
9 Schumer	Y	Y	Y	Y	Y	Y	Y	N
10 Towns	?	?	?	?	Y	Y	Y	Y
11 Owens	Y	Y	Y	Y	Y	Y	Y	N
12 Velázquez	Y	Y	Y	Y	Y	Y	Y	N
13 ***Molinari***	Y	Y	Y	Y	Y	Y	?	N
14 Maloney	Y	Y	Y	Y	Y	N	Y	N
15 Rangel	Y	Y	Y	Y	Y	Y	Y	N
16 Serrano	Y	Y	Y	Y	Y	Y	Y	N
17 Engel	Y	Y	Y	Y	Y	Y	+	Y
18 Lowey	?	?	?	?	Y	Y	N	N
19 ***Kelly***	Y	Y	Y	Y	Y	N	N	N
20 ***Gilman***	Y	Y	Y	Y	Y	Y	N	N
21 McNulty	Y	Y	Y	Y	Y	N	Y	Y
22 ***Solomon***	Y	Y	Y	Y	Y	N	N	N
23 ***Boehlert***	Y	Y	Y	Y	Y	Y	N	N
24 ***McHugh***	Y	Y	Y	Y	Y	Y	N	N
25 ***Walsh***	Y	Y	Y	Y	Y	?	N	N
26 Hinchey	Y	Y	Y	Y	Y	Y	Y	Y
27 ***Paxon***	Y	Y	Y	Y	Y	Y	N	N
28 Slaughter	Y	Y	Y	Y	Y	Y	Y	N
29 LaFalce	Y	Y	Y	Y	Y	Y	Y	Y
30 ***Quinn***	Y	Y	Y	Y	Y	Y	N	N
31 ***Houghton***	Y	Y	Y	Y	Y	Y	N	N

	204	205	206	207	208	209	210	211
NORTH CAROLINA								
1 Clayton	Y	Y	Y	Y	Y	Y	Y	N
2 Etheridge	Y	Y	Y	Y	Y	N	Y	N
3 ***Jones***	Y	Y	Y	Y	Y	Y	N	N
4 Price	Y	Y	Y	Y	Y	Y	N	N
5 ***Burr***	Y	?	Y	Y	Y	?	N	N
6 ***Coble***	Y	Y	N	Y	Y	Y	N	N
7 McIntyre	Y	Y	Y	Y	Y	Y	Y	N
8 Hefner	Y	Y	Y	Y	Y	Y	Y	N
9 ***Myrick***	Y	Y	Y	Y	Y	Y	N	N
10 ***Ballenger***	Y	Y	Y	Y	Y	Y	N	N
11 ***Taylor***	Y	Y	Y	Y	Y	Y	N	N
12 Watt	Y	Y	Y	Y	Y	Y	Y	N
NORTH DAKOTA								
AL Pomeroy	Y	Y	Y	Y	Y	Y	?	?
OHIO								
1 ***Chabot***	Y	Y	Y	Y	Y	Y	N	N
2 ***Portman***	Y	Y	Y	Y	Y	Y	N	N
3 Hall	Y	Y	Y	Y	Y	Y	Y	N
4 ***Oxley***	Y	Y	Y	Y	Y	Y	N	N
5 ***Gillmor***	Y	Y	Y	Y	Y	Y	N	N
6 Strickland	Y	Y	Y	Y	Y	Y	Y	N
7 ***Hobson***	Y	Y	Y	Y	Y	Y	N	N
8 ***Boehner***	Y	Y	Y	Y	Y	Y	N	N
9 Kaptur	Y	Y	Y	Y	Y	Y	Y	N
10 Kucinich	Y	Y	Y	Y	Y	N	N	N
11 Stokes	Y	Y	Y	Y	Y	Y	?	?
12 ***Kasich***	Y	Y	Y	Y	Y	Y	N	N
13 Brown	?	Y	Y	Y	Y	N	Y	N
14 Sawyer	Y	Y	Y	Y	Y	Y	N	N
15 ***Pryce***	Y	Y	Y	Y	Y	Y	N	N
16 ***Regula***	Y	Y	Y	Y	Y	Y	N	N
17 Traficant	Y	Y	Y	Y	Y	Y	N	N
18 ***Ney***	Y	Y	Y	Y	Y	N	N	N
19 ***LaTourette***	Y	Y	Y	Y	Y	Y	?	N
OKLAHOMA								
1 ***Largent***	Y	Y	Y	Y	?	?	N	N
2 ***Coburn***	Y	Y	Y	Y	Y	N	N	N
3 ***Watkins***	Y	Y	Y	Y	Y	Y	N	N
4 ***Watts***	Y	Y	Y	Y	Y	Y	N	N
5 ***Istook***	Y	Y	Y	Y	Y	Y	?	?
6 ***Lucas***	Y	Y	Y	Y	Y	?	N	N
OREGON								
1 Furse	Y	Y	Y	Y	Y	Y	Y	N
2 ***Smith***	Y	Y	Y	Y	Y	Y	N	N
3 Blumenauer	Y	Y	Y	Y	Y	Y	Y	N
4 DeFazio	Y	Y	Y	Y	Y	N	Y	N
5 Hooley	Y	Y	Y	Y	Y	Y	N	N
PENNSYLVANIA								
1 Foglietta	Y	Y	Y	Y	Y	Y	N	N
2 Fattah	Y	Y	Y	Y	Y	Y	?	?
3 Borski	Y	Y	Y	Y	Y	N	N	N
4 Klink	Y	Y	Y	Y	Y	Y	Y	?
5 ***Peterson***	Y	+	Y	Y	Y	Y	N	N
6 Holden	Y	Y	Y	Y	Y	Y	?	N
7 ***Weldon***	Y	Y	Y	Y	Y	Y	?	N
8 ***Greenwood***	Y	Y	Y	Y	Y	Y	N	N
9 ***Shuster***	Y	Y	Y	Y	Y	Y	N	N
10 ***McDade***	?	?	?	?	Y	Y	N	N
11 Kanjorski	Y	Y	Y	Y	Y	Y	N	N
12 Murtha	Y	Y	Y	Y	Y	?	N	N
13 ***Fox***	Y	Y	Y	Y	Y	N	N	N
14 Coyne	Y	Y	Y	Y	Y	Y	Y	N
15 McHale	Y	Y	Y	Y	Y	Y	N	N
16 ***Pitts***	Y	Y	Y	Y	Y	Y	N	N
17 ***Gekas***	Y	Y	?	Y	Y	?	N	N
18 Doyle	Y	Y	Y	Y	Y	Y	N	N
19 ***Goodling***	Y	Y	Y	Y	Y	Y	N	?
20 Mascara	Y	Y	Y	Y	Y	Y	N	N
21 ***English***	Y	Y	Y	Y	Y	N	N	N
RHODE ISLAND								
1 Kennedy	Y	Y	Y	Y	Y	Y	Y	N
2 Weygand	Y	Y	Y	Y	Y	Y	Y	N
SOUTH CAROLINA								
1 ***Sanford***	Y	Y	Y	Y	Y	Y	N	N
2 ***Spence***	Y	Y	Y	Y	Y	Y	N	N
3 ***Graham***	?	Y	Y	Y	Y	Y	N	N
4 ***Inglis***	Y	Y	Y	Y	Y	Y	N	N
5 Spratt	Y	Y	Y	Y	Y	Y	N	N
6 Clyburn	Y	Y	Y	Y	Y	Y	?	N
SOUTH DAKOTA								
AL ***Thune***	Y	Y	Y	Y	Y	Y	N	N
TENNESSEE								
1 ***Jenkins***	Y	Y	Y	Y	Y	Y	N	N
2 ***Duncan***	Y	Y	Y	Y	Y	Y	N	N

	204	205	206	207	208	209	210	
3 ***Wamp***	Y	Y	Y	Y	Y	N	N	N
4 ***Hilleary***	Y	Y	Y	Y	Y	N	N	N
5 Clement	Y	Y	Y	Y	Y	Y	N	N
6 Gordon	Y	Y	Y	Y	Y	?	N	N
7 ***Bryant***	Y	Y	Y	Y	Y	Y	N	N
8 Tanner	Y	Y	Y	Y	Y	Y	N	N
9 Ford	Y	Y	Y	Y	Y	Y	Y	N
TEXAS								
1 Sandlin	Y	Y	Y	Y	Y	Y	Y	N
2 Turner	Y	Y	Y	Y	Y	Y	Y	N
3 ***Johnson, Sam***	Y	Y	Y	Y	Y	Y	N	N
4 Hall	Y	Y	Y	Y	Y	Y	N	N
5 ***Sessions***	Y	Y	Y	Y	Y	Y	N	N
6 ***Barton***	Y	Y	Y	Y	?	?	N	N
7 ***Archer***	Y	Y	Y	Y	Y	Y	N	N
8 ***Brady***	Y	Y	Y	Y	Y	Y	N	N
9 Lampson	Y	Y	Y	Y	Y	Y	Y	N
10 Doggett	Y	Y	Y	Y	Y	Y	Y	N
11 Edwards	Y	Y	Y	Y	Y	Y	N	N
12 ***Granger***	Y	?	Y	Y	Y	Y	N	N
13 ***Thornberry***	Y	Y	Y	Y	Y	Y	N	N
14 ***Paul***	Y	Y	N	Y	N	Y	N	N
15 Hinojosa	Y	Y	Y	Y	Y	Y	Y	N
16 Reyes	Y	Y	Y	Y	Y	Y	Y	N
17 Stenholm	Y	Y	Y	Y	Y	Y	N	N
18 Jackson-Lee	Y	Y	Y	Y	Y	Y	Y	N
19 ***Combest***	Y	Y	Y	Y	Y	Y	N	N
20 Gonzalez	Y	Y	Y	Y	Y	Y	N	N
21 ***Smith***	Y	Y	Y	Y	Y	Y	N	N
22 ***DeLay***	?	Y	N	Y	Y	Y	N	N
23 ***Bonilla***	Y	Y	Y	Y	Y	Y	N	N
24 Frost	Y	Y	Y	Y	Y	N	Y	N
25 Bentsen	Y	Y	Y	Y	Y	Y	Y	N
26 ***Armey***	Y	Y	Y	Y	Y	?	N	N
27 Ortiz	Y	Y	Y	Y	Y	Y	N	N
28 Rodriguez	Y	Y	Y	Y	Y	Y	Y	N
29 Green	Y	Y	?	Y	Y	Y	N	N
30 Johnson, E.B.	Y	Y	Y	Y	Y	Y	Y	N
UTAH								
1 ***Hansen***	Y	Y	Y	Y	Y	Y	Y	N
2 ***Cook***	Y	Y	Y	Y	Y	Y	N	N
3 ***Cannon***	Y	Y	Y	Y	Y	Y	N	N
VERMONT								
AL *Sanders*	Y	Y	Y	Y	Y	Y	Y	N
VIRGINIA								
1 ***Bateman***	Y	Y	Y	Y	Y	Y	N	N
2 Pickett	Y	Y	Y	Y	Y	N	Y	N
3 Scott	Y	Y	Y	Y	Y	Y	Y	N
4 Sisisky	Y	Y	Y	Y	Y	Y	Y	N
5 Goode	Y	Y	Y	Y	Y	Y	N	N
6 ***Goodlatte***	Y	Y	Y	Y	Y	Y	N	N
7 ***Bliley***	Y	Y	Y	Y	Y	Y	N	N
8 Moran	+	+	+	+	Y	Y	Y	Y
9 Boucher	Y	Y	Y	Y	Y	Y	Y	N
10 ***Wolf***	Y	Y	Y	Y	Y	Y	N	N
11 ***Davis***	Y	Y	Y	Y	Y	Y	N	N
WASHINGTON								
1 ***White***	Y	Y	Y	Y	Y	Y	N	N
2 ***Metcalf***	Y	Y	Y	Y	Y	N	N	N
3 ***Smith, Linda***	Y	Y	Y	Y	Y	N	N	N
4 ***Hastings***	Y	Y	Y	Y	Y	Y	N	N
5 ***Nethercutt***	Y	Y	Y	Y	Y	Y	N	N
6 Dicks	Y	Y	Y	Y	Y	Y	N	N
7 McDermott	Y	Y	Y	Y	Y	N	Y	N
8 ***Dunn***	Y	Y	Y	Y	Y	Y	N	N
9 Smith, Adam	Y	Y	Y	Y	Y	Y	Y	?
WEST VIRGINIA								
1 Mollohan	Y	Y	Y	Y	Y	Y	N	N
2 Wise	Y	Y	Y	Y	Y	Y	Y	?
3 Rahall	Y	Y	Y	Y	Y	Y	N	N
WISCONSIN								
1 ***Neumann***	Y	Y	Y	Y	Y	Y	N	N
2 ***Klug***	Y	Y	Y	Y	Y	Y	N	?
3 Kind	Y	Y	Y	Y	Y	Y	N	N
4 Kleczka	Y	Y	Y	Y	Y	Y	?	N
5 Barrett	Y	Y	Y	Y	Y	Y	Y	N
6 ***Petri***	Y	Y	Y	Y	Y	Y	N	N
7 Obey	Y	Y	Y	Y	Y	Y	Y	Y
8 Johnson	Y	Y	Y	Y	Y	Y	Y	N
9 ***Sensenbrenner***	Y	Y	Y	Y	Y	Y	N	N
WYOMING								
AL ***Cubin***	Y	Y	Y	Y	Y	Y	N	N

Southern states - Ala., Ark., Fla., Ga., Ky., La., Miss., N.C., Okla., S.C., Tenn., Texas, Va.

HOUSE VOTES 212, 213, 214, 215, 216, 217

212. HR 1119. Fiscal 1998 Defense Authorization/Additional Amendments and Debate. Solomon, R-N.Y., amendment to the rule (H Res 169) to allow House floor consideration of certain additional amendments to and additional general debate on the bill to authorize $268.2 billion for defense programs in fiscal 1998. Adopted 329-94: R 146-76; D 182-18 (ND 139-7, SD 43-11); I 1-0, June 19, 1997.

213. HR 1119. Fiscal 1998 Defense Authorization/Rule. Adoption of the resolution (H Res 169) to provide House floor consideration of the bill to authorize $268.2 billion for defense programs in fiscal 1998. The bill authorizes $2.6 billion more than requested by the president. Adopted 322-101: R 176-46; D 146-54 (ND 115-30, SD 31-24); I 0-1, June 19, 1997.

214. HR 1119. Fiscal 1998 Defense Authorization/Overall Spending Cut. Sanders, I-Vt., amendment to cut the bill's overall authorization for defense programs by 5 percent in fiscal 1998, reducing it by $13.5 billion to a total of $254.8 billion. Rejected 89-332: R 13-211; D 75-121 (ND 68-73, SD 7-48); I 1-0, June 19, 1997.

215. HR 1119. Fiscal 1998 Defense Authorization/Defense Operations Reform. Spence, R-S.C., amendment to direct organizational, structural, business practice and acquisition reforms at the Defense Department, including a reduction of 124,000 in the agency's acquisition work force by fiscal 2002. It also would impose a 25 percent reduction in military headquarters staff by fiscal 2002, with a 10 percent reduction in fiscal 1998. Adopted 405-14: R 220-3; D 184-11 (ND 132-8, SD 52-3); I 1-0, June 19, 1997.

216. HR 1119. Fiscal 1998 Defense Authorization/Supercomputer Export Restrictions. Spence, R-S.C., amendment to restrict any export or re-export of U.S. supercomputers to countries that may violate non-proliferation agreements without the prior written approval of the Commerce, Defense, Energy and State departments and the Arms Control and Disarmament Agency. Adopted 332-88: R 195-29; D 136-59 (ND 92-48, SD 44-11); I 1-0, June 19, 1997.

217. HR 1119. Fiscal 1998 Defense Authorization/Overseas Military Hospital Abortions. Harman, D-Calif., amendment to repeal current law prohibiting overseas U.S. military hospitals and medical facilities from performing privately funded abortions for U.S. service members and their dependents. Rejected 196-224: R 34-189; D 161-35 (ND 114-27, SD 47-8); I 1-0, June 19, 1997. A "yea" was a vote in support of the president's position.

KEY

- Y Voted for (yea).
- # Paired for.
- + Announced for.
- N Voted against (nay).
- X Paired against.
- – Announced against.
- P Voted "present."
- C Voted "present" to avoid possible conflict of interest.
- ? Did not vote or otherwise make a position known.

Democrats ***Republicans***
Independent

	212	213	214	215	216	217
ALABAMA						
1 ***Callahan***	Y	Y	N	Y	Y	N
2 ***Everett***	Y	Y	N	Y	Y	N
3 ***Riley***	N	N	N	Y	Y	N
4 ***Aderholt***	N	N	N	Y	Y	N
5 Cramer	Y	Y	N	Y	Y	Y
6 ***Bachus***	N	N	N	Y	Y	N
7 Hilliard	Y	N	Y	Y	Y	Y
ALASKA						
AL ***Young***	N	N	N	Y	Y	N
ARIZONA						
1 ***Salmon***	N	N	N	Y	Y	N
2 Pastor	Y	Y	N	Y	Y	Y
3 ***Stump***	Y	Y	N	Y	Y	N
4 ***Shadegg***	N	Y	N	Y	Y	N
5 ***Kolbe***	Y	Y	N	Y	Y	Y
6 ***Hayworth***	Y	Y	N	Y	Y	N
ARKANSAS						
1 Berry	Y	Y	N	Y	Y	N
2 Snyder	Y	Y	N	Y	Y	Y
3 ***Hutchinson***	Y	Y	N	Y	Y	N
4 ***Dickey***	Y	Y	N	Y	Y	N
CALIFORNIA						
1 ***Riggs***	Y	Y	N	Y	Y	N
2 ***Herger***	Y	Y	?	Y	Y	N
3 Fazio	Y	Y	N	Y	N	Y
4 ***Doolittle***	Y	Y	N	Y	N	N
5 Matsui	Y	Y	N	Y	N	Y
6 Woolsey	Y	Y	Y	Y	N	Y
7 Miller	?	?	?	?	?	?
8 Pelosi	Y	Y	Y	Y	Y	Y
9 Dellums	Y	Y	Y	Y	Y	Y
10 Tauscher	Y	Y	N	Y	N	Y
11 ***Pombo***	?	?	?	?	?	?
12 Lantos	Y	Y	N	Y	Y	Y
13 Stark	Y	Y	Y	?	?	?
14 Eshoo	Y	Y	Y	Y	N	Y
15 ***Campbell***	Y	Y	Y	Y	Y	Y
16 Lofgren	Y	N	Y	Y	N	Y
17 Farr	Y	Y	Y	Y	N	Y
18 Condit	N	N	N	Y	Y	Y
19 ***Radanovich***	Y	Y	N	Y	Y	N
20 Dooley	Y	Y	?	Y	N	Y
21 ***Thomas***	N	Y	N	Y	N	Y
22 Capps	Y	Y	Y	Y	N	Y
23 ***Gallegly***	Y	Y	N	Y	Y	N
24 Sherman	Y	Y	N	Y	N	Y
25 ***McKeon***	N	N	N	Y	Y	N
26 Berman	Y	Y	N	Y	Y	Y
27 ***Rogan***	Y	Y	N	Y	Y	N
28 ***Dreier***	Y	Y	N	?	N	N
29 Waxman	Y	Y	Y	Y	Y	Y
30 Becerra	Y	Y	Y	Y	Y	Y
31 Martinez	Y	Y	N	Y	Y	Y
32 Dixon	Y	Y	N	Y	Y	Y
33 Roybal-Allard	Y	Y	N	Y	Y	Y
34 Torres	Y	Y	+	+	+	+
35 Waters	Y	N	Y	Y	Y	Y
36 Harman	Y	Y	N	Y	N	Y
37 Millender-McD.	Y	N	Y	Y	Y	Y
38 ***Horn***	Y	Y	N	Y	Y	Y
39 ***Royce***	N	Y	Y	Y	Y	N
40 ***Lewis***	N	Y	N	Y	Y	N
41 ***Kim***	Y	Y	N	Y	Y	N
42 Brown	Y	Y	Y	Y	Y	Y
43 ***Calvert***	Y	Y	N	Y	Y	N
44 ***Bono***	Y	Y	N	Y	Y	Y
45 ***Rohrabacher***	Y	N	Y	Y	N	N
46 Sanchez	Y	Y	N	Y	N	Y
47 ***Cox***	N	N	N	Y	Y	N
48 ***Packard***	Y	Y	N	Y	Y	N
49 ***Bilbray***	N	Y	N	Y	N	N
50 Filner	N	N	Y	Y	N	Y
51 ***Cunningham***	N	Y	N	Y	Y	N
52 ***Hunter***	N	Y	N	Y	Y	N
COLORADO						
1 DeGette	?	?	?	?	?	?
2 Skaggs	Y	Y	N	Y	Y	Y
3 ***McInnis***	Y	Y	N	Y	Y	Y
4 ***Schaffer***	N	Y	N	Y	Y	N
5 ***Hefley***	N	Y	N	Y	Y	N
6 ***Schaefer***	Y	Y	N	Y	Y	N
CONNECTICUT						
1 Kennelly	Y	Y	N	Y	N	Y
2 Gejdenson	Y	Y	N	Y	N	Y
3 DeLauro	Y	Y	N	Y	N	Y
4 ***Shays***	Y	Y	Y	Y	N	Y
5 Maloney	Y	Y	N	Y	Y	Y
6 ***Johnson***	N	N	N	Y	Y	Y
DELAWARE						
AL ***Castle***	Y	Y	N	Y	Y	Y
FLORIDA						
1 ***Scarborough***	N	Y	N	Y	Y	N
2 Boyd	Y	Y	N	Y	Y	Y
3 Brown	N	N	N	Y	Y	Y
4 ***Fowler***	N	N	N	Y	Y	Y
5 Thurman	N	N	N	Y	Y	Y
6 ***Stearns***	N	N	N	Y	Y	N
7 ***Mica***	Y	Y	N	Y	Y	N
8 ***McCollum***	Y	Y	N	Y	Y	N
9 ***Bilirakis***	N	Y	N	Y	Y	N
10 ***Young***	Y	Y	N	Y	Y	N
11 Davis	N	N	N	Y	N	Y
12 ***Canady***	N	Y	N	Y	Y	N
13 ***Miller***	N	Y	N	Y	Y	Y
14 ***Goss***	Y	Y	N	Y	Y	N
15 ***Weldon***	N	Y	N	Y	Y	N
16 ***Foley***	Y	Y	N	Y	Y	Y
17 Meek	Y	Y	Y	Y	Y	Y
18 ***Ros-Lehtinen***	Y	Y	N	Y	N	N
19 Wexler	Y	Y	N	Y	Y	Y
20 Deutsch	N	N	N	Y	Y	Y
21 ***Diaz-Balart***	Y	Y	N	Y	Y	N
22 ***Shaw***	N	N	N	Y	Y	Y
23 Hastings	N	N	Y	Y	Y	Y
GEORGIA						
1 ***Kingston***	N	Y	N	Y	Y	N
2 Bishop	N	N	N	Y	Y	Y
3 ***Collins***	N	N	N	Y	Y	N
4 McKinney	Y	Y	Y	Y	Y	Y
5 Lewis	Y	N	Y	Y	Y	Y
6 ***Gingrich***						
7 ***Barr***	Y	Y	N	Y	Y	N
8 ***Chambliss***	N	N	N	Y	Y	N
9 ***Deal***	N	N	N	Y	Y	N
10 ***Norwood***	N	N	N	Y	Y	N
11 ***Linder***	Y	Y	N	Y	Y	N
HAWAII						
1 Abercrombie	Y	Y	N	Y	Y	Y
2 Mink	Y	Y	Y	Y	Y	Y
IDAHO						
1 ***Chenoweth***	N	N	N	Y	Y	N
2 ***Crapo***	Y	N	N	Y	Y	N
ILLINOIS						
1 Rush	Y	N	Y	Y	Y	Y
2 Jackson	Y	Y	Y	N	N	Y
3 Lipinski	?	?	?	?	?	?
4 Gutierrez	Y	Y	Y	Y	Y	Y
5 Blagojevich	Y	Y	N	Y	Y	Y
6 ***Hyde***	Y	Y	N	Y	Y	N
7 Davis	Y	N	Y	N	Y	Y
8 ***Crane***	Y	Y	N	Y	Y	N
9 Yates	Y	N	Y	?	#	?
10 ***Porter***	Y	Y	N	Y	Y	Y
11 ***Weller***	N	N	N	Y	Y	N
12 Costello	Y	Y	N	Y	Y	N
13 ***Fawell***	Y	Y	N	Y	Y	Y
14 ***Hastert***	Y	Y	N	Y	Y	N
15 ***Ewing***	N	Y	N	Y	Y	N

ND Northern Democrats SD Southern Democrats

	212	213	214	215	216	217
16 **Manzullo**	Y	Y	N	Y	N	N
17 Evans	N	N	Y	N	Y	Y
18 **LaHood**	Y	Y	N	Y	Y	N
19 Poshard	Y	Y	N	Y	Y	N
20 **Shimkus**	N	N	N	Y	Y	N
INDIANA						
1 Visclosky	Y	Y	N	Y	Y	Y
2 **McIntosh**	Y	Y	N	Y	Y	N
3 Roemer	N	N	N	Y	Y	N
4 **Souder**	N	Y	N	Y	Y	N
5 **Buyer**	Y	Y	N	Y	Y	N
6 **Burton**	Y	Y	N	Y	Y	N
7 **Pease**	N	Y	N	Y	Y	N
8 **Hostettler**	N	N	N	Y	Y	N
9 Hamilton	Y	Y	N	Y	N	N
10 Carson	Y	Y	Y	Y	Y	Y
IOWA						
1 **Leach**	Y	Y	N	Y	Y	Y
2 **Nussle**	Y	Y	N	Y	Y	N
3 Boswell	Y	Y	N	Y	Y	Y
4 **Ganske**	Y	Y	N	Y	Y	N
5 **Latham**	Y	Y	N	Y	Y	N
KANSAS						
1 **Moran**	N	N	N	Y	Y	N
2 **Ryun**	N	Y	N	Y	Y	N
3 **Snowbarger**	N	N	N	Y	Y	N
4 **Tiahrt**	N	N	N	Y	Y	N
KENTUCKY						
1 **Whitfield**	?	?	N	Y	Y	N
2 **Lewis**	Y	Y	N	Y	Y	N
3 **Northup**	Y	Y	N	Y	Y	N
4 **Bunning**	N	Y	N	Y	Y	N
5 **Rogers**	N	Y	N	Y	Y	N
6 Baesler	Y	N	N	Y	Y	Y
LOUISIANA						
1 **Livingston**	Y	Y	N	Y	Y	N
2 Jefferson	N	Y	N	Y	Y	Y
3 **Tauzin**	N	Y	N	Y	Y	N
4 **McCrery**	Y	Y	N	Y	Y	N
5 **Cooksey**	Y	N	N	Y	Y	N
6 **Baker**	Y	Y	N	Y	Y	N
7 John	Y	Y	N	Y	Y	N
MAINE						
1 Allen	Y	Y	N	Y	Y	Y
2 Baldacci	Y	Y	N	Y	Y	Y
MARYLAND						
1 **Gilchrest**	Y	Y	Y	Y	Y	Y
2 **Ehrlich**	Y	Y	N	Y	Y	Y
3 Cardin	Y	N	N	Y	Y	Y
4 Wynn	Y	N	N	Y	Y	Y
5 Hoyer	Y	N	N	Y	Y	Y
6 **Bartlett**	N	N	N	N	N	N
7 Cummings	Y	Y	Y	Y	Y	Y
8 **Morella**	Y	Y	N	Y	Y	Y
MASSACHUSETTS						
1 Olver	Y	Y	Y	Y	N	Y
2 Neal	Y	Y	Y	N	N	Y
3 McGovern	Y	Y	Y	N	N	Y
4 Frank	Y	Y	Y	Y	N	Y
5 Meehan	Y	Y	Y	Y	N	Y
6 Tierney	Y	Y	Y	Y	N	Y
7 Markey	Y	N	Y	Y	Y	Y
8 Kennedy	Y	Y	Y	Y	N	Y
9 Moakley	Y	Y	N	N	N	N
10 Delahunt	Y	Y	Y	Y	N	Y
MICHIGAN						
1 Stupak	Y	Y	N	Y	Y	N
2 **Hoekstra**	Y	Y	N	Y	Y	N
3 **Ehlers**	Y	Y	N	Y	N	N
4 **Camp**	Y	Y	N	Y	Y	N
5 Barcia	Y	Y	N	Y	Y	N
6 **Upton**	Y	Y	N	Y	Y	N
7 **Smith**	N	Y	N	Y	N	N
8 Stabenow	Y	Y	N	Y	N	Y
9 Kildee	Y	Y	N	Y	Y	N
10 Bonior	Y	Y	Y	Y	Y	Y
11 **Knollenberg**	Y	Y	N	Y	Y	N
12 Levin	Y	Y	N	Y	N	Y
13 Rivers	Y	Y	Y	Y	N	Y
14 Conyers	Y	N	?	Y	Y	Y
15 Kilpatrick	Y	Y	Y	Y	Y	Y
16 Dingell	Y	N	N	Y	Y	Y
MINNESOTA						
1 **Gutknecht**	N	Y	N	Y	N	N
2 Minge	Y	Y	Y	Y	N	Y

	212	213	214	215	216	217
3 **Ramstad**	Y	Y	Y	Y	N	Y
4 Vento	Y	N	Y	Y	N	Y
5 Sabo	Y	Y	Y	Y	N	Y
6 Luther	Y	Y	Y	Y	N	Y
7 Peterson	Y	Y	N	Y	Y	N
8 Oberstar	Y	Y	?	?	?	?
MISSISSIPPI						
1 **Wicker**	Y	Y	N	Y	Y	N
2 Thompson	Y	N	N	Y	Y	Y
3 **Pickering**	N	Y	N	Y	Y	N
4 **Parker**	Y	Y	N	Y	Y	N
5 Taylor	N	N	N	Y	Y	N
MISSOURI						
1 Clay	Y	N	Y	Y	Y	Y
2 **Talent**	N	N	N	N	Y	N
3 Gephardt	Y	Y	?	?	?	?
4 Skelton	Y	Y	N	Y	Y	N
5 McCarthy	Y	Y	Y	Y	N	Y
6 Danner	N	Y	Y	Y	Y	N
7 **Blunt**	N	N	N	Y	Y	N
8 **Emerson**	Y	Y	N	Y	Y	N
9 **Hulshof**	Y	Y	N	Y	Y	N
MONTANA						
AL **Hill**	Y	Y	N	Y	Y	N
NEBRASKA						
1 **Bereuter**	Y	Y	N	Y	N	N
2 **Christensen**	N	N	N	Y	Y	N
3 **Barrett**	Y	Y	N	Y	N	N
NEVADA						
1 **Ensign**	Y	Y	N	Y	Y	N
2 **Gibbons**	N	N	N	Y	Y	N
NEW HAMPSHIRE						
1 **Sununu**	N	N	N	Y	Y	N
2 **Bass**	Y	Y	N	Y	Y	Y
NEW JERSEY						
1 Andrews	Y	Y	N	Y	Y	Y
2 **LoBiondo**	Y	Y	N	Y	Y	N
3 **Saxton**	Y	Y	N	Y	Y	N
4 **Smith**	N	Y	N	Y	Y	N
5 **Roukema**	Y	Y	Y	Y	Y	Y
6 Pallone	Y	N	N	Y	N	Y
7 **Franks**	Y	Y	N	Y	Y	Y
8 Pascrell	Y	Y	Y	Y	Y	Y
9 Rothman	Y	Y	N	Y	Y	Y
10 Payne	Y	N	Y	Y	Y	Y
11 **Frelinghuysen**	Y	Y	N	Y	Y	Y
12 **Pappas**	N	Y	N	Y	Y	N
13 Menendez	Y	Y	N	Y	Y	Y
NEW MEXICO						
1 **Schiff**	?	?	?	?	?	?
2 **Skeen**	Y	Y	N	Y	Y	N
3 **Redmond**	N	Y	N	Y	Y	N
NEW YORK						
1 **Forbes**	N	N	N	Y	N	N
2 **Lazio**	Y	Y	N	Y	Y	N
3 **King**	N	Y	N	Y	Y	N
4 McCarthy	N	N	N	Y	N	Y
5 Ackerman	Y	Y	?	?	X	?
6 Flake	Y	Y	N	Y	Y	Y
7 Manton	Y	Y	N	Y	Y	N
8 Nadler	Y	N	Y	Y	Y	Y
9 Schumer	Y	Y	N	Y	Y	Y
10 Towns	Y	N	Y	Y	Y	Y
11 Owens	Y	Y	Y	Y	Y	Y
12 Velázquez	Y	Y	Y	Y	Y	Y
13 **Molinari**	Y	Y	N	Y	Y	Y
14 Maloney	Y	N	Y	Y	Y	Y
15 Rangel	Y	N	Y	Y	Y	Y
16 Serrano	Y	Y	Y	Y	Y	Y
17 Engel	Y	Y	Y	Y	Y	Y
18 Lowey	Y	Y	Y	Y	Y	Y
19 **Kelly**	Y	Y	N	Y	N	Y
20 **Gilman**	Y	Y	N	Y	N	Y
21 McNulty	Y	Y	N	Y	Y	N
22 **Solomon**	Y	Y	N	Y	Y	N
23 **Boehlert**	Y	Y	N	Y	Y	N
24 **McHugh**	N	Y	N	Y	Y	?
25 **Walsh**	N	Y	N	Y	Y	N
26 Hinchey	Y	Y	Y	Y	Y	Y
27 **Paxon**	Y	Y	N	Y	Y	N
28 Slaughter	Y	Y	N	Y	Y	Y
29 LaFalce	Y	Y	N	Y	Y	Y
30 **Quinn**	Y	Y	N	Y	Y	N
31 **Houghton**	Y	Y	N	Y	N	Y

	212	213	214	215	216	217
NORTH CAROLINA						
1 Clayton	Y	N	N	Y	Y	Y
2 Etheridge	Y	N	N	Y	N	Y
3 **Jones**	N	N	N	Y	Y	N
4 Price	Y	Y	N	Y	N	Y
5 **Burr**	N	Y	N	Y	Y	N
6 **Coble**	Y	Y	N	Y	Y	N
7 McIntyre	N	N	N	Y	Y	N
8 Hefner	Y	N	N	Y	Y	Y
9 **Myrick**	N	N	N	Y	N	N
10 **Ballenger**	Y	Y	N	Y	Y	N
11 **Taylor**	Y	Y	N	?	?	?
12 Watt	Y	Y	Y	Y	N	Y
NORTH DAKOTA						
AL Pomeroy	?	?	?	?	?	?
OHIO						
1 **Chabot**	Y	Y	N	Y	N	N
2 **Portman**	Y	Y	N	Y	N	N
3 Hall	Y	Y	N	Y	N	N
4 **Oxley**	Y	Y	N	Y	Y	N
5 **Gillmor**	Y	Y	N	Y	N	N
6 Strickland	Y	Y	N	Y	Y	Y
7 **Hobson**	Y	Y	N	Y	Y	N
8 **Boehner**	Y	Y	N	Y	Y	N
9 Kaptur	Y	Y	N	?	Y	N
10 Kucinich	Y	Y	Y	Y	Y	N
11 Stokes	?	?	Y	Y	Y	Y
12 **Kasich**	Y	Y	N	Y	Y	N
13 Brown	Y	Y	Y	Y	Y	Y
14 Sawyer	Y	Y	N	Y	Y	Y
15 **Pryce**	Y	Y	N	Y	Y	Y
16 **Regula**	N	Y	N	Y	Y	N
17 Traficant	Y	Y	N	Y	Y	Y
18 **Ney**	N	Y	N	Y	Y	N
19 **LaTourette**	Y	Y	N	Y	Y	N
OKLAHOMA						
1 **Largent**	N	N	N	Y	Y	N
2 **Coburn**	N	N	N	Y	Y	N
3 **Watkins**	N	N	N	Y	Y	N
4 **Watts**	N	N	N	Y	Y	N
5 **Istook**	?	?	N	Y	Y	N
6 **Lucas**	N	N	N	Y	Y	N
OREGON						
1 Furse	Y	N	Y	Y	N	Y
2 **Smith**	Y	Y	N	Y	Y	N
3 Blumenauer	Y	N	Y	Y	N	Y
4 DeFazio	Y	N	Y	Y	N	Y
5 Hooley	Y	Y	Y	Y	N	Y
PENNSYLVANIA						
1 Foglietta	Y	?	N	Y	Y	Y
2 Fattah	Y	Y	Y	Y	Y	Y
3 Borski	Y	Y	N	N	Y	N
4 Klink	N	Y	N	Y	Y	N
5 **Peterson**	Y	Y	N	Y	Y	N
6 Holden	Y	Y	N	Y	Y	N
7 **Weldon**	Y	Y	N	Y	Y	N
8 **Greenwood**	Y	Y	N	Y	Y	Y
9 **Shuster**	Y	Y	N	Y	Y	N
10 **McDade**	Y	Y	N	Y	Y	N
11 Kanjorski	Y	Y	N	Y	Y	N
12 Murtha	Y	Y	N	Y	Y	N
13 **Fox**	Y	Y	N	Y	Y	N
14 Coyne	Y	Y	Y	Y	Y	Y
15 McHale	Y	Y	N	Y	Y	Y
16 **Pitts**	Y	Y	N	Y	Y	N
17 **Gekas**	N	Y	N	Y	Y	N
18 Doyle	Y	Y	N	Y	Y	N
19 **Goodling**	N	N	N	N	Y	N
20 Mascara	Y	Y	N	Y	Y	N
21 **English**	?	?	Y	Y	N	N
RHODE ISLAND						
1 Kennedy	Y	Y	N	Y	N	Y
2 Weygand	Y	Y	N	Y	–	N
SOUTH CAROLINA						
1 **Sanford**	Y	Y	N	Y	Y	N
2 **Spence**	Y	Y	N	Y	Y	N
3 **Graham**	Y	Y	N	Y	Y	N
4 **Inglis**	Y	Y	N	Y	Y	N
5 Spratt	Y	Y	N	Y	Y	Y
6 Clyburn	Y	N	N	Y	Y	Y
SOUTH DAKOTA						
AL **Thune**	Y	Y	N	Y	Y	N
TENNESSEE						
1 **Jenkins**	Y	Y	N	Y	Y	N
2 **Duncan**	Y	Y	Y	Y	Y	N

	212	213	214	215	216	217
3 **Wamp**	Y	Y	N	Y	Y	N
4 **Hilleary**	Y	Y	N	Y	Y	N
5 Clement	Y	Y	N	Y	Y	Y
6 Gordon	Y	Y	N	Y	Y	Y
7 **Bryant**	Y	Y	N	Y	Y	N
8 Tanner	Y	Y	N	Y	Y	Y
9 Ford	Y	Y	N	Y	Y	Y
TEXAS						
1 Sandlin	Y	N	N	Y	Y	Y
2 Turner	Y	Y	N	Y	Y	Y
3 **Johnson, Sam**	Y	Y	N	Y	Y	N
4 Hall	Y	N	N	N	N	N
5 **Sessions**	Y	Y	N	Y	Y	N
6 **Barton**	Y	Y	N	Y	Y	N
7 **Archer**	Y	Y	N	Y	Y	N
8 **Brady**	Y	Y	N	Y	N	N
9 Lampson	Y	Y	N	Y	Y	Y
10 Doggett	Y	Y	Y	Y	N	Y
11 Edwards	Y	Y	N	Y	Y	Y
12 **Granger**	Y	Y	N	Y	Y	N
13 **Thornberry**	Y	Y	N	Y	Y	N
14 **Paul**	Y	Y	Y	Y	N	N
15 Hinojosa	Y	Y	N	Y	Y	Y
16 Reyes	?	Y	N	N	Y	Y
17 Stenholm	Y	Y	N	Y	Y	N
18 Jackson-Lee	Y	N	N	Y	Y	Y
19 **Combest**	Y	Y	N	Y	Y	N
20 Gonzalez	Y	Y	N	Y	Y	Y
21 **Smith**	Y	Y	N	Y	Y	N
22 **DeLay**	Y	Y	N	Y	Y	N
23 **Bonilla**	Y	Y	N	Y	Y	N
24 Frost	Y	Y	N	Y	N	Y
25 Bentsen	Y	Y	N	Y	N	Y
26 **Armey**	Y	Y	N	Y	Y	N
27 Ortiz	Y	N	N	Y	Y	N
28 Rodriguez	Y	Y	N	Y	Y	Y
29 Green	N	N	N	Y	N	Y
30 Johnson, E.B.	Y	Y	N	Y	Y	Y
UTAH						
1 **Hansen**	N	N	N	Y	Y	N
2 **Cook**	N	N	N	Y	Y	N
3 **Cannon**	N	N	N	Y	Y	N
VERMONT						
AL *Sanders*	Y	N	Y	Y	Y	Y
VIRGINIA						
1 **Bateman**	Y	Y	N	Y	Y	N
2 Pickett	Y	N	N	Y	Y	Y
3 Scott	Y	Y	N	Y	Y	Y
4 Sisisky	Y	N	N	Y	Y	Y
5 Goode	Y	Y	N	Y	Y	N
6 **Goodlatte**	Y	Y	N	Y	N	N
7 **Bliley**	Y	Y	N	Y	Y	N
8 Moran	Y	N	N	N	N	Y
9 Boucher	Y	Y	N	Y	N	Y
10 **Wolf**	Y	Y	N	Y	Y	N
11 **Davis**	Y	Y	N	Y	N	N
WASHINGTON						
1 **White**	Y	N	N	Y	N	Y
2 **Metcalf**	Y	Y	N	Y	Y	N
3 **Smith, Linda**	Y	Y	N	Y	Y	N
4 **Hastings**	Y	Y	N	Y	Y	N
5 **Nethercutt**	Y	Y	N	Y	Y	N
6 Dicks	Y	Y	N	Y	Y	Y
7 McDermott	Y	N	Y	Y	N	Y
8 **Dunn**	Y	Y	N	Y	Y	Y
9 Smith, Adam	Y	Y	N	Y	N	Y
WEST VIRGINIA						
1 Mollohan	Y	Y	N	Y	Y	N
2 Wise	Y	Y	N	Y	Y	Y
3 Rahall	Y	Y	Y	Y	Y	N
WISCONSIN						
1 **Neumann**	Y	Y	N	Y	Y	N
2 **Klug**	Y	N	Y	Y	Y	Y
3 Kind	Y	Y	Y	Y	N	Y
4 Kleczka	Y	N	Y	Y	Y	N
5 Barrett	Y	N	Y	Y	Y	Y
6 **Petri**	Y	Y	Y	Y	N	N
7 Obey	Y	Y	Y	Y	N	Y
8 Johnson	Y	Y	N	Y	N	Y
9 **Sensenbrenner**	N	N	Y	Y	Y	N
WYOMING						
AL **Cubin**	N	Y	N	Y	Y	N

Southern states - Ala., Ark., Fla., Ga., Ky., La., Miss., N.C., Okla., S.C., Tenn., Texas, Va.

HOUSE VOTES 218, 219, 220, 221, 222, 223, 224, 225

218. Procedural Motion/Journal. Approval of the House Journal of Thursday, June 19, 1997. Approved 336-49: R 182-20; D 153-29 (ND 110-20, SD 43-9); I 1-0, June 20, 1997.

219. H Res 167. Fundraising Investigation Depositions/ Previous Question. Pryce, R-Ohio, motion to order the previous question (thus ending debate and the possibility of amendment) on the resolution to permit the chairman of the Government Reform and Oversight Committee, after consulting with the ranking minority member, to order the taking of sworn depositions anywhere within or outside the United States in connection with the committee's investigation of improper fundraising activities in the 1996 elections. Motion agreed to 217-196: R 216-0; D 1-195 (ND 1-141, SD 0-54); I 0-1, June 20, 1997.

220. H Res 167. Fundraising Investigation Depositions/ Adoption. Adoption of the resolution to permit the chairman of the Government Reform and Oversight Committee, after consulting with the ranking minority member, to order the taking of sworn depositions anywhere within or outside the United States in connection with the committee's investigation of improper fundraising activities in the 1996 elections. Adopted 216-194: R 212-1; D 4-192 (ND 1-141, SD 3-51); I 0-1, June 20, 1997.

221. HR 1119. Fiscal 1998 Defense Authorization/Trident D-5 Ballistic Missiles. Luther, D-Minn., amendment to cut the bill's $309 million authorization in fiscal 1998 for further production of the Trident D-5 submarine-launched ballistic missile. Rejected 145-253: R 32-176; D 112-77 (ND 98-38, SD 14-39); I 1-0, June 20, 1997.

222. HR 1119. Fiscal 1998 Defense Authorization/Colorado Oil Shale Reserves. Hefley, R-Colo., amendment to transfer jurisdiction of the Naval Oil Shale Reserves in Colorado from the Department of Energy to the Department of the Interior and require the agency to lease the land to the private sector for petroleum and natural gas exploration, development and production. Adopted 248-146: R 184-21; D 64-124 (ND 39-97, SD 25-27); I 0-1, June 20, 1997.

223. HR 1119. Fiscal 1998 Defense Authorization/Russian Ballistic Missile Certification. Weldon, R-Pa., amendment to require the president to certify whether it is possible for the United States to verify that no Russian ICBMs are targeted at the United States, determine the length of time it would take for a targeted Russian ICBM to be retargeted and determine whether a Russian ICBM would automatically be retargeted in the event of an accidental launch. Adopted 290-100: R 203-0; D 86-100 (ND 57-78, SD 29-22); I 1-0, June 20, 1997.

224. HR 1119. Fiscal 1998 Defense Authorization/Border Control Assistance. Traficant, D-Ohio, amendment to allow the secretary of Defense to assign up to 10,000 military personnel to assist the Immigration and Naturalization Service and the Customs Service in border control activities. Adopted 269-119: R 192-8; D 77-110 (ND 52-83, SD 25-27); I 0-1, June 20, 1997.

225. HR 1119. Fiscal 1998 Defense Authorization/Convicted Veteran Burials. Bachus, R-Ala., amendment to deny eligibility for burial with military honors in a national cemetery to any military service member who is convicted of a capital offense. The amendment would apply to Timothy McVeigh, convicted of murder in the 1995 bombing of the Alfred P. Murrah Federal Building in Oklahoma City. Adopted 416-0: R 221-0; D 194-0 (ND 140-0, SD 54-0); I 1-0, June 23, 1997.

KEY

- Y Voted for (yea).
- # Paired for.
- + Announced for.
- N Voted against (nay).
- X Paired against.
- – Announced against.
- P Voted "present."
- C Voted "present" to avoid possible conflict of interest.
- ? Did not vote or otherwise make a position known.

Democrats ***Republicans***
Independent

	218	219	220	221	222	223	224	225
ALABAMA								
1 ***Callahan***	Y	Y	Y	N	N	?	?	Y
2 ***Everett***	Y	Y	Y	N	N	Y	Y	Y
3 ***Riley***	Y	Y	Y	N	Y	Y	Y	Y
4 ***Aderholt***	Y	Y	Y	N	Y	Y	Y	Y
5 Cramer	Y	N	N	N	Y	Y	Y	Y
6 ***Bachus***	Y	Y	Y	N	Y	Y	Y	Y
7 Hilliard	N	N	N	Y	N	N	N	Y
ALASKA								
AL ***Young***	?	?	?	N	Y	Y	Y	Y
ARIZONA								
1 ***Salmon***	Y	Y	Y	N	Y	Y	Y	Y
2 Pastor	Y	N	N	Y	N	N	N	Y
3 ***Stump***	Y	Y	Y	N	Y	Y	N	Y
4 ***Shadegg***	Y	Y	Y	N	Y	Y	Y	Y
5 ***Kolbe***	?	Y	Y	N	Y	Y	N	Y
6 ***Hayworth***	Y	Y	Y	N	Y	Y	N	Y
ARKANSAS								
1 Berry	Y	N	N	N	N	Y	N	Y
2 Snyder	Y	N	N	N	Y	N	N	Y
3 ***Hutchinson***	Y	Y	Y	N	Y	Y	Y	Y
4 ***Dickey***	Y	Y	Y	N	Y	Y	Y	Y
CALIFORNIA								
1 ***Riggs***	?	Y	Y	N	Y	Y	Y	Y
2 ***Herger***	?	Y	?	N	Y	Y	Y	Y
3 Fazio	N	N	N	N	Y	N	N	Y
4 ***Doolittle***	?	?	?	?	?	?	?	Y
5 Matsui	Y	N	N	N	Y	N	N	Y
6 Woolsey	Y	N	N	Y	N	N	N	Y
7 Miller	?	?	?	?	?	?	?	Y
8 Pelosi	Y	N	N	Y	N	N	N	Y
9 Dellums	Y	N	N	Y	N	N	N	Y
10 Tauscher	Y	N	N	Y	Y	Y	Y	Y
11 ***Pombo***	?	?	?	?	?	?	?	Y
12 Lantos	Y	N	N	Y	N	Y	Y	Y
13 Stark	?	X	X	#	X	X	X	?
14 Eshoo	Y	N	N	Y	Y	Y	Y	+
15 ***Campbell***	Y	Y	Y	Y	Y	Y	Y	Y
16 Lofgren	Y	N	N	Y	N	N	N	Y
17 Farr	Y	N	N	Y	Y	Y	N	Y
18 Condit	Y	N	N	N	Y	Y	Y	Y
19 ***Radanovich***	Y	Y	Y	N	Y	Y	Y	Y
20 Dooley	Y	N	N	Y	Y	N	N	Y
21 ***Thomas***	Y	Y	Y	N	Y	Y	Y	Y
22 Capps	Y	N	N	Y	Y	N	N	Y
23 ***Gallegly***	Y	Y	Y	N	Y	Y	Y	Y
24 Sherman	Y	N	N	N	N	Y	Y	Y
25 ***McKeon***	Y	Y	Y	N	Y	Y	Y	Y
26 Berman	Y	N	N	Y	N	N	N	Y
27 ***Rogan***	Y	Y	Y	N	Y	Y	Y	Y
28 ***Dreier***	Y	Y	Y	N	Y	Y	Y	Y
29 Waxman	Y	N	N	Y	N	N	N	Y
30 Becerra	?	N	N	Y	N	N	N	Y
31 Martinez	?	N	N	N	Y	Y	N	Y
32 Dixon	?	N	N	N	Y	N	N	Y
33 Roybal-Allard	Y	N	N	N	N	N	N	Y
34 Torres	?	–	–	+	–	–	–	Y
35 Waters	?	N	N	Y	N	N	N	Y
36 Harman	Y	N	N	N	Y	Y	Y	Y
37 Millender-McD.	Y	N	N	N	Y	N	N	Y
38 ***Horn***	Y	Y	Y	N	Y	Y	Y	Y
39 ***Royce***	?	Y	Y	N	Y	Y	Y	Y
40 ***Lewis***	Y	Y	Y	N	Y	Y	Y	Y
41 ***Kim***	Y	Y	Y	N	Y	Y	Y	Y
42 Brown	N	N	N	?	?	?	?	Y
43 ***Calvert***	Y	Y	Y	N	Y	Y	Y	Y
44 ***Bono***	Y	Y	Y	N	Y	Y	Y	Y
45 ***Rohrabacher***	Y	Y	Y	Y	Y	Y	Y	Y
46 Sanchez	?	N	N	Y	N	Y	Y	Y
47 ***Cox***	Y	Y	Y	N	Y	Y	Y	?
48 ***Packard***	Y	Y	Y	N	Y	Y	Y	Y
49 ***Bilbray***	Y	Y	Y	N	Y	Y	Y	Y
50 Filner	N	N	N	Y	N	N	N	Y
51 ***Cunningham***	Y	Y	Y	N	Y	Y	Y	Y
52 ***Hunter***	Y	Y	Y	N	Y	Y	Y	Y
COLORADO								
1 DeGette	?	X	X	?	#	?	?	Y
2 Skaggs	Y	N	N	Y	Y	N	N	Y
3 ***McInnis***	Y	Y	Y	N	Y	Y	Y	Y
4 ***Schaffer***	N	Y	Y	N	Y	Y	Y	Y
5 ***Hefley***	N	Y	Y	N	Y	Y	Y	Y
6 ***Schaefer***	Y	Y	Y	N	Y	Y	Y	+
CONNECTICUT								
1 Kennelly	Y	N	N	N	N	Y	N	Y
2 Gejdenson	Y	N	N	N	N	Y	N	Y
3 DeLauro	Y	N	N	N	N	N	N	Y
4 ***Shays***	Y	Y	Y	Y	Y	Y	Y	Y
5 Maloney	Y	N	N	N	N	Y	Y	Y
6 ***Johnson***	Y	Y	Y	N	N	Y	Y	Y
DELAWARE								
AL ***Castle***	Y	Y	Y	N	Y	Y	Y	Y
FLORIDA								
1 ***Scarborough***	?	Y	Y	N	Y	Y	Y	Y
2 Boyd	Y	N	N	N	Y	Y	Y	Y
3 Brown	?	N	N	N	Y	N	N	Y
4 ***Fowler***	Y	Y	Y	N	Y	Y	Y	Y
5 Thurman	Y	N	N	N	Y	Y	Y	Y
6 ***Stearns***	N	Y	Y	N	Y	Y	Y	Y
7 ***Mica***	Y	Y	Y	N	Y	Y	Y	Y
8 ***McCollum***	Y	Y	Y	N	Y	Y	Y	Y
9 ***Bilirakis***	Y	Y	Y	N	Y	Y	Y	Y
10 ***Young***	Y	Y	Y	N	N	Y	Y	Y
11 Davis	Y	N	N	Y	N	Y	N	Y
12 ***Canady***	Y	Y	Y	N	Y	Y	?	Y
13 ***Miller***	Y	Y	Y	N	Y	Y	Y	Y
14 ***Goss***	+	+	+	–	+	+	+	Y
15 ***Weldon***	Y	Y	Y	N	?	?	?	Y
16 ***Foley***	Y	Y	Y	Y	Y	Y	Y	Y
17 Meek	N	N	N	N	N	N	N	Y
18 ***Ros-Lehtinen***	Y	Y	Y	N	Y	Y	Y	Y
19 Wexler	Y	N	N	Y	?	?	?	Y
20 Deutsch	Y	N	N	X	X	–	–	Y
21 ***Diaz-Balart***	Y	Y	Y	N	Y	Y	Y	Y
22 ***Shaw***	Y	Y	Y	N	Y	Y	Y	Y
23 Hastings	Y	N	N	N	N	N	N	Y
GEORGIA								
1 ***Kingston***	Y	Y	Y	N	Y	Y	Y	Y
2 Bishop	Y	N	N	N	Y	N	Y	Y
3 ***Collins***	Y	Y	Y	Y	N	Y	Y	Y
4 McKinney	Y	N	N	Y	N	Y	N	Y
5 Lewis	N	N	N	Y	N	N	N	Y
6 ***Gingrich***								
7 ***Barr***	Y	Y	Y	N	Y	Y	Y	Y
8 ***Chambliss***	Y	Y	Y	N	Y	Y	Y	Y
9 ***Deal***	Y	Y	Y	N	Y	Y	Y	Y
10 ***Norwood***	Y	Y	Y	Y	Y	Y	Y	Y
11 ***Linder***	Y	Y	Y	N	Y	Y	N	Y
HAWAII								
1 Abercrombie	N	N	N	Y	Y	Y	Y	Y
2 Mink	Y	N	N	Y	N	N	N	Y
IDAHO								
1 ***Chenoweth***	N	Y	Y	?	?	?	?	Y
2 ***Crapo***	?	Y	Y	N	N	Y	Y	Y
ILLINOIS								
1 Rush	N	N	N	Y	N	N	N	Y
2 Jackson	Y	N	N	Y	N	N	N	Y
3 Lipinski	?	?	?	?	?	?	?	?
4 Gutierrez	N	N	N	Y	N	Y	N	Y
5 Blagojevich	Y	N	N	Y	N	Y	N	Y
6 ***Hyde***	Y	Y	Y	N	N	Y	Y	Y
7 Davis	Y	N	N	Y	N	N	N	Y
8 ***Crane***	?	Y	Y	N	Y	Y	Y	Y
9 Yates	?	?	?	?	?	?	?	?
10 ***Porter***	?	Y	Y	Y	N	Y	Y	Y
11 ***Weller***	N	Y	Y	N	Y	Y	Y	Y
12 Costello	Y	N	N	Y	Y	Y	Y	Y
13 ***Fawell***	Y	Y	Y	N	Y	Y	Y	Y
14 ***Hastert***	Y	Y	Y	N	Y	Y	Y	Y
15 ***Ewing***	Y	Y	Y	N	Y	Y	?	Y

ND Northern Democrats SD Southern Democrats

	218	219	220	221	222	223	224	225
16 ***Manzullo***	Y	Y	Y	N	Y	Y	Y	Y
17 Evans	Y	N	N	Y	N	N	N	Y
18 ***LaHood***	Y	Y	Y	N	Y	Y	Y	Y
19 Poshard	N	N	N	Y	N	Y	Y	Y
20 ***Shimkus***	Y	Y	Y	N	Y	Y	Y	Y
INDIANA								
1 Visclosky	N	N	N	N	N	Y	N	Y
2 ***McIntosh***	Y	Y	#	X	#	#	#	?
3 Roemer	Y	N	N	Y	N	N	Y	Y
4 ***Souder***	Y	Y	Y	N	Y	Y	Y	Y
5 ***Buyer***	Y	Y	Y	?	?	?	?	Y
6 ***Burton***	Y	Y	Y	N	Y	Y	Y	Y
7 ***Pease***	Y	Y	Y	N	Y	Y	Y	Y
8 ***Hostettler***	Y	Y	Y	N	Y	Y	Y	Y
9 Hamilton	Y	N	N	N	N	N	N	Y
10 Carson	Y	N	N	Y	Y	Y	N	Y
IOWA								
1 ***Leach***	Y	Y	Y	Y	N	Y	Y	Y
2 ***Nussle***	N	Y	Y	Y	Y	Y	Y	Y
3 Boswell	Y	N	N	N	Y	Y	Y	Y
4 ***Ganske***	Y	Y	Y	N	N	Y	?	Y
5 ***Latham***	Y	Y	Y	Y	Y	Y	Y	Y
KANSAS								
1 ***Moran***	N	Y	Y	N	Y	Y	Y	Y
2 ***Ryun***	Y	Y	Y	N	Y	Y	Y	Y
3 ***Snowbarger***	Y	Y	Y	N	Y	Y	Y	Y
4 ***Tiahrt***	N	Y	Y	N	Y	+	Y	Y
KENTUCKY								
1 ***Whitfield***	Y	Y	Y	N	Y	Y	N	Y
2 ***Lewis***	Y	Y	Y	N	Y	Y	Y	Y
3 ***Northup***	Y	Y	Y	N	Y	Y	Y	Y
4 ***Bunning***	Y	Y	Y	N	N	Y	Y	Y
5 ***Rogers***	Y	Y	Y	N	Y	Y	Y	Y
6 Baesler	Y	N	N	N	N	Y	Y	Y
LOUISIANA								
1 ***Livingston***	Y	Y	Y	N	Y	Y	Y	Y
2 Jefferson	Y	N	N	N	Y	Y	Y	Y
3 ***Tauzin***	?	?	?	?	?	?	?	Y
4 ***McCrery***	Y	Y	Y	?	?	?	?	Y
5 ***Cooksey***	Y	Y	Y	–	+	+	+	Y
6 ***Baker***	Y	Y	Y	N	Y	Y	Y	Y
7 John	Y	N	N	N	Y	Y	Y	Y
MAINE								
1 Allen	Y	N	N	Y	N	N	N	Y
2 Baldacci	Y	N	N	Y	Y	N	N	Y
MARYLAND								
1 ***Gilchrest***	Y	Y	Y	N	Y	Y	Y	Y
2 ***Ehrlich***	Y	Y	Y	Y	Y	Y	N	Y
3 Cardin	Y	N	N	Y	Y	N	N	Y
4 Wynn	Y	N	N	Y	N	Y	N	Y
5 Hoyer	Y	N	N	N	Y	N	N	Y
6 ***Bartlett***	Y	Y	Y	N	Y	Y	Y	Y
7 Cummings	Y	N	N	Y	Y	N	Y	Y
8 ***Morella***	Y	Y	Y	Y	Y	Y	Y	Y
MASSACHUSETTS								
1 Olver	Y	N	N	N	N	N	N	Y
2 Neal	Y	N	N	N	N	N	N	Y
3 McGovern	Y	N	N	Y	N	N	N	Y
4 Frank	Y	N	N	Y	Y	N	N	Y
5 Meehan	Y	N	N	Y	N	Y	N	Y
6 Tierney	Y	N	N	Y	N	N	N	Y
7 Markey	?	N	N	Y	N	N	N	Y
8 Kennedy	Y	N	N	Y	N	N	N	Y
9 Moakley	Y	N	N	Y	N	N	Y	Y
10 Delahunt	Y	N	N	Y	N	N	N	Y
MICHIGAN								
1 Stupak	Y	N	N	Y	Y	N	N	Y
2 ***Hoekstra***	N	Y	Y	Y	N	Y	Y	Y
3 ***Ehlers***	Y	Y	Y	?	?	?	?	Y
4 ***Camp***	Y	Y	Y	Y	Y	Y	Y	Y
5 Barcia	Y	N	N	N	N	N	Y	Y
6 ***Upton***	Y	Y	Y	Y	Y	Y	Y	Y
7 ***Smith***	Y	Y	Y	N	Y	Y	Y	Y
8 Stabenow	Y	N	N	Y	N	Y	N	Y
9 Kildee	Y	N	N	Y	N	Y	N	Y
10 Bonior	Y	N	N	Y	N	N	N	Y
11 ***Knollenberg***	Y	Y	Y	N	Y	Y	Y	Y
12 Levin	Y	N	N	Y	Y	N	Y	Y
13 Rivers	Y	N	N	Y	N	Y	Y	Y
14 Conyers	?	N	N	Y	N	N	N	Y
15 Kilpatrick	Y	N	N	Y	N	N	N	+
16 Dingell	Y	N	N	Y	N	N	N	Y
MINNESOTA								
1 ***Gutknecht***	N	Y	Y	Y	Y	Y	Y	Y
2 Minge	Y	N	N	Y	N	Y	Y	Y

	218	219	220	221	222	223	224	225
3 ***Ramstad***	N	Y	Y	Y	Y	Y	Y	Y
4 Vento	Y	N	N	Y	N	N	N	Y
5 Sabo	N	N	N	Y	N	N	N	?
6 Luther	Y	N	N	Y	N	N	Y	Y
7 Peterson	Y	N	N	Y	N	Y	Y	Y
8 Oberstar	?	?	?	?	?	?	?	Y
MISSISSIPPI								
1 ***Wicker***	Y	Y	Y	N	Y	Y	Y	Y
2 Thompson	N	N	N	N	Y	N	N	Y
3 ***Pickering***	Y	Y	Y	N	Y	Y	Y	Y
4 ***Parker***	Y	Y	Y	N	N	Y	Y	Y
5 Taylor	N	N	Y	N	N	Y	Y	Y
MISSOURI								
1 Clay	N	N	N	?	?	?	?	Y
2 ***Talent***	Y	Y	Y	N	Y	Y	Y	Y
3 Gephardt	N	N	N	?	?	?	?	Y
4 Skelton	Y	N	N	N	Y	Y	Y	Y
5 McCarthy	Y	N	N	Y	N	N	Y	Y
6 Danner	Y	N	N	Y	Y	Y	Y	Y
7 ***Blunt***	?	Y	Y	N	Y	Y	Y	?
8 ***Emerson***	Y	Y	Y	N	Y	Y	Y	Y
9 ***Hulshof***	N	Y	Y	N	Y	Y	Y	Y
MONTANA								
AL ***Hill***	Y	Y	Y	N	Y	Y	Y	Y
NEBRASKA								
1 ***Bereuter***	Y	Y	Y	N	Y	Y	Y	Y
2 ***Christensen***	Y	Y	Y	N	Y	Y	Y	Y
3 ***Barrett***	Y	?	?	?	?	?	?	Y
NEVADA								
1 ***Ensign***	N	Y	Y	N	Y	Y	Y	Y
2 ***Gibbons***	Y	Y	Y	N	Y	Y	Y	Y
NEW HAMPSHIRE								
1 ***Sununu***	N	Y	Y	N	Y	Y	Y	Y
2 ***Bass***	Y	Y	Y	N	Y	Y	Y	Y
NEW JERSEY								
1 Andrews	Y	N	N	N	N	Y	Y	Y
2 ***LoBiondo***	N	Y	Y	Y	Y	Y	Y	Y
3 ***Saxton***	Y	Y	Y	N	Y	Y	Y	Y
4 ***Smith***	?	Y	Y	N	Y	Y	Y	Y
5 ***Roukema***	Y	Y	N	Y	Y	Y	Y	Y
6 Pallone	N	N	N	Y	N	Y	Y	Y
7 ***Franks***	?	Y	Y	Y	Y	Y	Y	Y
8 Pascrell	?	N	N	N	N	Y	Y	Y
9 Rothman	Y	N	N	Y	N	Y	N	Y
10 Payne	Y	N	N	Y	Y	N	N	Y
11 ***Frelinghuysen***	Y	Y	Y	N	Y	Y	Y	Y
12 ***Pappas***	Y	Y	Y	N	Y	Y	Y	Y
13 Menendez	?	N	N	Y	N	Y	N	Y
NEW MEXICO								
1 ***Schiff***	?	?	?	?	?	?	?	?
2 ***Skeen***	Y	Y	Y	N	Y	Y	Y	Y
3 ***Redmond***	Y	Y	Y	N	Y	Y	Y	Y
NEW YORK								
1 ***Forbes***	N	Y	Y	N	N	Y	Y	Y
2 ***Lazio***	Y	Y	Y	N	Y	Y	Y	Y
3 ***King***	Y	Y	Y	N	N	Y	Y	Y
4 McCarthy	Y	N	N	Y	N	Y	Y	Y
5 Ackerman	?	?	?	?	?	?	?	Y
6 Flake	Y	N	N	N	Y	N	Y	Y
7 Manton	Y	N	N	Y	N	N	Y	Y
8 Nadler	Y	N	N	Y	N	N	N	+
9 Schumer	?	N	N	N	N	Y	Y	?
10 Towns	Y	N	N	Y	Y	N	N	Y
11 Owens	Y	N	N	Y	N	N	Y	Y
12 Velázquez	Y	N	N	Y	N	N	N	Y
13 ***Molinari***	Y	Y	Y	N	Y	Y	Y	Y
14 Maloney	N	N	N	Y	Y	Y	Y	?
15 Rangel	Y	N	N	Y	N	N	Y	Y
16 Serrano	Y	N	N	Y	N	N	N	Y
17 Engel	+	N	N	N	N	N	Y	Y
18 Lowey	Y	N	N	Y	N	N	Y	Y
19 ***Kelly***	Y	Y	Y	Y	Y	Y	Y	Y
20 ***Gilman***	Y	Y	Y	N	N	Y	Y	Y
21 McNulty	N	N	N	N	N	Y	Y	Y
22 ***Solomon***	Y	Y	Y	N	Y	Y	Y	Y
23 ***Boehlert***	Y	Y	Y	N	Y	Y	Y	Y
24 ***McHugh***	Y	Y	Y	N	Y	Y	Y	Y
25 ***Walsh***	Y	Y	Y	N	Y	Y	Y	Y
26 Hinchey	Y	N	N	Y	N	Y	N	Y
27 ***Paxon***	Y	Y	Y	N	Y	Y	Y	Y
28 Slaughter	Y	N	N	Y	N	Y	N	Y
29 LaFalce	Y	N	N	Y	Y	Y	Y	Y
30 ***Quinn***	Y	Y	Y	N	Y	Y	Y	Y
31 ***Houghton***	Y	Y	Y	N	Y	Y	N	Y

	218	219	220	221	222	223	224	225
NORTH CAROLINA								
1 Clayton	?	?	?	?	?	?	?	Y
2 Etheridge	Y	N	N	N	N	N	Y	Y
3 ***Jones***	Y	Y	Y	N	Y	Y	Y	Y
4 Price	Y	N	N	Y	N	N	Y	Y
5 ***Burr***	?	Y	Y	N	Y	Y	Y	Y
6 ***Coble***	Y	Y	Y	Y	Y	Y	Y	Y
7 McIntyre	Y	N	N	N	Y	Y	Y	Y
8 Hefner	Y	N	N	N	N	N	Y	Y
9 ***Myrick***	Y	Y	Y	N	Y	Y	Y	Y
10 ***Ballenger***	Y	#	#	–	+	+	+	Y
11 ***Taylor***	?	?	?	?	?	?	?	Y
12 Watt	N	N	N	Y	N	N	N	Y
NORTH DAKOTA								
AL Pomeroy	?	?	?	?	?	?	?	Y
OHIO								
1 ***Chabot***	Y	Y	Y	N	Y	Y	Y	Y
2 ***Portman***	Y	Y	Y	N	Y	Y	Y	Y
3 Hall	Y	N	N	Y	Y	Y	Y	Y
4 ***Oxley***	Y	Y	Y	N	Y	Y	Y	Y
5 ***Gillmor***	N	Y	Y	N	?	?	?	Y
6 Strickland	Y	N	N	Y	N	Y	Y	Y
7 ***Hobson***	Y	Y	Y	Y	Y	Y	Y	Y
8 ***Boehner***	Y	Y	Y	N	+	+	+	Y
9 Kaptur	Y	N	N	N	N	Y	Y	Y
10 Kucinich	N	N	N	Y	N	Y	Y	Y
11 Stokes	Y	N	N	Y	?	?	?	Y
12 ***Kasich***	Y	Y	Y	N	Y	Y	Y	Y
13 Brown	N	N	N	Y	Y	?	?	Y
14 Sawyer	Y	N	N	N	N	N	N	Y
15 ***Pryce***	Y	Y	Y	N	Y	Y	Y	+
16 ***Regula***	Y	Y	Y	N	Y	Y	Y	Y
17 Traficant	Y	Y	Y	N	Y	Y	Y	Y
18 ***Ney***	Y	Y	Y	N	N	Y	Y	Y
19 ***LaTourette***	Y	Y	Y	N	Y	Y	Y	Y
OKLAHOMA								
1 ***Largent***	Y	Y	Y	?	?	?	?	Y
2 ***Coburn***	Y	Y	Y	?	?	?	?	Y
3 ***Watkins***	Y	Y	Y	N	Y	Y	Y	Y
4 ***Watts***	Y	Y	Y	N	Y	Y	Y	Y
5 ***Istook***	Y	Y	Y	N	Y	Y	Y	Y
6 ***Lucas***	Y	Y	Y	N	Y	Y	Y	Y
OREGON								
1 Furse	Y	N	N	?	N	N	N	Y
2 ***Smith***	?	Y	Y	N	Y	Y	Y	Y
3 Blumenauer	Y	N	N	Y	N	N	N	Y
4 DeFazio	N	N	N	Y	N	Y	N	Y
5 Hooley	Y	N	N	Y	Y	Y	N	Y
PENNSYLVANIA								
1 Foglietta	N	N	N	Y	N	N	N	Y
2 Fattah	Y	N	N	Y	N	N	Y	Y
3 Borski	N	N	N	N	N	N	N	Y
4 Klink	Y	N	N	Y	N	Y	Y	Y
5 ***Peterson***	Y	Y	Y	N	Y	Y	Y	Y
6 Holden	Y	N	N	N	N	Y	Y	Y
7 ***Weldon***	Y	Y	Y	N	Y	Y	Y	Y
8 ***Greenwood***	Y	Y	Y	Y	Y	Y	Y	Y
9 ***Shuster***	Y	Y	Y	N	Y	Y	Y	Y
10 ***McDade***	?	Y	Y	N	Y	Y	Y	Y
11 Kanjorski	Y	N	N	Y	N	N	N	Y
12 Murtha	Y	N	N	N	N	Y	N	Y
13 ***Fox***	N	Y	Y	N	Y	Y	Y	Y
14 Coyne	?	N	N	Y	N	N	N	Y
15 McHale	Y	N	N	Y	Y	Y	N	Y
16 ***Pitts***	Y	Y	Y	N	Y	Y	Y	Y
17 ***Gekas***	?	Y	Y	N	Y	Y	Y	Y
18 Doyle	Y	N	N	Y	N	Y	Y	Y
19 ***Goodling***	Y	Y	Y	N	Y	Y	Y	Y
20 Mascara	Y	N	N	Y	N	Y	Y	Y
21 ***English***	N	Y	Y	Y	Y	Y	Y	Y
RHODE ISLAND								
1 Kennedy	Y	N	N	N	Y	Y	N	Y
2 Weygand	Y	N	N	N	N	N	N	Y
SOUTH CAROLINA								
1 ***Sanford***	Y	Y	Y	N	Y	Y	Y	Y
2 ***Spence***	Y	Y	Y	N	N	Y	Y	Y
3 ***Graham***	Y	Y	Y	N	Y	Y	Y	Y
4 ***Inglis***	Y	Y	Y	N	Y	Y	Y	Y
5 Spratt	Y	N	N	N	N	Y	N	Y
6 Clyburn	Y	N	N	N	Y	N	Y	Y
SOUTH DAKOTA								
AL ***Thune***	Y	Y	Y	N	Y	Y	Y	Y
TENNESSEE								
1 ***Jenkins***	Y	Y	Y	N	Y	Y	Y	Y
2 ***Duncan***	Y	Y	Y	Y	Y	Y	Y	Y

	218	219	220	221	222	223	224	
3 ***Wamp***	N	Y	Y	N	Y	Y	Y	Y
4 ***Hilleary***	Y	Y	Y	N	Y	Y	Y	Y
5 Clement	Y	N	N	N	Y	Y	Y	Y
6 Gordon	Y	N	N	N	Y	Y	Y	?
7 ***Bryant***	Y	Y	Y	N	Y	Y	Y	Y
8 Tanner	Y	N	N	N	Y	Y	Y	Y
9 Ford	Y	N	N	Y	N	Y	N	Y
TEXAS								
1 Sandlin	Y	N	N	N	Y	+	Y	Y
2 Turner	Y	N	N	N	Y	N	Y	Y
3 ***Johnson, Sam***	?	?	?	?	?	?	?	Y
4 Hall	Y	N	Y	N	N	Y	Y	Y
5 ***Sessions***	Y	Y	Y	N	Y	Y	Y	Y
6 ***Barton***	Y	Y	Y	N	Y	Y	Y	Y
7 ***Archer***	Y	Y	Y	N	Y	Y	Y	Y
8 ***Brady***	Y	Y	Y	N	Y	Y	Y	Y
9 Lampson	Y	N	N	Y	Y	N	N	Y
10 Doggett	Y	N	N	Y	N	N	N	Y
11 Edwards	Y	N	N	N	N	Y	N	Y
12 ***Granger***	Y	Y	Y	N	Y	Y	Y	Y
13 ***Thornberry***	Y	Y	Y	N	Y	Y	Y	Y
14 ***Paul***	Y	Y	Y	Y	Y	Y	N	Y
15 Hinojosa	Y	N	N	N	Y	N	N	Y
16 Reyes	Y	N	N	N	Y	Y	N	Y
17 Stenholm	?	N	N	N	Y	Y	Y	Y
18 Jackson-Lee	Y	N	N	Y	N	N	N	Y
19 ***Combest***	Y	Y	Y	N	Y	Y	Y	Y
20 Gonzalez	Y	N	N	N	N	N	N	Y
21 ***Smith***	Y	Y	Y	N	Y	Y	Y	Y
22 ***DeLay***	Y	Y	Y	N	Y	Y	Y	Y
23 ***Bonilla***	Y	Y	+	N	Y	Y	P	Y
24 Frost	Y	N	N	N	N	Y	Y	Y
25 Bentsen	Y	N	N	Y	N	Y	N	Y
26 ***Armey***	Y	Y	Y	N	Y	Y	Y	Y
27 Ortiz	Y	N	N	N	Y	Y	N	Y
28 Rodriguez	Y	N	N	N	N	N	N	Y
29 Green	N	N	N	Y	Y	Y	N	Y
30 Johnson, E.B.	N	N	N	N	Y	N	N	Y
UTAH								
1 ***Hansen***	Y	Y	Y	N	Y	Y	Y	Y
2 ***Cook***	Y	Y	Y	N	Y	Y	Y	Y
3 ***Cannon***	Y	Y	Y	N	Y	Y	Y	Y
VERMONT								
AL *Sanders*	Y	N	N	Y	N	Y	N	Y
VIRGINIA								
1 ***Bateman***	Y	Y	Y	N	N	Y	Y	Y
2 Pickett	N	N	N	N	Y	Y	Y	Y
3 Scott	Y	N	N	N	N	Y	N	Y
4 Sisisky	Y	N	N	N	N	Y	Y	Y
5 Goode	Y	N	Y	N	N	Y	Y	Y
6 ***Goodlatte***	Y	Y	Y	Y	N	Y	Y	Y
7 ***Bliley***	Y	Y	Y	?	?	?	?	Y
8 Moran	Y	N	N	Y	N	N	N	Y
9 Boucher	Y	N	N	N	Y	Y	Y	Y
10 ***Wolf***	Y	Y	Y	N	Y	Y	Y	Y
11 ***Davis***	Y	Y	Y	N	N	Y	Y	Y
WASHINGTON								
1 ***White***	Y	Y	Y	N	Y	Y	Y	Y
2 ***Metcalf***	Y	Y	Y	N	Y	Y	Y	Y
3 ***Smith, Linda***	Y	Y	Y	N	Y	Y	Y	Y
4 ***Hastings***	Y	Y	Y	N	Y	Y	Y	Y
5 ***Nethercutt***	Y	+	+	–	+	+	+	Y
6 Dicks	Y	N	N	N	Y	Y	Y	Y
7 McDermott	N	N	N	Y	N	N	N	Y
8 ***Dunn***	?	Y	Y	N	Y	Y	Y	Y
9 Smith, Adam	Y	N	N	N	Y	Y	Y	Y
WEST VIRGINIA								
1 Mollohan	Y	N	N	N	N	N	N	?
2 Wise	Y	N	N	?	?	?	?	Y
3 Rahall	Y	N	N	#	+	+	+	Y
WISCONSIN								
1 ***Neumann***	Y	Y	Y	Y	Y	Y	Y	Y
2 ***Klug***	Y	Y	Y	Y	Y	Y	Y	Y
3 Kind	Y	N	N	Y	N	N	Y	Y
4 Kleczka	Y	N	N	Y	N	N	N	Y
5 Barrett	Y	N	N	Y	N	N	N	+
6 ***Petri***	Y	Y	Y	Y	Y	Y	Y	Y
7 Obey	Y	N	N	Y	N	N	Y	Y
8 Johnson	Y	N	N	Y	N	N	N	Y
9 ***Sensenbrenner***	Y	Y	Y	Y	Y	Y	Y	Y
WYOMING								
AL ***Cubin***	?	Y	Y	N	Y	Y	Y	Y

Southern states - Ala., Ark., Fla., Ga., Ky., La., Miss., N.C., Okla., S.C., Tenn., Texas, Va.

HOUSE VOTES 226, 227, 228, 229, 230, 231, 232, 233

226. HR 1119. Fiscal 1998 Defense Authorization/Missing Service Personnel Procedures. Talent, R-Mo., amendment to require military commanders to report and initiate searches for missing service personnel within 48 hours unless prevented by combat conditions, and require that recovered bodies that cannot be identified by visual means be examined by a credible forensic authority to determine whether they are the bodies of the missing personnel. Adopted 415-2: R 223-0; D 191-2 (ND 138-1, SD 53-1); I1-0, June 23, 1997.

227. HR 1119. Fiscal 1998 Defense Authorization/Gulf War Illnesses. Buyer, R-Ind., amendment to authorize $4.5 million in fiscal 1998 for the departments of Defense and Veterans Affairs to conduct clinical trials to evaluate treatments of Gulf War illnesses and require the agencies to develop a plan to provide health care to veterans suffering from symptoms of the illnesses and to monitor the services provided. Adopted 417-0: R 221-0; D 195-0 (ND 141-0, SD 54-0); I 1-0, June 23, 1997.

228. HR 1119. Fiscal 1998 Defense Authorization/B-2 Stealth Bomber. Dellums, D-Calif., amendment to eliminate the bill's $331 million authorization for advance procurement of the B-2 stealth bomber beyond the 21 aircraft previously authorized and redirect the funds to purchase equipment for the National Guard and Reserve. The amendment also prohibits other funds from being used for advanced procurement or production line expenses for more aircraft than previously authorized. Rejected 209-216: R 60-163; D 148-53 (ND 120-27, SD 28-26); I 1-0, June 23, 1997. A "yea" was a vote in support of the president's position.

229. HR 1119. Fiscal 1998 Defense Authorization/Military Depot Maintenance. Everett, R-Ala., amendment to strike the bill's provisions to prohibit the Department of Defense from entering into any contract for depot-level work at any depot facility that was identified for closure in 1995 by the Defense Base Closure and Realignment Commission, unless all other maintenance and repair facilities of that service are at 80 percent capacity. The amendment would effectively bar private contractors from performing maintenance work at Air Force maintenance depots in San Antonio and Sacramento, Calif. Rejected 145-278: R 25-197; D 119-81 (ND 94-52, SD 25-29); I 1-0, June 23, 1997. A "yea" was a vote in support of the president's position.

230. HR 1119. Fiscal 1998 Defense Authorization/Russian Missile Transfer. Rohrabacher, R-Calif., amendment to prohibit the transfer of the bill's Nunn-Lugar funding designated for Russia if Russia transfers an SS-N-22 missile system to China. Adopted 215-206: R 198-23; D 17-182 (ND 12-134, SD 5-48); I 0-1, June 23, 1997. A "nay" was a vote in support of the president's position.

231. H J Res 79. China MFN Disapproval/Passage. Passage of the joint resolution disapproving of President Clinton's decision to renew most-favored-nation status to China from July 3, 1997, to July 3, 1998. Rejected 173-259: R 79-147; D 93-112 (ND 74-76, SD 19-36); I 1-0, June 24, 1997. A "nay" was a vote in support of the president's position.

232. Procedural Motion/Journal. Approval of the House Journal of Monday, June 23, 1997. Approved 369-59: R 204-19; D 164-40 (ND 120-29, SD 44-11); I 1-0, June 24, 1997.

233. HR 1119. Fiscal 1998 Defense Authorization/Bosnia Troop Withdrawal Substitute. Hilleary, R-Tenn., substitute amendment to the Buyer, R-Ind., amendment to prohibit the obligation of funds for ground deployment of U.S. troops in Bosnia after Dec. 31, 1997, unless the president submits a report to Congress requesting an extension of funding. The Hilleary amendment would require the extension to be approved by a joint resolution of Congress and would permit deployment for an additional 180 days or until June 30, 1998. Rejected 196-231: R 174-49; D 21-182 (ND 15-133, SD 6-49); I 1-0, June 24, 1997. A "nay" was a vote in support of the president's position.

KEY

- Y Voted for (yea).
- # Paired for.
- \+ Announced for.
- N Voted against (nay).
- X Paired against.
- – Announced against.
- P Voted "present."
- C Voted "present" to avoid possible conflict of interest.
- ? Did not vote or otherwise make a position known.

Democrats ***Republicans***
Independent

	226	227	228	229	230	231	232	233
ALABAMA								
1 ***Callahan***	Y	Y	N	N	Y	N	Y	N
2 ***Everett***	Y	Y	N	Y	Y	Y	N	Y
3 ***Riley***	Y	Y	N	N	Y	Y	Y	Y
4 ***Aderholt***	Y	Y	N	N	Y	Y	Y	Y
5 Cramer	Y	Y	N	Y	N	N	Y	N
6 ***Bachus***	Y	Y	N	N	Y	N	Y	Y
7 Hilliard	Y	Y	Y	N	N	Y	N	N
ALASKA								
AL ***Young***	Y	Y	N	N	Y	N	Y	Y
ARIZONA								
1 ***Salmon***	Y	Y	N	N	Y	N	Y	Y
2 Pastor	Y	Y	Y	Y	Y	N	Y	N
3 ***Stump***	Y	Y	N	N	Y	N	Y	Y
4 ***Shadegg***	Y	Y	N	N	Y	N	Y	Y
5 ***Kolbe***	Y	Y	Y	N	N	N	Y	N
6 ***Hayworth***	Y	Y	N	N	Y	N	Y	Y
ARKANSAS								
1 Berry	Y	Y	Y	Y	N	N	Y	Y
2 Snyder	Y	Y	Y	Y	N	N	Y	N
3 ***Hutchinson***	Y	Y	N	N	Y	N	Y	Y
4 ***Dickey***	Y	Y	N	N	Y	Y	Y	Y
CALIFORNIA								
1 ***Riggs***	Y	?	N	Y	Y	N	Y	Y
2 ***Herger***	Y	Y	N	Y	Y	N	Y	Y
3 Fazio	Y	Y	N	Y	N	N	N	N
4 ***Doolittle***	Y	Y	N	Y	Y	Y	Y	Y
5 Matsui	Y	Y	N	Y	N	N	Y	N
6 Woolsey	Y	Y	Y	Y	N	Y	Y	N
7 Miller	Y	Y	Y	Y	N	Y	Y	N
8 Pelosi	Y	Y	Y	Y	N	Y	Y	N
9 Dellums	Y	Y	Y	Y	N	Y	Y	N
10 Tauscher	Y	Y	Y	Y	N	N	Y	N
11 ***Pombo***	Y	Y	N	Y	Y	Y	N	Y
12 Lantos	Y	Y	Y	Y	N	Y	Y	N
13 Stark	?	?	Y	Y	N	Y	N	N
14 Eshoo	+	+	Y	Y	N	N	Y	N
15 ***Campbell***	Y	Y	N	Y	Y	N	Y	Y
16 Lofgren	Y	Y	Y	Y	N	N	Y	N
17 Farr	Y	Y	Y	Y	N	N	Y	N
18 Condit	Y	Y	Y	Y	Y	Y	Y	Y
19 ***Radanovich***	Y	Y	N	Y	Y	N	Y	Y
20 Dooley	Y	Y	N	Y	N	N	Y	N
21 ***Thomas***	Y	Y	N	N	Y	N	Y	Y
22 Capps	Y	Y	Y	Y	N	N	Y	N
23 ***Gallegly***	Y	Y	N	N	Y	N	Y	Y
24 Sherman	Y	Y	N	Y	N	N	Y	N
25 ***McKeon***	Y	Y	N	Y	Y	N	Y	Y
26 Berman	Y	Y	N	Y	N	Y	Y	N
27 ***Rogan***	Y	Y	N	Y	Y	Y	Y	Y
28 ***Dreier***	Y	Y	N	N	Y	N	Y	Y
29 Waxman	Y	Y	Y	Y	N	Y	Y	N
30 Becerra	Y	Y	Y	Y	N	N	Y	N
31 Martinez	Y	Y	N	N	N	N	Y	N
32 Dixon	Y	Y	N	Y	N	N	Y	N
33 Roybal-Allard	Y	Y	Y	Y	N	N	Y	N
34 Torres	Y	Y	N	Y	N	Y	Y	?
35 Waters	Y	Y	N	N	N	Y	N	N
36 Harman	Y	Y	N	Y	N	N	Y	N
37 Millender-McD.	Y	Y	N	Y	N	N	Y	N
38 ***Horn***	Y	Y	N	N	N	Y	Y	Y
39 ***Royce***	Y	Y	N	N	Y	Y	Y	Y
40 ***Lewis***	Y	Y	N	N	Y	N	Y	N
41 ***Kim***	Y	Y	N	Y	Y	N	Y	Y
42 Brown	Y	Y	Y	Y	N	N	N	N
43 ***Calvert***	Y	Y	N	N	Y	N	Y	Y
44 ***Bono***	Y	Y	N	N	Y	Y	Y	N
45 ***Rohrabacher***	Y	Y	N	N	Y	Y	Y	Y
46 Sanchez	Y	Y	N	Y	N	Y	Y	N
47 ***Cox***	?	?	?	?	?	?	?	?
48 ***Packard***	Y	Y	N	N	Y	N	Y	Y
49 ***Bilbray***	Y	Y	N	N	Y	N	Y	Y
50 Filner	Y	Y	N	N	N	N	N	Y
51 ***Cunningham***	Y	Y	N	N	Y	N	Y	Y
52 ***Hunter***	Y	Y	N	N	Y	Y	Y	N
COLORADO								
1 DeGette	Y	Y	Y	N	N	N	Y	N
2 Skaggs	Y	Y	Y	Y	N	N	Y	N
3 ***McInnis***	Y	Y	N	N	Y	Y	Y	Y
4 ***Schaffer***	Y	Y	N	N	Y	Y	N	Y
5 ***Hefley***	Y	Y	N	N	Y	Y	N	Y
6 ***Schaefer***	Y	Y	N	N	Y	N	Y	Y
CONNECTICUT								
1 Kennelly	Y	Y	Y	Y	N	N	Y	N
2 Gejdenson	Y	Y	Y	Y	N	Y	Y	N
3 DeLauro	Y	Y	Y	Y	N	Y	Y	N
4 ***Shays***	Y	Y	Y	N	N	N	Y	Y
5 Maloney	Y	Y	N	Y	N	Y	Y	N
6 ***Johnson***	Y	Y	N	N	N	N	Y	Y
DELAWARE								
AL ***Castle***	Y	Y	Y	N	Y	N	Y	N
FLORIDA								
1 ***Scarborough***	Y	Y	N	N	Y	Y	Y	Y
2 Boyd	Y	Y	Y	Y	N	N	Y	Y
3 Brown	Y	Y	N	N	N	N	Y	N
4 ***Fowler***	Y	Y	N	N	Y	Y	Y	Y
5 Thurman	Y	Y	N	Y	N	N	Y	N
6 ***Stearns***	Y	Y	N	N	Y	Y	Y	Y
7 ***Mica***	Y	Y	N	N	Y	N	Y	Y
8 ***McCollum***	Y	Y	N	N	Y	N	Y	Y
9 ***Bilirakis***	Y	Y	N	N	Y	N	Y	Y
10 ***Young***	Y	Y	N	N	Y	N	Y	N
11 Davis	Y	Y	Y	Y	?	N	Y	N
12 ***Canady***	Y	Y	N	N	Y	N	Y	Y
13 ***Miller***	Y	Y	Y	N	Y	N	Y	Y
14 ***Goss***	Y	Y	N	N	Y	N	Y	Y
15 ***Weldon***	Y	Y	N	N	Y	Y	Y	+
16 ***Foley***	Y	Y	Y	N	Y	N	Y	Y
17 Meek	Y	Y	N	N	N	N	Y	N
18 ***Ros-Lehtinen***	Y	Y	Y	N	Y	Y	Y	Y
19 Wexler	Y	Y	Y	Y	N	Y	Y	N
20 Deutsch	Y	Y	Y	N	N	N	Y	N
21 ***Diaz-Balart***	Y	Y	N	N	Y	Y	Y	Y
22 ***Shaw***	Y	Y	N	N	Y	N	Y	N
23 Hastings	Y	Y	Y	N	N	Y	N	N
GEORGIA								
1 ***Kingston***	Y	Y	N	N	Y	Y	Y	Y
2 Bishop	Y	Y	N	N	Y	Y	Y	N
3 ***Collins***	Y	Y	N	N	Y	Y	Y	Y
4 McKinney	Y	Y	Y	N	N	Y	Y	N
5 Lewis	Y	Y	Y	N	N	Y	N	N
6 ***Gingrich***			N			N		
7 ***Barr***	Y	Y	N	N	Y	Y	Y	Y
8 ***Chambliss***	Y	Y	N	N	Y	Y	Y	Y
9 ***Deal***	Y	Y	N	N	Y	Y	Y	Y
10 ***Norwood***	Y	Y	N	N	Y	Y	Y	Y
11 ***Linder***	Y	Y	N	N	N	N	Y	N
HAWAII								
1 Abercrombie	Y	Y	Y	N	N	Y	N	N
2 Mink	Y	Y	Y	N	N	Y	Y	Y
IDAHO								
1 ***Chenoweth***	Y	Y	N	N	Y	Y	Y	Y
2 ***Crapo***	Y	Y	N	N	Y	Y	Y	Y
ILLINOIS								
1 Rush	Y	Y	Y	N	N	N	N	N
2 Jackson	Y	Y	Y	Y	N	Y	Y	N
3 Lipinski	?	?	?	?	?	Y	Y	Y
4 Gutierrez	Y	Y	Y	N	N	Y	Y	N
5 Blagojevich	Y	Y	Y	Y	N	N	Y	N
6 ***Hyde***	Y	Y	N	N	N	Y	Y	N
7 Davis	Y	Y	Y	N	N	Y	Y	N
8 ***Crane***	Y	Y	N	N	Y	N	Y	Y
9 Yates	?	?	?	?	?	?	?	?
10 ***Porter***	Y	Y	Y	N	N	N	Y	N
11 ***Weller***	Y	Y	N	N	Y	N	N	Y
12 Costello	Y	Y	Y	Y	Y	Y	N	N
13 ***Fawell***	Y	Y	N	N	Y	N	Y	N
14 ***Hastert***	Y	Y	N	N	N	N	Y	Y
15 ***Ewing***	Y	Y	N	N	Y	N	Y	Y

ND Northern Democrats SD Southern Democrats

	226	227	228	229	230	231	232	233
16 ***Manzullo***	Y	Y	N	N	Y	N	Y	Y
17 Evans	Y	Y	Y	N	N	Y	Y	Y
18 ***LaHood***	Y	Y	N	N	Y	N	Y	Y
19 Poshard	Y	Y	Y	N	Y	N	N	N
20 ***Shimkus***	Y	Y	N	N	Y	N	Y	Y
INDIANA								
1 Visclosky	Y	Y	N	Y	N	Y	N	N
2 ***McIntosh***	?	?	?	#	?	N	Y	Y
3 Roemer	Y	Y	Y	Y	N	N	Y	N
4 ***Souder***	Y	Y	N	N	Y	Y	Y	Y
5 ***Buyer***	Y	Y	N	N	Y	N	Y	N
6 ***Burton***	Y	Y	N	Y	Y	Y	Y	Y
7 ***Pease***	Y	Y	N	N	Y	N	Y	Y
8 ***Hostettler***	Y	Y	N	N	Y	Y	Y	N
9 Hamilton	Y	Y	Y	Y	N	N	Y	N
10 Carson	Y	Y	Y	N	Y	Y	Y	N
IOWA								
1 ***Leach***	Y	Y	Y	N	Y	N	?	N
2 ***Nussle***	Y	Y	Y	N	Y	N	Y	Y
3 Boswell	Y	Y	Y	N	N	N	Y	N
4 ***Ganske***	Y	Y	Y	N	Y	Y	Y	Y
5 ***Latham***	Y	Y	Y	N	Y	N	Y	Y
KANSAS								
1 ***Moran***	Y	Y	N	N	Y	N	N	Y
2 ***Ryun***	Y	Y	N	N	Y	N	Y	Y
3 ***Snowbarger***	Y	Y	N	N	Y	N	Y	Y
4 ***Tiahrt***	Y	Y	N	N	Y	Y	Y	Y
KENTUCKY								
1 ***Whitfield***	Y	Y	N	N	N	N	Y	Y
2 ***Lewis***	Y	Y	N	N	Y	Y	Y	Y
3 ***Northup***	Y	Y	N	N	Y	N	Y	Y
4 ***Bunning***	Y	Y	N	N	Y	Y	Y	Y
5 ***Rogers***	Y	Y	N	N	Y	Y	Y	Y
6 Baesler	Y	Y	Y	N	N	N	Y	N
LOUISIANA								
1 ***Livingston***	Y	Y	N	N	Y	N	Y	N
2 Jefferson	Y	Y	N	N	N	N	Y	N
3 ***Tauzin***	Y	Y	N	N	Y	N	Y	Y
4 ***McCrery***	Y	Y	N	N	Y	N	Y	Y
5 ***Cooksey***	Y	Y	N	N	Y	N	Y	Y
6 ***Baker***	Y	Y	N	N	Y	N	Y	Y
7 John	Y	Y	N	Y	N	N	Y	Y
MAINE								
1 Allen	Y	Y	Y	N	N	N	Y	N
2 Baldacci	Y	Y	Y	Y	N	N	Y	N
MARYLAND								
1 ***Gilchrest***	Y	Y	N	N	N	N	Y	Y
2 ***Ehrlich***	Y	Y	N	N	Y	Y	Y	Y
3 Cardin	Y	Y	Y	Y	N	Y	Y	N
4 Wynn	Y	Y	Y	N	N	Y	Y	N
5 Hoyer	Y	Y	N	Y	N	Y	Y	N
6 ***Bartlett***	Y	Y	N	N	Y	Y	Y	Y
7 Cummings	Y	Y	Y	N	N	Y	N	N
8 ***Morella***	Y	Y	Y	N	N	N	Y	N
MASSACHUSETTS								
1 Olver	Y	Y	Y	N	N	Y	N	N
2 Neal	Y	Y	Y	N	N	N	Y	Y
3 McGovern	Y	Y	Y	N	N	N	Y	N
4 Frank	Y	Y	Y	Y	N	Y	Y	Y
5 Meehan	Y	Y	Y	Y	N	N	Y	N
6 Tierney	Y	Y	Y	Y	N	Y	Y	Y
7 Markey	Y	Y	Y	N	N	Y	Y	Y
8 Kennedy	Y	Y	Y	N	N	Y	Y	N
9 Moakley	Y	Y	Y	Y	N	N	Y	N
10 Delahunt	Y	Y	Y	N	N	Y	Y	N
MICHIGAN								
1 Stupak	Y	Y	Y	Y	N	Y	N	N
2 ***Hoekstra***	Y	Y	Y	N	Y	N	Y	Y
3 ***Ehlers***	Y	Y	Y	N	Y	Y	Y	N
4 ***Camp***	Y	Y	Y	N	Y	N	Y	Y
5 Barcia	Y	Y	N	N	Y	Y	Y	Y
6 ***Upton***	Y	Y	Y	N	Y	Y	Y	Y
7 ***Smith***	Y	Y	Y	N	Y	Y	Y	N
8 Stabenow	Y	Y	Y	Y	N	N	Y	N
9 Kildee	Y	Y	Y	N	N	Y	Y	N
10 Bonior	Y	Y	Y	N	N	Y	Y	N
11 ***Knollenberg***	Y	Y	N	N	Y	N	Y	N
12 Levin	Y	Y	Y	Y	N	N	Y	N
13 Rivers	Y	Y	Y	N	N	Y	Y	N
14 Conyers	Y	Y	Y	N	N	N	Y	N
15 Kilpatrick	+	+	Y	Y	N	Y	N	N
16 Dingell	Y	Y	Y	Y	N	N	Y	N
MINNESOTA								
1 ***Gutknecht***	Y	Y	Y	N	Y	N	N	Y
2 Minge	Y	Y	Y	Y	N	N	Y	N

	226	227	228	229	230	231	232	233
3 ***Ramstad***	Y	Y	Y	N	Y	N	N	Y
4 Vento	Y	Y	Y	Y	N	Y	Y	N
5 Sabo	Y	Y	Y	Y	N	Y	N	N
6 Luther	Y	Y	Y	Y	N	N	Y	N
7 Peterson	Y	Y	Y	Y	N	N	Y	Y
8 Oberstar	Y	Y	Y	Y	N	N	N	N
MISSISSIPPI								
1 ***Wicker***	Y	Y	N	N	Y	N	N	N
2 Thompson	Y	Y	N	Y	N	Y	N	N
3 ***Pickering***	Y	Y	N	N	Y	Y	Y	Y
4 ***Parker***	Y	Y	N	N	Y	Y	Y	Y
5 Taylor	Y	Y	N	N	N	Y	N	N
MISSOURI								
1 Clay	Y	Y	Y	Y	N	Y	N	N
2 ***Talent***	Y	Y	N	N	Y	N	Y	Y
3 Gephardt	Y	Y	Y	Y	N	Y	N	N
4 Skelton	Y	Y	N	N	N	N	Y	N
5 McCarthy	Y	Y	Y	Y	N	N	Y	N
6 Danner	Y	Y	Y	N	Y	Y	Y	Y
7 ***Blunt***	?	?	?	X	?	Y	Y	N
8 ***Emerson***	Y	Y	N	N	Y	N	Y	N
9 ***Hulshof***	Y	Y	N	N	Y	N	N	Y
MONTANA								
AL ***Hill***	Y	Y	N	N	Y	N	Y	Y
NEBRASKA								
1 ***Bereuter***	Y	Y	Y	N	N	N	Y	Y
2 ***Christensen***	Y	Y	Y	N	Y	N	Y	Y
3 ***Barrett***	Y	Y	N	N	Y	N	Y	Y
NEVADA								
1 ***Ensign***	Y	Y	N	N	Y	Y	N	Y
2 ***Gibbons***	Y	Y	N	N	Y	Y	N	Y
NEW HAMPSHIRE								
1 ***Sununu***	Y	Y	Y	N	Y	N	N	Y
2 ***Bass***	Y	Y	Y	N	Y	N	?	Y
NEW JERSEY								
1 Andrews	Y	Y	Y	Y	N	N	Y	N
2 ***LoBiondo***	Y	Y	Y	N	Y	Y	N	Y
3 ***Saxton***	Y	Y	N	N	Y	N	N	Y
4 ***Smith***	Y	Y	N	N	N	Y	Y	N
5 ***Roukema***	Y	Y	Y	N	Y	N	Y	Y
6 Pallone	Y	Y	Y	N	N	N	Y	N
7 ***Franks***	Y	Y	Y	N	Y	N	Y	Y
8 Pascrell	Y	Y	Y	Y	Y	Y	N	N
9 Rothman	Y	Y	Y	Y	N	Y	Y	N
10 Payne	Y	Y	Y	N	N	Y	Y	N
11 ***Frelinghuysen***	Y	Y	N	N	Y	N	Y	N
12 ***Pappas***	Y	Y	N	N	Y	Y	Y	Y
13 Menendez	Y	Y	Y	N	N	Y	Y	N
NEW MEXICO								
1 ***Schiff***	?	?	?	?	?	?	?	?
2 ***Skeen***	Y	Y	N	N	Y	N	Y	N
3 ***Redmond***	Y	Y	N	N	Y	N	N	N
NEW YORK								
1 ***Forbes***	Y	Y	N	N	Y	Y	Y	Y
2 ***Lazio***	Y	Y	Y	N	Y	N	Y	N
3 ***King***	Y	Y	N	N	N	Y	Y	N
4 McCarthy	Y	Y	Y	N	Y	Y	Y	N
5 Ackerman	Y	Y	N	N	N	N	Y	N
6 Flake	Y	Y	Y	N	N	N	Y	N
7 Manton	?	Y	Y	N	N	N	Y	N
8 Nadler	+	+	Y	Y	N	Y	Y	N
9 Schumer	?	?	+	?	?	N	Y	?
10 Towns	Y	Y	Y	?	?	N	Y	N
11 Owens	?	Y	Y	Y	N	Y	Y	N
12 Velázquez	Y	Y	Y	Y	N	Y	Y	N
13 ***Molinari***	Y	Y	Y	N	Y	Y	Y	N
14 Maloney	?	?	?	?	?	N	N	N
15 Rangel	Y	Y	Y	Y	N	N	Y	N
16 Serrano	Y	Y	Y	Y	N	N	N	Y
17 Engel	Y	Y	Y	N	N	Y	Y	N
18 Lowey	Y	Y	Y	Y	N	N	Y	N
19 ***Kelly***	Y	Y	N	N	Y	N	Y	Y
20 ***Gilman***	Y	Y	N	N	Y	Y	Y	N
21 McNulty	Y	Y	Y	N	Y	N	N	N
22 ***Solomon***	Y	Y	N	N	Y	Y	Y	Y
23 ***Boehlert***	Y	Y	Y	Y	N	N	Y	N
24 ***McHugh***	Y	Y	N	N	Y	N	Y	N
25 ***Walsh***	Y	Y	N	N	Y	N	Y	Y
26 Hinchey	Y	Y	N	Y	N	Y	Y	N
27 ***Paxon***	Y	Y	?	N	Y	Y	Y	Y
28 Slaughter	Y	Y	Y	Y	N	N	Y	N
29 LaFalce	Y	Y	Y	Y	N	N	Y	N
30 ***Quinn***	Y	Y	Y	N	Y	N	Y	N
31 ***Houghton***	Y	Y	Y	?	?	N	Y	N

	226	227	228	229	230	231	232	233
NORTH CAROLINA								
1 Clayton	Y	Y	Y	N	N	Y	N	N
2 Etheridge	Y	Y	N	N	N	N	Y	N
3 ***Jones***	Y	Y	N	N	Y	Y	Y	Y
4 Price	Y	Y	Y	N	N	N	Y	N
5 ***Burr***	Y	Y	Y	N	Y	Y	Y	Y
6 ***Coble***	Y	Y	Y	N	Y	N	Y	Y
7 McIntyre	Y	Y	N	N	Y	Y	Y	N
8 Hefner	Y	Y	N	N	N	Y	N	N
9 ***Myrick***	Y	Y	N	N	Y	Y	Y	Y
10 ***Ballenger***	Y	Y	Y	N	Y	N	Y	Y
11 ***Taylor***	Y	Y	N	N	Y	N	Y	Y
12 Watt	Y	Y	Y	N	N	Y	N	N
NORTH DAKOTA								
AL Pomeroy	Y	Y	Y	Y	N	N	Y	N
OHIO								
1 ***Chabot***	Y	Y	Y	N	Y	N	Y	Y
2 ***Portman***	Y	Y	Y	N	Y	N	Y	Y
3 Hall	Y	Y	Y	N	Y	Y	Y	N
4 ***Oxley***	Y	Y	N	N	N	N	Y	N
5 ***Gillmor***	Y	Y	N	N	Y	Y	Y	N
6 Strickland	Y	Y	Y	Y	N	Y	?	N
7 ***Hobson***	Y	Y	N	N	Y	Y	Y	Y
8 ***Boehner***	Y	Y	N	N	Y	N	Y	N
9 Kaptur	Y	Y	Y	N	Y	Y	Y	N
10 Kucinich	Y	Y	Y	N	N	Y	N	N
11 Stokes	Y	Y	Y	N	N	Y	Y	N
12 ***Kasich***	Y	Y	Y	N	Y	Y	Y	Y
13 Brown	Y	Y	Y	Y	N	Y	N	N
14 Sawyer	Y	Y	Y	Y	N	N	Y	N
15 ***Pryce***	Y	Y	Y	N	Y	N	Y	Y
16 ***Regula***	Y	Y	Y	N	Y	N	Y	N
17 Traficant	Y	Y	N	N	Y	Y	Y	Y
18 ***Ney***	Y	Y	Y	N	Y	N	Y	Y
19 ***LaTourette***	Y	Y	Y	N	Y	N	Y	Y
OKLAHOMA								
1 ***Largent***	Y	Y	Y	N	Y	N	Y	Y
2 ***Coburn***	Y	Y	Y	N	Y	Y	Y	Y
3 ***Watkins***	Y	Y	N	N	Y	N	Y	Y
4 ***Watts***	Y	Y	N	N	Y	Y	N	Y
5 ***Istook***	Y	Y	N	N	Y	N	Y	Y
6 ***Lucas***	Y	Y	N	N	Y	N	Y	Y
OREGON								
1 Furse	Y	Y	Y	Y	N	N	Y	N
2 ***Smith***	Y	Y	N	N	Y	N	Y	Y
3 Blumenauer	Y	Y	Y	Y	N	N	Y	N
4 DeFazio	Y	Y	Y	Y	N	Y	N	Y
5 Hooley	Y	Y	Y	Y	N	N	Y	N
PENNSYLVANIA								
1 Foglietta	Y	Y	Y	Y	N	N	N	N
2 Fattah	Y	Y	Y	Y	N	N	Y	N
3 Borski	Y	Y	N	N	N	Y	N	N
4 Klink	Y	Y	Y	N	N	Y	Y	N
5 ***Peterson***	Y	Y	N	N	Y	N	Y	Y
6 Holden	Y	Y	N	N	N	N	Y	N
7 ***Weldon***	Y	Y	Y	N	N	N	Y	N
8 ***Greenwood***	Y	Y	Y	N	Y	N	Y	N
9 ***Shuster***	Y	Y	Y	N	?	N	Y	Y
10 ***McDade***	Y	?	N	N	N	N	Y	Y
11 Kanjorski	Y	Y	Y	N	N	N	Y	N
12 Murtha	N	Y	N	N	N	N	Y	N
13 ***Fox***	Y	Y	Y	N	Y	N	N	N
14 Coyne	Y	Y	Y	N	N	Y	Y	N
15 McHale	Y	Y	Y	Y	N	N	Y	N
16 ***Pitts***	Y	Y	N	N	Y	N	Y	Y
17 ***Gekas***	Y	Y	N	N	Y	N	Y	Y
18 Doyle	Y	Y	Y	N	N	N	Y	N
19 ***Goodling***	Y	Y	Y	N	Y	Y	Y	Y
20 Mascara	Y	Y	Y	N	N	Y	Y	N
21 ***English***	Y	Y	N	N	Y	N	N	Y
RHODE ISLAND								
1 Kennedy	Y	Y	Y	Y	N	Y	Y	N
2 Weygand	Y	Y	Y	Y	N	Y	Y	N
SOUTH CAROLINA								
1 ***Sanford***	Y	Y	Y	N	Y	Y	Y	Y
2 ***Spence***	Y	Y	N	N	Y	Y	Y	Y
3 ***Graham***	Y	Y	N	N	N	Y	Y	Y
4 ***Inglis***	Y	Y	N	N	Y	Y	Y	Y
5 Spratt	Y	Y	Y	Y	N	Y	Y	N
6 Clyburn	Y	Y	N	Y	N	Y	Y	N
SOUTH DAKOTA								
AL ***Thune***	Y	Y	N	N	Y	N	Y	Y
TENNESSEE								
1 ***Jenkins***	Y	Y	N	N	Y	N	Y	Y
2 ***Duncan***	Y	Y	Y	Y	Y	Y	Y	Y

	226	227	228	229	230	231	232	
3 ***Wamp***	Y	Y	Y	N	Y	Y	Y	Y
4 ***Hilleary***	Y	Y	N	Y	Y	Y	Y	Y
5 Clement	Y	Y	Y	N	N	N	Y	N
6 Gordon	?	?	?	?	?	Y	Y	N
7 ***Bryant***	Y	Y	N	N	Y	N	Y	+
8 Tanner	Y	Y	Y	Y	N	N	Y	N
9 Ford	Y	Y	Y	N	N	N	Y	N
TEXAS								
1 Sandlin	Y	Y	N	Y	N	N	Y	N
2 Turner	Y	Y	N	Y	N	N	Y	N
3 ***Johnson, Sam***	Y	Y	N	Y	Y	N	Y	Y
4 Hall	Y	Y	N	N	Y	N	Y	Y
5 ***Sessions***	Y	Y	N	Y	Y	N	N	Y
6 ***Barton***	Y	Y	Y	Y	Y	Y	Y	Y
7 ***Archer***	Y	Y	Y	N	Y	N	Y	Y
8 ***Brady***	Y	Y	N	Y	Y	N	Y	Y
9 Lampson	Y	Y	Y	Y	N	N	Y	N
10 Doggett	Y	Y	Y	Y	N	N	Y	N
11 Edwards	Y	Y	Y	Y	N	N	Y	N
12 ***Granger***	Y	Y	N	Y	Y	N	Y	Y
13 ***Thornberry***	Y	Y	N	Y	N	N	Y	Y
14 ***Paul***	Y	Y	Y	Y	Y	N	Y	Y
15 Hinojosa	Y	Y	N	Y	N	N	Y	N
16 Reyes	Y	Y	N	Y	N	N	Y	N
17 Stenholm	Y	Y	Y	N	Y	N	Y	N
18 Jackson-Lee	Y	Y	N	Y	N	N	Y	N
19 ***Combest***	Y	Y	Y	Y	Y	N	Y	Y
20 Gonzalez	Y	Y	N	Y	N	Y	Y	N
21 ***Smith***	Y	Y	N	Y	Y	N	Y	N
22 ***DeLay***	Y	Y	N	N	Y	N	Y	Y
23 ***Bonilla***	Y	Y	N	Y	Y	N	Y	Y
24 Frost	Y	Y	N	Y	N	N	Y	N
25 Bentsen	Y	Y	N	Y	N	N	Y	N
26 ***Armey***	Y	Y	N	N	Y	N	Y	N
27 Ortiz	Y	Y	N	N	N	N	Y	N
28 Rodriguez	Y	Y	N	Y	N	N	Y	N
29 Green	Y	Y	N	N	N	N	N	Y
30 Johnson, E.B.	Y	Y	N	N	N	N	N	N
UTAH								
1 ***Hansen***	Y	Y	N	N	Y	N	Y	Y
2 ***Cook***	Y	Y	N	N	Y	Y	Y	Y
3 ***Cannon***	Y	Y	N	N	Y	N	Y	Y
VERMONT								
AL *Sanders*	Y	Y	Y	Y	N	Y	Y	Y
VIRGINIA								
1 ***Bateman***	Y	Y	N	N	N	N	Y	N
2 Pickett	Y	Y	Y	N	N	N	N	N
3 Scott	Y	Y	Y	N	N	Y	Y	N
4 Sisisky	Y	Y	Y	N	N	Y	Y	N
5 Goode	Y	Y	Y	N	Y	Y	Y	Y
6 ***Goodlatte***	Y	Y	Y	N	Y	N	Y	Y
7 ***Bliley***	Y	Y	N	N	Y	N	Y	N
8 Moran	N	Y	Y	Y	N	N	Y	N
9 Boucher	Y	Y	Y	N	N	N	Y	N
10 ***Wolf***	Y	Y	N	N	Y	Y	Y	N
11 ***Davis***	Y	Y	N	N	Y	N	Y	N
WASHINGTON								
1 ***White***	Y	Y	Y	N	N	N	Y	N
2 ***Metcalf***	Y	Y	N	N	Y	N	Y	Y
3 ***Smith, Linda***	Y	Y	N	Y	Y	Y	Y	Y
4 ***Hastings***	Y	Y	N	N	Y	N	Y	Y
5 ***Nethercutt***	Y	Y	N	N	Y	N	Y	Y
6 Dicks	Y	Y	N	N	N	N	Y	N
7 McDermott	Y	Y	Y	Y	N	N	N	N
8 ***Dunn***	Y	Y	N	N	Y	N	Y	Y
9 Smith, Adam	Y	Y	Y	Y	N	N	Y	N
WEST VIRGINIA								
1 Mollohan	?	?	N	Y	N	Y	Y	N
2 Wise	Y	Y	Y	Y	N	N	Y	N
3 Rahall	Y	Y	Y	N	N	Y	Y	N
WISCONSIN								
1 ***Neumann***	Y	Y	N	N	Y	N	Y	Y
2 ***Klug***	Y	Y	Y	Y	Y	Y	Y	Y
3 Kind	Y	Y	Y	Y	N	N	Y	N
4 Kleczka	Y	Y	Y	Y	N	N	Y	N
5 Barrett	+	+	Y	Y	N	N	Y	N
6 ***Petri***	Y	Y	Y	N	Y	N	Y	Y
7 Obey	Y	Y	Y	Y	N	Y	Y	N
8 Johnson	Y	Y	Y	Y	N	N	Y	N
9 ***Sensenbrenner***	Y	Y	Y	N	Y	Y	Y	Y
WYOMING								
AL ***Cubin***	Y	Y	N	N	Y	Y	Y	Y

Southern states - Ala., Ark., Fla., Ga., Ky., La., Miss., N.C., Okla., S.C., Tenn., Texas, Va.

HOUSE VOTES 234, 235, 236, 237, 238, 239, 240, 241

234. HR 1119. Fiscal 1998 Defense Authorization/Bosnia Troop Withdrawal. Buyer, R-Ind., amendment to prohibit funding for U.S. ground troops in Bosnia after June 30, 1998. Adopted 278-148: R 220-2; D 57-146 (ND 37-111, SD 20-35); I 1-0, June 24, 1997. A "nay" was a vote in support of the president's position.

235. HR 1119. Fiscal 1998 Defense Authorization/Russian Missile Transfer. Separate vote requested by Dellums, D-Calif., on the Rohrabacher, R-Calif., amendment adopted June 23 in the Committee of the Whole (vote 230) to prohibit the transfer of the bill's Nunn-Lugar funding designated for Russia if Russia transfers an SS-N-22 missile system to China. Rejected 204-219: R 193-28; D 11-190 (ND 7-139, SD 4-51); I 0-1, June 25, 1997. A "nay" was a vote in support of the president's position.

236. HR 1119. Fiscal 1998 Defense Authorization/Passage. Passage of the bill to authorize $268.2 billion for defense programs in fiscal 1998, $2.6 billion more than the president requested. The bill also prohibits funding for U.S. ground troops in Bosnia after June 30, 1998, and effectively prohibits private contractors from performing maintenance work at Air Force maintenance depots in San Antonio and Sacramento, Calif. Passed 304-120: R 206-14; D 98-105 (ND 55-93, SD 43-12); I 0-1, June 25, 1997.

237. H Con Res 102. Cost of Government Spending/Adoption. Sessions, R-Texas, motion to suspend the rules and adopt the concurrent resolution to express the sense of Congress that the cost of government spending and regulatory programs should be reduced. Adopted 386-20: R 220-0; D 165-20 (ND 116-18, SD 49-2); I 1-0, June 25, 1997. A two-thirds majority of those present and voting (271 in this case) is required for adoption under suspension of the rules.

238. HR 2015, HR 2014. Fiscal 1998 Budget Reconciliation/Previous Question. Solomon, R-N.Y., motion to order the previous question (thus ending debate and the possibility of amendment) on adoption of the rule (H Res 174) to provide for House floor consideration of the bills to cut projected entitlement spending by about $137 billion and taxes by $85 billion over the next five years in order to provide for a balanced budget by fiscal 2002. The rule makes several self-executing changes to the spending bill (HR 2015), including an additional $1 billion to help pay the Medicare Part B premium for low-income seniors and increased savings of $10.6 billion from radio broadcast spectrum auctions. Motion agreed to 222-204: R 222-0; D 0-203 (ND 0-148, SD 0-55); I 0-1, June 25, 1997.

239. HR 2015, HR 2014. Fiscal 1998 Budget Reconciliation/Rule. Adoption of the rule (H Res 174) to provide for House floor consideration of bills to cut projected entitlement spending by about $137 billion and taxes by $85 billion over the next five years to provide for a balanced budget by fiscal 2002. The rule makes several self-executing changes to the spending bill (HR 2015), including an additional $1 billion to help pay the Medicare Part B premium for low-income seniors and an increased revenues of $10.6 billion from radio broadcast spectrum auctions. Adopted 228-200: R 222-2; D 6-197 (ND 4-145, SD 2-52); I 0-1, June 25, 1997.

240. HR 2015. Fiscal 1998 Budget Reconciliation — Spending/Recommit. Brown, D-Ohio, motion to recommit the bill to the Budget Committee with instructions to report it back with an amendment to substitute a Medicaid-based entitlement program for the bill's Child Health Assistance block grant program to expand health coverage to uninsured children and continue Medicaid eligibility for disabled children who lose Supplemental Security Income (SSI) benefits. Rejected 207-223: R 1-223; D 205-0 (ND 150-0,SD 55-0); I 1-0, June 25, 1997.

241. HR 2015. Fiscal 1998 Budget Reconciliation — Spending/Passage. Passage of the bill to cut total projected entitlement spending over five years by about $137 billion, including a $115 billion reduction in Medicare, in order to provide for a balanced budget by fiscal 2002. The bill increases the health insurance options available to Medicare beneficiaries beyond its fee-for-service program and permits up to 500,000 Medicare beneficiaries to establish tax-free medical savings accounts. The bill also includes a $14.4 billion block grant program to help states improve health coverage for uninsured children and restores Supplemental Security Income (SSI) and Medicaid benefits to certain legal immigrants. Passed 270-162: R 219-7; D 51-154 (ND 28-122, SD 23-32); I 0-1, June 25, 1997.

KEY

- Y Voted for (yea).
- # Paired for.
- + Announced for.
- N Voted against (nay).
- X Paired against.
- – Announced against.
- P Voted "present."
- C Voted "present" to avoid possible conflict of interest.
- ? Did not vote or otherwise make a position known.

Democrats ***Republicans***
Independent

	234	235	236	237	238	239	240	241
ALABAMA								
1 ***Callahan***	Y	Y	Y	Y	Y	Y	N	Y
2 ***Everett***	Y	Y	Y	Y	Y	Y	N	Y
3 ***Riley***	Y	Y	Y	Y	Y	Y	N	Y
4 ***Aderholt***	Y	Y	Y	Y	Y	Y	N	Y
5 Cramer	Y	Y	Y	Y	N	N	Y	Y
6 ***Bachus***	Y	Y	Y	Y	Y	Y	N	Y
7 Hilliard	N	N	N	Y	N	N	Y	N
ALASKA								
AL ***Young***	Y	Y	Y	Y	Y	Y	N	Y
ARIZONA								
1 ***Salmon***	Y	Y	Y	Y	Y	Y	N	N
2 Pastor	N	N	Y	Y	N	N	Y	N
3 ***Stump***	Y	Y	Y	Y	Y	Y	N	Y
4 ***Shadegg***	Y	Y	Y	Y	Y	Y	N	Y
5 ***Kolbe***	Y	N	Y	Y	Y	Y	N	Y
6 ***Hayworth***	Y	Y	Y	Y	Y	Y	N	Y
ARKANSAS								
1 Berry	Y	N	Y	Y	N	N	Y	N
2 Snyder	N	N	Y	Y	N	N	Y	Y
3 ***Hutchinson***	Y	Y	Y	Y	Y	Y	N	Y
4 ***Dickey***	Y	Y	Y	Y	Y	Y	N	Y
CALIFORNIA								
1 ***Riggs***	Y	Y	Y	Y	Y	Y	Y	Y
2 ***Herger***	Y	Y	Y	Y	Y	Y	N	Y
3 Fazio	N	N	N	?	N	N	Y	N
4 ***Doolittle***	Y	Y	Y	Y	Y	Y	N	Y
5 Matsui	N	N	N	Y	N	N	Y	N
6 Woolsey	N	N	N	Y	N	N	Y	N
7 Miller	Y	N	N	N	N	N	Y	N
8 Pelosi	N	N	N	P	N	N	Y	N
9 Dellums	N	N	N	N	N	N	Y	N
10 Tauscher	N	N	Y	Y	N	N	Y	Y
11 ***Pombo***	Y	Y	Y	Y	Y	Y	N	Y
12 Lantos	N	N	N	Y	N	N	Y	N
13 Stark	N	N	N	N	N	?	Y	N
14 Eshoo	Y	N	N	Y	?	N	Y	N
15 ***Campbell***	Y	Y	N	Y	Y	Y	N	Y
16 Lofgren	Y	N	N	P	N	N	Y	N
17 Farr	N	N	N	Y	N	N	Y	N
18 Condit	Y	Y	Y	Y	N	N	Y	Y
19 ***Radanovich***	Y	Y	#	Y	Y	Y	N	Y
20 Dooley	Y	N	Y	Y	N	N	Y	Y
21 ***Thomas***	Y	Y	Y	Y	Y	Y	N	Y
22 Capps	N	N	Y	Y	N	N	Y	Y
23 ***Gallegly***	Y	Y	Y	Y	Y	Y	N	Y
24 Sherman	Y	N	Y	Y	N	N	Y	N
25 ***McKeon***	Y	Y	Y	Y	Y	Y	N	Y
26 Berman	N	N	N	Y	N	N	Y	N
27 ***Rogan***	Y	Y	Y	Y	Y	Y	N	Y
28 ***Dreier***	Y	Y	Y	Y	Y	Y	N	Y
29 Waxman	N	N	N	?	N	N	Y	N
30 Becerra	N	N	N	P	N	N	Y	N
31 Martinez	N	N	N	Y	N	N	Y	Y
32 Dixon	N	N	Y	Y	N	N	Y	N
33 Roybal-Allard	N	N	N	N	N	N	Y	N
34 Torres	N	N	Y	P	N	N	Y	N
35 Waters	N	N	N	N	N	N	Y	N
36 Harman	Y	N	Y	Y	N	N	Y	Y
37 Millender-McD.	N	N	Y	Y	N	N	Y	N
38 ***Horn***	Y	N	Y	Y	Y	Y	N	Y
39 ***Royce***	Y	Y	N	Y	Y	Y	N	Y
40 ***Lewis***	Y	Y	Y	Y	Y	Y	N	Y
41 ***Kim***	Y	Y	Y	Y	Y	Y	N	Y
42 Brown	N	?	N	Y	N	N	Y	N
43 ***Calvert***	Y	Y	Y	Y	Y	Y	N	Y
44 ***Bono***	Y	Y	Y	Y	Y	Y	N	Y
45 ***Rohrabacher***	Y	Y	Y	Y	Y	Y	N	Y
46 Sanchez	Y	N	Y	Y	N	N	Y	Y
47 ***Cox***	?	?	?	?	?	?	?	?
48 ***Packard***	Y	Y	Y	Y	Y	Y	N	Y
49 ***Bilbray***	Y	Y	Y	Y	Y	Y	N	Y
50 Filner	Y	N	N	Y	N	N	Y	N
51 ***Cunningham***	Y	Y	Y	Y	Y	Y	N	Y
52 ***Hunter***	Y	Y	Y	Y	Y	Y	N	Y
COLORADO								
1 DeGette	N	N	N	Y	N	N	Y	N
2 Skaggs	N	N	N	Y	N	N	Y	N
3 ***McInnis***	Y	Y	Y	Y	Y	Y	N	Y
4 ***Schaffer***	Y	Y	Y	Y	Y	Y	N	Y
5 ***Hefley***	Y	Y	Y	Y	Y	Y	N	Y
6 ***Schaefer***	Y	Y	Y	Y	Y	Y	N	Y
CONNECTICUT								
1 Kennelly	N	N	Y	Y	N	N	Y	Y
2 Gejdenson	N	N	Y	Y	N	N	Y	N
3 DeLauro	N	N	Y	Y	N	N	Y	N
4 ***Shays***	Y	N	N	Y	Y	Y	N	Y
5 Maloney	Y	N	Y	Y	N	N	Y	Y
6 ***Johnson***	Y	N	Y	Y	Y	Y	N	Y
DELAWARE								
AL ***Castle***	Y	Y	Y	Y	Y	Y	N	Y
FLORIDA								
1 ***Scarborough***	Y	Y	Y	Y	Y	Y	N	Y
2 Boyd	Y	N	Y	Y	N	N	Y	Y
3 Brown	N	N	Y	P	N	N	Y	N
4 ***Fowler***	Y	Y	Y	Y	Y	Y	N	Y
5 Thurman	N	N	Y	Y	N	N	Y	Y
6 ***Stearns***	Y	Y	Y	Y	Y	Y	N	N
7 ***Mica***	Y	Y	Y	Y	Y	Y	N	Y
8 ***McCollum***	Y	Y	Y	Y	Y	Y	N	Y
9 ***Bilirakis***	Y	Y	Y	Y	Y	Y	N	Y
10 ***Young***	Y	Y	Y	Y	Y	Y	N	Y
11 Davis	N	N	Y	Y	N	N	Y	Y
12 ***Canady***	Y	Y	Y	Y	Y	Y	N	Y
13 ***Miller***	Y	Y	Y	Y	Y	Y	N	Y
14 ***Goss***	Y	Y	Y	Y	Y	Y	N	Y
15 ***Weldon***	Y	Y	Y	Y	Y	Y	N	Y
16 ***Foley***	Y	Y	Y	Y	Y	Y	N	Y
17 Meek	N	N	Y	Y	N	?	Y	N
18 ***Ros-Lehtinen***	Y	Y	Y	Y	Y	Y	N	Y
19 Wexler	N	N	N	Y	N	N	Y	N
20 Deutsch	N	N	N	Y	N	N	Y	N
21 ***Diaz-Balart***	Y	Y	Y	Y	Y	Y	N	Y
22 ***Shaw***	Y	Y	Y	Y	Y	Y	N	Y
23 Hastings	N	N	N	P	N	N	Y	N
GEORGIA								
1 ***Kingston***	Y	Y	Y	Y	Y	Y	N	Y
2 Bishop	Y	N	Y	Y	N	N	Y	Y
3 ***Collins***	Y	Y	Y	Y	Y	Y	N	Y
4 McKinney	N	N	N	Y	N	N	Y	N
5 Lewis	N	N	N	P	N	N	Y	N
6 ***Gingrich***								Y
7 ***Barr***	Y	Y	Y	Y	Y	Y	N	Y
8 ***Chambliss***	Y	Y	Y	Y	Y	Y	N	Y
9 ***Deal***	Y	Y	Y	Y	Y	Y	N	Y
10 ***Norwood***	Y	Y	Y	Y	Y	Y	N	Y
11 ***Linder***	Y	N	Y	Y	Y	Y	N	Y
HAWAII								
1 Abercrombie	N	–	Y	Y	N	N	Y	N
2 Mink	Y	N	Y	Y	N	N	Y	N
IDAHO								
1 ***Chenoweth***	Y	Y	Y	Y	Y	Y	?	Y
2 ***Crapo***	Y	Y	Y	Y	Y	Y	N	Y
ILLINOIS								
1 Rush	N	N	N	Y	N	N	Y	N
2 Jackson	N	N	N	N	N	N	Y	N
3 Lipinski	Y	Y	Y	Y	N	N	Y	N
4 Gutierrez	N	N	N	Y	N	N	Y	N
5 Blagojevich	N	N	Y	Y	N	N	Y	N
6 ***Hyde***	Y	N	Y	Y	Y	Y	N	Y
7 Davis	N	N	N	Y	N	N	Y	N
8 ***Crane***	Y	+	+	Y	Y	Y	N	Y
9 Yates	?	?	X	?	?	?	?	X
10 ***Porter***	Y	N	Y	Y	Y	Y	N	Y
11 ***Weller***	Y	Y	Y	Y	Y	Y	N	Y
12 Costello	Y	Y	Y	Y	N	N	Y	N
13 ***Fawell***	Y	Y	Y	Y	Y	Y	N	Y
14 ***Hastert***	Y	N	Y	Y	Y	Y	N	Y
15 ***Ewing***	Y	Y	Y	Y	Y	Y	N	Y

ND Northern Democrats SD Southern Democrats

Member	234	235	236	237	238	239	240	241
16 ***Manzullo***	Y	Y	Y	Y	Y	Y	N	Y
17 Evans	Y	N	N	Y	N	N	Y	N
18 ***LaHood***	Y	Y	Y	Y	Y	Y	N	Y
19 Poshard	Y	Y	Y	Y	N	N	Y	N
20 ***Shimkus***	Y	Y	Y	Y	Y	Y	N	Y
INDIANA								
1 Visclosky	N	N	Y	Y	N	N	Y	Y
2 ***McIntosh***	Y	N	Y	Y	Y	Y	N	N
3 Roemer	Y	N	N	Y	N	Y	Y	Y
4 ***Souder***	Y	Y	Y	Y	Y	Y	N	Y
5 ***Buyer***	Y	Y	Y	Y	Y	Y	N	Y
6 ***Burton***	Y	Y	Y	Y	Y	Y	N	Y
7 ***Pease***	Y	N	Y	Y	Y	Y	N	Y
8 ***Hostettler***	Y	Y	Y	Y	Y	Y	N	Y
9 Hamilton	N	N	Y	Y	N	N	Y	Y
10 Carson	N	N	N	P	N	N	Y	N
IOWA								
1 ***Leach***	Y	Y	Y	Y	Y	Y	N	Y
2 ***Nussle***	Y	Y	Y	Y	Y	Y	N	Y
3 Boswell	N	N	Y	Y	N	N	Y	Y
4 ***Ganske***	Y	N	Y	N	Y	Y	N	Y
5 ***Latham***	Y	Y	Y	Y	Y	Y	N	Y
KANSAS								
1 ***Moran***	Y	Y	Y	Y	Y	Y	N	N
2 ***Ryun***	Y	Y	Y	Y	Y	Y	N	Y
3 ***Snowbarger***	Y	Y	Y	Y	Y	Y	N	Y
4 ***Tiahrt***	Y	Y	Y	Y	Y	Y	N	Y
KENTUCKY								
1 ***Whitfield***	Y	N	Y	Y	Y	Y	N	Y
2 ***Lewis***	Y	Y	Y	Y	Y	Y	N	Y
3 ***Northup***	Y	Y	Y	Y	Y	Y	N	Y
4 ***Bunning***	Y	Y	Y	Y	Y	Y	N	Y
5 ***Rogers***	Y	Y	Y	Y	Y	Y	N	Y
6 Baesler	N	N	Y	Y	N	N	Y	Y
LOUISIANA								
1 ***Livingston***	Y	Y	Y	Y	Y	Y	N	Y
2 Jefferson	N	N	Y	Y	N	N	Y	N
3 ***Tauzin***	Y	Y	Y	Y	Y	Y	N	Y
4 ***McCrery***	Y	Y	Y	Y	Y	Y	N	Y
5 ***Cooksey***	Y	Y	Y	Y	Y	Y	N	Y
6 ***Baker***	Y	Y	Y	Y	Y	Y	N	Y
7 John	Y	N	Y	Y	N	N	Y	Y
MAINE								
1 Allen	N	N	Y	Y	N	N	Y	N
2 Baldacci	N	N	N	Y	N	Y	Y	N
MARYLAND								
1 ***Gilchrest***	Y	N	Y	Y	Y	Y	N	Y
2 ***Ehrlich***	Y	Y	Y	Y	Y	Y	N	Y
3 Cardin	N	N	N	Y	N	N	Y	N
4 Wynn	N	N	N	Y	N	N	Y	N
5 Hoyer	N	N	Y	Y	N	N	Y	N
6 ***Bartlett***	Y	Y	Y	Y	Y	Y	N	Y
7 Cummings	N	N	N	Y	N	N	Y	N
8 ***Morella***	Y	N	N	Y	Y	Y	N	Y
MASSACHUSETTS								
1 Olver	N	N	N	Y	N	N	Y	N
2 Neal	N	N	N	Y	N	N	Y	N
3 McGovern	N	N	N	Y	N	N	Y	N
4 Frank	Y	N	N	Y	N	N	Y	N
5 Meehan	N	N	Y	Y	N	N	Y	N
6 Tierney	Y	N	Y	N	N	N	Y	N
7 Markey	N	N	N	Y	N	N	Y	N
8 Kennedy	N	N	N	Y	N	N	Y	N
9 Moakley	N	N	N	Y	N	N	Y	N
10 Delahunt	N	N	N	?	N	N	Y	N
MICHIGAN								
1 Stupak	N	N	N	Y	N	N	Y	N
2 ***Hoekstra***	Y	Y	Y	Y	Y	Y	N	Y
3 ***Ehlers***	Y	Y	N	Y	Y	Y	N	Y
4 ***Camp***	Y	Y	Y	Y	Y	Y	N	Y
5 Barcia	Y	N	Y	Y	N	N	Y	Y
6 ***Upton***	Y	Y	Y	Y	Y	Y	N	Y
7 ***Smith***	Y	N	Y	Y	Y	Y	N	Y
8 Stabenow	N	N	N	Y	N	N	Y	N
9 Kildee	Y	N	Y	Y	N	N	Y	N
10 Bonior	N	N	N	N	N	N	Y	N
11 ***Knollenberg***	Y	Y	Y	Y	Y	Y	N	Y
12 Levin	N	N	N	Y	N	N	Y	N
13 Rivers	Y	N	N	Y	N	N	Y	N
14 Conyers	N	N	N	N	N	N	Y	N
15 Kilpatrick	N	N	N	Y	N	N	Y	N
16 Dingell	?	N	N	Y	N	N	Y	N
MINNESOTA								
1 ***Gutknecht***	Y	Y	Y	Y	Y	Y	N	Y
2 Minge	Y	N	N	Y	N	N	Y	Y
3 ***Ramstad***	Y	Y	N	Y	Y	Y	N	Y
4 Vento	N	N	N	Y	N	N	Y	N
5 Sabo	N	N	N	Y	N	N	Y	N
6 Luther	N	N	N	Y	N	N	Y	Y
7 Peterson	Y	N	Y	Y	N	N	Y	N
8 Oberstar	N	N	N	Y	N	N	Y	N
MISSISSIPPI								
1 ***Wicker***	Y	Y	Y	Y	Y	Y	N	Y
2 Thompson	Y	N	Y	Y	N	N	Y	N
3 ***Pickering***	Y	Y	Y	Y	Y	Y	N	Y
4 ***Parker***	Y	Y	Y	Y	Y	Y	N	Y
5 Taylor	Y	N	Y	Y	N	N	Y	Y
MISSOURI								
1 Clay	N	N	N	Y	N	N	Y	N
2 ***Talent***	?	Y	Y	Y	Y	Y	N	Y
3 Gephardt	N	N	N	Y	N	N	Y	N
4 Skelton	Y	N	Y	Y	N	N	Y	Y
5 McCarthy	Y	N	N	Y	N	N	Y	Y
6 Danner	Y	Y	N	Y	N	N	Y	Y
7 ***Blunt***	Y	Y	Y	Y	Y	Y	N	Y
8 ***Emerson***	Y	Y	Y	Y	Y	Y	N	Y
9 ***Hulshof***	Y	Y	Y	Y	Y	Y	N	Y
MONTANA								
AL ***Hill***	Y	Y	Y	Y	Y	Y	N	Y
NEBRASKA								
1 ***Bereuter***	Y	N	Y	Y	Y	Y	N	Y
2 ***Christensen***	Y	Y	Y	Y	Y	Y	N	Y
3 ***Barrett***	Y	Y	Y	Y	Y	Y	N	Y
NEVADA								
1 ***Ensign***	Y	Y	Y	Y	Y	N	N	Y
2 ***Gibbons***	Y	Y	Y	Y	Y	Y	N	Y
NEW HAMPSHIRE								
1 ***Sununu***	Y	Y	Y	Y	Y	Y	N	Y
2 ***Bass***	Y	Y	Y	Y	Y	Y	N	Y
NEW JERSEY								
1 Andrews	N	N	Y	Y	N	N	Y	N
2 ***LoBiondo***	Y	Y	N	Y	Y	Y	N	Y
3 ***Saxton***	Y	Y	Y	Y	Y	Y	N	Y
4 ***Smith***	Y	?	?	?	?	Y	N	Y
5 ***Roukema***	Y	Y	Y	Y	Y	N	N	Y
6 Pallone	N	N	Y	Y	N	N	Y	N
7 ***Franks***	Y	N	N	Y	Y	Y	N	Y
8 Pascrell	Y	N	Y	Y	N	N	Y	N
9 Rothman	N	N	Y	Y	N	N	Y	N
10 Payne	N	N	N	N	N	N	Y	N
11 ***Frelinghuysen***	Y	N	Y	Y	Y	Y	N	Y
12 ***Pappas***	Y	Y	Y	Y	Y	Y	N	Y
13 Menendez	Y	N	N	Y	N	N	Y	N
NEW MEXICO								
1 ***Schiff***	?	?	?	?	?	?	?	#
2 ***Skeen***	Y	N	Y	Y	Y	Y	N	Y
3 ***Redmond***	Y	Y	Y	Y	Y	Y	N	Y
NEW YORK								
1 ***Forbes***	Y	Y	Y	Y	Y	Y	N	Y
2 ***Lazio***	Y	Y	Y	Y	Y	Y	N	Y
3 ***King***	N	N	Y	Y	Y	Y	N	N
4 McCarthy	N	N	N	Y	N	N	Y	N
5 Ackerman	N	N	N	Y	N	N	Y	N
6 Flake	Y	N	Y	P	N	N	Y	N
7 Manton	Y	N	Y	Y	N	N	Y	N
8 Nadler	N	–	–	–	N	N	Y	N
9 Schumer	?	N	N	Y	N	N	Y	N
10 Towns	N	N	N	N	N	N	Y	N
11 Owens	Y	N	N	P	N	N	Y	N
12 Velázquez	N	N	N	N	N	N	Y	N
13 ***Molinari***	Y	Y	Y	Y	Y	Y	N	Y
14 Maloney	N	N	Y	Y	N	N	Y	N
15 Rangel	N	N	N	Y	N	N	Y	N
16 Serrano	Y	N	N	N	N	N	Y	N
17 Engel	N	–	N	Y	N	N	Y	N
18 Lowey	N	N	?	?	N	N	Y	N
19 ***Kelly***	Y	Y	Y	Y	Y	Y	N	Y
20 ***Gilman***	Y	Y	Y	Y	Y	Y	N	Y
21 McNulty	N	N	N	Y	N	N	Y	N
22 ***Solomon***	Y	Y	Y	Y	Y	Y	N	Y
23 ***Boehlert***	Y	N	Y	Y	Y	Y	N	Y
24 ***McHugh***	Y	?	?	?	?	Y	N	Y
25 ***Walsh***	Y	Y	Y	Y	Y	Y	N	Y
26 Hinchey	N	N	N	Y	N	N	Y	N
27 ***Paxon***	Y	Y	Y	Y	Y	Y	N	Y
28 Slaughter	N	N	Y	Y	N	N	Y	N
29 LaFalce	N	N	N	Y	N	N	Y	N
30 ***Quinn***	Y	Y	Y	Y	Y	Y	N	Y
31 ***Houghton***	N	N	Y	Y	Y	Y	N	Y
NORTH CAROLINA								
1 Clayton	N	N	N	N	N	N	Y	N
2 Etheridge	N	N	Y	Y	N	N	Y	Y
3 ***Jones***	Y	Y	Y	Y	Y	Y	N	Y
4 Price	N	N	Y	Y	N	N	Y	N
5 ***Burr***	Y	Y	Y	Y	Y	Y	N	Y
6 ***Coble***	Y	Y	Y	Y	Y	Y	N	Y
7 McIntyre	Y	Y	Y	Y	N	N	Y	Y
8 Hefner	N	N	Y	Y	N	N	Y	N
9 ***Myrick***	Y	Y	Y	Y	Y	Y	N	Y
10 ***Ballenger***	Y	Y	Y	Y	Y	Y	N	Y
11 ***Taylor***	Y	Y	Y	Y	Y	Y	N	Y
12 Watt	N	N	N	Y	N	N	Y	N
NORTH DAKOTA								
AL Pomeroy	N	N	Y	Y	?	N	Y	Y
OHIO								
1 ***Chabot***	Y	Y	Y	Y	Y	Y	N	Y
2 ***Portman***	Y	Y	Y	Y	Y	Y	N	Y
3 Hall	Y	N	Y	Y	N	N	Y	Y
4 ***Oxley***	Y	N	Y	Y	Y	Y	N	Y
5 ***Gillmor***	Y	Y	Y	Y	Y	Y	N	Y
6 Strickland	N	N	N	Y	N	N	Y	N
7 ***Hobson***	Y	Y	Y	Y	Y	Y	N	Y
8 ***Boehner***	Y	Y	Y	Y	Y	Y	N	Y
9 Kaptur	Y	Y	Y	P	N	N	Y	N
10 Kucinich	N	N	N	Y	N	N	Y	N
11 Stokes	N	N	N	?	N	N	Y	N
12 ***Kasich***	Y	Y	Y	Y	Y	Y	N	Y
13 Brown	N	N	N	Y	N	N	Y	N
14 Sawyer	N	N	N	Y	N	N	Y	N
15 ***Pryce***	Y	Y	Y	Y	Y	Y	N	Y
16 ***Regula***	Y	Y	Y	Y	Y	Y	N	Y
17 Traficant	Y	Y	Y	Y	N	Y	Y	Y
18 ***Ney***	Y	Y	Y	Y	Y	Y	N	Y
19 ***LaTourette***	Y	Y	Y	Y	Y	Y	N	Y
OKLAHOMA								
1 ***Largent***	Y	Y	Y	Y	Y	Y	N	Y
2 ***Coburn***	Y	Y	Y	Y	Y	P	N	Y
3 ***Watkins***	Y	Y	Y	Y	Y	Y	N	Y
4 ***Watts***	Y	Y	Y	Y	Y	Y	N	Y
5 ***Istook***	Y	Y	Y	Y	Y	Y	N	Y
6 ***Lucas***	Y	Y	Y	Y	Y	Y	N	Y
OREGON								
1 Furse	N	N	N	P	N	N	Y	N
2 ***Smith***	Y	Y	Y	Y	Y	Y	N	Y
3 Blumenauer	N	N	N	Y	N	N	Y	N
4 DeFazio	Y	N	N	Y	N	N	Y	N
5 Hooley	N	N	N	Y	N	N	Y	Y
PENNSYLVANIA								
1 Foglietta	N	N	N	Y	N	N	Y	N
2 Fattah	N	N	N	Y	N	N	Y	N
3 Borski	N	N	Y	Y	N	N	Y	N
4 Klink	N	N	N	Y	N	N	Y	N
5 ***Peterson***	Y	Y	Y	Y	Y	Y	N	Y
6 Holden	N	N	Y	Y	N	N	Y	Y
7 ***Weldon***	Y	N	Y	Y	Y	Y	N	Y
8 ***Greenwood***	Y	Y	Y	Y	Y	Y	N	Y
9 ***Shuster***	Y	Y	Y	Y	Y	Y	N	Y
10 ***McDade***	Y	N	Y	Y	Y	Y	N	Y
11 Kanjorski	N	N	N	N	N	N	Y	N
12 Murtha	N	N	Y	N	N	N	Y	N
13 ***Fox***	Y	Y	Y	Y	Y	Y	N	Y
14 Coyne	N	N	N	N	N	N	Y	N
15 McHale	N	N	Y	Y	N	N	Y	Y
16 ***Pitts***	Y	Y	Y	Y	Y	Y	N	Y
17 ***Gekas***	Y	Y	Y	Y	Y	Y	N	Y
18 Doyle	N	N	N	Y	N	N	Y	Y
19 ***Goodling***	Y	Y	Y	Y	Y	Y	N	Y
20 Mascara	N	N	N	Y	N	N	Y	N
21 ***English***	Y	Y	N	Y	Y	Y	N	Y
RHODE ISLAND								
1 Kennedy	N	N	Y	Y	N	N	Y	N
2 Weygand	N	N	Y	Y	N	N	Y	N
SOUTH CAROLINA								
1 ***Sanford***	Y	Y	Y	Y	Y	Y	N	Y
2 ***Spence***	Y	Y	Y	Y	Y	Y	N	Y
3 ***Graham***	Y	N	Y	Y	Y	Y	N	Y
4 ***Inglis***	Y	Y	Y	Y	Y	Y	N	Y
5 Spratt	Y	N	Y	Y	N	N	Y	Y
6 Clyburn	N	N	Y	Y	N	N	Y	N
SOUTH DAKOTA								
AL ***Thune***	Y	Y	Y	Y	Y	Y	N	Y
TENNESSEE								
1 ***Jenkins***	Y	Y	Y	Y	Y	Y	N	Y
2 ***Duncan***	Y	Y	Y	Y	Y	Y	N	Y
3 ***Wamp***	Y	Y	Y	Y	Y	Y	N	Y
4 ***Hilleary***	Y	Y	Y	Y	Y	Y	N	Y
5 Clement	N	N	Y	Y	N	N	Y	Y
6 Gordon	N	N	Y	Y	N	N	Y	Y
7 ***Bryant***	+	Y	Y	Y	Y	Y	N	Y
8 Tanner	N	N	Y	Y	N	N	Y	Y
9 Ford	N	N	Y	Y	N	N	Y	N
TEXAS								
1 Sandlin	N	N	Y	Y	N	N	Y	N
2 Turner	Y	N	Y	Y	N	N	Y	Y
3 ***Johnson, Sam***	Y	Y	Y	Y	Y	Y	N	Y
4 Hall	Y	Y	Y	Y	N	Y	Y	N
5 ***Sessions***	Y	Y	Y	Y	Y	Y	N	Y
6 ***Barton***	Y	Y	Y	?	Y	Y	N	Y
7 ***Archer***	Y	Y	Y	Y	Y	Y	N	Y
8 ***Brady***	+	Y	Y	Y	Y	Y	N	Y
9 Lampson	Y	N	Y	Y	N	N	Y	Y
10 Doggett	Y	N	N	Y	N	N	Y	N
11 Edwards	Y	N	Y	Y	N	N	Y	Y
12 ***Granger***	Y	Y	Y	Y	Y	Y	N	Y
13 ***Thornberry***	Y	N	Y	Y	Y	Y	N	Y
14 ***Paul***	Y	Y	N	Y	Y	Y	N	N
15 Hinojosa	N	N	Y	Y	N	N	Y	N
16 Reyes	N	N	Y	Y	N	N	Y	N
17 Stenholm	Y	N	Y	Y	N	N	Y	Y
18 Jackson-Lee	Y	N	N	Y	N	N	Y	N
19 ***Combest***	Y	Y	Y	Y	Y	Y	N	Y
20 Gonzalez	Y	N	Y	Y	N	N	Y	N
21 ***Smith***	Y	Y	Y	Y	Y	Y	N	Y
22 ***DeLay***	Y	Y	Y	Y	Y	Y	N	Y
23 ***Bonilla***	Y	Y	Y	Y	Y	Y	N	Y
24 Frost	N	N	Y	Y	N	N	Y	N
25 Bentsen	N	N	Y	Y	N	N	Y	Y
26 ***Armey***	Y	Y	Y	Y	Y	Y	N	Y
27 Ortiz	Y	N	Y	Y	N	N	Y	N
28 Rodriguez	N	N	N	Y	N	N	Y	N
29 Green	Y	N	Y	Y	N	N	Y	N
30 Johnson, E.B.	N	N	Y	P	N	N	Y	N
UTAH								
1 ***Hansen***	Y	Y	Y	Y	Y	Y	N	Y
2 ***Cook***	Y	Y	Y	Y	Y	Y	N	Y
3 ***Cannon***	Y	Y	Y	Y	Y	Y	N	Y
VERMONT								
AL *Sanders*	Y	N	N	Y	N	N	Y	N
VIRGINIA								
1 ***Bateman***	Y	N	Y	Y	Y	Y	N	Y
2 Pickett	N	N	Y	Y	N	N	Y	N
3 Scott	N	N	Y	N	N	N	Y	N
4 Sisisky	N	N	Y	Y	N	N	Y	Y
5 Goode	Y	Y	Y	Y	N	N	Y	Y
6 ***Goodlatte***	Y	Y	Y	Y	?	Y	N	Y
7 ***Bliley***	Y	Y	Y	Y	Y	Y	N	Y
8 Moran	N	N	N	Y	N	Y	Y	Y
9 Boucher	N	N	Y	Y	N	N	Y	N
10 ***Wolf***	Y	Y	Y	Y	Y	Y	N	Y
11 ***Davis***	Y	Y	Y	Y	Y	Y	N	Y
WASHINGTON								
1 ***White***	Y	N	Y	Y	Y	Y	N	Y
2 ***Metcalf***	Y	Y	Y	Y	Y	Y	N	N
3 ***Smith, Linda***	Y	Y	Y	Y	Y	Y	N	Y
4 ***Hastings***	Y	N	Y	Y	Y	Y	N	Y
5 ***Nethercutt***	Y	Y	Y	Y	Y	Y	N	Y
6 Dicks	N	N	Y	Y	N	N	Y	N
7 McDermott	N	N	N	N	N	N	Y	N
8 ***Dunn***	Y	Y	Y	?	Y	Y	N	Y
9 Smith, Adam	N	N	Y	Y	N	Y	Y	Y
WEST VIRGINIA								
1 Mollohan	N	N	Y	N	N	N	Y	N
2 Wise	N	N	Y	Y	N	N	Y	N
3 Rahall	N	N	N	Y	N	N	Y	N
WISCONSIN								
1 ***Neumann***	Y	?	?	?	Y	Y	N	Y
2 ***Klug***	Y	Y	N	Y	Y	Y	N	Y
3 Kind	N	N	N	Y	N	N	Y	N
4 Kleczka	Y	N	N	Y	N	N	Y	Y
5 Barrett	N	N	N	Y	N	N	Y	N
6 ***Petri***	Y	Y	N	Y	Y	Y	N	Y
7 Obey	N	N	N	?	N	N	Y	N
8 Johnson	N	N	Y	Y	N	N	Y	N
9 ***Sensenbrenner***	Y	Y	N	Y	Y	Y	N	Y
WYOMING								
AL ***Cubin***	Y	Y	Y	Y	Y	Y	N	Y

Southern states - Ala., Ark., Fla., Ga., Ky., La., Miss., N.C., Okla., S.C., Tenn., Texas, Va.

HOUSE VOTES 242, 243, 244, 245

242. H Res 176. Adjournment Resolution/Rule. Adoption of the resolution to provide for House floor consideration of and waive all points of order against the concurrent resolution to allow the adjournment of the House and the Senate until July 8 and July 7, respectively. The rule waives provisions under the Congressional Budget Act that require Congress to complete action on the 13 regular appropriations bills before July 4. Adopted 230-194: R 222-0; D 8-193 (ND 8-140, SD 0-53); I 0-1, June 26, 1997. (Subsequently, the concurrent resolution was adopted by voice vote.)

243. HR 2014. Fiscal 1998 Budget Reconciliation — Revenue/Democratic Tax Substitute. Rangel, D-N.Y., substitute amendment to provide a net tax cut of $84.9 billion over five years, including $133.7 billion in gross tax cuts offset by $49.3 billion in revenue increases. The substitute provides a refundable child tax credit that would not be reduced by the Earned Income Tax Credit, makes the HOPE scholarship higher education tax credit available for all four years of a college education, limits the increase in the exemption from the estate tax to family-owned businesses and sets a lifetime cap of $600,000 for capital gains eligible for favorable tax treatment. Rejected 197-235: R 0-227; D 196-8 (ND 144-5, SD 52-3); I 1-0, June 26, 1997.

244. HR 2014. Fiscal 1998 Budget Reconciliation — Revenue/Recommit. Peterson, D-Minn., motion to recommit the bill to the Budget Committee with instructions to report it back with an amendment to exempt certain percentages of non-corporate asset income from capital gains tax, increase the amount exempt from federal estate tax gradually from $700,000 to $1.2 million, provide a non-refundable tax credit for each child under age 17 and extend a tax credit of $1,500 per year for up to two years for higher education expenses. Rejected 164-268: R 0-227; D 164-40 (ND 115-34, SD 49-6); I 0-1, June 26, 1997.

245. HR 2014. Fiscal 1998 Budget Reconciliation — Revenue/Passage. Passage of the bill to provide a net tax cut of $85 billion over five years, including $133 billion in gross tax cuts offset by $48 billion in revenue increases. The bill establishes a tax credit for each child under age 17, lowers the top capital gains tax rate from 28 percent to 20 percent, raises the amount exempt from the federal estate tax gradually from $600,000 to $1 million and provides $31 billion in education tax incentives that include a non-refundable credit of up to $1,500 for each student each year for the first two years of college. Passed 253-179: R 226-1; D 27-177 (ND 14-135, SD 13-42); I 0-1, June 26, 1997. A "nay" was a vote in support of the president's position.

KEY

- Y Voted for (yea).
- # Paired for.
- + Announced for.
- N Voted against (nay).
- X Paired against.
- – Announced against.
- P Voted "present."
- C Voted "present" to avoid possible conflict of interest.
- ? Did not vote or otherwise make a position known.

Democrats ***Republicans***
Independent

	242	243	244	245
ALABAMA				
1 ***Callahan***	Y	N	N	Y
2 ***Everett***	Y	N	N	Y
3 ***Riley***	Y	N	N	Y
4 ***Aderholt***	Y	N	N	Y
5 Cramer	N	Y	Y	Y
6 ***Bachus***	Y	N	N	Y
7 Hilliard	N	Y	Y	N
ALASKA				
AL ***Young***	Y	N	N	Y
ARIZONA				
1 ***Salmon***	Y	N	N	Y
2 Pastor	Y	Y	Y	N
3 ***Stump***	Y	N	N	Y
4 ***Shadegg***	Y	N	N	Y
5 ***Kolbe***	Y	N	N	Y
6 ***Hayworth***	Y	N	N	Y
ARKANSAS				
1 Berry	N	Y	Y	N
2 Snyder	N	Y	Y	N
3 ***Hutchinson***	Y	N	N	Y
4 ***Dickey***	Y	N	N	Y
CALIFORNIA				
1 ***Riggs***	Y	N	N	Y
2 ***Herger***	Y	N	N	Y
3 Fazio	N	Y	Y	N
4 ***Doolittle***	Y	N	N	Y
5 Matsui	N	Y	Y	N
6 Woolsey	N	Y	Y	N
7 Miller	N	Y	N	N
8 Pelosi	N	Y	N	N
9 Dellums	N	Y	N	N
10 Tauscher	N	Y	Y	N
11 ***Pombo***	Y	N	N	Y
12 Lantos	N	Y	Y	N
13 Stark	N	Y	N	N
14 Eshoo	N	Y	Y	N
15 ***Campbell***	Y	N	N	N
16 Lofgren	N	Y	Y	N
17 Farr	N	Y	Y	N
18 Condit	N	Y	Y	Y
19 ***Radanovich***	Y	N	N	Y
20 Dooley	N	Y	Y	Y
21 ***Thomas***	Y	N	N	Y
22 Capps	N	Y	Y	N
23 ***Gallegly***	Y	N	N	Y
24 Sherman	N	Y	N	Y
25 ***McKeon***	Y	N	N	Y
26 Berman	N	Y	Y	N
27 ***Rogan***	Y	N	N	Y
28 ***Dreier***	Y	N	N	Y
29 Waxman	N	Y	N	N
30 Becerra	N	Y	N	N
31 Martinez	N	Y	Y	N
32 Dixon	Y	Y	Y	N
33 Roybal-Allard	N	Y	N	N
34 Torres	N	Y	N	N
35 Waters	N	Y	N	N
36 Harman	N	Y	Y	Y
37 Millender-McD.	N	Y	Y	N
38 ***Horn***	Y	N	N	Y
39 ***Royce***	Y	N	N	Y
40 ***Lewis***	Y	N	N	Y
41 ***Kim***	Y	N	N	Y
42 Brown	N	Y	Y	N
43 ***Calvert***	Y	N	N	Y
44 ***Bono***	Y	N	N	Y
45 ***Rohrabacher***	Y	N	N	Y
46 Sanchez	N	Y	Y	Y
47 ***Cox***	?	N	N	Y
48 ***Packard***	Y	N	N	Y
49 ***Bilbray***	Y	N	N	Y
50 Filner	N	Y	Y	N
51 ***Cunningham***	Y	N	N	Y
52 ***Hunter***	Y	N	N	Y
COLORADO				
1 DeGette	N	Y	Y	N
2 Skaggs	N	Y	Y	N
3 ***McInnis***	Y	N	N	Y
4 ***Schaffer***	Y	N	N	Y
5 ***Hefley***	Y	N	N	Y
6 ***Schaefer***	Y	N	N	Y
CONNECTICUT				
1 Kennelly	N	Y	Y	N
2 Gejdenson	N	Y	Y	N
3 DeLauro	N	Y	N	N
4 ***Shays***	Y	N	N	Y
5 Maloney	N	Y	Y	Y
6 ***Johnson***	Y	N	N	Y
DELAWARE				
AL ***Castle***	?	N	N	Y
FLORIDA				
1 ***Scarborough***	Y	N	N	Y
2 Boyd	N	Y	Y	N
3 Brown	N	Y	N	N
4 ***Fowler***	Y	N	N	Y
5 Thurman	N	Y	Y	N
6 ***Stearns***	Y	N	N	Y
7 ***Mica***	Y	N	N	Y
8 ***McCollum***	Y	N	N	Y
9 ***Bilirakis***	Y	N	N	Y
10 ***Young***	Y	N	N	Y
11 Davis	N	Y	Y	N
12 ***Canady***	Y	N	N	Y
13 ***Miller***	Y	N	N	Y
14 ***Goss***	Y	N	N	Y
15 ***Weldon***	Y	N	N	Y
16 ***Foley***	Y	N	N	Y
17 Meek	N	Y	N	N
18 ***Ros-Lehtinen***	Y	N	N	Y
19 Wexler	N	Y	Y	N
20 Deutsch	N	N	Y	N
21 ***Diaz-Balart***	Y	N	N	Y
22 ***Shaw***	Y	N	N	Y
23 Hastings	N	Y	Y	N
GEORGIA				
1 ***Kingston***	Y	N	N	Y
2 Bishop	N	Y	Y	N
3 ***Collins***	Y	N	N	Y
4 McKinney	N	Y	Y	N
5 Lewis	N	Y	N	N
6 ***Gingrich***		N	N	Y
7 ***Barr***	Y	N	N	Y
8 ***Chambliss***	Y	N	N	Y
9 ***Deal***	Y	N	N	Y
10 ***Norwood***	Y	N	N	Y
11 ***Linder***	Y	N	N	Y
HAWAII				
1 Abercrombie	N	Y	Y	N
2 Mink	N	Y	Y	N
IDAHO				
1 ***Chenoweth***	Y	N	N	Y
2 ***Crapo***	Y	N	N	Y
ILLINOIS				
1 Rush	?	Y	Y	N
2 Jackson	N	Y	N	N
3 Lipinski	N	N	N	Y
4 Gutierrez	N	Y	N	N
5 Blagojevich	N	Y	Y	N
6 ***Hyde***	Y	N	N	Y
7 Davis	N	Y	Y	N
8 ***Crane***	Y	N	N	Y
9 Yates	N	?	?	X
10 ***Porter***	Y	N	N	Y
11 ***Weller***	Y	N	N	Y
12 Costello	N	Y	Y	N
13 ***Fawell***	Y	N	N	Y
14 ***Hastert***	Y	N	N	Y
15 ***Ewing***	Y	N	N	Y

ND Northern Democrats SD Southern Democrats

	242	243	244	245
16 ***Manzullo***	Y	N	N	Y
17 Evans	N	Y	Y	N
18 ***LaHood***	Y	N	N	Y
19 Poshard	N	Y	Y	N
20 ***Shimkus***	Y	N	N	Y
INDIANA				
1 Visclosky	N	N	N	N
2 ***McIntosh***	Y	N	N	Y
3 Roemer	N	Y	Y	Y
4 ***Souder***	Y	N	N	Y
5 ***Buyer***	Y	N	N	Y
6 ***Burton***	Y	N	N	Y
7 ***Pease***	Y	N	N	Y
8 ***Hostettler***	Y	N	N	Y
9 Hamilton	N	Y	Y	N
10 Carson	N	Y	Y	N
IOWA				
1 ***Leach***	Y	N	N	Y
2 ***Nussle***	Y	N	N	Y
3 Boswell	Y	Y	Y	Y
4 ***Ganske***	Y	N	N	Y
5 ***Latham***	Y	N	N	Y
KANSAS				
1 ***Moran***	Y	N	N	Y
2 ***Ryun***	Y	N	N	Y
3 ***Snowbarger***	Y	N	N	Y
4 ***Tiahrt***	Y	N	N	Y
KENTUCKY				
1 ***Whitfield***	Y	N	N	Y
2 ***Lewis***	Y	N	N	Y
3 ***Northup***	Y	N	N	Y
4 ***Bunning***	Y	N	N	Y
5 ***Rogers***	Y	N	N	Y
6 Baesler	N	Y	Y	Y
LOUISIANA				
1 ***Livingston***	Y	N	N	Y
2 Jefferson	N	Y	Y	N
3 ***Tauzin***	Y	N	N	Y
4 ***McCrery***	Y	N	N	Y
5 ***Cooksey***	Y	N	N	Y
6 ***Baker***	Y	N	N	Y
7 John	N	Y	Y	Y
MAINE				
1 Allen	N	Y	Y	N
2 Baldacci	N	Y	Y	N
MARYLAND				
1 ***Gilchrest***	Y	N	N	Y
2 ***Ehrlich***	Y	N	N	Y
3 Cardin	N	Y	Y	N
4 Wynn	N	Y	Y	N
5 Hoyer	N	Y	Y	N
6 ***Bartlett***	Y	N	N	Y
7 Cummings	N	Y	Y	N
8 ***Morella***	Y	N	N	Y
MASSACHUSETTS				
1 Olver	N	Y	Y	N
2 Neal	N	Y	Y	N
3 McGovern	N	Y	N	N
4 Frank	N	Y	N	N
5 Meehan	N	?	?	?
6 Tierney	N	Y	N	N
7 Markey	N	Y	Y	N
8 Kennedy	N	Y	Y	N
9 Moakley	N	Y	Y	N
10 Delahunt	N	Y	Y	N
MICHIGAN				
1 Stupak	N	Y	Y	N
2 ***Hoekstra***	Y	N	N	Y
3 ***Ehlers***	Y	N	N	Y
4 ***Camp***	Y	N	N	Y
5 Barcia	N	Y	Y	N
6 ***Upton***	Y	N	N	Y
7 ***Smith***	Y	N	N	Y
8 Stabenow	N	Y	Y	N
9 Kildee	N	Y	Y	N
10 Bonior	N	Y	N	N
11 ***Knollenberg***	Y	N	N	Y
12 Levin	N	Y	Y	N
13 Rivers	N	Y	N	N
14 Conyers	N	Y	Y	N
15 Kilpatrick	N	Y	N	N
16 Dingell	N	Y	Y	N
MINNESOTA				
1 ***Gutknecht***	Y	N	N	Y
2 Minge	N	Y	Y	N
3 ***Ramstad***	Y	N	N	Y
4 Vento	N	Y	Y	N
5 Sabo	N	Y	Y	N
6 Luther	N	Y	Y	N
7 Peterson	N	Y	Y	N
8 Oberstar	N	Y	Y	N
MISSISSIPPI				
1 ***Wicker***	Y	N	N	Y
2 Thompson	N	Y	Y	N
3 ***Pickering***	Y	N	N	Y
4 ***Parker***	Y	N	N	Y
5 Taylor	N	Y	Y	Y
MISSOURI				
1 Clay	N	Y	Y	N
2 ***Talent***	Y	N	N	Y
3 Gephardt	N	Y	N	N
4 Skelton	N	Y	Y	Y
5 McCarthy	N	Y	Y	N
6 Danner	N	Y	Y	Y
7 ***Blunt***	Y	N	N	Y
8 ***Emerson***	Y	N	N	Y
9 ***Hulshof***	Y	N	N	Y
MONTANA				
AL ***Hill***	Y	N	N	Y
NEBRASKA				
1 ***Bereuter***	Y	N	N	Y
2 ***Christensen***	Y	N	N	Y
3 ***Barrett***	Y	N	N	Y
NEVADA				
1 ***Ensign***	Y	N	N	Y
2 ***Gibbons***	Y	N	N	Y
NEW HAMPSHIRE				
1 ***Sununu***	Y	N	N	Y
2 ***Bass***	Y	N	N	Y
NEW JERSEY				
1 Andrews	N	Y	Y	N
2 ***LoBiondo***	Y	N	N	Y
3 ***Saxton***	Y	N	N	Y
4 ***Smith***	Y	N	N	Y
5 ***Roukema***	Y	N	N	Y
6 Pallone	N	Y	Y	N
7 ***Franks***	Y	N	N	Y
8 Pascrell	N	Y	Y	N
9 Rothman	N	Y	Y	N
10 Payne	N	Y	N	N
11 ***Frelinghuysen***	Y	N	N	Y
12 ***Pappas***	Y	N	N	Y
13 Menendez	N	Y	Y	N
NEW MEXICO				
1 ***Schiff***	?	?	?	#
2 ***Skeen***	Y	N	N	Y
3 ***Redmond***	Y	N	N	Y
NEW YORK				
1 ***Forbes***	Y	N	N	Y
2 ***Lazio***	Y	N	N	Y
3 ***King***	Y	N	N	Y
4 McCarthy	Y	Y	Y	Y
5 Ackerman	N	Y	Y	N
6 Flake	?	Y	Y	N
7 Manton	N	Y	Y	N
8 Nadler	N	Y	Y	N
9 Schumer	N	Y	Y	N
10 Towns	N	Y	Y	N
11 Owens	?	Y	Y	N
12 Velázquez	N	Y	N	N
13 ***Molinari***	Y	N	N	Y
14 Maloney	N	Y	Y	N
15 Rangel	N	Y	Y	N
16 Serrano	N	Y	Y	N
17 Engel	N	Y	Y	N
18 Lowey	N	Y	Y	N
19 ***Kelly***	Y	N	N	Y
20 ***Gilman***	Y	N	N	Y
21 McNulty	N	Y	Y	N
22 ***Solomon***	Y	N	N	Y
23 ***Boehlert***	Y	N	N	Y
24 ***McHugh***	Y	N	N	Y
25 ***Walsh***	Y	N	N	Y
26 Hinchey	N	Y	Y	N
27 ***Paxon***	Y	N	N	Y
28 Slaughter	N	Y	Y	N
29 LaFalce	N	Y	Y	N
30 ***Quinn***	Y	N	N	Y
31 ***Houghton***	Y	N	N	Y
NORTH CAROLINA				
1 Clayton	N	Y	Y	N
2 Etheridge	N	Y	Y	N
3 ***Jones***	Y	N	N	Y
4 Price	N	Y	Y	N
5 ***Burr***	Y	N	N	Y
6 ***Coble***	Y	N	N	Y
7 McIntyre	N	Y	Y	Y
8 Hefner	N	Y	Y	N
9 ***Myrick***	Y	N	N	Y
10 ***Ballenger***	Y	N	N	Y
11 ***Taylor***	Y	N	N	Y
12 Watt	N	Y	Y	N
NORTH DAKOTA				
AL Pomeroy	N	Y	Y	N
OHIO				
1 ***Chabot***	Y	N	N	Y
2 ***Portman***	Y	N	N	Y
3 Hall	N	Y	Y	N
4 ***Oxley***	Y	N	N	Y
5 ***Gillmor***	Y	N	N	Y
6 Strickland	N	Y	N	N
7 ***Hobson***	Y	N	N	Y
8 ***Boehner***	Y	N	N	Y
9 Kaptur	N	Y	Y	N
10 Kucinich	N	Y	N	N
11 Stokes	N	Y	Y	N
12 ***Kasich***	?	N	N	Y
13 Brown	N	Y	Y	N
14 Sawyer	N	Y	Y	N
15 ***Pryce***	Y	N	N	Y
16 ***Regula***	Y	N	N	Y
17 Traficant	Y	N	N	Y
18 ***Ney***	Y	N	N	Y
19 ***LaTourette***	Y	N	N	Y
OKLAHOMA				
1 ***Largent***	Y	N	N	Y
2 ***Coburn***	Y	N	N	Y
3 ***Watkins***	Y	N	N	Y
4 ***Watts***	Y	N	N	Y
5 ***Istook***	Y	N	N	Y
6 ***Lucas***	Y	N	N	Y
OREGON				
1 Furse	N	Y	Y	N
2 ***Smith***	Y	N	N	Y
3 Blumenauer	Y	Y	Y	N
4 DeFazio	N	N	N	N
5 Hooley	N	Y	Y	N
PENNSYLVANIA				
1 Foglietta	N	Y	N	N
2 Fattah	N	Y	Y	N
3 Borski	N	Y	N	N
4 Klink	Y	Y	Y	N
5 ***Peterson***	Y	N	N	Y
6 Holden	N	Y	Y	N
7 ***Weldon***	Y	N	N	Y
8 ***Greenwood***	Y	N	N	Y
9 ***Shuster***	Y	N	N	Y
10 ***McDade***	Y	N	N	Y
11 Kanjorski	N	Y	N	N
12 Murtha	Y	N	N	N
13 ***Fox***	Y	N	N	Y
14 Coyne	N	Y	Y	N
15 McHale	N	Y	Y	N
16 ***Pitts***	Y	N	N	Y
17 ***Gekas***	Y	N	N	Y
18 Doyle	N	Y	Y	N
19 ***Goodling***	Y	N	N	Y
20 Mascara	N	Y	Y	N
21 ***English***	Y	N	N	Y
RHODE ISLAND				
1 Kennedy	N	Y	N	N
2 Weygand	N	Y	Y	N
SOUTH CAROLINA				
1 ***Sanford***	Y	N	N	Y
2 ***Spence***	Y	N	N	Y
3 ***Graham***	Y	N	N	Y
4 ***Inglis***	Y	N	N	Y
5 Spratt	N	Y	Y	N
6 Clyburn	N	Y	Y	N
SOUTH DAKOTA				
AL ***Thune***	Y	N	N	Y
TENNESSEE				
1 ***Jenkins***	Y	N	N	Y
2 ***Duncan***	Y	N	N	Y
3 ***Wamp***	Y	N	N	Y
4 ***Hilleary***	Y	N	N	Y
5 Clement	N	Y	Y	Y
6 Gordon	N	Y	N	Y
7 ***Bryant***	Y	N	N	Y
8 Tanner	N	Y	Y	N
9 Ford	N	Y	Y	N
TEXAS				
1 Sandlin	N	Y	Y	Y
2 Turner	N	Y	Y	Y
3 ***Johnson, Sam***	Y	N	N	Y
4 Hall	N	N	Y	Y
5 ***Sessions***	Y	N	N	Y
6 ***Barton***	Y	N	N	Y
7 ***Archer***	Y	N	N	Y
8 ***Brady***	Y	N	N	Y
9 Lampson	N	Y	Y	N
10 Doggett	N	Y	Y	N
11 Edwards	N	Y	Y	N
12 ***Granger***	Y	N	N	Y
13 ***Thornberry***	Y	N	N	Y
14 ***Paul***	Y	N	N	Y
15 Hinojosa	N	Y	Y	N
16 Reyes	N	Y	Y	N
17 Stenholm	N	Y	Y	N
18 Jackson-Lee	N	Y	Y	N
19 ***Combest***	Y	N	N	Y
20 Gonzalez	?	Y	Y	N
21 ***Smith***	Y	N	N	Y
22 ***DeLay***	Y	N	N	Y
23 ***Bonilla***	Y	N	N	Y
24 Frost	N	Y	Y	N
25 Bentsen	?	Y	Y	N
26 ***Armey***	Y	N	N	Y
27 Ortiz	N	Y	Y	N
28 Rodriguez	N	Y	Y	N
29 Green	N	Y	Y	N
30 Johnson, E.B.	N	Y	Y	N
UTAH				
1 ***Hansen***	Y	N	N	Y
2 ***Cook***	Y	N	N	Y
3 ***Cannon***	Y	N	N	Y
VERMONT				
AL *Sanders*	N	Y	N	N
VIRGINIA				
1 ***Bateman***	Y	N	N	Y
2 Pickett	N	Y	Y	Y
3 Scott	N	Y	N	N
4 Sisisky	N	Y	Y	Y
5 Goode	N	Y	Y	Y
6 ***Goodlatte***	Y	N	N	Y
7 ***Bliley***	Y	N	N	Y
8 Moran	N	N	N	N
9 Boucher	N	Y	Y	N
10 ***Wolf***	Y	N	N	Y
11 ***Davis***	Y	N	N	Y
WASHINGTON				
1 ***White***	Y	N	N	Y
2 ***Metcalf***	Y	N	N	Y
3 ***Smith, Linda***	Y	N	N	Y
4 ***Hastings***	Y	N	N	Y
5 ***Nethercutt***	Y	N	N	Y
6 Dicks	N	Y	Y	Y
7 McDermott	N	Y	Y	N
8 ***Dunn***	Y	N	N	Y
9 Smith, Adam	N	Y	Y	N
WEST VIRGINIA				
1 Mollohan	N	Y	Y	N
2 Wise	N	Y	Y	N
3 Rahall	N	Y	Y	N
WISCONSIN				
1 ***Neumann***	Y	N	N	Y
2 ***Klug***	Y	N	N	Y
3 Kind	N	Y	Y	N
4 Kleczka	N	Y	Y	N
5 Barrett	N	Y	N	N
6 ***Petri***	Y	N	N	Y
7 Obey	N	Y	Y	N
8 Johnson	N	Y	Y	N
9 ***Sensenbrenner***	Y	N	N	Y
WYOMING				
AL ***Cubin***	?	N	N	Y

Southern states - Ala., Ark., Fla., Ga., Ky., La., Miss., N.C., Okla., S.C., Tenn., Texas, Va.

HOUSE VOTES 246, 247, 248, 249, 250, 251, 252, 253

246. HR 849. Relocation Assistance for Illegal Aliens/ Passage. Passage of the bill to prohibit illegal aliens from receiving compensation under the program that provides federal relocation assistance to people displaced from their homes by any federally financed project or program, except in cases of exceptional and extremely unusual hardship. Passed 399-0: R 207-0; D 191-0 (ND 139-0, SD 52-0); I 1-0, July 8, 1997. Bills on the corrections calendar require a three-fifths majority of those present and voting (240 in this case) for passage.

247. S J Res 29. Franklin Roosevelt Memorial Statue/ Passage. Hansen, R-Utah, motion to suspend the rules and pass the joint resolution to direct the Department of the Interior to design and construct a statue or similar structure at the Franklin Delano Roosevelt Memorial in Washington that depicts Roosevelt in a wheelchair in order to show his disability. Passed 363-39: R 178-31; D 184-8 (ND 135-5, SD 49-3); I 1-0, July 8, 1997. A two-thirds majority of those present and voting (268 in this case) is required for passage under suspension of the rules.

248. HR 1658. Atlantic Striped Bass Conservation Reauthorization/Passage. Peterson, R-Pa., motion to suspend the rules and pass the bill to reauthorize the Atlantic Striped Bass Conservation Act (PL 98-613) through fiscal 2000 and authorize $1.05 million each year to conduct annual studies and assessments of Atlantic striped bass populations. Passed 399-8: R 204-8; D 194-0 (ND 142-0, SD 52-0); I 1-0, July 8, 1997. A two-thirds majority of those present and voting (272 in this case) is required for passage under suspension of the rules.

249. HR 748. Financial Transactions With Terrorist States/ Passage. McCollum, R-Fla., motion to suspend the rules and pass the bill to prohibit U.S. citizens and companies from conducting any financial transaction with countries that have been identified by the State Department as active sponsors of terrorism. The bill provides exceptions for humanitarian aid, news reporting or broadcasts, emergency medical services and payment of intellectual property and filing fees. Passed 377-33: R 212-3; D 164-30 (ND 120-22, SD 44-8); I 1-0, July 8, 1997. A two-thirds majority of those present and voting (274 in this case) is required for passage under suspension of the rules.

250. HR 2016. Fiscal 1998 Military Construction Appropriations/Passage. Passage of the bill to provide $9.2 billion for military construction, family housing and military base realignment and closures for the Department of Defense in fiscal 1998. The bill provides $800 million more than the $8.4 billion requested by the president and $610 million less than the $9.8 billion provided in fiscal 1997. Passed 395-14: R 211-6; D 183-8 (ND 132-8, SD 51-0); I 1-0, July 8, 1997.

251. HR 858. Forest Management/Passage. Passage of the bill to authorize a five-year land management pilot project on federal land in the Plumas, Lassen and Tahoe national forests in California in order to reduce the risk of catastrophic wildfires in the region. The bill requires the project to comply fully with existing federal environmental laws and California spotted owl guidelines. Passed 429-1: R 224-1; D 204-0 (ND 151-0, SD 53-0); I 1-0, July 9, 1997.

252. HR 1775. Fiscal 1998 Intelligence Authorization/Rule. Adoption of the rule (H Res 179) to provide for House floor consideration of the bill to authorize a classified amount for the activities of the CIA, National Security Agency, Defense Intelligence Agency and other U.S. intelligence agencies in fiscal 1998. The amount has been estimated to be about $30 billion. Adopted 425-2: R 222-0; D 202-2 (ND 148-2, SD 54-0); I 1-0, July 9, 1997.

253. HR 1775. Fiscal 1998 Intelligence Authorization/5 Percent Cut. Sanders, I-Vt., amendment to trim the bill's total authorization 5 percent through an across-the-board cut, except for the CIA Retirement and Disability Fund. Rejected 142-289: R 27-198; D 114-91 (ND 95-56, SD 19-35); I 1-0, July 9, 1997.

KEY

- Y Voted for (yea).
- # Paired for.
- + Announced for.
- N Voted against (nay).
- X Paired against.
- – Announced against.
- P Voted "present."
- C Voted "present" to avoid possible conflict of interest.
- ? Did not vote or otherwise make a position known.

Democrats ***Republicans***
Independent

	246	247	248	249	250	251	252	253
ALABAMA								
1 ***Callahan***	Y	Y	Y	Y	Y	Y	Y	N
2 ***Everett***	Y	Y	Y	Y	Y	Y	Y	N
3 ***Riley***	Y	Y	Y	Y	Y	Y	Y	N
4 ***Aderholt***	Y	Y	Y	Y	Y	Y	Y	N
5 Cramer	Y	Y	Y	Y	Y	Y	Y	N
6 ***Bachus***	Y	Y	Y	Y	Y	Y	Y	N
7 Hilliard	Y	Y	Y	N	Y	Y	Y	Y
ALASKA								
AL ***Young***	Y	Y	Y	Y	Y	Y	Y	N
ARIZONA								
1 ***Salmon***	Y	N	Y	Y	Y	Y	Y	N
2 Pastor	+	+	Y	Y	Y	Y	Y	Y
3 ***Stump***	Y	N	Y	Y	Y	Y	Y	N
4 ***Shadegg***	?	?	?	?	?	Y	Y	N
5 ***Kolbe***	Y	Y	Y	Y	Y	Y	Y	N
6 ***Hayworth***	+	+	Y	Y	Y	Y	Y	N
ARKANSAS								
1 Berry	Y	Y	Y	Y	Y	Y	Y	N
2 Snyder	Y	Y	Y	N	Y	Y	Y	N
3 ***Hutchinson***	Y	Y	Y	Y	Y	Y	Y	N
4 ***Dickey***	Y	Y	Y	Y	Y	Y	Y	N
CALIFORNIA								
1 ***Riggs***	?	?	?	?	?	Y	Y	N
2 ***Herger***	Y	Y	Y	Y	Y	Y	Y	N
3 Fazio	Y	Y	Y	Y	?	Y	Y	N
4 ***Doolittle***	Y	N	Y	Y	Y	Y	Y	N
5 Matsui	Y	Y	Y	Y	Y	Y	Y	N
6 Woolsey	Y	Y	Y	Y	Y	Y	Y	Y
7 Miller	Y	Y	Y	N	Y	Y	Y	Y
8 Pelosi	Y	Y	Y	N	Y	Y	Y	N
9 Dellums	?	?	?	?	?	Y	Y	Y
10 Tauscher	Y	Y	Y	N	Y	Y	Y	Y
11 ***Pombo***	Y	Y	Y	Y	Y	Y	Y	N
12 Lantos	?	?	?	?	?	Y	Y	N
13 Stark	Y	Y	Y	Y	N	Y	Y	Y
14 Eshoo	Y	Y	Y	Y	Y	Y	Y	Y
15 ***Campbell***	Y	Y	Y	N	N	Y	Y	Y
16 Lofgren	Y	Y	Y	N	Y	Y	Y	Y
17 Farr	Y	Y	Y	N	Y	Y	Y	Y
18 Condit	Y	Y	Y	Y	Y	Y	Y	Y
19 ***Radanovich***	Y	N	Y	Y	Y	Y	Y	N
20 Dooley	Y	Y	Y	Y	Y	Y	Y	N
21 ***Thomas***	Y	Y	Y	Y	Y	Y	Y	N
22 Capps	Y	Y	Y	Y	Y	Y	Y	Y
23 ***Gallegly***	Y	N	Y	Y	Y	Y	Y	N
24 Sherman	+	+	+	+	Y	Y	Y	N
25 ***McKeon***	Y	Y	Y	Y	Y	Y	Y	N
26 Berman	Y	N	Y	Y	Y	Y	Y	N
27 ***Rogan***	Y	Y	Y	Y	Y	Y	Y	N
28 ***Dreier***	Y	Y	Y	Y	Y	Y	Y	N
29 Waxman	Y	Y	Y	Y	Y	Y	Y	Y
30 Becerra	?	?	?	?	?	Y	Y	Y
31 Martinez	Y	Y	Y	Y	Y	Y	Y	Y
32 Dixon	Y	Y	Y	Y	Y	Y	Y	N
33 Roybal-Allard	Y	Y	Y	Y	Y	Y	Y	Y
34 Torres	Y	Y	Y	N	Y	Y	Y	Y
35 Waters	Y	Y	Y	N	Y	Y	Y	Y
36 Harman	Y	Y	Y	N	Y	Y	Y	N
37 Millender-McD.	Y	Y	Y	Y	Y	Y	Y	Y
38 ***Horn***	Y	Y	Y	Y	Y	Y	Y	N
39 ***Royce***	Y	N	N	Y	N	Y	Y	Y
40 ***Lewis***	Y	N	Y	Y	Y	Y	Y	N
41 ***Kim***	Y	Y	Y	Y	Y	Y	Y	N
42 Brown	Y	Y	Y	Y	Y	Y	Y	Y
43 ***Calvert***	Y	Y	Y	Y	Y	Y	Y	N
44 ***Bono***	Y	Y	Y	Y	Y	Y	Y	N
45 ***Rohrabacher***	Y	N	Y	Y	Y	Y	Y	Y
46 Sanchez	Y	Y	Y	Y	Y	Y	Y	Y
47 ***Cox***	?	?	?	?	Y	?	?	?
48 ***Packard***	Y	Y	Y	Y	Y	Y	Y	N
49 ***Bilbray***	?	?	?	?	Y	Y	Y	N
50 Filner	Y	Y	Y	Y	Y	Y	Y	Y
51 ***Cunningham***	Y	Y	Y	Y	Y	Y	Y	N
52 ***Hunter***	?	?	?	?	Y	Y	Y	N
COLORADO								
1 DeGette	Y	Y	Y	Y	Y	Y	Y	Y
2 Skaggs	Y	N	Y	N	Y	Y	Y	N
3 ***McInnis***	Y	Y	Y	Y	Y	Y	Y	N
4 ***Schaffer***	Y	N	Y	Y	Y	Y	Y	N
5 ***Hefley***	Y	N	Y	Y	Y	Y	Y	N
6 ***Schaefer***	Y	Y	Y	Y	Y	Y	Y	N
CONNECTICUT								
1 Kennelly	Y	Y	Y	Y	Y	Y	Y	N
2 Gejdenson	+	+	+	?	+	Y	Y	N
3 DeLauro	Y	Y	Y	Y	Y	Y	Y	Y
4 ***Shays***	Y	Y	Y	Y	Y	Y	Y	Y
5 Maloney	Y	Y	Y	Y	Y	Y	Y	Y
6 ***Johnson***	Y	Y	Y	Y	Y	Y	Y	N
DELAWARE								
AL ***Castle***	Y	Y	Y	Y	Y	Y	Y	N
FLORIDA								
1 ***Scarborough***	?	N	N	Y	Y	Y	Y	N
2 Boyd	Y	Y	Y	Y	Y	Y	Y	N
3 Brown	Y	Y	Y	Y	Y	Y	Y	Y
4 ***Fowler***	Y	Y	Y	Y	Y	Y	Y	N
5 Thurman	Y	Y	Y	Y	Y	Y	Y	N
6 ***Stearns***	Y	Y	Y	Y	Y	Y	Y	N
7 ***Mica***	+	+	+	Y	Y	Y	Y	N
8 ***McCollum***	Y	Y	Y	Y	Y	Y	Y	N
9 ***Bilirakis***	Y	Y	Y	Y	Y	Y	Y	N
10 ***Young***	Y	Y	Y	Y	Y	Y	Y	N
11 Davis	Y	Y	Y	Y	Y	Y	Y	N
12 ***Canady***	Y	Y	Y	Y	Y	Y	Y	N
13 ***Miller***	Y	Y	Y	Y	Y	Y	Y	N
14 ***Goss***	Y	Y	Y	Y	Y	Y	Y	N
15 ***Weldon***	Y	Y	Y	Y	Y	Y	Y	N
16 ***Foley***	Y	Y	N	Y	Y	Y	Y	Y
17 Meek	Y	Y	Y	N	Y	Y	Y	N
18 ***Ros-Lehtinen***	Y	Y	Y	Y	Y	Y	Y	N
19 Wexler	Y	Y	Y	Y	Y	Y	Y	N
20 Deutsch	Y	Y	Y	Y	Y	Y	Y	N
21 ***Diaz-Balart***	Y	Y	Y	Y	Y	Y	Y	N
22 ***Shaw***	Y	Y	Y	Y	Y	Y	Y	N
23 Hastings	Y	Y	Y	N	Y	Y	Y	Y
GEORGIA								
1 ***Kingston***	Y	Y	Y	Y	Y	Y	Y	N
2 Bishop	Y	Y	Y	Y	Y	Y	Y	N
3 ***Collins***	Y	Y	Y	Y	Y	Y	Y	N
4 McKinney	Y	Y	Y	N	Y	Y	Y	Y
5 Lewis	Y	Y	Y	N	Y	Y	Y	Y
6 ***Gingrich***								
7 ***Barr***	Y	N	N	Y	Y	Y	Y	N
8 ***Chambliss***	Y	Y	Y	Y	Y	Y	Y	N
9 ***Deal***	Y	Y	Y	Y	Y	Y	Y	N
10 ***Norwood***	Y	Y	Y	Y	Y	Y	Y	Y
11 ***Linder***	Y	Y	Y	Y	Y	Y	Y	N
HAWAII								
1 Abercrombie	Y	Y	Y	Y	Y	Y	Y	Y
2 Mink	Y	Y	Y	Y	Y	Y	Y	Y
IDAHO								
1 ***Chenoweth***	Y	N	Y	Y	Y	Y	Y	Y
2 ***Crapo***	Y	Y	Y	Y	Y	Y	Y	N
ILLINOIS								
1 Rush	?	?	?	?	Y	Y	Y	Y
2 Jackson	Y	Y	Y	Y	Y	Y	Y	Y
3 Lipinski	Y	Y	Y	Y	Y	Y	Y	N
4 Gutierrez	Y	Y	Y	Y	Y	Y	Y	Y
5 Blagojevich	Y	Y	Y	Y	Y	Y	Y	N
6 ***Hyde***	Y	Y	Y	Y	Y	Y	Y	N
7 Davis	Y	Y	Y	Y	Y	Y	Y	Y
8 ***Crane***	Y	Y	Y	Y	Y	Y	Y	N
9 Yates	Y	Y	Y	N	?	Y	Y	Y
10 ***Porter***	Y	Y	Y	Y	Y	Y	Y	Y
11 ***Weller***	Y	Y	Y	Y	Y	Y	Y	N
12 Costello	Y	Y	Y	Y	Y	Y	Y	Y
13 ***Fawell***	Y	Y	Y	Y	Y	Y	Y	N
14 ***Hastert***	Y	Y	Y	Y	Y	Y	?	N
15 ***Ewing***	Y	Y	Y	Y	?	Y	Y	N

ND Northern Democrats SD Southern Democrats

	246	247	248	249	250	251	252	253
16 ***Manzullo***	Y	Y	N	Y	Y	Y	Y	Y
17 Evans	Y	Y	Y	Y	Y	Y	Y	Y
18 ***LaHood***	Y	Y	Y	N	Y	Y	Y	N
19 Poshard	Y	Y	Y	Y	Y	Y	Y	Y
20 ***Shimkus***	Y	Y	Y	Y	Y	Y	Y	N
INDIANA								
1 Visclosky	Y	Y	Y	Y	Y	Y	Y	N
2 ***McIntosh***	Y	N	Y	Y	Y	Y	Y	N
3 Roemer	Y	Y	Y	Y	Y	Y	Y	Y
4 ***Souder***	Y	Y	Y	Y	Y	Y	Y	N
5 ***Buyer***	Y	Y	Y	Y	Y	Y	Y	N
6 ***Burton***	Y	N	Y	Y	Y	Y	Y	N
7 ***Pease***	Y	Y	Y	Y	Y	Y	Y	N
8 ***Hostettler***	+	–	Y	Y	Y	Y	Y	N
9 Hamilton	Y	Y	Y	N	Y	Y	Y	N
10 Carson	Y	Y	Y	Y	Y	Y	Y	Y
IOWA								
1 ***Leach***	Y	Y	Y	Y	Y	Y	Y	N
2 ***Nussle***	Y	Y	Y	Y	Y	Y	Y	Y
3 Boswell	Y	Y	Y	Y	Y	Y	Y	N
4 ***Ganske***	Y	Y	Y	Y	Y	Y	Y	N
5 ***Latham***	Y	Y	Y	Y	Y	Y	Y	N
KANSAS								
1 ***Moran***	Y	Y	Y	Y	Y	Y	Y	N
2 ***Ryun***	Y	Y	Y	Y	Y	Y	Y	N
3 ***Snowbarger***	Y	Y	Y	Y	Y	Y	Y	N
4 ***Tiahrt***	Y	N	Y	Y	Y	Y	Y	N
KENTUCKY								
1 ***Whitfield***	Y	Y	Y	Y	Y	Y	Y	N
2 ***Lewis***	Y	Y	Y	Y	Y	Y	Y	N
3 ***Northup***	Y	Y	Y	Y	Y	Y	Y	N
4 ***Bunning***	Y	Y	Y	Y	Y	Y	Y	N
5 ***Rogers***	Y	Y	Y	Y	Y	Y	Y	N
6 Baesler	Y	Y	Y	Y	?	Y	Y	N
LOUISIANA								
1 ***Livingston***	Y	N	Y	Y	Y	Y	Y	N
2 Jefferson	Y	Y	Y	Y	Y	Y	Y	N
3 ***Tauzin***	Y	Y	Y	Y	Y	Y	Y	N
4 ***McCrery***	Y	Y	Y	Y	Y	Y	Y	N
5 ***Cooksey***	Y	Y	Y	Y	Y	Y	Y	N
6 ***Baker***	Y	Y	Y	Y	Y	Y	Y	N
7 John	Y	Y	Y	Y	Y	Y	Y	N
MAINE								
1 Allen	Y	Y	Y	Y	Y	Y	Y	Y
2 Baldacci	Y	Y	Y	Y	Y	Y	Y	Y
MARYLAND								
1 ***Gilchrest***	Y	Y	Y	Y	Y	Y	Y	N
2 ***Ehrlich***	Y	Y	Y	Y	Y	Y	Y	N
3 Cardin	Y	Y	Y	Y	Y	Y	Y	N
4 Wynn	Y	Y	Y	Y	Y	Y	Y	N
5 Hoyer	Y	Y	Y	Y	Y	Y	Y	N
6 ***Bartlett***	Y	N	Y	Y	Y	Y	Y	N
7 Cummings	Y	Y	Y	Y	Y	Y	Y	Y
8 ***Morella***	Y	Y	Y	Y	Y	Y	Y	Y
MASSACHUSETTS								
1 Olver	Y	Y	Y	Y	Y	Y	Y	Y
2 Neal	Y	Y	Y	Y	Y	Y	Y	Y
3 McGovern	Y	Y	Y	Y	Y	Y	Y	Y
4 Frank	Y	Y	Y	Y	N	Y	Y	Y
5 Meehan	Y	Y	Y	Y	Y	Y	Y	Y
6 Tierney	Y	Y	Y	Y	Y	Y	Y	Y
7 Markey	Y	Y	Y	Y	N	Y	Y	Y
8 Kennedy	Y	Y	Y	Y	Y	Y	Y	Y
9 Moakley	Y	Y	Y	Y	Y	Y	Y	Y
10 Delahunt	Y	Y	Y	P	Y	Y	Y	Y
MICHIGAN								
1 Stupak	Y	Y	Y	Y	Y	Y	Y	Y
2 ***Hoekstra***	Y	Y	Y	Y	Y	Y	Y	Y
3 ***Ehlers***	Y	Y	Y	Y	Y	Y	Y	N
4 ***Camp***	Y	Y	Y	Y	Y	Y	Y	Y
5 Barcia	Y	Y	Y	Y	Y	Y	Y	Y
6 ***Upton***	Y	Y	Y	Y	N	Y	Y	Y
7 ***Smith***	Y	N	Y	Y	Y	Y	Y	N
8 Stabenow	Y	Y	Y	Y	Y	Y	Y	Y
9 Kildee	Y	Y	Y	Y	Y	Y	Y	N
10 Bonior	Y	Y	Y	N	Y	Y	N	Y
11 ***Knollenberg***	Y	Y	Y	Y	Y	Y	Y	N
12 Levin	Y	Y	Y	Y	Y	Y	Y	N
13 Rivers	Y	Y	Y	Y	Y	Y	Y	Y
14 Conyers	Y	Y	Y	N	N	Y	Y	Y
15 Kilpatrick	Y	Y	Y	Y	Y	Y	Y	Y
16 Dingell	Y	N	Y	N	Y	Y	Y	N
MINNESOTA								
1 ***Gutknecht***	Y	Y	Y	Y	Y	Y	Y	Y
2 Minge	Y	Y	Y	N	N	Y	Y	Y

	246	247	248	249	250	251	252	253
3 ***Ramstad***	Y	Y	Y	Y	N	Y	Y	Y
4 Vento	Y	Y	Y	N	Y	Y	Y	Y
5 Sabo	Y	Y	Y	Y	Y	Y	Y	N
6 Luther	Y	Y	Y	Y	Y	Y	Y	Y
7 Peterson	Y	Y	Y	Y	Y	Y	Y	Y
8 Oberstar	Y	Y	Y	Y	N	Y	Y	Y
MISSISSIPPI								
1 ***Wicker***	Y	Y	Y	Y	Y	Y	Y	N
2 Thompson	Y	Y	Y	Y	Y	Y	Y	N
3 ***Pickering***	Y	Y	Y	Y	Y	Y	Y	N
4 ***Parker***	Y	Y	Y	Y	Y	Y	Y	N
5 Taylor	Y	N	Y	Y	Y	Y	Y	N
MISSOURI								
1 Clay	Y	Y	Y	Y	Y	Y	Y	Y
2 ***Talent***	Y	Y	Y	Y	Y	Y	Y	N
3 Gephardt	Y	Y	Y	Y	Y	Y	Y	Y
4 Skelton	Y	N	Y	Y	Y	Y	Y	N
5 McCarthy	Y	Y	Y	Y	Y	Y	Y	Y
6 Danner	Y	Y	Y	Y	Y	Y	Y	Y
7 ***Blunt***	Y	Y	Y	Y	Y	Y	Y	N
8 ***Emerson***	Y	Y	Y	Y	Y	Y	Y	N
9 ***Hulshof***	Y	Y	Y	Y	Y	Y	Y	N
MONTANA								
AL ***Hill***	Y	Y	Y	Y	Y	Y	Y	Y
NEBRASKA								
1 ***Bereuter***	Y	Y	Y	Y	Y	Y	Y	N
2 ***Christensen***	Y	Y	Y	Y	Y	Y	Y	N
3 ***Barrett***	Y	Y	Y	Y	Y	Y	Y	N
NEVADA								
1 ***Ensign***	Y	Y	Y	Y	Y	Y	Y	Y
2 ***Gibbons***	Y	Y	Y	?	Y	Y	Y	N
NEW HAMPSHIRE								
1 ***Sununu***	Y	Y	Y	Y	Y	Y	Y	N
2 ***Bass***	Y	Y	Y	Y	Y	Y	Y	N
NEW JERSEY								
1 Andrews	Y	Y	Y	Y	Y	Y	Y	N
2 ***LoBiondo***	Y	Y	Y	Y	Y	Y	Y	N
3 ***Saxton***	Y	Y	Y	Y	Y	Y	Y	N
4 ***Smith***	?	?	?	?	?	Y	Y	N
5 ***Roukema***	Y	Y	Y	Y	Y	Y	?	N
6 Pallone	Y	Y	Y	Y	Y	Y	Y	N
7 ***Franks***	Y	Y	Y	Y	Y	Y	Y	N
8 Pascrell	Y	Y	Y	Y	Y	Y	Y	N
9 Rothman	Y	Y	Y	Y	Y	Y	Y	N
10 Payne	Y	Y	Y	N	Y	Y	Y	Y
11 ***Frelinghuysen***	Y	Y	Y	Y	Y	Y	Y	N
12 ***Pappas***	Y	Y	Y	Y	Y	Y	Y	N
13 Menendez	Y	Y	?	Y	Y	Y	Y	N
NEW MEXICO								
1 ***Schiff***	?	?	?	?	?	?	?	?
2 ***Skeen***	Y	Y	Y	Y	Y	Y	Y	N
3 ***Redmond***	Y	Y	Y	Y	Y	Y	Y	N
NEW YORK								
1 ***Forbes***	Y	Y	Y	Y	Y	Y	Y	N
2 ***Lazio***	Y	Y	Y	Y	Y	Y	Y	N
3 ***King***	Y	Y	Y	Y	Y	Y	Y	N
4 McCarthy	Y	Y	Y	Y	Y	Y	Y	N
5 Ackerman	Y	Y	Y	Y	Y	Y	Y	N
6 Flake	Y	Y	Y	Y	Y	Y	Y	N
7 Manton	Y	Y	Y	Y	Y	Y	Y	N
8 Nadler	Y	Y	Y	Y	Y	Y	Y	Y
9 Schumer	Y	Y	Y	Y	Y	Y	Y	Y
10 Towns	Y	Y	Y	Y	Y	Y	Y	Y
11 Owens	?	?	Y	Y	Y	Y	Y	Y
12 Velázquez	Y	Y	Y	Y	Y	Y	Y	Y
13 ***Molinari***	Y	Y	Y	Y	Y	Y	Y	N
14 Maloney	Y	Y	Y	Y	Y	Y	Y	Y
15 Rangel	Y	Y	Y	Y	Y	Y	Y	Y
16 Serrano	Y	Y	Y	Y	Y	Y	Y	Y
17 Engel	Y	Y	Y	Y	Y	Y	Y	N
18 Lowey	?	?	?	?	?	Y	Y	N
19 ***Kelly***	Y	Y	Y	Y	Y	Y	Y	N
20 ***Gilman***	+	+	+	+	+	Y	Y	N
21 McNulty	Y	Y	Y	Y	Y	Y	Y	N
22 ***Solomon***	?	?	?	?	?	Y	Y	N
23 ***Boehlert***	Y	Y	Y	Y	Y	Y	Y	N
24 ***McHugh***	Y	Y	Y	Y	Y	Y	Y	N
25 ***Walsh***	Y	Y	Y	Y	Y	Y	Y	N
26 Hinchey	Y	Y	Y	Y	Y	Y	Y	Y
27 ***Paxon***	Y	Y	Y	Y	Y	Y	Y	N
28 Slaughter	Y	Y	Y	Y	Y	Y	Y	Y
29 LaFalce	Y	Y	Y	N	Y	Y	Y	N
30 ***Quinn***	Y	Y	Y	Y	Y	Y	Y	N
31 ***Houghton***	Y	Y	Y	Y	Y	Y	Y	N

	246	247	248	249	250	251	252	253
NORTH CAROLINA								
1 Clayton	Y	Y	Y	Y	Y	Y	Y	Y
2 Etheridge	Y	Y	Y	Y	Y	Y	Y	N
3 ***Jones***	Y	Y	Y	Y	Y	Y	Y	N
4 Price	Y	Y	Y	Y	Y	Y	Y	N
5 ***Burr***	Y	Y	Y	Y	Y	Y	Y	N
6 ***Coble***	Y	N	Y	Y	Y	Y	Y	N
7 McIntyre	Y	Y	Y	Y	Y	Y	Y	N
8 Hefner	Y	Y	Y	Y	Y	Y	Y	N
9 ***Myrick***	Y	Y	Y	Y	Y	Y	Y	N
10 ***Ballenger***	Y	Y	Y	Y	Y	Y	Y	N
11 ***Taylor***	?	?	?	Y	?	Y	Y	N
12 Watt	Y	Y	Y	Y	Y	Y	Y	Y
NORTH DAKOTA								
AL Pomeroy	Y	Y	Y	Y	Y	Y	Y	N
OHIO								
1 ***Chabot***	Y	Y	Y	Y	Y	Y	Y	Y
2 ***Portman***	Y	Y	Y	Y	Y	Y	Y	N
3 Hall	Y	Y	Y	Y	Y	Y	?	N
4 ***Oxley***	Y	Y	Y	Y	Y	Y	Y	N
5 ***Gillmor***	Y	Y	Y	Y	Y	Y	Y	N
6 Strickland	Y	Y	Y	Y	Y	Y	Y	Y
7 ***Hobson***	Y	Y	Y	Y	Y	Y	Y	N
8 ***Boehner***	Y	Y	Y	Y	Y	Y	Y	N
9 Kaptur	Y	Y	Y	Y	Y	Y	Y	N
10 Kucinich	Y	Y	Y	Y	Y	Y	Y	Y
11 Stokes	Y	Y	Y	Y	Y	Y	Y	Y
12 ***Kasich***	Y	Y	Y	Y	Y	Y	Y	N
13 Brown	?	?	?	?	?	Y	Y	Y
14 Sawyer	Y	Y	Y	Y	Y	Y	Y	N
15 ***Pryce***	Y	Y	Y	Y	Y	Y	Y	N
16 ***Regula***	Y	Y	Y	Y	Y	Y	Y	N
17 Traficant	Y	Y	Y	Y	Y	Y	Y	Y
18 ***Ney***	Y	Y	Y	Y	Y	Y	Y	N
19 ***LaTourette***	?	?	?	?	?	Y	Y	N
OKLAHOMA								
1 ***Largent***	?	?	Y	Y	?	Y	Y	N
2 ***Coburn***	Y	N	Y	?	Y	Y	Y	Y
3 ***Watkins***	Y	Y	Y	Y	Y	Y	Y	N
4 ***Watts***	Y	Y	Y	Y	Y	Y	Y	N
5 ***Istook***	Y	Y	Y	Y	Y	Y	Y	N
6 ***Lucas***	Y	Y	Y	Y	Y	Y	Y	N
OREGON								
1 Furse	Y	Y	Y	Y	Y	Y	Y	Y
2 ***Smith***	Y	Y	Y	Y	Y	Y	Y	N
3 Blumenauer	Y	Y	Y	N	Y	Y	Y	Y
4 DeFazio	Y	Y	Y	Y	Y	Y	N	Y
5 Hooley	Y	Y	Y	Y	Y	Y	Y	Y
PENNSYLVANIA								
1 Foglietta	Y	Y	Y	Y	Y	Y	Y	Y
2 Fattah	?	?	Y	Y	?	Y	Y	Y
3 Borski	Y	Y	Y	Y	Y	Y	Y	N
4 Klink	Y	Y	Y	Y	Y	Y	Y	N
5 ***Peterson***	Y	Y	Y	Y	Y	Y	Y	N
6 Holden	Y	Y	Y	Y	Y	Y	Y	N
7 ***Weldon***	Y	Y	Y	Y	Y	Y	Y	N
8 ***Greenwood***	Y	Y	Y	Y	Y	Y	Y	N
9 ***Shuster***	Y	N	Y	Y	Y	Y	Y	N
10 ***McDade***	Y	Y	Y	Y	Y	Y	Y	N
11 Kanjorski	Y	Y	Y	Y	?	Y	Y	Y
12 Murtha	Y	Y	Y	Y	?	Y	Y	N
13 ***Fox***	Y	Y	Y	Y	Y	Y	Y	N
14 Coyne	Y	Y	Y	Y	Y	Y	Y	Y
15 McHale	Y	Y	Y	Y	Y	Y	Y	N
16 ***Pitts***	Y	Y	Y	Y	Y	Y	Y	N
17 ***Gekas***	Y	Y	Y	Y	Y	Y	Y	N
18 Doyle	Y	Y	Y	Y	Y	Y	Y	N
19 ***Goodling***	Y	Y	Y	Y	Y	Y	Y	N
20 Mascara	Y	Y	Y	Y	Y	Y	Y	N
21 ***English***	Y	Y	Y	Y	Y	Y	Y	N
RHODE ISLAND								
1 Kennedy	+	Y	Y	Y	Y	Y	Y	N
2 Weygand	Y	Y	Y	Y	Y	Y	Y	N
SOUTH CAROLINA								
1 ***Sanford***	+	+	?	Y	Y	Y	Y	N
2 ***Spence***	Y	Y	Y	Y	Y	Y	Y	N
3 ***Graham***	Y	Y	Y	Y	Y	Y	Y	N
4 ***Inglis***	?	?	?	Y	Y	Y	Y	N
5 Spratt	Y	Y	Y	Y	Y	Y	Y	N
6 Clyburn	Y	Y	Y	Y	Y	Y	Y	Y
SOUTH DAKOTA								
AL ***Thune***	Y	Y	Y	Y	Y	Y	Y	N
TENNESSEE								
1 ***Jenkins***	Y	Y	Y	Y	Y	Y	Y	N
2 ***Duncan***	Y	Y	Y	Y	Y	Y	Y	Y

	246	247	248	249	250	251	252	
3 ***Wamp***	Y	Y	Y	Y	Y	Y	Y	N
4 ***Hilleary***	?	?	?	Y	Y	Y	Y	N
5 Clement	Y	Y	Y	Y	Y	Y	Y	N
6 Gordon	Y	Y	Y	Y	Y	Y	Y	N
7 ***Bryant***	+	Y	Y	Y	Y	Y	Y	N
8 Tanner	Y	Y	Y	Y	Y	Y	Y	Y
9 Ford	Y	Y	Y	Y	Y	Y	Y	Y
TEXAS								
1 Sandlin	Y	Y	Y	Y	Y	Y	Y	N
2 Turner	Y	Y	Y	Y	Y	Y	Y	N
3 ***Johnson, Sam***	Y	N	Y	Y	Y	Y	Y	N
4 Hall	Y	N	Y	Y	Y	Y	Y	Y
5 ***Sessions***	Y	N	Y	Y	Y	Y	Y	N
6 ***Barton***	Y	N	Y	Y	Y	Y	Y	N
7 ***Archer***	Y	Y	Y	Y	Y	Y	Y	N
8 ***Brady***	Y	Y	Y	Y	Y	Y	Y	N
9 Lampson	Y	Y	Y	Y	Y	Y	Y	N
10 Doggett	Y	Y	Y	Y	Y	Y	Y	Y
11 Edwards	?	?	?	?	?	?	?	?
12 ***Granger***	Y	Y	Y	Y	Y	Y	Y	N
13 ***Thornberry***	Y	N	Y	Y	Y	Y	Y	N
14 ***Paul***	Y	N	N	N	N	N	Y	Y
15 Hinojosa	Y	Y	Y	Y	Y	Y	Y	Y
16 Reyes	Y	Y	Y	Y	Y	Y	Y	N
17 Stenholm	Y	Y	Y	Y	Y	Y	Y	Y
18 Jackson-Lee	Y	Y	Y	Y	Y	Y	Y	Y
19 ***Combest***	Y	N	Y	Y	Y	Y	Y	N
20 Gonzalez	Y	Y	Y	Y	Y	Y	Y	Y
21 ***Smith***	Y	Y	Y	Y	Y	Y	Y	N
22 ***DeLay***	Y	N	Y	Y	Y	Y	Y	N
23 ***Bonilla***	Y	N	Y	Y	Y	Y	Y	N
24 Frost	?	?	?	?	?	Y	Y	N
25 Bentsen	Y	Y	Y	Y	Y	Y	Y	Y
26 ***Armey***	Y	Y	Y	Y	Y	Y	Y	N
27 Ortiz	Y	Y	Y	Y	Y	Y	Y	N
28 Rodriguez	Y	Y	Y	Y	Y	Y	Y	N
29 Green	Y	Y	Y	Y	Y	Y	Y	Y
30 Johnson, E.B.	Y	Y	Y	Y	Y	Y	Y	Y
UTAH								
1 ***Hansen***	Y	Y	Y	Y	Y	Y	Y	N
2 ***Cook***	Y	Y	Y	Y	Y	Y	Y	N
3 ***Cannon***	Y	Y	Y	Y	Y	Y	Y	N
VERMONT								
AL *Sanders*	Y	Y	Y	Y	Y	Y	Y	Y
VIRGINIA								
1 ***Bateman***	Y	Y	Y	Y	Y	Y	Y	N
2 Pickett	Y	Y	Y	Y	Y	Y	Y	N
3 Scott	Y	Y	Y	N	Y	Y	Y	N
4 Sisisky	?	?	?	?	?	Y	Y	N
5 Goode	Y	Y	Y	Y	Y	Y	Y	N
6 ***Goodlatte***	Y	Y	Y	Y	Y	Y	Y	N
7 ***Bliley***	Y	Y	Y	Y	Y	Y	Y	N
8 Moran	Y	N	Y	N	Y	Y	Y	N
9 Boucher	Y	Y	Y	Y	Y	?	Y	N
10 ***Wolf***	Y	Y	Y	Y	Y	Y	Y	N
11 ***Davis***	Y	Y	Y	Y	Y	Y	Y	N
WASHINGTON								
1 ***White***	Y	Y	Y	Y	Y	Y	Y	N
2 ***Metcalf***	Y	Y	Y	Y	Y	Y	Y	Y
3 ***Smith, Linda***	Y	Y	Y	Y	Y	Y	Y	N
4 ***Hastings***	Y	Y	Y	Y	Y	Y	Y	N
5 ***Nethercutt***	Y	Y	Y	Y	Y	Y	Y	N
6 Dicks	Y	Y	Y	Y	Y	Y	Y	N
7 McDermott	Y	Y	Y	N	Y	Y	Y	Y
8 ***Dunn***	Y	Y	Y	Y	Y	Y	Y	N
9 Smith, Adam	Y	Y	Y	Y	Y	Y	Y	N
WEST VIRGINIA								
1 Mollohan	Y	Y	Y	Y	Y	Y	Y	N
2 Wise	Y	Y	Y	Y	Y	Y	Y	N
3 Rahall	Y	Y	Y	N	N	Y	Y	N
WISCONSIN								
1 ***Neumann***	Y	Y	N	Y	Y	Y	?	Y
2 ***Klug***	Y	Y	Y	Y	Y	Y	Y	N
3 Kind	Y	Y	Y	Y	Y	Y	Y	Y
4 Kleczka	Y	Y	Y	Y	Y	Y	Y	Y
5 Barrett	Y	Y	Y	Y	N	Y	Y	Y
6 ***Petri***	Y	Y	Y	Y	Y	Y	Y	Y
7 Obey	Y	N	Y	N	Y	Y	Y	Y
8 Johnson	Y	Y	Y	Y	Y	Y	Y	Y
9 ***Sensenbrenner***	Y	N	N	Y	N	Y	Y	Y
WYOMING								
AL ***Cubin***	Y	Y	Y	Y	Y	Y	Y	N

Southern states - Ala., Ark., Fla., Ga., Ky., La., Miss., N.C., Okla., S.C., Tenn., Texas, Va.

HOUSE VOTES 254, 255, 256, 257, 258, 259, 260, 261

254. HR 1775. Fiscal 1998 Intelligence Authorization/Unclassified Statement of Appropriations. Conyers, D-Mich., amendment to require the president, at the time of his annual budget request, to submit to Congress a separate, unclassified statement of the appropriations and proposed appropriations for the current fiscal year for intelligence activities and the amount requested for the next fiscal year. Rejected 192-237: R 18-207; D 173-30 (ND 132-17, SD 41-13); I 1-0, July 9, 1997.

255. HR 1775. Fiscal 1998 Intelligence Authorization/Cut to President's Request. Frank, D-Mass., amendment to trim the bill's total authorization by 0.7 percent through an across-the-board cut, except for the CIA Retirement and Disability Fund, reducing the total authorization level to the president's request. Rejected 182-238: R 23-199; D 158-39 (ND 122-23, SD 36-16); I 1-0, July 9, 1997.

256. Procedural Motion/Journal. Approval of the House Journal of Wednesday, July 9, 1997. Approved 364-49: R 201-17; D 163-32 (ND 117-26, SD 46-6); I 0-0, July 10, 1997.

257. HR 2015. Fiscal 1998 Budget Reconciliation — Spending/Motion To Instruct. Spratt, D-S.C., motion to instruct House conferees to oppose the Senate provision raising the age for Medicare eligibility from 65 to 67 and cover all workers under the Temporary Assistance for Needy Families program with the same protections as other workers, including the Fair Labor Standards Act, OSHA and anti-discrimination laws. Motion agreed to 414-14: R 210-14; D 203-0 (ND 148-0, SD 55-0); I 1-0, July 10, 1997.

258. HR 2014. Fiscal 1998 Budget Reconciliation — Revenue/Motion To Instruct. Rangel, D-N.Y., motion to instruct the House conferees to provide a $500-per-child tax credit to working families, support a HOPE Scholarship credit for the first two years of a college education, include tax benefits for families paying tuition costs for the second two years of a college education out of wage and salary income and oppose the indexing of capital assets. Motion rejected 199-233: R 0-226; D 198-7 (ND 147-3, SD 51-4); I 1-0, July 10, 1997.

259. HR 2107. Fiscal 1998 Interior Appropriations/Rule. Adoption of the rule (H Res 181) to provide for House floor consideration of the bill to provide $13 billion in new budget authority for the Department of the Interior and related agencies for fiscal 1998. The rule did not waive a point of order against the $10 million of funding in the bill for the National Endowment for the Arts because its authorization had expired. Adopted 217-216: R 212-15; D 5-200 (ND 2-148, SD 3-52); I 0-1, July 10, 1997.

260. HR 2107. Fiscal 1998 Interior Appropriations/Payment in Lieu of Taxes Program. Sanders, I-Vt., amendment to increase funding for the Payments In Lieu of Taxes program, which provides federal payments to make up for the taxes localities might otherwise collect if federal lands were not federally owned, by $19 million to $132.5 million. The amendment offsets the increase by reducing funding for the Department of Energy's fossil energy research and development program by $47.5 million and applies the remaining $28.5 million to deficit reduction. Rejected 199-230: R 95-131; D 103-99 (ND 79-69, SD 24-30); I 1-0, July 10, 1997.

261. HR 2107. Fiscal 1998 Interior Appropriations/Susan B. Anthony House Repairs. Maloney, D-N.Y., amendment to increase funding for National Park Service construction by $500,000 to repair the Susan B. Anthony House in New York. The increase would be offset by a reduction of $500,000 in National Wildlife Refuge funding. Rejected 77-351: R 9-217; D 67-134 (ND 55-92, SD 12-42); I 1-0, July 10, 1997.

KEY

- Y Voted for (yea).
- # Paired for.
- + Announced for.
- N Voted against (nay).
- X Paired against.
- – Announced against.
- P Voted "present."
- C Voted "present" to avoid possible conflict of interest.
- ? Did not vote or otherwise make a position known.

—

Democrats ***Republicans***
Independent

	254	255	256	257	258	259	260	261
ALABAMA								
1 ***Callahan***	N	N	Y	Y	N	Y	N	N
2 ***Everett***	N	N	Y	Y	N	Y	N	N
3 ***Riley***	N	N	Y	Y	N	Y	N	N
4 ***Aderholt***	N	N	Y	Y	N	Y	N	N
5 Cramer	N	N	Y	Y	Y	N	N	N
6 ***Bachus***	N	N	Y	Y	N	Y	N	N
7 Hilliard	Y	Y	N	Y	Y	N	Y	N
ALASKA								
AL ***Young***	N	N	?	Y	N	Y	N	N
ARIZONA								
1 ***Salmon***	N	N	Y	Y	N	Y	Y	N
2 Pastor	Y	Y	Y	Y	Y	N	Y	N
3 ***Stump***	N	N	Y	Y	N	Y	Y	N
4 ***Shadegg***	N	N	Y	N	N	Y	Y	N
5 ***Kolbe***	N	N	Y	N	N	Y	Y	N
6 ***Hayworth***	N	N	Y	Y	N	Y	Y	N
ARKANSAS								
1 Berry	Y	Y	Y	Y	Y	N	Y	Y
2 Snyder	Y	Y	Y	Y	Y	N	Y	N
3 ***Hutchinson***	N	N	N	Y	N	Y	Y	N
4 ***Dickey***	N	N	Y	Y	N	Y	Y	N
CALIFORNIA								
1 ***Riggs***	Y	Y	?	N	N	Y	Y	N
2 ***Herger***	N	N	Y	Y	N	Y	Y	N
3 Fazio	Y	Y	N	Y	Y	N	Y	Y
4 ***Doolittle***	N	N	Y	Y	N	Y	Y	N
5 Matsui	Y	Y	Y	Y	Y	N	N	N
6 Woolsey	Y	Y	Y	Y	Y	N	N	N
7 Miller	Y	Y	Y	Y	Y	N	N	N
8 Pelosi	Y	Y	Y	Y	Y	N	N	N
9 Dellums	Y	Y	Y	Y	Y	N	Y	N
10 Tauscher	Y	Y	Y	Y	Y	N	N	N
11 ***Pombo***	N	N	?	Y	N	Y	Y	N
12 Lantos	Y	Y	Y	Y	Y	N	Y	N
13 Stark	Y	Y	Y	Y	Y	N	N	N
14 Eshoo	Y	Y	Y	Y	Y	N	Y	Y
15 ***Campbell***	N	Y	Y	N	N	Y	Y	N
16 Lofgren	Y	Y	Y	Y	Y	N	N	N
17 Farr	Y	Y	Y	Y	Y	N	Y	Y
18 Condit	Y	Y	Y	Y	Y	Y	Y	N
19 ***Radanovich***	N	N	Y	Y	N	Y	N	N
20 Dooley	Y	Y	Y	Y	Y	N	N	?
21 ***Thomas***	N	N	Y	Y	N	Y	Y	N
22 Capps	Y	Y	Y	Y	Y	N	Y	N
23 ***Gallegly***	N	N	Y	Y	N	Y	Y	N
24 Sherman	Y	N	Y	Y	Y	N	Y	Y
25 ***McKeon***	N	N	Y	Y	N	Y	N	N
26 Berman	Y	?	Y	Y	Y	N	N	N
27 ***Rogan***	N	N	Y	Y	N	Y	N	N
28 ***Dreier***	N	N	Y	Y	N	Y	N	N
29 Waxman	Y	Y	Y	Y	Y	N	N	Y
30 Becerra	Y	Y	?	Y	Y	N	Y	Y
31 Martinez	Y	N	Y	Y	Y	N	N	N
32 Dixon	Y	N	?	Y	Y	N	N	N
33 Roybal-Allard	Y	Y	Y	Y	Y	N	Y	Y
34 Torres	Y	Y	Y	Y	Y	N	Y	N
35 Waters	Y	Y	N	Y	Y	N	Y	Y
36 Harman	Y	N	Y	Y	Y	N	?	?
37 Millender-McD.	Y	Y	Y	Y	Y	N	Y	Y
38 ***Horn***	Y	N	Y	Y	N	N	Y	Y
39 ***Royce***	N	Y	Y	Y	N	Y	N	N
40 ***Lewis***	N	N	Y	Y	N	Y	N	N
41 ***Kim***	N	N	Y	Y	N	Y	N	N
42 Brown	Y	Y	N	Y	Y	N	N	Y
43 ***Calvert***	N	N	Y	Y	N	Y	N	N
44 ***Bono***	N	N	Y	Y	N	Y	Y	N
45 ***Rohrabacher***	Y	Y	Y	N	N	Y	Y	N
46 Sanchez	Y	Y	Y	Y	Y	N	N	N
47 ***Cox***	N	N	Y	Y	N	Y	Y	N
48 ***Packard***	N	N	Y	Y	N	Y	N	N
49 ***Bilbray***	N	N	Y	Y	N	Y	Y	N
50 Filner	Y	Y	N	Y	Y	N	Y	Y
51 ***Cunningham***	N	N	N	Y	N	Y	Y	N
52 ***Hunter***	N	N	Y	Y	N	Y	N	N
COLORADO								
1 DeGette	Y	Y	Y	Y	Y	N	Y	Y
2 Skaggs	Y	Y	Y	?	Y	N	N	N
3 ***McInnis***	N	N	Y	Y	N	Y	Y	N
4 ***Schaffer***	N	N	N	Y	N	Y	Y	N
5 ***Hefley***	N	N	N	Y	N	Y	Y	N
6 ***Schaefer***	N	N	Y	Y	N	Y	N	N
CONNECTICUT								
1 Kennelly	Y	Y	Y	Y	Y	N	Y	Y
2 Gejdenson	Y	Y	Y	Y	Y	N	N	Y
3 DeLauro	Y	Y	Y	Y	Y	N	N	N
4 ***Shays***	Y	Y	Y	N	N	Y	Y	N
5 Maloney	Y	Y	Y	Y	Y	N	N	Y
6 ***Johnson***	N	N	Y	Y	N	Y	N	N
DELAWARE								
AL ***Castle***	N	N	Y	Y	N	N	N	N
FLORIDA								
1 ***Scarborough***	N	N	Y	N	N	Y	Y	N
2 Boyd	Y	Y	Y	Y	Y	N	Y	N
3 Brown	Y	Y	Y	Y	Y	N	Y	N
4 ***Fowler***	N	N	Y	N	N	Y	Y	N
5 Thurman	Y	Y	Y	Y	Y	N	N	Y
6 ***Stearns***	N	N	Y	Y	N	Y	Y	N
7 ***Mica***	N	N	Y	Y	N	Y	N	N
8 ***McCollum***	N	N	Y	Y	N	Y	Y	N
9 ***Bilirakis***	N	N	Y	Y	N	Y	N	N
10 ***Young***	N	N	Y	Y	N	Y	N	N
11 Davis	Y	Y	Y	Y	Y	N	Y	N
12 ***Canady***	N	N	Y	Y	N	Y	Y	N
13 ***Miller***	N	N	Y	Y	N	Y	Y	N
14 ***Goss***	N	N	Y	Y	N	Y	Y	N
15 ***Weldon***	N	N	Y	Y	N	Y	Y	N
16 ***Foley***	N	N	Y	Y	N	Y	Y	N
17 Meek	Y	Y	Y	Y	Y	N	Y	N
18 ***Ros-Lehtinen***	N	N	Y	Y	N	Y	N	Y
19 Wexler	Y	?	Y	Y	Y	N	Y	N
20 Deutsch	Y	N	Y	Y	N	N	Y	N
21 ***Diaz-Balart***	N	N	?	Y	N	Y	N	Y
22 ***Shaw***	N	N	Y	Y	N	Y	N	N
23 Hastings	Y	Y	N	Y	Y	N	Y	Y
GEORGIA								
1 ***Kingston***	N	N	Y	Y	N	Y	Y	N
2 Bishop	N	N	Y	Y	Y	N	Y	N
3 ***Collins***	N	?	Y	Y	N	Y	Y	N
4 McKinney	Y	Y	Y	Y	Y	N	Y	N
5 Lewis	Y	Y	N	Y	Y	N	N	N
6 ***Gingrich***						Y		
7 ***Barr***	N	N	Y	N	N	Y	N	N
8 ***Chambliss***	N	N	Y	Y	N	Y	N	N
9 ***Deal***	N	N	Y	Y	N	Y	Y	N
10 ***Norwood***	N	N	Y	Y	N	Y	Y	N
11 ***Linder***	N	N	Y	Y	N	Y	N	N
HAWAII								
1 Abercrombie	Y	Y	N	Y	Y	N	Y	Y
2 Mink	Y	Y	Y	Y	Y	N	N	Y
IDAHO								
1 ***Chenoweth***	Y	N	Y	Y	N	Y	Y	N
2 ***Crapo***	Y	N	Y	Y	N	Y	Y	N
ILLINOIS								
1 Rush	Y	Y	N	Y	Y	N	Y	Y
2 Jackson	Y	Y	Y	Y	Y	N	Y	Y
3 Lipinski	N	N	Y	Y	N	N	N	Y
4 Gutierrez	Y	Y	N	Y	Y	N	Y	Y
5 Blagojevich	Y	Y	Y	Y	Y	N	N	Y
6 ***Hyde***	N	N	Y	Y	N	Y	N	N
7 Davis	Y	Y	Y	Y	Y	N	Y	Y
8 ***Crane***	N	N	?	Y	N	Y	N	N
9 Yates	?	#	Y	Y	Y	N	?	?
10 ***Porter***	N	Y	Y	N	N	Y	N	N
11 ***Weller***	N	N	N	Y	N	Y	Y	N
12 Costello	Y	Y	N	Y	Y	N	N	N
13 ***Fawell***	N	N	N	Y	N	Y	N	Y
14 ***Hastert***	N	N	Y	Y	N	Y	N	N
15 ***Ewing***	N	N	Y	Y	N	Y	N	N

ND Northern Democrats SD Southern Democrats

	254	255	256	257	258	259	260	261
16 ***Manzullo***	N	N	Y	Y	N	Y	Y	N
17 Evans	Y	Y	Y	Y	Y	N	Y	N
18 ***LaHood***	N	N	Y	Y	N	Y	N	N
19 Poshard	Y	Y	N	Y	Y	N	N	N
20 ***Shimkus***	N	N	Y	Y	N	Y	N	N
INDIANA								
1 Visclosky	N	N	N	Y	Y	N	N	N
2 ***McIntosh***	N	N	Y	Y	N	Y	N	N
3 Roemer	Y	Y	Y	Y	Y	N	N	N
4 ***Souder***	N	N	?	Y	N	Y	N	Y
5 ***Buyer***	N	N	Y	Y	N	Y	N	N
6 ***Burton***	N	N	Y	?	N	Y	N	N
7 ***Pease***	N	N	Y	Y	N	Y	N	N
8 ***Hostettler***	N	N	Y	Y	N	Y	N	N
9 Hamilton	Y	Y	Y	Y	Y	N	N	N
10 Carson	Y	Y	Y	Y	Y	N	Y	Y
IOWA								
1 ***Leach***	Y	Y	Y	Y	N	N	Y	Y
2 ***Nussle***	N	N	Y	Y	N	Y	Y	N
3 Boswell	Y	Y	Y	Y	Y	N	Y	N
4 ***Ganske***	N	N	Y	Y	N	Y	Y	N
5 ***Latham***	N	N	Y	Y	N	Y	Y	N
KANSAS								
1 ***Moran***	N	N	N	Y	N	Y	Y	N
2 ***Ryun***	N	N	Y	Y	N	Y	N	N
3 ***Snowbarger***	N	N	Y	Y	N	Y	N	N
4 ***Tiahrt***	N	N	N	Y	N	Y	N	N
KENTUCKY								
1 ***Whitfield***	N	N	Y	Y	N	Y	N	N
2 ***Lewis***	N	N	Y	Y	N	Y	Y	N
3 ***Northup***	N	N	Y	Y	N	Y	N	N
4 ***Bunning***	N	N	Y	Y	N	Y	N	N
5 ***Rogers***	N	N	Y	Y	N	Y	Y	N
6 Baesler	Y	N	Y	Y	Y	N	N	N
LOUISIANA								
1 ***Livingston***	N	N	Y	Y	N	Y	N	N
2 Jefferson	N	Y	?	Y	Y	N	Y	Y
3 ***Tauzin***	N	N	Y	Y	N	Y	N	N
4 ***McCrery***	N	N	Y	Y	N	Y	N	N
5 ***Cooksey***	N	N	Y	Y	N	Y	N	N
6 ***Baker***	N	N	Y	Y	N	Y	N	N
7 John	N	N	Y	Y	Y	N	N	N
MAINE								
1 Allen	Y	Y	Y	Y	Y	N	Y	N
2 Baldacci	Y	Y	Y	Y	Y	N	Y	N
MARYLAND								
1 ***Gilchrest***	N	N	P	Y	N	Y	N	N
2 ***Ehrlich***	N	N	Y	N	N	Y	Y	N
3 Cardin	N	N	Y	Y	Y	N	N	N
4 Wynn	N	N	Y	Y	Y	N	N	N
5 Hoyer	N	N	Y	Y	Y	N	N	Y
6 ***Bartlett***	N	N	Y	Y	N	Y	N	N
7 Cummings	Y	Y	Y	Y	Y	N	N	Y
8 ***Morella***	Y	Y	Y	Y	N	N	Y	Y
MASSACHUSETTS								
1 Olver	Y	Y	N	Y	Y	N	Y	Y
2 Neal	Y	Y	Y	Y	Y	N	N	N
3 McGovern	Y	Y	Y	Y	Y	N	N	N
4 Frank	Y	Y	Y	Y	Y	N	N	N
5 Meehan	Y	Y	Y	Y	Y	N	N	N
6 Tierney	Y	Y	Y	Y	Y	N	N	N
7 Markey	Y	Y	?	?	Y	N	N	N
8 Kennedy	Y	Y	Y	Y	Y	N	N	N
9 Moakley	Y	Y	Y	Y	Y	N	N	Y
10 Delahunt	Y	Y	Y	Y	Y	N	Y	N
MICHIGAN								
1 Stupak	Y	Y	N	Y	Y	N	Y	N
2 ***Hoekstra***	N	N	Y	Y	N	Y	Y	N
3 ***Ehlers***	N	N	Y	Y	N	Y	N	N
4 ***Camp***	N	Y	Y	Y	N	Y	N	N
5 Barcia	Y	Y	Y	Y	Y	N	Y	N
6 ***Upton***	N	Y	Y	Y	N	Y	N	N
7 ***Smith***	N	N	Y	Y	N	Y	Y	N
8 Stabenow	Y	Y	Y	Y	Y	N	N	Y
9 Kildee	Y	Y	Y	Y	Y	N	N	N
10 Bonior	Y	Y	N	Y	Y	N	Y	Y
11 ***Knollenberg***	N	N	Y	Y	N	Y	N	N
12 Levin	Y	Y	Y	Y	Y	N	N	N
13 Rivers	Y	Y	Y	Y	Y	N	Y	N
14 Conyers	Y	Y	Y	Y	Y	N	Y	Y
15 Kilpatrick	Y	Y	Y	Y	Y	N	Y	N
16 Dingell	Y	Y	Y	Y	Y	N	N	N
MINNESOTA								
1 ***Gutknecht***	N	N	N	Y	N	Y	Y	N
2 Minge	Y	Y	Y	Y	Y	N	Y	N

	254	255	256	257	258	259	260	261
3 ***Ramstad***	N	Y	N	Y	N	N	Y	N
4 Vento	Y	Y	Y	Y	Y	N	N	Y
5 Sabo	Y	Y	N	Y	Y	N	N	N
6 Luther	Y	Y	Y	Y	Y	N	Y	N
7 Peterson	Y	Y	?	Y	Y	N	Y	N
8 Oberstar	Y	Y	N	Y	Y	N	Y	N
MISSISSIPPI								
1 ***Wicker***	N	N	Y	Y	N	Y	N	N
2 Thompson	Y	Y	N	Y	Y	N	Y	N
3 ***Pickering***	N	N	Y	Y	N	Y	Y	N
4 ***Parker***	N	N	Y	Y	N	Y	Y	N
5 Taylor	N	N	N	Y	Y	Y	Y	N
MISSOURI								
1 Clay	Y	Y	N	Y	Y	N	Y	N
2 ***Talent***	N	N	Y	Y	N	Y	N	N
3 Gephardt	Y	Y	N	Y	Y	N	N	Y
4 Skelton	N	N	Y	Y	Y	N	Y	N
5 McCarthy	Y	Y	Y	Y	Y	N	Y	N
6 Danner	Y	Y	Y	Y	N	N	Y	N
7 ***Blunt***	N	N	Y	Y	N	Y	N	N
8 ***Emerson***	N	N	Y	Y	N	Y	Y	N
9 ***Hulshof***	N	N	Y	Y	N	Y	Y	N
MONTANA								
AL ***Hill***	N	N	Y	Y	N	Y	Y	N
NEBRASKA								
1 ***Bereuter***	N	N	Y	Y	N	Y	Y	N
2 ***Christensen***	Y	N	Y	Y	N	Y	Y	N
3 ***Barrett***	N	N	Y	Y	N	Y	N	N
NEVADA								
1 ***Ensign***	Y	Y	N	Y	N	Y	Y	N
2 ***Gibbons***	N	N	N	Y	N	Y	Y	N
NEW HAMPSHIRE								
1 ***Sununu***	N	N	Y	Y	N	Y	Y	N
2 ***Bass***	?	N	Y	Y	N	Y	Y	Y
NEW JERSEY								
1 Andrews	Y	N	Y	Y	Y	N	Y	Y
2 ***LoBiondo***	N	N	N	Y	N	N	Y	N
3 ***Saxton***	N	N	Y	Y	N	N	N	N
4 ***Smith***	N	N	Y	Y	N	Y	N	N
5 ***Roukema***	N	Y	Y	Y	N	N	N	N
6 Pallone	Y	Y	N	Y	Y	N	N	N
7 ***Franks***	N	N	Y	Y	N	N	N	N
8 Pascrell	Y	Y	N	Y	Y	N	Y	N
9 Rothman	Y	Y	Y	Y	Y	N	Y	N
10 Payne	Y	Y	Y	Y	Y	N	Y	Y
11 ***Frelinghuysen***	N	N	Y	Y	N	Y	N	N
12 ***Pappas***	N	N	Y	Y	N	Y	Y	N
13 Menendez	Y	Y	Y	Y	Y	N	Y	N
NEW MEXICO								
1 ***Schiff***	?	?	?	?	?	?	?	?
2 ***Skeen***	N	N	Y	Y	N	Y	N	N
3 ***Redmond***	N	N	Y	Y	N	Y	N	N
NEW YORK								
1 ***Forbes***	N	N	Y	Y	N	N	N	N
2 ***Lazio***	N	N	Y	Y	N	N	N	N
3 ***King***	N	N	Y	Y	N	Y	N	N
4 McCarthy	Y	Y	Y	Y	Y	N	Y	N
5 Ackerman	Y	Y	Y	Y	Y	N	Y	Y
6 Flake	Y	Y	Y	Y	Y	N	Y	N
7 Manton	Y	?	?	Y	Y	N	Y	Y
8 Nadler	Y	Y	Y	Y	Y	N	N	Y
9 Schumer	Y	Y	Y	Y	Y	N	N	Y
10 Towns	?	?	Y	Y	Y	N	Y	Y
11 Owens	Y	Y	Y	Y	Y	N	Y	Y
12 Velázquez	Y	Y	Y	Y	Y	N	Y	Y
13 ***Molinari***	N	N	Y	Y	N	Y	N	N
14 Maloney	Y	Y	Y	Y	Y	N	Y	Y
15 Rangel	Y	Y	Y	Y	Y	N	Y	Y
16 Serrano	Y	Y	Y	Y	Y	N	Y	Y
17 Engel	N	Y	Y	Y	Y	N	N	Y
18 Lowey	Y	Y	Y	Y	Y	N	N	Y
19 ***Kelly***	N	N	Y	Y	N	Y	N	N
20 ***Gilman***	N	N	Y	Y	N	Y	N	Y
21 McNulty	Y	N	Y	Y	Y	N	Y	Y
22 ***Solomon***	N	N	Y	Y	N	Y	N	N
23 ***Boehlert***	N	N	Y	Y	N	Y	Y	N
24 ***McHugh***	N	N	Y	Y	N	Y	Y	N
25 ***Walsh***	N	N	Y	Y	N	Y	N	N
26 Hinchey	Y	Y	N	Y	Y	N	Y	Y
27 ***Paxon***	N	N	Y	Y	N	Y	N	N
28 Slaughter	Y	+	+	+	+	-	+	+
29 LaFalce	Y	Y	N	Y	Y	N	Y	Y
30 ***Quinn***	N	N	Y	Y	N	N	N	N
31 ***Houghton***	N	N	Y	Y	N	N	Y	N

	254	255	256	257	258	259	260	261
NORTH CAROLINA								
1 Clayton	Y	Y	Y	Y	Y	N	Y	N
2 Etheridge	N	Y	Y	Y	Y	N	N	N
3 ***Jones***	N	N	Y	Y	N	Y	Y	N
4 Price	Y	Y	Y	Y	Y	N	N	N
5 ***Burr***	N	N	Y	Y	N	Y	Y	N
6 ***Coble***	N	N	Y	Y	N	Y	Y	N
7 McIntyre	N	N	Y	Y	Y	N	Y	N
8 Hefner	Y	Y	Y	Y	Y	N	N	Y
9 ***Myrick***	N	N	Y	Y	N	Y	N	N
10 ***Ballenger***	N	N	Y	Y	N	Y	Y	N
11 ***Taylor***	N	N	Y	Y	N	Y	N	N
12 Watt	Y	Y	Y	Y	Y	N	Y	N
NORTH DAKOTA								
AL Pomeroy	Y	Y	Y	Y	Y	N	N	N
OHIO								
1 ***Chabot***	Y	Y	Y	Y	N	Y	Y	N
2 ***Portman***	N	N	Y	Y	N	Y	Y	N
3 Hall	N	Y	Y	Y	Y	N	N	Y
4 ***Oxley***	N	?	Y	Y	N	Y	N	N
5 ***Gillmor***	N	N	Y	Y	N	Y	N	N
6 Strickland	Y	Y	Y	Y	Y	N	Y	N
7 ***Hobson***	N	N	Y	Y	N	Y	N	N
8 ***Boehner***	N	N	Y	Y	N	Y	N	N
9 Kaptur	N	N	Y	Y	Y	N	Y	N
10 Kucinich	Y	Y	N	Y	Y	N	Y	Y
11 Stokes	Y	Y	Y	Y	Y	N	N	N
12 ***Kasich***	N	N	Y	Y	N	Y	Y	N
13 Brown	Y	Y	Y	Y	Y	N	Y	N
14 Sawyer	Y	Y	Y	Y	Y	N	N	N
15 ***Pryce***	N	N	Y	Y	N	Y	N	N
16 ***Regula***	N	N	Y	Y	N	Y	N	N
17 Traficant	Y	Y	Y	Y	N	Y	Y	N
18 ***Ney***	N	N	Y	Y	N	Y	N	N
19 ***LaTourette***	N	N	Y	Y	N	Y	Y	N
OKLAHOMA								
1 ***Largent***	N	Y	Y	Y	N	Y	N	N
2 ***Coburn***	N	N	Y	Y	N	Y	N	N
3 ***Watkins***	N	N	Y	Y	N	Y	N	N
4 ***Watts***	N	N	Y	Y	N	Y	N	N
5 ***Istook***	Y	N	Y	Y	N	Y	N	N
6 ***Lucas***	N	N	Y	Y	N	Y	N	N
OREGON								
1 Furse	Y	Y	Y	Y	Y	N	Y	N
2 ***Smith***	N	N	Y	Y	N	Y	Y	N
3 Blumenauer	Y	Y	Y	Y	Y	N	Y	N
4 DeFazio	Y	Y	N	Y	Y	N	Y	Y
5 Hooley	Y	Y	Y	Y	Y	N	Y	N
PENNSYLVANIA								
1 Foglietta	Y	Y	?	?	Y	N	N	N
2 Fattah	Y	?	?	Y	Y	N	N	N
3 Borski	Y	Y	N	Y	Y	N	N	N
4 Klink	N	N	Y	Y	Y	N	N	N
5 ***Peterson***	N	N	Y	Y	N	Y	Y	N
6 Holden	N	N	Y	Y	Y	N	N	N
7 ***Weldon***	N	N	Y	Y	N	Y	N	N
8 ***Greenwood***	N	N	Y	Y	N	Y	N	N
9 ***Shuster***	N	N	Y	Y	N	Y	N	N
10 ***McDade***	N	X	Y	Y	N	Y	N	N
11 Kanjorski	Y	Y	Y	Y	Y	N	N	N
12 Murtha	N	N	Y	Y	Y	N	N	N
13 ***Fox***	Y	Y	N	Y	N	Y	N	N
14 Coyne	Y	Y	Y	Y	Y	N	N	Y
15 McHale	Y	N	Y	Y	Y	N	N	N
16 ***Pitts***	N	N	Y	Y	N	Y	N	N
17 ***Gekas***	N	N	Y	Y	N	Y	N	N
18 Doyle	N	Y	Y	Y	Y	N	N	N
19 ***Goodling***	N	N	Y	Y	N	Y	N	N
20 Mascara	N	N	Y	Y	Y	N	N	N
21 ***English***	N	N	N	Y	N	Y	N	N
RHODE ISLAND								
1 Kennedy	Y	Y	Y	Y	Y	N	Y	N
2 Weygand	Y	Y	Y	Y	Y	N	Y	N
SOUTH CAROLINA								
1 ***Sanford***	N	Y	Y	N	N	Y	N	N
2 ***Spence***	N	N	Y	Y	N	Y	N	N
3 ***Graham***	N	N	Y	Y	N	Y	N	N
4 ***Inglis***	N	N	Y	Y	N	Y	N	N
5 Spratt	Y	Y	Y	Y	Y	N	Y	N
6 Clyburn	Y	Y	Y	Y	Y	N	Y	N
SOUTH DAKOTA								
AL ***Thune***	N	N	Y	Y	N	Y	Y	N
TENNESSEE								
1 ***Jenkins***	N	N	Y	Y	N	Y	N	N
2 ***Duncan***	Y	Y	Y	Y	N	Y	Y	N

	254	255	256	257	258	259	260	
3 ***Wamp***	N	N	N	Y	N	Y	N	N
4 ***Hilleary***	N	N	N	Y	N	Y	N	N
5 Clement	Y	N	Y	Y	Y	N	N	N
6 Gordon	Y	Y	Y	Y	Y	N	N	Y
7 ***Bryant***	N	N	Y	Y	N	Y	Y	N
8 Tanner	N	Y	Y	Y	Y	N	Y	N
9 Ford	Y	Y	Y	Y	Y	N	Y	N
TEXAS								
1 Sandlin	N	N	Y	Y	Y	N	N	N
2 Turner	Y	N	Y	Y	Y	N	N	N
3 ***Johnson, Sam***	N	?	Y	N	N	Y	N	N
4 Hall	Y	Y	Y	Y	N	Y	N	N
5 ***Sessions***	N	N	Y	Y	N	Y	N	N
6 ***Barton***	N	N	Y	N	N	Y	N	N
7 ***Archer***	N	N	Y	Y	N	Y	N	N
8 ***Brady***	N	N	Y	Y	N	Y	N	N
9 Lampson	Y	Y	Y	Y	Y	N	N	N
10 Doggett	Y	Y	Y	Y	Y	N	N	N
11 Edwards	?	?	?	Y	Y	N	N	Y
12 ***Granger***	N	N	Y	Y	N	Y	N	N
13 ***Thornberry***	N	N	Y	Y	N	Y	N	N
14 ***Paul***	Y	Y	Y	Y	N	Y	Y	N
15 Hinojosa	Y	N	Y	Y	Y	N	N	N
16 Reyes	Y	?	Y	Y	Y	N	N	N
17 Stenholm	Y	Y	Y	Y	Y	Y	N	N
18 Jackson-Lee	Y	Y	Y	Y	Y	N	N	Y
19 ***Combest***	N	N	Y	Y	N	Y	N	N
20 Gonzalez	Y	Y	Y	Y	Y	N	N	N
21 ***Smith***	N	N	Y	Y	N	Y	N	N
22 ***DeLay***	N	N	Y	Y	N	Y	N	N
23 ***Bonilla***	N	N	Y	Y	N	Y	N	N
24 Frost	Y	N	Y	Y	Y	N	N	Y
25 Bentsen	Y	Y	Y	Y	Y	N	N	Y
26 ***Armey***	N	N	?	?	N	Y	N	N
27 Ortiz	N	N	Y	Y	Y	N	N	N
28 Rodriguez	N	Y	Y	Y	Y	N	N	N
29 Green	Y	Y	Y	Y	Y	N	N	N
30 Johnson, E.B.	Y	Y	Y	Y	Y	N	N	Y
UTAH								
1 ***Hansen***	N	N	Y	Y	N	Y	N	N
2 ***Cook***	N	N	Y	Y	N	N	N	N
3 ***Cannon***	N	N	Y	Y	N	Y	Y	N
VERMONT								
AL *Sanders*	Y	Y	?	Y	Y	N	Y	Y
VIRGINIA								
1 ***Bateman***	N	N	Y	Y	N	Y	N	N
2 Pickett	N	N	N	Y	N	N	N	N
3 Scott	Y	N	Y	Y	Y	N	N	Y
4 Sisisky	N	N	Y	Y	Y	N	N	N
5 Goode	Y	Y	Y	Y	N	N	Y	N
6 ***Goodlatte***	Y	Y	Y	Y	N	Y	Y	N
7 ***Bliley***	N	N	Y	Y	N	Y	N	N
8 Moran	Y	Y	?	Y	Y	N	N	N
9 Boucher	Y	Y	Y	Y	Y	N	?	?
10 ***Wolf***	N	N	Y	Y	N	Y	N	N
11 ***Davis***	N	N	Y	Y	N	Y	N	N
WASHINGTON								
1 ***White***	N	N	Y	Y	N	Y	N	N
2 ***Metcalf***	Y	N	Y	Y	N	Y	Y	N
3 ***Smith, Linda***	N	N	Y	Y	N	Y	N	N
4 ***Hastings***	N	N	Y	Y	N	Y	N	N
5 ***Nethercutt***	N	N	Y	Y	N	Y	Y	N
6 Dicks	Y	N	Y	Y	Y	N	N	N
7 McDermott	Y	Y	N	Y	Y	N	N	N
8 ***Dunn***	N	N	Y	Y	N	Y	N	N
9 Smith, Adam	Y	N	Y	Y	Y	N	Y	Y
WEST VIRGINIA								
1 Mollohan	N	N	Y	Y	Y	N	N	N
2 Wise	N	N	Y	Y	Y	N	N	N
3 Rahall	N	N	Y	Y	Y	N	Y	N
WISCONSIN								
1 ***Neumann***	N	N	Y	Y	N	Y	Y	N
2 ***Klug***	N	Y	Y	Y	N	Y	Y	N
3 Kind	Y	Y	Y	Y	Y	N	Y	N
4 Kleczka	Y	Y	Y	Y	Y	N	Y	N
5 Barrett	Y	Y	Y	Y	Y	N	Y	N
6 ***Petri***	Y	Y	Y	Y	N	Y	Y	N
7 Obey	Y	Y	N	Y	Y	N	Y	N
8 Johnson	Y	Y	Y	Y	Y	N	Y	N
9 ***Sensenbrenner***	N	Y	Y	Y	N	Y	Y	N
WYOMING								
AL ***Cubin***	N	N	Y	Y	N	Y	Y	N

Southern states - Ala., Ark., Fla., Ga., Ky., La., Miss., N.C., Okla., S.C., Tenn., Texas, Va.

HOUSE VOTES 262, 263, 264, 265, 266, 267, 268, 269

262. HR 2107. Fiscal 1998 Interior Appropriations/Logging Roads Construction. Dicks, D-Wash., amendment to the Porter, R-Ill., amendment to reduce funding for the Forest Service to support construction of new timber logging roads by $5.6 million. The Dicks amendment would also reduce funding for the Purchaser Credit Program, which gives timber credits to companies as payment for building new forest roads, from $50 million to $25 million. The Porter amendment would have reduced road funding by $41.5 million and cut funding for the Purchaser Credit Program to $1. Adopted 211-209: R 160-61; D 51-147 (ND 26-119, SD 25-28); I 0-1, July 10, 1997.

263. HR 2107. Fiscal 1998 Interior Appropriations/Logging Roads Construction. Porter, R-Ill., amendment, as amended, to reduce funding for the Forest Service to support the construction of new timber logging roads by $5.6 million. The amendment would also reduce funding for the Purchaser Credit Program, which gives timber credits to companies as payment for building new forest roads, from $50 million to $25 million. Adopted 246-179: R 79-146; D 166-33 (ND 130-16, SD 36-17); I 1-0, July 10, 1997.

264. HR 2107. Fiscal 1998 Interior Appropriations/Clean Coal Technology Program. Klug, R-Wis., amendment to increase the bill's rescission of the Department of Energy's Clean Coal Technology program, which researches and develops advanced coal-based technologies, by $292 million, for a total reduction of $392 million. Rejected 173-243: R 95-121; D 77-122 (ND 63-82, SD 14-40); I 1-0, July 11, 1997.

265. HR 2107. Fiscal 1998 Interior Appropriations/Fossil Energy Research and Development. Royce, R-Calif., amendment to reduce the bill's funding for the Department of Energy's fossil energy research and development program by $21 million, to $291.1 million. Rejected 175-246: R 101-118; D 73-128 (ND 63-84, SD 10-44); I 1-0, July 11, 1997.

266. HR 2107. Fiscal 1998 Interior Appropriations/Arts Block Grant Program. Ehlers, R-Mich., amendment to terminate the National Endowment for the Arts and provide $80 million in block grants to states for arts funding. The amendment would direct 37 percent of the funding to state arts commissions, 60 percent to local school boards to fund school-based art activities and 3 percent for administrative costs. It also would prohibit the use of funds to support obscene or pornographic art. Rejected 155-271: R 149-75; D 6-195 (ND 3-144, SD 3-51); I 0-1, July 11, 1997. A "nay" was a vote in support of the president's position.

267. HR 1818. Juvenile Crime Block Grants/Passage. Riggs, R-Calif., motion to suspend the rules and pass the bill to consolidate juvenile crime prevention funding, including boot camps, gang prevention and mentoring programs, into block grants to the states. The bill would also reauthorize programs to serve runaway and homeless youth and the National Missing Children Center. Motion agreed to 413-14: R 212-13; D 200-1 (ND 147-1, SD 53-0); I 1-0, July 15, 1997. A two-thirds majority of those present and voting (285 in this case) is required for passage under suspension of the rules.

268. HR 2035. Naval Vessel Sale/Passage. Gilman, R-N.Y., motion to suspend the rules and pass the bill to authorize the Navy to sell 14 surplus naval vessels to certain foreign countries, including Egypt, Taiwan, Mexico, Israel, Malaysia, Thailand, Brazil and Chile. Motion agreed to 426-1: R 225-0; D 200-1 (ND 148-0, SD 52-1); I 1-0, July 15, 1997. A two-thirds majority of those present and voting (285 in this case) is required for passage under suspension of the rules.

269. Procedural Motion/Journal. Approval of the House Journal of Monday, July 14, 1997. Approved 373-50: R 203-20; D 169-30 (ND 125-21, SD 44-9); I 1-0, July 15, 1997.

KEY

- Y Voted for (yea).
- # Paired for.
- + Announced for.
- N Voted against (nay).
- X Paired against.
- – Announced against.
- P Voted "present."
- C Voted "present" to avoid possible conflict of interest.
- ? Did not vote or otherwise make a position known.

Democrats ***Republicans***
Independent

	262	263	264	265	266	267	268	269
ALABAMA								
1 ***Callahan***	Y	N	N	N	Y	Y	Y	Y
2 ***Everett***	Y	N	N	N	Y	Y	Y	N
3 ***Riley***	Y	N	N	N	Y	Y	Y	Y
4 ***Aderholt***	Y	N	N	N	Y	Y	Y	Y
5 Cramer	Y	N	N	N	N	Y	Y	Y
6 ***Bachus***	Y	N	N	Y	Y	Y	Y	Y
7 Hilliard	Y	N	N	N	N	Y	Y	N
ALASKA								
AL ***Young***	Y	N	?	?	Y	?	?	?
ARIZONA								
1 ***Salmon***	Y	Y	Y	Y	N	Y	Y	Y
2 Pastor	N	Y	N	N	N	Y	Y	Y
3 ***Stump***	Y	N	Y	Y	N	N	Y	Y
4 ***Shadegg***	Y	N	Y	Y	N	N	Y	Y
5 ***Kolbe***	Y	Y	N	N	N	Y	Y	Y
6 ***Hayworth***	Y	N	Y	Y	N	Y	Y	Y
ARKANSAS								
1 Berry	Y	N	Y	Y	N	Y	Y	Y
2 Snyder	N	Y	Y	N	N	Y	Y	Y
3 ***Hutchinson***	Y	N	N	Y	Y	Y	Y	Y
4 ***Dickey***	Y	N	N	Y	Y	Y	Y	Y
CALIFORNIA								
1 ***Riggs***	Y	N	+	+	N	Y	Y	Y
2 ***Herger***	Y	N	N	N	N	Y	Y	Y
3 Fazio	N	Y	N	N	N	Y	Y	N
4 ***Doolittle***	Y	N	?	?	?	Y	Y	Y
5 Matsui	N	Y	N	N	N	Y	Y	Y
6 Woolsey	N	Y	Y	Y	N	+	+	+
7 Miller	N	Y	Y	Y	N	Y	Y	Y
8 Pelosi	N	Y	?	N	N	Y	Y	Y
9 Dellums	N	Y	Y	Y	N	Y	Y	Y
10 Tauscher	N	Y	Y	Y	N	Y	Y	Y
11 ***Pombo***	Y	N	N	N	Y	N	Y	N
12 Lantos	N	Y	Y	N	N	Y	Y	Y
13 Stark	N	Y	Y	Y	N	Y	Y	Y
14 Eshoo	N	Y	Y	Y	N	+	+	+
15 ***Campbell***	N	Y	Y	Y	N	Y	Y	Y
16 Lofgren	N	Y	N	N	N	Y	Y	Y
17 Farr	N	Y	?	?	?	Y	Y	Y
18 Condit	N	Y	Y	Y	N	Y	Y	Y
19 ***Radanovich***	Y	N	N	Y	Y	Y	Y	Y
20 Dooley	N	Y	N	N	N	Y	Y	Y
21 ***Thomas***	Y	N	N	N	Y	Y	Y	Y
22 Capps	N	Y	Y	N	N	Y	Y	Y
23 ***Gallegly***	Y	N	N	Y	Y	Y	Y	Y
24 Sherman	N	Y	Y	Y	N	Y	Y	Y
25 ***McKeon***	Y	N	Y	N	Y	Y	Y	Y
26 Berman	?	?	?	?	?	Y	Y	Y
27 ***Rogan***	N	Y	Y	Y	Y	Y	Y	Y
28 ***Dreier***	Y	N	N	N	Y	Y	Y	Y
29 Waxman	N	Y	Y	Y	N	Y	Y	?
30 Becerra	?	?	Y	Y	N	Y	Y	N
31 Martinez	?	?	N	N	N	Y	Y	Y
32 Dixon	N	Y	N	N	N	Y	Y	Y
33 Roybal-Allard	N	Y	Y	Y	N	Y	Y	Y
34 Torres	N	Y	N	Y	N	Y	?	Y
35 Waters	N	Y	N	N	N	Y	Y	N
36 Harman	N	Y	Y	Y	N	Y	Y	Y
37 Millender-McD.	N	Y	N	N	N	Y	Y	Y
38 ***Horn***	N	Y	Y	Y	Y	Y	Y	Y
39 ***Royce***	N	Y	Y	Y	Y	N	Y	Y
40 ***Lewis***	Y	N	N	N	Y	Y	Y	Y
41 ***Kim***	Y	Y	N	N	Y	Y	Y	Y
42 Brown	N	Y	N	N	N	Y	Y	N
43 ***Calvert***	Y	N	N	N	Y	Y	Y	Y
44 ***Bono***	Y	N	N	N	N	Y	Y	Y
45 ***Rohrabacher***	N	Y	Y	Y	Y	Y	Y	Y
46 Sanchez	–	Y	N	N	N	Y	Y	Y
47 ***Cox***	N	Y	Y	Y	N	Y	Y	Y
48 ***Packard***	Y	N	N	N	Y	Y	Y	Y
49 ***Bilbray***	N	Y	Y	Y	Y	Y	Y	Y
50 Filner	N	Y	Y	Y	N	Y	Y	N
51 ***Cunningham***	Y	N	N	N	Y	Y	Y	N
52 ***Hunter***	Y	N	N	Y	Y	Y	Y	Y
COLORADO								
1 DeGette	N	Y	Y	Y	N	Y	Y	Y
2 Skaggs	N	Y	N	N	N	Y	Y	Y
3 ***McInnis***	Y	N	Y	N	Y	Y	Y	Y
4 ***Schaffer***	Y	N	N	N	N	Y	Y	Y
5 ***Hefley***	Y	N	Y	Y	N	Y	Y	N
6 ***Schaefer***	Y	N	N	N	Y	Y	Y	Y
CONNECTICUT								
1 Kennelly	N	Y	N	N	N	Y	Y	Y
2 Gejdenson	N	Y	Y	Y	N	Y	Y	Y
3 DeLauro	N	Y	Y	N	N	Y	Y	Y
4 ***Shays***	N	Y	Y	Y	Y	Y	Y	Y
5 Maloney	N	Y	N	N	N	Y	Y	Y
6 ***Johnson***	N	Y	Y	N	Y	Y	Y	Y
DELAWARE								
AL ***Castle***	N	Y	Y	Y	N	Y	Y	Y
FLORIDA								
1 ***Scarborough***	N	Y	Y	Y	N	N	Y	Y
2 Boyd	Y	Y	N	N	Y	Y	Y	Y
3 Brown	N	Y	Y	N	N	?	?	?
4 ***Fowler***	?	N	Y	Y	Y	Y	Y	Y
5 Thurman	Y	Y	N	N	N	Y	Y	Y
6 ***Stearns***	Y	N	Y	Y	N	Y	Y	Y
7 ***Mica***	Y	N	N	N	Y	Y	Y	Y
8 ***McCollum***	Y	Y	Y	Y	Y	Y	Y	Y
9 ***Bilirakis***	N	Y	N	N	Y	Y	Y	Y
10 ***Young***	Y	Y	N	N	Y	Y	Y	Y
11 Davis	N	Y	Y	Y	N	Y	Y	Y
12 ***Canady***	Y	N	N	Y	Y	Y	Y	Y
13 ***Miller***	N	Y	Y	Y	Y	Y	Y	Y
14 ***Goss***	N	Y	Y	Y	Y	Y	Y	Y
15 ***Weldon***	Y	N	Y	Y	Y	Y	Y	?
16 ***Foley***	N	Y	Y	Y	N	Y	Y	Y
17 Meek	N	Y	N	N	N	Y	Y	N
18 ***Ros-Lehtinen***	?	N	Y	Y	Y	Y	Y	Y
19 Wexler	N	Y	Y	Y	N	Y	Y	Y
20 Deutsch	N	Y	Y	Y	N	Y	Y	Y
21 ***Diaz-Balart***	Y	N	N	N	Y	Y	Y	Y
22 ***Shaw***	N	Y	Y	Y	Y	Y	Y	Y
23 Hastings	N	Y	Y	Y	N	Y	Y	N
GEORGIA								
1 ***Kingston***	Y	Y	Y	Y	N	Y	Y	N
2 Bishop	Y	N	N	N	N	Y	Y	Y
3 ***Collins***	Y	N	Y	Y	Y	Y	Y	Y
4 McKinney	N	Y	Y	Y	N	Y	Y	Y
5 Lewis	N	Y	Y	Y	N	Y	Y	N
6 ***Gingrich***					Y			
7 ***Barr***	Y	N	Y	Y	N	Y	Y	Y
8 ***Chambliss***	Y	N	N	N	Y	Y	Y	Y
9 ***Deal***	Y	N	Y	Y	Y	Y	Y	Y
10 ***Norwood***	Y	N	N	Y	Y	Y	Y	Y
11 ***Linder***	Y	N	N	N	Y	Y	Y	Y
HAWAII								
1 Abercrombie	N	Y	N	N	N	Y	Y	N
2 Mink	N	Y	N	N	N	Y	Y	Y
IDAHO								
1 ***Chenoweth***	Y	N	?	N	Y	N	Y	N
2 ***Crapo***	Y	N	N	N	Y	Y	Y	Y
ILLINOIS								
1 Rush	N	Y	N	N	N	Y	Y	N
2 Jackson	N	Y	N	N	N	Y	Y	Y
3 Lipinski	Y	Y	N	N	Y	Y	Y	Y
4 Gutierrez	N	Y	N	N	N	Y	Y	N
5 Blagojevich	N	Y	Y	Y	N	Y	Y	Y
6 ***Hyde***	Y	N	N	N	Y	Y	Y	Y
7 Davis	N	Y	N	N	N	N	Y	Y
8 ***Crane***	Y	N	N	Y	N	Y	Y	Y
9 Yates	?	?	N	N	N	Y	Y	Y
10 ***Porter***	N	Y	Y	Y	Y	Y	Y	Y
11 ***Weller***	Y	N	N	N	Y	Y	Y	N
12 Costello	N	Y	N	N	N	Y	Y	N
13 ***Fawell***	N	Y	Y	Y	Y	Y	Y	Y
14 ***Hastert***	Y	N	N	N	Y	Y	Y	Y
15 ***Ewing***	N	Y	N	N	Y	Y	Y	Y

ND Northern Democrats SD Southern Democrats

	262	263	264	265	266	267	268	269
16 ***Manzullo***	Y	N	N	Y	N	Y	Y	Y
17 Evans	N	Y	N	N	N	Y	Y	Y
18 ***LaHood***	Y	N	N	N	Y	Y	Y	Y
19 Poshard	N	Y	N	N	N	Y	Y	N
20 ***Shimkus***	Y	N	N	N	Y	Y	Y	Y
INDIANA								
1 Visclosky	N	Y	N	N	N	Y	Y	N
2 ***McIntosh***	N	N	N	Y	N	Y	Y	Y
3 Roemer	N	Y	N	N	N	Y	Y	Y
4 ***Souder***	Y	N	N	Y	N	Y	Y	Y
5 ***Buyer***	Y	N	N	N	Y	Y	Y	Y
6 ***Burton***	Y	N	N	N	N	Y	Y	Y
7 ***Pease***	N	Y	N	N	Y	Y	Y	Y
8 ***Hostettler***	Y	N	?	?	N	N	Y	Y
9 Hamilton	N	Y	N	N	N	Y	Y	Y
10 Carson	N	Y	Y	Y	N	Y	Y	Y
IOWA								
1 ***Leach***	N	Y	Y	Y	Y	Y	Y	Y
2 ***Nussle***	Y	N	Y	Y	Y	Y	Y	Y
3 Boswell	Y	N	N	Y	N	Y	Y	Y
4 ***Ganske***	N	Y	Y	Y	Y	Y	Y	Y
5 ***Latham***	Y	N	Y	Y	Y	Y	Y	Y
KANSAS								
1 ***Moran***	Y	N	Y	Y	Y	Y	Y	N
2 ***Ryun***	Y	N	Y	Y	N	Y	Y	Y
3 ***Snowbarger***	Y	N	N	N	Y	Y	Y	Y
4 ***Tiahrt***	Y	N	Y	Y	N	Y	Y	N
KENTUCKY								
1 ***Whitfield***	Y	N	N	N	Y	Y	Y	Y
2 ***Lewis***	Y	N	N	N	Y	Y	Y	Y
3 ***Northup***	Y	Y	N	N	Y	Y	Y	Y
4 ***Bunning***	Y	N	N	N	Y	Y	Y	Y
5 ***Rogers***	Y	N	N	N	Y	Y	Y	Y
6 Baesler	Y	N	N	N	N	Y	Y	Y
LOUISIANA								
1 ***Livingston***	Y	N	N	N	N	Y	Y	Y
2 Jefferson	N	Y	N	N	N	Y	Y	Y
3 ***Tauzin***	Y	N	N	N	N	Y	Y	Y
4 ***McCrery***	Y	N	Y	N	N	Y	Y	Y
5 ***Cooksey***	Y	N	Y	N	N	Y	Y	Y
6 ***Baker***	Y	N	N	N	Y	Y	Y	Y
7 John	Y	N	N	N	N	Y	Y	Y
MAINE								
1 Allen	N	Y	Y	Y	N	Y	Y	Y
2 Baldacci	N	Y	N	Y	N	Y	Y	Y
MARYLAND								
1 ***Gilchrest***	Y	Y	Y	N	Y	Y	Y	Y
2 ***Ehrlich***	Y	N	Y	Y	Y	Y	Y	Y
3 Cardin	N	Y	N	N	N	Y	Y	Y
4 Wynn	Y	Y	N	N	N	Y	Y	Y
5 Hoyer	N	Y	N	N	N	Y	Y	Y
6 ***Bartlett***	Y	N	N	N	N	Y	Y	Y
7 Cummings	N	Y	N	N	N	Y	Y	Y
8 ***Morella***	N	Y	Y	Y	N	Y	Y	Y
MASSACHUSETTS								
1 Olver	N	Y	Y	Y	N	Y	Y	Y
2 Neal	N	Y	Y	Y	N	Y	Y	Y
3 McGovern	N	Y	Y	Y	N	Y	Y	Y
4 Frank	N	Y	Y	N	N	Y	Y	Y
5 Meehan	N	Y	Y	Y	N	Y	Y	Y
6 Tierney	N	Y	Y	Y	N	Y	Y	Y
7 Markey	N	Y	Y	Y	N	Y	Y	?
8 Kennedy	N	Y	Y	Y	N	Y	Y	Y
9 Moakley	N	Y	N	N	N	Y	Y	Y
10 Delahunt	N	Y	Y	N	N	Y	Y	Y
MICHIGAN								
1 Stupak	Y	N	N	N	N	Y	Y	N
2 ***Hoekstra***	N	Y	Y	Y	Y	Y	Y	Y
3 ***Ehlers***	N	Y	Y	Y	Y	Y	Y	Y
4 ***Camp***	Y	N	Y	N	Y	Y	Y	Y
5 Barcia	Y	N	Y	Y	N	Y	Y	Y
6 ***Upton***	N	Y	Y	Y	Y	Y	Y	Y
7 ***Smith***	Y	Y	Y	Y	Y	Y	Y	Y
8 Stabenow	N	Y	Y	Y	N	Y	Y	Y
9 Kildee	N	Y	N	N	N	Y	Y	Y
10 Bonior	N	Y	?	?	?	Y	Y	Y
11 ***Knollenberg***	N	N	N	N	Y	Y	Y	Y
12 Levin	N	Y	Y	Y	N	Y	Y	Y
13 Rivers	N	Y	Y	Y	N	Y	Y	Y
14 Conyers	N	Y	N	N	N	Y	Y	Y
15 Kilpatrick	N	Y	N	N	N	Y	Y	Y
16 Dingell	Y	Y	N	N	N	Y	Y	Y
MINNESOTA								
1 ***Gutknecht***	N	Y	Y	Y	Y	Y	Y	N
2 Minge	N	Y	+	Y	N	Y	Y	Y

	262	263	264	265	266	267	268	269
3 ***Ramstad***	N	Y	Y	Y	N	Y	Y	N
4 Vento	N	Y	Y	Y	N	Y	Y	Y
5 Sabo	N	Y	N	N	N	Y	Y	N
6 Luther	N	Y	Y	Y	N	Y	Y	Y
7 Peterson	Y	N	Y	Y	N	Y	Y	Y
8 Oberstar	Y	N	N	N	N	Y	Y	Y
MISSISSIPPI								
1 ***Wicker***	Y	N	N	N	Y	Y	Y	N
2 Thompson	Y	N	N	N	N	Y	Y	N
3 ***Pickering***	Y	N	N	N	Y	Y	Y	Y
4 ***Parker***	Y	N	N	N	Y	Y	Y	Y
5 Taylor	Y	N	N	N	N	Y	N	N
MISSOURI								
1 Clay	N	Y	N	N	N	Y	Y	N
2 ***Talent***	Y	N	Y	Y	N	Y	Y	Y
3 Gephardt	N	Y	N	N	N	Y	Y	Y
4 Skelton	Y	N	N	N	Y	Y	Y	Y
5 McCarthy	N	Y	N	Y	N	Y	Y	Y
6 Danner	Y	N	N	Y	N	Y	Y	Y
7 ***Blunt***	Y	N	Y	Y	Y	N	Y	Y
8 ***Emerson***	Y	N	N	Y	N	Y	Y	Y
9 ***Hulshof***	N	Y	Y	Y	N	Y	Y	N
MONTANA								
AL ***Hill***	Y	N	N	N	Y	Y	Y	Y
NEBRASKA								
1 ***Bereuter***	Y	N	N	N	Y	Y	Y	Y
2 ***Christensen***	Y	Y	Y	Y	Y	Y	Y	Y
3 ***Barrett***	Y	N	N	N	Y	Y	Y	Y
NEVADA								
1 ***Ensign***	Y	N	Y	Y	Y	Y	Y	N
2 ***Gibbons***	Y	N	Y	N	Y	Y	Y	Y
NEW HAMPSHIRE								
1 ***Sununu***	Y	N	Y	Y	Y	Y	Y	N
2 ***Bass***	Y	N	Y	Y	Y	Y	Y	Y
NEW JERSEY								
1 Andrews	N	Y	Y	Y	N	Y	Y	Y
2 ***LoBiondo***	N	Y	Y	Y	N	Y	Y	N
3 ***Saxton***	N	Y	Y	Y	N	Y	Y	Y
4 ***Smith***	N	Y	Y	Y	Y	Y	Y	Y
5 ***Roukema***	N	Y	Y	Y	N	Y	Y	Y
6 Pallone	N	Y	Y	Y	N	Y	Y	N
7 ***Franks***	N	Y	Y	Y	N	Y	Y	?
8 Pascrell	N	Y	N	N	N	Y	Y	N
9 Rothman	N	Y	Y	Y	N	Y	Y	Y
10 Payne	N	Y	N	N	N	Y	Y	Y
11 ***Frelinghuysen***	N	Y	Y	Y	N	Y	Y	Y
12 ***Pappas***	N	Y	Y	N	Y	Y	Y	Y
13 Menendez	N	Y	Y	Y	N	Y	Y	Y
NEW MEXICO								
1 ***Schiff***	?	?	?	?	?	?	?	?
2 ***Skeen***	Y	N	N	N	Y	Y	Y	Y
3 ***Redmond***	Y	N	N	N	Y	Y	Y	N
NEW YORK								
1 ***Forbes***	N	Y	N	N	N	Y	Y	Y
2 ***Lazio***	N	Y	N	Y	N	Y	Y	Y
3 ***King***	Y	N	N	N	N	Y	Y	Y
4 McCarthy	N	Y	Y	Y	N	Y	Y	Y
5 Ackerman	N	Y	N	N	N	Y	Y	Y
6 Flake	N	Y	N	N	N	Y	Y	Y
7 Manton	N	Y	N	N	N	Y	Y	Y
8 Nadler	N	Y	Y	Y	N	Y	Y	Y
9 Schumer	N	Y	Y	Y	N	Y	Y	Y
10 Towns	N	Y	Y	N	N	Y	Y	Y
11 Owens	N	Y	Y	Y	N	Y	Y	Y
12 Velázquez	N	Y	Y	Y	N	Y	Y	Y
13 ***Molinari***	?	N	?	?	?	Y	Y	Y
14 Maloney	N	Y	N	N	N	Y	Y	Y
15 Rangel	N	Y	N	N	N	Y	Y	Y
16 Serrano	N	Y	N	N	N	Y	Y	Y
17 Engel	N	Y	N	N	N	+	Y	Y
18 Lowey	N	Y	Y	Y	N	Y	Y	Y
19 ***Kelly***	N	Y	Y	Y	N	Y	Y	Y
20 ***Gilman***	N	Y	N	N	N	Y	Y	Y
21 McNulty	N	Y	Y	Y	N	Y	Y	Y
22 ***Solomon***	Y	N	N	N	Y	Y	Y	Y
23 ***Boehlert***	N	Y	?	N	N	Y	Y	Y
24 ***McHugh***	Y	Y	N	Y	Y	Y	Y	Y
25 ***Walsh***	N	Y	N	N	N	Y	Y	Y
26 Hinchey	N	Y	Y	Y	N	Y	Y	Y
27 ***Paxon***	Y	N	Y	Y	Y	Y	Y	Y
28 Slaughter	–	+	+	+	–	Y	Y	Y
29 LaFalce	N	Y	N	Y	N	Y	Y	Y
30 ***Quinn***	N	Y	Y	Y	N	Y	Y	Y
31 ***Houghton***	N	N	N	N	N	Y	Y	Y

	262	263	264	265	266	267	268	269
NORTH CAROLINA								
1 Clayton	N	Y	N	N	N	Y	Y	Y
2 Etheridge	N	Y	N	N	N	Y	Y	Y
3 ***Jones***	Y	N	Y	Y	N	Y	Y	Y
4 Price	N	Y	N	N	N	Y	Y	Y
5 ***Burr***	Y	N	Y	N	Y	Y	Y	Y
6 ***Coble***	Y	N	Y	Y	Y	N	Y	Y
7 McIntyre	Y	N	Y	Y	N	Y	Y	Y
8 Hefner	Y	Y	N	N	N	Y	Y	Y
9 ***Myrick***	Y	N	N	N	N	Y	Y	Y
10 ***Ballenger***	Y	N	N	N	Y	Y	Y	Y
11 ***Taylor***	Y	N	Y	Y	Y	Y	Y	Y
12 Watt	N	Y	N	N	N	Y	Y	Y
NORTH DAKOTA								
AL Pomeroy	Y	Y	N	N	N	Y	Y	Y
OHIO								
1 ***Chabot***	N	Y	Y	Y	N	Y	Y	Y
2 ***Portman***	N	Y	Y	Y	Y	Y	Y	Y
3 Hall	N	Y	N	N	N	Y	Y	Y
4 ***Oxley***	Y	N	N	N	Y	Y	Y	Y
5 ***Gillmor***	N	Y	N	N	Y	Y	Y	Y
6 Strickland	N	Y	N	N	N	Y	Y	Y
7 ***Hobson***	Y	N	N	N	Y	Y	Y	Y
8 ***Boehner***	Y	N	N	N	Y	Y	Y	Y
9 Kaptur	Y	N	N	N	N	Y	Y	Y
10 Kucinich	N	Y	N	N	N	Y	Y	N
11 Stokes	N	Y	N	N	N	Y	Y	Y
12 ***Kasich***	N	Y	Y	Y	N	Y	Y	Y
13 Brown	N	Y	Y	N	N	Y	Y	Y
14 Sawyer	N	Y	N	N	N	Y	Y	Y
15 ***Pryce***	+	N	N	N	Y	Y	Y	Y
16 ***Regula***	Y	N	N	N	Y	Y	Y	Y
17 Traficant	Y	N	N	N	Y	Y	Y	Y
18 ***Ney***	Y	Y	N	N	Y	Y	Y	Y
19 ***LaTourette***	Y	Y	N	N	N	Y	Y	Y
OKLAHOMA								
1 ***Largent***	Y	N	N	N	Y	Y	Y	Y
2 ***Coburn***	Y	N	N	N	Y	Y	Y	Y
3 ***Watkins***	Y	N	N	N	Y	Y	Y	Y
4 ***Watts***	Y	N	N	N	Y	Y	Y	N
5 ***Istook***	Y	N	N	N	N	Y	Y	Y
6 ***Lucas***	Y	N	N	N	Y	Y	Y	Y
OREGON								
1 Furse	N	Y	Y	Y	N	Y	Y	Y
2 ***Smith***	Y	N	N	N	Y	Y	Y	Y
3 Blumenauer	N	Y	Y	Y	N	Y	Y	Y
4 DeFazio	Y	Y	Y	Y	N	Y	Y	N
5 Hooley	N	Y	Y	Y	N	Y	Y	Y
PENNSYLVANIA								
1 Foglietta	N	Y	N	N	N	Y	Y	N
2 Fattah	N	Y	N	N	N	Y	Y	Y
3 Borski	N	Y	N	N	N	Y	Y	N
4 Klink	Y	N	N	N	N	Y	Y	Y
5 ***Peterson***	Y	N	N	N	N	Y	Y	Y
6 Holden	Y	N	N	N	N	Y	Y	Y
7 ***Weldon***	N	Y	?	?	Y	Y	Y	Y
8 ***Greenwood***	N	Y	N	N	N	Y	Y	Y
9 ***Shuster***	?	?	N	N	N	Y	Y	Y
10 ***McDade***	Y	N	N	N	Y	Y	Y	Y
11 Kanjorski	N	Y	N	N	N	Y	Y	Y
12 Murtha	Y	N	N	N	N	Y	Y	Y
13 ***Fox***	N	Y	N	N	N	Y	Y	Y
14 Coyne	N	Y	N	N	N	Y	Y	Y
15 McHale	N	Y	N	N	N	Y	Y	Y
16 ***Pitts***	Y	N	Y	Y	N	Y	Y	Y
17 ***Gekas***	Y	N	N	N	Y	Y	Y	Y
18 Doyle	Y	N	N	N	N	Y	Y	Y
19 ***Goodling***	Y	Y	N	Y	Y	Y	Y	Y
20 Mascara	Y	N	N	N	N	Y	Y	Y
21 ***English***	Y	Y	N	N	Y	Y	Y	N
RHODE ISLAND								
1 Kennedy	N	Y	Y	Y	N	Y	Y	?
2 Weygand	N	Y	Y	Y	N	Y	Y	Y
SOUTH CAROLINA								
1 ***Sanford***	N	Y	Y	Y	Y	N	Y	Y
2 ***Spence***	Y	N	N	N	Y	Y	Y	Y
3 ***Graham***	Y	N	N	N	Y	Y	Y	Y
4 ***Inglis***	Y	N	Y	Y	N	Y	Y	Y
5 Spratt	N	Y	N	N	N	Y	Y	Y
6 Clyburn	N	Y	N	N	N	Y	Y	N
SOUTH DAKOTA								
AL ***Thune***	Y	N	Y	Y	Y	Y	Y	Y
TENNESSEE								
1 ***Jenkins***	Y	N	N	N	Y	Y	Y	Y
2 ***Duncan***	Y	N	N	Y	Y	Y	Y	Y

	262	263	264	265	266	267	268	
3 ***Wamp***	Y	Y	N	N	Y	Y	Y	Y
4 ***Hilleary***	Y	N	N	N	N	Y	Y	Y
5 Clement	?	?	N	N	N	Y	Y	Y
6 Gordon	N	Y	Y	N	N	Y	Y	Y
7 ***Bryant***	Y	N	Y	Y	N	Y	Y	Y
8 Tanner	Y	Y	Y	Y	Y	Y	Y	Y
9 Ford	N	Y	N	N	N	Y	Y	Y
TEXAS								
1 Sandlin	Y	N	N	N	N	Y	Y	Y
2 Turner	Y	N	N	N	N	Y	Y	Y
3 ***Johnson, Sam***	N	N	N	N	N	Y	Y	Y
4 Hall	Y	N	N	N	Y	Y	Y	Y
5 ***Sessions***	Y	N	N	N	Y	Y	Y	N
6 ***Barton***	Y	N	N	N	N	Y	Y	Y
7 ***Archer***	Y	N	Y	N	Y	Y	Y	Y
8 ***Brady***	Y	N	?	N	N	Y	Y	Y
9 Lampson	N	Y	N	N	N	Y	Y	Y
10 Doggett	N	Y	Y	N	N	Y	Y	Y
11 Edwards	Y	Y	N	N	N	Y	Y	Y
12 ***Granger***	Y	N	Y	N	Y	Y	Y	Y
13 ***Thornberry***	Y	Y	Y	N	N	Y	Y	Y
14 ***Paul***	N	Y	Y	Y	N	N	Y	Y
15 Hinojosa	N	Y	N	N	N	Y	Y	Y
16 Reyes	N	N	N	N	N	+	+	+
17 Stenholm	Y	N	N	N	N	Y	Y	N
18 Jackson-Lee	N	Y	N	N	N	Y	Y	Y
19 ***Combest***	Y	N	N	N	N	Y	Y	Y
20 Gonzalez	N	Y	N	N	N	Y	Y	Y
21 ***Smith***	Y	Y	N	N	Y	Y	Y	Y
22 ***DeLay***	Y	N	N	N	Y	Y	Y	Y
23 ***Bonilla***	Y	N	N	N	N	Y	Y	Y
24 Frost	Y	Y	N	N	N	Y	Y	Y
25 Bentsen	N	Y	N	N	N	Y	Y	Y
26 ***Armey***	Y	N	Y	Y	Y	Y	Y	Y
27 Ortiz	Y	Y	N	N	N	Y	Y	Y
28 Rodriguez	Y	Y	N	N	N	Y	Y	Y
29 Green	N	Y	N	N	N	Y	Y	Y
30 Johnson, E.B.	Y	Y	N	N	N	Y	Y	Y
UTAH								
1 ***Hansen***	Y	N	?	?	?	Y	Y	Y
2 ***Cook***	N	Y	N	N	Y	Y	Y	Y
3 ***Cannon***	Y	N	Y	Y	N	Y	Y	Y
VERMONT								
AL *Sanders*	N	Y	Y	Y	N	Y	Y	Y
VIRGINIA								
1 ***Bateman***	Y	N	N	N	Y	Y	Y	Y
2 Pickett	Y	N	N	N	N	Y	Y	N
3 Scott	N	Y	N	N	N	Y	Y	Y
4 Sisisky	Y	N	N	N	N	Y	Y	Y
5 Goode	Y	N	N	Y	N	Y	Y	Y
6 ***Goodlatte***	Y	N	N	Y	Y	Y	Y	Y
7 ***Bliley***	Y	N	N	N	Y	Y	Y	Y
8 Moran	N	Y	Y	N	N	Y	Y	Y
9 Boucher	?	?	?	?	?	Y	Y	Y
10 ***Wolf***	N	Y	N	N	Y	Y	Y	Y
11 ***Davis***	N	Y	N	N	Y	Y	Y	Y
WASHINGTON								
1 ***White***	Y	Y	Y	Y	N	Y	Y	Y
2 ***Metcalf***	Y	Y	N	Y	Y	N	Y	Y
3 ***Smith, Linda***	Y	N	Y	Y	N	Y	Y	Y
4 ***Hastings***	Y	N	Y	N	Y	Y	Y	Y
5 ***Nethercutt***	Y	N	N	N	Y	Y	Y	Y
6 Dicks	Y	Y	N	N	N	Y	Y	Y
7 McDermott	N	Y	N	N	N	Y	Y	N
8 ***Dunn***	Y	N	N	Y	Y	Y	Y	Y
9 Smith, Adam	Y	Y	Y	Y	N	Y	Y	Y
WEST VIRGINIA								
1 Mollohan	Y	N	N	N	N	Y	Y	Y
2 Wise	Y	N	N	N	N	Y	Y	Y
3 Rahall	Y	Y	N	N	N	Y	Y	Y
WISCONSIN								
1 ***Neumann***	Y	Y	Y	Y	N	Y	Y	Y
2 ***Klug***	N	Y	Y	Y	Y	Y	Y	Y
3 Kind	N	Y	Y	Y	N	Y	Y	Y
4 Kleczka	N	Y	Y	Y	N	Y	Y	Y
5 Barrett	N	Y	Y	Y	N	Y	Y	Y
6 ***Petri***	Y	Y	Y	Y	Y	Y	Y	Y
7 Obey	Y	Y	Y	Y	N	Y	Y	Y
8 Johnson	Y	Y	Y	Y	N	Y	Y	Y
9 ***Sensenbrenner***	N	Y	Y	Y	Y	N	Y	Y
WYOMING								
AL ***Cubin***	Y	N	N	N	Y	Y	Y	Y

Southern states - Ala., Ark., Fla., Ga., Ky., La., Miss., N.C., Okla., S.C., Tenn., Texas, Va.

HOUSE VOTES 270, 271, 272, 273, 274, 275, 276, 277

270. HR 2107. Fiscal 1998 Interior Appropriations/National Endowment for the Humanities. Chabot, R-Ohio, amendment to eliminate the bill's $110 million for the National Endowment for the Humanities. Rejected 96-328: R 92-132; D 4-195 (ND 1-145, SD 3-50); I 0-1, July 15, 1997.

271. HR 2107. Fiscal 1998 Interior Appropriations/Deficit-Reduction Lockbox. Crapo, R-Idaho, amendment to establish a "lockbox" mechanism that would take half the net savings made by floor amendments when any appropriations bill passes the House or Senate and preserve the money for deficit reduction by reducing overall spending caps and prohibiting reallocation of those savings to other spending programs. Adopted 314-109: R 211-11; D 103-97 (ND 65-82, SD 38-15); I 0-1, July 15, 1997.

272. HR 2017. Fiscal 1998 Interior Appropriations/Tribal Trust Lands. Istook, R-Okla., amendment to prohibit the Bureau of Indian Affairs from placing any federal land into tribal trust. Rejected 208-216: R 178-45; D 30-170 (ND 15-132, SD 15-38); I 0-1, July 15, 1997. A "nay" was a vote in support of the president's position.

273. HR 2107. Fiscal 1998 Interior Appropriations/Biosphere and World Heritage Programs. Coburn, R-Okla., amendment to prohibit funding for the U.S. Man and Biosphere Program or the World Heritage Program administered by the U.N. Educational, Scientific and Cultural Organization. Adopted 222-203: R 202-22; D 20-180 (ND 9-138, SD 11-42); I 0-1, July 15, 1997.

274. HR 2107. Fiscal 1998 Interior Appropriations/Canaveral National Seashore Designation. Weldon, R-Fla., amendment to prohibit the National Park Service from designating any portion of the Canaveral National Seashore in Florida as a "clothing optional" or "nude beach" area if the designation would be contrary to local county ordinance. Adopted 396-25: R 219-0; D 176-25 (ND 127-22, SD 49-3); I 1-0, July 15, 1997.

275. HR 2107. Fiscal 1998 Interior Appropriations/Passage. Passage of the bill to provide $13 billion in new budget authority for the Department of Interior and related agencies for fiscal 1998. The bill provides $562 million less than provided in fiscal 1997 and $147 million less than requested by the president. Passed 238-192: R 208-18; D 30-173 (ND 15-135, SD 15-38); I 0-1, July 15, 1997. A "nay" was a vote in support of the president's position.

276. HR 2158. Fiscal 1998 VA-HUD Appropriations/VA Medical Care. Obey, D-Wis., amendment to increase the bill's funding for Department of Veterans Affairs medical care by $48 million and decrease funding for the Federal Emergency Management Agency's emergency-management planning and assistance programs by $60 million. Adopted 322-110: R 131-94; D 190-16 (ND 144-7, SD 46-9); I 1-0, July 16, 1997.

277. HR 2158. Fiscal 1998 VA-HUD Appropriations/FEMA Windstorm Simulation Center. Stokes, D-Ohio, amendment to eliminate the bill's earmark of $60 million in Federal Emergency Management Agency funding for the planning and construction of a full-scale windstorm simulation center in Idaho. Adopted 244-187: R 49-176; D 194-11 (ND 146-4, SD 48-7); I 1-0, July 16, 1997.

KEY

- Y Voted for (yea).
- # Paired for.
- + Announced for.
- N Voted against (nay).
- X Paired against.
- – Announced against.
- P Voted "present."
- C Voted "present" to avoid possible conflict of interest.
- ? Did not vote or otherwise make a position known.

Democrats ***Republicans***
Independent

	270	271	272	273	274	275	276	277
ALABAMA								
1 ***Callahan***	N	Y	Y	Y	Y	Y	Y	N
2 ***Everett***	N	Y	Y	Y	Y	Y	Y	N
3 ***Riley***	Y	Y	Y	Y	Y	Y	Y	N
4 ***Aderholt***	Y	Y	Y	Y	Y	Y	Y	N
5 Cramer	N	Y	Y	N	Y	N	Y	Y
6 ***Bachus***	N	Y	Y	Y	Y	Y	N	N
7 Hilliard	N	N	N	N	Y	Y	N	Y
ALASKA								
AL ***Young***	?	?	?	?	?	?	?	?
ARIZONA								
1 ***Salmon***	Y	Y	Y	Y	Y	Y	Y	N
2 Pastor	N	N	N	N	Y	N	Y	Y
3 ***Stump***	Y	Y	Y	Y	Y	Y	N	N
4 ***Shadegg***	Y	Y	Y	Y	Y	Y	N	N
5 ***Kolbe***	N	Y	N	N	Y	Y	N	N
6 ***Hayworth***	Y	Y	N	Y	Y	Y	Y	N
ARKANSAS								
1 Berry	N	Y	N	Y	Y	N	Y	N
2 Snyder	N	N	N	N	Y	N	Y	Y
3 ***Hutchinson***	N	Y	Y	Y	Y	Y	N	Y
4 ***Dickey***	N	Y	Y	Y	Y	Y	N	N
CALIFORNIA								
1 ***Riggs***	N	Y	N	Y	Y	Y	N	N
2 ***Herger***	Y	Y	Y	Y	?	Y	Y	N
3 Fazio	N	N	N	N	Y	N	Y	Y
4 ***Doolittle***	Y	Y	Y	Y	Y	Y	N	N
5 Matsui	N	Y	N	N	Y	N	Y	Y
6 Woolsey	–	–	–	–	+	N	Y	Y
7 Miller	N	Y	N	N	N	N	Y	Y
8 Pelosi	N	N	N	N	N	N	Y	Y
9 Dellums	N	N	N	N	N	N	Y	Y
10 Tauscher	N	Y	N	N	Y	N	Y	Y
11 ***Pombo***	Y	Y	Y	Y	Y	Y	N	N
12 Lantos	N	N	N	N	Y	N	Y	Y
13 Stark	N	N	N	N	Y	N	Y	Y
14 Eshoo	–	+	–	–	+	N	Y	Y
15 ***Campbell***	N	Y	N	Y	Y	Y	Y	Y
16 Lofgren	N	N	N	N	Y	N	Y	Y
17 Farr	N	N	N	N	N	N	Y	Y
18 Condit	Y	Y	N	Y	Y	N	Y	Y
19 ***Radanovich***	Y	Y	Y	Y	Y	Y	N	N
20 Dooley	N	Y	N	N	Y	N	Y	Y
21 ***Thomas***	N	Y	Y	Y	Y	Y	N	N
22 Capps	N	Y	N	N	Y	N	Y	Y
23 ***Gallegly***	N	Y	N	Y	Y	Y	Y	N
24 Sherman	N	Y	N	N	Y	Y	Y	Y
25 ***McKeon***	Y	Y	Y	Y	Y	Y	N	N
26 Berman	N	N	N	N	Y	N	Y	Y
27 ***Rogan***	Y	Y	Y	Y	Y	Y	Y	N
28 ***Dreier***	Y	Y	Y	Y	Y	Y	N	N
29 Waxman	N	N	N	N	Y	N	Y	Y
30 Becerra	N	N	N	N	N	N	Y	Y
31 Martinez	N	Y	N	N	Y	N	Y	Y
32 Dixon	N	N	N	N	Y	N	Y	Y
33 Roybal-Allard	N	N	N	N	Y	N	Y	Y
34 Torres	N	N	N	N	Y	N	Y	?
35 Waters	N	N	N	N	N	N	N	Y
36 Harman	N	Y	N	N	Y	N	N	N
37 Millender-McD.	N	N	N	N	Y	N	Y	Y
38 ***Horn***	N	Y	N	N	Y	Y	Y	Y
39 ***Royce***	Y	Y	N	Y	Y	N	Y	Y
40 ***Lewis***	N	Y	?	Y	Y	Y	N	N
41 ***Kim***	N	Y	Y	Y	Y	Y	Y	N
42 Brown	N	N	N	N	N	N	Y	Y
43 ***Calvert***	N	Y	Y	Y	Y	Y	Y	N
44 ***Bono***	Y	N	N	Y	Y	Y	Y	N
45 ***Rohrabacher***	Y	Y	N	Y	Y	Y	Y	Y
46 Sanchez	N	Y	N	N	Y	N	Y	Y
47 ***Cox***	Y	Y	Y	Y	Y	Y	N	Y
48 ***Packard***	N	Y	N	Y	Y	Y	N	N
49 ***Bilbray***	N	Y	N	Y	Y	Y	N	N
50 Filner	N	N	N	N	Y	N	Y	Y
51 ***Cunningham***	Y	Y	Y	Y	Y	Y	Y	N
52 ***Hunter***	Y	Y	N	Y	Y	Y	N	N
COLORADO								
1 DeGette	N	N	N	N	Y	N	Y	Y
2 Skaggs	N	N	N	N	Y	N	Y	Y
3 ***McInnis***	N	Y	Y	Y	Y	Y	Y	N
4 ***Schaffer***	Y	Y	N	Y	Y	Y	Y	N
5 ***Hefley***	N	Y	Y	Y	Y	Y	Y	Y
6 ***Schaefer***	N	Y	Y	Y	Y	Y	Y	N
CONNECTICUT								
1 Kennelly	N	Y	N	N	Y	N	Y	Y
2 Gejdenson	N	Y	N	N	Y	N	Y	Y
3 DeLauro	N	Y	N	N	Y	N	Y	Y
4 ***Shays***	N	Y	Y	N	Y	Y	Y	Y
5 Maloney	N	Y	N	N	Y	N	Y	Y
6 ***Johnson***	N	N	Y	N	+	N	Y	Y
DELAWARE								
AL ***Castle***	N	Y	N	N	Y	N	Y	Y
FLORIDA								
1 ***Scarborough***	Y	Y	Y	Y	?	Y	N	N
2 Boyd	N	N	Y	N	Y	N	Y	Y
3 Brown	?	?	?	?	?	?	Y	N
4 ***Fowler***	N	Y	Y	Y	Y	Y	N	N
5 Thurman	N	Y	N	N	Y	N	Y	Y
6 ***Stearns***	Y	Y	Y	Y	Y	Y	N	N
7 ***Mica***	N	Y	Y	Y	Y	Y	Y	N
8 ***McCollum***	N	Y	Y	Y	Y	N	N	N
9 ***Bilirakis***	N	Y	Y	Y	Y	Y	Y	N
10 ***Young***	N	N	Y	Y	Y	Y	Y	N
11 Davis	N	Y	N	N	Y	N	Y	Y
12 ***Canady***	Y	Y	Y	Y	Y	Y	Y	Y
13 ***Miller***	N	Y	Y	Y	+	Y	N	N
14 ***Goss***	N	Y	N	Y	Y	Y	N	N
15 ***Weldon***	Y	Y	Y	Y	Y	Y	N	N
16 ***Foley***	N	Y	N	Y	Y	N	N	N
17 Meek	N	N	N	N	Y	N	N	N
18 ***Ros-Lehtinen***	N	Y	N	Y	Y	Y	N	N
19 Wexler	N	Y	N	N	Y	N	N	Y
20 Deutsch	N	Y	N	N	Y	Y	N	N
21 ***Diaz-Balart***	N	Y	N	Y	Y	Y	N	N
22 ***Shaw***	N	Y	N	Y	Y	Y	N	N
23 Hastings	N	N	N	N	N	N	N	N
GEORGIA								
1 ***Kingston***	Y	Y	Y	Y	Y	Y	N	N
2 Bishop	N	Y	N	N	Y	N	Y	Y
3 ***Collins***	Y	Y	Y	Y	Y	Y	Y	Y
4 McKinney	N	Y	N	N	Y	N	Y	Y
5 Lewis	N	N	N	N	Y	N	Y	Y
6 ***Gingrich***						Y		
7 ***Barr***	Y	Y	Y	Y	Y	Y	Y	Y
8 ***Chambliss***	Y	Y	Y	Y	Y	Y	Y	Y
9 ***Deal***	Y	Y	Y	Y	Y	Y	Y	N
10 ***Norwood***	Y	Y	Y	Y	Y	Y	Y	Y
11 ***Linder***	Y	Y	Y	Y	Y	Y	Y	N
HAWAII								
1 Abercrombie	N	N	N	N	Y	N	Y	Y
2 Mink	N	N	N	N	Y	N	Y	Y
IDAHO								
1 ***Chenoweth***	Y	Y	Y	Y	Y	Y	N	N
2 ***Crapo***	Y	Y	Y	Y	Y	Y	N	N
ILLINOIS								
1 Rush	N	N	N	N	Y	N	Y	Y
2 Jackson	N	N	N	N	Y	N	Y	Y
3 Lipinski	N	Y	Y	N	Y	Y	Y	Y
4 Gutierrez	N	N	N	N	Y	N	Y	Y
5 Blagojevich	N	Y	N	N	Y	N	Y	Y
6 ***Hyde***	Y	Y	Y	Y	Y	Y	N	N
7 Davis	N	N	N	N	Y	N	Y	Y
8 ***Crane***	Y	Y	Y	Y	Y	Y	Y	Y
9 Yates	N	N	N	N	N	N	Y	Y
10 ***Porter***	N	Y	Y	N	Y	Y	Y	Y
11 ***Weller***	N	Y	Y	Y	Y	Y	Y	N
12 Costello	N	Y	Y	N	Y	N	Y	Y
13 ***Fawell***	N	Y	Y	N	Y	N	N	N
14 ***Hastert***	Y	Y	N	Y	Y	Y	N	N
15 ***Ewing***	N	N	Y	Y	Y	Y	Y	N

ND Northern Democrats SD Southern Democrats

	270	271	272	273	274	275	276	277
16 ***Manzullo***	Y	Y	Y	Y	Y	Y	Y	N
17 Evans	N	N	N	N	Y	N	Y	Y
18 ***LaHood***	N	Y	Y	Y	Y	Y	Y	N
19 Poshard	N	Y	Y	N	Y	N	Y	Y
20 ***Shimkus***	N	Y	Y	Y	Y	Y	Y	N
INDIANA								
1 Visclosky	N	N	Y	N	Y	N	Y	Y
2 ***McIntosh***	Y	Y	Y	Y	Y	N	N	N
3 Roemer	N	Y	Y	N	Y	N	Y	Y
4 ***Souder***	Y	Y	Y	Y	Y	Y	N	N
5 ***Buyer***	Y	?	Y	Y	Y	Y	Y	N
6 ***Burton***	Y	Y	N	Y	Y	Y	N	N
7 ***Pease***	Y	Y	Y	Y	Y	Y	Y	N
8 ***Hostettler***	Y	Y	Y	Y	Y	Y	Y	N
9 Hamilton	N	Y	N	N	Y	Y	Y	Y
10 Carson	N	N	N	N	Y	N	Y	Y
IOWA								
1 ***Leach***	N	Y	Y	N	Y	N	N	Y
2 ***Nussle***	Y	Y	Y	Y	Y	Y	N	N
3 Boswell	N	Y	N	N	Y	N	N	N
4 ***Ganske***	N	Y	Y	Y	Y	N	N	N
5 ***Latham***	Y	Y	Y	Y	Y	Y	N	N
KANSAS								
1 ***Moran***	N	Y	Y	Y	Y	Y	N	N
2 ***Ryun***	Y	Y	Y	Y	Y	Y	N	N
3 ***Snowbarger***	N	Y	Y	Y	Y	Y	N	N
4 ***Tiahrt***	Y	Y	Y	Y	Y	Y	N	N
KENTUCKY								
1 ***Whitfield***	N	Y	Y	Y	Y	Y	Y	Y
2 ***Lewis***	N	Y	Y	Y	Y	Y	Y	N
3 ***Northup***	N	Y	Y	Y	Y	Y	Y	N
4 ***Bunning***	N	Y	Y	Y	Y	Y	N	N
5 ***Rogers***	N	N	Y	Y	Y	Y	Y	N
6 Baesler	N	Y	Y	N	Y	N	Y	Y
LOUISIANA								
1 ***Livingston***	N	N	Y	Y	Y	Y	N	N
2 Jefferson	N	N	N	N	Y	N	Y	Y
3 ***Tauzin***	N	Y	N	Y	Y	Y	N	N
4 ***McCrery***	N	Y	Y	Y	Y	Y	N	N
5 ***Cooksey***	N	Y	N	Y	?	Y	N	N
6 ***Baker***	N	Y	Y	Y	Y	Y	N	N
7 John	N	Y	Y	N	Y	N	Y	Y
MAINE								
1 Allen	N	N	N	N	Y	N	Y	Y
2 Baldacci	N	Y	N	N	Y	N	Y	Y
MARYLAND								
1 ***Gilchrest***	N	Y	Y	N	Y	Y	N	N
2 ***Ehrlich***	Y	Y	Y	Y	Y	Y	N	N
3 Cardin	N	Y	N	N	Y	N	Y	Y
4 Wynn	N	Y	N	N	Y	N	Y	Y
5 Hoyer	N	N	N	N	Y	Y	Y	Y
6 ***Bartlett***	Y	Y	Y	Y	Y	Y	Y	N
7 Cummings	N	N	N	N	Y	N	Y	Y
8 ***Morella***	N	Y	N	N	Y	N	Y	Y
MASSACHUSETTS								
1 Olver	N	N	N	N	N	N	Y	Y
2 Neal	N	Y	N	N	N	N	Y	Y
3 McGovern	N	N	N	N	Y	N	Y	Y
4 Frank	N	N	N	N	N	N	Y	Y
5 Meehan	N	Y	N	N	N	N	Y	Y
6 Tierney	N	N	N	N	N	N	Y	Y
7 Markey	N	N	N	N	Y	?	Y	Y
8 Kennedy	N	Y	N	N	Y	N	Y	Y
9 Moakley	N	N	N	N	Y	N	Y	Y
10 Delahunt	N	Y	N	N	Y	N	Y	Y
MICHIGAN								
1 Stupak	N	Y	N	N	Y	N	Y	Y
2 ***Hoekstra***	N	Y	Y	Y	Y	Y	Y	Y
3 ***Ehlers***	N	Y	Y	N	Y	Y	Y	N
4 ***Camp***	N	Y	Y	Y	Y	Y	Y	Y
5 Barcia	N	Y	N	Y	Y	Y	Y	Y
6 ***Upton***	N	Y	Y	Y	Y	Y	Y	Y
7 ***Smith***	N	Y	Y	Y	Y	Y	Y	Y
8 Stabenow	N	Y	N	N	Y	N	Y	Y
9 Kildee	N	Y	N	N	Y	N	Y	Y
10 Bonior	N	N	N	N	Y	N	Y	Y
11 ***Knollenberg***	N	N	Y	Y	Y	Y	N	N
12 Levin	N	Y	N	N	Y	N	Y	Y
13 Rivers	N	Y	N	N	Y	N	Y	Y
14 Conyers	?	?	?	?	Y	N	N	Y
15 Kilpatrick	N	N	N	N	Y	N	Y	Y
16 Dingell	N	N	N	N	Y	N	Y	Y
MINNESOTA								
1 ***Gutknecht***	Y	Y	N	Y	Y	Y	N	N
2 Minge	N	Y	N	N	Y	N	Y	Y

	270	271	272	273	274	275	276	277
3 ***Ramstad***	N	Y	N	N	Y	N	Y	Y
4 Vento	N	Y	N	N	Y	N	Y	Y
5 Sabo	N	N	N	N	N	N	Y	Y
6 Luther	N	Y	N	N	Y	N	Y	Y
7 Peterson	N	Y	N	Y	Y	N	Y	Y
8 Oberstar	N	N	N	N	Y	N	N	Y
MISSISSIPPI								
1 ***Wicker***	N	Y	N	Y	Y	Y	Y	N
2 Thompson	N	Y	N	N	Y	Y	N	Y
3 ***Pickering***	N	Y	N	Y	Y	Y	Y	N
4 ***Parker***	N	Y	N	Y	Y	Y	N	N
5 Taylor	Y	Y	N	Y	Y	Y	Y	Y
MISSOURI								
1 Clay	N	N	N	N	Y	N	Y	Y
2 ***Talent***	Y	Y	Y	Y	Y	Y	Y	Y
3 Gephardt	?	N	N	N	Y	N	Y	Y
4 Skelton	N	Y	Y	Y	Y	Y	Y	Y
5 McCarthy	N	Y	N	N	Y	N	Y	Y
6 Danner	N	Y	Y	Y	Y	N	Y	Y
7 ***Blunt***	N	Y	Y	Y	Y	Y	Y	N
8 ***Emerson***	Y	Y	Y	Y	Y	Y	Y	N
9 ***Hulshof***	N	Y	Y	Y	Y	Y	Y	N
MONTANA								
AL ***Hill***	N	Y	Y	Y	Y	Y	Y	N
NEBRASKA								
1 ***Bereuter***	N	Y	N	N	Y	Y	Y	N
2 ***Christensen***	Y	Y	Y	Y	Y	Y	Y	N
3 ***Barrett***	N	Y	Y	Y	Y	Y	Y	N
NEVADA								
1 ***Ensign***	N	Y	N	Y	Y	Y	Y	Y
2 ***Gibbons***	N	Y	N	Y	Y	Y	Y	N
NEW HAMPSHIRE								
1 ***Sununu***	N	Y	Y	Y	Y	Y	Y	Y
2 ***Bass***	N	Y	Y	Y	Y	Y	Y	N
NEW JERSEY								
1 Andrews	N	Y	N	N	Y	N	Y	Y
2 ***LoBiondo***	N	Y	Y	Y	Y	Y	Y	N
3 ***Saxton***	N	Y	Y	N	Y	Y	Y	N
4 ***Smith***	N	Y	Y	Y	Y	Y	Y	N
5 ***Roukema***	N	Y	Y	N	Y	Y	Y	Y
6 Pallone	N	Y	N	N	N	N	Y	Y
7 ***Franks***	N	Y	Y	Y	Y	Y	Y	N
8 Pascrell	N	Y	N	N	Y	N	Y	Y
9 Rothman	N	Y	Y	N	Y	N	Y	Y
10 Payne	N	N	N	N	N	N	Y	Y
11 ***Frelinghuysen***	N	Y	Y	Y	Y	Y	Y	Y
12 ***Pappas***	N	Y	Y	Y	Y	Y	Y	N
13 Menendez	N	Y	N	N	Y	N	Y	Y
NEW MEXICO								
1 ***Schiff***	?	?	?	?	?	?	?	?
2 ***Skeen***	N	Y	N	Y	Y	Y	Y	N
3 ***Redmond***	N	Y	N	Y	Y	Y	Y	N
NEW YORK								
1 ***Forbes***	N	Y	Y	Y	Y	Y	Y	N
2 ***Lazio***	N	Y	N	N	Y	N	Y	N
3 ***King***	Y	Y	Y	Y	Y	Y	Y	N
4 McCarthy	N	Y	N	N	Y	N	Y	Y
5 Ackerman	N	N	N	N	N	N	Y	Y
6 Flake	N	N	N	N	Y	N	Y	Y
7 Manton	N	N	N	N	Y	N	Y	Y
8 Nadler	N	N	N	N	N	N	Y	Y
9 Schumer	N	Y	N	N	Y	N	Y	Y
10 Towns	N	N	N	N	Y	N	Y	Y
11 Owens	N	N	N	N	Y	N	Y	Y
12 Velázquez	N	N	N	N	Y	N	Y	Y
13 ***Molinari***	N	Y	Y	Y	Y	Y	Y	N
14 Maloney	N	Y	N	N	Y	N	Y	Y
15 Rangel	N	N	N	N	Y	N	Y	Y
16 Serrano	N	N	N	N	Y	N	Y	Y
17 Engel	N	N	N	N	N	N	Y	Y
18 Lowey	N	N	N	N	Y	N	Y	Y
19 ***Kelly***	N	Y	Y	Y	Y	Y	Y	Y
20 ***Gilman***	N	Y	N	N	Y	Y	Y	Y
21 McNulty	N	N	N	N	Y	N	Y	Y
22 ***Solomon***	Y	Y	Y	Y	Y	Y	Y	N
23 ***Boehlert***	N	Y	N	N	Y	Y	Y	Y
24 ***McHugh***	N	Y	Y	Y	Y	N	Y	N
25 ***Walsh***	N	Y	Y	Y	Y	Y	Y	N
26 Hinchey	N	N	N	N	Y	N	Y	Y
27 ***Paxon***	Y	Y	Y	Y	Y	Y	N	N
28 Slaughter	N	N	N	N	Y	N	Y	Y
29 LaFalce	–	–	–	–	Y	N	Y	Y
30 ***Quinn***	N	Y	Y	Y	Y	N	Y	N
31 ***Houghton***	N	Y	N	N	Y	Y	N	N

	270	271	272	273	274	275	276	277
NORTH CAROLINA								
1 Clayton	N	Y	N	N	Y	N	Y	Y
2 Etheridge	N	Y	N	N	Y	N	Y	Y
3 ***Jones***	Y	Y	Y	Y	Y	Y	Y	Y
4 Price	N	Y	Y	N	Y	N	Y	Y
5 ***Burr***	N	Y	Y	Y	Y	Y	N	N
6 ***Coble***	Y	Y	Y	Y	Y	Y	Y	N
7 McIntyre	N	Y	N	Y	Y	Y	Y	N
8 Hefner	N	Y	N	N	Y	N	Y	Y
9 ***Myrick***	Y	Y	Y	Y	?	Y	N	N
10 ***Ballenger***	N	Y	Y	Y	Y	Y	N	N
11 ***Taylor***	Y	Y	Y	Y	Y	Y	N	N
12 Watt	N	N	N	N	Y	N	Y	Y
NORTH DAKOTA								
AL Pomeroy	N	Y	N	N	Y	N	Y	Y
OHIO								
1 ***Chabot***	Y	Y	Y	Y	Y	Y	Y	Y
2 ***Portman***	N	Y	Y	Y	Y	Y	Y	N
3 Hall	N	Y	N	N	Y	N	Y	Y
4 ***Oxley***	N	Y	Y	Y	Y	Y	N	N
5 ***Gillmor***	N	Y	Y	Y	Y	Y	Y	Y
6 Strickland	N	Y	N	N	Y	N	Y	Y
7 ***Hobson***	N	N	Y	Y	Y	Y	Y	N
8 ***Boehner***	Y	Y	Y	Y	Y	Y	N	N
9 Kaptur	N	N	N	N	Y	N	Y	Y
10 Kucinich	N	N	N	N	Y	N	Y	Y
11 Stokes	N	N	N	N	Y	N	Y	Y
12 ***Kasich***	Y	Y	Y	Y	Y	Y	Y	Y
13 Brown	N	Y	N	N	Y	N	Y	Y
14 Sawyer	N	N	N	N	Y	N	Y	Y
15 ***Pryce***	N	Y	N	Y	Y	Y	Y	N
16 ***Regula***	N	Y	N	Y	Y	Y	Y	N
17 Traficant	N	Y	Y	Y	Y	Y	Y	Y
18 ***Ney***	N	Y	Y	Y	Y	Y	Y	N
19 ***LaTourette***	N	Y	N	N	Y	N	N	N
OKLAHOMA								
1 ***Largent***	Y	Y	Y	Y	Y	Y	Y	N
2 ***Coburn***	Y	Y	Y	Y	Y	Y	N	N
3 ***Watkins***	N	Y	Y	Y	Y	Y	N	N
4 ***Watts***	N	Y	Y	Y	Y	Y	Y	N
5 ***Istook***	Y	Y	Y	Y	Y	Y	N	N
6 ***Lucas***	N	Y	Y	Y	Y	Y	N	N
OREGON								
1 Furse	N	N	N	N	N	N	Y	Y
2 ***Smith***	N	Y	Y	Y	Y	Y	N	N
3 Blumenauer	N	N	N	N	Y	N	Y	Y
4 DeFazio	N	Y	N	N	Y	N	Y	Y
5 Hooley	N	Y	N	N	Y	N	Y	Y
PENNSYLVANIA								
1 Foglietta	N	N	N	N	Y	N	Y	Y
2 Fattah	N	N	N	N	Y	N	Y	Y
3 Borski	N	N	N	N	Y	N	Y	Y
4 Klink	N	Y	N	N	Y	Y	Y	Y
5 ***Peterson***	N	Y	Y	Y	Y	Y	Y	N
6 Holden	N	Y	Y	Y	Y	Y	Y	Y
7 ***Weldon***	N	Y	Y	Y	Y	Y	Y	N
8 ***Greenwood***	N	Y	Y	Y	Y	Y	Y	Y
9 ***Shuster***	Y	N	Y	Y	Y	Y	N	N
10 ***McDade***	N	Y	Y	Y	Y	Y	Y	N
11 Kanjorski	N	N	Y	N	Y	N	Y	Y
12 Murtha	N	N	N	N	Y	Y	N	N
13 ***Fox***	N	Y	Y	Y	Y	Y	Y	N
14 Coyne	N	N	N	N	Y	N	Y	Y
15 McHale	N	Y	N	N	Y	N	Y	Y
16 ***Pitts***	N	Y	Y	Y	Y	Y	N	N
17 ***Gekas***	Y	Y	Y	Y	Y	Y	N	N
18 Doyle	N	Y	Y	Y	Y	Y	Y	Y
19 ***Goodling***	Y	Y	Y	Y	Y	Y	Y	N
20 Mascara	N	Y	Y	Y	Y	Y	Y	Y
21 ***English***	N	Y	Y	N	Y	Y	Y	N
RHODE ISLAND								
1 Kennedy	N	N	N	N	N	N	Y	Y
2 Weygand	N	Y	Y	N	Y	N	Y	Y
SOUTH CAROLINA								
1 ***Sanford***	N	Y	Y	Y	Y	Y	Y	Y
2 ***Spence***	N	N	Y	Y	Y	Y	N	N
3 ***Graham***	Y	Y	Y	Y	Y	Y	N	N
4 ***Inglis***	Y	Y	Y	Y	Y	Y	N	N
5 Spratt	N	Y	N	N	Y	N	N	Y
6 Clyburn	N	Y	N	N	Y	Y	N	Y
SOUTH DAKOTA								
AL ***Thune***	Y	Y	Y	Y	Y	Y	Y	N
TENNESSEE								
1 ***Jenkins***	N	Y	Y	Y	Y	Y	Y	N
2 ***Duncan***	Y	Y	Y	Y	Y	Y	Y	Y

	270	271	272	273	274	275	276	
3 ***Wamp***	N	Y	Y	Y	Y	Y	N	N
4 ***Hilleary***	Y	Y	Y	Y	Y	Y	Y	N
5 Clement	N	Y	Y	N	Y	Y	Y	Y
6 Gordon	N	Y	Y	N	Y	Y	Y	Y
7 ***Bryant***	Y	Y	Y	Y	Y	Y	Y	Y
8 Tanner	N	Y	Y	N	Y	Y	Y	Y
9 Ford	N	Y	N	N	Y	N	Y	Y
TEXAS								
1 Sandlin	N	Y	Y	Y	Y	N	Y	Y
2 Turner	N	Y	N	Y	Y	N	Y	Y
3 ***Johnson, Sam***	?	?	?	?	Y	Y	N	N
4 Hall	Y	Y	Y	Y	?	Y	Y	Y
5 ***Sessions***	Y	Y	Y	Y	Y	Y	Y	Y
6 ***Barton***	Y	Y	Y	Y	Y	Y	N	N
7 ***Archer***	Y	Y	Y	Y	Y	Y	N	N
8 ***Brady***	Y	Y	Y	Y	Y	Y	N	N
9 Lampson	N	Y	N	N	Y	N	Y	Y
10 Doggett	N	Y	Y	N	Y	N	Y	Y
11 Edwards	N	N	Y	N	Y	N	Y	Y
12 ***Granger***	N	Y	Y	Y	Y	Y	Y	N
13 ***Thornberry***	Y	Y	Y	Y	Y	Y	N	N
14 ***Paul***	Y	Y	Y	Y	Y	N	Y	Y
15 Hinojosa	N	Y	N	N	Y	N	Y	Y
16 Reyes	–	+	–	–	+	–	Y	Y
17 Stenholm	Y	Y	Y	Y	Y	Y	Y	Y
18 Jackson-Lee	N	N	N	N	Y	N	Y	Y
19 ***Combest***	Y	Y	Y	Y	Y	Y	Y	Y
20 Gonzalez	N	N	N	N	Y	N	Y	Y
21 ***Smith***	N	Y	Y	Y	Y	Y	Y	N
22 ***DeLay***	Y	Y	N	Y	Y	Y	N	N
23 ***Bonilla***	N	Y	Y	Y	Y	Y	Y	N
24 Frost	N	Y	N	N	Y	N	Y	Y
25 Bentsen	N	Y	N	N	Y	N	Y	Y
26 ***Armey***	Y	Y	Y	Y	Y	Y	N	N
27 Ortiz	N	Y	N	N	Y	Y	Y	Y
28 Rodriguez	N	N	N	N	Y	N	Y	Y
29 Green	N	Y	N	Y	Y	N	Y	Y
30 Johnson, E.B.	N	N	N	N	Y	N	Y	Y
UTAH								
1 ***Hansen***	Y	Y	Y	Y	Y	Y	N	N
2 ***Cook***	N	Y	Y	Y	Y	Y	N	N
3 ***Cannon***	N	Y	N	Y	Y	Y	Y	N
VERMONT								
AL *Sanders*	N	N	N	N	Y	N	Y	Y
VIRGINIA								
1 ***Bateman***	N	N	N	Y	Y	Y	N	N
2 Pickett	N	Y	N	N	Y	N	N	N
3 Scott	N	Y	N	Y	N	N	Y	Y
4 Sisisky	N	Y	Y	Y	Y	Y	Y	Y
5 Goode	N	Y	Y	Y	Y	Y	Y	Y
6 ***Goodlatte***	Y	Y	Y	Y	Y	Y	Y	Y
7 ***Bliley***	N	Y	Y	Y	Y	Y	N	N
8 Moran	N	N	N	N	N	Y	Y	Y
9 Boucher	N	N	N	N	Y	N	Y	Y
10 ***Wolf***	N	Y	Y	Y	Y	Y	N	N
11 ***Davis***	N	Y	Y	N	Y	Y	Y	N
WASHINGTON								
1 ***White***	N	Y	Y	Y	Y	Y	N	N
2 ***Metcalf***	N	Y	Y	Y	Y	Y	Y	N
3 ***Smith, Linda***	Y	Y	Y	Y	Y	Y	Y	N
4 ***Hastings***	Y	Y	Y	Y	Y	Y	Y	N
5 ***Nethercutt***	N	Y	Y	Y	Y	Y	N	N
6 Dicks	N	N	N	N	Y	Y	Y	Y
7 McDermott	N	N	N	N	N	N	Y	Y
8 ***Dunn***	N	Y	Y	Y	Y	Y	N	N
9 Smith, Adam	N	N	N	N	Y	N	Y	Y
WEST VIRGINIA								
1 Mollohan	N	N	N	N	Y	Y	N	N
2 Wise	N	N	N	N	Y	N	Y	Y
3 Rahall	N	N	Y	N	Y	Y	Y	Y
WISCONSIN								
1 ***Neumann***	Y	Y	Y	Y	Y	Y	N	Y
2 ***Klug***	N	Y	Y	Y	Y	N	Y	Y
3 Kind	N	Y	N	N	Y	N	Y	Y
4 Kleczka	N	Y	N	N	Y	N	Y	Y
5 Barrett	N	Y	N	N	Y	N	Y	Y
6 ***Petri***	Y	Y	Y	Y	Y	Y	Y	Y
7 Obey	N	N	N	N	Y	N	Y	Y
8 Johnson	N	N	N	N	Y	N	Y	Y
9 ***Sensenbrenner***	Y	Y	Y	Y	Y	N	Y	Y
WYOMING								
AL ***Cubin***	Y	?	Y	Y	Y	Y	Y	N

Southern states - Ala., Ark., Fla., Ga., Ky., La., Miss., N.C., Okla., S.C., Tenn., Texas, Va.

HOUSE VOTES 278, 279, 280, 281, 282, 283, 284, 285

278. HR 2158. Fiscal 1998 VA-HUD Appropriations/International Space Station. Sensenbrenner, R-Wis., amendment to limit the total NASA may spend on development and operations of the international space station to $1.876 billion in fiscal 1998. Rejected 200-227: R 131-93; D 68-134 (ND 66-83, SD 2-51); I 1-0, July 16, 1997.

279. HR 2158. Fiscal 1998 VA-HUD Appropriations/Recommit. Kennedy, D-Mass., motion to recommit the bill to the Appropriations Committee with instructions to report it back with an amendment to increase the bill's total funding level by $160 million, including increases of $60 million for homeless programs, $45 million for Community Development Block Grants, $25 million for Brownfields, $10 million for the Youthbuild program and $20 million for support service coordinators for the elderly and disabled. Motion rejected 193-235: R 1-222; D 191-13 (ND 143-6, SD 48-7); I 1-0, July 16, 1997.

280. HR 2158. Fiscal 1998 VA-HUD Appropriations/Passage. Passage of the bill to provide about $91.7 billion in new budget authority for the departments of Veterans Affairs and Housing and Urban Development in fiscal 1998. The bill would provide $5.8 billion more than the $85.9 billion provided in fiscal 1997 and $670 million more than the president's request of $91.0 billion. Passed 397-31: R 200-24; D 196-7 (ND 142-6, SD 54-1); I 1-0, July 16, 1997.

281. HR 2160. Fiscal 1998 Agriculture Appropriations/Resolve Into Committee of the Whole. Skeen, R-N.M., motion to resolve the House into the Committee of the Whole for consideration of the bill to provide $49.6 billion in new budget authority for agriculture programs, rural development, the Food and Drug Administration and related agencies in fiscal 1998. Motion agreed to 259-165: R 219-0; D 40-164 (ND 27-123, SD 13-41); I 0-1, July 17, 1997.

282. HR 2160. Fiscal 1998 Agriculture Appropriations/Table Reconsideration of Vote. Kingston, R-Ga., motion to table the Frank, D-Mass., motion to reconsider the vote by which the House agreed to resolve the House into the Committee of the Whole for consideration of the bill to provide $49.6 billion in new budget authority for agriculture programs, rural development, the Food and Drug Administration and related agencies in fiscal 1998. Motion agreed to 238-188: R 220-0; D 18-187 (ND 12-138, SD 6-49); I 0-1, July 17, 1997.

283. HR 2160. Fiscal 1998 Agriculture Appropriations/Motion To Rise. Slaughter, D-N.Y., motion to rise from the Committee of the Whole. Motion rejected 191-233: R 0-221; D 190-12 (ND 141-6, SD 49-6); I 1-0, July 17, 1997.

284. HR 2160. Fiscal 1998 Agriculture Appropriations/Motion To Rise. Kaptur, D-Ohio, motion to rise from the Committee of the Whole. Motion rejected 189-232: R 0-219; D 188-13 (ND 140-7, SD 48-6); I 1-0, July 17, 1997.

285. HR 2160. Fiscal 1998 Agriculture Appropriations/Motion To Rise. DeLauro, D-Conn., motion to rise from the Committee of the Whole. Motion agreed to 344-73: R 164-54; D 179-19 (ND 136-8, SD 43-11); I 1-0, July 17, 1997.

KEY

- Y Voted for (yea).
- # Paired for.
- \+ Announced for.
- N Voted against (nay).
- X Paired against.
- – Announced against.
- P Voted "present."
- C Voted "present" to avoid possible conflict of interest.
- ? Did not vote or otherwise make a position known.

Democrats ***Republicans***
Independent

	278	279	280	281	282	283	284	285
ALABAMA								
1 ***Callahan***	N	N	Y	Y	Y	N	N	N
2 ***Everett***	N	N	Y	Y	Y	N	N	N
3 ***Riley***	N	N	Y	Y	Y	N	N	N
4 ***Aderholt***	N	N	Y	Y	Y	N	N	N
5 Cramer	N	N	Y	N	N	N	N	N
6 ***Bachus***	N	N	Y	Y	Y	N	N	Y
7 Hilliard	N	Y	Y	N	N	Y	Y	Y
ALASKA								
AL ***Young***	?	?	?	?	?	?	?	?
ARIZONA								
1 ***Salmon***	Y	N	N	Y	Y	N	N	Y
2 Pastor	N	N	Y	N	N	Y	Y	Y
3 ***Stump***	N	N	Y	Y	Y	N	N	N
4 ***Shadegg***	Y	N	Y	Y	Y	N	N	Y
5 ***Kolbe***	N	N	Y	Y	Y	N	N	Y
6 ***Hayworth***	Y	N	Y	Y	Y	N	N	Y
ARKANSAS								
1 Berry	N	Y	Y	N	N	Y	Y	Y
2 Snyder	N	N	Y	N	N	Y	Y	Y
3 ***Hutchinson***	Y	N	Y	Y	Y	N	N	Y
4 ***Dickey***	N	N	Y	Y	Y	N	N	Y
CALIFORNIA								
1 ***Riggs***	Y	N	Y	Y	Y	N	N	N
2 ***Herger***	Y	N	Y	Y	Y	N	N	Y
3 Fazio	N	Y	Y	N	N	Y	Y	Y
4 ***Doolittle***	N	N	Y	Y	Y	N	N	Y
5 Matsui	N	?	Y	Y	N	Y	Y	Y
6 Woolsey	Y	Y	?	N	N	Y	Y	Y
7 Miller	Y	Y	Y	N	N	Y	Y	Y
8 Pelosi	Y	Y	Y	N	N	Y	Y	Y
9 Dellums	Y	Y	Y	Y	N	Y	Y	Y
10 Tauscher	N	Y	Y	N	N	Y	Y	Y
11 ***Pombo***	Y	N	Y	Y	Y	N	N	Y
12 Lantos	N	Y	Y	N	N	Y	Y	Y
13 Stark	Y	Y	Y	N	N	Y	Y	Y
14 Eshoo	Y	Y	Y	N	N	Y	Y	Y
15 ***Campbell***	Y	N	N	Y	Y	N	N	N
16 Lofgren	N	Y	Y	N	N	Y	Y	Y
17 Farr	N	Y	Y	N	N	Y	Y	Y
18 Condit	Y	Y	Y	N	N	Y	Y	Y
19 ***Radanovich***	N	N	Y	Y	Y	N	?	N
20 Dooley	N	Y	Y	N	N	Y	Y	Y
21 ***Thomas***	Y	N	Y	Y	Y	N	N	N
22 Capps	N	Y	Y	N	N	Y	Y	Y
23 ***Gallegly***	N	N	Y	Y	Y	N	N	Y
24 Sherman	N	Y	Y	N	N	Y	Y	Y
25 ***McKeon***	N	N	Y	Y	Y	N	N	Y
26 Berman	N	Y	Y	N	N	?	?	?
27 ***Rogan***	N	N	Y	Y	Y	N	N	Y
28 ***Dreier***	N	N	Y	Y	Y	N	N	N
29 Waxman	Y	Y	Y	N	N	Y	Y	Y
30 Becerra	N	Y	Y	N	N	Y	Y	Y
31 Martinez	N	Y	Y	N	N	Y	Y	?
32 Dixon	N	Y	Y	N	N	Y	Y	Y
33 Roybal-Allard	N	Y	Y	N	N	Y	Y	Y
34 Torres	?	Y	Y	N	N	Y	Y	Y
35 Waters	N	Y	Y	N	N	Y	Y	Y
36 Harman	N	Y	Y	N	N	Y	Y	Y
37 Millender-McD.	N	Y	Y	N	N	Y	Y	Y
38 ***Horn***	N	N	Y	Y	Y	N	N	Y
39 ***Royce***	Y	N	N	Y	Y	N	N	N
40 ***Lewis***	N	N	Y	Y	Y	N	N	N
41 ***Kim***	N	N	Y	Y	Y	N	N	Y
42 Brown	N	Y	Y	N	N	?	Y	Y
43 ***Calvert***	N	N	Y	Y	Y	N	N	Y
44 ***Bono***	N	N	Y	Y	Y	N	N	Y
45 ***Rohrabacher***	Y	N	N	Y	Y	N	N	Y
46 Sanchez	N	Y	Y	N	N	Y	Y	Y
47 ***Cox***	Y	N	N	Y	Y	N	N	Y
48 ***Packard***	N	N	Y	Y	Y	N	N	Y
49 ***Bilbray***	Y	N	Y	Y	Y	N	N	N
50 Filner	N	Y	N	N	N	Y	Y	Y
51 ***Cunningham***	Y	N	Y	Y	Y	N	N	N
52 ***Hunter***	Y	N	Y	Y	Y	N	N	Y
COLORADO								
1 DeGette	N	Y	Y	N	N	Y	Y	Y
2 Skaggs	N	Y	Y	N	N	Y	Y	Y
3 ***McInnis***	Y	N	Y	Y	Y	N	N	Y
4 ***Schaffer***	Y	N	Y	Y	Y	N	N	N
5 ***Hefley***	Y	N	N	Y	Y	N	N	Y
6 ***Schaefer***	Y	N	Y	Y	Y	N	N	Y
CONNECTICUT								
1 Kennelly	N	Y	Y	N	N	Y	Y	Y
2 Gejdenson	N	Y	Y	N	N	Y	Y	Y
3 DeLauro	N	Y	Y	N	N	Y	Y	Y
4 ***Shays***	Y	N	Y	Y	Y	N	N	Y
5 Maloney	N	Y	Y	N	N	Y	Y	Y
6 ***Johnson***	N	Y	Y	Y	Y	N	N	N
DELAWARE								
AL ***Castle***	N	N	Y	Y	Y	N	N	N
FLORIDA								
1 ***Scarborough***	N	N	N	Y	Y	N	N	N
2 Boyd	N	N	Y	N	N	Y	Y	Y
3 Brown	N	Y	Y	N	N	Y	Y	Y
4 ***Fowler***	N	N	Y	Y	Y	N	N	N
5 Thurman	N	Y	Y	N	N	Y	Y	Y
6 ***Stearns***	Y	N	Y	Y	Y	N	?	N
7 ***Mica***	N	N	Y	Y	Y	N	N	Y
8 ***McCollum***	N	N	Y	Y	Y	N	N	Y
9 ***Bilirakis***	Y	N	Y	Y	Y	N	N	N
10 ***Young***	Y	N	Y	Y	Y	N	N	Y
11 Davis	N	Y	Y	Y	N	Y	Y	Y
12 ***Canady***	Y	N	Y	Y	Y	N	N	Y
13 ***Miller***	Y	N	N	Y	Y	N	N	Y
14 ***Goss***	N	N	Y	Y	Y	N	N	N
15 ***Weldon***	N	N	Y	Y	Y	N	N	Y
16 ***Foley***	N	N	Y	Y	Y	N	N	Y
17 Meek	N	Y	Y	N	N	Y	Y	Y
18 ***Ros-Lehtinen***	Y	N	Y	Y	Y	N	N	Y
19 Wexler	N	Y	Y	N	N	Y	Y	Y
20 Deutsch	N	Y	Y	N	N	Y	Y	Y
21 ***Diaz-Balart***	Y	N	Y	Y	Y	N	N	Y
22 ***Shaw***	N	N	Y	Y	Y	N	N	Y
23 Hastings	N	Y	Y	N	N	Y	Y	Y
GEORGIA								
1 ***Kingston***	Y	N	N	Y	Y	N	N	N
2 Bishop	N	N	Y	N	N	Y	Y	Y
3 ***Collins***	Y	N	Y	Y	Y	N	N	Y
4 McKinney	N	Y	Y	N	N	Y	Y	Y
5 Lewis	N	Y	Y	N	N	Y	Y	Y
6 ***Gingrich***								
7 ***Barr***	Y	N	N	Y	Y	N	N	Y
8 ***Chambliss***	N	N	Y	Y	Y	N	N	Y
9 ***Deal***	Y	N	Y	Y	Y	N	N	N
10 ***Norwood***	Y	N	Y	Y	Y	N	N	Y
11 ***Linder***	Y	N	Y	Y	Y	N	N	Y
HAWAII								
1 Abercrombie	N	Y	Y	N	N	Y	Y	Y
2 Mink	N	Y	Y	N	N	Y	Y	Y
IDAHO								
1 ***Chenoweth***	Y	N	Y	Y	Y	N	N	N
2 ***Crapo***	Y	N	Y	Y	Y	N	N	N
ILLINOIS								
1 Rush	N	Y	Y	N	N	Y	Y	Y
2 Jackson	N	Y	Y	N	N	Y	Y	Y
3 Lipinski	Y	N	Y	Y	N	Y	N	Y
4 Gutierrez	Y	Y	Y	N	N	N	Y	Y
5 Blagojevich	N	Y	Y	N	N	Y	Y	Y
6 ***Hyde***	N	N	Y	Y	Y	N	N	Y
7 Davis	N	Y	Y	N	N	Y	Y	N
8 ***Crane***	Y	N	N	Y	Y	N	N	N
9 Yates	Y	Y	Y	N	N	Y	Y	Y
10 ***Porter***	Y	N	Y	Y	Y	N	N	Y
11 ***Weller***	N	N	Y	Y	Y	N	N	N
12 Costello	Y	Y	Y	N	N	Y	Y	Y
13 ***Fawell***	Y	N	Y	Y	Y	N	N	N
14 ***Hastert***	Y	N	Y	Y	?	N	N	Y

ND Northern Democrats SD Southern Democrats

	278	279	280	281	282	283	284	285
15 **Ewing**	Y	N	Y	Y	Y	N	N	Y
16 **Manzullo**	Y	N	Y	Y	Y	N	N	Y
17 Evans	Y	Y	Y	Y	N	Y	Y	Y
18 **LaHood**	Y	N	Y	Y	Y	N	N	Y
19 Poshard	Y	Y	Y	N	N	Y	Y	Y
20 **Shimkus**	Y	N	Y	Y	Y	N	N	Y
INDIANA								
1 Visclosky	Y	Y	Y	N	N	Y	Y	Y
2 **McIntosh**	Y	N	N	Y	Y	N	N	Y
3 Roemer	Y	Y	N	N	N	Y	Y	Y
4 **Souder**	Y	N	Y	Y	?	N	N	?
5 **Buyer**	Y	N	Y	Y	Y	N	N	Y
6 **Burton**	Y	N	Y	Y	Y	N	N	Y
7 **Pease**	Y	N	Y	Y	Y	N	N	N
8 **Hostettler**	Y	N	N	Y	Y	N	N	Y
9 Hamilton	Y	Y	Y	Y	Y	N	N	N
10 Carson	Y	Y	Y	N	N	Y	Y	Y
IOWA								
1 **Leach**	Y	N	Y	Y	Y	N	N	Y
2 **Nussle**	Y	N	Y	Y	Y	N	N	Y
3 Boswell	N	N	Y	N	N	Y	Y	Y
4 **Ganske**	Y	N	Y	Y	Y	N	N	N
5 **Latham**	Y	N	Y	Y	Y	N	N	Y
KANSAS								
1 **Moran**	Y	N	Y	Y	Y	N	N	Y
2 **Ryun**	N	N	Y	Y	Y	N	N	Y
3 **Snowbarger**	N	N	Y	Y	Y	N	N	Y
4 **Tiahrt**	N	N	Y	Y	Y	N	N	Y
KENTUCKY								
1 **Whitfield**	Y	N	Y	Y	Y	N	N	N
2 **Lewis**	N	N	Y	Y	Y	N	N	Y
3 **Northup**	N	N	Y	Y	Y	N	N	Y
4 **Bunning**	N	N	Y	Y	Y	N	N	Y
5 **Rogers**	N	N	Y	Y	Y	N	N	Y
6 Baesler	N	Y	Y	Y	N	Y	Y	N
LOUISIANA								
1 **Livingston**	N	N	Y	Y	Y	N	N	Y
2 Jefferson	N	Y	Y	N	N	Y	Y	Y
3 **Tauzin**	Y	N	Y	Y	Y	N	N	?
4 **McCrery**	Y	N	Y	Y	Y	N	N	N
5 **Cooksey**	N	N	Y	Y	Y	N	N	Y
6 **Baker**	N	N	Y	Y	Y	N	N	Y
7 John	N	Y	Y	N	N	Y	Y	Y
MAINE								
1 Allen	N	Y	Y	N	N	Y	Y	Y
2 Baldacci	N	Y	Y	Y	N	Y	Y	Y
MARYLAND								
1 **Gilchrest**	N	N	Y	Y	Y	N	N	Y
2 **Ehrlich**	N	N	Y	Y	Y	N	N	Y
3 Cardin	N	Y	Y	Y	N	N	N	N
4 Wynn	N	Y	Y	N	N	Y	Y	Y
5 Hoyer	N	Y	Y	N	N	Y	Y	Y
6 **Bartlett**	Y	N	Y	Y	Y	N	N	Y
7 Cummings	N	Y	Y	N	N	Y	Y	Y
8 **Morella**	Y	N	Y	Y	Y	N	N	Y
MASSACHUSETTS								
1 Olver	Y	Y	Y	N	N	Y	Y	Y
2 Neal	N	Y	Y	Y	N	Y	Y	Y
3 McGovern	N	Y	Y	N	N	Y	Y	Y
4 Frank	Y	Y	Y	N	Y	Y	Y	Y
5 Meehan	Y	Y	Y	N	N	Y	Y	Y
6 Tierney	Y	Y	Y	N	N	Y	Y	Y
7 Markey	Y	N	N	N	N	?	?	Y
8 Kennedy	N	Y	N	N	N	Y	Y	Y
9 Moakley	Y	Y	Y	Y	N	Y	Y	Y
10 Delahunt	Y	Y	Y	N	N	Y	Y	Y
MICHIGAN								
1 Stupak	Y	Y	Y	N	N	Y	Y	Y
2 **Hoekstra**	Y	N	N	Y	Y	N	N	Y
3 **Ehlers**	Y	-	Y	Y	Y	N	N	N
4 **Camp**	Y	N	Y	Y	Y	N	N	Y
5 Barcia	N	Y	Y	N	N	Y	Y	Y
6 **Upton**	Y	N	Y	Y	Y	N	N	Y
7 **Smith**	Y	N	Y	Y	Y	N	N	N
8 Stabenow	Y	Y	Y	N	N	Y	Y	Y
9 Kildee	N	Y	Y	N	N	Y	Y	Y
10 Bonior	N	Y	Y	N	N	Y	Y	Y
11 **Knollenberg**	N	N	Y	Y	Y	N	N	Y
12 Levin	Y	Y	Y	N	N	Y	Y	Y
13 Rivers	Y	Y	Y	N	N	N	N	N
14 Conyers	N	Y	Y	?	N	Y	Y	Y
15 Kilpatrick	N	Y	Y	N	N	Y	Y	Y
16 Dingell	Y	Y	Y	N	N	Y	Y	Y
MINNESOTA								
1 **Gutknecht**	Y	N	Y	Y	Y	N	N	?
2 Minge	Y	Y	N	N	N	Y	Y	Y

	278	279	280	281	282	283	284	285
3 **Ramstad**	Y	N	Y	Y	Y	N	N	N
4 Vento	Y	Y	Y	N	N	Y	Y	Y
5 Sabo	N	Y	Y	N	N	Y	Y	Y
6 Luther	Y	Y	Y	N	N	Y	Y	Y
7 Peterson	N	Y	Y	N	N	Y	Y	Y
8 Oberstar	Y	Y	Y	Y	N	Y	Y	Y
MISSISSIPPI								
1 **Wicker**	N	N	Y	Y	Y	N	N	Y
2 Thompson	N	Y	Y	Y	N	Y	Y	Y
3 **Pickering**	Y	N	Y	Y	Y	N	N	Y
4 **Parker**	N	N	Y	Y	Y	N	N	Y
5 Taylor	N	N	Y	Y	N	N	N	N
MISSOURI								
1 Clay	N	Y	Y	N	N	Y	Y	Y
2 **Talent**	Y	N	Y	Y	Y	N	N	Y
3 Gephardt	N	Y	Y	Y	N	Y	Y	Y
4 Skelton	Y	Y	Y	Y	Y	Y	Y	Y
5 McCarthy	Y	Y	Y	N	N	Y	Y	Y
6 Danner	Y	Y	Y	Y	N	Y	Y	Y
7 **Blunt**	Y	N	Y	Y	Y	N	N	Y
8 **Emerson**	Y	N	Y	Y	Y	N	N	N
9 **Hulshof**	N	N	Y	Y	Y	N	N	Y
MONTANA								
AL **Hill**	Y	N	Y	Y	Y	N	N	Y
NEBRASKA								
1 **Bereuter**	Y	N	Y	Y	Y	N	N	Y
2 **Christensen**	Y	N	Y	Y	Y	N	N	Y
3 **Barrett**	N	N	Y	Y	Y	N	N	Y
NEVADA								
1 **Ensign**	Y	N	Y	Y	Y	N	N	Y
2 **Gibbons**	Y	N	Y	Y	Y	N	N	Y
NEW HAMPSHIRE								
1 **Sununu**	Y	N	Y	Y	Y	N	N	Y
2 **Bass**	Y	N	Y	Y	Y	N	N	Y
NEW JERSEY								
1 Andrews	N	Y	Y	N	N	Y	Y	Y
2 **LoBiondo**	Y	N	Y	Y	Y	N	N	Y
3 **Saxton**	N	N	Y	Y	Y	N	N	N
4 **Smith**	Y	N	Y	Y	Y	N	N	Y
5 **Roukema**	Y	N	Y	?	?	N	N	Y
6 Pallone	Y	Y	Y	N	N	Y	Y	Y
7 **Franks**	N	N	Y	Y	Y	N	N	Y
8 Pascrell	N	Y	Y	N	N	Y	Y	Y
9 Rothman	N	Y	Y	N	N	Y	Y	Y
10 Payne	N	Y	Y	N	N	Y	Y	?
11 **Frelinghuysen**	N	N	Y	Y	Y	N	N	N
12 **Pappas**	Y	N	Y	Y	Y	N	N	Y
13 Menendez	Y	Y	Y	N	N	Y	Y	Y
NEW MEXICO								
1 **Schiff**	?	?	?	?	?	?	?	?
2 **Skeen**	N	N	Y	Y	Y	N	N	N
3 **Redmond**	N	N	Y	Y	Y	N	N	Y
NEW YORK								
1 **Forbes**	N	N	Y	+	+	-	-	+
2 **Lazio**	Y	N	Y	Y	Y	N	N	Y
3 **King**	N	N	Y	Y	Y	N	N	Y
4 McCarthy	N	Y	Y	N	N	Y	Y	N
5 Ackerman	N	Y	Y	N	N	Y	Y	Y
6 Flake	N	Y	Y	N	N	Y	Y	Y
7 Manton	N	Y	Y	N	N	Y	Y	?
8 Nadler	Y	Y	Y	N	N	Y	Y	Y
9 Schumer	Y	Y	Y	N	N	Y	Y	Y
10 Towns	N	Y	Y	N	N	Y	Y	Y
11 Owens	N	Y	Y	N	N	Y	Y	Y
12 Velázquez	N	Y	Y	N	N	Y	Y	Y
13 **Molinari**	Y	N	Y	?	Y	N	N	Y
14 Maloney	N	Y	Y	N	N	Y	Y	Y
15 Rangel	?	Y	Y	N	N	Y	Y	Y
16 Serrano	Y	Y	Y	N	N	Y	Y	Y
17 Engel	N	Y	Y	N	N	Y	Y	Y
18 Lowey	Y	Y	Y	N	N	Y	Y	Y
19 **Kelly**	Y	N	Y	Y	Y	N	N	Y
20 **Gilman**	Y	N	Y	Y	Y	N	N	Y
21 McNulty	Y	Y	Y	N	N	Y	Y	Y
22 **Solomon**	Y	?	?	Y	Y	N	N	N
23 **Boehlert**	Y	N	Y	?	Y	N	N	Y
24 **McHugh**	N	N	Y	Y	Y	N	?	?
25 **Walsh**	N	N	Y	Y	Y	N	N	N
26 Hinchey	N	Y	Y	N	N	Y	Y	Y
27 **Paxon**	Y	N	Y	Y	Y	N	N	Y
28 Slaughter	Y	Y	Y	N	N	Y	Y	Y
29 LaFalce	Y	Y	Y	Y	N	Y	Y	Y
30 **Quinn**	Y	N	Y	Y	Y	N	N	Y
31 **Houghton**	N	N	Y	?	Y	N	N	N

	278	279	280	281	282	283	284	285
NORTH CAROLINA								
1 Clayton	N	Y	Y	N	N	Y	Y	Y
2 Etheridge	N	Y	Y	N	N	Y	Y	N
3 **Jones**	Y	N	Y	Y	Y	N	N	Y
4 Price	N	Y	Y	Y	Y	Y	Y	Y
5 **Burr**	N	N	Y	Y	Y	N	N	Y
6 **Coble**	Y	N	Y	Y	Y	N	N	Y
7 McIntyre	N	Y	Y	Y	Y	N	N	N
8 Hefner	Y	Y	Y	N	N	Y	Y	Y
9 **Myrick**	N	N	Y	Y	Y	N	N	Y
10 **Ballenger**	Y	N	Y	Y	Y	N	N	Y
11 **Taylor**	Y	N	Y	Y	Y	N	N	Y
12 Watt	N	Y	Y	N	N	Y	Y	Y
NORTH DAKOTA								
AL Pomeroy	Y	Y	Y	N	Y	Y	Y	Y
OHIO								
1 **Chabot**	Y	N	Y	Y	Y	N	N	Y
2 **Portman**	+	N	Y	Y	Y	N	N	Y
3 Hall	N	Y	Y	Y	N	Y	Y	Y
4 **Oxley**	N	N	Y	Y	Y	?	N	?
5 **Gillmor**	Y	N	Y	Y	Y	N	N	Y
6 Strickland	Y	Y	Y	N	N	Y	Y	Y
7 **Hobson**	N	N	Y	Y	Y	N	N	N
8 **Boehner**	N	N	Y	Y	Y	N	N	Y
9 Kaptur	Y	Y	Y	N	N	Y	Y	Y
10 Kucinich	N	Y	Y	N	N	Y	Y	Y
11 Stokes	N	N	Y	N	N	Y	Y	?
12 **Kasich**	Y	N	Y	Y	Y	?	N	Y
13 Brown	Y	Y	Y	N	N	Y	Y	Y
14 Sawyer	N	Y	Y	N	N	Y	Y	N
15 **Pryce**	N	N	Y	Y	Y	N	N	Y
16 **Regula**	N	N	Y	Y	Y	N	N	N
17 Traficant	Y	Y	Y	Y	Y	N	N	N
18 **Ney**	N	N	Y	Y	Y	?	N	Y
19 **LaTourette**	N	N	Y	Y	Y	N	N	?
OKLAHOMA								
1 **Largent**	Y	N	N	Y	Y	N	N	Y
2 **Coburn**	Y	N	Y	Y	Y	N	N	N
3 **Watkins**	Y	N	Y	Y	Y	N	N	N
4 **Watts**	Y	N	Y	Y	Y	N	N	Y
5 **Istook**	Y	N	N	Y	Y	N	N	Y
6 **Lucas**	Y	N	Y	Y	Y	N	N	Y
OREGON								
1 Furse	N	Y	Y	N	?	?	?	?
2 **Smith**	N	N	Y	Y	Y	N	N	Y
3 Blumenauer	Y	Y	Y	N	N	Y	Y	Y
4 DeFazio	Y	Y	Y	N	N	Y	Y	Y
5 Hooley	Y	Y	Y	N	N	Y	Y	Y
PENNSYLVANIA								
1 Foglietta	N	Y	Y	N	N	Y	Y	Y
2 Fattah	Y	Y	Y	N	N	Y	?	?
3 Borski	Y	Y	Y	Y	N	Y	Y	Y
4 Klink	Y	Y	Y	Y	Y	Y	Y	Y
5 **Peterson**	Y	N	Y	Y	Y	N	N	N
6 Holden	Y	Y	Y	Y	Y	Y	Y	Y
7 **Weldon**	Y	N	Y	Y	Y	N	N	Y
8 **Greenwood**	N	N	Y	Y	Y	N	N	Y
9 **Shuster**	Y	N	Y	Y	Y	N	N	Y
10 **McDade**	N	N	Y	Y	Y	N	N	Y
11 Kanjorski	Y	Y	Y	Y	Y	Y	Y	Y
12 Murtha	N	Y	?	Y	Y	Y	Y	Y
13 **Fox**	N	N	Y	Y	Y	N	N	Y
14 Coyne	Y	Y	Y	N	N	Y	Y	Y
15 McHale	N	Y	Y	N	N	Y	Y	Y
16 **Pitts**	Y	N	Y	Y	Y	N	N	Y
17 **Gekas**	Y	N	Y	Y	Y	N	N	Y
18 Doyle	Y	Y	Y	Y	Y	Y	Y	Y
19 **Goodling**	N	N	Y	Y	Y	N	?	Y
20 Mascara	Y	Y	Y	N	N	Y	Y	Y
21 **English**	Y	N	Y	Y	Y	N	N	N
RHODE ISLAND								
1 Kennedy	N	Y	N	N	N	Y	Y	Y
2 Weygand	N	+	+	N	N	Y	Y	Y
SOUTH CAROLINA								
1 **Sanford**	Y	N	N	Y	Y	N	N	N
2 **Spence**	Y	N	Y	Y	Y	N	N	Y
3 **Graham**	N	N	Y	Y	Y	N	N	Y
4 **Inglis**	Y	N	Y	Y	Y	N	N	Y
5 Spratt	?	Y	Y	N	N	Y	Y	Y
6 Clyburn	N	Y	Y	N	N	Y	Y	Y
SOUTH DAKOTA								
AL **Thune**	Y	N	Y	Y	Y	N	N	Y

	278	279	280	281	282	283	284	
TENNESSEE								
1 **Jenkins**	Y	N	Y	Y	Y	N	N	Y
2 **Duncan**	Y	N	N	Y	Y	N	N	Y
3 **Wamp**	Y	N	Y	Y	Y	N	N	Y
4 **Hilleary**	Y	N	Y	Y	Y	N	N	N
5 Clement	N	Y	Y	N	N	Y	Y	Y
6 Gordon	N	Y	Y	N	N	N	N	N
7 **Bryant**	Y	N	Y	Y	Y	N	N	Y
8 Tanner	N	Y	Y	N	N	Y	Y	Y
9 Ford	N	Y	Y	N	N	Y	?	Y
TEXAS								
1 Sandlin	N	Y	Y	N	N	Y	Y	Y
2 Turner	N	N	Y	N	N	Y	Y	Y
3 **Johnson, Sam**	Y	N	N	Y	Y	N	N	Y
4 Hall	N	Y	Y	Y	N	Y	Y	N
5 **Sessions**	N	N	Y	Y	Y	N	N	Y
6 **Barton**	N	N	Y	Y	Y	N	N	Y
7 **Archer**	N	N	Y	Y	Y	N	N	Y
8 **Brady**	N	N	Y	Y	Y	N	N	Y
9 Lampson	N	Y	Y	N	N	Y	Y	Y
10 Doggett	N	Y	N	N	Y	Y	Y	Y
11 Edwards	N	Y	Y	N	N	Y	Y	Y
12 **Granger**	N	N	Y	Y	Y	N	N	Y
13 **Thornberry**	N	N	N	Y	Y	N	N	Y
14 **Paul**	Y	N	N	Y	Y	N	N	Y
15 Hinojosa	N	Y	Y	N	N	Y	Y	Y
16 Reyes	N	Y	Y	N	N	Y	Y	Y
17 Stenholm	N	Y	Y	Y	N	Y	Y	Y
18 Jackson-Lee	N	Y	Y	N	N	Y	Y	Y
19 **Combest**	Y	N	Y	Y	Y	N	N	Y
20 Gonzalez	?	Y	Y	?	N	Y	Y	Y
21 **Smith**	Y	N	Y	?	Y	N	N	Y
22 **DeLay**	N	N	Y	Y	Y	N	N	Y
23 **Bonilla**	N	N	Y	Y	Y	N	N	Y
24 Frost	N	Y	Y	N	N	Y	Y	Y
25 Bentsen	N	Y	Y	N	N	Y	Y	Y
26 **Armey**	N	N	Y	Y	Y	N	N	Y
27 Ortiz	N	Y	Y	Y	N	Y	Y	Y
28 Rodriguez	N	Y	Y	N	N	Y	Y	Y
29 Green	N	Y	Y	N	N	Y	Y	N
30 Johnson, E.B.	N	Y	Y	N	N	Y	Y	Y
UTAH								
1 **Hansen**	N	N	Y	Y	Y	N	N	Y
2 **Cook**	Y	N	Y	Y	Y	N	N	N
3 **Cannon**	Y	N	Y	Y	Y	N	N	Y
VERMONT								
AL Sanders	Y	Y	Y	N	N	Y	Y	Y
VIRGINIA								
1 **Bateman**	N	N	Y	Y	Y	N	N	Y
2 Pickett	N	Y	Y	Y	Y	N	N	N
3 Scott	N	Y	Y	N	N	Y	Y	N
4 Sisisky	N	Y	Y	Y	Y	Y	Y	Y
5 Goode	Y	N	Y	Y	Y	N	N	N
6 **Goodlatte**	Y	N	Y	Y	Y	N	N	Y
7 **Bliley**	Y	N	Y	Y	Y	N	N	Y
8 Moran	N	Y	Y	N	N	Y	Y	?
9 Boucher	N	Y	Y	Y	N	Y	Y	Y
10 **Wolf**	N	N	Y	Y	Y	N	N	Y
11 **Davis**	Y	N	Y	Y	Y	N	N	N
WASHINGTON								
1 **White**	N	N	Y	Y	Y	N	N	Y
2 **Metcalf**	N	N	Y	Y	Y	N	N	Y
3 **Smith, Linda**	N	N	Y	Y	Y	N	N	Y
4 **Hastings**	N	N	Y	Y	Y	N	N	Y
5 **Nethercutt**	Y	N	Y	Y	Y	N	N	Y
6 Dicks	N	Y	Y	N	N	Y	Y	Y
7 McDermott	N	Y	Y	N	N	Y	Y	Y
8 **Dunn**	N	N	Y	Y	Y	N	N	Y
9 Smith, Adam	N	Y	Y	N	N	Y	Y	Y
WEST VIRGINIA								
1 Mollohan	N	N	Y	Y	Y	Y	N	Y
2 Wise	N	Y	Y	Y	N	Y	Y	Y
3 Rahall	N	Y	Y	Y	Y	N	N	N
WISCONSIN								
1 **Neumann**	Y	N	Y	Y	Y	N	?	Y
2 **Klug**	Y	N	N	Y	Y	N	N	Y
3 Kind	Y	Y	Y	N	N	Y	Y	Y
4 Kleczka	Y	Y	Y	N	N	Y	Y	Y
5 Barrett	Y	Y	Y	N	N	Y	Y	Y
6 **Petri**	Y	N	N	Y	?	N	N	N
7 Obey	Y	Y	Y	N	N	Y	Y	Y
8 Johnson	N	Y	Y	N	N	Y	Y	Y
9 **Sensenbrenner**	Y	N	N	Y	Y	N	N	Y
WYOMING								
AL **Cubin**	Y	N	Y	Y	Y	N	N	Y

Southern states - Ala., Ark., Fla., Ga., Ky., La., Miss., N.C., Okla., S.C., Tenn., Texas, Va.

HOUSE VOTES 286, 287, 288, 289, 290, 291, 292, 293

286. HR 1853. Vocational-Technical Education/Gender Equity. Mink, D-Hawaii, amendment to require states and localities to spend a minimum of 10.5 percent of federal vocational education funds on programs that promote gender equity and assist displaced homemakers, single parents and single pregnant women. The amendment also would require each state to establish a sex-equity coordinator, as required under current law. Rejected 207-214: R 10-212; D 196-2 (ND 146-0, SD 50-2); I 1-0, July 22, 1997.

287. HR 1853. Vocational-Technical Education/Workforce Development Coordinator. Kennedy, D-Mass., amendment to allow local recipients of vocational education grants to use funds for a work force development coordinator, who would work with local businesses to develop a vocational education curriculum. Rejected 189-230: R 3-217; D 185-13 (ND 138-7, SD 47-6); I 1-0, July 22, 1997.

288. HR 1853. Vocational-Technical Education/Recommit. Mink, D-Hawaii, motion to recommit the bill to the Education and the Workforce Committee with instructions to report it back with an amendment to require states and localities to continue to fund at fiscal 1997 levels vocational education programs that promote gender equity and assist displaced homemakers, single parents and single pregnant women. Motion rejected 207-220: R 7-217; D 199-3 (ND 147-1, SD 52-2); I 1-0, July 22, 1997.

289. HR 1853. Vocational-Technical Education/Passage. Passage of the bill to reauthorize the Carl D. Perkins Vocational and Applied Technology Education Act through fiscal 2002 and provide an authorization of $1.3 billion for the program in fiscal 1998. The bill gradually changes the formula by which federal vocational education funds are allocated to states and distributed within each state. Passed 414-12: R 217-6; D 196-6 (ND 142-6, SD 54-0); I 1-0, July 22, 1997.

290. HR 765. Wild Horse Preservation/Passage. Hansen, R-Utah, motion to suspend the rules and pass the bill to direct the National Park Service to maintain a herd of 100 to 110 wild horses at the Cape Lookout National Seashore in North Carolina. Motion agreed to 416-6: R 216-5; D 199-1 (ND 146-1, SD 53-0); I 1-0, July 22, 1997. A two-thirds majority of those present and voting (282 in this case) is required for passage under suspension of the rules. A "nay" was a vote in support of the president's position.

291. HR 1944. Warner Canyon Ski Hill Land Exchange/Passage. Chenoweth, R-Idaho, motion to suspend the rules and pass the bill to authorize the Forest Service to transfer approximately 295 acres of national forest comprising the Warner Canyon Ski Hill to Lake County, Ore., in exchange for 320 acres of land owned by the county within the Hart Mountain National Antelope Refuge. Motion agreed to 423-0: R 223-0; D 199-0 (ND 146-0, SD 53-0); I 1-0, July 22, 1997. A two-thirds majority of those present and voting (282 in this case) is required for passage under suspension of the rules.

292. HR 1663. Emigrant Wilderness Dam Maintenance/Passage. Chenoweth, R-Idaho, motion to suspend the rules and pass the bill to require the Forest Service to allow a private organization to operate and maintain 18 dams and concrete weirs in the Emigrant Wilderness Area in California. The bill requires the private organization to pay the expenses to maintain and operate the dams. Motion agreed to 424-2: R 221-2; D 202-0 (ND 147-0, SD 55-0); I 1-0, July 22, 1997. A two-thirds majority of those present and voting (284 in this case) is required for passage under suspension of the rules.

293. HR 1661. Trademark Law Treaty Implementation/Passage. Coble, R-N.C., motion to suspend the rules and pass the bill to harmonize U.S. trademark registration requirements with those of other nations in the World Trade Organization to comply with a 1994 international trademark treaty. The bill includes provisions that would provide U.S. manufacturers with the same 10-year patent protections in foreign countries as other competitors in those countries. Motion agreed to 425-0: R 223-0; D 201-0 (ND 146-0, SD 55-0); I 1-0, July 22, 1997. A two-thirds majority of those present and voting (284 in this case) is required for passage under suspension of the rules. A "yea" was a vote in support of the president's position.

KEY

Y Voted for (yea).
\# Paired for.
\+ Announced for.
N Voted against (nay).
X Paired against.
\- Announced against.
P Voted "present."
C Voted "present" to avoid possible conflict of interest.
? Did not vote or otherwise make a position known.

Democrats ***Republicans***
Independent

	286	287	288	289	290	291	292	293
ALABAMA								
1 ***Callahan***	N	N	N	Y	Y	Y	Y	Y
2 ***Everett***	N	N	N	Y	Y	Y	Y	Y
3 ***Riley***	N	N	N	Y	Y	Y	Y	Y
4 ***Aderholt***	N	N	N	Y	Y	Y	Y	Y
5 Cramer	Y	Y	Y	Y	Y	Y	Y	Y
6 ***Bachus***	N	N	N	Y	Y	Y	Y	Y
7 Hilliard	Y	Y	Y	Y	Y	Y	Y	Y
ALASKA								
AL ***Young***	?	?	?	?	?	?	?	?
ARIZONA								
1 ***Salmon***	N	N	N	Y	Y	Y	Y	Y
2 Pastor	Y	Y	Y	Y	Y	Y	Y	Y
3 ***Stump***	N	N	N	Y	Y	Y	N	Y
4 ***Shadegg***	N	N	N	Y	Y	Y	Y	Y
5 ***Kolbe***	N	N	N	Y	Y	Y	Y	Y
6 ***Hayworth***	N	N	N	Y	Y	Y	Y	Y
ARKANSAS								
1 Berry	Y	Y	Y	Y	Y	Y	Y	Y
2 Snyder	Y	Y	Y	Y	Y	Y	Y	Y
3 ***Hutchinson***	N	N	N	Y	Y	Y	Y	Y
4 ***Dickey***	N	N	N	N	Y	Y	Y	Y
CALIFORNIA								
1 ***Riggs***	N	N	N	Y	Y	Y	Y	Y
2 ***Herger***	N	N	N	Y	Y	Y	Y	Y
3 Fazio	Y	Y	Y	Y	Y	Y	Y	Y
4 ***Doolittle***	N	N	N	Y	Y	Y	Y	Y
5 Matsui	Y	Y	Y	Y	Y	Y	Y	Y
6 Woolsey	Y	Y	Y	Y	Y	Y	Y	Y
7 Miller	Y	Y	Y	Y	Y	Y	Y	Y
8 Pelosi	Y	Y	Y	Y	Y	Y	Y	Y
9 Dellums	Y	Y	Y	Y	Y	Y	Y	Y
10 Tauscher	Y	Y	Y	Y	Y	Y	Y	Y
11 ***Pombo***	N	N	N	Y	Y	Y	Y	Y
12 Lantos	Y	Y	Y	Y	Y	Y	Y	Y
13 Stark	Y	Y	Y	N	Y	Y	Y	Y
14 Eshoo	Y	Y	Y	Y	Y	Y	Y	Y
15 ***Campbell***	N	N	N	N	N	Y	Y	Y
16 Lofgren	Y	Y	Y	Y	Y	Y	Y	Y
17 Farr	Y	Y	Y	Y	Y	Y	Y	Y
18 Condit	Y	N	Y	Y	Y	Y	Y	Y
19 ***Radanovich***	N	N	N	Y	Y	Y	Y	Y
20 Dooley	Y	Y	Y	Y	Y	Y	Y	Y
21 ***Thomas***	N	?	N	Y	Y	Y	Y	Y
22 Capps	Y	Y	Y	Y	Y	Y	Y	Y
23 ***Gallegly***	N	N	N	Y	Y	Y	Y	Y
24 Sherman	Y	Y	Y	Y	Y	Y	Y	Y
25 ***McKeon***	N	N	N	Y	Y	Y	Y	Y
26 Berman	Y	Y	Y	Y	Y	Y	Y	Y
27 ***Rogan***	N	N	N	Y	Y	Y	Y	Y
28 ***Dreier***	N	N	N	Y	Y	Y	Y	Y
29 Waxman	Y	Y	Y	Y	Y	Y	Y	Y
30 Becerra	Y	Y	Y	Y	Y	Y	Y	Y
31 Martinez	Y	Y	Y	Y	Y	Y	Y	Y
32 Dixon	Y	Y	Y	Y	Y	Y	Y	Y
33 Roybal-Allard	Y	Y	Y	Y	Y	Y	Y	Y
34 Torres	Y	Y	Y	Y	Y	Y	Y	Y
35 Waters	Y	Y	Y	Y	Y	Y	Y	Y
36 Harman	Y	Y	Y	Y	Y	Y	Y	Y
37 Millender-McD.	Y	Y	Y	Y	Y	Y	Y	Y
38 ***Horn***	Y	N	Y	Y	Y	Y	Y	Y
39 ***Royce***	N	N	N	N	Y	Y	Y	Y
40 ***Lewis***	N	N	N	Y	Y	Y	Y	Y
41 ***Kim***	N	N	N	Y	Y	Y	Y	Y
42 Brown	Y	Y	Y	Y	Y	Y	Y	Y
43 ***Calvert***	N	N	N	Y	Y	Y	Y	Y
44 ***Bono***	N	N	N	Y	Y	Y	Y	Y
45 ***Rohrabacher***	N	N	N	N	Y	Y	Y	Y
46 Sanchez	Y	Y	Y	Y	Y	Y	Y	Y
47 ***Cox***	N	?	N	Y	Y	Y	Y	Y
48 ***Packard***	N	N	N	Y	Y	Y	Y	Y
49 ***Bilbray***	N	N	N	Y	Y	Y	Y	Y
50 Filner	Y	Y	Y	Y	Y	Y	Y	Y
51 ***Cunningham***	N	N	N	Y	Y	Y	Y	Y
52 ***Hunter***	N	N	N	Y	Y	Y	Y	Y
COLORADO								
1 DeGette	Y	Y	Y	Y	Y	Y	Y	Y
2 Skaggs	Y	Y	Y	Y	Y	Y	Y	Y
3 ***McInnis***	N	N	N	Y	Y	Y	Y	Y
4 ***Schaffer***	N	N	N	Y	Y	Y	Y	Y
5 ***Hefley***	N	N	N	Y	Y	Y	Y	Y
6 ***Schaefer***	N	N	N	Y	Y	Y	Y	Y
CONNECTICUT								
1 Kennelly	Y	Y	Y	Y	Y	Y	Y	Y
2 Gejdenson	Y	Y	Y	Y	Y	Y	Y	Y
3 DeLauro	Y	Y	Y	Y	Y	Y	Y	Y
4 ***Shays***	Y	N	Y	Y	Y	Y	Y	Y
5 Maloney	Y	?	Y	Y	Y	Y	Y	Y
6 ***Johnson***	Y	N	Y	Y	Y	Y	Y	Y
DELAWARE								
AL ***Castle***	N	N	N	Y	Y	Y	Y	Y
FLORIDA								
1 ***Scarborough***	N	N	N	Y	N	Y	Y	Y
2 Boyd	Y	N	Y	Y	Y	Y	Y	Y
3 Brown	Y	Y	Y	Y	Y	Y	Y	Y
4 ***Fowler***	N	N	N	Y	Y	Y	Y	Y
5 Thurman	Y	Y	Y	Y	Y	Y	Y	Y
6 ***Stearns***	N	N	N	Y	Y	Y	Y	Y
7 ***Mica***	N	N	N	Y	Y	Y	Y	Y
8 ***McCollum***	N	N	N	Y	Y	Y	Y	Y
9 ***Bilirakis***	N	N	N	Y	Y	Y	Y	Y
10 ***Young***	N	N	N	Y	Y	Y	Y	Y
11 Davis	Y	Y	Y	Y	Y	Y	Y	Y
12 ***Canady***	N	N	N	Y	Y	Y	Y	Y
13 ***Miller***	N	N	N	Y	Y	Y	Y	Y
14 ***Goss***	N	N	N	Y	Y	Y	Y	Y
15 ***Weldon***	N	N	N	Y	Y	Y	Y	Y
16 ***Foley***	N	N	N	Y	Y	Y	Y	Y
17 Meek	Y	Y	Y	Y	Y	Y	Y	Y
18 ***Ros-Lehtinen***	N	N	N	Y	Y	Y	Y	Y
19 Wexler	Y	Y	Y	Y	Y	Y	Y	Y
20 Deutsch	Y	Y	Y	Y	Y	Y	Y	Y
21 ***Diaz-Balart***	N	N	N	Y	Y	Y	Y	Y
22 ***Shaw***	N	N	N	Y	Y	Y	Y	Y
23 Hastings	Y	Y	Y	Y	Y	Y	Y	Y
GEORGIA								
1 ***Kingston***	N	N	N	Y	Y	Y	Y	Y
2 Bishop	Y	Y	Y	Y	Y	Y	Y	Y
3 ***Collins***	N	N	N	Y	Y	Y	Y	Y
4 McKinney	Y	Y	Y	Y	Y	?	Y	Y
5 Lewis	Y	Y	Y	Y	Y	Y	Y	Y
6 ***Gingrich***			N					
7 ***Barr***	N	N	N	Y	Y	Y	Y	Y
8 ***Chambliss***	N	N	N	Y	Y	Y	Y	Y
9 ***Deal***	N	N	N	Y	Y	Y	Y	Y
10 ***Norwood***	N	N	N	Y	Y	Y	Y	Y
11 ***Linder***	N	N	N	Y	Y	Y	Y	Y
HAWAII								
1 Abercrombie	Y	Y	Y	Y	Y	Y	Y	Y
2 Mink	Y	Y	Y	N	Y	Y	Y	Y
IDAHO								
1 ***Chenoweth***	N	N	N	Y	Y	Y	Y	Y
2 ***Crapo***	N	N	N	Y	Y	Y	Y	Y
ILLINOIS								
1 Rush	Y	Y	Y	Y	Y	?	Y	Y
2 Jackson	Y	Y	Y	Y	Y	Y	Y	Y
3 Lipinski	Y	N	Y	Y	Y	Y	Y	Y
4 Gutierrez	Y	Y	Y	Y	Y	Y	Y	Y
5 Blagojevich	Y	Y	Y	Y	Y	Y	Y	Y
6 ***Hyde***	N	N	N	Y	Y	Y	Y	Y
7 Davis	Y	Y	Y	Y	Y	Y	Y	Y
8 ***Crane***	N	N	N	Y	Y	Y	Y	Y
9 Yates	Y	Y	Y	Y	?	?	?	?
10 ***Porter***	N	N	N	Y	Y	Y	Y	Y
11 ***Weller***	N	N	N	Y	Y	Y	Y	Y
12 Costello	Y	Y	Y	Y	Y	Y	Y	Y
13 ***Fawell***	N	N	N	Y	Y	Y	Y	Y
14 ***Hastert***	N	N	N	Y	Y	Y	Y	Y
15 ***Ewing***	N	N	N	Y	Y	Y	Y	Y

ND Northern Democrats SD Southern Democrats

	286	287	288	289	290	291	292	293
16 **Manzullo**	N	N	N	Y	Y	Y	Y	Y
17 Evans	Y	Y	Y	Y	Y	Y	Y	Y
18 **LaHood**	N	N	N	Y	Y	Y	Y	Y
19 Poshard	Y	Y	Y	Y	Y	Y	Y	Y
20 **Shimkus**	N	N	N	Y	Y	Y	Y	Y
INDIANA								
1 Visclosky	Y	Y	Y	Y	Y	Y	Y	Y
2 **McIntosh**	N	N	N	Y	Y	Y	Y	Y
3 Roemer	Y	Y	Y	Y	Y	Y	Y	Y
4 **Souder**	N	N	N	Y	Y	Y	Y	Y
5 **Buyer**	N	N	N	Y	Y	Y	Y	Y
6 **Burton**	N	N	N	Y	Y	Y	Y	Y
7 **Pease**	N	N	N	Y	Y	Y	Y	Y
8 **Hostettler**	N	N	N	Y	Y	Y	Y	Y
9 Hamilton	Y	Y	Y	Y	Y	Y	Y	Y
10 Carson	Y	Y	Y	Y	N	Y	Y	Y
IOWA								
1 **Leach**	Y	N	N	Y	Y	Y	Y	Y
2 **Nussle**	N	N	N	Y	Y	Y	Y	Y
3 Boswell	Y	Y	Y	Y	Y	Y	Y	Y
4 **Ganske**	N	N	N	Y	Y	Y	Y	Y
5 **Latham**	N	N	N	Y	Y	Y	Y	Y
KANSAS								
1 **Moran**	N	N	N	Y	Y	Y	Y	Y
2 **Ryun**	N	N	N	Y	Y	Y	Y	Y
3 **Snowbarger**	N	N	N	Y	Y	Y	Y	Y
4 **Tiahrt**	N	N	N	Y	Y	Y	Y	Y
KENTUCKY								
1 **Whitfield**	N	N	N	Y	Y	Y	Y	Y
2 **Lewis**	N	N	N	Y	Y	Y	Y	Y
3 **Northup**	N	N	N	Y	Y	Y	Y	Y
4 **Bunning**	N	N	N	Y	Y	Y	Y	Y
5 **Rogers**	N	N	N	Y	Y	Y	Y	Y
6 Baesler	Y	Y	Y	Y	Y	Y	Y	Y
LOUISIANA								
1 **Livingston**	N	N	N	Y	Y	Y	Y	Y
2 Jefferson	Y	?	Y	Y	Y	Y	Y	Y
3 **Tauzin**	N	N	N	Y	Y	Y	Y	Y
4 **McCrery**	N	N	N	Y	Y	Y	Y	Y
5 **Cooksey**	N	N	N	Y	Y	Y	Y	Y
6 **Baker**	N	N	N	Y	Y	Y	Y	Y
7 John	Y	Y	Y	Y	?	Y	Y	Y
MAINE								
1 Allen	Y	Y	Y	Y	Y	Y	Y	Y
2 Baldacci	Y	Y	Y	Y	Y	Y	Y	Y
MARYLAND								
1 **Gilchrest**	N	N	N	Y	Y	Y	Y	Y
2 **Ehrlich**	N	N	N	Y	Y	Y	Y	Y
3 Cardin	Y	Y	Y	Y	Y	Y	Y	Y
4 Wynn	Y	Y	Y	Y	Y	Y	Y	Y
5 Hoyer	Y	Y	Y	Y	Y	Y	Y	Y
6 **Bartlett**	N	N	N	Y	Y	Y	Y	Y
7 Cummings	Y	Y	Y	Y	Y	Y	Y	Y
8 **Morella**	Y	N	Y	Y	Y	Y	Y	Y
MASSACHUSETTS								
1 Olver	Y	Y	Y	N	Y	Y	Y	Y
2 Neal	Y	Y	Y	Y	Y	Y	Y	Y
3 McGovern	Y	Y	Y	Y	Y	Y	Y	Y
4 Frank	Y	Y	Y	Y	Y	Y	Y	Y
5 Meehan	Y	Y	Y	Y	Y	Y	Y	Y
6 Tierney	Y	Y	Y	Y	Y	Y	Y	Y
7 Markey	Y	Y	Y	Y	Y	Y	Y	Y
8 Kennedy	Y	Y	Y	Y	Y	Y	Y	Y
9 Moakley	Y	Y	Y	Y	Y	Y	Y	Y
10 Delahunt	Y	Y	Y	Y	Y	Y	Y	Y
MICHIGAN								
1 Stupak	Y	Y	Y	Y	Y	Y	Y	Y
2 **Hoekstra**	N	N	N	Y	Y	Y	Y	Y
3 **Ehlers**	N	N	N	Y	Y	Y	Y	Y
4 **Camp**	N	N	N	Y	Y	Y	Y	Y
5 Barcia	Y	Y	Y	Y	Y	Y	Y	Y
6 **Upton**	N	N	N	Y	Y	Y	Y	Y
7 **Smith**	N	N	N	Y	Y	Y	Y	Y
8 Stabenow	+	-	Y	Y	Y	Y	Y	Y
9 Kildee	Y	Y	Y	Y	Y	Y	Y	Y
10 Bonior	Y	Y	Y	N	Y	Y	Y	Y
11 **Knollenberg**	N	N	N	Y	Y	Y	Y	Y
12 Levin	Y	Y	Y	Y	Y	Y	Y	Y
13 Rivers	Y	Y	Y	Y	Y	Y	Y	Y
14 Conyers	Y	Y	Y	Y	Y	Y	Y	Y
15 Kilpatrick	Y	Y	Y	Y	Y	Y	Y	Y
16 Dingell	?	N	Y	Y	Y	Y	Y	Y
MINNESOTA								
1 **Gutknecht**	N	N	N	Y	Y	Y	Y	Y
2 Minge	Y	Y	Y	Y	Y	Y	Y	Y

	286	287	288	289	290	291	292	293
3 **Ramstad**	N	N	N	Y	Y	Y	Y	Y
4 Vento	Y	Y	Y	Y	Y	Y	Y	Y
5 Sabo	Y	Y	Y	Y	Y	Y	Y	Y
6 Luther	Y	Y	Y	Y	Y	Y	Y	Y
7 Peterson	Y	Y	Y	Y	Y	Y	Y	Y
8 Oberstar	Y	?	Y	Y	Y	Y	Y	Y
MISSISSIPPI								
1 **Wicker**	N	N	N	Y	Y	Y	Y	Y
2 Thompson	Y	Y	Y	Y	Y	Y	Y	Y
3 **Pickering**	N	N	N	Y	Y	Y	Y	Y
4 **Parker**	N	?	?	?	?	?	?	?
5 Taylor	N	Y	N	Y	Y	Y	Y	Y
MISSOURI								
1 Clay	Y	Y	Y	Y	Y	Y	Y	Y
2 **Talent**	N	N	N	Y	Y	Y	Y	Y
3 Gephardt	Y	?	?	?	?	?	?	?
4 Skelton	Y	Y	Y	Y	Y	Y	Y	Y
5 McCarthy	Y	Y	Y	Y	Y	Y	Y	Y
6 Danner	Y	Y	Y	Y	Y	Y	Y	Y
7 **Blunt**	N	N	N	Y	Y	Y	Y	Y
8 **Emerson**	N	N	N	Y	Y	Y	Y	Y
9 **Hulshof**	N	N	N	Y	Y	Y	Y	Y
MONTANA								
AL **Hill**	N	N	N	Y	Y	Y	Y	Y
NEBRASKA								
1 **Bereuter**	N	N	N	Y	Y	Y	Y	Y
2 **Christensen**	N	N	N	Y	Y	Y	Y	Y
3 **Barrett**	N	N	N	Y	Y	Y	Y	Y
NEVADA								
1 **Ensign**	Y	Y	N	Y	Y	Y	Y	Y
2 **Gibbons**	N	N	N	Y	Y	Y	Y	Y
NEW HAMPSHIRE								
1 **Sununu**	N	N	N	Y	Y	Y	Y	Y
2 **Bass**	N	N	N	Y	Y	Y	Y	Y
NEW JERSEY								
1 Andrews	Y	Y	Y	Y	Y	Y	Y	Y
2 **LoBiondo**	N	N	N	Y	Y	Y	Y	Y
3 **Saxton**	N	N	N	Y	Y	Y	Y	Y
4 **Smith**	N	N	N	Y	Y	Y	Y	Y
5 **Roukema**	N	N	N	Y	Y	Y	Y	Y
6 Pallone	Y	Y	Y	Y	Y	Y	Y	Y
7 **Franks**	N	N	N	Y	Y	Y	Y	Y
8 Pascrell	Y	Y	Y	Y	Y	Y	Y	Y
9 Rothman	Y	Y	Y	Y	Y	Y	Y	Y
10 Payne	Y	Y	Y	Y	Y	Y	Y	Y
11 **Frelinghuysen**	N	N	N	Y	Y	Y	Y	Y
12 **Pappas**	N	N	N	Y	Y	Y	Y	Y
13 Menendez	Y	Y	Y	Y	Y	Y	Y	Y
NEW MEXICO								
1 **Schiff**	?	?	?	?	?	?	?	?
2 **Skeen**	N	N	N	Y	Y	Y	Y	Y
3 **Redmond**	N	N	N	Y	Y	Y	Y	Y
NEW YORK								
1 **Forbes**	N	N	N	Y	Y	Y	Y	Y
2 **Lazio**	N	N	N	Y	Y	Y	Y	Y
3 **King**	N	N	N	Y	Y	Y	Y	Y
4 McCarthy	Y	Y	Y	Y	Y	Y	Y	Y
5 Ackerman	Y	Y	Y	Y	Y	Y	Y	Y
6 Flake	Y	Y	Y	Y	Y	Y	Y	Y
7 Manton	Y	Y	Y	Y	Y	Y	Y	Y
8 Nadler	Y	Y	Y	Y	Y	Y	Y	Y
9 Schumer	Y	Y	Y	Y	Y	Y	Y	Y
10 Towns	Y	Y	Y	Y	Y	Y	Y	Y
11 Owens	Y	Y	Y	N	Y	Y	Y	Y
12 Velázquez	Y	Y	Y	Y	Y	Y	Y	Y
13 **Molinari**	N	N	N	Y	Y	Y	Y	Y
14 Maloney	Y	Y	Y	Y	Y	Y	Y	Y
15 Rangel	Y	Y	Y	Y	Y	Y	Y	Y
16 Serrano	Y	Y	Y	Y	Y	Y	Y	Y
17 Engel	Y	Y	Y	Y	Y	Y	Y	Y
18 Lowey	Y	Y	Y	Y	Y	Y	Y	Y
19 **Kelly**	N	N	N	Y	Y	Y	Y	Y
20 **Gilman**	Y	N	Y	Y	Y	Y	Y	Y
21 McNulty	Y	Y	Y	Y	Y	Y	Y	Y
22 **Solomon**	N	N	N	Y	Y	Y	Y	Y
23 **Boehlert**	N	N	N	Y	Y	Y	Y	Y
24 **McHugh**	Y	N	N	Y	Y	Y	Y	Y
25 **Walsh**	N	N	N	Y	Y	Y	Y	Y
26 Hinchey	Y	Y	Y	Y	Y	Y	Y	Y
27 **Paxon**	N	N	N	Y	Y	Y	Y	Y
28 Slaughter	Y	Y	Y	Y	Y	Y	Y	Y
29 LaFalce	Y	Y	Y	Y	Y	Y	Y	Y
30 **Quinn**	N	N	N	Y	Y	Y	Y	Y
31 **Houghton**	Y	N	Y	Y	Y	Y	Y	Y

	286	287	288	289	290	291	292	293
NORTH CAROLINA								
1 Clayton	Y	Y	Y	Y	Y	Y	Y	Y
2 Etheridge	Y	Y	Y	Y	Y	Y	Y	Y
3 **Jones**	N	N	N	Y	Y	Y	Y	Y
4 Price	Y	Y	Y	Y	Y	Y	Y	Y
5 **Burr**	N	N	N	Y	Y	Y	Y	Y
6 **Coble**	N	N	N	Y	Y	Y	Y	Y
7 McIntyre	?	N	Y	Y	Y	Y	Y	Y
8 Hefner	Y	Y	Y	Y	Y	Y	Y	Y
9 **Myrick**	N	N	N	Y	Y	Y	Y	Y
10 **Ballenger**	N	N	N	Y	Y	Y	Y	Y
11 **Taylor**	N	N	N	Y	Y	Y	Y	Y
12 Watt	Y	Y	Y	Y	Y	Y	Y	Y
NORTH DAKOTA								
AL Pomeroy	Y	Y	Y	Y	Y	Y	Y	Y
OHIO								
1 **Chabot**	N	N	N	Y	Y	Y	Y	Y
2 **Portman**	N	N	N	Y	Y	Y	Y	Y
3 Hall	Y	Y	Y	Y	Y	Y	Y	Y
4 **Oxley**	N	?	N	Y	Y	Y	Y	Y
5 **Gillmor**	N	N	N	Y	Y	Y	Y	Y
6 Strickland	Y	Y	Y	Y	Y	Y	Y	Y
7 **Hobson**	N	N	N	Y	Y	Y	Y	Y
8 **Boehner**	N	N	N	Y	Y	Y	Y	Y
9 Kaptur	Y	Y	Y	Y	Y	Y	Y	Y
10 Kucinich	Y	Y	Y	Y	Y	Y	Y	Y
11 Stokes	Y	Y	Y	Y	Y	Y	Y	Y
12 **Kasich**	N	N	N	Y	Y	Y	Y	Y
13 Brown	Y	Y	Y	Y	Y	Y	Y	Y
14 Sawyer	Y	Y	Y	Y	Y	Y	Y	Y
15 **Pryce**	N	N	N	Y	Y	Y	Y	Y
16 **Regula**	N	N	N	Y	Y	Y	Y	Y
17 Traficant	Y	N	N	Y	Y	Y	Y	Y
18 **Ney**	?	Y	N	Y	Y	Y	Y	Y
19 **LaTourette**	N	N	N	Y	Y	Y	Y	Y
OKLAHOMA								
1 **Largent**	N	N	N	Y	Y	Y	Y	Y
2 **Coburn**	N	N	N	Y	Y	Y	Y	Y
3 **Watkins**	Y	N	Y	Y	Y	Y	Y	Y
4 **Watts**	N	N	N	Y	Y	Y	Y	Y
5 **Istook**	N	N	N	Y	Y	Y	Y	Y
6 **Lucas**	N	N	N	Y	Y	Y	Y	Y
OREGON								
1 Furse	Y	Y	Y	Y	Y	Y	Y	Y
2 **Smith**	N	N	N	Y	Y	Y	Y	Y
3 Blumenauer	Y	Y	Y	Y	Y	Y	Y	Y
4 DeFazio	Y	N	Y	Y	Y	Y	Y	Y
5 Hooley	Y	Y	Y	Y	Y	Y	Y	Y
PENNSYLVANIA								
1 Foglietta	Y	Y	Y	Y	Y	?	?	?
2 Fattah	?	Y	Y	Y	Y	Y	Y	Y
3 Borski	Y	Y	Y	Y	Y	Y	Y	Y
4 Klink	Y	Y	Y	Y	Y	Y	Y	Y
5 **Peterson**	N	N	N	Y	Y	Y	Y	Y
6 Holden	Y	Y	Y	Y	Y	Y	Y	Y
7 **Weldon**	N	N	N	Y	Y	Y	Y	Y
8 **Greenwood**	N	N	N	Y	Y	Y	Y	Y
9 **Shuster**	N	N	N	Y	Y	Y	Y	Y
10 **McDade**	?	?	?	?	?	?	?	?
11 Kanjorski	Y	Y	Y	Y	Y	Y	Y	Y
12 Murtha	Y	N	Y	Y	Y	Y	Y	Y
13 **Fox**	N	Y	N	Y	Y	Y	Y	Y
14 Coyne	Y	Y	Y	Y	Y	Y	Y	Y
15 McHale	Y	Y	Y	Y	Y	Y	Y	Y
16 **Pitts**	N	N	N	Y	Y	Y	Y	Y
17 **Gekas**	N	N	N	Y	Y	Y	Y	Y
18 Doyle	Y	Y	Y	Y	Y	Y	Y	Y
19 **Goodling**	N	N	N	Y	Y	Y	Y	Y
20 Mascara	Y	Y	Y	Y	Y	Y	Y	Y
21 **English**	N	N	N	Y	Y	Y	Y	Y
RHODE ISLAND								
1 Kennedy	+	+	+	+	+	Y	Y	Y
2 Weygand	Y	Y	Y	Y	Y	Y	Y	Y
SOUTH CAROLINA								
1 **Sanford**	N	N	N	Y	N	Y	Y	Y
2 **Spence**	N	N	N	Y	Y	Y	Y	Y
3 **Graham**	N	N	N	Y	Y	Y	Y	Y
4 **Inglis**	N	N	N	Y	Y	Y	Y	Y
5 Spratt	Y	Y	Y	Y	Y	Y	Y	Y
6 Clyburn	Y	Y	Y	Y	Y	Y	Y	Y
SOUTH DAKOTA								
AL **Thune**	N	N	N	Y	Y	Y	Y	Y
TENNESSEE								
1 **Jenkins**	N	N	N	Y	Y	Y	Y	Y
2 **Duncan**	N	N	N	Y	Y	Y	Y	Y

	286	287	288	289	290	291	292	
3 **Wamp**	N	N	N	Y	Y	Y	Y	Y
4 **Hilleary**	N	N	N	Y	Y	Y	Y	Y
5 Clement	Y	Y	Y	Y	Y	Y	Y	Y
6 Gordon	Y	Y	Y	Y	Y	Y	Y	Y
7 **Bryant**	N	N	N	Y	Y	Y	Y	Y
8 Tanner	Y	Y	Y	Y	Y	Y	Y	Y
9 Ford	Y	Y	Y	Y	Y	Y	Y	Y
TEXAS								
1 Sandlin	Y	Y	Y	Y	Y	Y	Y	Y
2 Turner	Y	Y	Y	Y	Y	Y	Y	Y
3 **Johnson, Sam**	N	N	N	Y	Y	Y	Y	Y
4 Hall	Y	Y	Y	Y	Y	Y	Y	Y
5 **Sessions**	N	N	N	Y	Y	Y	Y	Y
6 **Barton**	N	N	N	Y	Y	Y	Y	Y
7 **Archer**	?	N	N	Y	Y	Y	Y	Y
8 **Brady**	N	N	N	Y	Y	Y	Y	Y
9 Lampson	Y	Y	Y	Y	Y	Y	Y	Y
10 Doggett	Y	Y	Y	Y	Y	Y	Y	Y
11 Edwards	Y	Y	Y	Y	Y	Y	Y	Y
12 **Granger**	N	N	N	Y	Y	Y	Y	Y
13 **Thornberry**	N	N	N	Y	?	Y	Y	Y
14 **Paul**	N	N	N	N	N	Y	N	Y
15 Hinojosa	Y	Y	Y	Y	Y	Y	Y	Y
16 Reyes	Y	Y	Y	Y	Y	Y	Y	Y
17 Stenholm	Y	N	Y	Y	Y	Y	Y	Y
18 Jackson-Lee	Y	Y	Y	Y	Y	Y	Y	Y
19 **Combest**	N	N	N	Y	Y	Y	Y	Y
20 Gonzalez	?	Y	Y	Y	Y	Y	Y	Y
21 **Smith**	N	N	N	Y	Y	Y	Y	Y
22 **DeLay**	N	N	N	Y	Y	Y	Y	Y
23 **Bonilla**	N	N	N	Y	Y	Y	Y	Y
24 Frost	?	?	?	?	?	?	Y	Y
25 Bentsen	Y	Y	Y	Y	Y	Y	Y	Y
26 **Armey**	N	N	N	Y	Y	Y	Y	Y
27 Ortiz	Y	Y	Y	Y	Y	Y	Y	Y
28 Rodriguez	Y	Y	Y	Y	Y	Y	Y	Y
29 Green	Y	Y	Y	Y	Y	Y	Y	Y
30 Johnson, E.B.	Y	Y	Y	Y	Y	Y	Y	Y
UTAH								
1 **Hansen**	N	N	N	Y	Y	Y	Y	Y
2 **Cook**	N	N	N	Y	Y	Y	Y	Y
3 **Cannon**	N	N	N	Y	Y	Y	Y	Y
VERMONT								
AL *Sanders*	Y	Y	Y	Y	Y	Y	Y	Y
VIRGINIA								
1 **Bateman**	N	N	N	Y	Y	Y	Y	Y
2 Pickett	Y	N	Y	Y	Y	Y	Y	Y
3 Scott	Y	Y	Y	Y	Y	Y	Y	Y
4 Sisisky	Y	N	Y	Y	Y	Y	Y	Y
5 Goode	N	N	N	Y	Y	Y	Y	Y
6 **Goodlatte**	N	N	N	Y	Y	Y	Y	Y
7 **Bliley**	N	N	N	Y	Y	Y	Y	Y
8 Moran	Y	Y	Y	Y	Y	Y	Y	Y
9 Boucher	Y	Y	Y	Y	Y	Y	Y	Y
10 **Wolf**	N	N	N	Y	Y	Y	Y	Y
11 **Davis**	N	N	N	Y	Y	Y	Y	Y
WASHINGTON								
1 **White**	N	N	N	Y	Y	Y	Y	Y
2 **Metcalf**	N	N	N	Y	Y	Y	Y	Y
3 **Smith, Linda**	N	N	N	Y	Y	Y	Y	Y
4 **Hastings**	N	N	N	Y	Y	Y	Y	Y
5 **Nethercutt**	N	N	N	Y	Y	Y	Y	Y
6 Dicks	Y	Y	Y	Y	Y	Y	Y	Y
7 McDermott	Y	Y	Y	N	Y	Y	Y	Y
8 **Dunn**	N	N	N	Y	Y	Y	Y	Y
9 Smith, Adam	Y	Y	Y	Y	Y	Y	Y	Y
WEST VIRGINIA								
1 Mollohan	?	?	?	?	?	?	?	?
2 Wise	Y	Y	Y	Y	Y	Y	Y	Y
3 Rahall	Y	Y	Y	Y	Y	Y	Y	Y
WISCONSIN								
1 **Neumann**	N	N	N	Y	Y	Y	Y	Y
2 **Klug**	N	N	N	Y	Y	Y	Y	Y
3 Kind	Y	Y	Y	Y	Y	Y	Y	Y
4 Kleczka	Y	N	Y	Y	Y	Y	Y	Y
5 Barrett	Y	Y	Y	Y	Y	Y	Y	Y
6 **Petri**	N	N	N	Y	Y	Y	Y	Y
7 Obey	Y	Y	Y	Y	Y	Y	Y	Y
8 Johnson	Y	Y	Y	Y	Y	Y	Y	?
9 **Sensenbrenner**	N	N	N	N	N	Y	Y	Y
WYOMING								
AL **Cubin**	N	N	N	Y	+	Y	Y	Y

Southern states - Ala., Ark., Fla., Ga., Ky., La., Miss., N.C., Okla., S.C., Tenn., Texas, Va.

HOUSE VOTES 294, 295, 296, 297, 298, 299, 300, 301

294. H Con Res 81. Peace in Cyprus/Adoption. Gilman, R-N.Y., motion to suspend the rules and adopt the concurrent resolution to express the sense of the House reaffirming that the political division in Cyprus is unacceptable and detrimental to the interests of the United States. Motion agreed to 417-4: R 216-4; D 200-0 (ND 145-0, SD 55-0); I 1-0, July 22, 1997. A two-thirds majority of those present and voting (281 in this case) is required for passage under suspension of the rules.

295. H Con Res 88. Congratulate El Salvador/Adoption. Gilman, R-N.Y., motion to suspend the rules and adopt the concurrent resolution to congratulate the government and people of El Salvador for successfully completing free and democratic elections and reaffirm that the United States is committed to encouraging democracy and peaceful development throughout Central America. Motion agreed to 419-3: R 217-2; D 201-1 (ND 146-1, SD 55-0); I 1-0, July 22, 1997. A two-thirds majority of those present and voting (282 in this case) is required for adoption under suspension of the rules.

296. H Res 175. Violence in Congo/Adoption. Gilman, R-N.Y., motion to suspend the rules and adopt the resolution to condemn the current fighting in the Republic of Congo, urge the warring parties to reach a lasting cease-fire that would allow for humanitarian relief and call on all private militiamen to disarm and disband immediately. Motion rejected 279-147: R 79-143; D 199-4 (ND 146-2, SD 53-2); I 1-0, July 22, 1997. A two-thirds majority of those present and voting (284 in this case) is required for adoption under suspension of the rules.

297. H Con Res 99. Military Coup in Sierra Leone/Adoption. Gilman, R-N.Y., motion to suspend the rules and adopt the concurrent resolution to condemn the leaders and members of the military coup that overthrew the elected government of Sierra Leone. Motion agreed to 418-1: R 217-1; D 200-0 (ND 146-0, SD 54-0); I 1-0, July 22, 1997. A two-thirds majority of those present and voting (280 in this case) is required for adoption under suspension of the rules.

298. H Res 191. European Commission Merger Interference/Adoption. Gilman, R-N.Y., motion to suspend the rules and adopt the resolution to express the sense of the House that any disapproval by the European Commission of the merger of Boeing Co. and McDonnell Douglas Corp. would constitute an unwarranted and unprecedented interference in a U.S. business transaction. Motion agreed to 416-2: R 216-0; D 199-2 (ND 145-2, SD 54-0); I 1-0, July 22, 1997. A two-thirds majority of those present and voting (279 in this case) is required for adoption under suspension of the rules.

299. HR 1585. Breast Cancer Research Postage Stamp/Passage. McHugh, R-N.Y., motion to suspend the rules and pass the bill to direct the Postal Service to establish a special alternative postage rate (up to 25 percent above current rate) for first-class mail that patrons may use voluntarily to contribute toward funding for breast cancer research. The bill would allocate 70 percent of the proceeds for the National Institutes of Health and 30 percent for the Defense Department solely for breast cancer research, minus Postal Service administrative costs. Motion agreed to 422-3: R 219-3; D 202-0 (ND 147-0, SD 55-0); I 1-0, July 22, 1997. A two-thirds majority of those present and voting (284 in this case) is required for passage under suspension of the rules.

300. HR 2003. Budget Enforcement/Recommit. Thurman, D-Fla., motion to recommit the bill to the Ways and Means Committee with instructions to report it back with an amendment to provide that the first $100 billion of any budget surplus be used to take Social Security off budget, change the Medicare sequestration formula to limit Medicare Part-B premium increases and limit the total amount of spending sequestration to the amount total entitlement spending exceeds the total entitlement spending cap. Motion rejected 148-279: R 58-165; D 90-113 (ND 53-96, SD 37-17); I 0-1, July 23, 1997.

301. HR 2003. Budget Enforcement/Passage. Passage of the bill to establish in law spending, revenue and deficit targets agreed to in the 1997 bipartisan budget agreement for each of fiscal years 1998 through 2002 and to reform the budget process to provide enforcement mechanisms to ensure that the targets are actually implemented. The bill calls for automatic cuts in individual entitlement programs and a temporary suspension of tax cuts if the targets are breached. Rejected 81-347: R 46-178; D 35-168 (ND 20-129, SD 15-39); I 0-1, July 23, 1997.

KEY

- Y Voted for (yea).
- # Paired for.
- + Announced for.
- N Voted against (nay).
- X Paired against.
- – Announced against.
- P Voted "present."
- C Voted "present" to avoid possible conflict of interest.
- ? Did not vote or otherwise make a position known.

Democrats ***Republicans***
Independent

	294	295	296	297	298	299	300	301
ALABAMA								
1 ***Callahan***	Y	Y	N	Y	Y	Y	N	N
2 ***Everett***	Y	Y	N	Y	Y	Y	N	N
3 ***Riley***	Y	Y	Y	Y	Y	Y	N	N
4 ***Aderholt***	Y	Y	N	Y	Y	Y	N	N
5 Cramer	Y	Y	Y	Y	Y	Y	Y	N
6 ***Bachus***	Y	Y	N	Y	Y	Y	N	N
7 Hilliard	Y	Y	Y	Y	Y	Y	Y	N
ALASKA								
AL ***Young***	?	?	?	?	?	?	?	?
ARIZONA								
1 ***Salmon***	Y	Y	N	Y	Y	Y	N	N
2 Pastor	Y	Y	Y	Y	Y	Y	N	N
3 ***Stump***	Y	Y	N	Y	Y	Y	N	N
4 ***Shadegg***	Y	Y	N	Y	Y	Y	N	N
5 ***Kolbe***	Y	Y	N	Y	Y	Y	N	Y
6 ***Hayworth***	Y	Y	N	Y	Y	Y	N	N
ARKANSAS								
1 Berry	Y	Y	Y	Y	Y	Y	N	N
2 Snyder	Y	Y	Y	Y	Y	Y	N	N
3 ***Hutchinson***	?	?	Y	Y	Y	Y	?	?
4 ***Dickey***	Y	Y	N	Y	Y	Y	N	N
CALIFORNIA								
1 ***Riggs***	Y	Y	Y	Y	Y	Y	Y	N
2 ***Herger***	Y	Y	N	Y	Y	Y	N	N
3 Fazio	Y	Y	Y	Y	Y	Y	N	N
4 ***Doolittle***	Y	Y	Y	Y	Y	Y	N	N
5 Matsui	Y	Y	Y	Y	Y	Y	N	N
6 Woolsey	Y	Y	Y	Y	Y	Y	Y	N
7 Miller	Y	Y	Y	Y	Y	Y	Y	N
8 Pelosi	Y	Y	Y	Y	Y	Y	N	N
9 Dellums	Y	Y	Y	Y	Y	Y	N	N
10 Tauscher	Y	Y	Y	Y	Y	Y	Y	Y
11 ***Pombo***	Y	Y	Y	Y	Y	Y	N	N
12 Lantos	Y	Y	Y	Y	Y	Y	Y	N
13 Stark	Y	Y	Y	Y	N	Y	?	?
14 Eshoo	Y	Y	Y	Y	Y	Y	Y	N
15 ***Campbell***	Y	Y	Y	Y	Y	Y	Y	Y
16 Lofgren	Y	Y	Y	Y	Y	Y	N	N
17 Farr	Y	Y	Y	Y	Y	Y	Y	N
18 Condit	Y	Y	Y	Y	Y	Y	Y	Y
19 ***Radanovich***	Y	Y	Y	Y	Y	Y	N	N
20 Dooley	Y	Y	Y	Y	Y	Y	Y	Y
21 ***Thomas***	Y	Y	Y	Y	Y	Y	N	N
22 Capps	Y	Y	Y	Y	Y	Y	N	N
23 ***Gallegly***	Y	Y	N	Y	Y	Y	N	N
24 Sherman	Y	Y	Y	Y	Y	Y	Y	N
25 ***McKeon***	Y	Y	N	Y	Y	Y	N	N
26 Berman	Y	Y	Y	?	?	?	N	N
27 ***Rogan***	Y	Y	Y	Y	Y	Y	N	N
28 ***Dreier***	Y	Y	N	Y	Y	Y	N	N
29 Waxman	?	Y	Y	Y	Y	Y	N	N
30 Becerra	Y	Y	Y	Y	Y	Y	N	N
31 Martinez	Y	Y	Y	Y	Y	Y	N	N
32 Dixon	Y	Y	Y	Y	Y	Y	N	N
33 Roybal-Allard	Y	Y	Y	Y	Y	Y	N	N
34 Torres	Y	Y	Y	Y	Y	Y	N	N
35 Waters	?	?	Y	Y	Y	Y	N	N
36 Harman	Y	Y	Y	Y	Y	Y	Y	Y
37 Millender-McD.	Y	Y	Y	Y	Y	Y	N	N
38 ***Horn***	Y	Y	Y	Y	Y	Y	Y	Y
39 ***Royce***	Y	Y	Y	?	?	?	N	Y
40 ***Lewis***	Y	Y	Y	Y	Y	Y	N	N
41 ***Kim***	Y	Y	Y	Y	Y	Y	N	N
42 Brown	Y	Y	Y	Y	Y	Y	Y	N
43 ***Calvert***	Y	Y	Y	Y	Y	Y	N	N
44 ***Bono***	Y	Y	Y	Y	Y	Y	N	N
45 ***Rohrabacher***	Y	Y	Y	Y	Y	Y	N	Y
46 Sanchez	Y	Y	Y	Y	Y	Y	Y	Y
47 ***Cox***	Y	Y	Y	Y	Y	Y	N	N
48 ***Packard***	Y	Y	N	Y	Y	Y	N	N
49 ***Bilbray***	Y	Y	N	Y	Y	Y	N	N
50 Filner	Y	Y	Y	Y	Y	Y	N	N
51 ***Cunningham***	Y	Y	N	Y	Y	Y	N	N
52 ***Hunter***	Y	Y	N	Y	?	Y	Y	N
COLORADO								
1 DeGette	Y	Y	Y	Y	Y	Y	N	N
2 Skaggs	Y	Y	Y	Y	Y	Y	Y	N
3 ***McInnis***	Y	Y	Y	Y	Y	Y	N	Y
4 ***Schaffer***	Y	Y	N	Y	Y	Y	Y	Y
5 ***Hefley***	Y	Y	N	Y	Y	Y	N	N
6 ***Schaefer***	Y	Y	N	Y	Y	Y	Y	N
CONNECTICUT								
1 Kennelly	Y	Y	Y	Y	Y	Y	N	N
2 Gejdenson	Y	Y	Y	Y	Y	Y	N	N
3 DeLauro	Y	Y	Y	Y	Y	Y	N	N
4 ***Shays***	Y	Y	Y	Y	Y	Y	N	N
5 Maloney	Y	Y	Y	Y	Y	Y	Y	N
6 ***Johnson***	Y	Y	Y	Y	Y	Y	N	N
DELAWARE								
AL ***Castle***	Y	Y	Y	Y	Y	Y	Y	Y
FLORIDA								
1 ***Scarborough***	Y	Y	N	Y	Y	Y	N	N
2 Boyd	Y	Y	Y	Y	Y	Y	Y	Y
3 Brown	Y	Y	Y	Y	Y	Y	Y	N
4 ***Fowler***	Y	Y	N	Y	Y	Y	N	N
5 Thurman	Y	Y	Y	Y	Y	Y	Y	N
6 ***Stearns***	Y	Y	Y	Y	Y	Y	Y	N
7 ***Mica***	Y	Y	Y	Y	Y	Y	N	N
8 ***McCollum***	Y	+	N	Y	Y	Y	Y	N
9 ***Bilirakis***	Y	Y	N	Y	Y	Y	Y	N
10 ***Young***	Y	Y	N	Y	Y	Y	N	N
11 Davis	Y	Y	Y	Y	Y	Y	Y	Y
12 ***Canady***	Y	Y	N	Y	Y	Y	Y	N
13 ***Miller***	Y	Y	Y	Y	Y	Y	N	N
14 ***Goss***	Y	Y	N	Y	Y	Y	N	N
15 ***Weldon***	Y	Y	N	Y	Y	Y	N	N
16 ***Foley***	Y	Y	N	Y	Y	Y	N	N
17 Meek	Y	Y	Y	Y	Y	Y	N	N
18 ***Ros-Lehtinen***	Y	Y	Y	Y	Y	Y	Y	N
19 Wexler	Y	Y	Y	Y	Y	Y	Y	N
20 Deutsch	Y	Y	Y	Y	Y	Y	Y	Y
21 ***Diaz-Balart***	Y	Y	Y	Y	Y	Y	N	N
22 ***Shaw***	Y	Y	Y	Y	Y	Y	N	N
23 Hastings	Y	Y	Y	Y	Y	Y	N	N
GEORGIA								
1 ***Kingston***	Y	Y	Y	Y	Y	Y	N	Y
2 Bishop	Y	Y	Y	Y	Y	Y	Y	N
3 ***Collins***	N	Y	N	Y	Y	Y	N	N
4 McKinney	Y	Y	Y	Y	Y	Y	Y	Y
5 Lewis	Y	Y	Y	Y	Y	Y	N	N
6 ***Gingrich***								
7 ***Barr***	N	Y	N	P	Y	Y	N	N
8 ***Chambliss***	Y	Y	N	Y	Y	Y	N	Y
9 ***Deal***	N	Y	N	Y	Y	Y	Y	N
10 ***Norwood***	Y	Y	N	Y	Y	Y	Y	Y
11 ***Linder***	Y	Y	Y	Y	Y	Y	N	N
HAWAII								
1 Abercrombie	Y	Y	Y	Y	Y	Y	Y	N
2 Mink	Y	Y	Y	Y	Y	Y	Y	N
IDAHO								
1 ***Chenoweth***	Y	Y	N	Y	Y	Y	Y	N
2 ***Crapo***	Y	Y	Y	Y	Y	Y	N	N
ILLINOIS								
1 Rush	Y	Y	Y	Y	Y	Y	Y	N
2 Jackson	Y	Y	Y	Y	Y	Y	N	N
3 Lipinski	Y	Y	Y	Y	Y	Y	N	N
4 Gutierrez	Y	Y	Y	Y	Y	Y	N	N
5 Blagojevich	Y	Y	Y	Y	Y	Y	N	N
6 ***Hyde***	Y	Y	N	Y	Y	Y	N	N
7 Davis	Y	Y	Y	Y	Y	Y	N	N
8 ***Crane***	Y	Y	N	Y	Y	Y	N	N
9 Yates	?	?	?	?	?	?	Y	N
10 ***Porter***	Y	Y	Y	Y	Y	Y	Y	Y
11 ***Weller***	Y	Y	N	Y	Y	Y	Y	N
12 Costello	Y	Y	Y	Y	Y	Y	N	N
13 ***Fawell***	Y	Y	N	Y	Y	Y	N	Y
14 ***Hastert***	Y	Y	Y	Y	Y	Y	N	N
15 ***Ewing***	Y	Y	N	Y	Y	Y	N	N

ND Northern Democrats SD Southern Democrats

	294	295	296	297	298	299	300	301
16 ***Manzullo***	Y	Y	N	Y	Y	Y	N	N
17 Evans	Y	Y	Y	Y	Y	Y	N	N
18 ***LaHood***	Y	Y	N	Y	Y	Y	N	N
19 Poshard	Y	Y	Y	Y	Y	Y	N	N
20 ***Shimkus***	Y	Y	Y	Y	Y	Y	Y	N
INDIANA								
1 Visclosky	Y	Y	Y	Y	Y	Y	Y	Y
2 ***McIntosh***	Y	Y	Y	Y	Y	Y	Y	N
3 Roemer	Y	Y	Y	Y	Y	Y	Y	Y
4 ***Souder***	Y	Y	N	Y	Y	Y	N	N
5 ***Buyer***	Y	Y	N	Y	Y	Y	N	N
6 ***Burton***	Y	Y	N	Y	Y	Y	N	N
7 ***Pease***	Y	Y	N	Y	Y	Y	Y	N
8 ***Hostettler***	Y	Y	N	Y	Y	Y	N	N
9 Hamilton	Y	Y	Y	Y	Y	Y	Y	Y
10 Carson	Y	Y	Y	Y	Y	Y	Y	N
IOWA								
1 ***Leach***	Y	Y	Y	Y	Y	Y	Y	N
2 ***Nussle***	Y	Y	N	Y	Y	Y	N	N
3 Boswell	Y	Y	N	Y	Y	Y	Y	N
4 ***Ganske***	Y	Y	N	Y	Y	Y	Y	N
5 ***Latham***	Y	Y	N	Y	Y	Y	N	N
KANSAS								
1 ***Moran***	Y	Y	N	Y	Y	Y	N	N
2 ***Ryun***	Y	Y	N	Y	Y	Y	N	N
3 ***Snowbarger***	Y	Y	N	Y	Y	Y	N	N
4 ***Tiahrt***	Y	Y	N	Y	Y	Y	N	N
KENTUCKY								
1 ***Whitfield***	Y	Y	N	Y	Y	Y	N	N
2 ***Lewis***	Y	Y	N	Y	Y	Y	N	N
3 ***Northup***	Y	Y	N	Y	Y	Y	N	N
4 ***Bunning***	Y	Y	N	Y	Y	Y	N	N
5 ***Rogers***	Y	Y	N	Y	Y	Y	N	N
6 Baesler	Y	Y	Y	Y	Y	Y	Y	N
LOUISIANA								
1 ***Livingston***	Y	Y	N	Y	Y	Y	N	Y
2 Jefferson	Y	Y	Y	Y	Y	Y	Y	N
3 ***Tauzin***	Y	Y	N	Y	Y	Y	Y	Y
4 ***McCrery***	Y	Y	N	Y	Y	Y	N	N
5 ***Cooksey***	Y	Y	N	Y	Y	Y	N	N
6 ***Baker***	Y	Y	N	Y	Y	Y	N	N
7 John	Y	Y	Y	Y	Y	Y	Y	Y
MAINE								
1 Allen	Y	Y	Y	Y	Y	Y	Y	N
2 Baldacci	Y	Y	Y	Y	Y	Y	N	N
MARYLAND								
1 ***Gilchrest***	Y	Y	Y	Y	Y	Y	Y	N
2 ***Ehrlich***	Y	Y	Y	Y	Y	Y	N	N
3 Cardin	Y	Y	Y	Y	Y	Y	N	N
4 Wynn	Y	Y	Y	Y	Y	Y	N	N
5 Hoyer	Y	Y	Y	Y	Y	Y	N	N
6 ***Bartlett***	Y	Y	N	Y	Y	Y	N	N
7 Cummings	Y	Y	Y	Y	Y	Y	N	N
8 ***Morella***	Y	Y	Y	Y	Y	Y	Y	Y
MASSACHUSETTS								
1 Olver	Y	Y	Y	Y	Y	Y	N	N
2 Neal	Y	Y	Y	Y	Y	Y	N	N
3 McGovern	Y	Y	Y	Y	Y	Y	N	N
4 Frank	Y	Y	Y	Y	Y	Y	N	N
5 Meehan	Y	Y	Y	Y	Y	Y	Y	Y
6 Tierney	Y	Y	Y	Y	Y	Y	N	N
7 Markey	Y	Y	Y	Y	Y	Y	N	N
8 Kennedy	Y	Y	Y	Y	Y	Y	N	N
9 Moakley	Y	Y	Y	Y	Y	Y	N	N
10 Delahunt	Y	Y	Y	Y	Y	Y	N	N
MICHIGAN								
1 Stupak	Y	Y	Y	Y	Y	Y	Y	N
2 ***Hoekstra***	Y	Y	N	Y	Y	Y	N	Y
3 ***Ehlers***	Y	Y	Y	Y	Y	Y	N	Y
4 ***Camp***	Y	Y	N	Y	Y	Y	Y	N
5 Barcia	Y	Y	Y	Y	Y	Y	Y	Y
6 ***Upton***	Y	Y	N	Y	Y	Y	Y	Y
7 ***Smith***	Y	Y	N	Y	Y	Y	N	N
8 Stabenow	Y	Y	Y	Y	Y	Y	Y	N
9 Kildee	Y	Y	Y	Y	Y	Y	N	N
10 Bonior	Y	Y	Y	Y	Y	Y	N	N
11 ***Knollenberg***	Y	Y	Y	Y	Y	Y	N	N
12 Levin	Y	Y	Y	Y	Y	Y	N	N
13 Rivers	Y	Y	Y	Y	Y	Y	N	N
14 Conyers	Y	Y	Y	Y	Y	Y	N	N
15 Kilpatrick	Y	Y	Y	Y	Y	Y	N	N
16 Dingell	Y	Y	Y	Y	Y	Y	N	N
MINNESOTA								
1 ***Gutknecht***	Y	Y	N	Y	Y	Y	Y	Y
2 Minge	Y	Y	Y	Y	Y	Y	Y	Y

	294	295	296	297	298	299	300	301
3 ***Ramstad***	Y	Y	N	Y	Y	Y	Y	Y
4 Vento	Y	Y	Y	Y	Y	Y	N	N
5 Sabo	Y	Y	Y	Y	Y	Y	N	N
6 Luther	Y	Y	Y	Y	Y	Y	Y	Y
7 Peterson	Y	Y	Y	Y	Y	Y	Y	Y
8 Oberstar	Y	Y	Y	Y	N	Y	N	N
MISSISSIPPI								
1 ***Wicker***	Y	Y	N	Y	Y	Y	N	N
2 Thompson	Y	Y	Y	Y	Y	Y	Y	N
3 ***Pickering***	Y	Y	N	Y	Y	Y	N	N
4 ***Parker***	?	?	?	?	?	Y	N	N
5 Taylor	Y	Y	N	Y	Y	Y	Y	Y
MISSOURI								
1 Clay	Y	Y	Y	Y	Y	Y	N	N
2 ***Talent***	Y	Y	N	Y	Y	Y	Y	N
3 Gephardt	?	Y	Y	Y	Y	Y	N	N
4 Skelton	Y	Y	Y	Y	Y	Y	N	N
5 McCarthy	Y	Y	Y	Y	Y	Y	Y	N
6 Danner	Y	Y	Y	Y	Y	Y	Y	N
7 ***Blunt***	Y	Y	N	Y	Y	Y	N	Y
8 ***Emerson***	?	Y	N	Y	Y	Y	N	N
9 ***Hulshof***	Y	Y	N	Y	Y	Y	N	N
MONTANA								
AL ***Hill***	Y	Y	N	Y	Y	Y	Y	N
NEBRASKA								
1 ***Bereuter***	Y	Y	Y	Y	Y	Y	N	N
2 ***Christensen***	Y	Y	N	Y	Y	Y	N	N
3 ***Barrett***	Y	Y	Y	Y	Y	Y	N	N
NEVADA								
1 ***Ensign***	Y	Y	N	Y	Y	Y	P	N
2 ***Gibbons***	Y	Y	N	Y	Y	Y	N	N
NEW HAMPSHIRE								
1 ***Sununu***	Y	Y	N	Y	Y	Y	N	N
2 ***Bass***	Y	Y	N	Y	Y	Y	Y	Y
NEW JERSEY								
1 Andrews	Y	Y	Y	Y	Y	Y	Y	Y
2 ***LoBiondo***	Y	Y	N	Y	Y	Y	N	N
3 ***Saxton***	Y	Y	N	Y	Y	Y	N	N
4 ***Smith***	Y	Y	Y	Y	Y	Y	N	N
5 ***Roukema***	Y	?	?	?	?	Y	N	N
6 Pallone	Y	Y	Y	Y	Y	Y	?	?
7 ***Franks***	Y	Y	Y	Y	Y	Y	N	N
8 Pascrell	Y	Y	Y	Y	Y	Y	N	N
9 Rothman	Y	Y	Y	Y	Y	Y	N	N
10 Payne	Y	Y	Y	Y	Y	Y	N	N
11 ***Frelinghuysen***	Y	Y	N	Y	Y	Y	N	N
12 ***Pappas***	Y	Y	N	Y	Y	Y	N	N
13 Menendez	Y	Y	Y	Y	Y	Y	N	N
NEW MEXICO								
1 ***Schiff***	?	?	?	?	?	?	?	?
2 ***Skeen***	Y	Y	N	Y	Y	Y	N	N
3 ***Redmond***	Y	Y	N	Y	Y	Y	N	N
NEW YORK								
1 ***Forbes***	Y	Y	N	Y	Y	Y	Y	Y
2 ***Lazio***	Y	Y	Y	Y	Y	Y	Y	N
3 ***King***	Y	Y	N	Y	Y	Y	N	N
4 McCarthy	Y	Y	Y	Y	Y	Y	Y	N
5 Ackerman	Y	Y	Y	Y	Y	Y	N	N
6 Flake	Y	Y	Y	Y	Y	Y	N	N
7 Manton	Y	Y	Y	Y	Y	Y	Y	N
8 Nadler	Y	Y	Y	Y	Y	Y	N	N
9 Schumer	Y	Y	Y	Y	Y	Y	N	N
10 Towns	Y	Y	Y	Y	Y	Y	N	N
11 Owens	Y	Y	Y	Y	Y	Y	N	N
12 Velázquez	Y	Y	Y	Y	Y	Y	N	N
13 ***Molinari***	Y	Y	Y	Y	Y	Y	N	N
14 Maloney	Y	Y	Y	Y	Y	Y	Y	N
15 Rangel	Y	Y	Y	Y	Y	Y	N	N
16 Serrano	Y	Y	Y	Y	Y	Y	N	N
17 Engel	Y	Y	Y	Y	Y	Y	N	N
18 Lowey	Y	Y	Y	Y	Y	Y	N	N
19 ***Kelly***	Y	Y	N	Y	Y	Y	N	N
20 ***Gilman***	Y	Y	Y	Y	Y	Y	N	N
21 McNulty	Y	Y	Y	Y	Y	Y	N	N
22 ***Solomon***	Y	Y	Y	?	Y	Y	N	N
23 ***Boehlert***	Y	Y	N	Y	Y	Y	N	N
24 ***McHugh***	Y	Y	N	Y	Y	Y	N	N
25 ***Walsh***	Y	Y	N	Y	Y	Y	N	N
26 Hinchey	Y	Y	Y	Y	Y	Y	N	N
27 ***Paxon***	Y	Y	N	Y	Y	Y	Y	N
28 Slaughter	Y	Y	Y	?	Y	Y	N	N
29 LaFalce	Y	Y	Y	Y	Y	Y	N	N
30 ***Quinn***	Y	Y	N	Y	Y	Y	N	N
31 ***Houghton***	Y	Y	Y	Y	Y	Y	Y	Y

	294	295	296	297	298	299	300	301
NORTH CAROLINA								
1 Clayton	Y	Y	Y	Y	Y	Y	N	N
2 Etheridge	Y	Y	Y	Y	Y	Y	Y	N
3 ***Jones***	Y	Y	N	Y	Y	Y	N	N
4 Price	Y	Y	Y	Y	Y	Y	N	N
5 ***Burr***	Y	Y	N	Y	Y	Y	N	N
6 ***Coble***	Y	Y	N	Y	Y	Y	N	N
7 McIntyre	Y	Y	Y	Y	Y	Y	Y	Y
8 Hefner	Y	Y	Y	?	?	Y	Y	Y
9 ***Myrick***	Y	Y	Y	Y	Y	Y	N	N
10 ***Ballenger***	Y	Y	N	Y	+	+	Y	Y
11 ***Taylor***	Y	Y	N	Y	Y	Y	Y	Y
12 Watt	Y	Y	Y	Y	Y	Y	N	N
NORTH DAKOTA								
AL Pomeroy	Y	Y	Y	Y	Y	Y	N	N
OHIO								
1 ***Chabot***	Y	Y	Y	Y	Y	Y	Y	N
2 ***Portman***	Y	Y	Y	Y	?	Y	Y	N
3 Hall	Y	Y	Y	Y	Y	Y	N	N
4 ***Oxley***	Y	Y	Y	Y	Y	Y	N	N
5 ***Gillmor***	Y	Y	Y	Y	Y	Y	N	N
6 Strickland	Y	Y	Y	Y	Y	Y	N	N
7 ***Hobson***	Y	Y	Y	Y	Y	Y	N	N
8 ***Boehner***	Y	Y	Y	Y	Y	Y	N	N
9 Kaptur	Y	Y	Y	Y	Y	Y	Y	N
10 Kucinich	Y	N	Y	Y	Y	Y	N	N
11 Stokes	Y	Y	Y	Y	Y	Y	N	N
12 ***Kasich***	Y	Y	N	Y	Y	Y	N	N
13 Brown	Y	Y	Y	Y	Y	Y	N	N
14 Sawyer	Y	Y	Y	Y	Y	Y	N	N
15 ***Pryce***	Y	Y	Y	Y	Y	Y	N	N
16 ***Regula***	Y	Y	Y	Y	Y	Y	Y	Y
17 Traficant	Y	Y	N	Y	Y	Y	N	N
18 ***Ney***	Y	Y	N	Y	Y	Y	N	N
19 ***LaTourette***	Y	Y	Y	Y	Y	Y	Y	N
OKLAHOMA								
1 ***Largent***	Y	Y	Y	Y	Y	Y	Y	Y
2 ***Coburn***	Y	Y	N	Y	Y	Y	Y	Y
3 ***Watkins***	Y	Y	N	Y	Y	Y	N	N
4 ***Watts***	Y	Y	N	Y	Y	Y	N	N
5 ***Istook***	Y	Y	N	Y	Y	Y	N	N
6 ***Lucas***	Y	Y	N	Y	Y	Y	N	N
OREGON								
1 Furse	Y	Y	Y	Y	Y	Y	Y	N
2 ***Smith***	Y	Y	Y	Y	Y	Y	N	N
3 Blumenauer	Y	Y	Y	Y	Y	Y	Y	Y
4 DeFazio	Y	Y	Y	Y	Y	Y	Y	Y
5 Hooley	Y	Y	Y	Y	Y	Y	Y	N
PENNSYLVANIA								
1 Foglietta	?	?	?	?	?	?	N	N
2 Fattah	Y	Y	Y	Y	Y	Y	N	N
3 Borski	Y	Y	Y	Y	Y	Y	N	N
4 Klink	Y	Y	Y	Y	Y	Y	N	N
5 ***Peterson***	Y	Y	Y	Y	Y	Y	N	N
6 Holden	Y	Y	Y	Y	Y	Y	Y	N
7 ***Weldon***	Y	Y	Y	Y	?	Y	Y	N
8 ***Greenwood***	Y	Y	N	Y	Y	Y	Y	N
9 ***Shuster***	Y	Y	N	Y	Y	Y	N	N
10 ***McDade***	?	?	?	?	?	?	N	N
11 Kanjorski	Y	Y	Y	Y	Y	Y	Y	N
12 Murtha	Y	Y	Y	Y	Y	Y	Y	N
13 ***Fox***	Y	Y	N	Y	Y	Y	Y	N
14 Coyne	Y	Y	Y	Y	Y	Y	N	N
15 McHale	Y	Y	Y	Y	Y	Y	Y	Y
16 ***Pitts***	Y	Y	Y	Y	Y	Y	N	N
17 ***Gekas***	Y	Y	Y	Y	Y	Y	N	Y
18 Doyle	Y	Y	Y	Y	Y	Y	Y	Y
19 ***Goodling***	?	Y	N	Y	Y	Y	N	Y
20 Mascara	Y	Y	Y	Y	Y	Y	N	N
21 ***English***	Y	Y	N	Y	Y	Y	N	N
RHODE ISLAND								
1 Kennedy	Y	Y	Y	Y	Y	Y	N	N
2 Weygand	Y	Y	Y	Y	Y	Y	Y	N
SOUTH CAROLINA								
1 ***Sanford***	Y	Y	N	Y	Y	N	Y	Y
2 ***Spence***	Y	Y	N	Y	Y	Y	N	N
3 ***Graham***	Y	Y	N	Y	Y	Y	N	Y
4 ***Inglis***	Y	Y	N	Y	Y	Y	Y	Y
5 Spratt	Y	Y	Y	Y	Y	Y	N	N
6 Clyburn	Y	Y	Y	Y	Y	Y	Y	N
SOUTH DAKOTA								
AL ***Thune***	Y	Y	Y	Y	Y	Y	N	N
TENNESSEE								
1 ***Jenkins***	Y	Y	N	Y	Y	Y	N	N
2 ***Duncan***	Y	Y	N	Y	Y	Y	Y	Y

	294	295	296	297	298	299	300	
3 ***Wamp***	Y	Y	N	Y	Y	Y	Y	Y
4 ***Hilleary***	Y	Y	N	Y	Y	Y	N	N
5 Clement	Y	Y	Y	Y	Y	Y	Y	N
6 Gordon	Y	Y	Y	Y	Y	Y	Y	N
7 ***Bryant***	Y	N	N	Y	Y	Y	N	N
8 Tanner	Y	Y	Y	Y	Y	Y	Y	Y
9 Ford	Y	Y	Y	Y	Y	Y	N	N
TEXAS								
1 Sandlin	Y	Y	Y	Y	Y	Y	Y	N
2 Turner	Y	Y	Y	Y	Y	Y	Y	Y
3 ***Johnson, Sam***	Y	?	N	Y	Y	Y	N	N
4 Hall	Y	Y	Y	Y	Y	Y	Y	Y
5 ***Sessions***	Y	Y	Y	Y	Y	Y	N	N
6 ***Barton***	Y	Y	N	Y	Y	Y	Y	Y
7 ***Archer***	Y	Y	Y	Y	Y	Y	N	N
8 ***Brady***	Y	Y	N	Y	Y	Y	Y	Y
9 Lampson	Y	Y	Y	Y	Y	Y	Y	N
10 Doggett	Y	Y	Y	Y	Y	Y	Y	Y
11 Edwards	Y	Y	Y	Y	Y	Y	Y	N
12 ***Granger***	Y	Y	N	Y	Y	Y	N	N
13 ***Thornberry***	Y	Y	N	Y	Y	Y	N	N
14 ***Paul***	N	N	N	N	Y	N	N	N
15 Hinojosa	Y	Y	Y	Y	Y	Y	Y	N
16 Reyes	Y	Y	Y	Y	Y	Y	N	N
17 Stenholm	Y	Y	Y	Y	Y	Y	Y	Y
18 Jackson-Lee	Y	Y	Y	Y	Y	Y	N	N
19 ***Combest***	Y	Y	N	Y	Y	Y	Y	Y
20 Gonzalez	Y	Y	Y	Y	Y	Y	?	?
21 ***Smith***	Y	Y	N	Y	Y	Y	N	Y
22 ***DeLay***	Y	Y	N	Y	Y	Y	N	N
23 ***Bonilla***	Y	Y	N	Y	Y	Y	N	N
24 Frost	Y	Y	Y	Y	Y	Y	N	N
25 Bentsen	Y	Y	Y	Y	Y	Y	Y	N
26 ***Armey***	Y	Y	Y	?	Y	Y	N	N
27 Ortiz	Y	Y	Y	Y	Y	Y	N	N
28 Rodriguez	Y	Y	Y	Y	Y	Y	N	N
29 Green	Y	Y	Y	Y	Y	Y	Y	N
30 Johnson, E.B.	Y	Y	Y	Y	Y	Y	N	N
UTAH								
1 ***Hansen***	Y	Y	N	Y	Y	Y	N	N
2 ***Cook***	Y	Y	N	Y	Y	Y	N	N
3 ***Cannon***	Y	Y	N	Y	Y	Y	N	N
VERMONT								
AL *Sanders*	Y	Y	Y	Y	Y	Y	N	N
VIRGINIA								
1 ***Bateman***	Y	Y	Y	Y	Y	Y	N	N
2 Pickett	Y	Y	Y	Y	Y	Y	Y	N
3 Scott	Y	Y	Y	Y	Y	Y	N	N
4 Sisisky	Y	Y	Y	Y	Y	Y	Y	Y
5 Goode	Y	Y	N	Y	Y	Y	Y	Y
6 ***Goodlatte***	Y	Y	N	Y	Y	Y	N	N
7 ***Bliley***	Y	Y	Y	Y	Y	Y	N	Y
8 Moran	Y	Y	Y	Y	Y	Y	N	N
9 Boucher	Y	Y	Y	Y	Y	Y	N	N
10 ***Wolf***	Y	Y	Y	Y	Y	Y	N	N
11 ***Davis***	Y	Y	N	Y	Y	Y	N	N
WASHINGTON								
1 ***White***	Y	Y	Y	Y	Y	Y	N	N
2 ***Metcalf***	Y	Y	Y	Y	Y	Y	N	N
3 ***Smith, Linda***	Y	Y	Y	Y	Y	Y	N	N
4 ***Hastings***	Y	Y	N	Y	Y	Y	N	N
5 ***Nethercutt***	Y	Y	N	Y	?	Y	N	N
6 Dicks	Y	Y	Y	Y	Y	Y	N	N
7 McDermott	Y	Y	Y	Y	Y	Y	N	N
8 ***Dunn***	Y	Y	Y	Y	Y	Y	N	N
9 Smith, Adam	Y	Y	Y	Y	Y	Y	Y	N
WEST VIRGINIA								
1 Mollohan	?	?	?	?	?	?	N	N
2 Wise	Y	Y	Y	Y	Y	Y	N	N
3 Rahall	Y	Y	Y	Y	Y	Y	N	N
WISCONSIN								
1 ***Neumann***	Y	Y	N	Y	Y	Y	Y	Y
2 ***Klug***	Y	Y	Y	Y	Y	Y	Y	Y
3 Kind	Y	Y	Y	Y	Y	Y	Y	Y
4 Kleczka	Y	Y	Y	Y	Y	Y	Y	N
5 Barrett	Y	Y	Y	Y	Y	Y	Y	Y
6 ***Petri***	Y	Y	Y	Y	Y	Y	N	Y
7 Obey	Y	Y	Y	Y	Y	Y	N	N
8 Johnson	Y	Y	Y	Y	Y	Y	N	N
9 ***Sensenbrenner***	Y	Y	N	Y	Y	N	N	Y
WYOMING								
AL ***Cubin***	Y	Y	N	Y	Y	Y	N	N

Southern states - Ala., Ark., Fla., Ga., Ky., La., Miss., N.C., Okla., S.C., Tenn., Texas, Va.

HOUSE VOTES 302, 303, 304, 305, 306, 307, 308, 309

302. HR 2169. Fiscal 1998 Transportation Appropriations/ Passage. Passage of the bill to provide $12.5 billion in new budget authority for the Department of Transportation and related agencies in fiscal 1998, and to authorize a total of $42.5 billion in expenditures for fiscal 1998. The bill provides $402 million more than the $12.1 billion provided in fiscal 1997 and $10 million more than the president's request. The authorization exceeds the fiscal 1997 level by $4.5 billion and the president's request by $2.3 billion. Passed 424-5: R 220-4; D 203-1 (ND 148-1, SD 55-0); I 1-0, July 23, 1997.

303. Procedural Motion/Adjourn. DeLauro, D-Conn., motion to adjourn. Motion rejected 122-279: R 0-204; D 121-75 (ND 90-53, SD 31-22); I 1-0, July 23, 1997.

304. Procedural Motion/Adjourn. Jackson-Lee, D-Texas, motion to adjourn. Motion rejected 105-311: R 0-215; D 105-96 (ND 81-65, SD 24-31); I 0-0, July 23, 1997.

305. HR 2160. Fiscal 1998 Agriculture Appropriations/ Previous Question on Amendment to Rule. Hastings, R-Wash., motion to order the previous question (thus ending debate and the possibility of amendment) on the Hastings, R-Wash., amendment to make in order one additional amendment to the rule (H Res 193) to provide for further House floor consideration of the bill to provide $49.6 billion in new budget authority for agriculture programs, rural development, the Food and Drug Administration and related agencies in fiscal 1998. Motion agreed to 269-160: R 224-0; D 45-159 (ND 36-113, SD 9-46); I 0-1, July 23, 1997.

306. HR 2160. Fiscal 1998 Agriculture Appropriations/Rule. Adoption of the rule (H Res 193) to provide for further House floor consideration of the bill to provide $49.6 billion in new budget authority for agriculture programs, rural development, the Food and Drug Administration and related agencies in fiscal 1998. Adopted 226-202: R 223-0; D 3-201 (ND 1-148, SD 2-53); I 0-1, July 23, 1997.

307. Procedural Motion/Adjourn. Obey, D-Wis., motion to adjourn. Motion rejected 64-322: R 0-209; D 63-113 (ND 52-73, SD 11-40); I 1-0, July 24, 1997.

308. HR 2160. Fiscal 1998 Agriculture Appropriations/ Women, Infants and Children Program. Obey, D-Wis., amendment to increase funding for the Women, Infants and Children (WIC) supplemental nutrition program by $23.7 million and reduce funding for federal crop insurance sales commissions by $36 million. Rejected 195-230: R 36-186; D 158-44 (ND 131-16, SD 27-28); I 1-0, July 24, 1997.

309. HR 2160. Fiscal 1998 Agriculture Appropriations/FDA Tobacco Initiative. Meehan, D-Mass., amendment to increase funding for the Food and Drug Administration's tobacco initiative by $10 million and reduce funding for federal crop insurance sales commissions by $14 million. Rejected 177-248: R 41-179; D 135-69 (ND 120-29, SD 15-40); I 1-0, July 24, 1997.

KEY

- Y Voted for (yea).
- # Paired for.
- + Announced for.
- N Voted against (nay).
- X Paired against.
- – Announced against.
- P Voted "present."
- C Voted "present" to avoid possible conflict of interest.
- ? Did not vote or otherwise make a position known.

Democrats ***Republicans***
Independent

	302	303	304	305	306	307	308	309
ALABAMA								
1 ***Callahan***	Y	N	N	Y	Y	N	N	Y
2 ***Everett***	Y	N	N	Y	Y	N	N	N
3 ***Riley***	Y	N	N	Y	Y	N	N	N
4 ***Aderholt***	Y	N	N	Y	Y	N	N	N
5 Cramer	Y	N	N	N	N	N	N	N
6 ***Bachus***	Y	N	N	Y	Y	N	N	Y
7 Hilliard	Y	N	N	N	N	N	Y	N
ALASKA								
AL ***Young***	?	?	?	?	?	?	?	?
ARIZONA								
1 ***Salmon***	Y	N	N	Y	Y	N	Y	Y
2 Pastor	Y	Y	N	Y	N	N	Y	Y
3 ***Stump***	Y	N	N	Y	Y	N	N	N
4 ***Shadegg***	Y	N	N	Y	Y	N	N	N
5 ***Kolbe***	Y	N	N	Y	Y	N	N	N
6 ***Hayworth***	Y	N	N	Y	Y	N	N	Y
ARKANSAS								
1 Berry	Y	Y	Y	N	N	Y	N	N
2 Snyder	Y	Y	Y	Y	N	N	N	N
3 ***Hutchinson***	Y	N	N	Y	Y	N	N	N
4 ***Dickey***	Y	N	N	Y	Y	N	N	Y
CALIFORNIA								
1 ***Riggs***	Y	N	N	Y	Y	N	Y	Y
2 ***Herger***	Y	N	N	Y	Y	N	N	N
3 Fazio	Y	Y	Y	N	N	Y	N	N
4 ***Doolittle***	Y	?	N	Y	Y	N	N	N
5 Matsui	Y	Y	Y	N	N	?	Y	Y
6 Woolsey	Y	Y	Y	N	N	Y	Y	Y
7 Miller	Y	Y	Y	N	N	Y	Y	Y
8 Pelosi	Y	Y	?	N	N	Y	Y	Y
9 Dellums	Y	Y	Y	Y	N	Y	Y	Y
10 Tauscher	Y	Y	Y	N	N	N	Y	Y
11 ***Pombo***	Y	N	N	Y	Y	N	N	N
12 Lantos	Y	N	Y	N	N	Y	Y	Y
13 Stark	?	?	?	?	?	?	?	?
14 Eshoo	Y	Y	Y	N	N	?	Y	Y
15 ***Campbell***	N	N	N	Y	Y	N	Y	Y
16 Lofgren	Y	N	N	N	N	N	Y	Y
17 Farr	Y	Y	Y	N	N	Y	N	N
18 Condit	Y	N	N	N	N	N	N	N
19 ***Radanovich***	Y	N	N	Y	Y	?	N	N
20 Dooley	Y	N	N	N	N	?	Y	N
21 ***Thomas***	Y	N	N	Y	Y	N	N	N
22 Capps	Y	Y	N	N	N	N	Y	Y
23 ***Gallegly***	Y	N	N	Y	Y	N	N	Y
24 Sherman	Y	N	N	N	N	N	Y	Y
25 ***McKeon***	Y	N	N	Y	Y	N	N	N
26 Berman	Y	Y	N	N	N	?	Y	Y
27 ***Rogan***	Y	N	N	Y	Y	N	N	N
28 ***Dreier***	Y	N	N	Y	Y	N	N	N
29 Waxman	Y	Y	Y	N	N	Y	Y	Y
30 Becerra	Y	Y	Y	N	N	N	Y	Y
31 Martinez	Y	?	N	N	N	N	Y	N
32 Dixon	Y	N	N	N	N	N	Y	Y
33 Roybal-Allard	Y	N	N	N	N	N	Y	Y
34 Torres	Y	Y	Y	N	N	Y	Y	Y
35 Waters	Y	Y	Y	Y	N	Y	Y	Y
36 Harman	Y	Y	Y	N	N	N	Y	Y
37 Millender-McD.	Y	Y	Y	N	N	Y	Y	Y
38 ***Horn***	Y	N	N	Y	Y	N	Y	Y
39 ***Royce***	Y	N	N	Y	Y	N	N	Y
40 ***Lewis***	Y	N	N	Y	Y	N	N	N
41 ***Kim***	Y	N	N	Y	Y	N	N	N
42 Brown	Y	Y	N	N	N	Y	Y	Y
43 ***Calvert***	Y	N	N	Y	Y	N	N	N
44 ***Bono***	Y	N	N	Y	Y	N	N	N
45 ***Rohrabacher***	Y	N	N	Y	Y	N	N	N
46 Sanchez	Y	N	N	N	N	N	Y	Y
47 ***Cox***	Y	N	N	Y	Y	?	N	N
48 ***Packard***	Y	N	N	Y	Y	N	N	N
49 ***Bilbray***	Y	N	N	Y	Y	N	N	Y
50 Filner	Y	Y	Y	N	N	Y	Y	Y
51 ***Cunningham***	Y	?	N	Y	Y	N	N	N
52 ***Hunter***	Y	N	N	Y	Y	N	N	N
COLORADO								
1 DeGette	Y	Y	Y	Y	N	Y	Y	Y
2 Skaggs	Y	Y	Y	N	N	?	Y	Y
3 ***McInnis***	Y	N	N	Y	Y	N	N	N
4 ***Schaffer***	Y	N	?	Y	Y	N	N	N
5 ***Hefley***	Y	N	N	Y	Y	N	N	N
6 ***Schaefer***	Y	N	N	Y	Y	N	N	N
CONNECTICUT								
1 Kennelly	Y	Y	Y	N	N	?	Y	Y
2 Gejdenson	Y	Y	Y	N	N	Y	Y	Y
3 DeLauro	Y	Y	Y	N	N	Y	Y	Y
4 ***Shays***	Y	N	N	Y	Y	N	Y	Y
5 Maloney	Y	N	N	N	N	N	Y	Y
6 ***Johnson***	Y	N	N	Y	Y	N	Y	Y
DELAWARE								
AL ***Castle***	Y	N	N	Y	Y	N	Y	Y
FLORIDA								
1 ***Scarborough***	Y	N	N	Y	Y	N	N	Y
2 Boyd	Y	N	N	N	N	N	N	N
3 Brown	Y	Y	Y	Y	N	Y	Y	N
4 ***Fowler***	Y	?	?	Y	Y	N	N	N
5 Thurman	Y	N	N	N	N	?	Y	N
6 ***Stearns***	Y	N	N	Y	Y	N	N	N
7 ***Mica***	Y	N	N	Y	Y	N	N	N
8 ***McCollum***	Y	N	N	Y	Y	N	N	N
9 ***Bilirakis***	Y	N	N	Y	Y	N	Y	N
10 ***Young***	Y	N	N	Y	Y	N	Y	N
11 Davis	Y	N	N	Y	N	?	Y	Y
12 ***Canady***	Y	N	N	Y	Y	N	N	N
13 ***Miller***	Y	N	N	Y	Y	N	N	Y
14 ***Goss***	Y	N	N	Y	Y	N	N	N
15 ***Weldon***	Y	N	N	Y	Y	N	N	N
16 ***Foley***	Y	N	N	Y	Y	N	N	N
17 Meek	Y	Y	Y	N	N	N	Y	N
18 ***Ros-Lehtinen***	Y	N	N	Y	Y	N	Y	N
19 Wexler	Y	Y	Y	N	N	N	Y	Y
20 Deutsch	Y	Y	Y	N	N	N	Y	Y
21 ***Diaz-Balart***	Y	N	N	Y	Y	?	Y	N
22 ***Shaw***	Y	N	N	Y	Y	N	N	N
23 Hastings	Y	Y	Y	N	N	Y	Y	N
GEORGIA								
1 ***Kingston***	Y	N	N	Y	Y	N	N	N
2 Bishop	Y	Y	Y	N	N	N	N	N
3 ***Collins***	Y	N	N	Y	Y	N	N	N
4 McKinney	Y	N	N	Y	N	N	Y	Y
5 Lewis	Y	Y	Y	N	N	Y	Y	Y
6 ***Gingrich***								
7 ***Barr***	Y	N	N	Y	Y	N	N	N
8 ***Chambliss***	Y	N	N	Y	Y	N	N	N
9 ***Deal***	Y	N	N	Y	Y	N	N	N
10 ***Norwood***	Y	?	?	Y	Y	?	N	N
11 ***Linder***	Y	N	N	Y	Y	N	N	N
HAWAII								
1 Abercrombie	Y	Y	Y	N	N	Y	Y	N
2 Mink	Y	Y	Y	N	N	Y	Y	Y
IDAHO								
1 ***Chenoweth***	Y	N	N	Y	Y	?	N	N
2 ***Crapo***	Y	N	N	Y	Y	N	N	N
ILLINOIS								
1 Rush	Y	Y	Y	Y	N	N	Y	Y
2 Jackson	Y	N	N	Y	N	N	Y	Y
3 Lipinski	Y	Y	N	N	N	N	Y	Y
4 Gutierrez	Y	Y	N	N	N	N	Y	Y
5 Blagojevich	Y	N	N	Y	N	N	Y	Y
6 ***Hyde***	Y	N	N	Y	Y	?	?	N
7 Davis	Y	Y	Y	N	N	Y	Y	Y
8 ***Crane***	Y	?	?	Y	Y	?	N	N
9 Yates	Y	Y	Y	N	N	Y	Y	Y
10 ***Porter***	Y	N	N	Y	?	N	Y	Y
11 ***Weller***	Y	N	N	Y	Y	N	N	N
12 Costello	Y	Y	Y	N	N	N	Y	N
13 ***Fawell***	Y	N	N	Y	Y	N	Y	Y
14 ***Hastert***	Y	N	N	Y	Y	N	N	?
15 ***Ewing***	Y	N	N	Y	Y	N	N	N

ND Northern Democrats SD Southern Democrats

	302	303	304	305	306	307	308	309
16 *Manzullo*	Y	N	N	Y	Y	N	N	N
17 Evans	Y	Y	Y	N	N	Y	Y	Y
18 *LaHood*	Y	N	N	Y	Y	N	N	N
19 Poshard	Y	N	N	N	N	N	Y	N
20 *Shimkus*	Y	N	N	Y	Y	N	N	N
INDIANA								
1 Visclosky	Y	N	N	N	N	N	Y	Y
2 *McIntosh*	Y	N	N	Y	Y	N	N	N
3 Roemer	Y	N	N	N	N	?	Y	Y
4 *Souder*	Y	?	N	Y	Y	N	N	N
5 *Buyer*	Y	?	N	Y	Y	N	N	N
6 *Burton*	Y	N	N	Y	Y	N	N	N
7 *Pease*	Y	N	N	Y	Y	N	N	N
8 *Hostettler*	N	N	N	Y	Y	N	N	N
9 Hamilton	Y	N	N	Y	N	N	N	N
10 Carson	Y	Y	Y	Y	N	Y	Y	Y
IOWA								
1 *Leach*	Y	?	?	Y	Y	N	N	Y
2 *Nussle*	Y	N	N	Y	Y	N	N	N
3 Boswell	Y	Y	Y	Y	N	?	N	N
4 *Ganske*	Y	?	?	Y	Y	N	N	N
5 *Latham*	Y	N	N	Y	Y	N	N	N
KANSAS								
1 *Moran*	Y	N	N	Y	Y	N	N	N
2 *Ryun*	Y	N	N	Y	Y	N	N	N
3 *Snowbarger*	Y	N	?	Y	Y	N	N	Y
4 *Tiahrt*	Y	N	N	Y	Y	N	N	N
KENTUCKY								
1 *Whitfield*	Y	N	N	Y	Y	?	N	N
2 *Lewis*	Y	N	N	Y	Y	N	N	N
3 *Northup*	Y	N	N	Y	Y	N	N	N
4 *Bunning*	Y	N	N	Y	Y	N	N	N
5 *Rogers*	Y	N	N	Y	Y	N	N	N
6 Baesler	Y	N	N	N	N	N	N	N
LOUISIANA								
1 *Livingston*	Y	N	N	Y	Y	N	N	?
2 Jefferson	Y	Y	Y	N	N	Y	N	N
3 *Tauzin*	Y	N	N	Y	Y	N	N	N
4 *McCrery*	Y	?	N	Y	Y	N	N	N
5 *Cooksey*	Y	N	N	Y	Y	N	N	N
6 *Baker*	Y	N	N	Y	Y	N	N	N
7 John	Y	Y	Y	N	N	N	N	N
MAINE								
1 Allen	Y	N	N	N	N	N	Y	Y
2 Baldacci	Y	N	N	Y	N	N	Y	Y
MARYLAND								
1 *Gilchrest*	Y	N	N	Y	Y	?	N	N
2 *Ehrlich*	Y	N	N	Y	Y	N	N	N
3 Cardin	Y	N	N	N	N	?	Y	Y
4 Wynn	Y	N	Y	N	N	N	Y	N
5 Hoyer	Y	Y	Y	Y	N	?	Y	Y
6 *Bartlett*	Y	N	N	Y	Y	N	N	N
7 Cummings	Y	Y	Y	N	N	N	Y	Y
8 *Morella*	Y	N	N	Y	N	N	Y	Y
MASSACHUSETTS								
1 Olver	Y	Y	Y	N	N	Y	Y	Y
2 Neal	Y	Y	Y	N	N	?	?	Y
3 McGovern	Y	Y	Y	N	N	N	Y	Y
4 Frank	Y	?	?	Y	N	Y	Y	Y
5 Meehan	Y	N	Y	N	N	N	Y	Y
6 Tierney	Y	Y	Y	N	N	N	Y	Y
7 Markey	Y	Y	Y	N	N	?	Y	Y
8 Kennedy	Y	Y	Y	N	N	N	Y	Y
9 Moakley	Y	Y	Y	N	N	Y	Y	Y
10 Delahunt	Y	Y	Y	Y	N	Y	Y	Y
MICHIGAN								
1 Stupak	Y	N	N	Y	N	N	Y	Y
2 *Hoekstra*	Y	N	N	Y	Y	N	N	N
3 *Ehlers*	Y	N	N	Y	Y	N	Y	N
4 *Camp*	Y	N	N	Y	Y	N	N	N
5 Barcia	Y	N	N	N	N	N	N	N
6 *Upton*	Y	N	N	Y	Y	N	N	N
7 *Smith*	Y	N	N	Y	Y	N	N	N
8 Stabenow	Y	N	N	N	N	N	N	N
9 Kildee	Y	N	N	N	N	N	Y	Y
10 Bonior	Y	Y	Y	N	N	Y	Y	N
11 *Knollenberg*	Y	N	N	Y	Y	N	N	N
12 Levin	Y	Y	Y	N	N	N	Y	Y
13 Rivers	Y	N	N	N	N	N	Y	Y
14 Conyers	Y	?	Y	N	N	Y	Y	Y
15 Kilpatrick	Y	Y	Y	N	N	Y	Y	N
16 Dingell	N	Y	Y	N	N	?	?	?
MINNESOTA								
1 *Gutknecht*	Y	N	N	Y	Y	N	N	N
2 Minge	Y	N	N	N	N	N	N	N

	302	303	304	305	306	307	308	309
3 *Ramstad*	Y	N	N	Y	Y	N	Y	Y
4 Vento	Y	Y	Y	Y	N	Y	Y	Y
5 Sabo	Y	Y	Y	N	N	Y	Y	Y
6 Luther	Y	N	N	N	N	N	Y	Y
7 Peterson	Y	N	N	N	N	N	N	N
8 Oberstar	Y	Y	Y	N	N	N	Y	Y
MISSISSIPPI								
1 *Wicker*	Y	N	N	Y	Y	N	N	N
2 Thompson	Y	Y	Y	N	N	Y	N	N
3 *Pickering*	Y	N	N	Y	Y	N	N	N
4 *Parker*	Y	N	N	Y	Y	N	N	N
5 Taylor	Y	N	N	N	N	N	N	N
MISSOURI								
1 Clay	Y	Y	Y	N	N	Y	Y	Y
2 *Talent*	Y	N	N	Y	Y	N	N	N
3 Gephardt	Y	Y	Y	N	N	Y	Y	Y
4 Skelton	Y	N	N	N	N	N	N	N
5 McCarthy	Y	N	N	N	N	–	Y	Y
6 Danner	Y	N	N	N	N	N	N	N
7 *Blunt*	Y	N	N	Y	Y	N	N	N
8 *Emerson*	Y	N	N	Y	Y	N	N	N
9 *Hulshof*	Y	N	N	Y	Y	N	N	N
MONTANA								
AL *Hill*	Y	N	N	Y	Y	N	N	N
NEBRASKA								
1 *Bereuter*	Y	N	N	Y	Y	N	Y	N
2 *Christensen*	Y	?	N	Y	Y	N	N	N
3 *Barrett*	Y	N	N	Y	Y	N	N	N
NEVADA								
1 *Ensign*	Y	?	N	Y	Y	N	Y	Y
2 *Gibbons*	Y	N	N	Y	Y	N	Y	N
NEW HAMPSHIRE								
1 *Sununu*	Y	N	N	Y	Y	?	Y	N
2 *Bass*	Y	N	N	Y	Y	N	Y	N
NEW JERSEY								
1 Andrews	Y	Y	Y	N	N	Y	Y	Y
2 *LoBiondo*	Y	N	N	Y	Y	N	Y	N
3 *Saxton*	Y	N	N	Y	Y	N	Y	N
4 *Smith*	Y	N	N	Y	Y	N	N	Y
5 *Roukema*	Y	N	N	Y	N	N	Y	Y
6 Pallone	?	?	?	?	?	Y	Y	Y
7 *Franks*	Y	N	N	Y	Y	N	Y	Y
8 Pascrell	Y	Y	N	N	N	Y	Y	Y
9 Rothman	Y	N	N	N	N	N	Y	Y
10 Payne	Y	Y	Y	N	N	N	Y	Y
11 *Frelinghuysen*	Y	N	N	Y	Y	N	Y	Y
12 *Pappas*	Y	N	N	Y	Y	N	Y	Y
13 Menendez	Y	Y	N	N	N	N	Y	Y
NEW MEXICO								
1 *Schiff*	?	?	?	?	?	?	?	?
2 *Skeen*	Y	N	N	Y	Y	N	N	N
3 *Redmond*	Y	N	N	Y	Y	N	N	N
NEW YORK								
1 *Forbes*	Y	N	N	Y	Y	N	Y	N
2 *Lazio*	Y	N	N	Y	Y	N	N	N
3 *King*	Y	N	N	Y	Y	N	N	N
4 McCarthy	Y	Y	Y	N	N	Y	Y	Y
5 Ackerman	Y	Y	Y	N	N	N	Y	Y
6 Flake	Y	Y	Y	N	N	N	Y	Y
7 Manton	Y	Y	?	N	N	N	Y	N
8 Nadler	Y	Y	Y	N	N	N	Y	Y
9 Schumer	Y	N	N	N	N	N	Y	Y
10 Towns	Y	Y	Y	N	N	N	Y	N
11 Owens	Y	Y	Y	N	N	Y	Y	Y
12 Velázquez	Y	Y	Y	Y	N	N	Y	Y
13 *Molinari*	Y	N	N	Y	Y	?	?	?
14 Maloney	Y	Y	Y	N	N	N	Y	Y
15 Rangel	Y	Y	Y	N	N	?	Y	Y
16 Serrano	Y	?	N	N	N	Y	Y	Y
17 Engel	Y	Y	Y	N	N	+	Y	Y
18 Lowey	Y	Y	Y	N	N	Y	Y	Y
19 *Kelly*	Y	N	N	Y	Y	N	Y	Y
20 *Gilman*	Y	N	N	Y	Y	N	Y	Y
21 McNulty	Y	Y	Y	N	N	N	Y	Y
22 *Solomon*	Y	N	N	Y	Y	N	N	N
23 *Boehlert*	Y	N	N	Y	Y	N	Y	N
24 *McHugh*	Y	N	N	Y	Y	N	N	N
25 *Walsh*	Y	N	N	Y	Y	N	N	N
26 Hinchey	Y	Y	Y	N	N	Y	Y	Y
27 *Paxon*	Y	N	N	Y	Y	?	N	N
28 Slaughter	Y	?	Y	N	N	Y	Y	Y
29 LaFalce	Y	N	N	N	N	N	Y	Y
30 *Quinn*	Y	N	N	Y	Y	N	Y	Y
31 *Houghton*	Y	N	N	Y	Y	N	N	N

	302	303	304	305	306	307	308	309
NORTH CAROLINA								
1 Clayton	Y	Y	Y	N	N	N	Y	N
2 Etheridge	Y	N	N	N	N	N	N	N
3 *Jones*	Y	N	N	Y	Y	N	N	N
4 Price	Y	N	N	N	N	N	Y	N
5 *Burr*	Y	N	N	Y	Y	N	N	N
6 *Coble*	Y	N	N	Y	Y	N	N	N
7 McIntyre	Y	N	N	N	N	N	N	N
8 Hefner	Y	Y	Y	N	N	Y	Y	N
9 *Myrick*	Y	?	N	Y	Y	N	N	N
10 *Ballenger*	Y	N	N	Y	Y	N	N	N
11 *Taylor*	Y	N	N	Y	Y	N	N	N
12 Watt	Y	Y	Y	N	N	N	Y	N
NORTH DAKOTA								
AL Pomeroy	Y	N	N	Y	N	?	N	N
OHIO								
1 *Chabot*	Y	N	N	Y	Y	N	Y	N
2 *Portman*	Y	N	N	Y	Y	N	N	N
3 Hall	Y	Y	Y	Y	N	N	Y	Y
4 *Oxley*	Y	?	N	Y	Y	N	N	N
5 *Gillmor*	Y	N	N	Y	Y	N	N	N
6 Strickland	Y	Y	N	N	N	N	Y	N
7 *Hobson*	Y	N	N	Y	Y	N	N	N
8 *Boehner*	Y	N	N	Y	Y	N	N	N
9 Kaptur	Y	Y	Y	N	N	?	#	Y
10 Kucinich	Y	N	N	N	N	N	Y	Y
11 Stokes	Y	Y	N	N	N	?	Y	N
12 *Kasich*	Y	?	N	Y	Y	N	N	N
13 Brown	Y	Y	Y	N	N	Y	Y	Y
14 Sawyer	Y	Y	N	Y	N	?	Y	Y
15 *Pryce*	Y	N	N	Y	Y	N	N	N
16 *Regula*	Y	N	N	Y	Y	N	N	N
17 Traficant	Y	N	N	Y	Y	N	Y	Y
18 *Ney*	Y	N	N	Y	Y	N	N	N
19 *LaTourette*	Y	?	N	Y	Y	N	N	Y
OKLAHOMA								
1 *Largent*	Y	N	N	Y	Y	N	N	N
2 *Coburn*	Y	N	N	Y	Y	N	N	N
3 *Watkins*	Y	N	N	Y	Y	N	N	N
4 *Watts*	Y	N	N	Y	Y	N	N	N
5 *Istook*	Y	N	N	Y	Y	N	N	N
6 *Lucas*	Y	N	N	Y	Y	N	N	N
OREGON								
1 Furse	Y	Y	Y	N	N	Y	Y	Y
2 *Smith*	Y	N	N	Y	Y	N	N	N
3 Blumenauer	Y	N	N	N	N	?	Y	Y
4 DeFazio	Y	Y	Y	N	N	Y	Y	Y
5 Hooley	Y	N	N	N	N	?	N	Y
PENNSYLVANIA								
1 Foglietta	Y	N	N	Y	N	?	Y	Y
2 Fattah	Y	N	N	N	N	N	Y	Y
3 Borski	Y	N	N	N	N	N	Y	Y
4 Klink	Y	Y	Y	Y	N	Y	Y	N
5 *Peterson*	Y	N	N	Y	Y	N	N	N
6 Holden	Y	?	N	Y	N	N	N	Y
7 *Weldon*	Y	N	N	Y	Y	N	Y	Y
8 *Greenwood*	Y	N	N	Y	Y	N	N	?
9 *Shuster*	Y	N	N	Y	Y	N	N	N
10 *McDade*	Y	N	N	Y	Y	N	N	N
11 Kanjorski	Y	N	N	Y	N	N	Y	Y
12 Murtha	Y	N	N	Y	N	N	N	N
13 *Fox*	Y	N	N	Y	Y	N	Y	Y
14 Coyne	Y	Y	Y	N	N	Y	Y	Y
15 McHale	Y	N	N	N	N	N	Y	Y
16 *Pitts*	Y	N	N	Y	Y	N	N	N
17 *Gekas*	Y	N	N	Y	Y	N	N	N
18 Doyle	Y	N	N	Y	N	N	N	N
19 *Goodling*	Y	N	N	Y	Y	N	N	N
20 Mascara	Y	N	N	N	N	N	N	Y
21 *English*	Y	N	N	Y	Y	N	N	Y
RHODE ISLAND								
1 Kennedy	Y	Y	Y	N	N	Y	Y	Y
2 Weygand	Y	Y	Y	N	N	Y	Y	Y
SOUTH CAROLINA								
1 *Sanford*	N	N	N	Y	Y	N	N	N
2 *Spence*	Y	N	N	Y	Y	N	N	N
3 *Graham*	?	?	N	Y	Y	?	N	N
4 *Inglis*	Y	N	N	Y	Y	N	N	N
5 Spratt	Y	Y	N	Y	N	N	N	N
6 Clyburn	Y	Y	Y	N	N	N	N	N
SOUTH DAKOTA								
AL *Thune*	Y	N	N	Y	Y	N	N	N
TENNESSEE								
1 *Jenkins*	Y	N	N	Y	Y	N	N	N
2 *Duncan*	Y	N	N	Y	Y	N	N	Y

	302	303	304	305	306	307	308	
3 *Wamp*	Y	N	N	Y	Y	N	N	N
4 *Hilleary*	Y	?	N	Y	Y	N	N	N
5 Clement	Y	?	N	N	N	N	Y	N
6 Gordon	Y	N	N	N	N	N	N	N
7 *Bryant*	Y	N	N	Y	Y	N	N	N
8 Tanner	Y	N	N	N	N	N	N	N
9 Ford	Y	?	N	Y	N	N	N	Y
TEXAS								
1 Sandlin	Y	Y	N	N	N	Y	N	N
2 Turner	Y	Y	Y	N	N	N	N	N
3 *Johnson, Sam*	Y	N	N	Y	Y	?	N	N
4 Hall	Y	N	N	N	N	N	N	N
5 *Sessions*	Y	N	N	Y	Y	N	N	N
6 *Barton*	Y	N	N	?	?	?	X	?
7 *Archer*	Y	N	?	Y	Y	N	N	N
8 *Brady*	Y	N	N	Y	Y	?	N	N
9 Lampson	Y	Y	N	N	N	?	Y	Y
10 Doggett	Y	Y	Y	N	N	Y	Y	Y
11 Edwards	Y	N	N	N	N	N	N	N
12 *Granger*	Y	N	N	Y	Y	N	N	N
13 *Thornberry*	Y	N	N	Y	Y	N	N	N
14 *Paul*	N	N	N	Y	Y	N	N	N
15 Hinojosa	Y	N	N	N	N	N	N	N
16 Reyes	Y	N	N	N	N	N	Y	Y
17 Stenholm	Y	N	N	N	N	N	N	N
18 Jackson-Lee	Y	Y	Y	Y	N	N	Y	Y
19 *Combest*	Y	N	N	Y	Y	N	N	N
20 Gonzalez	Y	Y	Y	N	N	N	N	Y
21 *Smith*	Y	N	N	Y	Y	N	N	Y
22 *DeLay*	Y	?	?	Y	Y	N	N	N
23 *Bonilla*	Y	N	N	Y	Y	N	N	N
24 Frost	Y	Y	Y	N	N	Y	N	N
25 Bentsen	Y	N	N	N	N	N	Y	Y
26 *Armey*	Y	N	N	Y	Y	N	N	N
27 Ortiz	Y	Y	N	Y	N	N	Y	Y
28 Rodriguez	Y	Y	Y	N	N	N	Y	N
29 Green	Y	N	N	N	N	N	Y	Y
30 Johnson, E.B.	Y	Y	Y	N	N	?	Y	N
UTAH								
1 *Hansen*	Y	N	N	Y	Y	N	N	Y
2 *Cook*	Y	N	N	Y	Y	N	N	Y
3 *Cannon*	Y	N	N	Y	Y	N	N	N
VERMONT								
AL *Sanders*	Y	Y	?	N	N	Y	Y	Y
VIRGINIA								
1 *Bateman*	Y	?	?	Y	Y	N	N	N
2 Pickett	Y	Y	N	N	Y	N	N	N
3 Scott	Y	N	N	N	N	N	Y	N
4 Sisisky	Y	Y	N	N	N	N	N	N
5 Goode	Y	N	N	Y	Y	N	N	N
6 *Goodlatte*	Y	N	N	Y	Y	N	N	N
7 *Bliley*	Y	?	Y	Y	Y	N	N	N
8 Moran	Y	Y	N	N	N	Y	Y	Y
9 Boucher	Y	Y	Y	N	N	N	Y	N
10 *Wolf*	Y	N	N	Y	Y	N	N	N
11 *Davis*	Y	N	N	Y	Y	N	Y	Y
WASHINGTON								
1 *White*	Y	N	N	Y	Y	N	N	N
2 *Metcalf*	Y	N	N	Y	Y	N	N	N
3 *Smith, Linda*	Y	N	N	Y	Y	N	N	Y
4 *Hastings*	Y	N	N	Y	Y	N	N	N
5 *Nethercutt*	Y	N	N	Y	Y	N	N	N
6 Dicks	Y	N	N	Y	N	N	Y	Y
7 McDermott	Y	N	N	N	N	?	Y	Y
8 *Dunn*	Y	N	N	Y	Y	N	N	N
9 Smith, Adam	Y	Y	Y	N	N	N	Y	Y
WEST VIRGINIA								
1 Mollohan	Y	N	N	Y	N	N	N	N
2 Wise	Y	Y	N	Y	N	N	Y	Y
3 Rahall	Y	N	N	Y	N	N	Y	N
WISCONSIN								
1 *Neumann*	Y	N	N	Y	Y	N	N	N
2 *Klug*	Y	N	N	Y	Y	N	N	N
3 Kind	Y	N	N	N	N	?	Y	Y
4 Kleczka	Y	N	N	N	N	N	Y	Y
5 Barrett	Y	Y	Y	N	N	N	Y	Y
6 *Petri*	Y	N	N	Y	Y	N	N	N
7 Obey	Y	Y	Y	N	N	Y	Y	Y
8 Johnson	Y	Y	Y	Y	N	N	Y	Y
9 *Sensenbrenner*	Y	N	N	Y	Y	N	N	N
WYOMING								
AL *Cubin*	Y	N	N	Y	Y	N	N	N

Southern states - Ala., Ark., Fla., Ga., Ky., La., Miss., N.C., Okla., S.C., Tenn., Texas, Va.

HOUSE VOTES 310, 311, 312, 313, 314, 315, 316

310. HR 2160. Fiscal 1998 Agriculture Appropriations/ Tobacco Crop Insurance. Lowey, D-N.Y., amendment to prohibit the use of funds in the bill to pay the salaries of personnel who provide tobacco crop insurance or non-insured crop disaster assistance for tobacco, effectively ending the federal crop insurance subsidy for tobacco. Rejected 209-216: R 88-133; D 120-83 (ND 108-40, SD 12-43); I 1-0, July 24, 1997.

311. HR 2160. Fiscal 1998 Agriculture Appropriations/Food for North Korea. Cox, R-Calif., amendment to prohibit the use of funds in the bill to provide food to North Korea, except for humanitarian assistance distributed directly by the U.N. World Food Program or other non-governmental organizations. Adopted 418-0: R 219-0; D 198-0 (ND 144-0, SD 54-0); I 1-0, July 24, 1997.

312. HR 2160. Fiscal 1998 Agriculture Appropriations/Sugar Loan Program. Miller, R-Fla., amendment to prohibit the use of funds in the bill to pay the salaries and expenses of Department of Agriculture personnel who issue non-recourse loans to sugar beet or sugar cane processors, effectively ending the non-recourse loan program for sugar. Rejected 175-253: R 103-120; D 71-133 (ND 64-86, SD 7-47); I 1-0, July 24, 1997.

313. HR 2160. Fiscal 1998 Agriculture Appropriations/Motion to Rise. Slaughter, D-N.Y., motion to rise from the Committee of the Whole. Motion rejected 158-265: R 0-222; D 157-43 (ND 124-25, SD 33-18); I 1-0, July 24, 1997.

314. HR 2160. Fiscal 1998 Agriculture Appropriations/Peanut Price Supports. Neumann, R-Wis., amendment to prohibit the use of funds in the bill to pay the salaries and expenses of Department of Agriculture personnel who maintain a quota price for peanuts in excess of $550 per ton, effectively establishing the maximum market price for peanuts at that level. Rejected 185-242: R 100-123; D 84-119 (ND 80-69, SD 4-50); I 1-0, July 24, 1997.

315. HR 2160. Fiscal 1998 Agriculture Appropriations/Strike Enacting Clause. Obey, D-Wis., motion to strike the enacting clause, thus killing the bill. Motion rejected 125-300: R 1-222; D 123-78 (ND 105-42, SD 18-36); I 1-0, July 24, 1997.

316. HR 2160. Fiscal 1998 Agriculture Appropriations/Market Access Program. Chabot, R-Ohio, amendment to prohibit the use of funds in the bill to pay the salaries and expenses of Department of Agriculture personnel who administer the Market Access Program, effectively defunding the program, which provides grants to businesses and trade associations to promote exports of agricultural products. Rejected 150-277: R 85-137; D 64-140 (ND 60-90, SD 4-50); I 1-0, July 24, 1997.

KEY

- Y Voted for (yea).
- # Paired for.
- \+ Announced for.
- N Voted against (nay).
- X Paired against.
- \- Announced against.
- P Voted "present."
- C Voted "present" to avoid possible conflict of interest.
- ? Did not vote or otherwise make a position known.

Democrats ***Republicans***
Independent

	310	311	312	313	314	315	316
ALABAMA							
1 ***Callahan***	Y	Y	N	N	Y	N	Y
2 ***Everett***	N	Y	N	N	N	N	N
3 ***Riley***	N	Y	N	N	N	N	N
4 ***Aderholt***	N	Y	N	N	N	N	N
5 Cramer	N	Y	N	N	N	N	N
6 ***Bachus***	Y	Y	N	N	N	N	Y
7 Hilliard	N	Y	N	Y	N	Y	N
ALASKA							
AL ***Young***	?	?	?	?	?	?	?
ARIZONA							
1 ***Salmon***	Y	Y	Y	N	Y	N	Y
2 Pastor	N	Y	N	Y	N	Y	N
3 ***Stump***	N	Y	N	N	N	N	N
4 ***Shadegg***	N	Y	Y	N	Y	N	Y
5 ***Kolbe***	N	Y	Y	N	Y	N	Y
6 ***Hayworth***	Y	Y	Y	N	Y	N	Y
ARKANSAS							
1 Berry	N	Y	N	Y	N	N	N
2 Snyder	Y	Y	N	Y	N	N	N
3 ***Hutchinson***	N	Y	Y	N	Y	N	Y
4 ***Dickey***	N	Y	Y	N	Y	N	N
CALIFORNIA							
1 ***Riggs***	Y	Y	N	N	N	N	N
2 ***Herger***	N	Y	N	N	N	N	N
3 Fazio	N	Y	N	Y	N	Y	N
4 ***Doolittle***	N	Y	N	N	N	N	N
5 Matsui	N	Y	N	N	N	Y	N
6 Woolsey	Y	Y	N	Y	N	Y	N
7 Miller	Y	Y	Y	Y	N	Y	N
8 Pelosi	Y	Y	N	Y	N	Y	N
9 Dellums	Y	Y	N	Y	N	Y	N
10 Tauscher	Y	Y	Y	Y	Y	Y	N
11 ***Pombo***	N	Y	N	N	N	N	N
12 Lantos	Y	Y	Y	Y	Y	Y	Y
13 Stark	?	?	?	?	?	?	?
14 Eshoo	Y	Y	Y	Y	Y	Y	N
15 ***Campbell***	Y	Y	Y	N	Y	N	Y
16 Lofgren	Y	Y	N	Y	Y	Y	N
17 Farr	Y	Y	N	Y	N	N	N
18 Condit	N	Y	N	N	N	N	N
19 ***Radanovich***	N	Y	Y	N	N	N	N
20 Dooley	N	Y	N	N	Y	N	N
21 ***Thomas***	N	Y	N	N	N	N	N
22 Capps	Y	Y	Y	Y	Y	N	N
23 ***Gallegly***	N	Y	Y	N	Y	N	N
24 Sherman	Y	Y	N	Y	Y	N	N
25 ***McKeon***	Y	Y	N	N	N	N	N
26 Berman	Y	Y	Y	Y	Y	Y	N
27 ***Rogan***	-	Y	Y	N	N	N	Y
28 ***Dreier***	N	Y	Y	N	Y	N	N
29 Waxman	Y	Y	Y	Y	Y	Y	Y
30 Becerra	Y	Y	N	Y	N	Y	N
31 Martinez	N	Y	N	N	N	N	N
32 Dixon	N	Y	N	Y	N	Y	N
33 Roybal-Allard	Y	Y	N	Y	N	N	N
34 Torres	Y	Y	N	Y	N	Y	N
35 Waters	Y	Y	N	Y	Y	?	N
36 Harman	Y	Y	N	Y	N	N	N
37 Millender-McD.	N	Y	N	Y	N	Y	N
38 ***Horn***	Y	Y	Y	N	Y	N	Y
39 ***Royce***	Y	Y	Y	N	Y	N	Y
40 ***Lewis***	N	?	N	N	N	N	N
41 ***Kim***	N	Y	Y	N	Y	N	N
42 Brown	Y	Y	N	Y	Y	Y	N
43 ***Calvert***	N	Y	N	N	N	N	N
44 ***Bono***	N	Y	N	N	N	N	N
45 ***Rohrabacher***	Y	Y	Y	N	Y	N	Y
46 Sanchez	N	Y	N	Y	N	N	N
47 ***Cox***	Y	Y	Y	N	Y	N	Y
48 ***Packard***	N	Y	N	N	N	N	N
49 ***Bilbray***	Y	Y	Y	N	Y	N	Y
50 Filner	Y	Y	N	Y	N	Y	N
51 ***Cunningham***	N	Y	N	N	N	N	Y
52 ***Hunter***	N	Y	N	N	N	N	N
COLORADO							
1 DeGette	Y	?	Y	Y	Y	Y	Y
2 Skaggs	N	Y	N	Y	Y	N	N
3 ***McInnis***	Y	Y	N	N	N	N	N
4 ***Schaffer***	N	Y	N	N	N	N	N
5 ***Hefley***	Y	Y	N	N	N	N	Y
6 ***Schaefer***	N	Y	N	N	N	N	N
CONNECTICUT							
1 Kennelly	Y	Y	Y	Y	Y	Y	N
2 Gejdenson	Y	Y	Y	Y	?	N	Y
3 DeLauro	Y	Y	Y	Y	Y	Y	Y
4 ***Shays***	Y	Y	Y	N	Y	N	Y
5 Maloney	Y	Y	Y	Y	Y	N	Y
6 ***Johnson***	Y	Y	Y	N	Y	N	N
DELAWARE							
AL ***Castle***	Y	Y	Y	N	Y	N	Y
FLORIDA							
1 ***Scarborough***	Y	Y	Y	N	N	N	Y
2 Boyd	N	Y	N	N	N	N	N
3 Brown	N	Y	N	Y	N	Y	N
4 ***Fowler***	N	Y	N	N	N	N	Y
5 Thurman	N	Y	N	Y	N	N	N
6 ***Stearns***	N	Y	N	N	N	N	Y
7 ***Mica***	N	Y	N	N	N	N	N
8 ***McCollum***	N	Y	N	N	N	N	N
9 ***Bilirakis***	N	Y	Y	N	N	N	N
10 ***Young***	Y	Y	Y	N	N	N	N
11 Davis	N	Y	N	Y	N	Y	N
12 ***Canady***	Y	Y	N	N	N	N	N
13 ***Miller***	Y	Y	Y	N	Y	N	Y
14 ***Goss***	Y	Y	Y	N	Y	N	Y
15 ***Weldon***	Y	Y	N	N	N	N	N
16 ***Foley***	N	Y	N	N	N	N	N
17 Meek	N	Y	N	?	N	N	N
18 ***Ros-Lehtinen***	N	Y	Y	N	Y	N	N
19 Wexler	Y	Y	N	Y	N	Y	N
20 Deutsch	Y	Y	Y	Y	Y	Y	N
21 ***Diaz-Balart***	N	Y	N	N	N	N	N
22 ***Shaw***	Y	Y	Y	N	Y	N	Y
23 Hastings	N	Y	N	Y	N	Y	N
GEORGIA							
1 ***Kingston***	N	Y	Y	N	N	N	N
2 Bishop	N	Y	N	Y	N	N	N
3 ***Collins***	N	Y	Y	N	Y	N	Y
4 McKinney	Y	Y	Y	Y	N	Y	N
5 Lewis	Y	Y	Y	?	N	Y	Y
6 ***Gingrich***							
7 ***Barr***	N	Y	Y	N	Y	N	Y
8 ***Chambliss***	N	Y	N	N	N	N	N
9 ***Deal***	N	Y	N	N	N	N	N
10 ***Norwood***	N	Y	N	N	N	N	N
11 ***Linder***	N	Y	Y	N	N	N	Y
HAWAII							
1 Abercrombie	N	Y	N	Y	N	Y	N
2 Mink	N	Y	N	Y	N	Y	N
IDAHO							
1 ***Chenoweth***	N	Y	N	N	N	N	N
2 ***Crapo***	N	Y	N	N	N	N	N
ILLINOIS							
1 Rush	Y	Y	Y	Y	Y	Y	N
2 Jackson	Y	Y	Y	Y	Y	Y	Y
3 Lipinski	Y	Y	N	N	N	N	Y
4 Gutierrez	Y	Y	N	Y	Y	Y	Y
5 Blagojevich	Y	Y	Y	Y	Y	Y	Y
6 ***Hyde***	N	Y	N	N	N	N	Y
7 Davis	Y	Y	Y	Y	Y	Y	N
8 ***Crane***	N	Y	Y	N	Y	N	Y
9 Yates	Y	Y	Y	Y	N	Y	Y
10 ***Porter***	Y	Y	Y	N	Y	N	Y
11 ***Weller***	N	Y	N	N	N	N	N
12 Costello	Y	Y	N	N	N	N	N
13 ***Fawell***	Y	Y	Y	N	Y	N	Y
14 ***Hastert***	N	Y	N	N	N	N	Y
15 ***Ewing***	N	Y	N	N	N	N	N

ND Northern Democrats SD Southern Democrats

	310	311	312	313	314	315	316
16 ***Manzullo***	Y	Y	Y	N	Y	N	Y
17 Evans	Y	Y	N	N	N	Y	N
18 ***LaHood***	N	Y	N	N	N	N	N
19 Poshard	Y	Y	N	N	N	N	N
20 ***Shimkus***	N	Y	N	N	N	N	N
INDIANA							
1 Visclosky	Y	?	Y	Y	Y	Y	Y
2 ***McIntosh***	N	Y	N	N	Y	N	Y
3 Roemer	Y	Y	N	N	Y	N	N
4 ***Souder***	Y	Y	Y	N	Y	N	Y
5 ***Buyer***	N	Y	N	N	N	N	N
6 ***Burton***	N	Y	N	N	Y	N	N
7 ***Pease***	N	Y	N	N	N	N	N
8 ***Hostettler***	N	Y	Y	N	Y	N	Y
9 Hamilton	N	Y	N	N	N	N	N
10 Carson	Y	Y	N	Y	N	N	Y
IOWA							
1 ***Leach***	Y	Y	N	N	N	N	N
2 ***Nussle***	N	Y	N	N	N	N	N
3 Boswell	Y	Y	N	Y	N	N	N
4 ***Ganske***	Y	Y	N	N	Y	N	N
5 ***Latham***	N	Y	N	N	N	N	N
KANSAS							
1 ***Moran***	N	Y	Y	N	Y	N	N
2 ***Ryun***	Y	Y	N	N	Y	N	N
3 ***Snowbarger***	Y	Y	Y	N	Y	N	Y
4 ***Tiahrt***	Y	Y	N	N	Y	N	Y
KENTUCKY							
1 ***Whitfield***	N	Y	N	N	N	N	N
2 ***Lewis***	N	Y	N	N	N	N	N
3 ***Northup***	N	Y	Y	N	Y	N	N
4 ***Bunning***	N	Y	N	N	N	N	N
5 ***Rogers***	N	Y	N	N	N	N	N
6 Baesler	N	Y	N	N	N	N	N
LOUISIANA							
1 ***Livingston***	N	Y	N	N	N	N	N
2 Jefferson	N	Y	N	Y	N	Y	N
3 ***Tauzin***	N	Y	N	N	N	N	N
4 ***McCrery***	N	Y	N	N	N	N	N
5 ***Cooksey***	Y	Y	N	N	N	N	N
6 ***Baker***	N	Y	N	N	N	N	N
7 John	N	Y	N	Y	N	N	N
MAINE							
1 Allen	Y	Y	Y	Y	Y	Y	N
2 Baldacci	Y	Y	N	Y	N	Y	N
MARYLAND							
1 ***Gilchrest***	Y	Y	Y	N	N	N	N
2 ***Ehrlich***	N	Y	Y	N	Y	N	Y
3 Cardin	Y	Y	Y	N	Y	N	Y
4 Wynn	N	Y	N	Y	N	N	N
5 Hoyer	N	Y	Y	Y	N	Y	N
6 ***Bartlett***	Y	Y	Y	N	N	N	N
7 Cummings	Y	Y	Y	Y	N	Y	Y
8 ***Morella***	Y	Y	Y	N	Y	N	Y
MASSACHUSETTS							
1 Olver	Y	Y	Y	Y	Y	Y	Y
2 Neal	Y	Y	Y	Y	Y	Y	Y
3 McGovern	Y	Y	Y	Y	Y	Y	Y
4 Frank	Y	Y	Y	Y	Y	Y	Y
5 Meehan	Y	Y	Y	Y	Y	Y	Y
6 Tierney	Y	Y	Y	Y	Y	Y	Y
7 Markey	Y	Y	Y	Y	Y	Y	Y
8 Kennedy	Y	Y	Y	N	Y	Y	Y
9 Moakley	Y	Y	Y	Y	Y	Y	Y
10 Delahunt	Y	Y	N	Y	N	Y	Y
MICHIGAN							
1 Stupak	Y	Y	N	Y	N	Y	Y
2 ***Hoekstra***	Y	Y	Y	N	Y	N	Y
3 ***Ehlers***	Y	Y	N	N	Y	N	Y
4 ***Camp***	N	Y	N	N	N	N	N
5 Barcia	N	Y	N	N	N	N	N
6 ***Upton***	Y	Y	Y	N	Y	N	N
7 ***Smith***	N	Y	N	N	N	N	N
8 Stabenow	Y	Y	N	Y	N	N	N
9 Kildee	Y	Y	N	Y	N	Y	N
10 Bonior	N	Y	N	Y	N	Y	N
11 ***Knollenberg***	N	Y	N	N	Y	N	Y
12 Levin	Y	Y	N	Y	Y	Y	N
13 Rivers	Y	Y	N	Y	Y	N	Y
14 Conyers	Y	Y	Y	Y	Y	Y	Y
15 Kilpatrick	N	Y	N	Y	N	Y	N
16 Dingell	?	?	N	Y	N	Y	N
MINNESOTA							
1 ***Gutknecht***	Y	Y	N	N	N	N	Y
2 Minge	Y	Y	N	N	N	N	N
3 ***Ramstad***	Y	Y	Y	N	Y	N	Y
4 Vento	Y	Y	N	Y	Y	Y	Y
5 Sabo	Y	Y	N	Y	N	Y	N
6 Luther	Y	Y	Y	N	Y	N	Y
7 Peterson	N	Y	N	Y	N	N	N
8 Oberstar	N	Y	N	N	N	Y	N
MISSISSIPPI							
1 ***Wicker***	N	Y	N	N	N	N	N
2 Thompson	N	Y	N	Y	N	N	N
3 ***Pickering***	N	Y	N	N	N	N	N
4 ***Parker***	N	Y	N	N	N	N	N
5 Taylor	Y	Y	N	N	Y	N	Y
MISSOURI							
1 Clay	N	Y	N	Y	Y	Y	N
2 ***Talent***	Y	Y	N	N	N	N	Y
3 Gephardt	N	Y	N	Y	N	?	N
4 Skelton	N	Y	N	N	N	N	N
5 McCarthy	N	Y	Y	N	N	Y	N
6 Danner	N	Y	N	Y	Y	N	N
7 ***Blunt***	–	Y	N	N	N	N	N
8 ***Emerson***	N	Y	N	N	N	N	N
9 ***Hulshof***	N	Y	N	N	Y	N	N
MONTANA							
AL ***Hill***	Y	Y	N	N	N	N	N
NEBRASKA							
1 ***Bereuter***	Y	Y	N	N	N	N	N
2 ***Christensen***	Y	Y	N	N	Y	N	N
3 ***Barrett***	N	Y	N	N	N	N	N
NEVADA							
1 ***Ensign***	Y	Y	Y	N	Y	N	Y
2 ***Gibbons***	Y	Y	Y	N	Y	N	Y
NEW HAMPSHIRE							
1 ***Sununu***	Y	Y	Y	N	Y	N	Y
2 ***Bass***	Y	Y	Y	N	Y	N	Y
NEW JERSEY							
1 Andrews	Y	Y	Y	Y	Y	Y	Y
2 ***LoBiondo***	Y	Y	Y	N	Y	N	Y
3 ***Saxton***	N	Y	Y	N	N	N	N
4 ***Smith***	Y	Y	Y	N	Y	N	N
5 ***Roukema***	Y	Y	Y	N	Y	N	Y
6 Pallone	Y	Y	Y	Y	Y	Y	Y
7 ***Franks***	Y	Y	Y	N	Y	N	Y
8 Pascrell	Y	Y	Y	Y	Y	Y	Y
9 Rothman	Y	Y	N	Y	N	N	Y
10 Payne	Y	Y	Y	Y	Y	Y	Y
11 ***Frelinghuysen***	Y	Y	Y	N	Y	N	Y
12 ***Pappas***	Y	Y	Y	N	Y	N	N
13 Menendez	Y	Y	N	Y	Y	N	N
NEW MEXICO							
1 ***Schiff***	?	?	?	?	?	?	?
2 ***Skeen***	N	Y	N	N	N	N	N
3 ***Redmond***	N	Y	N	N	N	N	N
NEW YORK							
1 ***Forbes***	N	Y	Y	N	Y	N	N
2 ***Lazio***	Y	Y	Y	N	Y	N	Y
3 ***King***	Y	Y	N	N	Y	N	Y
4 McCarthy	Y	Y	Y	Y	Y	Y	Y
5 Ackerman	Y	Y	N	?	N	Y	N
6 Flake	N	Y	N	Y	N	Y	N
7 Manton	N	Y	N	Y	N	Y	N
8 Nadler	Y	Y	Y	Y	Y	Y	Y
9 Schumer	Y	Y	Y	Y	Y	Y	Y
10 Towns	N	Y	N	Y	N	Y	N
11 Owens	Y	Y	N	Y	N	Y	Y
12 Velázquez	Y	Y	Y	Y	Y	Y	Y
13 ***Molinari***	?	?	?	?	?	?	?
14 Maloney	Y	Y	Y	Y	Y	Y	Y
15 Rangel	?	Y	N	Y	N	Y	N
16 Serrano	Y	Y	N	Y	N	Y	N
17 Engel	Y	Y	Y	Y	Y	Y	Y
18 Lowey	Y	Y	Y	Y	Y	Y	Y
19 ***Kelly***	Y	Y	Y	N	Y	N	Y
20 ***Gilman***	Y	Y	N	N	Y	N	N
21 McNulty	Y	Y	Y	Y	Y	Y	N
22 ***Solomon***	N	Y	N	N	N	N	N
23 ***Boehlert***	N	Y	Y	N	Y	N	N
24 ***McHugh***	Y	Y	Y	N	Y	N	N
25 ***Walsh***	N	Y	N	N	N	N	N
26 Hinchey	Y	Y	Y	Y	Y	Y	Y
27 ***Paxon***	N	Y	Y	N	N	N	N
28 Slaughter	Y	Y	Y	Y	Y	Y	N
29 LaFalce	Y	Y	Y	Y	Y	Y	N
30 ***Quinn***	Y	Y	Y	N	Y	N	N
31 ***Houghton***	N	Y	N	N	N	N	N
NORTH CAROLINA							
1 Clayton	N	Y	N	Y	N	Y	N
2 Etheridge	N	Y	N	N	N	N	N
3 ***Jones***	N	Y	N	N	N	N	N
4 Price	N	Y	N	N	N	N	N
5 ***Burr***	N	Y	N	N	N	N	N
6 ***Coble***	N	Y	N	N	N	N	Y
7 McIntyre	N	Y	N	N	N	N	N
8 Hefner	N	Y	N	Y	N	N	N
9 ***Myrick***	N	Y	N	N	N	N	Y
10 ***Ballenger***	N	Y	N	N	N	N	N
11 ***Taylor***	N	?	N	N	N	N	N
12 Watt	N	Y	N	Y	N	N	N
NORTH DAKOTA							
AL Pomeroy	N	Y	N	Y	N	Y	N
OHIO							
1 ***Chabot***	Y	Y	Y	N	Y	N	Y
2 ***Portman***	N	Y	Y	N	Y	N	Y
3 Hall	Y	Y	Y	N	Y	N	N
4 ***Oxley***	N	Y	N	N	N	N	N
5 ***Gillmor***	Y	Y	N	N	Y	N	Y
6 Strickland	N	Y	N	Y	Y	N	N
7 ***Hobson***	Y	Y	Y	N	Y	N	Y
8 ***Boehner***	N	Y	N	N	Y	N	?
9 Kaptur	N	Y	N	Y	N	N	N
10 Kucinich	Y	Y	Y	Y	Y	Y	Y
11 Stokes	N	Y	N	Y	N	Y	N
12 ***Kasich***	Y	Y	Y	N	Y	N	Y
13 Brown	Y	Y	Y	Y	Y	Y	Y
14 Sawyer	N	Y	Y	Y	Y	Y	N
15 ***Pryce***	Y	Y	Y	N	Y	N	Y
16 ***Regula***	N	Y	Y	N	Y	N	N
17 Traficant	Y	Y	N	N	N	N	N
18 ***Ney***	N	Y	Y	N	N	N	Y
19 ***LaTourette***	N	Y	Y	N	Y	N	N
OKLAHOMA							
1 ***Largent***	N	Y	Y	N	N	N	Y
2 ***Coburn***	N	Y	N	N	N	N	N
3 ***Watkins***	N	Y	N	N	N	N	N
4 ***Watts***	N	Y	N	N	N	N	N
5 ***Istook***	N	Y	N	N	N	N	Y
6 ***Lucas***	N	Y	N	N	N	N	N
OREGON							
1 Furse	Y	Y	N	Y	N	Y	N
2 ***Smith***	N	Y	N	N	N	N	N
3 Blumenauer	Y	?	Y	Y	Y	Y	N
4 DeFazio	Y	Y	Y	Y	Y	Y	N
5 Hooley	Y	Y	N	Y	N	N	N
PENNSYLVANIA							
1 Foglietta	Y	Y	N	Y	Y	Y	Y
2 Fattah	Y	Y	N	N	Y	Y	N
3 Borski	Y	Y	Y	Y	Y	Y	Y
4 Klink	N	Y	N	Y	N	Y	Y
5 ***Peterson***	N	Y	N	N	N	N	N
6 Holden	Y	Y	N	Y	Y	Y	N
7 ***Weldon***	Y	Y	Y	N	Y	N	Y
8 ***Greenwood***	Y	Y	Y	N	Y	N	N
9 ***Shuster***	Y	Y	N	N	Y	N	N
10 ***McDade***	N	Y	Y	N	N	N	N
11 Kanjorski	Y	Y	Y	Y	Y	Y	Y
12 Murtha	N	Y	N	N	Y	N	N
13 ***Fox***	Y	Y	Y	N	Y	N	Y
14 Coyne	Y	?	N	Y	Y	Y	Y
15 McHale	Y	Y	Y	Y	Y	Y	N
16 ***Pitts***	N	Y	Y	N	Y	N	Y
17 ***Gekas***	N	Y	Y	N	Y	N	N
18 Doyle	Y	Y	Y	Y	Y	N	Y
19 ***Goodling***	Y	Y	Y	N	Y	N	N
20 Mascara	Y	Y	Y	Y	Y	Y	Y
21 ***English***	Y	Y	Y	N	Y	N	N
RHODE ISLAND							
1 Kennedy	Y	Y	Y	Y	N	?	Y
2 Weygand	Y	Y	N	Y	Y	Y	Y
SOUTH CAROLINA							
1 ***Sanford***	N	Y	Y	?	Y	N	Y
2 ***Spence***	N	Y	N	N	N	N	N
3 ***Graham***	N	Y	N	N	N	N	N
4 ***Inglis***	N	Y	Y	N	Y	N	Y
5 Spratt	N	Y	N	Y	N	Y	N
6 Clyburn	N	Y	N	Y	N	N	N
SOUTH DAKOTA							
AL ***Thune***	N	Y	N	N	N	N	N
TENNESSEE							
1 ***Jenkins***	N	+	N	N	N	N	N
2 ***Duncan***	Y	Y	Y	N	Y	N	Y
3 ***Wamp***	Y	Y	Y	N	Y	N	Y
4 ***Hilleary***	N	Y	Y	N	N	N	Y
5 Clement	N	Y	Y	Y	Y	N	N
6 Gordon	N	Y	Y	N	N	N	N
7 ***Bryant***	N	Y	N	N	N	N	N
8 Tanner	N	Y	N	Y	N	N	N
9 Ford	N	Y	N	Y	N	N	N
TEXAS							
1 Sandlin	N	Y	N	Y	N	Y	N
2 Turner	N	Y	N	Y	N	N	N
3 ***Johnson, Sam***	N	Y	N	N	N	N	N
4 Hall	N	Y	N	N	N	N	N
5 ***Sessions***	N	Y	N	N	N	N	N
6 ***Barton***	?	?	?	?	?	?	?
7 ***Archer***	N	Y	Y	N	Y	N	Y
8 ***Brady***	N	Y	N	N	N	N	N
9 Lampson	Y	Y	N	N	N	N	N
10 Doggett	Y	Y	Y	Y	Y	Y	Y
11 Edwards	Y	Y	N	Y	N	Y	N
12 ***Granger***	N	Y	N	N	N	N	N
13 ***Thornberry***	N	Y	N	N	N	N	N
14 ***Paul***	Y	Y	Y	N	Y	Y	Y
15 Hinojosa	N	Y	N	Y	N	N	N
16 Reyes	N	Y	N	?	N	N	N
17 Stenholm	N	Y	N	N	N	N	N
18 Jackson-Lee	Y	Y	N	Y	N	N	N
19 ***Combest***	N	Y	N	N	N	N	N
20 Gonzalez	N	Y	N	?	?	?	?
21 ***Smith***	Y	Y	N	N	N	N	N
22 ***DeLay***	N	Y	Y	N	Y	N	Y
23 ***Bonilla***	N	Y	N	N	N	N	N
24 Frost	N	Y	N	Y	N	Y	N
25 Bentsen	Y	Y	N	N	N	N	N
26 ***Armey***	N	Y	Y	N	Y	N	Y
27 Ortiz	N	Y	N	N	N	N	N
28 Rodriguez	N	Y	N	Y	N	Y	N
29 Green	N	Y	N	N	N	N	N
30 Johnson, E.B.	N	Y	N	Y	N	N	N
UTAH							
1 ***Hansen***	Y	Y	Y	N	N	N	N
2 ***Cook***	Y	Y	Y	N	Y	N	N
3 ***Cannon***	Y	?	N	N	Y	N	Y
VERMONT							
AL *Sanders*	Y	Y	Y	Y	Y	Y	Y
VIRGINIA							
1 ***Bateman***	N	Y	N	N	N	N	N
2 Pickett	N	Y	N	N	N	N	N
3 Scott	N	Y	N	N	N	N	N
4 Sisisky	N	Y	P	N	N	N	N
5 Goode	N	?	N	N	N	N	N
6 ***Goodlatte***	N	Y	Y	N	N	N	N
7 ***Bliley***	N	Y	N	N	N	N	N
8 Moran	Y	Y	Y	Y	N	Y	Y
9 Boucher	N	Y	N	Y	N	Y	N
10 ***Wolf***	Y	Y	Y	N	Y	N	Y
11 ***Davis***	N	Y	Y	N	N	N	Y
WASHINGTON							
1 ***White***	Y	Y	Y	N	Y	N	N
2 ***Metcalf***	Y	Y	N	N	N	N	N
3 ***Smith, Linda***	Y	Y	Y	N	Y	N	N
4 ***Hastings***	N	Y	N	N	N	N	N
5 ***Nethercutt***	N	Y	N	N	N	N	N
6 Dicks	N	Y	N	Y	N	Y	N
7 McDermott	Y	Y	Y	Y	Y	Y	Y
8 ***Dunn***	Y	Y	Y	N	N	N	N
9 Smith, Adam	Y	Y	N	Y	Y	N	Y
WEST VIRGINIA							
1 Mollohan	N	Y	N	N	N	N	N
2 Wise	N	?	N	N	N	N	N
3 Rahall	N	Y	N	N	N	N	N
WISCONSIN							
1 ***Neumann***	N	Y	Y	N	Y	N	Y
2 ***Klug***	Y	Y	Y	N	Y	N	N
3 Kind	Y	Y	Y	Y	Y	Y	Y
4 Kleczka	Y	Y	N	Y	N	Y	Y
5 Barrett	Y	Y	Y	Y	Y	Y	Y
6 ***Petri***	Y	Y	Y	N	Y	N	N
7 Obey	Y	Y	N	Y	Y	Y	N
8 Johnson	N	Y	N	Y	N	Y	N
9 ***Sensenbrenner***	Y	Y	Y	N	Y	N	Y
WYOMING							
AL ***Cubin***	N	Y	N	N	N	N	N

Southern states - Ala., Ark., Fla., Ga., Ky., La., Miss., N.C., Okla., S.C., Tenn., Texas, Va.

HOUSE VOTES 317, 318, 319, 320, 321, 322, 323

317. HR 2160. Fiscal 1998 Agriculture Appropriations/Previous Question on Recommittal. Yates, D-Ill., motion to order the previous question (thus ending debate and the possibility of amendment) on the Schumer, D-N.Y., motion to recommit to the Appropriations Committee (thus killing) the bill to provide $49.6 billion in new budget authority for agriculture programs, rural development, the Food and Drug Administration and related agencies in fiscal 1998. Motion agreed to 423-4: R 222-1; D 200-3 (ND 147-2, SD 53-1); I 1-0, July 24, 1997. A "nay" was a vote in support of the president's position.

318. HR 2160. Fiscal 1998 Agriculture Appropriations/Reconsideration of Vote. Hastings, R-Wash., motion to table the Roybal-Allard, D-Calif., motion to reconsider the vote by which the House agreed to order the previous question (thus ending debate and the possibility of amendment) on the Schumer, D-N.Y., motion to recommit to the Appropriations Committee (thus killing) the bill to provide $49.6 billion in new budget authority for agriculture programs, rural development, the Food and Drug Administration and related agencies in fiscal 1998. Motion agreed to 258-165: R 220-0; D 38-164 (ND 18-132, SD 20-32); I 0-1, July 24, 1997.

319. HR 2160. Fiscal 1998 Agriculture Appropriations/Recommit. Schumer, D-N.Y., motion to recommit to the Appropriations Committee (thus killing) the bill to provide $49.6 billion in new budget authority for agriculture programs, rural development, the Food and Drug Administration and related agencies in fiscal 1998. Motion rejected 56-363: R 0-220; D 55-143 (ND 49-97, SD 6-46); I 1-0, July 24, 1997.

320. HR 2160. Fiscal 1998 Agriculture Appropriations/Reconsideration of Vote. Hastings, R-Wash., motion to table the Obey, D-Wis., motion to reconsider the vote by which the House rejected the Schumer, D-N.Y., motion to recommit to the Appropriations Committee (thus killing) the bill to provide $49.6 billion in new budget authority for agriculture programs, rural development, the Food and Drug Administration and related agencies in fiscal 1998. Motion agreed to 285-139: R 222-0; D 63-138 (ND 30-118, SD 33-20); I 0-1, July 24, 1997.

321. HR 2160. Fiscal 1998 Agriculture Appropriations/Passage. Passage of the bill to provide $49.6 billion in new budget authority for agriculture programs, rural development, the Food and Drug Administration and related agencies in fiscal 1998. The bill would provide $4.3 billion less than the fiscal 1997 level of $53.9 billion and $2.7 billion less than the president's request of $52.3 billion. Passed 392-32: R 212-9; D 179-23 (ND 129-21, SD 50-2); I 1-0, July 24, 1997.

322. HR 2160. Fiscal 1998 Agriculture Appropriations/Reconsideration of Vote. Hastings, R-Wash., motion to table the Obey, D-Wis., motion to reconsider the vote by which the House passed the bill to provide $49.6 billion in new budget authority for agriculture programs, rural development, the Food and Drug Administration and related agencies in fiscal 1998. Motion agreed to 284-132: R 217-0; D 67-131 (ND 39-106, SD 28-25); I 0-1, July 24, 1997.

323. Procedural Motion/Adjourn. Bonior, D-Mich., motion to adjourn. Motion rejected 96-315: R 2-213; D 94-101 (ND 71-72, SD 23-29); I 0-1, July 24, 1997.

KEY

- Y Voted for (yea).
- # Paired for.
- + Announced for.
- N Voted against (nay).
- X Paired against.
- – Announced against.
- P Voted "present."
- C Voted "present" to avoid possible conflict of interest.
- ? Did not vote or otherwise make a position known.

Democrats ***Republicans***
Independent

	317	318	319	320	321	322	323
ALABAMA							
1 ***Callahan***	Y	Y	N	Y	Y	Y	N
2 ***Everett***	Y	Y	N	Y	Y	Y	N
3 ***Riley***	Y	Y	N	Y	Y	Y	N
4 ***Aderholt***	Y	Y	N	Y	Y	Y	N
5 Cramer	Y	Y	N	Y	Y	Y	N
6 ***Bachus***	Y	Y	N	Y	?	Y	N
7 Hilliard	Y	N	N	N	Y	N	N
ALASKA							
AL ***Young***	?	?	?	?	?	?	?
ARIZONA							
1 ***Salmon***	Y	Y	N	Y	N	Y	N
2 Pastor	Y	N	N	N	Y	N	N
3 ***Stump***	Y	Y	N	Y	Y	Y	N
4 ***Shadegg***	Y	Y	N	Y	Y	Y	N
5 ***Kolbe***	Y	Y	N	Y	Y	Y	N
6 ***Hayworth***	Y	Y	N	Y	Y	Y	N
ARKANSAS							
1 Berry	Y	Y	N	Y	Y	Y	Y
2 Snyder	Y	N	N	Y	Y	Y	N
3 ***Hutchinson***	Y	Y	N	Y	Y	Y	N
4 ***Dickey***	Y	Y	N	Y	Y	Y	N
CALIFORNIA							
1 ***Riggs***	Y	Y	N	Y	Y	Y	N
2 ***Herger***	Y	Y	N	Y	Y	Y	N
3 Fazio	Y	N	N	N	Y	N	Y
4 ***Doolittle***	Y	Y	N	Y	Y	Y	N
5 Matsui	Y	N	Y	N	Y	N	Y
6 Woolsey	Y	N	N	N	Y	N	Y
7 Miller	Y	N	Y	N	N	N	N
8 Pelosi	Y	N	Y	N	Y	N	Y
9 Dellums	Y	N	Y	N	Y	N	Y
10 Tauscher	Y	N	N	Y	Y	N	Y
11 ***Pombo***	Y	Y	N	Y	Y	Y	N
12 Lantos	Y	N	Y	N	Y	N	Y
13 Stark	?	?	?	?	?	?	?
14 Eshoo	Y	N	N	N	Y	N	N
15 ***Campbell***	Y	Y	N	Y	N	Y	N
16 Lofgren	Y	N	N	N	N	N	N
17 Farr	Y	N	N	Y	Y	Y	Y
18 Condit	Y	Y	N	Y	Y	Y	N
19 ***Radanovich***	Y	Y	N	Y	Y	Y	?
20 Dooley	Y	N	N	Y	Y	Y	Y
21 ***Thomas***	Y	Y	N	Y	Y	?	N
22 Capps	Y	Y	N	Y	Y	Y	Y
23 ***Gallegly***	Y	Y	N	Y	Y	Y	N
24 Sherman	Y	N	N	N	Y	N	N
25 ***McKeon***	Y	Y	N	Y	Y	Y	N
26 Berman	Y	N	N	N	Y	Y	N
27 ***Rogan***	Y	Y	N	Y	Y	Y	N
28 ***Dreier***	Y	Y	N	Y	Y	Y	N
29 Waxman	Y	N	Y	N	Y	N	Y
30 Becerra	Y	N	N	N	Y	N	N
31 Martinez	Y	N	N	Y	Y	Y	Y
32 Dixon	Y	N	N	N	Y	Y	N
33 Roybal-Allard	Y	N	Y	N	Y	N	N
34 Torres	Y	N	Y	N	Y	N	Y
35 Waters	?	N	Y	N	Y	N	Y
36 Harman	Y	N	?	N	Y	N	?
37 Millender-McD.	Y	N	N	N	Y	N	N
38 ***Horn***	Y	Y	N	Y	Y	Y	N
39 ***Royce***	Y	Y	N	Y	N	Y	N
40 ***Lewis***	Y	Y	N	Y	Y	Y	N
41 ***Kim***	Y	Y	N	Y	Y	Y	N
42 Brown	Y	N	Y	N	Y	?	N
43 ***Calvert***	Y	Y	N	Y	Y	Y	N
44 ***Bono***	N	Y	N	Y	Y	Y	N
45 ***Rohrabacher***	Y	Y	N	Y	N	Y	N
46 Sanchez	Y	N	Y	Y	Y	Y	N
47 ***Cox***	Y	Y	N	Y	Y	Y	N
48 ***Packard***	Y	Y	N	Y	Y	Y	N
49 ***Bilbray***	Y	Y	N	Y	Y	Y	N
50 Filner	Y	N	N	Y	Y	Y	Y
51 ***Cunningham***	Y	Y	N	Y	Y	Y	N
52 ***Hunter***	Y	Y	N	Y	Y	Y	N
COLORADO							
1 DeGette	Y	N	Y	N	Y	N	Y
2 Skaggs	Y	N	Y	N	Y	N	Y
3 ***McInnis***	Y	Y	N	Y	Y	Y	N
4 ***Schaffer***	Y	Y	N	Y	Y	Y	N
5 ***Hefley***	Y	Y	N	Y	Y	Y	N
6 ***Schaefer***	Y	Y	N	Y	Y	Y	N
CONNECTICUT							
1 Kennelly	Y	N	N	N	Y	?	Y
2 Gejdenson	Y	N	N	Y	Y	Y	Y
3 DeLauro	Y	N	N	N	Y	N	Y
4 ***Shays***	Y	Y	N	Y	Y	Y	N
5 Maloney	Y	N	N	N	Y	N	N
6 ***Johnson***	Y	Y	N	Y	Y	Y	N
DELAWARE							
AL ***Castle***	Y	Y	N	Y	Y	Y	N
FLORIDA							
1 ***Scarborough***	Y	Y	N	Y	N	Y	?
2 Boyd	N	N	N	Y	Y	Y	N
3 Brown	Y	Y	N	Y	Y	N	Y
4 ***Fowler***	Y	Y	N	Y	Y	?	?
5 Thurman	Y	Y	N	Y	Y	Y	Y
6 ***Stearns***	Y	Y	N	Y	Y	Y	N
7 ***Mica***	Y	Y	N	Y	Y	Y	N
8 ***McCollum***	Y	Y	N	Y	Y	Y	N
9 ***Bilirakis***	Y	Y	N	Y	Y	Y	N
10 ***Young***	Y	Y	N	Y	Y	Y	N
11 Davis	Y	N	N	N	Y	N	Y
12 ***Canady***	Y	Y	N	Y	Y	Y	N
13 ***Miller***	Y	Y	N	Y	Y	Y	N
14 ***Goss***	Y	Y	N	Y	Y	Y	N
15 ***Weldon***	Y	Y	N	Y	Y	Y	N
16 ***Foley***	Y	Y	N	Y	Y	Y	N
17 Meek	Y	N	Y	N	Y	N	Y
18 ***Ros-Lehtinen***	Y	Y	N	Y	Y	Y	N
19 Wexler	Y	?	?	?	?	?	?
20 Deutsch	Y	N	N	N	Y	N	N
21 ***Diaz-Balart***	Y	Y	N	Y	Y	Y	N
22 ***Shaw***	Y	Y	N	Y	Y	Y	N
23 Hastings	Y	N	N	N	Y	N	Y
GEORGIA							
1 ***Kingston***	Y	Y	N	Y	Y	Y	N
2 Bishop	Y	Y	N	Y	Y	N	N
3 ***Collins***	Y	Y	N	Y	Y	Y	N
4 McKinney	Y	Y	?	N	Y	Y	Y
5 Lewis	Y	N	N	N	Y	N	Y
6 ***Gingrich***							
7 ***Barr***	Y	Y	N	Y	Y	Y	N
8 ***Chambliss***	Y	Y	N	Y	Y	Y	N
9 ***Deal***	Y	Y	N	Y	Y	Y	N
10 ***Norwood***	Y	Y	N	Y	Y	Y	N
11 ***Linder***	Y	Y	N	Y	Y	?	?
HAWAII							
1 Abercrombie	Y	N	N	N	Y	N	Y
2 Mink	Y	N	N	N	Y	N	Y
IDAHO							
1 ***Chenoweth***	Y	Y	N	Y	Y	Y	N
2 ***Crapo***	Y	Y	N	Y	Y	Y	N
ILLINOIS							
1 Rush	Y	N	Y	N	Y	N	Y
2 Jackson	Y	N	Y	N	N	N	Y
3 Lipinski	Y	Y	P	N	Y	Y	N
4 Gutierrez	Y	N	Y	N	Y	N	N
5 Blagojevich	Y	N	Y	N	Y	N	N
6 ***Hyde***	Y	Y	N	Y	Y	Y	N
7 Davis	Y	N	N	N	Y	N	N
8 ***Crane***	Y	Y	N	Y	Y	Y	N
9 Yates	Y	N	Y	N	Y	?	?
10 ***Porter***	Y	Y	N	Y	Y	Y	N
11 ***Weller***	Y	Y	N	Y	Y	Y	N
12 Costello	Y	Y	N	Y	Y	Y	N
13 ***Fawell***	Y	?	N	Y	Y	Y	N
14 ***Hastert***	Y	Y	N	Y	Y	Y	N
15 ***Ewing***	Y	Y	N	Y	Y	Y	N

ND Northern Democrats SD Southern Democrats

	317	318	319	320	321	322	323
16 ***Manzullo***	Y	Y	N	Y	Y	Y	N
17 Evans	Y	N	N	Y	Y	Y	N
18 ***LaHood***	Y	Y	N	Y	Y	Y	N
19 Poshard	Y	Y	N	Y	Y	Y	N
20 ***Shimkus***	Y	Y	N	Y	Y	Y	N
INDIANA							
1 Visclosky	Y	N	N	N	Y	N	N
2 ***McIntosh***	Y	Y	N	Y	Y	Y	N
3 Roemer	Y	N	N	Y	Y	Y	N
4 ***Souder***	Y	Y	N	Y	Y	Y	N
5 ***Buyer***	Y	Y	N	Y	Y	Y	N
6 ***Burton***	Y	Y	N	Y	Y	Y	N
7 ***Pease***	Y	Y	N	Y	Y	Y	N
8 ***Hostettler***	Y	Y	N	Y	Y	Y	N
9 Hamilton	Y	Y	N	Y	Y	Y	N
10 Carson	Y	N	N	Y	Y	N	Y
IOWA							
1 ***Leach***	Y	Y	N	Y	Y	Y	N
2 ***Nussle***	Y	Y	N	Y	Y	Y	N
3 Boswell	Y	Y	N	Y	Y	Y	N
4 ***Ganske***	Y	Y	N	Y	Y	Y	N
5 ***Latham***	Y	Y	N	Y	Y	Y	N
KANSAS							
1 ***Moran***	Y	Y	N	Y	Y	Y	N
2 ***Ryun***	Y	Y	N	Y	Y	Y	N
3 ***Snowbarger***	Y	Y	N	Y	Y	Y	N
4 ***Tiahrt***	Y	Y	N	Y	Y	Y	N
KENTUCKY							
1 ***Whitfield***	Y	Y	N	Y	Y	Y	N
2 ***Lewis***	Y	Y	N	Y	Y	Y	N
3 ***Northup***	Y	Y	N	Y	Y	Y	N
4 ***Bunning***	Y	Y	N	Y	Y	Y	N
5 ***Rogers***	Y	Y	N	Y	Y	Y	N
6 Baesler	Y	N	N	Y	Y	Y	N
LOUISIANA							
1 ***Livingston***	Y	Y	N	Y	Y	Y	N
2 Jefferson	Y	N	Y	N	Y	N	Y
3 ***Tauzin***	Y	Y	N	Y	Y	Y	N
4 ***McCrery***	Y	Y	N	Y	Y	Y	N
5 ***Cooksey***	Y	Y	N	Y	Y	Y	N
6 ***Baker***	Y	Y	N	Y	Y	Y	N
7 John	Y	Y	N	Y	Y	Y	Y
MAINE							
1 Allen	Y	N	N	N	Y	N	N
2 Baldacci	Y	N	N	Y	Y	N	?
MARYLAND							
1 ***Gilchrest***	Y	Y	N	Y	Y	Y	N
2 ***Ehrlich***	Y	Y	?	Y	Y	Y	?
3 Cardin	Y	N	Y	N	N	N	N
4 Wynn	Y	N	N	N	Y	N	N
5 Hoyer	Y	N	N	N	Y	?	?
6 ***Bartlett***	Y	Y	N	Y	Y	Y	N
7 Cummings	Y	N	Y	N	Y	N	N
8 ***Morella***	Y	Y	N	Y	Y	Y	N
MASSACHUSETTS							
1 Olver	Y	N	N	N	N	N	?
2 Neal	Y	N	Y	N	N	N	Y
3 McGovern	Y	N	Y	N	N	N	Y
4 Frank	N	N	Y	N	N	N	Y
5 Meehan	Y	N	Y	N	N	N	N
6 Tierney	Y	Y	N	N	N	N	N
7 Markey	Y	N	Y	N	Y	N	Y
8 Kennedy	Y	N	Y	N	N	N	N
9 Moakley	Y	N	Y	Y	Y	N	Y
10 Delahunt	Y	N	N	N	Y	N	Y
MICHIGAN							
1 Stupak	Y	N	N	N	Y	N	Y
2 ***Hoekstra***	Y	Y	N	Y	Y	Y	N
3 ***Ehlers***	Y	Y	N	Y	Y	Y	N
4 ***Camp***	Y	Y	N	Y	Y	Y	N
5 Barcia	Y	Y	N	Y	Y	Y	N
6 ***Upton***	Y	Y	N	Y	Y	Y	N
7 ***Smith***	Y	Y	N	Y	Y	Y	N
8 Stabenow	Y	N	N	N	Y	N	N
9 Kildee	Y	N	N	N	Y	Y	N
10 Bonior	Y	N	N	N	Y	N	Y
11 ***Knollenberg***	Y	Y	N	Y	Y	Y	N
12 Levin	Y	N	N	N	Y	?	N
13 Rivers	Y	N	N	N	Y	N	N
14 Conyers	Y	N	Y	N	N	N	Y
15 Kilpatrick	Y	N	N	N	Y	N	Y
16 Dingell	Y	N	N	N	Y	N	Y
MINNESOTA							
1 ***Gutknecht***	Y	Y	N	Y	Y	Y	N
2 Minge	Y	N	N	Y	Y	Y	N

	317	318	319	320	321	322	323
3 ***Ramstad***	Y	Y	N	Y	Y	Y	N
4 Vento	Y	N	N	N	Y	N	Y
5 Sabo	Y	N	N	N	Y	N	Y
6 Luther	Y	N	Y	N	Y	N	N
7 Peterson	Y	Y	N	Y	Y	Y	Y
8 Oberstar	Y	N	Y	N	Y	N	Y
MISSISSIPPI							
1 ***Wicker***	Y	Y	N	Y	Y	Y	N
2 Thompson	Y	Y	N	Y	Y	N	Y
3 ***Pickering***	Y	Y	N	Y	Y	Y	N
4 ***Parker***	Y	Y	N	Y	Y	Y	N
5 Taylor	Y	Y	N	Y	N	Y	N
MISSOURI							
1 Clay	Y	N	N	N	Y	N	Y
2 ***Talent***	Y	Y	N	Y	Y	Y	N
3 Gephardt	Y	N	N	Y	Y	Y	Y
4 Skelton	Y	Y	N	Y	Y	Y	N
5 McCarthy	Y	N	N	N	Y	N	N
6 Danner	Y	N	N	N	Y	N	N
7 ***Blunt***	Y	Y	N	Y	Y	Y	N
8 ***Emerson***	Y	Y	N	Y	Y	Y	N
9 ***Hulshof***	Y	Y	N	Y	Y	Y	N
MONTANA							
AL ***Hill***	Y	Y	N	Y	Y	Y	N
NEBRASKA							
1 ***Bereuter***	Y	Y	N	Y	Y	Y	N
2 ***Christensen***	Y	Y	N	Y	Y	Y	N
3 ***Barrett***	Y	Y	N	Y	Y	Y	N
NEVADA							
1 ***Ensign***	Y	Y	N	Y	N	Y	N
2 ***Gibbons***	Y	Y	N	Y	Y	Y	N
NEW HAMPSHIRE							
1 ***Sununu***	Y	Y	N	Y	Y	Y	N
2 ***Bass***	Y	Y	N	Y	Y	Y	N
NEW JERSEY							
1 Andrews	Y	N	N	N	N	N	Y
2 ***LoBiondo***	Y	Y	N	Y	Y	Y	N
3 ***Saxton***	Y	Y	N	Y	Y	Y	N
4 ***Smith***	Y	Y	N	Y	Y	Y	N
5 ***Roukema***	Y	Y	N	Y	Y	Y	N
6 Pallone	Y	N	Y	N	Y	Y	Y
7 ***Franks***	Y	Y	N	Y	N	Y	N
8 Pascrell	Y	N	N	N	Y	Y	Y
9 Rothman	Y	N	N	N	Y	Y	N
10 Payne	Y	N	Y	N	Y	N	Y
11 ***Frelinghuysen***	Y	Y	N	Y	Y	Y	N
12 ***Pappas***	Y	Y	N	Y	Y	Y	N
13 Menendez	Y	N	N	N	N	N	N
NEW MEXICO							
1 ***Schiff***	?	?	?	?	?	?	?
2 ***Skeen***	Y	Y	N	Y	Y	Y	N
3 ***Redmond***	Y	Y	N	Y	Y	Y	N
NEW YORK							
1 ***Forbes***	Y	Y	N	Y	Y	Y	N
2 ***Lazio***	Y	?	N	Y	Y	Y	N
3 ***King***	Y	Y	N	Y	Y	Y	N
4 McCarthy	Y	N	N	N	Y	N	N
5 Ackerman	Y	N	N	N	Y	N	N
6 Flake	Y	N	N	N	Y	Y	Y
7 Manton	Y	N	N	N	Y	N	Y
8 Nadler	Y	N	N	N	Y	Y	Y
9 Schumer	Y	N	Y	N	N	N	N
10 Towns	Y	N	N	N	Y	N	N
11 Owens	Y	N	Y	N	N	N	Y
12 Velázquez	Y	N	Y	N	N	N	?
13 ***Molinari***	?	?	?	?	?	?	?
14 Maloney	Y	N	N	N	Y	N	N
15 Rangel	Y	N	N	N	N	N	N
16 Serrano	Y	N	N	N	Y	N	N
17 Engel	Y	N	N	N	Y	N	N
18 Lowey	Y	N	Y	N	Y	N	Y
19 ***Kelly***	Y	Y	N	Y	Y	Y	N
20 ***Gilman***	Y	Y	?	Y	Y	Y	N
21 McNulty	Y	N	Y	N	Y	N	Y
22 ***Solomon***	Y	Y	N	Y	Y	Y	N
23 ***Boehlert***	Y	Y	N	Y	Y	Y	N
24 ***McHugh***	Y	Y	N	Y	Y	Y	N
25 ***Walsh***	Y	Y	N	Y	Y	Y	N
26 Hinchey	Y	N	?	N	Y	N	Y
27 ***Paxon***	Y	Y	N	Y	Y	Y	N
28 Slaughter	Y	N	N	N	Y	N	N
29 LaFalce	Y	N	Y	?	Y	N	Y
30 ***Quinn***	Y	Y	N	Y	Y	Y	N
31 ***Houghton***	Y	Y	N	Y	Y	Y	N

	317	318	319	320	321	322	323
NORTH CAROLINA							
1 Clayton	Y	?	N	Y	Y	N	Y
2 Etheridge	Y	Y	N	Y	Y	Y	N
3 ***Jones***	Y	Y	N	Y	Y	Y	N
4 Price	Y	Y	N	Y	Y	Y	N
5 ***Burr***	Y	Y	N	Y	Y	Y	N
6 ***Coble***	Y	Y	N	Y	Y	Y	N
7 McIntyre	Y	Y	N	Y	Y	Y	N
8 Hefner	Y	N	N	Y	Y	N	?
9 ***Myrick***	Y	Y	N	Y	Y	Y	N
10 ***Ballenger***	Y	Y	–	+	Y	Y	N
11 ***Taylor***	Y	Y	N	Y	Y	Y	N
12 Watt	Y	N	N	N	Y	N	Y
NORTH DAKOTA							
AL Pomeroy	Y	N	N	N	Y	Y	Y
OHIO							
1 ***Chabot***	Y	Y	N	Y	Y	Y	N
2 ***Portman***	Y	Y	N	Y	Y	Y	N
3 Hall	Y	N	N	Y	Y	N	Y
4 ***Oxley***	Y	Y	N	Y	Y	Y	N
5 ***Gillmor***	Y	Y	N	Y	Y	Y	Y
6 Strickland	Y	N	N	N	Y	N	Y
7 ***Hobson***	Y	Y	N	Y	Y	Y	N
8 ***Boehner***	Y	Y	N	Y	Y	Y	N
9 Kaptur	Y	Y	N	N	Y	N	N
10 Kucinich	Y	N	Y	N	N	N	N
11 Stokes	Y	N	Y	N	Y	N	Y
12 ***Kasich***	Y	Y	N	Y	Y	Y	N
13 Brown	Y	N	Y	N	Y	N	Y
14 Sawyer	Y	N	N	N	Y	N	N
15 ***Pryce***	Y	Y	N	Y	Y	Y	N
16 ***Regula***	Y	Y	N	Y	Y	Y	N
17 Traficant	Y	Y	N	Y	Y	Y	N
18 ***Ney***	Y	Y	N	Y	Y	Y	N
19 ***LaTourette***	Y	Y	N	Y	Y	Y	N
OKLAHOMA							
1 ***Largent***	Y	Y	N	Y	Y	Y	N
2 ***Coburn***	Y	Y	N	Y	Y	Y	N
3 ***Watkins***	Y	Y	N	Y	Y	Y	N
4 ***Watts***	Y	Y	N	Y	Y	Y	N
5 ***Istook***	Y	Y	N	Y	Y	Y	N
6 ***Lucas***	Y	Y	N	Y	Y	Y	N
OREGON							
1 Furse	Y	N	N	N	Y	N	Y
2 ***Smith***	Y	Y	N	Y	Y	Y	N
3 Blumenauer	Y	N	N	N	Y	Y	Y
4 DeFazio	N	N	P	N	Y	Y	Y
5 Hooley	Y	N	N	N	Y	N	N
PENNSYLVANIA							
1 Foglietta	Y	Y	N	N	Y	N	Y
2 Fattah	Y	Y	N	N	Y	N	N
3 Borski	Y	N	N	N	Y	N	N
4 Klink	Y	N	N	N	Y	N	N
5 ***Peterson***	Y	Y	N	Y	Y	Y	N
6 Holden	Y	N	N	N	Y	N	N
7 ***Weldon***	Y	Y	N	Y	Y	Y	N
8 ***Greenwood***	Y	Y	N	Y	Y	?	N
9 ***Shuster***	Y	Y	N	Y	Y	Y	N
10 ***McDade***	Y	?	N	Y	Y	Y	N
11 Kanjorski	Y	N	N	N	Y	N	N
12 Murtha	Y	Y	N	N	Y	Y	N
13 ***Fox***	Y	Y	N	Y	Y	Y	N
14 Coyne	Y	N	Y	N	N	N	Y
15 McHale	Y	N	N	N	Y	Y	N
16 ***Pitts***	Y	Y	N	Y	Y	Y	N
17 ***Gekas***	Y	Y	N	Y	Y	Y	N
18 Doyle	Y	N	N	N	Y	N	N
19 ***Goodling***	Y	Y	N	Y	Y	Y	N
20 Mascara	Y	N	N	N	Y	N	N
21 ***English***	Y	Y	N	Y	Y	Y	N
RHODE ISLAND							
1 Kennedy	Y	N	Y	N	Y	N	N
2 Weygand	Y	N	N	N	Y	N	Y
SOUTH CAROLINA							
1 ***Sanford***	Y	Y	N	Y	Y	Y	N
2 ***Spence***	Y	Y	N	Y	Y	Y	?
3 ***Graham***	Y	Y	N	Y	Y	Y	N
4 ***Inglis***	Y	Y	N	Y	Y	Y	N
5 Spratt	Y	N	N	N	?	Y	Y
6 Clyburn	Y	N	Y	N	Y	N	Y
SOUTH DAKOTA							
AL ***Thune***	Y	Y	N	Y	Y	Y	N
TENNESSEE							
1 ***Jenkins***	Y	Y	N	Y	Y	Y	N
2 ***Duncan***	Y	Y	N	Y	Y	Y	N

	317	318	319	320	321	322	323
3 ***Wamp***	Y	Y	N	Y	Y	Y	N
4 ***Hilleary***	Y	Y	N	Y	Y	Y	?
5 Clement	Y	N	N	N	Y	N	N
6 Gordon	Y	N	N	N	Y	N	N
7 ***Bryant***	Y	Y	N	Y	Y	Y	N
8 Tanner	Y	Y	N	Y	Y	Y	N
9 Ford	Y	N	Y	N	Y	N	Y
TEXAS							
1 Sandlin	Y	N	N	Y	Y	Y	N
2 Turner	Y	N	N	Y	Y	Y	N
3 ***Johnson, Sam***	Y	Y	N	Y	Y	Y	N
4 Hall	Y	Y	N	Y	Y	Y	N
5 ***Sessions***	Y	Y	N	Y	Y	Y	N
6 ***Barton***	?	?	?	?	?	?	N
7 ***Archer***	Y	Y	N	Y	Y	?	N
8 ***Brady***	Y	Y	N	Y	Y	Y	N
9 Lampson	Y	N	N	Y	Y	N	Y
10 Doggett	Y	N	Y	N	N	N	Y
11 Edwards	Y	N	N	N	Y	N	N
12 ***Granger***	Y	Y	N	Y	Y	Y	N
13 ***Thornberry***	Y	Y	N	Y	Y	Y	N
14 ***Paul***	Y	Y	N	Y	N	Y	N
15 Hinojosa	Y	N	N	N	Y	Y	N
16 Reyes	Y	N	N	Y	Y	Y	N
17 Stenholm	Y	Y	N	Y	Y	Y	N
18 Jackson-Lee	Y	N	N	Y	Y	N	N
19 ***Combest***	Y	Y	N	Y	Y	Y	N
20 Gonzalez	?	?	?	?	?	?	?
21 ***Smith***	Y	Y	N	Y	Y	Y	N
22 ***DeLay***	Y	Y	N	Y	Y	Y	N
23 ***Bonilla***	Y	Y	N	Y	Y	Y	N
24 Frost	Y	N	N	N	Y	N	Y
25 Bentsen	Y	N	N	Y	Y	Y	N
26 ***Armey***	Y	Y	N	Y	Y	Y	N
27 Ortiz	Y	N	N	Y	Y	Y	N
28 Rodriguez	Y	N	N	N	Y	N	Y
29 Green	Y	Y	Y	N	Y	Y	N
30 Johnson, E.B.	Y	N	N	N	Y	N	Y
UTAH							
1 ***Hansen***	Y	Y	N	Y	Y	Y	N
2 ***Cook***	Y	Y	N	Y	Y	Y	N
3 ***Cannon***	Y	Y	N	Y	?	?	?
VERMONT							
AL *Sanders*	Y	N	Y	N	Y	N	N
VIRGINIA							
1 ***Bateman***	Y	Y	N	Y	Y	?	?
2 Pickett	Y	Y	N	Y	Y	Y	N
3 Scott	Y	N	N	Y	Y	Y	N
4 Sisisky	Y	Y	N	Y	Y	Y	Y
5 Goode	Y	Y	N	Y	Y	Y	N
6 ***Goodlatte***	Y	Y	N	Y	Y	Y	N
7 ***Bliley***	Y	Y	N	Y	Y	Y	N
8 Moran	Y	N	Y	Y	Y	Y	N
9 Boucher	Y	N	N	Y	Y	N	Y
10 ***Wolf***	Y	Y	N	Y	Y	Y	N
11 ***Davis***	Y	Y	N	Y	Y	Y	N
WASHINGTON							
1 ***White***	Y	Y	N	Y	Y	Y	N
2 ***Metcalf***	Y	Y	N	Y	Y	Y	N
3 ***Smith, Linda***	Y	Y	N	Y	Y	Y	N
4 ***Hastings***	Y	Y	N	Y	Y	Y	N
5 ***Nethercutt***	Y	Y	N	Y	Y	Y	N
6 Dicks	Y	N	Y	N	Y	Y	Y
7 McDermott	Y	N	Y	N	N	N	Y
8 ***Dunn***	Y	Y	N	Y	Y	Y	N
9 Smith, Adam	Y	N	Y	?	Y	N	Y
WEST VIRGINIA							
1 Mollohan	Y	N	N	Y	Y	Y	N
2 Wise	Y	Y	N	Y	Y	Y	N
3 Rahall	Y	Y	N	Y	Y	Y	N
WISCONSIN							
1 ***Neumann***	Y	Y	N	Y	Y	Y	N
2 ***Klug***	Y	Y	N	Y	Y	Y	N
3 Kind	Y	N	Y	N	Y	N	N
4 Kleczka	Y	N	Y	Y	Y	Y	?
5 Barrett	Y	N	Y	N	Y	N	Y
6 ***Petri***	Y	Y	N	Y	Y	Y	N
7 Obey	Y	N	N	N	Y	N	Y
8 Johnson	Y	N	N	Y	Y	Y	Y
9 ***Sensenbrenner***	Y	Y	N	Y	N	Y	N
WYOMING							
AL ***Cubin***	Y	Y	N	Y	Y	Y	Y

Southern states - Ala., Ark., Fla., Ga., Ky., La., Miss., N.C., Okla., S.C., Tenn., Texas, Va.

HOUSE VOTES 324, 325, 326, 327, 328, 329, 330, 331

324. HR 2209. Fiscal 1998 Legislative Branch Appropriations/Previous Question. Pryce, R-Ohio, motion to order the previous question (thus ending debate and the possibility of amendment) on adoption of the rule (H Res 197) to provide for House floor consideration of the bill to provide $1.7 billion in new budget authority for the legislative branch in fiscal 1998. Motion agreed to 222-201: R 221-0; D 1-200 (ND 1-146, SD 0-54); I 0-1, July 25, 1997.

325. HR 2209. Fiscal 1998 Legislative Branch Appropriations/Rule. Adoption of the rule (H Res 197) to provide for House floor consideration of the bill to provide $1.7 billion in new budget authority for the legislative branch in fiscal 1998. Adopted 218-203: R 215-5; D 3-197 (ND 2-145, SD 1-52); I 0-1, July 25, 1997.

326. HR 2203. Fiscal 1998 Energy and Water Appropriations/Appalachian Regional Commission. Klug, R-Wis., amendment to reduce by $90 million funding for the Appalachian Regional Commission, which funds economic development programs and road projects for the 13 states in the Appalachian region. Rejected 97-328: R 73-150; D 24-177 (ND 21-126, SD 3-51); I 0-1, July 25, 1997.

327. HR 2203. Fiscal 1998 Energy and Water Appropriations/Pyroprocessing. Markey, D-Mass., amendment to eliminate the bill's $45 million for research and development programs related to pyroprocessing, an experimental process designed to transform unstable nuclear waste into a form that could be placed safely into long-term storage. The amendment would reduce the bill's overall appropriation for energy supply by $33 million and atomic energy defense activities by $12 million. Rejected 134-290: R 27-196; D 106-94 (ND 94-52, SD 12-42); I 1-0, July 25, 1997.

328. HR 2203. Fiscal 1998 Energy and Water Appropriations/Animas-La Plata Irrigation Project. Fazio, D-Calif., substitute amendment to the Petri, R-Wis., amendment to prohibit the use of funds in the bill to pay the salaries of federal employees to work on the Animas-La Plata irrigation project in Colorado and New Mexico, except for activities that are required under current law or related to the Colorado Ute Indian Water Rights settlement. The Petri amendment would prohibit the use of funds to buy land or begin construction, without Fazio's broad exceptions. Adopted 223-201: R 153-70; D 70-130 (ND 40-106, SD 30-24); I 0-1, July 25, 1997. (Subsequently, the Petri amendment, as amended, was adopted by voice vote.)

329. HR 2203. Fiscal 1998 Energy and Water Appropriations/Passage. Passage of the bill to provide $20.4 billion in new budget authority for energy and water development during fiscal 1998. The bill would provide $987 million less than was provided in fiscal 1997 and $2.6 billion less than requested by the president. Passed 418-7: R 217-7; D 200-0 (ND 147-0, SD 53-0); I 1-0, July 25, 1997.

330. HR 1119. Fiscal 1998 Defense Authorization/Motion To Instruct. Dellums, D-Calif., motion to instruct the House conferees to limit the amount spent by the United States as its share of the total cost of admitting new member nations to NATO at $2 billion or 10 percent of the total cost, whichever is less. Motion agreed to 414-0: R 217-0; D 196-0 (ND 144-0, SD 52-0); I 1-0, July 25, 1997.

331. HR 1119. Fiscal 1998 Defense Authorization/Closed Conference. Spence, R-S.C., motion to close portions of the conference to the public during consideration of national security issues. Motion agreed to 409-1: R 212-0; D 196-1 (ND 144-1, SD 52-0); I 1-0, July 25, 1997.

KEY

- Y Voted for (yea).
- # Paired for.
- \+ Announced for.
- N Voted against (nay).
- X Paired against.
- – Announced against.
- P Voted "present."
- C Voted "present" to avoid possible conflict of interest.
- ? Did not vote or otherwise make a position known.

—

Democrats ***Republicans***
Independent

	324	325	326	327	328	329	330	331
ALABAMA								
1 ***Callahan***	Y	Y	N	N	Y	Y	Y	Y
2 ***Everett***	Y	Y	N	N	Y	Y	Y	Y
3 ***Riley***	Y	Y	N	N	Y	Y	Y	Y
4 ***Aderholt***	Y	Y	N	N	Y	Y	Y	Y
5 Cramer	N	N	N	N	N	Y	Y	Y
6 ***Bachus***	Y	Y	N	N	N	Y	Y	Y
7 Hilliard	N	N	N	N	Y	Y	Y	Y
ALASKA								
AL ***Young***	?	?	?	?	?	?	?	?
ARIZONA								
1 ***Salmon***	Y	Y	Y	N	N	Y	Y	Y
2 Pastor	N	N	N	N	Y	Y	Y	Y
3 ***Stump***	Y	Y	N	N	Y	Y	Y	Y
4 ***Shadegg***	Y	Y	Y	N	Y	Y	Y	Y
5 ***Kolbe***	Y	Y	N	N	Y	Y	Y	Y
6 ***Hayworth***	Y	Y	Y	N	Y	Y	Y	Y
ARKANSAS								
1 Berry	N	N	N	N	N	Y	Y	Y
2 Snyder	N	N	N	Y	Y	Y	Y	Y
3 ***Hutchinson***	Y	Y	N	N	N	Y	Y	Y
4 ***Dickey***	Y	Y	N	N	Y	Y	Y	Y
CALIFORNIA								
1 ***Riggs***	Y	Y	N	N	N	Y	Y	Y
2 ***Herger***	Y	Y	N	N	Y	Y	Y	?
3 Fazio	N	N	N	N	Y	Y	Y	Y
4 ***Doolittle***	Y	Y	N	N	Y	Y	Y	Y
5 Matsui	N	N	N	Y	N	Y	Y	Y
6 Woolsey	N	N	N	Y	N	Y	Y	Y
7 Miller	?	?	?	?	?	?	?	?
8 Pelosi	N	N	N	Y	N	Y	?	?
9 Dellums	N	N	N	Y	N	Y	Y	Y
10 Tauscher	N	N	N	N	N	Y	Y	Y
11 ***Pombo***	Y	Y	N	N	Y	Y	Y	Y
12 Lantos	N	N	N	N	N	Y	Y	Y
13 Stark	?	?	?	?	?	?	?	?
14 Eshoo	N	N	N	Y	N	Y	Y	Y
15 ***Campbell***	Y	Y	Y	N	N	Y	Y	Y
16 Lofgren	N	N	N	N	N	Y	Y	Y
17 Farr	N	N	N	Y	N	Y	Y	Y
18 Condit	N	N	Y	Y	N	Y	Y	Y
19 ***Radanovich***	Y	Y	N	N	Y	Y	Y	Y
20 Dooley	N	N	N	N	Y	Y	Y	Y
21 ***Thomas***	Y	Y	N	N	Y	Y	Y	Y
22 Capps	N	N	N	Y	N	Y	Y	Y
23 ***Gallegly***	Y	Y	N	N	Y	Y	Y	?
24 Sherman	N	N	Y	Y	N	Y	Y	Y
25 ***McKeon***	Y	Y	Y	N	Y	Y	Y	Y
26 Berman	N	N	N	N	N	Y	Y	Y
27 ***Rogan***	Y	Y	N	N	Y	Y	?	Y
28 ***Dreier***	Y	Y	N	N	Y	Y	Y	Y
29 Waxman	N	N	N	Y	N	Y	Y	Y
30 Becerra	N	N	N	Y	N	Y	Y	Y
31 Martinez	?	?	?	?	?	?	?	?
32 Dixon	N	N	N	N	N	Y	Y	Y
33 Roybal-Allard	N	N	N	Y	N	Y	Y	Y
34 Torres	N	N	N	N	N	Y	?	Y
35 Waters	N	N	N	N	N	Y	Y	Y
36 Harman	N	N	Y	N	Y	Y	Y	Y
37 Millender-McD.	N	N	N	N	N	Y	Y	Y
38 ***Horn***	Y	Y	N	N	N	Y	Y	Y
39 ***Royce***	Y	Y	Y	Y	N	N	Y	Y
40 ***Lewis***	Y	Y	N	N	Y	Y	Y	Y
41 ***Kim***	Y	Y	N	N	N	Y	Y	Y
42 Brown	N	N	N	N	N	Y	Y	Y
43 ***Calvert***	Y	Y	N	N	Y	Y	Y	Y
44 ***Bono***	Y	Y	N	N	Y	Y	Y	Y
45 ***Rohrabacher***	Y	Y	Y	N	Y	Y	Y	Y
46 Sanchez	N	N	N	Y	N	Y	Y	Y
47 ***Cox***	Y	Y	Y	N	Y	Y	Y	Y
48 ***Packard***	Y	Y	N	N	Y	Y	Y	Y
49 ***Bilbray***	Y	Y	N	N	Y	Y	Y	Y
50 Filner	N	N	N	Y	N	Y	Y	Y
51 ***Cunningham***	Y	Y	Y	Y	Y	Y	Y	Y
52 ***Hunter***	Y	Y	N	N	Y	Y	Y	Y
COLORADO								
1 DeGette	N	N	Y	Y	N	Y	Y	Y
2 Skaggs	N	N	Y	Y	Y	Y	Y	Y
3 ***McInnis***	Y	Y	N	N	Y	Y	Y	Y
4 ***Schaffer***	Y	Y	Y	N	Y	Y	Y	Y
5 ***Hefley***	Y	Y	Y	N	Y	Y	Y	Y
6 ***Schaefer***	Y	Y	N	N	Y	Y	Y	Y
CONNECTICUT								
1 Kennelly	N	N	N	Y	N	Y	Y	Y
2 Gejdenson	N	N	N	Y	N	Y	Y	Y
3 DeLauro	N	N	N	Y	N	Y	Y	Y
4 ***Shays***	Y	Y	Y	Y	N	Y	Y	Y
5 Maloney	N	N	Y	Y	N	Y	Y	Y
6 ***Johnson***	Y	Y	N	N	N	Y	Y	Y
DELAWARE								
AL ***Castle***	Y	Y	Y	Y	N	Y	Y	Y
FLORIDA								
1 ***Scarborough***	Y	Y	N	Y	Y	Y	Y	Y
2 Boyd	N	N	N	N	Y	Y	Y	Y
3 Brown	N	N	N	N	N	Y	Y	Y
4 ***Fowler***	Y	Y	N	N	Y	Y	Y	Y
5 Thurman	N	N	N	N	Y	Y	Y	Y
6 ***Stearns***	Y	Y	Y	N	N	Y	Y	Y
7 ***Mica***	Y	Y	N	N	Y	Y	Y	Y
8 ***McCollum***	Y	Y	Y	N	N	Y	Y	Y
9 ***Bilirakis***	Y	Y	N	N	Y	Y	Y	Y
10 ***Young***	Y	Y	N	N	Y	Y	Y	Y
11 Davis	N	N	Y	Y	N	Y	Y	Y
12 ***Canady***	Y	Y	N	N	Y	Y	Y	Y
13 ***Miller***	Y	Y	Y	Y	N	Y	Y	Y
14 ***Goss***	Y	Y	Y	N	Y	Y	Y	Y
15 ***Weldon***	Y	Y	N	N	Y	Y	Y	Y
16 ***Foley***	Y	Y	Y	Y	N	Y	Y	Y
17 Meek	N	N	N	N	N	?	?	?
18 ***Ros-Lehtinen***	Y	Y	N	N	Y	Y	+	+
19 Wexler	N	N	N	Y	N	Y	Y	Y
20 Deutsch	N	N	N	Y	N	Y	Y	Y
21 ***Diaz-Balart***	Y	Y	N	N	Y	Y	Y	Y
22 ***Shaw***	Y	Y	Y	N	Y	Y	Y	Y
23 Hastings	N	N	N	N	N	Y	Y	Y
GEORGIA								
1 ***Kingston***	Y	Y	Y	Y	Y	Y	Y	Y
2 Bishop	N	N	N	N	Y	Y	Y	Y
3 ***Collins***	Y	Y	N	N	N	Y	Y	Y
4 McKinney	N	N	N	Y	N	Y	Y	Y
5 Lewis	N	N	N	Y	N	Y	Y	Y
6 ***Gingrich***								
7 ***Barr***	Y	Y	N	N	Y	Y	Y	Y
8 ***Chambliss***	Y	Y	N	N	N	Y	Y	Y
9 ***Deal***	Y	Y	N	N	N	Y	Y	Y
10 ***Norwood***	Y	Y	N	N	N	Y	Y	Y
11 ***Linder***	Y	?	N	N	Y	Y	Y	Y
HAWAII								
1 Abercrombie	N	N	N	Y	Y	Y	Y	Y
2 Mink	N	N	N	Y	Y	Y	Y	Y
IDAHO								
1 ***Chenoweth***	Y	Y	N	N	Y	Y	Y	?
2 ***Crapo***	Y	Y	N	N	Y	Y	Y	Y
ILLINOIS								
1 Rush	N	N	N	N	N	Y	Y	Y
2 Jackson	N	N	N	N	N	Y	Y	Y
3 Lipinski	N	N	N	N	N	Y	?	?
4 Gutierrez	N	N	N	N	N	Y	Y	Y
5 Blagojevich	N	N	Y	N	N	Y	Y	Y
6 ***Hyde***	Y	Y	N	N	Y	Y	Y	Y
7 Davis	N	N	N	N	N	Y	Y	Y
8 ***Crane***	?	?	Y	N	Y	Y	Y	Y
9 Yates	N	N	N	N	N	Y	Y	Y
10 ***Porter***	Y	Y	Y	N	Y	Y	Y	Y
11 ***Weller***	Y	Y	N	N	Y	Y	Y	Y
12 Costello	N	N	N	N	N	Y	Y	Y
13 ***Fawell***	Y	Y	N	N	Y	Y	Y	Y
14 ***Hastert***	Y	Y	N	N	Y	Y	Y	Y
15 ***Ewing***	Y	Y	N	N	Y	Y	Y	Y

ND Northern Democrats SD Southern Democrats

	324	325	326	327	328	329	330	331
16 ***Manzullo***	Y	Y	Y	N	N	Y	Y	Y
17 Evans	N	N	N	Y	N	Y	Y	Y
18 ***LaHood***	Y	Y	N	N	Y	Y	Y	Y
19 Poshard	N	N	N	N	N	Y	Y	Y
20 ***Shimkus***	Y	Y	Y	N	Y	Y	Y	Y
INDIANA								
1 Visclosky	N	N	N	N	Y	Y	Y	Y
2 ***McIntosh***	Y	Y	Y	N	Y	Y	Y	Y
3 Roemer	N	Y	N	Y	N	Y	Y	Y
4 ***Souder***	Y	Y	Y	N	N	Y	Y	Y
5 ***Buyer***	Y	Y	N	N	?	Y	?	?
6 ***Burton***	Y	Y	N	N	Y	Y	Y	?
7 ***Pease***	Y	Y	N	N	Y	Y	Y	Y
8 ***Hostettler***	Y	Y	Y	N	Y	Y	Y	Y
9 Hamilton	N	N	N	N	Y	Y	Y	Y
10 Carson	N	N	N	N	Y	Y	Y	Y
IOWA								
1 ***Leach***	Y	Y	N	N	N	Y	Y	Y
2 ***Nussle***	?	Y	Y	N	Y	Y	Y	Y
3 Boswell	N	N	N	Y	N	Y	Y	Y
4 ***Ganske***	Y	Y	Y	Y	N	Y	Y	Y
5 ***Latham***	Y	Y	N	N	Y	Y	Y	Y
KANSAS								
1 ***Moran***	Y	Y	N	N	Y	Y	Y	Y
2 ***Ryun***	Y	Y	Y	N	N	Y	Y	Y
3 ***Snowbarger***	Y	Y	N	N	Y	Y	?	?
4 ***Tiahrt***	Y	Y	Y	N	Y	Y	Y	Y
KENTUCKY								
1 ***Whitfield***	Y	Y	N	N	N	Y	Y	Y
2 ***Lewis***	Y	Y	N	N	Y	Y	Y	Y
3 ***Northup***	Y	Y	N	N	N	Y	Y	Y
4 ***Bunning***	Y	Y	N	N	Y	Y	Y	Y
5 ***Rogers***	Y	Y	N	N	Y	Y	Y	Y
6 Baesler	N	N	N	N	Y	Y	Y	Y
LOUISIANA								
1 ***Livingston***	Y	Y	N	N	Y	Y	Y	Y
2 Jefferson	N	N	N	N	Y	Y	Y	Y
3 ***Tauzin***	Y	Y	N	N	Y	Y	Y	Y
4 ***McCrery***	Y	Y	N	N	Y	Y	Y	Y
5 ***Cooksey***	Y	Y	N	N	Y	Y	Y	Y
6 ***Baker***	Y	Y	N	N	Y	Y	?	?
7 John	N	N	N	N	Y	Y	Y	Y
MAINE								
1 Allen	N	N	N	Y	N	Y	Y	Y
2 Baldacci	N	N	N	Y	Y	Y	Y	Y
MARYLAND								
1 ***Gilchrest***	Y	Y	N	N	N	Y	Y	Y
2 ***Ehrlich***	Y	Y	Y	N	N	Y	Y	Y
3 Cardin	N	N	N	Y	N	Y	Y	Y
4 Wynn	N	N	N	N	Y	Y	Y	Y
5 Hoyer	N	N	N	N	Y	Y	Y	Y
6 ***Bartlett***	Y	Y	N	N	Y	Y	Y	Y
7 Cummings	N	N	N	N	N	Y	Y	Y
8 ***Morella***	Y	Y	Y	Y	N	Y	Y	Y
MASSACHUSETTS								
1 Olver	N	N	N	Y	N	Y	Y	Y
2 Neal	N	N	N	Y	N	Y	Y	Y
3 McGovern	N	N	N	Y	N	Y	Y	Y
4 Frank	N	N	N	Y	N	Y	Y	Y
5 Meehan	N	N	Y	Y	N	Y	Y	Y
6 Tierney	N	N	N	Y	N	Y	Y	Y
7 Markey	N	N	Y	Y	N	Y	Y	Y
8 Kennedy	N	N	Y	Y	N	Y	Y	Y
9 Moakley	N	N	N	Y	Y	Y	Y	Y
10 Delahunt	N	N	Y	Y	N	Y	Y	Y
MICHIGAN								
1 Stupak	N	N	N	N	N	Y	Y	Y
2 ***Hoekstra***	Y	Y	N	N	N	Y	Y	Y
3 ***Ehlers***	Y	Y	Y	N	N	Y	Y	Y
4 ***Camp***	Y	Y	Y	N	Y	Y	Y	Y
5 Barcia	N	N	Y	N	N	Y	Y	Y
6 ***Upton***	Y	Y	Y	N	N	Y	Y	Y
7 ***Smith***	Y	Y	Y	?	N	N	Y	Y
8 Stabenow	N	N	N	Y	N	Y	Y	Y
9 Kildee	N	N	N	Y	Y	Y	Y	Y
10 Bonior	N	N	N	Y	N	Y	Y	Y
11 ***Knollenberg***	Y	Y	N	N	Y	Y	Y	Y
12 Levin	N	N	N	Y	N	Y	Y	Y
13 Rivers	N	N	N	Y	N	Y	Y	Y
14 Conyers	N	N	N	Y	Y	Y	Y	Y
15 Kilpatrick	N	N	N	Y	Y	Y	Y	Y
16 Dingell	N	N	N	N	N	Y	Y	Y
MINNESOTA								
1 ***Gutknecht***	Y	Y	N	N	Y	Y	Y	Y
2 Minge	N	N	Y	Y	N	Y	Y	Y

	324	325	326	327	328	329	330	331
3 ***Ramstad***	Y	Y	Y	Y	N	Y	Y	Y
4 Vento	N	N	N	Y	N	Y	Y	Y
5 Sabo	N	N	N	Y	N	Y	Y	Y
6 Luther	N	N	Y	Y	N	Y	Y	Y
7 Peterson	N	N	Y	Y	N	Y	Y	Y
8 Oberstar	N	N	N	N	N	Y	Y	Y
MISSISSIPPI								
1 ***Wicker***	Y	Y	N	N	Y	Y	Y	Y
2 Thompson	N	N	N	N	N	Y	Y	Y
3 ***Pickering***	Y	Y	N	N	Y	Y	Y	Y
4 ***Parker***	Y	Y	N	N	Y	Y	Y	Y
5 Taylor	N	Y	N	N	N	Y	Y	Y
MISSOURI								
1 Clay	N	N	N	N	N	Y	Y	Y
2 ***Talent***	Y	Y	Y	N	Y	Y	Y	Y
3 Gephardt	N	N	N	Y	N	Y	Y	Y
4 Skelton	N	N	N	N	Y	Y	Y	Y
5 McCarthy	N	N	Y	Y	N	Y	Y	Y
6 Danner	N	N	N	N	N	Y	Y	Y
7 ***Blunt***	Y	Y	N	Y	Y	Y	Y	Y
8 ***Emerson***	Y	Y	N	N	Y	Y	Y	Y
9 ***Hulshof***	Y	Y	Y	N	N	Y	Y	Y
MONTANA								
AL ***Hill***	Y	Y	Y	N	Y	Y	Y	Y
NEBRASKA								
1 ***Bereuter***	Y	Y	Y	N	Y	Y	Y	Y
2 ***Christensen***	Y	Y	Y	N	Y	Y	Y	Y
3 ***Barrett***	Y	Y	N	N	Y	Y	Y	Y
NEVADA								
1 ***Ensign***	Y	Y	Y	N	Y	N	Y	Y
2 ***Gibbons***	Y	Y	N	N	Y	N	Y	Y
NEW HAMPSHIRE								
1 ***Sununu***	Y	Y	Y	Y	N	Y	Y	Y
2 ***Bass***	Y	Y	Y	Y	N	Y	Y	Y
NEW JERSEY								
1 Andrews	N	N	Y	Y	N	Y	Y	Y
2 ***LoBiondo***	Y	N	N	Y	N	Y	Y	Y
3 ***Saxton***	Y	Y	N	N	N	Y	Y	Y
4 ***Smith***	?	?	?	N	N	Y	Y	Y
5 ***Roukema***	Y	Y	Y	N	Y	Y	Y	Y
6 Pallone	N	N	N	Y	N	Y	Y	Y
7 ***Franks***	Y	Y	N	Y	N	Y	Y	Y
8 Pascrell	N	N	N	Y	N	Y	Y	Y
9 Rothman	N	N	N	Y	N	Y	Y	Y
10 Payne	N	N	N	Y	N	Y	Y	Y
11 ***Frelinghuysen***	Y	Y	N	N	Y	Y	Y	Y
12 ***Pappas***	Y	Y	Y	N	N	Y	Y	Y
13 Menendez	N	N	N	Y	N	Y	Y	Y
NEW MEXICO								
1 ***Schiff***	?	?	?	?	?	?	?	?
2 ***Skeen***	Y	Y	N	N	Y	Y	Y	Y
3 ***Redmond***	Y	Y	N	N	Y	Y	Y	Y
NEW YORK								
1 ***Forbes***	Y	N	N	N	N	Y	Y	Y
2 ***Lazio***	Y	Y	N	N	N	Y	Y	Y
3 ***King***	Y	N	N	N	Y	Y	Y	Y
4 McCarthy	N	N	N	Y	N	Y	Y	Y
5 Ackerman	N	N	N	Y	Y	Y	Y	Y
6 Flake	N	N	N	N	N	Y	Y	Y
7 Manton	N	N	N	N	N	Y	Y	Y
8 Nadler	N	N	N	Y	N	Y	Y	Y
9 Schumer	N	N	N	Y	N	Y	Y	Y
10 Towns	N	N	N	N	N	Y	Y	Y
11 Owens	N	N	N	Y	N	Y	Y	Y
12 Velázquez	N	N	N	Y	N	Y	Y	Y
13 ***Molinari***	?	?	?	?	?	?	?	?
14 Maloney	N	N	N	Y	N	Y	Y	Y
15 Rangel	N	N	N	Y	N	Y	Y	Y
16 Serrano	N	N	N	Y	N	Y	Y	Y
17 Engel	N	N	N	Y	N	Y	Y	Y
18 Lowey	N	N	N	Y	N	Y	Y	Y
19 ***Kelly***	Y	Y	N	N	N	Y	Y	Y
20 ***Gilman***	Y	Y	N	N	N	Y	Y	Y
21 McNulty	N	N	N	N	N	Y	Y	Y
22 ***Solomon***	Y	Y	N	N	Y	Y	Y	Y
23 ***Boehlert***	Y	Y	N	Y	N	Y	Y	Y
24 ***McHugh***	Y	Y	N	N	Y	Y	Y	Y
25 ***Walsh***	Y	Y	N	Y	Y	Y	Y	Y
26 Hinchey	N	N	N	Y	N	Y	Y	Y
27 ***Paxon***	Y	Y	Y	N	Y	Y	Y	Y
28 Slaughter	N	N	N	N	N	Y	Y	Y
29 LaFalce	N	N	N	Y	Y	Y	Y	Y
30 ***Quinn***	Y	N	N	N	Y	Y	Y	Y
31 ***Houghton***	Y	Y	N	N	N	Y	Y	Y

	324	325	326	327	328	329	330	331
NORTH CAROLINA								
1 Clayton	N	N	N	N	N	Y	Y	Y
2 Etheridge	N	N	N	Y	N	Y	Y	Y
3 ***Jones***	Y	Y	N	N	Y	Y	Y	Y
4 Price	N	N	N	Y	N	Y	Y	Y
5 ***Burr***	Y	Y	N	N	Y	Y	Y	Y
6 ***Coble***	Y	Y	Y	Y	N	Y	Y	Y
7 McIntyre	N	N	N	N	Y	Y	Y	Y
8 Hefner	N	N	N	Y	Y	Y	Y	Y
9 ***Myrick***	Y	Y	N	N	Y	Y	Y	Y
10 ***Ballenger***	Y	Y	N	N	Y	Y	Y	Y
11 ***Taylor***	Y	?	N	N	Y	Y	Y	Y
12 Watt	N	N	N	N	N	Y	Y	Y
NORTH DAKOTA								
AL Pomeroy	N	N	N	Y	Y	Y	Y	Y
OHIO								
1 ***Chabot***	Y	Y	Y	Y	N	Y	Y	Y
2 ***Portman***	Y	Y	N	Y	N	Y	Y	Y
3 Hall	N	N	N	Y	N	Y	Y	Y
4 ***Oxley***	Y	Y	Y	N	Y	Y	Y	Y
5 ***Gillmor***	Y	Y	N	N	Y	Y	Y	Y
6 Strickland	N	N	N	Y	N	Y	Y	Y
7 ***Hobson***	Y	Y	N	N	N	Y	Y	Y
8 ***Boehner***	Y	Y	N	N	Y	Y	Y	?
9 Kaptur	N	N	N	?	?	Y	Y	Y
10 Kucinich	N	N	N	Y	N	Y	Y	Y
11 Stokes	N	N	N	Y	N	Y	Y	Y
12 ***Kasich***	Y	Y	Y	Y	N	Y	Y	Y
13 Brown	N	N	N	Y	N	Y	Y	Y
14 Sawyer	N	N	N	N	Y	Y	Y	Y
15 ***Pryce***	Y	Y	N	N	Y	Y	Y	Y
16 ***Regula***	Y	Y	N	N	Y	Y	Y	Y
17 Traficant	Y	Y	N	N	Y	Y	Y	Y
18 ***Ney***	Y	Y	N	N	N	Y	Y	Y
19 ***LaTourette***	Y	Y	N	N	Y	Y	Y	Y
OKLAHOMA								
1 ***Largent***	Y	Y	Y	N	N	Y	Y	Y
2 ***Coburn***	Y	Y	Y	N	N	Y	Y	Y
3 ***Watkins***	Y	Y	N	N	Y	Y	?	?
4 ***Watts***	Y	Y	N	N	Y	Y	Y	Y
5 ***Istook***	Y	Y	Y	N	Y	Y	Y	Y
6 ***Lucas***	Y	Y	N	N	Y	Y	Y	Y
OREGON								
1 Furse	N	N	Y	Y	Y	Y	Y	Y
2 ***Smith***	Y	Y	N	N	Y	Y	Y	Y
3 Blumenauer	?	?	?	?	?	?	?	?
4 DeFazio	N	N	N	Y	N	Y	Y	N
5 Hooley	N	N	Y	Y	N	Y	Y	Y
PENNSYLVANIA								
1 Foglietta	N	N	N	Y	Y	Y	Y	Y
2 Fattah	N	N	N	Y	Y	Y	Y	Y
3 Borski	N	N	N	Y	Y	Y	Y	Y
4 Klink	N	N	N	N	Y	Y	Y	Y
5 ***Peterson***	Y	Y	N	N	Y	Y	Y	Y
6 Holden	N	N	N	N	Y	Y	Y	Y
7 ***Weldon***	Y	Y	N	N	N	Y	Y	Y
8 ***Greenwood***	Y	Y	N	N	N	Y	Y	Y
9 ***Shuster***	Y	Y	N	N	Y	Y	Y	Y
10 ***McDade***	Y	Y	N	N	Y	Y	Y	Y
11 Kanjorski	N	N	N	N	Y	Y	Y	Y
12 Murtha	N	N	N	N	Y	Y	Y	Y
13 ***Fox***	Y	Y	N	N	N	Y	Y	Y
14 Coyne	N	N	N	Y	N	Y	Y	Y
15 McHale	N	N	N	N	Y	Y	Y	Y
16 ***Pitts***	Y	Y	N	N	Y	Y	Y	Y
17 ***Gekas***	Y	Y	N	N	Y	Y	Y	Y
18 Doyle	N	N	N	N	Y	Y	Y	Y
19 ***Goodling***	Y	Y	N	N	Y	Y	Y	Y
20 Mascara	N	N	N	N	Y	Y	Y	Y
21 ***English***	Y	N	N	N	Y	Y	Y	Y
RHODE ISLAND								
1 Kennedy	N	N	N	Y	Y	Y	Y	Y
2 Weygand	N	N	N	Y	N	Y	Y	Y
SOUTH CAROLINA								
1 ***Sanford***	Y	Y	Y	Y	N	Y	Y	Y
2 ***Spence***	Y	Y	N	N	Y	Y	Y	Y
3 ***Graham***	Y	Y	N	N	Y	Y	Y	Y
4 ***Inglis***	Y	Y	Y	N	N	Y	Y	Y
5 Spratt	N	N	N	Y	Y	Y	Y	Y
6 Clyburn	N	N	N	N	N	Y	Y	Y
SOUTH DAKOTA								
AL ***Thune***	Y	Y	Y	N	Y	Y	Y	Y
TENNESSEE								
1 ***Jenkins***	Y	Y	N	N	Y	Y	Y	Y
2 ***Duncan***	Y	Y	N	Y	N	Y	Y	Y

	324	325	326	327	328	329	330	
3 ***Wamp***	Y	Y	N	N	Y	Y	Y	Y
4 ***Hilleary***	Y	Y	N	N	Y	Y	Y	Y
5 Clement	N	N	N	N	N	Y	Y	Y
6 Gordon	N	N	N	N	Y	Y	Y	?
7 ***Bryant***	Y	Y	N	N	Y	Y	Y	Y
8 Tanner	N	N	N	N	N	Y	Y	Y
9 Ford	N	N	N	Y	Y	Y	Y	Y
TEXAS								
1 Sandlin	N	N	N	N	Y	Y	Y	Y
2 Turner	N	N	N	N	Y	Y	Y	Y
3 ***Johnson, Sam***	Y	Y	Y	N	Y	Y	Y	Y
4 Hall	N	N	Y	N	Y	Y	Y	Y
5 ***Sessions***	Y	Y	Y	N	Y	Y	Y	Y
6 ***Barton***	Y	Y	N	N	Y	Y	Y	Y
7 ***Archer***	Y	Y	Y	N	Y	Y	Y	Y
8 ***Brady***	Y	Y	N	N	Y	Y	Y	Y
9 Lampson	N	N	N	N	Y	Y	Y	Y
10 Doggett	N	N	Y	Y	N	Y	?	Y
11 Edwards	N	N	N	N	Y	Y	Y	Y
12 ***Granger***	Y	Y	N	N	Y	Y	Y	Y
13 ***Thornberry***	Y	Y	N	N	Y	Y	Y	Y
14 ***Paul***	Y	Y	Y	Y	N	N	Y	Y
15 Hinojosa	N	N	N	N	Y	Y	Y	Y
16 Reyes	N	N	N	N	Y	Y	Y	Y
17 Stenholm	N	N	N	N	Y	Y	Y	Y
18 Jackson-Lee	N	N	N	N	Y	Y	Y	Y
19 ***Combest***	Y	Y	N	N	Y	Y	Y	Y
20 Gonzalez	?	?	?	?	?	?	?	?
21 ***Smith***	Y	Y	N	N	Y	Y	Y	Y
22 ***DeLay***	Y	Y	Y	N	Y	Y	Y	Y
23 ***Bonilla***	Y	Y	N	N	Y	Y	Y	Y
24 Frost	N	N	N	N	Y	Y	Y	Y
25 Bentsen	N	N	N	N	N	Y	Y	Y
26 ***Armey***	Y	Y	Y	N	Y	Y	Y	Y
27 Ortiz	N	N	N	N	Y	Y	Y	Y
28 Rodriguez	N	N	N	N	Y	Y	Y	Y
29 Green	N	N	N	N	Y	Y	Y	Y
30 Johnson, E.B.	N	–	N	N	Y	Y	Y	Y
UTAH								
1 ***Hansen***	Y	Y	N	N	Y	Y	Y	Y
2 ***Cook***	Y	Y	N	N	N	Y	Y	Y
3 ***Cannon***	Y	Y	Y	N	Y	Y	Y	Y
VERMONT								
AL *Sanders*	N	N	N	Y	N	Y	Y	Y
VIRGINIA								
1 ***Bateman***	Y	Y	N	N	Y	Y	Y	Y
2 Pickett	N	N	N	N	Y	Y	Y	Y
3 Scott	N	N	N	N	N	Y	Y	Y
4 Sisisky	N	N	N	N	Y	Y	Y	Y
5 Goode	N	N	N	N	N	Y	Y	Y
6 ***Goodlatte***	Y	Y	N	N	N	Y	Y	Y
7 ***Bliley***	Y	Y	N	N	Y	Y	Y	Y
8 Moran	N	N	N	N	Y	Y	Y	Y
9 Boucher	N	N	N	N	N	Y	Y	Y
10 ***Wolf***	Y	Y	Y	N	Y	Y	Y	Y
11 ***Davis***	Y	Y	N	N	Y	Y	?	Y
WASHINGTON								
1 ***White***	Y	Y	Y	N	Y	Y	Y	Y
2 ***Metcalf***	Y	Y	N	N	N	Y	Y	Y
3 ***Smith, Linda***	Y	Y	Y	N	Y	Y	Y	Y
4 ***Hastings***	Y	Y	N	N	Y	Y	Y	Y
5 ***Nethercutt***	Y	Y	N	N	Y	Y	Y	Y
6 Dicks	N	N	N	N	Y	Y	Y	Y
7 McDermott	N	N	N	Y	N	Y	Y	Y
8 ***Dunn***	Y	Y	Y	N	Y	Y	Y	Y
9 Smith, Adam	N	N	N	Y	N	Y	Y	Y
WEST VIRGINIA								
1 Mollohan	N	N	N	N	Y	Y	Y	Y
2 Wise	N	N	N	N	Y	Y	Y	Y
3 Rahall	N	N	N	Y	Y	Y	Y	Y
WISCONSIN								
1 ***Neumann***	Y	Y	Y	N	N	Y	Y	?
2 ***Klug***	Y	Y	Y	Y	N	N	Y	Y
3 Kind	N	N	Y	Y	N	Y	Y	Y
4 Kleczka	N	N	Y	Y	N	Y	Y	Y
5 Barrett	N	N	N	Y	N	Y	Y	Y
6 ***Petri***	Y	Y	N	N	N	Y	Y	Y
7 Obey	N	N	N	Y	N	Y	Y	Y
8 Johnson	N	N	N	N	N	Y	Y	Y
9 ***Sensenbrenner***	Y	Y	Y	Y	N	N	Y	Y
WYOMING								
AL ***Cubin***	Y	Y	N	N	Y	Y	Y	?

Southern states - Ala., Ark., Fla., Ga., Ky., La., Miss., N.C., Okla., S.C., Tenn., Texas, Va.

HOUSE VOTES 332, 333, 334, 335, 336, 337, 338, 339

332. HR 2209. Fiscal 1998 Legislative Branch Appropriations/Joint Tax Committee. Fazio, D-Calif., amendment to reduce funds in the bill for the Joint Committee on Taxation by $283,000, thereby preventing an increase in committee staff. The amendment instead would provide a 2.8 percent cost of living adjustment for current staff. Rejected 199-213: R 11-208; D 187-5 (ND 137-4, SD 50-1); I 1-0, July 28, 1997.

333. HR 2209. Fiscal 1998 Legislative Branch Appropriations/Government Printing Office. Klug, R-Wis., amendment to reduce by 350, to 3,550, the number of full-time equivalent positions in the Government Printing Office. Rejected 170-242: R 155-62; D 15-179 (ND 10-132, SD 5-47); I 0-1, July 28, 1997.

334. HR 2209. Fiscal 1998 Legislative Branch Appropriations/Recommit. Gejdenson, D-Conn., motion to recommit the bill to the Appropriations Committee with instructions to report it back with an amendment to eliminate funding in the bill for a $7.9 million reserve that would be allocated by the House Oversight Committee to meet unanticipated committee staffing and expense needs. Motion rejected 198-220: R 2-219; D 195-1 (ND 143-1, SD 52-0); I 1-0, July 28, 1997.

335. HR 2209. Fiscal 1998 Legislative Branch Appropriations/Passage. Passage of the bill to provide $1.7 billion in new budget authority for the legislative branch in fiscal 1998. The bill provides $10 million less than in fiscal 1997. Passed 214-203: R 213-7; D 1-195 (ND 1-144, SD 0-51); I 0-1, July 28, 1997.

336. HR 2266. Fiscal 1998 Defense Appropriations/B-2 Bomber. Obey, D-Wis., amendment to cut the $331 million provided in the bill for advance procurement of the B-2 Stealth Bomber beyond the 21 aircraft previously authorized. The amendment would increase funding for the Army Research and Development account by $105 million and the Defense Health Program for breast cancer research by $12 million, and would apply the remaining $214 million to deficit reduction. Rejected 200-222: R 55-165; D 144-57 (ND 118-30, SD 26-27); I 1-0, July 29, 1997. A "yea" was a vote in support of the president's position.

337. HR 2266. Fiscal 1998 Defense Appropriations/Spending Freeze. Shays, R-Conn., amendment to reduce the bill's overall appropriation by $3.87 billion, to $244.47 billion. Rejected 137-290: R 37-186; D 99-104 (ND 89-61, SD 10-43); I 1-0, July 29, 1997.

338. HR 2266. Fiscal 1998 Defense Appropriations/Passage. Passage of the bill to provide $248.3 billion in new budget authority for the Department of Defense in fiscal 1998. The bill provides $3.87 billion more than was provided in fiscal 1997 and $4.4 billion more than the $243.9 billion requested by the president. The bill also prohibits funding for U.S. ground troops in Bosnia after June 30, 1998, unless Congress approves an extension. Passed 322-105: R 200-22; D 122-82 (ND 73-77, SD 49-5); I 0-1, July 29, 1997. A "nay" was a vote in support of the president's position.

339. H Con Res 75. Violent Criminal Sentencing/Adoption. McCollum, R-Fla., motion to suspend the rules and adopt the concurrent resolution to commend the 25 states that require convicted felons to serve at least 85 percent of their prison sentences, encourage all remaining states to adopt legislation to increase time served by violent felons, and re-emphasize congressional support for the requirement that individuals convicted of violent federal crimes serve at least 85 percent of their sentences. Motion agreed to 400-24: R 221-0; D 179-23 (ND 130-19, SD 49-4); I 0-1, July 29, 1997. A two-thirds majority of those present and voting (283 in this case) is required for adoption under suspension of the rules.

KEY

Y Voted for (yea).
\# Paired for.
\+ Announced for.
N Voted against (nay).
X Paired against.
– Announced against.
P Voted "present."
C Voted "present" to avoid possible conflict of interest.
? Did not vote or otherwise make a position known.

Democrats ***Republicans***
Independent

	332	333	334	335	336	337	338	339
ALABAMA								
1 ***Callahan***	N	Y	N	Y	N	N	Y	Y
2 ***Everett***	N	Y	N	Y	N	N	Y	Y
3 ***Riley***	N	Y	N	Y	?	N	Y	Y
4 ***Aderholt***	N	Y	N	Y	N	N	Y	Y
5 Cramer	Y	N	Y	N	N	N	Y	Y
6 ***Bachus***	N	Y	N	Y	N	N	Y	Y
7 Hilliard	Y	N	Y	N	Y	Y	N	N
ALASKA								
AL ***Young***	?	?	?	?	?	?	?	?
ARIZONA								
1 ***Salmon***	N	Y	N	Y	N	N	Y	Y
2 Pastor	Y	N	Y	N	Y	N	Y	Y
3 ***Stump***	N	Y	N	Y	N	N	Y	Y
4 ***Shadegg***	N	Y	N	Y	N	N	Y	Y
5 ***Kolbe***	N	Y	N	Y	Y	N	Y	Y
6 ***Hayworth***	N	Y	N	Y	N	N	Y	Y
ARKANSAS								
1 Berry	Y	N	Y	N	Y	Y	N	Y
2 Snyder	Y	N	Y	N	Y	N	Y	P
3 ***Hutchinson***	N	Y	N	Y	N	N	Y	Y
4 ***Dickey***	N	N	N	Y	N	N	Y	Y
CALIFORNIA								
1 ***Riggs***	N	Y	N	Y	N	Y	N	Y
2 ***Herger***	N	Y	N	Y	N	N	Y	Y
3 Fazio	Y	N	Y	N	N	N	Y	Y
4 ***Doolittle***	N	Y	N	Y	N	N	Y	Y
5 Matsui	Y	N	Y	N	N	Y	Y	Y
6 Woolsey	Y	N	Y	N	Y	Y	Y	Y
7 Miller	Y	N	Y	N	Y	Y	N	Y
8 Pelosi	Y	N	Y	N	Y	Y	N	Y
9 Dellums	Y	N	Y	N	Y	Y	N	N
10 Tauscher	Y	N	Y	N	Y	N	Y	Y
11 ***Pombo***	N	N	N	Y	N	N	Y	Y
12 Lantos	?	?	Y	N	Y	Y	Y	Y
13 Stark	Y	N	Y	N	Y	Y	N	N
14 Eshoo	Y	N	Y	N	Y	Y	N	Y
15 ***Campbell***	N	Y	N	Y	N	Y	N	Y
16 Lofgren	Y	N	Y	N	Y	Y	N	Y
17 Farr	Y	N	Y	N	Y	Y	Y	Y
18 Condit	N	Y	Y	N	Y	N	Y	Y
19 ***Radanovich***	N	N	N	Y	N	N	Y	Y
20 Dooley	Y	N	Y	N	N	N	Y	Y
21 ***Thomas***	N	Y	N	Y	N	N	Y	Y
22 Capps	Y	N	Y	N	Y	Y	Y	Y
23 ***Gallegly***	N	N	N	Y	Y	N	Y	Y
24 Sherman	Y	N	Y	N	N	N	Y	Y
25 ***McKeon***	N	N	N	Y	N	N	Y	Y
26 Berman	Y	N	Y	N	N	Y	Y	Y
27 ***Rogan***	N	Y	N	Y	N	N	Y	Y
28 ***Dreier***	N	Y	N	Y	N	N	Y	Y
29 Waxman	Y	N	Y	N	Y	Y	N	Y
30 Becerra	Y	N	Y	N	Y	Y	N	Y
31 Martinez	Y	N	Y	N	N	N	Y	Y
32 Dixon	Y	N	Y	N	N	N	Y	Y
33 Roybal-Allard	Y	N	Y	N	Y	Y	Y	Y
34 Torres	?	?	?	?	N	N	N	Y
35 Waters	Y	N	Y	N	N	Y	Y	Y
36 Harman	?	?	Y	N	N	N	Y	Y
37 Millender-McD.	Y	N	Y	N	N	N	Y	Y
38 ***Horn***	N	N	N	Y	N	N	Y	Y
39 ***Royce***	Y	Y	N	Y	N	Y	N	Y
40 ***Lewis***	N	N	N	Y	N	N	Y	Y
41 ***Kim***	N	Y	N	Y	N	N	Y	Y
42 Brown	N	N	Y	N	N	Y	N	Y
43 ***Calvert***	N	N	N	Y	N	N	Y	Y
44 ***Bono***	N	N	N	Y	N	N	N	Y
45 ***Rohrabacher***	N	Y	N	Y	N	Y	Y	Y
46 Sanchez	?	?	?	?	N	N	Y	Y
47 ***Cox***	N	Y	N	Y	N	N	Y	Y
48 ***Packard***	N	N	N	Y	N	N	Y	Y
49 ***Bilbray***	N	Y	N	Y	N	N	Y	Y
50 Filner	Y	N	Y	N	N	Y	N	Y
51 ***Cunningham***	N	Y	N	Y	N	N	Y	Y
52 ***Hunter***	N	N	N	Y	N	N	?	Y
COLORADO								
1 DeGette	Y	N	Y	N	Y	Y	N	Y
2 Skaggs	Y	N	Y	N	Y	Y	Y	Y
3 ***McInnis***	?	?	?	?	?	N	Y	Y
4 ***Schaffer***	Y	Y	N	Y	N	N	Y	Y
5 ***Hefley***	Y	Y	N	Y	N	N	Y	Y
6 ***Schaefer***	N	Y	N	Y	N	N	Y	Y
CONNECTICUT								
1 Kennelly	Y	N	Y	N	Y	N	Y	Y
2 Gejdenson	Y	N	Y	N	Y	N	Y	Y
3 DeLauro	Y	N	Y	N	Y	N	Y	Y
4 ***Shays***	N	Y	N	Y	Y	Y	N	Y
5 Maloney	Y	N	Y	N	N	N	Y	Y
6 ***Johnson***	N	N	N	Y	N	N	Y	Y
DELAWARE								
AL ***Castle***	N	Y	N	Y	Y	Y	Y	Y
FLORIDA								
1 ***Scarborough***	N	Y	N	Y	N	N	Y	Y
2 Boyd	Y	N	Y	N	Y	N	Y	Y
3 Brown	Y	N	Y	N	N	N	Y	Y
4 ***Fowler***	N	Y	N	Y	N	N	Y	Y
5 Thurman	Y	N	Y	N	N	N	Y	Y
6 ***Stearns***	N	Y	N	Y	N	N	Y	Y
7 ***Mica***	N	Y	N	Y	N	N	Y	Y
8 ***McCollum***	N	Y	N	Y	N	N	Y	Y
9 ***Bilirakis***	N	Y	N	Y	N	N	Y	Y
10 ***Young***	N	N	N	Y	N	N	Y	Y
11 Davis	Y	N	Y	N	Y	?	Y	Y
12 ***Canady***	N	N	N	Y	N	N	Y	Y
13 ***Miller***	N	Y	N	Y	Y	N	Y	Y
14 ***Goss***	N	Y	N	Y	N	N	Y	Y
15 ***Weldon***	N	N	N	Y	N	N	Y	Y
16 ***Foley***	N	Y	N	Y	Y	Y	Y	Y
17 Meek	Y	N	Y	?	N	N	Y	Y
18 ***Ros-Lehtinen***	N	Y	N	Y	Y	N	Y	Y
19 Wexler	?	?	?	?	?	N	Y	Y
20 Deutsch	Y	N	Y	N	Y	N	Y	Y
21 ***Diaz-Balart***	N	N	N	Y	N	N	Y	Y
22 ***Shaw***	N	N	N	Y	N	N	Y	Y
23 Hastings	Y	N	Y	N	N	Y	Y	Y
GEORGIA								
1 ***Kingston***	N	Y	N	Y	N	N	Y	Y
2 Bishop	Y	N	Y	N	N	N	Y	Y
3 ***Collins***	N	Y	N	Y	N	N	Y	Y
4 McKinney	Y	N	Y	N	Y	Y	N	Y
5 Lewis	Y	N	Y	N	Y	N	Y	N
6 ***Gingrich***	N							
7 ***Barr***	N	Y	N	Y	N	N	Y	Y
8 ***Chambliss***	N	Y	N	Y	N	N	Y	Y
9 ***Deal***	N	Y	N	Y	N	N	Y	Y
10 ***Norwood***	N	Y	N	Y	N	N	Y	Y
11 ***Linder***	N	Y	N	Y	N	N	Y	Y
HAWAII								
1 Abercrombie	Y	N	Y	N	Y	N	Y	Y
2 Mink	Y	N	Y	N	Y	Y	Y	Y
IDAHO								
1 ***Chenoweth***	N	Y	N	Y	N	N	Y	Y
2 ***Crapo***	N	Y	N	Y	N	N	Y	Y
ILLINOIS								
1 Rush	?	?	?	N	Y	Y	N	N
2 Jackson	Y	N	Y	N	Y	Y	N	N
3 Lipinski	Y	N	Y	N	Y	N	Y	Y
4 Gutierrez	Y	N	Y	N	Y	Y	N	Y
5 Blagojevich	Y	Y	Y	N	Y	N	Y	Y
6 ***Hyde***	N	Y	N	Y	N	N	Y	Y
7 Davis	Y	N	Y	N	Y	Y	N	Y
8 ***Crane***	N	Y	N	Y	N	N	Y	Y
9 Yates	?	?	?	?	Y	Y	N	Y
10 ***Porter***	N	Y	N	Y	Y	Y	Y	Y
11 ***Weller***	N	Y	N	Y	N	N	Y	Y
12 Costello	Y	N	Y	N	Y	Y	Y	Y
13 ***Fawell***	N	Y	N	Y	N	N	Y	Y
14 ***Hastert***	N	Y	N	Y	N	N	Y	Y
15 ***Ewing***	N	Y	N	Y	N	N	Y	Y

ND Northern Democrats SD Southern Democrats

	332	333	334	335	336	337	338	339
16 ***Manzullo***	N	Y	N	Y	N	N	Y	Y
17 Evans	Y	N	Y	N	Y	Y	N	Y
18 ***LaHood***	N	Y	N	Y	N	N	Y	Y
19 Poshard	Y	N	Y	N	Y	Y	Y	Y
20 ***Shimkus***	N	Y	N	Y	N	N	Y	Y
INDIANA								
1 Visclosky	Y	N	Y	N	N	N	Y	Y
2 ***McIntosh***	N	Y	N	Y	N	N	Y	Y
3 Roemer	Y	N	Y	N	Y	N	Y	Y
4 ***Souder***	N	Y	N	Y	N	N	Y	Y
5 ***Buyer***	N	Y	N	Y	N	N	Y	Y
6 ***Burton***	N	Y	N	Y	N	N	Y	Y
7 ***Pease***	N	Y	N	Y	N	N	Y	Y
8 ***Hostettler***	N	Y	N	Y	N	N	Y	Y
9 Hamilton	Y	N	Y	N	Y	N	Y	Y
10 Carson	Y	N	Y	N	Y	Y	Y	N
IOWA								
1 ***Leach***	N	Y	N	Y	Y	Y	Y	Y
2 ***Nussle***	N	Y	N	Y	N	Y	Y	Y
3 Boswell	Y	Y	Y	N	Y	N	Y	Y
4 ***Ganske***	N	Y	N	Y	Y	Y	N	Y
5 ***Latham***	N	Y	N	Y	Y	N	Y	Y
KANSAS								
1 ***Moran***	N	N	N	Y	N	N	Y	Y
2 ***Ryun***	N	Y	N	Y	N	N	Y	Y
3 ***Snowbarger***	N	Y	N	Y	N	N	Y	Y
4 ***Tiahrt***	N	Y	N	Y	N	N	Y	Y
KENTUCKY								
1 ***Whitfield***	Y	Y	N	Y	N	N	Y	Y
2 ***Lewis***	N	N	N	Y	N	N	Y	Y
3 ***Northup***	N	N	N	Y	N	N	Y	Y
4 ***Bunning***	N	N	N	Y	N	N	Y	Y
5 ***Rogers***	N	N	N	Y	N	N	Y	Y
6 Baesler	Y	N	Y	N	N	N	Y	Y
LOUISIANA								
1 ***Livingston***	N	N	N	Y	N	N	Y	Y
2 Jefferson	Y	N	Y	N	N	N	Y	Y
3 ***Tauzin***	N	N	N	Y	N	N	Y	Y
4 ***McCrery***	N	N	N	Y	N	N	Y	Y
5 ***Cooksey***	N	Y	N	Y	N	N	Y	Y
6 ***Baker***	N	N	N	Y	N	N	Y	Y
7 John	Y	N	Y	N	N	N	Y	Y
MAINE								
1 Allen	Y	N	Y	N	Y	N	Y	Y
2 Baldacci	Y	N	Y	N	Y	Y	N	Y
MARYLAND								
1 ***Gilchrest***	N	N	N	Y	N	N	Y	Y
2 ***Ehrlich***	N	Y	N	Y	N	N	Y	Y
3 Cardin	Y	N	Y	N	Y	N	N	Y
4 Wynn	Y	N	Y	N	Y	N	Y	Y
5 Hoyer	Y	N	Y	N	N	N	Y	Y
6 ***Bartlett***	N	N	N	Y	N	N	Y	Y
7 Cummings	Y	N	Y	N	?	Y	N	N
8 ***Morella***	N	N	N	Y	Y	Y	N	Y
MASSACHUSETTS								
1 Olver	Y	N	Y	N	Y	Y	N	N
2 Neal	Y	N	Y	N	Y	Y	N	Y
3 McGovern	Y	N	Y	N	Y	Y	N	Y
4 Frank	Y	N	Y	N	Y	Y	N	Y
5 Meehan	Y	Y	Y	N	Y	Y	Y	Y
6 Tierney	Y	N	Y	N	Y	Y	Y	Y
7 Markey	Y	N	Y	N	Y	Y	N	Y
8 Kennedy	Y	N	Y	N	Y	Y	N	Y
9 Moakley	Y	N	Y	N	Y	N	Y	Y
10 Delahunt	Y	N	Y	N	Y	Y	N	Y
MICHIGAN								
1 Stupak	Y	N	Y	N	Y	Y	N	Y
2 ***Hoekstra***	N	Y	N	Y	Y	Y	N	Y
3 ***Ehlers***	N	Y	N	Y	Y	Y	N	Y
4 ***Camp***	N	Y	N	Y	Y	Y	N	Y
5 Barcia	Y	N	Y	N	N	Y	Y	Y
6 ***Upton***	+	+	N	Y	Y	Y	N	Y
7 ***Smith***	−	+	N	Y	Y	Y	N	Y
8 Stabenow	Y	N	Y	N	Y	Y	N	Y
9 Kildee	Y	N	Y	N	Y	N	Y	Y
10 Bonior	Y	N	Y	N	Y	Y	N	Y
11 ***Knollenberg***	N	N	N	Y	N	N	Y	Y
12 Levin	Y	N	Y	N	Y	Y	Y	Y
13 Rivers	Y	N	Y	N	Y	Y	N	Y
14 Conyers	Y	N	Y	N	Y	Y	N	N
15 Kilpatrick	Y	N	Y	N	Y	Y	N	N
16 Dingell	Y	N	Y	N	?	N	N	Y
MINNESOTA								
1 ***Gutknecht***	N	N	N	Y	N	Y	Y	Y
2 Minge	Y	Y	Y	N	Y	Y	N	Y

	332	333	334	335	336	337	338	339
3 ***Ramstad***	N	Y	N	Y	Y	Y	N	Y
4 Vento	Y	N	Y	N	Y	Y	N	Y
5 Sabo	Y	N	Y	N	Y	Y	N	N
6 Luther	Y	Y	Y	N	Y	Y	N	Y
7 Peterson	N	Y	Y	N	Y	Y	N	Y
8 Oberstar	Y	N	Y	N	Y	Y	N	N
MISSISSIPPI								
1 ***Wicker***	N	N	N	Y	N	N	Y	Y
2 Thompson	Y	N	Y	N	N	N	Y	Y
3 ***Pickering***	N	Y	N	Y	N	N	Y	Y
4 ***Parker***	N	Y	N	Y	N	N	Y	Y
5 Taylor	N	Y	Y	N	N	N	Y	Y
MISSOURI								
1 Clay	Y	N	Y	N	Y	Y	N	N
2 ***Talent***	N	Y	N	Y	N	N	Y	Y
3 Gephardt	Y	N	Y	N	Y	N	N	Y
4 Skelton	Y	N	Y	N	N	N	Y	Y
5 McCarthy	Y	N	Y	N	Y	Y	N	Y
6 Danner	Y	N	Y	N	Y	Y	N	Y
7 ***Blunt***	N	Y	N	Y	N	N	Y	Y
8 ***Emerson***	N	Y	N	Y	N	N	Y	Y
9 ***Hulshof***	Y	Y	N	N	N	N	Y	Y
MONTANA								
AL ***Hill***	N	Y	N	N	N	N	Y	Y
NEBRASKA								
1 ***Bereuter***	N	Y	N	Y	Y	N	Y	Y
2 ***Christensen***	N	Y	N	Y	N	N	Y	Y
3 ***Barrett***	N	Y	N	Y	N	N	Y	Y
NEVADA								
1 ***Ensign***	N	Y	N	N	N	Y	Y	Y
2 ***Gibbons***	N	Y	N	Y	N	N	Y	Y
NEW HAMPSHIRE								
1 ***Sununu***	N	Y	N	Y	Y	N	Y	Y
2 ***Bass***	N	Y	N	Y	Y	N	Y	Y
NEW JERSEY								
1 Andrews	Y	N	Y	N	Y	N	Y	Y
2 ***LoBiondo***	N	Y	N	Y	Y	Y	N	Y
3 ***Saxton***	N	N	N	Y	N	N	Y	Y
4 ***Smith***	N	N	N	Y	N	N	Y	Y
5 ***Roukema***	Y	Y	N	Y	Y	Y	N	Y
6 Pallone	Y	N	Y	N	Y	N	Y	Y
7 ***Franks***	N	Y	N	Y	Y	Y	N	Y
8 Pascrell	Y	N	Y	N	Y	N	Y	Y
9 Rothman	Y	N	Y	N	Y	N	Y	Y
10 Payne	Y	N	Y	N	Y	Y	N	N
11 ***Frelinghuysen***	N	N	N	Y	N	N	Y	Y
12 ***Pappas***	N	Y	N	Y	N	N	Y	Y
13 Menendez	Y	N	Y	N	Y	N	Y	Y
NEW MEXICO								
1 ***Schiff***	?	?	?	?	?	?	?	?
2 ***Skeen***	N	N	N	Y	N	N	Y	Y
3 ***Redmond***	N	N	N	Y	N	N	Y	Y
NEW YORK								
1 ***Forbes***	−	+	−	+	−	−	+	+
2 ***Lazio***	N	Y	N	Y	Y	N	Y	Y
3 ***King***	N	Y	Y	Y	N	N	Y	Y
4 McCarthy	Y	Y	Y	N	Y	N	N	Y
5 Ackerman	?	?	?	?	N	Y	N	Y
6 Flake	Y	N	Y	N	Y	N	Y	Y
7 Manton	Y	N	Y	N	N	N	Y	Y
8 Nadler	Y	N	Y	N	Y	Y	N	Y
9 Schumer	Y	N	Y	N	Y	Y	N	Y
10 Towns	?	?	?	?	Y	N	N	N
11 Owens	Y	N	Y	N	Y	Y	N	Y
12 Velázquez	Y	N	Y	N	Y	Y	N	N
13 ***Molinari***	N	N	N	Y	N	Y	Y	Y
14 Maloney	Y	N	Y	N	Y	Y	N	Y
15 Rangel	Y	N	Y	N	Y	Y	N	N
16 Serrano	Y	N	Y	N	Y	Y	N	N
17 Engel	Y	N	Y	N	Y	Y	N	Y
18 Lowey	Y	N	Y	N	Y	Y	N	Y
19 ***Kelly***	N	Y	N	Y	N	Y	Y	Y
20 ***Gilman***	N	N	N	Y	N	N	Y	Y
21 McNulty	Y	N	Y	N	Y	Y	N	Y
22 ***Solomon***	N	Y	N	Y	N	N	Y	Y
23 ***Boehlert***	N	N	N	Y	Y	N	Y	Y
24 ***McHugh***	N	N	N	Y	N	N	Y	Y
25 ***Walsh***	N	Y	N	Y	N	N	Y	Y
26 Hinchey	Y	N	Y	N	N	Y	N	Y
27 ***Paxon***	N	Y	N	Y	N	N	Y	Y
28 Slaughter	Y	N	Y	N	Y	Y	Y	Y
29 LaFalce	Y	N	Y	N	Y	Y	N	Y
30 ***Quinn***	N	Y	Y	Y	Y	N	Y	Y
31 ***Houghton***	N	Y	N	?	Y	N	Y	Y

	332	333	334	335	336	337	338	339
NORTH CAROLINA								
1 Clayton	Y	N	Y	N	Y	Y	Y	Y
2 Etheridge	Y	N	Y	N	N	N	Y	Y
3 ***Jones***	N	Y	N	Y	N	N	Y	Y
4 Price	Y	N	Y	N	Y	N	Y	Y
5 ***Burr***	N	Y	N	Y	Y	N	Y	Y
6 ***Coble***	N	Y	N	Y	Y	N	Y	Y
7 McIntyre	Y	N	Y	N	N	N	Y	Y
8 Hefner	Y	N	Y	N	N	N	Y	Y
9 ***Myrick***	N	Y	N	Y	N	N	Y	Y
10 ***Ballenger***	N	Y	N	Y	Y	N	Y	Y
11 ***Taylor***	N	Y	N	Y	N	N	Y	Y
12 Watt	Y	N	Y	N	Y	Y	N	N
NORTH DAKOTA								
AL Pomeroy	Y	N	Y	N	N	N	Y	Y
OHIO								
1 ***Chabot***	Y	Y	N	Y	Y	Y	Y	Y
2 ***Portman***	N	+	N	Y	Y	Y	Y	Y
3 Hall	Y	N	Y	N	Y	N	Y	Y
4 ***Oxley***	N	Y	N	Y	N	N	Y	Y
5 ***Gillmor***	N	N	N	Y	N	N	Y	Y
6 Strickland	Y	Y	Y	N	Y	N	Y	Y
7 ***Hobson***	N	N	N	Y	N	N	Y	Y
8 ***Boehner***	N	Y	N	Y	N	N	Y	Y
9 Kaptur	Y	Y	Y	N	Y	N	Y	Y
10 Kucinich	Y	N	Y	N	Y	Y	N	Y
11 Stokes	Y	N	Y	N	Y	Y	Y	N
12 ***Kasich***	N	Y	N	Y	Y	N	Y	Y
13 Brown	Y	N	Y	N	Y	Y	N	Y
14 Sawyer	Y	N	Y	N	Y	N	N	Y
15 ***Pryce***	N	Y	N	Y	Y	N	Y	Y
16 ***Regula***	N	N	N	Y	Y	N	Y	Y
17 Traficant	N	N	N	Y	N	N	Y	Y
18 ***Ney***	N	N	N	Y	+	+	Y	Y
19 ***LaTourette***	N	N	N	Y	+	N	Y	Y
OKLAHOMA								
1 ***Largent***	Y	Y	N	Y	Y	N	Y	Y
2 ***Coburn***	N	Y	N	N	Y	N	?	?
3 ***Watkins***	N	N	N	Y	N	N	Y	Y
4 ***Watts***	N	Y	N	Y	N	N	Y	Y
5 ***Istook***	N	Y	N	Y	N	N	Y	Y
6 ***Lucas***	N	N	N	Y	N	N	Y	Y
OREGON								
1 Furse	Y	N	Y	N	Y	Y	N	Y
2 ***Smith***	N	Y	N	Y	N	N	Y	Y
3 Blumenauer	Y	N	Y	N	Y	Y	N	Y
4 DeFazio	Y	N	Y	N	Y	Y	N	?
5 Hooley	Y	N	Y	N	Y	Y	N	Y
PENNSYLVANIA								
1 Foglietta	Y	N	Y	N	?	?	?	?
2 Fattah	Y	N	Y	N	Y	Y	N	Y
3 Borski	Y	N	Y	N	N	N	Y	Y
4 Klink	Y	N	Y	N	N	N	Y	Y
5 ***Peterson***	N	Y	N	Y	N	N	Y	Y
6 Holden	Y	N	Y	N	N	N	Y	Y
7 ***Weldon***	N	N	N	Y	Y	N	Y	Y
8 ***Greenwood***	N	N	N	Y	Y	Y	Y	Y
9 ***Shuster***	N	N	N	Y	N	N	Y	Y
10 ***McDade***	N	N	N	Y	N	N	Y	Y
11 Kanjorski	Y	N	Y	N	Y	Y	Y	Y
12 Murtha	Y	N	Y	N	N	N	Y	Y
13 ***Fox***	N	Y	N	Y	N	Y	Y	Y
14 Coyne	Y	N	Y	N	Y	Y	N	Y
15 McHale	Y	N	Y	N	Y	N	Y	Y
16 ***Pitts***	N	Y	N	Y	N	N	Y	Y
17 ***Gekas***	N	Y	N	Y	N	N	Y	Y
18 Doyle	Y	N	Y	N	Y	Y	N	Y
19 ***Goodling***	N	Y	N	Y	Y	N	Y	Y
20 Mascara	Y	N	Y	N	Y	N	Y	Y
21 ***English***	N	Y	N	Y	N	Y	N	Y
RHODE ISLAND								
1 Kennedy	Y	N	Y	N	Y	N	Y	Y
2 Weygand	Y	N	Y	N	Y	N	Y	Y
SOUTH CAROLINA								
1 ***Sanford***	N	Y	N	N	Y	Y	N	Y
2 ***Spence***	N	N	N	Y	N	N	Y	Y
3 ***Graham***	N	N	N	Y	N	N	Y	Y
4 ***Inglis***	N	Y	N	Y	N	N	Y	Y
5 Spratt	?	N	Y	N	Y	N	Y	Y
6 Clyburn	Y	N	Y	N	N	N	Y	Y
SOUTH DAKOTA								
AL ***Thune***	N	Y	N	Y	N	N	Y	Y
TENNESSEE								
1 ***Jenkins***	N	N	N	Y	N	N	Y	Y
2 ***Duncan***	N	Y	N	Y	Y	Y	Y	Y

	332	333	334	335	336	337	338	
3 ***Wamp***	N	Y	N	Y	Y	N	Y	Y
4 ***Hilleary***	N	Y	N	Y	N	N	Y	Y
5 Clement	Y	N	Y	N	Y	N	Y	Y
6 Gordon	Y	N	Y	N	Y	N	Y	Y
7 ***Bryant***	N	Y	N	Y	N	N	Y	Y
8 Tanner	Y	N	Y	N	Y	N	Y	Y
9 Ford	Y	N	Y	N	Y	N	Y	Y
TEXAS								
1 Sandlin	Y	N	Y	N	N	N	Y	Y
2 Turner	Y	Y	Y	N	N	N	Y	Y
3 ***Johnson, Sam***	N	N	N	Y	N	N	Y	Y
4 Hall	Y	Y	Y	N	N	N	Y	Y
5 ***Sessions***	N	Y	N	Y	N	N	Y	Y
6 ***Barton***	N	N	N	Y	N	N	Y	Y
7 ***Archer***	N	Y	N	Y	N	N	Y	Y
8 ***Brady***	N	Y	N	Y	N	N	Y	Y
9 Lampson	Y	N	Y	N	Y	N	Y	Y
10 Doggett	Y	N	Y	N	Y	Y	N	Y
11 Edwards	Y	N	Y	N	Y	N	Y	Y
12 ***Granger***	N	Y	N	Y	N	N	Y	Y
13 ***Thornberry***	?	?	N	Y	N	N	Y	Y
14 ***Paul***	Y	Y	N	N	Y	Y	N	Y
15 Hinojosa	Y	N	Y	N	N	N	Y	Y
16 Reyes	Y	N	Y	N	N	N	Y	Y
17 Stenholm	Y	Y	Y	N	Y	N	Y	Y
18 Jackson-Lee	Y	N	Y	N	N	Y	Y	Y
19 ***Combest***	N	Y	N	Y	Y	N	Y	Y
20 Gonzalez	?	?	?	?	?	?	?	?
21 ***Smith***	N	Y	N	Y	N	N	Y	Y
22 ***DeLay***	N	Y	N	Y	N	N	Y	Y
23 ***Bonilla***	N	Y	N	Y	N	N	Y	Y
24 Frost	Y	N	Y	N	N	N	Y	Y
25 Bentsen	Y	N	Y	N	N	Y	Y	Y
26 ***Armey***	N	Y	N	Y	N	N	Y	Y
27 Ortiz	Y	N	Y	N	N	N	Y	Y
28 Rodriguez	Y	N	Y	N	N	N	Y	Y
29 Green	Y	N	Y	N	N	Y	Y	Y
30 Johnson, E.B.	Y	N	Y	N	N	N	Y	Y
UTAH								
1 ***Hansen***	N	Y	N	Y	N	N	Y	Y
2 ***Cook***	N	N	N	Y	N	N	Y	Y
3 ***Cannon***	N	Y	N	Y	N	N	Y	Y
VERMONT								
AL *Sanders*	Y	N	Y	N	Y	Y	N	N
VIRGINIA								
1 ***Bateman***	N	N	N	Y	N	N	Y	Y
2 Pickett	Y	N	Y	N	Y	N	Y	Y
3 Scott	Y	N	Y	N	Y	N	Y	N
4 Sisisky	Y	N	Y	N	Y	N	Y	Y
5 Goode	Y	Y	Y	N	Y	N	Y	Y
6 ***Goodlatte***	N	Y	N	Y	N	N	Y	Y
7 ***Bliley***	N	Y	N	Y	N	N	Y	Y
8 Moran	Y	N	Y	N	Y	N	Y	Y
9 Boucher	?	?	?	?	Y	N	Y	Y
10 ***Wolf***	N	N	N	Y	N	N	Y	Y
11 ***Davis***	N	N	N	Y	N	N	Y	Y
WASHINGTON								
1 ***White***	−	+	−	+	Y	N	Y	?
2 ***Metcalf***	−	−	−	+	N	Y	Y	Y
3 ***Smith, Linda***	N	Y	N	N	Y	N	Y	?
4 ***Hastings***	N	Y	N	Y	N	N	Y	Y
5 ***Nethercutt***	N	Y	N	Y	N	N	Y	Y
6 Dicks	Y	N	Y	N	N	N	Y	Y
7 McDermott	+	−	+	−	Y	Y	N	N
8 ***Dunn***	N	Y	N	Y	N	N	Y	Y
9 Smith, Adam	Y	N	Y	N	Y	N	Y	Y
WEST VIRGINIA								
1 Mollohan	Y	N	Y	N	N	N	Y	Y
2 Wise	Y	N	Y	N	Y	N	Y	Y
3 Rahall	Y	N	Y	N	Y	N	N	Y
WISCONSIN								
1 ***Neumann***	Y	Y	N	Y	N	Y	N	Y
2 ***Klug***	N	Y	N	Y	Y	Y	N	Y
3 Kind	Y	N	Y	N	Y	Y	N	Y
4 Kleczka	Y	N	Y	N	Y	Y	N	Y
5 Barrett	Y	N	Y	N	Y	Y	N	Y
6 ***Petri***	Y	Y	N	Y	Y	Y	Y	Y
7 Obey	Y	N	Y	N	Y	Y	N	Y
8 Johnson	+	N	Y	N	Y	N	N	Y
9 ***Sensenbrenner***	N	Y	N	Y	Y	Y	N	Y
WYOMING								
AL ***Cubin***	N	N	N	Y	N	N	Y	Y

Southern states - Ala., Ark., Fla., Ga., Ky., La., Miss., N.C., Okla., S.C., Tenn., Texas, Va.

HOUSE VOTES 340, 341, 342, 343, 345, 346, 347, 348 *

340. HR 1348. War Crimes Expansion/Passage. Jenkins, R-Tenn., motion to suspend the rules and pass the bill to expand the federal definition of a war crime under the War Crimes Act of 1996 (PL 104-192) to include "grave breaches" of the Geneva Convention, certain articles of the Hague Convention and other conventions or protocols to which the United States becomes a signatory. Motion agreed to 391-32: R 218-2; D 172-30 (ND 122-26, SD 50-4); I 1-0, July 29, 1997. A two-thirds majority of those present and voting (282 in this case) is required for passage under suspension of the rules.

341. H Res 201. Expedited Floor Procedures/Previous Question. Linder, R-Ga., motion to order the previous question (thus ending debate and the possibility of amendment) on adoption of the resolution to waive through Aug. 3, 1997, the requirement of a two-thirds majority to consider rules governing House floor consideration on the same day as reported by the Rules Committee. Motion agreed to 226-201: R 222-0; D 4-200 (ND 3-147, SD 1-53); I 0-1, July 30, 1997.

342. H Res 201. Expedited Floor Procedures/Adoption. Adoption of the resolution to waive through Aug. 3, 1997, the requirement of a two-thirds majority to consider rules governing House floor consideration on the same day as reported by the Rules Committee. Adopted 237-187: R 216-4; D 21-182 (ND 16-134, SD 5-48); I 0-1, July 30, 1997.

343. HR 2015. Fiscal 1998 Budget Reconciliation — Spending/Previous Question. Solomon, R-N.Y., motion to order the previous question (thus ending debate and the possibility of amendment) on adoption of the rule (H Res 202) providing for House floor consideration of the bill to cut projected entitlement spending by about $140 billion, including a $115 billion reduction in Medicare, in order to provide for a balanced budget by fiscal 2002. Motion agreed to 226-197: R 220-0; D 6-196 (ND 5-143, SD 1-53); I 0-1, July 30, 1997.

* **345. HR 2015. Fiscal 1998 Budget Reconciliation — Spending/Conference Report.** Adoption of the conference report on the bill to cut projected entitlement spending by $140 billion, establishing a balanced budget by fiscal 2002. The bill would reduce Medicare funding by $115 billion; increase health insurance options available to Medicare beneficiaries beyond fee-for-service programs; and permit up to 390,000 Medicare beneficiaries to establish tax-free medical savings accounts. The bill also would include a $24 billion block grant program to help states improve health coverage for uninsured children, funded in part by a federal tobacco tax increase of 15 cents per pack over five years, and restore Supplemental Security Income (SSI) and Medicaid benefits to certain legal immigrants. Adopted (thus sent to the Senate) 346-85: R 193-32; D 153-52 (ND 109-42, SD 44-10); I 0-1, July 30, 1997. A "yea" was a vote in support of the president's position.

346. HR 2159. Fiscal 1998 Foreign Operations Appropriations/OPIC. Royce, R-Calif., amendment to cut $11.2 million from the $32 million in the bill for the operating expenses of the Overseas Private Investment Corporation, reflecting the operating expense level in fiscal 1994. Rejected 156-272: R 117-106; D 38-166 (ND 34-116, SD 4-50); I 1-0, July 30, 1997.

347. HR 2159. Fiscal 1998 Foreign Operations Appropriations/Export and Investment Assistance. Paul, R-Texas, amendment to eliminate the bill's funding for all federal export and investment assistance, including $632 million for the Export-Import Bank, $32 million for the Overseas Private Investment Corporation and $40 million for the Trade and Development Agency. Rejected 40-387: R 37-185; D 3-201 (ND 2-148, SD 1-53); I 0-1, July 30, 1997.

348. Condemn Jerusalem Terrorist Bombing/Adoption. Adoption of the concurrent resolution to condemn the two terrorist bombings in Jerusalem on July 30, 1997, as vicious assaults against the peace process and Israelis, and to express condolences to the families of the victims. Adopted 427-1: R 222-1; D 204-0 (ND 150-0, SD 54-0); I 1-0, July 30, 1997.

** NOTE: Omitted votes are quorum calls. CQ does not include quroum calls in its vote charts.*

KEY

Y Voted for (yea).
\# Paired for.
\+ Announced for.
N Voted against (nay).
X Paired against.
– Announced against.
P Voted "present."
C Voted "present" to avoid possible conflict of interest.
? Did not vote or otherwise make a position known.

Democrats ***Republicans***
Independent

	340	341	342	343	345	346	347	348
ALABAMA								
1 ***Callahan***	Y	Y	Y	Y	Y	N	N	Y
2 ***Everett***	Y	Y	Y	Y	Y	N	N	Y
3 ***Riley***	Y	Y	?	Y	Y	N	N	Y
4 ***Aderholt***	Y	Y	Y	Y	Y	N	N	Y
5 Cramer	Y	N	Y	N	Y	N	N	Y
6 ***Bachus***	Y	Y	Y	Y	Y	Y	Y	Y
7 Hilliard	Y	N	N	N	N	N	N	Y
ALASKA								
AL ***Young***	?	?	?	?	?	?	?	?
ARIZONA								
1 ***Salmon***	Y	Y	Y	Y	N	Y	N	Y
2 Pastor	Y	N	N	N	Y	N	N	Y
3 ***Stump***	Y	Y	Y	Y	Y	N	N	Y
4 ***Shadegg***	Y	Y	Y	Y	N	Y	Y	Y
5 ***Kolbe***	Y	Y	Y	Y	Y	N	N	Y
6 ***Hayworth***	Y	Y	Y	Y	Y	Y	Y	Y
ARKANSAS								
1 Berry	Y	N	N	N	N	N	N	Y
2 Snyder	Y	N	N	N	Y	N	N	Y
3 ***Hutchinson***	Y	Y	Y	Y	Y	Y	N	Y
4 ***Dickey***	Y	Y	Y	Y	N	Y	N	Y
CALIFORNIA								
1 ***Riggs***	Y	Y	Y	Y	Y	Y	N	Y
2 ***Herger***	Y	Y	Y	Y	Y	N	N	Y
3 Fazio	Y	N	N	N	Y	N	N	Y
4 ***Doolittle***	Y	Y	N	Y	N	N	Y	Y
5 Matsui	Y	N	N	N	Y	N	N	Y
6 Woolsey	Y	N	N	N	Y	Y	N	Y
7 Miller	N	N	N	N	Y	N	N	Y
8 Pelosi	Y	N	N	N	Y	N	N	Y
9 Dellums	N	N	N	N	N	Y	N	Y
10 Tauscher	Y	N	Y	Y	Y	N	N	Y
11 ***Pombo***	Y	Y	Y	Y	N	N	Y	Y
12 Lantos	Y	N	N	N	Y	N	N	Y
13 Stark	Y	N	N	N	N	?	?	?
14 Eshoo	Y	N	N	N	Y	Y	N	Y
15 ***Campbell***	Y	Y	Y	Y	Y	Y	Y	Y
16 Lofgren	Y	N	N	N	Y	N	N	Y
17 Farr	Y	N	N	N	Y	Y	N	Y
18 Condit	Y	Y	Y	N	Y	Y	N	Y
19 ***Radanovich***	Y	Y	Y	Y	Y	Y	N	Y
20 Dooley	Y	N	Y	N	Y	N	N	Y
21 ***Thomas***	?	Y	Y	Y	Y	N	N	Y
22 Capps	Y	N	N	N	Y	N	N	Y
23 ***Gallegly***	Y	Y	Y	Y	Y	N	N	Y
24 Sherman	Y	N	N	N	Y	N	N	Y
25 ***McKeon***	Y	Y	Y	Y	Y	Y	N	Y
26 Berman	Y	N	N	N	Y	N	N	Y
27 ***Rogan***	Y	Y	Y	Y	Y	Y	N	Y
28 ***Dreier***	Y	Y	Y	Y	Y	N	N	Y
29 Waxman	Y	N	N	N	N	N	N	Y
30 Becerra	Y	N	N	N	Y	N	N	Y
31 Martinez	Y	N	N	N	Y	N	N	Y
32 Dixon	Y	N	N	N	Y	N	N	Y
33 Roybal-Allard	Y	N	N	N	Y	N	N	Y
34 Torres	Y	N	Y	N	Y	N	N	Y
35 Waters	N	N	N	N	N	N	N	Y
36 Harman	Y	N	N	Y	Y	N	N	Y
37 Millender-McD.	Y	N	N	N	Y	N	N	Y
38 ***Horn***	Y	Y	Y	Y	Y	Y	N	Y
39 ***Royce***	Y	Y	Y	Y	N	Y	Y	Y
40 ***Lewis***	Y	Y	Y	Y	Y	N	N	Y
41 ***Kim***	Y	Y	Y	Y	Y	N	N	Y
42 Brown	Y	N	N	N	Y	N	N	Y
43 ***Calvert***	Y	Y	Y	Y	Y	N	N	Y
44 ***Bono***	Y	Y	Y	Y	Y	N	N	Y
45 ***Rohrabacher***	Y	Y	Y	Y	N	Y	Y	Y
46 Sanchez	Y	N	N	N	Y	N	N	Y
47 ***Cox***	Y	Y	Y	Y	Y	Y	N	Y
48 ***Packard***	Y	Y	Y	Y	Y	N	N	Y
49 ***Bilbray***	Y	Y	Y	Y	Y	N	N	Y
50 Filner	Y	N	N	N	N	N	N	Y
51 ***Cunningham***	Y	Y	Y	Y	Y	Y	N	Y
52 ***Hunter***	Y	Y	Y	Y	Y	Y	Y	Y
COLORADO								
1 DeGette	Y	N	N	N	Y	N	N	Y
2 Skaggs	Y	N	N	N	Y	N	N	Y
3 ***McInnis***	Y	Y	Y	Y	Y	Y	N	Y
4 ***Schaffer***	Y	Y	Y	Y	Y	Y	N	Y
5 ***Hefley***	Y	Y	Y	Y	Y	Y	N	Y
6 ***Schaefer***	Y	Y	Y	Y	Y	Y	N	Y
CONNECTICUT								
1 Kennelly	Y	N	N	N	Y	N	N	Y
2 Gejdenson	Y	N	N	N	Y	N	N	Y
3 DeLauro	Y	N	N	N	Y	N	N	Y
4 ***Shays***	Y	Y	Y	Y	Y	Y	N	Y
5 Maloney	Y	N	N	N	Y	N	N	Y
6 ***Johnson***	Y	Y	Y	Y	Y	N	N	Y
DELAWARE								
AL ***Castle***	Y	Y	Y	Y	Y	N	N	Y
FLORIDA								
1 ***Scarborough***	?	Y	Y	Y	N	Y	Y	Y
2 Boyd	Y	N	N	N	Y	N	N	Y
3 Brown	Y	N	N	N	Y	N	N	Y
4 ***Fowler***	Y	Y	Y	Y	Y	Y	N	Y
5 Thurman	Y	N	N	N	Y	N	N	Y
6 ***Stearns***	Y	Y	Y	Y	Y	Y	Y	Y
7 ***Mica***	Y	Y	Y	Y	N	Y	N	Y
8 ***McCollum***	Y	Y	Y	?	Y	N	N	Y
9 ***Bilirakis***	Y	Y	Y	Y	Y	N	N	Y
10 ***Young***	Y	Y	Y	Y	Y	N	N	Y
11 Davis	Y	N	N	N	Y	N	N	Y
12 ***Canady***	Y	Y	Y	Y	Y	Y	N	Y
13 ***Miller***	Y	Y	Y	Y	Y	Y	N	Y
14 ***Goss***	Y	Y	Y	Y	Y	Y	N	Y
15 ***Weldon***	Y	Y	Y	Y	N	N	N	Y
16 ***Foley***	Y	Y	Y	Y	Y	Y	N	Y
17 Meek	Y	N	N	N	Y	N	N	Y
18 ***Ros-Lehtinen***	Y	Y	Y	Y	Y	Y	N	Y
19 Wexler	Y	N	Y	N	Y	N	N	Y
20 Deutsch	Y	N	N	N	Y	N	N	Y
21 ***Diaz-Balart***	Y	?	Y	Y	Y	Y	N	Y
22 ***Shaw***	Y	Y	+	Y	Y	Y	N	Y
23 Hastings	Y	N	N	N	N	N	N	Y
GEORGIA								
1 ***Kingston***	Y	Y	Y	Y	N	Y	N	Y
2 Bishop	Y	N	N	N	Y	N	N	Y
3 ***Collins***	Y	Y	Y	Y	Y	Y	N	Y
4 McKinney	N	N	N	N	Y	Y	N	Y
5 Lewis	N	N	N	N	Y	Y	N	Y
6 ***Gingrich***					Y			
7 ***Barr***	Y	Y	Y	Y	Y	Y	Y	Y
8 ***Chambliss***	Y	Y	Y	Y	Y	Y	N	Y
9 ***Deal***	Y	Y	Y	Y	Y	Y	Y	Y
10 ***Norwood***	Y	Y	Y	Y	Y	Y	N	Y
11 ***Linder***	Y	Y	Y	Y	Y	Y	N	Y
HAWAII								
1 Abercrombie	?	N	N	N	Y	N	N	Y
2 Mink	Y	N	N	N	N	N	N	Y
IDAHO								
1 ***Chenoweth***	Y	Y	Y	Y	Y	Y	Y	Y
2 ***Crapo***	Y	Y	Y	Y	Y	Y	Y	Y
ILLINOIS								
1 Rush	N	N	N	N	N	N	N	Y
2 Jackson	N	N	N	N	N	Y	N	Y
3 Lipinski	Y	N	Y	N	Y	Y	N	Y
4 Gutierrez	Y	N	N	N	N	N	N	Y
5 Blagojevich	Y	N	N	?	Y	Y	N	Y
6 ***Hyde***	Y	Y	Y	Y	Y	N	N	Y
7 Davis	N	N	N	N	N	N	N	Y
8 ***Crane***	Y	Y	Y	Y	Y	Y	N	Y
9 Yates	Y	N	N	N	N	N	N	Y
10 ***Porter***	Y	Y	Y	Y	Y	N	N	Y
11 ***Weller***	Y	Y	Y	Y	Y	N	N	Y
12 Costello	Y	N	N	N	Y	Y	N	Y
13 ***Fawell***	Y	Y	Y	Y	Y	Y	N	Y
14 ***Hastert***	Y	Y	Y	Y	Y	Y	N	Y
15 ***Ewing***	Y	Y	Y	Y	Y	N	N	Y

ND Northern Democrats SD Southern Democrats

	340	341	342	343	345	346	347	348
16 ***Manzullo***	Y	Y	Y	Y	Y	N	N	Y
17 Evans	Y	N	N	N	Y	N	N	Y
18 ***LaHood***	Y	Y	Y	Y	Y	N	N	Y
19 Poshard	Y	N	N	N	Y	Y	N	Y
20 ***Shimkus***	Y	Y	Y	Y	Y	N	N	Y
INDIANA								
1 Visclosky	Y	N	N	N	Y	Y	N	Y
2 ***McIntosh***	Y	Y	Y	?	N	Y	Y	Y
3 Roemer	Y	N	Y	N	Y	Y	N	Y
4 ***Souder***	Y	Y	Y	Y	Y	Y	N	Y
5 ***Buyer***	Y	Y	Y	Y	Y	Y	N	Y
6 ***Burton***	Y	Y	Y	Y	Y	Y	Y	Y
7 ***Pease***	Y	Y	Y	Y	Y	Y	Y	Y
8 ***Hostettler***	Y	Y	Y	Y	Y	Y	Y	Y
9 Hamilton	Y	N	N	N	Y	N	N	Y
10 Carson	N	N	N	N	Y	N	N	Y
IOWA								
1 ***Leach***	Y	Y	Y	Y	Y	Y	N	Y
2 ***Nussle***	Y	Y	Y	Y	Y	N	N	Y
3 Boswell	Y	N	Y	N	Y	Y	N	Y
4 ***Ganske***	Y	Y	Y	Y	Y	Y	N	Y
5 ***Latham***	Y	Y	Y	Y	Y	N	N	Y
KANSAS								
1 ***Moran***	Y	Y	Y	Y	N	N	N	Y
2 ***Ryun***	Y	Y	Y	Y	N	Y	Y	Y
3 ***Snowbarger***	Y	Y	Y	Y	N	N	N	Y
4 ***Tiahrt***	Y	Y	Y	Y	N	Y	N	Y
KENTUCKY								
1 ***Whitfield***	Y	Y	Y	Y	Y	Y	N	Y
2 ***Lewis***	Y	Y	Y	Y	Y	N	N	Y
3 ***Northup***	Y	Y	Y	Y	Y	N	N	Y
4 ***Bunning***	Y	Y	Y	Y	Y	N	N	Y
5 ***Rogers***	Y	Y	Y	Y	Y	N	N	Y
6 Baesler	Y	N	N	N	N	N	N	Y
LOUISIANA								
1 ***Livingston***	Y	Y	Y	Y	Y	N	N	Y
2 Jefferson	Y	N	N	N	Y	N	N	Y
3 ***Tauzin***	Y	Y	Y	Y	Y	N	N	Y
4 ***McCrery***	Y	Y	Y	Y	Y	N	N	Y
5 ***Cooksey***	Y	Y	Y	Y	Y	N	N	Y
6 ***Baker***	Y	Y	Y	Y	Y	N	N	Y
7 John	Y	N	N	N	Y	N	N	Y
MAINE								
1 Allen	Y	N	N	N	Y	N	N	Y
2 Baldacci	Y	N	N	N	Y	N	N	Y
MARYLAND								
1 ***Gilchrest***	Y	Y	Y	Y	Y	N	N	Y
2 ***Ehrlich***	Y	Y	Y	Y	Y	Y	N	Y
3 Cardin	Y	N	N	N	Y	N	N	Y
4 Wynn	Y	N	N	N	Y	N	N	Y
5 Hoyer	Y	N	N	N	Y	N	N	Y
6 ***Bartlett***	Y	Y	Y	Y	Y	Y	Y	Y
7 Cummings	N	N	N	N	Y	N	N	Y
8 ***Morella***	Y	Y	Y	Y	Y	N	N	Y
MASSACHUSETTS								
1 Olver	N	N	N	N	Y	N	N	Y
2 Neal	Y	N	N	N	Y	N	N	Y
3 McGovern	N	N	N	N	N	N	N	Y
4 Frank	N	N	N	N	N	N	N	Y
5 Meehan	Y	N	N	N	Y	Y	N	Y
6 Tierney	N	N	N	N	Y	N	N	Y
7 Markey	N	N	N	N	N	Y	Y	Y
8 Kennedy	Y	N	N	N	N	N	N	Y
9 Moakley	Y	N	N	N	N	N	N	Y
10 Delahunt	N	N	N	N	N	N	N	Y
MICHIGAN								
1 Stupak	Y	N	N	N	Y	N	N	Y
2 ***Hoekstra***	Y	Y	Y	Y	Y	Y	Y	Y
3 ***Ehlers***	Y	Y	Y	Y	Y	N	N	Y
4 ***Camp***	Y	Y	Y	Y	Y	N	N	Y
5 Barcia	Y	N	N	N	Y	N	N	Y
6 ***Upton***	Y	Y	Y	Y	Y	N	N	Y
7 ***Smith***	Y	Y	Y	Y	Y	Y	Y	Y
8 Stabenow	Y	N	N	N	Y	N	N	Y
9 Kildee	Y	N	N	N	Y	N	N	Y
10 Bonior	?	N	N	N	Y	Y	N	Y
11 ***Knollenberg***	Y	Y	Y	Y	Y	N	N	Y
12 Levin	Y	N	N	N	Y	N	N	Y
13 Rivers	Y	N	N	N	Y	Y	N	Y
14 Conyers	N	N	N	N	N	Y	N	Y
15 Kilpatrick	N	N	N	N	N	N	N	Y
16 Dingell	Y	N	N	N	Y	N	N	Y
MINNESOTA								
1 ***Gutknecht***	Y	Y	Y	Y	Y	Y	N	Y
2 Minge	Y	N	N	N	Y	N	N	Y

	340	341	342	343	345	346	347	348
3 ***Ramstad***	Y	Y	Y	Y	Y	Y	N	Y
4 Vento	Y	N	N	N	Y	N	N	Y
5 Sabo	Y	N	N	N	Y	N	N	Y
6 Luther	Y	N	N	N	Y	Y	N	Y
7 Peterson	Y	Y	Y	Y	Y	Y	N	Y
8 Oberstar	Y	N	N	N	N	N	N	Y
MISSISSIPPI								
1 ***Wicker***	Y	Y	Y	Y	Y	N	N	Y
2 Thompson	Y	N	N	N	Y	N	N	Y
3 ***Pickering***	Y	Y	Y	Y	Y	N	N	Y
4 ***Parker***	Y	Y	Y	Y	Y	N	N	Y
5 Taylor	Y	N	N	N	N	Y	Y	Y
MISSOURI								
1 Clay	N	N	N	N	N	N	N	Y
2 ***Talent***	Y	Y	Y	Y	Y	Y	N	Y
3 Gephardt	Y	N	N	N	N	N	N	Y
4 Skelton	Y	N	N	N	Y	N	N	Y
5 McCarthy	Y	N	N	N	Y	N	N	Y
6 Danner	Y	N	Y	N	Y	N	N	Y
7 ***Blunt***	Y	Y	Y	Y	N	N	N	Y
8 ***Emerson***	Y	Y	Y	Y	Y	N	N	Y
9 ***Hulshof***	Y	Y	Y	Y	Y	Y	N	Y
MONTANA								
AL ***Hill***	Y	Y	Y	Y	Y	N	N	Y
NEBRASKA								
1 ***Bereuter***	Y	Y	Y	Y	Y	N	N	Y
2 ***Christensen***	Y	Y	N	Y	Y	N	N	Y
3 ***Barrett***	Y	Y	Y	Y	Y	N	N	Y
NEVADA								
1 ***Ensign***	Y	Y	N	Y	Y	Y	Y	Y
2 ***Gibbons***	Y	Y	Y	Y	Y	Y	N	Y
NEW HAMPSHIRE								
1 ***Sununu***	Y	Y	Y	Y	Y	Y	N	Y
2 ***Bass***	Y	Y	Y	Y	Y	Y	N	Y
NEW JERSEY								
1 Andrews	Y	N	N	N	Y	Y	N	Y
2 ***LoBiondo***	Y	Y	Y	Y	Y	Y	N	Y
3 ***Saxton***	Y	Y	Y	Y	Y	N	N	Y
4 ***Smith***	Y	Y	Y	Y	Y	Y	N	Y
5 ***Roukema***	Y	Y	Y	Y	Y	N	N	Y
6 Pallone	Y	N	N	N	Y	Y	N	Y
7 ***Franks***	Y	Y	Y	Y	Y	Y	N	Y
8 Pascrell	Y	N	Y	N	Y	Y	N	Y
9 Rothman	Y	N	N	N	Y	N	N	Y
10 Payne	N	N	N	N	N	N	N	Y
11 ***Frelinghuysen***	Y	Y	Y	Y	Y	N	N	Y
12 ***Pappas***	N	Y	Y	Y	Y	Y	N	Y
13 Menendez	Y	N	N	N	Y	N	N	Y
NEW MEXICO								
1 ***Schiff***	?	?	?	?	?	?	?	?
2 ***Skeen***	Y	Y	Y	Y	Y	N	N	Y
3 ***Redmond***	Y	Y	Y	Y	Y	N	N	Y
NEW YORK								
1 ***Forbes***	+	+	+	+	+	+	−	+
2 ***Lazio***	Y	?	?	Y	Y	N	N	Y
3 ***King***	Y	Y	Y	Y	Y	N	N	Y
4 McCarthy	Y	N	N	N	Y	N	N	Y
5 Ackerman	Y	N	N	N	Y	N	N	Y
6 Flake	Y	N	N	N	Y	N	N	Y
7 Manton	Y	N	Y	N	Y	N	N	Y
8 Nadler	Y	N	N	N	N	N	N	Y
9 Schumer	Y	N	N	N	Y	N	N	Y
10 Towns	N	N	N	N	N	N	N	Y
11 Owens	Y	N	N	N	N	N	N	Y
12 Velázquez	N	N	N	N	N	N	N	Y
13 ***Molinari***	Y	Y	Y	Y	Y	Y	N	Y
14 Maloney	Y	N	N	N	Y	N	N	Y
15 Rangel	N	N	N	N	N	N	N	Y
16 Serrano	N	N	N	N	N	N	N	Y
17 Engel	Y	N	N	N	N	N	N	Y
18 Lowey	Y	N	N	N	Y	N	N	Y
19 ***Kelly***	Y	Y	Y	Y	Y	N	N	Y
20 ***Gilman***	Y	Y	Y	Y	Y	N	N	Y
21 McNulty	Y	N	N	N	N	N	N	Y
22 ***Solomon***	Y	Y	Y	Y	Y	Y	?	Y
23 ***Boehlert***	Y	Y	Y	Y	Y	N	N	Y
24 ***McHugh***	Y	Y	Y	Y	Y	Y	N	Y
25 ***Walsh***	Y	Y	Y	Y	Y	N	N	Y
26 Hinchey	Y	N	N	N	Y	N	N	Y
27 ***Paxon***	Y	Y	Y	Y	Y	Y	N	Y
28 Slaughter	Y	N	N	N	Y	N	N	Y
29 LaFalce	Y	N	N	N	Y	N	N	Y
30 ***Quinn***	Y	Y	Y	Y	Y	N	N	Y
31 ***Houghton***	Y	Y	Y	?	Y	N	N	Y

	340	341	342	343	345	346	347	348
NORTH CAROLINA								
1 Clayton	Y	N	N	N	Y	N	N	Y
2 Etheridge	Y	N	N	N	N	N	N	Y
3 ***Jones***	Y	Y	Y	Y	N	Y	N	Y
4 Price	Y	N	N	N	Y	N	N	Y
5 ***Burr***	Y	Y	Y	Y	N	Y	N	Y
6 ***Coble***	Y	Y	Y	Y	N	Y	Y	Y
7 McIntyre	Y	N	N	N	N	Y	N	Y
8 Hefner	Y	N	N	N	Y	N	N	Y
9 ***Myrick***	Y	Y	Y	Y	Y	Y	N	Y
10 ***Ballenger***	Y	Y	Y	Y	N	N	N	Y
11 ***Taylor***	Y	Y	Y	Y	Y	?	?	Y
12 Watt	N	N	N	N	N	N	N	Y
NORTH DAKOTA								
AL Pomeroy	Y	N	N	N	Y	N	N	Y
OHIO								
1 ***Chabot***	Y	Y	Y	Y	Y	Y	Y	Y
2 ***Portman***	Y	Y	Y	Y	Y	Y	N	Y
3 Hall	Y	N	N	N	Y	N	N	Y
4 ***Oxley***	Y	Y	Y	Y	Y	N	N	Y
5 ***Gillmor***	Y	Y	Y	Y	Y	Y	N	Y
6 Strickland	Y	N	N	N	Y	Y	N	Y
7 ***Hobson***	Y	Y	Y	Y	Y	Y	N	Y
8 ***Boehner***	Y	Y	Y	Y	Y	N	N	Y
9 Kaptur	Y	N	N	N	N	Y	N	Y
10 Kucinich	N	N	N	N	N	Y	N	Y
11 Stokes	Y	N	N	N	N	N	N	Y
12 ***Kasich***	Y	Y	Y	Y	Y	Y	N	Y
13 Brown	Y	N	N	N	Y	N	N	Y
14 Sawyer	Y	N	N	N	Y	N	N	Y
15 ***Pryce***	Y	Y	Y	Y	Y	Y	N	Y
16 ***Regula***	Y	Y	Y	Y	Y	N	N	Y
17 Traficant	Y	Y	Y	Y	Y	Y	Y	Y
18 ***Ney***	Y	Y	Y	Y	Y	Y	N	Y
19 ***LaTourette***	Y	Y	Y	Y	Y	Y	N	Y
OKLAHOMA								
1 ***Largent***	Y	Y	Y	Y	N	Y	N	Y
2 ***Coburn***	?	Y	Y	Y	N	Y	Y	Y
3 ***Watkins***	Y	Y	Y	Y	Y	Y	N	Y
4 ***Watts***	Y	Y	Y	Y	Y	Y	N	Y
5 ***Istook***	Y	Y	N	Y	N	Y	Y	Y
6 ***Lucas***	Y	Y	Y	Y	Y	N	N	Y
OREGON								
1 Furse	Y	N	N	N	Y	N	N	Y
2 ***Smith***	Y	Y	Y	Y	Y	N	N	Y
3 Blumenauer	Y	N	N	N	N	N	N	Y
4 DeFazio	Y	N	N	N	N	Y	N	Y
5 Hooley	Y	N	Y	N	Y	N	N	Y
PENNSYLVANIA								
1 Foglietta	?	?	?	?	Y	N	N	Y
2 Fattah	Y	N	N	?	Y	N	N	Y
3 Borski	Y	N	N	N	N	N	N	Y
4 Klink	Y	N	N	N	Y	N	N	Y
5 ***Peterson***	Y	Y	Y	Y	Y	N	N	Y
6 Holden	Y	N	N	N	Y	N	N	Y
7 ***Weldon***	Y	Y	Y	Y	Y	Y	N	Y
8 ***Greenwood***	Y	Y	Y	Y	Y	Y	N	Y
9 ***Shuster***	Y	Y	Y	Y	Y	Y	N	Y
10 ***McDade***	Y	Y	Y	Y	Y	N	N	Y
11 Kanjorski	N	N	N	N	Y	Y	N	Y
12 Murtha	N	N	N	N	Y	N	N	Y
13 ***Fox***	Y	Y	Y	Y	Y	Y	N	Y
14 Coyne	Y	N	N	N	Y	N	N	Y
15 McHale	Y	N	N	N	Y	Y	N	Y
16 ***Pitts***	Y	Y	Y	Y	Y	Y	N	Y
17 ***Gekas***	Y	Y	Y	Y	Y	N	N	Y
18 Doyle	Y	N	N	N	Y	Y	N	Y
19 ***Goodling***	Y	Y	Y	Y	Y	Y	N	Y
20 Mascara	Y	N	N	N	Y	N	N	Y
21 ***English***	Y	Y	Y	Y	Y	N	N	Y
RHODE ISLAND								
1 Kennedy	Y	N	N	N	N	N	N	Y
2 Weygand	Y	N	N	N	Y	N	N	Y
SOUTH CAROLINA								
1 ***Sanford***	Y	Y	Y	Y	N	Y	Y	Y
2 ***Spence***	Y	Y	Y	Y	Y	N	N	Y
3 ***Graham***	Y	Y	?	Y	N	Y	N	Y
4 ***Inglis***	Y	Y	Y	Y	Y	N	N	Y
5 Spratt	Y	N	N	N	Y	N	N	Y
6 Clyburn	Y	N	N	N	Y	N	N	Y
SOUTH DAKOTA								
AL ***Thune***	Y	Y	Y	Y	Y	Y	N	Y
TENNESSEE								
1 ***Jenkins***	Y	Y	Y	Y	Y	N	N	Y
2 ***Duncan***	Y	Y	Y	Y	Y	Y	Y	Y

	340	341	342	343	345	346	347	
3 ***Wamp***	Y	Y	Y	Y	Y	Y	Y	Y
4 ***Hilleary***	Y	Y	Y	Y	N	Y	Y	Y
5 Clement	Y	N	N	N	Y	N	N	Y
6 Gordon	Y	N	Y	N	Y	N	N	Y
7 ***Bryant***	Y	Y	Y	?	N	N	N	Y
8 Tanner	Y	N	Y	N	Y	N	N	Y
9 Ford	Y	N	N	N	Y	N	N	Y
TEXAS								
1 Sandlin	Y	N	N	N	Y	N	N	Y
2 Turner	Y	N	N	N	Y	N	N	Y
3 ***Johnson, Sam***	Y	Y	Y	Y	Y	N	N	Y
4 Hall	Y	N	N	N	Y	N	N	Y
5 ***Sessions***	Y	Y	Y	Y	Y	N	N	Y
6 ***Barton***	Y	Y	Y	Y	N	N	N	Y
7 ***Archer***	Y	Y	Y	Y	Y	N	N	Y
8 ***Brady***	Y	Y	Y	Y	Y	N	N	Y
9 Lampson	Y	N	N	N	Y	N	N	Y
10 Doggett	Y	N	N	N	Y	N	N	Y
11 Edwards	Y	N	N	N	Y	N	N	Y
12 ***Granger***	Y	Y	Y	Y	Y	N	N	Y
13 ***Thornberry***	Y	Y	Y	Y	Y	N	N	Y
14 ***Paul***	N	Y	Y	Y	N	Y	Y	N
15 Hinojosa	Y	N	N	N	Y	N	N	Y
16 Reyes	Y	N	N	N	Y	N	N	Y
17 Stenholm	Y	N	Y	N	Y	N	N	Y
18 Jackson-Lee	Y	N	N	N	Y	N	N	Y
19 ***Combest***	Y	Y	Y	Y	Y	N	N	Y
20 Gonzalez	?	?	?	?	?	?	?	?
21 ***Smith***	Y	Y	Y	Y	Y	Y	N	Y
22 ***DeLay***	Y	Y	Y	Y	Y	N	Y	Y
23 ***Bonilla***	Y	Y	Y	Y	N	N	N	Y
24 Frost	Y	N	N	N	Y	N	N	Y
25 Bentsen	Y	N	N	N	Y	N	N	Y
26 ***Armey***	Y	Y	Y	Y	Y	Y	N	Y
27 Ortiz	Y	N	?	N	Y	N	N	Y
28 Rodriguez	Y	N	N	N	Y	N	N	Y
29 Green	Y	N	N	N	Y	N	N	Y
30 Johnson, E.B.	Y	N	N	N	Y	N	N	Y
UTAH								
1 ***Hansen***	Y	Y	Y	Y	Y	N	N	Y
2 ***Cook***	Y	Y	Y	Y	Y	Y	N	Y
3 ***Cannon***	Y	Y	Y	Y	Y	N	N	Y
VERMONT								
AL *Sanders*	Y	N	N	N	N	Y	N	Y
VIRGINIA								
1 ***Bateman***	Y	Y	Y	Y	Y	N	N	Y
2 Pickett	Y	N	N	N	Y	N	N	Y
3 Scott	N	N	N	N	Y	N	N	Y
4 Sisisky	Y	N	N	N	Y	N	N	Y
5 Goode	Y	Y	N	Y	N	N	N	Y
6 ***Goodlatte***	Y	Y	Y	Y	Y	Y	N	Y
7 ***Bliley***	Y	Y	Y	Y	Y	N	N	Y
8 Moran	Y	N	N	N	Y	N	N	Y
9 Boucher	Y	N	N	N	N	N	N	Y
10 ***Wolf***	Y	Y	Y	Y	Y	N	N	Y
11 ***Davis***	Y	Y	Y	Y	Y	N	N	Y
WASHINGTON								
1 ***White***	?	Y	Y	Y	Y	N	N	Y
2 ***Metcalf***	Y	Y	Y	Y	Y	N	N	Y
3 ***Smith, Linda***	Y	Y	Y	Y	N	Y	Y	Y
4 ***Hastings***	Y	Y	Y	Y	Y	N	N	Y
5 ***Nethercutt***	Y	Y	Y	Y	Y	Y	N	?
6 Dicks	Y	N	N	N	Y	N	N	Y
7 McDermott	N	N	N	N	N	N	N	Y
8 ***Dunn***	Y	Y	Y	Y	Y	N	N	Y
9 Smith, Adam	Y	N	Y	N	Y	N	N	Y
WEST VIRGINIA								
1 Mollohan	Y	N	N	N	N	N	N	Y
2 Wise	Y	N	N	N	Y	N	N	Y
3 Rahall	Y	N	N	N	N	N	N	Y
WISCONSIN								
1 ***Neumann***	Y	Y	Y	Y	Y	Y	N	Y
2 ***Klug***	Y	Y	Y	Y	Y	Y	N	Y
3 Kind	Y	N	Y	N	Y	N	N	Y
4 Kleczka	Y	N	Y	N	Y	N	N	Y
5 Barrett	Y	N	N	N	Y	Y	N	Y
6 ***Petri***	Y	Y	Y	Y	Y	Y	Y	Y
7 Obey	Y	N	N	N	N	Y	N	Y
8 Johnson	Y	N	N	N	Y	N	N	Y
9 ***Sensenbrenner***	Y	Y	Y	Y	Y	Y	Y	Y
WYOMING								
AL ***Cubin***	Y	Y	Y	Y	Y	Y	N	Y

Southern states - Ala., Ark., Fla., Ga., Ky., La., Miss., N.C., Okla., S.C., Tenn., Texas, Va.

HOUSE VOTES 350, 351, 352, 353, 354 *

*** 350. HR 2014. Fiscal 1998 Budget Reconciliation — Revenue/ Conference Report.** Adoption of the conference report on the bill to provide a net tax cut of $100.4 billion over five years, including $151.6 billion in gross tax cuts offset by $51.2 billion in revenue increases. The bill would establish a tax credit for each child under age 17, lower the top capital gains tax rate from 28 percent to 20 percent, raise the amount exempt from the federal estate tax gradually from $600,000 to $1 million and provide $39.4 billion in education tax incentives that include a non-refundable credit of up to $1,500 for each student per year for the first two years of college. Adopted (thus sent to the Senate) 389-43: R 225-1; D 164-41 (ND 114-37, SD 50-4); I 0-1, July 31, 1997. A "yea" was a vote in support of the president's position.

351. Adjournment Resolution/Adoption. Adoption of the concurrent resolution to allow the adjournment of the House and the Senate until Sept. 3 and Sept. 2, respectively. Adopted 403-16: R 219-2; D 184-14 (ND 137-9, SD 47-5); I 0-0, July 31, 1997.

352. HR 2209. Fiscal 1998 Legislative Branch Appropriations/ Motion To Instruct. Serrano, D-N.Y., motion to instruct the House conferees to limit the bill's increase in funding for the Joint Committee on Taxation to 4.64 percent. Motion rejected 202-208: R 11-206; D 190-2 (ND 137-2, SD 53-0); I 1-0, Sept. 3, 1997.

353. HR 2160. Fiscal 1998 Agriculture Appropriations/Motion To Instruct. Kaptur, D-Ohio, amendment to instruct the House conferees to agree to the $34 million funding level for the Food and Drug Administration's tobacco initiative included in the Senate's version of the legislation. Motion agreed to 299-125: R 107-117; D 191-8 (ND 145-0, SD 46-8); I 1-0, Sept. 3, 1997.

354. HR 2266. Fiscal 1998 Defense Appropriations/Close Portion of Conference. Young, R-Fla., motion to close portions of the conference to the public during consideration of national security issues. Motion agreed to 420-4: R 223-0; D 196-4 (ND 143-3, SD 53-1); I 1-0, Sept. 3, 1997.

** NOTE: Vote 349 was a quorum call. CQ does not include quorum calls in its vote charts.*

[1] Susan Molinari, R-N.Y., resigned on Aug. 1, 1997.

KEY

Y Voted for (yea).
Paired for.
+ Announced for.
N Voted against (nay).
X Paired against.
– Announced against.
P Voted "present."
C Voted "present" to avoid possible conflict of interest.
? Did not vote or otherwise make a position known.

Democrats ***Republicans***
Independent

	350	351	352	353	354
ALABAMA					
1 ***Callahan***	Y	Y	N	N	Y
2 ***Everett***	Y	Y	N	N	Y
3 ***Riley***	Y	Y	N	N	Y
4 ***Aderholt***	Y	Y	N	N	Y
5 Cramer	Y	Y	Y	Y	Y
6 ***Bachus***	Y	Y	N	Y	Y
7 Hilliard	N	Y	Y	Y	Y
ALASKA					
AL ***Young***	?	?	N	N	Y
ARIZONA					
1 ***Salmon***	Y	Y	N	Y	Y
2 Pastor	Y	Y	Y	Y	Y
3 ***Stump***	Y	Y	N	N	Y
4 ***Shadegg***	Y	Y	N	N	Y
5 ***Kolbe***	Y	Y	N	Y	Y
6 ***Hayworth***	Y	Y	N	Y	Y
ARKANSAS					
1 Berry	Y	Y	Y	Y	Y
2 Snyder	Y	Y	Y	Y	Y
3 ***Hutchinson***	Y	Y	N	Y	Y
4 ***Dickey***	Y	Y	N	N	Y
CALIFORNIA					
1 ***Riggs***	Y	Y	N	Y	Y
2 ***Herger***	Y	Y	N	N	Y
3 Fazio	Y	Y	Y	Y	Y
4 ***Doolittle***	Y	Y	N	N	Y
5 Matsui	N	Y	Y	Y	Y
6 Woolsey	Y	Y	Y	Y	Y
7 Miller	Y	?	Y	Y	Y
8 Pelosi	Y	Y	Y	Y	Y
9 Dellums	N	Y	Y	Y	Y
10 Tauscher	Y	Y	Y	Y	Y
11 ***Pombo***	Y	Y	N	N	Y
12 Lantos	Y	Y	?	?	Y
13 Stark	N	Y	Y	Y	N
14 Eshoo	Y	Y	Y	Y	Y
15 ***Campbell***	N	Y	N	Y	Y
16 Lofgren	Y	N	Y	Y	Y
17 Farr	Y	Y	Y	Y	Y
18 Condit	Y	Y	Y	Y	Y
19 ***Radanovich***	Y	Y	N	N	Y
20 Dooley	Y	Y	Y	Y	Y
21 ***Thomas***	Y	Y	N	N	Y
22 Capps	Y	Y	?	Y	Y
23 ***Gallegly***	Y	Y	?	N	Y
24 Sherman	Y	N	Y	Y	Y
25 ***McKeon***	Y	Y	N	N	Y
26 Berman	Y	Y	?	Y	Y
27 ***Rogan***	Y	Y	N	N	Y
28 ***Dreier***	Y	Y	N	N	Y
29 Waxman	N	Y	Y	Y	Y
30 Becerra	Y	Y	Y	Y	Y
31 Martinez	Y	Y	Y	Y	Y
32 Dixon	Y	Y	?	?	?
33 Roybal-Allard	Y	Y	Y	Y	Y
34 Torres	Y	Y	Y	Y	Y
35 Waters	N	Y	Y	Y	Y
36 Harman	Y	Y	Y	Y	Y
37 Millender-McD.	Y	Y	Y	Y	Y
38 ***Horn***	Y	Y	N	Y	Y
39 ***Royce***	Y	Y	N	Y	Y
40 ***Lewis***	Y	Y	N	N	Y
41 ***Kim***	Y	Y	N	N	Y
42 Brown	Y	Y	Y	Y	Y
43 ***Calvert***	Y	Y	N	Y	Y
44 ***Bono***	Y	Y	N	N	Y
45 ***Rohrabacher***	Y	Y	?	N	Y
46 Sanchez	Y	N	Y	Y	Y
47 ***Cox***	Y	Y	N	N	Y
48 ***Packard***	Y	Y	N	N	Y
49 ***Bilbray***	Y	Y	N	N	Y
50 Filner	N	Y	Y	Y	Y
51 ***Cunningham***	Y	N	N	N	Y
52 ***Hunter***	Y	Y	N	N	Y
COLORADO					
1 DeGette	Y	Y	Y	Y	Y
2 Skaggs	Y	Y	Y	Y	Y
3 ***McInnis***	Y	Y	?	N	Y
4 ***Schaffer***	Y	N	N	N	Y
5 ***Hefley***	Y	Y	N	N	Y
6 ***Schaefer***	Y	Y	N	N	Y
CONNECTICUT					
1 Kennelly	Y	Y	Y	Y	Y
2 Gejdenson	Y	Y	Y	Y	Y
3 DeLauro	Y	Y	Y	Y	Y
4 ***Shays***	Y	Y	N	Y	Y
5 Maloney	Y	?	Y	Y	Y
6 ***Johnson***	Y	Y	N	Y	Y
DELAWARE					
AL ***Castle***	Y	Y	N	Y	Y
FLORIDA					
1 ***Scarborough***	Y	Y	N	N	Y
2 Boyd	Y	Y	Y	N	Y
3 Brown	Y	Y	Y	Y	Y
4 ***Fowler***	Y	Y	N	Y	Y
5 Thurman	Y	Y	Y	Y	Y
6 ***Stearns***	Y	Y	Y	N	Y
7 ***Mica***	Y	Y	N	N	Y
8 ***McCollum***	Y	Y	?	?	?
9 ***Bilirakis***	Y	Y	N	Y	Y
10 ***Young***	Y	Y	N	Y	Y
11 Davis	Y	Y	Y	Y	Y
12 ***Canady***	Y	Y	N	Y	Y
13 ***Miller***	Y	Y	N	Y	Y
14 ***Goss***	Y	Y	N	Y	Y
15 ***Weldon***	Y	Y	N	N	?
16 ***Foley***	Y	Y	N	Y	Y
17 Meek	Y	Y	Y	Y	Y
18 ***Ros-Lehtinen***	Y	Y	N	Y	Y
19 Wexler	Y	Y	Y	Y	Y
20 Deutsch	Y	Y	Y	Y	Y
21 ***Diaz-Balart***	Y	Y	N	Y	Y
22 ***Shaw***	Y	Y	N	Y	Y
23 Hastings	N	N	Y	Y	Y
GEORGIA					
1 ***Kingston***	Y	Y	N	N	Y
2 Bishop	Y	Y	Y	Y	Y
3 ***Collins***	Y	Y	N	N	Y
4 McKinney	Y	Y	Y	Y	Y
5 Lewis	Y	Y	Y	Y	Y
6 ***Gingrich***	Y				
7 ***Barr***	Y	Y	N	N	Y
8 ***Chambliss***	Y	Y	N	N	Y
9 ***Deal***	Y	Y	N	N	Y
10 ***Norwood***	Y	Y	N	N	Y
11 ***Linder***	Y	Y	N	Y	Y
HAWAII					
1 Abercrombie	Y	Y	Y	Y	Y
2 Mink	Y	Y	Y	Y	Y
IDAHO					
1 ***Chenoweth***	Y	Y	Y	N	Y
2 ***Crapo***	Y	Y	N	Y	Y
ILLINOIS					
1 Rush	N	Y	?	?	Y
2 Jackson	N	Y	Y	Y	Y
3 Lipinski	Y	Y	Y	Y	Y
4 Gutierrez	N	Y	Y	Y	Y
5 Blagojevich	Y	Y	Y	Y	Y
6 ***Hyde***	Y	Y	N	N	Y
7 Davis	N	Y	Y	Y	Y
8 ***Crane***	Y	Y	N	N	Y
9 Yates	N	Y	Y	Y	?
10 ***Porter***	Y	Y	N	Y	Y
11 ***Weller***	Y	Y	N	N	Y
12 Costello	Y	Y	Y	Y	Y
13 ***Fawell***	Y	Y	N	Y	Y
14 ***Hastert***	Y	Y	N	Y	Y

ND Northern Democrats SD Southern Democrats

	350	351	352	353	354
15 ***Ewing***	Y	Y	N	Y	Y
16 ***Manzullo***	Y	Y	N	Y	Y
17 Evans	Y	Y	Y	Y	Y
18 ***LaHood***	Y	Y	N	Y	Y
19 Poshard	Y	Y	Y	Y	Y
20 ***Shimkus***	Y	Y	N	Y	Y
INDIANA					
1 Visclosky	N	Y	Y	Y	Y
2 ***McIntosh***	Y	Y	N	N	Y
3 Roemer	Y	Y	Y	Y	Y
4 ***Souder***	Y	Y	N	N	Y
5 ***Buyer***	Y	Y	N	N	Y
6 ***Burton***	Y	Y	N	N	Y
7 ***Pease***	Y	Y	N	N	Y
8 ***Hostettler***	Y	Y	N	N	Y
9 Hamilton	Y	Y	Y	Y	Y
10 Carson	Y	Y	Y	Y	Y
IOWA					
1 ***Leach***	Y	Y	N	Y	Y
2 ***Nussle***	Y	Y	N	Y	Y
3 Boswell	Y	Y	Y	Y	Y
4 ***Ganske***	Y	Y	N	Y	Y
5 ***Latham***	Y	Y	N	N	Y
KANSAS					
1 ***Moran***	Y	Y	N	Y	Y
2 ***Ryun***	Y	Y	N	N	Y
3 ***Snowbarger***	Y	Y	N	N	Y
4 ***Tiahrt***	Y	Y	N	Y	Y
KENTUCKY					
1 ***Whitfield***	Y	Y	N	N	Y
2 ***Lewis***	Y	Y	N	N	Y
3 ***Northup***	Y	Y	N	N	Y
4 ***Bunning***	Y	Y	N	N	Y
5 ***Rogers***	Y	Y	N	N	Y
6 Baesler	Y	Y	Y	N	Y
LOUISIANA					
1 ***Livingston***	Y	Y	N	N	Y
2 Jefferson	Y	Y	Y	Y	Y
3 ***Tauzin***	Y	Y	N	Y	Y
4 ***McCrery***	Y	Y	N	N	Y
5 ***Cooksey***	Y	Y	N	N	Y
6 ***Baker***	Y	Y	N	N	Y
7 John	Y	Y	Y	Y	Y
MAINE					
1 Allen	Y	Y	Y	Y	Y
2 Baldacci	Y	Y	Y	Y	Y
MARYLAND					
1 ***Gilchrest***	Y	Y	N	Y	Y
2 ***Ehrlich***	Y	Y	N	Y	Y
3 Cardin	Y	Y	Y	Y	Y
4 Wynn	Y	Y	Y	Y	Y
5 Hoyer	Y	Y	Y	Y	Y
6 ***Bartlett***	Y	Y	N	N	Y
7 Cummings	N	Y	Y	Y	Y
8 ***Morella***	Y	Y	N	Y	Y
MASSACHUSETTS					
1 Olver	Y	N	Y	Y	Y
2 Neal	Y	Y	Y	Y	Y
3 McGovern	Y	Y	Y	Y	Y
4 Frank	N	Y	Y	Y	Y
5 Meehan	Y	?	Y	Y	Y
6 Tierney	Y	Y	Y	Y	Y
7 Markey	N	Y	Y	Y	Y
8 Kennedy	N	Y	Y	Y	Y
9 Moakley	Y	Y	Y	Y	Y
10 Delahunt	N	Y	Y	Y	Y
MICHIGAN					
1 Stupak	Y	Y	Y	Y	Y
2 ***Hoekstra***	Y	Y	N	Y	Y
3 ***Ehlers***	Y	Y	N	Y	Y
4 ***Camp***	Y	Y	N	Y	Y
5 Barcia	Y	Y	Y	Y	Y
6 ***Upton***	Y	Y	Y	Y	Y
7 ***Smith***	Y	Y	Y	Y	Y
8 Stabenow	Y	Y	Y	Y	Y
9 Kildee	Y	Y	Y	Y	Y
10 Bonior	Y	Y	Y	Y	Y
11 ***Knollenberg***	Y	Y	N	N	Y
12 Levin	Y	Y	Y	Y	Y
13 Rivers	Y	Y	Y	Y	Y
14 Conyers	N	Y	Y	Y	N
15 Kilpatrick	N	Y	Y	Y	Y
16 Dingell	Y	Y	Y	Y	Y
MINNESOTA					
1 ***Gutknecht***	Y	?	N	Y	Y
2 Minge	Y	N	Y	Y	Y

	350	351	352	353	354
3 ***Ramstad***	Y	Y	N	Y	Y
4 Vento	Y	Y	Y	Y	Y
5 Sabo	Y	Y	Y	Y	Y
6 Luther	Y	Y	Y	Y	Y
7 Peterson	Y	Y	N	Y	Y
8 Oberstar	N	Y	Y	Y	Y
MISSISSIPPI					
1 ***Wicker***	Y	Y	N	N	Y
2 Thompson	Y	Y	Y	Y	Y
3 ***Pickering***	Y	Y	N	N	Y
4 ***Parker***	Y	Y	N	N	Y
5 Taylor	Y	N	Y	Y	Y
MISSOURI					
1 Clay	N	Y	Y	?	?
2 ***Talent***	Y	Y	N	Y	Y
3 Gephardt	N	Y	Y	Y	Y
4 Skelton	Y	Y	Y	Y	Y
5 McCarthy	Y	Y	Y	Y	Y
6 Danner	Y	Y	Y	Y	Y
7 ***Blunt***	Y	Y	N	N	Y
8 ***Emerson***	Y	Y	N	Y	Y
9 ***Hulshof***	Y	Y	Y	Y	Y
MONTANA					
AL ***Hill***	Y	Y	N	Y	Y
NEBRASKA					
1 ***Bereuter***	Y	Y	N	Y	Y
2 ***Christensen***	Y	Y	N	Y	Y
3 ***Barrett***	Y	Y	N	Y	Y
NEVADA					
1 ***Ensign***	Y	Y	–	Y	Y
2 ***Gibbons***	Y	Y	N	Y	Y
NEW HAMPSHIRE					
1 ***Sununu***	Y	Y	N	Y	Y
2 ***Bass***	Y	Y	N	Y	Y
NEW JERSEY					
1 Andrews	Y	Y	Y	Y	Y
2 ***LoBiondo***	Y	Y	N	Y	Y
3 ***Saxton***	Y	Y	N	Y	Y
4 ***Smith***	Y	Y	N	Y	Y
5 ***Roukema***	Y	Y	?	Y	Y
6 Pallone	Y	Y	Y	Y	Y
7 ***Franks***	Y	Y	N	Y	Y
8 Pascrell	Y	Y	Y	Y	Y
9 Rothman	Y	Y	Y	Y	Y
10 Payne	N	Y	?	Y	Y
11 ***Frelinghuysen***	Y	Y	N	Y	Y
12 ***Pappas***	Y	Y	N	Y	Y
13 Menendez	Y	Y	Y	Y	Y
NEW MEXICO					
1 ***Schiff***	?	?	?	?	?
2 ***Skeen***	Y	Y	N	N	Y
3 ***Redmond***	Y	Y	N	N	Y
NEW YORK					
1 ***Forbes***	Y	Y	N	Y	Y
2 ***Lazio***	Y	Y	N	Y	Y
3 ***King***	Y	Y	N	Y	Y
4 McCarthy	Y	Y	Y	Y	Y
5 Ackerman	Y	?	Y	Y	Y
6 Flake	Y	Y	Y	Y	Y
7 Manton	Y	Y	Y	Y	Y
8 Nadler	Y	Y	Y	Y	Y
9 Schumer	Y	Y	Y	Y	Y
10 Towns	N	Y	?	?	?
11 Owens	Y	Y	Y	Y	Y
12 Velázquez	N	Y	Y	Y	Y
13 ***Molinari*** [1]	Y	Y			
14 Maloney	Y	Y	Y	Y	Y
15 Rangel	Y	Y	Y	Y	Y
16 Serrano	N	Y	Y	Y	Y
17 Engel	Y	Y	+	Y	Y
18 Lowey	Y	Y	Y	Y	Y
19 ***Kelly***	Y	Y	N	Y	Y
20 ***Gilman***	Y	Y	N	Y	Y
21 McNulty	N	Y	Y	Y	Y
22 ***Solomon***	Y	Y	N	N	Y
23 ***Boehlert***	Y	Y	N	Y	Y
24 ***McHugh***	Y	Y	N	Y	Y
25 ***Walsh***	Y	Y	N	N	Y
26 Hinchey	Y	Y	?	Y	Y
27 ***Paxon***	Y	Y	N	N	Y
28 Slaughter	Y	Y	Y	Y	Y
29 LaFalce	Y	Y	Y	Y	Y
30 ***Quinn***	Y	Y	N	Y	Y
31 ***Houghton***	Y	Y	N	Y	Y

	350	351	352	353	354
NORTH CAROLINA					
1 Clayton	Y	Y	Y	Y	Y
2 Etheridge	Y	Y	Y	N	Y
3 ***Jones***	Y	Y	N	N	Y
4 Price	Y	Y	Y	N	Y
5 ***Burr***	Y	Y	N	N	Y
6 ***Coble***	Y	Y	N	N	Y
7 McIntyre	Y	Y	Y	N	Y
8 Hefner	Y	Y	Y	N	Y
9 ***Myrick***	Y	Y	N	N	Y
10 ***Ballenger***	Y	Y	N	N	Y
11 ***Taylor***	Y	Y	Y	N	Y
12 Watt	N	Y	Y	Y	N
NORTH DAKOTA					
AL Pomeroy	Y	Y	Y	Y	Y
OHIO					
1 ***Chabot***	Y	Y	Y	Y	Y
2 ***Portman***	Y	Y	N	Y	Y
3 Hall	Y	Y	?	?	?
4 ***Oxley***	Y	Y	N	Y	Y
5 ***Gillmor***	Y	Y	N	N	Y
6 Strickland	Y	Y	Y	Y	Y
7 ***Hobson***	Y	Y	N	Y	Y
8 ***Boehner***	Y	Y	N	N	Y
9 Kaptur	N	Y	Y	Y	Y
10 Kucinich	N	N	Y	Y	Y
11 Stokes	N	Y	Y	Y	Y
12 ***Kasich***	Y	Y	N	Y	Y
13 Brown	Y	Y	Y	Y	Y
14 Sawyer	Y	Y	Y	Y	Y
15 ***Pryce***	Y	Y	N	Y	Y
16 ***Regula***	Y	Y	N	Y	Y
17 Traficant	Y	Y	Y	Y	Y
18 ***Ney***	Y	Y	N	Y	Y
19 ***LaTourette***	Y	Y	N	Y	Y
OKLAHOMA					
1 ***Largent***	Y	Y	Y	N	Y
2 ***Coburn***	Y	Y	Y	N	Y
3 ***Watkins***	Y	Y	N	N	Y
4 ***Watts***	Y	Y	N	N	Y
5 ***Istook***	Y	Y	?	Y	Y
6 ***Lucas***	Y	Y	N	N	Y
OREGON					
1 Furse	Y	Y	?	Y	Y
2 ***Smith***	Y	Y	N	N	Y
3 Blumenauer	N	Y	Y	Y	Y
4 DeFazio	N	N	Y	Y	N
5 Hooley	Y	N	Y	Y	Y
PENNSYLVANIA					
1 Foglietta	Y	Y	Y	Y	Y
2 Fattah	Y	Y	Y	Y	Y
3 Borski	N	Y	Y	Y	Y
4 Klink	Y	Y	Y	Y	Y
5 ***Peterson***	Y	Y	N	Y	Y
6 Holden	Y	Y	Y	Y	Y
7 ***Weldon***	Y	Y	N	Y	Y
8 ***Greenwood***	Y	Y	N	Y	Y
9 ***Shuster***	Y	Y	N	N	Y
10 ***McDade***	Y	?	N	Y	Y
11 Kanjorski	Y	Y	Y	Y	Y
12 Murtha	Y	Y	Y	Y	Y
13 ***Fox***	Y	Y	N	Y	Y
14 Coyne	Y	Y	Y	Y	Y
15 McHale	Y	Y	Y	Y	Y
16 ***Pitts***	Y	Y	N	N	Y
17 ***Gekas***	Y	Y	N	N	Y
18 Doyle	Y	Y	Y	Y	Y
19 ***Goodling***	Y	Y	N	Y	Y
20 Mascara	Y	Y	Y	Y	Y
21 ***English***	Y	Y	N	Y	Y
RHODE ISLAND					
1 Kennedy	N	Y	Y	Y	Y
2 Weygand	Y	Y	Y	Y	Y
SOUTH CAROLINA					
1 ***Sanford***	Y	Y	N	N	Y
2 ***Spence***	Y	Y	N	N	Y
3 ***Graham***	Y	Y	N	N	Y
4 ***Inglis***	Y	Y	N	N	Y
5 Spratt	Y	Y	Y	Y	Y
6 Clyburn	Y	Y	Y	Y	Y
SOUTH DAKOTA					
AL ***Thune***	Y	Y	N	Y	Y

	350	351	352	353	354
TENNESSEE					
1 ***Jenkins***	Y	Y	N	N	Y
2 ***Duncan***	Y	Y	N	Y	Y
3 ***Wamp***	Y	Y	N	Y	Y
4 ***Hilleary***	Y	Y	N	N	Y
5 Clement	Y	Y	Y	Y	Y
6 Gordon	Y	Y	Y	Y	Y
7 ***Bryant***	Y	Y	N	Y	Y
8 Tanner	Y	Y	?	Y	Y
9 Ford	Y	Y	Y	Y	Y
TEXAS					
1 Sandlin	Y	Y	Y	Y	Y
2 Turner	Y	Y	Y	Y	Y
3 ***Johnson, Sam***	Y	Y	N	N	Y
4 Hall	Y	Y	Y	Y	Y
5 ***Sessions***	Y	Y	N	N	Y
6 ***Barton***	Y	Y	N	Y	Y
7 ***Archer***	Y	Y	N	N	Y
8 ***Brady***	Y	Y	N	N	Y
9 Lampson	Y	Y	Y	Y	Y
10 Doggett	Y	Y	Y	Y	Y
11 Edwards	Y	?	Y	Y	Y
12 ***Granger***	Y	Y	N	N	Y
13 ***Thornberry***	Y	Y	N	N	Y
14 ***Paul***	Y	Y	N	N	Y
15 Hinojosa	Y	Y	Y	Y	Y
16 Reyes	Y	Y	Y	Y	Y
17 Stenholm	Y	Y	Y	Y	Y
18 Jackson-Lee	Y	N	Y	Y	Y
19 ***Combest***	Y	Y	N	N	Y
20 Gonzalez	?	?	?	?	?
21 ***Smith***	Y	Y	N	Y	Y
22 ***DeLay***	Y	Y	N	N	Y
23 ***Bonilla***	Y	Y	N	N	Y
24 Frost	Y	Y	Y	Y	Y
25 Bentsen	Y	?	Y	Y	Y
26 ***Armey***	Y	Y	N	N	Y
27 Ortiz	Y	Y	Y	Y	Y
28 Rodriguez	Y	Y	Y	Y	Y
29 Green	Y	N	Y	Y	Y
30 Johnson, E.B.	Y	Y	Y	Y	Y
UTAH					
1 ***Hansen***	Y	Y	N	Y	Y
2 ***Cook***	Y	Y	N	Y	Y
3 ***Cannon***	Y	Y	N	Y	Y
VERMONT					
AL *Sanders*	N	?	Y	Y	Y
VIRGINIA					
1 ***Bateman***	Y	Y	N	N	Y
2 Pickett	Y	Y	Y	Y	Y
3 Scott	N	Y	Y	Y	Y
4 Sisisky	Y	Y	Y	Y	Y
5 Goode	Y	N	Y	N	Y
6 ***Goodlatte***	Y	Y	N	N	Y
7 ***Bliley***	Y	Y	N	N	Y
8 Moran	Y	Y	Y	Y	Y
9 Boucher	Y	Y	Y	N	Y
10 ***Wolf***	Y	Y	N	N	Y
11 ***Davis***	Y	Y	N	Y	Y
WASHINGTON					
1 ***White***	Y	Y	N	N	Y
2 ***Metcalf***	Y	Y	N	Y	Y
3 ***Smith, Linda***	Y	Y	?	N	Y
4 ***Hastings***	Y	?	N	N	Y
5 ***Nethercutt***	Y	Y	N	N	Y
6 Dicks	Y	Y	Y	Y	Y
7 McDermott	N	Y	Y	Y	Y
8 ***Dunn***	Y	Y	N	N	Y
9 Smith, Adam	Y	?	Y	Y	Y
WEST VIRGINIA					
1 Mollohan	Y	Y	Y	Y	Y
2 Wise	Y	Y	?	Y	Y
3 Rahall	N	Y	Y	Y	Y
WISCONSIN					
1 ***Neumann***	Y	Y	Y	Y	Y
2 ***Klug***	Y	Y	Y	Y	Y
3 Kind	Y	Y	Y	Y	Y
4 Kleczka	Y	Y	N	Y	Y
5 Barrett	Y	Y	Y	Y	Y
6 ***Petri***	Y	Y	N	Y	Y
7 Obey	N	N	Y	Y	Y
8 Johnson	Y	Y	Y	Y	Y
9 ***Sensenbrenner***	Y	Y	N	Y	Y
WYOMING					
AL ***Cubin***	Y	?	N	N	Y

Southern states - Ala., Ark., Fla., Ga., Ky., La., Miss., N.C., Okla., S.C., Tenn., Texas, Va.

HOUSE VOTES 355, 356, 357, 358, 359

355. Procedural Motion/Adjourn. Miller, D-Calif., motion to adjourn. Motion rejected 53-371: R 0-220; D 53-150 (ND 43-106, SD 10-44); I 0-1, Sept. 4, 1997.

356. HR 2159. Fiscal 1998 Foreign Operations Appropriations/Aid to India. Burton, R-Ind., amendment to cut the bill's development assistance to India by $14 million to $41.8 million, 25 percent less than the president's fiscal 1998 request. Rejected 82-342: R 73-149; D 9-192 (ND 8-142, SD 1-50); I 0-1, Sept. 4, 1997.

357. HR 2159. Fiscal 1998 Foreign Operations Appropriations/African Development Fund. Campbell, R-Calif., amendment to increase the bill's funding for the African Development Fund by $25 million to $50 million, offset by a reduction of $25 million from the Economic Support Fund. Adopted 273-150: R 76-145; D 196-5 (ND 145-2, SD 51-3); I 1-0, Sept. 4, 1997.

358. HR 2159. Fiscal 1998 Foreign Operations Appropriations/International Family Planning. Paul, R-Texas, amendment to cut the bill's $385 million in funding for international family planning and population control activities. Rejected 147-278: R 132-87; D 15-190 (ND 10-141, SD 5-49); I 0-1, Sept. 4, 1997.

359. HR 2159. Fiscal 1998 Foreign Operations Appropriations/Trophy Hunting. Fox, R-Pa., amendment to prohibit any development assistance funds in the bill from being used to directly support or promote trophy hunting or the international commercial trade in elephant ivory, elephant hides or rhinoceros horns. Rejected 159-267: R 31-190; D 128-76 (ND 110-41, SD 18-35); I 0-1, Sept. 4, 1997.

[1] *Susan Molinari, R-N.Y., resigned on Aug. 1, 1997.*

KEY

- Y Voted for (yea).
- \# Paired for.
- \+ Announced for.
- N Voted against (nay).
- X Paired against.
- – Announced against.
- P Voted "present."
- C Voted "present" to avoid possible conflict of interest.
- ? Did not vote or otherwise make a position known.

Democrats ***Republicans***
Independent

	355	356	357	358	359
ALABAMA					
1 ***Callahan***	N	N	N	N	N
2 ***Everett***	N	N	N	Y	N
3 ***Riley***	N	Y	N	Y	N
4 ***Aderholt***	N	Y	N	Y	N
5 Cramer	N	N	Y	N	N
6 ***Bachus***	N	N	Y	Y	N
7 Hilliard	N	?	Y	N	N
ALASKA					
AL ***Young***	N	N	N	N	N
ARIZONA					
1 ***Salmon***	N	Y	N	Y	N
2 Pastor	N	N	Y	N	Y
3 ***Stump***	N	Y	N	Y	N
4 ***Shadegg***	N	Y	N	Y	N
5 ***Kolbe***	N	N	Y	N	N
6 ***Hayworth***	N	N	N	Y	N
ARKANSAS					
1 Berry	N	N	Y	N	N
2 Snyder	N	N	Y	N	Y
3 ***Hutchinson***	N	Y	Y	Y	Y
4 ***Dickey***	N	N	N	Y	N
CALIFORNIA					
1 ***Riggs***	N	Y	Y	N	N
2 ***Herger***	N	Y	N	Y	N
3 Fazio	Y	Y	Y	N	Y
4 ***Doolittle***	N	Y	N	Y	N
5 Matsui	N	N	Y	N	Y
6 Woolsey	Y	N	Y	N	Y
7 Miller	Y	Y	Y	N	Y
8 Pelosi	Y	N	Y	N	Y
9 Dellums	N	N	Y	N	Y
10 Tauscher	N	N	Y	N	Y
11 ***Pombo***	N	Y	Y	Y	N
12 Lantos	N	N	Y	N	Y
13 Stark	Y	N	Y	N	Y
14 Eshoo	Y	N	Y	N	Y
15 ***Campbell***	N	N	Y	N	N
16 Lofgren	N	N	Y	N	Y
17 Farr	Y	Y	?	N	Y
18 Condit	N	Y	Y	N	N
19 ***Radanovich***	N	Y	Y	N	N
20 Dooley	N	N	Y	N	Y
21 ***Thomas***	N	N	Y	N	N
22 Capps	N	N	Y	N	Y
23 ***Gallegly***	N	N	N	N	Y
24 Sherman	N	N	Y	N	Y
25 ***McKeon***	N	Y	Y	Y	N
26 Berman	N	N	Y	N	Y
27 ***Rogan***	N	Y	N	N	Y
28 ***Dreier***	N	N	Y	N	N
29 Waxman	N	?	Y	N	Y
30 Becerra	N	N	?	N	N
31 Martinez	N	N	Y	N	N
32 Dixon	N	N	Y	N	Y
33 Roybal-Allard	N	N	Y	N	Y
34 Torres	Y	N	Y	N	Y
35 Waters	Y	N	Y	N	Y
36 Harman	N	N	Y	N	Y
37 Millender-McD.	Y	N	Y	N	Y
38 ***Horn***	N	N	Y	N	N
39 ***Royce***	N	N	Y	Y	N
40 ***Lewis***	N	N	N	N	N
41 ***Kim***	N	N	N	N	N
42 Brown	N	N	Y	N	N
43 ***Calvert***	N	N	Y	N	N
44 ***Bono***	?	N	N	Y	Y
45 ***Rohrabacher***	N	Y	N	N	N
46 Sanchez	N	N	Y	N	N
47 ***Cox***	N	Y	?	Y	N
48 ***Packard***	N	N	N	N	N
49 ***Bilbray***	N	N	N	N	N
50 Filner	Y	N	Y	N	Y
51 ***Cunningham***	N	Y	N	N	N
52 ***Hunter***	N	Y	N	Y	N
COLORADO					
1 DeGette	Y	N	Y	N	Y
2 Skaggs	N	N	Y	N	Y
3 ***McInnis***	N	N	Y	N	N
4 ***Schaffer***	N	Y	N	Y	N
5 ***Hefley***	N	N	N	Y	N
6 ***Schaefer***	N	Y	N	Y	N
CONNECTICUT					
1 Kennelly	N	N	Y	N	Y
2 Gejdenson	Y	N	Y	N	Y
3 DeLauro	Y	N	Y	N	Y
4 ***Shays***	N	N	Y	N	Y
5 Maloney	N	N	Y	N	Y
6 ***Johnson***	N	N	Y	N	N
DELAWARE					
AL ***Castle***	N	N	Y	N	Y
FLORIDA					
1 ***Scarborough***	N	Y	Y	Y	N
2 Boyd	N	N	Y	N	N
3 Brown	Y	N	Y	N	N
4 ***Fowler***	N	N	N	N	N
5 Thurman	N	N	Y	N	N
6 ***Stearns***	N	N	N	Y	N
7 ***Mica***	N	N	Y	Y	N
8 ***McCollum***	?	?	?	?	?
9 ***Bilirakis***	N	N	N	Y	N
10 ***Young***	N	N	Y	Y	N
11 Davis	Y	N	Y	N	N
12 ***Canady***	N	Y	Y	Y	N
13 ***Miller***	N	N	N	N	N
14 ***Goss***	N	N	N	N	N
15 ***Weldon***	N	N	N	Y	N
16 ***Foley***	N	N	N	N	N
17 Meek	N	N	Y	N	Y
18 ***Ros-Lehtinen***	N	Y	Y	N	Y
19 Wexler	Y	N	Y	N	Y
20 Deutsch	Y	N	Y	N	Y
21 ***Diaz-Balart***	N	Y	Y	N	Y
22 ***Shaw***	N	N	Y	N	N
23 Hastings	Y	N	Y	N	Y
GEORGIA					
1 ***Kingston***	N	N	Y	Y	N
2 Bishop	N	N	Y	N	N
3 ***Collins***	N	N	N	Y	N
4 McKinney	N	N	Y	N	Y
5 Lewis	Y	N	Y	N	Y
6 ***Gingrich***					N
7 ***Barr***	N	N	N	Y	N
8 ***Chambliss***	N	N	N	Y	N
9 ***Deal***	N	Y	N	Y	N
10 ***Norwood***	N	N	N	Y	N
11 ***Linder***	N	N	N	Y	N
HAWAII					
1 Abercrombie	N	N	Y	N	Y
2 Mink	Y	N	Y	N	Y
IDAHO					
1 ***Chenoweth***	N	Y	N	N	N
2 ***Crapo***	N	Y	N	Y	N
ILLINOIS					
1 Rush	N	N	Y	N	N
2 Jackson	N	N	Y	N	Y
3 Lipinski	N	N	N	Y	N
4 Gutierrez	N	N	Y	N	Y
5 Blagojevich	N	N	Y	N	Y
6 ***Hyde***	N	N	N	Y	N
7 Davis	Y	N	Y	N	N
8 ***Crane***	N	Y	Y	Y	Y
9 Yates	Y	N	Y	N	Y
10 ***Porter***	N	Y	N	N	N
11 ***Weller***	N	N	Y	Y	N
12 Costello	N	N	Y	Y	N
13 ***Fawell***	N	Y	N	N	Y
14 ***Hastert***	N	Y	N	Y	N

ND Northern Democrats SD Southern Democrats

	355	356	357	358	359
15 *Ewing*	N	N	N	N	N
16 *Manzullo*	N	N	N	Y	N
17 Evans	N	N	Y	N	Y
18 *LaHood*	N	N	N	Y	N
19 Poshard	N	N	Y	Y	N
20 *Shimkus*	N	N	N	Y	N
INDIANA					
1 Visclosky	N	N	Y	N	Y
2 *McIntosh*	N	Y	N	Y	N
3 Roemer	N	N	Y	N	N
4 *Souder*	N	N	N	Y	N
5 *Buyer*	N	Y	N	Y	N
6 *Burton*	N	Y	N	Y	N
7 *Pease*	N	Y	N	Y	N
8 *Hostettler*	N	Y	N	Y	Y
9 Hamilton	N	N	Y	N	N
10 Carson	N	N	Y	N	Y
IOWA					
1 *Leach*	N	N	Y	N	Y
2 *Nussle*	N	Y	Y	Y	Y
3 Boswell	Y	N	Y	N	N
4 *Ganske*	N	N	N	N	N
5 *Latham*	N	N	N	Y	N
KANSAS					
1 *Moran*	N	N	N	Y	N
2 *Ryun*	N	N	N	Y	N
3 *Snowbarger*	N	N	N	Y	N
4 *Tiahrt*	N	N	N	Y	N
KENTUCKY					
1 *Whitfield*	N	N	N	Y	N
2 *Lewis*	N	Y	N	Y	N
3 *Northup*	N	N	N	Y	N
4 *Bunning*	N	Y	N	Y	N
5 *Rogers*	N	N	N	Y	N
6 Baesler	N	N	Y	N	N
LOUISIANA					
1 *Livingston*	N	N	N	Y	N
2 Jefferson	Y	N	Y	N	N
3 *Tauzin*	N	N	N	Y	N
4 *McCrery*	N	N	N	N	N
5 *Cooksey*	N	N	Y	Y	N
6 *Baker*	N	N	N	Y	N
7 John	N	N	Y	Y	N
MAINE					
1 Allen	N	N	Y	N	Y
2 Baldacci	N	N	Y	N	Y
MARYLAND					
1 *Gilchrest*	N	N	Y	N	N
2 *Ehrlich*	N	N	N	N	N
3 Cardin	N	N	Y	N	Y
4 Wynn	N	N	Y	N	Y
5 Hoyer	N	N	Y	N	N
6 *Bartlett*	N	Y	N	Y	N
7 Cummings	N	N	Y	N	Y
8 *Morella*	N	N	Y	N	Y
MASSACHUSETTS					
1 Olver	N	N	Y	N	Y
2 Neal	N	N	Y	N	Y
3 McGovern	N	N	Y	N	Y
4 Frank	N	N	Y	N	Y
5 Meehan	N	N	Y	N	Y
6 Tierney	N	N	Y	N	Y
7 Markey	N	N	Y	N	Y
8 Kennedy	N	N	Y	N	Y
9 Moakley	N	N	Y	N	Y
10 Delahunt	N	N	Y	N	N
MICHIGAN					
1 Stupak	N	N	Y	N	N
2 *Hoekstra*	N	N	N	Y	N
3 *Ehlers*	N	N	Y	N	N
4 *Camp*	N	N	N	Y	N
5 Barcia	N	N	Y	Y	N
6 *Upton*	N	N	Y	N	N
7 *Smith*	N	N	Y	Y	Y
8 Stabenow	Y	N	Y	N	Y
9 Kildee	N	N	Y	Y	Y
10 Bonior	Y	Y	Y	N	Y
11 *Knollenberg*	N	N	N	N	N
12 Levin	N	N	Y	N	Y
13 Rivers	N	N	Y	N	Y
14 Conyers	Y	N	?	N	Y
15 Kilpatrick	Y	N	Y	N	Y
16 Dingell	Y	N	Y	N	N
MINNESOTA					
1 *Gutknecht*	N	N	Y	N	N
2 Minge	N	N	Y	N	N

	355	356	357	358	359
3 *Ramstad*	N	Y	Y	N	N
4 Vento	N	N	Y	N	Y
5 Sabo	N	N	Y	N	Y
6 Luther	N	N	Y	N	Y
7 Peterson	N	Y	Y	Y	N
8 Oberstar	Y	N	Y	Y	Y
MISSISSIPPI					
1 *Wicker*	N	N	N	Y	N
2 Thompson	N	?	Y	N	N
3 *Pickering*	N	N	N	Y	N
4 *Parker*	N	N	N	Y	N
5 Taylor	N	Y	N	Y	N
MISSOURI					
1 Clay	Y	N	Y	N	Y
2 *Talent*	N	N	N	Y	N
3 Gephardt	Y	N	Y	N	Y
4 Skelton	N	N	Y	Y	N
5 McCarthy	N	N	Y	N	Y
6 Danner	N	N	Y	N	N
7 *Blunt*	N	N	Y	Y	N
8 *Emerson*	N	N	N	Y	N
9 *Hulshof*	N	N	N	Y	N
MONTANA					
AL *Hill*	N	Y	N	N	N
NEBRASKA					
1 *Bereuter*	N	N	Y	N	N
2 *Christensen*	N	N	Y	Y	N
3 *Barrett*	N	Y	Y	N	N
NEVADA					
1 *Ensign*	N	N	Y	Y	Y
2 *Gibbons*	N	Y	N	N	N
NEW HAMPSHIRE					
1 *Sununu*	N	N	N	N	N
2 *Bass*	N	N	N	N	N
NEW JERSEY					
1 Andrews	Y	N	Y	N	Y
2 *LoBiondo*	N	N	Y	Y	N
3 *Saxton*	N	N	Y	N	N
4 *Smith*	N	N	Y	?	Y
5 *Roukema*	N	N	N	N	Y
6 Pallone	Y	N	Y	N	Y
7 *Franks*	N	N	Y	N	N
8 Pascrell	N	N	Y	N	Y
9 Rothman	N	N	Y	N	N
10 Payne	Y	N	Y	N	Y
11 *Frelinghuysen*	N	N	N	N	Y
12 *Pappas*	N	N	Y	Y	N
13 Menendez	N	N	Y	N	N
NEW MEXICO					
1 *Schiff*	?	?	?	?	?
2 *Skeen*	N	N	N	N	N
3 *Redmond*	N	N	Y	Y	N
NEW YORK					
1 *Forbes*	N	N	N	Y	N
2 *Lazio*	?	N	N	N	Y
3 *King*	N	Y	N	Y	N
4 McCarthy	N	N	Y	N	Y
5 Ackerman	N	N	Y	N	Y
6 Flake	Y	N	Y	N	N
7 Manton	?	N	N	N	Y
8 Nadler	N	N	Y	N	Y
9 Schumer	N	N	Y	N	Y
10 Towns	Y	Y	Y	N	Y
11 Owens	Y	N	Y	N	N
12 Velázquez	N	N	Y	N	Y
13 Vacant[1]					
14 Maloney	Y	N	Y	N	Y
15 Rangel	N	N	Y	N	Y
16 Serrano	N	N	Y	N	Y
17 Engel	–	N	Y	N	Y
18 Lowey	Y	N	Y	N	Y
19 *Kelly*	N	N	N	N	Y
20 *Gilman*	N	N	Y	N	Y
21 McNulty	Y	N	Y	N	Y
22 *Solomon*	N	Y	N	Y	N
23 *Boehlert*	N	N	Y	N	N
24 *McHugh*	N	N	N	N	N
25 *Walsh*	N	N	N	N	N
26 Hinchey	N	N	Y	N	Y
27 *Paxon*	N	Y	N	Y	N
28 Slaughter	Y	N	Y	N	Y
29 LaFalce	N	N	Y	N	Y
30 *Quinn*	N	N	Y	Y	N
31 *Houghton*	N	N	Y	N	Y

	355	356	357	358	359
NORTH CAROLINA					
1 Clayton	N	N	Y	N	Y
2 Etheridge	N	N	Y	N	Y
3 *Jones*	N	Y	N	Y	N
4 Price	N	N	Y	N	Y
5 *Burr*	N	N	N	Y	N
6 *Coble*	N	N	N	Y	N
7 McIntyre	N	–	Y	N	N
8 Hefner	Y	N	Y	N	N
9 *Myrick*	N	Y	N	Y	N
10 *Ballenger*	N	Y	Y	N	N
11 *Taylor*	?	Y	N	Y	N
12 Watt	N	N	Y	N	N
NORTH DAKOTA					
AL Pomeroy	N	N	Y	N	Y
OHIO					
1 *Chabot*	N	N	Y	Y	N
2 *Portman*	N	N	Y	Y	Y
3 Hall	N	N	Y	N	Y
4 *Oxley*	N	N	N	N	N
5 *Gillmor*	N	N	N	Y	N
6 Strickland	N	N	Y	N	N
7 *Hobson*	N	N	N	N	N
8 *Boehner*	N	N	N	Y	N
9 Kaptur	Y	N	Y	N	Y
10 Kucinich	N	N	Y	Y	Y
11 Stokes	N	N	Y	N	Y
12 *Kasich*	N	N	Y	Y	Y
13 Brown	N	N	Y	N	Y
14 Sawyer	N	N	Y	N	Y
15 *Pryce*	N	–	–	–	–
16 *Regula*	N	N	N	N	N
17 Traficant	N	N	Y	N	N
18 *Ney*	N	N	Y	Y	N
19 *LaTourette*	N	N	N	N	N
OKLAHOMA					
1 *Largent*	N	Y	N	Y	N
2 *Coburn*	N	Y	Y	Y	N
3 *Watkins*	N	N	N	Y	N
4 *Watts*	N	Y	Y	Y	N
5 *Istook*	N	Y	N	Y	N
6 *Lucas*	N	N	Y	Y	N
OREGON					
1 Furse	N	N	Y	N	Y
2 *Smith*	N	N	N	N	N
3 Blumenauer	N	N	Y	N	Y
4 DeFazio	Y	N	Y	N	Y
5 Hooley	N	N	Y	N	Y
PENNSYLVANIA					
1 Foglietta	Y	N	?	N	Y
2 Fattah	N	N	Y	N	Y
3 Borski	N	N	Y	N	Y
4 Klink	N	N	Y	N	Y
5 *Peterson*	N	N	N	N	N
6 Holden	N	Y	Y	N	N
7 *Weldon*	?	N	Y	Y	Y
8 *Greenwood*	N	N	Y	N	–
9 *Shuster*	N	Y	N	N	N
10 *McDade*	N	N	Y	N	P
11 Kanjorski	N	N	Y	N	N
12 Murtha	N	N	Y	N	N
13 *Fox*	N	N	Y	N	Y
14 Coyne	Y	N	Y	N	Y
15 McHale	N	N	Y	N	Y
16 *Pitts*	N	Y	N	Y	N
17 *Gekas*	N	N	N	N	N
18 Doyle	N	N	Y	N	N
19 *Goodling*	N	Y	Y	Y	Y
20 Mascara	N	N	Y	N	N
21 *English*	N	N	Y	?	N
RHODE ISLAND					
1 Kennedy	Y	N	Y	N	Y
2 Weygand	N	N	Y	N	Y
SOUTH CAROLINA					
1 *Sanford*	N	N	Y	N	N
2 *Spence*	N	N	N	N	N
3 *Graham*	N	N	N	Y	N
4 *Inglis*	N	N	N	Y	N
5 Spratt	N	N	Y	N	Y
6 Clyburn	N	N	Y	N	N
SOUTH DAKOTA					
AL *Thune*	N	Y	N	Y	N

	355	356	357	358	359
TENNESSEE					
1 *Jenkins*	N	Y	N	Y	N
2 *Duncan*	N	Y	N	Y	N
3 *Wamp*	N	Y	Y	Y	N
4 *Hilleary*	N	Y	N	Y	N
5 Clement	N	N	Y	N	Y
6 Gordon	N	N	Y	N	N
7 *Bryant*	N	Y	N	Y	N
8 Tanner	N	N	Y	N	N
9 Ford	N	N	Y	N	Y
TEXAS					
1 Sandlin	N	N	Y	N	N
2 Turner	N	N	Y	N	N
3 *Johnson, Sam*	N	N	N	Y	N
4 Hall	N	N	N	Y	N
5 *Sessions*	N	Y	N	Y	N
6 *Barton*	N	Y	N	Y	N
7 *Archer*	N	N	N	Y	N
8 *Brady*	N	Y	N	Y	N
9 Lampson	N	N	Y	N	Y
10 Doggett	Y	N	Y	N	Y
11 Edwards	N	N	Y	N	N
12 *Granger*	N	Y	N	N	N
13 *Thornberry*	N	N	N	Y	N
14 *Paul*	N	Y	N	Y	Y
15 Hinojosa	N	N	Y	N	N
16 Reyes	N	N	Y	N	N
17 Stenholm	N	N	N	Y	N
18 Jackson-Lee	N	N	Y	N	Y
19 *Combest*	N	N	N	Y	N
20 Gonzalez	?	?	?	?	?
21 *Smith*	N	N	Y	N	N
22 *DeLay*	N	Y	N	Y	N
23 *Bonilla*	N	N	N	Y	N
24 Frost	Y	N	Y	N	N
25 Bentsen	N	N	Y	N	Y
26 *Armey*	N	N	N	Y	N
27 Ortiz	N	N	Y	N	N
28 Rodriguez	N	N	Y	N	N
29 Green	N	N	Y	N	N
30 Johnson, E.B.	N	N	Y	N	N
UTAH					
1 *Hansen*	N	N	N	N	N
2 *Cook*	N	N	Y	N	Y
3 *Cannon*	N	N	N	Y	N
VERMONT					
AL *Sanders*	N	N	Y	N	N
VIRGINIA					
1 *Bateman*	N	N	N	N	N
2 Pickett	N	N	Y	N	N
3 Scott	N	N	Y	N	Y
4 Sisisky	N	N	Y	N	N
5 Goode	N	N	Y	Y	N
6 *Goodlatte*	N	N	Y	Y	N
7 *Bliley*	N	N	N	Y	N
8 Moran	N	N	Y	N	N
9 Boucher	N	N	Y	N	?
10 *Wolf*	N	Y	N	?	N
11 *Davis*	N	N	Y	N	Y
WASHINGTON					
1 *White*	N	N	N	N	N
2 *Metcalf*	N	N	Y	Y	N
3 *Smith, Linda*	N	Y	N	Y	N
4 *Hastings*	N	Y	N	Y	N
5 *Nethercutt*	N	N	N	N	N
6 Dicks	N	N	Y	N	Y
7 McDermott	Y	N	Y	N	Y
8 *Dunn*	N	N	N	N	N
9 Smith, Adam	Y	N	Y	N	Y
WEST VIRGINIA					
1 Mollohan	N	N	Y	N	N
2 Wise	N	N	Y	N	N
3 Rahall	N	N	Y	Y	N
WISCONSIN					
1 *Neumann*	N	?	?	?	?
2 *Klug*	N	Y	Y	N	N
3 Kind	N	N	Y	N	Y
4 Kleczka	N	N	Y	N	N
5 Barrett	N	N	Y	N	N
6 *Petri*	N	N	Y	Y	N
7 Obey	N	N	Y	N	N
8 Johnson	N	N	Y	N	N
9 *Sensenbrenner*	N	N	Y	Y	N
WYOMING					
AL *Cubin*	N	N	N	N	N

Southern states - Ala., Ark., Fla., Ga., Ky., La., Miss., N.C., Okla., S.C., Tenn., Texas, Va.

HOUSE VOTES 360, 361, 362, 363, 364, 365

360. HR 2159. Fiscal 1998 Foreign Operations Appropriations/School of the Americas. Torres, D-Calif., amendment to prohibit funding in the bill for the Army's School of the Americas. Rejected 210-217: R 47-174; D 162-43 (ND 134-17, SD 28-26); I 1-0, Sept. 4, 1997.

361. HR 2159. Fiscal 1998 Foreign Operations Appropriations/NATO Expansion Payments. Stearns, R-Fla., amendment to express the sense of Congress that all member nations of the North Atlantic Treaty Organization (NATO) should contribute proportionately to pay for the Partnership for Peace program and other costs associated with NATO expansion. Adopted 425-0: R 221-0; D 203-0 (ND 149-0, SD 54-0); I 1-0, Sept. 4, 1997.

362. HR 2159. Fiscal 1998 Foreign Operations Appropriations/Overseas Abortion Funding. Gilman, R-N.Y., amendment to the Smith, R-N.J., amendment to allow organizations that do not promote abortion as a method of family planning but use their own funds to perform abortions to remain eligible for international family planning funding. The amendment also would prohibit funding for lobbying for or against abortion, and for the U.N. Population Fund unless the president certifies that the organization has ceased all activity in China. Rejected 210-218: R 38-185; D 171-33 (ND 125-26, SD 46-7); I 1-0, Sept. 4, 1997.

363. HR 2159. Fiscal 1998 Foreign Operations Appropriations/International Family Planning Funding Restrictions. Smith, R-N.J., amendment to prohibit funding to any private, non-governmental or multilateral organization that directly or indirectly performs abortions in a foreign country, except in cases of rape, incest or when the life of the mother is endangered. The amendment also would prohibit funding for any foreign organization that lobbies for or against abortion, and for the U.N. Population Fund unless the organization ceases all activities in China. Adopted 234-191: R 192-29; D 42-161 (ND 33-117, SD 9-44); I 0-1, Sept. 4, 1997. A "nay" was a vote in support of the president's position.

364. HR 2159. Fiscal 1998 Foreign Operations Appropriations/Passage. Passage of the bill to provide about $12.3 billion for foreign operations and export financing in fiscal 1998. The bill would provide $86,730 less than in fiscal 1997 and $4.6 billion less than the president's request. Passed 375-49: R 185-35; D 190-13 (ND 143-7, SD 47-6); I 0-1, Sept. 4, 1997.

365. Procedural Motion/Journal. Approval of the House Journal of Wednesday, Sept. 3, 1997. Approved 363-46: R 198-15; D 164-31 (ND 120-23, SD 44-8); I 1-0, Sept. 4, 1997.

[1] *Susan Molinari, R-N.Y., resigned on Aug. 1, 1997.*

KEY

- Y Voted for (yea).
- # Paired for.
- + Announced for.
- N Voted against (nay).
- X Paired against.
- – Announced against.
- P Voted "present."
- C Voted "present" to avoid possible conflict of interest.
- ? Did not vote or otherwise make a position known.

Democrats ***Republicans***
Independent

	360	361	362	363	364	365
ALABAMA						
1 ***Callahan***	N	Y	N	Y	Y	Y
2 ***Everett***	N	Y	N	Y	Y	Y
3 ***Riley***	N	Y	N	Y	Y	Y
4 ***Aderholt***	N	Y	N	Y	Y	Y
5 Cramer	N	Y	Y	Y	Y	Y
6 ***Bachus***	N	Y	N	Y	Y	Y
7 Hilliard	N	Y	Y	N	Y	N
ALASKA						
AL ***Young***	N	Y	N	Y	Y	?
ARIZONA						
1 ***Salmon***	Y	Y	N	Y	?	Y
2 Pastor	Y	Y	Y	N	Y	N
3 ***Stump***	N	Y	N	Y	N	Y
4 ***Shadegg***	N	Y	N	Y	Y	Y
5 ***Kolbe***	N	Y	Y	N	Y	Y
6 ***Hayworth***	N	Y	N	Y	Y	Y
ARKANSAS						
1 Berry	N	Y	Y	Y	N	Y
2 Snyder	N	Y	Y	N	Y	Y
3 ***Hutchinson***	N	Y	N	Y	Y	Y
4 ***Dickey***	N	Y	N	Y	Y	Y
CALIFORNIA						
1 ***Riggs***	N	Y	N	Y	Y	Y
2 ***Herger***	N	Y	N	Y	Y	Y
3 Fazio	Y	Y	Y	N	Y	N
4 ***Doolittle***	N	Y	N	Y	N	Y
5 Matsui	Y	Y	Y	N	Y	Y
6 Woolsey	Y	Y	Y	N	Y	Y
7 Miller	Y	Y	Y	N	Y	N
8 Pelosi	Y	Y	Y	N	Y	Y
9 Dellums	Y	Y	Y	N	Y	Y
10 Tauscher	Y	Y	Y	N	Y	Y
11 ***Pombo***	N	Y	N	Y	N	N
12 Lantos	Y	Y	Y	N	Y	?
13 Stark	Y	Y	Y	N	Y	Y
14 Eshoo	Y	Y	Y	N	Y	Y
15 ***Campbell***	Y	Y	Y	N	N	Y
16 Lofgren	Y	Y	Y	N	Y	Y
17 Farr	Y	Y	Y	N	Y	Y
18 Condit	N	Y	Y	Y	N	Y
19 ***Radanovich***	N	Y	N	Y	Y	Y
20 Dooley	Y	Y	Y	N	Y	Y
21 ***Thomas***	N	Y	Y	Y	Y	Y
22 Capps	Y	Y	Y	N	Y	Y
23 ***Gallegly***	N	Y	N	Y	Y	Y
24 Sherman	Y	Y	Y	N	Y	Y
25 ***McKeon***	N	?	N	Y	Y	Y
26 Berman	Y	Y	Y	N	Y	Y
27 ***Rogan***	N	Y	N	Y	Y	Y
28 ***Dreier***	N	Y	N	Y	Y	Y
29 Waxman	Y	Y	Y	N	Y	Y
30 Becerra	Y	Y	Y	N	Y	Y
31 Martinez	N	Y	Y	N	Y	Y
32 Dixon	Y	Y	Y	N	Y	Y
33 Roybal-Allard	Y	Y	Y	N	Y	Y
34 Torres	Y	Y	Y	N	Y	Y
35 Waters	Y	Y	Y	N	Y	N
36 Harman	Y	Y	Y	N	Y	?
37 Millender-McD.	N	Y	Y	N	Y	Y
38 ***Horn***	N	Y	Y	N	Y	Y
39 ***Royce***	N	Y	N	Y	N	Y
40 ***Lewis***	N	Y	Y	Y	Y	Y
41 ***Kim***	N	Y	N	Y	Y	Y
42 Brown	Y	Y	Y	N	Y	N
43 ***Calvert***	N	Y	N	Y	Y	Y
44 ***Bono***	N	Y	N	Y	Y	?
45 ***Rohrabacher***	N	Y	N	Y	N	Y
46 Sanchez	Y	Y	Y	N	Y	Y
47 ***Cox***	N	Y	N	Y	Y	Y
48 ***Packard***	N	Y	N	Y	Y	Y
49 ***Bilbray***	?	Y	Y	N	Y	Y
50 Filner	Y	Y	Y	N	Y	N
51 ***Cunningham***	N	Y	N	Y	Y	Y
52 ***Hunter***	N	Y	N	Y	Y	Y
COLORADO						
1 DeGette	Y	Y	Y	N	Y	Y
2 Skaggs	Y	Y	Y	N	Y	Y
3 ***McInnis***	N	Y	N	Y	Y	Y
4 ***Schaffer***	Y	Y	N	Y	N	N
5 ***Hefley***	N	Y	N	Y	N	N
6 ***Schaefer***	N	Y	N	Y	N	Y
CONNECTICUT						
1 Kennelly	Y	Y	Y	N	Y	Y
2 Gejdenson	Y	Y	Y	N	Y	Y
3 DeLauro	Y	Y	Y	N	Y	Y
4 ***Shays***	Y	Y	Y	N	Y	Y
5 Maloney	Y	Y	Y	N	Y	Y
6 ***Johnson***	Y	Y	Y	N	Y	Y
DELAWARE						
AL ***Castle***	N	Y	Y	N	Y	Y
FLORIDA						
1 ***Scarborough***	Y	Y	N	Y	Y	Y
2 Boyd	N	Y	Y	N	Y	Y
3 Brown	N	Y	Y	N	Y	Y
4 ***Fowler***	N	Y	Y	Y	Y	Y
5 Thurman	Y	Y	Y	N	Y	Y
6 ***Stearns***	N	Y	N	Y	N	Y
7 ***Mica***	N	Y	N	Y	Y	Y
8 ***McCollum***	?	?	N	Y	Y	Y
9 ***Bilirakis***	N	Y	N	Y	Y	Y
10 ***Young***	N	Y	N	Y	N	?
11 Davis	N	Y	Y	N	Y	Y
12 ***Canady***	N	Y	N	Y	Y	Y
13 ***Miller***	N	Y	N	Y	Y	Y
14 ***Goss***	N	Y	N	Y	Y	Y
15 ***Weldon***	N	Y	N	Y	Y	Y
16 ***Foley***	Y	Y	Y	Y	Y	Y
17 Meek	N	Y	Y	N	Y	Y
18 ***Ros-Lehtinen***	N	Y	N	Y	Y	Y
19 Wexler	Y	Y	Y	N	Y	Y
20 Deutsch	N	Y	Y	N	Y	Y
21 ***Diaz-Balart***	N	Y	N	Y	Y	Y
22 ***Shaw***	N	Y	Y	Y	Y	Y
23 Hastings	N	Y	Y	N	Y	Y
GEORGIA						
1 ***Kingston***	N	Y	N	Y	Y	Y
2 Bishop	N	Y	Y	N	Y	Y
3 ***Collins***	N	Y	N	Y	Y	Y
4 McKinney	Y	Y	Y	N	Y	Y
5 Lewis	Y	Y	Y	N	Y	Y
6 ***Gingrich***	N					
7 ***Barr***	N	Y	N	Y	N	Y
8 ***Chambliss***	N	Y	N	Y	Y	Y
9 ***Deal***	N	Y	N	Y	N	Y
10 ***Norwood***	N	Y	N	Y	N	Y
11 ***Linder***	N	Y	N	Y	Y	Y
HAWAII						
1 Abercrombie	Y	Y	Y	N	Y	N
2 Mink	Y	Y	Y	N	Y	Y
IDAHO						
1 ***Chenoweth***	N	Y	N	Y	N	Y
2 ***Crapo***	N	Y	N	Y	Y	Y
ILLINOIS						
1 Rush	Y	Y	Y	N	Y	Y
2 Jackson	Y	Y	Y	N	Y	Y
3 Lipinski	Y	Y	N	Y	Y	Y
4 Gutierrez	Y	Y	Y	N	Y	Y
5 Blagojevich	Y	Y	Y	N	Y	Y
6 ***Hyde***	N	Y	N	Y	Y	Y
7 Davis	Y	Y	Y	N	Y	Y
8 ***Crane***	N	Y	N	Y	Y	Y
9 Yates	Y	Y	Y	N	Y	?
10 ***Porter***	Y	Y	Y	N	Y	Y
11 ***Weller***	N	Y	N	Y	Y	N
12 Costello	Y	Y	N	Y	Y	Y
13 ***Fawell***	Y	Y	Y	N	Y	Y
14 ***Hastert***	N	Y	N	Y	Y	Y
15 ***Ewing***	N	Y	N	Y	Y	Y

ND Northern Democrats SD Southern Democrats

	360	361	362	363	364	365
16 ***Manzullo***	N	Y	N	Y	Y	Y
17 Evans	Y	Y	Y	N	Y	Y
18 ***LaHood***	N	Y	N	Y	Y	Y
19 Poshard	Y	Y	N	Y	Y	N
20 ***Shimkus***	N	Y	N	Y	Y	Y
INDIANA						
1 Visclosky	N	Y	Y	N	Y	N
2 ***McIntosh***	N	Y	N	Y	Y	Y
3 Roemer	Y	Y	N	Y	N	Y
4 ***Souder***	N	Y	N	Y	Y	Y
5 ***Buyer***	N	Y	N	Y	Y	?
6 ***Burton***	N	Y	N	Y	Y	Y
7 ***Pease***	N	Y	N	Y	Y	Y
8 ***Hostettler***	N	Y	N	Y	N	Y
9 Hamilton	N	Y	Y	Y	Y	Y
10 Carson	Y	Y	Y	N	N	Y
IOWA						
1 ***Leach***	Y	Y	Y	N	Y	Y
2 ***Nussle***	Y	Y	N	Y	Y	Y
3 Boswell	N	Y	Y	N	Y	Y
4 ***Ganske***	N	Y	N	Y	Y	Y
5 ***Latham***	N	Y	N	Y	Y	Y
KANSAS						
1 ***Moran***	Y	Y	N	Y	N	N
2 ***Ryun***	N	Y	N	Y	Y	Y
3 ***Snowbarger***	N	Y	N	Y	Y	Y
4 ***Tiahrt***	N	Y	N	Y	Y	Y
KENTUCKY						
1 ***Whitfield***	N	Y	N	Y	Y	Y
2 ***Lewis***	N	Y	N	Y	Y	Y
3 ***Northup***	N	Y	N	Y	Y	Y
4 ***Bunning***	Y	Y	N	Y	Y	Y
5 ***Rogers***	N	Y	N	Y	N	Y
6 Baesler	Y	Y	Y	N	Y	Y
LOUISIANA						
1 ***Livingston***	N	Y	N	Y	Y	Y
2 Jefferson	Y	Y	Y	N	Y	Y
3 ***Tauzin***	N	Y	N	Y	Y	Y
4 ***McCrery***	N	Y	N	Y	Y	Y
5 ***Cooksey***	N	Y	N	Y	Y	Y
6 ***Baker***	N	Y	N	Y	Y	Y
7 John	N	Y	N	Y	N	Y
MAINE						
1 Allen	Y	Y	Y	N	Y	Y
2 Baldacci	Y	Y	Y	N	Y	Y
MARYLAND						
1 ***Gilchrest***	Y	Y	Y	N	Y	Y
2 ***Ehrlich***	N	Y	Y	N	Y	Y
3 Cardin	Y	Y	Y	N	Y	Y
4 Wynn	Y	Y	Y	N	Y	N
5 Hoyer	N	Y	Y	N	Y	Y
6 ***Bartlett***	N	Y	N	Y	Y	Y
7 Cummings	Y	Y	Y	N	Y	Y
8 ***Morella***	Y	Y	Y	N	Y	Y
MASSACHUSETTS						
1 Olver	Y	Y	Y	N	Y	Y
2 Neal	Y	Y	Y	Y	Y	Y
3 McGovern	Y	Y	Y	N	Y	Y
4 Frank	Y	Y	Y	N	Y	Y
5 Meehan	Y	Y	Y	N	Y	Y
6 Tierney	Y	Y	Y	N	Y	Y
7 Markey	Y	Y	Y	N	Y	Y
8 Kennedy	Y	Y	Y	N	Y	Y
9 Moakley	Y	?	Y	Y	Y	Y
10 Delahunt	Y	Y	Y	N	Y	Y
MICHIGAN						
1 Stupak	Y	Y	N	Y	Y	N
2 ***Hoekstra***	N	Y	N	Y	Y	Y
3 ***Ehlers***	Y	Y	N	Y	Y	Y
4 ***Camp***	Y	Y	N	Y	Y	Y
5 Barcia	Y	Y	N	Y	Y	Y
6 ***Upton***	Y	Y	N	Y	Y	Y
7 ***Smith***	Y	Y	N	Y	Y	Y
8 Stabenow	Y	Y	Y	N	Y	Y
9 Kildee	Y	Y	N	Y	Y	Y
10 Bonior	Y	Y	Y	Y	Y	Y
11 ***Knollenberg***	N	Y	N	Y	Y	Y
12 Levin	Y	Y	Y	N	Y	Y
13 Rivers	Y	Y	Y	N	Y	Y
14 Conyers	Y	Y	Y	N	N	Y
15 Kilpatrick	Y	Y	Y	N	Y	Y
16 Dingell	N	Y	Y	N	Y	Y
MINNESOTA						
1 ***Gutknecht***	Y	Y	N	Y	Y	N
2 Minge	Y	Y	Y	N	N	Y

	360	361	362	363	364	365
3 ***Ramstad***	Y	Y	Y	N	Y	N
4 Vento	Y	Y	Y	N	Y	Y
5 Sabo	Y	Y	Y	N	Y	N
6 Luther	Y	Y	Y	N	Y	Y
7 Peterson	Y	Y	N	Y	Y	Y
8 Oberstar	Y	Y	N	Y	Y	N
MISSISSIPPI						
1 ***Wicker***	N	Y	N	Y	Y	Y
2 Thompson	Y	Y	Y	N	Y	N
3 ***Pickering***	N	Y	N	Y	Y	Y
4 ***Parker***	N	Y	N	Y	Y	Y
5 Taylor	N	Y	N	Y	N	N
MISSOURI						
1 Clay	Y	Y	Y	N	Y	N
2 ***Talent***	Y	Y	N	Y	Y	Y
3 Gephardt	Y	Y	Y	N	Y	N
4 Skelton	N	Y	N	Y	Y	Y
5 McCarthy	Y	Y	Y	N	Y	Y
6 Danner	N	Y	Y	Y	Y	Y
7 ***Blunt***	N	Y	N	Y	Y	Y
8 ***Emerson***	N	Y	N	Y	Y	Y
9 ***Hulshof***	Y	Y	N	Y	Y	N
MONTANA						
AL ***Hill***	N	Y	N	Y	Y	N
NEBRASKA						
1 ***Bereuter***	N	Y	N	Y	Y	Y
2 ***Christensen***	N	Y	N	Y	Y	Y
3 ***Barrett***	N	Y	N	Y	N	Y
NEVADA						
1 ***Ensign***	N	Y	N	Y	Y	N
2 ***Gibbons***	Y	Y	Y	Y	Y	N
NEW HAMPSHIRE						
1 ***Sununu***	N	Y	N	Y	Y	Y
2 ***Bass***	N	Y	Y	N	Y	Y
NEW JERSEY						
1 Andrews	N	Y	Y	N	Y	Y
2 ***LoBiondo***	Y	Y	N	Y	Y	N
3 ***Saxton***	N	Y	N	Y	Y	Y
4 ***Smith***	Y	Y	N	Y	Y	Y
5 ***Roukema***	Y	Y	Y	N	Y	Y
6 Pallone	Y	Y	Y	N	Y	Y
7 ***Franks***	Y	Y	Y	N	Y	Y
8 Pascrell	Y	Y	Y	N	Y	N
9 Rothman	Y	?	Y	N	Y	Y
10 Payne	Y	Y	Y	N	Y	Y
11 ***Frelinghuysen***	N	Y	Y	N	Y	Y
12 ***Pappas***	N	Y	N	Y	Y	Y
13 Menendez	N	Y	Y	N	Y	Y
NEW MEXICO						
1 ***Schiff***	?	?	?	?	?	?
2 ***Skeen***	N	Y	Y	Y	Y	Y
3 ***Redmond***	N	Y	N	Y	Y	Y
NEW YORK						
1 ***Forbes***	Y	Y	N	Y	Y	Y
2 ***Lazio***	Y	Y	Y	N	Y	Y
3 ***King***	N	Y	N	Y	Y	?
4 McCarthy	Y	Y	Y	N	Y	Y
5 Ackerman	Y	Y	Y	N	Y	Y
6 Flake	Y	Y	Y	N	Y	Y
7 Manton	Y	Y	N	Y	Y	Y
8 Nadler	Y	Y	Y	?	Y	Y
9 Schumer	Y	Y	Y	N	Y	Y
10 Towns	Y	Y	Y	N	Y	?
11 Owens	Y	Y	Y	N	Y	Y
12 Velazquéz	Y	Y	Y	N	Y	Y
13 Vacant[1]						
14 Maloney	Y	Y	Y	N	Y	N
15 Rangel	Y	Y	Y	N	Y	Y
16 Serrano	Y	Y	Y	N	Y	Y
17 Engel	Y	Y	Y	N	Y	Y
18 Lowey	Y	Y	Y	N	Y	N
19 ***Kelly***	Y	Y	Y	N	Y	Y
20 ***Gilman***	N	Y	Y	N	Y	Y
21 McNulty	Y	Y	Y	N	Y	N
22 ***Solomon***	N	Y	N	Y	N	Y
23 ***Boehlert***	Y	Y	Y	N	Y	Y
24 ***McHugh***	N	Y	N	Y	Y	Y
25 ***Walsh***	Y	Y	N	Y	Y	Y
26 Hinchey	Y	Y	Y	N	Y	Y
27 ***Paxon***	N	Y	N	Y	Y	Y
28 Slaughter	Y	Y	Y	N	Y	N
29 LaFalce	N	Y	N	Y	Y	Y
30 ***Quinn***	Y	Y	N	Y	Y	Y
31 ***Houghton***	?	Y	Y	N	Y	Y

	360	361	362	363	364	365
NORTH CAROLINA						
1 Clayton	Y	Y	Y	N	Y	?
2 Etheridge	Y	Y	Y	N	Y	Y
3 ***Jones***	N	Y	N	?	N	Y
4 Price	Y	Y	Y	N	Y	Y
5 ***Burr***	N	Y	N	Y	Y	Y
6 ***Coble***	Y	Y	N	Y	Y	Y
7 McIntyre	N	Y	N	Y	Y	Y
8 Hefner	Y	Y	Y	N	Y	Y
9 ***Myrick***	N	Y	N	Y	Y	Y
10 ***Ballenger***	N	Y	N	Y	Y	Y
11 ***Taylor***	Y	Y	N	Y	Y	?
12 Watt	Y	Y	Y	N	Y	Y
NORTH DAKOTA						
AL Pomeroy	Y	Y	Y	N	Y	Y
OHIO						
1 ***Chabot***	N	Y	N	Y	Y	Y
2 ***Portman***	N	Y	N	Y	Y	Y
3 Hall	Y	Y	N	Y	Y	Y
4 ***Oxley***	N	Y	N	Y	Y	Y
5 ***Gillmor***	N	Y	N	Y	Y	Y
6 Strickland	Y	Y	Y	N	Y	Y
7 ***Hobson***	N	Y	Y	N	Y	Y
8 ***Boehner***	N	Y	N	Y	Y	Y
9 Kaptur	Y	Y	N	Y	Y	Y
10 Kucinich	Y	Y	N	Y	Y	N
11 Stokes	Y	Y	Y	N	Y	?
12 ***Kasich***	N	Y	N	Y	Y	Y
13 Brown	Y	Y	Y	N	Y	Y
14 Sawyer	Y	Y	Y	N	Y	Y
15 ***Pryce***	−	+	+	−	+	?
16 ***Regula***	N	Y	Y	Y	Y	Y
17 Traficant	Y	Y	N	Y	N	Y
18 ***Ney***	N	Y	N	Y	Y	Y
19 ***LaTourette***	Y	Y	N	Y	Y	Y
OKLAHOMA						
1 ***Largent***	N	Y	N	Y	Y	Y
2 ***Coburn***	Y	Y	N	Y	N	Y
3 ***Watkins***	N	Y	N	Y	N	Y
4 ***Watts***	N	Y	N	Y	Y	Y
5 ***Istook***	N	Y	N	Y	Y	Y
6 ***Lucas***	N	Y	N	Y	N	Y
OREGON						
1 Furse	Y	Y	Y	N	Y	?
2 ***Smith***	N	Y	N	Y	Y	Y
3 Blumenauer	Y	Y	Y	N	Y	Y
4 DeFazio	Y	Y	Y	N	Y	N
5 Hooley	Y	Y	Y	N	Y	Y
PENNSYLVANIA						
1 Foglietta	Y	Y	Y	N	Y	?
2 Fattah	Y	Y	Y	N	Y	Y
3 Borski	Y	Y	N	Y	Y	N
4 Klink	Y	Y	N	Y	Y	Y
5 ***Peterson***	N	Y	N	Y	N	Y
6 Holden	Y	Y	N	Y	Y	Y
7 ***Weldon***	N	Y	N	Y	Y	Y
8 ***Greenwood***	Y	Y	Y	N	?	Y
9 ***Shuster***	N	Y	N	Y	Y	Y
10 ***McDade***	N	Y	N	Y	Y	?
11 Kanjorski	Y	Y	N	Y	Y	Y
12 Murtha	N	Y	N	Y	Y	Y
13 ***Fox***	Y	Y	N	Y	Y	N
14 Coyne	Y	Y	Y	N	Y	Y
15 McHale	Y	Y	Y	N	Y	Y
16 ***Pitts***	N	Y	N	Y	Y	Y
17 ***Gekas***	N	Y	N	Y	Y	Y
18 Doyle	Y	Y	N	Y	Y	Y
19 ***Goodling***	Y	Y	N	Y	N	?
20 Mascara	Y	Y	N	Y	Y	Y
21 ***English***	Y	Y	N	Y	Y	N
RHODE ISLAND						
1 Kennedy	Y	Y	Y	N	Y	Y
2 Weygand	Y	Y	N	Y	Y	Y
SOUTH CAROLINA						
1 ***Sanford***	N	Y	N	Y	Y	Y
2 ***Spence***	N	Y	N	Y	Y	Y
3 ***Graham***	N	Y	N	Y	Y	Y
4 ***Inglis***	N	Y	N	Y	Y	Y
5 Spratt	N	Y	Y	N	Y	Y
6 Clyburn	N	Y	Y	N	Y	N
SOUTH DAKOTA						
AL ***Thune***	N	Y	N	Y	Y	Y
TENNESSEE						
1 ***Jenkins***	N	Y	N	Y	Y	Y
2 ***Duncan***	Y	Y	N	Y	N	Y

	360	361	362	363	364	365
3 ***Wamp***	N	Y	N	Y	Y	Y
4 ***Hilleary***	N	Y	N	Y	N	N
5 Clement	Y	Y	Y	N	Y	Y
6 Gordon	Y	Y	Y	N	Y	Y
7 ***Bryant***	N	Y	N	Y	Y	Y
8 Tanner	N	Y	Y	N	N	Y
9 Ford	Y	Y	Y	N	N	Y
TEXAS						
1 Sandlin	N	Y	Y	N	Y	Y
2 Turner	Y	Y	Y	N	Y	Y
3 ***Johnson, Sam***	N	Y	N	Y	Y	Y
4 Hall	N	Y	N	Y	N	Y
5 ***Sessions***	N	Y	N	?	Y	Y
6 ***Barton***	N	Y	N	Y	N	Y
7 ***Archer***	N	Y	N	Y	Y	Y
8 ***Brady***	N	Y	N	Y	Y	Y
9 Lampson	Y	Y	Y	N	Y	Y
10 Doggett	Y	Y	Y	N	Y	N
11 Edwards	N	Y	Y	N	Y	Y
12 ***Granger***	N	Y	N	Y	Y	Y
13 ***Thornberry***	N	Y	N	Y	Y	Y
14 ***Paul***	Y	Y	N	Y	N	Y
15 Hinojosa	Y	Y	Y	N	Y	Y
16 Reyes	N	Y	Y	N	Y	Y
17 Stenholm	N	Y	N	Y	Y	N
18 Jackson-Lee	Y	Y	Y	N	Y	Y
19 ***Combest***	N	Y	N	Y	N	Y
20 Gonzalez	?	?	?	?	?	?
21 ***Smith***	N	Y	N	Y	?	Y
22 ***DeLay***	N	Y	N	Y	Y	?
23 ***Bonilla***	N	Y	N	Y	Y	Y
24 Frost	Y	Y	Y	N	Y	Y
25 Bentsen	Y	Y	Y	N	Y	Y
26 ***Armey***	N	Y	N	Y	Y	Y
27 Ortiz	N	Y	N	Y	Y	Y
28 Rodriguez	Y	Y	Y	N	Y	Y
29 Green	Y	Y	Y	N	Y	Y
30 Johnson, E.B.	Y	Y	Y	N	Y	N
UTAH						
1 ***Hansen***	N	Y	N	Y	N	Y
2 ***Cook***	N	Y	N	Y	Y	Y
3 ***Cannon***	N	Y	N	Y	Y	Y
VERMONT						
AL *Sanders*	Y	Y	Y	N	N	Y
VIRGINIA						
1 ***Bateman***	N	Y	N	Y	Y	Y
2 Pickett	N	Y	Y	N	Y	N
3 Scott	N	Y	Y	N	Y	Y
4 Sisisky	N	Y	Y	N	Y	Y
5 Goode	Y	Y	N	Y	Y	Y
6 ***Goodlatte***	N	Y	N	Y	Y	Y
7 ***Bliley***	N	Y	N	Y	Y	Y
8 Moran	Y	Y	Y	N	Y	Y
9 Boucher	Y	Y	?	?	?	?
10 ***Wolf***	N	Y	N	Y	Y	Y
11 ***Davis***	N	Y	Y	N	Y	?
WASHINGTON						
1 ***White***	N	Y	Y	N	Y	Y
2 ***Metcalf***	N	Y	N	Y	Y	Y
3 ***Smith, Linda***	N	Y	N	Y	Y	Y
4 ***Hastings***	N	Y	N	Y	N	Y
5 ***Nethercutt***	N	Y	N	Y	Y	Y
6 Dicks	N	Y	Y	N	Y	?
7 McDermott	Y	Y	Y	N	Y	Y
8 ***Dunn***	N	Y	Y	Y	Y	Y
9 Smith, Adam	Y	Y	Y	N	Y	Y
WEST VIRGINIA						
1 Mollohan	N	Y	N	Y	Y	Y
2 Wise	N	Y	Y	N	Y	Y
3 Rahall	Y	Y	N	Y	N	Y
WISCONSIN						
1 ***Neumann***	?	?	−	+	+	?
2 ***Klug***	Y	Y	Y	N	Y	Y
3 Kind	Y	Y	Y	N	+	Y
4 Kleczka	Y	Y	Y	Y	Y	Y
5 Barrett	Y	Y	Y	N	Y	Y
6 ***Petri***	Y	Y	N	Y	N	Y
7 Obey	Y	Y	Y	N	Y	Y
8 Johnson	Y	Y	Y	N	Y	Y
9 ***Sensenbrenner***	Y	Y	N	Y	N	Y
WYOMING						
AL ***Cubin***	N	Y	N	Y	Y	Y

Southern states - Ala., Ark., Fla., Ga., Ky., La., Miss., N.C., Okla., S.C., Tenn., Texas, Va.

HOUSE VOTES 366, 367, 368, 369, 370, 371, 372, 373

366. Procedural Motion/Adjourn. Miller, D-Calif., motion to adjourn. Rejected 44-339: R 1-198; D 43-141 (ND 30-104, SD 13-37); I 0-0, Sept. 5, 1997.

367. HR 2264. Fiscal 1998 Labor-HHS Appropriations/Wage and Hour Enforcement Bureau. McIntosh, R-Ind., amendment to reduce funding for the Wage and Hour Enforcement Bureau by $4.3 million and redirect the funds to the Individuals with Disabilities Education Act program. Rejected 167-260: R 164-59; D 3-200 (ND 0-151, SD 3-49); I 0-1, Sept. 5, 1997.

368. HR 1119. Defense Authorization/Motion to Instruct. Traficant, D-Ohio, motion to instruct House conferees to insist upon House provisions to allow the secretary of Defense to assign up to 10,000 military personnel to assist the Immigration and Naturalization Service and the Customs Service in border-control activities. Approved 261-150: R 191-20; D 70-129 (ND 49-98, SD 21-31); I 0-1, Sept. 5, 1997.

369. HR 2264. Fiscal 1998 Labor-HHS Appropriations/OSHA Funding. Blunt, R-Mo., amendment to reduce funding levels for the Occupational Health and Safety Administration by $11.25 million and transfer the same amount to vocational and adult education programs. Rejected 160-237: R 155-56; D 5-180 (ND 0-135, SD 5-45); I 0-1, Sept. 8, 1997.

370. HR 2264. Fiscal 1998 Labor-HHS Appropriations/OSHA Funding. Norwood, R-Ga., amendment that would reduce funding levels for the Occupational Health and Safety Administration by $11.25 million and transfer the same amount to programs under the Individuals with Disabilities Education Act. Rejected 157-240: R 152-59; D 5-180 (ND 0-134, SD 5-46); I 0-1, Sept. 8, 1997.

371. Procedural Motion/Adjourn. Miller, D-Calif., motion to adjourn. Motion rejected 43-347: R 2-208; D 41-139 (ND 34-98, SD 7-41); I 0-0, Sept. 9, 1997.

372. Procedural Motion/Adjourn. Doggett, D-Texas, motion to adjourn. Motion rejected 29-367: R 0-216; D 29-151 (ND 23-108, SD 6-43); I 0-0, Sept. 9, 1997.

373. HR 2264. Fiscal 1998 Labor-HHS Appropriations/OSHA Funding. Souder, R-Ind., amendment to transfer $23 million from Occupational Safety and Health Administration (OSHA) accounts that enforce compliance with OSHA rules to an account that aids companies in complying with OSHA rules. Rejected 164-255: R 156-64; D 8-190 (ND 2-143, SD 6-47); I 0-1, Sept. 9, 1997.

KEY

- Y Voted for (yea).
- # Paired for.
- + Announced for.
- N Voted against (nay).
- X Paired against.
- – Announced against.
- P Voted "present."
- C Voted "present" to avoid possible conflict of interest.
- ? Did not vote or otherwise make a position known.

Democrats ***Republicans***
Independent

	366	367	368	369	370	371	372	373
ALABAMA								
1 ***Callahan***	N	Y	?	Y	Y	N	N	N
2 ***Everett***	N	Y	?	Y	Y	N	N	Y
3 ***Riley***	N	Y	Y	Y	Y	N	N	Y
4 ***Aderholt***	N	Y	Y	Y	Y	N	N	Y
5 Cramer	N	N	Y	N	N	N	N	Y
6 ***Bachus***	?	Y	Y	Y	Y	N	N	Y
7 Hilliard	N	N	N	?	?	?	?	?
ALASKA								
AL ***Young***	?	Y	?	Y	Y	?	N	N
ARIZONA								
1 ***Salmon***	N	Y	Y	Y	Y	N	N	Y
2 Pastor	N	N	N	N	N	N	N	N
3 ***Stump***	N	Y	N	Y	Y	Y	N	Y
4 ***Shadegg***	N	Y	Y	Y	Y	N	N	Y
5 ***Kolbe***	N	Y	N	Y	N	N	N	N
6 ***Hayworth***	N	Y	N	Y	Y	N	N	Y
ARKANSAS								
1 Berry	Y	N	N	N	N	Y	Y	N
2 Snyder	N	N	N	N	N	N	N	N
3 ***Hutchinson***	N	Y	Y	Y	Y	N	N	Y
4 ***Dickey***	N	Y	Y	N	N	N	N	N
CALIFORNIA								
1 ***Riggs***	N	Y	Y	Y	Y	?	?	Y
2 ***Herger***	?	Y	Y	Y	Y	N	N	N
3 Fazio	N	N	N	N	N	N	N	N
4 ***Doolittle***	N	Y	N	Y	Y	N	N	Y
5 Matsui	N	N	N	N	N	Y	?	N
6 Woolsey	Y	N	N	N	N	Y	Y	N
7 Miller	Y	N	N	?	?	Y	Y	N
8 Pelosi	?	N	?	N	?	Y	Y	N
9 Dellums	?	N	N	?	?	?	?	?
10 Tauscher	N	N	Y	N	N	N	N	N
11 ***Pombo***	?	Y	N	Y	Y	N	N	Y
12 Lantos	N	N	Y	N	N	N	N	N
13 Stark	Y	N	N	N	N	Y	Y	N
14 Eshoo	Y	N	Y	N	N	Y	Y	N
15 ***Campbell***	N	N	Y	N	N	N	N	Y
16 Lofgren	N	N	N	N	N	N	N	N
17 Farr	Y	N	N	N	N	Y	Y	N
18 Condit	N	N	Y	N	N	N	N	N
19 ***Radanovich***	?	Y	Y	Y	?	Y	N	Y
20 Dooley	N	N	N	N	N	N	N	N
21 ***Thomas***	N	N	Y	Y	?	N	N	N
22 Capps	N	N	N	–	–	N	N	N
23 ***Gallegly***	N	Y	Y	?	?	N	N	Y
24 Sherman	N	N	Y	N	N	N	N	N
25 ***McKeon***	N	Y	Y	Y	Y	N	N	Y
26 Berman	N	N	N	N	N	N	N	N
27 ***Rogan***	N	Y	Y	Y	Y	N	N	Y
28 ***Dreier***	N	Y	Y	Y	Y	N	N	Y
29 Waxman	N	N	?	N	N	N	N	N
30 Becerra	N	N	N	N	N	N	N	N
31 Martinez	?	N	Y	N	N	N	N	N
32 Dixon	?	N	N	N	N	N	N	N
33 Roybal-Allard	N	N	N	N	N	N	N	N
34 Torres	?	N	N	N	N	Y	Y	N
35 Waters	Y	N	N	N	N	Y	N	N
36 Harman	N	N	Y	N	N	N	N	N
37 Millender-McD.	Y	N	N	N	N	Y	N	N
38 ***Horn***	N	Y	Y	N	N	N	N	N
39 ***Royce***	N	Y	Y	Y	Y	N	N	Y
40 ***Lewis***	N	N	?	N	N	N	N	N
41 ***Kim***	N	N	Y	N	Y	N	N	N
42 Brown	?	N	N	N	N	N	?	N
43 ***Calvert***	N	Y	Y	Y	Y	N	N	Y
44 ***Bono***	?	Y	Y	Y	Y	N	?	Y
45 ***Rohrabacher***	N	Y	Y	Y	Y	N	N	Y
46 Sanchez	N	N	Y	N	N	N	N	N
47 ***Cox***	?	Y	Y	Y	Y	?	N	?
48 ***Packard***	N	Y	Y	Y	Y	N	N	Y
49 ***Bilbray***	N	Y	Y	Y	Y	N	N	N
50 Filner	Y	N	N	N	N	Y	Y	N
51 ***Cunningham***	N	Y	Y	Y	Y	N	N	N
52 ***Hunter***	N	Y	Y	Y	Y	N	N	Y
COLORADO								
1 DeGette	N	N	N	N	N	Y	N	N
2 Skaggs	N	N	N	N	N	?	N	N
3 ***McInnis***	N	Y	N	?	?	N	N	Y
4 ***Schaffer***	N	Y	Y	Y	Y	N	N	Y
5 ***Hefley***	N	Y	Y	Y	Y	N	N	Y
6 ***Schaefer***	N	Y	Y	Y	Y	N	N	Y
CONNECTICUT								
1 Kennelly	N	N	N	N	N	N	N	N
2 Gejdenson	Y	N	N	N	N	Y	Y	N
3 DeLauro	Y	N	N	N	N	Y	Y	N
4 ***Shays***	N	N	Y	N	N	N	N	N
5 Maloney	N	N	Y	N	N	N	N	N
6 ***Johnson***	N	N	Y	N	N	N	N	N
DELAWARE								
AL ***Castle***	N	N	Y	N	N	N	N	N
FLORIDA								
1 ***Scarborough***	N	Y	Y	Y	#	N	N	Y
2 Boyd	Y	N	Y	N	N	N	N	N
3 Brown	?	N	N	N	N	N	N	N
4 ***Fowler***	N	Y	N	Y	Y	N	N	Y
5 Thurman	N	N	Y	N	N	Y	Y	N
6 ***Stearns***	N	Y	Y	Y	Y	N	N	Y
7 ***Mica***	N	Y	Y	Y	Y	N	N	Y
8 ***McCollum***	N	Y	?	Y	Y	?	N	Y
9 ***Bilirakis***	N	Y	Y	Y	Y	N	N	Y
10 ***Young***	N	N	Y	?	?	N	N	N
11 Davis	Y	N	N	N	N	Y	Y	N
12 ***Canady***	N	Y	Y	Y	Y	N	N	Y
13 ***Miller***	N	N	?	N	N	N	N	N
14 ***Goss***	N	Y	Y	Y	N	N	N	Y
15 ***Weldon***	N	Y	Y	Y	Y	N	N	Y
16 ***Foley***	N	N	Y	Y	N	N	N	Y
17 Meek	Y	N	N	N	N	N	?	N
18 ***Ros-Lehtinen***	N	N	Y	N	N	N	N	N
19 Wexler	N	N	Y	N	N	N	N	N
20 Deutsch	Y	N	Y	N	N	N	N	N
21 ***Diaz-Balart***	N	N	Y	N	N	N	N	N
22 ***Shaw***	?	N	Y	Y	N	N	N	N
23 Hastings	Y	N	N	N	N	Y	Y	N
GEORGIA								
1 ***Kingston***	N	Y	Y	Y	Y	N	N	Y
2 Bishop	Y	N	Y	N	N	N	N	N
3 ***Collins***	N	Y	Y	Y	Y	N	N	Y
4 McKinney	N	N	N	N	N	N	N	N
5 Lewis	Y	N	N	N	N	Y	Y	N
6 ***Gingrich***						N		
7 ***Barr***	N	Y	Y	Y	Y	N	N	Y
8 ***Chambliss***	N	Y	Y	Y	Y	N	N	Y
9 ***Deal***	?	Y	Y	Y	Y	N	N	Y
10 ***Norwood***	N	Y	Y	Y	Y	N	?	Y
11 ***Linder***	N	Y	N	Y	Y	N	N	Y
HAWAII								
1 Abercrombie	?	N	N	N	N	N	N	N
2 Mink	Y	N	N	N	N	Y	Y	N
IDAHO								
1 ***Chenoweth***	N	Y	N	Y	Y	–	N	Y
2 ***Crapo***	N	Y	N	Y	Y	N	N	Y
ILLINOIS								
1 Rush	N	N	N	N	N	N	N	N
2 Jackson	N	N	N	N	N	Y	N	N
3 Lipinski	N	N	?	N	N	N	N	N
4 Gutierrez	Y	N	N	N	N	N	N	N
5 Blagojevich	N	N	N	N	N	N	N	N
6 ***Hyde***	N	N	Y	N	N	N	N	N
7 Davis	N	N	N	N	N	N	N	N
8 ***Crane***	?	Y	Y	Y	Y	?	N	Y
9 Yates	N	N	N	N	?	Y	N	N
10 ***Porter***	N	N	Y	N	N	N	N	N
11 ***Weller***	?	Y	Y	Y	N	N	N	Y
12 Costello	N	N	Y	N	N	N	N	N
13 ***Fawell***	N	N	Y	N	N	N	N	N
14 ***Hastert***	N	Y	Y	Y	N	N	N	Y
15 ***Ewing***	N	N	Y	N	N	N	N	Y

ND Northern Democrats SD Southern Democrats

	366	367	368	369	370	371	372	373
16 **Manzullo**	N	Y	Y	Y	Y	N	N	Y
17 Evans	N	N	N	N	N	N	N	N
18 **LaHood**	N	N	Y	N	N	N	N	N
19 Poshard	N	N	Y	N	N	N	N	N
20 **Shimkus**	N	Y	Y	N	N	N	N	Y
INDIANA								
1 Visclosky	N	N	N	N	N	N	N	N
2 **McIntosh**	N	Y	Y	Y	Y	N	N	Y
3 Roemer	N	N	Y	N	N	N	N	N
4 **Souder**	N	Y	Y	Y	Y	N	N	Y
5 **Buyer**	N	Y	N	Y	Y	N	N	Y
6 **Burton**	N	Y	Y	Y	Y	N	N	Y
7 **Pease**	N	Y	Y	N	N	N	N	Y
8 **Hostettler**	N	Y	Y	Y	Y	N	?	Y
9 Hamilton	N	N	N	N	N	N	N	N
10 Carson	N	N	N	-	-	-	-	-
IOWA								
1 **Leach**	N	N	Y	N	N	?	N	N
2 **Nussle**	N	Y	Y	Y	Y	N	N	Y
3 Boswell	Y	N	Y	N	N	N	N	N
4 **Ganske**	N	N	Y	Y	Y	N	N	Y
5 **Latham**	N	Y	Y	Y	Y	N	N	Y
KANSAS								
1 **Moran**	N	Y	Y	Y	Y	N	N	Y
2 **Ryun**	N	Y	N	Y	Y	N	N	Y
3 **Snowbarger**	N	Y	Y	Y	Y	N	N	Y
4 **Tiahrt**	N	Y	Y	Y	Y	N	N	Y
KENTUCKY								
1 **Whitfield**	N	N	N	?	Y	N	N	N
2 **Lewis**	N	Y	Y	Y	Y	N	N	Y
3 **Northup**	N	Y	Y	N	N	N	N	N
4 **Bunning**	N	Y	Y	Y	Y	N	N	Y
5 **Rogers**	N	Y	Y	Y	Y	N	N	N
6 Baesler	N	N	Y	N	N	N	?	N
LOUISIANA								
1 **Livingston**	N	N	Y	N	N	N	N	N
2 Jefferson	Y	N	N	?	N	N	N	N
3 **Tauzin**	N	Y	Y	N	Y	N	N	Y
4 **McCrery**	?	Y	Y	N	Y	N	N	Y
5 **Cooksey**	?	Y	Y	?	Y	N	N	Y
6 **Baker**	N	Y	?	?	?	?	?	?
7 John	N	N	Y	N	N	N	N	N
MAINE								
1 Allen	N	N	N	N	N	Y	Y	N
2 Baldacci	N	N	N	N	N	N	N	N
MARYLAND								
1 **Gilchrest**	N	Y	Y	N	Y	N	N	N
2 **Ehrlich**	N	Y	Y	Y	Y	N	N	Y
3 Cardin	N	N	N	N	N	N	N	N
4 Wynn	N	N	N	N	N	N	N	N
5 Hoyer	N	N	N	N	N	?	?	N
6 **Bartlett**	N	Y	Y	Y	Y	N	N	Y
7 Cummings	N	N	Y	N	N	N	N	N
8 **Morella**	N	N	Y	N	N	N	N	N
MASSACHUSETTS								
1 Olver	N	N	N	N	N	Y	N	N
2 Neal	N	N	N	N	N	N	N	N
3 McGovern	?	N	N	N	N	N	N	N
4 Frank	N	N	N	N	N	N	Y	N
5 Meehan	N	N	N	N	N	N	N	N
6 Tierney	N	N	N	N	N	N	?	N
7 Markey	Y	N	N	N	N	N	N	N
8 Kennedy	Y	N	N	N	N	N	?	N
9 Moakley	?	N	Y	N	N	N	N	N
10 Delahunt	?	N	N	N	N	N	?	N
MICHIGAN								
1 Stupak	N	N	N	N	N	N	N	N
2 **Hoekstra**	N	Y	Y	Y	Y	N	N	Y
3 **Ehlers**	N	Y	N	Y	Y	N	N	N
4 **Camp**	N	Y	Y	Y	Y	N	N	N
5 Barcia	N	N	Y	?	?	?	N	N
6 **Upton**	N	Y	Y	Y	Y	N	N	Y
7 **Smith**	N	Y	Y	N	Y	N	N	Y
8 Stabenow	N	N	N	N	N	N	N	N
9 Kildee	N	N	N	N	N	N	N	N
10 Bonior	N	N	N	N	N	Y	N	N
11 **Knollenberg**	N	N	Y	?	?	N	N	N
12 Levin	N	N	Y	N	N	N	N	N
13 Rivers	N	N	Y	N	N	N	N	N
14 Conyers	Y	N	N	N	N	?	Y	N
15 Kilpatrick	N	N	Y	N	N	N	N	N
16 Dingell	Y	N	N	?	?	Y	Y	N
MINNESOTA								
1 **Gutknecht**	N	Y	Y	Y	Y	N	N	Y
2 Minge	N	N	Y	N	N	N	N	N

	366	367	368	369	370	371	372	373
3 **Ramstad**	N	Y	Y	Y	Y	N	N	Y
4 Vento	N	N	N	N	N	N	N	N
5 Sabo	N	N	N	N	N	N	N	N
6 Luther	N	N	Y	N	N	N	N	N
7 Peterson	N	N	Y	N	N	N	N	N
8 Oberstar	?	N	Y	N	N	?	?	?
MISSISSIPPI								
1 **Wicker**	N	Y	Y	Y	Y	?	N	Y
2 Thompson	N	N	N	N	N	N	N	N
3 **Pickering**	N	Y	Y	Y	Y	N	N	Y
4 **Parker**	?	Y	?	Y	Y	?	N	N
5 Taylor	N	Y	Y	Y	Y	N	N	Y
MISSOURI								
1 Clay	Y	N	N	N	N	N	N	N
2 **Talent**	N	Y	Y	Y	Y	N	N	Y
3 Gephardt	Y	N	N	?	?	Y	?	N
4 Skelton	N	N	N	N	N	N	N	N
5 McCarthy	N	N	?	-	N	N	N	N
6 Danner	N	N	Y	N	N	N	N	N
7 **Blunt**	N	Y	Y	Y	Y	N	N	Y
8 **Emerson**	N	Y	Y	Y	Y	N	N	Y
9 **Hulshof**	N	Y	Y	Y	Y	N	N	Y
MONTANA								
AL **Hill**	N	Y	Y	Y	Y	N	N	Y
NEBRASKA								
1 **Bereuter**	?	N	Y	Y	Y	N	N	Y
2 **Christensen**	N	Y	Y	Y	Y	N	N	Y
3 **Barrett**	N	N	Y	Y	N	N	N	Y
NEVADA								
1 **Ensign**	N	Y	Y	Y	Y	N	N	Y
2 **Gibbons**	N	Y	Y	Y	Y	N	N	-
NEW HAMPSHIRE								
1 **Sununu**	N	Y	Y	Y	Y	?	N	Y
2 **Bass**	N	Y	Y	Y	Y	N	N	Y
NEW JERSEY								
1 Andrews	Y	N	Y	N	N	Y	N	N
2 **LoBiondo**	N	N	Y	N	N	N	N	N
3 **Saxton**	N	N	Y	N	N	N	N	Y
4 **Smith**	N	N	Y	N	N	N	N	N
5 **Roukema**	N	N	Y	N	N	N	N	N
6 Pallone	N	N	Y	N	N	Y	Y	N
7 **Franks**	N	N	Y	N	N	N	N	N
8 Pascrell	N	N	Y	N	N	N	?	N
9 Rothman	N	N	N	N	N	N	N	N
10 Payne	N	N	N	N	N	N	N	N
11 **Frelinghuysen**	N	N	Y	?	Y	N	N	Y
12 **Pappas**	N	N	Y	N	N	N	N	Y
13 Menendez	N	N	N	N	N	N	N	N
NEW MEXICO								
1 **Schiff**	?	?	?	?	?	?	?	?
2 **Skeen**	N	N	Y	Y	Y	N	N	Y
3 **Redmond**	N	Y	Y	Y	Y	N	N	Y
NEW YORK								
1 **Forbes**	N	N	Y	?	N	N	N	N
2 **Lazio**	N	N	Y	N	N	N	N	N
3 **King**	N	N	Y	N	N	N	N	N
4 McCarthy	N	N	Y	N	N	N	N	N
5 Ackerman	N	N	N	N	N	N	N	N
6 Flake	N	N	N	N	?	N	N	N
7 Manton	N	N	Y	N	N	Y	Y	N
8 Nadler	N	N	N	N	N	?	N	N
9 Schumer	N	N	Y	N	N	?	?	N
10 Towns	Y	N	Y	?	?	?	?	?
11 Owens	?	N	Y	N	N	?	?	?
12 Velázquez	N	N	N	-	-	-	-	N
13 Vacant								
14 Maloney	N	N	Y	N	N	Y	N	N
15 Rangel	Y	N	N	?	?	?	?	N
16 Serrano	N	N	N	?	?	?	?	?
17 Engel	-	N	N	N	N	?	?	N
18 Lowey	Y	N	Y	N	N	Y	Y	N
19 **Kelly**	N	N	Y	N	N	N	N	Y
20 **Gilman**	N	N	Y	N	N	N	N	N
21 McNulty	Y	N	Y	N	N	Y	Y	N
22 **Solomon**	N	Y	?	Y	Y	N	N	Y
23 **Boehlert**	N	N	Y	N	N	N	N	N
24 **McHugh**	N	N	Y	N	N	?	N	N
25 **Walsh**	Y	N	Y	N	N	N	N	N
26 Hinchey	N	N	N	N	N	?	N	N
27 **Paxon**	N	Y	Y	Y	Y	N	N	Y
28 Slaughter	?	N	N	N	?	Y	Y	N
29 LaFalce	Y	N	Y	N	N	Y	N	N
30 **Quinn**	N	N	Y	?	?	?	?	?
31 **Houghton**	?	N	N	N	?	N	N	N

	366	367	368	369	370	371	372	373
NORTH CAROLINA								
1 Clayton	N	N	N	N	N	N	N	N
2 Etheridge	N	N	Y	N	N	N	N	N
3 **Jones**	N	Y	Y	Y	Y	N	N	Y
4 Price	N	N	Y	N	N	N	N	N
5 **Burr**	N	Y	Y	Y	Y	N	?	Y
6 **Coble**	N	Y	Y	Y	Y	N	N	Y
7 McIntyre	N	N	Y	N	Y	N	N	N
8 Hefner	?	N	N	N	N	?	N	N
9 **Myrick**	N	Y	Y	Y	Y	N	N	Y
10 **Ballenger**	N	+	+	Y	Y	N	N	Y
11 **Taylor**	N	Y	Y	Y	Y	N	N	N
12 Watt	N	N	N	N	N	N	N	N
NORTH DAKOTA								
AL Pomeroy	N	N	N	N	N	?	?	N
OHIO								
1 **Chabot**	N	Y	Y	Y	Y	N	N	Y
2 **Portman**	N	Y	Y	Y	Y	N	N	Y
3 Hall	N	N	Y	N	N	N	N	N
4 **Oxley**	?	Y	Y	Y	Y	N	N	N
5 **Gillmor**	N	Y	Y	N	N	N	N	N
6 Strickland	N	N	Y	N	N	N	N	N
7 **Hobson**	N	Y	Y	Y	N	N	N	N
8 **Boehner**	N	Y	Y	Y	Y	N	N	Y
9 Kaptur	N	N	Y	N	N	N	N	N
10 Kucinich	N	N	Y	N	N	N	N	N
11 Stokes	N	N	N	N	N	N	N	N
12 **Kasich**	N	Y	Y	?	Y	N	N	Y
13 Brown	N	N	N	N	N	N	N	N
14 Sawyer	N	N	N	N	N	N	N	N
15 **Pryce**	?	?	?	Y	Y	N	N	Y
16 **Regula**	N	Y	Y	N	N	N	N	N
17 Traficant	N	N	Y	N	N	N	N	Y
18 **Ney**	N	Y	Y	N	N	N	N	N
19 **LaTourette**	?	N	Y	N	N	N	N	N
OKLAHOMA								
1 **Largent**	N	Y	Y	Y	Y	N	N	Y
2 **Coburn**	N	Y	Y	Y	Y	N	N	Y
3 **Watkins**	N	Y	Y	Y	Y	N	N	Y
4 **Watts**	N	Y	Y	Y	Y	N	N	Y
5 **Istook**	N	Y	?	Y	Y	N	N	Y
6 **Lucas**	N	Y	N	Y	Y	N	N	Y
OREGON								
1 Furse	Y	N	N	N	N	Y	N	N
2 **Smith**	N	Y	Y	Y	Y	N	N	Y
3 Blumenauer	N	N	N	N	N	N	N	N
4 DeFazio	Y	N	N	N	N	Y	Y	N
5 Hooley	N	N	N	N	N	N	N	N
PENNSYLVANIA								
1 Foglietta	?	N	N	N	?	?	?	N
2 Fattah	N	N	N	N	N	N	N	N
3 Borski	N	N	N	N	N	N	N	N
4 Klink	Y	N	Y	?	?	N	N	N
5 **Peterson**	N	Y	Y	Y	Y	N	N	Y
6 Holden	N	N	Y	N	N	N	N	N
7 **Weldon**	?	N	Y	N	N	?	N	N
8 **Greenwood**	N	N	Y	N	N	N	N	Y
9 **Shuster**	N	Y	Y	?	?	N	N	Y
10 **McDade**	?	N	Y	N	N	?	N	N
11 Kanjorski	N	N	N	N	N	N	N	N
12 Murtha	N	N	N	?	N	N	N	N
13 **Fox**	N	N	Y	N	N	N	N	N
14 Coyne	Y	N	N	N	N	Y	Y	N
15 McHale	N	N	N	N	N	N	N	N
16 **Pitts**	N	Y	Y	Y	Y	N	N	Y
17 **Gekas**	N	N	Y	N	N	N	N	N
18 Doyle	N	N	Y	N	N	N	N	Y
19 **Goodling**	N	N	Y	N	N	?	N	Y
20 Mascara	N	N	Y	N	N	N	N	N
21 **English**	N	N	Y	N	N	N	N	N
RHODE ISLAND								
1 Kennedy	?	N	N	-	N	N	N	N
2 Weygand	N	N	N	?	N	?	N	N
SOUTH CAROLINA								
1 **Sanford**	N	Y	Y	Y	Y	N	N	Y
2 **Spence**	N	Y	Y	Y	Y	N	N	Y
3 **Graham**	N	Y	?	Y	Y	N	N	Y
4 **Inglis**	N	Y	Y	Y	Y	N	N	Y
5 Spratt	N	N	N	N	N	N	N	N
6 Clyburn	N	N	N	N	N	N	N	N
SOUTH DAKOTA								
AL **Thune**	N	Y	Y	Y	Y	N	N	Y
TENNESSEE								
1 **Jenkins**	N	Y	Y	Y	Y	N	N	Y
2 **Duncan**	N	Y	Y	Y	Y	N	N	Y

	366	367	368	369	370	371	372	
3 **Wamp**	N	Y	Y	Y	Y	N	N	Y
4 **Hilleary**	N	Y	Y	Y	Y	N	N	Y
5 Clement	Y	N	Y	N	N	N	N	N
6 Gordon	N	N	Y	N	N	N	N	N
7 **Bryant**	N	Y	Y	Y	Y	N	N	Y
8 Tanner	N	N	Y	Y	N	N	N	Y
9 Ford	Y	N	N	N	N	Y	N	N
TEXAS								
1 Sandlin	N	N	Y	N	N	N	N	N
2 Turner	N	N	Y	N	N	N	N	N
3 **Johnson, Sam**	N	Y	Y	Y	Y	N	N	Y
4 Hall	N	Y	Y	Y	Y	N	N	Y
5 **Sessions**	?	Y	N	Y	Y	N	N	Y
6 **Barton**	?	Y	Y	Y	Y	N	N	Y
7 **Archer**	?	Y	Y	Y	Y	N	?	Y
8 **Brady**	N	Y	Y	Y	Y	N	N	Y
9 Lampson	N	N	N	N	N	N	N	N
10 Doggett	N	N	N	N	N	Y	Y	N
11 Edwards	N	N	N	N	N	N	N	N
12 **Granger**	N	Y	Y	Y	Y	N	N	Y
13 **Thornberry**	N	Y	Y	Y	Y	N	N	Y
14 **Paul**	N	Y	N	Y	Y	N	N	Y
15 Hinojosa	N	N	N	N	N	N	N	N
16 Reyes	Y	N	N	N	N	?	?	N
17 Stenholm	N	?	?	Y	Y	?	N	Y
18 Jackson-Lee	N	N	N	?	X	N	N	N
19 **Combest**	N	Y	Y	Y	Y	N	N	Y
20 Gonzalez	?	?	?	?	?	?	?	?
21 **Smith**	N	Y	Y	Y	Y	N	N	Y
22 **DeLay**	N	Y	Y	Y	Y	N	N	Y
23 **Bonilla**	N	Y	N	Y	Y	N	N	N
24 Frost	N	N	N	N	N	N	N	N
25 Bentsen	N	N	N	N	N	N	N	N
26 **Armey**	N	Y	Y	Y	Y	N	N	Y
27 Ortiz	N	N	N	N	N	N	N	N
28 Rodriguez	N	N	N	N	N	N	N	N
29 Green	N	N	N	N	N	N	N	N
30 Johnson, E.B.	Y	N	N	N	N	N	N	N
UTAH								
1 **Hansen**	N	Y	Y	?	?	N	N	Y
2 **Cook**	N	Y	Y	Y	Y	N	N	Y
3 **Cannon**	N	Y	N	Y	Y	N	N	?
VERMONT								
AL Sanders	?	N	N	N	N	?	?	N
VIRGINIA								
1 **Bateman**	?	N	Y	N	N	N	?	N
2 Pickett	N	N	Y	?	?	N	N	N
3 Scott	N	N	N	N	N	N	N	N
4 Sisisky	N	N	Y	N	N	N	N	N
5 Goode	N	Y	Y	Y	Y	N	N	Y
6 **Goodlatte**	N	Y	Y	Y	Y	N	N	Y
7 **Bliley**	N	Y	Y	?	?	N	N	Y
8 Moran	?	N	N	N	N	?	?	N
9 Boucher	?	?	?	N	N	?	N	N
10 **Wolf**	N	N	Y	N	N	N	N	N
11 **Davis**	N	N	Y	N	N	N	N	N
WASHINGTON								
1 **White**	N	Y	Y	Y	Y	N	N	Y
2 **Metcalf**	N	Y	N	N	N	N	N	N
3 **Smith, Linda**	N	N	?	Y	Y	N	N	Y
4 **Hastings**	N	Y	Y	Y	Y	N	N	Y
5 **Nethercutt**	N	N	Y	Y	Y	N	N	Y
6 Dicks	N	N	Y	N	N	N	N	N
7 McDermott	Y	N	N	N	N	Y	Y	N
8 **Dunn**	N	Y	Y	Y	Y	N	N	Y
9 Smith, Adam	N	N	N	N	N	N	N	N
WEST VIRGINIA								
1 Mollohan	N	N	N	N	N	N	N	N
2 Wise	N	N	Y	N	N	N	N	N
3 Rahall	N	N	Y	N	N	N	N	N
WISCONSIN								
1 **Neumann**	N	Y	Y	Y	Y	N	N	Y
2 **Klug**	N	Y	Y	Y	Y	N	N	Y
3 Kind	N	N	Y	N	N	N	N	N
4 Kleczka	?	N	N	N	N	N	N	N
5 Barrett	N	N	N	N	N	N	N	N
6 **Petri**	N	N	Y	N	N	N	N	N
7 Obey	N	N	N	N	N	N	N	N
8 Johnson	N	N	N	N	N	N	N	N
9 **Sensenbrenner**	N	Y	Y	Y	Y	N	N	Y
WYOMING								
AL **Cubin**	?	Y	Y	Y	Y	N	N	Y

Southern states - Ala., Ark., Fla., Ga., Ky., La., Miss., N.C., Okla., S.C., Tenn., Texas, Va.

HOUSE VOTES 374, 376, 377, 378, 379, 380, 381, 382 *

374. HR 2264. Fiscal 1998 Labor-HHS Appropriations/Motion to Rise. McIntosh, R-Ind., motion to rise from the Committee of the Whole. Motion rejected 42-375: R 39-181; D 3-193 (ND 3-142, SD 0-51); I 0-1, Sept. 9, 1997.

*** 376. HR 2264. Fiscal 1998 Labor-HHS Appropriations/Civic Education.** Burton, R-Ind., amendment that would increase by $1 million funding for the "We the People . . . Project Citizen" civic education program on the Constitution and Bill of Rights. Adopted 417-3: R 220-3; D 196-0 (ND 144-0, SD 52-0); I 1-0, Sept. 9, 1997.

377. HR 2264. Fiscal 1998 Labor-HHS Appropriations/AIDS Drug Assistance Programs. Coburn, R-Okla., amendment to increase funding by $34.9 million for state AIDS Drug Assistance Programs that support low-income people with HIV who do not qualify for Medicaid. It also would make corresponding reductions in spending for refugee assistance, the Department of Health and Human Services' policy research and general management accounts and the Health Care Policy and Research account. Rejected 141-282: R 135-89; D 6-192 (ND 4-141, SD 2-51); I 0-1, Sept. 9, 1997.

378. HR 2264. Fiscal 1998 Labor-HHS Appropriations/Parental Consent. Castle, R-Del., substitute amendment to the pending Istook, R-Okla., amendment to prohibit the use of federal funds by any organization unless it encourages family participation in the decision of minors to seek family planning services and provides counseling to minors on how to resist being coerced into sexual activity. The Istook amendment would require parental notification. Adopted 220-201: R 46-178; D 173-23 (ND 127-17, SD 46-6); I 1-0, Sept. 9, 1997.

379. HR 2264. Fiscal 1998 Labor-HHS Appropriations/Federally Funded Family Planning Services. Istook, R-Okla., amendment, as amended, to prohibit the use of federal funds by any organization unless it encourages family participation in the decision of minors to seek family planning services and provides counseling to minors on how to resist being coerced into sexual activity. Adopted 254-169: R 73-152; D 180-17 (ND 132-12, SD 48-5); I 1-0, Sept. 9, 1997.

380. Procedural Motion/Adjourn. Miller, D-Calif., motion to adjourn. Rejected 37-370: R 0-218; D 37-151 (ND 29-109, SD 8-42); I 0-1, Sept. 10, 1997.

381. Procedural Motion/Journal. Approval of House Journal of Tuesday, Sept. 9, 1997. Approved 352-58: R 196-20; D 155-38 (ND 112-30, SD 43-8); I 1-0, Sept. 10, 1997.

382. Procedural Motion/Adjourn. McDermott, D-Wash., motion to adjourn. Rejected 36-368: R 1-209; D 35-158 (ND 26-116, SD 9-42); I 0-1, Sept. 10, 1997.

** NOTE: Omitted votes are quorum calls. CQ does not include quorum calls in its vote charts.*

KEY

- Y Voted for (yea).
- # Paired for.
- \+ Announced for.
- N Voted against (nay).
- X Paired against.
- – Announced against.
- P Voted "present."
- C Voted "present" to avoid possible conflict of interest.
- ? Did not vote or otherwise make a position known.

Democrats ***Republicans***
Independent

	374	376	377	378	379	380	381	382
ALABAMA								
1 ***Callahan***	N	Y	N	N	N	N	Y	N
2 ***Everett***	N	Y	N	N	N	N	N	N
3 ***Riley***	Y	Y	Y	N	N	N	Y	N
4 ***Aderholt***	Y	Y	Y	N	N	N	Y	N
5 Cramer	N	Y	N	Y	Y	N	Y	N
6 ***Bachus***	Y	Y	Y	N	N	N	Y	N
7 Hilliard	?	?	?	?	?	N	N	N
ALASKA								
AL ***Young***	N	Y	N	N	N	N	Y	N
ARIZONA								
1 ***Salmon***	N	Y	Y	N	N	N	Y	N
2 Pastor	N	Y	N	Y	Y	N	Y	N
3 ***Stump***	N	Y	Y	N	N	N	Y	N
4 ***Shadegg***	Y	Y	Y	N	N	N	Y	N
5 ***Kolbe***	N	Y	N	Y	Y	N	Y	N
6 ***Hayworth***	N	Y	Y	N	N	N	Y	N
ARKANSAS								
1 Berry	N	?	N	Y	Y	Y	Y	Y
2 Snyder	N	Y	N	Y	Y	N	Y	N
3 ***Hutchinson***	N	Y	Y	N	Y	N	Y	?
4 ***Dickey***	N	Y	?	N	N	N	N	N
CALIFORNIA								
1 ***Riggs***	N	Y	N	Y	Y	N	Y	N
2 ***Herger***	Y	Y	Y	N	N	N	Y	N
3 Fazio	N	Y	N	Y	Y	N	N	N
4 ***Doolittle***	Y	Y	Y	N	N	N	Y	N
5 Matsui	N	Y	N	Y	Y	N	Y	N
6 Woolsey	N	Y	N	Y	Y	Y	Y	Y
7 Miller	N	Y	N	Y	Y	Y	N	Y
8 Pelosi	N	Y	N	Y	Y	Y	Y	Y
9 Dellums	?	?	?	?	?	?	?	?
10 Tauscher	N	Y	N	Y	Y	N	Y	N
11 ***Pombo***	N	Y	Y	N	N	N	N	N
12 Lantos	N	Y	N	Y	Y	N	Y	N
13 Stark	N	Y	N	Y	Y	N	Y	N
14 Eshoo	N	Y	N	Y	Y	Y	Y	Y
15 ***Campbell***	N	Y	N	Y	Y	N	Y	N
16 Lofgren	N	Y	N	Y	Y	N	Y	N
17 Farr	N	Y	N	Y	Y	Y	Y	Y
18 Condit	N	Y	N	Y	Y	N	Y	N
19 ***Radanovich***	N	Y	Y	N	N	N	Y	N
20 Dooley	N	Y	N	Y	Y	N	Y	N
21 ***Thomas***	N	N	N	Y	Y	N	Y	N
22 Capps	N	Y	N	Y	Y	N	Y	N
23 ***Gallegly***	N	Y	Y	N	Y	N	Y	N
24 Sherman	N	Y	N	Y	Y	N	Y	N
25 ***McKeon***	N	Y	Y	N	N	N	?	N
26 Berman	N	Y	N	Y	Y	N	Y	N
27 ***Rogan***	Y	Y	Y	N	N	N	N	N
28 ***Dreier***	N	Y	Y	N	Y	N	Y	N
29 Waxman	N	Y	N	Y	Y	Y	Y	?
30 Becerra	N	?	N	Y	Y	N	Y	N
31 Martinez	N	Y	N	Y	Y	N	Y	N
32 Dixon	N	Y	N	Y	Y	?	Y	N
33 Roybal-Allard	N	Y	N	Y	Y	N	Y	N
34 Torres	N	?	N	Y	Y	Y	Y	N
35 Waters	N	Y	N	Y	Y	?	?	?
36 Harman	N	Y	N	Y	Y	N	Y	N
37 Millender-McD.	N	Y	N	Y	Y	N	Y	N
38 ***Horn***	N	Y	N	Y	Y	N	Y	N
39 ***Royce***	Y	Y	Y	N	N	N	Y	N
40 ***Lewis***	N	Y	N	Y	Y	N	Y	N
41 ***Kim***	N	Y	N	N	Y	N	Y	N
42 Brown	?	Y	N	Y	Y	N	N	N
43 ***Calvert***	N	Y	Y	N	N	N	Y	N
44 ***Bono***	?	Y	Y	N	N	?	?	N
45 ***Rohrabacher***	N	Y	Y	N	N	N	Y	N
46 Sanchez	N	Y	N	Y	Y	N	Y	N
47 ***Cox***	N	Y	N	N	N	N	Y	N
48 ***Packard***	N	Y	N	N	N	N	Y	N
49 ***Bilbray***	N	Y	N	Y	N	N	Y	N
50 Filner	N	Y	N	Y	Y	Y	N	Y
51 ***Cunningham***	N	Y	Y	N	N	N	Y	N
52 ***Hunter***	N	Y	Y	N	N	N	Y	N
COLORADO								
1 DeGette	N	Y	N	Y	Y	N	Y	N
2 Skaggs	N	Y	N	Y	Y	N	Y	N
3 ***McInnis***	N	Y	Y	N	N	N	Y	N
4 ***Schaffer***	Y	Y	Y	N	N	N	N	N
5 ***Hefley***	N	Y	Y	N	N	N	N	N
6 ***Schaefer***	N	Y	N	N	N	N	Y	N
CONNECTICUT								
1 Kennelly	N	Y	N	Y	Y	N	Y	N
2 Gejdenson	N	Y	N	Y	Y	Y	Y	Y
3 DeLauro	N	Y	N	Y	Y	Y	N	Y
4 ***Shays***	N	Y	N	Y	Y	N	Y	N
5 Maloney	N	Y	N	Y	Y	N	Y	N
6 ***Johnson***	N	Y	N	Y	Y	N	Y	N
DELAWARE								
AL ***Castle***	N	Y	N	Y	Y	N	Y	N
FLORIDA								
1 ***Scarborough***	Y	Y	Y	N	N	N	Y	N
2 Boyd	N	Y	N	Y	Y	Y	Y	Y
3 Brown	N	Y	N	Y	Y	N	Y	N
4 ***Fowler***	N	Y	N	Y	Y	N	Y	N
5 Thurman	N	Y	N	Y	Y	N	Y	Y
6 ***Stearns***	N	Y	Y	N	N	N	N	N
7 ***Mica***	N	Y	Y	N	N	N	Y	N
8 ***McCollum***	N	Y	N	N	N	N	Y	?
9 ***Bilirakis***	N	Y	N	N	N	N	Y	N
10 ***Young***	N	Y	N	N	N	N	Y	N
11 Davis	N	Y	N	Y	Y	Y	Y	Y
12 ***Canady***	N	Y	Y	N	N	N	Y	N
13 ***Miller***	N	Y	N	Y	Y	N	Y	N
14 ***Goss***	N	Y	Y	N	N	N	Y	N
15 ***Weldon***	Y	Y	Y	N	Y	N	Y	?
16 ***Foley***	?	Y	N	Y	Y	N	Y	N
17 Meek	N	Y	N	Y	Y	N	Y	N
18 ***Ros-Lehtinen***	N	Y	N	N	N	N	Y	N
19 Wexler	N	Y	N	Y	Y	N	Y	N
20 Deutsch	N	Y	N	Y	Y	N	Y	N
21 ***Diaz-Balart***	N	Y	N	N	N	N	Y	N
22 ***Shaw***	N	Y	N	N	Y	N	Y	N
23 Hastings	N	Y	N	Y	Y	Y	Y	Y
GEORGIA								
1 ***Kingston***	N	Y	N	N	Y	N	Y	N
2 Bishop	N	Y	N	Y	Y	N	Y	N
3 ***Collins***	N	Y	Y	N	N	N	Y	N
4 McKinney	N	Y	N	Y	Y	N	Y	N
5 Lewis	N	Y	N	?	Y	Y	N	Y
6 ***Gingrich***								
7 ***Barr***	Y	Y	Y	N	N	N	Y	N
8 ***Chambliss***	N	Y	Y	N	Y	N	Y	N
9 ***Deal***	N	Y	Y	N	Y	N	Y	N
10 ***Norwood***	Y	Y	Y	N	N	N	Y	N
11 ***Linder***	N	Y	N	N	Y	N	Y	N
HAWAII								
1 Abercrombie	N	Y	N	Y	Y	N	N	N
2 Mink	N	Y	N	Y	Y	Y	Y	Y
IDAHO								
1 ***Chenoweth***	Y	Y	Y	N	N	N	Y	?
2 ***Crapo***	N	Y	Y	N	N	?	?	N
ILLINOIS								
1 Rush	N	Y	N	Y	Y	N	Y	N
2 Jackson	N	Y	N	Y	Y	N	Y	N
3 Lipinski	N	Y	N	N	N	N	Y	N
4 Gutierrez	N	Y	N	Y	Y	N	Y	N
5 Blagojevich	N	Y	N	Y	Y	N	Y	N
6 ***Hyde***	N	Y	N	N	N	N	Y	N
7 Davis	N	Y	N	Y	Y	?	?	N
8 ***Crane***	N	Y	Y	N	N	?	Y	N
9 Yates	Y	Y	N	Y	Y	Y	Y	N
10 ***Porter***	N	Y	N	Y	Y	N	Y	N
11 ***Weller***	N	Y	Y	N	Y	N	N	N
12 Costello	N	Y	N	N	N	N	N	N
13 ***Fawell***	N	Y	N	Y	Y	N	N	N
14 ***Hastert***	Y	Y	Y	N	N	N	Y	?
15 ***Ewing***	N	Y	Y	N	N	N	Y	N

ND Northern Democrats SD Southern Democrats

	374	376	377	378	379	380	381	382
16 **Manzullo**	Y	Y	Y	N	N	N	Y	N
17 Evans	N	Y	N	Y	Y	N	Y	N
18 **LaHood**	N	Y	N	N	N	N	Y	N
19 Poshard	N	Y	N	N	N	N	N	N
20 **Shimkus**	Y	Y	N	N	N	N	Y	N
INDIANA								
1 Visclosky	N	Y	N	N	Y	N	N	N
2 **McIntosh**	Y	Y	Y	N	N	N	Y	N
3 Roemer	N	Y	N	Y	Y	N	Y	N
4 **Souder**	Y	Y	Y	N	N	N	Y	N
5 **Buyer**	N	Y	N	Y	Y	N	Y	Y
6 **Burton**	N	Y	Y	N	N	N	Y	N
7 **Pease**	N	Y	N	N	N	N	Y	N
8 **Hostettler**	Y	Y	Y	N	N	N	Y	N
9 Hamilton	N	Y	N	Y	Y	N	Y	N
10 Carson	–	+	–	+	+	–	+	–
IOWA								
1 **Leach**	N	Y	N	Y	Y	N	Y	N
2 **Nussle**	N	Y	Y	N	N	N	Y	N
3 Boswell	N	Y	N	Y	Y	N	Y	N
4 **Ganske**	N	Y	Y	Y	Y	N	Y	N
5 **Latham**	N	Y	N	N	N	N	Y	N
KANSAS								
1 **Moran**	N	Y	Y	N	Y	N	Y	N
2 **Ryun**	Y	Y	Y	N	N	N	Y	N
3 **Snowbarger**	Y	Y	Y	N	N	N	Y	N
4 **Tiahrt**	Y	Y	Y	N	N	N	Y	N
KENTUCKY								
1 **Whitfield**	N	Y	N	N	N	N	Y	N
2 **Lewis**	N	Y	Y	N	N	N	Y	N
3 **Northup**	N	Y	N	N	N	N	Y	N
4 **Bunning**	N	Y	Y	N	N	N	Y	N
5 **Rogers**	N	Y	N	N	N	N	Y	N
6 Baesler	N	Y	N	Y	Y	N	Y	?
LOUISIANA								
1 **Livingston**	N	Y	N	N	N	?	Y	N
2 Jefferson	N	Y	N	Y	Y	N	Y	N
3 **Tauzin**	N	Y	Y	N	Y	N	Y	N
4 **McCrery**	N	Y	N	N	Y	N	Y	N
5 **Cooksey**	N	Y	Y	?	N	N	Y	N
6 **Baker**	N	Y	Y	N	N	N	Y	N
7 John	N	Y	N	Y	Y	N	Y	N
MAINE								
1 Allen	N	Y	N	Y	Y	Y	Y	Y
2 Baldacci	N	Y	N	Y	Y	N	Y	N
MARYLAND								
1 **Gilchrest**	N	Y	N	Y	Y	N	Y	N
2 **Ehrlich**	N	Y	Y	Y	Y	N	Y	N
3 Cardin	N	Y	N	Y	Y	N	Y	N
4 Wynn	N	Y	N	Y	Y	N	N	N
5 Hoyer	N	Y	N	Y	Y	N	Y	N
6 **Bartlett**	N	Y	Y	N	N	N	Y	N
7 Cummings	N	Y	N	Y	Y	N	Y	?
8 **Morella**	N	Y	N	Y	Y	?	?	?
MASSACHUSETTS								
1 Olver	N	Y	N	Y	Y	Y	Y	Y
2 Neal	N	Y	N	Y	Y	N	Y	N
3 McGovern	N	Y	N	Y	Y	N	Y	N
4 Frank	N	Y	N	Y	Y	N	Y	Y
5 Meehan	N	Y	N	Y	Y	Y	Y	N
6 Tierney	N	Y	N	Y	Y	N	Y	N
7 Markey	N	Y	N	Y	Y	N	Y	N
8 Kennedy	N	Y	N	Y	Y	N	Y	N
9 Moakley	N	Y	N	Y	Y	N	Y	N
10 Delahunt	N	Y	N	Y	Y	Y	N	N
MICHIGAN								
1 Stupak	N	Y	Y	Y	Y	N	N	Y
2 **Hoekstra**	N	Y	Y	N	N	N	Y	N
3 **Ehlers**	N	Y	N	N	N	N	Y	N
4 **Camp**	N	Y	Y	N	N	N	Y	N
5 Barcia	N	Y	N	N	N	N	Y	N
6 **Upton**	N	Y	Y	Y	Y	N	Y	N
7 **Smith**	N	Y	Y	N	N	N	Y	N
8 Stabenow	N	Y	N	Y	Y	N	Y	N
9 Kildee	N	Y	N	N	N	N	Y	N
10 Bonior	N	Y	N	Y	Y	Y	N	Y
11 **Knollenberg**	N	Y	N	N	Y	N	Y	N
12 Levin	N	Y	N	Y	Y	N	Y	N
13 Rivers	N	Y	N	Y	Y	N	Y	N
14 Conyers	N	Y	N	Y	Y	?	Y	Y
15 Kilpatrick	N	Y	N	Y	Y	N	Y	N
16 Dingell	N	Y	N	Y	Y	Y	Y	Y
MINNESOTA								
1 **Gutknecht**	N	Y	N	N	N	N	N	N
2 Minge	N	Y	N	Y	Y	N	Y	N

	374	376	377	378	379	380	381	382
3 **Ramstad**	N	Y	Y	Y	Y	N	N	N
4 Vento	N	Y	N	Y	Y	N	Y	N
5 Sabo	Y	Y	N	Y	Y	N	N	N
6 Luther	N	Y	N	Y	Y	N	Y	N
7 Peterson	N	Y	N	N	N	N	Y	N
8 Oberstar	N	Y	N	N	Y	N	N	N
MISSISSIPPI								
1 **Wicker**	N	Y	Y	N	N	N	Y	N
2 Thompson	N	Y	N	Y	Y	N	N	N
3 **Pickering**	N	Y	Y	N	N	N	Y	?
4 **Parker**	N	Y	Y	N	N	N	Y	N
5 Taylor	N	Y	Y	N	N	N	N	N
MISSOURI								
1 Clay	N	Y	N	Y	Y	?	?	N
2 **Talent**	N	Y	Y	N	N	N	Y	N
3 Gephardt	N	Y	N	Y	Y	Y	N	Y
4 Skelton	N	Y	N	N	N	N	Y	N
5 McCarthy	N	Y	N	Y	Y	N	Y	N
6 Danner	N	Y	N	Y	Y	N	Y	N
7 **Blunt**	N	Y	Y	N	Y	N	Y	N
8 **Emerson**	N	Y	Y	N	N	N	Y	N
9 **Hulshof**	N	Y	Y	N	Y	N	Y	N
MONTANA								
AL **Hill**	N	Y	Y	N	N	?	Y	N
NEBRASKA								
1 **Bereuter**	N	Y	N	N	N	N	Y	N
2 **Christensen**	N	Y	Y	N	N	N	Y	N
3 **Barrett**	N	Y	N	N	N	N	Y	N
NEVADA								
1 **Ensign**	N	N	Y	N	N	N	N	N
2 **Gibbons**	N	Y	Y	Y	Y	N	Y	N
NEW HAMPSHIRE								
1 **Sununu**	N	Y	Y	N	Y	N	N	N
2 **Bass**	N	N	Y	Y	Y	N	Y	N
NEW JERSEY								
1 Andrews	N	Y	N	Y	Y	N	Y	N
2 **LoBiondo**	N	Y	N	N	N	N	N	N
3 **Saxton**	N	Y	N	N	N	N	Y	N
4 **Smith**	N	Y	N	N	N	?	?	N
5 **Roukema**	N	Y	N	Y	Y	N	Y	?
6 Pallone	N	Y	N	Y	Y	Y	N	Y
7 **Franks**	N	Y	N	Y	Y	N	Y	N
8 Pascrell	N	Y	N	Y	Y	N	N	N
9 Rothman	N	Y	N	Y	Y	N	Y	N
10 Payne	N	Y	N	Y	Y	?	?	N
11 **Frelinghuysen**	N	Y	N	Y	Y	N	Y	N
12 **Pappas**	Y	Y	Y	N	N	N	Y	N
13 Menendez	N	Y	N	Y	Y	N	N	N
NEW MEXICO								
1 **Schiff**	?	?	?	?	?	?	?	?
2 **Skeen**	N	Y	N	Y	Y	N	Y	N
3 **Redmond**	N	Y	Y	N	N	N	Y	N
NEW YORK								
1 **Forbes**	N	Y	Y	N	N	N	Y	N
2 **Lazio**	N	Y	N	Y	Y	N	Y	N
3 **King**	N	Y	N	N	N	N	Y	N
4 McCarthy	N	Y	N	Y	Y	N	Y	N
5 Ackerman	N	Y	N	Y	Y	N	Y	N
6 Flake	N	Y	N	?	?	N	Y	N
7 Manton	N	Y	N	Y	Y	N	Y	N
8 Nadler	N	Y	N	?	?	N	Y	N
9 Schumer	N	Y	N	Y	Y	N	Y	N
10 Towns	?	?	?	?	?	N	Y	N
11 Owens	?	?	?	Y	Y	?	?	?
12 Velázquez	N	Y	–	+	+	N	N	N
13 Vacant								
14 Maloney	N	Y	N	Y	Y	N	Y	N
15 Rangel	N	Y	N	Y	Y	?	?	?
16 Serrano	?	?	?	?	?	N	Y	N
17 Engel	N	Y	Y	Y	Y	N	Y	N
18 Lowey	N	Y	N	Y	Y	Y	Y	N
19 **Kelly**	N	Y	N	Y	Y	N	Y	N
20 **Gilman**	N	Y	N	Y	Y	N	Y	N
21 McNulty	N	Y	N	Y	Y	Y	Y	Y
22 **Solomon**	?	Y	Y	N	N	N	Y	N
23 **Boehlert**	N	Y	N	Y	Y	N	Y	N
24 **McHugh**	N	Y	N	N	N	N	Y	N
25 **Walsh**	N	Y	N	N	N	N	Y	N
26 Hinchey	N	Y	N	Y	Y	Y	N	Y
27 **Paxon**	N	Y	Y	N	N	N	Y	N
28 Slaughter	N	Y	N	Y	Y	?	?	?
29 LaFalce	N	Y	N	N	N	Y	Y	N
30 **Quinn**	N	Y	N	N	N	N	Y	N
31 **Houghton**	N	Y	N	Y	Y	N	?	?

	374	376	377	378	379	380	381	382
NORTH CAROLINA								
1 Clayton	N	Y	N	Y	Y	?	?	N
2 Etheridge	N	Y	N	Y	Y	N	Y	N
3 **Jones**	Y	Y	Y	N	N	N	Y	N
4 Price	N	Y	N	Y	Y	N	Y	N
5 **Burr**	N	Y	Y	N	Y	N	?	N
6 **Coble**	N	Y	Y	N	N	N	Y	N
7 McIntyre	N	Y	N	N	Y	N	Y	N
8 Hefner	N	Y	N	Y	Y	N	Y	N
9 **Myrick**	N	Y	Y	N	N	N	?	N
10 **Ballenger**	N	Y	Y	N	Y	N	Y	N
11 **Taylor**	N	Y	Y	N	N	N	Y	N
12 Watt	N	Y	N	Y	Y	N	N	N
NORTH DAKOTA								
AL Pomeroy	N	Y	N	Y	Y	N	Y	N
OHIO								
1 **Chabot**	N	Y	Y	N	N	N	Y	N
2 **Portman**	N	Y	N	N	N	N	Y	N
3 Hall	N	Y	N	N	N	N	Y	N
4 **Oxley**	N	Y	N	Y	Y	N	Y	N
5 **Gillmor**	N	Y	Y	N	Y	N	Y	N
6 Strickland	Y	Y	N	Y	Y	N	N	N
7 **Hobson**	N	Y	Y	Y	Y	N	Y	N
8 **Boehner**	N	?	Y	N	N	N	Y	N
9 Kaptur	N	Y	N	Y	Y	N	Y	N
10 Kucinich	N	Y	N	Y	Y	N	N	N
11 Stokes	N	Y	N	Y	Y	N	Y	N
12 **Kasich**	N	Y	Y	N	Y	N	Y	N
13 Brown	N	Y	N	Y	Y	N	N	N
14 Sawyer	N	Y	N	Y	Y	N	Y	N
15 **Pryce**	N	Y	N	Y	Y	N	Y	N
16 **Regula**	N	Y	N	Y	Y	N	Y	N
17 Traficant	N	Y	N	N	Y	N	Y	N
18 **Ney**	N	Y	N	Y	Y	N	Y	N
19 **LaTourette**	N	Y	N	Y	Y	N	Y	N
OKLAHOMA								
1 **Largent**	Y	Y	Y	N	N	N	Y	N
2 **Coburn**	Y	Y	Y	N	N	N	Y	N
3 **Watkins**	N	Y	Y	N	N	N	Y	N
4 **Watts**	N	Y	Y	N	N	N	N	N
5 **Istook**	N	Y	Y	N	N	N	Y	N
6 **Lucas**	N	Y	Y	N	N	N	Y	N
OREGON								
1 Furse	N	Y	N	Y	Y	N	N	Y
2 **Smith**	N	Y	Y	N	N	N	Y	N
3 Blumenauer	N	Y	N	Y	Y	N	Y	N
4 DeFazio	N	Y	N	Y	Y	Y	N	?
5 Hooley	N	Y	N	Y	Y	N	Y	N
PENNSYLVANIA								
1 Foglietta	N	Y	N	Y	Y	?	N	N
2 Fattah	N	Y	N	Y	Y	N	Y	N
3 Borski	N	Y	N	Y	Y	N	N	N
4 Klink	N	Y	Y	Y	Y	N	Y	N
5 **Peterson**	N	Y	Y	N	N	N	Y	N
6 Holden	N	Y	N	N	Y	N	Y	N
7 **Weldon**	N	Y	N	N	N	N	Y	?
8 **Greenwood**	N	Y	N	Y	Y	N	Y	N
9 **Shuster**	N	Y	Y	Y	N	N	Y	N
10 **McDade**	N	Y	N	N	Y	N	Y	N
11 Kanjorski	N	Y	N	Y	Y	N	Y	N
12 Murtha	N	Y	N	N	Y	N	Y	N
13 **Fox**	N	Y	N	N	Y	N	N	N
14 Coyne	N	Y	N	Y	Y	Y	Y	Y
15 McHale	N	Y	N	Y	Y	N	Y	N
16 **Pitts**	Y	Y	Y	N	N	N	Y	N
17 **Gekas**	N	Y	N	Y	Y	N	Y	?
18 Doyle	N	Y	Y	N	N	N	Y	N
19 **Goodling**	N	Y	N	N	N	N	Y	N
20 Mascara	N	Y	N	Y	Y	N	Y	N
21 **English**	N	Y	Y	N	N	N	N	N
RHODE ISLAND								
1 Kennedy	N	Y	N	Y	Y	N	Y	N
2 Weygand	N	Y	N	Y	Y	N	Y	Y
SOUTH CAROLINA								
1 **Sanford**	N	Y	Y	N	N	N	Y	N
2 **Spence**	N	Y	Y	N	N	N	Y	N
3 **Graham**	Y	Y	Y	N	N	N	Y	N
4 **Inglis**	N	Y	N	N	N	N	Y	N
5 Spratt	N	Y	N	Y	Y	?	Y	N
6 Clyburn	N	Y	N	Y	Y	?	?	?
SOUTH DAKOTA								
AL **Thune**	Y	Y	Y	N	N	N	N	N
TENNESSEE								
1 **Jenkins**	N	Y	N	N	N	N	Y	N
2 **Duncan**	Y	Y	Y	N	N	N	Y	N

	374	376	377	378	379	380	381	382
3 **Wamp**	Y	Y	Y	N	N	N	N	N
4 **Hilleary**	Y	Y	Y	N	N	N	N	N
5 Clement	N	Y	N	Y	Y	N	Y	N
6 Gordon	N	Y	N	Y	Y	N	Y	N
7 **Bryant**	Y	Y	Y	N	N	N	Y	N
8 Tanner	N	Y	N	Y	Y	N	Y	N
9 Ford	N	Y	N	Y	Y	Y	Y	Y
TEXAS								
1 Sandlin	N	Y	N	Y	Y	N	Y	N
2 Turner	N	Y	N	Y	Y	N	Y	N
3 **Johnson, Sam**	?	Y	Y	N	N	N	Y	?
4 Hall	N	Y	N	N	N	N	Y	N
5 **Sessions**	N	Y	Y	N	N	N	Y	N
6 **Barton**	Y	Y	Y	N	Y	N	Y	N
7 **Archer**	N	Y	Y	N	N	N	Y	?
8 **Brady**	N	Y	Y	N	N	N	Y	N
9 Lampson	N	Y	N	Y	Y	N	Y	N
10 Doggett	N	Y	N	Y	Y	Y	N	Y
11 Edwards	N	Y	N	Y	Y	N	Y	?
12 **Granger**	N	Y	Y	N	Y	N	Y	N
13 **Thornberry**	N	Y	Y	Y	Y	N	Y	N
14 **Paul**	N	Y	Y	N	N	N	Y	N
15 Hinojosa	N	Y	N	Y	Y	N	Y	N
16 Reyes	N	Y	N	Y	Y	Y	Y	N
17 Stenholm	N	Y	N	N	N	N	N	N
18 Jackson-Lee	N	Y	N	Y	Y	N	Y	N
19 **Combest**	Y	Y	Y	N	N	N	?	N
20 Gonzalez	?	?	?	?	?	?	?	?
21 **Smith**	N	Y	N	N	N	N	Y	?
22 **DeLay**	N	Y	Y	N	N	N	Y	N
23 **Bonilla**	N	Y	Y	N	N	N	Y	N
24 Frost	N	Y	N	Y	Y	N	Y	N
25 Bentsen	?	Y	N	Y	Y	N	Y	N
26 **Armey**	N	Y	Y	N	N	N	Y	N
27 Ortiz	?	Y	N	N	N	N	Y	N
28 Rodriguez	N	Y	N	Y	Y	N	Y	N
29 Green	N	Y	N	Y	Y	N	Y	N
30 Johnson, E.B.	N	Y	N	Y	Y	N	Y	Y
UTAH								
1 **Hansen**	N	Y	Y	N	N	N	Y	N
2 **Cook**	N	Y	Y	N	N	N	Y	N
3 **Cannon**	Y	Y	Y	N	N	N	Y	N
VERMONT								
AL *Sanders*	N	Y	N	Y	Y	N	Y	N
VIRGINIA								
1 **Bateman**	N	Y	N	N	N	N	Y	N
2 Pickett	N	Y	N	Y	Y	N	N	N
3 Scott	N	Y	N	Y	Y	N	Y	N
4 Sisisky	N	Y	N	Y	Y	N	Y	N
5 Goode	N	Y	Y	N	N	N	Y	N
6 **Goodlatte**	N	Y	N	N	N	N	Y	N
7 **Bliley**	N	Y	N	N	N	N	Y	N
8 Moran	N	Y	N	Y	Y	?	?	N
9 Boucher	N	Y	N	Y	Y	N	Y	N
10 **Wolf**	?	Y	N	N	N	N	Y	N
11 **Davis**	N	Y	N	Y	Y	N	Y	?
WASHINGTON								
1 **White**	N	Y	Y	N	N	N	Y	N
2 **Metcalf**	N	Y	N	N	N	N	Y	N
3 **Smith, Linda**	Y	?	Y	N	N	N	Y	N
4 **Hastings**	N	Y	Y	N	N	N	Y	N
5 **Nethercutt**	N	Y	Y	N	Y	N	Y	N
6 Dicks	N	Y	N	Y	Y	N	Y	Y
7 McDermott	N	Y	N	Y	Y	Y	N	Y
8 **Dunn**	N	Y	Y	N	Y	N	Y	N
9 Smith, Adam	N	Y	N	Y	Y	N	Y	N
WEST VIRGINIA								
1 Mollohan	N	Y	N	N	N	N	Y	N
2 Wise	N	Y	N	Y	Y	?	Y	N
3 Rahall	N	Y	N	N	N	N	Y	N
WISCONSIN								
1 **Neumann**	Y	Y	Y	N	N	N	Y	N
2 **Klug**	N	Y	N	Y	Y	N	Y	N
3 Kind	N	Y	N	Y	Y	N	Y	N
4 Kleczka	N	Y	N	Y	Y	N	Y	N
5 Barrett	N	Y	N	Y	Y	N	Y	Y
6 **Petri**	N	Y	N	N	N	N	Y	N
7 Obey	N	Y	N	Y	Y	N	Y	N
8 Johnson	N	Y	N	Y	Y	Y	Y	N
9 **Sensenbrenner**	N	Y	N	N	N	N	Y	N
WYOMING								
AL **Cubin**	N	Y	Y	N	N	N	Y	N

Southern states - Ala., Ark., Fla., Ga., Ky., La., Miss., N.C., Okla., S.C., Tenn., Texas, Va.

HOUSE VOTES 384, 385, 386, 387, 388 *

384. HR 2264. Fiscal 1998 Labor-HHS Appropriations/Motion to Rise. Miller, D-Calif., motion to rise from the Committee of the Whole. Rejected 40-369: R 0-219; D 40-149 (ND 34-106, SD 6-43); I 0-1, Sept. 10, 1997.

385. HR 2264. Fiscal 1998 Labor-HHS Appropriations/Impact Aid. Hayworth, R-Ariz., amendment to provide an additional $18 million for construction costs for schools that receive Impact Aid payments, offset by an $18 million cut from National Labor Relations Board salaries and expenses. Rejected 170-253: R 164-58; D 6-194 (ND 0-146, SD 6-48); I 0-1, Sept. 10, 1997.

386. HR 2264. Fiscal 1998 Labor-HHS Appropriations/Goals 2000. Schaffer, R-Colo., amendment to transfer $40 million in funding from Goals 2000 to education programs for high-risk youth. Rejected 185-238: R 180-42; D 5-195 (ND 0-146, SD 5-49); I 0-1, Sept. 10, 1997.

387. HR 2264. Fiscal 1998 Labor-HHS Appropriations/Motion to Rise. Miller, D-Calif., motion to rise from the Committee of the Whole. Rejected 39-362: R 0-217; D 39-144 (ND 33-104, SD 6-40); I 0-1, Sept. 11, 1997.

388. HR 2264. Fiscal 1998 Labor-HHS Appropriations/Abortion Funding. Hyde, R-Ill., amendment to clarify existing law prohibiting certain federally funded abortions by requiring that Medicaid funds could not be used either to pay for abortions or to pay for health plans that cover abortions. Adopted 270-150: R 212-11; D 58-138 (ND 37-109, SD 21-29); I 0-1, Sept. 11, 1997.

** NOTE: Vote 383 was a quorum call. CQ does not include quorum calls in its vote charts.*

KEY

- Y Voted for (yea).
- # Paired for.
- \+ Announced for.
- N Voted against (nay).
- X Paired against.
- – Announced against.
- P Voted "present."
- C Voted "present" to avoid possible conflict of interest.
- ? Did not vote or otherwise make a position known.

Democrats ***Republicans***
Independent

	384	385	386	387	388
ALABAMA					
1 ***Callahan***	N	N	N	N	Y
2 ***Everett***	N	Y	Y	N	Y
3 ***Riley***	N	Y	Y	N	Y
4 ***Aderholt***	N	Y	Y	N	Y
5 Cramer	N	N	N	N	Y
6 ***Bachus***	N	Y	Y	N	Y
7 Hilliard	N	N	N	?	?
ALASKA					
AL ***Young***	N	Y	Y	N	Y
ARIZONA					
1 ***Salmon***	N	Y	Y	N	Y
2 Pastor	Y	N	N	Y	N
3 ***Stump***	N	Y	Y	N	Y
4 ***Shadegg***	N	Y	Y	N	Y
5 ***Kolbe***	N	+	+	N	Y
6 ***Hayworth***	N	Y	Y	N	Y
ARKANSAS					
1 Berry	?	N	N	Y	Y
2 Snyder	N	N	N	N	Y
3 ***Hutchinson***	N	N	Y	N	Y
4 ***Dickey***	N	Y	N	N	Y
CALIFORNIA					
1 ***Riggs***	N	Y	Y	N	Y
2 ***Herger***	N	Y	Y	N	Y
3 Fazio	?	N	N	N	N
4 ***Doolittle***	N	Y	Y	N	Y
5 Matsui	?	N	N	N	N
6 Woolsey	Y	N	N	Y	N
7 Miller	Y	N	N	Y	N
8 Pelosi	Y	N	N	Y	N
9 Dellums	?	?	?	?	X
10 Tauscher	?	N	N	N	N
11 ***Pombo***	N	Y	Y	N	Y
12 Lantos	N	N	N	N	N
13 Stark	N	N	N	N	N
14 Eshoo	Y	N	N	Y	N
15 ***Campbell***	N	N	Y	N	N
16 Lofgren	N	N	N	N	N
17 Farr	Y	N	N	Y	N
18 Condit	N	N	N	N	N
19 ***Radanovich***	?	Y	Y	N	Y
20 Dooley	?	N	N	?	N
21 ***Thomas***	N	Y	Y	N	Y
22 Capps	N	N	N	N	N
23 ***Gallegly***	N	Y	Y	N	Y
24 Sherman	N	N	N	N	N
25 ***McKeon***	N	Y	Y	N	Y
26 Berman	N	N	N	N	N
27 ***Rogan***	N	Y	Y	N	Y
28 ***Dreier***	N	Y	Y	N	Y
29 Waxman	Y	?	?	Y	N
30 Becerra	?	N	N	N	N
31 Martinez	N	N	N	N	N
32 Dixon	N	N	N	N	N
33 Roybal-Allard	N	N	N	N	N
34 Torres	?	N	N	N	N
35 Waters	N	N	N	?	N
36 Harman	N	N	N	N	N
37 Millender-McD.	N	N	N	Y	N
38 ***Horn***	N	N	N	N	N
39 ***Royce***	N	Y	Y	N	Y
40 ***Lewis***	N	N	N	N	Y
41 ***Kim***	N	N	Y	N	Y
42 Brown	Y	N	N	N	N
43 ***Calvert***	N	Y	Y	N	Y
44 ***Bono***	N	Y	Y	N	Y
45 ***Rohrabacher***	N	Y	Y	N	Y
46 Sanchez	N	N	N	?	N
47 ***Cox***	N	Y	Y	N	Y
48 ***Packard***	N	Y	N	N	Y
49 ***Bilbray***	N	Y	Y	N	Y
50 Filner	Y	N	N	Y	N
51 ***Cunningham***	N	Y	Y	N	Y
52 ***Hunter***	N	?	?	N	Y
COLORADO					
1 DeGette	N	N	N	N	N
2 Skaggs	N	N	N	N	N
3 ***McInnis***	N	Y	Y	N	Y
4 ***Schaffer***	N	Y	Y	N	Y
5 ***Hefley***	N	Y	Y	N	Y
6 ***Schaefer***	N	Y	Y	N	Y
CONNECTICUT					
1 Kennelly	N	N	N	N	N
2 Gejdenson	Y	N	N	Y	N
3 DeLauro	Y	N	N	Y	N
4 ***Shays***	N	N	Y	N	N
5 Maloney	N	N	N	N	N
6 ***Johnson***	N	N	N	N	N
DELAWARE					
AL ***Castle***	N	N	N	N	Y
FLORIDA					
1 ***Scarborough***	N	Y	Y	?	Y
2 Boyd	N	N	N	N	N
3 Brown	N	N	N	N	N
4 ***Fowler***	N	Y	Y	N	Y
5 Thurman	N	N	N	N	Y
6 ***Stearns***	N	Y	Y	N	Y
7 ***Mica***	N	Y	Y	N	Y
8 ***McCollum***	N	Y	Y	N	Y
9 ***Bilirakis***	N	N	N	N	Y
10 ***Young***	N	N	N	N	Y
11 Davis	?	N	N	Y	N
12 ***Canady***	N	N	Y	N	Y
13 ***Miller***	N	N	N	N	Y
14 ***Goss***	N	Y	Y	N	Y
15 ***Weldon***	N	Y	Y	N	Y
16 ***Foley***	N	N	Y	N	Y
17 Meek	N	N	N	?	N
18 ***Ros-Lehtinen***	N	N	Y	N	Y
19 Wexler	N	N	N	N	N
20 Deutsch	N	N	N	Y	N
21 ***Diaz-Balart***	N	N	Y	N	Y
22 ***Shaw***	N	N	Y	N	Y
23 Hastings	Y	N	N	?	–
GEORGIA					
1 ***Kingston***	N	Y	Y	N	Y
2 Bishop	N	N	N	N	N
3 ***Collins***	N	Y	Y	N	Y
4 McKinney	?	N	N	N	N
5 Lewis	Y	N	N	?	N
6 ***Gingrich***					
7 ***Barr***	N	Y	Y	?	Y
8 ***Chambliss***	N	Y	Y	N	Y
9 ***Deal***	N	Y	Y	N	Y
10 ***Norwood***	N	Y	Y	?	Y
11 ***Linder***	N	Y	Y	N	Y
HAWAII					
1 Abercrombie	N	N	N	N	N
2 Mink	Y	N	N	Y	N
IDAHO					
1 ***Chenoweth***	N	Y	Y	N	Y
2 ***Crapo***	N	Y	Y	N	Y
ILLINOIS					
1 Rush	N	N	N	?	N
2 Jackson	N	N	N	N	N
3 Lipinski	N	N	N	N	Y
4 Gutierrez	?	N	N	Y	N
5 Blagojevich	N	N	N	N	N
6 ***Hyde***	N	N	Y	N	Y
7 Davis	N	N	N	?	N
8 ***Crane***	N	Y	Y	N	Y
9 Yates	N	N	N	N	N
10 ***Porter***	N	N	N	N	Y
11 ***Weller***	N	N	Y	N	Y
12 Costello	N	N	N	N	Y
13 ***Fawell***	N	N	N	N	Y
14 ***Hastert***	N	Y	Y	N	Y
15 ***Ewing***	N	Y	Y	N	Y

ND Northern Democrats SD Southern Democrats

	384	385	386	387	388
16 *Manzullo*	N	Y	Y	N	Y
17 Evans	N	N	N	N	N
18 *LaHood*	N	Y	Y	N	Y
19 Poshard	N	N	N	N	Y
20 *Shimkus*	N	N	Y	N	Y
INDIANA					
1 Visclosky	N	N	N	N	N
2 *McIntosh*	N	Y	Y	N	Y
3 Roemer	N	N	N	?	Y
4 *Souder*	N	Y	Y	N	Y
5 *Buyer*	N	Y	N	N	Y
6 *Burton*	N	Y	?	N	Y
7 *Pease*	N	N	Y	N	Y
8 *Hostettler*	N	Y	Y	N	Y
9 Hamilton	N	N	N	N	Y
10 Carson	-	-	-	Y	N
IOWA					
1 *Leach*	N	N	N	N	Y
2 *Nussle*	N	Y	Y	N	Y
3 Boswell	N	N	N	N	N
4 *Ganske*	N	Y	Y	N	Y
5 *Latham*	N	Y	Y	N	Y
KANSAS					
1 *Moran*	N	Y	Y	N	Y
2 *Ryun*	N	Y	Y	N	Y
3 *Snowbarger*	N	Y	Y	N	Y
4 *Tiahrt*	N	Y	Y	N	Y
KENTUCKY					
1 *Whitfield*	N	Y	Y	N	Y
2 *Lewis*	N	Y	Y	N	Y
3 *Northup*	N	Y	N	N	Y
4 *Bunning*	N	Y	Y	N	Y
5 *Rogers*	N	Y	Y	N	Y
6 Baesler	N	N	N	N	Y
LOUISIANA					
1 *Livingston*	N	N	N	N	Y
2 Jefferson	N	N	N	N	N
3 *Tauzin*	N	Y	Y	N	Y
4 *McCrery*	N	Y	Y	N	Y
5 *Cooksey*	N	Y	Y	N	Y
6 *Baker*	?	Y	Y	N	Y
7 John	N	N	N	N	Y
MAINE					
1 Allen	Y	N	N	?	N
2 Baldacci	N	N	N	N	N
MARYLAND					
1 *Gilchrest*	N	?	N	N	Y
2 *Ehrlich*	N	Y	Y	N	Y
3 Cardin	N	N	N	N	N
4 Wynn	N	N	N	N	N
5 Hoyer	Y	N	N	N	N
6 *Bartlett*	N	Y	Y	N	Y
7 Cummings	N	N	N	N	N
8 *Morella*	N	N	N	N	N
MASSACHUSETTS					
1 Olver	Y	N	N	Y	N
2 Neal	N	N	N	N	Y
3 McGovern	N	N	N	N	N
4 Frank	Y	N	N	Y	N
5 Meehan	Y	N	N	Y	N
6 Tierney	N	N	N	N	N
7 Markey	N	N	N	N	N
8 Kennedy	N	N	N	N	N
9 Moakley	N	N	N	N	Y
10 Delahunt	Y	N	N	?	?
MICHIGAN					
1 Stupak	Y	N	N	Y	Y
2 *Hoekstra*	N	Y	Y	N	Y
3 *Ehlers*	N	N	Y	N	Y
4 *Camp*	N	N	Y	N	Y
5 Barcia	N	N	N	N	Y
6 *Upton*	N	N	N	N	Y
7 *Smith*	N	Y	Y	-	Y
8 Stabenow	N	N	N	N	N
9 Kildee	N	N	N	N	Y
10 Bonior	Y	N	?	?	Y
11 *Knollenberg*	N	Y	Y	N	Y
12 Levin	N	N	N	N	N
13 Rivers	N	N	N	N	N
14 Conyers	Y	?	N	?	N
15 Kilpatrick	N	N	N	N	N
16 Dingell	Y	N	N	Y	N
MINNESOTA					
1 *Gutknecht*	N	Y	Y	N	Y
2 Minge	?	N	N	N	Y

	384	385	386	387	388
3 *Ramstad*	N	Y	N	N	Y
4 Vento	Y	N	N	Y	N
5 Sabo	N	N	N	N	N
6 Luther	N	N	N	N	N
7 Peterson	N	N	N	N	Y
8 Oberstar	N	N	N	N	Y
MISSISSIPPI					
1 *Wicker*	N	Y	Y	N	Y
2 Thompson	N	N	N	N	N
3 *Pickering*	N	Y	Y	N	Y
4 *Parker*	N	Y	Y	N	Y
5 Taylor	N	Y	Y	N	Y
MISSOURI					
1 Clay	N	N	N	N	N
2 *Talent*	N	Y	Y	N	Y
3 Gephardt	Y	N	N	Y	Y
4 Skelton	N	N	N	N	Y
5 McCarthy	N	N	N	N	N
6 Danner	N	N	N	N	Y
7 *Blunt*	N	N	Y	N	Y
8 *Emerson*	N	Y	Y	N	Y
9 *Hulshof*	N	Y	Y	N	Y
MONTANA					
AL *Hill*	N	Y	Y	N	Y
NEBRASKA					
1 *Bereuter*	N	Y	N	N	Y
2 *Christensen*	N	Y	Y	N	Y
3 *Barrett*	N	Y	N	N	Y
NEVADA					
1 *Ensign*	N	Y	Y	N	Y
2 *Gibbons*	N	Y	Y	N	Y
NEW HAMPSHIRE					
1 *Sununu*	N	Y	Y	N	Y
2 *Bass*	N	Y	Y	N	Y
NEW JERSEY					
1 Andrews	Y	N	N	N	N
2 *LoBiondo*	N	N	Y	N	Y
3 *Saxton*	N	Y	Y	N	Y
4 *Smith*	N	N	Y	N	Y
5 *Roukema*	N	N	Y	N	N
6 Pallone	Y	N	N	Y	N
7 *Franks*	N	N	Y	N	Y
8 Pascrell	N	N	N	N	Y
9 Rothman	N	N	N	N	N
10 Payne	N	N	N	N	?
11 *Frelinghuysen*	N	Y	N	N	N
12 *Pappas*	N	Y	Y	N	Y
13 Menendez	N	N	N	N	N
NEW MEXICO					
1 *Schiff*	?	?	?	?	?
2 *Skeen*	N	Y	Y	N	Y
3 *Redmond*	N	Y	Y	N	Y
NEW YORK					
1 *Forbes*	N	N	N	N	Y
2 *Lazio*	N	N	N	N	Y
3 *King*	N	N	Y	N	Y
4 McCarthy	N	N	N	N	N
5 Ackerman	N	N	N	N	N
6 Flake	N	N	N	?	Y
7 Manton	N	N	N	N	Y
8 Nadler	N	N	N	N	N
9 Schumer	N	N	N	N	N
10 Towns	N	N	N	N	N
11 Owens	Y	N	N	Y	N
12 Velázquez	N	N	N	N	N
13 Vacant					
14 Maloney	N	N	N	N	N
15 Rangel	N	N	N	Y	N
16 Serrano	N	N	N	N	N
17 Engel	N	N	N	N	N
18 Lowey	N	N	N	Y	N
19 *Kelly*	N	Y	N	N	N
20 *Gilman*	N	N	N	N	N
21 McNulty	Y	N	N	Y	Y
22 *Solomon*	N	Y	Y	?	?
23 *Boehlert*	N	N	N	N	N
24 *McHugh*	N	Y	N	N	Y
25 *Walsh*	N	N	N	N	Y
26 Hinchey	Y	N	N	Y	N
27 *Paxon*	N	Y	Y	N	Y
28 Slaughter	Y	N	N	Y	N
29 LaFalce	N	N	N	N	Y
30 *Quinn*	N	N	N	N	Y
31 *Houghton*	N	N	Y	N	Y

	384	385	386	387	388
NORTH CAROLINA					
1 Clayton	N	N	N	?	N
2 Etheridge	N	N	N	N	Y
3 *Jones*	N	Y	Y	N	Y
4 Price	N	N	N	N	N
5 *Burr*	N	Y	Y	?	Y
6 *Coble*	N	Y	Y	N	Y
7 McIntyre	N	Y	N	N	Y
8 Hefner	N	N	N	N	Y
9 *Myrick*	N	Y	Y	N	Y
10 *Ballenger*	N	Y	Y	N	Y
11 *Taylor*	N	Y	Y	N	Y
12 Watt	N	N	N	?	N
NORTH DAKOTA					
AL Pomeroy	N	N	N	N	Y
OHIO					
1 *Chabot*	N	Y	Y	N	Y
2 *Portman*	N	Y	Y	N	Y
3 Hall	N	N	N	N	+
4 *Oxley*	?	N	N	N	Y
5 *Gillmor*	N	Y	Y	N	Y
6 Strickland	N	N	N	N	N
7 *Hobson*	N	N	Y	N	Y
8 *Boehner*	N	Y	Y	?	Y
9 Kaptur	N	N	N	N	N
10 Kucinich	N	N	N	N	Y
11 Stokes	N	N	N	N	N
12 *Kasich*	N	Y	Y	N	Y
13 Brown	N	N	N	Y	N
14 Sawyer	N	N	N	N	N
15 *Pryce*	N	Y	N	N	Y
16 *Regula*	N	N	N	N	Y
17 Traficant	N	N	N	N	Y
18 *Ney*	N	Y	Y	N	Y
19 *LaTourette*	N	N	Y	N	Y
OKLAHOMA					
1 *Largent*	N	Y	Y	N	Y
2 *Coburn*	N	Y	Y	N	Y
3 *Watkins*	N	Y	Y	N	Y
4 *Watts*	N	Y	Y	N	Y
5 *Istook*	N	Y	Y	N	Y
6 *Lucas*	N	Y	Y	N	Y
OREGON					
1 Furse	Y	N	N	N	N
2 *Smith*	N	Y	Y	N	Y
3 Blumenauer	N	N	N	N	N
4 DeFazio	Y	N	N	Y	N
5 Hooley	N	N	N	N	N
PENNSYLVANIA					
1 Foglietta	N	?	?	N	N
2 Fattah	N	N	N	N	N
3 Borski	N	N	N	N	?
4 Klink	N	N	N	N	Y
5 *Peterson*	N	Y	Y	N	Y
6 Holden	N	N	N	N	Y
7 *Weldon*	N	N	N	N	Y
8 *Greenwood*	N	Y	Y	N	N
9 *Shuster*	N	N	N	N	Y
10 *McDade*	N	N	N	N	Y
11 Kanjorski	N	N	N	N	Y
12 Murtha	N	N	N	N	Y
13 *Fox*	N	N	N	N	Y
14 Coyne	Y	N	N	Y	N
15 McHale	N	N	N	N	Y
16 *Pitts*	N	Y	Y	N	Y
17 *Gekas*	N	N	N	N	Y
18 Doyle	N	N	N	N	Y
19 *Goodling*	N	Y	Y	N	Y
20 Mascara	N	N	N	N	Y
21 *English*	?	N	Y	N	Y
RHODE ISLAND					
1 Kennedy	?	N	N	N	N
2 Weygand	N	N	N	N	Y
SOUTH CAROLINA					
1 *Sanford*	N	Y	Y	N	Y
2 *Spence*	N	Y	Y	N	Y
3 *Graham*	N	Y	Y	N	Y
4 *Inglis*	N	Y	Y	N	Y
5 Spratt	Y	N	N	N	Y
6 Clyburn	N	N	N	N	N
SOUTH DAKOTA					
AL *Thune*	N	Y	Y	N	Y
TENNESSEE					
1 *Jenkins*	N	Y	Y	N	Y
2 *Duncan*	N	Y	Y	N	Y

	384	385	386	387	388
3 *Wamp*	N	Y	Y	N	Y
4 *Hilleary*	N	Y	Y	N	Y
5 Clement	N	N	N	N	Y
6 Gordon	N	N	N	N	Y
7 *Bryant*	N	Y	Y	N	Y
8 Tanner	N	Y	N	N	Y
9 Ford	N	N	N	Y	N
TEXAS					
1 Sandlin	N	N	N	N	N
2 Turner	N	N	Y	N	Y
3 *Johnson, Sam*	N	Y	Y	N	Y
4 Hall	N	Y	Y	N	Y
5 *Sessions*	N	Y	Y	N	Y
6 *Barton*	N	Y	Y	N	Y
7 *Archer*	N	Y	Y	N	Y
8 *Brady*	N	Y	Y	N	Y
9 Lampson	N	N	N	N	Y
10 Doggett	Y	N	N	Y	N
11 Edwards	N	N	N	N	Y
12 *Granger*	N	Y	Y	N	Y
13 *Thornberry*	N	Y	Y	N	Y
14 *Paul*	N	Y	Y	N	Y
15 Hinojosa	N	N	N	N	N
16 Reyes	N	N	N	N	N
17 Stenholm	?	Y	Y	N	Y
18 Jackson-Lee	N	N	N	?	N
19 *Combest*	N	Y	Y	N	Y
20 Gonzalez	?	?	?	?	?
21 *Smith*	N	Y	Y	N	Y
22 *DeLay*	N	Y	Y	N	Y
23 *Bonilla*	N	Y	Y	?	#
24 Frost	N	N	N	N	N
25 Bentsen	N	N	N	N	N
26 *Armey*	N	Y	Y	N	Y
27 Ortiz	N	N	N	N	Y
28 Rodriguez	Y	N	N	N	N
29 Green	N	N	N	N	?
30 Johnson, E.B.	Y	N	N	Y	N
UTAH					
1 *Hansen*	N	Y	Y	N	Y
2 *Cook*	N	Y	Y	N	Y
3 *Cannon*	N	Y	Y	N	Y
VERMONT					
AL *Sanders*	N	N	N	N	N
VIRGINIA					
1 *Bateman*	?	N	N	N	Y
2 Pickett	N	N	N	N	N
3 Scott	N	N	N	N	N
4 Sisisky	N	N	N	N	N
5 Goode	N	Y	Y	N	Y
6 *Goodlatte*	N	Y	Y	N	Y
7 *Bliley*	N	Y	Y	N	Y
8 Moran	?	N	N	?	?
9 Boucher	N	N	N	N	N
10 *Wolf*	N	N	N	N	Y
11 *Davis*	?	N	N	N	Y
WASHINGTON					
1 *White*	N	Y	Y	N	Y
2 *Metcalf*	N	Y	Y	N	Y
3 *Smith, Linda*	N	N	Y	N	Y
4 *Hastings*	N	Y	Y	N	Y
5 *Nethercutt*	N	Y	Y	N	Y
6 Dicks	N	N	N	N	N
7 McDermott	Y	N	N	Y	N
8 *Dunn*	N	Y	Y	N	Y
9 Smith, Adam	N	N	N	?	N
WEST VIRGINIA					
1 Mollohan	N	N	N	N	Y
2 Wise	N	N	N	?	N
3 Rahall	N	N	N	N	Y
WISCONSIN					
1 *Neumann*	N	Y	Y	N	Y
2 *Klug*	N	Y	N	N	Y
3 Kind	N	N	N	Y	N
4 Kleczka	N	N	N	N	Y
5 Barrett	N	N	N	N	N
6 *Petri*	N	N	Y	N	Y
7 Obey	N	N	N	N	Y
8 Johnson	N	N	N	N	Y
9 *Sensenbrenner*	N	N	Y	N	Y
WYOMING					
AL *Cubin*	N	Y	Y	N	Y

Southern states - Ala., Ark., Fla., Ga., Ky., La., Miss., N.C., Okla., S.C., Tenn., Texas, Va.

HOUSE VOTES 389, 390, 391, 392

389. HR 2264. Fiscal 1998 Labor-HHS Appropriations/Public Broadcasting. Hefley, R-Colo., amendment to cut by $50 million the fiscal 2000 appropriation for the Corporation for Public Broadcasting. Rejected 155-265: R 151-70; D 4-194 (ND 2-144, SD 2-50); I 0-1, Sept. 11, 1997.

390. HR 2264. Fiscal 1998 Labor-HHS Appropriations/Public Broadcasting. Crane, R-Ill., amendment to eliminate the $300 million fiscal 2000 appropriation for the Corporation for Public Broadcasting. Rejected 78-345: R 78-145; D 0-199 (ND 0-147, SD 0-52); I 0-1, Sept. 11, 1997.

391. HR 2264. Fiscal 1998 Labor-HHS Appropriations/Needle Exchange Programs. Hastert, R-Ill., amendment to prohibit the use of funds in the bill to carry out or promote any program that distributes sterile needles for illegal drug use. Adopted 266-158: R 207-16; D 59-141 (ND 33-115, SD 26-26); I 0-1, Sept. 11, 1997.

392. HR 2264. Fiscal 1998 Labor-HHS Appropriations/National Labor Relations Board. Hostettler, R-Ind., amendment to adjust the standard for determining which companies fall under the jurisdiction of the National Labor Relations Board by allowing companies to conduct a larger volume of business without being subject to the board. Rejected 176-235: R 172-46; D 4-188 (ND 0-142, SD 4-46); I 0-1, Sept. 11, 1997.

KEY

- Y Voted for (yea).
- # Paired for.
- + Announced for.
- N Voted against (nay).
- X Paired against.
- – Announced against.
- P Voted "present."
- C Voted "present" to avoid possible conflict of interest.
- ? Did not vote or otherwise make a position known.

Democrats ***Republicans***
Independent

	389	390	391	392
ALABAMA				
1 ***Callahan***	N	N	Y	Y
2 ***Everett***	N	N	Y	Y
3 ***Riley***	Y	Y	Y	Y
4 ***Aderholt***	Y	N	Y	Y
5 Cramer	N	N	Y	N
6 ***Bachus***	N	N	Y	Y
7 Hilliard	?	N	N	N
ALASKA				
AL ***Young***	N	N	Y	Y
ARIZONA				
1 ***Salmon***	Y	Y	Y	Y
2 Pastor	N	N	N	N
3 ***Stump***	Y	Y	Y	Y
4 ***Shadegg***	Y	Y	Y	?
5 ***Kolbe***	N	N	N	Y
6 ***Hayworth***	Y	Y	Y	Y
ARKANSAS				
1 Berry	N	N	N	N
2 Snyder	N	N	N	N
3 ***Hutchinson***	Y	N	Y	Y
4 ***Dickey***	Y	N	Y	Y
CALIFORNIA				
1 ***Riggs***	Y	N	Y	N
2 ***Herger***	Y	Y	Y	Y
3 Fazio	N	N	N	N
4 ***Doolittle***	Y	Y	Y	Y
5 Matsui	N	N	N	N
6 Woolsey	N	N	N	N
7 Miller	N	N	N	N
8 Pelosi	N	N	N	N
9 Dellums	?	?	X	?
10 Tauscher	N	N	N	N
11 ***Pombo***	Y	Y	Y	Y
12 Lantos	N	N	N	N
13 Stark	N	N	N	N
14 Eshoo	N	N	N	N
15 ***Campbell***	Y	Y	N	N
16 Lofgren	N	N	N	N
17 Farr	N	N	N	N
18 Condit	Y	N	Y	N
19 ***Radanovich***	Y	Y	Y	Y
20 Dooley	N	N	N	N
21 ***Thomas***	Y	N	N	Y
22 Capps	N	N	N	N
23 ***Gallegly***	Y	N	Y	Y
24 Sherman	N	N	N	N
25 ***McKeon***	Y	N	Y	Y
26 Berman	N	N	N	N
27 ***Rogan***	Y	N	Y	Y
28 ***Dreier***	Y	Y	Y	Y
29 Waxman	N	N	N	N
30 Becerra	?	N	N	N
31 Martinez	N	N	N	N
32 Dixon	N	N	N	N
33 Roybal-Allard	N	N	N	N
34 Torres	N	N	N	N
35 Waters	N	N	N	N
36 Harman	N	N	N	N
37 Millender-McD.	N	N	N	N
38 ***Horn***	N	N	N	N
39 ***Royce***	Y	Y	Y	Y
40 ***Lewis***	N	N	Y	N

	389	390	391	392
41 ***Kim***	Y	N	Y	Y
42 Brown	N	N	N	?
43 ***Calvert***	N	N	Y	Y
44 ***Bono***	Y	Y	Y	Y
45 ***Rohrabacher***	Y	Y	Y	Y
46 Sanchez	N	N	N	N
47 ***Cox***	Y	Y	Y	?
48 ***Packard***	N	N	Y	Y
49 ***Bilbray***	N	N	Y	Y
50 Filner	N	N	N	N
51 ***Cunningham***	Y	N	Y	Y
52 ***Hunter***	Y	Y	Y	Y
COLORADO				
1 DeGette	N	N	N	N
2 Skaggs	N	N	N	N
3 ***McInnis***	Y	N	Y	Y
4 ***Schaffer***	Y	Y	Y	Y
5 ***Hefley***	Y	N	Y	Y
6 ***Schaefer***	Y	N	Y	Y
CONNECTICUT				
1 Kennelly	N	N	N	N
2 Gejdenson	N	N	N	N
3 DeLauro	N	N	N	N
4 ***Shays***	N	N	N	N
5 Maloney	N	N	N	N
6 ***Johnson***	N	N	N	Y
DELAWARE				
AL ***Castle***	N	N	Y	N
FLORIDA				
1 ***Scarborough***	Y	Y	Y	Y
2 Boyd	N	N	Y	N
3 Brown	N	N	N	?
4 ***Fowler***	Y	N	Y	Y
5 Thurman	N	N	N	N
6 ***Stearns***	Y	Y	Y	Y
7 ***Mica***	Y	N	Y	Y
8 ***McCollum***	Y	N	Y	Y
9 ***Bilirakis***	Y	N	Y	N
10 ***Young***	N	N	N	N
11 Davis	N	N	Y	N
12 ***Canady***	Y	Y	Y	Y
13 ***Miller***	Y	Y	Y	Y
14 ***Goss***	Y	N	Y	Y
15 ***Weldon***	Y	Y	Y	Y
16 ***Foley***	Y	N	N	N
17 Meek	N	?	?	?
18 ***Ros-Lehtinen***	Y	N	Y	?
19 Wexler	N	N	N	N
20 Deutsch	N	N	N	N
21 ***Diaz-Balart***	Y	N	Y	N
22 ***Shaw***	N	N	Y	Y
23 Hastings	?	?	?	N
GEORGIA				
1 ***Kingston***	Y	Y	Y	Y
2 Bishop	N	N	N	N
3 ***Collins***	Y	Y	Y	Y
4 McKinney	N	N	N	N
5 Lewis	N	N	N	?
6 ***Gingrich***				
7 ***Barr***	Y	Y	Y	Y
8 ***Chambliss***	Y	Y	Y	Y
9 ***Deal***	Y	N	Y	Y
10 ***Norwood***	Y	Y	Y	Y
11 ***Linder***	Y	Y	Y	Y
HAWAII				
1 Abercrombie	N	N	N	N
2 Mink	N	N	N	N
IDAHO				
1 ***Chenoweth***	Y	N	Y	Y
2 ***Crapo***	Y	N	Y	Y
ILLINOIS				
1 Rush	N	N	N	–
2 Jackson	N	N	N	N
3 Lipinski	N	N	Y	N
4 Gutierrez	N	N	N	N
5 Blagojevich	N	N	N	N
6 ***Hyde***	Y	N	Y	N
7 Davis	N	N	N	N
8 ***Crane***	Y	Y	Y	Y
9 Yates	N	N	N	N
10 ***Porter***	N	N	Y	N
11 ***Weller***	Y	N	Y	N
12 Costello	N	N	Y	N
13 ***Fawell***	N	N	Y	Y
14 ***Hastert***	Y	N	Y	Y
15 ***Ewing***	N	N	Y	Y

ND Northern Democrats SD Southern Democrats

	389	390	391	392
16 ***Manzullo***	Y	Y	Y	Y
17 Evans	N	N	N	N
18 ***LaHood***	N	N	Y	Y
19 Poshard	N	N	Y	N
20 ***Shimkus***	Y	N	Y	Y
INDIANA				
1 Visclosky	N	N	Y	N
2 ***McIntosh***	Y	Y	Y	Y
3 Roemer	N	N	Y	N
4 ***Souder***	Y	N	Y	Y
5 ***Buyer***	Y	N	Y	Y
6 ***Burton***	Y	Y	Y	Y
7 ***Pease***	Y	N	Y	Y
8 ***Hostettler***	Y	Y	Y	Y
9 Hamilton	N	N	Y	N
10 Carson	N	N	N	N
IOWA				
1 ***Leach***	N	N	N	N
2 ***Nussle***	Y	N	Y	Y
3 Boswell	N	N	Y	N
4 ***Ganske***	Y	N	N	Y
5 ***Latham***	N	N	Y	Y
KANSAS				
1 ***Moran***	N	N	Y	Y
2 ***Ryun***	Y	Y	Y	Y
3 ***Snowbarger***	Y	Y	Y	Y
4 ***Tiahrt***	Y	Y	Y	Y
KENTUCKY				
1 ***Whitfield***	N	N	Y	Y
2 ***Lewis***	Y	N	Y	Y
3 ***Northup***	N	N	Y	Y
4 ***Bunning***	Y	N	Y	Y
5 ***Rogers***	N	N	Y	Y
6 Baesler	N	N	Y	N
LOUISIANA				
1 ***Livingston***	Y	N	Y	N
2 Jefferson	N	N	N	N
3 ***Tauzin***	N	N	Y	Y
4 ***McCrery***	Y	N	N	Y
5 ***Cooksey***	N	N	N	Y
6 ***Baker***	N	N	Y	?
7 John	N	N	Y	N
MAINE				
1 Allen	N	N	N	N
2 Baldacci	N	N	N	N
MARYLAND				
1 ***Gilchrest***	N	N	Y	N
2 ***Ehrlich***	Y	Y	Y	Y
3 Cardin	N	N	N	N
4 Wynn	N	N	N	N
5 Hoyer	N	N	N	N
6 ***Bartlett***	Y	Y	Y	Y
7 Cummings	N	N	N	N
8 ***Morella***	N	N	N	N
MASSACHUSETTS				
1 Olver	N	N	N	N
2 Neal	N	N	N	N
3 McGovern	N	N	N	N
4 Frank	N	N	N	N
5 Meehan	N	N	N	N
6 Tierney	N	N	N	N
7 Markey	N	N	N	N
8 Kennedy	N	N	N	N
9 Moakley	N	N	N	N
10 Delahunt	?	?	N	N
MICHIGAN				
1 Stupak	N	N	Y	N
2 ***Hoekstra***	Y	N	Y	Y
3 ***Ehlers***	N	N	Y	Y
4 ***Camp***	Y	N	Y	Y
5 Barcia	N	N	Y	N
6 ***Upton***	N	N	Y	Y
7 ***Smith***	Y	N	Y	Y
8 Stabenow	N	N	N	N
9 Kildee	N	N	Y	N
10 Bonior	N	N	N	N
11 ***Knollenberg***	N	N	Y	N
12 Levin	N	N	N	N
13 Rivers	N	N	N	N
14 Conyers	N	N	N	N
15 Kilpatrick	N	N	N	N
16 Dingell	N	N	N	N
MINNESOTA				
1 ***Gutknecht***	Y	N	Y	Y
2 Minge	N	N	Y	N
3 ***Ramstad***	N	N	Y	Y
4 Vento	N	N	N	N
5 Sabo	N	N	N	N
6 Luther	N	N	Y	N
7 Peterson	N	N	Y	N
8 Oberstar	N	N	Y	N
MISSISSIPPI				
1 ***Wicker***	Y	N	Y	Y
2 Thompson	N	N	N	?
3 ***Pickering***	Y	N	Y	Y
4 ***Parker***	Y	N	Y	Y
5 Taylor	N	N	Y	Y
MISSOURI				
1 Clay	N	N	N	N
2 ***Talent***	Y	Y	Y	Y
3 Gephardt	N	N	N	N
4 Skelton	N	N	Y	N
5 McCarthy	N	N	Y	?
6 Danner	N	N	Y	N
7 ***Blunt***	Y	N	Y	Y
8 ***Emerson***	Y	N	Y	Y
9 ***Hulshof***	Y	N	Y	Y
MONTANA				
AL ***Hill***	Y	N	Y	Y
NEBRASKA				
1 ***Bereuter***	N	N	Y	Y
2 ***Christensen***	Y	Y	Y	?
3 ***Barrett***	Y	Y	Y	N
NEVADA				
1 ***Ensign***	Y	Y	Y	Y
2 ***Gibbons***	Y	N	Y	Y
NEW HAMPSHIRE				
1 ***Sununu***	Y	N	Y	Y
2 ***Bass***	N	N	Y	Y
NEW JERSEY				
1 Andrews	N	N	N	N
2 ***LoBiondo***	Y	Y	Y	N
3 ***Saxton***	N	N	Y	N
4 ***Smith***	Y	N	Y	N
5 ***Roukema***	N	N	Y	N
6 Pallone	N	N	N	N
7 ***Franks***	N	N	Y	N
8 Pascrell	N	N	Y	N
9 Rothman	N	N	N	N
10 Payne	?	?	?	?
11 ***Frelinghuysen***	N	N	N	Y
12 ***Pappas***	Y	N	Y	N
13 Menendez	N	N	N	N
NEW MEXICO				
1 ***Schiff***	?	?	?	?
2 ***Skeen***	N	N	Y	Y
3 ***Redmond***	N	N	Y	Y
NEW YORK				
1 ***Forbes***	N	N	Y	N
2 ***Lazio***	N	N	Y	N
3 ***King***	N	N	Y	N
4 McCarthy	N	N	N	N
5 Ackerman	N	N	N	N
6 Flake	N	N	N	N
7 Manton	N	N	N	N
8 Nadler	N	N	N	N
9 Schumer	N	N	N	N
10 Towns	N	N	N	N
11 Owens	N	N	N	N
12 Velázquez	N	N	N	N
13 Vacant				
14 Maloney	N	N	N	N
15 Rangel	N	N	N	?
16 Serrano	N	N	N	N
17 Engel	N	N	N	N
18 Lowey	N	N	N	N
19 ***Kelly***	N	N	Y	N
20 ***Gilman***	N	N	Y	N
21 McNulty	N	N	Y	N
22 ***Solomon***	?	Y	Y	Y
23 ***Boehlert***	N	N	Y	N
24 ***McHugh***	N	N	Y	Y
25 ***Walsh***	N	N	Y	Y
26 Hinchey	N	N	N	N
27 ***Paxon***	Y	Y	Y	Y
28 Slaughter	N	N	N	N
29 LaFalce	N	N	Y	N
30 ***Quinn***	N	N	Y	N
31 ***Houghton***	N	N	N	N
NORTH CAROLINA				
1 Clayton	N	N	N	N
2 Etheridge	N	N	Y	N
3 ***Jones***	Y	Y	Y	Y
4 Price	N	N	N	N
5 ***Burr***	N	N	Y	Y
6 ***Coble***	Y	N	Y	Y
7 McIntyre	N	N	Y	N
8 Hefner	N	N	Y	N
9 ***Myrick***	Y	Y	Y	Y
10 ***Ballenger***	Y	N	Y	Y
11 ***Taylor***	?	?	?	?
12 Watt	N	N	N	N
NORTH DAKOTA				
AL Pomeroy	N	N	N	N
OHIO				
1 ***Chabot***	Y	Y	Y	Y
2 ***Portman***	Y	N	Y	Y
3 Hall	N	N	Y	?
4 ***Oxley***	Y	N	Y	N
5 ***Gillmor***	N	N	Y	Y
6 Strickland	N	N	Y	N
7 ***Hobson***	Y	N	Y	N
8 ***Boehner***	Y	Y	Y	Y
9 Kaptur	N	N	N	N
10 Kucinich	N	N	N	N
11 Stokes	N	N	N	N
12 ***Kasich***	Y	Y	Y	Y
13 Brown	N	N	N	N
14 Sawyer	N	N	N	N
15 ***Pryce***	Y	N	Y	Y
16 ***Regula***	N	N	Y	Y
17 Traficant	Y	N	Y	N
18 ***Ney***	N	N	Y	N
19 ***LaTourette***	N	N	Y	N
OKLAHOMA				
1 ***Largent***	Y	Y	Y	Y
2 ***Coburn***	Y	Y	Y	Y
3 ***Watkins***	Y	N	Y	Y
4 ***Watts***	Y	N	Y	Y
5 ***Istook***	Y	Y	Y	Y
6 ***Lucas***	N	N	Y	Y
OREGON				
1 Furse	N	N	N	N
2 ***Smith***	N	N	Y	Y
3 Blumenauer	N	N	N	N
4 DeFazio	N	N	N	N
5 Hooley	N	N	N	N
PENNSYLVANIA				
1 Foglietta	N	N	N	N
2 Fattah	N	N	N	N
3 Borski	?	?	?	?
4 Klink	N	N	Y	N
5 ***Peterson***	Y	N	Y	Y
6 Holden	N	N	Y	N
7 ***Weldon***	N	N	Y	N
8 ***Greenwood***	N	N	N	Y
9 ***Shuster***	Y	Y	Y	Y
10 ***McDade***	N	N	Y	N
11 Kanjorski	N	N	N	N
12 Murtha	N	N	Y	?
13 ***Fox***	N	N	Y	N
14 Coyne	N	N	N	N
15 McHale	N	N	N	N
16 ***Pitts***	Y	Y	Y	Y
17 ***Gekas***	N	N	Y	N
18 Doyle	N	N	Y	N
19 ***Goodling***	Y	N	Y	Y
20 Mascara	N	N	Y	N
21 ***English***	N	N	Y	N
RHODE ISLAND				
1 Kennedy	N	N	N	N
2 Weygand	N	N	N	N
SOUTH CAROLINA				
1 ***Sanford***	Y	Y	Y	Y
2 ***Spence***	Y	N	Y	Y
3 ***Graham***	Y	Y	Y	Y
4 ***Inglis***	Y	Y	Y	Y
5 Spratt	N	N	Y	N
6 Clyburn	N	N	N	N
SOUTH DAKOTA				
AL ***Thune***	N	N	Y	Y
TENNESSEE				
1 ***Jenkins***	Y	N	Y	Y
2 ***Duncan***	Y	N	Y	Y
3 ***Wamp***	Y	Y	Y	Y
4 ***Hilleary***	Y	Y	Y	Y
5 Clement	N	N	Y	N
6 Gordon	N	N	Y	N
7 ***Bryant***	Y	Y	Y	Y
8 Tanner	N	N	Y	N
9 Ford	N	N	N	N
TEXAS				
1 Sandlin	N	N	Y	N
2 Turner	N	N	Y	N
3 ***Johnson, Sam***	Y	Y	Y	Y
4 Hall	N	N	Y	Y
5 ***Sessions***	Y	Y	Y	Y
6 ***Barton***	Y	Y	Y	Y
7 ***Archer***	Y	Y	Y	Y
8 ***Brady***	Y	Y	Y	Y
9 Lampson	N	N	N	N
10 Doggett	N	N	N	N
11 Edwards	N	N	Y	N
12 ***Granger***	N	N	Y	Y
13 ***Thornberry***	Y	Y	Y	Y
14 ***Paul***	Y	Y	Y	Y
15 Hinojosa	N	N	Y	N
16 Reyes	N	N	Y	N
17 Stenholm	Y	N	Y	Y
18 Jackson-Lee	N	N	N	N
19 ***Combest***	Y	Y	Y	Y
20 Gonzalez	?	?	?	?
21 ***Smith***	Y	N	Y	Y
22 ***DeLay***	Y	Y	Y	Y
23 ***Bonilla***	?	?	#	?
24 Frost	N	N	N	N
25 Bentsen	N	N	Y	N
26 ***Armey***	Y	Y	Y	Y
27 Ortiz	N	N	Y	N
28 Rodriguez	N	N	Y	N
29 Green	N	N	Y	N
30 Johnson, E.B.	N	N	N	N
UTAH				
1 ***Hansen***	Y	N	Y	Y
2 ***Cook***	N	N	Y	Y
3 ***Cannon***	Y	Y	Y	Y
VERMONT				
AL *Sanders*	N	N	N	N
VIRGINIA				
1 ***Bateman***	–	N	Y	N
2 Pickett	N	N	N	N
3 Scott	N	N	N	N
4 Sisisky	Y	N	Y	N
5 Goode	N	N	Y	Y
6 ***Goodlatte***	Y	N	Y	Y
7 ***Bliley***	Y	N	Y	Y
8 Moran	N	N	N	N
9 Boucher	N	N	N	N
10 ***Wolf***	N	N	Y	Y
11 ***Davis***	N	N	Y	Y
WASHINGTON				
1 ***White***	Y	N	Y	Y
2 ***Metcalf***	Y	Y	Y	N
3 ***Smith, Linda***	Y	N	Y	N
4 ***Hastings***	Y	Y	Y	Y
5 ***Nethercutt***	Y	N	Y	Y
6 Dicks	N	N	N	N
7 McDermott	N	N	N	N
8 ***Dunn***	Y	Y	Y	Y
9 Smith, Adam	N	N	N	N
WEST VIRGINIA				
1 Mollohan	N	N	Y	N
2 Wise	N	N	Y	N
3 Rahall	N	N	N	N
WISCONSIN				
1 ***Neumann***	Y	Y	Y	Y
2 ***Klug***	Y	N	Y	Y
3 Kind	N	N	N	N
4 Kleczka	N	N	Y	N
5 Barrett	N	N	N	N
6 ***Petri***	Y	Y	Y	N
7 Obey	N	N	N	N
8 Johnson	N	N	Y	N
9 ***Sensenbrenner***	Y	Y	Y	Y
WYOMING				
AL ***Cubin***	Y	N	Y	Y

Southern states - Ala., Ark., Fla., Ga., Ky., La., Miss., N.C., Okla., S.C., Tenn., Texas, Va.

HOUSE VOTES 393, 394, 395, 396, 397, 398

393. HR 2016. Fiscal 1998 Military Construction Appropriations/Previous Question. Linder, R-Ga., motion to order the previous question (thus ending debate and the possibility of amendment) on adoption of the rule (H Res 228) to provide for House floor consideration of the conference report on HR 2016, which would appropriate $9.2 billion for domestic and overseas military construction projects, military family housing and base realignment and closure accounts. The rule waived all points of order against the conference report. Motion agreed to 238-189: R 225-0; D 13-188 (ND 6-142, SD 7-46); I 0-1, Sept. 16, 1997.

394. HR 2016. Fiscal 1998 Military Construction Appropriations/Conference Report. Adoption of the conference report on the bill to provide $9.2 billion for military construction programs in fiscal 1998. The conference report would provide $610 million less than provided in fiscal 1997 and $800 million more than requested by President Clinton. Adopted (thus sent to the Senate) 413-12, Sept. 16, 1997.

395. S 910. Earthquake Hazards Reduction/Passage. Sensenbrenner, R-Wis., motion to suspend the rules and pass the bill to authorize $212 million over the next two years for the 1997 Earthquake Hazards Reduction Act, which develops emergency responses to earthquakes, performs geological research and develops building standards to minimize the impact of earthquakes. Motion agreed to 421-0: R 220-0; D 200-0 (ND 147-0, SD 53-0); I 1-0, Sept. 16, 1997. A two-thirds majority of those present and voting (281 in this case) is required for adoption under suspension of the rules.

396. H Con Res 134. Patriarch Bartholomew/Adoption. Ney, R-Ohio, motion to suspend the rules and adopt the concurrent resolution to authorize the use of the Capitol rotunda for a ceremony at which members of Congress can greet His All Holiness Patriarch Bartholomew, the 270th Ecumenical Patriarch of Constantinople, on Oct. 21, 1997. Motion agreed to 421-0: R 224-0; D 196-0 (ND 143-0, SD 53-0); I 1-0, Sept. 16, 1997. A two-thirds majority of those present and voting (281 in this case) is required for adoption under suspension of the rules.

397. S 562. Senior Citizen Home Equity Protection/Passage. Lazio, R-N.Y., motion to suspend the rules and pass the bill to authorize the Department of Housing and Urban Development to issue rules to prevent the charging of excess fees for advising senior citizens seeking to obtain reverse mortgages, which allow senior citizens to borrow against the equity in their homes. Motion agreed to 422-1: R 220-1; D 201-0 (ND 148-0, SD 53-0); I 1-0, Sept. 16, 1997. A two-thirds majority of those present and voting (282 in this case) is required for adoption under suspension of the rules.

398. HR 2264. Fiscal 1998 Labor-HHS Appropriations/National Education Testing. Goodling, R-Pa., amendment to prohibit the use of any funds in the bill to develop new national student tests in reading or math. Adopted 295-125: R 220-3; D 75-121 (ND 47-97, SD 28-24); I 0-1, Sept. 16, 1997. A "nay" was a vote in support of the president's position.

KEY

Y	Voted for (yea).
#	Paired for.
+	Announced for.
N	Voted against (nay).
X	Paired against.
-	Announced against.
P	Voted "present."
C	Voted "present" to avoid possible conflict of interest.
?	Did not vote or otherwise make a position known.

Democrats ***Republicans***
Independent

	393	394	395	396	397	398
ALABAMA						
1 ***Callahan***	Y	Y	Y	Y	Y	Y
2 ***Everett***	Y	Y	Y	Y	Y	Y
3 ***Riley***	Y	Y	Y	Y	Y	Y
4 ***Aderholt***	Y	Y	Y	Y	Y	Y
5 Cramer	N	Y	Y	Y	Y	N
6 ***Bachus***	Y	Y	Y	Y	Y	Y
7 Hilliard	N	Y	Y	Y	Y	Y
ALASKA						
AL ***Young***	Y	Y	Y	Y	Y	?
ARIZONA						
1 ***Salmon***	Y	Y	Y	Y	Y	Y
2 Pastor	N	Y	Y	Y	Y	Y
3 ***Stump***	Y	Y	Y	Y	Y	Y
4 ***Shadegg***	Y	Y	Y	Y	Y	Y
5 ***Kolbe***	Y	Y	Y	Y	Y	Y
6 ***Hayworth***	Y	Y	Y	Y	Y	Y
ARKANSAS						
1 Berry	N	Y	Y	Y	Y	N
2 Snyder	N	Y	Y	Y	Y	N
3 ***Hutchinson***	Y	Y	Y	Y	Y	Y
4 ***Dickey***	Y	Y	Y	Y	Y	Y
CALIFORNIA						
1 ***Riggs***	Y	Y	Y	Y	Y	Y
2 ***Herger***	Y	Y	Y	Y	Y	Y
3 Fazio	N	Y	Y	Y	Y	N
4 ***Doolittle***	Y	Y	Y	Y	Y	Y
5 Matsui	N	Y	Y	Y	Y	Y
6 Woolsey	N	Y	Y	Y	Y	N
7 Miller	N	Y	Y	Y	Y	N
8 Pelosi	N	Y	Y	Y	?	-
9 Dellums	N	Y	Y	Y	Y	Y
10 Tauscher	N	Y	Y	Y	Y	N
11 ***Pombo***	Y	Y	Y	Y	Y	Y
12 Lantos	N	Y	Y	Y	Y	N
13 Stark	N	N	Y	Y	Y	N
14 Eshoo	N	Y	Y	Y	Y	N
15 ***Campbell***	Y	N	Y	Y	Y	Y
16 Lofgren	N	Y	Y	Y	Y	N
17 Farr	N	Y	Y	Y	Y	N
18 Condit	N	Y	Y	Y	Y	N
19 ***Radanovich***	Y	Y	Y	Y	Y	Y
20 Dooley	N	Y	Y	Y	Y	N
21 ***Thomas***	Y	Y	Y	Y	Y	Y
22 Capps	N	Y	Y	Y	Y	N
23 ***Gallegly***	Y	Y	Y	Y	Y	Y
24 Sherman	N	Y	Y	Y	Y	N
25 ***McKeon***	Y	Y	Y	Y	Y	Y
26 Berman	N	Y	Y	Y	Y	N
27 ***Rogan***	Y	Y	Y	Y	Y	Y
28 ***Dreier***	Y	Y	Y	Y	Y	Y
29 Waxman	N	Y	Y	Y	Y	N
30 Becerra	N	Y	Y	Y	Y	+
31 Martinez	N	Y	Y	Y	Y	?
32 Dixon	Y	Y	Y	Y	Y	Y
33 Roybal-Allard	N	Y	Y	Y	Y	Y
34 Torres	N	Y	Y	Y	Y	?
35 Waters	N	Y	Y	?	Y	Y
36 Harman	N	Y	Y	Y	Y	N
37 Millender-McD.	N	+	Y	Y	Y	Y
38 ***Horn***	Y	Y	Y	Y	Y	N
39 ***Royce***	Y	N	Y	Y	Y	Y
40 ***Lewis***	Y	Y	Y	Y	Y	Y
41 ***Kim***	Y	Y	Y	Y	Y	Y
42 Brown	N	Y	Y	Y	Y	N
43 ***Calvert***	Y	Y	Y	Y	Y	Y
44 ***Bono***	Y	Y	Y	Y	Y	Y
45 ***Rohrabacher***	Y	Y	Y	Y	Y	Y
46 Sanchez	N	Y	Y	Y	Y	Y
47 ***Cox***	Y	Y	Y	Y	Y	Y
48 ***Packard***	Y	Y	Y	Y	Y	Y
49 ***Bilbray***	Y	Y	Y	Y	Y	Y
50 Filner	N	N	Y	Y	Y	N
51 ***Cunningham***	Y	Y	Y	Y	Y	Y
52 ***Hunter***	Y	Y	Y	Y	Y	Y
COLORADO						
1 DeGette	N	Y	Y	Y	Y	N
2 Skaggs	N	Y	Y	Y	Y	N
3 ***McInnis***	Y	Y	Y	Y	Y	Y
4 ***Schaffer***	Y	Y	Y	Y	Y	Y
5 ***Hefley***	Y	Y	Y	Y	Y	Y
6 ***Schaefer***	Y	Y	Y	Y	Y	Y
CONNECTICUT						
1 Kennelly	N	Y	Y	?	Y	N
2 Gejdenson	N	Y	Y	Y	Y	N
3 DeLauro	N	Y	Y	Y	Y	N
4 ***Shays***	Y	Y	Y	Y	Y	Y
5 Maloney	N	Y	Y	Y	Y	N
6 ***Johnson***	Y	Y	Y	Y	Y	N
DELAWARE						
AL ***Castle***	Y	Y	Y	Y	Y	Y
FLORIDA						
1 ***Scarborough***	Y	Y	Y	Y	Y	Y
2 Boyd	N	Y	Y	Y	Y	Y
3 Brown	?	?	?	?	?	Y
4 ***Fowler***	Y	Y	Y	Y	Y	Y
5 Thurman	N	Y	Y	Y	Y	N
6 ***Stearns***	Y	Y	Y	Y	Y	Y
7 ***Mica***	Y	Y	Y	Y	Y	Y
8 ***McCollum***	Y	N	Y	Y	Y	Y
9 ***Bilirakis***	Y	Y	Y	Y	Y	Y
10 ***Young***	Y	Y	Y	Y	Y	Y
11 Davis	N	Y	Y	Y	Y	N
12 ***Canady***	Y	Y	Y	Y	Y	Y
13 ***Miller***	Y	Y	Y	Y	Y	Y
14 ***Goss***	Y	Y	Y	Y	Y	Y
15 ***Weldon***	Y	Y	Y	Y	?	Y
16 ***Foley***	Y	Y	Y	Y	Y	Y
17 Meek	N	Y	Y	Y	Y	Y
18 ***Ros-Lehtinen***	Y	Y	Y	Y	Y	Y
19 Wexler	N	Y	Y	Y	Y	N
20 Deutsch	N	Y	Y	Y	Y	N
21 ***Diaz-Balart***	Y	Y	Y	Y	Y	Y
22 ***Shaw***	Y	Y	Y	Y	Y	Y
23 Hastings	N	Y	Y	Y	Y	Y
GEORGIA						
1 ***Kingston***	Y	Y	Y	Y	Y	Y
2 Bishop	Y	Y	Y	Y	Y	Y
3 ***Collins***	Y	Y	Y	Y	Y	Y
4 McKinney	N	Y	Y	Y	Y	Y
5 Lewis	N	Y	Y	Y	Y	Y
6 ***Gingrich***						
7 ***Barr***	Y	Y	Y	Y	Y	Y
8 ***Chambliss***	Y	Y	Y	Y	Y	Y
9 ***Deal***	Y	Y	Y	Y	Y	Y
10 ***Norwood***	Y	Y	Y	Y	Y	Y
11 ***Linder***	Y	Y	Y	Y	Y	Y
HAWAII						
1 Abercrombie	N	Y	Y	Y	+	Y
2 Mink	N	Y	Y	Y	Y	Y
IDAHO						
1 ***Chenoweth***	Y	Y	Y	Y	Y	Y
2 ***Crapo***	Y	Y	Y	Y	Y	Y
ILLINOIS						
1 Rush	N	Y	Y	Y	Y	Y
2 Jackson	N	Y	Y	Y	Y	Y
3 Lipinski	N	Y	Y	Y	Y	Y
4 Gutierrez	N	Y	Y	Y	Y	Y
5 Blagojevich	N	Y	Y	Y	Y	N
6 ***Hyde***	Y	Y	Y	Y	Y	Y
7 Davis	N	Y	Y	Y	Y	Y
8 ***Crane***	Y	Y	Y	Y	Y	Y
9 Yates	N	Y	Y	Y	Y	?
10 ***Porter***	Y	Y	Y	Y	Y	Y
11 ***Weller***	Y	Y	Y	Y	?	Y
12 Costello	N	Y	Y	Y	Y	N
13 ***Fawell***	Y	Y	Y	Y	Y	Y
14 ***Hastert***	Y	Y	Y	Y	Y	Y
15 ***Ewing***	Y	Y	Y	Y	Y	Y

ND Northern Democrats SD Southern Democrats

	393	394	395	396	397	398
16 **Manzullo**	Y	Y	Y	Y	Y	Y
17 Evans	?	?	Y	Y	Y	Y
18 **LaHood**	Y	Y	Y	Y	Y	Y
19 Poshard	N	Y	Y	Y	Y	N
20 **Shimkus**	Y	Y	Y	Y	Y	Y
INDIANA						
1 Visclosky	N	Y	Y	Y	Y	N
2 **McIntosh**	Y	Y	Y	Y	Y	Y
3 Roemer	N	Y	Y	Y	Y	Y
4 **Souder**	Y	Y	?	Y	Y	Y
5 **Buyer**	Y	Y	Y	Y	Y	Y
6 **Burton**	Y	Y	Y	Y	Y	Y
7 **Pease**	Y	Y	Y	Y	Y	Y
8 **Hostettler**	Y	Y	Y	Y	Y	Y
9 Hamilton	N	Y	Y	Y	Y	Y
10 Carson	N	Y	Y	Y	Y	Y
IOWA						
1 **Leach**	Y	Y	Y	Y	Y	Y
2 **Nussle**	Y	Y	Y	Y	Y	Y
3 Boswell	Y	Y	Y	Y	Y	N
4 **Ganske**	Y	Y	Y	Y	Y	Y
5 **Latham**	Y	Y	Y	Y	Y	Y
KANSAS						
1 **Moran**	Y	Y	Y	Y	Y	Y
2 **Ryun**	Y	Y	Y	Y	Y	Y
3 **Snowbarger**	Y	Y	Y	Y	Y	Y
4 **Tiahrt**	Y	Y	Y	Y	Y	Y
KENTUCKY						
1 **Whitfield**	Y	Y	Y	Y	Y	Y
2 **Lewis**	Y	Y	Y	Y	Y	Y
3 **Northup**	Y	Y	Y	Y	Y	Y
4 **Bunning**	Y	Y	Y	Y	Y	Y
5 **Rogers**	Y	Y	Y	Y	Y	Y
6 Baesler	N	Y	Y	Y	Y	N
LOUISIANA						
1 **Livingston**	Y	Y	Y	Y	Y	Y
2 Jefferson	N	Y	Y	Y	Y	Y
3 **Tauzin**	Y	Y	Y	Y	Y	Y
4 **McCrery**	Y	Y	Y	Y	Y	Y
5 **Cooksey**	Y	Y	Y	Y	Y	Y
6 **Baker**	Y	Y	Y	Y	Y	Y
7 John	N	Y	Y	Y	Y	Y
MAINE						
1 Allen	N	Y	Y	Y	Y	N
2 Baldacci	N	Y	Y	Y	Y	N
MARYLAND						
1 **Gilchrest**	Y	Y	Y	Y	Y	Y
2 **Ehrlich**	Y	Y	Y	Y	Y	Y
3 Cardin	N	Y	Y	Y	Y	N
4 Wynn	N	Y	Y	Y	Y	N
5 Hoyer	N	Y	Y	Y	Y	N
6 **Bartlett**	Y	Y	Y	Y	Y	Y
7 Cummings	N	Y	Y	Y	Y	Y
8 **Morella**	Y	Y	Y	Y	Y	Y
MASSACHUSETTS						
1 Olver	N	Y	Y	?	Y	N
2 Neal	N	Y	Y	Y	?	N
3 McGovern	N	Y	Y	Y	Y	N
4 Frank	N	Y	Y	Y	Y	N
5 Meehan	N	Y	Y	Y	Y	N
6 Tierney	N	Y	Y	Y	Y	N
7 Markey	Y	Y	Y	Y	Y	N
8 Kennedy	N	Y	Y	Y	Y	N
9 Moakley	N	Y	Y	Y	Y	N
10 Delahunt	N	Y	Y	Y	Y	N
MICHIGAN						
1 Stupak	N	Y	Y	Y	Y	N
2 **Hoekstra**	Y	Y	Y	Y	Y	Y
3 **Ehlers**	Y	Y	Y	Y	+	?
4 **Camp**	Y	Y	Y	Y	Y	Y
5 Barcia	N	Y	Y	Y	Y	Y
6 **Upton**	Y	N	Y	Y	Y	Y
7 **Smith**	Y	Y	Y	Y	Y	Y
8 Stabenow	N	Y	Y	Y	Y	N
9 Kildee	N	Y	Y	Y	Y	N
10 Bonior	N	Y	?	?	Y	Y
11 **Knollenberg**	Y	Y	Y	Y	Y	Y
12 Levin	N	Y	Y	Y	Y	N
13 Rivers	N	Y	Y	Y	Y	N
14 Conyers	N	Y	Y	Y	Y	Y
15 Kilpatrick	N	Y	Y	Y	Y	Y
16 Dingell	N	Y	Y	Y	Y	N
MINNESOTA						
1 **Gutknecht**	Y	Y	Y	Y	Y	Y
2 Minge	N	N	Y	Y	Y	N

	393	394	395	396	397	398
3 **Ramstad**	Y	Y	Y	Y	Y	Y
4 Vento	N	Y	Y	Y	Y	N
5 Sabo	N	Y	Y	Y	Y	N
6 Luther	N	Y	Y	Y	Y	N
7 Peterson	N	Y	Y	Y	Y	Y
8 Oberstar	N	Y	Y	Y	Y	N
MISSISSIPPI						
1 **Wicker**	Y	Y	Y	Y	Y	Y
2 Thompson	N	Y	Y	Y	Y	Y
3 **Pickering**	Y	Y	Y	Y	Y	Y
4 **Parker**	Y	Y	?	Y	Y	Y
5 Taylor	Y	Y	Y	Y	Y	Y
MISSOURI						
1 Clay	N	Y	Y	Y	Y	Y
2 **Talent**	Y	Y	Y	Y	Y	Y
3 Gephardt	N	Y	?	?	Y	N
4 Skelton	N	Y	Y	Y	Y	Y
5 McCarthy	N	Y	Y	Y	Y	N
6 Danner	N	Y	Y	Y	Y	Y
7 **Blunt**	Y	Y	Y	Y	Y	Y
8 **Emerson**	Y	Y	Y	Y	Y	Y
9 **Hulshof**	Y	Y	Y	Y	Y	Y
MONTANA						
AL **Hill**	Y	Y	Y	Y	Y	Y
NEBRASKA						
1 **Bereuter**	Y	Y	Y	Y	Y	Y
2 **Christensen**	Y	Y	Y	Y	Y	Y
3 **Barrett**	Y	Y	Y	Y	Y	Y
NEVADA						
1 **Ensign**	Y	Y	Y	Y	Y	Y
2 **Gibbons**	Y	Y	Y	Y	Y	Y
NEW HAMPSHIRE						
1 **Sununu**	Y	Y	?	Y	Y	Y
2 **Bass**	Y	Y	Y	Y	Y	Y
NEW JERSEY						
1 Andrews	N	Y	Y	Y	Y	N
2 **LoBiondo**	Y	Y	Y	Y	Y	Y
3 **Saxton**	Y	Y	Y	Y	Y	Y
4 **Smith**	Y	Y	Y	Y	Y	Y
5 **Roukema**	Y	Y	Y	Y	Y	Y
6 Pallone	N	Y	Y	Y	Y	N
7 **Franks**	Y	Y	Y	Y	Y	Y
8 Pascrell	N	Y	Y	?	Y	N
9 Rothman	N	Y	Y	Y	Y	N
10 Payne	N	Y	Y	Y	Y	N
11 **Frelinghuysen**	Y	Y	Y	Y	Y	Y
12 **Pappas**	Y	Y	Y	Y	Y	Y
13 Menendez	N	Y	Y	Y	Y	Y
NEW MEXICO						
1 **Schiff**	?	?	?	?	?	?
2 **Skeen**	Y	Y	Y	Y	Y	Y
3 **Redmond**	Y	Y	Y	Y	Y	Y
NEW YORK						
1 **Forbes**	Y	Y	Y	Y	Y	N
2 **Lazio**	Y	Y	Y	Y	Y	Y
3 **King**	Y	Y	Y	Y	Y	Y
4 McCarthy	N	Y	Y	Y	Y	N
5 Ackerman	N	Y	Y	Y	Y	N
6 Flake	N	Y	Y	Y	Y	?
7 Manton	N	Y	Y	Y	Y	Y
8 Nadler	N	?	Y	Y	Y	N
9 Schumer	N	Y	Y	Y	Y	N
10 Towns	N	Y	Y	Y	Y	Y
11 Owens	N	Y	Y	Y	Y	Y
12 Velázquez	N	Y	Y	Y	Y	Y
13 Vacant						
14 Maloney	N	Y	Y	Y	Y	N
15 Rangel	N	Y	?	?	Y	Y
16 Serrano	N	Y	Y	Y	Y	Y
17 Engel	N	Y	Y	Y	Y	N
18 Lowey	N	Y	Y	Y	Y	N
19 **Kelly**	Y	Y	Y	Y	Y	Y
20 **Gilman**	Y	Y	Y	Y	Y	Y
21 McNulty	N	Y	Y	Y	Y	N
22 **Solomon**	Y	Y	Y	Y	Y	Y
23 **Boehlert**	Y	Y	Y	Y	Y	Y
24 **McHugh**	Y	Y	Y	Y	Y	Y
25 **Walsh**	Y	Y	Y	Y	Y	Y
26 Hinchey	N	Y	Y	Y	Y	N
27 **Paxon**	Y	Y	Y	Y	Y	Y
28 Slaughter	N	Y	Y	Y	Y	N
29 LaFalce	N	Y	Y	Y	Y	N
30 **Quinn**	Y	Y	Y	Y	Y	Y
31 **Houghton**	Y	Y	Y	Y	Y	Y

	393	394	395	396	397	398
NORTH CAROLINA						
1 Clayton	N	Y	Y	Y	Y	Y
2 Etheridge	N	Y	Y	Y	Y	N
3 **Jones**	Y	Y	Y	Y	Y	Y
4 Price	N	Y	Y	Y	Y	N
5 **Burr**	Y	Y	Y	Y	Y	Y
6 **Coble**	Y	Y	Y	Y	Y	Y
7 McIntyre	Y	Y	Y	Y	Y	N
8 Hefner	Y	Y	Y	Y	Y	N
9 **Myrick**	Y	Y	Y	Y	Y	Y
10 **Ballenger**	Y	Y	Y	Y	Y	Y
11 **Taylor**	Y	Y	Y	Y	Y	Y
12 Watt	N	Y	Y	Y	Y	Y
NORTH DAKOTA						
AL Pomeroy	N	Y	Y	Y	Y	N
OHIO						
1 **Chabot**	Y	Y	Y	Y	Y	Y
2 **Portman**	Y	Y	Y	Y	Y	Y
3 Hall	N	Y	Y	Y	Y	N
4 **Oxley**	Y	Y	Y	Y	Y	Y
5 **Gillmor**	Y	Y	Y	Y	Y	Y
6 Strickland	N	Y	Y	Y	Y	Y
7 **Hobson**	Y	Y	Y	Y	Y	Y
8 **Boehner**	Y	Y	Y	Y	Y	Y
9 Kaptur	N	Y	Y	Y	Y	Y
10 Kucinich	N	Y	Y	Y	Y	N
11 Stokes	N	Y	Y	Y	Y	Y
12 **Kasich**	Y	Y	Y	Y	Y	Y
13 Brown	N	Y	Y	Y	Y	N
14 Sawyer	N	Y	Y	Y	Y	N
15 **Pryce**	Y	Y	Y	Y	Y	Y
16 **Regula**	Y	Y	Y	Y	Y	Y
17 Traficant	Y	Y	Y	Y	Y	Y
18 **Ney**	Y	Y	Y	Y	Y	Y
19 **LaTourette**	Y	Y	Y	Y	Y	Y
OKLAHOMA						
1 **Largent**	Y	Y	Y	Y	Y	Y
2 **Coburn**	Y	Y	Y	Y	Y	Y
3 **Watkins**	Y	Y	Y	Y	Y	Y
4 **Watts**	Y	Y	Y	Y	Y	Y
5 **Istook**	Y	Y	Y	Y	Y	Y
6 **Lucas**	Y	Y	Y	Y	Y	Y
OREGON						
1 Furse	?	?	?	?	?	?
2 **Smith**	Y	Y	Y	Y	Y	?
3 Blumenauer	N	Y	Y	Y	Y	N
4 DeFazio	N	Y	Y	Y	Y	Y
5 Hooley	N	Y	Y	Y	Y	N
PENNSYLVANIA						
1 Foglietta	?	Y	Y	Y	Y	N
2 Fattah	N	Y	Y	Y	Y	N
3 Borski	N	Y	Y	Y	Y	N
4 Klink	N	Y	Y	Y	Y	Y
5 **Peterson**	Y	Y	Y	Y	Y	Y
6 Holden	N	Y	Y	Y	Y	Y
7 **Weldon**	Y	Y	Y	Y	Y	Y
8 **Greenwood**	Y	Y	+	Y	Y	Y
9 **Shuster**	Y	Y	Y	Y	Y	Y
10 **McDade**	Y	Y	Y	Y	Y	Y
11 Kanjorski	N	Y	Y	Y	Y	N
12 Murtha	Y	Y	Y	Y	Y	Y
13 **Fox**	Y	Y	Y	Y	Y	Y
14 Coyne	N	Y	Y	Y	Y	N
15 McHale	N	Y	Y	Y	Y	N
16 **Pitts**	Y	Y	Y	Y	Y	Y
17 **Gekas**	Y	Y	Y	Y	Y	Y
18 Doyle	N	Y	Y	Y	Y	Y
19 **Goodling**	Y	Y	Y	Y	Y	Y
20 Mascara	N	Y	Y	Y	Y	N
21 **English**	Y	Y	Y	Y	Y	Y
RHODE ISLAND						
1 Kennedy	N	Y	Y	Y	Y	N
2 Weygand	N	Y	Y	Y	Y	N
SOUTH CAROLINA						
1 **Sanford**	Y	Y	Y	Y	Y	Y
2 **Spence**	Y	Y	Y	Y	Y	Y
3 **Graham**	Y	Y	Y	Y	Y	Y
4 **Inglis**	Y	Y	Y	Y	Y	Y
5 Spratt	N	Y	Y	Y	Y	N
6 Clyburn	N	Y	Y	Y	Y	Y
SOUTH DAKOTA						
AL **Thune**	Y	Y	Y	Y	Y	Y
TENNESSEE						
1 **Jenkins**	Y	Y	Y	Y	Y	Y
2 **Duncan**	Y	Y	Y	Y	Y	Y

	393	394	395	396	397	398
3 **Wamp**	Y	Y	Y	Y	Y	Y
4 **Hilleary**	Y	Y	Y	Y	Y	Y
5 Clement	N	Y	Y	Y	Y	N
6 Gordon	N	Y	Y	Y	Y	N
7 **Bryant**	Y	Y	Y	Y	Y	Y
8 Tanner	N	Y	Y	Y	Y	N
9 Ford	N	Y	Y	Y	Y	N
TEXAS						
1 Sandlin	N	Y	Y	Y	Y	N
2 Turner	N	Y	Y	Y	Y	Y
3 **Johnson, Sam**	Y	Y	Y	Y	Y	Y
4 Hall	Y	Y	Y	Y	Y	Y
5 **Sessions**	Y	Y	Y	Y	Y	Y
6 **Barton**	Y	Y	Y	Y	Y	Y
7 **Archer**	Y	Y	Y	Y	Y	Y
8 **Brady**	Y	Y	Y	Y	Y	Y
9 Lampson	N	Y	Y	Y	Y	N
10 Doggett	N	Y	Y	Y	Y	N
11 Edwards	N	Y	Y	Y	Y	Y
12 **Granger**	Y	Y	Y	Y	Y	Y
13 **Thornberry**	Y	N	Y	Y	Y	Y
14 **Paul**	Y	N	Y	Y	N	Y
15 Hinojosa	N	Y	Y	Y	Y	+
16 Reyes	N	Y	Y	Y	Y	Y
17 Stenholm	Y	Y	Y	Y	Y	Y
18 Jackson-Lee	N	Y	Y	Y	Y	Y
19 **Combest**	Y	Y	Y	Y	Y	Y
20 Gonzalez	?	?	?	?	?	?
21 **Smith**	Y	?	Y	Y	Y	Y
22 **DeLay**	Y	Y	Y	Y	Y	Y
23 **Bonilla**	Y	Y	Y	Y	Y	Y
24 Frost	N	Y	Y	Y	Y	N
25 Bentsen	N	Y	Y	Y	Y	N
26 **Armey**	Y	Y	Y	Y	Y	Y
27 Ortiz	N	Y	Y	Y	Y	+
28 Rodriguez	N	Y	Y	Y	Y	Y
29 Green	N	Y	Y	Y	Y	Y
30 Johnson, E.B.	N	Y	Y	Y	Y	Y
UTAH						
1 **Hansen**	Y	Y	Y	Y	Y	Y
2 **Cook**	Y	Y	Y	Y	Y	Y
3 **Cannon**	Y	Y	Y	Y	Y	Y
VERMONT						
AL Sanders	N	Y	Y	Y	Y	N
VIRGINIA						
1 **Bateman**	Y	Y	Y	Y	Y	Y
2 Pickett	N	Y	Y	Y	Y	Y
3 Scott	N	Y	Y	Y	Y	Y
4 Sisisky	N	Y	Y	Y	Y	Y
5 Goode	N	Y	Y	Y	Y	Y
6 **Goodlatte**	Y	Y	Y	Y	Y	Y
7 **Bliley**	Y	Y	Y	Y	Y	Y
8 Moran	N	Y	Y	Y	Y	N
9 Boucher	Y	Y	Y	Y	Y	N
10 **Wolf**	Y	Y	Y	Y	Y	Y
11 **Davis**	Y	Y	Y	Y	Y	Y
WASHINGTON						
1 **White**	Y	Y	?	Y	Y	Y
2 **Metcalf**	Y	Y	Y	?	?	Y
3 **Smith, Linda**	Y	Y	Y	Y	Y	Y
4 **Hastings**	Y	Y	Y	Y	Y	Y
5 **Nethercutt**	Y	Y	Y	Y	Y	Y
6 Dicks	Y	Y	Y	Y	Y	N
7 McDermott	N	Y	Y	Y	Y	N
8 **Dunn**	Y	Y	Y	Y	Y	Y
9 Smith, Adam	N	Y	Y	Y	Y	N
WEST VIRGINIA						
1 Mollohan	N	Y	Y	Y	Y	Y
2 Wise	N	Y	Y	Y	Y	N
3 Rahall	N	Y	Y	Y	Y	N
WISCONSIN						
1 **Neumann**	Y	Y	Y	Y	Y	Y
2 **Klug**	Y	Y	Y	Y	Y	Y
3 Kind	N	Y	Y	Y	Y	N
4 Kleczka	N	Y	Y	Y	Y	Y
5 Barrett	N	N	Y	Y	Y	N
6 **Petri**	Y	Y	Y	Y	Y	Y
7 Obey	N	Y	Y	Y	Y	N
8 Johnson	N	Y	Y	Y	Y	N
9 **Sensenbrenner**	Y	N	Y	Y	Y	Y
WYOMING						
AL **Cubin**	Y	N	Y	Y	Y	Y

Southern states - Ala., Ark., Fla., Ga., Ky., La., Miss., N.C., Okla., S.C., Tenn., Texas, Va.

HOUSE VOTES 399, 400, 401, 402, 403, 404

399. HR 2264. Fiscal 1998 Labor-HHS Appropriations/Teamsters Election. Hoekstra, R-Mich., amendment to prohibit the use of federal funds for a court-appointed election officer to oversee any future Teamsters election. Adopted 225-195: R 201-20; D 24-174 (ND 10-135, SD 14-39); I 0-1, Sept. 16, 1997.

400. Procedural Motion/Adjourn. Miller, D-Calif., motion to adjourn. Motion rejected 43-355: R 0-210; D 43-145 (ND 34-103, SD 9-42); I 0-0, Sept. 17, 1997.

401. Procedural Motion/Adjourn. DeLauro, D-Conn., motion to adjourn. Motion rejected 39-364: R 1-209; D 38-154 (ND 34-107, SD 4-47); I 0-1, Sept. 17, 1997.

402. HR 2264. Fiscal 1998 Labor-HHS Appropriations/Passage. Passage of the bill to provide $80 billion in discretionary budget authority for the departments of Labor, Health and Human Services (HHS), and Education and related agencies — $5.4 billion more than fiscal 1997 — and to provide a total of $279.2 billion, including mandatory spending, which is $8 billion less than fiscal 1997. Passed 346-80: R 147-77; D 198-3 (ND 146-1, SD 52-2); I 1-0, Sept. 17, 1997.

403. HR 2378. Fiscal 1998 Treasury-Postal Appropriations/Passage. Passage of the bill to provide $25.4 billion in fiscal 1998 for the Treasury Department, U.S. Postal Service, various offices of the Executive Office of the President and certain independent agencies. Passed 231-192: R 102-119; D 129-72 (ND 100-47, SD 29-25); I 0-1, Sept. 17, 1997.

404. Procedural Motion/Adjourn. Miller, D-Calif., motion to adjourn. Motion rejected 57-359: R 8-212; D 49-146 (ND 41-102, SD 8-44); I 0-1, Sept. 17, 1997.

KEY

Y Voted for (yea).
\# Paired for.
\+ Announced for.
N Voted against (nay).
X Paired against.
\- Announced against.
P Voted "present."
C Voted "present" to avoid possible conflict of interest.
? Did not vote or otherwise make a position known.

Democrats ***Republicans***
Independent

	399	400	401	402	403	404
ALABAMA						
1 ***Callahan***	Y	N	N	Y	Y	N
2 ***Everett***	Y	N	N	N	N	N
3 ***Riley***	Y	N	N	N	N	N
4 ***Aderholt***	Y	N	N	N	N	N
5 Cramer	N	N	N	Y	N	N
6 ***Bachus***	Y	N	N	N	N	N
7 Hilliard	N	?	N	Y	Y	N
ALASKA						
AL ***Young***	?	?	N	Y	Y	N
ARIZONA						
1 ***Salmon***	Y	N	N	N	N	N
2 Pastor	N	N	N	Y	Y	Y
3 ***Stump***	Y	N	N	N	N	N
4 ***Shadegg***	Y	N	N	Y	N	Y
5 ***Kolbe***	Y	N	?	Y	Y	N
6 ***Hayworth***	Y	N	N	Y	N	N
ARKANSAS						
1 Berry	Y	Y	Y	Y	N	Y
2 Snyder	N	N	N	Y	N	N
3 ***Hutchinson***	Y	N	N	N	N	N
4 ***Dickey***	Y	N	N	Y	N	N
CALIFORNIA						
1 ***Riggs***	Y	?	N	Y	N	N
2 ***Herger***	Y	N	N	N	N	N
3 Fazio	N	N	N	Y	Y	Y
4 ***Doolittle***	Y	N	N	N	Y	N
5 Matsui	N	N	N	Y	Y	N
6 Woolsey	N	Y	Y	Y	Y	Y
7 Miller	N	Y	Y	Y	Y	Y
8 Pelosi	N	Y	Y	Y	Y	Y
9 Dellums	N	?	N	Y	Y	N
10 Tauscher	N	N	N	Y	N	?
11 ***Pombo***	Y	N	N	N	N	N
12 Lantos	N	N	N	Y	Y	N
13 Stark	N	N	N	Y	Y	Y
14 Eshoo	N	Y	Y	Y	Y	Y
15 ***Campbell***	Y	N	N	Y	N	N
16 Lofgren	N	N	N	N	N	N
17 Farr	N	N	N	Y	Y	N
18 Condit	Y	N	N	?	N	N
19 ***Radanovich***	Y	N	N	N	N	N
20 Dooley	N	N	N	Y	Y	N
21 ***Thomas***	Y	N	N	Y	Y	N
22 Capps	N	N	N	Y	N	N
23 ***Gallegly***	Y	N	N	Y	Y	N
24 Sherman	N	N	N	Y	N	N
25 ***McKeon***	Y	N	N	Y	Y	N
26 Berman	N	N	N	Y	Y	Y
27 ***Rogan***	Y	N	N	Y	N	N
28 ***Dreier***	Y	N	N	Y	Y	N
29 Waxman	N	Y	?	Y	Y	Y
30 Becerra	–	Y	?	Y	N	N
31 Martinez	?	Y	?	Y	Y	N
32 Dixon	N	?	N	Y	Y	N
33 Roybal-Allard	N	?	N	Y	Y	N
34 Torres	?	N	Y	Y	Y	Y
35 Waters	N	Y	Y	Y	Y	Y
36 Harman	N	N	N	Y	Y	N
37 Millender-McD.	N	N	N	Y	Y	N
38 ***Horn***	N	N	N	Y	Y	N
39 ***Royce***	Y	N	N	N	N	N
40 ***Lewis***	Y	N	N	Y	Y	?
41 ***Kim***	Y	N	N	Y	Y	N
42 Brown	N	?	?	Y	Y	N
43 ***Calvert***	Y	N	N	Y	Y	N
44 ***Bono***	Y	N	N	Y	N	N
45 ***Rohrabacher***	Y	N	?	N	N	N
46 Sanchez	N	N	N	Y	N	N
47 ***Cox***	Y	N	N	N	N	N
48 ***Packard***	Y	N	N	Y	Y	N
49 ***Bilbray***	Y	N	N	Y	Y	N
50 Filner	N	Y	Y	Y	Y	Y
51 ***Cunningham***	Y	N	N	Y	N	N
52 ***Hunter***	Y	N	N	Y	Y	N
COLORADO						
1 DeGette	N	N	N	Y	Y	N
2 Skaggs	N	N	N	Y	Y	Y
3 ***McInnis***	Y	?	N	N	N	N
4 ***Schaffer***	Y	N	N	N	N	N
5 ***Hefley***	Y	N	N	N	N	N
6 ***Schaefer***	Y	N	N	N	N	N
CONNECTICUT						
1 Kennelly	N	N	N	Y	N	N
2 Gejdenson	N	Y	Y	Y	N	N
3 DeLauro	N	Y	Y	Y	N	Y
4 ***Shays***	Y	N	N	Y	N	N
5 Maloney	N	N	N	Y	N	N
6 ***Johnson***	Y	N	N	Y	N	N
DELAWARE						
AL ***Castle***	Y	N	?	Y	Y	N
FLORIDA						
1 ***Scarborough***	Y	N	N	N	N	N
2 Boyd	Y	N	N	Y	Y	N
3 Brown	N	N	N	Y	Y	N
4 ***Fowler***	Y	N	N	Y	Y	N
5 Thurman	N	N	N	Y	N	N
6 ***Stearns***	Y	N	N	N	N	N
7 ***Mica***	Y	N	N	N	Y	N
8 ***McCollum***	Y	N	N	N	Y	N
9 ***Bilirakis***	Y	N	N	Y	Y	N
10 ***Young***	Y	N	N	Y	Y	N
11 Davis	N	Y	Y	Y	N	Y
12 ***Canady***	Y	N	N	Y	N	N
13 ***Miller***	Y	N	N	Y	Y	N
14 ***Goss***	Y	N	N	Y	–	–
15 ***Weldon***	Y	N	N	N	Y	N
16 ***Foley***	Y	N	N	Y	N	N
17 Meek	N	N	N	Y	Y	N
18 ***Ros-Lehtinen***	N	N	N	Y	Y	N
19 Wexler	N	N	N	Y	Y	N
20 Deutsch	N	Y	Y	Y	N	Y
21 ***Diaz-Balart***	N	N	?	Y	Y	N
22 ***Shaw***	Y	N	N	Y	Y	N
23 Hastings	N	Y	N	Y	Y	N
GEORGIA						
1 ***Kingston***	Y	N	N	Y	Y	N
2 Bishop	N	N	N	Y	Y	N
3 ***Collins***	Y	N	N	N	N	N
4 McKinney	N	N	N	Y	N	N
5 Lewis	N	Y	N	Y	Y	Y
6 ***Gingrich***						
7 ***Barr***	Y	N	N	N	N	N
8 ***Chambliss***	Y	N	N	Y	N	N
9 ***Deal***	Y	N	N	Y	N	N
10 ***Norwood***	Y	?	N	N	N	N
11 ***Linder***	Y	N	N	N	N	N
HAWAII						
1 Abercrombie	N	N	N	Y	Y	N
2 Mink	N	Y	Y	Y	Y	Y
IDAHO						
1 ***Chenoweth***	Y	?	N	N	N	N
2 ***Crapo***	?	?	N	N	Y	N
ILLINOIS						
1 Rush	N	?	N	Y	Y	N
2 Jackson	N	N	N	Y	Y	Y
3 Lipinski	N	N	N	Y	Y	N
4 Gutierrez	N	N	Y	+	N	N
5 Blagojevich	N	N	N	Y	Y	N
6 ***Hyde***	Y	N	N	Y	Y	N
7 Davis	N	N	N	Y	Y	N
8 ***Crane***	Y	N	N	N	N	N
9 Yates	?	?	?	?	?	?
10 ***Porter***	Y	N	N	Y	Y	N
11 ***Weller***	N	N	N	Y	N	N
12 Costello	N	N	N	Y	N	N
13 ***Fawell***	Y	N	?	Y	Y	N
14 ***Hastert***	Y	N	N	Y	Y	N
15 ***Ewing***	Y	N	N	Y	N	N

ND Northern Democrats SD Southern Democrats

	399	400	401	402	403	404
16 ***Manzullo***	Y	N	N	N	N	N
17 Evans	N	N	N	Y	N	N
18 ***LaHood***	N	N	N	Y	N	N
19 Poshard	N	N	N	Y	N	N
20 ***Shimkus***	Y	N	N	Y	N	N
INDIANA						
1 Visclosky	N	N	N	Y	N	N
2 ***McIntosh***	Y	N	N	N	N	N
3 Roemer	N	N	N	Y	Y	N
4 ***Souder***	Y	N	?	N	N	N
5 ***Buyer***	Y	N	N	Y	Y	N
6 ***Burton***	Y	N	N	N	Y	N
7 ***Pease***	Y	N	N	N	N	N
8 ***Hostettler***	Y	?	N	N	N	N
9 Hamilton	N	N	N	Y	N	N
10 Carson	N	N	N	Y	N	N
IOWA						
1 ***Leach***	Y	N	?	Y	Y	N
2 ***Nussle***	Y	N	?	Y	Y	N
3 Boswell	N	N	N	Y	N	N
4 ***Ganske***	Y	N	N	Y	Y	N
5 ***Latham***	Y	N	N	Y	Y	N
KANSAS						
1 ***Moran***	Y	N	N	N	N	N
2 ***Ryun***	Y	N	N	N	N	N
3 ***Snowbarger***	Y	N	N	N	N	N
4 ***Tiahrt***	Y	N	N	N	N	N
KENTUCKY						
1 ***Whitfield***	Y	N	N	Y	N	N
2 ***Lewis***	Y	N	N	Y	N	N
3 ***Northup***	Y	N	N	Y	N	N
4 ***Bunning***	Y	N	N	Y	N	N
5 ***Rogers***	Y	N	N	Y	Y	N
6 Baesler	N	N	N	Y	N	N
LOUISIANA						
1 ***Livingston***	Y	?	N	Y	Y	N
2 Jefferson	N	Y	?	Y	Y	N
3 ***Tauzin***	Y	N	N	Y	Y	N
4 ***McCrery***	Y	?	N	Y	Y	N
5 ***Cooksey***	Y	N	N	N	N	N
6 ***Baker***	Y	N	N	Y	N	N
7 John	Y	N	N	Y	N	N
MAINE						
1 Allen	N	Y	Y	Y	N	Y
2 Baldacci	N	Y	N	Y	N	N
MARYLAND						
1 ***Gilchrest***	Y	N	N	Y	Y	N
2 ***Ehrlich***	Y	N	N	Y	Y	N
3 Cardin	N	N	N	Y	Y	Y
4 Wynn	N	N	N	Y	Y	N
5 Hoyer	N	N	N	Y	Y	N
6 ***Bartlett***	Y	N	N	N	Y	N
7 Cummings	N	N	N	Y	Y	N
8 ***Morella***	N	N	N	Y	Y	N
MASSACHUSETTS						
1 Olver	N	Y	Y	Y	Y	Y
2 Neal	N	N	N	Y	Y	?
3 McGovern	N	N	N	Y	Y	N
4 Frank	N	Y	Y	Y	Y	Y
5 Meehan	N	N	?	Y	Y	N
6 Tierney	N	Y	Y	Y	Y	N
7 Markey	N	N	N	Y	Y	Y
8 Kennedy	N	N	N	Y	Y	N
9 Moakley	N	N	N	Y	Y	Y
10 Delahunt	N	Y	Y	Y	Y	Y
MICHIGAN						
1 Stupak	Y	Y	Y	Y	Y	N
2 ***Hoekstra***	Y	N	N	N	Y	N
3 ***Ehlers***	Y	N	N	Y	Y	N
4 ***Camp***	Y	N	N	Y	Y	N
5 Barcia	N	N	N	Y	N	N
6 ***Upton***	Y	N	N	Y	Y	N
7 ***Smith***	Y	N	N	N	N	N
8 Stabenow	N	N	N	Y	N	?
9 Kildee	N	N	N	Y	N	N
10 Bonior	N	?	Y	Y	Y	Y
11 ***Knollenberg***	Y	N	N	Y	Y	N
12 Levin	N	N	N	Y	Y	Y
13 Rivers	N	N	N	Y	N	N
14 Conyers	N	?	Y	Y	Y	Y
15 Kilpatrick	N	N	N	Y	Y	N
16 Dingell	N	Y	Y	Y	Y	Y
MINNESOTA						
1 ***Gutknecht***	Y	N	N	Y	N	N
2 Minge	Y	N	N	Y	N	N

	399	400	401	402	403	404
3 ***Ramstad***	Y	N	N	Y	N	N
4 Vento	N	Y	Y	Y	Y	Y
5 Sabo	N	N	N	Y	Y	N
6 Luther	Y	N	N	Y	N	N
7 Peterson	N	N	N	Y	N	N
8 Oberstar	N	N	N	Y	+	N
MISSISSIPPI						
1 ***Wicker***	Y	N	N	Y	Y	N
2 Thompson	N	N	N	Y	N	N
3 ***Pickering***	Y	N	N	Y	Y	N
4 ***Parker***	Y	N	N	Y	Y	N
5 Taylor	Y	N	N	N	N	N
MISSOURI						
1 Clay	N	N	N	Y	Y	N
2 ***Talent***	Y	N	?	N	N	N
3 Gephardt	N	Y	Y	Y	Y	Y
4 Skelton	Y	N	N	Y	Y	N
5 McCarthy	N	N	N	Y	N	N
6 Danner	N	N	N	Y	N	N
7 ***Blunt***	Y	N	N	Y	Y	N
8 ***Emerson***	Y	N	N	Y	N	Y
9 ***Hulshof***	Y	N	N	Y	N	N
MONTANA						
AL ***Hill***	Y	N	N	N	N	N
NEBRASKA						
1 ***Bereuter***	Y	N	N	Y	Y	N
2 ***Christensen***	Y	N	N	Y	N	N
3 ***Barrett***	Y	N	N	Y	Y	N
NEVADA						
1 ***Ensign***	Y	N	N	Y	N	N
2 ***Gibbons***	Y	N	N	Y	N	N
NEW HAMPSHIRE						
1 ***Sununu***	Y	N	N	Y	N	N
2 ***Bass***	Y	N	N	Y	Y	N
NEW JERSEY						
1 Andrews	N	Y	Y	Y	Y	Y
2 ***LoBiondo***	Y	N	N	Y	N	N
3 ***Saxton***	Y	N	N	Y	N	N
4 ***Smith***	Y	N	N	Y	Y	N
5 ***Roukema***	Y	N	N	Y	N	N
6 Pallone	N	Y	Y	Y	Y	Y
7 ***Franks***	Y	N	N	Y	N	N
8 Pascrell	N	N	N	Y	N	N
9 Rothman	N	N	N	Y	N	N
10 Payne	N	N	N	Y	Y	N
11 ***Frelinghuysen***	N	N	N	Y	Y	N
12 ***Pappas***	Y	N	N	Y	N	N
13 Menendez	N	N	N	Y	N	N
NEW MEXICO						
1 ***Schiff***	?	?	?	?	?	?
2 ***Skeen***	Y	N	N	Y	Y	N
3 ***Redmond***	Y	N	N	Y	N	N
NEW YORK						
1 ***Forbes***	N	N	N	Y	N	N
2 ***Lazio***	N	N	N	Y	N	N
3 ***King***	N	N	N	Y	Y	N
4 McCarthy	N	N	N	Y	Y	N
5 Ackerman	N	?	N	Y	Y	?
6 Flake	?	?	N	Y	Y	N
7 Manton	N	N	N	Y	Y	N
8 Nadler	N	N	N	Y	Y	N
9 Schumer	N	N	N	Y	N	N
10 Towns	N	Y	Y	Y	Y	Y
11 Owens	N	Y	Y	Y	Y	Y
12 Velázquez	N	N	N	Y	Y	N
13 Vacant						
14 Maloney	N	N	N	Y	Y	N
15 Rangel	N	N	?	Y	Y	N
16 Serrano	N	N	N	Y	Y	N
17 Engel	N	N	N	Y	Y	N
18 Lowey	N	Y	Y	Y	N	Y
19 ***Kelly***	Y	N	N	Y	Y	N
20 ***Gilman***	N	N	N	Y	Y	N
21 McNulty	N	Y	Y	Y	Y	Y
22 ***Solomon***	?	N	N	Y	Y	N
23 ***Boehlert***	N	N	N	Y	Y	N
24 ***McHugh***	N	N	N	Y	Y	N
25 ***Walsh***	Y	N	N	Y	Y	N
26 Hinchey	N	N	N	Y	Y	Y
27 ***Paxon***	Y	N	N	N	Y	N
28 Slaughter	N	Y	Y	Y	N	Y
29 LaFalce	N	Y	N	Y	Y	N
30 ***Quinn***	N	N	N	Y	Y	N
31 ***Houghton***	N	?	N	Y	Y	?

	399	400	401	402	403	404
NORTH CAROLINA						
1 Clayton	N	N	N	Y	Y	Y
2 Etheridge	N	N	N	Y	N	N
3 ***Jones***	Y	N	N	N	N	N
4 Price	N	N	N	Y	N	N
5 ***Burr***	Y	N	N	Y	N	N
6 ***Coble***	Y	N	N	N	N	N
7 McIntyre	Y	N	N	Y	N	N
8 Hefner	N	Y	N	Y	Y	?
9 ***Myrick***	Y	N	N	N	N	N
10 ***Ballenger***	Y	N	N	Y	Y	N
11 ***Taylor***	Y	?	N	Y	Y	N
12 Watt	N	N	N	Y	Y	N
NORTH DAKOTA						
AL Pomeroy	Y	N	N	Y	Y	N
OHIO						
1 ***Chabot***	Y	N	N	N	N	N
2 ***Portman***	Y	N	N	Y	N	N
3 Hall	N	N	N	Y	Y	N
4 ***Oxley***	Y	N	?	Y	Y	N
5 ***Gillmor***	Y	N	N	Y	Y	N
6 Strickland	N	N	N	Y	N	N
7 ***Hobson***	Y	N	N	Y	Y	N
8 ***Boehner***	Y	N	?	Y	Y	N
9 Kaptur	N	?	Y	Y	Y	Y
10 Kucinich	N	N	N	Y	N	N
11 Stokes	N	N	N	Y	Y	N
12 ***Kasich***	Y	N	N	?	Y	N
13 Brown	N	Y	Y	Y	Y	N
14 Sawyer	N	N	N	Y	Y	N
15 ***Pryce***	Y	P	N	Y	N	N
16 ***Regula***	Y	N	N	Y	Y	N
17 Traficant	Y	N	N	Y	Y	N
18 ***Ney***	Y	N	Y	Y	Y	N
19 ***LaTourette***	Y	N	N	Y	Y	N
OKLAHOMA						
1 ***Largent***	Y	N	?	N	N	Y
2 ***Coburn***	Y	N	N	N	N	Y
3 ***Watkins***	Y	N	N	Y	N	N
4 ***Watts***	Y	N	N	Y	N	N
5 ***Istook***	Y	?	N	N	N	N
6 ***Lucas***	Y	N	N	Y	N	N
OREGON						
1 Furse	?	?	?	?	?	?
2 ***Smith***	?	N	N	Y	Y	N
3 Blumenauer	N	N	N	Y	Y	N
4 DeFazio	N	Y	Y	Y	N	Y
5 Hooley	N	N	N	Y	N	N
PENNSYLVANIA						
1 Foglietta	N	?	?	Y	?	?
2 Fattah	N	N	N	Y	Y	N
3 Borski	N	N	N	Y	Y	N
4 Klink	N	N	N	Y	Y	N
5 ***Peterson***	Y	N	N	Y	N	N
6 Holden	N	N	N	Y	Y	N
7 ***Weldon***	N	N	N	Y	Y	N
8 ***Greenwood***	Y	N	N	Y	Y	N
9 ***Shuster***	Y	N	N	N	Y	N
10 ***McDade***	N	N	N	Y	Y	N
11 Kanjorski	N	N	N	Y	Y	N
12 Murtha	N	N	N	Y	Y	N
13 ***Fox***	N	N	N	Y	N	N
14 Coyne	N	Y	Y	Y	Y	Y
15 McHale	N	N	N	Y	Y	N
16 ***Pitts***	Y	N	N	N	N	N
17 ***Gekas***	Y	N	N	Y	Y	N
18 Doyle	N	N	N	Y	Y	N
19 ***Goodling***	Y	N	N	Y	N	Y
20 Mascara	N	N	N	Y	Y	N
21 ***English***	N	N	N	Y	N	?
RHODE ISLAND						
1 Kennedy	N	N	N	Y	N	N
2 Weygand	N	N	N	Y	N	N
SOUTH CAROLINA						
1 ***Sanford***	Y	N	N	N	N	Y
2 ***Spence***	Y	N	N	Y	Y	N
3 ***Graham***	Y	N	N	N	N	N
4 ***Inglis***	Y	?	N	N	N	N
5 Spratt	N	N	N	Y	N	Y
6 Clyburn	N	N	N	Y	Y	N
SOUTH DAKOTA						
AL ***Thune***	Y	N	N	Y	N	N
TENNESSEE						
1 ***Jenkins***	Y	N	N	Y	N	N
2 ***Duncan***	Y	N	N	Y	N	N

	399	400	401	402	403	404
3 ***Wamp***	Y	N	N	N	N	N
4 ***Hilleary***	Y	N	N	N	N	Y
5 Clement	N	N	N	Y	Y	N
6 Gordon	Y	N	N	Y	N	N
7 ***Bryant***	Y	N	N	N	N	N
8 Tanner	Y	N	N	Y	Y	N
9 Ford	N	Y	N	Y	N	Y
TEXAS						
1 Sandlin	N	N	N	Y	N	N
2 Turner	Y	N	N	Y	N	N
3 ***Johnson, Sam***	Y	N	?	N	Y	N
4 Hall	Y	N	N	Y	N	N
5 ***Sessions***	Y	N	N	N	N	N
6 ***Barton***	Y	?	N	N	Y	Y
7 ***Archer***	Y	N	N	N	Y	N
8 ***Brady***	Y	N	N	N	N	N
9 Lampson	N	N	N	Y	N	N
10 Doggett	Y	Y	Y	Y	Y	Y
11 Edwards	Y	N	N	Y	Y	N
12 ***Granger***	Y	N	N	N	N	N
13 ***Thornberry***	Y	N	N	N	N	N
14 ***Paul***	Y	N	N	N	N	N
15 Hinojosa	N	N	N	Y	N	N
16 Reyes	N	?	?	Y	N	N
17 Stenholm	Y	N	N	Y	N	N
18 Jackson-Lee	N	N	N	Y	Y	N
19 ***Combest***	Y	N	N	N	Y	N
20 Gonzalez	?	?	?	?	?	?
21 ***Smith***	Y	N	N	Y	Y	N
22 ***DeLay***	Y	N	N	Y	Y	N
23 ***Bonilla***	Y	N	N	Y	Y	N
24 Frost	Y	N	N	Y	Y	N
25 Bentsen	N	N	N	Y	Y	N
26 ***Armey***	Y	N	?	Y	Y	N
27 Ortiz	+	N	N	Y	Y	N
28 Rodriguez	N	N	N	Y	Y	N
29 Green	N	N	N	Y	Y	N
30 Johnson, E.B.	N	N	N	Y	Y	N
UTAH						
1 ***Hansen***	Y	N	N	Y	Y	N
2 ***Cook***	Y	N	N	Y	Y	N
3 ***Cannon***	Y	N	N	Y	N	N
VERMONT						
AL *Sanders*	N	?	N	Y	N	N
VIRGINIA						
1 ***Bateman***	Y	N	N	Y	Y	N
2 Pickett	N	N	N	Y	Y	N
3 Scott	N	N	N	Y	Y	N
4 Sisisky	N	N	N	Y	Y	N
5 Goode	Y	N	N	N	N	N
6 ***Goodlatte***	Y	N	N	N	N	N
7 ***Bliley***	Y	N	N	Y	Y	N
8 Moran	N	?	?	Y	Y	?
9 Boucher	N	N	N	Y	Y	N
10 ***Wolf***	Y	N	N	Y	Y	N
11 ***Davis***	Y	N	N	Y	?	N
WASHINGTON						
1 ***White***	Y	N	N	Y	?	?
2 ***Metcalf***	N	N	?	Y	N	N
3 ***Smith, Linda***	Y	N	N	Y	?	N
4 ***Hastings***	Y	N	N	N	Y	N
5 ***Nethercutt***	Y	N	N	Y	N	N
6 Dicks	N	N	N	Y	Y	?
7 McDermott	N	Y	Y	Y	Y	N
8 ***Dunn***	Y	N	N	Y	Y	N
9 Smith, Adam	N	N	N	Y	N	N
WEST VIRGINIA						
1 Mollohan	N	N	N	Y	Y	N
2 Wise	N	?	?	Y	N	N
3 Rahall	N	N	N	Y	Y	N
WISCONSIN						
1 ***Neumann***	Y	N	N	N	N	N
2 ***Klug***	Y	N	N	Y	N	N
3 Kind	N	N	N	Y	N	N
4 Kleczka	N	N	N	Y	Y	N
5 Barrett	Y	N	N	Y	N	Y
6 ***Petri***	Y	N	N	N	N	N
7 Obey	Y	N	N	Y	Y	N
8 Johnson	Y	N	N	Y	N	N
9 ***Sensenbrenner***	Y	N	N	N	N	N
WYOMING						
AL ***Cubin***	Y	N	N	N	N	N

Southern states - Ala., Ark., Fla., Ga., Ky., La., Miss., N.C., Okla., S.C., Tenn., Texas, Va.

HOUSE VOTES 405, 406, 407, 408, 409, 410

405. Procedural Motion/Adjourn. Doggett, D-Texas, motion to adjourn. Motion rejected 41-370: R 0-218; D 41-151 (ND 34-108, SD 7-43); I 0-1, Sept. 18, 1997.

406. Procedural Motion/Journal. Approval of House Journal of Wednesday, Sept. 17, 1997. Approved 337-78: R 181-39; D 155-39 (ND 110-31, SD 45-8); I 1-0, Sept. 18, 1997.

407. H Res 168. House Ethics Reform Recommendations/ Previous Question. Solomon, R-N.Y., motion to order the previous question (thus ending debate and the possibility of amendment) on adoption of the rule (H Res 230) to provide for House floor consideration of the resolution (H Res 168) to revamp ethics rules of the House Committee on Standards of Official Conduct by, among other things, allowing non-members with "personal knowledge" of a violation to file a complaint with the committee, giving subcommittees more leeway to expand ethics probes and improving due process for members before the committee. Motion agreed to 227-191: R 220-0; D 7-190 (ND 7-137, SD 0-53); I 0-1, Sept. 18, 1997.

408. H Res 168. House Ethics Reform Recommendations/ Application. Livingston, R-La., amendment to apply the rules in H Res 168 to all complaints filed during the 105th Congress and each subsequent Congress. Adopted 420-0: R 219-0; D 200-0 (ND 147-0, SD 53-0); I 1-0, Sept. 18, 1997.

409. H Res 168. House Ethics Reform Recommendations/ Outside Complaints. Murtha, D-Pa., amendment to require that a member of the House sponsor a complaint from an outside group or non-member before it could be filed officially. Adopted 228-193: R 197-22; D 31-170 (ND 22-126, SD 9-44); I 0-1, Sept. 18, 1997.

410. H Res 168. House Ethics Reform Recommendations/ Complaint Dismissals. Tauzin, R-La., amendment to dismiss a complaint filed with the House Committee on Standards for Official Conduct after 180 calendar days if the committee is deadlocked and a motion to establish an investigative subcommittee does not prevail. Rejected 181-236; R 175-42; D 6-193 (ND 4-143, SD 2-50); I 0-1, Sept. 18, 1997.

KEY

Y	Voted for (yea).
#	Paired for.
+	Announced for.
N	Voted against (nay).
X	Paired against.
–	Announced against.
P	Voted "present."
C	Voted "present" to avoid possible conflict of interest.
?	Did not vote or otherwise make a position known.

Democrats ***Republicans***
Independent

	405	406	407	408	409	410
ALABAMA						
1 ***Callahan***	N	Y	Y	Y	Y	Y
2 ***Everett***	N	N	Y	Y	Y	Y
3 ***Riley***	N	Y	Y	Y	Y	Y
4 ***Aderholt***	N	Y	Y	Y	Y	Y
5 Cramer	N	Y	N	Y	N	N
6 ***Bachus***	N	Y	Y	Y	Y	Y
7 Hilliard	N	N	N	Y	N	N
ALASKA						
AL ***Young***	N	Y	Y	Y	Y	?
ARIZONA						
1 ***Salmon***	N	N	Y	Y	Y	Y
2 Pastor	N	Y	N	Y	Y	N
3 ***Stump***	N	Y	Y	Y	Y	Y
4 ***Shadegg***	N	N	Y	Y	Y	Y
5 ***Kolbe***	N	Y	Y	Y	Y	Y
6 ***Hayworth***	N	Y	Y	Y	Y	Y
ARKANSAS						
1 Berry	Y	Y	N	Y	N	N
2 Snyder	N	Y	N	Y	N	N
3 ***Hutchinson***	N	Y	Y	Y	N	Y
4 ***Dickey***	N	Y	Y	Y	Y	Y
CALIFORNIA						
1 ***Riggs***	N	Y	Y	Y	Y	Y
2 ***Herger***	N	Y	Y	Y	Y	Y
3 Fazio	N	?	N	Y	N	N
4 ***Doolittle***	N	Y	Y	Y	Y	Y
5 Matsui	N	Y	N	Y	N	N
6 Woolsey	Y	Y	N	Y	N	N
7 Miller	Y	N	N	Y	N	N
8 Pelosi	Y	Y	N	Y	N	N
9 Dellums	N	Y	N	Y	N	N
10 Tauscher	N	Y	N	Y	N	N
11 ***Pombo***	N	N	Y	Y	Y	Y
12 Lantos	N	Y	N	Y	N	N
13 Stark	Y	Y	N	Y	N	N
14 Eshoo	Y	Y	N	Y	N	N
15 ***Campbell***	N	Y	Y	Y	Y	Y
16 Lofgren	N	Y	N	Y	N	N
17 Farr	N	Y	N	Y	Y	N
18 Condit	N	Y	N	Y	Y	Y
19 ***Radanovich***	N	Y	Y	Y	Y	Y
20 Dooley	N	Y	N	Y	N	N
21 ***Thomas***	N	Y	Y	Y	Y	Y
22 Capps	N	Y	N	Y	N	N
23 ***Gallegly***	N	Y	Y	Y	Y	Y
24 Sherman	N	Y	N	Y	N	N
25 ***McKeon***	N	Y	Y	Y	Y	Y
26 Berman	N	Y	N	Y	N	N
27 ***Rogan***	N	Y	Y	Y	Y	Y
28 ***Dreier***	N	Y	Y	Y	Y	Y
29 Waxman	Y	Y	N	Y	N	N
30 Becerra	?	N	N	Y	N	N
31 Martinez	Y	Y	N	Y	N	N
32 Dixon	N	Y	N	Y	N	N
33 Roybal-Allard	N	?	N	Y	N	N
34 Torres	Y	Y	N	Y	Y	N
35 Waters	Y	N	N	Y	N	N
36 Harman	N	Y	N	Y	N	N
37 Millender-McD.	N	Y	N	Y	N	N
38 ***Horn***	N	Y	Y	Y	Y	Y
39 ***Royce***	N	Y	Y	Y	Y	Y
40 ***Lewis***	N	Y	Y	Y	Y	N
41 ***Kim***	N	Y	Y	P	P	P
42 Brown	N	N	N	Y	N	N
43 ***Calvert***	N	Y	Y	Y	Y	Y
44 ***Bono***	N	Y	Y	Y	Y	Y
45 ***Rohrabacher***	N	Y	Y	Y	Y	Y
46 Sanchez	N	Y	N	Y	N	N
47 ***Cox***	N	Y	Y	Y	Y	Y
48 ***Packard***	N	Y	Y	Y	Y	N
49 ***Bilbray***	N	Y	Y	Y	Y	Y
50 Filner	Y	N	N	Y	N	N
51 ***Cunningham***	N	Y	Y	Y	Y	Y
52 ***Hunter***	?	?	Y	Y	Y	Y
COLORADO						
1 DeGette	N	Y	N	Y	N	N
2 Skaggs	N	Y	N	Y	N	N
3 ***McInnis***	N	Y	Y	Y	Y	Y
4 ***Schaffer***	N	N	Y	Y	N	N
5 ***Hefley***	N	N	Y	Y	Y	Y
6 ***Schaefer***	N	Y	Y	Y	Y	Y
CONNECTICUT						
1 Kennelly	N	Y	N	Y	N	N
2 Gejdenson	Y	N	N	Y	N	N
3 DeLauro	Y	Y	N	Y	N	N
4 ***Shays***	N	Y	Y	Y	N	N
5 Maloney	N	Y	N	Y	N	N
6 ***Johnson***	N	Y	Y	Y	N	N
DELAWARE						
AL ***Castle***	N	Y	Y	Y	N	N
FLORIDA						
1 ***Scarborough***	N	Y	Y	Y	Y	N
2 Boyd	N	Y	N	Y	N	N
3 Brown	N	Y	N	Y	N	N
4 ***Fowler***	N	Y	Y	Y	Y	Y
5 Thurman	N	Y	N	Y	N	N
6 ***Stearns***	N	Y	Y	Y	Y	Y
7 ***Mica***	N	Y	Y	Y	Y	Y
8 ***McCollum***	N	Y	Y	Y	?	Y
9 ***Bilirakis***	N	Y	Y	Y	Y	Y
10 ***Young***	N	Y	Y	Y	Y	N
11 Davis	?	Y	N	Y	N	N
12 ***Canady***	N	N	Y	Y	N	Y
13 ***Miller***	N	Y	Y	Y	Y	Y
14 ***Goss***	–	+	+	+	+	+
15 ***Weldon***	N	Y	Y	Y	Y	Y
16 ***Foley***	N	Y	Y	Y	Y	Y
17 Meek	?	?	?	?	?	?
18 ***Ros-Lehtinen***	?	Y	Y	Y	Y	Y
19 Wexler	N	Y	N	Y	N	N
20 Deutsch	Y	Y	N	Y	N	N
21 ***Diaz-Balart***	N	Y	Y	Y	Y	Y
22 ***Shaw***	N	Y	Y	Y	Y	N
23 Hastings	Y	Y	N	Y	N	?
GEORGIA						
1 ***Kingston***	N	Y	Y	Y	Y	Y
2 Bishop	N	Y	N	Y	Y	N
3 ***Collins***	N	Y	Y	Y	Y	Y
4 McKinney	N	Y	N	Y	N	N
5 Lewis	Y	N	N	Y	N	N
6 ***Gingrich***						
7 ***Barr***	N	Y	Y	Y	Y	Y
8 ***Chambliss***	N	N	Y	Y	Y	Y
9 ***Deal***	N	Y	Y	Y	Y	Y
10 ***Norwood***	N	Y	Y	Y	Y	Y
11 ***Linder***	N	Y	Y	Y	Y	Y
HAWAII						
1 Abercrombie	N	N	N	Y	Y	N
2 Mink	Y	Y	N	Y	Y	N
IDAHO						
1 ***Chenoweth***	N	Y	Y	Y	Y	Y
2 ***Crapo***	N	Y	Y	Y	Y	Y
ILLINOIS						
1 Rush	N	?	N	Y	N	N
2 Jackson	N	Y	N	Y	N	N
3 Lipinski	N	Y	N	Y	Y	N
4 Gutierrez	N	Y	N	Y	N	N
5 Blagojevich	N	Y	N	Y	N	N
6 ***Hyde***	N	Y	Y	Y	Y	Y
7 Davis	N	Y	N	Y	N	N
8 ***Crane***	N	Y	Y	Y	Y	Y
9 Yates	?	N	N	Y	N	N
10 ***Porter***	N	Y	Y	Y	Y	–
11 ***Weller***	N	N	Y	Y	Y	Y
12 Costello	N	N	N	Y	N	N
13 ***Fawell***	N	Y	Y	Y	Y	Y
14 ***Hastert***	N	Y	Y	Y	Y	Y
15 ***Ewing***	N	Y	Y	Y	Y	Y

ND Northern Democrats SD Southern Democrats

	405	406	407	408	409	410
16 ***Manzullo***	N	N	Y	Y	Y	Y
17 Evans	Y	Y	N	Y	N	N
18 ***LaHood***	N	N	Y	Y	Y	Y
19 Poshard	N	N	N	Y	N	N
20 ***Shimkus***	N	Y	Y	Y	Y	N
INDIANA						
1 Visclosky	N	N	N	Y	N	N
2 ***McIntosh***	N	N	Y	Y	Y	Y
3 Roemer	N	Y	N	Y	N	N
4 ***Souder***	N	N	Y	Y	Y	Y
5 ***Buyer***	N	Y	Y	Y	Y	Y
6 ***Burton***	N	Y	Y	Y	Y	Y
7 ***Pease***	N	Y	Y	Y	Y	Y
8 ***Hostettler***	N	Y	Y	Y	Y	Y
9 Hamilton	N	Y	N	Y	N	N
10 Carson	N	Y	N	Y	N	N
IOWA						
1 ***Leach***	N	Y	Y	Y	N	N
2 ***Nussle***	N	N	Y	Y	Y	Y
3 Boswell	N	Y	?	Y	N	N
4 ***Ganske***	N	Y	Y	Y	Y	Y
5 ***Latham***	N	Y	Y	Y	Y	N
KANSAS						
1 ***Moran***	N	N	Y	Y	N	Y
2 ***Ryun***	N	N	Y	Y	Y	Y
3 ***Snowbarger***	N	N	Y	Y	Y	Y
4 ***Tiahrt***	N	Y	Y	Y	Y	Y
KENTUCKY						
1 ***Whitfield***	N	Y	Y	Y	Y	Y
2 ***Lewis***	N	Y	Y	Y	Y	Y
3 ***Northup***	N	Y	Y	Y	Y	Y
4 ***Bunning***	N	Y	Y	Y	Y	Y
5 ***Rogers***	N	Y	Y	Y	Y	Y
6 Baesler	N	Y	N	Y	N	N
LOUISIANA						
1 ***Livingston***	N	Y	Y	Y	N	N
2 Jefferson	N	Y	N	Y	N	N
3 ***Tauzin***	N	Y	Y	Y	Y	Y
4 ***McCrery***	N	Y	Y	Y	Y	N
5 ***Cooksey***	N	Y	Y	Y	Y	Y
6 ***Baker***	N	Y	Y	Y	Y	Y
7 John	N	Y	N	Y	N	N
MAINE						
1 Allen	Y	Y	N	Y	N	N
2 Baldacci	N	Y	N	Y	N	N
MARYLAND						
1 ***Gilchrest***	N	Y	Y	Y	Y	Y
2 ***Ehrlich***	N	Y	Y	Y	Y	Y
3 Cardin	N	Y	N	Y	N	N
4 Wynn	N	Y	N	Y	N	N
5 Hoyer	N	Y	N	Y	N	N
6 ***Bartlett***	N	Y	Y	Y	Y	Y
7 Cummings	N	Y	N	Y	N	N
8 ***Morella***	N	Y	Y	Y	N	N
MASSACHUSETTS						
1 Olver	Y	Y	N	Y	N	N
2 Neal	N	Y	N	Y	N	N
3 McGovern	N	Y	N	Y	N	N
4 Frank	Y	N	Y	Y	N	N
5 Meehan	N	Y	Y	Y	N	N
6 Tierney	Y	Y	N	Y	N	N
7 Markey	N	N	N	Y	N	N
8 Kennedy	N	Y	N	Y	N	N
9 Moakley	N	Y	N	Y	N	N
10 Delahunt	Y	Y	Y	Y	N	N
MICHIGAN						
1 Stupak	Y	N	?	Y	N	N
2 ***Hoekstra***	N	Y	Y	Y	Y	Y
3 ***Ehlers***	N	Y	Y	Y	Y	Y
4 ***Camp***	N	Y	Y	Y	Y	Y
5 Barcia	N	Y	N	Y	N	N
6 ***Upton***	N	Y	Y	Y	Y	Y
7 ***Smith***	N	Y	Y	Y	N	Y
8 Stabenow	N	Y	N	Y	N	N
9 Kildee	N	Y	N	Y	N	N
10 Bonior	Y	Y	N	Y	N	N
11 ***Knollenberg***	N	Y	Y	Y	Y	Y
12 Levin	N	N	N	Y	N	N
13 Rivers	N	Y	N	Y	N	N
14 Conyers	Y	Y	N	?	N	N
15 Kilpatrick	N	N	N	Y	N	N
16 Dingell	Y	Y	N	Y	N	N
MINNESOTA						
1 ***Gutknecht***	N	N	Y	Y	Y	Y
2 Minge	N	Y	N	Y	N	N

	405	406	407	408	409	410
3 ***Ramstad***	N	N	Y	Y	N	N
4 Vento	Y	Y	N	Y	N	N
5 Sabo	N	N	N	Y	N	N
6 Luther	N	Y	N	Y	N	N
7 Peterson	N	?	N	Y	N	N
8 Oberstar	–	+	–	+	–	–
MISSISSIPPI						
1 ***Wicker***	N	Y	Y	Y	Y	Y
2 Thompson	N	N	N	Y	N	N
3 ***Pickering***	N	Y	Y	?	Y	Y
4 ***Parker***	N	Y	Y	Y	Y	Y
5 Taylor	N	N	N	Y	Y	N
MISSOURI						
1 Clay	N	N	N	Y	Y	?
2 ***Talent***	N	Y	Y	Y	Y	N
3 Gephardt	?	?	?	?	?	?
4 Skelton	N	Y	N	Y	Y	Y
5 McCarthy	N	Y	N	Y	N	N
6 Danner	N	Y	N	Y	N	N
7 ***Blunt***	N	Y	Y	Y	Y	Y
8 ***Emerson***	N	Y	Y	Y	Y	N
9 ***Hulshof***	N	N	Y	Y	Y	N
MONTANA						
AL ***Hill***	N	Y	Y	Y	Y	Y
NEBRASKA						
1 ***Bereuter***	N	Y	Y	Y	Y	N
2 ***Christensen***	N	Y	Y	Y	Y	Y
3 ***Barrett***	N	Y	Y	Y	Y	Y
NEVADA						
1 ***Ensign***	N	N	Y	Y	Y	Y
2 ***Gibbons***	N	N	Y	Y	Y	Y
NEW HAMPSHIRE						
1 ***Sununu***	N	N	Y	Y	Y	Y
2 ***Bass***	N	Y	Y	Y	Y	Y
NEW JERSEY						
1 Andrews	?	?	N	Y	N	N
2 ***LoBiondo***	N	N	Y	Y	N	N
3 ***Saxton***	N	Y	Y	Y	Y	N
4 ***Smith***	N	Y	Y	Y	Y	Y
5 ***Roukema***	N	N	Y	Y	Y	N
6 Pallone	Y	N	N	Y	N	N
7 ***Franks***	N	N	Y	Y	N	N
8 Pascrell	N	Y	N	Y	Y	N
9 Rothman	N	Y	N	Y	N	N
10 Payne	N	Y	N	Y	N	N
11 ***Frelinghuysen***	N	Y	Y	Y	Y	N
12 ***Pappas***	N	Y	Y	Y	Y	N
13 Menendez	N	N	N	Y	N	N
NEW MEXICO						
1 ***Schiff***	?	?	?	?	?	?
2 ***Skeen***	N	Y	Y	Y	Y	Y
3 ***Redmond***	N	Y	Y	Y	Y	Y
NEW YORK						
1 ***Forbes***	N	Y	Y	Y	Y	N
2 ***Lazio***	N	Y	Y	Y	Y	Y
3 ***King***	N	Y	Y	Y	Y	Y
4 McCarthy	Y	Y	N	Y	N	N
5 Ackerman	N	Y	N	Y	N	N
6 Flake	N	Y	N	Y	Y	N
7 Manton	N	Y	N	Y	N	N
8 Nadler	N	Y	N	Y	N	N
9 Schumer	N	N	N	Y	N	N
10 Towns	Y	Y	N	Y	N	N
11 Owens	N	N	N	Y	N	N
12 Velázquez	N	N	N	Y	N	N
13 Vacant						
14 Maloney	N	N	N	Y	N	N
15 Rangel	?	?	N	Y	N	N
16 Serrano	N	Y	N	Y	N	N
17 Engel	N	Y	N	Y	N	N
18 Lowey	Y	Y	N	Y	N	N
19 ***Kelly***	N	Y	Y	Y	Y	Y
20 ***Gilman***	N	Y	Y	Y	Y	Y
21 McNulty	Y	N	N	Y	N	N
22 ***Solomon***	N	Y	Y	Y	Y	Y
23 ***Boehlert***	N	Y	Y	Y	Y	Y
24 ***McHugh***	N	Y	Y	Y	N	Y
25 ***Walsh***	N	Y	Y	Y	Y	N
26 Hinchey	?	Y	N	Y	N	N
27 ***Paxon***	N	?	Y	Y	Y	Y
28 Slaughter	Y	Y	N	Y	N	N
29 LaFalce	N	N	Y	N	N	N
30 ***Quinn***	N	N	Y	Y	Y	N
31 ***Houghton***	N	Y	Y	Y	Y	Y

	405	406	407	408	409	410
NORTH CAROLINA						
1 Clayton	?	Y	N	Y	N	N
2 Etheridge	N	Y	N	Y	N	N
3 ***Jones***	N	Y	Y	Y	Y	Y
4 Price	N	Y	N	Y	N	N
5 ***Burr***	?	?	Y	Y	Y	Y
6 ***Coble***	N	Y	Y	Y	Y	Y
7 McIntyre	N	Y	N	Y	N	N
8 Hefner	N	Y	N	Y	N	N
9 ***Myrick***	N	Y	Y	Y	Y	Y
10 ***Ballenger***	N	Y	Y	Y	Y	Y
11 ***Taylor***	N	Y	Y	Y	Y	Y
12 Watt	N	Y	N	Y	N	N
NORTH DAKOTA						
AL Pomeroy	N	Y	N	Y	N	N
OHIO						
1 ***Chabot***	N	N	Y	Y	N	N
2 ***Portman***	N	Y	Y	Y	Y	Y
3 Hall	N	N	N	Y	Y	N
4 ***Oxley***	?	Y	Y	Y	Y	Y
5 ***Gillmor***	N	N	Y	Y	Y	Y
6 Strickland	N	N	N	Y	N	N
7 ***Hobson***	N	Y	Y	Y	Y	Y
8 ***Boehner***	N	Y	Y	Y	Y	Y
9 Kaptur	Y	Y	N	Y	N	N
10 Kucinich	N	N	N	Y	N	N
11 Stokes	N	Y	N	Y	N	N
12 ***Kasich***	N	Y	Y	Y	Y	Y
13 Brown	N	Y	N	Y	N	N
14 Sawyer	N	Y	N	Y	N	N
15 ***Pryce***	N	Y	Y	Y	Y	Y
16 ***Regula***	N	Y	Y	Y	Y	Y
17 Traficant	N	N	Y	Y	Y	Y
18 ***Ney***	N	Y	Y	Y	Y	Y
19 ***LaTourette***	N	Y	Y	Y	Y	Y
OKLAHOMA						
1 ***Largent***	?	Y	?	Y	Y	?
2 ***Coburn***	N	Y	Y	Y	Y	Y
3 ***Watkins***	N	Y	Y	Y	Y	Y
4 ***Watts***	N	N	Y	Y	Y	Y
5 ***Istook***	N	Y	Y	Y	Y	Y
6 ***Lucas***	N	Y	Y	Y	Y	Y
OREGON						
1 Furse	?	?	?	?	?	?
2 ***Smith***	N	Y	Y	Y	Y	Y
3 Blumenauer	N	Y	N	Y	N	N
4 DeFazio	Y	N	N	Y	N	N
5 Hooley	N	Y	N	Y	N	N
PENNSYLVANIA						
1 Foglietta	?	?	?	Y	Y	N
2 Fattah	N	N	?	Y	N	N
3 Borski	N	N	N	Y	Y	N
4 Klink	N	Y	N	Y	Y	N
5 ***Peterson***	N	Y	Y	Y	Y	Y
6 Holden	N	Y	N	Y	N	N
7 ***Weldon***	N	Y	?	Y	?	?
8 ***Greenwood***	N	Y	Y	Y	N	N
9 ***Shuster***	N	Y	Y	Y	Y	Y
10 ***McDade***	N	Y	Y	Y	Y	Y
11 Kanjorski	N	Y	Y	Y	Y	N
12 Murtha	N	Y	Y	Y	Y	Y
13 ***Fox***	N	N	Y	Y	N	N
14 Coyne	Y	Y	N	Y	N	N
15 McHale	N	Y	N	Y	N	N
16 ***Pitts***	N	N	Y	Y	Y	Y
17 ***Gekas***	N	Y	Y	Y	Y	N
18 Doyle	N	Y	N	Y	N	N
19 ***Goodling***	N	Y	Y	Y	Y	Y
20 Mascara	N	Y	N	Y	N	N
21 ***English***	N	N	Y	Y	Y	Y
RHODE ISLAND						
1 Kennedy	N	Y	N	Y	N	N
2 Weygand	N	Y	N	Y	N	N
SOUTH CAROLINA						
1 ***Sanford***	N	N	Y	Y	Y	Y
2 ***Spence***	N	Y	Y	Y	Y	Y
3 ***Graham***	N	Y	Y	Y	Y	Y
4 ***Inglis***	N	Y	Y	Y	Y	N
5 Spratt	N	Y	N	Y	N	N
6 Clyburn	Y	N	N	Y	N	N
SOUTH DAKOTA						
AL ***Thune***	N	N	Y	Y	Y	Y
TENNESSEE						
1 ***Jenkins***	N	Y	Y	Y	Y	Y
2 ***Duncan***	N	Y	Y	Y	Y	N

	405	406	407	408	409	410
3 ***Wamp***	N	N	Y	Y	Y	N
4 ***Hilleary***	N	N	Y	Y	Y	Y
5 Clement	N	Y	N	Y	Y	N
6 Gordon	N	Y	N	Y	N	N
7 ***Bryant***	N	Y	Y	Y	Y	Y
8 Tanner	N	Y	N	Y	Y	N
9 Ford	Y	Y	N	Y	N	N
TEXAS						
1 Sandlin	N	Y	N	Y	N	N
2 Turner	N	Y	N	Y	N	N
3 ***Johnson, Sam***	N	Y	?	Y	Y	Y
4 Hall	N	Y	N	Y	N	N
5 ***Sessions***	N	Y	Y	Y	Y	Y
6 ***Barton***	N	Y	Y	Y	Y	Y
7 ***Archer***	N	Y	Y	Y	Y	Y
8 ***Brady***	N	N	Y	Y	Y	Y
9 Lampson	N	Y	N	Y	N	N
10 Doggett	Y	N	N	Y	N	N
11 Edwards	N	Y	N	Y	N	N
12 ***Granger***	N	Y	Y	?	Y	Y
13 ***Thornberry***	N	Y	Y	Y	Y	Y
14 ***Paul***	N	Y	Y	Y	Y	Y
15 Hinojosa	N	Y	N	Y	N	N
16 Reyes	N	Y	N	Y	N	N
17 Stenholm	N	N	N	Y	N	N
18 Jackson-Lee	N	Y	N	Y	N	N
19 ***Combest***	N	Y	Y	Y	Y	Y
20 Gonzalez	?	?	?	?	?	?
21 ***Smith***	N	Y	Y	Y	Y	Y
22 ***DeLay***	N	Y	Y	Y	Y	Y
23 ***Bonilla***	?	?	?	?	?	?
24 Frost	N	Y	N	Y	N	N
25 Bentsen	N	Y	N	Y	N	N
26 ***Armey***	N	Y	Y	Y	Y	Y
27 Ortiz	N	Y	N	Y	Y	N
28 Rodriguez	N	Y	N	Y	N	N
29 Green	N	Y	N	Y	N	N
30 Johnson, E.B.	N	Y	N	Y	N	N
UTAH						
1 ***Hansen***	N	Y	Y	Y	Y	Y
2 ***Cook***	N	Y	Y	Y	Y	Y
3 ***Cannon***	N	Y	Y	Y	Y	Y
VERMONT						
AL *Sanders*	N	Y	N	Y	N	N
VIRGINIA						
1 ***Bateman***	N	Y	Y	Y	Y	Y
2 Pickett	N	N	N	Y	Y	N
3 Scott	N	Y	N	Y	N	N
4 Sisisky	N	Y	N	Y	Y	Y
5 Goode	N	Y	N	Y	N	N
6 ***Goodlatte***	N	Y	Y	Y	Y	Y
7 ***Bliley***	N	Y	Y	Y	Y	Y
8 Moran	?	Y	N	Y	Y	N
9 Boucher	N	Y	N	Y	Y	Y
10 ***Wolf***	N	Y	Y	Y	N	N
11 ***Davis***	N	Y	Y	Y	N	Y
WASHINGTON						
1 ***White***	N	Y	Y	Y	Y	Y
2 ***Metcalf***	N	N	Y	Y	Y	Y
3 ***Smith, Linda***	N	Y	Y	Y	Y	N
4 ***Hastings***	N	Y	Y	Y	Y	Y
5 ***Nethercutt***	N	Y	Y	Y	Y	N
6 Dicks	N	Y	N	Y	N	N
7 McDermott	Y	N	N	Y	N	N
8 ***Dunn***	N	Y	Y	Y	Y	Y
9 Smith, Adam	N	Y	N	Y	N	N
WEST VIRGINIA						
1 Mollohan	N	Y	Y	Y	Y	N
2 Wise	N	Y	N	Y	Y	N
3 Rahall	N	Y	N	Y	Y	N
WISCONSIN						
1 ***Neumann***	N	Y	Y	?	?	?
2 ***Klug***	N	Y	Y	Y	N	N
3 Kind	N	Y	N	Y	N	N
4 Kleczka	N	Y	N	Y	N	N
5 Barrett	N	Y	N	Y	N	N
6 ***Petri***	N	Y	Y	Y	N	N
7 Obey	N	Y	N	Y	N	N
8 Johnson	N	Y	N	Y	N	N
9 ***Sensenbrenner***	N	Y	Y	Y	Y	N
WYOMING						
AL ***Cubin***	N	Y	Y	Y	Y	Y

Southern states - Ala., Ark., Fla., Ga., Ky., La., Miss., N.C., Okla., S.C., Tenn., Texas, Va.

HOUSE VOTES 411, 412, 413, 414, 415

411. H Res 168. House Ethics Reform Recommendations/ Investigation Expansion Powers. Bunning, R-Ky., amendment to require that the power to expand the scope of investigations and issue subpoenas lie with the full House Committee on Official Standards and Official Conduct and not with its investigative subcommittees. Adopted 221-194: R 194-23; D 27-170 (ND 21-124, SD 6-46); I 0-1, Sept. 18, 1997.

412. H Res 168. House Ethics Reform Recommendations/ Recommit. Cardin, D-Md., motion to recommit to the Ethics Reform Task Force the bill to revamp ethics rules of the House Committee on Standards and Official Conduct. Rejected 176-236: R 1-216; D 174-20 (ND 131-12, SD 43-8); I 1-0, Sept. 18, 1997.

413. H Res 168. House Ethics Reform Recommendations/ Adoption. Adoption of resolution to revamp ethics rules of the House Committee on Standards and Official Conduct by, among other things, requiring that outside groups and non-members be sponsored by a member of the House, allowing the chairman and ranking member to establish an investigative subcommittee without a vote of the full committee and take measures to improve due process for the respondents to complaints. Adopted 258-154: R 210-6; D 48-147 (ND 32-111, SD 16-36); I 0-1, Sept. 18, 1997.

414. H Res 233. Ban Former Member Robert K. Dornan, R-Calif., from Floor/Motion To Table. Stearns, R-Fla., motion to table (kill) the resolution to bar former House member Robert K. Dornan, R-Calif., from the House floor until the resolution of the contested election between him and Rep. Loretta Sanchez, D-Calif. Motion rejected 86-291: R 86-107; D 0-183 (ND 0-136, SD 0-47); I 0-1, Sept. 18, 1997.

415. H Res 233. Ban Former Member Robert K. Dornan, R-Calif., from Floor/Adoption. Adoption of the resolution to bar former House member Robert K. Dornan, R-Calif., from the House floor until the resolution of the contested election between him and Rep. Loretta Sanchez, D-Calif. Adopted 289-65: R 111-64; D 177-1 (ND 133-0, SD 44-1); I 1-0, Sept. 18, 1997.

KEY

Y Voted for (yea).
\# Paired for.
\+ Announced for.
N Voted against (nay).
X Paired against.
– Announced against.
P Voted "present."
C Voted "present" to avoid possible conflict of interest.
? Did not vote or otherwise make a position known.

Democrats ***Republicans***
Independent

	411	412	413	414	415
ALABAMA					
1 ***Callahan***	Y	N	Y	?	?
2 ***Everett***	Y	N	Y	Y	N
3 ***Riley***	Y	N	Y	Y	Y
4 ***Aderholt***	Y	N	Y	Y	Y
5 Cramer	Y	N	Y	?	?
6 ***Bachus***	Y	N	Y	N	Y
7 Hilliard	N	?	N	N	Y
ALASKA					
AL ***Young***	?	?	?	?	?
ARIZONA					
1 ***Salmon***	Y	N	Y	Y	?
2 Pastor	N	N	Y	N	Y
3 ***Stump***	Y	N	Y	Y	N
4 ***Shadegg***	Y	N	Y	Y	N
5 ***Kolbe***	Y	N	Y	N	Y
6 ***Hayworth***	Y	N	Y	N	Y
ARKANSAS					
1 Berry	N	Y	Y	?	?
2 Snyder	N	Y	N	N	Y
3 ***Hutchinson***	N	N	Y	N	Y
4 ***Dickey***	Y	N	Y	N	Y
CALIFORNIA					
1 ***Riggs***	Y	N	Y	N	N
2 ***Herger***	Y	N	Y	Y	N
3 Fazio	N	Y	N	N	Y
4 ***Doolittle***	Y	N	Y	Y	N
5 Matsui	N	Y	N	N	Y
6 Woolsey	N	Y	N	?	Y
7 Miller	N	Y	N	N	Y
8 Pelosi	N	Y	N	N	Y
9 Dellums	N	Y	N	N	Y
10 Tauscher	N	Y	N	N	Y
11 ***Pombo***	Y	N	Y	Y	N
12 Lantos	N	Y	N	N	Y
13 Stark	N	Y	N	N	Y
14 Eshoo	N	Y	N	N	Y
15 ***Campbell***	Y	N	Y	Y	N
16 Lofgren	N	Y	N	N	Y
17 Farr	N	Y	N	N	Y
18 Condit	Y	N	Y	N	Y
19 ***Radanovich***	Y	N	Y	Y	N
20 Dooley	N	Y	N	N	Y
21 ***Thomas***	Y	N	N	Y	P
22 Capps	N	Y	N	N	Y
23 ***Gallegly***	Y	N	Y	?	?
24 Sherman	N	Y	N	N	Y
25 ***McKeon***	Y	N	Y	Y	N
26 Berman	N	Y	N	N	?
27 ***Rogan***	Y	N	Y	Y	N
28 ***Dreier***	Y	N	Y	Y	N
29 Waxman	N	Y	N	N	Y
30 Becerra	N	Y	N	N	Y
31 Martinez	Y	Y	N	N	Y
32 Dixon	N	Y	N	N	Y
33 Roybal-Allard	N	Y	N	N	Y
34 Torres	N	Y	N	N	Y
35 Waters	N	Y	N	N	Y
36 Harman	N	Y	Y	N	Y
37 Millender-McD.	N	Y	N	N	Y
38 ***Horn***	Y	N	Y	N	Y
39 ***Royce***	Y	N	Y	Y	N
40 ***Lewis***	N	N	Y	Y	N
41 ***Kim***	P	P	P	Y	N
42 Brown	N	Y	Y	N	Y
43 ***Calvert***	Y	N	Y	Y	?
44 ***Bono***	Y	N	Y	Y	N
45 ***Rohrabacher***	Y	N	Y	Y	N
46 Sanchez	N	Y	N	P	P
47 ***Cox***	Y	N	Y	Y	N
48 ***Packard***	Y	N	Y	Y	N
49 ***Bilbray***	Y	N	Y	?	?
50 Filner	N	Y	N	N	Y
51 ***Cunningham***	Y	N	Y	Y	N
52 ***Hunter***	Y	N	Y	Y	N
COLORADO					
1 DeGette	N	Y	N	N	Y
2 Skaggs	N	Y	N	N	Y
3 ***McInnis***	Y	N	Y	?	?
4 ***Schaffer***	N	N	N	Y	N
5 ***Hefley***	Y	N	Y	Y	N
6 ***Schaefer***	Y	N	Y	Y	N
CONNECTICUT					
1 Kennelly	N	Y	N	N	Y
2 Gejdenson	N	Y	N	N	Y
3 DeLauro	N	Y	N	N	Y
4 ***Shays***	Y	N	N	N	Y
5 Maloney	N	Y	N	N	Y
6 ***Johnson***	Y	N	Y	N	Y
DELAWARE					
AL ***Castle***	N	N	Y	N	Y
FLORIDA					
1 ***Scarborough***	Y	N	Y	Y	N
2 Boyd	N	Y	N	N	Y
3 Brown	N	Y	N	N	Y
4 ***Fowler***	Y	N	Y	?	?
5 Thurman	N	Y	N	N	Y
6 ***Stearns***	Y	N	Y	Y	N
7 ***Mica***	N	N	Y	Y	P
8 ***McCollum***	Y	N	Y	Y	N
9 ***Bilirakis***	Y	N	Y	N	N
10 ***Young***	Y	N	Y	N	Y
11 Davis	N	Y	N	N	Y
12 ***Canady***	Y	N	Y	N	Y
13 ***Miller***	Y	N	Y	N	Y
14 ***Goss***	+	–	+	–	+
15 ***Weldon***	Y	N	Y	Y	Y
16 ***Foley***	Y	N	Y	Y	?
17 Meek	?	?	?	?	?
18 ***Ros-Lehtinen***	Y	N	Y	N	Y
19 Wexler	N	Y	N	N	Y
20 Deutsch	N	Y	N	N	Y
21 ***Diaz-Balart***	Y	N	Y	N	Y
22 ***Shaw***	Y	N	Y	N	Y
23 Hastings	?	?	?	?	?
GEORGIA					
1 ***Kingston***	Y	N	Y	Y	N
2 Bishop	Y	Y	Y	N	Y
3 ***Collins***	Y	N	Y	?	?
4 McKinney	N	Y	N	N	Y
5 Lewis	N	Y	N	N	Y
6 ***Gingrich***					
7 ***Barr***	Y	N	Y	Y	N
8 ***Chambliss***	Y	N	Y	?	?
9 ***Deal***	Y	N	Y	?	?
10 ***Norwood***	Y	N	Y	Y	N
11 ***Linder***	Y	N	Y	Y	?
HAWAII					
1 Abercrombie	Y	N	+	N	Y
2 Mink	Y	Y	Y	N	Y
IDAHO					
1 ***Chenoweth***	Y	N	Y	Y	N
2 ***Crapo***	Y	N	Y	Y	N
ILLINOIS					
1 Rush	N	Y	N	N	Y
2 Jackson	N	Y	N	N	Y
3 Lipinski	?	?	?	?	?
4 Gutierrez	N	Y	N	N	Y
5 Blagojevich	N	Y	N	N	Y
6 ***Hyde***	Y	N	Y	Y	N
7 Davis	N	Y	N	N	Y
8 ***Crane***	Y	N	Y	Y	N
9 Yates	N	Y	N	N	Y
10 ***Porter***	–	+	+	–	+
11 ***Weller***	Y	N	Y	N	Y
12 Costello	Y	Y	N	N	Y
13 ***Fawell***	Y	N	Y	Y	?
14 ***Hastert***	Y	N	+	N	Y
15 ***Ewing***	Y	N	Y	Y	Y

ND Northern Democrats SD Southern Democrats

	411	412	413	414	415
16 ***Manzullo***	Y	N	Y	N	Y
17 Evans	N	Y	N	N	Y
18 ***LaHood***	Y	N	Y	N	Y
19 Poshard	N	Y	N	N	Y
20 ***Shimkus***	Y	N	Y	N	Y
INDIANA					
1 Visclosky	N	Y	N	N	Y
2 ***McIntosh***	Y	N	Y	Y	N
3 Roemer	N	Y	Y	N	Y
4 ***Souder***	Y	N	Y	N	Y
5 ***Buyer***	Y	N	N	Y	N
6 ***Burton***	Y	N	Y	Y	N
7 ***Pease***	Y	N	Y	Y	Y
8 ***Hostettler***	Y	N	Y	Y	N
9 Hamilton	N	Y	N	N	Y
10 Carson	N	Y	N	N	Y
IOWA					
1 ***Leach***	N	N	Y	N	Y
2 ***Nussle***	Y	N	Y	N	Y
3 Boswell	N	Y	N	N	Y
4 ***Ganske***	Y	N	Y	?	?
5 ***Latham***	Y	N	Y	N	?
KANSAS					
1 ***Moran***	Y	N	Y	N	Y
2 ***Ryun***	Y	N	Y	Y	N
3 ***Snowbarger***	Y	N	Y	Y	N
4 ***Tiahrt***	Y	N	Y	Y	N
KENTUCKY					
1 ***Whitfield***	Y	N	N	Y	N
2 ***Lewis***	Y	N	Y	Y	N
3 ***Northup***	Y	N	Y	N	Y
4 ***Bunning***	Y	N	Y	?	?
5 ***Rogers***	Y	N	Y	Y	Y
6 Baesler	N	N	Y	N	Y
LOUISIANA					
1 ***Livingston***	N	N	Y	Y	Y
2 Jefferson	N	Y	N	N	Y
3 ***Tauzin***	Y	N	Y	Y	Y
4 ***McCrery***	Y	N	Y	?	?
5 ***Cooksey***	Y	N	Y	?	?
6 ***Baker***	?	?	?	?	?
7 John	N	Y	Y	N	Y
MAINE					
1 Allen	N	Y	N	N	Y
2 Baldacci	N	Y	N	N	Y
MARYLAND					
1 ***Gilchrest***	Y	N	Y	N	Y
2 ***Ehrlich***	Y	N	Y	N	Y
3 Cardin	N	Y	N	N	Y
4 Wynn	N	Y	N	N	?
5 Hoyer	N	Y	N	N	Y
6 ***Bartlett***	Y	N	Y	Y	N
7 Cummings	N	Y	N	N	Y
8 ***Morella***	N	N	Y	N	Y
MASSACHUSETTS					
1 Olver	N	Y	N	N	Y
2 Neal	Y	Y	N	N	Y
3 McGovern	N	Y	N	N	Y
4 Frank	N	Y	N	N	Y
5 Meehan	N	Y	N	?	?
6 Tierney	N	Y	N	N	Y
7 Markey	Y	Y	N	N	Y
8 Kennedy	N	Y	N	N	Y
9 Moakley	N	Y	N	?	?
10 Delahunt	Y	Y	Y	N	Y
MICHIGAN					
1 Stupak	N	Y	Y	N	Y
2 ***Hoekstra***	Y	N	Y	N	?
3 ***Ehlers***	Y	N	Y	P	P
4 ***Camp***	Y	N	Y	N	N
5 Barcia	Y	Y	Y	N	Y
6 ***Upton***	Y	N	Y	N	Y
7 ***Smith***	Y	N	Y	Y	?
8 Stabenow	N	Y	N	N	Y
9 Kildee	N	Y	N	N	Y
10 Bonior	N	Y	N	N	Y
11 ***Knollenberg***	Y	N	Y	N	Y
12 Levin	N	Y	N	?	?
13 Rivers	N	Y	N	N	Y
14 Conyers	N	Y	N	N	Y
15 Kilpatrick	N	Y	N	N	Y
16 Dingell	N	Y	Y	N	Y
MINNESOTA					
1 ***Gutknecht***	Y	N	Y	N	?
2 Minge	N	Y	Y	N	Y
3 ***Ramstad***	N	N	Y	N	Y
4 Vento	N	Y	N	N	Y
5 Sabo	N	Y	N	N	Y
6 Luther	N	Y	N	?	Y
7 Peterson	N	Y	Y	N	Y
8 Oberstar	–	+	–	–	+
MISSISSIPPI					
1 ***Wicker***	Y	N	Y	Y	N
2 Thompson	N	Y	N	?	?
3 ***Pickering***	Y	N	Y	Y	N
4 ***Parker***	Y	N	Y	N	Y
5 Taylor	N	N	Y	?	Y
MISSOURI					
1 Clay	?	?	?	?	?
2 ***Talent***	N	N	Y	N	Y
3 Gephardt	?	?	?	?	?
4 Skelton	Y	Y	Y	N	Y
5 McCarthy	N	Y	Y	N	Y
6 Danner	N	Y	Y	N	Y
7 ***Blunt***	Y	N	Y	N	Y
8 ***Emerson***	Y	N	Y	N	Y
9 ***Hulshof***	Y	N	Y	N	Y
MONTANA					
AL ***Hill***	Y	N	Y	N	Y
NEBRASKA					
1 ***Bereuter***	Y	N	Y	N	Y
2 ***Christensen***	Y	N	Y	N	Y
3 ***Barrett***	Y	N	Y	N	Y
NEVADA					
1 ***Ensign***	Y	N	Y	N	Y
2 ***Gibbons***	Y	N	Y	N	Y
NEW HAMPSHIRE					
1 ***Sununu***	Y	N	Y	N	Y
2 ***Bass***	Y	N	Y	N	Y
NEW JERSEY					
1 Andrews	N	Y	Y	N	Y
2 ***LoBiondo***	N	N	Y	N	Y
3 ***Saxton***	Y	N	Y	Y	N
4 ***Smith***	Y	N	Y	Y	N
5 ***Roukema***	Y	N	Y	N	Y
6 Pallone	N	Y	N	N	Y
7 ***Franks***	N	N	N	N	Y
8 Pascrell	N	Y	Y	N	Y
9 Rothman	N	Y	N	N	Y
10 Payne	N	Y	N	N	Y
11 ***Frelinghuysen***	N	N	Y	N	Y
12 ***Pappas***	Y	N	Y	N	Y
13 Menendez	N	Y	N	N	Y
NEW MEXICO					
1 ***Schiff***	?	?	?	?	?
2 ***Skeen***	Y	N	Y	N	Y
3 ***Redmond***	Y	N	Y	Y	N
NEW YORK					
1 ***Forbes***	N	N	Y	N	Y
2 ***Lazio***	Y	N	Y	N	Y
3 ***King***	Y	N	Y	N	Y
4 McCarthy	N	Y	N	N	Y
5 Ackerman	N	Y	N	N	Y
6 Flake	N	?	N	N	Y
7 Manton	N	Y	N	?	?
8 Nadler	N	Y	N	N	Y
9 Schumer	N	Y	N	N	Y
10 Towns	N	Y	N	N	Y
11 Owens	N	Y	N	N	Y
12 Velázquez	N	Y	N	N	Y
13 Vacant					
14 Maloney	N	Y	N	N	Y
15 Rangel	N	Y	N	N	Y
16 Serrano	N	Y	N	N	Y
17 Engel	N	Y	N	N	Y
18 Lowey	N	Y	N	N	Y
19 ***Kelly***	Y	N	Y	N	Y
20 ***Gilman***	Y	N	Y	N	Y
21 McNulty	N	Y	N	N	Y
22 ***Solomon***	Y	N	Y	Y	P
23 ***Boehlert***	Y	N	Y	N	Y
24 ***McHugh***	Y	N	Y	N	Y
25 ***Walsh***	Y	N	Y	N	Y
26 Hinchey	N	Y	N	?	?
27 ***Paxon***	Y	N	Y	Y	N
28 Slaughter	N	Y	N	N	Y
29 LaFalce	N	Y	Y	N	Y
30 ***Quinn***	N	N	Y	N	Y
31 ***Houghton***	Y	N	Y	N	Y
NORTH CAROLINA					
1 Clayton	N	Y	N	N	Y
2 Etheridge	N	Y	N	N	Y
3 ***Jones***	Y	N	Y	N	Y
4 Price	N	Y	N	N	Y
5 ***Burr***	Y	N	Y	?	?
6 ***Coble***	Y	N	Y	?	?
7 McIntyre	N	Y	N	N	Y
8 Hefner	N	Y	N	N	Y
9 ***Myrick***	Y	N	Y	?	Y
10 ***Ballenger***	Y	N	Y	?	N
11 ***Taylor***	N	N	Y	N	?
12 Watt	N	Y	N	N	Y
NORTH DAKOTA					
AL Pomeroy	N	Y	N	N	Y
OHIO					
1 ***Chabot***	N	Y	Y	Y	N
2 ***Portman***	Y	N	Y	N	Y
3 Hall	Y	Y	Y	N	Y
4 ***Oxley***	Y	N	Y	N	Y
5 ***Gillmor***	Y	N	Y	N	Y
6 Strickland	N	Y	N	N	Y
7 ***Hobson***	Y	N	Y	N	Y
8 ***Boehner***	Y	N	Y	N	Y
9 Kaptur	Y	Y	N	N	Y
10 Kucinich	N	Y	N	N	Y
11 Stokes	Y	Y	N	N	Y
12 ***Kasich***	Y	N	Y	N	Y
13 Brown	N	Y	N	N	Y
14 Sawyer	N	Y	N	N	Y
15 ***Pryce***	Y	N	Y	N	?
16 ***Regula***	Y	N	Y	N	Y
17 Traficant	Y	N	Y	N	P
18 ***Ney***	Y	N	Y	P	P
19 ***LaTourette***	N	N	Y	?	?
OKLAHOMA					
1 ***Largent***	Y	N	Y	Y	?
2 ***Coburn***	Y	N	Y	?	?
3 ***Watkins***	Y	N	Y	N	Y
4 ***Watts***	Y	N	Y	N	Y
5 ***Istook***	Y	N	Y	N	Y
6 ***Lucas***	Y	N	Y	Y	Y
OREGON					
1 Furse	?	?	?	?	?
2 ***Smith***	Y	N	Y	Y	Y
3 Blumenauer	N	N	N	N	?
4 DeFazio	N	Y	N	N	Y
5 Hooley	N	Y	N	N	Y
PENNSYLVANIA					
1 Foglietta	?	?	?	?	?
2 Fattah	N	Y	N	N	Y
3 Borski	Y	N	Y	N	Y
4 Klink	Y	N	Y	N	Y
5 ***Peterson***	Y	N	Y	N	Y
6 Holden	N	Y	Y	N	Y
7 ***Weldon***	?	?	?	?	?
8 ***Greenwood***	Y	N	Y	N	Y
9 ***Shuster***	Y	N	Y	Y	?
10 ***McDade***	Y	N	Y	N	Y
11 Kanjorski	Y	N	Y	N	Y
12 Murtha	Y	N	Y	N	Y
13 ***Fox***	N	N	Y	N	Y
14 Coyne	N	Y	N	N	Y
15 McHale	Y	Y	N	N	Y
16 ***Pitts***	Y	N	Y	N	Y
17 ***Gekas***	N	N	Y	Y	N
18 Doyle	N	Y	Y	N	Y
19 ***Goodling***	Y	N	Y	N	Y
20 Mascara	N	Y	Y	N	Y
21 ***English***	Y	N	Y	N	Y
RHODE ISLAND					
1 Kennedy	N	Y	N	N	Y
2 Weygand	N	Y	N	N	Y
SOUTH CAROLINA					
1 ***Sanford***	Y	N	Y	N	Y
2 ***Spence***	Y	N	Y	Y	N
3 ***Graham***	Y	N	Y	N	Y
4 ***Inglis***	Y	N	Y	N	Y
5 Spratt	N	Y	N	N	Y
6 Clyburn	N	Y	N	N	Y
SOUTH DAKOTA					
AL ***Thune***	Y	N	Y	N	Y
TENNESSEE					
1 ***Jenkins***	Y	N	Y	N	Y
2 ***Duncan***	Y	N	Y	Y	N
3 ***Wamp***	Y	N	Y	?	?
4 ***Hilleary***	Y	N	Y	N	Y
5 Clement	N	N	Y	N	+
6 Gordon	N	Y	N	N	Y
7 ***Bryant***	Y	N	Y	?	?
8 Tanner	Y	N	Y	?	?
9 Ford	N	Y	N	N	Y
TEXAS					
1 Sandlin	N	Y	N	N	Y
2 Turner	N	Y	N	N	Y
3 ***Johnson, Sam***	Y	N	Y	Y	N
4 Hall	Y	Y	Y	N	N
5 ***Sessions***	Y	N	Y	Y	?
6 ***Barton***	Y	N	Y	Y	N
7 ***Archer***	Y	N	Y	?	?
8 ***Brady***	Y	N	Y	N	N
9 Lampson	N	Y	N	N	Y
10 Doggett	N	Y	N	N	Y
11 Edwards	N	Y	N	N	Y
12 ***Granger***	Y	N	Y	N	Y
13 ***Thornberry***	Y	N	Y	Y	Y
14 ***Paul***	Y	N	Y	Y	N
15 Hinojosa	N	Y	N	N	Y
16 Reyes	N	Y	Y	N	Y
17 Stenholm	N	Y	Y	N	?
18 Jackson-Lee	N	Y	N	N	Y
19 ***Combest***	Y	N	Y	N	Y
20 Gonzalez	?	?	?	?	?
21 ***Smith***	Y	N	Y	N	Y
22 ***DeLay***	Y	N	Y	N	Y
23 ***Bonilla***	?	?	?	?	?
24 Frost	N	Y	Y	N	Y
25 Bentsen	N	Y	N	N	Y
26 ***Armey***	Y	N	Y	N	Y
27 Ortiz	Y	Y	Y	N	Y
28 Rodriguez	N	Y	Y	N	Y
29 Green	N	Y	N	N	Y
30 Johnson, E.B.	N	Y	N	N	Y
UTAH					
1 ***Hansen***	Y	N	Y	N	Y
2 ***Cook***	Y	N	Y	N	Y
3 ***Cannon***	Y	N	Y	?	?
VERMONT					
AL *Sanders*	N	Y	N	N	Y
VIRGINIA					
1 ***Bateman***	N	N	Y	N	Y
2 Pickett	N	N	N	N	?
3 Scott	N	Y	N	N	Y
4 Sisisky	Y	N	Y	N	Y
5 Goode	N	Y	N	N	Y
6 ***Goodlatte***	Y	N	Y	N	Y
7 ***Bliley***	Y	N	Y	Y	N
8 Moran	N	Y	N	N	Y
9 Boucher	N	N	Y	N	Y
10 ***Wolf***	N	N	Y	Y	N
11 ***Davis***	Y	N	Y	N	Y
WASHINGTON					
1 ***White***	Y	N	Y	?	?
2 ***Metcalf***	Y	N	Y	Y	Y
3 ***Smith, Linda***	Y	N	Y	Y	?
4 ***Hastings***	Y	N	Y	N	Y
5 ***Nethercutt***	Y	N	Y	Y	Y
6 Dicks	Y	N	Y	N	Y
7 McDermott	N	Y	N	N	Y
8 ***Dunn***	Y	N	Y	Y	Y
9 Smith, Adam	N	?	?	?	?
WEST VIRGINIA					
1 Mollohan	Y	N	Y	N	Y
2 Wise	N	Y	N	N	Y
3 Rahall	N	N	Y	N	Y
WISCONSIN					
1 ***Neumann***	?	?	?	?	?
2 ***Klug***	Y	N	Y	N	?
3 Kind	N	Y	N	N	Y
4 Kleczka	N	Y	Y	N	Y
5 Barrett	N	Y	N	N	Y
6 ***Petri***	N	N	Y	N	Y
7 Obey	N	Y	N	N	?
8 Johnson	N	Y	Y	N	Y
9 ***Sensenbrenner***	Y	N	Y	N	?
WYOMING					
AL ***Cubin***	Y	N	Y	Y	N

Southern states - Ala., Ark., Fla., Ga., Ky., La., Miss., N.C., Okla., S.C., Tenn., Texas, Va.

HOUSE VOTES 416, 417, 418, 419, 420, 421, 422, 423

416. HR 2343. RTC Oversight Board Elimination/Passage. Passage of the bill on the Corrections Calendar to abolish the Thrift Depositor Protection Oversight Board, which oversaw the now-dissolved Resolution Trust Corporation, transferring the board's remaining responsibilities to the Treasury Department. Motion agreed to 420-0: R 223-0; D 196-0 (ND 147-0, SD 49-0); I 1-0, Sept. 23, 1997. A three-fifths majority of those present and voting (252 in this case) is required for passage of a bill on the Corrections Calendar.

417. HR 2414. Fifty-State Commemorative Coin Program/Passage. Castle, R-Del., motion to suspend the rules and pass the bill to establish a 10-year commemorative coin program starting in 1999 to honor each of the 50 states on the reverse side of quarters. Motion agreed to 413-6: R 217-5; D 195-1 (ND 147-1, SD 48-0); I 1-0, Sept. 23, 1997. A two-thirds majority of those present and voting (280 in this case) is required for passage under suspension of the rules.

418. S 996. District Court Arbitration/Passage. Coble, R-N.C., motion to suspend the rules and pass the bill to permanently reauthorize a pilot program in 20 U.S. district courts that allows certain cases to be heard before arbiters instead of going to trial. Motion agreed to 421-0: R 223-0; D 197-0 (ND 148-0, SD 49-0); I 1-0, Sept. 23, 1997. A two-thirds majority of those present and voting (281 in this case) is required for passage under suspension of the rules.

419. HR 2027. U.S.-Canadian Border Entry/Passage. Smith, R-Texas, motion to suspend the rules and pass the bill to establish a pilot program to allow recreational boaters traveling from Canada to the United States to enter the country by showing just a U.S. passport. Motion agreed to 412-5: R 222-0; D 189-5 (ND 141-3, SD 48-2); I 1-0, Sept. 23, 1997. A two-thirds majority of those present and voting (278 in this case) is required for passage under suspension of the rules.

420. HR 1683. Sexual Offender Registration/Passage. McCollum, R-Fla., motion to suspend the rules and pass the bill to expand registration requirements for convicted sex offenders to ensure that those convicted of sexual crimes against children in a federal or military court are included in state registries and that communities are notified when such offenders are to reside there. Motion agreed to 415-2: R 222-0; D 192-2 (ND 144-0, SD 48-2); I 1-0, Sept. 23, 1997. A two-thirds majority of those present and voting (278 in this case) is required for passage under suspension of the rules.

421. HR 643. Carl B. Stokes U.S. Courthouse/Passage. Kim, R-Calif., motion to suspend the rules and pass the bill to designate a U.S. courthouse to be constructed in Cleveland as the Carl B. Stokes U.S. Courthouse. Motion agreed to 420-0: R 224-0; D 195-0 (ND 144-0, SD 51-0); I 1-0, Sept. 23, 1997. A two-thirds majority of those present and voting (280 in this case) is required for passage under suspension of the rules.

422. HR 824. Howard T. Markey National Courts Building/Passage. Kim, R-Calif., motion to suspend the rules and pass the bill to rename the National Courts Building located in the District of Columbia the Howard T. Markey National Courts Building. Motion agreed to 420-0: R 221-0; D 198-0 (ND 145-0, SD 53-0); I 1-0, Sept. 23, 1997. A two-thirds majority of those present and voting (280 in this case) is required for passage under suspension of the rules.

423. S 871. Oklahoma City National Memorial/Passage. Hansen, R-Utah, motion to suspend the rules and pass the bill to authorize $5 million for the construction of an Oklahoma City National Memorial as a unit of the National Park System and to establish a trust to administer the memorial. Motion agreed to 414-7: R 215-7; D 198-0 (ND 145-0, SD 53-0); I 1-0, Sept. 23, 1997. A two-thirds majority of those present and voting (281 in this case) is required for passage under suspension of the rules.

KEY

- Y Voted for (yea).
- # Paired for.
- + Announced for.
- N Voted against (nay).
- X Paired against.
- – Announced against.
- P Voted "present."
- C Voted "present" to avoid possible conflict of interest.
- ? Did not vote or otherwise make a position known.

Democrats ***Republicans***
Independent

	416	417	418	419	420	421	422	423
ALABAMA								
1 ***Callahan***	Y	Y	Y	Y	Y	Y	Y	Y
2 ***Everett***	Y	Y	Y	Y	Y	Y	Y	Y
3 ***Riley***	Y	Y	Y	Y	Y	Y	Y	Y
4 ***Aderholt***	Y	Y	Y	Y	Y	Y	Y	Y
5 Cramer	Y	Y	Y	Y	Y	Y	Y	Y
6 ***Bachus***	Y	Y	Y	Y	Y	Y	Y	Y
7 Hilliard	Y	Y	Y	Y	Y	Y	Y	Y
ALASKA								
AL ***Young***	Y	Y	Y	Y	Y	Y	Y	Y
ARIZONA								
1 ***Salmon***	Y	Y	Y	Y	Y	Y	Y	Y
2 Pastor	Y	Y	Y	Y	Y	Y	Y	Y
3 ***Stump***	Y	Y	Y	Y	Y	Y	Y	Y
4 ***Shadegg***	Y	Y	Y	Y	Y	Y	Y	Y
5 ***Kolbe***	Y	Y	Y	Y	Y	Y	Y	Y
6 ***Hayworth***	Y	Y	Y	Y	Y	Y	Y	Y
ARKANSAS								
1 Berry	Y	Y	Y	Y	Y	Y	Y	Y
2 Snyder	Y	Y	Y	Y	Y	Y	Y	Y
3 ***Hutchinson***	Y	Y	Y	Y	Y	Y	Y	Y
4 ***Dickey***	Y	Y	Y	Y	Y	Y	Y	Y
CALIFORNIA								
1 ***Riggs***	Y	Y	Y	Y	Y	Y	Y	Y
2 ***Herger***	Y	Y	Y	Y	Y	Y	Y	Y
3 Fazio	Y	Y	Y	Y	Y	Y	Y	Y
4 ***Doolittle***	Y	Y	Y	Y	Y	Y	Y	Y
5 Matsui	Y	Y	Y	Y	Y	Y	Y	Y
6 Woolsey	+	+	+	Y	Y	Y	Y	Y
7 Miller	Y	Y	Y	Y	Y	Y	Y	Y
8 Pelosi	?	Y	Y	Y	Y	Y	Y	Y
9 Dellums	Y	Y	Y	Y	Y	Y	Y	Y
10 Tauscher	Y	Y	Y	Y	Y	Y	Y	Y
11 ***Pombo***	Y	Y	Y	Y	Y	Y	Y	Y
12 Lantos	Y	Y	Y	Y	Y	Y	Y	Y
13 Stark	Y	Y	Y	Y	Y	Y	Y	Y
14 Eshoo	+	+	+	Y	Y	Y	Y	Y
15 ***Campbell***	Y	Y	Y	Y	Y	Y	Y	N
16 Lofgren	+	+	+	Y	Y	Y	Y	Y
17 Farr	Y	Y	Y	Y	Y	Y	Y	Y
18 Condit	Y	Y	Y	Y	Y	Y	Y	Y
19 ***Radanovich***	Y	Y	Y	Y	Y	Y	Y	Y
20 Dooley	Y	Y	Y	Y	Y	Y	Y	Y
21 ***Thomas***	Y	Y	Y	Y	Y	Y	Y	Y
22 Capps	Y	Y	Y	Y	Y	Y	Y	Y
23 ***Gallegly***	Y	Y	Y	Y	Y	Y	Y	Y
24 Sherman	Y	Y	Y	Y	Y	Y	Y	Y
25 ***McKeon***	Y	Y	Y	Y	Y	Y	Y	Y
26 Berman	Y	Y	Y	Y	Y	Y	Y	Y
27 ***Rogan***	Y	Y	Y	Y	Y	Y	Y	N
28 ***Dreier***	Y	Y	Y	Y	Y	Y	Y	Y
29 Waxman	Y	Y	Y	Y	Y	Y	Y	Y
30 Becerra	Y	Y	Y	N	Y	Y	Y	Y
31 Martinez	Y	Y	Y	Y	Y	Y	Y	Y
32 Dixon	Y	Y	Y	Y	Y	Y	Y	Y
33 Roybal-Allard	Y	Y	Y	Y	Y	Y	Y	Y
34 Torres	Y	Y	Y	?	?	Y	Y	Y
35 Waters	Y	Y	Y	N	Y	?	Y	Y
36 Harman	Y	Y	Y	Y	Y	Y	Y	Y
37 Millender-McD.	Y	Y	Y	Y	Y	Y	Y	Y
38 ***Horn***	Y	Y	Y	Y	Y	Y	Y	Y
39 ***Royce***	Y	Y	Y	Y	Y	Y	Y	Y
40 ***Lewis***	Y	Y	Y	Y	Y	Y	Y	Y
41 ***Kim***	Y	Y	Y	Y	Y	Y	Y	Y
42 Brown	Y	Y	Y	Y	Y	Y	Y	Y
43 ***Calvert***	Y	Y	Y	Y	Y	Y	Y	Y
44 ***Bono***	Y	Y	Y	Y	Y	Y	Y	Y
45 ***Rohrabacher***	Y	Y	Y	Y	Y	Y	Y	Y
46 Sanchez	Y	Y	Y	Y	Y	Y	Y	Y
47 ***Cox***	Y	?	Y	Y	Y	Y	Y	Y
48 ***Packard***	Y	Y	Y	Y	Y	Y	Y	Y
49 ***Bilbray***	Y	Y	Y	?	Y	Y	Y	Y
50 Filner	Y	Y	Y	Y	Y	Y	Y	Y
51 ***Cunningham***	Y	Y	Y	Y	Y	Y	Y	Y
52 ***Hunter***	Y	Y	Y	Y	Y	Y	Y	Y
COLORADO								
1 DeGette	Y	Y	Y	Y	Y	Y	Y	Y
2 Skaggs	Y	Y	Y	Y	Y	Y	Y	Y
3 ***McInnis***	Y	Y	Y	Y	Y	Y	Y	Y
4 ***Schaffer***	Y	Y	Y	Y	?	Y	Y	Y
5 ***Hefley***	Y	Y	Y	Y	Y	Y	Y	Y
6 ***Schaefer***	Y	Y	Y	Y	Y	Y	Y	Y
CONNECTICUT								
1 Kennelly	Y	Y	Y	Y	Y	Y	Y	Y
2 Gejdenson	Y	Y	Y	Y	Y	Y	Y	Y
3 DeLauro	Y	Y	Y	Y	Y	Y	Y	Y
4 ***Shays***	Y	Y	Y	Y	Y	Y	Y	Y
5 Maloney	Y	Y	Y	Y	Y	Y	Y	Y
6 ***Johnson***	Y	Y	Y	Y	Y	Y	Y	Y
DELAWARE								
AL ***Castle***	Y	Y	Y	Y	Y	Y	Y	Y
FLORIDA								
1 ***Scarborough***	Y	Y	Y	Y	Y	Y	Y	Y
2 Boyd	Y	Y	Y	Y	Y	Y	Y	Y
3 Brown	Y	Y	Y	Y	Y	Y	Y	Y
4 ***Fowler***	Y	Y	Y	Y	Y	Y	Y	Y
5 Thurman	Y	Y	Y	Y	Y	Y	Y	Y
6 ***Stearns***	Y	Y	Y	Y	Y	Y	Y	Y
7 ***Mica***	Y	Y	Y	Y	Y	Y	Y	Y
8 ***McCollum***	Y	Y	Y	Y	Y	Y	Y	Y
9 ***Bilirakis***	Y	Y	Y	Y	Y	Y	Y	Y
10 ***Young***	Y	Y	Y	Y	Y	Y	Y	Y
11 Davis	Y	Y	Y	Y	Y	Y	Y	Y
12 ***Canady***	Y	Y	Y	Y	Y	Y	Y	Y
13 ***Miller***	Y	Y	Y	Y	Y	Y	Y	Y
14 ***Goss***	Y	Y	Y	Y	Y	Y	Y	Y
15 ***Weldon***	Y	Y	Y	Y	Y	Y	Y	Y
16 ***Foley***	Y	Y	Y	Y	Y	Y	Y	Y
17 Meek	Y	Y	Y	Y	Y	Y	Y	Y
18 ***Ros-Lehtinen***	Y	Y	Y	Y	Y	Y	Y	Y
19 Wexler	Y	Y	Y	Y	Y	Y	Y	Y
20 Deutsch	Y	Y	Y	Y	Y	Y	Y	Y
21 ***Diaz-Balart***	Y	Y	Y	Y	Y	Y	Y	Y
22 ***Shaw***	Y	Y	Y	Y	Y	Y	Y	Y
23 Hastings	?	?	?	?	?	?	?	?
GEORGIA								
1 ***Kingston***	Y	Y	Y	Y	Y	Y	Y	Y
2 Bishop	Y	Y	Y	Y	Y	Y	Y	Y
3 ***Collins***	Y	Y	Y	Y	Y	Y	Y	Y
4 McKinney	Y	Y	Y	Y	Y	Y	Y	Y
5 Lewis	Y	Y	Y	Y	Y	Y	Y	Y
6 ***Gingrich***								
7 ***Barr***	Y	Y	Y	Y	Y	Y	Y	Y
8 ***Chambliss***	Y	Y	Y	Y	Y	Y	Y	Y
9 ***Deal***	Y	Y	Y	Y	Y	Y	Y	Y
10 ***Norwood***	Y	Y	Y	Y	Y	Y	Y	Y
11 ***Linder***	Y	Y	Y	Y	Y	Y	Y	Y
HAWAII								
1 Abercrombie	Y	Y	Y	Y	Y	Y	Y	Y
2 Mink	Y	Y	Y	Y	Y	Y	Y	Y
IDAHO								
1 ***Chenoweth***	Y	Y	Y	Y	Y	Y	Y	N
2 ***Crapo***	Y	Y	Y	Y	Y	Y	Y	Y
ILLINOIS								
1 Rush	Y	Y	Y	Y	Y	Y	Y	Y
2 Jackson	Y	Y	Y	Y	Y	Y	Y	Y
3 Lipinski	Y	Y	Y	Y	Y	Y	Y	Y
4 Gutierrez	Y	Y	Y	Y	Y	Y	Y	Y
5 Blagojevich	Y	Y	Y	Y	Y	Y	Y	Y
6 ***Hyde***	Y	Y	Y	Y	Y	Y	Y	Y
7 Davis	Y	Y	Y	Y	Y	Y	Y	Y
8 ***Crane***	Y	Y	Y	Y	Y	Y	Y	Y
9 Yates	Y	Y	Y	?	?	?	?	?
10 ***Porter***	Y	Y	Y	Y	Y	Y	Y	Y
11 ***Weller***	Y	Y	Y	Y	Y	Y	Y	Y
12 Costello	Y	Y	Y	Y	Y	Y	Y	Y
13 ***Fawell***	Y	Y	Y	Y	Y	Y	Y	Y
14 ***Hastert***	Y	Y	Y	Y	Y	Y	Y	Y
15 ***Ewing***	Y	Y	?	Y	Y	Y	Y	Y

ND Northern Democrats SD Southern Democrats

	416	417	418	419	420	421	422	423
16 ***Manzullo***	Y	Y	Y	Y	Y	Y	Y	Y
17 Evans	Y	Y	Y	Y	Y	Y	Y	Y
18 ***LaHood***	Y	Y	Y	Y	Y	Y	Y	Y
19 Poshard	Y	Y	Y	Y	Y	Y	Y	Y
20 ***Shimkus***	Y	Y	Y	Y	Y	Y	Y	Y
INDIANA								
1 Visclosky	Y	Y	Y	Y	Y	Y	Y	Y
2 ***McIntosh***	Y	Y	Y	Y	Y	Y	Y	N
3 Roemer	Y	Y	Y	Y	Y	Y	Y	Y
4 ***Souder***	Y	Y	Y	Y	Y	Y	Y	Y
5 ***Buyer***	Y	Y	Y	Y	Y	Y	Y	Y
6 ***Burton***	Y	Y	Y	Y	Y	Y	Y	Y
7 ***Pease***	Y	Y	Y	Y	Y	Y	Y	Y
8 ***Hostettler***	Y	Y	Y	Y	Y	Y	Y	Y
9 Hamilton	Y	Y	Y	Y	Y	Y	Y	Y
10 Carson	Y	Y	Y	N	Y	Y	Y	Y
IOWA								
1 ***Leach***	Y	Y	Y	Y	Y	Y	Y	Y
2 ***Nussle***	Y	Y	Y	Y	Y	Y	Y	Y
3 Boswell	Y	Y	Y	Y	Y	Y	Y	Y
4 ***Ganske***	Y	N	Y	Y	Y	Y	Y	Y
5 ***Latham***	Y	Y	Y	Y	Y	Y	Y	Y
KANSAS								
1 ***Moran***	Y	Y	Y	Y	Y	Y	Y	Y
2 ***Ryun***	Y	Y	Y	Y	Y	Y	Y	Y
3 ***Snowbarger***	Y	Y	Y	Y	Y	Y	Y	Y
4 ***Tiahrt***	Y	Y	Y	Y	Y	Y	Y	Y
KENTUCKY								
1 ***Whitfield***	Y	Y	Y	Y	Y	Y	Y	Y
2 ***Lewis***	Y	Y	Y	Y	Y	Y	Y	Y
3 ***Northup***	Y	Y	Y	Y	Y	Y	Y	Y
4 ***Bunning***	Y	Y	Y	Y	Y	Y	Y	Y
5 ***Rogers***	Y	Y	Y	Y	Y	Y	Y	Y
6 Baesler	Y	Y	Y	Y	Y	Y	Y	Y
LOUISIANA								
1 ***Livingston***	Y	Y	Y	Y	Y	Y	Y	Y
2 Jefferson	Y	Y	Y	Y	Y	Y	Y	Y
3 ***Tauzin***	Y	Y	Y	Y	Y	Y	Y	Y
4 ***McCrery***	Y	Y	Y	Y	Y	Y	Y	Y
5 ***Cooksey***	Y	Y	Y	Y	Y	Y	Y	Y
6 ***Baker***	Y	Y	Y	Y	Y	Y	Y	Y
7 John	?	?	?	Y	Y	?	Y	Y
MAINE								
1 Allen	Y	Y	Y	Y	Y	Y	Y	Y
2 Baldacci	Y	Y	Y	Y	Y	Y	Y	Y
MARYLAND								
1 ***Gilchrest***	Y	Y	Y	Y	Y	Y	Y	Y
2 ***Ehrlich***	Y	Y	Y	Y	Y	Y	Y	Y
3 Cardin	Y	Y	Y	Y	Y	Y	Y	Y
4 Wynn	Y	Y	Y	Y	Y	Y	Y	Y
5 Hoyer	Y	Y	Y	Y	Y	Y	Y	Y
6 ***Bartlett***	Y	Y	Y	Y	Y	Y	Y	Y
7 Cummings	Y	Y	Y	Y	Y	Y	Y	Y
8 ***Morella***	Y	Y	Y	Y	Y	Y	Y	Y
MASSACHUSETTS								
1 Olver	Y	Y	Y	Y	Y	Y	Y	Y
2 Neal	Y	Y	Y	Y	Y	Y	Y	Y
3 McGovern	Y	Y	Y	Y	Y	Y	Y	Y
4 Frank	Y	Y	Y	?	?	?	?	?
5 Meehan	Y	Y	Y	Y	Y	Y	Y	Y
6 Tierney	Y	Y	Y	Y	Y	Y	Y	Y
7 Markey	Y	Y	Y	Y	Y	Y	Y	Y
8 Kennedy	Y	Y	Y	Y	Y	Y	Y	Y
9 Moakley	Y	Y	Y	Y	Y	Y	Y	Y
10 Delahunt	Y	Y	Y	Y	Y	Y	Y	Y
MICHIGAN								
1 Stupak	Y	Y	Y	Y	Y	Y	Y	Y
2 ***Hoekstra***	Y	Y	Y	Y	Y	Y	Y	Y
3 ***Ehlers***	Y	Y	Y	Y	Y	Y	Y	Y
4 ***Camp***	Y	Y	Y	Y	Y	Y	Y	Y
5 Barcia	Y	Y	Y	Y	Y	Y	Y	Y
6 ***Upton***	Y	Y	Y	Y	Y	Y	Y	Y
7 ***Smith***	Y	Y	Y	Y	Y	Y	Y	Y
8 Stabenow	Y	Y	Y	Y	Y	Y	Y	Y
9 Kildee	Y	Y	Y	Y	Y	Y	Y	Y
10 Bonior	Y	Y	Y	Y	Y	Y	Y	Y
11 ***Knollenberg***	Y	Y	Y	Y	Y	Y	Y	Y
12 Levin	Y	Y	Y	Y	Y	Y	Y	Y
13 Rivers	Y	Y	Y	Y	Y	Y	Y	Y
14 Conyers	Y	Y	Y	Y	Y	Y	Y	Y
15 Kilpatrick	Y	Y	Y	Y	Y	Y	Y	Y
16 Dingell	Y	Y	Y	Y	Y	Y	Y	Y
MINNESOTA								
1 ***Gutknecht***	Y	Y	Y	Y	Y	Y	Y	Y
2 Minge	Y	Y	Y	Y	Y	Y	Y	Y

	416	417	418	419	420	421	422	423
3 ***Ramstad***	Y	Y	Y	Y	Y	Y	Y	Y
4 Vento	Y	Y	Y	Y	Y	Y	Y	Y
5 Sabo	Y	Y	Y	Y	Y	Y	Y	Y
6 Luther	Y	Y	Y	Y	Y	Y	Y	Y
7 Peterson	Y	Y	Y	Y	Y	Y	Y	Y
8 Oberstar	Y	Y	Y	Y	Y	Y	Y	Y
MISSISSIPPI								
1 ***Wicker***	Y	Y	Y	Y	Y	Y	Y	Y
2 Thompson	Y	Y	Y	?	?	?	Y	Y
3 ***Pickering***	Y	Y	Y	Y	Y	Y	Y	Y
4 ***Parker***	Y	Y	Y	Y	Y	Y	Y	Y
5 Taylor	Y	Y	Y	Y	Y	Y	Y	Y
MISSOURI								
1 Clay	Y	Y	Y	Y	Y	Y	Y	Y
2 ***Talent***	Y	Y	Y	Y	Y	Y	Y	Y
3 Gephardt	Y	Y	Y	Y	Y	Y	Y	Y
4 Skelton	Y	Y	Y	Y	Y	Y	Y	Y
5 McCarthy	Y	Y	Y	Y	Y	Y	Y	Y
6 Danner	Y	Y	Y	Y	Y	Y	Y	Y
7 ***Blunt***	Y	Y	Y	Y	Y	Y	Y	Y
8 ***Emerson***	Y	Y	Y	Y	Y	Y	Y	+
9 ***Hulshof***	Y	Y	Y	Y	Y	Y	Y	Y
MONTANA								
AL ***Hill***	Y	Y	Y	Y	Y	Y	Y	Y
NEBRASKA								
1 ***Bereuter***	Y	Y	Y	Y	Y	Y	Y	Y
2 ***Christensen***	Y	Y	Y	Y	Y	Y	Y	Y
3 ***Barrett***	Y	Y	Y	Y	Y	Y	Y	Y
NEVADA								
1 ***Ensign***	Y	Y	Y	Y	Y	Y	Y	Y
2 ***Gibbons***	Y	Y	Y	Y	Y	Y	Y	Y
NEW HAMPSHIRE								
1 ***Sununu***	Y	Y	Y	Y	Y	Y	Y	Y
2 ***Bass***	Y	Y	Y	Y	Y	Y	Y	Y
NEW JERSEY								
1 Andrews	Y	Y	Y	Y	Y	Y	Y	Y
2 ***LoBiondo***	Y	N	Y	Y	Y	Y	Y	Y
3 ***Saxton***	Y	Y	Y	Y	Y	Y	Y	Y
4 ***Smith***	Y	Y	Y	Y	Y	Y	Y	Y
5 ***Roukema***	Y	N	Y	Y	Y	Y	Y	Y
6 Pallone	Y	Y	Y	Y	Y	Y	Y	Y
7 ***Franks***	Y	Y	Y	Y	Y	Y	Y	Y
8 Pascrell	Y	Y	Y	Y	Y	Y	Y	Y
9 Rothman	Y	Y	Y	Y	Y	Y	Y	Y
10 Payne	Y	Y	Y	Y	Y	Y	Y	Y
11 ***Frelinghuysen***	Y	Y	Y	Y	Y	Y	Y	Y
12 ***Pappas***	Y	Y	Y	Y	Y	Y	Y	Y
13 Menendez	Y	Y	Y	Y	Y	Y	Y	Y
NEW MEXICO								
1 ***Schiff***	?	?	?	?	?	?	?	?
2 ***Skeen***	Y	Y	Y	Y	Y	Y	Y	Y
3 ***Redmond***	Y	Y	Y	Y	Y	Y	Y	Y
NEW YORK								
1 ***Forbes***	Y	Y	Y	Y	Y	Y	Y	Y
2 ***Lazio***	Y	Y	Y	Y	Y	Y	Y	Y
3 ***King***	Y	Y	Y	Y	Y	Y	Y	Y
4 McCarthy	Y	Y	Y	Y	Y	Y	Y	Y
5 Ackerman	Y	Y	Y	Y	Y	Y	Y	Y
6 Flake	Y	Y	Y	?	?	?	?	?
7 Manton	Y	Y	Y	Y	Y	Y	Y	Y
8 Nadler	Y	Y	Y	Y	Y	Y	Y	Y
9 Schumer	Y	Y	Y	Y	Y	Y	Y	Y
10 Towns	Y	Y	Y	Y	Y	Y	Y	Y
11 Owens	Y	Y	Y	Y	Y	Y	Y	Y
12 Velázquez	Y	Y	Y	Y	Y	Y	Y	Y
13 Vacant								
14 Maloney	Y	Y	Y	Y	Y	Y	Y	Y
15 Rangel	Y	Y	Y	Y	Y	Y	Y	Y
16 Serrano	Y	Y	Y	?	?	?	?	?
17 Engel	Y	Y	Y	Y	Y	Y	Y	Y
18 Lowey	Y	Y	Y	+	+	+	+	+
19 ***Kelly***	Y	Y	Y	Y	Y	Y	Y	Y
20 ***Gilman***	Y	Y	Y	Y	Y	Y	Y	Y
21 McNulty	Y	Y	Y	Y	Y	Y	Y	Y
22 ***Solomon***	Y	Y	Y	Y	Y	Y	Y	Y
23 ***Boehlert***	Y	Y	Y	Y	Y	Y	Y	Y
24 ***McHugh***	Y	Y	Y	Y	Y	Y	Y	Y
25 ***Walsh***	Y	Y	Y	Y	Y	Y	Y	Y
26 Hinchey	Y	Y	Y	Y	Y	Y	Y	Y
27 ***Paxon***	Y	Y	Y	Y	Y	Y	Y	Y
28 Slaughter	Y	N	Y	Y	Y	Y	Y	Y
29 LaFalce	Y	Y	Y	Y	Y	Y	Y	Y
30 ***Quinn***	Y	Y	Y	Y	Y	Y	Y	Y
31 ***Houghton***	Y	Y	Y	Y	Y	Y	Y	Y

	416	417	418	419	420	421	422	423
NORTH CAROLINA								
1 Clayton	Y	Y	Y	Y	Y	Y	Y	Y
2 Etheridge	Y	Y	Y	Y	Y	Y	Y	Y
3 ***Jones***	Y	Y	Y	Y	Y	Y	Y	Y
4 Price	Y	Y	Y	Y	Y	Y	Y	Y
5 ***Burr***	Y	Y	Y	Y	Y	Y	Y	Y
6 ***Coble***	Y	Y	Y	Y	Y	Y	Y	Y
7 McIntyre	Y	Y	Y	Y	Y	Y	Y	Y
8 Hefner	?	?	?	Y	Y	Y	Y	Y
9 ***Myrick***	Y	Y	Y	Y	Y	Y	Y	Y
10 ***Ballenger***	Y	Y	Y	Y	Y	Y	Y	Y
11 ***Taylor***	Y	?	Y	Y	Y	Y	Y	Y
12 Watt	Y	Y	Y	N	N	Y	Y	Y
NORTH DAKOTA								
AL Pomeroy	Y	Y	Y	Y	Y	Y	Y	Y
OHIO								
1 ***Chabot***	Y	Y	Y	Y	Y	Y	Y	Y
2 ***Portman***	Y	Y	Y	Y	Y	Y	?	Y
3 Hall	Y	Y	Y	Y	Y	Y	Y	Y
4 ***Oxley***	Y	Y	Y	Y	Y	Y	Y	Y
5 ***Gillmor***	Y	Y	Y	Y	Y	Y	Y	Y
6 Strickland	Y	Y	Y	Y	Y	Y	Y	Y
7 ***Hobson***	Y	Y	Y	Y	Y	Y	Y	Y
8 ***Boehner***	Y	Y	Y	Y	Y	Y	Y	Y
9 Kaptur	Y	Y	Y	Y	Y	Y	Y	Y
10 Kucinich	Y	Y	Y	Y	Y	Y	Y	Y
11 Stokes	Y	Y	Y	Y	Y	Y	Y	Y
12 ***Kasich***	Y	Y	Y	Y	Y	Y	Y	Y
13 Brown	Y	Y	Y	Y	Y	Y	Y	Y
14 Sawyer	Y	Y	Y	Y	Y	Y	Y	Y
15 ***Pryce***	Y	Y	Y	Y	Y	Y	Y	Y
16 ***Regula***	Y	Y	Y	Y	Y	Y	Y	Y
17 Traficant	Y	Y	Y	Y	Y	Y	Y	Y
18 ***Ney***	Y	Y	Y	Y	Y	Y	Y	Y
19 ***LaTourette***	Y	Y	Y	Y	Y	Y	Y	Y
OKLAHOMA								
1 ***Largent***	Y	Y	Y	Y	Y	Y	Y	Y
2 ***Coburn***	Y	N	Y	Y	Y	Y	?	?
3 ***Watkins***	Y	Y	Y	Y	Y	Y	Y	Y
4 ***Watts***	Y	Y	Y	Y	Y	Y	Y	Y
5 ***Istook***	Y	Y	Y	Y	Y	Y	Y	Y
6 ***Lucas***	Y	Y	Y	Y	Y	Y	Y	Y
OREGON								
1 Furse	Y	Y	Y	Y	Y	Y	Y	Y
2 ***Smith***	Y	Y	Y	Y	Y	Y	Y	Y
3 Blumenauer	Y	Y	Y	Y	Y	Y	Y	Y
4 DeFazio	Y	Y	Y	Y	Y	Y	Y	Y
5 Hooley	Y	Y	Y	Y	Y	Y	Y	Y
PENNSYLVANIA								
1 Foglietta	Y	Y	Y	?	?	?	?	?
2 Fattah	Y	Y	Y	Y	Y	Y	Y	Y
3 Borski	Y	Y	Y	Y	Y	Y	Y	Y
4 Klink	Y	Y	Y	Y	Y	Y	Y	Y
5 ***Peterson***	Y	Y	Y	Y	Y	Y	Y	Y
6 Holden	Y	Y	Y	Y	Y	Y	Y	Y
7 ***Weldon***	Y	Y	Y	Y	Y	Y	Y	Y
8 ***Greenwood***	Y	Y	Y	Y	Y	Y	Y	Y
9 ***Shuster***	Y	Y	Y	Y	Y	Y	Y	Y
10 ***McDade***	Y	Y	Y	Y	Y	Y	Y	Y
11 Kanjorski	Y	Y	Y	Y	Y	Y	Y	Y
12 Murtha	Y	Y	Y	Y	Y	Y	Y	Y
13 ***Fox***	Y	Y	Y	Y	Y	Y	Y	Y
14 Coyne	Y	Y	Y	Y	Y	Y	Y	Y
15 McHale	Y	Y	Y	Y	Y	Y	Y	Y
16 ***Pitts***	Y	Y	Y	Y	Y	Y	Y	Y
17 ***Gekas***	Y	Y	Y	Y	Y	Y	Y	Y
18 Doyle	Y	Y	Y	Y	Y	Y	Y	Y
19 ***Goodling***	Y	Y	Y	Y	Y	Y	Y	Y
20 Mascara	Y	Y	Y	Y	Y	Y	Y	Y
21 ***English***	Y	Y	Y	Y	Y	Y	Y	Y
RHODE ISLAND								
1 Kennedy	Y	Y	Y	Y	Y	Y	Y	Y
2 Weygand	Y	Y	Y	Y	Y	Y	Y	Y
SOUTH CAROLINA								
1 ***Sanford***	Y	Y	Y	Y	Y	Y	Y	N
2 ***Spence***	Y	Y	Y	Y	Y	Y	Y	Y
3 ***Graham***	Y	Y	Y	Y	Y	Y	Y	Y
4 ***Inglis***	Y	Y	Y	Y	Y	Y	Y	Y
5 Spratt	Y	Y	Y	Y	Y	Y	Y	Y
6 Clyburn	Y	Y	Y	Y	Y	Y	Y	Y
SOUTH DAKOTA								
AL ***Thune***	Y	Y	Y	Y	Y	Y	Y	Y
TENNESSEE								
1 ***Jenkins***	Y	Y	Y	Y	Y	Y	Y	Y
2 ***Duncan***	Y	Y	Y	Y	Y	Y	Y	Y

	416	417	418	419	420	421	422	
3 ***Wamp***	Y	Y	Y	Y	Y	Y	Y	Y
4 ***Hilleary***	Y	Y	Y	Y	Y	Y	Y	Y
5 Clement	Y	Y	Y	Y	Y	Y	Y	Y
6 Gordon	Y	Y	Y	Y	Y	Y	Y	Y
7 ***Bryant***	Y	Y	Y	Y	Y	Y	Y	Y
8 Tanner	Y	Y	Y	Y	Y	Y	Y	Y
9 Ford	Y	Y	Y	Y	Y	Y	Y	Y
TEXAS								
1 Sandlin	Y	Y	Y	Y	Y	Y	Y	Y
2 Turner	Y	Y	Y	Y	Y	Y	Y	Y
3 ***Johnson, Sam***	Y	Y	Y	?	Y	Y	?	Y
4 Hall	Y	Y	Y	Y	Y	Y	Y	Y
5 ***Sessions***	Y	Y	Y	Y	Y	Y	Y	Y
6 ***Barton***	Y	Y	Y	Y	Y	Y	Y	Y
7 ***Archer***	Y	Y	Y	Y	Y	Y	Y	Y
8 ***Brady***	Y	Y	Y	Y	Y	Y	Y	Y
9 Lampson	Y	Y	Y	Y	Y	Y	Y	Y
10 Doggett	Y	Y	Y	Y	Y	Y	Y	Y
11 Edwards	?	?	?	Y	Y	Y	Y	Y
12 ***Granger***	Y	Y	Y	Y	Y	Y	Y	Y
13 ***Thornberry***	Y	N	Y	Y	Y	Y	Y	Y
14 ***Paul***	Y	Y	Y	Y	P	Y	Y	N
15 Hinojosa	Y	?	Y	Y	Y	Y	Y	Y
16 Reyes	Y	Y	Y	?	?	Y	Y	Y
17 Stenholm	Y	Y	Y	Y	Y	Y	Y	Y
18 Jackson-Lee	Y	Y	Y	Y	Y	Y	Y	Y
19 ***Combest***	Y	Y	Y	Y	Y	Y	Y	Y
20 Gonzalez	?	?	?	?	?	?	?	?
21 ***Smith***	Y	Y	Y	Y	Y	Y	Y	Y
22 ***DeLay***	Y	Y	Y	Y	Y	Y	Y	Y
23 ***Bonilla***	?	?	?	?	?	?	?	?
24 Frost	Y	Y	Y	Y	Y	Y	Y	Y
25 Bentsen	Y	Y	Y	Y	Y	Y	Y	Y
26 ***Armey***	Y	Y	Y	Y	Y	Y	Y	Y
27 Ortiz	?	?	?	Y	Y	Y	Y	Y
28 Rodriguez	Y	Y	Y	?	?	Y	Y	Y
29 Green	Y	Y	Y	Y	Y	Y	Y	Y
30 Johnson, E.B.	Y	Y	Y	Y	Y	Y	Y	Y
UTAH								
1 ***Hansen***	Y	Y	Y	Y	Y	Y	Y	Y
2 ***Cook***	Y	Y	Y	Y	Y	Y	Y	Y
3 ***Cannon***	Y	Y	Y	Y	Y	Y	Y	Y
VERMONT								
AL *Sanders*	Y	Y	Y	Y	Y	Y	Y	Y
VIRGINIA								
1 ***Bateman***	Y	Y	Y	Y	Y	Y	Y	Y
2 Pickett	Y	Y	Y	Y	Y	Y	Y	Y
3 Scott	Y	Y	Y	N	N	Y	Y	Y
4 Sisisky	Y	Y	Y	Y	Y	Y	Y	Y
5 Goode	Y	Y	Y	Y	Y	Y	Y	Y
6 ***Goodlatte***	Y	Y	Y	Y	Y	Y	Y	Y
7 ***Bliley***	Y	Y	Y	Y	Y	Y	Y	Y
8 Moran	Y	Y	Y	Y	Y	Y	Y	Y
9 Boucher	Y	Y	Y	Y	Y	Y	Y	Y
10 ***Wolf***	Y	Y	Y	Y	Y	Y	Y	Y
11 ***Davis***	Y	Y	Y	Y	Y	Y	Y	Y
WASHINGTON								
1 ***White***	Y	Y	Y	Y	Y	Y	Y	Y
2 ***Metcalf***	Y	Y	Y	Y	Y	Y	Y	Y
3 ***Smith, Linda***	?	Y	Y	Y	Y	Y	Y	Y
4 ***Hastings***	Y	Y	Y	Y	Y	Y	Y	Y
5 ***Nethercutt***	Y	Y	Y	Y	Y	Y	Y	Y
6 Dicks	Y	Y	Y	Y	Y	Y	Y	Y
7 McDermott	Y	Y	Y	Y	Y	Y	Y	Y
8 ***Dunn***	Y	Y	Y	Y	Y	Y	Y	Y
9 Smith, Adam	Y	Y	Y	Y	Y	Y	Y	Y
WEST VIRGINIA								
1 Mollohan	Y	Y	Y	Y	Y	Y	Y	Y
2 Wise	Y	Y	Y	Y	Y	Y	Y	Y
3 Rahall	Y	Y	Y	Y	Y	Y	Y	Y
WISCONSIN								
1 ***Neumann***	Y	Y	Y	Y	Y	Y	Y	Y
2 ***Klug***	Y	Y	Y	Y	Y	Y	Y	Y
3 Kind	Y	Y	Y	Y	Y	Y	Y	Y
4 Kleczka	Y	Y	Y	Y	Y	Y	Y	Y
5 Barrett	Y	Y	Y	Y	Y	Y	Y	Y
6 ***Petri***	Y	Y	Y	Y	Y	Y	Y	Y
7 Obey	Y	Y	Y	Y	Y	Y	Y	Y
8 Johnson	Y	Y	Y	Y	Y	Y	Y	Y
9 ***Sensenbrenner***	Y	Y	Y	Y	Y	Y	Y	N
WYOMING								
AL ***Cubin***	Y	Y	Y	Y	Y	Y	Y	Y

Southern states - Ala., Ark., Fla., Ga., Ky., La., Miss., N.C., Okla., S.C., Tenn., Texas, Va.

HOUSE VOTES 424, 425, 426, 427, 428, 429, 430, 431

424. HR 1420. National Wildlife Refuge System/Passage. Young, R-Alaska, motion to suspend the rules and approve the Senate amendments to the bill to establish a mission of conservation for the National Wildlife Refuge System and allow public recreational use of a refuge only when the use is compatible with the conservation and established purpose of an individual refuge. Motion agreed to (thus cleared for the president) 419-1: R 220-1; D 198-0 (ND 145-0, SD 53-0); I 1-0, Sept. 23, 1997. A two-thirds majority of those present and voting (280 in this case) is required for passage under suspension of the rules.

425. HR 1948. Hood Bay Land Exchange/Passage. Young, R-Alaska, motion to suspend the rules and pass the bill to provide for a transfer of land on Admiralty Island National Monument in Alaska from the Alaska Pulp Corp. to the U.S. Forest Service in exchange for the government's reversionary interest on land the company owns near Sitka, Alaska. Motion agreed to 420-0: R 222-0; D 197-0 (ND 145-0, SD 52-0); I 1-0, Sept. 23, 1997. A two-thirds majority of those present and voting (280 in this case) is required for passage under suspension of the rules.

426. Procedural Motion/Adjourn. Miller, D-Calif., motion to adjourn. Motion rejected 59-342: R 1-207; D 58-134 (ND 47-94, SD 11-40); I 0-1, Sept. 24, 1997.

427. Procedural Motion/Journal. Approval of the House Journal of Tuesday, Sept. 23, 1997. Approved 324-81: R 184-25; D 139-56 (ND 102-42, SD 37-14); I 1-0, Sept. 24, 1997.

428. Procedural Motion/Motion to Table. McInnis, R-Colo., motion to table (kill) the Doggett, D-Texas, motion to reconsider the call of the chair on ordering the yeas and nays on the Gephardt, D-Mo., motion to adjourn. Motion agreed to 217-197: R 215-0; D 2-196 (ND 1-144, SD 1-52); I 0-1, Sept. 24, 1997.

429. Procedural Motion/Adjourn. Gephardt, D-Mo., motion to adjourn. Motion rejected 124-293: R 3-213; D 120-80 (ND 94-54, SD 26-26); I 1-0, Sept. 24, 1997.

430. HR 2209. Fiscal 1998 Legislative Branch Appropriations/ Previous Question. McInnis, R-Colo., motion to order the previous question (thus ending debate and the possibility for amendment) on adoption of the rule (H Res 238) to waive points of order against and provide for House floor consideration of the conference report to provide $2.25 billion for the operations of the legislative branch in fiscal 1998. Motion agreed to 237-186: R 222-0; D 15-185 (ND 12-135, SD 3-50); I 0-1, Sept. 24, 1997.

431. HR 2209. Fiscal 1998 Legislative Branch Appropriations/ Rule. Adoption of the rule (H Res 238) to waive points of order against and provide for House consideration of the conference report to provide $2.25 billion for the operations of the legislative branch in fiscal 1998. Adopted 408-5: R 217-2; D 190-3 (ND 139-2, SD 51-1); I 1-0, Sept. 24, 1997.

KEY

- Y Voted for (yea).
- # Paired for.
- \+ Announced for.
- N Voted against (nay).
- X Paired against.
- – Announced against.
- P Voted "present."
- C Voted "present" to avoid possible conflict of interest.
- ? Did not vote or otherwise make a position known.

Democrats ***Republicans***
Independent

	424	425	426	427	428	429	430	431
ALABAMA								
1 ***Callahan***	Y	Y	N	Y	Y	N	Y	Y
2 ***Everett***	Y	Y	N	Y	Y	N	Y	Y
3 ***Riley***	Y	Y	N	Y	Y	N	Y	Y
4 ***Aderholt***	Y	Y	N	N	Y	N	Y	Y
5 Cramer	Y	Y	N	Y	N	N	N	Y
6 ***Bachus***	Y	Y	N	Y	Y	N	Y	Y
7 Hilliard	Y	Y	N	N	N	Y	N	Y
ALASKA								
AL ***Young***	Y	Y	?	?	Y	N	Y	Y
ARIZONA								
1 ***Salmon***	Y	Y	N	N	Y	N	Y	Y
2 Pastor	Y	Y	N	Y	N	N	N	Y
3 ***Stump***	Y	Y	N	Y	Y	N	Y	Y
4 ***Shadegg***	Y	Y	N	Y	Y	N	Y	Y
5 ***Kolbe***	Y	Y	N	Y	Y	N	Y	Y
6 ***Hayworth***	Y	Y	N	Y	Y	N	Y	Y
ARKANSAS								
1 Berry	Y	Y	Y	Y	N	Y	N	Y
2 Snyder	Y	Y	N	Y	N	Y	N	Y
3 ***Hutchinson***	Y	Y	N	Y	Y	?	Y	Y
4 ***Dickey***	Y	Y	N	Y	Y	N	Y	Y
CALIFORNIA								
1 ***Riggs***	Y	Y	?	?	?	?	Y	Y
2 ***Herger***	Y	Y	N	Y	Y	N	Y	Y
3 Fazio	Y	Y	Y	N	N	Y	N	Y
4 ***Doolittle***	Y	Y	N	Y	Y	N	Y	Y
5 Matsui	Y	Y	N	Y	N	Y	N	Y
6 Woolsey	Y	Y	?	Y	N	Y	N	Y
7 Miller	Y	Y	Y	N	N	Y	N	Y
8 Pelosi	Y	Y	Y	Y	N	Y	N	Y
9 Dellums	Y	Y	N	Y	N	Y	?	?
10 Tauscher	Y	Y	N	Y	N	Y	N	Y
11 ***Pombo***	Y	Y	N	N	Y	N	Y	Y
12 Lantos	Y	Y	N	Y	N	N	N	Y
13 Stark	Y	Y	N	Y	N	Y	N	Y
14 Eshoo	Y	Y	N	Y	N	Y	N	Y
15 ***Campbell***	Y	Y	N	Y	Y	N	Y	Y
16 Lofgren	Y	Y	N	Y	N	N	N	Y
17 Farr	Y	Y	Y	Y	N	Y	N	Y
18 Condit	Y	Y	N	Y	N	N	N	Y
19 ***Radanovich***	Y	Y	N	Y	Y	N	Y	Y
20 Dooley	Y	Y	N	Y	N	N	N	Y
21 ***Thomas***	Y	Y	?	Y	Y	N	Y	Y
22 Capps	Y	Y	N	Y	N	N	N	Y
23 ***Gallegly***	Y	Y	N	Y	Y	N	Y	Y
24 Sherman	Y	Y	N	Y	N	N	N	Y
25 ***McKeon***	Y	Y	N	Y	Y	N	Y	Y
26 Berman	Y	Y	N	Y	N	N	N	?
27 ***Rogan***	Y	Y	N	Y	Y	N	Y	Y
28 ***Dreier***	Y	Y	N	Y	Y	N	Y	Y
29 Waxman	Y	Y	Y	Y	N	Y	N	Y
30 Becerra	Y	Y	Y	N	N	Y	N	Y
31 Martinez	Y	Y	Y	N	N	Y	N	Y
32 Dixon	Y	Y	N	Y	N	N	N	Y
33 Roybal-Allard	Y	Y	N	Y	N	Y	N	Y
34 Torres	Y	Y	?	?	?	Y	N	Y
35 Waters	Y	Y	N	N	N	Y	N	Y
36 Harman	Y	Y	Y	Y	N	Y	N	Y
37 Millender-McD.	Y	Y	N	Y	N	N	N	Y
38 ***Horn***	Y	Y	N	Y	Y	N	Y	Y
39 ***Royce***	Y	Y	N	Y	Y	N	Y	Y
40 ***Lewis***	Y	Y	N	Y	Y	N	Y	Y
41 ***Kim***	Y	Y	N	Y	Y	N	Y	Y
42 Brown	Y	Y	N	N	N	N	N	?
43 ***Calvert***	Y	Y	N	Y	Y	N	Y	Y
44 ***Bono***	Y	Y	?	Y	Y	N	Y	Y
45 ***Rohrabacher***	Y	Y	N	Y	Y	N	Y	Y
46 Sanchez	Y	Y	N	Y	N	Y	N	Y
47 ***Cox***	Y	Y	N	Y	Y	N	Y	Y
48 ***Packard***	Y	Y	N	Y	Y	N	Y	Y
49 ***Bilbray***	Y	Y	N	Y	Y	N	Y	Y
50 Filner	Y	Y	Y	N	N	Y	N	Y
51 ***Cunningham***	Y	Y	N	Y	Y	N	Y	Y
52 ***Hunter***	Y	Y	?	?	?	?	?	?
COLORADO								
1 DeGette	Y	Y	N	Y	?	Y	N	?
2 Skaggs	Y	Y	N	Y	N	N	N	?
3 ***McInnis***	Y	Y	N	Y	Y	N	Y	Y
4 ***Schaffer***	Y	Y	N	N	Y	N	Y	Y
5 ***Hefley***	Y	Y	N	Y	Y	N	Y	Y
6 ***Schaefer***	Y	Y	N	Y	Y	N	Y	Y
CONNECTICUT								
1 Kennelly	Y	Y	Y	N	N	Y	?	?
2 Gejdenson	Y	Y	Y	Y	N	Y	N	Y
3 DeLauro	Y	Y	Y	N	N	Y	N	Y
4 ***Shays***	Y	Y	N	Y	Y	N	Y	Y
5 Maloney	Y	Y	Y	Y	N	Y	N	Y
6 ***Johnson***	Y	Y	N	Y	Y	N	Y	Y
DELAWARE								
AL ***Castle***	Y	Y	N	Y	Y	N	Y	Y
FLORIDA								
1 ***Scarborough***	?	Y	N	Y	Y	?	Y	N
2 Boyd	Y	Y	N	Y	N	N	N	Y
3 Brown	Y	Y	N	N	N	Y	N	Y
4 ***Fowler***	Y	Y	N	Y	Y	N	Y	Y
5 Thurman	Y	Y	N	Y	N	N	N	Y
6 ***Stearns***	Y	Y	N	N	Y	N	Y	Y
7 ***Mica***	Y	Y	N	Y	Y	N	Y	Y
8 ***McCollum***	Y	Y	N	Y	Y	?	Y	Y
9 ***Bilirakis***	Y	Y	N	Y	Y	N	Y	Y
10 ***Young***	Y	Y	?	?	Y	N	Y	Y
11 Davis	Y	Y	Y	Y	N	Y	N	Y
12 ***Canady***	Y	Y	N	Y	Y	N	Y	Y
13 ***Miller***	Y	Y	N	Y	Y	N	Y	Y
14 ***Goss***	Y	Y	N	Y	Y	N	Y	Y
15 ***Weldon***	Y	Y	N	Y	Y	N	Y	Y
16 ***Foley***	Y	Y	N	Y	Y	N	Y	Y
17 Meek	Y	Y	N	N	N	Y	N	Y
18 ***Ros-Lehtinen***	Y	Y	N	Y	Y	N	Y	Y
19 Wexler	Y	Y	Y	Y	N	Y	N	Y
20 Deutsch	Y	Y	Y	Y	N	Y	N	Y
21 ***Diaz-Balart***	Y	Y	?	?	Y	N	Y	Y
22 ***Shaw***	Y	Y	N	Y	Y	N	Y	Y
23 Hastings	?	?	?	?	?	?	?	?
GEORGIA								
1 ***Kingston***	Y	Y	N	N	Y	N	Y	Y
2 Bishop	Y	Y	N	Y	N	N	N	Y
3 ***Collins***	Y	Y	N	?	Y	N	Y	Y
4 McKinney	Y	Y	N	Y	N	N	N	Y
5 Lewis	Y	?	Y	N	N	Y	N	Y
6 ***Gingrich***								
7 ***Barr***	Y	Y	N	Y	Y	N	Y	Y
8 ***Chambliss***	Y	Y	N	Y	Y	N	Y	Y
9 ***Deal***	Y	Y	N	Y	Y	N	Y	Y
10 ***Norwood***	Y	Y	N	N	Y	N	Y	Y
11 ***Linder***	Y	Y	N	Y	Y	N	Y	Y
HAWAII								
1 Abercrombie	Y	Y	N	N	N	N	N	Y
2 Mink	Y	Y	Y	Y	N	Y	N	Y
IDAHO								
1 ***Chenoweth***	Y	Y	N	+	Y	N	Y	Y
2 ***Crapo***	Y	Y	?	Y	Y	N	Y	Y
ILLINOIS								
1 Rush	Y	Y	N	Y	N	Y	N	Y
2 Jackson	Y	Y	N	Y	N	Y	N	Y
3 Lipinski	Y	Y	N	Y	N	Y	N	Y
4 Gutierrez	Y	Y	?	N	N	Y	N	?
5 Blagojevich	Y	Y	N	Y	N	N	N	Y
6 ***Hyde***	Y	Y	?	?	Y	N	Y	Y
7 Davis	Y	Y	N	Y	N	Y	N	Y
8 ***Crane***	Y	Y	?	?	Y	N	Y	Y
9 Yates	?	?	?	Y	N	Y	N	Y
10 ***Porter***	Y	Y	N	Y	?	N	Y	Y
11 ***Weller***	Y	Y	N	N	Y	N	Y	Y
12 Costello	Y	Y	N	N	N	Y	N	Y
13 ***Fawell***	Y	Y	N	Y	?	N	Y	Y
14 ***Hastert***	Y	Y	N	Y	Y	N	Y	Y
15 ***Ewing***	Y	Y	N	Y	Y	N	Y	Y

ND Northern Democrats SD Southern Democrats

	424	425	426	427	428	429	430	431
16 ***Manzullo***	Y	Y	N	Y	Y	N	Y	Y
17 Evans	Y	Y	N	N	N	Y	N	Y
18 ***LaHood***	Y	Y	N	Y	Y	N	Y	Y
19 Poshard	Y	Y	N	N	N	N	N	Y
20 ***Shimkus***	Y	Y	N	N	Y	N	Y	Y
INDIANA								
1 Visclosky	Y	Y	N	N	N	N	N	Y
2 ***McIntosh***	Y	Y	N	N	Y	N	Y	Y
3 Roemer	Y	Y	N	Y	N	N	N	Y
4 ***Souder***	Y	Y	N	N	Y	N	Y	Y
5 ***Buyer***	Y	Y	N	Y	Y	N	Y	?
6 ***Burton***	Y	Y	N	Y	Y	N	Y	Y
7 ***Pease***	Y	Y	N	Y	Y	N	Y	Y
8 ***Hostettler***	Y	Y	?	?	Y	N	Y	Y
9 Hamilton	Y	Y	N	Y	N	N	Y	Y
10 Carson	Y	Y	N	Y	N	N	N	Y
IOWA								
1 ***Leach***	Y	Y	N	Y	Y	N	Y	Y
2 ***Nussle***	Y	Y	N	Y	Y	N	Y	Y
3 Boswell	Y	Y	N	Y	N	N	N	Y
4 ***Ganske***	Y	Y	N	Y	Y	N	Y	Y
5 ***Latham***	Y	Y	N	Y	Y	N	Y	Y
KANSAS								
1 ***Moran***	Y	Y	N	Y	Y	N	Y	Y
2 ***Ryun***	Y	Y	N	Y	Y	N	Y	Y
3 ***Snowbarger***	Y	Y	N	N	Y	N	Y	Y
4 ***Tiahrt***	Y	Y	N	Y	Y	N	Y	Y
KENTUCKY								
1 ***Whitfield***	Y	Y	N	?	Y	N	Y	Y
2 ***Lewis***	Y	Y	N	Y	Y	N	Y	Y
3 ***Northup***	Y	Y	N	Y	Y	N	Y	Y
4 ***Bunning***	Y	Y	N	Y	Y	N	Y	Y
5 ***Rogers***	Y	Y	N	Y	Y	N	Y	Y
6 Baesler	Y	Y	N	Y	N	N	Y	Y
LOUISIANA								
1 ***Livingston***	Y	Y	N	Y	?	N	Y	Y
2 Jefferson	Y	Y	Y	Y	N	Y	N	Y
3 ***Tauzin***	Y	Y	N	Y	Y	N	Y	Y
4 ***McCrery***	Y	Y	?	?	Y	N	Y	Y
5 ***Cooksey***	Y	Y	N	Y	Y	N	Y	Y
6 ***Baker***	Y	Y	N	Y	Y	N	Y	Y
7 John	Y	Y	N	Y	N	Y	N	Y
MAINE								
1 Allen	Y	Y	Y	Y	N	Y	N	Y
2 Baldacci	Y	Y	N	Y	N	N	N	Y
MARYLAND								
1 ***Gilchrest***	Y	Y	N	Y	Y	N	Y	Y
2 ***Ehrlich***	Y	Y	N	Y	Y	N	Y	Y
3 Cardin	Y	Y	N	Y	N	Y	N	Y
4 Wynn	Y	Y	N	Y	?	?	N	Y
5 Hoyer	Y	Y	Y	?	?	Y	N	?
6 ***Bartlett***	Y	Y	N	Y	Y	N	Y	Y
7 Cummings	Y	Y	N	Y	N	Y	N	Y
8 ***Morella***	Y	Y	N	Y	Y	N	Y	Y
MASSACHUSETTS								
1 Olver	Y	Y	Y	N	N	Y	N	Y
2 Neal	Y	Y	N	Y	N	Y	N	Y
3 McGovern	Y	Y	N	N	N	Y	N	Y
4 Frank	?	?	?	?	?	?	N	Y
5 Meehan	Y	Y	N	Y	N	Y	N	N
6 Tierney	Y	Y	Y	Y	N	Y	N	Y
7 Markey	Y	Y	N	Y	N	Y	N	Y
8 Kennedy	Y	Y	N	Y	N	Y	N	Y
9 Moakley	Y	Y	N	Y	N	Y	N	Y
10 Delahunt	Y	Y	Y	Y	N	Y	N	Y
MICHIGAN								
1 Stupak	Y	Y	Y	N	N	Y	N	Y
2 ***Hoekstra***	Y	Y	N	Y	Y	N	Y	Y
3 ***Ehlers***	Y	Y	N	Y	Y	N	Y	Y
4 ***Camp***	Y	Y	N	Y	Y	N	Y	Y
5 Barcia	Y	Y	N	Y	N	N	N	Y
6 ***Upton***	Y	Y	N	Y	Y	N	Y	Y
7 ***Smith***	Y	Y	N	Y	Y	N	Y	+
8 Stabenow	Y	Y	N	Y	N	Y	N	Y
9 Kildee	Y	Y	N	Y	N	N	N	Y
10 Bonior	Y	Y	Y	?	N	Y	N	Y
11 ***Knollenberg***	Y	Y	N	Y	Y	N	Y	Y
12 Levin	Y	Y	Y	Y	N	Y	N	Y
13 Rivers	Y	Y	N	Y	N	N	N	Y
14 Conyers	Y	Y	Y	?	N	Y	N	Y
15 Kilpatrick	Y	Y	Y	N	N	Y	N	Y
16 Dingell	Y	Y	?	Y	N	Y	Y	Y
MINNESOTA								
1 ***Gutknecht***	Y	Y	N	N	Y	N	Y	Y
2 Minge	Y	Y	N	Y	N	N	N	Y
3 ***Ramstad***	Y	Y	N	N	Y	N	Y	Y
4 Vento	Y	Y	Y	N	N	Y	N	Y
5 Sabo	Y	Y	N	N	N	N	Y	Y
6 Luther	Y	Y	N	Y	N	N	N	Y
7 Peterson	Y	Y	N	Y	N	N	N	Y
8 Oberstar	Y	Y	N	N	N	Y	N	Y
MISSISSIPPI								
1 ***Wicker***	Y	Y	N	Y	Y	N	Y	Y
2 Thompson	Y	Y	N	N	N	Y	N	Y
3 ***Pickering***	Y	Y	N	Y	Y	N	Y	Y
4 ***Parker***	Y	Y	N	Y	Y	N	Y	Y
5 Taylor	Y	Y	N	N	Y	N	N	Y
MISSOURI								
1 Clay	Y	Y	N	N	N	Y	N	Y
2 ***Talent***	Y	Y	N	Y	Y	N	Y	Y
3 Gephardt	Y	Y	Y	N	N	Y	N	Y
4 Skelton	Y	Y	N	Y	N	N	N	Y
5 McCarthy	Y	Y	N	Y	N	N	N	Y
6 Danner	Y	Y	N	Y	N	?	N	Y
7 ***Blunt***	Y	Y	N	Y	Y	N	Y	Y
8 ***Emerson***	+	+	N	Y	Y	N	Y	Y
9 ***Hulshof***	Y	Y	N	N	Y	N	Y	Y
MONTANA								
AL ***Hill***	Y	Y	N	Y	Y	N	Y	Y
NEBRASKA								
1 ***Bereuter***	Y	Y	N	Y	Y	N	Y	Y
2 ***Christensen***	Y	Y	N	Y	Y	N	Y	Y
3 ***Barrett***	Y	Y	N	Y	Y	N	Y	Y
NEVADA								
1 ***Ensign***	Y	Y	N	N	Y	N	Y	Y
2 ***Gibbons***	Y	Y	N	N	Y	N	Y	Y
NEW HAMPSHIRE								
1 ***Sununu***	Y	Y	N	Y	Y	N	Y	Y
2 ***Bass***	Y	Y	N	Y	Y	N	Y	Y
NEW JERSEY								
1 Andrews	Y	Y	Y	Y	N	Y	N	Y
2 ***LoBiondo***	Y	Y	N	N	Y	N	Y	Y
3 ***Saxton***	Y	Y	N	Y	?	N	Y	Y
4 ***Smith***	Y	Y	N	Y	Y	N	Y	Y
5 ***Roukema***	Y	Y	N	Y	Y	N	Y	Y
6 Pallone	Y	Y	Y	Y	N	Y	N	Y
7 ***Franks***	Y	Y	N	Y	Y	N	Y	Y
8 Pascrell	Y	Y	N	Y	N	N	N	Y
9 Rothman	Y	Y	N	Y	N	Y	N	Y
10 Payne	Y	Y	N	Y	N	Y	N	Y
11 ***Frelinghuysen***	Y	Y	N	Y	Y	N	Y	Y
12 ***Pappas***	Y	Y	N	Y	Y	N	Y	Y
13 Menendez	Y	Y	N	N	N	Y	N	Y
NEW MEXICO								
1 ***Schiff***	?	?	?	?	?	?	?	?
2 ***Skeen***	Y	Y	N	Y	Y	N	Y	Y
3 ***Redmond***	Y	Y	N	Y	Y	N	+	+
NEW YORK								
1 ***Forbes***	Y	Y	?	?	Y	N	Y	Y
2 ***Lazio***	Y	Y	N	Y	Y	N	Y	Y
3 ***King***	Y	Y	N	Y	Y	N	Y	Y
4 McCarthy	Y	Y	N	N	N	Y	N	Y
5 Ackerman	Y	Y	N	N	N	Y	N	Y
6 Flake	?	?	N	Y	N	Y	?	?
7 Manton	Y	Y	N	Y	N	N	N	Y
8 Nadler	Y	Y	N	Y	N	Y	N	Y
9 Schumer	Y	Y	?	?	?	Y	N	Y
10 Towns	Y	Y	N	Y	N	Y	N	Y
11 Owens	Y	Y	Y	Y	N	N	N	Y
12 Velázquez	Y	Y	N	Y	N	Y	N	Y
13 Vacant								
14 Maloney	Y	Y	N	N	N	Y	N	Y
15 Rangel	Y	Y	N	Y	N	N	N	Y
16 Serrano	?	?	N	Y	N	N	N	Y
17 Engel	Y	Y	N	Y	N	N	Y	Y
18 Lowey	+	+	Y	Y	N	Y	N	Y
19 ***Kelly***	Y	Y	N	Y	Y	N	Y	Y
20 ***Gilman***	Y	Y	N	Y	Y	?	Y	Y
21 McNulty	Y	Y	Y	N	N	Y	N	Y
22 ***Solomon***	Y	Y	N	Y	Y	N	Y	Y
23 ***Boehlert***	Y	Y	N	Y	Y	N	Y	Y
24 ***McHugh***	Y	Y	N	Y	Y	N	Y	Y
25 ***Walsh***	Y	Y	N	Y	Y	N	Y	Y
26 Hinchey	Y	Y	N	N	N	Y	N	Y
27 ***Paxon***	Y	Y	N	Y	Y	N	Y	Y
28 Slaughter	Y	Y	Y	Y	N	Y	N	Y
29 LaFalce	Y	Y	N	N	N	Y	N	Y
30 ***Quinn***	Y	Y	N	Y	Y	N	Y	Y
31 ***Houghton***	Y	Y	N	Y	Y	N	Y	Y
NORTH CAROLINA								
1 Clayton	Y	Y	N	N	N	Y	N	Y
2 Etheridge	Y	Y	N	Y	N	Y	N	Y
3 ***Jones***	Y	Y	N	Y	Y	N	Y	Y
4 Price	Y	Y	N	Y	N	N	N	Y
5 ***Burr***	Y	Y	?	Y	Y	N	Y	Y
6 ***Coble***	Y	Y	N	Y	Y	N	Y	Y
7 McIntyre	Y	Y	N	Y	N	N	N	Y
8 Hefner	Y	Y	?	?	N	Y	N	Y
9 ***Myrick***	Y	Y	N	Y	Y	N	Y	Y
10 ***Ballenger***	Y	Y	N	Y	Y	N	Y	Y
11 ***Taylor***	Y	Y	N	Y	Y	N	Y	Y
12 Watt	Y	Y	N	Y	N	N	N	Y
NORTH DAKOTA								
AL Pomeroy	Y	Y	N	Y	N	Y	N	Y
OHIO								
1 ***Chabot***	Y	Y	N	Y	Y	N	Y	Y
2 ***Portman***	Y	Y	N	Y	Y	N	Y	Y
3 Hall	Y	Y	N	Y	N	N	Y	Y
4 ***Oxley***	Y	Y	N	Y	?	N	Y	Y
5 ***Gillmor***	Y	Y	N	N	Y	N	Y	Y
6 Strickland	Y	Y	Y	N	N	Y	N	N
7 ***Hobson***	Y	Y	N	Y	Y	N	Y	Y
8 ***Boehner***	Y	Y	N	Y	Y	N	Y	Y
9 Kaptur	Y	Y	Y	Y	N	Y	N	Y
10 Kucinich	Y	Y	N	N	N	N	N	Y
11 Stokes	Y	Y	?	Y	N	N	N	Y
12 ***Kasich***	Y	Y	N	Y	Y	N	Y	Y
13 Brown	Y	Y	Y	N	N	Y	N	Y
14 Sawyer	Y	Y	Y	N	N	Y	N	Y
15 ***Pryce***	Y	Y	N	Y	Y	N	Y	Y
16 ***Regula***	Y	Y	N	Y	Y	N	Y	Y
17 Traficant	Y	Y	N	Y	Y	N	Y	Y
18 ***Ney***	Y	Y	N	Y	Y	N	Y	Y
19 ***LaTourette***	Y	Y	N	Y	Y	N	Y	Y
OKLAHOMA								
1 ***Largent***	Y	Y	N	Y	?	?	Y	N
2 ***Coburn***	?	?	N	Y	Y	N	Y	Y
3 ***Watkins***	Y	Y	N	Y	Y	N	Y	?
4 ***Watts***	Y	Y	N	Y	Y	N	Y	Y
5 ***Istook***	Y	Y	N	Y	Y	N	Y	Y
6 ***Lucas***	Y	Y	N	Y	Y	N	Y	Y
OREGON								
1 Furse	Y	Y	Y	N	N	Y	N	Y
2 ***Smith***	Y	Y	N	Y	Y	N	Y	Y
3 Blumenauer	Y	Y	Y	Y	N	N	N	Y
4 DeFazio	Y	Y	Y	N	N	Y	N	Y
5 Hooley	Y	Y	N	N	N	N	N	Y
PENNSYLVANIA								
1 Foglietta	?	?	?	?	N	Y	?	?
2 Fattah	Y	Y	Y	Y	N	Y	N	Y
3 Borski	Y	Y	N	N	N	Y	N	Y
4 Klink	Y	Y	N	Y	N	N	Y	Y
5 ***Peterson***	Y	Y	N	?	Y	N	Y	Y
6 Holden	Y	Y	N	Y	N	N	Y	Y
7 ***Weldon***	Y	Y	N	Y	Y	N	Y	Y
8 ***Greenwood***	Y	Y	N	Y	Y	Y	Y	Y
9 ***Shuster***	Y	Y	N	Y	Y	N	Y	Y
10 ***McDade***	Y	Y	Y	Y	Y	N	Y	Y
11 Kanjorski	Y	Y	N	Y	N	N	N	Y
12 Murtha	Y	Y	Y	Y	N	N	Y	Y
13 ***Fox***	Y	Y	N	N	Y	N	Y	Y
14 Coyne	Y	Y	Y	Y	N	Y	N	Y
15 McHale	Y	Y	N	Y	N	N	N	Y
16 ***Pitts***	Y	Y	N	Y	Y	N	Y	Y
17 ***Gekas***	Y	Y	N	Y	Y	N	Y	Y
18 Doyle	Y	Y	?	Y	N	N	N	Y
19 ***Goodling***	Y	Y	N	Y	Y	?	Y	Y
20 Mascara	Y	Y	N	Y	N	N	N	Y
21 ***English***	Y	Y	N	N	Y	N	Y	Y
RHODE ISLAND								
1 Kennedy	Y	Y	N	Y	N	Y	N	Y
2 Weygand	Y	Y	N	Y	N	Y	N	Y
SOUTH CAROLINA								
1 ***Sanford***	Y	Y	N	N	Y	N	Y	Y
2 ***Spence***	Y	Y	N	Y	Y	N	Y	Y
3 ***Graham***	Y	Y	?	Y	Y	N	Y	Y
4 ***Inglis***	Y	Y	N	Y	Y	N	Y	Y
5 Spratt	Y	Y	Y	Y	N	Y	N	Y
6 Clyburn	Y	Y	N	N	N	N	N	Y
SOUTH DAKOTA								
AL ***Thune***	Y	Y	N	N	Y	N	Y	Y
TENNESSEE								
1 ***Jenkins***	Y	Y	N	Y	Y	N	Y	Y
2 ***Duncan***	Y	Y	N	Y	Y	N	Y	Y
3 ***Wamp***	Y	Y	N	Y	Y	N	Y	Y
4 ***Hilleary***	Y	Y	N	N	Y	Y	Y	Y
5 Clement	Y	Y	N	Y	N	?	N	Y
6 Gordon	Y	Y	N	N	N	N	N	Y
7 ***Bryant***	Y	Y	N	Y	Y	N	Y	Y
8 Tanner	Y	Y	N	Y	N	N	N	Y
9 Ford	Y	Y	N	Y	N	Y	N	Y
TEXAS								
1 Sandlin	Y	Y	N	Y	N	N	N	Y
2 Turner	Y	Y	Y	Y	N	N	N	Y
3 ***Johnson, Sam***	Y	Y	N	Y	Y	N	Y	Y
4 Hall	Y	Y	N	Y	N	N	N	Y
5 ***Sessions***	Y	Y	N	Y	Y	N	Y	Y
6 ***Barton***	Y	Y	N	Y	Y	N	Y	Y
7 ***Archer***	Y	Y	N	Y	Y	N	Y	Y
8 ***Brady***	Y	Y	N	Y	Y	N	Y	Y
9 Lampson	Y	Y	N	Y	N	Y	N	Y
10 Doggett	Y	Y	Y	N	N	Y	N	Y
11 Edwards	Y	Y	N	Y	N	N	N	Y
12 ***Granger***	Y	Y	?	Y	Y	N	Y	Y
13 ***Thornberry***	Y	Y	N	Y	Y	N	Y	Y
14 ***Paul***	N	Y	N	Y	Y	N	Y	Y
15 Hinojosa	Y	Y	N	N	N	Y	N	Y
16 Reyes	Y	Y	N	Y	N	Y	N	Y
17 Stenholm	Y	Y	N	N	N	N	N	Y
18 Jackson-Lee	Y	Y	N	Y	N	Y	N	Y
19 ***Combest***	Y	Y	N	Y	Y	N	Y	Y
20 Gonzalez	?	?	?	?	?	?	?	?
21 ***Smith***	Y	Y	N	Y	Y	N	Y	Y
22 ***DeLay***	Y	Y	N	Y	Y	N	Y	Y
23 ***Bonilla***	?	?	?	?	?	?	?	?
24 Frost	Y	Y	N	Y	N	N	N	Y
25 Bentsen	Y	Y	N	N	N	Y	N	Y
26 ***Armey***	Y	Y	N	?	Y	N	Y	Y
27 Ortiz	Y	Y	N	Y	N	N	N	Y
28 Rodriguez	Y	Y	N	Y	N	Y	N	Y
29 Green	Y	Y	N	Y	N	N	N	N
30 Johnson, E.B.	Y	Y	N	Y	N	Y	N	Y
UTAH								
1 ***Hansen***	Y	Y	N	Y	Y	N	Y	Y
2 ***Cook***	Y	Y	N	Y	Y	N	Y	Y
3 ***Cannon***	Y	Y	N	Y	Y	Y	Y	Y
VERMONT								
AL *Sanders*	Y	Y	N	Y	N	Y	N	Y
VIRGINIA								
1 ***Bateman***	Y	Y	N	Y	Y	N	Y	Y
2 Pickett	Y	Y	N	N	N	N	N	Y
3 Scott	Y	Y	Y	Y	N	Y	N	Y
4 Sisisky	Y	Y	N	Y	N	N	N	Y
5 Goode	Y	Y	Y	Y	N	N	N	Y
6 ***Goodlatte***	Y	Y	N	Y	Y	N	Y	Y
7 ***Bliley***	Y	Y	N	Y	?	N	Y	Y
8 Moran	Y	Y	?	?	N	N	Y	Y
9 Boucher	Y	Y	N	Y	N	N	Y	?
10 ***Wolf***	Y	Y	N	N	Y	N	Y	Y
11 ***Davis***	Y	Y	N	Y	Y	N	Y	Y
WASHINGTON								
1 ***White***	Y	Y	N	Y	Y	N	Y	Y
2 ***Metcalf***	Y	Y	N	Y	Y	N	Y	Y
3 ***Smith, Linda***	Y	Y	N	Y	Y	N	Y	Y
4 ***Hastings***	Y	Y	N	Y	Y	N	Y	Y
5 ***Nethercutt***	Y	Y	N	Y	Y	N	Y	Y
6 Dicks	Y	Y	N	Y	N	N	N	Y
7 McDermott	Y	Y	Y	N	N	Y	N	Y
8 ***Dunn***	Y	Y	N	Y	Y	N	Y	Y
9 Smith, Adam	Y	Y	N	Y	N	Y	N	Y
WEST VIRGINIA								
1 Mollohan	Y	Y	N	Y	N	N	Y	Y
2 Wise	Y	Y	N	Y	N	N	N	Y
3 Rahall	Y	Y	N	Y	N	N	Y	Y
WISCONSIN								
1 ***Neumann***	Y	Y	N	Y	Y	N	Y	Y
2 ***Klug***	Y	Y	N	Y	Y	N	Y	Y
3 Kind	Y	Y	Y	Y	N	Y	N	Y
4 Kleczka	Y	Y	N	Y	N	N	N	Y
5 Barrett	Y	Y	Y	N	N	Y	N	Y
6 ***Petri***	Y	Y	N	Y	Y	N	Y	Y
7 Obey	Y	Y	Y	Y	N	Y	Y	Y
8 Johnson	Y	Y	Y	N	N	Y	N	Y
9 ***Sensenbrenner***	Y	Y	N	Y	Y	N	Y	Y
WYOMING								
AL ***Cubin***	Y	Y	N	Y	Y	N	Y	Y

Southern states - Ala., Ark., Fla., Ga., Ky., La., Miss., N.C., Okla., S.C., Tenn., Texas, Va.

HOUSE VOTES 432, 433, 434, 435, 436, 437, 438, 439

432. HR 2209. Fiscal 1998 Legislative Branch Appropriations/Conference Report. Adoption of the conference report on the bill to provide $2.25 billion in new budget authority for the legislative branch in fiscal 1998. The conference report would provide $45.8 million more than provided in fiscal 1997 and $145.9 million less than requested by President Clinton. Adopted (thus sent to the Senate) 309-106: R 158-56; D 150-50 (ND 113-35, SD 37-15); I 1-0, Sept. 24, 1997.

433. Procedural Motion/Adjourn. Tierney, D-Mass., motion to adjourn. Motion rejected 82-325: R 3-211; D 79-114 (ND 65-78, SD 14-36); I 0-0, Sept. 24, 1997.

434. Procedural Motion/Adjourn. Miller, D-Calif., motion to adjourn. Motion rejected 66-348: R 2-215; D 64-132 (ND 54-89, SD 10-43); I 0-1, Sept. 24, 1997.

435. HR 2378. Fiscal 1998 Treasury-Postal Service Appropriations/Previous Question. Hoyer, D-Md., motion to order the previous question (thus ending debate and the possibility of amendment) on the Hoyer motion to instruct conferees to increase funding for the Exploited Child Unit of the National Center for Missing and Exploited Children. A "nay" vote would have allowed Smith, R-Wash., to offer an amendment to block a cost of living adjustment for members of Congress. Motion agreed to 229-199: R 114-110; D 115-88 (ND 88-62, SD 27-26); I 0-1, Sept. 24, 1997.

436. HR 2378. Fiscal 1998 Treasury-Postal Service Appropriations/Motion to Instruct. Hoyer, D-Md., motion to instruct conferees to increase funding for the Exploited Child Unit of the National Center for Missing and Exploited Children. Motion agreed to 412-2: R 213-2; D 198-0 (ND 146-0, SD 52-0); I 1-0, Sept. 24, 1997.

437. Procedural Motion/Adjourn. Eshoo, D-Calif., motion to adjourn. Motion rejected 70-342: R 6-210; D 64-132 (ND 56-87, SD 8-45); I 0-0, Sept. 24, 1997.

438. Procedural Motion/Adjourn. Mink, D-Hawaii, motion to adjourn. Motion rejected 71-337: R 5-207; D 66-129 (ND 59-84, SD 7-45); I 0-1, Sept. 25, 1997.

439. Procedural Motion/Journal. Approval of the House Journal of Wednesday, Sept. 24, 1997. Approved 331-78: R 180-32; D 150-46 (ND 110-35, SD 40-11); I 1-0, Sept. 25, 1997.

KEY

- Y Voted for (yea).
- # Paired for.
- + Announced for.
- N Voted against (nay).
- X Paired against.
- – Announced against.
- P Voted "present."
- C Voted "present" to avoid possible conflict of interest.
- ? Did not vote or otherwise make a position known.

Democrats ***Republicans***
Independent

	432	433	434	435	436	437	438	439
ALABAMA								
1 ***Callahan***	Y	N	N	Y	Y	N	N	Y
2 ***Everett***	Y	N	N	N	Y	N	N	N
3 ***Riley***	N	N	N	N	Y	N	N	N
4 ***Aderholt***	Y	N	N	N	Y	N	N	Y
5 Cramer	Y	N	N	N	Y	N	N	N
6 ***Bachus***	Y	N	N	Y	Y	N	N	Y
7 Hilliard	Y	N	N	Y	Y	N	N	?
ALASKA								
AL ***Young***	Y	N	N	Y	Y	?	?	?
ARIZONA								
1 ***Salmon***	N	N	N	N	P	Y	Y	N
2 Pastor	Y	N	N	N	+	N	Y	Y
3 ***Stump***	N	N	N	N	Y	N	N	Y
4 ***Shadegg***	N	N	N	N	P	Y	Y	N
5 ***Kolbe***	Y	N	N	Y	Y	N	N	Y
6 ***Hayworth***	N	N	N	N	Y	N	N	Y
ARKANSAS								
1 Berry	N	Y	Y	N	Y	Y	Y	Y
2 Snyder	Y	N	N	N	Y	N	N	Y
3 ***Hutchinson***	N	N	N	N	Y	N	N	Y
4 ***Dickey***	Y	N	N	Y	Y	N	N	Y
CALIFORNIA								
1 ***Riggs***	Y	N	?	N	Y	N	N	Y
2 ***Herger***	Y	N	N	N	Y	N	N	?
3 Fazio	Y	Y	Y	Y	Y	Y	Y	N
4 ***Doolittle***	Y	N	N	Y	Y	?	N	Y
5 Matsui	Y	N	N	Y	Y	N	N	Y
6 Woolsey	Y	Y	Y	Y	Y	?	Y	Y
7 Miller	N	Y	Y	Y	?	Y	Y	N
8 Pelosi	Y	Y	Y	Y	Y	?	Y	Y
9 Dellums	Y	N	Y	Y	Y	N	?	Y
10 Tauscher	N	Y	Y	N	Y	Y	Y	Y
11 ***Pombo***	Y	N	N	Y	Y	N	N	N
12 Lantos	Y	N	N	Y	Y	N	N	Y
13 Stark	N	Y	N	Y	Y	N	N	Y
14 Eshoo	N	Y	Y	Y	Y	Y	Y	Y
15 ***Campbell***	Y	N	N	Y	Y	N	N	Y
16 Lofgren	N	N	N	N	Y	N	N	Y
17 Farr	Y	Y	N	Y	Y	Y	Y	Y
18 Condit	N	N	N	Y	Y	N	N	Y
19 ***Radanovich***	N	N	N	N	Y	N	N	Y
20 Dooley	Y	N	N	Y	Y	N	N	Y
21 ***Thomas***	Y	N	N	Y	Y	N	N	Y
22 Capps	Y	N	N	N	Y	Y	N	Y
23 ***Gallegly***	Y	N	N	Y	Y	N	N	Y
24 Sherman	N	N	N	N	Y	N	N	Y
25 ***McKeon***	Y	N	N	Y	Y	N	N	Y
26 Berman	Y	?	?	Y	Y	N	N	Y
27 ***Rogan***	Y	N	N	N	Y	N	–	+
28 ***Dreier***	Y	N	N	Y	Y	N	N	Y
29 Waxman	Y	Y	Y	Y	Y	Y	Y	Y
30 Becerra	N	Y	Y	Y	Y	Y	Y	N
31 Martinez	Y	?	Y	Y	Y	Y	Y	Y
32 Dixon	Y	N	N	Y	Y	N	?	?
33 Roybal-Allard	Y	N	N	Y	Y	N	N	Y
34 Torres	Y	Y	Y	Y	Y	Y	Y	Y
35 Waters	Y	Y	N	Y	Y	N	Y	N
36 Harman	N	Y	Y	Y	Y	Y	Y	Y
37 Millender-McD.	Y	N	N	Y	Y	N	N	Y
38 ***Horn***	Y	N	N	Y	Y	N	N	Y
39 ***Royce***	N	N	N	N	Y	N	N	Y
40 ***Lewis***	Y	N	N	Y	Y	N	N	Y
41 ***Kim***	Y	N	N	Y	Y	N	N	Y
42 Brown	Y	N	N	Y	Y	N	Y	N
43 ***Calvert***	Y	N	N	Y	Y	N	N	Y
44 ***Bono***	Y	N	N	Y	Y	?	N	Y
45 ***Rohrabacher***	Y	N	N	Y	Y	N	N	Y
46 Sanchez	Y	N	N	N	Y	N	N	Y
47 ***Cox***	N	N	N	Y	Y	N	N	?
48 ***Packard***	Y	N	N	Y	Y	N	N	Y
49 ***Bilbray***	Y	N	N	Y	Y	N	N	Y
50 Filner	Y	Y	Y	Y	Y	Y	Y	N
51 ***Cunningham***	Y	N	N	Y	Y	N	N	Y
52 ***Hunter***	?	?	?	?	?	N	?	Y
COLORADO								
1 DeGette	Y	N	N	N	Y	N	N	Y
2 Skaggs	Y	N	N	Y	Y	N	N	Y
3 ***McInnis***	Y	N	N	N	Y	N	?	?
4 ***Schaffer***	N	N	N	N	Y	N	N	N
5 ***Hefley***	N	N	N	Y	Y	N	N	N
6 ***Schaefer***	N	N	N	Y	Y	N	N	Y
CONNECTICUT								
1 Kennelly	Y	Y	Y	N	Y	Y	Y	Y
2 Gejdenson	N	Y	Y	N	Y	Y	N	N
3 DeLauro	Y	Y	Y	N	Y	Y	Y	N
4 ***Shays***	N	N	N	N	Y	N	N	Y
5 Maloney	N	N	N	N	Y	N	N	Y
6 ***Johnson***	Y	N	N	N	Y	N	N	Y
DELAWARE								
AL ***Castle***	Y	N	N	Y	Y	N	N	Y
FLORIDA								
1 ***Scarborough***	N	N	?	N	P	Y	Y	Y
2 Boyd	Y	N	N	N	Y	N	N	Y
3 Brown	Y	N	N	Y	Y	N	N	Y
4 ***Fowler***	Y	N	N	Y	Y	N	N	Y
5 Thurman	N	N	N	N	Y	N	N	N
6 ***Stearns***	N	N	N	N	Y	N	N	N
7 ***Mica***	Y	N	N	N	Y	N	N	Y
8 ***McCollum***	Y	N	N	Y	Y	N	N	Y
9 ***Bilirakis***	N	N	N	Y	Y	N	N	Y
10 ***Young***	Y	N	N	Y	Y	N	N	Y
11 Davis	Y	Y	Y	N	Y	Y	Y	?
12 ***Canady***	Y	N	N	N	Y	N	N	Y
13 ***Miller***	Y	N	N	Y	Y	N	N	Y
14 ***Goss***	Y	N	N	Y	Y	N	N	Y
15 ***Weldon***	Y	N	N	Y	Y	N	N	Y
16 ***Foley***	Y	N	N	Y	Y	N	N	Y
17 Meek	Y	N	N	Y	Y	Y	N	N
18 ***Ros-Lehtinen***	Y	N	N	Y	Y	N	N	Y
19 Wexler	Y	?	N	Y	Y	N	N	Y
20 Deutsch	N	Y	Y	N	Y	Y	Y	Y
21 ***Diaz-Balart***	Y	N	N	Y	Y	N	N	Y
22 ***Shaw***	Y	N	N	Y	Y	N	N	Y
23 Hastings	?	?	?	?	?	?	?	?
GEORGIA								
1 ***Kingston***	Y	N	N	Y	Y	N	N	N
2 Bishop	Y	N	N	Y	Y	N	N	Y
3 ***Collins***	Y	N	?	Y	Y	N	N	Y
4 McKinney	Y	N	N	N	Y	N	N	Y
5 Lewis	Y	Y	Y	Y	Y	Y	Y	N
6 ***Gingrich***				Y				
7 ***Barr***	N	N	N	Y	Y	N	N	Y
8 ***Chambliss***	Y	N	N	N	Y	N	N	Y
9 ***Deal***	Y	N	N	Y	Y	N	N	Y
10 ***Norwood***	Y	N	?	N	Y	N	N	Y
11 ***Linder***	Y	N	N	Y	Y	N	N	Y
HAWAII								
1 Abercrombie	Y	N	N	N	Y	N	N	N
2 Mink	Y	Y	Y	N	Y	Y	Y	Y
IDAHO								
1 ***Chenoweth***	N	N	N	N	Y	N	N	?
2 ***Crapo***	Y	N	N	Y	Y	N	N	Y
ILLINOIS								
1 Rush	N	N	N	Y	Y	N	N	Y
2 Jackson	Y	N	N	Y	Y	N	Y	Y
3 Lipinski	Y	N	N	Y	Y	N	N	Y
4 Gutierrez	N	?	Y	N	Y	N	Y	N
5 Blagojevich	Y	N	N	N	Y	N	N	Y
6 ***Hyde***	Y	?	N	Y	Y	N	N	Y
7 Davis	N	N	N	N	Y	N	N	Y
8 ***Crane***	Y	N	N	Y	Y	N	?	?
9 Yates	Y	Y	N	Y	Y	?	Y	Y
10 ***Porter***	Y	N	N	Y	Y	N	N	Y
11 ***Weller***	N	N	N	N	Y	N	N	N
12 Costello	N	N	N	N	Y	N	N	N
13 ***Fawell***	Y	N	N	Y	Y	?	N	Y
14 ***Hastert***	Y	N	N	Y	Y	N	N	Y
15 ***Ewing***	Y	N	N	Y	Y	N	N	Y

ND Northern Democrats SD Southern Democrats

	432	433	434	435	436	437	438	439
16 *Manzullo*	Y	N	N	N	Y	N	N	N
17 Evans	Y	Y	Y	N	Y	Y	Y	Y
18 *LaHood*	Y	N	N	Y	Y	N	N	Y
19 Poshard	N	N	N	N	Y	N	N	N
20 *Shimkus*	N	N	N	N	N	N	N	Y
INDIANA								
1 Visclosky	Y	Y	N	N	Y	Y	N	N
2 *McIntosh*	Y	N	N	N	Y	N	N	?
3 Roemer	N	N	N	N	Y	N	N	Y
4 *Souder*	N	N	N	N	P	Y	N	N
5 *Buyer*	Y	?	N	Y	Y	?	N	Y
6 *Burton*	Y	N	N	Y	Y	N	?	Y
7 *Pease*	N	N	N	N	Y	N	N	Y
8 *Hostettler*	N	Y	Y	N	Y	Y	Y	Y
9 Hamilton	Y	N	N	N	Y	N	N	Y
10 Carson	N	N	N	N	Y	N	N	Y
IOWA								
1 *Leach*	Y	N	N	N	Y	N	N	Y
2 *Nussle*	N	N	N	N	Y	N	N	Y
3 Boswell	Y	N	N	N	Y	N	N	Y
4 *Ganske*	Y	N	N	Y	Y	N	N	Y
5 *Latham*	Y	N	N	Y	Y	N	N	Y
KANSAS								
1 *Moran*	N	N	N	N	Y	N	N	N
2 *Ryun*	Y	N	N	N	Y	N	N	Y
3 *Snowbarger*	Y	N	N	N	Y	N	N	N
4 *Tiahrt*	Y	N	N	N	Y	N	N	Y
KENTUCKY								
1 *Whitfield*	Y	N	N	N	Y	N	N	Y
2 *Lewis*	N	N	N	N	Y	N	N	Y
3 *Northup*	Y	N	N	N	Y	N	N	Y
4 *Bunning*	N	N	N	N	Y	N	N	Y
5 *Rogers*	Y	N	N	Y	Y	N	N	Y
6 Baesler	Y	?	N	N	Y	N	N	Y
LOUISIANA								
1 *Livingston*	Y	N	N	Y	Y	N	N	Y
2 Jefferson	Y	Y	Y	Y	Y	Y	Y	Y
3 *Tauzin*	Y	N	N	Y	Y	N	N	Y
4 *McCrery*	Y	N	N	Y	Y	N	N	Y
5 *Cooksey*	Y	?	N	N	Y	N	N	Y
6 *Baker*	Y	N	N	N	Y	N	N	Y
7 John	Y	N	N	N	Y	N	N	Y
MAINE								
1 Allen	Y	Y	Y	N	Y	?	Y	Y
2 Baldacci	Y	N	N	N	Y	N	N	Y
MARYLAND								
1 *Gilchrest*	Y	N	N	Y	Y	N	N	Y
2 *Ehrlich*	Y	N	N	Y	Y	N	N	Y
3 Cardin	Y	Y	Y	Y	Y	Y	N	Y
4 Wynn	Y	N	N	Y	Y	N	N	Y
5 Hoyer	Y	N	Y	Y	Y	Y	Y	Y
6 *Bartlett*	Y	Y	N	N	Y	N	N	Y
7 Cummings	Y	N	?	Y	Y	N	?	?
8 *Morella*	Y	N	N	Y	Y	N	N	Y
MASSACHUSETTS								
1 Olver	Y	Y	Y	Y	Y	Y	Y	Y
2 Neal	Y	Y	Y	Y	Y	N	N	Y
3 McGovern	Y	Y	Y	N	Y	Y	N	N
4 Frank	Y	Y	Y	Y	Y	Y	Y	Y
5 Meehan	Y	Y	N	N	Y	Y	N	Y
6 Tierney	Y	Y	Y	N	Y	Y	Y	Y
7 Markey	Y	?	?	Y	Y	N	Y	Y
8 Kennedy	Y	Y	N	Y	Y	N	N	Y
9 Moakley	Y	Y	Y	Y	Y	Y	N	Y
10 Delahunt	Y	Y	Y	Y	Y	Y	Y	Y
MICHIGAN								
1 Stupak	N	Y	Y	Y	Y	Y	Y	N
2 *Hoekstra*	Y	N	N	Y	Y	N	N	Y
3 *Ehlers*	Y	N	N	Y	Y	N	N	Y
4 *Camp*	Y	N	N	Y	Y	N	N	Y
5 Barcia	N	N	N	N	Y	N	N	Y
6 *Upton*	Y	N	N	Y	Y	N	N	Y
7 *Smith*	N	N	N	N	Y	?	N	Y
8 Stabenow	N	N	N	N	Y	N	Y	Y
9 Kildee	Y	N	N	N	Y	N	N	Y
10 Bonior	Y	Y	Y	Y	Y	Y	Y	N
11 *Knollenberg*	Y	N	N	Y	Y	N	N	Y
12 Levin	Y	Y	Y	Y	Y	N	Y	Y
13 Rivers	Y	N	N	N	Y	N	N	Y
14 Conyers	N	Y	Y	Y	Y	Y	Y	Y
15 Kilpatrick	Y	Y	N	N	Y	Y	Y	N
16 Dingell	Y	N	N	Y	Y	N	N	Y
MINNESOTA								
1 *Gutknecht*	Y	N	N	N	Y	N	N	N
2 Minge	N	N	N	N	Y	N	N	Y

	432	433	434	435	436	437	438	439
3 *Ramstad*	N	N	N	N	Y	N	N	N
4 Vento	Y	?	?	Y	Y	Y	Y	N
5 Sabo	Y	?	N	Y	Y	?	N	N
6 Luther	N	N	N	N	Y	N	N	Y
7 Peterson	?	N	N	N	Y	N	N	?
8 Oberstar	Y	N	N	Y	Y	Y	N	N
MISSISSIPPI								
1 *Wicker*	Y	N	N	Y	Y	N	N	Y
2 Thompson	N	Y	N	Y	Y	N	N	N
3 *Pickering*	Y	N	N	Y	Y	N	N	N
4 *Parker*	?	N	N	Y	Y	N	N	Y
5 Taylor	N	N	N	N	Y	N	N	N
MISSOURI								
1 Clay	Y	Y	N	Y	Y	N	N	N
2 *Talent*	Y	N	N	N	Y	N	N	Y
3 Gephardt	Y	Y	Y	Y	Y	Y	Y	N
4 Skelton	N	N	N	N	Y	N	N	Y
5 McCarthy	Y	N	N	N	Y	N	Y	Y
6 Danner	Y	N	N	N	Y	N	N	Y
7 *Blunt*	N	N	N	Y	Y	N	N	Y
8 *Emerson*	?	N	N	N	Y	N	N	Y
9 *Hulshof*	N	N	N	N	Y	?	N	Y
MONTANA								
AL *Hill*	N	N	N	N	Y	N	N	N
NEBRASKA								
1 *Bereuter*	Y	N	N	N	Y	N	N	Y
2 *Christensen*	Y	N	N	N	Y	N	N	N
3 *Barrett*	Y	N	N	N	Y	N	N	Y
NEVADA								
1 *Ensign*	N	N	N	N	Y	N	N	N
2 *Gibbons*	N	N	N	N	Y	N	?	?
NEW HAMPSHIRE								
1 *Sununu*	Y	N	N	N	Y	N	N	Y
2 *Bass*	Y	N	N	N	Y	N	N	Y
NEW JERSEY								
1 Andrews	Y	Y	Y	N	Y	Y	?	Y
2 *LoBiondo*	N	N	N	N	Y	N	N	N
3 *Saxton*	Y	N	N	N	Y	N	N	Y
4 *Smith*	Y	N	N	Y	Y	N	N	Y
5 *Roukema*	N	?	?	N	Y	N	N	Y
6 Pallone	Y	Y	Y	Y	Y	Y	Y	N
7 *Franks*	Y	N	N	N	Y	N	N	Y
8 Pascrell	Y	Y	N	N	Y	N	N	Y
9 Rothman	Y	N	N	N	Y	N	N	Y
10 Payne	Y	N	N	Y	Y	N	N	Y
11 *Frelinghuysen*	Y	N	N	Y	Y	N	N	Y
12 *Pappas*	Y	N	N	N	Y	N	N	Y
13 Menendez	Y	N	N	Y	Y	N	N	Y
NEW MEXICO								
1 *Schiff*	?	?	?	?	?	?	?	?
2 *Skeen*	Y	N	N	Y	Y	N	N	Y
3 *Redmond*	Y	N	N	N	Y	N	N	Y
NEW YORK								
1 *Forbes*	Y	N	N	N	Y	?	N	Y
2 *Lazio*	Y	N	N	Y	Y	N	N	Y
3 *King*	Y	N	N	Y	Y	N	N	Y
4 McCarthy	Y	N	N	N	Y	N	N	Y
5 Ackerman	Y	Y	N	Y	Y	N	N	Y
6 Flake	?	?	N	Y	Y	N	N	Y
7 Manton	Y	N	N	Y	Y	N	?	?
8 Nadler	Y	Y	?	Y	Y	Y	?	Y
9 Schumer	N	N	N	N	Y	N	?	?
10 Towns	Y	Y	Y	Y	Y	Y	Y	N
11 Owens	Y	N	N	Y	Y	Y	N	Y
12 Velázquez	Y	N	N	Y	Y	N	Y	Y
13 Vacant								
14 Maloney	Y	Y	N	Y	Y	Y	N	N
15 Rangel	Y	N	?	Y	Y	N	Y	Y
16 Serrano	Y	N	N	Y	Y	N	N	Y
17 Engel	Y	N	N	Y	Y	N	N	Y
18 Lowey	Y	Y	Y	Y	Y	Y	Y	Y
19 *Kelly*	Y	N	N	N	Y	N	N	N
20 *Gilman*	Y	N	N	Y	Y	N	N	Y
21 McNulty	Y	Y	Y	Y	Y	Y	Y	N
22 *Solomon*	Y	N	N	Y	Y	N	?	Y
23 *Boehlert*	Y	N	N	Y	Y	N	N	Y
24 *McHugh*	Y	N	N	Y	Y	N	N	Y
25 *Walsh*	Y	N	N	N	Y	N	N	Y
26 Hinchey	Y	N	Y	Y	Y	Y	Y	N
27 *Paxon*	Y	N	N	Y	Y	N	N	Y
28 Slaughter	N	Y	Y	N	Y	Y	Y	Y
29 LaFalce	Y	N	N	Y	Y	Y	N	Y
30 *Quinn*	Y	N	N	Y	Y	N	N	Y
31 *Houghton*	Y	N	N	Y	Y	N	N	?

	432	433	434	435	436	437	438	439
NORTH CAROLINA								
1 Clayton	Y	N	N	Y	Y	N	N	N
2 Etheridge	Y	N	N	N	Y	N	N	Y
3 *Jones*	N	N	N	N	Y	N	N	Y
4 Price	Y	N	N	N	Y	N	N	Y
5 *Burr*	N	?	N	N	Y	N	N	Y
6 *Coble*	?	N	N	Y	Y	N	N	Y
7 McIntyre	Y	N	N	N	Y	N	N	Y
8 Hefner	Y	Y	Y	Y	Y	N	N	Y
9 *Myrick*	N	Y	N	N	Y	N	N	Y
10 *Ballenger*	Y	N	N	Y	Y	N	N	Y
11 *Taylor*	Y	?	N	Y	Y	N	N	Y
12 Watt	Y	N	N	Y	Y	N	N	Y
NORTH DAKOTA								
AL Pomeroy	Y	N	N	N	Y	N	Y	N
OHIO								
1 *Chabot*	N	N	N	N	Y	N	N	N
2 *Portman*	?	N	N	N	Y	N	N	Y
3 Hall	Y	N	N	Y	Y	?	N	Y
4 *Oxley*	Y	N	N	Y	Y	N	N	Y
5 *Gillmor*	Y	N	N	N	Y	N	N	Y
6 Strickland	N	Y	Y	N	Y	Y	N	N
7 *Hobson*	Y	N	N	Y	Y	N	N	Y
8 *Boehner*	Y	N	N	Y	Y	N	N	Y
9 Kaptur	Y	Y	Y	N	?	Y	Y	Y
10 Kucinich	N	N	N	N	Y	N	N	Y
11 Stokes	Y	N	?	Y	Y	N	N	N
12 *Kasich*	?	N	N	N	Y	N	N	Y
13 Brown	Y	Y	Y	Y	Y	Y	Y	Y
14 Sawyer	Y	Y	Y	Y	Y	Y	Y	N
15 *Pryce*	Y	N	N	Y	Y	N	N	Y
16 *Regula*	Y	N	N	Y	Y	N	N	Y
17 Traficant	N	N	N	N	Y	N	N	Y
18 *Ney*	Y	N	N	Y	?	N	N	Y
19 *LaTourette*	Y	N	N	Y	Y	N	N	Y
OKLAHOMA								
1 *Largent*	N	N	N	N	Y	Y	Y	Y
2 *Coburn*	N	N	N	N	N	N	N	Y
3 *Watkins*	N	N	N	N	Y	N	N	Y
4 *Watts*	N	N	N	N	Y	N	N	N
5 *Istook*	Y	N	N	N	Y	N	N	Y
6 *Lucas*	Y	N	N	N	Y	N	N	Y
OREGON								
1 Furse	Y	Y	Y	Y	Y	Y	Y	Y
2 *Smith*	?	N	N	Y	Y	N	N	Y
3 Blumenauer	Y	Y	N	Y	Y	N	N	Y
4 DeFazio	N	Y	Y	N	Y	Y	Y	N
5 Hooley	N	N	N	N	Y	N	N	Y
PENNSYLVANIA								
1 Foglietta	?	?	?	?	?	?	?	?
2 Fattah	Y	Y	N	Y	Y	N	Y	Y
3 Borski	Y	Y	Y	Y	Y	Y	Y	N
4 Klink	Y	N	N	Y	Y	N	N	Y
5 *Peterson*	Y	N	N	N	Y	N	N	Y
6 Holden	Y	N	N	N	Y	N	N	Y
7 *Weldon*	Y	?	?	Y	?	N	N	Y
8 *Greenwood*	Y	?	N	Y	Y	N	?	Y
9 *Shuster*	Y	N	N	Y	Y	N	N	Y
10 *McDade*	Y	N	N	Y	Y	N	N	Y
11 Kanjorski	Y	N	N	Y	Y	N	N	Y
12 Murtha	Y	N	N	Y	Y	N	N	Y
13 *Fox*	N	N	N	N	Y	N	N	N
14 Coyne	Y	Y	Y	Y	Y	Y	?	Y
15 McHale	N	N	N	N	?	?	N	Y
16 *Pitts*	Y	N	N	N	Y	N	N	Y
17 *Gekas*	Y	?	N	N	Y	N	N	Y
18 Doyle	Y	N	N	Y	Y	N	N	Y
19 *Goodling*	N	N	N	N	Y	N	N	Y
20 Mascara	Y	N	N	N	Y	N	N	Y
21 *English*	Y	N	N	N	Y	N	N	N
RHODE ISLAND								
1 Kennedy	Y	Y	N	N	Y	N	N	Y
2 Weygand	Y	N	N	N	Y	N	N	Y
SOUTH CAROLINA								
1 *Sanford*	N	N	N	N	Y	N	N	Y
2 *Spence*	Y	N	N	Y	?	N	N	Y
3 *Graham*	?	N	N	N	Y	N	N	Y
4 *Inglis*	?	N	N	N	Y	N	N	Y
5 Spratt	?	N	N	Y	Y	N	N	Y
6 Clyburn	N	Y	N	Y	Y	N	N	N
SOUTH DAKOTA								
AL *Thune*	Y	N	N	N	Y	N	N	N
TENNESSEE								
1 *Jenkins*	Y	N	N	N	Y	N	N	Y
2 *Duncan*	Y	N	N	N	Y	N	N	Y

	432	433	434	435	436	437	438	
3 *Wamp*	Y	N	N	N	Y	N	N	N
4 *Hilleary*	N	N	N	N	Y	N	N	N
5 Clement	N	N	N	Y	Y	N	N	Y
6 Gordon	Y	N	N	N	Y	N	N	Y
7 *Bryant*	N	N	N	N	Y	N	N	Y
8 Tanner	Y	N	N	Y	Y	N	N	Y
9 Ford	Y	Y	Y	N	Y	Y	N	Y
TEXAS								
1 Sandlin	Y	N	N	N	Y	N	N	Y
2 Turner	N	N	N	N	Y	N	N	Y
3 *Johnson, Sam*	Y	N	N	Y	Y	N	?	Y
4 Hall	N	N	N	N	Y	N	N	Y
5 *Sessions*	Y	N	N	N	Y	N	N	N
6 *Barton*	N	N	N	Y	Y	N	N	Y
7 *Archer*	Y	N	N	Y	Y	N	?	?
8 *Brady*	N	N	N	N	Y	N	N	N
9 Lampson	N	Y	Y	N	Y	N	N	Y
10 Doggett	N	Y	Y	Y	Y	Y	Y	N
11 Edwards	Y	N	N	Y	Y	N	N	Y
12 *Granger*	Y	N	N	N	Y	N	N	Y
13 *Thornberry*	Y	N	N	N	Y	N	N	Y
14 *Paul*	N	N	N	N	Y	N	N	Y
15 Hinojosa	Y	N	N	N	Y	N	N	Y
16 Reyes	Y	N	N	N	Y	N	?	Y
17 Stenholm	N	N	N	N	Y	N	N	Y
18 Jackson-Lee	Y	N	N	Y	Y	N	Y	Y
19 *Combest*	Y	N	N	N	Y	N	N	Y
20 Gonzalez	?	?	?	?	?	?	?	?
21 *Smith*	Y	N	N	Y	Y	N	N	Y
22 *DeLay*	Y	N	N	Y	Y	N	N	Y
23 *Bonilla*	?	?	?	?	?	?	?	?
24 Frost	Y	?	N	Y	Y	N	N	Y
25 Bentsen	Y	N	N	Y	Y	N	N	Y
26 *Armey*	?	N	N	Y	Y	N	N	Y
27 Ortiz	Y	N	N	Y	Y	N	N	Y
28 Rodriguez	Y	Y	N	N	Y	N	N	Y
29 Green	N	N	N	N	Y	N	N	N
30 Johnson, E.B.	N	Y	Y	Y	Y	N	N	Y
UTAH								
1 *Hansen*	Y	N	N	Y	Y	N	N	Y
2 *Cook*	Y	N	N	N	Y	N	N	Y
3 *Cannon*	Y	N	N	N	Y	N	N	Y
VERMONT								
AL Sanders	Y	?	N	N	Y	?	N	Y
VIRGINIA								
1 *Bateman*	Y	N	N	Y	Y	N	N	Y
2 Pickett	Y	N	N	Y	Y	N	N	N
3 Scott	Y	Y	N	Y	Y	N	N	Y
4 Sisisky	Y	N	N	Y	Y	N	N	Y
5 Goode	N	N	N	N	P	N	N	Y
6 *Goodlatte*	Y	N	N	Y	Y	N	N	Y
7 *Bliley*	Y	N	N	Y	Y	N	N	Y
8 Moran	Y	N	N	Y	Y	N	N	Y
9 Boucher	Y	N	N	Y	Y	N	N	Y
10 *Wolf*	Y	N	N	Y	Y	N	N	Y
11 *Davis*	Y	N	N	Y	Y	N	N	Y
WASHINGTON								
1 *White*	Y	N	N	N	Y	N	N	Y
2 *Metcalf*	Y	N	N	N	Y	N	N	Y
3 *Smith, Linda*	N	N	N	N	P	N	N	N
4 *Hastings*	N	N	N	Y	Y	N	N	Y
5 *Nethercutt*	Y	N	N	N	Y	N	N	Y
6 Dicks	Y	N	N	Y	Y	N	N	Y
7 McDermott	Y	Y	Y	Y	Y	Y	Y	N
8 *Dunn*	Y	N	N	Y	Y	N	N	Y
9 Smith, Adam	Y	N	N	N	Y	N	N	Y
WEST VIRGINIA								
1 Mollohan	Y	N	N	Y	Y	N	N	Y
2 Wise	Y	N	N	N	Y	N	N	Y
3 Rahall	Y	N	N	Y	Y	N	N	Y
WISCONSIN								
1 *Neumann*	N	N	N	N	Y	N	N	Y
2 *Klug*	Y	N	N	Y	Y	N	N	Y
3 Kind	N	Y	Y	N	Y	Y	Y	Y
4 Kleczka	Y	N	N	Y	Y	N	N	Y
5 Barrett	N	Y	Y	N	Y	Y	Y	Y
6 *Petri*	Y	N	N	N	Y	N	N	Y
7 Obey	Y	Y	Y	Y	Y	Y	Y	Y
8 Johnson	Y	Y	Y	N	Y	N	N	Y
9 *Sensenbrenner*	N	N	N	N	Y	N	N	Y
WYOMING								
AL *Cubin*	Y	N	N	N	Y	N	N	?

Southern states - Ala., Ark., Fla., Ga., Ky., La., Miss., N.C., Okla., S.C., Tenn., Texas, Va.

HOUSE VOTES 440, 441, 442, 443, 444, 445, 446, 447

440. Procedural Motion/Adjourn. Woolsey, D-Calif., motion to adjourn. Motion rejected 82-334: R 7-210; D 75-124 (ND 64-85, SD 11-39); I 0-0, Sept. 25, 1997.

441. HR 2266. Fiscal 1998 Defense Appropriations/Rule. Adoption of the rule (H Res 242) to waive points of order against and provide for House floor consideration of the conference report to provide $247.7 billion in new budget authority to sustain military personnel, develop and purchase military hardware and maintain the operational readiness of U.S. military forces in fiscal 1998. Adopted 419-3: R 218-1; D 200-2 (ND 148-1, SD 52-1); I 1-0, Sept. 25, 1997.

442. HR 2266. Fiscal 1998 Defense Appropriations/Conference Report. Adoption of the conference report on the bill to provide $247.7 billion in new budget authority to sustain military personnel, develop and purchase military hardware and maintain the operational readiness of the U.S. military. The conference report would provide $5.3 billion more than the current appropriations level and $3.8 billion more than the administration's request. The conference report would cut off funding for U.S. troops in Bosnia after June 30, but would permit the president to request further funding. The measure provides nearly $46 billion for weapons procurement. Adopted (thus sent to the Senate) 356-65: R 202-17; D 154-47 (ND 106-43, SD 48-4); I 0-1, Sept. 25, 1997.

443. HR 2267. Fiscal 1998 Commerce, Justice, State Appropriations/Legal Expenses. Hyde, R-Ill., amendment to allow any defendant who prevails in a federal prosecution an opportunity to recover legal expenses unless the government can establish that it was substantially justified in initiating and prosecuting the case or that an award of attorneys' fees would be unjust. Adopted 340-84: R 215-6; D 125-77 (ND 83-66, SD 42-11); I 0-1, Sept. 25, 1997. A "nay" was a vote in support of the president's position.

444. HR 2267. Fiscal 1998 Commerce, Justice, State Appropriations/Juvenile Crime. Scott, D-Va., amendment to transfer $259 million from prison "truth in sentencing" grant construction funds to several juvenile crime prevention programs such as Boys and Girls Clubs. Rejected 129-291: R 10-206; D 118-85 (ND 92-58, SD 26-27); I 1-0, Sept. 25, 1997.

445. HR 2267. Fiscal 1998 Commerce, Justice, State Appropriations/Drug Courts. Waters, D-Calif., amendment to transfer the $30 million increase for the State Prison Grant Program to the Drug Courts Program. Rejected 162-259: R 12-205; D 149-54 (ND 121-29, SD 28-25); I 1-0, Sept. 25, 1997.

446. HR 2267. Fiscal 1998 Commerce, Justice, State Appropriations/Advanced Technology Program. Coburn, R-Okla., amendment to provide an additional $74 million to juvenile justice programs by removing funding allocated for new grants issued by the Advanced Technology Program. Rejected 163-261: R 147-73; D 16-187 (ND 13-137, SD 3-50); I 0-1, Sept. 25, 1997.

447. HR 2267. Fiscal 1998 Commerce, Justice, State Appropriations/Abortions in Federal Prisons. Norton, D-D.C., amendment to delete the language in the bill prohibiting federal funds from being used for abortions for women in federal prisons. Rejected 155-264: R 16-201; D 138-63 (ND 107-41, SD 31-22); I 1-0, Sept. 25, 1997.

KEY

- Y Voted for (yea).
- # Paired for.
- \+ Announced for.
- N Voted against (nay).
- X Paired against.
- – Announced against.
- P Voted "present."
- C Voted "present" to avoid possible conflict of interest.
- ? Did not vote or otherwise make a position known.

Democrats ***Republicans***
Independent

	440	441	442	443	444	445	446	447
ALABAMA								
1 ***Callahan***	N	Y	Y	Y	N	N	N	N
2 ***Everett***	N	Y	Y	Y	N	N	N	N
3 ***Riley***	N	Y	Y	Y	N	N	N	N
4 ***Aderholt***	N	Y	Y	Y	N	N	Y	N
5 Cramer	N	Y	Y	Y	N	N	N	N
6 ***Bachus***	N	Y	Y	Y	N	N	Y	N
7 Hilliard	N	Y	Y	Y	Y	Y	N	Y
ALASKA								
AL ***Young***	N	Y	Y	Y	N	N	N	N
ARIZONA								
1 ***Salmon***	Y	Y	Y	Y	N	N	Y	N
2 Pastor	Y	Y	Y	Y	Y	Y	N	Y
3 ***Stump***	N	Y	Y	Y	N	N	Y	N
4 ***Shadegg***	Y	Y	Y	Y	N	N	Y	N
5 ***Kolbe***	N	Y	Y	Y	N	N	Y	N
6 ***Hayworth***	N	Y	Y	Y	N	N	Y	N
ARKANSAS								
1 Berry	Y	Y	N	Y	N	N	Y	N
2 Snyder	N	Y	Y	Y	Y	N	N	N
3 ***Hutchinson***	N	Y	Y	Y	N	?	Y	N
4 ***Dickey***	N	Y	Y	Y	N	N	Y	N
CALIFORNIA								
1 ***Riggs***	N	Y	N	N	N	N	Y	N
2 ***Herger***	N	Y	Y	Y	N	N	N	N
3 Fazio	Y	Y	Y	Y	Y	Y	N	Y
4 ***Doolittle***	N	Y	Y	Y	N	N	Y	N
5 Matsui	N	Y	Y	N	Y	Y	N	Y
6 Woolsey	Y	Y	N	N	Y	Y	N	Y
7 Miller	Y	Y	N	N	Y	Y	N	Y
8 Pelosi	Y	Y	Y	N	Y	Y	N	Y
9 Dellums	N	Y	N	N	?	Y	N	?
10 Tauscher	Y	Y	Y	N	N	N	N	Y
11 ***Pombo***	N	Y	Y	Y	N	N	Y	N
12 Lantos	N	Y	Y	Y	Y	Y	N	Y
13 Stark	N	Y	N	Y	Y	Y	N	Y
14 Eshoo	Y	Y	N	N	Y	Y	N	Y
15 ***Campbell***	N	Y	N	Y	N	N	Y	Y
16 Lofgren	N	Y	N	N	Y	Y	Y	Y
17 Farr	Y	Y	N	Y	Y	Y	N	Y
18 Condit	N	Y	Y	Y	N	N	N	Y
19 ***Radanovich***	N	Y	Y	Y	N	N	Y	–
20 Dooley	N	Y	Y	Y	Y	Y	N	Y
21 ***Thomas***	N	Y	Y	Y	N	N	Y	?
22 Capps	N	Y	Y	Y	N	Y	N	Y
23 ***Gallegly***	N	Y	Y	Y	N	N	N	N
24 Sherman	N	Y	Y	N	N	N	N	Y
25 ***McKeon***	N	Y	Y	Y	N	N	Y	N
26 Berman	N	Y	Y	N	Y	Y	N	Y
27 ***Rogan***	–	+	+	+	–	–	–	+
28 ***Dreier***	N	Y	Y	Y	N	N	Y	N
29 Waxman	Y	Y	Y	N	Y	Y	N	Y
30 Becerra	Y	Y	N	Y	Y	Y	N	Y
31 Martinez	Y	Y	Y	N	Y	Y	N	Y
32 Dixon	N	Y	Y	Y	Y	Y	N	Y
33 Roybal-Allard	N	Y	Y	Y	Y	Y	N	Y
34 Torres	Y	Y	N	N	Y	Y	N	Y
35 Waters	Y	Y	Y	Y	Y	Y	N	Y
36 Harman	Y	Y	Y	Y	N	Y	N	Y
37 Millender-McD.	N	Y	Y	Y	Y	Y	N	Y
38 ***Horn***	N	Y	Y	Y	Y	Y	Y	Y
39 ***Royce***	N	Y	N	Y	N	N	Y	N
40 ***Lewis***	N	Y	Y	Y	N	N	Y	N

	440	441	442	443	444	445	446	447
41 ***Kim***	N	Y	Y	Y	N	N	N	N
42 Brown	N	Y	N	N	N	Y	N	Y
43 ***Calvert***	N	Y	Y	Y	N	N	Y	N
44 ***Bono***	N	Y	Y	Y	N	N	Y	N
45 ***Rohrabacher***	N	Y	Y	Y	N	N	Y	N
46 Sanchez	N	Y	Y	N	Y	Y	N	Y
47 ***Cox***	?	Y	Y	Y	N	N	Y	N
48 ***Packard***	N	Y	Y	Y	N	N	N	N
49 ***Bilbray***	N	Y	Y	Y	Y	N	N	N
50 Filner	Y	Y	N	Y	Y	Y	N	Y
51 ***Cunningham***	N	Y	Y	Y	Y	N	N	N
52 ***Hunter***	N	Y	Y	Y	N	N	Y	N
COLORADO								
1 DeGette	N	?	N	N	Y	Y	N	Y
2 Skaggs	N	Y	Y	N	Y	Y	N	Y
3 ***McInnis***	?	?	?	?	?	?	?	?
4 ***Schaffer***	N	Y	Y	Y	N	N	Y	N
5 ***Hefley***	N	Y	Y	Y	N	N	Y	N
6 ***Schaefer***	N	Y	Y	Y	N	N	Y	N
CONNECTICUT								
1 Kennelly	Y	Y	Y	N	N	Y	N	Y
2 Gejdenson	Y	Y	Y	N	Y	Y	N	Y
3 DeLauro	Y	Y	Y	N	Y	Y	N	Y
4 ***Shays***	N	Y	N	Y	N	Y	Y	Y
5 Maloney	N	Y	Y	Y	N	N	N	Y
6 ***Johnson***	N	Y	Y	Y	N	N	N	Y
DELAWARE								
AL ***Castle***	N	Y	Y	Y	N	N	N	N
FLORIDA								
1 ***Scarborough***	Y	Y	Y	Y	N	N	Y	N
2 Boyd	N	Y	Y	Y	Y	Y	N	Y
3 Brown	N	Y	Y	Y	Y	Y	N	Y
4 ***Fowler***	N	Y	Y	Y	N	N	Y	N
5 Thurman	N	Y	Y	Y	Y	Y	N	N
6 ***Stearns***	N	Y	Y	Y	N	N	Y	N
7 ***Mica***	N	Y	Y	Y	N	N	N	N
8 ***McCollum***	N	Y	Y	Y	N	N	Y	N
9 ***Bilirakis***	N	Y	Y	Y	N	N	Y	N
10 ***Young***	N	Y	Y	Y	N	N	Y	N
11 Davis	Y	Y	Y	N	Y	Y	N	Y
12 ***Canady***	N	Y	Y	Y	N	?	Y	N
13 ***Miller***	N	Y	Y	Y	N	N	Y	N
14 ***Goss***	N	Y	Y	Y	N	N	Y	N
15 ***Weldon***	?	Y	Y	Y	N	N	Y	N
16 ***Foley***	N	Y	Y	Y	N	N	Y	N
17 Meek	N	Y	Y	Y	Y	Y	N	Y
18 ***Ros-Lehtinen***	N	Y	Y	Y	N	N	N	N
19 Wexler	N	Y	Y	Y	Y	Y	N	Y
20 Deutsch	Y	Y	Y	Y	N	N	N	Y
21 ***Diaz-Balart***	N	Y	Y	Y	N	N	N	N
22 ***Shaw***	N	Y	Y	Y	N	N	N	N
23 Hastings	?	?	?	?	?	?	?	?
GEORGIA								
1 ***Kingston***	N	Y	Y	Y	N	N	Y	N
2 Bishop	N	Y	Y	Y	Y	Y	N	Y
3 ***Collins***	N	Y	Y	N	?	?	?	?
4 McKinney	N	Y	N	N	Y	Y	N	Y
5 Lewis	Y	Y	Y	N	Y	Y	N	Y
6 ***Gingrich***								
7 ***Barr***	N	Y	Y	Y	N	N	Y	N
8 ***Chambliss***	N	Y	Y	Y	N	N	Y	N
9 ***Deal***	N	Y	Y	Y	N	N	Y	N
10 ***Norwood***	N	Y	Y	Y	N	N	Y	N
11 ***Linder***	N	?	Y	Y	N	N	Y	N
HAWAII								
1 Abercrombie	Y	Y	Y	Y	Y	Y	N	Y
2 Mink	Y	Y	Y	N	Y	Y	N	Y
IDAHO								
1 ***Chenoweth***	N	Y	N	Y	N	N	Y	N
2 ***Crapo***	N	Y	Y	Y	N	N	Y	N
ILLINOIS								
1 Rush	N	Y	N	Y	Y	Y	N	Y
2 Jackson	Y	Y	N	Y	Y	Y	N	Y
3 Lipinski	N	Y	Y	Y	N	N	N	N
4 Gutierrez	N	Y	N	N	Y	Y	N	Y
5 Blagojevich	N	Y	Y	N	N	Y	Y	Y
6 ***Hyde***	N	Y	Y	Y	N	N	N	N
7 Davis	Y	Y	N	Y	Y	Y	N	Y
8 ***Crane***	N	Y	Y	Y	N	N	Y	?
9 Yates	N	Y	N	N	Y	Y	N	Y
10 ***Porter***	N	Y	Y	Y	N	N	N	Y
11 ***Weller***	N	Y	Y	Y	N	N	Y	N
12 Costello	N	Y	Y	Y	N	N	N	N
13 ***Fawell***	N	Y	Y	Y	N	N	N	Y
14 ***Hastert***	N	Y	Y	Y	N	N	N	N
15 ***Ewing***	N	Y	Y	Y	N	N	Y	N

ND Northern Democrats SD Southern Democrats

	440	441	442	443	444	445	446	447
16 ***Manzullo***	N	Y	Y	Y	N	N	Y	N
17 Evans	Y	Y	Y	Y	N	Y	N	Y
18 ***LaHood***	N	Y	Y	Y	N	N	N	N
19 Poshard	N	Y	Y	Y	N	N	N	N
20 ***Shimkus***	N	Y	Y	Y	N	N	Y	N
INDIANA								
1 Visclosky	Y	Y	Y	Y	N	N	Y	N
2 ***McIntosh***	N	Y	Y	Y	N	N	Y	N
3 Roemer	N	Y	Y	Y	N	N	N	N
4 ***Souder***	N	Y	Y	Y	N	N	Y	N
5 ***Buyer***	N	Y	Y	Y	N	?	N	N
6 ***Burton***	N	Y	Y	Y	N	N	N	N
7 ***Pease***	N	Y	Y	Y	N	N	N	N
8 ***Hostettler***	Y	Y	Y	Y	N	N	Y	N
9 Hamilton	N	Y	Y	N	N	N	N	N
10 Carson	N	Y	Y	Y	Y	Y	N	Y
IOWA								
1 ***Leach***	N	Y	Y	Y	Y	N	Y	N
2 ***Nussle***	N	Y	Y	Y	N	N	Y	N
3 Boswell	N	Y	Y	Y	N	N	N	Y
4 ***Ganske***	N	Y	N	Y	N	N	Y	N
5 ***Latham***	N	Y	Y	Y	N	N	N	N
KANSAS								
1 ***Moran***	N	Y	Y	Y	N	N	Y	N
2 ***Ryun***	N	Y	Y	Y	N	N	Y	N
3 ***Snowbarger***	N	Y	Y	Y	N	N	Y	N
4 ***Tiahrt***	N	Y	Y	Y	N	N	Y	N
KENTUCKY								
1 ***Whitfield***	N	Y	Y	Y	N	N	Y	N
2 ***Lewis***	N	Y	Y	Y	N	N	Y	N
3 ***Northup***	N	Y	Y	Y	N	N	Y	N
4 ***Bunning***	N	Y	Y	Y	N	N	N	N
5 ***Rogers***	N	Y	Y	Y	N	N	N	N
6 Baesler	N	Y	Y	Y	N	N	N	N
LOUISIANA								
1 ***Livingston***	N	Y	Y	Y	?	N	N	N
2 Jefferson	Y	Y	Y	Y	Y	Y	N	Y
3 ***Tauzin***	N	?	Y	Y	N	N	N	N
4 ***McCrery***	N	Y	Y	Y	N	N	Y	N
5 ***Cooksey***	N	Y	Y	Y	N	N	Y	N
6 ***Baker***	N	Y	Y	Y	N	N	N	N
7 John	N	Y	Y	Y	N	N	N	N
MAINE								
1 Allen	Y	Y	Y	N	Y	Y	N	Y
2 Baldacci	N	Y	Y	N	Y	Y	N	Y
MARYLAND								
1 ***Gilchrest***	N	Y	Y	Y	N	N	N	N
2 ***Ehrlich***	N	Y	Y	Y	N	N	Y	N
3 Cardin	N	Y	Y	N	N	Y	N	Y
4 Wynn	N	Y	Y	Y	Y	Y	N	Y
5 Hoyer	Y	Y	Y	?	N	Y	N	Y
6 ***Bartlett***	N	Y	Y	Y	N	N	N	N
7 Cummings	N	Y	Y	Y	Y	Y	N	Y
8 ***Morella***	N	Y	N	Y	N	Y	N	Y
MASSACHUSETTS								
1 Olver	Y	Y	Y	N	Y	Y	N	Y
2 Neal	N	Y	Y	Y	Y	Y	N	N
3 McGovern	Y	Y	N	N	Y	Y	N	Y
4 Frank	Y	Y	N	N	Y	Y	N	Y
5 Meehan	N	Y	Y	Y	Y	Y	N	Y
6 Tierney	Y	Y	Y	Y	Y	Y	N	Y
7 Markey	Y	Y	Y	N	Y	Y	N	Y
8 Kennedy	N	Y	N	N	Y	Y	N	Y
9 Moakley	N	Y	Y	Y	Y	Y	N	N
10 Delahunt	Y	Y	N	N	Y	Y	N	Y
MICHIGAN								
1 Stupak	Y	Y	Y	N	Y	Y	N	N
2 ***Hoekstra***	N	Y	N	Y	N	N	Y	N
3 ***Ehlers***	N	Y	N	Y	Y	Y	N	N
4 ***Camp***	N	Y	Y	Y	N	N	Y	N
5 Barcia	N	Y	Y	Y	N	N	N	N
6 ***Upton***	N	Y	Y	Y	Y	Y	Y	N
7 ***Smith***	N	Y	Y	Y	N	N	Y	N
8 Stabenow	N	Y	Y	Y	N	Y	N	Y
9 Kildee	N	Y	Y	Y	N	Y	N	N
10 Bonior	Y	Y	Y	N	Y	Y	N	N
11 ***Knollenberg***	N	Y	Y	Y	N	N	N	N
12 Levin	Y	Y	Y	N	N	Y	N	Y
13 Rivers	N	Y	N	N	N	Y	N	Y
14 Conyers	Y	Y	N	?	Y	Y	N	Y
15 Kilpatrick	Y	Y	Y	Y	Y	Y	N	Y
16 Dingell	N	Y	Y	N	N	N	N	N
MINNESOTA								
1 ***Gutknecht***	N	Y	Y	Y	N	N	Y	Y
2 Minge	N	Y	N	Y	Y	Y	Y	N

	440	441	442	443	444	445	446	447
3 ***Ramstad***	N	Y	N	Y	N	Y	Y	N
4 Vento	Y	Y	N	Y	Y	Y	N	Y
5 Sabo	N	Y	Y	Y	Y	Y	N	Y
6 Luther	N	Y	N	Y	Y	Y	Y	Y
7 Peterson	N	Y	Y	Y	N	N	N	N
8 Oberstar	N	Y	N	Y	Y	Y	N	N
MISSISSIPPI								
1 ***Wicker***	N	Y	Y	Y	N	N	Y	N
2 Thompson	N	Y	Y	Y	Y	Y	N	Y
3 ***Pickering***	N	Y	Y	Y	N	N	Y	N
4 ***Parker***	N	Y	Y	Y	N	N	Y	N
5 Taylor	N	Y	Y	Y	N	N	N	N
MISSOURI								
1 Clay	N	Y	Y	N	Y	Y	N	Y
2 ***Talent***	N	Y	Y	Y	Y	N	Y	N
3 Gephardt	Y	Y	Y	N	N	?	?	?
4 Skelton	N	Y	Y	Y	N	Y	N	N
5 McCarthy	Y	Y	Y	N	N	Y	N	Y
6 Danner	N	Y	Y	Y	N	N	Y	N
7 ***Blunt***	N	Y	Y	Y	N	N	Y	N
8 ***Emerson***	N	Y	Y	Y	N	N	Y	N
9 ***Hulshof***	N	Y	Y	Y	N	N	Y	N
MONTANA								
AL ***Hill***	N	Y	Y	Y	N	N	Y	N
NEBRASKA								
1 ***Bereuter***	N	Y	Y	N	N	N	N	N
2 ***Christensen***	N	Y	Y	Y	N	N	Y	N
3 ***Barrett***	N	Y	Y	Y	N	N	N	N
NEVADA								
1 ***Ensign***	N	Y	Y	Y	N	Y	Y	N
2 ***Gibbons***	?	?	?	?	?	?	?	?
NEW HAMPSHIRE								
1 ***Sununu***	N	Y	Y	Y	N	N	Y	N
2 ***Bass***	N	Y	Y	Y	N	N	Y	N
NEW JERSEY								
1 Andrews	Y	Y	Y	N	N	N	Y	Y
2 ***LoBiondo***	N	Y	N	Y	N	N	Y	N
3 ***Saxton***	N	Y	Y	Y	N	N	N	N
4 ***Smith***	N	Y	Y	Y	N	N	Y	N
5 ***Roukema***	N	Y	N	Y	N	N	Y	Y
6 Pallone	Y	Y	Y	N	Y	Y	N	Y
7 ***Franks***	N	Y	N	Y	N	N	N	Y
8 Pascrell	N	Y	Y	Y	N	Y	N	N
9 Rothman	N	Y	Y	N	N	N	N	Y
10 Payne	Y	Y	N	Y	Y	Y	N	Y
11 ***Frelinghuysen***	N	Y	Y	Y	N	N	Y	Y
12 ***Pappas***	N	Y	Y	Y	N	N	Y	N
13 Menendez	N	Y	Y	N	N	Y	N	Y
NEW MEXICO								
1 ***Schiff***	?	?	?	?	?	?	?	?
2 ***Skeen***	N	Y	Y	Y	N	N	Y	N
3 ***Redmond***	N	Y	Y	Y	N	N	N	N
NEW YORK								
1 ***Forbes***	N	Y	Y	Y	N	N	N	N
2 ***Lazio***	N	Y	Y	Y	N	N	N	N
3 ***King***	N	Y	Y	Y	N	N	N	N
4 McCarthy	N	Y	Y	Y	Y	Y	N	Y
5 Ackerman	Y	Y	Y	Y	N	Y	N	Y
6 Flake	N	Y	Y	Y	Y	Y	N	N
7 Manton	N	N	Y	Y	N	Y	N	N
8 Nadler	N	Y	N	N	N	Y	N	Y
9 Schumer	N	Y	Y	N	N	N	N	Y
10 Towns	Y	Y	Y	Y	Y	Y	N	Y
11 Owens	Y	Y	?	Y	Y	Y	N	Y
12 Velázquez	Y	Y	Y	Y	Y	Y	N	Y
13 Vacant								
14 Maloney	N	Y	Y	Y	N	Y	N	Y
15 Rangel	Y	Y	Y	N	Y	Y	N	Y
16 Serrano	N	Y	Y	Y	Y	Y	N	Y
17 Engel	N	Y	Y	Y	N	Y	Y	Y
18 Lowey	Y	Y	N	N	N	N	N	Y
19 ***Kelly***	N	Y	Y	Y	N	N	N	Y
20 ***Gilman***	N	Y	Y	Y	N	N	N	Y
21 McNulty	Y	Y	N	N	Y	Y	N	N
22 ***Solomon***	Y	Y	?	Y	N	N	Y	N
23 ***Boehlert***	N	Y	Y	Y	N	N	N	Y
24 ***McHugh***	N	Y	Y	Y	N	N	Y	N
25 ***Walsh***	N	Y	Y	Y	N	N	N	N
26 Hinchey	?	Y	N	N	Y	Y	N	Y
27 ***Paxon***	N	Y	Y	Y	N	N	Y	N
28 Slaughter	N	Y	Y	N	Y	Y	N	Y
29 LaFalce	N	Y	Y	Y	Y	Y	N	N
30 ***Quinn***	N	Y	Y	Y	Y	N	Y	N
31 ***Houghton***	N	Y	Y	Y	N	N	N	Y

	440	441	442	443	444	445	446	447
NORTH CAROLINA								
1 Clayton	N	Y	Y	Y	Y	Y	N	Y
2 Etheridge	N	Y	Y	Y	N	N	N	N
3 ***Jones***	N	Y	Y	Y	N	N	Y	N
4 Price	N	Y	Y	Y	N	Y	N	Y
5 ***Burr***	N	Y	Y	Y	N	N	N	N
6 ***Coble***	N	Y	Y	Y	N	N	Y	N
7 McIntyre	N	Y	Y	Y	N	N	Y	N
8 Hefner	?	Y	Y	Y	N	Y	N	N
9 ***Myrick***	Y	Y	Y	Y	N	N	Y	N
10 ***Ballenger***	N	Y	Y	Y	N	N	Y	N
11 ***Taylor***	N	Y	Y	Y	?	N	N	N
12 Watt	N	Y	N	Y	Y	Y	N	Y
NORTH DAKOTA								
AL Pomeroy	Y	Y	Y	Y	N	N	N	N
OHIO								
1 ***Chabot***	N	Y	Y	Y	N	N	Y	N
2 ***Portman***	N	Y	Y	Y	N	Y	N	N
3 Hall	N	Y	Y	Y	N	Y	N	N
4 ***Oxley***	?	Y	Y	Y	N	N	N	N
5 ***Gillmor***	N	Y	Y	Y	N	N	Y	N
6 Strickland	Y	Y	Y	Y	N	N	Y	Y
7 ***Hobson***	N	Y	Y	Y	N	N	Y	N
8 ***Boehner***	N	Y	Y	Y	N	N	N	N
9 Kaptur	Y	Y	Y	Y	Y	Y	N	N
10 Kucinich	N	Y	N	N	N	N	N	N
11 Stokes	N	Y	Y	N	Y	Y	N	Y
12 ***Kasich***	N	Y	Y	Y	N	N	Y	N
13 Brown	Y	Y	N	N	Y	Y	N	Y
14 Sawyer	Y	Y	Y	N	Y	Y	N	Y
15 ***Pryce***	N	Y	Y	Y	N	N	N	N
16 ***Regula***	N	Y	Y	Y	N	N	N	N
17 Traficant	N	Y	Y	Y	N	N	Y	N
18 ***Ney***	N	Y	Y	Y	N	N	Y	N
19 ***LaTourette***	N	Y	Y	N	N	N	N	N
OKLAHOMA								
1 ***Largent***	?	Y	?	Y	N	N	Y	N
2 ***Coburn***	N	Y	Y	Y	N	Y	Y	N
3 ***Watkins***	N	Y	Y	Y	N	N	Y	N
4 ***Watts***	N	Y	Y	Y	N	N	Y	N
5 ***Istook***	N	Y	Y	Y	N	N	Y	N
6 ***Lucas***	N	Y	Y	Y	N	N	Y	N
OREGON								
1 Furse	N	Y	N	N	Y	Y	N	Y
2 ***Smith***	N	Y	Y	Y	N	N	N	N
3 Blumenauer	N	Y	N	N	Y	Y	N	Y
4 DeFazio	Y	Y	N	Y	Y	Y	Y	Y
5 Hooley	N	Y	N	Y	Y	Y	N	Y
PENNSYLVANIA								
1 Foglietta	?	?	?	Y	Y	Y	N	Y
2 Fattah	Y	Y	N	Y	Y	Y	N	Y
3 Borski	Y	Y	Y	Y	N	Y	N	N
4 Klink	N	Y	Y	Y	N	Y	N	N
5 ***Peterson***	N	Y	Y	Y	N	N	Y	N
6 Holden	N	Y	Y	Y	N	N	N	N
7 ***Weldon***	N	N	Y	Y	N	N	N	N
8 ***Greenwood***	N	Y	Y	Y	N	N	Y	Y
9 ***Shuster***	N	Y	Y	Y	N	N	N	N
10 ***McDade***	N	Y	Y	Y	N	N	N	N
11 Kanjorski	N	Y	Y	Y	Y	Y	N	N
12 Murtha	N	Y	Y	Y	N	N	N	N
13 ***Fox***	N	Y	Y	Y	N	N	Y	N
14 Coyne	Y	Y	Y	N	Y	Y	N	Y
15 McHale	N	Y	Y	Y	N	N	N	N
16 ***Pitts***	N	Y	Y	Y	N	N	Y	N
17 ***Gekas***	N	Y	Y	Y	N	N	N	N
18 Doyle	N	Y	Y	Y	Y	Y	N	N
19 ***Goodling***	N	Y	Y	Y	N	N	Y	N
20 Mascara	N	Y	Y	Y	N	Y	N	N
21 ***English***	N	Y	Y	Y	N	N	N	N
RHODE ISLAND								
1 Kennedy	N	Y	Y	N	Y	Y	N	Y
2 Weygand	N	Y	Y	Y	Y	Y	N	N
SOUTH CAROLINA								
1 ***Sanford***	N	Y	N	Y	N	N	Y	N
2 ***Spence***	N	Y	Y	Y	?	N	Y	N
3 ***Graham***	N	Y	Y	Y	N	N	Y	N
4 ***Inglis***	N	Y	Y	Y	N	N	Y	N
5 Spratt	N	Y	Y	Y	N	Y	N	N
6 Clyburn	Y	Y	Y	Y	Y	Y	N	Y
SOUTH DAKOTA								
AL ***Thune***	N	Y	Y	Y	N	N	Y	N
TENNESSEE								
1 ***Jenkins***	N	Y	Y	Y	N	N	N	N
2 ***Duncan***	N	Y	Y	Y	N	N	Y	N

	440	441	442	443	444	445	446	
3 ***Wamp***	N	Y	Y	Y	N	N	Y	N
4 ***Hilleary***	Y	Y	Y	Y	N	N	Y	N
5 Clement	?	Y	Y	Y	N	N	N	N
6 Gordon	N	Y	Y	Y	N	N	N	N
7 ***Bryant***	N	Y	Y	Y	N	N	Y	N
8 Tanner	N	Y	Y	Y	N	N	N	N
9 Ford	Y	Y	Y	Y	Y	Y	N	Y
TEXAS								
1 Sandlin	N	Y	Y	N	Y	Y	N	Y
2 Turner	N	Y	Y	N	Y	N	N	N
3 ***Johnson, Sam***	N	Y	Y	Y	N	N	N	N
4 Hall	N	Y	Y	Y	N	N	N	N
5 ***Sessions***	N	Y	Y	Y	N	N	Y	N
6 ***Barton***	N	Y	Y	Y	Y	Y	Y	N
7 ***Archer***	N	Y	Y	Y	?	N	Y	N
8 ***Brady***	N	Y	Y	Y	N	N	N	N
9 Lampson	N	Y	Y	N	N	N	N	N
10 Doggett	Y	Y	N	N	Y	Y	N	Y
11 Edwards	?	Y	Y	Y	N	N	N	N
12 ***Granger***	N	Y	Y	Y	N	N	Y	N
13 ***Thornberry***	N	Y	Y	Y	N	N	Y	N
14 ***Paul***	N	Y	N	Y	Y	Y	N	N
15 Hinojosa	N	Y	?	N	N	Y	N	Y
16 Reyes	N	Y	Y	Y	Y	N	N	N
17 Stenholm	N	Y	Y	Y	N	Y	N	N
18 Jackson-Lee	Y	Y	Y	Y	Y	Y	N	Y
19 ***Combest***	N	Y	Y	Y	N	N	Y	N
20 Gonzalez	?	?	?	?	?	?	?	?
21 ***Smith***	N	Y	Y	Y	N	N	N	N
22 ***DeLay***	N	Y	Y	Y	N	N	Y	N
23 ***Bonilla***	?	?	?	?	?	?	?	?
24 Frost	N	Y	Y	N	Y	Y	N	Y
25 Bentsen	N	Y	Y	N	N	N	N	Y
26 ***Armey***	N	Y	Y	Y	N	N	Y	N
27 Ortiz	N	N	Y	Y	N	N	N	N
28 Rodriguez	Y	Y	Y	Y	Y	Y	N	Y
29 Green	N	Y	Y	Y	N	N	Y	Y
30 Johnson, E.B.	Y	Y	Y	N	Y	Y	N	Y
UTAH								
1 ***Hansen***	N	Y	Y	Y	N	N	N	N
2 ***Cook***	N	Y	Y	Y	N	N	N	N
3 ***Cannon***	N	Y	Y	Y	N	N	Y	N
VERMONT								
AL *Sanders*	?	Y	N	N	Y	Y	N	Y
VIRGINIA								
1 ***Bateman***	N	Y	Y	Y	N	N	N	N
2 Pickett	N	Y	Y	Y	N	N	N	Y
3 Scott	N	Y	Y	Y	Y	Y	N	Y
4 Sisisky	N	Y	Y	Y	N	Y	N	Y
5 Goode	N	Y	Y	Y	N	N	N	N
6 ***Goodlatte***	N	Y	Y	Y	N	N	Y	N
7 ***Bliley***	N	Y	Y	Y	N	N	N	N
8 Moran	N	Y	Y	Y	N	N	N	Y
9 Boucher	N	Y	Y	Y	N	N	N	Y
10 ***Wolf***	N	Y	Y	Y	N	N	Y	N
11 ***Davis***	N	Y	Y	Y	N	N	N	N
WASHINGTON								
1 ***White***	N	Y	Y	Y	N	N	Y	N
2 ***Metcalf***	N	Y	Y	Y	N	N	Y	N
3 ***Smith, Linda***	N	Y	Y	Y	N	N	Y	N
4 ***Hastings***	N	Y	Y	Y	N	N	Y	N
5 ***Nethercutt***	N	Y	Y	Y	N	Y	N	N
6 Dicks	N	Y	Y	Y	N	Y	N	Y
7 McDermott	Y	Y	N	N	Y	Y	N	Y
8 ***Dunn***	N	Y	Y	Y	N	N	Y	N
9 Smith, Adam	N	Y	Y	N	N	Y	N	Y
WEST VIRGINIA								
1 Mollohan	N	Y	Y	Y	Y	Y	N	N
2 Wise	N	Y	Y	Y	N	N	N	Y
3 Rahall	N	Y	Y	Y	N	N	N	N
WISCONSIN								
1 ***Neumann***	N	Y	Y	Y	N	N	Y	N
2 ***Klug***	N	Y	N	Y	N	N	Y	N
3 Kind	Y	Y	N	N	Y	Y	N	Y
4 Kleczka	N	Y	Y	Y	N	Y	N	N
5 Barrett	Y	Y	N	N	Y	Y	Y	Y
6 ***Petri***	N	Y	Y	N	N	N	N	N
7 Obey	Y	Y	N	Y	Y	Y	Y	?
8 Johnson	Y	Y	Y	N	N	N	N	N
9 ***Sensenbrenner***	N	Y	N	N	N	N	N	N
WYOMING								
AL ***Cubin***	N	Y	Y	Y	N	N	Y	N

Southern states - Ala., Ark., Fla., Ga., Ky., La., Miss., N.C., Okla., S.C., Tenn., Texas, Va.

HOUSE VOTES 448, 449, 450, 451, 452

448. HR 2267. Fiscal 1998 Commerce, Justice, State Appropriations/Motion to Rise. Tierney, D-Mass., motion to rise from the Committee of the Whole. Motion rejected 102-315: R 3-211; D 99-103 (ND 76-73, SD 23-30); I 0-1, Sept. 25, 1997.

449. HR 2267. Fiscal 1998 Commerce, Justice, State Appropriations/Legal Services Corporation. Fox, R-Pa., and Mollohan, D-W.Va., amendment to increase funding for the Legal Services Corporation from $141 million to $250 million. Adopted 246-176: R 45-173; D 200-3 (ND 151-0, SD 49-3); I 1-0, Sept. 25, 1997. A "yea" was a vote in support of the president's position.

450. HR 2267. Fiscal 1998 Commerce, Justice, State Appropriations/Motion to Rise. Gephardt, D-Mo., motion to rise from the Committee of the Whole. Motion rejected 119-293: R 3-210; D 116-82 (ND 86-60, SD 30-22); I 0-1, Sept. 25, 1997.

451. HR 2267. Fiscal 1998 Commerce, Justice, State Appropriations/Decision of the Chair. Kolbe, R-Ariz., motion to sustain the ruling of the chair that the Sanders, I-Vt., amendment was out of order. The Sanders amendment would have increased by $1 million the fiscal 1998 funding for the Office of the U.S. Trade Representative to better equip the agency to defend national, local, tribal and territorial law adversely affected by international agreements. Ruling of the chair upheld 231-188: R 218-0; D 13-187 (ND 12-136, SD 1-51); I 0-1, Sept. 25, 1997. (Subsequently, a unanimous consent agreement was reached to consider the Sanders amendment.)

452. HR 2267. Fiscal 1998 Commerce, Justice, State Appropriations/International Agreements. Sanders, I-Vt., amendment to increase by $1 million the fiscal 1998 funding for the Office of the U.S. Trade Representative to better equip the agency to defend national, state, local and territorial law adversely affected by international agreements. The increase would be offset by a $1 million cut in the Commerce Department's general administration account for salaries and expenses. Adopted 356-64: R 164-54; D 191-10 (ND 142-6, SD 49-4); I 1-0, Sept. 25, 1997.

KEY

- Y Voted for (yea).
- # Paired for.
- + Announced for.
- N Voted against (nay).
- X Paired against.
- – Announced against.
- P Voted "present."
- C Voted "present" to avoid possible conflict of interest.
- ? Did not vote or otherwise make a position known.

Democrats ***Republicans***
Independent

	448	449	450	451	452
ALABAMA					
1 ***Callahan***	N	N	N	Y	N
2 ***Everett***	N	N	N	Y	N
3 ***Riley***	N	N	N	Y	Y
4 ***Aderholt***	N	N	N	Y	Y
5 Cramer	N	Y	Y	N	Y
6 ***Bachus***	N	N	N	Y	Y
7 Hilliard	Y	Y	Y	N	Y
ALASKA					
AL ***Young***	?	N	N	Y	?
ARIZONA					
1 ***Salmon***	Y	N	N	Y	Y
2 Pastor	N	Y	N	N	Y
3 ***Stump***	N	N	N	Y	Y
4 ***Shadegg***	N	N	N	Y	Y
5 ***Kolbe***	N	N	N	Y	N
6 ***Hayworth***	N	N	N	Y	Y
ARKANSAS					
1 Berry	Y	Y	Y	N	N
2 Snyder	Y	Y	Y	N	N
3 ***Hutchinson***	N	N	N	Y	Y
4 ***Dickey***	N	N	N	Y	N
CALIFORNIA					
1 ***Riggs***	N	N	N	Y	Y
2 ***Herger***	N	?	?	Y	Y
3 Fazio	Y	Y	Y	N	Y
4 ***Doolittle***	N	N	N	Y	Y
5 Matsui	N	Y	?	N	N
6 Woolsey	Y	Y	Y	N	Y
7 Miller	?	Y	Y	N	Y
8 Pelosi	Y	Y	Y	N	Y
9 Dellums	Y	Y	Y	N	Y
10 Tauscher	Y	Y	Y	N	Y
11 ***Pombo***	N	N	N	Y	Y
12 Lantos	N	Y	Y	N	Y
13 Stark	N	Y	N	N	Y
14 Eshoo	Y	Y	Y	N	Y
15 ***Campbell***	N	N	N	Y	N
16 Lofgren	N	Y	N	N	Y
17 Farr	Y	Y	Y	N	Y
18 Condit	Y	Y	Y	N	Y
19 ***Radanovich***	N	N	?	Y	Y
20 Dooley	N	Y	N	N	N
21 ***Thomas***	N	N	N	Y	N
22 Capps	N	Y	Y	N	Y
23 ***Gallegly***	N	N	N	Y	Y
24 Sherman	N	Y	N	N	Y
25 ***McKeon***	N	N	N	Y	Y
26 Berman	N	Y	N	Y	Y
27 ***Rogan***	–	–	–	+	+
28 ***Dreier***	N	N	N	Y	N
29 Waxman	Y	Y	Y	N	Y
30 Becerra	Y	Y	Y	N	Y
31 Martinez	Y	Y	?	N	Y
32 Dixon	N	Y	N	N	Y
33 Roybal-Allard	Y	Y	Y	N	Y
34 Torres	Y	Y	Y	N	Y
35 Waters	N	Y	N	N	Y
36 Harman	N	Y	Y	N	Y
37 Millender-McD.	Y	Y	Y	N	Y
38 ***Horn***	N	Y	N	Y	N
39 ***Royce***	N	N	N	Y	Y
40 ***Lewis***	N	Y	N	Y	Y
41 ***Kim***	N	N	N	Y	Y
42 Brown	N	Y	N	N	Y
43 ***Calvert***	N	N	N	Y	Y
44 ***Bono***	N	N	N	Y	Y
45 ***Rohrabacher***	N	N	N	Y	Y
46 Sanchez	N	Y	Y	N	Y
47 ***Cox***	N	N	N	Y	Y
48 ***Packard***	N	N	N	Y	N
49 ***Bilbray***	N	Y	N	Y	N
50 Filner	Y	Y	Y	N	Y
51 ***Cunningham***	N	N	N	Y	Y
52 ***Hunter***	N	N	N	Y	Y
COLORADO					
1 DeGette	N	Y	N	N	Y
2 Skaggs	N	Y	N	N	Y
3 ***McInnis***	?	N	N	Y	Y
4 ***Schaffer***	N	N	N	Y	Y
5 ***Hefley***	N	N	N	Y	Y
6 ***Schaefer***	N	N	N	Y	Y
CONNECTICUT					
1 Kennelly	Y	Y	Y	N	Y
2 Gejdenson	Y	Y	Y	N	Y
3 DeLauro	Y	Y	Y	N	Y
4 ***Shays***	N	Y	N	Y	Y
5 Maloney	N	Y	Y	N	Y
6 ***Johnson***	N	Y	N	Y	N
DELAWARE					
AL ***Castle***	N	Y	N	Y	Y
FLORIDA					
1 ***Scarborough***	N	N	?	Y	Y
2 Boyd	N	Y	N	N	Y
3 Brown	N	Y	N	N	Y
4 ***Fowler***	N	Y	N	Y	Y
5 Thurman	N	Y	Y	N	Y
6 ***Stearns***	N	N	N	Y	Y
7 ***Mica***	N	N	N	Y	Y
8 ***McCollum***	N	Y	N	Y	Y
9 ***Bilirakis***	N	N	N	Y	Y
10 ***Young***	N	N	N	Y	Y
11 Davis	Y	Y	Y	N	Y
12 ***Canady***	N	Y	N	Y	Y
13 ***Miller***	N	N	N	Y	N
14 ***Goss***	N	N	N	Y	N
15 ***Weldon***	N	N	N	Y	Y
16 ***Foley***	N	N	N	Y	Y
17 Meek	N	Y	Y	N	Y
18 ***Ros-Lehtinen***	N	Y	N	Y	Y
19 Wexler	N	Y	Y	N	Y
20 Deutsch	Y	Y	Y	N	Y
21 ***Diaz-Balart***	N	Y	N	Y	Y
22 ***Shaw***	N	N	N	Y	N
23 Hastings	?	?	?	?	?
GEORGIA					
1 ***Kingston***	N	N	N	Y	Y
2 Bishop	Y	Y	Y	N	Y
3 ***Collins***	?	?	?	?	?
4 McKinney	Y	Y	Y	N	Y
5 Lewis	Y	Y	Y	N	Y
6 ***Gingrich***					
7 ***Barr***	N	N	N	Y	Y
8 ***Chambliss***	N	Y	N	Y	Y
9 ***Deal***	N	N	N	Y	Y
10 ***Norwood***	N	N	N	Y	Y
11 ***Linder***	N	N	N	Y	Y
HAWAII					
1 Abercrombie	Y	Y	Y	N	Y
2 Mink	Y	Y	Y	N	Y
IDAHO					
1 ***Chenoweth***	–	N	N	Y	Y
2 ***Crapo***	N	N	N	Y	Y
ILLINOIS					
1 Rush	N	Y	N	N	Y
2 Jackson	Y	Y	Y	N	Y
3 Lipinski	N	Y	N	N	Y
4 Gutierrez	Y	Y	Y	N	Y
5 Blagojevich	N	Y	N	N	Y
6 ***Hyde***	N	Y	N	Y	N
7 Davis	N	Y	N	N	Y
8 ***Crane***	N	N	N	Y	N
9 Yates	Y	Y	?	Y	Y
10 ***Porter***	N	Y	N	Y	N
11 ***Weller***	N	N	N	Y	Y
12 Costello	N	Y	N	N	Y
13 ***Fawell***	N	Y	N	Y	N
14 ***Hastert***	N	N	N	Y	N
15 ***Ewing***	N	Y	N	Y	Y

ND Northern Democrats SD Southern Democrats

	448	449	450	451	452
16 ***Manzullo***	N	N	N	Y	N
17 Evans	Y	Y	Y	N	Y
18 ***LaHood***	N	Y	N	Y	N
19 Poshard	N	Y	N	N	Y
20 ***Shimkus***	N	N	N	Y	Y
INDIANA					
1 Visclosky	N	Y	N	N	Y
2 ***McIntosh***	N	N	N	Y	Y
3 Roemer	N	Y	N	N	Y
4 ***Souder***	N	N	N	Y	Y
5 ***Buyer***	?	N	N	Y	Y
6 ***Burton***	N	N	N	Y	Y
7 ***Pease***	N	N	N	Y	Y
8 ***Hostettler***	Y	N	N	Y	Y
9 Hamilton	N	Y	N	N	N
10 Carson	Y	Y	Y	N	Y
IOWA					
1 ***Leach***	?	Y	N	Y	N
2 ***Nussle***	N	N	N	Y	N
3 Boswell	N	Y	N	N	Y
4 ***Ganske***	N	N	N	Y	Y
5 ***Latham***	N	N	N	Y	N
KANSAS					
1 ***Moran***	N	N	N	Y	Y
2 ***Ryun***	N	N	N	Y	Y
3 ***Snowbarger***	N	N	N	Y	Y
4 ***Tiahrt***	N	N	N	Y	Y
KENTUCKY					
1 ***Whitfield***	N	N	N	Y	Y
2 ***Lewis***	N	N	N	Y	Y
3 ***Northup***	N	N	N	Y	Y
4 ***Bunning***	N	N	N	Y	Y
5 ***Rogers***	N	N	N	Y	N
6 Baesler	N	Y	N	N	Y
LOUISIANA					
1 ***Livingston***	N	N	N	Y	N
2 Jefferson	Y	Y	Y	N	Y
3 ***Tauzin***	N	Y	N	Y	Y
4 ***McCrery***	N	Y	N	Y	N
5 ***Cooksey***	N	N	N	Y	Y
6 ***Baker***	N	N	N	Y	N
7 John	N	Y	N	N	Y
MAINE					
1 Allen	Y	Y	Y	N	Y
2 Baldacci	Y	Y	N	N	Y
MARYLAND					
1 ***Gilchrest***	Y	Y	N	Y	N
2 ***Ehrlich***	N	N	N	Y	Y
3 Cardin	N	Y	Y	Y	Y
4 Wynn	N	Y	N	N	?
5 Hoyer	Y	Y	?	Y	N
6 ***Bartlett***	N	N	N	Y	Y
7 Cummings	?	Y	Y	N	Y
8 ***Morella***	N	N	N	Y	N
MASSACHUSETTS					
1 Olver	Y	Y	Y	N	Y
2 Neal	Y	Y	Y	N	Y
3 McGovern	N	Y	N	N	Y
4 Frank	Y	Y	Y	N	Y
5 Meehan	Y	Y	Y	N	Y
6 Tierney	Y	Y	Y	N	Y
7 Markey	Y	Y	Y	N	Y
8 Kennedy	N	Y	N	N	Y
9 Moakley	N	Y	N	N	Y
10 Delahunt	Y	Y	Y	N	Y
MICHIGAN					
1 Stupak	Y	Y	Y	N	Y
2 ***Hoekstra***	N	N	N	Y	Y
3 ***Ehlers***	N	Y	N	Y	Y
4 ***Camp***	N	Y	N	Y	Y
5 Barcia	N	Y	N	N	Y
6 ***Upton***	N	Y	N	Y	Y
7 ***Smith***	N	N	N	Y	Y
8 Stabenow	Y	Y	N	N	Y
9 Kildee	N	Y	N	N	Y
10 Bonior	Y	Y	Y	N	Y
11 ***Knollenberg***	N	N	N	Y	N
12 Levin	Y	Y	Y	N	N
13 Rivers	N	Y	N	N	Y
14 Conyers	Y	Y	Y	N	Y
15 Kilpatrick	Y	Y	Y	N	Y
16 Dingell	N	Y	N	N	Y
MINNESOTA					
1 ***Gutknecht***	N	N	N	Y	Y
2 Minge	N	Y	N	N	Y

	448	449	450	451	452
3 ***Ramstad***	N	Y	N	Y	Y
4 Vento	Y	Y	Y	N	Y
5 Sabo	N	Y	N	N	Y
6 Luther	N	Y	N	N	Y
7 Peterson	N	Y	N	N	Y
8 Oberstar	N	Y	Y	N	Y
MISSISSIPPI					
1 ***Wicker***	N	N	N	Y	Y
2 Thompson	Y	Y	Y	N	Y
3 ***Pickering***	N	N	N	Y	Y
4 ***Parker***	N	N	N	Y	Y
5 Taylor	Y	N	Y	N	Y
MISSOURI					
1 Clay	N	Y	Y	N	Y
2 ***Talent***	N	N	N	Y	Y
3 Gephardt	Y	Y	Y	Y	Y
4 Skelton	Y	Y	Y	N	Y
5 McCarthy	Y	Y	Y	N	Y
6 Danner	Y	Y	N	N	Y
7 ***Blunt***	N	N	N	Y	Y
8 ***Emerson***	N	N	N	Y	Y
9 ***Hulshof***	N	Y	N	Y	Y
MONTANA					
AL ***Hill***	N	N	?	Y	Y
NEBRASKA					
1 ***Bereuter***	N	N	N	Y	N
2 ***Christensen***	N	N	N	Y	N
3 ***Barrett***	N	N	N	Y	N
NEVADA					
1 ***Ensign***	N	N	N	Y	Y
2 ***Gibbons***	?	?	?	?	?
NEW HAMPSHIRE					
1 ***Sununu***	N	N	N	Y	Y
2 ***Bass***	N	N	N	Y	Y
NEW JERSEY					
1 Andrews	Y	Y	Y	N	Y
2 ***LoBiondo***	N	N	N	Y	Y
3 ***Saxton***	N	N	N	Y	Y
4 ***Smith***	N	N	N	Y	Y
5 ***Roukema***	N	N	N	Y	N
6 Pallone	Y	Y	Y	N	Y
7 ***Franks***	N	Y	N	Y	Y
8 Pascrell	N	Y	N	Y	Y
9 Rothman	Y	Y	N	N	Y
10 Payne	N	Y	Y	N	Y
11 ***Frelinghuysen***	N	Y	N	Y	N
12 ***Pappas***	N	N	N	Y	Y
13 Menendez	Y	Y	Y	N	Y
NEW MEXICO					
1 ***Schiff***	?	?	?	?	?
2 ***Skeen***	N	N	N	Y	N
3 ***Redmond***	N	N	N	Y	Y
NEW YORK					
1 ***Forbes***	N	Y	N	Y	Y
2 ***Lazio***	?	?	?	?	?
3 ***King***	N	N	N	Y	N
4 McCarthy	N	Y	Y	N	Y
5 Ackerman	N	Y	Y	?	Y
6 Flake	N	Y	Y	?	?
7 Manton	N	Y	N	N	Y
8 Nadler	Y	Y	Y	N	Y
9 Schumer	N	Y	N	N	Y
10 Towns	Y	Y	Y	N	Y
11 Owens	Y	Y	Y	N	Y
12 Velázquez	Y	Y	Y	N	Y
13 Vacant					
14 Maloney	N	Y	Y	N	Y
15 Rangel	Y	Y	Y	N	Y
16 Serrano	Y	Y	Y	N	Y
17 Engel	N	Y	N	N	Y
18 Lowey	N	Y	Y	N	Y
19 ***Kelly***	N	Y	N	Y	Y
20 ***Gilman***	N	Y	N	Y	Y
21 McNulty	Y	Y	Y	N	Y
22 ***Solomon***	N	N	N	Y	Y
23 ***Boehlert***	N	Y	N	Y	Y
24 ***McHugh***	N	N	N	Y	Y
25 ***Walsh***	N	Y	N	Y	Y
26 Hinchey	Y	Y	Y	N	Y
27 ***Paxon***	N	N	N	Y	Y
28 Slaughter	N	Y	N	Y	Y
29 LaFalce	Y	Y	Y	N	Y
30 ***Quinn***	N	Y	N	Y	Y
31 ***Houghton***	N	Y	N	Y	N

	448	449	450	451	452
NORTH CAROLINA					
1 Clayton	Y	Y	?	N	Y
2 Etheridge	Y	Y	Y	N	Y
3 ***Jones***	N	N	N	Y	Y
4 Price	N	Y	Y	N	Y
5 ***Burr***	N	N	N	Y	Y
6 ***Coble***	N	N	N	Y	Y
7 McIntyre	N	Y	N	N	Y
8 Hefner	Y	Y	Y	N	Y
9 ***Myrick***	N	N	N	Y	Y
10 ***Ballenger***	N	N	N	Y	N
11 ***Taylor***	N	N	Y	Y	Y
12 Watt	Y	Y	N	N	Y
NORTH DAKOTA					
AL Pomeroy	Y	Y	Y	N	Y
OHIO					
1 ***Chabot***	N	N	N	Y	Y
2 ***Portman***	N	N	N	Y	Y
3 Hall	N	Y	N	N	Y
4 ***Oxley***	N	N	N	Y	N
5 ***Gillmor***	N	N	N	Y	Y
6 Strickland	Y	Y	Y	N	Y
7 ***Hobson***	N	N	N	Y	Y
8 ***Boehner***	N	N	N	Y	Y
9 Kaptur	Y	Y	Y	N	Y
10 Kucinich	N	Y	N	N	Y
11 Stokes	N	Y	N	N	Y
12 ***Kasich***	N	N	N	Y	Y
13 Brown	Y	Y	Y	N	Y
14 Sawyer	N	Y	Y	N	Y
15 ***Pryce***	N	Y	N	Y	Y
16 ***Regula***	N	Y	N	Y	Y
17 Traficant	N	Y	N	Y	Y
18 ***Ney***	N	Y	N	Y	Y
19 ***LaTourette***	N	Y	?	Y	Y
OKLAHOMA					
1 ***Largent***	N	N	Y	Y	Y
2 ***Coburn***	N	N	N	Y	Y
3 ***Watkins***	N	N	N	Y	Y
4 ***Watts***	N	N	N	Y	Y
5 ***Istook***	N	N	N	Y	Y
6 ***Lucas***	N	N	N	Y	Y
OREGON					
1 Furse	Y	Y	Y	N	Y
2 ***Smith***	N	N	N	Y	Y
3 Blumenauer	N	Y	N	N	Y
4 DeFazio	Y	Y	Y	N	Y
5 Hooley	Y	Y	N	N	Y
PENNSYLVANIA					
1 Foglietta	Y	Y	?	?	?
2 Fattah	Y	Y	Y	Y	Y
3 Borski	Y	Y	Y	N	Y
4 Klink	N	Y	N	N	Y
5 ***Peterson***	N	N	N	Y	Y
6 Holden	N	Y	N	N	Y
7 ***Weldon***	N	Y	N	?	Y
8 ***Greenwood***	N	Y	N	Y	Y
9 ***Shuster***	N	N	N	Y	Y
10 ***McDade***	N	N	N	Y	Y
11 Kanjorski	N	Y	Y	Y	Y
12 Murtha	N	Y	N	Y	Y
13 ***Fox***	N	Y	N	Y	Y
14 Coyne	Y	Y	Y	N	Y
15 McHale	N	Y	N	N	Y
16 ***Pitts***	N	N	N	Y	Y
17 ***Gekas***	N	N	N	Y	N
18 Doyle	N	Y	N	N	Y
19 ***Goodling***	N	N	N	Y	Y
20 Mascara	N	Y	N	N	Y
21 ***English***	N	N	N	Y	Y
RHODE ISLAND					
1 Kennedy	Y	Y	Y	N	Y
2 Weygand	N	Y	N	N	Y
SOUTH CAROLINA					
1 ***Sanford***	N	N	N	Y	N
2 ***Spence***	N	N	N	Y	Y
3 ***Graham***	N	N	N	Y	Y
4 ***Inglis***	N	N	N	Y	Y
5 Spratt	N	Y	N	Y	Y
6 Clyburn	Y	Y	Y	N	Y
SOUTH DAKOTA					
AL ***Thune***	N	N	N	Y	Y
TENNESSEE					
1 ***Jenkins***	N	N	N	Y	Y
2 ***Duncan***	N	N	N	Y	Y

	448	449	450	451	452
3 ***Wamp***	N	N	N	Y	Y
4 ***Hilleary***	N	N	Y	Y	Y
5 Clement	N	+	N	N	Y
6 Gordon	N	Y	N	N	Y
7 ***Bryant***	N	N	N	Y	Y
8 Tanner	Y	Y	Y	N	Y
9 Ford	Y	Y	Y	N	Y
TEXAS					
1 Sandlin	N	Y	N	N	Y
2 Turner	N	Y	N	N	Y
3 ***Johnson, Sam***	N	N	?	Y	Y
4 Hall	N	N	N	Y	Y
5 ***Sessions***	N	N	N	Y	Y
6 ***Barton***	N	N	N	Y	Y
7 ***Archer***	N	N	N	Y	N
8 ***Brady***	N	N	N	Y	Y
9 Lampson	N	Y	N	N	Y
10 Doggett	Y	Y	Y	N	Y
11 Edwards	Y	Y	Y	N	Y
12 ***Granger***	N	N	N	Y	N
13 ***Thornberry***	N	N	N	Y	Y
14 ***Paul***	N	N	N	Y	Y
15 Hinojosa	N	Y	Y	N	Y
16 Reyes	N	Y	N	N	Y
17 Stenholm	Y	Y	Y	N	Y
18 Jackson-Lee	N	Y	Y	N	Y
19 ***Combest***	N	N	N	Y	Y
20 Gonzalez	?	?	?	?	?
21 ***Smith***	N	N	N	Y	Y
22 ***DeLay***	N	N	N	Y	N
23 ***Bonilla***	?	?	?	?	?
24 Frost	Y	Y	N	N	Y
25 Bentsen	N	Y	Y	N	Y
26 ***Armey***	N	N	N	Y	Y
27 Ortiz	N	Y	N	N	Y
28 Rodriguez	N	Y	N	N	Y
29 Green	N	Y	N	N	Y
30 Johnson, E.B.	Y	Y	Y	N	Y
UTAH					
1 ***Hansen***	?	?	?	?	?
2 ***Cook***	N	N	N	Y	Y
3 ***Cannon***	N	N	N	Y	N
VERMONT					
AL *Sanders*	N	Y	N	N	Y
VIRGINIA					
1 ***Bateman***	N	N	N	Y	N
2 Pickett	N	Y	N	N	N
3 Scott	N	Y	Y	N	Y
4 Sisisky	N	Y	N	N	Y
5 Goode	N	N	N	N	Y
6 ***Goodlatte***	N	N	N	Y	Y
7 ***Bliley***	N	N	N	Y	Y
8 Moran	N	Y	N	N	N
9 Boucher	N	Y	N	?	Y
10 ***Wolf***	N	N	N	Y	Y
11 ***Davis***	N	N	N	Y	N
WASHINGTON					
1 ***White***	N	Y	N	Y	N
2 ***Metcalf***	N	N	N	Y	Y
3 ***Smith, Linda***	N	N	N	Y	Y
4 ***Hastings***	N	N	N	Y	N
5 ***Nethercutt***	N	Y	N	Y	N
6 Dicks	N	Y	N	N	N
7 McDermott	Y	Y	Y	N	Y
8 ***Dunn***	N	N	N	Y	N
9 Smith, Adam	N	Y	N	N	Y
WEST VIRGINIA					
1 Mollohan	N	Y	N	N	Y
2 Wise	N	Y	N	N	Y
3 Rahall	N	Y	N	Y	Y
WISCONSIN					
1 ***Neumann***	N	N	N	Y	Y
2 ***Klug***	N	Y	N	Y	Y
3 Kind	Y	Y	Y	N	Y
4 Kleczka	N	Y	N	N	Y
5 Barrett	Y	Y	Y	N	Y
6 ***Petri***	N	N	N	Y	Y
7 Obey	Y	Y	Y	Y	Y
8 Johnson	Y	Y	Y	N	Y
9 ***Sensenbrenner***	N	N	N	Y	Y
WYOMING					
AL ***Cubin***	N	N	N	Y	N

Southern states - Ala., Ark., Fla., Ga., Ky., La., Miss., N.C., Okla., S.C., Tenn., Texas, Va.

HOUSE VOTES 453, 454, 455, 456

453. HR 2267. Fiscal 1998 Commerce, Justice, State Appropriations/Motion to Rise. Becerra, D-Calif., motion to rise from the Committee of the Whole. Motion rejected 107-294: R 3-200; D 104-93 (ND 87-58, SD 17-35); I 0-1, Sept. 25, 1997.

454. HR 2267. Fiscal 1998 Commerce, Justice, State Appropriations/Motion to Rise. Becerra, D-Calif., motion to rise from the Committee of the Whole. Motion rejected 103-281: R 2-188; D 101-93 (ND 82-60, SD 19-33); I 0-0, Sept. 25, 1997.

455. HR 2267. Fiscal 1998 Commerce, Justice, State Appropriations/Economic Development Administration. Hefley, R-Colo., amendment to cut by $90 million fiscal 1998 funding for the Economic Development Administration, bringing the agency's appropriation level in line with the Senate's at $271 million. Rejected 107-305: R 106-104; D 1-200 (ND 1-147, SD 0-53); I 0-1, Sept. 25, 1997.

456. HR 2267. Fiscal 1998 Commerce, Justice, State Appropriations/Advanced Technology Program. Hostettler, R-Ind., amendment to eliminate the Advanced Technology Program by reducing fiscal 1998 funding by $175 million, thereby leaving the agency $10 million to administer remaining obligations and close out operations. Rejected 177-235: R 168-44; D 9-190 (ND 7-139, SD 2-51); I 0-1, Sept. 25, 1997.

KEY

- Y Voted for (yea).
- # Paired for.
- + Announced for.
- N Voted against (nay).
- X Paired against.
- – Announced against.
- P Voted "present."
- C Voted "present" to avoid possible conflict of interest.
- ? Did not vote or otherwise make a position known.

Democrats *Republicans*
Independent

	453	454	455	456
ALABAMA				
1 ***Callahan***	N	N	N	Y
2 ***Everett***	N	N	N	Y
3 ***Riley***	N	N	N	Y
4 ***Aderholt***	N	N	N	Y
5 Cramer	N	N	N	N
6 ***Bachus***	N	N	Y	Y
7 Hilliard	Y	Y	N	N
ALASKA				
AL ***Young***	?	?	?	?
ARIZONA				
1 ***Salmon***	N	?	?	Y
2 Pastor	Y	N	N	N
3 ***Stump***	N	N	Y	Y
4 ***Shadegg***	N	N	Y	Y
5 ***Kolbe***	N	N	Y	Y
6 ***Hayworth***	N	N	Y	Y
ARKANSAS				
1 Berry	Y	Y	N	Y
2 Snyder	Y	Y	N	N
3 ***Hutchinson***	N	N	N	Y
4 ***Dickey***	N	N	N	Y
CALIFORNIA				
1 ***Riggs***	N	N	Y	Y
2 ***Herger***	N	N	N	Y
3 Fazio	Y	Y	N	N
4 ***Doolittle***	Y	Y	Y	Y
5 Matsui	N	N	N	N
6 Woolsey	Y	Y	N	N
7 Miller	Y	Y	N	N
8 Pelosi	Y	?	N	N
9 Dellums	Y	Y	N	N
10 Tauscher	Y	Y	N	N
11 ***Pombo***	N	N	N	Y
12 Lantos	Y	Y	N	N
13 Stark	Y	Y	N	Y
14 Eshoo	Y	Y	N	N
15 ***Campbell***	N	N	N	Y
16 Lofgren	N	N	N	N
17 Farr	Y	Y	N	N
18 Condit	Y	N	Y	Y
19 ***Radanovich***	N	N	+	Y
20 Dooley	N	?	N	N
21 ***Thomas***	N	N	Y	Y
22 Capps	Y	N	N	N
23 ***Gallegly***	N	N	N	N
24 Sherman	N	N	N	N
25 ***McKeon***	N	N	N	Y
26 Berman	N	N	N	N
27 ***Rogan***	–	–	+	+
28 ***Dreier***	N	N	Y	Y
29 Waxman	Y	Y	N	N
30 Becerra	Y	Y	N	N
31 Martinez	Y	Y	N	N
32 Dixon	N	N	N	N
33 Roybal-Allard	Y	Y	N	N
34 Torres	Y	Y	N	N
35 Waters	Y	Y	N	N
36 Harman	Y	Y	N	N
37 Millender-McD.	Y	Y	N	N
38 ***Horn***	N	N	N	Y
39 ***Royce***	N	N	Y	Y
40 ***Lewis***	N	N	N	N
41 ***Kim***	N	N	N	N
42 Brown	N	N	N	N
43 ***Calvert***	N	N	N	N
44 ***Bono***	N	N	Y	Y
45 ***Rohrabacher***	N	N	Y	Y
46 Sanchez	Y	Y	N	N
47 ***Cox***	N	N	Y	Y
48 ***Packard***	N	N	N	N
49 ***Bilbray***	N	N	Y	N
50 Filner	Y	Y	N	N
51 ***Cunningham***	N	N	Y	Y
52 ***Hunter***	N	N	Y	Y
COLORADO				
1 DeGette	Y	Y	N	N
2 Skaggs	N	N	N	N
3 ***McInnis***	N	N	Y	Y
4 ***Schaffer***	N	N	Y	Y
5 ***Hefley***	N	N	Y	Y
6 ***Schaefer***	N	N	Y	Y
CONNECTICUT				
1 Kennelly	Y	Y	N	N
2 Gejdenson	Y	Y	N	N
3 DeLauro	Y	Y	N	N
4 ***Shays***	N	N	N	Y
5 Maloney	N	N	N	N
6 ***Johnson***	N	N	N	N
DELAWARE				
AL ***Castle***	N	N	N	N
FLORIDA				
1 ***Scarborough***	N	?	?	Y
2 Boyd	N	N	N	N
3 Brown	N	N	N	N
4 ***Fowler***	N	N	Y	Y
5 Thurman	Y	Y	N	N
6 ***Stearns***	N	N	Y	Y
7 ***Mica***	N	N	Y	Y
8 ***McCollum***	N	N	Y	Y
9 ***Bilirakis***	N	N	Y	Y
10 ***Young***	N	?	N	N
11 Davis	Y	Y	N	N
12 ***Canady***	N	N	N	Y
13 ***Miller***	N	N	Y	Y
14 ***Goss***	N	N	Y	Y
15 ***Weldon***	N	N	Y	Y
16 ***Foley***	N	N	Y	Y
17 Meek	N	N	N	N
18 ***Ros-Lehtinen***	N	N	N	N
19 Wexler	N	N	N	N
20 Deutsch	Y	Y	N	N
21 ***Diaz-Balart***	N	?	N	N
22 ***Shaw***	N	N	N	Y
23 Hastings	?	?	?	?
GEORGIA				
1 ***Kingston***	N	N	N	Y
2 Bishop	Y	Y	N	N
3 ***Collins***	?	?	?	?
4 McKinney	Y	Y	N	N
5 Lewis	Y	Y	N	N
6 ***Gingrich***				
7 ***Barr***	N	N	Y	Y
8 ***Chambliss***	N	N	N	Y
9 ***Deal***	N	N	Y	Y
10 ***Norwood***	N	N	Y	Y
11 ***Linder***	N	?	Y	Y
HAWAII				
1 Abercrombie	Y	Y	N	N
2 Mink	Y	Y	N	N
IDAHO				
1 ***Chenoweth***	Y	Y	N	Y
2 ***Crapo***	N	N	N	Y
ILLINOIS				
1 Rush	N	N	N	N
2 Jackson	Y	N	N	N
3 Lipinski	N	N	N	N
4 Gutierrez	Y	Y	N	N
5 Blagojevich	N	N	N	N
6 ***Hyde***	?	N	Y	N
7 Davis	N	N	N	N
8 ***Crane***	N	N	Y	Y
9 Yates	?	?	?	?
10 ***Porter***	N	N	Y	N
11 ***Weller***	N	N	N	Y
12 Costello	N	N	N	N
13 ***Fawell***	?	N	Y	N
14 ***Hastert***	N	N	Y	Y
15 ***Ewing***	?	?	N	N

ND Northern Democrats SD Southern Democrats

	453	454	455	456
16 ***Manzullo***	N	?	Y	Y
17 Evans	Y	Y	N	N
18 ***LaHood***	N	N	N	N
19 Poshard	N	N	N	N
20 ***Shimkus***	N	N	N	Y
INDIANA				
1 Visclosky	N	N	N	N
2 ***McIntosh***	N	N	Y	Y
3 Roemer	?	N	N	N
4 ***Souder***	N	N	Y	Y
5 ***Buyer***	N	N	N	Y
6 ***Burton***	N	N	Y	Y
7 ***Pease***	N	N	N	Y
8 ***Hostettler***	N	N	Y	Y
9 Hamilton	N	N	N	N
10 Carson	N	Y	N	N
IOWA				
1 ***Leach***	N	N	Y	N
2 ***Nussle***	N	N	Y	Y
3 Boswell	N	N	N	N
4 ***Ganske***	N	N	N	Y
5 ***Latham***	N	N	N	Y
KANSAS				
1 ***Moran***	N	N	N	Y
2 ***Ryun***	N	N	Y	Y
3 ***Snowbarger***	N	N	Y	Y
4 ***Tiahrt***	N	N	Y	Y
KENTUCKY				
1 ***Whitfield***	?	N	N	Y
2 ***Lewis***	N	N	N	Y
3 ***Northup***	N	N	N	Y
4 ***Bunning***	N	N	N	Y
5 ***Rogers***	N	N	N	N
6 Baesler	N	N	N	N
LOUISIANA				
1 ***Livingston***	N	N	N	Y
2 Jefferson	Y	Y	N	N
3 ***Tauzin***	N	N	N	N
4 ***McCrery***	N	N	?	?
5 ***Cooksey***	N	N	N	Y
6 ***Baker***	N	N	N	Y
7 John	N	N	N	N
MAINE				
1 Allen	Y	Y	N	N
2 Baldacci	N	N	N	N
MARYLAND				
1 ***Gilchrest***	N	N	N	N
2 ***Ehrlich***	N	N	Y	Y
3 Cardin	N	N	N	N
4 Wynn	?	N	N	N
5 Hoyer	Y	Y	N	N
6 ***Bartlett***	N	N	Y	N
7 Cummings	Y	?	N	N
8 ***Morella***	N	?	N	N
MASSACHUSETTS				
1 Olver	Y	Y	N	N
2 Neal	N	Y	N	N
3 McGovern	Y	Y	N	N
4 Frank	Y	Y	N	N
5 Meehan	Y	Y	N	N
6 Tierney	Y	Y	N	N
7 Markey	Y	Y	N	N
8 Kennedy	N	N	N	N
9 Moakley	Y	Y	N	N
10 Delahunt	Y	Y	N	N
MICHIGAN				
1 Stupak	Y	Y	N	N
2 ***Hoekstra***	N	N	Y	Y
3 ***Ehlers***	N	N	Y	N
4 ***Camp***	N	N	N	N
5 Barcia	N	N	N	N
6 ***Upton***	N	N	N	Y
7 ***Smith***	N	N	Y	Y
8 Stabenow	N	N	N	N
9 Kildee	N	N	N	N
10 Bonior	Y	Y	N	N
11 ***Knollenberg***	N	N	N	N
12 Levin	Y	Y	N	N
13 Rivers	N	N	N	N
14 Conyers	Y	Y	N	N
15 Kilpatrick	N	Y	N	N
16 Dingell	N	N	N	N
MINNESOTA				
1 ***Gutknecht***	N	N	Y	Y
2 Minge	N	N	N	Y

	453	454	455	456
3 ***Ramstad***	N	N	Y	Y
4 Vento	Y	Y	N	N
5 Sabo	N	N	N	N
6 Luther	N	N	N	Y
7 Peterson	Y	Y	N	Y
8 Oberstar	Y	Y	N	N
MISSISSIPPI				
1 ***Wicker***	?	?	N	Y
2 Thompson	Y	Y	N	N
3 ***Pickering***	N	N	N	Y
4 ***Parker***	N	?	N	Y
5 Taylor	Y	Y	N	N
MISSOURI				
1 Clay	Y	Y	N	N
2 ***Talent***	N	N	Y	Y
3 Gephardt	Y	Y	N	N
4 Skelton	Y	Y	N	N
5 McCarthy	Y	Y	N	N
6 Danner	N	N	N	N
7 ***Blunt***	N	N	Y	Y
8 ***Emerson***	N	N	N	Y
9 ***Hulshof***	N	N	N	Y
MONTANA				
AL ***Hill***	N	N	N	Y
NEBRASKA				
1 ***Bereuter***	N	N	Y	Y
2 ***Christensen***	?	N	Y	Y
3 ***Barrett***	N	N	Y	Y
NEVADA				
1 ***Ensign***	N	N	Y	Y
2 ***Gibbons***	?	?	?	?
NEW HAMPSHIRE				
1 ***Sununu***	N	N	Y	Y
2 ***Bass***	N	N	N	Y
NEW JERSEY				
1 Andrews	Y	Y	N	Y
2 ***LoBiondo***	N	N	N	Y
3 ***Saxton***	N	N	N	N
4 ***Smith***	N	N	N	Y
5 ***Roukema***	N	N	Y	Y
6 Pallone	Y	Y	N	N
7 ***Franks***	N	N	N	Y
8 Pascrell	N	N	N	N
9 Rothman	N	N	N	N
10 Payne	Y	N	N	N
11 ***Frelinghuysen***	N	N	N	Y
12 ***Pappas***	N	N	N	Y
13 Menendez	Y	N	N	N
NEW MEXICO				
1 ***Schiff***	?	?	?	?
2 ***Skeen***	N	N	N	N
3 ***Redmond***	N	N	N	Y
NEW YORK				
1 ***Forbes***	N	N	N	Y
2 ***Lazio***	?	?	?	?
3 ***King***	N	N	N	N
4 McCarthy	N	N	N	N
5 Ackerman	Y	Y	N	N
6 Flake	?	?	?	?
7 Manton	N	N	N	N
8 Nadler	Y	Y	N	N
9 Schumer	N	N	N	?
10 Towns	Y	Y	N	N
11 Owens	Y	Y	N	N
12 Velázquez	Y	Y	N	N
13 Vacant				
14 Maloney	Y	Y	N	N
15 Rangel	Y	Y	N	N
16 Serrano	Y	Y	N	N
17 Engel	Y	Y	N	N
18 Lowey	Y	Y	N	N
19 ***Kelly***	N	N	N	N
20 ***Gilman***	N	N	N	N
21 McNulty	Y	Y	N	N
22 ***Solomon***	N	N	?	Y
23 ***Boehlert***	N	N	N	N
24 ***McHugh***	N	N	N	Y
25 ***Walsh***	N	N	N	N
26 Hinchey	Y	Y	N	N
27 ***Paxon***	N	N	Y	Y
28 Slaughter	Y	Y	N	N
29 LaFalce	Y	Y	N	N
30 ***Quinn***	N	N	?	?
31 ***Houghton***	N	N	N	N

	453	454	455	456
NORTH CAROLINA				
1 Clayton	Y	Y	N	N
2 Etheridge	N	N	N	N
3 ***Jones***	N	N	N	Y
4 Price	N	N	N	N
5 ***Burr***	N	N	N	N
6 ***Coble***	N	N	Y	Y
7 McIntyre	N	N	N	Y
8 Hefner	N	Y	N	N
9 ***Myrick***	N	N	Y	Y
10 ***Ballenger***	–	–	+	Y
11 ***Taylor***	N	?	?	?
12 Watt	N	N	N	N
NORTH DAKOTA				
AL Pomeroy	Y	Y	N	N
OHIO				
1 ***Chabot***	N	N	Y	Y
2 ***Portman***	N	N	N	Y
3 Hall	N	N	N	?
4 ***Oxley***	?	?	Y	?
5 ***Gillmor***	?	?	N	Y
6 Strickland	Y	Y	N	N
7 ***Hobson***	N	N	Y	Y
8 ***Boehner***	N	N	Y	Y
9 Kaptur	Y	Y	N	N
10 Kucinich	N	N	N	N
11 Stokes	N	N	N	N
12 ***Kasich***	N	N	Y	Y
13 Brown	Y	Y	N	N
14 Sawyer	Y	Y	N	N
15 ***Pryce***	N	N	Y	Y
16 ***Regula***	N	N	N	N
17 Traficant	N	N	N	N
18 ***Ney***	N	N	N	Y
19 ***LaTourette***	N	N	N	N
OKLAHOMA				
1 ***Largent***	?	?	Y	Y
2 ***Coburn***	?	?	Y	Y
3 ***Watkins***	N	N	N	Y
4 ***Watts***	N	N	Y	Y
5 ***Istook***	N	N	Y	Y
6 ***Lucas***	N	N	N	Y
OREGON				
1 Furse	Y	Y	N	N
2 ***Smith***	?	?	N	?
3 Blumenauer	N	N	N	N
4 DeFazio	Y	Y	N	N
5 Hooley	N	N	N	N
PENNSYLVANIA				
1 Foglietta	?	?	?	?
2 Fattah	Y	Y	N	N
3 Borski	Y	Y	N	N
4 Klink	N	N	N	N
5 ***Peterson***	N	N	N	Y
6 Holden	N	N	N	N
7 ***Weldon***	N	N	Y	N
8 ***Greenwood***	N	N	Y	Y
9 ***Shuster***	N	N	N	Y
10 ***McDade***	N	?	N	?
11 Kanjorski	N	N	N	N
12 Murtha	N	N	N	N
13 ***Fox***	N	N	Y	Y
14 Coyne	Y	Y	N	N
15 McHale	N	N	N	N
16 ***Pitts***	N	N	Y	Y
17 ***Gekas***	N	N	Y	N
18 Doyle	?	?	N	N
19 ***Goodling***	N	N	Y	Y
20 Mascara	N	N	N	N
21 ***English***	N	N	N	N
RHODE ISLAND				
1 Kennedy	Y	Y	N	N
2 Weygand	N	N	N	N
SOUTH CAROLINA				
1 ***Sanford***	N	N	Y	Y
2 ***Spence***	N	N	N	Y
3 ***Graham***	N	N	N	Y
4 ***Inglis***	N	N	Y	Y
5 Spratt	N	N	N	N
6 Clyburn	Y	Y	N	N
SOUTH DAKOTA				
AL ***Thune***	N	N	Y	Y
TENNESSEE				
1 ***Jenkins***	N	N	N	Y
2 ***Duncan***	N	N	N	Y

	453	454	455	456
3 ***Wamp***	?	?	N	Y
4 ***Hilleary***	N	?	N	Y
5 Clement	N	N	N	N
6 Gordon	N	N	N	N
7 ***Bryant***	N	N	N	Y
8 Tanner	N	N	N	N
9 Ford	Y	Y	N	N
TEXAS				
1 Sandlin	N	N	N	N
2 Turner	N	N	N	N
3 ***Johnson, Sam***	?	?	Y	Y
4 Hall	N	N	N	N
5 ***Sessions***	N	N	Y	Y
6 ***Barton***	N	N	Y	Y
7 ***Archer***	N	?	Y	Y
8 ***Brady***	N	N	Y	Y
9 Lampson	N	N	N	N
10 Doggett	Y	Y	N	N
11 Edwards	Y	Y	N	N
12 ***Granger***	N	N	Y	Y
13 ***Thornberry***	N	?	Y	Y
14 ***Paul***	N	N	Y	Y
15 Hinojosa	N	N	N	N
16 Reyes	N	N	N	N
17 Stenholm	N	N	N	N
18 Jackson-Lee	N	Y	N	N
19 ***Combest***	N	N	N	Y
20 Gonzalez	?	?	?	?
21 ***Smith***	N	N	N	Y
22 ***DeLay***	N	N	Y	Y
23 ***Bonilla***	?	?	?	?
24 Frost	N	N	N	N
25 Bentsen	N	N	N	N
26 ***Armey***	?	?	Y	Y
27 Ortiz	?	N	N	N
28 Rodriguez	N	N	N	N
29 Green	N	N	N	N
30 Johnson, E.B.	N	N	N	N
UTAH				
1 ***Hansen***	?	?	?	?
2 ***Cook***	N	N	N	N
3 ***Cannon***	N	N	Y	Y
VERMONT				
AL *Sanders*	N	?	N	N
VIRGINIA				
1 ***Bateman***	N	N	N	N
2 Pickett	N	N	N	N
3 Scott	N	N	N	N
4 Sisisky	N	N	N	N
5 Goode	N	N	N	N
6 ***Goodlatte***	N	N	Y	Y
7 ***Bliley***	N	?	Y	Y
8 Moran	N	?	N	N
9 Boucher	N	N	N	N
10 ***Wolf***	N	?	N	Y
11 ***Davis***	N	?	N	N
WASHINGTON				
1 ***White***	N	N	Y	Y
2 ***Metcalf***	N	N	N	Y
3 ***Smith, Linda***	N	N	N	Y
4 ***Hastings***	N	N	Y	Y
5 ***Nethercutt***	N	N	Y	Y
6 Dicks	N	N	N	N
7 McDermott	Y	Y	N	N
8 ***Dunn***	N	N	Y	Y
9 Smith, Adam	Y	N	N	N
WEST VIRGINIA				
1 Mollohan	N	N	N	N
2 Wise	N	N	N	N
3 Rahall	N	?	N	N
WISCONSIN				
1 ***Neumann***	N	N	Y	Y
2 ***Klug***	N	N	Y	Y
3 Kind	N	N	N	N
4 Kleczka	N	?	N	N
5 Barrett	Y	Y	N	Y
6 ***Petri***	Y	N	Y	N
7 Obey	Y	Y	N	N
8 Johnson	N	Y	N	N
9 ***Sensenbrenner***	N	N	Y	N
WYOMING				
AL ***Cubin***	N	?	N	Y

Southern states - Ala., Ark., Fla., Ga., Ky., La., Miss., N.C., Okla., S.C., Tenn., Texas, Va.

HOUSE VOTES 457, 458, 459, 460, 461, 462, 463, 464

457. HR 2267. Fiscal 1998 Commerce, Justice, State Appropriations/Foreign Terrorist Organizations. Gilman, R-N.Y., amendment to withhold 2 percent, or $7.3 million, of the State Department's salaries and expenses budget until it designates foreign terrorist organizations as directed in the 1996 anti-terrorism law (PL 104-132). Adopted 396-6: R 214-1; D 181-5 (ND 136-4, SD 45-1); I 1-0, Sept. 26, 1997.

458. HR 2267. Fiscal 1998 Commerce, Justice, State Appropriations/U.N. Payments. Bartlett, R-Md., en bloc amendment prohibiting the payment of $54 million allocated in the bill for debt payments to international organizations and conferences of the United Nations, and prohibiting the payment of $46 million allocated in the bill for debt payments to the U.N.'s international peacekeeping activities. Rejected 165-242: R 157-57; D 8-184 (ND 3-141, SD 5-43); I 0-1, Sept. 26, 1997.

459. HR 2267. Fiscal 1998 Commerce, Justice, State Appropriations/Teamsters Election. Hoekstra, R-Mich., amendment prohibiting funds in the bill from being used to pay any expenses of a Teamsters union election. Adopted 213-189: R 195-16; D 18-172 (ND 4-138, SD 14-34); I 0-1, Sept. 26, 1997.

460. Procedural Motion/Adjourn. Miller, D-Calif., motion to adjourn. Motion rejected 55-339: R 3-205; D 52-134 (ND 41-94, SD 11-40); I 0-0, Sept. 29, 1997.

461. H J Res 94. Fiscal 1998 Continuing Appropriations/Passage. Passage of the joint resolution to provide continuing appropriations through Oct. 23 for fiscal 1998 spending bills not yet enacted. The continuing resolution generally sets spending levels at fiscal 1997 spending levels. The measure extends until Oct. 23 several other policies and programs, such as the Overseas Private Investment Corporation and the Export-Import Bank. Passed 355-57: R 167-52; D 187-5 (ND 139-1, SD 48-4); I 1-0, Sept. 29, 1997.

462. S 1211. Au Pair Program/Passage. Campbell, R-Calif., motion to suspend the rules and pass the bill to permanently extend the au pair program, which gives English-speaking Western Europeans between the ages of 18 and 25 the opportunity to live with an American family and assist in child care for that family for one year. Motion agreed to (thus cleared for the president) 377-33: R 188-30; D 188-3 (ND 138-1, SD 50-2); I 1-0, Sept. 29, 1997. A two-thirds majority of those present and voting (274 in this case) is required for passage under suspension of the rules.

463. HR 2261. Small Business Programs Reauthorization/Passage. Talent, R-Mo., motion to suspend the rules and pass the bill to reauthorize programs operated by the Small Business Administration through fiscal 2000. The measure authorizes $11 billion for the 7(a) loan program in fiscal 1998, with funding levels increasing in subsequent years. It authorizes $3 billion for the 504 loan program in fiscal 1998, with $3.5 billion and $4.5 billion authorized in subsequent years. The measure reauthorizes sundry technical assistance programs, doubling the authorization level for Women's Business Centers from $4 million to $8 million in each fiscal year through 2000. Motion agreed to 397-17: R 203-17; D 193-0 (ND 141-0, SD 52-0); I 1-0, Sept. 29, 1997. A two-thirds majority of those present and voting (276 in this case) is required under suspension of the rules.

464. HR 2472. Energy Policy and Conservation Extension/Passage. Crapo, R-Idaho, motion to suspend the rules and pass the bill to extend, through fiscal 1998, authorization for the operation of the Strategic Petroleum Reserve and U.S. participation in the International Energy Program, both of which are provisions under the 1975 Energy and Policy Conservation Act. Motion agreed to 405-8: R 211-8; D 193-0 (ND 141-0, SD 52-0); I 1-0, Sept. 29, 1997. A two-thirds majority of those present and voting (276 in this case) is required for passage under suspension of the rules.

KEY

- Y Voted for (yea).
- # Paired for.
- + Announced for.
- N Voted against (nay).
- X Paired against.
- – Announced against.
- P Voted "present."
- C Voted "present" to avoid possible conflict of interest.
- ? Did not vote or otherwise make a position known.

Democrats ***Republicans***
Independent

	457	458	459	460	461	462	463	464
ALABAMA								
1 ***Callahan***	Y	Y	Y	N	Y	Y	Y	Y
2 ***Everett***	Y	Y	Y	N	N	Y	Y	Y
3 ***Riley***	Y	Y	Y	N	N	Y	Y	Y
4 ***Aderholt***	Y	Y	Y	N	Y	Y	Y	Y
5 Cramer	Y	N	N	N	Y	Y	Y	Y
6 ***Bachus***	Y	Y	Y	N	Y	?	Y	Y
7 Hilliard	Y	N	N	N	Y	N	Y	Y
ALASKA								
AL ***Young***	Y	N	?	?	Y	Y	Y	Y
ARIZONA								
1 ***Salmon***	Y	Y	Y	N	N	N	Y	Y
2 Pastor	Y	N	N	Y	Y	Y	Y	Y
3 ***Stump***	Y	Y	Y	N	N	N	N	Y
4 ***Shadegg***	Y	Y	Y	Y	N	Y	Y	Y
5 ***Kolbe***	Y	N	Y	N	Y	Y	Y	Y
6 ***Hayworth***	Y	Y	Y	N	N	Y	Y	Y
ARKANSAS								
1 Berry	Y	N	Y	Y	Y	Y	Y	Y
2 Snyder	Y	N	N	N	Y	Y	Y	Y
3 ***Hutchinson***	Y	Y	Y	N	Y	Y	Y	Y
4 ***Dickey***	Y	Y	Y	N	Y	Y	Y	Y
CALIFORNIA								
1 ***Riggs***	Y	Y	Y	N	Y	N	Y	Y
2 ***Herger***	Y	Y	Y	?	N	N	Y	Y
3 Fazio	Y	N	N	?	Y	Y	Y	Y
4 ***Doolittle***	Y	Y	Y	N	N	Y	Y	N
5 Matsui	Y	N	N	N	Y	Y	Y	Y
6 Woolsey	Y	N	N	Y	Y	Y	Y	Y
7 Miller	N	N	N	Y	Y	Y	Y	Y
8 Pelosi	Y	N	N	Y	Y	Y	Y	Y
9 Dellums	N	N	N	N	Y	Y	Y	Y
10 Tauscher	Y	N	N	Y	Y	Y	Y	Y
11 ***Pombo***	Y	Y	Y	N	Y	N	Y	Y
12 Lantos	Y	N	N	N	Y	Y	Y	Y
13 Stark	Y	N	N	N	Y	Y	Y	Y
14 Eshoo	Y	N	N	Y	Y	Y	Y	Y
15 ***Campbell***	Y	N	Y	N	N	Y	N	Y
16 Lofgren	Y	N	N	N	Y	Y	Y	Y
17 Farr	Y	N	N	Y	Y	Y	Y	Y
18 Condit	Y	N	Y	N	Y	Y	Y	Y
19 ***Radanovich***	Y	Y	Y	N	Y	Y	Y	Y
20 Dooley	Y	N	N	N	Y	Y	Y	Y
21 ***Thomas***	Y	N	Y	N	Y	Y	Y	Y
22 Capps	Y	N	?	N	Y	Y	Y	Y
23 ***Gallegly***	Y	N	Y	N	N	Y	Y	Y
24 Sherman	Y	N	N	N	Y	Y	Y	Y
25 ***McKeon***	Y	Y	Y	N	N	Y	Y	Y
26 Berman	?	?	?	N	Y	Y	Y	Y
27 ***Rogan***	Y	Y	Y	N	Y	Y	Y	Y
28 ***Dreier***	Y	Y	Y	N	Y	Y	N	Y
29 Waxman	Y	N	N	N	Y	Y	Y	Y
30 Becerra	Y	N	N	Y	Y	Y	Y	Y
31 Martinez	Y	N	N	Y	Y	Y	Y	Y
32 Dixon	Y	N	N	N	Y	Y	Y	Y
33 Roybal-Allard	Y	N	N	N	Y	Y	Y	Y
34 Torres	Y	N	N	Y	Y	Y	Y	Y
35 Waters	P	N	N	N	Y	N	Y	Y
36 Harman	?	X	?	?	?	?	?	?
37 Millender-McD.	Y	N	N	N	Y	Y	Y	Y
38 ***Horn***	Y	N	Y	N	N	Y	Y	Y
39 ***Royce***	Y	Y	Y	N	N	N	N	N
40 ***Lewis***	Y	N	Y	N	Y	Y	Y	Y
41 ***Kim***	Y	Y	Y	N	Y	Y	Y	Y
42 Brown	Y	N	N	N	Y	Y	Y	Y
43 ***Calvert***	Y	Y	Y	N	Y	Y	Y	Y
44 ***Bono***	Y	Y	Y	?	N	Y	Y	Y
45 ***Rohrabacher***	Y	Y	Y	N	N	Y	N	N
46 Sanchez	Y	N	N	Y	Y	Y	Y	Y
47 ***Cox***	Y	Y	Y	?	Y	Y	N	Y
48 ***Packard***	Y	N	Y	N	Y	Y	Y	Y
49 ***Bilbray***	Y	Y	Y	N	N	Y	Y	Y
50 Filner	Y	N	N	Y	Y	Y	Y	Y
51 ***Cunningham***	Y	Y	Y	N	Y	Y	Y	Y
52 ***Hunter***	Y	Y	Y	N	N	N	Y	Y
COLORADO								
1 DeGette	Y	N	N	N	Y	Y	Y	Y
2 Skaggs	Y	N	N	N	Y	Y	Y	Y
3 ***McInnis***	?	?	?	N	N	Y	Y	Y
4 ***Schaffer***	Y	Y	Y	N	N	N	Y	Y
5 ***Hefley***	Y	Y	Y	N	N	N	Y	Y
6 ***Schaefer***	Y	Y	Y	N	N	Y	Y	Y
CONNECTICUT								
1 Kennelly	Y	N	N	N	Y	Y	Y	Y
2 Gejdenson	Y	N	N	Y	Y	Y	Y	Y
3 DeLauro	Y	N	N	Y	Y	Y	Y	Y
4 ***Shays***	Y	N	Y	N	Y	Y	Y	Y
5 Maloney	Y	N	N	N	Y	Y	Y	Y
6 ***Johnson***	Y	N	Y	N	Y	Y	Y	Y
DELAWARE								
AL ***Castle***	Y	N	Y	N	Y	Y	Y	Y
FLORIDA								
1 ***Scarborough***	Y	Y	Y	N	N	N	Y	Y
2 Boyd	Y	N	Y	N	Y	Y	Y	Y
3 Brown	Y	N	N	N	Y	Y	Y	Y
4 ***Fowler***	Y	Y	Y	N	Y	Y	Y	Y
5 Thurman	Y	N	N	Y	Y	Y	Y	Y
6 ***Stearns***	Y	Y	Y	N	N	N	Y	Y
7 ***Mica***	Y	Y	Y	N	Y	Y	Y	Y
8 ***McCollum***	Y	Y	Y	N	Y	Y	Y	Y
9 ***Bilirakis***	Y	Y	Y	N	Y	Y	Y	Y
10 ***Young***	Y	Y	Y	?	?	?	?	?
11 Davis	Y	N	N	Y	Y	Y	Y	Y
12 ***Canady***	Y	Y	Y	N	Y	Y	N	Y
13 ***Miller***	Y	Y	Y	N	Y	Y	N	Y
14 ***Goss***	Y	Y	Y	N	Y	Y	Y	Y
15 ***Weldon***	Y	Y	Y	N	Y	Y	Y	Y
16 ***Foley***	Y	Y	Y	N	Y	+	+	+
17 Meek	?	?	?	N	Y	Y	Y	Y
18 ***Ros-Lehtinen***	Y	Y	N	N	Y	Y	Y	Y
19 Wexler	Y	N	N	?	Y	Y	Y	Y
20 Deutsch	Y	N	N	Y	Y	Y	Y	Y
21 ***Diaz-Balart***	Y	N	N	N	Y	Y	Y	Y
22 ***Shaw***	Y	Y	Y	N	Y	Y	Y	Y
23 Hastings	?	?	?	Y	Y	Y	Y	Y
GEORGIA								
1 ***Kingston***	Y	Y	Y	N	Y	Y	Y	Y
2 Bishop	Y	N	N	N	Y	Y	Y	Y
3 ***Collins***	?	#	#	N	N	Y	Y	Y
4 McKinney	N	N	N	N	Y	Y	Y	Y
5 Lewis	Y	N	N	Y	Y	Y	Y	Y
6 ***Gingrich***								
7 ***Barr***	Y	Y	Y	N	N	N	N	Y
8 ***Chambliss***	Y	Y	Y	N	N	Y	Y	Y
9 ***Deal***	Y	Y	Y	N	N	Y	Y	Y
10 ***Norwood***	Y	Y	Y	N	N	Y	Y	Y
11 ***Linder***	Y	Y	Y	N	Y	Y	Y	Y
HAWAII								
1 Abercrombie	Y	N	N	Y	Y	Y	Y	Y
2 Mink	Y	N	N	Y	Y	Y	Y	Y
IDAHO								
1 ***Chenoweth***	Y	Y	Y	–	N	N	Y	+
2 ***Crapo***	Y	Y	Y	N	Y	Y	Y	Y
ILLINOIS								
1 Rush	Y	N	N	N	Y	Y	Y	Y
2 Jackson	Y	N	N	N	Y	Y	Y	Y
3 Lipinski	Y	N	N	N	Y	Y	Y	Y
4 Gutierrez	Y	N	N	Y	Y	Y	Y	Y
5 Blagojevich	Y	N	N	N	Y	Y	Y	Y
6 ***Hyde***	Y	N	Y	N	Y	Y	Y	Y
7 Davis	Y	N	N	N	Y	Y	Y	Y
8 ***Crane***	Y	Y	Y	?	Y	Y	Y	Y
9 Yates	Y	N	N	N	Y	Y	Y	Y
10 ***Porter***	Y	N	Y	N	Y	Y	Y	Y
11 ***Weller***	Y	Y	N	N	Y	Y	Y	Y
12 Costello	Y	N	N	N	Y	Y	Y	Y
13 ***Fawell***	Y	N	Y	N	Y	Y	Y	Y
14 ***Hastert***	Y	Y	Y	N	Y	Y	Y	Y
15 ***Ewing***	Y	Y	Y	N	N	Y	Y	Y

ND Northern Democrats SD Southern Democrats

	457	458	459	460	461	462	463	464
16 *Manzullo*	Y	Y	+	N	N	?	Y	Y
17 Evans	Y	N	N	Y	Y	Y	Y	Y
18 *LaHood*	Y	N	N	N	Y	N	Y	Y
19 Poshard	Y	N	N	N	Y	Y	Y	Y
20 *Shimkus*	Y	Y	Y	N	Y	Y	Y	Y
INDIANA								
1 Visclosky	Y	N	N	Y	Y	Y	Y	Y
2 *McIntosh*	Y	Y	Y	?	Y	Y	N	Y
3 Roemer	Y	N	N	N	Y	Y	Y	Y
4 *Souder*	Y	Y	Y	?	Y	Y	Y	Y
5 *Buyer*	?	?	?	N	Y	Y	Y	Y
6 *Burton*	Y	Y	?	N	Y	Y	Y	Y
7 *Pease*	Y	Y	Y	N	Y	Y	Y	Y
8 *Hostettler*	Y	+	Y	N	Y	Y	N	N
9 Hamilton	Y	N	N	N	Y	Y	Y	Y
10 Carson	Y	N	N	N	Y	Y	Y	Y
IOWA								
1 *Leach*	Y	N	Y	N	Y	Y	Y	Y
2 *Nussle*	Y	Y	Y	N	Y	Y	Y	Y
3 Boswell	Y	N	N	N	Y	Y	Y	Y
4 *Ganske*	Y	N	Y	N	Y	N	Y	Y
5 *Latham*	Y	N	Y	N	Y	Y	Y	Y
KANSAS								
1 *Moran*	Y	Y	Y	N	Y	N	Y	Y
2 *Ryun*	Y	Y	Y	N	Y	Y	Y	Y
3 *Snowbarger*	Y	Y	Y	N	Y	Y	Y	Y
4 *Tiahrt*	?	?	?	N	Y	Y	Y	N
KENTUCKY								
1 *Whitfield*	Y	Y	Y	N	Y	Y	Y	Y
2 *Lewis*	Y	Y	Y	N	Y	Y	Y	Y
3 *Northup*	Y	Y	Y	N	Y	Y	Y	Y
4 *Bunning*	Y	Y	Y	N	Y	Y	Y	Y
5 *Rogers*	Y	N	Y	N	Y	Y	Y	Y
6 Baesler	Y	N	N	N	Y	Y	Y	Y
LOUISIANA								
1 *Livingston*	Y	N	Y	N	Y	Y	Y	Y
2 Jefferson	Y	N	N	Y	Y	Y	Y	Y
3 *Tauzin*	Y	Y	Y	N	Y	Y	Y	Y
4 *McCrery*	Y	Y	Y	N	Y	Y	Y	Y
5 *Cooksey*	Y	Y	Y	?	?	?	?	?
6 *Baker*	Y	Y	Y	N	N	Y	Y	Y
7 John	Y	N	Y	N	Y	Y	Y	Y
MAINE								
1 Allen	Y	N	N	Y	Y	Y	Y	Y
2 Baldacci	Y	N	N	N	Y	Y	Y	Y
MARYLAND								
1 *Gilchrest*	Y	N	Y	N	Y	Y	Y	Y
2 *Ehrlich*	Y	Y	Y	?	Y	Y	Y	Y
3 Cardin	Y	N	N	N	Y	Y	Y	Y
4 Wynn	Y	N	N	N	Y	Y	Y	Y
5 Hoyer	Y	N	N	N	Y	Y	Y	Y
6 *Bartlett*	Y	Y	Y	N	N	Y	Y	Y
7 Cummings	Y	N	N	N	Y	Y	Y	Y
8 *Morella*	Y	N	N	N	Y	Y	Y	Y
MASSACHUSETTS								
1 Olver	Y	N	N	Y	Y	Y	Y	Y
2 Neal	Y	N	N	?	?	?	?	?
3 McGovern	Y	N	N	N	Y	Y	Y	Y
4 Frank	Y	N	N	Y	Y	?	?	?
5 Meehan	Y	N	N	Y	Y	Y	Y	Y
6 Tierney	Y	N	N	Y	Y	Y	Y	Y
7 Markey	Y	N	N	Y	Y	Y	Y	Y
8 Kennedy	Y	N	N	N	Y	Y	Y	Y
9 Moakley	Y	N	N	N	Y	Y	Y	Y
10 Delahunt	Y	N	N	Y	Y	Y	Y	Y
MICHIGAN								
1 Stupak	Y	N	N	Y	Y	Y	Y	Y
2 *Hoekstra*	Y	Y	Y	N	Y	Y	Y	Y
3 *Ehlers*	Y	N	Y	N	Y	Y	Y	Y
4 *Camp*	Y	Y	Y	N	Y	Y	Y	Y
5 Barcia	Y	Y	N	?	?	?	Y	Y
6 *Upton*	Y	Y	Y	N	Y	Y	Y	Y
7 *Smith*	Y	Y	Y	N	Y	Y	Y	Y
8 Stabenow	Y	N	N	N	Y	Y	Y	Y
9 Kildee	Y	N	N	N	Y	Y	Y	Y
10 Bonior	P	N	N	N	Y	Y	Y	Y
11 *Knollenberg*	Y	N	Y	N	Y	Y	Y	Y
12 Levin	Y	N	N	N	Y	Y	Y	Y
13 Rivers	Y	N	N	N	Y	Y	Y	Y
14 Conyers	?	N	N	?	?	?	?	?
15 Kilpatrick	Y	N	N	N	Y	Y	Y	Y
16 Dingell	Y	N	N	N	Y	Y	Y	Y
MINNESOTA								
1 *Gutknecht*	Y	Y	Y	N	Y	Y	Y	Y
2 Minge	N	N	N	N	Y	Y	Y	Y

	457	458	459	460	461	462	463	464
3 *Ramstad*	Y	N	Y	N	Y	Y	Y	Y
4 Vento	Y	N	N	Y	Y	?	Y	Y
5 Sabo	Y	N	N	N	Y	Y	Y	Y
6 Luther	Y	N	N	N	Y	Y	Y	Y
7 Peterson	Y	N	N	N	Y	Y	Y	Y
8 Oberstar	Y	N	N	N	Y	Y	Y	Y
MISSISSIPPI								
1 *Wicker*	Y	Y	Y	N	Y	Y	Y	Y
2 Thompson	Y	N	N	N	Y	Y	Y	Y
3 *Pickering*	Y	Y	Y	N	Y	Y	Y	Y
4 *Parker*	Y	N	Y	N	Y	Y	Y	Y
5 Taylor	Y	Y	Y	N	N	Y	Y	Y
MISSOURI								
1 Clay	Y	N	N	N	Y	Y	Y	Y
2 *Talent*	Y	Y	Y	N	Y	Y	Y	Y
3 Gephardt	Y	N	N	?	?	?	?	?
4 Skelton	Y	N	Y	N	Y	Y	Y	Y
5 McCarthy	Y	N	N	N	Y	Y	Y	Y
6 Danner	Y	Y	N	N	Y	Y	Y	Y
7 *Blunt*	Y	Y	Y	N	Y	N	Y	Y
8 *Emerson*	Y	Y	Y	N	Y	Y	Y	Y
9 *Hulshof*	Y	Y	Y	N	Y	N	Y	Y
MONTANA								
AL *Hill*	Y	Y	Y	?	Y	Y	Y	Y
NEBRASKA								
1 *Bereuter*	Y	N	Y	N	Y	N	Y	Y
2 *Christensen*	Y	Y	Y	N	Y	Y	Y	Y
3 *Barrett*	Y	Y	Y	N	Y	Y	Y	Y
NEVADA								
1 *Ensign*	Y	Y	Y	–	–	Y	Y	Y
2 *Gibbons*	?	#	?	N	Y	Y	Y	Y
NEW HAMPSHIRE								
1 *Sununu*	Y	Y	Y	N	Y	Y	Y	N
2 *Bass*	Y	N	Y	N	Y	Y	Y	Y
NEW JERSEY								
1 Andrews	Y	N	N	Y	Y	Y	Y	Y
2 *LoBiondo*	Y	Y	Y	N	Y	Y	Y	Y
3 *Saxton*	Y	N	Y	N	Y	Y	Y	Y
4 *Smith*	Y	N	Y	N	Y	Y	Y	Y
5 *Roukema*	Y	N	Y	N	N	Y	N	Y
6 Pallone	Y	N	N	+	+	Y	Y	Y
7 *Franks*	Y	N	Y	N	Y	Y	Y	Y
8 Pascrell	Y	N	N	N	Y	Y	Y	Y
9 Rothman	Y	N	N	N	Y	Y	Y	Y
10 Payne	Y	N	N	N	Y	Y	Y	Y
11 *Frelinghuysen*	Y	N	Y	N	Y	Y	Y	Y
12 *Pappas*	Y	Y	Y	N	Y	Y	Y	Y
13 Menendez	Y	N	N	N	Y	Y	Y	Y
NEW MEXICO								
1 *Schiff*	?	?	?	?	?	?	?	?
2 *Skeen*	Y	Y	Y	N	Y	Y	Y	Y
3 *Redmond*	Y	Y	Y	N	Y	Y	Y	Y
NEW YORK								
1 *Forbes*	Y	N	N	N	Y	Y	Y	Y
2 *Lazio*	?	?	?	N	Y	Y	Y	Y
3 *King*	Y	N	N	N	Y	Y	Y	Y
4 McCarthy	Y	N	N	N	Y	Y	Y	Y
5 Ackerman	Y	N	N	N	Y	Y	Y	Y
6 Flake	Y	N	N	?	?	?	?	?
7 Manton	Y	N	N	N	Y	Y	Y	Y
8 Nadler	Y	N	N	N	Y	Y	Y	Y
9 Schumer	?	?	?	N	Y	Y	Y	Y
10 Towns	Y	N	N	?	Y	Y	Y	Y
11 Owens	?	?	?	?	Y	Y	Y	Y
12 Velázquez	Y	N	N	Y	Y	Y	Y	Y
13 Vacant								
14 Maloney	Y	N	N	N	Y	Y	Y	Y
15 Rangel	Y	N	N	?	?	?	?	?
16 Serrano	Y	N	N	N	Y	Y	Y	Y
17 Engel	Y	N	N	N	Y	Y	Y	Y
18 Lowey	Y	N	N	Y	Y	Y	Y	Y
19 *Kelly*	Y	N	Y	N	Y	Y	Y	Y
20 *Gilman*	Y	N	N	N	Y	Y	Y	Y
21 McNulty	Y	N	N	N	Y	Y	Y	Y
22 *Solomon*	Y	Y	?	N	Y	Y	Y	Y
23 *Boehlert*	Y	N	N	N	Y	Y	Y	Y
24 *McHugh*	Y	N	N	N	Y	Y	Y	Y
25 *Walsh*	Y	N	Y	N	Y	Y	Y	Y
26 Hinchey	Y	N	N	?	?	?	?	?
27 *Paxon*	Y	Y	Y	N	Y	Y	Y	Y
28 Slaughter	Y	N	N	Y	Y	Y	Y	Y
29 LaFalce	Y	N	N	Y	Y	Y	Y	Y
30 *Quinn*	?	X	?	?	?	?	?	?
31 *Houghton*	Y	N	N	N	Y	Y	Y	Y

	457	458	459	460	461	462	463	464
NORTH CAROLINA								
1 Clayton	Y	N	N	N	Y	Y	Y	Y
2 Etheridge	Y	N	N	N	Y	Y	Y	Y
3 *Jones*	Y	Y	Y	N	N	Y	N	Y
4 Price	Y	N	N	N	Y	Y	Y	Y
5 *Burr*	Y	Y	Y	N	Y	Y	Y	Y
6 *Coble*	Y	Y	Y	N	N	N	Y	Y
7 McIntyre	Y	Y	Y	N	Y	Y	Y	Y
8 Hefner	Y	N	N	?	?	?	?	?
9 *Myrick*	Y	Y	Y	N	Y	Y	Y	Y
10 *Ballenger*	Y	N	Y	N	Y	Y	Y	Y
11 *Taylor*	?	?	?	N	Y	Y	Y	Y
12 Watt	Y	N	N	N	Y	Y	Y	Y
NORTH DAKOTA								
AL Pomeroy	Y	N	Y	N	Y	Y	Y	Y
OHIO								
1 *Chabot*	Y	Y	Y	N	Y	Y	Y	Y
2 *Portman*	Y	Y	Y	N	Y	Y	Y	Y
3 Hall	Y	N	N	N	Y	Y	Y	Y
4 *Oxley*	Y	N	Y	N	Y	Y	Y	Y
5 *Gillmor*	Y	Y	Y	N	N	Y	Y	Y
6 Strickland	Y	N	?	N	Y	Y	Y	Y
7 *Hobson*	Y	Y	Y	N	Y	Y	Y	Y
8 *Boehner*	Y	Y	Y	N	Y	Y	Y	Y
9 Kaptur	Y	N	N	Y	Y	Y	Y	Y
10 Kucinich	P	N	N	N	Y	Y	Y	Y
11 Stokes	Y	N	N	?	Y	Y	Y	Y
12 *Kasich*	Y	N	Y	N	Y	Y	Y	Y
13 Brown	Y	N	N	?	Y	Y	Y	Y
14 Sawyer	Y	N	N	N	Y	Y	Y	Y
15 *Pryce*	Y	N	Y	N	Y	Y	Y	Y
16 *Regula*	Y	N	Y	N	Y	Y	Y	Y
17 Traficant	Y	Y	Y	N	N	Y	Y	Y
18 *Ney*	Y	Y	Y	N	Y	Y	Y	Y
19 *LaTourette*	Y	N	Y	N	Y	Y	Y	Y
OKLAHOMA								
1 *Largent*	Y	Y	Y	N	N	Y	Y	Y
2 *Coburn*	Y	Y	Y	Y	N	Y	Y	Y
3 *Watkins*	Y	Y	Y	?	?	?	?	?
4 *Watts*	Y	Y	Y	N	Y	Y	Y	Y
5 *Istook*	Y	Y	Y	N	Y	Y	Y	Y
6 *Lucas*	Y	Y	Y	N	Y	Y	Y	Y
OREGON								
1 Furse	Y	N	N	N	Y	Y	Y	Y
2 *Smith*	Y	Y	Y	N	Y	Y	Y	Y
3 Blumenauer	Y	N	N	N	Y	Y	Y	Y
4 DeFazio	Y	N	N	Y	Y	Y	Y	Y
5 Hooley	Y	N	N	N	Y	Y	Y	Y
PENNSYLVANIA								
1 Foglietta	Y	N	N	?	?	?	?	?
2 Fattah	Y	N	N	?	?	?	?	?
3 Borski	Y	N	N	N	Y	Y	Y	Y
4 Klink	Y	N	N	N	Y	Y	Y	Y
5 *Peterson*	Y	Y	Y	N	Y	Y	Y	Y
6 Holden	Y	N	N	N	Y	Y	Y	Y
7 *Weldon*	Y	N	N	N	Y	Y	Y	Y
8 *Greenwood*	Y	N	Y	N	Y	Y	Y	Y
9 *Shuster*	Y	Y	Y	N	Y	Y	Y	Y
10 *McDade*	Y	Y	N	N	Y	Y	Y	Y
11 Kanjorski	Y	N	N	N	Y	Y	Y	Y
12 Murtha	Y	N	N	N	Y	Y	Y	Y
13 *Fox*	Y	N	N	N	Y	Y	Y	Y
14 Coyne	Y	N	N	Y	Y	Y	Y	Y
15 McHale	Y	N	N	N	Y	Y	Y	Y
16 *Pitts*	Y	Y	Y	N	Y	Y	Y	Y
17 *Gekas*	Y	N	Y	?	Y	Y	Y	Y
18 Doyle	Y	N	N	N	Y	Y	Y	Y
19 *Goodling*	Y	Y	Y	N	Y	Y	Y	Y
20 Mascara	Y	N	N	N	Y	Y	Y	Y
21 *English*	Y	Y	N	N	Y	Y	Y	Y
RHODE ISLAND								
1 Kennedy	?	?	?	N	Y	Y	Y	Y
2 Weygand	+	–	–	N	Y	Y	Y	Y
SOUTH CAROLINA								
1 *Sanford*	Y	Y	Y	N	N	N	N	Y
2 *Spence*	Y	Y	Y	N	Y	Y	Y	Y
3 *Graham*	Y	N	Y	N	N	Y	Y	Y
4 *Inglis*	Y	Y	Y	N	Y	Y	Y	Y
5 Spratt	?	?	?	N	Y	Y	Y	Y
6 Clyburn	Y	N	N	N	Y	N	Y	Y
SOUTH DAKOTA								
AL *Thune*	Y	Y	Y	N	Y	Y	Y	Y
TENNESSEE								
1 *Jenkins*	Y	Y	Y	–	+	Y	Y	Y
2 *Duncan*	Y	Y	Y	N	N	N	Y	Y

	457	458	459	460	461	462	463	464
3 *Wamp*	Y	Y	Y	N	N	N	Y	Y
4 *Hilleary*	Y	Y	Y	Y	N	N	Y	Y
5 Clement	Y	N	N	N	Y	Y	Y	Y
6 Gordon	Y	N	Y	N	Y	Y	Y	Y
7 *Bryant*	Y	Y	Y	N	Y	Y	Y	Y
8 Tanner	Y	N	Y	N	Y	Y	Y	Y
9 Ford	Y	N	N	Y	Y	Y	Y	Y
TEXAS								
1 Sandlin	Y	N	N	N	Y	Y	Y	Y
2 Turner	Y	N	Y	N	Y	Y	Y	Y
3 *Johnson, Sam*	Y	Y	Y	N	Y	Y	Y	Y
4 Hall	Y	Y	Y	N	N	Y	Y	Y
5 *Sessions*	Y	Y	Y	N	Y	N	Y	Y
6 *Barton*	Y	Y	Y	N	N	N	Y	Y
7 *Archer*	Y	Y	Y	N	Y	Y	Y	Y
8 *Brady*	Y	Y	Y	N	Y	Y	Y	Y
9 Lampson	Y	N	N	N	Y	Y	Y	Y
10 Doggett	Y	N	Y	Y	Y	Y	Y	Y
11 Edwards	Y	N	Y	N	Y	Y	Y	Y
12 *Granger*	Y	Y	Y	N	Y	Y	Y	Y
13 *Thornberry*	Y	Y	Y	N	Y	Y	Y	Y
14 *Paul*	N	Y	Y	N	N	N	N	N
15 Hinojosa	Y	N	N	N	Y	Y	Y	Y
16 Reyes	?	?	?	N	Y	Y	Y	Y
17 Stenholm	Y	Y	Y	?	?	?	?	?
18 Jackson-Lee	?	?	X	Y	Y	Y	Y	Y
19 *Combest*	Y	Y	Y	N	N	Y	Y	Y
20 Gonzalez	?	?	?	?	?	?	?	?
21 *Smith*	Y	Y	Y	N	Y	Y	Y	Y
22 *DeLay*	Y	Y	Y	N	N	Y	Y	Y
23 *Bonilla*	?	?	?	N	Y	Y	Y	Y
24 Frost	Y	N	Y	N	Y	Y	Y	Y
25 Bentsen	?	?	?	N	Y	Y	Y	Y
26 *Armey*	Y	Y	Y	N	Y	Y	Y	Y
27 Ortiz	Y	N	N	N	Y	Y	Y	Y
28 Rodriguez	Y	N	N	Y	Y	Y	Y	Y
29 Green	Y	N	N	N	Y	Y	Y	Y
30 Johnson, E.B.	P	N	N	N	Y	Y	Y	Y
UTAH								
1 *Hansen*	?	?	?	N	Y	Y	Y	Y
2 *Cook*	Y	Y	Y	N	Y	Y	Y	Y
3 *Cannon*	Y	Y	Y	N	Y	Y	Y	Y
VERMONT								
AL *Sanders*	Y	N	N	?	Y	Y	Y	Y
VIRGINIA								
1 *Bateman*	Y	N	Y	N	Y	Y	Y	Y
2 Pickett	Y	N	N	N	N	Y	Y	Y
3 Scott	Y	N	N	N	Y	Y	Y	Y
4 Sisisky	Y	N	N	N	Y	Y	Y	Y
5 Goode	Y	Y	Y	N	N	Y	Y	Y
6 *Goodlatte*	Y	Y	Y	N	Y	Y	Y	Y
7 *Bliley*	Y	N	Y	N	Y	Y	Y	Y
8 Moran	P	N	N	N	Y	Y	Y	Y
9 Boucher	Y	N	N	N	Y	Y	Y	Y
10 *Wolf*	Y	Y	Y	N	Y	Y	Y	Y
11 *Davis*	Y	N	Y	N	Y	Y	Y	Y
WASHINGTON								
1 *White*	Y	Y	Y	N	Y	Y	Y	Y
2 *Metcalf*	Y	Y	N	N	N	Y	Y	Y
3 *Smith, Linda*	Y	Y	Y	N	Y	Y	Y	Y
4 *Hastings*	Y	Y	Y	N	Y	Y	N	Y
5 *Nethercutt*	Y	Y	Y	N	Y	Y	Y	Y
6 Dicks	?	?	?	N	Y	Y	Y	Y
7 McDermott	Y	N	N	Y	Y	Y	Y	Y
8 *Dunn*	Y	Y	Y	N	Y	Y	Y	Y
9 Smith, Adam	Y	N	N	N	Y	Y	Y	Y
WEST VIRGINIA								
1 Mollohan	Y	N	N	N	Y	Y	Y	Y
2 Wise	Y	N	N	N	Y	Y	Y	Y
3 Rahall	N	N	N	N	Y	Y	Y	Y
WISCONSIN								
1 *Neumann*	Y	Y	Y	N	N	N	N	N
2 *Klug*	Y	Y	Y	N	Y	Y	Y	Y
3 Kind	Y	N	N	Y	Y	Y	Y	Y
4 Kleczka	Y	N	N	N	Y	Y	Y	Y
5 Barrett	Y	N	N	Y	Y	Y	Y	Y
6 *Petri*	Y	N	Y	N	Y	N	Y	Y
7 Obey	Y	N	N	Y	Y	Y	Y	Y
8 Johnson	Y	N	N	N	Y	Y	Y	Y
9 *Sensenbrenner*	Y	Y	Y	N	N	N	Y	Y
WYOMING								
AL *Cubin*	Y	Y	Y	N	N	Y	Y	Y

Southern states - Ala., Ark., Fla., Ga., Ky., La., Miss., N.C., Okla., S.C., Tenn., Texas, Va.

HOUSE VOTES 465, 466, 467, 468, 469, 470, 471, 472

465. Procedural Motion/Adjourn. Velázquez, D-N.Y., motion to adjourn. Motion rejected 132-285: R 4-219; D 127-66 (ND 96-44, SD 31-22); I 1-0, Sept. 30, 1997.

466. Procedural Motion/Journal. Approval of House Journal of Monday, Sept. 29, 1997. Approved 360-56: R 202-19; D 157-37 (ND 111-33, SD 46-4); I 1-0, Sept. 30, 1997.

467. HR 2203. Fiscal 1998 Energy and Water Appropriations/ Rule. Adoption of the rule (H Res 254) to waive points of order against and provide for House floor consideration of the conference report to provide $21.2 billion in new budget authority for operations of the Department of Energy and related programs in fiscal 1998. The measure provides $2.3 billion less than the president's request. Adopted 415-3: R 219-3; D 195-0 (ND 143-0, SD 52-0); I 1-0, Sept. 30, 1997.

468. HR 2203. Fiscal 1998 Energy and Water Appropriations/ Conference Report. Adoption of the conference report on the bill to provide $21.2 billion in new budget authority for energy and water development programs in fiscal 1998. The conference report would provide $162 million more than provided in fiscal 1997 and $2.3 billion less than requested by the administration. Adopted (thus sent to the Senate) 404-17: R 205-16; D 198-1 (ND 146-1, SD 52-0); I 1-0, Sept. 30, 1997.

469. HR 1370. Export-Import Bank Reauthorization/Previous Question. Dreier, R-Calif., motion to order the previous question (thus ending debate and the possibility of amendment) on adoption of the rule (H Res 255) to provide for House floor consideration of the bill to reauthorize the Export-Import Bank through fiscal 2001. Motion agreed to 423-3: R 223-0; D 199-3 (ND 148-1, SD 51-2); I 1-0, Sept. 30, 1997.

470. HR 1370. Export-Import Bank Reauthorization/Motion To Rise. McDermott, D-Wash., motion to rise from the Committee of the Whole. Motion rejected 128-291: R 3-218; D 125-72 (ND 95-50, SD 30-22); I 0-1, Sept. 30, 1997.

471. HR 1370. Export-Import Bank Reauthorization/Motion To Rise. DeLauro, D-Conn., motion to rise from the Committee of the Whole. Motion rejected 162-257: R 3-215; D 158-42 (ND 117-29, SD 41-13); I 1-0, Sept. 30, 1997.

472. HR 1370. Export-Import Bank Reauthorization/U.S. Business in China. Evans, D-Ill., amendment to direct the Export-Import Bank to give preference to those U.S. firms seeking assistance for activities in China who have adopted and adhered to a code of conduct consistent with internationally recognized human and workers' rights. Adopted 241-182: R 59-163; D 181-19 (ND 138-8, SD 43-11); I 1-0, Sept. 30, 1997.

KEY

- Y Voted for (yea).
- # Paired for.
- + Announced for.
- N Voted against (nay).
- X Paired against.
- – Announced against.
- P Voted "present."
- C Voted "present" to avoid possible conflict of interest.
- ? Did not vote or otherwise make a position known.

—

Democrats ***Republicans***
Independent

	465	466	467	468	469	470	471	472
ALABAMA								
1 ***Callahan***	N	Y	Y	Y	Y	N	N	N
2 ***Everett***	N	Y	Y	Y	Y	N	N	N
3 ***Riley***	N	Y	Y	Y	Y	N	N	N
4 ***Aderholt***	N	Y	Y	Y	Y	N	N	Y
5 Cramer	Y	Y	Y	Y	Y	N	Y	Y
6 ***Bachus***	N	Y	Y	Y	Y	N	N	N
7 Hilliard	N	?	Y	Y	Y	Y	Y	Y
ALASKA								
AL ***Young***	N	Y	Y	Y	Y	N	N	N
ARIZONA								
1 ***Salmon***	N	N	Y	Y	Y	N	N	N
2 Pastor	N	Y	Y	Y	Y	Y	Y	Y
3 ***Stump***	N	Y	Y	Y	Y	N	N	N
4 ***Shadegg***	N	Y	Y	Y	Y	Y	Y	N
5 ***Kolbe***	N	Y	Y	Y	Y	N	N	N
6 ***Hayworth***	N	Y	Y	Y	Y	N	N	Y
ARKANSAS								
1 Berry	Y	Y	Y	Y	Y	Y	Y	N
2 Snyder	Y	Y	Y	Y	Y	Y	Y	N
3 ***Hutchinson***	N	Y	Y	Y	Y	N	N	N
4 ***Dickey***	N	Y	Y	Y	Y	N	N	N
CALIFORNIA								
1 ***Riggs***	N	Y	Y	Y	Y	N	N	N
2 ***Herger***	N	Y	Y	Y	Y	N	N	N
3 Fazio	Y	Y	Y	Y	Y	Y	Y	Y
4 ***Doolittle***	N	Y	Y	Y	Y	N	N	N
5 Matsui	Y	Y	Y	Y	Y	Y	Y	Y
6 Woolsey	Y	Y	Y	Y	Y	Y	Y	Y
7 Miller	Y	N	Y	Y	Y	Y	Y	Y
8 Pelosi	?	?	?	Y	Y	Y	Y	Y
9 Dellums	?	?	?	?	Y	N	Y	Y
10 Tauscher	Y	Y	Y	Y	Y	Y	Y	Y
11 ***Pombo***	N	N	Y	Y	Y	N	N	N
12 Lantos	N	Y	Y	Y	Y	N	Y	Y
13 Stark	Y	N	Y	Y	Y	Y	Y	Y
14 Eshoo	Y	Y	Y	Y	Y	Y	Y	Y
15 ***Campbell***	N	Y	Y	N	Y	N	N	N
16 Lofgren	Y	Y	Y	Y	Y	N	N	Y
17 Farr	Y	Y	+	Y	Y	Y	Y	Y
18 Condit	N	Y	Y	Y	Y	N	Y	Y
19 ***Radanovich***	N	Y	Y	Y	Y	N	N	N
20 Dooley	N	Y	Y	Y	Y	N	N	N
21 ***Thomas***	N	Y	Y	Y	Y	N	N	N
22 Capps	Y	Y	Y	Y	Y	Y	Y	Y
23 ***Gallegly***	N	Y	Y	Y	Y	N	N	N
24 Sherman	N	Y	Y	Y	Y	Y	Y	Y
25 ***McKeon***	N	Y	Y	Y	Y	N	N	N
26 Berman	N	Y	Y	Y	Y	N	?	Y
27 ***Rogan***	N	Y	Y	Y	Y	N	N	N
28 ***Dreier***	N	Y	Y	Y	Y	N	N	N
29 Waxman	Y	Y	Y	Y	Y	Y	Y	Y
30 Becerra	Y	N	Y	Y	Y	Y	Y	Y
31 Martinez	Y	Y	Y	Y	Y	Y	Y	Y
32 Dixon	N	Y	Y	Y	Y	N	Y	Y
33 Roybal-Allard	Y	Y	Y	Y	Y	Y	Y	Y
34 Torres	Y	Y	Y	Y	Y	Y	Y	Y
35 Waters	Y	N	Y	Y	Y	Y	N	Y
36 Harman	Y	Y	Y	Y	Y	Y	Y	Y
37 Millender-McD.	Y	Y	Y	Y	Y	Y	Y	Y
38 ***Horn***	N	Y	Y	Y	Y	N	N	Y
39 ***Royce***	N	Y	Y	N	Y	N	N	Y
40 ***Lewis***	N	Y	Y	Y	Y	N	N	?
41 ***Kim***	N	Y	Y	Y	Y	N	N	N
42 Brown	Y	N	Y	?	Y	N	Y	?
43 ***Calvert***	N	Y	Y	Y	Y	N	N	N
44 ***Bono***	N	Y	Y	Y	Y	N	N	Y
45 ***Rohrabacher***	N	Y	Y	Y	Y	N	N	Y
46 Sanchez	Y	Y	Y	Y	Y	Y	Y	Y
47 ***Cox***	N	Y	Y	?	Y	N	N	Y
48 ***Packard***	N	Y	Y	Y	Y	N	N	N
49 ***Bilbray***	N	Y	Y	Y	Y	N	N	N
50 Filner	Y	N	Y	Y	Y	Y	Y	Y
51 ***Cunningham***	N	Y	Y	Y	Y	N	N	N
52 ***Hunter***	N	Y	?	Y	Y	N	N	Y
COLORADO								
1 DeGette	Y	Y	Y	Y	Y	?	Y	Y
2 Skaggs	N	Y	Y	Y	Y	N	Y	Y
3 ***McInnis***	N	Y	Y	Y	Y	N	N	Y
4 ***Schaffer***	N	N	Y	Y	Y	N	N	N
5 ***Hefley***	N	N	Y	Y	Y	N	N	Y
6 ***Schaefer***	N	Y	Y	Y	Y	N	N	N
CONNECTICUT								
1 Kennelly	Y	Y	Y	Y	Y	Y	Y	Y
2 Gejdenson	Y	N	Y	Y	Y	Y	Y	Y
3 DeLauro	Y	N	Y	Y	Y	Y	Y	Y
4 ***Shays***	N	Y	Y	N	Y	N	N	N
5 Maloney	Y	Y	Y	Y	Y	Y	Y	Y
6 ***Johnson***	N	Y	Y	Y	Y	N	N	N
DELAWARE								
AL ***Castle***	N	Y	Y	Y	Y	N	N	N
FLORIDA								
1 ***Scarborough***	N	Y	Y	Y	Y	N	N	Y
2 Boyd	Y	Y	Y	Y	Y	Y	Y	N
3 Brown	Y	Y	Y	Y	Y	N	N	Y
4 ***Fowler***	N	Y	Y	Y	Y	N	N	N
5 Thurman	Y	Y	Y	Y	Y	Y	Y	Y
6 ***Stearns***	N	Y	Y	Y	Y	N	N	Y
7 ***Mica***	N	Y	Y	Y	Y	N	N	N
8 ***McCollum***	N	Y	Y	Y	Y	N	N	N
9 ***Bilirakis***	N	Y	Y	Y	Y	N	N	N
10 ***Young***	N	Y	Y	Y	Y	N	?	?
11 Davis	Y	Y	Y	Y	Y	Y	Y	N
12 ***Canady***	N	Y	Y	Y	Y	N	N	N
13 ***Miller***	N	Y	Y	Y	Y	N	N	N
14 ***Goss***	N	Y	Y	Y	Y	N	N	N
15 ***Weldon***	N	Y	Y	Y	Y	N	N	N
16 ***Foley***	N	Y	Y	Y	Y	N	N	N
17 Meek	Y	Y	Y	Y	Y	?	N	Y
18 ***Ros-Lehtinen***	N	Y	Y	Y	Y	N	N	Y
19 Wexler	Y	Y	Y	Y	Y	N	Y	Y
20 Deutsch	Y	Y	Y	Y	Y	Y	Y	Y
21 ***Diaz-Balart***	N	Y	Y	Y	Y	N	N	Y
22 ***Shaw***	N	Y	Y	Y	Y	N	N	N
23 Hastings	Y	Y	Y	Y	Y	Y	Y	Y
GEORGIA								
1 ***Kingston***	N	Y	Y	Y	Y	N	N	Y
2 Bishop	Y	Y	?	Y	Y	Y	Y	Y
3 ***Collins***	N	Y	Y	Y	Y	N	N	N
4 McKinney	N	Y	Y	Y	N	Y	Y	Y
5 Lewis	Y	N	Y	Y	Y	Y	Y	Y
6 ***Gingrich***								
7 ***Barr***	N	Y	?	Y	Y	N	N	N
8 ***Chambliss***	N	Y	Y	Y	Y	N	N	N
9 ***Deal***	N	Y	Y	N	Y	N	N	N
10 ***Norwood***	N	Y	Y	Y	Y	?	N	N
11 ***Linder***	N	Y	Y	Y	Y	N	N	N
HAWAII								
1 Abercrombie	Y	N	Y	Y	Y	Y	Y	Y
2 Mink	Y	Y	Y	Y	Y	Y	Y	Y
IDAHO								
1 ***Chenoweth***	N	Y	Y	N	Y	N	N	N
2 ***Crapo***	N	Y	Y	Y	Y	N	N	N
ILLINOIS								
1 Rush	Y	N	Y	Y	Y	N	Y	Y
2 Jackson	N	Y	Y	Y	Y	Y	Y	Y
3 Lipinski	Y	Y	Y	Y	Y	N	N	Y
4 Gutierrez	Y	Y	Y	Y	Y	?	Y	Y
5 Blagojevich	Y	Y	Y	Y	Y	Y	N	Y
6 ***Hyde***	N	Y	Y	Y	Y	N	N	N
7 Davis	Y	Y	Y	Y	Y	Y	Y	Y
8 ***Crane***	N	Y	Y	Y	Y	N	N	N
9 Yates	N	Y	Y	Y	Y	?	Y	Y
10 ***Porter***	N	Y	Y	Y	Y	N	N	N
11 ***Weller***	N	N	Y	Y	Y	N	N	Y
12 Costello	N	N	Y	Y	Y	N	N	Y
13 ***Fawell***	N	N	Y	Y	Y	N	N	N
14 ***Hastert***	N	?	Y	Y	Y	N	N	N
15 ***Ewing***	N	Y	Y	Y	Y	N	N	N

ND Northern Democrats   SD Southern Democrats

	465	466	467	468	469	470	471	472
16 ***Manzullo***	N	Y	Y	Y	Y	N	N	N
17 Evans	Y	Y	Y	Y	Y	N	Y	Y
18 ***LaHood***	N	Y	Y	Y	Y	N	N	N
19 Poshard	N	N	Y	Y	Y	Y	Y	Y
20 ***Shimkus***	N	Y	Y	Y	Y	N	N	Y
INDIANA								
1 Visclosky	N	N	Y	Y	Y	N	N	Y
2 ***McIntosh***	N	Y	Y	Y	Y	N	N	Y
3 Roemer	N	Y	Y	Y	Y	N	N	N
4 ***Souder***	N	Y	Y	Y	Y	N	N	Y
5 ***Buyer***	N	Y	Y	Y	Y	N	N	N
6 ***Burton***	N	Y	Y	Y	Y	N	N	Y
7 ***Pease***	N	Y	Y	Y	Y	N	N	N
8 ***Hostettler***	N	Y	Y	Y	Y	N	N	N
9 Hamilton	N	Y	Y	Y	Y	N	N	N
10 Carson	N	Y	Y	Y	Y	Y	Y	Y
IOWA								
1 ***Leach***	N	Y	Y	Y	Y	N	N	N
2 ***Nussle***	N	N	Y	Y	Y	N	N	N
3 Boswell	Y	Y	Y	Y	Y	N	N	Y
4 ***Ganske***	N	Y	Y	Y	Y	N	N	Y
5 ***Latham***	N	Y	Y	Y	Y	N	N	N
KANSAS								
1 ***Moran***	N	N	Y	Y	Y	N	N	N
2 ***Ryun***	N	Y	Y	Y	Y	N	N	N
3 ***Snowbarger***	N	Y	Y	Y	Y	N	N	N
4 ***Tiahrt***	N	Y	Y	Y	Y	?	N	N
KENTUCKY								
1 ***Whitfield***	N	Y	Y	Y	Y	N	N	N
2 ***Lewis***	N	Y	Y	Y	Y	N	N	N
3 ***Northup***	N	Y	Y	Y	Y	N	N	N
4 ***Bunning***	N	Y	Y	Y	Y	N	N	Y
5 ***Rogers***	N	Y	Y	Y	Y	N	N	N
6 Baesler	N	Y	Y	Y	Y	N	N	Y
LOUISIANA								
1 ***Livingston***	?	Y	Y	Y	Y	N	N	N
2 Jefferson	Y	Y	Y	Y	Y	Y	Y	Y
3 ***Tauzin***	N	Y	Y	Y	Y	N	N	N
4 ***McCrery***	N	Y	Y	Y	Y	N	N	N
5 ***Cooksey***	N	Y	Y	Y	Y	N	N	N
6 ***Baker***	N	Y	Y	Y	Y	N	N	N
7 John	N	Y	Y	Y	Y	Y	Y	N
MAINE								
1 Allen	Y	Y	Y	Y	Y	Y	Y	Y
2 Baldacci	Y	Y	Y	Y	Y	Y	Y	Y
MARYLAND								
1 ***Gilchrest***	N	Y	Y	Y	Y	N	N	Y
2 ***Ehrlich***	N	Y	Y	Y	Y	N	N	N
3 Cardin	N	Y	?	Y	Y	Y	Y	Y
4 Wynn	Y	Y	Y	Y	Y	Y	Y	Y
5 Hoyer	Y	Y	Y	Y	Y	Y	Y	Y
6 ***Bartlett***	N	Y	Y	Y	Y	N	N	N
7 Cummings	N	Y	Y	Y	Y	Y	Y	Y
8 ***Morella***	N	Y	Y	Y	Y	N	N	N
MASSACHUSETTS								
1 Olver	Y	Y	Y	Y	Y	Y	Y	Y
2 Neal	Y	Y	Y	Y	Y	Y	Y	Y
3 McGovern	Y	N	Y	Y	Y	Y	Y	Y
4 Frank	Y	Y	Y	Y	Y	Y	Y	Y
5 Meehan	Y	Y	Y	Y	Y	Y	Y	Y
6 Tierney	Y	Y	Y	Y	Y	Y	Y	Y
7 Markey	Y	N	Y	Y	Y	Y	Y	Y
8 Kennedy	N	Y	Y	Y	Y	N	N	Y
9 Moakley	N	Y	Y	Y	Y	Y	Y	Y
10 Delahunt	Y	Y	Y	Y	Y	Y	?	Y
MICHIGAN								
1 Stupak	Y	N	Y	Y	Y	Y	Y	Y
2 ***Hoekstra***	N	Y	Y	N	Y	N	N	N
3 ***Ehlers***	N	Y	Y	Y	Y	N	N	Y
4 ***Camp***	N	Y	Y	Y	Y	N	N	N
5 Barcia	N	Y	Y	Y	Y	N	N	Y
6 ***Upton***	N	Y	Y	Y	Y	N	N	Y
7 ***Smith***	N	Y	Y	Y	Y	N	N	Y
8 Stabenow	Y	Y	Y	Y	Y	Y	Y	Y
9 Kildee	N	Y	Y	Y	Y	N	N	Y
10 Bonior	Y	N	Y	Y	Y	Y	Y	Y
11 ***Knollenberg***	N	Y	Y	Y	Y	N	N	N
12 Levin	Y	Y	Y	Y	Y	Y	Y	Y
13 Rivers	Y	Y	Y	Y	Y	N	Y	Y
14 Conyers	Y	Y	Y	Y	Y	N	Y	Y
15 Kilpatrick	Y	N	Y	Y	Y	Y	Y	Y
16 Dingell	Y	Y	Y	Y	Y	Y	Y	Y
MINNESOTA								
1 ***Gutknecht***	N	N	Y	Y	Y	N	N	N
2 Minge	?	Y	Y	Y	Y	N	N	Y

	465	466	467	468	469	470	471	472
3 ***Ramstad***	N	N	Y	N	Y	N	N	N
4 Vento	Y	N	Y	Y	Y	Y	Y	Y
5 Sabo	N	N	Y	Y	Y	N	N	Y
6 Luther	Y	Y	Y	Y	Y	N	Y	Y
7 Peterson	Y	Y	Y	Y	Y	Y	Y	N
8 Oberstar	N	N	Y	Y	Y	Y	N	Y
MISSISSIPPI								
1 ***Wicker***	N	Y	Y	Y	Y	N	?	N
2 Thompson	N	N	Y	Y	Y	Y	Y	Y
3 ***Pickering***	N	Y	Y	Y	Y	N	N	N
4 ***Parker***	N	Y	Y	Y	Y	N	N	N
5 Taylor	N	N	Y	Y	N	N	N	Y
MISSOURI								
1 Clay	N	N	Y	Y	Y	N	N	Y
2 ***Talent***	N	Y	Y	Y	Y	N	N	Y
3 Gephardt	?	?	Y	Y	Y	Y	Y	Y
4 Skelton	N	Y	Y	Y	Y	N	N	Y
5 McCarthy	N	Y	Y	Y	Y	Y	Y	Y
6 Danner	N	Y	Y	Y	Y	Y	Y	Y
7 ***Blunt***	N	Y	Y	Y	Y	N	N	N
8 ***Emerson***	N	Y	Y	Y	Y	N	N	N
9 ***Hulshof***	N	N	Y	Y	Y	N	N	N
MONTANA								
AL ***Hill***	N	N	Y	Y	Y	N	N	N
NEBRASKA								
1 ***Bereuter***	N	Y	Y	Y	Y	N	N	N
2 ***Christensen***	N	Y	Y	Y	Y	N	N	N
3 ***Barrett***	N	Y	Y	Y	Y	N	N	N
NEVADA								
1 ***Ensign***	N	N	N	N	Y	Y	Y	Y
2 ***Gibbons***	N	N	N	N	Y	N	N	Y
NEW HAMPSHIRE								
1 ***Sununu***	N	Y	Y	N	Y	N	N	N
2 ***Bass***	N	Y	Y	Y	Y	N	N	N
NEW JERSEY								
1 Andrews	Y	Y	Y	Y	Y	Y	Y	Y
2 ***LoBiondo***	N	N	Y	Y	Y	N	N	Y
3 ***Saxton***	–	+	+	+	+	N	N	N
4 ***Smith***	N	Y	Y	Y	Y	N	N	Y
5 ***Roukema***	N	Y	Y	Y	Y	?	N	N
6 Pallone	+	–	+	+	+	+	+	+
7 ***Franks***	N	Y	Y	Y	Y	N	N	Y
8 Pascrell	Y	Y	Y	Y	Y	Y	Y	Y
9 Rothman	–	+	+	+	Y	Y	Y	Y
10 Payne	Y	Y	Y	Y	Y	Y	Y	Y
11 ***Frelinghuysen***	N	Y	Y	Y	Y	N	N	N
12 ***Pappas***	N	Y	Y	Y	Y	N	N	Y
13 Menendez	Y	N	Y	Y	Y	N	Y	Y
NEW MEXICO								
1 ***Schiff***	?	?	?	?	?	?	?	?
2 ***Skeen***	N	Y	Y	Y	Y	N	N	N
3 ***Redmond***	N	Y	Y	Y	Y	N	N	N
NEW YORK								
1 ***Forbes***	N	Y	Y	Y	Y	N	N	Y
2 ***Lazio***	N	Y	Y	Y	Y	N	N	N
3 ***King***	N	Y	Y	Y	Y	N	N	Y
4 McCarthy	Y	Y	Y	Y	Y	N	Y	Y
5 Ackerman	Y	Y	Y	Y	Y	Y	Y	Y
6 Flake	?	?	?	Y	Y	N	N	N
7 Manton	N	Y	Y	Y	Y	N	N	Y
8 Nadler	N	Y	Y	Y	?	?	?	?
9 Schumer	?	N	Y	Y	Y	Y	Y	Y
10 Towns	Y	Y	Y	Y	Y	Y	Y	Y
11 Owens	Y	Y	Y	Y	Y	Y	Y	Y
12 Velázquez	Y	N	Y	Y	Y	Y	Y	Y
13 Vacant								
14 Maloney	Y	Y	Y	Y	Y	Y	Y	Y
15 Rangel	Y	Y	Y	Y	Y	Y	Y	Y
16 Serrano	N	Y	Y	Y	Y	Y	Y	Y
17 Engel	Y	Y	Y	Y	Y	N	Y	Y
18 Lowey	Y	N	Y	Y	Y	Y	Y	Y
19 ***Kelly***	N	Y	N	Y	Y	N	N	N
20 ***Gilman***	N	Y	Y	Y	Y	N	N	Y
21 McNulty	Y	N	Y	Y	Y	Y	Y	Y
22 ***Solomon***	N	Y	Y	Y	Y	N	N	N
23 ***Boehlert***	N	Y	Y	Y	Y	N	N	N
24 ***McHugh***	N	Y	Y	Y	Y	N	N	Y
25 ***Walsh***	N	Y	Y	Y	Y	N	N	N
26 Hinchey	Y	N	Y	Y	Y	Y	Y	Y
27 ***Paxon***	N	Y	Y	Y	Y	N	N	N
28 Slaughter	Y	Y	Y	Y	Y	Y	Y	Y
29 LaFalce	Y	Y	?	Y	Y	N	Y	Y
30 ***Quinn***	N	Y	Y	Y	Y	N	N	Y
31 ***Houghton***	N	Y	Y	Y	Y	N	N	N

	465	466	467	468	469	470	471	472
NORTH CAROLINA								
1 Clayton	Y	?	Y	?	Y	Y	Y	Y
2 Etheridge	Y	Y	Y	Y	Y	Y	Y	Y
3 ***Jones***	N	Y	Y	Y	Y	N	N	Y
4 Price	Y	Y	Y	Y	Y	?	Y	Y
5 ***Burr***	N	Y	Y	Y	Y	N	?	Y
6 ***Coble***	N	Y	Y	Y	Y	N	N	N
7 McIntyre	Y	Y	Y	Y	Y	Y	N	Y
8 Hefner	Y	Y	Y	Y	Y	Y	Y	Y
9 ***Myrick***	N	Y	Y	Y	Y	N	N	N
10 ***Ballenger***	N	Y	Y	Y	Y	N	N	N
11 ***Taylor***	N	Y	Y	Y	Y	N	N	N
12 Watt	N	Y	Y	Y	Y	Y	Y	Y
NORTH DAKOTA								
AL Pomeroy	Y	Y	Y	Y	Y	Y	Y	Y
OHIO								
1 ***Chabot***	N	Y	Y	Y	Y	N	N	N
2 ***Portman***	N	Y	Y	Y	Y	N	N	N
3 Hall	Y	Y	Y	Y	Y	N	Y	Y
4 ***Oxley***	N	Y	Y	Y	Y	N	?	N
5 ***Gillmor***	N	Y	Y	Y	Y	N	N	N
6 Strickland	Y	Y	Y	Y	Y	Y	Y	Y
7 ***Hobson***	N	Y	Y	Y	Y	N	N	N
8 ***Boehner***	N	Y	Y	Y	Y	N	N	N
9 Kaptur	Y	Y	Y	Y	Y	Y	Y	Y
10 Kucinich	N	N	Y	Y	Y	N	N	Y
11 Stokes	Y	Y	Y	Y	Y	N	N	?
12 ***Kasich***	N	Y	Y	Y	Y	N	N	N
13 Brown	Y	Y	Y	Y	Y	Y	Y	Y
14 Sawyer	Y	Y	Y	Y	Y	Y	Y	Y
15 ***Pryce***	N	Y	Y	Y	Y	N	N	N
16 ***Regula***	N	Y	Y	Y	Y	N	N	N
17 Traficant	N	Y	Y	Y	Y	N	N	Y
18 ***Ney***	N	Y	Y	Y	Y	N	N	Y
19 ***LaTourette***	N	Y	Y	Y	Y	N	?	Y
OKLAHOMA								
1 ***Largent***	Y	Y	Y	Y	Y	N	N	Y
2 ***Coburn***	Y	?	Y	Y	Y	N	?	Y
3 ***Watkins***	N	Y	Y	Y	Y	N	N	N
4 ***Watts***	Y	Y	Y	Y	Y	N	N	N
5 ***Istook***	N	Y	Y	Y	Y	N	N	N
6 ***Lucas***	N	Y	Y	Y	Y	N	N	N
OREGON								
1 Furse	Y	Y	Y	Y	Y	Y	Y	Y
2 ***Smith***	N	Y	Y	?	Y	N	N	N
3 Blumenauer	Y	Y	Y	Y	Y	N	Y	Y
4 DeFazio	Y	N	Y	Y	N	Y	Y	Y
5 Hooley	N	N	Y	Y	Y	Y	Y	Y
PENNSYLVANIA								
1 Foglietta	?	Y	Y	Y	Y	?	?	?
2 Fattah	Y	Y	Y	Y	Y	Y	Y	Y
3 Borski	Y	N	Y	Y	Y	Y	Y	Y
4 Klink	?	Y	Y	Y	Y	N	N	Y
5 ***Peterson***	N	Y	Y	Y	Y	N	N	N
6 Holden	N	Y	Y	Y	Y	N	N	Y
7 ***Weldon***	N	Y	Y	Y	Y	N	N	N
8 ***Greenwood***	N	Y	Y	Y	Y	N	N	N
9 ***Shuster***	N	Y	Y	Y	Y	N	N	Y
10 ***McDade***	N	Y	Y	Y	Y	N	N	Y
11 Kanjorski	Y	Y	Y	Y	Y	N	Y	Y
12 Murtha	Y	Y	Y	Y	Y	N	Y	Y
13 ***Fox***	N	N	Y	Y	Y	N	N	N
14 Coyne	Y	Y	Y	Y	Y	Y	Y	Y
15 McHale	N	Y	Y	Y	Y	N	Y	Y
16 ***Pitts***	N	Y	Y	Y	Y	N	N	N
17 ***Gekas***	N	Y	Y	Y	Y	N	N	N
18 Doyle	N	Y	Y	Y	Y	N	N	Y
19 ***Goodling***	N	Y	Y	Y	Y	N	N	Y
20 Mascara	N	Y	Y	Y	Y	N	N	Y
21 ***English***	N	N	Y	?	Y	N	N	N
RHODE ISLAND								
1 Kennedy	Y	Y	Y	Y	Y	Y	Y	Y
2 Weygand	N	Y	Y	Y	Y	Y	Y	Y
SOUTH CAROLINA								
1 ***Sanford***	N	Y	Y	N	Y	N	N	Y
2 ***Spence***	N	Y	Y	Y	Y	N	N	N
3 ***Graham***	N	Y	Y	Y	Y	N	N	N
4 ***Inglis***	N	Y	Y	Y	Y	N	N	Y
5 Spratt	Y	Y	Y	Y	Y	Y	Y	Y
6 Clyburn	Y	Y	Y	Y	Y	Y	Y	Y
SOUTH DAKOTA								
AL ***Thune***	N	Y	Y	Y	Y	N	N	Y
TENNESSEE								
1 ***Jenkins***	N	Y	Y	Y	Y	N	N	Y
2 ***Duncan***	N	Y	Y	Y	Y	N	N	Y

	465	466	467	468	469	470	471	
3 ***Wamp***	N	Y	Y	Y	Y	N	N	Y
4 ***Hilleary***	Y	N	Y	Y	Y	Y	Y	N
5 Clement	N	Y	Y	Y	Y	N	Y	Y
6 Gordon	N	Y	Y	Y	Y	N	Y	N
7 ***Bryant***	N	Y	Y	Y	Y	N	N	Y
8 Tanner	N	Y	Y	Y	Y	N	Y	N
9 Ford	Y	Y	Y	Y	Y	Y	Y	Y
TEXAS								
1 Sandlin	N	Y	Y	Y	Y	N	N	Y
2 Turner	N	Y	Y	Y	Y	Y	Y	Y
3 ***Johnson, Sam***	N	Y	Y	Y	Y	N	N	N
4 Hall	N	Y	Y	Y	Y	N	N	N
5 ***Sessions***	N	N	Y	Y	Y	N	?	?
6 ***Barton***	N	Y	Y	Y	Y	N	N	N
7 ***Archer***	N	Y	Y	Y	Y	?	N	N
8 ***Brady***	N	Y	Y	Y	Y	N	N	N
9 Lampson	?	?	Y	Y	Y	N	Y	Y
10 Doggett	Y	N	Y	Y	Y	Y	Y	Y
11 Edwards	N	Y	Y	Y	Y	N	Y	Y
12 ***Granger***	N	Y	Y	Y	Y	N	N	N
13 ***Thornberry***	N	Y	Y	Y	Y	N	N	N
14 ***Paul***	N	Y	Y	N	Y	N	N	Y
15 Hinojosa	Y	Y	Y	Y	Y	Y	Y	Y
16 Reyes	Y	Y	Y	Y	Y	Y	Y	Y
17 Stenholm	N	Y	Y	Y	Y	Y	Y	N
18 Jackson-Lee	Y	Y	Y	Y	Y	Y	Y	Y
19 ***Combest***	N	Y	Y	Y	Y	N	N	N
20 Gonzalez	?	?	?	?	?	?	?	?
21 ***Smith***	N	Y	Y	Y	Y	N	N	N
22 ***DeLay***	N	Y	Y	Y	Y	N	N	N
23 ***Bonilla***	N	Y	Y	Y	Y	N	N	N
24 Frost	N	Y	Y	Y	Y	Y	Y	Y
25 Bentsen	N	Y	Y	Y	Y	N	N	N
26 ***Armey***	N	?	Y	Y	Y	N	N	N
27 Ortiz	Y	Y	Y	Y	Y	N	N	Y
28 Rodriguez	Y	Y	Y	Y	Y	N	Y	Y
29 Green	N	Y	Y	Y	Y	Y	Y	Y
30 Johnson, E.B.	N	Y	Y	Y	Y	N	Y	Y
UTAH								
1 ***Hansen***	N	Y	Y	Y	?	N	N	N
2 ***Cook***	N	Y	Y	Y	Y	N	N	N
3 ***Cannon***	N	Y	Y	Y	Y	N	N	N
VERMONT								
AL *Sanders*	Y	Y	Y	Y	Y	N	Y	Y
VIRGINIA								
1 ***Bateman***	N	Y	Y	Y	Y	N	N	N
2 Pickett	N	?	?	?	Y	N	N	N
3 Scott	Y	Y	Y	Y	Y	N	N	Y
4 Sisisky	N	Y	Y	Y	Y	N	N	Y
5 Goode	Y	Y	Y	Y	Y	N	N	Y
6 ***Goodlatte***	N	Y	Y	Y	Y	N	N	N
7 ***Bliley***	N	Y	Y	Y	Y	N	N	N
8 Moran	Y	Y	Y	Y	?	N	Y	Y
9 Boucher	N	Y	Y	Y	Y	N	Y	Y
10 ***Wolf***	N	Y	Y	Y	Y	N	N	Y
11 ***Davis***	N	Y	Y	Y	Y	N	N	N
WASHINGTON								
1 ***White***	N	Y	Y	Y	Y	N	N	N
2 ***Metcalf***	N	Y	Y	Y	Y	N	N	N
3 ***Smith, Linda***	N	Y	Y	Y	Y	N	N	Y
4 ***Hastings***	N	Y	Y	Y	Y	N	N	N
5 ***Nethercutt***	N	Y	Y	Y	Y	N	N	N
6 Dicks	N	?	Y	Y	Y	N	Y	N
7 McDermott	Y	N	Y	Y	Y	Y	Y	N
8 ***Dunn***	N	Y	Y	Y	Y	N	N	N
9 Smith, Adam	Y	Y	Y	Y	Y	Y	Y	N
WEST VIRGINIA								
1 Mollohan	N	Y	Y	Y	Y	N	Y	Y
2 Wise	N	Y	Y	Y	Y	N	Y	Y
3 Rahall	N	Y	Y	Y	Y	N	N	Y
WISCONSIN								
1 ***Neumann***	N	Y	Y	N	Y	N	N	N
2 ***Klug***	N	Y	Y	N	Y	N	N	N
3 Kind	Y	Y	Y	Y	Y	Y	Y	Y
4 Kleczka	N	Y	Y	N	Y	N	N	Y
5 Barrett	Y	Y	Y	Y	Y	Y	Y	Y
6 ***Petri***	N	Y	Y	N	Y	N	N	Y
7 Obey	?	Y	Y	Y	Y	Y	Y	Y
8 Johnson	Y	Y	Y	Y	Y	Y	Y	Y
9 ***Sensenbrenner***	N	Y	Y	N	Y	N	N	N
WYOMING								
AL ***Cubin***	N	Y	Y	Y	Y	N	N	N

Southern states - Ala., Ark., Fla., Ga., Ky., La., Miss., N.C., Okla., S.C., Tenn., Texas, Va.

HOUSE VOTES 473, 474, 475, 476, 477, 478, 479, 480

473. HR 1370. Export-Import Bank Reauthorization/Renaming the Bank. LaFalce, D-N.Y., amendment to rename the Export-Import Bank the "United States Export Bank." Adopted 362-56: R 173-45; D 188-11 (ND 140-6, SD 48-5); I 1-0, Sept. 30, 1997.

474. HR 2378. Fiscal 1998 Treasury-Postal Service Appropriations/Conference Report. Adoption of the conference report on the bill to provide $25.4 billion in new mandatory and discretionary budget authority for the Treasury Department, Postal Service and other general government functions, including the Executive Office of the President in fiscal 1998. The conference report would provide $1.3 billion more than in fiscal 1997 and $262 million less than requested by President Clinton. Adopted (thus sent to the Senate) 220-207: R 107-118; D 113-88 (ND 86-62, SD 27-26); I 0-1, Sept. 30, 1997.

475. HR 2267. Fiscal 1998 Commerce, Justice, State Appropriations/Sampling in 2000 Census. Mollohan, D-W.Va., amendment to strike the bill's language restricting the use of Census Bureau funds for statistical sampling. The amendment prohibits the use of fiscal 1998 funds to make irreversible plans or preparations for the use of sampling or statistical adjustment in taking the census for purposes of congressional apportionment. The amendment also creates a three-person board to observe and monitor all aspects of Census 2000. Rejected 197-228: R 3-219; D 193-9 (ND 142-6, SD 51-3); I 1-0, Sept. 30, 1997. A "yea" vote was in support of the president's position.

476. HR 2267. Fiscal 1998 Commerce, Justice, State Appropriations/Passage. Passage of the bill to provide $31.8 billion in new budget authority for the departments of Commerce, Justice, State and the federal judiciary in fiscal 1998, $3.9 billion less than the administration's request. The measure appropriates $5.3 billion for the Violent Crime Reduction Trust Fund; $17.6 billion for the Justice Department; about $5.1 billion for the State Department; and $4.2 billion for the Commerce Department. The measure provides $382 million for the 2000 Census and bans the use of funds for statistical sampling. Passed 227-199: R 174-49; D 53-149 (ND 40-108, SD 13-41); I 0-1, Sept. 30, 1997.

477. H Res 244. Subpoena Enforcement in *Dornan v. Sanchez*/Rule. Adoption of the rule (H Res 253) to waive points of order against and provide for House floor consideration of the resolution to demand that the Office of the U.S. Attorney for the Central District of California file criminal charges against Hermandad Mexicana Nacional for failure to comply with a subpoena issued under the Federal Contested Election Act, if the U.S. Attorney determines that such an action is appropriate according to the law and the facts. Adopted 221-202: R 220-0; D 1-201 (ND 1-147, SD 0-54); I 0-1, Sept. 30, 1997.

478. H Res 244. Subpoena Enforcement in *Dornan v. Sanchez*/Adoption. Adoption of the resolution to demand that the Office of the U.S. Attorney for the Central District of California file criminal charges against Hermandad Mexicana Nacional for failure to comply with a subpoena issued under the Federal Contested Election Act, if the U.S. Attorney determines that such action is appropriate according to the law and the facts. Adopted 219-203: R 218-1; D 1-201 (ND 1-147, SD 0-54); I 0-1, Oct. 1, 1997 (in the session that began and the Congressional Record dated Sept. 30).

479. Procedural Motion/Adjourn. Scarborough, R-Fla., motion to adjourn. Motion agreed to 206-183: R 196-6; D 10-176 (ND 6-127, SD 4-49); I 0-1, Oct. 1, 1997 (in the session that began and the Congressional Record dated Sept. 30).

480. HR 1757. Fiscal 1998-99 State Department Authorization/Motion To Instruct. Doggett, D-Texas, motion to instruct conferees to reject a Senate provision that would place private claimants against frozen Iraqi assets ahead of U.S. government claimants, including Persian Gulf War veterans. Motion agreed to 412-5: R 211-5; D 200-0 (ND 146-0, SD 54-0); I 1-0, Oct. 1, 1997.

KEY

- Y Voted for (yea).
- \# Paired for.
- \+ Announced for.
- N Voted against (nay).
- X Paired against.
- \- Announced against.
- P Voted "present."
- C Voted "present" to avoid possible conflict of interest.
- ? Did not vote or otherwise make a position known.

Democrats ***Republicans***
Independent

	473	474	475	476	477	478	479	480
ALABAMA								
1 ***Callahan***	N	Y	N	Y	Y	Y	?	Y
2 ***Everett***	Y	N	N	Y	Y	Y	Y	Y
3 ***Riley***	Y	N	N	N	Y	Y	Y	Y
4 ***Aderholt***	N	N	N	Y	Y	Y	Y	Y
5 Cramer	Y	N	Y	Y	N	N	N	Y
6 ***Bachus***	Y	N	N	N	Y	Y	Y	Y
7 Hilliard	Y	Y	Y	N	N	N	N	Y
ALASKA								
AL ***Young***	Y	Y	N	Y	?	?	?	Y
ARIZONA								
1 ***Salmon***	Y	N	N	N	Y	Y	Y	Y
2 Pastor	Y	+	Y	Y	N	N	N	Y
3 ***Stump***	N	N	N	N	Y	Y	Y	Y
4 ***Shadegg***	N	N	N	Y	Y	Y	Y	Y
5 ***Kolbe***	Y	Y	N	Y	Y	Y	Y	Y
6 ***Hayworth***	Y	N	N	Y	Y	Y	Y	Y
ARKANSAS								
1 Berry	N	N	Y	N	N	N	N	Y
2 Snyder	N	N	Y	N	N	N	N	Y
3 ***Hutchinson***	Y	N	N	Y	Y	Y	Y	Y
4 ***Dickey***	Y	Y	N	Y	Y	Y	Y	Y
CALIFORNIA								
1 ***Riggs***	Y	N	N	Y	Y	Y	Y	Y
2 ***Herger***	Y	N	N	Y	Y	Y	Y	Y
3 Fazio	Y	Y	Y	N	N	N	N	?
4 ***Doolittle***	N	Y	N	N	Y	Y	Y	Y
5 Matsui	Y	Y	Y	Y	N	N	N	Y
6 Woolsey	Y	Y	Y	N	N	N	N	Y
7 Miller	Y	Y	Y	Y	N	N	N	Y
8 Pelosi	?	Y	Y	N	N	N	N	Y
9 Dellums	Y	Y	Y	N	N	N	N	Y
10 Tauscher	Y	N	Y	N	N	N	N	Y
11 ***Pombo***	N	N	N	N	Y	Y	Y	Y
12 Lantos	Y	Y	Y	N	N	N	?	Y
13 Stark	Y	Y	Y	N	N	N	N	Y
14 Eshoo	Y	Y	Y	Y	N	N	N	Y
15 ***Campbell***	Y	N	N	N	Y	Y	Y	Y
16 Lofgren	Y	N	Y	Y	N	N	N	Y
17 Farr	Y	Y	Y	Y	N	N	N	Y
18 Condit	Y	N	Y	Y	N	N	Y	Y
19 ***Radanovich***	N	N	N	N	Y	Y	Y	Y
20 Dooley	Y	Y	Y	N	N	N	?	Y
21 ***Thomas***	Y	Y	N	Y	Y	Y	Y	Y
22 Capps	Y	N	Y	N	N	N	N	Y
23 ***Gallegly***	Y	Y	N	Y	Y	Y	Y	Y
24 Sherman	Y	N	Y	Y	N	N	N	Y
25 ***McKeon***	Y	Y	N	Y	Y	Y	Y	Y
26 Berman	Y	Y	Y	Y	N	N	?	Y
27 ***Rogan***	N	N	N	Y	Y	Y	Y	Y
28 ***Dreier***	Y	Y	N	Y	Y	Y	Y	Y
29 Waxman	Y	Y	Y	Y	N	N	N	?
30 Becerra	Y	Y	Y	N	N	N	N	Y
31 Martinez	Y	Y	Y	N	N	N	?	Y
32 Dixon	Y	Y	Y	Y	N	N	Y	Y
33 Roybal-Allard	Y	Y	Y	N	N	N	N	Y
34 Torres	Y	Y	Y	N	N	N	N	Y
35 Waters	Y	Y	Y	N	N	N	N	Y
36 Harman	Y	Y	Y	N	N	N	N	Y
37 Millender-McD.	Y	Y	Y	N	N	N	N	Y
38 ***Horn***	Y	Y	N	Y	Y	Y	Y	Y
39 ***Royce***	N	N	N	N	Y	Y	Y	Y
40 ***Lewis***	Y	Y	N	Y	Y	Y	Y	Y
41 ***Kim***	Y	N	N	Y	Y	Y	Y	Y
42 Brown	Y	Y	Y	Y	N	N	N	Y
43 ***Calvert***	Y	Y	N	Y	Y	Y	?	Y
44 ***Bono***	N	Y	N	Y	Y	Y	Y	Y
45 ***Rohrabacher***	N	N	N	N	Y	Y	Y	Y
46 Sanchez	Y	N	Y	N	P	P	N	Y
47 ***Cox***	N	Y	N	N	Y	Y	Y	Y
48 ***Packard***	N	Y	N	Y	Y	Y	N	Y
49 ***Bilbray***	Y	Y	N	Y	Y	Y	Y	Y
50 Filner	Y	Y	Y	N	N	N	N	Y
51 ***Cunningham***	?	Y	N	Y	Y	Y	Y	Y
52 ***Hunter***	Y	Y	N	Y	Y	Y	Y	Y
COLORADO								
1 DeGette	Y	N	Y	N	N	N	N	Y
2 Skaggs	Y	Y	Y	Y	N	N	N	Y
3 ***McInnis***	N	Y	N	N	Y	Y	N	?
4 ***Schaffer***	N	N	N	N	Y	Y	N	Y
5 ***Hefley***	Y	N	N	N	Y	Y	?	Y
6 ***Schaefer***	N	N	N	Y	Y	Y	Y	Y
CONNECTICUT								
1 Kennelly	Y	N	Y	N	N	N	N	Y
2 Gejdenson	Y	N	Y	N	N	N	N	Y
3 DeLauro	Y	N	Y	N	N	N	N	Y
4 ***Shays***	Y	N	Y	N	Y	Y	Y	Y
5 Maloney	Y	N	Y	N	N	N	N	Y
6 ***Johnson***	Y	N	Y	Y	Y	Y	Y	Y
DELAWARE								
AL ***Castle***	Y	Y	N	Y	Y	Y	Y	Y
FLORIDA								
1 ***Scarborough***	N	N	N	N	Y	Y	Y	N
2 Boyd	Y	Y	Y	N	N	N	N	Y
3 Brown	Y	Y	Y	N	N	N	N	Y
4 ***Fowler***	Y	Y	N	Y	Y	Y	Y	Y
5 Thurman	Y	N	Y	N	N	N	N	Y
6 ***Stearns***	N	N	N	Y	Y	Y	Y	N
7 ***Mica***	Y	N	N	Y	Y	Y	Y	Y
8 ***McCollum***	Y	Y	N	Y	Y	Y	Y	Y
9 ***Bilirakis***	Y	Y	N	Y	Y	Y	Y	Y
10 ***Young***	?	?	?	?	?	?	?	?
11 Davis	Y	N	Y	N	N	N	N	Y
12 ***Canady***	Y	N	N	Y	Y	Y	?	Y
13 ***Miller***	Y	Y	N	Y	Y	Y	Y	Y
14 ***Goss***	Y	N	N	Y	Y	Y	Y	Y
15 ***Weldon***	Y	Y	N	Y	Y	Y	Y	Y
16 ***Foley***	Y	Y	N	Y	Y	Y	Y	Y
17 Meek	Y	Y	Y	N	N	N	N	Y
18 ***Ros-Lehtinen***	Y	Y	N	Y	Y	Y	Y	?
19 Wexler	Y	Y	Y	N	N	N	N	Y
20 Deutsch	Y	N	Y	N	N	N	N	Y
21 ***Diaz-Balart***	Y	Y	N	Y	Y	Y	Y	Y
22 ***Shaw***	Y	Y	N	Y	Y	Y	Y	Y
23 Hastings	Y	Y	Y	N	N	N	N	Y
GEORGIA								
1 ***Kingston***	N	Y	N	Y	Y	Y	Y	Y
2 Bishop	Y	Y	Y	N	N	N	N	Y
3 ***Collins***	Y	N	N	Y	Y	Y	Y	Y
4 McKinney	N	N	Y	N	N	N	N	Y
5 Lewis	Y	N	Y	N	N	N	N	Y
6 ***Gingrich***		Y			Y	Y		
7 ***Barr***	N	N	N	Y	Y	Y	Y	N
8 ***Chambliss***	Y	N	N	Y	Y	Y	Y	Y
9 ***Deal***	Y	N	N	Y	Y	Y	Y	Y
10 ***Norwood***	Y	N	N	N	Y	Y	Y	Y
11 ***Linder***	Y	Y	N	Y	Y	Y	Y	?
HAWAII								
1 Abercrombie	Y	Y	Y	Y	N	N	N	Y
2 Mink	N	Y	Y	N	N	N	N	Y
IDAHO								
1 ***Chenoweth***	?	N	N	N	Y	Y	Y	Y
2 ***Crapo***	Y	Y	N	N	Y	Y	Y	Y
ILLINOIS								
1 Rush	Y	Y	Y	N	N	N	N	Y
2 Jackson	Y	Y	Y	N	N	N	N	Y
3 Lipinski	Y	Y	Y	N	N	N	N	Y
4 Gutierrez	Y	N	Y	Y	N	N	N	Y
5 Blagojevich	Y	Y	Y	N	N	N	N	Y
6 ***Hyde***	Y	Y	N	Y	Y	Y	Y	Y
7 Davis	Y	N	Y	N	N	N	N	Y
8 ***Crane***	Y	N	N	N	Y	Y	?	Y
9 Yates	Y	Y	?	?	?	?	?	Y
10 ***Porter***	Y	Y	N	Y	Y	Y	Y	Y
11 ***Weller***	Y	N	N	Y	Y	Y	Y	Y
12 Costello	Y	N	Y	N	N	N	N	Y
13 ***Fawell***	Y	Y	N	Y	Y	Y	Y	Y
14 ***Hastert***	N	Y	N	Y	Y	Y	Y	Y
15 ***Ewing***	Y	Y	N	Y	Y	Y	Y	Y

ND Northern Democrats SD Southern Democrats

	473	474	475	476	477	478	479	480
16 ***Manzullo***	Y	N	N	N	Y	Y	Y	Y
17 Evans	Y	N	Y	N	N	N	N	Y
18 ***LaHood***	Y	N	N	Y	Y	Y	Y	Y
19 Poshard	Y	N	Y	N	N	N	N	Y
20 ***Shimkus***	Y	N	N	Y	Y	Y	Y	Y
INDIANA								
1 Visclosky	Y	N	Y	Y	N	N	N	+
2 ***McIntosh***	N	Y	N	N	Y	Y	Y	Y
3 Roemer	Y	N	Y	N	N	N	N	Y
4 ***Souder***	Y	N	N	Y	Y	Y	Y	Y
5 ***Buyer***	Y	Y	N	Y	Y	Y	Y	Y
6 ***Burton***	N	Y	N	N	Y	Y	Y	Y
7 ***Pease***	Y	N	N	Y	Y	Y	Y	Y
8 ***Hostettler***	Y	N	N	N	Y	Y	Y	Y
9 Hamilton	Y	N	Y	Y	N	N	N	Y
10 Carson	Y	N	Y	N	N	N	N	Y
IOWA								
1 ***Leach***	Y	Y	N	Y	Y	Y	Y	Y
2 ***Nussle***	Y	N	N	Y	Y	Y	Y	Y
3 Boswell	Y	N	Y	N	N	N	N	Y
4 ***Ganske***	N	Y	N	Y	Y	Y	Y	Y
5 ***Latham***	Y	Y	N	Y	Y	Y	Y	Y
KANSAS								
1 ***Moran***	Y	N	N	N	Y	Y	Y	Y
2 ***Ryun***	Y	N	N	N	Y	Y	Y	Y
3 ***Snowbarger***	Y	N	N	Y	Y	Y	Y	Y
4 ***Tiahrt***	Y	N	N	Y	Y	Y	Y	Y
KENTUCKY								
1 ***Whitfield***	N	N	N	Y	Y	Y	N	Y
2 ***Lewis***	Y	N	N	Y	Y	Y	Y	Y
3 ***Northup***	Y	N	N	Y	Y	Y	Y	Y
4 ***Bunning***	Y	N	N	Y	Y	Y	?	Y
5 ***Rogers***	Y	Y	N	Y	Y	Y	Y	Y
6 Baesler	Y	N	Y	Y	N	N	Y	Y
LOUISIANA								
1 ***Livingston***	Y	Y	N	Y	Y	Y	Y	Y
2 Jefferson	Y	Y	Y	N	N	N	N	Y
3 ***Tauzin***	Y	Y	N	Y	Y	Y	Y	Y
4 ***McCrery***	Y	Y	N	Y	Y	Y	Y	Y
5 ***Cooksey***	Y	N	?	Y	Y	Y	Y	Y
6 ***Baker***	Y	N	N	Y	Y	Y	?	Y
7 John	Y	N	Y	N	N	N	N	Y
MAINE								
1 Allen	Y	N	Y	N	N	N	N	Y
2 Baldacci	Y	N	Y	Y	N	N	N	Y
MARYLAND								
1 ***Gilchrest***	?	Y	N	Y	Y	Y	Y	Y
2 ***Ehrlich***	Y	Y	N	N	Y	Y	Y	Y
3 Cardin	Y	Y	Y	N	N	N	N	Y
4 Wynn	Y	Y	Y	N	N	N	N	Y
5 Hoyer	Y	Y	Y	Y	N	N	N	Y
6 ***Bartlett***	Y	N	N	N	Y	Y	Y	Y
7 Cummings	Y	Y	Y	N	N	N	N	Y
8 ***Morella***	Y	Y	Y	Y	Y	Y	Y	Y
MASSACHUSETTS								
1 Olver	Y	Y	Y	N	N	N	N	Y
2 Neal	Y	Y	Y	N	N	N	N	Y
3 McGovern	Y	N	Y	N	N	N	N	Y
4 Frank	Y	Y	Y	N	N	N	N	Y
5 Meehan	Y	Y	Y	N	N	N	N	Y
6 Tierney	Y	N	Y	N	N	N	N	Y
7 Markey	Y	Y	Y	N	N	N	?	Y
8 Kennedy	Y	Y	Y	N	N	N	N	Y
9 Moakley	?	Y	Y	N	N	N	?	Y
10 Delahunt	Y	Y	Y	N	N	N	N	Y
MICHIGAN								
1 Stupak	Y	Y	Y	N	N	N	N	Y
2 ***Hoekstra***	Y	Y	N	Y	Y	Y	Y	Y
3 ***Ehlers***	Y	Y	N	Y	Y	Y	Y	Y
4 ***Camp***	Y	Y	N	Y	Y	Y	Y	Y
5 Barcia	Y	N	Y	N	N	N	N	Y
6 ***Upton***	Y	Y	N	Y	Y	Y	Y	Y
7 ***Smith***	Y	N	N	Y	Y	Y	Y	Y
8 Stabenow	Y	N	Y	N	N	N	N	Y
9 Kildee	Y	N	Y	N	N	N	N	Y
10 Bonior	Y	N	Y	N	N	N	N	Y
11 ***Knollenberg***	Y	Y	N	Y	Y	Y	Y	Y
12 Levin	Y	Y	Y	N	N	N	N	Y
13 Rivers	Y	N	Y	N	N	N	N	Y
14 Conyers	Y	Y	Y	N	N	N	Y	?
15 Kilpatrick	Y	Y	Y	N	N	N	N	Y
16 Dingell	Y	Y	Y	N	N	N	N	Y
MINNESOTA								
1 ***Gutknecht***	Y	N	N	Y	Y	Y	Y	Y
2 Minge	Y	N	Y	N	N	N	N	Y

	473	474	475	476	477	478	479	480
3 ***Ramstad***	Y	N	N	Y	Y	Y	Y	Y
4 Vento	N	Y	Y	N	N	N	N	Y
5 Sabo	Y	Y	Y	N	N	N	N	Y
6 Luther	Y	N	Y	Y	N	N	N	Y
7 Peterson	Y	N	Y	N	N	N	Y	Y
8 Oberstar	Y	Y	Y	N	N	N	N	Y
MISSISSIPPI								
1 ***Wicker***	Y	Y	N	Y	Y	Y	Y	Y
2 Thompson	Y	Y	Y	N	N	N	N	Y
3 ***Pickering***	Y	Y	N	Y	Y	Y	Y	Y
4 ***Parker***	Y	Y	N	Y	Y	Y	Y	Y
5 Taylor	Y	N	N	N	N	N	N	Y
MISSOURI								
1 Clay	Y	Y	Y	N	N	N	?	Y
2 ***Talent***	Y	N	N	Y	Y	Y	Y	Y
3 Gephardt	Y	N	Y	N	N	N	N	Y
4 Skelton	Y	Y	Y	Y	N	N	N	Y
5 McCarthy	Y	N	Y	Y	N	N	N	Y
6 Danner	Y	N	Y	Y	N	N	N	Y
7 ***Blunt***	Y	Y	N	N	Y	Y	Y	Y
8 ***Emerson***	Y	N	N	Y	Y	Y	?	Y
9 ***Hulshof***	Y	N	N	Y	Y	Y	Y	Y
MONTANA								
AL ***Hill***	Y	N	N	N	Y	Y	Y	Y
NEBRASKA								
1 ***Bereuter***	Y	N	N	Y	Y	Y	Y	?
2 ***Christensen***	Y	N	N	Y	Y	Y	Y	Y
3 ***Barrett***	Y	Y	N	Y	Y	Y	Y	Y
NEVADA								
1 ***Ensign***	Y	N	N	N	Y	Y	Y	Y
2 ***Gibbons***	Y	N	N	N	Y	Y	Y	+
NEW HAMPSHIRE								
1 ***Sununu***	Y	N	N	Y	Y	Y	Y	Y
2 ***Bass***	Y	N	N	Y	Y	Y	Y	Y
NEW JERSEY								
1 Andrews	N	N	Y	N	N	N	N	Y
2 ***LoBiondo***	Y	N	N	Y	Y	Y	Y	Y
3 ***Saxton***	Y	Y	N	Y	Y	Y	Y	Y
4 ***Smith***	Y	Y	N	Y	Y	Y	Y	Y
5 ***Roukema***	Y	Y	–	?	Y	?	?	Y
6 Pallone	+	Y	Y	Y	N	N	N	Y
7 ***Franks***	Y	N	N	Y	Y	Y	Y	Y
8 Pascrell	Y	N	Y	N	N	N	N	Y
9 Rothman	Y	N	Y	N	N	N	N	Y
10 Payne	Y	Y	Y	N	N	N	N	Y
11 ***Frelinghuysen***	Y	Y	N	Y	Y	Y	Y	Y
12 ***Pappas***	Y	N	N	Y	Y	Y	Y	Y
13 Menendez	Y	N	Y	N	N	N	N	Y
NEW MEXICO								
1 ***Schiff***	?	?	?	?	?	?	?	?
2 ***Skeen***	Y	Y	N	Y	Y	Y	Y	Y
3 ***Redmond***	Y	Y	N	Y	Y	Y	Y	Y
NEW YORK								
1 ***Forbes***	Y	N	N	Y	Y	N	Y	Y
2 ***Lazio***	Y	N	N	Y	Y	Y	Y	Y
3 ***King***	Y	Y	N	Y	Y	Y	Y	Y
4 McCarthy	Y	Y	Y	N	N	N	N	Y
5 Ackerman	Y	Y	Y	N	N	N	N	Y
6 Flake	Y	Y	Y	N	N	N	Y	Y
7 Manton	Y	Y	Y	N	N	N	?	Y
8 Nadler	?	Y	Y	N	N	N	N	Y
9 Schumer	Y	N	?	?	?	?	?	Y
10 Towns	Y	Y	Y	N	N	N	N	Y
11 Owens	Y	Y	Y	N	N	N	N	Y
12 Velázquez	Y	N	Y	N	N	N	N	Y
13 Vacant								
14 Maloney	Y	–	Y	N	N	N	N	Y
15 Rangel	?	Y	Y	N	N	N	N	Y
16 Serrano	Y	Y	Y	N	N	N	N	Y
17 Engel	Y	Y	Y	N	N	N	N	Y
18 Lowey	Y	N	Y	N	N	N	N	Y
19 ***Kelly***	Y	N	N	Y	Y	Y	Y	Y
20 ***Gilman***	Y	Y	N	Y	Y	Y	N	Y
21 McNulty	Y	Y	Y	N	N	N	N	Y
22 ***Solomon***	N	Y	N	Y	Y	Y	Y	Y
23 ***Boehlert***	Y	Y	N	Y	Y	Y	Y	Y
24 ***McHugh***	Y	Y	N	Y	Y	Y	Y	Y
25 ***Walsh***	Y	N	N	Y	Y	Y	Y	Y
26 Hinchey	Y	+	Y	N	N	N	N	Y
27 ***Paxon***	N	Y	N	Y	Y	Y	Y	Y
28 Slaughter	Y	N	Y	N	N	N	N	Y
29 LaFalce	Y	Y	Y	N	N	N	?	Y
30 ***Quinn***	Y	Y	N	Y	Y	Y	Y	Y
31 ***Houghton***	N	Y	N	Y	?	?	?	Y

	473	474	475	476	477	478	479	480
NORTH CAROLINA								
1 Clayton	Y	Y	Y	N	N	N	N	Y
2 Etheridge	Y	N	Y	N	N	N	N	Y
3 ***Jones***	Y	N	N	N	Y	Y	Y	Y
4 Price	Y	N	Y	Y	N	N	N	Y
5 ***Burr***	N	N	N	N	Y	Y	Y	Y
6 ***Coble***	N	N	N	Y	Y	Y	Y	Y
7 McIntyre	Y	N	Y	N	N	N	N	Y
8 Hefner	Y	Y	Y	Y	N	N	N	Y
9 ***Myrick***	Y	N	N	Y	Y	Y	Y	Y
10 ***Ballenger***	Y	Y	N	Y	Y	Y	Y	Y
11 ***Taylor***	Y	Y	N	Y	Y	Y	Y	N
12 Watt	Y	Y	Y	N	N	N	N	Y
NORTH DAKOTA								
AL Pomeroy	Y	N	Y	N	N	N	?	Y
OHIO								
1 ***Chabot***	N	N	N	N	Y	Y	Y	Y
2 ***Portman***	Y	Y	N	Y	Y	Y	Y	Y
3 Hall	Y	Y	Y	Y	N	N	?	Y
4 ***Oxley***	Y	Y	N	Y	?	?	?	Y
5 ***Gillmor***	Y	N	N	Y	Y	Y	Y	Y
6 Strickland	Y	N	Y	N	N	N	N	Y
7 ***Hobson***	Y	Y	N	Y	Y	Y	Y	Y
8 ***Boehner***	Y	Y	N	Y	Y	Y	?	Y
9 Kaptur	Y	N	Y	N	N	N	N	Y
10 Kucinich	Y	N	Y	N	N	N	N	Y
11 Stokes	Y	Y	Y	N	N	N	?	?
12 ***Kasich***	Y	N	N	Y	Y	Y	Y	Y
13 Brown	Y	N	Y	N	N	N	N	Y
14 Sawyer	Y	N	Y	N	N	N	N	Y
15 ***Pryce***	Y	Y	N	Y	Y	Y	Y	Y
16 ***Regula***	Y	Y	N	Y	Y	Y	Y	Y
17 Traficant	N	N	N	Y	Y	Y	N	Y
18 ***Ney***	Y	Y	N	Y	Y	Y	Y	Y
19 ***LaTourette***	Y	Y	N	Y	Y	Y	Y	Y
OKLAHOMA								
1 ***Largent***	N	N	N	N	Y	Y	?	Y
2 ***Coburn***	Y	N	N	N	Y	Y	Y	Y
3 ***Watkins***	Y	N	N	Y	Y	Y	Y	Y
4 ***Watts***	Y	N	N	Y	Y	Y	Y	Y
5 ***Istook***	Y	N	N	N	Y	Y	Y	Y
6 ***Lucas***	?	N	N	N	Y	Y	Y	Y
OREGON								
1 Furse	Y	Y	Y	N	N	N	N	Y
2 ***Smith***	Y	Y	N	Y	?	?	?	?
3 Blumenauer	Y	Y	Y	N	N	N	N	Y
4 DeFazio	N	N	Y	N	N	N	N	Y
5 Hooley	Y	N	Y	N	N	N	N	Y
PENNSYLVANIA								
1 Foglietta	Y	Y	Y	N	N	N	?	Y
2 Fattah	Y	Y	Y	N	N	N	N	Y
3 Borski	Y	Y	Y	Y	N	N	?	Y
4 Klink	Y	Y	Y	Y	N	N	N	Y
5 ***Peterson***	Y	N	N	Y	Y	Y	Y	Y
6 Holden	?	N	Y	Y	N	N	N	Y
7 ***Weldon***	Y	Y	N	Y	Y	Y	Y	Y
8 ***Greenwood***	Y	Y	N	Y	Y	Y	?	Y
9 ***Shuster***	Y	Y	N	Y	Y	Y	?	Y
10 ***McDade***	Y	Y	N	Y	?	Y	?	Y
11 Kanjorski	N	Y	Y	Y	N	N	N	Y
12 Murtha	Y	Y	Y	Y	N	N	?	Y
13 ***Fox***	Y	N	N	Y	Y	Y	Y	Y
14 Coyne	Y	Y	Y	N	N	N	N	Y
15 McHale	Y	Y	Y	Y	N	N	N	Y
16 ***Pitts***	Y	N	N	Y	Y	Y	Y	Y
17 ***Gekas***	Y	N	N	Y	Y	Y	Y	Y
18 Doyle	Y	Y	Y	Y	N	N	N	Y
19 ***Goodling***	Y	N	N	Y	Y	Y	Y	Y
20 Mascara	Y	N	Y	N	N	N	N	Y
21 ***English***	Y	N	N	Y	Y	Y	Y	Y
RHODE ISLAND								
1 Kennedy	Y	N	Y	N	N	N	N	Y
2 Weygand	Y	N	Y	N	N	N	N	Y
SOUTH CAROLINA								
1 ***Sanford***	Y	N	N	N	Y	Y	Y	Y
2 ***Spence***	Y	Y	N	Y	Y	Y	Y	Y
3 ***Graham***	Y	N	N	N	Y	Y	Y	Y
4 ***Inglis***	Y	N	N	Y	Y	Y	Y	Y
5 Spratt	Y	N	Y	N	N	N	N	Y
6 Clyburn	Y	Y	Y	N	N	N	Y	Y
SOUTH DAKOTA								
AL ***Thune***	N	N	N	Y	Y	Y	Y	Y
TENNESSEE								
1 ***Jenkins***	N	N	N	Y	Y	Y	Y	Y
2 ***Duncan***	N	N	N	N	Y	Y	Y	Y

	473	474	475	476	477	478	479	
3 ***Wamp***	N	N	N	Y	Y	Y	Y	Y
4 ***Hilleary***	N	N	N	N	Y	Y	Y	Y
5 Clement	Y	Y	Y	N	N	N	N	Y
6 Gordon	?	N	Y	N	N	N	N	Y
7 ***Bryant***	Y	N	N	Y	Y	Y	Y	Y
8 Tanner	Y	Y	Y	Y	N	N	N	Y
9 Ford	Y	N	Y	N	N	N	N	Y
TEXAS								
1 Sandlin	Y	N	Y	N	N	N	N	Y
2 Turner	Y	N	Y	N	N	N	N	Y
3 ***Johnson, Sam***	N	Y	N	N	Y	Y	Y	N
4 Hall	N	N	N	Y	N	N	N	Y
5 ***Sessions***	Y	N	N	Y	Y	Y	Y	Y
6 ***Barton***	Y	Y	N	Y	Y	Y	Y	Y
7 ***Archer***	Y	Y	N	Y	Y	Y	Y	Y
8 ***Brady***	Y	N	N	Y	Y	Y	Y	Y
9 Lampson	Y	N	Y	N	N	N	N	Y
10 Doggett	Y	Y	Y	N	N	N	N	Y
11 Edwards	Y	N	Y	N	N	N	N	Y
12 ***Granger***	Y	N	N	Y	Y	Y	Y	?
13 ***Thornberry***	Y	N	N	Y	Y	Y	Y	Y
14 ***Paul***	N	N	N	N	Y	Y	?	Y
15 Hinojosa	Y	–	Y	N	N	N	N	Y
16 Reyes	Y	N	Y	Y	N	N	N	Y
17 Stenholm	Y	N	Y	Y	N	N	N	Y
18 Jackson-Lee	Y	Y	Y	N	N	N	N	Y
19 ***Combest***	Y	N	N	N	Y	Y	Y	Y
20 Gonzalez	?	?	?	?	?	?	?	?
21 ***Smith***	Y	Y	N	Y	Y	Y	Y	Y
22 ***DeLay***	N	Y	N	Y	Y	Y	Y	Y
23 ***Bonilla***	Y	Y	N	Y	Y	Y	Y	Y
24 Frost	Y	Y	Y	N	N	N	N	Y
25 Bentsen	Y	Y	Y	N	N	N	N	Y
26 ***Armey***	N	Y	N	Y	Y	Y	Y	Y
27 Ortiz	Y	Y	Y	Y	N	N	N	Y
28 Rodriguez	Y	N	Y	N	N	N	N	Y
29 Green	Y	Y	Y	N	N	N	N	Y
30 Johnson, E.B.	Y	Y	Y	N	N	N	N	Y
UTAH								
1 ***Hansen***	Y	Y	N	Y	Y	?	?	Y
2 ***Cook***	Y	N	N	Y	Y	Y	Y	Y
3 ***Cannon***	N	Y	N	Y	Y	Y	Y	Y
VERMONT								
AL *Sanders*	Y	N	Y	N	N	N	N	Y
VIRGINIA								
1 ***Bateman***	Y	Y	N	Y	Y	Y	Y	Y
2 Pickett	Y	Y	Y	N	N	N	Y	Y
3 Scott	Y	Y	Y	N	N	N	N	Y
4 Sisisky	Y	Y	Y	Y	N	N	N	Y
5 Goode	N	N	N	Y	N	N	Y	Y
6 ***Goodlatte***	Y	N	N	Y	Y	Y	Y	Y
7 ***Bliley***	Y	Y	N	Y	Y	Y	Y	?
8 Moran	Y	Y	Y	Y	N	N	N	Y
9 Boucher	Y	Y	Y	Y	N	N	?	Y
10 ***Wolf***	Y	Y	N	Y	Y	Y	Y	Y
11 ***Davis***	N	Y	N	Y	Y	Y	Y	Y
WASHINGTON								
1 ***White***	Y	N	N	Y	Y	Y	Y	Y
2 ***Metcalf***	Y	N	N	Y	Y	Y	Y	Y
3 ***Smith, Linda***	?	N	N	N	Y	Y	Y	Y
4 ***Hastings***	Y	Y	N	Y	Y	Y	Y	Y
5 ***Nethercutt***	N	Y	N	Y	Y	Y	Y	Y
6 Dicks	Y	Y	Y	Y	N	N	?	Y
7 McDermott	Y	Y	?	?	N	N	N	Y
8 ***Dunn***	Y	Y	N	Y	Y	Y	?	Y
9 Smith, Adam	Y	N	Y	N	N	N	N	Y
WEST VIRGINIA								
1 Mollohan	Y	Y	Y	Y	N	N	N	Y
2 Wise	Y	N	Y	Y	N	N	N	Y
3 Rahall	Y	Y	Y	Y	N	N	Y	Y
WISCONSIN								
1 ***Neumann***	N	N	N	N	Y	Y	?	Y
2 ***Klug***	Y	N	N	Y	Y	Y	Y	Y
3 Kind	Y	N	N	Y	N	N	N	Y
4 Kleczka	Y	Y	N	N	N	N	N	Y
5 Barrett	Y	N	N	Y	N	N	N	Y
6 ***Petri***	Y	N	N	Y	Y	Y	N	Y
7 Obey	Y	Y	N	N	N	N	N	Y
8 Johnson	Y	N	N	Y	N	N	N	Y
9 ***Sensenbrenner***	Y	N	N	N	Y	Y	Y	Y
WYOMING								
AL ***Cubin***	Y	N	N	Y	Y	Y	Y	Y

Southern states - Ala., Ark., Fla., Ga., Ky., La., Miss., N.C., Okla., S.C., Tenn., Texas, Va.

HOUSE VOTES 481, 482, 483, 484, 485

481. Procedural Motion/Adjourn. Condit, D-Calif., motion to adjourn. Motion rejected 112-295: R 2-210; D 109-85 (ND 88-53, SD 21-32); I 1-0, Oct. 1, 1997.

482. S 1161. Refugee Assistance Authorization/Passage. Smith, R-Texas, motion to suspend the rules and pass the bill to reauthorize, through fiscal 1999, a program providing grants to private organizations that help refugees adjust to life in the United States. Motion rejected 230-193: R 197-24; D 33-168 (ND 24-123, SD 9-45); I 0-1, Oct. 1, 1997. A two-thirds majority of those present and voting (282 in this case) is required for passage under suspension of the rules.

483. Procedural Motion/Adjourn. Nadler, D-N.Y., motion to adjourn. Motion rejected 207-213: R 13-207; D 193-6 (ND 143-2, SD 50-4); I 1-0, Oct. 1, 1997.

484. H Con Res 131. Importance of Oceans/Adoption. Saxton, R-N.J., motion to suspend the rules and adopt the resolution to acknowledge the paramount importance of the oceans to the economy, environment and national security of the United States, and to promote greater knowledge of the oceans. Motion rejected 237-175: R 213-1; D 24-173 (ND 16-128, SD 8-45); I 0-1, Oct. 1, 1997. A two-thirds majority of those present and voting (275 in this case) is required for adoption under suspension of the rules.

485. HR 2233. Coral Reef Conservation/Passage. Saxton, R-N.J., motion to suspend the rules and pass the bill to direct the Commerce Department to spend $1 million annually during the next five years to provide financial assistance in coral reef conservation. Motion rejected 230-181: R 198-20; D 32-160 (ND 21-120, SD 11-40); I 0-1, Oct. 1, 1997. A two-thirds majority of those present and voting (274 in this case) is required for passage under suspension of the rules.

KEY

- Y Voted for (yea).
- # Paired for.
- + Announced for.
- N Voted against (nay).
- X Paired against.
- – Announced against.
- P Voted "present."
- C Voted "present" to avoid possible conflict of interest.
- ? Did not vote or otherwise make a position known.

Democrats ***Republicans***
Independent

	481	482	483	484	485
ALABAMA					
1 ***Callahan***	N	Y	N	Y	N
2 ***Everett***	N	N	N	Y	N
3 ***Riley***	N	Y	N	Y	Y
4 ***Aderholt***	N	Y	N	Y	Y
5 Cramer	N	N	Y	N	N
6 ***Bachus***	N	Y	Y	Y	Y
7 Hilliard	N	N	Y	N	N
ALASKA					
AL ***Young***	N	Y	N	Y	Y
ARIZONA					
1 ***Salmon***	N	Y	N	Y	Y
2 Pastor	Y	N	Y	N	N
3 ***Stump***	N	Y	N	Y	N
4 ***Shadegg***	N	Y	N	Y	Y
5 ***Kolbe***	N	Y	N	Y	Y
6 ***Hayworth***	N	Y	N	Y	Y
ARKANSAS					
1 Berry	N	N	Y	N	N
2 Snyder	N	N	Y	N	N
3 ***Hutchinson***	N	Y	N	Y	Y
4 ***Dickey***	N	Y	N	Y	Y
CALIFORNIA					
1 ***Riggs***	N	Y	N	Y	Y
2 ***Herger***	N	Y	?	Y	Y
3 Fazio	?	N	Y	N	N
4 ***Doolittle***	N	Y	N	Y	Y
5 Matsui	Y	N	Y	N	N
6 Woolsey	Y	N	Y	N	N
7 Miller	Y	N	Y	N	N
8 Pelosi	Y	N	Y	N	?
9 Dellums	N	N	Y	N	N
10 Tauscher	Y	N	Y	N	N
11 ***Pombo***	N	Y	N	Y	Y
12 Lantos	N	N	Y	N	N
13 Stark	Y	N	Y	N	N
14 Eshoo	Y	N	Y	Y	N
15 ***Campbell***	N	Y	N	Y	Y
16 Lofgren	Y	N	Y	N	N
17 Farr	Y	N	Y	Y	?
18 Condit	Y	N	Y	N	N
19 ***Radanovich***	N	Y	N	Y	Y
20 Dooley	N	N	Y	N	N
21 ***Thomas***	N	Y	N	?	Y
22 Capps	Y	N	Y	N	N
23 ***Gallegly***	N	?	?	?	?
24 Sherman	Y	Y	Y	?	?
25 ***McKeon***	N	Y	N	Y	Y
26 Berman	?	?	?	?	?
27 ***Rogan***	N	Y	N	Y	Y
28 ***Dreier***	N	Y	N	Y	Y
29 Waxman	?	N	Y	N	N
30 Becerra	Y	N	Y	N	N
31 Martinez	?	N	Y	N	N
32 Dixon	N	N	Y	N	N
33 Roybal-Allard	Y	N	Y	N	N
34 Torres	Y	N	Y	N	N
35 Waters	Y	N	Y	N	N
36 Harman	Y	Y	Y	N	N
37 Millender-McD.	N	N	Y	N	N
38 ***Horn***	N	Y	Y	Y	Y
39 ***Royce***	N	N	N	Y	N
40 ***Lewis***	N	Y	N	Y	Y
41 ***Kim***	N	Y	N	Y	Y
42 Brown	Y	N	Y	N	N
43 ***Calvert***	N	Y	N	Y	Y
44 ***Bono***	N	Y	N	Y	Y
45 ***Rohrabacher***	?	Y	N	Y	Y
46 Sanchez	Y	Y	Y	N	Y
47 ***Cox***	Y	Y	N	Y	Y
48 ***Packard***	N	Y	N	Y	Y
49 ***Bilbray***	N	Y	N	Y	Y
50 Filner	Y	Y	Y	Y	Y
51 ***Cunningham***	N	Y	N	Y	Y
52 ***Hunter***	N	Y	N	?	Y
COLORADO					
1 DeGette	Y	N	Y	N	N
2 Skaggs	Y	N	Y	N	N
3 ***McInnis***	?	Y	N	Y	Y
4 ***Schaffer***	N	Y	N	Y	Y
5 ***Hefley***	N	Y	N	Y	Y
6 ***Schaefer***	N	N	N	Y	Y
CONNECTICUT					
1 Kennelly	?	Y	Y	N	Y
2 Gejdenson	Y	N	Y	N	N
3 DeLauro	Y	N	Y	N	N
4 ***Shays***	N	Y	Y	Y	Y
5 Maloney	N	Y	?	N	Y
6 ***Johnson***	N	Y	N	Y	Y
DELAWARE					
AL ***Castle***	N	Y	N	Y	Y
FLORIDA					
1 ***Scarborough***	N	N	N	Y	Y
2 Boyd	Y	N	Y	Y	N
3 Brown	N	N	Y	N	N
4 ***Fowler***	N	Y	N	Y	Y
5 Thurman	Y	N	Y	N	N
6 ***Stearns***	N	Y	N	Y	?
7 ***Mica***	N	Y	N	Y	Y
8 ***McCollum***	N	Y	N	Y	Y
9 ***Bilirakis***	N	Y	N	Y	Y
10 ***Young***	N	Y	N	Y	Y
11 Davis	Y	N	Y	N	N
12 ***Canady***	?	Y	N	Y	Y
13 ***Miller***	N	Y	N	Y	Y
14 ***Goss***	N	Y	N	Y	Y
15 ***Weldon***	N	Y	?	Y	?
16 ***Foley***	N	Y	N	Y	Y
17 Meek	N	N	Y	N	N
18 ***Ros-Lehtinen***	?	?	?	?	?
19 Wexler	Y	Y	Y	N	Y
20 Deutsch	Y	N	Y	+	+
21 ***Diaz-Balart***	N	Y	N	?	Y
22 ***Shaw***	N	Y	Y	Y	Y
23 Hastings	Y	Y	Y	N	Y
GEORGIA					
1 ***Kingston***	N	Y	N	Y	Y
2 Bishop	N	Y	Y	N	N
3 ***Collins***	N	N	N	Y	N
4 McKinney	N	Y	Y	N	?
5 Lewis	Y	N	Y	N	N
6 ***Gingrich***					
7 ***Barr***	N	Y	N	Y	N
8 ***Chambliss***	N	Y	N	Y	Y
9 ***Deal***	N	Y	N	Y	Y
10 ***Norwood***	N	Y	N	Y	Y
11 ***Linder***	?	Y	N	Y	Y
HAWAII					
1 Abercrombie	Y	N	Y	Y	Y
2 Mink	Y	N	Y	N	N
IDAHO					
1 ***Chenoweth***	N	Y	N	Y	N
2 ***Crapo***	N	Y	N	Y	Y
ILLINOIS					
1 Rush	N	N	Y	N	N
2 Jackson	N	N	Y	N	N
3 Lipinski	N	N	Y	N	N
4 Gutierrez	Y	N	Y	N	N
5 Blagojevich	N	N	Y	N	N
6 ***Hyde***	N	Y	N	Y	Y
7 Davis	N	N	Y	N	Y
8 ***Crane***	N	Y	N	Y	Y
9 Yates	N	N	Y	N	N
10 ***Porter***	N	Y	N	Y	Y
11 ***Weller***	N	Y	N	Y	Y
12 Costello	N	N	Y	N	N
13 ***Fawell***	N	Y	N	Y	Y
14 ***Hastert***	N	Y	N	Y	Y
15 ***Ewing***	N	Y	N	Y	Y

ND Northern Democrats SD Southern Democrats

	481	482	483	484	485
16 ***Manzullo***	N	Y	N	Y	Y
17 Evans	Y	N	Y	N	N
18 ***LaHood***	N	Y	N	Y	Y
19 Poshard	N	N	Y	N	N
20 ***Shimkus***	N	Y	N	Y	Y
INDIANA					
1 Visclosky	N	N	Y	N	N
2 ***McIntosh***	N	Y	N	Y	Y
3 Roemer	N	N	Y	N	Y
4 ***Souder***	N	Y	N	Y	Y
5 ***Buyer***	?	Y	N	Y	Y
6 ***Burton***	N	Y	N	Y	Y
7 ***Pease***	N	Y	N	Y	Y
8 ***Hostettler***	N	Y	N	Y	Y
9 Hamilton	N	Y	Y	Y	Y
10 Carson	Y	N	Y	N	N
IOWA					
1 ***Leach***	N	Y	N	Y	Y
2 ***Nussle***	N	Y	N	Y	Y
3 Boswell	N	N	Y	N	N
4 ***Ganske***	N	Y	N	Y	Y
5 ***Latham***	N	Y	N	Y	Y
KANSAS					
1 ***Moran***	N	Y	N	Y	Y
2 ***Ryun***	N	Y	N	Y	Y
3 ***Snowbarger***	N	Y	N	Y	Y
4 ***Tiahrt***	N	Y	N	Y	Y
KENTUCKY					
1 ***Whitfield***	N	Y	N	Y	Y
2 ***Lewis***	N	Y	N	Y	Y
3 ***Northup***	N	Y	N	Y	Y
4 ***Bunning***	N	Y	N	Y	Y
5 ***Rogers***	N	Y	N	Y	N
6 Baesler	Y	N	Y	Y	Y
LOUISIANA					
1 ***Livingston***	N	Y	N	Y	Y
2 Jefferson	Y	N	Y	N	N
3 ***Tauzin***	N	Y	N	Y	Y
4 ***McCrery***	N	Y	N	Y	Y
5 ***Cooksey***	N	N	N	Y	Y
6 ***Baker***	?	Y	N	Y	Y
7 John	N	N	Y	Y	Y
MAINE					
1 Allen	Y	N	Y	N	N
2 Baldacci	Y	N	Y	N	N
MARYLAND					
1 ***Gilchrest***	N	Y	N	Y	Y
2 ***Ehrlich***	N	Y	N	Y	Y
3 Cardin	N	Y	Y	N	Y
4 Wynn	N	N	Y	N	N
5 Hoyer	N	N	Y	N	N
6 ***Bartlett***	N	Y	N	Y	Y
7 Cummings	Y	N	Y	N	N
8 ***Morella***	N	Y	N	Y	Y
MASSACHUSETTS					
1 Olver	Y	N	Y	N	N
2 Neal	Y	N	Y	N	N
3 McGovern	Y	N	Y	N	N
4 Frank	Y	N	Y	N	N
5 Meehan	Y	N	Y	N	N
6 Tierney	Y	N	Y	N	N
7 Markey	Y	N	Y	N	N
8 Kennedy	Y	N	Y	N	N
9 Moakley	Y	N	Y	N	N
10 Delahunt	Y	Y	Y	Y	Y
MICHIGAN					
1 Stupak	Y	N	Y	N	N
2 ***Hoekstra***	N	Y	N	Y	Y
3 ***Ehlers***	N	Y	N	Y	Y
4 ***Camp***	N	Y	N	Y	Y
5 Barcia	N	N	Y	N	N
6 ***Upton***	N	Y	N	Y	Y
7 ***Smith***	N	Y	N	Y	Y
8 Stabenow	N	N	Y	N	N
9 Kildee	N	Y	Y	N	Y
10 Bonior	Y	N	Y	N	N
11 ***Knollenberg***	N	Y	N	Y	Y
12 Levin	Y	N	Y	N	N
13 Rivers	N	N	Y	N	N
14 Conyers	?	N	Y	N	N
15 Kilpatrick	Y	N	Y	N	N
16 Dingell	Y	Y	Y	N	N
MINNESOTA					
1 ***Gutknecht***	N	Y	N	Y	Y
2 Minge	N	N	Y	N	Y

	481	482	483	484	485
3 ***Ramstad***	N	Y	N	Y	Y
4 Vento	Y	N	Y	N	N
5 Sabo	N	N	Y	N	N
6 Luther	N	Y	Y	N	Y
7 Peterson	Y	N	Y	N	N
8 Oberstar	Y	N	Y	N	N
MISSISSIPPI					
1 ***Wicker***	N	Y	N	Y	Y
2 Thompson	N	N	Y	N	N
3 ***Pickering***	N	N	N	Y	N
4 ***Parker***	N	N	N	Y	Y
5 Taylor	N	N	Y	N	N
MISSOURI					
1 Clay	N	N	Y	N	N
2 ***Talent***	N	Y	N	Y	Y
3 Gephardt	Y	N	Y	N	N
4 Skelton	?	N	Y	N	N
5 McCarthy	N	N	Y	N	N
6 Danner	N	N	Y	N	N
7 ***Blunt***	N	Y	N	Y	Y
8 ***Emerson***	N	Y	N	Y	Y
9 ***Hulshof***	N	Y	N	Y	Y
MONTANA					
AL ***Hill***	N	Y	N	Y	Y
NEBRASKA					
1 ***Bereuter***	N	Y	N	Y	Y
2 ***Christensen***	N	Y	N	Y	Y
3 ***Barrett***	N	Y	N	Y	Y
NEVADA					
1 ***Ensign***	Y	Y	N	Y	Y
2 ***Gibbons***	–	Y	N	Y	Y
NEW HAMPSHIRE					
1 ***Sununu***	N	Y	N	Y	N
2 ***Bass***	N	Y	N	Y	Y
NEW JERSEY					
1 Andrews	Y	N	Y	N	N
2 ***LoBiondo***	N	Y	Y	Y	Y
3 ***Saxton***	N	Y	Y	Y	Y
4 ***Smith***	N	N	Y	Y	Y
5 ***Roukema***	N	N	Y	Y	Y
6 Pallone	Y	N	Y	Y	N
7 ***Franks***	N	Y	N	Y	Y
8 Pascrell	N	Y	Y	N	N
9 Rothman	N	Y	Y	N	N
10 Payne	Y	N	Y	N	N
11 ***Frelinghuysen***	N	Y	N	Y	Y
12 ***Pappas***	N	Y	N	Y	Y
13 Menendez	N	Y	Y	N	N
NEW MEXICO					
1 ***Schiff***	?	?	?	?	?
2 ***Skeen***	N	Y	N	Y	Y
3 Redmond	N	Y	N	Y	Y
NEW YORK					
1 ***Forbes***	N	Y	Y	?	Y
2 ***Lazio***	N	Y	N	Y	Y
3 ***King***	N	Y	Y	Y	Y
4 McCarthy	Y	N	Y	N	N
5 Ackerman	Y	?	?	?	?
6 Flake	N	N	Y	Y	N
7 Manton	Y	N	Y	N	N
8 Nadler	Y	Y	Y	N	N
9 Schumer	Y	Y	Y	N	N
10 Towns	Y	Y	Y	N	N
11 Owens	Y	N	Y	N	N
12 Velázquez	Y	N	Y	N	N
13 Vacant					
14 Maloney	Y	N	Y	Y	N
15 Rangel	Y	N	Y	N	N
16 Serrano	Y	N	Y	N	N
17 Engel	Y	N	Y	N	N
18 Lowey	Y	?	?	?	?
19 ***Kelly***	N	Y	N	Y	Y
20 ***Gilman***	N	Y	N	Y	Y
21 McNulty	Y	Y	Y	Y	Y
22 ***Solomon***	N	N	N	Y	Y
23 ***Boehlert***	N	Y	N	Y	Y
24 ***McHugh***	N	Y	N	Y	Y
25 ***Walsh***	N	Y	N	Y	Y
26 Hinchey	Y	N	Y	Y	Y
27 ***Paxon***	N	Y	Y	Y	Y
28 Slaughter	Y	N	Y	N	N
29 LaFalce	?	N	Y	N	N
30 ***Quinn***	N	Y	N	Y	Y
31 ***Houghton***	N	Y	N	Y	?

	481	482	483	484	485
NORTH CAROLINA					
1 Clayton	Y	N	Y	N	N
2 Etheridge	N	N	Y	N	N
3 ***Jones***	N	N	Y	+	+
4 Price	N	N	Y	N	N
5 ***Burr***	N	Y	N	Y	Y
6 ***Coble***	N	N	N	Y	Y
7 McIntyre	N	N	Y	Y	Y
8 Hefner	Y	N	Y	N	N
9 ***Myrick***	N	N	N	Y	Y
10 ***Ballenger***	N	Y	N	Y	Y
11 ***Taylor***	N	Y	N	Y	Y
12 Watt	N	N	Y	N	N
NORTH DAKOTA					
AL Pomeroy	Y	N	Y	?	?
OHIO					
1 ***Chabot***	N	Y	N	Y	N
2 ***Portman***	N	Y	N	Y	Y
3 Hall	N	Y	Y	N	N
4 ***Oxley***	N	Y	N	Y	Y
5 ***Gillmor***	N	Y	N	Y	Y
6 Strickland	Y	N	Y	N	N
7 ***Hobson***	N	Y	N	Y	Y
8 ***Boehner***	N	Y	N	Y	Y
9 Kaptur	Y	N	Y	N	N
10 Kucinich	N	N	Y	Y	Y
11 Stokes	?	?	?	?	?
12 ***Kasich***	N	Y	N	Y	Y
13 Brown	Y	N	Y	N	N
14 Sawyer	N	N	Y	N	Y
15 ***Pryce***	N	Y	N	Y	Y
16 ***Regula***	N	Y	N	Y	Y
17 Traficant	N	N	N	Y	Y
18 ***Ney***	N	Y	N	?	Y
19 ***LaTourette***	N	Y	N	Y	Y
OKLAHOMA					
1 ***Largent***	N	N	Y	Y	Y
2 ***Coburn***	N	Y	N	Y	Y
3 ***Watkins***	N	Y	N	Y	N
4 ***Watts***	N	Y	N	?	Y
5 ***Istook***	N	N	N	Y	Y
6 ***Lucas***	N	Y	N	Y	Y
OREGON					
1 Furse	Y	N	Y	N	N
2 ***Smith***	?	Y	N	Y	Y
3 Blumenauer	Y	N	Y	Y	Y
4 DeFazio	Y	N	Y	N	N
5 Hooley	N	Y	Y	N	Y
PENNSYLVANIA					
1 Foglietta	?	N	?	N	?
2 Fattah	Y	N	Y	N	N
3 Borski	Y	N	Y	N	N
4 Klink	N	N	N	N	N
5 ***Peterson***	N	Y	N	Y	Y
6 Holden	N	N	Y	N	N
7 ***Weldon***	N	Y	N	Y	Y
8 ***Greenwood***	N	Y	N	Y	Y
9 ***Shuster***	N	N	N	Y	Y
10 ***McDade***	N	N	N	Y	Y
11 Kanjorski	Y	N	Y	N	N
12 Murtha	Y	N	Y	N	N
13 ***Fox***	N	Y	N	Y	Y
14 Coyne	N	Y	Y	N	N
15 McHale	N	N	Y	N	N
16 ***Pitts***	N	Y	N	Y	Y
17 ***Gekas***	?	Y	N	Y	Y
18 Doyle	Y	N	Y	N	N
19 ***Goodling***	N	Y	N	Y	Y
20 Mascara	N	N	Y	N	N
21 ***English***	N	Y	N	Y	Y
RHODE ISLAND					
1 Kennedy	Y	N	Y	N	N
2 Weygand	Y	Y	Y	Y	Y
SOUTH CAROLINA					
1 ***Sanford***	N	Y	N	Y	N
2 ***Spence***	N	Y	N	Y	Y
3 ***Graham***	N	Y	N	Y	Y
4 ***Inglis***	N	Y	N	Y	Y
5 Spratt	N	N	Y	N	N
6 Clyburn	N	N	Y	N	N
SOUTH DAKOTA					
AL ***Thune***	N	Y	N	Y	N
TENNESSEE					
1 ***Jenkins***	N	N	N	Y	Y
2 ***Duncan***	N	N	N	Y	N

	481	482	483	484	485
3 ***Wamp***	N	N	Y	Y	Y
4 ***Hilleary***	N	N	N	Y	Y
5 Clement	N	N	Y	N	N
6 Gordon	N	N	Y	N	N
7 ***Bryant***	N	Y	N	Y	N
8 Tanner	N	N	N	N	N
9 Ford	Y	N	Y	N	N
TEXAS					
1 Sandlin	N	Y	Y	Y	Y
2 Turner	Y	N	Y	N	N
3 ***Johnson, Sam***	?	Y	N	Y	Y
4 Hall	N	N	N	N	N
5 ***Sessions***	N	Y	N	Y	Y
6 ***Barton***	N	?	N	Y	Y
7 ***Archer***	N	Y	N	Y	Y
8 ***Brady***	N	Y	N	Y	Y
9 Lampson	Y	N	Y	N	Y
10 Doggett	Y	N	Y	N	N
11 Edwards	Y	N	Y	N	N
12 ***Granger***	?	?	?	?	?
13 ***Thornberry***	N	Y	N	Y	Y
14 ***Paul***	N	N	N	N	N
15 Hinojosa	N	N	Y	N	N
16 Reyes	N	N	Y	N	N
17 Stenholm	Y	N	Y	N	N
18 Jackson-Lee	Y	Y	Y	N	N
19 ***Combest***	N	Y	N	Y	Y
20 Gonzalez	?	?	?	?	?
21 ***Smith***	N	Y	N	?	Y
22 ***DeLay***	N	Y	N	Y	Y
23 ***Bonilla***	N	Y	N	Y	N
24 Frost	Y	N	Y	N	N
25 Bentsen	Y	N	Y	N	Y
26 ***Armey***	N	Y	N	Y	Y
27 Ortiz	N	N	Y	Y	N
28 Rodriguez	N	N	Y	N	N
29 Green	N	Y	Y	N	Y
30 Johnson, E.B.	Y	N	Y	N	N
UTAH					
1 ***Hansen***	N	Y	N	Y	Y
2 ***Cook***	N	Y	N	Y	Y
3 ***Cannon***	N	Y	N	Y	Y
VERMONT					
AL *Sanders*	Y	N	Y	N	N
VIRGINIA					
1 ***Bateman***	N	Y	N	Y	Y
2 Pickett	N	Y	N	Y	Y
3 Scott	N	N	Y	N	N
4 Sisisky	N	Y	Y	N	N
5 Goode	N	N	N	Y	Y
6 ***Goodlatte***	N	Y	N	Y	Y
7 ***Bliley***	?	Y	N	Y	Y
8 Moran	?	N	Y	N	?
9 Boucher	N	N	Y	N	N
10 ***Wolf***	N	Y	N	Y	Y
11 ***Davis***	N	Y	N	Y	Y
WASHINGTON					
1 ***White***	N	Y	N	Y	Y
2 ***Metcalf***	N	Y	N	Y	Y
3 ***Smith, Linda***	N	Y	N	Y	Y
4 ***Hastings***	N	Y	N	Y	Y
5 ***Nethercutt***	N	Y	N	Y	Y
6 Dicks	N	N	N	Y	N
7 McDermott	Y	N	Y	?	?
8 ***Dunn***	N	Y	N	Y	Y
9 Smith, Adam	N	N	Y	N	N
WEST VIRGINIA					
1 Mollohan	N	N	Y	N	N
2 Wise	N	N	Y	N	N
3 Rahall	N	N	Y	N	N
WISCONSIN					
1 ***Neumann***	N	N	N	Y	N
2 ***Klug***	N	Y	N	Y	Y
3 Kind	N	N	Y	N	N
4 Kleczka	N	N	Y	N	N
5 Barrett	Y	N	Y	N	N
6 ***Petri***	N	Y	N	Y	Y
7 Obey	Y	Y	Y	N	N
8 Johnson	N	N	Y	N	N
9 ***Sensenbrenner***	N	N	N	Y	N
WYOMING					
AL ***Cubin***	N	Y	N	Y	Y

Southern states - Ala., Ark., Fla., Ga., Ky., La., Miss., N.C., Okla., S.C., Tenn., Texas, Va.

HOUSE VOTES 486, 487, 488, 489

486. Procedural Motion/Adjourn. Schumer, D-N.Y., motion to adjourn. Motion rejected 202-211: R 8-208; D 193-3 (ND 142-1, SD 51-2); I 1-0, Oct. 1, 1997.

487. HR 2007. Canadian River Reclamation Project/Passage. Thornberry, R-Texas, motion to suspend the rules and pass the bill to direct the Interior Department to allow use of the distribution system for the Texas-based Canadian River reclamation project to transport water from other sources to areas that receive project water. Motion rejected 226-176: R 202-7; D 24-168 (ND 10-130, SD 14-38); I 0-1, Oct. 1, 1997. A two-thirds majority of those present and voting (268 in this case) is required for passage under suspension of the rules.

488. HR 1476. Miccosukee Settlement Act/Passage. Thornberry, R-Texas, motion to suspend the rules and pass the bill to direct the Interior Department to assist in land exchange between the Florida Department of Transportation and the federal government trust that will hold certain lands for the Miccosukee Tribe. Motion rejected 229-176: R 204-8; D 25-167 (ND 14-126, SD 11-41); I 0-1, Oct. 1, 1997. A two-thirds majority of those present and voting (270 in this case) is required for passage under suspension of the rules.

489. HR 1262. SEC Authorization/Passage. Oxley, R-Ohio, motion to suspend the rules and pass the bill to reauthorize, through fiscal 1999, the Securities and Exchange Commission. The bill authorizes spending of $320 million in fiscal 1998 and $343 million in the following year, while limiting, to $100,000 per year, the amount of money the SEC can spend on meetings with foreign governmental officials. Motion rejected 230-170: R 196-14; D 34-155 (ND 21-117, SD 13-38); I 0-1, Oct. 1, 1997. A two-thirds majority of those present and voting (267 in this case) is required for passage under suspension of the rules.

KEY

- Y Voted for (yea).
- # Paired for.
- + Announced for.
- N Voted against (nay).
- X Paired against.
- – Announced against.
- P Voted "present."
- C Voted "present" to avoid possible conflict of interest.
- ? Did not vote or otherwise make a position known.

Democrats ***Republicans***
Independent

	486	487	488	489
ALABAMA				
1 ***Callahan***	N	Y	Y	Y
2 ***Everett***	N	Y	Y	Y
3 ***Riley***	N	Y	Y	Y
4 ***Aderholt***	N	Y	Y	Y
5 Cramer	Y	N	N	Y
6 ***Bachus***	Y	?	Y	Y
7 Hilliard	Y	N	N	N
ALASKA				
AL ***Young***	N	Y	Y	Y
ARIZONA				
1 ***Salmon***	N	Y	Y	Y
2 Pastor	Y	N	N	N
3 ***Stump***	N	Y	Y	N
4 ***Shadegg***	N	Y	Y	Y
5 ***Kolbe***	N	Y	Y	Y
6 ***Hayworth***	N	Y	Y	Y
ARKANSAS				
1 Berry	Y	Y	N	N
2 Snyder	Y	N	N	N
3 ***Hutchinson***	N	Y	Y	Y
4 ***Dickey***	N	Y	Y	Y
CALIFORNIA				
1 ***Riggs***	N	Y	Y	Y
2 ***Herger***	N	Y	Y	Y
3 Fazio	Y	N	N	N
4 ***Doolittle***	N	Y	Y	Y
5 Matsui	Y	N	N	N
6 Woolsey	Y	N	N	N
7 Miller	Y	N	N	N
8 Pelosi	Y	N	N	N
9 Dellums	Y	N	?	?
10 Tauscher	Y	N	N	N
11 ***Pombo***	N	Y	Y	Y
12 Lantos	Y	N	N	N
13 Stark	Y	N	N	N
14 Eshoo	Y	N	Y	N
15 ***Campbell***	N	Y	Y	Y
16 Lofgren	Y	N	N	N
17 Farr	Y	N	Y	N
18 Condit	Y	N	N	N
19 ***Radanovich***	N	Y	Y	Y
20 Dooley	Y	Y	N	N
21 ***Thomas***	N	Y	Y	Y
22 Capps	Y	N	N	N
23 ***Gallegly***	?	?	?	?
24 Sherman	?	?	?	?
25 ***McKeon***	N	Y	Y	Y
26 Berman	?	?	?	?
27 ***Rogan***	N	Y	Y	Y
28 ***Dreier***	N	Y	Y	Y
29 Waxman	Y	N	N	N
30 Becerra	Y	N	N	N
31 Martinez	Y	N	N	N
32 Dixon	Y	N	N	Y
33 Roybal-Allard	Y	N	N	N
34 Torres	Y	N	N	N
35 Waters	Y	P	N	N
36 Harman	Y	N	N	N
37 Millender-McD.	Y	N	N	N
38 ***Horn***	N	Y	Y	Y
39 ***Royce***	N	N	Y	Y
40 ***Lewis***	N	Y	Y	Y
41 ***Kim***	N	Y	Y	Y
42 Brown	Y	N	N	N
43 ***Calvert***	N	Y	Y	Y
44 ***Bono***	N	Y	Y	Y
45 ***Rohrabacher***	N	Y	Y	Y
46 Sanchez	Y	N	N	N
47 ***Cox***	N	Y	Y	Y
48 ***Packard***	N	Y	Y	Y
49 ***Bilbray***	N	Y	Y	Y
50 Filner	Y	N	N	N
51 ***Cunningham***	N	Y	Y	Y
52 ***Hunter***	N	Y	Y	Y
COLORADO				
1 DeGette	Y	N	N	N
2 Skaggs	Y	?	N	Y
3 ***McInnis***	N	Y	Y	Y
4 ***Schaffer***	N	Y	Y	Y
5 ***Hefley***	N	Y	N	N
6 ***Schaefer***	N	N	N	Y
CONNECTICUT				
1 Kennelly	Y	N	Y	N
2 Gejdenson	Y	N	N	N
3 DeLauro	Y	N	N	N
4 ***Shays***	N	Y	Y	Y
5 Maloney	Y	N	N	Y
6 ***Johnson***	N	Y	Y	Y
DELAWARE				
AL ***Castle***	N	Y	Y	Y
FLORIDA				
1 ***Scarborough***	N	Y	Y	Y
2 Boyd	Y	N	N	N
3 Brown	Y	N	Y	N
4 ***Fowler***	N	Y	Y	Y
5 Thurman	Y	N	Y	N
6 ***Stearns***	N	?	Y	Y
7 ***Mica***	N	Y	Y	Y
8 ***McCollum***	N	Y	Y	Y
9 ***Bilirakis***	N	Y	Y	?
10 ***Young***	N	Y	Y	Y
11 Davis	Y	N	Y	N
12 ***Canady***	N	Y	Y	Y
13 ***Miller***	N	Y	Y	Y
14 ***Goss***	N	Y	Y	Y
15 ***Weldon***	N	Y	Y	Y
16 ***Foley***	N	Y	Y	Y
17 Meek	Y	N	Y	N
18 ***Ros-Lehtinen***	?	?	?	?
19 Wexler	Y	?	?	?
20 Deutsch	+	–	+	–
21 ***Diaz-Balart***	N	?	?	?
22 ***Shaw***	Y	Y	Y	Y
23 Hastings	Y	N	Y	N
GEORGIA				
1 ***Kingston***	N	Y	Y	Y
2 Bishop	Y	N	N	N
3 ***Collins***	?	Y	Y	Y
4 McKinney	Y	N	N	N
5 Lewis	Y	N	N	N
6 ***Gingrich***	N			
7 ***Barr***	N	Y	Y	Y
8 ***Chambliss***	N	Y	Y	Y
9 ***Deal***	N	Y	Y	Y
10 ***Norwood***	N	Y	Y	Y
11 ***Linder***	N	Y	Y	Y
HAWAII				
1 Abercrombie	Y	N	Y	Y
2 Mink	Y	N	N	N
IDAHO				
1 ***Chenoweth***	N	Y	N	N
2 ***Crapo***	N	N	Y	Y
ILLINOIS				
1 Rush	Y	N	N	Y
2 Jackson	Y	N	N	N
3 Lipinski	Y	N	N	N
4 Gutierrez	Y	N	N	N
5 Blagojevich	Y	N	N	N
6 ***Hyde***	N	Y	Y	Y
7 Davis	Y	Y	Y	Y
8 ***Crane***	N	Y	Y	Y
9 Yates	Y	N	N	?
10 ***Porter***	N	Y	Y	Y
11 ***Weller***	N	Y	Y	Y
12 Costello	Y	N	N	N
13 ***Fawell***	?	Y	Y	Y
14 ***Hastert***	N	Y	Y	Y
15 ***Ewing***	N	Y	Y	Y

ND Northern Democrats SD Southern Democrats

	486	487	488	489
16 ***Manzullo***	N	Y	Y	N
17 Evans	Y	N	N	N
18 ***LaHood***	N	Y	Y	Y
19 Poshard	Y	N	N	N
20 ***Shimkus***	N	Y	Y	Y
INDIANA				
1 Visclosky	Y	N	N	N
2 ***McIntosh***	N	Y	Y	?
3 Roemer	Y	Y	Y	Y
4 ***Souder***	N	Y	Y	Y
5 ***Buyer***	N	Y	Y	Y
6 ***Burton***	N	?	Y	Y
7 ***Pease***	N	Y	Y	Y
8 ***Hostettler***	N	Y	Y	Y
9 Hamilton	Y	Y	Y	Y
10 Carson	Y	N	N	N
IOWA				
1 ***Leach***	N	Y	Y	Y
2 ***Nussle***	N	Y	Y	Y
3 Boswell	Y	N	N	N
4 ***Ganske***	N	Y	Y	Y
5 ***Latham***	N	Y	Y	Y
KANSAS				
1 ***Moran***	N	Y	Y	Y
2 ***Ryun***	N	Y	Y	Y
3 ***Snowbarger***	N	Y	Y	Y
4 ***Tiahrt***	N	Y	Y	Y
KENTUCKY				
1 ***Whitfield***	N	Y	Y	Y
2 ***Lewis***	N	Y	Y	N
3 ***Northup***	N	Y	Y	Y
4 ***Bunning***	N	Y	Y	Y
5 ***Rogers***	N	Y	Y	Y
6 Baesler	Y	Y	N	Y
LOUISIANA				
1 ***Livingston***	N	Y	Y	Y
2 Jefferson	Y	N	N	N
3 ***Tauzin***	N	Y	Y	Y
4 ***McCrery***	N	Y	Y	N
5 ***Cooksey***	N	Y	Y	Y
6 ***Baker***	N	Y	Y	N
7 John	Y	Y	Y	Y
MAINE				
1 Allen	Y	N	N	N
2 Baldacci	Y	N	N	N
MARYLAND				
1 ***Gilchrest***	N	Y	Y	Y
2 ***Ehrlich***	N	Y	Y	Y
3 Cardin	Y	N	N	Y
4 Wynn	Y	N	N	N
5 Hoyer	Y	N	N	N
6 ***Bartlett***	N	Y	Y	Y
7 Cummings	Y	N	N	N
8 ***Morella***	N	Y	Y	Y
MASSACHUSETTS				
1 Olver	Y	N	N	N
2 Neal	Y	N	N	N
3 McGovern	Y	N	N	N
4 Frank	Y	N	N	N
5 Meehan	Y	N	N	N
6 Tierney	Y	N	N	N
7 Markey	Y	N	N	N
8 Kennedy	Y	N	N	N
9 Moakley	Y	N	N	N
10 Delahunt	Y	Y	Y	Y
MICHIGAN				
1 Stupak	Y	N	N	N
2 ***Hoekstra***	N	Y	Y	Y
3 ***Ehlers***	N	+	Y	Y
4 ***Camp***	N	Y	Y	Y
5 Barcia	Y	N	N	N
6 ***Upton***	N	Y	Y	Y
7 ***Smith***	N	Y	Y	Y
8 Stabenow	Y	N	N	N
9 Kildee	Y	N	Y	N
10 Bonior	Y	N	N	N
11 ***Knollenberg***	N	Y	Y	Y
12 Levin	Y	N	N	N
13 Rivers	Y	N	N	N
14 Conyers	Y	N	N	N
15 Kilpatrick	Y	N	N	N
16 Dingell	Y	N	N	N
MINNESOTA				
1 ***Gutknecht***	N	Y	Y	Y
2 Minge	Y	N	N	N
3 ***Ramstad***	N	Y	Y	Y
4 Vento	Y	N	N	N
5 Sabo	Y	N	N	N
6 Luther	Y	N	N	N
7 Peterson	Y	Y	N	N
8 Oberstar	Y	N	N	N
MISSISSIPPI				
1 ***Wicker***	N	Y	Y	Y
2 Thompson	Y	N	N	N
3 ***Pickering***	N	Y	Y	Y
4 ***Parker***	N	Y	Y	Y
5 Taylor	Y	N	N	N
MISSOURI				
1 Clay	Y	N	N	N
2 ***Talent***	N	Y	Y	Y
3 Gephardt	Y	N	N	?
4 Skelton	Y	N	N	N
5 McCarthy	Y	N	N	N
6 Danner	Y	N	N	Y
7 ***Blunt***	N	Y	Y	Y
8 ***Emerson***	N	Y	Y	Y
9 ***Hulshof***	N	Y	Y	Y
MONTANA				
AL ***Hill***	N	Y	Y	Y
NEBRASKA				
1 ***Bereuter***	N	Y	Y	Y
2 ***Christensen***	N	Y	Y	Y
3 ***Barrett***	N	Y	Y	Y
NEVADA				
1 ***Ensign***	N	Y	Y	Y
2 ***Gibbons***	N	Y	Y	Y
NEW HAMPSHIRE				
1 ***Sununu***	N	Y	Y	Y
2 ***Bass***	N	Y	Y	Y
NEW JERSEY				
1 Andrews	Y	N	N	N
2 ***LoBiondo***	Y	Y	Y	Y
3 ***Saxton***	Y	Y	Y	Y
4 ***Smith***	N	Y	Y	Y
5 ***Roukema***	Y	Y	Y	Y
6 Pallone	Y	N	N	N
7 ***Franks***	N	Y	Y	Y
8 Pascrell	Y	N	N	N
9 Rothman	Y	N	N	Y
10 Payne	Y	N	N	N
11 ***Frelinghuysen***	N	Y	Y	Y
12 ***Pappas***	N	Y	Y	Y
13 Menendez	Y	N	N	N
NEW MEXICO				
1 ***Schiff***	?	?	?	?
2 ***Skeen***	N	N	Y	Y
3 ***Redmond***	N	Y	Y	Y
NEW YORK				
1 ***Forbes***	Y	?	?	?
2 ***Lazio***	N	Y	Y	Y
3 ***King***	Y	?	?	?
4 McCarthy	Y	N	N	N
5 Ackerman	?	?	?	?
6 Flake	Y	N	Y	Y
7 Manton	Y	N	N	Y
8 Nadler	Y	N	N	?
9 Schumer	Y	N	N	Y
10 Towns	Y	N	N	Y
11 Owens	Y	N	N	N
12 Velázquez	Y	N	N	N
13 Vacant				
14 Maloney	Y	N	N	N
15 Rangel	Y	N	N	N
16 Serrano	Y	N	N	N
17 Engel	Y	N	N	N
18 Lowey	?	?	?	?
19 ***Kelly***	N	Y	Y	Y
20 ***Gilman***	?	Y	Y	Y
21 McNulty	Y	?	?	?
22 ***Solomon***	N	Y	Y	Y
23 ***Boehlert***	N	Y	Y	Y
24 ***McHugh***	N	Y	Y	Y
25 ***Walsh***	N	Y	Y	Y
26 Hinchey	Y	N	N	N
27 ***Paxon***	N	Y	Y	Y
28 Slaughter	Y	N	N	N
29 LaFalce	Y	Y	N	Y
30 ***Quinn***	N	Y	Y	Y
31 ***Houghton***	?	?	?	?
NORTH CAROLINA				
1 Clayton	Y	N	N	N
2 Etheridge	Y	N	N	N
3 ***Jones***	–	+	+	+
4 Price	Y	N	N	N
5 ***Burr***	N	?	?	?
6 ***Coble***	N	Y	N	Y
7 McIntyre	Y	Y	Y	Y
8 Hefner	Y	N	N	N
9 ***Myrick***	N	Y	Y	Y
10 ***Ballenger***	N	Y	Y	Y
11 ***Taylor***	?	Y	Y	Y
12 Watt	Y	N	N	N
NORTH DAKOTA				
AL Pomeroy	?	?	?	?
OHIO				
1 ***Chabot***	N	Y	Y	Y
2 ***Portman***	N	Y	Y	Y
3 Hall	Y	Y	Y	Y
4 ***Oxley***	N	Y	Y	Y
5 ***Gillmor***	N	Y	Y	Y
6 Strickland	Y	N	N	N
7 ***Hobson***	N	Y	Y	Y
8 ***Boehner***	N	Y	Y	Y
9 Kaptur	Y	N	N	N
10 Kucinich	Y	Y	Y	Y
11 Stokes	?	?	?	?
12 ***Kasich***	N	Y	Y	Y
13 Brown	Y	N	N	N
14 Sawyer	Y	N	N	N
15 ***Pryce***	N	Y	Y	Y
16 ***Regula***	N	Y	Y	Y
17 Traficant	N	N	Y	Y
18 ***Ney***	N	Y	Y	Y
19 ***LaTourette***	N	Y	Y	Y
OKLAHOMA				
1 ***Largent***	Y	Y	Y	Y
2 ***Coburn***	N	Y	Y	Y
3 ***Watkins***	N	Y	Y	Y
4 ***Watts***	N	Y	Y	Y
5 ***Istook***	N	Y	Y	Y
6 ***Lucas***	N	Y	Y	Y
OREGON				
1 Furse	Y	N	N	N
2 ***Smith***	N	Y	Y	Y
3 Blumenauer	Y	N	N	N
4 DeFazio	Y	N	N	N
5 Hooley	Y	Y	Y	Y
PENNSYLVANIA				
1 Foglietta	?	?	?	?
2 Fattah	Y	N	N	N
3 Borski	Y	N	N	N
4 Klink	Y	N	N	N
5 ***Peterson***	N	Y	Y	Y
6 Holden	Y	N	N	N
7 ***Weldon***	N	Y	?	?
8 ***Greenwood***	N	Y	Y	Y
9 ***Shuster***	N	Y	Y	Y
10 ***McDade***	N	Y	Y	Y
11 Kanjorski	Y	N	N	N
12 Murtha	Y	N	N	N
13 ***Fox***	N	Y	Y	Y
14 Coyne	Y	N	N	N
15 McHale	Y	N	N	N
16 ***Pitts***	N	Y	Y	Y
17 ***Gekas***	N	Y	Y	Y
18 Doyle	Y	N	N	N
19 ***Goodling***	N	Y	Y	Y
20 Mascara	Y	N	N	N
21 ***English***	N	Y	Y	Y
RHODE ISLAND				
1 Kennedy	Y	N	N	N
2 Weygand	Y	N	N	N
SOUTH CAROLINA				
1 ***Sanford***	N	Y	Y	Y
2 ***Spence***	N	Y	Y	Y
3 ***Graham***	N	?	?	?
4 ***Inglis***	N	?	?	?
5 Spratt	Y	N	N	N
6 Clyburn	Y	N	N	N
SOUTH DAKOTA				
AL ***Thune***	N	Y	Y	Y
TENNESSEE				
1 ***Jenkins***	N	Y	Y	Y
2 ***Duncan***	N	Y	Y	N
3 ***Wamp***	?	?	?	?
4 ***Hilleary***	N	Y	Y	Y
5 Clement	Y	N	N	N
6 Gordon	Y	N	N	N
7 ***Bryant***	N	Y	Y	Y
8 Tanner	Y	N	N	N
9 Ford	Y	N	N	N
TEXAS				
1 Sandlin	Y	Y	Y	Y
2 Turner	Y	N	N	N
3 ***Johnson, Sam***	N	Y	Y	Y
4 Hall	N	Y	N	Y
5 ***Sessions***	N	Y	Y	Y
6 ***Barton***	N	Y	Y	Y
7 ***Archer***	N	Y	Y	Y
8 ***Brady***	N	Y	Y	Y
9 Lampson	Y	N	N	N
10 Doggett	Y	N	N	N
11 Edwards	Y	N	N	N
12 ***Granger***	?	?	?	?
13 ***Thornberry***	N	Y	Y	Y
14 ***Paul***	N	Y	Y	N
15 Hinojosa	Y	N	N	N
16 Reyes	Y	N	N	N
17 Stenholm	Y	Y	N	N
18 Jackson-Lee	Y	Y	N	N
19 ***Combest***	N	Y	Y	Y
20 Gonzalez	?	?	?	?
21 ***Smith***	N	Y	Y	Y
22 ***DeLay***	N	Y	Y	Y
23 ***Bonilla***	N	Y	Y	N
24 Frost	Y	N	N	N
25 Bentsen	Y	Y	N	Y
26 ***Armey***	N	Y	Y	Y
27 Ortiz	Y	Y	N	N
28 Rodriguez	Y	Y	N	N
29 Green	Y	Y	N	Y
30 Johnson, E.B.	Y	N	N	Y
UTAH				
1 ***Hansen***	N	Y	Y	Y
2 ***Cook***	N	Y	Y	Y
3 ***Cannon***	N	Y	Y	Y
VERMONT				
AL *Sanders*	Y	N	N	N
VIRGINIA				
1 ***Bateman***	N	Y	Y	Y
2 Pickett	N	Y	Y	Y
3 Scott	Y	N	N	N
4 Sisisky	Y	N	Y	?
5 Goode	Y	Y	Y	Y
6 ***Goodlatte***	N	Y	Y	Y
7 ***Bliley***	N	Y	Y	Y
8 Moran	Y	N	N	Y
9 Boucher	Y	N	N	Y
10 ***Wolf***	N	Y	Y	Y
11 ***Davis***	N	Y	Y	Y
WASHINGTON				
1 ***White***	N	Y	Y	Y
2 ***Metcalf***	N	Y	Y	N
3 ***Smith, Linda***	N	Y	Y	Y
4 ***Hastings***	N	Y	Y	Y
5 ***Nethercutt***	N	Y	Y	Y
6 Dicks	Y	N	N	N
7 McDermott	?	?	?	?
8 ***Dunn***	N	Y	Y	Y
9 Smith, Adam	Y	N	N	N
WEST VIRGINIA				
1 Mollohan	Y	N	N	N
2 Wise	Y	N	N	Y
3 Rahall	Y	N	N	N
WISCONSIN				
1 ***Neumann***	N	N	N	N
2 ***Klug***	N	Y	Y	Y
3 Kind	Y	N	N	N
4 Kleczka	Y	N	N	N
5 Barrett	Y	N	N	N
6 ***Petri***	N	N	N	N
7 Obey	Y	N	N	N
8 Johnson	Y	N	?	N
9 ***Sensenbrenner***	N	N	N	N
WYOMING				
AL ***Cubin***	N	Y	N	Y

Southern states - Ala., Ark., Fla., Ga., Ky., La., Miss., N.C., Okla., S.C., Tenn., Texas, Va.

HOUSE VOTES 490, 491, 492, 493, 494, 495, 496, 497

490. HR 2160. Fiscal 1998 Agriculture Appropriations/Rule. Adoption of the rule (H Res 232) to waive points of order against and provide for House floor consideration of the conference report on the bill to provide $49.7 billion in new budget authority for agriculture programs, rural development, the Food and Drug Administration, and related agencies in fiscal 1998. The conference report would provide $4.1 billion less than the fiscal 1997 level of $53.9 billion and $2.6 billion less than the president's request of $52.3 billion. Adopted 367-34: R 194-19; D 172-15 (ND 128-9, SD 44-6); I 1-0, Oct. 6, 1997.

491. HR 2160. Fiscal 1998 Agriculture Appropriations/Conference Report. Adoption of the conference report on the bill to provide $49.7 billion in new budget authority for agriculture programs, rural development, the Food and Drug Administration, and related agencies in fiscal 1998. The conference report would provide $4.1 billion less than the fiscal 1997 level of $53.9 billion and $2.6 billion less than the president's request of $52.3 billion. Adopted (thus sent to the Senate) 399-18: R 210-10; D 188-8 (ND 139-6, SD 49-2); I 1-0, Oct. 6, 1997.

492. HR 1370. Export-Import Bank Reauthorization/Passage. Passage of the bill to reauthorize the Export-Import Bank through fiscal 2001. Passed 378-38: R 186-33; D 191-5 (ND 139-5, SD 52-0); I 1-0, Oct. 6, 1997. Subsequently, S 1026, a similar Senate-passed bill was passed in lieu after being amended to contain the text of HR 1370 as passed by the House; and HR 1370 was laid on the table.

493. HR 1127. National Monument Designation/Congressional Consent. Vento, D-Minn., amendment to strike the bill's provision to require the president to obtain congressional approval for proposed national monuments in excess of 50,000 acres. The amendment instead would establish a one-year delay from the time the president announces a monument designation to when the designation actually would take effect. Rejected 201-224: R 22-202; D 178-22 (ND 139-10, SD 39-12); I 1-0, Oct. 7, 1997.

494. HR 1127. National Monument Designation/Hansen Substitute. Hansen, R-Utah, substitute amendment to allow the president to designate national monuments in excess of 50,000 acres but require termination of the monument within two years unless Congress adopts a joint resolution approving the monument. The substitute also would require the president to notify the governor of the state in which the monument is to be located and seek the governor's written comments at least 30 days prior to the monument declaration. Adopted 222-202: R 199-25; D 23-176 (ND 11-137, SD 12-39); I 0-1, Oct. 7, 1997.

495. HR 1127. National Monument Designation/Passage. Passage of the bill to allow the president to unilaterally designate national monuments but require termination of a monument in excess of 50,000 acres within two years unless Congress adopts a joint resolution approving the monument. The bill also would require the president to notify the governor of the state in which the monument is to be located and seek the governor's written comments at least 30 days prior to the monument declaration. Passed 229-197: R 202-23; D 27-173 (ND 11-138, SD 16-35); I 0-1, Oct. 7, 1997. A "nay" was a vote in support of the president's position.

496. HR 2159. Fiscal 1998 Foreign Operations Appropriations/Motion To Instruct. Largent, R-Okla., motion to instruct the House conferees to insist on the House provision to prohibit funding to any private, non-governmental or multilateral organization that directly or indirectly performs abortions in a foreign country, except in cases of rape, incest or when the life of the mother is endangered. Motion agreed to 233-194: R 193-32; D 40-161 (ND 31-118, SD 9-43); I 0-1, Oct. 7, 1997.

497. HR 629. Texas Low-Level Radioactive Waste Disposal Compact/Passage. Passage of the bill to give congressional approval to a compact between Texas, Maine and Vermont that allows them to dispose of their low-level radioactive waste at a proposed site in Sierra Blanca, Texas. Passed 309-107: R 189-36; D 119-71 (ND 79-61, SD 40-10); I 1-0, Oct. 7, 1997.

KEY

- Y Voted for (yea).
- # Paired for.
- \+ Announced for.
- N Voted against (nay).
- X Paired against.
- – Announced against.
- P Voted "present."
- C Voted "present" to avoid possible conflict of interest.
- ? Did not vote or otherwise make a position known.

Democrats ***Republicans***
Independent

	490	491	492	493	494	495	496	497
ALABAMA								
1 ***Callahan***	Y	Y	Y	N	Y	Y	Y	Y
2 ***Everett***	Y	Y	Y	N	Y	Y	Y	Y
3 ***Riley***	Y	Y	Y	N	Y	Y	Y	Y
4 ***Aderholt***	Y	Y	Y	N	Y	Y	Y	Y
5 Cramer	Y	Y	Y	Y	Y	Y	Y	Y
6 ***Bachus***	Y	Y	Y	N	Y	Y	Y	N
7 Hilliard	?	?	?	?	?	?	?	?
ALASKA								
AL ***Young***	N	Y	Y	N	Y	Y	Y	Y
ARIZONA								
1 ***Salmon***	Y	N	Y	N	Y	Y	Y	Y
2 Pastor	Y	Y	Y	Y	N	N	N	?
3 ***Stump***	Y	Y	Y	N	Y	Y	Y	Y
4 ***Shadegg***	N	Y	N	N	Y	Y	Y	Y
5 ***Kolbe***	Y	Y	Y	N	Y	Y	N	Y
6 ***Hayworth***	Y	Y	N	N	Y	Y	Y	Y
ARKANSAS								
1 Berry	Y	Y	Y	N	N	Y	Y	Y
2 Snyder	Y	Y	Y	Y	N	N	N	Y
3 ***Hutchinson***	Y	Y	Y	N	Y	Y	Y	Y
4 ***Dickey***	Y	Y	Y	N	Y	Y	Y	Y
CALIFORNIA								
1 ***Riggs***	Y	Y	Y	N	Y	Y	Y	Y
2 ***Herger***	Y	Y	Y	N	Y	Y	Y	Y
3 Fazio	Y	Y	Y	Y	N	N	N	Y
4 ***Doolittle***	Y	Y	Y	N	Y	Y	Y	N
5 Matsui	Y	Y	Y	Y	N	N	N	?
6 Woolsey	Y	Y	Y	Y	Y	N	N	Y
7 Miller	N	N	Y	Y	N	N	N	Y
8 Pelosi	?	Y	Y	Y	N	N	N	Y
9 Dellums	Y	Y	Y	Y	N	N	N	N
10 Tauscher	Y	Y	Y	Y	N	N	N	Y
11 ***Pombo***	?	?	?	N	N	Y	Y	N
12 Lantos	Y	Y	Y	Y	N	N	N	N
13 Stark	Y	Y	Y	Y	N	N	N	Y
14 Eshoo	Y	Y	Y	Y	N	N	N	Y
15 ***Campbell***	Y	N	N	N	Y	Y	N	Y
16 Lofgren	Y	N	Y	Y	N	N	N	Y
17 Farr	Y	Y	Y	Y	N	N	N	Y
18 Condit	N	Y	Y	N	Y	Y	N	Y
19 ***Radanovich***	Y	Y	N	N	Y	Y	Y	Y
20 Dooley	?	Y	Y	Y	Y	Y	N	Y
21 ***Thomas***	Y	Y	Y	N	Y	Y	Y	Y
22 Capps	Y	Y	Y	Y	N	N	N	N
23 ***Gallegly***	Y	Y	Y	N	Y	Y	Y	Y
24 Sherman	Y	Y	Y	Y	N	N	?	Y
25 ***McKeon***	Y	Y	Y	N	Y	Y	Y	Y
26 Berman	Y	Y	Y	Y	Y	N	N	Y
27 ***Rogan***	Y	Y	N	N	Y	Y	Y	N
28 ***Dreier***	Y	Y	Y	N	Y	Y	Y	Y
29 Waxman	Y	Y	Y	Y	N	N	N	?
30 Becerra	?	?	Y	Y	?	?	N	?
31 Martinez	Y	Y	Y	Y	N	N	N	Y
32 Dixon	?	Y	Y	Y	N	N	N	N
33 Roybal-Allard	Y	Y	Y	Y	N	N	N	N
34 Torres	Y	Y	Y	Y	N	N	N	N
35 Waters	Y	Y	Y	Y	N	N	N	Y
36 Harman	Y	Y	Y	Y	N	N	N	Y
37 Millender-McD.	Y	Y	Y	Y	N	N	N	N
38 ***Horn***	Y	Y	Y	N	Y	Y	N	Y
39 ***Royce***	?	N	N	N	Y	Y	Y	Y
40 ***Lewis***	?	Y	Y	?	Y	Y	N	N
41 ***Kim***	Y	Y	Y	N	Y	Y	Y	Y
42 Brown	Y	Y	Y	Y	N	N	N	Y
43 ***Calvert***	Y	Y	Y	N	Y	Y	Y	N
44 ***Bono***	Y	Y	Y	N	Y	Y	Y	Y
45 ***Rohrabacher***	N	N	N	N	Y	Y	Y	Y
46 Sanchez	Y	Y	Y	Y	N	N	N	N
47 ***Cox***	Y	Y	N	N	Y	Y	Y	Y
48 ***Packard***	Y	Y	Y	N	Y	Y	Y	Y
49 ***Bilbray***	?	Y	Y	N	Y	Y	N	Y
50 Filner	Y	Y	Y	Y	N	N	N	N
51 ***Cunningham***	Y	Y	Y	N	Y	Y	Y	Y
52 ***Hunter***	?	Y	Y	N	Y	Y	Y	N
COLORADO								
1 DeGette	Y	Y	Y	Y	N	N	N	Y
2 Skaggs	Y	Y	Y	Y	N	N	N	Y
3 ***McInnis***	Y	Y	Y	N	Y	Y	Y	Y
4 ***Schaffer***	Y	Y	Y	N	Y	Y	Y	Y
5 ***Hefley***	?	Y	Y	N	Y	Y	Y	Y
6 ***Schaefer***	Y	Y	Y	N	Y	Y	Y	Y
CONNECTICUT								
1 Kennelly	Y	Y	Y	Y	N	N	N	N
2 Gejdenson	Y	Y	Y	Y	N	N	N	N
3 DeLauro	Y	Y	Y	Y	N	N	N	N
4 ***Shays***	Y	Y	Y	Y	N	N	N	N
5 Maloney	Y	Y	Y	Y	N	N	N	N
6 ***Johnson***	Y	Y	Y	Y	N	N	N	N
DELAWARE								
AL ***Castle***	Y	Y	Y	Y	Y	Y	N	N
FLORIDA								
1 ***Scarborough***	N	N	N	N	Y	Y	Y	Y
2 Boyd	Y	Y	Y	N	Y	Y	N	Y
3 Brown	?	?	?	Y	N	N	N	Y
4 ***Fowler***	Y	Y	Y	N	Y	Y	Y	Y
5 Thurman	N	Y	Y	Y	N	N	N	?
6 ***Stearns***	Y	N	N	N	Y	Y	Y	Y
7 ***Mica***	Y	Y	Y	N	Y	Y	Y	Y
8 ***McCollum***	Y	Y	Y	N	Y	Y	Y	Y
9 ***Bilirakis***	Y	Y	N	N	Y	Y	Y	Y
10 ***Young***	Y	Y	Y	N	N	Y	Y	Y
11 Davis	Y	Y	Y	Y	N	N	N	Y
12 ***Canady***	Y	Y	Y	N	Y	Y	Y	Y
13 ***Miller***	Y	Y	N	N	Y	Y	Y	Y
14 ***Goss***	Y	Y	Y	N	Y	Y	Y	Y
15 ***Weldon***	Y	Y	Y	N	Y	Y	Y	Y
16 ***Foley***	Y	Y	Y	N	Y	Y	Y	Y
17 Meek	?	Y	Y	Y	N	N	N	Y
18 ***Ros-Lehtinen***	Y	Y	Y	N	Y	Y	Y	N
19 Wexler	Y	Y	Y	Y	N	N	N	Y
20 Deutsch	N	Y	Y	Y	N	N	N	Y
21 ***Diaz-Balart***	Y	Y	Y	N	Y	Y	Y	N
22 ***Shaw***	Y	Y	Y	N	Y	Y	Y	Y
23 Hastings	Y	Y	Y	Y	N	N	N	Y
GEORGIA								
1 ***Kingston***	Y	Y	Y	N	Y	Y	Y	Y
2 Bishop	Y	Y	Y	N	Y	Y	N	Y
3 ***Collins***	Y	Y	Y	N	Y	Y	Y	Y
4 McKinney	?	Y	Y	Y	N	N	N	N
5 Lewis	Y	Y	Y	Y	N	N	N	N
6 ***Gingrich***							Y	
7 ***Barr***	?	Y	N	N	Y	Y	Y	Y
8 ***Chambliss***	Y	Y	Y	N	Y	Y	Y	Y
9 ***Deal***	N	Y	Y	N	Y	Y	Y	N
10 ***Norwood***	N	Y	Y	N	Y	Y	Y	Y
11 ***Linder***	Y	Y	Y	N	Y	Y	Y	Y
HAWAII								
1 Abercrombie	Y	Y	Y	Y	N	N	N	Y
2 Mink	Y	Y	Y	Y	N	N	N	Y
IDAHO								
1 ***Chenoweth***	Y	Y	Y	N	N	Y	Y	Y
2 ***Crapo***	Y	Y	Y	N	Y	Y	Y	Y
ILLINOIS								
1 Rush	Y	Y	Y	Y	N	N	N	N
2 Jackson	Y	Y	Y	Y	N	N	N	N
3 Lipinski	Y	Y	Y	Y	N	N	Y	N
4 Gutierrez	Y	Y	Y	Y	N	N	N	N
5 Blagojevich	Y	Y	Y	Y	N	N	N	N
6 ***Hyde***	Y	Y	Y	N	Y	Y	Y	Y
7 Davis	Y	Y	Y	Y	N	N	N	N
8 ***Crane***	Y	Y	Y	N	Y	Y	Y	Y
9 Yates	Y	Y	Y	Y	N	N	N	N
10 ***Porter***	Y	Y	Y	Y	N	N	N	Y
11 ***Weller***	Y	Y	Y	N	Y	Y	Y	N
12 Costello	N	Y	Y	Y	N	N	Y	N
13 ***Fawell***	Y	Y	Y	Y	Y	Y	N	Y
14 ***Hastert***	Y	Y	Y	N	Y	Y	Y	Y
15 ***Ewing***	Y	Y	Y	N	Y	N	Y	Y

ND Northern Democrats SD Southern Democrats

	490	491	492	493	494	495	496	497
16 *Manzullo*	Y	?	Y	N	Y	Y	Y	Y
17 Evans	Y	Y	Y	Y	N	N	N	N
18 *LaHood*	Y	Y	Y	N	Y	Y	Y	N
19 Poshard	N	Y	Y	Y	N	N	Y	N
20 *Shimkus*	Y	Y	Y	N	Y	Y	Y	Y
INDIANA								
1 Visclosky	Y	Y	Y	Y	N	N	N	–
2 *McIntosh*	Y	Y	N	N	Y	Y	Y	Y
3 Roemer	Y	Y	Y	Y	N	N	Y	Y
4 *Souder*	N	Y	Y	N	Y	Y	Y	N
5 *Buyer*	Y	Y	Y	N	Y	Y	Y	Y
6 *Burton*	Y	Y	Y	N	Y	Y	Y	Y
7 *Pease*	Y	Y	Y	N	Y	N	Y	Y
8 *Hostettler*	Y	Y	N	N	Y	Y	Y	Y
9 Hamilton	Y	Y	Y	Y	N	N	Y	Y
10 Carson	Y	Y	Y	Y	N	N	N	Y
IOWA								
1 *Leach*	Y	Y	Y	Y	N	N	N	Y
2 *Nussle*	N	Y	Y	N	Y	Y	Y	Y
3 Boswell	Y	Y	Y	N	Y	Y	N	Y
4 *Ganske*	N	Y	N	N	Y	Y	Y	Y
5 *Latham*	Y	Y	Y	N	Y	Y	Y	Y
KANSAS								
1 *Moran*	Y	Y	Y	N	Y	Y	Y	Y
2 *Ryun*	Y	Y	Y	N	Y	Y	Y	Y
3 *Snowbarger*	Y	Y	Y	N	Y	Y	Y	Y
4 *Tiahrt*	Y	Y	Y	N	Y	Y	Y	Y
KENTUCKY								
1 *Whitfield*	N	Y	?	N	Y	Y	Y	Y
2 *Lewis*	Y	Y	Y	N	Y	Y	Y	Y
3 *Northup*	Y	Y	Y	N	Y	Y	Y	Y
4 *Bunning*	Y	Y	Y	N	Y	Y	Y	Y
5 *Rogers*	Y	Y	Y	N	Y	Y	Y	Y
6 Baesler	N	Y	Y	N	N	Y	N	N
LOUISIANA								
1 *Livingston*	Y	Y	Y	N	Y	Y	P	Y
2 Jefferson	Y	Y	Y	Y	?	?	N	?
3 *Tauzin*	Y	Y	Y	N	Y	Y	Y	Y
4 *McCrery*	Y	Y	Y	N	Y	Y	Y	Y
5 *Cooksey*	Y	Y	Y	N	?	Y	Y	Y
6 *Baker*	Y	Y	Y	N	Y	Y	Y	Y
7 John	Y	Y	Y	Y	N	N	Y	Y
MAINE								
1 Allen	Y	Y	Y	Y	N	N	N	Y
2 Baldacci	?	Y	Y	Y	N	N	N	Y
MARYLAND								
1 *Gilchrest*	Y	Y	Y	N	Y	Y	N	Y
2 *Ehrlich*	Y	Y	Y	N	Y	Y	N	Y
3 Cardin	Y	Y	Y	Y	N	N	N	?
4 Wynn	Y	Y	Y	Y	N	N	N	Y
5 Hoyer	Y	Y	Y	Y	N	N	N	Y
6 *Bartlett*	Y	Y	Y	N	Y	Y	Y	Y
7 Cummings	Y	Y	Y	Y	N	N	N	N
8 *Morella*	Y	Y	Y	Y	N	N	N	N
MASSACHUSETTS								
1 Olver	Y	Y	Y	Y	N	N	N	N
2 Neal	Y	Y	Y	Y	N	N	Y	?
3 McGovern	Y	Y	Y	Y	N	N	N	N
4 Frank	Y	Y	Y	Y	N	N	N	N
5 Meehan	Y	Y	Y	Y	N	N	N	N
6 Tierney	Y	Y	Y	Y	N	N	N	N
7 Markey	Y	Y	Y	Y	N	N	N	N
8 Kennedy	Y	Y	Y	Y	N	N	N	N
9 Moakley	Y	Y	Y	Y	N	N	Y	N
10 Delahunt	Y	Y	Y	Y	N	N	N	N
MICHIGAN								
1 Stupak	Y	Y	Y	Y	N	Y	Y	Y
2 *Hoekstra*	Y	Y	N	N	Y	Y	Y	Y
3 *Ehlers*	Y	Y	Y	N	Y	N	Y	Y
4 *Camp*	Y	Y	Y	N	Y	Y	Y	Y
5 Barcia	Y	Y	Y	Y	Y	Y	Y	Y
6 *Upton*	Y	Y	Y	N	Y	Y	N	Y
7 *Smith*	Y	Y	N	N	Y	Y	Y	Y
8 Stabenow	Y	Y	Y	Y	N	N	N	Y
9 Kildee	Y	Y	Y	Y	N	N	Y	Y
10 Bonior	Y	Y	N	Y	N	N	Y	Y
11 *Knollenberg*	Y	Y	Y	N	Y	Y	Y	Y
12 Levin	Y	Y	Y	Y	N	N	N	Y
13 Rivers	Y	Y	Y	Y	N	N	N	Y
14 Conyers	?	N	Y	Y	N	N	N	N
15 Kilpatrick	Y	Y	Y	Y	N	N	N	Y
16 Dingell	Y	Y	Y	Y	N	N	N	Y
MINNESOTA								
1 *Gutknecht*	Y	Y	Y	N	Y	Y	Y	Y
2 Minge	N	Y	Y	Y	N	N	N	Y

	490	491	492	493	494	495	496	497
3 *Ramstad*	Y	Y	Y	Y	N	N	N	Y
4 Vento	Y	Y	Y	Y	N	N	N	Y
5 Sabo	Y	Y	Y	Y	N	N	N	Y
6 Luther	Y	Y	Y	Y	N	N	N	Y
7 Peterson	N	Y	Y	N	Y	Y	Y	Y
8 Oberstar	Y	Y	Y	N	Y	Y	Y	Y
MISSISSIPPI								
1 *Wicker*	Y	Y	Y	N	Y	Y	Y	Y
2 Thompson	Y	Y	Y	?	?	?	?	Y
3 *Pickering*	Y	Y	Y	N	Y	Y	Y	Y
4 *Parker*	Y	Y	Y	N	Y	Y	Y	Y
5 Taylor	N	N	Y	Y	N	N	Y	Y
MISSOURI								
1 Clay	Y	Y	Y	Y	N	N	N	Y
2 *Talent*	Y	Y	Y	N	Y	Y	Y	Y
3 Gephardt	?	?	?	Y	N	N	N	Y
4 Skelton	Y	Y	Y	Y	Y	Y	Y	Y
5 McCarthy	Y	Y	Y	Y	N	N	N	Y
6 Danner	Y	Y	Y	N	Y	Y	Y	Y
7 *Blunt*	Y	Y	Y	N	Y	Y	Y	Y
8 *Emerson*	Y	Y	Y	N	Y	Y	Y	Y
9 *Hulshof*	Y	Y	Y	N	Y	Y	Y	Y
MONTANA								
AL *Hill*	Y	Y	Y	N	Y	Y	Y	Y
NEBRASKA								
1 *Bereuter*	Y	Y	Y	N	Y	Y	Y	Y
2 *Christensen*	Y	Y	Y	N	Y	Y	Y	Y
3 *Barrett*	Y	Y	Y	N	Y	Y	Y	Y
NEVADA								
1 *Ensign*	Y	N	Y	N	Y	Y	Y	N
2 *Gibbons*	Y	Y	Y	N	Y	Y	N	N
NEW HAMPSHIRE								
1 *Sununu*	N	Y	Y	N	Y	Y	Y	Y
2 *Bass*	Y	Y	N	N	Y	Y	N	Y
NEW JERSEY								
1 Andrews	Y	N	N	Y	N	N	N	N
2 *LoBiondo*	Y	Y	Y	Y	N	N	Y	N
3 *Saxton*	Y	Y	Y	Y	N	N	Y	Y
4 *Smith*	Y	Y	Y	Y	N	N	Y	N
5 *Roukema*	Y	Y	Y	Y	N	N	N	Y
6 Pallone	Y	Y	Y	Y	N	N	N	N
7 *Franks*	Y	Y	Y	Y	N	N	N	N
8 Pascrell	Y	Y	Y	Y	N	N	N	N
9 Rothman	Y	Y	Y	Y	N	N	N	N
10 Payne	Y	Y	Y	Y	N	N	N	N
11 *Frelinghuysen*	Y	Y	Y	N	Y	Y	N	Y
12 *Pappas*	Y	Y	Y	N	Y	Y	Y	N
13 Menendez	Y	Y	Y	Y	N	N	N	N
NEW MEXICO								
1 *Schiff*	?	?	?	?	?	?	?	?
2 *Skeen*	Y	Y	Y	N	Y	Y	Y	N
3 *Redmond*	Y	Y	Y	N	Y	Y	Y	Y
NEW YORK								
1 *Forbes*	Y	Y	Y	Y	N	N	Y	N
2 *Lazio*	Y	Y	Y	Y	N	N	N	Y
3 *King*	Y	Y	Y	Y	N	Y	Y	Y
4 McCarthy	Y	Y	Y	Y	N	N	N	Y
5 Ackerman	Y	Y	Y	Y	N	N	N	N
6 Flake	Y	Y	Y	Y	N	N	N	Y
7 Manton	Y	Y	Y	Y	N	N	Y	Y
8 Nadler	Y	Y	Y	Y	N	N	N	N
9 Schumer	?	?	?	Y	N	N	N	N
10 Towns	Y	Y	Y	Y	N	N	N	Y
11 Owens	?	?	?	Y	N	N	N	Y
12 Velázquez	Y	Y	Y	Y	N	N	N	N
13 Vacant								
14 Maloney	?	Y	?	Y	N	N	N	N
15 Rangel	Y	Y	?	Y	N	N	N	?
16 Serrano	Y	Y	Y	Y	N	N	N	Y
17 Engel	Y	Y	Y	Y	N	N	N	Y
18 Lowey	Y	Y	Y	Y	N	N	N	Y
19 *Kelly*	Y	Y	Y	Y	N	N	N	N
20 *Gilman*	+	Y	+	Y	N	N	N	N
21 McNulty	Y	Y	Y	Y	N	N	N	N
22 *Solomon*	Y	Y	N	N	Y	Y	Y	Y
23 *Boehlert*	Y	Y	Y	N	Y	Y	N	Y
24 *McHugh*	Y	Y	Y	N	Y	Y	Y	Y
25 *Walsh*	Y	Y	Y	N	N	N	Y	Y
26 Hinchey	Y	Y	Y	Y	N	N	N	N
27 *Paxon*	Y	Y	Y	N	Y	Y	Y	Y
28 Slaughter	Y	Y	Y	Y	N	N	N	N
29 LaFalce	Y	Y	Y	?	?	N	Y	Y
30 *Quinn*	Y	Y	Y	N	N	N	Y	Y
31 *Houghton*	Y	Y	Y	Y	Y	Y	N	Y

	490	491	492	493	494	495	496	497
NORTH CAROLINA								
1 Clayton	Y	Y	Y	+	N	N	N	Y
2 Etheridge	Y	Y	Y	Y	N	N	N	Y
3 *Jones*	N	Y	N	N	Y	Y	Y	Y
4 Price	Y	Y	Y	Y	N	N	N	N
5 *Burr*	N	Y	Y	N	Y	Y	Y	Y
6 *Coble*	N	Y	N	N	Y	Y	Y	Y
7 McIntyre	Y	Y	Y	Y	N	N	Y	Y
8 Hefner	Y	Y	Y	Y	N	N	N	Y
9 *Myrick*	Y	Y	Y	N	Y	Y	Y	Y
10 *Ballenger*	N	Y	Y	N	Y	Y	Y	Y
11 *Taylor*	Y	Y	Y	N	Y	Y	Y	Y
12 Watt	Y	Y	Y	Y	N	N	N	N
NORTH DAKOTA								
AL Pomeroy	Y	Y	Y	Y	N	N	N	Y
OHIO								
1 *Chabot*	Y	Y	N	N	Y	Y	Y	Y
2 *Portman*	Y	Y	Y	N	Y	Y	Y	Y
3 Hall	Y	Y	Y	Y	N	N	Y	?
4 *Oxley*	Y	Y	Y	N	Y	Y	Y	Y
5 *Gillmor*	Y	Y	Y	N	Y	Y	Y	Y
6 Strickland	Y	Y	Y	Y	N	N	N	N
7 *Hobson*	Y	Y	Y	N	Y	Y	N	Y
8 *Boehner*	Y	Y	Y	N	Y	Y	Y	Y
9 Kaptur	Y	Y	Y	Y	N	N	Y	Y
10 Kucinich	Y	N	Y	Y	N	N	Y	N
11 Stokes	Y	Y	Y	Y	N	N	N	Y
12 *Kasich*	Y	Y	Y	N	Y	Y	Y	N
13 Brown	Y	Y	Y	Y	N	N	N	Y
14 Sawyer	Y	Y	Y	Y	N	N	N	Y
15 *Pryce*	Y	Y	Y	N	Y	Y	N	Y
16 *Regula*	Y	Y	Y	N	Y	Y	Y	Y
17 Traficant	Y	Y	Y	N	Y	Y	Y	Y
18 *Ney*	Y	Y	Y	N	Y	Y	Y	Y
19 *LaTourette*	Y	Y	Y	N	Y	Y	Y	Y
OKLAHOMA								
1 *Largent*	N	Y	N	N	Y	Y	Y	Y
2 *Coburn*	?	?	?	N	Y	Y	Y	Y
3 *Watkins*	Y	Y	Y	N	Y	Y	Y	Y
4 *Watts*	Y	Y	N	N	Y	Y	Y	Y
5 *Istook*	Y	Y	Y	N	Y	Y	Y	Y
6 *Lucas*	Y	Y	Y	N	Y	Y	Y	Y
OREGON								
1 Furse	Y	Y	Y	Y	N	N	N	Y
2 *Smith*	#	?	?	N	Y	Y	Y	Y
3 Blumenauer	Y	Y	Y	Y	N	N	N	Y
4 DeFazio	N	N	N	Y	N	N	N	N
5 Hooley	Y	Y	Y	Y	N	N	N	N
PENNSYLVANIA								
1 Foglietta	?	?	?	Y	N	N	N	Y
2 Fattah	Y	Y	Y	Y	N	N	N	Y
3 Borski	Y	Y	Y	Y	N	N	Y	Y
4 Klink	N	Y	Y	N	N	Y	Y	Y
5 *Peterson*	Y	Y	Y	N	Y	Y	Y	Y
6 Holden	Y	Y	Y	N	N	N	Y	N
7 *Weldon*	Y	Y	Y	N	Y	Y	Y	Y
8 *Greenwood*	?	?	?	N	Y	Y	N	Y
9 *Shuster*	Y	Y	Y	N	Y	Y	Y	Y
10 *McDade*	Y	Y	Y	N	Y	Y	Y	N
11 Kanjorski	Y	Y	Y	Y	N	N	Y	N
12 Murtha	Y	Y	Y	N	N	N	Y	N
13 *Fox*	Y	Y	Y	Y	N	N	Y	Y
14 Coyne	Y	Y	Y	Y	N	N	N	N
15 McHale	N	Y	Y	Y	N	N	N	Y
16 *Pitts*	Y	Y	Y	N	Y	Y	Y	Y
17 *Gekas*	Y	Y	Y	N	Y	Y	Y	Y
18 Doyle	Y	Y	Y	N	N	N	Y	N
19 *Goodling*	Y	Y	Y	N	Y	Y	Y	Y
20 Mascara	Y	Y	Y	Y	N	N	Y	Y
21 *English*	Y	Y	Y	Y	N	N	Y	N
RHODE ISLAND								
1 Kennedy	Y	Y	Y	Y	N	N	N	N
2 Weygand	+	+	+	+	–	–	+	N
SOUTH CAROLINA								
1 *Sanford*	Y	Y	N	N	Y	Y	Y	Y
2 *Spence*	Y	Y	Y	N	Y	Y	Y	Y
3 *Graham*	N	Y	Y	N	Y	Y	Y	Y
4 *Inglis*	Y	Y	Y	N	Y	Y	Y	Y
5 Spratt	Y	Y	Y	Y	N	N	N	Y
6 Clyburn	Y	Y	Y	Y	N	N	N	Y
SOUTH DAKOTA								
AL *Thune*	Y	Y	Y	N	Y	Y	Y	Y
TENNESSEE								
1 *Jenkins*	Y	Y	Y	N	Y	Y	Y	Y
2 *Duncan*	Y	Y	N	N	Y	Y	Y	Y

	490	491	492	493	494	495	496	
3 *Wamp*	Y	Y	N	N	Y	Y	Y	Y
4 *Hilleary*	Y	Y	N	N	Y	Y	Y	Y
5 Clement	Y	Y	Y	Y	N	N	N	Y
6 Gordon	Y	Y	Y	Y	N	N	N	Y
7 *Bryant*	Y	Y	Y	N	Y	Y	Y	Y
8 Tanner	Y	Y	Y	Y	Y	Y	N	?
9 Ford	Y	Y	Y	Y	N	N	N	Y
TEXAS								
1 Sandlin	Y	Y	Y	Y	Y	Y	N	Y
2 Turner	Y	Y	Y	N	N	Y	N	Y
3 *Johnson, Sam*	Y	Y	Y	N	Y	Y	Y	Y
4 Hall	Y	Y	Y	N	Y	Y	Y	Y
5 *Sessions*	Y	Y	Y	N	Y	Y	Y	Y
6 *Barton*	N	Y	Y	N	Y	Y	Y	Y
7 *Archer*	Y	Y	Y	N	Y	Y	Y	Y
8 *Brady*	Y	Y	Y	N	Y	Y	Y	Y
9 Lampson	Y	Y	Y	Y	N	N	N	Y
10 Doggett	Y	N	Y	Y	N	N	N	N
11 Edwards	Y	Y	Y	N	Y	Y	N	Y
12 *Granger*	Y	Y	Y	N	Y	Y	Y	Y
13 *Thornberry*	Y	Y	Y	N	Y	Y	Y	Y
14 *Paul*	Y	N	N	N	N	Y	Y	N
15 Hinojosa	Y	Y	Y	Y	N	N	N	N
16 Reyes	Y	Y	Y	Y	N	N	N	N
17 Stenholm	N	Y	Y	N	Y	Y	Y	Y
18 Jackson-Lee	Y	Y	Y	Y	N	N	N	Y
19 *Combest*	Y	Y	Y	N	Y	Y	Y	Y
20 Gonzalez	?	?	?	?	?	?	?	?
21 *Smith*	Y	Y	Y	N	Y	Y	Y	Y
22 *DeLay*	Y	Y	Y	N	Y	Y	Y	Y
23 *Bonilla*	Y	Y	Y	N	Y	Y	Y	N
24 Frost	Y	Y	Y	Y	N	N	N	Y
25 Bentsen	Y	Y	Y	Y	N	N	N	Y
26 *Armey*	Y	Y	N	N	Y	Y	Y	Y
27 Ortiz	Y	Y	Y	N	Y	Y	Y	N
28 Rodriguez	Y	Y	Y	Y	N	N	N	N
29 Green	Y	Y	Y	Y	N	Y	N	Y
30 Johnson, E.B.	Y	Y	Y	Y	N	N	N	Y
UTAH								
1 *Hansen*	Y	Y	Y	N	Y	Y	Y	Y
2 *Cook*	Y	Y	Y	N	Y	Y	Y	Y
3 *Cannon*	Y	Y	Y	N	Y	Y	Y	Y
VERMONT								
AL Sanders	Y	Y	Y	Y	N	N	N	Y
VIRGINIA								
1 *Bateman*	Y	Y	Y	N	Y	Y	Y	Y
2 Pickett	Y	Y	Y	N	Y	Y	N	Y
3 Scott	Y	Y	Y	Y	N	N	N	Y
4 Sisisky	Y	Y	Y	N	Y	Y	N	Y
5 Goode	N	Y	Y	N	Y	Y	Y	Y
6 *Goodlatte*	Y	Y	Y	N	Y	Y	Y	Y
7 *Bliley*	Y	Y	Y	N	Y	Y	Y	Y
8 Moran	Y	Y	Y	Y	N	N	N	Y
9 Boucher	Y	?	Y	Y	N	N	N	Y
10 *Wolf*	Y	Y	Y	N	Y	Y	Y	Y
11 *Davis*	Y	Y	Y	Y	N	N	N	N
WASHINGTON								
1 *White*	Y	Y	Y	N	Y	Y	N	Y
2 *Metcalf*	Y	Y	Y	N	Y	Y	Y	Y
3 *Smith, Linda*	Y	Y	Y	N	Y	Y	Y	Y
4 *Hastings*	Y	Y	Y	N	Y	Y	Y	Y
5 *Nethercutt*	Y	Y	Y	N	Y	Y	Y	N
6 Dicks	?	Y	Y	Y	N	N	N	Y
7 McDermott	Y	Y	N	Y	N	N	N	?
8 *Dunn*	Y	Y	Y	N	Y	Y	Y	Y
9 Smith, Adam	Y	Y	Y	Y	N	N	N	Y
WEST VIRGINIA								
1 Mollohan	Y	Y	Y	Y	N	N	Y	N
2 Wise	Y	Y	Y	Y	N	N	N	?
3 Rahall	+	Y	Y	Y	N	N	Y	Y
WISCONSIN								
1 *Neumann*	Y	Y	Y	N	Y	Y	Y	Y
2 *Klug*	N	Y	Y	N	Y	Y	N	Y
3 Kind	Y	Y	Y	Y	N	N	N	Y
4 Kleczka	Y	Y	Y	Y	N	N	Y	N
5 Barrett	Y	Y	Y	Y	N	N	N	Y
6 *Petri*	Y	Y	N	N	Y	Y	Y	N
7 Obey	Y	Y	Y	Y	N	N	N	Y
8 Johnson	Y	Y	N	Y	N	N	N	Y
9 *Sensenbrenner*	Y	N	N	N	Y	Y	Y	N
WYOMING								
AL *Cubin*	X	N	Y	N	Y	Y	Y	Y

Southern states - Ala., Ark., Fla., Ga., Ky., La., Miss., N.C., Okla., S.C., Tenn., Texas, Va.

HOUSE VOTES 498, 499, 500, 501, 502, 503, 504, 505

498. HR 901. U.N. Land Designation/Ramsar Convention Exemption. Vento, D-Minn., amendment to exempt from the bill's requirements all sites nominated for international designation under the Convention on Wetlands of International Importance Especially as Waterfowl Habitats, commonly known as the Ramsar Convention. Rejected 195-220: R 26-191; D 168-29 (ND 132-14, SD 36-15); I 1-0, Oct. 7, 1997.

499. HR 1122. Abortion Procedure Ban/Previous Question. Myrick, R-N.C., motion to order the previous question (thus ending debate and the possibility of amendment) on adoption of the rule (H Res 262) to provide for House floor consideration of the bill to impose penalties on doctors who perform certain abortion procedures, in which the person performing the abortion partially delivers the fetus before completing the abortion. An exception would be granted where the procedure was necessary to save the life of the woman. Motion agreed to 280-144: R 217-6; D 63-137 (ND 39-108, SD 24-29); I 0-1, Oct. 8, 1997.

500. HR 1122. Abortion Procedure Ban/Agreeing to Senate Amendments. Canady, R-Fla., motion to agree to the Senate amendments to allow a doctor facing a penalty under the bill to have a hearing before a state medical board to determine whether the procedure was necessary and to clarify the definition of the outlawed procedure. The bill would impose penalties on doctors who perform certain abortion procedures, in which the person performing the abortion partially delivers the fetus before completing the abortion. The bill provides an exception when the procedure was necessary to save the life of the woman. Motion agreed to (thus clearing the bill for the president) 296-132: R 217-8; D 79-123 (ND 52-97, SD 27-26); I 0-1, Oct. 8, 1997. A "nay" was a vote in support of the president's position.

501. HR 901. U.N. Land Designation/California Coast Ranges Biosphere Reserve. Farr, D-Calif., amendment to exempt the California Coast Ranges Biosphere Reserves from the bill's provisions, which terminate existing biosphere reserves in the United States unless explicitly authorized by Congress. Rejected 200-226: R 14-209; D 185-17 (ND 145-5, SD 40-12); I 1-0, Oct. 8, 1997.

502. HR 901. U.N. Land Designation/Foreign Company Commercial Land Development. Vento, D-Minn., amendment to require Congress to approve any lease or other agreement with foreign companies or their U.S. subsidiaries that involves the commercial use or development of U.S. lands. Adopted 242-182: R 43-179; D 198-3 (ND 146-2, SD 52-1); I 1-0, Oct. 8, 1997.

503. HR 901. U.N. Land Designation/Biosphere Reserves Termination. Miller, D-Calif., amendment to strike the bill's provision that would terminate all existing biosphere reserves unless a reserve is explicitly authorized by Congress before Dec. 31, 2000. Rejected 199-227: R 17-205; D 181-22 (ND 144-6, SD 37-16); I 1-0, Oct. 8, 1997.

504. HR 901. U.N. Land Designation/Passage. Passage of the bill to prohibit federal officials from nominating U.S. lands for protection under U.N. Educational, Scientific and Cultural Organization conservation programs without previous congressional approval. The bill also would terminate all existing U.S. lands in the U.N. Biosphere Reserves program unless certain conditions are met, including congressional authorization for each reserve by Dec. 31, 2000. Passed 236-191: R 203-21; D 33-169 (ND 16-133, SD 17-36); I 0-1, Oct. 8, 1997. A "nay" was a vote in support of the president's position.

505. HR 2158. Fiscal 1998 VA-HUD Appropriations/Conference Report. Adoption of the conference report on the bill to provide \$90.7 billion in new budget authority for the departments of Veterans Affairs and Housing and Urban Development in fiscal 1998. The bill would provide \$4.8 billion more than the \$85.9 billion provided in fiscal 1997 and \$255 million less than the president's request of \$91.0 billion. Adopted (thus sent to the Senate) 405-21: R 207-17; D 197-4 (ND 144-4, SD 53-0); I 1-0, Oct. 8, 1997.

KEY

- Y Voted for (yea).
- # Paired for.
- \+ Announced for.
- N Voted against (nay).
- X Paired against.
- – Announced against.
- P Voted "present."
- C Voted "present" to avoid possible conflict of interest.
- ? Did not vote or otherwise make a position known.

Democrats ***Republicans***
Independent

	498	499	500	501	502	503	504	505
ALABAMA								
1 ***Callahan***	N	Y	Y	N	N	N	Y	Y
2 ***Everett***	N	Y	Y	N	N	N	Y	Y
3 ***Riley***	N	Y	Y	N	N	N	Y	Y
4 ***Aderholt***	N	Y	Y	N	N	N	Y	Y
5 Cramer	N	Y	Y	N	Y	Y	Y	Y
6 ***Bachus***	N	Y	Y	N	N	N	Y	Y
7 Hilliard	?	?	?	?	?	?	?	?
ALASKA								
AL ***Young***	N	Y	Y	N	N	N	Y	Y
ARIZONA								
1 ***Salmon***	N	Y	Y	N	N	N	Y	Y
2 Pastor	Y	N	N	Y	Y	Y	N	Y
3 ***Stump***	N	Y	Y	N	N	N	Y	Y
4 ***Shadegg***	N	Y	Y	N	N	N	Y	Y
5 ***Kolbe***	N	N	N	N	N	N	Y	Y
6 ***Hayworth***	N	Y	Y	N	N	N	Y	Y
ARKANSAS								
1 Berry	N	Y	Y	N	Y	N	Y	Y
2 Snyder	Y	N	N	Y	Y	Y	N	Y
3 ***Hutchinson***	N	Y	Y	N	N	N	Y	Y
4 ***Dickey***	N	Y	Y	N	N	N	Y	Y
CALIFORNIA								
1 ***Riggs***	N	Y	Y	N	Y	N	Y	Y
2 ***Herger***	N	Y	Y	N	N	N	Y	Y
3 Fazio	Y	N	N	Y	Y	Y	N	Y
4 ***Doolittle***	N	Y	Y	N	N	N	Y	Y
5 Matsui	Y	N	N	Y	Y	Y	N	Y
6 Woolsey	Y	N	N	Y	Y	Y	N	Y
7 Miller	Y	N	N	Y	Y	Y	N	Y
8 Pelosi	Y	N	N	Y	Y	Y	N	Y
9 Dellums	Y	N	N	Y	Y	Y	N	Y
10 Tauscher	Y	N	N	Y	Y	Y	N	Y
11 ***Pombo***	N	Y	Y	N	N	N	Y	Y
12 Lantos	Y	N	N	Y	Y	Y	N	Y
13 Stark	Y	N	N	Y	Y	Y	N	Y
14 Eshoo	Y	N	N	Y	Y	Y	N	Y
15 ***Campbell***	N	Y	N	N	N	N	Y	N
16 Lofgren	Y	N	N	Y	Y	Y	N	Y
17 Farr	Y	N	N	Y	Y	Y	N	+
18 Condit	N	Y	Y	Y	Y	N	Y	Y
19 ***Radanovich***	?	Y	Y	N	N	N	Y	Y
20 Dooley	Y	N	N	Y	N	Y	N	Y
21 ***Thomas***	N	Y	Y	N	N	N	Y	Y
22 Capps	Y	N	N	Y	Y	Y	N	Y
23 ***Gallegly***	N	Y	Y	N	N	N	Y	Y
24 Sherman	Y	N	N	Y	Y	Y	N	Y
25 ***McKeon***	N	Y	Y	N	N	N	Y	Y
26 Berman	Y	N	N	Y	Y	Y	N	Y
27 ***Rogan***	N	Y	Y	N	N	N	Y	Y
28 ***Dreier***	N	Y	Y	N	Y	N	Y	Y
29 Waxman	Y	N	N	Y	Y	Y	N	Y
30 Becerra	Y	N	N	Y	Y	Y	N	Y
31 Martinez	N	N	Y	N	Y	Y	Y	Y
32 Dixon	Y	N	N	Y	Y	Y	N	Y
33 Roybal-Allard	Y	N	N	Y	Y	Y	N	Y
34 Torres	Y	N	N	Y	Y	Y	N	Y
35 Waters	Y	N	N	Y	Y	Y	N	Y
36 Harman	Y	N	N	Y	Y	Y	N	Y
37 Millender-McD.	Y	N	N	Y	Y	Y	N	Y
38 ***Horn***	Y	N	N	Y	Y	Y	Y	Y
39 ***Royce***	N	Y	Y	N	N	N	Y	N
40 ***Lewis***	N	Y	Y	N	N	N	Y	Y
41 ***Kim***	N	Y	Y	N	N	N	Y	Y
42 Brown	Y	N	N	Y	Y	Y	N	Y
43 ***Calvert***	N	Y	Y	N	N	N	Y	Y
44 ***Bono***	N	Y	Y	N	N	N	Y	Y
45 ***Rohrabacher***	N	Y	Y	N	Y	N	Y	Y
46 Sanchez	Y	N	N	Y	Y	Y	N	Y
47 ***Cox***	N	Y	Y	N	N	N	Y	N
48 ***Packard***	N	Y	Y	N	N	N	Y	Y
49 ***Bilbray***	N	Y	Y	Y	N	N	Y	Y
50 Filner	Y	N	N	Y	Y	Y	N	Y
51 ***Cunningham***	N	Y	Y	N	N	N	Y	Y
52 ***Hunter***	N	Y	Y	N	N	N	Y	Y
COLORADO								
1 DeGette	Y	N	N	Y	Y	Y	N	Y
2 Skaggs	Y	N	N	Y	Y	Y	N	Y
3 ***McInnis***	N	Y	Y	N	N	N	Y	Y
4 ***Schaffer***	N	Y	Y	N	N	N	Y	Y
5 ***Hefley***	N	Y	Y	N	N	N	Y	Y
6 ***Schaefer***	N	Y	Y	N	N	N	Y	Y
CONNECTICUT								
1 Kennelly	?	N	N	Y	Y	Y	N	Y
2 Gejdenson	Y	N	N	Y	Y	Y	N	Y
3 DeLauro	Y	N	N	Y	Y	Y	N	Y
4 ***Shays***	Y	N	Y	Y	N	Y	N	Y
5 Maloney	Y	N	Y	Y	Y	Y	N	Y
6 ***Johnson***	Y	Y	N	–	Y	Y	N	Y
DELAWARE								
AL ***Castle***	Y	Y	Y	Y	Y	Y	N	Y
FLORIDA								
1 ***Scarborough***	N	Y	Y	N	N	N	Y	N
2 Boyd	Y	N	Y	Y	Y	Y	N	Y
3 Brown	Y	N	N	Y	Y	Y	N	Y
4 ***Fowler***	N	Y	Y	N	N	N	Y	Y
5 Thurman	Y	N	N	Y	Y	Y	N	Y
6 ***Stearns***	?	Y	Y	N	N	N	Y	Y
7 ***Mica***	N	Y	Y	N	Y	N	Y	Y
8 ***McCollum***	N	Y	Y	N	Y	N	Y	Y
9 ***Bilirakis***	?	Y	Y	N	Y	N	Y	Y
10 ***Young***	N	Y	Y	N	N	N	Y	Y
11 Davis	Y	Y	Y	Y	Y	Y	N	Y
12 ***Canady***	N	Y	Y	N	N	N	Y	Y
13 ***Miller***	N	Y	Y	N	N	N	Y	Y
14 ***Goss***	N	Y	Y	N	N	N	Y	Y
15 ***Weldon***	N	Y	Y	N	N	N	Y	Y
16 ***Foley***	N	Y	Y	N	Y	N	Y	Y
17 Meek	Y	N	N	?	Y	Y	N	Y
18 ***Ros-Lehtinen***	N	Y	Y	N	N	N	Y	Y
19 Wexler	Y	N	N	Y	Y	Y	N	Y
20 Deutsch	Y	N	N	Y	Y	Y	N	Y
21 ***Diaz-Balart***	N	Y	Y	N	?	N	Y	Y
22 ***Shaw***	N	Y	Y	N	N	N	Y	Y
23 Hastings	Y	N	N	Y	Y	Y	N	Y
GEORGIA								
1 ***Kingston***	N	Y	Y	N	N	N	Y	Y
2 Bishop	N	N	Y	N	Y	N	Y	Y
3 ***Collins***	N	Y	Y	N	N	N	Y	Y
4 McKinney	Y	N	N	Y	Y	Y	N	Y
5 Lewis	Y	N	N	Y	Y	N	N	Y
6 ***Gingrich***			Y					
7 ***Barr***	N	Y	Y	N	N	N	Y	Y
8 ***Chambliss***	N	Y	Y	N	N	N	Y	Y
9 ***Deal***	N	Y	Y	N	N	N	Y	Y
10 ***Norwood***	N	Y	Y	N	N	N	Y	Y
11 ***Linder***	N	Y	Y	N	N	N	Y	Y
HAWAII								
1 Abercrombie	Y	N	N	Y	Y	Y	N	Y
2 Mink	Y	N	N	Y	Y	Y	N	Y
IDAHO								
1 ***Chenoweth***	N	Y	Y	N	N	N	Y	Y
2 ***Crapo***	N	Y	Y	N	N	N	Y	Y
ILLINOIS								
1 Rush	Y	N	N	Y	Y	Y	N	N
2 Jackson	Y	N	N	Y	Y	Y	N	Y
3 Lipinski	Y	Y	Y	Y	Y	Y	N	Y
4 Gutierrez	Y	N	N	Y	Y	Y	N	Y
5 Blagojevich	Y	N	N	Y	Y	Y	N	Y
6 ***Hyde***	N	Y	Y	N	N	N	Y	Y
7 Davis	Y	N	N	Y	Y	Y	N	Y
8 ***Crane***	N	Y	Y	N	N	N	Y	N
9 Yates	?	N	N	Y	Y	Y	N	Y
10 ***Porter***	Y	Y	Y	Y	N	Y	N	Y
11 ***Weller***	N	Y	Y	N	N	N	Y	Y
12 Costello	Y	Y	Y	Y	Y	Y	N	Y
13 ***Fawell***	Y	Y	Y	N	N	Y	N	Y
14 ***Hastert***	N	Y	Y	N	N	N	Y	Y
15 ***Ewing***	Y	Y	Y	N	N	N	Y	Y

ND Northern Democrats SD Southern Democrats

	498	499	500	501	502	503	504	505
16 ***Manzullo***	N	Y	Y	N	N	N	Y	Y
17 Evans	Y	N	N	Y	Y	Y	N	Y
18 ***LaHood***	N	Y	Y	N	N	N	Y	Y
19 Poshard	Y	Y	Y	Y	Y	Y	N	Y
20 ***Shimkus***	N	Y	Y	N	N	N	Y	Y
INDIANA								
1 Visclosky	+	+	Y	Y	Y	Y	N	Y
2 ***McIntosh***	N	Y	Y	N	N	N	Y	N
3 Roemer	Y	Y	Y	Y	Y	Y	Y	N
4 ***Souder***	N	Y	Y	N	N	N	Y	N
5 ***Buyer***	N	Y	Y	N	Y	N	Y	Y
6 ***Burton***	?	Y	Y	N	N	N	Y	Y
7 ***Pease***	N	Y	Y	N	N	N	Y	Y
8 ***Hostettler***	N	Y	Y	N	N	N	Y	N
9 Hamilton	Y	Y	Y	Y	Y	Y	N	Y
10 Carson	Y	N	N	Y	Y	Y	N	Y
IOWA								
1 ***Leach***	Y	Y	Y	Y	Y	Y	N	Y
2 ***Nussle***	N	Y	Y	N	N	N	Y	Y
3 Boswell	N	Y	Y	N	Y	Y	Y	Y
4 ***Ganske***	N	Y	Y	N	Y	N	Y	Y
5 ***Latham***	N	Y	Y	N	N	N	Y	Y
KANSAS								
1 ***Moran***	N	Y	Y	N	N	N	Y	Y
2 ***Ryun***	N	Y	Y	N	N	N	Y	Y
3 ***Snowbarger***	N	Y	Y	N	N	N	Y	Y
4 ***Tiahrt***	N	Y	Y	N	N	N	Y	Y
KENTUCKY								
1 ***Whitfield***	N	Y	Y	N	N	N	Y	Y
2 ***Lewis***	–	+	+	–	–	–	+	+
3 ***Northup***	N	Y	Y	N	N	N	Y	Y
4 ***Bunning***	N	Y	Y	N	N	N	Y	Y
5 ***Rogers***	N	Y	Y	N	N	N	Y	Y
6 Baesler	N	Y	Y	N	Y	N	Y	Y
LOUISIANA								
1 ***Livingston***	N	Y	Y	N	N	N	Y	Y
2 Jefferson	Y	Y	Y	Y	Y	Y	N	Y
3 ***Tauzin***	N	Y	Y	N	N	N	Y	Y
4 ***McCrery***	N	Y	Y	N	N	N	Y	Y
5 ***Cooksey***	?	Y	Y	N	?	N	Y	Y
6 ***Baker***	N	Y	Y	N	N	N	Y	Y
7 John	Y	Y	Y	Y	N	N	Y	Y
MAINE								
1 Allen	Y	N	N	Y	Y	Y	N	Y
2 Baldacci	Y	N	N	Y	Y	Y	N	Y
MARYLAND								
1 ***Gilchrest***	Y	Y	Y	Y	Y	N	N	Y
2 ***Ehrlich***	N	Y	Y	N	N	N	Y	N
3 Cardin	Y	N	N	Y	Y	Y	N	Y
4 Wynn	Y	N	N	Y	Y	Y	N	Y
5 Hoyer	Y	N	N	Y	Y	Y	N	Y
6 ***Bartlett***	N	Y	Y	N	N	N	Y	Y
7 Cummings	Y	N	N	Y	Y	Y	N	Y
8 ***Morella***	Y	N	N	Y	Y	Y	N	Y
MASSACHUSETTS								
1 Olver	Y	N	N	Y	Y	Y	N	Y
2 Neal	Y	N	Y	Y	Y	Y	N	Y
3 McGovern	Y	N	N	Y	Y	Y	N	Y
4 Frank	Y	N	N	Y	Y	Y	N	Y
5 Meehan	Y	N	N	Y	Y	Y	N	Y
6 Tierney	Y	N	N	Y	Y	Y	N	Y
7 Markey	Y	N	N	Y	Y	Y	N	Y
8 Kennedy	Y	N	N	Y	Y	Y	N	Y
9 Moakley	?	N	Y	Y	Y	Y	N	Y
10 Delahunt	Y	N	N	Y	Y	Y	N	Y
MICHIGAN								
1 Stupak	N	Y	Y	Y	Y	Y	N	Y
2 ***Hoekstra***	N	Y	Y	N	N	N	Y	N
3 ***Ehlers***	Y	Y	Y	N	N	Y	N	Y
4 ***Camp***	N	Y	Y	N	Y	N	Y	Y
5 Barcia	N	Y	Y	Y	N	N	Y	Y
6 ***Upton***	N	Y	Y	N	Y	N	Y	N
7 ***Smith***	N	Y	Y	N	N	N	Y	N
8 Stabenow	Y	N	N	Y	Y	Y	N	Y
9 Kildee	Y	Y	Y	Y	Y	Y	N	Y
10 Bonior	Y	Y	Y	Y	Y	Y	N	Y
11 ***Knollenberg***	N	Y	Y	N	N	N	Y	Y
12 Levin	Y	N	N	Y	Y	Y	N	Y
13 Rivers	Y	N	N	Y	Y	Y	N	Y
14 Conyers	Y	N	N	N	?	Y	N	Y
15 Kilpatrick	Y	N	N	Y	Y	Y	N	Y
16 Dingell	Y	Y	Y	Y	Y	Y	N	Y
MINNESOTA								
1 ***Gutknecht***	N	Y	Y	N	Y	N	Y	Y
2 Minge	Y	Y	Y	Y	Y	Y	N	N

	498	499	500	501	502	503	504	505
3 ***Ramstad***	Y	Y	Y	Y	Y	Y	Y	Y
4 Vento	Y	N	N	Y	Y	Y	N	Y
5 Sabo	Y	N	N	Y	Y	Y	N	Y
6 Luther	Y	N	N	Y	Y	Y	N	Y
7 Peterson	N	Y	Y	Y	Y	N	Y	Y
8 Oberstar	N	Y	Y	Y	Y	Y	Y	Y
MISSISSIPPI								
1 ***Wicker***	N	Y	Y	N	N	N	Y	Y
2 Thompson	Y	N	N	Y	Y	Y	N	Y
3 ***Pickering***	N	Y	Y	N	N	N	Y	Y
4 ***Parker***	N	Y	Y	N	N	N	Y	Y
5 Taylor	N	Y	Y	N	Y	N	Y	Y
MISSOURI								
1 Clay	Y	N	N	Y	Y	Y	N	Y
2 ***Talent***	N	Y	Y	N	N	N	Y	Y
3 Gephardt	Y	?	?	?	?	?	?	Y
4 Skelton	N	Y	Y	Y	Y	N	Y	Y
5 McCarthy	Y	N	N	Y	Y	Y	N	Y
6 Danner	N	Y	Y	N	Y	N	Y	Y
7 ***Blunt***	N	Y	Y	N	N	N	Y	Y
8 ***Emerson***	N	Y	Y	N	N	N	Y	Y
9 ***Hulshof***	N	Y	Y	N	N	N	Y	Y
MONTANA								
AL ***Hill***	N	Y	Y	N	N	N	Y	Y
NEBRASKA								
1 ***Bereuter***	N	Y	Y	Y	N	N	N	Y
2 ***Christensen***	N	Y	Y	N	N	N	N	Y
3 ***Barrett***	N	Y	Y	N	N	N	N	Y
NEVADA								
1 ***Ensign***	N	Y	Y	N	N	N	Y	Y
2 ***Gibbons***	N	Y	Y	N	N	N	Y	Y
NEW HAMPSHIRE								
1 ***Sununu***	N	Y	Y	N	N	N	Y	Y
2 ***Bass***	N	Y	Y	N	Y	N	Y	Y
NEW JERSEY								
1 Andrews	Y	N	N	Y	Y	Y	N	Y
2 ***LoBiondo***	N	Y	Y	N	N	N	Y	Y
3 ***Saxton***	Y	Y	Y	Y	Y	Y	N	Y
4 ***Smith***	Y	Y	Y	N	N	N	Y	Y
5 ***Roukema***	Y	Y	Y	N	Y	Y	N	Y
6 Pallone	Y	N	N	Y	Y	Y	N	Y
7 ***Franks***	N	Y	Y	N	Y	Y	N	Y
8 Pascrell	Y	Y	Y	Y	Y	Y	Y	Y
9 Rothman	Y	N	N	Y	Y	Y	?	Y
10 Payne	Y	?	?	Y	Y	Y	N	Y
11 ***Frelinghuysen***	Y	Y	Y	N	Y	Y	N	Y
12 ***Pappas***	N	Y	Y	N	N	N	Y	Y
13 Menendez	Y	N	N	Y	Y	Y	N	Y
NEW MEXICO								
1 ***Schiff***	?	?	?	?	?	?	?	?
2 ***Skeen***	N	Y	Y	N	N	N	Y	Y
3 ***Redmond***	N	Y	Y	N	N	N	Y	Y
NEW YORK								
1 ***Forbes***	Y	Y	Y	N	N	N	Y	Y
2 ***Lazio***	N	Y	Y	N	N	N	Y	Y
3 ***King***	N	Y	Y	N	N	N	Y	Y
4 McCarthy	Y	N	N	Y	Y	Y	N	Y
5 Ackerman	Y	N	N	Y	Y	Y	N	Y
6 Flake	Y	Y	Y	Y	Y	Y	N	Y
7 Manton	Y	Y	Y	Y	Y	Y	N	Y
8 Nadler	Y	N	N	Y	Y	Y	N	Y
9 Schumer	Y	N	N	Y	Y	Y	N	Y
10 Towns	Y	N	N	Y	?	Y	N	Y
11 Owens	Y	N	N	Y	Y	Y	N	Y
12 Velázquez	Y	N	N	Y	Y	Y	N	Y
13 Vacant								
14 Maloney	Y	N	N	Y	Y	Y	N	Y
15 Rangel	Y	N	Y	Y	Y	Y	Y	?
16 Serrano	Y	N	N	Y	Y	Y	N	Y
17 Engel	Y	N	N	Y	Y	Y	N	Y
18 Lowey	Y	N	N	Y	Y	Y	N	Y
19 ***Kelly***	Y	Y	Y	Y	Y	N	Y	Y
20 ***Gilman***	Y	N	N	N	Y	Y	N	Y
21 McNulty	Y	Y	Y	Y	Y	Y	N	Y
22 ***Solomon***	N	Y	Y	N	N	N	Y	Y
23 ***Boehlert***	N	Y	N	N	Y	N	Y	Y
24 ***McHugh***	N	Y	Y	N	N	N	Y	Y
25 ***Walsh***	Y	Y	Y	N	Y	N	Y	Y
26 Hinchey	Y	N	N	Y	Y	Y	N	Y
27 ***Paxon***	N	Y	Y	N	N	N	Y	Y
28 Slaughter	Y	N	N	Y	Y	Y	N	Y
29 LaFalce	Y	Y	Y	Y	Y	Y	N	Y
30 ***Quinn***	N	Y	Y	N	Y	N	Y	Y
31 ***Houghton***	N	Y	Y	Y	Y	N	N	Y

	498	499	500	501	502	503	504	505
NORTH CAROLINA								
1 Clayton	Y	N	N	Y	Y	Y	N	Y
2 Etheridge	+	Y	Y	Y	Y	Y	N	Y
3 ***Jones***	N	Y	Y	N	Y	N	Y	Y
4 Price	Y	N	N	Y	Y	Y	N	Y
5 ***Burr***	N	Y	Y	N	N	N	Y	Y
6 ***Coble***	N	Y	Y	N	N	N	Y	Y
7 McIntyre	N	Y	Y	N	Y	N	Y	Y
8 Hefner	Y	Y	Y	Y	Y	Y	N	Y
9 ***Myrick***	N	Y	Y	N	N	N	Y	Y
10 ***Ballenger***	N	Y	Y	N	N	N	Y	N
11 ***Taylor***	N	Y	Y	N	N	N	Y	Y
12 Watt	Y	N	N	Y	Y	Y	N	Y
NORTH DAKOTA								
AL Pomeroy	Y	Y	Y	Y	Y	Y	Y	Y
OHIO								
1 ***Chabot***	N	Y	Y	N	Y	N	Y	Y
2 ***Portman***	N	Y	Y	N	Y	N	Y	Y
3 Hall	Y	Y	Y	Y	Y	Y	N	Y
4 ***Oxley***	N	Y	Y	N	N	N	Y	Y
5 ***Gillmor***	N	Y	Y	N	N	N	Y	Y
6 Strickland	Y	Y	Y	Y	Y	Y	N	Y
7 ***Hobson***	N	Y	Y	N	N	N	Y	Y
8 ***Boehner***	?	Y	Y	N	N	N	Y	Y
9 Kaptur	Y	Y	Y	Y	Y	Y	N	Y
10 Kucinich	Y	Y	Y	Y	Y	Y	N	Y
11 Stokes	Y	N	N	Y	Y	Y	N	Y
12 ***Kasich***	N	Y	Y	N	N	?	Y	Y
13 Brown	Y	N	N	Y	Y	Y	N	Y
14 Sawyer	Y	N	N	Y	Y	Y	N	Y
15 ***Pryce***	N	Y	Y	N	N	N	Y	Y
16 ***Regula***	N	Y	Y	N	Y	N	Y	Y
17 Traficant	N	Y	Y	N	Y	N	Y	Y
18 ***Ney***	N	Y	Y	N	N	N	Y	Y
19 ***LaTourette***	Y	Y	Y	N	N	?	Y	Y
OKLAHOMA								
1 ***Largent***	N	Y	Y	N	N	N	Y	Y
2 ***Coburn***	N	Y	Y	N	N	N	Y	Y
3 ***Watkins***	N	Y	Y	N	N	N	Y	Y
4 ***Watts***	N	Y	Y	N	N	N	Y	Y
5 ***Istook***	N	Y	Y	N	N	N	Y	Y
6 ***Lucas***	N	Y	Y	N	N	N	Y	Y
OREGON								
1 Furse	Y	N	N	Y	Y	Y	N	Y
2 ***Smith***	N	Y	Y	N	N	N	Y	Y
3 Blumenauer	Y	N	N	Y	Y	Y	N	Y
4 DeFazio	Y	N	N	Y	Y	Y	N	Y
5 Hooley	Y	N	N	Y	Y	Y	N	Y
PENNSYLVANIA								
1 Foglietta	?	?	Y	Y	Y	Y	N	?
2 Fattah	Y	N	N	Y	Y	Y	N	Y
3 Borski	Y	Y	Y	Y	Y	Y	N	Y
4 Klink	N	Y	Y	Y	Y	Y	Y	Y
5 ***Peterson***	N	Y	Y	N	N	N	Y	N
6 Holden	N	Y	Y	Y	Y	Y	Y	Y
7 ***Weldon***	Y	Y	Y	N	Y	Y	Y	Y
8 ***Greenwood***	N	N	N	N	N	N	N	Y
9 ***Shuster***	N	Y	Y	N	N	N	Y	Y
10 ***McDade***	?	Y	Y	N	N	N	Y	Y
11 Kanjorski	Y	Y	Y	Y	Y	Y	N	N
12 Murtha	N	Y	Y	Y	Y	Y	N	Y
13 ***Fox***	Y	Y	Y	N	Y	N	Y	Y
14 Coyne	Y	N	N	Y	Y	Y	N	Y
15 McHale	Y	N	Y	Y	Y	Y	N	Y
16 ***Pitts***	N	Y	Y	N	N	N	Y	Y
17 ***Gekas***	N	Y	Y	N	N	N	Y	Y
18 Doyle	N	Y	Y	Y	Y	Y	Y	Y
19 ***Goodling***	N	Y	Y	N	N	N	Y	Y
20 Mascara	Y	Y	Y	Y	Y	Y	N	Y
21 ***English***	Y	Y	Y	N	Y	N	N	Y
RHODE ISLAND								
1 Kennedy	Y	N	Y	Y	Y	Y	N	Y
2 Weygand	Y	Y	Y	Y	Y	Y	N	Y
SOUTH CAROLINA								
1 ***Sanford***	Y	Y	Y	Y	Y	Y	Y	N
2 ***Spence***	N	Y	Y	N	N	N	Y	Y
3 ***Graham***	N	Y	Y	N	N	N	Y	Y
4 ***Inglis***	N	Y	Y	N	N	N	Y	Y
5 Spratt	Y	Y	Y	Y	Y	Y	N	Y
6 Clyburn	Y	N	N	Y	Y	Y	N	Y
SOUTH DAKOTA								
AL ***Thune***	N	Y	Y	N	N	N	Y	Y
TENNESSEE								
1 ***Jenkins***	N	Y	Y	N	N	N	Y	Y
2 ***Duncan***	N	Y	Y	N	Y	N	Y	Y

	498	499	500	501	502	503	504	
3 ***Wamp***	N	Y	Y	N	N	N	Y	Y
4 ***Hilleary***	N	Y	Y	N	N	N	Y	Y
5 Clement	Y	Y	Y	Y	Y	Y	N	Y
6 Gordon	N	Y	Y	Y	Y	Y	N	Y
7 ***Bryant***	N	Y	Y	N	N	N	Y	Y
8 Tanner	N	Y	Y	Y	Y	N	Y	Y
9 Ford	Y	N	N	Y	Y	Y	N	Y
TEXAS								
1 Sandlin	Y	Y	Y	Y	Y	N	Y	Y
2 Turner	N	Y	Y	N	Y	N	Y	Y
3 ***Johnson, Sam***	N	Y	Y	N	N	N	Y	Y
4 Hall	N	Y	Y	N	Y	N	Y	Y
5 ***Sessions***	N	Y	Y	N	N	N	Y	Y
6 ***Barton***	N	Y	Y	N	N	N	Y	Y
7 ***Archer***	N	Y	Y	N	N	N	Y	Y
8 ***Brady***	N	Y	Y	N	N	N	Y	Y
9 Lampson	Y	Y	Y	Y	Y	Y	N	Y
10 Doggett	Y	N	N	Y	Y	Y	N	Y
11 Edwards	N	N	N	Y	Y	Y	Y	Y
12 ***Granger***	N	Y	Y	N	N	N	Y	Y
13 ***Thornberry***	N	Y	Y	N	N	N	Y	Y
14 ***Paul***	N	Y	Y	N	N	N	Y	N
15 Hinojosa	Y	N	Y	Y	Y	Y	N	Y
16 Reyes	Y	Y	Y	Y	Y	Y	N	Y
17 Stenholm	N	Y	Y	N	Y	N	Y	Y
18 Jackson-Lee	Y	N	N	Y	Y	Y	N	Y
19 ***Combest***	N	Y	Y	N	N	N	Y	Y
20 Gonzalez	?	?	?	?	?	?	?	?
21 ***Smith***	N	Y	Y	N	N	N	Y	Y
22 ***DeLay***	N	Y	Y	N	N	N	Y	Y
23 ***Bonilla***	N	Y	Y	N	N	N	Y	Y
24 Frost	Y	N	N	Y	Y	Y	N	Y
25 Bentsen	Y	N	N	Y	Y	Y	N	Y
26 ***Armey***	N	Y	Y	N	N	N	Y	Y
27 Ortiz	Y	Y	Y	Y	Y	Y	N	Y
28 Rodriguez	Y	N	N	Y	Y	Y	N	Y
29 Green	N	N	N	Y	Y	N	Y	Y
30 Johnson, E.B.	Y	N	N	Y	Y	Y	N	Y
UTAH								
1 ***Hansen***	N	Y	Y	N	N	N	Y	Y
2 ***Cook***	N	Y	Y	N	Y	N	Y	Y
3 ***Cannon***	N	Y	Y	N	N	N	Y	Y
VERMONT								
AL *Sanders*	Y	N	N	Y	Y	Y	N	Y
VIRGINIA								
1 ***Bateman***	N	Y	Y	N	N	N	Y	Y
2 Pickett	N	Y	N	N	Y	N	Y	Y
3 Scott	Y	N	N	Y	Y	Y	N	Y
4 Sisisky	Y	Y	Y	N	Y	N	Y	Y
5 Goode	N	Y	Y	N	Y	N	Y	Y
6 ***Goodlatte***	N	Y	Y	N	Y	N	Y	Y
7 ***Bliley***	N	Y	Y	N	N	N	Y	Y
8 Moran	?	N	Y	Y	Y	Y	N	Y
9 Boucher	Y	N	N	Y	Y	Y	N	Y
10 ***Wolf***	N	Y	Y	N	N	N	Y	Y
11 ***Davis***	N	Y	Y	N	N	N	Y	Y
WASHINGTON								
1 ***White***	N	Y	Y	N	N	N	Y	Y
2 ***Metcalf***	N	Y	Y	N	Y	N	Y	Y
3 ***Smith, Linda***	N	Y	Y	N	N	N	Y	Y
4 ***Hastings***	N	Y	Y	N	N	N	Y	Y
5 ***Nethercutt***	N	?	Y	N	N	N	Y	Y
6 Dicks	Y	N	N	Y	Y	Y	N	Y
7 McDermott	Y	N	N	Y	Y	Y	N	Y
8 ***Dunn***	N	Y	Y	N	N	N	Y	Y
9 Smith, Adam	Y	N	N	Y	Y	Y	N	Y
WEST VIRGINIA								
1 Mollohan	Y	Y	Y	Y	Y	Y	N	Y
2 Wise	Y	N	N	Y	Y	Y	N	Y
3 Rahall	Y	Y	Y	Y	Y	Y	N	Y
WISCONSIN								
1 ***Neumann***	N	Y	Y	N	N	N	Y	N
2 ***Klug***	Y	Y	Y	N	Y	N	N	Y
3 Kind	Y	N	Y	Y	Y	Y	N	Y
4 Kleczka	Y	Y	Y	Y	Y	Y	N	Y
5 Barrett	Y	N	Y	Y	Y	Y	N	Y
6 ***Petri***	N	Y	Y	N	N	N	Y	Y
7 Obey	Y	N	Y	Y	Y	Y	N	Y
8 Johnson	Y	N	Y	Y	Y	Y	N	Y
9 ***Sensenbrenner***	N	Y	Y	N	N	N	Y	Y
WYOMING								
AL ***Cubin***	N	Y	Y	N	N	N	Y	Y

Southern states - Ala., Ark., Fla., Ga., Ky., La., Miss., N.C., Okla., S.C., Tenn., Texas, Va.

HOUSE VOTES 506, 507, 508, 509, 510

506. HR 1757. Fiscal 1998-99 State Department Authorization/Motion to Instruct. Callahan, R-Ala., motion to instruct House conferees to insist on the House provision to prohibit funding to any private, non-governmental or multilateral organization that directly or indirectly performs abortions in a foreign country, except in cases of rape, incest, or when the life of the mother is endangered. Motion agreed to 236-190: R 191-32; D 45-157 (ND 35-114, SD 10-43); I 0-1, Oct. 8, 1997.

507. HR 2169. Fiscal 1998 Transportation Appropriations/Rule. Adoption of the rule (H Res 263) to waive points of order against and provide for House floor consideration of the conference report on the bill to provide $13.1 billion in new budget authority for the Department of Transportation and related agencies in fiscal 1998, and to authorize a total of $42.2 billion in expenditures for fiscal 1998. Adopted 413-4: R 218-1; D 194-3 (ND 144-2, SD 50-1); I 1-0, Oct. 9, 1997.

508. HR 2607. Fiscal 1998 District of Columbia Appropriations/Rule. Adoption of the rule (H Res 264) to provide for House floor consideration of the bill to provide $828 million in new budget authority for the District of Columbia in fiscal 1998. Adopted 370-50: R 220-1; D 149-49 (ND 114-33, SD 35-16); I 1-0, Oct. 9, 1997.

509. Procedural Motion/Journal. Approval of the House Journal of Wednesday, Oct. 8, 1997. Approved 352-58: R 197-18; D 154-40 (ND 114-30, SD 40-10); I 1-0, Oct. 9, 1997.

510. HR 2169. Fiscal 1998 Transportation Appropriations/Conference Report. Adoption of the conference report on the bill to provide $13.1 billion in new budget authority for the Department of Transportation and related agencies in fiscal 1998, and to authorize a total of $42.2 billion in expenditures for fiscal 1998. The bill provides $2 billion more than the $11.1 billion provided in fiscal 1997 and $52 million less than the president's request. Adopted (thus sent to the Senate) 401-21: R 210-12; D 190-9 (ND 141-6, SD 49-3); I 1-0, Oct. 9, 1997.

KEY

- Y Voted for (yea).
- # Paired for.
- + Announced for.
- N Voted against (nay).
- X Paired against.
- – Announced against.
- P Voted "present."
- C Voted "present" to avoid possible conflict of interest.
- ? Did not vote or otherwise make a position known.

Democrats ***Republicans***
Independent

	506	507	508	509	510
ALABAMA					
1 ***Callahan***	Y	Y	Y	Y	Y
2 ***Everett***	Y	Y	Y	N	Y
3 ***Riley***	Y	Y	Y	Y	Y
4 ***Aderholt***	Y	Y	Y	Y	Y
5 Cramer	Y	Y	Y	Y	Y
6 ***Bachus***	Y	Y	Y	Y	Y
7 Hilliard	?	?	?	?	?
ALASKA					
AL ***Young***	Y	?	?	?	Y
ARIZONA					
1 ***Salmon***	Y	Y	Y	N	Y
2 Pastor	N	Y	Y	N	Y
3 ***Stump***	Y	Y	Y	Y	Y
4 ***Shadegg***	Y	Y	Y	Y	Y
5 ***Kolbe***	N	Y	Y	Y	Y
6 ***Hayworth***	Y	Y	Y	Y	Y
ARKANSAS					
1 Berry	Y	Y	Y	Y	Y
2 Snyder	N	Y	Y	Y	Y
3 ***Hutchinson***	Y	Y	Y	Y	Y
4 ***Dickey***	Y	Y	Y	Y	Y
CALIFORNIA					
1 ***Riggs***	Y	Y	Y	Y	Y
2 ***Herger***	Y	Y	Y	Y	Y
3 Fazio	N	Y	N	N	Y
4 ***Doolittle***	Y	Y	Y	Y	Y
5 Matsui	N	Y	Y	Y	Y
6 Woolsey	N	Y	Y	Y	Y
7 Miller	N	?	?	?	Y
8 Pelosi	N	Y	Y	Y	Y
9 Dellums	N	Y	Y	Y	Y
10 Tauscher	N	Y	Y	Y	Y
11 ***Pombo***	Y	Y	Y	N	Y
12 Lantos	N	Y	Y	Y	Y
13 Stark	N	Y	N	Y	Y
14 Eshoo	N	Y	Y	Y	Y
15 ***Campbell***	N	Y	Y	Y	N
16 Lofgren	N	Y	Y	Y	Y
17 Farr	N	Y	Y	Y	Y
18 Condit	N	Y	Y	Y	Y
19 ***Radanovich***	Y	Y	Y	Y	Y
20 Dooley	N	Y	Y	Y	Y
21 ***Thomas***	N	Y	Y	Y	Y
22 Capps	N	Y	Y	Y	Y
23 ***Gallegly***	Y	Y	Y	Y	Y
24 Sherman	N	Y	N	Y	Y
25 ***McKeon***	Y	Y	Y	?	Y
26 Berman	N	Y	Y	Y	Y
27 ***Rogan***	Y	Y	Y	Y	Y
28 ***Dreier***	Y	Y	Y	Y	Y
29 Waxman	N	Y	Y	Y	?
30 Becerra	N	Y	Y	N	Y
31 Martinez	N	Y	Y	Y	Y
32 Dixon	N	Y	N	Y	Y
33 Roybal-Allard	N	Y	Y	Y	Y
34 Torres	Y	Y	Y	Y	Y
35 Waters	N	Y	N	?	Y
36 Harman	N	Y	Y	Y	Y
37 Millender-McD.	N	Y	Y	Y	Y
38 ***Horn***	N	Y	N	Y	Y
39 ***Royce***	Y	Y	Y	Y	Y
40 ***Lewis***	Y	Y	Y	Y	Y
41 ***Kim***	Y	Y	Y	Y	Y
42 Brown	N	Y	Y	N	Y
43 ***Calvert***	Y	Y	Y	Y	Y
44 ***Bono***	Y	Y	Y	Y	Y
45 ***Rohrabacher***	Y	Y	Y	Y	Y
46 Sanchez	N	Y	Y	Y	Y
47 ***Cox***	Y	Y	Y	Y	Y
48 ***Packard***	Y	Y	Y	Y	Y
49 ***Bilbray***	N	Y	Y	Y	Y
50 Filner	N	Y	N	N	Y
51 ***Cunningham***	Y	Y	Y	Y	Y
52 ***Hunter***	Y	Y	Y	?	Y
COLORADO					
1 DeGette	N	Y	N	Y	Y
2 Skaggs	N	Y	Y	Y	Y
3 ***McInnis***	Y	Y	Y	Y	Y
4 ***Schaffer***	Y	Y	Y	N	Y
5 ***Hefley***	Y	Y	Y	N	Y
6 ***Schaefer***	Y	Y	Y	Y	Y
CONNECTICUT					
1 Kennelly	N	Y	Y	Y	Y
2 Gejdenson	N	Y	Y	Y	Y
3 DeLauro	N	Y	Y	Y	Y
4 ***Shays***	N	Y	Y	Y	Y
5 Maloney	N	Y	Y	Y	Y
6 ***Johnson***	N	Y	Y	Y	Y
DELAWARE					
AL ***Castle***	N	Y	Y	Y	Y
FLORIDA					
1 ***Scarborough***	Y	Y	Y	Y	N
2 Boyd	N	Y	Y	Y	Y
3 Brown	N	?	?	?	?
4 ***Fowler***	Y	Y	Y	Y	Y
5 Thurman	N	Y	Y	Y	Y
6 ***Stearns***	Y	Y	Y	Y	Y
7 ***Mica***	Y	Y	Y	Y	Y
8 ***McCollum***	Y	Y	Y	Y	Y
9 ***Bilirakis***	Y	Y	Y	Y	Y
10 ***Young***	Y	Y	Y	Y	Y
11 Davis	N	Y	Y	Y	Y
12 ***Canady***	Y	Y	Y	Y	Y
13 ***Miller***	Y	Y	Y	Y	Y
14 ***Goss***	Y	Y	Y	Y	Y
15 ***Weldon***	Y	Y	Y	Y	Y
16 ***Foley***	Y	Y	Y	Y	Y
17 Meek	N	Y	N	N	Y
18 ***Ros-Lehtinen***	Y	Y	Y	Y	Y
19 Wexler	N	Y	N	N	N
20 Deutsch	N	Y	N	N	Y
21 ***Diaz-Balart***	Y	Y	Y	Y	Y
22 ***Shaw***	Y	Y	Y	Y	Y
23 Hastings	N	Y	N	N	Y
GEORGIA					
1 ***Kingston***	Y	Y	Y	Y	Y
2 Bishop	N	Y	Y	Y	Y
3 ***Collins***	Y	Y	Y	Y	Y
4 McKinney	N	Y	N	Y	Y
5 Lewis	N	Y	N	N	Y
6 ***Gingrich***					
7 ***Barr***	Y	Y	Y	Y	Y
8 ***Chambliss***	Y	?	?	?	?
9 ***Deal***	Y	Y	Y	Y	Y
10 ***Norwood***	Y	Y	Y	Y	Y
11 ***Linder***	Y	Y	Y	Y	Y
HAWAII					
1 Abercrombie	N	+	+	+	Y
2 Mink	N	Y	N	Y	Y
IDAHO					
1 ***Chenoweth***	Y	Y	Y	Y	Y
2 ***Crapo***	Y	Y	Y	Y	Y
ILLINOIS					
1 Rush	N	Y	Y	Y	Y
2 Jackson	N	Y	Y	Y	Y
3 Lipinski	Y	Y	Y	Y	Y
4 Gutierrez	N	Y	Y	N	Y
5 Blagojevich	N	Y	Y	Y	Y
6 ***Hyde***	Y	Y	Y	Y	Y
7 Davis	N	Y	Y	Y	Y
8 ***Crane***	Y	Y	Y	Y	Y
9 Yates	N	Y	Y	Y	Y
10 ***Porter***	N	Y	Y	Y	Y
11 ***Weller***	Y	Y	Y	N	Y
12 Costello	Y	Y	Y	N	Y
13 ***Fawell***	N	Y	Y	?	Y
14 ***Hastert***	Y	Y	Y	Y	Y
15 ***Ewing***	Y	Y	Y	Y	Y

ND Northern Democrats SD Southern Democrats

	506	507	508	509	510
16 ***Manzullo***	Y	Y	Y	?	Y
17 Evans	N	Y	Y	N	Y
18 ***LaHood***	Y	Y	Y	Y	Y
19 Poshard	Y	Y	Y	N	Y
20 ***Shimkus***	Y	Y	Y	Y	Y
INDIANA					
1 Visclosky	N	Y	Y	N	Y
2 ***McIntosh***	Y	Y	Y	Y	Y
3 Roemer	Y	Y	Y	Y	Y
4 ***Souder***	Y	Y	Y	Y	Y
5 ***Buyer***	Y	Y	Y	Y	Y
6 ***Burton***	Y	Y	Y	Y	Y
7 ***Pease***	Y	Y	Y	Y	Y
8 ***Hostettler***	Y	Y	Y	Y	N
9 Hamilton	Y	Y	Y	Y	Y
10 Carson	N	Y	Y	Y	Y
IOWA					
1 ***Leach***	N	Y	Y	Y	Y
2 ***Nussle***	Y	Y	Y	Y	Y
3 Boswell	N	Y	Y	Y	Y
4 ***Ganske***	Y	Y	Y	Y	Y
5 ***Latham***	Y	Y	Y	Y	Y
KANSAS					
1 ***Moran***	Y	Y	Y	Y	Y
2 ***Ryun***	Y	Y	Y	Y	Y
3 ***Snowbarger***	Y	Y	Y	Y	Y
4 ***Tiahrt***	Y	Y	Y	?	Y
KENTUCKY					
1 ***Whitfield***	Y	Y	Y	Y	Y
2 ***Lewis***	+	+	+	+	+
3 ***Northup***	Y	Y	Y	Y	Y
4 ***Bunning***	Y	Y	Y	Y	Y
5 ***Rogers***	Y	Y	Y	Y	Y
6 Baesler	N	Y	N	Y	Y
LOUISIANA					
1 ***Livingston***	Y	Y	Y	Y	Y
2 Jefferson	N	Y	N	Y	Y
3 ***Tauzin***	Y	Y	Y	Y	Y
4 ***McCrery***	Y	Y	Y	Y	Y
5 ***Cooksey***	Y	Y	Y	Y	Y
6 ***Baker***	Y	Y	Y	Y	Y
7 John	Y	Y	Y	Y	Y
MAINE					
1 Allen	N	Y	Y	Y	Y
2 Baldacci	N	Y	Y	Y	Y
MARYLAND					
1 ***Gilchrest***	N	Y	Y	Y	Y
2 ***Ehrlich***	N	Y	Y	Y	Y
3 Cardin	N	Y	Y	Y	Y
4 Wynn	N	Y	Y	Y	Y
5 Hoyer	N	Y	N	Y	Y
6 ***Bartlett***	Y	Y	Y	Y	Y
7 Cummings	N	Y	Y	Y	Y
8 ***Morella***	N	Y	Y	Y	Y
MASSACHUSETTS					
1 Olver	N	Y	N	Y	Y
2 Neal	Y	Y	Y	Y	Y
3 McGovern	N	Y	N	N	Y
4 Frank	N	Y	N	Y	Y
5 Meehan	N	Y	N	Y	Y
6 Tierney	N	Y	N	Y	Y
7 Markey	N	Y	N	Y	Y
8 Kennedy	N	Y	N	Y	Y
9 Moakley	Y	Y	Y	Y	Y
10 Delahunt	N	Y	N	Y	Y
MICHIGAN					
1 Stupak	Y	Y	Y	N	N
2 ***Hoekstra***	Y	Y	Y	Y	N
3 ***Ehlers***	Y	Y	Y	Y	N
4 ***Camp***	Y	Y	Y	Y	N
5 Barcia	Y	N	Y	Y	Y
6 ***Upton***	N	Y	Y	Y	N
7 ***Smith***	Y	Y	Y	Y	N
8 Stabenow	N	Y	Y	Y	N
9 Kildee	Y	Y	Y	Y	Y
10 Bonior	Y	Y	N	?	?
11 ***Knollenberg***	Y	Y	Y	Y	Y
12 Levin	N	Y	Y	Y	N
13 Rivers	N	Y	N	Y	Y
14 Conyers	N	Y	N	Y	N
15 Kilpatrick	N	Y	N	N	N
16 Dingell	N	?	?	?	N
MINNESOTA					
1 ***Gutknecht***	Y	Y	Y	N	Y
2 Minge	N	Y	Y	Y	Y

	506	507	508	509	510
3 ***Ramstad***	N	Y	Y	N	Y
4 Vento	N	Y	N	Y	Y
5 Sabo	N	Y	Y	N	Y
6 Luther	N	Y	Y	Y	Y
7 Peterson	Y	Y	Y	Y	Y
8 Oberstar	Y	N	Y	N	Y
MISSISSIPPI					
1 ***Wicker***	Y	Y	Y	N	Y
2 Thompson	N	Y	Y	N	Y
3 ***Pickering***	Y	Y	Y	Y	Y
4 ***Parker***	Y	Y	Y	Y	Y
5 Taylor	Y	Y	N	N	Y
MISSOURI					
1 Clay	?	Y	Y	N	Y
2 ***Talent***	Y	Y	Y	Y	Y
3 Gephardt	N	Y	N	?	Y
4 Skelton	Y	Y	Y	Y	Y
5 McCarthy	N	Y	Y	Y	Y
6 Danner	Y	Y	Y	Y	Y
7 ***Blunt***	Y	Y	Y	Y	Y
8 ***Emerson***	Y	Y	Y	Y	Y
9 ***Hulshof***	Y	Y	Y	N	Y
MONTANA					
AL ***Hill***	Y	Y	Y	N	Y
NEBRASKA					
1 ***Bereuter***	Y	Y	Y	Y	Y
2 ***Christensen***	Y	Y	Y	Y	Y
3 ***Barrett***	Y	Y	Y	Y	Y
NEVADA					
1 ***Ensign***	Y	Y	Y	N	Y
2 ***Gibbons***	N	Y	Y	N	Y
NEW HAMPSHIRE					
1 ***Sununu***	Y	Y	Y	Y	Y
2 ***Bass***	N	Y	Y	Y	Y
NEW JERSEY					
1 Andrews	N	Y	N	Y	Y
2 ***LoBiondo***	Y	Y	Y	N	Y
3 ***Saxton***	Y	+	+	?	Y
4 ***Smith***	Y	?	Y	Y	Y
5 ***Roukema***	N	Y	Y	Y	Y
6 Pallone	N	Y	Y	N	Y
7 ***Franks***	N	Y	Y	Y	Y
8 Pascrell	N	Y	Y	N	Y
9 Rothman	N	Y	N	Y	Y
10 Payne	N	Y	N	N	Y
11 ***Frelinghuysen***	N	Y	Y	Y	Y
12 ***Pappas***	Y	Y	Y	Y	Y
13 Menendez	N	Y	Y	N	Y
NEW MEXICO					
1 ***Schiff***	?	?	?	?	?
2 ***Skeen***	Y	Y	Y	Y	Y
3 ***Redmond***	Y	Y	Y	Y	Y
NEW YORK					
1 ***Forbes***	Y	Y	Y	Y	Y
2 ***Lazio***	N	Y	Y	Y	Y
3 ***King***	Y	Y	Y	Y	Y
4 McCarthy	N	Y	Y	Y	Y
5 Ackerman	N	Y	Y	Y	Y
6 Flake	Y	Y	Y	Y	Y
7 Manton	Y	Y	Y	Y	Y
8 Nadler	N	Y	Y	Y	Y
9 Schumer	–	Y	Y	Y	Y
10 Towns	N	Y	Y	N	Y
11 Owens	N	Y	N	Y	Y
12 Velázquez	N	Y	Y	Y	Y
13 Vacant					
14 Maloney	N	Y	Y	Y	Y
15 Rangel	N	Y	N	N	Y
16 Serrano	N	Y	Y	Y	Y
17 Engel	N	Y	Y	Y	Y
18 Lowey	N	Y	Y	Y	Y
19 ***Kelly***	N	Y	Y	Y	Y
20 ***Gilman***	N	Y	Y	Y	Y
21 McNulty	N	Y	Y	N	Y
22 ***Solomon***	Y	Y	Y	Y	Y
23 ***Boehlert***	N	Y	Y	Y	Y
24 ***McHugh***	Y	Y	Y	Y	Y
25 ***Walsh***	Y	Y	Y	Y	Y
26 Hinchey	N	Y	N	N	Y
27 ***Paxon***	Y	Y	Y	Y	Y
28 Slaughter	N	Y	N	Y	Y
29 LaFalce	Y	Y	Y	Y	Y
30 ***Quinn***	Y	Y	Y	Y	Y
31 ***Houghton***	N	Y	Y	Y	Y

	506	507	508	509	510
NORTH CAROLINA					
1 Clayton	N	Y	N	Y	Y
2 Etheridge	N	Y	Y	Y	Y
3 ***Jones***	Y	Y	Y	Y	Y
4 Price	N	Y	Y	Y	Y
5 ***Burr***	Y	Y	Y	?	Y
6 ***Coble***	Y	Y	Y	Y	Y
7 McIntyre	Y	Y	Y	Y	Y
8 Hefner	N	Y	Y	Y	Y
9 ***Myrick***	Y	Y	Y	Y	Y
10 ***Ballenger***	Y	Y	Y	Y	Y
11 ***Taylor***	Y	Y	Y	Y	Y
12 Watt	N	Y	Y	?	Y
NORTH DAKOTA					
AL Pomeroy	N	Y	Y	Y	Y
OHIO					
1 ***Chabot***	Y	Y	Y	Y	Y
2 ***Portman***	Y	Y	Y	Y	Y
3 Hall	Y	Y	Y	Y	Y
4 ***Oxley***	Y	+	Y	Y	Y
5 ***Gillmor***	Y	Y	Y	Y	Y
6 Strickland	N	Y	Y	Y	Y
7 ***Hobson***	N	Y	Y	Y	Y
8 ***Boehner***	Y	Y	Y	Y	Y
9 Kaptur	Y	Y	Y	Y	Y
10 Kucinich	Y	Y	N	N	Y
11 Stokes	N	Y	N	N	Y
12 ***Kasich***	Y	Y	Y	Y	Y
13 Brown	N	Y	Y	Y	Y
14 Sawyer	N	Y	Y	Y	Y
15 ***Pryce***	N	Y	Y	Y	Y
16 ***Regula***	Y	Y	Y	Y	Y
17 Traficant	Y	Y	Y	Y	Y
18 ***Ney***	Y	Y	Y	Y	Y
19 ***LaTourette***	Y	Y	Y	Y	Y
OKLAHOMA					
1 ***Largent***	Y	Y	Y	Y	?
2 ***Coburn***	?	Y	Y	Y	N
3 ***Watkins***	Y	Y	Y	Y	Y
4 ***Watts***	Y	Y	Y	Y	Y
5 ***Istook***	Y	Y	Y	Y	Y
6 ***Lucas***	Y	Y	Y	Y	Y
OREGON					
1 Furse	N	Y	Y	Y	Y
2 ***Smith***	Y	Y	Y	Y	Y
3 Blumenauer	N	Y	Y	Y	Y
4 DeFazio	N	Y	Y	N	Y
5 Hooley	N	Y	Y	Y	Y
PENNSYLVANIA					
1 Foglietta	N	?	Y	N	Y
2 Fattah	N	Y	Y	Y	Y
3 Borski	Y	Y	Y	N	Y
4 Klink	Y	Y	Y	Y	Y
5 ***Peterson***	Y	Y	Y	Y	Y
6 Holden	Y	Y	Y	Y	Y
7 ***Weldon***	Y	Y	Y	Y	Y
8 ***Greenwood***	N	Y	Y	Y	Y
9 ***Shuster***	Y	Y	Y	Y	Y
10 ***McDade***	Y	Y	Y	Y	Y
11 Kanjorski	Y	Y	Y	Y	Y
12 Murtha	Y	?	?	?	?
13 ***Fox***	Y	Y	Y	N	Y
14 Coyne	N	Y	Y	Y	Y
15 McHale	N	Y	Y	Y	Y
16 ***Pitts***	Y	Y	Y	Y	Y
17 ***Gekas***	Y	Y	Y	Y	Y
18 Doyle	Y	Y	Y	Y	Y
19 ***Goodling***	Y	Y	Y	Y	Y
20 Mascara	Y	Y	Y	Y	Y
21 ***English***	Y	Y	Y	N	Y
RHODE ISLAND					
1 Kennedy	N	Y	N	Y	?
2 Weygand	Y	Y	Y	Y	Y
SOUTH CAROLINA					
1 ***Sanford***	Y	Y	Y	Y	N
2 ***Spence***	Y	Y	Y	Y	Y
3 ***Graham***	Y	Y	Y	Y	Y
4 ***Inglis***	Y	Y	Y	Y	Y
5 Spratt	N	Y	Y	Y	Y
6 Clyburn	N	Y	Y	N	Y
SOUTH DAKOTA					
AL ***Thune***	Y	Y	Y	Y	Y
TENNESSEE					
1 ***Jenkins***	Y	Y	Y	Y	Y
2 ***Duncan***	Y	Y	Y	Y	Y

	506	507	508	509	510
3 ***Wamp***	Y	Y	Y	Y	Y
4 ***Hilleary***	Y	Y	Y	N	Y
5 Clement	N	Y	Y	Y	Y
6 Gordon	N	Y	Y	Y	Y
7 ***Bryant***	Y	Y	Y	Y	Y
8 Tanner	N	?	?	?	Y
9 Ford	N	Y	N	Y	Y
TEXAS					
1 Sandlin	N	Y	Y	Y	Y
2 Turner	N	Y	Y	Y	Y
3 ***Johnson, Sam***	Y	Y	Y	Y	Y
4 Hall	Y	Y	Y	Y	Y
5 ***Sessions***	Y	Y	Y	N	Y
6 ***Barton***	Y	?	Y	Y	Y
7 ***Archer***	Y	Y	Y	Y	Y
8 ***Brady***	Y	Y	Y	Y	Y
9 Lampson	N	Y	Y	Y	Y
10 Doggett	N	Y	Y	Y	Y
11 Edwards	N	Y	Y	Y	Y
12 ***Granger***	Y	N	Y	Y	N
13 ***Thornberry***	Y	Y	Y	Y	Y
14 ***Paul***	Y	Y	Y	Y	N
15 Hinojosa	N	Y	Y	Y	Y
16 Reyes	N	Y	Y	Y	Y
17 Stenholm	Y	Y	Y	Y	Y
18 Jackson-Lee	N	Y	N	Y	Y
19 ***Combest***	Y	Y	Y	Y	Y
20 Gonzalez	?	?	?	?	?
21 ***Smith***	Y	Y	Y	Y	Y
22 ***DeLay***	Y	Y	Y	Y	Y
23 ***Bonilla***	Y	Y	Y	Y	Y
24 Frost	N	N	Y	Y	N
25 Bentsen	N	Y	N	Y	Y
26 ***Armey***	Y	Y	Y	Y	Y
27 Ortiz	Y	Y	Y	Y	Y
28 Rodriguez	N	Y	Y	Y	Y
29 Green	N	Y	N	Y	Y
30 Johnson, E.B.	N	Y	Y	Y	N
UTAH					
1 ***Hansen***	Y	Y	Y	Y	Y
2 ***Cook***	Y	Y	Y	Y	Y
3 ***Cannon***	Y	Y	Y	Y	Y
VERMONT					
AL *Sanders*	N	Y	Y	Y	Y
VIRGINIA					
1 ***Bateman***	Y	Y	Y	Y	Y
2 Pickett	N	Y	Y	N	Y
3 Scott	N	Y	N	N	Y
4 Sisisky	Y	Y	Y	Y	Y
5 Goode	Y	Y	N	Y	Y
6 ***Goodlatte***	Y	Y	Y	Y	Y
7 ***Bliley***	Y	Y	Y	Y	Y
8 Moran	N	Y	Y	Y	Y
9 Boucher	N	Y	Y	Y	Y
10 ***Wolf***	Y	Y	Y	Y	Y
11 ***Davis***	N	Y	Y	Y	Y
WASHINGTON					
1 ***White***	N	Y	Y	Y	Y
2 ***Metcalf***	Y	Y	Y	Y	Y
3 ***Smith, Linda***	Y	Y	Y	Y	Y
4 ***Hastings***	Y	Y	Y	Y	Y
5 ***Nethercutt***	Y	Y	Y	Y	Y
6 Dicks	N	Y	Y	Y	Y
7 McDermott	N	Y	Y	N	Y
8 ***Dunn***	Y	Y	Y	Y	Y
9 Smith, Adam	N	Y	Y	Y	Y
WEST VIRGINIA					
1 Mollohan	Y	Y	Y	Y	Y
2 Wise	N	Y	Y	Y	Y
3 Rahall	Y	Y	Y	Y	Y
WISCONSIN					
1 ***Neumann***	Y	Y	Y	Y	Y
2 ***Klug***	N	Y	Y	Y	Y
3 Kind	N	Y	Y	Y	Y
4 Kleczka	Y	Y	Y	Y	Y
5 Barrett	N	Y	Y	Y	Y
6 ***Petri***	Y	Y	Y	Y	Y
7 Obey	Y	Y	Y	Y	Y
8 Johnson	N	Y	Y	Y	Y
9 ***Sensenbrenner***	Y	Y	Y	Y	Y
WYOMING					
AL ***Cubin***	Y	Y	Y	Y	Y

Southern states - Ala., Ark., Fla., Ga., Ky., La., Miss., N.C., Okla., S.C., Tenn., Texas, Va.

HOUSE VOTES 511, 512, 513, 514

511. HR 2607. Fiscal 1998 District of Columbia Appropriations/School Contractor Wages. Sabo, D-Minn., amendment to strike the bill's provision that permits a waiver of the Davis-Bacon Act, which requires the payment of locally prevailing wages on federally funded construction projects, for contractors who perform repairs and construction of District of Columbia schools. Adopted 234-188: R 38-183; D 195-5 (ND 149-0, SD 46-5); I 1-0, Oct. 9, 1997.

512. HR 2607. Fiscal 1998 District of Columbia Appropriations/Senate Bill Substitute. Moran, D-Va., substitute amendment to provide $820 million in new budget authority for the District of Columbia in fiscal 1998. The substitute would eliminate a number of legislative riders contained in the bill, including a provision to establish an educational scholarship program to allow low-income students from the District of Columbia to attend private schools or public schools in the Virginia or Maryland suburbs. Rejected 197-212: R 8-208; D 188-4 (ND 141-2, SD 47-2); I 1-0, Oct. 9, 1997.

513. HR 2607. Fiscal 1998 District of Columbia Appropriations/Passage. Passage of the bill to provide $828 million in new budget authority for the District of Columbia in fiscal 1998. The bill would provide $109 million more than the $719 million provided in fiscal 1997 and $51 million more than the $777 million requested by the city. The bill contains a number of legislative riders, including a provision to establish an educational scholarship program to allow low-income students from the District of Columbia to attend private schools or public schools in the Virginia or Maryland suburbs. Passed 203-202: R 203-11; D 0-190 (ND 0-142, SD 0-48); I 0-1, Oct. 9, 1997. A "nay" was a vote in support of the president's position.

514. HR 2607. Fiscal 1998 District of Columbia Appropriations/Reconsideration of Vote. Hansen, R-Utah, motion to table (kill) the Frank, D-Mass., motion to reconsider the vote by which the House passed the bill to provide $828 million in new budget authority for the District of Columbia in fiscal 1998. Motion agreed to 162-135: R 161-0; D 1-134 (ND 1-98, SD 0-36); I 0-1, Oct. 9, 1997.

KEY

- Y Voted for (yea).
- # Paired for.
- + Announced for.
- N Voted against (nay).
- X Paired against.
- – Announced against.
- P Voted "present."
- C Voted "present" to avoid possible conflict of interest.
- ? Did not vote or otherwise make a position known.

Democrats ***Republicans***
Independent

	511	512	513	514
ALABAMA				
1 ***Callahan***	N	N	Y	?
2 ***Everett***	N	N	Y	?
3 ***Riley***	N	N	Y	Y
4 ***Aderholt***	N	N	Y	Y
5 Cramer	Y	Y	N	N
6 ***Bachus***	N	N	Y	Y
7 Hilliard	?	?	?	?
ALASKA				
AL ***Young***	Y	N	Y	Y
ARIZONA				
1 ***Salmon***	N	N	Y	Y
2 Pastor	Y	Y	N	?
3 ***Stump***	N	N	Y	Y
4 ***Shadegg***	N	N	Y	Y
5 ***Kolbe***	N	N	Y	Y
6 ***Hayworth***	N	N	Y	Y
ARKANSAS				
1 Berry	Y	Y	N	?
2 Snyder	Y	Y	N	?
3 ***Hutchinson***	N	N	N	Y
4 ***Dickey***	N	N	Y	Y
CALIFORNIA				
1 ***Riggs***	N	N	Y	Y
2 ***Herger***	N	N	Y	Y
3 Fazio	Y	Y	N	N
4 ***Doolittle***	N	N	Y	Y
5 Matsui	Y	Y	N	N
6 Woolsey	Y	Y	N	N
7 Miller	Y	?	?	?
8 Pelosi	Y	Y	N	N
9 Dellums	Y	Y	N	N
10 Tauscher	Y	Y	N	?
11 ***Pombo***	N	N	Y	Y
12 Lantos	Y	Y	N	N
13 Stark	Y	Y	N	?
14 Eshoo	Y	Y	N	N
15 ***Campbell***	N	N	N	Y
16 Lofgren	Y	Y	N	N
17 Farr	Y	Y	N	N
18 Condit	Y	N	N	N
19 ***Radanovich***	N	N	Y	Y
20 Dooley	Y	?	?	?
21 ***Thomas***	N	N	Y	Y
22 Capps	Y	Y	N	N
23 ***Gallegly***	N	N	Y	?
24 Sherman	Y	Y	N	N
25 ***McKeon***	N	N	Y	Y
26 Berman	#	#	?	?
27 ***Rogan***	N	N	Y	Y
28 ***Dreier***	N	?	?	?
29 Waxman	Y	Y	N	N
30 Becerra	Y	Y	N	N
31 Martinez	Y	Y	N	?
32 Dixon	Y	Y	N	N
33 Roybal-Allard	Y	Y	N	N
34 Torres	Y	?	?	?
35 Waters	Y	Y	N	N
36 Harman	Y	Y	N	?
37 Millender-McD.	Y	Y	N	N
38 ***Horn***	Y	N	Y	Y
39 ***Royce***	N	N	Y	Y
40 ***Lewis***	Y	X	#	?
41 ***Kim***	N	N	Y	Y
42 Brown	Y	Y	N	N
43 ***Calvert***	N	N	Y	?
44 ***Bono***	N	N	Y	?
45 ***Rohrabacher***	N	N	Y	Y
46 Sanchez	Y	Y	N	N
47 ***Cox***	N	N	Y	Y
48 ***Packard***	N	N	Y	?
49 ***Bilbray***	Y	N	Y	Y
50 Filner	Y	Y	N	N
51 ***Cunningham***	N	N	Y	Y
52 ***Hunter***	N	N	Y	Y
COLORADO				
1 DeGette	Y	Y	N	N
2 Skaggs	Y	Y	N	N
3 ***McInnis***	N	N	Y	Y
4 ***Schaffer***	N	N	Y	Y
5 ***Hefley***	N	N	Y	Y
6 ***Schaefer***	N	N	Y	Y
CONNECTICUT				
1 Kennelly	Y	Y	N	?
2 Gejdenson	Y	Y	?	?
3 DeLauro	Y	Y	N	N
4 ***Shays***	Y	N	Y	Y
5 Maloney	Y	Y	N	?
6 ***Johnson***	Y	Y	Y	Y
DELAWARE				
AL ***Castle***	N	N	N	Y
FLORIDA				
1 ***Scarborough***	N	N	Y	Y
2 Boyd	Y	Y	N	N
3 Brown	?	?	?	?
4 ***Fowler***	N	N	Y	?
5 Thurman	Y	Y	N	N
6 ***Stearns***	N	N	Y	Y
7 ***Mica***	N	N	Y	Y
8 ***McCollum***	N	N	Y	?
9 ***Bilirakis***	N	N	Y	Y
10 ***Young***	N	N	Y	Y
11 Davis	Y	Y	N	N
12 ***Canady***	N	N	Y	Y
13 ***Miller***	N	N	Y	?
14 ***Goss***	N	N	Y	Y
15 ***Weldon***	N	N	Y	Y
16 ***Foley***	N	N	Y	Y
17 Meek	Y	Y	N	N
18 ***Ros-Lehtinen***	N	N	Y	?
19 Wexler	Y	Y	N	N
20 Deutsch	Y	Y	N	–
21 ***Diaz-Balart***	Y	N	Y	?
22 ***Shaw***	N	N	Y	Y
23 Hastings	Y	Y	N	?
GEORGIA				
1 ***Kingston***	N	N	Y	?
2 Bishop	Y	Y	N	N
3 ***Collins***	N	N	Y	Y
4 McKinney	Y	Y	N	N
5 Lewis	Y	Y	N	N
6 ***Gingrich***		N	Y	
7 ***Barr***	N	N	Y	Y
8 ***Chambliss***	X	X	?	?
9 ***Deal***	N	N	Y	?
10 ***Norwood***	N	N	Y	?
11 ***Linder***	N	N	Y	Y
HAWAII				
1 Abercrombie	Y	Y	N	N
2 Mink	Y	Y	N	N
IDAHO				
1 ***Chenoweth***	N	N	Y	Y
2 ***Crapo***	N	N	Y	Y
ILLINOIS				
1 Rush	Y	Y	N	?
2 Jackson	Y	Y	N	N
3 Lipinski	Y	N	N	?
4 Gutierrez	?	Y	N	?
5 Blagojevich	Y	Y	N	?
6 ***Hyde***	N	N	Y	?
7 Davis	Y	Y	N	N
8 ***Crane***	N	N	Y	Y
9 Yates	Y	Y	N	?
10 ***Porter***	N	N	Y	Y
11 ***Weller***	Y	N	Y	Y
12 Costello	Y	Y	N	?
13 ***Fawell***	N	Y	Y	Y
14 ***Hastert***	N	N	Y	Y
15 ***Ewing***	Y	N	Y	?

ND Northern Democrats SD Southern Democrats

	511	512	513	514
16 Manzullo	N	N	Y	Y
17 Evans	Y	Y	N	N
18 LaHood	Y	N	Y	Y
19 Poshard	Y	Y	N	?
20 Shimkus	Y	N	Y	Y
INDIANA				
1 Visclosky	Y	Y	N	N
2 McIntosh	N	N	Y	Y
3 Roemer	Y	Y	N	N
4 Souder	N	N	Y	Y
5 Buyer	N	?	?	?
6 Burton	N	N	Y	Y
7 Pease	N	N	Y	Y
8 Hostettler	N	N	Y	Y
9 Hamilton	Y	Y	N	N
10 Carson	Y	Y	N	N
IOWA				
1 Leach	N	Y	N	Y
2 Nussle	N	N	Y	Y
3 Boswell	Y	Y	N	?
4 Ganske	N	N	Y	?
5 Latham	N	N	Y	Y
KANSAS				
1 Moran	N	N	Y	Y
2 Ryun	N	N	Y	Y
3 Snowbarger	N	N	Y	Y
4 Tiahrt	N	N	Y	Y
KENTUCKY				
1 Whitfield	N	N	Y	Y
2 Lewis	–	–	+	+
3 Northup	N	N	Y	Y
4 Bunning	N	N	Y	Y
5 Rogers	N	N	Y	?
6 Baesler	Y	Y	N	?
LOUISIANA				
1 Livingston	N	N	Y	Y
2 Jefferson	Y	Y	N	N
3 Tauzin	N	N	Y	Y
4 McCrery	N	N	Y	Y
5 Cooksey	N	N	Y	?
6 Baker	N	?	?	?
7 John	N	Y	N	?
MAINE				
1 Allen	Y	Y	N	N
2 Baldacci	Y	#	X	N
MARYLAND				
1 Gilchrest	N	N	Y	Y
2 Ehrlich	N	N	Y	Y
3 Cardin	Y	Y	N	N
4 Wynn	Y	Y	N	N
5 Hoyer	Y	Y	N	N
6 Bartlett	N	N	Y	Y
7 Cummings	Y	Y	N	N
8 Morella	N	Y	N	?
MASSACHUSETTS				
1 Olver	Y	Y	N	?
2 Neal	Y	Y	N	?
3 McGovern	Y	Y	N	N
4 Frank	Y	Y	N	N
5 Meehan	Y	Y	N	?
6 Tierney	Y	Y	N	?
7 Markey	Y	Y	N	N
8 Kennedy	Y	Y	N	?
9 Moakley	Y	Y	N	N
10 Delahunt	Y	Y	N	N
MICHIGAN				
1 Stupak	Y	Y	N	N
2 Hoekstra	N	N	Y	Y
3 Ehlers	N	N	Y	Y
4 Camp	N	N	Y	Y
5 Barcia	Y	Y	N	N
6 Upton	N	N	Y	Y
7 Smith	N	N	Y	Y
8 Stabenow	Y	Y	N	N
9 Kildee	Y	Y	N	N
10 Bonior	Y	Y	N	N
11 Knollenberg	N	N	Y	Y
12 Levin	Y	Y	N	N
13 Rivers	Y	Y	N	N
14 Conyers	Y	Y	N	N
15 Kilpatrick	Y	Y	N	N
16 Dingell	Y	Y	N	N
MINNESOTA				
1 Gutknecht	N	N	Y	Y
2 Minge	Y	Y	N	N

	511	512	513	514
3 Ramstad	N	Y	N	Y
4 Vento	Y	Y	N	?
5 Sabo	Y	Y	N	N
6 Luther	Y	Y	N	?
7 Peterson	Y	Y	N	N
8 Oberstar	Y	Y	N	?
MISSISSIPPI				
1 Wicker	N	N	Y	?
2 Thompson	Y	Y	N	?
3 Pickering	N	N	Y	Y
4 Parker	N	N	Y	?
5 Taylor	N	N	N	N
MISSOURI				
1 Clay	Y	Y	N	?
2 Talent	N	N	Y	Y
3 Gephardt	Y	Y	N	N
4 Skelton	Y	Y	N	?
5 McCarthy	Y	+	–	+
6 Danner	Y	Y	N	N
7 Blunt	N	N	Y	?
8 Emerson	N	N	Y	?
9 Hulshof	N	N	Y	Y
MONTANA				
AL Hill	Y	N	Y	Y
NEBRASKA				
1 Bereuter	N	N	Y	Y
2 Christensen	N	N	Y	Y
3 Barrett	N	N	Y	?
NEVADA				
1 Ensign	N	N	Y	Y
2 Gibbons	N	N	Y	Y
NEW HAMPSHIRE				
1 Sununu	N	N	Y	Y
2 Bass	N	N	Y	?
NEW JERSEY				
1 Andrews	Y	Y	N	N
2 LoBiondo	Y	N	N	Y
3 Saxton	Y	N	Y	Y
4 Smith	Y	N	Y	Y
5 Roukema	Y	Y	N	Y
6 Pallone	Y	Y	N	N
7 Franks	Y	N	N	Y
8 Pascrell	Y	Y	N	N
9 Rothman	Y	Y	N	?
10 Payne	Y	Y	N	N
11 Frelinghuysen	N	N	Y	?
12 Pappas	Y	N	Y	Y
13 Menendez	Y	Y	N	?
NEW MEXICO				
1 Schiff	?	?	?	?
2 Skeen	N	N	Y	Y
3 Redmond	N	N	Y	Y
NEW YORK				
1 Forbes	Y	N	Y	?
2 Lazio	Y	N	Y	Y
3 King	Y	N	Y	Y
4 McCarthy	Y	Y	N	?
5 Ackerman	Y	Y	N	?
6 Flake	Y	Y	N	N
7 Manton	Y	Y	N	N
8 Nadler	Y	Y	N	N
9 Schumer	Y	+	–	–
10 Towns	Y	Y	N	N
11 Owens	Y	Y	N	?
12 Velázquez	Y	Y	N	?
13 Vacant				
14 Maloney	Y	Y	N	N
15 Rangel	Y	Y	N	N
16 Serrano	Y	Y	N	N
17 Engel	Y	Y	N	N
18 Lowey	Y	Y	N	N
19 Kelly	Y	N	Y	Y
20 Gilman	Y	N	Y	Y
21 McNulty	Y	Y	N	N
22 Solomon	?	N	Y	Y
23 Boehlert	Y	Y	N	Y
24 McHugh	Y	Y	?	?
25 Walsh	Y	N	Y	Y
26 Hinchey	Y	Y	N	?
27 Paxon	N	N	Y	Y
28 Slaughter	Y	Y	N	N
29 LaFalce	Y	Y	N	N
30 Quinn	Y	N	Y	Y
31 Houghton	Y	N	Y	Y

	511	512	513	514
NORTH CAROLINA				
1 Clayton	Y	Y	N	N
2 Etheridge	Y	Y	N	N
3 Jones	N	N	Y	Y
4 Price	Y	Y	N	N
5 Burr	N	N	Y	Y
6 Coble	N	N	Y	?
7 McIntyre	Y	Y	N	N
8 Hefner	?	?	?	?
9 Myrick	N	N	Y	?
10 Ballenger	N	N	Y	Y
11 Taylor	N	N	Y	Y
12 Watt	Y	Y	N	N
NORTH DAKOTA				
AL Pomeroy	Y	Y	N	?
OHIO				
1 Chabot	N	N	Y	?
2 Portman	N	N	Y	Y
3 Hall	Y	#	X	?
4 Oxley	N	N	Y	Y
5 Gillmor	N	N	Y	Y
6 Strickland	Y	Y	N	N
7 Hobson	N	N	Y	Y
8 Boehner	N	N	Y	?
9 Kaptur	Y	Y	N	N
10 Kucinich	Y	Y	N	N
11 Stokes	Y	Y	N	N
12 Kasich	N	N	Y	Y
13 Brown	Y	Y	N	N
14 Sawyer	Y	Y	N	?
15 Pryce	N	N	Y	Y
16 Regula	Y	N	Y	Y
17 Traficant	Y	Y	N	Y
18 Ney	Y	N	Y	Y
19 LaTourette	Y	N	Y	?
OKLAHOMA				
1 Largent	N	N	Y	?
2 Coburn	N	N	Y	?
3 Watkins	N	N	Y	Y
4 Watts	N	N	Y	?
5 Istook	N	N	Y	Y
6 Lucas	N	N	Y	Y
OREGON				
1 Furse	Y	Y	N	N
2 Smith	N	?	?	?
3 Blumenauer	Y	Y	N	N
4 DeFazio	Y	Y	N	N
5 Hooley	Y	Y	N	?
PENNSYLVANIA				
1 Foglietta	Y	Y	N	?
2 Fattah	Y	Y	N	N
3 Borski	Y	Y	N	?
4 Klink	Y	Y	N	N
5 Peterson	N	N	Y	Y
6 Holden	Y	Y	N	?
7 Weldon	Y	N	Y	Y
8 Greenwood	Y	N	Y	Y
9 Shuster	N	N	Y	?
10 McDade	Y	N	Y	?
11 Kanjorski	Y	Y	N	N
12 Murtha	Y	Y	N	?
13 Fox	Y	N	Y	Y
14 Coyne	Y	Y	N	N
15 McHale	Y	Y	N	N
16 Pitts	N	N	Y	Y
17 Gekas	N	N	Y	?
18 Doyle	Y	Y	N	?
19 Goodling	N	N	Y	+
20 Mascara	Y	Y	N	?
21 English	Y	N	Y	Y
RHODE ISLAND				
1 Kennedy	Y	Y	N	?
2 Weygand	Y	Y	N	N
SOUTH CAROLINA				
1 Sanford	N	N	Y	Y
2 Spence	N	N	Y	?
3 Graham	N	N	Y	?
4 Inglis	N	N	Y	Y
5 Spratt	Y	Y	N	N
6 Clyburn	Y	Y	N	?
SOUTH DAKOTA				
AL Thune	N	N	Y	Y
TENNESSEE				
1 Jenkins	N	N	Y	?
2 Duncan	N	N	N	?

	511	512	513	514
3 Wamp	N	N	Y	?
4 Hilleary	N	N	Y	Y
5 Clement	Y	+	–	–
6 Gordon	Y	Y	N	N
7 Bryant	N	N	Y	?
8 Tanner	Y	Y	N	?
9 Ford	Y	Y	N	?
TEXAS				
1 Sandlin	Y	Y	N	N
2 Turner	Y	Y	N	N
3 Johnson, Sam	N	N	Y	Y
4 Hall	N	N	N	?
5 Sessions	N	N	Y	Y
6 Barton	N	N	?	?
7 Archer	N	N	Y	Y
8 Brady	N	N	Y	Y
9 Lampson	Y	Y	N	N
10 Doggett	Y	?	?	?
11 Edwards	Y	Y	?	?
12 Granger	N	N	Y	Y
13 Thornberry	N	N	Y	Y
14 Paul	N	N	P	Y
15 Hinojosa	Y	Y	N	N
16 Reyes	Y	Y	N	N
17 Stenholm	N	Y	N	N
18 Jackson-Lee	Y	Y	N	N
19 Combest	N	N	Y	Y
20 Gonzalez	?	?	?	?
21 Smith	N	N	Y	Y
22 DeLay	N	N	Y	Y
23 Bonilla	N	N	Y	?
24 Frost	Y	Y	N	N
25 Bentsen	Y	Y	N	N
26 Armey	N	N	Y	Y
27 Ortiz	Y	Y	N	N
28 Rodriguez	Y	Y	N	N
29 Green	Y	Y	N	N
30 Johnson, E.B.	Y	Y	N	N
UTAH				
1 Hansen	N	N	Y	Y
2 Cook	N	N	Y	Y
3 Cannon	N	N	Y	?
VERMONT				
AL Sanders	Y	Y	N	N
VIRGINIA				
1 Bateman	N	N	Y	Y
2 Pickett	Y	Y	N	N
3 Scott	Y	Y	N	N
4 Sisisky	Y	Y	N	?
5 Goode	N	Y	N	N
6 Goodlatte	N	N	Y	?
7 Bliley	N	N	Y	Y
8 Moran	Y	Y	N	N
9 Boucher	Y	Y	N	N
10 Wolf	N	X	#	?
11 Davis	N	N	Y	Y
WASHINGTON				
1 White	N	N	Y	Y
2 Metcalf	Y	N	Y	?
3 Smith, Linda	Y	N	Y	Y
4 Hastings	?	?	?	?
5 Nethercutt	N	P	Y	Y
6 Dicks	Y	Y	N	?
7 McDermott	Y	Y	N	?
8 Dunn	N	N	Y	Y
9 Smith, Adam	Y	Y	N	N
WEST VIRGINIA				
1 Mollohan	Y	Y	N	N
2 Wise	Y	Y	N	N
3 Rahall	Y	Y	N	N
WISCONSIN				
1 Neumann	N	N	Y	?
2 Klug	N	N	Y	Y
3 Kind	Y	Y	N	N
4 Kleczka	Y	Y	N	N
5 Barrett	Y	Y	N	N
6 Petri	Y	N	Y	?
7 Obey	Y	Y	N	N
8 Johnson	Y	Y	N	N
9 Sensenbrenner	N	N	Y	?
WYOMING				
AL Cubin	N	N	Y	Y

Southern states - Ala., Ark., Fla., Ga., Ky., La., Miss., N.C., Okla., S.C., Tenn., Texas, Va.

HOUSE VOTES 515, 516, 517, 518, 519, 520

515. HR 2204. Fiscal 1998-99 Coast Guard Authorization/Previous Question. Diaz-Balart, R-Fla., motion to order the previous question (thus ending debate and the possibility of amendment) on adoption of the rule (H Res 265) to provide for floor consideration of the bill to authorize $3.9 billion for Coast Guard programs in fiscal 1998 and $4.1 billion in fiscal 1999. Motion agreed to 223-196: R 217-2; D 6-193 (ND 6-141, SD 0-52); I 0-1, Oct. 21, 1997. (Subsequently, the rule was adopted by voice vote.)

516. HR 2464. International Adoption Vaccinations/Passage. Smith, R-Texas, motion to suspend the rules and pass the bill to exempt foreign children under age 10 who are adopted by U.S. citizens from immigration vaccination requirements. Motion agreed to 420-0: R 219-0; D 200-0 (ND 148-0, SD 52-0); I 1-0, Oct. 21, 1997. A two-thirds majority of those present and voting (280 in this case) is required for passage under suspension of the rules.

517. HR 1962. White House Chief Financial Officer/Passage. Horn, R-Calif., motion to suspend the rules and pass the bill to establish the position of chief financial officer within the Executive Office of the President. Motion agreed to 413-3: R 213-2; D 199-1 (ND 147-1, SD 52-0); I 1-0, Oct. 21, 1997. A two-thirds majority of those present and voting (278 in this case) is required for passage under suspension of the rules.

518. HR 1534. Private Property Rights/Local Land Use Decision Appeals. Boehlert, R-N.Y., substitute amendment to eliminate the bill's provisions that would allow a private property owner to appeal local land use decisions in the federal courts while retaining provisions that allow expedited federal court consideration of land use disputes involving the federal government. Rejected 178-242: R 36-184; D 141-58 (ND 119-27, SD 22-31); I 1-0, Oct. 22, 1997.

519. HR 1534. Private Property Rights/Passage. Passage of the bill to establish guidelines for allowing private property owners to appeal local, state and federal land use decisions in federal courts. The bill would require federal courts to consider all cases qualifying as "takings" under the Fifth Amendment to the Constitution. Passed 248-178: R 193-30; D 55-147 (ND 25-124, SD 30-23); I 0-1, Oct. 22, 1997. A "nay" was a vote in support of the president's position.

520. HR 2247. Amtrak Subsidies/Rule. Adoption of the rule (H Res 270) to provide for floor consideration of the bill to authorize subsidies to Amtrak of $3.37 billion through fiscal 2000 and streamline operations of the railway, steering Amtrak toward private control by 2002. Adopted 226-200: R 220-2; D 6-197 (ND 3-146, SD 3-51); I 0-1, Oct. 22, 1997.

KEY

- Y Voted for (yea).
- # Paired for.
- + Announced for.
- N Voted against (nay).
- X Paired against.
- – Announced against.
- P Voted "present."
- C Voted "present" to avoid possible conflict of interest.
- ? Did not vote or otherwise make a position known.

Democrats ***Republicans***
Independent

	515	516	517	518	519	520
ALABAMA						
1 ***Callahan***	Y	Y	Y	N	Y	Y
2 ***Everett***	Y	Y	Y	N	Y	Y
3 ***Riley***	Y	Y	Y	N	Y	Y
4 ***Aderholt***	Y	Y	Y	N	Y	Y
5 Cramer	N	Y	Y	N	Y	N
6 ***Bachus***	Y	Y	Y	N	Y	Y
7 Hilliard	N	Y	Y	N	Y	N
ALASKA						
AL ***Young***	Y	Y	Y	N	Y	Y
ARIZONA						
1 ***Salmon***	Y	Y	Y	N	Y	Y
2 Pastor	N	Y	Y	Y	N	N
3 ***Stump***	Y	Y	Y	N	Y	Y
4 ***Shadegg***	?	Y	Y	N	Y	Y
5 ***Kolbe***	Y	Y	Y	N	Y	Y
6 ***Hayworth***	Y	Y	Y	N	Y	Y
ARKANSAS						
1 Berry	N	Y	Y	N	Y	N
2 Snyder	N	Y	Y	Y	N	N
3 ***Hutchinson***	Y	Y	Y	N	Y	Y
4 ***Dickey***	Y	Y	Y	N	Y	Y
CALIFORNIA						
1 ***Riggs***	Y	Y	Y	N	Y	Y
2 ***Herger***	Y	Y	Y	N	Y	Y
3 Fazio	N	Y	Y	N	Y	N
4 ***Doolittle***	Y	Y	Y	N	Y	Y
5 Matsui	N	Y	Y	Y	N	N
6 Woolsey	N	Y	Y	Y	N	N
7 Miller	N	Y	Y	Y	N	N
8 Pelosi	N	Y	Y	Y	N	N
9 Dellums	?	?	?	Y	N	N
10 Tauscher	N	Y	Y	N	N	N
11 ***Pombo***	Y	Y	Y	N	Y	Y
12 Lantos	?	?	?	?	?	?
13 Stark	N	Y	Y	?	N	N
14 Eshoo	N	Y	Y	Y	N	N
15 ***Campbell***	Y	Y	Y	N	Y	Y
16 Lofgren	N	Y	Y	Y	N	N
17 Farr	N	Y	Y	Y	N	N
18 Condit	N	Y	Y	N	Y	N
19 ***Radanovich***	Y	Y	Y	N	Y	Y
20 Dooley	N	Y	Y	N	Y	Y
21 ***Thomas***	Y	Y	Y	N	Y	Y
22 Capps	N	Y	Y	Y	N	N
23 ***Gallegly***	Y	Y	Y	N	Y	Y
24 Sherman	N	Y	Y	Y	N	N
25 ***McKeon***	Y	Y	Y	N	Y	Y
26 Berman	N	Y	Y	Y	N	N
27 ***Rogan***	Y	Y	Y	N	Y	Y
28 ***Dreier***	Y	Y	Y	N	Y	Y
29 Waxman	N	Y	Y	Y	N	N
30 Becerra	N	Y	Y	Y	N	N
31 Martinez	N	Y	Y	?	Y	N
32 Dixon	N	Y	Y	Y	N	N
33 Roybal-Allard	N	Y	Y	Y	N	N
34 Torres	N	Y	Y	Y	N	N
35 Waters	N	Y	Y	Y	N	N
36 Harman	N	Y	Y	N	Y	N
37 Millender-McD.	N	Y	Y	Y	N	N
38 ***Horn***	Y	Y	Y	Y	N	Y
39 ***Royce***	Y	Y	Y	N	Y	Y
40 ***Lewis***	Y	Y	Y	N	Y	Y
41 ***Kim***	Y	Y	Y	N	Y	Y
42 Brown	N	Y	Y	?	N	N
43 ***Calvert***	Y	Y	Y	N	Y	Y
44 ***Bono***	?	?	?	N	Y	Y
45 ***Rohrabacher***	Y	Y	Y	N	Y	Y
46 Sanchez	N	Y	Y	Y	Y	N
47 ***Cox***	Y	Y	Y	N	Y	Y
48 ***Packard***	Y	Y	Y	N	Y	Y
49 ***Bilbray***	Y	Y	Y	N	N	Y
50 Filner	N	Y	Y	Y	N	N
51 ***Cunningham***	Y	Y	Y	N	Y	N
52 ***Hunter***	Y	Y	Y	N	Y	Y
COLORADO						
1 DeGette	N	Y	Y	Y	N	N
2 Skaggs	N	Y	Y	Y	N	N
3 ***McInnis***	Y	Y	Y	N	Y	Y
4 ***Schaffer***	Y	Y	Y	N	Y	Y
5 ***Hefley***	Y	Y	Y	N	Y	N
6 ***Schaefer***	Y	Y	Y	N	Y	Y
CONNECTICUT						
1 Kennelly	N	Y	Y	N	N	N
2 Gejdenson	N	Y	Y	N	N	N
3 DeLauro	N	Y	Y	Y	N	N
4 ***Shays***	N	Y	Y	+	N	Y
5 Maloney	N	Y	Y	Y	N	N
6 ***Johnson***	Y	Y	Y	Y	N	Y
DELAWARE						
AL ***Castle***	Y	Y	Y	Y	N	Y
FLORIDA						
1 ***Scarborough***	Y	Y	Y	Y	Y	Y
2 Boyd	N	Y	Y	N	Y	N
3 Brown	N	Y	Y	Y	N	N
4 ***Fowler***	Y	Y	?	N	Y	Y
5 Thurman	N	Y	Y	Y	N	N
6 ***Stearns***	Y	Y	Y	N	Y	Y
7 ***Mica***	Y	Y	Y	N	Y	Y
8 ***McCollum***	Y	Y	Y	N	Y	Y
9 ***Bilirakis***	Y	Y	Y	N	Y	Y
10 ***Young***	Y	Y	Y	N	Y	Y
11 Davis	N	Y	Y	Y	N	N
12 ***Canady***	Y	Y	Y	N	Y	Y
13 ***Miller***	Y	Y	Y	Y	Y	Y
14 ***Goss***	Y	Y	Y	Y	N	Y
15 ***Weldon***	Y	Y	Y	N	Y	Y
16 ***Foley***	Y	Y	Y	N	Y	Y
17 Meek	N	Y	Y	Y	N	N
18 ***Ros-Lehtinen***	Y	Y	Y	N	Y	Y
19 Wexler	N	Y	Y	N	N	N
20 Deutsch	N	Y	Y	N	Y	N
21 ***Diaz-Balart***	Y	Y	Y	N	Y	Y
22 ***Shaw***	Y	Y	Y	Y	Y	Y
23 Hastings	N	Y	Y	Y	N	N
GEORGIA						
1 ***Kingston***	Y	Y	Y	N	Y	Y
2 Bishop	N	Y	Y	N	Y	N
3 ***Collins***	Y	Y	Y	N	Y	Y
4 McKinney	N	Y	Y	Y	N	N
5 Lewis	N	Y	Y	Y	N	N
6 ***Gingrich***				N	Y	
7 ***Barr***	Y	Y	Y	N	Y	Y
8 ***Chambliss***	Y	Y	Y	?	?	?
9 ***Deal***	Y	Y	Y	N	Y	Y
10 ***Norwood***	Y	Y	Y	N	Y	Y
11 ***Linder***	Y	Y	Y	N	Y	Y
HAWAII						
1 Abercrombie	N	Y	Y	Y	N	N
2 Mink	N	Y	Y	Y	N	N
IDAHO						
1 ***Chenoweth***	Y	Y	Y	N	Y	Y
2 ***Crapo***	Y	Y	Y	N	Y	Y
ILLINOIS						
1 Rush	N	Y	Y	Y	N	N
2 Jackson	N	Y	Y	Y	N	N
3 Lipinski	N	Y	Y	Y	N	N
4 Gutierrez	N	Y	Y	Y	N	N
5 Blagojevich	N	Y	Y	Y	N	N
6 ***Hyde***	Y	?	?	N	Y	Y
7 Davis	N	Y	Y	Y	N	N
8 ***Crane***	Y	Y	Y	N	Y	Y
9 Yates	N	Y	Y	Y	N	N
10 ***Porter***	Y	Y	Y	Y	N	Y
11 ***Weller***	Y	Y	Y	N	Y	Y
12 Costello	N	Y	Y	Y	N	N
13 ***Fawell***	Y	Y	Y	Y	N	Y
14 ***Hastert***	Y	Y	Y	N	Y	Y
15 ***Ewing***	Y	Y	Y	Y	N	Y

ND Northern Democrats SD Southern Democrats

	515	516	517	518	519	520
16 ***Manzullo***	Y	Y	Y	N	Y	Y
17 Evans	N	Y	Y	N	N	N
18 ***LaHood***	Y	Y	Y	N	Y	Y
19 Poshard	N	Y	Y	Y	N	N
20 ***Shimkus***	Y	Y	Y	N	Y	Y
INDIANA						
1 Visclosky	N	Y	Y	Y	N	N
2 ***McIntosh***	?	?	?	?	?	?
3 Roemer	N	Y	Y	Y	Y	N
4 ***Souder***	Y	Y	Y	N	Y	Y
5 ***Buyer***	Y	Y	Y	N	Y	Y
6 ***Burton***	Y	Y	Y	N	Y	Y
7 ***Pease***	Y	Y	Y	N	Y	Y
8 ***Hostettler***	Y	Y	Y	N	Y	Y
9 Hamilton	N	Y	Y	Y	Y	N
10 Carson	N	Y	Y	Y	N	N
IOWA						
1 ***Leach***	Y	Y	Y	Y	Y	Y
2 ***Nussle***	Y	Y	Y	N	Y	Y
3 Boswell	N	Y	Y	N	Y	N
4 ***Ganske***	Y	Y	Y	Y	N	Y
5 ***Latham***	Y	Y	Y	N	Y	Y
KANSAS						
1 ***Moran***	Y	Y	Y	N	Y	Y
2 ***Ryun***	Y	Y	Y	N	Y	Y
3 ***Snowbarger***	Y	Y	Y	N	Y	Y
4 ***Tiahrt***	Y	Y	Y	N	Y	Y
KENTUCKY						
1 ***Whitfield***	Y	Y	Y	N	Y	Y
2 ***Lewis***	Y	Y	Y	N	Y	Y
3 ***Northup***	Y	Y	Y	N	Y	Y
4 ***Bunning***	Y	Y	Y	N	Y	Y
5 ***Rogers***	Y	Y	Y	N	Y	Y
6 Baesler	N	Y	Y	N	Y	N
LOUISIANA						
1 ***Livingston***	Y	Y	Y	N	Y	Y
2 Jefferson	?	?	?	N	Y	N
3 ***Tauzin***	Y	Y	Y	N	Y	Y
4 ***McCrery***	Y	Y	Y	N	Y	Y
5 ***Cooksey***	Y	Y	Y	N	Y	Y
6 ***Baker***	Y	Y	Y	N	Y	Y
7 John	N	Y	Y	N	Y	N
MAINE						
1 Allen	N	Y	Y	N	N	N
2 Baldacci	N	Y	Y	Y	Y	N
MARYLAND						
1 ***Gilchrest***	Y	Y	Y	Y	N	Y
2 ***Ehrlich***	Y	Y	Y	N	Y	Y
3 Cardin	N	Y	Y	Y	N	Y
4 Wynn	N	Y	Y	Y	N	N
5 Hoyer	N	Y	Y	N	Y	N
6 ***Bartlett***	Y	Y	Y	N	Y	Y
7 Cummings	N	Y	Y	Y	N	N
8 ***Morella***	Y	Y	Y	Y	N	Y
MASSACHUSETTS						
1 Olver	N	Y	Y	Y	N	N
2 Neal	?	?	?	Y	N	N
3 McGovern	N	Y	Y	Y	N	N
4 Frank	N	Y	Y	Y	N	N
5 Meehan	N	Y	Y	Y	N	N
6 Tierney	N	Y	Y	Y	N	N
7 Markey	N	Y	Y	Y	N	N
8 Kennedy	N	Y	Y	Y	N	N
9 Moakley	N	Y	Y	Y	N	N
10 Delahunt	N	Y	Y	Y	N	N
MICHIGAN						
1 Stupak	N	Y	Y	Y	N	N
2 ***Hoekstra***	Y	Y	Y	N	Y	Y
3 ***Ehlers***	Y	Y	Y	Y	N	Y
4 ***Camp***	Y	Y	Y	N	Y	Y
5 Barcia	N	Y	Y	N	Y	N
6 ***Upton***	Y	Y	Y	N	Y	Y
7 ***Smith***	Y	Y	Y	N	Y	Y
8 Stabenow	N	Y	Y	Y	N	N
9 Kildee	N	Y	Y	Y	N	N
10 Bonior	N	Y	Y	Y	N	N
11 ***Knollenberg***	Y	Y	Y	N	Y	Y
12 Levin	N	Y	Y	Y	N	N
13 Rivers	N	Y	Y	Y	N	N
14 Conyers	N	Y	Y	N	N	N
15 Kilpatrick	N	Y	Y	Y	N	N
16 Dingell	N	Y	Y	N	N	N
MINNESOTA						
1 ***Gutknecht***	Y	Y	Y	N	Y	Y
2 Minge	N	Y	Y	Y	N	N

	515	516	517	518	519	520
3 ***Ramstad***	Y	Y	Y	Y	N	Y
4 Vento	N	Y	Y	Y	N	N
5 Sabo	N	Y	Y	Y	N	N
6 Luther	N	Y	Y	Y	N	N
7 Peterson	N	Y	Y	N	Y	N
8 Oberstar	N	Y	Y	N	N	N
MISSISSIPPI						
1 ***Wicker***	Y	Y	Y	N	Y	Y
2 Thompson	N	Y	Y	N	Y	N
3 ***Pickering***	Y	Y	Y	N	Y	Y
4 ***Parker***	Y	Y	Y	?	Y	Y
5 Taylor	N	Y	Y	N	Y	N
MISSOURI						
1 Clay	N	Y	Y	Y	N	N
2 ***Talent***	Y	Y	?	N	Y	Y
3 Gephardt	N	Y	Y	Y	N	N
4 Skelton	N	Y	Y	N	Y	N
5 McCarthy	N	Y	Y	Y	N	N
6 Danner	N	Y	Y	N	Y	N
7 ***Blunt***	Y	Y	Y	N	Y	Y
8 ***Emerson***	Y	Y	Y	N	Y	Y
9 ***Hulshof***	Y	Y	Y	N	Y	Y
MONTANA						
AL ***Hill***	Y	Y	Y	N	Y	Y
NEBRASKA						
1 ***Bereuter***	Y	Y	Y	Y	N	Y
2 ***Christensen***	Y	Y	Y	N	Y	Y
3 ***Barrett***	Y	Y	?	N	Y	Y
NEVADA						
1 ***Ensign***	Y	Y	Y	N	Y	Y
2 ***Gibbons***	Y	Y	Y	N	Y	Y
NEW HAMPSHIRE						
1 ***Sununu***	Y	Y	Y	Y	Y	Y
2 ***Bass***	Y	Y	Y	Y	N	Y
NEW JERSEY						
1 Andrews	N	Y	Y	Y	N	N
2 ***LoBiondo***	Y	Y	Y	N	Y	Y
3 ***Saxton***	Y	Y	Y	Y	N	Y
4 ***Smith***	Y	Y	Y	Y	N	Y
5 ***Roukema***	N	Y	Y	Y	N	Y
6 Pallone	N	Y	Y	N	N	N
7 ***Franks***	Y	Y	Y	N	Y	Y
8 Pascrell	N	Y	Y	N	Y	N
9 Rothman	N	Y	Y	N	Y	N
10 Payne	N	Y	Y	Y	N	N
11 ***Frelinghuysen***	Y	Y	Y	Y	N	Y
12 ***Pappas***	Y	Y	Y	N	Y	Y
13 Menendez	N	Y	Y	Y	N	N
NEW MEXICO						
1 ***Schiff***	?	?	?	?	?	?
2 ***Skeen***	Y	Y	Y	N	Y	Y
3 ***Redmond***	Y	Y	Y	N	Y	Y
NEW YORK						
1 ***Forbes***	Y	Y	Y	Y	N	Y
2 ***Lazio***	Y	Y	Y	Y	N	Y
3 ***King***	Y	Y	Y	N	Y	Y
4 McCarthy	N	Y	Y	Y	N	N
5 Ackerman	N	Y	Y	Y	N	N
6 Flake	N	Y	Y	N	N	N
7 Manton	N	Y	N	Y	N	N
8 Nadler	N	Y	Y	Y	N	N
9 Schumer	N	Y	Y	Y	N	N
10 Towns	N	Y	Y	Y	N	N
11 Owens	N	Y	Y	Y	N	N
12 Velázquez	N	Y	Y	Y	N	N
13 Vacant						
14 Maloney	N	Y	Y	Y	N	N
15 Rangel	N	Y	Y	Y	N	N
16 Serrano	Y	Y	Y	Y	N	N
17 Engel	N	Y	Y	Y	N	N
18 Lowey	N	Y	Y	Y	N	N
19 ***Kelly***	Y	Y	Y	Y	N	Y
20 ***Gilman***	Y	Y	Y	Y	N	Y
21 McNulty	N	Y	Y	Y	N	N
22 ***Solomon***	Y	Y	Y	N	Y	Y
23 ***Boehlert***	Y	Y	Y	Y	N	Y
24 ***McHugh***	Y	Y	Y	N	Y	Y
25 ***Walsh***	Y	Y	Y	Y	N	Y
26 Hinchey	N	Y	Y	Y	N	N
27 ***Paxon***	Y	Y	Y	N	Y	Y
28 Slaughter	N	Y	Y	Y	N	N
29 LaFalce	N	Y	Y	Y	N	N
30 ***Quinn***	Y	Y	Y	N	Y	Y
31 ***Houghton***	Y	Y	Y	N	Y	Y

	515	516	517	518	519	520
NORTH CAROLINA						
1 Clayton	N	Y	Y	Y	N	N
2 Etheridge	N	Y	Y	Y	Y	N
3 ***Jones***	Y	Y	Y	N	Y	Y
4 Price	N	Y	Y	Y	N	N
5 ***Burr***	Y	Y	Y	N	Y	Y
6 ***Coble***	Y	Y	N	N	Y	Y
7 McIntyre	N	Y	Y	N	Y	N
8 Hefner	N	Y	Y	Y	N	N
9 ***Myrick***	Y	Y	Y	N	Y	Y
10 ***Ballenger***	Y	Y	Y	N	Y	Y
11 ***Taylor***	Y	Y	Y	N	Y	Y
12 Watt	N	Y	Y	Y	N	N
NORTH DAKOTA						
AL Pomeroy	N	Y	Y	Y	N	N
OHIO						
1 ***Chabot***	Y	Y	Y	N	Y	Y
2 ***Portman***	Y	Y	Y	Y	N	Y
3 Hall	Y	Y	Y	Y	Y	N
4 ***Oxley***	Y	Y	Y	N	Y	Y
5 ***Gillmor***	?	?	?	N	Y	Y
6 Strickland	Y	Y	Y	?	?	?
7 ***Hobson***	Y	Y	Y	N	Y	Y
8 ***Boehner***	Y	Y	Y	N	Y	Y
9 Kaptur	N	Y	Y	Y	N	N
10 Kucinich	N	Y	Y	Y	N	N
11 Stokes	N	Y	Y	Y	N	N
12 ***Kasich***	Y	Y	Y	N	Y	Y
13 Brown	N	Y	Y	Y	N	N
14 Sawyer	N	Y	Y	Y	N	N
15 ***Pryce***	Y	Y	Y	N	Y	Y
16 ***Regula***	Y	Y	Y	N	Y	Y
17 Traficant	Y	Y	Y	N	Y	Y
18 ***Ney***	Y	Y	Y	N	Y	Y
19 ***LaTourette***	Y	Y	Y	Y	Y	Y
OKLAHOMA						
1 ***Largent***	Y	Y	Y	N	Y	Y
2 ***Coburn***	Y	Y	Y	N	Y	Y
3 ***Watkins***	Y	Y	?	N	Y	Y
4 ***Watts***	?	?	?	N	Y	Y
5 ***Istook***	Y	Y	Y	N	Y	Y
6 ***Lucas***	Y	Y	Y	N	Y	Y
OREGON						
1 Furse	N	Y	Y	Y	N	N
2 ***Smith***	Y	Y	Y	N	Y	Y
3 Blumenauer	N	Y	Y	Y	N	N
4 DeFazio	N	Y	Y	Y	N	N
5 Hooley	N	Y	Y	N	N	N
PENNSYLVANIA						
1 Foglietta	?	Y	Y	Y	N	N
2 Fattah	N	Y	Y	Y	N	N
3 Borski	N	Y	Y	Y	N	N
4 Klink	N	Y	Y	Y	N	N
5 ***Peterson***	Y	Y	Y	N	Y	Y
6 Holden	Y	Y	Y	N	Y	N
7 ***Weldon***	Y	Y	Y	+	Y	Y
8 ***Greenwood***	Y	Y	Y	Y	N	Y
9 ***Shuster***	Y	Y	Y	N	Y	Y
10 ***McDade***	Y	Y	Y	N	Y	Y
11 Kanjorski	N	Y	Y	Y	N	N
12 Murtha	Y	Y	Y	Y	Y	N
13 ***Fox***	Y	Y	Y	Y	Y	Y
14 Coyne	N	Y	Y	Y	N	N
15 McHale	N	Y	Y	Y	N	N
16 ***Pitts***	Y	Y	Y	N	Y	Y
17 ***Gekas***	Y	Y	Y	N	Y	Y
18 Doyle	N	Y	Y	Y	Y	N
19 ***Goodling***	Y	Y	Y	N	Y	Y
20 Mascara	N	Y	Y	Y	Y	N
21 ***English***	Y	Y	Y	N	Y	Y
RHODE ISLAND						
1 Kennedy	N	Y	Y	Y	N	N
2 Weygand	N	Y	Y	Y	Y	N
SOUTH CAROLINA						
1 ***Sanford***	Y	Y	Y	Y	N	Y
2 ***Spence***	Y	Y	Y	N	Y	Y
3 ***Graham***	Y	Y	Y	N	Y	Y
4 ***Inglis***	Y	Y	Y	N	Y	Y
5 Spratt	N	Y	Y	Y	N	N
6 Clyburn	N	Y	Y	N	N	N
SOUTH DAKOTA						
AL ***Thune***	Y	Y	Y	N	Y	Y
TENNESSEE						
1 ***Jenkins***	Y	Y	Y	N	Y	Y
2 ***Duncan***	Y	Y	Y	N	Y	Y

	515	516	517	518	519	520
3 ***Wamp***	Y	Y	Y	N	Y	Y
4 ***Hilleary***	Y	Y	Y	N	Y	Y
5 Clement	N	Y	Y	N	Y	N
6 Gordon	N	Y	Y	N	Y	N
7 ***Bryant***	Y	Y	Y	N	Y	Y
8 Tanner	N	Y	Y	N	Y	N
9 Ford	–	+	Y	N	Y	N
TEXAS						
1 Sandlin	N	Y	Y	N	Y	N
2 Turner	N	Y	Y	N	Y	N
3 ***Johnson, Sam***	Y	Y	Y	N	Y	Y
4 Hall	N	Y	Y	N	Y	Y
5 ***Sessions***	Y	Y	Y	N	Y	Y
6 ***Barton***	Y	Y	Y	N	Y	Y
7 ***Archer***	Y	Y	Y	N	Y	Y
8 ***Brady***	Y	Y	Y	N	Y	Y
9 Lampson	N	Y	Y	Y	N	N
10 Doggett	N	Y	?	N	N	N
11 Edwards	N	Y	Y	N	Y	N
12 ***Granger***	Y	Y	Y	N	Y	Y
13 ***Thornberry***	Y	Y	Y	N	Y	Y
14 ***Paul***	Y	Y	N	N	Y	Y
15 Hinojosa	N	Y	Y	N	Y	N
16 Reyes	N	Y	Y	Y	N	N
17 Stenholm	N	Y	Y	N	Y	Y
18 Jackson-Lee	N	Y	Y	+	–	N
19 ***Combest***	Y	Y	Y	N	Y	Y
20 Gonzalez	?	?	?	?	?	?
21 ***Smith***	Y	Y	Y	N	Y	Y
22 ***DeLay***	Y	Y	Y	N	Y	Y
23 ***Bonilla***	Y	Y	Y	N	Y	Y
24 Frost	N	Y	Y	N	Y	N
25 Bentsen	N	Y	Y	Y	N	N
26 ***Armey***	Y	Y	Y	N	Y	Y
27 Ortiz	N	Y	Y	N	Y	N
28 Rodriguez	N	Y	Y	Y	N	N
29 Green	N	Y	Y	N	Y	N
30 Johnson, E.B.	N	Y	Y	Y	N	N
UTAH						
1 ***Hansen***	Y	Y	Y	N	Y	Y
2 ***Cook***	Y	Y	Y	N	Y	Y
3 ***Cannon***	Y	Y	Y	N	Y	Y
VERMONT						
AL *Sanders*	N	Y	Y	Y	N	N
VIRGINIA						
1 ***Bateman***	Y	Y	Y	N	Y	Y
2 Pickett	N	Y	Y	N	Y	N
3 Scott	N	Y	Y	Y	Y	N
4 Sisisky	N	Y	Y	N	Y	N
5 Goode	N	Y	Y	N	Y	Y
6 ***Goodlatte***	Y	Y	Y	N	Y	Y
7 ***Bliley***	Y	Y	Y	N	Y	Y
8 Moran	N	Y	Y	Y	N	N
9 Boucher	N	Y	Y	Y	N	N
10 ***Wolf***	Y	Y	Y	N	Y	Y
11 ***Davis***	Y	Y	Y	N	Y	Y
WASHINGTON						
1 ***White***	Y	Y	Y	N	Y	Y
2 ***Metcalf***	Y	Y	Y	N	Y	Y
3 ***Smith, Linda***	Y	Y	Y	N	Y	Y
4 ***Hastings***	Y	Y	Y	N	Y	Y
5 ***Nethercutt***	Y	Y	Y	N	Y	Y
6 Dicks	N	Y	Y	Y	N	N
7 McDermott	N	Y	Y	Y	N	N
8 ***Dunn***	Y	Y	Y	N	Y	Y
9 Smith, Adam	N	Y	Y	Y	N	N
WEST VIRGINIA						
1 Mollohan	N	Y	Y	Y	N	N
2 Wise	N	Y	Y	Y	N	N
3 Rahall	N	Y	Y	N	N	N
WISCONSIN						
1 ***Neumann***	Y	Y	Y	N	Y	Y
2 ***Klug***	Y	Y	Y	Y	N	Y
3 Kind	N	Y	Y	Y	N	N
4 Kleczka	N	Y	Y	Y	N	N
5 Barrett	N	Y	Y	Y	N	N
6 ***Petri***	Y	Y	Y	N	Y	Y
7 Obey	N	Y	Y	Y	N	N
8 Johnson	N	Y	Y	Y	N	N
9 ***Sensenbrenner***	Y	Y	Y	Y	Y	Y
WYOMING						
AL ***Cubin***	?	?	?	?	?	?

Southern states - Ala., Ark., Fla., Ga., Ky., La., Miss., N.C., Okla., S.C., Tenn., Texas, Va.

HOUSE VOTES 521, 522, 523, 524, 525

521. Procedural Motion/Journal. Approval of the House Journal of Wednesday, Oct. 22, 1997. Approved 364-52: R 199-18; D 164-34 (ND 118-26, SD 46-8); I 1-0, Oct. 23, 1997.

522. HR 2646. Education Savings Accounts/Rule. Adoption of the rule (H Res 274) to provide for floor consideration of the bill to expand contribution limits for education individual retirement accounts to $2,500 a year per child to be spent tax-free for education expenses for elementary and secondary school students. Adopted 287-135: R 220-0; D 67-134 (ND 42-105, SD 25-29); I 0-1, Oct. 23, 1997.

523. HR 2646. Education Savings Accounts/Public School Improvement Bonds. Rangel, D-N.Y., substitute amendment to increase the cap on the amount of funding that public schools may use to issue interest-free bonds for facility improvement or construction projects, purchase of educational equipment, curriculum development and teacher training from $400 million to $4 billion in fiscal 1998 and 1999. Rejected 199-224: R 2-220; D 196-4 (ND 143-3, SD 53-1); I 1-0, Oct. 23, 1997.

524. HR 2646. Education Savings Accounts/Passage. Passage of the bill to expand contribution limits for education individual retirement accounts to $2,500 a year per child to be spent tax-free for education expenses for elementary and secondary school students. Passed 230-198: R 215-8; D 15-189 (ND 7-143, SD 8-46); I 0-1, Oct. 23, 1997. A "nay" was a vote in support of the president's position.

525. Robert K. Dornan Election Challenge/Adoption. Adoption of the privileged resolution to dismiss the complaint by former Rep. Robert K. Dornan, R-Calif., contesting the election of Loretta Sanchez, D-Calif., by Oct. 29, 1997, unless the House Oversight Committee reports a recommendation for final disposition of the contest before that date. Rejected 204-222: R 1-221; D 202-1 (ND 148-1, SD 54-0); I 1-0, Oct. 23, 1997.

KEY

Y Voted for (yea).
Paired for.
+ Announced for.
N Voted against (nay).
X Paired against.
– Announced against.
P Voted "present."
C Voted "present" to avoid possible conflict of interest.
? Did not vote or otherwise make a position known.

Democrats ***Republicans***
Independent

	521	522	523	524	525
ALABAMA					
1 ***Callahan***	Y	Y	N	Y	N
2 ***Everett***	N	Y	N	Y	N
3 ***Riley***	Y	Y	N	Y	N
4 ***Aderholt***	Y	Y	N	Y	N
5 Cramer	Y	Y	Y	N	Y
6 ***Bachus***	Y	Y	N	Y	N
7 Hilliard	N	N	Y	N	Y
ALASKA					
AL ***Young***	Y	Y	N	Y	N
ARIZONA					
1 ***Salmon***	N	Y	N	Y	N
2 Pastor	Y	Y	Y	N	Y
3 ***Stump***	Y	Y	N	Y	N
4 ***Shadegg***	Y	Y	N	Y	N
5 ***Kolbe***	Y	Y	N	Y	N
6 ***Hayworth***	Y	Y	N	Y	N
ARKANSAS					
1 Berry	Y	N	Y	N	Y
2 Snyder	Y	Y	Y	N	Y
3 ***Hutchinson***	Y	Y	N	Y	N
4 ***Dickey***	N	Y	N	Y	N
CALIFORNIA					
1 ***Riggs***	Y	Y	N	Y	N
2 ***Herger***	Y	Y	N	Y	N
3 Fazio	Y	N	Y	N	Y
4 ***Doolittle***	Y	Y	N	Y	N
5 Matsui	Y	N	Y	N	Y
6 Woolsey	Y	N	Y	N	Y
7 Miller	N	N	Y	N	Y
8 Pelosi	Y	N	Y	N	Y
9 Dellums	Y	Y	Y	N	Y
10 Tauscher	Y	Y	Y	Y	Y
11 ***Pombo***	N	Y	N	Y	N
12 Lantos	Y	N	Y	N	Y
13 Stark	Y	N	Y	N	Y
14 Eshoo	Y	Y	Y	N	Y
15 ***Campbell***	Y	Y	N	Y	N
16 Lofgren	Y	N	Y	N	Y
17 Farr	N	Y	Y	N	Y
18 Condit	Y	Y	Y	Y	Y
19 ***Radanovich***	Y	Y	N	Y	N
20 Dooley	Y	N	Y	N	Y
21 ***Thomas***	Y	Y	N	Y	N
22 Capps	Y	Y	#	N	Y
23 ***Gallegly***	Y	Y	N	Y	N
24 Sherman	Y	N	Y	N	Y
25 ***McKeon***	Y	Y	N	Y	N
26 Berman	Y	Y	?	N	Y
27 ***Rogan***	Y	Y	N	Y	N
28 ***Dreier***	Y	Y	N	Y	N
29 Waxman	Y	N	Y	N	Y
30 Becerra	N	N	Y	N	Y
31 Martinez	Y	N	Y	N	Y
32 Dixon	?	N	Y	N	Y
33 Roybal-Allard	Y	N	Y	N	Y
34 Torres	Y	N	Y	N	Y
35 Waters	N	N	Y	N	Y
36 Harman	Y	?	Y	N	Y
37 Millender-McD.	Y	N	Y	N	Y
38 ***Horn***	Y	Y	N	Y	N
39 ***Royce***	Y	Y	N	Y	N
40 ***Lewis***	Y	Y	N	Y	N
41 ***Kim***	Y	Y	N	Y	N
42 Brown	?	?	Y	N	Y
43 ***Calvert***	Y	Y	N	Y	N
44 ***Bono***	?	Y	N	Y	N
45 ***Rohrabacher***	Y	Y	N	Y	N
46 Sanchez	Y	Y	Y	N	P
47 ***Cox***	Y	Y	N	Y	N
48 ***Packard***	Y	Y	N	Y	N
49 ***Bilbray***	Y	Y	N	Y	N
50 Filner	N	N	Y	N	Y
51 ***Cunningham***	Y	Y	N	Y	N
52 ***Hunter***	Y	Y	N	Y	N
COLORADO					
1 DeGette	Y	N	Y	N	Y
2 Skaggs	Y	Y	Y	N	Y
3 ***McInnis***	Y	Y	N	Y	N
4 ***Schaffer***	N	Y	N	Y	N
5 ***Hefley***	N	Y	N	Y	N
6 ***Schaefer***	Y	Y	N	Y	N
CONNECTICUT					
1 Kennelly	Y	Y	Y	N	Y
2 Gejdenson	Y	N	Y	N	Y
3 DeLauro	Y	N	Y	N	Y
4 ***Shays***	Y	Y	N	Y	N
5 Maloney	Y	N	Y	N	Y
6 ***Johnson***	Y	Y	Y	N	N
DELAWARE					
AL ***Castle***	Y	Y	N	Y	N
FLORIDA					
1 ***Scarborough***	Y	Y	N	Y	N
2 Boyd	Y	Y	Y	Y	Y
3 Brown	Y	N	Y	N	Y
4 ***Fowler***	Y	Y	N	Y	N
5 Thurman	Y	N	Y	N	Y
6 ***Stearns***	Y	Y	N	Y	N
7 ***Mica***	Y	Y	N	Y	N
8 ***McCollum***	Y	Y	N	Y	N
9 ***Bilirakis***	Y	Y	N	Y	N
10 ***Young***	Y	Y	N	Y	N
11 Davis	Y	Y	Y	N	Y
12 ***Canady***	Y	Y	N	Y	N
13 ***Miller***	Y	Y	N	Y	N
14 ***Goss***	Y	Y	N	Y	N
15 ***Weldon***	Y	Y	N	Y	N
16 ***Foley***	Y	Y	N	Y	N
17 Meek	Y	N	Y	N	Y
18 ***Ros-Lehtinen***	Y	Y	N	Y	N
19 Wexler	Y	N	Y	N	Y
20 Deutsch	Y	N	Y	N	Y
21 ***Diaz-Balart***	Y	Y	N	Y	N
22 ***Shaw***	Y	Y	N	Y	N
23 Hastings	Y	N	Y	N	Y
GEORGIA					
1 ***Kingston***	Y	Y	N	Y	N
2 Bishop	Y	Y	Y	Y	Y
3 ***Collins***	Y	Y	N	Y	N
4 McKinney	Y	N	Y	N	Y
5 Lewis	N	N	Y	N	Y
6 ***Gingrich***				Y	N
7 ***Barr***	Y	Y	N	Y	N
8 ***Chambliss***	Y	Y	N	Y	N
9 ***Deal***	Y	Y	N	Y	N
10 ***Norwood***	Y	Y	N	Y	N
11 ***Linder***	Y	?	N	Y	N
HAWAII					
1 Abercrombie	N	N	Y	N	Y
2 Mink	Y	N	Y	N	Y
IDAHO					
1 ***Chenoweth***	N	Y	N	Y	N
2 ***Crapo***	Y	Y	N	Y	N
ILLINOIS					
1 Rush	Y	N	Y	N	Y
2 Jackson	Y	N	Y	N	Y
3 Lipinski	Y	N	N	Y	Y
4 Gutierrez	N	N	Y	N	Y
5 Blagojevich	Y	N	Y	N	Y
6 ***Hyde***	Y	Y	N	Y	N
7 Davis	Y	Y	Y	N	Y
8 ***Crane***	Y	Y	N	Y	N
9 Yates	Y	N	Y	N	Y
10 ***Porter***	Y	Y	N	Y	N
11 ***Weller***	N	Y	N	Y	N
12 Costello	Y	N	Y	N	Y
13 ***Fawell***	Y	Y	N	Y	N
14 ***Hastert***	Y	Y	N	Y	N
15 ***Ewing***	Y	Y	N	Y	N

ND Northern Democrats SD Southern Democrats

	521	522	523	524	525
16 ***Manzullo***	Y	Y	N	Y	N
17 Evans	N	N	Y	N	Y
18 ***LaHood***	Y	Y	N	Y	N
19 Poshard	N	N	Y	N	Y
20 ***Shimkus***	Y	Y	N	Y	N
INDIANA					
1 Visclosky	N	N	–	–	+
2 ***McIntosh***	?	?	?	?	?
3 Roemer	Y	N	Y	N	Y
4 ***Souder***	?	Y	N	Y	N
5 ***Buyer***	Y	Y	N	Y	N
6 ***Burton***	Y	Y	N	Y	N
7 ***Pease***	Y	Y	N	Y	N
8 ***Hostettler***	Y	Y	N	Y	N
9 Hamilton	Y	Y	Y	N	Y
10 Carson	Y	Y	Y	N	Y
IOWA					
1 ***Leach***	Y	Y	N	Y	N
2 ***Nussle***	Y	Y	N	Y	N
3 Boswell	Y	N	Y	N	Y
4 ***Ganske***	Y	Y	N	Y	N
5 ***Latham***	Y	Y	N	Y	N
KANSAS					
1 ***Moran***	N	Y	N	Y	N
2 ***Ryun***	Y	Y	N	Y	–
3 ***Snowbarger***	Y	Y	N	Y	N
4 ***Tiahrt***	Y	Y	N	Y	N
KENTUCKY					
1 ***Whitfield***	Y	Y	N	Y	N
2 ***Lewis***	Y	Y	N	Y	N
3 ***Northup***	Y	Y	N	Y	N
4 ***Bunning***	Y	Y	N	Y	N
5 ***Rogers***	Y	Y	N	Y	N
6 Baesler	Y	Y	Y	N	Y
LOUISIANA					
1 ***Livingston***	Y	Y	N	Y	N
2 Jefferson	Y	N	Y	N	Y
3 ***Tauzin***	Y	Y	N	Y	N
4 ***McCrery***	Y	Y	N	Y	N
5 ***Cooksey***	Y	Y	N	Y	N
6 ***Baker***	Y	Y	N	Y	N
7 John	Y	Y	Y	N	Y
MAINE					
1 Allen	Y	N	Y	N	Y
2 Baldacci	Y	Y	Y	N	Y
MARYLAND					
1 ***Gilchrest***	Y	Y	N	Y	N
2 ***Ehrlich***	Y	Y	N	Y	N
3 Cardin	Y	N	Y	N	Y
4 Wynn	Y	Y	Y	N	Y
5 Hoyer	Y	N	Y	N	Y
6 ***Bartlett***	Y	Y	N	Y	N
7 Cummings	Y	N	Y	N	Y
8 ***Morella***	Y	Y	N	N	N
MASSACHUSETTS					
1 Olver	Y	N	Y	N	Y
2 Neal	Y	Y	Y	N	Y
3 McGovern	Y	N	Y	N	Y
4 Frank	Y	N	Y	N	Y
5 Meehan	Y	N	Y	N	Y
6 Tierney	Y	N	Y	N	Y
7 Markey	Y	N	Y	N	Y
8 Kennedy	Y	Y	Y	N	Y
9 Moakley	Y	Y	Y	N	Y
10 Delahunt	Y	N	Y	N	Y
MICHIGAN					
1 Stupak	N	N	Y	N	Y
2 ***Hoekstra***	Y	Y	N	Y	N
3 ***Ehlers***	Y	Y	N	Y	N
4 ***Camp***	Y	Y	N	Y	N
5 Barcia	Y	N	Y	N	Y
6 ***Upton***	Y	Y	N	Y	N
7 ***Smith***	Y	Y	N	Y	N
8 Stabenow	Y	N	Y	N	Y
9 Kildee	Y	Y	Y	N	Y
10 Bonior	?	N	Y	N	Y
11 ***Knollenberg***	Y	Y	N	Y	N
12 Levin	Y	Y	Y	N	Y
13 Rivers	Y	N	Y	N	Y
14 Conyers	Y	N	Y	N	Y
15 Kilpatrick	Y	N	Y	N	Y
16 Dingell	Y	?	Y	N	Y
MINNESOTA					
1 ***Gutknecht***	N	Y	N	Y	N
2 Minge	Y	N	Y	N	Y
3 ***Ramstad***	N	Y	N	Y	N
4 Vento	N	N	Y	N	Y
5 Sabo	N	N	N	N	Y
6 Luther	Y	N	Y	N	Y
7 Peterson	Y	N	N	N	Y
8 Oberstar	Y	N	Y	N	Y
MISSISSIPPI					
1 ***Wicker***	N	Y	N	Y	N
2 Thompson	N	N	Y	N	Y
3 ***Pickering***	Y	Y	N	Y	N
4 ***Parker***	Y	Y	N	Y	N
5 Taylor	N	N	Y	Y	Y
MISSOURI					
1 Clay	N	N	Y	N	Y
2 ***Talent***	Y	Y	N	Y	N
3 Gephardt	N	N	Y	N	Y
4 Skelton	Y	Y	Y	N	Y
5 McCarthy	Y	Y	Y	N	Y
6 Danner	Y	Y	Y	Y	Y
7 ***Blunt***	Y	Y	N	Y	N
8 ***Emerson***	Y	Y	N	Y	N
9 ***Hulshof***	N	Y	N	Y	N
MONTANA					
AL ***Hill***	Y	Y	N	Y	N
NEBRASKA					
1 ***Bereuter***	Y	Y	N	Y	N
2 ***Christensen***	Y	Y	N	Y	N
3 ***Barrett***	Y	Y	N	N	N
NEVADA					
1 ***Ensign***	N	Y	N	Y	N
2 ***Gibbons***	N	Y	N	Y	N
NEW HAMPSHIRE					
1 ***Sununu***	Y	Y	N	Y	N
2 ***Bass***	Y	Y	N	Y	N
NEW JERSEY					
1 Andrews	Y	N	Y	N	Y
2 ***LoBiondo***	N	Y	N	N	N
3 ***Saxton***	Y	Y	N	Y	N
4 ***Smith***	Y	Y	N	Y	N
5 ***Roukema***	Y	Y	N	Y	N
6 Pallone	N	N	Y	N	Y
7 ***Franks***	Y	Y	N	Y	N
8 Pascrell	N	Y	Y	N	Y
9 Rothman	Y	N	Y	N	Y
10 Payne	Y	N	Y	N	Y
11 ***Frelinghuysen***	Y	Y	N	Y	N
12 ***Pappas***	Y	Y	N	Y	N
13 Menendez	N	Y	Y	N	Y
NEW MEXICO					
1 ***Schiff***	?	?	?	?	?
2 ***Skeen***	Y	Y	N	Y	N
3 ***Redmond***	Y	Y	N	Y	N
NEW YORK					
1 ***Forbes***	Y	Y	N	Y	Y
2 ***Lazio***	Y	Y	N	Y	N
3 ***King***	Y	Y	N	Y	N
4 McCarthy	Y	Y	Y	N	Y
5 Ackerman	Y	N	Y	N	Y
6 Flake	?	?	?	Y	Y
7 Manton	Y	Y	Y	N	Y
8 Nadler	Y	N	Y	N	Y
9 Schumer	?	Y	Y	N	Y
10 Towns	Y	N	Y	N	Y
11 Owens	Y	N	Y	N	Y
12 Velázquez	N	N	Y	N	Y
13 Vacant					
14 Maloney	N	N	Y	N	Y
15 Rangel	Y	Y	Y	N	Y
16 Serrano	Y	N	Y	N	Y
17 Engel	Y	Y	Y	N	Y
18 Lowey	Y	N	Y	N	Y
19 ***Kelly***	Y	Y	N	Y	N
20 ***Gilman***	Y	Y	N	Y	N
21 McNulty	?	N	Y	N	Y
22 ***Solomon***	Y	Y	N	Y	N
23 ***Boehlert***	Y	Y	N	N	N
24 ***McHugh***	Y	Y	Y	N	N
25 ***Walsh***	Y	Y	N	Y	N
26 Hinchey	N	N	Y	N	Y
27 ***Paxon***	Y	Y	N	Y	N
28 Slaughter	N	N	Y	N	Y
29 LaFalce	Y	Y	Y	N	Y
30 ***Quinn***	Y	Y	N	Y	N
31 ***Houghton***	?	?	?	?	?
NORTH CAROLINA					
1 Clayton	Y	Y	Y	N	Y
2 Etheridge	Y	N	Y	N	Y
3 ***Jones***	Y	Y	N	Y	N
4 Price	Y	Y	Y	N	Y
5 ***Burr***	Y	Y	N	Y	N
6 ***Coble***	Y	Y	N	Y	N
7 McIntyre	Y	Y	Y	N	Y
8 Hefner	Y	N	Y	N	Y
9 ***Myrick***	Y	Y	N	Y	N
10 ***Ballenger***	Y	Y	N	Y	N
11 ***Taylor***	Y	Y	N	Y	N
12 Watt	Y	N	Y	N	Y
NORTH DAKOTA					
AL Pomeroy	Y	Y	Y	N	Y
OHIO					
1 ***Chabot***	Y	Y	N	Y	N
2 ***Portman***	Y	Y	N	Y	N
3 Hall	Y	Y	Y	Y	Y
4 ***Oxley***	Y	Y	N	Y	N
5 ***Gillmor***	Y	Y	N	Y	N
6 Strickland	Y	N	Y	N	Y
7 ***Hobson***	Y	Y	N	Y	N
8 ***Boehner***	Y	Y	N	Y	N
9 Kaptur	Y	N	Y	N	Y
10 Kucinich	N	N	Y	N	Y
11 Stokes	Y	N	Y	N	Y
12 ***Kasich***	Y	Y	N	Y	N
13 Brown	Y	N	Y	N	Y
14 Sawyer	Y	N	Y	N	Y
15 ***Pryce***	Y	Y	N	Y	N
16 ***Regula***	Y	Y	N	Y	N
17 Traficant	Y	Y	Y	N	N
18 ***Ney***	Y	Y	N	Y	N
19 ***LaTourette***	Y	Y	N	Y	N
OKLAHOMA					
1 ***Largent***	Y	Y	N	Y	N
2 ***Coburn***	Y	Y	N	Y	N
3 ***Watkins***	Y	Y	N	Y	N
4 ***Watts***	Y	Y	N	Y	N
5 ***Istook***	?	Y	N	Y	N
6 ***Lucas***	Y	Y	N	Y	N
OREGON					
1 Furse	Y	N	Y	N	Y
2 ***Smith***	Y	Y	N	Y	N
3 Blumenauer	Y	Y	Y	N	Y
4 DeFazio	N	N	Y	N	Y
5 Hooley	Y	Y	Y	N	Y
PENNSYLVANIA					
1 Foglietta	?	N	?	N	Y
2 Fattah	Y	N	Y	N	Y
3 Borski	N	N	Y	N	Y
4 Klink	Y	Y	Y	N	Y
5 ***Peterson***	Y	Y	N	Y	N
6 Holden	Y	N	Y	N	Y
7 ***Weldon***	Y	Y	N	Y	N
8 ***Greenwood***	Y	Y	N	Y	N
9 ***Shuster***	Y	Y	N	Y	N
10 ***McDade***	?	Y	N	Y	N
11 Kanjorski	Y	N	Y	N	Y
12 Murtha	Y	Y	Y	N	Y
13 ***Fox***	N	Y	N	Y	N
14 Coyne	Y	N	Y	N	Y
15 McHale	Y	N	Y	Y	Y
16 ***Pitts***	Y	Y	N	Y	N
17 ***Gekas***	Y	Y	N	Y	N
18 Doyle	Y	N	Y	N	Y
19 ***Goodling***	Y	Y	N	Y	N
20 Mascara	Y	N	Y	N	Y
21 ***English***	N	Y	N	Y	N
RHODE ISLAND					
1 Kennedy	Y	N	Y	N	Y
2 Weygand	Y	N	Y	N	Y
SOUTH CAROLINA					
1 ***Sanford***	Y	Y	N	Y	N
2 ***Spence***	Y	Y	N	Y	N
3 ***Graham***	Y	Y	N	Y	N
4 ***Inglis***	Y	Y	N	Y	N
5 Spratt	Y	Y	Y	N	Y
6 Clyburn	N	N	Y	N	Y
SOUTH DAKOTA					
AL ***Thune***	Y	Y	N	Y	N
TENNESSEE					
1 ***Jenkins***	Y	Y	N	Y	N
2 ***Duncan***	Y	Y	N	Y	N
3 ***Wamp***	Y	Y	N	Y	N
4 ***Hilleary***	Y	Y	N	Y	N
5 Clement	Y	Y	Y	Y	Y
6 Gordon	Y	Y	Y	N	Y
7 ***Bryant***	Y	Y	N	Y	N
8 Tanner	Y	N	Y	Y	Y
9 Ford	Y	Y	Y	N	Y
TEXAS					
1 Sandlin	Y	Y	Y	N	Y
2 Turner	Y	N	Y	N	Y
3 ***Johnson, Sam***	Y	Y	N	Y	N
4 Hall	Y	Y	N	Y	Y
5 ***Sessions***	Y	Y	N	Y	N
6 ***Barton***	Y	Y	N	Y	N
7 ***Archer***	Y	Y	N	Y	N
8 ***Brady***	Y	Y	N	Y	N
9 Lampson	Y	Y	Y	N	Y
10 Doggett	Y	N	Y	N	Y
11 Edwards	Y	N	Y	N	Y
12 ***Granger***	Y	Y	N	Y	N
13 ***Thornberry***	Y	Y	N	Y	N
14 ***Paul***	Y	Y	N	N	N
15 Hinojosa	Y	Y	Y	N	Y
16 Reyes	Y	Y	Y	N	Y
17 Stenholm	Y	N	Y	N	Y
18 Jackson-Lee	Y	N	Y	N	Y
19 ***Combest***	Y	Y	N	Y	N
20 Gonzalez	?	?	?	?	?
21 ***Smith***	Y	Y	N	Y	N
22 ***DeLay***	Y	Y	N	Y	N
23 ***Bonilla***	Y	Y	N	Y	N
24 Frost	Y	Y	Y	N	Y
25 Bentsen	Y	Y	Y	N	Y
26 ***Armey***	Y	Y	N	Y	N
27 Ortiz	Y	Y	Y	N	Y
28 Rodriguez	Y	N	Y	N	Y
29 Green	N	N	Y	N	Y
30 Johnson, E.B.	N	N	Y	N	Y
UTAH					
1 ***Hansen***	Y	Y	N	Y	N
2 ***Cook***	Y	Y	N	Y	N
3 ***Cannon***	Y	Y	N	Y	N
VERMONT					
AL *Sanders*	Y	N	Y	N	Y
VIRGINIA					
1 ***Bateman***	Y	Y	N	N	N
2 Pickett	N	N	Y	N	Y
3 Scott	Y	N	Y	N	Y
4 Sisisky	Y	Y	Y	N	Y
5 Goode	Y	Y	Y	Y	Y
6 ***Goodlatte***	Y	Y	N	Y	N
7 ***Bliley***	Y	?	N	Y	N
8 Moran	Y	Y	Y	Y	Y
9 Boucher	Y	N	Y	N	Y
10 ***Wolf***	Y	Y	N	Y	N
11 ***Davis***	Y	Y	N	Y	N
WASHINGTON					
1 ***White***	Y	Y	N	Y	N
2 ***Metcalf***	?	Y	N	Y	N
3 ***Smith, Linda***	Y	Y	N	Y	N
4 ***Hastings***	Y	Y	N	Y	N
5 ***Nethercutt***	Y	Y	N	Y	N
6 Dicks	Y	N	Y	N	Y
7 McDermott	N	N	Y	N	Y
8 ***Dunn***	Y	Y	N	Y	N
9 Smith, Adam	Y	N	Y	N	Y
WEST VIRGINIA					
1 Mollohan	Y	Y	Y	N	Y
2 Wise	Y	N	Y	N	Y
3 Rahall	Y	Y	Y	N	Y
WISCONSIN					
1 ***Neumann***	Y	Y	N	Y	N
2 ***Klug***	Y	Y	N	Y	N
3 Kind	Y	N	Y	N	Y
4 Kleczka	Y	Y	Y	N	Y
5 Barrett	Y	N	Y	N	Y
6 ***Petri***	Y	Y	N	Y	N
7 Obey	Y	N	Y	N	Y
8 Johnson	Y	N	Y	N	Y
9 ***Sensenbrenner***	Y	Y	N	Y	N
WYOMING					
AL ***Cubin***	?	?	X	?	?

Southern states - Ala., Ark., Fla., Ga., Ky., La., Miss., N.C., Okla., S.C., Tenn., Texas, Va.

HOUSE VOTES 526, 527, 528, 529, 530, 531, 532, 533

526. Procedural Motion/Journal. Approval of the House Journal of Thursday, Oct. 23, 1997. Approved 318-56: R 175-15; D 143-41 (ND 101-31, SD 42-10); I 0-0, Oct. 24, 1997.

527. HR 2107. Fiscal 1998 Interior Appropriations/Rule. Adoption of the rule (H Res 277) to waive points of order against and provide for House floor consideration of the conference report on the bill to provide $13,789,438,000 in new budget authority for the Department of the Interior and related agencies for fiscal 1998. Adopted 247-166: R 153-60; D 94-105 (ND 60-85, SD 34-20); I 0-1, Oct. 24, 1997.

528. HR 2247. Amtrak Subsidies/Motion To Rise. Bonior, D-Mich., motion to rise from the Committee of the Whole. Motion rejected 195-214: R 3-206; D 191-8 (ND 140-5, SD 51-3); I 1-0, Oct. 24, 1997.

529. HR 2247. Amtrak Subsidies/Labor Protection. Quinn, R-N.Y., substitute amendment to the LaTourette, R-Ohio, amendment. Quinn's substitute would clarify that existing Amtrak labor protections that would be ended by the bill still would apply to freight and transit rail employees. The provisions would repeal severance benefits for fired or relocated railroad workers and allow Amtrak to contract out more of its work. The LaTourette amendment would restore the statutory protections against contracting out and for severance pay but would allow labor and management to bargain collectively on labor issues. Rejected 195-223: R 190-26; D 5-196 (ND 2-145, SD 3-51); I 0-1, Oct. 24, 1997.

530. Procedural Motion/Adjourn. Bonior, D-Mich., motion to adjourn. Motion rejected 168-244: R 3-208; D 164-36 (ND 122-24, SD 42-12); I 1-0, Oct. 24, 1997.

531. HR 2107. Fiscal 1998 Interior Appropriations/Conference Report. Adoption of the conference report on the bill to provide $13,789,438,000 in new budget authority for the Department of the Interior and related agencies for fiscal 1998. The bill provides $275,003,000 more than was provided in fiscal 1997 and $10,508,000 less than requested by the president. Adopted (thus sent to the Senate) 233-171: R 130-77; D 103-93 (ND 67-77, SD 36-16); I 0-1, Oct. 24, 1997.

532. Procedural Motion/Adjourn. Ensign, R-Nev., motion to adjourn. Motion rejected 52-359: R 2-216; D 50-142 (ND 40-99, SD 10-43); I 0-1, Oct. 28, 1997.

533. HR 1119. Fiscal 1998 Defense Authorization/Rule. Adoption of the rule (H Res 278) to waive points of order against and provide for House floor consideration of the conference report on the bill to authorize $268,301,837,000 for defense programs in fiscal 1998, $2,605,203,000 more than the president requested. Adopted 353-59: R 214-4; D 139-54 (ND 96-44, SD 43-10); I 0-1, Oct. 28, 1997.

[1] *Walter Capps, D-Calif., died Oct. 28.*

KEY

Y Voted for (yea).
\# Paired for.
\+ Announced for.
N Voted against (nay).
X Paired against.
– Announced against.
P Voted "present."
C Voted "present" to avoid possible conflict of interest.
? Did not vote or otherwise make a position known.

Democrats ***Republicans***
Independent

	526	527	528	529	530	531	532	533
ALABAMA								
1 ***Callahan***	Y	Y	N	?	?	?	N	Y
2 ***Everett***	N	N	N	Y	N	?	N	N
3 ***Riley***	Y	N	N	Y	N	N	N	Y
4 ***Aderholt***	Y	N	N	Y	N	N	N	Y
5 Cramer	Y	Y	Y	N	Y	Y	N	Y
6 ***Bachus***	Y	N	N	Y	N	N	N	Y
7 Hilliard	N	Y	Y	N	Y	Y	N	N
ALASKA								
AL ***Young***	?	Y	N	N	N	Y	N	Y
ARIZONA								
1 ***Salmon***	Y	N	N	Y	N	N	N	Y
2 Pastor	Y	Y	Y	N	Y	Y	Y	Y
3 ***Stump***	Y	N	N	Y	N	N	N	Y
4 ***Shadegg***	Y	Y	N	Y	N	N	N	Y
5 ***Kolbe***	?	Y	N	Y	N	Y	N	Y
6 ***Hayworth***	Y	Y	N	Y	N	N	N	Y
ARKANSAS								
1 Berry	Y	Y	Y	N	Y	Y	N	Y
2 Snyder	Y	N	Y	N	Y	Y	N	Y
3 ***Hutchinson***	Y	N	N	Y	N	N	N	Y
4 ***Dickey***	?	?	?	?	?	?	N	Y
CALIFORNIA								
1 ***Riggs***	?	Y	N	Y	N	Y	N	Y
2 ***Herger***	Y	N	N	Y	N	Y	?	Y
3 Fazio	N	N	Y	N	Y	Y	Y	N
4 ***Doolittle***	?	N	N	Y	N	N	N	Y
5 Matsui	Y	Y	Y	N	Y	Y	N	N
6 Woolsey	Y	Y	Y	N	Y	Y	N	N
7 Miller	N	N	Y	N	Y	N	Y	Y
8 Pelosi	Y	N	Y	N	Y	?	Y	Y
9 Dellums	?	N	Y	N	Y	N	Y	Y
10 Tauscher	N	Y	Y	N	Y	Y	N	N
11 ***Pombo***	?	Y	N	Y	N	Y	N	Y
12 Lantos	Y	Y	Y	N	Y	N	Y	N
13 Stark	Y	N	Y	N	Y	N	Y	?
14 Eshoo	Y	Y	Y	N	Y	Y	Y	N
15 ***Campbell***	Y	Y	N	Y	N	N	N	Y
16 Lofgren	Y	Y	Y	N	Y	Y	N	N
17 Farr	Y	Y	Y	N	Y	Y	N	Y
18 Condit	Y	N	Y	N	Y	N	N	Y
19 ***Radanovich***	Y	Y	N	Y	N	Y	N	Y
20 Dooley	Y	Y	Y	Y	N	Y	N	Y
21 ***Thomas***	Y	Y	N	Y	N	Y	N	Y
22 Capps [1]	Y	N	Y	N	Y	Y		
23 ***Gallegly***	Y	Y	N	Y	N	Y	N	Y
24 Sherman	Y	Y	Y	N	N	Y	N	Y
25 ***McKeon***	Y	Y	N	Y	N	Y	N	Y
26 Berman	Y	N	Y	N	Y	N	N	N
27 ***Rogan***	Y	N	N	Y	N	N	N	Y
28 ***Dreier***	Y	Y	N	Y	N	Y	N	Y
29 Waxman	Y	Y	Y	N	Y	N	N	N
30 Becerra	N	N	Y	N	Y	N	N	N
31 Martinez	?	N	Y	N	Y	Y	Y	N
32 Dixon	?	?	Y	N	Y	N	N	Y
33 Roybal-Allard	?	N	Y	N	Y	N	N	Y
34 Torres	?	N	Y	N	Y	Y	Y	Y
35 Waters	?	Y	Y	N	Y	Y	N	N
36 Harman	Y	Y	Y	N	Y	Y	N	Y
37 Millender-McD.	Y	N	Y	N	Y	Y	Y	Y
38 ***Horn***	Y	Y	N	Y	N	Y	N	Y
39 ***Royce***	Y	N	N	Y	N	N	N	Y
40 ***Lewis***	Y	Y	N	Y	N	Y	N	Y
41 ***Kim***	Y	Y	N	Y	N	Y	N	Y
42 Brown	?	?	?	N	Y	Y	?	?
43 ***Calvert***	Y	N	N	Y	N	Y	N	Y
44 ***Bono***	?	?	?	Y	N	Y	?	Y
45 ***Rohrabacher***	?	N	N	Y	N	N	N	Y
46 Sanchez	Y	N	Y	N	Y	N	N	Y
47 ***Cox***	Y	Y	N	Y	N	N	N	Y
48 ***Packard***	Y	Y	N	Y	N	Y	N	Y
49 ***Bilbray***	Y	Y	N	Y	N	Y	N	Y
50 Filner	N	N	Y	N	Y	N	Y	N
51 ***Cunningham***	Y	N	N	Y	N	N	N	N
52 ***Hunter***	?	?	N	Y	N	Y	?	Y
COLORADO								
1 DeGette	Y	N	Y	N	Y	N	Y	N
2 Skaggs	Y	Y	Y	N	Y	Y	N	Y
3 ***McInnis***	Y	Y	N	Y	N	Y	N	Y
4 ***Schaffer***	N	N	N	Y	N	N	N	Y
5 ***Hefley***	N	N	N	Y	N	N	N	Y
6 ***Schaefer***	Y	N	N	Y	N	N	N	Y
CONNECTICUT								
1 Kennelly	Y	Y	Y	N	Y	Y	N	Y
2 Gejdenson	Y	N	Y	N	Y	N	N	Y
3 DeLauro	N	Y	Y	N	Y	Y	N	Y
4 ***Shays***	Y	N	N	Y	N	Y	N	Y
5 Maloney	Y	N	Y	N	Y	N	N	Y
6 ***Johnson***	Y	Y	N	Y	N	Y	N	Y
DELAWARE								
AL ***Castle***	Y	Y	N	Y	N	Y	N	Y
FLORIDA								
1 ***Scarborough***	?	N	?	Y	N	X	N	Y
2 Boyd	Y	N	Y	N	Y	Y	N	Y
3 Brown	Y	N	Y	N	Y	N	N	Y
4 ***Fowler***	Y	Y	N	Y	N	Y	N	Y
5 Thurman	Y	N	Y	N	Y	N	N	Y
6 ***Stearns***	?	N	N	Y	N	N	N	Y
7 ***Mica***	Y	Y	N	Y	N	Y	N	Y
8 ***McCollum***	Y	Y	N	Y	N	N	N	Y
9 ***Bilirakis***	Y	?	?	?	?	Y	N	Y
10 ***Young***	?	Y	N	N	N	Y	N	Y
11 Davis	Y	Y	Y	N	Y	Y	N	Y
12 ***Canady***	Y	Y	N	Y	N	Y	N	Y
13 ***Miller***	Y	Y	N	Y	N	Y	N	Y
14 ***Goss***	Y	Y	N	Y	N	Y	N	Y
15 ***Weldon***	Y	N	N	Y	N	N	N	+
16 ***Foley***	Y	Y	N	Y	N	Y	N	Y
17 Meek	N	Y	Y	N	Y	Y	N	Y
18 ***Ros-Lehtinen***	Y	Y	N	N	N	Y	N	Y
19 Wexler	Y	Y	Y	N	N	N	N	N
20 Deutsch	Y	Y	Y	N	Y	Y	Y	N
21 ***Diaz-Balart***	Y	Y	N	N	N	Y	N	Y
22 ***Shaw***	Y	Y	N	Y	N	Y	N	Y
23 Hastings	Y	Y	Y	N	Y	N	Y	Y
GEORGIA								
1 ***Kingston***	Y	Y	N	Y	N	Y	N	Y
2 Bishop	Y	Y	Y	N	Y	Y	N	Y
3 ***Collins***	Y	Y	N	Y	N	Y	N	Y
4 McKinney	Y	N	Y	N	Y	N	N	N
5 Lewis	N	N	Y	N	Y	Y	Y	Y
6 ***Gingrich***				Y				
7 ***Barr***	Y	N	N	Y	N	N	N	Y
8 ***Chambliss***	Y	Y	N	Y	N	Y	N	Y
9 ***Deal***	Y	Y	N	Y	N	Y	N	Y
10 ***Norwood***	Y	Y	N	Y	Y	Y	N	Y
11 ***Linder***	Y	Y	N	Y	N	Y	N	Y
HAWAII								
1 Abercrombie	N	N	Y	N	N	Y	N	Y
2 Mink	Y	N	Y	N	Y	Y	Y	Y
IDAHO								
1 ***Chenoweth***	+	–	–	+	–	–	N	Y
2 ***Crapo***	Y	Y	N	N	N	Y	N	Y
ILLINOIS								
1 Rush	Y	N	Y	N	Y	N	N	N
2 Jackson	Y	Y	Y	N	Y	Y	Y	N
3 Lipinski	Y	N	Y	N	Y	N	N	Y
4 Gutierrez	N	N	Y	N	Y	N	N	Y
5 Blagojevich	Y	N	Y	N	Y	N	N	Y
6 ***Hyde***	Y	Y	N	Y	N	Y	N	Y
7 Davis	Y	N	Y	N	Y	N	N	N
8 ***Crane***	?	N	N	Y	N	N	N	Y
9 Yates	Y	Y	Y	N	Y	Y	N	?
10 ***Porter***	?	Y	N	Y	N	Y	N	Y
11 ***Weller***	N	Y	N	N	N	Y	N	Y
12 Costello	N	Y	Y	N	Y	N	N	Y
13 ***Fawell***	?	Y	?	Y	N	Y	N	Y
14 ***Hastert***	Y	Y	N	Y	N	Y	N	Y
15 ***Ewing***	Y	Y	N	Y	N	?	N	Y

ND Northern Democrats SD Southern Democrats

	526	527	528	529	530	531	532	533
16 *Manzullo*	Y	N	N	Y	N	N	N	Y
17 Evans	Y	N	Y	N	Y	N	N	Y
18 *LaHood*	Y	Y	N	Y	N	?	N	Y
19 Poshard	Y	N	Y	N	Y	N	N	Y
20 *Shimkus*	Y	Y	N	Y	N	N	N	Y
INDIANA								
1 Visclosky	N	Y	Y	N	N	Y	N	Y
2 *McIntosh*	?	?	?	?	?	?	?	?
3 Roemer	Y	N	Y	N	N	N	N	Y
4 *Souder*	?	?	?	Y	N	N	N	Y
5 *Buyer*	Y	Y	N	Y	N	Y	N	Y
6 *Burton*	Y	N	N	N	N	N	N	Y
7 *Pease*	Y	N	N	Y	N	N	N	Y
8 *Hostettler*	Y	N	N	Y	N	N	N	Y
9 Hamilton	Y	Y	N	N	N	Y	N	Y
10 Carson	Y	N	Y	N	Y	N	Y	Y
IOWA								
1 *Leach*	?	Y	N	N	N	?	N	Y
2 *Nussle*	Y	Y	N	Y	N	Y	N	Y
3 Boswell	Y	N	Y	N	Y	Y	N	Y
4 *Ganske*	Y	Y	N	Y	N	Y	N	Y
5 *Latham*	Y	Y	N	Y	N	N	N	Y
KANSAS								
1 *Moran*	Y	N	N	Y	N	N	N	Y
2 *Ryun*	?	?	?	+	?	–	N	Y
3 *Snowbarger*	Y	Y	N	Y	N	N	N	Y
4 *Tiahrt*	Y	Y	N	N	N	N	N	Y
KENTUCKY								
1 *Whitfield*	?	Y	N	Y	N	Y	N	Y
2 *Lewis*	Y	N	N	Y	N	N	N	Y
3 *Northup*	Y	Y	N	Y	N	Y	N	Y
4 *Bunning*	Y	N	N	Y	N	N	N	Y
5 *Rogers*	Y	Y	N	Y	N	Y	N	Y
6 Baesler	Y	Y	Y	N	N	Y	N	Y
LOUISIANA								
1 *Livingston*	Y	Y	N	Y	N	Y	N	Y
2 Jefferson	N	N	Y	N	Y	Y	Y	Y
3 *Tauzin*	Y	Y	N	Y	N	Y	N	Y
4 *McCrery*	?	Y	N	Y	N	Y	N	Y
5 *Cooksey*	?	Y	N	Y	N	?	N	Y
6 *Baker*	Y	Y	N	Y	N	Y	N	Y
7 John	Y	Y	Y	N	Y	Y	N	Y
MAINE								
1 Allen	Y	Y	Y	N	Y	Y	Y	Y
2 Baldacci	N	N	Y	N	Y	Y	N	Y
MARYLAND								
1 *Gilchrest*	Y	Y	N	Y	N	Y	N	Y
2 *Ehrlich*	Y	Y	N	Y	N	N	N	Y
3 Cardin	Y	N	Y	Y	Y	Y	N	N
4 Wynn	Y	Y	Y	N	Y	Y	N	Y
5 Hoyer	Y	Y	Y	N	Y	Y	Y	Y
6 *Bartlett*	Y	Y	N	Y	N	N	N	Y
7 Cummings	Y	Y	Y	N	Y	Y	N	N
8 *Morella*	?	Y	N	Y	N	N	N	Y
MASSACHUSETTS								
1 Olver	Y	N	Y	N	Y	Y	Y	N
2 Neal	Y	Y	Y	N	Y	N	N	Y
3 McGovern	N	N	Y	N	Y	N	N	Y
4 Frank	Y	Y	Y	N	Y	Y	Y	N
5 Meehan	Y	N	Y	N	Y	N	N	Y
6 Tierney	Y	N	Y	N	Y	N	N	Y
7 Markey	?	N	Y	N	Y	N	Y	N
8 Kennedy	Y	N	Y	N	Y	N	?	Y
9 Moakley	Y	Y	Y	N	Y	N	N	Y
10 Delahunt	Y	N	Y	N	Y	N	N	N
MICHIGAN								
1 Stupak	N	N	Y	N	Y	Y	N	Y
2 *Hoekstra*	Y	N	N	Y	N	N	N	Y
3 *Ehlers*	Y	Y	N	Y	N	Y	N	Y
4 *Camp*	Y	Y	N	Y	N	N	N	Y
5 Barcia	Y	Y	Y	N	Y	Y	N	Y
6 *Upton*	Y	Y	N	Y	N	Y	N	Y
7 *Smith*	Y	Y	N	Y	N	Y	N	Y
8 Stabenow	Y	N	Y	N	Y	N	N	Y
9 Kildee	Y	Y	Y	N	N	N	N	Y
10 Bonior	N	N	Y	N	Y	N	?	Y
11 *Knollenberg*	Y	Y	N	Y	N	Y	N	Y
12 Levin	Y	Y	Y	N	Y	N	N	Y
13 Rivers	Y	N	Y	N	Y	N	N	N
14 Conyers	Y	N	Y	N	Y	N	Y	?
15 Kilpatrick	Y	N	Y	N	Y	N	N	Y
16 Dingell	Y	Y	Y	N	Y	N	N	N
MINNESOTA								
1 *Gutknecht*	N	Y	N	Y	N	Y	N	Y
2 Minge	Y	N	Y	N	N	N	N	Y

	526	527	528	529	530	531	532	533
3 *Ramstad*	N	Y	N	Y	N	Y	N	Y
4 Vento	Y	N	Y	N	Y	N	N	Y
5 Sabo	N	N	Y	N	Y	Y	N	Y
6 Luther	Y	N	Y	N	Y	N	N	N
7 Peterson	Y	N	Y	N	Y	N	Y	Y
8 Oberstar	N	Y	Y	N	Y	Y	N	Y
MISSISSIPPI								
1 *Wicker*	N	Y	N	Y	N	Y	N	Y
2 Thompson	N	Y	Y	N	Y	Y	N	N
3 *Pickering*	Y	N	N	Y	N	N	N	Y
4 *Parker*	Y	Y	N	Y	N	?	N	Y
5 Taylor	N	N	N	Y	N	N	Y	Y
MISSOURI								
1 Clay	N	N	Y	N	Y	Y	N	N
2 *Talent*	Y	N	N	Y	N	N	N	Y
3 Gephardt	N	N	Y	N	?	X	Y	Y
4 Skelton	Y	Y	Y	N	Y	N	N	Y
5 McCarthy	Y	N	Y	N	Y	N	N	Y
6 Danner	Y	Y	Y	N	N	Y	N	Y
7 *Blunt*	Y	Y	N	Y	N	N	N	Y
8 *Emerson*	Y	Y	N	Y	N	Y	N	Y
9 *Hulshof*	N	N	N	N	N	N	N	?
MONTANA								
AL *Hill*	Y	Y	N	Y	N	Y	N	Y
NEBRASKA								
1 *Bereuter*	?	?	?	?	?	?	N	Y
2 *Christensen*	Y	N	N	Y	N	N	N	Y
3 *Barrett*	Y	Y	N	Y	N	Y	N	Y
NEVADA								
1 *Ensign*	N	N	Y	Y	Y	N	Y	N
2 *Gibbons*	N	N	Y	Y	N	N	Y	Y
NEW HAMPSHIRE								
1 *Sununu*	Y	Y	N	Y	N	Y	N	Y
2 *Bass*	Y	Y	N	Y	N	Y	N	Y
NEW JERSEY								
1 Andrews	Y	Y	?	N	Y	N	?	?
2 *LoBiondo*	N	Y	N	Y	N	Y	N	Y
3 *Saxton*	Y	Y	N	Y	N	Y	N	Y
4 *Smith*	Y	Y	N	N	N	N	N	Y
5 *Roukema*	Y	Y	N	Y	N	Y	N	?
6 Pallone	N	N	Y	N	Y	N	Y	Y
7 *Franks*	Y	Y	N	Y	N	Y	N	Y
8 Pascrell	N	N	Y	N	Y	N	N	Y
9 Rothman	Y	N	Y	N	N	N	N	Y
10 Payne	?	?	?	?	?	?	?	?
11 *Frelinghuysen*	Y	Y	N	Y	N	Y	N	Y
12 *Pappas*	Y	Y	N	Y	N	Y	N	Y
13 Menendez	N	N	Y	N	Y	Y	N	Y
NEW MEXICO								
1 *Schiff*	?	?	?	?	?	?	?	?
2 *Skeen*	Y	Y	N	Y	N	Y	N	Y
3 *Redmond*	Y	Y	N	Y	N	Y	N	Y
NEW YORK								
1 *Forbes*	Y	Y	?	Y	N	Y	N	Y
2 *Lazio*	Y	Y	N	N	N	Y	N	Y
3 *King*	Y	Y	Y	N	N	Y	N	Y
4 McCarthy	+	+	+	–	–	+	Y	N
5 Ackerman	Y	N	Y	N	Y	Y	N	N
6 Flake	Y	Y	Y	N	Y	Y	N	?
7 Manton	Y	Y	Y	N	Y	Y	N	Y
8 Nadler	?	Y	Y	N	Y	N	N	Y
9 Schumer	Y	N	Y	N	Y	N	?	?
10 Towns	?	N	Y	N	Y	Y	N	Y
11 Owens	?	N	Y	N	Y	Y	Y	N
12 Velázquez	N	N	Y	N	Y	N	N	Y
13 Vacant								
14 Maloney	N	N	Y	N	Y	N	N	Y
15 Rangel	?	?	?	X	?	#	N	N
16 Serrano	Y	Y	Y	N	Y	Y	Y	N
17 Engel	Y	Y	Y	N	Y	N	N	Y
18 Lowey	Y	N	Y	N	Y	N	N	N
19 *Kelly*	Y	Y	N	N	N	Y	N	Y
20 *Gilman*	Y	Y	N	N	N	Y	N	Y
21 McNulty	N	N	Y	N	Y	N	Y	Y
22 *Solomon*	Y	Y	N	Y	N	Y	N	Y
23 *Boehlert*	Y	Y	N	Y	N	Y	N	Y
24 *McHugh*	Y	Y	N	Y	N	Y	N	Y
25 *Walsh*	Y	Y	N	Y	N	Y	N	Y
26 Hinchey	N	N	Y	N	Y	N	Y	N
27 *Paxon*	Y	N	N	Y	N	N	N	Y
28 Slaughter	Y	N	Y	N	Y	N	N	Y
29 LaFalce	Y	N	Y	N	Y	N	Y	N
30 *Quinn*	Y	Y	N	Y	N	Y	N	Y
31 *Houghton*	?	?	?	Y	N	?	N	?

	526	527	528	529	530	531	532	533
NORTH CAROLINA								
1 Clayton	Y	N	Y	N	Y	Y	N	Y
2 Etheridge	Y	Y	Y	N	Y	Y	N	Y
3 *Jones*	Y	N	N	Y	N	N	N	Y
4 Price	Y	N	Y	N	Y	Y	N	Y
5 *Burr*	Y	N	N	Y	N	Y	N	Y
6 *Coble*	Y	Y	N	Y	N	N	N	?
7 McIntyre	Y	Y	Y	N	Y	Y	N	Y
8 Hefner	Y	Y	Y	N	Y	Y	Y	Y
9 *Myrick*	Y	N	N	Y	N	N	N	Y
10 *Ballenger*	?	Y	N	Y	N	N	N	Y
11 *Taylor*	Y	Y	N	Y	N	Y	N	Y
12 Watt	Y	N	Y	N	Y	N	N	Y
NORTH DAKOTA								
AL Pomeroy	Y	Y	Y	N	Y	Y	N	Y
OHIO								
1 *Chabot*	Y	N	N	Y	N	N	N	Y
2 *Portman*	Y	Y	N	Y	N	Y	N	Y
3 Hall	Y	Y	Y	N	N	Y	N	Y
4 *Oxley*	Y	Y	N	Y	N	Y	N	Y
5 *Gillmor*	?	Y	N	N	N	Y	N	Y
6 Strickland	Y	N	Y	N	Y	Y	N	Y
7 *Hobson*	Y	Y	N	Y	N	Y	N	Y
8 *Boehner*	Y	Y	N	Y	N	Y	N	Y
9 Kaptur	Y	Y	Y	N	N	Y	Y	Y
10 Kucinich	N	N	N	N	N	N	N	N
11 Stokes	?	Y	Y	N	Y	Y	N	Y
12 *Kasich*	?	Y	N	Y	N	N	N	N
13 Brown	?	N	Y	N	Y	N	N	N
14 Sawyer	Y	Y	Y	N	Y	Y	N	Y
15 *Pryce*	Y	Y	N	Y	N	Y	N	Y
16 *Regula*	Y	Y	N	Y	N	Y	N	Y
17 Traficant	Y	Y	N	N	N	Y	N	Y
18 *Ney*	Y	Y	N	N	?	Y	N	Y
19 *LaTourette*	Y	Y	N	N	N	Y	N	Y
OKLAHOMA								
1 *Largent*	Y	N	N	Y	N	N	N	Y
2 *Coburn*	Y	N	N	Y	Y	N	N	Y
3 *Watkins*	Y	Y	N	Y	N	Y	N	Y
4 *Watts*	Y	N	N	Y	N	N	N	Y
5 *Istook*	Y	N	N	Y	N	–	N	Y
6 *Lucas*	Y	Y	N	Y	N	Y	N	Y
OREGON								
1 Furse	Y	N	Y	N	Y	N	Y	N
2 *Smith*	?	?	?	#	?	#	N	Y
3 Blumenauer	Y	N	Y	N	Y	N	N	Y
4 DeFazio	N	N	Y	N	Y	N	P	N
5 Hooley	Y	N	Y	N	Y	N	N	Y
PENNSYLVANIA								
1 Foglietta	?	Y	Y	N	Y	?	?	Y
2 Fattah	Y	N	Y	N	Y	Y	N	Y
3 Borski	N	Y	Y	N	Y	N	?	?
4 Klink	Y	Y	N	N	N	Y	N	Y
5 *Peterson*	Y	Y	N	Y	?	Y	N	Y
6 Holden	Y	N	Y	N	N	N	N	Y
7 *Weldon*	?	Y	?	N	N	Y	?	Y
8 *Greenwood*	Y	Y	N	Y	N	Y	N	Y
9 *Shuster*	Y	Y	N	Y	N	Y	N	Y
10 *McDade*	?	Y	N	N	N	Y	N	Y
11 Kanjorski	Y	Y	Y	N	N	N	?	Y
12 Murtha	Y	Y	Y	N	N	Y	N	Y
13 *Fox*	N	Y	N	N	N	Y	N	Y
14 Coyne	Y	N	Y	N	Y	Y	Y	Y
15 McHale	Y	N	Y	N	N	Y	N	Y
16 *Pitts*	Y	N	N	Y	N	N	N	Y
17 *Gekas*	?	Y	N	Y	?	Y	N	Y
18 Doyle	Y	Y	Y	N	N	Y	N	Y
19 *Goodling*	Y	N	?	Y	N	N	N	Y
20 Mascara	Y	Y	Y	N	N	Y	N	Y
21 *English*	N	Y	N	N	N	Y	N	Y
RHODE ISLAND								
1 Kennedy	Y	N	Y	N	Y	N	Y	Y
2 Weygand	Y	N	Y	N	Y	N	Y	Y
SOUTH CAROLINA								
1 *Sanford*	Y	N	N	Y	N	N	N	Y
2 *Spence*	Y	Y	N	Y	N	Y	N	Y
3 *Graham*	Y	N	N	Y	N	N	N	Y
4 *Inglis*	Y	N	N	Y	N	N	N	Y
5 Spratt	Y	N	Y	N	N	N	N	Y
6 Clyburn	N	Y	Y	N	Y	Y	N	N
SOUTH DAKOTA								
AL *Thune*	Y	Y	N	Y	N	Y	N	Y
TENNESSEE								
1 *Jenkins*	Y	N	N	Y	N	Y	N	Y
2 *Duncan*	Y	N	N	Y	N	N	N	Y

	526	527	528	529	530	531	532	
3 *Wamp*	Y	Y	N	Y	N	Y	N	Y
4 *Hilleary*	N	N	N	Y	N	N	N	Y
5 Clement	Y	Y	Y	N	Y	Y	N	Y
6 Gordon	Y	Y	Y	N	Y	Y	N	N
7 *Bryant*	Y	N	N	Y	N	N	N	Y
8 Tanner	Y	N	Y	N	N	Y	N	Y
9 Ford	Y	Y	Y	N	Y	?	Y	Y
TEXAS								
1 Sandlin	Y	Y	Y	N	Y	?	N	Y
2 Turner	Y	Y	Y	N	N	Y	N	Y
3 *Johnson, Sam*	Y	N	N	Y	N	N	N	Y
4 Hall	Y	N	N	N	N	N	N	Y
5 *Sessions*	N	Y	N	Y	N	N	N	Y
6 *Barton*	Y	Y	N	Y	N	N	N	Y
7 *Archer*	?	Y	N	Y	N	Y	N	Y
8 *Brady*	Y	N	N	Y	N	N	N	Y
9 Lampson	Y	N	Y	N	Y	N	N	Y
10 Doggett	N	N	Y	N	Y	N	Y	N
11 Edwards	Y	Y	Y	N	Y	Y	N	Y
12 *Granger*	Y	Y	N	Y	?	Y	?	Y
13 *Thornberry*	Y	Y	N	Y	N	N	N	Y
14 *Paul*	Y	N	N	N	N	N	N	Y
15 Hinojosa	Y	Y	Y	N	Y	N	N	Y
16 Reyes	Y	Y	Y	N	Y	Y	N	Y
17 Stenholm	Y	N	Y	Y	Y	N	N	Y
18 Jackson-Lee	Y	Y	Y	N	Y	Y	N	Y
19 *Combest*	Y	Y	N	Y	N	N	N	Y
20 Gonzalez	?	?	?	?	?	?	?	?
21 *Smith*	Y	Y	N	Y	N	Y	N	Y
22 *DeLay*	Y	Y	N	Y	N	N	N	Y
23 *Bonilla*	Y	Y	N	Y	N	Y	N	Y
24 Frost	Y	Y	Y	N	Y	N	Y	Y
25 Bentsen	Y	N	Y	N	N	Y	N	N
26 *Armey*	Y	Y	N	Y	N	Y	N	Y
27 Ortiz	Y	Y	Y	N	N	Y	N	Y
28 Rodriguez	Y	Y	Y	N	Y	Y	N	N
29 Green	Y	N	Y	N	N	N	N	Y
30 Johnson, E.B.	N	Y	Y	N	Y	N	Y	Y
UTAH								
1 *Hansen*	Y	Y	N	Y	N	Y	N	Y
2 *Cook*	Y	Y	N	Y	N	Y	N	Y
3 *Cannon*	Y	Y	N	Y	N	Y	N	Y
VERMONT								
AL *Sanders*	?	N	Y	N	Y	N	N	N
VIRGINIA								
1 *Bateman*	Y	Y	N	Y	N	Y	N	Y
2 Pickett	N	Y	Y	N	Y	Y	?	Y
3 Scott	Y	N	Y	N	Y	Y	N	Y
4 Sisisky	?	Y	N	N	N	Y	N	Y
5 Goode	Y	Y	Y	Y	N	Y	N	Y
6 *Goodlatte*	Y	Y	N	Y	N	Y	N	Y
7 *Bliley*	Y	N	N	Y	N	Y	N	Y
8 Moran	?	Y	Y	N	Y	Y	N	Y
9 Boucher	Y	Y	Y	N	Y	Y	N	?
10 *Wolf*	Y	Y	N	Y	N	Y	N	Y
11 *Davis*	Y	Y	N	Y	N	Y	N	Y
WASHINGTON								
1 *White*	Y	Y	N	Y	N	Y	N	Y
2 *Metcalf*	Y	Y	N	N	N	Y	N	Y
3 *Smith, Linda*	Y	N	N	N	N	Y	N	Y
4 *Hastings*	Y	Y	N	Y	N	Y	N	Y
5 *Nethercutt*	Y	Y	N	Y	N	Y	N	Y
6 Dicks	Y	Y	Y	N	Y	Y	N	Y
7 McDermott	N	N	Y	N	Y	N	Y	N
8 *Dunn*	Y	Y	N	Y	N	Y	N	Y
9 Smith, Adam	Y	N	Y	N	Y	N	N	Y
WEST VIRGINIA								
1 Mollohan	?	?	?	?	?	?	?	?
2 Wise	N	Y	Y	N	Y	Y	Y	Y
3 Rahall	Y	Y	N	N	N	Y	N	Y
WISCONSIN								
1 *Neumann*	Y	Y	N	N	N	N	N	Y
2 *Klug*	Y	Y	N	?	?	?	N	Y
3 Kind	Y	N	Y	N	Y	N	N	N
4 Kleczka	?	Y	Y	N	N	Y	N	Y
5 Barrett	Y	N	Y	N	Y	N	N	N
6 *Petri*	Y	Y	N	Y	N	N	N	Y
7 Obey	Y	Y	Y	N	Y	Y	Y	N
8 Johnson	N	Y	Y	N	N	N	Y	N
9 *Sensenbrenner*	Y	Y	N	Y	N	N	N	Y
WYOMING								
AL *Cubin*	?	?	?	?	?	?	?	?

Southern states - Ala., Ark., Fla., Ga., Ky., La., Miss., N.C., Okla., S.C., Tenn., Texas, Va.

HOUSE VOTES 534, 535, 536, 537, 538, 539, 540, 541

534. HR 1119. Fiscal 1998 Defense Authorization/Conference Report. Adoption of the conference report on the bill to authorize $268,301,837,000 for defense programs in fiscal 1998, $2,605,203,000 more than the president requested. The bill would prohibit funding for U.S. ground troops in Bosnia after June 30, 1998, unless the president certified to Congress that the operation was in the interest of U.S. national security, and would establish new competitive bidding rules for private contractors working at Air Force maintenance depots in San Antonio and Sacramento, Calif. Adopted (thus sent to the Senate) 286-123: R 192-22; D 94-100 (ND 53-88, SD 41-12); I 0-1, Oct. 28, 1997. A "nay" was a vote in support of the president's position.

535. Procedural Motion/Adjourn. Ensign, R-Nev., motion to adjourn. Motion rejected 29-374: R 4-204; D 25-169 (ND 21-120, SD 4-49); I 0-1, Oct. 29, 1997.

536. HR 1270. Temporary Nuclear Waste Repository/Rule. Adoption of the rule (H Res 283) to provide for floor consideration of the bill to establish a temporary nuclear waste storage site at Yucca Mountain, Nev. Adopted 259-155: R 191-24; D 68-130 (ND 33-112, SD 35-18); I 0-1, Oct. 29, 1997.

537. H Res 287. Robert K. Dornan Election Challenge/Motion To Table. Solomon, R-N.Y., motion to table the Gephardt, D-Mo., privileged resolution to dismiss the complaint by former Rep. Robert K. Dornan, R-Calif., contesting the election of Loretta Sanchez, D-Calif., by Oct. 31, 1997, unless the House Oversight Committee reports a recommendation for final disposition of the contest before that date. Motion agreed to 218-200: R 217-1; D 1-198 (ND 1-145, SD 0-53); I 0-1, Oct. 29, 1997.

538. H Res 139. Federal Education Funding/Adoption. Goodling, R-Pa., motion to suspend the rules and adopt the resolution to express the sense of the House that the Department of Education, states and local education agencies should work together to ensure that 90 percent of federal elementary and secondary education funding actually is spent for children in the classroom. Motion agreed to 310-99: R 216-0; D 94-98 (ND 63-76, SD 31-22); I 0-1, Oct. 29, 1997. A two-thirds majority of those present and voting (273 in this case) is required for adoption under suspension of the rules.

539. HR 1484. J. Roy Rowland U.S. Courthouse/Passage. Kim, R-Calif., motion to suspend the rules and pass the bill to designate the U.S. courthouse in Dublin, Ga., as the J. Roy Rowland U.S. Courthouse. Motion agreed to 414-0: R 215-0; D 198-0 (ND 145-0, SD 53-0); I 1-0, Oct. 29, 1997. A two-thirds majority of those present and voting (276 in this case) is required for passage under suspension of the rules.

540. HR 1479. David W. Dyer U.S. Courthouse/Passage. Kim, R-Calif., motion to suspend the rules and pass the bill to designate the U.S. courthouse in Miami as the David W. Dyer U.S. Courthouse. Motion agreed to 411-0: R 216-0; D 194-0 (ND 142-0, SD 52-0); I 1-0, Oct. 29, 1997. A two-thirds majority of those present and voting (274 in this case) is required for passage under suspension of the rules.

541. HR 2267. Fiscal 1998 Commerce, Justice, State Appropriations/Motion To Instruct. Rohrabacher, R-Calif., motion to instruct House conferees to disagree with the Senate amendment to permanently extend section 245(i) of the Immigration and Nationality Act, which permits immigrants who have illegally overstayed their visas to remain in the United States while seeking permanent legal status after paying a $1,000 fine. Motion rejected 153-268: R 148-71; D 5-196 (ND 2-145, SD 3-51); I 0-1, Oct. 29, 1997.

[1]*Walter Capps, D-Calif., died Oct. 28.*

KEY

- Y Voted for (yea).
- # Paired for.
- \+ Announced for.
- N Voted against (nay).
- X Paired against.
- – Announced against.
- P Voted "present."
- C Voted "present" to avoid possible conflict of interest.
- ? Did not vote or otherwise make a position known.

Democrats ***Republicans***
Independent

	534	535	536	537	538	539	540	541
ALABAMA								
1 ***Callahan***	Y	N	Y	Y	Y	Y	Y	Y
2 ***Everett***	N	N	Y	Y	Y	Y	Y	Y
3 ***Riley***	Y	N	Y	Y	Y	Y	Y	?
4 ***Aderholt***	Y	N	Y	Y	Y	Y	Y	Y
5 Cramer	Y	N	Y	N	Y	Y	Y	N
6 ***Bachus***	Y	N	Y	Y	Y	Y	Y	N
7 Hilliard	N	N	N	N	N	Y	Y	N
ALASKA								
AL ***Young***	Y	?	N	Y	Y	Y	Y	N
ARIZONA								
1 ***Salmon***	Y	N	Y	Y	Y	Y	Y	Y
2 Pastor	Y	N	Y	N	Y	Y	Y	N
3 ***Stump***	Y	N	Y	Y	Y	Y	Y	Y
4 ***Shadegg***	Y	N	Y	Y	Y	Y	Y	Y
5 ***Kolbe***	Y	N	?	?	Y	Y	Y	N
6 ***Hayworth***	Y	N	Y	Y	Y	Y	Y	Y
ARKANSAS								
1 Berry	Y	N	Y	N	Y	Y	Y	N
2 Snyder	Y	N	N	N	Y	Y	Y	N
3 ***Hutchinson***	Y	N	Y	Y	Y	Y	Y	Y
4 ***Dickey***	Y	?	N	Y	Y	Y	Y	Y
CALIFORNIA								
1 ***Riggs***	Y	N	Y	Y	Y	Y	Y	Y
2 ***Herger***	N	N	Y	Y	Y	Y	Y	Y
3 Fazio	N	N	Y	N	Y	Y	Y	N
4 ***Doolittle***	N	N	Y	Y	Y	Y	Y	Y
5 Matsui	N	N	?	?	Y	Y	Y	N
6 Woolsey	N	N	N	N	N	Y	Y	N
7 Miller	N	N	N	N	N	Y	Y	N
8 Pelosi	N	?	?	N	N	Y	Y	N
9 Dellums	N	Y	N	N	N	Y	Y	N
10 Tauscher	N	N	N	N	Y	Y	Y	N
11 ***Pombo***	N	N	N	Y	Y	Y	Y	N
12 Lantos	N	N	N	N	Y	Y	Y	N
13 Stark	?	Y	N	N	N	Y	Y	N
14 Eshoo	N	Y	Y	N	N	Y	Y	N
15 ***Campbell***	N	N	Y	Y	Y	Y	Y	Y
16 Lofgren	N	N	N	N	Y	Y	Y	N
17 Farr	N	N	Y	N	N	Y	Y	N
18 Condit	N	N	Y	N	Y	Y	Y	N
19 ***Radanovich***	Y	N	N	Y	Y	Y	Y	Y
20 Dooley	N	N	Y	N	Y	Y	Y	N
21 ***Thomas***	Y	N	Y	Y	Y	?	Y	N
22 Vacant [1]								
23 ***Gallegly***	Y	N	Y	Y	Y	Y	Y	Y
24 Sherman	N	N	N	N	N	Y	Y	N
25 ***McKeon***	Y	N	Y	Y	Y	Y	Y	Y
26 Berman	N	N	N	N	Y	Y	Y	N
27 ***Rogan***	Y	?	Y	Y	Y	Y	Y	Y
28 ***Dreier***	Y	N	Y	Y	Y	Y	Y	Y
29 Waxman	N	N	N	N	N	Y	Y	N
30 Becerra	N	N	N	N	N	Y	Y	N
31 Martinez	N	?	N	N	N	Y	Y	N
32 Dixon	N	N	N	N	N	Y	Y	N
33 Roybal-Allard	N	N	N	N	N	Y	Y	N
34 Torres	N	Y	N	N	N	Y	Y	N
35 Waters	Y	N	N	N	?	Y	Y	N
36 Harman	Y	N	N	N	Y	Y	Y	N
37 Millender-McD.	N	N	N	N	Y	Y	Y	N
38 ***Horn***	Y	N	Y	Y	Y	Y	Y	Y
39 ***Royce***	N	N	Y	Y	Y	Y	Y	Y
40 ***Lewis***	Y	Y	Y	Y	Y	Y	Y	Y
41 ***Kim***	Y	N	Y	Y	Y	Y	Y	N
42 Brown	?	?	?	N	N	Y	Y	N
43 ***Calvert***	Y	N	Y	Y	Y	Y	Y	Y
44 ***Bono***	Y	?	Y	Y	Y	Y	Y	Y
45 ***Rohrabacher***	Y	N	Y	Y	Y	Y	Y	Y
46 Sanchez	Y	N	Y	P	Y	Y	Y	N
47 ***Cox***	Y	N	Y	Y	Y	Y	Y	Y
48 ***Packard***	Y	N	Y	Y	Y	Y	Y	Y
49 ***Bilbray***	Y	N	Y	Y	Y	Y	Y	Y
50 Filner	N	Y	N	N	N	Y	Y	N
51 ***Cunningham***	N	N	N	Y	Y	Y	Y	Y
52 ***Hunter***	Y	N	Y	Y	Y	Y	Y	Y
COLORADO								
1 DeGette	N	Y	N	N	N	Y	Y	N
2 Skaggs	N	N	N	N	N	Y	Y	N
3 ***McInnis***	Y	N	Y	Y	Y	Y	Y	N
4 ***Schaffer***	Y	N	Y	Y	Y	Y	Y	Y
5 ***Hefley***	Y	N	Y	Y	Y	Y	Y	Y
6 ***Schaefer***	Y	N	Y	Y	Y	Y	Y	Y
CONNECTICUT								
1 Kennelly	Y	N	Y	N	Y	Y	Y	N
2 Gejdenson	Y	N	Y	N	N	Y	Y	N
3 DeLauro	Y	N	N	N	N	Y	Y	N
4 ***Shays***	N	N	Y	Y	Y	Y	Y	N
5 Maloney	Y	N	N	N	Y	Y	Y	N
6 ***Johnson***	Y	N	Y	Y	Y	Y	Y	N
DELAWARE								
AL ***Castle***	Y	N	Y	Y	Y	Y	Y	N
FLORIDA								
1 ***Scarborough***	Y	?	?	Y	Y	Y	Y	Y
2 Boyd	Y	N	Y	N	Y	Y	Y	Y
3 Brown	Y	N	N	N	N	Y	Y	N
4 ***Fowler***	Y	N	Y	Y	Y	Y	Y	Y
5 Thurman	Y	N	Y	N	Y	Y	Y	N
6 ***Stearns***	Y	N	Y	Y	Y	Y	Y	Y
7 ***Mica***	Y	N	Y	Y	Y	Y	Y	Y
8 ***McCollum***	Y	N	Y	Y	Y	Y	Y	Y
9 ***Bilirakis***	Y	N	Y	Y	Y	Y	Y	Y
10 ***Young***	Y	N	Y	Y	Y	Y	Y	Y
11 Davis	Y	N	Y	N	Y	Y	Y	N
12 ***Canady***	Y	N	Y	Y	Y	Y	?	Y
13 ***Miller***	Y	N	Y	Y	Y	Y	Y	Y
14 ***Goss***	Y	N	Y	Y	Y	Y	Y	Y
15 ***Weldon***	+	–	+	+	+	+	+	+
16 ***Foley***	Y	N	Y	Y	Y	Y	Y	Y
17 Meek	Y	N	?	?	?	?	?	N
18 ***Ros-Lehtinen***	Y	N	Y	Y	Y	Y	Y	N
19 Wexler	N	N	Y	N	N	Y	Y	N
20 Deutsch	N	N	Y	N	N	Y	+	N
21 ***Diaz-Balart***	Y	N	Y	Y	Y	Y	Y	N
22 ***Shaw***	Y	N	Y	Y	Y	Y	Y	Y
23 Hastings	N	N	N	N	N	Y	Y	N
GEORGIA								
1 ***Kingston***	Y	N	N	Y	Y	Y	Y	Y
2 Bishop	Y	N	N	N	Y	Y	Y	N
3 ***Collins***	Y	N	Y	Y	Y	Y	Y	Y
4 McKinney	N	N	N	N	N	Y	Y	N
5 Lewis	Y	Y	N	N	N	Y	Y	N
6 ***Gingrich***								
7 ***Barr***	Y	N	Y	Y	Y	Y	Y	Y
8 ***Chambliss***	Y	N	Y	Y	Y	Y	Y	Y
9 ***Deal***	Y	N	Y	Y	Y	Y	Y	Y
10 ***Norwood***	Y	N	Y	Y	Y	Y	Y	Y
11 ***Linder***	Y	N	Y	Y	Y	Y	Y	Y
HAWAII								
1 Abercrombie	Y	N	N	N	N	Y	Y	N
2 Mink	Y	Y	N	N	N	Y	Y	N
IDAHO								
1 ***Chenoweth***	N	N	Y	Y	Y	Y	Y	N
2 ***Crapo***	N	N	Y	Y	Y	Y	Y	N
ILLINOIS								
1 Rush	N	N	Y	N	N	Y	Y	N
2 Jackson	N	Y	N	N	N	Y	Y	N
3 Lipinski	N	N	Y	N	Y	Y	Y	N
4 Gutierrez	N	N	N	N	N	Y	Y	N
5 Blagojevich	Y	N	N	N	N	Y	Y	N
6 ***Hyde***	Y	N	Y	Y	Y	Y	Y	N
7 Davis	N	N	N	N	N	Y	Y	N
8 ***Crane***	Y	N	Y	Y	Y	?	Y	N
9 Yates	?	?	N	N	N	Y	Y	N
10 ***Porter***	Y	N	Y	Y	Y	Y	Y	Y
11 ***Weller***	Y	N	Y	Y	Y	Y	Y	N
12 Costello	N	N	N	N	Y	Y	Y	N
13 ***Fawell***	Y	N	Y	Y	Y	Y	Y	Y
14 ***Hastert***	Y	N	Y	Y	Y	Y	Y	Y
15 ***Ewing***	Y	N	Y	Y	+	Y	Y	Y

ND Northern Democrats SD Southern Democrats

	534	535	536	537	538	539	540	541
16 *Manzullo*	Y	N	Y	Y	Y	Y	Y	Y
17 Evans	Y	N	N	N	?	Y	Y	N
18 *LaHood*	Y	N	Y	Y	Y	Y	Y	N
19 Poshard	N	N	N	N	Y	Y	Y	N
20 *Shimkus*	Y	N	Y	Y	Y	Y	Y	Y
INDIANA								
1 Visclosky	Y	N	Y	N	N	Y	Y	N
2 *McIntosh*	?	?	?	?	?	?	?	?
3 Roemer	Y	N	N	N	Y	Y	Y	Y
4 *Souder*	Y	N	N	Y	Y	Y	Y	N
5 *Buyer*	Y	N	Y	Y	Y	Y	Y	N
6 *Burton*	Y	N	Y	Y	Y	?	Y	Y
7 *Pease*	Y	N	Y	Y	Y	Y	Y	Y
8 *Hostettler*	Y	N	Y	Y	Y	Y	Y	Y
9 Hamilton	Y	N	Y	N	?	Y	Y	N
10 Carson	Y	N	N	N	?	Y	Y	N
IOWA								
1 *Leach*	Y	N	Y	Y	Y	Y	Y	N
2 *Nussle*	Y	N	Y	Y	Y	Y	Y	N
3 Boswell	Y	N	Y	N	Y	Y	Y	N
4 *Ganske*	N	N	Y	Y	Y	Y	Y	Y
5 *Latham*	Y	N	Y	Y	Y	Y	Y	N
KANSAS								
1 *Moran*	Y	N	Y	Y	Y	Y	Y	Y
2 *Ryun*	Y	N	Y	Y	Y	Y	Y	Y
3 *Snowbarger*	Y	N	Y	Y	Y	Y	Y	Y
4 *Tiahrt*	Y	N	Y	Y	Y	Y	Y	Y
KENTUCKY								
1 *Whitfield*	Y	N	Y	Y	Y	Y	Y	Y
2 *Lewis*	Y	N	Y	Y	Y	Y	Y	Y
3 *Northup*	Y	N	Y	Y	Y	Y	Y	Y
4 *Bunning*	Y	N	Y	Y	Y	Y	Y	Y
5 *Rogers*	Y	N	Y	Y	Y	Y	Y	N
6 Baesler	Y	N	N	N	Y	Y	Y	N
LOUISIANA								
1 *Livingston*	Y	N	Y	Y	Y	Y	Y	N
2 Jefferson	Y	Y	N	N	N	Y	Y	N
3 *Tauzin*	Y	N	Y	Y	Y	Y	Y	Y
4 *McCrery*	Y	N	Y	Y	Y	Y	Y	Y
5 *Cooksey*	Y	N	Y	Y	Y	Y	Y	Y
6 *Baker*	Y	N	Y	Y	Y	Y	Y	Y
7 John	Y	N	Y	N	Y	Y	Y	N
MAINE								
1 Allen	Y	N	N	N	Y	Y	Y	N
2 Baldacci	Y	N	N	N	Y	Y	Y	N
MARYLAND								
1 *Gilchrest*	Y	N	?	Y	Y	Y	Y	N
2 *Ehrlich*	Y	N	Y	Y	Y	Y	Y	Y
3 Cardin	N	N	N	N	Y	Y	Y	N
4 Wynn	Y	N	N	N	N	Y	Y	N
5 Hoyer	Y	N	N	N	?	Y	Y	N
6 *Bartlett*	Y	N	Y	Y	Y	Y	Y	Y
7 Cummings	N	N	N	N	N	Y	Y	N
8 *Morella*	N	N	Y	Y	Y	Y	Y	N
MASSACHUSETTS								
1 Olver	N	Y	N	N	N	Y	Y	N
2 Neal	N	N	N	N	N	Y	Y	N
3 McGovern	N	N	N	N	Y	Y	Y	N
4 Frank	N	N	N	N	N	Y	Y	N
5 Meehan	Y	N	N	N	N	Y	Y	N
6 Tierney	Y	N	N	N	N	Y	Y	N
7 Markey	N	Y	N	N	N	Y	Y	N
8 Kennedy	N	N	N	N	N	Y	Y	N
9 Moakley	N	N	N	N	N	Y	Y	N
10 Delahunt	N	Y	N	N	N	Y	Y	N
MICHIGAN								
1 Stupak	N	N	Y	N	N	Y	Y	N
2 *Hoekstra*	Y	N	Y	Y	Y	Y	Y	N
3 *Ehlers*	Y	N	Y	Y	Y	Y	Y	N
4 *Camp*	Y	N	Y	Y	Y	Y	Y	N
5 Barcia	Y	N	Y	N	?	Y	Y	N
6 *Upton*	Y	N	Y	Y	Y	Y	Y	N
7 *Smith*	N	N	Y	Y	Y	Y	Y	Y
8 Stabenow	Y	N	N	N	Y	Y	Y	N
9 Kildee	Y	N	Y	N	N	Y	Y	N
10 Bonior	Y	N	Y	N	N	Y	Y	N
11 *Knollenberg*	Y	N	+	Y	Y	Y	Y	N
12 Levin	Y	N	Y	N	N	Y	Y	N
13 Rivers	N	N	N	N	N	Y	Y	N
14 Conyers	N	?	N	N	N	?	?	N
15 Kilpatrick	N	N	N	N	Y	Y	Y	N
16 Dingell	N	N	Y	N	N	Y	Y	N
MINNESOTA								
1 *Gutknecht*	Y	N	Y	Y	Y	Y	Y	Y
2 Minge	N	N	N	N	Y	Y	Y	N

	534	535	536	537	538	539	540	541
3 *Ramstad*	N	N	Y	Y	Y	Y	Y	N
4 Vento	N	N	N	N	N	Y	Y	N
5 Sabo	N	N	Y	N	Y	Y	Y	N
6 Luther	N	N	N	N	Y	Y	Y	N
7 Peterson	Y	N	Y	N	Y	Y	Y	N
8 Oberstar	N	N	N	N	Y	Y	Y	N
MISSISSIPPI								
1 *Wicker*	Y	N	Y	Y	Y	Y	Y	Y
2 Thompson	Y	N	N	N	N	Y	Y	N
3 *Pickering*	Y	N	Y	Y	Y	Y	Y	Y
4 *Parker*	Y	N	Y	Y	Y	Y	Y	Y
5 Taylor	Y	N	Y	N	Y	Y	Y	Y
MISSOURI								
1 Clay	N	N	N	N	N	Y	?	N
2 *Talent*	Y	?	N	Y	Y	Y	Y	N
3 Gephardt	Y	Y	N	N	N	Y	Y	N
4 Skelton	Y	N	Y	N	Y	Y	Y	N
5 McCarthy	N	N	N	N	N	Y	Y	N
6 Danner	N	N	Y	N	Y	Y	Y	N
7 *Blunt*	Y	N	Y	Y	Y	Y	Y	Y
8 *Emerson*	Y	N	Y	Y	Y	Y	Y	Y
9 *Hulshof*	Y	N	Y	Y	Y	Y	Y	Y
MONTANA								
AL *Hill*	Y	N	Y	Y	+	Y	Y	Y
NEBRASKA								
1 *Bereuter*	Y	N	Y	Y	Y	Y	Y	Y
2 *Christensen*	Y	N	N	Y	Y	Y	Y	Y
3 *Barrett*	Y	N	Y	Y	Y	Y	Y	Y
NEVADA								
1 *Ensign*	Y	Y	N	Y	Y	Y	Y	Y
2 *Gibbons*	Y	Y	N	Y	Y	Y	Y	Y
NEW HAMPSHIRE								
1 *Sununu*	Y	N	Y	Y	Y	Y	Y	Y
2 *Bass*	Y	N	Y	Y	Y	Y	Y	Y
NEW JERSEY								
1 Andrews	?	Y	N	N	N	Y	Y	N
2 *LoBiondo*	N	N	Y	Y	Y	Y	Y	Y
3 *Saxton*	Y	N	Y	Y	Y	Y	Y	N
4 *Smith*	Y	N	N	Y	Y	Y	Y	N
5 *Roukema*	N	N	Y	Y	Y	Y	Y	Y
6 Pallone	Y	N	N	N	N	Y	Y	N
7 *Franks*	N	N	Y	Y	Y	Y	Y	Y
8 Pascrell	Y	?	N	N	Y	Y	Y	N
9 Rothman	Y	N	N	N	Y	Y	Y	N
10 Payne	?	?	?	?	?	?	?	?
11 *Frelinghuysen*	Y	N	Y	Y	Y	Y	Y	Y
12 *Pappas*	Y	N	Y	Y	Y	Y	Y	N
13 Menendez	Y	N	N	N	N	Y	Y	N
NEW MEXICO								
1 *Schiff*	?	?	?	?	?	?	?	?
2 *Skeen*	Y	N	Y	Y	Y	Y	Y	Y
3 *Redmond*	Y	N	Y	Y	Y	Y	Y	N
NEW YORK								
1 *Forbes*	Y	N	Y	N	Y	Y	Y	N
2 *Lazio*	Y	N	Y	Y	Y	Y	Y	N
3 *King*	Y	N	Y	Y	Y	Y	Y	N
4 McCarthy	Y	N	Y	N	Y	Y	Y	N
5 Ackerman	N	Y	N	N	N	Y	Y	N
6 Flake	?	?	N	N	Y	Y	Y	N
7 Manton	N	N	Y	N	N	Y	Y	N
8 Nadler	N	N	N	N	N	Y	Y	N
9 Schumer	?	N	N	N	Y	Y	Y	N
10 Towns	N	N	N	N	N	Y	Y	N
11 Owens	N	N	N	N	N	Y	Y	N
12 Velázquez	N	N	N	N	N	Y	Y	N
13 Vacant								
14 Maloney	Y	N	N	N	Y	Y	Y	N
15 Rangel	N	N	N	N	?	Y	Y	N
16 Serrano	N	N	N	N	N	Y	?	N
17 Engel	N	N	N	N	N	Y	Y	N
18 Lowey	N	N	N	N	Y	Y	Y	N
19 *Kelly*	?	−	+	+	+	+	+	−
20 *Gilman*	Y	N	Y	?	Y	Y	Y	N
21 McNulty	Y	Y	N	N	N	Y	Y	N
22 *Solomon*	Y	N	Y	Y	Y	Y	Y	Y
23 *Boehlert*	Y	N	Y	Y	Y	Y	Y	N
24 *McHugh*	Y	N	Y	Y	Y	Y	Y	N
25 *Walsh*	Y	N	Y	Y	Y	Y	Y	N
26 Hinchey	N	N	N	N	Y	Y	Y	N
27 *Paxon*	Y	N	Y	Y	Y	Y	Y	Y
28 Slaughter	N	N	N	N	N	Y	Y	N
29 LaFalce	N	Y	N	N	Y	Y	Y	N
30 *Quinn*	Y	N	Y	Y	Y	Y	Y	N
31 *Houghton*	?	?	?	?	?	?	?	?

	534	535	536	537	538	539	540	541
NORTH CAROLINA								
1 Clayton	Y	N	Y	N	N	Y	Y	N
2 Etheridge	Y	N	Y	N	Y	Y	Y	N
3 *Jones*	Y	N	Y	Y	Y	Y	Y	Y
4 Price	Y	N	Y	N	Y	Y	Y	N
5 *Burr*	?	N	Y	Y	Y	Y	Y	N
6 *Coble*	Y	N	Y	Y	Y	Y	Y	Y
7 McIntyre	Y	N	Y	N	Y	Y	Y	N
8 Hefner	Y	N	Y	N	Y	Y	Y	N
9 *Myrick*	Y	?	Y	Y	Y	Y	Y	N
10 *Ballenger*	Y	N	Y	Y	Y	Y	Y	N
11 *Taylor*	?	N	N	Y	Y	Y	Y	Y
12 Watt	N	N	Y	N	N	Y	Y	N
NORTH DAKOTA								
AL Pomeroy	Y	N	Y	N	Y	Y	Y	N
OHIO								
1 *Chabot*	Y	N	Y	Y	Y	Y	Y	N
2 *Portman*	Y	N	Y	Y	Y	Y	Y	N
3 Hall	Y	N	N	N	Y	Y	Y	N
4 *Oxley*	Y	N	Y	Y	Y	Y	Y	N
5 *Gillmor*	Y	N	Y	Y	Y	Y	Y	Y
6 Strickland	Y	N	Y	N	Y	Y	Y	N
7 *Hobson*	Y	N	Y	Y	Y	Y	Y	Y
8 *Boehner*	Y	N	Y	Y	Y	Y	Y	Y
9 Kaptur	Y	N	N	N	N	Y	Y	N
10 Kucinich	N	N	N	N	N	Y	Y	N
11 Stokes	N	?	?	?	?	?	?	?
12 *Kasich*	Y	N	N	Y	Y	Y	Y	Y
13 Brown	N	N	N	N	N	Y	Y	N
14 Sawyer	N	N	N	N	N	Y	?	N
15 *Pryce*	Y	N	Y	Y	Y	Y	+	Y
16 *Regula*	Y	N	Y	Y	Y	Y	Y	N
17 Traficant	N	N	Y	Y	Y	Y	Y	Y
18 *Ney*	Y	N	Y	Y	Y	Y	Y	Y
19 *LaTourette*	Y	N	Y	Y	Y	Y	Y	N
OKLAHOMA								
1 *Largent*	Y	N	N	Y	Y	Y	Y	Y
2 *Coburn*	Y	N	Y	Y	Y	Y	?	Y
3 *Watkins*	Y	N	Y	Y	Y	Y	Y	Y
4 *Watts*	Y	N	N	Y	Y	Y	Y	N
5 *Istook*	Y	N	Y	Y	Y	Y	Y	Y
6 *Lucas*	Y	N	N	Y	Y	Y	Y	Y
OREGON								
1 Furse	N	N	N	N	?	Y	Y	N
2 *Smith*	?	N	N	Y	Y	Y	Y	Y
3 Blumenauer	N	N	N	N	N	Y	Y	N
4 DeFazio	N	Y	N	N	Y	Y	Y	P
5 Hooley	N	N	N	N	Y	Y	Y	N
PENNSYLVANIA								
1 Foglietta	N	Y	N	N	N	?	?	N
2 Fattah	N	Y	N	N	?	?	?	N
3 Borski	?	N	N	N	Y	Y	Y	N
4 Klink	Y	N	Y	N	Y	Y	Y	N
5 *Peterson*	Y	N	Y	Y	Y	Y	Y	Y
6 Holden	Y	N	N	N	Y	Y	Y	N
7 *Weldon*	Y	N	Y	Y	Y	Y	?	Y
8 *Greenwood*	Y	N	Y	Y	Y	Y	Y	Y
9 *Shuster*	?	N	Y	Y	Y	Y	Y	Y
10 *McDade*	?	N	Y	Y	Y	?	Y	N
11 Kanjorski	Y	N	Y	N	N	Y	Y	N
12 Murtha	Y	N	N	N	Y	Y	Y	N
13 *Fox*	Y	N	N	Y	Y	Y	Y	N
14 Coyne	N	N	N	N	N	Y	Y	N
15 McHale	Y	N	N	N	Y	Y	Y	N
16 *Pitts*	Y	N	Y	Y	Y	Y	Y	Y
17 *Gekas*	Y	?	Y	Y	Y	Y	Y	N
18 Doyle	Y	N	N	N	Y	Y	Y	N
19 *Goodling*	Y	N	Y	Y	Y	Y	Y	Y
20 Mascara	Y	N	N	N	Y	Y	Y	N
21 *English*	Y	?	N	Y	Y	Y	Y	N
RHODE ISLAND								
1 Kennedy	Y	N	N	N	N	Y	Y	N
2 Weygand	Y	N	N	N	N	Y	Y	N
SOUTH CAROLINA								
1 *Sanford*	Y	N	Y	Y	Y	Y	Y	Y
2 *Spence*	Y	N	Y	Y	Y	Y	Y	Y
3 *Graham*	Y	N	Y	Y	Y	Y	Y	Y
4 *Inglis*	Y	N	Y	Y	Y	Y	Y	Y
5 Spratt	Y	N	Y	N	N	Y	Y	N
6 Clyburn	Y	N	Y	N	N	Y	Y	N
SOUTH DAKOTA								
AL *Thune*	Y	N	Y	Y	Y	Y	Y	Y
TENNESSEE								
1 *Jenkins*	Y	N	Y	Y	Y	Y	Y	N
2 *Duncan*	?	N	Y	Y	Y	Y	Y	Y

	534	535	536	537	538	539	540	
3 *Wamp*	Y	N	N	Y	Y	Y	Y	Y
4 *Hilleary*	Y	Y	Y	Y	Y	Y	Y	Y
5 Clement	Y	N	Y	N	Y	Y	Y	N
6 Gordon	N	Y	Y	N	Y	Y	Y	N
7 *Bryant*	Y	N	N	Y	Y	Y	Y	Y
8 Tanner	Y	N	Y	N	Y	Y	Y	N
9 Ford	N	Y	N	N	N	Y	Y	N
TEXAS								
1 Sandlin	Y	N	Y	N	Y	Y	Y	N
2 Turner	Y	N	Y	N	Y	Y	Y	N
3 *Johnson, Sam*	Y	?	Y	Y	Y	Y	Y	Y
4 Hall	Y	N	Y	N	Y	Y	Y	N
5 *Sessions*	N	N	Y	Y	Y	Y	Y	Y
6 *Barton*	Y	N	Y	Y	Y	Y	Y	Y
7 *Archer*	Y	N	Y	Y	Y	Y	Y	Y
8 *Brady*	Y	N	Y	Y	Y	Y	Y	Y
9 Lampson	N	N	Y	N	Y	Y	Y	N
10 Doggett	N	N	N	N	N	Y	Y	N
11 Edwards	Y	N	Y	N	Y	Y	Y	N
12 *Granger*	Y	?	Y	Y	Y	Y	Y	N
13 *Thornberry*	Y	N	Y	Y	Y	Y	Y	N
14 *Paul*	N	N	Y	Y	Y	Y	Y	N
15 Hinojosa	Y	N	Y	N	N	Y	Y	N
16 Reyes	Y	N	N	N	N	Y	Y	N
17 Stenholm	Y	N	Y	N	Y	Y	Y	N
18 Jackson-Lee	N	N	N	N	Y	Y	Y	N
19 *Combest*	Y	N	Y	Y	Y	Y	Y	Y
20 Gonzalez	?	?	?	?	?	?	?	?
21 *Smith*	Y	N	Y	Y	Y	Y	Y	Y
22 *DeLay*	Y	N	Y	Y	Y	Y	Y	Y
23 *Bonilla*	N	N	Y	Y	Y	Y	Y	N
24 Frost	Y	N	Y	N	N	Y	Y	N
25 Bentsen	Y	N	Y	N	Y	Y	Y	N
26 *Armey*	Y	N	Y	Y	Y	Y	Y	N
27 Ortiz	Y	N	N	N	N	Y	Y	N
28 Rodriguez	N	?	N	N	N	Y	Y	N
29 Green	Y	N	Y	N	Y	Y	Y	N
30 Johnson, E.B.	Y	N	Y	N	N	Y	Y	N
UTAH								
1 *Hansen*	Y	?	N	Y	Y	Y	Y	Y
2 *Cook*	Y	N	Y	Y	Y	Y	Y	N
3 *Cannon*	Y	N	Y	Y	Y	Y	Y	N
VERMONT								
AL Sanders	N	N	N	N	N	Y	Y	N
VIRGINIA								
1 *Bateman*	Y	N	Y	Y	Y	Y	Y	Y
2 Pickett	Y	N	Y	N	Y	Y	Y	N
3 Scott	Y	N	N	N	N	Y	Y	N
4 Sisisky	Y	N	Y	N	Y	Y	Y	N
5 Goode	Y	N	Y	N	Y	Y	Y	Y
6 *Goodlatte*	Y	N	Y	Y	Y	Y	Y	Y
7 *Bliley*	Y	N	Y	Y	Y	Y	Y	Y
8 Moran	Y	N	N	N	Y	Y	Y	N
9 Boucher	?	N	Y	N	Y	Y	Y	N
10 *Wolf*	Y	N	?	Y	Y	Y	Y	Y
11 *Davis*	Y	N	Y	Y	?	Y	Y	N
WASHINGTON								
1 *White*	Y	N	Y	Y	Y	Y	Y	N
2 *Metcalf*	Y	N	Y	Y	Y	Y	Y	N
3 *Smith, Linda*	Y	N	Y	Y	Y	Y	Y	Y
4 *Hastings*	Y	N	Y	Y	?	?	Y	Y
5 *Nethercutt*	Y	N	Y	Y	Y	Y	Y	Y
6 Dicks	Y	N	Y	N	Y	Y	Y	N
7 McDermott	N	Y	N	N	N	Y	Y	N
8 *Dunn*	Y	N	Y	Y	Y	Y	Y	Y
9 Smith, Adam	Y	N	N	N	Y	Y	Y	N
WEST VIRGINIA								
1 Mollohan	?	N	Y	N	Y	Y	Y	N
2 Wise	N	N	N	N	N	Y	Y	N
3 Rahall	N	N	N	N	Y	Y	Y	N
WISCONSIN								
1 *Neumann*	Y	N	N	Y	Y	Y	Y	Y
2 *Klug*	N	N	Y	Y	Y	Y	Y	Y
3 Kind	N	N	N	N	N	Y	Y	N
4 Kleczka	N	N	N	N	Y	Y	Y	N
5 Barrett	N	N	N	N	Y	Y	Y	N
6 *Petri*	Y	N	Y	Y	Y	Y	Y	Y
7 Obey	N	Y	N	N	Y	Y	Y	N
8 Johnson	N	N	N	N	Y	Y	Y	N
9 *Sensenbrenner*	N	N	Y	Y	Y	Y	Y	Y
WYOMING								
AL *Cubin*	?	?	?	?	?	?	?	?

Southern states - Ala., Ark., Fla., Ga., Ky., La., Miss., N.C., Okla., S.C., Tenn., Texas, Va.

HOUSE VOTES 542, 543, 544, 545, 546, 547, 548, 549

542. HR 1270. Temporary Nuclear Waste Repository/Question of Consideration. Question of whether the House should consider the bill to establish a temporary nuclear waste storage site at Yucca Mountain, Nev. A point of order had been raised that the bill violated the unfunded mandates law (PL 104-4). Agreed to consider 312-105: R 196-22; D 116-82 (ND 75-70, SD 41-12); I 0-1, Oct. 29, 1997.

543. HR 1270. Temporary Nuclear Waste Repository/Indian Tribe Assistance. Kildee, D-Mich., amendment to allow Indian tribes whose reservation boundaries are contiguous with land used for the waste repositories to receive federal assistance and program-activity reviewing rights provided under the bill. Adopted 408-10: R 208-10; D 199-0 (ND 146-0, SD 53-0); I 1-0, Oct. 29, 1997.

544. HR 1270. Temporary Nuclear Waste Repository/Foreign Nuclear Waste. Traficant, D-Ohio, amendment to allow only nuclear waste produced in the United States to be stored in the repository established by the bill. Adopted 407-11: R 215-1; D 191-10 (ND 139-8, SD 52-2); I 1-0, Oct. 29, 1997.

545. HR 2493. Grazing Fees and Rangeland Management/Rule. Adoption of the resolution (H Res 284) to provide for House floor consideration of the bill to establish a statutory formula to calculate rancher fees for grazing cattle and other livestock on lands administered by the Bureau of Land Management and the Forest Service. Adopted 277-139: R 219-0; D 58-138 (ND 34-109, SD 24-29); I 0-1, Oct. 30, 1997.

546. HR 2493. Grazing Fees and Rangeland Management/State Equivalent Fees. Klug, R-Wis., amendment to the Vento, D-Minn., amendment to modify the bill's grazing fee formula to require producers to pay a rate equal to the state grazing fee for the particular state in which the federal lands are located. Rejected 205-219: R 48-174; D 156-45 (ND 132-17, SD 24-28); I 1-0, Oct. 30, 1997.

547. HR 2493. Grazing Fees and Rangeland Management/Large Producer Fees. Vento, D-Minn., amendment to modify the bill's grazing fee formula to require large producers to pay either the average grazing fee for the particular state where the federal lands are located or the bill's grazing fee formula plus a 25 percent federal fee, whichever is higher. The amendment allows small producers to pay according to the bill's grazing fee formula for federal land use. Rejected 208-212: R 45-174; D 162-38 (ND 136-13, SD 26-25); I 1-0, Oct. 30, 1997.

548. HR 2493. Grazing Fees and Rangeland Management/Animal Unit Months Definition. Vento, D-Minn., amendment to eliminate a provision in the bill that redefines an animal unit month (AUM), the amount of forage needed to feed livestock for a month and the basis by which ranchers are assigned grazing fees. The bill would change the number of sheep or goats that constitute an AUM, effectively reducing the grazing fee for sheep or goats by about one-third. Rejected 176-244: R 24-194; D 151-50 (ND 126-21, SD 25-29); I 1-0, Oct. 30, 1997.

549. HR 2493. Grazing Fees and Rangeland Management/Passage. Passage of the bill to establish a statutory formula to calculate rancher fees to graze cattle and other livestock on lands administered by the Bureau of Land Management and the Forest Service. The bill increases federal fees for grazing cattle on public lands but decreases grazing fees for sheep and goats. Passed 242-182: R 199-22; D 43-159 (ND 17-131, SD 26-28); I 0-1, Oct. 30, 1997.

KEY

- Y Voted for (yea).
- \# Paired for.
- \+ Announced for.
- N Voted against (nay).
- X Paired against.
- − Announced against.
- P Voted "present."
- C Voted "present" to avoid possible conflict of interest.
- ? Did not vote or otherwise make a position known.

Democrats ***Republicans***
Independent

	542	543	544	545	546	547	548	549
ALABAMA								
1 ***Callahan***	Y	Y	Y	Y	N	N	N	Y
2 ***Everett***	Y	Y	Y	Y	N	N	N	Y
3 ***Riley***	Y	Y	Y	Y	N	N	N	Y
4 ***Aderholt***	Y	Y	Y	Y	N	N	N	Y
5 Cramer	Y	Y	Y	Y	N	N	N	Y
6 ***Bachus***	Y	Y	Y	Y	N	N	N	Y
7 Hilliard	Y	Y	Y	N	Y	Y	Y	Y
ALASKA								
AL ***Young***	N	Y	Y	Y	N	N	N	Y
ARIZONA								
1 ***Salmon***	Y	Y	Y	Y	N	N	N	Y
2 Pastor	Y	Y	Y	Y	Y	Y	N	Y
3 ***Stump***	Y	N	Y	Y	N	N	N	Y
4 ***Shadegg***	Y	Y	Y	Y	N	N	N	Y
5 ***Kolbe***	Y	Y	Y	Y	N	N	N	Y
6 ***Hayworth***	Y	Y	Y	Y	N	N	N	Y
ARKANSAS								
1 Berry	Y	Y	Y	Y	N	N	N	Y
2 Snyder	Y	Y	Y	N	Y	Y	Y	N
3 ***Hutchinson***	Y	Y	Y	Y	N	N	N	Y
4 ***Dickey***	Y	Y	Y	Y	Y	N	N	Y
CALIFORNIA								
1 ***Riggs***	Y	Y	Y	Y	N	N	N	Y
2 ***Herger***	Y	Y	Y	Y	N	N	N	Y
3 Fazio	Y	Y	Y	Y	N	N	N	Y
4 ***Doolittle***	Y	Y	Y	Y	N	N	N	Y
5 Matsui	N	Y	Y	Y	Y	Y	Y	N
6 Woolsey	N	Y	N	N	Y	Y	Y	N
7 Miller	N	Y	Y	N	Y	Y	Y	N
8 Pelosi	N	Y	Y	?	Y	Y	Y	N
9 Dellums	N	Y	Y	N	Y	Y	Y	N
10 Tauscher	N	Y	Y	N	Y	Y	Y	N
11 ***Pombo***	N	Y	Y	Y	N	N	N	Y
12 Lantos	N	Y	Y	N	Y	Y	Y	N
13 Stark	Y	Y	Y	N	Y	Y	Y	N
14 Eshoo	Y	Y	Y	N	Y	Y	Y	N
15 ***Campbell***	N	Y	?	Y	Y	Y	Y	N
16 Lofgren	Y	Y	N	N	Y	Y	Y	N
17 Farr	Y	Y	Y	N	Y	Y	N	N
18 Condit	Y	Y	Y	Y	N	N	N	Y
19 ***Radanovich***	N	Y	Y	Y	N	N	N	Y
20 Dooley	Y	Y	Y	Y	N	N	N	Y
21 ***Thomas***	Y	Y	Y	Y	N	N	N	Y
22 Vacant								
23 ***Gallegly***	Y	Y	Y	Y	N	N	N	Y
24 Sherman	N	Y	Y	N	Y	Y	N	N
25 ***McKeon***	N	Y	Y	Y	N	N	N	Y
26 Berman	Y	?	?	Y	Y	Y	Y	N
27 ***Rogan***	Y	Y	Y	Y	N	N	N	Y
28 ***Dreier***	Y	Y	Y	Y	N	N	N	Y
29 Waxman	N	Y	N	N	Y	Y	Y	N
30 Becerra	N	Y	Y	N	Y	Y	Y	N
31 Martinez	N	Y	N	Y	N	N	N	Y
32 Dixon	Y	Y	Y	?	Y	Y	Y	N
33 Roybal-Allard	N	Y	Y	N	Y	Y	Y	N
34 Torres	?	Y	Y	N	Y	Y	Y	N
35 Waters	N	Y	Y	N	Y	Y	Y	N
36 Harman	N	Y	Y	N	Y	Y	Y	N
37 Millender-McD.	N	Y	Y	N	Y	Y	Y	N
38 ***Horn***	Y	Y	Y	Y	Y	Y	Y	Y
39 ***Royce***	Y	Y	Y	Y	N	N	N	Y
40 ***Lewis***	N	?	Y	Y	N	N	N	Y
41 ***Kim***	Y	Y	Y	Y	N	N	N	Y
42 Brown	Y	Y	Y	N	Y	Y	Y	N
43 ***Calvert***	Y	Y	Y	Y	N	N	N	Y
44 ***Bono***	Y	Y	Y	Y	N	?	N	Y
45 ***Rohrabacher***	Y	Y	Y	Y	Y	Y	N	Y
46 Sanchez	N	Y	Y	Y	Y	Y	Y	N
47 ***Cox***	Y	Y	Y	Y	Y	N	N	Y
48 ***Packard***	Y	Y	Y	Y	N	N	N	Y
49 ***Bilbray***	Y	Y	Y	Y	N	N	N	Y
50 Filner	N	Y	Y	N	Y	Y	Y	N
51 ***Cunningham***	Y	Y	Y	Y	N	N	N	Y
52 ***Hunter***	Y	Y	Y	Y	N	N	N	Y
COLORADO								
1 DeGette	N	Y	Y	N	Y	Y	Y	N
2 Skaggs	N	Y	Y	N	N	Y	Y	N
3 ***McInnis***	Y	Y	Y	Y	N	N	N	Y
4 ***Schaffer***	Y	Y	Y	Y	N	N	N	Y
5 ***Hefley***	Y	N	Y	Y	N	N	N	Y
6 ***Schaefer***	Y	Y	Y	Y	N	N	N	Y
CONNECTICUT								
1 Kennelly	Y	Y	Y	N	Y	Y	Y	N
2 Gejdenson	Y	Y	Y	N	Y	Y	N	N
3 DeLauro	N	Y	Y	N	Y	Y	Y	N
4 ***Shays***	Y	Y	Y	Y	Y	Y	Y	N
5 Maloney	N	Y	Y	N	Y	Y	Y	N
6 ***Johnson***	Y	Y	Y	Y	Y	Y	Y	N
DELAWARE								
AL ***Castle***	Y	Y	Y	Y	Y	Y	N	Y
FLORIDA								
1 ***Scarborough***	N	Y	Y	Y	Y	Y	N	N
2 Boyd	Y	Y	Y	Y	N	N	N	Y
3 Brown	Y	Y	Y	Y	Y	Y	Y	N
4 ***Fowler***	Y	Y	Y	Y	N	N	?	Y
5 Thurman	Y	Y	Y	Y	N	N	Y	Y
6 ***Stearns***	Y	Y	Y	Y	N	N	N	Y
7 ***Mica***	Y	Y	Y	Y	N	N	N	Y
8 ***McCollum***	Y	Y	Y	Y	N	N	N	Y
9 ***Bilirakis***	Y	Y	Y	Y	Y	Y	N	Y
10 ***Young***	Y	Y	Y	?	N	N	N	Y
11 Davis	Y	Y	Y	N	Y	Y	Y	N
12 ***Canady***	Y	Y	Y	Y	N	N	N	Y
13 ***Miller***	Y	Y	Y	Y	Y	Y	N	Y
14 ***Goss***	Y	Y	Y	Y	Y	N	N	Y
15 ***Weldon***	+	+	+	+	−	−	−	+
16 ***Foley***	Y	Y	Y	Y	N	N	N	Y
17 Meek	N	Y	Y	N	N	Y	Y	N
18 ***Ros-Lehtinen***	Y	Y	Y	Y	Y	N	N	Y
19 Wexler	Y	Y	Y	N	Y	Y	Y	N
20 Deutsch	Y	Y	Y	N	+	+	Y	N
21 ***Diaz-Balart***	Y	Y	Y	Y	N	N	N	Y
22 ***Shaw***	Y	Y	Y	Y	N	N	N	Y
23 Hastings	N	Y	Y	N	Y	Y	N	N
GEORGIA								
1 ***Kingston***	N	Y	Y	Y	Y	Y	N	Y
2 Bishop	Y	Y	Y	Y	N	N	N	Y
3 ***Collins***	Y	Y	Y	Y	N	N	N	Y
4 McKinney	N	Y	Y	N	Y	Y	Y	N
5 Lewis	N	Y	Y	N	Y	Y	Y	N
6 ***Gingrich***								Y
7 ***Barr***	Y	N	Y	Y	N	N	N	Y
8 ***Chambliss***	Y	Y	Y	Y	N	N	N	Y
9 ***Deal***	Y	Y	Y	Y	N	?	N	Y
10 ***Norwood***	Y	Y	Y	Y	N	N	N	Y
11 ***Linder***	Y	Y	Y	Y	N	N	?	Y
HAWAII								
1 Abercrombie	N	Y	Y	N	Y	Y	Y	N
2 Mink	N	Y	Y	N	Y	Y	Y	N
IDAHO								
1 ***Chenoweth***	Y	Y	Y	Y	N	N	N	Y
2 ***Crapo***	Y	Y	Y	Y	N	N	N	Y
ILLINOIS								
1 Rush	Y	Y	Y	N	Y	Y	Y	N
2 Jackson	N	Y	Y	N	Y	Y	Y	N
3 Lipinski	Y	Y	Y	Y	Y	Y	Y	Y
4 Gutierrez	N	Y	Y	N	Y	Y	Y	N
5 Blagojevich	N	Y	Y	N	Y	Y	Y	N
6 ***Hyde***	?	Y	Y	Y	N	N	N	Y
7 Davis	N	Y	Y	N	Y	Y	Y	N
8 ***Crane***	Y	Y	Y	Y	N	N	N	Y
9 Yates	?	?	?	N	Y	Y	Y	N
10 ***Porter***	Y	Y	Y	Y	Y	Y	N	Y
11 ***Weller***	Y	Y	Y	Y	N	N	N	Y
12 Costello	Y	Y	Y	N	Y	Y	N	N
13 ***Fawell***	Y	Y	Y	?	Y	Y	N	Y
14 ***Hastert***	Y	N	Y	Y	N	N	N	Y
15 ***Ewing***	Y	N	Y	Y	N	N	N	Y

ND Northern Democrats SD Southern Democrats

	542	543	544	545	546	547	548	549
16 **Manzullo**	Y	Y	?	Y	N	N	N	Y
17 Evans	N	Y	Y	N	Y	Y	Y	N
18 **LaHood**	Y	Y	Y	Y	N	N	N	Y
19 Poshard	Y	Y	Y	N	Y	Y	N	N
20 **Shimkus**	Y	Y	Y	Y	N	N	N	Y
INDIANA								
1 Visclosky	Y	Y	Y	Y	Y	Y	Y	N
2 **McIntosh**	?	?	?	Y	N	N	N	Y
3 Roemer	N	Y	Y	N	Y	Y	Y	N
4 **Souder**	N	Y	Y	Y	N	N	N	Y
5 **Buyer**	Y	Y	Y	Y	N	N	N	Y
6 **Burton**	Y	Y	Y	Y	N	N	N	Y
7 **Pease**	Y	Y	Y	Y	Y	Y	Y	N
8 **Hostettler**	Y	N	Y	Y	N	N	N	Y
9 Hamilton	Y	Y	Y	N	Y	Y	Y	N
10 Carson	N	Y	Y	N	Y	Y	Y	N
IOWA								
1 **Leach**	Y	Y	Y	Y	Y	Y	Y	Y
2 **Nussle**	Y	Y	Y	Y	N	N	N	Y
3 Boswell	Y	Y	Y	Y	N	N	N	Y
4 **Ganske**	Y	Y	Y	Y	N	N	Y	Y
5 **Latham**	Y	Y	Y	Y	N	N	N	Y
KANSAS								
1 **Moran**	Y	Y	Y	Y	N	N	N	Y
2 **Ryun**	Y	Y	Y	Y	N	N	N	Y
3 **Snowbarger**	Y	Y	Y	Y	N	N	N	Y
4 **Tiahrt**	Y	Y	Y	Y	N	N	N	Y
KENTUCKY								
1 **Whitfield**	Y	Y	Y	Y	N	N	N	Y
2 **Lewis**	Y	Y	Y	Y	N	N	N	Y
3 **Northup**	Y	Y	Y	Y	N	N	N	Y
4 **Bunning**	Y	Y	Y	Y	N	N	N	Y
5 **Rogers**	Y	Y	Y	Y	N	N	N	Y
6 Baesler	N	Y	Y	Y	N	N	N	Y
LOUISIANA								
1 **Livingston**	Y	Y	Y	Y	N	N	N	Y
2 Jefferson	N	Y	Y	N	Y	Y	Y	N
3 **Tauzin**	Y	?	Y	Y	N	N	N	Y
4 **McCrery**	Y	Y	Y	Y	N	N	N	Y
5 **Cooksey**	N	Y	Y	Y	N	N	N	Y
6 **Baker**	Y	Y	Y	Y	N	N	N	Y
7 John	Y	Y	Y	Y	N	N	N	Y
MAINE								
1 Allen	Y	Y	Y	N	Y	Y	Y	N
2 Baldacci	Y	Y	Y	N	Y	Y	Y	N
MARYLAND								
1 **Gilchrest**	Y	Y	Y	Y	N	N	N	Y
2 **Ehrlich**	Y	Y	Y	Y	N	N	N	Y
3 Cardin	Y	Y	Y	N	Y	Y	Y	N
4 Wynn	Y	Y	Y	Y	Y	Y	Y	N
5 Hoyer	Y	Y	Y	N	Y	Y	Y	N
6 **Bartlett**	Y	Y	Y	Y	N	N	N	Y
7 Cummings	N	Y	Y	N	Y	Y	Y	N
8 **Morella**	Y	?	?	Y	Y	Y	Y	N
MASSACHUSETTS								
1 Olver	Y	Y	Y	N	Y	Y	Y	N
2 Neal	Y	Y	Y	N	Y	Y	Y	N
3 McGovern	N	Y	Y	N	Y	Y	Y	N
4 Frank	Y	Y	N	N	Y	Y	Y	N
5 Meehan	N	Y	Y	N	Y	Y	Y	N
6 Tierney	N	Y	Y	N	Y	Y	Y	N
7 Markey	N	Y	Y	N	Y	Y	Y	N
8 Kennedy	N	Y	Y	N	Y	Y	Y	N
9 Moakley	N	Y	Y	N	?	Y	Y	N
10 Delahunt	N	Y	Y	N	Y	Y	Y	N
MICHIGAN								
1 Stupak	Y	Y	Y	Y	Y	Y	Y	N
2 **Hoekstra**	Y	Y	Y	Y	Y	Y	N	Y
3 **Ehlers**	Y	Y	Y	Y	N	N	N	Y
4 **Camp**	Y	Y	Y	Y	N	N	N	Y
5 Barcia	Y	Y	Y	Y	N	Y	N	Y
6 **Upton**	Y	Y	Y	Y	Y	Y	Y	Y
7 **Smith**	Y	Y	Y	Y	Y	Y	N	Y
8 Stabenow	Y	Y	Y	Y	Y	Y	Y	N
9 Kildee	Y	Y	Y	N	Y	Y	Y	N
10 Bonior	Y	Y	Y	N	Y	Y	Y	N
11 **Knollenberg**	Y	Y	Y	Y	N	N	N	Y
12 Levin	Y	Y	Y	N	Y	Y	Y	N
13 Rivers	Y	Y	Y	Y	Y	Y	Y	N
14 Conyers	Y	Y	Y	N	Y	Y	?	N
15 Kilpatrick	N	Y	Y	N	Y	Y	Y	N
16 Dingell	Y	?	Y	N	Y	Y	Y	N
MINNESOTA								
1 **Gutknecht**	Y	Y	Y	Y	N	N	N	Y
2 Minge	Y	Y	Y	Y	Y	N	N	Y

	542	543	544	545	546	547	548	549
3 **Ramstad**	Y	Y	Y	Y	Y	Y	Y	N
4 Vento	Y	Y	Y	N	Y	Y	Y	N
5 Sabo	Y	Y	Y	N	Y	Y	Y	N
6 Luther	Y	Y	Y	N	Y	Y	Y	N
7 Peterson	Y	Y	Y	Y	N	N	N	Y
8 Oberstar	Y	Y	Y	N	N	Y	Y	Y
MISSISSIPPI								
1 **Wicker**	Y	Y	Y	Y	N	N	N	Y
2 Thompson	Y	Y	Y	N	Y	Y	N	Y
3 **Pickering**	Y	Y	Y	Y	N	N	N	Y
4 **Parker**	Y	Y	Y	Y	N	N	N	Y
5 Taylor	Y	Y	Y	N	N	Y	N	N
MISSOURI								
1 Clay	N	Y	Y	N	Y	Y	Y	N
2 **Talent**	N	Y	Y	Y	N	N	N	Y
3 Gephardt	N	Y	Y	N	Y	Y	Y	N
4 Skelton	Y	Y	Y	Y	Y	Y	Y	N
5 McCarthy	Y	Y	Y	N	Y	Y	Y	N
6 Danner	Y	Y	Y	Y	N	–	–	+
7 **Blunt**	Y	Y	Y	Y	N	N	N	Y
8 **Emerson**	Y	Y	Y	Y	N	N	N	Y
9 **Hulshof**	Y	Y	Y	Y	N	N	N	Y
MONTANA								
AL **Hill**	Y	Y	Y	Y	N	N	N	Y
NEBRASKA								
1 **Bereuter**	Y	Y	Y	Y	N	N	Y	Y
2 **Christensen**	N	Y	Y	Y	N	N	N	Y
3 **Barrett**	Y	Y	Y	Y	N	N	N	Y
NEVADA								
1 **Ensign**	N	Y	Y	Y	N	N	N	Y
2 **Gibbons**	N	Y	Y	Y	N	N	N	Y
NEW HAMPSHIRE								
1 **Sununu**	Y	Y	Y	Y	N	N	N	Y
2 **Bass**	Y	Y	Y	Y	Y	N	N	Y
NEW JERSEY								
1 Andrews	N	Y	Y	N	Y	Y	Y	N
2 **LoBiondo**	Y	Y	Y	Y	Y	Y	Y	N
3 **Saxton**	Y	Y	Y	Y	N	N	N	Y
4 **Smith**	Y	Y	Y	Y	Y	Y	N	N
5 **Roukema**	Y	Y	Y	Y	Y	Y	Y	Y
6 Pallone	Y	Y	Y	N	Y	Y	Y	N
7 **Franks**	?	Y	Y	Y	Y	Y	Y	N
8 Pascrell	N	Y	Y	N	Y	Y	Y	N
9 Rothman	N	Y	Y	N	Y	Y	Y	N
10 Payne	?	Y	Y	N	Y	Y	Y	N
11 **Frelinghuysen**	Y	Y	Y	Y	Y	Y	Y	N
12 **Pappas**	Y	Y	Y	Y	Y	Y	Y	N
13 Menendez	Y	Y	Y	N	Y	Y	Y	N
NEW MEXICO								
1 **Schiff**	?	?	?	?	?	?	?	?
2 **Skeen**	Y	Y	Y	Y	N	N	N	N
3 **Redmond**	Y	Y	Y	Y	N	N	N	N
NEW YORK								
1 **Forbes**	Y	Y	Y	Y	Y	Y	Y	N
2 **Lazio**	Y	Y	Y	Y	N	Y	N	N
3 **King**	Y	Y	Y	Y	N	N	N	Y
4 McCarthy	Y	Y	Y	Y	Y	Y	Y	N
5 Ackerman	N	Y	Y	N	Y	Y	Y	N
6 Flake	Y	Y	Y	N	Y	Y	N	N
7 Manton	Y	Y	Y	Y	Y	Y	Y	Y
8 Nadler	N	Y	Y	N	Y	Y	Y	N
9 Schumer	N	Y	Y	N	Y	Y	Y	N
10 Towns	Y	Y	Y	N	Y	Y	Y	N
11 Owens	N	Y	Y	N	Y	Y	Y	N
12 Velázquez	N	Y	Y	N	Y	Y	Y	N
13 Vacant								
14 Maloney	N	Y	Y	N	Y	Y	Y	N
15 Rangel	N	Y	Y	N	Y	Y	Y	N
16 Serrano	N	Y	Y	N	Y	Y	Y	N
17 Engel	N	Y	Y	Y	Y	Y	Y	N
18 Lowey	N	Y	Y	N	Y	Y	Y	N
19 **Kelly**	+	+	+	Y	N	Y	N	Y
20 **Gilman**	Y	Y	?	Y	Y	N	N	Y
21 McNulty	N	Y	Y	N	Y	Y	Y	N
22 **Solomon**	Y	N	Y	Y	N	N	N	Y
23 **Boehlert**	Y	Y	Y	Y	N	N	N	Y
24 **McHugh**	Y	Y	Y	Y	N	N	N	Y
25 **Walsh**	Y	Y	Y	Y	N	N	N	Y
26 Hinchey	N	Y	Y	N	Y	Y	Y	N
27 **Paxon**	Y	Y	Y	Y	N	N	N	Y
28 Slaughter	N	Y	Y	N	Y	Y	Y	N
29 LaFalce	N	Y	Y	Y	Y	Y	Y	N
30 **Quinn**	Y	Y	Y	Y	N	N	N	Y
31 **Houghton**	?	Y	Y	Y	N	N	N	Y

	542	543	544	545	546	547	548	549
NORTH CAROLINA								
1 Clayton	Y	Y	Y	N	Y	Y	Y	N
2 Etheridge	Y	Y	Y	N	N	N	N	Y
3 **Jones**	Y	Y	Y	Y	N	N	N	Y
4 Price	Y	Y	Y	N	Y	Y	Y	N
5 **Burr**	Y	Y	Y	Y	N	N	N	Y
6 **Coble**	Y	N	Y	Y	Y	N	N	Y
7 McIntyre	Y	Y	Y	Y	N	N	N	Y
8 Hefner	Y	Y	Y	N	N	N	N	Y
9 **Myrick**	Y	Y	Y	Y	N	N	N	Y
10 **Ballenger**	Y	Y	Y	Y	N	N	N	Y
11 **Taylor**	Y	Y	Y	Y	N	N	N	Y
12 Watt	N	Y	Y	N	Y	Y	Y	N
NORTH DAKOTA								
AL Pomeroy	Y	Y	Y	Y	N	N	N	Y
OHIO								
1 **Chabot**	Y	Y	Y	Y	Y	Y	Y	Y
2 **Portman**	Y	Y	Y	Y	Y	Y	N	Y
3 Hall	Y	Y	Y	?	N	N	N	N
4 **Oxley**	Y	Y	Y	Y	N	N	N	Y
5 **Gillmor**	Y	Y	Y	Y	N	Y	N	Y
6 Strickland	Y	Y	Y	N	Y	Y	Y	N
7 **Hobson**	Y	Y	Y	Y	N	N	N	Y
8 **Boehner**	Y	Y	Y	Y	N	N	N	Y
9 Kaptur	Y	Y	Y	Y	Y	Y	Y	N
10 Kucinich	N	Y	Y	N	Y	Y	Y	N
11 Stokes	?	?	?	N	Y	Y	?	?
12 **Kasich**	Y	Y	Y	Y	Y	N	N	Y
13 Brown	Y	Y	Y	N	Y	Y	Y	N
14 Sawyer	Y	Y	Y	N	Y	Y	Y	N
15 **Pryce**	Y	Y	Y	Y	N	N	N	Y
16 **Regula**	Y	Y	Y	Y	N	N	Y	Y
17 Traficant	Y	Y	Y	Y	N	N	N	Y
18 **Ney**	Y	Y	Y	Y	N	N	N	Y
19 **LaTourette**	Y	Y	Y	Y	N	N	N	N
OKLAHOMA								
1 **Largent**	Y	Y	Y	Y	N	N	N	Y
2 **Coburn**	N	Y	Y	Y	N	N	?	Y
3 **Watkins**	Y	Y	Y	Y	N	N	N	?
4 **Watts**	N	Y	Y	Y	N	N	N	Y
5 **Istook**	Y	Y	Y	Y	N	N	N	Y
6 **Lucas**	N	Y	Y	Y	N	N	N	Y
OREGON								
1 Furse	N	Y	N	N	Y	Y	Y	N
2 **Smith**	Y	Y	Y	Y	N	N	N	Y
3 Blumenauer	N	Y	Y	N	Y	Y	Y	N
4 DeFazio	N	Y	Y	N	Y	Y	Y	N
5 Hooley	N	Y	Y	N	Y	Y	Y	N
PENNSYLVANIA								
1 Foglietta	N	Y	Y	?	Y	Y	Y	N
2 Fattah	Y	Y	Y	N	Y	Y	Y	N
3 Borski	Y	Y	Y	Y	Y	Y	Y	N
4 Klink	Y	Y	N	N	Y	Y	Y	N
5 **Peterson**	Y	Y	Y	Y	N	N	N	Y
6 Holden	N	Y	Y	Y	N	N	N	Y
7 **Weldon**	Y	Y	Y	Y	?	?	?	?
8 **Greenwood**	Y	Y	Y	Y	Y	Y	N	N
9 **Shuster**	Y	Y	Y	Y	N	N	N	Y
10 **McDade**	Y	Y	Y	?	Y	Y	N	Y
11 Kanjorski	Y	Y	N	N	Y	Y	Y	N
12 Murtha	Y	Y	Y	Y	N	N	N	Y
13 **Fox**	Y	Y	Y	Y	Y	Y	Y	N
14 Coyne	Y	Y	Y	N	Y	Y	Y	N
15 McHale	N	Y	Y	Y	Y	Y	Y	N
16 **Pitts**	Y	Y	Y	Y	N	N	N	Y
17 **Gekas**	N	Y	Y	Y	N	N	N	Y
18 Doyle	Y	Y	Y	N	Y	Y	Y	N
19 **Goodling**	Y	Y	Y	Y	N	N	N	Y
20 Mascara	Y	Y	Y	Y	Y	Y	Y	N
21 **English**	N	Y	Y	Y	N	N	N	Y
RHODE ISLAND								
1 Kennedy	N	Y	Y	N	Y	Y	Y	N
2 Weygand	N	Y	Y	N	Y	Y	Y	N
SOUTH CAROLINA								
1 **Sanford**	Y	N	Y	Y	Y	Y	Y	N
2 **Spence**	Y	Y	Y	Y	N	N	N	Y
3 **Graham**	Y	Y	Y	Y	N	N	N	Y
4 **Inglis**	Y	Y	Y	Y	Y	Y	N	Y
5 Spratt	Y	Y	Y	Y	Y	Y	Y	N
6 Clyburn	Y	Y	N	N	Y	Y	Y	N
SOUTH DAKOTA								
AL **Thune**	Y	Y	Y	Y	N	N	N	Y
TENNESSEE								
1 **Jenkins**	Y	Y	Y	Y	N	N	N	Y
2 **Duncan**	Y	Y	Y	Y	N	Y	Y	Y

	542	543	544	545	546	547	548	
3 **Wamp**	Y	Y	Y	Y	N	Y	Y	Y
4 **Hilleary**	Y	Y	Y	Y	N	N	N	Y
5 Clement	Y	Y	Y	Y	Y	Y	Y	N
6 Gordon	Y	Y	Y	N	N	Y	Y	N
7 **Bryant**	N	Y	Y	Y	N	N	N	Y
8 Tanner	Y	Y	Y	Y	N	N	N	Y
9 Ford	N	Y	Y	N	Y	Y	Y	N
TEXAS								
1 Sandlin	Y	Y	Y	Y	N	N	N	Y
2 Turner	Y	Y	Y	Y	N	N	N	Y
3 **Johnson, Sam**	Y	Y	Y	Y	N	N	N	Y
4 Hall	Y	Y	Y	Y	N	N	N	Y
5 **Sessions**	Y	Y	Y	Y	N	N	N	Y
6 **Barton**	Y	N	Y	Y	N	N	N	Y
7 **Archer**	Y	Y	Y	Y	N	N	N	Y
8 **Brady**	Y	Y	Y	Y	N	N	N	Y
9 Lampson	N	Y	Y	N	Y	Y	Y	N
10 Doggett	N	Y	Y	N	Y	Y	Y	N
11 Edwards	Y	Y	Y	?	N	N	N	Y
12 **Granger**	Y	Y	Y	Y	N	?	?	?
13 **Thornberry**	Y	Y	Y	Y	N	N	N	Y
14 **Paul**	N	Y	Y	Y	N	Y	N	N
15 Hinojosa	?	Y	Y	Y	N	N	N	Y
16 Reyes	N	Y	Y	Y	N	N	N	Y
17 Stenholm	Y	Y	Y	Y	N	N	N	Y
18 Jackson-Lee	N	Y	Y	N	+	+	Y	N
19 **Combest**	Y	Y	Y	Y	N	N	N	Y
20 Gonzalez	?	?	?	?	?	?	?	?
21 **Smith**	Y	Y	?	Y	N	N	N	Y
22 **DeLay**	Y	Y	Y	Y	N	N	N	Y
23 **Bonilla**	Y	Y	Y	Y	N	N	N	Y
24 Frost	Y	Y	Y	Y	N	N	N	Y
25 Bentsen	Y	Y	Y	N	N	N	N	N
26 **Armey**	Y	Y	Y	Y	N	N	N	Y
27 Ortiz	Y	Y	Y	Y	N	N	N	Y
28 Rodriguez	Y	Y	Y	N	Y	Y	N	Y
29 Green	Y	Y	Y	N	Y	Y	Y	N
30 Johnson, E.B.	Y	Y	N	N	N	N	N	N
UTAH								
1 **Hansen**	N	Y	Y	Y	N	N	N	Y
2 **Cook**	Y	Y	Y	Y	Y	Y	N	Y
3 **Cannon**	Y	Y	N	Y	N	N	N	Y
VERMONT								
AL *Sanders*	N	Y	Y	N	Y	Y	Y	N
VIRGINIA								
1 **Bateman**	Y	Y	Y	Y	N	N	N	Y
2 Pickett	Y	Y	Y	Y	N	N	N	Y
3 Scott	Y	Y	Y	N	Y	?	N	N
4 Sisisky	Y	Y	Y	Y	N	N	N	Y
5 Goode	Y	Y	Y	Y	N	N	N	Y
6 **Goodlatte**	Y	Y	Y	Y	N	N	N	Y
7 **Bliley**	Y	Y	Y	Y	N	N	N	Y
8 Moran	Y	?	Y	N	Y	Y	Y	N
9 Boucher	Y	Y	Y	Y	Y	Y	Y	N
10 **Wolf**	Y	Y	Y	Y	N	N	N	Y
11 **Davis**	Y	Y	Y	Y	Y	Y	N	Y
WASHINGTON								
1 **White**	Y	Y	Y	Y	N	N	N	Y
2 **Metcalf**	Y	Y	Y	?	N	N	N	Y
3 **Smith, Linda**	Y	Y	Y	Y	N	N	N	Y
4 **Hastings**	Y	Y	Y	Y	N	N	N	Y
5 **Nethercutt**	Y	Y	Y	Y	N	N	N	Y
6 Dicks	Y	Y	Y	N	Y	Y	Y	N
7 McDermott	N	Y	Y	?	Y	Y	Y	N
8 **Dunn**	Y	Y	Y	Y	N	N	N	Y
9 Smith, Adam	N	Y	Y	?	Y	Y	Y	N
WEST VIRGINIA								
1 Mollohan	Y	Y	Y	Y	N	N	Y	N
2 Wise	?	Y	Y	?	Y	Y	Y	N
3 Rahall	Y	Y	Y	N	Y	Y	Y	N
WISCONSIN								
1 **Neumann**	Y	Y	Y	Y	Y	Y	Y	Y
2 **Klug**	Y	Y	Y	Y	Y	Y	N	N
3 Kind	Y	Y	Y	N	Y	Y	Y	N
4 Kleczka	Y	Y	Y	N	Y	Y	Y	N
5 Barrett	Y	Y	Y	N	Y	Y	Y	N
6 **Petri**	Y	Y	Y	Y	Y	Y	N	Y
7 Obey	Y	Y	Y	N	Y	Y	Y	N
8 Johnson	Y	Y	Y	Y	N	Y	N	Y
9 **Sensenbrenner**	Y	Y	Y	Y	Y	Y	N	Y
WYOMING								
AL **Cubin**	?	?	?	?	?	?	?	?

Southern states - Ala., Ark., Fla., Ga., Ky., La., Miss., N.C., Okla., S.C., Tenn., Texas, Va.

HOUSE VOTES 550, 551, 552, 553, 554, 555, 556, 557

550. HR 1270. Temporary Nuclear Waste Repository/Risk Assessment. Ensign, R-Nev., amendment to require the Department of Energy to complete a scientifically objective risk assessment prior to carrying out any provision in the bill. Rejected 135-290: R 34-186; D 101-103 (ND 90-60, SD 11-43); I 0-1, Oct. 30, 1997.

551. HR 1270. Temporary Nuclear Waste Repository/State Emergency Response Team Certification. Gibbons, R-Nev., amendment to require certification from the governor of each state through which nuclear waste will be transported that a prepared emergency response team exists to manage any accident that may occur during waste transport. Rejected 112-312: R 45-175; D 67-136 (ND 60-90, SD 7-46); I 0-1, Oct. 30, 1997.

552. HR 1270. Temporary Nuclear Waste Repository/Waste Transportation Planning. Ensign, R-Nev., amendment to prohibit the Department of Energy from planning nuclear waste transportation routes unless sufficient funds have been appropriated during the fiscal year to support emergency response teams in states through which waste is being transported. Rejected 118-305: R 37-181; D 81-123 (ND 72-78, SD 9-45); I 0-1, Oct. 30, 1997.

553. HR 1270. Temporary Nuclear Waste Repository/Radiation Exposure Standards. Markey, D-Mass., amendment to allow the Environmental Protection Agency to develop radiation exposure standards, eliminating the bill's provision that establishes a statutory standard for annual radiation exposure. Rejected 151-273: R 19-200; D 131-73 (ND 111-39, SD 20-34); I 1-0, Oct. 30, 1997.

554. HR 1270. Temporary Nuclear Waste Repository/Electricity Fee Cap. Gibbons, R-Nev., amendment to eliminate the bill's provision that caps the fees imposed upon electricity produced at nuclear facilities. Rejected 67-357: R 9-211; D 58-145 (ND 50-100, SD 8-45); I 0-1, Oct. 30, 1997.

555. HR 1270. Temporary Nuclear Waste Repository/Buy American. Traficant, D-Ohio, amendment to express the sense of Congress that all materials and services purchased under the bill should be made in the United States. Adopted 407-2: R 219-0; D 187-2 (ND 137-2, SD 50-0); I 1-0, Oct. 30, 1997.

556. HR 1270. Temporary Nuclear Waste Repository/Motion To Recommit. Markey, D-Mass., motion to recommit the bill to the Commerce Committee with instructions to report it back with an amendment to ensure that trucking or railroad contractors transporting nuclear waste under the bill are not indemnified for any liability resulting from negligence, gross negligence or willful misconduct in a nuclear waste transportation accident. Motion rejected 142-283: R 10-212; D 131-71 (ND 111-37, SD 20-34); I 1-0, Oct. 30, 1997.

557. HR 1270. Temporary Nuclear Waste Repository/Passage. Passage of the bill to establish a temporary nuclear waste storage site at Yucca Mountain, Nev. Passed 307-120: R 200-22; D 107-97 (ND 61-89, SD 46-8); I 0-1, Oct. 30, 1997. A "nay" was a vote in support of the president's position.

KEY

- Y Voted for (yea).
- \# Paired for.
- \+ Announced for.
- N Voted against (nay).
- X Paired against.
- – Announced against.
- P Voted "present."
- C Voted "present" to avoid possible conflict of interest.
- ? Did not vote or otherwise make a position known.

Democrats ***Republicans***
Independent

	550	551	552	553	554	555	556	557
ALABAMA								
1 ***Callahan***	N	N	N	N	N	Y	N	Y
2 ***Everett***	N	N	N	N	N	Y	N	Y
3 ***Riley***	N	N	N	N	N	Y	N	Y
4 ***Aderholt***	N	N	N	N	N	Y	N	Y
5 Cramer	N	N	N	N	N	Y	N	Y
6 ***Bachus***	N	N	N	N	N	Y	N	Y
7 Hilliard	N	N	N	N	N	Y	N	Y
ALASKA								
AL ***Young***	Y	Y	Y	N	Y	Y	N	Y
ARIZONA								
1 ***Salmon***	N	N	N	N	N	Y	N	Y
2 Pastor	N	N	N	N	N	P	N	Y
3 ***Stump***	N	N	N	N	N	Y	N	Y
4 ***Shadegg***	N	N	N	N	N	Y	N	Y
5 ***Kolbe***	N	N	N	N	N	Y	N	Y
6 ***Hayworth***	N	N	N	N	N	Y	N	Y
ARKANSAS								
1 Berry	N	N	N	N	N	Y	N	Y
2 Snyder	N	N	N	N	N	Y	N	Y
3 ***Hutchinson***	N	Y	Y	N	N	Y	N	Y
4 ***Dickey***	N	N	N	N	N	Y	N	Y
CALIFORNIA								
1 ***Riggs***	N	N	N	N	N	Y	N	Y
2 ***Herger***	N	Y	N	?	N	Y	N	N
3 Fazio	N	N	N	N	N	Y	N	Y
4 ***Doolittle***	N	N	N	N	N	Y	N	Y
5 Matsui	Y	N	N	Y	N	Y	Y	Y
6 Woolsey	Y	Y	Y	Y	Y	Y	Y	N
7 Miller	Y	Y	Y	Y	Y	Y	Y	N
8 Pelosi	Y	Y	Y	Y	Y	Y	Y	N
9 Dellums	Y	Y	Y	Y	Y	Y	Y	N
10 Tauscher	N	Y	Y	Y	N	Y	Y	N
11 ***Pombo***	Y	Y	N	N	N	Y	N	N
12 Lantos	Y	Y	Y	Y	N	Y	Y	N
13 Stark	Y	Y	Y	Y	Y	Y	Y	N
14 Eshoo	Y	Y	Y	Y	Y	Y	Y	N
15 ***Campbell***	N	N	Y	Y	N	Y	N	Y
16 Lofgren	Y	N	N	Y	N	Y	Y	N
17 Farr	N	Y	N	Y	N	Y	Y	N
18 Condit	Y	N	N	N	N	Y	N	N
19 ***Radanovich***	N	N	N	N	N	Y	N	N
20 Dooley	N	N	N	N	N	Y	N	Y
21 ***Thomas***	N	N	Y	N	N	Y	N	Y
22 Vacant								
23 ***Gallegly***	N	N	N	N	N	Y	N	Y
24 Sherman	Y	N	Y	Y	N	Y	Y	N
25 ***McKeon***	Y	Y	Y	N	N	Y	Y	N
26 Berman	Y	N	Y	Y	Y	Y	Y	N
27 ***Rogan***	N	N	N	N	N	Y	N	Y
28 ***Dreier***	N	N	N	N	N	Y	N	Y
29 Waxman	Y	Y	Y	Y	Y	Y	Y	N
30 Becerra	Y	Y	Y	Y	Y	P	Y	N
31 Martinez	N	N	N	N	Y	P	Y	N
32 Dixon	N	N	Y	Y	Y	Y	Y	N
33 Roybal-Allard	Y	Y	Y	Y	Y	P	Y	N
34 Torres	Y	Y	Y	Y	Y	P	Y	N
35 Waters	Y	N	N	Y	Y	Y	Y	N
36 Harman	N	N	N	N	N	Y	Y	N
37 Millender-McD.	Y	Y	Y	Y	Y	Y	Y	N
38 ***Horn***	N	N	N	N	N	Y	N	Y
39 ***Royce***	N	N	N	N	N	Y	N	Y
40 ***Lewis***	N	N	N	N	N	Y	N	N
41 ***Kim***	N	N	N	N	N	Y	N	Y
42 Brown	Y	N	N	Y	N	Y	Y	N
43 ***Calvert***	N	N	N	N	N	Y	N	Y
44 ***Bono***	N	N	N	N	N	Y	N	Y
45 ***Rohrabacher***	N	N	N	N	N	Y	N	Y
46 Sanchez	Y	N	Y	Y	N	Y	Y	N
47 ***Cox***	N	N	N	N	N	Y	N	Y
48 ***Packard***	N	N	N	N	N	Y	N	Y
49 ***Bilbray***	N	N	N	N	N	Y	N	Y
50 Filner	Y	Y	Y	Y	Y	P	Y	N
51 ***Cunningham***	Y	N	N	N	N	Y	N	Y
52 ***Hunter***	N	N	N	N	N	Y	N	Y
COLORADO								
1 DeGette	Y	N	Y	Y	Y	Y	Y	N
2 Skaggs	N	N	N	Y	N	Y	Y	N
3 ***McInnis***	N	Y	N	N	N	Y	N	Y
4 ***Schaffer***	N	N	N	N	N	Y	N	Y
5 ***Hefley***	N	N	N	N	N	Y	N	Y
6 ***Schaefer***	N	N	N	N	N	Y	N	Y
CONNECTICUT								
1 Kennelly	Y	N	N	Y	Y	Y	Y	Y
2 Gejdenson	N	N	N	Y	Y	Y	Y	Y
3 DeLauro	Y	N	Y	Y	Y	Y	Y	N
4 ***Shays***	Y	Y	Y	Y	Y	Y	Y	N
5 Maloney	Y	N	N	Y	N	Y	Y	Y
6 ***Johnson***	N	N	N	N	N	Y	N	Y
DELAWARE								
AL ***Castle***	N	N	N	N	N	Y	N	Y
FLORIDA								
1 ***Scarborough***	N	N	N	N	N	Y	N	Y
2 Boyd	N	N	N	N	N	Y	N	Y
3 Brown	N	Y	N	N	N	Y	Y	Y
4 ***Fowler***	N	N	N	N	N	Y	N	Y
5 Thurman	Y	N	N	N	N	Y	Y	Y
6 ***Stearns***	N	Y	N	N	N	Y	N	Y
7 ***Mica***	N	N	N	N	N	+	N	Y
8 ***McCollum***	N	N	N	N	N	Y	N	Y
9 ***Bilirakis***	N	N	N	N	N	Y	N	Y
10 ***Young***	N	N	N	N	N	Y	N	Y
11 Davis	N	N	N	N	N	Y	N	Y
12 ***Canady***	N	N	N	N	N	Y	N	Y
13 ***Miller***	N	N	N	N	N	Y	N	Y
14 ***Goss***	N	N	N	N	N	Y	N	Y
15 ***Weldon***	–	–	–	–	–	–	+	–
16 ***Foley***	N	N	N	N	N	Y	N	Y
17 Meek	N	N	N	N	N	Y	Y	Y
18 ***Ros-Lehtinen***	N	N	N	N	N	Y	N	Y
19 Wexler	N	N	N	N	N	Y	N	Y
20 Deutsch	N	N	N	N	N	Y	N	Y
21 ***Diaz-Balart***	N	N	N	N	N	Y	N	Y
22 ***Shaw***	N	N	N	N	N	Y	N	Y
23 Hastings	N	N	N	N	N	Y	Y	N
GEORGIA								
1 ***Kingston***	Y	Y	Y	N	N	Y	N	Y
2 Bishop	Y	N	N	N	N	Y	N	Y
3 ***Collins***	N	Y	N	N	N	Y	N	Y
4 McKinney	Y	Y	Y	Y	Y	Y	Y	N
5 Lewis	Y	Y	Y	Y	Y	Y	Y	N
6 ***Gingrich***								Y
7 ***Barr***	Y	Y	Y	N	N	Y	N	Y
8 ***Chambliss***	N	N	N	N	N	Y	N	Y
9 ***Deal***	N	Y	N	N	N	Y	N	Y
10 ***Norwood***	N	N	N	N	N	Y	N	Y
11 ***Linder***	N	Y	Y	N	N	Y	N	Y
HAWAII								
1 Abercrombie	Y	Y	Y	Y	N	Y	Y	N
2 Mink	Y	Y	Y	Y	Y	Y	Y	N
IDAHO								
1 ***Chenoweth***	N	N	N	N	N	Y	N	Y
2 ***Crapo***	N	N	N	N	N	Y	N	Y
ILLINOIS								
1 Rush	N	N	N	N	N	Y	N	Y
2 Jackson	Y	Y	Y	Y	Y	Y	Y	N
3 Lipinski	N	N	N	N	N	Y	N	Y
4 Gutierrez	Y	N	Y	Y	N	P	Y	N
5 Blagojevich	Y	Y	Y	Y	N	Y	Y	N
6 ***Hyde***	N	N	N	N	N	Y	N	Y
7 Davis	Y	Y	Y	Y	Y	Y	Y	N
8 ***Crane***	N	N	N	N	N	Y	N	Y
9 Yates	Y	N	N	Y	N	Y	Y	N
10 ***Porter***	N	N	N	N	N	Y	N	Y
11 ***Weller***	N	N	N	N	N	Y	N	Y
12 Costello	N	N	N	Y	N	Y	N	Y
13 ***Fawell***	N	N	N	N	N	?	N	Y
14 ***Hastert***	N	N	N	N	N	Y	N	Y
15 ***Ewing***	N	N	N	N	N	Y	N	Y

ND Northern Democrats SD Southern Democrats

	550	551	552	553	554	555	556	557
16 ***Manzullo***	N	N	N	N	N	Y	N	Y
17 Evans	Y	Y	Y	Y	Y	Y	Y	N
18 ***LaHood***	N	N	N	N	N	Y	N	Y
19 Poshard	N	N	N	Y	N	Y	N	Y
20 ***Shimkus***	N	N	N	N	N	Y	N	Y
INDIANA								
1 Visclosky	N	N	N	N	N	Y	Y	Y
2 ***McIntosh***	Y	N	?	N	N	Y	N	N
3 Roemer	Y	Y	N	Y	N	Y	Y	N
4 ***Souder***	Y	Y	Y	Y	Y	Y	Y	N
5 ***Buyer***	N	N	N	N	N	Y	N	Y
6 ***Burton***	N	N	N	N	N	Y	N	Y
7 ***Pease***	Y	Y	N	N	N	Y	N	N
8 ***Hostettler***	N	Y	N	N	N	Y	N	Y
9 Hamilton	Y	N	N	N	N	Y	Y	N
10 Carson	Y	Y	Y	Y	Y	Y	Y	N
IOWA								
1 ***Leach***	N	N	N	N	N	Y	N	Y
2 ***Nussle***	N	N	N	N	N	Y	N	Y
3 Boswell	Y	N	Y	Y	N	Y	Y	N
4 ***Ganske***	N	N	N	N	N	Y	N	Y
5 ***Latham***	N	N	N	N	N	Y	N	Y
KANSAS								
1 ***Moran***	Y	Y	Y	N	N	Y	N	Y
2 ***Ryun***	N	N	N	N	N	Y	N	Y
3 ***Snowbarger***	N	N	N	N	N	Y	N	Y
4 ***Tiahrt***	N	N	N	N	N	Y	N	Y
KENTUCKY								
1 ***Whitfield***	N	N	N	N	N	Y	N	Y
2 ***Lewis***	N	N	N	N	N	Y	N	Y
3 ***Northup***	N	N	N	N	N	Y	N	Y
4 ***Bunning***	N	N	N	N	N	Y	N	Y
5 ***Rogers***	N	N	N	N	N	Y	N	Y
6 Baesler	Y	Y	Y	Y	N	Y	Y	N
LOUISIANA								
1 ***Livingston***	N	N	N	Y	N	Y	N	Y
2 Jefferson	N	?	Y	Y	N	Y	Y	Y
3 ***Tauzin***	?	?	?	N	N	Y	N	Y
4 ***McCrery***	N	N	N	N	N	Y	N	Y
5 ***Cooksey***	Y	Y	Y	Y	Y	Y	N	Y
6 ***Baker***	N	N	N	N	N	Y	N	Y
7 John	N	N	N	N	–	Y	N	Y
MAINE								
1 Allen	N	N	N	Y	N	Y	N	Y
2 Baldacci	Y	N	N	Y	N	Y	N	Y
MARYLAND								
1 ***Gilchrest***	N	Y	Y	N	N	Y	N	Y
2 ***Ehrlich***	N	N	N	N	N	Y	N	Y
3 Cardin	N	N	Y	N	N	Y	Y	Y
4 Wynn	Y	N	N	N	N	Y	N	Y
5 Hoyer	N	N	N	N	N	Y	N	Y
6 ***Bartlett***	N	N	?	N	N	Y	N	Y
7 Cummings	N	Y	N	Y	N	Y	Y	N
8 ***Morella***	N	N	N	N	N	Y	N	Y
MASSACHUSETTS								
1 Olver	Y	N	N	Y	N	Y	N	Y
2 Neal	Y	N	N	Y	N	Y	Y	Y
3 McGovern	Y	Y	Y	Y	Y	Y	Y	N
4 Frank	N	N	N	Y	N	Y	N	Y
5 Meehan	Y	Y	Y	Y	N	Y	Y	N
6 Tierney	Y	Y	Y	Y	Y	Y	Y	N
7 Markey	Y	Y	Y	Y	Y	Y	Y	N
8 Kennedy	N	Y	Y	Y	N	Y	Y	N
9 Moakley	Y	Y	Y	Y	N	Y	Y	N
10 Delahunt	Y	Y	Y	Y	Y	Y	Y	N
MICHIGAN								
1 Stupak	N	N	N	N	N	Y	N	Y
2 ***Hoekstra***	N	N	N	N	N	Y	N	Y
3 ***Ehlers***	N	Y	N	N	N	Y	N	Y
4 ***Camp***	N	N	N	N	N	Y	N	Y
5 Barcia	N	N	N	N	N	Y	N	Y
6 ***Upton***	N	N	N	N	N	Y	N	Y
7 ***Smith***	N	N	N	N	N	Y	N	Y
8 Stabenow	N	N	Y	Y	N	Y	N	Y
9 Kildee	N	N	N	N	N	Y	N	Y
10 Bonior	N	N	N	N	N	Y	?	Y
11 ***Knollenberg***	N	N	N	N	N	Y	N	Y
12 Levin	N	N	N	N	N	Y	N	Y
13 Rivers	Y	N	Y	Y	N	Y	Y	N
14 Conyers	Y	N	N	Y	Y	N	Y	N
15 Kilpatrick	N	N	N	N	N	Y	N	Y
16 Dingell	N	N	N	N	N	Y	Y	Y
MINNESOTA								
1 ***Gutknecht***	N	N	N	N	N	Y	N	Y
2 Minge	N	N	N	N	N	Y	N	Y

	550	551	552	553	554	555	556	557
3 ***Ramstad***	N	N	N	Y	N	Y	N	Y
4 Vento	N	N	Y	Y	Y	Y	Y	Y
5 Sabo	N	N	N	Y	N	Y	Y	N
6 Luther	Y	N	Y	Y	N	Y	Y	Y
7 Peterson	Y	N	N	N	N	Y	N	Y
8 Oberstar	Y	N	N	Y	N	Y	Y	Y
MISSISSIPPI								
1 ***Wicker***	N	N	N	N	N	Y	N	Y
2 Thompson	N	N	N	Y	N	Y	Y	Y
3 ***Pickering***	N	N	N	N	N	Y	N	Y
4 ***Parker***	N	N	N	N	N	Y	N	Y
5 Taylor	N	N	N	Y	N	Y	N	Y
MISSOURI								
1 Clay	Y	Y	N	Y	Y	Y	Y	N
2 ***Talent***	Y	Y	Y	Y	N	Y	Y	N
3 Gephardt	N	Y	Y	Y	N	Y	Y	N
4 Skelton	N	N	N	N	N	Y	N	Y
5 McCarthy	Y	N	Y	Y	N	Y	Y	Y
6 Danner	N	N	N	N	N	Y	N	Y
7 ***Blunt***	N	N	N	N	N	Y	N	Y
8 ***Emerson***	N	N	N	N	N	Y	N	Y
9 ***Hulshof***	Y	N	N	N	N	Y	N	Y
MONTANA								
AL ***Hill***	Y	Y	Y	N	N	Y	N	Y
NEBRASKA								
1 ***Bereuter***	N	N	N	N	?	Y	N	Y
2 ***Christensen***	Y	N	Y	N	N	Y	N	Y
3 ***Barrett***	N	N	N	N	N	Y	N	Y
NEVADA								
1 ***Ensign***	Y	Y	Y	Y	Y	Y	Y	N
2 ***Gibbons***	Y	Y	Y	Y	Y	Y	Y	N
NEW HAMPSHIRE								
1 ***Sununu***	N	N	N	N	N	Y	N	Y
2 ***Bass***	N	N	N	N	N	Y	N	Y
NEW JERSEY								
1 Andrews	Y	N	Y	Y	N	Y	Y	N
2 ***LoBiondo***	N	Y	N	Y	N	Y	N	Y
3 ***Saxton***	N	Y	N	N	N	Y	N	Y
4 ***Smith***	Y	Y	Y	Y	N	Y	Y	N
5 ***Roukema***	N	N	N	N	N	Y	N	Y
6 Pallone	N	Y	Y	Y	Y	Y	Y	N
7 ***Franks***	N	Y	N	Y	N	Y	N	Y
8 Pascrell	Y	Y	Y	Y	N	Y	Y	N
9 Rothman	Y	Y	Y	Y	N	Y	Y	N
10 Payne	Y	Y	Y	Y	Y	Y	Y	N
11 ***Frelinghuysen***	N	N	N	N	N	Y	N	Y
12 ***Pappas***	N	Y	Y	N	N	Y	N	Y
13 Menendez	N	N	N	Y	N	P	N	Y
NEW MEXICO								
1 ***Schiff***	?	?	?	?	?	?	?	?
2 ***Skeen***	N	N	N	N	N	Y	N	Y
3 ***Redmond***	N	N	N	N	N	Y	N	Y
NEW YORK								
1 ***Forbes***	N	Y	Y	Y	N	Y	N	Y
2 ***Lazio***	N	N	N	N	N	Y	N	Y
3 ***King***	N	N	N	N	N	Y	N	Y
4 McCarthy	N	N	N	Y	N	Y	Y	Y
5 Ackerman	Y	Y	Y	Y	N	Y	Y	N
6 Flake	Y	Y	Y	Y	N	Y	Y	Y
7 Manton	N	N	N	N	N	Y	N	Y
8 Nadler	Y	Y	Y	Y	Y	Y	Y	N
9 Schumer	Y	Y	Y	Y	N	Y	Y	N
10 Towns	Y	N	N	N	N	Y	N	Y
11 Owens	Y	Y	Y	Y	Y	Y	Y	N
12 Velázquez	N	N	N	Y	N	P	Y	N
13 Vacant								
14 Maloney	Y	Y	Y	Y	Y	Y	Y	Y
15 Rangel	Y	Y	N	Y	N	Y	Y	N
16 Serrano	Y	N	Y	Y	Y	P	Y	N
17 Engel	Y	N	Y	Y	N	Y	Y	Y
18 Lowey	Y	Y	Y	Y	Y	Y	Y	N
19 ***Kelly***	Y	Y	Y	N	N	Y	N	N
20 ***Gilman***	N	N	N	N	N	Y	N	Y
21 McNulty	Y	Y	Y	Y	Y	Y	Y	N
22 ***Solomon***	N	N	N	N	N	Y	N	Y
23 ***Boehlert***	N	N	N	Y	N	Y	N	Y
24 ***McHugh***	N	N	N	N	N	Y	N	Y
25 ***Walsh***	N	N	N	Y	N	Y	N	Y
26 Hinchey	Y	Y	Y	Y	Y	Y	Y	N
27 ***Paxon***	N	N	N	N	N	Y	N	Y
28 Slaughter	N	Y	N	Y	N	Y	Y	N
29 LaFalce	Y	Y	Y	Y	Y	Y	Y	N
30 ***Quinn***	N	Y	N	N	N	Y	N	Y
31 ***Houghton***	N	N	N	N	N	Y	N	Y

	550	551	552	553	554	555	556	557
NORTH CAROLINA								
1 Clayton	N	N	N	Y	Y	Y	Y	Y
2 Etheridge	N	N	N	N	N	Y	N	Y
3 ***Jones***	N	N	N	N	N	Y	N	Y
4 Price	N	N	N	Y	N	Y	N	Y
5 ***Burr***	N	N	N	N	N	Y	N	Y
6 ***Coble***	N	N	N	N	N	Y	N	Y
7 McIntyre	N	N	N	N	N	Y	N	Y
8 Hefner	N	N	N	Y	N	Y	Y	Y
9 ***Myrick***	N	N	N	N	N	Y	N	Y
10 ***Ballenger***	N	N	N	N	N	Y	N	Y
11 ***Taylor***	N	N	N	?	?	?	N	Y
12 Watt	N	N	N	Y	Y	Y	N	Y
NORTH DAKOTA								
AL Pomeroy	N	N	N	N	N	Y	N	Y
OHIO								
1 ***Chabot***	N	N	N	N	N	Y	N	Y
2 ***Portman***	N	N	N	Y	N	Y	N	Y
3 Hall	N	N	N	Y	N	Y	Y	N
4 ***Oxley***	N	N	N	N	N	Y	N	Y
5 ***Gillmor***	N	N	N	N	N	Y	N	Y
6 Strickland	N	N	N	Y	N	Y	Y	Y
7 ***Hobson***	N	N	N	N	N	Y	N	Y
8 ***Boehner***	N	N	N	N	N	Y	N	Y
9 Kaptur	N	N	N	Y	N	Y	Y	N
10 Kucinich	Y	Y	Y	Y	Y	Y	Y	N
11 Stokes	Y	Y	Y	Y	Y	Y	Y	N
12 ***Kasich***	Y	Y	Y	N	N	Y	N	N
13 Brown	N	N	N	Y	N	Y	Y	Y
14 Sawyer	N	N	N	Y	N	Y	Y	Y
15 ***Pryce***	N	Y	Y	N	N	Y	N	Y
16 ***Regula***	N	N	N	N	N	Y	N	Y
17 Traficant	N	N	N	N	N	Y	N	Y
18 ***Ney***	N	Y	Y	N	N	Y	Y	N
19 ***LaTourette***	N	N	N	N	N	Y	N	Y
OKLAHOMA								
1 ***Largent***	N	N	N	N	N	Y	N	Y
2 ***Coburn***	N	N	Y	N	N	Y	N	?
3 ***Watkins***	?	Y	Y	N	N	Y	N	N
4 ***Watts***	Y	Y	Y	Y	N	Y	N	Y
5 ***Istook***	Y	N	N	N	N	Y	N	Y
6 ***Lucas***	Y	Y	Y	Y	Y	Y	N	N
OREGON								
1 Furse	Y	Y	Y	Y	Y	N	Y	N
2 ***Smith***	N	?	N	N	N	Y	N	Y
3 Blumenauer	Y	Y	Y	Y	N	Y	Y	N
4 DeFazio	Y	Y	Y	Y	Y	Y	Y	N
5 Hooley	Y	Y	Y	Y	Y	Y	Y	N
PENNSYLVANIA								
1 Foglietta	Y	N	N	N	N	Y	?	N
2 Fattah	N	N	N	Y	N	Y	Y	Y
3 Borski	N	N	N	N	N	Y	Y	Y
4 Klink	N	N	N	N	N	Y	Y	Y
5 ***Peterson***	N	N	N	N	N	Y	N	Y
6 Holden	N	N	N	N	N	Y	N	Y
7 ***Weldon***	?	?	?	?	?	?	?	?
8 ***Greenwood***	N	N	N	N	N	Y	N	Y
9 ***Shuster***	N	N	N	N	N	Y	N	Y
10 ***McDade***	N	N	N	N	N	Y	N	Y
11 Kanjorski	N	N	N	N	N	Y	Y	Y
12 Murtha	N	N	N	N	N	Y	N	Y
13 ***Fox***	N	N	N	N	N	Y	N	Y
14 Coyne	Y	N	N	Y	N	Y	Y	N
15 McHale	Y	N	N	Y	N	Y	Y	N
16 ***Pitts***	N	N	N	N	N	Y	N	Y
17 ***Gekas***	N	N	N	N	N	Y	N	Y
18 Doyle	Y	N	Y	N	N	Y	N	Y
19 ***Goodling***	Y	N	N	N	N	Y	N	Y
20 Mascara	Y	N	N	N	N	Y	N	Y
21 ***English***	Y	Y	Y	N	N	Y	N	N
RHODE ISLAND								
1 Kennedy	Y	N	Y	Y	Y	Y	Y	N
2 Weygand	Y	Y	Y	Y	N	Y	Y	N
SOUTH CAROLINA								
1 ***Sanford***	N	N	N	N	N	Y	N	Y
2 ***Spence***	N	N	N	N	N	Y	N	Y
3 ***Graham***	N	N	N	N	N	Y	N	Y
4 ***Inglis***	N	N	N	N	N	Y	N	Y
5 Spratt	N	N	N	N	N	Y	N	Y
6 Clyburn	N	N	N	N	N	Y	N	Y
SOUTH DAKOTA								
AL ***Thune***	N	Y	Y	N	N	Y	N	Y
TENNESSEE								
1 ***Jenkins***	N	N	N	N	N	Y	N	Y
2 ***Duncan***	N	N	N	N	N	Y	N	Y

	550	551	552	553	554	555	556	
3 ***Wamp***	N	N	N	N	N	Y	N	Y
4 ***Hilleary***	Y	N	Y	N	N	Y	N	Y
5 Clement	N	N	N	N	N	Y	N	Y
6 Gordon	N	N	N	N	N	Y	N	Y
7 ***Bryant***	Y	Y	Y	N	N	Y	N	Y
8 Tanner	N	N	N	N	N	Y	N	Y
9 Ford	Y	Y	Y	Y	N	Y	N	Y
TEXAS								
1 Sandlin	N	N	N	N	N	Y	N	Y
2 Turner	N	N	N	N	N	Y	N	Y
3 ***Johnson, Sam***	N	N	?	N	N	Y	N	Y
4 Hall	N	N	N	N	N	Y	N	Y
5 ***Sessions***	N	N	N	N	N	Y	N	Y
6 ***Barton***	N	N	N	N	N	Y	N	Y
7 ***Archer***	N	N	N	N	N	Y	N	Y
8 ***Brady***	N	N	N	N	N	Y	N	Y
9 Lampson	Y	Y	Y	Y	Y	Y	Y	N
10 Doggett	Y	N	Y	Y	Y	Y	Y	N
11 Edwards	N	N	N	N	N	Y	N	Y
12 ***Granger***	N	N	N	N	N	Y	N	Y
13 ***Thornberry***	N	N	N	N	N	Y	N	Y
14 ***Paul***	Y	Y	Y	N	N	Y	Y	N
15 Hinojosa	N	N	N	N	N	P	Y	Y
16 Reyes	Y	Y	Y	N	Y	P	Y	N
17 Stenholm	Y	N	N	N	N	Y	N	Y
18 Jackson-Lee	Y	N	Y	Y	Y	Y	Y	Y
19 ***Combest***	N	N	N	N	N	Y	N	Y
20 Gonzalez	?	?	?	?	?	?	?	?
21 ***Smith***	N	N	N	N	N	Y	N	Y
22 ***DeLay***	N	N	N	N	N	Y	N	Y
23 ***Bonilla***	Y	N	N	N	N	Y	N	N
24 Frost	N	N	N	Y	N	Y	N	Y
25 Bentsen	N	N	N	Y	N	Y	Y	Y
26 ***Armey***	N	N	N	N	N	Y	N	Y
27 Ortiz	N	N	N	N	N	P	N	Y
28 Rodriguez	N	N	N	Y	N	P	Y	Y
29 Green	N	N	N	Y	N	Y	Y	Y
30 Johnson, E.B.	N	N	N	Y	N	Y	Y	Y
UTAH								
1 ***Hansen***	Y	Y	Y	?	Y	Y	N	N
2 ***Cook***	N	N	N	N	N	Y	N	Y
3 ***Cannon***	Y	Y	Y	N	Y	Y	N	Y
VERMONT								
AL *Sanders*	N	N	N	Y	N	Y	Y	N
VIRGINIA								
1 ***Bateman***	N	N	N	N	N	Y	N	Y
2 Pickett	N	N	N	N	N	Y	N	Y
3 Scott	N	N	N	N	N	Y	N	Y
4 Sisisky	N	N	N	N	N	Y	N	Y
5 Goode	N	N	N	N	N	Y	N	Y
6 ***Goodlatte***	N	N	N	N	N	Y	N	Y
7 ***Bliley***	N	N	N	N	N	Y	N	Y
8 Moran	N	N	N	Y	N	Y	N	N
9 Boucher	N	N	N	N	N	Y	N	Y
10 ***Wolf***	N	Y	Y	Y	N	Y	Y	Y
11 ***Davis***	N	N	N	N	N	Y	N	Y
WASHINGTON								
1 ***White***	N	N	N	N	N	Y	N	Y
2 ***Metcalf***	N	N	N	N	N	Y	N	Y
3 ***Smith, Linda***	N	N	N	N	N	Y	N	Y
4 ***Hastings***	N	N	N	N	N	Y	N	Y
5 ***Nethercutt***	N	N	N	N	N	Y	N	Y
6 Dicks	N	N	N	Y	N	Y	N	Y
7 McDermott	Y	Y	Y	Y	Y	Y	Y	N
8 ***Dunn***	N	N	N	N	N	Y	N	Y
9 Smith, Adam	N	N	N	Y	N	Y	Y	N
WEST VIRGINIA								
1 Mollohan	N	N	N	N	N	Y	N	Y
2 Wise	N	N	Y	Y	N	Y	N	N
3 Rahall	Y	Y	Y	Y	Y	P	Y	N
WISCONSIN								
1 ***Neumann***	Y	N	N	N	N	Y	N	Y
2 ***Klug***	Y	N	N	N	N	Y	N	Y
3 Kind	N	N	N	N	N	Y	Y	Y
4 Kleczka	Y	Y	N	Y	N	Y	Y	N
5 Barrett	Y	N	N	Y	N	Y	Y	N
6 ***Petri***	N	N	N	N	N	Y	N	Y
7 Obey	Y	Y	N	Y	N	Y	Y	Y
8 Johnson	N	N	N	N	N	Y	N	Y
9 ***Sensenbrenner***	N	N	N	N	N	Y	N	Y
WYOMING								
AL ***Cubin***	?	?	?	?	?	?	?	?

Southern states - Ala., Ark., Fla., Ga., Ky., La., Miss., N.C., Okla., S.C., Tenn., Texas, Va.

HOUSE VOTES 558, 559, 560, 561, 562, 563, 564, 565

558. H Res 290. Robert K. Dornan Election Challenge/Motion To Table. Solomon, R-N.Y., motion to table the Menendez, D-N.J., privileged resolution to dismiss the complaint by former Rep. Robert K. Dornan, R-Calif., contesting the election of Loretta Sanchez, D-Calif., by Oct. 31, 1997, unless the House Oversight Committee reports a recommendation for final disposition of the contest before that date. Motion agreed to 212-198: R 211-1; D 1-196 (ND 1-143, SD 0-53); I 0-1, Oct. 30, 1997.

559. H Res 291. Robert K. Dornan Election Challenge/Motion To Table. Solomon, R-N.Y., motion to table the Roybal-Allard, D-Calif., privileged resolution to dismiss the complaint by former Rep. Robert K. Dornan, R-Calif., contesting the election of Loretta Sanchez, D-Calif., by Oct. 31, 1997, unless the House Oversight Committee reports a recommendation for final disposition of the contest before that date. Motion agreed to 216-200: R 215-2; D 1-197 (ND 1-143, SD 0-54); I 0-1, Oct. 30,1997.

560. H Res 292. Robert K. Dornan Election Challenge/Motion To Table. Solomon, R-N.Y., motion to table the Norton, D-D.C., privileged resolution to dismiss the complaint by former Rep. Robert K. Dornan, R-Calif., contesting the election of Loretta Sanchez, D-Calif., by Oct. 31, 1997, unless the House Oversight Committee reports a recommendation for final disposition of the contest before that date. Motion agreed to 214-187: R 213-1; D 1-185 (ND 1-135, SD 0-50); I 0-1, Oct. 30, 1997.

561. H Res 293. Robert K. Dornan Election Challenge/Motion To Table. Solomon, R-N.Y., motion to table the Condit, D-Calif., privileged resolution to dismiss the complaint by former Rep. Robert K. Dornan, R-Calif., contesting the election of Loretta Sanchez, D-Calif., by Oct. 31, 1997, unless the House Oversight Committee reports a recommendation for final disposition of the contest before that date. Motion agreed to 212-190: R 211-1; D 1-188 (ND 1-136, SD 0-52); I 0-1, Oct. 30, 1997.

562. H Res 294. Robert K. Dornan Election Challenge/Motion To Table. Solomon, R-N.Y., motion to table the Becerra, D-Calif., privileged resolution to dismiss the complaint by former Rep. Robert K. Dornan, R-Calif., contesting the election of Loretta Sanchez, D-Calif., by Oct. 31, 1997, unless the House Oversight Committee reports a recommendation for final disposition of the contest before that date. Motion agreed to 217-193: R 215-1; D 2-192 (ND 1-140, SD 1-52); I 0-0, Oct. 30, 1997.

563. H Res 295. Robert K. Dornan Election Challenge/Motion To Table. Solomon, R-N.Y., motion to table the Hooley, D-Ore., privileged resolution to dismiss the complaint by former Rep. Robert K. Dornan, R-Calif., contesting the election of Loretta Sanchez, D-Calif., by Oct. 31, 1997, unless the House Oversight Committee reports a recommendation for final disposition of the contest before that date. Motion agreed to 212-197: R 210-1; D 2-195 (ND 1-143, SD 1-52); I 0-1, Oct. 30, 1997.

564. H Res 296. Robert K. Dornan Election Challenge/Motion To Table. Solomon, R-N.Y., motion to table the Waters, D-Calif., privileged resolution to dismiss the complaint by former Rep. Robert K. Dornan, R-Calif., contesting the election of Loretta Sanchez, D-Calif., by Oct. 31, 1997, unless the House Oversight Committee reports a recommendation for final disposition of the contest before that date. Motion agreed to 214-196: R 212-1; D 2-194 (ND 1-142, SD 1-52); I 0-1, Oct. 30, 1997.

565. H Res 297. Robert K. Dornan Election Challenge/Motion To Table. Solomon, R-N.Y., motion to table the Dooley, D-Calif., privileged resolution to dismiss the complaint by former Rep. Robert K. Dornan, R-Calif., contesting the election of Loretta Sanchez, D-Calif., by Oct. 31, 1997, unless the House Oversight Committee reports a recommendation for final disposition of the contest before that date. Motion agreed to 208-192: R 206-2; D 2-189 (ND 1-138, SD 1-51); I 0-1, Oct. 30, 1997.

KEY

- Y Voted for (yea).
- # Paired for.
- + Announced for.
- N Voted against (nay).
- X Paired against.
- – Announced against.
- P Voted "present."
- C Voted "present" to avoid possible conflict of interest.
- ? Did not vote or otherwise make a position known.

Democrats ***Republicans***
Independent

	558	559	560	561	562	563	564	565
ALABAMA								
1 ***Callahan***	Y	Y	Y	Y	Y	Y	Y	Y
2 ***Everett***	Y	Y	Y	Y	Y	Y	Y	Y
3 ***Riley***	Y	Y	Y	Y	Y	Y	Y	Y
4 ***Aderholt***	Y	Y	Y	Y	Y	Y	Y	Y
5 Cramer	N	N	N	N	N	N	N	N
6 ***Bachus***	Y	Y	Y	Y	Y	Y	Y	Y
7 Hilliard	N	N	N	N	N	N	N	N
ALASKA								
AL ***Young***	?	Y	Y	Y	Y	?	?	Y
ARIZONA								
1 ***Salmon***	Y	Y	Y	Y	Y	Y	Y	Y
2 Pastor	N	N	N	N	N	N	N	N
3 ***Stump***	Y	Y	Y	Y	Y	Y	Y	Y
4 ***Shadegg***	Y	P	P	P	P	P	Y	N
5 ***Kolbe***	Y	Y	Y	Y	Y	Y	Y	Y
6 ***Hayworth***	Y	Y	Y	Y	Y	Y	Y	Y
ARKANSAS								
1 Berry	N	N	N	N	N	N	N	N
2 Snyder	N	N	N	N	N	N	N	N
3 ***Hutchinson***	Y	Y	Y	Y	Y	Y	Y	Y
4 ***Dickey***	Y	Y	Y	Y	Y	Y	Y	Y
CALIFORNIA								
1 ***Riggs***	Y	Y	Y	Y	Y	Y	Y	Y
2 ***Herger***	Y	Y	Y	Y	Y	Y	Y	Y
3 Fazio	N	N	N	N	N	N	N	N
4 ***Doolittle***	?	Y	Y	Y	Y	Y	Y	Y
5 Matsui	N	N	N	N	N	N	N	N
6 Woolsey	N	N	?	N	N	N	N	N
7 Miller	N	N	N	N	N	N	N	N
8 Pelosi	N	N	?	N	N	N	N	N
9 Dellums	N	N	N	N	N	N	N	N
10 Tauscher	N	N	N	N	N	N	N	N
11 ***Pombo***	Y	Y	Y	Y	Y	Y	Y	Y
12 Lantos	N	N	N	N	N	N	N	N
13 Stark	N	N	N	N	N	N	N	N
14 Eshoo	N	N	N	N	N	N	N	N
15 ***Campbell***	Y	Y	Y	Y	Y	Y	Y	Y
16 Lofgren	N	N	N	N	N	N	N	N
17 Farr	N	N	N	N	N	N	N	N
18 Condit	N	N	N	N	N	N	N	N
19 ***Radanovich***	Y	Y	Y	Y	Y	Y	Y	Y
20 Dooley	N	N	N	?	N	N	N	N
21 ***Thomas***	Y	Y	Y	Y	Y	?	Y	Y
22 Vacant								
23 ***Gallegly***	Y	Y	Y	Y	Y	Y	Y	Y
24 Sherman	N	N	N	N	N	N	N	N
25 ***McKeon***	Y	Y	Y	Y	Y	Y	Y	Y
26 Berman	N	N	N	N	N	N	N	N
27 ***Rogan***	Y	Y	Y	Y	Y	Y	Y	Y
28 ***Dreier***	Y	Y	Y	Y	Y	Y	Y	Y
29 Waxman	N	N	?	?	?	N	N	N
30 Becerra	N	N	N	N	N	N	N	N
31 Martinez	N	N	N	?	N	N	N	N
32 Dixon	N	N	N	N	N	N	N	N
33 Roybal-Allard	N	N	N	N	N	N	N	N
34 Torres	N	N	N	N	N	N	N	N
35 Waters	N	N	N	N	N	N	N	N
36 Harman	N	N	N	N	N	N	N	N
37 Millender-McD.	N	N	–	N	N	N	N	N
38 ***Horn***	Y	Y	Y	Y	Y	Y	Y	Y
39 ***Royce***	Y	Y	Y	Y	Y	Y	Y	Y
40 ***Lewis***	Y	Y	Y	Y	Y	Y	Y	Y
41 ***Kim***	Y	Y	Y	Y	Y	Y	Y	Y
42 Brown	N	N	N	N	N	N	N	N
43 ***Calvert***	Y	Y	Y	Y	Y	Y	Y	Y
44 ***Bono***	Y	N	Y	Y	Y	Y	Y	?
45 ***Rohrabacher***	Y	Y	Y	Y	Y	Y	Y	Y
46 Sanchez	P	P	P	?	P	P	N	P
47 ***Cox***	Y	?	?	Y	Y	Y	Y	Y
48 ***Packard***	Y	Y	Y	Y	Y	Y	Y	Y
49 ***Bilbray***	Y	Y	Y	Y	Y	Y	Y	Y
50 Filner	N	N	N	N	N	N	N	N
51 ***Cunningham***	Y	Y	Y	Y	Y	Y	Y	Y
52 ***Hunter***	Y	Y	Y	Y	Y	Y	Y	Y
COLORADO								
1 DeGette	N	N	N	N	N	N	N	N
2 Skaggs	N	N	N	N	N	N	N	N
3 ***McInnis***	Y	Y	Y	?	Y	Y	Y	Y
4 ***Schaffer***	Y	Y	Y	Y	Y	Y	Y	Y
5 ***Hefley***	Y	Y	Y	Y	Y	Y	Y	Y
6 ***Schaefer***	Y	Y	Y	Y	Y	Y	Y	Y
CONNECTICUT								
1 Kennelly	N	N	N	N	N	N	N	N
2 Gejdenson	N	N	N	N	N	N	N	N
3 DeLauro	N	N	N	N	N	N	N	N
4 ***Shays***	Y	Y	Y	Y	Y	Y	Y	Y
5 Maloney	N	N	N	N	N	N	N	N
6 ***Johnson***	Y	Y	Y	Y	Y	Y	Y	Y
DELAWARE								
AL ***Castle***	Y	Y	Y	Y	Y	Y	Y	Y
FLORIDA								
1 ***Scarborough***	Y	Y	Y	Y	Y	Y	Y	Y
2 Boyd	N	N	N	N	N	N	N	N
3 Brown	N	N	N	N	N	N	N	N
4 ***Fowler***	Y	Y	Y	Y	Y	Y	Y	Y
5 Thurman	N	N	N	N	N	N	N	N
6 ***Stearns***	Y	Y	Y	Y	Y	Y	Y	Y
7 ***Mica***	Y	Y	Y	Y	Y	Y	Y	Y
8 ***McCollum***	Y	Y	Y	Y	Y	Y	Y	Y
9 ***Bilirakis***	Y	Y	Y	Y	Y	Y	Y	Y
10 ***Young***	Y	Y	Y	Y	Y	Y	Y	Y
11 Davis	N	N	?	N	N	N	N	N
12 ***Canady***	Y	Y	Y	Y	Y	Y	Y	Y
13 ***Miller***	Y	Y	Y	Y	Y	Y	Y	Y
14 ***Goss***	Y	Y	Y	Y	Y	Y	Y	Y
15 ***Weldon***	+	+	+	+	+	+	+	+
16 ***Foley***	Y	Y	Y	?	Y	Y	Y	Y
17 Meek	?	N	?	N	N	N	N	N
18 ***Ros-Lehtinen***	Y	Y	Y	Y	Y	Y	Y	Y
19 Wexler	N	N	N	N	N	N	N	N
20 Deutsch	N	N	N	N	N	N	N	N
21 ***Diaz-Balart***	Y	Y	Y	Y	Y	Y	Y	Y
22 ***Shaw***	Y	Y	Y	Y	Y	Y	Y	Y
23 Hastings	N	N	N	N	N	N	N	N
GEORGIA								
1 ***Kingston***	Y	Y	Y	Y	Y	Y	Y	Y
2 Bishop	N	N	N	N	?	N	N	N
3 ***Collins***	Y	Y	Y	Y	Y	Y	Y	Y
4 McKinney	N	N	N	N	N	N	N	?
5 Lewis	N	N	N	N	N	N	N	N
6 ***Gingrich***								
7 ***Barr***	?	Y	Y	Y	Y	Y	Y	Y
8 ***Chambliss***	Y	Y	Y	Y	Y	Y	Y	Y
9 ***Deal***	Y	Y	Y	Y	Y	Y	Y	Y
10 ***Norwood***	Y	Y	Y	Y	Y	Y	Y	Y
11 ***Linder***	Y	Y	Y	Y	Y	Y	Y	Y
HAWAII								
1 Abercrombie	N	N	N	N	N	N	N	N
2 Mink	N	N	N	N	N	N	N	N
IDAHO								
1 ***Chenoweth***	Y	Y	Y	Y	Y	Y	Y	Y
2 ***Crapo***	Y	Y	Y	?	Y	Y	Y	Y
ILLINOIS								
1 Rush	N	N	N	N	N	N	N	N
2 Jackson	N	N	N	N	N	N	N	N
3 Lipinski	N	N	N	N	N	N	N	N
4 Gutierrez	N	N	N	N	N	N	N	N
5 Blagojevich	N	N	N	N	N	N	N	N
6 ***Hyde***	Y	Y	Y	Y	Y	Y	Y	Y
7 Davis	N	N	N	N	N	N	N	N
8 ***Crane***	Y	Y	Y	Y	Y	Y	Y	Y
9 Yates	N	?	?	?	?	?	?	?
10 ***Porter***	Y	Y	Y	Y	Y	Y	Y	Y
11 ***Weller***	Y	Y	Y	Y	Y	Y	Y	Y
12 Costello	N	N	N	N	N	N	N	N
13 ***Fawell***	Y	Y	Y	Y	Y	Y	Y	Y
14 ***Hastert***	Y	Y	Y	Y	Y	Y	Y	Y
15 ***Ewing***	Y	Y	Y	Y	Y	Y	Y	Y

ND Northern Democrats SD Southern Democrats

	558	559	560	561	562	563	564	565
16 ***Manzullo***	Y	Y	Y	Y	Y	Y	Y	Y
17 Evans	N	N	N	N	N	N	N	N
18 ***LaHood***	Y	Y	Y	Y	Y	Y	Y	Y
19 Poshard	N	N	N	N	N	N	N	N
20 ***Shimkus***	Y	Y	Y	Y	Y	Y	Y	Y
INDIANA								
1 Visclosky	N	N	N	N	N	N	N	N
2 ***McIntosh***	Y	Y	Y	?	Y	Y	Y	Y
3 Roemer	N	N	N	N	N	N	N	N
4 ***Souder***	P	?	?	?	?	?	?	?
5 ***Buyer***	Y	Y	Y	Y	Y	Y	Y	Y
6 ***Burton***	Y	Y	?	Y	Y	?	Y	Y
7 ***Pease***	Y	Y	Y	Y	Y	Y	Y	Y
8 ***Hostettler***	Y	Y	Y	Y	Y	Y	Y	Y
9 Hamilton	N	N	N	N	N	N	N	N
10 Carson	N	N	N	N	N	N	N	N
IOWA								
1 ***Leach***	?	Y	Y	Y	Y	Y	Y	Y
2 ***Nussle***	Y	Y	Y	Y	Y	Y	Y	Y
3 Boswell	N	N	N	N	N	N	N	N
4 ***Ganske***	Y	Y	Y	Y	Y	Y	Y	Y
5 ***Latham***	Y	Y	Y	Y	Y	Y	Y	Y
KANSAS								
1 ***Moran***	Y	Y	Y	Y	Y	Y	Y	Y
2 ***Ryun***	Y	Y	Y	Y	Y	Y	Y	Y
3 ***Snowbarger***	Y	Y	Y	Y	Y	Y	Y	Y
4 ***Tiahrt***	Y	Y	Y	Y	Y	P	P	P
KENTUCKY								
1 ***Whitfield***	Y	Y	Y	Y	Y	Y	Y	Y
2 ***Lewis***	Y	Y	Y	Y	Y	Y	Y	Y
3 ***Northup***	Y	Y	Y	Y	Y	Y	Y	Y
4 ***Bunning***	Y	Y	Y	Y	Y	Y	Y	Y
5 ***Rogers***	Y	Y	Y	Y	Y	Y	Y	Y
6 Baesler	N	N	N	N	N	N	N	N
LOUISIANA								
1 ***Livingston***	Y	Y	Y	Y	Y	Y	Y	Y
2 Jefferson	N	N	N	N	N	N	N	N
3 ***Tauzin***	Y	Y	Y	Y	Y	Y	Y	Y
4 ***McCrery***	Y	Y	Y	Y	Y	Y	Y	Y
5 ***Cooksey***	Y	Y	Y	Y	Y	Y	Y	Y
6 ***Baker***	Y	Y	Y	Y	Y	Y	Y	Y
7 John	N	N	N	N	N	N	N	N
MAINE								
1 Allen	N	N	N	N	N	N	N	N
2 Baldacci	N	N	N	N	N	N	N	?
MARYLAND								
1 ***Gilchrest***	Y	Y	Y	Y	Y	Y	Y	Y
2 ***Ehrlich***	Y	Y	Y	Y	Y	Y	Y	?
3 Cardin	N	N	N	N	N	N	N	N
4 Wynn	N	N	N	N	N	N	N	N
5 Hoyer	N	N	N	N	N	N	N	N
6 ***Bartlett***	Y	Y	Y	Y	Y	Y	Y	Y
7 Cummings	N	N	N	N	N	N	N	N
8 ***Morella***	Y	Y	Y	Y	Y	Y	Y	Y
MASSACHUSETTS								
1 Olver	N	N	N	N	N	N	N	N
2 Neal	N	N	N	N	N	N	N	N
3 McGovern	N	N	N	N	N	N	N	N
4 Frank	N	N	N	N	N	N	N	N
5 Meehan	N	N	N	N	N	N	N	N
6 Tierney	N	N	N	N	N	N	N	N
7 Markey	N	N	N	N	N	N	N	N
8 Kennedy	N	N	N	N	N	N	N	N
9 Moakley	N	?	?	?	?	?	?	?
10 Delahunt	N	N	N	N	N	N	N	N
MICHIGAN								
1 Stupak	N	N	N	N	N	N	N	N
2 ***Hoekstra***	Y	Y	Y	Y	Y	Y	Y	Y
3 ***Ehlers***	Y	Y	Y	Y	Y	Y	Y	Y
4 ***Camp***	Y	Y	Y	Y	Y	Y	Y	Y
5 Barcia	N	N	N	N	N	N	N	N
6 ***Upton***	Y	Y	Y	Y	Y	Y	Y	Y
7 ***Smith***	Y	Y	Y	Y	Y	Y	Y	Y
8 Stabenow	N	N	N	N	N	N	N	N
9 Kildee	N	N	N	N	N	N	N	N
10 Bonior	N	N	N	N	N	N	N	N
11 ***Knollenberg***	Y	Y	Y	Y	Y	Y	Y	Y
12 Levin	N	N	N	N	N	N	N	N
13 Rivers	N	N	N	N	N	N	N	N
14 Conyers	N	N	N	N	?	N	N	N
15 Kilpatrick	N	N	N	N	N	N	N	N
16 Dingell	N	N	N	N	N	N	N	N
MINNESOTA								
1 ***Gutknecht***	Y	Y	Y	Y	Y	Y	Y	Y
2 Minge	N	N	N	N	N	N	N	N

	558	559	560	561	562	563	564	565
3 ***Ramstad***	Y	Y	Y	Y	Y	Y	Y	Y
4 Vento	N	N	N	N	N	N	N	N
5 Sabo	N	N	N	N	N	N	N	N
6 Luther	N	N	N	N	N	N	N	N
7 Peterson	N	N	N	N	N	N	N	N
8 Oberstar	N	N	N	N	?	N	N	N
MISSISSIPPI								
1 ***Wicker***	Y	Y	Y	Y	Y	Y	Y	Y
2 Thompson	N	N	N	N	N	N	N	N
3 ***Pickering***	Y	Y	Y	Y	Y	Y	Y	Y
4 ***Parker***	Y	Y	Y	Y	Y	Y	Y	Y
5 Taylor	N	N	?	P	Y	Y	Y	Y
MISSOURI								
1 Clay	N	N	N	N	N	N	N	N
2 ***Talent***	Y	Y	Y	Y	Y	Y	Y	Y
3 Gephardt	N	N	N	N	N	N	N	N
4 Skelton	N	N	N	N	N	N	?	?
5 McCarthy	N	N	N	N	N	N	N	N
6 Danner	N	N	N	N	N	N	N	N
7 ***Blunt***	Y	Y	Y	Y	Y	Y	Y	Y
8 ***Emerson***	Y	Y	Y	Y	Y	Y	Y	Y
9 ***Hulshof***	Y	Y	Y	Y	Y	Y	Y	Y
MONTANA								
AL ***Hill***	Y	Y	Y	Y	Y	Y	Y	Y
NEBRASKA								
1 ***Bereuter***	Y	Y	?	Y	Y	Y	Y	?
2 ***Christensen***	Y	Y	Y	Y	Y	Y	Y	Y
3 ***Barrett***	Y	Y	+	+	+	+	+	+
NEVADA								
1 ***Ensign***	Y	Y	Y	Y	Y	Y	Y	Y
2 ***Gibbons***	Y	Y	Y	Y	Y	Y	Y	Y
NEW HAMPSHIRE								
1 ***Sununu***	Y	Y	Y	Y	Y	Y	Y	Y
2 ***Bass***	Y	Y	Y	Y	Y	Y	Y	Y
NEW JERSEY								
1 Andrews	N	N	N	N	N	N	N	N
2 ***LoBiondo***	Y	Y	Y	Y	Y	Y	Y	Y
3 ***Saxton***	Y	Y	Y	Y	Y	?	Y	Y
4 ***Smith***	Y	Y	Y	Y	Y	Y	Y	Y
5 ***Roukema***	Y	Y	Y	Y	Y	Y	Y	Y
6 Pallone	N	N	–	N	N	N	N	N
7 ***Franks***	Y	Y	Y	Y	Y	Y	Y	Y
8 Pascrell	N	N	N	N	N	N	N	N
9 Rothman	N	N	N	N	N	N	N	N
10 Payne	?	?	?	?	?	?	?	?
11 ***Frelinghuysen***	Y	Y	Y	Y	Y	Y	Y	Y
12 ***Pappas***	Y	Y	Y	Y	Y	Y	Y	Y
13 Menendez	N	N	N	?	N	N	N	N
NEW MEXICO								
1 ***Schiff***	?	?	?	?	?	?	?	?
2 ***Skeen***	Y	Y	Y	Y	Y	Y	Y	Y
3 ***Redmond***	Y	Y	Y	Y	Y	Y	Y	Y
NEW YORK								
1 ***Forbes***	N	N	N	N	N	N	N	N
2 ***Lazio***	Y	Y	Y	Y	?	Y	Y	Y
3 ***King***	Y	Y	Y	Y	Y	Y	Y	Y
4 McCarthy	N	N	N	N	N	N	N	N
5 Ackerman	N	N	N	N	N	N	N	N
6 Flake	N	N	N	N	N	N	N	N
7 Manton	?	?	?	?	?	?	?	?
8 Nadler	N	N	N	N	N	N	N	N
9 Schumer	N	N	N	?	N	N	N	N
10 Towns	N	N	N	N	N	N	N	N
11 Owens	N	N	?	?	N	N	N	N
12 Velázquez	N	N	N	N	N	N	N	N
13 Vacant								
14 Maloney	N	N	?	N	N	N	N	N
15 Rangel	N	N	?	?	N	N	N	N
16 Serrano	N	N	N	N	N	N	N	N
17 Engel	N	N	N	N	N	N	N	N
18 Lowey	N	N	N	N	N	N	N	N
19 ***Kelly***	Y	Y	Y	Y	Y	Y	Y	Y
20 ***Gilman***	Y	Y	Y	Y	Y	Y	Y	Y
21 McNulty	N	N	N	N	N	N	?	?
22 ***Solomon***	Y	Y	Y	Y	Y	Y	Y	Y
23 ***Boehlert***	Y	Y	Y	Y	Y	Y	Y	Y
24 ***McHugh***	Y	Y	Y	Y	Y	Y	Y	Y
25 ***Walsh***	Y	Y	Y	Y	Y	Y	Y	Y
26 Hinchey	N	N	N	N	N	N	N	N
27 ***Paxon***	Y	Y	Y	Y	Y	Y	Y	Y
28 Slaughter	N	N	N	N	N	N	N	N
29 LaFalce	N	N	N	N	N	N	N	N
30 ***Quinn***	Y	Y	Y	Y	Y	Y	Y	Y
31 ***Houghton***	?	?	Y	Y	Y	Y	Y	Y

	558	559	560	561	562	563	564	565
NORTH CAROLINA								
1 Clayton	N	N	?	N	N	N	N	N
2 Etheridge	N	N	N	N	N	N	N	N
3 ***Jones***	Y	Y	Y	Y	Y	Y	Y	Y
4 Price	N	N	N	N	N	N	N	N
5 ***Burr***	Y	Y	Y	Y	Y	Y	Y	Y
6 ***Coble***	Y	Y	Y	Y	Y	Y	Y	Y
7 McIntyre	N	N	N	N	N	N	N	N
8 Hefner	N	N	N	N	N	N	N	N
9 ***Myrick***	Y	Y	Y	Y	Y	Y	Y	Y
10 ***Ballenger***	Y	Y	Y	Y	Y	Y	Y	Y
11 ***Taylor***	Y	Y	Y	Y	Y	Y	Y	Y
12 Watt	N	N	N	N	N	N	N	N
NORTH DAKOTA								
AL Pomeroy	N	N	N	N	N	N	N	N
OHIO								
1 ***Chabot***	Y	Y	Y	Y	Y	Y	Y	Y
2 ***Portman***	Y	Y	Y	Y	Y	Y	Y	Y
3 Hall	N	N	N	N	N	N	N	?
4 ***Oxley***	Y	Y	Y	Y	Y	Y	Y	?
5 ***Gillmor***	Y	Y	Y	Y	Y	Y	Y	Y
6 Strickland	N	N	N	N	N	N	N	N
7 ***Hobson***	Y	Y	Y	Y	Y	Y	Y	Y
8 ***Boehner***	Y	Y	Y	Y	Y	Y	Y	Y
9 Kaptur	N	N	N	N	N	N	N	N
10 Kucinich	N	N	N	N	N	N	N	N
11 Stokes	N	N	N	N	N	N	N	N
12 ***Kasich***	Y	Y	Y	Y	Y	Y	Y	?
13 Brown	N	N	N	N	N	N	N	N
14 Sawyer	N	N	N	N	N	N	N	N
15 ***Pryce***	Y	Y	Y	Y	Y	Y	?	?
16 ***Regula***	Y	Y	Y	Y	Y	Y	Y	Y
17 Traficant	Y	Y	Y	Y	Y	Y	Y	Y
18 ***Ney***	Y	Y	Y	Y	Y	Y	Y	Y
19 ***LaTourette***	Y	Y	Y	Y	Y	Y	Y	Y
OKLAHOMA								
1 ***Largent***	Y	Y	Y	Y	Y	Y	Y	Y
2 ***Coburn***	P	P	P	P	P	P	P	P
3 ***Watkins***	Y	Y	Y	Y	Y	Y	Y	Y
4 ***Watts***	Y	Y	Y	Y	Y	Y	Y	Y
5 ***Istook***	Y	Y	Y	Y	Y	Y	Y	Y
6 ***Lucas***	Y	Y	Y	Y	Y	Y	Y	Y
OREGON								
1 Furse	N	N	N	N	N	N	N	N
2 ***Smith***	Y	Y	Y	Y	Y	Y	Y	?
3 Blumenauer	N	N	N	N	N	N	N	N
4 DeFazio	N	N	N	N	N	N	N	N
5 Hooley	N	N	N	N	N	N	N	N
PENNSYLVANIA								
1 Foglietta	?	?	?	?	?	?	?	?
2 Fattah	N	N	N	N	N	N	N	N
3 Borski	N	N	N	N	N	N	N	N
4 Klink	N	N	N	N	N	N	N	N
5 ***Peterson***	Y	Y	Y	Y	Y	Y	Y	Y
6 Holden	N	N	N	N	N	N	N	N
7 ***Weldon***	?	?	?	?	?	?	?	?
8 ***Greenwood***	Y	Y	Y	Y	Y	Y	Y	Y
9 ***Shuster***	Y	Y	Y	Y	Y	Y	Y	Y
10 ***McDade***	Y	Y	Y	Y	Y	Y	Y	Y
11 Kanjorski	N	N	N	N	N	N	N	N
12 Murtha	N	N	N	N	N	N	N	?
13 ***Fox***	Y	Y	Y	Y	Y	Y	Y	Y
14 Coyne	N	N	N	N	N	N	N	N
15 McHale	?	N	N	N	N	N	N	N
16 ***Pitts***	Y	Y	Y	Y	Y	Y	Y	Y
17 ***Gekas***	?	Y	Y	Y	Y	?	?	Y
18 Doyle	N	N	N	N	N	N	N	N
19 ***Goodling***	Y	Y	Y	Y	Y	Y	Y	Y
20 Mascara	N	N	N	N	N	N	N	N
21 ***English***	Y	Y	Y	Y	Y	Y	Y	Y
RHODE ISLAND								
1 Kennedy	N	N	N	N	N	N	N	N
2 Weygand	N	N	N	N	N	N	N	N
SOUTH CAROLINA								
1 ***Sanford***	Y	Y	Y	Y	Y	Y	Y	Y
2 ***Spence***	Y	Y	Y	Y	Y	Y	Y	Y
3 ***Graham***	Y	Y	Y	Y	Y	Y	Y	Y
4 ***Inglis***	Y	Y	Y	Y	Y	Y	Y	Y
5 Spratt	N	N	N	N	N	N	N	N
6 Clyburn	N	N	N	N	N	N	N	N
SOUTH DAKOTA								
AL ***Thune***	Y	Y	Y	Y	Y	Y	Y	Y
TENNESSEE								
1 ***Jenkins***	Y	Y	Y	Y	Y	Y	Y	?
2 ***Duncan***	Y	Y	Y	Y	Y	Y	Y	Y

	558	559	560	561	562	563	564	
3 ***Wamp***	Y	Y	P	P	P	P	P	P
4 ***Hilleary***	Y	Y	Y	Y	Y	Y	Y	Y
5 Clement	N	N	N	N	N	N	N	N
6 Gordon	N	N	N	N	N	N	N	N
7 ***Bryant***	Y	Y	Y	Y	Y	Y	Y	Y
8 Tanner	N	N	N	N	N	N	N	N
9 Ford	N	N	N	N	N	N	N	N
TEXAS								
1 Sandlin	N	N	N	N	N	N	N	N
2 Turner	N	N	N	N	N	N	N	N
3 ***Johnson, Sam***	Y	Y	Y	Y	Y	Y	Y	Y
4 Hall	N	N	N	N	N	N	N	N
5 ***Sessions***	Y	Y	Y	Y	Y	Y	Y	Y
6 ***Barton***	Y	Y	Y	Y	Y	Y	Y	Y
7 ***Archer***	Y	Y	Y	Y	Y	Y	?	?
8 ***Brady***	Y	Y	Y	Y	Y	Y	Y	Y
9 Lampson	N	N	N	N	N	N	N	N
10 Doggett	N	N	N	N	N	N	N	N
11 Edwards	N	N	N	N	N	N	N	N
12 ***Granger***	Y	Y	Y	Y	Y	Y	Y	Y
13 ***Thornberry***	Y	Y	Y	Y	Y	Y	Y	Y
14 ***Paul***	Y	Y	Y	Y	Y	Y	Y	Y
15 Hinojosa	N	N	N	N	N	N	N	N
16 Reyes	N	N	N	N	N	N	N	N
17 Stenholm	N	N	N	N	N	N	N	N
18 Jackson-Lee	N	N	N	N	N	N	N	N
19 ***Combest***	Y	Y	Y	Y	Y	Y	Y	Y
20 Gonzalez	?	?	?	?	?	?	?	?
21 ***Smith***	Y	Y	Y	Y	Y	Y	Y	Y
22 ***DeLay***	?	Y	Y	Y	Y	Y	Y	Y
23 ***Bonilla***	Y	Y	Y	Y	Y	Y	Y	Y
24 Frost	N	N	N	N	N	?	?	?
25 Bentsen	N	N	N	N	N	N	N	N
26 ***Armey***	Y	Y	?	Y	Y	Y	Y	Y
27 Ortiz	N	N	N	N	N	N	N	N
28 Rodriguez	N	N	N	N	N	N	N	N
29 Green	N	N	N	N	N	N	N	N
30 Johnson, E.B.	N	N	N	N	N	N	N	N
UTAH								
1 ***Hansen***	Y	Y	Y	Y	Y	Y	Y	Y
2 ***Cook***	Y	Y	Y	Y	Y	Y	Y	Y
3 ***Cannon***	Y	Y	Y	Y	Y	Y	Y	Y
VERMONT								
AL *Sanders*	N	N	N	N	?	N	N	N
VIRGINIA								
1 ***Bateman***	Y	Y	Y	Y	Y	Y	Y	Y
2 Pickett	N	N	N	N	N	N	N	N
3 Scott	N	N	N	N	N	N	N	N
4 Sisisky	N	N	N	N	N	N	N	N
5 Goode	N	N	N	N	N	N	N	N
6 ***Goodlatte***	Y	Y	Y	Y	Y	Y	Y	Y
7 ***Bliley***	Y	Y	Y	Y	Y	Y	Y	Y
8 Moran	N	N	N	?	N	N	N	N
9 Boucher	N	N	N	N	N	N	N	N
10 ***Wolf***	Y	Y	Y	Y	Y	Y	Y	Y
11 ***Davis***	Y	Y	Y	Y	Y	Y	Y	Y
WASHINGTON								
1 ***White***	Y	Y	Y	Y	Y	Y	Y	Y
2 ***Metcalf***	?	Y	Y	Y	Y	Y	Y	Y
3 ***Smith, Linda***	Y	Y	Y	Y	Y	Y	Y	Y
4 ***Hastings***	Y	Y	Y	Y	Y	Y	Y	Y
5 ***Nethercutt***	Y	Y	Y	Y	Y	Y	Y	Y
6 Dicks	N	N	N	N	N	N	N	N
7 McDermott	N	N	N	N	N	N	N	N
8 ***Dunn***	Y	Y	Y	Y	Y	Y	Y	Y
9 Smith, Adam	N	N	N	N	N	N	N	N
WEST VIRGINIA								
1 Mollohan	N	N	N	N	N	N	N	N
2 Wise	N	N	N	N	N	N	N	N
3 Rahall	N	N	N	N	N	N	N	N
WISCONSIN								
1 ***Neumann***	Y	Y	Y	Y	Y	Y	Y	Y
2 ***Klug***	Y	Y	Y	Y	Y	Y	Y	Y
3 Kind	N	N	N	N	N	N	N	N
4 Kleczka	?	N	N	N	N	N	N	N
5 Barrett	N	N	N	N	N	N	N	N
6 ***Petri***	Y	Y	Y	Y	Y	Y	Y	Y
7 Obey	N	N	N	N	N	N	N	N
8 Johnson	N	N	N	N	N	N	N	N
9 ***Sensenbrenner***	Y	Y	Y	Y	Y	Y	Y	Y
WYOMING								
AL ***Cubin***	?	?	?	?	?	?	?	?

Southern states - Ala., Ark., Fla., Ga., Ky., La., Miss., N.C., Okla., S.C., Tenn., Texas, Va.

HOUSE VOTES 566, 567, 568, 569, 570, 571, 572, 573

566. HR 2746. Private School Vouchers/Previous Question. Myrick, R-N.C., motion to order the previous question (thus ending debate and the possibility of amendment) on the rule (H Res 288) to provide for floor consideration of the bill to authorize states to use certain federal elementary and secondary education funds to provide scholarships to low-income families to send their children to public, private or religious schools. The rule would also provide for House floor consideration of the bill (HR 2616) to authorize $100 million in fiscal 1998 for federal grants to states and localities to help start new public charter schools. Motion agreed to 222-195: R 219-0; D 3-194 (ND 3-141, SD 0-53); I 0-1, Oct. 31, 1997.

567. HR 2746. Private School Vouchers/Rule. Adoption of the rule (H Res 288) to provide for floor consideration of the bill to authorize states to use certain federal elementary and secondary education funds to provide scholarships to low-income families to send their children to public, private or religious schools. The rule also provides for House floor consideration of the bill (HR 2616) to authorize $100 million in fiscal 1998 for federal grants to states and localities to help start new public charter schools. Adopted 214-198: R 212-8; D 2-189 (ND 2-137, SD 0-52); I 0-1, Oct. 31, 1997.

568. HR 2746. Private School Vouchers/Recommit. Etheridge, D-N.C., motion to recommit the bill to the Education and the Workforce Committee with instructions to report it back only after the committee conducts a hearing and holds a full committee markup on the bill. Motion rejected 203-215: R 9-212; D 193-3 (ND 140-2, SD 53-1); I 1-0, Nov. 4, 1997.

569. HR 2746. Private School Vouchers/Passage. Passage of the bill to authorize states to use certain federal elementary and secondary education funds to provide scholarships to low-income families to send their children to public, private or religious schools. Rejected 191-228: R 187-35; D 4-192 (ND 2-140, SD 2-52); I 0-1, Nov. 4, 1997. A "nay" was a vote in support of the president's position.

570. HR 2644. Caribbean and Central American Trade/Passage. Crane, R-Ill., motion to suspend the rules and pass the bill to provide Caribbean and Central American countries duty-free trade benefits similar to those accorded to Mexico under the North American Free Trade Agreement on certain products. Motion rejected 182-234: R 136-83; D 46-150 (ND 32-111, SD 14-39); I 0-1, Nov. 4, 1997.

571. HR 1493. Illegal Immigrant Prisoners/Passage. Gallegly, R-Calif., motion to suspend the rules and pass the bill to authorize the Immigration and Naturalization Service to screen local jails and prisons for illegal aliens before their arraignment and enable law enforcement officials to deport criminal illegal immigrants immediately after they are released. Motion agreed to 410-2: R 215-2; D 194-0 (ND 141-0, SD 53-0); I 1-0, Nov. 4, 1997. A two-thirds majority of those present and voting (275 in this case) is required for passage under suspension of the rules.

572. S 587. Colorado Land Exchange/Passage. Hansen, R-Utah, motion to suspend the rules and pass the bill to authorize the transfer of 560 acres of land managed by the Bureau of Land Management in Hinsdale County, Colo., to Lake City Ranches Ltd. in exchange for lands of equal value within the Handies Peak or Red Cloud Peak Wilderness study areas and the Alpine Loop Backcountry Bi-way. Motion agreed to (thus cleared for the president) 406-0: R 213-0; D 192-0 (ND 140-0, SD 52-0); I 1-0, Nov. 4, 1997. A two-thirds majority of those present and voting (271 in this case) is required for passage under suspension of the rules.

573. HR 1839. Salvage Vehicle Standards/Passage. Bliley, R-Va., motion to suspend the rules and pass the bill to establish national uniform standards for the state titling, transferring or registration of salvage, non-repairable and rebuilt motor vehicles. Motion agreed to 336-72: R 212-3; D 124-68 (ND 78-62, SD 46-6); I 0-1, Nov. 4, 1997. A two-thirds majority of those present and voting (272 in this case) is required for passage under suspension of the rules.

KEY

Y Voted for (yea).
Paired for.
\+ Announced for.
N Voted against (nay).
X Paired against.
– Announced against.
P Voted "present."
C Voted "present" to avoid possible conflict of interest.
? Did not vote or otherwise make a position known.

Democrats ***Republicans***
Independent

	566	567	568	569	570	571	572	573
ALABAMA								
1 ***Callahan***	Y	Y	N	Y	Y	Y	Y	Y
2 ***Everett***	Y	Y	N	Y	N	Y	Y	Y
3 ***Riley***	Y	Y	X	#	#	?	+	+
4 ***Aderholt***	Y	Y	N	Y	N	Y	Y	Y
5 Cramer	N	N	Y	N	N	Y	Y	Y
6 ***Bachus***	Y	Y	N	Y	Y	Y	Y	Y
7 Hilliard	N	N	Y	N	N	Y	Y	Y
ALASKA								
AL ***Young***	Y	Y	N	Y	N	Y	?	?
ARIZONA								
1 ***Salmon***	Y	Y	N	Y	Y	Y	Y	Y
2 Pastor	N	Y	Y	N	Y	Y	Y	Y
3 ***Stump***	Y	Y	N	Y	Y	Y	Y	Y
4 ***Shadegg***	Y	Y	N	Y	Y	Y	Y	Y
5 ***Kolbe***	Y	Y	N	Y	Y	Y	Y	Y
6 ***Hayworth***	Y	Y	N	Y	Y	Y	Y	Y
ARKANSAS								
1 Berry	N	N	Y	N	Y	Y	Y	Y
2 Snyder	N	N	Y	N	N	Y	Y	Y
3 ***Hutchinson***	Y	Y	N	N	N	Y	Y	Y
4 ***Dickey***	Y	Y	N	Y	N	Y	Y	Y
CALIFORNIA								
1 ***Riggs***	Y	Y	N	Y	N	Y	Y	Y
2 ***Herger***	Y	Y	N	Y	Y	Y	Y	Y
3 Fazio	N	N	Y	N	Y	Y	Y	N
4 ***Doolittle***	Y	Y	N	Y	N	Y	Y	Y
5 Matsui	N	N	Y	N	Y	Y	Y	Y
6 Woolsey	N	N	Y	N	N	Y	Y	N
7 Miller	N	N	Y	N	N	Y	Y	N
8 Pelosi	N	N	Y	N	Y	Y	?	N
9 Dellums	N	N	Y	N	N	Y	Y	N
10 Tauscher	N	N	Y	N	N	Y	Y	Y
11 ***Pombo***	Y	Y	N	Y	N	Y	Y	Y
12 Lantos	N	N	Y	N	N	Y	Y	Y
13 Stark	N	N	Y	N	N	Y	Y	N
14 Eshoo	N	N	Y	N	Y	Y	Y	Y
15 ***Campbell***	Y	Y	N	Y	Y	Y	Y	Y
16 Lofgren	N	N	Y	N	N	Y	Y	Y
17 Farr	N	N	Y	N	N	Y	Y	Y
18 Condit	N	N	Y	N	N	Y	Y	Y
19 ***Radanovich***	Y	Y	N	Y	N	Y	Y	Y
20 Dooley	N	N	Y	N	Y	Y	Y	Y
21 ***Thomas***	Y	Y	N	Y	Y	Y	Y	Y
22 Vacant								
23 ***Gallegly***	?	?	N	Y	N	Y	Y	Y
24 Sherman	N	N	Y	N	N	Y	Y	Y
25 ***McKeon***	Y	Y	N	Y	Y	Y	?	?
26 Berman	N	N	Y	N	Y	Y	Y	N
27 ***Rogan***	Y	Y	N	Y	Y	Y	Y	Y
28 ***Dreier***	Y	Y	N	Y	Y	Y	Y	Y
29 Waxman	N	N	Y	N	N	Y	?	?
30 Becerra	N	N	Y	N	N	Y	Y	N
31 Martinez	N	N	Y	N	N	Y	Y	Y
32 Dixon	N	N	Y	N	Y	Y	Y	Y
33 Roybal-Allard	N	N	Y	N	N	Y	Y	N
34 Torres	N	N	Y	N	N	Y	Y	Y
35 Waters	N	N	Y	N	N	Y	Y	N
36 Harman	N	N	Y	N	N	Y	Y	Y
37 Millender-McD.	N	N	Y	N	N	Y	Y	Y
38 ***Horn***	Y	N	Y	N	Y	Y	Y	Y
39 ***Royce***	Y	Y	N	Y	N	Y	Y	Y
40 ***Lewis***	Y	Y	N	Y	Y	Y	?	?
41 ***Kim***	Y	Y	N	Y	Y	Y	Y	Y
42 Brown	N	N	Y	N	N	Y	Y	Y
43 ***Calvert***	Y	Y	N	Y	Y	Y	Y	Y
44 ***Bono***	Y	Y	N	Y	N	Y	Y	Y
45 ***Rohrabacher***	Y	Y	N	Y	N	Y	Y	Y
46 Sanchez	N	N	Y	N	Y	Y	Y	Y
47 ***Cox***	Y	Y	N	Y	Y	Y	?	Y
48 ***Packard***	Y	Y	N	Y	Y	Y	Y	Y
49 ***Bilbray***	Y	Y	N	Y	Y	Y	Y	Y
50 Filner	N	N	Y	N	N	Y	Y	N
51 ***Cunningham***	?	?	N	Y	Y	Y	Y	Y
52 ***Hunter***	Y	Y	N	Y	N	Y	Y	Y
COLORADO								
1 DeGette	N	N	Y	N	N	Y	Y	N
2 Skaggs	N	N	Y	N	Y	Y	Y	N
3 ***McInnis***	Y	Y	N	Y	N	Y	Y	Y
4 ***Schaffer***	Y	Y	N	Y	N	Y	Y	Y
5 ***Hefley***	Y	Y	N	Y	N	Y	Y	Y
6 ***Schaefer***	Y	Y	N	Y	N	Y	Y	Y
CONNECTICUT								
1 Kennelly	N	N	Y	N	Y	Y	Y	N
2 Gejdenson	N	N	Y	N	N	Y	Y	N
3 DeLauro	N	N	Y	N	N	Y	Y	N
4 ***Shays***	Y	Y	N	Y	Y	Y	Y	Y
5 Maloney	N	N	Y	N	N	Y	Y	N
6 ***Johnson***	Y	Y	Y	N	Y	Y	Y	Y
DELAWARE								
AL ***Castle***	Y	N	N	N	Y	Y	Y	Y
FLORIDA								
1 ***Scarborough***	Y	Y	N	Y	N	Y	Y	N
2 Boyd	N	N	Y	N	N	Y	Y	Y
3 Brown	N	N	Y	N	N	Y	Y	Y
4 ***Fowler***	Y	Y	N	Y	Y	Y	Y	Y
5 Thurman	N	N	Y	N	N	Y	Y	Y
6 ***Stearns***	Y	Y	N	Y	N	Y	Y	Y
7 ***Mica***	Y	Y	N	Y	N	Y	Y	Y
8 ***McCollum***	Y	Y	N	Y	Y	Y	Y	Y
9 ***Bilirakis***	Y	Y	N	Y	N	Y	Y	Y
10 ***Young***	Y	Y	N	Y	N	Y	Y	Y
11 Davis	N	N	Y	N	Y	Y	Y	Y
12 ***Canady***	Y	Y	N	Y	N	Y	Y	Y
13 ***Miller***	Y	Y	N	Y	Y	Y	Y	Y
14 ***Goss***	Y	Y	N	Y	Y	Y	Y	Y
15 ***Weldon***	+	+	N	Y	Y	Y	Y	Y
16 ***Foley***	?	?	N	Y	Y	Y	Y	Y
17 Meek	N	N	Y	N	N	Y	Y	Y
18 ***Ros-Lehtinen***	Y	Y	N	Y	N	N	Y	Y
19 Wexler	N	N	Y	N	Y	Y	Y	Y
20 Deutsch	X	X	Y	N	Y	Y	Y	Y
21 ***Diaz-Balart***	Y	Y	N	Y	N	Y	Y	Y
22 ***Shaw***	Y	Y	N	Y	Y	Y	Y	Y
23 Hastings	N	N	Y	N	N	Y	Y	Y
GEORGIA								
1 ***Kingston***	Y	Y	N	Y	N	Y	Y	Y
2 Bishop	N	N	Y	N	N	Y	Y	Y
3 ***Collins***	Y	Y	N	N	Y	Y	Y	Y
4 McKinney	N	N	Y	N	Y	Y	Y	N
5 Lewis	N	N	Y	N	N	Y	Y	N
6 ***Gingrich***	Y	Y	N	Y				
7 ***Barr***	Y	Y	N	Y	N	Y	Y	Y
8 ***Chambliss***	Y	Y	N	Y	N	Y	Y	Y
9 ***Deal***	Y	Y	N	Y	N	Y	Y	Y
10 ***Norwood***	Y	Y	N	Y	N	Y	Y	Y
11 ***Linder***	Y	Y	N	Y	Y	Y	Y	Y
HAWAII								
1 Abercrombie	N	N	Y	N	N	Y	Y	N
2 Mink	N	N	Y	N	N	Y	Y	N
IDAHO								
1 ***Chenoweth***	Y	Y	N	Y	N	Y	Y	Y
2 ***Crapo***	Y	Y	N	Y	N	Y	Y	Y
ILLINOIS								
1 Rush	N	N	Y	N	N	Y	Y	Y
2 Jackson	N	N	Y	N	N	Y	Y	N
3 Lipinski	Y	?	N	Y	N	Y	Y	Y
4 Gutierrez	N	?	Y	N	N	Y	Y	N
5 Blagojevich	N	N	Y	N	N	Y	Y	N
6 ***Hyde***	Y	Y	N	Y	Y	Y	Y	Y
7 Davis	N	N	Y	N	N	Y	Y	N
8 ***Crane***	Y	Y	N	Y	Y	Y	Y	Y
9 Yates	N	N	Y	N	N	Y	?	?
10 ***Porter***	Y	Y	?	X	#	?	Y	Y
11 ***Weller***	Y	Y	N	Y	Y	Y	?	Y
12 Costello	N	N	Y	N	N	Y	Y	Y
13 ***Fawell***	Y	Y	N	N	?	Y	?	?
14 ***Hastert***	Y	Y	N	Y	Y	Y	Y	Y
15 ***Ewing***	Y	Y	N	Y	Y	+	Y	Y

ND Northern Democrats SD Southern Democrats

	566	567	568	569	570	571	572	573
16 ***Manzullo***	Y	Y	N	Y	Y	Y	Y	Y
17 Evans	N	N	Y	N	N	Y	Y	N
18 ***LaHood***	Y	Y	N	N	Y	Y	Y	Y
19 Poshard	N	N	Y	N	N	Y	Y	Y
20 ***Shimkus***	Y	Y	N	Y	Y	Y	Y	Y
INDIANA								
1 Visclosky	–	–	Y	N	N	Y	Y	Y
2 ***McIntosh***	#	#	N	Y	Y	Y	?	?
3 Roemer	N	N	Y	N	Y	Y	Y	Y
4 ***Souder***	Y	Y	N	Y	N	Y	Y	Y
5 ***Buyer***	Y	Y	N	Y	Y	Y	Y	Y
6 ***Burton***	Y	Y	N	Y	N	Y	Y	Y
7 ***Pease***	Y	Y	N	Y	Y	Y	Y	Y
8 ***Hostettler***	Y	Y	N	Y	Y	Y	Y	Y
9 Hamilton	N	N	Y	N	Y	Y	Y	Y
10 Carson	N	N	Y	N	N	Y	Y	N
IOWA								
1 ***Leach***	Y	Y	Y	N	Y	Y	Y	Y
2 ***Nussle***	Y	Y	N	Y	Y	Y	Y	Y
3 Boswell	N	N	Y	N	N	Y	Y	N
4 ***Ganske***	Y	Y	N	Y	Y	Y	Y	Y
5 ***Latham***	Y	Y	N	Y	Y	Y	Y	Y
KANSAS								
1 ***Moran***	Y	Y	N	N	Y	Y	Y	Y
2 ***Ryun***	Y	Y	N	Y	Y	Y	Y	Y
3 ***Snowbarger***	Y	Y	N	Y	Y	Y	Y	Y
4 ***Tiahrt***	Y	Y	N	Y	N	Y	Y	Y
KENTUCKY								
1 ***Whitfield***	Y	Y	N	Y	N	Y	Y	Y
2 ***Lewis***	Y	Y	N	Y	N	Y	Y	Y
3 ***Northup***	Y	Y	N	Y	Y	Y	Y	Y
4 ***Bunning***	Y	Y	N	Y	N	Y	Y	Y
5 ***Rogers***	Y	Y	N	Y	N	Y	Y	Y
6 Baesler	N	N	Y	N	N	Y	Y	Y
LOUISIANA								
1 ***Livingston***	Y	Y	N	Y	Y	Y	Y	Y
2 Jefferson	N	?	Y	N	Y	Y	Y	Y
3 ***Tauzin***	Y	Y	N	Y	N	Y	Y	Y
4 ***McCrery***	Y	Y	N	Y	Y	Y	Y	Y
5 ***Cooksey***	Y	Y	N	Y	X	Y	Y	Y
6 ***Baker***	Y	Y	N	Y	Y	Y	Y	Y
7 John	N	N	N	Y	N	Y	Y	Y
MAINE								
1 Allen	N	N	Y	N	N	Y	Y	Y
2 Baldacci	N	N	Y	N	N	Y	Y	Y
MARYLAND								
1 ***Gilchrest***	Y	Y	N	Y	Y	Y	Y	Y
2 ***Ehrlich***	Y	Y	N	Y	Y	Y	Y	Y
3 Cardin	N	N	Y	N	N	Y	Y	N
4 Wynn	N	N	Y	N	Y	Y	Y	Y
5 Hoyer	N	N	Y	N	Y	Y	Y	Y
6 ***Bartlett***	Y	Y	N	Y	N	Y	Y	Y
7 Cummings	N	N	Y	N	Y	Y	Y	N
8 ***Morella***	Y	N	Y	N	Y	Y	Y	Y
MASSACHUSETTS								
1 Olver	N	N	Y	N	N	Y	Y	N
2 Neal	N	N	Y	N	N	Y	Y	N
3 McGovern	N	N	Y	N	N	Y	Y	Y
4 Frank	N	N	Y	N	N	Y	Y	N
5 Meehan	N	N	Y	N	Y	Y	Y	N
6 Tierney	N	N	Y	N	N	Y	Y	N
7 Markey	N	N	Y	N	N	Y	Y	N
8 Kennedy	N	N	Y	N	Y	Y	Y	N
9 Moakley	N	N	Y	N	N	Y	Y	Y
10 Delahunt	N	N	Y	N	N	Y	Y	Y
MICHIGAN								
1 Stupak	N	N	Y	N	N	Y	Y	Y
2 ***Hoekstra***	Y	Y	N	Y	Y	Y	Y	Y
3 ***Ehlers***	Y	Y	N	Y	Y	Y	Y	Y
4 ***Camp***	Y	Y	N	Y	Y	Y	Y	Y
5 Barcia	N	N	?	N	N	Y	Y	Y
6 ***Upton***	Y	Y	N	Y	Y	Y	Y	Y
7 ***Smith***	Y	Y	N	Y	N	Y	Y	Y
8 Stabenow	N	N	Y	N	N	Y	Y	Y
9 Kildee	N	N	Y	N	N	Y	Y	Y
10 Bonior	N	N	Y	N	N	?	Y	Y
11 ***Knollenberg***	Y	Y	N	Y	Y	Y	Y	Y
12 Levin	N	N	Y	N	N	Y	Y	Y
13 Rivers	N	N	Y	N	N	Y	Y	Y
14 Conyers	N	N	Y	N	N	Y	Y	N
15 Kilpatrick	N	N	Y	N	N	Y	Y	N
16 Dingell	N	N	Y	N	N	Y	Y	N
MINNESOTA								
1 ***Gutknecht***	Y	Y	N	Y	N	Y	Y	Y
2 Minge	N	N	Y	N	Y	Y	Y	Y

	566	567	568	569	570	571	572	573
3 ***Ramstad***	Y	N	Y	N	Y	Y	Y	Y
4 Vento	N	N	Y	N	N	Y	Y	Y
5 Sabo	N	N	Y	N	N	Y	Y	Y
6 Luther	N	N	Y	N	Y	Y	Y	Y
7 Peterson	N	N	Y	N	Y	Y	Y	Y
8 Oberstar	N	N	Y	N	N	Y	Y	Y
MISSISSIPPI								
1 ***Wicker***	Y	Y	N	Y	Y	Y	Y	Y
2 Thompson	N	N	Y	N	N	Y	Y	Y
3 ***Pickering***	Y	Y	N	Y	Y	Y	Y	Y
4 ***Parker***	Y	Y	N	Y	N	Y	Y	Y
5 Taylor	N	N	Y	N	N	Y	Y	Y
MISSOURI								
1 Clay	N	N	Y	N	N	Y	Y	?
2 ***Talent***	Y	Y	N	Y	Y	Y	Y	Y
3 Gephardt	?	?	Y	N	N	Y	?	?
4 Skelton	N	N	Y	N	N	Y	Y	Y
5 McCarthy	N	N	Y	N	Y	Y	Y	N
6 Danner	N	N	Y	N	N	Y	Y	Y
7 ***Blunt***	Y	Y	N	N	Y	Y	Y	Y
8 ***Emerson***	Y	Y	N	Y	Y	Y	Y	Y
9 ***Hulshof***	Y	Y	N	Y	Y	Y	Y	Y
MONTANA								
AL ***Hill***	Y	Y	N	Y	Y	Y	Y	Y
NEBRASKA								
1 ***Bereuter***	Y	N	Y	N	Y	Y	Y	Y
2 ***Christensen***	Y	Y	N	Y	Y	Y	Y	Y
3 ***Barrett***	Y	Y	N	N	Y	Y	Y	Y
NEVADA								
1 ***Ensign***	Y	Y	Y	Y	N	Y	Y	Y
2 ***Gibbons***	Y	Y	N	Y	N	Y	Y	Y
NEW HAMPSHIRE								
1 ***Sununu***	Y	Y	N	Y	Y	Y	Y	Y
2 ***Bass***	Y	Y	N	Y	Y	Y	Y	Y
NEW JERSEY								
1 Andrews	N	N	Y	N	N	Y	Y	N
2 ***LoBiondo***	Y	Y	N	N	N	Y	Y	Y
3 ***Saxton***	Y	Y	N	N	N	Y	Y	Y
4 ***Smith***	Y	Y	N	N	N	Y	Y	Y
5 ***Roukema***	Y	N	Y	N	Y	Y	Y	Y
6 Pallone	N	N	Y	N	N	Y	Y	N
7 ***Franks***	Y	Y	N	Y	N	Y	Y	Y
8 Pascrell	N	N	Y	N	N	Y	Y	Y
9 Rothman	N	N	Y	N	N	Y	Y	N
10 Payne	?	?	?	?	?	?	?	?
11 ***Frelinghuysen***	Y	Y	N	N	Y	Y	Y	Y
12 ***Pappas***	Y	Y	N	Y	Y	Y	Y	Y
13 Menendez	N	N	?	?	?	?	?	?
NEW MEXICO								
1 ***Schiff***	?	?	?	?	?	?	?	?
2 ***Skeen***	Y	Y	N	Y	Y	Y	Y	Y
3 ***Redmond***	Y	Y	N	Y	Y	Y	Y	Y
NEW YORK								
1 ***Forbes***	Y	Y	N	Y	N	Y	Y	Y
2 ***Lazio***	Y	Y	N	Y	Y	Y	Y	Y
3 ***King***	Y	Y	N	Y	Y	Y	?	?
4 McCarthy	N	N	Y	N	N	Y	Y	Y
5 Ackerman	?	?	Y	?	?	?	?	?
6 Flake	Y	?	N	Y	Y	Y	?	?
7 Manton	N	N	Y	N	N	Y	Y	N
8 Nadler	N	N	Y	N	N	Y	Y	N
9 Schumer	N	N	Y	N	Y	Y	Y	N
10 Towns	N	N	?	?	Y	?	Y	Y
11 Owens	N	N	Y	N	N	Y	Y	N
12 Velázquez	N	N	Y	N	N	Y	Y	N
13 Vacant								
14 Maloney	N	N	Y	N	N	Y	Y	N
15 Rangel	N	N	Y	N	Y	Y	Y	Y
16 Serrano	N	N	Y	N	N	Y	Y	N
17 Engel	N	N	Y	N	N	Y	Y	Y
18 Lowey	N	N	Y	N	Y	Y	Y	Y
19 ***Kelly***	Y	Y	N	Y	Y	Y	Y	Y
20 ***Gilman***	Y	Y	N	Y	Y	Y	Y	Y
21 McNulty	?	?	?	?	?	?	?	?
22 ***Solomon***	Y	Y	N	Y	N	Y	Y	Y
23 ***Boehlert***	Y	N	N	N	Y	Y	Y	Y
24 ***McHugh***	Y	N	N	N	Y	Y	Y	Y
25 ***Walsh***	Y	Y	N	Y	N	Y	Y	Y
26 Hinchey	N	N	Y	N	N	Y	Y	N
27 ***Paxon***	Y	Y	N	Y	Y	Y	Y	Y
28 Slaughter	N	N	#	–	–	+	Y	N
29 LaFalce	N	N	Y	N	N	Y	Y	N
30 ***Quinn***	Y	Y	N	N	N	Y	Y	Y
31 ***Houghton***	Y	Y	N	N	Y	Y	Y	Y

	566	567	568	569	570	571	572	573
NORTH CAROLINA								
1 Clayton	N	N	Y	N	N	Y	Y	Y
2 Etheridge	N	N	Y	N	N	Y	Y	Y
3 ***Jones***	Y	Y	N	Y	Y	Y	Y	Y
4 Price	N	N	Y	N	N	Y	Y	Y
5 ***Burr***	Y	Y	N	Y	Y	Y	Y	Y
6 ***Coble***	Y	Y	N	Y	Y	Y	Y	Y
7 McIntyre	N	N	Y	N	N	Y	Y	Y
8 Hefner	N	N	Y	N	N	Y	Y	Y
9 ***Myrick***	Y	Y	N	Y	N	Y	Y	Y
10 ***Ballenger***	Y	Y	N	Y	Y	Y	Y	Y
11 ***Taylor***	Y	Y	N	Y	Y	?	Y	Y
12 Watt	N	N	Y	N	N	Y	Y	N
NORTH DAKOTA								
AL Pomeroy	N	N	Y	N	N	Y	Y	Y
OHIO								
1 ***Chabot***	Y	Y	N	Y	Y	Y	Y	Y
2 ***Portman***	Y	Y	N	Y	Y	Y	Y	Y
3 Hall	N	N	Y	N	Y	Y	Y	Y
4 ***Oxley***	Y	Y	N	Y	Y	Y	Y	Y
5 ***Gillmor***	Y	Y	N	Y	Y	Y	Y	Y
6 Strickland	N	N	Y	N	N	Y	Y	Y
7 ***Hobson***	Y	Y	N	Y	Y	Y	Y	Y
8 ***Boehner***	Y	Y	N	Y	N	Y	Y	Y
9 Kaptur	N	N	Y	N	N	Y	Y	N
10 Kucinich	N	N	Y	N	N	Y	Y	N
11 Stokes	N	N	Y	N	N	Y	Y	Y
12 ***Kasich***	Y	Y	N	Y	Y	Y	Y	Y
13 Brown	N	N	Y	N	N	Y	Y	Y
14 Sawyer	N	N	Y	N	N	Y	Y	N
15 ***Pryce***	Y	Y	N	Y	Y	Y	Y	Y
16 ***Regula***	Y	Y	N	N	Y	Y	Y	Y
17 Traficant	Y	Y	Y	N	N	Y	Y	Y
18 ***Ney***	Y	Y	N	N	Y	Y	Y	Y
19 ***LaTourette***	Y	Y	N	Y	Y	Y	Y	Y
OKLAHOMA								
1 ***Largent***	Y	Y	N	Y	Y	Y	Y	Y
2 ***Coburn***	Y	Y	?	?	?	?	?	?
3 ***Watkins***	Y	Y	N	Y	Y	Y	Y	Y
4 ***Watts***	Y	Y	N	Y	Y	Y	Y	Y
5 ***Istook***	Y	Y	N	Y	N	Y	Y	Y
6 ***Lucas***	Y	Y	N	Y	N	Y	Y	Y
OREGON								
1 Furse	N	N	Y	N	N	Y	Y	N
2 ***Smith***	Y	Y	N	Y	N	Y	Y	Y
3 Blumenauer	N	N	Y	N	Y	Y	Y	Y
4 DeFazio	N	N	Y	N	N	Y	Y	Y
5 Hooley	N	N	Y	N	N	Y	Y	Y
PENNSYLVANIA								
1 Foglietta	?	?	?	?	?	?	?	?
2 Fattah	N	N	Y	N	Y	Y	Y	N
3 Borski	N	N	Y	N	N	Y	Y	N
4 Klink	N	?	Y	N	N	Y	Y	N
5 ***Peterson***	Y	Y	N	Y	N	Y	Y	Y
6 Holden	N	N	?	?	N	Y	Y	Y
7 ***Weldon***	Y	Y	N	Y	N	Y	Y	Y
8 ***Greenwood***	Y	Y	N	Y	Y	Y	Y	Y
9 ***Shuster***	Y	Y	N	Y	N	Y	?	?
10 ***McDade***	Y	Y	?	N	N	?	Y	Y
11 Kanjorski	N	N	Y	N	N	Y	Y	Y
12 Murtha	N	N	Y	N	N	Y	Y	Y
13 ***Fox***	Y	Y	N	Y	N	Y	Y	Y
14 Coyne	N	N	Y	N	N	Y	Y	Y
15 McHale	N	N	Y	N	N	Y	Y	N
16 ***Pitts***	Y	Y	N	Y	Y	Y	Y	Y
17 ***Gekas***	Y	Y	N	Y	N	Y	Y	Y
18 Doyle	N	N	Y	N	N	Y	Y	Y
19 ***Goodling***	Y	Y	N	Y	N	+	Y	Y
20 Mascara	N	N	Y	N	N	Y	Y	Y
21 ***English***	Y	Y	N	N	Y	Y	Y	Y
RHODE ISLAND								
1 Kennedy	N	N	Y	N	N	Y	Y	Y
2 Weygand	N	N	Y	N	N	Y	Y	Y
SOUTH CAROLINA								
1 ***Sanford***	Y	Y	N	Y	Y	Y	Y	N
2 ***Spence***	Y	Y	N	Y	N	Y	Y	Y
3 ***Graham***	Y	Y	N	Y	N	Y	Y	Y
4 ***Inglis***	Y	Y	N	Y	N	Y	Y	Y
5 Spratt	N	N	Y	N	N	Y	Y	Y
6 Clyburn	N	N	Y	N	N	Y	Y	Y
SOUTH DAKOTA								
AL ***Thune***	Y	Y	N	N	Y	Y	Y	Y
TENNESSEE								
1 ***Jenkins***	Y	Y	N	N	N	Y	Y	Y
2 ***Duncan***	Y	Y	N	Y	N	Y	Y	Y

	566	567	568	569	570	571	572	
3 ***Wamp***	Y	Y	N	Y	N	Y	Y	Y
4 ***Hilleary***	Y	Y	N	Y	N	Y	Y	Y
5 Clement	N	N	Y	N	Y	Y	Y	Y
6 Gordon	N	N	Y	N	N	Y	Y	Y
7 ***Bryant***	Y	Y	N	Y	Y	Y	Y	Y
8 Tanner	N	N	Y	N	Y	Y	Y	Y
9 Ford	N	N	Y	N	N	Y	Y	N
TEXAS								
1 Sandlin	N	N	Y	N	N	Y	Y	Y
2 Turner	N	N	Y	N	N	Y	Y	Y
3 ***Johnson, Sam***	Y	Y	N	Y	Y	Y	Y	Y
4 Hall	N	N	Y	Y	N	Y	Y	Y
5 ***Sessions***	Y	Y	N	Y	Y	Y	Y	Y
6 ***Barton***	Y	Y	N	Y	Y	Y	Y	Y
7 ***Archer***	Y	Y	N	Y	Y	Y	Y	Y
8 ***Brady***	Y	Y	N	Y	Y	Y	Y	Y
9 Lampson	N	N	Y	N	N	Y	Y	Y
10 Doggett	N	N	Y	N	N	Y	Y	Y
11 Edwards	N	N	Y	N	?	Y	Y	Y
12 ***Granger***	Y	Y	N	Y	Y	Y	Y	Y
13 ***Thornberry***	Y	Y	N	Y	Y	Y	Y	Y
14 ***Paul***	Y	Y	N	Y	N	N	Y	N
15 Hinojosa	N	N	Y	N	N	Y	?	?
16 Reyes	N	N	Y	N	N	Y	Y	Y
17 Stenholm	N	N	Y	N	Y	Y	Y	Y
18 Jackson-Lee	N	N	Y	N	Y	Y	Y	Y
19 ***Combest***	Y	Y	N	Y	Y	Y	Y	Y
20 Gonzalez	?	?	?	?	?	?	?	?
21 ***Smith***	Y	Y	N	Y	Y	Y	Y	Y
22 ***DeLay***	Y	Y	N	Y	Y	Y	Y	Y
23 ***Bonilla***	Y	Y	N	Y	Y	Y	Y	Y
24 Frost	N	N	Y	N	N	Y	Y	Y
25 Bentsen	N	N	Y	N	Y	Y	Y	Y
26 ***Armey***	Y	Y	N	Y	Y	Y	Y	Y
27 Ortiz	N	N	Y	N	N	Y	Y	N
28 Rodriguez	N	N	Y	N	N	Y	Y	Y
29 Green	N	N	Y	N	N	Y	Y	Y
30 Johnson, E.B.	N	N	Y	N	Y	Y	Y	Y
UTAH								
1 ***Hansen***	Y	Y	N	Y	N	Y	Y	Y
2 ***Cook***	Y	Y	N	Y	N	Y	Y	Y
3 ***Cannon***	?	Y	N	N	Y	Y	Y	Y
VERMONT								
AL *Sanders*	N	N	Y	N	N	Y	Y	N
VIRGINIA								
1 ***Bateman***	Y	Y	N	Y	Y	Y	Y	Y
2 Pickett	N	N	Y	N	Y	?	Y	Y
3 Scott	N	N	Y	N	N	Y	?	?
4 Sisisky	N	N	Y	N	N	Y	Y	Y
5 Goode	N	N	Y	N	N	Y	Y	Y
6 ***Goodlatte***	Y	Y	N	N	Y	Y	Y	Y
7 ***Bliley***	Y	Y	N	Y	Y	Y	Y	Y
8 Moran	N	N	Y	N	Y	Y	Y	Y
9 Boucher	N	N	Y	N	N	Y	Y	N
10 ***Wolf***	Y	Y	N	Y	N	Y	Y	Y
11 ***Davis***	Y	Y	N	N	Y	Y	Y	Y
WASHINGTON								
1 ***White***	Y	Y	N	Y	Y	Y	Y	Y
2 ***Metcalf***	Y	Y	N	Y	N	Y	Y	Y
3 ***Smith, Linda***	Y	Y	N	Y	N	Y	Y	Y
4 ***Hastings***	Y	Y	N	Y	Y	Y	Y	Y
5 ***Nethercutt***	Y	Y	N	Y	Y	Y	Y	Y
6 Dicks	N	N	Y	N	Y	Y	Y	N
7 McDermott	N	N	Y	N	Y	Y	Y	N
8 ***Dunn***	Y	Y	N	Y	Y	Y	Y	Y
9 Smith, Adam	N	N	Y	N	N	Y	Y	Y
WEST VIRGINIA								
1 Mollohan	N	N	Y	N	N	Y	Y	Y
2 Wise	N	N	Y	N	?	?	Y	Y
3 Rahall	N	N	Y	N	N	Y	Y	Y
WISCONSIN								
1 ***Neumann***	Y	Y	N	Y	N	Y	Y	Y
2 ***Klug***	Y	Y	N	N	Y	Y	Y	Y
3 Kind	N	N	Y	N	N	Y	Y	Y
4 Kleczka	N	N	Y	N	N	Y	Y	Y
5 Barrett	N	N	Y	N	N	Y	Y	Y
6 ***Petri***	Y	Y	N	Y	Y	Y	Y	Y
7 Obey	N	N	Y	N	N	Y	Y	Y
8 Johnson	N	?	Y	N	N	Y	Y	Y
9 ***Sensenbrenner***	Y	Y	N	Y	Y	Y	Y	Y
WYOMING								
AL ***Cubin***	?	?	?	?	?	?	?	?

Southern states - Ala., Ark., Fla., Ga., Ky., La., Miss., N.C., Okla., S.C., Tenn., Texas, Va.

HOUSE VOTES 574, 575, 577, 578, 579, 580, 581, 582 *

574. HR 948. Ottawa and Chippewa Indian Recognition/Passage. Saxton, R-N.J., motion to suspend the rules and pass the bill to reaffirm federal recognition of the Burt Lake Band of Ottawa and Chippewa Indians in Michigan and allow its members to apply for services and benefits available to federally recognized Indian tribes. Motion rejected 240-167: R 58-157; D 181-10 (ND 133-6, SD 48-4); I 1-0, Nov. 4, 1997. A two-thirds majority of those present and voting (272 in this case) is required for passage under suspension of the rules.

575. Procedural Motion/Journal. Approval of the House Journal of Tuesday, Nov. 4, 1997. Approved 353-48: R 197-14; D 155-34 (ND 114-25, SD 41-9); I 1-0, Nov. 5, 1997.

*** 577. HR 2676. Internal Revenue Service Overhaul/Passage.** Passage of the bill to restructure the management of the Internal Revenue Service by establishing an oversight board to oversee the agency's operations. The bill would shift the burden of proof from the taxpayer to the IRS in cases before the U.S. Tax Court and allow taxpayers to sue the federal government for civil damages caused by IRS employees who negligently disregard tax laws. Passed 426-4: R 225-0; D 200-4 (ND 146-4, SD 54-0); I 1-0, Nov. 5, 1997. A "yea" was a vote in support of the president's position.

578. H Res 302. U.S.-China Policy/Rule. Adoption of the resolution to provide for House floor consideration of nine measures concerning U.S. policy toward China: HR 2358, to increase the number of U.S. diplomats in China monitoring human rights; HR 2195, to enforce the ban on slave labor products made in Chinese prison camps; H Res 188, to request the president to enforce sanctions on Chinese missile exports to Iran; HR 967, to ban travel to the United States by Chinese officials who engage in religious persecution; HR 2570, to ban travel to the United States by Chinese officials involved in forced abortions and sterilizations; HR 2386, to require the Defense Department to conduct a study for a missile defense system to protect Taiwan; HR 2605, to direct U.S. representatives at the World Bank and International Monetary Fund to vote against certain loans for China; HR 2647, to authorize the president to monitor, restrict or ban commercial activities by the People's Liberation Army of China in the United States; and HR 2232, to authorize increased funding for Radio Free Asia and Voice of America broadcasting in China. Adopted 237-184: R 222-0; D 15-183 (ND 10-136, SD 5-47); I 0-1, Nov. 5, 1997.

579. HR 2358. China Human Rights Monitors/Technology Exports. Gilman, R-N.Y., amendment to change the U.S.-China Agreement for Nuclear Cooperation (PL 99-183), which restricts the sale of nuclear technology to China unless the president certifies that China has stopped selling such technology to any country developing nuclear weapons, by extending the congressional review period from 30 to 120 legislative days and adding expedited procedures for disapproval. Adopted 394-29: R 209-13; D 184-16 (ND 136-11, SD 48-5); I 1-0, Nov. 5, 1997.

580. HR 2358. China Human Rights Monitors/Passage. Passage of the bill to authorize $2.2 million in fiscal 1998 and 1999 to fund additional State Department personnel at diplomatic posts in China to monitor human rights. Passed 416-5: R 220-1; D 195-4 (ND 143-3, SD 52-1); I 1-0, Nov. 5, 1997. A "nay" was a vote in support of the president's position.

581. HR 2195. Chinese Prison Labor/Table Appeal of Ruling of Chair. Crane, R-Ill., motion to table (kill) the Taylor, D-Miss., appeal of the ruling of the chair that the Taylor motion to recommit with instructions was not germane. The Taylor motion would instruct the Ways and Means Committee to report the bill back with an amendment to require that the total amount of tariffs paid to China for U.S. exports be adjusted quarterly to equal the total amount China pays in tariffs to the United States for Chinese exports. Motion agreed to 217-202: R 214-6; D 3-195 (ND 3-143, SD 0-52); I 0-1, Nov. 5, 1997.

582. HR 2195. Chinese Prison Labor/Passage. Passage of the bill to authorize $2 million in fiscal 1998 and 1999 for the Customs Service and State Department to monitor and enforce the current U.S. ban on Chinese exports made with forced prison labor. Passed 419-2: R 221-0; D 197-2 (ND 145-1, SD 52-1); I 1-0, Nov. 5, 1997.

** Omitted votes are quorum calls. CQ does not include quorum calls in its vote charts.*

[1] Rep. Vito J. Fossella, R-N.Y., was sworn in Nov. 5. The first vote for which he was eligible was vote 576.

KEY

- Y Voted for (yea).
- # Paired for.
- \+ Announced for.
- N Voted against (nay).
- X Paired against.
- – Announced against.
- P Voted "present."
- C Voted "present" to avoid possible conflict of interest.
- ? Did not vote or otherwise make a position known.

Democrats ***Republicans***
Independent

	574	575	577	578	579	580	581	582
ALABAMA								
1 ***Callahan***	N	Y	Y	Y	Y	Y	Y	Y
2 ***Everett***	N	N	Y	Y	Y	Y	Y	Y
3 ***Riley***	–	+	+	#	+	+	+	+
4 ***Aderholt***	N	Y	Y	Y	Y	Y	Y	Y
5 Cramer	Y	Y	Y	N	Y	Y	N	Y
6 ***Bachus***	N	Y	Y	Y	Y	Y	Y	Y
7 Hilliard	Y	N	Y	N	Y	Y	N	Y
ALASKA								
AL ***Young***	?	?	Y	Y	Y	Y	?	?
ARIZONA								
1 ***Salmon***	Y	?	Y	Y	Y	Y	Y	Y
2 Pastor	Y	Y	Y	N	Y	Y	N	Y
3 ***Stump***	N	Y	Y	Y	N	Y	Y	Y
4 ***Shadegg***	Y	Y	Y	Y	Y	Y	Y	Y
5 ***Kolbe***	Y	Y	Y	Y	N	Y	Y	Y
6 ***Hayworth***	Y	Y	Y	Y	Y	Y	Y	Y
ARKANSAS								
1 Berry	Y	Y	Y	N	Y	Y	N	Y
2 Snyder	Y	Y	Y	N	N	Y	N	Y
3 ***Hutchinson***	N	?	Y	Y	Y	Y	Y	Y
4 ***Dickey***	Y	Y	Y	Y	Y	Y	Y	Y
CALIFORNIA								
1 ***Riggs***	N	?	Y	Y	+	Y	Y	Y
2 ***Herger***	N	Y	Y	Y	Y	Y	Y	Y
3 Fazio	Y	N	Y	N	N	Y	N	Y
4 ***Doolittle***	N	Y	Y	Y	Y	Y	Y	Y
5 Matsui	Y	Y	N	N	Y	Y	N	Y
6 Woolsey	Y	Y	Y	N	Y	Y	N	Y
7 Miller	Y	N	Y	N	Y	Y	N	Y
8 Pelosi	Y	Y	Y	Y	Y	Y	N	Y
9 Dellums	Y	?	Y	N	Y	Y	N	Y
10 Tauscher	Y	N	Y	N	Y	Y	N	Y
11 ***Pombo***	N	Y	Y	Y	Y	Y	Y	Y
12 Lantos	Y	Y	Y	N	Y	Y	N	Y
13 Stark	Y	Y	N	N	Y	Y	N	Y
14 Eshoo	Y	Y	Y	Y	Y	Y	N	Y
15 ***Campbell***	Y	Y	Y	Y	Y	Y	Y	Y
16 Lofgren	Y	Y	Y	N	Y	Y	N	Y
17 Farr	Y	Y	Y	N	Y	Y	N	Y
18 Condit	Y	Y	Y	N	Y	Y	N	Y
19 ***Radanovich***	Y	Y	Y	Y	Y	Y	Y	Y
20 Dooley	Y	Y	Y	N	N	Y	N	Y
21 ***Thomas***	N	Y	Y	Y	Y	Y	Y	Y
22 Vacant								
23 ***Gallegly***	Y	Y	Y	Y	Y	Y	Y	Y
24 Sherman	Y	Y	Y	N	Y	Y	N	Y
25 ***McKeon***	?	Y	Y	Y	Y	Y	Y	Y
26 Berman	Y	Y	Y	N	Y	Y	N	Y
27 ***Rogan***	N	Y	Y	Y	Y	Y	Y	Y
28 ***Dreier***	Y	Y	Y	Y	N	Y	Y	Y
29 Waxman	?	Y	Y	N	Y	Y	N	Y
30 Becerra	Y	N	Y	N	Y	Y	N	Y
31 Martinez	Y	Y	Y	N	Y	Y	N	Y
32 Dixon	Y	?	Y	N	Y	Y	N	Y
33 Roybal-Allard	Y	Y	Y	N	Y	Y	N	Y
34 Torres	Y	Y	Y	N	Y	Y	N	Y
35 Waters	Y	?	Y	N	Y	Y	N	Y
36 Harman	Y	Y	Y	Y	Y	Y	N	Y
37 Millender-McD.	Y	Y	Y	N	Y	Y	N	Y
38 ***Horn***	N	Y	Y	Y	Y	Y	Y	Y
39 ***Royce***	N	?	Y	Y	Y	Y	Y	Y
40 ***Lewis***	?	Y	Y	Y	Y	Y	Y	Y
41 ***Kim***	Y	Y	Y	Y	Y	Y	Y	Y
42 Brown	Y	N	Y	N	N	N	N	N
43 ***Calvert***	Y	Y	Y	Y	Y	Y	Y	Y
44 ***Bono***	Y	Y	Y	Y	Y	Y	Y	Y
45 ***Rohrabacher***	Y	Y	Y	Y	Y	Y	N	Y
46 Sanchez	Y	Y	Y	N	Y	Y	N	Y
47 ***Cox***	Y	Y	Y	Y	Y	Y	Y	Y
48 ***Packard***	N	Y	Y	Y	Y	Y	Y	Y
49 ***Bilbray***	Y	Y	Y	Y	Y	Y	N	Y
50 Filner	Y	N	Y	N	Y	Y	N	Y
51 ***Cunningham***	N	Y	Y	Y	Y	Y	Y	Y
52 ***Hunter***	N	Y	Y	Y	Y	Y	N	Y
COLORADO								
1 DeGette	Y	Y	Y	N	Y	Y	N	Y
2 Skaggs	Y	Y	Y	N	N	Y	Y	Y
3 ***McInnis***	N	Y	Y	Y	Y	Y	Y	Y
4 ***Schaffer***	N	N	Y	Y	Y	Y	Y	Y
5 ***Hefley***	N	N	Y	Y	Y	Y	Y	Y
6 ***Schaefer***	N	Y	Y	Y	Y	Y	Y	Y
CONNECTICUT								
1 Kennelly	N	Y	Y	N	N	Y	N	Y
2 Gejdenson	Y	Y	Y	N	Y	Y	N	Y
3 DeLauro	N	N	Y	N	Y	Y	N	Y
4 ***Shays***	N	Y	Y	Y	N	Y	Y	Y
5 Maloney	Y	Y	Y	N	Y	Y	N	Y
6 ***Johnson***	N	Y	Y	Y	N	Y	Y	Y
DELAWARE								
AL ***Castle***	N	Y	Y	Y	Y	Y	Y	Y
FLORIDA								
1 ***Scarborough***	N	Y	Y	Y	Y	Y	Y	Y
2 Boyd	Y	Y	Y	N	Y	Y	N	Y
3 Brown	Y	Y	Y	?	Y	Y	N	Y
4 ***Fowler***	N	Y	Y	Y	Y	Y	Y	Y
5 Thurman	Y	Y	Y	N	Y	Y	N	Y
6 ***Stearns***	N	Y	Y	Y	Y	Y	?	Y
7 ***Mica***	N	Y	Y	Y	Y	Y	Y	Y
8 ***McCollum***	Y	Y	Y	Y	Y	Y	Y	Y
9 ***Bilirakis***	N	Y	Y	Y	Y	Y	Y	Y
10 ***Young***	N	Y	Y	Y	Y	Y	Y	Y
11 Davis	Y	Y	Y	N	Y	Y	N	Y
12 ***Canady***	Y	Y	Y	Y	Y	Y	Y	Y
13 ***Miller***	N	Y	Y	Y	Y	Y	Y	Y
14 ***Goss***	N	Y	Y	Y	Y	Y	Y	Y
15 ***Weldon***	N	Y	Y	Y	Y	Y	Y	Y
16 ***Foley***	Y	Y	Y	Y	Y	Y	Y	Y
17 Meek	Y	?	Y	N	N	Y	N	Y
18 ***Ros-Lehtinen***	Y	Y	Y	Y	Y	Y	Y	Y
19 Wexler	Y	Y	Y	N	Y	Y	N	Y
20 Deutsch	Y	Y	Y	Y	Y	Y	N	Y
21 ***Diaz-Balart***	Y	Y	Y	Y	Y	Y	Y	Y
22 ***Shaw***	N	Y	Y	Y	Y	Y	Y	Y
23 Hastings	Y	N	Y	N	N	Y	N	Y
GEORGIA								
1 ***Kingston***	N	Y	Y	Y	Y	?	Y	Y
2 Bishop	Y	Y	Y	N	Y	Y	N	Y
3 ***Collins***	N	Y	Y	Y	Y	Y	Y	Y
4 McKinney	Y	Y	Y	X	?	?	?	?
5 Lewis	Y	N	Y	N	Y	Y	N	Y
6 ***Gingrich***			Y					
7 ***Barr***	N	?	Y	Y	Y	Y	Y	Y
8 ***Chambliss***	Y	Y	Y	Y	Y	Y	Y	Y
9 ***Deal***	N	Y	Y	Y	Y	Y	Y	Y
10 ***Norwood***	N	Y	Y	Y	Y	Y	Y	Y
11 ***Linder***	Y	Y	Y	Y	Y	Y	Y	Y
HAWAII								
1 Abercrombie	Y	N	Y	Y	Y	Y	N	Y
2 Mink	Y	Y	Y	N	Y	Y	N	Y
IDAHO								
1 ***Chenoweth***	N	Y	Y	Y	Y	Y	Y	Y
2 ***Crapo***	N	Y	Y	Y	Y	Y	Y	Y
ILLINOIS								
1 Rush	Y	Y	Y	N	Y	Y	N	Y
2 Jackson	Y	Y	Y	N	Y	Y	N	Y
3 Lipinski	Y	N	Y	N	Y	Y	N	Y
4 Gutierrez	Y	Y	Y	N	Y	Y	N	Y
5 Blagojevich	Y	Y	Y	N	Y	Y	N	Y
6 ***Hyde***	N	?	Y	Y	Y	Y	Y	Y
7 Davis	Y	?	Y	N	Y	Y	N	Y
8 ***Crane***	Y	?	Y	Y	N	Y	Y	Y
9 Yates	?	Y	Y	N	?	?	?	?
10 ***Porter***	N	Y	Y	Y	Y	Y	Y	Y
11 ***Weller***	Y	N	Y	Y	Y	Y	Y	Y
12 Costello	Y	Y	Y	N	Y	Y	N	Y
13 ***Fawell***	?	Y	Y	Y	Y	Y	Y	Y
14 ***Hastert***	N	Y	Y	Y	Y	Y	Y	Y
15 ***Ewing***	N	Y	Y	Y	Y	Y	Y	Y

ND Northern Democrats SD Southern Democrats

	574	575	577	578	579	580	581	582
16 ***Manzullo***	N	Y	Y	Y	N	Y	Y	Y
17 Evans	Y	Y	Y	N	Y	Y	N	Y
18 ***LaHood***	N	Y	Y	Y	N	Y	Y	Y
19 Poshard	Y	Y	Y	N	Y	Y	N	Y
20 ***Shimkus***	N	Y	Y	Y	Y	Y	Y	Y
INDIANA								
1 Visclosky	N	N	Y	N	Y	Y	N	Y
2 ***McIntosh***	?	Y	Y	Y	Y	Y	Y	Y
3 Roemer	N	Y	Y	N	N	Y	N	Y
4 ***Souder***	Y	Y	Y	Y	Y	Y	Y	Y
5 ***Buyer***	N	Y	Y	Y	Y	Y	Y	Y
6 ***Burton***	N	Y	Y	Y	Y	Y	Y	Y
7 ***Pease***	N	Y	Y	Y	Y	Y	Y	Y
8 ***Hostettler***	N	Y	Y	Y	Y	Y	Y	Y
9 Hamilton	Y	Y	Y	N	N	Y	Y	Y
10 Carson	Y	Y	Y	N	Y	Y	N	Y
IOWA								
1 ***Leach***	Y	Y	Y	Y	Y	Y	Y	Y
2 ***Nussle***	N	N	Y	Y	Y	Y	Y	Y
3 Boswell	Y	?	Y	N	Y	Y	N	Y
4 ***Ganske***	N	Y	Y	Y	Y	Y	Y	Y
5 ***Latham***	N	Y	Y	Y	Y	Y	Y	Y
KANSAS								
1 ***Moran***	N	N	Y	Y	Y	Y	Y	Y
2 ***Ryun***	N	Y	Y	Y	Y	Y	Y	Y
3 ***Snowbarger***	N	Y	Y	Y	Y	Y	Y	Y
4 ***Tiahrt***	N	Y	Y	Y	Y	Y	Y	Y
KENTUCKY								
1 ***Whitfield***	N	Y	Y	Y	Y	Y	Y	Y
2 ***Lewis***	N	Y	Y	Y	Y	Y	Y	Y
3 ***Northup***	N	Y	Y	Y	Y	Y	Y	Y
4 ***Bunning***	N	Y	Y	Y	?	?	Y	Y
5 ***Rogers***	N	Y	Y	Y	Y	Y	Y	Y
6 Baesler	Y	Y	Y	N	Y	Y	N	Y
LOUISIANA								
1 ***Livingston***	Y	Y	Y	Y	Y	Y	Y	Y
2 Jefferson	Y	?	Y	N	Y	Y	N	Y
3 ***Tauzin***	Y	Y	Y	Y	Y	Y	Y	Y
4 ***McCrery***	N	Y	Y	Y	Y	Y	Y	Y
5 ***Cooksey***	N	?	Y	Y	Y	Y	Y	Y
6 ***Baker***	N	Y	Y	Y	Y	Y	Y	Y
7 John	Y	Y	Y	N	Y	Y	N	Y
MAINE								
1 Allen	Y	Y	Y	N	Y	Y	N	Y
2 Baldacci	Y	Y	Y	N	Y	Y	N	Y
MARYLAND								
1 ***Gilchrest***	N	Y	Y	Y	Y	Y	Y	Y
2 ***Ehrlich***	N	Y	Y	Y	Y	Y	Y	Y
3 Cardin	Y	Y	Y	N	Y	Y	N	Y
4 Wynn	Y	Y	Y	N	Y	Y	N	Y
5 Hoyer	Y	Y	N	N	Y	Y	N	Y
6 ***Bartlett***	N	Y	Y	Y	Y	Y	N	Y
7 Cummings	Y	Y	Y	N	Y	Y	N	Y
8 ***Morella***	N	Y	Y	?	Y	Y	Y	Y
MASSACHUSETTS								
1 Olver	Y	Y	Y	N	Y	Y	N	Y
2 Neal	Y	Y	Y	N	Y	Y	N	Y
3 McGovern	Y	Y	Y	N	Y	Y	N	Y
4 Frank	Y	Y	Y	N	Y	Y	N	Y
5 Meehan	Y	Y	Y	N	Y	Y	N	Y
6 Tierney	Y	Y	Y	N	Y	Y	N	Y
7 Markey	Y	Y	Y	N	Y	Y	N	Y
8 Kennedy	Y	Y	Y	N	Y	Y	N	Y
9 Moakley	Y	Y	Y	N	Y	Y	Y	Y
10 Delahunt	Y	?	Y	N	Y	Y	N	Y
MICHIGAN								
1 Stupak	Y	N	Y	N	Y	Y	N	Y
2 ***Hoekstra***	N	Y	Y	Y	Y	Y	Y	Y
3 ***Ehlers***	N	Y	Y	Y	Y	Y	Y	Y
4 ***Camp***	N	Y	Y	Y	Y	Y	Y	Y
5 Barcia	Y	Y	Y	N	Y	Y	N	Y
6 ***Upton***	N	Y	Y	Y	Y	Y	Y	Y
7 ***Smith***	N	Y	Y	Y	Y	Y	N	Y
8 Stabenow	Y	Y	Y	Y	Y	Y	N	Y
9 Kildee	Y	Y	Y	N	Y	Y	N	Y
10 Bonior	Y	N	Y	N	Y	Y	N	Y
11 ***Knollenberg***	Y	Y	Y	Y	Y	Y	Y	Y
12 Levin	N	Y	Y	N	Y	Y	N	Y
13 Rivers	Y	Y	Y	N	Y	Y	N	Y
14 Conyers	Y	Y	Y	?	Y	Y	N	Y
15 Kilpatrick	Y	Y	Y	N	Y	?	N	Y
16 Dingell	Y	Y	Y	N	N	N	N	Y
MINNESOTA								
1 ***Gutknecht***	N	N	Y	Y	Y	Y	Y	Y
2 Minge	Y	Y	Y	N	Y	Y	N	Y

	574	575	577	578	579	580	581	582
3 ***Ramstad***	N	N	Y	Y	Y	Y	Y	Y
4 Vento	Y	N	Y	N	Y	Y	N	Y
5 Sabo	Y	N	Y	N	Y	Y	N	Y
6 Luther	Y	Y	Y	N	Y	Y	N	Y
7 Peterson	Y	Y	Y	N	Y	Y	N	Y
8 Oberstar	Y	N	Y	N	Y	Y	N	Y
MISSISSIPPI								
1 ***Wicker***	N	Y	Y	Y	Y	Y	Y	Y
2 Thompson	Y	N	Y	N	Y	Y	N	Y
3 ***Pickering***	N	Y	Y	Y	Y	Y	Y	Y
4 ***Parker***	N	Y	Y	Y	Y	Y	Y	Y
5 Taylor	Y	N	Y	N	Y	Y	N	Y
MISSOURI								
1 Clay	?	N	Y	N	Y	Y	N	Y
2 ***Talent***	N	Y	Y	Y	Y	Y	Y	Y
3 Gephardt	?	N	Y	N	Y	Y	N	Y
4 Skelton	Y	Y	Y	N	Y	Y	N	Y
5 McCarthy	Y	Y	Y	N	Y	Y	N	Y
6 Danner	Y	Y	Y	N	Y	Y	N	Y
7 ***Blunt***	N	Y	Y	Y	N	Y	Y	Y
8 ***Emerson***	Y	Y	Y	Y	Y	Y	Y	Y
9 ***Hulshof***	N	N	Y	Y	Y	Y	Y	Y
MONTANA								
AL ***Hill***	Y	Y	Y	Y	Y	Y	Y	Y
NEBRASKA								
1 ***Bereuter***	N	Y	Y	Y	N	Y	Y	Y
2 ***Christensen***	N	Y	Y	Y	Y	Y	Y	Y
3 ***Barrett***	N	Y	Y	Y	Y	Y	Y	Y
NEVADA								
1 ***Ensign***	Y	N	Y	Y	Y	Y	Y	Y
2 ***Gibbons***	N	N	Y	Y	Y	Y	Y	Y
NEW HAMPSHIRE								
1 ***Sununu***	N	Y	Y	Y	Y	Y	Y	Y
2 ***Bass***	Y	Y	Y	Y	Y	Y	Y	Y
NEW JERSEY								
1 Andrews	Y	Y	Y	N	Y	Y	N	Y
2 ***LoBiondo***	N	N	Y	Y	Y	Y	Y	Y
3 ***Saxton***	Y	Y	Y	Y	Y	Y	Y	Y
4 ***Smith***	Y	Y	Y	Y	Y	Y	Y	Y
5 ***Roukema***	N	Y	Y	Y	Y	Y	Y	Y
6 Pallone	Y	Y	Y	N	Y	Y	N	Y
7 ***Franks***	N	Y	Y	Y	Y	Y	Y	Y
8 Pascrell	Y	Y	Y	N	Y	Y	N	Y
9 Rothman	Y	Y	Y	N	Y	Y	N	Y
10 Payne	?	Y	Y	N	N	Y	N	Y
11 ***Frelinghuysen***	Y	Y	Y	Y	Y	Y	Y	Y
12 ***Pappas***	N	Y	Y	Y	Y	Y	Y	Y
13 Menendez	?	N	Y	N	Y	Y	N	Y
NEW MEXICO								
1 ***Schiff***	?	?	?	?	?	?	?	?
2 ***Skeen***	N	Y	Y	Y	Y	Y	Y	Y
3 ***Redmond***	N	Y	Y	Y	Y	Y	Y	Y
NEW YORK								
1 ***Forbes***	Y	Y	Y	Y	Y	Y	Y	Y
2 ***Lazio***	N	Y	Y	Y	Y	Y	Y	Y
3 ***King***	?	Y	Y	Y	Y	Y	Y	Y
4 McCarthy	Y	Y	Y	Y	Y	Y	N	Y
5 Ackerman	?	Y	Y	N	Y	Y	N	Y
6 Flake	?	?	Y	?	?	?	?	?
7 Manton	Y	Y	Y	N	Y	Y	N	Y
8 Nadler	Y	Y	Y	N	Y	Y	N	Y
9 Schumer	Y	Y	Y	?	?	?	?	?
10 Towns	Y	Y	Y	N	Y	Y	N	Y
11 Owens	Y	Y	Y	N	Y	Y	N	Y
12 Velázquez	Y	Y	Y	N	Y	Y	N	Y
13 ***Fossella*** [1]			Y	Y	Y	Y	Y	Y
14 Maloney	Y	Y	Y	N	Y	Y	N	Y
15 Rangel	Y	Y	Y	N	Y	Y	N	Y
16 Serrano	Y	Y	Y	N	Y	Y	N	Y
17 Engel	Y	+	Y	N	Y	Y	N	Y
18 Lowey	Y	Y	Y	N	Y	Y	N	Y
19 ***Kelly***	Y	Y	Y	Y	Y	Y	Y	Y
20 ***Gilman***	Y	Y	Y	Y	Y	Y	Y	Y
21 McNulty	?	N	Y	N	Y	Y	N	Y
22 ***Solomon***	N	Y	Y	Y	Y	Y	Y	Y
23 ***Boehlert***	Y	Y	Y	Y	Y	Y	Y	Y
24 ***McHugh***	N	Y	Y	Y	Y	Y	Y	Y
25 ***Walsh***	N	Y	Y	Y	Y	Y	Y	Y
26 Hinchey	Y	N	Y	N	Y	Y	N	Y
27 ***Paxon***	N	Y	Y	Y	Y	Y	Y	Y
28 Slaughter	Y	Y	Y	N	Y	Y	N	Y
29 LaFalce	Y	Y	Y	N	Y	Y	N	Y
30 ***Quinn***	N	Y	Y	Y	Y	Y	Y	Y
31 ***Houghton***	Y	Y	Y	Y	N	Y	Y	Y

	574	575	577	578	579	580	581	582
NORTH CAROLINA								
1 Clayton	Y	N	Y	N	Y	Y	N	Y
2 Etheridge	Y	Y	Y	N	Y	Y	N	Y
3 ***Jones***	Y	Y	Y	Y	Y	Y	Y	Y
4 Price	Y	Y	Y	N	Y	Y	N	Y
5 ***Burr***	N	Y	Y	Y	Y	Y	Y	Y
6 ***Coble***	N	Y	Y	Y	Y	Y	Y	Y
7 McIntyre	Y	?	Y	N	Y	Y	N	Y
8 Hefner	Y	Y	Y	N	Y	Y	N	Y
9 ***Myrick***	Y	Y	Y	Y	Y	Y	Y	Y
10 ***Ballenger***	N	Y	Y	Y	Y	Y	Y	Y
11 ***Taylor***	N	Y	Y	Y	Y	Y	Y	Y
12 Watt	Y	Y	Y	N	Y	Y	N	Y
NORTH DAKOTA								
AL Pomeroy	Y	Y	Y	N	Y	Y	N	Y
OHIO								
1 ***Chabot***	N	Y	Y	Y	Y	Y	Y	Y
2 ***Portman***	N	Y	Y	Y	Y	Y	Y	Y
3 Hall	?	Y	Y	N	Y	Y	N	Y
4 ***Oxley***	Y	Y	Y	Y	Y	Y	Y	Y
5 ***Gillmor***	Y	Y	Y	Y	N	Y	Y	Y
6 Strickland	Y	Y	Y	N	Y	Y	N	Y
7 ***Hobson***	N	Y	Y	Y	Y	Y	Y	Y
8 ***Boehner***	N	Y	Y	Y	Y	Y	Y	Y
9 Kaptur	Y	?	Y	N	Y	Y	N	Y
10 Kucinich	Y	N	Y	N	Y	Y	N	Y
11 Stokes	Y	Y	Y	N	Y	Y	N	Y
12 ***Kasich***	N	Y	Y	Y	Y	Y	Y	Y
13 Brown	Y	N	Y	N	Y	Y	N	Y
14 Sawyer	Y	Y	Y	N	N	Y	N	Y
15 ***Pryce***	N	Y	Y	Y	Y	Y	Y	Y
16 ***Regula***	N	Y	Y	Y	Y	Y	Y	Y
17 Traficant	N	Y	Y	Y	Y	Y	N	Y
18 ***Ney***	Y	Y	Y	Y	Y	Y	Y	Y
19 ***LaTourette***	N	Y	Y	Y	Y	Y	Y	Y
OKLAHOMA								
1 ***Largent***	N	Y	Y	Y	Y	Y	Y	Y
2 ***Coburn***	?	?	Y	Y	Y	Y	Y	Y
3 ***Watkins***	N	Y	Y	Y	Y	Y	Y	Y
4 ***Watts***	N	Y	Y	Y	Y	Y	Y	Y
5 ***Istook***	N	Y	Y	Y	Y	Y	Y	Y
6 ***Lucas***	N	Y	Y	Y	Y	Y	Y	Y
OREGON								
1 Furse	Y	Y	Y	Y	Y	Y	N	Y
2 ***Smith***	N	Y	Y	Y	Y	Y	Y	Y
3 Blumenauer	Y	Y	Y	N	Y	Y	N	Y
4 DeFazio	Y	N	Y	N	Y	Y	N	Y
5 Hooley	Y	Y	Y	N	Y	Y	N	Y
PENNSYLVANIA								
1 Foglietta	?	?	Y	?	N	Y	?	?
2 Fattah	Y	Y	Y	N	Y	Y	N	Y
3 Borski	Y	N	Y	N	Y	Y	N	Y
4 Klink	Y	Y	Y	N	Y	Y	N	Y
5 ***Peterson***	Y	Y	Y	Y	Y	Y	Y	Y
6 Holden	Y	Y	Y	N	Y	Y	N	Y
7 ***Weldon***	N	Y	Y	Y	Y	Y	?	Y
8 ***Greenwood***	N	Y	Y	Y	Y	Y	Y	?
9 ***Shuster***	?	Y	Y	Y	Y	Y	Y	Y
10 ***McDade***	N	Y	Y	Y	Y	Y	Y	Y
11 Kanjorski	Y	Y	Y	N	Y	N	N	Y
12 Murtha	Y	Y	Y	N	Y	Y	N	Y
13 ***Fox***	N	N	Y	Y	Y	Y	Y	Y
14 Coyne	Y	Y	Y	N	Y	Y	N	Y
15 McHale	Y	Y	Y	N	Y	Y	N	Y
16 ***Pitts***	Y	Y	Y	Y	Y	Y	Y	Y
17 ***Gekas***	Y	Y	Y	Y	Y	Y	Y	Y
18 Doyle	Y	Y	Y	N	Y	Y	N	Y
19 ***Goodling***	Y	Y	Y	Y	Y	Y	Y	Y
20 Mascara	Y	Y	Y	N	Y	Y	N	Y
21 ***English***	Y	N	Y	Y	N	Y	Y	Y
RHODE ISLAND								
1 Kennedy	Y	Y	Y	N	Y	Y	N	Y
2 Weygand	Y	Y	Y	N	Y	Y	N	Y
SOUTH CAROLINA								
1 ***Sanford***	N	Y	Y	Y	Y	Y	Y	Y
2 ***Spence***	N	?	Y	Y	Y	Y	Y	Y
3 ***Graham***	N	Y	Y	Y	Y	Y	Y	Y
4 ***Inglis***	N	Y	Y	Y	Y	Y	Y	Y
5 Spratt	Y	Y	Y	N	Y	Y	N	Y
6 Clyburn	Y	N	Y	N	Y	Y	N	Y
SOUTH DAKOTA								
AL ***Thune***	N	Y	Y	Y	Y	+	Y	Y
TENNESSEE								
1 ***Jenkins***	Y	Y	Y	Y	Y	Y	Y	Y
2 ***Duncan***	N	Y	Y	Y	Y	Y	Y	Y

	574	575	577	578	579	580	581	
3 ***Wamp***	N	Y	Y	Y	Y	Y	Y	Y
4 ***Hilleary***	N	Y	Y	Y	Y	Y	Y	Y
5 Clement	Y	Y	Y	N	Y	Y	N	Y
6 Gordon	Y	Y	Y	N	Y	Y	N	Y
7 ***Bryant***	N	Y	Y	Y	Y	Y	Y	Y
8 Tanner	Y	Y	Y	N	Y	Y	N	Y
9 Ford	Y	Y	Y	N	Y	Y	?	Y
TEXAS								
1 Sandlin	Y	Y	Y	N	Y	Y	N	Y
2 Turner	Y	Y	Y	N	Y	Y	N	Y
3 ***Johnson, Sam***	Y	?	Y	Y	Y	Y	Y	Y
4 Hall	N	Y	Y	Y	N	Y	N	Y
5 ***Sessions***	N	Y	Y	Y	Y	Y	Y	Y
6 ***Barton***	N	Y	Y	Y	Y	Y	Y	Y
7 ***Archer***	N	Y	Y	Y	Y	Y	Y	Y
8 ***Brady***	N	Y	Y	Y	Y	Y	Y	Y
9 Lampson	Y	Y	Y	N	Y	Y	N	Y
10 Doggett	Y	Y	Y	N	Y	Y	N	Y
11 Edwards	Y	Y	Y	N	Y	Y	N	Y
12 ***Granger***	Y	Y	Y	Y	Y	Y	Y	Y
13 ***Thornberry***	N	Y	Y	Y	Y	Y	Y	Y
14 ***Paul***	N	Y	Y	Y	Y	N	Y	P
15 Hinojosa	?	Y	Y	N	Y	Y	N	Y
16 Reyes	Y	Y	Y	N	Y	Y	N	Y
17 Stenholm	N	Y	Y	N	Y	Y	N	Y
18 Jackson-Lee	Y	Y	Y	N	Y	Y	N	Y
19 ***Combest***	N	Y	Y	Y	Y	Y	Y	Y
20 Gonzalez	?	?	?	?	?	?	?	?
21 ***Smith***	Y	Y	Y	Y	Y	Y	Y	Y
22 ***DeLay***	N	Y	Y	Y	Y	Y	Y	Y
23 ***Bonilla***	Y	Y	Y	Y	Y	Y	Y	Y
24 Frost	Y	Y	Y	N	Y	Y	N	Y
25 Bentsen	Y	Y	Y	N	Y	Y	N	Y
26 ***Armey***	N	Y	Y	Y	Y	Y	Y	Y
27 Ortiz	Y	Y	Y	Y	Y	Y	N	Y
28 Rodriguez	Y	Y	Y	N	Y	Y	N	Y
29 Green	Y	Y	Y	N	Y	Y	N	Y
30 Johnson, E.B.	Y	N	Y	N	Y	Y	N	Y
UTAH								
1 ***Hansen***	N	Y	Y	Y	Y	Y	Y	Y
2 ***Cook***	Y	Y	Y	Y	Y	Y	Y	Y
3 ***Cannon***	N	Y	Y	Y	Y	Y	Y	Y
VERMONT								
AL *Sanders*	Y	Y	Y	N	Y	Y	N	Y
VIRGINIA								
1 ***Bateman***	N	Y	Y	Y	Y	Y	Y	Y
2 Pickett	Y	N	Y	N	Y	N	N	N
3 Scott	?	?	Y	N	Y	Y	N	Y
4 Sisisky	Y	Y	Y	N	Y	Y	N	Y
5 Goode	N	Y	Y	Y	Y	Y	N	Y
6 ***Goodlatte***	N	Y	Y	Y	Y	Y	Y	Y
7 ***Bliley***	Y	Y	Y	Y	Y	Y	Y	Y
8 Moran	N	Y	Y	Y	N	Y	N	Y
9 Boucher	Y	Y	Y	N	Y	Y	N	Y
10 ***Wolf***	N	Y	Y	Y	Y	Y	Y	Y
11 ***Davis***	N	Y	Y	Y	Y	Y	?	Y
WASHINGTON								
1 ***White***	N	Y	Y	Y	Y	Y	Y	Y
2 ***Metcalf***	N	Y	Y	Y	Y	Y	Y	Y
3 ***Smith, Linda***	N	Y	Y	Y	Y	Y	Y	Y
4 ***Hastings***	N	Y	Y	Y	Y	Y	Y	Y
5 ***Nethercutt***	N	Y	Y	Y	Y	Y	Y	Y
6 Dicks	Y	Y	Y	N	Y	Y	N	Y
7 McDermott	Y	N	N	N	Y	Y	N	Y
8 ***Dunn***	N	Y	Y	Y	Y	Y	Y	Y
9 Smith, Adam	Y	Y	Y	N	Y	Y	N	Y
WEST VIRGINIA								
1 Mollohan	Y	?	Y	N	Y	Y	N	Y
2 Wise	Y	Y	Y	N	Y	Y	N	Y
3 Rahall	Y	Y	Y	N	Y	Y	N	Y
WISCONSIN								
1 ***Neumann***	N	Y	Y	Y	Y	Y	N	Y
2 ***Klug***	N	Y	Y	Y	Y	Y	Y	Y
3 Kind	Y	Y	Y	Y	Y	Y	N	Y
4 Kleczka	Y	Y	Y	N	Y	Y	N	Y
5 Barrett	Y	Y	Y	N	Y	Y	N	Y
6 ***Petri***	N	Y	Y	?	Y	Y	Y	Y
7 Obey	Y	Y	Y	N	Y	Y	N	Y
8 Johnson	Y	Y	Y	Y	Y	Y	N	Y
9 ***Sensenbrenner***	N	Y	Y	Y	Y	Y	Y	Y
WYOMING								
AL ***Cubin***	?	?	?	?	?	?	?	?

Southern states - Ala., Ark., Fla., Ga., Ky., La., Miss., N.C., Okla., S.C., Tenn., Texas, Va.

HOUSE VOTES 583, 584, 585, 586, 587, 588, 589, 590

583. H Res 307. Robert K. Dornan Election Challenge/Motion To Table. Thomas, R-Calif., motion to table the Furse, D-Ore., privileged resolution to dismiss the complaint by former Rep. Robert K. Dornan, R-Calif., contesting the election of Loretta Sanchez, D-Calif., by Nov. 7, 1997, unless the House Oversight Committee reports a recommendation for final disposition of the contest before that date. Motion agreed to 217-194: R 216-1; D 1-192 (ND 1-140, SD 0-52); I 0-1, Nov. 5, 1997.

584. Procedural Motion/Adjourn. Armey, R-Texas, motion to adjourn. Motion agreed to 216-192: R 214-2; D 2-189 (ND 2-137, SD 0-52); I 0-1, Nov. 5, 1997.

585. Procedural Motion/Adjourn. Menendez, D-N.J., motion to adjourn. Motion rejected 85-315: R 3-208; D 82-106 (ND 66-73, SD 16-33); I 0-1, Nov. 6, 1997.

586. Procedural Motion/Adjourn. Reyes, D-Texas, motion to adjourn. Motion rejected 100-309: R 3-211; D 97-97 (ND 74-68, SD 23-29); I 0-1, Nov. 6, 1997.

587. H Res 305. Expedited Floor Procedures/Previous Question. Solomon, R-N.Y., motion to order the previous question (thus ending debate and the possibility of amendment) on adoption of the resolution to waive through Nov. 10, 1997, the requirement of a two-thirds majority to consider rules governing floor consideration on the same day as reported by the Rules Committee, allow legislation to be considered under suspension of the rules at any time, restrict members other than the majority or minority leader from offering resolutions as a question of privileges of the House and allow the Speaker to postpone consideration of such resolutions already introduced for the remainder of the first session of the 105th Congress. Motion agreed to 224-198: R 221-0; D 3-197 (ND 3-145, SD 0-52); I 0-1, Nov. 6, 1997.

588. H Res 305. Expedited Floor Procedures/Reconsideration of Vote. Solomon, R-N.Y., motion to table (kill) the Wise, D-W.Va., motion to reconsider the vote by which the House ordered the previous question (thus ending debate and the possibility of amendment) on adoption of the resolution to waive through Nov. 10, 1997, the requirement of a two-thirds majority to consider rules governing floor consideration on the same day as reported by the Rules Committee, allow legislation to be considered under suspension of the rules at any time, restrict members other than the majority or minority leader from offering resolutions as a question of privileges of the House and allow the Speaker to postpone consideration of such resolutions already introduced for the remainder of the first session of the 105th Congress. Motion agreed to 222-200: R 221-0; D 1-199 (ND 1-147, SD 0-52); I 0-1, Nov. 6, 1997.

589. H Res 305. Expedited Floor Procedures/Adoption. Adoption of the resolution to waive through Nov. 10, 1997, the requirement of a two-thirds majority to consider rules governing House floor consideration on the same day as reported by the Rules Committee, allow legislation to be considered under suspension of the rules at any time, restrict members other than the majority or minority leader from offering resolutions as a question of privileges of the House and allow the Speaker to postpone consideration of such resolutions already introduced for the remainder of the first session of the 105th Congress. Motion agreed to 219-195: R 217-0; D 2-194 (ND 2-142, SD 0-52); I 0-1, Nov. 6, 1997.

590. H Res 305. Expedited Floor Procedures/Reconsideration of Vote. Solomon, R-N.Y., motion to table (kill) the Frank, D-Mass., motion to reconsider the vote by which the House adopted the resolution to waive through Nov. 10, 1997, the requirement of a two-thirds majority to consider rules governing floor consideration on the same day as reported by the Rules Committee, allow legislation to be considered under suspension of the rules at any time, restrict members other than the majority or minority leader from offering resolutions as a question of privileges of the House and allow the Speaker to postpone consideration of such resolutions already introduced for the remainder of the first session of the 105th Congress. Motion agreed to 218-201: R 217-0; D 1-200 (ND 1-147, SD 0-53); I 0-1, Nov. 6, 1997.

KEY

- Y Voted for (yea).
- # Paired for.
- \+ Announced for.
- N Voted against (nay).
- X Paired against.
- – Announced against.
- P Voted "present."
- C Voted "present" to avoid possible conflict of interest.
- ? Did not vote or otherwise make a position known.

Democrats ***Republicans***
Independent

	583	584	585	586	587	588	589	590
ALABAMA								
1 ***Callahan***	Y	Y	N	N	Y	Y	Y	Y
2 ***Everett***	Y	Y	N	N	Y	Y	Y	Y
3 ***Riley***	+	+	–	–	+	+	#	+
4 ***Aderholt***	Y	Y	N	N	Y	Y	Y	Y
5 Cramer	N	N	N	N	N	N	N	N
6 ***Bachus***	Y	Y	N	N	Y	Y	Y	Y
7 Hilliard	N	N	N	N	N	N	N	N
ALASKA								
AL ***Young***	?	?	?	N	Y	Y	Y	Y
ARIZONA								
1 ***Salmon***	Y	Y	N	N	Y	Y	Y	Y
2 Pastor	N	N	N	N	N	N	N	N
3 ***Stump***	Y	Y	N	N	Y	Y	Y	Y
4 ***Shadegg***	Y	Y	N	N	Y	Y	Y	Y
5 ***Kolbe***	Y	Y	N	N	Y	Y	Y	Y
6 ***Hayworth***	Y	Y	N	N	Y	Y	Y	Y
ARKANSAS								
1 Berry	N	N	Y	Y	N	N	N	N
2 Snyder	N	N	Y	Y	N	N	N	N
3 ***Hutchinson***	Y	Y	N	N	Y	Y	Y	Y
4 ***Dickey***	Y	Y	N	N	Y	Y	Y	Y
CALIFORNIA								
1 ***Riggs***	Y	Y	N	N	Y	Y	Y	Y
2 ***Herger***	Y	Y	?	N	Y	Y	Y	Y
3 Fazio	N	N	Y	?	N	N	N	N
4 ***Doolittle***	Y	Y	N	N	Y	Y	Y	Y
5 Matsui	N	N	N	N	N	N	N	N
6 Woolsey	N	N	Y	Y	N	N	N	N
7 Miller	N	N	Y	Y	N	N	N	N
8 Pelosi	N	N	Y	Y	N	N	N	N
9 Dellums	N	N	?	Y	?	N	N	N
10 Tauscher	N	N	Y	N	N	N	N	N
11 ***Pombo***	Y	Y	N	N	Y	Y	Y	Y
12 Lantos	N	?	Y	Y	N	N	N	N
13 Stark	?	?	Y	Y	N	N	N	N
14 Eshoo	N	N	Y	Y	N	N	N	N
15 ***Campbell***	Y	Y	N	N	Y	Y	Y	Y
16 Lofgren	N	N	N	N	N	N	N	N
17 Farr	N	N	Y	Y	N	N	N	N
18 Condit	N	N	N	N	N	N	N	N
19 ***Radanovich***	Y	Y	N	N	Y	Y	Y	Y
20 Dooley	N	N	N	N	N	N	N	N
21 ***Thomas***	Y	Y	N	N	Y	Y	Y	Y
22 Vacant								
23 ***Gallegly***	Y	Y	N	N	Y	Y	Y	Y
24 Sherman	N	N	N	N	N	N	N	N
25 ***McKeon***	Y	Y	Y	N	Y	Y	Y	Y
26 Berman	N	N	N	Y	N	N	N	N
27 ***Rogan***	Y	Y	N	N	Y	Y	Y	Y
28 ***Dreier***	Y	Y	N	N	Y	Y	Y	Y
29 Waxman	N	?	N	N	N	N	N	N
30 Becerra	N	N	Y	Y	N	N	N	N
31 Martinez	N	N	N	Y	N	N	N	N
32 Dixon	N	N	?	N	N	N	N	N
33 Roybal-Allard	N	N	?	?	N	N	N	N
34 Torres	N	N	Y	Y	N	N	N	N
35 Waters	N	N	N	Y	N	N	N	N
36 Harman	N	N	N	Y	N	N	N	N
37 Millender-McD.	N	N	Y	Y	N	N	N	N
38 ***Horn***	Y	Y	N	N	Y	Y	Y	Y
39 ***Royce***	Y	Y	N	N	Y	Y	Y	Y
40 ***Lewis***	Y	Y	N	N	Y	Y	Y	Y
41 ***Kim***	Y	Y	N	N	Y	Y	Y	Y
42 Brown	N	N	N	N	N	N	?	N
43 ***Calvert***	Y	Y	N	N	Y	Y	Y	Y
44 ***Bono***	?	?	?	?	Y	Y	Y	Y
45 ***Rohrabacher***	Y	Y	N	N	Y	Y	Y	Y
46 Sanchez	P	?	Y	Y	N	N	N	N
47 ***Cox***	?	?	N	N	Y	Y	Y	Y
48 ***Packard***	Y	Y	N	N	Y	Y	Y	Y
49 ***Bilbray***	Y	Y	N	N	Y	Y	Y	Y
50 Filner	N	N	Y	Y	N	N	N	N
51 ***Cunningham***	Y	Y	N	N	Y	Y	Y	Y
52 ***Hunter***	Y	Y	N	?	Y	Y	Y	Y
COLORADO								
1 DeGette	N	N	N	Y	N	N	N	N
2 Skaggs	N	N	N	N	N	N	?	N
3 ***McInnis***	Y	Y	N	N	Y	Y	Y	Y
4 ***Schaffer***	Y	N	N	N	Y	Y	Y	Y
5 ***Hefley***	Y	Y	N	N	Y	Y	Y	Y
6 ***Schaefer***	Y	Y	N	N	Y	Y	Y	Y
CONNECTICUT								
1 Kennelly	N	N	Y	Y	N	N	N	N
2 Gejdenson	N	N	Y	Y	N	N	N	N
3 DeLauro	N	N	Y	Y	N	N	N	N
4 ***Shays***	Y	Y	N	N	Y	Y	Y	Y
5 Maloney	N	N	N	N	N	N	N	N
6 ***Johnson***	Y	Y	N	N	Y	Y	Y	Y
DELAWARE								
AL ***Castle***	Y	Y	N	N	Y	Y	Y	Y
FLORIDA								
1 ***Scarborough***	?	?	?	N	Y	Y	Y	Y
2 Boyd	N	N	N	N	N	N	N	N
3 Brown	N	N	Y	Y	N	N	N	N
4 ***Fowler***	?	?	N	N	Y	Y	Y	Y
5 Thurman	N	N	Y	Y	N	N	N	N
6 ***Stearns***	Y	Y	N	N	Y	Y	Y	Y
7 ***Mica***	Y	Y	–	–	+	+	+	+
8 ***McCollum***	Y	Y	N	N	Y	Y	Y	Y
9 ***Bilirakis***	Y	Y	N	N	Y	Y	Y	Y
10 ***Young***	Y	Y	N	N	Y	Y	Y	Y
11 Davis	N	N	N	N	N	N	N	N
12 ***Canady***	Y	Y	N	N	Y	Y	Y	Y
13 ***Miller***	Y	Y	N	N	Y	Y	Y	Y
14 ***Goss***	Y	Y	N	N	Y	Y	Y	Y
15 ***Weldon***	Y	Y	N	N	Y	Y	Y	Y
16 ***Foley***	Y	Y	N	N	Y	Y	+	Y
17 Meek	N	N	Y	Y	N	N	N	N
18 ***Ros-Lehtinen***	Y	Y	N	N	Y	Y	Y	Y
19 Wexler	N	N	N	N	N	N	N	N
20 Deutsch	N	N	Y	Y	N	N	N	N
21 ***Diaz-Balart***	Y	Y	N	N	Y	Y	Y	Y
22 ***Shaw***	Y	Y	N	N	Y	Y	Y	Y
23 Hastings	N	N	Y	Y	N	N	N	N
GEORGIA								
1 ***Kingston***	Y	Y	N	N	Y	Y	Y	Y
2 Bishop	N	N	?	Y	N	N	N	N
3 ***Collins***	Y	Y	?	N	Y	Y	Y	Y
4 McKinney	?	?	?	?	?	?	X	?
5 Lewis	N	N	?	?	N	N	N	N
6 ***Gingrich***								
7 ***Barr***	Y	Y	N	N	Y	Y	Y	Y
8 ***Chambliss***	Y	Y	N	Y	Y	Y	Y	Y
9 ***Deal***	Y	Y	N	N	Y	Y	Y	Y
10 ***Norwood***	Y	?	N	N	Y	Y	Y	Y
11 ***Linder***	Y	Y	N	N	Y	Y	Y	Y
HAWAII								
1 Abercrombie	N	N	N	N	N	N	N	N
2 Mink	N	N	?	?	N	N	N	N
IDAHO								
1 ***Chenoweth***	Y	Y	N	N	Y	Y	Y	Y
2 ***Crapo***	Y	Y	N	N	Y	Y	Y	Y
ILLINOIS								
1 Rush	N	N	Y	N	N	N	N	N
2 Jackson	N	N	Y	Y	N	N	N	N
3 Lipinski	N	N	N	N	N	N	N	N
4 Gutierrez	N	N	N	N	N	N	N	N
5 Blagojevich	N	N	N	N	N	N	N	N
6 ***Hyde***	Y	Y	N	N	Y	Y	Y	Y
7 Davis	N	N	Y	N	N	N	N	N
8 ***Crane***	Y	Y	?	?	Y	Y	Y	Y
9 Yates	?	?	N	?	N	N	N	N
10 ***Porter***	Y	Y	N	?	Y	Y	Y	Y
11 ***Weller***	Y	Y	N	N	Y	Y	Y	Y
12 Costello	N	N	N	N	N	N	N	N
13 ***Fawell***	?	?	N	N	Y	Y	Y	Y
14 ***Hastert***	Y	Y	N	N	Y	Y	Y	Y
15 ***Ewing***	Y	Y	N	N	Y	Y	Y	Y

ND Northern Democrats SD Southern Democrats

	583	584	585	586	587	588	589	590
16 ***Manzullo***	Y	Y	N	N	Y	Y	Y	Y
17 Evans	N	N	Y	Y	N	N	N	N
18 ***LaHood***	Y	Y	N	N	Y	Y	Y	Y
19 Poshard	N	N	N	N	N	N	N	N
20 ***Shimkus***	Y	Y	N	N	Y	Y	Y	Y
INDIANA								
1 Visclosky	N	N	N	N	N	N	N	N
2 ***McIntosh***	Y	Y	N	N	Y	Y	Y	Y
3 Roemer	N	N	N	N	N	N	N	N
4 ***Souder***	Y	Y	N	N	Y	Y	Y	Y
5 ***Buyer***	Y	Y	N	N	Y	Y	Y	Y
6 ***Burton***	Y	Y	N	N	Y	Y	Y	Y
7 ***Pease***	Y	Y	N	N	Y	Y	Y	Y
8 ***Hostettler***	Y	Y	N	N	Y	Y	Y	Y
9 Hamilton	N	N	N	N	N	N	N	N
10 Carson	N	N	–	–	–	–	–	–
IOWA								
1 ***Leach***	Y	Y	?	?	Y	Y	?	?
2 ***Nussle***	Y	Y	N	N	Y	Y	Y	Y
3 Boswell	N	N	Y	N	N	N	N	N
4 ***Ganske***	Y	Y	N	N	Y	Y	Y	Y
5 ***Latham***	Y	Y	N	N	Y	Y	Y	Y
KANSAS								
1 ***Moran***	Y	Y	N	N	Y	Y	Y	Y
2 ***Ryun***	Y	Y	N	N	Y	Y	Y	Y
3 ***Snowbarger***	Y	Y	N	N	Y	Y	Y	Y
4 ***Tiahrt***	Y	Y	N	N	Y	Y	Y	Y
KENTUCKY								
1 ***Whitfield***	Y	Y	N	N	Y	Y	Y	Y
2 ***Lewis***	Y	Y	N	N	Y	Y	Y	Y
3 ***Northup***	Y	Y	N	N	Y	Y	Y	Y
4 ***Bunning***	Y	Y	N	N	Y	Y	Y	Y
5 ***Rogers***	Y	Y	N	N	Y	Y	Y	Y
6 Baesler	N	N	N	N	N	N	N	N
LOUISIANA								
1 ***Livingston***	Y	Y	N	N	Y	Y	Y	Y
2 Jefferson	N	N	?	Y	N	N	N	N
3 ***Tauzin***	Y	Y	N	N	Y	Y	Y	Y
4 ***McCrery***	Y	Y	?	N	Y	Y	Y	Y
5 ***Cooksey***	Y	Y	N	N	Y	Y	Y	Y
6 ***Baker***	Y	Y	N	N	Y	Y	Y	Y
7 John	N	N	N	N	N	N	N	N
MAINE								
1 Allen	N	N	N	N	N	N	N	N
2 Baldacci	N	N	N	N	N	N	?	N
MARYLAND								
1 ***Gilchrest***	Y	Y	N	N	Y	Y	Y	Y
2 ***Ehrlich***	Y	Y	N	N	Y	Y	Y	Y
3 Cardin	N	N	N	N	N	N	N	N
4 Wynn	N	N	N	N	N	N	N	N
5 Hoyer	N	N	N	N	N	N	N	N
6 ***Bartlett***	Y	Y	N	N	Y	Y	Y	Y
7 Cummings	N	N	Y	Y	N	N	N	N
8 ***Morella***	Y	Y	N	N	Y	Y	Y	Y
MASSACHUSETTS								
1 Olver	N	N	Y	Y	N	N	N	N
2 Neal	N	N	N	Y	N	N	N	N
3 McGovern	N	N	Y	Y	N	N	N	N
4 Frank	N	N	Y	Y	N	N	Y	N
5 Meehan	N	N	N	N	N	?	N	N
6 Tierney	N	N	N	Y	N	N	N	N
7 Markey	N	N	Y	Y	N	N	N	N
8 Kennedy	N	N	?	?	N	N	N	N
9 Moakley	?	?	N	Y	N	N	N	N
10 Delahunt	N	N	N	Y	N	N	N	N
MICHIGAN								
1 Stupak	N	N	Y	Y	N	N	N	N
2 ***Hoekstra***	Y	Y	N	N	Y	Y	Y	Y
3 ***Ehlers***	Y	Y	N	N	Y	Y	Y	Y
4 ***Camp***	Y	Y	N	N	Y	Y	Y	Y
5 Barcia	N	N	N	N	N	N	N	N
6 ***Upton***	Y	Y	N	N	Y	Y	Y	Y
7 ***Smith***	Y	Y	N	N	Y	Y	Y	Y
8 Stabenow	N	N	Y	Y	N	N	N	N
9 Kildee	N	N	N	N	N	N	N	N
10 Bonior	N	N	?	Y	N	N	N	N
11 ***Knollenberg***	Y	Y	N	N	Y	Y	Y	Y
12 Levin	N	N	Y	Y	N	N	N	N
13 Rivers	N	N	N	N	N	N	N	N
14 Conyers	N	Y	Y	Y	N	N	?	N
15 Kilpatrick	N	N	Y	Y	N	N	N	N
16 Dingell	N	N	Y	Y	N	N	N	N
MINNESOTA								
1 ***Gutknecht***	Y	Y	N	N	Y	Y	Y	Y
2 Minge	N	N	N	N	N	N	N	N

	583	584	585	586	587	588	589	590
3 ***Ramstad***	Y	Y	N	N	Y	Y	Y	Y
4 Vento	N	N	N	Y	N	N	N	N
5 Sabo	N	N	Y	Y	N	N	N	N
6 Luther	N	N	N	N	N	N	N	N
7 Peterson	N	N	Y	Y	N	N	N	N
8 Oberstar	N	N	Y	Y	N	N	N	N
MISSISSIPPI								
1 ***Wicker***	Y	Y	N	N	Y	Y	Y	Y
2 Thompson	N	N	Y	Y	N	N	N	N
3 ***Pickering***	Y	Y	N	N	Y	Y	Y	Y
4 ***Parker***	Y	Y	N	N	Y	Y	Y	Y
5 Taylor	N	N	N	N	N	N	N	N
MISSOURI								
1 Clay	N	N	N	N	N	N	N	N
2 ***Talent***	Y	Y	N	N	Y	Y	Y	Y
3 Gephardt	N	N	?	Y	N	N	N	N
4 Skelton	?	N	N	Y	N	N	N	N
5 McCarthy	N	N	Y	Y	N	N	N	N
6 Danner	N	N	N	N	N	N	N	N
7 ***Blunt***	Y	Y	N	N	Y	Y	Y	Y
8 ***Emerson***	Y	Y	N	N	Y	Y	Y	Y
9 ***Hulshof***	Y	Y	N	N	Y	Y	Y	Y
MONTANA								
AL ***Hill***	Y	Y	N	N	Y	Y	Y	Y
NEBRASKA								
1 ***Bereuter***	Y	Y	N	N	Y	Y	Y	Y
2 ***Christensen***	Y	Y	N	N	Y	Y	Y	Y
3 ***Barrett***	Y	Y	N	N	Y	Y	Y	Y
NEVADA								
1 ***Ensign***	Y	Y	N	N	Y	Y	Y	Y
2 ***Gibbons***	Y	Y	N	N	Y	Y	Y	Y
NEW HAMPSHIRE								
1 ***Sununu***	Y	Y	N	N	Y	Y	Y	Y
2 ***Bass***	Y	Y	N	N	Y	Y	Y	Y
NEW JERSEY								
1 Andrews	N	N	Y	Y	N	N	N	N
2 ***LoBiondo***	Y	Y	N	N	Y	Y	Y	Y
3 ***Saxton***	Y	Y	N	N	Y	Y	Y	Y
4 ***Smith***	Y	Y	N	N	Y	Y	Y	Y
5 ***Roukema***	Y	Y	N	N	Y	Y	Y	Y
6 Pallone	N	N	Y	Y	N	N	N	N
7 ***Franks***	Y	Y	N	N	Y	Y	Y	Y
8 Pascrell	N	N	N	N	N	N	N	N
9 Rothman	N	N	N	N	N	N	N	N
10 Payne	N	N	Y	Y	N	N	N	N
11 ***Frelinghuysen***	Y	Y	N	N	Y	Y	Y	Y
12 ***Pappas***	Y	Y	N	N	Y	Y	Y	Y
13 Menendez	N	N	Y	Y	N	N	N	N
NEW MEXICO								
1 ***Schiff***	?	?	?	?	?	?	?	?
2 ***Skeen***	Y	Y	N	N	Y	Y	Y	Y
3 ***Redmond***	Y	Y	N	N	Y	Y	Y	Y
NEW YORK								
1 ***Forbes***	N	N	–	–	–	+	+	+
2 ***Lazio***	Y	Y	N	N	Y	Y	Y	Y
3 ***King***	Y	Y	N	N	Y	Y	Y	Y
4 McCarthy	N	N	N	N	N	N	N	N
5 Ackerman	N	N	N	Y	N	N	N	N
6 Flake	?	?	N	N	N	N	N	N
7 Manton	N	N	N	N	N	N	N	N
8 Nadler	N	N	Y	Y	N	N	N	N
9 Schumer	N	N	N	N	N	N	N	N
10 Towns	N	N	?	Y	N	N	N	N
11 Owens	N	N	Y	Y	N	N	N	N
12 Velázquez	N	N	Y	Y	N	N	N	N
13 ***Fossella***	Y	Y	N	N	Y	Y	Y	Y
14 Maloney	N	N	N	N	N	N	N	N
15 Rangel	N	N	?	?	N	N	N	N
16 Serrano	N	N	N	N	N	N	N	N
17 Engel	N	N	Y	Y	N	N	N	N
18 Lowey	N	N	N	Y	N	N	N	N
19 ***Kelly***	Y	Y	N	N	Y	Y	Y	Y
20 ***Gilman***	Y	Y	N	N	Y	Y	Y	Y
21 McNulty	N	N	Y	Y	N	N	N	N
22 ***Solomon***	Y	Y	N	N	Y	Y	Y	Y
23 ***Boehlert***	Y	Y	N	N	Y	Y	Y	Y
24 ***McHugh***	Y	Y	N	N	Y	Y	Y	Y
25 ***Walsh***	Y	Y	N	N	Y	Y	Y	Y
26 Hinchey	N	N	Y	Y	N	N	N	N
27 ***Paxon***	Y	Y	N	N	Y	Y	Y	Y
28 Slaughter	N	N	Y	Y	N	N	N	N
29 LaFalce	N	N	Y	Y	N	N	N	N
30 ***Quinn***	Y	Y	N	N	Y	Y	Y	Y
31 ***Houghton***	Y	Y	N	N	Y	Y	Y	Y

	583	584	585	586	587	588	589	590
NORTH CAROLINA								
1 Clayton	N	N	N	Y	N	N	N	N
2 Etheridge	N	N	N	Y	N	N	N	N
3 ***Jones***	Y	Y	N	N	Y	Y	Y	Y
4 Price	N	N	N	N	N	N	N	N
5 ***Burr***	Y	Y	N	?	Y	Y	Y	Y
6 ***Coble***	Y	Y	N	N	Y	Y	Y	Y
7 McIntyre	N	N	N	N	N	N	N	N
8 Hefner	N	N	N	Y	N	N	N	N
9 ***Myrick***	Y	Y	N	N	Y	Y	Y	Y
10 ***Ballenger***	Y	Y	N	N	Y	Y	Y	Y
11 ***Taylor***	Y	Y	N	N	Y	Y	Y	Y
12 Watt	N	N	N	N	N	N	N	N
NORTH DAKOTA								
AL Pomeroy	N	N	Y	N	N	N	N	N
OHIO								
1 ***Chabot***	Y	Y	N	N	Y	Y	Y	Y
2 ***Portman***	Y	Y	–	–	+	+	+	+
3 Hall	?	?	Y	N	N	N	N	N
4 ***Oxley***	Y	Y	?	N	Y	Y	?	Y
5 ***Gillmor***	Y	Y	N	N	Y	Y	Y	Y
6 Strickland	N	N	Y	Y	N	N	N	N
7 ***Hobson***	Y	Y	N	N	Y	Y	Y	Y
8 ***Boehner***	Y	Y	N	N	Y	Y	Y	Y
9 Kaptur	N	N	N	N	N	N	N	N
10 Kucinich	N	N	N	N	N	N	N	N
11 Stokes	N	?	N	N	N	N	N	N
12 ***Kasich***	Y	Y	N	N	Y	Y	Y	Y
13 Brown	N	N	Y	Y	Y	N	N	N
14 Sawyer	N	N	N	Y	N	N	N	N
15 ***Pryce***	Y	Y	N	N	Y	Y	Y	Y
16 ***Regula***	Y	Y	N	N	Y	Y	Y	Y
17 Traficant	Y	Y	N	N	Y	Y	Y	Y
18 ***Ney***	Y	Y	N	N	Y	Y	Y	Y
19 ***LaTourette***	Y	Y	N	N	Y	Y	Y	Y
OKLAHOMA								
1 ***Largent***	Y	Y	N	N	Y	Y	Y	Y
2 ***Coburn***	Y	Y	N	N	Y	Y	Y	?
3 ***Watkins***	Y	Y	N	N	Y	Y	?	Y
4 ***Watts***	Y	Y	N	N	Y	Y	Y	?
5 ***Istook***	Y	Y	N	N	Y	Y	Y	Y
6 ***Lucas***	Y	Y	N	N	Y	Y	Y	Y
OREGON								
1 Furse	N	N	Y	Y	N	N	N	N
2 ***Smith***	?	?	N	N	Y	Y	Y	Y
3 Blumenauer	N	N	Y	Y	N	N	N	N
4 DeFazio	N	N	Y	Y	N	N	N	N
5 Hooley	N	N	N	N	N	N	N	N
PENNSYLVANIA								
1 Foglietta	?	?	?	?	N	N	?	N
2 Fattah	N	N	N	N	N	N	N	N
3 Borski	N	N	N	N	N	N	N	N
4 Klink	N	N	N	N	N	N	N	N
5 ***Peterson***	Y	Y	N	N	Y	Y	Y	Y
6 Holden	N	N	N	N	N	N	N	N
7 ***Weldon***	Y	Y	N	N	Y	Y	Y	Y
8 ***Greenwood***	Y	Y	N	N	Y	Y	Y	Y
9 ***Shuster***	Y	Y	N	N	Y	Y	Y	Y
10 ***McDade***	Y	Y	N	N	Y	Y	Y	Y
11 Kanjorski	N	N	N	N	N	N	N	N
12 Murtha	?	?	N	N	N	N	N	N
13 ***Fox***	Y	Y	N	N	Y	Y	Y	Y
14 Coyne	N	N	Y	Y	N	N	N	N
15 McHale	N	N	N	N	N	N	N	N
16 ***Pitts***	Y	Y	N	N	Y	Y	Y	Y
17 ***Gekas***	Y	Y	N	N	Y	Y	Y	Y
18 Doyle	N	N	N	N	N	N	N	N
19 ***Goodling***	Y	Y	N	N	Y	Y	Y	Y
20 Mascara	N	N	N	N	N	N	N	N
21 ***English***	Y	Y	N	N	Y	Y	Y	Y
RHODE ISLAND								
1 Kennedy	N	N	Y	Y	N	N	N	N
2 Weygand	N	N	N	N	N	N	N	N
SOUTH CAROLINA								
1 ***Sanford***	Y	Y	N	N	Y	Y	Y	Y
2 ***Spence***	Y	Y	N	N	Y	Y	Y	Y
3 ***Graham***	Y	Y	N	N	Y	Y	Y	Y
4 ***Inglis***	Y	Y	N	N	Y	Y	Y	Y
5 Spratt	N	N	Y	Y	N	N	N	N
6 Clyburn	N	N	Y	Y	N	N	N	N
SOUTH DAKOTA								
AL ***Thune***	Y	Y	N	N	Y	Y	Y	Y
TENNESSEE								
1 ***Jenkins***	Y	Y	N	N	Y	Y	Y	Y
2 ***Duncan***	Y	Y	N	N	Y	Y	Y	Y

	583	584	585	586	587	588	589	
3 ***Wamp***	Y	Y	N	N	Y	Y	Y	Y
4 ***Hilleary***	Y	Y	Y	Y	Y	Y	Y	Y
5 Clement	?	?	Y	Y	N	N	N	N
6 Gordon	N	N	N	N	N	N	N	N
7 ***Bryant***	Y	Y	N	N	Y	Y	Y	Y
8 Tanner	N	N	N	N	N	N	N	N
9 Ford	N	N	N	N	N	N	N	N
TEXAS								
1 Sandlin	N	N	N	N	N	N	N	N
2 Turner	N	N	N	N	N	N	N	N
3 ***Johnson, Sam***	Y	Y	N	N	Y	Y	Y	Y
4 Hall	N	N	N	N	N	N	N	N
5 ***Sessions***	Y	Y	N	N	Y	Y	Y	Y
6 ***Barton***	Y	Y	N	N	Y	Y	Y	Y
7 ***Archer***	Y	Y	N	N	Y	Y	Y	?
8 ***Brady***	Y	Y	N	Y	Y	Y	Y	Y
9 Lampson	N	N	N	Y	N	N	N	N
10 Doggett	N	N	Y	Y	N	N	N	N
11 Edwards	N	N	N	N	N	N	N	N
12 ***Granger***	Y	Y	N	N	Y	Y	Y	Y
13 ***Thornberry***	Y	Y	N	?	Y	Y	Y	Y
14 ***Paul***	Y	Y	?	N	Y	Y	Y	Y
15 Hinojosa	N	N	Y	Y	N	N	N	N
16 Reyes	N	N	Y	Y	N	N	N	N
17 Stenholm	N	N	N	N	N	N	N	N
18 Jackson-Lee	N	N	Y	Y	N	N	N	N
19 ***Combest***	Y	Y	N	N	Y	Y	Y	Y
20 Gonzalez	?	?	?	?	?	?	?	?
21 ***Smith***	Y	Y	N	N	Y	Y	Y	Y
22 ***DeLay***	Y	Y	N	N	Y	Y	Y	Y
23 ***Bonilla***	Y	Y	N	N	Y	Y	Y	Y
24 Frost	N	N	N	N	N	N	N	N
25 Bentsen	N	N	N	N	N	N	N	N
26 ***Armey***	Y	Y	N	N	Y	Y	Y	Y
27 Ortiz	N	N	N	N	N	N	N	N
28 Rodriguez	N	N	N	N	N	N	N	N
29 Green	N	N	N	N	N	N	N	N
30 Johnson, E.B.	N	N	Y	Y	N	N	N	N
UTAH								
1 ***Hansen***	Y	Y	N	N	Y	Y	Y	Y
2 ***Cook***	Y	Y	N	N	Y	Y	Y	Y
3 ***Cannon***	Y	Y	N	N	Y	Y	Y	Y
VERMONT								
AL *Sanders*	N	N	N	N	N	N	N	N
VIRGINIA								
1 ***Bateman***	Y	Y	N	N	Y	Y	Y	Y
2 Pickett	N	N	N	N	N	N	N	N
3 Scott	N	N	N	N	N	N	N	N
4 Sisisky	N	N	N	N	N	N	N	N
5 Goode	N	N	N	N	N	N	N	N
6 ***Goodlatte***	Y	Y	N	N	Y	Y	Y	Y
7 ***Bliley***	Y	Y	N	N	Y	Y	Y	Y
8 Moran	N	N	N	N	?	?	?	N
9 Boucher	N	N	?	Y	N	N	N	N
10 ***Wolf***	Y	Y	N	N	Y	Y	Y	Y
11 ***Davis***	Y	Y	N	N	Y	Y	Y	Y
WASHINGTON								
1 ***White***	Y	Y	N	N	Y	Y	Y	Y
2 ***Metcalf***	Y	Y	Y	N	Y	Y	Y	Y
3 ***Smith, Linda***	Y	Y	N	N	Y	Y	Y	Y
4 ***Hastings***	Y	Y	N	N	Y	Y	Y	Y
5 ***Nethercutt***	Y	Y	N	N	Y	Y	Y	Y
6 Dicks	N	N	Y	N	N	N	N	N
7 McDermott	N	N	Y	Y	N	N	N	N
8 ***Dunn***	Y	Y	N	N	Y	Y	Y	Y
9 Smith, Adam	N	N	Y	N	N	N	N	?
WEST VIRGINIA								
1 Mollohan	N	N	N	N	N	N	N	N
2 Wise	N	N	Y	Y	Y	N	N	N
3 Rahall	N	N	N	N	N	N	N	N
WISCONSIN								
1 ***Neumann***	Y	Y	N	N	Y	Y	Y	Y
2 ***Klug***	Y	Y	N	N	Y	Y	Y	Y
3 Kind	N	N	Y	N	N	N	N	N
4 Kleczka	N	N	N	N	N	N	N	N
5 Barrett	N	N	Y	Y	N	N	N	N
6 ***Petri***	Y	Y	N	N	Y	Y	Y	Y
7 Obey	N	N	Y	Y	N	N	N	N
8 Johnson	N	N	Y	Y	N	N	N	N
9 ***Sensenbrenner***	Y	Y	N	N	Y	Y	Y	Y
WYOMING								
AL ***Cubin***	?	?	?	?	?	?	?	?

Southern states - Ala., Ark., Fla., Ga., Ky., La., Miss., N.C., Okla., S.C., Tenn., Texas, Va.

HOUSE VOTES 591, 592, 593, 594, 595, 596, 597, 598

591. Procedural Motion/Adjourn. Martinez, D-Calif., motion to adjourn. Motion rejected 79-333: R 0-217; D 79-115 (ND 58-84, SD 21-31); I 0-1, Nov. 6, 1997.

592. H Res 188. Chinese Missile Exports to Iran/Adoption. Adoption of the resolution to urge the president to sanction China for transferring C-802 cruise missiles to Iran. Such presidential action would be in accordance with the Iran-Iraq Arms Non-Proliferation Act of 1992 (PL 102-484), which imposes U.S. sanctions on countries that transfer advanced conventional weapons to Iran or Iraq. Adopted 414-8: R 220-1; D 193-7 (ND 142-5, SD 51-2); I 1-0, Nov. 6, 1997.

593. H Res 188. Chinese Missile Exports to Iran/Reconsideration of Vote. Latham, R-Iowa, motion to table (kill) the Velázquez, D-N.Y., motion to reconsider the vote by which the House adopted the resolution to urge the president to sanction China for transferring C-802 cruise missiles to Iran. Such presidential action would be in accordance with the Iran-Iraq Arms Non-Proliferation Act of 1992 (PL 102-484), which imposes U.S. sanctions on countries that transfer advanced conventional weapons to Iran or Iraq. Motion agreed to 240-176: R 219-0; D 21-175 (ND 6-138, SD 15-37); I 0-1, Nov. 6, 1997.

594. Procedural Motion/Adjourn. Torres, D-Calif., motion to adjourn. Motion rejected 74-336: R 0-215; D 74-120 (ND 57-84, SD 17-36); I 0-1, Nov. 6, 1997.

595. HR 967. Religious Persecution in China/Passage. Passage of the bill to deny U.S. visas to Chinese officials involved in government-created organizations that formulate or implement policies that repress practices of free religious expression. Passed 366-54: R 217-3; D 148-51 (ND 105-41, SD 43-10); I 1-0, Nov. 6, 1997. A "nay" was a vote in support of the president's position.

596. HR 967. Religious Persecution in China/Reconsideration of Vote. Kolbe, R-Ariz., motion to table (kill) the Wise, D-W.Va., motion to reconsider the vote by which the House passed the bill to deny U.S. visas to Chinese officials involved in government-created organizations that formulate or implement policies that repress practices of free religious expression. Motion agreed to 227-185: R 217-0; D 10-184 (ND 5-138, SD 5-46); I 0-1, Nov. 6, 1997.

597. Procedural Motion/Adjourn. Mink, D-Hawaii, motion to adjourn. Motion rejected 75-333: R 2-209; D 73-123 (ND 60-84, SD 13-39); I 0-1, Nov. 6, 1997.

598. HR 2570. Forced Abortions in China/Passage. Passage of the bill to deny U.S. visas to Chinese officials known to be involved in the establishment or enforcement of population control activities resulting in forced abortion or sterilization. Passed 415-1: R 221-0; D 193-1 (ND 141-1, SD 52-0); I 1-0, Nov. 6, 1997. A "nay" was a vote in support of the president's position.

KEY

Y Voted for (yea).
\# Paired for.
\+ Announced for.
N Voted against (nay).
X Paired against.
\- Announced against.
P Voted "present."
C Voted "present" to avoid possible conflict of interest.
? Did not vote or otherwise make a position known.

Democrats ***Republicans***
Independent

	591	592	593	594	595	596	597	598
ALABAMA								
1 ***Callahan***	N	Y	Y	N	Y	Y	N	Y
2 ***Everett***	N	Y	Y	N	Y	Y	N	Y
3 ***Riley***	-	+	+	-	+	+	-	+
4 ***Aderholt***	N	Y	Y	N	Y	Y	N	Y
5 Cramer	N	Y	N	N	Y	N	N	Y
6 ***Bachus***	N	Y	Y	N	Y	Y	N	Y
7 Hilliard	N	Y	N	N	N	N	N	Y
ALASKA								
AL ***Young***	N	Y	Y	N	Y	Y	N	Y
ARIZONA								
1 ***Salmon***	N	Y	Y	N	Y	Y	N	Y
2 Pastor	Y	Y	N	N	Y	N	N	Y
3 ***Stump***	N	Y	Y	N	Y	Y	N	Y
4 ***Shadegg***	N	Y	Y	N	Y	Y	N	Y
5 ***Kolbe***	N	Y	Y	N	Y	Y	N	Y
6 ***Hayworth***	N	Y	Y	N	Y	Y	N	Y
ARKANSAS								
1 Berry	Y	Y	Y	Y	Y	N	N	Y
2 Snyder	N	Y	N	N	Y	N	N	Y
3 ***Hutchinson***	N	Y	Y	N	Y	Y	?	Y
4 ***Dickey***	N	Y	Y	N	Y	Y	N	Y
CALIFORNIA								
1 ***Riggs***	N	Y	Y	N	Y	?	N	Y
2 ***Herger***	N	Y	Y	N	Y	Y	N	Y
3 Fazio	Y	Y	N	Y	N	N	Y	Y
4 ***Doolittle***	N	Y	Y	N	Y	Y	N	Y
5 Matsui	N	Y	N	N	Y	N	N	Y
6 Woolsey	Y	Y	N	Y	Y	N	Y	Y
7 Miller	Y	Y	N	Y	Y	N	Y	Y
8 Pelosi	N	Y	N	Y	Y	N	Y	Y
9 Dellums	?	Y	N	N	N	N	N	Y
10 Tauscher	N	Y	N	N	Y	N	N	?
11 ***Pombo***	N	Y	Y	N	Y	Y	N	Y
12 Lantos	Y	Y	N	Y	Y	N	Y	?
13 Stark	Y	Y	N	Y	Y	N	N	Y
14 Eshoo	Y	Y	N	Y	Y	N	Y	Y
15 ***Campbell***	N	Y	Y	N	Y	Y	N	Y
16 Lofgren	N	Y	N	N	N	N	N	Y
17 Farr	N	Y	N	N	Y	N	N	Y
18 Condit	N	Y	Y	N	Y	N	N	Y
19 ***Radanovich***	N	Y	Y	N	Y	Y	N	Y
20 Dooley	N	Y	N	N	Y	N	N	Y
21 ***Thomas***	N	Y	Y	?	Y	Y	N	Y
22 Vacant								
23 ***Gallegly***	N	Y	Y	N	Y	Y	N	Y
24 Sherman	N	Y	N	N	N	N	N	Y
25 ***McKeon***	N	Y	Y	N	Y	Y	N	Y
26 Berman	N	Y	N	N	N	N	N	Y
27 ***Rogan***	N	Y	Y	N	Y	Y	N	Y
28 ***Dreier***	N	Y	Y	N	Y	Y	N	Y
29 Waxman	Y	Y	N	Y	N	N	Y	?
30 Becerra	Y	Y	N	?	N	N	?	Y
31 Martinez	Y	Y	Y	?	N	N	N	Y
32 Dixon	N	Y	N	N	Y	N	N	Y
33 Roybal-Allard	Y	Y	N	Y	N	N	Y	Y
34 Torres	Y	Y	N	Y	Y	N	Y	Y
35 Waters	Y	Y	N	Y	N	?	Y	Y
36 Harman	Y	Y	N	Y	Y	N	Y	Y
37 Millender-McD.	?	Y	N	Y	N	N	N	Y
38 ***Horn***	N	Y	Y	N	Y	Y	N	Y
39 ***Royce***	N	Y	Y	N	Y	Y	N	Y
40 ***Lewis***	N	Y	Y	?	Y	Y	N	Y
41 ***Kim***	N	Y	Y	N	Y	Y	N	Y
42 Brown	?	?	?	?	N	N	N	N
43 ***Calvert***	N	Y	Y	N	Y	Y	N	Y
44 ***Bono***	N	Y	Y	N	Y	Y	N	Y
45 ***Rohrabacher***	N	Y	Y	N	Y	Y	N	Y
46 Sanchez	Y	Y	N	Y	Y	N	Y	Y
47 ***Cox***	N	Y	Y	N	Y	Y	N	Y
48 ***Packard***	N	Y	Y	N	Y	Y	N	Y
49 ***Bilbray***	N	Y	Y	N	Y	Y	N	Y
50 Filner	Y	Y	N	Y	Y	N	Y	Y
51 ***Cunningham***	N	Y	Y	N	Y	Y	N	Y
52 ***Hunter***	?	Y	Y	N	Y	Y	N	Y
COLORADO								
1 DeGette	N	Y	N	N	Y	N	N	Y
2 Skaggs	N	N	N	N	N	N	N	Y
3 ***McInnis***	N	Y	Y	N	Y	Y	N	Y
4 ***Schaffer***	N	Y	Y	N	Y	Y	Y	Y
5 ***Hefley***	N	Y	Y	N	Y	Y	N	Y
6 ***Schaefer***	N	Y	Y	N	Y	Y	N	Y
CONNECTICUT								
1 Kennelly	Y	Y	N	Y	N	N	Y	Y
2 Gejdenson	Y	Y	N	Y	N	Y	Y	Y
3 DeLauro	Y	Y	N	Y	N	N	Y	Y
4 ***Shays***	N	Y	Y	N	Y	Y	N	Y
5 Maloney	N	Y	N	N	Y	N	N	Y
6 ***Johnson***	N	Y	Y	N	N	Y	N	Y
DELAWARE								
AL ***Castle***	N	Y	Y	N	Y	Y	N	Y
FLORIDA								
1 ***Scarborough***	N	Y	Y	N	Y	Y	N	Y
2 Boyd	Y	Y	Y	N	Y	Y	N	Y
3 Brown	Y	Y	N	Y	Y	N	Y	Y
4 ***Fowler***	N	Y	Y	N	Y	Y	N	Y
5 Thurman	Y	Y	N	Y	Y	N	Y	Y
6 ***Stearns***	N	Y	Y	N	Y	Y	N	Y
7 ***Mica***	-	+	+	-	+	+	-	Y
8 ***McCollum***	N	Y	Y	N	Y	Y	N	Y
9 ***Bilirakis***	N	Y	Y	N	Y	Y	N	Y
10 ***Young***	N	Y	Y	N	Y	Y	N	Y
11 Davis	Y	Y	Y	Y	N	?	Y	Y
12 ***Canady***	N	Y	Y	N	Y	Y	N	Y
13 ***Miller***	N	Y	Y	N	Y	Y	?	Y
14 ***Goss***	N	Y	Y	N	Y	Y	N	Y
15 ***Weldon***	N	Y	Y	N	Y	Y	N	Y
16 ***Foley***	N	Y	Y	N	Y	Y	N	Y
17 Meek	Y	Y	N	Y	Y	N	Y	Y
18 ***Ros-Lehtinen***	N	Y	Y	N	Y	Y	N	+
19 Wexler	N	Y	Y	N	N	N	N	Y
20 Deutsch	Y	Y	N	Y	Y	N	Y	Y
21 ***Diaz-Balart***	N	Y	Y	N	Y	Y	N	Y
22 ***Shaw***	N	Y	Y	N	Y	Y	N	Y
23 Hastings	Y	Y	Y	Y	N	N	Y	Y
GEORGIA								
1 ***Kingston***	N	Y	Y	N	Y	Y	N	Y
2 Bishop	N	Y	N	Y	Y	N	N	Y
3 ***Collins***	N	Y	Y	N	Y	Y	N	Y
4 McKinney	?	?	?	?	?	?	?	?
5 Lewis	Y	Y	N	Y	Y	N	Y	Y
6 ***Gingrich***								
7 ***Barr***	N	Y	Y	N	Y	Y	?	Y
8 ***Chambliss***	N	Y	Y	N	Y	Y	N	Y
9 ***Deal***	N	Y	Y	N	Y	Y	N	Y
10 ***Norwood***	N	Y	Y	N	Y	Y	N	Y
11 ***Linder***	N	Y	Y	N	Y	Y	N	Y
HAWAII								
1 Abercrombie	N	Y	N	N	Y	Y	N	Y
2 Mink	Y	Y	N	Y	N	N	Y	Y
IDAHO								
1 ***Chenoweth***	N	Y	Y	N	Y	Y	N	Y
2 ***Crapo***	N	Y	Y	N	Y	Y	N	Y
ILLINOIS								
1 Rush	N	Y	N	Y	N	N	N	Y
2 Jackson	Y	Y	N	Y	Y	N	Y	Y
3 Lipinski	N	Y	N	N	Y	N	N	Y
4 Gutierrez	N	Y	N	?	?	?	N	Y
5 Blagojevich	N	Y	N	N	Y	N	N	Y
6 ***Hyde***	N	Y	Y	N	Y	Y	N	Y
7 Davis	N	Y	N	N	N	N	N	Y
8 ***Crane***	N	Y	Y	N	Y	Y	N	Y
9 Yates	?	N	N	N	N	N	Y	?
10 ***Porter***	N	Y	Y	N	Y	Y	N	Y
11 ***Weller***	N	Y	Y	N	Y	Y	N	Y
12 Costello	N	Y	N	N	Y	N	N	Y
13 ***Fawell***	N	Y	Y	N	Y	Y	N	Y
14 ***Hastert***	N	Y	Y	N	Y	Y	N	Y
15 ***Ewing***	N	Y	Y	N	Y	Y	N	Y

ND Northern Democrats SD Southern Democrats

	591	592	593	594	595	596	597	598
16 ***Manzullo***	N	Y	Y	N	Y	Y	N	Y
17 Evans	Y	Y	N	Y	Y	N	Y	Y
18 ***LaHood***	N	Y	Y	N	Y	Y	N	Y
19 Poshard	N	Y	N	N	Y	N	N	Y
20 ***Shimkus***	N	Y	Y	N	Y	Y	N	Y
INDIANA								
1 Visclosky	N	Y	N	N	Y	N	N	Y
2 ***McIntosh***	N	Y	Y	N	Y	Y	N	Y
3 Roemer	N	Y	Y	N	Y	Y	N	Y
4 ***Souder***	N	Y	Y	N	Y	Y	N	Y
5 ***Buyer***	N	Y	Y	N	Y	Y	N	Y
6 ***Burton***	N	Y	Y	N	Y	Y	N	Y
7 ***Pease***	N	Y	Y	N	Y	Y	N	Y
8 ***Hostettler***	N	Y	Y	N	Y	Y	N	Y
9 Hamilton	N	N	N	N	N	N	N	Y
10 Carson	–	+	–	–	+	–	–	+
IOWA								
1 ***Leach***	?	Y	Y	N	Y	Y	N	Y
2 ***Nussle***	N	Y	Y	?	Y	Y	N	Y
3 Boswell	N	Y	N	N	Y	N	N	Y
4 ***Ganske***	N	Y	Y	N	Y	Y	N	Y
5 ***Latham***	N	Y	Y	N	Y	Y	N	Y
KANSAS								
1 ***Moran***	N	Y	Y	N	Y	Y	N	Y
2 ***Ryun***	N	Y	Y	N	Y	Y	N	Y
3 ***Snowbarger***	N	Y	Y	N	Y	Y	N	Y
4 ***Tiahrt***	N	Y	Y	N	Y	Y	N	Y
KENTUCKY								
1 ***Whitfield***	N	Y	Y	N	Y	Y	N	Y
2 ***Lewis***	N	Y	Y	N	Y	Y	N	Y
3 ***Northup***	?	Y	Y	N	Y	Y	N	Y
4 ***Bunning***	N	Y	Y	N	Y	Y	N	Y
5 ***Rogers***	N	Y	Y	N	Y	Y	N	Y
6 Baesler	N	Y	N	N	Y	N	N	Y
LOUISIANA								
1 ***Livingston***	N	Y	Y	N	Y	Y	N	Y
2 Jefferson	Y	Y	N	Y	N	N	Y	Y
3 ***Tauzin***	?	Y	Y	N	Y	Y	N	Y
4 ***McCrery***	N	Y	Y	N	Y	Y	N	Y
5 ***Cooksey***	N	Y	Y	N	Y	Y	N	Y
6 ***Baker***	N	Y	Y	N	Y	Y	N	Y
7 John	N	Y	Y	N	Y	?	N	Y
MAINE								
1 Allen	N	Y	N	N	Y	N	N	Y
2 Baldacci	N	Y	N	?	Y	N	N	Y
MARYLAND								
1 ***Gilchrest***	N	Y	Y	N	Y	Y	N	Y
2 ***Ehrlich***	N	Y	Y	N	Y	Y	N	Y
3 Cardin	N	Y	N	N	Y	N	N	Y
4 Wynn	N	Y	N	N	Y	N	N	Y
5 Hoyer	N	Y	N	Y	Y	?	Y	Y
6 ***Bartlett***	N	Y	Y	N	Y	Y	N	Y
7 Cummings	N	Y	N	N	Y	N	?	Y
8 ***Morella***	N	Y	Y	N	Y	Y	N	Y
MASSACHUSETTS								
1 Olver	Y	Y	N	Y	Y	N	Y	Y
2 Neal	N	Y	N	N	?	?	?	?
3 McGovern	N	Y	N	N	N	N	N	Y
4 Frank	Y	Y	N	Y	N	N	Y	Y
5 Meehan	Y	Y	N	Y	Y	N	Y	Y
6 Tierney	Y	Y	N	N	Y	N	N	Y
7 Markey	Y	Y	N	Y	Y	N	Y	Y
8 Kennedy	Y	Y	N	Y	Y	N	?	Y
9 Moakley	?	Y	N	N	Y	N	Y	Y
10 Delahunt	N	Y	N	Y	Y	N	Y	Y
MICHIGAN								
1 Stupak	Y	Y	N	Y	Y	N	N	Y
2 ***Hoekstra***	N	Y	Y	N	Y	Y	N	Y
3 ***Ehlers***	N	Y	Y	N	Y	Y	N	Y
4 ***Camp***	N	Y	Y	N	Y	Y	N	Y
5 Barcia	N	Y	N	N	Y	N	N	Y
6 ***Upton***	N	Y	Y	N	Y	Y	N	Y
7 ***Smith***	N	Y	Y	N	Y	Y	N	Y
8 Stabenow	N	Y	?	N	Y	N	N	Y
9 Kildee	N	Y	N	N	Y	N	N	Y
10 Bonior	Y	Y	N	Y	Y	N	Y	Y
11 ***Knollenberg***	N	Y	Y	N	Y	Y	N	Y
12 Levin	N	Y	N	N	Y	N	N	Y
13 Rivers	N	Y	N	N	Y	N	N	Y
14 Conyers	Y	Y	N	Y	?	?	Y	Y
15 Kilpatrick	N	Y	N	?	Y	N	Y	Y
16 Dingell	Y	Y	N	Y	N	N	Y	Y
MINNESOTA								
1 ***Gutknecht***	N	Y	Y	N	Y	Y	N	Y
2 Minge	N	Y	N	N	N	N	N	Y

	591	592	593	594	595	596	597	598
3 ***Ramstad***	N	Y	Y	N	Y	Y	N	Y
4 Vento	N	Y	N	Y	N	N	Y	Y
5 Sabo	Y	Y	N	Y	N	N	Y	Y
6 Luther	N	Y	N	N	Y	N	N	Y
7 Peterson	Y	Y	N	Y	Y	N	Y	Y
8 Oberstar	Y	Y	N	N	Y	N	N	Y
MISSISSIPPI								
1 ***Wicker***	N	Y	Y	N	Y	Y	N	Y
2 Thompson	Y	Y	N	N	N	N	N	Y
3 ***Pickering***	N	Y	Y	N	Y	Y	N	Y
4 ***Parker***	N	Y	Y	N	Y	Y	N	Y
5 Taylor	N	Y	Y	N	Y	N	N	Y
MISSOURI								
1 Clay	N	Y	N	N	N	N	N	?
2 ***Talent***	N	Y	Y	N	Y	Y	?	Y
3 Gephardt	Y	Y	N	Y	Y	N	Y	Y
4 Skelton	?	Y	N	Y	Y	N	Y	Y
5 McCarthy	N	Y	N	N	Y	N	N	Y
6 Danner	N	Y	N	N	Y	N	N	Y
7 ***Blunt***	N	Y	Y	N	Y	Y	N	Y
8 ***Emerson***	N	Y	Y	N	Y	Y	N	Y
9 ***Hulshof***	N	Y	Y	N	Y	Y	N	Y
MONTANA								
AL ***Hill***	N	Y	Y	N	Y	Y	N	Y
NEBRASKA								
1 ***Bereuter***	N	Y	?	?	Y	Y	N	Y
2 ***Christensen***	N	Y	Y	N	Y	Y	N	Y
3 ***Barrett***	N	Y	Y	N	Y	Y	N	Y
NEVADA								
1 ***Ensign***	N	Y	Y	N	Y	Y	N	Y
2 ***Gibbons***	N	Y	Y	N	Y	Y	N	Y
NEW HAMPSHIRE								
1 ***Sununu***	N	Y	Y	N	Y	Y	N	Y
2 ***Bass***	N	Y	Y	N	Y	Y	N	Y
NEW JERSEY								
1 Andrews	Y	Y	N	Y	Y	N	Y	Y
2 ***LoBiondo***	N	Y	Y	N	Y	Y	N	Y
3 ***Saxton***	N	Y	Y	N	Y	Y	N	Y
4 ***Smith***	N	Y	Y	N	Y	Y	N	Y
5 ***Roukema***	N	Y	Y	N	Y	Y	N	Y
6 Pallone	Y	Y	N	Y	Y	N	Y	Y
7 ***Franks***	N	Y	Y	N	Y	Y	N	Y
8 Pascrell	N	Y	N	N	Y	N	Y	Y
9 Rothman	N	Y	N	N	Y	N	N	Y
10 Payne	Y	Y	Y	Y	N	N	Y	Y
11 ***Frelinghuysen***	N	Y	Y	N	Y	Y	N	Y
12 ***Pappas***	N	Y	Y	N	Y	Y	N	Y
13 Menendez	Y	Y	N	Y	Y	N	Y	Y
NEW MEXICO								
1 ***Schiff***	?	?	?	?	?	?	?	?
2 ***Skeen***	N	Y	Y	N	Y	Y	N	Y
3 ***Redmond***	N	Y	Y	N	Y	Y	N	Y
NEW YORK								
1 ***Forbes***	–	+	+	–	+	+	–	Y
2 ***Lazio***	N	Y	Y	N	Y	Y	N	Y
3 ***King***	N	Y	Y	N	Y	Y	N	Y
4 McCarthy	N	Y	N	N	Y	N	N	Y
5 Ackerman	N	Y	N	N	N	N	N	Y
6 Flake	N	Y	N	N	Y	N	N	Y
7 Manton	N	Y	N	N	Y	N	N	Y
8 Nadler	N	Y	?	Y	N	N	N	Y
9 Schumer	N	Y	N	N	Y	N	N	Y
10 Towns	Y	Y	N	Y	Y	N	Y	Y
11 Owens	Y	Y	N	Y	Y	N	Y	Y
12 Velázquez	Y	Y	N	N	N	N	Y	Y
13 ***Fossella***	N	Y	Y	N	Y	Y	N	Y
14 Maloney	N	Y	N	N	N	N	N	Y
15 Rangel	N	Y	N	?	N	N	Y	Y
16 Serrano	N	Y	N	N	N	N	N	Y
17 Engel	Y	Y	N	Y	Y	N	Y	Y
18 Lowey	N	Y	N	N	Y	N	N	Y
19 ***Kelly***	N	Y	Y	N	Y	Y	N	Y
20 ***Gilman***	N	Y	Y	N	Y	Y	N	Y
21 McNulty	Y	Y	N	Y	Y	N	Y	Y
22 ***Solomon***	N	Y	Y	N	Y	?	N	Y
23 ***Boehlert***	N	Y	Y	N	Y	Y	N	Y
24 ***McHugh***	N	Y	Y	N	Y	Y	N	Y
25 ***Walsh***	N	Y	Y	N	Y	Y	N	Y
26 Hinchey	Y	Y	N	Y	Y	N	Y	Y
27 ***Paxon***	N	Y	Y	N	Y	Y	N	Y
28 Slaughter	Y	Y	?	Y	Y	N	Y	Y
29 LaFalce	Y	N	N	Y	N	N	Y	Y
30 ***Quinn***	N	Y	Y	N	Y	Y	?	Y
31 ***Houghton***	N	N	Y	N	Y	Y	N	Y

	591	592	593	594	595	596	597	598
NORTH CAROLINA								
1 Clayton	N	Y	N	Y	Y	N	N	Y
2 Etheridge	N	Y	N	N	Y	N	N	Y
3 ***Jones***	N	Y	Y	N	Y	Y	N	Y
4 Price	N	Y	N	N	Y	N	N	Y
5 ***Burr***	N	Y	?	N	Y	Y	N	Y
6 ***Coble***	N	Y	Y	N	Y	Y	N	Y
7 McIntyre	N	Y	Y	N	Y	Y	N	Y
8 Hefner	Y	Y	N	Y	Y	N	N	Y
9 ***Myrick***	N	Y	Y	N	Y	Y	N	Y
10 ***Ballenger***	N	Y	Y	N	Y	Y	N	Y
11 ***Taylor***	N	Y	Y	N	Y	Y	N	Y
12 Watt	N	Y	N	N	N	N	N	Y
NORTH DAKOTA								
AL Pomeroy	N	Y	N	N	Y	N	N	Y
OHIO								
1 ***Chabot***	N	Y	Y	N	Y	Y	N	Y
2 ***Portman***	–	+	+	–	+	+	–	Y
3 Hall	N	Y	N	N	Y	N	N	Y
4 ***Oxley***	N	Y	Y	N	Y	Y	N	Y
5 ***Gillmor***	N	Y	Y	N	Y	Y	N	Y
6 Strickland	N	Y	N	Y	Y	N	Y	Y
7 ***Hobson***	N	Y	Y	N	Y	Y	N	Y
8 ***Boehner***	N	Y	Y	N	Y	?	N	Y
9 Kaptur	Y	Y	N	N	Y	N	N	Y
10 Kucinich	N	Y	N	N	N	N	N	Y
11 Stokes	N	Y	N	N	N	?	N	Y
12 ***Kasich***	N	Y	Y	N	Y	Y	N	Y
13 Brown	Y	Y	N	N	Y	N	N	Y
14 Sawyer	N	Y	N	N	Y	N	N	Y
15 ***Pryce***	N	Y	Y	N	Y	Y	N	Y
16 ***Regula***	N	Y	Y	N	Y	Y	N	Y
17 Traficant	N	Y	Y	N	Y	Y	N	Y
18 ***Ney***	N	Y	Y	N	Y	Y	N	Y
19 ***LaTourette***	N	Y	Y	N	Y	Y	N	?
OKLAHOMA								
1 ***Largent***	N	Y	Y	N	Y	Y	N	Y
2 ***Coburn***	N	Y	Y	?	Y	Y	N	Y
3 ***Watkins***	N	Y	Y	N	Y	Y	N	Y
4 ***Watts***	N	Y	Y	N	Y	Y	N	Y
5 ***Istook***	N	Y	Y	N	Y	Y	N	Y
6 ***Lucas***	N	Y	Y	N	Y	Y	N	Y
OREGON								
1 Furse	Y	Y	N	Y	Y	N	Y	?
2 ***Smith***	N	Y	Y	N	Y	Y	N	Y
3 Blumenauer	N	Y	N	N	Y	N	N	Y
4 DeFazio	Y	Y	N	N	Y	N	Y	Y
5 Hooley	N	Y	N	N	Y	N	N	Y
PENNSYLVANIA								
1 Foglietta	?	?	?	?	Y	N	?	Y
2 Fattah	N	Y	N	N	N	N	N	Y
3 Borski	N	Y	N	N	Y	N	N	Y
4 Klink	N	Y	N	N	Y	N	N	Y
5 ***Peterson***	N	Y	Y	N	Y	Y	N	Y
6 Holden	N	Y	N	N	Y	N	N	Y
7 ***Weldon***	N	Y	Y	N	Y	Y	?	Y
8 ***Greenwood***	N	Y	Y	N	Y	Y	N	Y
9 ***Shuster***	N	Y	Y	N	Y	Y	N	Y
10 ***McDade***	N	Y	Y	N	Y	Y	N	Y
11 Kanjorski	N	Y	N	N	Y	N	N	Y
12 Murtha	N	N	N	N	Y	N	N	Y
13 ***Fox***	N	Y	Y	N	Y	Y	N	Y
14 Coyne	Y	Y	N	Y	Y	N	Y	Y
15 McHale	N	Y	N	N	Y	N	N	Y
16 ***Pitts***	N	Y	Y	N	Y	Y	N	Y
17 ***Gekas***	N	Y	Y	N	Y	Y	?	Y
18 Doyle	N	Y	N	N	Y	N	N	Y
19 ***Goodling***	N	Y	Y	N	Y	Y	N	Y
20 Mascara	N	Y	N	N	Y	N	N	Y
21 ***English***	N	Y	Y	N	Y	Y	N	Y
RHODE ISLAND								
1 Kennedy	Y	Y	N	Y	Y	N	N	Y
2 Weygand	N	Y	N	N	Y	Y	N	Y
SOUTH CAROLINA								
1 ***Sanford***	N	Y	Y	N	Y	Y	N	Y
2 ***Spence***	N	Y	Y	N	Y	Y	N	Y
3 ***Graham***	N	Y	Y	N	Y	Y	N	Y
4 ***Inglis***	N	Y	Y	N	Y	Y	N	Y
5 Spratt	N	Y	N	Y	Y	N	N	Y
6 Clyburn	Y	Y	N	Y	N	N	Y	Y
SOUTH DAKOTA								
AL ***Thune***	N	Y	Y	N	Y	Y	N	Y
TENNESSEE								
1 ***Jenkins***	N	Y	Y	N	Y	Y	N	Y
2 ***Duncan***	N	Y	Y	?	Y	Y	N	Y

	591	592	593	594	595	596	597	
3 ***Wamp***	N	Y	Y	N	Y	Y	N	Y
4 ***Hilleary***	N	Y	Y	N	Y	Y	Y	Y
5 Clement	Y	Y	N	Y	Y	N	Y	Y
6 Gordon	N	Y	N	N	Y	N	N	Y
7 ***Bryant***	N	Y	Y	N	Y	Y	N	Y
8 Tanner	N	Y	N	N	Y	N	N	Y
9 Ford	N	Y	N	N	Y	N	N	Y
TEXAS								
1 Sandlin	N	Y	N	N	Y	N	N	Y
2 Turner	N	Y	Y	N	Y	N	N	Y
3 ***Johnson, Sam***	N	Y	Y	N	?	?	?	Y
4 Hall	N	Y	Y	N	Y	Y	N	Y
5 ***Sessions***	N	Y	Y	N	Y	Y	N	Y
6 ***Barton***	N	Y	Y	N	Y	Y	?	Y
7 ***Archer***	N	Y	Y	N	Y	Y	N	Y
8 ***Brady***	N	Y	Y	N	Y	Y	N	Y
9 Lampson	N	Y	Y	N	Y	N	N	Y
10 Doggett	Y	Y	N	Y	Y	N	Y	Y
11 Edwards	N	Y	N	N	Y	N	N	Y
12 ***Granger***	N	Y	Y	N	Y	Y	N	Y
13 ***Thornberry***	N	Y	Y	N	Y	Y	N	Y
14 ***Paul***	N	Y	Y	N	N	Y	N	Y
15 Hinojosa	Y	Y	N	N	Y	N	N	Y
16 Reyes	Y	Y	N	Y	Y	N	N	Y
17 Stenholm	N	Y	?	N	Y	N	N	Y
18 Jackson-Lee	Y	Y	N	N	Y	N	Y	Y
19 ***Combest***	N	Y	Y	N	Y	Y	N	Y
20 Gonzalez	?	?	?	?	?	?	?	?
21 ***Smith***	N	Y	Y	N	Y	Y	N	Y
22 ***DeLay***	N	Y	Y	N	Y	Y	N	Y
23 ***Bonilla***	N	Y	Y	N	Y	Y	N	Y
24 Frost	N	Y	N	N	Y	N	N	Y
25 Bentsen	N	Y	Y	N	Y	N	N	Y
26 ***Armey***	N	Y	Y	N	Y	Y	N	Y
27 Ortiz	Y	Y	N	N	Y	N	N	Y
28 Rodriguez	Y	Y	Y	N	Y	N	N	Y
29 Green	N	Y	N	N	Y	N	N	Y
30 Johnson, E.B.	Y	N	N	N	N	N	N	Y
UTAH								
1 ***Hansen***	N	Y	Y	N	Y	Y	N	Y
2 ***Cook***	N	Y	Y	N	Y	Y	N	Y
3 ***Cannon***	N	Y	Y	N	Y	Y	N	Y
VERMONT								
AL *Sanders*	N	Y	N	N	Y	N	N	Y
VIRGINIA								
1 ***Bateman***	N	Y	Y	N	Y	Y	N	+
2 Pickett	N	Y	N	N	N	N	?	?
3 Scott	?	Y	N	N	Y	N	Y	Y
4 Sisisky	N	Y	N	N	Y	N	N	Y
5 Goode	N	Y	Y	N	Y	Y	N	Y
6 ***Goodlatte***	N	Y	Y	N	Y	Y	N	Y
7 ***Bliley***	N	Y	Y	N	Y	Y	N	Y
8 Moran	N	N	N	N	Y	N	N	Y
9 Boucher	N	Y	N	N	Y	N	N	Y
10 ***Wolf***	N	Y	Y	N	Y	Y	N	Y
11 ***Davis***	N	Y	Y	N	Y	Y	N	Y
WASHINGTON								
1 ***White***	N	Y	Y	N	Y	Y	?	Y
2 ***Metcalf***	N	Y	Y	N	Y	Y	N	Y
3 ***Smith, Linda***	N	Y	Y	N	Y	Y	N	Y
4 ***Hastings***	N	Y	Y	N	Y	Y	N	Y
5 ***Nethercutt***	N	Y	Y	N	Y	Y	N	Y
6 Dicks	N	Y	N	N	Y	N	N	Y
7 McDermott	Y	Y	N	Y	N	N	Y	Y
8 ***Dunn***	N	Y	Y	N	Y	Y	N	Y
9 Smith, Adam	N	Y	N	N	N	N	N	Y
WEST VIRGINIA								
1 Mollohan	N	Y	N	N	Y	N	N	Y
2 Wise	Y	Y	N	Y	Y	N	Y	Y
3 Rahall	N	Y	N	N	Y	N	N	Y
WISCONSIN								
1 ***Neumann***	N	Y	Y	N	Y	Y	N	Y
2 ***Klug***	N	Y	Y	N	Y	Y	N	Y
3 Kind	N	Y	N	N	Y	N	N	Y
4 Kleczka	N	Y	N	N	Y	N	N	Y
5 Barrett	Y	Y	N	N	N	N	Y	Y
6 ***Petri***	N	Y	Y	N	Y	Y	N	Y
7 Obey	Y	Y	N	Y	Y	N	Y	Y
8 Johnson	N	Y	Y	N	Y	N	Y	Y
9 ***Sensenbrenner***	N	Y	Y	N	Y	Y	N	Y
WYOMING								
AL ***Cubin***	?	?	?	?	?	?	?	?

Southern states - Ala., Ark., Fla., Ga., Ky., La., Miss., N.C., Okla., S.C., Tenn., Texas, Va.

HOUSE VOTES 599, 600, 601, 602, 603, 604, 605

599. HR 2570. Forced Abortions in China/Reconsideration of Vote. Fowler, R-Fla., motion to table (kill) the Lofgren, D-Calif., motion to reconsider the vote by which the House passed the bill to deny U.S. visas to Chinese officials known to be involved in the establishment or enforcement of population control activities resulting in forced abortion or sterilization. Motion agreed to 245-171: R 220-0; D 25-170 (ND 13-130, SD 12-40); I 0-1, Nov. 6, 1997.

600. Procedural Motion/Adjourn. Doggett, D-Texas, motion to adjourn. Motion rejected 66-350: R 0-222; D 66-127 (ND 51-91, SD 15-36); I 0-1, Nov. 6, 1997.

601. HR 2386. Taiwan Missile Defense System/Passage. Passage of the bill to require the Defense Department to conduct a study on a plan for developing an anti-ballistic missile defense system to help protect Taiwan and express the sense of Congress that the president should approve the sale of an appropriate defense system to Taiwan in accordance with the results of the study, if requested by Taiwan. Passed 301-116: R 213-7; D 88-108 (ND 56-87, SD 32-21); I 0-1, Nov. 6, 1997. A "nay" was a vote in support of the president's position.

602. HR 2386. Taiwan Missile Defense System/Reconsideration of Vote. Bereuter, R-Neb., motion to table (kill) the Pallone, D-N.J., motion to reconsider the vote by which the House passed the bill to require the Defense Department to conduct a study on a plan for developing an anti-ballistic missile defense system to help protect Taiwan and express the sense of Congress that the president should approve the sale of an appropriate defense system to Taiwan in accordance with the results of the study, if requested by Taiwan. Motion agreed to 245-175: R 223-0; D 22-174 (ND 11-132, SD 11-42); I 0-1, Nov. 6, 1997.

603. Procedural Motion/Adjourn. Gejdenson, D-Conn., motion to adjourn. Motion rejected 91-321: R 5-212; D 86-108 (ND 69-73, SD 17-35); I 0-1, Nov. 6, 1997.

604. HR 2605. International Loans to China/Appeal Ruling of Chair. Cox, R-Calif., motion to table (kill) the Taylor, D-Miss., appeal of the ruling of the chair that the Taylor motion to recommit with instructions was not germane. The Taylor motion would instruct the Ways and Means Committee to report the bill back with an amendment to require the total amount of tariffs paid to China for U.S. exports to be adjusted quarterly to equal the total amount China pays in tariffs to the U.S. for Chinese exports. Motion agreed to 220-192: R 218-0; D 2-191 (ND 2-138, SD 0-53); I 0-1, Nov. 6, 1997.

605. HR 2605. International Loans to China/Passage. Passage of the bill to require U.S. representatives to international financial institutions, including the World Bank and International Monetary Fund, to oppose the extension of concessional loans to any entity in China. Passed 354-59: R 211-9; D 142-50 (ND 99-40, SD 43-10); I 1-0, Nov. 6, 1997. A "nay" was a vote in support of the president's position.

KEY

- Y Voted for (yea).
- # Paired for.
- + Announced for.
- N Voted against (nay).
- X Paired against.
- – Announced against.
- P Voted "present."
- C Voted "present" to avoid possible conflict of interest.
- ? Did not vote or otherwise make a position known.

Democrats ***Republicans***
Independent

	599	600	601	602	603	604	605
ALABAMA							
1 ***Callahan***	Y	N	Y	Y	N	Y	Y
2 ***Everett***	Y	N	Y	Y	?	Y	Y
3 ***Riley***	+	–	#	+	–	+	+
4 ***Aderholt***	Y	N	Y	Y	N	Y	Y
5 Cramer	Y	N	Y	N	N	N	Y
6 ***Bachus***	Y	N	Y	Y	N	Y	Y
7 Hilliard	N	N	Y	N	N	N	Y
ALASKA							
AL ***Young***	Y	N	Y	Y	?	?	?
ARIZONA							
1 ***Salmon***	Y	N	Y	Y	N	Y	Y
2 Pastor	N	N	N	N	Y	N	N
3 ***Stump***	Y	N	Y	Y	N	Y	Y
4 ***Shadegg***	Y	N	Y	Y	N	Y	Y
5 ***Kolbe***	Y	N	Y	Y	N	Y	N
6 ***Hayworth***	Y	N	Y	Y	N	Y	Y
ARKANSAS							
1 Berry	N	N	N	N	Y	N	Y
2 Snyder	N	N	N	N	N	N	N
3 ***Hutchinson***	Y	N	Y	Y	N	Y	Y
4 ***Dickey***	Y	N	Y	Y	N	Y	Y
CALIFORNIA							
1 ***Riggs***	Y	N	Y	Y	N	Y	Y
2 ***Herger***	Y	N	Y	Y	N	Y	Y
3 Fazio	N	N	N	N	Y	N	N
4 ***Doolittle***	Y	N	Y	Y	Y	Y	Y
5 Matsui	N	N	N	N	N	N	Y
6 Woolsey	N	Y	N	N	Y	N	Y
7 Miller	N	Y	N	N	Y	?	?
8 Pelosi	N	Y	N	N	Y	N	Y
9 Dellums	N	N	N	N	N	N	Y
10 Tauscher	Y	N	Y	N	N	N	N
11 ***Pombo***	Y	N	Y	Y	N	Y	Y
12 Lantos	?	Y	Y	N	Y	N	Y
13 Stark	Y	Y	N	N	Y	?	?
14 Eshoo	N	Y	N	Y	Y	N	N
15 ***Campbell***	Y	N	Y	Y	N	Y	N
16 Lofgren	N	Y	N	N	N	N	N
17 Farr	N	Y	N	N	Y	N	N
18 Condit	Y	N	Y	Y	N	N	Y
19 ***Radanovich***	Y	N	Y	Y	N	Y	Y
20 Dooley	N	N	N	N	N	N	N
21 ***Thomas***	Y	N	Y	Y	N	Y	Y
22 Vacant							
23 ***Gallegly***	Y	N	Y	Y	N	Y	Y
24 Sherman	N	N	Y	Y	N	N	Y
25 ***McKeon***	Y	N	Y	Y	N	Y	Y
26 Berman	N	N	N	N	N	N	N
27 ***Rogan***	Y	N	Y	Y	N	Y	Y
28 ***Dreier***	Y	N	Y	Y	N	Y	Y
29 Waxman	N	Y	N	N	Y	N	N
30 Becerra	N	Y	N	N	Y	N	N
31 Martinez	N	N	Y	N	N	N	Y
32 Dixon	N	N	N	N	N	?	?
33 Roybal-Allard	N	N	N	N	Y	N	Y
34 Torres	N	Y	Y	N	Y	N	Y
35 Waters	N	Y	N	N	N	N	Y
36 Harman	?	Y	N	N	Y	N	Y
37 Millender-McD.	N	N	N	N	N	?	N
38 ***Horn***	Y	N	Y	Y	N	Y	Y
39 ***Royce***	Y	N	Y	Y	N	Y	Y
40 ***Lewis***	Y	N	Y	Y	N	Y	Y
41 ***Kim***	Y	N	Y	Y	N	Y	Y
42 Brown	N	Y	N	N	Y	N	N
43 ***Calvert***	Y	N	Y	Y	N	Y	Y
44 ***Bono***	Y	N	Y	Y	N	Y	Y
45 ***Rohrabacher***	Y	N	Y	Y	N	Y	Y
46 Sanchez	N	Y	Y	N	Y	N	Y
47 ***Cox***	Y	N	Y	Y	N	Y	Y
48 ***Packard***	Y	N	Y	Y	N	Y	Y
49 ***Bilbray***	Y	N	Y	Y	N	Y	Y
50 Filner	N	Y	N	N	Y	N	Y
51 ***Cunningham***	Y	N	Y	Y	N	Y	Y
52 ***Hunter***	Y	N	Y	Y	N	Y	Y
COLORADO							
1 DeGette	N	N	Y	N	Y	N	Y
2 Skaggs	N	N	N	N	N	Y	N
3 ***McInnis***	Y	N	Y	Y	N	Y	Y
4 ***Schaffer***	Y	N	Y	Y	N	Y	Y
5 ***Hefley***	Y	N	Y	Y	N	Y	Y
6 ***Schaefer***	Y	N	Y	Y	N	Y	Y
CONNECTICUT							
1 Kennelly	N	N	N	N	Y	N	Y
2 Gejdenson	N	Y	N	N	Y	N	Y
3 DeLauro	N	Y	?	N	Y	N	Y
4 ***Shays***	Y	N	Y	Y	N	Y	Y
5 Maloney	N	N	Y	N	N	N	Y
6 ***Johnson***	?	N	Y	Y	N	Y	Y
DELAWARE							
AL ***Castle***	Y	N	N	Y	N	Y	N
FLORIDA							
1 ***Scarborough***	Y	N	Y	Y	N	Y	Y
2 Boyd	Y	N	Y	Y	N	N	Y
3 Brown	N	Y	Y	N	Y	N	Y
4 ***Fowler***	Y	N	Y	Y	N	Y	Y
5 Thurman	N	Y	N	N	Y	N	N
6 ***Stearns***	Y	N	Y	Y	N	Y	Y
7 ***Mica***	Y	N	Y	Y	N	Y	Y
8 ***McCollum***	Y	N	Y	Y	N	Y	Y
9 ***Bilirakis***	Y	N	Y	Y	N	Y	Y
10 ***Young***	Y	N	Y	Y	N	Y	Y
11 Davis	Y	Y	N	N	Y	N	N
12 ***Canady***	Y	N	Y	Y	N	Y	Y
13 ***Miller***	Y	N	Y	Y	N	Y	Y
14 ***Goss***	Y	N	Y	Y	N	Y	Y
15 ***Weldon***	Y	N	Y	Y	N	Y	Y
16 ***Foley***	Y	N	Y	Y	N	Y	Y
17 Meek	N	Y	Y	N	Y	N	N
18 ***Ros-Lehtinen***	Y	N	Y	Y	N	Y	Y
19 Wexler	N	N	Y	N	N	N	Y
20 Deutsch	N	Y	Y	N	Y	N	Y
21 ***Diaz-Balart***	Y	N	Y	Y	N	Y	Y
22 ***Shaw***	Y	N	Y	Y	N	Y	Y
23 Hastings	N	Y	Y	N	N	N	Y
GEORGIA							
1 ***Kingston***	Y	N	Y	Y	N	Y	Y
2 Bishop	N	N	Y	N	N	N	Y
3 ***Collins***	Y	N	Y	Y	?	Y	Y
4 McKinney	?	?	X	?	?	?	?
5 Lewis	N	Y	N	N	Y	N	Y
6 ***Gingrich***							
7 ***Barr***	Y	N	Y	Y	N	?	Y
8 ***Chambliss***	Y	N	Y	Y	N	Y	Y
9 ***Deal***	Y	N	Y	Y	N	Y	Y
10 ***Norwood***	Y	N	Y	Y	N	Y	Y
11 ***Linder***	Y	N	?	Y	N	Y	Y
HAWAII							
1 Abercrombie	N	N	Y	Y	N	N	Y
2 Mink	N	Y	N	N	Y	N	N
IDAHO							
1 ***Chenoweth***	Y	N	Y	Y	N	Y	Y
2 ***Crapo***	Y	N	Y	Y	N	Y	Y
ILLINOIS							
1 Rush	N	N	N	N	Y	N	?
2 Jackson	N	N	N	N	Y	N	Y
3 Lipinski	N	N	Y	N	N	N	Y
4 Gutierrez	N	?	Y	N	N	N	N
5 Blagojevich	N	N	N	N	N	N	N
6 ***Hyde***	Y	N	Y	Y	N	Y	Y
7 Davis	N	N	N	N	N	N	Y
8 ***Crane***	Y	N	Y	Y	N	Y	Y
9 Yates	?	?	?	?	?	?	?
10 ***Porter***	Y	N	Y	Y	N	Y	Y
11 ***Weller***	Y	N	Y	Y	N	Y	Y
12 Costello	N	N	N	N	N	N	Y
13 ***Fawell***	Y	N	Y	Y	N	Y	Y
14 ***Hastert***	Y	N	Y	Y	N	Y	N
15 ***Ewing***	Y	N	Y	Y	?	Y	N

ND Northern Democrats SD Southern Democrats

	599	600	601	602	603	604	605
16 ***Manzullo***	Y	N	Y	Y	N	Y	N
17 Evans	N	Y	N	N	Y	N	Y
18 ***LaHood***	Y	N	Y	Y	N	Y	N
19 Poshard	N	N	N	N	N	N	Y
20 ***Shimkus***	Y	N	Y	Y	N	Y	Y
INDIANA							
1 Visclosky	N	N	N	N	N	N	Y
2 ***McIntosh***	Y	N	Y	Y	N	Y	Y
3 Roemer	Y	N	N	N	N	N	N
4 ***Souder***	Y	N	Y	?	?	Y	Y
5 ***Buyer***	Y	N	Y	Y	N	Y	Y
6 ***Burton***	Y	N	Y	Y	N	Y	Y
7 ***Pease***	Y	N	Y	Y	N	Y	Y
8 ***Hostettler***	Y	N	Y	Y	N	Y	Y
9 Hamilton	N	N	N	N	N	Y	N
10 Carson	-	-	-	-	-	-	+
IOWA							
1 ***Leach***	Y	N	Y	Y	N	Y	Y
2 ***Nussle***	Y	N	Y	Y	N	Y	Y
3 Boswell	Y	N	Y	Y	N	N	Y
4 ***Ganske***	Y	N	Y	Y	N	Y	Y
5 ***Latham***	Y	N	Y	Y	N	Y	Y
KANSAS							
1 ***Moran***	Y	N	Y	Y	N	Y	Y
2 ***Ryun***	Y	N	Y	Y	N	Y	Y
3 ***Snowbarger***	Y	N	Y	Y	N	Y	Y
4 ***Tiahrt***	Y	N	Y	Y	N	Y	Y
KENTUCKY							
1 ***Whitfield***	Y	N	Y	Y	?	Y	Y
2 ***Lewis***	Y	N	Y	Y	N	Y	Y
3 ***Northup***	Y	N	Y	Y	N	Y	Y
4 ***Bunning***	Y	N	Y	Y	N	Y	Y
5 ***Rogers***	Y	N	Y	Y	N	Y	Y
6 Baesler	Y	N	Y	Y	N	N	Y
LOUISIANA							
1 ***Livingston***	Y	N	Y	Y	N	Y	Y
2 Jefferson	N	Y	N	N	?	N	N
3 ***Tauzin***	Y	N	Y	Y	N	Y	Y
4 ***McCrery***	Y	N	Y	Y	N	Y	Y
5 ***Cooksey***	Y	N	Y	Y	N	Y	Y
6 ***Baker***	Y	N	Y	Y	N	Y	Y
7 John	Y	N	Y	Y	N	N	Y
MAINE							
1 Allen	N	N	N	N	N	N	Y
2 Baldacci	N	N	N	N	N	N	Y
MARYLAND							
1 ***Gilchrest***	Y	N	Y	Y	N	Y	Y
2 ***Ehrlich***	Y	N	Y	Y	N	Y	Y
3 Cardin	N	N	N	N	N	N	Y
4 Wynn	N	N	N	N	N	N	Y
5 Hoyer	N	N	N	N	Y	N	Y
6 ***Bartlett***	Y	N	Y	Y	N	Y	Y
7 Cummings	N	N	N	N	N	N	Y
8 ***Morella***	Y	N	N	Y	N	Y	N
MASSACHUSETTS							
1 Olver	N	Y	N	N	Y	N	N
2 Neal	?	?	?	?	?	?	?
3 McGovern	N	N	N	N	N	N	Y
4 Frank	N	Y	N	N	Y	N	Y
5 Meehan	N	N	N	N	?	N	Y
6 Tierney	N	N	N	Y	N	N	Y
7 Markey	N	Y	N	N	Y	N	Y
8 Kennedy	N	?	N	N	N	N	Y
9 Moakley	N	N	N	N	Y	N	Y
10 Delahunt	N	N	N	N	Y	N	Y
MICHIGAN							
1 Stupak	N	Y	Y	N	Y	N	Y
2 ***Hoekstra***	Y	N	Y	Y	N	Y	Y
3 ***Ehlers***	Y	N	Y	Y	N	Y	Y
4 ***Camp***	Y	N	Y	Y	N	Y	Y
5 Barcia	N	N	Y	N	?	N	Y
6 ***Upton***	Y	N	Y	Y	N	Y	Y
7 ***Smith***	Y	N	Y	Y	N	Y	Y
8 Stabenow	N	N	N	N	N	N	N
9 Kildee	N	N	Y	N	N	N	Y
10 Bonior	N	Y	N	N	Y	N	Y
11 ***Knollenberg***	Y	N	Y	Y	N	Y	Y
12 Levin	N	N	N	N	Y	N	Y
13 Rivers	Y	N	Y	N	N	N	Y
14 Conyers	N	Y	N	N	Y	N	N
15 Kilpatrick	N	N	Y	N	Y	N	Y
16 Dingell	N	Y	N	N	Y	N	N
MINNESOTA							
1 ***Gutknecht***	Y	N	Y	Y	N	Y	Y
2 Minge	Y	N	N	N	N	N	N

	599	600	601	602	603	604	605
3 ***Ramstad***	Y	N	Y	Y	N	Y	Y
4 Vento	N	Y	N	N	?	N	Y
5 Sabo	N	Y	N	?	Y	N	N
6 Luther	Y	N	N	N	N	N	Y
7 Peterson	N	Y	Y	N	Y	N	Y
8 Oberstar	N	Y	N	N	N	N	Y
MISSISSIPPI							
1 ***Wicker***	Y	N	Y	Y	N	Y	Y
2 Thompson	N	N	Y	N	Y	N	Y
3 ***Pickering***	Y	N	Y	Y	N	Y	Y
4 ***Parker***	Y	N	Y	Y	N	Y	Y
5 Taylor	Y	N	Y	Y	N	N	Y
MISSOURI							
1 Clay	?	N	Y	N	N	N	Y
2 ***Talent***	Y	N	Y	Y	N	Y	Y
3 Gephardt	N	Y	Y	N	Y	?	?
4 Skelton	N	Y	N	N	Y	N	Y
5 McCarthy	N	N	Y	N	N	N	Y
6 Danner	N	N	Y	N	N	N	Y
7 ***Blunt***	Y	N	Y	Y	N	Y	Y
8 ***Emerson***	Y	N	Y	Y	N	Y	Y
9 ***Hulshof***	Y	N	Y	Y	N	Y	Y
MONTANA							
AL ***Hill***	Y	N	Y	Y	N	Y	Y
NEBRASKA							
1 ***Bereuter***	?	N	Y	Y	N	Y	Y
2 ***Christensen***	Y	N	Y	Y	N	Y	Y
3 ***Barrett***	Y	N	Y	Y	N	Y	Y
NEVADA							
1 ***Ensign***	Y	N	Y	Y	N	Y	Y
2 ***Gibbons***	Y	N	Y	Y	N	Y	Y
NEW HAMPSHIRE							
1 ***Sununu***	Y	N	Y	Y	N	Y	Y
2 ***Bass***	Y	N	Y	Y	N	Y	Y
NEW JERSEY							
1 Andrews	N	Y	Y	N	Y	N	Y
2 ***LoBiondo***	Y	N	Y	Y	N	Y	Y
3 ***Saxton***	Y	N	Y	Y	N	Y	Y
4 ***Smith***	Y	N	Y	Y	N	Y	Y
5 ***Roukema***	Y	N	Y	Y	N	Y	Y
6 Pallone	N	Y	Y	N	Y	N	Y
7 ***Franks***	Y	N	Y	Y	N	Y	Y
8 Pascrell	N	N	Y	N	N	N	Y
9 Rothman	Y	N	Y	N	N	N	Y
10 Payne	N	Y	N	N	Y	N	N
11 ***Frelinghuysen***	Y	N	Y	Y	N	Y	Y
12 ***Pappas***	Y	N	Y	Y	N	Y	Y
13 Menendez	N	Y	Y	N	Y	N	Y
NEW MEXICO							
1 ***Schiff***	?	?	?	?	?	?	?
2 ***Skeen***	Y	N	Y	Y	N	Y	Y
3 ***Redmond***	Y	N	Y	Y	N	Y	Y
NEW YORK							
1 ***Forbes***	Y	N	Y	Y	N	Y	Y
2 ***Lazio***	Y	N	Y	Y	N	Y	Y
3 ***King***	Y	N	Y	Y	N	Y	Y
4 McCarthy	Y	N	Y	Y	Y	N	Y
5 Ackerman	N	N	N	N	N	N	N
6 Flake	N	Y	?	?	?	?	?
7 Manton	N	N	Y	N	N	N	Y
8 Nadler	N	N	Y	N	N	N	N
9 Schumer	N	N	Y	N	N	N	Y
10 Towns	N	Y	Y	N	Y	N	Y
11 Owens	N	?	Y	N	Y	N	Y
12 Velázquez	N	Y	N	N	Y	N	N
13 ***Fossella***	Y	N	Y	Y	N	Y	Y
14 Maloney	N	N	Y	N	N	N	Y
15 Rangel	N	Y	Y	N	N	N	?
16 Serrano	N	N	N	N	N	N	N
17 Engel	N	N	Y	N	Y	N	N
18 Lowey	N	N	N	N	N	N	N
19 ***Kelly***	Y	N	Y	Y	N	Y	Y
20 ***Gilman***	Y	N	Y	Y	N	Y	Y
21 McNulty	N	Y	Y	N	Y	N	Y
22 ***Solomon***	?	N	Y	Y	N	Y	Y
23 ***Boehlert***	Y	N	Y	Y	N	Y	Y
24 ***McHugh***	Y	N	Y	Y	N	Y	Y
25 ***Walsh***	Y	N	Y	Y	N	Y	Y
26 Hinchey	N	Y	N	N	Y	N	N
27 ***Paxon***	Y	N	Y	Y	N	Y	Y
28 Slaughter	N	N	Y	N	Y	N	N
29 LaFalce	N	Y	N	N	Y	N	N
30 ***Quinn***	Y	N	Y	Y	N	Y	Y
31 ***Houghton***	Y	N	N	Y	N	Y	?

	599	600	601	602	603	604	605
NORTH CAROLINA							
1 Clayton	N	?	N	N	N	N	Y
2 Etheridge	N	N	Y	N	N	N	Y
3 ***Jones***	Y	N	Y	Y	N	Y	Y
4 Price	N	N	N	N	N	N	Y
5 ***Burr***	Y	N	Y	Y	N	Y	Y
6 ***Coble***	Y	N	Y	Y	N	Y	Y
7 McIntyre	Y	N	Y	Y	Y	N	Y
8 Hefner	N	Y	N	N	N	N	Y
9 ***Myrick***	Y	N	Y	Y	N	Y	Y
10 ***Ballenger***	Y	?	?	Y	N	Y	Y
11 ***Taylor***	Y	N	Y	Y	N	Y	Y
12 Watt	N	N	N	N	N	N	N
NORTH DAKOTA							
AL Pomeroy	N	N	Y	N	N	N	Y
OHIO							
1 ***Chabot***	Y	N	Y	Y	N	Y	Y
2 ***Portman***	Y	N	Y	Y	N	Y	Y
3 Hall	N	N	Y	N	N	N	Y
4 ***Oxley***	Y	N	Y	Y	N	Y	Y
5 ***Gillmor***	Y	N	N	Y	Y	Y	Y
6 Strickland	N	Y	Y	Y	N	N	Y
7 ***Hobson***	Y	N	Y	Y	N	Y	Y
8 ***Boehner***	Y	N	?	Y	N	?	Y
9 Kaptur	N	N	Y	N	N	N	Y
10 Kucinich	N	N	N	N	N	N	Y
11 Stokes	N	?	?	?	N	N	Y
12 ***Kasich***	Y	N	Y	Y	N	Y	Y
13 Brown	N	Y	Y	N	Y	N	Y
14 Sawyer	N	N	N	N	N	N	Y
15 ***Pryce***	Y	N	Y	Y	N	Y	Y
16 ***Regula***	Y	N	Y	Y	N	Y	Y
17 Traficant	Y	N	Y	Y	N	N	Y
18 ***Ney***	Y	N	Y	Y	N	Y	Y
19 ***LaTourette***	Y	N	Y	Y	N	?	?
OKLAHOMA							
1 ***Largent***	Y	N	Y	Y	N	Y	Y
2 ***Coburn***	Y	N	?	Y	N	Y	Y
3 ***Watkins***	Y	N	Y	Y	N	Y	Y
4 ***Watts***	Y	N	Y	Y	N	Y	Y
5 ***Istook***	Y	N	Y	Y	N	Y	Y
6 ***Lucas***	Y	N	Y	Y	N	Y	Y
OREGON							
1 Furse	N	N	N	N	Y	N	N
2 ***Smith***	Y	N	Y	Y	N	?	?
3 Blumenauer	N	N	N	N	Y	N	Y
4 DeFazio	N	Y	Y	N	Y	N	Y
5 Hooley	N	N	Y	N	N	N	Y
PENNSYLVANIA							
1 Foglietta	?	?	?	?	?	?	?
2 Fattah	N	N	N	N	Y	N	Y
3 Borski	N	N	N	N	Y	N	Y
4 Klink	N	N	Y	N	N	N	Y
5 ***Peterson***	Y	N	Y	Y	N	Y	Y
6 Holden	N	N	Y	N	N	N	Y
7 ***Weldon***	Y	N	Y	Y	?	Y	Y
8 ***Greenwood***	Y	N	?	Y	N	Y	Y
9 ***Shuster***	Y	?	Y	Y	N	Y	Y
10 ***McDade***	Y	N	Y	Y	N	Y	Y
11 Kanjorski	N	N	N	N	N	N	Y
12 Murtha	N	N	N	N	Y	N	Y
13 ***Fox***	Y	N	Y	Y	N	Y	Y
14 Coyne	N	Y	N	N	N	N	N
15 McHale	N	N	Y	N	N	N	Y
16 ***Pitts***	Y	N	Y	Y	Y	Y	Y
17 ***Gekas***	Y	N	Y	Y	N	Y	Y
18 Doyle	N	N	Y	N	N	N	Y
19 ***Goodling***	Y	N	Y	Y	N	Y	Y
20 Mascara	N	N	Y	N	N	N	Y
21 ***English***	Y	N	Y	Y	N	Y	N
RHODE ISLAND							
1 Kennedy	N	N	N	N	Y	N	Y
2 Weygand	N	N	Y	N	Y	N	Y
SOUTH CAROLINA							
1 ***Sanford***	Y	N	N	Y	N	Y	Y
2 ***Spence***	Y	N	Y	Y	N	Y	Y
3 ***Graham***	Y	N	Y	Y	N	Y	Y
4 ***Inglis***	Y	N	Y	Y	N	Y	Y
5 Spratt	N	N	N	N	Y	N	Y
6 Clyburn	N	Y	Y	N	Y	N	Y
SOUTH DAKOTA							
AL ***Thune***	Y	N	Y	Y	N	Y	Y
TENNESSEE							
1 ***Jenkins***	+	N	Y	Y	N	Y	Y
2 ***Duncan***	Y	N	Y	Y	N	Y	Y

	599	600	601	602	603	604	605
3 ***Wamp***	Y	N	Y	Y	N	Y	Y
4 ***Hilleary***	Y	N	Y	Y	Y	Y	Y
5 Clement	N	Y	N	N	Y	N	Y
6 Gordon	N	N	N	N	N	N	Y
7 ***Bryant***	Y	N	Y	Y	N	Y	Y
8 Tanner	N	N	Y	N	N	N	Y
9 Ford	N	N	N	N	N	N	Y
TEXAS							
1 Sandlin	N	N	Y	Y	N	N	Y
2 Turner	Y	N	Y	Y	N	N	Y
3 ***Johnson, Sam***	Y	N	Y	Y	Y	Y	Y
4 Hall	Y	N	Y	Y	N	N	Y
5 ***Sessions***	Y	N	Y	Y	N	Y	Y
6 ***Barton***	Y	N	Y	Y	N	Y	Y
7 ***Archer***	Y	N	N	Y	N	Y	Y
8 ***Brady***	Y	N	Y	Y	N	Y	Y
9 Lampson	N	N	Y	N	N	N	Y
10 Doggett	N	Y	N	N	Y	N	Y
11 Edwards	N	N	N	N	N	N	Y
12 ***Granger***	Y	N	Y	Y	N	?	Y
13 ***Thornberry***	Y	N	Y	Y	N	Y	Y
14 ***Paul***	Y	N	N	Y	N	Y	Y
15 Hinojosa	N	N	Y	N	N	N	Y
16 Reyes	?	?	Y	N	N	N	Y
17 Stenholm	N	N	Y	Y	N	N	Y
18 Jackson-Lee	N	N	Y	N	N	N	Y
19 ***Combest***	Y	N	Y	Y	N	Y	Y
20 Gonzalez	?	?	?	?	?	?	?
21 ***Smith***	Y	N	Y	Y	N	Y	Y
22 ***DeLay***	Y	N	Y	Y	N	Y	Y
23 ***Bonilla***	Y	N	Y	Y	N	Y	Y
24 Frost	N	N	Y	N	Y	N	Y
25 Bentsen	Y	N	N	N	N	N	N
26 ***Armey***	Y	N	Y	Y	N	Y	Y
27 Ortiz	N	N	Y	N	N	N	Y
28 Rodriguez	N	Y	Y	N	N	N	Y
29 Green	N	N	Y	N	N	N	Y
30 Johnson, E.B.	N	N	Y	N	Y	N	N
UTAH							
1 ***Hansen***	Y	N	Y	Y	N	Y	Y
2 ***Cook***	Y	N	Y	Y	N	Y	Y
3 ***Cannon***	Y	N	Y	Y	N	Y	Y
VERMONT							
AL *Sanders*	N	N	N	N	N	N	Y
VIRGINIA							
1 ***Bateman***	Y	N	Y	Y	N	Y	Y
2 Pickett	N	Y	N	N	Y	N	N
3 Scott	N	Y	N	N	Y	N	Y
4 Sisisky	Y	N	Y	Y	N	N	Y
5 Goode	Y	N	Y	Y	N	N	Y
6 ***Goodlatte***	Y	N	Y	Y	N	Y	Y
7 ***Bliley***	Y	N	Y	Y	N	Y	Y
8 Moran	N	N	N	N	N	N	N
9 Boucher	N	N	N	N	N	N	Y
10 ***Wolf***	Y	N	Y	Y	N	Y	Y
11 ***Davis***	Y	N	Y	Y	N	Y	Y
WASHINGTON							
1 ***White***	Y	N	Y	Y	N	Y	Y
2 ***Metcalf***	Y	N	Y	Y	N	Y	Y
3 ***Smith, Linda***	Y	N	Y	Y	N	Y	Y
4 ***Hastings***	Y	N	Y	Y	N	Y	Y
5 ***Nethercutt***	Y	N	Y	Y	N	Y	Y
6 Dicks	N	N	N	N	Y	N	N
7 McDermott	N	Y	N	N	Y	N	N
8 ***Dunn***	Y	N	Y	Y	N	Y	Y
9 Smith, Adam	N	N	N	N	Y	N	N
WEST VIRGINIA							
1 Mollohan	N	N	Y	N	N	N	Y
2 Wise	N	Y	Y	N	Y	N	Y
3 Rahall	N	N	Y	N	N	N	Y
WISCONSIN							
1 ***Neumann***	Y	N	Y	Y	N	Y	Y
2 ***Klug***	Y	N	Y	Y	N	Y	Y
3 Kind	Y	N	Y	Y	N	N	Y
4 Kleczka	N	N	N	N	N	N	Y
5 Barrett	Y	Y	N	N	Y	N	Y
6 ***Petri***	Y	N	Y	Y	N	Y	Y
7 Obey	N	N	N	N	Y	N	N
8 Johnson	N	N	N	N	N	N	Y
9 ***Sensenbrenner***	Y	N	Y	Y	N	Y	Y
WYOMING							
AL ***Cubin***	?	?	?	?	?	?	?

Southern states - Ala., Ark., Fla., Ga., Ky., La., Miss., N.C., Okla., S.C., Tenn., Texas, Va.

HOUSE VOTES 606, 607, 608, 609, 610, 611, 612, 613

606. Procedural Motion/Journal. Pallone, D-N.J., motion to adjourn. Motion rejected 38-308: R 1-181; D 37-127 (ND 27-92, SD 10-35); I 0-0, Nov. 7, 1997.

607. S 858. Fiscal 1998 Intelligence Authorization/Conference Report. Adoption of the conference report on the bill to authorize a classified amount for the activities of the CIA, National Security Agency, Defense Intelligence Agency and other U.S. intelligence agencies in fiscal 1998. The amount has been estimated to be nearly $27 billion. Adopted (thus cleared for the president) 385-36: R 217-4; D 168-31 (ND 116-29, SD 52-2); I 0-1, Nov. 7, 1997.

608. HR 2616. Charter Schools Authorization/Motion To Rise. Menendez, D-N.J., motion to rise from the Committee of the Whole. Motion rejected 71-348: R 0-222; D 70-126 (ND 58-87, SD 12-39); I 1-0, Nov. 7, 1997.

609. HR 2616. Charter Schools Authorization/Motion To Rise. Velázquez, D-N.Y., motion to rise from the Committee of the Whole. Motion rejected 75-334: R 1-209; D 74-124 (ND 59-85, SD 15-39); I 0-1, Nov. 7, 1997.

610. HR 2616. Charter Schools Authorization/State Funding Priority. Tierney, D-Mass., amendment to eliminate the bill's provisions that grant priority for certain federal funding to states that give charter schools financial autonomy, expand the number of charter schools established each year and periodically review the performance of charter schools. Rejected 164-260: R 5-216; D 158-44 (ND 121-27, SD 37-17); I 1-0, Nov. 7, 1997.

611. HR 2616. Charter Schools Authorization/Passage. Passage of the bill to authorize $100 million in fiscal 1998 to provide federal assistance to states for establishing new charter schools and evaluating existing charter schools. Passed 367-57: R 215-8; D 151-49 (ND 107-41, SD 44-8); I 1-0, Nov. 7, 1997.

612. HR 2616. Charter Schools Authorization/Reconsideration of Vote. Riggs, R-Calif., motion to table (kill) the Doggett, D-Texas, motion to reconsider the vote by which the House passed the bill to authorize $100 million in fiscal 1998 to provide federal assistance to states for establishing new charter schools and evaluating existing charter schools. Motion agreed to 256-163: R 217-1; D 39-161 (ND 25-121, SD 14-40); I 0-1, Nov. 7, 1997.

613. Procedural Motion/Adjourn. Becerra, D-Calif., motion to adjourn. Motion rejected 61-348: R 0-215; D 61-133 (ND 48-95, SD 13-38); I 0-0, Nov. 7, 1997.

KEY

- Y Voted for (yea).
- # Paired for.
- + Announced for.
- N Voted against (nay).
- X Paired against.
- – Announced against.
- P Voted "present."
- C Voted "present" to avoid possible conflict of interest.
- ? Did not vote or otherwise make a position known.

Democrats ***Republicans***
Independent

	606	607	608	609	610	611	612	613
ALABAMA								
1 ***Callahan***	N	Y	N	N	N	Y	Y	?
2 ***Everett***	N	Y	N	N	N	Y	Y	N
3 ***Riley***	–	+	–	–	–	+	+	+
4 ***Aderholt***	N	Y	N	N	N	Y	Y	N
5 Cramer	N	Y	N	N	Y	Y	Y	N
6 ***Bachus***	N	Y	N	N	N	Y	Y	N
7 Hilliard	N	Y	N	N	Y	?	N	N
ALASKA								
AL ***Young***	?	Y	N	N	N	Y	Y	N
ARIZONA								
1 ***Salmon***	N	Y	N	N	N	Y	Y	N
2 Pastor	N	Y	N	N	N	Y	N	N
3 ***Stump***	N	Y	N	N	N	Y	Y	N
4 ***Shadegg***	N	Y	N	N	N	Y	Y	N
5 ***Kolbe***	?	Y	N	N	N	Y	Y	N
6 ***Hayworth***	N	Y	N	N	N	Y	Y	N
ARKANSAS								
1 Berry	N	Y	N	N	Y	Y	N	Y
2 Snyder	N	Y	N	N	N	Y	N	N
3 ***Hutchinson***	N	Y	N	N	N	Y	Y	N
4 ***Dickey***	N	Y	N	?	N	Y	Y	N
CALIFORNIA								
1 ***Riggs***	?	Y	N	N	N	Y	Y	N
2 ***Herger***	N	Y	N	N	N	Y	Y	N
3 Fazio	Y	Y	Y	Y	Y	Y	N	Y
4 ***Doolittle***	?	Y	N	N	N	Y	Y	N
5 Matsui	N	Y	N	N	Y	Y	N	N
6 Woolsey	Y	N	Y	Y	Y	Y	N	Y
7 Miller	?	N	Y	Y	Y	Y	N	Y
8 Pelosi	Y	Y	Y	Y	Y	Y	N	Y
9 Dellums	?	N	Y	Y	Y	Y	N	?
10 Tauscher	N	Y	N	N	Y	Y	Y	N
11 ***Pombo***	?	Y	N	N	N	Y	Y	N
12 Lantos	N	Y	N	N	Y	Y	N	Y
13 Stark	?	?	Y	Y	Y	Y	N	Y
14 Eshoo	N	Y	N	N	Y	Y	N	N
15 ***Campbell***	N	Y	N	N	Y	Y	Y	N
16 Lofgren	N	N	Y	Y	Y	Y	N	N
17 Farr	?	Y	Y	Y	Y	Y	N	Y
18 Condit	N	Y	N	N	N	Y	N	N
19 ***Radanovich***	?	Y	N	N	N	Y	?	N
20 Dooley	N	Y	N	N	Y	Y	N	N
21 ***Thomas***	N	Y	N	N	N	Y	Y	N
22 Vacant								
23 ***Gallegly***	N	Y	N	N	N	Y	Y	N
24 Sherman	N	Y	N	N	Y	Y	N	N
25 ***McKeon***	N	Y	N	N	N	Y	Y	N
26 Berman	N	Y	N	?	N	Y	Y	N
27 ***Rogan***	N	Y	N	N	N	Y	Y	N
28 ***Dreier***	N	Y	N	N	N	Y	Y	N
29 Waxman	?	Y	N	N	Y	Y	Y	N
30 Becerra	?	N	Y	Y	Y	N	N	Y
31 Martinez	N	Y	N	N	Y	N	Y	N
32 Dixon	?	Y	N	N	Y	Y	N	N
33 Roybal-Allard	N	Y	Y	Y	Y	N	N	Y
34 Torres	Y	N	Y	Y	Y	N	N	Y
35 Waters	N	N	N	N	Y	N	N	Y
36 Harman	?	Y	N	N	N	Y	N	N
37 Millender-McD	?	Y	Y	Y	Y	Y	Y	Y
38 ***Horn***	N	Y	N	N	N	Y	Y	N
39 ***Royce***	N	Y	N	N	N	Y	?	N
40 ***Lewis***	N	Y	N	N	N	Y	Y	N
41 ***Kim***	N	Y	N	N	N	Y	Y	N
42 Brown	N	Y	N	?	Y	Y	N	N
43 ***Calvert***	N	Y	N	N	N	Y	Y	N
44 ***Bono***	?	Y	?	?	N	Y	Y	N
45 ***Rohrabacher***	N	Y	N	N	N	Y	Y	N
46 Sanchez	N	Y	Y	Y	Y	Y	N	Y
47 ***Cox***	?	Y	N	N	N	Y	Y	N
48 ***Packard***	N	Y	N	N	N	Y	Y	N
49 ***Bilbray***	N	Y	N	N	N	Y	Y	N
50 Filner	Y	N	Y	Y	Y	Y	N	Y
51 ***Cunningham***	N	Y	N	N	N	Y	Y	N
52 ***Hunter***	N	Y	N	N	N	Y	Y	N
COLORADO								
1 DeGette	N	Y	N	N	Y	Y	Y	N
2 Skaggs	N	Y	Y	Y	Y	Y	N	N
3 ***McInnis***	N	Y	N	N	N	Y	Y	N
4 ***Schaffer***	N	Y	N	N	N	N	Y	N
5 ***Hefley***	N	Y	N	N	N	N	Y	N
6 ***Schaefer***	N	Y	N	N	N	Y	Y	N
CONNECTICUT								
1 Kennelly	Y	Y	Y	N	Y	Y	N	Y
2 Gejdenson	Y	Y	Y	Y	N	Y	N	Y
3 DeLauro	?	Y	Y	Y	N	Y	N	Y
4 ***Shays***	N	Y	N	N	Y	Y	Y	N
5 Maloney	N	Y	N	N	N	Y	N	N
6 ***Johnson***	N	Y	N	N	Y	Y	Y	N
DELAWARE								
AL ***Castle***	N	Y	N	N	N	Y	Y	N
FLORIDA								
1 ***Scarborough***	?	Y	N	N	?	Y	Y	N
2 Boyd	N	Y	N	N	N	Y	Y	N
3 Brown	?	Y	Y	Y	N	Y	N	Y
4 ***Fowler***	N	Y	N	N	N	Y	Y	N
5 Thurman	Y	Y	N	N	N	Y	N	Y
6 ***Stearns***	N	Y	N	N	N	Y	Y	N
7 ***Mica***	N	Y	N	N	N	Y	Y	N
8 ***McCollum***	N	Y	N	N	N	Y	Y	?
9 ***Bilirakis***	N	Y	N	N	N	Y	Y	N
10 ***Young***	?	Y	N	N	N	Y	Y	N
11 Davis	?	Y	N	N	N	Y	Y	N
12 ***Canady***	?	Y	N	N	N	Y	Y	N
13 ***Miller***	N	Y	N	N	N	Y	Y	N
14 ***Goss***	N	Y	N	N	N	Y	Y	N
15 ***Weldon***	?	Y	N	N	N	Y	Y	N
16 ***Foley***	?	Y	N	N	N	?	Y	N
17 Meek	?	Y	Y	Y	N	N	N	Y
18 ***Ros-Lehtinen***	N	Y	N	N	N	Y	Y	N
19 Wexler	?	Y	?	N	N	N	N	N
20 Deutsch	Y	Y	Y	Y	Y	N	N	Y
21 ***Diaz-Balart***	N	Y	N	N	N	Y	Y	N
22 ***Shaw***	?	Y	N	N	N	Y	Y	N
23 Hastings	Y	Y	Y	Y	Y	Y	N	Y
GEORGIA								
1 ***Kingston***	N	Y	N	N	N	Y	Y	N
2 Bishop	N	Y	N	N	Y	Y	N	N
3 ***Collins***	N	Y	N	N	N	Y	?	N
4 McKinney	?	N	Y	Y	Y	Y	Y	N
5 Lewis	Y	Y	Y	Y	Y	Y	N	Y
6 ***Gingrich***								
7 ***Barr***	N	Y	N	N	N	Y	Y	N
8 ***Chambliss***	N	Y	N	N	N	Y	Y	N
9 ***Deal***	N	Y	N	N	N	Y	Y	N
10 ***Norwood***	N	Y	N	N	N	Y	Y	N
11 ***Linder***	N	Y	N	?	N	Y	Y	?
HAWAII								
1 Abercrombie	N	Y	N	N	Y	N	N	N
2 Mink	Y	Y	Y	Y	Y	N	N	Y
IDAHO								
1 ***Chenoweth***	?	N	N	N	N	N	Y	N
2 ***Crapo***	?	Y	N	N	N	Y	Y	N
ILLINOIS								
1 Rush	?	N	N	N	Y	N	N	N
2 Jackson	N	N	Y	Y	Y	Y	N	N
3 Lipinski	N	Y	N	N	N	Y	Y	N
4 Gutierrez	N	N	N	N	Y	Y	N	N
5 Blagojevich	N	Y	N	Y	Y	Y	N	N
6 ***Hyde***	N	Y	N	?	N	N	Y	N
7 Davis	N	N	N	N	N	N	N	N
8 ***Crane***	?	Y	N	N	N	Y	Y	N
9 Yates	?	?	?	?	?	?	?	?
10 ***Porter***	?	Y	N	N	N	Y	Y	N
11 ***Weller***	?	Y	N	N	N	Y	Y	N
12 Costello	N	Y	N	N	Y	Y	N	N
13 ***Fawell***	N	Y	N	N	N	Y	Y	N
14 ***Hastert***	N	Y	N	?	N	Y	Y	N
15 ***Ewing***	N	Y	N	N	N	Y	Y	N

ND Northern Democrats SD Southern Democrats

	606	607	608	609	610	611	612	613
16 **Manzullo**	?	Y	N	N	N	N	Y	N
17 Evans	Y	Y	Y	Y	Y	Y	N	Y
18 **LaHood**	N	Y	N	N	N	Y	Y	N
19 Poshard	N	Y	N	N	Y	Y	N	N
20 **Shimkus**	N	Y	N	N	N	Y	Y	N
INDIANA								
1 Visclosky	N	Y	N	N	Y	Y	N	N
2 **McIntosh**	?	Y	N	N	N	Y	Y	N
3 Roemer	N	Y	N	N	N	Y	Y	N
4 **Souder**	N	Y	N	N	N	Y	Y	N
5 **Buyer**	N	Y	N	N	N	Y	Y	N
6 **Burton**	?	Y	N	N	N	Y	Y	N
7 **Pease**	N	Y	N	N	N	Y	Y	N
8 **Hostettler**	N	Y	N	N	N	N	Y	N
9 Hamilton	N	Y	N	N	N	Y	N	N
10 Carson	–	Y	Y	N	N	N	N	N
IOWA								
1 **Leach**	?	Y	N	?	N	Y	Y	N
2 **Nussle**	N	Y	N	N	N	Y	Y	N
3 Boswell	N	Y	N	N	Y	N	N	N
4 **Ganske**	N	Y	N	N	N	Y	Y	N
5 **Latham**	N	Y	N	N	N	Y	Y	N
KANSAS								
1 **Moran**	N	Y	N	N	N	Y	Y	N
2 **Ryun**	N	Y	N	N	N	Y	Y	N
3 **Snowbarger**	N	Y	N	N	N	Y	Y	N
4 **Tiahrt**	N	Y	N	?	N	Y	Y	N
KENTUCKY								
1 **Whitfield**	N	Y	N	N	N	Y	Y	N
2 **Lewis**	N	Y	N	N	N	Y	Y	N
3 **Northup**	N	Y	N	N	N	Y	Y	N
4 **Bunning**	N	Y	N	N	N	Y	Y	N
5 **Rogers**	N	Y	N	N	N	Y	Y	N
6 Baesler	N	Y	N	N	Y	Y	Y	N
LOUISIANA								
1 **Livingston**	?	Y	N	?	N	Y	Y	N
2 Jefferson	Y	Y	Y	Y	Y	Y	N	Y
3 **Tauzin**	?	Y	N	N	N	Y	Y	N
4 **McCrery**	?	Y	N	?	N	Y	Y	N
5 **Cooksey**	?	?	N	N	N	Y	Y	N
6 **Baker**	N	Y	N	N	N	Y	Y	N
7 John	N	Y	N	N	N	Y	Y	N
MAINE								
1 Allen	N	Y	N	N	Y	Y	N	N
2 Baldacci	N	Y	N	Y	Y	Y	N	N
MARYLAND								
1 **Gilchrest**	N	Y	N	N	N	Y	Y	N
2 **Ehrlich**	?	Y	N	N	N	Y	Y	N
3 Cardin	N	Y	N	N	Y	Y	N	N
4 Wynn	N	Y	N	N	Y	Y	N	N
5 Hoyer	N	Y	N	N	Y	Y	N	N
6 **Bartlett**	N	Y	N	N	N	Y	Y	N
7 Cummings	N	Y	N	N	Y	Y	N	N
8 **Morella**	N	Y	N	N	N	Y	Y	?
MASSACHUSETTS								
1 Olver	?	N	Y	Y	Y	N	N	Y
2 Neal	?	?	N	N	Y	N	N	N
3 McGovern	N	N	N	N	Y	N	N	N
4 Frank	Y	N	Y	Y	Y	N	N	Y
5 Meehan	N	Y	N	N	Y	N	N	Y
6 Tierney	N	N	N	N	Y	N	N	N
7 Markey	Y	?	N	Y	Y	N	N	?
8 Kennedy	N	Y	N	N	Y	N	N	N
9 Moakley	N	Y	N	N	Y	N	N	N
10 Delahunt	Y	Y	N	Y	Y	N	N	N
MICHIGAN								
1 Stupak	N	Y	Y	Y	Y	N	N	Y
2 **Hoekstra**	N	Y	N	N	N	Y	Y	?
3 **Ehlers**	N	Y	N	N	N	Y	+	N
4 **Camp**	N	N	N	N	N	Y	Y	N
5 Barcia	N	Y	N	N	Y	Y	Y	N
6 **Upton**	N	Y	N	N	N	Y	Y	N
7 **Smith**	N	Y	N	N	N	Y	Y	N
8 Stabenow	N	Y	N	N	Y	N	N	N
9 Kildee	N	Y	N	N	Y	Y	N	N
10 Bonior	Y	N	Y	Y	Y	N	N	Y
11 **Knollenberg**	N	Y	N	N	N	Y	Y	N
12 Levin	N	Y	N	N	Y	Y	N	N
13 Rivers	N	Y	N	N	Y	N	N	N
14 Conyers	Y	N	Y	Y	Y	Y	N	Y
15 Kilpatrick	N	Y	N	N	Y	N	N	N
16 Dingell	?	Y	Y	Y	Y	N	N	Y
MINNESOTA								
1 **Gutknecht**	N	Y	N	N	N	Y	Y	N
2 Minge	N	N	N	N	Y	Y	Y	N

	606	607	608	609	610	611	612	613
3 **Ramstad**	N	Y	N	N	N	Y	Y	N
4 Vento	N	N	N	N	Y	N	N	N
5 Sabo	Y	Y	N	N	Y	Y	N	N
6 Luther	N	Y	N	N	Y	Y	Y	N
7 Peterson	Y	Y	Y	Y	Y	Y	N	Y
8 Oberstar	?	N	Y	Y	Y	Y	N	N
MISSISSIPPI								
1 **Wicker**	?	Y	N	N	N	Y	Y	N
2 Thompson	N	Y	N	N	Y	?	N	N
3 **Pickering**	N	Y	N	N	N	Y	Y	N
4 **Parker**	?	Y	N	N	N	Y	Y	N
5 Taylor	N	Y	N	N	N	Y	Y	N
MISSOURI								
1 Clay	N	Y	N	N	Y	N	N	N
2 **Talent**	N	Y	?	?	N	Y	Y	N
3 Gephardt	Y	Y	Y	Y	N	Y	N	Y
4 Skelton	N	Y	N	N	Y	Y	N	N
5 McCarthy	N	Y	N	N	Y	Y	N	N
6 Danner	N	Y	N	N	Y	Y	N	N
7 **Blunt**	N	Y	N	N	N	Y	Y	N
8 **Emerson**	N	Y	N	N	N	Y	Y	N
9 **Hulshof**	N	Y	N	N	N	Y	Y	N
MONTANA								
AL **Hill**	N	Y	N	N	N	Y	Y	N
NEBRASKA								
1 **Bereuter**	N	Y	N	N	N	Y	Y	N
2 **Christensen**	N	Y	N	N	N	Y	Y	N
3 **Barrett**	N	Y	N	N	N	Y	Y	N
NEVADA								
1 **Ensign**	N	Y	N	N	N	Y	Y	N
2 **Gibbons**	N	Y	N	N	N	Y	Y	N
NEW HAMPSHIRE								
1 **Sununu**	N	Y	N	N	N	Y	Y	N
2 **Bass**	N	Y	N	N	N	Y	Y	N
NEW JERSEY								
1 Andrews	Y	Y	N	N	Y	Y	N	Y
2 **LoBiondo**	N	Y	N	N	Y	Y	Y	N
3 **Saxton**	N	Y	N	N	N	Y	Y	N
4 **Smith**	N	Y	N	N	N	Y	Y	N
5 **Roukema**	N	Y	N	N	N	Y	Y	N
6 Pallone	Y	Y	Y	Y	Y	Y	N	Y
7 **Franks**	N	Y	N	N	N	Y	Y	N
8 Pascrell	N	Y	N	N	Y	Y	?	N
9 Rothman	N	Y	N	N	Y	Y	N	N
10 Payne	?	N	Y	Y	Y	N	N	Y
11 **Frelinghuysen**	N	Y	N	N	N	Y	Y	N
12 **Pappas**	N	Y	N	N	N	Y	Y	N
13 Menendez	N	Y	Y	Y	Y	Y	Y	Y
NEW MEXICO								
1 **Schiff**	?	?	?	?	?	?	?	?
2 **Skeen**	?	Y	N	N	N	Y	Y	N
3 **Redmond**	N	Y	N	N	N	Y	Y	?
NEW YORK								
1 **Forbes**	?	Y	N	N	N	Y	Y	N
2 **Lazio**	N	Y	N	N	N	Y	Y	N
3 **King**	N	Y	N	N	N	Y	Y	N
4 McCarthy	N	Y	Y	N	Y	Y	Y	N
5 Ackerman	?	Y	Y	?	Y	Y	N	N
6 Flake	?	Y	N	N	Y	Y	N	N
7 Manton	?	Y	N	N	Y	Y	N	N
8 Nadler	N	Y	Y	Y	Y	Y	N	N
9 Schumer	N	Y	N	N	Y	Y	N	N
10 Towns	Y	Y	Y	Y	Y	Y	N	Y
11 Owens	?	N	Y	Y	Y	+	N	Y
12 Velázquez	Y	N	Y	Y	Y	Y	N	Y
13 **Fossella**	N	Y	N	N	N	Y	Y	N
14 Maloney	N	Y	Y	Y	Y	Y	N	N
15 Rangel	?	Y	Y	Y	Y	Y	N	Y
16 Serrano	?	N	N	N	Y	Y	N	Y
17 Engel	–	Y	N	N	Y	Y	N	N
18 Lowey	N	Y	N	N	Y	Y	N	N
19 **Kelly**	N	Y	N	N	N	Y	Y	N
20 **Gilman**	?	Y	N	N	N	Y	Y	N
21 McNulty	Y	Y	Y	Y	Y	Y	N	Y
22 **Solomon**	N	Y	N	N	N	Y	Y	N
23 **Boehlert**	N	Y	N	N	N	Y	Y	N
24 **McHugh**	N	Y	N	N	N	Y	Y	N
25 **Walsh**	N	Y	N	N	N	Y	Y	N
26 Hinchey	N	N	Y	Y	Y	N	N	Y
27 **Paxon**	N	Y	N	N	N	Y	Y	N
28 Slaughter	N	Y	?	N	Y	N	N	?
29 LaFalce	?	Y	Y	Y	Y	Y	N	Y
30 **Quinn**	N	Y	N	N	N	Y	Y	N
31 **Houghton**	N	Y	N	N	N	Y	Y	N

	606	607	608	609	610	611	612	613
NORTH CAROLINA								
1 Clayton	?	Y	N	N	Y	Y	N	Y
2 Etheridge	Y	Y	N	Y	Y	Y	N	N
3 **Jones**	N	Y	N	N	N	Y	Y	?
4 Price	N	Y	N	N	Y	Y	N	N
5 **Burr**	N	Y	N	N	N	Y	Y	N
6 **Coble**	N	Y	N	N	N	Y	Y	N
7 McIntyre	N	Y	N	N	N	Y	Y	?
8 Hefner	?	Y	N	Y	Y	Y	N	Y
9 **Myrick**	N	Y	N	N	N	Y	Y	N
10 **Ballenger**	N	Y	N	N	N	Y	N	?
11 **Taylor**	?	Y	N	N	N	Y	Y	N
12 Watt	N	N	N	Y	Y	N	N	Y
NORTH DAKOTA								
AL Pomeroy	N	Y	Y	Y	Y	Y	N	N
OHIO								
1 **Chabot**	N	Y	N	N	N	Y	Y	N
2 **Portman**	N	Y	N	N	N	Y	Y	N
3 Hall	?	Y	N	N	N	Y	N	N
4 **Oxley**	N	Y	N	?	N	Y	Y	N
5 **Gillmor**	N	Y	N	N	N	Y	Y	N
6 Strickland	N	Y	Y	Y	Y	Y	Y	N
7 **Hobson**	N	Y	N	N	N	Y	Y	N
8 **Boehner**	N	Y	N	N	N	Y	Y	N
9 Kaptur	?	Y	?	N	Y	Y	N	N
10 Kucinich	N	Y	N	N	Y	N	N	N
11 Stokes	N	?	N	?	Y	N	N	?
12 **Kasich**	?	Y	N	N	N	Y	Y	N
13 Brown	N	Y	Y	Y	Y	N	N	N
14 Sawyer	N	Y	N	N	Y	Y	N	N
15 **Pryce**	?	Y	N	N	N	Y	Y	N
16 **Regula**	N	Y	N	N	N	Y	Y	N
17 Traficant	N	Y	N	N	N	Y	Y	N
18 **Ney**	N	Y	N	N	N	Y	?	N
19 **LaTourette**	N	Y	N	N	N	Y	Y	N
OKLAHOMA								
1 **Largent**	?	Y	N	N	N	Y	Y	N
2 **Coburn**	N	Y	N	N	N	Y	Y	N
3 **Watkins**	N	Y	N	N	N	Y	Y	N
4 **Watts**	N	Y	N	N	N	Y	Y	N
5 **Istook**	N	Y	N	N	N	Y	Y	N
6 **Lucas**	N	Y	N	N	N	Y	Y	N
OREGON								
1 Furse	N	N	Y	Y	Y	Y	N	N
2 **Smith**	N	Y	N	N	N	Y	Y	N
3 Blumenauer	Y	Y	Y	Y	Y	N	N	N
4 DeFazio	N	N	?	Y	Y	N	N	Y
5 Hooley	N	Y	Y	N	Y	Y	N	N
PENNSYLVANIA								
1 Foglietta	?	Y	?	?	?	Y	?	?
2 Fattah	N	Y	N	Y	N	Y	N	N
3 Borski	N	Y	N	N	N	Y	N	N
4 Klink	N	Y	N	N	N	N	?	?
5 **Peterson**	N	Y	N	N	N	Y	Y	N
6 Holden	N	Y	N	N	N	Y	Y	N
7 **Weldon**	N	Y	N	N	N	Y	Y	N
8 **Greenwood**	?	Y	N	N	N	Y	?	N
9 **Shuster**	N	Y	N	N	N	Y	Y	N
10 **McDade**	?	?	N	N	N	Y	Y	N
11 Kanjorski	N	Y	N	N	N	Y	Y	N
12 Murtha	N	Y	Y	N	N	Y	Y	N
13 **Fox**	N	Y	N	N	N	Y	Y	N
14 Coyne	Y	Y	Y	Y	Y	N	N	Y
15 McHale	N	Y	N	N	N	Y	Y	N
16 **Pitts**	N	Y	N	N	N	Y	Y	N
17 **Gekas**	N	Y	N	N	N	Y	Y	N
18 Doyle	N	Y	N	N	N	Y	Y	N
19 **Goodling**	N	Y	N	N	N	Y	Y	N
20 Mascara	N	Y	N	N	N	Y	Y	N
21 **English**	N	Y	N	N	N	Y	Y	N
RHODE ISLAND								
1 Kennedy	N	Y	Y	Y	Y	Y	N	Y
2 Weygand	N	Y	N	N	Y	Y	N	N
SOUTH CAROLINA								
1 **Sanford**	N	Y	N	N	N	Y	Y	N
2 **Spence**	N	Y	N	N	N	Y	Y	N
3 **Graham**	?	Y	N	N	N	Y	Y	N
4 **Inglis**	N	Y	N	N	N	Y	Y	N
5 Spratt	?	Y	N	Y	Y	Y	N	Y
6 Clyburn	Y	Y	N	N	N	Y	N	Y
SOUTH DAKOTA								
AL **Thune**	N	Y	N	N	N	Y	Y	N
TENNESSEE								
1 **Jenkins**	N	Y	N	N	N	Y	Y	N
2 **Duncan**	N	N	N	N	N	Y	Y	N

	606	607	608	609	610	611	612	613
3 **Wamp**	N	Y	N	N	N	Y	Y	N
4 **Hilleary**	N	Y	N	Y	N	Y	Y	N
5 Clement	N	Y	N	N	Y	Y	N	N
6 Gordon	N	Y	N	N	N	Y	N	N
7 **Bryant**	N	Y	N	N	N	Y	Y	N
8 Tanner	N	Y	N	N	Y	Y	N	N
9 Ford	N	Y	N	N	Y	Y	N	N
TEXAS								
1 Sandlin	N	Y	N	N	Y	Y	N	N
2 Turner	N	Y	N	N	Y	Y	Y	N
3 **Johnson, Sam**	?	?	N	?	?	Y	Y	N
4 Hall	N	Y	N	N	N	Y	Y	N
5 **Sessions**	N	Y	N	N	N	Y	Y	N
6 **Barton**	N	Y	N	N	N	Y	Y	?
7 **Archer**	N	Y	N	N	N	Y	Y	N
8 **Brady**	N	Y	N	N	N	Y	Y	N
9 Lampson	N	Y	N	N	Y	Y	N	N
10 Doggett	Y	Y	Y	Y	Y	Y	N	?
11 Edwards	N	Y	N	N	Y	Y	N	N
12 **Granger**	?	Y	N	N	N	Y	Y	N
13 **Thornberry**	N	Y	N	N	N	Y	Y	N
14 **Paul**	N	N	N	N	Y	N	Y	N
15 Hinojosa	N	Y	N	Y	Y	N	N	N
16 Reyes	N	Y	Y	N	Y	N	Y	N
17 Stenholm	N	Y	N	N	N	Y	N	N
18 Jackson-Lee	?	Y	Y	N	Y	Y	N	N
19 **Combest**	N	Y	N	N	N	Y	Y	N
20 Gonzalez	?	?	?	?	?	?	?	?
21 **Smith**	N	Y	N	N	N	Y	Y	N
22 **DeLay**	N	Y	N	N	N	Y	Y	N
23 **Bonilla**	Y	Y	N	N	N	Y	Y	N
24 Frost	N	Y	N	N	Y	Y	N	N
25 Bentsen	N	Y	N	N	Y	Y	N	N
26 **Armey**	N	Y	N	?	?	Y	Y	N
27 Ortiz	N	Y	N	N	N	Y	Y	N
28 Rodriguez	N	Y	Y	Y	Y	Y	N	N
29 Green	N	Y	N	N	Y	Y	N	N
30 Johnson, E.B.	Y	Y	?	N	N	Y	N	N
UTAH								
1 **Hansen**	N	Y	N	N	N	Y	Y	N
2 **Cook**	N	Y	N	N	N	Y	Y	N
3 **Cannon**	N	Y	N	N	N	N	Y	N
VERMONT								
AL *Sanders*	?	N	Y	N	Y	Y	N	?
VIRGINIA								
1 **Bateman**	N	Y	N	N	N	Y	Y	N
2 Pickett	N	Y	N	N	Y	Y	N	N
3 Scott	N	Y	Y	Y	Y	N	N	N
4 Sisisky	N	Y	?	N	Y	Y	N	N
5 Goode	N	Y	N	N	N	N	Y	N
6 **Goodlatte**	N	Y	N	N	N	Y	Y	N
7 **Bliley**	N	Y	N	N	N	Y	Y	N
8 Moran	N	Y	N	N	Y	Y	N	N
9 Boucher	Y	Y	N	N	Y	Y	Y	?
10 **Wolf**	N	Y	N	N	N	Y	Y	N
11 **Davis**	N	Y	N	N	N	Y	Y	N
WASHINGTON								
1 **White**	N	Y	N	N	N	Y	Y	N
2 **Metcalf**	N	Y	N	N	N	Y	Y	N
3 **Smith, Linda**	N	Y	N	N	N	Y	Y	N
4 **Hastings**	N	Y	N	?	N	Y	Y	N
5 **Nethercutt**	N	Y	N	N	N	Y	Y	N
6 Dicks	N	N	Y	N	Y	Y	N	N
7 McDermott	Y	N	Y	Y	Y	N	N	Y
8 **Dunn**	N	Y	N	N	N	Y	Y	N
9 Smith, Adam	Y	Y	N	Y	N	Y	N	Y
WEST VIRGINIA								
1 Mollohan	?	Y	Y	N	Y	Y	N	N
2 Wise	Y	Y	Y	Y	Y	Y	Y	Y
3 Rahall	N	Y	N	N	Y	N	Y	N
WISCONSIN								
1 **Neumann**	N	Y	N	N	N	Y	Y	N
2 **Klug**	N	Y	N	N	N	Y	Y	N
3 Kind	N	Y	N	N	Y	Y	N	N
4 Kleczka	?	Y	N	N	Y	Y	N	N
5 Barrett	N	Y	N	Y	Y	Y	N	Y
6 **Petri**	N	Y	N	N	N	Y	Y	N
7 Obey	N	Y	Y	N	N	Y	N	Y
8 Johnson	N	Y	N	N	Y	Y	N	N
9 **Sensenbrenner**	N	Y	N	N	N	Y	Y	N
WYOMING								
AL **Cubin**	?	?	?	?	?	?	?	?

Southern states - Ala., Ark., Fla., Ga., Ky., La., Miss., N.C., Okla., S.C., Tenn., Texas, Va.

HOUSE VOTES 614, 615, 616, 617, 618, 619, 620, 621

614. HR 2647. Chinese Military Companies/Passage. Passage of the bill to allow the president to investigate, regulate and prohibit activities of companies in the United States controlled by or associated with China's People's Liberation Army without first declaring a national emergency as required by the International Emergency Economic Powers Act. Passed 408-10: R 216-2; D 191-8 (ND 139-6, SD 52-2); I 1-0, Nov. 7, 1997. A "nay" was a vote in support of the president's position.

615. HR 2264. Fiscal 1998 Labor-HHS Appropriations/Conference Report. Adoption of the conference report on the bill to provide $80.4 billion in discretionary budget authority for the departments of Labor, Health and Human Services, and Education, and related agencies — $5.7 billion more than fiscal 1997 — and to provide a total of $268.0 billion, including mandatory spending, which is $10.7 billion less than provided in fiscal 1997. Adopted (thus sent to the Senate) 352-65: R 157-60; D 194-5 (ND 142-3, SD 52-2); I 1-0, Nov. 7, 1997.

616. Procedural Motion/Journal. Approval of the House Journal of Friday, Nov. 7, 1997. Approved 345-56: R 193-16; D 151-40 (ND 108-29, SD 43-11); I 1-0, Nov. 8, 1997.

617. HR 2631. Line-Item Veto Disapproval/Passage. Packard, R-Calif., motion to suspend the rules and pass the bill to disapprove President Clinton's line-item vetoes of 38 projects, totaling $287 million, in the fiscal 1998 military construction appropriations bill (HR 2016 — PL 105-45). Motion agreed to 352-64: R 193-23; D 158-41 (ND 109-36, SD 49-5); I 1-0, Nov. 8, 1997. A two-thirds majority of those present and voting (278 in this case) is required for passage under suspension of the rules. A "nay" was a vote in support of the president's position.

618. HR 2534. Agricultural Research and Education/Passage. Smith, R-Ore., motion to suspend the rules and pass the bill to authorize $14.7 billion through fiscal 2002 for the Department of Agriculture's research, education and extension programs. The bill streamlines or eliminates certain existing programs and establishes some new research initiatives. Motion agreed to 291-125: R 208-8; D 83-116 (ND 46-99, SD 37-17); I 0-1, Nov. 8, 1997. A two-thirds majority of those present and voting (278 in this case) is required for passage under suspension of the rules.

619. HR 2813. Robert R. Ingram Medal of Honor/Passage. Fowler, R-Fla., motion to suspend the rules and pass the bill to waive time limitations against granting the Medal of Honor for Robert R. Ingram of Jacksonville, Fla., a Vietnam War veteran. Motion agreed to 412-0: R 215-0; D 197-0 (ND 144-0, SD 53-0); I 0-0, Nov. 8, 1997. A two-thirds majority of those present and voting (275 in this case) is required for passage under suspension of the rules.

620. H Res 315. Robert K. Dornan Election Challenge/Motion To Table. Solomon, R-N.Y., motion to table (kill) the Gephardt, D-Mo., privileged resolution to dismiss the complaint by former Rep. Robert K. Dornan, R-Calif., contesting the election of Loretta Sanchez, D-Calif. The resolution calls for state authorities to continue their investigation into questionable voter registration activities and for the House Oversight Committee to examine voter registration procedures. Motion agreed to 215-193: R 214-1; D 1-192 (ND 1-139, SD 0-53); I 0-0, Nov. 8, 1997.

621. Procedural Motion/Adjourn. Armey, R-Texas, motion to adjourn. Motion agreed to 233-170: R 210-4; D 23-166 (ND 16-120, SD 7-46); I 0-0, Nov. 8, 1997.

KEY

Y Voted for (yea).
Paired for.
+ Announced for.
N Voted against (nay).
X Paired against.
– Announced against.
P Voted "present."
C Voted "present" to avoid possible conflict of interest.
? Did not vote or otherwise make a position known.

Democrats ***Republicans***
Independent

	614	615	616	617	618	619	620	621
ALABAMA								
1 ***Callahan***	?	Y	Y	Y	Y	Y	Y	Y
2 ***Everett***	Y	N	N	Y	Y	Y	Y	Y
3 ***Riley***	–	?	?	+	+	+	+	+
4 ***Aderholt***	Y	N	Y	Y	Y	Y	Y	Y
5 Cramer	Y	Y	Y	Y	Y	Y	N	N
6 ***Bachus***	Y	N	Y	Y	Y	Y	Y	Y
7 Hilliard	Y	Y	N	Y	N	Y	N	N
ALASKA								
AL ***Young***	Y	Y	?	Y	Y	Y	Y	Y
ARIZONA								
1 ***Salmon***	Y	N	Y	N	Y	Y	Y	Y
2 Pastor	Y	Y	Y	Y	Y	Y	N	Y
3 ***Stump***	Y	N	Y	Y	Y	Y	Y	Y
4 ***Shadegg***	?	Y	Y	Y	Y	Y	Y	Y
5 ***Kolbe***	Y	Y	Y	Y	Y	Y	Y	Y
6 ***Hayworth***	Y	Y	Y	Y	Y	Y	Y	Y
ARKANSAS								
1 Berry	Y	Y	Y	Y	Y	Y	N	N
2 Snyder	Y	Y	Y	Y	N	Y	N	N
3 ***Hutchinson***	Y	N	Y	Y	Y	Y	Y	Y
4 ***Dickey***	Y	Y	N	N	Y	Y	Y	Y
CALIFORNIA								
1 ***Riggs***	Y	Y	Y	Y	Y	Y	Y	Y
2 ***Herger***	Y	Y	Y	Y	Y	Y	Y	Y
3 Fazio	Y	Y	N	Y	N	Y	N	N
4 ***Doolittle***	Y	N	Y	Y	Y	Y	Y	Y
5 Matsui	Y	Y	Y	Y	N	Y	N	N
6 Woolsey	Y	Y	Y	Y	N	Y	N	N
7 Miller	Y	Y	N	Y	N	Y	N	N
8 Pelosi	Y	Y	Y	Y	N	Y	N	N
9 Dellums	Y	Y	Y	Y	N	Y	N	N
10 Tauscher	Y	Y	Y	Y	Y	Y	N	N
11 ***Pombo***	Y	N	Y	Y	Y	Y	Y	Y
12 Lantos	Y	Y	Y	Y	N	Y	?	N
13 Stark	Y	Y	Y	N	N	Y	N	N
14 Eshoo	Y	Y	Y	Y	N	Y	N	N
15 ***Campbell***	Y	Y	Y	Y	N	Y	Y	Y
16 Lofgren	N	Y	Y	Y	N	Y	N	N
17 Farr	Y	Y	Y	Y	Y	Y	N	N
18 Condit	Y	Y	Y	Y	Y	Y	N	N
19 ***Radanovich***	Y	N	Y	Y	Y	Y	Y	Y
20 Dooley	Y	Y	Y	N	Y	Y	N	N
21 ***Thomas***	Y	Y	Y	Y	Y	Y	Y	Y
22 Vacant								
23 ***Gallegly***	Y	Y	Y	Y	Y	Y	Y	Y
24 Sherman	Y	Y	Y	N	N	Y	N	N
25 ***McKeon***	Y	Y	Y	Y	Y	Y	Y	Y
26 Berman	Y	Y	Y	Y	N	Y	N	Y
27 ***Rogan***	Y	Y	Y	Y	Y	Y	Y	Y
28 ***Dreier***	Y	Y	Y	Y	Y	Y	Y	Y
29 Waxman	Y	Y	Y	N	N	Y	N	?
30 Becerra	Y	Y	N	Y	N	Y	N	N
31 Martinez	Y	Y	Y	Y	N	Y	N	N
32 Dixon	Y	Y	Y	Y	N	Y	N	N
33 Roybal-Allard	Y	Y	Y	N	N	Y	N	N
34 Torres	Y	Y	?	Y	N	Y	N	N
35 Waters	Y	Y	N	N	N	Y	N	N
36 Harman	Y	Y	?	N	N	Y	N	?
37 Millender-McD.	Y	Y	Y	Y	N	Y	N	N
38 ***Horn***	Y	Y	Y	Y	Y	Y	Y	Y
39 ***Royce***	Y	N	Y	N	N	Y	Y	Y
40 ***Lewis***	Y	Y	Y	Y	Y	Y	Y	Y
41 ***Kim***	Y	Y	Y	Y	Y	Y	Y	Y
42 Brown	N	Y	N	N	Y	Y	N	N
43 ***Calvert***	Y	Y	Y	Y	Y	Y	Y	Y
44 ***Bono***	Y	Y	Y	Y	Y	Y	Y	Y
45 ***Rohrabacher***	Y	N	Y	N	Y	Y	Y	Y
46 Sanchez	Y	Y	Y	N	N	Y	P	N
47 ***Cox***	Y	N	?	Y	Y	Y	Y	Y
48 ***Packard***	Y	Y	Y	Y	Y	Y	Y	Y
49 ***Bilbray***	Y	Y	N	Y	Y	Y	Y	N
50 Filner	+	Y	N	N	N	Y	N	N
51 ***Cunningham***	Y	Y	Y	Y	Y	Y	Y	Y
52 ***Hunter***	Y	Y	Y	Y	Y	Y	Y	Y
COLORADO								
1 DeGette	Y	Y	Y	N	N	Y	N	N
2 Skaggs	N	Y	Y	N	N	Y	N	N
3 ***McInnis***	Y	Y	Y	Y	Y	Y	Y	Y
4 ***Schaffer***	Y	N	N	Y	Y	?	Y	N
5 ***Hefley***	Y	N	N	Y	Y	Y	Y	Y
6 ***Schaefer***	Y	N	Y	Y	Y	Y	Y	Y
CONNECTICUT								
1 Kennelly	Y	Y	Y	Y	Y	Y	N	N
2 Gejdenson	Y	Y	Y	Y	N	Y	N	N
3 DeLauro	Y	Y	Y	Y	N	Y	N	N
4 ***Shays***	Y	Y	Y	N	N	Y	Y	Y
5 Maloney	Y	Y	Y	Y	Y	Y	N	N
6 ***Johnson***	Y	Y	Y	Y	Y	Y	Y	N
DELAWARE								
AL ***Castle***	Y	Y	?	Y	Y	Y	Y	Y
FLORIDA								
1 ***Scarborough***	Y	N	Y	Y	Y	Y	Y	Y
2 Boyd	Y	Y	Y	Y	Y	Y	N	N
3 Brown	Y	Y	Y	Y	N	Y	N	N
4 ***Fowler***	Y	Y	Y	Y	Y	Y	Y	Y
5 Thurman	Y	Y	Y	Y	Y	Y	N	N
6 ***Stearns***	Y	N	Y	Y	Y	Y	Y	Y
7 ***Mica***	Y	N	Y	Y	Y	Y	Y	Y
8 ***McCollum***	?	X	Y	Y	Y	Y	Y	Y
9 ***Bilirakis***	Y	Y	Y	Y	Y	Y	Y	Y
10 ***Young***	Y	?	Y	Y	Y	Y	Y	Y
11 Davis	Y	Y	Y	N	N	Y	N	Y
12 ***Canady***	Y	Y	Y	Y	Y	Y	Y	Y
13 ***Miller***	Y	Y	Y	N	Y	Y	Y	Y
14 ***Goss***	Y	Y	Y	Y	Y	Y	Y	Y
15 ***Weldon***	Y	N	Y	Y	Y	Y	Y	Y
16 ***Foley***	Y	Y	Y	Y	Y	Y	Y	Y
17 Meek	Y	Y	N	Y	N	Y	N	Y
18 ***Ros-Lehtinen***	Y	Y	Y	Y	Y	?	?	?
19 Wexler	Y	Y	Y	N	N	Y	N	N
20 Deutsch	Y	Y	Y	N	N	Y	N	N
21 ***Diaz-Balart***	Y	Y	Y	Y	Y	Y	Y	Y
22 ***Shaw***	Y	Y	?	Y	Y	Y	Y	Y
23 Hastings	Y	Y	N	Y	N	Y	N	N
GEORGIA								
1 ***Kingston***	Y	Y	N	Y	Y	Y	Y	Y
2 Bishop	Y	Y	Y	Y	Y	Y	N	N
3 ***Collins***	Y	N	Y	Y	Y	Y	Y	Y
4 McKinney	Y	Y	Y	N	N	Y	N	N
5 Lewis	Y	Y	N	Y	N	Y	N	N
6 ***Gingrich***				Y	Y		Y	
7 ***Barr***	Y	N	Y	Y	Y	Y	Y	Y
8 ***Chambliss***	Y	Y	Y	Y	Y	Y	Y	Y
9 ***Deal***	Y	Y	Y	Y	Y	Y	Y	Y
10 ***Norwood***	Y	N	Y	Y	Y	Y	Y	Y
11 ***Linder***	Y	Y	Y	Y	Y	Y	Y	Y
HAWAII								
1 Abercrombie	Y	Y	N	Y	N	Y	N	Y
2 Mink	Y	Y	Y	Y	N	Y	N	N
IDAHO								
1 ***Chenoweth***	Y	N	Y	Y	Y	Y	Y	Y
2 ***Crapo***	Y	N	Y	Y	Y	Y	Y	Y
ILLINOIS								
1 Rush	Y	Y	Y	N	N	Y	N	N
2 Jackson	Y	Y	Y	Y	N	Y	N	N
3 Lipinski	Y	Y	Y	Y	N	Y	N	N
4 Gutierrez	Y	Y	N	Y	N	Y	N	?
5 Blagojevich	Y	Y	Y	Y	N	Y	N	N
6 ***Hyde***	Y	Y	Y	Y	Y	Y	Y	Y
7 Davis	Y	Y	Y	Y	N	Y	N	N
8 ***Crane***	Y	N	Y	Y	Y	Y	Y	Y
9 Yates	?	?	N	?	?	?	?	?
10 ***Porter***	Y	Y	Y	Y	Y	Y	Y	Y
11 ***Weller***	Y	Y	N	Y	Y	Y	Y	Y
12 Costello	Y	Y	?	Y	Y	Y	N	N
13 ***Fawell***	Y	Y	Y	Y	Y	Y	Y	Y
14 ***Hastert***	Y	Y	Y	Y	Y	Y	Y	Y
15 ***Ewing***	Y	Y	Y	N	Y	Y	Y	Y

ND Northern Democrats SD Southern Democrats

	614	615	616	617	618	619	620	621
16 ***Manzullo***	Y	N	Y	Y	Y	Y	Y	Y
17 Evans	Y	Y	Y	Y	Y	Y	N	N
18 ***LaHood***	Y	Y	Y	N	Y	Y	Y	Y
19 Poshard	Y	Y	Y	N	Y	Y	N	N
20 ***Shimkus***	Y	Y	Y	Y	Y	Y	Y	Y
INDIANA								
1 Visclosky	Y	Y	N	Y	N	Y	N	N
2 ***McIntosh***	Y	N	?	?	?	?	?	?
3 Roemer	Y	Y	Y	Y	Y	Y	N	N
4 ***Souder***	Y	Y	Y	Y	Y	Y	Y	Y
5 ***Buyer***	Y	Y	Y	Y	Y	Y	Y	Y
6 ***Burton***	?	Y	Y	Y	Y	Y	Y	Y
7 ***Pease***	Y	Y	Y	Y	Y	Y	Y	Y
8 ***Hostettler***	Y	N	Y	Y	Y	Y	Y	Y
9 Hamilton	N	Y	Y	Y	Y	Y	N	Y
10 Carson	Y	Y	Y	N	N	Y	N	N
IOWA								
1 ***Leach***	Y	?	Y	N	Y	Y	Y	Y
2 ***Nussle***	Y	Y	Y	N	Y	Y	Y	Y
3 Boswell	Y	Y	Y	N	Y	Y	N	N
4 ***Ganske***	Y	Y	Y	N	Y	Y	Y	?
5 ***Latham***	Y	Y	Y	Y	Y	Y	Y	Y
KANSAS								
1 ***Moran***	Y	N	Y	Y	Y	Y	Y	Y
2 ***Ryun***	Y	N	Y	Y	Y	Y	Y	Y
3 ***Snowbarger***	Y	N	Y	Y	Y	Y	Y	Y
4 ***Tiahrt***	Y	N	Y	Y	Y	Y	Y	Y
KENTUCKY								
1 ***Whitfield***	Y	Y	Y	Y	Y	Y	Y	Y
2 ***Lewis***	Y	Y	Y	Y	Y	Y	Y	Y
3 ***Northup***	Y	Y	Y	Y	Y	Y	Y	Y
4 ***Bunning***	Y	Y	Y	Y	Y	Y	Y	Y
5 ***Rogers***	Y	Y	Y	Y	Y	Y	Y	Y
6 Baesler	Y	Y	Y	Y	Y	Y	N	N
LOUISIANA								
1 ***Livingston***	Y	Y	Y	Y	Y	Y	Y	Y
2 Jefferson	Y	Y	Y	Y	N	Y	N	N
3 ***Tauzin***	Y	Y	Y	Y	Y	Y	Y	Y
4 ***McCrery***	Y	Y	Y	Y	Y	Y	Y	Y
5 ***Cooksey***	Y	Y	Y	Y	Y	Y	Y	Y
6 ***Baker***	Y	Y	Y	Y	Y	Y	Y	Y
7 John	Y	Y	Y	Y	Y	Y	N	Y
MAINE								
1 Allen	Y	Y	Y	Y	Y	Y	N	N
2 Baldacci	Y	Y	N	Y	Y	Y	N	N
MARYLAND								
1 ***Gilchrest***	Y	Y	Y	Y	Y	Y	Y	Y
2 ***Ehrlich***	Y	Y	Y	Y	Y	Y	Y	Y
3 Cardin	Y	Y	Y	Y	Y	Y	N	N
4 Wynn	Y	Y	Y	Y	N	Y	N	N
5 Hoyer	Y	Y	Y	Y	Y	Y	N	N
6 ***Bartlett***	Y	N	Y	Y	Y	Y	Y	Y
7 Cummings	Y	Y	Y	Y	N	Y	N	N
8 ***Morella***	Y	Y	Y	Y	Y	Y	Y	Y
MASSACHUSETTS								
1 Olver	Y	Y	Y	Y	Y	Y	N	N
2 Neal	Y	Y	Y	Y	N	Y	N	N
3 McGovern	Y	Y	Y	Y	N	Y	N	N
4 Frank	Y	?	Y	N	N	?	?	?
5 Meehan	Y	Y	Y	N	N	Y	N	N
6 Tierney	Y	Y	Y	Y	N	Y	N	N
7 Markey	Y	Y	N	N	N	Y	N	N
8 Kennedy	Y	Y	?	?	?	Y	N	N
9 Moakley	Y	Y	Y	Y	N	Y	N	N
10 Delahunt	Y	Y	N	Y	N	Y	N	N
MICHIGAN								
1 Stupak	Y	N	N	N	Y	Y	N	N
2 ***Hoekstra***	Y	?	?	Y	Y	Y	Y	Y
3 ***Ehlers***	Y	Y	Y	Y	Y	Y	Y	Y
4 ***Camp***	Y	Y	Y	Y	Y	Y	Y	Y
5 Barcia	Y	Y	Y	Y	Y	Y	N	N
6 ***Upton***	Y	Y	Y	N	Y	Y	Y	Y
7 ***Smith***	Y	Y	Y	N	Y	Y	Y	?
8 Stabenow	Y	Y	?	Y	Y	Y	N	N
9 Kildee	Y	Y	Y	Y	N	Y	N	N
10 Bonior	Y	Y	N	Y	N	Y	N	N
11 ***Knollenberg***	Y	Y	Y	Y	Y	Y	Y	Y
12 Levin	Y	Y	Y	Y	N	Y	N	N
13 Rivers	Y	Y	Y	N	N	Y	N	N
14 Conyers	Y	N	Y	N	N	Y	N	Y
15 Kilpatrick	Y	Y	Y	Y	N	Y	N	N
16 Dingell	Y	Y	Y	Y	N	Y	N	N
MINNESOTA								
1 ***Gutknecht***	Y	Y	N	Y	Y	Y	Y	Y
2 Minge	Y	Y	Y	N	Y	Y	N	N

	614	615	616	617	618	619	620	621
3 ***Ramstad***	Y	Y	N	N	Y	Y	Y	Y
4 Vento	Y	Y	Y	N	N	Y	N	N
5 Sabo	Y	Y	N	Y	N	Y	N	N
6 Luther	Y	Y	Y	N	Y	Y	N	N
7 Peterson	Y	N	Y	Y	Y	Y	N	N
8 Oberstar	Y	Y	N	Y	N	Y	N	N
MISSISSIPPI								
1 ***Wicker***	Y	Y	Y	Y	Y	Y	Y	Y
2 Thompson	Y	Y	N	Y	Y	Y	N	N
3 ***Pickering***	Y	Y	Y	Y	Y	Y	Y	Y
4 ***Parker***	Y	Y	Y	Y	Y	Y	Y	Y
5 Taylor	Y	N	N	Y	Y	Y	N	Y
MISSOURI								
1 Clay	Y	Y	N	Y	N	Y	N	N
2 ***Talent***	Y	N	Y	Y	Y	Y	Y	Y
3 Gephardt	Y	Y	N	Y	Y	Y	N	N
4 Skelton	Y	Y	Y	Y	Y	Y	N	?
5 McCarthy	Y	Y	Y	N	N	Y	N	N
6 Danner	Y	Y	Y	Y	N	Y	N	N
7 ***Blunt***	Y	N	Y	Y	Y	Y	Y	Y
8 ***Emerson***	Y	Y	Y	Y	Y	Y	Y	Y
9 ***Hulshof***	Y	Y	N	Y	Y	Y	Y	Y
MONTANA								
AL ***Hill***	Y	N	N	Y	Y	Y	Y	Y
NEBRASKA								
1 ***Bereuter***	Y	Y	?	Y	Y	Y	Y	Y
2 ***Christensen***	Y	Y	Y	Y	Y	Y	Y	Y
3 ***Barrett***	Y	Y	Y	Y	Y	Y	Y	Y
NEVADA								
1 ***Ensign***	Y	Y	N	N	Y	Y	Y	Y
2 ***Gibbons***	Y	Y	Y	Y	Y	Y	Y	Y
NEW HAMPSHIRE								
1 ***Sununu***	Y	Y	Y	Y	Y	Y	Y	Y
2 ***Bass***	Y	Y	Y	Y	Y	Y	Y	Y
NEW JERSEY								
1 Andrews	Y	Y	Y	N	N	Y	N	N
2 ***LoBiondo***	Y	Y	N	Y	Y	Y	Y	Y
3 ***Saxton***	Y	Y	Y	Y	Y	Y	Y	Y
4 ***Smith***	Y	Y	Y	Y	Y	Y	Y	Y
5 ***Roukema***	Y	Y	Y	N	Y	Y	Y	Y
6 Pallone	Y	Y	N	Y	N	Y	N	N
7 ***Franks***	Y	Y	Y	N	N	Y	Y	Y
8 Pascrell	Y	Y	N	Y	N	Y	N	N
9 Rothman	Y	Y	?	N	N	Y	N	N
10 Payne	Y	Y	Y	Y	N	Y	N	N
11 ***Frelinghuysen***	Y	Y	Y	Y	Y	Y	Y	Y
12 ***Pappas***	Y	Y	Y	Y	Y	Y	Y	Y
13 Menendez	Y	Y	N	Y	N	Y	N	N
NEW MEXICO								
1 ***Schiff***	?	?	?	?	?	?	?	?
2 ***Skeen***	Y	Y	Y	Y	Y	Y	Y	Y
3 ***Redmond***	Y	Y	Y	Y	Y	Y	Y	Y
NEW YORK								
1 ***Forbes***	Y	Y	Y	Y	N	Y	N	Y
2 ***Lazio***	Y	Y	Y	Y	Y	Y	Y	Y
3 ***King***	Y	Y	Y	Y	Y	Y	Y	Y
4 McCarthy	Y	Y	Y	Y	Y	Y	N	?
5 Ackerman	Y	Y	Y	Y	N	Y	N	N
6 Flake	Y	?	Y	Y	N	?	?	?
7 Manton	Y	Y	Y	Y	N	Y	?	?
8 Nadler	N	Y	Y	Y	N	Y	N	N
9 Schumer	Y	Y	Y	Y	N	Y	N	N
10 Towns	Y	Y	Y	N	N	Y	N	Y
11 Owens	Y	Y	Y	N	N	Y	N	Y
12 Velázquez	Y	Y	N	Y	N	Y	N	N
13 ***Fossella***	Y	Y	Y	Y	Y	Y	Y	Y
14 Maloney	Y	Y	?	Y	N	Y	N	N
15 Rangel	Y	Y	Y	Y	N	Y	N	N
16 Serrano	Y	Y	Y	Y	N	Y	N	N
17 Engel	Y	Y	Y	N	N	Y	N	N
18 Lowey	Y	Y	Y	Y	N	Y	N	N
19 ***Kelly***	Y	Y	Y	Y	Y	Y	Y	Y
20 ***Gilman***	Y	Y	Y	Y	Y	Y	Y	Y
21 McNulty	Y	Y	N	Y	N	Y	N	N
22 ***Solomon***	Y	Y	Y	Y	Y	Y	Y	Y
23 ***Boehlert***	Y	Y	Y	Y	N	Y	Y	Y
24 ***McHugh***	Y	Y	Y	Y	Y	Y	Y	Y
25 ***Walsh***	Y	Y	?	?	?	?	?	?
26 Hinchey	Y	Y	?	Y	Y	Y	N	Y
27 ***Paxon***	Y	N	Y	Y	Y	Y	Y	Y
28 Slaughter	Y	Y	Y	Y	N	Y	N	N
29 LaFalce	Y	Y	Y	Y	Y	Y	N	Y
30 ***Quinn***	?	#	?	?	?	Y	Y	Y
31 ***Houghton***	N	Y	Y	Y	Y	Y	Y	Y

	614	615	616	617	618	619	620	621
NORTH CAROLINA								
1 Clayton	Y	Y	Y	Y	Y	?	?	?
2 Etheridge	Y	Y	Y	Y	Y	Y	N	N
3 ***Jones***	Y	N	Y	Y	Y	Y	Y	Y
4 Price	Y	Y	Y	Y	Y	Y	N	N
5 ***Burr***	Y	Y	Y	Y	Y	Y	Y	Y
6 ***Coble***	Y	N	Y	Y	Y	Y	Y	Y
7 McIntyre	Y	Y	Y	Y	Y	Y	N	N
8 Hefner	Y	Y	Y	Y	Y	Y	N	N
9 ***Myrick***	Y	Y	Y	?	?	?	?	?
10 ***Ballenger***	Y	Y	Y	+	+	Y	Y	Y
11 ***Taylor***	Y	Y	?	?	?	?	?	?
12 Watt	Y	Y	Y	Y	N	Y	N	N
NORTH DAKOTA								
AL Pomeroy	Y	Y	Y	Y	Y	Y	N	N
OHIO								
1 ***Chabot***	Y	N	Y	N	Y	Y	Y	Y
2 ***Portman***	Y	Y	Y	Y	Y	Y	Y	Y
3 Hall	Y	Y	Y	Y	Y	Y	N	Y
4 ***Oxley***	Y	Y	Y	Y	Y	Y	Y	Y
5 ***Gillmor***	Y	?	?	?	?	?	?	?
6 Strickland	Y	Y	N	N	N	Y	N	N
7 ***Hobson***	Y	Y	Y	Y	Y	Y	Y	Y
8 ***Boehner***	Y	Y	Y	Y	Y	Y	Y	Y
9 Kaptur	Y	Y	Y	Y	N	Y	N	N
10 Kucinich	Y	Y	N	Y	N	Y	N	N
11 Stokes	Y	Y	Y	Y	N	Y	N	N
12 ***Kasich***	Y	Y	Y	Y	Y	Y	Y	Y
13 Brown	Y	Y	N	N	N	Y	N	N
14 Sawyer	Y	Y	Y	Y	N	Y	N	N
15 ***Pryce***	Y	Y	Y	Y	Y	Y	Y	Y
16 ***Regula***	Y	Y	Y	Y	Y	Y	Y	Y
17 Traficant	Y	Y	Y	Y	Y	Y	Y	Y
18 ***Ney***	Y	Y	Y	Y	Y	Y	Y	Y
19 ***LaTourette***	Y	Y	Y	Y	Y	Y	Y	Y
OKLAHOMA								
1 ***Largent***	Y	N	Y	Y	Y	Y	Y	Y
2 ***Coburn***	Y	N	Y	Y	Y	Y	Y	Y
3 ***Watkins***	Y	Y	Y	Y	Y	Y	Y	Y
4 ***Watts***	Y	Y	Y	Y	Y	Y	Y	Y
5 ***Istook***	Y	N	Y	Y	Y	Y	Y	Y
6 ***Lucas***	Y	Y	Y	Y	Y	Y	Y	Y
OREGON								
1 Furse	Y	Y	Y	Y	N	Y	N	N
2 ***Smith***	Y	Y	Y	Y	Y	Y	Y	Y
3 Blumenauer	+	+	+	+	+	+	+	+
4 DeFazio	Y	Y	N	Y	N	Y	N	N
5 Hooley	Y	Y	Y	Y	Y	Y	N	N
PENNSYLVANIA								
1 Foglietta	Y	Y	?	?	?	Y	N	N
2 Fattah	?	Y	?	Y	N	Y	N	N
3 Borski	Y	Y	N	Y	N	Y	?	?
4 Klink	Y	Y	Y	Y	Y	Y	N	Y
5 ***Peterson***	Y	Y	Y	Y	Y	Y	Y	Y
6 Holden	Y	Y	Y	Y	Y	?	?	?
7 ***Weldon***	Y	Y	Y	Y	Y	Y	Y	Y
8 ***Greenwood***	Y	Y	Y	N	Y	Y	Y	Y
9 ***Shuster***	Y	Y	Y	Y	Y	Y	Y	Y
10 ***McDade***	Y	Y	?	Y	Y	Y	Y	Y
11 Kanjorski	Y	Y	Y	Y	Y	Y	N	Y
12 Murtha	Y	Y	Y	Y	N	Y	N	Y
13 ***Fox***	Y	Y	N	Y	Y	Y	Y	Y
14 Coyne	Y	Y	Y	Y	Y	Y	N	N
15 McHale	Y	Y	Y	Y	N	Y	N	N
16 ***Pitts***	Y	Y	Y	Y	Y	Y	Y	Y
17 ***Gekas***	Y	Y	Y	Y	Y	Y	Y	Y
18 Doyle	Y	Y	Y	Y	Y	Y	N	N
19 ***Goodling***	Y	Y	Y	Y	Y	Y	?	Y
20 Mascara	Y	Y	Y	Y	Y	Y	N	N
21 ***English***	Y	Y	N	Y	Y	Y	Y	Y
RHODE ISLAND								
1 Kennedy	Y	Y	Y	Y	N	Y	N	N
2 Weygand	Y	Y	?	Y	N	Y	N	N
SOUTH CAROLINA								
1 ***Sanford***	Y	N	Y	N	N	Y	Y	Y
2 ***Spence***	Y	Y	Y	Y	Y	Y	Y	Y
3 ***Graham***	Y	Y	Y	Y	Y	Y	Y	Y
4 ***Inglis***	Y	N	Y	Y	Y	Y	Y	Y
5 Spratt	Y	Y	N	Y	Y	Y	N	N
6 Clyburn	Y	Y	N	Y	Y	Y	N	N
SOUTH DAKOTA								
AL ***Thune***	Y	Y	Y	Y	Y	Y	Y	Y
TENNESSEE								
1 ***Jenkins***	Y	Y	Y	Y	Y	Y	Y	Y
2 ***Duncan***	Y	Y	Y	N	Y	Y	Y	Y

	614	615	616	617	618	619	620	
3 ***Wamp***	Y	N	Y	Y	Y	Y	P	N
4 ***Hilleary***	Y	N	Y	Y	Y	Y	Y	Y
5 Clement	Y	Y	Y	Y	Y	Y	N	N
6 Gordon	Y	Y	Y	Y	Y	Y	N	N
7 ***Bryant***	Y	N	Y	Y	Y	Y	Y	Y
8 Tanner	Y	Y	Y	Y	Y	Y	N	N
9 Ford	Y	Y	Y	Y	Y	Y	N	N
TEXAS								
1 Sandlin	Y	Y	Y	Y	Y	Y	N	N
2 Turner	Y	Y	Y	Y	Y	Y	N	N
3 ***Johnson, Sam***	Y	N	Y	Y	Y	Y	Y	Y
4 Hall	Y	Y	Y	Y	Y	Y	N	N
5 ***Sessions***	Y	N	N	Y	Y	Y	Y	Y
6 ***Barton***	Y	N	Y	Y	Y	Y	Y	Y
7 ***Archer***	Y	N	?	Y	Y	Y	Y	Y
8 ***Brady***	Y	N	Y	Y	Y	Y	Y	Y
9 Lampson	Y	Y	Y	Y	Y	Y	N	N
10 Doggett	Y	Y	Y	N	N	Y	N	N
11 Edwards	Y	Y	Y	Y	Y	Y	N	N
12 ***Granger***	Y	Y	Y	Y	Y	Y	Y	Y
13 ***Thornberry***	Y	Y	Y	Y	Y	Y	Y	Y
14 ***Paul***	N	N	Y	Y	N	Y	Y	Y
15 Hinojosa	Y	Y	Y	Y	Y	Y	N	N
16 Reyes	Y	Y	Y	Y	Y	Y	N	N
17 Stenholm	Y	Y	Y	Y	Y	Y	N	N
18 Jackson-Lee	Y	Y	Y	Y	N	Y	N	N
19 ***Combest***	Y	Y	Y	Y	Y	Y	Y	Y
20 Gonzalez	?	?	?	?	?	?	?	?
21 ***Smith***	Y	Y	Y	Y	Y	Y	Y	Y
22 ***DeLay***	Y	Y	Y	Y	Y	Y	Y	Y
23 ***Bonilla***	Y	Y	Y	Y	Y	Y	Y	Y
24 Frost	Y	Y	Y	Y	Y	Y	N	N
25 Bentsen	Y	Y	Y	Y	Y	Y	N	N
26 ***Armey***	Y	Y	Y	Y	Y	Y	Y	Y
27 Ortiz	Y	Y	Y	Y	Y	Y	N	Y
28 Rodriguez	Y	Y	Y	Y	Y	Y	N	N
29 Green	Y	Y	Y	Y	Y	Y	N	N
30 Johnson, E.B.	Y	Y	N	Y	N	Y	N	N
UTAH								
1 ***Hansen***	Y	Y	Y	Y	Y	Y	Y	Y
2 ***Cook***	Y	Y	Y	Y	Y	Y	Y	Y
3 ***Cannon***	Y	N	Y	Y	Y	Y	Y	Y
VERMONT								
AL *Sanders*	Y	Y	Y	Y	N	?	?	?
VIRGINIA								
1 ***Bateman***	Y	Y	Y	Y	Y	Y	Y	Y
2 Pickett	N	Y	N	Y	Y	Y	N	Y
3 Scott	Y	Y	N	Y	N	Y	N	N
4 Sisisky	Y	Y	Y	Y	Y	Y	N	N
5 Goode	Y	N	Y	Y	Y	Y	N	N
6 ***Goodlatte***	Y	N	Y	Y	Y	Y	Y	Y
7 ***Bliley***	Y	Y	Y	Y	Y	Y	Y	Y
8 Moran	N	Y	Y	Y	N	Y	N	N
9 Boucher	Y	Y	Y	Y	Y	Y	N	Y
10 ***Wolf***	Y	Y	Y	Y	Y	Y	Y	Y
11 ***Davis***	Y	Y	Y	Y	Y	Y	Y	Y
WASHINGTON								
1 ***White***	Y	Y	Y	Y	Y	Y	Y	Y
2 ***Metcalf***	Y	Y	Y	Y	Y	Y	Y	Y
3 ***Smith, Linda***	Y	Y	Y	Y	Y	Y	Y	Y
4 ***Hastings***	Y	N	Y	Y	Y	Y	Y	Y
5 ***Nethercutt***	Y	Y	Y	Y	Y	Y	Y	Y
6 Dicks	N	Y	Y	Y	N	Y	N	N
7 McDermott	?	?	?	?	?	?	?	?
8 ***Dunn***	Y	Y	Y	Y	Y	Y	Y	Y
9 Smith, Adam	Y	Y	Y	Y	Y	Y	N	N
WEST VIRGINIA								
1 Mollohan	Y	Y	Y	Y	Y	Y	N	N
2 Wise	Y	Y	Y	Y	Y	Y	N	N
3 Rahall	Y	Y	Y	Y	Y	Y	N	Y
WISCONSIN								
1 ***Neumann***	Y	N	?	?	?	?	?	?
2 ***Klug***	?	?	?	?	?	?	?	?
3 Kind	Y	Y	Y	N	Y	Y	N	N
4 Kleczka	Y	Y	Y	Y	N	Y	N	?
5 Barrett	Y	Y	Y	N	N	Y	N	Y
6 ***Petri***	Y	N	Y	N	Y	Y	Y	Y
7 Obey	Y	Y	Y	Y	N	Y	N	N
8 Johnson	Y	Y	Y	N	Y	Y	N	N
9 ***Sensenbrenner***	Y	N	Y	N	Y	Y	Y	Y
WYOMING								
AL ***Cubin***	?	?	?	?	?	?	?	?

Southern states - Ala., Ark., Fla., Ga., Ky., La., Miss., N.C., Okla., S.C., Tenn., Texas, Va.

HOUSE VOTES 622, 623, 624, 625, 626, 627, 628, 629

622. H Res 318. Robert K. Dornan Election Challenge/Motion To Table. Boehner, R-Ohio, motion to table (kill) the Gephardt, D-Mo., privileged resolution to dismiss the complaint by former Rep. Robert K. Dornan, R-Calif., contesting the election of Loretta Sanchez, D-Calif. The resolution calls for state authorities to continue their investigation into questionable voter registration activities and for the House Oversight Committee to examine voter registration procedures. Motion agreed to 218-194: R 216-1; D 2-192 (ND 2-138, SD 0-54); I 0-1, Nov. 9, 1997.

623. HR 2232. Radio Free Asia/Passage. Passage of the bill to authorize $82 million through fiscal 1999 for Radio Free Asia and Voice of America radio broadcasting to China and construction of facilities to increase broadcasting capabilities. Passed 401-21: R 211-8; D 190-12 (ND 138-10, SD 52-2); I 0-1, Nov. 9, 1997.

624. HR 1129. Foreign Microenterprise Development/Passage. Gilman, R-N.Y., motion to suspend the rules and pass the bill to authorize the president to provide assistance through non-governmental organizations and credit institutions to developing countries for establishing microenterprises to give local entrepreneurs access to credit and business services. Motion agreed to 393-21: R 196-18; D 196-3 (ND 145-1, SD 51-2); I 1-0, Nov. 9, 1997. A two-thirds majority of those present and voting (276 in this case) is required for passage under suspension of the rules.

625. H Con Res 22. Religious Rights in Germany/Adoption. Gilman, R-N.Y., motion to suspend the rules and adopt the concurrent resolution to condemn German officials who have practiced religious discrimination against Scientologists and urge the German government to take action to protect the rights of minority religious groups. Motion rejected 101-318: R 42-177; D 59-140 (ND 43-102, SD 16-38); I 0-1, Nov. 9, 1997. A two-thirds majority of those present and voting (280 in this case) is required for adoption under suspension of the rules.

626. H Con Res 139. EXPO 2000/Adoption. Bereuter, R-Neb., motion to suspend the rules and adopt the concurrent resolution to express the sense of Congress that the U.S. should participate fully in EXPO 2000, a global town hall meeting to occur in 2000 in Germany to mark the new millennium. Motion agreed to 415-2: R 214-1; D 200-1 (ND 148-0, SD 52-1); I 1-0, Nov. 9, 1997. A two-thirds majority of those present and voting (278 in this case) is required for adoption under suspension of the rules.

627. HR 2920. U.S. Land Border Control/Passage. Smith, R-Texas, motion to suspend the rules and pass the bill to extend the deadline by which a border crossing card entry-exit system at land border entry points from Canada and Mexico must be operational under the 1996 immigration law (PL 104-208) until Oct. 1, 1999. Motion agreed to 325-90: R 205-11; D 119-79 (ND 101-44, SD 18-35); I 1-0, Nov. 10, 1997 (in the session that began and the Congressional Record dated Nov. 9). A two-thirds majority of those present and voting (277 in this case) is required for passage under suspension of the rules.

628. H Res 311. Adjournment Preparation Resolution/Adoption. Adoption of the resolution to prepare for the sine die adjournment of the first session of the 105th Congress. Adopted 257-159: R 213-5; D 44-153 (ND 34-109, SD 10-44); I 0-1, Nov. 10, 1997 (in the session that began and the Congressional Record dated Nov. 9).

629. S 738. Amtrak Subsidies/Rule. Adoption of the rule (H Res 319) to provide for floor consideration of the bill to authorize subsidies to Amtrak of $5.2 billion through fiscal 2002 and streamline operations of the railway, steering Amtrak toward private control by 2002. Adopted 324-72: R 208-1; D 115-71 (ND 81-54, SD 34-17); I 1-0, Nov. 12, 1997.

[1] *Rep. Thomas M. Foglietta, D-Pa., resigned Nov. 12. The last vote for which he was eligible was vote 628.*

KEY

- Y Voted for (yea).
- \# Paired for.
- \+ Announced for.
- N Voted against (nay).
- X Paired against.
- – Announced against.
- P Voted "present."
- C Voted "present" to avoid possible conflict of interest.
- ? Did not vote or otherwise make a position known.

Democrats ***Republicans*** *Independent*

	622	623	624	625	626	627	628	629
ALABAMA								
1 ***Callahan***	Y	Y	Y	N	Y	Y	Y	N
2 ***Everett***	Y	Y	Y	N	Y	Y	Y	Y
3 ***Riley***	+	+	+	–	+	+	+	+
4 ***Aderholt***	Y	Y	Y	N	Y	Y	Y	Y
5 Cramer	N	Y	Y	N	Y	Y	Y	Y
6 ***Bachus***	Y	Y	Y	N	Y	Y	Y	Y
7 Hilliard	N	Y	Y	Y	Y	N	N	Y
ALASKA								
AL ***Young***	Y	Y	Y	N	Y	Y	Y	Y
ARIZONA								
1 ***Salmon***	Y	Y	?	Y	Y	N	N	Y
2 Pastor	N	Y	Y	Y	Y	N	Y	N
3 ***Stump***	Y	Y	N	N	Y	Y	Y	Y
4 ***Shadegg***	Y	Y	N	N	Y	N	Y	Y
5 ***Kolbe***	Y	Y	Y	N	Y	Y	Y	Y
6 ***Hayworth***	Y	Y	Y	N	Y	Y	Y	Y
ARKANSAS								
1 Berry	N	Y	Y	N	Y	N	N	Y
2 Snyder	N	Y	Y	N	Y	N	N	Y
3 ***Hutchinson***	Y	Y	Y	Y	Y	Y	Y	Y
4 ***Dickey***	Y	Y	Y	N	Y	Y	Y	Y
CALIFORNIA								
1 ***Riggs***	Y	Y	Y	N	Y	Y	Y	Y
2 ***Herger***	Y	Y	Y	N	Y	Y	Y	Y
3 Fazio	N	Y	Y	N	Y	Y	N	N
4 ***Doolittle***	Y	Y	Y	Y	Y	Y	Y	Y
5 Matsui	N	Y	Y	N	Y	N	N	N
6 Woolsey	N	Y	Y	N	Y	Y	N	Y
7 Miller	N	Y	Y	N	Y	N	N	Y
8 Pelosi	N	Y	Y	N	Y	N	Y	N
9 Dellums	N	Y	Y	Y	Y	N	Y	N
10 Tauscher	N	Y	Y	N	Y	Y	N	N
11 ***Pombo***	Y	Y	N	N	Y	Y	Y	Y
12 Lantos	N	Y	Y	N	Y	N	Y	?
13 Stark	N	Y	Y	N	Y	N	N	?
14 Eshoo	N	Y	Y	N	Y	Y	N	N
15 ***Campbell***	Y	Y	Y	N	Y	Y	Y	Y
16 Lofgren	N	Y	Y	N	Y	Y	N	N
17 Farr	N	Y	Y	N	Y	Y	N	Y
18 Condit	?	Y	Y	N	Y	Y	N	N
19 ***Radanovich***	Y	Y	Y	N	Y	Y	Y	?
20 Dooley	N	Y	Y	N	Y	N	N	N
21 ***Thomas***	Y	Y	Y	N	Y	Y	Y	Y
22 Vacant								
23 ***Gallegly***	Y	Y	Y	N	Y	Y	Y	Y
24 Sherman	N	Y	Y	Y	Y	N	N	N
25 ***McKeon***	Y	Y	Y	N	Y	Y	Y	Y
26 Berman	N	Y	Y	N	Y	Y	N	N
27 ***Rogan***	Y	Y	Y	Y	Y	Y	Y	Y
28 ***Dreier***	Y	Y	Y	Y	Y	Y	Y	Y
29 Waxman	N	Y	Y	N	Y	Y	N	N
30 Becerra	N	Y	Y	Y	Y	N	N	N
31 Martinez	Y	Y	Y	Y	Y	N	?	N
32 Dixon	N	Y	Y	N	Y	Y	Y	Y
33 Roybal-Allard	N	Y	Y	N	Y	N	N	Y
34 Torres	N	Y	Y	Y	Y	N	N	Y
35 Waters	N	Y	Y	Y	Y	N	N	Y
36 Harman	N	Y	Y	N	Y	N	N	N
37 Millender-McD.	N	Y	Y	Y	Y	N	N	Y
38 ***Horn***	Y	Y	Y	Y	Y	Y	Y	Y
39 ***Royce***	Y	Y	Y	Y	Y	Y	Y	Y
40 ***Lewis***	Y	Y	Y	Y	Y	Y	Y	Y

	622	623	624	625	626	627	628	629
41 ***Kim***	Y	Y	Y	Y	Y	Y	Y	Y
42 Brown	N	Y	Y	N	Y	N	N	N
43 ***Calvert***	Y	Y	Y	Y	Y	Y	Y	Y
44 ***Bono***	?	Y	+	Y	Y	Y	Y	Y
45 ***Rohrabacher***	Y	Y	Y	Y	Y	N	Y	Y
46 Sanchez	N	Y	Y	N	Y	N	N	Y
47 ***Cox***	Y	Y	Y	Y	Y	Y	Y	Y
48 ***Packard***	Y	Y	Y	N	Y	Y	Y	Y
49 ***Bilbray***	Y	Y	Y	Y	Y	N	Y	Y
50 Filner	N	Y	Y	N	Y	N	N	Y
51 ***Cunningham***	Y	Y	Y	Y	Y	Y	Y	Y
52 ***Hunter***	Y	Y	Y	N	Y	N	Y	Y
COLORADO								
1 DeGette	N	Y	Y	Y	Y	Y	N	N
2 Skaggs	N	Y	Y	N	Y	Y	N	N
3 ***McInnis***	Y	Y	Y	N	Y	Y	Y	Y
4 ***Schaffer***	Y	Y	Y	Y	Y	N	Y	Y
5 ***Hefley***	Y	Y	N	N	Y	Y	Y	Y
6 ***Schaefer***	Y	Y	Y	N	Y	Y	Y	Y
CONNECTICUT								
1 Kennelly	N	Y	Y	Y	Y	Y	Y	Y
2 Gejdenson	N	Y	Y	Y	Y	Y	N	N
3 DeLauro	N	Y	Y	Y	Y	Y	N	Y
4 ***Shays***	Y	Y	Y	N	Y	Y	N	Y
5 Maloney	N	Y	Y	Y	Y	Y	Y	Y
6 ***Johnson***	Y	Y	Y	Y	Y	Y	Y	Y
DELAWARE								
AL ***Castle***	Y	Y	Y	N	Y	Y	Y	Y
FLORIDA								
1 ***Scarborough***	Y	Y	N	Y	Y	N	N	?
2 Boyd	N	Y	+	N	Y	Y	N	Y
3 Brown	N	Y	Y	Y	Y	N	N	Y
4 ***Fowler***	Y	Y	Y	N	Y	Y	Y	Y
5 Thurman	N	Y	Y	N	Y	Y	N	Y
6 ***Stearns***	?	Y	N	N	Y	Y	Y	Y
7 ***Mica***	Y	Y	Y	N	Y	Y	Y	Y
8 ***McCollum***	Y	Y	Y	N	Y	Y	Y	Y
9 ***Bilirakis***	Y	Y	Y	Y	Y	Y	Y	Y
10 ***Young***	Y	Y	N	N	Y	Y	Y	Y
11 Davis	N	Y	Y	N	Y	Y	Y	Y
12 ***Canady***	Y	Y	Y	N	Y	Y	Y	Y
13 ***Miller***	Y	Y	Y	N	Y	Y	Y	Y
14 ***Goss***	Y	Y	Y	N	Y	Y	Y	Y
15 ***Weldon***	Y	Y	Y	N	Y	Y	Y	Y
16 ***Foley***	Y	Y	Y	Y	Y	Y	Y	Y
17 Meek	N	Y	Y	Y	Y	N	N	Y
18 ***Ros-Lehtinen***	Y	Y	Y	Y	Y	Y	Y	Y
19 Wexler	N	Y	Y	Y	Y	Y	N	N
20 Deutsch	N	Y	Y	Y	Y	Y	N	N
21 ***Diaz-Balart***	Y	Y	Y	Y	Y	Y	Y	Y
22 ***Shaw***	Y	Y	Y	N	Y	Y	Y	Y
23 Hastings	N	Y	Y	Y	Y	N	N	Y
GEORGIA								
1 ***Kingston***	Y	Y	Y	N	Y	Y	Y	Y
2 Bishop	N	Y	Y	Y	Y	N	N	Y
3 ***Collins***	Y	Y	N	N	Y	Y	Y	Y
4 McKinney	N	Y	Y	Y	Y	N	Y	Y
5 Lewis	N	Y	Y	N	Y	N	N	Y
6 ***Gingrich***								
7 ***Barr***	Y	Y	N	N	N	Y	Y	Y
8 ***Chambliss***	Y	Y	Y	N	Y	Y	Y	Y
9 ***Deal***	Y	Y	N	N	Y	N	Y	Y
10 ***Norwood***	Y	Y	Y	N	Y	?	Y	?
11 ***Linder***	Y	Y	Y	N	Y	Y	Y	Y
HAWAII								
1 Abercrombie	N	Y	Y	Y	Y	N	N	Y
2 Mink	N	Y	Y	N	Y	N	N	Y
IDAHO								
1 ***Chenoweth***	Y	Y	N	N	Y	Y	Y	Y
2 ***Crapo***	Y	Y	Y	N	Y	Y	Y	Y
ILLINOIS								
1 Rush	N	Y	Y	Y	Y	N	N	?
2 Jackson	N	Y	Y	Y	Y	N	Y	N
3 Lipinski	N	Y	Y	N	Y	Y	Y	Y
4 Gutierrez	N	Y	Y	Y	Y	N	N	Y
5 Blagojevich	N	Y	Y	N	Y	Y	Y	Y
6 ***Hyde***	Y	Y	Y	N	Y	Y	Y	Y
7 Davis	N	Y	Y	Y	Y	N	N	N
8 ***Crane***	Y	Y	Y	N	Y	Y	Y	Y
9 Yates	?	?	?	?	?	?	?	Y
10 ***Porter***	Y	Y	Y	N	Y	Y	Y	Y
11 ***Weller***	Y	Y	Y	Y	Y	Y	Y	Y
12 Costello	N	Y	Y	N	Y	Y	N	Y
13 ***Fawell***	Y	Y	Y	N	Y	Y	Y	Y
14 ***Hastert***	Y	Y	Y	N	Y	Y	Y	Y
15 ***Ewing***	Y	Y	Y	N	Y	?	Y	Y

ND Northern Democrats SD Southern Democrats

	622	623	624	625	626	627	628	629
16 ***Manzullo***	Y	Y	Y	N	Y	Y	Y	Y
17 Evans	N	Y	Y	N	Y	N	N	N
18 ***LaHood***	Y	Y	Y	N	Y	Y	Y	Y
19 Poshard	N	Y	Y	N	Y	Y	N	Y
20 ***Shimkus***	Y	Y	Y	N	Y	Y	Y	Y
INDIANA								
1 Visclosky	N	Y	Y	N	Y	Y	N	N
2 ***McIntosh***	Y	Y	Y	N	Y	Y	Y	?
3 Roemer	N	Y	Y	Y	Y	Y	N	N
4 ***Souder***	Y	Y	Y	N	Y	Y	Y	Y
5 ***Buyer***	Y	Y	Y	N	Y	Y	Y	Y
6 ***Burton***	Y	Y	Y	N	Y	?	?	Y
7 ***Pease***	Y	Y	Y	N	Y	Y	Y	Y
8 ***Hostettler***	Y	Y	Y	N	Y	Y	Y	Y
9 Hamilton	N	Y	Y	N	Y	Y	N	Y
10 Carson	N	Y	Y	Y	Y	N	N	Y
IOWA								
1 ***Leach***	Y	Y	Y	N	Y	Y	Y	Y
2 ***Nussle***	Y	Y	Y	N	Y	Y	Y	Y
3 Boswell	N	Y	Y	N	Y	Y	N	Y
4 ***Ganske***	Y	Y	Y	N	Y	Y	Y	Y
5 ***Latham***	Y	Y	Y	N	Y	Y	Y	Y
KANSAS								
1 ***Moran***	Y	Y	Y	N	Y	Y	Y	Y
2 ***Ryun***	Y	Y	Y	N	Y	Y	Y	Y
3 ***Snowbarger***	Y	Y	Y	N	Y	Y	Y	Y
4 ***Tiahrt***	Y	Y	Y	Y	Y	Y	Y	Y
KENTUCKY								
1 ***Whitfield***	Y	Y	Y	N	?	Y	Y	Y
2 ***Lewis***	Y	Y	Y	N	Y	Y	Y	Y
3 ***Northup***	Y	Y	Y	N	Y	Y	Y	Y
4 ***Bunning***	Y	Y	Y	N	Y	Y	Y	Y
5 ***Rogers***	Y	Y	Y	N	Y	Y	Y	Y
6 Baesler	N	Y	Y	N	Y	N	N	N
LOUISIANA								
1 ***Livingston***	Y	Y	Y	N	Y	Y	Y	Y
2 Jefferson	N	Y	Y	N	Y	N	Y	N
3 ***Tauzin***	Y	Y	Y	N	Y	Y	Y	Y
4 ***McCrery***	Y	Y	Y	N	Y	?	?	Y
5 ***Cooksey***	Y	Y	Y	N	Y	Y	Y	?
6 ***Baker***	Y	Y	Y	N	Y	Y	Y	Y
7 John	N	Y	Y	N	Y	Y	Y	?
MAINE								
1 Allen	N	Y	Y	N	Y	Y	Y	N
2 Baldacci	N	Y	Y	N	Y	Y	N	Y
MARYLAND								
1 ***Gilchrest***	Y	Y	Y	N	Y	Y	Y	Y
2 ***Ehrlich***	Y	Y	Y	N	Y	Y	Y	Y
3 Cardin	N	Y	Y	P	Y	Y	N	Y
4 Wynn	N	Y	Y	Y	Y	N	Y	Y
5 Hoyer	N	Y	Y	P	Y	Y	N	N
6 ***Bartlett***	Y	Y	Y	N	Y	Y	Y	Y
7 Cummings	N	Y	Y	Y	Y	N	N	N
8 ***Morella***	Y	Y	Y	N	Y	Y	Y	?
MASSACHUSETTS								
1 Olver	N	Y	Y	N	Y	Y	N	N
2 Neal	N	Y	Y	N	Y	Y	N	?
3 McGovern	N	Y	Y	N	Y	Y	Y	Y
4 Frank	N	Y	Y	N	Y	Y	Y	Y
5 Meehan	N	Y	Y	N	Y	Y	N	?
6 Tierney	N	Y	Y	N	Y	Y	N	N
7 Markey	N	Y	Y	N	Y	Y	N	N
8 Kennedy	N	Y	Y	N	Y	Y	Y	N
9 Moakley	N	Y	Y	N	Y	Y	Y	N
10 Delahunt	N	Y	Y	Y	Y	Y	Y	N
MICHIGAN								
1 Stupak	N	Y	Y	N	Y	Y	N	N
2 ***Hoekstra***	?	Y	Y	N	Y	Y	Y	Y
3 ***Ehlers***	Y	Y	Y	N	Y	Y	Y	Y
4 ***Camp***	Y	Y	Y	N	Y	Y	Y	Y
5 Barcia	N	Y	Y	N	Y	Y	Y	Y
6 ***Upton***	Y	Y	Y	N	Y	Y	Y	Y
7 ***Smith***	Y	Y	Y	N	Y	Y	Y	Y
8 Stabenow	N	Y	Y	N	Y	Y	Y	N
9 Kildee	N	Y	Y	Y	Y	Y	Y	Y
10 Bonior	N	Y	Y	Y	Y	Y	N	N
11 ***Knollenberg***	Y	Y	Y	N	Y	Y	Y	Y
12 Levin	N	Y	Y	N	Y	Y	N	Y
13 Rivers	N	Y	Y	N	Y	Y	N	Y
14 Conyers	?	Y	Y	Y	Y	N	N	N
15 Kilpatrick	N	Y	Y	Y	Y	Y	N	Y
16 Dingell	N	Y	Y	N	Y	?	?	?
MINNESOTA								
1 ***Gutknecht***	Y	Y	Y	Y	Y	Y	Y	Y
2 Minge	N	Y	Y	N	Y	Y	Y	Y

	622	623	624	625	626	627	628	629
3 ***Ramstad***	Y	Y	Y	N	Y	Y	Y	Y
4 Vento	N	Y	Y	N	Y	Y	N	Y
5 Sabo	N	Y	Y	N	Y	Y	Y	N
6 Luther	N	Y	Y	N	Y	Y	N	Y
7 Peterson	N	Y	Y	N	Y	Y	N	N
8 Oberstar	N	Y	Y	N	Y	Y	N	Y
MISSISSIPPI								
1 ***Wicker***	Y	Y	Y	Y	Y	Y	Y	Y
2 Thompson	N	Y	Y	Y	Y	N	N	Y
3 ***Pickering***	Y	Y	+	–	Y	Y	Y	Y
4 ***Parker***	Y	Y	Y	N	Y	Y	Y	Y
5 Taylor	N	Y	N	N	Y	N	N	N
MISSOURI								
1 Clay	N	N	Y	Y	Y	N	N	Y
2 ***Talent***	Y	Y	Y	N	Y	Y	Y	Y
3 Gephardt	N	Y	Y	Y	Y	Y	N	?
4 Skelton	N	Y	Y	N	Y	N	N	Y
5 McCarthy	N	Y	Y	N	Y	Y	N	Y
6 Danner	N	Y	Y	N	Y	Y	Y	Y
7 ***Blunt***	Y	Y	Y	N	Y	Y	Y	Y
8 ***Emerson***	Y	Y	Y	N	?	Y	Y	Y
9 ***Hulshof***	Y	Y	Y	Y	Y	Y	Y	Y
MONTANA								
AL ***Hill***	Y	Y	N	N	Y	Y	Y	Y
NEBRASKA								
1 ***Bereuter***	Y	Y	Y	N	Y	Y	Y	Y
2 ***Christensen***	Y	Y	Y	Y	Y	Y	Y	Y
3 ***Barrett***	Y	Y	Y	N	Y	Y	Y	Y
NEVADA								
1 ***Ensign***	Y	Y	Y	Y	Y	Y	Y	Y
2 ***Gibbons***	Y	Y	Y	N	Y	Y	Y	Y
NEW HAMPSHIRE								
1 ***Sununu***	Y	Y	Y	N	Y	Y	Y	Y
2 ***Bass***	Y	Y	Y	N	Y	Y	Y	Y
NEW JERSEY								
1 Andrews	N	Y	Y	Y	Y	Y	N	Y
2 ***LoBiondo***	Y	Y	Y	N	Y	N	Y	Y
3 ***Saxton***	Y	Y	Y	N	Y	Y	Y	Y
4 ***Smith***	Y	Y	Y	N	Y	Y	Y	Y
5 ***Roukema***	Y	?	?	?	?	?	N	Y
6 Pallone	N	Y	Y	Y	Y	Y	N	Y
7 ***Franks***	Y	Y	Y	N	Y	Y	Y	Y
8 Pascrell	N	Y	Y	N	Y	Y	Y	Y
9 Rothman	N	Y	Y	Y	Y	N	N	Y
10 Payne	N	Y	Y	Y	Y	N	N	Y
11 ***Frelinghuysen***	Y	Y	Y	N	Y	Y	Y	Y
12 ***Pappas***	Y	Y	Y	Y	Y	Y	Y	Y
13 Menendez	N	Y	Y	Y	Y	Y	N	–
NEW MEXICO								
1 ***Schiff***	?	?	?	?	?	?	?	?
2 ***Skeen***	Y	Y	Y	N	Y	N	Y	Y
3 ***Redmond***	Y	Y	Y	N	Y	Y	Y	Y
NEW YORK								
1 ***Forbes***	N	Y	Y	N	Y	Y	Y	Y
2 ***Lazio***	Y	Y	Y	N	Y	Y	Y	Y
3 ***King***	Y	Y	Y	N	Y	Y	Y	Y
4 McCarthy	N	Y	Y	N	Y	Y	Y	Y
5 Ackerman	?	Y	Y	N	Y	Y	N	N
6 Flake	?	Y	Y	Y	Y	?	?	?
7 Manton	N	Y	Y	N	Y	Y	N	Y
8 Nadler	N	Y	Y	N	Y	Y	N	Y
9 Schumer	?	Y	Y	N	Y	Y	N	?
10 Towns	N	Y	Y	Y	Y	Y	N	?
11 Owens	N	Y	Y	Y	Y	N	N	?
12 Velázquez	N	N	Y	N	Y	N	N	N
13 ***Fossella***	Y	Y	Y	N	Y	Y	Y	Y
14 Maloney	N	Y	Y	Y	Y	Y	N	Y
15 Rangel	N	N	Y	N	Y	N	Y	Y
16 Serrano	N	N	Y	N	Y	N	N	Y
17 Engel	N	Y	Y	Y	Y	Y	N	Y
18 Lowey	N	Y	Y	N	Y	Y	N	Y
19 ***Kelly***	Y	Y	Y	Y	Y	Y	Y	Y
20 ***Gilman***	Y	Y	Y	Y	Y	Y	Y	Y
21 McNulty	N	Y	Y	N	Y	Y	N	Y
22 ***Solomon***	Y	Y	Y	N	Y	Y	Y	Y
23 ***Boehlert***	Y	Y	Y	N	Y	Y	Y	Y
24 ***McHugh***	Y	Y	Y	N	Y	Y	Y	Y
25 ***Walsh***	Y	Y	Y	N	Y	Y	Y	Y
26 Hinchey	N	Y	Y	N	Y	Y	N	Y
27 ***Paxon***	Y	Y	Y	N	Y	Y	Y	Y
28 Slaughter	N	N	Y	Y	Y	Y	N	Y
29 LaFalce	N	Y	Y	N	Y	Y	N	N
30 ***Quinn***	Y	Y	Y	N	Y	Y	Y	Y
31 ***Houghton***	Y	Y	Y	N	Y	Y	Y	?

	622	623	624	625	626	627	628	629
NORTH CAROLINA								
1 Clayton	N	Y	Y	Y	Y	N	N	Y
2 Etheridge	N	Y	Y	N	Y	N	N	N
3 ***Jones***	Y	Y	Y	N	Y	Y	Y	Y
4 Price	N	Y	Y	N	Y	N	N	N
5 ***Burr***	Y	Y	Y	N	Y	Y	Y	Y
6 ***Coble***	Y	Y	N	N	Y	Y	Y	Y
7 McIntyre	N	Y	Y	N	Y	Y	Y	Y
8 Hefner	N	Y	Y	N	Y	N	N	N
9 ***Myrick***	Y	Y	Y	N	Y	Y	Y	Y
10 ***Ballenger***	Y	Y	Y	N	Y	Y	Y	Y
11 ***Taylor***	?	?	?	N	Y	Y	Y	Y
12 Watt	N	N	Y	Y	Y	N	N	N
NORTH DAKOTA								
AL Pomeroy	N	Y	Y	N	Y	Y	Y	Y
OHIO								
1 ***Chabot***	Y	N	Y	Y	Y	Y	Y	Y
2 ***Portman***	Y	Y	Y	Y	+	Y	Y	Y
3 Hall	N	Y	Y	Y	Y	Y	Y	N
4 ***Oxley***	Y	Y	?	N	Y	Y	Y	Y
5 ***Gillmor***	?	?	?	?	?	?	Y	Y
6 Strickland	N	Y	Y	N	Y	N	N	Y
7 ***Hobson***	Y	Y	Y	N	Y	Y	Y	Y
8 ***Boehner***	Y	Y	Y	N	Y	Y	Y	Y
9 Kaptur	N	Y	Y	N	Y	Y	N	Y
10 Kucinich	N	Y	Y	P	Y	Y	N	Y
11 Stokes	?	N	Y	Y	Y	N	Y	Y
12 ***Kasich***	Y	Y	Y	N	Y	Y	Y	Y
13 Brown	N	Y	?	N	Y	Y	N	N
14 Sawyer	N	Y	Y	N	Y	Y	N	Y
15 ***Pryce***	Y	Y	Y	Y	Y	Y	Y	+
16 ***Regula***	Y	Y	Y	N	Y	Y	Y	Y
17 Traficant	Y	Y	N	N	Y	N	Y	Y
18 ***Ney***	Y	Y	Y	Y	Y	Y	Y	Y
19 ***LaTourette***	Y	Y	Y	Y	Y	Y	Y	Y
OKLAHOMA								
1 ***Largent***	Y	Y	Y	N	Y	?	Y	Y
2 ***Coburn***	Y	Y	Y	N	Y	N	Y	Y
3 ***Watkins***	Y	Y	Y	N	Y	Y	Y	Y
4 ***Watts***	Y	Y	Y	N	Y	Y	Y	Y
5 ***Istook***	Y	Y	Y	N	Y	Y	Y	Y
6 ***Lucas***	Y	Y	Y	N	Y	Y	Y	Y
OREGON								
1 Furse	N	Y	Y	N	Y	Y	N	Y
2 ***Smith***	Y	Y	Y	N	Y	Y	?	?
3 Blumenauer	N	Y	Y	N	Y	Y	N	Y
4 DeFazio	N	N	Y	N	Y	Y	N	Y
5 Hooley	N	Y	Y	N	Y	Y	N	N
PENNSYLVANIA								
1 Foglietta[1]	?	Y	Y	N	Y	?	?	
2 Fattah	N	N	Y	Y	Y	N	N	Y
3 Borski	N	Y	Y	N	Y	Y	N	Y
4 Klink	N	Y	Y	N	Y	Y	N	Y
5 ***Peterson***	Y	Y	Y	N	Y	Y	Y	Y
6 Holden	N	Y	Y	N	Y	Y	N	Y
7 ***Weldon***	Y	Y	Y	N	Y	Y	Y	Y
8 ***Greenwood***	Y	Y	Y	N	Y	Y	Y	Y
9 ***Shuster***	Y	N	Y	N	Y	Y	Y	Y
10 ***McDade***	Y	Y	Y	N	Y	Y	Y	Y
11 Kanjorski	N	Y	Y	N	Y	Y	N	N
12 Murtha	N	Y	Y	N	Y	Y	?	Y
13 ***Fox***	Y	Y	Y	Y	Y	Y	Y	Y
14 Coyne	N	Y	Y	N	Y	Y	N	N
15 McHale	N	Y	Y	N	Y	Y	N	N
16 ***Pitts***	Y	Y	Y	N	Y	Y	Y	Y
17 ***Gekas***	Y	Y	Y	N	Y	Y	Y	Y
18 Doyle	N	Y	Y	N	Y	Y	N	Y
19 ***Goodling***	Y	Y	Y	N	Y	Y	?	Y
20 Mascara	N	Y	Y	N	Y	Y	N	Y
21 ***English***	Y	Y	Y	P	Y	Y	Y	Y
RHODE ISLAND								
1 Kennedy	N	Y	?	N	Y	N	N	N
2 Weygand	N	Y	Y	N	Y	Y	N	Y
SOUTH CAROLINA								
1 ***Sanford***	Y	N	Y	Y	Y	Y	Y	Y
2 ***Spence***	Y	Y	N	N	Y	Y	Y	Y
3 ***Graham***	Y	Y	Y	N	Y	Y	Y	Y
4 ***Inglis***	Y	Y	Y	N	Y	Y	Y	Y
5 Spratt	N	Y	Y	N	Y	Y	N	Y
6 Clyburn	N	Y	Y	Y	Y	N	N	Y
SOUTH DAKOTA								
AL ***Thune***	Y	Y	Y	N	Y	Y	Y	Y
TENNESSEE								
1 ***Jenkins***	Y	Y	?	N	Y	Y	Y	Y
2 ***Duncan***	Y	N	Y	N	Y	Y	Y	Y

	622	623	624	625	626	627	628	
3 ***Wamp***	P	Y	Y	N	Y	Y	N	Y
4 ***Hilleary***	Y	Y	Y	N	Y	Y	Y	Y
5 Clement	N	Y	Y	N	Y	Y	Y	N
6 Gordon	N	Y	Y	N	Y	Y	Y	?
7 ***Bryant***	Y	Y	Y	N	Y	Y	Y	Y
8 Tanner	N	Y	Y	N	Y	Y	N	N
9 Ford	N	Y	Y	Y	Y	N	N	N
TEXAS								
1 Sandlin	N	Y	Y	N	Y	N	N	Y
2 Turner	N	Y	Y	N	Y	N	N	Y
3 ***Johnson, Sam***	Y	?	Y	N	Y	?	Y	Y
4 Hall	N	Y	Y	N	Y	Y	Y	N
5 ***Sessions***	Y	Y	N	N	Y	Y	Y	Y
6 ***Barton***	Y	Y	N	N	Y	Y	?	Y
7 ***Archer***	Y	Y	Y	N	Y	Y	Y	Y
8 ***Brady***	Y	Y	Y	N	Y	Y	Y	?
9 Lampson	N	Y	Y	N	Y	Y	N	Y
10 Doggett	N	Y	Y	N	Y	N	N	N
11 Edwards	N	Y	Y	N	?	N	N	N
12 ***Granger***	Y	Y	Y	N	Y	Y	Y	Y
13 ***Thornberry***	Y	Y	Y	N	Y	Y	Y	Y
14 ***Paul***	Y	N	N	N	Y	Y	Y	Y
15 Hinojosa	N	Y	Y	N	Y	N	N	Y
16 Reyes	N	Y	Y	N	Y	N	N	Y
17 Stenholm	N	Y	Y	N	Y	N	N	N
18 Jackson-Lee	N	Y	Y	Y	N	N	N	Y
19 ***Combest***	Y	Y	Y	N	Y	Y	Y	?
20 Gonzalez	?	?	?	?	?	?	?	?
21 ***Smith***	Y	Y	Y	N	Y	Y	Y	Y
22 ***DeLay***	Y	Y	Y	N	?	Y	Y	Y
23 ***Bonilla***	Y	N	N	N	Y	Y	Y	Y
24 Frost	N	Y	Y	Y	Y	N	Y	?
25 Bentsen	N	Y	Y	N	Y	N	N	Y
26 ***Armey***	Y	Y	Y	N	?	Y	Y	Y
27 Ortiz	N	Y	Y	N	Y	N	N	Y
28 Rodriguez	N	Y	Y	N	Y	N	N	Y
29 Green	N	Y	Y	N	Y	N	N	Y
30 Johnson, E.B.	N	Y	Y	Y	Y	N	N	Y
UTAH								
1 ***Hansen***	Y	Y	Y	N	Y	Y	Y	?
2 ***Cook***	Y	Y	Y	N	Y	Y	Y	Y
3 ***Cannon***	Y	Y	Y	N	Y	Y	Y	Y
VERMONT								
AL *Sanders*	N	N	Y	N	Y	Y	N	Y
VIRGINIA								
1 ***Bateman***	Y	Y	Y	N	Y	Y	Y	Y
2 Pickett	N	N	Y	N	Y	Y	N	N
3 Scott	N	Y	Y	N	Y	N	N	Y
4 Sisisky	N	Y	Y	N	Y	Y	N	Y
5 Goode	N	Y	N	N	Y	Y	N	Y
6 ***Goodlatte***	Y	Y	Y	N	Y	Y	Y	Y
7 ***Bliley***	Y	Y	Y	N	Y	Y	Y	Y
8 Moran	N	Y	Y	N	Y	Y	N	Y
9 Boucher	N	Y	Y	N	Y	?	N	Y
10 ***Wolf***	Y	Y	Y	N	Y	Y	Y	Y
11 ***Davis***	Y	Y	Y	Y	Y	Y	Y	Y
WASHINGTON								
1 ***White***	Y	Y	Y	N	Y	Y	Y	?
2 ***Metcalf***	Y	Y	?	Y	Y	Y	Y	?
3 ***Smith, Linda***	Y	Y	Y	N	+	Y	Y	Y
4 ***Hastings***	Y	Y	Y	N	Y	Y	Y	Y
5 ***Nethercutt***	Y	Y	Y	N	Y	Y	Y	Y
6 Dicks	N	Y	Y	N	Y	Y	N	Y
7 McDermott	?	?	?	?	?	?	?	?
8 ***Dunn***	Y	Y	Y	N	Y	Y	Y	?
9 Smith, Adam	N	Y	Y	N	Y	Y	Y	?
WEST VIRGINIA								
1 Mollohan	N	N	Y	N	Y	Y	N	Y
2 Wise	N	Y	Y	N	Y	Y	N	Y
3 Rahall	N	Y	Y	N	Y	Y	N	Y
WISCONSIN								
1 ***Neumann***	Y	N	Y	N	Y	Y	Y	Y
2 ***Klug***	?	?	?	?	?	?	?	Y
3 Kind	N	Y	Y	N	Y	Y	N	Y
4 Kleczka	?	Y	Y	N	Y	N	N	N
5 Barrett	N	Y	Y	N	Y	Y	Y	N
6 ***Petri***	Y	Y	Y	N	Y	Y	Y	Y
7 Obey	N	N	Y	N	Y	Y	N	N
8 Johnson	N	Y	Y	N	Y	Y	N	Y
9 ***Sensenbrenner***	Y	N	Y	N	Y	Y	Y	Y
WYOMING								
AL ***Cubin***	?	?	?	?	?	?	?	?

Southern states - Ala., Ark., Fla., Ga., Ky., La., Miss., N.C., Okla., S.C., Tenn., Texas, Va.

HOUSE VOTES 630, 631, 632, 633, 634, 635, 636, 637

630. H Res 314. Expedited Floor Procedures/Adoption. Adoption of the resolution to waive through Nov. 14, 1997, the requirement of a two-thirds majority to consider rules governing floor consideration on the same day as reported by the Rules Committee and allow legislation to be considered under suspension of the rules at any time. Adopted 213-193: R 212-0; D 1-192 (ND 1-140, SD 0-52); I 0-1, Nov. 12, 1997.

631. HR 2159. Fiscal 1998 Foreign Operations Appropriations/Conference Report. Adoption of the conference report on the bill to provide about $13 billion for foreign operations and export financing in fiscal 1998. The conference report would provide approximately $530 million more than the fiscal 1997 level and $4.0 billion less than the president's request. Adopted (thus sent to the Senate) 333-76: R 150-64; D 182-12 (ND 134-6, SD 48-6); I 1-0, Nov. 13, 1997 (in the session that began and the Congressional Record dated Nov. 12).

632. H Res 301. Broadcast of Committee Witnesses/Adoption. Adoption of the resolution to repeal the House rule that allows a subpoenaed witness testifying at a public House committee hearing to request not to be photographed or broadcast by radio or television. Adopted 241-165: R 206-7; D 35-157 (ND 20-119, SD 15-38); I 0-1, Nov. 13, 1997 (in the session that began and the Congressional Record dated Nov. 12).

633. H Res 326. New Subcommittee on Census/Previous Question. Linder, R-Ga., motion to order the previous question (thus ending debate and the possibility of amendment) on the resolution to allow a temporary increase in the number of subcommittees each committee may have under House rules in order to allow the Government Reform and Oversight Committee to create a new Subcommittee on the Census for the duration of the 105th Congress. Motion agreed to 220-194: R 219-0; D 1-193 (ND 1-141, SD 0-52); I 0-1, Nov. 13, 1997.

634. H Res 326. New Subcommittee on Census/Adoption. Adoption of the resolution to allow a temporary increase in the number of subcommittees each committee may have under House rules in order to allow the Government Reform and Oversight Committee to create a new Subcommittee on the Census for the duration of the 105th Congress. Adopted 219-195: R 217-1; D 2-193 (ND 2-141, SD 0-52); I 0-1, Nov. 13, 1997.

635. HR 867. Foster Children Adoption/Passage. Shaw, R-Fla., motion to suspend the rules and adopt the rule (H Res 327) to concur in Senate amendments and make further amendments. The bill would give states and local authorities more discretion to permanently remove foster children from abusive homes and authorize $20 million annually from fiscal 1999 through 2003 for states that increase adoptions from the foster care system. Motion agreed to (thus sent to the Senate) 406-7: R 212-5; D 193-2 (ND 143-1, SD 50-1); I 1-0, Nov. 13, 1997. A two-thirds majority of those present and voting (276 in this case) is required for adoption under suspension of the rules.

636. HR 2267. Fiscal 1998 Commerce, Justice, State Appropriations/Rule. Adoption of the rule (H Res 330) to provide for floor consideration of and waive all points of order against the conference report on the bill to provide $31.8 billion in new budget authority for the departments of Commerce, Justice and State, the judiciary and related agencies for fiscal 1998. The conference report would provide approximately $1.5 billion more than the $29.7 billion provided in fiscal 1997 and $4.5 billion less than the $35.7 billion requested by the president. Adopted 285-113: R 209-1; D 76-111 (ND 57-82, SD 19-29); I 0-1, Nov. 13, 1997.

637. H Con Res 137. Iraq War Crimes Tribunal/Adoption. Gilman, R-N.Y., motion to suspend the rules and adopt the concurrent resolution to express the sense of Congress that the president should endorse and work toward the formation of an international war crimes tribunal to prosecute Saddam Hussein and other members of the Iraqi government for crimes against humanity. Motion agreed to 396-2: R 209-1; D 186-1 (ND 137-0, SD 49-1); I 1-0, Nov. 13, 1997. A two-thirds majority of those present and voting (266 in this case) is required for adoption under suspension of the rules.

KEY

Y Voted for (yea).
Paired for.
+ Announced for.
N Voted against (nay).
X Paired against.
– Announced against.
P Voted "present."
C Voted "present" to avoid possible conflict of interest.
? Did not vote or otherwise make a position known.

Democrats ***Republicans***
Independent

	630	631	632	633	634	635	636	637
ALABAMA								
1 ***Callahan***	Y	Y	Y	Y	Y	Y	Y	Y
2 ***Everett***	Y	Y	Y	Y	Y	Y	Y	Y
3 ***Riley***	+	–	+	+	+	+	#	+
4 ***Aderholt***	Y	N	Y	Y	Y	Y	Y	Y
5 Cramer	N	Y	N	N	N	Y	Y	Y
6 ***Bachus***	Y	Y	N	Y	Y	Y	Y	Y
7 Hilliard	N	Y	N	N	N	Y	N	Y
ALASKA								
AL ***Young***	Y	?	?	Y	Y	Y	Y	Y
ARIZONA								
1 ***Salmon***	Y	Y	Y	Y	Y	Y	Y	Y
2 Pastor	N	Y	N	N	N	Y	N	Y
3 ***Stump***	Y	N	Y	Y	Y	Y	Y	Y
4 ***Shadegg***	Y	Y	Y	Y	Y	Y	Y	Y
5 ***Kolbe***	Y	Y	Y	Y	Y	Y	Y	Y
6 ***Hayworth***	Y	Y	Y	Y	Y	Y	Y	Y
ARKANSAS								
1 Berry	N	N	N	N	N	Y	Y	Y
2 Snyder	N	Y	Y	N	N	Y	?	N
3 ***Hutchinson***	Y	Y	Y	Y	Y	Y	Y	Y
4 ***Dickey***	Y	Y	Y	Y	Y	Y	?	?
CALIFORNIA								
1 ***Riggs***	Y	Y	Y	?	Y	Y	Y	Y
2 ***Herger***	Y	N	Y	Y	Y	Y	Y	Y
3 Fazio	N	Y	N	N	N	Y	Y	Y
4 ***Doolittle***	Y	N	Y	Y	Y	Y	Y	Y
5 Matsui	N	Y	N	?	?	?	Y	Y
6 Woolsey	N	Y	N	N	N	Y	N	Y
7 Miller	N	Y	N	N	N	Y	?	?
8 Pelosi	N	Y	N	?	N	Y	N	?
9 Dellums	N	Y	N	N	N	Y	N	?
10 Tauscher	N	Y	Y	N	N	Y	N	Y
11 ***Pombo***	Y	N	Y	Y	Y	Y	Y	Y
12 Lantos	N	Y	N	N	N	Y	Y	?
13 Stark	?	?	?	?	?	?	?	?
14 Eshoo	N	Y	N	N	N	Y	Y	Y
15 ***Campbell***	Y	Y	Y	Y	Y	Y	Y	Y
16 Lofgren	N	Y	N	N	N	Y	Y	Y
17 Farr	N	Y	N	N	N	Y	Y	Y
18 Condit	N	N	N	N	N	Y	N	Y
19 ***Radanovich***	?	?	?	Y	Y	Y	Y	Y
20 Dooley	N	Y	N	N	N	Y	Y	Y
21 ***Thomas***	Y	Y	Y	Y	Y	Y	Y	Y
22 Vacant								
23 ***Gallegly***	Y	Y	Y	Y	Y	Y	Y	Y
24 Sherman	N	Y	Y	N	N	Y	Y	Y
25 ***McKeon***	Y	Y	Y	Y	Y	Y	Y	Y
26 Berman	N	Y	Y	N	N	Y	Y	Y
27 ***Rogan***	Y	Y	Y	Y	Y	Y	Y	Y
28 ***Dreier***	Y	Y	Y	Y	N	Y	Y	Y
29 Waxman	N	Y	?	N	N	Y	N	Y
30 Becerra	N	Y	N	N	N	Y	N	Y
31 Martinez	N	Y	N	N	N	Y	N	Y
32 Dixon	N	Y	N	N	N	Y	Y	Y
33 Roybal-Allard	N	Y	N	N	N	Y	N	Y
34 Torres	N	Y	N	N	N	Y	N	Y
35 Waters	N	Y	N	N	N	Y	N	Y
36 Harman	N	Y	Y	N	N	Y	Y	Y
37 Millender-McD.	N	Y	N	?	?	Y	N	Y
38 ***Horn***	Y	Y	Y	Y	Y	Y	Y	Y
39 ***Royce***	Y	N	Y	Y	Y	Y	Y	Y
40 ***Lewis***	Y	Y	Y	Y	Y	Y	Y	Y
41 ***Kim***	Y	Y	Y	Y	Y	Y	Y	Y
42 Brown	N	Y	N	N	N	Y	N	Y
43 ***Calvert***	Y	Y	Y	Y	Y	Y	Y	Y
44 ***Bono***	Y	Y	Y	Y	Y	Y	Y	Y
45 ***Rohrabacher***	Y	N	Y	Y	Y	Y	Y	Y
46 Sanchez	N	Y	Y	N	N	Y	N	Y
47 ***Cox***	Y	Y	Y	Y	Y	Y	Y	Y
48 ***Packard***	Y	Y	Y	Y	Y	Y	Y	Y
49 ***Bilbray***	Y	N	Y	Y	Y	Y	Y	Y
50 Filner	N	Y	N	N	N	Y	N	Y
51 ***Cunningham***	Y	Y	Y	Y	Y	Y	Y	Y
52 ***Hunter***	Y	Y	Y	Y	Y	Y	Y	Y
COLORADO								
1 DeGette	N	Y	N	N	N	Y	N	Y
2 Skaggs	N	Y	N	N	N	Y	Y	Y
3 ***McInnis***	Y	Y	Y	Y	Y	Y	?	?
4 ***Schaffer***	Y	Y	Y	Y	Y	Y	Y	Y
5 ***Hefley***	Y	N	Y	Y	Y	Y	Y	Y
6 ***Schaefer***	Y	Y	Y	Y	Y	Y	Y	Y
CONNECTICUT								
1 Kennelly	N	Y	N	N	N	Y	N	Y
2 Gejdenson	N	Y	N	N	N	Y	N	Y
3 DeLauro	N	Y	N	N	N	Y	N	Y
4 ***Shays***	Y	Y	Y	Y	Y	Y	Y	Y
5 Maloney	N	Y	Y	N	N	?	N	Y
6 ***Johnson***	Y	Y	Y	Y	Y	Y	Y	Y
DELAWARE								
AL ***Castle***	Y	Y	Y	Y	Y	Y	Y	Y
FLORIDA								
1 ***Scarborough***	?	N	Y	Y	Y	Y	Y	Y
2 Boyd	N	Y	N	N	N	Y	N	Y
3 Brown	N	Y	N	N	N	Y	N	Y
4 ***Fowler***	Y	Y	Y	Y	Y	Y	?	?
5 Thurman	N	Y	N	N	N	Y	N	Y
6 ***Stearns***	Y	N	Y	Y	Y	Y	Y	Y
7 ***Mica***	Y	N	Y	Y	Y	Y	Y	Y
8 ***McCollum***	Y	Y	Y	Y	Y	Y	Y	Y
9 ***Bilirakis***	Y	Y	Y	Y	Y	Y	Y	Y
10 ***Young***	Y	N	Y	Y	Y	Y	Y	Y
11 Davis	N	Y	Y	N	N	Y	Y	Y
12 ***Canady***	Y	Y	Y	Y	Y	Y	Y	Y
13 ***Miller***	Y	Y	Y	Y	Y	Y	Y	Y
14 ***Goss***	Y	Y	Y	Y	Y	Y	Y	Y
15 ***Weldon***	Y	N	Y	Y	Y	Y	Y	Y
16 ***Foley***	Y	Y	Y	Y	Y	Y	Y	Y
17 Meek	N	Y	N	N	N	Y	N	Y
18 ***Ros-Lehtinen***	Y	Y	Y	Y	Y	Y	Y	Y
19 Wexler	N	Y	N	N	N	Y	?	?
20 Deutsch	N	Y	N	N	N	Y	N	Y
21 ***Diaz-Balart***	Y	Y	Y	Y	Y	Y	Y	Y
22 ***Shaw***	Y	Y	Y	Y	Y	Y	Y	Y
23 Hastings	N	Y	N	N	N	Y	N	Y
GEORGIA								
1 ***Kingston***	Y	Y	Y	Y	Y	Y	Y	Y
2 Bishop	N	Y	N	N	N	Y	N	Y
3 ***Collins***	Y	Y	Y	Y	Y	Y	Y	Y
4 McKinney	N	Y	N	N	N	Y	N	Y
5 Lewis	N	Y	N	N	N	Y	N	Y
6 ***Gingrich***			Y					
7 ***Barr***	Y	N	Y	Y	Y	Y	Y	Y
8 ***Chambliss***	Y	Y	Y	Y	Y	Y	Y	Y
9 ***Deal***	Y	Y	Y	Y	Y	Y	Y	Y
10 ***Norwood***	?	?	?	Y	Y	Y	Y	Y
11 ***Linder***	Y	Y	Y	Y	Y	Y	Y	Y
HAWAII								
1 Abercrombie	N	Y	N	N	N	Y	N	Y
2 Mink	N	Y	N	?	?	N	N	Y
IDAHO								
1 ***Chenoweth***	Y	N	Y	Y	Y	Y	Y	Y
2 ***Crapo***	Y	Y	Y	Y	Y	Y	Y	Y
ILLINOIS								
1 Rush	N	Y	N	N	N	Y	N	Y
2 Jackson	N	Y	N	N	N	Y	Y	Y
3 Lipinski	N	Y	Y	N	N	Y	?	?
4 Gutierrez	N	Y	N	N	N	Y	N	Y
5 Blagojevich	N	Y	N	N	N	Y	N	Y
6 ***Hyde***	Y	N	Y	Y	Y	Y	Y	Y
7 Davis	N	Y	N	N	N	Y	N	Y
8 ***Crane***	Y	N	Y	Y	Y	Y	Y	Y
9 Yates	N	?	?	N	N	Y	X	?
10 ***Porter***	Y	Y	Y	Y	Y	Y	Y	Y
11 ***Weller***	Y	Y	Y	Y	Y	Y	Y	Y
12 Costello	N	Y	N	N	N	Y	Y	Y
13 ***Fawell***	Y	Y	Y	Y	Y	Y	Y	Y
14 ***Hastert***	Y	Y	Y	Y	Y	Y	Y	Y
15 ***Ewing***	Y	Y	Y	Y	Y	Y	Y	Y

ND Northern Democrats SD Southern Democrats

	630	631	632	633	634	635	636	637
16 **Manzullo**	Y	Y	Y	Y	Y	N	Y	Y
17 Evans	N	Y	N	N	N	Y	N	Y
18 **LaHood**	Y	N	Y	Y	Y	N	Y	Y
19 Poshard	N	Y	N	N	N	Y	Y	Y
20 **Shimkus**	Y	Y	Y	Y	Y	Y	Y	Y
INDIANA								
1 Visclosky	N	Y	N	N	N	Y	N	Y
2 **McIntosh**	Y	Y	Y	Y	Y	Y	Y	Y
3 Roemer	N	N	Y	N	N	Y	?	?
4 **Souder**	Y	Y	Y	Y	Y	Y	Y	Y
5 **Buyer**	Y	N	Y	Y	?	?	Y	Y
6 **Burton**	Y	Y	Y	Y	Y	Y	Y	Y
7 **Pease**	Y	N	Y	Y	Y	Y	Y	Y
8 **Hostettler**	Y	N	Y	Y	Y	Y	Y	Y
9 Hamilton	N	Y	N	N	N	Y	Y	Y
10 Carson	N	Y	N	N	N	Y	N	Y
IOWA								
1 **Leach**	Y	Y	Y	Y	Y	Y	Y	Y
2 **Nussle**	Y	Y	Y	Y	Y	Y	?	?
3 Boswell	N	Y	Y	N	N	Y	Y	Y
4 **Ganske**	Y	Y	Y	Y	Y	Y	Y	Y
5 **Latham**	Y	Y	Y	Y	Y	Y	Y	Y
KANSAS								
1 **Moran**	Y	N	Y	Y	Y	Y	Y	Y
2 **Ryun**	Y	N	Y	Y	Y	Y	Y	Y
3 **Snowbarger**	Y	Y	Y	Y	Y	Y	Y	Y
4 **Tiahrt**	Y	N	Y	Y	Y	Y	Y	Y
KENTUCKY								
1 **Whitfield**	Y	Y	Y	Y	Y	Y	Y	Y
2 **Lewis**	Y	Y	Y	Y	Y	Y	Y	Y
3 **Northup**	Y	Y	Y	Y	Y	Y	Y	Y
4 **Bunning**	Y	Y	Y	Y	Y	Y	Y	Y
5 **Rogers**	Y	N	Y	Y	Y	Y	Y	Y
6 Baesler	N	Y	Y	N	N	Y	Y	Y
LOUISIANA								
1 **Livingston**	Y	Y	Y	Y	Y	Y	Y	Y
2 Jefferson	N	Y	N	N	N	Y	N	Y
3 **Tauzin**	Y	Y	Y	Y	Y	Y	Y	Y
4 **McCrery**	Y	Y	Y	Y	Y	Y	Y	Y
5 **Cooksey**	?	Y	Y	Y	Y	Y	Y	Y
6 **Baker**	Y	?	?	Y	Y	Y	?	Y
7 John	?	Y	N	N	N	?	?	Y
MAINE								
1 Allen	N	Y	N	N	N	Y	Y	Y
2 Baldacci	N	Y	N	N	N	Y	N	Y
MARYLAND								
1 **Gilchrest**	Y	Y	Y	Y	Y	Y	Y	Y
2 **Ehrlich**	Y	Y	Y	Y	Y	Y	Y	Y
3 Cardin	N	Y	N	N	N	Y	N	Y
4 Wynn	N	Y	N	N	N	Y	N	Y
5 Hoyer	N	Y	N	N	N	Y	Y	Y
6 **Bartlett**	Y	N	Y	Y	?	Y	Y	Y
7 Cummings	N	Y	N	N	N	Y	N	Y
8 **Morella**	Y	Y	Y	Y	Y	Y	Y	Y
MASSACHUSETTS								
1 Olver	N	Y	N	N	N	Y	N	Y
2 Neal	?	?	?	N	N	Y	N	Y
3 McGovern	N	Y	N	N	N	Y	Y	Y
4 Frank	N	Y	N	N	N	Y	Y	Y
5 Meehan	?	?	?	N	N	Y	N	Y
6 Tierney	N	Y	N	N	N	Y	Y	Y
7 Markey	N	?	?	N	N	Y	Y	Y
8 Kennedy	N	Y	N	N	N	Y	Y	Y
9 Moakley	N	Y	N	N	N	Y	Y	Y
10 Delahunt	N	Y	N	N	N	Y	Y	Y
MICHIGAN								
1 Stupak	N	Y	N	N	N	Y	N	Y
2 **Hoekstra**	Y	N	Y	Y	Y	Y	Y	Y
3 **Ehlers**	Y	Y	Y	Y	Y	Y	?	?
4 **Camp**	Y	Y	Y	Y	Y	Y	Y	Y
5 Barcia	N	P	N	N	N	Y	Y	Y
6 **Upton**	Y	Y	Y	Y	Y	Y	Y	Y
7 **Smith**	Y	Y	Y	Y	Y	Y	Y	Y
8 Stabenow	N	Y	N	N	N	Y	N	Y
9 Kildee	N	Y	Y	N	N	Y	N	Y
10 Bonior	N	Y	N	N	N	Y	N	Y
11 **Knollenberg**	Y	Y	Y	Y	Y	Y	Y	Y
12 Levin	N	Y	N	N	N	Y	N	Y
13 Rivers	N	Y	Y	N	N	Y	N	Y
14 Conyers	N	Y	N	N	N	Y	N	Y
15 Kilpatrick	N	Y	N	N	N	Y	N	Y
16 Dingell	N	Y	N	N	N	Y	Y	Y
MINNESOTA								
1 **Gutknecht**	Y	N	Y	Y	Y	Y	Y	Y
2 Minge	N	N	Y	N	N	Y	Y	Y

	630	631	632	633	634	635	636	637
3 **Ramstad**	Y	Y	Y	Y	Y	Y	Y	Y
4 Vento	N	Y	N	N	N	Y	Y	Y
5 Sabo	N	Y	N	N	N	Y	Y	Y
6 Luther	N	Y	Y	N	N	Y	N	Y
7 Peterson	N	Y	N	N	N	Y	N	Y
8 Oberstar	N	Y	N	N	N	Y	Y	Y
MISSISSIPPI								
1 **Wicker**	Y	Y	Y	Y	Y	Y	Y	Y
2 Thompson	N	Y	N	N	N	Y	N	Y
3 **Pickering**	Y	N	Y	Y	Y	Y	Y	Y
4 **Parker**	Y	Y	Y	Y	Y	Y	Y	Y
5 Taylor	N	N	Y	N	N	Y	N	Y
MISSOURI								
1 Clay	N	Y	N	N	N	Y	N	Y
2 **Talent**	Y	Y	Y	Y	Y	Y	Y	Y
3 Gephardt	?	?	?	?	?	?	N	Y
4 Skelton	N	Y	Y	N	N	Y	Y	Y
5 McCarthy	N	Y	N	N	N	Y	N	Y
6 Danner	N	Y	N	N	N	Y	N	Y
7 **Blunt**	Y	N	Y	Y	Y	Y	Y	Y
8 **Emerson**	Y	N	N	Y	Y	Y	Y	Y
9 **Hulshof**	Y	N	Y	Y	Y	Y	Y	Y
MONTANA								
AL **Hill**	Y	Y	Y	Y	Y	Y	Y	Y
NEBRASKA								
1 **Bereuter**	Y	Y	Y	Y	Y	Y	Y	Y
2 **Christensen**	Y	Y	Y	Y	Y	Y	Y	Y
3 **Barrett**	Y	N	N	Y	Y	Y	Y	Y
NEVADA								
1 **Ensign**	Y	N	Y	Y	Y	Y	N	Y
2 **Gibbons**	Y	Y	Y	Y	Y	Y	Y	Y
NEW HAMPSHIRE								
1 **Sununu**	Y	N	Y	Y	Y	Y	Y	Y
2 **Bass**	Y	Y	Y	Y	Y	Y	Y	Y
NEW JERSEY								
1 Andrews	N	Y	N	N	N	Y	N	Y
2 **LoBiondo**	Y	Y	Y	Y	Y	Y	Y	Y
3 **Saxton**	Y	Y	Y	Y	Y	Y	Y	Y
4 **Smith**	Y	N	Y	Y	Y	Y	Y	Y
5 **Roukema**	Y	Y	N	Y	Y	Y	Y	Y
6 Pallone	N	Y	N	N	N	Y	N	Y
7 **Franks**	Y	Y	Y	Y	Y	Y	Y	Y
8 Pascrell	N	Y	N	N	N	Y	N	Y
9 Rothman	N	Y	N	N	N	Y	N	Y
10 Payne	N	Y	N	N	N	Y	N	Y
11 **Frelinghuysen**	Y	Y	Y	Y	Y	Y	Y	Y
12 **Pappas**	Y	Y	Y	Y	Y	Y	Y	Y
13 Menendez	N	Y	N	N	N	Y	N	Y
NEW MEXICO								
1 **Schiff**	?	?	?	?	?	?	?	?
2 **Skeen**	Y	Y	Y	Y	Y	Y	Y	Y
3 **Redmond**	Y	Y	Y	Y	Y	Y	Y	Y
NEW YORK								
1 **Forbes**	Y	Y	Y	Y	Y	Y	Y	Y
2 **Lazio**	Y	Y	Y	Y	Y	Y	Y	Y
3 **King**	Y	Y	Y	Y	Y	Y	Y	Y
4 McCarthy	N	Y	Y	N	N	Y	N	Y
5 Ackerman	N	Y	N	N	N	Y	Y	Y
6 Flake	?	?	?	?	?	?	?	?
7 Manton	N	Y	N	N	N	Y	N	Y
8 Nadler	N	Y	N	N	N	Y	N	Y
9 Schumer	?	Y	N	N	N	Y	N	Y
10 Towns	?	Y	N	N	N	Y	N	Y
11 Owens	?	Y	N	N	N	Y	N	Y
12 Velázquez	N	Y	N	N	N	Y	N	Y
13 **Fossella**	Y	Y	Y	Y	Y	Y	Y	Y
14 Maloney	N	Y	N	N	N	Y	N	Y
15 Rangel	N	Y	N	N	N	Y	N	Y
16 Serrano	N	Y	N	N	N	Y	N	Y
17 Engel	N	Y	N	N	N	Y	N	Y
18 Lowey	N	Y	N	N	N	Y	N	Y
19 **Kelly**	Y	Y	Y	Y	Y	Y	Y	Y
20 **Gilman**	Y	Y	Y	Y	Y	Y	Y	Y
21 McNulty	N	Y	N	N	N	Y	Y	Y
22 **Solomon**	Y	N	Y	Y	Y	Y	Y	Y
23 **Boehlert**	Y	Y	Y	Y	Y	Y	Y	Y
24 **McHugh**	Y	Y	Y	Y	Y	Y	Y	Y
25 **Walsh**	Y	Y	Y	Y	Y	Y	Y	Y
26 Hinchey	N	Y	N	N	N	Y	N	Y
27 **Paxon**	Y	Y	Y	Y	Y	Y	Y	Y
28 Slaughter	N	Y	N	N	N	Y	Y	Y
29 LaFalce	N	Y	N	N	N	Y	?	?
30 **Quinn**	Y	Y	Y	Y	Y	Y	Y	Y
31 **Houghton**	?	?	?	?	?	?	?	?

	630	631	632	633	634	635	636	637
NORTH CAROLINA								
1 Clayton	N	Y	N	N	N	Y	Y	Y
2 Etheridge	N	Y	N	N	N	Y	Y	Y
3 **Jones**	Y	N	Y	Y	Y	Y	Y	Y
4 Price	N	Y	N	N	N	Y	Y	Y
5 **Burr**	Y	Y	Y	Y	Y	Y	Y	Y
6 **Coble**	Y	Y	Y	Y	Y	Y	Y	Y
7 McIntyre	N	Y	Y	N	N	Y	Y	Y
8 Hefner	N	Y	N	N	N	Y	N	Y
9 **Myrick**	?	N	Y	Y	Y	Y	?	?
10 **Ballenger**	Y	Y	Y	Y	Y	Y	Y	Y
11 **Taylor**	Y	Y	?	Y	Y	Y	?	?
12 Watt	N	Y	N	N	N	Y	N	Y
NORTH DAKOTA								
AL Pomeroy	N	Y	N	N	N	Y	Y	Y
OHIO								
1 **Chabot**	Y	N	Y	Y	Y	Y	Y	Y
2 **Portman**	Y	Y	Y	Y	Y	Y	Y	Y
3 Hall	N	Y	?	N	N	Y	Y	Y
4 **Oxley**	Y	Y	Y	Y	Y	Y	Y	Y
5 **Gillmor**	Y	Y	Y	Y	Y	Y	Y	Y
6 Strickland	N	Y	N	N	N	Y	N	Y
7 **Hobson**	Y	Y	Y	Y	Y	Y	Y	Y
8 **Boehner**	Y	Y	Y	Y	Y	Y	Y	Y
9 Kaptur	N	Y	N	N	N	Y	N	Y
10 Kucinich	N	N	N	N	N	Y	N	Y
11 Stokes	N	Y	N	N	N	Y	N	Y
12 **Kasich**	Y	Y	Y	Y	Y	Y	Y	Y
13 Brown	N	Y	N	N	N	Y	N	Y
14 Sawyer	N	Y	?	N	N	Y	Y	Y
15 **Pryce**	+	+	?	Y	Y	Y	?	?
16 **Regula**	Y	Y	Y	Y	Y	Y	Y	Y
17 Traficant	Y	N	Y	Y	Y	Y	Y	Y
18 **Ney**	Y	Y	Y	Y	Y	Y	Y	Y
19 **LaTourette**	Y	Y	Y	Y	Y	Y	Y	Y
OKLAHOMA								
1 **Largent**	Y	Y	N	Y	Y	Y	Y	Y
2 **Coburn**	Y	N	Y	Y	Y	Y	Y	Y
3 **Watkins**	Y	N	Y	Y	Y	Y	?	?
4 **Watts**	Y	N	Y	Y	Y	Y	Y	Y
5 **Istook**	Y	Y	Y	Y	Y	Y	Y	Y
6 **Lucas**	Y	N	Y	Y	Y	Y	Y	Y
OREGON								
1 Furse	N	?	N	N	N	Y	?	?
2 **Smith**	?	?	?	?	?	?	?	?
3 Blumenauer	N	Y	N	N	N	Y	?	?
4 DeFazio	N	Y	Y	N	N	Y	N	Y
5 Hooley	N	Y	N	N	N	Y	N	Y
PENNSYLVANIA								
1 Vacant								
2 Fattah	N	Y	N	N	N	Y	N	Y
3 Borski	N	Y	N	N	N	Y	N	Y
4 Klink	N	Y	N	N	N	Y	N	Y
5 **Peterson**	Y	N	Y	Y	Y	Y	Y	Y
6 Holden	N	Y	N	N	N	Y	Y	Y
7 **Weldon**	Y	Y	Y	Y	Y	?	Y	Y
8 **Greenwood**	Y	Y	Y	Y	Y	Y	Y	Y
9 **Shuster**	Y	?	?	Y	Y	Y	Y	Y
10 **McDade**	Y	Y	Y	Y	Y	Y	Y	Y
11 Kanjorski	N	Y	N	N	N	Y	Y	Y
12 Murtha	N	Y	N	N	N	Y	Y	Y
13 **Fox**	Y	Y	Y	Y	Y	Y	Y	Y
14 Coyne	N	Y	N	N	N	Y	N	Y
15 McHale	N	Y	N	N	Y	Y	Y	Y
16 **Pitts**	Y	Y	Y	Y	Y	Y	Y	Y
17 **Gekas**	Y	Y	Y	Y	Y	Y	Y	Y
18 Doyle	N	Y	N	N	N	Y	Y	Y
19 **Goodling**	Y	N	Y	Y	Y	Y	Y	Y
20 Mascara	N	Y	N	N	N	Y	Y	Y
21 **English**	Y	Y	Y	Y	Y	Y	Y	Y
RHODE ISLAND								
1 Kennedy	N	Y	N	N	N	Y	N	Y
2 Weygand	N	Y	N	N	N	Y	Y	Y
SOUTH CAROLINA								
1 **Sanford**	Y	N	Y	Y	Y	Y	Y	Y
2 **Spence**	Y	Y	Y	Y	Y	Y	Y	Y
3 **Graham**	Y	N	Y	Y	Y	Y	Y	Y
4 **Inglis**	Y	N	Y	Y	Y	Y	Y	Y
5 Spratt	N	Y	N	N	N	Y	Y	Y
6 Clyburn	N	Y	N	N	N	Y	N	Y
SOUTH DAKOTA								
AL **Thune**	Y	Y	Y	Y	Y	Y	Y	Y
TENNESSEE								
1 **Jenkins**	Y	Y	Y	Y	Y	Y	Y	Y
2 **Duncan**	Y	N	Y	Y	Y	Y	Y	Y

	630	631	632	633	634	635	636	
3 **Wamp**	Y	Y	Y	Y	Y	N	Y	Y
4 **Hilleary**	Y	N	Y	Y	Y	Y	Y	Y
5 Clement	N	Y	Y	N	N	Y	Y	Y
6 Gordon	N	Y	?	N	N	N	N	Y
7 **Bryant**	Y	Y	Y	Y	Y	Y	Y	Y
8 Tanner	N	N	Y	N	N	Y	Y	Y
9 Ford	N	Y	N	N	N	Y	N	Y
TEXAS								
1 Sandlin	N	Y	Y	N	N	Y	N	Y
2 Turner	N	Y	Y	N	N	Y	Y	Y
3 **Johnson, Sam**	Y	N	Y	Y	Y	Y	Y	Y
4 Hall	N	N	Y	N	N	Y	Y	Y
5 **Sessions**	Y	N	Y	Y	Y	Y	Y	Y
6 **Barton**	Y	N	Y	Y	Y	Y	Y	Y
7 **Archer**	Y	N	Y	Y	Y	Y	Y	Y
8 **Brady**	?	N	Y	Y	Y	Y	Y	Y
9 Lampson	N	Y	Y	N	N	Y	N	Y
10 Doggett	N	Y	Y	N	N	Y	N	Y
11 Edwards	N	Y	Y	N	N	Y	Y	Y
12 **Granger**	Y	Y	Y	Y	Y	Y	Y	Y
13 **Thornberry**	Y	N	Y	Y	Y	Y	Y	Y
14 **Paul**	Y	N	N	Y	Y	N	Y	N
15 Hinojosa	N	Y	N	N	N	Y	N	Y
16 Reyes	N	Y	N	N	N	Y	N	Y
17 Stenholm	N	Y	Y	N	N	Y	Y	Y
18 Jackson-Lee	N	Y	N	N	N	Y	N	Y
19 **Combest**	?	?	?	?	?	?	?	?
20 Gonzalez	?	?	?	?	?	?	?	?
21 **Smith**	Y	Y	Y	Y	Y	Y	Y	Y
22 **DeLay**	Y	Y	Y	Y	Y	Y	Y	Y
23 **Bonilla**	Y	Y	Y	Y	Y	Y	Y	Y
24 Frost	?	Y	N	N	N	Y	N	Y
25 Bentsen	N	Y	N	N	N	Y	N	Y
26 **Armey**	Y	Y	Y	Y	Y	?	Y	Y
27 Ortiz	N	Y	N	N	N	Y	?	?
28 Rodriguez	N	Y	N	N	N	Y	N	Y
29 Green	N	Y	N	N	N	Y	?	?
30 Johnson, E.B.	N	Y	N	–	–	+	N	Y
UTAH								
1 **Hansen**	?	N	Y	Y	Y	Y	Y	Y
2 **Cook**	Y	Y	Y	Y	Y	Y	Y	Y
3 **Cannon**	Y	N	Y	Y	Y	N	Y	Y
VERMONT								
AL Sanders	N	Y	N	N	N	Y	N	Y
VIRGINIA								
1 **Bateman**	Y	Y	Y	Y	Y	Y	Y	Y
2 Pickett	N	N	N	N	N	Y	?	?
3 Scott	N	Y	N	?	?	?	N	Y
4 Sisisky	N	Y	N	N	N	Y	Y	Y
5 Goode	N	N	Y	N	N	Y	Y	Y
6 **Goodlatte**	Y	Y	Y	Y	Y	Y	Y	Y
7 **Bliley**	Y	Y	Y	Y	Y	Y	Y	Y
8 Moran	N	Y	N	N	N	Y	Y	Y
9 Boucher	N	Y	N	N	N	Y	Y	Y
10 **Wolf**	Y	Y	Y	Y	Y	Y	Y	Y
11 **Davis**	Y	Y	?	Y	Y	Y	Y	Y
WASHINGTON								
1 **White**	?	?	?	?	?	?	?	?
2 **Metcalf**	Y	Y	Y	Y	Y	Y	Y	Y
3 **Smith, Linda**	Y	Y	Y	Y	Y	Y	Y	Y
4 **Hastings**	Y	N	Y	Y	Y	Y	Y	Y
5 **Nethercutt**	Y	Y	Y	Y	Y	Y	Y	Y
6 Dicks	N	Y	N	N	N	Y	Y	Y
7 McDermott	N	Y	N	N	N	Y	N	Y
8 **Dunn**	Y	Y	Y	Y	Y	Y	Y	Y
9 Smith, Adam	N	Y	N	N	N	Y	Y	Y
WEST VIRGINIA								
1 Mollohan	N	Y	N	N	N	Y	Y	Y
2 Wise	N	Y	N	N	N	Y	?	Y
3 Rahall	N	N	N	N	N	Y	Y	Y
WISCONSIN								
1 **Neumann**	Y	Y	Y	Y	Y	Y	Y	Y
2 **Klug**	Y	Y	Y	Y	Y	Y	Y	Y
3 Kind	N	Y	Y	N	N	Y	Y	Y
4 Kleczka	N	Y	N	N	N	Y	Y	Y
5 Barrett	N	Y	N	N	N	Y	Y	Y
6 **Petri**	Y	N	Y	Y	Y	Y	Y	Y
7 Obey	N	Y	N	N	N	Y	Y	Y
8 Johnson	N	Y	N	N	N	Y	Y	Y
9 **Sensenbrenner**	Y	N	Y	Y	Y	Y	Y	Y
WYOMING								
AL **Cubin**	?	?	?	?	?	?	?	?

Southern states - Ala., Ark., Fla., Ga., Ky., La., Miss., N.C., Okla., S.C., Tenn., Texas, Va.

HOUSE VOTES 638, 639, 640

638. S Con Res 68. Sine Die Adjournment/Adoption. Adoption of the concurrent resolution to allow the sine die adjournment of the House and Senate for the first session of the 105th Congress. Adopted 205-193: R 204-4; D 1-188 (ND 1-138, SD 0-50); I 0-1, Nov. 13, 1997.

639. HR 2267. Fiscal 1998 Commerce, Justice, State Appropriations/Recommit. Obey, D-Wis., motion to recommit to the House Appropriations Committee (thus killing) the conference report on the bill to provide $31.8 billion in new budget authority for the departments of Commerce, Justice and State, the judiciary and related agencies for fiscal 1998. Motion rejected 171-216: R 3-200; D 167-16 (ND 125-12, SD 42-4); I 1-0, Nov. 13, 1997.

640. HR 2267. Fiscal 1998 Commerce, Justice, State Appropriations/Conference Report. Adoption of the conference report on the bill to provide $31.8 billion in new budget authority for the departments of Commerce, Justice, and State, the judiciary and related agencies for fiscal 1998. The conference report provides $1.9 billion more than the amount provided in fiscal 1997 and $4.1 billion less than the $35.7 billion requested by the president. Adopted (thus sent to the Senate) 282-110: R 160-46; D 122-63 (ND 93-44, SD 29-19); I 0-1, Nov. 13, 1997.

Note: Vote 640 was the last roll-call vote taken by the House in the first session of the 105th Congress.

KEY

- Y Voted for (yea).
- # Paired for.
- + Announced for.
- N Voted against (nay).
- X Paired against.
- – Announced against.
- P Voted "present."
- C Voted "present" to avoid possible conflict of interest.
- ? Did not vote or otherwise make a position known.

Democrats ***Republicans*** *Independent*

	638	639	640
ALABAMA			
1 ***Callahan***	Y	N	Y
2 ***Everett***	Y	N	Y
3 ***Riley***	+	–	#
4 ***Aderholt***	Y	N	Y
5 Cramer	N	Y	Y
6 ***Bachus***	Y	N	Y
7 Hilliard	N	Y	N
ALASKA			
AL ***Young***	Y	N	Y
ARIZONA			
1 ***Salmon***	Y	?	N
2 Pastor	N	Y	Y
3 ***Stump***	Y	N	N
4 ***Shadegg***	Y	N	Y
5 ***Kolbe***	Y	N	Y
6 ***Hayworth***	Y	N	Y
ARKANSAS			
1 Berry	N	Y	Y
2 Snyder	N	Y	Y
3 ***Hutchinson***	Y	N	Y
4 ***Dickey***	?	?	?
CALIFORNIA			
1 ***Riggs***	Y	N	Y
2 ***Herger***	Y	N	N
3 Fazio	N	Y	Y
4 ***Doolittle***	Y	N	N
5 Matsui	N	Y	Y
6 Woolsey	N	Y	Y
7 Miller	?	?	?
8 Pelosi	N	Y	Y
9 Dellums	N	Y	N
10 Tauscher	N	Y	Y
11 ***Pombo***	Y	N	N
12 Lantos	N	Y	Y
13 Stark	?	?	?
14 Eshoo	N	Y	Y
15 ***Campbell***	Y	N	N
16 Lofgren	N	Y	Y
17 Farr	N	Y	Y
18 Condit	N	Y	Y
19 ***Radanovich***	Y	N	Y
20 Dooley	N	Y	Y
21 ***Thomas***	Y	N	Y
22 Vacant			
23 ***Gallegly***	Y	N	Y
24 Sherman	N	Y	Y
25 ***McKeon***	Y	N	Y
26 Berman	N	Y	Y
27 ***Rogan***	Y	N	Y
28 ***Dreier***	Y	N	Y
29 Waxman	N	?	?
30 Becerra	N	Y	N
31 Martinez	N	Y	Y
32 Dixon	N	Y	Y
33 Roybal-Allard	N	Y	Y
34 Torres	N	Y	Y
35 Waters	N	Y	N
36 Harman	N	Y	Y
37 Millender-McD.	N	Y	N
38 ***Horn***	Y	N	Y
39 ***Royce***	Y	N	N
40 ***Lewis***	Y	N	Y
41 ***Kim***	Y	N	Y
42 Brown	N	Y	Y
43 ***Calvert***	Y	N	Y
44 ***Bono***	Y	N	Y
45 ***Rohrabacher***	Y	N	N
46 Sanchez	N	Y	Y
47 ***Cox***	Y	N	N
48 ***Packard***	Y	N	Y
49 ***Bilbray***	Y	N	Y
50 Filner	N	Y	N
51 ***Cunningham***	Y	N	Y
52 ***Hunter***	Y	N	Y
COLORADO			
1 DeGette	N	Y	N
2 Skaggs	N	Y	Y
3 ***McInnis***	?	?	?
4 ***Schaffer***	Y	N	Y
5 ***Hefley***	Y	N	N
6 ***Schaefer***	Y	N	N
CONNECTICUT			
1 Kennelly	N	Y	Y
2 Gejdenson	N	Y	N
3 DeLauro	N	Y	N
4 ***Shays***	Y	N	Y
5 Maloney	N	Y	Y
6 ***Johnson***	Y	N	Y
DELAWARE			
AL ***Castle***	Y	N	Y
FLORIDA			
1 ***Scarborough***	Y	?	N
2 Boyd	N	Y	Y
3 Brown	N	Y	N
4 ***Fowler***	?	?	?
5 Thurman	N	Y	N
6 ***Stearns***	Y	N	N
7 ***Mica***	Y	N	Y
8 ***McCollum***	Y	N	Y
9 ***Bilirakis***	Y	N	Y
10 ***Young***	Y	N	Y
11 Davis	N	Y	Y
12 ***Canady***	Y	N	Y
13 ***Miller***	Y	N	Y
14 ***Goss***	Y	N	Y
15 ***Weldon***	Y	N	Y
16 ***Foley***	Y	N	Y
17 Meek	N	Y	N
18 ***Ros-Lehtinen***	Y	N	Y
19 Wexler	?	?	?
20 Deutsch	N	Y	Y
21 ***Diaz-Balart***	Y	N	Y
22 ***Shaw***	Y	N	Y
23 Hastings	N	Y	N
GEORGIA			
1 ***Kingston***	Y	N	Y
2 Bishop	N	Y	Y
3 ***Collins***	Y	N	Y
4 McKinney	N	?	N
5 Lewis	N	Y	N
6 ***Gingrich***			
7 ***Barr***	Y	N	N
8 ***Chambliss***	Y	N	Y
9 ***Deal***	Y	N	N
10 ***Norwood***	Y	N	Y
11 ***Linder***	Y	N	Y
HAWAII			
1 Abercrombie	N	Y	Y
2 Mink	N	Y	Y
IDAHO			
1 ***Chenoweth***	Y	N	N
2 ***Crapo***	Y	N	N
ILLINOIS			
1 Rush	N	Y	N
2 Jackson	N	Y	N
3 Lipinski	?	?	?
4 Gutierrez	N	Y	Y
5 Blagojevich	N	?	?
6 ***Hyde***	Y	N	Y
7 Davis	N	Y	N
8 ***Crane***	Y	N	N
9 Yates	?	?	X
10 ***Porter***	Y	N	Y
11 ***Weller***	Y	N	Y
12 Costello	N	N	Y
13 ***Fawell***	Y	N	Y
14 ***Hastert***	Y	N	Y
15 ***Ewing***	Y	?	?

ND Northern Democrats SD Southern Democrats

	638	639	640
16 ***Manzullo***	Y	N	N
17 Evans	N	Y	Y
18 ***LaHood***	Y	N	Y
19 Poshard	N	N	Y
20 ***Shimkus***	Y	N	Y
INDIANA			
1 Visclosky	N	Y	Y
2 ***McIntosh***	Y	?	?
3 Roemer	?	?	X
4 ***Souder***	?	N	Y
5 ***Buyer***	Y	N	Y
6 ***Burton***	Y	N	Y
7 ***Pease***	Y	N	N
8 ***Hostettler***	Y	N	N
9 Hamilton	N	Y	Y
10 Carson	N	Y	Y
IOWA			
1 ***Leach***	Y	Y	Y
2 ***Nussle***	?	?	?
3 Boswell	N	Y	Y
4 ***Ganske***	Y	N	Y
5 ***Latham***	Y	N	Y
KANSAS			
1 ***Moran***	Y	N	N
2 ***Ryun***	Y	N	N
3 ***Snowbarger***	Y	N	Y
4 ***Tiahrt***	Y	N	Y
KENTUCKY			
1 ***Whitfield***	Y	?	Y
2 ***Lewis***	Y	N	Y
3 ***Northup***	Y	N	Y
4 ***Bunning***	Y	N	Y
5 ***Rogers***	Y	N	Y
6 Baesler	N	?	?
LOUISIANA			
1 ***Livingston***	Y	N	Y
2 Jefferson	N	Y	N
3 ***Tauzin***	Y	N	Y
4 ***McCrery***	Y	N	Y
5 ***Cooksey***	Y	N	Y
6 ***Baker***	?	?	?
7 John	N	N	Y
MAINE			
1 Allen	N	Y	Y
2 Baldacci	N	Y	Y
MARYLAND			
1 ***Gilchrest***	Y	N	Y
2 ***Ehrlich***	Y	N	Y
3 Cardin	N	Y	Y
4 Wynn	N	Y	Y
5 Hoyer	N	Y	Y
6 ***Bartlett***	Y	N	N
7 Cummings	N	Y	N
8 ***Morella***	Y	N	Y
MASSACHUSETTS			
1 Olver	N	Y	N
2 Neal	N	?	?
3 McGovern	N	Y	Y
4 Frank	N	Y	Y
5 Meehan	N	Y	N
6 Tierney	N	Y	Y
7 Markey	N	Y	Y
8 Kennedy	N	Y	N
9 Moakley	N	Y	Y
10 Delahunt	N	Y	Y
MICHIGAN			
1 Stupak	N	Y	N
2 ***Hoekstra***	Y	N	Y
3 ***Ehlers***	?	?	?
4 ***Camp***	Y	N	Y
5 Barcia	N	Y	Y
6 ***Upton***	Y	N	Y
7 ***Smith***	Y	N	Y
8 Stabenow	N	Y	Y
9 Kildee	N	Y	Y
10 Bonior	N	Y	N
11 ***Knollenberg***	Y	N	Y
12 Levin	N	Y	N
13 Rivers	N	Y	N
14 Conyers	N	Y	N
15 Kilpatrick	N	Y	N
16 Dingell	N	Y	Y
MINNESOTA			
1 ***Gutknecht***	Y	N	Y
2 Minge	N	Y	Y
3 ***Ramstad***	Y	N	Y
4 Vento	N	Y	Y
5 Sabo	N	Y	Y
6 Luther	N	Y	Y
7 Peterson	N	Y	Y
8 Oberstar	N	Y	Y
MISSISSIPPI			
1 ***Wicker***	Y	N	Y
2 Thompson	N	Y	N
3 ***Pickering***	Y	N	Y
4 ***Parker***	Y	N	Y
5 Taylor	N	N	N
MISSOURI			
1 Clay	N	Y	N
2 ***Talent***	Y	N	Y
3 Gephardt	N	Y	N
4 Skelton	N	Y	Y
5 McCarthy	N	Y	Y
6 Danner	N	Y	Y
7 ***Blunt***	Y	N	N
8 ***Emerson***	Y	N	Y
9 ***Hulshof***	N	N	Y
MONTANA			
AL ***Hill***	N	N	Y
NEBRASKA			
1 ***Bereuter***	Y	N	Y
2 ***Christensen***	Y	N	N
3 ***Barrett***	Y	N	Y
NEVADA			
1 ***Ensign***	Y	N	N
2 ***Gibbons***	Y	N	N
NEW HAMPSHIRE			
1 ***Sununu***	Y	N	Y
2 ***Bass***	Y	N	Y
NEW JERSEY			
1 Andrews	N	Y	Y
2 ***LoBiondo***	Y	N	Y
3 ***Saxton***	Y	N	Y
4 ***Smith***	Y	N	Y
5 ***Roukema***	Y	Y	Y
6 Pallone	N	Y	Y
7 ***Franks***	Y	N	Y
8 Pascrell	N	Y	Y
9 Rothman	N	Y	Y
10 Payne	N	Y	N
11 ***Frelinghuysen***	Y	N	Y
12 ***Pappas***	Y	N	Y
13 Menendez	N	Y	Y
NEW MEXICO			
1 ***Schiff***	?	?	?
2 ***Skeen***	Y	N	Y
3 ***Redmond***	Y	N	Y
NEW YORK			
1 ***Forbes***	Y	N	Y
2 ***Lazio***	Y	N	Y
3 ***King***	Y	?	?
4 McCarthy	N	Y	Y
5 Ackerman	?	?	?
6 Flake	?	?	?
7 Manton	N	Y	Y
8 Nadler	N	Y	N
9 Schumer	N	Y	Y
10 Towns	N	Y	N
11 Owens	N	Y	N
12 Velázquez	N	Y	N
13 ***Fossella***	Y	N	Y
14 Maloney	N	Y	N
15 Rangel	N	Y	N
16 Serrano	N	Y	N
17 Engel	N	Y	N
18 Lowey	N	Y	Y
19 ***Kelly***	Y	N	Y
20 ***Gilman***	?	N	Y
21 McNulty	N	Y	Y
22 ***Solomon***	Y	N	Y
23 ***Boehlert***	Y	N	Y
24 ***McHugh***	Y	N	Y
25 ***Walsh***	Y	N	Y
26 Hinchey	N	Y	N
27 ***Paxon***	Y	N	Y
28 Slaughter	N	Y	Y
29 LaFalce	?	?	?
30 ***Quinn***	Y	N	Y
31 ***Houghton***	?	?	?
NORTH CAROLINA			
1 Clayton	N	Y	N
2 Etheridge	N	Y	Y
3 ***Jones***	Y	N	N
4 Price	N	Y	Y
5 ***Burr***	Y	N	Y
6 ***Coble***	Y	Y	N
7 McIntyre	N	N	Y
8 Hefner	N	Y	Y
9 ***Myrick***	?	?	?
10 ***Ballenger***	Y	N	Y
11 ***Taylor***	?	?	?
12 Watt	N	Y	N
NORTH DAKOTA			
AL Pomeroy	N	Y	Y
OHIO			
1 ***Chabot***	Y	N	N
2 ***Portman***	Y	N	Y
3 Hall	N	Y	Y
4 ***Oxley***	Y	N	Y
5 ***Gillmor***	Y	N	Y
6 Strickland	N	Y	Y
7 ***Hobson***	Y	N	Y
8 ***Boehner***	Y	N	Y
9 Kaptur	N	Y	N
10 Kucinich	N	N	N
11 Stokes	N	Y	N
12 ***Kasich***	Y	N	Y
13 Brown	N	Y	N
14 Sawyer	N	Y	Y
15 ***Pryce***	?	?	?
16 ***Regula***	Y	N	Y
17 Traficant	Y	N	N
18 ***Ney***	Y	N	Y
19 ***LaTourette***	Y	N	Y
OKLAHOMA			
1 ***Largent***	Y	N	N
2 ***Coburn***	Y	N	N
3 ***Watkins***	?	?	?
4 ***Watts***	Y	N	N
5 ***Istook***	Y	N	N
6 ***Lucas***	Y	N	N
OREGON			
1 Furse	?	Y	N
2 ***Smith***	?	?	?
3 Blumenauer	?	?	?
4 DeFazio	N	Y	N
5 Hooley	N	Y	Y
PENNSYLVANIA			
1 Vacant			
2 Fattah	N	Y	N
3 Borski	N	Y	Y
4 Klink	N	N	Y
5 ***Peterson***	Y	N	Y
6 Holden	N	N	Y
7 ***Weldon***	Y	N	Y
8 ***Greenwood***	Y	N	Y
9 ***Shuster***	Y	?	?
10 ***McDade***	Y	N	Y
11 Kanjorski	N	N	Y
12 Murtha	N	N	Y
13 ***Fox***	Y	N	Y
14 Coyne	N	Y	N
15 McHale	N	Y	Y
16 ***Pitts***	Y	N	Y
17 ***Gekas***	Y	N	Y
18 Doyle	N	N	Y
19 ***Goodling***	N	N	Y
20 Mascara	N	N	Y
21 ***English***	Y	N	Y
RHODE ISLAND			
1 Kennedy	N	Y	N
2 Weygand	N	Y	Y
SOUTH CAROLINA			
1 ***Sanford***	Y	N	N
2 ***Spence***	Y	N	Y
3 ***Graham***	Y	N	Y
4 ***Inglis***	Y	N	N
5 Spratt	N	Y	Y
6 Clyburn	N	Y	N
SOUTH DAKOTA			
AL ***Thune***	Y	N	Y
TENNESSEE			
1 ***Jenkins***	Y	N	Y
2 ***Duncan***	Y	N	N
3 ***Wamp***	N	N	Y
4 ***Hilleary***	Y	N	N
5 Clement	N	Y	Y
6 Gordon	N	Y	Y
7 ***Bryant***	Y	N	N
8 Tanner	N	Y	Y
9 Ford	N	Y	N
TEXAS			
1 Sandlin	N	Y	Y
2 Turner	N	Y	Y
3 ***Johnson, Sam***	Y	N	Y
4 Hall	N	Y	Y
5 ***Sessions***	Y	N	Y
6 ***Barton***	Y	N	Y
7 ***Archer***	Y	N	Y
8 ***Brady***	Y	N	Y
9 Lampson	N	Y	Y
10 Doggett	N	?	Y
11 Edwards	N	Y	Y
12 ***Granger***	Y	N	Y
13 ***Thornberry***	Y	N	Y
14 ***Paul***	Y	N	N
15 Hinojosa	N	Y	Y
16 Reyes	N	Y	Y
17 Stenholm	N	Y	Y
18 Jackson-Lee	N	Y	N
19 ***Combest***	?	?	?
20 Gonzalez	?	?	?
21 ***Smith***	Y	N	Y
22 ***DeLay***	Y	N	Y
23 ***Bonilla***	Y	N	Y
24 Frost	N	Y	N
25 Bentsen	N	Y	Y
26 ***Armey***	Y	N	Y
27 Ortiz	?	?	#
28 Rodriguez	N	Y	N
29 Green	?	?	?
30 Johnson, E.B.	N	Y	N
UTAH			
1 ***Hansen***	Y	N	Y
2 ***Cook***	Y	N	Y
3 ***Cannon***	Y	N	Y
VERMONT			
AL *Sanders*	N	Y	N
VIRGINIA			
1 ***Bateman***	Y	N	Y
2 Pickett	?	?	?
3 Scott	N	Y	N
4 Sisisky	N	Y	Y
5 Goode	N	N	Y
6 ***Goodlatte***	Y	N	Y
7 ***Bliley***	Y	N	Y
8 Moran	N	Y	Y
9 Boucher	N	?	?
10 ***Wolf***	Y	N	Y
11 ***Davis***	Y	N	Y
WASHINGTON			
1 ***White***	?	?	?
2 ***Metcalf***	Y	N	Y
3 ***Smith, Linda***	Y	N	N
4 ***Hastings***	Y	N	Y
5 ***Nethercutt***	Y	N	Y
6 Dicks	N	Y	Y
7 McDermott	N	Y	N
8 ***Dunn***	Y	N	Y
9 Smith, Adam	N	Y	Y
WEST VIRGINIA			
1 Mollohan	N	N	Y
2 Wise	N	Y	Y
3 Rahall	N	N	Y
WISCONSIN			
1 ***Neumann***	Y	N	N
2 ***Klug***	Y	N	Y
3 Kind	N	Y	Y
4 Kleczka	N	Y	Y
5 Barrett	N	Y	Y
6 ***Petri***	Y	N	N
7 Obey	N	Y	Y
8 Johnson	N	Y	Y
9 ***Sensenbrenner***	Y	N	N
WYOMING			
AL ***Cubin***	?	?	?

Southern states - Ala., Ark., Fla., Ga., Ky., La., Miss., N.C., Okla., S.C., Tenn., Texas, Va.

House Roll Call Votes By Subject

A

B

C

D

E

F

G

H

N

O

P

R

S

T

U

V

W

Y

Bill Number Index

House Bills

Senate Bills

CQ

Appendix S

SENATE ROLL CALL VOTES

SENATE VOTES 1, 2, 3, 4

	1	2	3	4
ALABAMA				
Sessions	Y	Y	Y	Y
Shelby	Y	Y	Y	Y
ALASKA				
Murkowski	Y	Y	Y	Y
Stevens	Y	Y	Y	Y
ARIZONA				
Kyl	Y	Y	Y	Y
McCain	Y	Y	Y	Y
ARKANSAS				
Hutchinson	Y	Y	Y	Y
Bumpers	Y	Y	Y	Y
CALIFORNIA				
Boxer	Y	Y	Y	Y
Feinstein	Y	Y	Y	Y
COLORADO				
Allard	Y	Y	Y	Y
Campbell	Y	Y	Y	Y
CONNECTICUT				
Dodd	Y	Y	Y	Y
Lieberman	Y	Y	Y	Y
DELAWARE				
Roth	Y	Y	Y	Y
Biden	Y	Y	Y	Y
FLORIDA				
Mack	Y	Y	Y	Y
Graham	Y	Y	Y	Y
GEORGIA				
Coverdell	Y	Y	Y	Y
Cleland	Y	Y	Y	Y
HAWAII				
Akaka	Y	Y	Y	Y
Inouye	Y	Y	?	Y
IDAHO				
Craig	Y	Y	Y	Y
Kempthorne	Y	Y	Y	Y
ILLINOIS				
Durbin	Y	Y	Y	Y
Moseley-Braun	Y	Y	Y	Y
INDIANA				
Coats	Y	Y	Y	Y
Lugar	Y	Y	Y	Y
IOWA				
Grassley	Y	Y	Y	Y
Harkin	Y	Y	Y	Y
KANSAS				
Brownback	Y	Y	Y	N
Roberts	Y	Y	Y	Y
KENTUCKY				
McConnell	Y	Y	Y	Y
Ford	Y	Y	Y	Y
LOUISIANA				
Breaux	Y	Y	Y	Y
Landrieu	Y	Y	Y	Y
MAINE				
Collins	Y	Y	Y	Y
Snowe	Y	Y	Y	Y
MARYLAND				
Mikulski	Y	Y	Y	Y
Sarbanes	Y	Y	Y	Y
MASSACHUSETTS				
Kennedy	Y	Y	Y	Y
Kerry	Y	Y	Y	Y
MICHIGAN				
Abraham	Y	Y	Y	Y
Levin	Y	Y	Y	Y
MINNESOTA				
Grams	Y	Y	Y	Y
Wellstone	Y	Y	Y	Y
MISSISSIPPI				
Cochran	Y	Y	Y	Y
Lott	Y	Y	Y	Y
MISSOURI				
Ashcroft	Y	Y	Y	Y
Bond	Y	Y	Y	?
MONTANA				
Burns	Y	Y	Y	Y
Baucus	Y	Y	Y	Y
NEBRASKA				
Hagel	Y	Y	Y	Y
Kerrey	Y	Y	Y	Y
NEVADA				
Bryan	Y	Y	Y	Y
Reid	Y	Y	Y	Y
NEW HAMPSHIRE				
Gregg	Y	Y	Y	Y
Smith	Y	Y	Y	Y
NEW JERSEY				
Lautenberg	Y	Y	Y	Y
Torricelli	Y	Y	Y	Y
NEW MEXICO				
Domenici	Y	Y	Y	Y
Bingaman	Y	Y	Y	Y
NEW YORK				
D'Amato	Y	Y	Y	?
Moynihan	Y	Y	Y	Y
NORTH CAROLINA				
Faircloth	Y	Y	Y	Y
Helms	Y	Y	Y	Y
NORTH DAKOTA				
Conrad	Y	Y	Y	Y
Dorgan	Y	Y	Y	Y
OHIO				
DeWine	Y	Y	Y	Y
Glenn	Y	Y	Y	Y
OKLAHOMA				
Inhofe	Y	Y	Y	N
Nickles	Y	Y	Y	Y
OREGON				
Smith	Y	Y	Y	Y
Wyden	Y	Y	Y	Y
PENNSYLVANIA				
Santorum	Y	Y	Y	Y
Specter	Y	Y	Y	Y
RHODE ISLAND				
Chafee	Y	Y	Y	Y
Reed	Y	Y	Y	Y
SOUTH CAROLINA				
Thurmond	Y	Y	Y	Y
Hollings	Y	Y	Y	Y
SOUTH DAKOTA				
Daschle	Y	Y	Y	Y
Johnson	Y	Y	Y	Y
TENNESSEE				
Frist	Y	Y	Y	Y
Thompson	Y	Y	Y	Y
TEXAS				
Gramm	Y	Y	Y	Y
Hutchison	Y	Y	Y	?
UTAH				
Bennett	Y	Y	Y	Y
Hatch	Y	Y	Y	Y
VERMONT				
Jeffords	Y	Y	Y	Y
Leahy	Y	Y	Y	Y
VIRGINIA				
Warner	Y	Y	Y	Y
Robb	Y	Y	Y	Y
WASHINGTON				
Gorton	Y	Y	Y	Y
Murray	Y	Y	Y	Y
WEST VIRGINIA				
Byrd	Y	Y	Y	Y
Rockefeller	+	+	Y	Y
WISCONSIN				
Feingold	Y	Y	Y	Y
Kohl	Y	Y	Y	Y
WYOMING				
Enzi	Y	Y	Y	Y
Thomas	Y	Y	Y	Y

ND Northern Democrats SD Southern Democrats

Southern states - Ala., Ark., Fla., Ga., Ky., La., Miss., N.C., Okla., S.C., Tenn., Texas, Va.

KEY

- Y Voted for (yea).
- # Paired for.
- + Announced for.
- N Voted against (nay).
- X Paired against.
- – Announced against.
- P Voted "present."
- C Voted "present" to avoid possible conflict of interest.
- ? Did not vote or otherwise make a position known.

Democrats ***Republicans***

1. Albright Nomination/Confirmation. Confirmation of President Clinton's nomination of Madeleine K. Albright of the District of Columbia to be secretary of State. Confirmed 99-0: R 55-0; D 44-0 (ND 36-0, SD 8-0), Jan. 22, 1997. A "yea" was a vote in support of the president's position.

2. Cohen Nomination/Confirmation. Confirmation of President Clinton's nomination of William S. Cohen of Maine to be secretary of Defense. Confirmed 99-0: R 55-0; D 44-0 (ND 36-0, SD 8-0), Jan. 22, 1997. A "yea" was a vote in support of the president's position.

3. Cuomo Nomination/Confirmation. Confirmation of President Clinton's nomination of Andrew M. Cuomo of New York to be secretary of Housing and Urban Development. Confirmed 99-0: R 55-0; D 44-0 (ND 36-0, SD 8-0), Jan. 29, 1997. A "yea" was a vote in support of the president's position.

4. Daley Nomination/Confirmation. Confirmation of President Clinton's nomination of William M. Daley of Illinois to be secretary of Commerce. Confirmed 95-2: R 50-2; D 45-0 (ND 37-0, SD 8-0), Jan. 30, 1997. A "yea" was a vote in support of the president's position.

SENATE VOTES 5, 6, 7, 8, 9, 10, 11

	5	6	7	8	9	10	11
ALABAMA							
Sessions	Y	Y	Y	Y	Y	Y	Y
Shelby	Y	Y	Y	Y	Y	Y	Y
ALASKA							
Murkowski	Y	Y	Y	Y	Y	Y	Y
Stevens	Y	Y	Y	Y	Y	Y	Y
ARIZONA							
Kyl	Y	Y	Y	Y	Y	Y	N
McCain	Y	Y	Y	Y	Y	Y	Y
ARKANSAS							
Hutchinson	Y	Y	Y	Y	Y	Y	Y
Bumpers	Y	Y	N	N	Y	N	Y
CALIFORNIA							
Boxer	Y	Y	N	N	Y	N	Y
Feinstein	Y	Y	N	N	Y	N	Y
COLORADO							
Allard	Y	Y	Y	Y	Y	Y	N
Campbell	Y	Y	Y	Y	Y	Y	N
CONNECTICUT							
Dodd	Y	Y	N	N	Y	N	Y
Lieberman	Y	Y	N	N	Y	N	Y
DELAWARE							
Roth	Y	Y	Y	Y	Y	Y	Y
Biden	Y	Y	Y	Y	Y	N	Y
FLORIDA							
Mack	Y	Y	Y	Y	Y	Y	N
Graham	Y	Y	Y	Y	Y	Y	Y
GEORGIA							
Coverdell	Y	Y	Y	Y	Y	Y	Y
Cleland	Y	Y	N	N	Y	N	Y
HAWAII							
Akaka	Y	Y	N	N	Y	N	Y
Inouye	Y	Y	N	N	Y	N	Y
IDAHO							
Craig	Y	Y	Y	Y	Y	Y	N
Kempthorne	Y	Y	Y	Y	Y	Y	N
ILLINOIS							
Durbin	Y	Y	N	N	Y	N	Y
Moseley-Braun	Y	Y	Y	N	Y	Y	Y
INDIANA							
Coats	Y	Y	Y	Y	Y	Y	N
Lugar	Y	Y	Y	Y	Y	Y	Y
IOWA							
Grassley	Y	Y	Y	Y	Y	Y	Y
Harkin	Y	Y	N	N	Y	N	Y
KANSAS							
Brownback	Y	Y	Y	Y	Y	Y	N
Roberts	Y	Y	Y	Y	Y	Y	N
KENTUCKY							
McConnell	Y	Y	Y	Y	Y	Y	Y
Ford	Y	Y	N	N	Y	N	Y
LOUISIANA							
Breaux	Y	Y	N	N	Y	N	?
Landrieu	Y	Y	N	N	Y	N	Y
MAINE							
Collins	Y	Y	Y	Y	Y	Y	Y
Snowe	Y	Y	Y	Y	Y	Y	Y
MARYLAND							
Mikulski	Y	Y	N	N	Y	N	Y
Sarbanes	Y	Y	N	N	Y	N	Y
MASSACHUSETTS							
Kennedy	Y	Y	N	N	Y	N	Y
Kerry	Y	Y	N	N	Y	N	Y
MICHIGAN							
Abraham	Y	Y	Y	Y	Y	Y	Y
Levin	Y	Y	N	N	Y	N	Y
MINNESOTA							
Grams	Y	Y	Y	Y	Y	Y	Y
Wellstone	Y	Y	N	N	Y	N	Y
MISSISSIPPI							
Cochran	Y	Y	Y	Y	Y	Y	Y
Lott	Y	Y	Y	Y	Y	Y	Y
MISSOURI							
Ashcroft	Y	Y	Y	Y	Y	Y	Y
Bond	Y	Y	Y	Y	Y	Y	N
MONTANA							
Burns	Y	Y	Y	Y	Y	Y	Y
Baucus	Y	Y	Y	Y	Y	Y	Y
NEBRASKA							
Hagel	Y	Y	Y	Y	Y	Y	Y
Kerrey	Y	Y	N	N	Y	N	Y
NEVADA							
Bryan	Y	Y	Y	Y	Y	Y	Y
Reid	Y	Y	Y	Y	Y	Y	Y
NEW HAMPSHIRE							
Gregg	Y	Y	Y	Y	Y	Y	Y
Smith	Y	Y	Y	Y	Y	Y	Y
NEW JERSEY							
Lautenberg	Y	Y	N	N	Y	N	N
Torricelli	Y	Y	N	N	Y	N	Y
NEW MEXICO							
Domenici	Y	Y	Y	Y	Y	Y	Y
Bingaman	Y	Y	N	Y	Y	N	Y
NEW YORK							
D'Amato	Y	Y	Y	Y	Y	Y	Y
Moynihan	Y	Y	N	N	Y	N	Y
NORTH CAROLINA							
Faircloth	Y	Y	Y	Y	Y	Y	Y
Helms	Y	Y	Y	Y	Y	Y	Y
NORTH DAKOTA							
Conrad	Y	Y	N	N	Y	N	Y
Dorgan	Y	Y	Y	N	Y	Y	Y
OHIO							
DeWine	Y	Y	Y	Y	Y	Y	Y
Glenn	Y	Y	N	N	Y	N	Y
OKLAHOMA							
Inhofe	Y	Y	Y	Y	Y	Y	Y
Nickles	Y	Y	Y	Y	Y	Y	Y
OREGON							
Smith	Y	Y	Y	Y	Y	Y	Y
Wyden	Y	Y	Y	N	Y	Y	Y
PENNSYLVANIA							
Santorum	Y	Y	?	Y	Y	Y	Y
Specter	Y	Y	Y	N	Y	Y	Y
RHODE ISLAND							
Chafee	Y	Y	Y	Y	Y	Y	Y
Reed	Y	Y	N	N	Y	N	Y
SOUTH CAROLINA							
Thurmond	?	?	Y	Y	Y	Y	Y
Hollings	Y	Y	Y	Y	Y	Y	Y
SOUTH DAKOTA							
Daschle	Y	Y	N	N	Y	N	Y
Johnson	Y	Y	N	N	Y	N	Y
TENNESSEE							
Frist	Y	Y	Y	Y	Y	Y	Y
Thompson	Y	Y	Y	Y	Y	Y	Y
TEXAS							
Gramm	Y	Y	Y	Y	Y	Y	Y
Hutchison	Y	Y	Y	Y	Y	Y	Y
UTAH							
Bennett	Y	?	Y	Y	Y	Y	N
Hatch	Y	Y	Y	Y	Y	Y	N
VERMONT							
Jeffords	Y	Y	Y	Y	Y	Y	Y
Leahy	Y	Y	N	N	Y	N	?
VIRGINIA							
Warner	Y	Y	Y	Y	Y	Y	Y
Robb	Y	Y	Y	Y	Y	Y	Y
WASHINGTON							
Gorton	Y	Y	Y	Y	Y	Y	Y
Murray	?	Y	N	N	Y	N	Y
WEST VIRGINIA							
Byrd	Y	Y	N	N	Y	N	Y
Rockefeller	Y	Y	N	N	Y	N	Y
WISCONSIN							
Feingold	Y	Y	N	Y	Y	N	Y
Kohl	Y	Y	N	Y	Y	N	Y
WYOMING							
Enzi	Y	Y	Y	Y	Y	Y	N
Thomas	Y	Y	Y	Y	Y	Y	N

KEY

- Y Voted for (yea).
- # Paired for.
- \+ Announced for.
- N Voted against (nay).
- X Paired against.
- \- Announced against.
- P Voted "present."
- C Voted "present" to avoid possible conflict of interest.
- ? Did not vote or otherwise make a position known.

Democrats *Republicans*

ND Northern Democrats SD Southern Democrats

Southern states - Ala., Ark., Fla., Ga., Ky., La., Miss., N.C., Okla., S.C., Tenn., Texas, Va.

5. S Res 47. Breast Cancer Screening/Adoption. Adoption of the resolution to express the sense of the Senate that accurate guidelines are needed to determine whether it is beneficial for women in their 40s to have mammography screenings for breast cancer, and to urge the National Cancer Institute to consider reissuing guidelines it rescinded in 1993 that recommended mammograms for women in their 40s. Adopted 98-0: R 54-0; D 44-0 (ND 36-0, SD 8-0), Feb. 4, 1997.

6. Slater Nomination/Confirmation. Confirmation of President Clinton's nomination of Rodney E. Slater of Arkansas to be secretary of Transportation. Confirmed 98-0: R 53-0; D 45-0 (ND 37-0, SD 8-0), Feb. 6, 1997. A "yea" was a vote in support of the president's position.

7. S J Res 1. Balanced-Budget Constitutional Amendment/ Economic Emergency. Craig, R-Idaho, motion to table (kill) the Durbin, D-Ill., amendment to allow a waiver of balanced-budget requirements during a recession or serious economic emergency, as declared by a majority of both chambers of Congress and approved by the president. Under the balanced-budget amendment, a three-fifths vote of both chambers would be required to allow the federal government's spending to exceed revenue. Motion agreed to 64-35: R 54-0; D 10-35 (ND 7-30, SD 3-5), Feb. 10, 1997.

8. S J Res 1. Balanced-Budget Constitutional Amendment/ Children's Health. Hatch, R-Utah, motion to table (kill) the Wellstone, D-Minn., amendment to state that it is the policy of the United States that federal outlays affecting education, nutrition and health programs for poor children shall not be disproportionately reduced to achieve a balanced budget. Motion agreed to 64-36: R 54-1; D 10-35 (ND 7-30, SD 3-5), Feb. 11, 1997.

9. Richardson Nomination/Confirmation. Confirmation of President Clinton's nomination of Bill Richardson of New Mexico to be the permanent representative to the United Nations. Confirmed 100-0: R 55-0; D 45-0 (ND 37-0, SD 8-0), Feb. 11, 1997. A "yea" was a vote in support of the president's position.

10. S J Res 1. Balanced-Budget Constitutional Amendment/ Military Spending. Hatch, R-Utah, motion to table (kill) the Dodd, D-Conn., amendment to allow deficit spending if Congress passes a joint resolution by simple majority vote declaring an imminent and serious military threat to national security. Motion agreed to 64-36: R 55-0; D 9-36 (ND 6-31, SD 3-5), Feb. 12, 1997.

11. S Res 55. Milk Pricing Formula/Adoption. Adoption of the resolution to express the sense of the Senate that Agriculture Secretary Dan Glickman should consider modifying the formula used to establish minimum milk prices by removing cheese prices, as established by the National Cheese Exchange in Green Bay, Wis., as a factor. Adopted 83-15: R 41-14; D 42-1 (ND 35-1, SD 7-0), Feb. 13, 1997.

SENATE VOTES 12, 13, 14, 15, 16, 17, 18

	12	13	14	15	16	17	18
ALABAMA							
Sessions	Y	N	Y	Y	N	Y	Y
Shelby	Y	N	Y	Y	N	Y	Y
ALASKA							
Murkowski	Y	N	Y	Y	N	Y	Y
Stevens	Y	Y	Y	Y	N	Y	Y
ARIZONA							
Kyl	Y	N	Y	Y	N	Y	Y
McCain	Y	N	N	Y	N	N	Y
ARKANSAS							
Hutchinson	Y	N	Y	Y	N	Y	Y
Bumpers	N	Y	N	N	Y	N	N
CALIFORNIA							
Boxer	N	Y	N	N	Y	N	N
Feinstein	Y	Y	N	N	Y	N	N
COLORADO							
Allard	Y	N	Y	Y	N	Y	Y
Campbell	Y	Y	Y	Y	N	Y	Y
CONNECTICUT							
Dodd	N	Y	N	Y	Y	Y	N
Lieberman	N	Y	N	N	Y	N	N
DELAWARE							
Roth	Y	Y	Y	Y	N	Y	Y
Biden	Y	Y	N	N	Y	N	N
FLORIDA							
Mack	Y	N	Y	Y	N	Y	Y
Graham	Y	Y	N	Y	N	N	Y
GEORGIA							
Coverdell	Y	N	Y	Y	N	Y	Y
Cleland	N	Y	N	N	Y	N	N
HAWAII							
Akaka	N	Y	N	N	Y	N	N
Inouye	?	?	?	N	Y	N	N
IDAHO							
Craig	Y	N	Y	Y	N	Y	Y
Kempthorne	Y	N	Y	Y	N	Y	Y
ILLINOIS							
Durbin	N	Y	N	N	Y	N	N
Moseley-Braun	Y	Y	N	Y	N	N	N
INDIANA							
Coats	Y	N	Y	Y	N	Y	Y
Lugar	Y	N	Y	Y	N	Y	Y
IOWA							
Grassley	Y	N	Y	Y	N	Y	Y
Harkin	Y	Y	N	N	N	N	N
KANSAS							
Brownback	Y	N	Y	Y	N	Y	Y
Roberts	Y	N	Y	Y	N	Y	Y
KENTUCKY							
McConnell	Y	N	Y	Y	N	Y	Y
Ford	N	N	N	N	Y	N	N
LOUISIANA							
Breaux	N	N	N	N	Y	N	N
Landrieu	N	Y	N	N	Y	N	N
MAINE							
Collins	Y	Y	Y	Y	N	Y	Y
Snowe	Y	Y	Y	Y	N	Y	Y
MARYLAND							
Mikulski	N	Y	N	N	Y	N	N
Sarbanes	N	Y	N	N	Y	N	N
MASSACHUSETTS							
Kennedy	N	Y	N	N	Y	N	N
Kerry	N	Y	N	N	Y	N	N
MICHIGAN							
Abraham	Y	N	Y	Y	N	Y	Y
Levin	N	Y	N	N	Y	N	N
MINNESOTA							
Grams	Y	N	Y	Y	N	Y	Y
Wellstone	N	Y	N	N	Y	N	N
MISSISSIPPI							
Cochran	Y	N	Y	Y	N	Y	Y
Lott	Y	N	Y	Y	N	Y	Y
MISSOURI							
Ashcroft	Y	N	Y	Y	N	Y	Y
Bond	Y	N	Y	Y	N	Y	Y
MONTANA							
Burns	Y	N	Y	Y	N	Y	Y
Baucus	Y	Y	N	Y	Y	N	Y
NEBRASKA							
Hagel	Y	N	Y	Y	N	Y	Y
Kerrey	N	Y	Y	Y	Y	Y	N
NEVADA							
Bryan	Y	Y	N	Y	N	N	N
Reid	Y	Y	N	Y	N	N	Y
NEW HAMPSHIRE							
Gregg	Y	Y	Y	Y	N	Y	Y
Smith	Y	N	Y	Y	N	Y	Y
NEW JERSEY							
Lautenberg	N	Y	N	N	Y	N	N
Torricelli	N	Y	N	N	Y	N	N
NEW MEXICO							
Domenici	Y	N	Y	Y	N	Y	Y
Bingaman	N	Y	N	N	Y	N	N
NEW YORK							
D'Amato	Y	N	Y	Y	N	Y	Y
Moynihan	N	Y	N	N	Y	N	N
NORTH CAROLINA							
Faircloth	?	N	Y	Y	N	Y	Y
Helms	Y	N	Y	Y	N	Y	Y
NORTH DAKOTA							
Conrad	N	Y	N	N	Y	N	N
Dorgan	N	Y	N	N	Y	N	N
OHIO							
DeWine	Y	N	Y	Y	N	Y	Y
Glenn	N	Y	N	N	Y	N	N
OKLAHOMA							
Inhofe	?	N	Y	Y	N	Y	Y
Nickles	Y	N	Y	Y	N	Y	Y
OREGON							
Smith	Y	Y	Y	Y	N	Y	Y
Wyden	Y	Y	N	Y	N	N	N
PENNSYLVANIA							
Santorum	Y	N	Y	Y	N	Y	Y
Specter	?	Y	N	Y	N	N	Y
RHODE ISLAND							
Chafee	Y	Y	Y	Y	N	Y	Y
Reed	N	Y	N	N	Y	N	N
SOUTH CAROLINA							
Thurmond	Y	N	Y	Y	N	Y	Y
Hollings	N	Y	N	N	N	N	N
SOUTH DAKOTA							
Daschle	N	Y	N	N	Y	N	N
Johnson	N	Y	N	N	Y	N	N
TENNESSEE							
Frist	Y	N	Y	Y	N	Y	Y
Thompson	Y	N	Y	Y	N	Y	Y
TEXAS							
Gramm	Y	N	Y	Y	N	Y	Y
Hutchison	Y	N	Y	Y	N	Y	Y
UTAH							
Bennett	?	N	Y	Y	N	Y	Y
Hatch	Y	N	Y	Y	N	Y	Y
VERMONT							
Jeffords	Y	Y	Y	Y	N	Y	Y
Leahy	N	Y	N	N	Y	N	N
VIRGINIA							
Warner	Y	Y	Y	Y	N	Y	Y
Robb	Y	Y	Y	Y	N	Y	Y
WASHINGTON							
Gorton	Y	N	Y	Y	N	Y	Y
Murray	N	Y	N	Y	Y	Y	N
WEST VIRGINIA							
Byrd	N	Y	N	Y	Y	Y	N
Rockefeller	N	Y	N	Y	Y	Y	N
WISCONSIN							
Feingold	N	Y	N	N	Y	N	N
Kohl	N	Y	N	N	Y	N	Y
WYOMING							
Enzi	Y	N	Y	Y	N	Y	Y
Thomas	Y	N	Y	Y	N	Y	Y

KEY

- Y Voted for (yea).
- # Paired for.
- \+ Announced for.
- N Voted against (nay).
- X Paired against.
- – Announced against.
- P Voted "present."
- C Voted "present" to avoid possible conflict of interest.
- ? Did not vote or otherwise make a position known.

Democrats ***Republicans***

ND Northern Democrats SD Southern Democrats

Southern states - Ala., Ark., Fla., Ga., Ky., La., Miss., N.C., Okla., S.C., Tenn., Texas, Va.

12. S J Res. 1 Balanced-Budget Constitutional Amendment/ Budget Estimates. Hatch, R-Utah, motion to table (kill) the Byrd, D-W.Va., amendment to implement the constitutional amendment by law and strike a provision to "enforce and implement the article by appropriate legislation" that may rely on estimates of federal outlays and receipts for budgeting purposes. Motion agreed to 61-34: R 51-0; D 10-34 (ND 8-28, SD 2-6), Feb. 24, 1997.

13. H J Res 36. International Family Planning Aid/Passage. Passage of the joint resolution to authorize the early release of $385 million for international family planning activities beginning March 1. Passed 53-46: R 11-44; D 42-2 (ND 36-0, SD 6-2), Feb. 25, 1997. A "yea" was a vote in support of the president's position.

14. S J Res 1. Balanced-Budget Constitutional Amendment/ Social Security. Hatch, R-Utah, motion to table (kill) the Reid, D-Nev., amendment to exempt Social Security trust funds from budget calculations under the balanced-budget amendment. Motion agreed to 55-44: R 53-2; D 2-42 (ND 1-35, SD 1-7), Feb. 25, 1997.

15. S J Res 1. Balanced-Budget Constitutional Amendment/ Feinstein Substitute. Hatch, R-Utah, motion to table (kill) the Feinstein, D-Calif., substitute amendment to permit Congress to raise the federal debt limit by majority vote, waive balanced-budget requirements by joint resolution when the United States is experiencing an economic emergency or natural disaster, exempt Social Security and capital spending from budget calculations one year after the amendment takes effect and permit a capital budget. Motion agreed to 67-33: R 55-0; D 12-33 (ND 10-27, SD 2-6), Feb. 26, 1997.

16. S J Res 1. Balanced-Budget Constitutional Amendment/ Capital Budget. Torricelli, D-N.J., amendment to exclude capital spending from budget calculations, allow Congress to waive balanced-budget requirements when a declaration of war is in effect or by passing a joint resolution declaring an "imminent and serious military threat to national security" or that the country "is in a period of economic recession or significant economic hardship." Rejected 37-63: R 1-54; D 36-9 (ND 31-6, SD 5-3), Feb. 26, 1997.

17. S J Res 1. Balanced-Budget Constitutional Amendment/ Dorgan Substitute. Hatch, R-Utah, motion to table (kill) the Dorgan, D-N.D., substitute amendment to exempt Social Security from budget calculations. Motion agreed to 59-41: R 53-2; D 6-39 (ND 5-32, SD 1-7), Feb. 26, 1997.

18. S J Res 1. Balanced-Budget Constitutional Amendment/ Disaster Relief. Hatch, R-Utah, motion to table (kill) the Boxer, D-Calif., amendment to allow Congress to waive spending restrictions by a majority vote if the president declares a major disaster has occurred or an emergency exists. Motion agreed to 60-40: R 55-0; D 5-40 (ND 3-34, SD 2-6), Feb. 26, 1997.

SENATE VOTES 19, 20, 21, 22, 23

	19	20	21	22	23
ALABAMA					
Sessions	Y	Y	Y	Y	Y
Shelby	Y	Y	Y	Y	Y
ALASKA					
Murkowski	Y	Y	Y	Y	Y
Stevens	Y	Y	Y	Y	Y
ARIZONA					
Kyl	Y	Y	Y	Y	Y
McCain	Y	Y	Y	Y	Y
ARKANSAS					
Hutchinson	Y	Y	Y	Y	Y
Bumpers	N	N	N	N	N
CALIFORNIA					
Boxer	N	N	N	N	N
Feinstein	N	N	N	N	N
COLORADO					
Allard	Y	Y	Y	Y	Y
Campbell	Y	Y	Y	Y	Y
CONNECTICUT					
Dodd	N	N	N	N	N
Lieberman	N	N	N	N	N
DELAWARE					
Roth	Y	Y	Y	Y	Y
Biden	—	N	Y	N	Y
FLORIDA					
Mack	Y	Y	Y	Y	Y
Graham	N	Y	Y	Y	Y
GEORGIA					
Coverdell	Y	Y	Y	Y	Y
Cleland	N	N	N	N	N
HAWAII					
Akaka	N	N	N	N	N
Inouye	N	N	N	N	N
IDAHO					
Craig	Y	Y	Y	Y	Y
Kempthorne	Y	Y	Y	Y	Y
ILLINOIS					
Durbin	Y	N	N	N	N
Moseley-Braun	N	N	Y	N	Y
INDIANA					
Coats	Y	Y	Y	Y	Y
Lugar	Y	Y	Y	Y	Y
IOWA					
Grassley	Y	Y	Y	Y	Y
Harkin	N	Y	Y	N	Y
KANSAS					
Brownback	Y	Y	Y	Y	Y
Roberts	Y	Y	Y	Y	Y
KENTUCKY					
McConnell	Y	Y	Y	Y	Y
Ford	N	N	N	N	N
LOUISIANA					
Breaux	N	N	Y	N	N
Landrieu	-	N	Y	Y	N
MAINE					
Collins	Y	Y	Y	Y	Y
Snowe	Y	Y	Y	Y	Y
MARYLAND					
Mikulski	N	N	N	N	N
Sarbanes	N	N	N	N	N
MASSACHUSETTS					
Kennedy	N	N	N	N	N
Kerry	N	N	N	N	N
MICHIGAN					
Abraham	Y	Y	Y	Y	Y
Levin	N	N	N	N	N
MINNESOTA					
Grams	Y	Y	Y	Y	Y
Wellstone	N	N	N	N	N
MISSISSIPPI					
Cochran	Y	Y	Y	Y	Y
Lott	Y	Y	Y	Y	Y
MISSOURI					
Ashcroft	Y	Y	Y	Y	Y
Bond	Y	Y	Y	Y	Y
MONTANA					
Burns	Y	Y	Y	Y	Y
Baucus	N	N	Y	N	Y
NEBRASKA					
Hagel	Y	Y	Y	Y	Y
Kerrey	Y	N	N	N	N
NEVADA					
Bryan	N	Y	Y	Y	Y
Reid	N	N	Y	N	Y
NEW HAMPSHIRE					
Gregg	Y	Y	Y	Y	Y
Smith	Y	Y	Y	Y	Y
NEW JERSEY					
Lautenberg	N	N	N	N	N
Torricelli	N	N	N	N	N
NEW MEXICO					
Domenici	Y	Y	Y	Y	Y
Bingaman	N	N	N	N	Y
NEW YORK					
D'Amato	Y	Y	Y	Y	Y
Moynihan	N	N	N	N	N
NORTH CAROLINA					
Faircloth	Y	Y	Y	Y	Y
Helms	Y	Y	Y	Y	Y
NORTH DAKOTA					
Conrad	N	N	N	N	N
Dorgan	N	N	Y	N	N
OHIO					
DeWine	Y	Y	Y	Y	Y
Glenn	N	N	N	N	N
OKLAHOMA					
Inhofe	Y	Y	Y	Y	?
Nickles	Y	Y	Y	Y	Y
OREGON					
Smith	Y	Y	Y	Y	Y
Wyden	Y	Y	Y	N	Y
PENNSYLVANIA					
Santorum	Y	Y	Y	Y	Y
Specter	Y	Y	Y	Y	Y
RHODE ISLAND					
Chafee	Y	Y	Y	Y	Y
Reed	N	N	N	N	N
SOUTH CAROLINA					
Thurmond	Y	Y	Y	Y	Y
Hollings	N	N	Y	N	N
SOUTH DAKOTA					
Daschle	N	N	N	N	N
Johnson	N	Y	N	N	N
TENNESSEE					
Frist	Y	Y	Y	Y	Y
Thompson	Y	Y	Y	Y	Y
TEXAS					
Gramm	Y	Y	Y	Y	Y
Hutchison	Y	Y	Y	Y	Y
UTAH					
Bennett	Y	Y	Y	Y	Y
Hatch	Y	Y	Y	Y	Y
VERMONT					
Jeffords	Y	Y	Y	Y	Y
Leahy	N	N	N	N	N
VIRGINIA					
Warner	Y	Y	Y	Y	Y
Robb	N	Y	Y	Y	Y
WASHINGTON					
Gorton	Y	Y	Y	Y	Y
Murray	N	N	N	N	N
WEST VIRGINIA					
Byrd	N	N	N	Y	N
Rockefeller	N	N	N	N	N
WISCONSIN					
Feingold	N	N	N	N	N
Kohl	Y	N	Y	N	Y
WYOMING					
Enzi	Y	Y	Y	Y	Y
Thomas	Y	Y	Y	Y	Y

KEY

- Y Voted for (yea).
- # Paired for.
- \+ Announced for.
- N Voted against (nay).
- X Paired against.
- – Announced against.
- P Voted "present."
- C Voted "present" to avoid possible conflict of interest.
- ? Did not vote or otherwise make a position known.

Democrats *Republicans*

ND Northern Democrats SD Southern Democrats

Southern states - Ala., Ark., Fla., Ga., Ky., La., Miss., N.C., Okla., S.C., Tenn., Texas, Va.

19. S J Res 1. Balanced-Budget Constitutional Amendment/ Debt Limit. Hatch, R-Utah, motion to table (kill) the Graham, D-Fla., amendment to require a three-fifths vote to increase the federal debt. Motion agreed to 59-39: R 55-0; D 4-39 (ND 4-32, SD 0-7), Feb. 27, 1997.

20. S J Res 1. Balanced-Budget Constitutional Amendment/ Judicial Review. Hatch, R-Utah, motion to table (kill) the Kennedy, D-Mass., amendment to give Congress exclusive authority to enforce the provisions of the balanced-budget amendment, unless it passes legislation specifically granting judicial review authority to the courts. Motion agreed to 61-39: R 55-0; D 6-39 (ND 4-33, SD 2-6), Feb. 27, 1997.

21. S J Res 1. Balanced-Budget Constitutional Amendment/ Three-Year Ratification. Hatch, R-Utah, motion to table (kill) the Feingold, D-Wis., amendment to require ratification by the states within three years of the amendment's submission to them, instead of seven. Motion agreed to 69-31: R 55-0; D 14-31 (ND 9-28, SD 5-3), Feb. 27, 1997.

22. S J Res 1. Balanced-Budget Constitutional Amendment/ Budget Surplus. Kyl, R-Ariz., motion to table (kill) the Feingold, D-Wis., amendment to allow budget surpluses to accumulate and be available to be allocated later. Motion agreed to 60-40: R 55-0; D 5-40 (ND 2-35, SD 3-5), Feb. 27, 1997.

23. S J Res 1. Balanced-Budget Constitutional Amendment/ Referral. Hatch, R-Utah, motion to table (kill) the Bumpers, D-Ark., motion to refer the joint resolution to the Budget Committee with instructions to report it back at the earliest possible date with an amendment to make it out of order to consider a budget resolution in which outlays exceed receipts for any fiscal year beginning in 2002. Motion agreed to 65-34: R 54-0; D 11-34 (ND 9-28, SD 2-6), Feb. 27, 1997.

SENATE VOTES 24, 25, 26, 27

	24	25	26	27
ALABAMA				
Sessions	Y	Y	Y	Y
Shelby	Y	Y	Y	Y
ALASKA				
Murkowski	Y	Y	Y	Y
Stevens	Y	Y	Y	Y
ARIZONA				
Kyl	Y	Y	Y	Y
McCain	Y	Y	Y	Y
ARKANSAS				
Hutchinson	Y	Y	Y	Y
Bumpers	N	Y	Y	Y
CALIFORNIA				
Boxer	N	Y	Y	Y
Feinstein	N	Y	Y	Y
COLORADO				
Allard	Y	Y	N	N
Campbell	Y	Y	Y	Y
CONNECTICUT				
Dodd	N	Y	Y	Y
Lieberman	N	Y	Y	Y
DELAWARE				
Roth	Y	Y	Y	Y
Biden	Y	N	Y	Y
FLORIDA				
Mack	Y	Y	Y	Y
Graham	Y	Y	Y	Y
GEORGIA				
Coverdell	Y	Y	Y	Y
Cleland	Y	Y	Y	Y
HAWAII				
Akaka	N	Y	Y	Y
Inouye	N	N	Y	Y
IDAHO				
Craig	Y	N	Y	Y
Kempthorne	Y	N	Y	Y
ILLINOIS				
Durbin	N	Y	Y	Y
Moseley-Braun	Y	Y	Y	Y
INDIANA				
Coats	Y	Y	Y	Y
Lugar	Y	Y	Y	Y
IOWA				
Grassley	Y	Y	Y	Y
Harkin	Y	Y	Y	Y
KANSAS				
Brownback	Y	Y	Y	Y
Roberts	Y	Y	Y	Y
KENTUCKY				
McConnell	Y	Y	Y	Y
Ford	N	N	Y	Y
LOUISIANA				
Breaux	Y	Y	Y	Y
Landrieu	Y	Y	Y	Y
MAINE				
Collins	Y	Y	Y	Y
Snowe	Y	N	Y	Y
MARYLAND				
Mikulski	N	Y	Y	Y
Sarbanes	N	Y	Y	Y
MASSACHUSETTS				
Kennedy	N	Y	Y	Y
Kerry	N	Y	Y	Y
MICHIGAN				
Abraham	Y	Y	Y	Y
Levin	N	Y	Y	Y
MINNESOTA				
Grams	Y	Y	Y	Y
Wellstone	N	N	Y	Y
MISSISSIPPI				
Cochran	Y	Y	Y	Y
Lott	Y	Y	N	Y
MISSOURI				
Ashcroft	Y	N	Y	Y
Bond	Y	Y	Y	Y
MONTANA				
Burns	Y	Y	Y	Y
Baucus	Y	Y	Y	Y
NEBRASKA				
Hagel	Y	Y	Y	Y
Kerrey	N	Y	Y	Y
NEVADA				
Bryan	Y	Y	Y	Y
Reid	N	Y	Y	Y
NEW HAMPSHIRE				
Gregg	Y	Y	Y	Y
Smith	Y	N	Y	Y
NEW JERSEY				
Lautenberg	N	Y	Y	Y
Torricelli	N	Y	Y	Y
NEW MEXICO				
Domenici	Y	Y	Y	Y
Bingaman	N	Y	Y	Y
NEW YORK				
D'Amato	Y	Y	Y	Y
Moynihan	N	Y	Y	Y
NORTH CAROLINA				
Faircloth	Y	N	Y	Y
Helms	Y	N	Y	Y
NORTH DAKOTA				
Conrad	N	N	Y	Y
Dorgan	N	N	Y	Y
OHIO				
DeWine	Y	Y	Y	Y
Glenn	N	Y	Y	Y
OKLAHOMA				
Inhofe	Y	Y	Y	Y
Nickles	Y	Y	Y	Y
OREGON				
Smith	Y	Y	Y	Y
Wyden	N	Y	Y	Y
PENNSYLVANIA				
Santorum	Y	Y	Y	Y
Specter	Y	Y	Y	Y
RHODE ISLAND				
Chafee	Y	Y	Y	Y
Reed	N	Y	Y	Y
SOUTH CAROLINA				
Thurmond	Y	Y	Y	Y
Hollings	N	N	Y	Y
SOUTH DAKOTA				
Daschle	N	Y	Y	Y
Johnson	N	Y	Y	Y
TENNESSEE				
Frist	Y	Y	Y	Y
Thompson	Y	Y	Y	Y
TEXAS				
Gramm	Y	Y	Y	Y
Hutchison	Y	Y	Y	Y
UTAH				
Bennett	Y	Y	Y	Y
Hatch	Y	Y	Y	Y
VERMONT				
Jeffords	Y	Y	Y	Y
Leahy	N	Y	Y	Y
VIRGINIA				
Warner	Y	Y	Y	Y
Robb	Y	Y	Y	Y
WASHINGTON				
Gorton	Y	Y	Y	Y
Murray	N	Y	Y	Y
WEST VIRGINIA				
Byrd	N	N	Y	Y
Rockefeller	N	Y	Y	Y
WISCONSIN				
Feingold	N	N	Y	Y
Kohl	Y	Y	Y	Y
WYOMING				
Enzi	Y	Y	Y	Y
Thomas	Y	Y	Y	Y

KEY

- Y Voted for (yea).
- # Paired for.
- + Announced for.
- N Voted against (nay).
- X Paired against.
- – Announced against.
- P Voted "present."
- C Voted "present" to avoid possible conflict of interest.
- ? Did not vote or otherwise make a position known.

Democrats *Republicans*

ND Northern Democrats SD Southern Democrats

Southern states - Ala., Ark., Fla., Ga., Ky., La., Miss., N.C., Okla., S.C., Tenn., Texas, Va.

24. S J Res 1. Balanced-Budget Constitutional Amendment/ Passage. Passage of the joint resolution to propose a constitutional amendment to balance the budget by the year 2002 or two years after ratification by three-fourths of the states, whichever is later. Rejected 66-34: R 55-0; D 11-34 (ND 6-31, SD 5-3), March 4, 1997. (A two-thirds majority vote of those present and voting (67 in this case) is required to pass a joint resolution proposing an amendment to the Constitution.) A "nay" was a vote in support of the president's position.

25. S J Res 5. Barshefsky Waiver/Trade Agreements. McCain, R-Ariz., motion to table (kill) the Hollings, D-S.C., amendment to require congressional approval of international trade agreements that amend or repeal U.S. laws. Motion agreed to 84-16: R 48-7; D 36-9 (ND 30-7, SD 6-2), March 5, 1997. A "yea" was a vote in support of the president's position.

26. S J Res 5. Barshefsky Waiver/Passage. Passage of the joint resolution to waive a provision of U.S. trade law and authorize the president to appoint Charlene Barshefsky as U.S. trade representative. The law prohibits appointment of anyone who has ever represented foreign interests. Passed 98-2: R 53-2; D 45-0 (ND 37-0, SD 8-0), March 5, 1997. A "yea" was a vote in support of the president's position.

27. Barshefsky Nomination/Confirmation. Confirmation of President Clinton's nomination of Charlene Barshefsky of the District of Columbia to be U.S. trade representative. Confirmed 99-1: R 54-1; D 45-0 (ND 37-0, SD 8-0), March 5, 1997. A "yea" was a vote in support of the president's position.

SENATE VOTES 28, 29, 30

	28	29	30
ALABAMA			
Sessions	Y	Y	Y
Shelby	Y	Y	Y
ALASKA			
Murkowski	Y	Y	Y
Stevens	Y	Y	Y
ARIZONA			
Kyl	Y	Y	Y
McCain	Y	Y	Y
ARKANSAS			
Hutchinson	Y	Y	Y
Bumpers	Y	Y	Y
CALIFORNIA			
Boxer	Y	Y	Y
Feinstein	Y	Y	Y
COLORADO			
Allard	Y	Y	Y
Campbell	Y	Y	Y
CONNECTICUT			
Dodd	C	C	Y
Lieberman	Y	Y	Y
DELAWARE			
Roth	Y	Y	Y
Biden	Y	Y	Y
FLORIDA			
Mack	Y	Y	Y
Graham	Y	Y	Y
GEORGIA			
Coverdell	Y	Y	Y
Cleland	Y	Y	Y
HAWAII			
Akaka	Y	Y	Y
Inouye	Y	Y	Y
IDAHO			
Craig	Y	Y	Y
Kempthorne	Y	Y	Y
ILLINOIS			
Durbin	Y	Y	Y
Moseley-Braun	Y	Y	Y
INDIANA			
Coats	Y	Y	Y
Lugar	Y	Y	Y
IOWA			
Grassley	Y	Y	Y
Harkin	Y	Y	Y
KANSAS			
Brownback	Y	Y	Y
Roberts	Y	Y	Y
KENTUCKY			
McConnell	Y	Y	Y
Ford	Y	Y	Y
LOUISIANA			
Breaux	Y	Y	Y
Landrieu	Y	Y	Y
MAINE			
Collins	Y	Y	Y
Snowe	Y	Y	Y
MARYLAND			
Mikulski	Y	Y	Y
Sarbanes	Y	Y	Y
MASSACHUSETTS			
Kennedy	Y	Y	Y
Kerry	Y	Y	Y
MICHIGAN			
Abraham	Y	Y	Y
Levin	Y	Y	Y
MINNESOTA			
Grams	Y	Y	N
Wellstone	Y	Y	Y
MISSISSIPPI			
Cochran	Y	Y	Y
Lott	Y	Y	Y
MISSOURI			
Ashcroft	Y	Y	Y
Bond	Y	Y	Y
MONTANA			
Burns	Y	Y	Y
Baucus	Y	Y	Y
NEBRASKA			
Hagel	Y	Y	Y
Kerrey	Y	Y	Y
NEVADA			
Bryan	Y	Y	Y
Reid	Y	Y	Y
NEW HAMPSHIRE			
Gregg	Y	Y	Y
Smith	Y	Y	Y
NEW JERSEY			
Lautenberg	Y	Y	Y
Torricelli	Y	Y	Y
NEW MEXICO			
Domenici	Y	Y	Y
Bingaman	Y	Y	Y
NEW YORK			
D'Amato	Y	Y	Y
Moynihan	Y	Y	Y
NORTH CAROLINA			
Faircloth	Y	Y	Y
Helms	Y	Y	Y
NORTH DAKOTA			
Conrad	Y	Y	Y
Dorgan	Y	Y	Y
OHIO			
DeWine	Y	Y	Y
Glenn	Y	Y	Y
OKLAHOMA			
Inhofe	Y	Y	Y
Nickles	Y	Y	Y
OREGON			
Smith	Y	Y	Y
Wyden	Y	Y	Y
PENNSYLVANIA			
Santorum	Y	Y	Y
Specter	Y	Y	Y
RHODE ISLAND			
Chafee	Y	Y	Y
Reed	Y	Y	Y
SOUTH CAROLINA			
Thurmond	Y	Y	Y
Hollings	Y	Y	Y
SOUTH DAKOTA			
Daschle	Y	Y	Y
Johnson	Y	Y	Y
TENNESSEE			
Frist	Y	Y	Y
Thompson	Y	Y	Y
TEXAS			
Gramm	Y	Y	Y
Hutchison	Y	Y	Y
UTAH			
Bennett	Y	Y	Y
Hatch	Y	Y	Y
VERMONT			
Jeffords	Y	Y	Y
Leahy	Y	Y	Y
VIRGINIA			
Warner	Y	Y	Y
Robb	Y	Y	Y
WASHINGTON			
Gorton	Y	Y	Y
Murray	Y	Y	Y
WEST VIRGINIA			
Byrd	Y	Y	Y
Rockefeller	Y	Y	Y
WISCONSIN			
Feingold	Y	Y	Y
Kohl	Y	Y	Y
WYOMING			
Enzi	Y	Y	Y
Thomas	Y	Y	Y

KEY

- Y Voted for (yea).
- # Paired for.
- + Announced for.
- N Voted against (nay).
- X Paired against.
- \- Announced against.
- P Voted "present."
- C Voted "present" to avoid possible conflict of interest.
- ? Did not vote or otherwise make a position known.

Democrats ***Republicans***

ND Northern Democrats SD Southern Democrats

Southern states - Ala., Ark., Fla., Ga., Ky., La., Miss., N.C., Okla., S.C., Tenn., Texas, Va.

28. S Res 39. Governmental Affairs Investigation/Improper Activities. Lott, R-Miss., amendment to include "improper" fundraising activities in the scope of the Governmental Affairs Committee's investigation into the 1996 presidential and congressional election campaigns. The underlying resolution would have included only "illegal" activities. Adopted 99-0: R 55-0; D 44-0 (ND 36-0, SD 8-0), March 11, 1997.

29. S Res 39. Governmental Affairs Investigation/Adoption. Adoption of the resolution to authorize $4,350,000 for the Governmental Affairs Committee's investigation into illegal and improper activities in connection with the 1996 congressional and presidential election campaigns. The committee has until Dec. 31, 1997, to complete its probe, and is required to submit a final report by Jan. 31, 1998. Adopted 99-0: R 55-0; D 44-0 (ND 36-0, SD 8-0), March 11, 1997.

30. Peña Nomination/Confirmation. Confirmation of President Clinton's nomination of Federico F. Peña of Colorado to be secretary of Energy. Confirmed 99-1: R 54-1; D 45-0 (ND 37-0, SD 8-0), March 12, 1997. A "yea" was a vote in support of the president's position.

SENATE VOTES 31, 32, 33, 34, 35

	31	32	33	34	35
ALABAMA					
Sessions	N	Y	Y	N	Y
Shelby	N	Y	Y	N	Y
ALASKA					
Murkowski	N	Y	Y	Y	Y
Stevens	N	Y	Y	Y	Y
ARIZONA					
Kyl	N	Y	Y	N	Y
McCain	N	Y	Y	Y	Y
ARKANSAS					
Hutchinson	N	Y	Y	N	N
Bumpers	N	N	N	Y	Y
CALIFORNIA					
Boxer	Y	N	N	Y	Y
Feinstein	Y	N	N	Y	Y
COLORADO					
Allard	N	Y	Y	N	Y
Campbell	N	Y	Y	Y	Y
CONNECTICUT					
Dodd	Y	C	C	Y	Y
Lieberman	Y	N	N	Y	Y
DELAWARE					
Roth	Y	Y	Y	Y	Y
Biden	Y	N	N	Y	Y
FLORIDA					
Mack	N	Y	Y	Y	Y
Graham	Y	N	N	Y	Y
GEORGIA					
Coverdell	N	Y	Y	N	Y
Cleland	Y	N	N	Y	Y
HAWAII					
Akaka	Y	N	N	Y	Y
Inouye	Y	N	N	Y	Y
IDAHO					
Craig	N	Y	Y	N	Y
Kempthorne	N	Y	Y	Y	Y
ILLINOIS					
Durbin	N	N	N	Y	Y
Moseley-Braun	N	N	N	Y	Y
INDIANA					
Coats	N	Y	Y	Y	Y
Lugar	N	Y	Y	Y	Y

	31	32	33	34	35
IOWA					
Grassley	N	Y	Y	N	Y
Harkin	Y	N	N	Y	Y
KANSAS					
Brownback	N	Y	Y	N	N
Roberts	N	Y	Y	Y	Y
KENTUCKY					
McConnell	N	Y	Y	N	Y
Ford	Y	N	N	Y	Y
LOUISIANA					
Breaux	Y	N	N	Y	Y
Landrieu	Y	N	N	Y	Y
MAINE					
Collins	N	Y	Y	Y	Y
Snowe	N	Y	Y	Y	Y
MARYLAND					
Mikulski	Y	N	N	Y	Y
Sarbanes	Y	N	N	Y	Y
MASSACHUSETTS					
Kennedy	N	N	N	Y	Y
Kerry	Y	N	N	Y	Y
MICHIGAN					
Abraham	N	Y	Y	Y	Y
Levin	Y	N	N	Y	Y
MINNESOTA					
Grams	N	Y	Y	N	Y
Wellstone	Y	N	Y	Y	Y
MISSISSIPPI					
Cochran	Y	Y	Y	Y	Y
Lott	N	Y	Y	N	Y
MISSOURI					
Ashcroft	N	Y	Y	N	Y
Bond	N	Y	Y	Y	Y
MONTANA					
Burns	?	Y	Y	N	Y
Baucus	Y	N	N	Y	Y
NEBRASKA					
Hagel	N	Y	Y	N	Y
Kerrey	N	N	N	Y	Y
NEVADA					
Bryan	Y	N	N	Y	Y
Reid	Y	N	N	Y	Y

	31	32	33	34	35
NEW HAMPSHIRE					
Gregg	N	Y	Y	N	Y
Smith	N	Y	Y	Y	N
NEW JERSEY					
Lautenberg	Y	N	N	Y	Y
Torricelli	N	N	N	Y	N
NEW MEXICO					
Domenici	N	Y	Y	Y	Y
Bingaman	Y	N	N	Y	Y
NEW YORK					
D'Amato	N	Y	Y	Y	Y
Moynihan	N	N	Y	Y	Y
NORTH CAROLINA					
Faircloth	N	Y	Y	N	Y
Helms	N	Y	Y	N	Y
NORTH DAKOTA					
Conrad	Y	N	N	Y	Y
Dorgan	Y	N	N	Y	Y
OHIO					
DeWine	N	Y	Y	Y	Y
Glenn	Y	N	N	?	Y
OKLAHOMA					
Inhofe	N	Y	Y	Y	Y
Nickles	N	Y	Y	N	Y
OREGON					
Smith	N	Y	Y	Y	Y
Wyden	Y	N	N	Y	Y
PENNSYLVANIA					
Santorum	N	Y	Y	Y	Y
Specter	Y	Y	Y	Y	Y
RHODE ISLAND					
Chafee	N	Y	Y	Y	Y
Reed	Y	N	N	Y	Y
SOUTH CAROLINA					
Thurmond	N	Y	Y	N	Y
Hollings	Y	N	N	Y	Y
SOUTH DAKOTA					
Daschle	Y	N	N	Y	Y
Johnson	Y	N	N	Y	Y
TENNESSEE					
Frist	N	Y	Y	N	Y
Thompson	N	Y	Y	Y	Y

KEY

- Y Voted for (yea).
- # Paired for.
- + Announced for.
- N Voted against (nay).
- X Paired against.
- – Announced against.
- P Voted "present."
- C Voted "present" to avoid possible conflict of interest.
- ? Did not vote or otherwise make a position known.

Democrats *Republicans*

	31	32	33	34	35
TEXAS					
Gramm	N	Y	Y	N	Y
Hutchison	N	Y	Y	Y	Y
UTAH					
Bennett	N	Y	Y	Y	Y
Hatch	N	Y	Y	Y	Y
VERMONT					
Jeffords	Y	Y	Y	Y	Y
Leahy	N	N	N	Y	Y
VIRGINIA					
Warner	N	Y	Y	Y	?
Robb	Y	N	N	Y	Y
WASHINGTON					
Gorton	N	Y	Y	Y	Y
Murray	Y	N	N	Y	Y
WEST VIRGINIA					
Byrd	Y	N	N	Y	Y
Rockefeller	N	N	N	Y	Y
WISCONSIN					
Feingold	N	N	Y	Y	Y
Kohl	N	N	N	Y	Y
WYOMING					
Enzi	N	Y	Y	N	Y
Thomas	N	Y	Y	Y	N

ND Northern Democrats SD Southern Democrats

Southern states - Ala., Ark., Fla., Ga., Ky., La., Miss., N.C., Okla., S.C., Tenn., Texas, Va.

31. S J Res 18. Spending-Limit Constitutional Amendment/Passage. Passage of the joint resolution to propose a constitutional amendment to allow Congress and the states to set "reasonable limits" on campaign spending. The Supreme Court ruled in the 1976 *Buckley v. Valeo* case that restricting campaign spending infringed on the First Amendment rights of free speech. Rejected 38-61: R 4-50; D 34-11 (ND 27-10, SD 7-1), March 18, 1997. (A two-thirds majority vote of those present and voting (66 in this case) is required to pass a joint resolution proposing an amendment to the Constitution.)

32. S J Res 22. Independent Counsel Investigation/Passage. Passage of the joint resolution to express the sense of Congress that the attorney general should appoint an independent counsel to investigate allegations of illegal fundraising in the 1996 presidential election campaign. Passed 55-44; R 55-0; D 0-44 (ND 0-36, SD 0-8), March 19, 1997.

33. S J Res 23. Attorney General's Judgment/Motion To Table. Lott, R-Miss., motion to table (kill) the joint resolution expressing the sense of Congress that the attorney general should "exercise her best professional judgment" on whether to appoint an independent counsel to investigate alleged criminal misconduct in presidential or congressional election campaigns. Motion agreed to 58-41: R 55-0; D 3-41 (ND 3-33, SD 0-8), March 19, 1997.

34. Garland Nomination/Confirmation. Confirmation of President Clinton's nomination of Merrick B. Garland of Maryland to be United States Circuit judge for the District of Columbia Circuit. Confirmed 76-23: R 32-23; D 44-0 (ND 36-0, SD 8-0), March 19, 1997. A "yea" was a vote in support of the president's position.

35. H J Res 58. Mexico Anti-Drug Certification/Coverdell-Feinstein Substitute. Coverdell, R-Ga., substitute amendment to require the president to report to Congress by Sept. 1, 1997, on the extent of U.S. and Mexican progress toward combating drug trafficking and related crimes. The joint resolution would have decertified Mexico as an ally in the fight against drugs unless six criteria were met in 90 days. Adopted 94-5: R 50-4; D 44-1 (ND 36-1, SD 8-0), March 20, 1997. (Subsequently, the joint resolution was passed by voice vote.)

SENATE VOTES 36, 37, 38, 39

	36	37	38	39
ALABAMA				
Sessions	Y	Y	N	N
Shelby	Y	Y	N	N
ALASKA				
Murkowski	Y	Y	N	N
Stevens	Y	Y	N	N
ARIZONA				
Kyl	Y	Y	N	N
McCain	Y	Y	N	N
ARKANSAS				
Hutchinson	Y	?	?	?
Bumpers	Y	Y	Y	Y
CALIFORNIA				
Boxer	N	?	?	?
Feinstein	N	?	?	?
COLORADO				
Allard	Y	Y	N	N
Campbell	N	Y	N	N
CONNECTICUT				
Dodd	Y	N	N	Y
Lieberman	Y	N	N	Y
DELAWARE				
Roth	Y	Y	N	N
Biden	Y	N	Y	N
FLORIDA				
Mack	Y	Y	N	N
Graham	Y	Y	N	Y
GEORGIA				
Coverdell	Y	Y	N	N
Cleland	N	Y	N	N
HAWAII				
Akaka	Y	N	Y	Y
Inouye	N	N	Y	?
IDAHO				
Craig	Y	Y	N	N
Kempthorne	Y	Y	N	N
ILLINOIS				
Durbin	N	N	Y	Y
Moseley-Braun	Y	N	N	Y
INDIANA				
Coats	N	Y	N	N
Lugar	Y	Y	N	N
IOWA				
Grassley	Y	Y	N	N
Harkin	N	N	Y	Y
KANSAS				
Brownback	Y	Y	N	N
Roberts	Y	Y	N	N
KENTUCKY				
McConnell	Y	Y	N	N
Ford	N	Y	Y	N
LOUISIANA				
Breaux	N	N	Y	Y
Landrieu	N	N	Y	Y
MAINE				
Collins	Y	Y	N	Y
Snowe	Y	Y	N	Y
MARYLAND				
Mikulski	N	N	N	Y
Sarbanes	N	N	N	Y
MASSACHUSETTS				
Kennedy	Y	N	Y	Y
Kerry	Y	N	Y	Y
MICHIGAN				
Abraham	Y	Y	N	N
Levin	Y	N	N	Y
MINNESOTA				
Grams	?	?	?	?
Wellstone	?	?	?	?
MISSISSIPPI				
Cochran	Y	Y	N	N
Lott	Y	Y	N	N
MISSOURI				
Ashcroft	Y	Y	N	N
Bond	Y	Y	N	N
MONTANA				
Burns	Y	Y	N	N
Baucus	N	N	Y	Y
NEBRASKA				
Hagel	Y	Y	N	N
Kerrey	N	N	N	Y
NEVADA				
Bryan	N	N	Y	Y
Reid	N	N	Y	Y
NEW HAMPSHIRE				
Gregg	Y	Y	N	N
Smith	Y	Y	N	N
NEW JERSEY				
Lautenberg	Y	N	Y	Y
Torricelli	Y	N	Y	Y
NEW MEXICO				
Domenici	Y	Y	N	Y
Bingaman	Y	N	Y	Y
NEW YORK				
D'Amato	Y	Y	N	N
Moynihan	N	N	Y	Y
NORTH CAROLINA				
Faircloth	Y	Y	N	N
Helms	Y	Y	N	N
NORTH DAKOTA				
Conrad	?	?	?	?
Dorgan	?	?	?	?
OHIO				
DeWine	Y	Y	N	N
Glenn	N	N	Y	Y
OKLAHOMA				
Inhofe	Y	Y	N	N
Nickles	Y	Y	N	N
OREGON				
Smith	Y	Y	N	N
Wyden	N	Y	Y	N
PENNSYLVANIA				
Santorum	Y	Y	N	Y
Specter	Y	Y	N	N
RHODE ISLAND				
Chafee	Y	Y	N	N
Reed	N	N	Y	Y
SOUTH CAROLINA				
Thurmond	Y	Y	N	N
Hollings	Y	N	N	N
SOUTH DAKOTA				
Daschle	N	N	Y	Y
Johnson	Y	Y	N	Y
TENNESSEE				
Frist	Y	Y	N	N
Thompson	Y	Y	N	N
TEXAS				
Gramm	Y	Y	N	N
Hutchison	Y	Y	N	N
UTAH				
Bennett	Y	Y	N	N
Hatch	Y	Y	N	N
VERMONT				
Jeffords	Y	Y	N	N
Leahy	Y	N	N	N
VIRGINIA				
Warner	Y	Y	N	N
Robb	Y	N	N	Y
WASHINGTON				
Gorton	Y	Y	N	N
Murray	Y	Y	Y	N
WEST VIRGINIA				
Byrd	Y	N	N	Y
Rockefeller	N	N	Y	Y
WISCONSIN				
Feingold	N	N	N	Y
Kohl	Y	N	N	Y
WYOMING				
Enzi	Y	Y	N	N
Thomas	Y	Y	N	N

KEY

- Y Voted for (yea).
- # Paired for.
- \+ Announced for.
- N Voted against (nay).
- X Paired against.
- \- Announced against.
- P Voted "present."
- C Voted "present" to avoid possible conflict of interest.
- ? Did not vote or otherwise make a position known.

Democrats *Republicans*

ND Northern Democrats SD Southern Democrats

Southern states - Ala., Ark., Fla., Ga., Ky., La., Miss., N.C., Okla., S.C., Tenn., Texas, Va.

36. S 104. Interim Nuclear Waste Repository/Governor's Consent. Murkowski, R-Alaska, motion to table (kill) the Reid, D-Nev., amendment to ban transportation of radioactive waste through a state without prior written consent from the state's governor. Motion agreed to 72-24: R 52-2; D 20-22 (ND 16-18, SD 4-4), April 10, 1997.

37. S 104. Interim Nuclear Waste Repository/Oak Ridge Reservation. Thompson, R-Tenn., amendment to prohibit the president from choosing the Oak Ridge Reservation in Tennessee as the alternate site for the interim nuclear waste repository. The bill directs the president to choose an alternate nuclear waste dump site if Yucca Mountain in Nevada is deemed unsuitable. Adopted 60-33: R 53-0; D 7-33 (ND 3-29, SD 4-4), April 10, 1997.

38. S 104. Interim Nuclear Waste Repository/Absolve Department of Energy. Bumpers, D-Ark., amendment to express the sense of the Senate that a court ruling on whether the Department of Energy has met its obligation to dispose of radioactive waste should take into account delaying factors beyond the department's control. Rejected 24-69: R 0-53; D 24-16 (ND 20-12, SD 4-4), April 10, 1997.

39. S 104. Interim Nuclear Waste Repository/Alternate Sites. Bingaman, D-N.M., amendment to allow the president to choose any site in the country as an alternate for interim nuclear waste disposal should Yucca Mountain, Nevada, be deemed unsuitable. Rejected 36-56: R 4-49; D 32-7 (ND 27-4, SD 5-3), April 10, 1997.

SENATE VOTES 40, 41, 42, 43, 44, 45

	40	41	42	43	44	45
ALABAMA						
Sessions	Y	Y	Y	Y	Y	Y
Shelby	Y	Y	Y	Y	Y	Y
ALASKA						
Murkowski	Y	Y	Y	Y	Y	Y
Stevens	Y	Y	Y	Y	Y	Y
ARIZONA						
Kyl	Y	Y	Y	Y	Y	Y
McCain	Y	Y	Y	Y	Y	Y
ARKANSAS						
Hutchinson	Y	Y	Y	Y	Y	Y
Bumpers	N	N	N	Y	Y	N
CALIFORNIA						
Boxer	N	N	N	Y	Y	N
Feinstein	N	N	N	Y	Y	N
COLORADO						
Allard	Y	Y	Y	Y	Y	Y
Campbell	N	Y	N	Y	Y	Y
CONNECTICUT						
Dodd	N	Y	N	Y	Y	N
Lieberman	N	Y	N	Y	Y	Y
DELAWARE						
Roth	Y	Y	Y	Y	Y	Y
Biden	N	N	N	Y	Y	N
FLORIDA						
Mack	Y	Y	Y	Y	Y	Y
Graham	Y	Y	Y	Y	Y	N
GEORGIA						
Coverdell	Y	Y	Y	Y	Y	Y
Cleland	N	N	Y	Y	Y	N
HAWAII						
Akaka	N	N	N	Y	Y	N
Inouye	N	Y	N	Y	Y	N
IDAHO						
Craig	Y	Y	Y	Y	Y	Y
Kempthorne	Y	Y	Y	Y	Y	Y
ILLINOIS						
Durbin	N	N	N	Y	Y	N
Moseley-Braun	Y	N	Y	Y	Y	N
INDIANA						
Coats	?	?	N	Y	Y	Y
Lugar	Y	Y	Y	Y	Y	Y

	40	41	42	43	44	45
IOWA						
Grassley	Y	Y	Y	Y	Y	Y
Harkin	N	N	Y	Y	Y	N
KANSAS						
Brownback	Y	Y	Y	Y	Y	Y
Roberts	Y	Y	Y	Y	Y	Y
KENTUCKY						
McConnell	Y	Y	Y	Y	Y	Y
Ford	N	N	N	Y	Y	N
LOUISIANA						
Breaux	N	Y	N	Y	Y	N
Landrieu	N	N	N	Y	Y	N
MAINE						
Collins	Y	Y	Y	Y	Y	Y
Snowe	Y	Y	Y	Y	Y	Y
MARYLAND						
Mikulski	N	Y	N	Y	Y	N
Sarbanes	N	Y	N	Y	Y	N
MASSACHUSETTS						
Kennedy	N	N	N	Y	Y	N
Kerry	N	N	N	Y	Y	N
MICHIGAN						
Abraham	Y	Y	Y	Y	Y	Y
Levin	N	Y	Y	Y	Y	N
MINNESOTA						
Grams	Y	Y	Y	Y	Y	Y
Wellstone	N	N	N	Y	Y	N
MISSISSIPPI						
Cochran	Y	Y	Y	Y	Y	?
Lott	Y	Y	Y	Y	Y	Y
MISSOURI						
Ashcroft	Y	N	Y	Y	Y	Y
Bond	Y	Y	Y	Y	Y	+
MONTANA						
Burns	Y	Y	Y	Y	Y	Y
Baucus	N	N	N	Y	Y	N
NEBRASKA						
Hagel	Y	Y	Y	Y	Y	Y
Kerrey	N	N	N	Y	Y	N
NEVADA						
Bryan	N	N	N	Y	Y	N
Reid	N	N	N	Y	Y	N

	40	41	42	43	44	45
NEW HAMPSHIRE						
Gregg	Y	Y	Y	Y	Y	Y
Smith	Y	Y	Y	Y	Y	Y
NEW JERSEY						
Lautenberg	N	N	N	Y	Y	N
Torricelli	N	N	N	Y	Y	N
NEW MEXICO						
Domenici	Y	Y	Y	Y	Y	Y
Bingaman	N	N	N	Y	Y	N
NEW YORK						
D'Amato	Y	Y	Y	Y	Y	Y
Moynihan	N	N	N	Y	Y	N
NORTH CAROLINA						
Faircloth	Y	Y	Y	?	?	?
Helms	Y	Y	Y	Y	Y	Y
NORTH DAKOTA						
Conrad	N	N	N	Y	Y	N
Dorgan	N	N	N	Y	Y	N
OHIO						
DeWine	Y	Y	Y	Y	Y	Y
Glenn	N	N	N	Y	Y	N
OKLAHOMA						
Inhofe	Y	Y	Y	Y	Y	Y
Nickles	Y	Y	Y	Y	Y	Y
OREGON						
Smith	Y	Y	Y	?	Y	Y
Wyden	N	N	Y	Y	Y	N
PENNSYLVANIA						
Santorum	Y	Y	Y	Y	Y	Y
Specter	Y	Y	Y	Y	Y	Y
RHODE ISLAND						
Chafee	N	Y	Y	Y	Y	Y
Reed	N	N	N	Y	Y	N
SOUTH CAROLINA						
Thurmond	Y	Y	Y	Y	Y	Y
Hollings	Y	Y	Y	Y	Y	N
SOUTH DAKOTA						
Daschle	N	N	N	Y	Y	N
Johnson	Y	Y	Y	Y	Y	N
TENNESSEE						
Frist	Y	Y	Y	Y	Y	Y
Thompson	Y	Y	Y	Y	Y	Y

KEY

- Y Voted for (yea).
- # Paired for.
- + Announced for.
- N Voted against (nay).
- X Paired against.
- – Announced against.
- P Voted "present."
- C Voted "present" to avoid possible conflict of interest.
- ? Did not vote or otherwise make a position known.

Democrats ***Republicans***

	40	41	42	43	44	45
TEXAS						
Gramm	Y	Y	Y	Y	Y	Y
Hutchison	Y	Y	Y	Y	Y	Y
UTAH						
Bennett	Y	Y	Y	Y	Y	Y
Hatch	Y	Y	Y	Y	Y	Y
VERMONT						
Jeffords	Y	Y	Y	Y	Y	Y
Leahy	Y	Y	Y	Y	Y	N
VIRGINIA						
Warner	Y	Y	Y	Y	Y	Y
Robb	N	Y	Y	Y	Y	N
WASHINGTON						
Gorton	Y	Y	Y	Y	Y	Y
Murray	Y	N	Y	Y	Y	N
WEST VIRGINIA						
Byrd	N	N	N	Y	Y	N
Rockefeller	?	?	?	?	Y	N
WISCONSIN						
Feingold	N	N	N	Y	Y	N
Kohl	Y	Y	Y	Y	Y	N
WYOMING						
Enzi	Y	Y	Y	Y	Y	Y
Thomas	Y	Y	Y	Y	Y	Y

ND Northern Democrats SD Southern Democrats

Southern states - Ala., Ark., Fla., Ga., Ky., La., Miss., N.C., Okla., S.C., Tenn., Texas, Va.

40. S 104. Interim Nuclear Waste Repository/Halt Construction. Murkowski, R-Alaska, motion to table (kill) the Bingaman, D-N.M., amendment to halt all activities related to construction of an interim nuclear waste storage facility at Yucca Mountain, Nevada, if the site is deemed unsuitable as a permanent repository. Motion agreed to 59-39: R 52-2; D 7-37 (ND 5-31, SD 2-6), April 15, 1997. A "nay" was a vote in support of the president's position.

41. S 104. Interim Nuclear Waste Repository/Fee Cap. Murkowski, R-Alaska, amendment to cap the nuclear waste user fee paid by nuclear energy consumers at 1 mill per kilowatt hour, unless a cap waiver is approved by Congress. Adopted 66-32: R 53-1; D 13-31 (ND 9-27, SD 4-4), April 15, 1997.

42. S 104. Interim Nuclear Waste Repository/Passage. Passage of the bill to establish an interim high-level nuclear waste repository at Yucca Mountain, Nevada. The bill gives the president until March 1, 1999, to halt construction of the temporary waste site if it is deemed unsuitable as a permanent repository. The president would then have 18 months to choose an alternate site, which Congress would have two years to approve. If an alternate is not agreed upon, construction would automatically begin at the Nevada site. Passed 65-34: R 53-2; D 12-32 (ND 8-28, SD 4-4), April 15, 1997. A "nay" was a vote in support of the president's position.

43. S 522. Tax Return Browsing/Passage. Passage of the bill to make it unlawful for federal employees and others to inspect income tax returns or return information without authorization. Violators could be subject to a $1,000 fine and up to one year in prison. In addition, federal officers and employees could be dismissed from employment. Passed 97-0: R 53-0; D 44-0 (ND 36-0, SD 8-0), April 15, 1997.

44. HR 1003. Assisted Suicide Funding Ban/Passage. Passage of the bill to prohibit the use of federal funds for assisted suicide, euthanasia or mercy killing. Passed (thus cleared for the president) 99-0: R 54-0; D 45-0 (ND 37-0, SD 8-0), April 16, 1997.

45. S 495. Domestic Chemical Weapons Ban/Passage. Passage of the bill to make it a crime to develop, produce, acquire or possess chemical or biological weapons and to establish criminal and civil penalties for violations. The bill would direct the president to impose sanctions on any foreign government that uses chemical or biological weapons in violation of international law. Passed 53-44: R 52-0; D 1-44 (ND 1-36, SD 0-8), April 17, 1997. A "nay" was a vote in support of the president's position.

SENATE VOTES 46, 47, 48, 49, 50, 51

	46	47	48	49	50	51
ALABAMA						
Sessions	N	N	N	N	N	N
Shelby	N	N	N	N	N	N
ALASKA						
Murkowski	N	N	N	N	N	Y
Stevens	Y	Y	Y	Y	Y	Y
ARIZONA						
Kyl	N	N	N	N	N	N
McCain	Y	Y	Y	N	Y	Y
ARKANSAS						
Hutchinson	N	N	N	N	N	N
Bumpers	Y	Y	Y	Y	Y	Y
CALIFORNIA						
Boxer	Y	Y	Y	Y	Y	Y
Feinstein	Y	Y	Y	Y	Y	Y
COLORADO						
Allard	N	N	N	N	N	N
Campbell	N	N	N	N	N	N
CONNECTICUT						
Dodd	Y	Y	Y	Y	Y	Y
Lieberman	Y	Y	Y	Y	Y	Y
DELAWARE						
Roth	Y	Y	Y	Y	Y	Y
Biden	Y	Y	Y	Y	Y	Y
FLORIDA						
Mack	N	N	N	N	N	N
Graham	Y	Y	Y	Y	Y	Y
GEORGIA						
Coverdell	N	N	N	N	N	N
Cleland	Y	Y	Y	Y	Y	Y
HAWAII						
Akaka	Y	Y	Y	Y	Y	Y
Inouye	Y	Y	Y	Y	Y	Y
IDAHO						
Craig	N	N	N	N	N	N
Kempthorne	N	N	N	N	N	N
ILLINOIS						
Durbin	Y	Y	Y	Y	Y	Y
Moseley-Braun	Y	Y	Y	Y	Y	Y
INDIANA						
Coats	Y	Y	Y	N	Y	Y
Lugar	Y	Y	Y	Y	Y	Y
IOWA						
Grassley	N	N	N	N	N	N
Harkin	Y	Y	Y	Y	Y	Y
KANSAS						
Brownback	N	N	N	N	N	N
Roberts	Y	Y	Y	N	Y	Y
KENTUCKY						
McConnell	N	N	N	N	N	Y
Ford	Y	Y	Y	Y	Y	Y
LOUISIANA						
Breaux	Y	Y	Y	Y	Y	Y
Landrieu	Y	Y	Y	Y	Y	Y
MAINE						
Collins	Y	Y	Y	Y	Y	Y
Snowe	Y	Y	Y	Y	Y	Y
MARYLAND						
Mikulski	Y	Y	Y	Y	Y	Y
Sarbanes	Y	Y	Y	Y	Y	Y
MASSACHUSETTS						
Kennedy	Y	Y	Y	Y	Y	Y
Kerry	Y	Y	Y	Y	Y	Y
MICHIGAN						
Abraham	Y	N	N	N	N	Y
Levin	Y	Y	Y	Y	Y	Y
MINNESOTA						
Grams	N	N	N	N	N	N
Wellstone	Y	Y	Y	Y	Y	Y
MISSISSIPPI						
Cochran	Y	Y	Y	Y	Y	Y
Lott	N	N	N	N	N	Y
MISSOURI						
Ashcroft	N	N	N	N	N	N
Bond	Y	N	N	N	N	N
MONTANA						
Burns	N	N	N	N	N	N
Baucus	Y	Y	Y	Y	Y	Y
NEBRASKA						
Hagel	Y	Y	Y	N	Y	Y
Kerrey	Y	Y	Y	Y	Y	Y
NEVADA						
Bryan	Y	Y	Y	Y	Y	Y
Reid	Y	Y	Y	Y	Y	Y
NEW HAMPSHIRE						
Gregg	Y	Y	N	N	N	Y
Smith	N	N	N	N	N	N
NEW JERSEY						
Lautenberg	Y	Y	Y	Y	Y	Y
Torricelli	Y	Y	Y	Y	Y	Y
NEW MEXICO						
Domenici	Y	Y	Y	N	Y	Y
Bingaman	Y	Y	Y	Y	Y	Y
NEW YORK						
D'Amato	Y	Y	Y	Y	Y	Y
Moynihan	Y	Y	Y	Y	Y	Y
NORTH CAROLINA						
Faircloth	N	N	N	N	N	N
Helms	N	N	N	N	N	N
NORTH DAKOTA						
Conrad	Y	Y	Y	Y	Y	Y
Dorgan	Y	Y	Y	Y	Y	Y
OHIO						
DeWine	Y	Y	Y	N	Y	Y
Glenn	Y	Y	Y	Y	Y	Y
OKLAHOMA						
Inhofe	N	N	N	N	N	N
Nickles	Y	N	N	N	N	N
OREGON						
Smith	Y	Y	Y	N	Y	Y
Wyden	Y	Y	Y	Y	Y	Y
PENNSYLVANIA						
Santorum	Y	N	Y	N	N	Y
Specter	Y	Y	Y	Y	Y	Y
RHODE ISLAND						
Chafee	Y	Y	Y	Y	Y	Y
Reed	Y	Y	Y	Y	Y	Y
SOUTH CAROLINA						
Thurmond	N	N	N	N	N	N
Hollings	Y	Y	Y	Y	Y	Y
SOUTH DAKOTA						
Daschle	Y	Y	Y	Y	Y	Y
Johnson	Y	Y	Y	Y	Y	Y
TENNESSEE						
Frist	Y	Y	Y	Y	Y	Y
Thompson	N	N	N	N	N	N
TEXAS						
Gramm	N	N	N	N	N	N
Hutchison	N	N	N	N	N	N
UTAH						
Bennett	N	N	N	N	N	N
Hatch	Y	Y	Y	N	Y	Y
VERMONT						
Jeffords	Y	Y	Y	Y	Y	Y
Leahy	Y	Y	Y	Y	Y	Y
VIRGINIA						
Warner	Y	N	N	N	Y	Y
Robb	Y	Y	Y	Y	Y	Y
WASHINGTON						
Gorton	Y	Y	Y	N	Y	Y
Murray	Y	Y	Y	Y	Y	Y
WEST VIRGINIA						
Byrd	Y	Y	Y	Y	Y	Y
Rockefeller	Y	Y	Y	Y	Y	Y
WISCONSIN						
Feingold	Y	Y	Y	Y	Y	Y
Kohl	Y	Y	Y	Y	Y	Y
WYOMING						
Enzi	N	N	N	N	N	Y
Thomas	N	N	N	N	N	Y

KEY

- Y Voted for (yea).
- # Paired for.
- + Announced for.
- N Voted against (nay).
- X Paired against.
- – Announced against.
- P Voted "present."
- C Voted "present" to avoid possible conflict of interest.
- ? Did not vote or otherwise make a position known.

Democrats *Republicans*

ND Northern Democrats SD Southern Democrats

Southern states - Ala., Ark., Fla., Ga., Ky., La., Miss., N.C., Okla., S.C., Tenn., Texas, Va.

46. S Res 75. Chemical Weapons Treaty/Terrorist Nations. Biden, D-Del., motion to strike the language deferring ratification of the Chemical Weapons Convention until the president certifies to Congress that countries with offensive chemical weapons programs have ratified or acceded to the convention. Motion agreed to 71-29: R 26-29; D 45-0 (ND 37-0, SD 8-0), April 24, 1997.

47. S Res 75. Chemical Weapons Treaty/ Russian Compliance. Biden, D-Del., motion to strike language deferring ratification of the Chemical Weapons Convention until the president certifies to Congress that Russia has ratified the treaty, complied with certain bilateral weapons agreements and ceased all chemical weapons activity. Motion agreed to 66-34: R 21-34; D 45-0 (ND 37-0, SD 8-0), April 24, 1997.

48. S Res 75. Chemical Weapons Treaty/Effective Verification. Biden, D-Del., motion to strike the language deferring ratification of the Chemical Weapons Convention until the president certifies to Congress that the Central Intelligence Agency has a "high degree of confidence" that it can detect militarily significant violations of the treaty in a timely fashion. Motion agreed to 66-34: R 21-34; D 45-0 (ND 37-0, SD 8-0), April 24, 1997.

49. S Res 75. Chemical Weapons Treaty/Inspector Ban. Biden, D-Del., motion to strike the language prohibiting the inspection of U.S. chemical plants by inspectors from nations that have sponsored terrorism or violated U.S. non-proliferation laws. Motion agreed to 56-44: R 11-44; D 45-0 (ND 37-0, SD 8-0), April 24, 1997.

50. S Res 75. Chemical Weapons Treaty/Information Sharing. Biden, D-Del., motion to strike the language deferring ratification of the Chemical Weapons Convention until the president certifies to Congress that the treaty has been amended to remove the provision facilitating exchange of chemical weapons defense technology and prohibiting restrictions on chemical trading. Motion agreed to 66-34: R 21-34; D 45-0 (ND 37-0, SD 8-0), April 24, 1997.

51. S Res 75. Chemical Weapons Treaty/Adoption. Adoption of the resolution of ratification of the treaty to prohibit development, production, acquisition, stockpiling, transfer or use of chemical weapons. Adopted 74-26: R 29-26; D 45-0 (ND 37-0, SD 8-0), April 24, 1997. A two-thirds majority of those present and voting (67 in this case) is required for adoption of resolutions of ratification. A "yea" was a vote in support of the president's position.

SENATE VOTES 52, 53, 54, 55

	52	53	54	55
ALABAMA				
Sessions	Y	Y	Y	Y
Shelby	N	N	Y	Y
ALASKA				
Murkowski	Y	Y	Y	Y
Stevens	Y	Y	Y	Y
ARIZONA				
Kyl	Y	Y	Y	Y
McCain	Y	Y	Y	Y
ARKANSAS				
Hutchinson	Y	Y	Y	Y
Bumpers	N	N	Y	Y
CALIFORNIA				
Boxer	N	N	Y	Y
Feinstein	N	N	Y	Y
COLORADO				
Allard	Y	Y	N	Y
Campbell	Y	Y	N	Y
CONNECTICUT				
Dodd	N	N	Y	Y
Lieberman	N	Y	Y	Y
DELAWARE				
Roth	Y	Y	Y	Y
Biden	N	N	Y	Y
FLORIDA				
Mack	Y	Y	Y	Y
Graham	N	N	Y	Y
GEORGIA				
Coverdell	Y	Y	Y	Y
Cleland	N	N	Y	Y
HAWAII				
Akaka	N	N	Y	Y
Inouye	N	?	?	Y
IDAHO				
Craig	Y	Y	N	Y
Kempthorne	Y	Y	Y	Y
ILLINOIS				
Durbin	N	N	Y	Y
Moseley-Braun	N	N	Y	Y
INDIANA				
Coats	Y	Y	Y	Y
Lugar	Y	Y	N	Y

	52	53	54	55
IOWA				
Grassley	Y	Y	Y	Y
Harkin	N	N	Y	Y
KANSAS				
Brownback	Y	Y	Y	Y
Roberts	Y	Y	N	Y
KENTUCKY				
McConnell	Y	Y	Y	Y
Ford	N	N	Y	Y
LOUISIANA				
Breaux	N	N	Y	Y
Landrieu	N	N	Y	Y
MAINE				
Collins	Y	Y	Y	Y
Snowe	Y	Y	Y	Y
MARYLAND				
Mikulski	N	N	Y	Y
Sarbanes	N	N	Y	Y
MASSACHUSETTS				
Kennedy	N	N	Y	Y
Kerry	N	N	Y	Y
MICHIGAN				
Abraham	Y	Y	Y	Y
Levin	N	N	Y	Y
MINNESOTA				
Grams	Y	Y	Y	Y
Wellstone	N	N	Y	Y
MISSISSIPPI				
Cochran	Y	Y	Y	Y
Lott	Y	Y	Y	Y
MISSOURI				
Ashcroft	Y	Y	Y	Y
Bond	?	Y	Y	Y
MONTANA				
Burns	Y	Y	Y	Y
Baucus	N	N	Y	Y
NEBRASKA				
Hagel	Y	Y	N	Y
Kerrey	N	N	Y	Y
NEVADA				
Bryan	N	N	Y	Y
Reid	N	N	Y	Y

	52	53	54	55
NEW HAMPSHIRE				
Gregg	Y	Y	Y	Y
Smith	Y	Y	N	Y
NEW JERSEY				
Lautenberg	N	N	Y	Y
Torricelli	N	N	Y	Y
NEW MEXICO				
Domenici	Y	Y	Y	Y
Bingaman	N	N	Y	Y
NEW YORK				
D'Amato	Y	Y	Y	Y
Moynihan	N	N	+	Y
NORTH CAROLINA				
Faircloth	Y	Y	N	Y
Helms	Y	Y	N	Y
NORTH DAKOTA				
Conrad	N	N	Y	Y
Dorgan	N	N	Y	Y
OHIO				
DeWine	Y	Y	Y	Y
Glenn	N	N	Y	Y
OKLAHOMA				
Inhofe	Y	Y	N	Y
Nickles	Y	Y	Y	Y
OREGON				
Smith	Y	Y	Y	Y
Wyden	N	N	Y	Y
PENNSYLVANIA				
Santorum	Y	Y	Y	Y
Specter	Y	Y	Y	Y
RHODE ISLAND				
Chafee	Y	Y	Y	Y
Reed	N	N	Y	Y
SOUTH CAROLINA				
Thurmond	Y	Y	Y	Y
Hollings	N	N	Y	Y
SOUTH DAKOTA				
Daschle	N	N	Y	Y
Johnson	N	N	Y	Y
TENNESSEE				
Frist	Y	Y	Y	Y
Thompson	Y	Y	N	N

KEY

- Y Voted for (yea).
- # Paired for.
- + Announced for.
- N Voted against (nay).
- X Paired against.
- – Announced against.
- P Voted "present."
- C Voted "present" to avoid possible conflict of interest.
- ? Did not vote or otherwise make a position known.

Democrats ***Republicans***

	52	53	54	55
TEXAS				
Gramm	Y	Y	N	Y
Hutchison	Y	Y	Y	Y
UTAH				
Bennett	Y	Y	Y	Y
Hatch	Y	Y	Y	Y
VERMONT				
Jeffords	Y	Y	Y	Y
Leahy	N	N	Y	Y
VIRGINIA				
Warner	Y	Y	Y	Y
Robb	N	N	Y	Y
WASHINGTON				
Gorton	Y	Y	Y	Y
Murray	N	N	Y	Y
WEST VIRGINIA				
Byrd	N	N	Y	Y
Rockefeller	N	N	Y	Y
WISCONSIN				
Feingold	N	N	Y	Y
Kohl	N	N	Y	Y
WYOMING				
Enzi	Y	Y	Y	Y
Thomas	Y	Y	N	Y

ND Northern Democrats SD Southern Democrats

Southern states - Ala., Ark., Fla., Ga., Ky., La., Miss., N.C., Okla., S.C., Tenn., Texas, Va.

52. S 543. Volunteer Liability Limitation/Cloture. Motion to invoke cloture (thus limiting debate) on the motion to proceed to the bill that pre-empts state law and exempts volunteers from civil liability if they are acting within the scope of their responsibilities. Motion rejected 53-46: R 53-1; D 0-45 (ND 0-37, SD 0-8), April 29, 1997. Three-fifths of the total Senate (60) is required to invoke cloture.

53. S 543. Volunteer Liability Limitation/Cloture. Motion to invoke cloture (thus limiting debate) on the motion to proceed to the bill that pre-empts state law and exempts volunteers from civil liability if they are acting within the scope of their responsibilities. Motion rejected 55-44: R 54-1; D 1-43 (ND 1-35, SD 0-8), April 30, 1997. Three-fifths of the total Senate (60) is required to invoke cloture.

54. Herman Nomination/Confirmation. Confirmation of President Clinton's nomination of Alexis M. Herman of Alabama to be secretary of Labor. Confirmed 85-13: R 42-13; D 43-0 (ND 35-0, SD 8-0), April 30, 1997. A "yea" was a vote in support of the president's position.

55. S 543. Volunteer Liability Limitation/Passage. Passage of the bill to pre-empt state law and exempt volunteers from civil liability if they are acting within the scope of their responsibilities. The bill was amended to remove an exemption concerning nonprofit groups, and to allow a state to opt out of the federal law if it determined that its own state laws protecting volunteers from frivolous lawsuits were adequate. Passed 99-1: R 54-1; D 45-0 (ND 37-0, SD 8-0), May 1, 1997.

SENATE VOTES 56, 57, 58, 59, 60, 61, 62, 63

	56	57	58	59	60	61	62	63
ALABAMA								
Sessions	Y	Y	Y	Y	N	Y	N	N
Shelby	Y	Y	Y	Y	N	Y	Y	Y
ALASKA								
Murkowski	Y	Y	Y	Y	Y	Y	Y	Y
Stevens	Y	Y	Y	Y	Y	Y	Y	Y
ARIZONA								
Kyl	Y	Y	Y	Y	N	Y	N	N
McCain	Y	Y	Y	Y	N	Y	N	Y
ARKANSAS								
Hutchinson	Y	Y	Y	N	N	Y	N	Y
Bumpers	Y	Y	Y	N	N	N	Y	Y
CALIFORNIA								
Boxer	Y	Y	Y	N	N	N	Y	Y
Feinstein	Y	Y	Y	N	N	N	Y	Y
COLORADO								
Allard	Y	Y	N	Y	Y	Y	N	Y
Campbell	Y	Y	Y	Y	Y	Y	Y	Y
CONNECTICUT								
Dodd	Y	Y	Y	N	Y	N	Y	N
Lieberman	Y	Y	Y	N	Y	N	Y	N
DELAWARE								
Roth	Y	Y	Y	N	Y	Y	N	Y
Biden	Y	Y	Y	N	Y	N	Y	Y
FLORIDA								
Mack	Y	Y	Y	Y	N	Y	N	Y
Graham	Y	Y	Y	N	N	N	Y	N
GEORGIA								
Coverdell	Y	Y	Y	Y	N	Y	N	Y
Cleland	Y	Y	Y	N	N	N	Y	Y
HAWAII								
Akaka	Y	Y	Y	N	Y	N	Y	Y
Inouye	Y	Y	Y	Y	Y	N	Y	Y
IDAHO								
Craig	Y	Y	Y	Y	N	Y	N	Y
Kempthorne	Y	Y	Y	Y	N	Y	N	Y
ILLINOIS								
Durbin	Y	Y	Y	N	Y	N	Y	N
Moseley-Braun	Y	Y	Y	N	Y	N	Y	N
INDIANA								
Coats	Y	Y	N	Y	N	Y	N	Y
Lugar	Y	Y	Y	Y	N	Y	Y	Y
IOWA								
Grassley	Y	Y	Y	Y	Y	Y	N	Y
Harkin	Y	Y	Y	N	Y	N	Y	Y
KANSAS								
Brownback	Y	Y	Y	Y	Y	Y	N	Y
Roberts	Y	Y	Y	Y	Y	Y	Y	Y
KENTUCKY								
McConnell	Y	Y	Y	Y	N	Y	N	Y
Ford	Y	Y	Y	N	N	N	Y	Y
LOUISIANA								
Breaux	Y	Y	Y	N	N	N	Y	Y
Landrieu	Y	Y	Y	N	N	N	Y	Y
MAINE								
Collins	Y	Y	Y	N	Y	Y	Y	Y
Snowe	Y	Y	Y	N	Y	Y	Y	Y
MARYLAND								
Mikulski	Y	Y	Y	N	Y	N	Y	N
Sarbanes	Y	Y	Y	N	Y	N	Y	N
MASSACHUSETTS								
Kennedy	Y	Y	Y	N	Y	N	Y	Y
Kerry	Y	Y	Y	N	Y	N	Y	Y
MICHIGAN								
Abraham	Y	Y	Y	Y	N	Y	N	Y
Levin	Y	Y	Y	N	N	N	Y	N
MINNESOTA								
Grams	Y	Y	Y	Y	Y	Y	N	Y
Wellstone	Y	Y	Y	N	Y	N	Y	Y
MISSISSIPPI								
Cochran	Y	Y	Y	Y	N	Y	Y	Y
Lott	Y	Y	Y	Y	N	Y	N	Y
MISSOURI								
Ashcroft	Y	Y	N	Y	N	Y	N	Y
Bond	Y	Y	Y	Y	N	Y	Y	Y
MONTANA								
Burns	Y	Y	Y	Y	Y	Y	N	Y
Baucus	Y	Y	Y	N	Y	N	Y	Y
NEBRASKA								
Hagel	Y	Y	Y	Y	Y	Y	N	N
Kerrey	Y	Y	Y	N	Y	N	Y	Y
NEVADA								
Bryan	Y	Y	Y	N	Y	N	Y	Y
Reid	Y	Y	Y	N	Y	N	Y	Y
NEW HAMPSHIRE								
Gregg	Y	Y	N	Y	Y	Y	N	N
Smith	Y	Y	N	Y	Y	Y	N	N
NEW JERSEY								
Lautenberg	Y	Y	Y	N	Y	N	Y	N
Torricelli	Y	Y	Y	N	Y	N	Y	Y
NEW MEXICO								
Domenici	Y	Y	Y	Y	Y	Y	Y	Y
Bingaman	?	Y	Y	N	Y	N	Y	Y
NEW YORK								
D'Amato	Y	Y	Y	Y	Y	Y	Y	Y
Moynihan	Y	Y	Y	N	Y	N	Y	Y
NORTH CAROLINA								
Faircloth	Y	Y	N	Y	N	Y	N	N
Helms	Y	Y	Y	Y	N	Y	N	N
NORTH DAKOTA								
Conrad	Y	Y	Y	Y	Y	N	Y	Y
Dorgan	Y	Y	Y	Y	Y	N	Y	Y
OHIO								
DeWine	Y	Y	Y	Y	N	Y	N	Y
Glenn	Y	Y	Y	N	N	N	Y	Y
OKLAHOMA								
Inhofe	Y	Y	N	Y	N	Y	N	Y
Nickles	Y	Y	N	Y	N	Y	N	N
OREGON								
Smith	Y	Y	Y	Y	N	Y	Y	Y
Wyden	Y	Y	Y	N	N	N	Y	Y
PENNSYLVANIA								
Santorum	Y	Y	Y	Y	N	Y	N	N
Specter	Y	Y	Y	Y	N	Y	Y	Y
RHODE ISLAND								
Chafee	Y	Y	Y	N	Y	Y	Y	Y
Reed	Y	Y	Y	N	Y	N	Y	Y
SOUTH CAROLINA								
Thurmond	Y	Y	Y	Y	N	Y	N	Y
Hollings	Y	Y	Y	N	N	N	Y	Y
SOUTH DAKOTA								
Daschle	Y	Y	Y	N	Y	N	Y	Y
Johnson	Y	Y	Y	N	Y	N	Y	Y
TENNESSEE								
Frist	Y	Y	Y	N	N	Y	N	Y
Thompson	Y	Y	Y	Y	N	Y	N	Y
TEXAS								
Gramm	Y	Y	N	Y	N	Y	N	N
Hutchison	?	Y	Y	Y	N	Y	N	Y
UTAH								
Bennett	Y	Y	Y	Y	Y	Y	Y	Y
Hatch	Y	Y	Y	Y	Y	Y	Y	Y
VERMONT								
Jeffords	Y	Y	Y	N	Y	Y	Y	Y
Leahy	Y	Y	Y	N	Y	N	Y	Y
VIRGINIA								
Warner	Y	Y	Y	Y	N	Y	N	Y
Robb	Y	Y	Y	N	N	N	Y	Y
WASHINGTON								
Gorton	Y	Y	Y	Y	Y	Y	Y	Y
Murray	Y	Y	Y	N	Y	N	Y	Y
WEST VIRGINIA								
Byrd	Y	Y	Y	N	Y	N	Y	N
Rockefeller	Y	Y	Y	N	Y	N	Y	Y
WISCONSIN								
Feingold	Y	Y	Y	N	N	N	N	N
Kohl	Y	Y	Y	N	N	N	N	N
WYOMING								
Enzi	Y	Y	N	Y	Y	Y	N	Y
Thomas	Y	Y	N	Y	Y	Y	N	Y

KEY

Y Voted for (yea).
Paired for.
+ Announced for.
N Voted against (nay).
X Paired against.
– Announced against.
P Voted "present."
C Voted "present" to avoid possible conflict of interest.
? Did not vote or otherwise make a position known.

Democrats *Republicans*

ND Northern Democrats SD Southern Democrats

Southern states - Ala., Ark., Fla., Ga., Ky., La., Miss., N.C., Okla., S.C., Tenn., Texas, Va.

56. S 672. Supplemental Fiscal 1997 Appropriations/Credit Availability. Grams, R-Minn., amendment to allow the Federal Reserve Board of Governors to facilitate increased credit allowances for residents in federally declared disaster areas. Adopted 98-0: R 54-0; D 44-0 (ND 36-0, SD 8-0), May 6, 1997.

57. S 672. Supplemental Fiscal 1997 Appropriations/Cloture. Motion to invoke cloture (thus limiting debate) on the bill to provide $8.4 billion in emergency spending primarily for flood relief and foreign peacekeeping operations. Motion agreed to 100-0: R 55-0; D 45-0 (ND 37-0, SD 8-0), May 7, 1997. Three-fifths of the total Senate (60) is required to invoke cloture.

58. S 672. Supplemental Fiscal 1997 Appropriations/Benefits for Legal Immigrants. D'Amato, R-N.Y., amendment to extend Supplemental Security Income and food stamps benefits for legal immigrants through Sept. 30, 1997. Under the 1996 welfare law (PL 104-193), legal immigrants would lose their benefits Aug. 22, 1997. Adopted 89-11: R 44-11; D 45-0 (ND 37-0, SD 8-0), May 7, 1997.

59. S 672. Supplemental Fiscal 1997 Appropriations/Highway Rights. Stevens, R-Alaska, motion to table (kill) the Bumpers, D-Ark., amendment to strike a section of the bill that would delete an Interior Department directive and allow states to claim rights-of-way on federal lands. Motion agreed to 51-49: R 48-7; D 3-42 (ND 3-34, SD 0-8), May 7, 1997.

60. S 672. Supplemental Fiscal 1997 Appropriations/Highway Funds. Stevens, R-Alaska, motion to table (kill) the Warner, R-Va., amendment to ensure that $794 million for highway improvement is distributed to states according to 1991 funding formulas. Motion agreed to 54-46: R 24-31; D 30-15 (ND 30-7, SD 0-8), May 8, 1997.

61. S 672. Supplemental Fiscal 1997 Appropriations/Automatic Continuing Resolution. Stevens, R-Alaska, motion to table (kill) the Byrd, D-W.Va., amendment to strike the section that would provide funding for federal programs that lack appropriations authority at the start of the next fiscal year at 100 percent of their fiscal 1997 levels until fiscal 1998 appropriations are enacted. Motion agreed to 55-45: R 55-0; D 0-45 (ND 0-37, SD 0-8), May 8, 1997. A "nay" was a vote in support of the president's position.

62. S 672. Supplemental Fiscal 1997 Appropriations/Spending Reduction. Stevens, R-Alaska, motion to table (kill) the Gramm, R-Texas, amendment to reduce all non-defense discretionary spending by the percentage necessary to offset the non-defense budget authority provided by the bill. Motion agreed to 62-38: R 19-36; D 43-2 (ND 35-2, SD 8-0), May 8, 1997.

63. S 672. Supplemental Fiscal 1997 Appropriations/Third Reading. Stevens, R-Alaska, motion to advance to third reading (thus ending the possibility of amendment) on the bill to provide about $8.4 billion in additional funds for fiscal 1997, including $5.6 billion in emergency disaster aid for flood-stricken regions and $1.8 billion to finance peacekeeping operations in Bosnia. Motion agreed to 78-22: R 45-10; D 33-12 (ND 26-11, SD 7-1), May 8, 1997.

SENATE VOTES 64, 65, 66, 67, 68, 69, 70

	64	65	66	67	68	69	70
ALABAMA							
Sessions	N	N	Y	Y	Y	N	N
Shelby	N	N	Y	Y	Y	N	N
ALASKA							
Murkowski	N	N	Y	Y	Y	N	N
Stevens	Y	Y	Y	Y	Y	N	N
ARIZONA							
Kyl	N	N	Y	Y	Y	N	N
McCain	N	N	Y	Y	Y	N	N
ARKANSAS							
Hutchinson	Y	Y	Y	Y	Y	N	N
Bumpers	Y	Y	Y	Y	N	N	Y
CALIFORNIA							
Boxer	Y	Y	Y	Y	N	Y	N
Feinstein	N	Y	Y	Y	N	Y	N
COLORADO							
Allard	N	N	Y	Y	Y	N	N
Campbell	Y	Y	Y	Y	Y	N	N
CONNECTICUT							
Dodd	Y	Y	Y	Y	N	N	Y
Lieberman	N	Y	Y	Y	N	N	Y
DELAWARE							
Roth	N	Y	Y	Y	Y	N	N
Biden	Y	Y	Y	Y	N	N	Y
FLORIDA							
Mack	Y	Y	Y	Y	Y	N	N
Graham	N	Y	Y	Y	N	N	Y
GEORGIA							
Coverdell	Y	Y	Y	Y	Y	N	N
Cleland	Y	Y	Y	Y	N	Y	Y
HAWAII							
Akaka	Y	Y	Y	Y	N	Y	Y
Inouye	Y	Y	Y	Y	N	Y	Y
IDAHO							
Craig	Y	Y	Y	Y	Y	N	N
Kempthorne	Y	Y	Y	Y	Y	N	N
ILLINOIS							
Durbin	Y	Y	Y	Y	N	Y	Y
Moseley-Braun	Y	Y	Y	Y	N	Y	Y
INDIANA							
Coats	Y	Y	Y	Y	Y	N	N
Lugar	N	Y	Y	Y	Y	N	N
IOWA							
Grassley	N	Y	Y	Y	Y	N	N
Harkin	Y	Y	Y	Y	N	N	Y
KANSAS							
Brownback	N	N	Y	Y	Y	N	N
Roberts	N	N	Y	Y	Y	N	N
KENTUCKY							
McConnell	Y	Y	Y	Y	Y	N	N
Ford	Y	Y	Y	Y	N	N	N
LOUISIANA							
Breaux	Y	Y	Y	Y	N	N	N
Landrieu	Y	Y	Y	Y	N	N	Y
MAINE							
Collins	Y	Y	Y	Y	Y	N	Y
Snowe	Y	Y	Y	Y	Y	N	Y
MARYLAND							
Mikulski	Y	Y	Y	Y	N	Y	Y
Sarbanes	Y	Y	Y	Y	N	Y	Y
MASSACHUSETTS							
Kennedy	Y	Y	Y	Y	N	Y	Y
Kerry	Y	Y	Y	Y	N	Y	Y
MICHIGAN							
Abraham	N	Y	Y	Y	Y	N	N
Levin	Y	Y	Y	Y	N	Y	Y
MINNESOTA							
Grams	N	N	Y	Y	Y	N	N
Wellstone	Y	Y	Y	Y	N	Y	Y
MISSISSIPPI							
Cochran	N	Y	Y	Y	Y	N	N
Lott	Y	Y	Y	Y	Y	N	N
MISSOURI							
Ashcroft	N	N	Y	Y	Y	N	N
Bond	N	N	Y	Y	Y	N	N
MONTANA							
Burns	N	Y	Y	Y	Y	N	N
Baucus	Y	Y	Y	Y	N	Y	Y
NEBRASKA							
Hagel	N	N	Y	Y	Y	N	N
Kerrey	Y	Y	Y	Y	N	Y	Y
NEVADA							
Bryan	N	Y	Y	Y	N	Y	Y
Reid	N	Y	Y	Y	N	N	N
NEW HAMPSHIRE							
Gregg	N	N	Y	Y	Y	N	N
Smith	N	N	Y	Y	Y	N	N
NEW JERSEY							
Lautenberg	Y	Y	Y	Y	N	Y	N
Torricelli	N	Y	Y	Y	N	Y	Y
NEW MEXICO							
Domenici	Y	N	Y	Y	Y	N	N
Bingaman	Y	Y	Y	Y	N	Y	Y
NEW YORK							
D'Amato	Y	Y	Y	Y	N	N	N
Moynihan	Y	Y	Y	Y	N	N	N
NORTH CAROLINA							
Faircloth	N	N	Y	Y	Y	N	N
Helms	N	N	Y	Y	Y	N	N
NORTH DAKOTA							
Conrad	N	Y	Y	Y	N	N	N
Dorgan	N	Y	Y	Y	N	N	N
OHIO							
DeWine	Y	Y	Y	Y	Y	N	N
Glenn	Y	Y	Y	Y	N	Y	N
OKLAHOMA							
Inhofe	N	N	Y	Y	Y	N	N
Nickles	N	N	Y	Y	Y	N	N
OREGON							
Smith	N	Y	Y	Y	Y	N	N
Wyden	Y	Y	Y	Y	N	Y	Y
PENNSYLVANIA							
Santorum	N	Y	Y	Y	Y	N	N
Specter	N	N	Y	Y	N	N	N
RHODE ISLAND							
Chafee	Y	Y	Y	Y	Y	Y	N
Reed	Y	Y	Y	Y	N	Y	Y
SOUTH CAROLINA							
Thurmond	N	N	Y	Y	Y	N	N
Hollings	N	Y	Y	Y	N	N	N
SOUTH DAKOTA							
Daschle	Y	Y	Y	Y	N	N	Y
Johnson	N	N	Y	Y	N	N	Y
TENNESSEE							
Frist	Y	Y	Y	Y	Y	N	N
Thompson	N	N	Y	Y	Y	N	N
TEXAS							
Gramm	N	N	Y	Y	Y	N	N
Hutchison	N	N	Y	Y	Y	N	N
UTAH							
Bennett	N	N	Y	Y	Y	N	N
Hatch	N	N	Y	Y	Y	N	N
VERMONT							
Jeffords	Y	Y	Y	Y	Y	Y	N
Leahy	Y	Y	Y	Y	N	Y	Y
VIRGINIA							
Warner	N	N	Y	Y	Y	N	N
Robb	Y	Y	Y	Y	N	Y	Y
WASHINGTON							
Gorton	N	N	N	Y	Y	N	N
Murray	Y	Y	Y	Y	N	Y	Y
WEST VIRGINIA							
Byrd	N	Y	Y	Y	N	N	Y
Rockefeller	?	?	?	Y	N	Y	Y
WISCONSIN							
Feingold	Y	Y	Y	Y	N	N	Y
Kohl	Y	Y	Y	Y	N	N	Y
WYOMING							
Enzi	N	N	Y	Y	Y	N	N
Thomas	N	N	Y	Y	Y	N	N

KEY

- Y Voted for (yea).
- # Paired for.
- + Announced for.
- N Voted against (nay).
- X Paired against.
- – Announced against.
- P Voted "present."
- C Voted "present" to avoid possible conflict of interest.
- ? Did not vote or otherwise make a position known.

Democrats *Republicans*

ND Northern Democrats SD Southern Democrats

Southern states - Ala., Ark., Fla., Ga., Ky., La., Miss., N.C., Okla., S.C., Tenn., Texas, Va.

64. S 717. Individuals with Disabilities Education Act Reauthorization/Disciplinary Rules. Jeffords, R-Vt., motion to table (kill) the Gorton, R-Wash., amendment to allow state and local boards of education to establish uniform discipline policies within their jurisdictions. Motion agreed to 51-48: R 18-37; D 33-11 (ND 27-9, SD 6-2), May 14, 1997.

65. S 717. Individuals with Disabilities Education Act Reauthorization/Court Review. Jeffords, R-Vt., motion to table (kill) the Smith, R-N.H., amendment to require a court making an award pursuant to the disability law to consider how it will affect students in the penalized district. Motion agreed to 68-31: R 25-30; D 43-1 (ND 35-1, SD 8-0), May 14, 1997.

66. HR 5. Individuals with Disabilities Education Act Reauthorization/Passage. Passage of the bill to authorize such sums as necessary for the Individuals with Disabilities Education Act, allow schools more flexibility to discipline disabled students and change the program's grant funding formula once the annual total appropriation exceeds $4.9 billion. Passed (thus cleared for the president) 98-1: R 54-1; D 44-0 (ND 36-0, SD 8-0), May 14, 1997. A "yea" was a vote in support of the president's position.

67. CFE Treaty Amendment/Adoption. Adoption of the resolution of ratification revising the Conventional Forces in Europe treaty to allow Russia to keep more weapons on its Baltic and Caucasian frontiers. The resolution requires the president to seek Senate approval for certain changes to the 1972 Anti-Ballistic Missile treaty. Adopted 100-0: R 55-0; D 45-0 (ND 37-0, SD 8-0), May 14, 1997. A two-thirds majority of those present and voting (67 in this case) is required for adoption of resolutions of ratification.

68. S 4. Compensatory Time, Flexible Credit/Cloture. Motion to invoke cloture (thus limiting debate) on the bill to amend the Fair Labor Standards Act of 1938 to allow private-sector employees to choose compensatory time off or flexible credit hour programs instead of overtime pay. Motion rejected 53-47: R 53-2; D 0-45 (ND 0-37, SD 0-8), May 15, 1997. Three-fifths of the total Senate (60) is required to invoke cloture.

69. HR 1122. Abortion Procedure Ban/Feinstein Substitute. Feinstein, D-Calif., substitute amendment to prohibit post-viability abortions except when necessary to save a woman's life or to prevent "serious adverse health consequences." Rejected 28-72: R 2-53; D 26-19 (ND 24-13, SD 2-6), May 15, 1997.

70. HR 1122. Abortion Procedure Ban/Daschle Substitute. Daschle, D-S.D., substitute amendment to ban post-viability abortions unless the mother's life is at risk or she faces "grievous" injury to her physical health. Rejected 36-64: R 2-53; D 34-11 (ND 29-8, SD 5-3), May 15, 1997. A "yea" was a vote in support of the president's position.

SENATE VOTES 71, 72, 73, 74, 75, 76, 77, 78

	71	72	73	74	75	76	77	78
ALABAMA								
Sessions	Y	Y	N	N	Y	Y	N	Y
Shelby	Y	Y	Y	N	Y	Y	N	Y
ALASKA								
Murkowski	Y	Y	N	N	Y	Y	Y	Y
Stevens	Y	Y	Y	N	Y	Y	Y	Y
ARIZONA								
Kyl	Y	Y	N	N	Y	Y	N	Y
McCain	Y	Y	N	N	Y	Y	N	Y
ARKANSAS								
Hutchinson	Y	Y	N	N	Y	Y	N	Y
Bumpers	N	N	Y	N	Y	N	Y	Y
CALIFORNIA								
Boxer	N	N	Y	N	Y	N	Y	Y
Feinstein	N	N	Y	N	Y	Y	Y	Y
COLORADO								
Allard	Y	Y	N	N	Y	Y	N	Y
Campbell	Y	Y	Y	N	Y	Y	N	Y
CONNECTICUT								
Dodd	N	N	Y	N	Y	N	Y	Y
Lieberman	N	N	Y	N	Y	Y	Y	Y
DELAWARE								
Roth	Y	Y	Y	N	Y	Y	N	Y
Biden	Y	N	Y	N	Y	N	Y	Y
FLORIDA								
Mack	Y	Y	Y	N	Y	Y	N	Y
Graham	N	N	Y	N	Y	N	Y	Y
GEORGIA								
Coverdell	Y	Y	N	N	Y	Y	N	Y
Cleland	N	Y	Y	N	Y	Y	Y	Y
HAWAII								
Akaka	N	N	Y	N	Y	N	Y	Y
Inouye	N	N	Y	N	Y	N	Y	Y
IDAHO								
Craig	Y	Y	N	N	Y	Y	N	Y
Kempthorne	Y	Y	N	N	Y	Y	?	Y
ILLINOIS								
Durbin	N	N	Y	N	Y	N	Y	Y
Moseley-Braun	N	N	Y	N	Y	N	Y	Y
INDIANA								
Coats	Y	Y	N	N	Y	Y	N	Y
Lugar	Y	Y	Y	N	Y	N	Y	Y
IOWA								
Grassley	Y	Y	N	N	Y	Y	Y	Y
Harkin	N	N	?	?	Y	N	Y	Y
KANSAS								
Brownback	Y	Y	N	N	Y	Y	N	Y
Roberts	Y	Y	Y	N	Y	Y	Y	Y
KENTUCKY								
McConnell	Y	Y	N	N	Y	Y	N	Y
Ford	Y	Y	Y	N	Y	Y	Y	Y
LOUISIANA								
Breaux	Y	Y	Y	N	Y	Y	Y	Y
Landrieu	Y	N	Y	N	Y	N	Y	Y
MAINE								
Collins	N	Y	Y	N	Y	Y	Y	Y
Snowe	N	Y	Y	N	Y	Y	Y	Y
MARYLAND								
Mikulski	N	N	Y	N	Y	N	Y	Y
Sarbanes	N	N	Y	N	Y	N	Y	Y
MASSACHUSETTS								
Kennedy	N	N	Y	N	Y	N	Y	Y
Kerry	N	N	Y	N	Y	N	Y	Y
MICHIGAN								
Abraham	Y	Y	N	N	Y	Y	N	Y
Levin	N	N	Y	N	Y	N	Y	Y
MINNESOTA								
Grams	Y	Y	N	N	Y	Y	N	Y
Wellstone	N	N	Y	N	Y	N	Y	Y
MISSISSIPPI								
Cochran	Y	Y	Y	N	Y	Y	Y	Y
Lott	Y	Y	Y	N	Y	Y	Y	Y
MISSOURI								
Ashcroft	Y	Y	N	N	Y	Y	N	Y
Bond	Y	Y	Y	N	Y	Y	Y	Y
MONTANA								
Burns	Y	Y	N	N	Y	Y	N	Y
Baucus	N	Y	Y	N	Y	N	Y	Y
NEBRASKA								
Hagel	Y	Y	Y	N	N	Y	Y	Y
Kerrey	N	N	Y	N	Y	N	Y	Y
NEVADA								
Bryan	N	N	Y	N	Y	N	Y	Y
Reid	Y	N	Y	Y	Y	N	Y	Y
NEW HAMPSHIRE								
Gregg	Y	Y	N	N	Y	Y	N	+
Smith	Y	Y	N	N	Y	Y	N	Y
NEW JERSEY								
Lautenberg	N	Y	Y	N	Y	N	Y	Y
Torricelli	N	N	Y	N	Y	N	Y	Y
NEW MEXICO								
Domenici	Y	Y	Y	N	Y	Y	Y	Y
Bingaman	N	N	Y	N	Y	N	Y	Y
NEW YORK								
D'Amato	Y	N	Y	N	Y	N	Y	Y
Moynihan	Y	N	Y	Y	Y	N	Y	Y
NORTH CAROLINA								
Faircloth	Y	Y	N	N	Y	Y	N	Y
Helms	Y	Y	N	N	Y	Y	N	+
NORTH DAKOTA								
Conrad	Y	N	Y	Y	Y	N	Y	Y
Dorgan	Y	N	Y	Y	Y	N	Y	Y
OHIO								
DeWine	Y	Y	Y	N	Y	N	Y	Y
Glenn	N	N	Y	N	Y	N	Y	Y
OKLAHOMA								
Inhofe	Y	Y	N	N	Y	Y	N	Y
Nickles	Y	Y	N	N	Y	Y	N	Y
OREGON								
Smith	Y	Y	Y	N	Y	N	Y	Y
Wyden	N	N	Y	N	Y	N	Y	Y
PENNSYLVANIA								
Santorum	Y	Y	N	N	Y	Y	N	Y
Specter	Y	N	Y	N	Y	N	Y	Y
RHODE ISLAND								
Chafee	N	Y	Y	N	Y	N	Y	Y
Reed	N	N	Y	N	Y	N	Y	Y
SOUTH CAROLINA								
Thurmond	Y	Y	Y	N	Y	Y	N	Y
Hollings	Y	N	Y	Y	Y	Y	Y	Y
SOUTH DAKOTA								
Daschle	Y	Y	Y	N	Y	N	Y	Y
Johnson	Y	Y	Y	N	Y	N	Y	Y
TENNESSEE								
Frist	Y	Y	Y	N	Y	Y	Y	Y
Thompson	Y	Y	Y	N	N	Y	Y	Y
TEXAS								
Gramm	Y	Y	N	N	Y	Y	N	Y
Hutchison	Y	Y	N	N	Y	Y	N	Y
UTAH								
Bennett	Y	Y	Y	N	Y	Y	Y	Y
Hatch	Y	Y	N	N	Y	N	N	Y
VERMONT								
Jeffords	N	N	Y	N	Y	N	Y	Y
Leahy	Y	N	Y	N	Y	N	Y	Y
VIRGINIA								
Warner	Y	Y	Y	N	Y	Y	Y	Y
Robb	N	Y	Y	Y	Y	Y	Y	Y
WASHINGTON								
Gorton	Y	Y	Y	N	Y	Y	Y	Y
Murray	N	N	Y	N	Y	N	Y	Y
WEST VIRGINIA								
Byrd	Y	N	Y	Y	Y	N	Y	Y
Rockefeller	N	Y	Y	N	Y	N	Y	Y
WISCONSIN								
Feingold	N	N	Y	Y	Y	N	Y	Y
Kohl	N	N	Y	N	Y	Y	Y	Y
WYOMING								
Enzi	Y	Y	N	N	Y	Y	N	Y
Thomas	Y	Y	N	N	Y	Y	N	Y

KEY

- Y Voted for (yea).
- # Paired for.
- + Announced for.
- N Voted against (nay).
- X Paired against.
- – Announced against.
- P Voted "present."
- C Voted "present" to avoid possible conflict of interest.
- ? Did not vote or otherwise make a position known.

Democrats *Republicans*

ND Northern Democrats SD Southern Democrats

Southern states - Ala., Ark., Fla., Ga., Ky., La., Miss., N.C., Okla., S.C., Tenn., Texas, Va.

71. H 1122. Abortion Procedure Ban/Passage. Passage of the bill to impose penalties on doctors who perform certain abortion procedures, in which the person performing the abortion partially delivers the fetus before completing the abortion. An exception would be granted where the procedure was necessary to save the life of the woman. The bill was amended to clarify the definition of the procedure and to allow an accused doctor a hearing before a state medical board prior to trial. Passed 64-36: R 51-4; D 13-32 (ND 9-28, SD 4-4), May 20, 1997. A "nay" was a vote in support of the president's position.

72. S Con Res 27. Fiscal 1998 Budget Resolution/Children's Programs. Domenici, R-N.M., motion to table (kill) the Dodd, D-Conn., amendment to raise discretionary spending caps by $15.8 billion over five years and express the sense of the Senate that there should be increased funding for children's programs, with offsets coming from ending corporate tax breaks. Motion agreed to 61-39: R 52-3; D 9-36 (ND 5-32, SD 4-4), May 20, 1997.

73. S Con Res 27. Fiscal 1998 Budget Resolution/Revenue Shortfalls. Domenici, R-N.M., motion to table (kill) the Allard, R-Colo., amendment to ensure that revenue shortfalls in 1999-2002 are offset by automatic reductions in discretionary spending. Motion agreed to 70-29: R 26-29; D 44-0 (ND 36-0, SD 8-0), May 20, 1997.

74. S Con Res 27. Fiscal 1998 Budget Resolution/Presidential Initiatives. Hollings, D-S.C., amendment to strike $85 billion in tax cuts and eliminate $31.2 billion in presidential initiatives, which with interest savings would produce additional deficit reduction of $130 billion over five years. Rejected 8-91: R 0-55; D 8-36 (ND 6-30, SD 2-6), May 20, 1997.

75. S Con Res 27. Fiscal 1998 Budget Resolution/Funding Levels. Domenici, R-N.M., amendment to reiterate that $16 billion would be spent over five years to provide additional health insurance for up to 5 million children. Adopted 98-2: R 53-2; D 45-0 (ND 37-0, SD 8-0), May 21, 1997.

76. S Con Res 27. Fiscal 1998 Budget Resolution/Children's Health Insurance. Domenici, R-N.M., motion to table (kill) the Hatch, R-Utah, amendment to raise an additional $30 billion in revenue by increasing the tobacco tax. Of that, $20 billion would be used to provide health insurance for low- and moderate-income children and $10 billion to reduce the deficit. Motion agreed to 55-45: R 47-8; D 8-37 (ND 3-34, SD 5-3), May 21, 1997. A "yea" was a vote in support of the president's position.

77. S Con Res 27. Fiscal 1998 Budget Resolution/Fiscal 1997 Levels. Lautenberg, D-N.J., motion to table (kill) the Gramm, R-Texas, amendment to limit non-defense discretionary spending to the levels proposed by President Clinton in his fiscal 1997 budget request and allow for a net tax cut of $161 billion over five years. Motion agreed to 68-31: R 23-31; D 45-0 (ND 37-0, SD 8-0), May 21, 1997.

78. S Con Res 27. Fiscal 1998 Budget Resolution/NIH Funding. Mack, R-Fla., amendment to express the sense of the Senate that funding for the National Institutes of Health should be increased by $2 billion in fiscal 1998. Adopted 98-0: R 53-0; D 45-0 (ND 37-0, SD 8-0), May 21, 1997.

SENATE VOTES 79, 80, 81, 82, 83, 84, 85

	79	80	81	82	83	84	85
ALABAMA							
Sessions	Y	N	Y	Y	Y	Y	N
Shelby	Y	N	Y	Y	Y	Y	N
ALASKA							
Murkowski	Y	Y	Y	Y	Y	Y	N
Stevens	Y	Y	Y	Y	Y	Y	Y
ARIZONA							
Kyl	Y	Y	Y	Y	Y	Y	N
McCain	Y	Y	Y	Y	Y	Y	N
ARKANSAS							
Hutchinson	Y	N	Y	Y	Y	Y	N
Bumpers	N	N	N	N	N	Y	Y
CALIFORNIA							
Boxer	N	N	N	Y	N	Y	Y
Feinstein	N	Y	Y	Y	N	Y	Y
COLORADO							
Allard	Y	Y	Y	Y	Y	Y	N
Campbell	N	Y	Y	Y	N	Y	Y
CONNECTICUT							
Dodd	N	N	N	Y	N	N	Y
Lieberman	Y	Y	Y	Y	N	Y	Y
DELAWARE							
Roth	Y	Y	Y	Y	N	N	N
Biden	N	Y	Y	Y	N	Y	Y
FLORIDA							
Mack	Y	Y	Y	Y	Y	Y	N
Graham	N	N	N	N	N	N	Y
GEORGIA							
Coverdell	Y	Y	Y	Y	Y	Y	N
Cleland	Y	Y	N	Y	N	Y	Y
HAWAII							
Akaka	N	N	N	N	N	Y	Y
Inouye	N	N	N	Y	N	Y	Y
IDAHO							
Craig	Y	Y	Y	Y	Y	Y	N
Kempthorne	Y	N	Y	Y	Y	Y	N
ILLINOIS							
Durbin	N	Y	Y	Y	N	N	Y
Moseley-Braun	N	Y	N	N	N	N	Y
INDIANA							
Coats	Y	N	?	?	?	?	?
Lugar	Y	Y	Y	Y	N	Y	Y
IOWA							
Grassley	Y	Y	Y	Y	Y	Y	N
Harkin	–	N	N	Y	Y	N	Y
KANSAS							
Brownback	Y	Y	Y	Y	Y	Y	N
Roberts	Y	Y	Y	Y	N	Y	Y
KENTUCKY							
McConnell	Y	N	Y	Y	Y	Y	N
Ford	Y	Y	Y	Y	N	N	Y
LOUISIANA							
Breaux	Y	Y	Y	Y	N	Y	Y
Landrieu	N	Y	Y	Y	N	Y	Y
MAINE							
Collins	Y	Y	Y	Y	N	Y	Y
Snowe	Y	Y	Y	Y	Y	Y	N
MARYLAND							
Mikulski	N	N	N	Y	N	Y	Y
Sarbanes	N	N	N	N	N	Y	Y
MASSACHUSETTS							
Kennedy	N	N	N	N	N	N	Y
Kerry	N	N	Y	Y	N	N	Y
MICHIGAN							
Abraham	Y	N	Y	Y	Y	Y	N
Levin	N	N	N	N	N	N	Y
MINNESOTA							
Grams	Y	N	Y	Y	Y	Y	N
Wellstone	N	N	N	Y	N	N	Y
MISSISSIPPI							
Cochran	Y	Y	Y	Y	N	Y	N
Lott	Y	Y	Y	Y	N	Y	N
MISSOURI							
Ashcroft	Y	N	Y	Y	Y	Y	N
Bond	Y	Y	Y	Y	Y	Y	Y
MONTANA							
Burns	Y	N	Y	Y	Y	Y	N
Baucus	N	N	Y	Y	N	Y	Y
NEBRASKA							
Hagel	Y	Y	Y	Y	Y	Y	N
Kerrey	N	N	Y	N	N	Y	Y
NEVADA							
Bryan	N	N	Y	N	N	Y	Y
Reid	N	N	N	N	N	Y	Y
NEW HAMPSHIRE							
Gregg	Y	Y	Y	Y	Y	Y	N
Smith	Y	Y	Y	Y	Y	Y	N
NEW JERSEY							
Lautenberg	N	Y	Y	Y	N	Y	Y
Torricelli	N	N	N	Y	N	Y	N
NEW MEXICO							
Domenici	Y	Y	Y	Y	N	Y	Y
Bingaman	N	N	Y	Y	N	Y	Y
NEW YORK							
D'Amato	N	Y	Y	Y	N	Y	N
Moynihan	N	Y	N	N	N	N	Y
NORTH CAROLINA							
Faircloth	Y	N	Y	Y	Y	Y	N
Helms	Y	N	Y	Y	Y	Y	N
NORTH DAKOTA							
Conrad	N	N	N	N	N	Y	Y
Dorgan	N	N	N	Y	N	Y	Y
OHIO							
DeWine	Y	N	Y	Y	N	Y	N
Glenn	N	N	N	N	N	N	N
OKLAHOMA							
Inhofe	Y	N	Y	Y	Y	Y	N
Nickles	Y	Y	Y	Y	Y	Y	N
OREGON							
Smith	Y	Y	Y	Y	Y	Y	Y
Wyden	N	N	N	Y	Y	Y	N
PENNSYLVANIA							
Santorum	Y	Y	Y	Y	Y	Y	N
Specter	N	N	Y	Y	N	Y	Y
RHODE ISLAND							
Chafee	Y	Y	Y	Y	N	N	Y
Reed	N	Y	N	Y	N	N	Y
SOUTH CAROLINA							
Thurmond	Y	N	Y	Y	Y	Y	N
Hollings	N	N	N	N	N	Y	Y
SOUTH DAKOTA							
Daschle	N	Y	Y	Y	N	Y	Y
Johnson	N	N	N	Y	N	Y	Y
TENNESSEE							
Frist	Y	Y	Y	Y	Y	Y	N
Thompson	Y	Y	Y	Y	Y	Y	N
TEXAS							
Gramm	Y	Y	Y	Y	Y	Y	N
Hutchison	Y	Y	Y	Y	Y	Y	N
UTAH							
Bennett	Y	Y	Y	Y	N	Y	Y
Hatch	Y	N	Y	Y	Y	Y	Y
VERMONT							
Jeffords	Y	N	Y	Y	N	Y	N
Leahy	N	N	Y	Y	N	Y	Y
VIRGINIA							
Warner	Y	N	Y	Y	Y	Y	N
Robb	N	N	Y	N	N	N	N
WASHINGTON							
Gorton	Y	Y	Y	Y	N	Y	Y
Murray	N	N	N	N	N	Y	Y
WEST VIRGINIA							
Byrd	N	N	N	N	N	Y	Y
Rockefeller	N	Y	Y	Y	N	Y	Y
WISCONSIN							
Feingold	N	Y	Y	N	N	Y	N
Kohl	N	Y	Y	Y	N	Y	N
WYOMING							
Enzi	Y	Y	Y	Y	Y	Y	N
Thomas	Y	N	Y	Y	Y	Y	N

KEY

- Y Voted for (yea).
- # Paired for.
- \+ Announced for.
- N Voted against (nay).
- X Paired against.
- – Announced against.
- P Voted "present."
- C Voted "present" to avoid possible conflict of interest.
- ? Did not vote or otherwise make a position known.

Democrats *Republicans*

ND Northern Democrats SD Southern Democrats

Southern states - Ala., Ark., Fla., Ga., Ky., La., Miss., N.C., Okla., S.C., Tenn., Texas, Va.

79. S Con Res 27. Fiscal 1998 Budget Resolution/School Infrastructure. Domenici, R-N.M., motion to table (kill) the Moseley-Braun, D-Ill., amendment to provide an additional $5 billion in revenue to help states and school districts repair and renovate dilapidated schools. Motion agreed to 56-43: R 52-3; D 4-40 (ND 1-35, SD 3-5), May 22, 1997.

80. S Con Res 27. Fiscal 1998 Budget Resolution/Highway Funds. Domenici, R-N.M., motion to table (kill) the Warner, R-Va., amendment to increase spending on transportation by $12 billion over five years. Motion agreed to 51-49: R 35-20; D 16-29 (ND 12-25, SD 4-4), May 22, 1997.

81. S Con Res 27. Fiscal 1998 Budget Resolution/Tax Increase. Domenici, R-N.M. motion to table (kill) the Bumpers, D-Ark., amendment to strike $85 billion in tax cuts and increase taxes by $30 billion over five years. Motion agreed to 73-26: R 54-0; D 19-26 (ND 15-22, SD 4-4), May 22, 1997.

82. S Con Res 27. Fiscal 1998 Budget Resolution/Tax Effectiveness. Domenici, R-N.M., motion to table (kill) the Bumpers, D-Ark., amendment to delay the effective dates of tax cuts until the federal budget is balanced. Motion agreed to 81-18: R 54-0; D 27-18 (ND 23-14, SD 4-4), May 22, 1997.

83. S Con Res 27. Fiscal 1998 Budget Resolution/Budget Act Waiver. Ashcroft, R-Mo., motion to waive the Budget Act with respect to the Lautenberg, D-N.J., point of order against the Ashcroft, R-Mo., amendment to require a three-fifths vote of both houses of Congress for any deficit spending after fiscal 2002. Motion rejected 41-58: R 39-15; D 2-43 (ND 2-35, SD 0-8), May 22, 1997. A three-fifths majority vote (60) of the total Senate is required to waive the Budget Act. (Subsequently, the chair upheld the Lautenberg point of order and the amendment fell.)

84. S Con Res 27. Fiscal 1998 Budget Resolution/Gasoline Taxes. Gramm, R-Texas, amendment to express the sense of the Senate that all revenues from federal gasoline taxes (including the 4.34 cents per gallon currently dedicated to deficit reduction) should be deposited into the Highway Trust Fund. Adopted 83-16: R 52-2; D 31-14 (ND 26-11, SD 5-3), May 22, 1997.

85. S Con Res 27. Fiscal 1998 Budget Resolution/Unified Budget. Lautenberg, D-N.J., motion to table (kill) the Inhofe, R-Okla., amendment to require a three-fifths vote for Senate consideration of any budget resolution after fiscal 2001 that would cause a deficit in the unified budget. Motion agreed to 52-47: R 13-41; D 39-6 (ND 32-5, SD 7-1), May 22, 1997.

SENATE VOTES 86, 87, 88, 89, 90, 91, 92

	86	87	88	89	90	91	92
ALABAMA							
Sessions	Y	N	Y	Y	N	Y	Y
Shelby	Y	N	Y	Y	Y	Y	Y
ALASKA							
Murkowski	Y	Y	Y	Y	Y	Y	Y
Stevens	Y	Y	Y	Y	Y	Y	Y
ARIZONA							
Kyl	Y	N	Y	Y	N	Y	N
McCain	Y	N	Y	Y	N	Y	Y
ARKANSAS							
Hutchinson	Y	N	Y	Y	N	Y	Y
Bumpers	N	N	N	N	Y	Y	N
CALIFORNIA							
Boxer	N	Y	N	N	Y	N	Y
Feinstein	Y	Y	N	N	Y	N	Y
COLORADO							
Allard	Y	N	Y	Y	N	Y	N
Campbell	Y	Y	Y	Y	Y	Y	Y
CONNECTICUT							
Dodd	Y	Y	N	N	Y	N	Y
Lieberman	Y	Y	N	N	Y	Y	Y
DELAWARE							
Roth	Y	Y	Y	Y	N	Y	Y
Biden	Y	Y	N	N	Y	Y	Y
FLORIDA							
Mack	Y	Y	Y	Y	Y	N	Y
Graham	Y	Y	N	N	Y	N	Y
GEORGIA							
Coverdell	Y	Y	Y	Y	N	Y	Y
Cleland	N	Y	N	N	Y	Y	Y
HAWAII							
Akaka	Y	Y	N	N	Y	N	Y
Inouye	Y	Y	N	N	Y	N	Y
IDAHO							
Craig	Y	N	Y	Y	Y	Y	Y
Kempthorne	Y	N	Y	Y	Y	Y	Y
ILLINOIS							
Durbin	N	Y	N	N	Y	N	Y
Moseley-Braun	Y	Y	N	N	Y	N	Y
INDIANA							
Coats	Y	Y	Y	Y	N	Y	N
Lugar	Y	Y	Y	Y	Y	Y	Y
IOWA							
Grassley	Y	Y	Y	Y	N	N	Y
Harkin	N	Y	N	N	Y	N	Y
KANSAS							
Brownback	Y	N	Y	Y	N	N	Y
Roberts	Y	Y	Y	Y	Y	Y	Y
KENTUCKY							
McConnell	Y	N	Y	Y	N	Y	Y
Ford	Y	Y	N	N	Y	Y	Y
LOUISIANA							
Breaux	Y	Y	N	N	Y	Y	Y
Landrieu	Y	Y	N	N	Y	Y	Y
MAINE							
Collins	Y	Y	Y	N	Y	N	Y
Snowe	Y	Y	Y	Y	Y	N	Y
MARYLAND							
Mikulski	Y	Y	N	N	Y	N	Y
Sarbanes	N	Y	N	N	Y	N	N
MASSACHUSETTS							
Kennedy	Y	Y	N	N	Y	N	N
Kerry	N	Y	N	N	Y	N	N
MICHIGAN							
Abraham	Y	N	Y	Y	Y	Y	Y
Levin	Y	Y	N	N	Y	N	Y
MINNESOTA							
Grams	Y	N	Y	Y	N	Y	N
Wellstone	N	Y	N	N	Y	N	N
MISSISSIPPI							
Cochran	Y	Y	Y	Y	Y	Y	Y
Lott	Y	Y	Y	Y	Y	Y	Y
MISSOURI							
Ashcroft	Y	N	Y	Y	N	Y	N
Bond	Y	Y	Y	Y	Y	Y	Y
MONTANA							
Burns	Y	N	Y	Y	Y	Y	Y
Baucus	Y	Y	N	N	Y	N	Y
NEBRASKA							
Hagel	Y	Y	Y	Y	Y	Y	Y
Kerrey	Y	Y	N	N	Y	N	Y
NEVADA							
Bryan	Y	Y	N	N	Y	Y	Y
Reid	Y	Y	N	N	Y	Y	Y
NEW HAMPSHIRE							
Gregg	Y	N	Y	Y	N	Y	Y
Smith	Y	N	Y	Y	N	Y	N
NEW JERSEY							
Lautenberg	Y	Y	N	N	Y	Y	Y
Torricelli	N	Y	N	N	Y	Y	Y
NEW MEXICO							
Domenici	Y	Y	Y	Y	Y	Y	Y
Bingaman	Y	Y	N	N	Y	N	Y
NEW YORK							
D'Amato	Y	Y	Y	Y	Y	N	Y
Moynihan	Y	Y	N	N	Y	N	N
NORTH CAROLINA							
Faircloth	Y	N	Y	Y	N	Y	N
Helms	Y	N	Y	Y	N	Y	N
NORTH DAKOTA							
Conrad	Y	N	N	N	Y	Y	Y
Dorgan	?	?	N	N	Y	Y	Y
OHIO							
DeWine	Y	Y	Y	Y	Y	N	Y
Glenn	Y	Y	N	N	Y	N	Y
OKLAHOMA							
Inhofe	Y	N	Y	Y	N	Y	N
Nickles	Y	N	Y	Y	N	Y	Y
OREGON							
Smith	Y	Y	Y	Y	Y	Y	Y
Wyden	Y	Y	N	N	Y	N	Y
PENNSYLVANIA							
Santorum	Y	N	Y	Y	N	N	Y
Specter	Y	Y	Y	N	Y	N	N
RHODE ISLAND							
Chafee	Y	Y	Y	N	Y	Y	Y
Reed	N	Y	N	N	Y	N	N
SOUTH CAROLINA							
Thurmond	Y	Y	Y	Y	N	Y	Y
Hollings	Y	N	N	N	Y	N	N
SOUTH DAKOTA							
Daschle	Y	Y	N	N	Y	Y	Y
Johnson	N	Y	N	N	Y	Y	Y
TENNESSEE							
Frist	Y	N	Y	Y	Y	Y	Y
Thompson	Y	N	Y	Y	N	Y	N
TEXAS							
Gramm	Y	N	Y	Y	N	Y	N
Hutchison	Y	N	Y	Y	N	Y	Y
UTAH							
Bennett	Y	Y	Y	Y	Y	Y	Y
Hatch	N	Y	Y	Y	Y	Y	Y
VERMONT							
Jeffords	Y	Y	Y	N	Y	N	Y
Leahy	Y	N	N	N	Y	Y	Y
VIRGINIA							
Warner	Y	N	Y	Y	N	Y	Y
Robb	Y	N	N	N	Y	N	Y
WASHINGTON							
Gorton	Y	Y	Y	Y	Y	Y	Y
Murray	N	Y	N	N	Y	N	Y
WEST VIRGINIA							
Byrd	N	Y	N	N	Y	Y	Y
Rockefeller	N	Y	N	N	Y	Y	Y
WISCONSIN							
Feingold	Y	Y	N	N	Y	N	Y
Kohl	Y	Y	Y	N	Y	N	Y
WYOMING							
Enzi	Y	N	Y	Y	N	Y	N
Thomas	Y	N	Y	Y	N	Y	N

ND Northern Democrats SD Southern Democrats

Southern states - Ala., Ark., Fla., Ga., Ky., La., Miss., N.C., Okla., S.C., Tenn., Texas, Va.

KEY

- Y Voted for (yea).
- # Paired for.
- + Announced for.
- N Voted against (nay).
- X Paired against.
- – Announced against.
- P Voted "present."
- C Voted "present" to avoid possible conflict of interest.
- ? Did not vote or otherwise make a position known.

Democrats *Republicans*

86. S Con Res 27. Fiscal 1998 Budget Resolution/Spectrum Auctions. McCain, R-Ariz., amendment to express the sense of the Senate that spending should be reduced if auctions of electromagnetic spectrum yield less revenue than anticipated. Adopted 84-15: R 54-1; D 30-14 (ND 24-12, SD 6-2), May 23, 1997.

87. S Con Res 27. Fiscal 1998 Budget Resolution/Budget Act Waiver. Domenici, R-N.M., motion to waive the Budget Act with respect to the Gramm, R-Texas, point of order against the concurrent resolution on grounds that it violates a previously established spending cap. Motion agreed to 66-33: R 27-28; D 39-5 (ND 34-2, SD 5-3), May 23, 1997. A three-fifths majority vote (60) of the total Senate is required to waive the Budget Act. (Subsequently, the Gramm point of order failed.)

88. S Con Res 27. Fiscal 1998 Budget Resolution/Revenue Windfall. Abraham, R-Mich., amendment to express the sense of the Senate that if actual revenues exceed projected revenues due to the effect of tax cuts, unforecast economic growth or for any other reason, the windfall should be reserved for additional tax cuts or deficit reduction. Adopted 56-44: R 55-0; D 1-44 (ND 1-36, SD 0-8), May 23, 1997.

89. S Con Res 27. Fiscal 1998 Budget Resolution/School Choice. Domenici. R-N.M., amendment to the Wellstone, D-Minn., amendment, to allow states to use federal education funds to assist children who have been victims of crime who want to change schools. The Wellstone amendment would increase funding for children's health and education programs by reducing tax benefits for wealthy individuals and certain corporations. Adopted 51-49: R 51-4; D 0-45 (ND 0-37, SD 0-8), May 23, 1997. (Subsequently, the Wellstone amendment as amended was adopted by voice vote.)

90. S Con Res 27. Fiscal 1998 Budget Resolution/Discretionary Spending. Domenici, R-N.M., motion to table (kill) the Grams, R-Minn., amendment to freeze non-defense discretionary spending and to require that the $225 billion in anticipated revenue receipts resulting from revised estimates of the Congressional Budget Office be applied equally to deficit reduction and tax relief. Motion agreed to 73-27: R 28-27; D 45-0 (ND 37-0, SD 8-0), May 23, 1997.

91. S Con Res 27. Fiscal 1998 Budget Resolution/NIH Funding. Stevens, R-Alaska, motion to table (kill) the Specter, R-Pa., amendment to increase funding for the National Institutes of Health by $1.1 billion, offset with unspecified cuts from other programs. Motion agreed to 63-37: R 45-10; D 18-27 (ND 13-24, SD 5-3), May 23, 1997.

92. H Con Res 84. Fiscal 1998 Budget Resolution/Adoption. Adoption of the concurrent resolution to adopt a five-year budget plan that would balance the budget by 2002 by cutting gross projected spending by approximately $320 billion and cutting taxes by a net $85 billion, for a net deficit reduction of $204.3 billion. Projected spending cuts would include reductions of $115 billion in Medicare, $13.6 billion in Medicaid and $138 billion in discretionary spending. The plan calls for additional funds to provide health insurance to currently uninsured children and to restore Supplemental Security Income and Medicaid benefits for some legal immigrants scheduled to lose their benefits under the 1996 welfare system overhaul (PL 104-193). The resolution sets binding levels for the fiscal year ending Sept. 30, 1998: budget authority, $1,702 billion; outlays, $1,692.3 billion; revenues, $1,601.8 billion; deficit, $90.5 billion. Adopted 78-22: R 41-14; D 37-8 (ND 31-6, SD 6-2), May 23, 1997. (Before passage the Senate struck all after the enacting clause and inserted the text of S Con Res 27 as amended.) A "yea" was a vote in support of the president's position.

SENATE VOTES 93, 94, 95, 96, 97

	93	94	95	96	97
ALABAMA					
Sessions	Y	Y	N	Y	Y
Shelby	Y	Y	Y	Y	Y
ALASKA					
Murkowski	Y	Y	Y	Y	Y
Stevens	Y	Y	Y	Y	Y
ARIZONA					
Kyl	Y	Y	N	N	Y
McCain	Y	Y	Y	Y	Y
ARKANSAS					
Hutchinson	Y	Y	Y	Y	Y
Bumpers	N	N	Y	N	N
CALIFORNIA					
Boxer	N	N	Y	Y	N
Feinstein	N	N	Y	Y	N
COLORADO					
Allard	Y	Y	Y	N	Y
Campbell	N	Y	Y	Y	Y
CONNECTICUT					
Dodd	N	N	N	Y	N
Lieberman	N	N	?	?	?
DELAWARE					
Roth	Y	Y	Y	Y	Y
Biden	N	N	N	Y	N
FLORIDA					
Mack	Y	Y	Y	Y	Y
Graham	N	N	N	Y	N
GEORGIA					
Coverdell	Y	Y	Y	Y	Y
Cleland	N	N	N	Y	N
HAWAII					
Akaka	N	N	N	Y	N
Inouye	N	N	N	Y	N
IDAHO					
Craig	Y	Y	Y	Y	Y
Kempthorne	Y	Y	Y	Y	Y
ILLINOIS					
Durbin	N	N	N	Y	N
Moseley-Braun	N	N	N	Y	N
INDIANA					
Coats	Y	Y	Y	N	N
Lugar	Y	Y	Y	Y	Y
IOWA					
Grassley	Y	Y	Y	Y	Y
Harkin	N	N	N	Y	N
KANSAS					
Brownback	Y	Y	Y	Y	Y
Roberts	Y	Y	Y	Y	Y
KENTUCKY					
McConnell	Y	Y	Y	Y	Y
Ford	N	N	N	Y	N
LOUISIANA					
Breaux	N	N	Y	Y	N
Landrieu	N	N	Y	Y	N
MAINE					
Collins	Y	Y	Y	Y	Y
Snowe	Y	Y	Y	Y	Y
MARYLAND					
Mikulski	N	N	N	Y	N
Sarbanes	N	N	N	N	N
MASSACHUSETTS					
Kennedy	N	N	N	N	N
Kerry	N	N	Y	N	N
MICHIGAN					
Abraham	Y	Y	Y	Y	Y
Levin	N	N	N	Y	N
MINNESOTA					
Grams	Y	Y	Y	N	Y
Wellstone	N	N	Y	N	N
MISSISSIPPI					
Cochran	Y	Y	Y	Y	Y
Lott	Y	Y	Y	Y	Y
MISSOURI					
Ashcroft	Y	Y	Y	N	Y
Bond	Y	Y	Y	Y	Y
MONTANA					
Burns	Y	Y	Y	Y	Y
Baucus	N	N	Y	Y	N
NEBRASKA					
Hagel	Y	Y	N	Y	Y
Kerrey	N	N	Y	Y	N
NEVADA					
Bryan	N	N	Y	Y	N
Reid	N	N	Y	Y	N
NEW HAMPSHIRE					
Gregg	Y	Y	N	Y	Y
Smith	Y	Y	N	N	Y
NEW JERSEY					
Lautenberg	N	N	N	Y	N
Torricelli	N	N	Y	Y	N
NEW MEXICO					
Domenici	Y	?	Y	Y	Y
Bingaman	N	N	N	Y	N
NEW YORK					
D'Amato	N	Y	Y	Y	Y
Moynihan	N	N	Y	N	N
NORTH CAROLINA					
Faircloth	Y	Y	N	N	Y
Helms	Y	Y	N	N	Y
NORTH DAKOTA					
Conrad	N	N	Y	Y	N
Dorgan	N	N	Y	Y	N
OHIO					
DeWine	Y	Y	Y	Y	Y
Glenn	N	N	Y	Y	N
OKLAHOMA					
Inhofe	Y	Y	Y	N	?
Nickles	Y	Y	N	Y	Y
OREGON					
Smith	Y	Y	Y	Y	Y
Wyden	N	N	Y	Y	N
PENNSYLVANIA					
Santorum	Y	Y	N	Y	?
Specter	N	Y	Y	N	Y
RHODE ISLAND					
Chafee	Y	Y	Y	Y	Y
Reed	-	?	Y	N	N
SOUTH CAROLINA					
Thurmond	Y	Y	Y	Y	Y
Hollings	N	N	N	N	N
SOUTH DAKOTA					
Daschle	N	N	Y	Y	N
Johnson	N	N	Y	Y	N
TENNESSEE					
Frist	Y	Y	Y	Y	Y
Thompson	Y	Y	Y	N	Y
TEXAS					
Gramm	Y	Y	N	N	Y
Hutchison	Y	Y	Y	Y	Y
UTAH					
Bennett	Y	Y	Y	Y	Y
Hatch	Y	Y	Y	Y	Y
VERMONT					
Jeffords	+	?	+	+	+
Leahy	N	N	N	Y	N
VIRGINIA					
Warner	Y	Y	Y	Y	Y
Robb	N	N	Y	Y	N
WASHINGTON					
Gorton	Y	Y	Y	Y	Y
Murray	N	N	Y	Y	N
WEST VIRGINIA					
Byrd	N	N	N	Y	N
Rockefeller	N	N	Y	Y	N
WISCONSIN					
Feingold	N	N	N	Y	N
Kohl	N	N	N	Y	N
WYOMING					
Enzi	Y	Y	Y	N	Y
Thomas	Y	Y	Y	N	Y

KEY

- Y Voted for (yea).
- # Paired for.
- + Announced for.
- N Voted against (nay).
- X Paired against.
- \- Announced against.
- P Voted "present."
- C Voted "present" to avoid possible conflict of interest.
- ? Did not vote or otherwise make a position known.

Democrats *Republicans*

ND Northern Democrats SD Southern Democrats

Southern states - Ala., Ark., Fla., Ga., Ky., La., Miss., N.C., Okla., S.C., Tenn., Texas, Va.

93. S 4. Compensatory Time, Flexible Credit/Cloture. Motion to invoke cloture (thus limiting debate) on the bill to amend the Fair Labor Standards Act of 1938 to allow private-sector employees to choose compensatory time off or flexible credit hour programs instead of overtime pay. Motion rejected 51-47: R 51-3; D 0-44 (ND 0-36, SD 0-8), June 4, 1997. Three-fifths of the total Senate (60) is required to invoke cloture.

94. Procedural Motion. Lott, R-Miss., motion to adjourn. Motion agreed to 53-44: R 53-0; D 0-44 (ND 0-36, SD 0-8), June 4, 1997.

95. HR 1469. Supplemental Fiscal 1997 Appropriations/Conference Report. Adoption of the conference report on the bill to provide about $8.6 billion in additional funds for fiscal 1997, including about $5.4 billion in emergency disaster aid for the flood-stricken Northwest and about $1.9 billion to finance military peacekeeping operations in Bosnia and the Middle East. The bill also includes provisions that automatically provide funding for federal programs that lack appropriations authority at the start of fiscal 1998 at 100 percent of their fiscal 1997 levels until fiscal 1998 appropriations are enacted and prohibit the Census Bureau from using statistical sampling in calculating the national population in 2000. Adopted 67-31: R 44-10; D 23-21 (ND 19-17, SD 4-4), June 5, 1997. A "nay" was a vote in support of the president's position.

96. H Con Res 84. Fiscal 1998 Budget Resolution/Conference Report. Adoption of the conference report on the concurrent resolution to adopt a five-year budget plan that would balance the budget by fiscal 2002 by cutting projected spending by approximately $322 billion, adding or restoring $32.7 billion in priority spending and cutting taxes by a net of $85 billion, for net deficit reduction of $204.3 billion. Projected spending cuts would include reductions of $115 billion in Medicare, $13.6 billion in Medicaid and approximately $139 billion in discretionary spending. The plan calls for additional spending to provide health insurance to currently uninsured children and to restore Supplemental Security Income and Medicaid benefits eliminated under the 1996 welfare system overhaul (PL 104-193). The resolution sets levels for the fiscal year ending Sept. 30, 1998: budget authority, $1,703.8 trillion; outlays, $1,692.3 trillion; revenues, $1,601.8 trillion; deficit, $90.5 billion. Adopted 76-22: R 40-14; D 36-8 (ND 30-6, SD 6-2), June 5, 1997. A "yea" was a vote in support of the president's position.

97. Procedural Motion. Lott, R-Miss., motion to adjourn. Motion agreed to 51-45: R 51-1; D 0-44 (ND 0-36, SD 0-8), June 5, 1997.

SENATE VOTES 98, 99, 100

	98	99	100
ALABAMA			
Sessions	Y	Y	N
Shelby	Y	Y	Y
ALASKA			
Murkowski	Y	Y	Y
Stevens	Y	Y	Y
ARIZONA			
Kyl	Y	Y	N
McCain	Y	Y	Y
ARKANSAS			
Hutchinson	Y	Y	Y
Bumpers	N	N	Y
CALIFORNIA			
Boxer	N	N	Y
Feinstein	N	N	Y
COLORADO			
Allard	Y	Y	N
Campbell	Y	Y	Y
CONNECTICUT			
Dodd	N	N	Y
Lieberman	N	N	Y
DELAWARE			
Roth	Y	Y	Y
Biden	N	N	Y
FLORIDA			
Mack	Y	Y	N
Graham	?	N	Y
GEORGIA			
Coverdell	Y	Y	Y
Cleland	N	N	Y
HAWAII			
Akaka	N	N	Y
Inouye	N	?	Y
IDAHO			
Craig	Y	Y	Y
Kempthorne	Y	Y	Y
ILLINOIS			
Durbin	N	N	Y
Moseley-Braun	?	N	Y
INDIANA			
Coats	Y	Y	N
Lugar	Y	Y	Y
IOWA			
Grassley	Y	Y	Y
Harkin	N	N	+
KANSAS			
Brownback	Y	Y	Y
Roberts	Y	Y	Y
KENTUCKY			
McConnell	Y	Y	Y
Ford	N	N	Y
LOUISIANA			
Breaux	?	N	Y
Landrieu	N	N	Y
MAINE			
Collins	Y	Y	Y
Snowe	Y	Y	Y
MARYLAND			
Mikulski	N	N	Y
Sarbanes	N	N	Y
MASSACHUSETTS			
Kennedy	N	N	Y
Kerry	N	N	Y
MICHIGAN			
Abraham	Y	Y	N
Levin	N	N	Y
MINNESOTA			
Grams	Y	Y	Y
Wellstone	N	N	Y
MISSISSIPPI			
Cochran	Y	Y	Y
Lott	Y	Y	N
MISSOURI			
Ashcroft	Y	Y	N
Bond	Y	Y	Y
MONTANA			
Burns	Y	Y	Y
Baucus	?	N	Y
NEBRASKA			
Hagel	Y	Y	N
Kerrey	?	N	Y
NEVADA			
Bryan	?	N	Y
Reid	N	N	Y
NEW HAMPSHIRE			
Gregg	Y	Y	N
Smith	Y	Y	N
NEW JERSEY			
Lautenberg	N	N	Y
Torricelli	N	N	Y
NEW MEXICO			
Domenici	Y	Y	Y
Bingaman	N	N	Y
NEW YORK			
D'Amato	Y	Y	Y
Moynihan	?	N	Y
NORTH CAROLINA			
Faircloth	Y	Y	N
Helms	Y	Y	N
NORTH DAKOTA			
Conrad	N	N	Y
Dorgan	N	N	Y
OHIO			
DeWine	Y	Y	Y
Glenn	N	N	Y
OKLAHOMA			
Inhofe	Y	Y	N
Nickles	Y	Y	N
OREGON			
Smith	Y	Y	Y
Wyden	N	N	Y
PENNSYLVANIA			
Santorum	Y	Y	N
Specter	Y	Y	Y
RHODE ISLAND			
Chafee	Y	Y	Y
Reed	N	N	Y
SOUTH CAROLINA			
Thurmond	Y	Y	Y
Hollings	N	N	Y
SOUTH DAKOTA			
Daschle	N	N	Y
Johnson	N	N	Y
TENNESSEE			
Frist	Y	Y	Y
Thompson	Y	Y	Y
TEXAS			
Gramm	Y	Y	N
Hutchison	Y	Y	Y
UTAH			
Bennett	Y	Y	Y
Hatch	Y	Y	Y
VERMONT			
Jeffords	Y	Y	Y
Leahy	N	N	Y
VIRGINIA			
Warner	Y	Y	Y
Robb	N	N	Y
WASHINGTON			
Gorton	Y	Y	Y
Murray	N	N	Y
WEST VIRGINIA			
Byrd	N	N	Y
Rockefeller	?	N	Y
WISCONSIN			
Feingold	N	N	N
Kohl	N	N	N
WYOMING			
Enzi	Y	Y	N
Thomas	Y	Y	N

KEY

- Y Voted for (yea).
- # Paired for.
- + Announced for.
- N Voted against (nay).
- X Paired against.
- – Announced against.
- P Voted "present."
- C Voted "present" to avoid possible conflict of interest.
- ? Did not vote or otherwise make a position known.

Democrats *Republicans*

ND Northern Democrats SD Southern Democrats

Southern states - Ala., Ark., Fla., Ga., Ky., La., Miss., N.C., Okla., S.C., Tenn., Texas, Va.

98. Procedural Motion. Lott, R-Miss., motion to adjourn. Motion agreed to 55-37: R 55-0; D 0-37 (ND 0-31, SD 0-6), June 10, 1997.

99. Procedural Motion. Lott, R-Miss., motion to adjourn. Motion agreed to 55-44: R 55-0; D 0-44 (ND 0-36, SD 0-8), June 11, 1997.

100. HR 1871. Fiscal 1997 Supplemental Appropriations/Passage. Passage of the bill to provide about $8.6 billion in additional funds for fiscal 1997, including about $5.6 billion in emergency disaster aid for 35 states and about $1.9 billion to finance military peacekeeping operations in Bosnia and the Middle East. Passed (thus cleared for the president) 78-21: R 36-19; D 42-2 (ND 34-2, SD 8-0), June 12, 1997. A "yea" was a vote in support of the president's position.

SENATE VOTES 101, 102, 103, 104, 105, 106

	101	102	103	104	105	106
ALABAMA						
Sessions	Y	N	Y	N	Y	Y
Shelby	Y	N	Y	N	Y	Y
ALASKA						
Murkowski	Y	N	Y	N	Y	Y
Stevens	Y	N	Y	N	Y	Y
ARIZONA						
Kyl	Y	N	Y	N	Y	Y
McCain	Y	N	Y	N	Y	Y
ARKANSAS						
Hutchinson	Y	N	Y	N	Y	Y
Bumpers	Y	Y	Y	Y	Y	Y
CALIFORNIA						
Boxer	Y	Y	Y	Y	Y	Y
Feinstein	Y	N	Y	N	Y	Y
COLORADO						
Allard	Y	N	Y	N	Y	Y
Campbell	Y	N	Y	N	Y	Y
CONNECTICUT						
Dodd	Y	Y	Y	N	Y	Y
Lieberman	Y	Y	Y	N	Y	Y
DELAWARE						
Roth	Y	N	Y	N	Y	Y
Biden	Y	N	Y	N	Y	Y
FLORIDA						
Mack	Y	N	Y	N	Y	Y
Graham	Y	N	Y	N	Y	Y
GEORGIA						
Coverdell	Y	N	Y	N	Y	Y
Cleland	Y	N	Y	N	Y	Y
HAWAII						
Akaka	Y	Y	Y	N	Y	Y
Inouye	Y	N	Y	N	Y	Y
IDAHO						
Craig	Y	N	Y	N	Y	Y
Kempthorne	Y	N	?	?	?	Y
ILLINOIS						
Durbin	Y	Y	Y	N	Y	Y
Moseley-Braun	Y	Y	Y	Y	Y	Y
INDIANA						
Coats	Y	N	Y	N	Y	Y
Lugar	Y	Y	Y	N	Y	Y
IOWA						
Grassley	Y	N	Y	N	Y	Y
Harkin	?	?	?	Y	N	Y
KANSAS						
Brownback	Y	N	Y	N	Y	Y
Roberts	Y	N	Y	?	?	Y
KENTUCKY						
McConnell	Y	N	Y	N	Y	Y
Ford	Y	N	Y	N	Y	Y
LOUISIANA						
Breaux	Y	N	Y	N	Y	Y
Landrieu	Y	Y	Y	N	Y	Y
MAINE						
Collins	Y	N	Y	N	Y	Y
Snowe	Y	N	Y	N	Y	Y
MARYLAND						
Mikulski	Y	N	Y	N	Y	Y
Sarbanes	Y	Y	Y	Y	N	Y
MASSACHUSETTS						
Kennedy	Y	Y	Y	Y	Y	Y
Kerry	Y	Y	Y	Y	Y	Y
MICHIGAN						
Abraham	Y	N	Y	N	Y	Y
Levin	Y	Y	Y	N	Y	Y
MINNESOTA						
Grams	Y	N	Y	N	Y	Y
Wellstone	Y	Y	Y	Y	N	Y
MISSISSIPPI						
Cochran	Y	N	Y	N	Y	Y
Lott	Y	N	Y	N	Y	Y
MISSOURI						
Ashcroft	Y	N	Y	N	Y	Y
Bond	Y	N	Y	N	Y	Y
MONTANA						
Burns	Y	N	Y	N	Y	Y
Baucus	Y	N	Y	Y	Y	Y
NEBRASKA						
Hagel	Y	N	Y	N	Y	Y
Kerrey	Y	Y	Y	Y	Y	Y
NEVADA						
Bryan	Y	N	Y	Y	Y	Y
Reid	Y	N	Y	Y	Y	Y
NEW HAMPSHIRE						
Gregg	Y	N	Y	N	Y	Y
Smith	Y	N	Y	N	Y	Y
NEW JERSEY						
Lautenberg	Y	Y	Y	N	Y	Y
Torricelli	Y	N	Y	N	Y	Y
NEW MEXICO						
Domenici	Y	N	Y	N	Y	Y
Bingaman	Y	Y	Y	Y	N	Y
NEW YORK						
D'Amato	Y	N	Y	N	Y	Y
Moynihan	Y	N	Y	N	Y	Y
NORTH CAROLINA						
Faircloth	Y	N	Y	N	Y	Y
Helms	Y	N	Y	N	Y	Y
NORTH DAKOTA						
Conrad	Y	N	Y	Y	Y	Y
Dorgan	Y	N	Y	Y	Y	Y
OHIO						
DeWine	Y	N	Y	N	Y	Y
Glenn	Y	Y	Y	N	Y	Y
OKLAHOMA						
Inhofe	Y	N	Y	N	Y	Y
Nickles	Y	N	Y	N	Y	Y
OREGON						
Smith	Y	N	Y	N	Y	Y
Wyden	Y	N	Y	Y	Y	Y
PENNSYLVANIA						
Santorum	Y	N	Y	N	Y	Y
Specter	Y	Y	Y	N	Y	Y
RHODE ISLAND						
Chafee	Y	Y	Y	N	Y	Y
Reed	Y	Y	Y	Y	Y	Y
SOUTH CAROLINA						
Thurmond	Y	N	Y	N	Y	Y
Hollings	Y	N	Y	N	Y	Y
SOUTH DAKOTA						
Daschle	?	?	?	?	?	?
Johnson	Y	N	?	?	?	?
TENNESSEE						
Frist	Y	N	Y	N	Y	Y
Thompson	Y	N	Y	N	Y	Y
TEXAS						
Gramm	Y	N	Y	N	Y	Y
Hutchison	Y	N	Y	N	Y	Y
UTAH						
Bennett	Y	N	Y	N	Y	Y
Hatch	Y	N	Y	N	Y	Y
VERMONT						
Jeffords	Y	Y	Y	N	Y	Y
Leahy	Y	Y	Y	Y	Y	Y
VIRGINIA						
Warner	Y	N	Y	N	Y	Y
Robb	Y	N	Y	N	Y	Y
WASHINGTON						
Gorton	Y	N	Y	N	Y	Y
Murray	Y	Y	Y	N	Y	Y
WEST VIRGINIA						
Byrd	Y	N	Y	N	N	Y
Rockefeller	Y	N	Y	Y	Y	Y
WISCONSIN						
Feingold	Y	Y	Y	Y	Y	Y
Kohl	Y	N	Y	Y	Y	Y
WYOMING						
Enzi	Y	N	Y	?	?	Y
Thomas	Y	N	Y	N	Y	Y

KEY

- Y Voted for (yea).
- # Paired for.
- + Announced for.
- N Voted against (nay).
- X Paired against.
- – Announced against.
- P Voted "present."
- C Voted "present" to avoid possible conflict of interest.
- ? Did not vote or otherwise make a position known.

Democrats ***Republicans***

ND Northern Democrats SD Southern Democrats

Southern states - Ala., Ark., Fla., Ga., Ky., La., Miss., N.C., Okla., S.C., Tenn., Texas, Va.

101. S 903. Fiscal 1998-99 State Department Authorization/ Haiti. DeWine, R-Ohio, amendment to require the secretary of State to deny visas to aliens who have ordered, carried out or assisted extrajudicial and political killings in Haiti. Adopted 98-0: R 55-0; D 43-0 (ND 35-0, SD 8-0), June 17, 1997.

102. S 903. Fiscal 1998-99 State Department Authorization/ U.N. Payment. Lugar, R-Ind., amendment to eliminate conditions for payment of $819 million in U.S. debt to the United Nations. The bill releases the funds only if the secretary of State certifies that the United Nations has not infringed on U.S. sovereignty and if it reduces the U.S. budget contribution from 25 percent to 20 percent by fiscal 2000. Rejected 25-73: R 4-51; D 21-22 (ND 19-16, SD 2-6), June 17, 1997.

103. S 903. Fiscal 1998-99 State Department Authorization/ Iranian Missiles. Bennett, R-Utah, amendment to express the sense of the Senate that the Clinton administration should enforce the provisions of the Iran-Iraq Arms Non-Proliferation Act of 1992 regarding Iran's acquisition of C-802 model cruise missiles from China. Adopted 96-0: R 54-0; D 42-0 (ND 34-0, SD 8-0), June 17, 1997.

104. S 903. Fiscal 1998-99 State Department Authorization/ Broadcasting Board. Feingold, D-Wis., amendment to ensure that the Broadcasting Board of Governors functions under the State Department instead of as a separate federal agency. The bill abolishes the U.S. Information Agency except for the Broadcasting Board of Governors, and establishes the board as a separate entity. Rejected 21-74: R 0-52; D 21-22 (ND 20-15, SD 1-7), June 17, 1997.

105. HR 1757. Fiscal 1998-99 State Department Authorization/Passage. Passage of the bill to abolish the Arms Control and Disarmament Agency, the U.S. Information Agency and the Agency for International Development, and to transfer most of the functions of those agencies to the State Department. The bill authorizes payment of $819 million owed by the United States to the United Nations, but requires the United Nations to comply with a series of conditions, including lowering the U.S. budget contribution from 25 percent to 20 percent by fiscal 2000. The bill authorizes $6.1 billion for fiscal 1998 and $5.9 billion for fiscal 1999 for the State Department and related agencies. The president requested $6.2 billion for fiscal 1998. Passed 90-5: R 52-0; D 38-5 (ND 30-5, SD 8-0), June 17, 1997. (Before passage the Senate struck all after the enacting clause and inserted the text of S 903 as amended.)

106. S 923. Veterans' Benefits Limitation for Capital Convictions/Passage. Passage of the bill to deny veterans' benefits to a person convicted of a federal capital offense. The bill is designed to deny veterans' benefits to Timothy McVeigh, convicted of murder in the 1995 bombing of the Alfred P. Murrah Federal Building in Oklahoma City. Passed 98-0: R 55-0; D 43-0 (ND 35-0, SD 8-0), June 18, 1997.

SENATE VOTES 107, 108, 109, 110

	107	108	109	110
ALABAMA				
Sessions	Y	N	Y	Y
Shelby	Y	N	Y	Y
ALASKA				
Murkowski	Y	N	Y	Y
Stevens	Y	N	Y	Y
ARIZONA				
Kyl	Y	N	Y	Y
McCain	Y	N	Y	Y
ARKANSAS				
Hutchinson	Y	N	Y	Y
Bumpers	Y	Y	Y	Y
CALIFORNIA				
Boxer	Y	Y	Y	Y
Feinstein	Y	Y	Y	Y
COLORADO				
Allard	Y	N	Y	Y
Campbell	Y	N	Y	Y
CONNECTICUT				
Dodd	Y	Y	Y	Y
Lieberman	Y	N	Y	Y
DELAWARE				
Roth	Y	N	Y	Y
Biden	Y	Y	Y	Y
FLORIDA				
Mack	Y	N	Y	Y
Graham	Y	Y	Y	Y
GEORGIA				
Coverdell	Y	N	Y	Y
Cleland	Y	Y	Y	Y
HAWAII				
Akaka	Y	Y	Y	Y
Inouye	Y	Y	Y	?
IDAHO				
Craig	Y	N	Y	Y
Kempthorne	Y	N	Y	Y
ILLINOIS				
Durbin	Y	Y	Y	Y
Moseley-Braun	Y	Y	Y	Y
INDIANA				
Coats	Y	N	Y	Y
Lugar	Y	N	Y	Y
IOWA				
Grassley	Y	N	Y	Y
Harkin	Y	Y	N	?
KANSAS				
Brownback	Y	N	Y	Y
Roberts	Y	N	Y	Y
KENTUCKY				
McConnell	Y	N	Y	Y
Ford	Y	N	Y	Y
LOUISIANA				
Breaux	Y	Y	Y	Y
Landrieu	Y	Y	Y	Y
MAINE				
Collins	Y	N	Y	Y
Snowe	Y	N	Y	Y
MARYLAND				
Mikulski	Y	Y	Y	?
Sarbanes	Y	Y	Y	Y
MASSACHUSETTS				
Kennedy	Y	Y	Y	Y
Kerry	Y	Y	Y	Y
MICHIGAN				
Abraham	Y	N	Y	Y
Levin	Y	Y	Y	Y
MINNESOTA				
Grams	Y	N	Y	Y
Wellstone	Y	Y	Y	Y
MISSISSIPPI				
Cochran	Y	N	Y	Y
Lott	Y	N	Y	Y
MISSOURI				
Ashcroft	Y	N	Y	Y
Bond	Y	N	Y	Y
MONTANA				
Burns	Y	N	Y	Y
Baucus	Y	Y	Y	Y
NEBRASKA				
Hagel	Y	N	Y	Y
Kerrey	Y	Y	Y	Y
NEVADA				
Bryan	Y	Y	Y	Y
Reid	Y	Y	Y	Y
NEW HAMPSHIRE				
Gregg	Y	N	Y	Y
Smith	Y	N	Y	Y
NEW JERSEY				
Lautenberg	Y	Y	Y	Y
Torricelli	Y	Y	Y	Y
NEW MEXICO				
Domenici	Y	N	Y	Y
Bingaman	Y	Y	Y	?
NEW YORK				
D'Amato	Y	N	Y	Y
Moynihan	Y	Y	Y	Y
NORTH CAROLINA				
Faircloth	Y	N	Y	Y
Helms	Y	N	Y	?
NORTH DAKOTA				
Conrad	Y	Y	Y	Y
Dorgan	Y	Y	Y	Y
OHIO				
DeWine	Y	N	Y	Y
Glenn	Y	Y	Y	Y
OKLAHOMA				
Inhofe	Y	N	Y	Y
Nickles	Y	N	Y	Y
OREGON				
Smith	Y	N	Y	Y
Wyden	Y	Y	Y	Y
PENNSYLVANIA				
Santorum	Y	N	Y	Y
Specter	Y	Y	Y	Y
RHODE ISLAND				
Chafee	Y	N	Y	Y
Reed	Y	Y	Y	Y
SOUTH CAROLINA				
Thurmond	Y	N	Y	Y
Hollings	Y	Y	Y	Y
SOUTH DAKOTA				
Daschle	?	?	?	?
Johnson	Y	Y	Y	Y
TENNESSEE				
Frist	Y	N	Y	Y
Thompson	Y	N	Y	Y
TEXAS				
Gramm	Y	N	Y	Y
Hutchison	Y	N	Y	Y
UTAH				
Bennett	Y	N	Y	Y
Hatch	Y	N	Y	Y
VERMONT				
Jeffords	Y	N	Y	Y
Leahy	Y	Y	Y	Y
VIRGINIA				
Warner	Y	N	Y	Y
Robb	Y	Y	Y	Y
WASHINGTON				
Gorton	Y	N	Y	Y
Murray	Y	Y	Y	Y
WEST VIRGINIA				
Byrd	Y	Y	Y	Y
Rockefeller	Y	Y	Y	Y
WISCONSIN				
Feingold	Y	Y	Y	Y
Kohl	Y	Y	Y	Y
WYOMING				
Enzi	Y	N	Y	Y
Thomas	Y	N	Y	Y

KEY

- Y Voted for (yea).
- # Paired for.
- + Announced for.
- N Voted against (nay).
- X Paired against.
- – Announced against.
- P Voted "present."
- C Voted "present" to avoid possible conflict of interest.
- ? Did not vote or otherwise make a position known.

Democrats *Republicans*

ND Northern Democrats SD Southern Democrats

Southern states - Ala., Ark., Fla., Ga., Ky., La., Miss., N.C., Okla., S.C., Tenn., Texas, Va.

107. S 858. Fiscal 1998 Intelligence Authorization/Tax Impact. Wellstone, D-Minn., amendment to express the sense of the Senate that tax bills enacted by Congress this year should be fair to taxpayers of different income levels and not provide disproportionate benefits to the highest-income taxpayers. Adopted 99-0: R 55-0; D 44-0 (ND 36-0, SD 8-0), June 19, 1997.

108. S 858. Fiscal 1998 Intelligence Authorization/Intelligence Budget. Torricelli, D-N.J., amendment to require the president to release the aggregate appropriation and budget request for all intelligence and intelligence-related activities. The intelligence budget currently is classified. Rejected 43-56: R 1-54; D 42-2 (ND 35-1, SD 7-1), June 19, 1997.

109. S 858. Fiscal 1998 Intelligence Authorization/Passage. Passage of the bill to authorize appropriations for fiscal 1998 for intelligence and related activities. The bill also authorizes appropriations totaling $196.9 million for the Central Intelligence Agency Retirement and Disability System, and $90.6 million for the Community Management Account of the Director of Central Intelligence. Passed 98-1: R 55-0; D 43-1 (ND 35-1, SD 8-0), June 19, 1997. A "nay" was a vote in support of the president's position.

110. S 936. Fiscal 1998 Defense Authorization/Bomb Demonstrations. Feinstein, D-Calif., amendment to prohibit the teaching or demonstration of bomb construction or use if the lesson is intended to further a criminal act. Violators are subject to fines and up to 20 years in prison. Adopted 94-0: R 54-0; D 40-0 (ND 32-0, SD 8-0), June 19, 1997.

SENATE VOTES 111, 112, 113, 114, 115, 116, 117

	111	112	113	114	115	116	117
ALABAMA							
Sessions	Y	Y	Y	N	N	N	N
Shelby	Y	Y	Y	N	N	N	N
ALASKA							
Murkowski	Y	Y	Y	N	N	N	Y
Stevens	Y	Y	Y	N	N	N	Y
ARIZONA							
Kyl	Y	Y	Y	N	N	N	N
McCain	Y	Y	N	Y	N	N	N
ARKANSAS							
Hutchinson	Y	Y	Y	N	N	N	N
Bumpers	N	N	Y	Y	N	Y	N
CALIFORNIA							
Boxer	N	N	N	Y	Y	Y	Y
Feinstein	N	Y	Y	N	N	Y	Y
COLORADO							
Allard	Y	Y	Y	N	N	N	N
Campbell	Y	Y	Y	N	N	N	N
CONNECTICUT							
Dodd	N	N	Y	Y	N	Y	N
Lieberman	Y	Y	Y	N	N	Y	Y
DELAWARE							
Roth	Y	Y	Y	N	N	N	N
Biden	N	N	N	Y	Y	Y	Y
FLORIDA							
Mack	Y	Y	Y	N	N	N	Y
Graham	Y	Y	Y	N	N	Y	Y
GEORGIA							
Coverdell	N	N	N	Y	N	N	N
Cleland	N	N	N	Y	Y	Y	Y
HAWAII							
Akaka	N	N	N	Y	Y	Y	Y
Inouye	N	N	N	Y	Y	Y	Y
IDAHO							
Craig	Y	Y	Y	N	N	N	N
Kempthorne	Y	Y	Y	N	N	N	N
ILLINOIS							
Durbin	N	N	N	Y	Y	Y	Y
Moseley-Braun	N	N	N	Y	N	Y	Y
INDIANA							
Coats	Y	Y	Y	N	N	N	N
Lugar	Y	Y	Y	N	N	N	N
IOWA							
Grassley	Y	Y	Y	N	N	N	Y
Harkin	N	N	Y	Y	Y	Y	Y
KANSAS							
Brownback	Y	Y	Y	N	N	N	N
Roberts	Y	Y	Y	N	N	N	N
KENTUCKY							
McConnell	Y	Y	Y	N	N	N	N
Ford	N	N	N	Y	Y	Y	Y
LOUISIANA							
Breaux	Y	Y	Y	N	N	Y	Y
Landrieu	N	N	Y	N	N	Y	Y
MAINE							
Collins	N	N	Y	Y	N	Y	N
Snowe	N	N	N	Y	N	Y	N
MARYLAND							
Mikulski	N	N	N	Y	Y	Y	N
Sarbanes	N	N	N	Y	Y	Y	Y
MASSACHUSETTS							
Kennedy	N	N	N	Y	Y	Y	Y
Kerry	N	N	Y	Y	N	Y	Y
MICHIGAN							
Abraham	Y	Y	N	Y	N	N	N
Levin	N	N	Y	Y	Y	Y	Y
MINNESOTA							
Grams	Y	Y	Y	N	N	N	N
Wellstone	N	N	N	Y	Y	Y	Y
MISSISSIPPI							
Cochran	Y	Y	Y	N	N	N	N
Lott	Y	Y	Y	N	N	N	N
MISSOURI							
Ashcroft	Y	Y	Y	N	N	N	N
Bond	Y	Y	Y	N	N	N	N
MONTANA							
Burns	Y	Y	Y	N	N	N	N
Baucus	Y	Y	Y	N	N	Y	N
NEBRASKA							
Hagel	Y	Y	Y	N	N	N	N
Kerrey	Y	Y	Y	N	N	Y	N
NEVADA							
Bryan	Y	Y	Y	N	N	Y	N
Reid	N	N	N	Y	Y	Y	Y
NEW HAMPSHIRE							
Gregg	Y	Y	Y	N	N	N	N
Smith	Y	Y	Y	N	N	N	N
NEW JERSEY							
Lautenberg	N	N	N	Y	Y	Y	Y
Torricelli	N	N	N	Y	N	Y	Y
NEW MEXICO							
Domenici	Y	Y	Y	N	N	N	N
Bingaman	N	N	Y	Y	N	Y	N
NEW YORK							
D'Amato	N	N	N	Y	N	Y	Y
Moynihan	Y	Y	Y	N	N	N	Y
NORTH CAROLINA							
Faircloth	Y	Y	Y	N	N	N	Y
Helms	Y	Y	Y	N	N	N	N
NORTH DAKOTA							
Conrad	Y	Y	Y	N	N	Y	Y
Dorgan	N	N	N	Y	Y	Y	Y
OHIO							
DeWine	Y	Y	Y	N	N	N	Y
Glenn	N	Y	Y	N	N	Y	N
OKLAHOMA							
Inhofe	Y	Y	Y	N	N	N	N
Nickles	Y	Y	Y	N	N	N	N
OREGON							
Smith	Y	Y	Y	N	N	N	N
Wyden	N	N	N	Y	N	Y	Y
PENNSYLVANIA							
Santorum	Y	Y	Y	N	N	N	N
Specter	N	N	N	Y	N	Y	Y
RHODE ISLAND							
Chafee	Y	Y	Y	N	N	Y	N
Reed	N	N	N	Y	Y	Y	Y
SOUTH CAROLINA							
Thurmond	Y	Y	Y	N	N	N	Y
Hollings	N	N	Y	N	Y	Y	Y
SOUTH DAKOTA							
Daschle	N	N	N	Y	Y	Y	Y
Johnson	N	N	N	Y	Y	Y	Y
TENNESSEE							
Frist	Y	Y	Y	N	N	N	N
Thompson	Y	Y	Y	N	N	N	N
TEXAS							
Gramm	Y	Y	Y	N	N	N	N
Hutchison	Y	Y	Y	N	N	N	N
UTAH							
Bennett	Y	Y	Y	N	N	N	N
Hatch	Y	Y	Y	N	N	N	N
VERMONT							
Jeffords	Y	Y	Y	N	N	N	Y
Leahy	N	N	N	Y	Y	Y	Y
VIRGINIA							
Warner	Y	Y	Y	N	N	N	Y
Robb	Y	Y	Y	N	N	Y	Y
WASHINGTON							
Gorton	Y	Y	Y	N	N	N	N
Murray	N	N	N	Y	Y	Y	Y
WEST VIRGINIA							
Byrd	N	N	N	Y	Y	N	N
Rockefeller	N	N	N	Y	Y	Y	Y
WISCONSIN							
Feingold	N	N	Y	N	Y	Y	N
Kohl	N	Y	Y	N	N	Y	Y
WYOMING							
Enzi	Y	Y	Y	N	N	N	N
Thomas	Y	Y	Y	N	N	N	N

ND Northern Democrats SD Southern Democrats

Southern states - Ala., Ark., Fla., Ga., Ky., La., Miss., N.C., Okla., S.C., Tenn., Texas, Va.

KEY

- Y Voted for (yea).
- # Paired for.
- + Announced for.
- N Voted against (nay).
- X Paired against.
- – Announced against.
- P Voted "present."
- C Voted "present" to avoid possible conflict of interest.
- ? Did not vote or otherwise make a position known.

Democrats *Republicans*

111. S 947. Fiscal 1998 Budget Reconciliation — Spending/Home Health Copayment. Roth, R-Del., motion to table (kill) the Kennedy, D-Mass., amendment to strike the section imposing a $5 copayment for some Medicare home health visits. Motion agreed to 59-41: R 50-5; D 9-36 (ND 6-31, SD 3-5), June 24, 1997. Following the vote, Moseley-Braun, D-Ill., asked and was granted unanimous consent to change her vote from "yea" to "nay." The change is reflected on this chart. The Congressional Record for June 24 should have reflected the change, but it did not.

112. S 947. Fiscal 1998 Budget Reconciliation — Spending/Medicare Eligibility. Roth, R-Del., motion to waive the Budget Act with respect to the Durbin, D-Ill., point of order against a provision that would gradually raise the Medicare eligibility age from 65 to 67 between 2003 and 2027. Motion agreed to 62-38: R 50-5; D 12-33 (ND 9-28, SD 3-5), June 24, 1997. A three-fifths majority (60) of the total Senate is required to waive the Budget Act. (Subsequently, the point of order was waived and the provision was retained.)

113. S 947. Fiscal 1998 Budget Reconciliation — Spending/Medicare Means Testing. Roth, R-Del., motion to table (kill) the Kennedy, D-Mass., amendment to strike the section that introduces a means-based formula to determine insurance premiums under Medicare Part B. Motion agreed to 70-30: R 49-6; D 21-24 (ND 15-22, SD 6-2), June 24, 1997.

114. S 947. Fiscal 1998 Budget Reconciliation — Spending/Means Test Effective Date. Kennedy, D-Mass., motion to waive the Budget Act with respect to the Domenici, R-N.M., point of order against the Kennedy amendment to delay means testing under Medicare Part B until January 2000. Motion rejected 37-63: R 7-48; D 30-15 (ND 27-10, SD 3-5), June 24, 1997. A three-fifths majority vote (60) of the Senate is required to waive the Budget Act. (Subsequently, the chair upheld the Domenici point of order and the Kennedy amendment fell.)

115. S 947. Fiscal 1998 Budget Reconciliation — Spending/Medicare Substitute. Reed, D-R.I., motion to waive the Budget Act with respect to the Domenici, R-N.M., point of order against the Reed substitute amendment to eliminate the age increase for Medicare eligibility, remove the $5 copayment for home health care visits and eliminate Medicare means testing. Motion rejected 25-75: R 0-55; D 25-20 (ND 22-15, SD 3-5), June 25, 1997. A three-fifths majority vote (60) of the Senate is required to waive the Budget Act. (Subsequently, the chair upheld the Domenici point of order and the amendment fell.)

116. S 947. Fiscal 1998 Budget Reconciliation — Spending/Food Stamps. Durbin, D-Ill., motion to waive the Budget Act with respect to the Domenici, R-N.M., point of order against the Durbin amendment to restore food stamps the 1996 welfare law cut for children of legal immigrants. Motion rejected 48-52: R 5-50; D 43-2 (ND 35-2, SD 8-0), June 25, 1997. A three-fifths majority vote (60) of the total Senate is required to waive the Budget Act. (Subsequently, the chair upheld the Domenici point of order and the amendment fell.)

117. S 947. Fiscal 1998 Budget Reconciliation — Spending/Health Research. D'Amato, R-N.Y., motion to waive the Budget Act with respect to the Domenici, R-N.M., point of order against the D'Amato amendment to establish a trust fund for health research from Medicare and Medicaid savings. Motion rejected 46-54: R 11-44; D 35-10 (ND 28-9, SD 7-1), June 25, 1997. A three-fifths majority vote (60) of the Senate is required to waive the Budget Act. (Subsequently, the chair upheld the Domenici point of order and the amendment fell.)

SENATE VOTES 118, 119, 120, 121, 122, 123, 124

	118	119	120	121	122	123	124
ALABAMA							
Sessions	N	N	Y	N	Y	Y	Y
Shelby	N	N	Y	N	Y	Y	N
ALASKA							
Murkowski	N	N	Y	N	Y	Y	Y
Stevens	N	Y	Y	N	Y	Y	Y
ARIZONA							
Kyl	N	N	Y	N	Y	Y	Y
McCain	N	N	Y	N	Y	Y	Y
ARKANSAS							
Hutchinson	N	N	Y	N	Y	Y	Y
Bumpers	Y	Y	N	Y	N	N	N
CALIFORNIA							
Boxer	Y	Y	N	Y	N	N	N
Feinstein	Y	Y	Y	Y	Y	Y	N
COLORADO							
Allard	N	N	Y	N	Y	Y	Y
Campbell	Y	N	Y	N	Y	Y	Y
CONNECTICUT							
Dodd	Y	Y	Y	Y	N	Y	N
Lieberman	Y	Y	Y	Y	N	Y	N
DELAWARE							
Roth	N	N	Y	N	Y	Y	Y
Biden	Y	Y	Y	Y	Y	N	N
FLORIDA							
Mack	N	N	Y	N	Y	Y	Y
Graham	Y	Y	N	Y	N	Y	Y
GEORGIA							
Coverdell	N	N	Y	N	Y	Y	Y
Cleland	Y	Y	N	Y	N	N	N
HAWAII							
Akaka	Y	Y	N	Y	N	N	N
Inouye	Y	Y	?	Y	N	N	N
IDAHO							
Craig	N	N	Y	N	Y	Y	Y
Kempthorne	N	N	Y	N	Y	Y	Y
ILLINOIS							
Durbin	Y	Y	N	Y	N	N	N
Moseley-Braun	Y	Y	N	Y	N	Y	N
INDIANA							
Coats	N	N	Y	N	Y	Y	Y
Lugar	N	Y	Y	N	Y	Y	Y
IOWA							
Grassley	N	N	Y	N	Y	Y	Y
Harkin	Y	Y	N	Y	N	N	N
KANSAS							
Brownback	N	N	Y	N	Y	Y	Y
Roberts	N	N	Y	N	Y	Y	Y
KENTUCKY							
McConnell	N	N	Y	N	Y	Y	Y
Ford	Y	Y	N	Y	N	Y	N
LOUISIANA							
Breaux	Y	Y	Y	Y	Y	Y	Y
Landrieu	Y	Y	Y	Y	Y	Y	N
MAINE							
Collins	N	Y	Y	Y	Y	Y	Y
Snowe	N	Y	Y	Y	Y	Y	Y
MARYLAND							
Mikulski	Y	Y	N	Y	N	N	N
Sarbanes	Y	Y	N	Y	N	N	N
MASSACHUSETTS							
Kennedy	Y	Y	N	Y	N	N	N
Kerry	Y	Y	N	Y	N	N	N
MICHIGAN							
Abraham	N	Y	Y	N	Y	Y	Y
Levin	Y	Y	N	Y	N	N	N
MINNESOTA							
Grams	N	N	Y	N	Y	Y	Y
Wellstone	Y	Y	N	Y	N	N	N
MISSISSIPPI							
Cochran	N	N	Y	N	Y	Y	Y
Lott	N	N	Y	N	Y	Y	Y
MISSOURI							
Ashcroft	N	N	Y	N	Y	Y	Y
Bond	N	N	Y	Y	Y	N	Y
MONTANA							
Burns	N	N	Y	N	Y	Y	Y
Baucus	Y	Y	N	Y	N	Y	Y
NEBRASKA							
Hagel	N	N	Y	N	Y	Y	Y
Kerrey	Y	Y	N	Y	Y	Y	Y
NEVADA							
Bryan	Y	Y	N	Y	N	Y	Y
Reid	Y	Y	N	Y	N	N	N
NEW HAMPSHIRE							
Gregg	N	N	Y	N	Y	Y	Y
Smith	N	N	Y	N	Y	Y	Y
NEW JERSEY							
Lautenberg	Y	Y	N	Y	N	Y	Y
Torricelli	Y	Y	N	Y	Y	Y	N
NEW MEXICO							
Domenici	N	N	Y	N	Y	Y	Y
Bingaman	Y	Y	N	Y	Y	N	Y
NEW YORK							
D'Amato	Y	Y	Y	Y	Y	N	N
Moynihan	Y	Y	N	Y	Y	N	Y
NORTH CAROLINA							
Faircloth	N	N	Y	N	Y	N	Y
Helms	N	N	Y	N	Y	Y	Y
NORTH DAKOTA							
Conrad	Y	Y	N	Y	N	Y	Y
Dorgan	Y	Y	N	Y	N	Y	N
OHIO							
DeWine	N	N	Y	N	Y	Y	Y
Glenn	Y	Y	Y	Y	N	Y	N
OKLAHOMA							
Inhofe	N	N	Y	N	Y	Y	Y
Nickles	N	N	Y	N	Y	Y	Y
OREGON							
Smith	N	Y	Y	N	Y	Y	Y
Wyden	Y	Y	N	Y	N	N	N
PENNSYLVANIA							
Santorum	N	N	Y	Y	Y	N	Y
Specter	Y	Y	Y	Y	Y	N	Y
RHODE ISLAND							
Chafee	Y	Y	Y	N	Y	Y	Y
Reed	Y	Y	N	Y	N	Y	N
SOUTH CAROLINA							
Thurmond	N	N	Y	N	Y	N	Y
Hollings	Y	Y	Y	Y	N	Y	Y
SOUTH DAKOTA							
Daschle	Y	Y	N	Y	N	N	N
Johnson	Y	Y	N	Y	N	N	N
TENNESSEE							
Frist	N	N	Y	N	Y	Y	Y
Thompson	N	N	Y	N	Y	Y	Y
TEXAS							
Gramm	N	N	Y	N	Y	Y	Y
Hutchison	N	N	Y	N	Y	Y	Y
UTAH							
Bennett	N	N	Y	N	Y	Y	Y
Hatch	N	N	Y	N	?	Y	Y
VERMONT							
Jeffords	Y	Y	Y	Y	Y	N	Y
Leahy	Y	Y	N	Y	N	Y	Y
VIRGINIA							
Warner	N	N	Y	N	Y	Y	N
Robb	Y	Y	Y	Y	N	Y	Y
WASHINGTON							
Gorton	N	N	Y	N	Y	Y	Y
Murray	Y	Y	N	Y	N	N	N
WEST VIRGINIA							
Byrd	N	Y	N	Y	N	N	N
Rockefeller	Y	Y	N	Y	N	Y	N
WISCONSIN							
Feingold	Y	Y	N	Y	N	Y	Y
Kohl	Y	Y	N	Y	N	Y	Y
WYOMING							
Enzi	N	N	Y	N	Y	Y	Y
Thomas	N	N	Y	N	Y	Y	Y

KEY

- Y Voted for (yea).
- # Paired for.
- \+ Announced for.
- N Voted against (nay).
- X Paired against.
- – Announced against.
- P Voted "present."
- C Voted "present" to avoid possible conflict of interest.
- ? Did not vote or otherwise make a position known.

Democrats *Republicans*

ND Northern Democrats SD Southern Democrats

Southern states - Ala., Ark., Fla., Ga., Ky., La., Miss., N.C., Okla., S.C., Tenn., Texas, Va.

118. S 947. Fiscal 1998 Budget Reconciliation — Spending/ Disabled Children. Dodd, D-Conn., motion to waive the Budget Act with respect to the Domenici, R-N.M., point of order against the Dodd amendment to revise the 1996 welfare law to provide Medicaid eligibility for disabled children who lose Supplemental Security Income benefits. Motion rejected 49-51: R 5-50; D 44-1 (ND 36-1, SD 8-0), June 25, 1997. A three-fifths majority vote (60) of the total Senate is required to waive the Budget Act. (Subsequently, the chair upheld the Domenici point of order and the amendment fell.)

119. S 947. Fiscal 1998 Budget Reconciliation — Spending/ Vocational Training. Levin, D-Mich., motion to waive the Budget Act with respect to the Domenici, R-N.M., point of order against the Levin amendment to allow 24 months of vocational education training to count as "work activity" under a federal assistance program for needy families. Under current law only 12 months can be counted. Motion rejected 55-45: R 10-45; D 45-0 (ND 37-0, SD 8-0), June 25, 1997. A three-fifths majority vote (60) of the total Senate is required to waive the Budget Act. (Subsequently, the chair upheld the Domenici point of order and the amendment fell.)

120. S 947. Fiscal 1998 Budget Reconciliation — Spending/ Private Contracts. Kyl, R-Ariz., motion to waive the Budget Act with respect to the Lautenberg, D-N.J., point of order against the Kyl amendment to allow physicians to enter into private contracts with Medicare beneficiaries if claims have not been filed for services. The administrator of the Health Care Financing Administration would have to report to Congress on the provision by Oct. 1, 2001. Motion agreed to 64-35: R 55-0; D 9-35 (ND 5-31, SD 4-4), June 25, 1997. A three-fifths vote (60) of the total Senate is required to waive the Budget Act. (Subsequently, the chair overruled the point of order and the Kyl amendment was adopted by voice vote.)

121. S 947. Fiscal 1998 Budget Reconciliation — Spending/ Premium Protections. Specter, R-Pa., motion to waive the Budget Act with respect to the Domenici, R-N.M., point of order against the Specter amendment to extend premium protections for low-income Medicare beneficiaries under the Medicaid program. Motion rejected 52-48: R 7-48; D 45-0 (ND 37-0, SD 8-0), June 25, 1997. A three-fifths majority vote (60) of the total Senate is required to waive the Budget Act. (Subsequently, the chair upheld the Domenici point of order and the amendment fell.)

122. S 947. Fiscal 1998 Budget Reconciliation — Spending/ Budget Act Waiver. Domenici, R-N.M., motion to waive the Budget Act with respect to the Rockefeller, D-W.Va., point of order against the bill to cut spending by $135.9 billion between fiscal 1998 and fiscal 2002. Motion agreed to 62-37: R 54-0; D 8-37 (ND 6-31, SD 2-6), June 25, 1997. A three-fifths majority vote (60) of the total Senate is required to waive the Budget Act. (Subsequently, the Rockefeller point of order was waived.)

123. S 947. Fiscal 1998 Budget Reconciliation — Spending/ Teaching Hospitals. Domenici, R-N.M., motion to table (kill) the Specter, R-Pa., amendment to strike the section limiting payments to hospitals under the Indirect Graduate Medical Education physician training program. Motion agreed to 71-29: R 48-7; D 23-22 (ND 17-20, SD 6-2), June 25, 1997.

124. S 947. Fiscal 1998 Budget Reconciliation — Spending/ Nursing Homes. Domenici, R-N.M., motion to table (kill) the Mikulski, D-Md., amendment to strike the section that repeals the "Boren amendment," which ensures a basic daily reimbursement rate for nursing homes under Medicaid. Motion agreed to 66-34: R 52-3; D 14-31 (ND 10-27, SD 4-4), June 25, 1997. Following the vote, Kohl, D-Wis., asked and was granted unanimous consent to change his vote from "nay" to "yea." The change is reflected on this chart.

SENATE VOTES 125, 126, 127, 128, 129, 130, 131

	125	126	127	128	129	130	131
ALABAMA							
Sessions	N	N	N	Y	N	Y	N
Shelby	N	N	N	Y	N	Y	N
ALASKA							
Murkowski	N	N	N	Y	N	Y	N
Stevens	N	N	N	Y	Y	Y	N
ARIZONA							
Kyl	N	N	N	Y	N	Y	N
McCain	N	N	N	Y	N	Y	N
ARKANSAS							
Hutchinson	N	N	N	Y	N	Y	N
Bumpers	Y	Y	Y	N	Y	N	Y
CALIFORNIA							
Boxer	Y	Y	Y	N	Y	N	Y
Feinstein	Y	Y	Y	N	Y	Y	Y
COLORADO							
Allard	N	N	N	Y	N	Y	N
Campbell	N	N	N	Y	Y	Y	N
CONNECTICUT							
Dodd	Y	Y	Y	N	Y	N	Y
Lieberman	Y	Y	Y	N	Y	Y	Y
DELAWARE							
Roth	N	N	N	Y	N	Y	N
Biden	Y	Y	N	N	N	Y	Y
FLORIDA							
Mack	N	N	N	Y	N	Y	N
Graham	Y	Y	Y	Y	N	Y	Y
GEORGIA							
Coverdell	N	N	N	Y	N	Y	N
Cleland	Y	Y	Y	N	N	Y	N
HAWAII							
Akaka	Y	Y	Y	N	Y	N	Y
Inouye	Y	Y	Y	N	Y	N	N
IDAHO							
Craig	N	N	N	Y	N	Y	N
Kempthorne	N	N	N	Y	N	Y	N
ILLINOIS							
Durbin	Y	Y	Y	N	Y	N	Y
Moseley-Braun	Y	Y	N	N	Y	Y	Y
INDIANA							
Coats	N	N	N	Y	N	Y	Y
Lugar	N	N	N	Y	N	Y	N
IOWA							
Grassley	N	N	N	Y	N	Y	N
Harkin	Y	Y	Y	N	Y	N	Y
KANSAS							
Brownback	N	N	N	Y	N	Y	N
Roberts	N	N	N	Y	N	Y	?
KENTUCKY							
McConnell	N	N	N	Y	N	Y	N
Ford	Y	Y	Y	N	N	Y	N
LOUISIANA							
Breaux	N	Y	Y	Y	N	Y	N
Landrieu	N	N	Y	N	Y	Y	N
MAINE							
Collins	N	N	N	Y	N	Y	Y
Snowe	N	N	N	Y	N	Y	Y
MARYLAND							
Mikulski	Y	Y	Y	N	Y	N	Y
Sarbanes	Y	Y	Y	N	Y	N	Y
MASSACHUSETTS							
Kennedy	Y	Y	Y	N	Y	N	Y
Kerry	Y	Y	Y	N	Y	N	Y
MICHIGAN							
Abraham	N	N	N	Y	N	Y	N
Levin	Y	Y	Y	N	Y	N	Y
MINNESOTA							
Grams	N	N	N	Y	N	N	N
Wellstone	Y	Y	Y	N	Y	N	Y
MISSISSIPPI							
Cochran	N	N	N	Y	N	Y	N
Lott	N	N	N	Y	N	Y	N
MISSOURI							
Ashcroft	N	N	N	Y	N	Y	N
Bond	N	N	N	Y	N	Y	N
MONTANA							
Burns	N	N	N	Y	N	Y	N
Baucus	Y	Y	N	Y	Y	Y	N
NEBRASKA							
Hagel	N	N	N	Y	N	Y	N
Kerrey	N	Y	N	Y	Y	Y	Y
NEVADA							
Bryan	N	Y	Y	N	Y	Y	N
Reid	Y	Y	Y	N	N	N	N
NEW HAMPSHIRE							
Gregg	N	N	N	Y	N	Y	Y
Smith	N	N	N	Y	N	Y	Y
NEW JERSEY							
Lautenberg	Y	Y	Y	N	Y	N	Y
Torricelli	Y	Y	Y	N	Y	N	Y
NEW MEXICO							
Domenici	N	N	N	Y	N	Y	N
Bingaman	Y	Y	Y	N	Y	N	N
NEW YORK							
D'Amato	N	N	N	Y	N	Y	N
Moynihan	N	Y	N	Y	Y	Y	N
NORTH CAROLINA							
Faircloth	N	N	N	Y	N	N	N
Helms	N	N	N	Y	N	N	N
NORTH DAKOTA							
Conrad	Y	Y	Y	N	N	Y	N
Dorgan	Y	Y	Y	N	N	N	N
OHIO							
DeWine	N	N	N	Y	N	Y	N
Glenn	?	Y	Y	N	Y	Y	Y
OKLAHOMA							
Inhofe	N	N	N	Y	N	Y	N
Nickles	N	N	N	Y	N	Y	N
OREGON							
Smith	N	N	N	Y	N	Y	N
Wyden	Y	Y	Y	N	Y	Y	Y
PENNSYLVANIA							
Santorum	N	N	N	Y	N	Y	N
Specter	N	N	N	N	Y	Y	N
RHODE ISLAND							
Chafee	Y	N	N	N	Y	Y	Y
Reed	Y	Y	Y	N	Y	N	Y
SOUTH CAROLINA							
Thurmond	N	N	N	Y	N	Y	N
Hollings	Y	Y	N	N	Y	N	N
SOUTH DAKOTA							
Daschle	Y	Y	Y	N	Y	N	N
Johnson	Y	N	Y	N	N	N	N
TENNESSEE							
Frist	N	N	N	Y	N	Y	N
Thompson	N	N	N	Y	N	Y	N
TEXAS							
Gramm	N	N	N	Y	N	Y	N
Hutchison	N	N	N	Y	N	Y	N
UTAH							
Bennett	N	N	N	Y	N	Y	N
Hatch	N	N	N	Y	N	Y	N
VERMONT							
Jeffords	Y	N	N	N	Y	Y	Y
Leahy	Y	Y	Y	N	Y	Y	Y
VIRGINIA							
Warner	N	N	N	Y	N	Y	N
Robb	N	Y	Y	N	Y	Y	Y
WASHINGTON							
Gorton	N	N	N	Y	N	Y	N
Murray	Y	Y	Y	N	Y	N	Y
WEST VIRGINIA							
Byrd	Y	Y	Y	N	N	N	N
Rockefeller	Y	Y	Y	N	Y	Y	Y
WISCONSIN							
Feingold	N	Y	Y	N	Y	Y	Y
Kohl	N	Y	N	N	N	Y	Y
WYOMING							
Enzi	N	N	N	Y	N	Y	N
Thomas	N	N	N	Y	N	Y	N

KEY

- Y Voted for (yea).
- # Paired for.
- + Announced for.
- N Voted against (nay).
- X Paired against.
- – Announced against.
- P Voted "present."
- C Voted "present" to avoid possible conflict of interest.
- ? Did not vote or otherwise make a position known.

Democrats *Republicans*

ND Northern Democrats SD Southern Democrats

Southern states - Ala., Ark., Fla., Ga., Ky., La., Miss., N.C., Okla., S.C., Tenn., Texas, Va.

125. S 947. Fiscal 1998 Budget Reconciliation — Spending/ Quality Services. Wellstone, D-Minn., motion to waive the Budget Act with respect to the Domenici, R-N.M., point of order against the Wellstone amendment to ensure actuarially sufficient reimbursement rates for hospitals and nursing facilities. Motion rejected 38-61: R 2-53; D 36-8 (ND 31-5, SD 5-3), June 25, 1997. A three-fifths majority vote (60) of the total Senate is required to waive the Budget Act. (Subsequently, the chair upheld the Domenici point of order and the amendment fell.) Following the vote, Frist, R-Tenn., asked and was granted unanimous consent to change his vote from "yea" to "nay." The change is reflected on this chart. The Congressional Record for June 25 should have reflected the change, but it did not.

126. S 947. Fiscal 1998 Budget Reconciliation — Spending/ Higher Education. Dodd, D-Conn., motion to waive the Budget Act with respect to the Domenici, R-N.M., point of order against the Kennedy, D-Mass., amendment to revise the 1965 Higher Education Act regarding the recovery of reserve funds, the repeal of direct loan origination fees and the extension of student aid programs. Motion rejected 43-57: R 0-55; D 43-2 (ND 36-1, SD 7-1), June 25, 1997. A three-fifths majority vote (60) of the total Senate is required to waive the Budget Act. (Subsequently, the chair upheld the Domenici point of order and the amendment fell.)

127. S 947. Fiscal 1998 Budget Reconciliation — Spending/ Health Benefits Transfer. Kennedy, D-Mass., motion to waive the Budget Act with respect to the Domenici, R-N.M., point of order against the Kennedy amendment to immediately transfer certain home health benefits from Medicare Part A to Medicare Part B. The bill would make similar transfers over seven years. Motion rejected 38-62: R 0-55; D 38-7 (ND 31-6, SD 7-1), June 25, 1997. A three-fifths majority vote (60) of the total Senate is required to waive the Budget Act. (Subsequently, the chair upheld the Domenici point of order and the amendment fell.)

128. S 947. Fiscal 1998 Budget Reconciliation — Spending/ Uninsured Children. Domenici, R-N.M., motion to table (kill) the Kennedy, D-Mass., amendment to revise the Social Security Act to include additional benefits for children with special needs, including physical, speech and language therapy, and mental health services. Motion agreed to 57-43: R 52-3; D 5-40 (ND 3-34, SD 2-6), June 25, 1997.

129. S 947. Fiscal 1998 Budget Reconciliation — Spending/ Abortion. Kerrey, D-Neb., amendment to strike from the children's health initiative the "Hyde Amendment" prohibiting the use of federal funds for abortions except in cases of rape, incest or threat to a woman's life. Rejected 39-61: R 5-50; D 34-11 (ND 30-7, SD 4-4), June 25, 1997.

130. S 947. Fiscal 1998 Budget Reconciliation — Spending/ Passage. Passage of the bill to cut spending by $135.9 billion between fiscal 1998 and fiscal 2002. The bill would cut the growth of Medicare by about $115 billion, gradually increase the Medicare eligibility age from 65 to 67 between 2003 and 2027 and introduce means-based testing to determine premiums under Medicare Part B. It would cut Medicaid spending by $13.6 billion, boost spending on children's health care by $16 billion. As part of the children's health initiative, the use of federal funds for abortions would be prohibited except in cases of rape or incest, or when a woman's life is threatened. Passed 73-27: R 52-3; D 21-24 (ND 15-22, SD 6-2), June 25, 1997.

131. S 949. Fiscal 1998 Budget Reconciliation — Revenue/ Mining. Gregg, R-N.H., motion to waive the Budget Act with respect to the Murkowski, R-Alaska, point of order against the Bumpers, D-Ark., amendment to revise the Internal Revenue Code and repeal the "depletion allowance" tax break available to hardrock mining companies. Motion rejected 36-63: R 7-47; D 29-16 (ND 26-11, SD 3-5), June 26, 1997. A three-fifths majority vote (60) of the total Senate is required to waive the Budget Act. (Subsequently, the chair upheld the Murkowski point of order and the amendment failed.)

SENATE VOTES 132, 133, 134, 135, 136, 137

	132	133	134	135	136	137
ALABAMA						
Sessions	N	N	N	N	N	N
Shelby	N	N	N	Y	N	Y
ALASKA						
Murkowski	N	N	N	Y	N	N
Stevens	N	N	N	Y	N	N
ARIZONA						
Kyl	N	N	N	N	N	N
McCain	N	N	N	Y	C	Y
ARKANSAS						
Hutchinson	N	N	N	N	N	N
Bumpers	N	Y	Y	Y	Y	Y
CALIFORNIA						
Boxer	Y	Y	Y	Y	N	Y
Feinstein	N	Y	Y	Y	N	Y
COLORADO						
Allard	N	N	N	Y	N	N
Campbell	N	N	N	Y	N	N
CONNECTICUT						
Dodd	N	Y	Y	Y	N	Y
Lieberman	N	N	Y	Y	N	Y
DELAWARE						
Roth	N	N	N	Y	N	N
Biden	N	Y	Y	Y	N	Y
FLORIDA						
Mack	N	N	N	Y	N	N
Graham	N	N	N	Y	N	N
GEORGIA						
Coverdell	N	N	N	N	N	N
Cleland	N	N	Y	Y	Y	N
HAWAII						
Akaka	Y	Y	Y	Y	N	N
Inouye	Y	Y	Y	Y	N	N
IDAHO						
Craig	N	N	N	N	N	N
Kempthorne	N	N	N	Y	N	N
ILLINOIS						
Durbin	Y	Y	Y	Y	N	Y
Moseley-Braun	N	Y	Y	Y	N	N
INDIANA						
Coats	N	N	N	N	N	N
Lugar	N	N	N	Y	N	Y
IOWA						
Grassley	N	N	N	Y	N	N
Harkin	Y	Y	Y	Y	N	Y
KANSAS						
Brownback	N	N	N	Y	N	N
Roberts	?	?	?	?	?	?
KENTUCKY						
McConnell	N	N	N	N	N	N
Ford	Y	Y	Y	N	N	N
LOUISIANA						
Breaux	N	N	N	Y	N	N
Landrieu	N	N	Y	Y	N	Y
MAINE						
Collins	N	N	N	Y	N	Y
Snowe	N	N	N	Y	N	N
MARYLAND						
Mikulski	Y	N	Y	Y	N	Y
Sarbanes	Y	Y	Y	Y	Y	Y
MASSACHUSETTS						
Kennedy	Y	Y	Y	Y	Y	Y
Kerry	N	Y	Y	Y	N	Y
MICHIGAN						
Abraham	N	N	N	Y	N	Y
Levin	Y	Y	Y	Y	N	Y
MINNESOTA						
Grams	N	N	N	N	N	N
Wellstone	Y	Y	Y	Y	Y	Y
MISSISSIPPI						
Cochran	N	N	N	Y	N	N
Lott	N	N	N	Y	N	N
MISSOURI						
Ashcroft	N	N	N	N	N	N
Bond	N	N	N	Y	N	Y
MONTANA						
Burns	N	N	N	Y	N	N
Baucus	N	N	N	Y	N	N
NEBRASKA						
Hagel	N	N	N	Y	N	N
Kerrey	N	N	N	Y	N	N
NEVADA						
Bryan	N	N	N	Y	N	N
Reid	N	Y	Y	Y	N	Y
NEW HAMPSHIRE						
Gregg	N	N	N	N	N	Y
Smith	N	N	N	N	N	N
NEW JERSEY						
Lautenberg	Y	Y	Y	Y	N	Y
Torricelli	N	Y	Y	Y	N	Y
NEW MEXICO						
Domenici	N	N	N	Y	N	N
Bingaman	N	Y	Y	Y	N	Y
NEW YORK						
D'Amato	N	?	N	Y	N	N
Moynihan	N	N	N	Y	N	N
NORTH CAROLINA						
Faircloth	N	N	N	N	N	N
Helms	N	N	N	N	Y	N
NORTH DAKOTA						
Conrad	Y	Y	Y	Y	N	N
Dorgan	Y	Y	Y	Y	N	Y
OHIO						
DeWine	N	N	N	Y	Y	Y
Glenn	N	Y	Y	Y	Y	Y
OKLAHOMA						
Inhofe	N	N	N	N	N	N
Nickles	N	N	N	N	N	N
OREGON						
Smith	N	N	N	Y	N	N
Wyden	N	Y	Y	Y	N	Y
PENNSYLVANIA						
Santorum	N	N	N	Y	N	Y
Specter	N	N	N	Y	N	Y
RHODE ISLAND						
Chafee	N	N	N	Y	N	N
Reed	Y	Y	Y	Y	N	Y
SOUTH CAROLINA						
Thurmond	N	N	N	N	Y	N
Hollings	Y	Y	Y	Y	N	N
SOUTH DAKOTA						
Daschle	Y	Y	Y	Y	N	Y
Johnson	Y	Y	Y	Y	N	Y
TENNESSEE						
Frist	N	N	N	Y	N	N
Thompson	N	N	N	N	N	N
TEXAS						
Gramm	N	N	N	N	N	N
Hutchison	N	N	N	Y	N	Y
UTAH						
Bennett	N	N	N	Y	N	N
Hatch	N	N	N	Y	Y	N
VERMONT						
Jeffords	N	N	N	Y	N	N
Leahy	Y	Y	Y	Y	N	Y
VIRGINIA						
Warner	N	N	N	Y	N	N
Robb	Y	Y	Y	Y	N	N
WASHINGTON						
Gorton	N	N	N	Y	N	Y
Murray	Y	Y	Y	Y	N	Y
WEST VIRGINIA						
Byrd	Y	Y	N	Y	Y	N
Rockefeller	Y	N	Y	Y	Y	N
WISCONSIN						
Feingold	Y	Y	Y	Y	N	Y
Kohl	N	Y	Y	Y	N	Y
WYOMING						
Enzi	N	N	N	Y	N	N
Thomas	N	N	N	Y	N	N

KEY

- Y Voted for (yea).
- # Paired for.
- \+ Announced for.
- N Voted against (nay).
- X Paired against.
- – Announced against.
- P Voted "present."
- C Voted "present" to avoid possible conflict of interest.
- ? Did not vote or otherwise make a position known.

Democrats *Republicans*

ND Northern Democrats SD Southern Democrats

Southern states - Ala., Ark., Fla., Ga., Ky., La., Miss., N.C., Okla., S.C., Tenn., Texas, Va.

132. S 949. Fiscal 1998 Budget Reconciliation — Revenue/ Capital Gains Cut Limit. Dorgan, D-N.D., amendment to impose a $1 million lifetime cap on capital gains reduction. Rejected 24-75: R 0-54; D 24-21 (ND 21-16, SD 3-5), June 26, 1997.

133. S 949. Fiscal 1998 Budget Reconciliation — Revenue/ Refer. Dorgan, D-N.D., motion to waive the Budget Act with respect to the Roth, R-Del., point of order against the Dorgan motion to refer the bill to the Budget Committee with instructions to report it back with an amendment to temporarily sunset certain tax cuts if revenues lost due to the bill exceed the budget agreement's restrictions and there is a deficit. Motion rejected 34-64: R 0-53; D 34-11 (ND 30-7, SD 4-4), June 26, 1997. A three-fifths majority vote (60) of the total Senate is required to waive the Budget Act. (Subsequently, the chair upheld the Roth point of order and the bill was not referred.)

134. S 949. Fiscal 1998 Budget Reconciliation — Revenue/ Daschle Substitute. Daschle, D-S.D., substitute amendment to revise the Internal Revenue Code and establish a $500-per-child tax credit refundable against payroll taxes, such as Social Security. The substitute also would expand the capital gains tax exclusion for small businesses and create a special estate tax exemption for certain family-owned businesses and farms. Rejected 38-61: R 0-54; D 38-7 (ND 32-5, SD 6-2), June 26, 1997.

135. S 949. Fiscal 1998 Budget Reconciliation — Revenue/ Children's Health. Roth, R-Del., motion to waive the Budget Act with respect to the Domenici, R-N.M., point of order against the Roth amendment to revise the Social Security Act and provide $8 billion to states between fiscal 1998 and fiscal 2002 to expand health insurance coverage for low-income children. Motion agreed to 80-19: R 36-18; D 44-1 (ND 37-0, SD 7-1), June 26, 1997. A three-fifths majority vote (60) of the total Senate is required to waive the Budget Act. (Subsequently, the chair overruled the Domenici point of order and the amendment was adopted by voice vote.)

136. S 949. Fiscal 1998 Budget Reconciliation — Revenue/ Alcohol Advertising. Byrd, D-W.Va., motion to waive the Budget Act with respect to the Roth, R-Del., point of order against the Byrd amendment to eliminate tax deductions for alcoholic beverage advertisement and promotion. Motion rejected 12-86: R 4-49; D 8-37 (ND 6-31, SD 2-6), June 26, 1997. A three-fifths majority vote (60) of the total Senate is required to waive the Budget Act. (Subsequently, the chair upheld the Roth point of order and the amendment fell.)

137. S 949. Fiscal 1998 Budget Reconciliation — Revenue/ Tobacco Products. Durbin, D-Ill., motion to waive the Budget Act with respect to the Roth, R-Del., point of order against the Durbin amendment to increase the tax deduction for medical insurance and to increase taxes on tobacco products including cigarettes, cigars, cigarette papers, smokeless tobacco and pipe tobacco. Motion rejected 41-58: R 12-42; D 29-16 (ND 27-10, SD 2-6), June 26, 1997. A three-fifths majority vote (60) of the total Senate is required to waive the Budget Act. (Subsequently, the chair upheld the Roth point of order and the amendment fell.)

SENATE VOTES 138, 139, 140, 141, 142, 143, 144, 145

	138	139	140	141	142	143	144	145
ALABAMA								
Sessions	Y	Y	N	Y	Y	N	Y	Y
Shelby	Y	Y	N	Y	Y	N	Y	Y
ALASKA								
Murkowski	Y	Y	N	Y	N	N	Y	Y
Stevens	Y	N	N	Y	N	N	Y	Y
ARIZONA								
Kyl	Y	Y	N	Y	Y	N	Y	Y
McCain	Y	Y	N	Y	Y	N	Y	Y
ARKANSAS								
Hutchinson	Y	Y	N	Y	Y	N	Y	Y
Bumpers	Y	N	Y	N	N	Y	N	N
CALIFORNIA								
Boxer	Y	N	Y	Y	N	Y	N	N
Feinstein	Y	N	Y	Y	N	N	N	N
COLORADO								
Allard	Y	Y	N	Y	Y	N	Y	Y
Campbell	Y	Y	N	Y	N	N	Y	Y
CONNECTICUT								
Dodd	Y	N	Y	Y	N	Y	N	N
Lieberman	Y	N	N	Y	N	Y	N	N
DELAWARE								
Roth	Y	N	N	Y	N	N	Y	Y
Biden	Y	N	Y	Y	N	Y	N	N
FLORIDA								
Mack	Y	N	N	Y	Y	N	Y	Y
Graham	Y	N	N	Y	N	Y	N	N
GEORGIA								
Coverdell	Y	Y	N	Y	Y	N	Y	Y
Cleland	Y	N	Y	Y	N	Y	N	N
HAWAII								
Akaka	Y	Y	Y	Y	N	Y	N	N
Inouye	Y	N	Y	Y	N	Y	N	N
IDAHO								
Craig	Y	N	N	Y	Y	N	Y	Y
Kempthorne	Y	Y	N	Y	Y	N	Y	Y
ILLINOIS								
Durbin	Y	N	?	Y	N	Y	N	N
Moseley-Braun	?	N	N	Y	N	Y	N	N
INDIANA								
Coats	Y	Y	Y	Y	Y	N	Y	Y
Lugar	Y	Y	N	Y	N	N	N	Y
IOWA								
Grassley	Y	N	N	Y	Y	N	Y	Y
Harkin	Y	N	Y	Y	N	Y	N	N
KANSAS								
Brownback	Y	Y	N	Y	Y	N	Y	Y
Roberts	?	Y	N	Y	N	N	Y	Y
KENTUCKY								
McConnell	Y	Y	N	Y	Y	N	Y	Y
Ford	Y	N	Y	Y	N	Y	N	N
LOUISIANA								
Breaux	Y	N	Y	Y	N	N	N	N
Landrieu	Y	N	Y	Y	N	Y	N	N
MAINE								
Collins	Y	Y	Y	Y	Y	Y	N	Y
Snowe	Y	Y	N	Y	N	Y	N	Y
MARYLAND								
Mikulski	Y	N	Y	Y	N	Y	N	N
Sarbanes	Y	N	Y	Y	N	Y	N	N
MASSACHUSETTS								
Kennedy	Y	N	Y	Y	N	Y	N	N
Kerry	Y	N	Y	Y	N	Y	N	N
MICHIGAN								
Abraham	Y	Y	N	Y	Y	N	Y	Y
Levin	Y	N	Y	Y	N	Y	N	N
MINNESOTA								
Grams	Y	Y	N	Y	Y	N	Y	Y
Wellstone	Y	Y	Y	N	N	Y	N	N
MISSISSIPPI								
Cochran	Y	N	N	Y	N	N	N	Y
Lott	Y	N	N	Y	Y	N	Y	Y
MISSOURI								
Ashcroft	Y	Y	N	Y	Y	N	Y	Y
Bond	Y	Y	N	Y	Y	N	N	Y
MONTANA								
Burns	Y	Y	N	Y	N	N	N	Y
Baucus	Y	N	N	Y	N	N	N	N
NEBRASKA								
Hagel	Y	Y	N	Y	Y	N	Y	Y
Kerrey	Y	N	N	Y	N	Y	N	N
NEVADA								
Bryan	Y	N	N	Y	N	Y	N	N
Reid	Y	N	Y	Y	N	Y	N	N
NEW HAMPSHIRE								
Gregg	Y	N	N	Y	Y	Y	Y	Y
Smith	Y	Y	N	Y	Y	N	Y	Y
NEW JERSEY								
Lautenberg	Y	N	Y	Y	N	Y	N	N
Torricelli	Y	N	Y	Y	N	Y	N	N
NEW MEXICO								
Domenici	Y	Y	N	Y	N	N	N	Y
Bingaman	Y	N	Y	Y	N	Y	N	N
NEW YORK								
D'Amato	Y	Y	N	Y	N	N	Y	Y
Moynihan	Y	N	N	Y	N	Y	N	N
NORTH CAROLINA								
Faircloth	Y	Y	N	Y	Y	N	Y	Y
Helms	Y	Y	N	Y	Y	N	Y	Y
NORTH DAKOTA								
Conrad	Y	Y	Y	Y	N	Y	N	N
Dorgan	Y	Y	Y	Y	N	Y	N	N
OHIO								
DeWine	Y	Y	N	Y	N	N	N	Y
Glenn	Y	N	Y	Y	N	Y	N	N
OKLAHOMA								
Inhofe	Y	Y	N	Y	Y	N	Y	Y
Nickles	Y	Y	N	Y	Y	N	Y	Y
OREGON								
Smith	Y	Y	N	Y	N	N	N	Y
Wyden	Y	N	Y	Y	N	Y	N	N
PENNSYLVANIA								
Santorum	Y	Y	N	Y	Y	N	Y	Y
Specter	Y	N	Y	Y	N	Y	N	Y
RHODE ISLAND								
Chafee	Y	N	N	Y	N	Y	N	Y
Reed	Y	N	Y	Y	N	Y	N	N
SOUTH CAROLINA								
Thurmond	Y	Y	N	Y	Y	N	Y	Y
Hollings	Y	N	Y	Y	Y	Y	N	N
SOUTH DAKOTA								
Daschle	Y	N	Y	Y	N	Y	N	N
Johnson	Y	Y	Y	Y	N	Y	N	N
TENNESSEE								
Frist	Y	Y	N	Y	Y	N	Y	Y
Thompson	Y	Y	N	Y	Y	N	Y	Y
TEXAS								
Gramm	Y	Y	N	Y	Y	N	Y	Y
Hutchison	Y	Y	N	Y	Y	N	Y	Y
UTAH								
Bennett	Y	N	N	Y	N	N	Y	Y
Hatch	Y	N	N	Y	Y	N	Y	Y
VERMONT								
Jeffords	Y	N	Y	Y	N	Y	N	Y
Leahy	Y	N	Y	Y	N	Y	N	N
VIRGINIA								
Warner	Y	Y	N	Y	N	N	Y	Y
Robb	Y	N	Y	Y	N	Y	N	Y
WASHINGTON								
Gorton	Y	N	N	Y	N	N	N	Y
Murray	Y	N	Y	Y	N	Y	N	N
WEST VIRGINIA								
Byrd	Y	N	N	Y	N	Y	N	N
Rockefeller	Y	N	N	Y	N	Y	N	N
WISCONSIN								
Feingold	Y	N	Y	Y	N	Y	N	N
Kohl	Y	N	Y	Y	N	Y	N	Y
WYOMING								
Enzi	Y	Y	N	Y	Y	N	Y	Y
Thomas	Y	Y	N	Y	Y	N	Y	Y

KEY

- Y Voted for (yea).
- # Paired for.
- \+ Announced for.
- N Voted against (nay).
- X Paired against.
- \- Announced against.
- P Voted "present."
- C Voted "present" to avoid possible conflict of interest.
- ? Did not vote or otherwise make a position known.

Democrats *Republicans*

ND Northern Democrats SD Southern Democrats

Southern states - Ala., Ark., Fla., Ga., Ky., La., Miss., N.C., Okla., S.C., Tenn., Texas, Va.

138. S 949. Fiscal 1998 Budget Reconciliation — Revenue/Health Insurance Deduction. Nickles, R-Okla., amendment to increase the tax deduction for health insurance for the self-employed through calendar year 2007, when the deduction would be 100 percent. Adopted 98-0: R 54-0; D 44-0 (ND 36-0, SD 8-0), June 27, 1997.

139. S 949. Fiscal 1998 Budget Reconciliation — Revenue/Child Credit Requirements. Gramm, R-Texas, amendment to eliminate the requirement that the $500-per-child tax credit be invested in a tuition program or education individual retirement account. Rejected 46-54: R 41-14; D 5-40 (ND 5-32, SD 0-8), June 27, 1997.

140. S 949. Fiscal 1998 Budget Reconciliation — Revenue/Payroll Tax. Kerry, D-Mass., motion to waive the Budget Act with respect to the Domenici, R-N.M., point of order against Kerry's amendment to allow payroll taxes, rather than income taxes, to count toward the calculation of tax liability for receipt of the $500-per-child tax credit. Motion rejected 39-60: R 4-51; D 35-9 (ND 28-8, SD 7-1), June 27, 1997. A three-fifths majority vote (60) of the total Senate is required to waive the Budget Act. (Subsequently, the chair upheld the point of order and the amendment fell.)

141. S 949. Fiscal 1998 Budget Reconciliation — Revenue/Budget Enforcement. Domenici, R-N.M., amendment to enforce balanced-budget provisions and extend the 1990 Budget Enforcement Act through fiscal 2002. Adopted 98-2: R 55-0; D 43-2 (ND 36-1, SD 7-1), June 27, 1997.

142. S 949. Fiscal 1998 Budget Reconciliation — Revenue/Sequesters. Gramm, R-Texas, motion to waive the Budget Act with respect to the Lautenberg, D-N.J., point of order against Gramm's amendment to require across-the-board sequesters of appropriated accounts if needed to meet deficit targets. Motion rejected 37-63: R 36-19; D 1-44 (ND 0-37, SD 1-7), June 27, 1997. A three-fifths majority vote (60) of the total Senate is required to waive the Budget Act. (Subsequently, the chair upheld the point of order and the amendment fell.)

143. S 949. Fiscal 1998 Budget Reconciliation — Revenue/Public Lands. Bumpers, D-Ark., motion to waive the Budget Act with respect to the Domenici, R-N.M., point of order against Bumpers' amendment to prohibit scoring revenue from sales of certain federal lands for budget purposes. Under current rules sales cannot be scored if they result in lost revenue. Motion rejected 48-52: R 6-49; D 42-3 (ND 35-2, SD 7-1), June 27, 1997. A three-fifths majority vote (60) of the total Senate is required to waive the Budget Act. (Subsequently, the chair upheld the point of order and the amendment fell.)

144. S 949. Fiscal 1998 Budget Reconciliation — Revenue/Taxes. Craig, R-Idaho, motion to waive the Budget Act with respect to the Lautenberg, D-N.J., point of order against Craig's amendment to create a 60-vote point of order against any measure that boosts taxes to pay for mandatory spending hikes. Motion rejected 42-58: R 42-13; D 0-45 (ND 0-37, SD 0-8), June 27, 1997. A three-fifths majority vote (60) of the total Senate is required to waive the Budget Act. (Subsequently, the chair upheld the point of order and the amendment fell.)

145. S 949. Fiscal 1998 Budget Reconciliation — Revenue/Targets. Brownback, R-Kan., motion to waive the Budget Act with respect to the Lautenberg, D-N.J., point of order against Brownback's second-degree amendment to create a 60-vote point of order against any measure that exceeds projected spending targets between fiscal 1998 and fiscal 2002. Motion rejected 57-43: R 55-0; D 2-43 (ND 1-36, SD 1-7), June 27, 1997. A three-fifths majority vote (60) of the total Senate is required to waive the Budget Act. (Subsequently, the chair upheld the point of order and the amendment fell.)

SENATE VOTES 146, 147, 148, 149, 150, 151, 152, 153

	146	147	148	149	150	151	152	153
ALABAMA								
Sessions	Y	Y	Y	N	Y	N	N	N
Shelby	Y	Y	Y	N	Y	N	N	N
ALASKA								
Murkowski	Y	Y	Y	N	Y	N	N	N
Stevens	Y	Y	Y	N	Y	N	Y	Y
ARIZONA								
Kyl	Y	Y	Y	N	Y	N	N	N
McCain	Y	Y	N	N	Y	N	Y	N
ARKANSAS								
Hutchinson	Y	Y	Y	N	Y	N	N	N
Bumpers	N	N	Y	Y	N	Y	Y	Y
CALIFORNIA								
Boxer	N	N	Y	Y	N	Y	Y	Y
Feinstein	N	N	Y	Y	N	Y	Y	Y
COLORADO								
Allard	Y	Y	N	N	Y	N	Y	Y
Campbell	Y	Y	Y	N	Y	N	Y	Y
CONNECTICUT								
Dodd	N	N	Y	Y	N	Y	Y	Y
Lieberman	N	N	Y	Y	Y	N	Y	Y
DELAWARE								
Roth	Y	Y	Y	N	Y	N	N	N
Biden	N	N	Y	Y	Y	N	Y	Y
FLORIDA								
Mack	Y	Y	Y	N	Y	N	N	Y
Graham	N	N	Y	N	N	N	Y	Y
GEORGIA								
Coverdell	Y	Y	Y	N	Y	N	Y	Y
Cleland	N	N	Y	Y	N	Y	Y	Y
HAWAII								
Akaka	N	N	Y	Y	N	Y	Y	Y
Inouye	N	N	Y	N	N	Y	Y	Y
IDAHO								
Craig	Y	Y	N	N	Y	N	N	N
Kempthorne	Y	Y	Y	N	Y	N	Y	N
ILLINOIS								
Durbin	N	N	Y	Y	N	Y	Y	Y
Moseley-Braun	N	N	Y	N	N	N	N	Y
INDIANA								
Coats	Y	Y	Y	N	Y	N	Y	N
Lugar	Y	Y	Y	N	Y	N	Y	N
IOWA								
Grassley	Y	Y	Y	N	Y	N	Y	N
Harkin	N	N	Y	Y	Y	Y	Y	Y
KANSAS								
Brownback	Y	Y	N	N	Y	N	Y	N
Roberts	Y	Y	Y	N	Y	N	Y	Y
KENTUCKY								
McConnell	Y	Y	Y	N	Y	N	Y	N
Ford	N	N	Y	N	N	Y	Y	Y
LOUISIANA								
Breaux	N	N	Y	N	Y	N	N	Y
Landrieu	N	N	Y	N	Y	N	Y	Y
MAINE								
Collins	Y	Y	Y	N	N	Y	Y	N
Snowe	Y	Y	Y	N	N	Y	Y	Y
MARYLAND								
Mikulski	N	N	Y	Y	N	N	Y	Y
Sarbanes	N	N	Y	Y	N	Y	Y	Y
MASSACHUSETTS								
Kennedy	N	N	Y	Y	N	Y	Y	Y
Kerry	N	N	Y	Y	N	Y	Y	Y
MICHIGAN								
Abraham	Y	Y	Y	N	Y	N	Y	N
Levin	N	N	Y	Y	N	Y	Y	Y
MINNESOTA								
Grams	Y	Y	Y	N	Y	N	Y	N
Wellstone	N	N	N	Y	N	Y	Y	Y
MISSISSIPPI								
Cochran	Y	Y	Y	N	Y	N	N	N
Lott	Y	Y	Y	N	Y	N	N	N
MISSOURI								
Ashcroft	Y	Y	N	N	Y	N	Y	N
Bond	Y	Y	Y	N	Y	N	N	N
MONTANA								
Burns	Y	Y	Y	N	Y	N	N	N
Baucus	N	N	Y	N	N	N	Y	Y
NEBRASKA								
Hagel	Y	Y	Y	N	Y	N	N	N
Kerrey	N	N	Y	N	N	N	N	Y
NEVADA								
Bryan	N	N	Y	N	N	N	Y	Y
Reid	N	N	Y	Y	N	Y	Y	Y
NEW HAMPSHIRE								
Gregg	Y	Y	Y	N	Y	N	Y	N
Smith	Y	Y	Y	N	Y	N	Y	N
NEW JERSEY								
Lautenberg	N	N	Y	Y	N	Y	Y	Y
Torricelli	N	N	Y	Y	Y	N	Y	Y
NEW MEXICO								
Domenici	Y	Y	Y	N	Y	N	Y	N
Bingaman	N	N	Y	Y	N	Y	Y	Y
NEW YORK								
D'Amato	Y	Y	Y	N	Y	N	Y	Y
Moynihan	N	N	Y	N	N	N	N	N
NORTH CAROLINA								
Faircloth	Y	Y	Y	N	Y	N	N	N
Helms	Y	Y	Y	N	Y	N	N	N
NORTH DAKOTA								
Conrad	Y	N	Y	N	N	Y	Y	Y
Dorgan	N	N	Y	Y	N	Y	Y	Y
OHIO								
DeWine	Y	Y	Y	N	Y	N	Y	N
Glenn	N	N	Y	Y	N	Y	Y	Y
OKLAHOMA								
Inhofe	Y	Y	Y	N	Y	N	N	N
Nickles	Y	Y	Y	N	Y	N	N	N
OREGON								
Smith	Y	Y	Y	N	Y	N	Y	Y
Wyden	N	N	Y	Y	N	N	Y	Y
PENNSYLVANIA								
Santorum	Y	Y	N	N	Y	N	Y	N
Specter	Y	Y	Y	N	Y	N	Y	Y
RHODE ISLAND								
Chafee	Y	N	Y	N	N	N	N	Y
Reed	N	N	Y	Y	N	Y	Y	Y
SOUTH CAROLINA								
Thurmond	Y	Y	Y	N	Y	N	Y	N
Hollings	N	N	Y	N	N	Y	Y	?
SOUTH DAKOTA								
Daschle	N	N	Y	Y	N	Y	Y	Y
Johnson	N	N	Y	Y	N	Y	Y	Y
TENNESSEE								
Frist	Y	Y	Y	N	Y	N	Y	N
Thompson	Y	Y	Y	N	Y	N	Y	N
TEXAS								
Gramm	Y	Y	N	N	Y	N	N	N
Hutchison	Y	Y	Y	N	Y	N	Y	Y
UTAH								
Bennett	Y	Y	Y	N	Y	N	N	N
Hatch	Y	Y	Y	N	Y	N	Y	N
VERMONT								
Jeffords	Y	Y	Y	N	N	Y	Y	Y
Leahy	N	N	Y	Y	Y	Y	Y	Y
VIRGINIA								
Warner	Y	Y	Y	N	Y	N	Y	Y
Robb	Y	N	Y	N	N	Y	Y	Y
WASHINGTON								
Gorton	Y	N	Y	N	Y	N	N	N
Murray	N	N	Y	Y	N	Y	Y	Y
WEST VIRGINIA								
Byrd	N	N	Y	N	N	Y	N	N
Rockefeller	N	N	Y	N	N	N	Y	Y
WISCONSIN								
Feingold	Y	N	Y	Y	N	Y	Y	Y
Kohl	Y	N	Y	Y	Y	N	Y	Y
WYOMING								
Enzi	Y	Y	Y	N	Y	N	N	Y
Thomas	Y	Y	Y	N	Y	N	N	N

KEY

- Y Voted for (yea).
- # Paired for.
- + Announced for.
- N Voted against (nay).
- X Paired against.
- \- Announced against.
- P Voted "present."
- C Voted "present" to avoid possible conflict of interest.
- ? Did not vote or otherwise make a position known.

Democrats ***Republicans***

ND Northern Democrats SD Southern Democrats

Southern states - Ala., Ark., Fla., Ga., Ky., La., Miss., N.C., Okla., S.C., Tenn., Texas, Va.

146. S 949. Fiscal 1998 Budget Reconciliation — Revenue/Enforcement. Frist, R-Tenn., motion to waive the Budget Act with respect to the Lautenberg, D-N.J., point of order against Frist's amendment to create a 60-vote point of order against a measure that would cause a deficit for fiscal 2002 or beyond. Motion rejected 59-41: R 55-0; D 4-41 (ND 3-34, SD 1-7), June 27, 1997. A three-fifths majority vote (60) of the total Senate is required to waive the Budget Act. (Subsequently, the chair upheld the point of order and the amendment fell.)

147. S 949. Fiscal 1998 Budget Reconciliation — Revenue/Windfalls. Abraham, R-Mich., motion to waive the Budget Act with respect to the Lautenberg, D-N.J., point of order against Abraham's amendment to require that unplanned revenue windfalls be used to decrease the deficit or reduce taxes. Motion rejected 53-47: R 53-2; D 0-45 (ND 0-37, SD 0-8), June 27, 1997. A three-fifths majority vote (60) of the total Senate is required to waive the Budget Act. (Subsequently, the chair upheld the point of order and the amendment fell.)

148. S 949. Fiscal 1998 Budget Reconciliation — Revenue/Debate. Byrd, D-W.Va., amendment to allow 30 hours of debate on reconciliation bills instead of 20, prohibit new first-degree amendments after 15 hours of debate and prohibit new second-degree amendments after 20 hours of debate. Adopted 92-8: R 48-7; D 44-1 (ND 36-1, SD 8-0), June 27, 1997.

149. S 949. Fiscal 1998 Budget Reconciliation — Revenue/Children's Health. Kennedy, D-Mass., motion to waive the Budget Act with respect to the Domenici, R-N.M., point of order against Kennedy's amendment to increase the excise tax on cigarettes by 43 cents per pack to provide $12 billion for children's health insurance programs through fiscal 2002. Motion rejected 30-70: R 0-55; D 30-15 (ND 28-9, SD 2-6), June 27, 1997. A three-fifths majority vote (60) of the total Senate is required to waive the Budget Act. (Subsequently, the chair upheld the point of order and the amendment fell.) A "yea" was a vote in support of the president's position.

150. S 949. Fiscal 1998 Budget Reconciliation — Revenue/Elementary Schools. Coverdell, R-Ga., amendment to expand the proposed education individual retirement account and allow tax credits to be spent penalty-free on elementary and secondary education expenses. Adopted 59-41: R 50-5; D 8-37 (ND 6-31, SD 2-6), June 27, 1997. (After the vote, Bond, R-Mo., was given unanimous consent to change his vote from "nay" to "yea." That change is reflected on this chart.)

151. S 949. Fiscal 1998 Budget Reconciliation — Revenue/IRA Plus Accounts. Bingaman, D-N.M., amendment to strike establishing non-deductible individual retirement "plus" accounts. Rejected 33-67: R 3-52; D 30-15 (ND 25-12, SD 5-3), June 27, 1997.

152. S 949. Fiscal 1998 Budget Reconciliation — Revenue/Child Care. Kohl, D-Wis., motion to waive the Budget Act with respect to the Roth, R-Del., point of order against Kohl's amendment to provide tax credits to employers who provide quality child care for dependents of their employees. Motion agreed to 72-28: R 32-23; D 40-5 (ND 33-4, SD 7-1), June 27, 1997. A three-fifths majority vote (60) of the total Senate is required to waive the Budget Act. (Subsequently, the chair overruled the point of order and the amendment was adopted by voice vote.)

153. S 949. Fiscal 1998 Budget Reconciliation — Revenue/Child Care. Jeffords, R-Vt., motion to waive the Budget Act with respect to the Roth, R-Del., point of order against Jeffords' amendment to expand tax credits for businesses with quality child care and mandate that home child care providers meet added requirements. Motion rejected 57-42: R 15-40; D 42-2 (ND 35-2, SD 7-0), June 27, 1997. A three-fifths majority vote (60) of the total Senate is required to waive the Budget Act. (Subsequently, the chair upheld the point of order and the amendment fell.)

SENATE VOTES 154, 155, 156, 157, 158, 159, 160

	154	155	156	157	158	159	160
ALABAMA							
Sessions	N	Y	N	N	N	Y	Y
Shelby	N	Y	N	N	N	Y	Y
ALASKA							
Murkowski	N	N	N	Y	N	N	Y
Stevens	Y	Y	N	Y	N	N	Y
ARIZONA							
Kyl	N	Y	N	N	N	Y	Y
McCain	Y	Y	N	N	N	Y	Y
ARKANSAS							
Hutchinson	N	N	N	Y	N	Y	Y
Bumpers	Y	N	Y	Y	Y	N	N
CALIFORNIA							
Boxer	Y	N	Y	Y	Y	N	Y
Feinstein	Y	N	Y	Y	Y	N	Y
COLORADO							
Allard	N	N	N	N	N	Y	Y
Campbell	N	N	N	Y	N	Y	Y
CONNECTICUT							
Dodd	Y	N	Y	Y	Y	N	Y
Lieberman	Y	Y	Y	Y	Y	N	Y
DELAWARE							
Roth	N	N	N	Y	N	N	Y
Biden	Y	N	Y	Y	Y	N	Y
FLORIDA							
Mack	Y	N	N	Y	N	Y	Y
Graham	Y	N	N	Y	Y	N	Y
GEORGIA							
Coverdell	N	Y	N	N	N	Y	Y
Cleland	Y	N	Y	Y	N	N	Y
HAWAII							
Akaka	Y	N	Y	Y	Y	N	Y
Inouye	Y	N	?	?	?	?	+
IDAHO							
Craig	N	N	N	N	N	Y	Y
Kempthorne	N	N	N	N	N	Y	Y
ILLINOIS							
Durbin	Y	N	Y	Y	Y	N	N
Moseley-Braun	Y	N	N	Y	Y	N	Y
INDIANA							
Coats	N	Y	N	Y	Y	Y	Y
Lugar	N	N	N	Y	N	N	Y
IOWA							
Grassley	Y	N	N	Y	N	N	Y
Harkin	Y	N	Y	Y	Y	N	N
KANSAS							
Brownback	N	N	N	N	N	Y	Y
Roberts	N	N	N	Y	N	Y	Y
KENTUCKY							
McConnell	N	N	N	Y	N	Y	Y
Ford	N	N	Y	Y	N	N	N
LOUISIANA							
Breaux	N	N	Y	Y	N	N	Y
Landrieu	N	N	Y	Y	N	N	Y
MAINE							
Collins	Y	Y	Y	Y	Y	N	Y
Snowe	Y	Y	Y	Y	Y	N	Y
MARYLAND							
Mikulski	Y	N	Y	Y	Y	Y	Y
Sarbanes	Y	N	Y	Y	Y	N	N
MASSACHUSETTS							
Kennedy	Y	Y	Y	Y	Y	N	N
Kerry	Y	N	Y	Y	Y	N	N
MICHIGAN							
Abraham	N	N	N	N	N	Y	Y
Levin	Y	N	Y	Y	Y	N	N
MINNESOTA							
Grams	N	N	N	N	N	Y	N
Wellstone	Y	N	Y	Y	Y	N	N
MISSISSIPPI							
Cochran	N	N	N	Y	N	N	Y
Lott	N	N	N	Y	N	Y	Y
MISSOURI							
Ashcroft	N	N	N	N	N	Y	Y
Bond	N	N	N	N	N	Y	Y
MONTANA							
Burns	Y	N	N	Y	N	Y	Y
Baucus	N	N	N	Y	N	N	Y
NEBRASKA							
Hagel	N	N	N	Y	N	N	Y
Kerrey	Y	N	N	Y	Y	N	Y
NEVADA							
Bryan	Y	N	N	Y	N	N	Y
Reid	Y	N	Y	Y	N	N	Y
NEW HAMPSHIRE							
Gregg	N	Y	N	N	Y	Y	Y
Smith	N	Y	N	N	N	Y	Y
NEW JERSEY							
Lautenberg	Y	Y	Y	Y	Y	N	Y
Torricelli	Y	N	Y	Y	Y	Y	Y
NEW MEXICO							
Domenici	N	N	Y	Y	N	N	Y
Bingaman	N	N	Y	Y	N	N	Y
NEW YORK							
D'Amato	Y	N	Y	Y	N	N	Y
Moynihan	Y	N	N	Y	N	N	Y
NORTH CAROLINA							
Faircloth	N	N	N	Y	N	Y	N
Helms	N	N	N	Y	N	Y	N
NORTH DAKOTA							
Conrad	Y	N	N	Y	N	N	Y
Dorgan	Y	N	Y	Y	N	N	Y
OHIO							
DeWine	Y	N	N	Y	N	Y	Y
Glenn	Y	N	Y	N	Y	N	N
OKLAHOMA							
Inhofe	N	Y	N	Y	N	Y	Y
Nickles	N	Y	N	Y	N	N	Y
OREGON							
Smith	N	N	N	Y	N	Y	Y
Wyden	Y	Y	Y	Y	Y	Y	Y
PENNSYLVANIA							
Santorum	N	Y	N	Y	N	Y	Y
Specter	Y	Y	Y	Y	Y	Y	Y
RHODE ISLAND							
Chafee	N	N	N	Y	N	N	Y
Reed	Y	N	Y	Y	Y	N	N
SOUTH CAROLINA							
Thurmond	N	N	N	Y	N	Y	Y
Hollings	?	?	?	?	?	?	–
SOUTH DAKOTA							
Daschle	Y	N	Y	Y	Y	N	Y
Johnson	Y	N	Y	Y	Y	N	Y
TENNESSEE							
Frist	Y	Y	N	N	N	Y	Y
Thompson	Y	Y	N	N	N	Y	Y
TEXAS							
Gramm	N	N	N	N	N	Y	N
Hutchison	Y	Y	N	Y	N	Y	Y
UTAH							
Bennett	N	N	N	Y	N	N	Y
Hatch	N	N	N	Y	N	N	Y
VERMONT							
Jeffords	Y	N	N	Y	Y	N	Y
Leahy	Y	Y	Y	Y	Y	N	Y
VIRGINIA							
Warner	N	Y	N	N	N	Y	Y
Robb	Y	Y	Y	Y	Y	N	N
WASHINGTON							
Gorton	N	Y	N	N	N	N	Y
Murray	Y	Y	Y	Y	Y	N	Y
WEST VIRGINIA							
Byrd	N	Y	N	Y	N	N	N
Rockefeller	Y	Y	N	Y	Y	N	Y
WISCONSIN							
Feingold	N	Y	Y	Y	Y	N	N
Kohl	Y	N	Y	Y	Y	N	Y
WYOMING							
Enzi	N	N	N	Y	N	Y	Y
Thomas	N	N	N	Y	N	Y	Y

KEY

Y Voted for (yea).
Paired for.
+ Announced for.
N Voted against (nay).
X Paired against.
– Announced against.
P Voted "present."
C Voted "present" to avoid possible conflict of interest.
? Did not vote or otherwise make a position known.

Democrats *Republicans*

ND Northern Democrats SD Southern Democrats

Southern states - Ala., Ark., Fla., Ga., Ky., La., Miss., N.C., Okla., S.C., Tenn., Texas, Va.

154. S 949. Fiscal 1998 Budget Reconciliation — Revenue/Medical Research. Harkin, D-Iowa, motion to waive the Budget Act with respect to the Nickles, R-Okla., point of order against Harkin's amendment to create a "National Fund for Health Research" with revenues that exceed Joint Tax Committee estimations. Motion rejected 51-48: R 14-41; D 37-7 (ND 33-4, SD 4-3), June 27, 1997. A three-fifths majority vote (60) of the total Senate is required to waive the Budget Act. (Subsequently, the chair upheld the point of order and the amendment fell.)

155. S 949. Fiscal 1998 Budget Reconciliation — Revenue/Ethanol. McCain, R-Ariz., amendment to strike sections extending and modifying subsidies for alcohol fuels including ethanol. Rejected 30-69: R 20-35; D 10-34 (ND 9-28, SD 1-6), June 27, 1997.

156. S 949. Fiscal 1998 Budget Reconciliation — Revenue/Earned-Income Tax Credit. Landrieu, D-La., motion to waive the Budget Act with respect to the Nickles, R-Okla., point of order against Landrieu's amendment to allow taxpayers with income tax liability to take the $500-per-child tax credit before the earned-income tax credit. Motion rejected 39-59: R 5-50; D 34-9 (ND 28-8, SD 6-1), June 27, 1997. A three-fifths majority vote (60) of the total Senate is required to waive the Budget Act. (Subsequently, the chair upheld the point of order and the amendment fell.)

157. S 949. Fiscal 1998 Budget Reconciliation — Revenue/Amtrak. Roth, R-Del., motion to waive the Budget Act with respect to the McCain, R-Ariz., point of order against the bill that provides $77 billion in net tax cuts over five years and dedicates funds for Amtrak in an "intercity passenger rail fund." Motion agreed to 77-21: R 35-20; D 42-1 (ND 35-1, SD 7-0), June 27, 1997. A three-fifths majority vote (60) of the total Senate is required to waive the Budget Act. (Subsequently, the chair overruled the point of order.)

158. S 949. Fiscal 1998 Budget Reconciliation — Revenue/Mining. Feingold, D-Wis., motion to waive the Budget Act with respect to the Roth, R-Del., point of order against Feingold's amendment to end the depletion allowance tax break for mining operations involving uranium, asbestos, lead and mercury. Motion rejected 37-61: R 6-49; D 31-12 (ND 28-8, SD 3-4), June 27, 1997. A three-fifths majority vote (60) of the total Senate is required to waive the Budget Act. (Subsequently, the chair upheld the point of order and the amendment fell.)

159. S 949. Fiscal 1998 Budget Reconciliation — Revenue/Inflation Indexing. Allard, R-Colo., amendment to require capital gains to be indexed for inflation. Rejected 41-57: R 38-17; D 3-40 (ND 3-33, SD 0-7), June 27, 1997.

160. HR 2014. Fiscal 1998 Budget Reconciliation — Revenue/Passage. Passage of the bill to provide a net tax cut of about $77 billion between fiscal 1998 and fiscal 2002. The bill would boost the 24-cents-per-pack cigarette tax by 20 cents to fund an $8 billion children's health initiative. The bill would reduce the top capital gains tax rate from 28 percent to 20 percent, establish a $500-per-child tax credit for children under 17, expand tax-deferred Individual Retirement Accounts, provide an education tax credit for college tuition and provide a greater break for estate taxes. Passed 80-18: R 51-4; D 29-14 (ND 25-11, SD 4-3), June 27, 1997. (Before passage the Senate struck all after the enacting clause and inserted the text of S 949 as amended.)

SENATE VOTES 161, 162, 163, 164, 165

	161	162	163	164	165
ALABAMA					
Sessions	Y	Y	Y	Y	Y
Shelby	Y	Y	Y	Y	Y
ALASKA					
Murkowski	Y	Y	N	Y	Y
Stevens	Y	Y	N	Y	Y
ARIZONA					
Kyl	Y	Y	Y	Y	N
McCain	?	Y	N	Y	N
ARKANSAS					
Hutchinson	?	Y	N	Y	Y
Bumpers	N	N	N	Y	Y
CALIFORNIA					
Boxer	N	N	Y	Y	Y
Feinstein	N	N	Y	Y	Y
COLORADO					
Allard	Y	Y	Y	Y	Y
Campbell	Y	Y	Y	Y	Y
CONNECTICUT					
Dodd	N	Y	N	Y	Y
Lieberman	N	Y	N	Y	N
DELAWARE					
Roth	?	Y	Y	Y	N
Biden	?	Y	N	Y	N
FLORIDA					
Mack	Y	Y	Y	Y	Y
Graham	N	Y	N	Y	Y
GEORGIA					
Coverdell	Y	Y	Y	Y	Y
Cleland	N	Y	N	Y	Y
HAWAII					
Akaka	N	N	N	Y	Y
Inouye	N	Y	N	Y	N
IDAHO					
Craig	Y	Y	Y	Y	Y
Kempthorne	Y	Y	Y	Y	Y
ILLINOIS					
Durbin	N	N	N	Y	Y
Moseley-Braun	N	N	N	Y	Y
INDIANA					
Coats	?	?	Y	Y	N
Lugar	N	Y	Y	Y	N

	161	162	163	164	165
IOWA					
Grassley	Y	Y	Y	Y	N
Harkin	N	N	N	Y	N
KANSAS					
Brownback	Y	Y	N	Y	Y
Roberts	Y	Y	N	Y	Y
KENTUCKY					
McConnell	Y	Y	Y	Y	Y
Ford	N	N	N	Y	Y
LOUISIANA					
Breaux	N	Y	N	Y	Y
Landrieu	?	Y	N	Y	Y
MAINE					
Collins	Y	Y	Y	Y	Y
Snowe	Y	Y	Y	Y	Y
MARYLAND					
Mikulski	?	?	?	?	?
Sarbanes	N	N	N	Y	Y
MASSACHUSETTS					
Kennedy	N	N	N	Y	N
Kerry	N	N	N	Y	N
MICHIGAN					
Abraham	Y	Y	Y	Y	Y
Levin	N	N	N	Y	N
MINNESOTA					
Grams	Y	Y	Y	Y	Y
Wellstone	N	N	Y	Y	N
MISSISSIPPI					
Cochran	N	Y	N	Y	Y
Lott	Y	Y	Y	Y	Y
MISSOURI					
Ashcroft	Y	Y	Y	Y	Y
Bond	Y	Y	N	Y	Y
MONTANA					
Burns	Y	Y	Y	Y	Y
Baucus	N	N	N	Y	Y
NEBRASKA					
Hagel	Y	Y	Y	Y	Y
Kerrey	N	Y	N	Y	N
NEVADA					
Bryan	N	Y	N	Y	N
Reid	N	N	N	Y	N

	161	162	163	164	165
NEW HAMPSHIRE					
Gregg	Y	Y	Y	Y	Y
Smith	Y	Y	N	Y	Y
NEW JERSEY					
Lautenberg	N	N	N	Y	Y
Torricelli	N	N	N	Y	Y
NEW MEXICO					
Domenici	Y	Y	Y	Y	Y
Bingaman	N	Y	N	Y	Y
NEW YORK					
D'Amato	Y	Y	Y	Y	Y
Moynihan	N	N	N	Y	Y
NORTH CAROLINA					
Faircloth	Y	Y	Y	Y	Y
Helms	Y	Y	Y	Y	Y
NORTH DAKOTA					
Conrad	N	N	N	Y	Y
Dorgan	N	N	N	Y	Y
OHIO					
DeWine	Y	Y	Y	Y	Y
Glenn	N	N	N	Y	N
OKLAHOMA					
Inhofe	Y	Y	Y	Y	Y
Nickles	Y	Y	Y	Y	Y
OREGON					
Smith	?	Y	Y	Y	N
Wyden	N	N	N	Y	N
PENNSYLVANIA					
Santorum	Y	Y	Y	Y	Y
Specter	Y	N	Y	Y	Y
RHODE ISLAND					
Chafee	Y	Y	Y	Y	N
Reed	N	N	N	Y	N
SOUTH CAROLINA					
Thurmond	Y	Y	N	Y	Y
Hollings	N	Y	N	Y	Y
SOUTH DAKOTA					
Daschle	N	N	N	Y	Y
Johnson	N	N	N	Y	Y
TENNESSEE					
Frist	Y	Y	Y	Y	Y
Thompson	Y	Y	Y	Y	Y

KEY

- Y Voted for (yea).
- # Paired for.
- \+ Announced for.
- N Voted against (nay).
- X Paired against.
- \- Announced against.
- P Voted "present."
- C Voted "present" to avoid possible conflict of interest.
- ? Did not vote or otherwise make a position known.

Democrats ***Republicans***

	161	162	163	164	165
TEXAS					
Gramm	Y	Y	Y	Y	N
Hutchison	Y	Y	Y	Y	Y
UTAH					
Bennett	Y	Y	N	Y	Y
Hatch	Y	Y	N	Y	Y
VERMONT					
Jeffords	?	N	Y	?	Y
Leahy	N	N	N	Y	N
VIRGINIA					
Warner	Y	Y	N	Y	N
Robb	N	Y	N	Y	N
WASHINGTON					
Gorton	N	Y	Y	Y	N
Murray	N	N	Y	Y	Y
WEST VIRGINIA					
Byrd	N	N	N	Y	N
Rockefeller	N	N	N	Y	N
WISCONSIN					
Feingold	N	N	N	Y	N
Kohl	N	N	N	Y	N
WYOMING					
Enzi	Y	Y	Y	Y	N
Thomas	Y	Y	Y	Y	N

ND Northern Democrats SD Southern Democrats

Southern states - Ala., Ark., Fla., Ga., Ky., La., Miss., N.C., Okla., S.C., Tenn., Texas, Va.

161. S 936. Fiscal 1998 Defense Authorization/Cloture. Motion to invoke cloture (thus limiting debate) on the bill to authorize $268.2 billion for defense programs in fiscal 1998, an increase of $2.6 billion from the president's request. The bill would authorize about $345 million to begin accelerated purchase of a nuclear-powered aircraft carrier. Motion rejected 46-45: R 46-3; D 0-42 (ND 0-35, SD 0-7), July 8, 1997. Three-fifths of the total Senate (60) is required to invoke cloture.

162. S 936. Fiscal 1998 Defense Authorization/School Breakfast. Thurmond, R-S.C., motion to table (kill) the Wellstone, D-Minn., amendment to require the Defense secretary to transfer $5 million to the Agriculture secretary each fiscal year between fiscal 1998 and 2002 to provide funds for the school breakfast program. Motion agreed to 65-33: R 52-2; D 13-31 (ND 7-29, SD 6-2), July 9, 1997.

163. S 936. Fiscal 1998 Defense Authorization/USS *Missouri*. Gorton, R-Wash., amendment to require the Navy secretary to reopen the competition to select a location for the retired battleship USS *Missouri*, disregarding all previous applications. The Navy had decided to send the historic ship to Honolulu. Rejected 46-53: R 42-13; D 4-40 (ND 4-32, SD 0-8), July 9, 1997.

164. S 936. Fiscal 1998 Defense Authorization/Mexican Elections. Dodd, D-Conn., amendment to express the sense of Congress that the July 6, 1997, elections in Mexico were free, fair and impartial and have been respected by President Ernesto Zedillo. Adopted 98-0: R 54-0; D 44-0 (ND 36-0, SD 8-0), July 9, 1997.

165. S 936. Fiscal 1998 Defense Authorization/Base Closures. Dorgan, D-N.D., amendment to the McCain, R-Ariz., amendment, to require the Defense secretary to report to Congress on the cost and savings attributable to the four base closing rounds before 1996 and to determine if additional base closures are needed. The McCain amendment would have authorized base closure rounds in 1999 and 2001. Adopted 66-33: R 42-13; D 24-20 (ND 17-19, SD 7-1), July 9, 1997. (Subsequently, the McCain amendment, as amended, was adopted by voice vote.)

SENATE VOTES 166, 167, 168, 169, 170

	166	167	168	169	170
ALABAMA					
Sessions	N	N	Y	N	Y
Shelby	Y	N	Y	N	Y
ALASKA					
Murkowski	Y	N	Y	Y	Y
Stevens	N	Y	Y	Y	Y
ARIZONA					
Kyl	N	N	Y	Y	Y
McCain	Y	N	Y	Y	Y
ARKANSAS					
Hutchinson	N	N	Y	Y	Y
Bumpers	Y	Y	N	N	Y
CALIFORNIA					
Boxer	Y	Y	N	N	N
Feinstein	Y	Y	N	Y	Y
COLORADO					
Allard	Y	N	Y	N	Y
Campbell	Y	N	N	Y	Y
CONNECTICUT					
Dodd	N	Y	N	N	Y
Lieberman	Y	Y	Y	N	Y
DELAWARE					
Roth	Y	N	Y	Y	Y
Biden	Y	Y	N	Y	N
FLORIDA					
Mack	N	N	Y	Y	Y
Graham	Y	Y	Y	Y	Y
GEORGIA					
Coverdell	N	N	Y	Y	Y
Cleland	Y	Y	N	Y	Y
HAWAII					
Akaka	Y	Y	N	Y	N
Inouye	N	Y	N	N	Y
IDAHO					
Craig	Y	N	Y	Y	Y
Kempthorne	Y	N	Y	N	Y
ILLINOIS					
Durbin	N	Y	N	Y	N
Moseley-Braun	Y	Y	N	N	N
INDIANA					
Coats	N	N	Y	Y	Y
Lugar	N	N	Y	N	Y
IOWA					
Grassley	Y	N	N	N	N
Harkin	Y	Y	N	Y	N
KANSAS					
Brownback	Y	N	Y	Y	Y
Roberts	N	N	Y	Y	Y
KENTUCKY					
McConnell	Y	N	Y	Y	Y
Ford	N	N	N	N	Y
LOUISIANA					
Breaux	Y	N	Y	N	Y
Landrieu	Y	Y	Y	Y	Y
MAINE					
Collins	N	Y	Y	Y	Y
Snowe	N	Y	Y	Y	Y
MARYLAND					
Mikulski	?	?	?	?	?
Sarbanes	Y	Y	N	Y	Y
MASSACHUSETTS					
Kennedy	Y	Y	N	Y	N
Kerry	Y	Y	N	N	Y
MICHIGAN					
Abraham	N	N	Y	N	Y
Levin	Y	Y	N	N	Y
MINNESOTA					
Grams	Y	N	Y	Y	Y
Wellstone	Y	Y	N	N	N
MISSISSIPPI					
Cochran	N	N	Y	Y	Y
Lott	N	N	Y	Y	Y
MISSOURI					
Ashcroft	Y	N	Y	Y	Y
Bond	Y	N	Y	Y	Y
MONTANA					
Burns	N	N	Y	Y	Y
Baucus	Y	Y	N	N	Y
NEBRASKA					
Hagel	Y	N	Y	Y	Y
Kerrey	Y	Y	N	Y	Y
NEVADA					
Bryan	Y	Y	Y	N	Y
Reid	Y	N	N	N	Y
NEW HAMPSHIRE					
Gregg	Y	N	Y	Y	Y
Smith	N	N	Y	N	Y
NEW JERSEY					
Lautenberg	Y	Y	N	N	Y
Torricelli	Y	Y	N	Y	Y
NEW MEXICO					
Domenici	Y	N	Y	Y	Y
Bingaman	Y	Y	N	Y	Y
NEW YORK					
D'Amato	Y	N	N	N	Y
Moynihan	Y	Y	N	N	Y
NORTH CAROLINA					
Faircloth	Y	N	Y	N	Y
Helms	Y	N	Y	N	Y
NORTH DAKOTA					
Conrad	Y	Y	N	Y	Y
Dorgan	Y	Y	N	Y	Y
OHIO					
DeWine	N	N	Y	Y	Y
Glenn	N	Y	Y	N	Y
OKLAHOMA					
Inhofe	N	N	Y	Y	Y
Nickles	Y	N	Y	Y	Y
OREGON					
Smith	Y	N	Y	N	Y
Wyden	Y	Y	N	Y	N
PENNSYLVANIA					
Santorum	Y	N	Y	Y	Y
Specter	N	Y	N	Y	Y
RHODE ISLAND					
Chafee	Y	Y	Y	Y	Y
Reed	Y	Y	N	N	N
SOUTH CAROLINA					
Thurmond	N	N	Y	Y	Y
Hollings	Y	Y	N	Y	Y
SOUTH DAKOTA					
Daschle	Y	Y	N	N	Y
Johnson	Y	Y	N	Y	N
TENNESSEE					
Frist	Y	N	Y	N	Y
Thompson	N	N	Y	Y	Y
TEXAS					
Gramm	Y	N	Y	Y	Y
Hutchison	Y	N	Y	Y	N
UTAH					
Bennett	Y	N	Y	Y	Y
Hatch	Y	N	Y	Y	Y
VERMONT					
Jeffords	Y	Y	N	Y	N
Leahy	Y	Y	N	Y	N
VIRGINIA					
Warner	Y	N	Y	N	Y
Robb	Y	Y	Y	N	Y
WASHINGTON					
Gorton	Y	Y	Y	N	Y
Murray	Y	Y	N	Y	Y
WEST VIRGINIA					
Byrd	Y	Y	N	Y	Y
Rockefeller	Y	Y	Y	Y	Y
WISCONSIN					
Feingold	N	Y	N	Y	N
Kohl	Y	Y	N	Y	Y
WYOMING					
Enzi	Y	N	Y	N	Y
Thomas	Y	N	Y	N	Y

KEY

- Y Voted for (yea).
- # Paired for.
- + Announced for.
- N Voted against (nay).
- X Paired against.
- – Announced against.
- P Voted "present."
- C Voted "present" to avoid possible conflict of interest.
- ? Did not vote or otherwise make a position known.

Democrats *Republicans*

ND Northern Democrats SD Southern Democrats

Southern states - Ala., Ark., Fla., Ga., Ky., La., Miss., N.C., Okla., S.C., Tenn., Texas, Va.

166. S 936. Fiscal 1998 Defense Authorization/Overseas Computer Sales. Grams, R-Minn., amendment to the Cochran, R-Miss., amendment, to require the comptroller general to study the risks that selling high-powered computers to certain countries may represent to national security. The Cochran amendment would have required certain computer companies to obtain export licenses from the Commerce secretary to sell high-powered computers to certain high-risk countries. Adopted 72-27: R 34-21; D 38-6 (ND 31-5, SD 7-1), July 10, 1997. (Subsequently, the Cochran amendment was adopted by voice vote.)

167. S 936. Fiscal 1998 Defense Authorization/Overseas Military Hospital Abortions. Murray, D-Wash., amendment to repeal current law prohibiting overseas U.S. military hospitals and medical facilities from performing privately funded abortions for U.S. service members and their dependents. Rejected 48-51: R 7-48; D 41-3 (ND 35-1, SD 6-2), July 10, 1997. A "yea" was a vote in support of the president's position.

168. S 936. Fiscal 1998 Defense Authorization/Veterans Benefits. Thurmond, R-S.C., motion to table (kill) the Wellstone, D-Minn., amendment to require the Defense secretary to transfer $400 million to the secretary of Veterans Affairs in fiscal 1998 for veterans' benefits. Motion agreed to 58-41: R 50-5; D 8-36 (ND 4-32, SD 4-4), July 10, 1997.

169. S 936. Fiscal 1998 Defense Authorization/Defense Procurement. Gramm, R-Texas, amendment to the Levin, D-Mich., amendment, to require the Defense Department to conduct a joint study into procurement practices with the federal agency that manages the production of goods by inmates at federal prisons. The Levin amendment would have eased the requirement that federal agencies purchase certain goods made in federal prisons. Adopted 62-37: R 38-17; D 24-20 (ND 20-16, SD 4-4), July 10, 1997. (Subsequently, the Levin amendment was adopted by voice vote.)

170. S 936. Fiscal 1998 Defense Authorization/Executive Pay. Thurmond, R-S.C., motion to table (kill) the Boxer, D-Calif., amendment to limit federal payments to executives at contracting companies to no more than the pay received each year by the president of the United States. Motion agreed to 83-16: R 52-3; D 31-13 (ND 23-13, SD 8-0), July 10, 1997. (After the vote, Coverdell, R-Ga., was given unanimous consent to change his vote from "nay" to "yea." That change is reflected on this chart.)

SENATE VOTES 171, 172, 173, 174, 175, 176, 177, 178

	171	172	173	174	175	176	177	178
ALABAMA								
Sessions	N	N	Y	?	N	Y	Y	Y
Shelby	N	N	Y	Y	N	Y	Y	Y
ALASKA								
Murkowski	N	N	Y	Y	N	Y	Y	Y
Stevens	N	N	Y	Y	N	Y	Y	Y
ARIZONA								
Kyl	N	N	Y	Y	N	Y	Y	Y
McCain	N	N	Y	Y	N	Y	N	Y
ARKANSAS								
Hutchinson	N	N	Y	Y	N	Y	Y	Y
Bumpers	Y	Y	Y	Y	Y	Y	N	Y
CALIFORNIA								
Boxer	Y	Y	Y	Y	Y	Y	N	Y
Feinstein	Y	N	Y	Y	N	Y	N	Y
COLORADO								
Allard	N	N	Y	Y	N	Y	Y	Y
Campbell	N	N	Y	Y	N	Y	Y	Y
CONNECTICUT								
Dodd	N	N	Y	?	N	Y	N	Y
Lieberman	N	N	Y	Y	N	Y	N	Y
DELAWARE								
Roth	N	N	Y	Y	N	Y	N	Y
Biden	Y	N	Y	?	N	Y	N	Y
FLORIDA								
Mack	N	N	Y	Y	N	Y	Y	Y
Graham	Y	N	Y	Y	N	Y	N	Y
GEORGIA								
Coverdell	N	N	Y	Y	N	Y	Y	Y
Cleland	Y	N	Y	N	N	Y	Y	Y
HAWAII								
Akaka	Y	N	Y	N	N	Y	Y	Y
Inouye	N	N	Y	Y	N	Y	Y	Y
IDAHO								
Craig	N	N	Y	Y	N	Y	Y	Y
Kempthorne	N	N	Y	Y	N	Y	Y	Y
ILLINOIS								
Durbin	Y	Y	Y	Y	Y	Y	N	Y
Moseley-Braun	Y	Y	Y	Y	N	Y	N	Y
INDIANA								
Coats	N	N	Y	Y	N	Y	Y	Y
Lugar	N	N	Y	Y	N	Y	Y	N
IOWA								
Grassley	N	Y	Y	Y	Y	Y	Y	Y
Harkin	Y	Y	N	N	Y	N	N	Y
KANSAS								
Brownback	N	N	Y	Y	N	Y	N	Y
Roberts	N	N	Y	Y	N	Y	Y	Y
KENTUCKY								
McConnell	N	N	Y	Y	N	Y	Y	Y
Ford	Y	N	Y	Y	N	Y	N	Y
LOUISIANA								
Breaux	Y	N	Y	Y	N	Y	Y	Y
Landrieu	Y	?	Y	Y	N	Y	Y	Y
MAINE								
Collins	N	N	Y	Y	N	Y	N	Y
Snowe	N	N	Y	Y	N	Y	N	Y
MARYLAND								
Mikulski	?	?	?	?	N	Y	N	Y
Sarbanes	Y	N	Y	Y	N	Y	N	Y
MASSACHUSETTS								
Kennedy	Y	N	Y	+	N	Y	N	Y
Kerry	Y	N	Y	Y	N	Y	N	Y
MICHIGAN								
Abraham	N	N	Y	Y	N	Y	Y	Y
Levin	Y	N	Y	Y	N	Y	N	Y
MINNESOTA								
Grams	N	N	Y	?	N	Y	Y	Y
Wellstone	Y	Y	N	N	Y	N	N	Y
MISSISSIPPI								
Cochran	N	N	Y	Y	N	Y	Y	Y
Lott	N	N	Y	Y	N	Y	Y	Y
MISSOURI								
Ashcroft	N	N	Y	Y	N	Y	Y	Y
Bond	N	N	Y	Y	N	Y	Y	Y
MONTANA								
Burns	N	N	Y	?	?	?	+	+
Baucus	Y	N	Y	Y	N	Y	Y	Y
NEBRASKA								
Hagel	N	N	Y	Y	N	Y	Y	Y
Kerrey	Y	Y	Y	N	N	Y	N	N
NEVADA								
Bryan	Y	Y	Y	Y	N	Y	Y	Y
Reid	Y	Y	Y	Y	N	Y	Y	Y
NEW HAMPSHIRE								
Gregg	N	N	Y	Y	N	Y	N	Y
Smith	N	N	Y	Y	N	Y	N	Y
NEW JERSEY								
Lautenberg	Y	Y	Y	N	N	Y	N	Y
Torricelli	Y	Y	Y	Y	Y	Y	N	Y
NEW MEXICO								
Domenici	N	N	Y	Y	N	Y	Y	Y
Bingaman	Y	N	Y	Y	N	Y	Y	N
NEW YORK								
D'Amato	N	N	Y	?	N	Y	Y	Y
Moynihan	Y	N	Y	Y	Y	Y	N	Y
NORTH CAROLINA								
Faircloth	N	N	Y	Y	N	Y	Y	Y
Helms	N	N	Y	Y	N	Y	Y	Y
NORTH DAKOTA								
Conrad	Y	N	Y	N	N	Y	Y	Y
Dorgan	Y	N	Y	N	Y	Y	Y	Y
OHIO								
DeWine	N	N	Y	Y	N	Y	Y	Y
Glenn	Y	N	Y	Y	Y	Y	N	Y
OKLAHOMA								
Inhofe	N	N	Y	Y	N	Y	Y	Y
Nickles	N	N	Y	Y	N	Y	Y	Y
OREGON								
Smith	N	N	Y	Y	N	Y	Y	Y
Wyden	Y	Y	Y	?	Y	Y	N	Y
PENNSYLVANIA								
Santorum	N	N	Y	?	N	Y	N	Y
Specter	N	N	Y	Y	N	Y	N	Y
RHODE ISLAND								
Chafee	Y	N	Y	Y	?	?	?	Y
Reed	Y	N	Y	Y	N	Y	N	Y
SOUTH CAROLINA								
Thurmond	N	N	Y	Y	N	Y	Y	Y
Hollings	Y	N	Y	N	N	Y	N	Y
SOUTH DAKOTA								
Daschle	Y	N	Y	Y	N	Y	Y	Y
Johnson	Y	Y	Y	Y	N	Y	N	Y
TENNESSEE								
Frist	N	N	Y	Y	N	Y	Y	Y
Thompson	N	N	Y	Y	Y	Y	Y	Y
TEXAS								
Gramm	N	N	Y	Y	N	Y	Y	Y
Hutchison	N	N	Y	Y	N	Y	Y	Y
UTAH								
Bennett	N	N	Y	?	N	Y	Y	Y
Hatch	N	N	Y	Y	N	Y	Y	Y
VERMONT								
Jeffords	Y	N	Y	Y	N	Y	Y	Y
Leahy	Y	Y	Y	Y	N	Y	N	Y
VIRGINIA								
Warner	N	N	Y	Y	N	Y	Y	Y
Robb	Y	N	Y	Y	N	Y	N	Y
WASHINGTON								
Gorton	N	N	Y	Y	N	Y	Y	Y
Murray	Y	N	Y	Y	N	Y	N	Y
WEST VIRGINIA								
Byrd	Y	Y	Y	N	Y	Y	N	N
Rockefeller	Y	Y	?	Y	N	Y	N	Y
WISCONSIN								
Feingold	Y	Y	N	N	Y	N	N	Y
Kohl	Y	Y	N	Y	Y	N	N	Y
WYOMING								
Enzi	N	N	Y	Y	N	Y	Y	Y
Thomas	N	N	Y	Y	N	Y	Y	Y

KEY

- Y Voted for (yea).
- # Paired for.
- + Announced for.
- N Voted against (nay).
- X Paired against.
- – Announced against.
- P Voted "present."
- C Voted "present" to avoid possible conflict of interest.
- ? Did not vote or otherwise make a position known.

Democrats *Republicans*

ND Northern Democrats SD Southern Democrats

Southern states - Ala., Ark., Fla., Ga., Ky., La., Miss., N.C., Okla., S.C., Tenn., Texas, Va.

171. S 936. Fiscal 1998 Defense Authorization/Space-Based Lasers. Bingaman, D-N.M., amendment to reduce the amount available for the space-based laser program by $118 million. Rejected 43-56: R 2-53; D 41-3 (ND 33-3, SD 8-0), July 11, 1997.

172. S 936. Fiscal 1998 Defense Authorization/Tactical Fighters. Feingold, D-Wis., amendment to require the Defense secretary to recommend canceling one of three new tactical fighter aircraft programs: the F/A-18 E/F, the F-22 or the Joint Strike Fighter. Rejected 19-79: R 1-54; D 18-25 (ND 17-19, SD 1-6), July 11, 1997.

173. S 936. Fiscal 1998 Defense Authorization/Passage. Passage of the bill to authorize $268 billion for defense-related activities in fiscal 1998, $2.6 billion more than President Clinton's request but $3.3 billion below last year's level in inflation-adjusted dollars. The bill also expresses the sense of Congress that U.S. troops should pull out of Bosnia by June 30, 1998, and requires the Defense Department to study whether additional base closure rounds are necessary. Passed 94-4: R 55-0; D 39-4 (ND 31-4, SD 8-0), July 11, 1997.

174. Klein Nomination/Cloture. Motion to invoke cloture (thus limiting debate) on the confirmation of President Clinton's nomination of Joel I. Klein of the District of Columbia to be assistant attorney general in the Justice Department's Antitrust Division. Motion agreed to 78-11: R 49-0; D 29-11 (ND 23-9, SD 6-2), July 14, 1997. Three-fifths of the total Senate (60) is required to invoke cloture. A "yea" was a vote in support of the president's position.

175. S 1005. Fiscal 1998 Defense Appropriations/Defense Company Mergers. Harkin, D-Iowa, amendment to prohibit the use of Defense Department funds for restructuring costs involving defense company mergers. Rejected 15-83: R 2-51; D 13-32 (ND 12-25, SD 1-7), July 15, 1997.

176. S 1005. Fiscal 1998 Defense Appropriations/Passage. Passage of the bill to provide $247.1 billion in new budget authority for defense-related programs in fiscal 1998. The bill provides $3.2 billion more than President Clinton requested and $3.1 billion more than provided in fiscal 1997. The bill includes a 2.8 percent pay raise for military personnel effective Jan. 1, 1998, $45.4 billion for military procurement and $82.7 billion for Defense Department operations. The bill also would require the Defense Department to report to Congress by Oct. 1, 1997, on the costs associated with expansion of NATO. Passed 94-4: R 53-0; D 41-4 (ND 33-4, SD 8-0), July 15, 1997.

177. S 1004. Fiscal 1998 Energy and Water Development Appropriations/Animas-La Plata Report. Campbell, R-Colo., motion to table (kill) the Feingold, D-Wis., amendment to prohibit construction spending until the Interior secretary submits a report to Congress detailing ways to reduce the cost of the Animas-La Plata irrigation project in southwestern Colorado. Construction could begin only after a new, scaled-down project was authorized. The project would divert water from the Animas River to high-plateau farmland. Motion agreed to 56-42: R 44-9; D 12-33 (ND 9-28, SD 3-5), July 15, 1997.

178. S 955. Fiscal 1998 Foreign Operations Appropriations/Russian Religious Freedom. Smith, R-Ore., amendment to the Smith amendment to withhold Russian aid unless President Clinton certifies to Congress that the Russian Federation has not enacted any statute or executive order discriminating against religious minorities. The second-degree amendment clarifies that the provision would be effective one day after enactment of the bill. Adopted 95-4: R 53-1; D 42-3 (ND 34-3, SD 8-0), July 16, 1997. (Subsequently, the Smith amendment was adopted by voice vote.) A "nay" was a vote in support of the president's position.

SENATE VOTES 179, 180, 181, 182, 183, 184, 185

	179	180	181	182	183	184	185
ALABAMA							
Sessions	Y	Y	Y	N	N	Y	Y
Shelby	Y	Y	N	N	N	N	Y
ALASKA							
Murkowski	Y	Y	N	N	N	N	Y
Stevens	Y	Y	N	Y	N	N	Y
ARIZONA							
Kyl	Y	Y	Y	Y	N	Y	Y
McCain	Y	Y	Y	Y	N	N	Y
ARKANSAS							
Hutchinson	Y	Y	Y	N	N	Y	Y
Bumpers	Y	Y	N	N	Y	N	Y
CALIFORNIA							
Boxer	Y	Y	N	N	Y	N	Y
Feinstein	Y	Y	N	N	Y	N	Y
COLORADO							
Allard	Y	Y	Y	Y	N	N	Y
Campbell	Y	Y	N	N	N	Y	Y
CONNECTICUT							
Dodd	Y	Y	N	Y	Y	N	Y
Lieberman	Y	Y	N	Y	N	N	Y
DELAWARE							
Roth	Y	Y	N	N	N	N	Y
Biden	Y	Y	N	N	Y	N	Y
FLORIDA							
Mack	Y	Y	N	N	N	Y	Y
Graham	Y	Y	N	N	N	N	Y
GEORGIA							
Coverdell	Y	Y	Y	N	N	N	Y
Cleland	Y	Y	N	Y	Y	N	Y
HAWAII							
Akaka	Y	Y	N	Y	Y	N	Y
Inouye	Y	Y	N	Y	Y	N	Y
IDAHO							
Craig	Y	Y	Y	N	N	N	N
Kempthorne	Y	Y	Y	N	N	N	N
ILLINOIS							
Durbin	Y	Y	N	N	Y	N	Y
Moseley-Braun	Y	Y	N	N	Y	N	Y
INDIANA							
Coats	Y	Y	Y	N	N	Y	Y
Lugar	Y	Y	N	Y	Y	N	Y
IOWA							
Grassley	Y	Y	N	N	N	N	Y
Harkin	Y	Y	N	Y	Y	N	Y
KANSAS							
Brownback	Y	Y	Y	N	N	N	Y
Roberts	Y	Y	Y	N	Y	N	Y
KENTUCKY							
McConnell	Y	Y	N	N	N	N	Y
Ford	Y	Y	N	N	N	N	Y
LOUISIANA							
Breaux	Y	Y	N	N	Y	N	Y
Landrieu	Y	Y	N	Y	Y	N	Y
MAINE							
Collins	Y	Y	Y	N	N	Y	Y
Snowe	Y	Y	N	N	N	Y	Y
MARYLAND							
Mikulski	Y	Y	N	Y	N	N	Y
Sarbanes	Y	Y	N	Y	Y	N	Y
MASSACHUSETTS							
Kennedy	Y	Y	N	Y	Y	N	Y
Kerry	Y	Y	N	N	Y	N	Y
MICHIGAN							
Abraham	Y	Y	N	N	N	N	Y
Levin	Y	Y	N	Y	Y	Y	Y
MINNESOTA							
Grams	Y	Y	Y	N	N	N	Y
Wellstone	Y	Y	Y	N	Y	Y	Y
MISSISSIPPI							
Cochran	Y	Y	N	Y	N	N	Y
Lott	Y	Y	Y	N	N	N	Y
MISSOURI							
Ashcroft	Y	Y	Y	N	N	Y	N
Bond	Y	Y	N	N	Y	N	Y
MONTANA							
Burns	+	+	–	?	?	?	+
Baucus	Y	Y	N	Y	Y	N	Y
NEBRASKA							
Hagel	Y	Y	N	Y	N	N	Y
Kerrey	Y	Y	N	Y	Y	N	Y
NEVADA							
Bryan	Y	Y	Y	Y	N	N	Y
Reid	Y	Y	Y	N	N	N	Y
NEW HAMPSHIRE							
Gregg	Y	Y	Y	N	N	N	Y
Smith	Y	Y	Y	N	N	Y	N
NEW JERSEY							
Lautenberg	Y	Y	N	N	Y	N	Y
Torricelli	Y	Y	N	N	N	Y	Y
NEW MEXICO							
Domenici	Y	Y	N	Y	N	N	Y
Bingaman	Y	Y	N	N	Y	N	Y
NEW YORK							
D'Amato	Y	Y	Y	N	N	Y	Y
Moynihan	Y	Y	N	Y	Y	N	Y
NORTH CAROLINA							
Faircloth	Y	Y	Y	N	N	Y	N
Helms	Y	Y	Y	N	N	Y	N
NORTH DAKOTA							
Conrad	Y	Y	N	N	Y	N	Y
Dorgan	Y	Y	Y	N	Y	N	Y
OHIO							
DeWine	Y	Y	Y	Y	N	Y	Y
Glenn	Y	Y	N	?	N	N	Y
OKLAHOMA							
Inhofe	Y	Y	Y	N	N	Y	Y
Nickles	Y	Y	Y	N	N	N	Y
OREGON							
Smith	Y	Y	N	N	N	N	Y
Wyden	Y	Y	Y	N	Y	N	Y
PENNSYLVANIA							
Santorum	Y	Y	N	N	N	N	Y
Specter	Y	Y	N	N	N	N	Y
RHODE ISLAND							
Chafee	Y	Y	N	Y	Y	N	Y
Reed	Y	Y	N	N	Y	N	Y
SOUTH CAROLINA							
Thurmond	Y	Y	N	N	N	N	Y
Hollings	Y	Y	Y	Y	N	Y	N
SOUTH DAKOTA							
Daschle	Y	Y	N	Y	Y	N	Y
Johnson	Y	Y	N	Y	Y	N	Y
TENNESSEE							
Frist	Y	Y	N	N	N	N	Y
Thompson	Y	Y	Y	Y	N	Y	Y
TEXAS							
Gramm	Y	Y	Y	Y	N	N	Y
Hutchison	Y	Y	Y	Y	N	N	Y
UTAH							
Bennett	Y	Y	N	N	N	N	Y
Hatch	Y	Y	N	N	N	N	Y
VERMONT							
Jeffords	Y	Y	N	Y	Y	N	Y
Leahy	Y	Y	N	Y	Y	Y	Y
VIRGINIA							
Warner	Y	Y	N	Y	N	N	Y
Robb	Y	Y	N	Y	N	N	Y
WASHINGTON							
Gorton	Y	Y	N	Y	N	N	Y
Murray	Y	Y	N	Y	Y	N	Y
WEST VIRGINIA							
Byrd	Y	Y	N	N	Y	N	N
Rockefeller	Y	Y	N	N	N	N	Y
WISCONSIN							
Feingold	Y	Y	Y	N	Y	Y	Y
Kohl	Y	Y	Y	Y	N	N	Y
WYOMING							
Enzi	Y	Y	N	N	N	N	Y
Thomas	Y	Y	Y	N	N	N	Y

KEY

- Y Voted for (yea).
- # Paired for.
- + Announced for.
- N Voted against (nay).
- X Paired against.
- – Announced against.
- P Voted "present."
- C Voted "present" to avoid possible conflict of interest.
- ? Did not vote or otherwise make a position known.

Democrats ***Republicans***

ND Northern Democrats SD Southern Democrats

Southern states - Ala., Ark., Fla., Ga., Ky., La., Miss., N.C., Okla., S.C., Tenn., Texas, Va.

179. S 1004. Fiscal 1998 Energy and Water Development Appropriations/Passage. Passage of the bill to provide $21.2 billion in new budget authority for energy and water programs in fiscal 1998. The bill provides $219.6 million more than the $20.9 billion provided in fiscal 1997 and $1.8 billion less than the $23 billion requested by the Clinton administration. Passed 99-0: R 54-0; D 45-0 (ND 37-0, SD 8-0), July 16, 1997.

180. S 955. Fiscal 1998 Foreign Operations Appropriations/Cambodian Democracy Report. McConnell, R-Ky., amendment to prohibit the use of funds for programs in Cambodia until the secretary of State reports to Congress on the state of Cambodian democracy. Adopted 99-0: R 54-0; D 45-0 (ND 37-0, SD 8-0), July 16, 1997.

181. S 955. Fiscal 1998 Foreign Operations Appropriations/OPIC Administrative Costs. Allard, R-Colo., amendment to reduce funding for administrative costs associated with the Overseas Private Investment Corporation's credit and insurance programs from $32 million to $21 million. Rejected 35-64: R 27-27; D 8-37 (ND 7-30, SD 1-7), July 16, 1997.

182. S 955. Fiscal 1998 Foreign Operations Appropriations/Drug Certification Process. Dodd, D-Conn., amendment to suspend the annual certification process for certain drug-producing and drug-transit countries in 1998 and 1999. The president could continue the suspension in 2000 if it would facilitate international narcotics-control programs. Rejected 38-60: R 16-38; D 22-22 (ND 18-18, SD 4-4), July 16, 1997. A "yea" was a vote in support of the president's position.

183. S 955. Fiscal 1998 Foreign Operations Appropriations/Family Remittances to Cuba. Bingaman, D-N.M., amendment to allow Cuban-Americans to send up to $200 each month to family members living in Cuba, allow limited travel to the island and allow the United States to participate in humanitarian relief operations following Cuban natural disasters. Rejected 38-61: R 5-49; D 33-12 (ND 29-8, SD 4-4), July 17, 1997.

184. S 955. Fiscal 1998 Foreign Operations Appropriations/China MFN. Hutchinson, R-Ark., amendment to express the sense of the Senate that China's most-favored-nation trade status (MFN) should be revoked. Rejected 22-77: R 16-38; D 6-39 (ND 5-32, SD 1-7), July 17, 1997.

185. S 955. Fiscal 1998 Foreign Operations Appropriations/Passage. Passage of the bill to provide $13.2 billion in new budget authority for foreign affairs programs in fiscal 1998. The bill provides $933.1 million more than the fiscal 1997 level and $116 million less than President Clinton's request. The bill includes Middle East earmarks of $3 billion for Israel, $2.1 billion for Egypt and $150 million for Jordan. Earmarks for Eastern Europe and the Baltic states total $485 million, and $800 million is slated for the independent states of the former Soviet Union. The bill also includes a one-time $3.5 billion appropriation to the International Monetary Fund to prevent global financial crises. Passed 91-8: R 48-6; D 43-2 (ND 36-1, SD 7-1), July 17, 1997.

SENATE VOTES 186, 187, 188

	186	187	188
ALABAMA			
Sessions	N	Y	Y
Shelby	N	Y	Y
ALASKA			
Murkowski	Y	Y	Y
Stevens	N	Y	Y
ARIZONA			
Kyl	Y	Y	Y
McCain	Y	Y	Y
ARKANSAS			
Hutchinson	Y	Y	Y
Bumpers	N	N	Y
CALIFORNIA			
Boxer	Y	Y	Y
Feinstein	Y	Y	Y
COLORADO			
Allard	N	Y	Y
Campbell	Y	Y	Y
CONNECTICUT			
Dodd	Y	Y	Y
Lieberman	Y	Y	Y
DELAWARE			
Roth	Y	Y	Y
Biden	Y	Y	Y
FLORIDA			
Mack	Y	Y	Y
Graham	Y	Y	Y
GEORGIA			
Coverdell	Y	Y	Y
Cleland	Y	N	Y
HAWAII			
Akaka	Y	Y	Y
Inouye	N	N	Y
IDAHO			
Craig	Y	Y	Y
Kempthorne	Y	Y	Y
ILLINOIS			
Durbin	Y	Y	Y
Moseley-Braun	Y	Y	Y
INDIANA			
Coats	Y	Y	Y
Lugar	Y	Y	Y
IOWA			
Grassley	Y	Y	Y
Harkin	Y	N	Y
KANSAS			
Brownback	Y	Y	Y
Roberts	Y	Y	Y
KENTUCKY			
McConnell	Y	Y	Y
Ford	Y	N	Y
LOUISIANA			
Breaux	Y	Y	Y
Landrieu	Y	Y	Y
MAINE			
Collins	Y	Y	Y
Snowe	Y	Y	Y
MARYLAND			
Mikulski	Y	Y	Y
Sarbanes	Y	Y	Y
MASSACHUSETTS			
Kennedy	Y	Y	Y
Kerry	Y	Y	Y
MICHIGAN			
Abraham	Y	Y	Y
Levin	N	Y	Y
MINNESOTA			
Grams	Y	Y	Y
Wellstone	Y	Y	Y
MISSISSIPPI			
Cochran	N	Y	Y
Lott	Y	Y	Y
MISSOURI			
Ashcroft	Y	Y	Y
Bond	Y	Y	Y
MONTANA			
Burns	Y	Y	Y
Baucus	Y	Y	Y
NEBRASKA			
Hagel	N	Y	Y
Kerrey	Y	N	Y
NEVADA			
Bryan	Y	Y	Y
Reid	Y	Y	Y
NEW HAMPSHIRE			
Gregg	Y	Y	Y
Smith	N	Y	Y
NEW JERSEY			
Lautenberg	Y	Y	Y
Torricelli	Y	Y	Y
NEW MEXICO			
Domenici	Y	Y	Y
Bingaman	N	Y	Y
NEW YORK			
D'Amato	Y	Y	Y
Moynihan	Y	Y	Y
NORTH CAROLINA			
Faircloth	Y	Y	Y
Helms	Y	Y	Y
NORTH DAKOTA			
Conrad	Y	N	Y
Dorgan	Y	N	Y
OHIO			
DeWine	Y	Y	Y
Glenn	N	Y	Y
OKLAHOMA			
Inhofe	N	Y	Y
Nickles	N	Y	Y
OREGON			
Smith	Y	Y	Y
Wyden	Y	N	Y
PENNSYLVANIA			
Santorum	Y	Y	Y
Specter	Y	Y	Y
RHODE ISLAND			
Chafee	Y	Y	Y
Reed	Y	Y	Y
SOUTH CAROLINA			
Thurmond	Y	Y	Y
Hollings	N	N	Y
SOUTH DAKOTA			
Daschle	Y	Y	Y
Johnson	Y	Y	Y
TENNESSEE			
Frist	Y	Y	Y
Thompson	N	Y	Y
TEXAS			
Gramm	Y	Y	Y
Hutchison	Y	Y	Y
UTAH			
Bennett	Y	Y	Y
Hatch	Y	Y	Y
VERMONT			
Jeffords	Y	Y	Y
Leahy	Y	Y	Y
VIRGINIA			
Warner	Y	Y	Y
Robb	Y	Y	Y
WASHINGTON			
Gorton	N	Y	Y
Murray	Y	Y	Y
WEST VIRGINIA			
Byrd	Y	N	Y
Rockefeller	Y	Y	Y
WISCONSIN			
Feingold	Y	N	Y
Kohl	Y	Y	Y
WYOMING			
Enzi	Y	Y	Y
Thomas	Y	Y	Y

KEY

- Y Voted for (yea).
- # Paired for.
- + Announced for.
- N Voted against (nay).
- X Paired against.
- – Announced against.
- P Voted "present."
- C Voted "present" to avoid possible conflict of interest.
- ? Did not vote or otherwise make a position known.

Democrats ***Republicans***

ND Northern Democrats SD Southern Democrats

Southern states - Ala., Ark., Fla., Ga., Ky., La., Miss., N.C., Okla., S.C., Tenn., Texas, Va.

186. S 1023. Fiscal 1998 Treasury-Postal Service-General Government Appropriations/Breast Cancer Research. Feinstein, D-Calif., amendment to facilitate voluntary contributions for breast cancer research by requiring the Postal Service to establish special-issue stamps costing 1 cent more than regular stamps and forward proceeds to the Department of Health and Human Services. Adopted 83-17: R 44-11; D 39-6 (ND 33-4, SD 6-2), July 17, 1997.

187. Klein Nomination/Confirmation. Confirmation of President Clinton's nomination of Joel I. Klein of the District of Columbia to be an assistant attorney general in the Justice Department's Antitrust Division. Confirmed 88-12: R 55-0; D 33-12 (ND 29-8, SD 4-4), July 17, 1997. A "yea" was a vote in support of the president's position.

188. Holder Nomination/Confirmation. Confirmation of President Clinton's nomination of Eric H. Holder Jr. of the District of Columbia to be deputy attorney general in the Justice Department. Confirmed 100-0: R 55-0; D 45-0 (ND 37-0, SD 8-0), July 17, 1997. A "yea" was a vote in support of the president's position.

SENATE VOTES 189, 190, 191, 192, 193, 194, 195, 196

	189	190	191	192	193	194	195	196
ALABAMA								
Sessions	Y	Y	Y	Y	Y	Y	Y	Y
Shelby	Y	Y	Y	Y	Y	Y	Y	Y
ALASKA								
Murkowski	N	Y	Y	Y	Y	Y	Y	Y
Stevens	Y	N	Y	Y	Y	Y	Y	Y
ARIZONA								
Kyl	Y	Y	Y	N	Y	N	N	N
McCain	Y	Y	Y	N	Y	Y	N	N
ARKANSAS								
Hutchinson	N	Y	Y	Y	N	Y	Y	N
Bumpers	N	N	Y	Y	N	Y	Y	N
CALIFORNIA								
Boxer	N	N	Y	Y	Y	Y	Y	N
Feinstein	N	N	Y	Y	Y	Y	Y	N
COLORADO								
Allard	Y	Y	Y	Y	Y	Y	Y	Y
Campbell	Y	N	Y	Y	Y	Y	Y	Y
CONNECTICUT								
Dodd	N	N	Y	Y	Y	Y	N	N
Lieberman	Y	N	Y	Y	Y	Y	Y	N
DELAWARE								
Roth	Y	Y	Y	Y	Y	Y	Y	Y
Biden	N	Y	Y	Y	Y	Y	N	Y
FLORIDA								
Mack	Y	Y	Y	Y	Y	Y	Y	N
Graham	N	N	Y	Y	Y	Y	N	Y
GEORGIA								
Coverdell	Y	Y	Y	Y	Y	Y	Y	Y
Cleland	Y	N	Y	Y	Y	Y	Y	Y
HAWAII								
Akaka	N	N	Y	Y	Y	Y	Y	Y
Inouye	N	N	Y	Y	Y	Y	Y	Y
IDAHO								
Craig	N	Y	Y	Y	Y	Y	Y	Y
Kempthorne	N	Y	Y	Y	Y	Y	Y	Y
ILLINOIS								
Durbin	N	N	Y	Y	N	Y	N	N
Moseley-Braun	N	N	Y	Y	Y	Y	Y	N
INDIANA								
Coats	Y	Y	Y	Y	Y	Y	Y	N
Lugar	N	Y	Y	Y	N	Y	Y	N
IOWA								
Grassley	Y	Y	Y	Y	Y	Y	Y	Y
Harkin	N	N	Y	Y	N	Y	Y	N
KANSAS								
Brownback	N	Y	Y	Y	Y	Y	Y	N
Roberts	Y	Y	Y	Y	Y	Y	Y	Y
KENTUCKY								
McConnell	Y	Y	Y	Y	Y	Y	Y	Y
Ford	N	Y	Y	Y	Y	Y	Y	Y
LOUISIANA								
Breaux	N	Y	Y	Y	Y	Y	N	Y
Landrieu	N	N	Y	Y	Y	Y	N	Y
MAINE								
Collins	Y	N	Y	Y	N	Y	Y	N
Snowe	Y	N	Y	Y	N	Y	Y	N
MARYLAND								
Mikulski	N	N	Y	Y	Y	Y	Y	Y
Sarbanes	N	N	Y	Y	Y	Y	N	Y
MASSACHUSETTS								
Kennedy	N	N	Y	Y	N	Y	N	N
Kerry	N	N	Y	Y	Y	Y	N	N
MICHIGAN								
Abraham	Y	Y	Y	Y	N	Y	Y	N
Levin	N	N	Y	Y	N	Y	Y	N
MINNESOTA								
Grams	N	Y	Y	Y	Y	Y	Y	Y
Wellstone	Y	N	Y	Y	N	Y	N	N
MISSISSIPPI								
Cochran	N	Y	Y	Y	Y	Y	Y	Y
Lott	N	Y	Y	Y	Y	Y	Y	Y
MISSOURI								
Ashcroft	N	Y	Y	Y	N	Y	Y	Y
Bond	N	Y	Y	Y	Y	Y	Y	Y
MONTANA								
Burns	N	Y	Y	Y	Y	Y	Y	Y
Baucus	N	N	Y	Y	N	Y	Y	Y
NEBRASKA								
Hagel	N	Y	Y	Y	Y	Y	Y	Y
Kerrey	N	N	Y	Y	Y	Y	N	Y
NEVADA								
Bryan	N	N	Y	Y	N	Y	Y	Y
Reid	N	Y	Y	Y	Y	Y	Y	N
NEW HAMPSHIRE								
Gregg	Y	Y	Y	Y	Y	Y	Y	N
Smith	N	Y	Y	Y	Y	Y	Y	N
NEW JERSEY								
Lautenberg	Y	N	Y	Y	N	Y	N	N
Torricelli	N	N	Y	Y	Y	Y	Y	N
NEW MEXICO								
Domenici	N	Y	Y	Y	Y	Y	Y	Y
Bingaman	N	N	Y	Y	Y	Y	N	N
NEW YORK								
D'Amato	Y	Y	Y	Y	Y	Y	Y	N
Moynihan	N	N	Y	Y	N	Y	N	Y
NORTH CAROLINA								
Faircloth	N	Y	Y	Y	Y	Y	Y	Y
Helms	N	Y	Y	Y	Y	Y	Y	Y
NORTH DAKOTA								
Conrad	N	Y	Y	Y	N	Y	Y	Y
Dorgan	N	Y	Y	Y	N	Y	Y	Y
OHIO								
DeWine	N	Y	Y	Y	Y	Y	Y	N
Glenn	Y	N	Y	Y	Y	Y	Y	N
OKLAHOMA								
Inhofe	N	Y	Y	Y	Y	Y	Y	Y
Nickles	N	Y	Y	Y	Y	Y	Y	Y
OREGON								
Smith	N	Y	Y	Y	Y	Y	Y	N
Wyden	N	N	Y	Y	N	Y	Y	N
PENNSYLVANIA								
Santorum	Y	Y	Y	Y	Y	Y	Y	N
Specter	N	N	Y	Y	N	Y	Y	N
RHODE ISLAND								
Chafee	Y	N	Y	Y	N	Y	N	N
Reed	N	N	Y	Y	N	Y	Y	N
SOUTH CAROLINA								
Thurmond	N	Y	Y	Y	Y	Y	Y	Y
Hollings	N	N	Y	Y	N	Y	Y	Y
SOUTH DAKOTA								
Daschle	N	N	Y	Y	Y	Y	Y	Y
Johnson	N	N	Y	Y	N	Y	Y	N
TENNESSEE								
Frist	Y	Y	Y	Y	Y	Y	Y	Y
Thompson	Y	Y	Y	Y	Y	Y	Y	Y
TEXAS								
Gramm	Y	Y	Y	Y	Y	Y	N	N
Hutchison	Y	Y	Y	Y	Y	Y	Y	N
UTAH								
Bennett	Y	Y	Y	Y	Y	Y	Y	N
Hatch	N	Y	Y	Y	Y	Y	Y	N
VERMONT								
Jeffords	N	N	Y	Y	N	Y	Y	Y
Leahy	N	N	Y	Y	N	Y	N	Y
VIRGINIA								
Warner	N	Y	Y	Y	N	Y	Y	Y
Robb	N	N	Y	Y	Y	Y	Y	Y
WASHINGTON								
Gorton	Y	Y	Y	Y	Y	Y	Y	N
Murray	Y	N	Y	Y	Y	Y	Y	N
WEST VIRGINIA								
Byrd	N	N	Y	Y	N	Y	Y	N
Rockefeller	?	?	?	Y	Y	Y	Y	N
WISCONSIN								
Feingold	Y	N	Y	Y	N	Y	Y	Y
Kohl	Y	N	Y	Y	N	Y	Y	Y
WYOMING								
Enzi	N	Y	Y	Y	Y	Y	Y	Y
Thomas	N	Y	Y	Y	N	Y	Y	N

KEY

- Y Voted for (yea).
- # Paired for.
- + Announced for.
- N Voted against (nay).
- X Paired against.
- – Announced against.
- P Voted "present."
- C Voted "present" to avoid possible conflict of interest.
- ? Did not vote or otherwise make a position known.

Democrats *Republicans*

ND Northern Democrats SD Southern Democrats

Southern states - Ala., Ark., Fla., Ga., Ky., La., Miss., N.C., Okla., S.C., Tenn., Texas, Va.

189. S 1023. Fiscal 1998 Treasury-Postal Service-General Government Appropriations/Energy Conservation. Stevens, R-Alaska, motion to table (kill) the Bingaman, D-N.M., amendment seeking to strike provisions of the bill that would revise the law mandating that federal agencies use energy conservation services offered by local utilities. Motion rejected 35-64: R 27-28; D 8-36 (ND 7-29, SD 1-7), July 22, 1997. (The Bingaman amendment was subsequently passed by voice vote.)

190. S 1023. Fiscal 1998 Treasury-Postal Service-General Government Appropriations/Abortion. DeWine, R-Ohio, amendment that would continue to prohibit federal health plans from covering elective abortions, except in cases where the life of the mother is threatened or those involving rape or incest. Adopted 54-45: R 48-7; D 6-38 (ND 4-32, SD 2-6), July 22, 1997.

191. S 1023. Fiscal 1998 Treasury-Postal Service-General Government Appropriations/Passage. Passage of the bill to provide $25.2 billion in new budget authority for the Treasury Department, the White House, postal subsidies and civil service benefits in fiscal 1998. The bill would provide $1.1 billion more than in fiscal 1997 and $455.9 million less than requested by President Clinton. Passed 99-0: R 55-0; D 44-0 (ND 36-0, SD 8-0), July 22, 1997.

192. HR 2016. Fiscal 1998 Military Construction Appropriations/Passage. Passage of the bill to provide $9.18 billion in new budget authority for military construction in fiscal 1998. The bill would provide $610 million less than in fiscal 1997 and $800 million more than requested by President Clinton. Passed 98-2: R 53-2; D 45-0 (ND 37-0, SD 8-0), July 22, 1997.

193. S 1034. Fiscal 1998 Veterans Affairs-Housing and Urban Development Appropriations/Space Station. Bond, R-Mo., motion to table (kill) the Bumpers, D-Ark., amendment that would reduce NASA appropriations for human space flight from $5.3 billion to $3.8 billion for the purpose of terminating the international space station program. Motion agreed to 69-31: R 44-11; D 25-20 (ND 19-18, SD 6-2), July 22, 1997.

194. HR 2158. Fiscal 1998 Veterans Affairs-Housing and Urban Development Appropriations/Passage. Passage of the bill to provide $90.9 billion in new budget authority for veterans, housing, space and science programs and agencies. The bill would provide $8.9 billion more than in fiscal 1997 and $70.9 million less than requested by President Clinton. Passed 99-1: R 54-1; D 45-0 (ND 37-0, SD 8-0), July 22, 1997. (Before passage, the Senate struck all after the enacting clause and inserted the text of S 1034.)

195. S Res 109. Condemnation of Canada. Adoption of the resolution expressing the sense of the Senate condemning the Canadian government's failure to accept responsibility for the illegal blockade by Canadian fishermen of a U.S. passenger vessel in the Canadian province of British Columbia. The resolution also calls on President Clinton to take appropriate actions compelling the Canadian government to prevent such harassment of U.S. citizens. Adopted 81-19: R 51-4; D 30-15 (ND 25-12, SD 5-3), July 23, 1997.

196. S 1033. Fiscal 1998 Agriculture Appropriations/Tobacco Crop Insurance. Cochran, R-Miss., motion to table (kill) the Durbin, D-Ill., amendment that would eliminate federal support for crop insurance for tobacco farmers. Motion agreed to 53-47: R 31-24; D 22-23 (ND 15-22, SD 7-1), July 23, 1997.

SENATE VOTES 197, 198, 199, 200, 201, 202, 203, 204

	197	198	199	200	201	202	203	204
ALABAMA								
Sessions	Y	Y	Y	Y	Y	Y	N	N
Shelby	Y	Y	Y	Y	Y	Y	Y	N
ALASKA								
Murkowski	N	Y	Y	Y	Y	N	N	N
Stevens	N	Y	Y	Y	Y	N	Y	N
ARIZONA								
Kyl	N	Y	N	Y	Y	Y	N	N
McCain	Y	Y	N	Y	Y	Y	N	N
ARKANSAS								
Hutchinson	N	Y	N	Y	Y	Y	N	N
Bumpers	Y	N	N	N	Y	N	Y	Y
CALIFORNIA								
Boxer	Y	N	Y	N	Y	N	Y	Y
Feinstein	Y	N	Y	N	Y	N	N	Y
COLORADO								
Allard	Y	Y	N	Y	Y	Y	Y	N
Campbell	N	Y	Y	Y	Y	Y	N	N
CONNECTICUT								
Dodd	Y	N	N	N	Y	N	N	Y
Lieberman	Y	N	N	N	Y	N	N	Y
DELAWARE								
Roth	N	Y	N	Y	Y	N	N	N
Biden	Y	N	?	Y	Y	N	N	Y
FLORIDA								
Mack	Y	N	Y	Y	Y	Y	N	N
Graham	Y	N	Y	N	Y	N	N	Y
GEORGIA								
Coverdell	Y	Y	Y	Y	Y	N	N	N
Cleland	Y	Y	Y	N	Y	N	Y	Y
HAWAII								
Akaka	Y	N	Y	N	Y	N	N	Y
Inouye	Y	Y	Y	N	Y	N	N	Y
IDAHO								
Craig	Y	Y	Y	Y	Y	Y	N	N
Kempthorne	Y	Y	Y	Y	Y	Y	N	N
ILLINOIS								
Durbin	Y	N	Y	N	Y	N	N	Y
Moseley-Braun	Y	Y	Y	N	Y	N	N	Y
INDIANA								
Coats	Y	Y	N	Y	Y	Y	N	N
Lugar	Y	N	N	Y	Y	Y	N	N
IOWA								
Grassley	Y	N	Y	Y	Y	Y	Y	N
Harkin	Y	N	Y	N	Y	N	N	Y
KANSAS								
Brownback	Y	Y	N	Y	Y	Y	N	N
Roberts	Y	Y	Y	Y	Y	Y	N	N
KENTUCKY								
McConnell	N	Y	Y	Y	Y	Y	N	N
Ford	N	Y	Y	N	Y	N	Y	Y
LOUISIANA								
Breaux	Y	Y	Y	N	Y	N	Y	Y
Landrieu	Y	Y	Y	N	Y	N	N	Y
MAINE								
Collins	Y	N	Y	Y	Y	Y	N	N
Snowe	Y	N	Y	Y	Y	Y	N	N
MARYLAND								
Mikulski	Y	N	N	N	Y	N	N	Y
Sarbanes	Y	N	Y	N	Y	N	N	Y
MASSACHUSETTS								
Kennedy	Y	N	N	-	+	-	-	Y
Kerry	Y	N	N	N	Y	N	N	Y
MICHIGAN								
Abraham	Y	Y	N	Y	Y	Y	N	N
Levin	Y	N	Y	N	Y	N	N	Y
MINNESOTA								
Grams	Y	Y	N	Y	Y	N	N	N
Wellstone	Y	N	N	N	Y	N	N	Y
MISSISSIPPI								
Cochran	N	Y	Y	Y	Y	N	Y	N
Lott	N	Y	Y	Y	Y	Y	Y	N
MISSOURI								
Ashcroft	Y	Y	N	Y	Y	Y	N	N
Bond	Y	N	Y	Y	Y	Y	N	N
MONTANA								
Burns	Y	Y	Y	Y	Y	N	N	N
Baucus	Y	N	Y	N	Y	N	Y	Y
NEBRASKA								
Hagel	Y	Y	Y	Y	Y	N	N	N
Kerrey	Y	N	Y	N	Y	N	N	Y
NEVADA								
Bryan	Y	Y	N	N	Y	N	N	Y
Reid	Y	Y	N	N	Y	N	N	Y
NEW HAMPSHIRE								
Gregg	N	N	N	Y	Y	Y	Y	N
Smith	Y	Y	N	Y	Y	Y	N	N
NEW JERSEY								
Lautenberg	Y	N	N	N	Y	N	N	Y
Torricelli	Y	N	N	N	Y	N	N	Y
NEW MEXICO								
Domenici	Y	Y	Y	Y	Y	Y	N	N
Bingaman	Y	N	N	N	Y	N	Y	Y
NEW YORK								
D'Amato	N	N	N	N	Y	N	Y	N
Moynihan	Y	Y	N	N	Y	N	N	Y
NORTH CAROLINA								
Faircloth	N	Y	N	Y	Y	Y	Y	N
Helms	N	Y	Y	Y	Y	Y	Y	N
NORTH DAKOTA								
Conrad	Y	N	Y	N	Y	N	Y	Y
Dorgan	Y	N	Y	N	Y	N	Y	Y
OHIO								
DeWine	Y	N	N	N	Y	N	N	N
Glenn	Y	N	N	Y	Y	N	N	Y
OKLAHOMA								
Inhofe	N	Y	Y	Y	Y	Y	N	N
Nickles	N	Y	N	Y	Y	Y	Y	N
OREGON								
Smith	Y	N	Y	Y	Y	Y	N	N
Wyden	Y	N	Y	N	Y	Y	Y	Y
PENNSYLVANIA								
Santorum	Y	Y	Y	Y	Y	Y	N	N
Specter	Y	N	Y	N	Y	N	N	N
RHODE ISLAND								
Chafee	Y	N	Y	Y	Y	Y	N	N
Reed	Y	N	N	N	Y	N	N	Y
SOUTH CAROLINA								
Thurmond	N	Y	Y	Y	Y	Y	N	N
Hollings	N	Y	N	N	Y	N	Y	Y
SOUTH DAKOTA								
Daschle	Y	Y	Y	N	Y	N	N	Y
Johnson	Y	N	N	Y	Y	N	N	Y
TENNESSEE								
Frist	N	Y	Y	Y	Y	N	N	N
Thompson	N	Y	N	Y	Y	Y	Y	N
TEXAS								
Gramm	N	Y	Y	Y	Y	Y	N	N
Hutchison	N	N	Y	Y	Y	N	N	N
UTAH								
Bennett	N	N	Y	Y	Y	N	N	N
Hatch	Y	Y	Y	Y	Y	Y	N	N
VERMONT								
Jeffords	Y	N	Y	N	Y	N	N	N
Leahy	Y	N	Y	N	Y	N	N	Y
VIRGINIA								
Warner	N	Y	Y	Y	Y	N	Y	N
Robb	Y	Y	N	N	Y	N	N	Y
WASHINGTON								
Gorton	Y	Y	Y	Y	Y	Y	N	N
Murray	Y	N	Y	N	Y	N	N	Y
WEST VIRGINIA								
Byrd	Y	N	N	N	Y	N	Y	Y
Rockefeller	Y	N	N	N	Y	N	N	Y
WISCONSIN								
Feingold	Y	N	N	N	Y	Y	Y	Y
Kohl	Y	N	N	N	Y	Y	Y	Y
WYOMING								
Enzi	Y	Y	Y	Y	Y	Y	N	N
Thomas	Y	Y	Y	Y	Y	Y	N	N

KEY

- Y Voted for (yea).
- # Paired for.
- + Announced for.
- N Voted against (nay).
- X Paired against.
- \- Announced against.
- P Voted "present."
- C Voted "present" to avoid possible conflict of interest.
- ? Did not vote or otherwise make a position known.

Democrats *Republicans*

ND Northern Democrats SD Southern Democrats

Southern states - Ala., Ark., Fla., Ga., Ky., La., Miss., N.C., Okla., S.C., Tenn., Texas, Va.

197. S 1033. Fiscal 1998 Agriculture Appropriations/Ethanol Tax. Harkin, D-Iowa, motion to table (kill) the Helms, R-N.C., amendment to the Harkin amendment that would assess an additional 3-cent tax on every gallon of ethanol produced, to be used by the Department of Health and Human Services for anti-smoking programs. The underlying Harkin amendment would fund Food and Drug Administration anti-smoking programs by increasing the federal marketing assessment on tobacco from 1.0 percent of the national price support level to 2.1 percent. Motion agreed to 76-24: R 33-22; D 43-2 (ND 37-0, SD 6-2), July 23, 1997.

198. S 1033. Fiscal 1998 Agriculture Appropriations/Tobacco Tax. Stevens, R-Alaska, motion to table (kill) the Harkin, D-Iowa, amendment that would raise the marketing assessment on tobacco from 1.0 percent of the national price support level to 2.1 percent in order to fully fund President Clinton's request of $34 million for the Food and Drug Administration's anti-smoking initiatives. Motion agreed to 52-48: R 40-15; D 12-33 (ND 6-31, SD 6-2), July 23, 1997.

199. S 1033. Fiscal 1998 Agriculture Appropriations/Overseas Market Promotion. Cochran, R-Miss., motion to table (kill) the Bryan, D-Nev., amendment that would reduce funding for subsidized overseas market promotion programs from $90 million to $70 million. Motion agreed to 59-40: R 37-18; D 22-22 (ND 17-19, SD 5-3), July 23, 1997.

200. S 1033. Fiscal 1998 Agriculture Appropriations/School Breakfast Programs. Cochran, R-Miss., motion to table (kill) the Wellstone, D-Minn., amendment to provide $5 million for outreach efforts and start-up grants for state school breakfast programs for low-income children. Motion agreed to 54-45: R 51-4; D 3-41 (ND 3-33, SD 0-8), July 24, 1997.

201. S 1033. Fiscal 1998 Agriculture Appropriations/Passage. Passage of the bill to provide $50.7 billion in new budget authority for the Agriculture Department (USDA), the Food and Drug Administration (FDA) and rural development programs in fiscal 1998. The bill provides $3.2 billion less than provided in fiscal 1997 and $1.6 billion less than requested by President Clinton. Passed 99-0: R 55-0; D 44-0 (ND 36-0, SD 8-0), July 24, 1997.

202. S 1022. Fiscal 1998 Commerce, Justice, State Appropriations/Advanced Technology Program. Brownback, R-Kan., amendment to prohibit any corporation with revenues exceeding $2.5 billion from participating in the Advanced Technology Program. Rejected 42-57: R 39-16; D 3-41 (ND 3-33, SD 0-8), July 24, 1997.

203. S 1022. Fiscal 1998 Commerce, Justice, State Appropriations/Democracy Program Funding. Stevens, R-Alaska, motion to table (kill) the Lugar, R-Ind., amendment that would redirect $30 million from the State Department's capital improvement account for the National Endowment for Democracy. Motion rejected 27-72: R 13-42; D 14-30 (ND 9-27, SD 5-3), July 24, 1997. (Subsequently, the Lugar amendment was adopted on a voice vote.)

204. S 1022. Fiscal 1998 Commerce, Justice, State Appropriations/9th U.S. Circuit Court of Appeals. Feinstein, D-Calif., amendment that would strike sections of the bill dividing the jurisdiction of the 9th U.S. Circuit Court of Appeals, mandating instead a 10-member commission to study reorganization of the U.S. Courts of Appeals, with emphasis on the 9th Circuit. Rejected 45-55: R 0-55; D 45-0 (ND 37-0, SD 8-0), July 24, 1997.

SENATE VOTES 205, 206, 207, 208, 209, 210, 211

	205	206	207	208	209	210	211
ALABAMA							
Sessions	Y	Y	Y	Y	N	Y	Y
Shelby	Y	Y	Y	Y	Y	Y	Y
ALASKA							
Murkowski	Y	Y	Y	Y	Y	Y	Y
Stevens	Y	Y	Y	Y	Y	Y	Y
ARIZONA							
Kyl	Y	Y	Y	Y	Y	Y	Y
McCain	Y	Y	Y	Y	Y	Y	Y
ARKANSAS							
Hutchinson	Y	Y	Y	Y	Y	Y	Y
Bumpers	Y	Y	Y	Y	Y	N	N
CALIFORNIA							
Boxer	Y	Y	Y	Y	Y	N	Y
Feinstein	?	Y	Y	Y	Y	Y	Y
COLORADO							
Allard	Y	Y	Y	Y	N	Y	Y
Campbell	Y	Y	Y	Y	Y	Y	Y
CONNECTICUT							
Dodd	Y	Y	Y	Y	Y	Y	Y
Lieberman	Y	Y	Y	Y	Y	Y	Y
DELAWARE							
Roth	Y	Y	Y	N	Y	Y	Y
Biden	Y	Y	Y	Y	Y	Y	Y
FLORIDA							
Mack	Y	Y	Y	Y	Y	Y	Y
Graham	Y	Y	Y	Y	Y	Y	Y
GEORGIA							
Coverdell	Y	Y	Y	Y	Y	Y	Y
Cleland	Y	Y	Y	Y	Y	Y	Y
HAWAII							
Akaka	Y	Y	Y	Y	Y	N	Y
Inouye	Y	Y	Y	Y	Y	Y	Y
IDAHO							
Craig	Y	Y	Y	Y	Y	Y	Y
Kempthorne	Y	Y	Y	Y	Y	Y	Y
ILLINOIS							
Durbin	Y	Y	Y	Y	Y	N	Y
Moseley-Braun	Y	Y	Y	Y	Y	N	Y
INDIANA							
Coats	Y	Y	Y	Y	N	Y	Y
Lugar	Y	Y	Y	Y	Y	Y	Y
IOWA							
Grassley	Y	Y	Y	Y	Y	Y	Y
Harkin	?	Y	Y	Y	Y	N	Y
KANSAS							
Brownback	Y	Y	Y	Y	Y	Y	Y
Roberts	Y	Y	Y	Y	Y	Y	Y
KENTUCKY							
McConnell	Y	Y	Y	Y	Y	Y	Y
Ford	Y	Y	Y	Y	N	Y	Y
LOUISIANA							
Breaux	Y	Y	Y	Y	Y	Y	Y
Landrieu	Y	Y	Y	Y	Y	Y	Y
MAINE							
Collins	Y	Y	Y	Y	Y	Y	Y
Snowe	Y	Y	Y	Y	Y	Y	Y
MARYLAND							
Mikulski	Y	Y	Y	Y	Y	Y	Y
Sarbanes	Y	Y	Y	Y	Y	N	N
MASSACHUSETTS							
Kennedy	Y	Y	Y	Y	Y	N	Y
Kerry	Y	Y	Y	Y	Y	Y	Y
MICHIGAN							
Abraham	Y	Y	Y	Y	Y	Y	Y
Levin	Y	Y	Y	Y	Y	Y	Y
MINNESOTA							
Grams	?	Y	Y	Y	N	Y	Y
Wellstone	Y	Y	Y	Y	N	N	N
MISSISSIPPI							
Cochran	Y	?	Y	Y	Y	Y	Y
Lott	Y	Y	Y	Y	Y	Y	Y
MISSOURI							
Ashcroft	Y	Y	Y	Y	N	Y	Y
Bond	Y	Y	Y	Y	Y	Y	Y
MONTANA							
Burns	Y	Y	Y	Y	Y	Y	Y
Baucus	Y	Y	Y	Y	Y	Y	Y
NEBRASKA							
Hagel	Y	Y	Y	Y	Y	Y	Y
Kerrey	Y	Y	Y	Y	Y	Y	Y
NEVADA							
Bryan	?	Y	Y	Y	Y	N	Y
Reid	?	Y	Y	Y	Y	N	Y
NEW HAMPSHIRE							
Gregg	Y	Y	Y	Y	Y	Y	Y
Smith	Y	Y	Y	Y	N	Y	Y
NEW JERSEY							
Lautenberg	Y	Y	Y	Y	Y	N	Y
Torricelli	Y	Y	Y	Y	Y	N	Y
NEW MEXICO							
Domenici	Y	Y	Y	Y	Y	Y	Y
Bingaman	Y	Y	Y	Y	Y	N	Y
NEW YORK							
D'Amato	Y	Y	Y	Y	Y	Y	Y
Moynihan	Y	Y	Y	Y	Y	Y	Y
NORTH CAROLINA							
Faircloth	Y	Y	?	?	N	Y	Y
Helms	Y	Y	Y	Y	N	Y	Y
NORTH DAKOTA							
Conrad	Y	Y	Y	Y	Y	Y	Y
Dorgan	Y	Y	Y	Y	Y	N	Y
OHIO							
DeWine	Y	Y	Y	Y	Y	Y	Y
Glenn	Y	Y	Y	Y	Y	N	N
OKLAHOMA							
Inhofe	Y	Y	Y	Y	N	Y	Y
Nickles	Y	Y	Y	Y	Y	Y	Y
OREGON							
Smith	Y	Y	Y	Y	Y	Y	Y
Wyden	Y	Y	Y	Y	Y	N	Y
PENNSYLVANIA							
Santorum	Y	Y	Y	Y	Y	Y	Y
Specter	Y	Y	Y	Y	Y	Y	Y
RHODE ISLAND							
Chafee	Y	Y	Y	Y	Y	Y	Y
Reed	Y	Y	Y	Y	Y	N	Y
SOUTH CAROLINA							
Thurmond	Y	Y	Y	Y	Y	Y	Y
Hollings	Y	Y	Y	Y	N	Y	N
SOUTH DAKOTA							
Daschle	Y	Y	Y	Y	Y	Y	Y
Johnson	Y	Y	Y	Y	Y	Y	Y
TENNESSEE							
Frist	Y	Y	Y	Y	Y	Y	Y
Thompson	Y	Y	Y	Y	N	Y	Y
TEXAS							
Gramm	Y	Y	Y	Y	N	Y	Y
Hutchison	Y	Y	Y	Y	Y	Y	Y
UTAH							
Bennett	Y	Y	Y	Y	Y	Y	Y
Hatch	Y	Y	Y	Y	Y	Y	Y
VERMONT							
Jeffords	Y	Y	Y	Y	Y	Y	Y
Leahy	Y	Y	Y	Y	Y	N	Y
VIRGINIA							
Warner	Y	Y	Y	Y	Y	Y	Y
Robb	Y	Y	Y	Y	Y	Y	N
WASHINGTON							
Gorton	Y	Y	Y	Y	Y	Y	Y
Murray	Y	Y	Y	Y	Y	N	Y
WEST VIRGINIA							
Byrd	Y	Y	Y	Y	Y	N	N
Rockefeller	Y	Y	Y	Y	Y	Y	Y
WISCONSIN							
Feingold	Y	Y	Y	Y	Y	N	N
Kohl	Y	Y	Y	Y	Y	Y	Y
WYOMING							
Enzi	Y	Y	Y	Y	N	Y	Y
Thomas	Y	Y	Y	Y	Y	Y	Y

KEY

- Y Voted for (yea).
- # Paired for.
- + Announced for.
- N Voted against (nay).
- X Paired against.
- – Announced against.
- P Voted "present."
- C Voted "present" to avoid possible conflict of interest.
- ? Did not vote or otherwise make a position known.

Democrats *Republicans*

ND Northern Democrats SD Southern Democrats

Southern states - Ala., Ark., Fla., Ga., Ky., La., Miss., N.C., Okla., S.C., Tenn., Texas, Va.

205. S Res 98. Conditions on U.N. Framework Convention on Climate Change/Passage. Adoption of the resolution specifying Senate conditions regarding treaty agreements on the U.N. Framework Convention on Climate Change to be negotiated in Kyoto, Japan, in December 1997. The resolution stipulates that any binding agreement on reducing greenhouse gas emissions include commitments by the nations of the developing world, such as China and India. Adopted 95-0: R 54-0; D 41-0 (ND 33-0, SD 8-0), July 25, 1997.

206. S 1022. Fiscal 1998 Commerce, Justice, State Appropriations/Passage. Passage of the bill to provide $31.6 billion in new budget authority for the departments of Commerce, Justice and State in fiscal 1998. The bill provides $1.4 billion more than in fiscal 1997 and $4.0 billion less than requested by President Clinton. Passed 99-0: R 54-0; D 45-0 (ND 37-0, SD 8-0), July 29, 1997.

207. S 39. International Dolphin Conservation Program/Passage. Passage of the bill to implement an international agreement to lift the embargo on Latin American tuna. The bill would redefine the "dolphin safe" label affixed to tuna cans. The definition could be loosened as early as March 1999 under a preliminary finding by the Commerce secretary that encircling nets do not have an adverse impact on dolphins. Passed 99-0: R 54-0; D 45-0 (ND 37-0, SD 8-0), July 30, 1997. (After passage, the Senate struck all after the enacting clause of HR 408, inserted the text of S 39 and passed the bill by unanimous consent.)

208. HR 2169. Fiscal 1998 Transportation Appropriations/Passage. Passage of the bill to provide $12.8 billion in new budget authority for the Department of Transportation and related agencies in fiscal 1998 and to authorize a total of $41.9 billion in expenditures for fiscal 1998. The bill provides $3.8 billion more than in fiscal 1997 and $1.6 billion more than requested by President Clinton. Passed 98-1: R 53-1; D 45-0 (ND 37-0, SD 8-0), July 30, 1997. (Before passage, the Senate struck all after the enacting clause and inserted the text of S 1048.)

209. HR 2015. Fiscal 1998 Budget Reconciliation — Spending/Conference Report. Adoption of the conference report on the bill to cut projected entitlement spending by $140 billion, establishing a balanced budget by fiscal 2002. The bill would reduce Medicare funding by $115 billion; increase health insurance options available to Medicare beneficiaries beyond fee-for-service programs; and permit up to 390,000 Medicare beneficiaries to establish tax-free medical savings accounts. The bill also would include a $24 billion block grant program to help states improve health coverage for uninsured children, funded in part by a federal tobacco tax increase of 15 cents per pack over five years, and restore Supplemental Security Income (SSI) and Medicaid benefits to certain legal immigrants. Adopted (thus cleared for the president) 85-15: R 43-12; D 42-3 (ND 36-1, SD 6-2), July 31, 1997. A "yea" was a vote in support of the president's position.

210. HR 2014. Fiscal 1998 Budget Reconciliation — Revenue/Procedural Motion. Roth, R-Del., motion to waive the Budget Act with respect to the conference report on HR 2014. Motion agreed to 78-22: R 55-0; D 23-22 (ND 16-21, SD 7-1), July 31, 1997. Three-fifths of the total Senate (60) is required to waive the Budget Act.

211. HR 2014. Fiscal 1998 Budget Reconciliation — Revenue/Conference Report. Adoption of the conference report on the bill to provide a net tax cut of $100.4 billion over five years, including $151.6 billion in gross tax cuts offset by $51.2 billion in revenue increases. The bill would establish a tax credit for each child under age 17, lower the top capital gains tax rate from 28 percent to 20 percent, raise the amount exempt from the federal estate tax gradually from $600,000 to $1 million and provide $39.4 billion in education tax incentives that include a non-refundable credit of up to $1,500 for each student per year for the first two years of college. Adopted (thus cleared for the president) 92-8: R 55-0; D 37-8 (ND 32-5, SD 5-3), July 31, 1997. A "yea" was a vote in support of the president's position.

SENATE VOTES 212, 213, 214, 215, 216, 217, 218, 219

KEY

- Y Voted for (yea).
- # Paired for.
- + Announced for.
- N Voted against (nay).
- X Paired against.
- – Announced against.
- P Voted "present."
- C Voted "present" to avoid possible conflict of interest.
- ? Did not vote or otherwise make a position known.

Democrats *Republicans*

	212	213	214	215	216	217	218	219
ALABAMA								
Sessions	Y	Y	Y	Y	Y	Y	Y	Y
Shelby	Y	Y	Y	Y	Y	Y	Y	Y
ALASKA								
Murkowski	?	?	?	?	?	?	?	?
Stevens	Y	N	Y	N	Y	Y	Y	Y
ARIZONA								
Kyl	N	Y	Y	Y	Y	Y	Y	Y
McCain	N	Y	Y	N	Y	Y	Y	Y
ARKANSAS								
Hutchinson	Y	Y	Y	Y	Y	Y	Y	Y
Bumpers	N	N	Y	N	Y	N	Y	Y
CALIFORNIA								
Boxer	N	N	Y	N	Y	N	Y	Y
Feinstein	N	Y	Y	N	Y	N	Y	Y
COLORADO								
Allard	N	Y	Y	Y	Y	Y	Y	Y
Campbell	N	N	Y	N	Y	Y	Y	Y
CONNECTICUT								
Dodd	N	N	Y	N	Y	N	Y	Y
Lieberman	N	N	Y	N	Y	N	Y	Y
DELAWARE								
Roth	N	N	Y	N	Y	Y	Y	Y
Biden	N	N	Y	N	Y	N	Y	Y
FLORIDA								
Mack	N	Y	Y	N	Y	Y	Y	Y
Graham	N	N	Y	N	Y	N	Y	Y
GEORGIA								
Coverdell	N	Y	Y	Y	Y	Y	Y	Y
Cleland	N	N	Y	N	Y	N	Y	Y
HAWAII								
Akaka	N	N	Y	N	Y	N	Y	Y
Inouye	N	N	?	N	Y	N	Y	Y
IDAHO								
Craig	N	N	Y	Y	Y	Y	Y	Y
Kempthorne	N	N	Y	Y	Y	Y	Y	Y
ILLINOIS								
Durbin	N	N	Y	N	Y	N	Y	Y
Moseley-Braun	N	N	Y	N	Y	N	Y	Y
INDIANA								
Coats	Y	N	Y	Y	Y	Y	Y	Y
Lugar	N	N	Y	N	Y	Y	Y	Y
IOWA								
Grassley	N	N	Y	Y	Y	Y	Y	Y
Harkin	N	N	Y	N	Y	N	Y	Y
KANSAS								
Brownback	Y	Y	Y	Y	Y	Y	Y	Y
Roberts	Y	Y	Y	Y	Y	Y	Y	Y
KENTUCKY								
McConnell	Y	Y	Y	N	Y	Y	Y	Y
Ford	Y	N	Y	N	Y	N	Y	Y
LOUISIANA								
Breaux	N	Y	Y	N	Y	Y	Y	Y
Landrieu	N	N	Y	N	Y	N	Y	Y
MAINE								
Collins	N	N	Y	N	Y	Y	Y	Y
Snowe	N	N	Y	N	Y	Y	Y	Y
MARYLAND								
Mikulski	N	N	Y	N	Y	N	Y	Y
Sarbanes	N	N	Y	N	Y	N	Y	Y
MASSACHUSETTS								
Kennedy	N	N	Y	N	Y	N	Y	Y
Kerry	N	N	Y	N	Y	N	Y	Y
MICHIGAN								
Abraham	N	N	Y	Y	Y	Y	Y	Y
Levin	N	N	Y	N	Y	N	Y	Y
MINNESOTA								
Grams	Y	N	Y	Y	Y	Y	Y	Y
Wellstone	N	N	Y	N	Y	N	Y	Y
MISSISSIPPI								
Cochran	Y	Y	Y	N	Y	Y	Y	Y
Lott	Y	Y	Y	Y	Y	Y	Y	Y
MISSOURI								
Ashcroft	Y	Y	N	Y	Y	Y	Y	Y
Bond	N	N	Y	Y	Y	Y	Y	Y
MONTANA								
Burns	Y	N	Y	Y	Y	Y	Y	Y
Baucus	N	N	Y	N	Y	N	Y	Y
NEBRASKA								
Hagel	Y	N	Y	Y	Y	Y	Y	Y
Kerrey	N	N	Y	N	Y	N	Y	Y
NEVADA								
Bryan	N	N	Y	N	Y	N	Y	Y
Reid	N	N	Y	N	Y	N	Y	Y
NEW HAMPSHIRE								
Gregg	N	N	Y	Y	Y	Y	Y	Y
Smith	Y	N	Y	Y	Y	Y	Y	Y
NEW JERSEY								
Lautenberg	N	N	Y	N	Y	N	Y	Y
Torricelli	N	N	Y	N	Y	N	Y	Y
NEW MEXICO								
Domenici	Y	N	Y	Y	Y	Y	Y	Y
Bingaman	N	N	Y	N	?	N	Y	Y
NEW YORK								
D'Amato	N	N	Y	Y	Y	Y	Y	Y
Moynihan	N	N	Y	N	Y	N	Y	Y
NORTH CAROLINA								
Faircloth	Y	Y	Y	Y	Y	Y	Y	Y
Helms	Y	Y	Y	Y	Y	Y	?	?
NORTH DAKOTA								
Conrad	N	N	Y	N	Y	N	Y	Y
Dorgan	N	N	Y	N	Y	N	Y	Y
OHIO								
DeWine	N	N	Y	Y	Y	Y	Y	Y
Glenn	N	N	Y	N	?	?	?	?
OKLAHOMA								
Inhofe	Y	Y	Y	Y	Y	Y	Y	Y
Nickles	N	Y	Y	Y	Y	Y	Y	Y
OREGON								
Smith	N	N	Y	N	Y	Y	Y	Y
Wyden	N	N	Y	N	Y	N	Y	Y
PENNSYLVANIA								
Santorum	Y	N	Y	Y	Y	Y	Y	Y
Specter	N	N	Y	N	Y	N	Y	Y
RHODE ISLAND								
Chafee	N	N	Y	?	Y	Y	?	?
Reed	N	N	Y	N	Y	N	Y	Y
SOUTH CAROLINA								
Thurmond	Y	Y	Y	N	Y	Y	Y	Y
Hollings	N	N	Y	N	Y	Y	Y	Y
SOUTH DAKOTA								
Daschle	N	N	Y	N	Y	N	Y	Y
Johnson	N	N	Y	N	Y	N	Y	Y
TENNESSEE								
Frist	Y	N	Y	Y	Y	Y	Y	Y
Thompson	N	N	Y	Y	Y	Y	Y	Y
TEXAS								
Gramm	Y	Y	Y	Y	Y	Y	Y	Y
Hutchison	Y	Y	Y	Y	Y	Y	Y	Y
UTAH								
Bennett	N	N	Y	Y	Y	Y	Y	Y
Hatch	N	Y	Y	Y	Y	Y	Y	Y
VERMONT								
Jeffords	N	N	N	N	Y	Y	Y	Y
Leahy	N	N	Y	N	Y	N	Y	Y
VIRGINIA								
Warner	?	N	Y	N	Y	Y	Y	Y
Robb	N	N	Y	N	Y	N	Y	Y
WASHINGTON								
Gorton	Y	Y	Y	Y	Y	Y	Y	Y
Murray	N	N	Y	N	Y	N	Y	Y
WEST VIRGINIA								
Byrd	N	N	Y	N	Y	Y	Y	Y
Rockefeller	N	N	Y	N	Y	N	Y	Y
WISCONSIN								
Feingold	N	N	Y	N	Y	N	Y	Y
Kohl	N	N	Y	N	Y	N	Y	Y
WYOMING								
Enzi	Y	N	N	Y	Y	Y	Y	Y
Thomas	Y	N	Y	Y	Y	Y	Y	Y

ND Northern Democrats SD Southern Democrats

Southern states - Ala., Ark., Fla., Ga., Ky., La., Miss., N.C., Okla., S.C., Tenn., Texas, Va.

212. S 1033. Fiscal 1998 Agriculture Appropriations/FDA Children's Tobacco Initiative. Cochran, R-Miss., motion to table (kill) the Harkin, D-Iowa, amendment to fund fully the Food and Drug Administration's initiative to curb teenage smoking at $34 million in fiscal 1998 by limiting funding to the Commodity Credit Corporation. The amendment also would rescind the offset should funding for the FDA tobacco initiative be provided through any tobacco settlement legislation. Motion rejected 28-70: R 27-26; D 1-44 (ND 0-37, SD 1-7), Sept. 3, 1997. (Subsequently, the Harkin amendment was adopted by voice vote.)

213. S 1061. Fiscal 1998 Labor-HHS Appropriations/Pell Grants. Kyl, R-Ariz., amendment to increase funding for Pell grants, which help pay college tuition for low-income individuals, by $528 million. The increase would be funded by an equal reduction in funding for the Low Income Home Energy Assistance Program, which provides heating assistance to low-income individuals. Rejected 25-74: R 23-31; D 2-43 (ND 1-36, SD 1-7), Sept. 3, 1997.

214. S 1061. Fiscal 1998 Labor-HHS Appropriations/Parkinson's Disease Research. Wellstone, D-Minn., and McCain, R-Ariz., amendment to instruct the director of the National Institutes of Health to establish a research and training program on Parkinson's disease. The measure would authorize $100 million in fiscal 1998 and unspecified amounts in fiscal 1999 and 2000. Adopted 95-3: R 51-3; D 44-0 (ND 36-0, SD 8-0), Sept. 3, 1997.

215. S 1061. Fiscal 1998 Labor-HHS Appropriations/Fetal Tissue Research. Coats, R-Ind., amendment to prohibit the use of funds authorized in the bill for Parkinson's disease research for any procedure that utilizes human fetal tissue, cells or organs obtained from an embryo or fetus during or after an induced abortion. The revision would not apply to fetal tissue, cells or organs obtained from a miscarriage or pregnancy outside of the womb. Rejected 38-60: R 38-15; D 0-45 (ND 0-37, SD 0-8), Sept. 4, 1997.

216. S 1061. Fiscal 1998 Labor-HHS Appropriations/Older Americans Act. D'Amato, R-N.Y., amendment to increase funding by $40 million in fiscal 1998 for senior citizens' health programs administered under the 1965 Older Americans Act. The increase would be offset by reducing administrative expenses in the departments of Labor, Health and Human Services, and Education. Adopted 97-0: R 54-0; D 43-0 (ND 35-0, SD 8-0), Sept. 4, 1997.

217. S 1061. Fiscal 1998 Labor-HHS Appropriations/Teamsters' Consent Decree. Nickles, R-Okla., motion to table (kill) the Kennedy, D-Mass., amendment to the pending Nickles amendment stipulating that no revision would affect the obligations of the United States under the 1989 consent decree in *United States v. International Brotherhood of Teamsters*. Motion agreed to 56-42: R 53-1; D 3-41 (ND 1-35, SD 2-6), Sept. 4, 1997.

218. Kennedy Nomination/Confirmation. Confirmation of President Clinton's nomination of Henry Harold Kennedy Jr. of the District of Columbia to be a district judge for the District of Columbia. Confirmed 96-0: R 52-0; D 44-0 (ND 36-0, SD 8-0), Sept. 4, 1997. A "yea" was a vote in support of the president's position.

219. Hull Nomination/Confirmation. Confirmation of President Clinton's nomination of Frank M. Hull of Georgia to be a judge on the 11th U.S. Circuit Court of Appeals. Confirmed 96-0: R 52-0; D 44-0 (ND 36-0, SD 8-0), Sept. 4, 1997. A "yea" was a vote in support of the president's position.

SENATE VOTES 220, 221, 222, 223, 224, 225, 226, 227

	220	221	222	223	224	225	226	227
ALABAMA								
Sessions	Y	+	Y	Y	N	Y	Y	Y
Shelby	Y	Y	Y	Y	Y	N	Y	Y
ALASKA								
Murkowski	?	Y	Y	N	N	Y	Y	Y
Stevens	Y	Y	Y	N	N	Y	Y	Y
ARIZONA								
Kyl	Y	Y	Y	Y	N	Y	Y	Y
McCain	?	Y	Y	Y	N	Y	Y	Y
ARKANSAS								
Hutchinson	Y	Y	Y	Y	N	Y	Y	Y
Bumpers	Y	Y	Y	N	Y	N	Y	Y
CALIFORNIA								
Boxer	Y	Y	Y	Y	Y	N	Y	Y
Feinstein	Y	Y	Y	Y	Y	N	Y	Y
COLORADO								
Allard	Y	Y	Y	Y	N	Y	Y	Y
Campbell	Y	Y	Y	Y	N	Y	Y	Y
CONNECTICUT								
Dodd	Y	Y	Y	Y	Y	N	Y	Y
Lieberman	Y	?	Y	N	Y	N	Y	Y
DELAWARE								
Roth	Y	?	Y	N	Y	N	Y	Y
Biden	Y	?	Y	N	Y	N	Y	Y
FLORIDA								
Mack	Y	Y	Y	Y	N	Y	Y	Y
Graham	Y	Y	Y	N	Y	N	Y	Y
GEORGIA								
Coverdell	Y	Y	Y	Y	N	Y	Y	Y
Cleland	N	Y	Y	N	Y	N	Y	Y
HAWAII								
Akaka	N	Y	Y	N	+	N	Y	Y
Inouye	Y	Y	Y	N	Y	N	Y	Y
IDAHO								
Craig	Y	Y	Y	Y	N	Y	Y	Y
Kempthorne	Y	Y	Y	Y	N	Y	Y	Y
ILLINOIS								
Durbin	N	Y	Y	N	Y	N	Y	Y
Moseley-Braun	Y	Y	Y	N	Y	N	Y	Y
INDIANA								
Coats	Y	Y	Y	Y	N	Y	Y	Y
Lugar	Y	Y	Y	Y	N	Y	Y	Y
IOWA								
Grassley	Y	Y	Y	N	N	Y	Y	Y
Harkin	Y	Y	Y	Y	Y	N	Y	Y
KANSAS								
Brownback	Y	Y	Y	Y	N	Y	Y	Y
Roberts	Y	Y	Y	Y	N	Y	Y	Y
KENTUCKY								
McConnell	Y	Y	Y	Y	N	Y	Y	N
Ford	?	Y	Y	N	N	Y	Y	Y
LOUISIANA								
Breaux	Y	Y	Y	N	Y	N	Y	Y
Landrieu	Y	Y	Y	N	Y	N	Y	Y
MAINE								
Collins	Y	Y	Y	Y	Y	N	Y	Y
Snowe	Y	Y	Y	N	Y	N	Y	Y
MARYLAND								
Mikulski	Y	Y	Y	Y	Y	N	Y	Y
Sarbanes	Y	Y	Y	N	Y	N	Y	Y
MASSACHUSETTS								
Kennedy	N	?	Y	N	Y	N	Y	Y
Kerry	Y	?	Y	N	Y	N	Y	Y
MICHIGAN								
Abraham	Y	Y	Y	Y	N	Y	Y	Y
Levin	Y	Y	Y	N	Y	N	Y	Y
MINNESOTA								
Grams	Y	Y	Y	Y	N	Y	Y	Y
Wellstone	Y	Y	Y	Y	Y	N	Y	Y
MISSISSIPPI								
Cochran	Y	Y	Y	N	Y	N	Y	Y
Lott	Y	Y	Y	Y	N	Y	Y	Y
MISSOURI								
Ashcroft	Y	N	Y	Y	N	Y	Y	Y
Bond	Y	Y	Y	N	N	Y	Y	Y
MONTANA								
Burns	Y	Y	Y	N	N	Y	Y	Y
Baucus	Y	Y	Y	N	Y	N	Y	Y
NEBRASKA								
Hagel	Y	Y	Y	Y	N	Y	Y	Y
Kerrey	Y	Y	Y	N	Y	N	Y	Y
NEVADA								
Bryan	Y	Y	Y	N	Y	N	Y	Y
Reid	Y	Y	Y	N	Y	N	Y	Y
NEW HAMPSHIRE								
Gregg	Y	Y	Y	Y	N	Y	Y	Y
Smith	Y	Y	Y	Y	N	Y	Y	Y
NEW JERSEY								
Lautenberg	Y	Y	Y	N	Y	N	Y	Y
Torricelli	Y	Y	Y	N	Y	N	Y	Y
NEW MEXICO								
Domenici	Y	N	Y	N	N	Y	Y	Y
Bingaman	Y	Y	Y	N	?	?	?	?
NEW YORK								
D'Amato	Y	Y	Y	N	Y	N	Y	Y
Moynihan	Y	Y	Y	N	Y	N	Y	Y
NORTH CAROLINA								
Faircloth	Y	?	Y	Y	N	Y	N	N
Helms	Y	N	Y	Y	N	Y	Y	N
NORTH DAKOTA								
Conrad	Y	Y	Y	N	Y	N	Y	Y
Dorgan	Y	Y	Y	N	Y	N	Y	Y
OHIO								
DeWine	Y	Y	Y	N	N	Y	Y	Y
Glenn	?	Y	Y	N	Y	N	Y	Y
OKLAHOMA								
Inhofe	Y	?	Y	Y	N	Y	Y	Y
Nickles	Y	N	Y	Y	N	Y	Y	Y
OREGON								
Smith	Y	?	Y	N	N	Y	Y	Y
Wyden	Y	Y	Y	N	Y	N	Y	Y
PENNSYLVANIA								
Santorum	?	Y	Y	N	N	Y	Y	Y
Specter	Y	Y	Y	Y	N	Y	Y	Y
RHODE ISLAND								
Chafee	Y	Y	Y	N	N	Y	Y	Y
Reed	N	Y	Y	N	Y	N	Y	Y
SOUTH CAROLINA								
Thurmond	Y	Y	Y	Y	N	Y	Y	Y
Hollings	Y	+	Y	Y	Y	N	Y	Y
SOUTH DAKOTA								
Daschle	Y	Y	Y	N	Y	N	Y	Y
Johnson	Y	Y	Y	Y	Y	N	Y	Y
TENNESSEE								
Frist	Y	Y	Y	N	N	Y	Y	Y
Thompson	Y	Y	Y	Y	N	Y	Y	Y
TEXAS								
Gramm	Y	Y	Y	Y	N	Y	Y	Y
Hutchison	Y	Y	Y	Y	N	Y	Y	Y
UTAH								
Bennett	Y	?	?	?	?	?	?	?
Hatch	Y	Y	Y	N	N	Y	Y	Y
VERMONT								
Jeffords	Y	Y	Y	N	N	Y	Y	Y
Leahy	Y	?	?	N	Y	N	Y	Y
VIRGINIA								
Warner	Y	Y	Y	Y	N	Y	Y	Y
Robb	Y	Y	Y	N	Y	N	Y	Y
WASHINGTON								
Gorton	Y	Y	Y	Y	N	N	Y	Y
Murray	Y	Y	Y	N	Y	N	Y	Y
WEST VIRGINIA								
Byrd	Y	Y	Y	N	Y	N	Y	Y
Rockefeller	Y	Y	Y	N	Y	N	Y	Y
WISCONSIN								
Feingold	Y	Y	Y	N	Y	N	Y	Y
Kohl	Y	Y	Y	Y	Y	N	Y	Y
WYOMING								
Enzi	Y	Y	Y	N	N	Y	Y	Y
Thomas	?	Y	Y	Y	N	Y	Y	Y

ND Northern Democrats SD Southern Democrats

Southern states - Ala., Ark., Fla., Ga., Ky., La., Miss., N.C., Okla., S.C., Tenn., Texas, Va.

KEY

- Y Voted for (yea).
- # Paired for.
- \+ Announced for.
- N Voted against (nay).
- X Paired against.
- \- Announced against.
- P Voted "present."
- C Voted "present" to avoid possible conflict of interest.
- ? Did not vote or otherwise make a position known.

Democrats ***Republicans***

220. S 830. Food and Drug Administration Overhaul /Cloture. Motion to invoke cloture (thus limiting debate) on the bill to revise Food and Drug Administration regulatory procedures regarding medical devices, pharmaceuticals, cosmetics and other products. Motion agreed to 89-5: R 51-0; D 38-5 (ND 32-4, SD 6-1), Sept. 5, 1997. A three-fifths majority vote (60) of the total Senate is required to invoke cloture.

221. S 1061. Fiscal 1998 Labor-HHS Appropriations/State Student Grants. Reed, D-R.I., amendment to provide $35 million for the State Student Incentive Grant program. The increase would be offset by transferring unobligated balances from other Education Department accounts. Adopted 84-4: R 45-4; D 39-0 (ND 32-0, SD 7-0), Sept. 8, 1997.

222. S Res 120. Mother Teresa Recognition/Passage. Nickles, R-Okla., sense of Senate resolution extending sympathies to the Missionaries of Charity regarding the death of Mother Teresa. It also establishes Sept. 13, 1997, as a national day of recognition. Adopted 98-0: R 54-0; D 44-0 (ND 36-0, SD 8-0), Sept. 9, 1997.

223. S 1061. Fiscal 1998 Labor-HHS Appropriations/Medical Training Programs. McCain, R-Ariz., motion to waive the Budget Act regarding his amendment revising the Balanced Budget Act of 1997. The revision would prohibit the secretary of Health and Human Services from entering into any agreement with any institution to provide incentive payments for reducing medical education training programs. Rejected 45-54: R 36-18; D 9-36 (ND 8-29, SD 1-7), Sept. 9, 1997. A three-fifths majority vote (60) of the total Senate is required to waive the Budget Act.

224. S 1061. Fiscal 1998 Labor-HHS Appropriations/Tobacco Settlement Attorneys' Fees. Durbin, D-Ill., motion to table (kill) the Sessions, R-Ala., amendment to limit plaintiffs' attorneys' fees in any agreement between states and tobacco companies regarding compensation for state Medicaid expenses incurred on tobacco-related illnesses. The amendment would limit those attorneys' fees to $250 per hour with an aggregate cap of $5 million per state. Motion rejected 48-49: R 6-48; D 42-1 (ND 35-0, SD 7-1), Sept. 10, 1997.

225. S 1061. Fiscal 1998 Labor-HHS Appropriations/Tobacco Settlement Attorneys' Fees. Sessions, R-Ala., motion to table (kill) the Wellstone, D-Minn., amendment to the Sessions amendment stipulating that its limits on attorneys' fees would not apply to previous agreements between states and private attorneys regarding tobacco-related litigation. Motion rejected 48-50: R 47-7; D 1-43 (ND 0-36, SD 1-7), Sept. 10, 1997. (Subsequently, the Wellstone amendment was adopted by voice vote.)

226. S 1061. Fiscal 1998 Labor-HHS Appropriations/Tobacco Settlement Attorneys' Fees. Durbin, D-Ill., amendment expressing the sense of the Senate that any attorneys' fees paid in connection with a state action against tobacco companies affected by federal tobacco settlement legislation should be publicly disclosed and should not displace spending in the settlement legislation intended for public health. Adopted 97-1: R 53-1; D 44-0 (ND 36-0, SD 8-0), Sept. 10, 1997.

227. S 1061. Fiscal 1998 Labor-HHS Appropriations/Tobacco Settlement Tax Credit. Durbin, D-Ill., amendment to repeal the tobacco industry settlement credit contained in the Balanced Budget Act of 1997 (PL 105-34). Adopted 95-3: R 51-3; D 44-0 (ND 36-0, SD 8-0), Sept. 10, 1997.

SENATE VOTES 228, 229, 230, 231, 232, 233, 234, 235

	228	229	230	231	232	233	234	235
ALABAMA								
Sessions	Y	N	Y	Y	N	Y	N	N
Shelby	Y	N	Y	Y	N	Y	N	Y
ALASKA								
Murkowski	Y	N	Y	Y	N	Y	Y	Y
Stevens	Y	N	Y	Y	N	Y	Y	Y
ARIZONA								
Kyl	Y	N	N	Y	N	Y	Y	Y
McCain	Y	N	N	Y	N	Y	Y	Y
ARKANSAS								
Hutchinson	Y	N	Y	Y	N	Y	N	Y
Bumpers	Y	Y	Y	Y	Y	N	Y	Y
CALIFORNIA								
Boxer	Y	Y	Y	Y	Y	N	Y	Y
Feinstein	Y	N	Y	Y	Y	Y	Y	Y
COLORADO								
Allard	Y	N	Y	Y	N	Y	N	Y
Campbell	Y	N	Y	Y	N	Y	Y	Y
CONNECTICUT								
Dodd	Y	N	Y	Y	Y	N	Y	Y
Lieberman	Y	N	Y	Y	Y	N	Y	Y
DELAWARE								
Roth	Y	N	Y	Y	N	Y	Y	Y
Biden	Y	N	Y	Y	Y	N	Y	Y
FLORIDA								
Mack	Y	N	Y	Y	N	Y	Y	Y
Graham	Y	N	Y	Y	Y	N	Y	Y
GEORGIA								
Coverdell	Y	N	Y	Y	N	Y	Y	Y
Cleland	Y	N	Y	Y	Y	N	Y	Y
HAWAII								
Akaka	Y	Y	Y	Y	Y	N	Y	Y
Inouye	Y	N	Y	Y	Y	N	Y	Y
IDAHO								
Craig	Y	N	Y	Y	N	Y	Y	Y
Kempthorne	Y	N	Y	Y	N	Y	Y	Y
ILLINOIS								
Durbin	Y	Y	Y	Y	Y	N	Y	Y
Moseley-Braun	Y	Y	Y	Y	Y	N	Y	Y
INDIANA								
Coats	Y	N	Y	Y	N	Y	Y	N
Lugar	Y	N	Y	Y	N	Y	Y	Y
IOWA								
Grassley	Y	N	Y	Y	N	Y	Y	Y
Harkin	Y	Y	Y	Y	Y	N	Y	Y
KANSAS								
Brownback	Y	N	Y	Y	N	Y	N	Y
Roberts	Y	N	Y	Y	N	Y	Y	Y
KENTUCKY								
McConnell	Y	N	Y	Y	N	Y	Y	Y
Ford	Y	N	Y	Y	Y	N	Y	Y
LOUISIANA								
Breaux	Y	N	Y	Y	Y	N	Y	Y
Landrieu	Y	N	Y	Y	Y	N	Y	Y
MAINE								
Collins	Y	N	Y	Y	N	Y	Y	Y
Snowe	Y	N	Y	Y	Y	Y	Y	Y
MARYLAND								
Mikulski	Y	Y	Y	Y	Y	N	Y	Y
Sarbanes	Y	Y	Y	Y	Y	N	Y	Y
MASSACHUSETTS								
Kennedy	Y	Y	Y	Y	Y	N	Y	Y
Kerry	Y	Y	Y	Y	Y	N	Y	Y
MICHIGAN								
Abraham	Y	N	Y	Y	N	Y	Y	Y
Levin	Y	Y	Y	Y	Y	N	Y	Y
MINNESOTA								
Grams	Y	N	N	Y	N	Y	N	Y
Wellstone	Y	Y	Y	Y	Y	N	Y	Y
MISSISSIPPI								
Cochran	Y	N	Y	Y	N	Y	Y	Y
Lott	Y	N	Y	Y	N	Y	Y	Y
MISSOURI								
Ashcroft	Y	N	N	Y	N	Y	N	N
Bond	Y	N	Y	Y	N	Y	Y	Y
MONTANA								
Burns	Y	N	Y	Y	N	Y	Y	Y
Baucus	Y	N	Y	Y	Y	N	Y	Y
NEBRASKA								
Hagel	Y	N	Y	Y	N	Y	N	Y
Kerrey	Y	N	Y	Y	Y	N	Y	Y
NEVADA								
Bryan	Y	Y	N	Y	Y	N	Y	Y
Reid	Y	Y	Y	Y	Y	N	Y	Y
NEW HAMPSHIRE								
Gregg	Y	N	Y	Y	N	Y	Y	Y
Smith	Y	N	Y	Y	N	Y	Y	N
NEW JERSEY								
Lautenberg	Y	Y	Y	Y	Y	N	Y	Y
Torricelli	Y	N	Y	Y	Y	N	Y	Y
NEW MEXICO								
Domenici	Y	N	Y	Y	N	Y	Y	Y
Bingaman	?	?	?	?	Y	N	Y	Y
NEW YORK								
D'Amato	Y	N	Y	Y	N	Y	Y	Y
Moynihan	Y	Y	Y	Y	Y	N	Y	Y
NORTH CAROLINA								
Faircloth	Y	N	Y	N	N	Y	Y	N
Helms	N	N	Y	N	N	Y	N	N
NORTH DAKOTA								
Conrad	Y	N	Y	Y	Y	N	Y	Y
Dorgan	Y	N	Y	Y	Y	N	Y	Y
OHIO								
DeWine	Y	N	Y	Y	N	Y	Y	Y
Glenn	Y	N	N	Y	Y	N	Y	Y
OKLAHOMA								
Inhofe	Y	N	Y	N	N	Y	N	N
Nickles	Y	N	Y	Y	N	Y	N	Y
OREGON								
Smith	Y	N	Y	Y	N	Y	Y	Y
Wyden	Y	Y	Y	Y	Y	N	Y	Y
PENNSYLVANIA								
Santorum	Y	N	Y	Y	N	Y	Y	Y
Specter	Y	Y	Y	Y	Y	Y	Y	Y
RHODE ISLAND								
Chafee	Y	N	Y	Y	Y	Y	Y	Y
Reed	Y	Y	Y	Y	Y	N	Y	Y
SOUTH CAROLINA								
Thurmond	Y	N	Y	Y	N	Y	Y	Y
Hollings	Y	Y	Y	Y	Y	Y	Y	Y
SOUTH DAKOTA								
Daschle	Y	N	Y	Y	Y	N	Y	Y
Johnson	Y	Y	Y	Y	Y	N	Y	Y
TENNESSEE								
Frist	Y	N	Y	Y	N	Y	Y	Y
Thompson	Y	N	Y	Y	N	Y	N	Y
TEXAS								
Gramm	Y	N	N	Y	N	Y	N	N
Hutchison	Y	N	Y	Y	N	Y	Y	Y
UTAH								
Bennett	Y	N	Y	Y	N	Y	Y	Y
Hatch	Y	N	Y	Y	N	Y	Y	Y
VERMONT								
Jeffords	Y	Y	N	Y	Y	Y	Y	Y
Leahy	Y	Y	Y	Y	Y	N	Y	Y
VIRGINIA								
Warner	Y	N	Y	Y	N	Y	Y	Y
Robb	Y	N	Y	Y	Y	N	Y	Y
WASHINGTON								
Gorton	Y	N	Y	Y	N	Y	Y	Y
Murray	Y	Y	Y	Y	Y	N	Y	Y
WEST VIRGINIA								
Byrd	Y	N	Y	Y	Y	Y	Y	Y
Rockefeller	Y	Y	Y	Y	Y	N	Y	Y
WISCONSIN								
Feingold	Y	Y	Y	Y	Y	N	Y	Y
Kohl	Y	Y	Y	Y	Y	N	Y	Y
WYOMING								
Enzi	Y	N	Y	Y	N	Y	Y	Y
Thomas	Y	N	Y	Y	N	Y	Y	Y

KEY

- Y Voted for (yea).
- # Paired for.
- + Announced for.
- N Voted against (nay).
- X Paired against.
- – Announced against.
- P Voted "present."
- C Voted "present" to avoid possible conflict of interest.
- ? Did not vote or otherwise make a position known.

Democrats *Republicans*

ND Northern Democrats SD Southern Democrats

Southern states - Ala., Ark., Fla., Ga., Ky., La., Miss., N.C., Okla., S.C., Tenn., Texas, Va.

228. S 1061. Fiscal 1998 Labor-HHS Appropriations/Domestic Violence. Murray, D-Wash., amendment to provide temporary waivers from work requirements in the 1996 Personal Responsibility and Work Opportunity Reconciliation Act for victims of domestic violence. Adopted 98-1: R 54-1; D 44-0 (ND 36-0, SD 8-0), Sept. 10, 1997.

229. S 1061. Fiscal 1998 Labor-HHS Appropriations/Head Start. Wellstone, D-Minn., motion to waive the Budget Act with respect to the Domenici, R-N.M., point of order against his amendment to increase funding for Head Start educational programs by $525 million and offset the increase with a similar reduction in the Defense Department fiscal 1998 budget. Motion rejected 27-72: R 2-53; D 25-19 (ND 23-13, SD 2-6), Sept. 10, 1997. A three-fifths majority vote (60) of the total Senate is required to waive the Budget Act. (Subsequently, the chair upheld the point of order and the amendment fell.)

230. S 1061. Fiscal 1998 Labor-HHS Appropriations/Food Research Funding. Coverdell, R-Ga., amendment to require the secretary of Health and Human Services to provide $5 million in fiscal 1998 for improved medical treatments, research and education regarding the E. coli bacteria and food safety. Adopted 91-8: R 49-6; D 42-2 (ND 34-2, SD 8-0), Sept. 10, 1997.

231. S 1061. Fiscal 1998 Labor-HHS Appropriations/Pell Grants and Child Literacy. Daschle, D-S.D., amendment expressing the sense of the Senate that the bill's fiscal 1998 funding levels for federal Pell grants should be increased by $700 million, and that another $260 million should be provided for a child literacy initiative. Adopted 96-3: R 52-3; D 44-0 (ND 36-0, SD 8-0), Sept. 10, 1997.

232. S 1061. Fiscal 1998 Labor-HHS Appropriations/Education Funding. Jeffords, R-Vt., motion to table (kill) the Gorton, R-Wash., amendment that would require the secretary of Education to award many funds for elementary and secondary education directly to local agencies to use as they see fit. Motion rejected 49-51: R 4-51; D 45-0 (ND 37-0, SD 8-0), Sept. 11, 1997. (Subsequently, the Gorton amendment was adopted on a voice vote.)

233. S 1061. Fiscal 1998 Labor-HHS Appropriations/Teamsters Election. Nickles, R-Okla., amendment to limit the use of taxpayer funds for any future Teamsters union leadership election. Adopted 58-42: R 55-0; D 3-42 (ND 2-35, SD 1-7), Sept. 11, 1997. A "nay" was a vote in support of the president's position.

234. S 1061. Fiscal 1998 Labor-HHS Appropriations/National Education Standards. Gregg, R-N.H., amendment establishing that the National Assessment Governing Board has exclusive authority over all policies for creating and implementing voluntary national tests for fourth-grade English reading and for eighth-grade mathematics. Adopted 87-13: R 42-13; D 45-0 (ND 37-0, SD 8-0), Sept. 11, 1997.

235. S 1061. Fiscal 1998 Labor-HHS Appropriations/Passage. Passage of the bill to provide $269 billion for labor, health and education programs and agencies in fiscal 1998. The bill provides $10.3 billion less than provided in fiscal 1997 and $645 million more than requested by President Clinton. Passed 92-8: R 47-8; D 45-0 (ND 37-0, SD 8-0), Sept. 11, 1997.

SENATE VOTES 236, 237, 238

KEY

Y Voted for (yea).
Paired for.
+ Announced for.
N Voted against (nay).
X Paired against.
– Announced against.
P Voted "present."
C Voted "present" to avoid possible conflict of interest.
? Did not vote or otherwise make a position known.

Democrats ***Republicans***

	236	237	238
ALABAMA			
Sessions	Y	Y	Y
Shelby	Y	Y	Y
ALASKA			
Murkowski	Y	Y	Y
Stevens	Y	Y	Y
ARIZONA			
Kyl	Y	Y	Y
McCain	Y	Y	Y
ARKANSAS			
Hutchinson	Y	Y	?
Bumpers	Y	Y	Y
CALIFORNIA			
Boxer	Y	Y	Y
Feinstein	Y	Y	Y
COLORADO			
Allard	Y	Y	Y
Campbell	Y	Y	Y
CONNECTICUT			
Dodd	Y	Y	Y
Lieberman	Y	Y	Y
DELAWARE			
Roth	Y	Y	Y
Biden	Y	Y	Y
FLORIDA			
Mack	Y	Y	Y
Graham	Y	Y	Y
GEORGIA			
Coverdell	Y	Y	Y
Cleland	Y	Y	Y
HAWAII			
Akaka	Y	Y	Y
Inouye	Y	Y	Y
IDAHO			
Craig	Y	Y	Y
Kempthorne	Y	Y	Y
ILLINOIS			
Durbin	Y	Y	Y
Moseley-Braun	Y	Y	Y
INDIANA			
Coats	Y	Y	Y
Lugar	Y	Y	Y
IOWA			
Grassley	Y	Y	Y
Harkin	Y	Y	Y
KANSAS			
Brownback	Y	Y	Y
Roberts	Y	Y	Y
KENTUCKY			
McConnell	Y	Y	Y
Ford	Y	Y	Y
LOUISIANA			
Breaux	Y	Y	Y
Landrieu	Y	Y	Y
MAINE			
Collins	Y	Y	Y
Snowe	Y	Y	Y
MARYLAND			
Mikulski	Y	Y	Y
Sarbanes	Y	Y	Y
MASSACHUSETTS			
Kennedy	Y	Y	Y
Kerry	Y	Y	Y
MICHIGAN			
Abraham	Y	Y	Y
Levin	Y	Y	Y
MINNESOTA			
Grams	Y	Y	Y
Wellstone	Y	Y	Y
MISSISSIPPI			
Cochran	Y	Y	Y
Lott	Y	Y	Y
MISSOURI			
Ashcroft	Y	Y	Y
Bond	Y	Y	Y
MONTANA			
Burns	Y	Y	Y
Baucus	Y	Y	Y
NEBRASKA			
Hagel	Y	Y	Y
Kerrey	Y	Y	Y
NEVADA			
Bryan	Y	Y	Y
Reid	Y	Y	Y
NEW HAMPSHIRE			
Gregg	Y	Y	Y
Smith	Y	Y	Y
NEW JERSEY			
Lautenberg	Y	Y	Y
Torricelli	Y	Y	Y
NEW MEXICO			
Domenici	Y	Y	Y
Bingaman	Y	Y	Y
NEW YORK			
D'Amato	Y	Y	Y
Moynihan	Y	Y	Y
NORTH CAROLINA			
Faircloth	Y	Y	N
Helms	Y	Y	Y
NORTH DAKOTA			
Conrad	Y	Y	Y
Dorgan	Y	Y	Y
OHIO			
DeWine	Y	Y	Y
Glenn	Y	Y	Y
OKLAHOMA			
Inhofe	Y	Y	Y
Nickles	Y	Y	Y
OREGON			
Smith	Y	Y	Y
Wyden	Y	Y	Y
PENNSYLVANIA			
Santorum	Y	Y	Y
Specter	Y	Y	Y
RHODE ISLAND			
Chafee	Y	Y	Y
Reed	Y	Y	Y
SOUTH CAROLINA			
Thurmond	Y	Y	Y
Hollings	Y	Y	Y
SOUTH DAKOTA			
Daschle	Y	Y	Y
Johnson	Y	Y	Y
TENNESSEE			
Frist	Y	Y	Y
Thompson	Y	Y	Y
TEXAS			
Gramm	Y	Y	Y
Hutchison	Y	Y	Y
UTAH			
Bennett	Y	Y	Y
Hatch	Y	Y	Y
VERMONT			
Jeffords	Y	Y	Y
Leahy	Y	Y	Y
VIRGINIA			
Warner	Y	Y	Y
Robb	Y	Y	Y
WASHINGTON			
Gorton	Y	Y	Y
Murray	Y	Y	Y
WEST VIRGINIA			
Byrd	Y	Y	Y
Rockefeller	Y	Y	Y
WISCONSIN			
Feingold	Y	Y	Y
Kohl	Y	Y	Y
WYOMING			
Enzi	Y	Y	Y
Thomas	Y	Y	Y

ND Northern Democrats SD Southern Democrats

Southern states - Ala., Ark., Fla., Ga., Ky., La., Miss., N.C., Okla., S.C., Tenn., Texas, Va.

236. Bataillon Nomination/Confirmation. Confirmation of President Clinton's nomination of Joseph F. Bataillon of Nebraska to be a U.S. district judge for the District of Nebraska. Confirmed 100-0: R 55-0; D 45-0 (ND 37-0, SD 8-0), Sept. 11, 1997. A "yea" was a vote in support of the president's position.

237. Droney Nomination/Confirmation. Confirmation of President Clinton's nomination of Christopher Droney of Connecticut to be a U.S. district judge for the District of Connecticut. Confirmed 100-0: R 55-0; D 45-0 (ND 37-0, SD 8-0), Sept. 11, 1997. A "yea" was a vote in support of the president's position.

238. Hall Nomination/Confirmation. Confirmation of President Clinton's nomination of Janet C. Hall of Connecticut to be a U.S. district judge for the District of Connecticut. Confirmed 98-1: R 53-1; D 45-0 (ND 37-0, SD 8-0), Sept. 11, 1997. A "yea" was a vote in support of the president's position.

SENATE VOTES 239, 240, 241, 242, 243, 244, 245, 246

	239	240	241	242	243	244	245	246
ALABAMA								
Sessions	Y	Y	Y	N	N	Y	Y	Y
Shelby	Y	Y	Y	N	N	Y	Y	Y
ALASKA								
Murkowski	Y	Y	N	N	N	N	Y	Y
Stevens	Y	Y	N	N	N	N	N	N
ARIZONA								
Kyl	Y	N	Y	N	N	Y	Y	Y
McCain	Y	N	Y	N	N	?	?	Y
ARKANSAS								
Hutchinson	Y	Y	Y	N	N	Y	Y	Y
Bumpers	Y	Y	N	Y	Y	N	N	N
CALIFORNIA								
Boxer	Y	Y	N	Y	Y	N	N	N
Feinstein	Y	Y	N	Y	Y	N	N	N
COLORADO								
Allard	Y	Y	Y	N	N	Y	Y	Y
Campbell	Y	Y	N	N	N	N	N	N
CONNECTICUT								
Dodd	Y	Y	N	Y	Y	N	N	N
Lieberman	Y	Y	N	Y	Y	N	N	N
DELAWARE								
Roth	Y	Y	N	Y	Y	N	N	N
Biden	Y	Y	N	Y	Y	N	N	N
FLORIDA								
Mack	Y	Y	Y	N	N	Y	Y	Y
Graham	Y	Y	N	Y	Y	N	N	N
GEORGIA								
Coverdell	Y	Y	N	N	N	Y	Y	Y
Cleland	Y	Y	N	Y	Y	N	N	N
HAWAII								
Akaka	N	Y	N	Y	Y	N	N	N
Inouye	Y	Y	N	Y	Y	N	N	N
IDAHO								
Craig	Y	Y	N	N	N	N	Y	Y
Kempthorne	Y	Y	N	N	N	N	Y	Y
ILLINOIS								
Durbin	Y	Y	N	Y	Y	N	N	N
Moseley-Braun	Y	Y	N	Y	Y	N	N	N
INDIANA								
Coats	Y	Y	Y	N	N	Y	Y	Y
Lugar	Y	Y	N	N	N	N	Y	Y
IOWA								
Grassley	Y	Y	N	N	N	N	Y	Y
Harkin	Y	Y	N	Y	Y	N	N	N
KANSAS								
Brownback	Y	Y	Y	Y	N	Y	Y	Y
Roberts	Y	Y	N	N	N	Y	Y	Y
KENTUCKY								
McConnell	Y	Y	Y	N	N	Y	Y	Y
Ford	Y	Y	N	Y	Y	N	N	N
LOUISIANA								
Breaux	Y	Y	N	N	N	N	Y	N
Landrieu	Y	Y	N	Y	Y	N	N	N
MAINE								
Collins	Y	Y	N	N	N	N	N	N
Snowe	Y	Y	N	N	N	N	N	N
MARYLAND								
Mikulski	Y	Y	N	Y	Y	N	N	N
Sarbanes	Y	Y	N	Y	Y	N	N	N
MASSACHUSETTS								
Kennedy	N	Y	N	Y	Y	N	N	N
Kerry	Y	Y	N	Y	Y	N	N	N
MICHIGAN								
Abraham	Y	Y	N	N	N	Y	Y	Y
Levin	Y	Y	N	N	N	N	N	N
MINNESOTA								
Grams	Y	Y	Y	N	N	Y	N	Y
Wellstone	N	Y	N	Y	Y	N	N	N
MISSISSIPPI								
Cochran	Y	Y	N	N	N	N	N	N
Lott	Y	Y	Y	N	N	Y	Y	Y
MISSOURI								
Ashcroft	Y	Y	Y	N	N	Y	Y	Y
Bond	Y	Y	N	N	N	N	N	Y
MONTANA								
Burns	Y	Y	N	N	N	N	Y	Y
Baucus	Y	Y	N	N	N	N	N	N
NEBRASKA								
Hagel	Y	Y	Y	N	N	Y	Y	Y
Kerrey	Y	Y	N	Y	Y	N	N	N
NEVADA								
Bryan	Y	Y	N	N	Y	N	N	N
Reid	Y	Y	N	Y	Y	N	N	N
NEW HAMPSHIRE								
Gregg	Y	Y	N	Y	Y	N	N	Y
Smith	Y	Y	Y	N	N	Y	Y	Y
NEW JERSEY								
Lautenberg	Y	Y	N	Y	Y	N	N	N
Torricelli	Y	Y	N	Y	Y	N	N	N
NEW MEXICO								
Domenici	Y	Y	N	N	N	N	N	N
Bingaman	Y	Y	N	Y	Y	N	N	N
NEW YORK								
D'Amato	?	Y	N	Y	Y	N	N	N
Moynihan	Y	Y	N	Y	Y	N	N	N
NORTH CAROLINA								
Faircloth	Y	Y	Y	N	N	Y	Y	Y
Helms	Y	Y	Y	N	N	Y	Y	Y
NORTH DAKOTA								
Conrad	Y	Y	N	Y	Y	N	N	N
Dorgan	Y	Y	N	Y	Y	N	N	N
OHIO								
DeWine	Y	Y	N	Y	Y	N	Y	Y
Glenn	Y	Y	N	Y	Y	N	N	N
OKLAHOMA								
Inhofe	Y	Y	Y	N	N	Y	Y	Y
Nickles	Y	Y	Y	N	N	Y	Y	Y
OREGON								
Smith	Y	Y	N	N	N	N	N	N
Wyden	Y	Y	N	Y	Y	N	N	N
PENNSYLVANIA								
Santorum	Y	Y	N	N	N	N	Y	Y
Specter	Y	Y	N	N	N	N	N	N
RHODE ISLAND								
Chafee	Y	Y	N	Y	Y	N	N	N
Reed	N	Y	N	Y	Y	N	N	N
SOUTH CAROLINA								
Thurmond	Y	Y	Y	N	N	Y	Y	Y
Hollings	Y	Y	N	Y	Y	N	N	N
SOUTH DAKOTA								
Daschle	Y	Y	N	Y	Y	N	N	N
Johnson	Y	Y	N	Y	Y	N	N	N
TENNESSEE								
Frist	Y	Y	N	Y	Y	Y	Y	Y
Thompson	Y	Y	Y	Y	Y	Y	Y	Y
TEXAS								
Gramm	Y	Y	Y	N	N	Y	Y	Y
Hutchison	Y	Y	N	N	N	N	Y	Y
UTAH								
Bennett	Y	Y	N	N	N	N	N	N
Hatch	Y	Y	N	N	N	N	N	N
VERMONT								
Jeffords	Y	Y	N	Y	Y	N	N	N
Leahy	Y	Y	N	Y	Y	N	N	N
VIRGINIA								
Warner	Y	Y	N	N	N	N	N	N
Robb	Y	Y	N	Y	Y	N	N	N
WASHINGTON								
Gorton	Y	Y	N	N	N	N	N	N
Murray	Y	Y	N	Y	Y	N	N	N
WEST VIRGINIA								
Byrd	?	Y	N	N	N	N	N	N
Rockefeller	Y	Y	N	Y	Y	N	N	N
WISCONSIN								
Feingold	Y	N	N	Y	Y	N	N	N
Kohl	Y	Y	N	Y	Y	N	N	N
WYOMING								
Enzi	Y	Y	Y	N	N	Y	Y	Y
Thomas	Y	Y	N	N	N	N	Y	Y

KEY

- Y Voted for (yea).
- # Paired for.
- + Announced for.
- N Voted against (nay).
- X Paired against.
- – Announced against.
- P Voted "present."
- C Voted "present" to avoid possible conflict of interest.
- ? Did not vote or otherwise make a position known.

Democrats *Republicans*

ND Northern Democrats SD Southern Democrats

Southern states - Ala., Ark., Fla., Ga., Ky., La., Miss., N.C., Okla., S.C., Tenn., Texas, Va.

239. S 830. Food and Drug Administration Overhaul/Cloture. Motion to invoke cloture (thus limiting debate) on the substitute amendment to the bill revising Food and Drug Administration regulatory procedures regarding medical devices, pharmaceuticals, cosmetics and other products. Motion agreed to 94-4: R 54-0; D 40-4 (ND 32-4, SD 8-0), Sept. 16, 1997. A three-fifths majority vote (60) of the total Senate is required to invoke cloture.

240. HR 2016. Fiscal 1998 Military Construction Appropriations/Conference Report. Adoption of the conference report on the bill to provide $9.2 billion for military construction programs in fiscal 1998. The conference report would provide $610 million less than provided in fiscal 1997 and $800 million more than requested by President Clinton. Adopted (thus cleared for the president) 97-3: R 53-2; D 44-1 (ND 36-1, SD 8-0), Sept. 17, 1997.

241. HR 2107. Fiscal 1998 Interior Appropriations/NEA Funding. Ashcroft, R-Mo., amendment to eliminate funding for programs and activities carried out by the National Endowment for the Arts. Rejected 23-77: R 23-32; D 0-45 (ND 0-37, SD 0-8), Sept. 17, 1997.

242. HR 2107. Fiscal 1998 Interior Appropriations/Logging Roads Program. Bryan, D-Nev., amendment to reduce funding for Forest Service road construction by $10 million and eliminate the Purchaser Credit Program. Rejected 49-51: R 9-46; D 40-5 (ND 33-4, SD 7-1), Sept. 17, 1997.

243. HR 2107. Fiscal 1998 Interior Appropriations/Reconsideration of Vote. Lott, R-Miss., motion to reconsider the vote by which the Senate rejected the Bryan, D-Nev., amendment to reduce funding for Forest Service road construction by $10 million and eliminate the Purchaser Credit Program. Motion Rejected 49-51: R 8-47; D 41-4 (ND 34-3, SD 7-1), Sept. 17, 1997.

244. HR 2107. Fiscal 1998 Interior Appropriations/NEA Funding. Abraham, R-Mich., amendment to reduce funding for the National Endowment for the Arts by one-third in fiscal 1998 with the goal of privatizing the agency within a three-year span. Money shifted from the NEA would provide additional construction funds for the National Park Service. Rejected 26-73: R 26-28; D 0-45 (ND 0-37, SD 0-8), Sept. 17, 1997. A "nay" was a vote in support of the president's position.

245. HR 2107. Fiscal 1998 Interior Appropriations/NEA Funding. Hutchinson, R-Ark., amendment to abolish the National Endowment for the Arts and transfer its fiscal 1998 funding directly to the states. Rejected 36-63: R 35-19; D 1-44 (ND 0-37, SD 1-7), Sept. 17, 1997. A "nay" was a vote in support of the president's position.

246. HR 2107. Fiscal 1998 Interior Appropriations/NEA Funding. Hutchison, R-Texas, amendment that would establish a $100 million state block grant program for the arts. The National Endowment for the Arts would be allowed to earmark 25 percent of the funds for major arts organizations. Rejected 39-61: R 39-16; D 0-45 (ND 0-37, SD 0-8), Sept. 18, 1997. A "nay" was a vote in support of the president's position.

SENATE VOTES 247, 248, 249, 250, 251

	247	248	249	250	251
ALABAMA					
Sessions	N	Y	Y	N	Y
Shelby	N	N	Y	Y	Y
ALASKA					
Murkowski	N	Y	Y	Y	Y
Stevens	?	N	Y	Y	Y
ARIZONA					
Kyl	N	Y	Y	Y	Y
McCain	Y	Y	Y	N	Y
ARKANSAS					
Hutchinson	N	N	Y	Y	Y
Bumpers	Y	N	N	Y	Y
CALIFORNIA					
Boxer	Y	N	N	Y	Y
Feinstein	Y	N	N	Y	Y
COLORADO					
Allard	N	Y	Y	N	Y
Campbell	N	Y	Y	Y	Y
CONNECTICUT					
Dodd	Y	N	N	Y	Y
Lieberman	Y	N	N	Y	Y
DELAWARE					
Roth	Y	N	Y	Y	Y
Biden	Y	N	N	Y	Y
FLORIDA					
Mack	N	Y	Y	Y	Y
Graham	Y	N	N	Y	Y
GEORGIA					
Coverdell	N	Y	Y	Y	Y
Cleland	Y	N	N	Y	Y
HAWAII					
Akaka	Y	?	?	?	?
Inouye	Y	N	Y	Y	Y
IDAHO					
Craig	N	Y	Y	Y	Y
Kempthorne	N	Y	Y	Y	Y
ILLINOIS					
Durbin	Y	Y	N	Y	Y
Moseley-Braun	Y	N	N	Y	Y
INDIANA					
Coats	N	N	N	Y	Y
Lugar	N	N	Y	Y	Y
IOWA					
Grassley	N	Y	Y	Y	Y
Harkin	Y	N	N	?	?
KANSAS					
Brownback	N	Y	Y	N	Y
Roberts	N	Y	Y	Y	Y
KENTUCKY					
McConnell	N	Y	Y	Y	Y
Ford	Y	N	N	Y	Y
LOUISIANA					
Breaux	Y	N	Y	Y	Y
Landrieu	Y	N	N	Y	Y
MAINE					
Collins	Y	N	N	Y	Y
Snowe	Y	N	N	Y	Y
MARYLAND					
Mikulski	Y	N	Y	Y	Y
Sarbanes	Y	N	N	Y	Y
MASSACHUSETTS					
Kennedy	Y	N	N	Y	Y
Kerry	Y	N	N	Y	Y
MICHIGAN					
Abraham	Y	Y	Y	Y	Y
Levin	Y	N	N	Y	Y
MINNESOTA					
Grams	N	Y	Y	N	Y
Wellstone	Y	–	–	+	+
MISSISSIPPI					
Cochran	N	N	Y	Y	Y
Lott	N	N	Y	Y	Y
MISSOURI					
Ashcroft	N	Y	Y	N	N
Bond	Y	N	Y	Y	Y
MONTANA					
Burns	N	N	Y	Y	Y
Baucus	Y	N	Y	Y	Y
NEBRASKA					
Hagel	N	N	Y	Y	Y
Kerrey	Y	N	N	Y	Y
NEVADA					
Bryan	Y	N	Y	Y	Y
Reid	Y	N	Y	Y	Y
NEW HAMPSHIRE					
Gregg	Y	N	N	Y	Y
Smith	N	Y	Y	Y	Y
NEW JERSEY					
Lautenberg	Y	N	N	Y	Y
Torricelli	Y	N	N	Y	Y
NEW MEXICO					
Domenici	Y	Y	Y	Y	Y
Bingaman	Y	Y	Y	Y	Y
NEW YORK					
D'Amato	Y	N	Y	Y	Y
Moynihan	Y	N	N	?	?
NORTH CAROLINA					
Faircloth	Y	Y	N	Y	N
Helms	N	Y	Y	Y	N
NORTH DAKOTA					
Conrad	N	N	N	Y	Y
Dorgan	N	N	Y	Y	Y
OHIO					
DeWine	Y	Y	N	Y	Y
Glenn	Y	N	N	N	Y
OKLAHOMA					
Inhofe	N	Y	Y	Y	Y
Nickles	N	Y	Y	Y	Y
OREGON					
Smith	N	N	Y	?	Y
Wyden	Y	Y	N	Y	Y
PENNSYLVANIA					
Santorum	N	Y	Y	N	Y
Specter	Y	N	Y	Y	Y
RHODE ISLAND					
Chafee	Y	N	Y	Y	Y
Reed	Y	N	N	Y	Y
SOUTH CAROLINA					
Thurmond	N	Y	Y	Y	Y
Hollings	Y	N	Y	N	Y
SOUTH DAKOTA					
Daschle	Y	N	Y	Y	Y
Johnson	Y	N	Y	Y	Y
TENNESSEE					
Frist	Y	N	Y	Y	Y
Thompson	Y	N	Y	Y	Y
TEXAS					
Gramm	N	N	Y	N	Y
Hutchison	N	Y	Y	Y	Y
UTAH					
Bennett	N	N	Y	Y	Y
Hatch	N	Y	Y	Y	Y
VERMONT					
Jeffords	Y	N	N	Y	Y
Leahy	Y	N	N	Y	Y
VIRGINIA					
Warner	N	N	Y	Y	Y
Robb	Y	N	N	Y	Y
WASHINGTON					
Gorton	N	N	Y	N	Y
Murray	Y	Y	N	Y	Y
WEST VIRGINIA					
Byrd	N	N	N	N	Y
Rockefeller	N	N	N	Y	Y
WISCONSIN					
Feingold	Y	N	N	N	Y
Kohl	Y	N	N	N	Y
WYOMING					
Enzi	N	Y	Y	Y	Y
Thomas	N	Y	Y	Y	Y

KEY

- Y Voted for (yea).
- # Paired for.
- + Announced for.
- N Voted against (nay).
- X Paired against.
- – Announced against.
- P Voted "present."
- C Voted "present" to avoid possible conflict of interest.
- ? Did not vote or otherwise make a position known.

Democrats *Republicans*

ND Northern Democrats SD Southern Democrats

Southern states - Ala., Ark., Fla., Ga., Ky., La., Miss., N.C., Okla., S.C., Tenn., Texas, Va.

247. HR 2107. Fiscal 1998 Interior Appropriations/American Heritage Rivers. D'Amato, R-N.Y., motion to table (kill) the Hutchinson, R-Ark., amendment to require congressional approval before President Clinton could implement the American Heritage Rivers Initiative, which he established by executive order. Motion agreed to 57-42: R 16-38; D 41-4 (ND 33-4, SD 8-0), Sept. 18, 1997.

248. HR 2107. Fiscal 1998 Interior Appropriations/Bureau of Indian Affairs. Kyl, R-Ariz., amendment to transfer $4.8 million from the Woodrow Wilson Center to the Bureau of Indian Affairs to fund increased anti-gang activities on Indian reservations. Rejected 34-64: R 30-25; D 4-39 (ND 4-31, SD 0-8), Sept. 18, 1997.

249. HR 2107. Fiscal 1998 Interior Appropriations/Constitutional Violations. Gorton, R-Wash., point of order against the Bumpers, D-Ark., amendment, which revises royalty and reclamation fees regarding mining operations on public lands, for violating the constitution by originating a revenue bill in the Senate and breaching the principles of the Supreme Court decision in *Buckly v. Valeo*. Point of order upheld 59-39: R 48-7; D 11-32 (ND 9-26, SD 2-6), Sept. 18, 1997.

250. HR 2107. Fiscal 1998 Interior Appropriations/Stampede Mine Site. Murkowski, R-Alaska, amendment that would require the secretary of the Interior to provide $500,000 within existing funds to the University of Alaska Fairbanks, School of Mineral Engineering in payment for facilities, equipment and interests destroyed by the federal government at the Stampede Mine site. Adopted 81-14: R 45-9; D 36-5 (ND 29-4, SD 7-1), Sept. 18, 1997.

251. HR 2107. Fiscal 1998 Interior Appropriations/Passage. Passage of the bill to provide $13.8 billion for the Interior Department and related agencies in fiscal 1998. The bill provides $241.9 million more than provided in fiscal 1997 and $43.6 million less than requested by President Clinton. Passed 93-3: R 52-3; D 41-0 (ND 33-0, SD 8-0), Sept. 18, 1997.

SENATE VOTES 252, 253, 254, 255, 256, 257, 258, 259

	252	253	254	255	256	257	258	259
ALABAMA								
Sessions	N	N	Y	Y	Y	Y	Y	Y
Shelby	N	Y	Y	Y	Y	N	Y	Y
ALASKA								
Murkowski	N	N	Y	Y	Y	Y	Y	Y
Stevens	N	N	Y	Y	Y	Y	Y	Y
ARIZONA								
Kyl	N	N	Y	Y	Y	N	Y	Y
McCain	N	N	Y	Y	Y	Y	Y	Y
ARKANSAS								
Hutchinson	N	N	Y	Y	Y	Y	Y	Y
Bumpers	Y	N	N	Y	Y	Y	N	Y
CALIFORNIA								
Boxer	Y	Y	N	Y	Y	Y	Y	Y
Feinstein	Y	Y	N	Y	Y	Y	Y	Y
COLORADO								
Allard	N	N	Y	Y	Y	N	Y	Y
Campbell	N	N	Y	Y	Y	Y	Y	Y
CONNECTICUT								
Dodd	N	N	Y	Y	Y	Y	Y	Y
Lieberman	Y	N	Y	Y	Y	Y	Y	Y
DELAWARE								
Roth	N	N	Y	Y	Y	Y	Y	Y
Biden	Y	N	N	Y	Y	Y	+	+
FLORIDA								
Mack	N	N	Y	Y	Y	Y	Y	Y
Graham	Y	Y	N	Y	Y	Y	Y	Y
GEORGIA								
Coverdell	N	N	Y	Y	Y	Y	Y	Y
Cleland	Y	Y	N	Y	Y	Y	Y	Y
HAWAII								
Akaka	Y	Y	N	Y	Y	Y	Y	Y
Inouye	Y	Y	N	Y	Y	Y	Y	Y
IDAHO								
Craig	N	N	Y	Y	Y	Y	Y	Y
Kempthorne	N	N	Y	Y	Y	Y	Y	Y
ILLINOIS								
Durbin	Y	Y	N	Y	Y	Y	Y	Y
Moseley-Braun	Y	Y	N	Y	Y	Y	Y	Y
INDIANA								
Coats	N	N	Y	Y	Y	N	Y	Y
Lugar	N	N	Y	Y	Y	Y	Y	Y
IOWA								
Grassley	N	N	Y	Y	Y	Y	Y	Y
Harkin	Y	Y	N	Y	Y	Y	N	Y
KANSAS								
Brownback	N	N	Y	Y	Y	N	Y	Y
Roberts	N	N	Y	Y	Y	Y	Y	Y
KENTUCKY								
McConnell	N	N	Y	Y	Y	Y	Y	Y
Ford	Y	Y	Y	Y	Y	Y	Y	Y
LOUISIANA								
Breaux	Y	Y	Y	Y	Y	Y	Y	Y
Landrieu	Y	N	Y	Y	Y	Y	Y	Y
MAINE								
Collins	N	N	Y	Y	Y	Y	Y	Y
Snowe	N	N	Y	Y	Y	Y	Y	Y
MARYLAND								
Mikulski	N	Y	Y	Y	Y	Y	?	?
Sarbanes	Y	Y	N	Y	Y	Y	Y	Y
MASSACHUSETTS								
Kennedy	N	N	N	N	N	Y	Y	Y
Kerry	Y	Y	N	Y	Y	Y	Y	Y
MICHIGAN								
Abraham	N	N	Y	Y	Y	Y	Y	Y
Levin	Y	Y	N	Y	Y	Y	Y	Y
MINNESOTA								
Grams	N	N	Y	Y	Y	Y	Y	Y
Wellstone	Y	Y	Y	Y	Y	Y	N	Y
MISSISSIPPI								
Cochran	N	N	Y	Y	Y	Y	Y	Y
Lott	N	N	Y	Y	Y	Y	Y	Y
MISSOURI								
Ashcroft	N	N	Y	Y	Y	Y	Y	Y
Bond	N	N	Y	Y	Y	Y	Y	Y
MONTANA								
Burns	N	N	Y	Y	Y	N	Y	Y
Baucus	Y	Y	N	Y	Y	Y	Y	Y
NEBRASKA								
Hagel	N	N	Y	Y	Y	Y	Y	Y
Kerrey	N	Y	N	Y	Y	Y	Y	Y
NEVADA								
Bryan	Y	Y	N	Y	Y	Y	Y	Y
Reid	Y	Y	N	Y	Y	Y	Y	Y
NEW HAMPSHIRE								
Gregg	N	N	Y	Y	Y	Y	Y	Y
Smith	N	N	Y	Y	Y	N	Y	Y
NEW JERSEY								
Lautenberg	Y	N	N	Y	Y	Y	Y	Y
Torricelli	Y	Y	N	Y	Y	Y	Y	Y
NEW MEXICO								
Domenici	N	N	Y	Y	Y	Y	Y	Y
Bingaman	Y	Y	N	Y	Y	Y	Y	Y
NEW YORK								
D'Amato	N	N	Y	Y	Y	Y	Y	Y
Moynihan	Y	N	N	Y	Y	Y	Y	Y
NORTH CAROLINA								
Faircloth	N	N	Y	Y	Y	Y	Y	Y
Helms	?	N	Y	Y	Y	Y	Y	Y
NORTH DAKOTA								
Conrad	Y	Y	N	Y	Y	Y	Y	Y
Dorgan	Y	Y	N	Y	Y	Y	Y	Y
OHIO								
DeWine	N	N	Y	Y	Y	Y	Y	Y
Glenn	Y	Y	N	Y	Y	Y	Y	Y
OKLAHOMA								
Inhofe	N	N	Y	Y	Y	N	Y	Y
Nickles	N	N	Y	Y	Y	Y	Y	Y
OREGON								
Smith	N	N	Y	Y	Y	Y	Y	Y
Wyden	Y	N	Y	Y	Y	Y	Y	Y
PENNSYLVANIA								
Santorum	N	N	Y	Y	Y	Y	Y	Y
Specter	N	Y	Y	Y	Y	Y	Y	Y
RHODE ISLAND								
Chafee	N	N	Y	Y	Y	Y	Y	Y
Reed	Y	Y	N	N	N	Y	Y	Y
SOUTH CAROLINA								
Thurmond	N	N	Y	Y	Y	Y	Y	Y
Hollings	Y	Y	Y	Y	Y	Y	Y	Y
SOUTH DAKOTA								
Daschle	Y	Y	N	Y	Y	Y	Y	Y
Johnson	Y	Y	N	Y	Y	Y	Y	Y
TENNESSEE								
Frist	N	N	Y	Y	Y	Y	Y	Y
Thompson	N	N	Y	Y	Y	Y	Y	Y
TEXAS								
Gramm	N	N	Y	Y	Y	N	Y	Y
Hutchison	N	Y	Y	Y	Y	Y	Y	Y
UTAH								
Bennett	N	N	Y	Y	Y	Y	Y	Y
Hatch	N	N	Y	Y	Y	Y	Y	Y
VERMONT								
Jeffords	N	N	Y	Y	Y	Y	Y	?
Leahy	Y	Y	N	Y	Y	Y	Y	Y
VIRGINIA								
Warner	N	N	Y	Y	Y	Y	Y	Y
Robb	Y	Y	N	Y	Y	Y	Y	Y
WASHINGTON								
Gorton	N	N	Y	Y	Y	Y	Y	Y
Murray	Y	Y	Y	Y	Y	Y	Y	Y
WEST VIRGINIA								
Byrd	Y	Y	N	Y	Y	Y	Y	Y
Rockefeller	Y	Y	N	Y	Y	Y	Y	Y
WISCONSIN								
Feingold	Y	Y	N	Y	Y	Y	N	Y
Kohl	N	Y	N	Y	Y	N	N	Y
WYOMING								
Enzi	N	N	Y	Y	Y	Y	Y	Y
Thomas	N	N	Y	Y	Y	Y	Y	Y

KEY

- Y Voted for (yea).
- # Paired for.
- \+ Announced for.
- N Voted against (nay).
- X Paired against.
- – Announced against.
- P Voted "present."
- C Voted "present" to avoid possible conflict of interest.
- ? Did not vote or otherwise make a position known.

Democrats *Republicans*

ND Northern Democrats SD Southern Democrats

Southern states - Ala., Ark., Fla., Ga., Ky., La., Miss., N.C., Okla., S.C., Tenn., Texas, Va.

252. S 830. Food and Drug Administration Overhaul/Conflict of Interest Standard. Durbin, D-Ill., amendment to apply FDA conflict-of-interest standards to entities accredited to conduct reviews of medical-device notifications. Rejected 40-59: R 0-54; D 40-5 (ND 32-5, SD 8-0), Sept. 23, 1997.

253. S 830. Food and Drug Administration Overhaul/Medical Device Tracking. Durbin, D-Ill., amendment to eliminate provisions in the bill limiting the ability of the Health and Human Services secretary to require tracking of medical devices. Rejected 39-61: R 3-52; D 36-9 (ND 30-7, SD 6-2), Sept. 23, 1997.

254. S 830. Food and Drug Administration Overhaul/Review Authority. Jeffords, R-Vt., motion to table (kill) the Reed, D-R.I., amendment that would allow the Food and Drug Administration to retain its review authority regarding the safety of certain medical devices in cases where the FDA finds product labels to be misleading or false. Motion agreed to 65-35: R 55-0; D 10-35 (ND 6-31, SD 4-4), Sept. 23, 1997.

255. S 830. Food and Drug Administration Overhaul/Committee Substitute Amendment. Committee substitute amendment to the bill to revise Food and Drug Administration regulatory procedures regarding medical devices, pharmaceuticals, cosmetics and other products. Adopted 98-2: R 55-0; D 43-2 (ND 35-2, SD 8-0), Sept. 23, 1997.

256. S 830. Food and Drug Administration Overhaul/Passage. Passage of the bill to reauthorize the 1992 Prescription Drug User Fee Act and revise Food and Drug Administration regulatory procedures regarding medical devices, pharmaceuticals, cosmetics and other products. Passed 98-2: R 55-0; D 43-2 (ND 35-2, SD 8-0), Sept. 24, 1997.

257. HR 2209. Fiscal 1998 Legislative Branch Appropriations/Conference Report. Adoption of the conference report on the bill to provide $2.25 billion in new budget authority for the legislative branch in fiscal 1998. The conference report would provide $45.8 million more than provided in fiscal 1997 and $145.9 million less than requested by President Clinton. Adopted (thus cleared for the president) 90-10: R 46-9; D 44-1 (ND 36-1, SD 8-0), Sept. 24, 1997.

258. HR 2266. Fiscal 1998 Defense Appropriations/Conference Report. Adoption of the conference report on the bill to provide $247.7 billion in new budget authority to sustain military personnel, develop and purchase military hardware and maintain the operational readiness of the U.S. military. The conference report would provide $5.3 billion more than the current appropriations level and $3.8 billion more than the administration's request. The conference report would cut off funding for U.S. troops in Bosnia after June 30, but would permit the president to request further funding. The measure provides nearly $46 billion for weapons procurement. Adopted (thus cleared for the president) 93-5: R 55-0; D 38-5 (ND 31-4, SD 7-1), Sept. 25, 1997.

259. Hayden Nomination/Confirmation. Confirmation of President Clinton's nomination of Katharine Sweeney Hayden of New Jersey to be a U.S. District Judge for the District of New Jersey. Confirmed 97-0: R 54-0; D 43-0 (ND 35-0, SD 8-0), Sept. 25, 1997. A "yea" was a vote in support of the president's position.

SENATE VOTES 260, 261, 262, 263, 264, 265

	260	261	262	263	264	265
ALABAMA						
Sessions	Y	Y	Y	N	N	N
Shelby	Y	Y	Y	Y	N	N
ALASKA						
Murkowski	Y	Y	Y	Y	Y	N
Stevens	Y	Y	Y	Y	Y	Y
ARIZONA						
Kyl	Y	Y	Y	N	N	N
McCain	Y	Y	Y	C	N	N
ARKANSAS						
Hutchinson	Y	Y	Y	Y	N	N
Bumpers	N	Y	Y	Y	Y	N
CALIFORNIA						
Boxer	N	Y	Y	N	N	N
Feinstein	N	Y	Y	Y	Y	N
COLORADO						
Allard	Y	Y	Y	N	N	N
Campbell	Y	Y	Y	N	Y	N
CONNECTICUT						
Dodd	N	Y	Y	Y	N	N
Lieberman	Y	Y	Y	Y	Y	N
DELAWARE						
Roth	Y	Y	Y	Y	Y	N
Biden	N	Y	Y	?	Y	N
FLORIDA						
Mack	Y	Y	Y	N	Y	N
Graham	N	Y	Y	Y	Y	N
GEORGIA						
Coverdell	Y	Y	Y	Y	N	N
Cleland	N	Y	Y	Y	N	N
HAWAII						
Akaka	N	Y	Y	Y	Y	N
Inouye	N	Y	Y	Y	Y	N
IDAHO						
Craig	Y	Y	Y	N	Y	N
Kempthorne	Y	Y	Y	N	Y	N
ILLINOIS						
Durbin	N	Y	Y	Y	Y	N
Moseley-Braun	N	Y	Y	Y	N	N
INDIANA						
Coats	Y	Y	Y	Y	Y	N
Lugar	Y	Y	Y	Y	Y	N
IOWA						
Grassley	Y	Y	Y	N	N	N
Harkin	N	Y	Y	Y	Y	N
KANSAS						
Brownback	Y	Y	Y	Y	N	N
Roberts	Y	Y	Y	Y	N	N
KENTUCKY						
McConnell	Y	Y	Y	Y	Y	N
Ford	N	Y	Y	Y	Y	N
LOUISIANA						
Breaux	Y	Y	Y	Y	Y	N
Landrieu	Y	Y	Y	?	Y	N
MAINE						
Collins	Y	Y	Y	N	N	N
Snowe	Y	Y	Y	Y	N	N
MARYLAND						
Mikulski	N	Y	Y	Y	Y	N
Sarbanes	N	Y	Y	Y	Y	?
MASSACHUSETTS						
Kennedy	N	Y	Y	Y	Y	N
Kerry	N	Y	Y	Y	Y	N
MICHIGAN						
Abraham	Y	Y	Y	Y	N	N
Levin	N	Y	Y	N	Y	N
MINNESOTA						
Grams	Y	Y	Y	Y	N	N
Wellstone	N	Y	Y	Y	N	N
MISSISSIPPI						
Cochran	Y	Y	Y	N	Y	N
Lott	Y	Y	Y	Y	Y	N
MISSOURI						
Ashcroft	Y	Y	Y	N	N	N
Bond	Y	Y	Y	Y	N	N
MONTANA						
Burns	Y	Y	Y	N	N	N
Baucus	N	Y	Y	Y	N	N
NEBRASKA						
Hagel	Y	Y	Y	Y	Y	N
Kerrey	N	Y	Y	Y	N	N
NEVADA						
Bryan	N	Y	Y	N	N	N
Reid	N	Y	Y	N	N	N
NEW HAMPSHIRE						
Gregg	Y	Y	Y	Y	N	N
Smith	Y	Y	Y	N	N	N
NEW JERSEY						
Lautenberg	N	Y	Y	Y	N	N
Torricelli	N	Y	Y	Y	Y	N
NEW MEXICO						
Domenici	Y	Y	Y	N	Y	N
Bingaman	N	Y	Y	Y	Y	N
NEW YORK						
D'Amato	Y	Y	Y	Y	N	N
Moynihan	Y	Y	Y	Y	Y	N
NORTH CAROLINA						
Faircloth	Y	Y	Y	Y	N	N
Helms	Y	Y	Y	Y	N	N
NORTH DAKOTA						
Conrad	N	Y	Y	Y	Y	N
Dorgan	N	Y	Y	Y	Y	N
OHIO						
DeWine	Y	Y	Y	Y	N	N
Glenn	N	Y	Y	Y	Y	N
OKLAHOMA						
Inhofe	Y	Y	Y	N	Y	N
Nickles	Y	Y	Y	Y	Y	N
OREGON						
Smith	Y	Y	Y	Y	Y	N
Wyden	N	Y	Y	Y	N	N
PENNSYLVANIA						
Santorum	Y	Y	Y	N	N	N
Specter	Y	Y	Y	Y	N	N
RHODE ISLAND						
Chafee	N	Y	Y	N	Y	N
Reed	N	Y	Y	Y	Y	N
SOUTH CAROLINA						
Thurmond	Y	Y	Y	Y	Y	N
Hollings	N	Y	Y	Y	N	N
SOUTH DAKOTA						
Daschle	N	Y	Y	Y	Y	N
Johnson	N	Y	Y	Y	N	N
TENNESSEE						
Frist	Y	Y	Y	Y	N	N
Thompson	Y	Y	Y	Y	Y	N
TEXAS						
Gramm	Y	Y	Y	N	N	N
Hutchison	Y	Y	Y	Y	Y	N
UTAH						
Bennett	Y	Y	Y	Y	Y	N
Hatch	Y	Y	Y	Y	Y	N
VERMONT						
Jeffords	Y	Y	Y	Y	Y	N
Leahy	?	?	?	?	N	N
VIRGINIA						
Warner	Y	Y	Y	Y	Y	N
Robb	N	Y	Y	N	Y	N
WASHINGTON						
Gorton	Y	Y	Y	N	Y	N
Murray	N	Y	Y	Y	N	N
WEST VIRGINIA						
Byrd	N	Y	Y	Y	Y	Y
Rockefeller	N	Y	Y	Y	Y	N
WISCONSIN						
Feingold	N	Y	Y	N	N	N
Kohl	N	Y	Y	N	Y	N
WYOMING						
Enzi	Y	Y	Y	Y	N	N
Thomas	Y	Y	Y	N	N	N

KEY

- Y Voted for (yea).
- # Paired for.
- + Announced for.
- N Voted against (nay).
- X Paired against.
- – Announced against.
- P Voted "present."
- C Voted "present" to avoid possible conflict of interest.
- ? Did not vote or otherwise make a position known.

Democrats *Republicans*

ND Northern Democrats SD Southern Democrats

Southern states - Ala., Ark., Fla., Ga., Ky., La., Miss., N.C., Okla., S.C., Tenn., Texas, Va.

260. S 1156. Fiscal 1998 District of Columbia Appropriations/Cloture. Motion to invoke cloture (thus limiting debate) on the Coats, R-Ind., amendment that would allocate $7 million in fiscal 1998 for educational scholarships to allow low-income kindergarten through 12th grade students from the District of Columbia to attend private schools or public schools in the Virginia or Maryland suburbs. Motion rejected 58-41: R 54-1; D 4-40 (ND 2-34, SD 2-6), Sept. 30, 1997.

261. H J Res 94. Fiscal 1998 Continuing Appropriations/Passage. Passage of the joint resolution to provide continuing appropriations through Oct. 23 for fiscal 1998 spending bills not yet enacted. The continuing resolution sets spending levels at fiscal 1997 levels unless Congress has agreed with an administration budget request for less than current levels. Passed 99-0: R 55-0; D 44-0 (ND 36-0, SD 8-0), Sept. 30, 1997.

262. HR 2203. Fiscal 1998 Energy and Water Development Appropriations/Conference Report. Adoption of the conference report on the bill to provide $21.2 billion in new budget authority for energy and water development programs in fiscal 1998. The conference report would provide $162 million more than provided in fiscal 1997 and $2.3 billion less than requested by the administration. Adopted (thus cleared for the president) 99-0: R 55-0; D 44-0 (ND 36-0, SD 8-0), Sept. 30, 1997.

263. S 1156. Fiscal 1998 District of Columbia Appropriations/Alcohol Sales. Byrd, D-W.Va., amendments that would restrict alcohol beverage advertising in the District of Columbia; increase the number of Alcohol Beverage Control Board inspectors in the District; and require the General Accounting Office to study the District's taxation of alcohol. Adopted 69-27: R 34-20; D 35-7 (ND 29-6, SD 6-1), Sept. 30, 1997.

264. HR 2378. Fiscal 1998 Treasury-Postal Appropriations/Conference Report. Adoption of the conference report on the bill to provide $25.4 billion in new mandatory and discretionary budget authority for the Treasury Department, the U.S. Postal Service and Executive Office of the President in fiscal 1998. The conference report would provide $1.3 billion more than in fiscal 1997 and $262 million less than requested by President Clinton. Adopted (thus cleared for the president) 55-45: R 26-29; D 29-16 (ND 23-14, SD 6-2), Oct. 1, 1997.

265. S 1156. Fiscal 1998 District of Columbia Appropriations/Motion to Table. Mack, R-Fla., motion to table (kill) the Mack amendment that would offer relief to certain immigrants who otherwise would be subject to removal from the United States. Motion rejected 2-97: R 1-54; D 1-43 (ND 1-35, SD 0-8), Oct. 1, 1997.

SENATE VOTES 266, 267, 268, 269, 270

	266	267	268	269	270
ALABAMA					
Sessions	Y	N	Y	Y	N
Shelby	Y	N	Y	Y	N
ALASKA					
Murkowski	Y	N	Y	Y	N
Stevens	Y	N	Y	Y	N
ARIZONA					
Kyl	Y	N	Y	Y	N
McCain	Y	Y	Y	Y	Y
ARKANSAS					
Hutchinson	Y	Y	Y	Y	N
Bumpers	N	Y	Y	Y	Y
CALIFORNIA					
Boxer	N	Y	Y	Y	Y
Feinstein	N	Y	Y	Y	Y
COLORADO					
Allard	Y	N	Y	Y	N
Campbell	Y	N	Y	Y	N
CONNECTICUT					
Dodd	N	Y	Y	Y	Y
Lieberman	N	Y	Y	Y	Y
DELAWARE					
Roth	Y	N	Y	Y	N
Biden	N	Y	Y	Y	Y
FLORIDA					
Mack	Y	N	Y	Y	?
Graham	N	Y	Y	Y	Y
GEORGIA					
Coverdell	Y	N	Y	Y	N
Cleland	N	Y	Y	Y	Y
HAWAII					
Akaka	N	Y	Y	Y	Y
Inouye	N	Y	Y	Y	Y
IDAHO					
Craig	Y	N	Y	Y	N
Kempthorne	Y	N	Y	Y	N
ILLINOIS					
Durbin	N	Y	Y	Y	Y
Moseley-Braun	N	Y	Y	Y	Y
INDIANA					
Coats	Y	N	Y	Y	N
Lugar	Y	N	Y	Y	N
IOWA					
Grassley	Y	N	Y	Y	N
Harkin	N	Y	Y	Y	Y
KANSAS					
Brownback	Y	N	Y	Y	N
Roberts	Y	N	Y	Y	N
KENTUCKY					
McConnell	Y	N	Y	Y	N
Ford	N	Y	Y	Y	Y
LOUISIANA					
Breaux	N	Y	Y	Y	Y
Landrieu	N	Y	Y	Y	Y
MAINE					
Collins	Y	Y	Y	Y	Y
Snowe	N	Y	Y	Y	Y
MARYLAND					
Mikulski	N	Y	Y	Y	Y
Sarbanes	N	Y	Y	Y	Y
MASSACHUSETTS					
Kennedy	N	Y	Y	Y	Y
Kerry	N	Y	Y	Y	Y
MICHIGAN					
Abraham	Y	N	Y	Y	N
Levin	N	Y	Y	Y	Y
MINNESOTA					
Grams	Y	N	Y	Y	N
Wellstone	N	Y	Y	Y	Y
MISSISSIPPI					
Cochran	Y	N	Y	Y	N
Lott	Y	N	Y	Y	N
MISSOURI					
Ashcroft	Y	N	Y	Y	N
Bond	Y	N	Y	Y	N
MONTANA					
Burns	Y	N	Y	Y	N
Baucus	N	Y	Y	Y	Y
NEBRASKA					
Hagel	Y	N	Y	Y	N
Kerrey	N	Y	Y	Y	Y
NEVADA					
Bryan	N	Y	Y	Y	Y
Reid	N	Y	Y	Y	Y
NEW HAMPSHIRE					
Gregg	Y	N	Y	Y	N
Smith	Y	N	Y	Y	N
NEW JERSEY					
Lautenberg	N	Y	Y	Y	Y
Torricelli	N	Y	Y	Y	Y
NEW MEXICO					
Domenici	Y	N	Y	Y	N
Bingaman	N	Y	Y	Y	Y
NEW YORK					
D'Amato	Y	N	Y	Y	N
Moynihan	N	Y	Y	Y	Y
NORTH CAROLINA					
Faircloth	Y	N	Y	Y	N
Helms	Y	N	Y	Y	N
NORTH DAKOTA					
Conrad	N	Y	Y	Y	Y
Dorgan	N	Y	Y	Y	Y
OHIO					
DeWine	Y	N	Y	Y	N
Glenn	N	Y	Y	Y	Y
OKLAHOMA					
Inhofe	Y	N	Y	Y	N
Nickles	Y	N	Y	Y	N
OREGON					
Smith	Y	N	Y	Y	N
Wyden	N	Y	Y	Y	Y
PENNSYLVANIA					
Santorum	Y	N	Y	Y	N
Specter	N	Y	Y	Y	Y
RHODE ISLAND					
Chafee	Y	Y	Y	Y	Y
Reed	N	Y	Y	Y	Y
SOUTH CAROLINA					
Thurmond	Y	N	Y	Y	N
Hollings	N	Y	Y	Y	Y
SOUTH DAKOTA					
Daschle	N	Y	Y	Y	Y
Johnson	N	Y	Y	Y	Y
TENNESSEE					
Frist	Y	N	Y	Y	N
Thompson	Y	Y	Y	Y	Y
TEXAS					
Gramm	Y	N	Y	Y	N
Hutchison	Y	N	Y	Y	N
UTAH					
Bennett	Y	N	Y	Y	N
Hatch	Y	N	Y	Y	N
VERMONT					
Jeffords	N	Y	Y	Y	Y
Leahy	N	Y	Y	Y	Y
VIRGINIA					
Warner	Y	N	Y	Y	N
Robb	N	Y	Y	Y	Y
WASHINGTON					
Gorton	Y	N	Y	Y	N
Murray	N	Y	Y	Y	Y
WEST VIRGINIA					
Byrd	N	Y	N	N	Y
Rockefeller	N	Y	Y	Y	Y
WISCONSIN					
Feingold	N	Y	Y	Y	Y
Kohl	N	Y	Y	Y	Y
WYOMING					
Enzi	Y	N	Y	Y	N
Thomas	Y	N	Y	Y	N

KEY

- Y Voted for (yea).
- # Paired for.
- \+ Announced for.
- N Voted against (nay).
- X Paired against.
- \- Announced against.
- P Voted "present."
- C Voted "present" to avoid possible conflict of interest.
- ? Did not vote or otherwise make a position known.

Democrats *Republicans*

ND Northern Democrats SD Southern Democrats

Southern states - Ala., Ark., Fla., Ga., Ky., La., Miss., N.C., Okla., S.C., Tenn., Texas, Va.

266. S 25. Campaign Finance Overhaul/Cloture. Motion to invoke cloture (thus limiting debate) on the Lott, R-Miss., amendment that would require labor organizations, banks or corporations to secure voluntary authorization from their members before using any membership dues, initiation fees or other payments to fund political activities. Motion rejected 52-48: R 52-3; D 0-45 (ND 0-37, SD 0-8), Oct. 7, 1997. Three-fifths of the total Senate (60) is required to invoke cloture. A "nay" was a vote in support of the president's position.

267. S 25. Campaign Finance Overhaul/Cloture. Motion to invoke cloture (thus limiting debate) on the bill to revise financing of federal political campaigns. Motion rejected 53-47: R 8-47; D 45-0 (ND 37-0, SD 8-0), Oct. 7, 1997. Three-fifths of the total Senate (60) is required to invoke cloture. A "yea" was a vote in support of the president's position.

268. S 1156. District of Colombia Appropriations/Cloture. Motion to invoke cloture (thus limiting debate) on the Mack, R-Fla., amendment that would offer relief to certain immigrants who otherwise would be subject to removal from the United States. Motion agreed to 99-1: R 55-0; D 44-1 (ND 36-1, SD 8-0), Oct. 7, 1997. Three-fifths of the total Senate (60) is required to invoke cloture.

269. S 1156. Fiscal 1998 District of Columbia Appropriations/Immigration. Mack, R-Fla., substitute amendment that would offer relief to certain immigrants who otherwise would be subject to removal from the United States. Adopted 99-1: R 55-0; D 44-1 (ND 36-1, SD 8-0), Oct. 7, 1997.

270. S 25. Campaign Finance Overhaul/Cloture. Motion to invoke cloture (thus limiting debate) on the bill to revise financing of federal political campaigns. Motion rejected 52-47: R 7-47; D 45-0 (ND 37-0, SD 8-0), Oct. 8, 1997. Three-fifths of the total Senate (60) is required to invoke cloture. A "yea" was a vote in support of the president's position.

SENATE VOTES 271, 272, 273, 274

	271	272	273	274
ALABAMA				
Sessions	Y	Y	N	Y
Shelby	Y	Y	N	Y
ALASKA				
Murkowski	Y	Y	N	Y
Stevens	Y	Y	N	Y
ARIZONA				
Kyl	Y	Y	N	Y
McCain	N	N	Y	Y
ARKANSAS				
Hutchinson	Y	Y	N	Y
Bumpers	Y	N	Y	N
CALIFORNIA				
Boxer	Y	N	Y	N
Feinstein	Y	N	Y	N
COLORADO				
Allard	Y	Y	N	Y
Campbell	Y	Y	N	Y
CONNECTICUT				
Dodd	Y	N	Y	N
Lieberman	Y	N	Y	N
DELAWARE				
Roth	Y	Y	N	Y
Biden	?	N	Y	N
FLORIDA				
Mack	?	?	?	?
Graham	Y	N	Y	N
GEORGIA				
Coverdell	Y	Y	N	Y
Cleland	Y	N	Y	N
HAWAII				
Akaka	Y	N	Y	N
Inouye	Y	Y	Y	N
IDAHO				
Craig	Y	Y	N	Y
Kempthorne	Y	Y	N	Y
ILLINOIS				
Durbin	Y	N	Y	N
Moseley-Braun	Y	N	Y	N
INDIANA				
Coats	Y	Y	N	Y
Lugar	Y	Y	N	Y
IOWA				
Grassley	Y	Y	N	Y
Harkin	Y	N	Y	N
KANSAS				
Brownback	Y	Y	N	Y
Roberts	Y	Y	N	Y
KENTUCKY				
McConnell	Y	Y	N	Y
Ford	Y	N	Y	N
LOUISIANA				
Breaux	Y	N	Y	N
Landrieu	Y	N	Y	N
MAINE				
Collins	Y	Y	Y	Y
Snowe	Y	Y	Y	N
MARYLAND				
Mikulski	Y	N	Y	N
Sarbanes	Y	N	Y	N
MASSACHUSETTS				
Kennedy	Y	N	Y	N
Kerry	Y	N	Y	N
MICHIGAN				
Abraham	Y	Y	N	Y
Levin	Y	N	Y	N
MINNESOTA				
Grams	Y	Y	N	Y
Wellstone	Y	N	Y	N
MISSISSIPPI				
Cochran	Y	Y	N	Y
Lott	Y	Y	N	Y
MISSOURI				
Ashcroft	Y	Y	N	Y
Bond	Y	Y	N	Y
MONTANA				
Burns	Y	Y	N	Y
Baucus	Y	N	Y	N
NEBRASKA				
Hagel	Y	Y	N	Y
Kerrey	Y	N	Y	N
NEVADA				
Bryan	Y	N	Y	N
Reid	Y	N	Y	N
NEW HAMPSHIRE				
Gregg	Y	Y	N	Y
Smith	Y	Y	N	Y
NEW JERSEY				
Lautenberg	Y	N	Y	N
Torricelli	Y	N	Y	N
NEW MEXICO				
Domenici	Y	Y	N	Y
Bingaman	Y	N	Y	N
NEW YORK				
D'Amato	N	Y	N	Y
Moynihan	Y	N	Y	N
NORTH CAROLINA				
Faircloth	Y	Y	N	Y
Helms	Y	Y	N	Y
NORTH DAKOTA				
Conrad	Y	N	Y	N
Dorgan	Y	N	Y	N
OHIO				
DeWine	Y	Y	N	Y
Glenn	Y	N	Y	N
OKLAHOMA				
Inhofe	Y	Y	N	Y
Nickles	Y	Y	N	Y
OREGON				
Smith	Y	Y	N	Y
Wyden	Y	N	Y	N
PENNSYLVANIA				
Santorum	Y	Y	N	Y
Specter	Y	Y	Y	N
RHODE ISLAND				
Chafee	Y	Y	Y	Y
Reed	Y	N	Y	N
SOUTH CAROLINA				
Thurmond	Y	Y	N	Y
Hollings	Y	N	Y	N
SOUTH DAKOTA				
Daschle	Y	N	Y	N
Johnson	Y	N	Y	N
TENNESSEE				
Frist	Y	Y	N	Y
Thompson	Y	N	Y	Y
TEXAS				
Gramm	N	Y	N	Y
Hutchison	Y	Y	N	Y
UTAH				
Bennett	N	Y	N	Y
Hatch	Y	Y	N	Y
VERMONT				
Jeffords	Y	Y	Y	N
Leahy	Y	N	Y	N
VIRGINIA				
Warner	Y	Y	N	Y
Robb	Y	N	Y	N
WASHINGTON				
Gorton	Y	Y	N	Y
Murray	Y	N	Y	N
WEST VIRGINIA				
Byrd	Y	Y	Y	N
Rockefeller	Y	N	Y	N
WISCONSIN				
Feingold	Y	N	Y	N
Kohl	Y	N	Y	N
WYOMING				
Enzi	Y	Y	N	Y
Thomas	Y	Y	N	Y

KEY

- Y Voted for (yea).
- # Paired for.
- + Announced for.
- N Voted against (nay).
- X Paired against.
- \- Announced against.
- P Voted "present."
- C Voted "present" to avoid possible conflict of interest.
- ? Did not vote or otherwise make a position known.

Democrats ***Republicans***

ND Northern Democrats SD Southern Democrats

Southern states - Ala., Ark., Fla., Ga., Ky., La., Miss., N.C., Okla., S.C., Tenn., Texas, Va.

271. Procedural Motion. Chafee, R-R.I., motion to instruct the sergeant-at-arms to request the attendance of absent senators. Motion agreed to 94-4: R 50-4; D 44-0 (ND 36-0, SD 8-0), Oct. 8, 1997.

272. Procedural Motion/Adjourn. Lott, R-Miss., motion to adjourn. Motion agreed to 54-45: R 52-2; D 2-43 (ND 2-35, SD 0-8), Oct. 8, 1997.

273. S 25. Campaign Finance Overhaul/Cloture. Motion to invoke cloture (thus limiting debate) on the bill to revise financing of federal political campaigns. Motion rejected 52-47: R 7-47; D 45-0 (ND 37-0, SD 8-0), Oct. 9, 1997. Three-fifths of the total Senate (60) is required to invoke cloture. A "yea" was a vote in support of the president's position.

274. S 25. Campaign Finance Overhaul/Cloture. Motion to invoke cloture (thus limiting debate) on the Lott, R-Miss., amendment that would require labor organizations, banks or corporations to secure voluntary authorization from their members before using any membership dues, initiation fees or other payments to fund political activities. Motion rejected 51-48: R 51-3; D 0-45 (ND 0-37, SD 0-8), Oct. 9, 1997. Three-fifths of the total Senate (60) is required to invoke cloture. A "nay" was a vote in support of the president's position.

SENATE VOTES 275, 276, 277

	275	276	277
ALABAMA			
Sessions	Y	Y	Y
Shelby	Y	Y	Y
ALASKA			
Murkowski	Y	Y	Y
Stevens	Y	Y	Y
ARIZONA			
Kyl	Y	Y	Y
McCain	N	Y	N
ARKANSAS			
Hutchinson	Y	Y	Y
Bumpers	N	Y	N
CALIFORNIA			
Boxer	N	Y	N
Feinstein	N	Y	N
COLORADO			
Allard	Y	Y	Y
Campbell	Y	Y	Y
CONNECTICUT			
Dodd	N	Y	N
Lieberman	N	Y	N
DELAWARE			
Roth	Y	Y	Y
Biden	N	Y	N
FLORIDA			
Mack	N	Y	N
Graham	N	Y	N
GEORGIA			
Coverdell	Y	Y	Y
Cleland	N	Y	N
HAWAII			
Akaka	N	Y	N
Inouye	N	Y	N
IDAHO			
Craig	Y	Y	Y
Kempthorne	Y	Y	Y
ILLINOIS			
Durbin	N	Y	N
Moseley-Braun	N	Y	N
INDIANA			
Coats	Y	Y	Y
Lugar	Y	Y	Y
IOWA			
Grassley	Y	Y	Y
Harkin	N	Y	N
KANSAS			
Brownback	Y	Y	Y
Roberts	Y	Y	Y
KENTUCKY			
McConnell	Y	Y	Y
Ford	N	Y	N
LOUISIANA			
Breaux	N	Y	N
Landrieu	N	Y	N
MAINE			
Collins	N	Y	N
Snowe	N	Y	N
MARYLAND			
Mikulski	N	Y	?
Sarbanes	N	Y	?
MASSACHUSETTS			
Kennedy	N	Y	N
Kerry	N	Y	N
MICHIGAN			
Abraham	Y	Y	Y
Levin	N	Y	N
MINNESOTA			
Grams	Y	Y	Y
Wellstone	N	Y	N
MISSISSIPPI			
Cochran	Y	Y	Y
Lott	Y	Y	Y
MISSOURI			
Ashcroft	Y	Y	Y
Bond	Y	Y	Y
MONTANA			
Burns	Y	Y	Y
Baucus	N	Y	N
NEBRASKA			
Hagel	Y	Y	Y
Kerrey	N	Y	N
NEVADA			
Bryan	N	Y	N
Reid	N	Y	N
NEW HAMPSHIRE			
Gregg	Y	Y	Y
Smith	Y	Y	Y
NEW JERSEY			
Lautenberg	N	Y	N
Torricelli	N	Y	N
NEW MEXICO			
Domenici	Y	Y	Y
Bingaman	N	Y	N
NEW YORK			
D'Amato	Y	Y	Y
Moynihan	N	Y	N
NORTH CAROLINA			
Faircloth	Y	Y	Y
Helms	Y	Y	Y
NORTH DAKOTA			
Conrad	N	Y	N
Dorgan	N	Y	N
OHIO			
DeWine	Y	Y	Y
Glenn	N	Y	N
OKLAHOMA			
Inhofe	Y	Y	Y
Nickles	Y	Y	Y
OREGON			
Smith	Y	Y	Y
Wyden	N	Y	N
PENNSYLVANIA			
Santorum	N	Y	N
Specter	N	Y	N
RHODE ISLAND			
Chafee	Y	Y	Y
Reed	N	Y	N
SOUTH CAROLINA			
Thurmond	Y	Y	Y
Hollings	N	Y	N
SOUTH DAKOTA			
Daschle	N	Y	N
Johnson	N	Y	N
TENNESSEE			
Frist	Y	Y	Y
Thompson	N	Y	N
TEXAS			
Gramm	Y	Y	Y
Hutchison	Y	Y	Y
UTAH			
Bennett	Y	Y	Y
Hatch	Y	Y	Y
VERMONT			
Jeffords	Y	Y	Y
Leahy	N	Y	N
VIRGINIA			
Warner	Y	Y	Y
Robb	N	Y	N
WASHINGTON			
Gorton	Y	Y	Y
Murray	N	Y	N
WEST VIRGINIA			
Byrd	N	Y	N
Rockefeller	N	Y	N
WISCONSIN			
Feingold	N	Y	N
Kohl	N	Y	N
WYOMING			
Enzi	Y	Y	Y
Thomas	Y	Y	Y

KEY

Y Voted for (yea).
Paired for.
\+ Announced for.
N Voted against (nay).
X Paired against.
\- Announced against.
P Voted "present."
C Voted "present" to avoid possible conflict of interest.
? Did not vote or otherwise make a position known.

Democrats ***Republicans***

ND Northern Democrats SD Southern Democrats

Southern states - Ala., Ark., Fla., Ga., Ky., La., Miss., N.C., Okla., S.C., Tenn., Texas, Va.

275. S 1173. Highway and Transit Reauthorization/Cloture. Motion to invoke cloture (thus limiting debate) on the Senate Environment and Public Works Committee amendment to the Intermodal Surface Transportation Efficiency Act of 1991, which would authorize $145 billion over fiscal years 1998-2003 for highway funding. Motion rejected 48-52: R 48-7; D 0-45 (ND 0-37, SD 0-8), Oct. 23, 1997. Three-fifths of the total Senate (60) is required to invoke cloture.

276. H J Res 97. Fiscal 1998 Continuing Appropriations/Passage. Passage of the joint resolution to provide continuing appropriations through Nov. 7 for fiscal 1998 spending bills not yet enacted. The continuing resolution would set spending levels for federal programs and agencies it covers at fiscal 1997 levels, except in circumstances where the president and Congress have agreed to lower levels of funding. Passed 100-0: R 55-0; D 45-0 (ND 37-0, SD 8-0), Oct. 23, 1997.

277. S 1173. Highway and Transit Reauthorization/Cloture. Motion to invoke cloture (thus limiting debate) on the Senate Environment and Public Works Committee amendment to the Intermodal Surface Transportation Efficiency Act of 1991, which would authorize $145 billion over fiscal years 1998-2003 for highway funding. Motion rejected 48-50: R 48-7; D 0-43 (ND 0-35, SD 0-8), Oct. 23, 1997. Three-fifths of the total Senate (60) is required to invoke cloture.

SENATE VOTES 278, 279 280, 281, 282

	278	279	280	281	282
ALABAMA					
Sessions	Y	Y	Y	Y	Y
Shelby	Y	Y	Y	Y	Y
ALASKA					
Murkowski	Y	Y	Y	Y	Y
Stevens	Y	Y	Y	Y	Y
ARIZONA					
Kyl	?	Y	Y	Y	Y
McCain	?	Y	Y	Y	N
ARKANSAS					
Hutchinson	Y	Y	Y	Y	Y
Bumpers	N	Y	Y	Y	N
CALIFORNIA					
Boxer	N	Y	Y	Y	N
Feinstein	N	Y	Y	Y	N
COLORADO					
Allard	Y	Y	Y	Y	Y
Campbell	Y	Y	Y	Y	Y
CONNECTICUT					
Dodd	N	Y	Y	Y	N
Lieberman	N	Y	Y	Y	N
DELAWARE					
Roth	Y	?	?	?	Y
Biden	N	?	?	?	N
FLORIDA					
Mack	N	Y	Y	Y	Y
Graham	N	Y	Y	Y	N
GEORGIA					
Coverdell	Y	Y	Y	Y	Y
Cleland	N	Y	Y	Y	N
HAWAII					
Akaka	N	Y	Y	Y	N
Inouye	N	Y	Y	Y	N
IDAHO					
Craig	Y	Y	Y	Y	Y
Kempthorne	Y	Y	Y	Y	Y
ILLINOIS					
Durbin	N	Y	Y	Y	N
Moseley-Braun	N	Y	Y	Y	N
INDIANA					
Coats	Y	Y	Y	Y	Y
Lugar	Y	Y	Y	Y	Y

	278	279	280	281	282
IOWA					
Grassley	Y	Y	Y	Y	Y
Harkin	?	Y	Y	Y	N
KANSAS					
Brownback	Y	Y	Y	Y	Y
Roberts	Y	Y	Y	Y	Y
KENTUCKY					
McConnell	Y	Y	Y	Y	Y
Ford	N	Y	Y	Y	N
LOUISIANA					
Breaux	N	Y	Y	Y	N
Landrieu	N	Y	Y	Y	N
MAINE					
Collins	N	Y	Y	Y	Y
Snowe	N	Y	Y	Y	N
MARYLAND					
Mikulski	N	?	?	?	N
Sarbanes	N	Y	Y	Y	N
MASSACHUSETTS					
Kennedy	N	?	?	Y	N
Kerry	N	Y	Y	Y	N
MICHIGAN					
Abraham	Y	Y	Y	Y	Y
Levin	N	Y	Y	Y	N
MINNESOTA					
Grams	Y	Y	Y	Y	Y
Wellstone	–	Y	Y	Y	N
MISSISSIPPI					
Cochran	Y	Y	Y	Y	Y
Lott	Y	Y	Y	Y	Y
MISSOURI					
Ashcroft	Y	Y	Y	Y	Y
Bond	Y	Y	Y	Y	Y
MONTANA					
Burns	Y	Y	Y	Y	Y
Baucus	N	Y	Y	Y	N
NEBRASKA					
Hagel	Y	Y	Y	Y	Y
Kerrey	N	Y	Y	Y	N
NEVADA					
Bryan	N	Y	Y	Y	N
Reid	N	Y	Y	Y	N

	278	279	280	281	282
NEW HAMPSHIRE					
Gregg	Y	Y	Y	Y	Y
Smith	Y	Y	Y	Y	Y
NEW JERSEY					
Lautenberg	N	+	+	+	N
Torricelli	N	Y	Y	Y	N
NEW MEXICO					
Domenici	?	Y	Y	Y	Y
Bingaman	N	Y	Y	Y	N
NEW YORK					
D'Amato	Y	?	?	?	Y
Moynihan	N	Y	Y	Y	N
NORTH CAROLINA					
Faircloth	Y	?	?	?	Y
Helms	Y	Y	Y	Y	Y
NORTH DAKOTA					
Conrad	N	Y	Y	Y	N
Dorgan	N	Y	Y	Y	N
OHIO					
DeWine	Y	Y	Y	Y	Y
Glenn	N	Y	Y	Y	N
OKLAHOMA					
Inhofe	?	Y	Y	Y	Y
Nickles	Y	Y	Y	Y	Y
OREGON					
Smith	Y	Y	Y	Y	Y
Wyden	N	?	?	?	N
PENNSYLVANIA					
Santorum	N	Y	Y	Y	Y
Specter	N	Y	Y	Y	N
RHODE ISLAND					
Chafee	Y	Y	Y	Y	Y
Reed	N	Y	Y	Y	N
SOUTH CAROLINA					
Thurmond	Y	Y	Y	Y	Y
Hollings	N	Y	Y	Y	N
SOUTH DAKOTA					
Daschle	N	Y	Y	Y	N
Johnson	N	Y	?	?	N
TENNESSEE					
Frist	Y	Y	Y	Y	Y
Thompson	N	Y	Y	Y	Y

KEY

- Y Voted for (yea).
- # Paired for.
- + Announced for.
- N Voted against (nay).
- X Paired against.
- – Announced against.
- P Voted "present."
- C Voted "present" to avoid possible conflict of interest.
- ? Did not vote or otherwise make a position known.

Democrats *Republicans*

	278	279	280	281	282
TEXAS					
Gramm	Y	Y	Y	Y	Y
Hutchison	Y	Y	Y	Y	Y
UTAH					
Bennett	Y	Y	Y	Y	Y
Hatch	?	Y	Y	Y	Y
VERMONT					
Jeffords	Y	Y	Y	Y	Y
Leahy	N	Y	Y	Y	N
VIRGINIA					
Warner	Y	?	?	?	Y
Robb	N	Y	Y	Y	N
WASHINGTON					
Gorton	Y	Y	Y	Y	Y
Murray	N	Y	Y	Y	N
WEST VIRGINIA					
Byrd	N	Y	Y	Y	N
Rockefeller	N	Y	Y	Y	N
WISCONSIN					
Feingold	N	Y	Y	Y	N
Kohl	N	Y	Y	Y	N
WYOMING					
Enzi	?	Y	Y	Y	Y
Thomas	Y	Y	Y	Y	Y

ND Northern Democrats SD Southern Democrats

Southern states - Ala., Ark., Fla., Ga., Ky., La., Miss., N.C., Okla., S.C., Tenn., Texas, Va.

278. S 1173. Highway and Transit Reauthorization/Cloture. Motion to invoke cloture (thus limiting debate) on the Senate Environment and Public Works Committee amendment to the bill reauthorizing Intermodal Surface Transportation Efficiency Act of 1991, which would authorize $145 billion over fiscal years 1998-2003 for highway and transit funding. Motion rejected 43-49: R 43-6; D 0-43 (ND 0-35, SD 0-8), Oct. 24, 1997. Three-fifths of the total Senate (60) is required to invoke cloture.

279. Algenon L. Marbley Nomination/Confirmation. Confirmation of President Clinton's nomination of Algenon L. Marbley of Ohio to be a U.S. district judge for the southern district of Ohio. Confirmed 91-0: R 51-0; D 40-0 (ND 32-0, SD 8-0), Oct. 27, 1997. A "yea" was a vote in support of the president's position.

280. Wyche Fowler Jr. Nomination/Confirmation. Confirmation of President Clinton's nomination of Wyche Fowler Jr. of Georgia to be U.S. ambassador to the Kingdom of Saudi Arabia. Confirmed 90-0: R 51-0; D 39-0 (ND 31-0, SD 8-0), Oct. 27, 1997. A "yea" was a vote in support of the president's position.

281. Thomas S. Foley Nomination/Confirmation. Confirmation of President Clinton's nomination of Thomas S. Foley of Washington to be U.S. ambassador to Japan. Confirmed 91-0: R 51-0; D 40-0 (ND 32-0, SD 8-0), Oct. 27, 1997. A "yea" was a vote in support of the president's position.

282. S 1173. Highway and Transit Reauthorization/Cloture. Motion to invoke cloture (thus limiting debate) on the Senate Environment and Public Works Committee amendment to the bill reauthorizing Intermodal Surface Transportation Efficiency Act of 1991, which would authorize $145 billion over fiscal years 1998-2003 for highway funding. Motion rejected 52-48: R 52-3; D 0-45 (ND 0-37, SD 0-8), Oct. 28, 1997. Three-fifths of the total Senate (60) is required to invoke cloture.

SENATE VOTES 283, 284, 285, 286, 287

	283	284	285	286	287
ALABAMA					
Sessions	Y	Y	Y	Y	N
Shelby	Y	Y	Y	Y	Y
ALASKA					
Murkowski	Y	Y	Y	Y	Y
Stevens	Y	Y	Y	Y	Y
ARIZONA					
Kyl	Y	Y	Y	Y	N
McCain	Y	Y	Y	Y	N
ARKANSAS					
Hutchinson	Y	Y	Y	Y	N
Bumpers	Y	Y	Y	Y	N
CALIFORNIA					
Boxer	N	Y	N	Y	Y
Feinstein	Y	Y	N	Y	Y
COLORADO					
Allard	Y	Y	Y	Y	Y
Campbell	Y	Y	N	Y	Y
CONNECTICUT					
Dodd	Y	Y	Y	Y	N
Lieberman	Y	Y	Y	Y	N
DELAWARE					
Roth	N	Y	Y	Y	Y
Biden	Y	Y	N	Y	Y
FLORIDA					
Mack	Y	Y	Y	Y	Y
Graham	Y	Y	Y	Y	Y
GEORGIA					
Coverdell	Y	Y	Y	Y	Y
Cleland	Y	Y	Y	Y	Y
HAWAII					
Akaka	Y	Y	Y	Y	Y
Inouye	Y	Y	Y	Y	Y
IDAHO					
Craig	Y	Y	Y	Y	Y
Kempthorne	Y	Y	Y	Y	Y
ILLINOIS					
Durbin	N	Y	Y	Y	N
Moseley-Braun	N	Y	Y	Y	Y
INDIANA					
Coats	Y	Y	?	?	?
Lugar	Y	Y	Y	Y	Y

	283	284	285	286	287
IOWA					
Grassley	Y	Y	Y	Y	N
Harkin	Y	Y	Y	?	Y
KANSAS					
Brownback	Y	Y	Y	Y	Y
Roberts	Y	Y	Y	Y	Y
KENTUCKY					
McConnell	Y	Y	Y	Y	Y
Ford	Y	Y	Y	Y	Y
LOUISIANA					
Breaux	Y	Y	N	Y	N
Landrieu	Y	Y	Y	Y	N
MAINE					
Collins	Y	Y	Y	Y	Y
Snowe	Y	Y	Y	Y	Y
MARYLAND					
Mikulski	Y	Y	?	Y	Y
Sarbanes	Y	Y	Y	Y	Y
MASSACHUSETTS					
Kennedy	?	Y	Y	Y	Y
Kerry	Y	Y	Y	Y	N
MICHIGAN					
Abraham	Y	Y	Y	Y	N
Levin	Y	Y	Y	Y	Y
MINNESOTA					
Grams	Y	Y	N	Y	N
Wellstone	N	Y	N	Y	N
MISSISSIPPI					
Cochran	Y	Y	Y	Y	Y
Lott	Y	Y	Y	Y	Y
MISSOURI					
Ashcroft	N	Y	Y	Y	N
Bond	Y	Y	N	Y	Y
MONTANA					
Burns	Y	N	Y	Y	Y
Baucus	Y	Y	Y	Y	Y
NEBRASKA					
Hagel	Y	Y	Y	Y	Y
Kerrey	Y	Y	N	Y	N
NEVADA					
Bryan	N	Y	N	Y	N
Reid	Y	Y	N	Y	Y

	283	284	285	286	287
NEW HAMPSHIRE					
Gregg	Y	Y	Y	Y	Y
Smith	N	Y	Y	Y	Y
NEW JERSEY					
Lautenberg	Y	Y	Y	Y	Y
Torricelli	Y	Y	N	Y	Y
NEW MEXICO					
Domenici	Y	Y	Y	Y	Y
Bingaman	Y	Y	Y	Y	Y
NEW YORK					
D'Amato	Y	Y	Y	Y	Y
Moynihan	Y	Y	N	Y	Y
NORTH CAROLINA					
Faircloth	N	Y	Y	Y	Y
Helms	N	Y	Y	Y	Y
NORTH DAKOTA					
Conrad	Y	Y	Y	Y	N
Dorgan	Y	Y	Y	Y	Y
OHIO					
DeWine	Y	Y	Y	Y	Y
Glenn	Y	Y	Y	Y	Y
OKLAHOMA					
Inhofe	Y	Y	Y	Y	Y
Nickles	Y	Y	Y	Y	N
OREGON					
Smith	Y	Y	Y	Y	Y
Wyden	N	Y	Y	Y	N
PENNSYLVANIA					
Santorum	Y	Y	Y	Y	Y
Specter	+	Y	Y	Y	Y
RHODE ISLAND					
Chafee	Y	Y	Y	Y	Y
Reed	Y	Y	Y	Y	Y
SOUTH CAROLINA					
Thurmond	Y	Y	Y	Y	N
Hollings	Y	Y	Y	Y	N
SOUTH DAKOTA					
Daschle	Y	Y	Y	Y	N
Johnson	Y	Y	Y	Y	N
TENNESSEE					
Frist	Y	Y	Y	Y	Y
Thompson	Y	Y	Y	Y	Y

KEY

- Y Voted for (yea).
- # Paired for.
- + Announced for.
- N Voted against (nay).
- X Paired against.
- \- Announced against.
- P Voted "present."
- C Voted "present" to avoid possible conflict of interest.
- ? Did not vote or otherwise make a position known.

Democrats *Republicans*

	283	284	285	286	287
TEXAS					
Gramm	N	Y	N	Y	N
Hutchison	Y	Y	N	Y	Y
UTAH					
Bennett	Y	Y	Y	Y	Y
Hatch	Y	Y	Y	Y	Y
VERMONT					
Jeffords	Y	Y	N	Y	Y
Leahy	Y	Y	N	Y	Y
VIRGINIA					
Warner	Y	Y	Y	Y	Y
Robb	Y	Y	Y	Y	N
WASHINGTON					
Gorton	Y	Y	Y	Y	Y
Murray	Y	Y	Y	Y	Y
WEST VIRGINIA					
Byrd	Y	Y	N	Y	Y
Rockefeller	Y	Y	N	Y	Y
WISCONSIN					
Feingold	N	Y	Y	Y	N
Kohl	N	Y	N	Y	N
WYOMING					
Enzi	Y	Y	Y	Y	Y
Thomas	Y	Y	Y	Y	N

ND Northern Democrats SD Southern Democrats

Southern states - Ala., Ark., Fla., Ga., Ky., La., Miss., N.C., Okla., S.C., Tenn., Texas, Va.

283. HR 2107. Fiscal 1998 Interior Appropriations/Conference Report. Adoption of the conference report on the bill to provide $13,789,438,000 in new budget authority for the Department of the Interior and related agencies for fiscal 1998. The bill provides $275,003,000 more than was provided in fiscal 1997 and $10,508,000 less than requested by the president. Adopted (thus cleared for the president) 84-14: R 48-6; D 36-8 (ND 28-8, SD 8-0), Oct. 28, 1997.

284. William E. Kennard Nomination/Confirmation. Confirmation of President Clinton's nomination of William E. Kennard of California to be chairman of the Federal Communications Commission. Confirmed 99-1: R 54-1; D 45-0 (ND 37-0, SD 8-0), Oct. 29, 1997. A "yea" was a vote in support of the president's position.

285. HR 1119. Fiscal 1998-99 Defense Authorization/Motion To Table. Lott, R-Miss., motion to table (kill) the Gramm, R-Texas, motion to postpone consideration of the conference report to the fiscal 1998-99 Department of Defense authorization bill. The Gramm motion, amended by Hutchison, R-Texas, would postpone until Jan. 18, 1998, Senate consideration of the conference report. Motion agreed to 78-20: R 48-6; D 30-14 (ND 23-13, SD 7-1), Oct. 29, 1997.

286. Charles J. Siragusa Nomination/Confirmation. Confirmation of President Clinton's nomination of Charles J. Siragusa of New York to be a U.S. district judge for the Western District of New York. Confirmed 98-0: R 54-0; D 44-0 (ND 36-0, SD 8-0), Oct. 30, 1997. A "yea" was a vote in support of the president's position.

287. S 1292. Line-Item Veto Disapproval/Passage. Passage of the bill to disapprove President Clinton's line-item vetoes of 36 projects, totaling $287 million, in the fiscal 1998 military construction appropriations bill (HR 2016 — PL 105-45). Passed 69-30: R 42-12; D 27-18 (ND 24-13, SD 3-5), Oct. 30, 1997. A "nay" was a vote in support of the president's position.

SENATE VOTES 288, 289, 290, 291, 292, 293, 294, 295

	288	289	290	291	292	293	294	295
ALABAMA								
Sessions	Y	Y	Y	Y	Y	Y	N	Y
Shelby	Y	Y	Y	Y	N	Y	N	Y
ALASKA								
Murkowski	Y	Y	Y	Y	Y	Y	Y	Y
Stevens	Y	Y	Y	Y	N	Y	?	Y
ARIZONA								
Kyl	Y	Y	Y	Y	Y	Y	Y	Y
McCain	Y	?	Y	Y	Y	Y	Y	Y
ARKANSAS								
Hutchinson	Y	Y	Y	Y	Y	Y	Y	Y
Bumpers	N	Y	Y	N	Y	Y	Y	Y
CALIFORNIA								
Boxer	N	Y	Y	N	N	Y	N	Y
Feinstein	N	Y	Y	N	N	Y	N	Y
COLORADO								
Allard	Y	Y	Y	Y	Y	Y	Y	Y
Campbell	Y	Y	Y	Y	N	Y	N	Y
CONNECTICUT								
Dodd	N	Y	Y	N	Y	Y	Y	Y
Lieberman	Y	Y	Y	Y	Y	Y	Y	Y
DELAWARE								
Roth	Y	Y	Y	Y	Y	Y	Y	Y
Biden	N	Y	?	N	Y	Y	Y	Y
FLORIDA								
Mack	Y	?	Y	Y	Y	Y	Y	Y
Graham	N	Y	Y	N	Y	Y	Y	Y
GEORGIA								
Coverdell	Y	Y	Y	Y	Y	Y	Y	Y
Cleland	N	Y	Y	N	Y	Y	Y	Y
HAWAII								
Akaka	N	Y	Y	N	Y	Y	Y	Y
Inouye	N	Y	Y	N	Y	Y	Y	Y
IDAHO								
Craig	Y	Y	Y	Y	Y	Y	Y	Y
Kempthorne	Y	Y	Y	Y	Y	Y	Y	Y
ILLINOIS								
Durbin	N	Y	Y	N	N	Y	N	Y
Moseley-Braun	N	Y	Y	N	N	Y	N	Y
INDIANA								
Coats	Y	Y	Y	Y	Y	Y	Y	Y
Lugar	Y	Y	Y	Y	Y	Y	Y	Y
IOWA								
Grassley	Y	Y	Y	Y	Y	Y	Y	Y
Harkin	N	Y	?	N	N	Y	N	Y
KANSAS								
Brownback	Y	Y	Y	Y	Y	Y	Y	Y
Roberts	Y	Y	Y	Y	Y	Y	Y	Y
KENTUCKY								
McConnell	Y	Y	Y	Y	Y	Y	Y	Y
Ford	N	Y	?	N	N	Y	N	Y
LOUISIANA								
Breaux	N	Y	Y	N	Y	Y	Y	Y
Landrieu	N	Y	Y	N	Y	Y	Y	Y
MAINE								
Collins	Y	Y	Y	Y	Y	Y	Y	Y
Snowe	Y	Y	Y	Y	N	Y	N	Y
MARYLAND								
Mikulski	N	Y	?	N	N	Y	N	?
Sarbanes	N	Y	Y	N	N	Y	N	Y
MASSACHUSETTS								
Kennedy	N	Y	Y	N	N	Y	N	Y
Kerry	N	Y	Y	N	Y	Y	Y	Y
MICHIGAN								
Abraham	Y	Y	Y	Y	Y	Y	Y	Y
Levin	N	Y	Y	N	N	Y	N	Y
MINNESOTA								
Grams	Y	Y	Y	Y	Y	Y	Y	Y
Wellstone	–	+	Y	N	N	Y	N	Y
MISSISSIPPI								
Cochran	Y	Y	Y	Y	Y	Y	Y	Y
Lott	Y	Y	Y	Y	Y	Y	Y	Y
MISSOURI								
Ashcroft	Y	Y	Y	Y	Y	Y	Y	Y
Bond	Y	Y	Y	Y	Y	Y	Y	Y
MONTANA								
Burns	Y	Y	Y	Y	N	Y	N	Y
Baucus	–	+	Y	N	Y	Y	Y	Y
NEBRASKA								
Hagel	Y	Y	Y	Y	Y	Y	Y	Y
Kerrey	N	Y	?	N	Y	Y	Y	Y
NEVADA								
Bryan	N	Y	Y	N	Y	Y	Y	Y
Reid	N	Y	Y	N	N	Y	N	Y
NEW HAMPSHIRE								
Gregg	Y	Y	Y	Y	Y	Y	Y	Y
Smith	Y	Y	Y	Y	N	Y	N	Y
NEW JERSEY								
Lautenberg	N	Y	Y	N	Y	Y	Y	Y
Torricelli	Y	Y	Y	Y	N	Y	N	Y
NEW MEXICO								
Domenici	Y	Y	Y	Y	Y	Y	Y	Y
Bingaman	N	Y	Y	N	Y	Y	Y	Y
NEW YORK								
D'Amato	Y	Y	?	Y	Y	Y	Y	Y
Moynihan	N	Y	Y	N	Y	Y	Y	Y
NORTH CAROLINA								
Faircloth	Y	Y	?	Y	N	Y	N	N
Helms	Y	Y	?	Y	Y	Y	N	Y
NORTH DAKOTA								
Conrad	N	Y	Y	N	N	Y	N	Y
Dorgan	N	Y	Y	N	N	Y	N	Y
OHIO								
DeWine	Y	Y	Y	Y	Y	Y	Y	Y
Glenn	N	Y	Y	N	Y	Y	Y	Y
OKLAHOMA								
Inhofe	Y	Y	Y	Y	N	Y	N	Y
Nickles	Y	Y	Y	Y	Y	Y	Y	Y
OREGON								
Smith	Y	Y	Y	Y	Y	Y	Y	Y
Wyden	N	Y	Y	N	Y	Y	Y	Y
PENNSYLVANIA								
Santorum	Y	Y	Y	Y	N	Y	Y	Y
Specter	Y	Y	Y	Y	N	Y	N	Y
RHODE ISLAND								
Chafee	N	Y	Y	N	Y	Y	Y	Y
Reed	N	Y	Y	N	N	Y	N	Y
SOUTH CAROLINA								
Thurmond	Y	Y	Y	Y	N	Y	N	Y
Hollings	N	N	Y	N	N	Y	N	Y
SOUTH DAKOTA								
Daschle	N	Y	Y	N	Y	Y	Y	Y
Johnson	N	Y	Y	N	Y	Y	Y	Y
TENNESSEE								
Frist	Y	Y	Y	Y	Y	Y	Y	Y
Thompson	Y	Y	Y	Y	Y	Y	Y	Y
TEXAS								
Gramm	Y	Y	Y	Y	Y	Y	Y	Y
Hutchison	Y	Y	Y	Y	Y	Y	Y	Y
UTAH								
Bennett	Y	Y	Y	Y	Y	Y	Y	Y
Hatch	Y	Y	Y	Y	Y	Y	Y	Y
VERMONT								
Jeffords	Y	Y	Y	Y	Y	Y	Y	Y
Leahy	N	Y	Y	N	Y	Y	Y	Y
VIRGINIA								
Warner	Y	Y	Y	Y	Y	Y	Y	Y
Robb	N	Y	Y	N	Y	Y	Y	Y
WASHINGTON								
Gorton	Y	Y	Y	Y	Y	Y	Y	Y
Murray	N	Y	Y	N	Y	Y	Y	Y
WEST VIRGINIA								
Byrd	N	Y	Y	N	N	Y	N	Y
Rockefeller	?	?	Y	N	Y	Y	Y	Y
WISCONSIN								
Feingold	N	Y	Y	N	N	Y	N	Y
Kohl	N	N	Y	N	Y	Y	Y	Y
WYOMING								
Enzi	Y	Y	Y	Y	N	Y	N	Y
Thomas	Y	Y	Y	Y	Y	Y	Y	Y

KEY

- Y Voted for (yea).
- # Paired for.
- \+ Announced for.
- N Voted against (nay).
- X Paired against.
- – Announced against.
- P Voted "present."
- C Voted "present" to avoid possible conflict of interest.
- ? Did not vote or otherwise make a position known.

Democrats *Republicans*

ND Northern Democrats SD Southern Democrats

Southern states - Ala., Ark., Fla., Ga., Ky., La., Miss., N.C., Okla., S.C., Tenn., Texas, Va.

288. HR 2646. Education Savings Accounts/Cloture. Motion to invoke cloture (thus limiting debate) on the bill allowing parents to invest up to $2,500 annually in savings accounts designated for education-related expenses. Withdrawals of both principal and interest from such accounts could be made without incurring tax liability. Motion rejected 56-41: R 54-1; D 2-40 (ND 2-32, SD 0-8), Oct. 31, 1997. Three-fifths of the total Senate (60) is required to invoke cloture.

289. HR 1119. Fiscal 1998 Defense Authorization/Cloture. Motion to invoke cloture (thus limiting debate) on the motion to proceed to the conference report to the bill authorizing $268.3 billion for defense programs in fiscal 1998, an increase of $2.6 billion from the president's request. The bill also includes several international initiatives and revises recommendations of the 1995 Base Closure and Realignment Commission. Motion agreed to 93-2: R 53-0; D 40-2 (ND 33-1, SD 7-1), Oct. 31, 1997. Three-fifths of the total Senate (60) is required to invoke cloture.

290. Charles O. Rossotti Nomination/Confirmation. Confirmation of President Clinton's nomination of Charles O. Rossotti of the District of Columbia to be commissioner of the Internal Revenue Service. Confirmed 92-0: R 52-0; D 40-0 (ND 33-0, SD 7-0), Nov. 3, 1997. A "yea" was a vote in support of the president's position.

291. HR 2646. Education Savings Accounts/Cloture. Motion to invoke cloture (thus limiting debate) on the bill allowing parents to invest up to $2,500 annually in savings accounts designated for education-related expenses. Withdrawals of both principal and interest from such accounts could be made without incurring tax liability. Motion rejected 56-44: R 54-1; D 2-43 (ND 2-35, SD 0-8), Nov. 4, 1997. Three-fifths of the total Senate (60) is required to invoke cloture.

292. S 1269. Fast Track/Cloture. Motion to invoke cloture (thus limiting debate) on the motion to proceed to the bill allowing the president to submit bills implementing trade pacts to Congress under expedited review procedures requiring up-or-down votes without amendments. Motion agreed to 69-31: R 43-12; D 26-19 (ND 20-17, SD 6-2), Nov. 4, 1997. Three-fifths of the total Senate (60) is required to invoke cloture.

293. James S. Gwin Nomination/Confirmation. Confirmation of President Clinton's nomination of James S. Gwin of Ohio to be U.S. district judge for the northern district of Ohio. Confirmed 100-0: R 55-0; D 45-0 (ND 37-0, SD 8-0), Nov. 5, 1997. A "yea" was a vote in support of the president's position.

294. S 1269. Fast Track/Motion To Proceed. Motion to proceed to the bill allowing the president to submit bills implementing trade pacts to Congress under expedited review procedures requiring up-or-down votes without amendments. Motion agreed to 68-31: R 42-12; D 26-19 (ND 20-17, SD 6-2), Nov. 5, 1997.

295. Ronald Lee Gilman Nomination/Confirmation. Confirmation of President Clinton's nomination of Ronald Lee Gilman of Tennessee to be a U.S. circuit judge for the 6th Circuit. Confirmed 98-1: R 54-1; D 44-0 (ND 36-0, SD 8-0), Nov. 6, 1997. A "yea" was a vote in support of the president's position.

SENATE VOTES 296, 297, 298

	296	297	298
ALABAMA			
Sessions	Y	Y	N
Shelby	Y	Y	Y
ALASKA			
Murkowski	Y	Y	Y
Stevens	N	Y	Y
ARIZONA			
Kyl	Y	Y	Y
McCain	Y	Y	?
ARKANSAS			
Hutchinson	Y	Y	Y
Bumpers	N	Y	Y
CALIFORNIA			
Boxer	N	Y	Y
Feinstein	N	Y	Y
COLORADO			
Allard	Y	Y	Y
Campbell	Y	?	?
CONNECTICUT			
Dodd	Y	Y	Y
Lieberman	Y	Y	Y
DELAWARE			
Roth	Y	Y	Y
Biden	Y	Y	Y
FLORIDA			
Mack	Y	Y	Y
Graham	Y	Y	Y
GEORGIA			
Coverdell	Y	N	Y
Cleland	Y	Y	Y
HAWAII			
Akaka	Y	Y	Y
Inouye	Y	Y	Y
IDAHO			
Craig	Y	N	Y
Kempthorne	Y	Y	Y
ILLINOIS			
Durbin	Y	Y	Y
Moseley-Braun	Y	Y	Y
INDIANA			
Coats	Y	Y	Y
Lugar	Y	Y	Y
IOWA			
Grassley	Y	Y	Y
Harkin	Y	Y	Y
KANSAS			
Brownback	Y	Y	Y
Roberts	Y	Y	Y
KENTUCKY			
McConnell	Y	Y	?
Ford	Y	Y	Y
LOUISIANA			
Breaux	Y	Y	Y
Landrieu	Y	Y	Y
MAINE			
Collins	Y	Y	Y
Snowe	Y	Y	Y
MARYLAND			
Mikulski	Y	Y	Y
Sarbanes	Y	Y	Y
MASSACHUSETTS			
Kennedy	Y	Y	Y
Kerry	Y	Y	Y
MICHIGAN			
Abraham	Y	Y	Y
Levin	Y	Y	Y
MINNESOTA			
Grams	N	N	Y
Wellstone	N	Y	+
MISSISSIPPI			
Cochran	Y	Y	Y
Lott	Y	Y	Y
MISSOURI			
Ashcroft	Y	Y	-
Bond	Y	Y	Y
MONTANA			
Burns	Y	N	Y
Baucus	Y	Y	Y
NEBRASKA			
Hagel	Y	Y	Y
Kerrey	Y	Y	Y
NEVADA			
Bryan	Y	Y	Y
Reid	Y	Y	Y
NEW HAMPSHIRE			
Gregg	Y	Y	Y
Smith	Y	Y	N
NEW JERSEY			
Lautenberg	Y	Y	Y
Torricelli	Y	Y	Y
NEW MEXICO			
Domenici	Y	Y	Y
Bingaman	Y	Y	Y
NEW YORK			
D'Amato	Y	Y	Y
Moynihan	Y	Y	Y
NORTH CAROLINA			
Faircloth	Y	N	Y
Helms	Y	Y	N
NORTH DAKOTA			
Conrad	Y	Y	Y
Dorgan	Y	Y	Y
OHIO			
DeWine	Y	Y	Y
Glenn	Y	Y	Y
OKLAHOMA			
Inhofe	Y	Y	N
Nickles	Y	Y	Y
OREGON			
Smith	Y	Y	Y
Wyden	Y	Y	Y
PENNSYLVANIA			
Santorum	Y	Y	Y
Specter	Y	Y	Y
RHODE ISLAND			
Chafee	Y	Y	Y
Reed	Y	Y	Y
SOUTH CAROLINA			
Thurmond	Y	Y	Y
Hollings	Y	Y	Y
SOUTH DAKOTA			
Daschle	Y	Y	Y
Johnson	Y	Y	Y
TENNESSEE			
Frist	Y	Y	Y
Thompson	Y	Y	Y
TEXAS			
Gramm	N	Y	Y
Hutchison	N	Y	Y
UTAH			
Bennett	Y	Y	Y
Hatch	Y	Y	Y
VERMONT			
Jeffords	Y	Y	Y
Leahy	Y	Y	Y
VIRGINIA			
Warner	Y	Y	Y
Robb	Y	Y	Y
WASHINGTON			
Gorton	Y	Y	Y
Murray	Y	Y	Y
WEST VIRGINIA			
Byrd	Y	Y	Y
Rockefeller	Y	Y	Y
WISCONSIN			
Feingold	N	Y	Y
Kohl	N	Y	Y
WYOMING			
Enzi	Y	N	Y
Thomas	Y	Y	Y

KEY

- Y Voted for (yea).
- # Paired for.
- \+ Announced for.
- N Voted against (nay).
- X Paired against.
- \- Announced against.
- P Voted "present."
- C Voted "present" to avoid possible conflict of interest.
- ? Did not vote or otherwise make a position known.

Democrats ***Republicans***

ND Northern Democrats SD Southern Democrats

Southern states - Ala., Ark., Fla., Ga., Ky., La., Miss., N.C., Okla., S.C., Tenn., Texas, Va.

296. HR 1119. Fiscal 1998 Defense Authorization/Conference Report. Adoption of the conference report on the bill to authorize $268,301,837,000 for defense programs in fiscal 1998, $2,605,203,000 more than the president requested. The bill would prohibit funding for U.S. ground troops in Bosnia after June 30, 1998, unless the president certified to Congress that the operation was in the interest of U.S. national security, and would establish new competitive bidding rules for private contractors performing maintenance work at Air Force maintenance depots in Sacramento, Calif., and San Antonio. Adopted (thus cleared for the president) 90-10: R 51-4; D 39-6 (ND 32-5, SD 7-1), Nov. 6, 1997. A "nay" was a vote in support of the president's position.

297. Christina A. Snyder Nomination/Confirmation. Confirmation of President Clinton's nomination of Christina A. Snyder of California to be a U.S. district judge for the Central District of California. Confirmed 93-6: R 48-6; D 45-0 (ND 37-0, SD 8-0), Nov. 7, 1997. A "yea" was a vote in support of the president's position.

298. HR 2264. Fiscal 1998 Labor-HHS Appropriations/Conference Report. Adoption of the conference report on the bill to provide $80.4 billion in discretionary budget authority for the departments of Labor, Health and Human Services, and Education, and related agencies — $5.7 billion more than fiscal 1997 — and to provide a total of $268.0 billion, including mandatory spending, which is $10.7 billion less than provided in fiscal 1997. Adopted (thus cleared for the president) 91-4: R 47-4; D 44-0 (ND 36-0, SD 8-0), Nov. 8, 1997.

Note: Vote 298 was the last roll-call vote taken by the Senate in the first session of the 105th Congress.

Senate Roll Call Votes By Subject

A

B

M

N

O

P

R

S

T

U

V

W

Bill Number Index

Senate Bills

House Bills

CQ

Appendix I

GENERAL INDEX

General Index

A

B

C

D

E

F

G

I

J

K

S